The Norton Anthology of Theory and Criticism

William E. Cain
MARY JEWETT GAISER PROFESSOR OF ENGLISH AND AMERICAN STUDIES
WELLESLEY COLLEGE

Laurie A. Finke
PROFESSOR OF WOMEN'S AND GENDER STUDIES
KENYON COLLEGE

Barbara E. Johnson
PROFESSOR OF ENGLISH AND COMPARATIVE LITERATURE
FREDRIC WERTHAM PROFESSOR OF LAW AND PSYCHIATRY IN SOCIETY
HARVARD UNIVERSITY

John McGowan
PROFESSOR OF ENGLISH AND COMPARATIVE LITERATURE
UNIVERSITY OF NORTH CAROLINA, CHAPEL HILL

Jeffrey J. Williams
ASSOCIATE PROFESSOR OF ENGLISH
UNIVERSITY OF MISSOURI

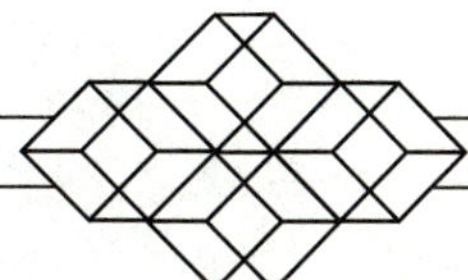

The Norton Anthology of Theory and Criticism

Vincent B. Leitch, *General Editor*
PROFESSOR AND PAUL AND CAROL DAUBE SUTTON CHAIR IN ENGLISH
UNIVERSITY OF OKLAHOMA

W · W · NORTON & COMPANY · New York · London

First Edition.

The text of this book is composed in Fairfield Medium
with the display set in Bernhard Modern.
Composition by Binghamton Valley Composition.
Manufacturing by R. R. Donnelley & Sons.

Editor: Peter Simon
Manuscript Editor: Alice Falk
Assistant Editor: Isobel Evans
Associate Managing Editor: Marian Johnson
Production Manager: Diane O'Connor
Cover and Text Design: Antonina Krass
Permissions Manager: Nancy Rodwan
Art Research: Neil Ryder Hoos

Library of Congress Cataloging-in-Publication Data

The Norton anthology of theory and criticism / Vincent B./Leitch, general editor.
p. cm.
Includes bibliographical references and index.

ISBN 0-393-97429-4

1. Criticism. 2. Literature—History and criticism. I. Leitch, Vincent B., Date
PN86 .N67 2001
801'.95—dc21
00-048057

W. W. Norton & Company, Inc., 500 Fifth Avenue, New York, NY 10110
www.wwnorton.com

W. W. Norton & Company Ltd., Castle House, 75/76 Wells Street, London W1T 3QT

12 13 14 15 16

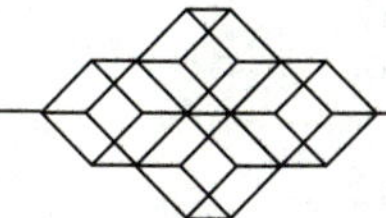

Contents

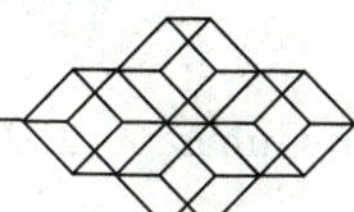

Alternative Table of Contents

Part I: Modern and Contemporary Schools and Movements

PHENOMENOLOGY AND HERMENEUTICS

POSTCOLONIAL THEORY AND CRITICISM

PSYCHOANALYSIS

RACE AND ETHNICITY STUDIES

READER-RESPONSE THEORY

STRUCTURALISM AND SEMIOTICS

Part II: Genres

EPIC AND ROMANCE

DRAMA

THE NOVEL

POETRY

Part III: Historical Periods

Part IV: Issues and Topics

AUTHORSHIP

THE BODY

THE CANON/TRADITION

DEFENSES OF CRITICISM

WOMEN'S LITERATURE

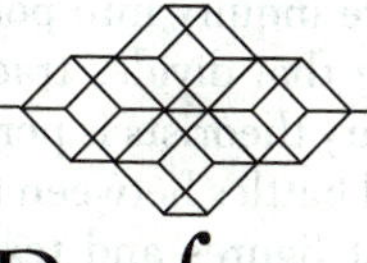

Preface

The most wide-ranging and comprehensive collection of its kind, *The Norton Anthology of Theory and Criticism* offers one or more selections from 148 figures, representing major developments from ancient to recent times, from Gorgias and Plato to bell hooks, Judith Butler, and Stuart Moulthrop. In contrast to comparable anthologies, it provides generous selections from previously underrepresented fields, such as rhetoric, medieval theory, and criticism by women and people of color, along with a full complement of works from canonical figures such as Aristotle, Immanuel Kant, Karl Marx, Cleanth Brooks, Mikhail Bakhtin, and Michel Foucault. From canonical authors, it includes classic texts as well as selections newly revalued. The standard works of Western theory and criticism from the ancient Greeks to the present are represented, as are texts from "forgotten" figures such as Moses Maimonides, Friedrich Schleiermacher, and Frantz Fanon. The anthology is particularly rich in modern and contemporary theory, providing materials from 93 writers and covering all the main schools and movements, ranging from Marxism, psychoanalysis, and formalism to poststructuralism, cultural studies, race and ethnicity studies, and many more. We have also drawn from vital minor currents, including body studies, media theory, theory of national literature and institutional analysis and history. This anthology consolidates the many gains won through the expansion of theory in recent decades.

In view of current changes, it is worth pausing for a moment to reconsider the configuration and meaning of "theory" itself. Today the term encompasses significant works not only of poetics, theory of criticism, and aesthetics as of old, but also of rhetoric, media and discourse theory, semiotics, race and ethnicity theory, gender theory, and visual and popular culture theory. But theory in its newer sense means still more than this broadly expanded body of topics and texts. It entails a mode of questioning and analysis that goes beyond the earlier New Critical research into the "literariness" of literature. Because of the effects of poststructuralism, cultural studies, and the new social movements, especially the women's and civil rights movements, theory now entails skepticism toward systems, institutions, and norms; a readiness to take critical stands and to engage in resistance; an interest in blind spots, contradictions, and distortions (often discovered to be ineradicable); and a habit of linking local and personal practices to the larger economic, political, historical, and ethical forces of culture. This theory—or "cultural critique," as it is more descriptively termed—is less concerned with elaborating conditions of possibility, as is Kantian critique, than with investigating and criticizing values, practices, categories, and representations embedded in cultural texts and surrounding institutions. To an earlier generation, such theory looks like advocacy rather than a disinterested, objective inquiry into poetics and the history of literature. This revealing fault line that divides traditionalist literary critics from large numbers of contemporary theorists is perhaps today's version of the old Renaissance and neoclassical battles between the ancients and the moderns.

The Table of Contents list figures and texts in chronological order. An Alternative Table of Contents recasts the chronological order, providing lists of figures in four categories commonly used in studying theory: schools and movements; major genres; historical periods; and key issues and topics. Additional ways of organizing the history and subject matter of theory and criticism are possible; the Alternative Table of Contents is meant to be suggestive and not comprehensive. Other figures in the anthology could be included in the existing categories. We decided against combining proponents and opponents in the popular schools and movements categories, as is sometimes done. Thus, for example, neither Leon Trotsky nor Mikhail Bakhtin appear under "Formalism" as its most celebrated critics. To list together antagonists and advocates would have created confusion and unduly multiplied the number of figures in our categories. Within each school and movement, of course, readers will encounter differences and disputes. One of the risks of the categories we employ in the Alternative Table of Contents is that their groupings of figures and topics from different periods and moments unavoidably deemphasize historical conflicts, evolution, and differences. That noted, the editors hope our readers find the Alternative Table of Contents suggestive and useful. Many ways of configuring the materials in the anthology are outlined in M. Keith Booker's manual for instructors, *Teaching with "The Norton Anthology of Theory and Criticism": A Guide for Instructors*, a rich source of planning options, classroom strategies, and examination and discussion questions.

The Introduction to Theory and Criticism that follows the two Tables of Contents consists of fifteen brief, semiautonomous sections that introduce students to the field of theory through its main historical periods, its major modern and contemporary schools and movements, its perennial issues and problems, and its key terms. We are aware of no source offering students a quicker, more wide-ranging, or more lucid bird's-eye view of the history and nature of the field. Sections have been subtitled for easy reference in making assignments and in following the trajectory of the discussion.

Each selection in the anthology is fully annotated so that students may focus on the texts and not have to consult reference sources for basic information. Headnotes to each figure cover a range of topics. To begin with, they provide helpful biographical information and historical background. They discuss sources and critical receptions as well as the relevance of the selections for theoretical questions. They highlight each selection's main arguments, where necessary defining key terms and concepts and pointing out related perennial problems in the field. They regularly refer to other works by the authors and note problems identified by later critics. They position the authors in relation to other figures in the anthology, picturing the history of theory not as a string of isolated pearls but as a mosaic in which each work fits into larger frames of ongoing discussions and arguments. Finally, an annotated selected bibliography is given for each figure, covering main texts and editions, biographical sources (when available), the best secondary sources and criticism, and bibliographies related to the author's works (where available).

In choosing the selections the editors have been guided by a range of criteria. We have looked for readable and teachable texts that reflect the scope of the history of theory. This does not mean, however, that challenging and difficult texts are missing. We have favored complete works and self-contained excerpts; snippets are the exception. Yet in a number of cases we have edited texts to focus on topics germane to the field and to save time, space for other selections, and the energy of readers. We have sought out the best editions and translations; for Plato, Aristotle, Longinus, Kant, and Hegel, we introduce new, highly regarded translations. From the outset we have followed the practice that no figure or selection could make it into the anthology without the agreement of at least half the editors. We have also made quite a few selections with an eye to pairing or triangulating—for example, we chose the famous closing section on writing from Plato's *Phaedrus*, having in mind Derrida's landmark critique of that text in his *Dissemination*. When they occur, such fruitful counterpoints are indicated in the headnotes and in the Alternative Table of Contents. Of course, innumerable combinations and permutations are possible, and our accounts cannot be exhaustive. But we have noted typographically all cross-references in the headnotes and footnotes by putting in small capitals the names of theorists and critics appearing in the anthology. While we have privileged standard works and contemporary classics of theory, we have also sought to resurrect forgotten texts and to discover overlooked gems. We believe you will be pleasantly surprised.

The Selected Bibliography of Theory and Criticism at the end of the anthology is the most comprehensive one in existence, containing works through the close of the twentieth century. It lists leading English-language sources in six main categories: Theory and Criticism Bibliographies; Anthologies of Theory and Criticism; Histories of Criticism and Theory; specialized Glossaries, Encyclopedias, and Handbooks; Introductions and Guides; and Modern and Contemporary Critical Schools and Movements. We have divided the three longest of these parts into convenient subcategories: into historical period in the lists both of anthologies and of histories of criticism and into sixteen autonomous profiles in the schools and movements section. To make the bibliography of schools and movements most useful to students, we have organized and briefly annotated the sources in short essays rather than lists, presenting each of the sixteen profiles in a five-paragraph format: (1) groundbreaking texts; (2) introductions, overviews, and histories; (3) anthologies and readers; (4) school- or movement-specific reference works (handbooks, dictionaries, encyclopedias, etc.); and (5) "crossover texts." This last category attests to the increasing frequency with which contemporary works of theory are not limited to one or two domains of influence. It can be argued that in recent years many of the most innovative writings have been hybrid, crossover texts, mixing and matching strands from numerous schools and movements, and we have sought to illustrate this significant trend judiciously.

In putting this anthology together, we have faced a number of challenges. One difficulty was coping with the impossibility of including every significant theorist. Our original list of 250 figures had to be shortened to 148: even a very long book such as this one imposes limits. A few of the lengthiest selections—by Longinus, John Dryden, Percy Bysshe Shelley, and Adrienne Rich, for instance—had to be trimmed, and each editor had favorite figures dropped. The enclosure of post–World War II theory in the university and its increased professionalization have meant that contemporary nonacademic critics, literary journalists, and writers have been largely excluded from the theory canon—a trend slowly being reversed, we hope. Theory remains resolutely Eurocentric, but we look forward to a time when it will go global. Our Selected Bibliography posed its own nagging challenges of inclusion and exclusion. To cite just one case, we had to be rigorously selective in the category of guides and introductions to theory, since there are so many available. We trust we have not missed any major resources. Our Subject Index errs on the side of fullness; we calculated that this would help more than hinder the reader seeking assistance.

The editors of this anthology were selected because of their scholarly expertise. They combine knowledge of canonical works with awareness of contemporary trends and extensive experience as teachers. Each was involved in constructing the anthology's contents and design, and each was responsible for refining selections, drafting headnotes, compiling bibliographies, and editing one another's work. In preparing the volume the editors have incurred obligations to many colleagues, whom we thank separately in the Acknowledgments. With their help, we believe we have made this a readable and teachable anthology replete with significant texts for our contemporaries, meaningful in the context of the history of theory, and able to enlighten and challenge today's students.

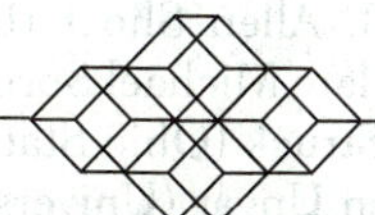

Acknowledgments

While putting this anthology together, we incurred numerous debts to many people, whom we would like to acknowledge publicly.

We thank the following for making valuable suggestions and corrections during various stages: Meryl Altman (DePauw University), Eyal Amiran (Michigan State University), Albert Russell Ascoli (University of California at Berkeley), Eve Tavor Bannet (University of Oklahoma), Patrick Brantlinger (Indiana University), Timothy Andres Brennan (University of Minnesota at Twin Cities), Diane Brown (Macalester College), Gerald L. Bruns (University of Notre Dame), Angie Chabram-Dernersesian (University of California at Davis), Michel Chaouli (Indiana University), King-Kok Cheung (University of California at Los Angeles), Verena Andermatt Conley (Harvard University), Eva L. Corredor (United States Naval Academy), Jane Cowles (Kenyon College), Jonathan Culler (Cornell University), Reed Way Dasenbrock (New Mexico State University), Robert Con Davis-Undiano (University of Oklahoma), Miriam Dean-Otting (Kenyon College), Sheila Delany (Simon Fraser University), Aparna Dharwadker (University of Wisconsin), Vinay Dharwadker (University of Wisconsin), Richard Dienst (Rutgers University), George Economou (University of Oklahoma), Richard Feldstein (Rhode Island College), Paul Fry (Yale University), Jane Gallop (University of Wisconsin at Milwaukee), Leela Gandhi (La Trobe University), Marjorie Garber (Harvard University), Valerie Green (Kenyon College), Stephen Greenblatt (Harvard University), Lawrence Grossberg (University of North Carolina at Chapel Hill), Catherine Hobbs (University of Oklahoma), Robert C. Holub (University of California at Berkeley), J. Paul Hunter (University of Chicago), Martin J. Irvine (Georgetown University), Arpad Kadarkay (University of Puget Sound), Walter Kalaidjian (Emory University), Elaine H. Kim (University of California at Berkeley), John Kirby (Purdue University), Maureen Konkle (University of Missouri), Helga Madland (University of Oklahoma), Steven Mailloux (University of California at Irvine), Donald G. Marshall (University of Illinois at Chicago), Bill McCulloch (Kenyon College), Louis A. Montrose (University of California at San Diego), Timothy Murphy (University of Oklahoma), Winston Napier (Clark University), Cary Nelson (University of Illinois at Urbana), Suzanne Nienaber (Kenyon College), Patrick O'Donnell (Michigan State University), James Paxson (University of Florida), Sarah Pessin, Alvina Quintana (University of Delaware), Royal Rhodes (Kenyon College), Elizabeth Richmond-Garza (University of Texas at Austin), Bruce Robbins (Rutgers University), Charles Ross (Purdue University), A. LaVonne Brown Ruoff (University of Illinois at Chicago), Dianne Sadoff (Miami University), José David Saldívar (University of California at Berkeley), Ramón Saldívar (Stanford University), Ronald Schleifer

(University of Oklahoma), R. Allen Shoaf (University of Florida), Brigid Slipka (Kenyon College), the late Michael Sprinker (State University of New York at Stony Brook), Peter Struck (Ohio State University), Gregory Ulmer (University of Florida), Steven Ungar (University of Iowa), H. Aram Veeser (City College of New York), Alan R. Velie (University of Oklahoma), Jerry W. Ward Jr. (Tougaloo College), Robyn R. Warhol (University of Vermont), Michael Warner (Rutgers University), Joel Weinsheimer (University of Minnesota at Twin Cities), Kathleen Welch (University of Oklahoma), Saranya Wheat (Kenyon College), Robyn Wiegman (Duke University), Martha Woodmansee (Case Western Reserve University), and Duncan Wu (Oxford University).

Several global readings of the Selected Bibliography of Theory and Criticism were provided by David Gorman (Northern Illinois University) and Wallace Martin (University of Toledo). We are particularly in the debt of Professor Martin, who graciously shared his own abundant bibliographic research on the history of theory and criticism.

All of these colleagues have helped make this anthology possible, and with much gratitude we thank them for their valuable time and effort. We single out Richard Dienst, David Gorman, Martin Irvine, John Kirby, and Donald Marshall for substantial contributions to this text.

M. Keith Booker (University of Arkansas at Fayetteville) has written a highly useful instructor's manual, *Teaching with "The Norton Anthology of Theory and Criticism": A Guide for Instructors*, which we strongly recommend to teachers. His contribution extended beyond the manual to text selections, headnotes, and bibliographical items.

The general editor thanks the editors, who have been passionately engaged in every facet of this work. It has been a wonderful collaboration.

The editors in turn would like to thank Vincent Leitch for his inspiration, guidance, and tireless work on this project from beginning to end.

At W. W. Norton, our editor, Peter Simon, guided this anthology with great professional care. Our exceptional copyeditor, Alice Falk, made significant contributions throughout this project, and Marian Johnson and Isobel Evans, managing editor and assistant editor, respectively, kept the complex publishing process moving smoothly. We thank them all.

We appreciate our supportive home universities, especially the libraries at Harvard University, Kenyon College, the University of Missouri, the University of North Carolina at Chapel Hill, the University of Oklahoma, and Wellesley College.

Thanks are also due our research assistants. In this regard the editors would like to thank Jeremy Countryman, Mary DiLucia, Melissa Feuerstein, Bill Johnson González, Tina Hall, Heidi Lynn Kyser-Genoist, Eric Leuschner, Lilian Porten, Marjut Ruti, Maggie Schmitt, and Mary Schwartz. The general editor would also like to acknowledge Christine Braunberger and Mitchell R. Lewis: the former designed the template of our schools and movements bibliographies, while the latter played an active role in every aspect of the project over a period of three years.

We would also like to extend a personal thanks to friends and families.

The Norton Anthology of Theory and Criticism

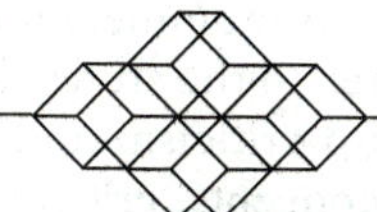

Introduction to Theory and Criticism

In recent decades, theory and criticism have grown ever more prominent in literary and cultural studies, treated less as aids to the study of literature and culture than as ends in themselves. As Jonathan Culler notes in *Framing the Sign: Criticism and Its Institutions* (1988), "Formerly the history of criticism was part of the history of literature (the story of changing conceptions of literature advanced by great writers), but . . . now the history of literature is part of the history of criticism." This dramatic reversal, which occurred gradually over the course of the twentieth century, means that the history of criticism and theory increasingly provides the general framework for studying literature and culture in colleges and universities. Some literary scholars and writers deplore the shift toward theory, regarding it as a turn away from literature and its central concerns. These "antitheorists," as they are called, advocate a return to studying literature for itself—yet however refreshing this position may at first appear, it has problems: it itself presupposes a definition of literature, and it promotes a certain way of scrutinizing literature ("for itself"). In other words, the antitheory position turns out to rely on unexamined—and debatable—theories of literature and criticism. What theory demonstrates, in this case and in others, is that there is no position free of theory, not even the one called "common sense."

The history of theory and criticism from ancient times to the present is one of contending ideas and opinions about such apparently self-evident topics as "literature" and "interpretation." Historically, interpretation has been conceptualized in a number of different ways: as, for example, objective textual analysis or moral assessment or emotional response or literary evaluation or cultural critique. The same is also true of literature, which has been defined in terms of its ability to represent reality, or to express its author's inner being, or to teach morality, or to cleanse our emotions, to name only a few common but conflicting formulations. The history of criticism and theory contains many such arguments. Taken together, the antitheorists themselves adhere to very different, often contradictory understandings of literature and interpretation. Such conflict points to the vitality, the excitement, and the complexity of the field of theory and criticism, whose expansive universe of perennial issues and problems engages ideas not only about literature, language, interpretation, genre, style, meaning, and tradition but also about subjectivity, ethnicity, race, gender, class, culture, nationality, ideology, institutions, and historical periods. In this anthology, students new to literary and cultural studies will discover a wide-ranging interdisciplinary and comparative field whose practitioners examine, formulate, and assess all manner of theories and problems related to the study of literature and culture.

In addition, students new to criticism and theory will encounter a rich array of technical terms and concepts, critical approaches and schools, and literary and cultural theories and theorists. From *signifier* to *deconstruction* to *cultural studies*, from Kant to Foucault, the field of theory and criticism is marked by a multitude of signposts sometimes unfamiliar to even the most widely read students. In this introduction as well as in the headnotes to each author, we help students make sense of this complex but rewarding field. We begin the introduction by surveying an array of notable answers to two central questions—what is interpretation? and what is literature?—in order to establish our bearings. Shifting direction, we then survey the historical development of theory and criticism, from the classical to the Romantic, after which we provide brief overviews of major schools and movements of the last century. Along the way, we discuss many of the theorists in this anthology, explain perennial problems and issues, define key concepts and terms, and illuminate the underlying structure of the field of theory and criticism, including its most significant conflicts.

WHAT IS INTERPRETATION?

Within the field of theory and criticism, various terms and concepts are applied to the encounter between the reader and the text. This transaction, which we will provisionally call "reading" or "interpretation," typically involves such activities as personal response, appreciation, evaluation, historical reception, explication, exegesis, and critique. Not surprisingly, the master words *interpretation* and *reading* are themselves debatable. In fact, in choosing a term or terms to characterize the encounter between text and reader, one takes a specific theoretical position regarding the exact nature of reading and interpretation.

Consider a few such keywords. Whereas *explication* and *exegesis* stress the objective labor of deciphering a text in a methodical way (line by line, in the case of a short poem), *personal response* and *appreciation* emphasize the intimate, casual, and subjective aspects of reading. *Critique* and *historical reception*, in turn, accentuate the distances in values and time between the interpreter and the work. An exegesis of a text is not the same as an appreciation or a critique. Exegesis presumes a dense and enigmatic text in need of elaborate explanation; appreciation implies a reader-friendly work just waiting to be enjoyed here and now; and critique presupposes a hidden set of questionable or dangerous premises and values undergirding a complex document. In the case of exegesis an interpreter needs to be a knowledgeable puzzle solver; appreciation positions the reader as an eager and sympathetic hedonist; and critique calls for a critic at once suspicious and ethical, committed to a set of values different from, or directly opposed to, those expressed in the text. In depicting the critical encounter, theories of reading and interpretation invariably assign characteristics to texts and allocate particular roles and tasks to readers.

Many of the selections in this anthology differ markedly in how they characterize interpretation and reading. For instance, Friedrich Schleiermacher draws a detailed account of interpretation both as historically informed grammatical explication and as psychological identification with the author. His view contrasts with the perspective of Fredric Jameson, who advocates an elaborate three-phase process of interpretation focused specifically on ideology critique of social contradictions, class antagonisms, and historical stages of social development manifested in texts. And Paul de Man instead pictures reading as a mode of exegesis wherein the reader's rewriting or restaging of the text replaces the original with an interpretive allegory: reading for him unavoidably becomes "misreading." That highly competent theorists can propose completely different models of reading fuels continued theoretical debate about interpretation.

One of the most familiar ways of reading is the mode of textual analysis developed by the New Critics, particularly Cleanth Brooks. During the mid–twentieth century, the New Criticism became the dominant critical practice in North American and British universities, and it remains influential today, especially in the introductory literature classroom. To interpret as a New Critic is to demonstrate through multiple (re)readings of poetic texts the intricacy of artistic forms. "Meaning" is found neither in a simple paraphrase of the text, nor in propositions extracted from it, but in carefully orchestrated and unified textual elements (for example, images, tropes, tones, and symbols). The literary work is (pre)conceived as an autonomous, highly coherent, dramatic artifact (a "well-wrought urn") separate from and above the life of the author and reader as well as separate from its social context and from everyday language. Textual inconsistencies are harmonized by being valorized as literary ambiguities, paradoxes, or ironies.

Yet there are problems with this seemingly sensible method. Various theorists have complained that it posits an overly aestheticized, narrow theory of meaning. The "close reading" or "practical criticism" advocated rules out a great deal, including personal response, authorial intention, propositional meaning, social and historical context, and ideology. It values retrospective analysis rather than the risky ongoing experience or actual process of trying to make sense of a work. It privileges freestanding spatial form over temporal flow and critical distance over the reader's personal participation. It makes textual unity mandatory, finessing gaps and loose ends. It favors well-made and compact rather than sprawling works and genres. The famous reading practice of New Criticism is a calculated emptying out of literary interpretation in order to highlight intrinsic artistic craft and form while ruling out such extrinsic matters as morality, psychology, and politics.

Even without sampling further the many theories of reading and interpretation presented in this anthology, we can readily see that there are no easy answers to the question "what is interpretation?" New Criticism has been singled out to demonstrate how a practice of reading might be questioned, but many of the other theories in this anthology could have served equally well. The problematic of interpretation/reading continues to be a major preoccupation in the field of criticism and theory. All who think critically have an opportunity to engage various theories of reading and to formulate their own views.

WHAT IS LITERATURE?

Another major question—"what is literature?"—can be, and regularly is, answered by associating *literature* with such key terms as *representation, expression, knowledge, poetic* or *rhetorical language, genre, text,* or *discourse.*

In our ordinary understanding, literature represents life; it holds up, as it were, a mirror to nature and is thus "mimetic." The expressive theory of literature, which regards literature as stemming from the author's inner being, similarly depends on a notion of mirroring, though here literature reflects the inner soul rather than the external world of the writer. The didactic theory, which sees literature as a source of knowledge, insight, wisdom, and perhaps prophecy, is compatible with both the mimetic and the expressive theory: literature can depict external and internal realities while at the same time disseminating valuable knowledge and clarifying emotions. The dominant view of literature as both mimetic and didactic, still alive today, arose with the ancient Greeks and was challenged by the Romantics and then the moderns. Though the theory of literature—or "poetics," as it is sometimes called—has been a contested topic throughout history, the debate has been especially fierce in modern and contemporary times.

Modern theorists often insist that the language of literature, unlike that of newspapers and science, foregrounds poetic effects (particularly tropes and figures) that range from alliteration, assonance, metaphor, and paradox to rhythm and rhyme. In this "formalist" theory of literature or poetics, neither depiction of external or internal reality nor knowledge about existence or refined emotion distinguishes literature from ordinary and scientific discourse: instead, "literariness" (or "poeticity") renders literature distinctive and special. The theory first emerged during the nineteenth century when poets such as Edgar Allan Poe and Gerard Manley Hopkins started exploring, sometimes extravagantly, the constituent materials of literature (especially sound effects), turning away from the notion of literature as simply a reliable recorder of nature or source of morality. A similar transformation followed in the visual arts; the postimpressionist painters focused on paint textures, brush strokes, and color intensities rather than seeking photographic realities. Writers and theorists at the time often felt that to justify literature by pointing to its accuracy and realism was to put it in competition with the sciences, social sciences, journalism, and photography—a competition they believed it could not win. Conversely, by emphasizing the literariness of literature, they would accord it a distinctive and elevated aesthetic status over competing domains and fields, ensuring its survival and dignity in challenging times. Such a formalist theory of literature prevailed in the early and mid–twentieth century among Anglo-American New Critics and Slavic formalists, many of whom are represented in this anthology.

A well-known heuristic device conveniently summarizes all the accounts of literature discussed up to this point. Developed by M. H. Abrams in *The Mirror and the Lamp: Romantic Theory and the Critical Tradition* (1953), this study aid pictures the literary "work" at the center of a triangular structure; the outer three points are occupied by the "universe," the "artist," and the "audience." Mimetic theory emphasizes the relations between the work and the universe; expressive theory foregrounds the link between work and

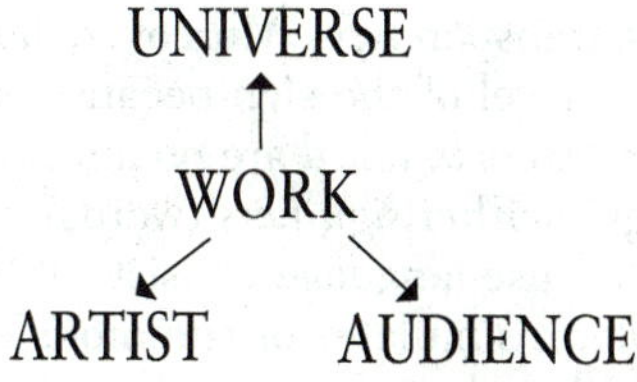

artist; didactic theory highlights the tie between work and audience. Formalist theory focuses on the work itself; as we have just seen, it characteristically deemphasizes connections between the text and the universe, artist, or audience. Until the early Romantic era, literary theory dealt largely with the poem's relationship to the universe and the audience; in the nineteenth century it focused on the artist; and in the twentieth century it turned to the work itself. Most theories of criticism and literature, argues Abrams, juggle these four major elements and orientations, tending to privilege one.

This classification scheme and its lessons have proven useful, especially in illustrating basic theoretical orientations and in delineating broad historical trends. But the famous diagram has limitations, as any theorist will tell you. Perhaps the most serious is that it stops with modernism: it predates the appearance of such influential postmodern theoretical movements as structuralism, poststructuralism, feminism, postcolonial theory, and cultural studies. Abrams maps out a progression from mimesis and didacticism to expressionism to formalism, but recent theory and criticism of literature have moved on to cultural critique. In the process, theorists have focused in turn on the imitation of reality and its lessons, on inner truths and visions, on poetic techniques and their orchestrations, and on sociohistorical and political representations and their values. In this historical development the "old" problems recede from view but never disappear; instead, they undergo reconfiguration and occupy new conceptual relations.

Consider, for instance, the structuralist or semiotic theory of literature that fits all literary texts into genre classifications. According to this perspective, a genre is defined by arbitrary sets of conventions, such as those governing the haiku—a poem of seventeen syllables in three lines of five, seven, and five syllables, respectively. These conventions distance literary writing from ordinary reality, even when the conventions are calculated to give the appearance of direct reportage. In seeing literature as genre consisting of complex sets of codes, the structuralist retains the formalist view of literature as a separate mode of discourse that follows its own artistic rules but adds the key sociological concept of *convention*. Because conventions are not only literary but also linguistic and cultural, literature and society are reconnected through discourse.

Poststructuralist and deconstructive accounts of literature go one step further by problematizing the notion of mirroring, which, as we have seen, undergirds expressive, didactic, and mimetic theories of literature. They do so through a close and technically complex examination of the workings of language—seen as distant and different from reality, for it necessarily contains distorting rhetorical and genre devices. Language is not a simple transparent medium. Any use of language, no matter how typical or everyday, employs *some* combination of historical conventions and figurative devices, which compromises its transparency. Moreover, language separates from "reality" at the very basic level of the sign because, strictly speaking, words are not things. The four letters *b, i, r, d* are not an actual feathered creature. In linguistic terminology, neither *signifiers* (words) nor *signifieds* (concepts) are *referents* (things). Because language consists of "floating signifiers" that are detached from reality, it simulates or summons things as they are. Language deals in effects rather than things. The gaps between signifiers, signifieds, and referents render the truthfulness and reliability of language *undecidable* (a technical term from mathematics borrowed by poststructuralism). Language is thus, to employ technical deconstructive terms, *text* or *textuality*, meaning a complex interweaving of self-referential, undecidable relationships. In extreme forms, this challenging theory of literature as textuality views language as thoroughly divorced from reality; in more moderate forms, language maintains a relation to reality, albeit a highly unstable one. At stake is literature's ability to reflect reality or impart reliable knowledge—and the uncertainty raises doubts about its truth claims and about earlier theories of literature. This area of inquiry is commonly labeled the "crisis of reference" (or "referentiality").

The dizzying deconstructive view of literature as text has been opposed by the widespread recent poststructuralist theory of literature as *discourse*, a term associated with the influential work of Michel Foucault. Discourse theorists explicitly trace the language of literature to its source in the spoken language of everyday social life. Conceived by its many advocates as anti-elitist, this materialist theory of discourse—whether it stems from the work of Foucault, Mikhail M. Bakhtin, black aestheticians, New Historicists, cultural materialists, queer theorists, psychoanalytic critics, or cultural studies scholars (all allotted space in this anthology and discussed later in the introduction)—insists that language is uttered by embodied subjects situated historically in contentious social spheres that are regulated by powerful institutions. Significantly, this theory of the *social* text—of language use as dialogical—gives new life to earlier views of literature as mimetic, expressive, and didactic.

Literature, according to these recent discourse theories, re-presents and refracts reality. Indeed, language itself constitutes reality; it also produces distortions. This is mimesis with a difference: literature represents reality; but reality is grounded in convention, not nature, and it is subject to illusion. Similarly, discourse theorists affirm that literature expresses the inner life of authors, but life is understood to be a regulated *social* phenomenon that differs with the time, location, and group of the author. In place of the solitary poet giving unique expression to truths universal to all humankind, we find in recent discourse theories an embattled "scriptor" creatively mixing and matching cultural codes derived from her or his situation, community, and tradition. In this account literature retains didactic as well as mimetic and expressive powers. The knowledge it conveys is of the "cultural unconscious"—that is, of the archive of historical words, symbols, codes, instincts, wishes, and conflicts characteristic of a people and its era. To treat discourse as social text pluralizes the theory of literature, making a single universal or totalizing theory of literature, good for all times and places, appear reductive. Literatures replace literature.

Theories of literature and theories of reading have affinities with one another. Here are four instances. First, the formalist idea of literature as a well-made artistic object corresponds to the notion of reading as careful explication and evaluation of dense poetic style. Second, when viewed as the spiritual expression of a gifted seer, poetry elicits a biographical approach to criticism focused on the poet's inner development. Third, dense historical symbolic works presuppose a theory of reading as exegesis or decipherment. Fourth, literature conceived as social text or discourse calls for cultural critique. While we can separate theories of literature from theories of interpretation, they often work hand in hand.

CLASSICAL THEORY AND CRITICISM

Anthologies covering the history of theory and criticism usually begin with the classical theorists, and rightly so, because their influence on its development has continued up to the present. The most influential classical theorists in Western culture are Plato and Aristotle, followed distantly by Horace. Recently, a renewed interest in rhetoric has brought Gorgias, Quintilian, and others into the picture—a change that illustrates the mutability of the canon of theory. Taken together, the classical theorists represent a wide range of opinions about literature and its significance developed over a millennium (from the fifth century B.C.E. to the fifth century C.E.). To sample their groundbreaking work, we will consider some of their opinions on two leading, often interrelated issues of their time: literary mimesis and didacticism.

On these two issues, Plato and his student Aristotle present the best-known views. Both agree that *mimēsis* (imitation or representation) is a key feature of poetry, but they conceive of and evaluate it quite differently. Plato has his spokesperson Socrates disapprove of poetry's imitation of reality on the grounds that poetry cannot depict truth and teach morality and that it is irrational—based on inspiration, not knowledge. As an idealist philosopher, he locates reality in a transcendent world of eternal Forms or Ideas that only reason can properly apprehend; this world is distinct from the illusory phenomenal world of our senses, which poetry represents. For Plato, the material world is at best an imperfect copy of the original transcendent world of Ideas, and poetry is but a degraded copy of a copy. He concludes that poetic representation threatens social stability by offering false images and unsuitable role models. In *Republic*, therefore, he has Socrates recommend that it be banished from the ideal society, except perhaps that poetry which praises the gods and avoids representing them in an unseemly fashion.

Plato takes this severe position in part because he is reacting against the views of earlier sophists such as Gorgias and Thrasymachus, whom he represents as less concerned with truth than with persuasion. They saw language as not simply representing reality but in effect producing reality by shaping the beliefs of an audience. As a result, in oratory as well as in poetry, what matters most is bringing a particular audience to hold a specific point of view, not imitating an absolute truth. Some sophists even boasted that in a debate they could argue any side of an issue and win. Later rhetoricians such as Quintilian emphasized that the good orator was also a morally good man, but truth and honesty apparently mattered little to fifth-century Greek sophists, who significantly influenced the formation of Plato's ethical position.

Less transcendental than Plato and Socrates, and more concerned with truth than the sophists, Aristotle asserts that poetic imitation can reveal truth precisely because it does not passively copy appearances: it is a more creative act. Poetry in this view is an organized whole, whose parts are organically related and subordinated to a single objective. Because he focuses on tragic drama, Aristotle takes plot as the key example of the organization of poetry. For him, plot is not a random sequence of incidents but a unified whole with a beginning, middle, and end structured by logical necessity. Unlike history, which is built on accidental details, poetry rises above the description of particulars to represent universal truths about nature. This new view of imitation springs from Aristotle's belief that human beings have a natural instinct for imitation, which is generally pleasurable and connected with learning.

Later developments in classical theory and criticism build on the groundbreaking work of the Greek rhetoricians, Plato, and Aristotle. Horace, a poet, follows Aristotle in asserting that poets can and must imitate nature, adding that it is also important for young poets to imitate great writers. As he approves of poetic imitation, Horace stresses the importance of morality and decorum. For him, the pleasures of imitation are best yoked with moral teaching: he declares that the primary function of poetry is to combine "pleasure with usefulness." This famous Horatian maxim has exerted considerable influence on all subsequent theorizing.

MEDIEVAL THEORY AND CRITICISM

Spanning the course of a millennium (from the fifth through the fifteenth century), medieval theory and criticism contain numerous documents related to the practices of reading and interpretation, to the theory of language, and to the nature and use of literature.

Much medieval literary theory evolved out of the interpretation of sacred Scriptures. Drawing on the Neoplatonism of Plotinus and his disciple Proclus, medieval writers explored how to read the Book of God's Word (the Bible) as a divinely authorized representation of the Book of God's Works (nature). Hugh of St. Victor, for instance, describes interpretation as the reflection, or imitation, of God's works in his words. For Hugh, the whole visible world is a book written by the finger of God. Thus in reading one discovers not a pale imitation of nature, as Plato believed, but the ways in which reading a text and reading the world are parallel activities.

This medieval theory of hermeneutics (the art and science of interpretation) is grounded in Augustine's notion that human language is a divinely ordained reflection of the Logos (the Word of God), which is said to guarantee the unity of meaning in the Bible and the book of nature, even if that meaning is not readily discernible. Language truthfully portrays the world as it is, in spite of the confusion caused by the multiplication of tongues at Babel. In other words, language is "transparent." According to Augustine, language exists only to convey a meaning that preexists it; it cannot be reflexive or playful (as it may be in poetry); and it must efface itself in pointing to the preexistent truth it represents.

Most medieval writers accepted the Augustinian theory of language, and they also shared Augustine's deep distrust of poetic fables and figurative language. But they constantly faced serious theoretical contradictions. Try as they might to assert the "truth" of language and the uselessness of poetic fictions, medieval writers could not overlook the presence of both poetry and fables in the master text of Christianity, the Bible. The most common if still not entirely satisfactory response was to argue that the transcendental majesty of God could be represented only indirectly, through poetic or figurative language. In this view, the heroic songs and psalms of the Old Testament, as well as Christ's parables in the New Testament, function as metaphoric mediations, creating similitudes between this world and the next. Such similitudes are necessary, Augustine argues, so that "by means of corporeal and temporal things we may comprehend the eternal and spiritual." Ultimately, the medieval defense of poetry was based on Macrobius's key distinction between fables that "merely gratify the ear" and those that "encourage the reader to good works."

In exploring such issues, medieval writers relied primarily on the textual techniques of exegesis. Particularly important were the exegetical genres of the gloss and the commentary, derived from the works of ancient grammarians and expanded for explication of the Bible. Glosses are elucidations of individual words or phrases, written in the margins or between the lines of a text; commentaries are much more extensive textual expositions, appearing at first as local and marginal remarks (like footnotes) but later produced as freestanding continuous texts (see, for example, Bernardus Sylvestris's twelfth-century *Commentary on the First Six Books of Virgil's "Aeneid"*). Known as the *enarratio poetarum* (exposition of the poets), these interpretive genres shaped the basic approach to all authoritative texts, which were transmitted in manuscripts filled with glosses and commentary that retained space for future textual exegesis.

The dominant technique of medieval gloss and commentary is allegory, a method of reading texts for their underlying esoteric meanings. Quintilian's definition of allegory as meaning "one thing in the words, another in the senses" was the basis of all medieval definitions of allegory; but what was for him a figure of speech became, when combined with the Augustinian belief that poetry is a revelation of an otherwise inaccessible transcendent world, a critical tool to explain and control the dissemination of meanings in sacred Scriptures. Only later would it become a literary genre. Following Quintilian, medieval writers eventually elaborated four levels of allegorical interpretation to be used in the study of the Bible: the *literal*, or historical; the *allegorical*, or spiritual; the *tropological*, or moral; and the *anagogical*, or mystical. In the New Testament story of Christ's raising of Lazarus from the dead, for example, the medieval exegete would recognize first that on the literal level, the story is a record of an event that actually took place. On the allegorical level, the story prefigures Christ's death, descent into hell, and resurrection. On the tropological level, it represents the sacrament of Penance, whereby the individual soul is raised from the death of sin. And on the anagogical level, it portrays the resurrection of the body after the Last Judgment.

By the twelfth century, medieval writers had extended allegorical biblical interpretation to the study of pagan mythologies and great classical works of art, such as Virgil's epic poem, the *Aeneid*. Medieval Christians could not literally accept pagan gods, nor could they simply read the stories as "fables," but they could see them as expressions of philosophical ideas. Eventually, allegorical interpretation was applied to contemporary writing, as in Dante's own reading of his *Divine Comedy* in "Letter to Can Grande." Although it slowly passed out of favor after the Middle Ages, allegorical interpretation reemerged as a significant influence in the late twentieth century—especially in the work of Northrop Frye and Fredric Jameson, both of whom developed schemes for interpreting texts based on multiple levels of interpretation.

Medieval theory and criticism, significantly, concerns itself with prescriptive poetics: that is, with how to write poetry. Inspired by Horace's *Ars Poetica,* this pragmatic criticism synthesizes classical views on rhetoric, grammar, and style, often taking the form of guides to composition. Perhaps the best-known medieval Horatian critic is Geoffrey of Vinsauf, who adopts and revises Horace's fundamental principle of decorum for a medieval audience. For Geoffrey, the poet's objective is not to invent new subject matter but to develop new ways of treating traditional themes. In this regard, the poet is like the medieval exegete, who preserves the past and develops intricate ways of extending it.

RENAISSANCE AND NEOCLASSICAL THEORY AND CRITICISM

While Renaissance and neoclassical literary theory and criticism display a renewed interest in Greek and Latin classics, they also manifest a new concern with vernacular languages and national literatures. Spanning the sixteenth, seventeenth, and eighteenth centuries, the debate between the ancients and the moderns began in Italy and extended throughout western Europe, setting the framework for much of the theory and criticism of the time—and addressing problems that are still with us today.

The defenders of the ancients directed attention to classical genres such as tragic drama and epic, holding them up as models for composition. At first, the ideal was not just to imitate the genres of antiquity but to use their languages, especially Latin. The argument for strictly adhering to classical forms grew out of a unique synthesis of Aristotle's *Poetics* and Horace's *Ars Poetica*. From the *Poetics*, Renaissance critics developed an appreciation for isolating and distinguishing genres, which they tended to treat prescriptively rather than descriptively. The most famous instance is the doctrine of the "three unities" (action, place and time), which extrapolates from Aristotle's notion of the unity of action to demand that dramas have not only one action but also one setting and a brief span of fictional time (not exceeding one day). Here Aristotle's original description of a body of preexisting Greek tragedies is turned into a set of rules for the writing of plays. This position, which first emerged in the commentaries on Aristotle by the Italian Renaissance critic Ludovico Castelvetro, found its most influential expression a century later in the critical writings of the neoclassical French dramatist Pierre Corneille and the English poet John Dryden—both of whom in their creative works were dedicated to their native languages and literatures and thus combined modern and ancient perspectives.

Joined to the doctrine of the three unities was a special Horatian concern with "verisimilitude." In practice, this meant depicting historical realities and facts and excluding fantastic beings and events (except those that could be explained by Christian beliefs, such as the actions of God and demons). Critics often pointed to significant passages in Horace that stressed the importance of decorum and of copying the techniques and strategies of one's accomplished literary predecessors. The general sense was that by imitating classics, modern Renaissance and neoclassical writers were also imitating nature. This position was strongly advocated by the Italian critic Julius Caesar Scaliger and was later summed up memorably in one of the many witty neoclassical couplets of Alexander Pope's *Essay on Criticism*. Pope notes that the youthful poet Virgil scorned to represent anything except nature when he set out to write his epic, the *Aeneid*: "But when t'examine ev'ry Part he came, / *Nature* and *Homer* were, he found, the *same*." Pope concludes from Virgil's example, "Learn hence for Ancient *Rules* a just Esteem; / To copy *Nature* is to copy *Them*."

In contrast to the ancients, the moderns not only appreciated but championed new literary forms that departed from the various classical genres. One among many examples is Giambattista Giraldi's defense of the new Renaissance romantic epic, epitomized by Ludovico Ariosto's *Orlando Furioso* and later by Edmund Spenser's *Faerie Queene*. Critics of these long poems pointed out that they lacked unity and verisimilitude and that they deviated markedly from the classical epic, but Giraldi praised the variety of Ariosto's poem as well as its "marvelous" incidents, claiming that it constituted a new genre not subject to classical rules. In a parallel move, Giacopo Mazzoni supported Dante's dream allegory in the *Divine Comedy*, stressing the importance of purely imaginary imitation. Informing both Mazzoni's and Giraldi's arguments is a view of the poet's creative powers as unbounded. Sir Philip Sidney captured the essence of this position, which set the stage for Shakespeare, when he stated, "Nature never set forth the earth in so rich tapestry as divers poets have done, neither with pleasant rivers, fruitful trees, sweet smelling flowers, nor whatsoever else may make the too much loved earth more lovely. Her world is brazen, the poets only deliver a golden."

With this defense of the unfettered powers of the poet also came a defense of the use of vernacular languages in place of Latin. Critics and poets began to believe that they could rival the great literary achievements of Greece and Rome with their respective native languages. This trend began as early as Dante, whose *Divine Comedy* was composed in Italian, but in the Renaissance it spread across western Europe. The Italian language was defended by Giraldi and Mazzoni, the French language by Joachim du Bellay and Pierre de Ronsard, and the English language by Sidney and George Puttenham. The turn to the vernacular reflected the growing national consciousness of the time and an increasing preoccupation with distinct national literary traditions.

ROMANTIC THEORY AND CRITICISM

The Romantic movement in the arts developed in the latter half of the eighteenth century, inspired in part by the American and French Revolutions, and flourished in the early nineteenth century, spreading throughout Europe and the New World. Although it manifests a variety of forms in specific social and historical contexts, the major characteristic of Romanticism is arguably its focus on the individual. Romantic theory was significantly influenced by the philosopher Immanuel Kant's attention to the ways in which subjectivity determines our apprehension of the world. It was also influenced by the developing regard for individual sensibility and originality, a concern first memorably manifested during the mid–eighteenth century in the critical work of the poet Edward Young.

In Romantic theory and criticism, emphasis on the individual led to an unprecedented focus on poetry as the personal expression of the poet—a development that aimed to counter the decorum, traditionalism, and preoccupation with genre characteristic of neoclassicism. Romantic poets such as Johann Wolfgang von Goethe, William Wordsworth, and Percy Bysshe Shelley all saw their art as intimately bound up with their personal impressions, moods, feelings, and sentiments, while Romantic critics such as Schleiermacher called for readers' sympathetic identification with the author.

In discussions of poetry, Romantics frequently drew attention to how the imagination transforms and synthesizes discrete sense perceptions, creating unique organic poems. Perhaps the most celebrated instance of this focus appears in *Biographia Literaria*, where Samuel Taylor Coleridge claims that the poet "diffuses a tone and spirit of unity, that blends, and (as it were) *fuses*, each into each, by that synthetic and magical power, to which we have exclusively appropriated the name of imagination." This Romantic view of the poem as an organic form developed by the individual imagination was contrary to the neoclassical dictate that artists must imitate previous works of art and follow the rules of their genre. As exemplified by Coleridge, Elizabeth Robinson Montagu, and others, it led to a renewed appreciation of the unique creative genius of Shakespeare, whose unusual and irregular plays were often criticized by neoclassical theorists for ignoring the unities of action, time, and place. Later the Romantic concept of organic form, shorn of theorizing about the author, would inspire early-twentieth-century formalist theories of intricate poetic structure and coherence.

The Romantic fascination with the synthesizing power of the imagination paralleled an abiding concern with the symbol, displayed most famously in the writings of Coleridge and Ralph Waldo Emerson. For the Romantics, the poetic symbol magically expressed universal ideas through particular concrete details, images, and metaphors. Unlike allegory, which they widely condemned as a mechanical imposition of meaning and morality onto poetry, the poetic symbol manifested its meaning organically, providing aesthetic pleasure and beauty as well as moral truth. According to Friedrich von Schiller, the process of reading a poem was an experience of "play"—a serious play that reconciled the particular and the general and brought an uplifting sense of freedom to the reader and the poet, saving them from the alienation and despair of the modern world. For the Romantics, poetry—through the symbol—humanized an increasingly dehumanized world.

The genre of choice during the Romantic era was the lyric poem, which displaced the epic poem favored by neoclassical writers (longer Romantic poems tended to be arrangements of lyric pieces, as in Wordsworth's *Prelude*). Of all the available genres, the lyric poem was best suited for the expression of individual emotion. Not uncommonly, the lyric appeared as a "fragment," a technique that further stressed the break with neoclassicism, which valued unity, wholeness, and rational design. Many lyrics aimed to attain a sublimity associated with robust imaginative grandeur, infinity, irrationality, and fear and terror, which was achieved less through sophisticated style and rhetoric (as in the classical writer Longinus, the earliest theorist of the sublime) than by the force of individual genius.

The long struggle of the novel to be regarded as a serious literary form as yet had little effect on theory and criticism, though this genre (especially the Gothic novel) thrived during the Romantic period. The classical hierarchy of literary genres—epic followed by tragic drama and then by lyric poetry—left little room for the humble and prosaic novel until Victorian times. And still today the novel cedes pride of place in literary history to epic poetry and tragic drama, though perhaps no longer to lyric poetry.

A final significant trait of Romantic theory was an emphasis on historical stages of development. The changing social, political, and economic conditions around them prompted many thinkers to ponder literary and cultural history. In theory and criticism, such attention led to repeated attempts—by Jean-Jacques Rousseau, G. W. F. Hegel, Thomas Love Peacock, Germaine de Staël, and others—to correlate specific forms of literature and the arts to specific historical periods. Often, poetry was identified—as it had earlier been by Giambattista Vico—with "primitive" forms of society, in which people were purportedly less rational and more intuitive. This concern with the dynamics of history was to have a significant impact on the influential work of Karl Marx.

MARXISM

From ancient times, literature and the arts have portrayed, and criticism and theory have discussed, differences in people's social class and history. But with the spread and maturation of capitalism through its various stages, economic and other disparities have more visibly polarized wealthy and poor classes, city residents and ghetto dwellers, inhabitants of the first and third worlds, whites and people of color, men and women. Class formations, class consciousness, and class tensions form part of the historical experience of modernization, and theory and criticism have been grappling with these and related issues for several centuries now.

Many of the current concepts, terms, and issues related to social class derive from Marxist criticism, a diverse and influential source for literary and cultural theory that stems from the work of the nineteenth-century German philosopher and economist Karl Marx. One of its grounding concepts is Marx's theory of "modes of production." According to Marx, human history is divided into seven successive historical modes of production—tribal hordes, Neolithic kinship societies, oriental despotism, ancient slaveholding societies, feudalism, capitalism, and communism. Class conflict within a specific mode of production follows a basic overall pattern. The capitalist or bourgeois mode of our time has been characterized mainly by the conflict between the industrial working class (the *proletariat*, or labor) and the owners and manipulators of the means of production (the *bourgeoisie*). Other classes, including the unemployed and criminals (the *lumpenproletariat*) as well as the dwindling aristocracy, watch this conflict from the historical sidelines. Sooner or later, Marx predicted, international labor will win and the communist mode of production will emerge triumphant, eventually leading to a society free from rampant inequalities, exploitation, and class struggle.

According to Marxist theory, the socioeconomic elements of society constitute its base (or foundation), while its cultural spheres—specifically its politics, law, religion, philosophy, and arts—compose its superstructure. *Ideology* consists of the ideas, beliefs, forms, and values of the ruling class that circulate through all the cultural spheres. Members of the working class who ascribe to bourgeois ideas and values exhibit "false consciousness," since such values ignore the socioeconomic realities of their own working-class lives. *Hegemony* designates the continuous ideological domination of all classes by the ruling class through such nonviolent stabilizing and consensus-building institutions as church, school, family, the media, the mainstream arts, trade unions, business interests, and technoscientific establishments. These institutions are what the celebrated Marxist theorist Louis Althusser calls "Ideological State Apparatuses" (ISAs): they manage social instability and conflict to impose and maintain hegemonic order, working for the most part outside of official state power.

Culture and the arts in the Marxist view are neither innocent entertainment nor independent of social forces; they play a significant role in transmitting ideology and shoring up the hegemonic order. This is not to say that artists and intellectuals are merely mouthpieces of the dominant social class, because many explicitly protest the ruling systems and implicitly address their contradictions and shortcomings. The ideological orientations of a literary work can be quite complicated: a text often contains mixed and contradictory messages that reflect its broad social milieu rather than its author's personal philosophy. From a Marxist perspective, artistic works frequently present fugitive, alternative, and counterhegemonic images sometimes suggesting liberatory possibilities and lending them a socially critical undertone.

Viewed from the vantage point of stylistics (the branch of linguistics that analyzes literary style), the conflicts of classes and groups in society produce what Bakhtin famously called "heteroglossia"—that is, the complex stratification of a language like English into different dialects, generational slangs, professional argots, speech genres, group codes, literary genres, and class mannerisms. Many novels (for example, James Joyce's *Ulysses*) incorporate such social conflicts in the form of heteroglot discourse, a carnivalization of different languages that revolt against official style.

With the rise of consumer and multinational capitalism, many have found Karl Marx's concepts of the *commodity, commodity fetishism,* and *commodification* increasingly useful for understanding culture and society, and thus the terms often appear in the writings of contemporary critics and theorists. Commodities are goods or services produced primarily for monetary exchange and profit—a carpenter may, for example, build a table to sell, not to use. For him, or her, this commodity has exchange value, not use value. Labor itself has come to be bought and sold in a money economy; rather than being applied by isolated workers to the production of goods for personal use, it is more typically used in the service of another to earn and then exchange money for items necessary for subsistence. The fetishism of the commodity describes both our fascination as we stand before a glittering array of products in a store and our forgetting the paid labor of workers that went into the products. This displacement of use value from the commodity—its transformation into cash exchange—results in the alienation of workers from their own labor: carpenters in the factory care little about the tables they assemble. Moreover, the extraction of profit by owners from their workers' labor results in exploitation, which is a key element of all commodity exchange. The term *commodification* names this whole accelerating phenomenon of producing goods and services not for their use value but their exchange value, a phenomenon that threatens to permeate every sphere of life in our time. Marxist critics complain that commodification promotes reification, the tendency to view people and human relations as things or objects with price tags. In the arts, for instance, commodification leads artists to hawk their works anxiously to gain profits in an impersonal, competitive market, and it has positioned critics as the hired advisers to moneyed collectors. Observing this process, theorists have begun to wonder if criticism and the arts can any longer possess a socially critical dimension.

Indeed, contemporary Marxist critics and cultural studies scholars (who are indebted to Marxism) increasingly worry about the co-optation by the market (and the media) of every form of resistance, ranging across the arts and popular culture. If outrageous radical vanguard movements such as surrealism and punk can become profitable commodities, is opposition to hegemony possible? The agencies of commodification and hegemonic incorporation threaten to defuse the radical force of all subversive artistic practices, transforming them into hot news stories and merchandise destined for the market economy. Marxist criticism and cultural studies frequently aim their critical inquiries at this system and its dynamics.

PSYCHOANALYSIS

It is often said that Sigmund Freud discovered the unconscious, but it is more accurate to say that he and other psychoanalysts mapped its spaces and mechanisms. The findings of psychoanalysis have filtered into literary and cultural criticism and theory, providing a battery of terms, concepts, and problems that reach beyond those critics who describe themselves as psychoanalytic.

According to psychoanalysis, the human psyche consists of unconscious and conscious spheres, with most of its contents lodged out of sight in the unconscious and covered over by a relatively smaller and less dense consciousness. The keys to the dark and inaccessible unconscious lie, psychoanalysts say, in free association, fantasies, slips of the tongue (so-called Freudian slips), and especially dreams, all of which reveal deeply buried, repressed, and self-censored wishes. The techniques used to interpret such unconscious materials, particularly dreams, have been useful to literary and cultural critics as well as psychoanalysts, since they are all in the business of deciphering cryptic symbolic texts.

The nightly formation of dreams, or the *dream-work* in Freudian terminology, involves the censorship of unconscious wishes (frequently sexual) that undergo four kinds of deliberate, positive distortion on their way to consciousness: condensation, displacement, symbolization, and secondary revision or elaboration. These unconscious processes explain why dreams usually emerge as garbled "nonsense." The task of the psychoanalyst is, with the help of the patient, to make sense of dream texts. Here, psychoanalysis asserts that nonsense is meaningful and that distortion is inescapable and creative. Both assertions are taken seriously by many critics and theorists as they work to understand texts, especially since literary discourses are often as seemingly nonsensical and distorted as dreams. Psychoanalytic decoding of symbols has proved particularly illuminating to critics, notably those followers of Carl Jung who have made inventories of archetypes—universal symbols such as the garden and the desert, water and fire, the hero and the monster, the river journey and the ordeal, birth and death—that they believe are stored in humanity's collective unconscious.

Many highly influential modern and postmodern theories of literature are indebted to psychoanalysis and its foundational concept of the unconscious. Two examples of such psychopoetics—Harold Bloom's "anxiety of influence" and French feminism's *écriture féminine*—illustrate the richness and complexity of psychoanalytic theories. According to Bloom, each major poet in the Anglo-American tradition from the early Romantics to the late modernists has suffered a devastating yet productive anxiety of influence, as the newcomer poet selects a role model both to imitate and to compete against, wishing ultimately to emerge as a major poet who triumphs over (but triumphs because of) the poetic precursor. Prior to the neoclassical and Romantic periods, literary influence was almost entirely beneficial (as in the case, say, of Spenser's influence on Milton). With the rise of the subjective lyric poem as a major genre, influence became baleful, involving the aspiring poet's primal repression of the precursor plus a series of later psychological defenses against this parent figure, including masochistic reversals, sublimations, introjections, regressions, and projections. These all entail what Bloom calls "misprision" (mistaking, misreading, misinterpreting), the inescapable and necessary creative *distortion* enacted unconsciously in the newcomer's poems in imitation of, and competition with, the loved but hated precursor. Bloom's complex psychopoetics has been criticized for focusing on competition instead of collaboration, for favoring canonical poets over less well known poets, and for omitting nearly all writing by women, but Bloom's critics have rarely questioned the usefulness of his theoretical understanding of distortion or of unconscious repression, two key psychoanalytical concepts widely used in the field of theory and criticism.

The literary theory of *écriture féminine* (feminine/female writing) derives from the work of the celebrated psychoanalyst Jacques Lacan, as creatively revised by the French feminist Hélène Cixous. According to Lacan's challenging theory, an infant moves during its earliest psychosocial development from an "Imaginary order"—a mother-centered, nonsubjugated, presymbolic, pre-oedipal space of bodily drives and rhythms (linked with the unconscious)—to a "Symbolic order" of separation between self and (m)other, of law and patriarchal social codes, and of loss and associated desire (linked with consciousness). *Écriture féminine* is a radical, disruptive mode of "feminine" writing that is opposed to patriarchal discourse with its rigid grammar, boundaries, and categories; tapping into the Imaginary, it gives voice to the unconscious, the body, the nonsubjective, and polymorphous drives. Even though such feminine writing can be produced by male as well as female writers (for example, by Jean Genet and James Joyce), it is a psychopoetics positioned by Cixous explicitly against patriarchal values and practices.

In both the anxiety of influence and *écriture féminine*, as in psychoanalysis generally, Freud's theory of the "Oedipus complex" plays a key role. According to this theory, an infant must successfully complete various stages of development (oral, anal, oedipal) to ensure later psychological well-being. In the oedipal stage, the (male) child must separate from the mother and identify with the father on his way to entering the Symbolic order. The Oedipal complex is displayed by those males whose failure to negotiate the oedipal stage of development leaves them deeply attached to their mothers and often feeling rivalry with their fathers. Bloom's theory of the anxiety of influence presents a parallel rivalry with the father. And *écriture féminine* is a feminist effort to reconceive the pre-oedipal sphere as a highly positive source of creativity and liberation, rather than simply an infantile domain of irrational instincts that we must all abandon.

Perhaps the most famous contemporary revision of Freudian oedipal theory appears in Gilles Deleuze and Félix Guattari's Marxist and psychoanalytical *Anti-Oedipus*, a book that criticizes many aspects of Freud's work—notably, the bourgeois presupposition that the nuclear family is the universal framework for all normal human development. According to Deleuze and Guattari, Freudian theory subjugates the disruptive unconscious—with its often antisocial desires and flows—to the hegemonic order of the patriarchal family, the rule of law, and the capitalist economy. Freud's psychoanalysis, focused as it is on the oedipal triangle, is unable to acknowledge the truly complex nature of subjectivity, seen by Deleuze and Guattari as an open-ended process of becoming in which multiple contradictory positions and roles coexist and clash.

FORMALISM

Formalist criticism rose to prominence in the early twentieth century, usually defining itself in opposition to subjectivist theories of literature such as Romanticism, which was perceived to be both solipsistic and relativistic. Formalist criticism is not interested in the feelings of poets, the individual responses of readers, or representations of "reality"; instead, it attends to artistic structure and form. The two best-known schools of formalist criticism are Anglo-American New Criticism and Russian formalism.

As discussed above, New Critics approach literature—particularly poetry—as an autonomous entity. They focus on the form of the literary object, self-consciously separating literary criticism from the study of sources, biography, reception, social and historical contexts, politics, and other "extrinsic" matters. They advocate intrinsic analysis or "close reading" that avoids paraphrase and thematic statements, examining instead the complex stylistic orchestrations that compose poetry. What New Critics seek in their studies of poetic form is a set of "organic" relationships of literary elements (images, symbols, tropes, features of genre and style, settings, and tones), whose overall unity often depends on ambiguity, paradox, or irony. This special state of aesthetic suspension—reminiscent of Kant's earlier "purposiveness without purpose" and Coleridge's "balance or reconciliation of opposite or discordant qualities"—is for them a defining feature of poetry. It distinguishes the literary from the more ordinary uses of language found in journalism, everyday speech, scientific writing, and so on, where direct communication, not highly wrought aesthetic form, is most important.

Similarly, Russian formalist critics such as Roman Jakobson and Boris Eichenbaum distinguish between the literary and the nonliterary. They view literature primarily as a verbal art, rather than as a reflection of reality or an expression of emotions. Separating literary criticism from such fields as psychology, sociology, and intellectual history, they focus on the distinguishing features of literature, its "literariness." What most separates literature from other modes of discourse is that it draws attention to its own medium, that is, to a complex texture of formal devices and strategies that include versification, style, and narrative structure. Whereas New Critics study the artful convergence of elements in a literary structure, Russian formalists examine the creative deviation of elements from the background of literary norms and conventions.

The importance of formalism, especially the Anglo-American variety, cannot be underestimated. Because it is the dominant mode of modern criticism against which much later theory typically defines itself in whole or in part, we will return to it later in this introduction.

READER-RESPONSE THEORY

Contemporary critical theory offers a rich panoply of types of readers—ideal readers, superreaders, implied readers, virtual readers, real readers, historical readers, resisting readers, critical readers, and more. Such terms are usually found in reader-response theory and reception aesthetics, realms that focus on theories of readers and meaning.

In reading a novel, one can sometimes extrapolate from it an implied reader, a figure whom the text seems to be addressing and who occasionally functions as a character in the work (for example, the characters to whom Marlow tells his story in Joseph Conrad's *Heart of Darkness*). An implied reader differs both from a virtual reader, to whom the text is vaguely addressed by the author, and from a historical reader, who actually reads the text at the time of its publication. The hypothetical perfect decoder of the work, who knows everything necessary to make sense of it, is the ideal reader; but the most original and innovative texts require a superreader, a special ideal reader endowed not only with extensive linguistic and literary knowledge but also with superior aesthetic sensibility. Both the critical and the resisting reader, situated in definite historical moments and possessing strong values and interests, find themselves opposing and interrogating texts (imagine an average American today reading Hitler's *Mein Kampf*). Real readers are people whose actual responses to novels, plays, poems, and other texts have been recorded by theorists and, in some cases, analyzed for their individual styles and for the personal psychological quirks that they reveal.

Theories of meaning accompany these accounts of various readers. Some reader-response theories construe meaning as an entity located in the text or in a paraphrase of the text and thus view readers as discovering objective textual meanings. But other reader-response theories argue that insofar as reading occurs through time and involves the continuous adjustment of perceptions, ideas, feelings, and evaluations, the meaning of a work is the moment-by-moment experience of it, not something separate or left over. Meaning is therefore a process, not a product; it is an event, not a retrospective reconstruction or intellectual reformulation. This subjectivist theory of meaning has several obvious limitations, however: it endorses the idea of reading as private consumption, and it construes *experience* as a straightforward, unconditioned, and knowable process.

Some reader-response theorists see meaning as a production dependent on preexisting social codes and protocols of interpretation. In this view, every interpretive community—for example, psychoanalytical critics—employs a particular set of interpretive strategies for (re)writing (that is, producing) texts and for constituting their properties, intentions, and meanings. Such preestablished strategies determine the shape of meaning, which thus is neither prior to nor independent of the act of interpretation.

The New Critics approach meaning quite differently. They warn against the "heresy of paraphrase," emphasizing that it is a mistake for a reader to paraphrase a work's content in order to distill its propositional meaning. Textual paraphrases usually end up being moral or utilitarian statements, putting literature on a level and in competition with other disciplines such as philosophy, religion, or politics. By invoking the "affective fallacy" and "intentional fallacy," two related and equally famous New Critical concepts, they forbid us to locate meaning in the emotional responses of the reader or in the intentions of the author, respectively. According to the New Critics, the literary artifact does not need the support of such external agents if it is well made. The sense of *meaning* becomes complex and abstract for these formalists. On the one hand, it is a secondary, relatively unimportant feature of literary structure; on the other, it is an aesthetic concept of organic unity that reconciles textual incongruities in the name of irony, paradox, or ambiguity. New Criticism is most celebrated for telling us what meaning is not: it is not propositional truth, nor the author's intention, nor a reader's response.

To help clarify the concept, some theorists, such as E. D. Hirsch Jr., have added the notion of significance. While significance changes, meaning does not. Here meaning is construed as a fixed, self-identical, reproducible object derived from the author's intention. Significance, which builds on meaning, adds the reader's personal associations, interests, values, and contexts. Over time a text may come to have a different significance but not a different meaning. The reader therefore operates on two levels, one subjective and one objective, with the latter seen as higher.

Meaning is often understood as having multiple levels, with the reader playing different roles as part of one complicated task. Consider approaches as different as the medieval division of textual meaning into four levels (literal, allegorical, moral, mystical), which emphasizes the spiritual realm, and Fredric Jameson's Marxist attention to three horizons of meaning (social stratification, class struggle, mode of production), which aims to discover the utopian elements of cultural texts. Such levels or horizons inevitably are set in hierarchies, a process that leads to disagreements among theorists as they argue over which should take priority.

No concepts of meaning or notions of the reader and the reading process should be taken at face value by students of theory. They should be thought of as complex problematics perennially at issue, likely to crop up at any point in discussions about criticism and interpretation.

STRUCTURALISM AND SEMIOTICS

Pioneering concepts and methods of structural linguistics and anthropology have strongly influenced how modern theory and criticism understand cultural phenomena. Out of structuralist methodology has come the discipline of semiotics or semiology, a field that studies sign systems, codes, and conventions of all kinds, ranging from human to animal languages, the language of fashion to the lexicon of food, the codes of diagnostic medicine to those of written literature. By extension, literary semiotics construes its primary object of analysis to be literature as a system, while social (or cultural) semiotics explores culture as a set of interlocking systems and subsystems.

The model for structuralist thinking is Ferdinand de Saussure's pioneering linguistics, which centers not on individual utterances but on the underlying rules and conventions that enable language to operate. Saussurean structuralism analyzes the social or collective dimensions of language, focusing on grammar rather than usage, rules rather than actual expressions, and *langue* (the system of language) rather than *parole* (actual speech). This linguistics is concerned with the infrastructure of language common to all speakers at a given time (which operates on an unconscious level), and not with surface phenomena or historical change. Thus it attends to the synchronic (that which exists now) not the diachronic (that which exists and changes over time).

In valuing deep structure over surface phenomena, structuralism strongly resembles Marxism and psychoanalysis, both of which examine underlying causes and transpersonal forces of complex systems, shifting attention away from individual human consciousness and choice. Structuralism thereby shares in the widespread and ongoing modern antihumanism that decenters the individual, portraying the self as a construct and a consequence of impersonal systems. Individuals neither originate nor control the conventions of their social existence, mental life, or mother tongue. Rather, they are created by social and cultural systems, within which they are subjects. For this reason, many contemporary theorists, especially structuralist, Marxist, and psychoanalytical critics, prefer the terms *subject* and *subjectivity* to *person* or *individual*.

To get a sense of the kinds of projects that structuralism and semiotics might undertake, consider the fashion system. As members of a society, people know which items of clothing, textures, colors, and styles go with which. In most Western societies today, sneakers don't fit with a tuxedo, a top hat doesn't work with jeans and a T-shirt, and a pair of red shoes, an orange skirt, and a purple blouse simply don't go together. Few people would be able to supply a complete written description of all the unconscious but well-known rules of dress, but such a list could be created—by structuralists and semioticians. Similarly, sophisticated readers as well as authors possess a considerable amount of knowledge in the form of not-quite-explicit conventions and rules of reading, which structuralist poetics aims to chart. Most stories can be reduced to one of a few underlying basic plots, and most characters are variations on a few types, which structuralist narratology aims to inventory.

POSTSTRUCTURALISM AND DECONSTRUCTION

In recent decades, poststructuralism has set the terms and the agenda for many of the major developments and debates in the field of theory and criticism. It has played a significant role in shaping the direction of other schools and movements, particularly feminist criticism, postcolonial theory, cultural studies, film studies, and queer theory. Originally a vanguard movement of French literary intellectuals and philosophers who came into prominence during the 1960s and 1970s and who all were critical of structuralism, it quickly spread to intellectuals around the globe. By the close of the twentieth century, poststructuralism had become the leading edge of postmodernism and was often labeled "postmodern theory."

We have already touched on some of the main features of poststructuralism. They include the problematizing of linguistic referentiality, an emphasis on heteroglossia, the decentering of the subject, the rejection of "reason" as universal or foundational, the criticism of humanism, and a stress on difference.

Poststructuralist accounts of literature often stem from deconstructive theory, especially its three interconnected concepts of textuality (or floating signifiers), rhetoricity, and intertextuality. Because the signifier (word) is disconnected from the signified (concept) and the referent (thing), language floats or slides in relation to reality, a condition made more severe with the additional sliding introduced into language by figurative language, such as metaphors and metonymies. Such rhetoricity (as it is called) adds layers of substitutions and supplements (more differences) to floating signifiers. Textuality and rhetoricity are conditioned by yet a third sliding or differential element, intertextuality—a text's dependence on prior words, concepts, connotations, codes, conventions, unconscious practices, and texts. Every text is an intertext that borrows, knowingly or not, from the immense archive of previous culture. The term *(inter)textuality*, with the parentheses, captures the sense of textuality as being conditioned by this inescapable historical intertext.

The technical term *dissemination* is commonly employed to name the deconstructive concept of textual meaning; rather than being simply ambiguous or paradoxical, as in earlier New Criticism, meaning here is sliding, abyssal, undecidable. The linguistic, rhetorical, and intertextual properties of language undermine or deconstruct stable meaning. Poststructuralist theories of language, whether they focus on floating signifiers, rhetoricity, intertextuality, dissemination, *écriture féminine*, or elsewhere, typically bring traditional mimetic, expressive, didactic, and formalist theories into crisis but do not flatly invalidate their claims. This "undecidability," a particular hallmark of Jacques Derrida's and Paul de Man's deconstruction, galvanizes opponents—particularly when joined to the related poststructuralist claim of the "death of the author," which explicitly disconnects the text from any grounding in authorial intention or psychology.

Deconstructive conceptions of reading as both misreading and misprision, discussed earlier, do not signal an end to textual interpretation but change its grounds. The redoubled reading typical of much deconstruction rests on claims of interest and insight, not of validity or truth. A reading or interpretation of a text does not prove but persuades: it is more or less compelling, productive, original, or useful. This pragmatic set of criteria links deconstruction with contemporary U.S. neopragmatism, an influential philosophy that insists on the contingency of all human arrangements and concepts.

Deconstruction originated in the name of a special difference (or *différance*), stemming from both structural linguistics and phenomenological philosophy. It denotes the structure of differences that defines both the sliding (differential) operation of the signifier-signified complex and, more abstractly, the being of entities that are already differentiated and divided because they necessarily exist in space and in time. Leftist-oriented deconstruction extends these concepts of ontological difference and differential meaning to include sociopolitical differences in class, gender, sexuality, race, and ethnicity. There is perhaps no more vexed term in contemporary poststructuralist theory than *difference*.

Deconstruction is not just a school but also an analytic procedure developed by Derrida, a historian of philosophy, that has become a methodological instrument widely used by all manner of literary and cultural theorists and critics. "A deconstruction" involves *inversion* and *reinscription* of a traditional philosophical opposition. First, one locates in a chosen text a significant conceptual opposition (for example, nature/culture, purity/contamination, animality/humanity, or male/female) at a moment of maximum instability. To invert the binary pair, one shows how the belated second term is actually indispensable and constitutively prior to the primary term. For instance, it is from the vantage point of culture that nature is named and defined; similarly, the idea of purity depends on the prior possibility of contamination. To reinscribe the terms of the opposition, one must destabilize and transform—deconstruct—the usual understanding of the concepts, especially their temporal and hierarchical relations. Thus Derrida famously deconstructed the speech/writing opposition by showing how writing precedes speech; characteristically, he reinscribes the concept of writing (*écriture* in French) to mean any and all forms of inscription and at the same time undercuts the privileging of speech as face-to-face spontaneous utterance.

Certain significant strands of poststructuralism focus on desire, the body, and subjectivity rather than on textuality, rhetoricity, and deconstruction. Two cases mentioned earlier (in the discussion of psychoanalytic criticism) are the theories of *écriture féminine* and the anti-oedipus. In this domain—where psychoanalysis, gender studies, cultural studies, and poststructuralism intersect—the problems of subject formation, gender identity, and political resistance link poststructuralism not only with cultural studies and feminist theory but also with postcolonial criticism, queer theory, and related movements and schools. By comparison, the deconstructive strands of poststructuralism concerned with the rhetoricity and undecidability of literary texts seem narrowly focused, conservative, formalistic, and apolitical. Poststructuralism in its political form is also interested in popular culture, minority literatures, radical politics, "deviant" subjectivities, and the dynamics of hegemonic institutions. A great deal of common ground, therefore, is shared by politically oriented poststructuralism, Marxism, and postmodern social activism such as the feminist, lesbian and gay rights, and ethnic civil rights movements. The commingling of approaches, disciplines, and movements can be quite confusing, but it has produced some of the most interesting and original criticism and theory of recent times.

FEMINISM AND QUEER THEORY

Feminist criticism is part of the broader feminist political movement that seeks to rectify sexist discrimination and inequalities. While there is no single feminist literary criticism, there are a half dozen interrelated projects: exposing masculinist stereotypes, distortions, and omissions in male-dominated literature; studying female creativity, genres, styles, themes, careers, and literary traditions; discovering and evaluating lost and neglected literary works by women; developing feminist theoretical concepts and methods; examining the forces that shape women's lives, literature, and criticism, ranging across psychology and politics, biology and cultural history; and creating new ideas of and roles for women, including new institutional arrangements. Feminist theory and criticism have brought revolutionary change to literary and cultural studies by expanding the canon, by critiquing sexist representations and values, by stressing the importance of gender and sexuality, and by proposing institutional and social reforms.

Theorists of a "feminist aesthetic" argue that women have a literature of their own, possessing its own images, themes, characters, forms, styles, and canons. In Elaine Showalter's pioneering account of British novelists from the early nineteenth century to the 1970s, for example, women writers form a subculture sharing distinctive economic, political, and professional realities, all of which help determine specific problems and artistic preoccupations that mark women's literature. Sandra M. Gilbert and Susan Gubar propose that nineteenth-century women writers had to negotiate alienation and psychological disease in order to attain literary authority, which they achieved by reclaiming the heritage of female creativity, remembering their lost foremothers, and refusing the debilitating cultural roles of *angel* and *monster* assigned to them by patriarchal society. Countering Harold Bloom's masculinist "anxiety of influence" (explained above), Gilbert and Gubar's "anxiety of authorship" depicts the precursor poet as a sister or mother whose example enables the creativity of the latecomer writer to develop collaboratively against the confining and sickening backdrop of forbidding male literary authority. Diseases common among women in male-dominated, misogynistic societies include agoraphobia, anorexia, bulimia, claustrophobia, hysteria, and madness in general, and they recur in the images, themes, and characters of women's literature.

As Judith Fetterley insists in *The Resisting Reader: A Feminist Approach to American Fiction* (1978), women read differently than men. She examines classic American fiction from Irving and Hawthorne to Hemingway and Mailer and points out that this is not "universal" but masculine literature, which forces women readers to identify against themselves. Such literature neither expresses nor legitimates women's experiences, and in reading it women have to think as men, identify with male viewpoints, accept male values and interests, and tolerate sexist hostility and oppression. Under such conditions, women must become "resisting readers" rather than assenting ones, using feminist criticism as one way both to challenge male domination of the institutions of literature and to change society.

As concepts such as the anxiety of authorship, *écriture féminine*, and the potential of the Imaginary order suggest, psychoanalysis is fundamental to a great deal of feminist theory and criticism. However, feminist psychoanalysis is typically revisionist: it has had to work through and criticize the "phallocentric" presuppositions and prejudices of Sigmund Freud, Jacques Lacan, and other pioneering psychoanalysts. For example, the feminine anxiety of authorship—in its opposition to the masculine anxiety of influence—reconfigures the "oedipal" relationship between writers as cooperative and nurturing rather than competitive and rivalrous. Similarly, *écriture féminine* transforms Lacan's idea of the Imaginary, casting it not simply as an infantile sphere of primary drives superseded on the way to the patriarchal Symbolic order but as a liberating domain of bodily rhythms and pulsations associated with the mother that permeates literature, especially modern experimental poetry. Moreover, the pre-Symbolic Imaginary order, a realm of bisexual/androgynous/polymorphous sexuality, opens the possibility of sexual liberation from the suffocating confines of the "compulsory heterosexuality" that dominates patriarchal culture.

Within feminist circles, there are political differences and conflicts of interest among women of color and white women, women from different classes, women of different sexualities, women belonging to different nations and groups, and women who are liberals, conservatives, radicals, and revolutionaries. Black women have complained that white middle-class women, in academia as well as in the mass media, often end up speaking for feminism or for all women, even though they tend to represent only their own interests. Third world women, abroad and at home (Latinas, aboriginals, Asian women), feel similarly silenced and unrepresented in mainstream social agendas, which rarely consider their needs or issues. Lesbian women have likewise organized themselves to ensure that their voices are heard. The "politics of difference" opens onto a world of differences and multiple identities among and within women themselves.

One of the main flash points among feminist critics has been identity politics, by which is meant a politics of difference based on some fixed or definable identity (as a middle-class white woman, a working-class black woman, a third world brown woman, and so on). Critics of identity politics have several major complaints. To begin with, defining feminist identity by giving priority to race or class or geography tends to essentialize these features, reducing people to social indicators whose "real essence" is determined by race or class or country of origin. Moreover, an emphasis on the multiplicity of female identities undermines the solidarity and united front of feminists. Advocates of the politics of difference respond, in turn, that the act of herding all women into one homogeneous category (Woman) is a reductive totalization and very unlikely to disturb the dominant order. They argue that alliances and coalitions, in strategic cooperation with other new social movements, will best and most democratically address issues of equality and recognition. In the spheres of theory and criticism, the politics of difference opposes universal notions of traditional humanism and promotes two key ideas: there are many women's literatures across the globe, and there are many modes of resistance and of resisting reading.

An influential field that has built on ideas from feminist criticism, gender studies, women's studies, and lesbian and gay studies is queer theory. It begins by criticizing the dominant heterosexual binary, masculine/feminine, which enthrones "the" two sexes and casts other sexualities as abnormal, illicit, or criminal. Queer theory attacks the homophobic and patriarchal basis of heterosexuality. It aims beyond lesbian and gay rights philosophies to study other so-called perverse, deviant, and alternative sexualities. For example, queer theorists investigate the historical developments of such categories as *sodomite*, *hermaphrodite*, and *homosexual*, as well as *woman* and *man*, stressing the socially constructed character of sexualities. Of particular interest are transgressive phenomena such as drag, camp, cross-dressing, and transsexuality, all of which highlight the nonbiological, performative aspects of gender construction. To be "masculine" or "feminine" requires practicing an array of rituals (which cross-dressers faithfully mimic and parody in the production of gender identity).

POSTCOLONIAL STUDIES AND RACE AND ETHNICITY STUDIES

Postcolonial studies is an interdisciplinary field that examines the global impact of European colonialism, from its beginnings in the fifteenth century up to the present. Broadly speaking, it aims to describe the mechanisms of colonial power, to recover excluded or marginalized "subaltern" voices, and to theorize the complexities of colonial and postcolonial identity, national belonging, and globalization.

One major issue concerns the nature of representation. Following the groundbreaking example of Edward Said's *Orientalism*, postcolonial critics have examined the ways in which Western representations of third world countries serve the political interests of their makers. Postcolonial critics problematize "objective" perception, pointing out the unbalanced power relations that typically shape the production of knowledge. They argue that the West has constructed the third world as an "Other." Such ideological projections typically become the negative terms of binary oppositions in which the positive terms are normative representations of the West. Further, these damaging stereotypes circulate through anthropological, historical, and literary texts, as well as mass media such as newspapers, television, and cinema.

A related line of inquiry in postcolonial theory studies how institutions of Western education function in the spread of imperialism. Historical documents such as Thomas Babington Macaulay's "Minute on Indian Education" show that education—including the study of English literature and the English language—plays a strategic part in ruling over colonized peoples. As it inculcates Western Eurocentric values, literary education supports a kind of "cultural colonization," creating a class of colonial subjects often burdened by a double consciousness and by divided loyalties. It helps Western colonizers rule by consent rather than by violence. The nature of this enterprise has led some—for example, Ngugi wă Thiong'o, Henry Owuor Anyumba, and Taban lo Liyong in "On the Abolition of the English Department"—to call for the dismantling of institutions of Western education in the third world.

The realization of the extent to which the cultures of colonizers and colonized interact has prompted reflections on the hybrid nature of culture. No culture, one argument goes, is ever pure. This insight is everywhere evident in our own era of globalized postindustrial capitalism: the nationalism that undergirds notions of pure culture is daily called into question by the international flows of commodities, money, information, technology, and workers. These dynamics of globalization, hybridization, and nationalism preoccupy scholars of postcolonial studies.

Postcolonial literary criticism focuses specifically on literatures produced by subjects in the context of colonial domination, most notably in Africa, Asia, and the Caribbean. Building on knowledge of the institutions of Western education and the hybrid nature of culture, the analysis of postcolonial literature characteristically explores the complex interactions and antagonisms between native, indigenous, "precolonial" cultures and the imperial cultures imposed on them.

The concerns of postcolonial literary studies overlap with those of race and ethnicity studies, a broad field that examines a wide array of topics (including literature) related to minority ethnic groups; in North America these would include African, Asian, Hispanic, and Native peoples, among others. Consider the case of African Americans, whose history has included deportation, slavery, oppression, and struggle. Some scholars argue that the black community in the United States has evolved a distinctive and separate way of life, neither Anglo-Saxon nor African. The character of African American arts is communal rather than individualistic, their psychology is repudiative rather than accommodative of racism, and their tradition is oral-musical rather than textual: they possess their own values, styles, customs, themes, techniques, and genres. In the past, mainstream white critics have found the black arts to be grotesque, humorous, entertaining, inferior. African American artists have responded variously; sometimes adopting white values and forms, or rejecting them outright, or blending them into a hybrid. Literary critics engaged in race and ethnicity studies analyze the nature and dynamics of minority literatures, usually focusing on one literature but occasionally examining as well the context of dominant cultures (thereby overlapping with postcolonial studies).

CULTURAL STUDIES AND NEW HISTORICISM

Theories concerned with literature and its interpretation almost inevitably touch on ideas about culture. If we define *culture* as the aggregate of language, knowledge, belief, morality, law, custom, and art collectively acquired by human beings, then it is easy to see how the contents and forms of culture supply the materials and procedures of literature and criticism. As a way of life (and sphere of struggle), culture obviously encompasses elements not only of elite but also of popular and mass arts and practices. Yet the contemporary recognition of "low-" and "middle-brow" culture is something new in the long history of modern cultural criticism, which for several centuries has focused mainly on exceptional and elite forms. In recent decades cultural critics have started paying serious attention to mass, popular, and everyday materials, usually in the context of their ideologies (dominant ideas and values). Those in the discipline now called cultural studies, in particular, have begun studying such discourses as television, cinema, advertising, rock music, magazines, minority literatures, and popular literature (thrillers, science fiction, romances, westerns, Gothic fiction), characteristically focusing on how such materials are produced, distributed, and consumed.

While researchers in cultural studies employ various methods, including surveys, field-based studies, textual interpretations, historical background studies, and participant observations, institutional analysis and ideology critique have been especially important. Critics interested in present-day popular romances, for instance, have examined the practices of institutions such as publishing companies and bookstores in shaping and maintaining the rules of the romance genre as well as in packaging and promoting successful reproductions of the form. Since institutions overlap and connect with satellite institutions, an investigation into one often leads to another. In the case of romance, one who began by scrutinizing the genre's presence in television soap operas and women's magazines would soon find links to publishers, literary agents, booksellers, television programmers, magazine editors, and authors. Because circuits of institutions play such important roles in creating, conditioning, and commodifying cultural discourses, their analysis is central to the enterprise of cultural studies.

Ideology critique critically examines the ideas, feelings, beliefs, values, and representations embedded in, and promoted by, the artifacts and practices of a culture or a group. It overlaps with institutional analysis. For instance, in *English in America*, Richard Ohmann describes how the institution of English studies itself disseminates not only the practical skills of analysis, organization, and literacy but also the values of detachment, caution, and cooperation, all of which aid the smooth operation of contemporary capitalist societies. Associated with the professional managerial classes, such attitudes and manners (ideology) are invisible yet ever present in English classrooms, as well as in places of employment.

Some literary critics have opposed cultural studies, particularly criticizing the twin displacements of the canon (the body of works traditionally accepted as "great") by popular culture and of poetic explication by sociological analyses, especially ideology critique. Because cultural studies deals with issues of conflict, domination, class struggle, minorities, state power, and ideology, they fault it for politicizing the discipline. Often this debate sets multiculturalism and analysis attentive to race, class, and gender against literary appreciation and close reading.

Yet many literary scholars have incorporated the concerns of cultural studies into the historical analysis of literature, examining class conflicts, hegemonic forces, and racial and gender codes in such texts as William Shakespeare's plays, Charles Dickens's novels, and Walt Whitman's poetry. Particularly important in this regard is the critical movement known as the "New Historicism" (a term coined in the early 1980s by Stephen Greenblatt). New Historicists study literary texts not as autonomous objects but as material products emerging out of specific social, cultural, and political contexts. This view of literature breaks down the traditional distinction between literary and nonliterary texts and forms. Typically, New Historicists demonstrate the ways in which the power relations of a particular era shape how literature is produced, distributed, and consumed, making use of a wide range of contemporary materials—everything from diaries and travel writings to legal documents to medical and penal records. Some dismiss such historical literary investigations as watered-down, co-opted cultural analysis, not cultural studies proper.

Cultural studies advocates argue that what counts as literature changes from one time, place, and group to another. Before the eighteenth century in western Europe, the word *literature* designated all books and writing. Only during the neoclassical and Romantic eras did literature come to be more narrowly defined as belles lettres. Perhaps contemporary debates over the concept of literature may be seen as staging a return to the older definition; in any case, they explicitly contest the aestheticizing or refining of literature typical of the modern age.

Cultural studies offers distinctive answers to the two key questions with which we began—what is interpretation? what is literature? First, literature consists of popular, mass, and minority genres as well as elite canonical works. It includes a wide array of discursive materials, from writings in standard literary genres to rap lyrics, blues poems, oral legends, diaries, magazines, movies, posters, romances, soap operas, and so on. With a different population or in another time or place, literature would be differently defined. There is one constant in this culturally relative definition: literature is symptomatic of the state of its society. Second, interpretation employs institutional analysis, ideology critique, and field-based research, as well as textual explication, exegesis, aesthetic appreciation, and personal response. For cultural studies, personhood (or subjectivity) involves three things: the operations of our unconscious, the effects of surrounding sociohistorical forces, and the multiple subject positions that each individual occupies. This complex view of subjectivity applies to the author, not just the critic: authored texts by definition contain unconscious and socially symptomatic materials unique to specific times, places, and persons. It is thus no surprise that cultural studies and formalist literary criticism are seen as opposed, antagonistic critical projects—one expansive and wide-ranging, the other contracted and tightly focused; one engaged with psychology, sociology, and politics, the other wedded to aesthetics and poetics.

There are very good reasons that, as Jonathan Culler observes, contemporary theory now frames the study of literature and culture in academic institutions. Theory raises and answers questions about a broad array of fundamental issues, some old and some new, pertaining to reading and interpretive strategies, literature and culture, tradition and nationalism, genre and gender, meaning and paraphrase, originality and intertextuality, authorial intention and the unconscious, literary education and social hegemony, standard language and heteroglossia, poetics and rhetoric, representation and truth, and so on. In addition, theory opens literary and cultural studies to neighboring disciplines and numerous national traditions. And it reinvigorates the field not only by reexamining the canonical list of great works and the tool kit of basic concepts and methods but also by recasting the received interpretations of old texts and frameworks and by revealing interesting new zones of meaning and possibilities for future critical inquiry.

Theorists are fond of pointing out that everyone has a theory, about the world as well as about literature and interpretation, and that theories must be examined, debated, and tested. Plato suggested long ago that the unexamined life is not worth living, providing a worthy credo for philosophers—and for students of theory and criticism.

Theory and Criticism

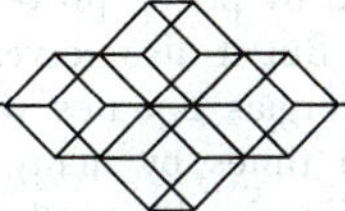

GORGIAS OF LEONTINI
ca. 483–376 B.C.E.

With its observations on the power of speech (*logos*), Gorgias's "Encomium of Helen" develops a classical rhetoric antithetical to Platonic poetics, one that anticipates JACQUES DERRIDA's twentieth-century critique of PLATO. Where Plato commends moral content, Gorgias praises elegant form; where Plato is didactic, Gorgias aims to persuade through performance; where Plato—and those who followed him, like AUGUSTINE—condemns rhetoric as dangerously false, Gorgias embraces it. Speech, Gorgias wrote in another fragment, "summons whoever wishes [to compete], but crowns the one who is able." The highly wrought style for which he is justly famous, with its frequent use of paradox, antithesis, balancing clauses, and rhyme, has its closest modern parallel in OSCAR WILDE's celebrated epigrammatic style. Like Wilde, Gorgias raises significant issues about the radical contingency of all truth claims, issues that have been central to contemporary theoretical debates.

Gorgias came from a Greek colony in Sicily and, by all accounts, lived to be more than one hundred years old. Nothing is known of his life until he came to Athens in 427 B.C.E. as part of an embassy from his native Leontini. There his dazzling oratorical style, whose force is difficult to capture in translation, made him something of a sensation; he quickly became one of the most influential of the sophists, a group of itinerant teachers who went from city to city earning their living by instructing others in subtle argumentation. Although later writers would credit them with philosophical doctrines, in particular a skepticism about the claims of reason to arrive at truth, the sophists were members of a profession and not a school of thought. That we today use the term *sophistry* to refer to plausible but fallacious arguments reflects the influence of the sophists' critics.

Gorgias confined himself almost exclusively to the teaching of oratory—rhetoric—which was the main road to success in Greek city-states. In the *Meno*, Plato writes that he admired Gorgias because he did not claim to be a teacher of *aretē*, or virtue; "in fact, he laughs at others he hears making such promises. He thinks one should make men skillful at speaking." Only fragments of Gorgias's rhetorical works survive, primarily in the form of commonplaces, or rhetorical exercises that were used to instruct others. The "Encomium of Helen" is an example of this genre, as is the longer fragment in defense of Palamides, a minor Greek hero at Troy. Gorgias concludes his defense of Helen, "I wished to write this speech for Helen's encomium and my amusement," suggesting that like the other fragments of his speeches that survive, it was an epideictic composition—a display piece intended to demonstrate the principles of rhetoric to his pupils, presumably accompanied by a verbal commentary that has not survived.

The extant "Encomium of Helen" illustrates Gorgias's flamboyant style, which Plato later parodied in Agathon's speech in the *Symposium*. The defense of Helen of Troy, a character long vilified by poets, proves a fitting challenge for the even most accomplished rhetorician. But it also serves as a pretext for a discussion of the power of speech, which Gorgias equates with the force of compulsion, an argument developed in modern times by many critics, most notably FRIEDRICH NIETZSCHE and PAUL DE MAN. Gorgias likens the power of speech to persuade to the power of magical charms or drugs to alter the mind or body. He has none of Plato's firm belief that right reasoning will ultimately lead to truth. Speech is as likely to lead to "evil persuasion" as to correct action. The elaborate antitheses and paradoxes of Gorgias's style may express the belief that since truth exists but is contingent, a clear expression of contrasts and alternatives is needed if one is to sift through the competing claims of persuasive speech. In the history of theory and criticism, rhetoric continually raises such problems as the truth status of language, the power and pleasure of persuasive discourse, and the reliability of figures and tropes.

BIBLIOGRAPHY

D. M. MacDowell has published the Greek text of the *Encomium on Helen* with a parallel English translation (1989). Michael Gagarin and Paul Woodruff include all the extant fragments attributed to Gorgias in *Early Greek Political Thought from Homer to the Sophists* (1995). Their translations are based on the Greek text established by Thomas Buchheim in his edition with German translation, *Reden, Fragmente, und Testimonien* (1989). The standard account of the sophists is *The Sophists* by W. K. C. Guthrie; the volume, published separately in 1971, was originally part of volume 3 of his *History of Greek Philosophy* (6 vols., 1962–81). George Kerferd offers a comprehensive interpretation of the whole movement in *The Sophistic Movement* (1981). Susan C. Jarratt's *Rereading the Sophists: Classical Rhetoric Refigured* (1991) reads the sophists with and against contemporary literary theories, including feminism and deconstruction. C. J. Classen's *Sophistik* (1976) includes a thorough and useful bibliography.

From Encomium of Helen[1]

[1] For a city the finest adornment (*kosmos*) is a good citizenry, for a body beauty, for a soul wisdom, for an action *aretē*,[2] and for a speech truth; and the opposites of these are indecorous. A man, woman, speech, deed, city or action that is worthy of praise should be honored with acclaim, but the unworthy should be branded with blame. For it is equally error and ignorance to blame the praiseworthy and praise the blameworthy. [2] The man who speaks correctly what ought to be said has a duty to refute those who find fault with Helen. Among those who listen to the poets a single-voiced, single-minded conviction has arisen about this woman, the notoriety of whose name is now a reminder of disasters. My only wish is to bring reason to the debate, eliminate the cause of her bad reputation, demonstrate that her detractors are lying, reveal the truth, and put an end to ignorance.

1. Translated by Michael Gagarin and Paul Woodruff, who occasionally include the Greek in parentheses.
2. Excellence or virtue (Greek).

[3] That the woman I speak of is by nature and birth the foremost of the foremost, men or women, is well known by all.[3] Clearly her mother was Leda and her father in fact a god, but in story a mortal: Zeus and Tyndareus. One was thought to be her father because he was, the other was reported to be because he said he was; one was mightiest of men, the other tyrant of all. [4] Born from such as these, she equaled the gods in beauty, not concealed but revealed. Many were the erotic passions she aroused in many men, and her one body brought many bodies full of great ambition for great deeds; some had abundant wealth, some the glory of an old noble lineage, some the vigor of personal valor, and some the power of acquired wisdom. All came for love that desires to conquer and from unconquerable desire for honor. [5] Who it was or why or how he took Helen and fulfilled his love, I shall not say. For to tell those who know something they know carries conviction, but does not bring pleasure. Now that my speech has passed over the past, it is to the beginning of my future speech that I proceed and propose the likely reasons for Helen's journey to Troy.

[6] Either she did what she did because of the will of fortune and the plan of the gods and the decree of necessity, or she was seized by force, or persuaded by words, ⟨or captured by love⟩. If she left for the first reason, then any who blame her deserve blame themselves, for a human's anticipation cannot restrain a god's inclination. For by nature the stronger is not restrained by the weaker but the weaker is ruled and led by the stronger: the stronger leads, the weaker follows. Now, a god is stronger than a human in strength, in wisdom, and in other respects; and so if blame must be attached to fortune and god, then Helen must be detached from her ill repute.

[7] If she was forcibly abducted and unlawfully violated and unjustly assaulted, it is clear that her abductor, her assaulter, engaged in crime; but she who was abducted and assaulted encountered misfortune. Thus, the undertaking undertaken by the barbarian was barbarous in word and law and deed and deserves blame in word, loss of rights in law, and punishment in deed. But she who was violated, from her country separated, from her friends isolated, surely (*eikotōs*) deserves compassion rather than slander. For he did and she suffered terrible things. It is right to pity her but hate him.

[8] If speech (*logos*) persuaded and deluded her mind, even against this it is not hard to defend her or free her from blame, as follows: speech is a powerful master and achieves the most divine feats with the smallest and least evident body.[4] It can stop fear, relieve pain, create joy, and increase pity. How this is so, I shall show; [9] and I must demonstrate this to my audience to change their opinion.

Poetry (*poiēsis*) as a whole I deem and name "speech (*logos*) with meter."

3. According to the Greek myth, Helen was the daughter of Zeus, who took the form of a swan before raping her mother, Leda. Before he would give her in marriage, Helen's human father, Tyndareus, made all the Greek princes swear an oath that if any wrong were done to her husband they would come to his aid. Thus the Trojan prince Paris's abduction of Helen from her husband, Menelaus, precipitated the Trojan War. Paris had been asked to judge the beauty of three goddesses; he declared the fairest to be Aphrodite, goddess of love, who had promised him the love of the world's most beautiful woman (i.e., Helen) if he chose her.

4. Gorgias seems to be describing speech as if it were a physical body, so small it cannot be seen, moving from person to person.

To its listeners poetry brings a fearful shuddering, a tearful pity, and a grieving desire, while through its words the soul feels its own feelings for good and bad fortune in the affairs and lives of others. Now, let me move from one argument to another. [10] Sacred incantations with words inject pleasure and reject pain, for in associating with the opinion of the mind, the power of an incantation enchants, persuades, and alters it through bewitchment. The twin arts of witchcraft and magic have been discovered, and these are illusions of mind and delusions of judgment. [11] How many men on how many subjects have persuaded and do persuade how many others by shaping a false speech! For if all men on all subjects had memory of the past, ⟨understanding⟩ of the present, and foresight into the future, speech would not be the same in the same way;[5] but as it is, to remember the past, to examine the present, or to prophesy the future is not easy; and so most men on most subjects make opinion an adviser to their minds. But opinion is perilous and uncertain, and brings those who use it to perilous and uncertain good fortune. [12] What reason is there, then, why Helen did not go just as unwillingly under the influence of speech as if she were seized by the violence of violators? For persuasion expelled her thought—persuasion, which has the same power, but not the same form as compulsion (*anankē*). A speech persuaded a soul that was persuaded, and forced it to be persuaded by what was said and to consent to what was done. The persuader, then, is the wrongdoer, because he compelled her, while she who was persuaded is wrongly blamed, because she was compelled by the speech. [13] To see that persuasion, when added to speech, indeed molds the mind as it wishes, one must first study the arguments of astronomers, who replace opinion with opinion: displacing one but implanting another, they make incredible, invisible matters apparent to the eyes of opinion. Second, compulsory debates with words,[6] where a single speech to a large crowd pleases and persuades because written with skill (*technē*), not spoken with truth. Third, contests of philosophical arguments, where it is shown that speed of thought also makes it easy to change a conviction based on opinion. [14] The power of speech has the same effect on the disposition of the soul as the disposition of drugs on the nature of bodies. Just as different drugs draw forth different humors from the body—some putting a stop to disease, others to life—so too with words: some cause pain, others joy, some strike fear, some stir the audience to boldness, some benumb and bewitch the soul with evil persuasion.

[15] The case has been made: if she was persuaded by speech, her fortune was evil, not her action. The fourth reason, I discuss in my fourth argument. If it was love that did all these things, she will easily escape blame for the error that is said to have occurred.

* * *

[19] So if Helen's eye, pleased by Alexander's[7] body, transmitted to her soul an eagerness and striving for love, why is that surprising? If love is a god, with the divine power of gods, how could a weaker person refuse and reject him? But if love is a human sickness and a mental weakness, it must not be blamed as mistake, but claimed as misfortune. For it came, as it came, snared

5. Text uncertain, but the sense clearly is "the same as it is now" [translators' note].
6. This expression probably designates speeches in law courts [translators' note].
7. Paris.

by the mind, not prepared by thought, under the compulsion of love, not the provision of art (*technē*).

[20] How then can the blame of Helen be considered just? Whether she did what she did, invaded by love, persuaded by speech, impelled by force or compelled by divine necessity, she escapes all blame entirely.

[21] With my speech I have removed this woman's ill repute; I have abided by the rule laid down at the beginning of my speech; I have tried to dispel the injustice of blame and the ignorance of opinion; I wished to write this speech for Helen's encomium and my amusement.

ca. 400 B.C.E.

PLATO

ca. 427–ca. 347 B.C.E.

A monumental figure in the history of Western philosophy, Plato looms nearly as large in the history of European literary theory. Indeed, for many literary scholars he marks the beginning of the tradition of literary theory, although his choice of the dialogue format, in which historical personages convey particular arguments, suggests that the issue he raises had already been debated before he took them up—as do the extant fragments of the writings of the pre-Socratic philosophers. The several dozen dialogues attributed to Plato engage almost every issue that interests philosophers: the nature of being; the question of how we come to know things; the proper ordering of human society; and the nature of justice, truth, the good, beauty, and love. Although Plato did not set out to write systematic literary theory—unlike his student ARISTOTLE, who produced a treatise on poetics—his consideration of philosophical issues in several of the dialogues leads him to reflect on poetry, and those reflections have often set the terms of literary debate in the West.

What binds together Plato's various discussions of poetry is a distrust of *mimēsis* (representation or imitation). According to Plato, all art—including poetry—is a mimesis of nature, a copy of objects in the physical world. But those objects in the material world, according to the idealist philosophy that Plato propounds, are themselves only mutable copies of timeless universals, called Forms or Ideas. Poetry is merely a copy of a copy, leading away from the truth rather than toward it. Philosophers and literary critics ever since, from PLOTINUS in the third century C.E. to JACQUES DERRIDA in the late twentieth century, have wrestled with the terms of Plato's critique of poetry, revising it or attempting to point out inconsistencies in his argument.

Plato was born about four years after the beginning of the twenty-five-year-long Peloponnesian War between Athens and Sparta and just after the death of the great Athenian statesman Pericles, who had overseen the city's artistic golden age. His parents both came from distinguished Athenian families, and his stepfather, an associate of Pericles, was an active participant in the political and cultural life of fifth-century Athens. Plato had two older brothers, Glaucon and Adeimantus, who appear as characters in his longest dialogue, *Republic* (ca. 375 B.C.E.). As a young man, growing up in a city at war and in constant political turmoil, he seems to have been destined for a political career. But after the Peloponnesian War ended in 405, with the defeat and humiliation of Athens, the excesses of Athenian political life under the oligarchical rule (404–403) of the so-called Thirty Tyrants and under the restored democracy left Plato disillusioned with political life. The execution in 399 of Socrates, on charges of impiety and corrupting the young, was a turning point in his life. The older philosopher was a close friend of Plato's family, and Plato's writings attest to Socrates' great influence on him. Indeed, the position of Socrates in European philosophy is unique. Though he apparently never wrote a word, his influence on subsequent thought through his followers, Plato in particular, is incalculable.

After Socrates' death Plato retired from Athenian political life and traveled for a number of years. In 388 he journeyed to Italy and Sicily, where he became the friend of Dionysius I, the ruler of Syracuse, and his brother-in-law Dion. The following year he returned to Athens, where he founded the Academy, an institution devoted to research and instruction in philosophy and the sciences; he taught there for the rest of his life. Plato envisioned the Academy as a school for statesmen where he could train a new kind of philosopher-ruler (or "guardian") according to the principles set forth in his *Republic*. Unlike the older sophist GORGIAS or Plato's contemporary rival Isocrates, who both taught the arts of rhetoric and persuasion, Plato focused primarily in the Academy on mathematics, logic, and philosophy. However, when Dionysius died in 367, Dion invited Plato to return to Syracuse to undertake the philosophical education of the new ruler, Dionysius II. Plato went, perhaps with the hope of putting the theory of *Republic* into practice; but philosophy proved no match for local politics and Dionysius's suspicions. Indeed, a return visit resulted in Plato's brief imprisonment; by 360 he was back at the Academy for good.

Plato is recognized as a master of the dialogue form and as one of the great prose stylists of the Greek language. His published writings, apparently all of which are preserved, consist of some twenty-six dramatic dialogues on philosophical and related themes. The central problematic posed by this form is that it becomes virtually impossible to attribute any statement directly to Plato: he never speaks in his own person. The only exceptions are a series of thirteen letters (whose authenticity is still a matter of scholarly debate) written in the last decades of Plato's life, most addressing the political situation in Syracuse. Only the seventh—and longest—letter takes up philosophical issues. For the most part, Plato places his arguments in the mouths of characters who may or may not be based on historical persons. The speakers can never be assumed to be voicing Plato's own views or the views of those whose names they bear. In almost all the dialogues, Socrates is the focal character and Plato's mouthpiece, but Plato's Socrates is not the historical Socrates. These complications, which thwart efforts to fix Plato's thought within a series of propositional statements, have attracted much attention, especially from late-twentieth-century poststructuralist philosophers like Derrida.

The chronology of Plato's dialogues is highly controversial, but most scholars divide the works roughly into three periods. The earliest works, begun after 399, include the *Apology of Socrates* and *Crito*, in which Plato defends Socrates against the charges that led to his death; *Gorgias*, in which Socrates' opponent is the sophist Gorgias; and *Ion* (one of our selections), which examines poetry as a kind of divine madness. Characteristic of these early Platonic dialogues is Socrates' disarming claim of ignorance and a formal technique of cross-examination called *elenchus*, a method of questioning designed to lead a learner through stages of reasoning and to expose the contradictions in an opponent's original statement. This method of "emptying out" the question by Socrates to reveal his opponents' ignorance is especially evident in his discussion of poetry with Ion, a rhapsode (professional reciter of epic poetry). The middle period, from 380 to 367, includes the *Symposium, Cratylus*, and *Republic*, all begun after the founding of the Academy; they develop the theory of Forms or Ideas anticipated in the early dialogues. The Forms constitute a realm of unchanging being to which the world of individual mutable objects is subordinate. Because the Forms are immutable, they are more real—and more true—than the changeable material world. The Form of the Good enjoys a unique status, for it is responsible for the being and intelligibility of the world as a whole. Plato's famous "Allegory of the Cave" in book 7 of *Republic* (one of our selections), a passage that has generated much interest among poststructuralist theorists, provides a memorable introduction to the Platonic theory of Forms, which is reiterated in book 10's equally well known critique of artistic imitation. *Cratylus* is of interest to theorists of language because the dispute in this dialogue concerns the "correctness" of names: do they point unproblematically to the "nature of things"—that is, to the Forms—as Hermogenes contends, or are they merely a matter of convention, as Cratylus argues? Socrates concludes that the matter is unresolvable, but that "no one with any understanding will commit himself or the education of his soul to names, or trust them or their givers to the point of firmly stating that he knows something." To the late period (366–360) belong *Timaeus*, which throughout the Middle Ages was Plato's most widely known work; *Critias; Sophist*; and *Phaedrus*, the latter closing with a notorious attack on writing.

In *Ion*, our opening selection, Plato's Socrates engages Ion in a debate about the nature of the rhapsode's knowledge of poetry, about the nature of poetry, and about the status of knowledge itself. Poetry, Socrates maintains, is not an art; it is a form of divine madness: "the poet is an airy thing, winged and holy, and he is not able to make poetry until he becomes inspired and goes out of his mind." This debate between the claims of inspiration and those of art would subsequently have a long history in European literary criticism. Is poetry primarily a craft with a set of rules that can be taught and learned, as HORACE, GEOFFREY OF VINSAUF, and ALEXANDER POPE argue, or is it primarily the result of inspiration or genius, as LONGINUS, PLOTINUS, FRIEDRICH VON SCHILLER, WILLIAM WORDSWORTH, RALPH WALDO EMERSON, and others, following Plato, have maintained?

Plato's Socrates goes a step further. Not only is poetry a form of divinely inspired madness, but so is criticism. "You are powerless to speak of Homer," he tells Ion, "on the basis of knowledge or mastery." Socrates uses the image of a magnet as a metaphor for divine inspiration: as a magnet attracts iron and passes that attraction along, so the gods inspire the artist, who inspires the interpreter, who, in turn, inspires the audience. For Plato's Socrates, the work of poet and critic is not divided between inspiration and rational analysis, as it is for most modern critics (see, for instance, MATTHEW ARNOLD and the New Critic CLEANTH BROOKS); rather, it lies on a continuum, and the work of the critic is no more rational than that of the poet, the critic's knowledge no more truthful.

However, it is helpful when reading Plato to remember that his dialogues don't always present a straightforward argument or arrive at a single unambiguous conclusion. The process of elenchus and Socrates' persistent irony often make it difficult to pin him down to any one position. In *Ion*, is Socrates making fun of the pomposity of the rhapsode, or does he seriously believe that whatever truth emerges from poetry and the interpretation of poetry results only from divine madness?

On the surface, it might seem that *Ion* treats poetry very differently than does the later *Republic*, our second selection, where Plato's Socrates argues that far from being divinely inspired, poets lie and ought to be banished from the ideal republic—or, at the very least, heavily censored and kept in check. But *Ion* presents a view of knowledge that is consistent with the weightier arguments in *Republic*. However divinely inspired, Socrates argues, poets' and critics' knowledge is of a different order than, and one decidedly inferior to, the knowledge of charioteers, fishermen, or philosophers. To the modern student of literature, this denigration of the poet's learning appears downright odd. Surely the standards by which the knowledge of a charioteer or a fisherman or a mathematician would be judged are irrelevant in judging the value of poetry. Why demand that the poet "know" about horses in the same way that a horseman "knows" about horses?

To understand Socrates' remarks about knowledge, the modern reader needs to understand the centrality of poetry to Greek education. In a culture in which literacy was a relatively new and suspect technology, knowledge was frequently encoded and passed on through the mnemonic devices of music and poetry. The instruction provided by the sophists and by Plato's main rival, Isocrates, was almost exclusively rhetorical and literary. Even in *Republic*, a book concerned with the ideal education of the guardians and citizens, Socrates divides schooling into physical training for the body and music and poetry for the soul. Socrates' criticism of poetry and its representations appears to be directed against a culture that believed literally "that poets know all crafts, all human affairs." In such a culture, Socrates' insistence makes more sense: a poet needs to know a horse the way a horseman knows a horse. In his Academy, however, Plato promoted a learning whose foundation was dialectics, dialogue, and philosophical reasoning.

Both the Allegory of the Cave and *Republic* 10's infamous critique of mimesis explore the nature of knowledge and its proper objects. The world we perceive through the senses, Socrates argues, is illusory and deceptive. It depends on a prior realm of separately existing Forms, organized beneath the Form of Good. The realm of Forms is accessible not through the senses, as is the world of appearances, but only through rigorous philosophic discussion and thought, based on mathematical reasoning. For Plato's Socrates, measuring, counting, and weighing all bring us closer to the realm of Forms than do poetry's pale representations of nature. All art and poetry, because they represent what is already an inferior representation of the true original (the Forms), can only lead further away from the truth, and further into a world of illusion and deception. Virtually every subsequent defense of poetry (memorable examples include those by Aristotle, SIR PHILIP SIDNEY, APHRA BEHN, and PERCY BYSSHE SHELLEY) has had to come to terms with Plato's devastating attack on poetry as inferior and deceptive mimesis.

Plato's *Phaedrus* (from which our final selection has been taken) has been of interest to contemporary literary theory for its discussion of the evils of writing. There Plato has Socrates relate the story of the invention of writing by the Egyptian god Theuth (Thoth), who offers it to King Thamus. Thamus declines the offer, deciding that humans are better off without writing because it substitutes an alien inscription—lifeless signs—for the authentic living presence of spoken language. Far from aiding memory, writing will cause it to atrophy. For Plato, the only good memory is *anamnēsis*, the recollection of spiritual truths through genuine, living wisdom: that is, through philosophy. Plato reiterates this point in his Seventh Letter, where he says: "anyone who is seriously studying high matters will be the last to write about them and thus expose his thought to the envy and criticism of men . . . [W]henever we see a book, whether the laws of a legislator or a composition on any other subject, we can be sure that if the author is really serious, the book does not contain his best thoughts; they are stored away with the fairest of his possessions. And if he has committed these serious thoughts to writing, it is because men, not the gods, 'have taken his wits away.' " Yet Plato's use of a myth in *Phaedrus* to frame his philosophical objections to writing raises questions of its own, since presumably myths suffer from the same defects as the texts of the sophists, rhetoricians, poets, and other purveyors of false wisdom whom Plato criticizes elsewhere. Derrida offers a celebrated unraveling of the logic of Plato's argument against writing in his *Dissemination* (see below), which may be the most significant encounter between a twentieth-century philosopher and Plato.

Plato is the progenitor of Western didactic criticism and theory: the idea that literature should serve moral and social functions. *Republic*, where he describes an ideal well-regulated community in which the educational curriculum promotes respect for law, reason, authority, self-discipline, and piety, has been especially influential. Although Plato's Socrates loves and regularly cites Homer's *Iliad* and *Odyssey*, he calls for the censorship of many passages in these works that represent sacrilegious, sentimental, unlawful, and irrational behavior. Above all else, he requires that literature teach goodness and grace. Plato's relentless application of this standard to all literature marks one of the most noteworthy beginnings of the ancient quarrel between philosophy and poetry.

BIBLIOGRAPHY

The standard Greek edition of the entire works of Plato, including those of dubious authorship, is *Platonis Opera*, edited by John Burnet (5 vols., 1900–1907). This edition is being updated by a team of scholars led by E. A. Duke (2 vols. to date, 1995–). For a handy one-volume English translation of selected dialogues by various translators, see *The Collected Dialogues of Plato*, edited by Edith Hamilton and Huntington Cairns (1961). *Plato: Complete Works*, edited by John M. Cooper (1997), is the most complete one-volume collection, with the best translations available (done by various hands). The best translation of *Republic* is Robin Wakefield's (1993).

A. E. Taylor's *Plato, the Man and His Work* (1926; 7th ed., 1969) contains a complete translation of Diogenes Laërtius's third-century C.E. life of Plato, which has served as the basis for modern reconstructions of the philosopher's life. Several books provide good introductions to Plato's aesthetic theory, including Whitney J. Oates, *Plato's View of Art* (1972); Iris Murdoch, *The Fire and the Sun: Why Plato Banished the Artists* (1977), which attempts to defend Plato's view of the arts; and Morriss Henry Partee, *Plato's Poetics: The Authority of Beauty* (1981). Gerald F. Else, *Plato and Aristotle on Poetry* (1986), is a comparative study of the aesthetic theory of Greece's two greatest philosophers. In *Postmodern Platos* (1985), Catherine H. Zuckert examines the centrality of Platonic thought to theorists from Friedrich Nietzsche to Jacques Derrida. Other books dealing with Plato's importance to poststructuralist criticism include Jasper Neel, *Plato, Derrida, and Writing* (1988), and *Plato and Postmodernism*, edited by Steven Shankman (1994). *The Cambridge Companion to Plato*, edited by Richard Kraut (1992), contains essays on several aspects of Plato's thought, including aesthetics. Andrea Wilson Nightingale's *Genres in Dialogue: Plato and the Construct of Philosophy* (1996) examines Plato's integration of Greek poetry and rhetoric into his dialogues. For an introduction to *Republic*, see Julia Annas, *An Introduction to Plato's "Republic"* (1981). On *Phaedrus* and Plato's discussions of rhetoric and writing, see Ronna Burger, *Plato's "Phaedrus": A Defense of a Philosophic Art of Writing* (1980); Charles Griswold Jr., *Self-Knowledge in Plato's "Phaedrus"* (1986); and David A. White, *Rhetoric and Reality in Plato's "Phaedrus"* (1993). For an advanced, close reading of this dialogue, see Seth Benardete's *Rhetoric of Morality and Philosophy: Plato's "Gorgias" and "Phaedrus"* (1994). For feminist readings of Plato, see *Feminist Interpretations of Plato*, edited by Nancy Tuala (1994). Two books that analyze the Platonic dialogue as a literary form are *Platonic Writings, Platonic Readings*, edited by Charles Griswold Jr. (1988), and Charles H. Kahn, *Plato and the Socratic Dialogue* (1996). The most complete and up-to-date bibliography can be found in *The Cambridge Companion to Plato* (cited above).

Ion[1]

[530] SOCRATES:[2] Ion! Hello. Where have you come from to visit us this time? From your home in Ephesus?

ION: No, no, Socrates. From Epidaurus, from the festival of Asclepius.[3]

1. Translated by Paul Woodruff, who sometimes adds clarifying words or phrases in square brackets; also in square brackets in the text are the Stephanus numbers used almost universally in citing Plato's works: they refer to the pages of a 1578 edition published by Henri Estienne.

2. Greek philosopher (469–399 B.C.E.) and Plato's spokesperson.

3. Greco-Roman hero and god of healing. Epidaurus: small Greek state on a peninsula of the Saronic Gulf, famed for its 4th-century B.C.E. temple of Asclepius.

SOCRATES: Don't tell me the Epidaurians hold a contest for *rhapsodes*[4] in honor of the god?

ION: They certainly do! They do it for every sort of poetry and music.

SOCRATES: Really! Did you enter the contest? And how did it go for you?

ION: First prize, Socrates! We carried it off.

SOCRATES: That's good to hear. Well, let's see that we win the games at Athens, next.

ION: We'll do it, Socrates, god willing.

SOCRATES: You know, Ion, many times I've envied you rhapsodes your profession. Physically, it is always fitting for you in your profession to be dressed up to look as beautiful as you can; and at the same time it is necessary for you to be at work with poets—many fine ones, and with Homer[5] above all, who's the best poet and the most divine—and you have to learn his thought, not just his verses! Now that is something to envy! I mean, no one would ever get to be a good rhapsode if he didn't understand what is meant by the poet. A rhapsode must come to present the poet's thought to his audience; and he can't do that beautifully unless he knows what the poet means. So this all deserves to be envied.

ION: That's true, Socrates. And that's the part of my profession that took the most work. I think I speak more beautifully than anyone else about Homer; neither Metrodorus of Lampsacus nor Stesimbrotus of Thasos nor Glaucon[6] nor anyone else past or present could offer as many beautiful thoughts about Homer as I can.

SOCRATES: That's good to hear, Ion. Surely you won't begrudge me a demonstration?

ION: Really, Socrates, its worth hearing how well I've got Homer dressed up. I think I'm worthy to be crowned by the Sons of Homer[7] with a golden crown.

SOCRATES: Really, I shall make time to hear that later. [531] Now I'd just like an answer to this: Are you so wonderfully clever about Homer alone—or also about Hesiod and Archilochus?[8]

ION: No, no. Only about Homer. That's good enough, I think.

SOCRATES: Is there any subject on which Homer and Hesiod both say the same things?

ION: Yes, I think so. A good many.

SOCRATES: Then, on those subjects, would you explain Homer's verse better and more beautifully than Hesiod's?

ION: Just the same Socrates, on those subjects, anyway, where they say the same things.

SOCRATES: And how about the subjects on which they do not say the same things? Divination, for example. Homer says something about it and so does Hesiod.

ION: Certainly.

4. Professional orators who recited poetry, especially that of Homer and the other epic poets.

5. Greek epic poet (ca. 8th c. B.C.E.), to whom the *Iliad* and the *Odyssey* are attributed.

6. Plato had an elder brother with this name. Metrodorus of Lampsacus (ca. 5th c. B.C.E.), interpreter of Homer. Stesimbrotus (active late 5th c. B.C.E.), biographer of Homer.

7. The Homeridae, a guild of rhapsodes devoted to reciting Homer's poetry who originally claimed to be his descendants.

8. Earliest Greek lyric poet (active ca. 650 B.C.E.). Hesiod (active ca. 700 B.C.E.), Greek epic didactic poet.

SOCRATES: Well. Take all the places where those two poets speak of divination, both where they agree and where they don't: who would explain those better and more beautifully, you, or one of the diviners if he's good?

ION: One of the diviners.

SOCRATES: Suppose *you* were a diviner: if you were really able to explain the places where the two poets agree, wouldn't you also know how to explain the places where they disagree?

ION: That's clear.

SOCRATES: Then what in the world is it that you're clever about in Homer but not in Hesiod and the other poets? Does Homer speak of any subjects that differ from those of *all* the other poets? Doesn't he mainly go through tales of war, and of how people deal with each other in society—good people and bad, ordinary folks and craftsmen? And of the gods, how *they* deal with each other and with men? And doesn't he recount what happens in heaven and in hell, and tell of the births of gods and heroes? Those are the subjects of Homer's poetry-making, aren't they?

ION: That's true, Socrates.

SOCRATES: And how about the other poets? Did they write on the same subjects?

ION: Yes, but Socrates, they didn't do it the way Homer did.

SOCRATES: How, then? Worse?

ION: Much worse.

SOCRATES: And Homer does it better?

ION: *Really* better.

SOCRATES: Well now, Ion, dear heart, when a number of people are discussing arithmetic, and one of them speaks best, I suppose *someone* will know how to pick out the good speaker.

ION: Yes.

SOCRATES: Will it be the same person who can pick out the bad speakers, or someone else?

ION: The same, of course.

SOCRATES: And that will be someone who has mastered arithmetic, right?

ION: Yes.

SOCRATES: Well. Suppose a number of people are discussing healthy nutrition, and one of them speaks best. Will one person know that the best speaker speaks best, and another that an inferior speaker speaks worse? Or will the same man know both?

ION: Obviously, the same man.

SOCRATES: Who is he? What do we call him?

ION: A doctor.

SOCRATES: So, to sum it up, this is what we're saying: when a number of people speak on the same subject, it's always the same person [532] who will know how to pick out good speakers and bad speakers. If he doesn't know how to pick out a bad speaker, he certainly won't know a good speaker—on the same subject, anyway.

ION: That's so.

SOCRATES: Then it turns out that the same person is "wonderfully clever" about both speakers.

ION: Yes.

SOCRATES: Now *you* claim that Homer and the other poets (including

Hesiod and Archilochus) speak on the same subjects, but not equally well. *He's* good, and they're inferior.

ION: Yes, and it's true.

SOCRATES: Now if you really do know who's speaking well, you'll know that the inferior speakers are speaking worse.

ION: Apparently so.

SOCRATES: You're superb! So if we say that Ion is equally clever about Homer and the other poets, we'll make no mistake. Because you agree yourself that the same person will be an adequate judge of all who speak on the same subjects, and that almost all the poets *do* treat the same subjects.

ION: Then how in the world do you explain what *I* do, Socrates? When someone discusses another poet I pay no attention, and I have no power to contribute anything worthwhile: I simply doze off. But let someone mention Homer and right away I'm wide awake and I'm paying attention and I have plenty to say.

SOCRATES: *That's* not hard to figure out, my friend. Anyone can tell that you are powerless to speak about Homer on the basis of the knowledge or mastery. Because if your ability came by mastery, you would be able to speak about all the other poets as well. Look, there is an art of poetry as a whole, isn't there?

ION: Yes.

SOCRATES: And now take the whole of *any* other subject: won't it have the same discipline throughout? And this goes for every subject that can be mastered. Do you need me to tell you what I mean by this, Ion?

ION: Lord, yes, I do, Socrates. I love to hear you wise men talk.

SOCRATES: I wish that were true, Ion. But wise? Surely you are the wise men, you rhapsodes and actors, you and the poets whose work you sing. As for me, I say nothing but the truth, as you'd expect from an ordinary man. I mean, even this question I asked you—look how commonplace and ordinary a matter it is. Anybody could understand what I meant: don't you use the same discipline throughout whenever you master the whole of a subject? Take this for discussion—painting is a subject to be mastered as a whole, isn't it?

ION: Yes.

SOCRATES: And there are many painters, good and bad, and there have been many in the past.

ION: Certainly.

SOCRATES: Have you ever known anyone who is clever at showing what's well painted and what's not in the work of Polygnotus,[9] but who's powerless to do that for other painters? [533] Someone who dozes off when the work of other painters is displayed, and is lost, and has nothing to contribute—but when he has to give judgment on Polygnotus or any other painter (so long as it's just *one*), he's wide awake and he's paying attention and he has plenty to say—have you ever known anyone like that?

ION: Good lord no, of course not!

SOCRATES: Well. Take sculpture. Have you ever known anyone who is clever at explaining which statues are well made in the case of Daedalus, son of Metion, or Epeius, son of Panopeus, or Theodorus of Samos,[1] or any

9. Greek painter from Thasos (ca. 500–ca. 440 B.C.E.), later an Athenian citizen.

1. Greek architect and sculptor (active ca. 550 B.C.E.). Daedalus: in Greek mythology, a consummately skilled Athenian artisan and artist. Epeius: mythological builder of the Trojan Horse.

other *single* sculptor, but who's lost when he's among the products of other sculptors, and he dozes off and has nothing to say?

ION: Good lord no. I haven't.

SOCRATES: And further, it is my opinion, you've never known anyone ever—not in flute-playing, not in cithara-playing, not in singing to the cithara, and not in rhapsodizing—you've never known a man who is clever at explaining Olympus or Thamyras or Orpheus or Phemius,[2] the rhapsode from Ithaca, but who has nothing to contribute about Ion, the rhapsode from Ephesus, and cannot tell when he does his work well and when he doesn't—you've never known a man like that.

ION: I have nothing to say against you on that point, Socrates. But *this* I know about myself: I speak about Homer more beautifully than anybody else and I have lots to say; and everybody says I do it well. But about the other poets I do not. Now see what that means.

SOCRATES: I do see, Ion, and I'm going to announce to you what I think that is. As I said earlier, that's not a subject you've mastered—speaking well about Homer; it's a divine power that moves you, as a "Magnetic" stone moves iron rings. (That's what Euripides called it; most people call it "Heraclian.")[3] This stone not only pulls those rings, if they're iron, it also puts power *in* the rings, so that they in turn can do just what the stone does—pull other rings—so that there's sometimes a very long chain of iron pieces and rings hanging from one another. And the power in all of them depends on this stone. In the same way, the Muse[4] makes some people inspired herself, and then through those who are inspired a chain of other enthusiasts is suspended. You know, none of the epic poets, if they're good, are masters of their subject; they are inspired, possessed, and that is how they utter all those beautiful poems. The same goes for lyric poets if they're good: just as the Corybantes[5] [534] are not in their right minds when they dance, lyric poets, too, are not in their right minds when they make those beautiful lyrics, but as soon as they sail into harmony and rhythm they are possessed by Bacchic frenzy. Just as Bacchus worshippers[6] when they are possessed draw honey and milk from rivers, but not when they are in their right minds—the soul of a lyric poet does this too, as they say themselves. For of course poets tell us that they gather songs at honey-flowing springs, from glades and gardens of the Muses, and that they bear songs to us as bees carry honey, flying like bees. And what they say is true. For a poet is an airy thing, winged and holy, and he is not able to make poetry until he becomes inspired and goes out of his mind and his intellect is no longer in him. As long as a human being has his intellect in his possession he will always lack the power to make poetry or sing prophecy. Therefore because it's not by mastery that they make poems or say many lovely things about their subjects (as you do about Homer)—but because it's by a divine gift—each poet is able to compose

2. Court singer in the palace of Odysseus in Homer's *Odyssey*. Olympus: Greek mountain, famed as the home of the gods. Thamyras: mythological Thracian bard who challenged the Muses. Orpheus: Greek musician unrivaled among mortals.

3. Natural magnets apparently came from Magnesia and Heraclia in Caria in Asia Minor, and were called after those places [translator's note]. Euripides (ca. 485–ca. 406 B.C.E.), Athenian tragedian.

4. One of the 9 daughters of Memory who preside over the arts and all intellectual pursuits.

5. Priests of the goddess Cybele, the Great Mother of the gods (whose worship spread west from Asia Minor); her followers engaged in wild and sometimes bloody dances.

6. Bacchus worshippers apparently danced themselves into a frenzy in which they found streams flowing with honey and milk (Euripides, *Bacchae* 708–11) [translator's note]. Bacchus: Greek and Roman god of wine (Bakchos is one of the names of Dionysus).

beautifully only that for which the Muse has aroused him: one can do dithyrambs, another encomia, one can do dance songs, another, epics, and yet another, iambics;[7] and each of them is worthless for the other types of poetry. You see, it's not mastery that enables them to speak those verses, but a divine power, since if they knew how to speak beautifully on one type of poetry by mastering the subject, they could do so for all the others also. That's why the god takes their intellect away from them when he uses them as his servants, as he does prophets and godly diviners, so that we who hear should know that *they* are not the ones who speak those verses that are of such high value, for their intellect is not in them: the god himself is the one who speaks, and he gives voice through them to us. The best evidence for this account is Tynnichus from Chalcis,[8] who never made a poem anyone would think worth mentioning, *except* for the praise-song everyone sings, almost the most beautiful lyric-poem there is, and simply, as he says himself, "an invention of the Muses." In this more than anything, then, I think, the god is showing us, so that we should be in no doubt about it, that these beautiful poems are not human, not even *from* human beings, but are divine and from gods; that poets are nothing but representatives of the gods, possessed by whoever possesses them. To show *that*, the god deliberately sang the most beautiful lyric poem [535] through the most worthless poet. Don't you think I'm right, Ion?

ION: Lord yes, *I* certainly do. Somehow you touch my soul with your words, Socrates, and I do think it's by a divine gift that good poets are able to present these poems to us from the gods.

SOCRATES: And you rhapsodes in turn present what the poets say.

ION: That's true too.

SOCRATES: So you turn out to be representatives of representatives.

ION: Quite right.

SOCRATES: Hold on, Ion; tell me this. Don't keep any secrets from *me*. When you recite epic poetry well and you have the most stunning effect on your spectators, either when you sing of Odysseus[9]—how he leapt into the doorway, his identity now obvious to the suitors, and he poured out arrows at his feet—or when you sing of Achilles charging at Hector, or when you sing a pitiful episode about Andromache or Hecuba or Priam,[1] are you at that time in your right mind, or do you get beside yourself? And doesn't your soul, in its enthusiasm, believe that it is present at the actions you describe, whether they're in Ithaca or in Troy or wherever the epic actually takes place?

ION: What a vivid example you've given me, Socrates! I won't keep secrets from *you*. Listen, when *I* tell a sad story, my eyes are full of tears; and when I tell a story that's frightening or awful, my hair stands on end with fear and my heart jumps.

SOCRATES: Well, Ion, should we say this man is in his right mind at times like these: when he's at festivals or celebrations, all dressed up in fancy clothes, with golden crowns, and he weeps, though he's lost none of his finery—or when he's standing among millions of friendly people and he's

7. A meter based on the syllabic pattern short-long; iambic trimeter was regularly used in the dialogue and set speeches of tragedy. "Encomia": hymns of praise. "Dithyrambs": choral poems originally sung in honor of Dionysus, later associated with highly excited music and impassioned language.
8. Greek poet known solely for his paean to Apollo, which does not survive.
9. King of Ithaca, the hero of Homer's *Odyssey*; he pours out arrows in *Odyssey* 22.
1. King of Troy; he appears in Homer's *Iliad*. Achilles: greatest Greek warrior of the Trojan War and central character of the *Iliad*. Hector: oldest son of Priam and the greatest of the Trojan warriors, slain by Achilles (see *Iliad* 22). Andromache: wife of Hector. Hecuba: wife of Priam and mother of Hector.

frightened, though no one is undressing him or doing him any harm? Is he in his right mind then?

ION: Lord no, Socrates. Not at all, to tell the truth.

SOCRATES: And you know that you have the same effects on most of your spectators too, don't you?

ION: I know very well that we do. I look down at them every time from up on the rostrum, and they're crying and looking terrified, and as the stories are told they are filled with amazement. You see I must keep my wits and pay close attention to them: if I start them crying, *I* will laugh as I take their money, but if *they* laugh, I shall cry at having lost money.

SOCRATES: And you know that this spectator is the last of the rings, don't you—the ones that I said take their power from each other by virtue of the Heraclian stone[the magnet]? The middle ring is you, [536] the rhapsode or actor, and the first one is the poet himself. The god pulls people's souls through all these wherever he wants, looping the power down from one to another. And just as if it hung from that stone, there's an enormous chain of choral dancers and dance teachers and assistant teachers hanging off to the sides of the rings that are suspended from the Muse. One poet is attached to one Muse, another to another (we say he is "possessed," and that's near enough, for he is *held*). From these first rings, from the poets, *they* are attached in their turn and inspired, some from one poet, some from another: some from Orpheus, some from Musaeus,[2] and many are possessed and held from Homer. You are one of *them*, Ion, and you are possessed from Homer. And when anyone sings the work of another poet, you're asleep and you're lost about what to say; but when any song of that poet is sounded, you are immediately awake, your soul is dancing, and you have plenty to say. You see it's not because you're a master of knowledge about Homer that you can say what you say, but because of a divine gift, because you are possessed. That's how it is with the Corybantes, who have sharp ears only for the specific song that belongs to whatever god possesses them; they have plenty of words and movements to go with *that* song; but they are quite lost if the music is different. That's how it is with you, Ion: when anyone mentions Homer, you have plenty to say, but if he mentions the others you are lost; and the explanation of this, for which you ask me—why it is that you have plenty to say about Homer but not about the others—is that it's not mastering the subject, but a divine gift, that makes you a wonderful singer of Homer's praises.

ION: You're a good speaker, Socrates. Still, I would be amazed if you could speak well enough to convince me that I am possessed or crazed when I praise Homer. I don't believe you'd think so if you heard me speaking on Homer.

SOCRATES: And I really do want to hear you, but not before you answer me this: on which of Homer's subjects do you speak well? I don't suppose you speak well on *all* of them.

ION: I do, Socrates, believe me, on every single one!

SOCRATES: Surely not on those subjects you happen to know nothing about, even if Homer does speak of them.

ION: And these subjects Homer speaks of, but I don't know about—what are they?

[537] SOCRATES: But doesn't Homer speak about professional subjects in

2. Mythical singer, closely connected with Orpheus.

many places, and say a great deal? Chariot driving, for example, I'll show you, if I can remember the lines.

Ion: No, I'll recite them. I *do* remember.

Socrates: Then tell me what Nestor says to his son Antilochus, when he advises him to take care at the turning post in the horse race they held for Patroclus'[3] funeral.

Ion: "Lean," he says,

> Lean yourself over on the smooth-planed chariot
> Just to the left of the pair. Then the horse on the right—
> Goad him, shout him on, easing the reins with your hands.
> At the post let your horse on the left stick tight to the turn
> So you seem to come right to the edge, with the hub
> Of your welded wheel. But escape cropping the stone . . .[4]

Socrates: That's enough. Who would know better, Ion, whether Homer speaks correctly or not in these particular verses—a doctor or a charioteer?

Ion: A charioteer, of course.

Socrates: Is that because he is a master of that profession, or for some other reason?

Ion: No. It's because he's a master of it.

Socrates: Then to each profession a god has granted the ability to know a certain function. I mean, the things navigation teaches us—we won't learn them from medicine as well, will we?

Ion: Of course not.

Socrates: And the things medicine teaches us we won't learn from architecture.

Ion: Of course not.

Socrates: And so it is for every other profession: what we learn by mastering one profession we won't learn by mastering another, right? But first, answer me this. Do you agree that there are different professions—that one is different from another?

Ion: Yes.

Socrates: And is this how you determine which ones are different? When *I* find that the knowledge [involved in one case] deals with different subjects from the knowledge [in another case], then I claim that one is a different profession from the other. Is that what you do?

Ion: Yes.

Socrates: I mean if there is some knowledge of the same subjects, then why should we say there are two different professions?—Especially when each of them would allow us to know the same subjects! Take these fingers: I know there are five of them, and you know the same thing about them that I do. Now suppose I asked you whether it's the same profession—arithmetic—that teaches you and me the same things, or whether it's two different ones. Of course you'd say it's the same one.

Ion: Yes.

[538] Socrates: Then tell me now what I was going to ask you earlier.

3. Achilles' dearest friend, slain by Hector. Nestor: the oldest of the Greek generals at Troy; in the *Iliad*, he often gives advice. His son Antilochus later died fighting at Troy.

4. *Iliad* 23.335–40 [translator's note].

Do you think it's the same way for every profession—the same profession must teach the same subjects, and a different profession, if it *is* different, must teach not the same subjects, but different ones?

ION: That's how I think it is, Socrates.

SOCRATES: Then a person who has not mastered a given profession will not be able to be a good judge of the things which belong to that profession, whether they are things said or things done.

ION: That's true.

SOCRATES: Then who will know better whether or not Homer speaks beautifully and well in the lines you quoted? You, or a charioteer?

ION: A charioteer.

SOCRATES: That's because you're a rhapsode, of course, and not a charioteer.

ION: Yes.

SOCRATES: And the rhapsode's profession is different from the charioteer's.

ION: Yes.

SOCRATES: If it's different, then its knowledge is of different subjects also.

ION: Yes.

SOCRATES: Then what about the time Homer tells how Hecamede, Nestor's woman, gave barley-medicine to Machaon to drink? He says something like this—

> Over wine of Pramnos she grated goat's milk cheese
> With a brazen grater. . . . And onion relish for the drink . . .[5]

Is Homer right or not: would a fine diagnosis here come from a doctor's profession or a rhapsode's?

ION: A doctor's.

SOCRATES: And what about the time Homer says:

> Leaden she plunged to the floor of the sea like a weight
> That is fixed to a field cow's horn. Given to the hunt
> It goes among ravenous fish, carrying death.[6]

Should we say it's for a fisherman's profession or a rhapsode's to tell whether or not he describes this beautifully and well?

ION: That's obvious, Socrates. It's for a fisherman's.

SOCRATES: All right, look. Suppose you were the one asking questions, and you asked me, "Socrates, since you're finding out which passages belong to each of the professions Homer treats—which are the passages that each profession should judge—come tell me this: which are the passages that belong to a diviner and to divination, passages he should be able to judge as to whether they're well or badly composed?" Look how easily I can give you a true answer. Often, in the *Odyssey*, he says things like what Theoclymenus says—the prophet of the sons of Melampus:

> [539] Are you mad? What evil is this that's upon you? Night
> Has enshrouded your hands, your faces, and down to your knees.
> Wailing spreads like fire, tears wash your cheeks.

5. *Iliad* 11.639–40 with 630 [translator's note]. Machaon: a fighter and healer in the *Iliad*.

6. *Iliad* 24.80–82 [translator's note].

Ghosts fill the dooryard, ghosts fill the hall, they rush
To the black gate of hell, they drop below darkness. Sunlight
Has died from a sky run over with evil mist.[7]

And often in the *Iliad*, as in the battle at the wall.[8] There he says:

There came to them a bird as they hungered to cross over.
An eagle, a high-flier, circled the army's left
With a blood-red serpent carried in its talons, a monster,
Alive, still breathing, it has not yet forgotten its warlust,
For it struck its captor on the breast, by the neck;
It was writhing back, but the eagle shot it groundwards
In agony of pain, and dropped it in the midst of the throng,
Then itself, with a scream, soared on a breath of the wind.[9]

I shall say that these passages and those like them belong to a diviner. They are for him to examine and judge.

ION: That's a true answer, Socrates.

SOCRATES: Well, *your* answers are true, too, Ion. Now *you* tell me—just as I picked out for you, from the *Odyssey* and the *Iliad*, passages that belong to a diviner and ones that belong to a doctor and ones that belong to a fisherman—in the same way, Ion, since you have more experience with Homer's work than I do, you pick out for me the passages that belong to the rhapsode and to his profession, the passages a rhapsode should be able to examine and to judge better than anyone else.

ION: My answer, Socrates, is "all of them."

SOCRATES: That's not *your* answer, Ion. Not "all of them." Or are you really so forgetful? But no, it would not befit a *rhapsode* to be forgetful.

[540] ION: What do you think I'm forgetting?

SOCRATES: Don't you remember you said that a rhapsode's profession is different from a charioteer's?

ION: I remember.

SOCRATES: And didn't you agree that because they are different they will know different subjects?

ION: Yes.

SOCRATES: So a rhapsode's profession, on *your* view, will not know everything, and neither will a rhapsode.

ION: But things like that are exceptions, Socrates.

SOCRATES: By "things like that" you mean that almost all the subjects of the other professions are exceptions, don't you? But then what sort of thing *will* a rhapsode know, if not everything?

ION: My opinion, anyhow, is that he'll know what it's fitting for a man or a woman to say—or for a slave or a freeman, or for a follower or a leader.

SOCRATES: So—what should a leader say when he's at sea and his ship is hit by a storm—do you mean a rhapsode will know better than a navigator?

ION: No, no. A navigator will know *that*.

7. *Odyssey* 20.351–57; line 354 is omitted by Plato [translator's note].

8. The city wall of Troy.

9. *Iliad* 12.200–207 [translator's note].

SOCRATES: And when he is in charge of a sick man, what should a leader say—will a rhapsode know better than a doctor?

ION: Not that, either.

SOCRATES: But he *will* know what a slave should say. Is that what you mean?

ION: Yes.

SOCRATES: For example, what should a slave who's a cowherd say to calm down his cattle when they're going wild—will a rhapsode know what a cowherd does not?

ION: Certainly not.

SOCRATES: And what a woman who spins yarn should say about working with wool?

ION: No.

SOCRATES: And what a man should say, if he's a general, to encourage his troops?

ION: Yes! That's the sort of thing a rhapsode will know.

SOCRATES: What? Is a rhapsode's profession the same as a general's?

ION: Well, *I* certainly would know what a general should say.

SOCRATES: Perhaps that's because you're also a general by profession, Ion. I mean, if you were somehow both a horseman and a cithara-player at the same time, you would know good riders from bad. But suppose I asked you: "Which profession teaches you good horsemanship—the one that makes you a horseman, or the one that makes you a cithara-player?"

ION: The horseman, I'd say.

SOCRATES: Then if you also knew good cithara-players from bad, the profession that taught you *that* would be the one which made you a cithara-player, not the one that made you a horseman. Wouldn't you agree?

ION: Yes.

SOCRATES: Now, since you know the business of a general, do you know this by being a good rhapsode?

ION: I don't think there's any difference.

[541] SOCRATES: What? Are you saying there's no difference? On your view is there one profession for rhapsodes and generals, or two?

ION: One, I think.

SOCRATES: So anyone who is a good rhapsode turns out to be a good general too.

ION: Certainly, Socrates.

SOCRATES: It also follows that anyone who turns out to be a good general is a good rhapsode too.

ION: No. This time I don't agree.

SOCRATES: But you do agree to this: anyone who is a good rhapsode is a good general too.

ION: I quite agree.

SOCRATES: And aren't you the best rhapsode in Greece?

ION: By far, Socrates.

SOCRATES: Are you also a general, Ion? Are you the best in Greece?

ION: Certainly, Socrates. That, too, I learned from Homer's poetry.

SOCRATES: Then why in heaven's name, Ion, when you're both the best general *and* the best rhapsode in Greece, do you go around the country giving rhapsodies but not commanding troops? Do you think Greece really needs a rhapsode who is crowned with a golden crown? And does not need a general?[1]

ION: Socrates, *my* city is governed and commanded by you [by Athens]; we don't need a general. Besides, neither your city nor Sparta would choose me for a general. You think you're good enough for that yourselves.

SOCRATES: Ion, you're superb. Don't you know Apollodorus of Cyzicus?

ION: What does *he* do?

SOCRATES: He's a foreigner who has often been chosen by Athens to be their general. And Phanosthenes of Andros and Heraclides of Clazomenae—they're also foreigners; they've demonstrated that they are worth noticing, and Athens appoints them to be generals or other sorts of officials. And do you think that *this* city, that makes such appointments, would not select Ion of Ephesus and honor him, if they thought he was worth noticing? Why? Aren't you people from Ephesus Athenians of long standing?[2] And isn't Ephesus a city that is second to none?

But *you*, Ion, you're doing me wrong, if what you say is true that what enables you to praise Homer is knowledge or mastery of a profession. You assured me that you knew many lovely things about Homer, you promised to give a demonstration; but you're cheating me, you're a long way from giving a demonstration. You aren't even willing to tell me what it is that you're so wonderfully clever *about*, though I've been begging you for ages. Really, you're just like Proteus,[3] you twist up and down and take many different shapes, till finally you've escaped me altogether by turning yourself into a general, [542] so as to avoid proving how wonderfully wise you are about Homer.

If you're really a master of your subject, and if, as I said earlier, you're cheating me of the demonstration you promised about Homer, then you're doing me wrong. But if you're not a master of your subject, if you're possessed by a divine gift from Homer, so that you make many lovely speeches about the poet without knowing anything—as *I* said about you—then you're not doing me wrong. So choose, how do you want us to think of you—as a *man* who does wrong, or as someone *divine*?

ION: There's a great difference, Socrates. It's much lovelier to be thought divine.

SOCRATES: Then *that* is how we think of you, Ion, the lovelier way: it's as someone divine, and not as master of a profession, that you are a singer of Homer's praises.

ca. 390 B.C.E.

1. The memory of Athens' defeat in the Peloponnesian War (which ended in 404 B.C.E.) was perhaps still fresh in Plato's mind when he wrote this dialogue.

2. For most of the 5th century, Ephesus, an important center of trade founded by Ionian colonists on the west coast of Asia Minor, belonged to an alliance led by Athens against the Persians.

3. Son of Poseidon (Greek god of the sea), who had both the power of prophecy and the power to change shape; when he was held fast, he would answer questions (see *Odyssey* 4.385–570).

From Republic[1]

From *Book II*

* * *

'All right, then let's devise a theoretical education for these people,[2] as if we were making up a story and weren't worried about time.'

'Yes, that's a good idea.'

'How shall we educate them, then? Or is it hard to improve on the educational system which has evolved over a long period of time? This, as you know, consists of exercise for the body and cultural studies for the mind.[3]

'Yes.'

'And shall we begin the cultural programme before the physical one?'

'Of course.'

'Cultural studies include literature, don't you think?' I asked.

'I do.'

'Aren't there two kinds of literature, true and false?'[4]

'Yes.'

[377] 'Should we include both kinds in our educational system, and start with the untrue kind?'

'I don't understand what you're getting at,' he said.

'Don't you realize,' I asked, 'that we start by telling children stories which are, by and large, untrue, though they contain elements of truth? And stories precede physical exercise in our education of children.'

'True.'

'Which is why I suggested that cultural studies should be taken up before physical exercise.'

'It was a good suggestion,' he said.

'Now, do you appreciate that the most important stage of any enterprise is the beginning, especially when something young and sensitive is involved? You see, that's when most of its formation takes place, and it absorbs every impression that anyone wants to stamp upon it.'

'You're absolutely right.'

'Shall we, then, casually allow our children to listen to any old stories, made up by just anyone, and to take into their minds views which, on the whole, contradict those we'll want them to have as adults?'

'No, we won't allow that at all.'

1. Translated by Robin Waterfield. The numbers in square brackets are the Stephanus numbers used almost universally in citing Plato's works; they refer to the pages of a 1578 edition published by Henri Estienne.

2. At this point in *Republic*, the philosopher Socrates (469–399 B.C.E., Plato's spokesperson) and Adeimantus are discussing what education the future rulers (or "guardians") of the perfect state should have. Socrates (speaking here) leads the discussion and Adeimantus follows (Socrates' other interlocutor in our selections from *Republic* is Adeimantus's brother Glaucon).

3. Nowadays we think of education, especially school education, in terms of information and skills above all. But it is important to realize that the kind of education Plato is offering here, which is primarily education of character (though reading, writing, and elementary arithmetic would be covered by the *grammatistēs*, the teacher responsible for literature, as it was in Athens), is *all* the education a contemporary Athenian child could expect: he would be taught by a *grammatistēs*, a *kitharistēs* (music and lyric poetry), and a *paidotribēs* (physical exercise). Higher (i.e. intellectual) education of any kind was a novelty, introduced by the sophists [translator's note]. Sophists: itinerant teachers of the 5th century B.C.E., they were Greece's first professional teachers (see GORGIAS).

4. I.e. fiction or non-fiction [translator's note].

'So our first job, apparently, is to oversee the work of the story-writers, and to accept any good story they write, but reject the others. We'll let nurses and mothers tell their children the acceptable ones, and we'll have them devote themselves far more to using these stories to form their children's minds than they do to using their hands to form their bodies. However, we'll have to disallow most of the stories they currently tell.'

'Which stories?' he asked.

'If we examine the grander kind of story,' I said, 'that will give us insights into the more lightweight kind as well, because the same principle must be involved and both kinds are bound to have the same effect, don't you think?'

'That sounds fine to me,' he replied, 'but I don't even understand which stories you're describing as grander.'

'The ones which Hesiod, Homer,[5] and their fellow poets tell us. In the past, it's always been the poets who've composed untrue stories to tell people, and it's no different nowadays.'

'Which stories?' he asked. 'And what's their defect, in your view?'

'There is no defect which one ought to condemn more quickly and more thoroughly,' I replied, 'especially if the lies have no redeeming feature.'

'Yes, but what *is* this defect?'

'Using the written word to give a distorted image of the nature of the gods and heroes, just as a painter might produce a portrait which completely fails to capture the likeness of the original.'

'Yes,' he said, 'it's quite right to find fault with that sort of thing. But how do they do that? What kinds of things do they say?'

'First and most important, since the subject is so important,' I said, 'there is no redeeming feature to the lies which Hesiod repeats, about Uranus' deeds and Cronus' revenge on Uranus. [378] Then there are Cronus' deeds and what his son did to him.[6] Now, I think that even if these stories are true, they oughtn't to be told so casually to young people and people who lack discrimination; it's better to keep silent, and if one absolutely has to speak, to make them esoteric secrets told to as few people as possible, who are to have sacrificed no mere piglet,[7] but something so large and rare that the smallest conceivable number of people get to hear them.'

'Yes,' he said, 'these stories are definitely dangerous.'

'And we must censor them in our community, Adeimantus,' I said. 'No young person is to hear stories which suggest that were he to commit the vilest of crimes, and were he to do his utmost to punish his father's crimes, he wouldn't be doing anything out of the ordinary, but would simply be behaving like the first and the greatest gods.'

'No, I absolutely agree,' he said. 'I share your view that these stories are unsuitable and shouldn't be repeated.'

5. Greek epic poet (ca. 8th c. B.C.E), to whom the *Iliad* and the *Odyssey* are attributed. Hesiod (active ca. 700 B.C.E.), Greek epic didactic poet.

6. Hesiod, *Theogony* 154–210, 453–506. Uranus (Heaven) hated his children and kept them packed in their mother Earth's womb, to her agony. One of the children, Cronus, was persuaded by Earth to castrate his father when he came to have sex with Earth. Cronus then became lord of creation. Cronus wanted to remain king, so he swallowed all of his children in case one of them might take over someday. Their mother Rhea, however, hid one of them away on Crete and gave Cronus a rock to swallow instead. In due course the child, Zeus, overthrew Cronus and established himself as king of the gods [translator's note].

7. A pig or piglet was a standard small sacrifice and was usual before initiation into the Eleusinian mysteries [translator's note]. "Eleusinian mysteries": secret cults at Eleusis in honor of Demeter, goddess of grain, and her daughter Persephone.

'And that's not all,' I said. 'The stories which have gods fighting and scheming and battling against one another are utterly unsuitable too, because they're just as untrue. If the prospective guardians of our community are to loathe casual quarrels with one another, we must take good care that battles between gods and giants[8] and all the other various tales of gods and heroes coming to blows with their relatives and friends don't occur in the stories they hear and the pictures they see. No, if we're somehow to convince them that fellow citizens never fall out with one another, that this is wrong, then that is the kind of story they must hear, from childhood onwards, from the community's elders of both sexes; and the poets they'll hear when they're older must be forced to tell equivalent stories in their poetry. But we'd better not admit into our community the story of Hera being tied up by her son, or the episode when Hephaestus[9] is hurled away by his father for trying to save his mother from a beating, or any of the battles between the gods which Homer has in his poetry, whether or not their intention is allegorical. The point is that a young person can't tell when something is allegorical and when it isn't, and any idea admitted by a person of that age tends to become almost ineradicable and permanent. All things considered, then, that is why a very great deal of importance should be placed upon ensuring that the first stories they hear are best adapted for their moral improvement.'

'Yes, that makes sense,' he said. 'But suppose we were once again to be asked, in this context as well, what stories we meant, how would we respond?'

'Adeimantus,' I said, 'you and I are not making up stories at the moment; we're founding a community. [379] Founders ought to know the broad outlines within which their poets are to compose stories, so that they can exclude any compositions which do not conform to those outlines; but they shouldn't themselves make stories up.'

'You're right,' he said. 'But that's precisely the point: what are these guidelines for talking about the gods?'

'They'd be something like this,' I said. 'Whatever the type of poetry—epic, lyric, or tragic—God must of course always be portrayed as he really is.'[1]

'Yes, he must.'

'Well, isn't God good, in fact, and shouldn't he be described as such?'

'Of course.'

'And nothing good is harmful, is it?'

'I don't think so.'

'Now, can anything harmless cause damage?'

'No, of course not.'

'Can anything incapable of causing damage do anything bad?'

'Again, no.'

'And something which never does bad couldn't be responsible for bad, could it?'

'Of course not.'

8. For example, the war between Zeus and the Titans, who were his father's siblings, and the later revolt by the giants, defeated by all the gods and Heracles. The Gigantomachia was a popular subject for sculpture.

9. Greek god of fire and metalworking. According to one legend, he was lamed when Zeus cast him out of heaven for defending his mother, Hera, queen of the gods (see *Iliad* 1.591–97). According to another myth, Hephaestus fashioned a throne for Hera with hidden chains, to punish her for rejecting him.

1. The Greek philosophers tend to talk equally of "God" and the "god": there is a single Divine of which the gods are various manifestations [translator's note].

'Well now, is goodness beneficial?'

'Yes.'

'And it's responsible for doing good, then?'

'Yes.'

'So goodness is not responsible for everything: it's responsible for things that are in a good state, but bad things cannot be attributed to it.'

'Exactly,' he said.

'The same goes for God too, then,' I said. 'Since he is good, he cannot be responsible for everything, as is commonly said. He is responsible only for a small part of human life, and many things cannot be attributed to him—I mean, there's far more bad than good in the world. He and he alone must be held responsible for the good things, but responsibility for bad things must be looked for elsewhere and not attributed to God.'

'I think you're absolutely right,' he said.

'So,' I said, 'we shouldn't connive at Homer or any other poet making the stupid mistake of saying about the gods, "Two jars sit on Zeus' threshold: one is full of good destinies, but the other is full of wretched destinies", and that if Zeus mixes the two up together and doles them out to someone, that person "sometimes meets with bad, sometimes with good", whereas if he doesn't mix them up, but allots the pernicious ones to someone in an unadulterated form, that person "is driven over the glorious earth by the evil of poverty".[2] Nor will we connive at them claiming that "Zeus is the dispenser of both good and evil".

'Moreover, we'll disapprove of the attribution of Pandarus' perjury and truce-breaking to the agency of Athena and Zeus,[3] and of the gods' quarrel and its resolution to Themis and Zeus;[4] [380] and we'll not allow the younger generation to hear the idea which Aeschylus[5] expresses as "When God wants to visit utter ruin on a household, he implants the cause in men." No, if plays are composed (such as the one these lines are from) about Niobe's afflictions, or about the trials and tribulations of the descendants of Pelops,[6] or about the Trojan War, the playwrights must either be prohibited from saying that God was responsible for these events, or if they do attribute them to God, they have to come up with an explanation which approximates to the one we're looking for at the moment, and say that what God did was right and good, in the sense that the people in question were being punished and therefore benefited; but poets should be prohibited from saying that these people were in a *bad* way as a result of being punished and that this was God's doing. The claim that the sinners were badly off because they were in need of punishment, and that in punishing them God was benefiting them, is permissible; but the claim that God, who is good, is responsible for any instance of badness is to be resisted as forcefully as possible by anyone who wants a well-regulated community, until it is never spoken and never heard

2. *Iliad* 24.527–32 [translator's note].

3. *Iliad* 4.20–72 [translator's note]. Pandarus: Trojan archer favored by Apollo. Athena: Greek goddess of wisdom and war and the patron god of Athens; in the passage cited, she takes on the form of a Trojan and persuades Pandarus to break the truce (as Zeus has bid her to do).

4. Perhaps *Iliad* 20.1–74 or 15.12–217 [translator's note] Themis: Greek goddess of justice, wisdom, and good counsel.

5. Greek tragedian (525–456 B.C.E.); from his *Niobe* (a lost play). Because Niobe, wife of a legendary king of Thebes, boasted that she had more children than the goddess Leto, Leto's children, Apollo and Artemis, killed her six sons and six daughters (see *Iliad* 24.602–17).

6. I.e., the ill-starred Atreus, Agamemnon, Orestes, and Electra: see especially Aeschylus's Oresteian trilogy [translator's note].

by anyone, of whatever age, whether the tale is told in verse or in prose. And the reasons are that the voicing of these views is sacrilege, they do us no good, and they are inconsistent with one another.'

'I approve of this law,' he said. 'I'll be right behind you when you cast your vote for it.'

'So now we have the first of the laws and guidelines which pertain to the gods,' I said. 'Any spoken words or composed works will have to conform to the principle that God is not responsible for everything, but only for good.'

'Well, I'm certainly happy with it,' he said.

'All right, then. What about a second principle, as follows? Do you think that God is a sorcerer and can by exercising his will vary his appearance from time to time, sometimes by actually changing and transforming his appearance into a large number of forms, and at other times by deluding us into thinking that's what he's done? Or do you think he's uniform and extremely unlikely to abandon his own appearance?'

'I'm not in a position to say just at the moment,' he replied.

'Look at it this way. Isn't it inevitable that if anything sheds its form, the change is due either to itself or to something else?'

'Yes.'

'Now, really good things are extremely unlikely to be altered or moved by an external agent, aren't they? For instance, a human body is altered by food, drink, and exercise, and plants are altered by the heat of the sun and by wind and phenomena like that; but the more healthy and strong a thing is, the less likely [381] it is to be altered.'

'Of course.'

'And the more courageous and intelligent a mind is, the less likely it is that an external agent would disturb it and alter it?'

'Yes.'

'Moreover, the same principle applies universally even to manufactured items, such as utensils, houses, and clothes: things which are well made and are in good condition are less likely to be altered by time and other phenomena.'

'True.'

'So anything which is in a good state—whether that is due to nature or human skill or both—can hardly be changed at all by an external agent.'

'That sounds right.'

'But God and the divine realm are of course in all respects as perfect as anything can be.'

'Of course.'

'From this point of view, then, God is extremely unlikely to have at his disposal a large number of forms.'

'Yes, extremely unlikely indeed.'

'Would he, however, change and alter himself internally, by his own resources?'

'If he changes in the first place,' he said, 'then obviously this must be how.'

'Well, does he enhance and improve himself, or does he worsen and debase himself?'

'If he changes,' he said, 'then it must be for the worse, since it's unthinkable that God's goodness and excellence are anything less than perfect.'

'You're absolutely right,' I said. 'And, Adeimantus, in this context, do you think that anyone—human or divine—deliberately makes himself deteriorate in any respect?'

'That's impossible,' he said.

'It is equally impossible, then,' I said, 'for God to want to change himself. Since, as we have found, the divine nature is as perfect and as good as anything could be, then any god retains his own form in a uniform, direct fashion for ever.'

'I think that's absolutely inevitable,' he said.

'It follows, Adeimantus,' I said, 'that none of our poets is to say, "The gods travel around human habitations disguised as all sorts of visitors from other lands."[7] Nor are they to tell lies about Proteus and Thetis,[8] or present Hera in a tragedy or any other kind of poem in an altered form, as a mendicant holy woman begging alms "for the life-giving children of the Argive river Inachus",[9] or repeat the mass of other similar lies that have been told. Furthermore, we should neutralize the poets' influence on mothers, which makes them scare their children with terrible stories about how some gods tend to prowl around during the hours of darkness in a wide variety of unfamiliar human guises, so that we stop the mothers blaspheming against the gods, and at the same time stop them making their children too timid.'

'Yes, we should,' he said.

'But even if it isn't in the gods' nature actually to change,' I said, 'do they magically delude us into seeing them appear in all kinds of guises?'

'It's not inconceivable,' he said.

[382] 'Well, would God willingly mask the truth behind appearance and deceive us by his words or actions?' I asked.

'I don't know,' he answered.

'Don't you know that a true falsehood (if you'll allow me the phrase) is loathed by everyone, divine or human?' I asked.

'What do you mean?' he asked.

'I mean,' I said, 'that no one chooses and wants to be deceived in the most important part of himself and about the most important things. The presence of falsehood there is his worst fear.'

'I still don't understand,' he said.

'That's because you think I'm trying to make a high-powered point,' I said. 'But all I'm saying is that no one is at all happy at being lied to and deceived in his mind about the facts; no one likes being ignorant, and the existence and presence of falsehood there are extremely unwelcome to everyone; they particularly hate it there.'

'They certainly do,' he said.

'Well, I might have been perfectly correct when I described this state a moment ago as true falsehood—the state of misapprehension caused by falsehood in the mind. I mean, a spoken lie is a kind of copy and subsequent reflection of the mental condition, and no pure lie, don't you think?'

'Yes.'

'Now, a genuine lie is hated by men as well as gods.'

7. *Odyssey* 17.485–86 [translator's note].

8. A sea nymph who was fated to bear a son mightier than his father; she married the hero Peleus and bore Achilles. Proteus: prophetic son of Poseidon, Greek god of the sea, who had the power to change shape.

9. Both a river and a river god. Argive: of Argos, a city-state on the Peloponnese. The "children" are presumably the river's tributaries with their "life-giving" water. The quotation is from *The Xantriai*, a lost play by Aeschylus.

'I think so.'

'What about a spoken lie? Aren't there occasions and situations when telling lies is helpful and doesn't therefore warrant hatred? What about when we're dealing with enemies, or with people we count as friends, but who are trying to do something bad because they've gone mad or have somehow taken leave of their senses? Isn't telling lies helpful under these circumstances as a preventative medicine? Moreover, consider those stories we were discussing not long ago: we cannot know the truth about events in the past, so we make something up which approximates as closely as possible to the truth, and that helps us, doesn't it?'

'Yes,' he said, 'you're quite right.'

'Which of these reasons, then, makes telling lies helpful to God? Would he make up something which resembles the truth because he doesn't know the past?'

'That's a ridiculous suggestion,' he said.

'So there's nothing of the lying poet in God.'

'I don't think so.'

'Would he lie out of fear for his enemies?'

'Hardly.'

'Because his friends have taken leave of their senses or gone mad?'

'Anyone witless or insane is no friend of God,' he said.

'So God has no reason to lie.'

'No.'

'So it is not in the nature of deities or gods to deceive.'

'Absolutely not,' he said.

'Whether acting or speaking, then, God is entirely uniform and truthful. He doesn't actually change himself, and he doesn't delude others either, during their sleeping or their waking hours, in how he appears or in what he says or in the signs he sends.'

[383] 'Listening to you speak,' he said, 'I find myself agreeing with you.'

'So do you agree,' I said, 'that this is the second principle to which religious discussions and literature must conform—that the gods are not shape-shifting wizards and do not mislead us by lying in what they say or do?'

'I agree.'

'Although there is much to commend in Homer, then, we won't approve of the passage when Zeus sends the dream to Agamemnon.[1] Likewise, we won't approve of the bit of Aeschylus[2] where Thetis says that at her wedding Apollo "celebrated in song how happy my children would make me—how they wouldn't know sickness and would live for many long years—and went on and on about how lucky I was and how the gods smiled on me, until he made my heart glad. And since Phoebus[3] is a god and abounds in prophetic skill, I expected his words to be true. But for all his singing, for all his sharing of our feast, for all these claims of his, it is he who has now killed my son." We'll come down hard on anyone who says anything like this about the gods: we'll refuse him a chorus and ban teachers from using his works to educate

1. Zeus sends a lying dream to Agamemnon that the capture of Troy is imminent in *Iliad* 2. Notice that Plato is not denying the existence of omens and portents, only that they can be false or that false ones can be sent by the gods; it is we who misinterpret the gods' messages [translator's note]. Agamemnon: king of Mycenae and commander of the Greek expedition against Troy.

2. From a lost play [translator's note].

3. Apollo, god of prophecy as well as healing and music.

our children. Otherwise, our guardians won't grow up to be religious people, or to be as godlike themselves as is humanly possible.'

'I'm in complete agreement with these principles,' he said, 'and would want them enshrined as laws.'

From *Book III*

[386] 'All right, then,' I said. 'If people are going to revere the gods, respect their parents, and not belittle friendship with one another, then apparently those are the kinds of stories they should and shouldn't hear about the gods, from childhood onwards.'

'I'm sure we're right about this,' he said.

'What about if they are to be brave? Won't they also need stories which are designed to make them fear death as little as possible? I mean, don't you think that courage and fearing death are mutually exclusive?'

'Yes, I certainly do,' he answered.

'What about the idea that Hades[4] doesn't just exist, but is terrifying? Do you think this goes with facing death fearlessly and with preferring death in battle to defeat and slavery?'

'Of course not.'

'So here's another aspect of story-telling for us to oversee, apparently. We must ask those who take on the job of telling stories not to denigrate Hades in the simple fashion they have been, but to speak well of it, because otherwise they'll not only be lying, but also not speaking in a way that is conducive to courage in battle.'

'Yes, we must,' he said.

'Then we'll start with the following lines,' I said, 'and delete everything which resembles them: "I'd rather be a slave labouring for someone else—someone without property, who can hardly make a living—than rule over all the spirits of the dead"; and "The vile, dank halls, which even the gods hate, might appear to men and gods"; and "Amazing! The soul, the likeness of a person, really does exist in Hades' halls, but it is completely witless"; and "He alone had consciousness, while the rest were darting shadows"; and "His soul flew from his body and went to Hades bewailing its fate, forfeiting courage and the glory of young manhood"; [387] and "Like a wisp of smoke, his soul went down to the underworld with a shrill cry"; and "As when bats flit about squeaking in the depths of an awful cave, when one of them loses its perch on the crowded rock, and they cling to one another, so the flock of souls went with shrill cries."[5] We'll implore Homer and the rest of the poets not to get cross if we strike these and all similar lines from their works. We'll explain that it's not because the lines are not good poetry and don't give pleasure to most people; on the contrary, the better poetry they are, the more they are to be kept from the ears of children and men who are to be autonomous and to be more afraid of losing this freedom than of death.'

'Absolutely.'

'Now, we'd better get rid of all the frightening and terrifying names which crop up here. I mean names like Cocytus and Styx,[6] ghost and wraith, and

4. The Greek underworld.

5. Quoted from, respectively, *Odyssey* 11.489–91, *Iliad* 20.64–66, *Iliad* 23.103–4, *Odyssey* 10.495, *Iliad* 16.856–57, *Iliad* 23.100–101, and *Odyssey* 24.6–9 [translator's note].

6. Two of the rivers of Hades—Lamentation and Hateful [translator's note].

so on—all the names which are designed to make everyone who hears them shudder. In another context, they may have a useful purpose to serve; but our worry is that this shivering might make our guardians too feverish and enervated.'

'It's a legitimate worry,' he remarked.

'Should we ban them, then?'

'Yes.'

'It's names which have the opposite effect that should be used in both prose and poetry, isn't it?'

'Clearly.'

'Shall we also remove the passages where eminent men weep and wail in mourning, then?'

'We have to,' he said. 'It follows from what we've already done.'

'Let's see whether or not we're right to remove them,' I said. 'We can agree that one good man will not regard death as a terrible thing for another good man—a friend of his—to suffer.'

'Yes, we can.'

'So a good man won't mourn as if the other person had suffered something terrible.'

'No.'

'Moreover, we can also agree that a good man is preeminently capable of providing himself with a good life entirely from his own resources, and is absolutely the last person to need anyone or anything else.'

'True.'

'So he'd be the last person to be overwhelmed by the loss of a son or a brother or some money and so on and so forth.'

'Yes, definitely.'

'He'll also be the last person to mourn, then, when some such disaster overtakes him: no one will endure it with more equanimity than him.'

'Very true.'

'We'd be right, then, not to have famous men mourning. We can allow women to do that (as long as they aren't admirable women) and any bad men there might be, [388] so that the people we claim to be training for guardianship of our land find all that sort of behavior distasteful.'

'That's right,' he said.

'So we have a further request to make of Homer and the rest of the poets. We'll ask them not to portray Achilles, who was the son of a goddess, "at one point lying on his side, then later on his back, and then on his front; and then getting to his feet and sailing, crazed with grief, over the sands of the bitter sea", or as "pouring handfuls of filthy ashes over his head",[7] or generally as weeping and wailing to the extent and in the fashion that the poet portrays him. And we'll ask them not to have Priam, a close relative of the gods by birth, "begging and rolling in the dung as he calls out to each man by name".[8] We'll be even more forceful, however, in our request that they don't portray the *gods* lamenting and saying things like, "Oh, poor me! How wretched I am to have borne the noblest of children!";[9] or at the very least they ought to stop short of giving such an inaccurate portrait of the greatest of the gods

7. *Iliad* 24.10–13, 18.23–24 [translator's note]. Achilles: the greatest of the Greek warriors at Troy and the central figure of the *Iliad*.
8. *Iliad* 22.414–15 [translator's note]. Priam: the last king of Troy, descended from Zeus.
9. *Iliad* 18.54 [translator's note]. The speaker is Thetis.

that they have him saying, "Alas! The man I now see being chased around Troy is dear to me, and my heart grieves", and "Alas that Sarpedon, the dearest of men to me, is destined to fall at the hands of Patroclus the son of Menoetius."[1]

'The point is, my dear Adeimantus, that if the young men of our community hear this kind of thing and take it seriously, rather than regarding it as despicable and absurd, they're hardly going to regard such behaviour as despicable in human beings like themselves and feel remorse when they also find themselves saying or doing these or similar things. Instead, they won't find it at all degrading to be constantly chanting laments and dirges for trivial incidents, and they won't resist doing so.'

'You're quite right,' he said.

'And what we've just been arguing, in effect—and at the moment no one's come up with a better argument, so we should stick to this one—is that we must prevent this happening.'

'Yes, we must.'

'Now, they'd better not be prone to laughter either. I mean, the stronger the laughter, the stronger the consequent emotional reaction too—that's almost inevitable.'

'I agree,' he said.

'We should, therefore, refuse admittance to any poetry which portrays eminent humans as being overcome by laughter, and [389] do so even more vigorously if it shows gods in that state.'

'Yes, indeed,' he said.

'So we'll also reject the lines of Homer where he says about the gods, "Unquenchable laughter arose among the blessed gods as they watched Hephaestus bustling about the house."[2] According to your argument, we should disallow this type of passage.'

'Yes, if you want to attribute the argument to me,' he said. 'At any rate, we should disallow it.'

'Next, they must rate honesty highly. You see, if we were right in what we were saying a short while ago, and the gods really have no use for falsehood, although it can serve as a type of medicine for us humans, then clearly lying should be entrusted to doctors, and laymen should have nothing to do with it.'

'Clearly,' he said.

'If it's anyone's job, then, it's the job of the rulers of our community: they can lie for the good of the community, when either an external or an internal threat makes it necessary. No one else, however, should have anything to do with lying. If an ordinary person lies to these rulers of ours, we'll count that as equivalent in misguidedness, if not worse, to a patient lying to his doctor about his physical condition, or someone misleading a ship's captain, with respect to his ship or crew, by telling him lies about his own state or that of one of his fellow crewmen.'

'You're absolutely right,' he said.

'So if anyone else is caught lying in our community—"any artisan, whether diviner or healer of ills or carpenter"[3]—he is to be punished on the grounds

1. *Iliad* 22.168–69 [Hector is being chased by Achilles], 16.433 [translator's note]. Sarpedon: a son of Zeus who fought with the Trojans. Patroclus: the best friend of Achilles.
2. *Iliad* 1.599–600 [translator's note].
3. *Odyssey* 17.383–84 [translator's note].

that he's introducing a practice which is just as liable to wreck and ruin a community as a ship.'

'Yes, it would,' he said, 'if what people did was influenced by what he had said.'

'Now, won't the young men of our community need self-discipline?'

'Of course.'

'And aren't the most important aspects of self-discipline, at least for the general rank and file, obedience to those in authority and establishing one's authority over the pleasures of drink, sex, and food?'

'I think so.'

'So I'm sure we'll approve of the kind of thing Homer has Diomedes say—"Sit down, shut up, and listen to me"[4]—and related passages, like "Exuding an aura of courage, the Greeks advanced in silence, respecting their leaders",[5] and so on and so forth.'

'Yes, we will.'

'Well, what about lines like "You're groggy with wine, you have the eyes of a dog and the heart of a deer"[6] and the next few lines? Are they all right? [390] And what about all the other impertinent things people have said to their rules in works of prose or poetry?'

'We won't approve of them.'

'That, I suppose, is because they don't encourage self-discipline in their audience, though they may well be enjoyable from another point of view. What do you think?'

'I agree,' he said.

'What about having your cleverest character saying that in his opinion the best thing in the world is when "The nearby tables are laden with bread and meat, and the steward draws wine from the mixing-bowl, brings it, and pours it into the cups"?[7] Do you think this is the right material for a young man to hear if he is to be self-controlled? Or "There is no death worse than death by starvation, no more wretched fate to face"?[8] And then there's the passage where, while everyone else—mortal and immortal—is asleep, Zeus stays awake to do some planning, but in no time at all it is driven completely out of his mind by his sexual desire, and he is so overwhelmed by the sight of Hera that he doesn't even want to go to their room, but wants to have sex with her there and then, on the ground, and he says that he's feeling more desire for her even than the first time they slept together, "without our parents knowing".[9] And the story of how Hephaestus ensnared Ares and Aphrodite for similar reasons is equally inappropriate material for them to hear.'[1]

'I couldn't agree with you more,' he said. 'It's quite unsuitable.'

'On the other hand,' I said, 'it's worth their paying attention to the portrayal

4. *Iliad* 4.412 [translator's note]. Diomedes: a lord of Argos who was one of the best Greek fighters at Troy.

5. A combination of *Iliad* 3.8 and 4.431 [translator's note].

6. *Iliad* 1.225; Achilles is insulting his leader Agamemnon by calling him a lecherous, cowardly drunk [translator's note].

7. *Odyssey* 9.8–10 [translator's note]. The lines are spoken by Odysseus, who is often described as clever or scheming.

8. *Odyssey* 12.342; the point is that this sentiment encouraged Odysseus's men to steal the Sun-god's cattle [translator's note].

9. *Iliad* 14.294–351; quotation, 296 [translator's note].

1. *Odyssey* 8.266–366 [translator's note]. When Hephaestus learned that his wife, Aphrodite, the Greek goddess of love and beauty, was committing adultery with Ares, the god of war, he fashioned a metal net and caught the pair in bed.

on stage or in writing of occasions when famous men express, by their words or actions, resistance to all kinds of temptations. For instance, there are the lines, "He struck his breast and spoke sternly to his heart: 'Patience, heart—you've put up with worse in the past.' " '[2]

'Absolutely,' he said.

'Then again, we shouldn't let them be mercenary or avaricious.'

'Of course not.'

'So they shouldn't repeat the verse "Gifts win over even gods and magnificent kings".[3] And we won't compliment Achilles' attendant Phoenix on his restraint in advising Achilles to accept the gifts he was being offered and help the Greeks in their fight, but not to refrain from his "wrath" unless he was bribed. It will also go against our wishes and our convictions for Achilles himself to be mercenary enough to accept Agamemnon's gifts and to refuse to release a corpse [391] until he'd been given a ransom.[4]

'Yes, it would be wrong to approve of that kind of behavior,' he said.

'Now, the fact that it's Homer makes me hesitate,' I said, 'but I'm not sure it's not actually sacrilegious for us to say things like this about Achilles and accept them when others say them. The same goes also for when Achilles says to Apollo, "There's no god more baneful than you—you with your aloofness. You misled me, and I'd pay you back if I could."[5] We shouldn't believe that he refused to obey the river-god either, and was ready to fight him, and that he said of his hair, which was dedicated to another river, the Spercheius, "I hereby give my hair to the hero Patroclus: may he take it with him",[6] when Patroclus was dead—we shouldn't believe that he did this. And we'll deny the truth of the stories that he dragged Hector around Patroclus' tomb and slaughtered prisoners on his funeral pyre.[7] And we won't allow our citizens to believe that Achilles—the child of a goddess and of Peleus (who was himself a model of self-discipline and a grandson of Zeus) and tutored by the sage Cheiron—was so full of turmoil that he suffered from the two conflicting diseases of mean-spirited avarice and disdain for gods and men.'

'You're right,' he said.

'Moreover,' I went on, 'we won't believe or tolerate the story about those horrific kidnap projects by Theseus and Peirithous, who were respectively the sons of Poseidon[8] and Zeus; and in general, we find it unthinkable that anyone with a god as a parent, or any hero, would be unscrupulous enough to do the terrible, sacrilegious things people falsely attribute to them. No, we should force the poets to deny either that the heroes did these things or that their parents were gods, but not to say both; and they should also be forcibly prevented from trying to persuade the young men of our community that the gods are the source of evil and that the heroes are no better than

2. *Odyssey* 20.17–18 [translator's note].

3. A proverb, possibly originating with Hesiod [translator's note].

4. Achilles accepts Agamemnon's gifts at *Iliad* 19.278–81; Priam brings him gifts to release Hector's body at *Iliad* 24.469–595 [translator's note].

5. *Iliad* 22.15, 20 [translator's note].

6. The river Scamander in *Iliad* 21.211–382; the river Spercheius, *Iliad* 23.151. The river was supposed to guarantee Achilles' safe return from the war; because it has failed to do so, Achilles tells it off and bitterly re-dedicates his hair to his dead companion Patroclus. It was a primitive Greek practice to dedicate your hair to a river; the fact that hair grows makes it an external manifestation of one's life-force, so in dedicating your hair, you are dedicating yourself [translator's note].

7. *Iliad* 24.14–18, 23.175–77 [translator's note].

8. Greek god of the sea. Theseus: legendary hero and king of Athens, who was assisted by his friend Peirithous both in carrying off Helen and in attempting to retrieve Persephone from the underworld.

ordinary people. We demonstrated earlier the impossibility of bad things originating with the gods; so, as we said then, these stories are not only sacrilegious, but also false.'

'Of course.'

'And they have a pernicious effect on their audience as well, in the sense that no one will find his own badness reprehensible once he's been persuaded that these things are and always have been done by "immediate descendants of the gods, close relatives of Zeus, people whose altar to Zeus, their father-protector, is high on Mount Ida, above the clouds" and "in whom the blood of deities is still fresh".[9] That's why we must put an end to stories of this nature: if we don't, they will engender [392] in the young men of our community a casual attitude towards badness.'

'I quite agree,' he said.

'Now,' I said, 'if we want to distinguish what in literature should be allowed and what should be censored, there's one further type of writing we should still look at, isn't there? I mean, we've discussed how gods must be portrayed—and deities, heroes, and the dead.

'Yes.'

'So wouldn't we be left with writing which has human beings as its subject?'

'Yes, obviously.'

'In fact, though, we can't evaluate this kind of writing at the moment.'

'Why not?'

'Because what we'd claim, I imagine, is that poets and prose-writers misrepresent people in extremely important ways, when—as they often do—they portray immoral people as happy and moral people as unhappy, and write about the rewards of undiscovered immorality and how morality is good for someone else, but disadvantageous to oneself. I suppose we'd proscribe assertions of that kind, and tell them that their poems and stories are to make the opposite points, don't you think?'

'I'm certain we would,' he said.

* * *

'It follows, then, that good use of language, harmony, grace, and rhythm all depend on goodness of character. I'm not talking about the state which is actually stupidity, but which we gloss as goodness of character; I'm talking about when the mind really had equipped the character with moral goodness and excellence.'

'Absolutely,' he[1] said.

'And shouldn't the young people of our community take every opportunity to cultivate these qualities, if they are to do their jobs?'

'Yes, they should.'

[401] 'Now, painting and related arts, and weaving, embroidery, architecture, and the manufacture of utensils in general, and also the physical structures of creatures and plants, are all pervaded by these qualities, in the sense that they may display grace or inelegance. And inelegance, lack of rhythm,

9. Both passages are from the *Niobe* of Aeschylus; Niobe is talking about her father Tantalus, a notorious criminal whose father was Zeus [translator's note]. Tantalus cooked his own son, Pelops, and served him to the gods.

1. Glaucon.

and disharmony are allied to abuse of language and a corrupt character, whereas their opposites are allied to and reflect a disciplined and good character.'

'Absolutely,' he said.

'Is it only the poets we should oversee, then, and compel to choose between imbuing their composition with the image of goodness of character or not practising their art in our community? Don't we also have to oversee artisans in general and stop them imbuing their portraits of animals, their edifices, and whatever else they may produce, with corruption, lack of self-restraint, meanness of spirit, and inelegance, and punish failure to comply with a ban on working in our community? Otherwise, during their upbringing our guardians will be surrounded by the pernicious pasturage of images of badness, which will be so common that they'll often be nibbling and feeding on them, day in and day out, a little at a time, until without realizing it they'll amass badness in their minds. No, we must look for craftsmen who have the innate gift of tracking down goodness and grace, so that the young people of our community can live in a salubrious region where everything is beneficial and where their eyes and ears meet no influences except those of fine works of art, whose effect is like a breeze which brings health from favorable regions, and which imperceptibly guides them, from childhood onwards, until they are assimilated to, familiar with, and in harmony with the beauty of reason.'

'Yes, that would be an outstandingly fine upbringing for them,' he said.

'Now, Glaucon,' I said, 'isn't the prime importance of cultural education due to the fact that rhythm and harmony sink more deeply into the mind than anything else and affect it more powerfully than anything else and bring grace in their train? For someone who is given a correct education, their product is grace; but in the opposite situation it is inelegance. And isn't its importance also due to the fact that a proper cultural education would enable a person to be very quick at noticing defects and flaws in the construction or nature of things? In other words, he'd find offensive the things he ought to find offensive. Fine things would be appreciated and enjoyed by him, and he'd accept them into his mind as nourishment and would therefore become truly good; [402] even when young, however, and still incapable of rationally understanding why, he would rightly condemn and loathe contemptible things. And then the rational mind would be greeted like an old friend when it did arrive, because anyone with this upbringing would be more closely affiliated with rationality than anyone else.'

'Yes,' he said, 'to my mind those are the kinds of reasons for cultural education.'

'It's analogous to the process of becoming literate, then,' I said. 'We weren't literate until we realized that, despite being few in number, the letters are fundamental wherever they occur, and until we appreciated their importance whether the word which contained them was great or small, and stopped thinking that we didn't need to take note of them, but tried hard to recognize them everywhere, on the grounds that literacy would elude us until we were capable of doing so.'

'True.'

'And we won't be able to tell which letters are which when they're reflected in water or a mirror either, until we can recognize the letters themselves, will we? It takes the same expertise and training, doesn't it?'

'Absolutely.'

'Then this is incredibly similar to what I've been saying. We won't be cultured either (and this doesn't apply only to us, but to the people we're claiming to educate for guardianship) until we recognize the types—self-discipline, courage, generosity, broadness of vision, and all the qualities which are allied and opposed to them—wherever they occur, and notice instances of their presence, whether it is the qualities themselves or their reflections that we are noticing, and don't underestimate them whether the situation in which they're occurring is great or small, but bear in mind that it takes the same expertise and training. Right?'

'Definitely,' he said.

'Now,' I went on, 'imagine a situation where someone combines beautiful mental characteristics with physical features which conform to the same principle and so are consistent and concordant with the beauty of his mind. Could there be a more beautiful sight for anyone capable of seeing it?'

'Hardly.'

'And the more beautiful a thing is, the more lovable it is?'

'Naturally.'

'Therefore, the more people are of this type, the more a cultured person will love them. If they're discordant, however, he will not love them.'

'No, he won't,' he said, 'if they have a mental defect; but if their flaw is physical, he'll put up with it and not refuse his affection.'

'I appreciate what you're saying,' I said. 'I know you are or were in love with someone like that, and I concede the point. But answer me this: can self-discipline and excessive pleasure go together?'

'Of course not,' he said. 'Pleasure deranges people just as effectively as distress.'

'Can excessive pleasure partner any of the other virtues?'

[403] 'No.'

'What about promiscuity and dissoluteness?'

'Yes, they're its chief partners.'

'Can you think of any pleasure which is greater and more intense than sexual pleasure?'

'No, I can't,' he said, 'and I can't think of any pleasure which is more manic either.'

'And authentic love is a disciplined and cultured love of someone who is restrained as well as good-looking. Yes?'

'Definitely,' he said.

'Authentic love should have no involvement, then, with anything manic or anything which bears the trace of dissoluteness, should it?'

'No, it shouldn't.'

'Doesn't it follow, then, that lovers and their boyfriends who love and are loved authentically should have no involvement with this pleasure and should have nothing to do with it?'

'That's right, Socrates,' he said. 'They most certainly should not.'

'So you'll apparently be making a regulation in the community we're founding to the effect that although a lover can (if he can persuade his boyfriend to let him) kiss and spend time with and touch his boyfriend, as he would his son—which is to say, for honourable reasons—still his relationship with anyone he cares for will basically be such that he never gives the impression that there is more to it than that. Otherwise, he'll be liable to condemnation for lacking culture and moral sensibility.'

'Exactly,' he said.

'Now, do you join me in thinking that we've completed our discussion of cultural studies?' I asked. 'At any rate, we've reached a good place to finish: I mean, it's good for cultural studies to lead ultimately to love of beauty.'

'I agree,' he said.

* * *

From *Book VII*

[514] 'Next,' I said, 'here's a situation which you can use as an analogy for the human condition—for our education or lack of it. Imagine people living in a cavernous cell down under the ground; at the far end of the cave, a long way off, there's an entrance open to the outside world. They've been there since childhood, with their legs and necks tied up in a way which keeps them in one place and allows them to look only straight ahead, but not to turn their heads. There's firelight burning a long way further up the cave behind them, and up the slope between the fire and the prisoners there's a road, beside which you should imagine a low wall has been built—like the partition which conjurors place between themselves and their audience and above which they show their tricks.'

'All right,' he[2] said.

'Imagine also that there are people on the other side of this wall who are carrying all sorts of artefacts. These artefacts, human statuettes, and animal models carved in stone and wood [515] and all kinds of materials stick out over the wall; and as you'd expect, some of the people talk as they carry these objects along, while others are silent.'

'This is a strange picture you're painting,' he said, 'with strange prisoners.'

'They're no different from us,' I said. 'I mean, in the first place, do you think they'd see anything of themselves and one another except the shadows cast by the fire on to the cave wall directly opposite them?

'Of course not,' he said. 'They're forced to spend their lives without moving their heads.'

'And what about the objects which were being carried along? Won't they only see their shadows as well?'

'Naturally.'

'Now, suppose they were able to talk to one another: don't you think they'd assume that their words applied to what they saw passing by in front of them?'[3]

'They couldn't think otherwise.'

"And what if sound echoed off the prison wall opposite them? When any of the passers-by spoke, don't you think they'd be bound to assume that the sound came from a passing shadow?'

2. Glaucon.
3. In Platonic terms, this shows the extent of the prisoners' delusion, since our words really refer to types [translator's note].

'I'm absolutely certain of it,' he said.

'All in all, then,' I said, 'the shadows of artefacts would constitute the only reality people in this situation would recognize.'

'That's absolutely inevitable,' he agreed.

'What do you think would happen, then,' I asked, 'if they were set free from their bonds and cured of their inanity? What would it be like if they found that happening to them? Imagine that one of them has been set free and is suddenly made to stand up, to turn his head and walk, and to look towards the firelight. It hurts him to do all this and he's too dazzled to be capable of making out the objects whose shadows he'd formerly been looking at. And suppose someone tells him that what he's been seeing all this time has no substance, and that he's now closer to reality and is seeing more accurately, because of the greater reality of the things in front of his eyes—what do you imagine his reaction would be? And what do you think he'd say if he were shown any of the passing objects and had to respond to being asked what it was? Don't you think he'd be bewildered and would think that there was more reality in what he'd been seeing before than in what he was being shown now?'

'Far more,' he said.

'And if he were forced to look at the actual firelight, don't you think it would hurt his eyes? Don't you think he'd turn away and run back to the things he could make out, and would take the truth of the matter to be that these things are clearer than what he was being shown?'

'Yes,' he agreed.

'And imagine him being dragged forcibly away from there up the rough, steep slope,' I went on, 'without being released until he's been pulled out into the sunlight. Wouldn't this treatment cause him pain and distress? [516] And once he's reached the sunlight, he wouldn't be able to see a single one of the things which are currently taken to be real, would he, because his eyes would be overwhelmed by the sun's beams?'

'No, he wouldn't,' he answered, 'not straight away.'

'He wouldn't be able to see things up on the surface of the earth, I suppose, until he'd got used to his situation. At first, it would be a shadows that he could most easily make out, then he'd move on to the reflections of people and so on in water,[4] and later he'd be able to see the actual things themselves. Next, he'd feast his eyes on the heavenly bodies and the heavens themselves, which would be easier at night: he'd look at the light of the stars and the moon, rather than at the sun and sunlight during the daytime.'

'Of course.'

'And at last, I imagine, he'd be able to discern and feast his eyes on the sun—not the displaced image of the sun in water or elsewhere, but the sun on its own, in its proper place.'[5]

'Yes, he'd inevitably come to that,' he said.

'After that, he'd start to think about the sun and he'd deduce that it is the source of the seasons and the yearly cycle, that the whole of the visible realm

4. The stage of looking at reflections and so on outside the cave does not differ in terms of objects from the stage of looking at the effigies in the cave. But it differs in that it is now more difficult for one to return to the safety of convention [translator's note].

5. The sun in the allegory is, of course, goodness [translator's note].

is its domain, and that in a sense everything which he and his peers used to see is its responsibility.'

'Yes, that would obviously be the next point he'd come to,' he agreed.

'Now, if he recalled the cell where he'd originally lived and what passed for knowledge there and his former fellow prisoners, don't you think he'd feel happy about his own altered circumstances, and sorry for them?'

'Definitely.'

'Suppose that the prisoners used to assign prestige and credit to one another, in the sense that they rewarded speed at recognizing the shadows as they passed, and the ability to remember which ones normally come earlier and later and at the same time as which other ones, and expertise at using this as a basis for guessing which ones would arrive next. Do you think our former prisoner would covet these honours and would envy the people who had status and power there, or would he much prefer, as Homer describes it, "being a slave labouring for someone else—someone without property",[6] and would put up with anything at all, in fact, rather than share their beliefs and their life?'

'Yes, I think he'd go through anything rather than live that way,' he said.

'Here's something else I'd like your opinion about,' I said. 'If he went back underground and sat down again in the same spot, wouldn't the sudden transition from the sunlight mean that his eyes would be overwhelmed by darkness?'

'Certainly,' he replied.

'Now, the process of adjustment would be quite long this time, and suppose that before his eyes had settled down and while he wasn't seeing well, [517] he had once again to compete against those same old prisoners at identifying those shadows. Wouldn't he make a fool of himself? Wouldn't they say that he'd come back from his upward journey with his eyes ruined, and that it wasn't even worth trying to go up there? And wouldn't they—if they could—grab hold of anyone who tried to set them free and take them up there and kill him?'[7]

'They certainly would,' he said.

'Well, my dear Glaucon,' I said, 'you should apply this allegory, as a whole, to what we were talking about before. The region which is accessible to sight should be equated with the prison cell, and the firelight there with the light of the sun. And if you think of the upward journey and the sight of things up on the surface of the earth as the mind's ascent to the intelligible realm, you won't be wrong—at least, *I* don't think you'd be wrong, and it's my impression that you want to hear. Only God knows if it's actually true, however. Anyway, it's my opinion that the last thing to be seen—and it isn't easy to see either—in the realm of knowledge is goodness; and the sight of the character of goodness leads one to deduce that it is responsible for everything that is right and fine, whatever the circumstances, and that in the visible realm it is the progenitor of light and of the source of light, and in the intelligible realm it is the source and provider of truth and knowledge. And I also think that the sight of it is a prerequisite for intelligent conduct either of one's own private affairs or of public business.'

'I couldn't agree more,' he said.

6. *Odyssey* 11.489 [translator's note]. In Homer, the comparison is between being a living slave and ruling over the dead—a passage that, according to *Republic* 3.386c (see above), should be deleted.

7. As Socrates was killed [translator's note], found guilty of impiety and corrupting Athens' youth.

'All right, then,' I said. 'I wonder if you also agree with me in not finding it strange that people who've travelled there don't want to engage in human business: there's nowhere else their minds would ever rather be than in the upper region—which is hardly surprising, if our allegory has got this aspect right as well.'

'No, it's not surprising,' he agreed.

'Well, what about this?' I asked. 'Imagine someone returning to the human world and all its misery after contemplating the divine realm. Do you think it's surprising if he seems awkward and ridiculous while he's still not seeing well, before he's had time to adjust to the darkness of his situation, and he's forced into a contest (in a lawcourt or wherever) about the shadows of morality or the statuettes which cast the shadows, and into a competition whose terms are the conceptions of morality held by people who have never seen morality itself?'

'No, that's not surprising in the slightest,' he said.

[518] 'In fact anyone with any sense,' I said, 'would remember that the eyes can become confused in two different ways, as a result of two different sets of circumstances: it can happen in the transition from light to darkness, and also in the transition from darkness to light. If he took the same facts into consideration when he also noticed someone's mind in such a state of confusion that it was incapable of making anything out, his reaction wouldn't be unthinking ridicule. Instead, he'd try to find out whether this person's mind was returning from a mode of existence which involves greater lucidity and had been blinded by the unfamiliar darkness, or whether it was moving from relative ignorance to relative lucidity and had been overwhelmed and dazzled by the increased brightness. Once he'd distinguished between the two conditions and modes of existence, he'd congratulate anyone he found in the second state, and feel sorry for anyone in the first state. If he did choose to laugh at someone in the second state, his amusement would be less absurd than when laughter is directed at someone returning from the light above.

'Yes,' he said, 'you're making a lot of sense.'

* * *

From *Book X*

[595] 'You know,' I said, 'the issue of poetry is the main consideration—among many others—which convinces me that the way we were trying to found our community was along absolutely the right lines.'

'What are you thinking of?' he[8] asked.

'That we flatly refused to admit any representational poetry.[9] I mean, its total unacceptability is even clearer, in my opinion, now that we've distinguished the different aspects of the mind.'

'How is it clearer?'

'Well, this is just between ourselves: please don't denounce me to the tragic playwrights and all the other representational poets. But it looks as though this whole genre of poetry deforms its audience's minds,[1] unless they have the antidote, which is recognition of what this kind of poetry is actually like.'

8. Glaucon.

9. Tragedy and epic; insofar as they are imitative, they are by definition removed from reality. The total ban here seems to contradict *Republic* 2 and 3, where Socrates encourages literary representation of behavior that is appropriate and good.

1. Poetry deforms minds in the sense that it feeds our lower mind and, by virtue of the fact that its

'What do you mean? What do you have in mind?' he asked.

'It's fairly clear,' I said, 'that all these fine tragedians trace their lineage back to Homer: they're Homer's students and disciples, ultimately. And this makes it difficult for me to say what I have to say, because I've had a kind of fascinated admiration for Homer ever since I was young. Still, we should value truth more than we value any person, so, as I say, I'd better speak out.'

'Yes,' he said.

'And you'll listen to what I have to say, or rather respond to any questions I ask?'

'Yes. Go ahead and ask them.'

'Can you tell me what representation basically is? You see, I don't quite understand its point myself.'

'And I suppose I do!' he said.

'It wouldn't surprise me if you did,' I said. 'Just because a person can't see very well, it doesn't mean that [596] he won't often see things before people with better eyesight than him.'

'That's true,' he said. 'All the same, I'd be too shy to explain any views I did have in front of you, so please try to come up with an answer yourself.'

'All right. Shall we get the enquiry going by drawing on familiar ideas? Our usual position is, as you know, that any given plurality of things which have a single name constitutes a single specific type.[2] Is that clear to you?'

'Yes.'

'So now let's take any plurality you want. Would it be all right with you if we said that there were, for instance, lots of beds and tables?'

'Of course.'

'But these items of furniture comprise only two types—the type of bed and the type of table.'

'Yes.'

'Now, we also invariably claim that the manufacture of either of these items of furniture involves the craftsman looking to the type and then making the beds or tables (or whatever) which we use. The point is that the type itself is not manufactured by any craftsman. How could it be?'

'It couldn't.'

'There's another kind of craftsman too. I wonder what you think of him.'

'What kind?'

'He makes everything—all the items which every single manufacturer makes.'

'He must be extraordinarily gifted.'

'Wait: you haven't heard the half of it yet. It's not just a case of his being able to manufacture all the artefacts there are: every plant too, every creature (himself included), the earth, the heavens, gods, and everything in the heavens and in Hades under the earth—all these are made and created by this one man!'

'He really must be extraordinarily clever,' he said.

'Don't you believe me?' I asked. 'Tell me, do you doubt that this kind of craftsman could exist under any circumstances, or do you admit the possibility that a person could—in one sense, at least—create all these things? I

domain is appearance, does not feed that inner organ which can perceive truth and reality [translator's note].

2. That is, the Idea or Form.

mean, don't you realize that you yourself could, under certain circumstances, create all these things?'

'What circumstances?' he asked.

'I'm not talking about anything complicated or rare,' I said. 'It doesn't take long to create the circumstances. The quickest method, I suppose, is to get hold of a mirror and carry it around with you everywhere. You'll soon be creating everything I mentioned a moment ago—the sun and the heavenly bodies, the earth, yourself, and all other creatures, plants, and so on.'

'Yes, but I'd be creating appearances, not actual real things,' he said.

'That's a good point,' I said. 'You've arrived just in time to save the argument. I mean, that's presumably the kind of craftsman a painter is. Yes?'

'Of course.'

'His creations aren't real, according to you; but do you agree that all the same there's a sense in which even a painter creates a bed?'

'Yes,' he said, 'he's another one who creates an apparent bed.'

[597] 'What about a joiner who specializes in making beds? Weren't we saying a short while ago that what he makes is a particular bed, not the type, which is (on our view) the real bed?'

'Yes, we were.'

'So if there's no reality to his creation, then it isn't real; it's similar to something real, but it isn't actually real. It looks as though it's wrong to attribute full reality to a joiner's or any artisan's product, doesn't it?'

'Yes,' he said, 'any serious student of this kind of argument would agree with you.'

'It shouldn't surprise us, then, if we find that even these products are obscure when compared with the truth.'

'No, it shouldn't.'

'Now, what about this representer we're trying to understand? Shall we see if these examples help us?' I asked.

'That's fine by me,' he said.

'Well, we've got these three beds. First, there's the real one, and we'd say, I imagine, that it is the product of divine craftsmanship. I mean, who else could have made it?'

'No one, surely.'

'Then there's the one the joiner makes.'

'Yes,' he said.

'And then there's the one the painter makes. Yes?'

'Yes, agreed.'

'These three, then—painter, joiner, God—are responsible for three different kinds of bed.'

'Yes, that's right.'

'Now, God has produced only that one real bed. The restriction to only one might have been his own choice, or it might just be impossible for him to make more than one. But God never has, and never could, create two or more such beds.'

'Why not?' he asked.

'Even if he were to make only two such beds,' I said, 'an extra one would emerge, and both the other two would be of that one's type. It, and not the two beds, would be the real bed.'

'Right,' he said.

'God realized this, I'm sure. He didn't want to be a kind of joiner, making a particular bed: he wanted to be a genuine creator and make a genuine bed. That's why he created a single real one.'

'I suppose that's right.'

'Shall we call him its progenitor, then, or something like that?'

'Yes, he deserves the name,' he said, 'since he's the maker of this and every other reality.'

'What about a joiner? Shall we call him a manufacturer of beds?'

'Yes.'

'And shall we also call a painter a manufacturer and maker of beds and so on?'

'No, definitely not.'

'What do you think he does with beds, then?'

'I think the most suitable thing to call him would be a representer of the others' creations,' he said.

'Well, in that case,' I said, 'you're using the term "representer" for someone who deals with things which are, in fact, two generations away from reality, aren't you?'

'Yes,' he said.

'The same goes for tragic playwrights, then, since they're representers: they're two generations away from the throne of truth, and so are all other representers.'

'I suppose so.'

'Well, in the context of what we're now saying about representation, I've got a further question about painters. [598] Is it, in any given instance, the actual reality that they try to represent, or is it the craftsmen's products?'

'The craftsmen's products,' he said.

'Here's another distinction you'd better make: do they try to represent them as they are, or as they appear to be?'

'What do you mean?' he asked.

'I'll tell you. Whether you look at a bed from the side or straight on or whatever, it's still just as much a bed as it ever was, isn't it? I mean, it doesn't actually alter it at all: it just *appears* to be different, doesn't it? And the same goes for anything else you can mention. Yes?'

'Yes,' he agreed. 'It seems different, but isn't actually.'

'So I want you to consider carefully which of these two alternatives painting is designed for in any and every instance. Is it designed to represent the facts of the real world or appearances? Does it represent appearance or truth?'

'Appearance,' he said.

'It follows that representation and truth are a considerable distance apart, and a representer is capable of making every product there is only because his contact with things is slight and is restricted to how they look. Consider what a painter does, for instance: we're saying that he doesn't have a clue about shoemaking or joinery, but he'll still paint pictures of artisans working at these and all other areas of expertise, and if he's good at painting he might paint a joiner, have people look at it from far away, and deceive them—if they're children or stupid adults—by making it look as though the joiner were real.'

'Naturally.'

'I think the important thing to bear in mind about cases like this, Glaucon, is that when people tell us they've met someone who's mastered every craft, and is the world's leading expert in absolutely every branch of human knowledge, we should reply that they're being rather silly. They seem to have met the kind of illusionist who's expert at representation and, thanks to their own inability to evaluate knowledge, ignorance, and representation, to have been so thoroughly taken in as to believe in his omniscience.'

'You're absolutely right,' he said.

'Now, we'd better investigate tragedy next,' I said, 'and its guru, Homer, because one does come across the claim that there's no area of expertise, and nothing relevant to human goodness and badness either—and nothing to do with the gods even—that these poets don't understand. It is said that a good poet must understand the issues he writes about, if his writing is to be successful, and that if he didn't understand them, he wouldn't be able to write about them. So we'd better try to decide between the alternatives. Either the people who come across these representational poets are being taken in and are failing to appreciate, when they see their products, that these products are [599] two steps away from reality and that it certainly doesn't take knowledge of the truth to create them (since what they're creating are appearances, not reality); or this view is valid, and in fact good poets are authorities on the subjects most people are convinced they're good at writing about.'

'Yes, this definitely needs looking into,' he said.

'Well, do you think that anyone who was capable of producing both originals and images would devote his energy to making images, and would make out that this is the best thing he's done with his life?'

'No, I don't.'

'I'm sure that if he really knew about the things he was copying in his representations, he'd put far more effort into producing real objects than he would into representations, and would try to leave behind a lot of fine products for people to remember him by, and would dedicate himself to being the recipient rather than the bestower of praise.'

'I agree,' he said. 'He'd gain a lot more prestige and do himself a great deal more good.'

'Well, let's concentrate our interrogation of Homer (or any other poet you like) on a single area. Let's not ask him whether he can tell us of any patients cured by any poet in ancient or modern times, as Asclepius[3] cured his patients, or of any students any of them left to continue his work, as Asclepius left his sons. And even these questions grant the possibility that a poet might have had some medical knowledge, instead of merely representing medical terminology. No, let's not bother to ask him about any other areas of expertise either. But we do have a right to ask Homer about the most important and glorious areas he undertakes to expound—warfare, tactics, politics, and human education. Let's ask him, politely, "Homer, maybe you aren't two steps away from knowing the truth about goodness; maybe you aren't involved in the manufacture of images (which is what we called representation). Perhaps you're actually only one step away, and you do have the ability to recognize which practices—in their private or their public

3. Hero and god of healing (in the *Iliad*, a mortal).

lives—improve people and which ones impair them. But in that case, just as Sparta has its Lycurgus[4] and communities of all different sizes have their various reformers, please tell us which community has you to thank for improvements to its government. Which community attributes the benefits of its good legal code to you? Italy and Sicily name Charondas in this respect, we Athenians name Solon.[5] Which country names you?" Will he have any reply to make?'

'I don't think so,' said Glaucon. 'Even the Homeridae'[6] themselves don't make that claim.'

[600] 'Well, does history record that there was any war fought in Homer's time whose success depended on his leadership or advice?'

'No.'

'Well then, are a lot of ingenious inventions attributed to him, as they are to Thales of Miletus and Anacharsis of Scythia?[7] I mean the kinds of inventions which have practical applications in the arts and crafts and elsewhere. He is, after all, supposed to be good at creating things.'

'No, there's not the slightest hint of that sort of thing.'

'All right, so there's no evidence of his having been a public benefactor, but what about in private? Is there any evidence that, during his lifetime, he was a mentor to people, and that they used to value him for his teaching and then handed down to their successors a particular Homeric way of life? This is what happened to Pythagoras:[8] he wasn't only held in extremely high regard for his teaching during his lifetime, but his successors even now call their way of life Pythagorean and somehow seem to stand out from all other people.'

'No, there's no hint of that sort of thing either,' he said. 'I mean, Homer's associate Creophylus'[9] cultural attainments would turn out to be even more derisory than his name suggests they are, Socrates, if the stories about Homer are true. You see, Creophylus is said to have more or less disregarded Homer during his lifetime.'

'Yes, that *is* what we're told,' I agreed. 'But, Glaucon, if Homer really had been an educational expert whose products were better people—which is to say, if he had knowledge in this sphere and his abilities were not limited to representation—don't you think he'd have been surrounded by hordes of associates, who would have admired him and valued his company highly? Look at Protagoras of Abdera, Prodicus of Ceos,[1] and all the rest of them: they can use their exclusive tuition to make their contemporaries believe that without them in charge of their education they won't be capable of managing

4. Traditional founder of the Spartan political, social, and legal systems.
5. Athenian statesman and poet (ca. 638–559 B.C.E.) who reformed the city's constitution. Charondas (6th c. B.C.E.), lawgiver of Catana and other colonies of Chalcis in Sicily.
6. The "guild" of people who claimed descent from Homer, in the sense of maintaining and perpetuating his poems, also claimed inside knowledge of all aspects of the poet's life and perpetuated a lot of apocryphal tales about him [translator's note]. *Homeridae* literally means "Sons of Homer."
7. Scythian prince (6th c. B.C.E.) who traveled widely in Greece and gained a reputation for wisdom; he was said to have invented the potter's wheel. Thales (6th c. B.C.E.) reputed founder of geometry and physical science, who calculated eclipses and discovered the solstice.
8. Greek philosopher and mathematician (6th c. B.C.E.).
9. Greek poet; his name literally means "meat-kin." Glaucon's meaning is that meat was a more important part of a coarse athlete's diet than a cultured intellectual's; and it would have been a sign of culture on Creophylus's part not to have neglected his mentor [translator's note].
1. Greek sophist, a contemporary of Socrates. Protagoras (5th c. B.C.E.), Greek philosopher, one of the most successful of the sophists.

their own estates, let alone their communities, and they're so appreciated for this expertise of theirs that their associates almost carry them around on their heads.[2] So if Homer or Hesiod had been able to help people's moral development, would their contemporaries have allowed them to go from town to town reciting their poems? Wouldn't they have kept a tighter grip on them than on their money, and tried to force them to stay with them in their homes? And if they couldn't persuade them to do that, wouldn't they have danced attendance on them wherever they went, until they'd gained as much from their teaching as they could?'

'I don't think anyone could disagree with you, Socrates,' he said.

'So shall we classify all poets, from Homer onwards, as representers of images of goodness (and of everything else which occurs in their poetry), and claim that they don't have any contact with the truth? The facts are as we said a short while ago: a painter creates an illusory shoemaker, when not only does he not understand anything about shoemaking, [601] but his audience doesn't either. They just base their conclusions on the colours and shapes they can see.'

'Yes.'

'And I should think we'll say that the same goes for a poet as well: he uses words and phrases to block in some of the colours of each area of expertise, although all he understands is how to represent things in a way which makes other superficial people, who base their conclusions on the words they can hear, think that he's written a really good poem about shoemaking or military command or whatever else it is that he's set to metre, rhythm, and music. It only takes these features to cast this powerful a spell: that's what they're for. But when the poets' work is stripped of its musical hues and expressed in plain words, I think you've seen what kind of impression it gives, so you know what I'm talking about.'

'I do,' he said.

'Isn't it,' I asked, 'like what noticeably happens when a young man has alluring features, without actually being good-looking, and then this charm of his deserts him?'

'Exactly,' he said.

'Now, here's another point to consider. An image-maker, a representer, understands only appearance, while reality is beyond him. Isn't that our position?'

'Yes.'

'Let's not leave the job half done: let's give this idea the consideration it deserves.'

'Go on,' he said.

'What a painter does, we're saying, is paint a picture of a horse's reins and a bit. Yes?'

'Yes.'

'While they're made by a saddler and a smith, aren't they?'

'Yes.'

'Does a painter know what the reins and the bit have to be like? Surely

2. As effigies and images of the gods were carried through the streets during a ritual procession [translator's note].

even their makers, the smith and the saddler, don't know this, do they? Only the horseman does, because he's the one who knows how to make use of them.'

'You're quite right.'

'In fact, won't we claim that it's a general principle?'

'What?'

'That whatever the object, there are three areas of expertise: usage, manufacture, and representation.'

'Yes.'

'Now, is there any other standard by which one assesses the goodness, fineness, and rightness of anything (whether it's a piece of equipment or a creature or an activity) than the use for which it was made, by man or by nature?'

'No.'

'It's absolutely inevitable, then, that no one knows the ins and outs of any object more than the person who makes use of it. He has to be the one to tell the manufacturer how well or badly the object he's using fares in actual usage. A pipe-player,[3] for example, tells a pipe-maker which of his pipes do what they're supposed to do when actually played, and goes on to instruct him in what kinds of pipes to make, and the pipe-maker does what he's told.'

'Of course.'

'So as far as good and bad pipes are concerned, it's a knowledgeable person who gives the orders, while the other obeys the orders and does the manufacturing. Right?'

'Yes.'

'Justified confidence, then, is what a pipe-maker has about goodness and badness (as a result of spending time with a knowledgeable person and having to listen to him), while knowledge is the province [602] of the person who makes use of the pipes.'

'Yes.'

'Which of these two categories does our representer belong to? Does he acquire knowledge about whether or not what he's painting is good or right from making use of the object, or does he acquire true belief because of having to spend time with a knowledgeable person and being told what to paint?'

'He doesn't fit either case.'

'As far as goodness and badness are concerned, then, a representer doesn't have either knowledge or true beliefs about whatever it is he's representing.'

'Apparently not.'

'How nicely placed a poetic representer is, then, to know what he's writing about!'

'Not really.'

'No, because all the same, despite his ignorance of the good and bad aspects of things, he'll go on representing them. But what he'll be representing, apparently, is whatever appeals to a large, if ignorant, audience.'

'Naturally.'

'Here are the points we seem to have reached a reasonable measure of agreement on, then: a representer knows nothing of value about the things

3. Or "flute player."

he represents; representation is a kind of game, and shouldn't be taken seriously; and those who compose tragedies in iambic and epic verse[4] are, without exception, outstanding examples of representers.'

'Yes.'

'So the province of representation is indeed two steps removed from truth, isn't it?' I said.

'Yes.'

'But on which of the many aspects of a person does it exert its influence?'

'What are you getting at?'

'Something like this. One and the same object appears to vary in size depending on whether we're looking at it from close up or far away.'

'Yes.'

'And the same objects look both bent and straight depending on whether we look at them when they're in water or out of it, and both concave and convex because sight gets misled by colouring. Our mind obviously contains the potential for every single kind of confusion like this. It's because illusory painting aims at this affliction in our natures that it can only be described as sorcery; and the same goes for conjuring and all trickery of that sort.'

'True.'

'Now, methods have evolved of combating this—measuring, counting, and weighing are the most elegant of them—and consequently of ending the reign within us of apparent size, number, and weight, and replacing them with something which calculates and measures, or even weighs. Right?'

'Of course.'

'And this, of course, is the job of the rational part of the mind, which is capable of performing calculations.'

'Yes.'

'Now, it's not uncommon for the mind to have made its measurements, and to be reporting that *x* is larger than *y* (or smaller than it, or the same size as it), but still to be receiving an impression which contradicts its measurements of these very objects.'

'Yes.'

'Well, didn't we say that it's impossible for a single thing to hold contradictory beliefs at the same time about the same objects?'

'Yes, we did, and we were right.'

[603] 'So the part of the mind whose views run counter to the measurements must be different from the part whose views fall in with the measurements.'

'Yes.'

'But it's the best part of the mind which accepts measurements and calculations.'

'Of course.'

'The part which opposes them, therefore, must be a low-grade part of the mind.'

'Necessarily.'

'Well, all that I've been saying has been intended to bring us to the point where we can agree that not only does painting—or rather representation in

4. The meter of epics is dactylic hexameter (a 6-foot line based on the syllabic patterns long-short-short); iambic trimeter (a 3-foot line based on the syllabic pattern short-long) was the most common meter of dialogue and set speeches in tragedies.

general—produce a product which is far from truth, but it also forms a close, warm, affectionate relationship with a part of us which is, in its turn, far from intelligence. And nothing healthy or authentic can emerge from this relationship.'

'Absolutely,' he said.

'A low-grade mother like representation, then, and an equally low-grade father produce low-grade children.'

'I suppose that's right.'

'Does this apply only to visual representation,' I asked, 'or to aural representation as well—in other words, to poetry?'

'I suppose it applies to poetry as well,' he said.

'Well, we'd better not rely on mere suppositions based on painting,' I said. 'Let's also get close enough to that part of the mind which poetic representation consorts with to see whether it's of low or high quality.'

'Yes, we should.'

'We'd better start by having certain ideas out in the open. We'd say that representational poetry represents people doing things, willingly or unwillingly, and afterwards thinking that they've been successful or unsuccessful, and throughout feeling distressed or happy. Have I missed anything out?'

'No, nothing.'

'Well, does a person remain internally unanimous throughout all this? We found that, in the case of sight, there's conflict and people have contradictory views within themselves at the same time about the same objects. Is it like that when one is doing things too? Is there internal conflict and dissent? But it occurs to me that there's really no need for us to decide where we stand on this issue now, because we've already done so, perfectly adequately, in an earlier phase of the discussion,[5] when we concluded that, at any given moment, our minds are teeming with countless thousands of these kinds of contradictions.'

'That's right,' he said.

'Yes,' I said. 'But that earlier discussion of ours was incomplete, and I think it's crucial that we finish it off now.'

'What have we left out?' he asked.

'If a good man meets with a misfortune such as losing a son or something else he values very highly, we've already said, as you know, that he'll endure this better than anyone else.

'Yes.'

'But here's something for us to think about. Will he feel no grief, or is that impossible? If it's impossible, is it just that he somehow keeps his pain within moderate bounds?'

'The second alternative is closer to the truth,' he said.

[604] 'But now I've got another question for you about him. Do you think he'll be more likely to fight and resist his distress when his peers can see him, or when he's all alone by himself in some secluded spot?'

'He'll endure pain far better when there are people who can see him, of course,' he said.

'When he's all alone, however, I imagine he won't stop himself expressing

5. In *Republic* 4.439b–444a, where Socrates argues that each mind or soul is divided into three distinct and sometimes warring parts (the rational, the spirited, and the desiring).

a lot of things he'd be ashamed of anyone hearing, and doing a lot of things he'd hate anyone to see him do.'

'That's right,' he agreed.

'Isn't it the case that reason and convention recommend resistance, while the actual event pushes him towards distress?'

'True.'

'When a person is simultaneously pulled in opposite directions in response to a single object, we're bound to conclude that he has two sides.'

'Of course.'

'One of which is prepared to let convention dictate the proper course of action, isn't it?'

'Can you explain how?'

'Convention tells us, as you know, that it's best to remain as unruffled as possible when disaster strikes and not to get upset, on the grounds that it's never clear whether an incident of this nature is good or bad, that nothing positive is gained by taking it badly, that no aspect of human life is worth bothering about a great deal, and that grief blocks our access to the very thing we need to have available as quickly as possible in these circumstances.'

'What do you have in mind?' he asked.

'The ability to think about the incident,' I replied, 'and, under the guidance of reason, to make the best possible use of one's situation, as one would in a game of dice when faced with how the dice had fallen. When children bump into things, they clutch the hurt spot and spend time crying; instead of behaving like that, we should constantly be training our minds to waste no time before trying to heal anything which is unwell, and help anything which has fallen get up from the floor—to banish mourning by means of medicine.'

'Yes, that's the best way to deal with misfortune,' he said.

'Now, our position is that the best part of our minds is perfectly happy to be guided by reason like this.'

'That goes without saying.'

'Whereas there's another part of our minds which urges us to remember the bad times and to express our grief, and which is insatiably greedy for tears. What can we say about it? That it's incapable of listening to reason, that it can't face hard work, that it goes hand in hand with being frightened of hardship?'

'Yes, that's right.'

'Now, although the petulant part of us is rich in a variety of representable possibilities, the intelligent and calm side of our characters is pretty well constant and unchanging. This makes it not only difficult to represent, but also difficult to understand when it is represented, particularly when the audience is the kind of motley crowd you find crammed into a theatre, because they're simply not acquainted with the experience that's being represented to them.'

[605] 'Absolutely.'

'Evidently, then, a representational poet has nothing to do with this part of the mind: his skill isn't made for its pleasure, because otherwise he'd lose his popular appeal. He's concerned with the petulant and varied side of our characters, because it's easy to represent.'

'Obviously.'

'So we're now in a position to see that we'd be perfectly justified in taking hold of him and placing him in the same category as a painter. He resembles a painter because his creations fall short of truth, and a further point of resemblance is that the part of the mind he communicates with is not the best part, but something else. Now we can see how right we'd be to refuse him admission into any community which is going to respect convention, because now we know which part of the mind he wakes up. He destroys the rational part by feeding and fattening up this other part, and this is equivalent to someone destroying the more civilized members of a community by presenting ruffians with political power. There's no difference, we'll claim, between this and what a representational poet does: at a personal level, he establishes a bad system of government in people's minds by gratifying their irrational side, which can't even recognize what size things are—an object which at one moment it calls big, it might call small the next moment—by creating images, and by being far removed from truth.'

'Yes.'

'However, we haven't yet made the most serious allegation against representational poetry. It has a terrifying capacity for deforming even good people. Only a very few escape.'

'Yes, that *is* terrifying. Does it really do that?'

'Here's my evidence: you can make up your mind. When Homer or another tragedian represents the grief of one of the heroes, they have him deliver a lengthy speech of lamentation or even have him sing a dirge and beat his breast; and when we listen to all this, even the best of us, as I'm sure you're aware, feels pleasure. We surrender ourselves, let ourselves be carried along, and share the hero's pain; and then we enthuse about the skill of any poet who makes us feel particularly strong feelings.'

'Yes, I'm aware of this, of course.'

'However, you also appreciate that when we're afflicted by trouble in our own lives, then we take pride in the opposite—in our ability to endure pain without being upset. We think that this is manly behaviour, and that only women behave in the way we were sanctioning earlier.'

'I realize that,' he said.

'So,' I said, 'instead of being repulsed by the sight of the kind of person we'd regret and deplore being ourselves, we enjoy the spectacle and sanction it. Is this a proper way to behave?'

'No, it certainly isn't,' he said. 'It's pretty unreasonable, I'd say.'

[606] 'I agree,' I said, 'and here's even more evidence.'

'What?'

'Consider this. What a poet satisfies and gratifies on these occasions is an aspect of ourselves which we forcibly restrain when tragedy strikes our own lives—an aspect which hungers after tears and the satisfaction of having cried until one can cry no more, since that is what it is in its nature to want to do. When the part of us which is inherently good has been inadequately trained in habits enjoined by reason, it relaxes its guard over this other part, the part which feels sad. Other people, not ourselves, are feeling these feelings, we tell ourselves, and it's no disgrace for us to sanction such behaviour and feel sorry for someone who, even while claiming to be good, is over-indulging in grief; and, we think, we are at least profiting from the pleasure, and there's no point in throwing away the pleasure by spurning the whole poem or play. You see, few people have the ability to work out that we ourselves are bound to store the harvest we reap from others: these occasions feed the feeling of sadness until it is too strong for us easily to restrain it when hardship occurs in our own lives.'

'You're absolutely right,' he said.

'And doesn't the same go for humour as well? If there are amusing things which you'd be ashamed to do yourself, but which give you a great deal of pleasure when you see them in a comic representation or hear about them in private company—when you don't find them loathsome and repulsive[6]—then isn't this exactly the same kind of behaviour as we uncovered when talking about feeling sad? There's a part of you which wants to make people laugh, but your reason restrains it, because you're afraid of being thought a vulgar clown. Nevertheless, you let it have its way on those other occasions, and you don't realize that the almost inevitable result of giving it energy in this other context is that you become a comedian in your own life.'

'Yes, that's very true,' he said.

'And the same goes for sex, anger, and all the desires and feelings of pleasure and distress which, we're saying, accompany everything we do: poetic representation has the same effect in all these cases too. It irrigates and tends to these things when they should be left to wither, and it makes them our rulers when they should be our subjects, because otherwise we won't live better and happier lives, but quite the opposite.'

'I can't deny the truth of what you're saying,' he said.

'Therefore, Glaucon,' I went on, 'when you come across people praising Homer and saying that he is the poet who has educated Greece,[7] that he's a good source for people to learn how to manage their affairs and gain culture in their lives, and that one should structure the whole of one's life in accordance with his precepts, [607] you ought to be kind and considerate: after all, they're doing the best they can. You should concede that Homer is a supreme poet and the original tragedian, but you should also recognize that the only poems we can admit into our community are hymns to the gods and eulogies of virtuous men. If you admit the entertaining Muse of lyric and epic poetry, then instead of law and the shared acceptance of reason as the best guide, the kings of your community will be pleasure and pain.'

'You're quite right,' he agreed.

'So,' I said, 'since we've been giving poetry another hearing, there's our defence: given its nature, we had good grounds for banishing it earlier from our community. No rational person could have done any different. However, poetry might accuse us of insensitivity and lack of culture, so we'd better also tell her that there's an ancient quarrel between poetry and philosophy. There are countless pieces of evidence for this enmity between them, but here are just a few: there's that "bitch yelping and baying at her master"; there's "featuring prominently in the idle chatter of fools"; there's "control by a crowd of know-alls"; there are those whose "subtle notions" lead them to realize that they do indeed have "notional incomes".[8] All the same, we

6. It is important to remember in this paragraph that Greek Old Comedy relied extremely heavily on very crude sexual humor [translator's note].

7. Herodotus said that Homer and Hesiod had described the form and function of the gods for the Greeks. In general, Homer was still in Plato's day considered an essential part of one's education, not only as poetry, but as a source of wisdom, morality, and all kinds of information. This is the background to Plato's attack [translator's note].

8. We know the author of none of these snatches of verse [translator's note].

ought to point out that if the kinds of poetry and representation which are designed merely to give pleasure can come up with a rational argument for their inclusion in a well-governed community, we'd be delighted—short of compromising the truth as we see it, which wouldn't be right—to bring them back from exile: after all, we know from our own experience all about their spell. I mean, haven't *you* ever fallen under the spell of poetry, Glaucon, especially when the spectacle is provided by Homer?'

'I certainly have.'

'Under these circumstances, then, if our allegations met a poetic rebuttal in lyric verse or whatever, would we be justified in letting poetry return?'

'Yes.'

'And I suppose we'd also allow people who champion poetry because they like it, even though they can't compose it, to speak on its behalf in prose, and to try to prove that there's more to poetry than mere pleasure—that it also has a beneficial effect on society and on human life in general. And we won't listen in a hostile frame of mind, because we'll be the winners if poetry turns out to be beneficial as well as enjoyable.'

'Of course we will,' he agreed.

'And if it doesn't, Glaucon, then we'll do what a lover does when he thinks that a love affair he's involved in is no good for him: he reluctantly detaches himself. Similarly, since we've been conditioned by our wonderful societies until we have a deep-seated love for this kind of poetry, [608] we'll be delighted if there proves to be nothing better and closer to the truth than it. As long as it is incapable of rebutting our allegations, however, then while we listen to poetry we'll be chanting these allegations of ours to ourselves as a precautionary incantation against being caught once more by that childish and pervasive love. Our message will be that the commitment appropriate for an important matter with access to the truth shouldn't be given to this kind of poetry. People should, instead, be worried about the possible effects, on one's own inner political system, of listening to it and should tread cautiously; and they should let our arguments guide their attitude towards poetry.'

'I couldn't agree more,' he said.

'You see, my dear Glaucon,' I said, 'what's in the balance here is absolutely crucial—far more so than people think. It's whether one becomes a good or a bad person, and consequently has the calibre not to be distracted by prestige, wealth, political power, or even poetry from applying oneself to morality and whatever else goodness involves.'

'Looking back over our discussion,' he said, 'I can only agree with you. And I think anyone else would do the same as well.'

* * *

ca. 375 B.C.E.

From Phaedrus[1]

* * *

SOCRATES: Well, then, that's enough about artfulness and artlessness in connection with speaking.

PHAEDRUS: Quite.

SOCRATES: What's left, then, is aptness and ineptness in connection with writing: What feature makes writing good, and what inept? Right?

PHAEDRUS: Yes.

SOCRATES: Well, do you know how best to please god when you either use words or discuss them in general?

PHAEDRUS: Not at all. Do you?

SOCRATES: I can tell you what I've heard the ancients said, though they alone know the truth. However, if we could discover that ourselves, would we still care about the speculations of other people?

PHAEDRUS: That's a silly question. Still, tell me what you say you've heard.

SOCRATES: Well, this is what I've heard. Among the ancient gods of Naucratis in Egypt there was one to whom the bird called the ibis is sacred. The name of that divinity was Theuth,[2] and it was he who first discovered number and calculation, geometry and astronomy, as well as the games of checkers and dice, and, above all else, writing.

Now the king of all Egypt at that time was Thamus, who lived in the great city in the upper region that the Greeks call Egyptian Thebes; Thamus they call Ammon.[3] Theuth came to exhibit his arts to him and urged him to disseminate them to all the Egyptians. Thamus asked him about the usefulness of each art, and while Theuth was explaining it, Thamus praised him for whatever he thought was right in his explanations and criticized him for whatever he thought was wrong.

The story goes that Thamus said much to Theuth, both for and against each art, which it would take too long to repeat. But when they came to writing, Theuth said: "O King, here is something that, once learned, will make the Egyptians wiser and will improve their memory; I have discovered a potion for memory and for wisdom." Thamus, however, replied: "O most expert Theuth, one man can give birth to the elements of an art, but only another can judge how they can benefit or harm those who will use them. And now, [275] since you are the father of writing, your affection for it has made you describe its effects as the opposite of what they really are. In fact, it will introduce forgetfulness into the soul of those who learn it: they will not practice using their memory because they will put their trust in writing, which is external and depends on signs that belong to others, instead of trying to remember from the inside, completely on their own. You have not discov-

1. Translated by Alexander Nehamas and Paul Woodruff. The participants in the dialogue are the philosopher Socrates (469–399 B.C.E., Plato's spokesperson) and Phaedrus (ca. 450–400 B.C.E.), a Socratic philosopher. The numbers in square brackets are the Stephanus numbers used almost universally in citing Plato's works; they refer to the pages of a 1578 edition published by Henri Estienne.

2. Also known as Thoth, whom the Greeks identified with Hermes, the messenger of the gods. Naucratis: a Greek trading colony in Egypt. The following story, which reworks elements of Greek and Egyptian mythology, is probably an invention of Plato's.

3. Chief god of the Egyptians, identified by the Greeks with an aspect of Zeus.

ered a potion for remembering, but for reminding; you provide your students with the appearance of wisdom, not with its reality. Your invention will enable them to hear many things without being properly taught, and they will imagine that they have come to know much while for the most part they will know nothing. And they will be difficult to get along with, since they will merely appear to be wise instead of really being so."

PHAEDRUS: Socrates, you're very good at making up stories from Egypt or wherever else you want!

SOCRATES: But, my friend, the priest of the temple of Zeus at Dodona[4] say that the first prophecies were the words of an oak. Everyone who lived at that time, not being as wise as you young ones are today, found it rewarding enough in their simplicity to listen to an oak or even a stone, so long as it was telling the truth, while it seems to make a difference to you, Phaedrus, who is speaking and where he comes from. Why, though, don't you just consider whether what he says is right or wrong?

PHAEDRUS: I deserved that, Socrates. And I agree that the Theban king was correct about writing.

SOCRATES: Well, then, those who think they can leave written instructions for an art, as well as those who accept them, thinking that writing can yield results that are clear or certain, must be quite naive and truly ignorant of Ammon's prophetic judgment: otherwise, how could they possibly think that words that have been written down can do more than remind those who already know what the writing is about?

PHAEDRUS: Quite right.

SOCRATES: You know, Phaedrus, writing shares a strange feature with painting. The offsprings of painting stand there as if they are alive, but if anyone asks them anything, they remain most solemnly silent. The same is true of written words. You'd think they were speaking as if they had some understanding, but if you question anything that has been said because you want to learn more, it continues to signify just that very same thing forever. When it has once been written down, every discourse rolls about everywhere, reaching indiscriminately those with understanding no less than those who have no business with it, and it doesn't know to whom it should speak and to whom it should not. And when it is faulted and attacked unfairly, it always needs its father's support; alone, it can neither defend itself nor come to its own support.

PHAEDRUS: You are absolutely right about that, too.

[276] SOCRATES: Now tell me, can we discern another kind of discourse, a legitimate brother of this one? Can we say how it comes about, and how it is by nature better and more capable?

PHAEDRUS: Which one is that? How do you think it comes about?

SOCRATES: It is a discourse that is written down, with knowledge, in the soul of the listener; it can defend itself, and it knows for whom it should speak and for whom it should remain silent.

PHAEDRUS: You mean the living, breathing discourse of the man who knows, of which the written one can be fairly called an image.

4. A sanctuary of Zeus in Epirus famous as the center of an oracle, which was said to speak through an oak tree (see *Odyssey* 14.327–28, 19.296–97; Herodotus 2.55.1).

SOCRATES: Absolutely right. And tell me this. Would a sensible farmer, who cared about his seeds and wanted them to yield fruit, plant them in all seriousness in the gardens of Adonis[5] in the middle of the summer and enjoy watching them bear fruit within seven days? Or would he do this as an amusement and in honor of the holiday, if he did it at all? Wouldn't he use his knowledge of farming to plant the seeds he cared for when it was appropriate and be content if they bore fruit seven months later?

PHAEDRUS: That's how he would handle those he was serious about, Socrates, quite differently from the others, as you say.

SOCRATES: Now what about the man who knows what is just, noble, and good? Shall we say that he is less sensible with his seeds than the farmer is with his?

PHAEDRUS: Certainly not.

SOCRATES: Therefore; he won't be serious about writing them in ink, sowing them, through a pen, with words that are as incapable of speaking in their own defense as they are of teaching the truth adequately.

PHAEDRUS: That wouldn't be likely.

SOCRATES: Certainly not. When he writes, it's likely he will sow gardens of letters for the sake of amusing himself, storing up reminders for himself "when he reaches forgetful old age" and for everyone who wants to follow in his footsteps, and will enjoy seeing them sweetly blooming. And when others turn to different amusements, watering themselves with drinking parties and everything else that goes along with them, he will rather spend his time amusing himself with the things I have just described.

PHAEDRUS: Socrates, you are contrasting a vulgar amusement with the very noblest—with the amusement of a man who can while away his time telling stories of justice and the other matters you mentioned.

SOCRATES: That's just how it is, Phaedrus. But it is much nobler to be serious about these matters, and use the art of dialectic.[6] The dialectician chooses a proper soul and plants and sows within it discourse accompanied by knowledge—discourse capable of helping itself as well as the man who planted it, [277] which is not barren but produces a seed from which more discourse grows in the character of others. Such discourse makes the seed forever immortal and renders the man who has it as happy as any human being can be.

PHAEDRUS: What you describe is really much nobler still.

SOCRATES: And now that we have agreed about this, Phaedrus, we are finally able to decide the issue.

PHAEDRUS: What issue is that?

SOCRATES: The issue which brought us to this point in the first place: We wanted to examine the attack made on Lysias[7] on account of his writing speeches, and to ask which speeches are written artfully and which not. Now, I think that we have answered that question clearly enough.

PHAEDRUS: So it seemed; but remind me again how we did it.

5. Pots or window boxes used for forcing plants during the festival of Adonis, a Greek mythological figure whose cult is associated with vegetation and fertility.

6. That is, use logic to investigate the nature of truth through critical analysis of concepts and hypotheses.

7. Athenian orator (ca. 459–ca. 380 B.C.E.), whose oration on love provides the occasion for the discussion in *Phaedrus*.

SOCRATES: First, you must know the truth concerning everything you are speaking or writing about; you must learn how to define each thing in itself; and, having defined it, you must know how to divide it into kinds until you reach something indivisible. Second, you must understand the nature of the soul, along the same lines; you must determine which kind of speech is appropriate to each kind of soul, prepare and arrange your speech accordingly, and offer a complex and elaborate speech to a complex soul and a simple speech to a simple one. Then, and only then, will you be able to use speech artfully, to the extent that its nature allows it to be used that way, either in order to teach or in order to persuade. This is the whole point of the argument we have been making.

PHAEDRUS: Absolutely. That is exactly how it seemed to us.

SOCRATES: Now how about whether it's noble or shameful to give or write a speech—when it could be fairly said to be grounds for reproach, and when not? Didn't what we said just a little while ago make it clear—

PHAEDRUS: What was that?

SOCRATES: That if Lysias or anybody else ever did or ever does write—privately or for the public, in the course of proposing some law—a political document which he believes to embody clear knowledge of lasting importance, then this writer deserves reproach, whether anyone says so or not. For to be unaware of the difference between a dream-image and the reality of what is just and unjust, good and bad, must truly be grounds for reproach even if the crowd praises it with one voice.

PHAEDRUS: It certainly must be.

SOCRATES: On the other hand, take a man who thinks that a written discourse on any subject can only be a great amusement, that no discourse worth serious attention has ever been written in verse or prose, and that those that are recited in public without questioning and explanation, in the manner of the rhapsodes,[8] are given only in order to produce conviction. [278] He believes that at their very best these can only serve as reminders to those who already know. And he also thinks that only what is said for the sake of understanding and learning, what is truly written in the soul concerning what is just, noble, and good can be clear, perfect, and worth serious attention: Such discourse should be called his own legitimate children, first the discourse he may have discovered already within himself and then its sons and brothers who may have grown naturally in other souls insofar as these are worthy; to the rest, he turns his back. Such a man, Phaedrus, would be just what you and I both would pray to become.

PHAEDRUS: I wish and pray for things to be just as you say.

SOCRATES: Well, then: our playful amusement regarding discourse is complete. Now you go and tell Lysias that we came to the spring which is sacred to the Nymphs[9] and heard words charging us to deliver a message to Lysias and anyone else who composes speeches, as well as to Homer and anyone else who has composed poetry either spoken or sung, and third, to Solon[1] and anyone else who writes political documents that he calls laws: If any one of you has composed these things with a knowledge of the truth, if you can

8. Professional orators who recited poetry, especially that of Homer and the other epic poets.
9. In Greek mythology, goddesses of lower rank, often associated with aspects of nature (the ocean, trees, etc.).
1. Athenian statesman and poet (ca. 638–559 B.C.E.), who reformed the city's constitution.

defend your writing when you are challenged, and if you can yourself make the argument that your writing is of little worth, then you must be called by a name derived not from these writings but rather from those things that you are seriously pursuing.

PHAEDRUS: What name, then, would you give such a man?

SOCRATES: To call him wise, Phaedrus, seems to me too much, and proper only for a god. To call him wisdom's lover—a philosopher—or something similar would fit him better and be more seemly.

PHAEDRUS: That would be quite appropriate.

SOCRATES: On the other hand, if a man has nothing more valuable than what he has composed or written, spending long hours twisting it around, pasting parts together and taking them apart—wouldn't you be right to call him a poet or a speech writer or an author of laws?

PHAEDRUS: Of course.

SOCRATES: Tell that, then, to your friend.

PHAEDRUS: And what about you? What shall you do? We must surely not forget your own friend.

SOCRATES: Whom do you mean?

PHAEDRUS: The beautiful Isocrates.[2] What are you going to tell him, Socrates? What shall we say he is?

SOCRATES: Isocrates is still young, Phaedrus. But I want to tell you [279] what I foresee for him.

PHAEDRUS: What is that?

SOCRATES: It seems to me that by his nature he can outdo anything that Lysias has accomplished in his speeches; and he also has a nobler character. So I wouldn't be at all surprised if, as he gets older and continues writing speeches of the sort he is composing now, he makes everyone who has ever attempted to compose a speech seem like a child in comparison. Even more so if such work no longer satisfies him and a higher, divine impulse leads him to more important things. For nature, my friend, has placed the love of wisdom in his mind.

That is the message I will carry to my beloved, Isocrates, from the gods of this place; and you have your own message for your Lysias.

PHAEDRUS: So it shall be. But let's be off, since the heat has died down a bit.

SOCRATES: Shouldn't we offer a prayer to the gods here before we leave?

PHAEDRUS: Of course.

SOCRATES: O dear Pan[3] and all the other gods of this place, grant that I may be beautiful inside. Let all my external possessions be in friendly harmony with what is within. May I consider the wise man rich. As for gold, let me have as much as a moderate man could bear and carry with him.

Do we need anything else, Phaedrus? I believe my prayer is enough for me.

PHAEDRUS: Make it a prayer for me as well. Friends have everything in common.

SOCRATES: Let's be off.

ca. 370 B.C.E.

2. Athenian orator, rhetorician, and teacher (436–338 B.C.E.), whose school attracted pupils from all over Greece and greatly influenced later methods of education.

3. Greek god of shepherds and flocks, usually depicted as part human, part goat; he is invoked because this conversation has taken place in the countryside.

ARISTOTLE
384–322 B.C.E.

Alongside his teacher PLATO, Aristotle is the great founding figure of Western philosophy and literary theory. Aristotle invented the scientific method of analysis and, in a wide-ranging series of treatises, codified the divisions of knowledge into disciplines and subdisciplines that carry on to the present day, such as physics, chemistry, zoology, biology, botany, psychology, politics, logic, and epistemology. Unlike Plato, who uses the dialogue to dramatize paths of thinking in a conversational literary form, Aristotle relies in his extant works on categorization and logical differentiation in a straightforward propositional manner. He focuses on the distinctive qualities of any given object of study, whether of plants or of poems, systematically describing their specific features and construction.

Plato and other ancient writers often commented on literary works, but Aristotle inaugurated the systematic and distinctive discipline of literary criticism and theory with the *Poetics*. It is perhaps the most influential work in the history of criticism and theory, shaping future considerations of genre, prosody, style, structure, and form. Its modern impact began in the Renaissance, when it was rediscovered from fragmentary manuscript sources and taken as a rulebook for literary composition. Its descriptions of formal unity influenced seventeenth-century European writers, such as the French dramatist PIERRE CORNEILLE, and eighteenth-century writers reviving its precepts as "neoclassicism." In twentieth-century literary theory the *Poetics* was foundational for formalist methods, which apply objective modes of analysis to linguistic artifacts and discern the structural attributes of literary works; it influenced a wide array of critics, ranging from the Russian formalists (like BORIS EICHENBAUM) and the American New Critics (like WILLIAM K. WIMSATT JR. and MONROE C. BEARDSLEY) to the archetypal critics (notably NORTHROP FRYE) and the French structuralists (like TZVETAN TODOROV).

Aristotle's *Rhetoric* suggests a different avenue for the study of literature. Rather than seeing literary works in terms of their distinctive features and internal construction, it opens for consideration their affective and political dimensions as forms of public speech. Because of its focus on types of public speaking, the *Rhetoric*'s influence on literary study has been less direct than that of the *Poetics*, but its emphasis on audience response undergirds subsequent theoretical approaches concerned with the reader, interpretation, and the political effects of literature. Although Aristotle himself does not favor one avenue of investigation over another, his distinction between poetics and rhetoric reflects a perennial division in literary theory: the split between theories concerned with the internal properties of literature and those concerned with literature's external effects, especially on readers and society.

Aristotle was born in Stagira in northern Greece, which was under the rule of Macedonia. His father, Nicomachus, was the personal physician to and a friend of Amyntus II, the king of Macedonia. Scholars speculate that his father's practice as a physician inculcated in Aristotle a pragmatic interest in biology and the natural world, and Aristotle's ties to the Macedonian court affected his subsequent career. In 367 B.C.E. Aristotle went to study at Plato's Academy in Athens, where he distinguished himself as one of Plato's best students and eventually became a teacher himself. In 347, around the time of Plato's death, Aristotle left Athens; he traveled first to Assos in Asia Minor, where he taught in a colony of Platonists for three years, and then to the island of Lesbos, where he did the biological research that grounded his later scientific treatises. In 344 or 343, Amyntas's son, King Philip, invited Aristotle to tutor his heir, Alexander (later known as Alexander the Great), who was then about thirteen years old. While he had contact with and received the patronage of Alexander until his death, Aristotle concluded his tutoring in 340, after which he probably lived in Macedonia or Stagira, perhaps then completing the *Rhetoric*. In 335, when Alexander acceded to the throne and departed for his campaigns in Asia, Aristotle returned to Athens and began his own school at the Lyceum. He taught poetics, rhetoric, politics, ethics, and metaphysics, and probably at this time worked on his famous treatises, including the *Politics*, the *Nicomachean Ethics*, and the *Poetics*. After the death of Alexander in 323, when public sentiment against Macedonia was rising, Aristotle left Athens to live in Chalcis on the island of Euboea, where he died in 322. For Aristotle the life of the philosopher was not reclusive and scholarly but unfolded in the midst of public affairs.

Only about a fifth of Aristotle's prodigious 150 reported works survive—transmitted, usually imperfectly, through manuscript copies in the Middle Ages. His treatises are known as "esoteric" works, because they were not copied by scribes to be distributed but were available only in libraries for study by others; some seem to be lecture notes or study guides rather than polished works. This accounts for their compressed style and sometimes abrupt transitions, frequent repetitions, and shorthand references to other works or writers. It also makes the works particularly difficult to date, since they were probably composed and revised over a period of time. The *Poetics*, very likely gathered from a set of incomplete notes, survived only in a few faulty copies. Scholars speculate that we have only half the original text and that the missing second half dealt with comedy.

Aristotle's early writings, now known only by the reports of ancient writers, were written in the form of dialogues, obviously showing the influence of Plato. His more mature works, however, depart from his teacher's model in a number of significant ways. Stylistically, he replaces the literary approach with systematic expositions of particular subjects, more in the form of technical manuals than dramatic accounts. Methodologically, Aristotle operates through analysis, which in its root sense entails examining objects by studying their component parts, and through differentiation and classification. For instance, in biology Aristotle starts with the most general category—living organisms; he then examines them according to what differentiates them—as plants, animals, and so on; further classifies them into particular species; and catalogues their distinctive traits. Philosophically, Aristotle grounds his research on a more pragmatic basis than Plato, looking at nature and the objects of the real world. In so doing, he tacitly rejects Plato's fundamental concept of transcendent Ideas or Forms that govern and generate reality. In his own terms, Aristotle often works from induction, drawing his general conclusions from the particular objects he observes, whereas Plato usually works from deduction, drawing particular conclusions from his general metaphysical concept of being.

The *Poetics* demonstrates Aristotle's analytical method, which here parallels that of his examinations of biology or zoology. Aristotle turns to the various categories of human artifacts, differentiating those made in language and eventually focusing on poetry and especially on the species-specific traits of epic and tragedy. He assumes a distinction between the wide class of objects that are humanly made and those that are naturally produced—between, say, a chair and a tree. (The Greek word for "poetry," *poiēsis*, is itself based on the verb "to make.") In treating poetry as a craft, Aristotle differs from Plato, who discusses poetry in terms of inspiration and the emotive transport of the poet—a strain that continues in nineteenth-century Romanticism, exemplified by WILLIAM WORDSWORTH's definition of poetry as "the spontaneous overflow of emotion." Aristotle limits his study of poetry to its observable kinds and its formal construction, more or less ignoring questions about its affective origins, which he regards as falling under the auspices of other pursuits, such as psychology or rhetoric.

Drawing on a wide range of literary examples, especially Sophocles' celebrated tragedy *Oedipus Rex*, Aristotle adduces six salient parts of tragedy, in order of their importance—plot, character, thought, diction, music, and spectacle. He spends the most time on the first, specifying the key features of good plots. Central to Aristotle is imitation (*mimēsis*), and he judges the best plots to have verisimilitude: they must be plausible (even if impossible). He also stresses a logically connected order (an appropriate starting point, elaboration, and a dramatic end or resolution), centered on one unified action rather than depicting multiple, divergent, or unnecessary actions. The best kind of resolution is one that shows a reversal (*peripeteia*) of position for the main character, as well as the character's recognition (*anagnōrisis*) of his or her fate. Aristotle reasons that the characters in tragedy should come from high positions, otherwise their tragic circumstances would not be remarkable; he also prescribes that their fates be linked to their own error (*hamartia*, literally "missing the mark," though frequently translated as "flaw"), rather than from some accident or wickedness. Aristotle concludes somewhat technically by classifying parts of speech (in his discussion of diction), sketching solutions to problems of interpretation, and comparing the genres of tragedy and epic.

Though rooted in the literature of its time (and focusing especially on a form of drama quite different from ours), the extant *Poetics* has continued to powerfully influence criticism. Aristotle's systematic categorization of genus and species and his comparison of tragedy and epic underlie all genre theory. Notably, they undergird modern considerations of the historical movement from epic to the novel, such as those of GYÖRGY LUKÁCS and MIKHAIL BAKHTIN. Perhaps most decisively, Aristotle's systematic description of plot and its component parts ground contemporary narrative theory, in particular the technical field of narratology.

His scientific examination of poetry has been championed by the New Critics Wimsatt and CLEANTH BROOKS as "Aristotle's answer" to Plato, responding both to Plato's view of poetry as a degraded imitation twice removed from the reality of eternal Ideas or Forms and to his suspicion of poetry as stirring emotions in a way that is dangerous for society. Instead of directly disagreeing with Plato, Aristotle implicitly validates poetry by examining it as a legitimate branch of study. Countering Plato's notion of poetry as degraded imitation, Aristotle sees poetry as a source of universal knowledge of human behavior: unlike history, which produces knowledge only of specific situations, poetry describes the actions of characters who might be any humans. Moreover, he claims that good poetry has a positive emotional effect on its audience, which he calls *katharsis*—perhaps the most important and variously interpreted word in the *Poetics*. Some commentators have interpreted the term in a medical sense, as a purgative that flushes out the audience's unwieldy emotion; others see it in terms of moral purification. More recently, critics have equated catharsis with ethical and intellectual clarification.

In other treatises, Aristotle analyzes natural objects in terms of four component "causes," schematized as material, formal, efficient, and final. If we apply this rubric to poetry, the material cause of a poem would be its raw material—language; the formal cause, the shape of the resulting object—the poem; its efficient cause, what makes it—the poet; and the final cause, the end use—its effects on an audience, emotionally as well as educationally and politically. Although Aristotle alludes to audience response in his discussion of catharsis, in the *Poetics* he is most concerned with the material and formal causes of poetry. This concentrated focus has strongly marked modern literary criticism—notably that of the New Critics, who explicitly disallow considerations of the audience as "the affective fallacy," in the phrase of Wimsatt and Beardsley. However, Aristotle is by no means so dismissive. Instead, he treats considerations of the audience—the final cause—as a different line of research, taken up in his *Rhetoric*.

We have come to understand rhetoric as the study of figures of speech, following the medieval and Renaissance traditions (and the modern practice of writers like PAUL DE MAN), but Aristotle defines it more broadly as the ability to see the available means of persuasion. In typical Aristotelian fashion, the *Rhetoric* begins in book 1 by differentiating three elements of persuasion in public speech: the arguments a speaker uses; the *ēthos* or character of the speaker; and the disposition of the audience. Additionally, it differentiates three species of public speeches: deliberative, which deal with future events, as in politics; judicial, which concern past events, as in law courts; and epideictic, which are concerned with the present as they praise or blame a person, as in a eulogy or declamatory attack. Aristotle stresses the importance of argument in part to challenge the then prevalent teachings of the sophists, such as GORGIAS in an earlier generation, who he believed used rhetoric irresponsibly, lacking concern for valid reasoning.

However, Aristotle also acknowledges the elements of persuasion outside the realm of reasoning, paying particular attention to the emotions that speeches induce in their audiences. In book 2, Aristotle adduces the first systematic study of affect, differentiating emotions such as anger, calmness, fear, confidence, shame, pity, indignation, envy, and emulation. In book 3, paralleling his examination of diction in the *Poetics*, Aristotle concludes with a discussion of *lexis* (variously translated as "style," "word choice," or "form of expression"). Perhaps the most important term in the *Rhetoric* is *telos*—the final cause, end, objective, or goal of persuasion—effected through emotion and style as well as argument. The *Rhetoric* highlights the public ends of language rather than its formal properties.

Although its influence has not been as sustained or decisive as that of the *Poetics*, the *Rhetoric* proposes what the twentieth-century philosopher MARTIN HEIDEGGER called the first work of hermeneutics; that is, it considers how response is a factor in interpretation. In its delineations of emotions, it presages the aesthetic tradition, whose concern is the affective dimensions of literary works, and it provides a grounding for reader-response theory, which centers on subjective audience interaction rather than the objective features of the work itself. Perhaps most significantly, it suggests the historical and political significance of literature in its role as public discourse.

Whether acknowledged or not, Aristotle's seminal distinction between poetics and rhetoric has been crucial in contemporary debates over the proper object of literary criticism. Against the tendency fostered by the New Critics and later the deconstructive critics who advocated a narrow linguistic study of literature, recent decades have witnessed a "rhetorical turn" toward methods favoring attention to the personal, historical, and social effects of literary texts. Some object that such approaches address topics outside the purview of literary study. That is, they urge a strict poetic view, arguing that literary criticism should focus on the distinctive attributes of literary works. But when we take account of his *Rhetoric* alongside the *Poetics*, we see that Aristotle does not disallow these other topics; he opens literary study to a consideration of its pedagogical and social ends as well as its distinctive formal properties.

BIBLIOGRAPHY

There are a vast number of editions and translations of Aristotle's works, from the medieval period to the present. Our text of the *Poetics* comes from *"Poetics" I, with the "Tractatus Coislinianus," A Hypothetical Reconstruction of "Poetics" II, and the Fragments of the "On the Poets,"* admirably translated and annotated by Richard Janko (1986), which is based on the standard edition of Rudolf Kassel, *Aristotelis "De Arte Poetica Liber"* (1965). Our selection from the *Rhetoric* is taken from the definitive present-day English version, *Aristotle "On Rhetoric": A Theory of Civic Discourse*, translated and annotated by George A. Kennedy (1991), which also includes useful commentary. It draws on an amalgam of Greek texts, including *Aristotelis "Ars Rhetorica,"* edited by W. David Ross (1959); *Aristote, "Rhétorique,"* edited by Médéric Dufour and André Wartelle (3 vols., 1960–73); and *Aristotelis "Ars Rhetorica,"* edited by Rudolf Kassel (1976). *The Complete Works of Aristotle*, edited by Jonathan Barnes (2 vols., 1984), contains the best compendium of Aristotle's works in English. *The Basic Works of Aristotle*, edited by Richard McKeon (1941), who was the leading American expositor of Aristotle through the mid–twentieth century, is an earlier but still useful compendium.

Jonathan Barnes's *Aristotle* (1982) is a brief, accessible overview of Aristotle's life and works. In a crowded field, Abraham Edel's *Aristotle and His Philosophy* (1982) and John M. Rist's *Mind of Aristotle* (1989) stand out as good basic introductions to Aristotle's biography and works. *The Cambridge Companion to Aristotle*, edited by Barnes (1995), contains chapters on important phases of Aristotle's philosophical project, including a survey of his life and work by Barnes.

On the *Poetics*, Stephen Halliwell's *Aristotle's "Poetics"* (1986) is the authoritative contemporary interpretation. Gerald F. Else, *Aristotle's "Poetics": The Argument* (1957), provides a detailed commentary on the text, and his *Plato and Aristotle on Poetry* (1986) is a useful comparative study. D. W. Lucas's *Aristotle—"Poetics"* (1968) offers significant commentary as well as the Kassel edition of the Greek text. Martha Nussbaum's *Fragility of Goodness: Luck and Ethics in Greek Philosophy* (1986) contains an influential modification of the argument about catharsis. *Aristotle's "Poetics" and English Literature: A Collection of Critical Essays*, edited by Elder Olson (1965), gathers views from the eighteenth century through the 1960s, highlighting the work of the Chicago Critics, or "Neo-Aristotelians," who promoted a formal method in literary study during the mid–twentieth century. Its last chapter, "Rhetoric and Poetic in the Philosophy of Aristotle," by Richard McKeon, a Chicago Critic, offers an illuminating discrimination of poetic and rhetorical approaches. McKeon's "Literary Criticism and the Concept of Imitation in Antiquity," in *Critics and Criticism: Essays in Method* (ed. R. S. Crane, 1952), is an important text on imitation. *Essays on Aristotle's "Poetics,"* edited by Amélie Oksenberg Rorty (1992), is an excellent contemporary collection by philosophers and scholars of Aristotle, clarifying concepts such as mimesis, catharsis, and comedy.

On the *Rhetoric*, W. M. A. Grimaldi's *Aristotle, "Rhetoric": A Commentary* (1980) is a useful exposition. *Essays on Aristotle's "Rhetoric"* (1996), edited by Amélie Oksenberg Rorty as a companion to her volume on the *Poetics*, provides an excellent range of contemporary interpretations and reevaluations of the text. Alexander Nehamas's "Pity and Fear in the *Rhetoric* and *Poetics*," in *Aristotle's "Rhetoric": Philosophical Essays* (ed. David J. Furley and Nehamas, 1994), cogently compares Aristotle's treatment of emotion in both texts and, in a provocative argument, claims that catharsis refers to the internal resolution of a tragic plot itself rather than to the response of the audience.

The "Poetics" of Aristotle and the "Tractatus Coislinianus": A Bibliography from about 900 till 1996, compiled by Omert J. Schrier (1998), testifies to the massive literature relating to the *Poetics*. *Aristotle's "Rhetoric": Five Centuries of Philological Research*, compiled by Keith V. Erickson (1975), covers the many studies of the *Rhetoric*. *The Cambridge Companion to Aristotle* contains an excellent bibliography on all of Aristotle's work, with individual sections on the *Poetics* and *Rhetoric*. Both Janko's edition of the *Poetics* and Kennedy's of the *Rhetoric* include selective bibliographies on their respective texts. The Rorty collections on the *Poetics* and *Rhetoric* also include good selective bibliographies.

Poetics[1]

[1, 1447a] Our topic is poetry in itself and its kinds, and what potential each has; how plots should be constructed if the composition is to turn out well;

1. Translated by Richard Janko, who sometimes adds clarifying words or phrases in square brackets and includes the Greek in parentheses. Also in square brackets in the text are the traditional chapter divisions inserted by Renaissance editors and the Bekker numbers used almost universally in citing Aristotle's works; they refer to the page numbers and columns of an 1831 edition by Immanuel Bekker.

also, from how many parts it is [constituted], and of what sort they are; and likewise all other aspects of the same enquiry. Let us first begin, following the natural [order], from first [principles].

Epic and tragic composition, and indeed comedy, dithyrambic composition,[2] and most sorts of music for wind and stringed instruments are all, [considered] as a whole, representations.[3] They differ from one another in three ways, by using for the representation (i) different media, (ii) different objects, or (iii) a manner that is different and not the same.

Some people use colours and forms for representations, making images of many objects (some by art, and some by practice), and others do so with sound; so too all the arts we mentioned produce a representation using rhythm, speech and melody, but use these either separately or mixed. E.g., the art of [playing] the oboe and lyre, and any other arts that have the same potential (e.g. that of [playing] the pan-pipes), use melody and rhythm alone, but the art of dancers [uses] rhythm by itself without melody; for they too can represent characters, sufferings and actions, by means of rhythms given form.

But the art of representation that uses unaccompanied words or verses [1447b] (whether it mixes these together or uses one single class of verse-form) has to the present day no name. For we have no common name for the mimes of Sophron and Xenarchus and the Socratic dialogues,[4] and would not have one even if someone were to compose the representation in [iambic] trimeters, elegiacs[5] or some other such verse. But people attach the word "poet" to the verse-form, and name some "elegiac poets" and other "epic poets," terming them poets not according to [whether they compose a] representation but indiscriminately, according to [their use of] verse. Thus if someone brings out a work of medicine or natural science in verse, they normally call him a poet; but there is nothing in common between Homer and Empedocles[6] except the verse-form. For this reason it is right to call the former a poet, but the latter a natural scientist rather than a poet. Likewise, if someone produced a representation by intermingling all the verse-forms, just as Chaeremon[7] composed his *Centaur* (a recitation which mixes all the verse-forms), he must still be termed a poet. This, then, is how we should define these matters.

Some arts use all the media we have mentioned (i.e. rhythm, song and verse), like the composition of dithyrambic poems, that of nomes,[8] and tragedy and comedy; they differ because the former use all the media at the same time, the latter [use them only] in certain parts. So these are what I mean

2. Greek choral poetry originally sung in honor of Dionysus, the god of wine worshipped in an ecstatic cult.
3. From the Greek *mimēsis*, translated as "representation" or "imitation."
4. The philosophical works of PLATO (ca. 427–ca. 327 B.C.E.), which are written as dialogues featuring his teacher, Socrates (469–399 B.C.E.), and one or more interlocutors. "Mimes": imitative performances usually featuring short scenes from daily life. Sophron of Syracuse (5th c. B.C.E.) wrote mimes in rhythmic prose; his son Xenarchus also wrote mimes.
5. A verse form consisting of couplets whose first line is in dactylic hexameter (i.e., a 6-foot line based on the syllabic pattern long-short-short), the meter of epic, and whose second line replaces the 3d and 6th foot with one long syllable. "Iambic trimeters": the verse form of most dialogue and set speeches in tragedies (a 3-foot line based on the pattern short-long).
6. Pre-Socratic Greek natural philosopher (ca. 493–433 B.C.E.), who wrote in epic meter (dactylic hexameter). Homer (ca. 8th c. B.C.E.), Greek epic poet to whom is attributed the *Iliad* and the *Odyssey*; the ancient Greeks also credited him with a number of lost shorter epics, including the comic *Magrites*.
7. Greek tragedian (mid-4th c. B.C.E.).
8. Originally, melodies (for lyre or flute) created to accompany epic texts; later, choral compositions.

by the differences between the arts in the media by which they produce the representation.

[2, 1448a] Since those who represent people in action, these people are necessarily either good or inferior. For characters almost always follow from these [qualities] alone; everyone differs in character because of vice and virtue. So they are either (i) better than we are, or (ii) worse, or (iii) such [as we are], just as the painters [represent them]; for Polygnotus used to make images of superior persons, Pauson of worse ones, and Dionysius[9] of those like [us].

Clearly each of the [kinds of] representation we mentioned will contain these differences, and will vary by representing objects which vary in this manner. For these divergences can arise in dancing and in playing the oboe and lyre. They can also arise in speeches and unaccompanied verse: e.g. (i) Homer [represents] better persons, (ii) Cleophon [represents] ones like [us], and (iii)Hegemon of Thasos, who was the first to compose parodies, and Nicochares[1] who composed the *Deiliad*, [represent] worse ones. [They can arise] likewise in dithyrambs and nomes: for just as Timotheus and Philoxenus [represented] Cyclopes,[2] [so] one may represent [people in different ways]. Tragedy too is distinguished from comedy by precisely this difference; comedy prefers to represent people who are worse than those who exist, tragedy people who are better.

[3]Again, a third difference among these [kinds] is the manner in which one can represent each of these things. For one can use the same media to represent the very same things, sometimes (a) by narrating (either (i) becoming another [person], as Homer does, or (ii) remaining the same person and not changing), or (b) by representing everyone as in action and activity.

Representation, then, has these three points of difference, as we said at the beginning, its media, its objects and its manner. Consequently, in one respect Sophocles is the same sort of representational artist as Homer, in that both represent good people, but in another he is like Aristophanes,[3] since both represent men in action and doing [things].

This is why, some say, their works are called "dramas," because they represent men "doing" (*drōntas*). For this reason too the Dorians[4] lay claim to both tragedy and comedy. The Megarians[5] here allege that comedy arose during the time of their democracy, and the Megarians in Sicily claim it; for Ephicharmus was from there, though he was not much prior to Chionides and Magnes.[6] Some of the Dorians in the Peloponnese lay claim to tragedy. They produce the names [of comedy and drama] as an indication [of their origins]: they say that they call villages *kōmai* but the Athenians call them *dēmoi*, on the assumption that comedians were so called not from their rev-

9. Painter from Colophon. Polygnotus (ca. 500–ca. 440 B.C.E.), one of the first great Greek painters. Pauson (late 5th c. B.C.E.), Athenian caricaturist.

1. Athenian comic poet (active ca. 390 B.C.E.), whose *Deiliad* (*deilos* means "cowardly") parodied heroic epic. Cleophon (4th c. B.C.E.), Athenian tragic poet. Hegemon (5th c. B.C.E.), poet whose parodies won competitions in Athens.

2. Mythical one-eyed giants. Timotheus of Miletus (ca. 450– ca. 360 B.C.E.) and Philoxenus of Cythera (ca. 435–ca. 380 B.C.E.) were both Greek dithyrambic poets.

3. Greatest poet of Greek Old Comedy (450–385 B.C.E.). Sophocles (ca. 496–406 B.C.E.), great Greek tragedian.

4. A people (probably originally from southwest Macedonia) that invaded Greece ca. 1100–1000 B.C.E., reaching south into the Peloponnese.

5. Residents of a Dorian city on the Isthmus of Corinth (west of Athens); it was a democracy in the 6th century B.C.E.

6. Aristotle names three early comic poets: Epicharmus was Sicilian (active early 5th c. B.C.E.) and wrote in Doric Greek, while Chionides (active ca. 485 B.C.E.) and Magnes (active ca. 470 B.C.E.) were Athenian.

elling (*kōmazein*), but because they wandered around the villages, ejected in disgrace from the town. [1448b] They also say that they term "doing" *dran*, but that the Athenians term it *prattein*.

Anyway, as for the points of difference in representation, and how many and what they are, let this account suffice.

[4] Two causes seem to have generated the art of poetry as a whole, and these are natural ones.

(i) Representation is natural to human beings from childhood. They differ from the other animals in this: man tends most towards representation and learns his first lessons through representation.

Also (ii) everyone delights in representations. An indication of this is what happens in fact: we delight in looking at the most detailed images of things which in themselves we see with pain, e.g. the shapes of the most despised wild animals even when dead. The cause of this is that learning is most pleasant, not only for philosophers but for others likewise (but they share in it to a small extent). For this reason they delight in seeing images, because it comes about that they learn as they observe, and infer what each thing is, e.g. that this person [represents] that one. For if one has not seen the thing [that is represented] before, [its image] will not produce pleasure as a representation, but because of its accomplishment, colour, or some other such cause.

Since by nature we are given to representation, melody and rhythm (that verses are parts of rhythms is obvious), from the beginning those by nature most disposed towards these generated poetry from their improvisations, developing it little by little. Poetry was split up according to their particular characters; the grander people represented fine actions, i.e. those of fine persons, the more ordinary people represented those of inferior ones, at first composing invectives, just as the others composed hymns and praise-poems. We do not know of any composition of this sort by anyone before Homer, but there were probably many [who composed invectives]. Beginning with Homer [such compositions] do exist, e.g. his *Margites* etc. In these the iambic verse-form arrived too, as is appropriate. This is why it is now called "iambic", because they used to lampoon (*iambizein*) each other in this verse-form. Thus some of the ancients became composers of heroic poems, others of lampoons.

Just as Homer was the greatest composer of serious poetry (not that he alone composed well, but because he alone composed dramatic representations), so too he was first to indicate the form of comedy, by dramatising not an invective but the laughable. For his *Margites* stands in the same relation to comedies as do the *Iliad* and *Odyssey* to tragedies. [1449a] When tragedy and comedy appeared, people were attracted to each [kind of] composition according to their own particular natures. Some became composers of comedies instead of lampoons, but others presented tragedies instead of epics, because comedy and tragedy are greater and more honourable in their forms than are lampoon and epic. To consider whether tragedy is now fully [developed] in its elements or not, as judged both in and of itself and in relation to its audiences, is a different topic.

Anyway, arising from an improvisatory beginning (both tragedy and comedy—tragedy from the leaders of the dithyramb, and comedy from the leaders of the phallic processions which even now continue as a custom in many of our cities), [tragedy] grew little by little, as [the poets] developed whatever [new part] of it had appeared; and, passing through many changes, tragedy came to a halt, since it had attained its own nature.

(i) Aeschylus[7] was first to increase the number of its actors from one to two; he reduced the [songs] of the chorus, and made speech play the main role. Sophocles [brought in] three actors and scenery.

(ii) Again, as for its magnitude, [starting] from trivial plots and laughable diction, because it had changed from a satyric [composition],[8] [tragedy only] became grand at a late date. Its verse-form altered from the tetrameter[9] to iambic verse. For at first [poets] used the tetrameter, because the composition was satyric and mainly danced; but when [spoken] diction came in, nature itself found the proper verse-form. The iambic is the verse most suited to speech; and indication of this is that in [everyday] speech with each other we use mostly iambic [rhythms], but rarely hexameters, and [only] when we depart from the intonations of [everyday] speech.

(iii) Again, as for the number of its episodes,[1] and how each of its other [parts] is said to have been elaborated, let them pass as described; it would probably be a major undertaking to go through their particulars.

[5] Comedy is, as we said, a representation of people who are rather inferior—not, however, with respect to every [kind of] vice, but the laughable is [only] a part of what is ugly. For the laughable is a sort of error and ugliness that is not painful and destructive, just as, evidently, a laughable mask is something ugly and distorted without pain.

The transformations of tragedy, and [the poets] who brought them about, have not been forgotten; but comedy was disregarded from the beginning, because it was not taken seriously. [1449b] For the magistrate granted a chorus of comic performers at a late date—they had been volunteers. The record of those termed its poets begins from [a time] when comedy already possessed some of its forms. It is unknown who introduced masks, prologues, a multiplicity of actors, etc. As for the composing of plots, Epicharmus and Phormis[2] [introduced it]. In the beginning it came from Sicily, and, of the poets at Athens, Crates[3] was the first to relinquish the form of the lampoon and compose generalised stories, i.e. plots.

Epic poetry follows tragedy insofar as it is a representation of serious people which uses speech in verse; but they differ in that [epic] has a single verse-form, and is narrative. Again, with respect to length, tragedy attempts as far as possible to keep within one revolution of the sun or [only] to exceed this a little, but epic is unbounded in time; it does differ in this respect, even though [the poets] at first composed in the same way in tragedies as in epics. As for their parts, some are the same, others are particular to tragedy. For this reason, whoever knows about good and inferior tragedies knows about

7. The earliest of the 3 great Greek tragedians (525–456 B.C.E.).

8. That is, like the satyr plays that formed part of the spring festival of Dionysus in early-5th-century B.C.E. Athens. Each of the poets competing wrote three tragedies and one satyr play; the latter presented grotesque versions of ancient legends, with the chorus dressed as satyrs (half-man, half-goat, and wearing a phallus).

9. That is, trochaic tetrameter (a 4-foot line based on the syllabic pattern long-short); though occasionally used for dialogue in tragedies, this fast-moving line was thought less stately than iambic meter. The choruses in tragedies used other meters.

1. The sections of a tragedy that are positioned between two choruses.

2. Syracusan writer of comedy, apparently a contemporary of Epicharmus.

3. Athenian comic poet (active ca. 450–ca. 430 B.C.E.).

epics too. Tragedy possesses all [the parts] that epic has, but those that it possesses are not all in epic.

[6] We will discuss representational art in hexameters, and comedy, later. Now let us discuss tragedy, taking up the definition of its essence that results from what we have said.

Tragedy is a representation of a serious, complete action which has magnitude, in embellished speech, with each of its elements [used] separately in the [various] parts [of the play]; [represented] by people acting and not by narration; accomplishing by means of pity and terror the catharsis[4] of such emotions.

By "embellished speech," I mean that which has rhythm and melody, i.e. song; by "with its elements separately," I mean that some [parts of it] are accomplished only by means of spoken verses, and others again by means of song.

Since people acting produce the representation, first (i) the ornament of spectacle will necessarily be a part of tragedy; and then (ii) song and (iii) diction, for these are the media in which they produce the representation. By "diction" I mean the construction of the [spoken] verses itself; by "song" I mean that of which the meaning is entirely obvious.

Since [tragedy] is a representation of an action, and is enacted by people acting, these people are necessarily of a certain sort according to their character and their reasoning. For it is because of these that we say that actions are of a certain sort, [1450a] and it is according to people's actions that they all succeed or fail. So (iv) the plot is the representation of the action; by "plot" here, I mean the construction of the incidents. By (v) the "characters," I mean that according to which we say that the people in action are of a certain sort. By (vi) "reasoning," I mean the way in which they use speech to demonstrate something or indeed to make some general statement.

So tragedy as a whole necessarily has six parts, according to which tragedy is of a certain sort. These are plot, characters, diction, reasoning, spectacle and song. The media in which [the poets] make the representation comprise two parts [i.e. diction and song], the manner in which they make the representation, one [i.e. spectacle], and the objects which they represent, three [i.e. plot, character and reasoning]; there are no others except these. Not a few of them, one might say, use these elements; for they may have instances of spectacle, character, plot, diction, song and reasoning likewise.

But the most important of these is the structure of the incidents. For (i) tragedy is a representation not of human beings but of action and life. Happiness and unhappiness lie in action, and the end [of life] is a sort of action, not a quality; people are of a certain sort according to their characters, but happy or the opposite according to their actions. So [the actors] do not act in order to represent the characters, but they include the characters for the sake of their actions. Consequently the incidents, i.e. the plot, are the end of tragedy, and the end is most important of all.

(ii) Again, without action a tragedy cannot exist, but without characters it may. For the tragedies of most recent [poets] lack character, and in general there are many such poets. E.g. too among the painters, how Zeuxis[5] relates

4. A much-debated Greek term, related to a verb meaning "to cleanse" or "purify"; usually left untranslated and understood as "purgation," it can also mean "clarification."

5. Greek painter from Heraclea in southern Italy; he was in Athens ca. 400 B.C.E.

to Polygnotus—Polygnotus is a good character-painter, but Zeuxis' painting contains no character at all.

(iii) Again, if [a poet] puts in sequence speeches full of character, well-composed in diction and reasoning, he will not achieve what was [agreed to be] the function of tragedy; a tragedy that employs these less adequately, but has a plot (i.e. structure of incidents), will achieve it much more.

(iv) In addition, the most important things with which a tragedy enthralls [us] are parts of plot—reversals and recognitions.

(v) A further indication is that people who try their hand at composing can be proficient in the diction and characters before they are able to structure the incidents; e.g. too almost all the early poets.

So plot is the origin and as it were the soul of tragedy, and the characters are secondary. It is very similar [1450b] in the case of painting too: if someone daubed [a surface] with the finest pigments indiscriminately, he would not give the same enjoyment as if he had sketched an image in black and white. Tragedy is a representation of an action, and for the sake of the action above all [a representation] of the people who are acting.

Reasoning comes third, i.e. being able to say what is possible and appropriate, which is its function in the case of the speeches of civic life and rhetoric. The old [poets] made people speak like citizens, but the recent ones make them speak like rhetoricians. Character is that which reveals decision, of whatever sort; this is why those speeches in which the speaker decides or avoids nothing at all do not have character. Reasoning, on the other hand, is that with which people demonstrate that something is or is not, or make some universal statement.

Diction is fourth. By "diction" I mean, as we said earlier, communication by means of language, which has the same potential in the case of both verse and [prose] speeches.

Of the remaining [parts], song is the most important of the embellishments. Spectacle is something enthralling, but is very artless and least particular to the art of poetic composition. The potential of tragedy exists even without a performance and actors; besides, the designer's art is more essential for the accomplishment of spectacular [effects] than is the poets'.

[7] Now that these definitions have been given, let us next discuss what sort of structure of the incidents there should be, since this is the first and most important [part] of tragedy. We have laid down that tragedy is the representation of a complete i.e. whole action which has some magnitude (for there can be a whole with no magnitude). A whole is that which has a beginning, a middle and a conclusion. A beginning is that which itself does not of necessity follow something else, but after which there naturally is, or comes into being, something else. A conclusion, conversely, is that which itself naturally follows something else, either of necessity or for the most part, but has nothing else after it. A middle is that which itself naturally follows something else, and has something else after it. Well-constructed plots, then, should neither begin from a random point nor conclude at a random point, but should use the elements we have mentioned [i.e. beginning, middle and conclusion].

Further, to be fine both an animal and every thing which is constructed from some [parts] should not only have these [parts] in order, but also possess a magnitude that is not random. For fineness lies in magnitude and order. For this reason a fine animal can be neither very small, for observation becomes confused when it approaches an imperceptible instant of time; nor [can it be] very large, for [1451a] observation cannot happen at the same time, but its unity and wholeness vanish from the observers' view, e.g. if there were an animal a thousand miles long. Consequently, just as in the case of bodies and of animals these should have magnitude, but [only] a magnitude that is easily seen as a whole, so too in the case of plots these should have length, but [only] a length that is easily memorable.

As for the limit on their length, one limit relates to performances and the perception [of them], not to the art [itself]. If the performance of a hundred tragedies were required [at one tragic competition], they would be performed "against the clock," as the saying goes! But as for the limit according to the nature of the thing [itself], the larger the plot is, the finer it is because of its magnitude, so long as the whole is still clear. To give a simple definition, in whatever magnitude a change from misfortune to good fortune, or from good fortune to misfortune, can come about by a sequence of events in accordance with probability or necessity—this is an adequate definition of its magnitude.

[8] A plot is not unified, as some suppose, if it concerns one single person. An indefinitely large number of things happens to one person, in some of which there is no unity. So too the actions of one person are many, but do not turn into a single action. For this reason, it seems, all those poets who composed a *Heracleid, a Theseid*[6] or similar poems are in error. They suppose that, because Heracles was a single person, his story too must be a single story. But, just as Homer is superior in other respects, it seems that he saw this clearly as well (whether by art or by nature). In composing the *Odyssey*, he did not put into his poem everything that happened to *Odysseus*,[7] e.g. that he was wounded on Parnassus and pretended to be insane during recruitment; whether one of these things happened did not make it necessary or probable that the other would happen. But he constructed the *Odyssey* around a single action of the kind we are discussing, and the *Iliad* similarly.

Therefore, just as in the other representational arts a single representation is of a single [thing], so too the plot, since it is a representation of action, ought to represent a single action, and a whole one at that; and its parts (the incidents) ought to be so constructed that, when some part is transposed or removed, the whole is disrupted and disturbed. Something which, whether it is present or not present, explains nothing [else], is no part of the whole.

[9] It is also obvious from what we have said that it is the function of a poet to relate not things that have happened, but things that may happen, i.e. that are possible in accordance with probability or necessity. For [1451b] the historian and the poet do not differ according to whether they write in verse or without verse—the writings of Herodotus[8] could be put into verse, but they would be no less a sort of history in verse than they are without verses. But the difference is that the former relates things that have happened, the latter things that may happen. For this reason poetry is a more philosophical and more serious thing than history; poetry tends to speak of

6. In ancient Greece, there were several epic *Heracleids* and *Theseids*—poems depicting, respectively, the heroes Heracles and Theseus.

7. The wily king of Ithaca whose efforts to return home to Greece after the Trojan War are chronicled in the *Odyssey*.

8. Greek historian (ca. 484–425 B.C.E.), chiefly of the Persian Wars; sometimes called "the father of history."

universals, history of particulars. A universal is the sort of thing that a certain kind of person may well say or do in accordance with probability or necessity—this is what poetry aims at, although it assigns names [to the people]. A particular is what Alcibiades[9] did or what he suffered.

In the case of comedy this has already become clear. When [comic poets] have composed a plot according to probability, only then do they supply the names at random; they do not, like the composers of lampoons, compose [poems] about particular individuals. In the case of tragedy [the poets] keep to actual names. The reason is that what is possible is believable; we do not believe that what has never happened is possible, but things which have happened are obviously possible—they would not have happened, if they were impossible. Nonetheless, even among tragedies some have only one or two well-known names, and the rest made up; and some have not one, e.g. Agathon's[1] *Antheus*. In this [drama] the incidents and the names alike are made up, and it is no less delightful. Consequently one must not seek to keep entirely to the traditional stories which tragedies are about. In fact it is ridiculous to seek to do so, since even the well-known [incidents] are known only to a few people, but even so everyone enjoys them.

So it is clear from these arguments that a poet must be a composer of plots rather than of verses, insofar as he is a poet according to representation, and represents actions. So even if it turns out that he is representing things that happened, he is no less a poet; for there is nothing to prevent some of the things that have happened from being the sort of things that may happen according to probability, i.e. that are possible, which is why he can make a poetic composition about them.

Among simple plots and actions, episodic [tragedies] are the worst. By "episodic" I mean a plot in which there is neither probability nor necessity that the episodes follow one another. Such [tragedies] are composed by inferior poets because of themselves, but by good ones because of the actors. For in composing competition-pieces, they extend the plot beyond its potential and [1452a] are often compelled to distort the sequence.

The representation is not only of a complete action but also of terrifying and pitiable [incidents]. These arise to a very great or a considerable extent when they happen contrary to expectation but because of one another. For they will be more amazing in this way than if [they happened] on their own, i.e. at random, since the most amazing even among random events are those which appear to have happened as it were on purpose, e.g. the way the statue of Mitys at Argos[2] killed the man who was the cause of Mitys' death, by falling on him as he looked at it. Such things do not seem to happen at random. Consequently plots of this kind are necessarily finer.

[10] Among plots, some are simple and some are complex; for the actions, of which plots are representations, are evidently of these kinds. By "simple," I mean an action which is, as we have defined it, continuous in its course and single, where the transformation comes about without reversal or recognition. By "complex," I mean an action as a result of which the transformation is accompanied by a recognition, a reversal or both. These should

9. Athenian politician and general (ca. 450–404 B.C.E.).
1. Innovative Athenian tragedian (d. ca. 401 B.C.E.); less than 40 lines of his works remain.
2. The providential punishment of the murderer of Mitys of Argos happened some time before or around 374 B.C.E. [translator's note].

arise from the actual structure of the plot, so it happens that they arise either by necessity or by probability as a result of the preceding events. It makes a great difference whether these [events] happen because of those or [only] after those.

[11] A reversal is a change of the actions to their opposite, as we said, and that, as we are arguing, in accordance with probability or necessity. E.g. in the *Oedipus,*[3] the man who comes to bring delight to Oedipus, and to rid him of his terror about his mother, does the opposite by revealing who Oedipus is; and in the *Lynceus,*[4] Lynceus is being led to his death, and Danaus follows to kill him, but it comes about as a result of the preceding actions that Danaus is killed and Lynceus is rescued.

A recognition, as the word itself indicates, is a change from ignorance to knowledge, and so to either friendship or enmity, among people defined in relation to good fortune or misfortune. A recognition is finest when it happens at the same time as a reversal, as does the one in the *Oedipus*. There are indeed other [kinds of] recognition. For it can happen in the manner stated regarding inanimate objects and random events; and one can recognise whether someone has done something or not done it. But the sort that most belongs to the plot, i.e. most belongs to the action, is that which we have mentioned: for such a recognition and reversal [1452b] will contain pity or terror (tragedy is considered to be a representation of actions of this sort), and in addition misfortune and good fortune will come about in the case of such events.

Since recognition is a recognition of people, some recognitions are by one person only of the other, when the identity of one of them is clear; but sometimes there must be a recognition of both persons. E.g. Iphigeneia is recognised by Orestes[5] as a result of her sending the letter, but it requires another recognition for him [to be recognised] by Iphigeneia. These, then, reversal and recognition, are two parts of plot. A third is suffering. Of these, we have discussed reversal and recognition. Suffering is a destructive or painful action, e.g. deaths in full view, agonies, woundings etc.

[12] Regarding the parts of tragedy, we stated earlier which ones should be used as elements. The quantitative parts, i.e. the separate parts into which it is divided, are as follows: (i) prologue, (ii) episode, (iii) exit and (iv) choral [part], with this divided into (a) processional and (b) stationary [song]—these are shared by all [dramas], and [songs sung] from the stage, i.e. dirges—these are particular [to some].

(i) A prologue is a whole part of a tragedy that is before the processional [song] of the chorus.

(ii) An episode is a whole part of a tragedy that is between whole choral songs.

(iii) An exit is a whole part of a tragedy after which there is no song of the chorus.

3. *Oedipus Rex* (ca. 430 B.C.E.), by Sophocles—a play to which Aristotle frequently refers as a model for his definition of tragedy. Unknowingly, Oedipus kills his father, Laius; takes his father's place as king of Thebes; and marries his mother, Jocasta. When he learns that he has not escaped the fate foretold, he gouges out his eyes and banishes himself, hence undergoing a reversal from king to outcast.

4. Lost tragedy by the orator and tragic poet Theodectes (ca. 375–334 B.C.E.), about the daughters of King Danaus of Argos, who ordered them to kill their husbands (all obeyed except Hypermestra, whose husband was Lynceus).

5. In *Iphigeneia in Tauris* (ca. 413 B.C.E.), by Euripides (ca. 485–ca. 406 B.C.E.), the youngest of the 3 great Greek tragedians.

(iv) Of the choral [part], (a) a processional is the first whole utterance of the chorus; (b) a stationary song is a song of the chorus without anapaestic[6] trochaic verse; and (c) a dirge is a lament shared by the chorus and [those] on stage.

Regarding the parts of tragedy, we stated earlier which ones should be used [as elements]; the quantitative ones, i.e the separate parts into which it is divided, are these.

[13] After what we have just been saying, we must perhaps discuss next what [poets] should aim at and what they should beware of in constructing plots, i.e. how tragedy will achieve its function. Since the construction of the finest tragedy should be not simple but complex, and moreover it should represent terrifying and pitiable events (for this is particular to representation of this sort), first, clearly, it should not show (i) decent men undergoing a change from good fortune to misfortune; for this is neither terrifying nor pitiable, but shocking. Nor [should it show] (ii) wicked men [passing] from misfortune to good fortune. This is most untragic of all, as it has nothing of what it should; for it is neither morally satisfying nor pitiable nor terrifying. [1453a] Nor, again, [should it show] (iii) a thoroughly villainous person falling from good fortune into misfortune: such a structure can contain moral satisfaction, but not pity or terror, for the former is [felt] for a person undeserving of his misfortune, and the latter for a person like [ourselves]. Consequently the outcome will be neither pitiable nor terrifying.

There remains, then, the person intermediate between these. Such a person is one who neither is superior [to us] in virtue and justice, nor undergoes a change to misfortune because of vice and wickedness, but because of some error, and who is one of those people with a great reputation and a good fortune, e.g. Oedipus, Thyestes[7] and distinguished men from similar families. Necessarily, then, a plot that is fine is single rather than (as some say) double, and involves a change not from misfortune to good fortune, but conversely, from good fortune to misfortune, not because of wickedness but because of a great error by a person like the one mentioned, or by a better person rather than a worse one.

An indication [that this is so] is what is coming about. At first the poets recounted stories at random, but now the finest tragedies are constructed around a few households, e.g. about Alcmeon, Oedipus, Orestes, Meleager, Thyestes, Telephus and the others, who happen to have had dreadful things done to them, or to have done them.[8] So the tragedy which is finest according to the [principles of the] art results from this structure. For this reason, people make the same error when they bring against Euripides the charge that he does this in his tragedies, and many of his [tragedies] end in misfortune; for this, as we said, is correct. A very important indication [that this is so is the following].

6. Based on a foot of the syllabic pattern short-short-long (sometimes known as marching meter because of its regularity).

7. Like Oedipus, a popular subject for Greek tragedy, though none survive; his story has numerous variants. He unknowingly ate the flesh of his own sons, served by his brother Atreus; and following the advice of an oracle, he committed incest with his daughter to beget the son who would avenge him.

8. Few of the tragedies involving these characters survive. Alcmaeon and Orestes kill their mothers, Eriphyle and Clytemnestra, to avenge their fathers' deaths and are driven mad by the Furies (female demons who punish kin-murderers); Meleager kills his uncles, and as a result his mother kills him; and Telephus, fated to kill his great-uncles, is exposed by his grandfather (a tragedy by Euripides told of Telephus's wound, received from Achilles as the Greeks were preparing to sail for Troy, that would not heal).

On stage, i.e. in performance, tragedies of this sort, if they are done correctly, are obviously the most tragic, and although Euripides manages badly in other respects, he is obviously the most tragic of poets.

The second[-best] structure is that which some say is first, the [tragedy] which has a double structure like the *Odyssey*, and which ends in opposite ways for the better and worse [persons]. This [structure] would seem to be first because of the weakness of the audiences; the poets follow the spectators, composing to suit their wishes. But this is not the pleasure [that comes] from tragedy, but is more particular to comedy. There the bitterest enemies in the story, e.g. Orestes and Aegisthus,[9] exit as friends at the conclusion, and nobody kills anyone else.

[14, 1453b] That which is terrifying and pitiable can arise from spectacle, but it can also arise from the structure of the incidents itself; this is superior and belongs to a better poet. For the plot should be constructed in such a way that, even without seeing it, someone who hears about the incidents will shudder and feel pity at the outcome, as someone may feel upon hearing the plot of the *Oedipus*. To produce this by means of spectacle is less artful and requires lavish production. Those [poets] who use spectacle to produce what is only monstrous and not terrifying have nothing in common with tragedy. For we should not seek every [kind of] pleasure from tragedy, but [only] the sort which is particular to it. Since the poet should use representation to produce the pleasure [arising] from pity and terror, it is obvious that this must be put into the incidents.

Let us consider, then, what sorts of occurrence arouse dread or compassion in us. These sorts of action against each another necessarily take place between friends, enemies or people who are neither. If it is one enemy [who does the action] to another, there is nothing pitiable, whether he does it or is [only] about to do it, except in the suffering itself. Nor [is it pitiable] if the people are neither [friends nor enemies]. But when suffering happen within friendly relationships, e.g. brother against brother, son against father, mother against son or son against mother, when someone kills someone else, is about to, or does something else of the same sort—these are what must be sought after.

[The poet] cannot undo the traditional stories, I mean e.g. that Clytaemestra is killed by Orestes or Eriphyle by Alcmeon; but he should invent for himself, i.e. use the inherited [stories], well. Let me explain more clearly what I mean by "well."

The action may arise (i) in the way the old [poets] made people act knowingly, i.e. in full knowledge, just as Euripides too made Medea[1] kill her children. Or (ii) they may be going to act, in full knowledge, but not do it. Or (iii) they may act, but do the dreadful deed in ignorance, and then recognise the friendly relationship later, as Sophocles' Oedipus [does]. This is outside the drama; but [they may do the deed] in the tragedy itself, as Astydamas' Alcmeon or Telegonus in the *Wounded Odysseus*[2] [do]. Again, fourth beside

9. Clytemnestra's lover (and Agamemnon's cousin), whom (in the version told in Aeschylus's *Agamemnon*) Orestes also kills.

1. A sorceress from Colchis. In *Medea* (431 B.C.E.), to avenge herself on Jason, who has deserted her for the daughter of a king, she kills his—and her—children.

2. A lost play by Sophocles in which Telegonus, the son of Odysseus and Circe, fatally wounds his father without knowing his identity. Astydamas (active ca. 390 B.C.E.), a prolific Athenian tragedian; *Alcmaeon* (and all but a few lines of his works) is lost.

these [ways] is (iv) to be about to do something deadly in ignorance [of one's relationship], but to recognise it before doing so. Beside these there is no other way; for the act is necessarily either done or not done, and those who act either have knowledge or do not.

Among these [ways], (i) to be about to act in full knowledge, but not do it, is the worst. For this is shocking and also not tragic, as there is no suffering. For this reason nobody composes in this way, [1445a] except rarely, e.g. Haemon against Creon in the *Antigone*.[3] (ii) To act is second[-worst]. (iii) To act in ignorance, but recognise [the relationship] afterwards, is better. This has nothing shocking in it, and the recognition is astonishing. (iv) The last [way] is the best. I mean e.g. the *Cresphontes*, where Merope is about to kill her son, but does not kill him and recognises him; the *Iphigeneia*, where [it is the same for] the sister and her brother; and the *Helle*,[4] where the son is about to hand over his mother but recognises her. This is why, as we said a while ago, tragedies are not about many families. [The poets] sought to produce this sort [of effect] in their plots, and discovered how to not by art but by chance; so they are obliged to concern themselves with those households in which such sufferings have happened.

As for the structure of the incidents, and what sort of plots there should be, let this suffice.

[15] Regarding characters, there are four things at which [the poet] should aim.

(i) First and foremost, the characters should be good. [The tragedy] will have character if, as we said, the speech or the action makes obvious a decision of whatever sort; it will have a good character, if it makes obvious a good decision. [Good character] can exist in every class [of person]; for a woman can be good, and a slave can, although the first of these [classes] may be inferior and the second wholly worthless.

(ii) Second, [they should be] appropriate. It is possible to be manly in character, but it is not appropriate for a woman to be so manly or clever.

(iii) Third, [the character should be life-]like. This is different from making the character good and appropriate in the way already stated.

(iv) Fourth, [the character should be] consistent. If the model for the representation is somebody inconsistent, and such a character is intended, even so it should be consistently inconsistent.

An example of unnecessary villainy of character is the Menelaus in the *Orestes*; of the unsuitable and inappropriate, the lament of Odysseus in the *Scylla*, and the speech of Melanippe;[5] and of the inconsistent, the *Iphigeneia at Aulis* (the girl who begs [for her life] does not seem at all like the later Iphigeneia).[6]

In the characters too, exactly as in the structure of the incidents, [the

3. By Sophocles (ca. 441 B.C.E.). Haemon, who loves Antigone, tries to kill his father (Creon, king of Thebes), who is responsible for her suicide.

4. Nothing more is known of this play. The *Cresphontes* (now lost) and *Iphigenia in Tauris* are both by Euripides.

5. In *Melanippe the Wise*, a lost play by Euripides; the heroine apparently argues with a philosophical sophistication inappropriate for a woman. Menelaus in the *Orestes*; in Euripides' play (408 B.C.E.), Menelaus basely refuses to help his nephew. *Scylla*: a lost dithyramb by Timotheus, in which Odysseus weeps in an unmanly way for his crew members killed by the monster Scylla.

6. That is, *Iphigenia at Tauris*. Euripides' play set at Aulis (ca. 405 B.C.E.) depicts Iphigenia about to be sacrificed by her father, Agamemnon, so that the Greeks may have fair winds as they sail to Troy; according to one version of the myth, she was saved by Artemis and transported far away to Tauris, where she becomes high priestess (and where Orestes later comes).

poet] ought always to seek what is either necessary or probable, so that it is either necessary or probable that a person of such-and-such a sort say or do things of the same sort, and it is either necessary or probable that this [incident] happen after that one.

It is obvious that the solutions of plots too should come about as a result of the plot itself, [1454b] and not from a contrivance, as in the *Medea* and in the passage about sailing home in the *Iliad.*[7] A contrivance must be used for matters outside the drama—either previous events which are beyond human knowledge, or later ones that need to be foretold or announced. For we grant that the gods can see everything. There should be nothing improbable in the incidents; otherwise, it should be outside the tragedy, e.g. that in Sophocles' *Oedipus*.

Since tragedy is a representation of people who are better than we are, [the poet] should emulate the good portrait-painters. In rendering people's particular shape, while making them [life-]like, they paint them as finer [than they are]. So too the poet, as he represents people who are angry, lazy, or have other such traits, should make them such in their characters, [but] decent [too]. E.g. Homer [made] Achilles[8] good as well as an example of stubbornness. [The poet] should guard against these things, as well as against [causing] reactions contrary to those that necessarily follow from the art of poetry. In fact one can often make errors in these; there is a sufficient account of them in my published work.

[16] We stated earlier what recognition is. As for the kinds of recognition, (i) the first is the least artful, which [poets] make most use of from lack of resourcefulness—recognition by signs. Of these, (a) some are congenital, e.g. "the spear-head that the earth-born bear," or [the birth-marks like] stars such as Carcinus[9] [made up] in his *Thyestes*. (b) Others are acquired. Of these (1) some are on the body, e.g. scars, and (2) others are external, e.g. necklaces, and e.g. [the recognition] by means of the dinghy in the *Tyro.*[1]

These can be used more or less well; e.g. Odysseus was recognised from his scar in one way by the nurse, and in another by the swineherds.[2] For the latter recognitions, and all similar ones, are less artful because of the [means of] proof; but those that result from a reversal, like that in the "Bath-scene," are better.

(ii) Second are those recognitions made up by the poet, which is why they are not artful. E.g. in the *Iphigeneia*, how Orestes makes it known that he is Orestes; for Iphigeneia is recognised by means of the letter, but he himself says what the poet wants, not what the plot does. For this reason, this recognition is not far from the error we [just] mentioned; Orestes could have brought some actual objects. Also "the shuttle's voice" in Sophocles' *Tereus.*[3]

7. In *Iliad* 8.155–81, only the arbitrary intervention of the goddess Athena prevents the Greeks from giving up the fight at Troy and going home. The *Medea*: after killing her children, Medea flies off in the chariot of the sun-god Helios, her grandfather; this "contrivance" is the *deus ex machina*.

8. The greatest warrior among the Greeks and the central character of the *Iliad*. He displays his "stubbornness" by long refusing to engage in the battle because of his anger with Agamemnon, the leader of the Greek forces.

9. Prolific Greek tragic poet (early 4th c. B.C.E.). The preceding quotation may be from Euripides' lost *Antigone*.

1. A lost play by Sophocles; Tyro's sons are abandoned in a small boat that leads to their later recognition.

2. Odysseus is recognized artfully (because inevitably) by his nurse when he shows them his scar in the "bath scene" (*Odyssey* 19.386–475); but his declaration of his identity to the swineherds, when he shows them the scar as proof (21.205–25), is manufactured by the poet.

3. A lost play. Philomela tells her sister the story of her rape by Tereus, who has torn out her tongue to silence her, by weaving a picture of it.

(iii) The third [kind of recognition] is by means of a memory, when someone reacts to something he sees, [1455a] like the one in Dicaeogenes' *Cypriots* where he bursts into tears upon seeing the painting, or the one in the "Tale told to Alcinous"[4] where Odysseus hears the lyre-player and weeps at his memories, as a result of which they recognise him.

(iv) Fourth is recognition resulting from an inference, e.g. in the *Libation Bearers*, on the grounds that "someone like [Electra] has come; but there is nobody like [her] except Orestes; it is he, then, who has come".[5] Or the recognition [proposed by] the sophist Polyidus concerning Iphigeneia: it would be reasonable, he said, for Orestes to infer that "his sister was sacrificed, and it [now] falls to him to be sacrificed himself." Or in Theodectes' *Tydeus*, on the grounds that "he came to find a son, but is to die himself." Or the recognition in the *Sons of Phineus*:[6] when the women see the place they infer their fate, on the grounds that "they are fated to be killed there, for [the boys] were left to perish there."

There is also a combined recognition resulting from a false inference by the audience, e.g. in *Odysseus the False Messenger*:[7] for the fact that [Odysseus could] bend the bow, but nobody else [could], is made up by the poet and is a premise, and [so is Odysseus'] saying that he would recognise the bow which he had not seen; but the way he is expected to make himself known by the former means, but does so by the latter, is a [case of] false inference.

(v) The best recognition of all is that which results from the incidents themselves, when our astonishment comes about by means of probable [incidents], e.g. in Sophocles' *Oedipus* and the *Iphigeneia*: it is probable that Iphigeneia would wish to dispatch a letter. For such recognitions alone are without made-up [incidents] and necklaces. Recognitions as a result of inference are second[-best].

[17] In constructing his plots and using diction to bring them to completion, [the poet] should put [the events] before his eyes as much as he can. In this way, seeing them very vividly as if he were actually present at the actions [he represents], he can discover what is suitable, and is least likely to miss contradictions. An indication of this is the [contradiction] for which Carcinus was criticised. His Amphiaraus comes up out of a shrine;[8] this would have been missed by anyone not seeing it as a spectator. But [the play] failed on stage, as the spectators were upset about it.

As far as possible, [the poet should] also bring [his plots] to completion with gestures. Given the same nature, those [poets] who experience the emotions [to be represented] are most believable, i.e. he who is agitated or furious [can represent] agitation and anger most truthfully. For this reason, the art of poetry belongs to the genius or the madman; of these, the first are adaptable, the second can step outside themselves.

As for his stories, both those [already] made up and those he composes himself, [1455b] he should set them out as universals, and only then introduce episodes, i.e. extend them. I mean that he might investigate what is

4. King of the Phaeacians and Odysseus's host in *Iliad* 7–12 (for the telltale weeping, see 8.521–34). Dicaeogenes (late 5th c. B.C.E.), a minor Greek tragedian.

5. Aeschylus, *Libation Bearers* (458 B.C.E.), lines 168–234.

6. Lost, as is *Tydeus*. Polyidus (early 4th c. B.C.E.), perhaps the poet and critic Polyidus of Selymbria.

7. A lost play by an unknown author.

8. In a lost play.

universal in them in the following way, e.g. [the story] of Iphigeneia: "a girl has been sacrificed and disappears in a way unclear to the people who sacrificed her. She is set down in another country, where there is a law that foreigners must be sacrificed to the goddess; this is the priesthood she is given. Some time later it turns out that the priestess' brother arrives. . . ." The fact that the oracle commanded him to go there, for some reason that is not a universal, and his purpose [in going], are outside the plot. "After he arrives, he is captured. When he is about to be sacrificed [by his sister], he makes himself known [to her]," either as Euripides or as Polyidus arranged it, "by saying—as would be probable—that it was not only his sister's fate to be sacrificed, but his own too. This leads to the rescue." After this [the poet] should now supply the names and introduce episodes. Take care that the episodes are particular [to the story], e.g. in Orestes' case his madness through which he is captured, and his rescue by means of the purification.

In dramas the episodes are brief, but epic is lengthened out with them. The story of the *Odyssey* is not long: "someone has been away from home for many years, with a god on the watch for him, and he is alone. Moreover affairs at home are such that his wealth is being consumed by [his wife's] suitors, and his son is being plotted against [by them]. He arrives after much distress, makes himself known to some people, and attacks. He is rescued, his enemies annihilated." This is what is proper [to the *Odyssey*]; its other [parts] are episodes.

[18] [Part] of every tragedy is the complication, and [part] is the solution. The [incidents] outside [the tragedy] and often some of those inside it are the complication, and the rest is the solution. By "complication," I mean the [tragedy] from the beginning up to the final part from which there is a transformation towards good fortune or misfortune; by "solution," the [tragedy] from the beginning of the transformation up to the end. E.g. in Theodectes' *Lynceus*, the prior incidents, the capture of the baby and then its parents' explanation is the complication, and the [tragedy] from the demand for the death penalty up to the end is the solution.

There are four kinds of tragedy (for we said that its parts too are of the same number): (i) the complex tragedy, the whole of which is reversal and recognition; (ii) the tragedy of suffering, e.g. the [tragedies called] *Ajax* and [1456a] *Ixion*;[9] (iii) the tragedy of character, e.g. the *Women of Phthia* and the *Peleus*;[1] (iv) the fourth [kind] is spectacle, e.g. the *Daughters of Phorcys*, the *Prometheus*[2] and [dramas set] in Hades. Preferably [the poet] should attempt to have all [the parts]; otherwise, the most important and the majority of them, especially given the way people belittle poets nowadays. Since there have been poets good at each part [of tragedy], they demand that a single [poet] surpass the particular good [quality] of each one; but it is not right to call a tragedy the same [as another] or different according to anything

9. No play of this name survives. Ixion was the first to murder kin and attempted to rape Hera, queen of the gods; as punishment for the second crime, he is chained forever to a wheel in the underworld. *Ajax*: Sophocles' play (ca. 445 B.C.E.) tells the story of the Greek warrior driven mad by Athena who then commits suicide out of shame.

1. Both lost works revolve around the family of Achilles, who was the son of Peleus and came from Phthia. *Women of Phthia* is by Sophocles; both Sophocles and Euripides wrote plays titled *Peleus*.

2. Perhaps Aeschylus's *Prometheus Bound*, whose hero speaks while bound to the rocks in the Caucasus. *Daughters of Phorcys*: perhaps by Aeschylus. Phorcys was a sea god, and his daughters were monsters: the 3 Graeae, old women who shared one tooth and one eye, and the 3 serpent-haired Gorgons, the sight of whom turned humans to stone.

so much as the plot, that is, [plots] with the same development and solution. Many [poets] develop [the plot] well and solve it badly, but one should harmonise both [parts].

[The poet] ought to remember what we have often said, and not compose a tragedy with an epic structure (by an "epic" structure, I mean one with more than one plot), e.g. if someone were to compose [a tragedy with] the whole plot of the *Iliad*. For there, the parts receive suitable magnitude because of the length [of the epic]; but in dramas the result is far from one's expectation.

An indication [that this is so is the following]: those [tragedians] who composed a *Sack of Troy* as a whole and not in part like Euripides, or a *Niobe*[3] and not like Aeschylus, either fail or compete badly, since even Agathon failed in this one respect. In reversals and in simple incidents, they aim to arouse the amazement which they desire; for this is tragic and morally satisfying. This is possible when someone who is clever but villainous is deceived, like Sisyphus,[4] or someone who is brave but unjust is defeated. This is even probable, as Agathon says; for it is probable that many things will happen even against probability.

[The poet] should regard the chorus as one of the actors. It should be a part of the whole, and contribute to the performance, not as in Euripides but as in Sophocles. In the rest the sung [parts] belong to the plot no more than they belong to another tragedy. For this reason they sing interludes; Agathon was first to begin this. Yet what difference is there between singing interludes and trying to adapt a speech, or a whole episode, from one [drama] to another?

[19] We have discussed the other elements [of tragedy]; it remains to discuss diction and reasoning. As for reasoning, what was said about it in my *Rhetoric*[5] should be assumed; for this is proper rather to that enquiry. All [the effects] that have to be produced by speech fall under reasoning. The types of these are (i) demonstration and refutation, (ii) the production of emotions [1456b] (e.g. pity, terror, anger, etc.), and again (iii) [arguments about things'] importance or unimportance.

In the incidents too [the poet] clearly should use some of the same elements when he needs to make things [e.g.] pitiable, dreadful, important or probable, except that there is this difference, that these [effects] should be apparent without a production, but those dependent on speech should be produced by the speaker and arise from speech. What would be the speaker's function, if the element were apparent even without [the use of] speech?

Among matters related to diction, one kind of investigation is the forms of the diction. Knowledge of this belongs to the art of delivery and to the person with mastery in it. [I mean] e.g. what is a command, what is a wish, a statement, a threat, a question, an answer, etc. No criticism at all made

3. There are no known epics concerning Niobe; Aeschylus's *Niobe* is lost. *Sack of Troy*: a poem in the epic cycle, by Lesches of Mytiline (ca. 7th c. B.C.E.) or Arctinus of Miletus (ca. 8th c. B.C.E.). Euripides treated some of the same events in his *Trojan Women* and *Hecuba*.

4. A sly trickster who murdered travelers and once even chained the god of death, he is punished eternally for betraying Zeus's secrets; he tries to roll a stone over the top of a steep hill, but always fails and must try again from the bottom. Aeschylus, Sophocles, and Euripides all wrote plays on Sisyphus.

5. In a discussion of types of argument; see *Rhetoric* 1356a–1358a.

against the art of poetry, that is based on knowledge or ignorance of these [forms], actually deserves to be taken seriously. What error could anybody consider there to be in "Sing, goddess, of the wrath," which Protagoras[6] criticises on the grounds that [Homer] supposes he is making a wish, but is giving an order? (For Protagoras says that telling someone to do something or not do it is an order.) For this reason let us leave this investigation aside, as it belongs to another art and not to that of poetry.

[20] The parts of diction in its entirety are as follows: (i) the element [i.e. letter], (ii) the syllable, (iii) the particle, (iv) the conjunction, (v) the name [i.e. noun or adjective], (vi) the verb, (vii) the inflection, (viii) the utterance.

(i) The element is an indivisible sound—not every [kind of] sound, but one from which it is natural for a composite sound to arise. For wild animals too make indivisible sounds, none of which I mean by an element. The types of this [kind of] sound are (a) the vowel, (b) the semi-vowel and (c) the consonant.

(a) A vowel is that which has an audible sound without a contact [between the parts of the mouth]. (b) A semi-vowel is that which has an audible sound with [such] a contact, e.g. *s* and *r*. (c) A consonant is that which has no audible sound in itself with [such] a contact, but becomes audible together with those elements that have a sound of some sort; e.g. *g* and *d*.

The elements differ according to the forms of the mouth, the places [in the mouth where they are produced], aspiration, non-aspiration, length, shortness, and also high, low or intermediate pitch. One must investigate the particulars of these matters in works on versification.

(ii) A syllable is a non-significant sound composed of a consonant and [an element] which has sound. In fact *gr* without an *a* is a syllable, and [it is also a syllable] with an *a*, as in *gra*. But the investigation of the differences between these also belongs to the art of versification.

(iii) A particle is (a) a non-significant sound which neither precludes, [1457a] nor brings about, the production of a single significant sound that by nature is composed of several sounds [i.e. an utterance], and which it is not appropriate to place at the beginning of an utterance on its own, e.g. *men, ētoi, de*. Or [it is] (b) a non-significant sound which by nature produces, as a result of [joining together] several sounds that are significant, a single significant sound [i.e. an utterance], e.g. "about," "concerning" etc.

(iv) A conjunction is a non-significant sound which makes clear the beginning of an utterance, its end or its dividing-point, and which by nature is placed both at the extremities and in the middle [of an utterance], e.g. "or," "because," "but."

(v) A name [i.e. noun or adjective] is a composite significant sound without [an indication of] time, no part of which is significant in itself. For in double names we do not use [any part] as being significant in and of itself: e.g. in "Theodore" [i.e. "gift of god"] *dore* is not significant.

(vi) A verb is a composite significant sound with [an indication of] time, no part of which is significant in itself, just as in the case of names. For "human being" or "white" does not signify when, but "walks" or "walked"

6. Pre-Socratic philosopher (5th c. B.C.E.), who was one of the most successful of the sophists, or itinerant teachers. "Sing . . .": the first words of the *Iliad*.

signifies this as well, present time in the first case, and past time in the second.

(vii) An inflection of a name or verb is either (a) the inflection according to the [part] that signifies "of him," "for him," etc., or (b) that according to the [part] that signifies "one" or "many," e.g. "person" or "persons," or (c) that according to the delivery, e.g. according to [whether it is] a question or an order; for "did he walk?" or "walk!" is an inflection of the verb according to these kinds.

(viii) An utterance is a composite significant sound, some parts of which signify something in themselves. For not every utterance is composed of verbs and names, e.g. the definition of a human being, but there can be an utterance without verbs. However, an utterance will always have a part that signifies something [in itself], e.g. "Cleon" in "Cleon walks."

An utterance can be single in two ways, either (a) by signifying one thing, or (b) by a conjunction of several things. E.g. the *Iliad* is one by a conjunction [of many things], but the definition of a human being is one by signifying one thing.

[21] The kinds of name are (i) single (by "single," I mean that which is not composed from [parts] that are significant, e.g. "earth"), and (ii) double. Of the double name, (a) one [kind] is composed of [a part] that is significant and [a part] that is non-significant, except that these [parts] are not significant and non-significant in the [double] name [itself]; (b) the other [kind] is composed of [parts] that are significant. There can be a triple and a quadruple name, even a multiple one: e.g. most of the names of the people of Marseilles, "Hermocaicoxanthus,[7] who prays to Zeus." [1457b] Every name is either (i) standard, (ii) exotic, (iii) a metaphor, (iv) an ornament, (v) made-up, (vi) lengthened, (vii) reduced or (viii) altered.

By (i) "standard," I mean a name which a particular people uses; by (ii) "exotic," I mean one which other people uses. Consequently it is obvious that it is possible for the same [name] to be both exotic and standard, but not for the same people. For *sigunon* ("spear") is standard for the Cypriots,[8] but exotic for us; and "spear" is standard for us, but exotic for the Cypriots.

(iii) A "metaphor" is the application [to something] of a name belonging to something else, either (a) from the genus to the species, or (b) from the species to the genus, or (c) from a species to [another] species, or (d) according to analogy.

By (a), "from genus to species," I mean e.g. "here stands my ship": for [the species] lying at anchor is a [part of the genus] standing. By (b), "from species to genus," I mean e.g. "truly has Odysseus done ten thousand deeds of worth": for [the species] "ten thousand" is [part of the genus] "many," and [Homer] uses it here instead of "a lot". By (c), "from species to species," I mean e.g. [killing a man by] "draining out his life with bronze" [i.e. a weapon], and [drawing water by] "cutting it with long-edged bronze" [i.e. a bowl]: for here [the poet] calls cutting "draining" and draining "cutting". Both are [species of the genus] "taking away." By (d), "analogy," I mean when *b* is to *a* as *d* is to *c*; for [the poet then] will say *d* instead of *b*, or *b* instead of *d*.

7. A comical name compounded from the names of three rivers (Hermus, Caïcus, and Xanthus) in western Asia Minor, where the founders of Marseilles (then called Massalia) originated.

8. That is, those speaking the dialect of Greek used on the island of Cyprus.

Sometimes too [poets] add [to the metaphor] the thing to which the name relates, instead of what it means. I mean e.g. that the wine-bowl stands to Dionysus as the shield does to Ares:[9] so [the poet] will call a wine-bowl "shield of Dionysus" and a shield "wine-bowl of Ares." Again, as old age stands to life, so the evening stands to the day: so [the poet] will call evening "old age of the day," as Empedocles does, and old age "the evening of life" or "the sunset of life."

There may be no current name for some of the things in the analogy, but even so they will be expressed in the same way. E.g. to scatter seed is to sow, and to scatter radiance from the sun has no name; but this has the same relation to the sun as sowing does to the seed. For this reason [the poet] says "sowing god-wrought radiance."

This manner of [making a] metaphor can be used in another way too. After terming something by a name that belongs to something else, one can deny to it one of the things particular to [that other thing], e.g. if [a poet] called a shield not "wine-bowl of Ares" but "wine-bowl without wine."

(iv) [An "ornament" is ***][1]

(v) A "made-up [name]" is one which is wholly unused by people, but which the poet supplies himself. There would seem to be some such names, e.g. "branchers" for "horns" or "prayerman" for "priest."

(vi)–(vii) As for lengthened [1458a] or shortened names, the former is one which uses a longer vowel than the one particular [to it], or an inserted syllable. The latter is one some [part] of which has been shortened. A lengthened [name] is e.g. *polēos* for *poleōs* "of the city," and *Pelēiadeō* for *Peleidou* "son of Peleus"; a shortened [name] is e.g. *kri* [for *krithē*] "barley," *dō* [for *dōma*] "mansion" and, in "one seeing comes from both [eyes]," *ops* [for *opsis*] "seeing."

(viii) An altered [name] is when [the poet] leaves some of the appellation [unaltered], but makes up some of it, e.g. "by her righter breast" instead of "right."

Among names [in] themselves, (a) some are masculine, (b) some are feminine, and (c) some are in between [i.e. neuter].[2] (a) Masculine names are those that end in *n, r, s* and the elements that are composed of *s*; there are two of these, *ps* and *x* [i.e. *ks*]. (b) Feminine names are (i) those that end in the vowels that are always long, i.e. in *ē* and *ō*, and (ii) those that end in *a* among the vowels that may be lengthened. Consequently the elements in which the masculine and feminine names end turn out to be equal in number [i.e. three], for *ps* and *x* are composite. No names end in a consonant, nor in a short vowel [that is always short]. There are only three names ending in *i*, "honey," "gum" and "pepper" (*meli, kommi, peperi*); there are five ending in *u*, "spear," "fleece," "mustard," "knee" and "city" (*doru, pōu, napu, gonu, astu*). The [names] that are in between end in these elements [*a, i* and *u*], and in *n*, [*r*] and *s*.

[22] The virtue of diction is to be clear and not commonplace. Diction made up of standard names is clearest, but is commonplace. An example is the poetry of Cleophon and that of Sthenelus.[3] Diction that uses unfamiliar

9. Greek god of war.
1. Aristotle distinguishes between ornamental and standard names, but his account here is missing in all surviving manuscripts.
2. Some editors condemn this paragraph (which contains much that is not true) as spurious.
3. Perhaps a tragic poet whose style was mocked by Aristophanes [translator's note].

names is grand and altered from the everyday. By "unfamiliar," I mean the exotic [name], metaphor, lengthening and everything that is contrary to what is standard. But if someone makes all [the names] of this sort, [his poem] will be either a riddle or gibberish. If [it is composed] of metaphors, it will be a riddle; if of exotic [names], gibberish. For it is the form of a riddle to use an impossible combination [of names] in saying things that are the case. This cannot be done with the combination of the other names, but is possible with metaphor, e.g. "I saw a man glue bronze on a man with fire," etc. Things [composed] of exotic names are gibberish. [The poet], then, should mix these [two kinds] in some way. The first (e.g. the exotic name, metaphor, ornament and the other kinds we mentioned) will produce that which is not everyday and commonplace, and the standard name will produce clarity.

Lengthenings, curtailments and alterations of names make no small contribution [1458b] towards making the diction clear and not everyday. These will produce what is not everyday, because of their variation from what is standard, as they are contrary to the norm, but clarity will come from what they have in common with the norm. Consequently those who criticize this manner of speech and ridicule the poet [for using it] are not correct to abuse him. E.g. old Euclides, to show that it is easy to compose if [a poet] is allowed to lengthen [names] as much as he wishes, composed as a lampoon in his words "I saw Epichares walking to Marathon" and "not mixing hellebore for him."[4] To use this manner in some obvious way is laughable. [The need for] due measure is shared by all the types [of unfamiliar names]. For [a poet] who purposely uses metaphors, exotic [names], and the other kinds unsuitably, with a view to arousing laughter, can accomplish the same [effect].

How much what is appropriate is superior [to what is inappropriate] can be observed, in the case of lengthened [names], by inserting the [standard] names into the verse [instead]. In the case of exotic [names], as well as metaphors and the other forms, someone who substitutes the standard names can see that what we are saying is true. E.g. when Euripides composed the same iambic verse as Aeschylus, and substituted only one name, an exotic name instead of the usual standard one, his verse seems fine, but Aeschylus' seems ordinary. For Aeschylus in his *Philoctetes*[5] composed the verse

> "the gangrene which eats at the flesh of my foot,"

but Euripides substituted "feasts on" for "eats at." Also, [in the verse]

> "now I am a paltry man, nothing worth and plain,"[6]

suppose that someone substituted the standard names to say

> "now I am a little man, a feeble one and ugly."

Compare too

> "setting down a squalid hassock and a paltry table,"[7]

4. The two phrases are unrelated; both contain words with arbitrarily lengthened syllables. Euclides: identity unknown; both an Athenian magistrate and a Megaran philosopher of that name were active ca. 400 B.C.E. Epichares: a common name in Athens. Marathon: a large Attic city on the northeast coast. "Hellebore": an herb thought to be a cure for madness.

5. A lost play (the *Philoctetes* of Sophocles but not Euripides survives). Philoctetes, who used the bow and arrows of Heracles, sailed with the Greeks for Troy but was left behind on an island because a wound on his foot, caused by snakebite, produced a horrible smell. He remained alone for 10 years, until on the advice of an oracle he and his bow were brought to Troy.

6. *Odyssey* 9.515.

7. *Odyssey* 20.259.

with

"setting down a nasty hassock and a little table,"

or "the headlands bellow" with "the headlands yell."

Again, Ariphrades[8] ridiculed the tragedians on the grounds that they use things which nobody would say in his [everyday] speech, e.g. "without the palace" and not "outside the palace," "of thee," "mine own," [1459a] "Achilles round" and not "around Achilles," etc. Because all such [names] are not among the standard ones, they produce what is not everyday in the diction. But Ariphrades was ignorant of this.

It is important to use each of the [kinds] mentioned suitably, both double names and exotic ones, but the metaphorical [kind] is the most important by far. This alone (a) cannot be acquired from someone else, and (b) is an indication of genius. For to make metaphors well is to observe what is like [something else].

Among names, double ones are most appropriate for dithyrambs, exotic ones for heroic [verses][9] and metaphors for iambic verses. In heroic verses all the [kinds] mentioned are useful. In iambic verses, because these represent [everyday] diction as far as possible, those [kinds] of names are appropriate which one can use in [prose] speeches too. These are the standard name, metaphor and ornament.

As for tragedy, i.e. representation by means of acting, let this account suffice us.

[23] As for the art of exposition and representation in verse, it is clear that, just as in tragedies, [the epic poet] should construct plots that are dramatic (i.e. [plots] about a single whole action that is complete, with a beginning, middle [parts] and end), so that it will produce the pleasure particular to it, as a single whole animal does. The constructions [of the incidents] should not be like histories; in these it is necessary to produce a description not of a single action, but of a single time, with all that happened during it to one or more people; each [event] relates to the others at random. Just as the sea-battle at Salamis and the battle against the Carthaginians in Sicily happened at the same time,[1] but did not contribute to the same end, so too in sequential [periods of] time one thing sometimes comes about after another, but from these there comes about no single end. But this is what the majority, almost, of [epic] poet do.

For this reason, as we said already, Homer appears marvellous compared to the others, in that he did not undertake to put into his composition even the [Trojan] war as a whole, although it has a beginning and an end. For the plot would probably have been too big and not easily seen as a whole; or, if it were moderate in magnitude, [it would have been too] complex in its variety [of incidents]. As it is, selecting a single part [of it], Homer has used many of them as episodes, e.g. he diversifies his composition with the "Catalogue of Ships"[2] and other episodes. The other [poets] compose about a single man, a single time, or a single action that has many parts, e.g. he who composed the [1459b] *Cypria* and the *Little Iliad*.[3] Consequently one or at most two

8. An unknown comic poet.

9. That is, verses in the meter of epic (dactylic hexameter).

1. According to Herodotus (7.166.1), the victory of the Greek fleet over the Persians at Salamis and the victory of the Sicilian Greeks led by Gelon over the Carthaginians occurred on the same day in 480 B.C.E.

2. *Iliad* 2.484–759.

3. Poems in the epic cycle, of unknown authorship: the *Cypria* related the origins of the Trojan War and the *Little Iliad* events after the end of the *Iliad*.

tragedies in each case are produced from the *Iliad* and the *Odyssey*; but many [are produced] from the *Cypria*, and from the *Little Iliad* more than eight, e.g. the *Judgment of Arms, Philoctetes, Neoptolemus, Eurypylus, Vagabondage, Laconian Women, Sack of Troy, Embarkation, Sinon,* and *Trojan Women.*[4]

[24] Again, epic must have the same kinds as tragedy, for [it must be] either (i) simple or (ii) complex, (iii) an epic of character or (iv) one of suffering. Its parts, except for song and spectacle, are the same; in fact it needs reversals, recognitions and sufferings. Again, the reasonings and diction should be fine.

Homer is first and foremost in the use of all of these. In fact each of his poems is constructed in each of the two ways—the *Iliad* is simple and full of suffering, the *Odyssey* is complex (for it is recognition right through) and full of character. In addition, he has surpassed all [others] in diction and reasoning.

Epic differs [from tragedy] in (i) the length of its [plot-]structure, and (ii) its verse.

(i) As for its length, the definition that we stated is sufficient; it should be possible to see at one view its beginning and end. This would be so, if the structures were smaller than the ancient ones, but reached [the length of] the number of tragedies presented at a single hearing.

For extending its magnitude, epic has an [advantage] very particular [to it]. In tragedy, it is not possible for many parts [of the action] to be presented as being done at the same time, but only the part of the actors on the stage. But in epic, because it is exposition, it is possible to put in many parts which are accomplished at the same time; with these—provided they are particular [to it]—the weight of the poem is increased. Consequently epic has this advantage [over tragedy], both (a) for [giving it] splendour, and (b) for diverting the listener and introducing episodes that are unlike [one another]. For likeness [in episodes] is soon boring and makes tragedies fail.

(ii) As for its verse-form, heroic verse has been found appropriate from experience. If anyone produced an expository representation in some other verse-form, or in many, it would obviously be unsuitable. Heroic verse is the stateliest and weightiest of the verse-forms. For this reason, it most readily admits exotic names, metaphors and lengthenings—for expository representation exceeds the other [kinds] in this too. But the iambic and tetrameter [1460a] verse-forms are [fast-]moving, as the first is related to action, and the second to dance. It would be still more odd if someone mixed them, as Chaeremon did. For this reason, nobody has composed a long structure in any verse other than the heroic; but, as we said, nature itself teaches [poets] to choose [the verse-form] that is appropriate to it.

Homer deserves acclaim for many things, but especially because he alone among [epic] poets is well aware of what he himself should do. The poet should say very little himself; for this is not the way in which [a poet] represents. The other [epic poets] do the performing themselves right through [the poem], but represent few [people speaking] and do so rarely.

4. Only Sophocles' *Philoctetes* and Euripides' *Trojan Women* are extant; some editors doubt that Aristotle is responsible for all the titles in this list.

But Homer, after a brief preamble, immediately brings on a man, a woman, or some other [person]—and none of them characterless, but [all] with character.

[The poet] should put what is amazing into his tragedies; but what is improbable, from which amazement arises most, is more admissible in epic because [the audience] does not see the person in action. For the passage about the pursuit of Hector[5] would obviously be laughable on the stage, with the Greeks standing still and not pursuing him, and Achilles forbidding them to do so, but it passes unnoticed in the epic verses. What is amazing is pleasant. An indication [of this is that] everyone narrates [stories] with additions, so as to please.

Homer above all has taught the other [poets] to tell untruths in the right way, that is, [by] a false inference. For if, whenever *p* exists or comes to be, *q* exists or comes to be, people suppose that if the latter (*q*) exists, the former (*p*) also exists or comes to be. But this [supposition] is untrue. For this reason, if the former (*p*) is untrue, but it follows from its existence that something else (*q*) exists or comes to be, [the poet] should add it [i.e. *q*]. Because we know that this (*q*) is true, our soul falsely infers that the former (*p*) exists too. An example of this is the passage in the "Bath-scene."[6]

Impossible [incidents] that are believable should be preferred to possible ones that are unbelievable, and stories should not be constructed from improbable parts, but above all should contain nothing improbable; otherwise, it should be outside the plot-structure, like Oedipus' not knowing how Laius was killed. But it should not be within the drama, like the people who narrate [the accident at] the Pythian games in the *Electra*, and the person who comes to Mysia from Tegea without speaking in the *Mysians*.[7] Consequently it is ridiculous to say that the plot would have been ruined [without the improbability]; such plots should not be constructed in the first place. But if one is set up, and it appears fairly logical, even an oddity can be admitted. For even the improbabilities in the *Odyssey* over the putting ashore [of Odysseus][8] would clearly not be tolerable, if an [1460b] inferior poet composed them. But as it is, the poet makes the oddity disappear by using his other good [qualities] for embellishment. [The poet] should take great pains with the diction in the slack parts [of the poem], i.e. those with neither character nor reasoning. For in turn excessively resplendent diction obscures characters and reasoning.

[25] As for the questions that are raised [about epic poetry] and their solutions, it may become obvious to how many kinds they belong, and of what sort they are, if we investigate them as follows.

(i) Since a poet represents, just like a painter or some other maker of images, at any moment he is necessarily representing one of three things, either (a) things as they were or are, or (b) things as people say and think [they were or are], or (c) things as they should be.

5. *Iliad* 22.131–207; Hector, eldest son of the king of Troy and the greatest Trojan warrior, initially flees Achilles.

6. That is, Penelope's false inference, from the disguised Odysseus's accurate description of some clothing, that his tale of being a Cretan who met her husband Odysseus is true (*Odyssey* 19.165–250).

7. A play of Aeschylus or Sophocles; Tegea in the Peloponnese is far distant from Mysia in northwest Asia Minor. *Electra*: Sophocles' tragedy (ca. 414 B.C.E.) contains a false account (lines 680–763) of Orestes' death in a chariot crash in the Pythian games, which were founded centuries after the events of the play.

8. *Odyssey* 13.116–25.

(ii) These things are expressed in diction in which there are exotic names, metaphors and many modifications of diction; we grant these to poets.

(iii) In addition, there is not the same [standard of] correctness in the art of civic life as in that of poetry, nor is there in any other art as in that of poetry. Error in the art of poetry itself is of two sorts, (a) error in the art itself, (b) error in it by coincidence. For if [an artist] decided to represent [a horse correctly, but erred in the representation because of his] lack of ability, the error belongs to the art itself; but if he decided to represent it incorrectly, and [represented] the horse with both right legs thrown forward, [it is] an error in the individual art (e.g. one in medicine or another art of whatever sort), not in the art of poetry itself.

Consequently one should consider and solve the criticisms that are among the questions raised [starting] from these [principles].

(i) First, some [criticisms should be solved] with reference to the art itself. [If] impossibilities have been produced, there is an error; but it is correct, if it attains the end of the art itself. The end has been stated [already, i.e.] if in this way it makes either that part [of the poem], or another part, more astonishing. An example is the pursuit of Hector.

However, if the end [of the art] could have been brought about better or no worse [without erring] according to the art concerned with these matters, the error is not correct. For [the poet] should, if possible, have made no errors at all.

(ii) Again, to which sort does the error belong, to those in the art [itself], or [to those in it] by coincidence? The error is less, if [an artist] did not know that a female deer has no horns, than if he painted without representing [anything].

(iii) In addition, if [the poet] is criticised for representing things that are not true, perhaps he is representing them [as] they should be, e.g. as Sophocles said that he himself portrayed people as they should be, but Euripides portrayed them as they are—there is the solution.

(iv) If [the solution] is in neither of these ways, then [it may be] on the grounds that people say [it is] so, e.g. the [stories] about the gods. These are perhaps neither better [told this way] nor true, but are possibly [lies] [1461a] as Xenophanes[9] thought; yet people say [it is] so.

(v) Some things are perhaps not better [than they should be], but were so, e.g. the passage about the weapons:

> "their spears, [set] upright on the butt-spike . . ."[1]

This was the custom then, as it is among the Illyrians even now.

(vi) As for whether someone's saying or action is fine or not so fine, one must consider not only what was said or done itself, to see whether it is good or inferior, but also the person saying or doing it, and to whom, at what time, by what means and to what end, e.g. whether it is to bring about a greater good, or to avert a greater evil.

(vii) Some [criticisms] must be resolved by looking at the diction, e.g. by [assuming] an exotic name in "the *oureis* first":[2] perhaps [Homer] means not

9. Pre-Socratic philosopher and poet (ca. 570–ca. 480 B.C.E.) who denounced immoral tales of the Greek gods.

1. *Iliad* 10.152–53.
2. *Iliad* 1.50, where the Greek word *ourēas* may derive either from *oreus* (mule) or *ouros* (sentinal).

"mules" but "sentinels." As for Dolon[3] "who was evil in form," [Homer may mean] not that his body was misproportioned, but that his face was ugly; for the Cretans call someone fair of face "well-formed." Also by "mix it purer" [he may mean] not "[mix the wine] stronger," as if for drunkards, but "mix it faster."

(viii) Some things are said with a metaphor, e.g. "all gods and men slept all night long," but [Homer] says at the same time "but when he gazed at the Trojan plain, [he marvelled at] the din of flutes and pipes." "All" is said for "many" with a metaphor; for "all" is a lot. So too "[this constellation] alone has no share [in the baths of Ocean]" is said with a metaphor; for what is best known is "alone."

(ix) [Some questions should be solved] with reference to the pronunciation, as Hippias of Thasaos[4] solved [the question of] "but grant that he gain his prayer" [instead of "we grant"], and "part rotted by rain" [instead of "not rotted"].

(x) Some [should be solved] by punctuation, e.g. Empedocles' "at once were things mortal born, that learnt before to be immortal, and things were mixed, pure before."

(xi) Some [should be solved] by [assuming] an ambiguity, [e.g.] in "more of the night has gone," "more" is ambiguous.

(xii) Some [should be solved] with reference to a habit of diction. People call mixed [wine] "wine," whence [Homer] composed "a greave of new-wrought tin" [i.e. of bronze, copper mixed with tin]; and they call men who work iron "bronze-smiths," whence his calling Ganymede[5] "wine-pourer of Zeus," although [gods] do not drink wine [but nectar]. This could also be [solved] with reference to a metaphor.

Whenever any name would seem to signify something contradictory, one should consider how many ways it may signify in the passage, e.g. in "there the brazen spear was held" consider how many ways it can mean "was stopped there," one way or another as best one may understand it, according to the exact opposite of what [1461b] Glaucon[6] says.

Again, some people illogically make some prior assumption, and judging it right themselves make inferences [from it]. If there is a contradiction to their own supposition, they criticise [the poet] as if he had said what they think. This has happened in the case of Icarius. People suppose that Icarius is a Lacedaemonian: so they think it odd that Telemachus[7] does not meet him when he goes to Lacedaemon. But perhaps it is as the Cephallenians say; they say that Odysseus took a wife from among them, and that [Penelope's father] was Icadius and not Icarius. It is probable that the question [has arisen] because of an error [by Homer's critics].

In general, (i) the impossibility should be explained with reference either to (a) the composition, or to (b) [making something] better [than it is], or to (c) opinion. In relation to [the needs of] the composition, a believable impos-

All the following examples in this passage come from the *Iliad*, sometimes abbreviating the original.

3. A Trojan scout killed by the Greeks (*Iliad* 10.314–457).

4. An unknown figure (possibly an individual who died in Athens in 404 B.C.E.).

5. A beautiful young Trojan prince seized and carried to Olympus by Zeus's eagle; he became a minor Greek god.

6. Perhaps the interpreter of Homer named by Plato in *Ion* 530d (see above).

7. Odysseus's son. Icarius: Penelope's father, from Sparta (Lacedaemonia).

sibility is preferable to an unbelievable possibility. For it may be impossible that there are people like those Zeuxis painted, but [it is] better [so]. For [the artist] should improve on his model.

(ii) Improbabilities [should be explained] with reference to what people say; for one must solve them in this way, and on the grounds that sometimes an improbability is no improbability: for it is probable that things will happen even against probability.

(iii) Sayings that are contradictory should be considered just like refutations in arguments, as to whether it is the same thing [that is meant], relates to the same thing, or is said in the same way. Consequently [these] must be solved with reference either to (a) what [the poet] himself says or to (b) what a sensible person may assume.

Criticism of improbability and wickedness is correct when, with no necessity at all to do so, [the poet] uses an improbability, as Euripides uses Aegeus,[8] or villainy, as Euripides uses Menelaus in the *Orestes*.

So the criticisms that people make are of five kinds—that things are impossible, improbable, harmful, contradictory, or incorrect in terms of [another] art. Solutions must be looked for among the items we have stated; there are twelve of them.

[26] One may be puzzled about which is better, epic or tragic representation. If the less vulgar representation is better, and the less vulgar is always that which relates to better spectators, it is very clear that the one which represents in all respects is vulgar. Assuming that [the spectators] will not react unless [each actor] adds something himself, they use a lot of movement, like inferior oboe-players who whirl about if they have to represent a discus, and drag the chorus-leader about if they are playing the *Scylla*. So tragedy is [a representation] of this sort. Compare too how the earlier actors regarded those who came after them. Mynniscus used to call Callippides a monkey, on the grounds that he went to great excesses, and the opinion about Pindarus[9] was similar. [1462a] As the later actors stand to them, so the whole art [of tragedy] stands to epic. So people say that epic relates to decent spectators, who have no need of gestures, but the tragic [art] relates to inferior ones. Therefore, if it is vulgar, clearly it would be worse [than epic].

So let us discuss these matters. (i) First, the charge is not against the art of [tragic] composition but against that of [the actors'] delivery. For [visual] signs can be overworked even in reciting an epic, as Sosistratus did, and in singing, as Mnasithesus of Opus[1] did.

(ii) Next, not all movement is to be rejected, unless dance is to be too, but [only] that of inferior [people], such as that for which Callippides was criticised, and others now are, on the grounds that they represent women who are not free born.

(iii) Again, tragedy can produce its own [effect] even without movement, as epic does. For it is obvious from reading it what sort [of tragedy] it is. So if tragedy is superior in all other things, this at any rate does not necessarily belong to it.

8. In *Medea* (lines 663–758). Aegeus, king of Athens, happens to pass through Corinth and see Medea; he promises her future asylum.

9. Presumably an actor. Mynniscus of Chacis (active ca. 460–420 B.C.E.), an actor known for roles in Aeschylus's plays. Callippides (active ca. 427–400 B.C.E.), a Greek actor.

1. Both unknown.

(i) Furthermore, [tragedy is superior] because it has everything that epic has; for it is even possible to use its verse [in tragedy].

(ii) Again, it also has as no small part of it music and spectacles, by means of which its pleasures are constructed very vividly.

(iii) Next, it has vividness in reading as well as in performance.

(iv) Again, [it has the advantage] that the end [1462b] of the representation is in a smaller length. What is more concentrated is more pleasurable than what is diluted with a lot of time [in performance]. I mean, e.g. [the effect] if someone put Sophocles' *Oedipus* into as many epic verses as the *Iliad*.

(v) Again, the epic poets' representation is less unified. An indication [of this is] that more than one tragedy comes from any [epic] representation. Consequently, if they compose a unified plot, it appears either docked, if it is briefly presented, or watery, if it accords with the length [appropriate to] the verse-form. [By "less unified"], I mean, e.g. [the effect] if it is composed of several [complete] actions, just as the *Iliad* and the *Odyssey* have many such parts, which have magnitude even in themselves. Yet these poems are as well constructed as [epics] may be, and are, as far as possible, representations of a single action.

So if tragedy is superior in all these ways, and also in [achieving] the function of the art (for tragedy and epic should produce not a random pleasure, but the one we have mentioned), it is obvious that it will be superior to epic as it achieves its end more than epic does.

So regarding tragedy and epic, in themselves, their kinds and their parts, as to how many there are and how they differ, and what are the causes of doing well or not [in them], and regarding questions raised and their solutions, let this account suffice.

ca. 330 B.C.E.

From Rhetoric[1]

From *Book I*

FROM CHAPTER 2

Let rhetoric be [defined as] an ability, in each [particular] case, to see the available means of persuasion. This is the function of no other art;[2] for each of the others is instructive and persuasive about its own subject: for example, medicine about health and disease and geometry about the properties of magnitudes and arithmetic about numbers and similarly in the case of the other arts and sciences. But rhetoric seems to be able to observe the persuasive about "the given," so to speak. That, too, is why we say it does not include technical knowledge of any particular, defined genus [of subjects].

Of the *pisteis*,[3] some are atechnic ["nonartistic"], some entechnic ["em-

1. Translated by George A. Kennedy, who sometimes adds clarifying words or phrases in square brackets. Also in square brackets in the text are the Bekker numbers used almost universally in citing Aristotle's works; they refer to the page numbers and columns of an 1831 edition by Immanuel Bekker.

2. In Greek, *technē*. Aristotle distinguishes between human arts, such as rhetoric or poetics, and sciences, such as physics or logic, which adduce verifiable results.

3. Proofs or means of persuasion (Greek).

bodied in art, artistic"]. I call atechnic those that are not provided by "us" [i.e., the potential speaker] but are preexisting: for example, witnesses, testimony of slaves taken under torture, contracts, and such like; and artistic whatever can be prepared by method and by "us"; thus, one must *use* the former and *invent* the latter. [1356a] Of the *pisteis* provided through speech there are three species: for some are in the character of the speaker, and some in disposing the listener in some way, and some in the argument itself, by showing or seeming to show something.

[There is persuasion] through character whenever the speech is spoken in such a way as to make the speaker worthy of credence; for we believe fair-minded people to a greater extent and more quickly [than we do others] on all subjects in general and completely so in cases where there is not exact knowledge but room for doubt. And this should result from the speech, not from a previous opinion that the speaker is a certain kind of person; for it is not the case, as some of the technical writers propose in their treatment of the art, that fair-mindedness on the part of the speaker makes no contribution to persuasiveness; rather, character is almost, so to speak, the controlling factor in persuasion.

[There is persuasion] through the hearers when they are led to feel emotion by the speech; for we do not give the same judgment when grieved and rejoicing or when being friendly and hostile. To this and only this we said contemporary technical writers try to give their attention. The details on this subject will be made clear when we speak about the emotions.

Persuasion occurs through the arguments when we show the truth or the apparent truth from whatever is persuasive in each case.

* * *

FROM CHAPTER 3

The species of rhetoric are three in number; for such is the number [of classes] to which the hearers of speeches belong. A speech [situation] consists of three things: a speaker and a subject on which he speaks and someone addressed, [1358b] and the objective[4] of the speech relates to the last (I mean the hearer). Now it is necessary for the hearer to be either a spectator or a judge, and [in the latter case] a judge of either past of future happenings. A member of a democratic assembly is an example of one judging about future happenings, a jury-man an example of one judging the past. A spectator is concerned with the ability [of the speaker]. Thus, there would necessarily be three genera of rhetorics, deliberative, judicial, demonstrative.[5] Deliberative advice is either protreptic ["exhortation"] or apotreptic ["dissuasion"]; for both those advising in private and those speaking in public always do one or the other of these. In the law court there is either accusation or defense; for it is necessary for the disputants to offer one or the other of these. In epideictic, there is either praise or blame. Each of these has its own "time": for the deliberative speaker, the future (for whether exhorting or dissuading he advises about future events); for the speaker in court, the past (for he always prosecutes or defends concerning what has been done); in epideictic the present is the most important; for all speakers praise or blame

4. In Greek, *telos*, also translated as "end" or "goal."

5. In Greek, *epideiktikon*, also translated as "epideictic."

in regard to existing qualities, but they often also make use of other things, both reminding [the audience] of the past and projecting the course of the future. The "end" of each of these is different, and there are three ends for three [species]: for the deliberative speaker [the end] is the advantageous and the harmful (for someone urging something advises it as the better course and one dissuading dissuades on the ground that it is worse), and he includes other factors as incidental: whether it is just or unjust, or honorable or disgraceful; for those speaking in the law courts [the end] is the just and the unjust, and they make other considerations incidental to these; for those praising and blaming [the end] is the honorable and the shameful, and these speakers bring up other considerations in reference to these qualities. Here is a sign that the end of each [species of rhetoric] is what has been said: sometimes one would not dispute other factors; for example, a judicial speaker [might not deny] that he has done something or done harm, but he would never agree that he has [intentionally] done wrong; for [if he admitted that,] there would be no need of a trial. Similarly, deliberative speakers often grant other factors, but they would never admit that they are advising things that are not advantageous [to the audience] or that they are dissuading [the audience] from what is beneficial; and often they do not insist that it is not unjust to enslave neighbors or those who have done no wrong. And similarly, those who praise or blame do not consider whether someone has done actions that are advantageous or harmful [to himself] [1359a] but often they include it even as a source of praise that he did what was honorable without regard to the cost to himself; for example, they praise Achilles because he went to the aid of his companion Patroclus[6] knowing that he himself must die, though he could have lived. To him, such a death was more honorable; but life was advantageous.

* * *

From *Book II*

FROM CHAPTER 1

These [topics, set forth in book I] are the proper sources of exhortation and dissuasion, praise and blame, and prosecution and defense, and the kinds of opinions and propositions useful for their persuasive expression; for enthymemes[7] are concerned with these matters and drawn from these sources, so the result is speaking in a specific way in each genus of speeches. But since rhetoric is concerned with making a judgment (people judge what is said in deliberation, and judicial proceedings are also a judgment), it is necessary not only to look to the argument, that it may be demonstrative and persuasive but also [for the speaker] to construct a view of himself as a certain kind of person and to prepare the judge; for it makes much difference in regard to persuasion (especially in deliberations but also in trials) that the speaker seem to be a certain kind of person and that his hearers suppose him to be disposed toward them in a certain way and in addition if they, too, happen

6. In stories of the Trojan War, Achilles' closest friend; Achilles rejoined the battle to avenge his death at the hands of the Trojan hero Hector.

7. Rhetorical argument by deduction, applying general principles to specific cases, that leaves one of its premises unstated. Enthymemes use a looser form of reasoning than syllogisms, which are technical logical arguments that follow a rigid 3-part procedure.

to be disposed in a certain way [favorably or unfavorably to him]. For the speaker to seem to have certain qualities is more useful in deliberation; for the audience to be disposed in a certain way [is more useful] in lawsuits, for things do not seem the same to those who are friendly and those who are hostile, nor [the same] to the angry and the calm but either altogether different or different in importance: [1378a] to one who is friendly, the person about whom he passes judgment seems not to do wrong or only in a small way; to one who is hostile, the opposite; and to a person feeling strong desire and being hopeful, if something in the future is a source of pleasure, it appears that it will come to pass and will be good; but to an unemotional person and one in a disagreeable state of mind, the opposite.

There are three reasons why speakers themselves are persuasive; for there are three things we trust other than logical demonstrations. These are practical wisdom and virtue and good will; for speakers make mistakes in what they say or advise through [failure to exhibit] either all or one of these; for either through lack of practical sense they do not form opinions rightly; or though forming opinions rightly they do not say what they think because of a bad character; or they are prudent and fair-minded but lack good will, so that it is possible for people not to give the best advice although they know [what] it [is]. These are the only possibilities. Therefore, a person seeming to have all these qualities is necessarily persuasive to the hearers. The means by which one might appear prudent and good are to be grasped from analysis of the virtues, for a person would present himself as being of a certain sort from the same sources that he would use to present another person; and good will and friendliness need to be described in a discussion of the emotions.

The emotions are those things through which, by undergoing change, people come to differ in their judgments and which are accompanied by pain and pleasure, for example, anger, pity, fear, and other such things and their opposites. There is need to divide the discussion of each into three headings. I mean, for example, in speaking of anger, what is their *state of mind* when people are angry and against *whom* are they usually angry, and for what sort of *reasons*; for if we understood one or two of these but not all, it would be impossible to create anger [in someone]. And similarly, in speaking of the other emotions.

* * *

From *Book III*

FROM CHAPTER 2

[1404b] Let the matters just discussed be regarded as understood, and let the virtue of style[8] be defined as "to be clear" (speech is a kind of sign, so if it does not make clear it will not perform its function)—and neither flat nor above the dignity of the subject, but appropriate. The poetic style is hardly flat, but it is not appropriate for speech. The use of nouns and verbs in their prevailing meaning makes for clarity; other kinds of words, as discussed in the *Poetics*,[9] makes the style ornamented rather than flat. To deviate [from

8. In Greek, *lexis*, literally "speech"; the word is variously translated "language," "word choice," and "expression," as well as "style."
9. See *Poetics* 21–22, 1457a–1459a (above).

prevailing usage] makes language seem more elevated; for people feel the same in regard to *lexis* as they do in regard to strangers compared with citizens. As a result, one should make the language unfamiliar, for people are admirers of what is far off, and what is marvelous is sweet. Many [kinds of words] accomplish this in verse and are appropriate there; for what is said [in poetry] about subjects and characters is more out of the ordinary, but in prose much less so; for the subject matter is less remarkable, since even in poetry it would be rather inappropriate if a slave used fine language or if a man were too young for his words, or if the subject were too trivial, but in these cases, too, propriety is a matter of contraction or expansion. As a result, authors should compose without being noticed and should seem to speak not artificially but naturally. (The latter is persuasive, the former the opposite; for [if artifice is obvious] people become resentful, as at someone plotting against them, just as they are at those adulterating wines.) An example is the success of Theodorus'[1] voice when contrasted with that of other actors; for his seems the voice of the actual character, but the others' those of somebody else. The "theft" is well done if one composes by choosing words from ordinary language. Euripides[2] does this and first showed the way.

* * *

ca. 340 B.C.E.

1. Renowned Athenian tragic actor (active ca. 370 B.C.E.).

2. Greek tragedian (ca. 485–ca. 406 B.C.E.).

HORACE
65–8 B.C.E.

It would be impossible to overestimate the importance of Horace's *Ars Poetica* (*Art of Poetry*) for the subsequent history of literary criticism. Since its composition in the first century B.C.E., this epigrammatic and sometimes enigmatic critical poem has exerted an almost continual influence over poets and literary critics alike—perhaps because its dicta, phrased in verse form, are so eminently quotable. Horace's injunction that poetry should both "instruct and delight" has been repeated so often that it has come be to known as the Horatian platitude. His practical approach to poetry as a craft, or *ars*, contrasts markedly with the more theoretical bent of his predecessors, especially ARISTOTLE and PLATO. In fact, unlike Plato, Horace holds the poet in very high regard, as his "Epistle to Augustus" suggests: "The poet forms the young child's stammering mouth, and turns his ear at a timely hour from obscene discourse; next he also shapes his heart with friendly precepts, castigating harshness, resentment, and wrath. He tells of deeds honorably done, instructs rising generations by the examples of famous men, and consoles the sick and helpless."

Horace describes himself in his youth as the impoverished son of a freed slave, yet he rose to great prominence in Rome, becoming both a leading member of the illustrious circle of poets patronized by the emperor Augustus (63 B.C.E.–14 C.E.) and one of Rome's greatest poets and satirists. Quintus Horatius Flaccus was born in Venusia, a Roman military colony in southeastern Italy on the border between Apulia and

Lucania. His father worked as an auctioneer and had a small landholding. It is possible that in his poetry (our main source for his biography) Horace somewhat exaggerates his family's poverty. His father was apparently wealthy enough to send his son to Rome for his schooling. At the age of nineteen Horace went to Athens to the university. There Marcus Brutus convinced him to join in his futile attempt to reestablish the Republic. He accompanied Brutus to Asia Minor and was appointed to the high post of military tribune. After the defeat of Brutus and Cassius at Philippi in 42 B.C.E. at the hands of Octavian—the future Augustus who would one day be the poet's patron—Horace returned to Rome, to find that his father's home and land had been confiscated. Despite this setback, he was able to obtain a pardon for his part in the rebellion and to purchase a position as *scriba quaestorius*, a keeper of records in the treasury. At this time, he also began his career as a poet. His abilities were recognized by Gaius Maecenas, a wealthy aristocrat and the most prominent literary patron in Rome, to whom he was introduced by the poet Virgil. He maintained a close friendship with Maecenas until the latter's death. Around 38 B.C.E., through Maecenas, Horace became a member of the small circle of writers who enjoyed the patronage of Octavian, now the emperor. Though he declined an offer to become the emperor's secretary, the emperor's support enabled Horace to do nothing but write poetry for the rest of his life. He died of a sudden illness on November 27, 8 B.C.E., only two months after the death of his patron and friend Maecenas, next to whose tomb he was buried.

Horace is celebrated for his poetry; between 39 and 10 B.C.E., he produced numerous epodes (lyric poems), odes, satires, and verse epistles (letters). Many of the epistles deal with the subject of poetry: the best-known are the "Epistle to Florus" (19); the "Epistle to Augustus" (12), which examines the role of poetry in the state and asserts the merits of contemporary (that is, Augustan) poetry; and the famous "Epistle to the Pisones."

QUINTILIAN was the first to give the title *ars poetica* (art of poetry) or *liber de arte poetica* (book of the poetic art) to Horace's letter to the Pisones, a prominent Roman family with interests in poetry and literary criticism. The *Ars Poetica* was written perhaps as late as 10 B.C.E., although the date remains controversial, as do the identities of the members of the Piso family—father and sons—whom the poem addresses. Most likely the senior Piso is Lucius Calpurnius Piso (48 B.C.E.–32 C.E.); the sons have not been identified. The *Ars Poetica* is less a formal verse epistle, however—the trappings of the letter form are superficial at best—than a long conversational poem about poetry, written by an experienced and famous poet of the day. This form was widely imitated by later poets—most notably by GEOFFREY OF VINSAUF in the twelfth century, PIERRE DE RONSARD in the sixteenth, Nicolas Boileau in the seventeenth, ALEXANDER POPE in the eighteenth, Lord Byron in the nineteenth, and Wallace Stevens in the twentieth. The genre of literary theory in verse form presents many challenges. Because of the requirements of versification, the structure of Horace's text—its organization and transitions—is often dictated less by logical argumentation than by verbal association and rhetorical tone. Translation of the *Ars Poetica* (476 lines long) is notoriously difficult. Many English translations imitate Horace's hexameter lines by using rhymed couplets, which tend to reduce Horace's urbane wit at best to a string of epigrammatic statements held together by the meter, at worst to doggerel. For this reason, we have chosen a prose translation here.

While heavily indebted to Greek literature, and in particular to Aristotle (especially the *Poetics* and *Rhetoric*), the *Ars Poetica* is neither a systematic exposition of a coherent theory of poetic composition nor a comprehensive textbook for aspiring writers. Instead, it is an argument for poetry as a craft. Poetry is not merely inspired madness (as in Plato) or genius; it is an art and, as such, has rules and conventions that require both instruction and practice. Horace understands the concept of *ars* in three ways: as a practiced mastery of a craft, as a systematic knowledge of theory and technique, and as a capacity for objective self-criticism. His urbane text counsels the aspiring young poet, in this case probably the elder Piso son, that the craft of poetry will require painstaking work and self-sacrifice to acquire.

Another key principle that dominates the whole of the *Ars Poetica* is decorum. Briefly defined, decorum is the discernment and use of appropriateness, propriety, proportion, and unity in the arts, whether in painting, sculpture, or poetry. This is the Horatian principle that most appealed to later French and English neoclassical critics (see, for example, Pope, below), who often applied standards of decorum more rigidly than Horace himself would have. For Horace, decorum required that the poet fit the part to the whole, the subject to the appropriate genre, and meter and language to both character and circumstance. A skillful poet, knowledgeable in the craft of poetry and observant of the principles of decorum, would produce the kind of poetry able to "delight and instruct" its audiences.

Among the many dicta for which Horace's text is most famous are the warning against the "purple patch" (*purpureus pannus*) and the declarations that "poetry resembles painting" (*ut pictura poesis*), "even Homer sometimes sleeps" (*idem dormitat Homerus*), and poetry should be "pleasing" and "useful" (*dulce et utile*). Purple patches are inappropriately placed ornate passages that violate the principle of decorum and thus should be avoided by writers. Later critics have built on Horace's likening of poetry to painting to explore the spatial as well as the temporal dimensions of literature (see below, for example, G. E. LESSING and Erich Auerbach). Because sometimes even a poet as great as Homer errs, Horace counsels tolerance of occasional small faults. The pleasures of poetry for readers and theater audiences should be joined to practical and moral instruction embodied in the work, though Horace seems more preoccupied with delight and careful craft than with moral uplift. It is to these and other pithy and suggestive observations that modern critics often turn when considering Horace.

Horace's critics have complained that the long epistle is disorganized, that it sometimes sacrifices sense for the sake of wit, and that it lacks grandeur, being preoccupied with audience response. Since its publication, however, the *Ars Poetica* has appealed to those literary critics interested in codifying the principles of poetic composition, in arguing the relative merits of craft and genius in poetry, and in debating whether the primary goal of literature is pleasure or instruction.

BIBLIOGRAPHY

The complete Latin works of Horace are collected in *Q. Horati Flacci Opera*, edited by D. R. Shackleton Bailey (1985). The standard Latin edition of the *Ars Poetica* with English commentary can be found in *Epistles Book II and Epistle to the Pisones*, edited by Niall Rudd (1989). This text also includes the important "Epistle to Augustus" and the "Epistle to Florus." *The Complete Works of Horace*, edited by Charles E. Passage (1983), offers an English translation of Horace's collected poetry, including the *Ars Poetica*. Very readable prose translations are also provided by D. A. Russell in *Ancient Literary Criticism* (1972) and by Leon Golden in O. B. Hardison and Leon Golden's *Horace for Students of Literature: The "Ars Poetica" and Its Tradition* (1995), which also includes a series of documents that demonstrate the influence of Horace's epistle throughout the history of Western literary criticism. A Latin *Life of Horace* exists; it is attributed to the Roman historian Suetonius (ca. 69–140 C.E.). A recent English biography is Peter Levi's *Horace: A Life* (1997).

D. A. Russell's essay on the *Ars Poetica* in *Horace* (ed. C. D. N. Costa, 1973) provides a useful and brief introduction to the poem. Charles O. Brink's monumental three-volume study, *Horace on Poetry* (1963–82), offers an indispensable advanced study of Horace's critical principles; it includes texts and commentaries on the *Ars Poetica*, the "Epistle to Augustus," and the "Epistle to Florus." Ross S. Kilpatrick, in *The Poetry of Criticism: Horace, Epistles II and the Ars Poetica* (1990), also focuses on Horace's writing on literature in a format more accessible to the beginning student of Horace. Bernard Frischer, in *Shifting Paradigms: New Approaches to Horace's "Ars Poetica"* (1991), presents a detailed statistical analysis of the epistle's many controversies.

Volume 3 of Brink's *Horace on Poetry* (cited above) contains an extensive bibliography of primary and secondary sources on Horace's literary criticism. For a more general work, see the bibliographical essay in *Homage to Horace: A Bimillenary Celebration* (ed. S. J. Harrison, 1995).

Ars Poetica[1]

Unity and Consistency

Imagine a painter who wanted to combine a horse's neck with a human head, and then clothe a miscellaneous collection of limbs with various kinds of feathers, so that what started out at the top as a beautiful woman ended in a hideously ugly fish. If you were invited, as friends, to the private view, could you help laughing? Let me tell you, my Piso[2] friends, a book whose different features are made up at random like a sick man's dreams, with no unified form to have a head or a tail, is exactly like that picture.

'Painters and poets have always enjoyed recognized[3] rights to venture on what they will.' [11] Yes, we know; indeed, we ask and grant this permission turn and turn about. But it doesn't mean that fierce and gentle can be united, snakes paired with birds or lambs with tigers.

Serious and ambitious designs often have a purple patch or two sewn on to them just to make a good show at a distance—a description of a grove and altar of Diana,[4] the meanderings of a stream running through pleasant meads, the River Rhine, the rainbow: [19] but the trouble is, it's not the place for them.

Maybe you know how to do a picture of a cypress tree? What's the good of that, if the man who is paying for the picture is a desperate ship-wrecked mariner swimming to safety? The job began as a wine-jar: the wheel runs round—why is that a tub that's coming out? In short, let it be what you will, but let it be simple and unified.

Skill Needed to Avoid Faults

Most of us poets—father and worthy sons—are deceived by appearances of correctness. I try to be concise, but I become obscure; my aim is smoothness, but sinews and spirit fail; professions of grandeur end in bombast; the over-cautious who fear the storm creep along the ground. Similarly, the writer who wants to give fantastic variety to his single theme [30] paints a dolphin in his woods and a wild boar in his sea. If art is wanting, the flight from blame leads to faults. The poorest smith near the School of Aemilius[5] will reproduce nails and mimic soft hair in bronze, though he has no luck with the over-all effect of his work, because he won't know how to organize the

1. Translated by D. A. Russell. In this prose translation of Horace's verse, subheads have been added by the translator.
2. Horace is thought to have addressed the *Ars* to Lucius Calpurnius Piso (48 B.C.E.–32 C.E.) and his sons, though none of the sons has been positively identified.
3. Or "equal" [translator's note].
4. Roman goddess of the hunt, the moon, and childbirth.
5. A school for gladiators, near the shops of bronze workers.

whole. If I were anxious to put anything together, I would as soon be that man as I would live with a mis-shapen nose when my black eyes and black hair had made me a beauty.

You writers must choose material equal to your powers. Consider long what your shoulders will bear and what they will refuse. The man who chooses his subject with full control will not be abandoned by eloquence or lucidity of arrangement.

As to arrangement: its excellence and charm, unless I'm very wrong, consist in saying at this moment what needs to be said at this moment, and postponing and temporarily omitting a great many things. An author who has undertaken a poem must be choosy—cling to one point and spurn another.

As to words: if you're delicate and cautious in arranging them, you will give distinction to your style if an ingenious combination makes a familiar word new. If it happens to be necessary to denote hidden mysteries by novel symbols, it will fall to you to invent terms the Cethegi in their loincloths[6] never heard—and the permission will be granted if you accept it modestly—and, moreover, your new and freshly invented words will receive credit, if sparingly derived from the Greek springs. Is the Roman to give Caecilius and Plautus privileges denied to Virgil and Varius?[7] Why am I unpopular if I can make a few acquisitions, when the tongue of Cato and Ennius[8] so enriched their native language and produced such a crop of new names for things?

Fashions in Words

It always has been, and always will be, lawful to produce a word stamped with the current mark. As woods change in leaf as the seasons slide on, and the first leaves fall, so the old generation of words dies out, and the newly born bloom and are strong like young men. We and our works are a debt owed to death. Here a land-locked sea protects fleets from the North wind—a royal achievement; here an old barren marsh where oars were piled feeds neighbouring cities and feels the weight of the plough; here again a river gives up a course that damaged the crops and learns a better way. But whatever they are, all mortal works will die; and still less can the glory and charm of words endure for a long life. Many words which have fallen will be born again, many now in repute will fall if usage[9] decrees: for in her hand is the power and the law and the canon of speech.

Metre and Subject

Histories of kings and generals, dreadful wars: it was Homer[1] who showed in what metre these could be narrated. Lines unequally yoked in pairs[2]

6. I.e., primitive Romans [translator's note].

7. Roman poet (ca. 74–14 B.C.E.), friend of Virgil and Horace; author of the tragedy *Thyestes*. Caecilius Statius (d. ca. 168 B.C.E.), former slave from Gaul who wrote Latin comedies. Plautus (d. ca. 184 B.C.E.), Roman comic dramatist whose plays were modeled on Greek New Comedy originals. Virgil (70–19 B.C.E.), Roman poet and friend of Horace.

8. Roman tragic and epic poet (ca. 239–169 B.C.E.) who tried to refine the Latin language according to Greek example. Cato (234–149 B.C.E.), Roman statesman, stern moralist, and prolific writer of treatises and history.

9. Or "need" [translator's note].

1. Greek epic poet (8th c. B.C.E.) to whom the *Iliad* and *Odyssey* are traditionally attributed.

2. In elegiac couplets, formed by a dactylic hexameter (a 6-foot line based on the syllabic pattern long-short-short) and a line replacing the 3d and 6th foot with one long syllable. The shorter second line gives the couplet a sense of falling off, thought to impart melancholy.

formed the setting first for lamentations, then for the expression of a vow fulfilled[3] though who first sent these tiny 'elegies' into the world is a grammarians' quarrel and still *sub judice*. Madness armed Archilochus with its own iambus;[4] [80] that too was the foot that the comic sock and tragic buskin held, because it was suitable for dialogue, able to subdue the shouts of the mob, and intended by nature for a life of action. To the lyre, the Muse granted the celebration of gods and the children of gods, victorious boxers, winning race-horses, young men's love, and generous wine. If I have neither the ability nor the knowledge to keep the duly assigned functions and tones of literature, why am I hailed as a poet? Why do I prefer to be ignorant than learn, out of sheer false shame? A comic subject will not be set out in tragic verse; [90] likewise, the Banquet of Thyestes[5] disdains being told in poetry of the private kind, that borders on the comic stage. Everything must keep the appropriate place to which it was allotted.

Nevertheless, comedy does sometimes raise her voice, and angry Chremes[6] perorates with swelling eloquence. Often too Telephus and Peleus[7] in tragedy lament in prosaic language, when they are both poor exiles and throw away their bombast and words half a yard long, if they are anxious to touch the spectator's heart with their complaint.

Emotion and Character

It is not enough for poetry to be beautiful; it must also be pleasing and lead the hearer's mind wherever it will. [101] The human face smiles in sympathy with smilers and comes to the help of those that weep. If you want me to cry, mourn first yourself; *then* your misfortunes will hurt me, Telephus and Peleus. If your words are given you ineptly, I shall fall asleep or laugh. Sad words suit a mournful countenance, threatening words an angry one; sportive words are for the playful, serious for the grave. For nature first shapes us within for any state of fortune—gives us pleasure or drives us to anger or casts us down to the ground with grievous sorrow and pains us—[111] and then expresses the emotions through the medium of the tongue. If the words are out of tune with the speaker's fortunes, the knights and infantry of Rome will raise a cackle. It will make a lot of difference whether the speaker is a god or a hero, an old man of ripe years or a hot youth, an influential matron or a hard-working nurse, a travelling merchant or the tiller of a green farm, a Colchian or an Assyrian, one nurtured at Thebes or at Argos.[8]

Choice and Handling of Myth

Either follow tradition or invent a consistent story. [120] If as a writer you are representing Achilles with all his honours, let him be active, irascible,

3. Horace is thinking of inscriptions accompanying dedications to gods [translator's note].
4. Metrical foot made of one short and one long syllable; iambic trimeter was the measure used in dialogue in both Greek comedies and Greek tragedies. Archilochus (ca. 7th c. B.C.E.), Ionian lyric poet thought to be the earliest writer of iambic verse.
5. In Greek mythology, Atreus murdered his brother Thyestes' son and served the boy to Thyestes, who had seduced Atreus's wife.
6. Miserly character in the comedies of Terence (Roman dramatist, ca. 190–ca. 159 B.C.E.).
7. Father of the Greek hero Achilles, the central character in the *Iliad*. Telephus: son of Heracles and Auge, wounded by Achilles' spear and cured by its rust.
8. The Argive Agamemnon shows reserve and dignity, while the Theban Creon is a headstrong tyrant. The Assyrian would be effeminate, as compared with the Colchian, but both would be barbarians (Assyria was an ancient empire of west Asia; Colchis bordered the Black Sea).

implacable, and fierce; let him say 'the laws are not for me' and set no limit to the claims that arms can make. Let Medea be proud and indomitable, Ino full of tears, Ixion treacherous, Io never at rest, Orestes full of gloom.[9] On the other hand, if you are putting something untried on the stage and venturing to shape a new character, let it be maintained to the end as it began and be true to itself. It is hard to put generalities in an individual way: you do better to reduce the song of Troy to acts than if you were the first to bring out something unknown and unsaid.[1] [131] The common stock will become your private property if you don't linger on the broad and vulgar round, or anxiously render word for word, a loyal interpreter, or again, in the process of imitation, find yourself in a tight corner from which shame, or the rule of the craft, won't let you move; or, once again, if you avoid a beginning like the cyclic poet[2]—

> Of Priam's fortune will I sing, and war
> well known to fame.

If he opens his mouth as wide as that, how *can* the promiser bring forth anything to match it? The mountains shall be in labour, and there shall be born—a silly mouse. [140] How much better was the way of that poet whose every endeavour is to the point!

> Tell me, O Muse, of him who, after Troy
> had fallen, saw the manners and the towns
> of many men.[3]

His plan is not to turn fire to smoke, but smoke to light, so as to relate magnificent wonders thereafter—Antiphates and the Cyclops, Scylla and Charybdis.[4] *He* doesn't start the Return of Diomedes from the death of Meleager,[5] nor begin the Trojan war from the twin egg;[6] he is always making good speed towards the end of the story, and carries his hearer right into the thick of it as though it were already known. [150] He leaves out anything which he thinks cannot be polished up satisfactorily by treatment, and tells his fables and mixes truth with falsehood in such a way that the middle squares with the beginning and the end with the middle.

Let me tell you what I and the public both want, if you're hoping for an applauding audience that will wait for the curtain and keep its seat until the epilogue-speaker says 'Pray clap your hands'.[7] You must mark the manners

9. Son of Agamemnon and Clytemnestra who avenges his father's murder by killing his mother and her lover; he is gloomy because the Furies hound him for the crime of matricide. Medea: enchantress of Greek myth who helps Jason gain the Golden Fleece, and, after he abandons her, murders their children in revenge. Ino: daughter of Cadmus, wife of Athamas; pursued by her enraged husband after plotting against her stepchildren, she leaped into the sea with her son. Ixion: king who slew his father-in-law and is bound to a perpetually revolving wheel in the underworld as punishment for his attempted seduction of Juno. Io: daughter of Inachus who was loved by Zeus and subsequently transformed into a cow, goaded by gadflies sent by the angry Hera, Zeus's wife.

1. I.e., to invent names and circumstances for a general theme is undesirable; if you object that the known myths are hackneyed, the remedy is in the treatment of them in a new way [translator's note].

2. That is, a poet of the epic cycle, writing poems in Homeric style and usually about events of the Trojan War.

3. *Odyssey* 1.1ff. [translator's note].

4. Characters from Homer's *Odyssey*: Antiphates, king of the Laestrygones; Cyclops, Greek mythological giant with one eye; Scylla, half-human sea monster that takes men from passing ships; Charybdis, a dangerous whirlpool in the waters between Sicily and Italy, regarded as a female monster.

5. Uncle of Diomedes, a Greek hero in the *Iliad*, and therefore of an older generation.

6. The offspring of Leda and Zeus were twins, Clytemnestra and Helen; Helen, taken from her husband by the Trojan prince Paris, is usually considered by poets to be the immediate cause of the Trojan War.

7. The comedies of the Roman playwrights Plautus and Terence close with *plaudite* (applaud!) or an equivalent phrase.

of each time of life, and assign the appropriate part to changing natures and ages. The child, just able to repeat words and planting his steps on the ground with confidence, is eager to play with his contemporaries, gets in and out of a temper without much cause, and changes hour by hour. [161] The beardless youth, his tutor at last out of the way, enjoys his horses and dogs and the grass of the sunny Park. Moulded like wax into vice, he is surly to would-be advisers, slow to provide for necessities, prodigal of money, up in the air, eager, and quick to abandon the objects of his sudden love. Soon interests change: the grown man's mind pursues wealth and influential connections, is enslaved to honour, and avoids doing anything he may soon be trying to change. [169] Many distresses surround the old man. He is acquisitive, and, poor man, daren't put his hand on what he has laid up; he is afraid to use it. He goes about his business timidly and coldly, procrastinating, letting things drag on in hope, lazy yet greedy of his future; he is awkward and grumbling, given to praising the days when he was a boy and to criticizing and finding fault with his juniors. Years as they come bring many blessings with them, and as they go take many away. To save yourself giving a young man an old man's role or a boy a grown man's, remember that your character should always remain faithful to what is associated with his age and suits it.

Some Rules for Dramatists[8]

Actions may be either performed on the stage or reported when performed. [180] What comes in through the ear is less effective in stirring the mind than what is put before our faithful eyes and told by the spectator to himself. However, you are not to bring on to the stage events which ought to be carried out within; you are to remove many things from sight, and let them be related in due course by the eloquence of an eye-witness. Don't let Medea murder the children before the people's gaze, or wicked Atreus cook human offal in public, or Procne be metamorphosed into a bird or Cadmus[9] into a snake. Anything you show me like that earns my incredulity and disgust.

A play that wants to be in demand and to be revived must not be shorter or longer than five acts.[1]

[191] There should be no god to intervene, unless the problem merits such a champion.[2]

No fourth character should attempt to speak.

The chorus should play an actor's part, and do a man's duty. It should not sing between the acts anything which has no relevance to or cohesion with the plot. It should side with the good and give them friendly counsel, restrain the angry, and approve those who scruple to go astray. It should praise a frugal table's fare, sound justice, law, and times of peace when the town's gates stand open. [200] It should keep secrets entrusted to it, and beg and pray the gods that Fortune may return to the wretched and abandon the proud.

8. Most of the precepts enumerated in this section may be found in ARISTOTLE's *Poetics* (see above).
9. Founder of Thebes; in Ovid's *Metamorphoses*, Cadmus and his wife are changed into serpents. Atreus: father of Agamemnon and Menelaus; he arranged the feast of Thyestes. Procne: wife of Tereus, who punished him for raping her sister by killing her own child and serving him to her husband; later all three were turned into birds.

1. Not Aristotelian; but Menander seems normally to have composed his comedies in five acts, separated by choral interludes [translator's note]. Menander (ca. 342–ca. 292 B.C.E.), a leading writer of Greek New Comedy.
2. The *deus ex machina* was a divine character lowered from above the stage to conveniently resolve the action at the end of a play.

Development of Tragedy

The flute used not to be, as it is now, bound with copper and a rival to the trumpet. It was slight and simple, with few apertures, but serviceable to accompany and aid the chorus and to fill with its music the still not too crowded benches, where a population of no great size gathered in numbers easily counted, honest and decent and modest. But when that same population won wars and began to extend its territory, when longer walls came to embrace the cities, and people indulged themselves on holidays by drinking in the daytime, and nobody blamed them, [211] then rhythm and tunes acquired greater licence. For what taste could the uneducated show, the holiday crowd of countrymen and townsmen, honest folk and rogues, all mixed up together? This is how the musician came to add movement and elaboration to his art, and to trail his robe as he roamed the stage. This is how even the austere lyre gained a stronger voice, while lofty eloquence produced strange utterance and thought that shrewdly grasped practical needs and prophesied the future grew indistinguishable from the oracles of Delphi.[3]

Satyr-Plays[4]

[220] The competitor in tragic poetry, who strove for a worthless goat,[5] next showed the rustic Satyrs, naked. Preserving his seriousness despite his keen wit, he made an attempt at a joke, because the audience, drunk and lawless at the end of the festival, had to be prevented from going away by tricks and pleasing innovations. But the way to recommend your laughing, joking satyrs, the way to turn seriousness to jest, is this: no god or hero you bring on the stage, if he was seen not long ago in royal gold and purple, must lower his language and move into a humble cottage; not, on the other hand, must his efforts to get off the ground lead him to try to grasp clouds and void. [231] Tragedy does not deserve to blurt out trivial lines, but she will modestly consort a little with the forward satyrs, like a respectable lady dancing because she must on a feast day.

As a Satyr-writer, my Piso friends, I shall not limit my liking to plain and proper terms, nor yet try to be so different from the tone of tragedy that there is no difference between Davus talking or bold Pythias, when she's just tricked Simon out of a talent,[6] and Silenus, at once guardian and servant of the god he has brought up. [240] I shall make up my poem of known elements, so that anyone may hope to do the same, but he'll sweat and labour to no purpose when he ventures: such is the force of arrangement and combination, such the splendour that commonplace words acquire. Your woodland Fauns, if you take my judgement, should beware of behaving as if they were born at the street corner and were creatures of the Forum—they

3. The oracle of Apollo, and the most important oracle in ancient Greece.

4. These featured Silenus and satyrs in burlesque episodes of myth; style and meter were those of tragedy, not comedy. The piece was commonly performed as a fourth play after three tragedies. Euripides' *Cyclops* [ca. 410 B.C.E.] is the only complete extant example. Aristotle believed satyr-plays were at the origin of tragedy; others, as Horace here, that they were a later refinement [translator's note]. Silenus: male spirit associated with Dionysus, later represented as a drunken old man. "Satyrs": woodland spirits, usually part human, part goat.

5. Horace believes that the Greek term *tragōidia*, literally, "goat song," took its name from the prize of a goat.

6. Typical New Comedy names: slave, maid or prostitute, old man [translator's note].

shouldn't play the gallant in languishing verse or crack dirty and disreputable jokes; possessors of horses[7] or ancestors or property take offence at this sort of thing and don't look kindly on work approved by the fried-peas-and-nuts public, or give it the prize.

The Need for Technical Perfection

[251] A long syllable following a short one makes an iambus.[8] He is a quick foot; this is why he ordered iambic lines to be called trimeters, although he was giving six beats to the line, and was the same in form from first to last. Not all that long ago, wanting to fall rather more slowly and weightily upon our ears, he admitted the stately spondees to family privileges—what a comfortable, easy-going foot he is!—but without being quite so complaisant as to give up the second and fourth positions in the line. Rarely does he appear in Accius'[9] noble trimeters, and his rarity in Ennius' [260] weighty lines as they fly out on the stage damns them with the shocking accusation of hasty and careless craftsmanship—or else sheer ignorance of the trade.

Of course, it's not every critic that notices lines that aren't tuneful, and Roman poets have enjoyed undeserved licence. But does that entitle *me* to make mistakes and scribble away carelessly? Or should I rather expect everyone to see my mistakes, and so play safe and cautious, keeping within the bounds of what I can hope to be pardoned for? In that case, all I've done is to avoid blame; I have not deserved praise.

Greek Models

Study Greek models night and day. [270] Your ancestors praised Plautus' metre and his humour. On both counts their admiration was too indulgent, not to say childish, if it's true that you and I know how to distinguish a witless jest from a subtle one and if we've skill in our fingers and ears to know what sounds are permitted.

Inventiveness of the Greeks in Drama

The hitherto unknown genre of the tragic Muse is said to be Thespis'[1] invention; he is supposed to have carried on a cart verses to be sung and acted by performers whose faces were smeared with wine-lees. After him came Aeschylus,[2] the inventor of the mask and splendid robe; he gave the stage a floor of modest boards, and taught the actors to talk big and give themselves height by their high boots. [281] Next came Old Comedy,[3] much praised, though its liberty degenerated into vice and violence deserving restraint of law; the law was accepted, and the chorus fell silent, its right of shameful insult removed.

7. In the Roman Republic, the *equites* (horsemen or "knights") formed a wealthy class almost equal to senators in social standing.
8. Horace's main theme in what preceded was propriety; in the next section it is perfection. He marks the transition by humorously giving some very elementary metrical instruction [translator's note]. A spondee is a metrical foot formed by two long syllables.
9. Roman playwright and literary critic (170–90 B.C.E.).
1. Pioneer of Greek tragedy (6th. c. B.C.E.) who introduced the actor's reply to the chorus.
2. Greek dramatist (525–456 B.C.E.) who introduced the third actor to the Greek stage.
3. The greatest writer of Old Comedy was Aristophanes (ca. 450–ca. 385 B.C.E.).

Inventiveness of the Romans

Our poets have left nothing unattempted. Not the least part of their glory was won by venturing to abandon the footsteps of the Greeks and celebrate our own affairs; some produced historical plays, some comedies in Roman dress. [289] Latium[4] would have been as famous for literature as for valour and deeds of arms if the poets had not, one and all, been put off by the labour and time of polishing their work. Children of Numa,[5] show your disapproval of any poem which long time and much correction have not disciplined and smoothed ten times over, to satisfy the well-pared nail.

The Poet[6]

Democritus[7] thinks native talent a happier thing than poor, miserable art, and banishes sane poets from his Helicon.[8] That's why so many don't bother to cut their nails or beard, but seek solitude and keep away from the bath. [299] For a man is sure to win the reward and name of poet if he never lets barber Licinus get hold of that head that three Anticyras[9] won't make sound. I'm a fool to purge my bile when spring comes round. I could write as good poetry as any; but nothing is worth that price, and so I'll play the part of the whetstone, that can sharpen the knife though it can't itself cut. In other words, without writing myself, I will teach function and duty—where the poet's resources come from, what nurtures and forms him, what is proper and what not, in what directions excellence and error lead.

Wisdom is the starting-point and source of correct writing. [310] Socratic books[1] will be able to point out to you your material, and once the material is provided the words will follow willingly enough. If a man has learned his duty to his country and his friends, the proper kind of love with which parent, brother, and guest should be cherished, the functions of a senator and a judge, the task of a general sent to the front—then he automatically understands how to give each character its proper attributes. My advice to the skilled imitator will be to keep his eye on the model of life and manners, and draw his speech living from there.

[319] Sometimes a play devoid of charm, weight, and skill, but attractive with its commonplaces and with the characters well drawn, gives the people keener pleasure and keeps them in their seats more effectively than lines empty of substance and harmonious trivialities.

Greek and Roman Attitudes

The Greeks have the gift of genius from the Muse, and the power of well-rounded speech. They covet nothing but praise. Roman boys do long sums and learn to divide their *as* into a hundred parts.[2]

4. Area of central Italy that included Rome.
5. Numa Pompilius, half-legendary second king of Rome (traditional dates, 715–673 B.C.E.).
6. From this point, the poem turns to topics concerned with the poet himself: inspiration, moral knowledge, care for posterity, commitment. This main theme continues to the end [translator's note].
7. Greek philosopher (460–370 B.C.E.).
8. Mountain sacred to the Muses.
9. Hellebore, proverbially a cure for madness, came from Anticyra [translator's note].
1. The Greek philosopher Socrates (469–399 B.C.E.) left no writings, but he was the most important speaker in the dialogues of his greatest pupil, PLATO (ca. 427–ca. 347 B.C.E.).
2. Twelve unciae = 1 as; 5 unciae = quincunx; one-third as = triens; one-half as = semis [translator's note]. An as was worth perhaps $3.

'Young Albinus,[3] subtract one uncia from a quincunx: what's left? . . . You could have told me by now . . . '

'A triens.'

'Excellent. You'll be able to look after your affairs. Now add an uncia. What is it now?'

'A semis.'

Once this rust and care for cash has tainted the soul, can we hope for poems to be written that deserve preserving with cedar oil and keeping safe in smooth cypress?

Poets aim either to do good or to give pleasure—or, thirdly, to say things which are both pleasing and serviceable for life.

Whatever advice you give, be brief, so that the teachable mind can take in your words quickly and retain them faithfully. Anything superfluous overflows from the full mind.

Whatever you invent for pleasure, let it be near to truth. We don't want a play to ask credence for anything it feels like, or draw a living child from the ogress's belly after lunch. The ranks of elder citizens chase things off the stage if there's no good meat in them, and the high-spirited youngsters won't vote for dry poetry. The man who combines pleasure with usefulness wins every suffrage, delighting the reader and also giving him advice; this is the book that earns money for the Sosii,[4] goes overseas and gives your celebrated writer a long lease of fame.

However, there are some mistakes we are ready to forgive. The string doesn't always give the note that the hand and mind intended: it often returns a high note when you ask for a low. The bow won't always hit what it threatens to hit. But when most features of a poem are brilliant, I shan't be offended by a few blemishes thrown around by carelessness or human negligence. But what then? If a copyist goes on making the same mistake however much he is warned, he is not forgiven; if a lyre-player always gets the same note wrong, people laugh at him; so, in my estimation, if a poet fails to come off a good deal, he's another Choerilus,[5] whom I admire with a smile if he's good two or three times. Why, I'm angry even if good Homer goes to sleep, though a doze is quite legitimate in a long piece of work.

Poetry is like painting. Some attracts you more if you stand near, some if you're further off. One picture likes a dark place, one will need to be seen in the light, because it's not afraid of the critic's sharp judgement. One gives pleasure once, one will please if you look it over ten times.

Dear elder son of Piso, though your father's words are forming you in the right way and you have wisdom of your own besides, take this piece of advice away with you and remember it. In some things, a tolerable mediocrity is properly allowed. A mediocre lawyer or advocate is a long way from the distinction of learned Messalla and doesn't know as much as Aulus Cascellius,[6] but he has his value. But neither men nor gods nor shop-fronts allow a poet to be mediocre. Just as music out of tune or thick ointment or Sardinian honey with your poppy[7] gives offence at a nice dinner, because the

3. Roman family name.
4. Booksellers (the Sosii were brothers and well-known booksellers).
5. Minor poet of the 4th c. B.C.E. who accompanied Alexander the Great on his campaigns and was paid to celebrate him.
6. Famous Augustan lawyer. Messalla Corvinus (64 B.C.E.–8 C.E.), Roman political leader, orator, author, soldier, and a patron of the arts.
7. Poppy seeds, when roasted and served with honey, were considered a delicacy; but they were spoiled if the honey had a bitter flavor.

meal could go on without them, so poetry, which was created and discovered for the pleasure of the mind, sinks right to the bottom the moment it declines a little from the top. The man who doesn't know how to play keeps away from the sporting gear in the park. [380] The man who's never been taught ball or discus or hoop keeps quiet, so that the packed spectators can't get a free laugh. But the man who doesn't know how to make verses still has a go. Why shouldn't he? He's free, and of free birth, he's assessed at an equestrian property rate, and he's not got a fault in the world.

You will never do or say anything if Minerva[8] is against you: your taste and intelligence guarantee us that. But if you do write something some day, let it find its way to critic Maecius'[9] ears, and your father's, and mine, and be stored up for eight years in your notebooks at home. You will be able to erase what you haven't published; words once uttered forget the way home.

Poetry and Its Social Uses and Value

[391] Orpheus,[1] who was a holy man and the interpreter of the gods, deterred the men of the forests from killing and from disgusting kinds of food. This is why he was said to tame tigers and rabid lions. This too is why Amphion,[2] the founder of the city of Thebes, was said to move rocks where he wished by the sound of the lyre and coaxing prayers. In days of old, wisdom consisted in separating public property from private, the sacred from the secular, in checking promiscuity, in laying down rules for the married, in building cities, in inscribing laws on wooden tablets. [400] And that is how honour and renown came to divine poets and poetry. After them came the great Homer and Tyrtaeus,[3] who sharpened masculine hearts for war by their verses. Oracles were uttered in verse. The path of life was pointed out in verse. Kings' favours were won by the Muses' tunes. Entertainment was found there also, and rest after long labour. So there is no call to be ashamed of the Muse with her skill on the lyre or of Apollo[4] the singer.

Art and Nature

Do good poems come by nature or by art? This is a common question. For my part, I don't see what study can do without a rich vein of talent, [410] nor what good can come of untrained genius. They need each other's help and work together in friendship. A boy who wants to reach the hoped-for goal in the race endures and does a lot, sweats and freezes, refrains from sex and wine. The clarinetist who is playing in honour of Apollo learns his lesson first and stands in awe of his master. But nowadays it's enough to say: 'I write marvellous poems. The itch take the hindmost! It's a disgrace for me to be left behind and admit I don't know something that, to be sure, I never learned.'

8. Roman goddess of handicrafts and war, whose attributes became conflated with those of the Greek goddess Athena.

9. Roman author of 12 epigrams of whom nothing is known except his name.

1. A holy man because he founded the Greek religion Orphism. His extraordinary musical powers—said to be able to charm not only wild beasts but also rocks and trees—made Orpheus a model of the poet.

2. Son of Zeus and Antiope, responsible in part for the miraculous construction of the walls of Thebes.

3. Poet of the 7th c. B.C.E.—according to tradition, a lame Attic schoolmaster—who composed war songs and martial elegies for the Spartans, who sang them while marching.

4. Son of Zeus and Leto, god of music and poetry.

[419] A poet who is rich in land and investments bids his flatterers 'come and better themselves'—just like an auctioneer collecting a crowd to buy his wares. But if he's a man who can set out a good dinner properly and go bail for a poor and impecunious client and get him out of a grim legal tangle, I shall be surprised if the lucky fellow knows how to distinguish a false friend from a true. If you have given a man a present, or if you want to, don't then lead him, full of joy, to your verses. He's bound to say 'Splendid, beautiful, just right'; he'll grow pale here, he'll drip dew from loving eyes, he'll jump about, he'll beat the ground with his foot. [431] Your mocker is more deeply stirred than your true admirer, just as hired mourners at a funeral say and do almost more than those who genuinely grieve. Kings are said to ply a man with many cups and test him with wine if they are trying to discover if he deserves their friendship. If you write poetry, the fox's hidden feelings will never escape you. If you read anything aloud to Quintilius,[5] he'd say 'pray change that, and that'. You would say you couldn't do better, [440] though you'd tried two or three times, to no purpose. Then he'd tell you to scratch it out and put the badly turned lines back on the anvil. If you preferred defending your error to amending it, he wasted no more words or trouble on preventing you from loving yourself and your handiwork without competition. A wise and good man will censure flabby lines, reprehend harsh ones, put a black line with a stroke of the pen besides unpolished ones, prune pretentious ornaments, force you to shed light on obscurities, convict you of ambiguity, mark down what must be changed. [450] He'll be an Aristarchus.[6] He won't say, 'Why should I offend a friend in trifles?' These trifles lead to serious troubles, if once you are ridiculed and get a bad reception.

The Mad Poet

Men of sense are afraid to touch a mad poet and give him a wide berth. He's like a man suffering from a nasty itch, or the jaundice, or fanaticism, or Diana's wrath.[7] Boys chase him and follow him round incautiously. And if, while he's belching out his lofty lines and wandering round, he happens to fall into a well or a pit, like a fowler intent on his birds, then, however long he shouts 'Help! Help! Fellow citizens, help!' there'll be no one to bother to pick him up. [461] And if anyone should trouble to help and let down a rope, my question will be, 'How do you know that he didn't throw himself down deliberately? Are you sure he wants to be saved?' And I shall tell the tale of the death of the Sicilian poet. Empedocles[8] wanted to be regarded as an immortal god, and so he jumped, cool as you like, into burning Etna.[9] Let poets have the right and privilege of death. To save a man against his will is the same as killing him. This isn't the only time he's done it. If he's pulled out now, he won't become human or lay aside his love of a notorious end.

[470] It's far from clear *why* he keeps writing poetry. Has the villain pissed on his father's ashes? Or disturbed the grim site of a lightning-strike? Any-

5. Roman critic of the 2d c. B.C.E.; the name is used here to denote someone with taste.
6. The great Alexandrian scholar [2d c. B.C.E.] marked spurious or doubtful lines in Homer with the sign which Horace here attributes to the good critic [translator's note].
7. Lunacy (as the word's derivation from *luna* suggests) was supposed to be caused by the moon goddess, Diana.
8. Sicilian philosopher and statesman (5th c. B.C.E.). The actual place and manner of his death is disputed.
9. Europe's highest active volcano, located in Sicily.

way, he's raving, and his harsh readings put learned and unlearned alike to flight, like a bear that's broken the bars of his cage. If he catches anyone, he holds on and kills him with reading. He's a real leech that won't let go of the skin till it's full of blood.

ca. 10 B.C.E.

LONGINUS
first century C.E.

Since the eighteenth century, the ancient Greek text *On Sublimity* has maintained a reputation as one of the most influential classical works in the tradition of European criticism, despite the uncertainty that surrounds its authorship and date of composition. A distinctive feature of this famous treatise is its favorable commentary on the role of emotion (*pathos*) in the practices of writing, oratory, and reading. According to the author of *On Sublimity* (*Peri Hupsous* in Greek), whom critics refer to as "Longinus," the presence of noble passion is essential for achieving sublimity (*hupsos*), by which he means an elevated and lofty style of writing that rises above the ordinary. From Longinus's author-centered perspective, writers and orators achieve greatness not just by rhetorical techniques but also by deep feelings, profound thoughts, and natural genius: "Sublimity is the echo of a noble mind." Often the experience of reading a great author or listening to a great speech leads us to a feeling of ecstasy or transport (*ekstasis*), which is distinct from the more rational effects of persuasion, the goal of rhetoric. For Longinus, sublimity uplifts the spirit of the reader, filling him or her with unexpected astonishment and pride, arousing noble thoughts, and suggesting more than words can convey.

The extant text of *On Sublimity* derives from a tenth-century medieval manuscript that offers conflicting statements as to the identity of the treatise's creator. For unknown reasons, the table of contents attributes the text to either "Dionysius or Longinus," while the title of the manuscript itself simply indicates that a certain "Dionysius Longinus" is the author. The first attribution suggests that the author is either the Augustan Age Dionysius of Halicarnassus or Cassius Longinus, the third-century pupil of PLOTINUS. For various detailed reasons, neither of these alternatives has convinced scholars. The principal argument against Dionysius is that *On Sublimity* does not comport with the style and general approach of his other works, whose authorship is not in question. The main point of contention against Longinus, who in the eighteenth century was universally held to be the author, is that textual evidence taken from the concluding chapter on the decline of literature suggests a date of composition no later than 100 C.E., thus ruling out a third-century author. The title of the manuscript offers no solution either, for nothing is known of a Dionysius Longinus. One of the few things that can be determined with some certainty is that the author must have been a Hellenized Jew or at least in contact with Jewish culture, since the opening of Genesis is cited as a worthy example of sublimity. Such a reference is quite distinctive: no other known pagan writer employs the Bible in this manner. While scholars continue to attribute *On Sublimity* to Cassius Longinus, they do so as a matter of convenience.

Despite seven lengthy gaps that make up approximately one-third of the original text, the intended organization of *On Sublimity* is reasonably certain. After the formal preface addressed to Postumius Terentianus (about whom we know nothing) and the enumeration of common faults that arise when authors attempt to achieve sublimity, Longinus provides some general marks of true sublimity. Then, in the eighth chapter, he proceeds to enumerate the five sources of sublimity: great thoughts, strong emotion, certain figures of thought and speech, noble diction, and dignified word arrangement. The remainder of the treatise, except for the anomalous short final chapter on the decline of literature (not included in our selection), concerns itself with detailed analytical discussion of each source in the order in which they are first listed, with illustrative digressions on Homer (8th c. B.C.E.), Demosthenes (384–322 B.C.E.), and PLATO (ca. 427–347 B.C.E.), among others. While the text on the second source, strong emotion, is no longer extant, the author's understanding of it is clear from many comments scattered throughout the treatise.

Often cited as a peak moment in *On Sublimity* is the digression on Plato and the orator Lysias (ca. 459–ca. 380 B.C.E.) near the end of the treatise, following the discussion of metaphors. The digression on genius, as it is known, is important because it provides a detailed and eloquent account of sublimity through a series of concise comparisons in which Homer, Plato, and Demosthenes figure as exemplary geniuses. (Many classical writers are mentioned in the text.) Longinus is prompted by the preference of Caecilius, a rival theorist of the sublime (1st c. B.C.E.), for Lysias over Plato. Lysias, Caecilius claims, is a more faultless, pure, and correct writer than Plato, who often gets carried away with his metaphors. Longinus responds by saying that flawless or impeccable mediocrity, which never reaches the heights of sublimity, is not to be preferred over erratic genius. The former, which concerns itself with exactitude, minutia, and correctness, remains within the domain of the familiar, the humble, the charming, and the customary; the latter ranges freely over the grandeur, the loftiness, and the vastness of nature, admiring such awe-inspiring phenomena as the Nile, the Danube, the Rhine, or indeed the ocean, rather than the lesser streams. For Longinus, the faults that geniuses sometimes manifest are excusable because they are inevitable in the pursuit of sublimity, which expresses the boundless thought of human beings and raises them to the "spiritual greatness of god." Freedom from error, per se, Longinus concludes, does not achieve the emotional intensity of sublimity, which strikes suddenly like the brilliance of lightning. Because of the grand manner in which Longinus makes his case here and throughout the treatise, ALEXANDER POPE would later say that Longinus "is himself that great Sublime he draws."

On Sublimity differs fundamentally from Platonic doctrine, which distrusted the frenzied and irrational flights of poetic inspiration and banned poetry from the ideal republic. Cleverly, Longinus points out that Plato does not practice what he preaches. In citing Plato as an example of a sublime writer, Longinus reinterprets the philosopher, highlighting the unconscious ways in which he too is "carried away by a sort of literary madness." *On Sublimity* also differs from HORACE, who in the *Ars Poetica* coolly stresses rhetorical strategies rather than the erratic genius of authors; Horace would have felt comfortable with the last three sources of the sublime, centered as they are on rhetoric, but probably not with the first two, which depend on the mind and heart of the author. In some respects, Longinus's treatise is more like ARISTOTLE's *Poetics*, for they both take note of the formal techniques and psychological effects of literature, Aristotle famously focusing on the emotional "catharsis" that an audience experiences during the performance of a tragedy. An important distinction between the two is that Longinus considers the emotional psychology of the author as well as that of the audience.

Longinus's text appears not to have been read during ancient or medieval times, perhaps because it was lost. It reemerged as an important text first in the Renaissance, with the Italian translation of Niccolò da Falgano in 1560, but especially with Nicolas Boileau's 1674 French rendering. The latter made *On Sublimity* a central text in European criticism throughout the eighteenth century and set the stage for many discussions of the sublime, including those by JOSEPH ADDISON, EDMUND BURKE, and, most notably, IMMANUEL KANT. With Kant's *Critique of Judgment* (1790), the theory of the sublime reached a level of analytical rigor considerably beyond Longinus, who, by comparison, is content merely to enact the sublime and work intuitively. Still, Longinus manages to anticipate many of Kant's major themes, especially his fascination with the uplifting sense of the "supersensible" (the transcendent). He also anticipates Romantic theories of literature, which focus on the creative genius of the author.

From a contemporary perspective, Longinus's view of the sublime has limitations. It focuses mainly on the profound feelings and thoughts of geniuses and audiences, without attending to the ways in which they are structured or determined by language. Longinus does discuss figurative language, rhetoric, and composition, but the ideas and emotions of the genius precede such linguistic "ornamentation." The audience's experience, moreover, is said to transcend words. Such a view contrasts with the influential rhetorical reading of the sublime by the deconstructive theorist PAUL DE MAN, who—especially in his "Phenomenality and Materiality in Kant" (1984)—underscores the figurative or tropological determination of consciousness. Another important limitation for contemporary theory is Longinus's emphasis on spiritual transcendence. Some late-twentieth-century theorists of postmodern culture, including FREDRIC JAMESON and JEAN-FRANÇOIS LYOTARD, conceive the sublime in materialist cultural terms—as disorienting experiences of unrepresentable new global systems and networks and as inconceivable cataclysmic modern historical events (such as the Holocaust). Such theorizing, however, could not have taken place without Longinus's groundbreaking analysis in *On Sublimity*, which thus will continue to be a key text for understanding the sublime.

BIBLIOGRAPHY

The original Greek text with valuable critical commentary can be found in *"Longinus" on the Sublime* (1964), edited by the leading Longinus scholar, D. A. Russell. English translations include W. R. Roberts's *Longinus on the Sublime* (1899); W. H. Fyfe's Loeb Classical Library edition (vol. 199, 1927); and, most notably, D. A. Russell's version in *Ancient Literary Criticism: The Principal Texts in New Translations* (1972) and in *Classical Literary Criticism* (1989), both edited by Russell and M. Winterbottom. Fyfe's translation has also been revised by Russell in the more recent Loeb edition (1995). Both of Russell's translations offer useful and authoritative introductions and annotations.

Works of criticism focusing on the English reception of Longinus include T. R. Henn's *Longinus and English Criticism* (1934) and S. H. Monk's *The Sublime: A Study of Critical Theories in Eighteenth-Century England* (1935). J. W. H. Atkins's *Literary Criticism in Antiquity, A Sketch of Its Development*, volume II, *Graeco-Roman* (1934) and G. M. A. Grube's *Greek and Roman Critics* (1965) offer comprehensive discussions of the text of *On Sublimity*, covering important social and historical contexts. M. H. Abrams's *The Mirror and the Lamp: Romantic Theory and the Critical Tradition* (1953) includes insightful comments on Longinus's relationship to the emergence of Romanticism, while Jules Brody's *Boileau and Longinus* (1958) concentrates on the poet-critic who with his late-seventeenth-century French translation contributed the most to Longinus's great reputation in Europe. *Classical Criticism*, volume 1 of *The Cambridge History of Literary Criticism*, includes an informative short piece on Longinus by D. A. Russell (ed. George A. Kennedy, 1989). For an overview of theories of the sublime, see *The Sublime: A Reader*, edited by Andrew Ashfield and Peter De Bolla (1993). For bibliographic information, see Demiotrio St. Marin's *Bibliography of the Essay on the Sublime* (1967) and Thomas Gwinup and Fidelia Dickinson's *Greek and Roman Authors: A Checklist of Criticism* (1982).

From On Sublimity[1]

Preface

My dear Postumius Terentianus,[2]

[1.1] You will recall that when we were reading together Caecilius'[3] monograph *On Sublimity*, we felt that it was inadequate to its high subject, and failed to touch the essential points. Nor indeed did it appear to offer the reader much practical help, though this ought to be a writer's principal object. Two things are required of any textbook: first, that it should explain what its subject is; second, and more important, that it should explain how and by what methods we can achieve it. Caecilius tries at immense length to explain to us what sort of thing 'the sublime' is, as though we did not know; but he has somehow passed over as unnecessary the question how we can develop our nature to some degree of greatness. [1.2] However, we ought perhaps not so much to blame our author for what he has left out as to commend him for his originality and enthusiasm.

You have urged me to set down a few notes on sublimity for your own use. Let us then consider whether there is anything in my observations which may be thought useful to public men. You must help me, my friend, by giving your honest opinion in detail, as both your natural candour and your friendship with me require. It was well said that what man has in common with the gods is 'doing good and telling the truth'.

[1.3] Your education dispenses me from any long preliminary definition. Sublimity is a kind of eminence or excellence of discourse. It is the source of the distinction of the very greatest poets and prose writers and the means by which they have given eternal life to their own fame. [1.4] For grandeur produces ecstasy rather than persuasion in the hearer; and the combination of wonder and astonishment always proves superior to the merely persuasive and pleasant. This is because persuasion is on the whole something we can control, whereas amazement and wonder exert invincible power and force and get the better of every hearer. Experience in invention and ability to order and arrange material cannot be detected in single passages; we begin to appreciate them only when we see the whole context. Sublimity, on the other hand, produced at the right moment, tears everything up like a whirlwind, and exhibits the orator's whole power at a single blow.

[2.1] Your own experience will lead you to these and similar considerations. The question from which I must begin is whether there is in fact an art of sublimity or profundity. Some people think it is a complete mistake to reduce things like this to technical rules. Greatness, the argument runs, is a natural product, and does not come by teaching. The only art is to be born like that. They believe moreover that natural products are very much weakened by being reduced to the bare bones of a textbook.

[2.2] In my view, these arguments can be refuted by considering three points:

1. Translated by D. A. Russell, who has also supplied the headings in the text. The chapter and section numbers, included in square brackets, date to the 16th century.
2. Nothing is known of Postumius Terentianus.
3. Caecilius of Calacte in Sicily (1st c. B.C.E.), Greek rhetorician. His monograph on sublimity is lost, but later references in Longinus's text suggest that the author neglected the role of strong noble emotion and generous use of metaphor, valuing the even tone of impeccably correct and faultless writers over the ecstasy, wonder, and astonishment of erratic geniuses.

(i) Though nature is on the whole a law unto herself in matters of emotion and elevation, she is not a random force and does not work altogether without method.

(ii) She is herself in every instance a first and primary element of creation, but it is method that is competent to provide and contribute quantities and appropriate occasions for everything, as well as perfect correctness in training and application.

(iii) Grandeur is particularly dangerous when left on its own, unaccompanied by knowledge, unsteadied, unballasted, abandoned to mere impulse and ignorant temerity. It often needs the curb as well as the spur.

[2.3] What Demosthenes[4] said of life in general is true also of literature: good fortune is the greatest of blessings, but good counsel comes next, and the lack of it destroys the other also. In literature, nature occupies the place of good fortune, and art that of good counsel. Most important of all, the very fact that some things in literature depend on nature alone can itself be learned only from art.

If the critic of students of this subject will bear these points in mind, he will, I believe, come to realize that the examination of the question before us is by no means useless or superfluous.

* * *

Some Marks of True Sublimity

At this stage, the question we must put to ourselves for discussion is how to avoid the faults which are so much tied up with sublimity. [6.1] The answer, my friend, is: by first of all achieving a genuine understanding and appreciation of true sublimity. This is difficult; literary judgement comes only as the final product of long experience. However, for the purposes of instruction, I think we can say that an understanding of all this can be acquired. I approach the problem in this way:

[7.1] In ordinary life, nothing is truly great which it is great to despise; wealth, honour, reputation, absolute power—anything in short which has a lot of external trappings—can never seem supremely good to the wise man because it is no small good to despise them. People who could have these advantages if they chose but disdain them out of magnanimity are admired much more than those who actually possess them. It is much the same with elevation in poetry and literature generally. We have to ask ourselves whether any particular example does not give a show of grandeur which, for all its accidental trappings, will, when dissected, prove vain and hollow, the kind of thing which it does a man more honour to despise than to admire. [7.2] It is our nature to be elevated and exalted by true sublimity. Filled with joy and pride, we come to believe we have created what we have only heard. [7.3] When a man of sense and literary experience hears something many times over, and it fails to dispose his mind to greatness or to leave him with more to reflect upon than was contained in the mere words, but comes instead to seem valueless on repeated inspection, this is not true sublimity; it endures only for the moment of hearing. Real sublimity contains much food for reflection, is difficult or rather impossible to resist, and makes a strong and ineffaceable impression on the memory. [7.4] In a word, reckon

4. *Orations* 23.113 [translator's note]. Demosthenes (384–322 B.C.E.), the greatest Athenian orator.

those things which please everybody all the time as genuinely and finely sublime. When people of different trainings, ways of life, tastes, ages, and manners all agree about something, the judgement and assent of so many distinct voices lends strength and irrefutability to the conviction that their admiration is rightly directed.

The Five Sources of Sublimity; The Plan of the Book

[8.1] There are, one may say, five most productive sources of sublimity. (Competence in speaking is assumed as a common foundation for all five; nothing is possible without it.)

(i) The first and most important is the power to conceive great thoughts; I defined this in my work on Xenophon.[5]

(ii) The second is strong and inspired emotion. (These two sources are for the most part natural; the remaining three involve art.)

(iii) Certain kinds of figures. (These may be divided into figures of thought and figures of speech.)

(iv) Noble diction. This has as subdivisions choice of words and the use of metaphorical and artificial language.[6]

(v) Finally, to round off the whole list, dignified and elevated word-arrangement.

Let us now examine the points which come under each of these heads.

I must first observe, however, that Caecilius has omitted some of the five—emotion, for example. [8.2] Now if he thought that sublimity and emotion were one and the same thing and always existed and developed together, he was wrong. Some emotions, such as pity, grief, and fear, are found divorced from sublimity and with a low effect. Conversely, sublimity often occurs apart from emotion. Of the innumerable examples of this I select Homer's bold account of the Aloadae:[7]

> Ossa upon Olympus they sought to heap; and on Ossa
> Pelion with its shaking forest, to make a path to heaven—

and the even more impressive sequel—

> and they would have finished their work . . . [8]

[8.3] In orators, encomia[9] and ceremonial or exhibition pieces always involve grandeur and sublimity, though they are generally devoid of emotion. Hence those orators who are best at conveying emotion are least good at encomia, and conversely the experts at encomia are not conveyers of emotion. [8.4] On the other hand, if Caecilius thought that emotion had no contribution to make to sublimity and therefore thought it not worth mentioning, he was again completely wrong. I should myself have no hesitation in saying that there is nothing so productive of grandeur as noble emotion in the right place. It inspires and possesses our words with a kind of madness and divine spirit.

5. Athenian historian and essayist (ca. 428–ca. 354 B.C.E.).
6. Or "and coined words" [translator's note].
7. In Greek mythology, the two sons of Poseidon (god of the sea) and Iphimedeia, wife of Aloeus.
8. *Odyssey* 11.315–17 [translator's note]. Ossa, Olympus, and Pelion are all mountains in northeastern Greece.
9. Formal poems (odes) or speeches in praise of a living person, object, or event, but not a god, delivered before a special audience. See, for example, GORGIAS's *Encomium of Helen* (above).

(i) Greatness of Thought

[9.1] The first source, natural greatness, is the most important. Even if it is a matter of endowment rather than acquisition, we must, so far as is possible, develop our minds in the direction of greatness and make them always pregnant with noble thoughts. You ask how this can be done. [9.2] I wrote elsewhere something like this: 'Sublimity is the echo of a noble mind.' This is why a mere idea, without verbal expression, is sometimes admired for its nobility—just as Ajax's silence in the Vision of the Dead is grand and indeed more sublime than any words could have been.[1] [9.3] First then we must state where sublimity comes from: the orator must not have low or ignoble thoughts. Those whose thoughts and habits are trivial and servile all their lives cannot possibly produce anything admirable or worthy of eternity. Words will be great if thoughts are weighty.

* * *

Selection and Organization of Material

[10.1] Now have we any other means of making our writing sublime? Every topic naturally includes certain elements which are inherent in its raw material. It follows that sublimity will be achieved if we consistently select the most important of these inherent features and learn to organize them as a unity by combining one with another. The first of these procedures attracts the reader by the selection of details, the second by the density of those selected.

Consider Sappho's[2] treatment of the feelings involved in the madness of being in love. She uses the attendant circumstances and draws on real life at every point. And in what does she show her quality? In her skill in selecting the outstanding details and making a unity of them:

> [10.2] To me he seems a peer of the gods, the man who sits facing you and hears your sweet voice
>
> and lovely laughter; it flutters my heart in my breast. When I see you only for a moment, I cannot speak;
>
> my tongue is broken, a subtle fire runs under my skin; my eyes cannot see, my ears hum;
>
> cold sweat pours off me; shivering grips me all over; I am paler than grass; I seem near to dying;
>
> but all must be endured . . . [3]

[10.3] Do you not admire the way in which she brings everything together—mind and body, hearing and tongue, eyes and skin? She seems to have lost them all, and to be looking for them as though they were external to her. She is cold and hot, mad and sane, frightened and near death, all by turns. The result is that we see in her not a single emotion, but a complex of emotions. Lovers experience all this; Sappho's excellence, as I have said, lies in her adoption and combination of the most striking details.

A similar point can be made about the descriptions of storms in Homer,

1. *Odyssey* 11.563. Note that this is not an example, but a simile illustrating the point that ideas in themselves can be grand [translator's note].

2. Greek lyric poet (b. ca. 612 B.C.E.).

3. Sappho, frag. 31 Lobel-Page.

who always picks out the most terrifying aspects. [10.4] The author of the *Arimaspea* on the other hand expects these lines to excite terror:

> This too is a great wonder to us in our hearts:
> there are men living on water, far from land, on the deep sea:
> miserable they are, for hard is their lot;
> they give their eyes to the stars, their lives to the sea;
> often they raise their hands in prayer to the gods,
> as their bowels heave in pain.[4]

Anyone can see that this is more polished than awe-inspiring. Now compare it with Homer [10.5] (I select one example out of many):

> He fell upon them as upon a swift ship falls a wave,
> huge, wind-reared by the clouds. The ship
> is curtained in foam, a hideous blast of wind
> roars in the sail. The sailors shudder in terror:
> they are carried away from under death, but only just.[5]

[10.6] Aratus[6] tried to transfer the same thought:

> A little plank wards off Hades.

But this is smooth and unimpressive, not frightening. Moreover, by saying 'a plank wards off Hades', he has got rid of the danger. The plank *does* keep death away. Homer, on the other hand, does not banish the cause of fear at a stroke; he gives a vivid picture of men, one might almost say, facing death many times with every wave that comes. Notice also the forced combination of naturally uncompoundable prepositions: *hupek*, 'from under'. Homer has tortured the words to correspond with the emotion of the moment, and expressed the emotion magnificently by thus crushing words together. He has in effect stamped the special character of the danger on the diction: 'they are carried away from under death'.

[10.7] Compare Archilochus on the shipwreck, and Demosthenes on the arrival of the news ('It was evening . . .').[7]

In short, one might say that these writers have taken only the very best pieces, polished them up and fitted them together. They have inserted nothing inflated, undignified, or pedantic. Such things ruin the whole effect, because they produce, as it were, gaps or crevices, and so spoil the impressive thoughts which have been built into a structure whose cohesion depends upon their mutual relations.

4. From a lost poem attributed to Aristeas of Proconnesus, a prophet of Apollo said to have traveled in Siberia in the 7th c. B.C.E. The lines perhaps express the surprised comment of innocent continentals, deep in Asia, on the tales they have heard about ships and seagoing [translator's note].

5. *Iliad* 15.624–28 [translator's note].

6. *Phaenomena* 299 [translator's note]. Aratus (ca. 315–ca. 240 B.C.E.), Greek poet who often wrote on philosophy and natural science.

7. The example from Archilochus cannot be certainly identified. That from Demosthenes (*On the Crown* 169) describes the alarm at Athens when news arrived of Philip's occupation of Elatea (339 B.C.E.): "It was evening when somebody brought the *prutaneis* [city magistrates] the news that Elatea was captured. Some of them got up in the middle of dinner and began to drive the traders from the stalls in the *agora* and burn the wicker hurdles. Other sent for the generals and gave instructions to the trumpeter. The town was full of uproar" [translator's note]. Archilochus (7th c. B.C.E.), earliest Greek lyric poet whose work survives. Philip II (359–336 B.C.E.), king of Macedon. Elatea: strategically located town, three days' march from Athens.

Amplification

[11.1] The quality called 'amplification' is connected with those we have been considering. It is found when the facts or the issues at stake allow many starts and pauses in each section. You wheel up one impressive unit after another to give a series of increasing importance. There are innumerable varieties of amplification: [11.2] it may be produced by commonplaces, by exaggeration or intensification of facts or arguments, or by a build-up of action or emotion. The orator should realize, however, that none of these will have its full effect without sublimity. Passages expressing pity or disparagement are no doubt an exception; but in any other instance of amplification, if you take away the sublime element, you take the soul away from the body. Without the strengthening influence of the sublimity, the effective element in the whole loses all its vigour and solidity.

[11.3] What is the difference between this precept and the point made above about the inclusion of vital details and their combination in a unity? What in general is the difference between amplification and sublimity? I must define my position briefly on these points, in order to make myself clear.

[12.1] I do not feel satisfied with the definition given by the rhetoricians: 'amplification is expression which adds grandeur to its subject'. This might just as well be a definition of sublimity or emotion or tropes. All these add grandeur of some kind. The difference lies, in my opinion, in the fact that sublimity depends on elevation, whereas amplification involves extension; sublimity exists often in a single thought, amplification cannot exist without a certain quantity and superfluity. [12.2] To give a general definition, amplification is an aggregation of all the details and topics which constitute a situation, strengthening the argument by dwelling on it; it differs from proof in that the latter demonstrates the point made . . .

* * *

Imitation of Earlier Writers as a Means to Sublimity

[13.2] Plato,[8] if we will read him with attention, illustrates yet another road to sublimity, besides those we have discussed. This is the way of imitation and emulation of great writers of the past. Here too, my friend, is an aim to which we must hold fast. Many are possessed by a spirit not their own. It is like what we are told of the Pythia[9] at Delphi: she is in contact with the tripod near the cleft in the ground which (so they say) exhales a divine vapour, and she is thereupon made pregnant by the supernatural power and forthwith prophesies as one inspired. Similarly, the genius of the ancients acts as a kind of oracular cavern, and effluences flow from it into the minds of their imitators. Even those previously not much inclined to prophesy become inspired and share the enthusiasm which comes from the greatness of others. [13.3] Was Herodotus the only 'most Homeric' writer? Surely Stesichorus[1] and Archilochus earned the name before him. So, more than any,

8. Greek philosopher (427–347 B.C.E.). For PLATO's comments on poetry, see above.

9. A priestess of Apollo and the most famous of his oracles (located on the slopes of Mt. Parnassus near the Greek city Delphi).

1. Greek choral poet (ca. 630–555 B.C.E.) who wrote narratives on epic themes. Herodotus (ca. 484–ca. 425 B.C.E.), Greek historian.

did Plato, who diverted to himself countless rills from the Homeric spring. (If Ammonius[2] had not selected and written up detailed examples of this, I might have had to prove the point myself.) [13.4] In all this process there is no plagiarism. It resembles rather the reproduction of good character in statues and works of art.[3] Plato could not have put such a brilliant finish on his philosophical doctrines or so often risen to poetical subjects and poetical language, if he had not tried, and tried wholeheartedly, to compete for the prize against Homer, like a young aspirant challenging an admired master. To break a lance in this way may well have been a brash and contentious thing to do, but the competition proved anything but valueless. As Hesiod says, 'this strife is good for men.'[4] Truly it is a noble contest and prize of honour, and one well worth winning, in which to be defeated by one's elders is itself no disgrace.

[14.1] We can apply this to ourselves. When we are working on something which needs loftiness of expression and greatness of thought, it is good to imagine how Homer would have said the same thing, or how Plato or Demosthenes or (in history) Thucydides[5] would have invested it with sublimity. These great figures, presented to us as objects of emulation and, as it were, shining before our gaze, will somehow elevate our minds to the greatness of which we form a mental image. [14.2] They will be even more effective if we ask ourselves 'How would Homer or Demosthenes have reacted to what I am saying, if he had been here? What would his feelings have been?' It makes it a great occasion if you imagine such a jury or audience for your own speech, and pretend that you are answering for what you write before judges and witnesses of such heroic stature. [14.3] Even more stimulating is the further thought: 'How will posterity take what I am writing?' If a man is afraid of saying anything which will outlast his own life and age, the conceptions of his mind are bound to be incomplete and abortive; they will miscarry and never be brought to birth whole and perfect for the day of posthumous fame.

Visualization (Phantasia)

[15.1] Another thing which is extremely productive of grandeur, magnificence and urgency, my young friend, is visualization (*phantasia*). I use this word for what some people call image-production. The term *phantasia* is used generally for anything which in any way suggests a thought productive of speech;[6] but the word has also come into fashion for the situation in which enthusiasm and emotion make the speaker *see* what he is saying and bring it *visually* before his audience. [15.2] It will not escape you that rhetorical visualization has a different intention from that of the poets: in poetry the aim is astonishment, in oratory it is clarity. Both, however, seek emotion and excitement.

2. Head of the Alexandrian library (2d c. B.C.E.) and author of commentaries on Homer and other Greek authors.
3. Text uncertain: perhaps "the reproduction of beauty of form . . ." [translator's note].
4. *Works and Days* 24: healthy rivalry contrasted with the strife that produces war [translator's note]. Hesiod (active ca. 700 B.C.E.), Greek didactic poet.
5. Greek historian (ca. 455–ca. 400 B.C.E.).
6. A Stoic definition [translator's note].

Mother, I beg you, do not drive them at me,
the women with the blood in their eyes and the snakes—
they are here, they are here, jumping right up to me.[7]

Or again:

O! O! She'll kill me. Where shall I escape?[8]

The poet himself saw the Erinyes,[9] and has as good as made his audience see what he imagined.

* * *

[15.8] The poetical examples, as I said, have a quality of exaggeration which belongs to fable and goes far beyond credibility. In an orator's visualizations, on the other hand, it is the element of fact and truth which makes for success; when the content of the passage is poetical and fabulous and does not shrink from any impossibility, the result is a shocking and outrageous abnormality. This is what happens with the shock orators of our own day; like tragic actors, these fine fellows *see* the Erinyes, and are incapable of understanding that when Orestes says

Let me go; you are one of my Erinyes,
you are hugging me tight, to throw me into Hell,[1]

he visualizes all this *because he is mad.*

[15.9] What then is the effect of rhetorical visualization? There is much it can do to bring urgency and passion into our words; but it is when it is closely involved with factual arguments that it enslaves the hearer as well as persuading him. 'Suppose you heard a shout this very moment outside the court, and someone said that the prison had been broken open and the prisoners had escaped—no one, young or old, would be so casual as not to give what help he could. And if someone then came forward and said "This is the man who let them out", our friend would never get a hearing; it would be the end of him.'[2] [15.10] There is a similar instance in Hyperides' defence of himself when he was on trial for the proposal to liberate the slaves which he put forward after the defeat.[3] 'It was not the proposer', he said, 'who drew up this decree: it was the battle of Chaeronea.' Here the orator uses a visualization actually in the moment of making his factual argument, with the result that his thought has taken him beyond the limits of mere persuasiveness. [15.11] Now our natural instinct is, in all such cases, to attend to the stronger influence, so that we are diverted from the demonstration to the astonishment caused by the visualization, which by its very brilliance conceals the factual aspect. This is a natural reaction: when two things are joined together, the stronger attracts to itself the force of the weaker.

[15.12] This will suffice for an account of sublimity of thought produced by greatness of mind, imitation, or visualization.[4]

7. Euripides, *Orestes* 255–57. Orestes sees the Furies [translator's note]. The Furies: hideous spirits, who avenge wrongs done to kindred, especially murder.

8. Euripides, *Iphigenia in Tauris* 291. Again Orestes and the Furies [translator's note].

9. That is, the Furies.

1. Euripides, *Orestes* 264–65 [translator's note].

2. Demosthenes, *Orations* 24.208 [translator's note].

3. I.e., after Philip's victory at Chaeronea (338 B.C.E.). The speech is not extant [translator's note]. Hyperides (389–322 B.C.E.), Greek orator, professional speech writer, and prosecutor. Chaeronea: northernmost town of Boeotia, where Philip defeated the Athenians and the Thebans.

4. Note that this is not a complete summary of chaps. 9–15 [translator's note].

(iii) Figures: An Example to Illustrate the Right Use of Figures[5]

[16.1] The next topic is that of figures. Properly handled, figures constitute, as I said, no small part of sublimity. It would be a vast, or rather infinite, labour to enumerate them all; what I shall do is to expound a few of those which generate sublimity, simply in order to confirm my point.

[16.2] Here is Demosthenes putting forward a demonstrative argument on behalf of his policy.[6] What would have been the natural way to put it? 'You have not done wrong, you who fought for the liberty of Greece; you have examples to prove this close at home: the men of Marathon, of Salamis, of Plataea did not do wrong.' But instead of this he was suddenly inspired to give voice to the oath by the heroes of Greece: 'By those who risked their lives at Marathon, you have not done wrong!' Observe what he effects by this single figure of conjuration, or 'apostrophe' as I call it here. He deifies his audience's ancestors, suggesting that it is right to take an oath by men who fell so bravely, as though they were gods. He inspires the judges with the temper of those who risked their lives. He transforms his demonstrations into an extraordinary piece of sublimity and passion, and into the convincingness of this unusual and amazing oath. At the same time he injects into his hearers' minds a healing specific, so as to lighten their hearts by these paeans of praise and make them as proud of the battle with Philip as of the triumphs[7] of Marathon and Salamis. In short, the figure enables him to run away with his audience.

* * *

The Relation between Figures and Sublimity

[17.1] At this point, my friend, I feel I ought not to pass over an observation of my own. It shall be very brief: figures are natural allies of sublimity and themselves profit wonderfully from the alliance. I will explain how this happens.

Playing tricks by means of figures is a peculiarly suspect procedure. It raises the suspicion of a trap, a deep design, a fallacy. It is to be avoided in addressing a judge who has power to decide, and especially in addressing tyrants, kings, governors, or anybody in a high place. Such a person immediately becomes angry if he is led astray like a foolish child by some skilful orator's figures. He takes the fallacy as indicating contempt for himself. He becomes like a wild animal. Even if he controls his temper, he is now completely conditioned against being convinced by what is said. A figure is therefore generally thought to be best when the fact that it is a figure is concealed.

[17.2] Thus sublimity and emotion are a defence and a marvellous aid against the suspicion which the use of figures engenders. The artifice of the trick is lost to sight in the surrounding brilliance of beauty and grandeur, and it escapes all suspicion. 'By the men of Marathon . . . ' is proof enough. For how did Demosthenes conceal the figure in that passage? By sheer bril-

5. The section on the second source of the sublime, strong emotion, is missing from the extant Greek manuscript.

6. The passage discussed is in *Orations* 18.208 [translator's note].

7. At Marathon, the Athenians aided by the Plataeans became the first Greeks to defeat the Persians (490 B.C.E.); near the island of Salamis, the Persian fleet was routed by combined Greek forces (480 B.C.E.).

liance, of course. As fainter lights disappear when the sunshine surrounds them, so the sophisms of rhetoric are dimmed when they are enveloped in encircling grandeur. [17.3] Something like this happens in painting: when light and shadow are juxtaposed in colours on the same plane, the light seems more prominent to the eye, and both stands out and actually appears much nearer. Similarly, in literature, emotional and sublime features seem closer to the mind's eye, both because of a certain natural kinship and because of their brilliance. Consequently, they always show up above the figures, and overshadow and eclipse their artifice.

* * *

Hyperbaton

* * *

[22.1] Hyperbaton is an arrangement of words or thoughts which differs from the normal sequence . . . [8] It is a very real mark of urgent emotion. People who in real life feel anger, fear, or indignation, or are distracted by jealousy or some other emotion (it is impossible to say how many emotions there are; they are without number), often put one thing forward and then rush off to another, irrationally inserting some remark, and then hark back again to their first point. They seem to be blown this way and that by their excitement, as if by a veering wind. They inflict innumerable variations on the expression, the thought, and the natural sequence. Thus hyperbaton is a means by which, in the best authors, imitation approaches the effect of nature. Art is perfect when it looks like nature, nature is felicitous when it embraces concealed art. Consider the words of Dionysius of Phocaea in Herodotus:[9] 'Now, for our affairs are on the razor's edge, men of Ionia, whether we are to be free or slaves—and worse than slaves, runaways—so if you will bear hardships now, you will suffer temporarily but be able to overcome your enemies.' [22.2] The natural order of thought would have been: 'Men of Ionia, now is the time for you to bear hardships, for our affairs are on the razor's edge.' The speaker has displaced 'men of Ionia'; he begins with the cause of fear, as though the alarm was so pressing that he did not even have time to address the audience by name. He has also diverted the order of thought. Before saying that they must suffer hardship themselves (that is the gist of his exhortation), he first gives the reason why it is necessary, by saying 'our affairs are on the razor's edge'. The result is that he seems to be giving not a premeditated speech but one forced on him by the circumstances.

[22.3] It is even more characteristic of Thucydides to show ingenuity in separating by transpositions even things which are by nature completely unified and indivisible.

Demosthenes is less wilful in this than Thucydides, but no one uses this kind of effect more lavishly. His transpositions produce not only a great sense of urgency but the appearance of extemporization, as he drags his hearers with him into the hazards of his long hyperbata. [22.4] He often holds in suspense the meaning which he set out to convey and, introducing one extra-

8. Probably a few words are missing here [translator's note].

9. *Histories* 6.11 [translator's note]. Dionysius of Phocaea: commander of Greek fleet in the battle of Lade (494 B.C.E.), which the Persians won. In the ancient world, defeated peoples were often enslaved.

neous item after another in an alien and unusual place before getting to the main point, throws the hearer into a panic lest the sentence collapse altogether, and forces him in his excitement to share the speaker's peril, before, at long last and beyond all expectation, appositely paying off at the end the long due conclusion; the very audacity and hazardousness of the hyperbata add to the astounding effect. There are so many examples that I forbear to give any.

* * *

Conclusion of the Section on Figures

[29.2] So much, my dear Terentianus, by way of digression on the theory of the use of those figures which conduce to sublimity. They all make style more emotional and excited, and emotion is as essential a part of sublimity as characterization is of charm.

(iv) Diction: General Remarks

[30.1] Thought and expression are of course very much involved with each other. We have therefore next to consider whether any topics still remain in the field of diction. The choice of correct and magnificent words is a source of immense power to entice and charm the hearer. This is something which all orators and other writers cultivate intensely. It makes grandeur, beauty, old-world charm, weight, force, strength, and a kind of lustre bloom upon our words as upon beautiful statues; it gives things life and makes them speak. But I suspect there is no need for me to make this point; you know it well. It is indeed true that beautiful words are the light that illuminates thought.

[30.2] Magniloquence, however, is not always serviceable: to dress up trivial material in grand and solemn language is like putting a huge tragic mask on a little child. In poetry and history, however . . . [1]

Use of Everyday Words

* * *

[31.1] Theopompus'[2] much-admired phrase seems to me to be particularly expressive because of the aptness of the analogy, though Caecilius manages to find fault with it: 'Philip was excellent at stomaching facts.' An idiomatic phrase is sometimes much more vivid than an ornament of speech, for it is immediately recognized from everyday experience, and the familiar is inevitably easier to credit. 'To stomach facts' is thus used vividly of a man who endures unpleasantness and squalor patiently, and indeed with pleasure, for the sake of gain. [31.2] There are similar things in Herodotus: 'Cleomenes in his madness cut his own flesh into little pieces with a knife till he had sliced himself to death', 'Pythes continued fighting on the ship until he was cut into joints.'[3] These phrases come within an inch of being vulgar, but they are so expressive that they avoid vulgarity.

1. Lacuna equivalent to about four pages [translator's note].
2. Greek historian (b. ca. 378 B.C.E.).
3. *Histories* 6.75, 7.181 [translator's note]. Cleomenes: king of Sparta (reigned ca. 519–480 B.C.E.). Pythes: soldier who fought against the Persians ca. 480 B.C.E.

Metaphors

[32.1] As regards number of metaphors, Caecilius seems to agree with the propounders of the rule that not more than two or at most three may be used of the same subject. Here too Demosthenes is our canon. The right occasions are when emotions come flooding in and bring the multiplication of metaphors with them as a necessary accompaniment. [32.2] 'Vile flatterers, mutilators of their countries, who have given away liberty as a drinking present, first to Philip and now to Alexander, measuring happiness by the belly and the basest impulses, overthrowing liberty and freedom from despotism, which Greeks of old regarded as the canons and standards of the good.'[4] In this passage the orator's anger against traitors obscures the multiplicity of his metaphors.

[32.3] This is why Aristotle and Theophrastus[5] say that there are ways of softening bold metaphors—namely by saying 'as if', 'as it were', 'if I may put it so', or 'if we may venture on a bold expression'. Apology, they say, is a remedy for audacity. [32.4] I accept this doctrine, but I would add—and I said the same about figures—that strong and appropriate emotions and genuine sublimity are a specific palliative for multiplied or daring metaphors, because their nature is to sweep and drive all these other things along with the surging tide of their movement. Indeed it might be truer to say that they *demand* the hazardous. They never allow the hearer leisure to count the metaphors, because he too shares the speaker's enthusiasm.

[32.5] At the same time, nothing gives distinction to commonplaces and descriptions so well as a continuous series of tropes.[6] This is the medium in which the description of man's bodily tabernacle is worked out so elaborately in Xenophon and yet more superlatively by Plato.[7] Thus Plato calls the head the 'citadel' of the body; the neck is an 'isthmus' constructed between the head and the chest; the vertebrae, he says, are fixed underneath 'like pivots'. Pleasure is a 'lure of evil' for mankind; the tongue is a 'taste-meter'. The heart is a 'knot of veins' and 'fountain of the blood that moves impetuously round', allocated to the 'guard-room'. The word he uses for the various passages of the canals is 'alleys'. 'Against the throbbing of the heart,' he continues, 'in the expectation of danger and in the excitation of anger, when it gets hot, they contrived a means of succour, implanting in us the lungs, soft, bloodless, and with cavities, a sort of cushion, so that when anger boils up in the heart, the latter's throbbing is against a yielding obstacle, so that it comes to no harm.' Again: he calls the seat of the desires 'the women's quarters', and the seat of anger 'the men's quarters'. The spleen is for him 'a napkin for the inner parts, which therefore grows big and festering through being filled with secretions'. 'And thereafter', he says again, 'they buried the whole under a canopy of flesh', putting the flesh on 'as a protection against dangers from without, like felting.' Blood he called 'fodder of the flesh'. For the purpose of nutrition, he says also, 'they irrigated the body, cutting channels as in gardens, so that the streams of the veins might flow as it were from an incoming stream, making the body an aqueduct'. Finally: when the end is at hand, the soul's 'ship's cables' are 'loosed', and she herself 'set free'.

4. Demosthenes 18.296 [translator's note].
5. Greek philosopher and naturalist (ca. 370–ca. 285 B.C.E.), pupil and successor of Aristotle.
6. Figures of speech.
7. Xenophon, *Memorabilia* 1.4.5ff.; Plato, *Timaeus* 65c–85e ("Longinus" picks various details out of this long passage, and runs them together) [translator's note].

[32.6] The passage contains countless similar examples; but these are enough to make my point, namely that tropes are naturally grand, that metaphors conduce to sublimity, and that passages involving emotion and description are the most suitable field for them. [32.7] At the same time, it is plain without my saying it that the use of tropes, like all other good things in literature, always tempts one to go too far. This is what people ridicule most in Plato, who is often carried away by a sort of literary madness into crude, harsh metaphors or allegorical fustian. 'It is not easy to understand that a city ought to be mixed like a bowl of wine, wherein the wine seethes with madness, but when chastened by another, sober god, and achieving a proper communion with him, produces a good and moderate drink.'[8] To call water 'a sober god', says the critic, and mixture 'chastening', is the language of a poet who is far from sober himself.

Digression: Genius versus Mediocrity

[32.8] Faults of this kind formed the subject of Caecilius' attack in his book on Lysias,[9] in which he had the audacity to declare Lysias in all respects superior to Plato. He has in fact given way without discrimination to two emotions: loving Lysias more deeply than he loves himself, he yet hates Plato with an even greater intensity. His motive, however, is desire to score a point, and his assumptions are not, as he believed, generally accepted. In preferring Lysias to Plato he thinks he is preferring a faultless and pure writer to one who makes many mistakes. But the facts are far from supporting his view.

[33.1] Let us consider a really pure and correct writer. We have then to ask ourselves in general terms whether grandeur attended by some faults of execution is to be preferred, in prose or poetry, to a modest success of impeccable soundness. We must also ask whether the greater *number* of good qualities or the greater good qualities ought properly to win the literary prizes. These questions are relevant to a discussion of sublimity, and urgently require an answer.

[33.2] I am certain in the first place that great geniuses are least 'pure'. Exactness in every detail involves a risk of meanness; with grandeur, as with great wealth, there ought to be something overlooked. It may also be inevitable that low or mediocre abilities should maintain themselves generally at a correct and safe level, simply because they take no risks and do not aim at the heights, whereas greatness, just because it is greatness, incurs danger.

[33.3] I am aware also of a second point. All human affairs are, in the nature of things, better known on their worse side; the memory of mistakes is ineffaceable, that of goodness is soon gone. [33.4] I have myself cited not a few mistakes in Homer and other great writers, not because I take pleasure in their slips, but because I consider them not so much voluntary mistakes as oversights let fall at random through inattention and with the negligence of genius. I do, however, think that the greater good qualities, even if not consistently maintained, are always more likely to win the prize—if for no other reason, because of the greatness of spirit they reveal. Apollonius makes no mistakes in the *Argonautica*; Theocritus[1] is very felicitous in the *Pastorals*,

8. *Laws* 773c–d [translator's note].
9. Greek orator (ca. 459–ca. 380 B.C.E.) who reacted against the grandiose manner of Gorgias, striving for common language, pure diction, and lucidity rather than powerful emotional appeals.

1. Greek poet (ca. 300–ca. 260 B.C.E.) whose works are the earliest example of pastoral poetry. Apollonius of Rhodes (b. ca. 295 B.C.E.), head of the Alexandrian library and poet; his *Argonautica* is the great epic of the Alexandrian period.

apart from a few passages not connected with the theme; but would you rather be Homer or Apollonius? [33.5] Is the Eratosthenes[2] of that flawless little poem *Erigone* a greater poet than Archilochus, with his abundant, uncontrolled flood, that bursting forth of the divine spirit which is so hard to bring under the rule of law? Take lyric poetry: would you rather be Bacchylides or Pindar?[3] Take tragedy: would you rather be Ion of Chios or Sophocles?[4] Ion and Bacchylides are impeccable, uniformly beautiful writers in the polished manner; but it is Pindar and Sophocles who sometimes set the world on fire with their vehemence, for all that their flame often goes out without reason and they collapse dismally. Indeed, no one in his senses would reckon all Ion's works put together as the equivalent of the one play *Oedipus*.

[34.1] If good points were totted up, not judged by their real value, Hyperides would in every way surpass Demosthenes. He is more versatile, and has more good qualities. He is second-best at everything, like a pentathlon competitor; always beaten by the others for first place, he remains the best of the non-specialists. [34.2] In fact, he reproduces all the good features of Demosthenes, except his word-arrangement, and also has for good measure the excellences and graces of Lysias. He knows how to talk simply where appropriate; he does not deliver himself of everything in the same tone, like Demosthenes. His expression of character has sweetness and delicacy. Urbanity, sophisticated sarcasm, good breeding, skill in handling irony, humour neither rude nor tasteless but flavoured with true Attic salt,[5] an ingenuity in attack with a strong comic element and a sharp sting to its apt fun—all this produces inimitable charm. He has moreover great talents for exciting pity, and a remarkable facility for narrating myths with copiousness and developing general topics with fluency. For example, while his account of Leto is in his more poetic manner, his Funeral Speech is an unrivalled example of the epideictic style.[6] [34.3] Demosthenes, by contrast, has no sense of character. He lacks fluency, smoothness, and capacity for the epideictic manner; in fact he is practically without all the qualities I have been describing. When he forces himself to be funny or witty, he makes people laugh at him rather than with him. When he wants to come near to being charming, he is furthest removed from it. If he had tried to write the little speech on Phryne or that on Athenogenes,[7] he would have been an even better advertisement for Hyperides. [34.4] Yet Hyperides' beauties, though numerous, are without grandeur: 'inert in the heart of a sober man', they leave the hearer at peace. Nobody feels frightened reading Hyperides.

But when Demosthenes begins to speak, he concentrates in himself excellences finished to the highest perfection of his sublime genius—the intensity of lofty speech, living emotions, abundance, acuteness, speed where speed

2. Eratosthenes of Cyrene (ca. 275–194 B.C.E.), Greek poet, critic, geographer, and astronomer.
3. Major Greek lyric poet (518–438 B.C.E.), known for his elaborate odes (encomia) celebrating victories in athletic and music contests. Bacchylides (ca. 524–ca. 452), Greek lyric poet also known for his odes.
4. One of the great Greek tragedians (ca. 496–406 B.C.E.), best known for his Oedipus trilogy. Ion of Chios (ca. 490–ca. 421 B.C.E.), Greek poet famed chiefly for his tragedies, none of which has survived.
5. Elegant wit.
6. The speech (*Deliacus*) in which the myth of Leto was told is lost; the Funeral Speech is extant (*Oration* 2) [translator's note]. "The epideictic style": speech designed for delivery at festivals and funeral orations; it is distinguished from forensic oratory (for law courts) and deliberative (political) oratory. Leto: the mother of the Greek deities Apollo and Artemis.
7. The first is lost; the second is *Oration* 3 (5) [translator's note]. Phryne (4th c. B.C.E.), celebrated Greek courtesan. Athenogenes: Athenian businessman who was the subject of Hyperides' "Against Athenogenes."

is vital, all his unapproachable vehemence and power. He concentrates it all in himself—they are divine gifts, it is almost blasphemous to call them human—and so outpoints all his rivals, compensating with the beauties he has even for those which he lacks. The crash of his thunder, the brilliance of his lightning make all other orators, of all ages, insignificant. It would be easier to open your eyes to an approaching thunderbolt than to face up to his unremitting emotional blows.

[35.1] To return to Plato and Lysias, there is, as I said, a further difference between them. Lysias is much inferior not only in the importance of the good qualities concerned but in their number; and at the same time he exceeds Plato in the number of his failings even more than he falls short in his good qualities.

[35.2] What then was the vision which inspired those divine writers who disdained exactness of detail and aimed at the greatest prizes in literature? Above all else, it was the understanding that nature made man to be no humble or lowly creature, but brought him into life and into the universe as into a great festival, to be both a spectator and an enthusiastic contestant in its competitions. She implanted in our minds from the start an irresistible desire for anything which is great and, in relation to ourselves, supernatural.

[35.3] The universe therefore is not wide enough for the range of human speculation and intellect. Our thoughts often travel beyond the boundaries of our surroundings. If anyone wants to know what we were born for, let him look round at life and contemplate the splendour, grandeur, and beauty in which it everywhere abounds. [35.4] It is a natural inclination that leads us to admire not the little streams, however pellucid and however useful, but the Nile, the Danube, the Rhine, and above all the Ocean. Nor do we feel so much awe before the little flame we kindle, because it keeps its light clear and pure, as before the fires of heaven, though they are often obscured. We do not think our flame more worthy of admiration than the craters of Etna,[8] whose eruptions bring up rocks and whole hills out of the depths, and sometimes pour forth rivers of the earth-born, spontaneous fire. [35.5] A single comment fits all these examples: the useful and necessary are readily available to man, it is the unusual that always excites our wonder.

[36.1] So when we come to great geniuses in literature—where, by contrast, grandeur is not divorced from service and utility—we have to conclude that such men, for all their faults, tower far above mortal stature. Other literary qualities prove their users to be human; sublimity raises us towards the spiritual greatness of god. Freedom from error does indeed save us from blame, but it is only greatness that wins admiration. [36.2] Need I add that every one of those great men redeems all his mistakes many times over by a single sublime stroke? Finally, if you picked out and put together all the mistakes in Homer, Demosthenes, Plato, and all the other really great men, the total would be found to be a minute fraction of the successes which those heroic figures have to their credit. Posterity and human experience—judges whose sanity envy cannot question—place the crown of victory on their heads. They keep their prize irrevocably, and will do so

so long as waters flow and tall trees flourish.[9]

8. An active volcano in Sicily.
9. "Epigram on the tomb of Midas," ascribed to Homer: see Plato, *Phaedrus* 264d [translator's note].

[36.3] It has been remarked that 'the failed Colossus is no better than the Doryphorus of Polyclitus'.[1] There are many ways of answering this. We may say that accuracy is admired in art and grandeur in nature, and it is *by nature* that man is endowed with the power of speech; or again that statues are expected to represent the human form, whereas, as I said, something higher than human is sought in literature.

[36.4] At this point I have a suggestion to make which takes us back to the beginning of the book. Impeccability is generally a product of art; erratic excellence comes from natural greatness; therefore, art must always come to the aid of nature, and the combination of the two may well be perfection.

It seemed necessary to settle this point for the sake of our inquiry; but everyone is at liberty to enjoy what he takes pleasure in.

* * *

(v) Word-Arrangement or Composition

[39.1] There remains the fifth of the factors contributing to sublimity which we originally enumerated. This was a certain kind of composition or word-arrangement. Having set out my conclusions on this subject fully in two books, I shall here add only so much as is essential for our present subject.

Effect of Rhythm

Harmony is a natural instrument not only of conviction and pleasure but also to a remarkable degree of grandeur and emotion. [39.2] The *aulos*[2] fills the audience with certain emotions and makes them somehow beside themselves and possessed. It sets a rhythm, it makes the hearer move to the rhythm and assimilate himself to the tune, 'untouched by the Muses though he be'.[3] The notes of the lyre, though they have no meaning, also, as you know, often cast a wonderful spell of harmony with their varied sounds and blended and mingled notes. [39.3] Yet all these are but spurious images and imitations of persuasion, not the genuine activities proper to human nature of which I spoke.[4] Composition, on the other hand, is a harmony of words, man's natural instrument, penetrating not only the ears but the very soul. It arouses all kinds of conceptions of words and thoughts and objects, beauty and melody—all things native and natural to mankind. The combination and variety of its sounds convey the speaker's emotions to the minds of those around him and make the hearers share them. It fits his great thoughts into a coherent structure by the way in which it builds up patterns of words. Shall we not then believe that by all these methods it bewitches us and elevates to grandeur, dignity, and sublimity both every thought which comes within its compass and ourselves as well, holding as it does complete domination over our minds? It is absurd to question facts so generally agreed. Experience is proof enough.

* * *

1. It is not certain whether "Longinus" means the Colossus of Rhodes or some other large statue. For the Doryphorus, famous for its proportions, see, e.g., G. M. A. Richter, *Handbook of Greek Art* (Phaidon, 1959), 110 [translator's note]. Polyclitus: a leading Greek sculptor of the second half of the 5th c. B.C.E. (a number of copies of his Doryphoros exist).
2. A reed instrument (often translated "pipe" or "flute").
3. Euripides, frag. 663 Nauck [translator's note].
4. Presumably in the work referred to in 39.1 [translator's note].

Effect of Period Structure

[40.1] I come now to a principle of particular importance for lending grandeur to our words. The beauty of the body depends on the way in which the limbs are joined together, each one when severed from the others having nothing remarkable about it, but the whole together forming a perfect unity. Similarly great thoughts which lack connection are themselves wasted and waste the total sublime effect, whereas if they co-operate to form a unity and are linked by the bonds of harmony, they come to life and speak just by virtue of the periodic structure.[5] It is indeed generally true that, in periods, grandeur results from the total contribution of many elements.

[40.2] I have shown elsewhere that many poets and other writers who are not naturally sublime, and may indeed be quite unqualified for grandeur, and who use in general common and everyday words which carry with them no special effect, nevertheless acquire magnificence and splendour, and avoid being thought low or mean, solely by the way in which they arrange and fit together their words. Philistus, Aristophanes[6] sometimes, Euripides generally, are among the many examples. [40.3] Thus Heracles says after the killing of the children:

> I'm full of troubles, there's no room for more.[7]

This is a very ordinary remark, but it has become sublime, as the situation demands. If you re-arrange it, it will become apparent that it is in the composition, not in the sense, that Euripides' greatness appears.

[40.4] Dirce is being pulled about by the bull:

> And where it could, it writhed and twisted round,
> dragging at everything, rock, woman, oak,
> juggling with them all.[8]

The conception is fine in itself, but it has been improved by the fact that the word-harmony is not hurried and does not run smoothly; the words are propped up by one another and rest on the intervals between them; set wide apart like that, they give the impression of solid strength.

* * *

Conclusion

[43.6] There is no urgent need to enumerate in detail features which produce a low effect. We have explained what makes style noble and sublime; the opposite qualities will obviously make it low and undignified.

* * *

1st century C.E.

5. A sentence (i.e., a "period") composed of intricately balanced main and dependent clauses, often artfully arranged to create a sense of anticipation.
6. Major Greek comic dramatist (ca. 450–ca. 385 B.C.E.). Philistus (ca. 430–356 B.C.E.), Greek historian of Sicily.
7. Euripides, *Hercules Furens* 1245 [translator's note].
8. From Euripides' lost *Antiope* (frag. 221 Nauck) [translator's note]. The quote describes how the mythical Dirce died. She was tied to the tail of a bull by Antiope's sons, who were attempting to avenge the mistreatment Dirce inflicted on their mother.

QUINTILIAN
ca. 30/35–ca. 100

Coming at the height of the classical period, Quintilian's *Institutio Oratoria* (*Institutes of Rhetoric*) stands as one of the most important statements of Roman rhetorical theory and practice. Its influence extends from medieval and Renaissance philosophers and literary figures, such as AUGUSTINE, HUGH OF ST. VICTOR, and John of Salisbury, to eighteenth-century critics like ALEXANDER POPE, who praised "Quintilian's copious work," wherein was found "the justest rules, and clearest method joined." Even today, it would be difficult to follow discussions of rhetorical language in more recent formalist and poststructuralist theorists such as ROMAN JAKOBSON, CLEANTH BROOKS, JACQUES DERRIDA, and PAUL DE MAN without the kind of technical knowledge of how tropes work so lucidly explained in Quintilian's rhetoric.

Describing the education of the rhetorician from childhood to adulthood, the *Institutio Oratoria* combines detailed accounts of various rhetorical techniques, including the invention and arrangement of discourse, and descriptions of the various figures of speech and thought; it adds philosophic speculation on the proper uses of rhetoric. Because he is a practitioner and teacher of rhetoric, Quintilian does not equate the rhetorician's task with the philosopher's. However, he was an astute enough observer of his own time to fear the potential for corruption and manipulation in rhetoric. The skills he teaches in the *Institutio Oratoria* might easily be used by "harlots, flatterers, and seducers." But unlike the Greek rhetorician GORGIAS, who noted that rhetoric might as easily be used to promote evil as virtue, Quintilian is not content to accept rhetoric's moral neutrality. He advocates the study of philosophy as a necessary component of a rhetorician's training to ensure that the good orator will also be a good person. Quintilian's teachings, then, contain an ethical imperative that he shares with PLATO, HORACE, LONGINUS, and Augustine. Its legacy, which has permeated the history of literary criticism, is the widely held idea that the study of literature is worthwhile because it can make us more virtuous and discriminating, while instilling in us proper moral values.

Marcus Fabius Quintilianus was born at Calagurris in Spain sometime between 30 and 35 C.E. His father, who may have been a Roman rhetorician, sent his son to Rome to study rhetoric. After finishing his education, Quintilian returned for a short while to his native Spain. However, by 68 he was back in the Roman capital teaching and practicing law. Quintilian became a famous teacher, the first rhetorician to found a public school and receive a state salary. Among his students was the celebrated Roman writer Pliny the Younger. When he retired from teaching in 88, he was appointed by the emperor Domitian as tutor to his two great-nephews and heirs. Quintilian's family life, however, seems to have been much less successful than his public one. The introduction to book 6 of the *Institutio Oratoria* contains a moving description of the death of his son, whom he intended as one of the beneficiaries of his pedagogical advice, as well as expressions of grief over the death of his wife at the age of nineteen and the loss of another son. The date of Quintilian's death is unknown, but it was very probably sometime around 100 C.E.

The *Institutio Oratoria*, the only extant text by Quintilian, was written during the last years of Domitian's reign (which ended with the emperor's murder in 96 C.E.) against a backdrop of political unrest; during this time, the emperor had turned to persecution to maintain his rule, executing people on the flimsiest of excuses and banishing all the philosophers from Rome for fear they would incite people to rebellion. Quintilian's continued favor with the emperor was, therefore, so remarkable that it has led some to question his integrity.

Institutio Oratoria, which might more accurately be translated *On the Teaching of*

Rhetoric, outlines (in twelve parts) a course of study enabling the "good man" (*vir bonus* in Latin—education among the Romans was reserved almost exclusively for elite men) to achieve success as an orator. Book 1 opens by describing how the very young should be educated in preparation for the study of rhetoric. Book 2 defines the nature and aims of rhetoric. Books 3 to 7 discuss such technical matters as invention, the different parts of a speech, and argumentative proofs. Books 8 to 10 deal with oratorical style, including various ornamental figures and tropes. Book 11 examines memorization and oral delivery, while the final section of book 12 portrays the perfect orator. Most of this material is not new; Quintilian's work distills the classical rhetorical tradition that precedes him, drawing heavily on Greek and Roman sources. ARISTOTLE's *Rhetoric* (see above) is an important precursor, but perhaps the most significant influence is the great Roman rhetorician and statesman Cicero (106–43 B.C.E.). While Quintilian's work fell out of favor shortly after his death, by the Middle Ages it had become, along with the anonymous *Rhetorica ad Herennium* (86–82 B.C.E., *Rhetoric Addressed to C. Herennius*), mistakenly attributed to Cicero, an influential source of rhetorical and poetic theory.

The three excerpts below illustrate important features of the *Institutio Oratoria*. Books 8 and 9 define and illustrate the use of the various tropes and figures that constitute the principal sources of rhetorical ornamentation. Book 12 makes the argument for the inclusion of ethics as a part of rhetorical instruction. Although Quintilian is interested primarily in the application of ornaments to rhetoric, not poetry, he frequently uses the poetry of Homer, Virgil, Horace, and others as examples; as a result, throughout the Middle Ages and Renaissance, his analysis of various tropes and figures was construed as advice for poets as well as rhetoricians on how to increase vividness and feeling, variety and interest, conviction and belief (see, for instance, GEOFFREY OF VINSAUF). Chapter 6 of book 8 describes the various tropes, which he defines as "the artistic alteration of a word or phrase from its proper meaning to another." He examines closely metaphor and synecdoche, mentioning simile, ellipsis, and metonymy and warning against their coarse or obscure use.

In book 9, Quintilian turns to a discussion of rhetorical figures, which he distinguishes from tropes. While a *trope* involves the substitution of one word for another, a *figure* does not necessarily entail any change either to the order or meaning of words; instead it is "a form of expression to which a new aspect is given by art." He further distinguishes between figures of speech and figures of thought, suggesting that for him and his contemporaries, thought and the language it is clothed in remain two separate and distinct entities, with language strictly subordinated to thought. A good example of his discussion of figures of thought is his cogent analysis of irony in sections 44 to 49 of book 9, chapter 2. This analysis, however, also reveals the cracks and instabilities in Quintilian's neat divisions between speech and thought: he ends up admitting that a single irony might be classified as trope, figure of speech, and figure of thought. Considerable confusion still surrounds these terms today, and often they are used interchangeably.

Unlike Augustine, Quintilian is not interested in exploring a linguistic theory of signs that might explain figurative language; his concern is the practical uses of rhetoric in oratory and poetry. He does, however, recognize that tropes such as metaphor are not merely optional ornaments of style; some are necessary to convey meaning. He also acknowledges, as many of our own contemporary critics do, that metaphoric language may be very much part of the mental processes by which we find meaning in our world. But unlike those contemporary theorists, Quintilian does not see figurative language as a threat to the stability of linguistic reference. For him, words have their primary "proper" (referential) uses; figurative uses are always secondary. For theorists like Paul de Man, however, processes such as metaphor and metonymy reveal a fundamental instability of linguistic reference and a slippage in signification.

Our final selection, from book 12, examines the moral education of the rhetorician. Quintilian takes exception to the view that virtue is acquired naturally; not only can it be taught, it must be taught. Here Quintilian distinguishes between the role of the philosopher and that of the orator in the state. Philosophers do not argue cases in the law courts or the Senate. Plato's imaginary Republic to the contrary, they do not govern. But though the two occupations are distinct, he urges the orator to learn what the philosopher has to teach. Orators must not only delight; they must also instruct their audiences. Quintilian quickly surveys the three main fields of philosophy—dialectics (or logic), ethics, and physics (which includes religion)—and maintains that all are relevant to the training of an orator. He seems to us today a philosophical pluralist when he advises his reader to swear allegiance to no particular brand of philosophy, but to pick and choose freely from those precepts that will perfect him both in "the glory of a virtuous life" and in eloquence.

Quintilian's injunctions remind us of the importance of rhetoric in Roman education (it was almost the entire curriculum for higher education), an education with a very practical end—the training of lawyers and statesmen capable of pleading cases in public. While a Roman citizen would not necessarily read Quintilian the better to appreciate beautiful poetry, subsequent critics in the Middle Ages, Renaissance, and beyond assimilated to their poetics both Quintilian's analysis of rhetorical technique and his ethical imperative that the rhetorician represent, as MATTHEW ARNOLD might have put it, "the best that has been thought and said."

BIBLIOGRAPHY

The standard Latin text for the *Institutio Oratoria*, the only existing text by Quintilian, is Michael Winterbottom's two-volume 1970 edition; the four-volume edition by H. E. Butler (1920–22) includes a facing English translation. A biographical sketch of Quintilian can be found in George A. Kennedy, *Quintilian* (1969), which also provides a useful introduction to the *Institutio Oratoria*. Charles Baldwin Sears's *Ancient Rhetoric and Poetic Interpreted from Representative Works* (1924) offers a helpful introduction to the relationships in classical literature between rhetoric and poetics and is still frequently cited in studies on Quintilian. Winterbottom's *Problems in Quintilian* (1970) presents a more advanced analysis of the *Institutio Oratoria*. Kennedy's *New History of Classical Rhetoric* (1974) and M. L. Clarke's *Rhetoric at Rome: A Historical Survey* (1996) both examine Quintilian's contributions to the history of rhetoric in ancient Rome. Roy Harris, in *Landmarks in Linguistic Thought: The Western Tradition from Socrates to Saussure* (1997), places Quintilian in the context of Western linguistic theory.

For a bibliography, see James J. Murphy's *Quintilian on the Teaching of Speaking and Writing* (1987). Lewis A. Sussman's *Major Declamations Ascribed to Quintilian* (1987) contains the most current and complete bibliography.

From Institutio Oratoria[1]

From *Book 8*

FROM CHAPTER 5

* * *

[35] I will now proceed to the next subject for discussion, which is, as I have said, that of *tropes*, or *modes*, as the most distinguished Roman rhetoricians call them. Rules for their use are given by the teachers of literature as well.

1. Translated by H. E. Butler.

But I postponed the discussion of the subject when I was dealing with literary education, because it seemed to me that the theme would have greater importance if handled in connexion with the ornaments of oratory, and that it ought to be reserved for treatment on a larger scale.

FROM CHAPTER 6

By a *trope* is meant the artistic alteration of a word or phrase from its proper meaning to another. This is a subject which has given rise to interminable disputes among the teachers of literature, who have quarrelled no less violently with the philosophers than among themselves over the problem of the *genera* and *species* into which *tropes* may be divided, their number and their correct classification. [2] I propose to disregard such quibbles as in no wise concerning the training of an orator, and to proceed to discuss those *tropes* which are most necessary and meet with most general acceptance, contenting myself merely with noting the fact that some *tropes* are employed to help out our meaning and others to adorn our style, that some arise from words used *properly* and others from words used *metaphorically*, and that the changes involved concern not merely individual words, but also our thoughts and the structure of our sentences. [3] In view of these facts I regard those writers as mistaken who have held that *tropes* necessarily involved the substitution of word for word. And I do not ignore the fact that as a rule the *tropes* employed to express our meaning involve ornament as well, though the converse is not the case, since there are some which are intended solely for the purpose of embellishment.

[4] Let us begin, then, with the commonest and by far the most beautiful of *tropes*, namely, *metaphor*, the Greek term for our *translatio*.[2] It is not merely so natural a turn of speech that it is often employed unconsciously or by uneducated persons, but it is in itself so attractive and elegant that however distinguished the language in which it is embedded it shines forth with a light that is all its own. [5] For if it be correctly and appropriately applied, it is quite impossible for its effect to be commonplace, mean or unpleasing. It adds to the copiousness of language by the interchange of words and by borrowing, and finally succeeds in accomplishing the supremely difficult task of providing a name for everything. A noun or a verb is transferred from the place to which it properly belongs to another where there is either no *literal* term or the *transferred* is better than the *literal*. [6] We do this either because it is necessary or to make our meaning clearer or, as I have already said, to produce a decorative effect. When it secures none of these results, our metaphor will be out of place. As an example of a necessary metaphor I may quote the following usages in vogue with peasants when they call a vinebud *gemma*, a gem (what other term is there which they could use?), or speak of the *crops being thirsty* or the *fruit suffering*. For the same reason we speak of a *hard* or *rough* man, there being no *literal* term for these temperaments. [7] On the other hand, when we say that a man is *kindled to anger* or *on fire with greed* or that he has *fallen into error*, we do so to enhance our meaning. For none of these things can be more literally described in its own words than in those which we import from elsewhere.

2. Transferred or figurative use of a word (Latin).

But it is a purely ornamental metaphor when we speak of *brilliance of style, splendour of birth, tempestuous public assemblies, thunderbolts of eloquence,* to which I may add the phrase employed by Cicero in his defence of Milo where he speaks of Clodius[3] as the *fountain*, and in another place as *the fertile field and material* of his client's *glory*. [8] It is even possible to express facts of a somewhat unseemly character by a judicious use of metaphor, as in the following passage.[4]

> "This do they lest too much indulgence make
> The field of generation slothful grow
> And choke its idle furrows."

On the whole *metaphor* is a shorter form of *simile*, while there is this further difference, that in the latter we compare some object to the thing which we wish to describe, whereas in the former this object is actually substituted for the thing. [9] It is a comparison when I say that a man did something *like a lion*, it is a metaphor when I say of him, *He is a lion*. Metaphors fall into four classes. In the first we substitute one living thing for another, as in the passage where the poet, speaking of a charioteer says,[5]

> "The steersman then
> With mighty effort wrenched his charger round."

or when Livy says that Scipio was continually *barked at* by Cato.[6] [10] Secondly, inanimate things may be substituted for inanimate, as in the Virgilian.

> "And gave his fleet the rein,"[7]

or inanimate may be substituted for animate, as in

> "Did the Argive bulwark fall by sword or fate?"[8]

or animate for inanimate, as in the following lines:

> "The shepherd sits unknowing on the height
> Listening the roar from some far mountain brow."

[11] But, above all, effects of extraordinary sublimity are produced when the theme is exalted by a bold and almost hazardous metaphor and inanimate objects are given life and action, as in the phrase

> "Araxes' flood that scorns a bridge,"[9]

[12] or in the passage of Cicero, already quoted, where he cries, "What was that sword of yours doing, Tubero, the sword you drew on the field of Pharsalus?[1] Against whose body did you aim its point? What meant those arms you bore?" Sometimes the effect is doubled, as in Virgil's.

> "And with venom arm the steel."[2]

3. Roman politician (b. 92 B.C.E.) who played a part in the exile of Cicero in 58 B.C.E. Cicero (106–43 B.C.E.), Roman statesman, orator, and author. Milo: Roman politician (d. 48 B.C.E.), who murdered Clodius in 52 B.C.E.; he was unsuccessfully defended by Cicero.

4. Virgil [70–19 B.C.E.], *Georgics* 3.135 [translator's note].

5. Probably from Ennius [translator's note]. Ennius (239–149 B.C.E.), Roman epic poet.

6. Roman statesman and stern moralist (234–149 B.C.E.). Livy (59 B.C.E.–17 C.E.), Roman historian. Scipio (185–129 B.C.E.), Roman general.

7. Virgil, *Aeneid* 6.1.

8. From an unknown tragedian [translator's note].

9. This and the previous passage are from Virgil's *Aeneid* (2.307, 8.728).

1. City in Thessaly, situated on the main road to central Greece; the site of Caesar's defeat in 48 B.C.E. of his former ally Pompey. Tubero (1st c. B.C.E.), jurist and annalist, who fought on the side of Pompey but was later reconciled to Caesar.

2. *Virgil, Aeneid* 9.773.

For both "to arm the steel" and "to arm with venom" are metaphors. [13] These four kinds of metaphor are further subdivided into a number of *species*, such as transference from rational beings to rational and from irrational to irrational and the reverse, in which the method is the same, and finally from the whole to its parts and from the parts to the whole. But I am not now teaching boys: my readers are old enough to discover the *species* for themselves when once they have been given the *genus*.

[14] While a temperate and timely use of metaphor is a real adornment to style, on the other hand, its frequent use serves merely to obscure our language and weary our audience, while if we introduce them in one continuous series, our language will become allegorical and enigmatic. There are also certain metaphors which fail from meanness, such as that of which I spoke above:[3]

"There is a rocky wart upon the mountain's brow."

or they may even be coarse. [15] For it does not follow that because Cicero was perfectly justified in talking of "the sink of the state," when he desired to indicate the foulness of certain men, we can approve the following passage from an ancient orator: "You have lanced the boils of the state." Indeed Cicero himself has demonstrated in the most admirable manner how important it is to avoid grossness in metaphor, such as is revealed by the following examples, which he quotes:—"The state was gelded by the death of Africanus," or "Glaucia,[4] the excrement of the senate-house." [16] He also points out that a metaphor must not be too great for its subject or, as is more frequently the case, too little, and that it must not be inappropriate. Anyone who realises that these are faults, will be able to detect instances of them only too frequently. But excess in the use of metaphor is also a fault, more especially if they are of the same species. [17] Metaphors may also be harsh, that is, far-fetched, as in phrases like "the snows of the head" or

"Jove with white snow the wintry Alps bespewed."[5]

The worst errors of all, however, originate in the fact that some authors regard it as permissible to use even in prose any metaphors that are allowed to poets, in spite of the fact that the latter aim solely at pleasing their readers and are compelled in many cases to employ metaphor by sheer metrical necessity. [18] For my own part I should not regard a phrase like "the shepherd of the people" as admissible in pleading, although it has the authority of Homer, nor would I venture to say that winged creatures "swim through the air," despite the fact that this metaphor has been most effectively employed by Virgil to describe the flight of bees and of Daedalus.[6] For metaphor should always either occupy a place already vacant, or if it fills the room of something else, should be more impressive than that which it displaces.

[19] What I have said above applies perhaps with even greater force to *synecdochē*. For while *metaphor* is designed to move the feelings, give special distinction to things and place them vividly before the eye, *synecdochē* has

3. Discussed earlier in this book (8.3.48).

4. A witty popular orator who died sometime after 99 B.C.E.; in 102 he was nearly expelled from the Senate by political enemies. Africanus: Scipio Africanus (236–184 B.C.E.), the Roman general who defeated the Carthaginian army during the Second Punic War.

5. From Furius, an old epic poet of the second century [translator's note].

6. In Greek mythology, an Athenian artist celebrated for his mechanical skill, who was said to have escaped Crete by fashioning wings of wax and feathers and flying to Sicily.

the power to give variety to our language by making us realise many things from one, the whole from a part, the *genus* from a *species*, things which follow from things which have preceded; or, on the other hand, the whole procedure may be reversed. It may, however, be more freely employed by poets than by orators. [20] For while in prose it is perfectly correct to use *mucro*, the point, for the whole sword, and *tectum*, roof, for a whole house, we may not employ *puppis*, stern, to describe a ship, nor *abies*, fir, to describe planks; and again, though *ferrum*, the steel, may be used to indicate a sword, *quadrupes* cannot be used in the sense of horse. It is where numbers are concerned that *synecdochē* can be most freely employed in prose. For example, Livy frequently says, "The Roman won the day," when he means that the *Romans* were victorious; on the other hand, Cicero in a letter to Brutus[7] says, "We have imposed on the people and are regarded as orators," when he is speaking of himself alone. [21] This form of *trope* is not only a rhetorical ornament, but is frequently employed in everyday speech. Some also apply the term *synecdochē* when something is assumed which has not actually been expressed, since one word is then discovered from other words, as in the sentence,

"The Arcadians to the gates began to rush;"[8]

when such omission creates a blemish, it is called an *ellipse*. [22] For my own part, I prefer to regard this as a figure, and shall therefore discuss it under that head. Again, one thing may be suggested by another, as in the line,

"Behold, the steers
Bring back the plough suspended from the yoke,"[9]

from which we infer the approach of night. I am not sure whether this is permissible to an orator except in arguments, when it serves as an indication of some fact. However, this has nothing to do with the question of style.

[23] It is but a short step from *synecdochē* to *metonymy*, which consists in the substitution of one name for another, and, as Cicero tells us, is called *hypallage* by the rhetoricians. These devices are employed to indicate an invention by substituting the name of the inventor, or a possession by substituting the name of the possessor. Virgil, for example, writes:

"Ceres by water spoiled,"

and Horace:

"Neptune admitted to the land
Protects the fleets from blasts of Aquilo."[1]

If, however, the process is reversed, the effect is harsh. [24] But it is important to enquire to what extent *tropes* of this kind should be employed by the orator. For though we often hear "Vulcan" used for fire and to say *vario Marte pugnatum est* for "they fought with varying success" is elegant and idiomatic, while *Venus*[2] is a more decent expression than *coitus*, it would be too bold for the severe style demanded in the courts to speak of *Liber* and *Ceres*[3]

7. Marcus Brutus (ca. 85–42 B.C.E.), Roman statesman and orator.
8. Virgil, *Aeneid* 11.142; the word "began" is omitted.
9. Virgil, *Eclogue* 2.66.
1. Virgil, *Aeneid* 1.177; HORACE (65–8 B.C.E.), *Ars Poetica* 63.
2. The Roman goddess of love. Vulcan: Roman god of fire and metalworking. Mars: Roman god of war.
3. Roman corn goddess. Liber: Roman god of fertility and especially of wine.

when we mean bread and wine. Again, while usage permits us to substitute that which contains for that which is contained, as in phrases such as "civilised cities," or "a cup was drunk to the lees," or "a happy age," [25] the converse procedure would rarely be ventured on by any save a poet: take, for example, the phrase:

"Ucalegon burns next."[4]

It is, however, perhaps more permissible to describe what is possessed by reference to its possessor, as, for example, to say of a man whose estate is being squandered, "the man is being eaten up." Of this form there are innumerable species. [26] For example, we say "sixty thousand men were slain by Hannibal at Cannae,"[5] and speak of "Virgil" when we mean "Virgil's poems"; again, we say that supplies have "come," when they have been "brought," that a "sacrilege," and not a "sacrilegious man" has been detected, and that a man possesses a knowledge of "arms," not of "the art of arms." [27] The type which indicates cause by effect is common both in poets and orators. As examples from poetry I may quote:

"Pale death with equal foot knocks at the poor man's door"

and

"There pale diseases dwell and sad old age;[6]

while the orator will speak of "headlong anger," "cheerful youth" or "slothful ease."

[28] The following type of *trope* has also some kinship with *synecdochē*. For when I speak of a man's "looks" instead of his "look," I use the plural for the singular, but my aim is not to enable one thing to be inferred from many (for the sense is clear enough), but I merely vary the form of the word. Again, when I call a "gilded roof," a "golden roof," I diverge a little from the truth, because gilding forms only a part of the roof. But to follow out these points is a task involving too much minute detail even for a work whose aim is not the training of an orator.

* * *

From *Book 9*

FROM CHAPTER 1

In my last book I spoke of *tropes*. I now come to *figures*, called σχήματα in Greek, a topic which is naturally and closely connected with the preceding. [2] For many authors have considered *figures* identical with *tropes*, because whether it be that the latter derive their name from having a certain form or from the fact that they effect alterations in language (a view which has also led to their being styled *motions*), it must be admitted that both these features are found in *figures* as well. Their employment is also the same. For they add force and charm to our matter. There are some again who call *tropes figures*, Artorius Proculus[7] among them. [3] Further the resemblance between the two is so close that it is not easy to distinguish between them. For although

4. Virgil, *Aeneid* 2.311. Ucalegon was a Trojan hero who also appears in book 3 of Homer's *Iliad*.
5. Village in Apulia, the site of a famous victory against Rome in 216 B.C.E. by Hannibal (247–182 B.C.E.), a great Carthaginian general.
6. The first passage is quoted from Horace, *Odes* 1.4.13, the second from Virgil, *Aeneid* 6.275.
7. Prominent Roman jurist (early 1st c. C.E.).

certain kinds differ, while retaining, a general resemblance (since both involve a departure from the simple and straightforward method of expression coupled with a certain rhetorical excellence), on the other hand some are distinguished by the narrowest possible dividing line: for example, while *irony* belongs to *figures of thought* just as much as to *tropes, periphrasis, hyperbaton* and *onomatopoea*[8] have been ranked by distinguished authors as *figures of speech* rather than *tropes*.

[4] It is therefore all the more necessary to point out the distinction between the two. The name of *trope* is applied to the transference of expressions from their natural and principal signification to another, with a view to the embellishment of style or, as the majority of grammarians define it, the transference of words and phrases from the place which is strictly theirs to another to which they do not properly belong. A *figure*, on the other hand, as is clear from the name itself, is the term employed when we give our language a conformation other than the obvious and ordinary. [5] Therefore the substitution of one word for another is placed among *tropes*, as for example in the case of *metaphor, metonymy, antonomasia, metalepsis, synecdochē, catachresis, allegory* and, as a rule, *hyperbole*,[9] which may, of course, be concerned either with words or things. *Onomatopoea* is the creation of a word and therefore involves substitution for the words which we should use but for such creation. [6] Again although *periphrasis* often includes the actual word whose place it supplies, it still uses a number of words in place of one. The *epithet* as a rule involves an element of *antonomasia* and consequently becomes a *trope* on account of this affinity. *Hyperbaton* is a change of order and for this reason many exclude it from *tropes*. None the less it transfers a word or part of a word from its own place to another. [7] None of these can be called *figures*. For a *figure* does not necessarily involve any alteration either of the order or the strict sense of words. As regards *irony*, I shall show elsewhere how in some of its forms it is a *trope*, in others a *figure*. For I admit that the name is common to both and am aware of the complicated and minute discussions to which it has given rise. They, however, have no bearing on my present task. For it makes no difference by which name either is called, so long as its stylistic value is apparent, since the meaning of things is not altered by a change of name. [8] For just as men remain the same, even though they adopt a new name, so these artifices will produce exactly the same effect, whether they are styled *tropes* or *figures*, since their values lie not in their names, but in their effect. * * * [9] It is best therefore in dealing with these topics to adopt the generally accepted terms and to understand the actual thing, by whatever name it is called. But we must note the fact that *trope* and *figure* are often combined in the expression of the same thought, since figures are introduced just as much by the metaphorical as by the literal use of words.

[10] There is, however, a considerable difference of opinion among authors as to the meaning of the name,[1] the number of *genera* and the nature

8. Use or invention of words that sound like their meaning (e.g., *buzz*). "Periphrasis": circumlocution. "Hyperbaton": separation of words usually belonging together or, more generally, any departure from ordinary word order.

9. Exaggerated or extravagant terms used for emphasis. "Antonomasia": descriptive phrase for proper name or a proper name for a quality associated with it (e.g., "the Bard" to refer to Shakespeare). "Metalepsis": attribution of a present effect to a remote cause. "Catachresis": an implied metaphor, using words wrenched from common usage. "Allegory": according to Quintilian, allegory "presents one thing in words and another in meaning" (8.6.44).

1. Figure.

and number of the *species* into which figures may be divided. The first point for consideration is, therefore, what is meant by a *figure*. For the term is used in two senses. In the first it is applied to any form in which thought is expressed, just as it is to bodies which, whatever their composition, must have some shape. [11] In the second and special sense, in which it is called a *schema*, it means a rational change in meaning or language from the ordinary and simple form, that is to say, a change analogous to that involved by sitting, lying down on something or looking back. Consequently when a student tends to continuous or at any rate excessive use of the same cases, tenses, rhythms or even feet, we are in the habit of instructing him to vary his *figures* with a view to the avoidance of monotony. [12] In so doing we speak as if every kind of language possessed a *figure*: for example *cursitare* and *lectitare*[2] are said to have the same figure, that is to say, they are identical in formation. Therefore in the first and common sense of the word everything is expressed by *figures*. If we are content with this view, there is good reason for the opinion expressed by Apollodorus (if we may trust the statement of Caecilius[3] on this point) to the effect that he found the rules laid down in this connexion quite incomprehensible. [13] If, on the other hand, the name is to be applied to certain attitudes, or I might say gestures of language, we must interpret *schema* in the sense of that which is poetically or rhetorically altered from the simple and obvious method of expression. It will then be true to distinguish between the style which is devoid of figures (or ἀσχημάτιστος) and that which is devoid of figures (or ἐσχηματισμένη). [14] But Zoilus[4] narrowed down the definition, since he restricted the term *schema* to cases when the speaker pretends to say something other than that which he actually does say. I know that this view meets with common acceptance: it is, in fact, for this reason that we speak of *figured* controversial themes, of which I shall shortly speak. We shall then take a *figure* to mean a form of expression to which a new aspect is given by art.

[15] Some writers have held that there is only one kind of *figure*, although they differ as regards the reasons which lead them to adopt this view. For some of them, on the ground that a change of words causes a corresponding change in the sense, assert that all *figures* are concerned with words, while others hold that *figures* are concerned solely with the sense, on the ground that words are adapted to things. Both these views are obviously quibbling. [16] For the same things are often put in different ways and the sense remains unaltered though the words are changed, while a *figure of thought* may include several *figures of speech*. For the former lies in the conception, the latter in the expression of our thought. The two are frequently combined, however, as in the following passage: "Now, Dolabella,[5] [I have no pity] either for you or for your children": for the device by which he turns from the judges to Dolabella is a *figure of thought*, while *iam iam* ("now") and *liberum* ("your children") are *figures of speech*.

[17] It is, however, to the best of my knowledge, generally agreed by the

2. Frequentative forms of the Latin verbs *curro* (run) and *lego* (read) [translator's note].
3. Teacher and writer of the Augustan era (active ca. 20 B.C.E.), the first to give public lectures on Virgil and other contemporary poets. Apollodorus (ca. 104–22 B.C.E.), influential rhetorician, best known for his oral teaching, whose theories are discussed elsewhere by Quintilian.
4. Cynic rhetor and philosopher (4th c. B.C.E.).
5. Roman commander (80–43 B.C.E.) who was declared a public enemy by the Senate and who committed suicide. He was the son-in-law of Cicero, who is being quoted; his two sons by Cicero's daughter, Tullia, probably died in infancy.

majority of authors that there are two classes of *figure*, namely *figures of thought*, that is of the mind, feeling or conceptions, since all these terms are used, and *figures of speech*, that is of words, diction, expression, language or style: the name by which they are known varies, but mere terminology is a matter of indifference. * * * We may therefore conclude that, like language itself, figures are necessarily concerned with thought and with words.

[19] As, however, in the natural course of things we conceive ideas before we express them, I must take *figures of thought* first. Their utility is at once great and manifold, and is revealed with the utmost clearness in every product of oratory. For although it may seem that proof is infinitesimally affected by the *figures* employed, none the less those same *figures* lend credibility to our arguments and steal their way secretly into the minds of the judges. [20] For just as in sword-play it is easy to see, parry, and ward off direct blows and simple and straightforward thrusts, while side-strokes and feints are less easy to observe and the task of the skilful swordsman is to give the impression that his design is quite other than it actually is, even so the oratory in which there is no guile fights by sheer weight and impetus alone; on the other hand, the fighter who feints and varies his assault is able to attack flank or back as he will, to lure his opponent's weapons from their guard and to outwit him by a slight inclination of the body. [21] Further, there is no more effective method of exciting the emotions than an apt use of figures. For if the expression of brow, eyes and hands has a powerful effect in stirring the passions, how much more effective must be the aspect of our style itself when composed to produce the result at which we aim? But, above all, *figures* serve to commend what we say to those that hear us, whether we seek to win approval for our character as pleaders, or to win favour for the cause which we plead, to relieve monotony by variation of our language, or to indicate our meaning in the safest or most seemly way.

[22] But before I proceed to demonstrate what *figures* best suit the different circumstances, I must point out that their number is far from being as great as some authorities make out. For I am not in the least disturbed by the various names which the Greeks more especially are so fond of inventing. [23] First of all, then, I must repudiate the views of those who hold that there are as many types of *figure* as there are kinds of emotion, on the ground, not that emotions are not qualities of the mind, but that a figure, in its strict, not its general sense, is not simply the expression of anything you choose to select. Consequently the expression in words of anger, grief, pity, fear, confidence or contempt is not a *figure*, any more than persuasion, threats, entreaty or excuse. [24] But superficial observers are deceived by the fact that they find *figures* in all passages dealing with such themes, and select examples of them from speeches; whereas in reality there is no department of oratory which does not admit such *figures*. But it is one thing to admit a *figure* and another to be a *figure*; I am not going to be frightened out of repeating the term with some frequency in my attempt to make the facts clear. [25] My opponents will, I know, direct my attention to special figures employed in expressing anger, in entreating for mercy, or appealing to pity, but it does not follow that expressions of anger, appeals to pity or entreaties for mercy are in themselves *figures*. Cicero, it is true, includes all ornaments of oratory under this head, and in so doing adopts, as it seems to me, a middle course. For he does not hold that all forms of expression are to be regarded

as *figures*, nor, on the other hand, would he restrict the term merely to those expressions whose form varies from ordinary use. But he regards as figurative all those expressions which are especially striking and most effective in stirring the emotions of the audience. He sets forth this view in two of his works.[6]

* * *

FROM CHAPTER 2

* * *

I have found some who speak of *irony* as *dissimulation*, but, in view of the fact that this latter name does not cover the whole range of this figure, I shall follow my general rule and rest content with the Greek term. *Irony* involving a *figure* does not differ from the *irony* which is a *trope*, as far as its *genus* is concerned, since in both cases we understand something which is the opposite of what is actually said; on the other hand, a careful consideration of the *species of irony* will soon reveal the fact that they differ. [45] In the first place, the *trope* is franker in its meaning, and, despite the fact that it implies something other than it says, makes no pretence about it. For the context as a rule is perfectly clear, as, for example, in the following passage from the Catilinarian orations. "Rejected by him, you migrated to your boon-companion, that excellent gentleman Metellus."[7] In this case the irony lies in two words, and is therefore a specially concise form of *trope*. [46] But in the *figurative* form of irony the speaker disguises his entire meaning, the disguise being apparent rather than confessed. For in the *trope* the conflict is purely verbal, while in the *figure* the meaning, and sometimes the whole aspect of our case, conflicts with the language and the tone of voice adopted; nay, a man's whole life may be coloured with *irony*, as was the case with Socrates,[8] who was called an *ironist* because he assumed the role of an ignorant man lost in wonder at the wisdom of others. Thus, as continued *metaphor* develops into *allegory*, so a sustained series of *tropes* develops into this *figure*. [47] There are, however, certain kinds of this *figure* which have no connexion with *tropes*. In the first place, there is the *figure* which derives its name from negation and is called by some ἀντίφρασις.[9] Here is an example: "I will not plead against you according to the rigour of the law, I will not press the point which I should perhaps be able to make good" or again, "Why should I mention his decrees, his acts of plunder, his acquisition, whether by cession or by force, of certain inheritances?" or "I say nothing of the first wrong inflicted by his lust" or "I do not even propose to produce the evidence given concerning the 600,000 sesterces"; or "I might say, etc."[1] [48] Such kinds of irony may even be sustained at times through whole sections of our argument, as, for instance, where Cicero says, "If I were to plead on this point as though there were some real charge to refute, I should speak at greater length." It is also *irony* when we assume the tone of command or concession, as in Virgil's

6. Cicero's *Orator* (46 B.C.E.) and *De Oratore* (55 B.C.E.).

7. Roman consul (d. ca. 59 B.C.E.) who, at the request of Cicero, was put in charge of quashing the conspiracy of the Roman patrician Cataline, which ended in Cataline's death in 62 B.C.E. Cicero published his speeches against Cataline, delivered in 63 when he was consul, in 60.

8. Greek philosopher (ca. 470–399 B.C.E.) whose teachings have survived primarily through the works of his followers, most notably the dialogues of PLATO.

9. *Antiphrasis* (Greek): irony of using words to mean the opposite of their literal sense.

1. The examples are all from Cicero. "Sesterces": Roman coins (worth several dollars each).

"Go!
Follow the winds to Italy;"[2]

[49] or when we concede to our opponents qualities which we are unwilling that they should seem to possess. This is specially effective when we possess these qualities and they do not, as in the following passage,

"Brand *me* as coward, Drances, since thy sword
Has slain such hosts of Trojans."[3]

A like result is produced by reversing this method when we pretend to own to faults which are not ours or which even recoil upon the heads of our opponents, as for example,

" 'Twas I that led the Dardan gallant on
To storm the bridal bed of Sparta's queen!"[4]

* * *

From *Book 12*

FROM CHAPTER 2

Since then the orator is a good man, and such goodness cannot be conceived as existing apart from virtue, virtue, despite the fact that it is in part derived from certain natural impulses, will require to be perfected by instruction. The orator must above all things devote his attention to the formation of moral character and must acquire a complete knowledge of all that is just and honourable. For without this knowledge no one can be either a good man or skilled in speaking, [2] unless indeed we agree with those who regard morality as intuitive and as owing nothing to instruction: indeed they go so far as to acknowledge that handicrafts, not excluding even those which are most despised among them, can only be acquired by the result of teaching, whereas virtue, which of all gifts to man is that which makes him most near akin to the immortal gods, comes to him without search or effort, as a natural concomitant of birth. But can the man who does not know what abstinence is, claim to be truly abstinent? [3] or brave, if he has never purged his soul of the fears of pain, death and superstition? or just, if he has never, in language approaching that of philosophy, discussed the nature of virtue and justice, or of the laws that have been given to mankind by nature or established among individual peoples and nations? What a contempt it argues for such themes to regard them as being so easy of comprehension! [4] However, I pass this by; for I am sure that no one with the least smattering of literary culture will have the slightest hesitation in agreeing with me. I will proceed to my next point, that no one will achieve sufficient skill even in speaking, unless he makes a thorough study of all the workings of nature and forms his character on the precepts of philosophy and the dictates of reason. [5] For it is with good cause that Lucius Crassus,[5] in the third book of the *de Oratore*, affirms that all that is said concerning equity, justice, truth and the

2. Virgil, *Aeneid* 4.381; Dido is speaking to Aeneas. She continues by praying for his destruction [translator's note]
3. Virgil, *Aeneid* 11.383. Turnus addresses Drances, who has been attacking him as the cause of the war and bidding him fight himself, if he would win Lavinia for his bride [translator's note].
4. Virgil, *Aeneid* 10.92. Juno ironically pretends to have brought about the rape of Helen [the precipitating event of Trojan War], which was in reality the work of Venus [translator's note].
5. Outstanding Roman orator (140–91 B.C.E.), main speaker of Cicero's *De Oratore*.

good, and their opposites, forms part of the studies of an orator, and that the philosophers, when they exert their powers of speaking to defend these virtues, are using the weapons of rhetoric, not their own. But he also confesses that the knowledge of these subjects must be sought from the philosophers for the reason that, in his opinion, philosophy has more effective possession of them. [6] And it is for the same reason that Cicero in several of his books and letters proclaims that eloquence has its fountain-head in the most secret springs of wisdom, and that consequently for a considerable time the instructors of morals and of eloquence were identical. Accordingly this exhortation of mine must not be taken to mean that I wish the orator to be a philosopher, since there is no other way of life that is further removed from the duties of a statesman and the tasks of an orator. [7] For what philosopher has ever been a frequent speaker in the courts or won renown in public assemblies? Nay, what philosopher has ever taken a prominent part in the government of the state, which forms the most frequent theme of their instructions? None the less I desire that he, whose character I am seeking to mould, should be a "wise man" in the Roman sense, that is, one who reveals himself as a true statesman, not in the discussions of the study, but in the actual practice and experience of life. [8] But inasmuch as the study of philosophy has been deserted by those who have turned to the pursuit of eloquence, and since philosophy no longer moves in its true sphere of action and in the broad daylight of the forum, but has retired first to porches and gymnasia and finally to the gatherings of the schools, all that is essential for an orator, and yet is not taught by the professors of eloquence, must undoubtedly be sought from those persons in whose possession it has remained. The authors who have discoursed on the nature of virtue must be read through and through, that the life of the orator may be wedded to the knowledge of things human and divine. [9] But how much greater and fairer would such subjects appear if those who taught them were also those who could give them most eloquent expression! O that the day may dawn when the perfect orator of our heart's desire shall claim for his own possession that science that has lost the affection of mankind through the arrogance of its claims and the vices of some that have brought disgrace upon its virtues, and shall restore it to its place in the domain of eloquence, as though he had been victorious in a trial for the restoration of stolen goods! [10] And since philosophy falls into three divisions, physics, ethics and dialectic,[6] which, I ask you, of these departments is not closely connected with the task of the orator?

Let us reverse the order just given and deal first with the third department which is entirely concerned with words. If it be true that to know the properties of each word, to clear away ambiguities, to unravel perplexities, to distinguish between truth and falsehood, to prove or to refute as may be desired, all form part of the functions of an orator, who is there that can doubt the truth of my contention? [11] I grant that we shall not have to employ dialectic with such minute attention to detail when we are pleading in the courts as when we are engaged in philosophical debate, since the orator's duty is not merely to instruct, but also to move and delight his audience; and to succeed in doing this he needs a strength, impetuosity and grace

6. Logic.

as well. For oratory is like a river: the current is stronger when it flows within deep banks and with a mighty flood, than when the waters are shallow and broken by the pebbles that bar their way. [12] And just as the trainers of the wrestling school do not impart the various *throws* to their pupils that those who have learnt them may make use of all of them in actual wrestling matches (for weight and strength and wind count for more than these), but that they may have a store from which to draw one or two of such tricks, as occasion may offer; [13] even so the science of dialectic, or if you prefer it of disputation, while it is often useful in definition, inference, differentiation, resolution of ambiguity, distinction and classification, as also in luring on or entangling our opponents, yet if it claim to assume the entire direction of the struggles of the forum, will merely stand in the way of arts superior to itself and by its very subtlety will exhaust the strength that has been pared down to suit its limitations. [14] As a result you will find that certain persons who show astonishing skill in philosophical debate, as soon as they quit the sphere of their quibbles, are as helpless in any case that demands more serious pleading as those small animals which, though nimble enough in a confined space, are easily captured in an open field.

[15] Proceeding to moral philosophy or ethics, we may note that it at any rate is entirely suited to the orator. For vast as is the variety of cases (since in them, as I have pointed out in previous books, we seek to discover certain points by conjecture, reach our conclusions in others by means of definition, dispose of others on legal grounds or by raising the question of competence, while other points are established by syllogism[7] and others involve contradictions or are diversely interpreted owing to some ambiguity of language), there is scarcely a single one which does not at some point or another involve the discussion of equity and virtue, while there are also, as everyone knows, not a few which turn entirely on questions of quality. [16] Again in deliberative assemblies how can we advise a policy without raising the question of what is honourable? Nay, even the third department of oratory, which is concerned with the tasks of praise and denunciation, must without a doubt deal with questions of right and wrong. [17] For the orator will assuredly have much to say on such topics as justice, fortitude, abstinence, self-control and piety. But the good man, who has come to the knowledge of these things not by mere hearsay, as though they were just words and names for his tongue to employ, but has grasped the meaning of virtue and acquired a true feeling for it, will never be perplexed when he has to think out a problem, but will speak out truly what he knows. [18] Since, however, *general* questions are always more important than special (for the particular is contained in the universal, while the universal is never to be regarded as something superimposed on the particular), everyone will readily admit that the studies of which we are speaking are pre-eminently concerned with general questions. [19] Further, since there are numerous points which require to be determined by appropriate and concise definitions (hence the *definitive basis* of cases), it is surely desirable that the orator should be instructed in such things by those who have devoted special attention to the subject. Again, does not every question of law turn either

7. A deductive argument in logic consisting of a major premise, a minor premise, and a conclusion; its validity depends entirely on its form.

on the precise meaning of words, the discussion of equity, or conjecture as to the intention—subjects which in part encroach on the domain of dialectic and in part on that of ethics? [20] Consequently all oratory involves a natural admixture of all these philosophic elements—at least, that is to say, all oratory that is worthy of the name. For mere garrulity that is ignorant of all such learning must needs go astray, since its guides are either non-existent or false.

Physics[8] on the other hand is far richer than the other branches of philosophy, if viewed from the standpoint of providing exercise in speaking, in proportion as a loftier inspiration is required to speak of things divine than of things human; and further it includes within its scope the whole of ethics, which as we have shown are essential to the very existence of oratory. [21] For, if the world is governed by providence, it will certainly be the duty of all good men to bear their part in the administration of the state. If the origin of our souls be divine, we must win our way towards virtue and abjure the service of the lusts of our earthly body. Are not these themes which the orator will frequently be called upon to handle? Again there are questions concerned with auguries and oracles or any other religious topic (all of them subjects that have often given rise to the most important debates in the senate) on which the orator will have to discourse, if he is also to be the statesman we would have him be. And finally, how can we conceive of any real eloquence at all proceeding from a man who is ignorant of all that is best in the world? [22] If our reason did not make these facts obvious, we should still be led by historical examples to believe their truth. For Pericles,[9] whose eloquence, despite the fact that it has left no visible record for posterity, was none the less, if we may believe the historians and that free-speaking tribe, the old comic poets, endowed with almost incredible force, is known to have been a pupil of the physicist Anaxagoras, while Demosthenes, greatest of all the orators of Greece, sat at the feet of Plato.[1] [23] As for Cicero, he has often proclaimed the fact that he owed less to the schools of rhetoric than to the walks of Academe: nor would he ever have developed such amazing fertility of talent, had he bounded his genius by the limits of the forum and not by the frontiers of nature herself.

But this leads me to another question as to which school of philosophy is like to prove of most service to oratory, although there are only a few that can be said to contend for this honour. [24] For in the first place Epicurus[2] banishes us from his presence without more ado, since he bids all his followers to fly from learning in the swiftest ship that they can find. Nor would Aristippus,[3] who regards the highest good as consisting in physical pleasure, be likely to exhort us to the toils entailed by our study. And what part can Pyrrho[4] have in the work that is before us? For he will have doubts as to whether there exist judges to address, accused to defend, or a senate where he can be called upon to speak his opinion. [25] Some authorities hold that the Academy[5] will be the most useful school, on the ground

8. I.e., natural philosophy in the widest sense [translator's note]. This includes religion.
9. Athenian statesman (ca. 495–429 B.C.E.).
1. Greek philosopher (427–347 B.C.E.). Anaxagoras (ca. 500–ca. 428 B.C.E.), Greek philosopher. Demosthenes (384–322 B.C.E.), Athenian orator and statesman.
2. Greek philosopher (341–270 B.C.E.).
3. Greek philosopher (ca. 435–ca. 356 B.C.E.).
4. Greek philosopher (365–275 B.C.E.).
5. Athenian school founded by Plato.

that its habit of disputing on both sides of a question approaches most nearly to the actual practice of the courts. And by way of proof they add the fact that this school has produced speakers highly renowned for their eloquence. The Peripatetics[6] also make it their boast that they have a form of study which is near akin to oratory. For it was with them in the main that originated the practice of declaiming on general questions by way of exercise. The Stoics,[7] though driven to admit that, generally speaking, their teachers have been deficient both in fullness and charm of eloquence, still contend that no men can prove more acutely or draw conclusions with greater subtlety than themselves. [26] But all these arguments take place within their own circle, for, as though they were tied by some solemn oath or held fast in the bonds of some superstitious belief, they consider that it is a crime to abandon a conviction once formed. On the other hand, there is no need for an orator to swear allegiance to any one philosophic code. [27] For he has a greater and nobler aim, to which he directs all his efforts with as much zeal as if he were a candidate for office, since he is to be made perfect not only in the glory of a virtuous life, but in that of eloquence as well. He will consequently select as his models of eloquence all the greatest masters of oratory, and will choose the noblest precepts and the most direct road to virtue as the means for the formation of an upright character. He will neglect no form of exercise, but will devote special attention to those which are of the highest and fairest nature. [28] For what subject can be found more fully adapted to a rich and weighty eloquence than the topics of virtue, politics, providence, the origin of the soul and friendship? The themes which tend to elevate mind and language alike are questions such as what things are truly good, what means there are of assuaging fear, restraining the passions and lifting us and the soul that came from heaven clear of the delusions of the common herd.

* * *

ca. 96 C.E.

6. Followers of ARISTOTLE (384–322 B.C.E.).
7. Members of an Athenian philosophical school founded by Zeno of Cyprus (335–263 B.C.E.).

PLOTINUS
ca. 204/5–270

Plotinus's "On the Intellectual Beauty," the eighth treatise of his Fifth Ennead (one of a group of fifty-four treatises), provides an influential theory of representation, Platonic in its origins, that challenges PLATO's notorious distrust of storytelling. Plotinus is the third-century founder and greatest philosopher of Neoplatonism—a philosophical system that locates reality in a transcendental spiritual realm that gives meaning to the visible world. Plotinus denies that art is merely the pale imitation of a more perfect nature. He argues instead that artists struggle to invest an inchoate matter with form and beauty, thus enabling both viewers and artists to transcend the sensible world and discover the more "real" intelligible world of Forms, with the ultimate goal of unification with the One (the transcendent source of all being). Plotinus's revisions of Plato, especially his description of an intellectual ascent from the corporeal world to the intelligible world of Forms, were transmitted through the Christian works of AUGUSTINE (354–430), MACROBIUS (b. ca. 360), and Boethius (480–524), later shaping the Christian Neoplatonism of the Middle Ages (see, for example, Bernardus Silvestrus, d. ca. 1160). Plotinus's influence, however, extends beyond the Middle Ages to a varied array of movements and figures, including Romantic theories of artistic creativity (see, for instance, FRIEDRICH VON SCHILLER, SAMUEL TAYLOR COLERIDGE, PERCY BYSSHE SHELLEY, and RALPH WALDO EMERSON), the more enigmatic twentieth-century psychoanalytic writings of HAROLD BLOOM, and many versions of contemporary New Age philosophy and religion.

Details of Plotinus's life can be reliably gleaned from a biography written by his disciple and editor, the Greek philosopher Porphyry. Although he complains that Plotinus "could never be induced to tell of his ancestry, his parentage or his birthplace," others record that he was born in either Lyco or Lycopolis in Egypt. His name is Roman, though his native language was Greek. At twenty-eight he was "caught by the passion for philosophy." He spent the next eleven years studying in Alexandria, Egypt, a famous center of learning, under Ammonius Saccas, a philosopher born of Christian parents who reverted to Greek paganism and who was supposed to have reconciled the doctrines of ARISTOTLE and Plato. During his Alexandrian sojourn, Plotinus also encountered the works of the Jewish philosopher Philo of Alexandria (ca. 20 B.C.E.–50 C.E.), as well as those of the Gnostics and Neopythagoreans. In 242/3 Plotinus joined the Emperor Gordian's expedition against Persia, as a means of learning about Eastern philosophy. When the campaign failed, he settled in Rome as a teacher. There he was the center of a circle of intellectuals that included men of letters and professional philosophers. Plotinus was also interested in social problems and tried to persuade the Emperor Gallienus to invest in a scheme to found a city (called Platonopolis) in Campania, Italy, to be governed by the principles set forth in Plato's *Republic*. He remained in Rome until his last illness, when he retired to Campania.

Plotinus, according to Porphyry, "remained a long time without writing." At about the age of fifty, he began to produce a series of philosophical essays in Greek that grew out of his seminars and were intended primarily for circulation among his pupils. Porphyry records that when he first came to know Plotinus there were twenty-one of these treatises. By the time of the philosopher's death there were fifty-four. After Plotinus's death, Porphyry was left with the task of editing the manuscripts, which he describes as "slovenly." Between 300 and 305, he arranged them into six sets or "enneads" (from the Greek *ennea*, "nine") of nine treatises, "an arrangement which pleased me by the happy combination of the perfect number six with the nines"—a reference to Pythagorean numerology, in which twice three is perfect harmony or unity and three threes produce the perfect plural. Porphyry's organization loosely binds together a series of seemingly discrete and unrelated treatises. If there is any other method of organization to the treatises of the *Enneads*, it is created through the recapitulation in each one of the basic elements of the Plotinian system. Such an arrangement, with its emphasis on unity and harmony within plurality, mirrors the philosophical idealism of Plotinus's thought. A strict dualist, Plotinus posits a fundamental split between the intelligible world—that is, the world of ideas and Ideal Forms—and the sensible world of matter. For Plotinus the intelligible world is unchanging and nonspatial; for this reason it is, more real than the sensible world of matter. The sensible world is the changeable image of the intelligible world, its extension in time and space.

The opening paragraphs of "On the Intellectual Beauty" illustrate Plotinus's tendency to reproduce his entire system within each treatise. In them he describes the ascent from the beauty of the corporeal world to the beautiful itself, expressed in terms of the Plotinian hierarchy. "On the Intellectual Beauty" challenges Plato's controversial view of art as an imitation twice removed from the real (the intelligible), and therefore a copy of a copy. Nature, Plotinus argues, is an emanation, and not a copy, of a higher reality, an ideal reality the artist may apprehend because the arts "run back up to the forming principles from which nature derives."

"The forming principles from which nature derives"—the intelligible world—can be mapped through a hierarchy of three principal causes, or *archai* (for a critique of the philosophical notion of *archē* as origin, beginning, or first principle, see JACQUES DERRIDA). In this scheme, agency is transmitted from (1) the Absolute Being, called the One or the Good, to creation through (2) the *nous* (Greek), or Intellect, from which emanates (3) the Soul of the world, that is, the soul of individual humans, animals, and finally matter. The One transcends essence and existence; it has neither number nor name. It is the source of everything and the goal toward which everything strives. (In later Christian Neoplatonism the One is God.) In the translation below, Plotinus refers to the One as the "Father which is beyond Intellect." Intellect (the *nous*) proceeds from the One; it is thought thinking itself, flanked by absolute knowledge and wisdom. The Intellect's thoughts are the Platonic Forms, the eternal and unchanging paradigms of which sensible things are imperfect images. These Forms, for Plotinus, are not ideas; they are substances and more real than the sensible things through which we come to understand them. Finally, the Soul, or *psuchē* (Greek), proceeds from the Intellect and mediates between the intelligible and the sensible world. Soul is the lowest intelligible cause; it forms and orders the sensible world. Humans stand midway between the two worlds; the body belongs to the sensible world, while the soul has its roots in the intelligible world.

The goal of philosophy for Plotinus is the soul's transcendence of the sensible, its ascent toward an intuition of the Intellect, and ultimately a complete and ecstatic union with the One. Since the more beautiful a thing is the closer it is to the One, art's beauty can provide a privileged glimpse of the One, but not as an exact copy or duplication of it. The ascent from the beauty of the corporeal world to the beautiful itself is expressed in terms of Plotinus's doctrine of intellectual ascent. The beauty of the work of art resides not in its materials or anything of the sensible world, but in the form art imparts to the work. This visible form is itself merely a pale reflection of the beauty that resides in art itself, "which is greater and more beautiful than anything in the external object." Far from being a dangerous misrepresentation of reality, as Plato states in the *Republic*, art—the contemplation of the beautiful and ultimately of beauty itself—can be the means by which individuals ascend toward ecstatic unification with the One. Plotinus claimed to have experienced this divine ecstasy on several occasions; he may be alluding to such an experience in sections 3 and 4 of our selection.

"On the Intellectual Beauty" is not Plotinus's only attempt to describe the place of art in his philosophic system. The sixth treatise of the First Ennead, "On Beauty," which builds on Diotima's speech in Plato's *Symposium*, covers much the same ground and was influential among artists, especially during the Renaissance. Of special significance for literary criticism is Plotinus's insistence that the Forms that beauty contemplates are not discursive forms of knowledge—theorems and propositions—but "beautiful images . . . not painted but real." Images in the intelligible world are not re-presentations of absent (or lost) referents but are fully present, like archetypes; only our embodiedness in the sensible world prevents us from apprehending them.

Ultimately, however, Plotinus's importance to literary criticism may lie less in what he says specifically about the arts than in the influence his philosophic idealism has exerted on subsequent thinking in the West. On the one hand, because Plotinus's Neoplatonism locates reality in a transcendent world of spirit rather than in an imperfect material world, his work appealed to the leaders of an emergent Christianity anxious to reconcile biblical narrative with mystical Christian doctrine. On the other, his emphasis in this treatise on intuitive knowledge at the expense of the rational and the discursive especially appealed to later Romantic poets and critics reacting against Enlightenment rationalism. Yet the plenitude promised by "On the Intellectual Beauty"—its belief in a prelinguistic realm of ideas that can stand outside of and provide an origin for the sensible world—has been the target of contemporary post-structuralist critiques of Western philosophy, which explore the deconstructive roles of absence and lack in constituting philosophical ideas and mystical religions.

BIBLIOGRAPHY

The standard Greek text of the *Enneads* can be found in *Plotini Opera* (3 vols., 1964–82), edited by Paul Henry and Hans-Rudolf Schwyzer. Stephen MacKenna's translation, *Plotinus: The Six Enneads* (1921–30), contains an English version not only of the entire *Enneads* but of Porphyry's *Life of Plotinus* as well. A. H. Armstrong's *Plotinus* (1953) remains a classic introduction to Plotinian philosophy. J. M. Rist, in *Plotinus: The Road to Reality* (1967), discusses specialized topics in Plotinus, including beauty. D. J. O'Meara's *Plotinus: An Introduction to the Enneads* (1993) is a more recent and highly recommended introduction to Plotinus. Lloyd P. Gerson's *Plotinus* (1994) offers an extensive and more advanced philosophical discussion of most aspects of his thought. Gerson's *Cambridge Companion to Plotinus* (1996) is an indispensible guide to research on the philosopher.

For bibliographies, see A. J. Blumenthal, "Plotinus in the Light of Twenty Years' Scholarship, 1951–1971," and K. Corrigan and P. O'Cleirigh, "The Course of Plotinian Scholarship from 1971–1986," both contained in *Aufstieg und Niedergang der romischen Welt* (ed. Wolfgang Haase, 1987). Gerson's bibliography in *The Cambridge Companion to Plotinus* is also helpful.

From the Fifth Ennead

Eighth Tractate
On the Intellectual Beauty[1]

1. It is a principle with us that one who has attained to the vision of the Intellectual[2] Beauty and grasped the beauty of the Authentic Intellect will be able also to come to understand the Father and Transcendent of that Divine Being. It concerns us, then, to try to see and say, for ourselves and as far as such matters may be told, how the Beauty of the divine Intellect and of the Intellectual Cosmos may be revealed to contemplation.

Let us go to the realm of magnitudes:—suppose two blocks of stone lying side by side: one is unpatterned, quite untouched by art; the other has been minutely wrought by the craftsman's hands into some statue of god or man, a Grace or a Muse,[3] or if a human being, not a portrait but a creation in which the sculptor's art has concentrated all loveliness.

Now it must be seen that the stone thus brought under the artist's hand to the beauty of form is beautiful not as stone—for so the crude block would be as pleasant—but in virtue of the Form or Idea introduced by the art. This form is not in the material; it is in the designer before ever it enters the stone;

1. Translated by Stephen MacKenna.
2. Plotinus uses the term "Intellectual" or "Intelligible" to refer to a transcendent realm that can be apprehended only by the understanding, not by the senses. The opening paragraphs illustrate the ascent from the beauty of the corporeal world to Beauty itself in terms of a mystical hierarchy.
3. One of the 9 Greek sister goddesses presiding over the arts and sciences. Grace: one of the 3 Greek sister goddesses of charm and beauty.

and the artificer holds it not by his equipment of eyes and hands but by his participation[4] in his art. The beauty, therefore, exists in a far higher state in the art; for it does not come over integrally into the work; that original beauty is not transferred; what comes over is a derivative and a minor: and even that shows itself upon the statue not integrally and with entire realization of intention but only in so far as it has subdued the resistance of the material.

Art, then, creating in the image of its own nature and content, and working by the Idea or Reason-Principle of the beautiful object it is to produce, must itself be beautiful in a far higher and purer degree since it is the seat and source of that beauty, indwelling in the art, which must naturally be more complete than any comeliness of the external. In the degree in which the beauty is diffused by entering into matter, it is so much the weaker than that concentrated in unity; everything that reaches outwards is the less for it, strength less strong, heat less hot, every power less potent, and so beauty less beautiful.

Then again every prime cause must be, within itself, more powerful than its effect can be: the musical does not derive from an unmusical source but from music; and so the art exhibited in the material work derives from an art yet higher.

Still the arts are not to be slighted on the ground that they create by imitation of natural objects; for, to begin with, these natural objects are themselves imitations; then, we must recognize that they give no bare reproduction of the thing seen but go back to the Reason-Principles from which Nature itself derives, and, furthermore, that much of their work is all their own; they are holders of beauty and add where nature is lacking. Thus Pheidias wrought the Zeus[5] upon no model among things of sense but by apprehending what form Zeus must take if he chose to become manifest to sight.

2. But let us leave the arts and consider those works produced by Nature and admitted to be naturally beautiful which the creations of art are charged with imitating, all reasoning life and unreasoning things alike, but especially the consummate among them, where the moulder and maker has subdued the material and given the form he desired. Now what is the beauty here? It has nothing to do with the blood or the menstrual process: either there is also a colour and form apart from all this or there is nothing unless sheer ugliness or (at best) a bare recipient, as it were the mere Matter of beauty.

Whence shone forth the beauty of Helen,[6] battle-sought; or of all those women like in loveliness to Aphrodite;[7] or of Aphrodite herself; or of any human being that has been perfect in beauty; or of any of these gods manifest to sight, or unseen but carrying what would be beauty if we saw?

In all these is it not the Idea, something of that realm but communicated to the produced from within the producer, just as in works of art, we held, it is communicated from the arts to their creations? Now we can surely not

4. A crucial term in the Greek philosopher PLATO (ca. 427–327 B.C.E.), who often describes sensible objects as "participating" in the Form of which they are the imperfect copy.

5. King of all Greek gods. The renowned statue of Zeus called *Olympian Zeus*, known only from descriptions made by ancient writers, was the most famous work of the Greek sculptor Pheidias (5th c. B.C.E.).

6. In Greek mythology, the most beautiful woman in the world. She was married to a Greek king, Menelaus, and her abduction by the Trojan prince Paris precipitated the Trojan War.

7. Greek goddess of love, beauty, and fertility.

believe that, while the made thing and the Idea thus impressed upon Matter are beautiful, yet the Idea not so alloyed but resting still with the creator—the Idea primal, immaterial, firmly a unity—is not Beauty.

If material extension were in itself the ground of beauty, then the creating principle, being without extension, could not be beautiful: but beauty cannot be made to depend upon magnitude since, whether in a large object or a small, the one Idea equally moves and forms the mind by its inherent power. A further indication is that as long as the object remains outside us we know nothing of it; it affects us by entry; but only as an Idea can it enter through the eyes which are not of scope to take an extended mass: we are, no doubt, simultaneously possessed of the magnitude which, however, we take in not as mass but by an elaboration upon the presented form.

Then again the principle producing the beauty must be, itself, ugly, neutral, or beautiful: ugly, it could not produce the opposite; neutral, why should its product be the one rather than the other? The Nature, then, which creates things so lovely must be itself of a far earlier beauty;[8] we, undisciplined in discernment of the inward, knowing nothing of it, run after the outer, never understanding that it is the inner which stirs us; we are in the case of one who sees his own reflection but not realizing whence it comes goes in pursuit of it.

But that the thing we are pursuing is something different and that the beauty is not in the concrete object is manifest from the beauty there is in matters of study, in conduct and custom; briefly, in soul or mind. And it is precisely here that the greater beauty lies, perceived whenever you look to the wisdom in a man and delight in it, not wasting attention on the face, which may be hideous, but passing all appearance by and catching only at the inner comeliness, the truly personal; if you are still unmoved and cannot acknowledge beauty under such conditions, then looking to your own inner being you will find no beauty to delight you and it will be futile in that state to seek the greater vision, for you will be questing it through the ugly and impure.

This is why such matters are not spoken of to everyone; you, if you are conscious of beauty within, remember.

3. Thus there is in the Nature-Principle itself an Ideal archetype of the beauty that is found in material forms and, of that archetype again, the still more beautiful archetype in Soul, source of that in Nature. In the proficient soul this is brighter and of more advanced loveliness: adorning the soul and bringing to it a light from that greater light which is Beauty primally, its immediate presence sets the soul reflecting upon the quality of this prior, the archetype which has no such entries, and is present nowhere but remains in itself alone, and thus is not even to be called a Reason-Principle but is the creative source of the very first Reason-Principle which is the Beauty to which Soul serves as Matter.

This prior, then, is the Intellectual-Principle, the veritable, abiding and not fluctuant since not taking intellectual quality from outside itself. By what image, thus, can we represent it? We have nowhere to go but to what is less. Only from itself can we take an image of it; that is, there can be no repre-

8. Plotinus refers here not to temporal but to spiritual priority; such beauty is closer to the One.

sentation of it, except in the sense that we represent gold by some portion of gold—purified, either actually or mentally, if it be impure—insisting at the same time that this is not the total thing gold, but merely the particular gold of a particular parcel. In the same way we learn in this matter from the purified Intellect in ourselves or, if you like, from the gods and the glory of the Intellect in them.

For assuredly all the gods are august and beautiful in a beauty beyond our speech. And what makes them so? Intellect; and especially Intellect operating within them (the divine sun and stars) to visibility. It is not through the loveliness of their corporeal forms: even those that have body are not gods by that beauty; it is in virtue of Intellect that they, too, are gods, and as gods beautiful. They do not veer between wisdom and folly: in the immunity of Intellect unmoving and pure, they are wise always, all-knowing, taking cognizance not of the human but of their own being and of all that lies within the contemplation of Intellect. Those of them whose dwelling is in the heavens are ever in this meditation—what task prevents them?—and from afar they look, too, into that further heaven by a lifting of the head. The gods belonging to that higher Heaven itself, they whose station is upon it and in it, see and know in virtue of their omnipresence to it. For all There is heaven; earth is heaven, and sea heaven; and animal and plant and man; all is the heavenly content of that heaven: and the gods in it, despising neither men nor anything else that is there where all is of the heavenly order, traverse all that country and all space in peace.

4. To 'live at ease'[9] is There; and to these divine beings verity is mother and nurse, existence and sustenance; all that is not of process but of authentic being they see, and themselves in all: for all is transparent, nothing dark, nothing resistant; every being is lucid to every other, in breadth and depth; light runs through light. And each of them contains all within itself, and at the same time sees all in every other, so that everywhere there is all, and all is all and each all, and infinite the glory. Each of them is great; the small is great; the sun, There, is all the stars; and every star, again, is all the stars and sun. While some one manner of being is dominant in each, all are mirrored in every other.

Movement There is pure (as self-caused), for the moving principle is not a separate thing to complicate it as it speeds.

So, too, Repose is not troubled, for there is no admixture of the unstable; and the Beauty is all beauty since it is not resident in what is not beautiful. Each There walks upon no alien soil; its place is its essential self; and, as each moves, so to speak, towards what is Above, it is attended by the very ground from which it starts: there is no distinguishing between the Being and the Place; all is Intellect, the Principle and the ground on which it stands, alike. Thus we might think that our visible sky (the ground or place of the stars), lit as it is, produces the light which reaches us from it, though of course this is really produced by the stars (as it were, by the Principles of light alone, not also by the ground as the analogy would require).

In our realm all is part rising from part and nothing can be more than partial; but There each being is an eternal product of a whole and is at once

9. A Homeric expression to describe the life of the gods; for example, see *Iliad* 6.138.

a whole and an individual manifesting as part but, to the keen vision There, known for the whole it is.

The myth of Lynceus[1] seeing into the very deeps of the earth tells us of those eyes in the divine. No weariness overtakes this vision which yet brings no such satiety as would call for its ending; for there never was a void to be filled so that, with the fullness and the attainment of purpose, the sense of sufficiency be induced: nor is there any such incongruity within the divine that one Being There could be repulsive to another: and of course all There are unchangeable. This absence of satisfaction means only a satisfaction leading to no distaste for that which produces it; to see is to look the more, since for them to continue in the contemplation of an infinite self and of infinite objects is but to acquiesce in the bidding of their nature.

Life, pure, is never a burden; how then could there be weariness There where the living is most noble? That very life is wisdom, not a wisdom built up by reasonings but complete from the beginning, suffering no lack which could set it inquiring, a wisdom primal, unborrowed, not something added to the Being, but its very essence. No wisdom, thus, is greater; this is the authentic knowing, assessor to the divine Intellect as projected into manifestation simultaneously with it; thus, in the symbolic saying, Justice is assessor to Zeus.

(Perfect wisdom:) for all the Principles of this order, dwelling There, are as it were visible images projected from themselves, so that all becomes an object of contemplation to contemplators immeasurably blessed. The greatness and power of the wisdom There we may know from this, that it embraces all the real Beings, and has made all and all follow it, and yet that it is itself those beings, which sprang into being with it, so that all is one and the essence There is wisdom. If we have failed to understand, it is that we have thought of knowledge as a mass of theorems and an accumulation of propositions, though that is false even for our sciences of the sense-realm. But in case this should be questioned, we may leave our own sciences for the present, and deal with the knowing in the Supreme at which Plato glances where he speaks of 'that knowledge which is not a stranger in something strange to it'[2]—though in what sense, he leaves us to examine and declare, if we boast ourselves worthy of the discussion. This is probably our best starting-point.

5. All that comes to be, work of nature or of craft, some wisdom has made: everywhere a wisdom presides at a making.

No doubt the wisdom of the artist may be the guide of the work; it is sufficient explanation of the wisdom exhibited in the arts; but the artist himself goes back, after all, to that wisdom in Nature which is embodied in himself; and this is not a wisdom built up of theorems but one totality, not a wisdom consisting of manifold detail co-ordinated into a unity but rather a unity working out into detail.

Now, if we could think of this as the primal wisdom, we need look no further, since, at that, we have discovered a principle which is neither a derivative nor a 'stranger in something strange to it'. But if we are told that,

1. One of the Argonauts, who was said to be so sharp-sighted that he could see things underground.
2. Plato, *Phaedrus* 247d–e.

while this Reason-Principle is in Nature, yet Nature itself is its source, we ask how Nature came to possess it; and, if Nature derived it from some other source, we ask what that other source may be; if, on the contrary, the principle is self-sprung, we need look no further: but if (as we assume) we are referred to the Intellectual-Principle we must make clear whether the Intellectual-Principle engendered the wisdom: if we learn that it did, we ask whence: if from itself, then inevitably it is itself Wisdom.

The true Wisdom, then (found to be identical with the Intellectual-Principle), is Real Being; and Real Being is Wisdom; it is wisdom that gives value to Real Being; and Being is Real in virtue of its origin in wisdom. It follows that all forms of existence not possessing wisdom are, indeed, Beings in right of the wisdom which went to their forming, but, as not in themselves possessing it, are not Real Beings.

We cannot, therefore, think that the divine Beings of that sphere, or the other supremely blessed There, need look to our apparatus of science: all of that realm (the very Beings themselves), all is noble image, such images as we may conceive to lie within the soul of the wise—but There not as inscription but as authentic existence. The ancients had this in mind when they declared the Ideas (Forms) to be Beings, Essentials.

6. Similarly, as it seems to me, the wise of Egypt—whether in precise knowledge or by a prompting of nature—indicated the truth where, in their effort towards philosophical statement, they left aside the writing-forms that take in the detail of words and sentences—those characters that represent sounds and convey the propositions of reasoning—and drew pictures instead, engraving in the temple-inscriptions a separate image for every separate item: thus they exhibited the absence of discursiveness in the Intellectual Realm.

For each manifestation of knowledge and wisdom is a distinct image, an object in itself, an immediate unity, not an aggregate of discursive reasoning and detailed willing. Later from this wisdom in unity there appears, in another form of being, an image, already less compact, which announces the original in terms of discourse and seeks the causes by which things are such that the wonder rises how a generated world can be so excellent.

For, one who knows must declare his wonder that this Wisdom, while not itself containing the causes by which Being exists and takes such excellence, yet imparts them to the entities produced in Being's realm. This excellence, whose necessity is scarcely or not at all manifest to search, exists, if we could but find it out, before all searching and reasoning.

What I say may be considered in one chief thing, and thence applied to all the particular entities:

7. Consider the universe: we are agreed that its existence and its nature come to it from beyond itself; are we, now, to imagine that its maker first thought it out in detail—the earth, and its necessary situation in the middle; water and, again, its position as lying upon the earth; all the other elements and objects up to the sky in due place and order; living beings with their appropriate forms as we know them, their inner organs and their outer limbs—and that having thus appointed every item beforehand, he then set about the execution?

Such designing was not even possible; how could the plan for a universe come to one that had never looked outward? Nor could he work on material gathered from elsewhere as our craftsmen do, using hands and tools; feet and hands are of the later order.

One way, only, remains: all things must exist in something else; of that prior—since there is no obstacle, all being continuous within the realm of reality—there has suddenly appeared a sign, an image, whether given forth directly or through the ministry of soul or of some phase of soul, matters nothing for the moment: thus the entire aggregate of existence springs from the divine world, in greater beauty There because There unmingled but mingled here.

From the beginning to end all is gripped by the Forms of the Intellectual Realm: Matter itself is held by the Ideas of the elements and to these Ideas are added other Ideas and others again, so that it is hard to work down to crude Matter beneath all that sheathing of Idea. Indeed since Matter itself is, in its degree, an Idea—the lowest—all this universe is Idea and there is nothing that is not Idea as the archetype was. And all is made silently, since nothing had part in the making but Being and Idea—a further reason why creation went without toil. The Exemplar was the Idea of an All and so an All must come into being.

Thus nothing stood in the way of the Idea, and even now it dominates, despite all the clash of things: the creation is not hindered on its way even now; it stands firm in virtue of being All. To me, moreover, it seems that if we ourselves were archetypes, Ideas, veritable Being, and the Idea with which we construct here were our veritable Essence, then our creative power, too, would toillessly effect its purpose: as man now stands, he does not produce in his work a true image of himself: become man, he has ceased to be the All; ceasing to be man—we read—'he soars aloft and administers the Cosmos entire';[3] restored to the All he is maker of the All.

But—to our immediate purpose—it is possible to give a reason why the earth is set in the midst and why it is round and why the ecliptic runs precisely as it does, but, looking to the creating principle, we cannot say that because this was the way therefore things were so planned: we can say only that because the Exemplar is what it is, therefore the things of this world are good; the causing principle, we might put it, reached the conclusion before all formal reasoning and not from any premises, not by sequence or plan but before either, since all of that order is later, all reason, demonstration, persuasion.

Since there is a Source, all the created must spring from it and in accordance with it; and we are rightly told not to go seeking the causes impelling a Source to produce, especially when this is the perfectly sufficient Source and identical with the Term: a Source which is Source and Term must be the All-Unity, complete in itself.

8. This then is Beauty primally: it is entire and omnipresent as an entirety; and therefore in none of its parts or members lacking in beauty; beautiful thus beyond denial. Certainly it cannot be anything (be, for example, Beauty) without being wholly that thing; it can be nothing which it is to possess partially or in which it utterly fails (and therefore it must entirely be Beauty entire).

3. Plato, *Phaedrus* 246c.

If this principle were not beautiful, what other could be? Its prior does not deign to be beautiful; that which is the first to manifest itself—Form and object of vision to the intellect—cannot but be lovely to see. It is to indicate this that Plato, drawing on something well within our observation, represents the Creator as approving the work he has achieved: the intention is to make us feel the lovable beauty of the archetype and of the Divine Idea; for to admire a representation is to admire the original upon which it was made.

It is not surprising if we fail to recognize what is passing within us: lovers, and those in general that admire beauty here, do not stay to reflect that it is to be traced, as of course it must be, to the Beauty There. That the admiration of the Demiurge[4] is to be referred to the Ideal Exemplar is deliberately made evident by the rest of the passage: 'He admired; and determined to bring the work into still closer likeness with the Exemplar';[5] he makes us feel the magnificent beauty of the Exemplar by telling us that the Beauty sprung from this world is, itself, a copy from That.

And indeed if the divine did not exist, the transcendently beautiful, in a beauty beyond all thought, what could be lovelier than the things we see? Certainly no reproach can rightly be brought against this world save only that it is not That.

9. Let us, then, make a mental picture of our universe: each member shall remain what it is, distinctly apart; yet all is to form, as far as possible, a complete unity so that whatever comes into view, say the outer orb of the heavens, shall bring immediately with it the vision, on the one plane, of the sun and of all the stars with earth and sea all living things as if exhibited upon a transparent globe.

Bring this vision actually before your sight, so that there shall be in your mind the gleaming representation of a sphere, a picture holding all the things of the universe moving or in repose or (as in reality) some at rest, some in motion. Keep this sphere before you, and from it imagine another, a sphere stripped of magnitude and of spatial differences; cast out your inborn sense of Matter, taking care not merely to attenuate it: call on God, maker of the sphere whose image you now hold, and pray Him to enter. And may He come bringing His own Universe with all the gods that dwell in it—He who is the one God and all the gods, where each is all, blending into a unity, distinct in powers but all one god in virtue of that one divine power of many facets.

More truly, this is the one God who is all the gods; for, in the coming to be of all those, this, the one, has suffered no diminishing. He and all have one existence, while each again is distinct. It is distinction by state without interval: there is no outward form to set one here and another there and to prevent any from being an entire identity; yet there is no sharing of parts from one to another. Nor is each of those divine wholes a power in fragment, a power totalling to the sum of the measurable segments: the divine is one all-power, reaching out to infinity, powerful to infinity: and so great is God that his very members are infinites. What place can be named to which He does not reach?

Great, too, is this firmament of ours and all the powers constellated within it, but it would be greater still, unspeakably, but that there is inbound in it

4. In Plato's *Timaeus*, a subordinate deity who fashions the physical world in the image of eternal ideas.

5. Plato, *Timaeus* 37c.

something of the petty power of body; no doubt the powers of fire and other bodily substances might themselves be thought very great, but in fact, it is through their failure in the true power that we see them burning, destroying, wearing things away, and slaving towards the production of life; they destroy because they are themselves in process of destruction, and they produce because they belong to the realm of the produced.

The power in that other world has merely Being and Beauty of Being. Beauty without Being could not be, nor Being voided of Beauty: abandoned of Beauty, Being loses something of its essence. Being is desirable because it is identical with Beauty; and Beauty is loved because it is Being. How then can we debate which is the cause of the other, where the nature is one? The very figment of Being needs some imposed image of Beauty to make it passable, and even to ensure its existence; it exists to the degree in which it has taken some share in the beauty of Idea; and the more deeply it has drawn on this, the less imperfect it is, precisely because the nature which is essentially the beautiful has entered into it the more intimately.

10. This is why Zeus, although the oldest of the gods and their sovereign, advances first (in the Phaedrus[6] myth) towards that vision, followed by gods and demigods and such souls as are of strength to see. That Being appears before them from some unseen place and rising loftily over them pours its light upon all things, so that all gleams in its radiance; it upholds some beings, and they see; the lower are dazzled and turn away, unfit to gaze upon that sun, the trouble falling the more heavily on those most remote.

Of those looking upon that Being and its content, and able to see, all take something but not all the same vision always: intently gazing, one sees the fount and principle of Justice, another is filled with the sight of Moral Wisdom, the original of that quality as found, sometimes at least, among men, copied by them in their degree from the divine virtue which, covering all the expanse, so to speak, of the Intellectual Realm is seen, last attainment of all, by those who have known already many splendid visions.

The gods see, each singly and all as one. So, too, the souls; they see all There in right of being sprung, themselves, of that universe and therefore including all from beginning to end and having their existence There if only by that phase which belongs inherently to the Divine, though often too they are There entire, those of them that have not incurred separation.

This vision Zeus takes and it is for such of us, also, as share his love and appropriate our part in the Beauty There, the final object of all seeing, the entire beauty upon all things; for all There sheds radiance, and floods those that have found their way thither so that they too become beautiful; thus it will often happen that men climbing heights where the soil has taken a yellow glow will themselves appear so, borrowing colour from the place on which they move. The colour flowering on that other height we speak of is Beauty; or rather all There is light and beauty, through and through, for the beauty is no mere bloom upon the surface.

To those that do not see entire, the immediate impression is alone taken into account; but those drunken with this wine, filled with the nectar, all their soul penetrated by this beauty, cannot remain mere gazers: no longer

6. Plato, *Phaedrus* 246e.

is there a spectator outside gazing on an outside spectacle; the clear-eyed hold the vision within themselves, though, for the most part, they have no idea that it is within but look towards it as to something beyond them and see it as an object of vision caught by a direction of the will.

All that one sees as a spectacle is still external; one must bring the vision within and see no longer in that mode of separation but as we know ourselves; thus a man filled with a god—possessed by Apollo[7] or by one of the Muses—need no longer look outside for his vision of the divine being; it is but finding the strength to see divinity within.

11. Similarly any one, unable to see himself, but possessed by that God, has but to bring that divine-within before his consciousness and at once he sees an image of himself, himself lifted to a better beauty: now let him ignore that image, lovely though it is, and sink into a perfect self-identity, no such separation remaining; at once he forms a multiple unity with the God silently present; in the degree of his power and will, the two become one; should he turn back to the former duality, still he is pure and remains very near to the God; he has but to look again and the same presence is there.

This conversion brings gain: at the first stage, that of separation, a man is aware of self; but retreating inwards, he becomes possessor of all; he puts sense away behind him in dread of the separated life and becomes one in the Divine; if he plans to see in separation, he sets himself outside.

The novice must hold himself constantly under some image of the Divine Being and seek in the light of a clear conception; knowing thus, in a deep conviction, whither he is going—into what a sublimity he penetrates—he must give himself forthwith to the inner and, radiant with the Divine Intellections (with which he is now one), be no longer the seer, but, as that place has made him, the seen.

Still, we will be told, one cannot be in beauty and yet fail to see it. The very contrary: to see the divine as something external is to be outside of it; to become it is to be most truly in beauty: since sight deals with the external, there can here be no vision unless in the sense of identification with the object.

And this identification amounts to a self-knowing, a self-consciousness, guarded by the fear of losing the self in the desire of a too wide awareness.

It must be remembered that sensations of the ugly and evil impress us more violently than those of what is agreeable and yet leave less knowledge as the residue of the shock: sickness makes the rougher mark, but health, tranquilly present, explains itself better; it takes the first place, it is the natural thing, it belongs to our being; illness is alien, unnatural, and thus makes itself felt by its very incongruity, while the other conditions are native and we take no notice. Such being our nature, we are most completely aware of ourselves when we are most completely identified with the object of our knowledge.

This is why in that other sphere, when we are deepest in that knowledge by intellection, we are aware of none; we are expecting some impression on sense, which has nothing to report since it has seen nothing and never could

7. Greek god associated with prophecy, music, and poetry.

in that order see anything. The unbelieving element is sense; it is the other, the Intellectual-Principle, that sees; and if this too doubted, it could not even credit its own existence, for it can never stand away and with bodily eyes apprehend itself as a visible object.

12. We have told how this vision is to be procured, whether by the mode of separation or in identity: now, seen in either way, what does it give to report?

The vision has been of God in travail of a beautiful offspring, God engendering a universe within himself in a painless labour and—rejoiced in what he has brought into being, proud of his children—keeping all closely by Him, for the pleasure He has in his radiance and in theirs.

Of this offspring—all beautiful, but most beautiful those that have remained within—only one has become manifest without; from him (Zeus, sovran over the visible universe), the youngest born, we may gather, as from some image, the greatness of the Father and of the Brothers that remain within the Father's house.

Still the manifested God cannot think that he has come forth in vain from the father; for through him another universe has arisen, beautiful as the image of beauty, and it could not be lawful that Beauty and Being should fail of a beautiful image.

This second Cosmos at every point copies the archetype: it has life and being in copy, and has beauty as springing from that diviner world. In its character of image it holds, too, that divine perpetuity without which it would only at times be truly representative and sometimes fail like a construction of art; for every image whose existence lies in the nature of things must stand during the entire existence of the archetype.

Hence it is false to put an end to the visible sphere as long as the Intellectual endures, or to found it upon a decision taken by its maker at some given moment.

That teaching shirks the penetration of such a making as is here involved: it fails to see that as long as the Supreme is radiant there can be no failing of its sequel but, that existing, all exists. And—since the necessity of conveying our meaning compels such terms—the Supreme has existed for ever and for ever will exist.

13. The God fettered (as in the Kronos[8] Myth) to an unchanging identity leaves the ordering of this universe to his son (to Zeus), for it could not be in his character to neglect his rule within the divine sphere, and, as though sated with the Authentic-Beauty, seek a lordship too recent and too poor for his might. Ignoring this lower world, Kronos (Intellectual-Principle) claims for himself his own father (Ouranos,[9] the Absolute, or One) with all the upward-tending between them: and he counts all that tends to the inferior, beginning from his son (Zeus, the All-Soul), as ranking beneath him. Thus he holds a mid-position determined on the one side by the differentiation implied in the severance from the very highest and, on the other, by that which keeps him apart from the link between himself and the lower: he

8. Pre-Hellenic Greek agricultural deity, the son of Ouranus (heaven) and Gaia (earth).

9. Personification of heaven in Greek mythology.

stands between a greater father and an inferior son. But since that father is too lofty to be thought of under the name of Beauty, the second God remains the primally beautiful.[1]

Soul also has beauty, but is less beautiful than Intellect as being its image and therefore, though beautiful in nature, taking increase of beauty by looking to that original. Since then the All-Soul—to use the more familiar term—since Aphrodite herself is so beautiful, what name can we give to that other? If Soul is so lovely in its own right, of what quality must that prior be? And since its being is derived, what must that power be from which the Soul takes the double beauty, the borrowed and the inherent?

We ourselves possess beauty when we are true to our own being; our ugliness is in going over to another order; our self-knowledge, that is to say, is our beauty; in self-ignorance we are ugly.

Thus beauty is of the Divine and comes Thence only.

Do these considerations suffice to a clear understanding of the Intellectual Sphere or must we make yet another attempt by another road?

ca. 260–70 ca. 300–305

1. Plotinus here explains the story of Ouranus, Kronos, and Zeus as symbolically referring to the Three Hypostases: the One, Intellect, and Soul. His version of their myths differs markedly from the power struggle usually recounted (see, e.g., Hesiod's *Theogony*).

AUGUSTINE OF HIPPO
354–430

"Scripture teaches nothing but charity, nor condemns anything except cupidity." Although this critical touchstone, articulated by St. Augustine in *On Christian Doctrine*, may strike modern readers as more theological than literary, it involved Augustine in some strikingly modern literary issues: for example, how signs function, how readers make meaning of texts, and how interpretations are validated. He offers a specifically Christian response to the problem of intentionality when he says of the Scriptures, "Whoever finds a lesson there useful to the building of charity, even though he has not said what the author may be shown to have intended in that place, has not been deceived, nor is he lying in any way."

Augustine was born in a North African Roman province in present-day Algeria—a backwater of the Roman Empire. Although his mother, Monica, was a devout Christian, his father was a pagan and thus their son was not baptized. He studied in the rhetoric schools of Carthage, where he was attracted to Manichaeism, an early Christian philosophy noted for its extreme metaphysical and moral dualism and its belief that evil is as powerful as good. The other great influence on his intellectual development was Greek philosophy, most notably the works of such Neoplatonists as PLOTINUS. Augustine taught in Carthage for seven years, from 376 to 383. He then went to Rome, where he set up as a teacher of rhetoric. By 384, at the age of thirty, he was a prominent enough scholar to be appointed municipal professor of rhetoric by the city of Milan. There, profoundly moved by the preaching of Ambrose, the bishop of Milan, he was baptized in 387. He resigned his position and returned to North

Africa, where, in 391, he became a priest. In 395 he was appointed bishop of Hippo, a position he held until his death.

Augustine was an extremely prolific writer (his bibliography numbers over one thousand works). Besides his celebrated *Confessions*, written around 400, and his magisterial philosophy of history, *City of God* (413–26), undertaken in the wake of the sack of Rome, he wrote many commentaries on the Bible and polemics against prominent heresies of the time, including Manichaeism. Two treaties that deal with the theory of criticism and biblical interpretation—*On Christian Doctrine* and *The Trinity*—were written after his appointment as bishop of Hippo. *On Christian Doctrine*, whose first three books were written around 395 (book 4 was added in 427), is a central text of medieval philosophy and aesthetics. *The Trinity*, completed in 416, deals with, among other things, key problems of signification: that is, how to establish meaning.

Augustine wrote at a time when Christianity was just beginning to establish itself, a time when there was no agreement on a fixed text for its Scriptures. The Bible consisted of scattered manuscript fragments (complete Bibles were rare), written variously in Hebrew, Greek, and Latin. Because of his early experiences with Manichaeism, Augustine recognized the need for some way to authorize the interpretation of Scriptures to prevent Christianity from fragmenting into sects. The existing hodgepodge of unconnected and sometimes contradictory narratives could not simply be taken as a group of literal documents. Only a method of interpreting figurative language could unravel the many difficult and obscure passages contained in various Scriptures, but to argue for a figurative reading of the sacred texts of Christianity required mechanisms to limit meaning to authorized interpretations. Drawing from many sources, including classical Platonic thinking about language (see PLATO), the rhetorical tradition in which he was trained (see QUINTILIAN), the epistles of St. Paul, and the early traditions of biblical criticism pioneered by Origen (180–254) in Greek and Sts. Jerome (ca. 347–420) and Ambrose (ca. 340–397) in Latin, Augustine fashioned a theory of signification that would dominate Western hermeneutics for ten centuries after his death. In the later Middle Ages, Augustinian sign theory would be further developed into a system of exegesis (a method for interpreting texts allegorically) by writers such as HUGH OF ST. VICTOR and THOMAS AQUINAS, as well as by vernacular poets such as DANTE.

Augustine's originality lay in linking the theory of signs to a theory of language, which to this point had been considered separately, and in bringing both theories to bear on the practice of interpreting Scriptures. His first principles, the basic elements of signification, were transmitted almost unchanged to the modern linguist FERDINAND DE SAUSSURE. Augustine distinguishes in *On Christian Doctrine* between things and signs: "A sign is a thing which causes us to think of something beyond the impression that the thing itself makes upon the senses." He further differentiates between natural and conventional signs: natural signs, such as smoke or the tracks of an animal, signify without intending to; conventional signs, such as words, are used by living beings to convey things they have sensed or understood. Conventional signs may be further distinguished as literal and figurative; for instance, "ox" may conventionally refer to a four-legged draft animal, but in the New Testament it also figuratively symbolizes one of the four evangelists. This careful survey of assumptions might seem, at first glance, somewhat obvious and simple, but it is necessary so that Augustine can posit a stable one-to-one correspondence between signs and the things they signify. The development of an adequate theory of conventional signs, especially the figurative, is one of the goals of Augustinian hermeneutics—as it is for much subsequent theory of interpretation, including modern semiotics. It is, however, a project undermined by signs' ability to carry multiple meanings (to function in richly figurative ways), a problem Augustine never adequately resolved.

The final book of *The Trinity* elucidates the problem of figurative signs in its analysis of a baffling theological concept: how the Godhead can unite three persons—the Father, the Son, and the Holy Spirit—in one. Here Augustine reprises and extends his analysis of signs in *On Christian Doctrine*. The Bible's explanations of mysteries of faith like the Trinity can only be shrouded in enigmatic allegory, a kind of narrative that, according to Quintilian, "means one thing in the words, another in the sense." The sign is supposed to point unidirectionally to a thing; however, figurative signs convert or "commute" (to use JACQUES DERRIDA's term) things into signs in a process that may be, for modern theorists, interminable. This process of commutation works to undermine the stable referentiality that Augustine seeks. *The Trinity* asserts the stability of the biblical sign to guarantee that the relationship between literal and figurative uses is as stable as the relationship between sign and thing. But Augustinian sign theory requires a mysterious transcendental signified (again Derrida's term), a prevocalic word that can stand outside of, initiate, and control the processes of figurative language: "We must, therefore, come to that word of man; . . . it precedes all the signs by which it is signified, and is begotten by the knowledge which remains in the mind . . . just as it is." Yet because allegory depends on the gap between signs and what they signify, there is always a danger, which Augustine does not fully acknowledge, that interpretation will reveal not a stable and fixed truth but a free play of signification. Instead he fills the gap opened up between sign and signifier with faith. Notwithstanding the theological nature of his solution to a problem that continues to vex contemporary linguistics, Augustine's rich remarks on signification laid the foundation for twentieth-century semiotics.

BIBLIOGRAPHY

Augustine's complete works in Latin can be found in his *Opera Omnia* (1830–38). More up-to-date editions of some works appear in the unfinished *Bibliothèque Augustinienne* (1947–). English translations of Augustine's major works, including Stephen McKenna's 1963 translation of *The Trinity*, are included in Catholic University's *Fathers of the Church* series (1947–). D. W. Robertson Jr.'s 1958 translation of *On Christian Doctrine* is usually favored by scholars. John Healey's 1940 translation of *The City of God* is widely cited, as is John K. Ryan's 1960 translation of *The Confessions*. Peter Brown's universally acclaimed biography, *Augustine of Hippo* (1967), is an excellent source of information on the saint's life. Eugene Portalie's *Guide to the Thought of St. Augustine* (1960) is an accessible and carefully indexed guide to Augustine's writings. D. W. Robertson's *Preface to Chaucer* (1963), controversial since its publication, is a learned and useful introduction to Augustinian aesthetics. Marcia L. Colish's *Mirror of Language: A Study in the Medieval Theory of Knowledge* (1968) cogently draws out the implications of Augustinian sign theory for later medieval theorists such as Thomas Aquinas and Dante. *Augustine: A Collection of Critical Essays* (1972), edited by R. A. Markus, provides a range of critical views. Augustine's influence on the later Middle Ages is examined in *Reading and Wisdom: The De doctrina christiana of Augustine in the Middle Ages*, edited by E. D. English (1995). The *Augustinus-Lexicon* (1985–), when completed (vol. 1 is currently available), will become the standard reference work, containing encyclopedic articles on Augustine's life, works, and doctrine. The *Fichier Augustinien* (1972) offers a comprehensive bibliography to 1970, with one supplemental volume (1978).

From On Christian Doctrine[1]

From *Book One*

II

[2] All doctrine concerns either things or signs, but things are learned by signs. Strictly speaking, I have here called a "thing" that which is not used to signify something else, like wood, stone, cattle, and so on; but not that wood concerning which we read that Moses cast it into bitter waters that their bitterness might be dispelled,[2] nor that stone which Jacob placed at his head,[3] nor that beast which Abraham sacrificed in place of his son.[4] For these are things in such a way that they are also signs of other things.[5] There are other signs whose whole use is in signifying, like words. For no one uses words except for the purpose of signifying something. From this may be understood what we call "signs"; they are things used to signify something. Thus every sign is also a thing, for that which is not a thing is nothing at all; but not every thing is also a sign. And thus in this distinction between things and signs, when we speak of things, we shall so speak that, although some of them may be used to signify something else, this fact shall not disturb the arrangement we have made to speak of things as such first and of signs later. We should bear in mind that now we are to consider what things are, not what they signify beyond themselves.

From *Book Two*

I

[1] Just as I began, when I was writing about things, by warning that no one should consider them except as they are, without reference to what they signify beyond themselves, now when I am discussing signs I wish it understood that no one should consider them for what they are but rather for their value as signs which signify something else. A sign is a thing which causes us to think of something beyond the impression the thing itself makes upon the senses. Thus if we see a track, we think of the animal that made the track; if we see smoke, we know that there is a fire which causes it; if we hear the voice of a living being, we attend to the emotion it expresses; and when a trumpet sounds, a soldier should know whether it is necessary to advance or to retreat, or whether the battle demands some other response.

[2] Among signs, some are natural and others are conventional. Those are natural which, without any desire or intention of signifying, make us aware of something beyond themselves, like smoke which signifies fire. It does this without any will to signify, for even when smoke appears alone, observation and memory of experience with things bring a recognition of an underlying fire. The track of a passing animal belongs to this class, and the face of one who is wrathful or sad signifies his emotion even when he does not wish to

1. Translated by D. W. Robertson Jr., who sometimes adds clarifying words or phrases in brackets.
2. Exodus 15.25.
3. Genesis 28.11.
4. Genesis 22.13.
5. According to St. Augustine, the "wood" is a sign of the cross. The "stone" and the "beast" represent the human nature of Christ [translator's note].

show that he is wrathful or sad, just as other emotions are signified by the expression even when we do not deliberately set out to show them. But it is not proposed here to discuss signs of this type. Since the class formed a division of my subject, I could not disregard it completely, and this notice of it will suffice.

II

[3] Conventional signs are those which living creatures show to one another for the purpose of conveying, in so far as they are able, the motion of their spirits or something which they have sensed or understood. Nor is there any other reason for signifying, or for giving signs, except for bringing forth and transferring to another mind the action of the mind in the person who makes the sign. We propose to consider and to discuss this class of signs in so far as men are concerned with it, for even signs given by God and contained in the Holy Scriptures are of this type also, since they were presented to us by the men who wrote them. Animals also have signs which they use among themselves, by means of which they indicate their appetites. For a cock who finds food makes a sign with his voice to the hen so that she runs to him. And the dove calls his mate with a cry or is called by her in turn, and there are many similar examples which may be adduced. Whether these signs, or the expression or cry of a man in pain, express the motion of the spirit without intention of signifying or are truly shown as signs is not in question here and does not pertain to our discussion, and we remove this division of the subject from this work as superfluous.

III

[4] Among the signs by means of which men express their meanings to one another, some pertain to the sense of sight, more to the sense of hearing, and very few to the other senses. For when we nod, we give a sign only to the sight of the person whom we wish by that sign to make a participant in our will. Some signify many things through the motions of their hands, and actors give signs to those who understand with the motions of all their members as if narrating things to their eyes. And banners and military standards visibly indicate the will of the captains. And all of these things are like so many visible words. More signs, as I have said, pertain to the ears, and most of these consist of words. But the trumpet, the flute, and the harp make sounds which are not only pleasing but also significant, although as compared with the number of verbal signs the number of signs of this kind are few. For words have come to be predominant among men for signifying whatever the mind conceives if they wish to communicate it to anyone. However, Our Lord gave a sign with the odor of the ointment with which His feet were anointed;[6] and the taste of the sacrament of His body and blood signified what He wished;[7]and when the woman was healed by touching the hem of His garment,[8] something was signified. Nevertheless, a multitude of innumerable signs by means of which men express their thoughts is made

6. In the gospel of St. John (12.3–8), Mary anoints Christ's feet with precious ointment. Later in *On Christian Doctrine*, Augustine interprets the "good odor" of the ointment as a sign of "good fame" (3.12.18).

7. Matthew 26.28; Luke 22.19–20.

8. Matthew 9.20–22.

up of words. And I could express the meaning of all signs of the type here touched upon in words, but I would not be able at all to make the meanings of words clear by these signs.

IV

[5] But because vibrations in the air soon pass away and remain no longer than they sound, signs of words have been constructed by means of letters. Thus words are shown to the eyes, not in themselves but through certain signs which stand for them. These signs could not be common to all peoples because of the sin of human dissension which arises when one people seizes the leadership for itself. A sign of this pride is that tower[9] erected in the heavens where impious men deserved that not only their minds but also their voices should be dissonant.

X

[15] There are two reasons why things written are not understood: they are obscured either by unknown or by ambiguous signs. For signs are either literal or figurative. They are called literal when they are used to designate those things on account of which they were instituted; thus we say *bos* [ox] when we mean an animal of a herd because all men using the Latin language call it by that name just as we do. Figurative signs occur when that thing which we designate by a literal sign is used to signify something else; thus we say "ox" and by that syllable understand the animal which is ordinarily designated by that word, but again by that animal we understand an evangelist, as is signified in the Scripture, according to the interpretation of the Apostle, when it says, "Thou shalt not muzzle the ox that treadeth out the corn."[1]

XI

[16] Against unknown literal signs the sovereign remedy is a knowledge of languages. And Latin-speaking men, whom we have here undertaken to instruct, need two others for a knowledge of the Divine Scriptures, Hebrew and Greek,[2] so that they may turn back to earlier exemplars if the infinite variety of Latin translations gives rise to any doubts. Again, in these books we frequently find untranslated Hebrew words, like *amen, alleluia, racha, hosanna,* and so on, of which some, although they could be translated, have been preserved from antiquity on account of their holier authority, like *amen* and *alleluia;* others, like the other two mentioned above, are said not to be translatable into another language. For there are some words in some languages which cannot be translated into other languages. And this is especially true of interjections which signify the motion of the spirit rather than any part of a rational concept. And these two belong to this class: *racha* is said to be an expression of indignation and *hosanna* an expression of delight. But a knowledge of these two languages is not necessary for these few things, which are easy to know and to discover, but, as we have said, it is necessary

9. The Tower of Babel; see Genesis 11.1–9.
1. Deuteronomy 25.4. St. Paul interprets oxen as apostles, those "who labor in the word and doctrine," in 1 Corinthians 9.9 and 1 Timothy 5.18.
2. Augustine himself admits to having little Greek and no Hebrew.

on account of the variety of translations. We can enumerate those who have translated the Scriptures from Hebrew into Greek, but those who have translated them into Latin are innumerable. In the early times of the faith when anyone found a Greek codex, and he thought that he had some facility in both languages, he attempted to translate it.

From *Book Three*

XXIX

[40] Lettered men should know, moreover, that all those modes of expression which the grammarians designate with the Greek word *tropes* were used by our authors, and more abundantly and copiously than those who do not know them and have learned about such expressions elsewhere are able to suppose or believe. Those who know these tropes, however, will recognize them in the sacred letters, and this knowledge will be of considerable assistance in understanding them. But it is not proper to teach them to the ignorant here, lest we seem to be teaching the art of grammar. I advise that they be learned elsewhere, although I have already advised the same thing before in the second book where I discussed the necessary knowledge of languages. For letters from which grammar takes its name—the Greeks call letters *grámmata*—are indeed signs of sounds made by the articulate voice with which we speak. And not only examples of all these tropes are found in reading the sacred books, but also the names of some of them, like *allegoria, aenigma, parabola.*[3] And yet almost all of these tropes, said to be learned in the liberal arts, find a place in the speech of those who have never heard the lectures of grammarians and are content with the usage of common speech. For who does not say, "So may you flourish"? And this is the trope called metaphor. Who does not use the word *piscina* [basin, pool, pond, tank, or other large container for water] for something which neither contains fish nor was constructed for the use of fish, when the word itself is derived from *piscis* [fish]? This trope is called catachresis.[4]

[41] It would be tedious to describe other examples of this kind. For the vulgar speech even extends to those tropes which are more remarkable because they imply the opposite of what is said, like that which is called irony or antiphrasis.[5] Now irony indicates by inflection what it wishes to be understood, as when we say to a man who is doing evil, "You are doing well." Antiphrasis, however, does not rely on inflection that it may signify the contrary, but either uses its own words whose origin is from the contrary, like *lucus,* "groove," so called *quod minime luceat,* "because it has very little light"; or it indicates that a thing is so when it wishes to imply the contrary, as when we seek to obtain what is not there and we are told. "There is plenty." Or, by adding words we may indicate that what we say is to be taken in a contrary sense, as when we say, "Beware of him, for he is a good man." And what unlearned man does not say such things without knowing at all what these tropes are or what they are called? Yet an awareness of them is nec-

3. Teaching moral lessons by means of extended metaphors. "Allegoria": saying one thing to mean another. "Aenigma": allusive or obscure speech.
4. A strained use of words.
5. From *anti*, meaning reverse, and *phrasis*, meaning diction: saying one thing and meaning the contrary.

essary to a solution of the ambiguities of the Scriptures, for when the sense is absurd if it is taken verbally, it is to be inquired whether or not what is said is expressed in this or that trope which we do not know; and in this way many hidden things are discovered.

ca. 395

From The Trinity[1]

From *Book Fifteen*

FROM CHAPTER 9

[15] We have spoken about these things because of what the Apostle has said: 'we see now through a mirror.'[2] But since he added 'in an enigma,' his meaning is unknown to many who are ignorant of that branch of literature in which these modes of speech are taught; they are called tropes by the Greeks, and we ourselves also use this Greek word in place of the Latin. For just as we are more accustomed to say *schemata*[3] than figures, so we are more accustomed to say tropes instead of modes. But to render the names of all the modes or tropes in Latin, so as to apply to each word its appropriate name, is very difficult and quite unusual. Therefore, some of our interpreters, reluctant to use the Greek word where the Apostle says 'which are by way of allegory,'[4] have translated it by a circumlocution, saying 'those which signify one thing by another.' But there are very many species of this trope or allegory, and among them is that which is also called an enigma.[5]

But the definition of a generic term itself must include all the species. And, therefore, just as every horse is an animal, but not every animal is a horse, so every enigma is an allegory, but not every allegory is an enigma. What, then, is an allegory except a trope in which one thing is understood from another, as when he writes to the Thessalonians: 'Therefore, let us not sleep as do the rest, but let us be wakeful and sober. For they who sleep, sleep at night, and they who are drunk are drunk at night. But let us, who are of the day, be sober'?[6] This allegory, however, is not an enigma, for unless one is very slow of comprehension, its meaning is clear. But, to explain it briefly, an enigma is an obscure allegory, such as: 'The horseleech has three daughters,'[7] and whatever expressions are similar to this. But where the Apostle[8] speaks of the allegory, he finds it not in the words but in the deed; for he pointed out that by the two sons of Abraham, the one by a slave-girl and the other by a free woman—he was not speaking figuratively, but of something that also took place—the two Testaments are to be understood; this was obscure before he explained it, and, hence, such an allegory, which is a general name, could also be specially called an enigma.

* * *

1. Translated by Stephen McKenna.
2. "These things" refers to Augustine's gloss, in the previous chapter, of 1 Corinthians 13.12, where the apostle Paul says: "We see now through a mirror in an enigma, but then face to face."
3. Another technical rhetorical term for tropes.
4. Galatians 4.24. An allegory says one thing but means another.
5. Allusive or obscure speech.
6. 1 Thessalonians 5.6–8.
7. Proverbs 30.15.
8. St. Paul, Galatians 4.22–24.

FROM CHAPTER 10

* * *

[18] Some thoughts, then, are speeches of the heart, and that a mouth is also there[9] is shown by the Lord when He says: 'What goes into the mouth doth not defile a man, but what comes out of the mouth, that defiles a man.'[1] In one sentence he has included the two different mouths of man, the one of the body, the other of the heart. For certainly these people[2] thought that a man is defiled by that which enters the mouth of the body, but the Lord said a man is defiled by that which comes out of the mouth of the heart. Such was the explanation that He Himself gave of what He had said. For a little later He spoke of this subject to His disciples: 'Are you also even yet without understanding? Do you not understand that whatever enters the mouth, passes into the belly and is cast out into the drain?' Here indeed He referred very clearly to the mouth of the body. But He indicates the mouth of the heart in that which follows: 'But the things that proceed out of the mouth come from the heart, and it is they that defile a man. For out of the heart come evil thoughts,' etc.[3] What clearer explanation can there be than this? Yet because we speak of thoughts as speeches of the heart, we do not, therefore, mean that they are not at the same time acts of sight, which arise from the sights of knowledge when they are true.

For when these take place outwardly through the body, then speech is one thing and sight another thing; but when we think inwardly, then both are one. Just as hearing and sight are two things, differing from each other in the senses of the body, but in the mind it is not one thing to see and another thing to hear; and, therefore, although speech is not seen outwardly, but is rather heard, yet the Holy Gospel says that the inner speeches, that is, the thoughts, were seen by the Lord and not heard: 'They said within themselves, "He blasphemes," ' and then it adds: 'And when Jesus had seen their thoughts.'[4] He saw, therefore, what they had said. For by His own thought He saw their thoughts which they alone thought that they saw.

[19] Whoever, then, can understand the word, not only before it sounds, but even before the images of its sounds are contemplated in thought—such a word belongs to no language, that is, to none of the so-called national languages, of which ours is the Latin—whoever, I say, can understand this, can already see through this mirror and in this enigma some likeness of that Word of whom it was said: 'In the beginning was the Word, and the Word was with God; and the Word was God.'[5]

For when we speak the truth, that is, speak of what we know, then the word which is born from the knowledge itself which we retain in the memory must be altogether of the same kind as that knowledge from which it is born. For the thought formed from that thing which we know is the word which we speak in our heart, and it is neither Greek, nor Latin, nor of any other language, but when we have to bring it to the knowledge of those to whom we are speaking, then some sign is assumed by which it may be made known. And generally this is a sound, but at times also a nod; the former is shown

9. That is, in the heart.
1. Matthew 15.11.
2. The scribes and pharisees (Matthew 15.1).
3. Matthew 15.10–20.
4. Matthew 9.2–4.
5. John 1.1.

to the ears, the latter to the eyes, in order that that word which we bear in our mind may also become known by bodily signs to the senses of the body. For even to nod, what else is it but to speak, as it were, in a visible manner? A witness for this opinion is found in the Sacred Scriptures, for we read as follows in the Gospel according to John: 'Amen, amen I say to you, one of you shall betray me. The disciples therefore looked at one another, uncertain of whom he was speaking. Now one of his disciples, he whom Jesus loved, was reclining at Jesus' bosom. Simon Peter therefore beckoned to him, and said to him, "Who is it of whom he speaks?" '[6] Behold, he spoke by beckoning what he did not venture to speak aloud. But we make use of these and other corporeal signs of this kind when we speak to the eyes or the ears of those who are present. But letters have also been found by which we can also speak to those who are absent; but the letters are the signs of words, while the words themselves in our speech are signs of the things of which we are thinking.

FROM CHAPTER 11

[20] Hence, the word which sounds without is a sign of the word that shines within, to which the name of word more properly belongs. For that which is produced by the mouth of the flesh is the sound of the word, and is itself also called the word, because that inner word assumed it in order that it might appear outwardly. For just as our word in some way becomes a bodily sound by assuming that in which it may be manifested to the senses of men, so the Word of God was made flesh by assuming that in which He might also be manifested to the senses of men. And just as our word becomes a sound and is not changed into a sound, so the Word of God indeed becomes flesh, but far be it from us that it should be changed into flesh. For by assuming it, not by being consumed in it, this word of ours becomes a sound, and that Word becomes flesh.

Whoever, then, desires to arrive at some kind of a likeness to the Word of God, although unlike it in many things, let him not behold our word which sounds in the ears, either when it is brought forth in sound, or when it is thought in silence. For all words, no matter in what language they may sound, are also thought in silence; and hymns run through our mind, even when the mouth of the body is silent; not only the numbers of the syllables, but also the melodies of the hymns, since they are corporeal and belong to that sense of the body called hearing, are present by their own kind of incorporeal images to those who think of them, and silently turn all of them over in their minds.

But we must pass by these things in order to arrive at that word of man, for by its likeness, of whatever sort it may be, the Word of God may in some manner be seen as in an enigma: not that which was spoken to this or that Prophet, and of which it was said: 'But the word of God increased and multiplied,'[7] and of which it was again said: 'Faith then by hearing, and hearing by the word of Christ,'[8] and again: 'When you received from us the word of God, you received it not as the word of man, but, as it truly is, the word of God.'[9] There are numberless instances in the Scriptures where similar state-

6. John 13.21–24.
7. Acts 6.7.
8. Romans 10.17.
9. 1 Thessalonians 2.13.

ments are made about the word of God, which is scattered in the sounds of many different languages through the hearts and mouths of men. But it is called the word of God, therefore, because a divine and not a human doctrine is handed down. But by means of this likeness we are endeavoring to see that Word of God, in whatever way we can, of whom it was said: 'The Word was God,' of whom it was said: 'All things were made through him,' of whom it was said: 'The Word was made flesh,'[1] of whom it was said: 'The word of God on high is the fountain of wisdom.'[2]

We must, therefore, come to that word of man, to the word of a living being endowed with reason, to the word of the image of God, not born of God but made by God; this word cannot be uttered in sound nor thought in the likeness of sound, such as must be done with the word of any language; it precedes all the signs by which it is signified, and is begotten by the knowledge which remains in the mind when this same knowledge is spoken inwardly, just as it is. For the sight of thought is very similar to the sight of knowledge. For, when it is spoken through a sound or through some bodily sign, it is not spoken just as it is, but as it can be seen or heard through the body. When, therefore, that which is in the knowledge is in the word, then it is a true word, and the truth which is expected from man, so that what is in the knowledge is also in the word, and what is not in the knowledge is not in the word; it is here that we recognize 'Yes, yes; no, no.'[3] In this way the likeness of the image that was made approaches, insofar, as it can, to the likeness of the image that was born, whereby God the Son is proclaimed as substantially like the Father in all things.

The following likeness in this enigma to the Word of God is also to be noted: just as it was said of that Word: 'All things were made through him,'[4] where it is declared that God made all things through His only-begotten Word, so there are no works of man which are not first spoken in the heart, and, therefore, it is written: 'The beginning of every work is the word.'[5] But even here when the word is true, then it is the beginning of a good work. But the word is true, if it is begotten from the knowledge of working well, so that here too the admonition may be preserved: 'Yes, yes; no, no.' If it is 'yes' in the knowledge by which one must live, it is also 'yes' in the word by which the work is to be fulfilled; if it is 'no' there, it is also 'no' here. Otherwise, such a word will be a lie, not the truth, and consequently a sin and not a right work.

In the likeness of our word, there is also this likeness of the Word of God, that our word can exist and yet no work may follow it; but there can be no work unless the word precedes, just as the Word of God could be, even though no creature existed, but no creature could be, except through that Word through whom all things were made. Therefore, not God the Father, not the Holy Spirit, not the Trinity itself, but the Son alone, who is the Word of God, was made flesh, although the Trinity brought this about, in order that by our word following and imitating His example, we might live rightly, that is, that we might have no lie either in the contemplation or in the work of our word. But this perfection of this image is to be at some time in the

1. John 1.1, 3, 14.
2. Ecclesiasticus 1.5.
3. Matthew 5.37: "But let your communication be, Yea, yea; Nay, nay: for whatsoever is more than these cometh of evil."
4. John 1.1.
5. Ecclesiasticus 37.20.

future. In order to obtain it, the good master instructs us by the Christian faith and the doctrine of godliness, that 'with face unveiled,' from the veil of the Law, which is the shadow of things to come, 'beholding the glory of the Lord,' that is, looking as it were through a mirror, 'we might be transformed into the same image from glory to glory, as through the Spirit of the Lord,'[6] according to our previous explanation of these words.

* * *

416

6. 2 Corinthians 3.18.

MACROBIUS
b. ca. 360

Throughout the Middle Ages and up until at least the end of the seventeenth century, Macrobius's *Commentary on the Dream of Scipio* was the authoritative text on the meaning of dreams, influencing poets and critics from DANTE and Chaucer down to Milton. In addition this account of dreams in general, and Scipio's dream in particular, engages with questions about the role of fables in philosophy and the figurative nature of the truth that have interested philosophers as diverse as FRIEDRICH NIETZSCHE, Richard Rorty, and JACQUES DERRIDA. When Macrobius wrote that "Philosophy does not discountenance all stories nor does it accept all," he defined for subsequent ages the Neoplatonic attitude toward literature. Some fables proclaim their falsity and deserve at best to be relegated to "children's nurseries." But others, those which present "a decent and dignified conception of holy truths . . . presented beneath a modest veil of allegory," are not only appropriate but necessary to philosophy. In this way Macrobius's commentary defends Cicero's inclusion of the "Dream of Scipio" in a serious philosophical treatise on good government.

In the oldest manuscripts the author of *Commentary on the Dream of Scipio* is called "Macrobius Ambrosius Theodosius, vir clarissimus et inlustris" (most famous and illustrious man), a title that, in the Roman world of late antiquity, was used only of someone holding the highest public office. Almost nothing else is known of his life except that he was not a native of Italy; he may have been from Africa; he had a son, Eustachius, to whom he dedicated his major works; and he flourished at the end of the fourth and beginning of the fifth century. Scholars have attempted, unsuccessfully, to identify him with various government functionaries also named Macrobius who are mentioned in legal texts of the period. Although he was a contemporary of St. AUGUSTINE, it is not clear whether Macrobius was a Christian. He never mentions Christianity and reveals in his writing a fondness for pagan antiquities. However, to hold high governmental positions in the fifth-century Roman world, he would have had to be at least a nominal Christian, and nothing in the texts attributed to him would contradict the beliefs of fifth-century Christianity.

Macrobius is the author of two works that have been wholly or partially preserved, the *Saturnalia* (ca. 395) and *Commentary on the Dream of Scipio* (ca. 400). A third treatise, *On the Differences and Similarities of the Greek and Latin Verb*, has been lost, though summaries of it survive in the later Middle Ages. Books 3 and 4 of *Saturnalia* are devoted to commentary on Virgil's works; they illustrate the tendency in the fourth-century Roman world to regard Virgil less as a great poet than as a philosopher, an authority of prodigious wisdom and learning, a role he plays in the *Commentary* as well.

At the conclusion of his *Republic*, the Roman statesman and philosopher Cicero (106–43 B.C.E.) recounts a dream of Scipio Africanus the Younger (Roman general and statesman, ca. 184–129 B.C.E), in which he meets his famous grandfather, Scipio Africanus the Elder (ca. 235–183 B.C.E.), the general who defeated Hannibal during the Second Punic War. In the course of the dream, Scipio the Elder shows his grandson a vision of the "celestial circles, orbits, and spheres, the movements of the planets, and the revolutions of the heavens." The *Republic*, a treatise on good government modeled on PLATO's *Republic*, was not known in the Middle Ages except for this brief fragment, which was preserved only because Macrobius wondered why Cicero would choose to include such a "fiction and dream" in a serious philosophical treatise. Macrobius defends the obviously fabulous "Dream of Scipio" from detractors who argued that "philosophers should refrain from using fiction since no kind of fiction has a place with those who profess to tell the truth."

Macrobius's *Commentary on the Dream of Scipio* is a fascinating example of an early commentary on a nonbiblical text; it greatly influenced the development of this medieval genre, an expository tradition that grew out of the late classical encyclopedic glosses of pagan texts. Commentaries were central to the medieval experience of reading any authoritative (that is, Latin) text, an integral part of the process of transmitting canonical works. Macrobius's commentary uses Scipio's dream as an occasion for an exposition of Neoplatonic doctrine and its relation to such subjects as arithmetic, astronomy, the music of the spheres, geography, and the immortality of the soul. Macrobius's philosophical Neoplatonism, however, his belief that reality must be located in a transcendental spiritual realm that gives meaning to the visible world, is of interest to literary critics primarily because it contends that the higher truths philosophy strives to discover can be accessed only through figurative language and allegorical veils.

"The Dream of Scipio" offers a wide-ranging account of dreams and their relationship to the fables required to make sense of transcendent truths such as the nature of the soul or God. Macrobius catalogues the various types of dreams, particularly the five varieties of "enigmatic dreams," demonstrating a systematic approach to dream interpretation that would dominate the understanding of dreams for centuries. Throughout the Middle Ages, this chapter on dreams was the most popular section of the *Commentary*. While its details differ from the later psychoanalytic approach to dreams, Macrobius's account shares with SIGMUND FREUD's analysis a belief that dreams function like narratives and can be used to uncover truths not visible to empirical observation.

BIBLIOGRAPHY

The standard Latin edition of Macrobius's works, *Macrobius*, was edited by Francis Eyssenhardt in 1893 and updated by J. Willis in 1963. *Commentary on the Dream of Scipio* was translated into English by William Harris Stahl in 1952. In 1969 Percival Vaughan Davies published an English translation of Macrobius's only other surviving work, *The Saturnalia*. Few studies focus on Macrobius as a figure in his own time. These include Thomas Whittaker in *Macrobius: or, Philosophy, Science, and Letters in the Year 400* (1923) and Herman de Ley in *Macrobius and Numenius: A Study of Macrobius, In Somnium Scipionis 1.c.12* (1972). T. R. Glover includes a chapter on Macrobius in *Life and Letters in the Fourth Century* (1968), as does Jane Chance in *Medieval Mythography: From Roman North Africa to the School of Chartres, A.D. 433–1177* (1994). Most literary studies track the influence of Macrobius's analysis of dreams on later medieval literature and criticism; among the best examples are Allison M. Peden's "Macrobius and Medieval Dream Literature" (1985) and Constance B.

Hieatt's "The Dreams of Troilus, Criseyde, and Chauntecleer: Chaucer's Manipulation of the Categories of Macrobius" (1988).

From Commentary on the Dream of Scipio[1]

Chapter III

[1] After these prefatory remarks, there remains another matter to be considered before taking up the text of *Scipio's Dream*. We must first describe the many varieties of dreams recorded by the ancients, who have classified and defined the various types that have appeared to men in their sleep, wherever they might be.[2] Then we shall be able to decide to which type the dream we are discussing belongs.

[2] All dreams may be classified under five main types: there is the enigmatic dream, in Greek *oneiros*, in Latin *somnium*; second, there is the prophetic vision, in Greek *horama*, in Latin *visio*; third, there is the oracular dream, in Greek *chrematismos*, in Latin *oraculum*; fourth, there is the nightmare, in Greek *enypnion*, in Latin *insomnium*; and last, the apparition, in Greek *phantasma*, which Cicero, when he has occasion to use the word, calls *visum*.

[3] The last two, the nightmare and the apparition, are not worth interpreting since they have no prophetic significance. [4] Nightmares may be caused by mental or physical distress, or anxiety about the future: the patient experiences in dreams vexations similar to those that disturb him during the day. As examples of the mental variety, we might mention the lover who dreams of possessing his sweetheart or of losing her, or the man who fears the plots or might of an enemy and is confronted with him in his dream or seems to be fleeing him. The physical variety might be illustrated by one who has overindulged in eating or drinking and dreams that he is either choking with food or unburdening himself, or by one who has been suffering from hunger or thirst and dreams that he is craving and searching for food or drink or has found it. Anxiety about the future would cause a man to dream that he is gaining a prominent position or office as he hoped or that he is being deprived of it as he feared.

[5] Since these dreams and others like them arise from some condition or circumstance that irritates a man during the day and consequently disturbs him when he falls asleep, they flee when he awakes and vanish into thin air. Thus the name *insomnium* was given, not because such dreams occur "in sleep"—in this respect nightmares are like other types—but because they are noteworthy only during their course and afterwards have no importance or meaning.

[6] Virgil, too, considers nightmares deceitful: "False are the dreams (*insomnia*) sent by departed spirits to their sky."[3] He used the word "sky" with reference to our mortal realm because the earth bears the same relation to the regions of the dead as the heavens bear to the earth. Again, in describ-

1. Translated by William Harris Stahl.
2. Macrobius's classification of dreams may have been derived from Artemidorus (late 2d c. C.E.), a Greek writer who traveled extensively to collect dreams and wrote a treatise, *Onirocriticon*, on the interpretation of dreams.
3. *Aeneid* 6.896.

ing the passion of love, whose concerns are always accompanied by nightmares, he says: "Oft to her heart rushes back the chief's valour, oft his glorious stock; his looks and words cling fast within her bosom, and the pang withholds calm rest from her limbs." And a moment later: "Anna, my sister, what dreams (*insomnia*) thrill me with fears?"[4]

[7] The apparition (*phantasma or visum*) comes upon one in the moment between wakefulness and slumber, in the so-called "first cloud of sleep." In this drowsy condition he thinks he is still fully awake and imagines he sees specters rushing at him or wandering vaguely about, differing from natural creatures in size and shape, and hosts of diverse things, either delightful or disturbing. To this class belongs the incubus,[5] which, according to popular belief, rushes upon people in sleep and presses them with a weight which they can feel. [8] The two types just described are of no assistance in foretelling the future; but by means of the other three we are gifted with the powers of divination.

We call a dream oracular in which a parent, or a pious or revered man, or a priest, or even a god clearly reveals what will or will not transpire, and what action to take or to avoid. [9] We call a dream a prophetic vision if it actually comes true. For example, a man dreams of the return of a friend who has been staying in a foreign land, thoughts of whom never enter his mind. He goes out and presently meets his friend and embraces him. Or in his dream he agrees to accept a deposit, and early the next day a man runs anxiously to him, charging him with the safekeeping of his money and committing secrets to his trust. [10] By an enigmatic dream we mean one that conceals with strange shapes and veils with ambiguity the true meaning of the information being offered, and requires an interpretation for its understanding. We need not explain further the nature of this dream since everyone knows from experience what it is. There are five varieties of it: personal, alien, social, public, and universal. [11] It is called personal when one dreams that he himself is doing or experiencing something; alien, when he dreams this about someone else; social, when his dream involves others and himself; public, when he dreams that some misfortune or benefit has befallen the city, forum, theater, public walls, or other public enterprise; universal, when he dreams that some change has taken place in the sun, moon, planets, sky, or regions of the earth.

[12] The dream which Scipio reports that he saw embraces the three reliable types mentioned above, and also has to do with all five varieties of the enigmatic dream. It is oracular since the two men who appeared before him and revealed his future, Aemilius Paulus and Scipio the Elder, were both his father,[6] both were pious and revered men, and both were affiliated with the priesthood. It is a prophetic vision since Scipio saw the regions of his abode after death and his future condition. It is an enigmatic dream because the truths revealed to him were couched in words that hid their profound meaning and could not be comprehended without skillful interpretation.

It also embraces the five varieties of the last type. [13] It is personal since Scipio himself was conducted to the regions above and learned of his future.

4. *Aeneid* 4.3–5, 9.

5. An evil spirit or demon, originating in personified representations of nightmares, who was supposed to have sexual intercourse with women while they were sleeping.

6. Scipio the Younger (ca. 184–129 B.C.E.), the natural son of Aemilius Paulus (d. 160 B.C.E.), a famous Roman general, was adopted sometime before 168 B.C.E. by Scipio Africanus, the eldest son of Scipio the Elder.

It is alien since he observed the estates to which the souls of others were destined. It is social since he learned that for men with merits similar to his the same places were being prepared as for himself. It is public since he foresaw the victory of Rome and the destruction of Carthage, his triumph on the Capitoline, and the coming civil strife.[7] And it is universal since by gazing up and down he was initiated into the wonders of the heavens, the great celestial circles, and the harmony of the revolving spheres,[8] things strange and unknown to mortals before this; in addition he witnessed the movements of the stars and planets and was able to survey the whole earth.

[14] It is incorrect to maintain that Scipio was not the proper person to have a dream that was both public and universal inasmuch as he had not yet attained the highest office but, as he himself admitted, was still ranked "not much higher than a private soldier."[9] The critics say that dreams concerning the welfare of the state are not to be considered significant unless military or civil officers dream them, or unless many plebeians have the same dream. [15] They cite the incident in Homer[1] when, before the assembled Greeks, Agamemnon disclosed a dream that he had had about a forthcoming battle. Nestor, who helped the army quite as much with his prudence as all the youth with their might, by way of instilling confidence in the dream said that in matters of general welfare they had to confide in the dream of a king, whereas they would repudiate the dream of anyone else. [16] However, the point in Scipio's favor was that although he had not yet held the consulship[2] or a military command, he—who himself was destined to lead that campaign—was dreaming about the coming destruction of Carthage, was witnessing the public triumph in his honor, and was even learning of the secrets of nature; for he excelled as much in philosophy as in deeds of courage.

[17] Because, in citing Virgil above as an authority for the unreliability of nightmares, we excerpted a verse from his description of the twin portals of dreams, someone may take the occasion to inquire why false dreams are allotted to the gate of ivory and trustworthy ones to the gate of horn.[3] He should avail himself of the help of Porphyry,[4] who, in his *Commentaries*, makes the following remarks on a passage in Homer[5] presenting the same distinction between gates: "All truth is concealed. [18] Nevertheless, the soul, when it is partially disengaged from bodily functions during sleep, at times gazes and at times peers intently at the truth, but does not apprehend it; and when it gazes it does not see with clear and direct vision, but rather with a dark obstructing veil interposed." [19] Virgil attests that this is natural in the following lines: "Behold—for all the cloud, which now, drawn over thy sight, dulls thy mortal vision and with dank pall enshrouds thee, I will tear away."[6] [20] If, during sleep, this veil permits the vision of the attentive soul to perceive the truth, it is thought to be made of horn, the nature of which is such that, when thinned, it becomes transparent. When the veil

7. Cicero was writing shortly before the civil war that was to end republican government in Rome. The Capitoline: a hill in Rome. Carthage: an African city (near modern Tunis) destroyed by the Romans in 146 B.C.E. in the Second Punic War.
8. The ancients believed that the universe consisted of a fixed Earth surrounded by eight or nine concentric spheres. The movement of the spheres was supposed to produce a perfectly harmonious music.
9. *Scipio's Dream* 2.1.
1. *Iliad* 2.56–83.
2. Highest regular office in the Roman Republic (held by 2 men for a 2-year term).
3. *Aeneid* 6.893–96.
4. A scholar, philosopher, and student of Neoplatonism (232–305 C.E.). He edited the *Enneads* of PLOTINUS and wrote a commentary on Homer.
5. *Odyssey* 19.562–67.
6. *Aeneid* 2.604–6.

dulls the vision and prevents its reaching the truth, it is thought to be made of ivory, the composition of which is so dense that no matter how thin a layer of it may be, it remains opaque.

ca. 400

HUGH OF ST. VICTOR

ca. 1097–1141

It is common for students of literature to question the utility of literary study and for their professors to defend it, articulating its place among the disciplines that constitute the contemporary university curriculum. Medieval writers wrestled with the same questions, especially writers concerned with the education of those who would join the ranks of the literate. And though their answers might sometimes seem alien to us, their inquiry touches on issues that continue to resonate with modern readers of literature. Indeed, every literary curriculum begins with Hugh of St. Victor's three questions in *The Didascalicon, or On the Study of Reading* (ca. 1125): what should the literate individual read, in what sequence, and in what manner?

A book about literacy, *The Didascalicon* is a clear and orderly compendium of the medieval arts: a guide for the study of texts, both sacred and profane, written at a time when a "new learning"—specialized, rational, and scientific—was threatening the established curriculum of the trivium (grammar, dialectic, and rhetoric). In answer to those who embraced dialectic and disputation for their own sake, Hugh insists, in the preface to *The Didascalicon*, on the importance of reading, which "holds first place in instruction." Later in the text, he elaborates on the importance of understanding how to read figurative language: "Following the shadow, one comes to the body: learn the figure, and you will come to the truth." Hugh's attempt to combine, in a single rigorous educational program, biblical interpretation, theology, and a comprehensive philosophy was ambitious; the breadth and scope of his synthesis would earn him the title of "a second Augustine" (see AUGUSTINE). *The Didascalicon* attempts to demonstrate how all knowledge—secular and religious—can be used as preparation for the study of the Bible, which, in turn, would lead to the contemplation of God.

The facts of Hugh's life have been the subject of some controversy among medieval scholars. The evidence available on his early life is fragmentary and often enigmatic. He was born most likely in the last decade of the eleventh century and educated somewhere in Saxony or the Low Countries. Around 1118 Hugh arrived at the abbey of St. Victor in Paris, where he took his monastic vows and ultimately became master of its school. He served as prior of the abbey from 1133 until his death in 1141. Founded in 1108 by William of Champeaux in reaction to the success of the Parisian schools of theology, which emphasized dialectic and debate, the abbey of St. Victor already had a tradition of learning by the time of Hugh's arrival, but it did not have a distinctive theological or philosophical project. It was ready to receive the kind of intellectual synthesis and direction provided by texts like Hugh's *Dindimus's Epitome of Philosophy* (written between 1118 and 1125) and *The Didascalicon*. His work, aimed primarily at teachers, laid the groundwork for the teaching program at St. Victor's and brought the abbey considerable renown; its curriculum was widely copied throughout Europe in the twelfth century, influencing medieval writers as diverse as John of Salisbury and THOMAS AQUINAS. Hugh is also known for his biblical commentaries and a number of mystical texts, the most important of which is the treatise *On the Sacraments of the Christian Faith* (ca. 1133).

The Didascalicon, Hugh's best-known work, belongs to a tradition of literature concerned with developing methods for the education of the individual. In the West the model of such didascalic literature is Augustine's *On Christian Doctrine* (see above), though the genre is considerably older, going back to Roman writers such as Cicero (106–43 B.C.E.) and QUINTILIAN and ultimately to the educational models propounded by PLATO and ARISTOTLE. *The Didascalicon*'s concern to integrate various areas of learning with the study of Scriptures and with the scientific pursuit of a whole complex of arts is characteristic of the twelfth-century renaissance, a period that saw the growth of towns, the development of vernacular literature, the revival of the classical poets, the recovery of Greek science and philosophy, and especially the origins of universities.

The first half of *The Didascalicon* describes the range of secular knowledge, dividing philosophy into four master categories: the theoretical, or speculative, which leads toward the contemplation of truth; the practical, which includes morality and ethics; the mechanical, which incorporates the "occupations of life"; and the logical, without which one cannot understand rationally the other three. This division owes more to an Aristotelianism derived by way of Boethius (480–524 C.E.) than to Plato or the Neoplatonism (see PLOTINUS) that had dominated intellectual life in Europe since the fifth century. Knowledge of the four branches of philosophy was, for Hugh, a necessary preparation for the contemplative life that is the ultimate goal of *The Didascalicon*; in the end, however, reason must be supplemented by revelation.

For Hugh, as for Augustine before him, the authority of biblical language derived from its special mode of signification that sets it apart from secular texts. The Bible is polysemous, allowing individual signs to carry several different meanings or senses. In explicating Scriptures, Hugh advises the reader to consider—in order—the letter, the sense, and the inner meaning of a text. The "letter" refers to such matters as grammar, style, and rhetoric. The "sense" refers to the most obvious meaning conveyed by the letter. The "inner meaning," or *sententia*, is the hidden or deeper senses contained in the literal level.

Whereas earlier, for Augustine, meaning could disseminate from a word in several and perhaps even unpredictable directions (so long as the reader adhered to the interpretive principle of charity), for Hugh, as for other twelfth century exegetes, meanings are organized systematically and hierarchically on three levels: the historical, the allegorical (which refers to the spiritual meaning), and the topological (which refers to moral messages). While this system of biblical interpretation was introduced in the West through the writings of John Cassian in the fourth century, it reached the height of its popularity in the twelfth century in treatises like *The Didascalicon*, although Hugh differs from most medieval exegetes in ascribing to Scriptures only three levels rather than four (compare, for example, Thomas Aquinas and DANTE). He also differs from other twelfth-century exegetes in his insistence that all three meanings cannot be dogmatically sought in every passage of Scriptures. Reacting against the allegorizing tendencies of many of his contemporaries, who often disregarded the literal sense of the text in favor of its other senses, Hugh asserted the importance of history—of the Bible's being the historical narrative of God's interactions with humanity—as the basis of all subsequent exegesis. His *Chronica* (written before 1141) was an attempt to write a history of the Jews that would illuminate the literal level of Scriptures.

Only after mastering the historical level of interpretation through the study of history, language, and geography are students ready to move on to the discipline of allegory, into which Hugh incorporated the field of theology. His *On the Sacraments of the Christian Faith*, the first great theological synthesis, or *summa*, of the Middle

Ages, is designed to provide the foundation for allegorical interpretation. Ultimately, students should be prepared to turn to the study of tropology, which concerned the moral and contemplative life. This Hugh examines most systematically in his two treatises on Noah's ark—*On the Moral Ark of Noah* and *On the Mystical Ark of Noah* (both written before 1141), which provide a methodical exposition of the stages of contemplative life.

Hugh's attempt to create an interpretive system that could order and control the proliferation of meanings attached to the Bible's figurative language reflects the widespread medieval tendency toward synopsis. But far from determining once and for all the significance of particular texts, new interpretations or "glosses" of the Bible proliferated in subsequent centuries at such a rate that by the fourteenth century, the term "gloss" was virtually synonymous with a lie, and much of the intellectual force of the later Protestant movement was directed against a system of commentary that had become overly complex and detached from the original narrative. Yet in its effort to come to terms with the difficulties of biblical language, Hugh's magisterial synthesis solidified conventions of interpretation that would influence subsequent literary criticism long after its particulars were forgotten. Like Augustine centuries before him and E. D. HIRSCH JR. centuries later, Hugh counsels interpreters to seek out the intention of the author first and relevant facts from the author's historical milieu and horizon second, two conventions of interpretation widely used and debated today.

BIBLIOGRAPHY

Hugh of St. Victor's Latin works are collected in the *Patrologia Latina*, vols. 175–77 (1879). Modern editions of individual Latin texts include *Didascalicon de studio legendi*, edited by Charles H. Buttimer (1939), and *Opera propaedeutica*, edited by Roger Baron (1966), which includes *Epitome Dindimi in philosopham*. English translations include *On the Sacraments of the Christian Faith*, by Roy J. Defarrari (1951); *The Divine Love: Two Treatises*, an anonymous translation by a sister of the Anglican Community of St. Mary the Virgin (1956; C.S.M.V); *Soliloquy on the Earnest Money of the Soul*, by Kevin Herbert (1956); *The Didascalicon: A Medieval Guide to the Arts* (1961), by Jerome Taylor, with valuable introduction and notes; and *Selected Spiritual Writings* (which includes the treatises on Noah), also translated by an anonymous sister of the C.S.M.V. (1962), with a useful introduction by Aelred Squire. While not exactly a typical biography, Jerome Taylor's *Origins and Early Life of Hugh of St. Victor: An Evaluation of the Tradition* (1957) presents a critical survey of the conflicting evidence available on Hugh's life.

John Philip Kleinz, in *The Theory of Knowledge of Hugh of St. Victor* (1944), examines Hugh's pedagogical works. Hugh's approach to biblical interpretation is treated in Beryl Smalley's *Study of the Bible in the Middle Ages* (1952). Roger Baron's French *Science et sagesse chez Hugues de Saint-Victor* (1957) is the best book-length study of Hugh's thought. For a modern commentary from a sympathetic, committed Christian, see Ivan Illich, *In the Vineyard of the Text: A Commentary of Hugh's Didascalicon* (1993). Rebecca Moore, in *Jews and Christians in the Life and Thought of Hugh of St. Victor* (1998), examines the respective influences of both the Jewish and Christian hermeneutic traditions on Hugh's writing. The bibliography in Taylor (cited above) is complete, though now dated. Readers may supplement it with the bibliography in Mark D. Jordan's entry on Hugh of St. Victor in the *Routledge Encyclopedia of Philosophy* (ed. Edward Craig, 1998).

From The Didascalicon[1]

From *Book One*

FROM CHAPTER ELEVEN: CONCERNING THE ORIGIN OF LOGIC

Having demonstrated the origin of the theoretical, the practical, and the mechanical arts,[2] we must now therefore investigate as well the derivation of the logical; and these I have left to the end because they were the last to be discovered. All the other arts were invented first; but that logic too should be invented was essential, for no man can fitly discuss things unless he first has learned the nature of correct and true discourse. For, as Boethius[3] declares, when the ancients first applied themselves to searching out the natures of things and the essentials of morality, they of necessity erred frequently, for they lacked discrimination in the use of words and concepts: "This is frequently the case with Epicurus,[4] who thinks that the universe consists of atoms, and who falsely maintains that pleasure is virtue. Clearly, such errors befell Epicurus and others because, being unskilled in argument, they transferred to the real world whatever conclusion they had reached by reasoning. This is a great error indeed, for real things do not precisely conform to the conclusions of our reasoning as they do to a mathematical count. In counting, whatever result obtains in the figure of one who computes correctly is sure to obtain in reality as well, so that if a count of one hundred is registered, one hundred objects will also necessarily be found as the basis for that count. In argument, however, such a relationship does not obtain with equal force, and whatever emerges in the course of a discussion does not find a fixed counterpart in nature, either. Thus it is that the man who brushes aside knowledge of argumentation falls of necessity into error when he searches out the nature of things. For unless he has first come to know for certain what form of reasoning keeps to the true course of argument, and what form keeps only to a seemingly true course, and unless he has learned what form of reasoning can be depended upon and what form must be held suspect, he cannot attain, by reasoning, the imperishable truth of things.

"Since, therefore, the ancients, having fallen often into many errors, came to certain conclusions and arguments which were false and contrary to each other; and since it seemed impossible, when contrary conclusions had been constructed concerning the same matter, either that both the conclusions which mutually inconsistent trains of reasoning had established should be true, or that there should be ambiguity concerning which train of reasoning should be credited, it was apparent that the true and whole nature of argument itself should be considered first. Once this was known, then they could also know whether the results discovered by argument were truly held. Hence, skill in the discipline of logic began—that discipline which provides

1. Translated by Jerome Taylor, who sometimes includes the original Latin in parentheses.
2. In previous and subsequent chapters Hugh divides all the arts into four branches: the theoretical, which strives for the contemplation of truth; the practical, which includes ethics and morality; the mechanical, which incorporates the "occupations of life"; and the logical, which "provides the knowledge necessary for correct speaking and argumentation."
3. Roman philosopher (480–524), best known for *The Consolation of Philosophy*, a frequently cited medieval text.
4. Greek moral and natural philosopher (341–270 B.C.E.).

ways of distinguishing between modes of argument and the trains of reasoning themselves, so that it can be known which trains of reasoning are sometimes true, sometimes false, which moreover are always false, and which never false."[5] And so logic came last in time, but is first in order. It is logic which ought to be read first by those beginning the study of philosophy, for it teaches the nature of words and concepts, without both of which no treatise of philosophy can be explained rationally.

Logic is so called from the Greek word *logos*, which has a double sense. For *logos* means either word (*sermo*) or reason, and hence logic can be called either a linguistic (*sermocinalis*) or a rational science. Rational logic, which is called argumentative, contains dialectic, and rhetoric, Linguistic logic stands as genus to grammar, dialectic, and rhetoric, thus containing argumentative logic as a subdivision. It is linguistic logic that we put fourth after the theoretical, practical, and mechanical. It must not be supposed, however, that this science is called logical, that is, linguistic, because before its discovery there were no words, or as if men before its time did not have conversations with one another.[6] For both spoken and written words existed previously, but the theory of spoken and written language was not yet reduced to an art; no rules for speaking or arguing correctly had yet been given. All sciences, indeed, were matters of use before they became matters of art. But when men subsequently considered that use can be transformed into art, and what was previously vague and subject to caprice can be brought into order by definite rules and precepts, they began, we are told, to reduce to art the habits which had arisen partly by chance, partly by nature—correcting what was bad in use, supplying what was missing, eliminating what was superfluous, and furthermore prescribing definite rules and precepts for each usage.

Such was the origin of all the arts; scanning them all, we find this true. Before there was grammar, men both wrote and spoke; before there was dialectic, they distinguished the true from the false by reasoning; before there was rhetoric, they discoursed upon civil laws; before there was arithmetic, there was knowledge of counting; before there was an art of music, they sang; before there was geometry, they measured fields; before there was astronomy, they marked off periods of time from the courses of the stars. But then came the arts, which, though they took their rise in usage, nonetheless excel it.[7]

This would be the place to set forth who were the inventors of the separate arts, when these persons flourished and where, and how the various disciplines made a start in their hands: first, however, I wish to distinguish the individual arts from one another by dividing philosophy into its parts, so to say. I should therefore briefly recapitulate the things I have said thus far, so that the transition to what follows may more easily be made.

5. Quoted from Boethius, *Commentaria in Porphyrium a se translatum* 2 (*Patrilogia Latina*, 64, 73A–B) [translator's note].

6. By contrast, Adelard of Bath, in *De eodem et diverso* (Willner, ed., p. 18), credits grammar with making speech possible for men, who "at first roamed the fields like beasts, without mutual intercourse and with their reason silent" [translator's note]. Adelard (12th c.), English scholastic philosopher.

7. Cf. Cicero, *De oratore* 1.42.187–88: "Almost all things now comprehended in the arts were once scattered and disordered. So in music, . . . in geometry, . . . in astronomy, . . . in grammar, all these things seemed unknown and without order. A certain art was therefore imposed on them from without . . . to tie together the disconnected and fragmentary material and delimit it in some kind of rational order" [translator's note]. Cicero (106–43 B.C.E), Roman statesman, orator, and author.

We have said that there are four branches of knowledge only, and that they contain all the rest: they are the theoretical, which strives for the contemplation of truth; the practical, which considers the regulation of morals; the mechanical, which supervises the occupations of this life; and the logical, which provides the knowledge necessary for correct speaking and clear argumentation.

* * *

From *Book Three*

CHAPTER THREE: WHICH ARTS ARE PRINCIPALLY TO BE READ

Out of all the sciences[8] above named, however, the ancients, in their studies, especially selected seven to be mastered by those who were to be educated. These seven they considered so to excel all the rest in usefulness that anyone who had been thoroughly schooled in them might afterward come to a knowledge of the others by his own inquiry and effort rather than by listening to a teacher. For these, one might say, constitute the best instruments, the best rudiments, by which the way is prepared for the mind's complete knowledge of philosophic truth. Therefore they are called by the name tri*vium* and quadri*vium*,[9] because by them, as by certain *ways* (*viae*), a quick mind enters into the secret places of wisdom.

In those days, no one was thought worthy the name of master who was unable to claim knowledge of these seven. Pythagoras,[1] too, is said to have maintained the following practice as a teacher: for seven years, according to the number of the seven liberal arts, no one of his pupils dared ask the reason behind statements made by him; instead, he was to give credence to the words of the master until he had heard him out, and then, having done this, he would be able to come at the reason of those things himself. We read that some men studied these seven with such zeal that they had them completely in memory, so that whatever writings they subsequently took in hand or whatever questions they proposed for solution or proof, they did not thumb the pages of books to hunt for rules and reasons which the liberal arts might afford for the resolution of a doubtful matter, but at once had the particulars ready by heart. Hence, it is a fact that in that time there were so many learned men that they alone wrote more than we are able to read. But the students of our day, whether from ignorance or from unwillingness, fail to hold to a fit method of study, and therefore we find many who study but few who are wise. Yet it seems to me that the student should take no less care not to expend his effort in useless studies than he should to avoid a lukewarm pursuit of good and useful ones. It is bad to pursue something good negligently; it is worse to expend many labors on an empty thing. But because not everyone is mature enough to know what is of advantage to him, I shall briefly indicate to the student which writings seem to me more useful than others, and then I shall add a few words on the method of study.

8. That Hugh uses the terms "art" and "science" interchangeably is evident from a comparison of the title and opening sentence of this chapter [translator's note].
9. A group of 4 studies consisting of arithmetic, music, geometry, and astronomy. "Trivium": a group of 3 studies consisting of grammar, rhetoric, and logic.
1. Greek philosopher and mathematician (6th c. B.C.E.).

CHAPTER EIGHT: CONCERNING ORDER IN EXPOUNDING A TEXT

One kind of order is observed in the disciplines, when I say, for instance, that grammar is more ancient than dialectic, or arithmetic comes before music; another kind in codices or anthologies, when I declare, for instance, that the Catilinarian orations are ahead of the *Jugurtha*;[2] another kind in narration, which moves in continuous series; and another kind in the exposition of a text.

Order in the disciplines is arranged to follow nature. In books it is arranged according to the person of the author or the nature of the subject matter.[3] In narration it follows an arrangement which is of two kinds—either natural, as when deeds are recounted in the order of their occurrence, or artificial, as when a subsequent event is related first and a prior event is told after it. In the exposition of a text, the order followed is adapted to inquiry.

Exposition includes three things: the letter, the sense, and the inner meaning. The letter is the fit arrangement of words, which we also call construction; the sense is a certain ready and obvious meaning which the letter presents on the surface; the inner meaning is the deeper understanding which can be found only through interpretation and commentary. Among these, the order of inquiry is first the letter, then the sense, and finally the inner meaning. And when this is done, the exposition is complete.

From *Book Five*

CHAPTER TWO: CONCERNING THE THREEFOLD UNDERSTANDING

First of all, it ought to be known that Sacred Scripture has three ways of conveying meaning—namely, history, allegory, and tropology.[4] To be sure, all things in the divine utterance must not be wrenched to an interpretation such that each of them is held to contain history, allegory, and tropology all at once. Even if a triple meaning can appropriately be assigned in many passages, nevertheless it is either difficult or impossible to see it everywhere. "On the zither and musical instruments of this type not all the parts which are handled ring out with musical sounds; only the strings do this. All the other things on the whole body of the zither are made as a frame to which may be attached, and across which may be stretched, those parts which the artist plays to produce sweetness of song."[5] Similarly, in the divine utterances are placed certain things which are intended to be understood spiritually only, certain things that emphasize the importance of moral conduct, and certain things said according to the simple sense of history. And yet, there

2. A history of the Jugurthine war in Rome, written by the Roman historian Sallust (ca. 86–ca. 35 B.C.E.). Catilinarian orations: a history of a conspiracy headed by the Roman statesman Cataline, also by Sallust. Hugh may be confusing Cicero's orations against Cataline with Sallust's *Bellum Catalinae*; however, his point is that we should study an author's texts in order.

3. That is, works may be selected for inclusion in a single codex either because they belong to a single author or connected group of authors, or because they treat a common subject [translator's note].

4. Unlike most medieval thinkers, Hugh leaves out the fourth, or anagogical, level of interpretation, the mystical sense concerned with the fate of souls after the Last Judgment (see, for example, Bernardus Silvestris, THOMAS AQUINAS, and DANTE).

5. Quoted verbatim from Isidore, *Quaestiones in Vetus Testamentum* Praefatio 4 (*Patrologia Latina*, v.82, p. 208), but independently applied by Hugh to Scripture [translator's note]. Isidore (ca. 570–636), Spanish prelate and scholar.

are some things which can suitably be expounded not only historically but allegorically and tropologically as well. Thus is it that, in a wonderful manner, all of Sacred Scripture is so suitably adjusted and arranged in all its parts through the Wisdom of God that whatever is contained in it either resounds with the sweetness of spiritual understanding in the manner of strings; or, containing utterances of mysteries set here and there in the course of a historical narrative or in the substance of a literal context, and, as it were, connecting these up into one object, it binds them together all at once as the wood does which curves under the taut strings; and, receiving their sound into itself, it reflects it more sweetly to our ears—a sound which the string alone has not yielded, but which the wood too has formed by the shape of its body. Thus also is honey more pleasing because enclosed in the comb, and whatever is sought with greater effort is also found with greater desire. It is necessary, therefore, so to handle the Sacred Scripture that we do not try to find history everywhere, nor allegory everywhere, nor tropology everywhere but rather that we assign individual things fittingly in their own places, as reason demands. Often, however, in one and the same literal context, all may be found together, as when a truth of history both hints at some mystical meaning by way of allegory, and equally shows by way of tropology how we ought to behave.

From *Book Six*

CHAPTER EIGHT: CONCERNING THE ORDER OF EXPOSITION

Exposition includes three things: the letter, the sense, and the deeper meaning (*sententia*). The letter is found in every discourse, for the very sounds are letters; but sense and a deeper meaning are not found together in every discourse. Some discourses contain only the letter and sense, some only the letter and a deeper meaning, some all these three together. But every discourse ought to contain at least two. That discourse in which something is so clearly signified by the mere telling that nothing else is left to be supplied for its understanding contains only letter and sense. But that discourse in which the hearer can conceive nothing from the mere telling unless an exposition is added thereto contains only the letter and a deeper meaning in which, on the one hand, something is plainly signified and, on the other, something else is left which must be supplied for its understanding and which is made clear by exposition.

CHAPTER NINE: CONCERNING THE LETTER

Sometimes the letter is perfect, when, in order to signify what is said, nothing more than what has been set down needs to be added or taken away—as, "All wisdom is from the Lord God";[6] sometimes it is compressed, when something is left which must be supplied—as, "The Ancient to the lady Elect";[7] sometimes it is in excess, when, either in order to inculcate an idea or because of a long parenthetical remark, the same thought is repeated or

6. Ecclesiasticus 1.1.
7. 2 John 1.1. John addresses his second epistle to "The elder unto the elect lady and her children, whom I love in the truth."

another and unnecessary one is added, as Paul, at the end of his Epistle to the Romans, says: "Now to him . . ." and then, after many parenthetical remarks, concludes, "to whom is honor and glory."[8] The other part of this passage seems to be in excess. I say "in excess," that is, not necessary for making the particular statement. Sometimes the literal text is such that unless it is stated in another form it seems to mean nothing or not to fit, as in the following: "The Lord, in heaven the throne of him,"[9] that is, "the throne of the Lord in heaven"; "the sons of men, the teeth of those are weapons and arrows,"[1] that is, "the teeth of the sons of men"; and "man, like grass the days of him,"[2] that is, "man's days": in these examples the nominative case of the noun and the genitive case of the pronoun are put for a single genitive of the noun; and there are many other things which are similar. To the letter belong construction and continuity.

CHAPTER TEN: CONCERNING THE SENSE

Some sense is fitting, other unfitting. Of unfitting sense, some is incredible, some impossible, some absurd, some false. You find many things of this kind in the Scriptures, like the following: "They have devoured Jacob."[3] And the following: "Under whom they stoop that bear up the world."[4] And the following: "My soul hath chosen hanging."[5] And there are many others.

There are certain places in Divine Scripture in which, although there is a clear meaning to the words, there nevertheless seems to be no sense, either because of an unaccustomed manner of expression or because of some circumstance which impedes the understanding of the reader, as is the case, for example, in that passage in which Isaias says: "In that day seven women shall take hold of one man, saying: We will eat our own bread, and wear our own apparel: only let us be called by thy name. Take away our reproach."[6] The words are plain and open. You understand well enough, "Seven women shall take hold of one man." You understand, "We will eat our own bread." You understand, "We will wear our own apparel." You understand, "Only let us be called by thy name." You understand, "Take away our reproach." But possibly you cannot understand what the sense of the whole thing together is. You do not know what the Prophet wanted to say, whether he promised good or threatened evil. For this reason it comes about that you think the passage, whose literal sense you do not see, has to be understood spiritually only. Therefore, you say that the seven women are the seven gifts of the Holy Spirit, and that these take hold of one man, that is, Christ, in whom it pleased all fulness of grace to dwell because he alone received these gifts without measure; and that he alone takes away their reproach so that they may find someone with whom to rest, because no one else alive asked for the gifts of the Holy Spirit.

See now, you have given a spiritual interpretation, and what the passage may mean to say literally you do not understand. But the Prophet could also

8. Romans 16.25–27.
9. Psalms 11.4 (psalms here are numbered as in the King James version).
1. Psalms 57.4.
2. Psalms 103.15.
3. Psalms 79.7.
4. Job 9.13.
5. Job 7.15. This and the previous example are adduced by Gregory the Great, *Moralium libri Epistula missoria* 3 (*Patrologia Latina* 75, 513 D), to show the impossibility of understanding all things in Scripture literally [translator's note]. Gregory (d. 604), pope and Father of the Church.
6. Isaiah 4.1.

mean something literal by these words.[7] For, since he had spoken above about the slaughter of the transgressing people, he now adds that so great would be the destruction of that same people and to such an extent were their men to be wiped out that seven women will hardly find one husband, for only one woman usually has one man; and, while now women are usually sought after by men, then, in contrary fashion, women will seek after men; and, so that one man may not hesitate to marry seven women at the same time, since he might not have the wherewithal to feed and clothe them, they say to him: "We will eat our own bread, and wear our own apparel." It will not be necessary for you to be concerned about our well-being, "only let us be called by thy name," so that you may be called our husband and *be* our husband so that we may not be heralded as rejected women, and die sterile, without children—which at that time was a great disgrace. And that is why they say, "Take away our reproach."

You find many things of this sort in the Scriptures, and especially in the Old Testament—things said according to the idiom of that language and which, although they are clear in that tongue, seem to mean nothing in our own.

CHAPTER ELEVEN: CONCERNING THE DEEPER MEANING

The divine deeper meaning can never be absurd, never false. Although in the sense, as has been said, many things are found to disagree, the deeper meaning admits no contradiction, is always harmonious, always true. Sometimes there is a single deeper meaning for a single expression; sometimes there are several deeper meanings for a single expression; sometimes there is a single deeper meaning for several expressions; sometimes there are several deeper meanings for several expressions. "When, therefore, we read the Divine Books, in such a great multitude of true concepts elicited from a few words and fortified by the sound rule of the catholic faith, let us prefer above all what it seems certain that the man we are reading thought. But if this is not evident, let us certainly prefer what the circumstances of the writing do not disallow and what is consonant with sound faith. But if even the circumstances of the writing cannot be explored and examined, let us at least prefer only what sound faith prescribes. For it is one thing not to see what the writer himself thought, another to stray from the rule of piety. If both these things are avoided, the harvest of the reader is a perfect one. But if both cannot be avoided, then, even though the will of the writer may be doubtful, it is not useless to have elicited a deeper meaning consonant with sound faith.[8] "So too, if, regarding matters which are obscure and farthest removed from our comprehension, we read some of the Divine Writings and find them susceptible, in sound faith, to many different meanings, let us not plunge ourselves into headlong assertion of any one of these meanings, so that if the truth is perhaps more carefully

7. The exclusively allegorical interpretation is Origen's; Jerome, in his commentary on Isaias, gives both a literal and allegorical interpretation; *Commentaria in Isaiam prophetam* 2.4 (*Patrologia Latina*, 24, 72–3) [translator's note]. Origen (185–232), a prolific early Christian writer, frequently cited by medieval authors. Jerome (ca. 340–420), Father of the Church, author of the Latin Vulgate translation of the Bible.

8. Quoted from Augustine, *The Literal Meaning of Genesis* (*De Genesis ad litteram*) 1.21 (*Patrologia Latina*, 34, 262) [translator's note]. AUGUSTINE (354–430), early Christian philosopher and Father of the Church.

opened up and destroys that meaning, we are overthrown; for so we should be battling not for the thought of the Divine Scriptures but for our own thought, and this is such a way that we wished the thought of the Scriptures to be identical with our own, whereas we ought rather to wish our thought identical with that of the Scriptures."[9]

ca. 1125

9. Quoted from Augustine, *The Literal Meaning of Genesis* 1.18 (*Patrologia Latina*, 34, 260) [translator's note].

MOSES MAIMONIDES (RABBI MOSES BEN MAIMON)

1135–1204

Moses Maimonides' *Guide of the Perplexed* brings into view what MATTHEW ARNOLD might call Hebraic ways of thinking about textual interpretation that continue to be relevant to literary theory today. As JACQUES DERRIDA declares in *Writing and Difference* (1967): "We live in the difference between the Jew and the Greek, which is perhaps the unity of what is called history." While Greek philosophy values the universal, the general, and the univocal, Jewish thought is more open to ambiguity, contradiction, and plurality of meaning. Where Greek thought separates interpretation from text, Jewish hermeneutics tends to see text and its interpretation as part of one process. Conflicts over these values have been central to contemporary debates, especially those on poststructuralism, even as the original theological issues that created them have become increasingly unfamiliar. Maimonides' importance for the Latin Middle Ages is twofold: he is among the handful of Jewish and Islamic scholars who reintroduced the works of ARISTOTLE, including Aristotelian literary criticism, to Europe; and he influenced Scholastic philosophers like THOMAS AQUINAS. But the significance of Jewish hermeneutics (the theory and practice of interpretation) for contemporary literary theory has not been as well understood as that of Christian hermeneutics, even though it is clear that Maimonides' methods of exegesis have strongly affected Jewish theorists who have shaped recent theoretical debates, such as SIGMUND FREUD, HAROLD BLOOM, and Derrida.

Maimonides resembles AUGUSTINE when he insists on the need for an allegorical interpretation of the Torah (the Jewish Scriptures). Like other Western theorists of interpretation, Maimonides worries about three principal problems: discovering the author's original intention, warding off ingenious overinterpretation, and finding deep as opposed to superficial meaning. And he too argues that esoteric meanings exist, though they can often only be glimpsed before fading back into obscurity—which, he believes, is as it should be. The meaning of sacred texts is not always accessible to the vulgar but can be understood only by the perfect (virtuous) person, one who is prone to being perplexed. This is the reader that Maimonides addresses.

Maimonides' approach will seem somewhat alien to students of a Western literary criticism based on Greek methods of interpretation—and their Christian derivatives—which separate the literary text from its commentary and which strive for a univocal, single, "correct" interpretation. Jewish hermeneutics, as exemplified by Maimonides' *Guide of the Perplexed*, treats text and interpretation as dual aspects of the same revelation that remains open to multiple textual meanings and endless indeterminacy.

Maimonides was born into an influential Jewish family in Cordova, in Muslim Spain, near the end of the *conviviencia*, the period from the eighth to the twelfth centuries when the three great religious cultures of the Middle Ages—Christian, Jewish, and Islamic—coexisted relatively peacefully on the Iberian Peninsula. His father, from whom he received his rabbinic instruction, was a noted Talmudist (a scholar of the collection of ancient Jewish law) as well as a mathematician and astronomer. In addition, Maimonides received a secular education from the most distinguished Arabic scholars of his day. He was thirteen years old when Cordova was captured by the Almohads, members of a fundamentalist Islamic sect, and his family was compelled to choose between Islam and exile. They chose the latter; after wandering around Spain for ten years, they took up residence in Fez in Morocco, where Maimonides devoted himself to studies in theology and medicine. Fez was also under the rule of the Almohads, and for a while the family tried to pass as Muslims. But Maimonides' growing reputation as a scholar (by sixteen he had already published a treatise on logical terminology) brought him under the scrutiny of the authorities. He was even tried for having lapsed from Islam, a capital crime; he escaped death only because an Arab friend interceded. In 1165 the family set sail for the Holy Land, then held by Christians. They finally settled in Egypt, where Maimonides lived for the rest of his life. In Cairo he went into business in precious stones; but when his brother, his business partner, was lost at sea with the family fortune, Maimonides turned to medicine to support himself, becoming physician to the court of the grand vizier. He describes his work there as grueling, yet in his spare time he became the unofficial leader of the Jewish community of Cairo, studied the Torah, and worked on his comprehensive code of Jewish law. His widespread reputation for learning made him one of the most celebrated Jews of the Middle Ages; England's King Richard invited Maimonides to become his royal physician. Maimonides' death was publicly mourned throughout the Jewish world, and his body was moved to the Holy Land, where his grave has been a pilgrimage site ever since.

Maimonides' writings are extensive and eclectic; they include lengthy and ambitious works in medicine, theology, and philosophy. He wrote several commentaries on traditional Jewish law. He began his *Commentary on the Mishnah* (1168)—the great legal code composed during the period between 10 and 220 C.E. that was designed to organize and regulate Jewish oral law—when he was just twenty-three, completing it ten years later. A second collection, the massive *Mishneh Torah* (1178), was meant to provide a complete classification of rabbinic law. This alone would have been an unprecedented undertaking; but the *Mishneh Torah* is more than simply a law code. In it Maimonides also included many interpretations, passages of exegesis, historical surveys, and explanations of difficult phrases and concepts. *The Guide of the Perplexed* (1190) turns from the codification of religious law to "the science of the law in its true sense." In this wide-ranging and occasionally baffling treatise, Maimonides attempts to reconcile faith with philosophical reason, Judaism with a newly recovered Aristotelianism. More specifically, he wants to demonstrate that Judaism is not irreconcilable with the understanding of physics and metaphysics articulated by the twelfth-century Aristotelians. In the course of his introduction, he argues that when their "internal" sense is properly understood, the *Account of the Beginning* (the Genesis story) refers to "natural science" (physics) and *The Account of the Chariot* (Ezekiel 1 and 10) to "divine science" (metaphysics).

Ostensibly written for his disciple, Joseph ben Judah, *The Guide* elucidates obscure parables and terms found in "the books of the prophets." Maimonides, whose interpretive skills were honed by his extensive investigations of the Mishnah, argues that to penetrate the meaning of Scriptures and the Talmud (the great collections of oral law compiled between the second and fifth centuries C.E.) requires a fully elaborated method of interpretation (a hermeneutic). In his introduction, he explains that the failures to understand (1) the polysemy (many meanings) of biblical language and (2) the biblical use of obscure parables (which maintain the secrets of divine knowledge) give rise to "perplexity" even in the learned. Significantly, biblical texts are full of terms that are difficult to understand because they are "equivocal"—they have more than one meaning; or "derivative"—they contain supplemental meanings derived from other terms; or "amphibolus"—they are understood as having sometimes one and sometimes many meanings. Maimonides illustrates his discussions with frequent quotations from the Bible.

A purely linguistic comprehension of the richness of biblical language, according to Maimonides, is insufficient for understanding the Torah and Talmud, for these texts are also full of parables designed to obscure the "secrets of the prophetic books." Such an understanding requires a more fully elaborated theory of narrative, which Maimonides sketches in his introduction, including a key distinction between those parables that must be interpreted word by word and those that must be interpreted holistically.

For Maimonides, contradictions, far from being philosophical flaws, are to be embraced and studied according to principles he sets forth at the end of the introduction, where he identifies seven types. Perhaps the most interesting of the contradictions in Maimonides' own hermeneutic is the essential tension in his introduction between the injunction to secrecy—his understanding that the secrets of that divine science "ought not to be taught even to one man, except if he be wise and able to understand by himself, in which case only the chapter headings may be transmitted to him"—and the need to pass those secrets from generation to generation by teaching them to others. In the context of a close-knit and homogeneous community, it might be possible to preserve secret knowledge by passing it on orally from teacher to student, master to disciple. But in the context of the Jewish Diaspora, which could separate teacher from pupil—as happened to Maimonides and his disciple Joseph—written texts become necessary for organizing and preserving such knowledge, even while running the risk that the teacher "in effect would be teaching them to thousands of men." To preserve from the ignorant and the vulgar "those truths especially requisite for [the pupil's] apprehension," Maimonides must adopt the very techniques of the texts he seeks to explain: he must conceal them by scattering them throughout the treatise and entangling them with contradictions so that the truths are "glimpsed and then again concealed."

Insofar as Maimonides' interpretive method strikes the modern student of literary criticism as perhaps too esoteric to illuminate literary issues, that response may suggest the extent to which Greek modes of thinking have determined Western literary criticism. Yet Jewish hermeneutics has continued to exert at least a covert influence on the development of the dominant tradition. Although it was translated from its original Arabic into Hebrew and Latin during the Middle Ages, *The Guide of the Perplexed* was, ironically, not eagerly accepted within the Jewish community, because it advocated the study of philosophy alongside the more important study of the Torah. But in the century following his death, Maimonides' influence spread widely among Jews and Christians alike. Maimonides and his famous predecessor Rashi (Rabbi Solomon ben Isaac, 1040–1105, a talmudic scholar from Troyes) were both important precursors of the Scholasticism of the High Middle Ages, affecting Christian exegetes such as HUGH OF ST. VICTOR and Thomas Aquinas. There are also elements in later Freudian analysis that elaborate and extend the rabbinic hermeneutics articulated by Maimonides. Finally, many of the issues that interest contemporary literary theorists such as Derrida and his Yale School disciples, most notably Harold Bloom—for example, the indeterminacy of interpretation or the continuity between literary text and interpretation—show the influence of Jewish approaches to interpretation.

BIBLIOGRAPHY

The modern Arabic edition of *The Guide of the Perplexed* (*Dalalat al-Ha'irin*) was compiled in 1929 by S. Munk and translated into English by Shlomo Pines (1963);

Joseph Kafih's three-volume edition (1972) offers parallel Arabic and Hebrew versions. Large sections of the *Mishneh Torah* as well as other writings by Maimonides are available in English translation in *The Maimonides Reader*, edited by Isadore Twersky (1972). The standard biography is Abraham Joshua Heschel's *Maimonides: A Biography* (1981). Leo Strauss's essay "The Literary Character of *The Guide for the Perplexed*," originally included in *Essays on Maimonides: An Octocentennial Volume* (ed. Salo W. Baron, 1941) and later reprinted in *Maimonides: A Collection of Critical Essays* (ed. Joseph A. Buijs, 1988), is an indispensable introduction to Maimonides' method in *The Guide*. In *Maimonides and Aquinas: A Contemporary Appraisal* (1979), Jacob Haberman documents Maimonides' contributions to medieval thought, while Susan A. Handelman, in *The Slayers of Moses: The Emergence of Rabbinic Interpretation in Modern Literary Theory* (1982), examines the relationship between early Jewish biblical hermeneutics and contemporary deconstructive literary theory. The collection of essays edited by Geoffrey H. Hartman and Sanford Budick, *Midrash and Literature* (1986), also examines the relationships between Jewish hermeneutics and literary theory. A excellent bibliography is appended to Buijs's *Maimonides* (cited above).

From The Guide of the Perplexed[1]

[*Introduction to the First Part*]

Cause me to know the way wherein I should walk,
For unto Thee have I lifted my soul.[2]

Unto you, O men, I call,
And my voice is to the sons of men.[3]

Incline thine ear, and hear the words of the wise,
And apply thy heart unto my knowledge.[4]

The first purpose of this Treatise is to explain the meanings of certain terms occurring in books of prophecy. Some of these terms are equivocal; hence the ignorant attribute to them only one or some of the meanings in which the term in question is used. Others are derivative terms; hence they attribute to them only the original meaning from which the other meaning is derived. Others are amphibolous terms,[5] so that at times they are believed to be univocal and at other times equivocal. It is not the purpose of this Treatise to make its totality understandable to the vulgar or to beginners in speculation, nor to teach those who have not engaged in any study other than the science of the Law—I mean the legalistic study of the Law. For the purpose of this Treatise and of all those like it is the science of Law in its true sense.[6] Or rather its purpose is to give indications to a religious man for whom the validity of our Law has become established in his soul and has become actual in his belief—such a man being perfect in his religion and character, and

1. Translated by Shlomo Pines, who occasionally supplies explanatory text in brackets.
2. Psalms 143.8.
3. Proverbs 8.4.
4. Proverbs 22.17.
5. Words understood as having sometimes one meaning and sometimes many meanings. "Equivocal": words with more than one meaning. "Derivative": words containing supplemental meanings derived from other words; words used figuratively.
6. In an earlier work, the *Mishneh Torah* (literally, "repetition of the Torah"), Maimonides collected, organized, and commented on the oral rabbinic law—called the Mishnah—that had evolved in the first centuries of the common era. In *The Guide of the Perplexed*, he turns his attention to the relationship between Jewish law and philosophy as well as to interpretive theory.

having studied the sciences of the philosophers and come to know what they signify. The human intellect having drawn him on and led him to dwell within its province, he must have felt distressed by the externals of the Law and by the meanings of the above-mentioned equivocal, derivative, or amphibolous terms, as he continued to understand them by himself or was made to understand them by others. Hence he would remain in a state of perplexity and confusion as to whether he should follow his intellect, renounce what he knew concerning the terms in question, and consequently consider that he has renounced the foundations of the Law. Or he should hold fast to his understanding of these terms and not let himself be drawn on together with his intellect, rather turning his back on it and moving away from it, while at the same time perceiving that he had brought loss to himself and harm to his religion. He would be left with those imaginary beliefs to which he owes his fear and difficulty and would not cease to suffer from heartache and great perplexity.

This Treatise also has a second purpose: namely, the explanation of very obscure parables occurring in the books of the prophets, but not explicitly identified there as such. Hence an ignorant or heedless individual might think that they possess only an external sense, but no internal one. However, even when one who truly possesses knowledge considers these parables and interprets them according to their external meaning, he too is overtaken by great perplexity. But if we explain these parables to him or if we draw his attention to their being parables, he will take the right road and be delivered from this perplexity. That is why I have called this Treatise "The Guide of the Perplexed."

I do not say that this Treatise will remove all difficulties for those who understand it. I do, however, say that it will remove most of the difficulties, and those of the greatest moment. A sensible man thus should not demand of me or hope that when we mention a subject, we shall make a complete exposition of it, or that when we engage in the explanation of the meaning of one of the parables, we shall set forth exhaustively all that is expressed in that parable. An intelligent man would be unable to do so even by speaking directly to an interlocutor. How then could he put it down in writing without becoming a butt for every ignoramus who, thinking that he has the necessary knowledge, would let fly at him the shafts of his ignorance? We have already explained in our legal compilations some general propositions concerning this subject and have drawn attention to many themes. Thus we have mentioned there that the *Account of the Beginning*[7] is identical with natural science, and the *Account of the Chariot*[8] with divine science; and have explained the rabbinic saying: *The Account of the Chariot ought not to be taught even to one man, except if he be wise and able to understand by himself, in which case only the chapter headings may be transmitted to him.*[9] Hence you should not ask of me here anything beyond *the chapter headings*. And

7. Literally, the *Work of the Beginning* [translator's note]. That is, the Genesis story.
8. Literally, the *Work of the Chariot* [translator's note]. That is, Ezekiel 1 and 10.
9. From the Babylonian Talmud, Hagigah, 11b, 13a [translator's note]. The Babylonian Talmud is one of the two great Talmuds, or collections of oral law; it was compiled between the 2d and 5th centuries C.E. (the Jerusalem Talmud was compiled between 220 C.E. and the end of the 4th c.). It is divided into six Orders; each Order has a number of tractates. Hagigah is one of the tractates, which are further divided into chapters and then paragraphs. More generally, the Talmud is divided into the Mishnah, which states the law, and the Gemara, which presents the discussion of it.

even those are not set down in order or arranged in coherent fashion in this Treatise, but rather are scattered and entangled with other subjects that are to be clarified. For my purpose is that the truths be glimpsed and then again be concealed, so as not to oppose that divine purpose which one cannot possibly oppose and which has concealed from the vulgar among the people those truths especially requisite for His apprehension. As He has said: *The secret of the Lord is with them that fear Him.*[1] Know that with regard to natural matters as well, it is impossible to give a clear exposition when teaching some of their principles as they are. For you know the saying of [the Sages], *may their memory be blessed: The Account of the Beginning ought not to be taught in the presence of two men.*[2] Now if someone explained all those matters in a book, he in effect would be *teaching* them to thousands of men. Hence these matters too occur in parables in the books of prophecy. The *Sages, may their memory be blessed*, following the trail of these books, likewise have spoken of them in riddles and parables, for there is a close connection between these matters and the divine science, and they too are secrets of that divine science.

You should not think that these great *secrets* are fully and completely known to anyone among us. They are not. But sometimes truth flashes out to us so that we think that it is day, and then matter and habit in their various forms conceal it so that we find ourselves again in an obscure night, almost as we were at first. We are like someone in a very dark night over whom lightning flashes time and time again. Among us there is one[3] for whom the lightning flashes time and time again, so that he is always, as it were, in unceasing light. Thus night appears to him as day. That is the degree of the great one among the prophets, to whom it was said: *But as for thee, stand thou here by Me,*[4] and of whom it was said: *that the skin of his face sent forth beams, and so on.*[5] Among them there is one to whom the lightning flashes only once in the whole of his night; that is the rank of those of whom it is said: *they prophesied, but they did so no more.*[6] There are others between whose lightning flashes there are greater or shorter intervals. Thereafter comes he who does not attain a degree in which his darkness is illumined by any lightning flash. It is illumined, however, by a polished body or something of that kind, stones or something else that give light in the darkness of the night. And even this small light that shines over us is not always there, but flashes and is hidden again, as if it were the *flaming sword which turned every way.*[7] It is in accord with these states that the degrees of the perfect vary. As for those who never even once see a light, but grope about in their night, of them it is said: *They know not, neither do they understand; They go about in darkness.*[8] The truth, in spite of the strength of its manifestation, is entirely hidden from them, as is said of them: *And now men see not the light which is bright in the skies.*[9] They are the vulgar among the people. There is then no occasion to mention them here in this Treatise.

Know that whenever one of the perfect wishes to mention, either orally or in writing, something that he understands of these *secrets*, according to the degree of his perfection, he is unable to explain with complete clarity and

1. Psalm 25.14.
2. Babylonian Talmud, Hagigah, 11b.
3. Or: there are those [translator's note].
4. Deuteronomy 5.31.
5. Exodus 34.29.
6. Numbers 11.25.
7. Genesis 3.24.
8. Psalm 82.5.
9. Job 37.21.

coherence even the portion that he has apprehended, as he could do with the other sciences whose teaching is generally recognized. Rather there will befall him when teaching another that which he had undergone when learning himself. I mean to say that the subject matter will appear, flash, and then be hidden again, as though this were the nature of this subject matter, be there much or little of it. For this reason, all the Sages possessing knowledge of God the Lord, knowers of the truth, when they aimed at teaching something of this subject matter, spoke of it only in parables and riddles. They even multiplied the parables and made them different in species and even in genus. In most cases the subject to be explained was placed in the beginning or in the middle or at the end of the parable; this happened where a parable appropriate for the intended subject from start to finish could not be found. Sometimes the subject intended to be taught to him who was to be instructed was divided—although it was one and the same subject—among many parables remote from one another. Even more obscure is the case of one and the same parable corresponding to several subjects, its beginning fitting one subject and its ending another. Sometimes the whole is a parable referring to two cognate subjects within the particular species of science in question. The situation is such that the exposition of one who wishes to teach without recourse to parables and riddles is so obscure and brief as to make obscurity and brevity serve in place of parables and riddles. The men of knowledge and the sages[1] are drawn, as it were, toward this purpose by the divine will just as they are drawn by their natural circumstances. Do you not see the following fact? God, may His mention be exalted, wished us to be perfected and the state of our societies to be improved by His laws regarding actions. Now this can come about only after the adoption of intellectual beliefs, the first of which being His apprehension, may He be exalted, according to our capacity. This, in its turn, cannot come about except through divine science, and this divine science cannot become actual except after a study of natural science. This is so since natural science borders on divine science, and its study precedes that of divine science in time as has been made clear to whoever has engaged in speculation on these matters. Hence God, may He be exalted, caused His book to open with the *Account of the Beginning*, which, as we have made clear, is natural science. And because of the greatness and importance of the subject and because our capacity falls short of apprehending the greatest of subjects as it really is, we are told about those profound matters—which divine wisdom has deemed necessary to convey to us—in parables and riddles and in very obscure words. As [the Sages], *may their memory be blessed*, have said: *It is impossible to tell mortals*[2] *of the power of the Account of the Beginning. For this reason Scripture tells you obscurely: In the beginning God created, and so on.*[3] They thus have drawn your attention to the fact that the above-mentioned subjects are *obscure*. You likewise know *Solomon's* saying: *That which was is far off, and exceeding deep; who can find it out?*[4] That which is said about all this is in

1. The Arabic term *al-ḥukamā'* often designates the philosophers [translator's note].
2. Literally, flesh and blood [translator's note].
3. Cf. Midrash Shnei Ketubim, Batei Midrashoth, IV [translator's note]. Midrash: literally, "to seek out the meaning" (Hebrew); an explanation of a text from the Torah (the 5 books of Moses; more generally known as the first 5 books of the Old Testament). The term may refer to a collection of such explanations or to a hermeneutic technique by which such explanations are produced. A midrash might explain a single word or a gap in the text. There are midrashim for every book of the Torah, and Maimonides here refers to a midrash on Genesis.
4. Ecclesiastes 7.24.

equivocal terms so that the multitude might comprehend them in accord with the capacity of their understanding and the weakness of their representation, whereas the perfect man, who is already informed, will comprehend them otherwise.

We had promised in the Commentary on the *Mishnah* that we would explain strange subjects in the "Book of Prophecy" and in the "Book of Correspondence"—the latter being a book in which we promised to explain all the difficult passages in the *Midrashim*[5] where the external sense manifestly contradicts the truth and departs from the intelligible. They are all parables. However, when, many years ago, we began these books and composed a part of them, our beginning to explain matters in this way did not commend itself to us. For we saw that if we should adhere to parables and to concealment of what ought to be concealed, we would not be deviating from the primary purpose. We would, as it were, have replaced one individual by another of the same species. If, on the other hand, we explained what ought to be explained, it would be unsuitable for the vulgar among the people. Now it was to the vulgar that we wanted to explain the import of the *Midrashim* and the external meanings of prophecy. We also saw that if an ignoramus among the multitude of Rabbanites[6] should engage in speculation on these *Midrashim*, he would find nothing difficult in them, inasmuch as a rash fool, devoid of any knowledge of the nature of being, does not find impossibilities hard to accept. If, however, a perfect man of virtue should engage in speculation on them, he cannot escape one of two courses: either he can take the speeches in question in their external sense and, in so doing, think ill of their author and regard him as an ignoramus—in this there is nothing that would upset the foundations of belief; or he can attribute to them an inner meaning, thereby extricating himself from his predicament and being able to think well of the author whether or not the inner meaning of the saying is clear to him. With regard to the meaning of prophecy, the exposition of its various degrees, and the elucidation of the parables occurring in the prophetic books, another manner of explanation is used in this Treatise. In view of these considerations, we have given up composing these two books in the way in which they were begun. We have confined ourselves to mentioning briefly the foundations of belief and general truths, while dropping hints that approach a clear exposition, just as we have set them forth in the great legal compilation, *Mishneh Torah*.[7]

My speech in the present Treatise is directed, as I have mentioned, to one who has philosophized and has knowledge of the true sciences, but believes at the same time in the matters pertaining to the Law and is perplexed as to their meaning because of the uncertain terms and the parables. We shall include in this Treatise some chapters in which there will be no mention of an equivocal term. Such a chapter will be preparatory for another, or it will hint at one of the meanings of an equivocal term that I might not wish to mention explicitly in that place, or it will explain one of the parables or hint

5. Maimonides uses here and subsequently the term *drashoth* [translator's note]. The Hebrew term (singular *derash* or *derasha*) refers to the meanings derived from the original text by means of a variety of rabbinic techniques.

6. Tenth-century teachers who began to use philosophy to supplement the written Torah and the oral Torah (Talmud) as a defense against rationalism. Though their philosophical thinking was not as sophisticated as Maimonides' use of Aristotle, they paved the way for him and other Jewish philosophers.

7. Maimonides' massive compilation of Jewish rabbinic law, written a decade before *The Guide of the Perplexed*.

at the fact that a certain story is a parable. Such a chapter may contain strange matters regarding which the contrary of the truth sometimes is believed, either because of the equivocality of the terms or because a parable is taken for the thing being represented or vice versa.

As I have mentioned parables, we shall make the following introductory remarks: Know that the key to the understanding of all that the prophets, peace be on them, have said, and to the knowledge of its truth, is an understanding of the parables, of their import, and of the meaning of the words occurring in them. You know what God, may He be exalted, has said: *And by the ministry of the prophets have I used similitudes.*[8] And you know that He has said: *Put forth a riddle and speak a parable.*[9] You know too that because of the frequent use prophets make of parables, the prophet has said: *They say of me: Is he not a maker of parables?*[1] You know how *Solomon* began his book: *To understand a proverb, and a figure; The words of the wise, and their dark sayings.*[2] And it said in the *Midrash: To what were the words of the Torah to be compared before the advent of Solomon? To a well the waters of which are at a great depth and cool, yet no man could drink of them. Now what did one clever man do? He joined cord with cord and rope with rope and drew them up and drank. Thus did Solomon say one parable after another and speak one word after another until he understood the meaning of the words of the Torah.*[3] That is literally what they say. I do not think that anyone possessing an unimpaired capacity imagines that the *words of the Torah* referred to here that one contrives to understand through understanding the meaning of parables are ordinances concerning the building of *tabernacles*, the *lulab*, and the *law of four trustees.*[4] Rather what this text has in view here is, without any doubt, the understanding of obscure matters. About this it has been said: *Our Rabbis say: a man who loses a sela or a pearl in his house can find the pearl by lighting a taper worth an issar.*[5] *In the same way this parable in itself is worth nothing, but by means of it you can understand the words of the Torah.*[6] This too is literally what they say. Now consider the explicit affirmation of [the Sages], *may their memory be blessed*, that the internal meaning of the *words of the Torah* is a *pearl* whereas the external meaning of all parables *is* worth *nothing*, and their comparison of the concealment of a subject by its parable's external meaning to a man who let drop a pearl in his house, which was dark and full of furniture. Now this pearl is there, but he does not see it and does not know where it is. It is as though it were no longer in his possession, as it is impossible for him to derive any benefit from it until, as has been mentioned, he lights a lamp—an act to which an understanding of the meaning of the parable corresponds. The Sage has said: *A word fitly spoken is like apples of gold in settings [maskiyyoth] of silver.*[7] Hear now an

8. Hosea 12.10.
9. Ezekiel 17.2.
1. Ezekiel 20.49.
2. Proverbs 1.6. Proverbs is one of the books of the Bible traditionally ascribed to Solomon.
3. Cf. Midrash on the Song of Songs, 1.1 [translator's note].
4. Maimonides, contrasting those parts of the Torah that can be taken as parables with those that are completely straightforward (not in need of special interpretation), gives three examples of straightforward ordinances. "Tabernacle": a sukkah or building constructed during the holiday of Sukkoth, which occurs after the High Holy Days and commemorates the Jews' wandering in the desert. "Lulab": a wand of sorts, fashioned of palm leaves, willow, and myrtle and waved in four directions during the holiday of Sukkoth. "The law of the four trustees": the four categories of legal guardian over someone else's property, which include the unpaid guardian, the borrower, the paid guardian, and the hirer.
5. A coin; ninety-six *issar* were worth a *sela*. "A *sela*": a silver coin [translator's note].
6. Cf. Midrash on the Song of Songs, 1.1 [translator's note].
7. Proverbs 25.11.

elucidation of the thought that he has set forth. The term *maskiyyoth* denotes filigree traceries; I mean to say traceries in which there are apertures with very small eyelets, like the handiwork of silversmiths. They are so called because a glance penetrates through them; for in the [Aramaic] *translation* of the Bible the Hebrew term *va-yashqeph*—meaning, he glanced—is translated *va-istekhe.*[8] The Sage accordingly said that a saying uttered with a view to two meanings is like an apple of gold overlaid with silver filigree-work having very small holes. Now see how marvellously this dictum describes a well-constructed parable. For he says that in a saying that has two meanings—he means an external and an internal one—the external meaning ought to be as beautiful as silver, while its internal meaning ought to be more beautiful than the external one, the former being in comparison to the latter as gold is to silver. Its external meaning also ought to contain in it something that indicates to someone considering it what is to be found in its internal meaning, as happens in the case of an apple of gold overlaid with silver filigree-work having very small holes. When looked at from a distance or with imperfect attention, it is deemed to be an apple of silver; but when a keen-sighted observer looks at it with full attention, its interior becomes clear to him and he knows that it is of gold. The parables of the prophets, peace be on them, are similar. Their external meaning contains wisdom that is useful in many respects, among which is the welfare of human societies, as is shown by the external meaning of *Proverbs* and of similar sayings. Their internal meaning, on the other hand, contains wisdom that is useful for beliefs concerned with the truth as it is.

Know that the prophetic parables are of two kinds. In some of these parables each word has a meaning, while in others the parable as a whole indicates the whole of the intended meaning. In such a parable very many words are to be found, not every one of which adds something to the intended meaning. They serve rather to embellish the parable and to render it more coherent or to conceal further the intended meaning; hence the speech proceeds in such a way as to accord with everything required by the parable's external meaning. Understand this well.

An example of the first kind of prophetic parable is the following text: *And behold a ladder set up on the earth, and so on.*[9] In this text, the word *ladder* indicates one subject; the words *set up on the earth* indicate a second subject; the words *and the top of it reached to heaven* indicate a third subject; the words *and behold the angels of God* indicate a fourth subject; the word *ascending* indicates a fifth subject; the words *and descending* indicate a sixth subject; and the words *And behold the Lord stood above it* indicate a seventh subject. Thus every word occurring in this parable refers to an additional subject in the complex of subjects represented by the parable as a whole.

An example of the second kind of prophetic parable is the following text: *For at the window of my house I looked forth through my lattice; And I beheld among the thoughtless ones, I discerned among the youths, A young man void of understanding, Passing through the street near her corner, And he went the way to her house; In the twilight, in the evening of the day, In the blackness*

8. A verbal form deriving from the same root as the word *maskiyyoth.* Genesis 26.8 [translator's note].

9. Genesis 28.12–13. After the word *earth,* the verses read: *and the top of it reached to heaven; and behold the angels of God ascending and descending on it. And behold the Lord stood above it* [translator's note].

of night and the darkness. And, behold, there met him a woman With the attire of a harlot, and wily of heart. She is riotous and rebellious, and so on.[1] *Now she is in the streets, now in the broad places, and so on.*[2] *So she caught him, and so on.*[3] *Sacrifices of peace-offerings were due from me, and so on.*[4] *Therefore came I forth to meet thee, and so on.*[5] *I have decked with the coverlets, and so on.*[6] *I have perfumed my bed, and so on.*[7] *Come, let us take our fill of love, and so on.*[8] *For my husband is not at home, and so on.*[9] *The bag of money, and so on.*[1] *With her much fair speech she causeth him to yield. With the blandishment of her lips she enticeth him away.*[2] The outcome of all this is a warning against the pursuit of bodily pleasures and desires. Accordingly he [Solomon] likens matter, which is the cause of all these bodily pleasures, *to a harlot* who is also a *married woman.* In fact his entire book is based on this allegory. And we shall explain in various chapters of this Treatise his wisdom in likening matter to a *married harlot,* and we shall explain how he concluded this book of his with a eulogy of the *woman* who is not a *harlot* but confines herself to attending to the welfare of her household and husband. For all the hindrances keeping man from his ultimate perfection, every deficiency affecting him and every disobedience, come to him from his matter alone, as we shall explain in this Treatise. This is the proposition that can be understood from this parable as a whole. I mean that man should not follow his bestial nature; I mean his matter, for the proximate matter of man is identical with the proximate matter of the other living beings. And as I have explained this to you and disclosed the secret of this parable, you should not hope [to find some signification corresponding to every subject occurring in the parable][3] so that you could say: what can be submitted for the words, *Sacrifices of peace-offerings were due from me; this day have I paid my vows?* What subject is indicated by the words, *I have decked my couch with coverlets?* And what subject is added to this general proposition by the words, *For my husband is not at home?* The same holds good for the other details in this *chapter.* For all of them only figure in the consistent development of the parable's external meaning, the circumstances described in it being of a kind typical for adulterers. Also the spoken words and other such details are of a kind typical of words spoken among adulterers. Understand this well from what I have said for it is a great and important principle with regard to matters that I wish to explain.

When, therefore, you find that in some chapter of this Treatise I have explained the meaning of a parable and have drawn your attention to the general proposition signified by it, you should not inquire into all the details occurring in the parable, nor should you wish to find significations corre-

1. The omitted words are: *her feet abide not in her house* [translator's note].
2. The omitted words are: *and lieth in wait at every corner* [translator's note].
3. The omitted words are: *and kissed him, and with impudent face she said unto him* [translator's note].
4. The omitted words are: *this day have I paid my vows* [translator's note].
5. The omitted words are: *diligently to seek thy face, and I have found thee* [translator's note].
6. The omitted words are: *my bed, with striped cloths of the yarn of Egypt* [translator's note].
7. The omitted words are: *with myrrh, aloes and cinnamon* [translator's note].
8. The omitted words are: *until the morning; let us solace ourselves with loves* [translator's note].
9. The omitted words are: *he is gone a long journey* [translator's note].
1. The omitted words are: *he has taken with him, and will come home at the full moon* [translator's note].
2. Proverbs 7.6–21.
3. The words enclosed in brackets appear in Ibn Tibbon's Hebrew translation, but not in the printed Arabic text. There is little doubt that in this case Ibn Tibbon's text is more correct [translator's note].

sponding to them. For doing so would lead you into one of two ways: either into turning aside from the parable's intended subject, or into assuming an obligation to interpret things not susceptible of interpretation and that have not been inserted with a view to interpretation. The assumption of such an obligation would result in extravagant fantasies such as are entertained and written about in our time by most of the sects of the world, since each of these sects desires to find certain significations for words whose author in no wise had in mind the significations wished by them. Your purpose, rather, should always be to know, regarding most parables, the whole that was intended to be known. In some matters it will suffice you to gather from my remarks that a given story is a parable, even if we explain nothing more; for once you know it is a parable, it will immediately become clear to you what it is a parable of. My remarking that it is a parable will be like someone's removing a screen from between the eye and a visible thing.

INSTRUCTION WITH RESPECT TO THIS TREATISE

If you wish to grasp the totality of what this Treatise contains, so that nothing of it will escape you, then you must connect its chapters one with another; and when reading a given chapter, your intention must be not only to understand the totality of the subject of that chapter, but also to grasp each word that occurs in it in the course of the speech, even if that word does not belong to the intention of the chapter. For the diction of this Treatise has not been chosen at haphazard, but with great exactness and exceeding precision, and with care to avoid failing to explain any obscure point. And nothing has been mentioned out of its place, save with a view to explaining some matter in its proper place. You therefore should not let your fantasies elaborate on what is said here, for that would hurt me and be of no use to yourself. You ought rather to learn everything that ought to be learned and constantly study this Treatise. For it then will elucidate for you most of the obscurities of the Law that appear as difficult to every intelligent man. I adjure—by God, may He be exalted!—every reader of this Treatise of mine not to comment upon a single word of it and not to explain to another anything in it save that which has been explained and commented upon in the words of the famous Sages of our Law who preceded me. But whatever he understands from this Treatise of those things that have not been said by any of our famous Sages other than myself should not be explained to another; nor should he hasten to refute me, for that which he understood me to say might be contrary to my intention. He thus would harm me in return for my having wanted to benefit him and would *repay evil for good.*[4] All into whose hands it falls should consider it well; and if it slakes his thirst, though it be on only one point from among the many that are obscure, he should thank God and be content with what he has understood. If, on the other hand, he finds nothing in this Treatise that might be of use to him in any respect, he should think of it as not having been composed at all. If anything in it, according to his way of thinking, appears to be in some way harmful, he should interpret it, even if in a farfetched way, in order to *pass a favorable judgment.*[5] For as we are enjoined to act in this way toward our vulgar ones, all the more should

4. Psalm 38.20.
5. Cf. Mishnah, Aboth, I 6 [translator's note]. Aboth, meaning literally "Father," is a tractate of the Mishnah.

this be so with respect to our erudite ones and Sages of our Law who are trying to help us to the truth as they apprehend it. I know that, among men generally, every beginner will derive benefit from some of the chapters of this Treatise, though he lacks even an inkling of what is involved in speculation. A perfect man, on the other hand, devoted to Law and, as I have mentioned, perplexed, will benefit from all its chapters. How greatly will he rejoice in them and how pleasant will it be to hear them! But those who are confused and whose brains have been polluted by false opinions and misleading ways deemed by them to be true sciences, and who hold themselves to be men of speculation without having any knowledge of anything that can truly be called science,[6] those will flee from many of its chapters. Indeed, these chapters will be very difficult for them to bear because they cannot apprehend their meaning and also because they would be led to recognize the falseness of the counterfeit money in their hands—their treasure and fortune held ready for future calamities. God, may He be exalted, knows that I have never ceased to be exceedingly apprehensive about setting down those things that I wish to set down in this Treatise. For they are concealed things; none of them has been set down in any book—written in the religious community[7] in these times of *Exile*—the books composed in these times being in our hands. How then can I now innovate and set them down? However, I have relied on two premises, the one being [the Sages'] saying in a similar case, *It is time to do something for the Lord, and so on;*[8] the second being their saying, *Let all thy acts be for the sake of Heaven.*[9] Upon these two premises have I relied when setting down what I have composed in some of the chapters of this Treatise.

To sum up: I am the man who when the concern pressed him and his way was straitened and he could find no other device by which to teach a demonstrated truth other than by giving satisfaction to a single virtuous man while displeasing ten thousand ignoramuses—I am he who prefers to address that single man by himself, and I do not heed the blame of those many creatures. For I claim to liberate that virtuous one from that into which he has sunk, and I shall guide him in his perplexity until he becomes perfect and he finds rest.

INTRODUCTION

One of seven causes should account for the contradictory or contrary statements to be found in any book or compilation.

The first cause. The author has collected the remarks of various people with differing opinions, but has omitted citing his authorities and has not attributed each remark to the one who said it. Contradictory or contrary statements can be found in such compilations because one of the two propositions is the opinion of one individual while the other proposition is the opinion of another individual.

6. In this phrase the same Arabic term is translated by two words: "knowledge" and "science" [translator's note].
7. Meaning the Jewish community [translator's note].
8. The verse continues as follows: *for they have infringed Thy Law.* Psalms 119.126; cf. Babylonian Talmud, Berakhoth, 63 [translator's note]. Berakhoth: a tractate of the Talmud.
9. Mishnah, Aboth, II 17.

The second cause. The author of a particular book has adopted a certain opinion that he later rejects; both his original and later statements are retained in the book.

The third cause. Not all the statements in question are to be taken in their external sense; some are to be taken in their external sense, while some others are parables and hence have an inner content. Alternatively, two apparently contradictory propositions may both be parables and when taken in their external sense may contradict, or be contrary to, one another.

The fourth cause. There is a proviso that, because of a certain necessity, has not been explicitly stated in its proper place; or the two subjects may differ, but one of them has not been explained in its proper place, so that a contradiction appears to have been said, whereas there is no contradiction.

The fifth cause arises from the necessity of teaching and making someone understand. For there may be a certain obscure matter that is difficult to conceive. One has to mention it or to take it as a premise in explaining something that is easy to conceive and that by rights ought to be taught before the former, since one always begins with what is easier. The teacher, accordingly, will have to be lax and, using any means that occur to him or gross speculation, will try to make that first matter somehow understood. He will not undertake to state the matter as it truly is in exact terms, but rather will leave it so in accord with the listener's imagination that the latter will understand only what he now wants him to understand. Afterwards, in the appropriate place, that obscure matter is stated in exact terms and explained as it truly is.

The sixth cause. The contradiction is concealed and becomes evident only after many premises. The greater the number of premises needed to make the contradiction evident, the more concealed it is. It thus may escape the author, who thinks there is no contradiction between his two original propositions. But if each proposition is considered separately—a true premise being joined to it and the necessary conclusion drawn—and this is done to every conclusion—a true premise being joined to it and the necessary conclusion drawn—, after many syllogisms the outcome of the matter will be that the two final conclusions are contradictory or contrary to each other. That is the kind of thing that escapes the attention of scholars who write books. If, however, the two original propositions are evidently contradictory, but the author has simply forgotten the first when writing down the second in another part of his compilation, this is a very great weakness, and that man should not be reckoned among those whose speeches deserve consideration.

The seventh cause. In speaking about very obscure matters it is necessary to conceal some parts and to disclose others. Sometimes in the case of certain dicta this necessity requires that the discussion proceed on the basis of a certain premise, whereas in another place necessity requires that the discussion proceed on the basis of another premise contradicting the first one. In such cases the vulgar must in no way be aware of the contradiction; the author accordingly uses some device to conceal it by all means.

The contradictions that are to be found in the *Mishnah* and the *Baraithoth*[1] are due to the first cause. Thus you will find that they constantly ask: *Does not the beginning [of the passage] constitute an objection against its end?* In such cases the answer is: *The beginning is the opinion of a certain rabbi and the end that of another rabbi*. You likewise will find that they say: *Rabbi [Judah ha-Nasi]*[2] *agreed with the opinion of a certain rabbi in this one matter and therefore cited it anonymously. In that other matter he agreed with the opinion of that other rabbi and therefore cited it anonymously*. You often will find them also saying: *Who is the author of this anonymous passage? Such and such rabbi. Who is the author of that passage of the Mishnah? Such and such rabbi*. Such cases are innumerable. The contradictions or divergences to be found in the *Talmud* are due to the first cause and to the second. Thus you find them constantly saying: *In this matter he agreed with this rabbi and in that with another rabbi*. They likewise say: *He agreed with him on one point and disagreed on another*. They also say: [*The two statements are made by*] *two Amoraim*[3] *who disagree as to the opinion of a certain rabbi*. All contradictions of this kind are due to the first cause. Contradictions due to the second cause are referred to when they say: *Rab abandoned this opinion. Raba*[4] *abandoned that opinion*. In such cases an inquiry is made as to which of the two statements is the later one. This is similar to their saying: *In the first recension [of the Talmud] by Rabbi Ashi*,[5] *he said one thing, and in the second another*. That some passages in every prophetic book, when taken in their external sense, appear to contradict or to be contrary to one another is due to the third cause and to the fourth. And it was with this in view that this entire introduction was written. You already know how often [the Sages], *may their memory be blessed*, say: *One verse says this and another verse says that*. They straightway establish that there is an apparent contradiction. Thereupon they explain that a proviso is lacking in the statement of the subject or that the two texts have different subjects. Thus, they say: *Solomon, it is not enough for you that your words contradict those of your father? They also contradict themselves, and so on*.[6] Cases of this are frequent in the sayings of the Sages, *may their memory be blessed*; however, most of the prophetic statements they refer to concern commandments or precepts regarding conduct. We, on the other hand, propose to draw attention to *verses* that are apparently contradictory with regard to opinions and beliefs. Part of this will be explained in some of the chapters of this Treatise, for this subject too belongs to *the mysteries of the Torah*. Whether contradictions due to the seventh cause are to be found in the books of the prophets is a matter for speculative study and investigation. Statements about this should not be a matter of conjecture. As for the divergences occurring in the books of the philosophers, or rather of those who know the truth, they are due to the fifth cause. On the other hand, the contradictions occurring in most of the books of authors and

1. A collection of extraneous rabbinic statements collected after the Mishnah but never incorporated into the Talmud.
2. Judah the Prince or Patriarch (135–ca. 220 C.E.), rabbi responsible for codifying the Mishnah out of the collected oral tradition, ca. 200 C.E.
3. Literally, "sayers" (Hebrew); rabbinic teachers whose opinions are preserved in the Talmud. They lived from the 3d to the 5th century C.E. in both Palestine and Babylonia.
4. Possibly Raba Bar Joseph bar Hama (299–352 C.E.), although the context suggests Maimonides may simply be referring by way of example to any rabbi or teacher. Rab: honorific given to Abba bar Aivu (3d c.), a student of Judah ha Nisi who founded a yeshiva (school) at Sura. That he is simply called Rab (or rabbi) reflects his status.
5. Babylonian teacher who died early in the 5th century C.E. He was head of the yeshiva at Sura and famous for his reading of the whole Talmud during two months of the year.
6. Babylonian Talmud, Shabbath, 30a [translator's note]. Shabbath: a tractate of the Talmud.

commentators other than those we have mentioned are due to the sixth cause. Likewise in the *Midrashim* and the *Haggadah*[7] there is to be found great contradiction due to this cause. That is why the Sages have said: *No questions should be asked about difficulties in the Haggadah.* There are also to be found therein contradictions due to the seventh cause. Divergences that are to be found in this Treatise are due to the fifth cause and the seventh. Know this, grasp its true meaning, and remember it very well so as not to become perplexed by some of its chapters.

And after these introductory remarks, I shall begin to mention the terms whose true meaning, as intended in every passage according to its context, must be indicated. This, then, will be a key permitting one to enter places the gates to which were locked. And when these gates are opened and these places are entered into, the souls will find rest therein, the eyes will be delighted, and the bodies will be eased of their toil and of their labor.

1190

7. Theological speculation, general ethical teachings that have not attained the status of law (*halachah*); parables, maxims, legends, and folklore.

GEOFFREY OF VINSAUF
ca. 1200

Geoffrey of Vinsauf is perhaps most familiar to students of English literature through the work of the poet Geoffrey Chaucer. In his *Nun's Priest's Tale*, Chaucer parodies Geoffrey of Vinsauf's lament on the death of Richard I in *Poetria Nova*: "O dear sovereign master, Geoffrey, you who movingly elegized the death of noble King Richard when he was slain by the arrow, would that I had your art and skill to rail at Friday as you did." Chaucer's mock praise suggests that even in the fourteenth century, Geoffrey of Vinsauf's best-known work, *Poetria Nova* (ca. 1200, *New Poetics*), had a reputation for stylistic extravagance. That Chaucer could so casually refer to it also suggests its popularity. Throughout the late Middle Ages, the *Poetria* was a widely read treatise on poetry; almost 200 extant manuscript copies, as well as a number of elaborate commentaries written between the thirteenth and fifteenth centuries, attest to its considerable influence on Latin and vernacular literature.

While most medieval literary criticism is concerned with the proper reading either of the ancient poets (see, for instance, Bernardus Silvestris and GIOVANNI BOCCACCIO) or of the Bible (see AUGUSTINE and THOMAS AQUINAS), Geoffrey's textbook for working poets is keenly interested in modernity and innovation. Not that he rejects the authority of tradition: indeed, his own treatise is explicitly modeled on HORACE's *Ars Poetica* (see above). But just as his "new" poetics reconceives and revises Horatian poetics, so aspiring poets, he maintains, best imitate tradition when they renew and refresh it. The rich texture of Geoffrey's citations calls to mind the later poststructuralist notion of intertextuality—the interanimation within a text of citations, references, echoes, and cultural languages—as described by contemporary theorists like ROLAND BARTHES. Written in Latin poetic verse that illustrates the principles Geoffrey is setting forth, *Poetria Nova* exhibits a Barthesian pleasure in the display of language for its own sake.

Geoffrey of Vinsauf was a poet and a teacher of rhetoric who lived in the last decades of the twelfth and the beginning of the thirteenth centuries. Few details of his life survive; even the dates of his birth and death are unrecorded. The manuscripts of the *Poetria Nova* attribute it to a "Galfridus Anglicus" (Geoffrey the Englishman) who studied in Paris and taught in "Hamton" (probably Northampton) and who, on at least one occasion, accompanied a mission to Rome in the service of either King Richard (reigned 1189–99) or King John (reigned 1199–1216) of England. Geoffrey seems in every way the product of the Anglo-Norman culture into which he was born, a hybrid of the English-French cultural exchange facilitated by the Norman conquest of England nearly a century earlier. Traditional, but less trustworthy, accounts of his life place his birth in Normandy, France, and his early education at St. Frideswide, Oxford. He is supposed to have returned to the Continent for further university study, first in Paris and later in Italy. A quarrel with a friend named Robert may have earned him the displeasure of a Bishop Adam so that he was forced to appeal to the archbishop of Canterbury for protection. The intercession of the archbishop enabled him to return to England as a tutor. His designation "Vinsauf" in English, or "de Vino Salvo" in Latin, comes from a treatise attributed to him on the keeping of wine. Topical references in the *Poetria Nova*—including a dedication to Innocent III (whose papacy extended from 1198 to 1216), allusions to the death of Richard I (1199), and a reference to Pope Innocent III's interdict on England (1208–13)—not only help date the poem and its revisions fairly precisely to the first decades of the thirteenth century, but provide a historical context for Geoffrey's life as well. He was writing during a period of renewed interest in literature at the Continental cathedral schools and was a contemporary of important members of the influential School of Chartres, especially Bernardus Silvestris and John of Salisbury, sharing important literary concerns with them.

Geoffrey is best known for *Poetria Nova*, but at least three other works have been securely attributed to him. *Documentum de Modo et Arte Dictandi et Versificandi* (*Instruction in the Method and Art of Speaking and Versifying*) is a long prose treatise on rhetoric and poetics, written earlier than the *Poetria Nova* but covering much the same material. While the *Poetria Nova* is a treatise and poem intended specifically for aspiring poets, the *Documentum* consists primarily of rhetorical exercises in essay writing and poetry. *Summa de Coloribus Rhetoricis* (*A Summary of the Colors of Rhetoric*) is a briefer work, primarily on figures of speech. The "Causa Magistri Gaufredi Vinesauf" ("The Apology of Master Geoffrey of Vinsauf") is one of a number of short poems of topical and political interest attributed to Geoffrey.

The title of Geoffrey's most popular book suggestively indicates the author's relation to tradition and innovation. *Poetria Nova* refers to the medieval traditions of rhetoric and of poetics. By the late twelfth century, Cicero's rhetorical treatise *De Inventione* (ca. 85 B.C.E., *On Invention*) had been added to the rhetoric curriculum of the schools, joining the standard rhetorical text, the *Rhetorica ad Herennium* (ca. 86–82 B.C.E., *Rhetoric Addressed to C. Herennius*), which had been falsely attributed to Cicero. *De Inventione* was called the "old rhetoric" (*rhetorica vetus*) and the *Ad Herennium* the "new rhetoric" (*rhetorica nova*). Horace's *Ars Poetica*, known as the *Poetria*, was the standard treatise on poetics. Geoffrey's *Poetria Nova* thus announces itself as a work rooted in the tradition of Horace, but carrying Horatian poetics forward in the same way that the *Ad Herennium* carries forward Cicero's *De Inventione*. Despite this gesture toward Horace, the *Poetria Nova* contains not a single citation from Horace, and its examples of figurative language are not culled from classical authors; rather, they are entirely invented by Geoffrey, a mark of his commitment to innovation and to a rethinking of traditional poetics. Unlike his predecessors, Geoffrey is less interested in carefully defining poetic techniques than in creatively illustrating them.

Though Geoffrey recognizes natural ability (*ingenium*) as a prerequisite for the poet, he is concerned in the *Poetria Nova* with the practical aspects of the poet's training. In the debate between the claims of genius or inspiration and of craft, Geoffrey follows Horace rather than PLATO (in *Ion*; see above) and LONGINUS, who portray an ecstatic poet moved to utterance by a supernatural agency. For Geoffrey, genius is necessary but useless without proper training and experience. His poet is an artisan—an architect, to use the metaphor he develops in the beginning of the treatise—rather than a vehicle for transcendent revelation. Yet his view of the poet as *artifex*, or creator, links him with the medieval tradition of Neoplatonism rooted in PLOTINUS's belief that artistic creation is a reflection of divine creation; at least this is how generations of commentators have read his opening remarks on poetry.

Geoffrey sees the poet's training as requiring a theoretical understanding of language and composition (*ars*), diligent practice (*usus*), and the reading and imitation of great authors (*imitatio*). His treatise, following the *Ad Herennium*, reduces the five divisions of rhetoric common in Roman treatises to four, leaving out techniques of invention (the choice of material): (1) disposition, or the ordering of material; (2) style, including amplification, abbreviation, and figures of speech and thought; (3) memory; and (4) delivery. The discussion of the figures of speech and thought, however, is by far the longest section of the *Poetria Nova*, occupying nearly four-fifths of the 2,100-line text. (Our selection includes the treatment of disposition and style.) Geoffrey shares with Horace the concept of decorum (i.e., the outer garment of ornamentation must suit the inner nature of the words) and with his medieval contemporaries a concern for distinguishing proper and figurative uses of language; but more than any other classical or medieval literary theorist, he displays a fascination with the texture of language for its own sake that, at times, seems modern. His discussion of amplification—which explains seven ways to lengthen a literary work—is a bravura performance.

The *Poetria Nova* demonstrates the fusion of poetics and rhetoric that characterized medieval thinking about poetry. This treatise and its imitators constituted the training manuals of most European poets from the thirteenth century through the Renaissance, and they remain to this day a primary source for technical discussion of poetic figures. More significantly, Geoffrey of Vinsauf revitalized a tradition of verse criticism, begun with Horace, that is carried on in English literature by ALEXANDER POPE's *Essay on Criticism* (1711; see below) in the eighteenth century, Lord Byron's "English Bards and Scottish Reviewers" (1809) and "Hints from Horace" (1811) in the nineteenth, and Wallace Stevens's "Notes toward a Supreme Fiction" (1947) in the twentieth.

BIBLIOGRAPHY

Latin editions of Geoffrey's *Poetria Nova*, *Documentum*, and *Summa* can all be found in *Les Arts poétiques du XIIe et du XIIIe siècles* (ed. Edmond Faral, 1924). Margaret F. Nims, *Poetria Nova of Geoffrey of Vinsauf* (1967), remains the standard English prose translation of *Poetria Nova*. Prose translations have also been done by Ernest Gallo in *The "Poetria Nova" and Its Sources in Early Rhetorical Doctrine* (1971) and by Jane Baltzell Kopp in *Three Medieval Rhetorical Arts* (ed. James Jerome Murphy, 1971). Roger Parr has made available an English version of *Documentum de Modo et Arte Dictandi et Versificandi* (1968).

The few details about Geoffrey's life that survive are found primarily in the "Causa Magistri Gaufredi" and have been summarized by Josiah Cox Russell in *The Dictionary of Writers of Thirteenth-Century England* (1967). Marjorie Curry Woods's edition and translation of one of the twelfth-century anonymous commentaries on the *Poetria Nova*, *An Early Commentary on the Poetria Nova of Geoffrey of Vinsauf* (1985), provides some interesting evidence about the earliest reception of Geoffrey's text. Walter Sedgwick, "The Style and Vocabulary of the Latin Arts of Poetry in the Twelfth and Thirteenth Centuries," *Speculum* 3 (1928), is a classic study of the *Poetria Nova*. Both Douglas Kelly, "The Theory of Composition in Medieval Narrative

Poetry and Geoffrey of Vinsauf's *Poetria Nova*," *Mediaeval Studies* 31 (1969), and Ernest Gallo, "The Grammarian's Rhetoric: *The Poetria Nova* of Geoffrey of Vinsauf in Medieval Eloquence," in *Studies in the Theory and Practice of Medieval Rhetoric* (ed. James J. Murphy, 1978), are important studies of the text. Alexandre Leupin's essay "Absolute Reflexivity: Geoffroi de Vinsauf," in *Medieval Texts and Contemporary Readers* (ed. Laurie A. Finke and Martin B. Shichtman, 1987), examines Geoffrey's obsession with modernity in his "new" poetics, linking the *Poetria Nova* with contemporary literary theory's interest in textuality. For bibliography on Geoffrey, consult James J. Murphy's *Medieval Rhetoric: A Select Bibliography* (1971).

From Poetria Nova[1]

I. General Remarks on Poetry
Divisions of the Present Treatise

If a man has a house to build, his impetuous hand does not rush into action. The measuring line of his mind first lays out the work, and he mentally outlines the successive steps in a definite order. The mind's hand[2] shapes the entire house before the body's hand builds it. Its mode of being is archetypal before it is actual. Poetic art may see in this analogy the law to be given to poets: let the poet's hand not be swift to take up the pen, nor his tongue be impatient to speak; (50)[3] trust neither hand nor tongue to the guidance of fortune. To ensure greater success for the work, let the discriminating mind, as a prelude to action, defer the operation of hand and tongue, and ponder long on the subject matter. Let the mind's interior compass first circle the whole extent of the material. Let a definite order chart in advance at what point the pen will take up its course, or where it will fix its Cadiz.[4] As a prudent workman, construct the whole fabric within the mind's citadel; let it exist in the mind before it is on the lips.

When due order has arranged the material in the hidden chamber of the mind, (60) let poetic art come forward to clothe the matter with words. Since poetry comes to serve, however, let it make due preparation for attendance upon its mistress. Let it take heed lest a head with tousled locks, or a body in rumpled garments, or any final details[5] prove displeasing, and lest in adorning one part it should in some way disfigure another. If any part is ill-groomed, the work as a whole incurs censure from that one part. A touch of gall makes all the honey bitter; a single blemish disfigures the entire face. Give careful thought to the material, therefore, that there may be no possible grounds for reproach. (70)

Let the poem's beginning, like a courteous attendant, introduce the subject with grace. Let the main section, like a diligent host, make provision for its worthy reception. Let the conclusion, like a herald when the race is over,

1. Translated by Margaret F. Nims, who sometimes includes explanatory material in square brackets in the text. The subheads are provided by Alex Preminger, O. B. Hardison Jr., and Kevin Kerrane (eds. of *Classical and Medieval Literary Criticism*, 1974).
2. Geoffrey makes frequent use of corporal metaphors [translator's note].
3. Numbers in parentheses refer to line numbers of the original Latin verse.
4. Limit. (To the Greeks and Romans, Cádiz [in Spain], the ancient Gades, was long the westernmost point of the known world.) [Translator's note.]
5. Geoffrey refers, again in a corporal metaphor (head, body, final details) to the three parts of a composition: beginning, middle, end [translator's note].

dismiss it honorably. In all of its parts let the whole method of presentation bring credit upon the poem, lest it falter in any section, lest its brightness suffer eclipse.

In order that the pen may know what a skillful ordering of material requires, the treatise to follow begins its course with a discussion of order. Since the following treatise begins its course with a discussion of order, its first concern is the path[6] that the ordering of material should follow. Its second care: with what scales[7] to establish a delicate balance if meaning is to be given the weight appropriate to it. The third task is to see that the body of words is not boorishly crude but urbane. The final concern is to ensure that a well-modulated voice enters the ears and feeds the hearing, a voice seasoned with the two spices of facial expression and gesture.[8]

From *II. Ordering the Material*

The material's order may follow two possible courses: at one time it advances along the pathway of art, at another it travels the smooth road of nature. Nature's smooth road points the way when "things" and "words" follow the same sequence, and the order of discourse does not depart from the order of occurrence. The poem travels the pathway of art if a more effective order presents first what was later in time, and defers the appearance of what was actually earlier. Now, when the natural order is thus transposed, later events incur no censure by their early appearance, nor do early events by their late introduction. Without contention, indeed, they willingly assume each other's place, and gracefully yield to each other with ready consent. Deft artistry inverts things in such a way that it does not pervert them; in transposing, it disposes the material to better effect. The order of art is more elegant than natural order, and in excellence far ahead, even though it puts last things first.[9]

The first branch of order has no offshoots; the second is prolific: from its marvelous stock, bough branches out into boughs, the single shoot into many, the one into eight. The air in this region of art may seem murky and the pathway rugged, the doors locked and the theory itself entangled with knots. Since that is so, the words that follow will serve as physicians for that disorder. Scan them well: here you will find a light to dispel the darkness, safe footing to traverse rugged ground, a key to unlock the doors, a finger to loose the knots. The way is thrown open; guide the reins of your mind as the nature of your course demands.

Let that part of the material which is first in the order of nature wait outside the gates of the work. Let the end, as a worthy precursor, be first to enter and take up its place in advance, as a guest of more honorable rank, or even as master. Nature has placed the end last in order, but art respectfully defers to it, leads it from its humble position and accords it the place of honor.

The place of honor at the beginning of a work does not reserve its luster

6. That is, natural order or the order of art [translator's note].
7. That is, amplified or abbreviated treatment, as the dignity of the subject demands [translator's note].
8. In *Poetria Nova* Geoffrey modifies the classical five divisions of rhetoric—invention, organization, style, memory, and delivery—leaving out invention.
9. Bernardus Silvestris (d. ca. 1160) makes a similar distinction between natural and artificial order.

for the end of the material only; rather, two parts share the glory: the end of the material and the middle. Art draws from either of these a graceful beginning. Art plays, as it were, the conjurer: causes the last to be first, the future to be present, the oblique to be straight, the remote to be near; what is rustic becomes urbane, what is old becomes new, public things are made private, black things white, and worthless things are made precious.

If a still more brilliant beginning is desired (while leaving the sequence of the material unchanged) make use of a proverb,[1] ensuring that it may not sink to a purely specific relevance, but raise its head high to some general truth. See that, while prizing the charm of the unusual, it may not concentrate its attention on the particular subject, but refuse, as if in disdain, to remain within its bosom. Let it take a stand above the given subject, but look with direct glance towards it. Let it say nothing directly about the subject, but derive its inspiration therefrom.

This kind of beginning is threefold, springing up from three shoots. The shoots are the first, the middle, and the last parts of the theme. From their stem a sprig, as it were, bursts forth, and is thus wont to be born, one might say, of three mothers. It remains in hiding, however, and when summoned it refuses to hear. It does not as a rule come forward when the mind bids it; it is of a somewhat haughty nature, and does not present itself readily nor to all. It is reluctant to appear, unless, indeed, it is compelled to do so.

Proverbs, in this way, add distinction to a poem. No less appropriately do exempla[2] occupy a position at the beginning of a work. The same quality, indeed, shines forth from exempla and proverbs, and the distinction conferred by the two is of equal value. In stylistic elegance, proverbs alone are on a par with exempla. Artistic theory has advanced other techniques [for the poem's beginning] but prefers these two; they have greater prestige. The others are of less worth and more recent appearance; the sanction of time favors the two forms mentioned. Thus the way that lies open is more restricted, its use more appropriate, its art superior, as we see both from artistic principle and from practice. . . .[3]

From *III. Amplification and Abbreviation*

For the opening of the poem, the principles of art outlined above have offered a variety of paths. The poem's development now invites you onward. Keeping to our image, direct your steps further along the road's course.

The way continues along two routes: there will be either a wide path or a narrow, either a river or a brook. You may advance at a leisurely pace or leap swiftly ahead. You may report the matter with brevity or draw it out in a lengthy discourse. The footing on either path is not without effort; if you wish to be wisely guided, entrust yourself to a reliable guide. Reflect upon the precepts below; they will guide your pen and teach the essentials for each path. The material to be molded, like the molding wax, is at first

1. The author understands by the term *proverbium* any general truth drawn from observation or experience [translator's note].

2. The term *exemplaris imago* (illustrative image) renders more precisely what Geoffrey understands by the term *exemplum*. All the exempla he offers as models in this treatise are exemplary images rather than stories [translator's note].

3. Here and elsewhere, ellipses marked by three periods represent the deletions of Preminger, Hardison, and Kerrane.

hard to the touch. If intense concentration enkindle native ability, the material is soon made pliant by the mind's fire, and submits to the hand in whatever way it requires, malleable to any form. The hand of the mind controls it, either to amplify or curtail.

A. Amplification

Repetition (*interpretatio, expolitio*).[4] If you choose an amplified form, proceed first of all by this step: although the meaning is one, let it not come content with one set of apparel. Let it vary its robes and assume different raiment. Let it take up again in other words what has already been said; let it reiterate, in a number of clauses, a single thought. Let one and the same thing be concealed under multiple forms—be varied and yet the same.

Periphrasis (*circuitio, circumlocutio*). Since a word, a short sound, passes swiftly through the ears, a step onward is taken when an expression made up of a long and leisurely sequence of sounds is substituted for a word. In order to amplify the poem, avoid calling things by their names; use other designations for them. Do not unveil the thing fully but suggest it by hints. Do not let your words move straight onward through the subject, but, circling it, take a long and winding path around what you were going to say briefly. Retard the tempo by thus increasing the number of words. This device lengthens brief forms of expression, since a short word abdicates in order that an extended sequence may be its heir. Since a concept is confined in one of three strongholds—in a noun, or a verb, or a combination of both—do not let the noun or verb or combination of both render the concept explicit, but let an amplified form stand in place of verb or noun or both.

Comparison (*collatio*). A third step is comparison, made in accord with one of two laws—either in a hidden or in an overt manner. Notice that some things are joined deftly enough, but certain signs reveal the point of juncture. A comparison which is made overtly presents a resemblance which signs explicitly point out. These signs are three: the words *more, less, equally*. A comparison that is made in a hidden way is introduced with no sign to point it out. It is introduced not under its own aspect but with dissembled mien, as if there were no comparison there at all, but the taking on, one might say, of a new form marvelously engrafted, where the new element fits as securely into the context as if it were born of the theme. The new term is, indeed, taken from elsewhere, but it seems to be taken from there; it is from outside and does not appear outside; it makes an appearance within and is not within; so it fluctuates inside and out, here and there, far and near; it stands apart, and yet is at hand. It is a kind of plant; if it is planted in the garden of the material the handling of the subject will be pleasanter. Here is the flowing water of a well-spring, where the source runs purer; here is the formula for a skillful juncture, where the elements joined flow together and touch each other as if they were not contiguous but continuous; as if the hand of nature had joined them rather than the hand of art. This type of comparison is more artistic; its use is much more distinguished.

4. The words in parentheses are the usual Latin terms for the techniques being discussed.

APOSTROPHE (*apostrophatio, exclamatio*). In order that you may travel the more spacious route, let apostrophe be a fourth mode of delay. By it you may cause the subject to linger on its way, and in it you may stroll for an hour. Take delight in apostrophe; without it the feast would be ample enough, but with it the courses of an excellent cuisine are multiplied. The splendor of dishes arriving in rich profusion and the leisured delay at the table are festive signs. With a variety of courses we feed the ear for a longer time and more lavishly. Here is food indeed for the ear when it arrives delicious and fragrant and costly. Example may serve to complement theory: the eye is a surer arbiter than the ear. One example is not enough; there will be an ample number; from this ample evidence learn what occasion suitably introduces apostrophe, what object it addresses, and in what form.

Rise up, apostrophe, before the man whose mind soars too high in prosperity, and rebuke him thus:

Why does joy so intense excite your spirit? Curb jubilation with due restraint and extend not its limits beyond what is meet [appropriate]. O soul, heedless of misfortune to come, imitate Janus[.][5]

* * *

DIGRESSION. If it is desirable to amplify the treatise yet more fully, go outside the bounds of the subject and withdraw from it a little; let the pen digress, but not so widely that it will be difficult to find the way back. This technique demands a talent marked by restraint, lest the bypath be longer than decorum allows. A kind of digression is made when I turn aside from the material at hand, bringing in first what is actually remote and altering the natural order. For sometimes, as I advance along the way, I leave the middle of the road, and with a kind of leap I fly off to the side, as it were; then I return to the point whence I had digressed. Lest this matter of digression be veiled in obscurity, I offer the following example:

The bond of a single love bound together two hearts; a strange cause divided them one from the other. But before they were parted, lips pressed kisses on lips; a mutual embrace holds and enfolds them both. From the fount of their eyes, tears flow down their cheeks, and sobs alternate with farewells. Love is a spur to grief, and grief a witness to the strength of love. Winter yields to spring. The air unclasps its robe of cloud, and heaven caresses the earth. Moist and warm, air sports with earth, and the feminine earth feels the masculine power of the air.[6] A flower, earth's child, bursts forth into the breeze and smiles at its mother. Their first foliage adorns the tips of the trees; seeds that were dead spring up into life; the promise of harvest to come lives first in the tender blade. Now is the season in which birds delight. This hour of time found the lovers apart, who yet through their love were not parted.

DESCRIPTION, pregnant with words, follows as a seventh means of amplifying the work. But although the path of description is wide, let it also be wise, let it be both lengthy and lovely. See that the words with due ceremony are wedded to the subject. If description is to be the food and ample refresh-

5. Roman god of doorways, associated with beginnings and represented by a double-faced head. With "O soul," Geoffrey gives an example of apostrophe, or rhetorical address.

6. The topos [stock rhetorical theme] of *Mater Terra* (mother earth) and *Pater Aether* (father air) appears frequently in classical and medieval times [translator's note].

ment of the mind, avoid too curt a brevity as well as trite conventionality. Examples of description, accompanied by novel figures, will be varied, that eye and ear may roam amid a variety of subjects.

If you wish to describe, in amplified form, a woman's beauty:

Let the compass of Nature first fashion a sphere for her head; let the color of gold give a glow to her hair, and lilies bloom high on her brow. Let her eyebrows resemble in dark beauty the blackberry, and a lovely and milk-white path separate their twin arches. Let her nose be straight, of moderate length, not too long nor too short for perfection. Let her eyes, those watch-fires of her brow, be radiant with emerald light, or with the brightness of stars. Let her countenance emulate dawn: not red, nor yet white—but at once neither of those colors and both. Let her mouth be bright, small in shape—as it were, a half-circle. Let her lips be rounded and full, but moderately so; let them glow, aflame, but with gentle fire. Let her teeth be snowy, regular, all of one size, and her breath like the fragrance of incense. Smoother than polished marble let Nature fashion her chin—Nature, so potent a sculptor. Let her neck be a precious column of milk-white beauty, holding high the perfection of her countenance. From her crystal throat let radiance gleam, to enchant the eye of the viewer and enslave his heart. Let her shoulders, conforming to beauty's law, not slope in unlovely descent, nor jut out with an awkward rise; rather, let them be gracefully straight. Let her arms be a joy to behold, charming in their grace and their length. Let soft and slim loveliness, a form shapely and white, a line long and straight, flow into her slender fingers. Let her beautiful hands take pride in those fingers. Let her breast, the image of snow, show side by side its twin virginal gems. Let her waist be close girt, and so slim that a hand may encircle it. For the other parts I am silent—here the mind's speech is more apt than the tongue's. Let her leg be of graceful length and her wonderfully tiny foot dance with joy at its smallness.

So let the radiant description descend from the top of her head to her toe, and the whole be polished to perfection.

If you wish to add to the loveliness thus pictured an account of attire:

Let her hair, braided and bound at her back, bind in its gold; let a circlet of gold gleam on her ivory brow. Let her face be free of adornment, lovely in its natural hue. Have a starry chain encircle her milk-white neck. Let the border of her robe gleam with fine linen; with gold let her mantle blaze. Let a zone, richly set with bright gems, bind her waist, and bracelets enrich her arms. Have gold encircle her slender fingers, and a jewel more splendid than gold shed its brilliant rays. Let artistry vie with materials in her fair attire; let no skill of hand or invention of mind be able to add aught to that apparel. But her beauty will be of more worth than richness of vesture. Who, in this torch, is unaware of the fires? Who does not find the flame? If Jupiter in those days of old had seen her, he would not, in Amphitryon's shape, have deluded Alcmena;[7] nor assumed the face of Diana to defraud you, Callisto,

7. In classical mythology, the wife of Amphitryon; the visit by Jupiter/Zeus (father and ruler of the gods) resulted in the birth of Hercules/Heracles (the Romans borrowed heavily from Greek mythology, often assimilating Greek gods to native Italian deities). What follows is a list of mortals and goddesses whom Zeus, in various forms, successfully pursued; many of them bore him children. Callisto was a follower of the huntress Artemis (identified with Diana), turned into a bear by either Hera or Artemis and made a constellation by Zeus; Io, daughter of the river-god Inachus, was changed into a cow by Zeus to protect her from Hera; Antiope bore the famous musician Amphion and

of your flower; nor would he have betrayed Io in the form of a cloud, nor Antiope in the shape of a satyr, nor the daughter of Agenor as a bull, nor you, Mnemosyne, as a shepherd; nor the daughter of Asopo in the guise of fire; nor you, Deo's daughter, in the form of a serpent; nor Leda as a swan; nor Danae in a shower of gold. This maiden alone would he cherish, and see all others in her. . . .

OPPOSITION (*oppositio, oppositum*). There remains yet another means of fostering the amplified style: any statement at all may assume two forms: one form makes a positive assertion, the other negates its opposite. The two modes harmonize in a single meaning; and thus two streams of sound flow forth, each flowing along with the other. Words flow in abundance from the two streams. Consider this example: *"That young man is wise."* Affirm the youthfulness of his countenance and deny its age: *"His is the appearance of youth and not of old age."* Affirm the maturity of his mind and deny its youthfulness: *"His is the mind of mature age and not of youth."* The account may perhaps continue along the same line: *"His is not the cheek of age but of youth;* *his is not the mind of youth but age."* Or, choosing details closely related to the theme, you may travel a rather long path, thus:

His face is not wrinkled, nor is his skin dry; his heart is not stricken with age, nor is his breath labored; his loins are not stiff, nor is his back bowed; physically he is a young man, mentally he is in advanced maturity.

In this way, plentiful harvest springs from a little seed; great rivers draw their source from a tiny spring; from a slender twig a great tree rises and spreads.

B. ABBREVIATION

If you wish to be brief, first prune away those devices mentioned above which contribute to an elaborate style; let the entire theme be confined within narrow limits. Compress it in accordance with the following formula. Let *emphasis* be spokesman, saying much in few words. Let *articulus*,[8] with staccato speech, cut short a lengthy account. The *ablative*,[9] when it appears alone without a pilot, effects a certain compression. Give no quarter to *repetition*. Let skillful *implication* convey the unsaid in the said. Introduce no *conjunction* as a link between clauses—let them proceed uncoupled (*asyndeton*).[1] Let the craftsman's skill effect a *fusion of many concepts in one*, so that many may be seen in a single glance of the mind. By such concision you may gird up a lengthy theme; in this bark you may cross a sea. This form of expression is preferable for a factual account, in order not to enshroud facts discreetly in mist, but rather to clear away mist and usher in sunlight. Combine these devices, therefore, when occasion warrants: emphasis, articulus, ablative absolute, deft implication of one thing in the rest,

his twin brother Zethus, dual rulers of Thebes; the daughter of Agenor, king of Phoenicia, was Europa, whom Zeus carried off after taking the form of a white bull; Mnemosyne (literally, "memory"; Greek) was the mother of the 9 Muses; when the river-god Asopus tried to prevent Zeus from abducting his daughter Aegina, Zeus drove him off with a thunderbolt; the daughter of Deo—another name for Demeter, goddess of agriculture—is Persephone (Zeus was also her father); Leda, the wife of Tyndareus, king of Sparta, bore Helen of Troy (as well as Clytemnestra, Castor, and Pollux); and Danaë, who was locked in a tower because of the prophecy that her son would kill her father, bore the hero Perseus.

8. A word by itself, or a short phrase in place of a sentence (Latin).

9. A grammatical case in Latin that appears in a number of independent constructions.

1. The omission of conjunctions between words, phrases, or clauses, as in this sentence.

omission of conjunctions between clauses, fusion of many concepts in one, avoidance of repetition. Draw on all of these, or at least on such as the subject allows. Here is a model of abbreviation; the whole technique is reflected in it:

Her husband abroad improving his fortunes, an adulterous wife bears a child. On his return after long delay, she pretends it begotten of snow.[2] Deceit is mutual. Slyly he waits. He whisks off, sells, and—reporting to the mother a like ridiculous tale—pretends the child melted by sun. . . .

From *IV. Ornaments of Style*

Whether it be brief or long, a discourse should always have both internal and external adornment, but with a distinction of ornament reflecting the distinction between the two orders. First examine the mind of a word, and only then its face; do not trust the adornment of its face alone. If internal ornament is not in harmony with external, a sense of propriety is lacking. Adorning the face of a word is painting a worthless picture: it is a false thing, its beauty fictitious; the word is a whitewashed wall and a hypocrite, pretending to be something whereas it is nothing. Its fair form conceals its deformity; it makes a brave outward show, but has nothing within. It is a picture[3] that charms one who stands at a distance, but displeases the viewer who stands at close range. Take care, then, not to be hasty, but be Argus[4] in relation to what you have said, and, Argus-eyed, examine the words in relation to the meaning proposed. If the meaning has dignity, let that dignity be preserved; see that no vulgar word may debase it. That all may be guided by precept: let rich meaning be honored by rich diction, lest a noble lady blush in pauper's rags.

In order that meaning may wear a precious garment, if a word is old, be its physician and give to the old a new vigor. Do not let the word invariably reside on its native soil[5]—such residence dishonors it. Let it avoid its natural location, travel about elsewhere, and take up a pleasant abode on the estate of another. There let it stay as a novel guest, and give pleasure by its very strangeness. If you provide this remedy, you will give to the word's face a new youth.

DIFFICULT ORNAMENT

METAPHOR (*translatio*). The method suggested above affords guidence in the artistic transposition of words. If an observation is to be made about man, I turn to an object which clearly resembles man [in the quality or state of being I wish to attribute to him]. When I see what that object's proper vesture is, in the aspect similar to man's, I borrow it, and fashion for myself a new garment in place of the old. For example, taking the words in their literal sense, gold is said to be yellow; milk, white; a rose, very red; honey, sweet-flowing; flames, glowing; snow, white. Say therefore: *snowy* teeth, *flaming* lips, *honied* taste, *rosy* countenance, *milky* brow, *golden* hair.

2. The story of the snow child was a popular theme in the Middle Ages [translator's note].

3. See HORACE, *Ars Poetica* (ca. 10 B.C.E.), lines 361–62: "Poetry is like painting. Some attracts you more if you stand near, some if you're further off."

4. That is, watchful; in Greek mythology, Argus had a hundred eyes.

5. The word's "native soil" (*proprium locum*) refers to its literal meaning rather than to its position in the sentence [translator's note].

These word-pairs are well suited to each other: teeth, snow; lips, flames; taste, honey; countenance, rose; brow, milk; hair, gold. And since here the linking of aspects that are similar sheds a pleasing light, if the subject of your discourse is not man, turn the reins of your mind to the human realm. With artistic tact, transpose a word which, in its literal sense, applies to man in an analogous situation. For example, if you should wish to say: "Springtime makes the earth beautiful; the first flowers grow up; the weather turns mild; storms cease; the sea is calm, its motion without violence; the vales are deep, the mountains lofty"; consider what words, in a literal sense, express the analogous situation in our human life. When you adorn something, you *paint*; when you enter on existence, you *are born*; affable in discourse, you *placate*; withdrawing from all activity, you *sleep*; motionless, you *stand on fixed foot*; sinking down, you *lie*; lifted into the air, you *rise*. The wording is a source of pleasure, then, if you say:

Springtime paints the earth with flowers: the first blossoms are born; the mild weather soothes; storms, dying down, slumber; the sea stands still, as if without movement; the valleys lie deep; the mountains rise aloft. . . .

Art has woven other garments of less price, yet they, too, have a dignified and appropriate use. There are in all ten[6] tropes, six in this group, four [in addition to metaphor, onomatopoeia, antonomasia,[7] and allegory] mentioned above. This decade of figures adorns expression in a way we term *difficult* in that a word is taken only in its figurative and not in its literal sense. All the tropes are of one general class, distinguished by the figurative status of the words and the uncommon meaning assigned them. Lest understanding be uncertain and hesitant here, the following examples will ensure confidence.

METONYMY (*denominatio*). Consider a statement of this kind: *The sick man seeks a physician; the grieving man, solace; the poor man, aid.* Expression attains a fuller flowering in this trope: *Illness is in need of a physician; grief is in need of solace; poverty is in need of aid.* There is a natural charm in this use of the abstract for the concrete, and so in the change of *sick man* to *sickness, grieving man* to *grief, poor man* to *poverty*.

What does fear produce? Pallor. What does anger cause? A flush. Or what, the vice of pride? A swelling up. We refashion the statement thus: *Fear grows pale, anger flushes; pride swells.* There is greater pleasure and satisfaction for the ear when I attribute to the cause what the effect claims as its own.

Let the comb's action groom the hair after the head has been washed. Let scissors trim away from the hair whatever is excessive, and let a razor give freshness to the face. In this way, art teaches us to attribute to the instrument, by a happy turn of expression, what is proper to the one who uses it. So from the resources of art springs a means of avoiding worn-out paths and of travelling a more distinguished route.

Again, a statement expressed in the following way adds luster to style: *We*

6. In his discussion of the tropes, the author follows the treatment in *Ad Herenniunm* 4.31.42–34.46. But Geoffrey lists only nine figures (anastrophe and transposition are included under hyperbaton), omitting the tenth, *circuitio* or periphrasis [translator's note]. *Rhetorical Herennium*: a rhetorical treatise (ca. 86–82 B.C.E.) wrongly attributed to the Roman statesman and orator Cicero. Anastrophe: inversion of normal word order for rhetorical emphasis (a kind of "hyperbaton," which is any rhetorical device involving unusual word order).

7. Use of a proper name to stand for an entire class which that name represents; also the use of an epithet for a proper name (e.g., referring to Shakespeare as "the Bard").

have robbed their bodies of steel, their coffers of silver, their fingers of gold. The point here is not that zeugma[8] adorns the words with its own figure of speech, but that when I am about to mention something, I withhold its form completely and mention only the material. Whereas a less elegant style mentions both, art is silent about one, and conveys both by a single term. This device brings with it three advantages: it curtails the number of words required, it constitutes a poetic adornment, and it is helpful to the meter. It curtails the number of words in that a single term is more succinct than a word-group; it constitutes a poetic adornment in that an expression of this kind is artistically more skillful; and it is helpful to the meter if an oblique case, whose form the meter rejects, requires such help. This is clear from the following example: *The finger rejoices in gold. Gold* is a shorter sound, *a ring of gold* is longer; the latter form names the object itself, the former conveys it more artfully; in the former [*aurum*] the meter admits of oblique cases, in the latter [*annulus auri*] it rejects them.

Instead of the thing contained, name that which contains it, choosing the word judiciously whether it be noun or adjective. Introduce a noun in this way: *tippling England; weaving Flanders; bragging Normandy.* Try out an adjective thus: *clamorous market-places; silent cloisters; lamenting prison; jubilant house; quiet night; laborious day.* Seek turns of expression like the following: *In time of sickness Salerno, with its medical skill, cures those who are ill. In civil causes Bologna arms the defenceless with laws. Paris, in the arts, dispenses bread to feed the strong. Orleans, in its cradle, rears tender youth on the milk of the authors.*

HYPERBOLE (*superlatio*). Give hyperbole rein, but see that its discourse does not run ineptly hither and yon. Let reason keep it in check, and its moderate use be a source of pleasure, that neither mind nor ear may shrink from excess. For example, employing this trope: *A rain of darts lashes the foe like hail; the shattered array of spears resembles a forest; a tide of blood flows like a wave of the sea, and bodies clog the valleys.* This mode of expression diminishes or heightens eulogy to a remarkable degree; and exaggeration is a source of pleasure when both ear and good usage commend it.

SYNECDOCHE (*intellectio*). If you intend to say: *I studied for three years,* you may, with happier effect, adorn the statement. The wording above is inelegant and trite; you may refine the inelegant, your file may renew the trite in this way: *The third summer came upon me in study; the third autumn found me engaged; the third winter embroiled me in cares; in study I passed through three spring times.* I word the statement more skillfully when, suppressing the whole, I imply that whole from the parts, in the way just exemplified. Part of the year may be wet. *The year is wet;* part may be dry: *The year is dry;* part may be hot. *The year is hot;* part may be mild: *The year is mild.* I attribute to the whole what characterizes a part of it. By this same mode of reckoning, you, Gion,[9] will be accounted turbid and clear, narrow and broad, brackish and sweet, because of some varied part of your course. Again, by the same figure, a day is to be accounted dry and yet rainy because of a part of it. Since both forms of this figure are pleasing, you may give pleasure by either form.

8. A figure of speech in which a single word, usually a verb or adjective, governs in a grammatically parallel way two or more other words (as in the previous sentence); often one use is literal and the other figurative.

9. The river Garonne in France.

CATACHRESIS (*abusio*). There is likewise an urbane imprecision of diction when a word is chosen which is neither literal nor precise in its context, but which is related to the literal word. For example, if one proposes to say: (1040): *The strength of the Ithacan is slight, but yet he has a mind of great wisdom,* let catachresis alter the wording thus: *Strength in Ulysses*[1] *is short, wisdom in his heart is long,* for there is a certain affinity between the words *long* and *great*, as between *short* and *slight*.

In the figures given above there is a common element of adornment and weightiness, arising from the fact that an object does not come before us with unveiled face, and accompanied by its natural voice; rather, an alien voice attends it, and so it shrouds itself in mist, as it were, but in a luminous mist. (1050)

HYPERBATON[2] (*transgressio*). A certain weightiness of style results also from the order of words alone, when units grammatically related are separated by their position, so that an inversion of this sort occurs (anastrophe [*perversio*]): *rege sub ipso; tempus ad illud; ea de causa; rebus in illis* [under the king himself; up to that time; for this reason; in those matters]; or a transposed order of this sort (transposition [*transjectio*]): *Dura creavit pestiferam fortuna famem* [harsh fortune produced a pestilent famine]; *Letalis egenam gente fames spoliavit humum* [deadly famine robbed the destitute soil of produce]. Here words related grammatically are separated by their position in the sentence. Juxtaposition of related words conveys the sense more readily, but their moderate separation sounds better to the ear and has greater elegance. (1060)

* * *

VARIOUS PRESCRIPTIONS

If you heed the directives carefully and suit words to content, you will speak with precise appropriateness in this way. If mention has perhaps arisen of an object, sex, age, condition, event, place, or time, it is regard for its distinctive quality that the object, sex, age, condition, event, time, or place claims as its due. Felicity in this matter is an admirable thing, for when I make an apt use of qualifying words [*determino*] I give the whole theme a finished completeness [*termino*]. An object described [*condita*] in its entirety is a dish well-seasoned [*condita*]. Note this prescription and heed its tenor; (1850) it is a prescription that is valid for prose as well as for verse. The same principle of art holds good for both, although in a different way.

Meter is straitened by laws, but prose roams along a freer way, for the public road of prose admits here and there wagons and carts, whereas the narrow path of a line of verse does not allow of things so inelegant. Verse wishes its very words to be graceful in appearance, lest the rustic form of a word embarrass by its ungainliness, and bring shame to the line. Meter desires to appear as a handmaid with hair adorned, with shining cheek, slim body, and peerless form. (1860) The charming gracefulness of verse cannot find a group of words of equal sweetness to the ear. A line of prose is a

1. Odysseus, king of Ithaca and the hero of Homer's *Odyssey*.
2. The translations under this heading do not reflect the unusual Latin word order (e.g., *rege sub ipso* literally reads "the king under himself").

coarser thing; it favors all words, observing no distinction except in the case of those which it keeps for the end of periods:[3] such words are those whose penultimate syllable carries the accent. It is not desirable that other words hold this final position. Aulus Gellius[4] reaches the same conclusion and subjoins his reason: lest otherwise the number of syllables be weak and insufficient to bring the line to a close. If the last word of a period should be, as it frequently is, of a different cursus,[5] nevertheless the one suggested above is preferable in as much as sounder opinion supports it—and my authority here is Aulus Gellius.[6] For the rest, the method of prose and verse does not differ; rather, the principles of art remain the same, whether in a composition bound by the laws of meter or in one independent of those laws, although what depends upon the principles of art is not always the same. In both prose and verse see that diction is controlled in such a way that words do not enter as dry things, but let their meaning confer a juicy savor upon them, and let them arrive succulent and rare. Let them say nothing in a childish way; see that they have dignity but not pomposity, lest what should be honorable becomes onerous. Do not let them enter with unsightly mien; rather, see that there is both internal and external adornment. Let the hand of artistic skill provide colors of both kinds.

* * *

ca. 1200

3. Sentences.
4. Author (ca. 130–180 C.E.) of the Latin work *Attic Nights*, whose 20 books treat many different topics.
5. Arrangement of accents.
6. The reference is to Aulus Gellius, *Attic Nights* 1.7.20 [translator's note].

THOMAS AQUINAS
1225–1274

Thomas Aquinas's *Summa Theologica*, with its compelling synthesis of faith and reason, of Platonism and Aristotelianism, of Hellenistic and Christian thought, marks the high point of the Scholastic philosophy and theology of the Middle Ages. But it may be difficult to imagine that Aquinas, the medieval philosopher most widely read today, could have much to say about poetics, which he relegates in the *Summa* to "the least of all the sciences." Yet when read against the backdrop of the so-called commentary tradition, the tradition of allegorical interpretation of biblical and secular texts, Aquinas's writings on biblical exegesis force a reevaluation of our portrait of the saint as a prosaic logician. Early in the *Summa*, Aquinas wrestles with a problem that has continued to perplex both literary critics and philosophers of language: how to reconcile the indeterminacy of figurative language (such as poetic metaphor) with a belief in the ability of language to guarantee stable reference and access to truth and reality. If language cannot guarantee that the intentions of its author—whether divine or human—can be known, then how can it function as a vehicle of knowledge? The centrality of this question to contemporary debates over the nature of language and signification makes Aquinas's uneasy resolution of it—his insistence on both the multiplicity of meaning and the stability of reference in the biblical text—all the more interesting.

Thomas Aquinas (Tommaso d'Aquino) was born in his father's castle in Roccasecea in central Italy, the youngest son of a noble family. At the age of five he was sent to the Benedictine monastery of Monte Cassino to begin his education, and in 1236 he entered the University of Naples. Some time between 1240 and 1243, against his parents' wishes, he decided to join the Dominican friars, an order founded in 1205 and dedicated to learning and preaching. On the way to Rome he was abducted by his brothers and imprisoned for two years at the castle of San Giovanni, where his family tried everything—including hiring a prostitute to seduce him—to break his will. When his family finally relented, Thomas took his vows; he was sent to Cologne, Germany, in 1244 where he continued his education under the direction of Albertus Magnus, the most famous scholar of the order. Thomas's taciturnity as a student earned him a reputation for dullness, though Albertus, on hearing him defend a difficult thesis, is reported to have said, "We call this young man a dumb ox, but his bellowing in doctrine will one day resound throughout the world."

In 1245 Thomas accompanied Albertus to Paris as a student. In 1248, when a new *studium generale* (a school founded by the Dominicans for the teaching of theology) was opened in Cologne, Albertus returned as its master. Thomas went with him to serve as a bachelor, or subregent, under him. While in Cologne, in 1250, he was ordained a priest by the city's archbishop. In 1252 Thomas was sent to Paris to fill the position of bachelor at the *studium generale* in that city. His primary duty was teaching the *Sentences* of Peter Lombard (ca. 1100–1160), the basic textbook for all theology courses in the Middle Ages, and his commentaries on that book would later furnish the materials and plan for his chief work, the *Summa Theologica*. In 1257 Thomas took the degree of doctor in theology from the University of Paris and was subsequently appointed regent (or master) in theology, a position he held until 1259. The years between 1259 and 1265 are not well documented; most likely he spent them teaching, preaching, writing, and traveling throughout Europe. In 1265 he went to Rome to serve as regent of the *studium generale* founded there, and in 1268 the order sent him back to the University of Paris. In 1274, while traveling to the Council of Lyons, he fell ill. He was taken to the monastery of Fossanova, where he died on March 7. He was canonized a saint on July 18, 1323.

Aquinas composed more than sixty books on philosophy, theology, ethics, and exegesis. His exegetical works include commentaries on various books of the Bible, including Job, the Psalms, Isaiah, Jeremiah, the Epistles of St. Paul, and his *Catena Aurea* (a commentary on all four Gospels). His philosophical works include thirteen commentaries on ARISTOTLE, which were instrumental in the efforts of Christian scholarship to assimilate the Greek philosopher's newly discovered works. His *Summa contra Gentiles* (1261–64) was a defense of the Christian faith against the Jews and Muslims of Spain, whose scholarship was central to the recovery of Aristotle's writing in thirteenth-century Europe. This work reveals the breadth and depth of his understanding of the Jewish and Islamic philosophy of the period, especially that of MAIMONIDES (1135–1204) and the great Islamic philosopher Avicenna (980–1037). Far and away his greatest work, however, is the twenty-two-volume *Summa Theologica* (1265–73), an encyclopedic compendium, left unfinished at his death, designed to organize systematically and to explicate all of Christian theology and philosophy.

In his prologue to the *Summa*, Aquinas explains, "we shall endeavor, confiding in the Divine assistance, to treat of these things that pertain to sacred doctrine with brevity and clearness, in so far as the subject to be treated will permit." The fourfold method Aquinas follows, a method identified with Scholasticism, is first to pose a yes or no question, next to offer all of the arguments for the no position, then to present the contrary argument, and finally to supply a complete defense of his own position by replying to the objections outlined at the beginning. This form is illustrated in the selection below.

Very early in the *Summa*, in articles 9 and 10 of question 1, "On Sacred Doctrine: What Kind It Is and What It Covers," Aquinas deals with problems of interpretation that have occupied literary critics from ancient and medieval Christian and Jewish exegetes down to poststructuralist theorists like JACQUES DERRIDA. He wishes not only to explain the obscurities and ambiguities of biblical texts but also to understand the theoretical consequences of figurative language in a text that claims privileged authorship. Aquinas, like other medieval religious writers, has inherited the Platonic distrust of poetry—which is, in part, a distrust of the multiplicity of meaning and the instability of linguistic reference. The divine text, he argues, must "make truth clear," while figurative language obscures truth. Yet Scriptures use figurative language frequently; thus Aquinas must struggle to reconcile this kind of unstable language with the authority and infallibility of the sacred biblical word.

While poetry uses metaphors "for the sake of lively description," Aquinas argues, Scriptures use them of necessity. While poetry promotes deception, Scriptures reveal spiritual truths through corporeal metaphors. He offers three defenses of Scriptures' use of figurative language, which will find their way into the Italian poet-critic BOCCACCIO's defense of poetry in the fourteenth century. For Aquinas, the figurative language of Scriptures exercises the thoughtful mind, serves as a defense against the "ridicule of the impious," and preserves readers from error because it appeals to the senses to guide them to the intelligible. Like AUGUSTINE, Aquinas endorses the possibility that the Bible contains multiple meanings, while maintaining that such multiplicity does not lead to indeterminacy. And, like his twelfth-century predecessors, HUGH OF ST. VICTOR and Bernardus Silvestris, he attempts to contain any uncontrolled proliferation of meaning by organizing these multiple meanings vertically and hierarchically in the now famous scheme that attaches different meanings to the literal, allegorical, moral, and anagogical (or mystical) senses and levels of the text.

What sets Aquinas apart from his predecessors is his decidedly non-Platonic insistence that all interpretation of biblical texts must proceed from the literal sense alone. Aquinas's claim that nothing necessary to faith is conveyed through the allegorical senses of the Bible that is not conveyed clearly and openly through the literal sense would seem at odds with his endorsement of multiple meanings, since the obvious consequence of literal reading would be to render the techniques of *allegoresis* redundant. Indeed, there are some scholars who have argued that Aquinas's literal reading of Scriptures led to the rejection of allegorical readings of the Bible during the Reformation. Yet in their effort to come to terms with the difficulties of biblical language, Aquinas and other medieval exegetes developed conventions of interpretation that would influence all subsequent literary criticism long after the fourfold scheme of allegory was forgotten. Among these conventions is the practice of searching for "hidden" meanings in the text and the tendency to value literary texts for their multiplicity and complexity of meaning.

Aquinas occupies a pivotal position between the Neoplatonic exegetes of the twelfth century, philosopher-theologians such as Hugh of St. Victor and Bernardus Silvestris who wrote in Latin for a primarily clerical audience, and Italian poet-critics such as DANTE and Boccaccio, who, writing in Italian, would literally invent vernacular literary criticism in the fourteenth. Twelfth-century exegetes (Hugh may be the exception here) believed, with Augustine, that meaning had been hidden in the biblical text by God, so they subordinated the literal sense of the text to its allegorical senses in much the same way that Neoplatonists subordinated the material world to the transcendental world of forms (see PLATO and PLOTINUS). The revival of interest in Aristotle in the thirteenth century had profound consequences for the study of signification in both biblical and secular texts. Aquinas's more Aristotelian analyses of Scriptures privilege the literal over allegorical sense; and because the literal sense was identified with the expression of the author's intention, his remarks on biblical commentary set the stage for the appreciation of the individual poet's style apparent in the landmark fourteenth-century Italian criticism of Dante and Boccaccio.

BIBLIOGRAPHY

Not all of Aquinas's works exist in critical editions, but the many volumes of the still-unfinished *Opera Omnia* (1882, *Complete Works*), edited by the Leonine Commission (commissioned by Pope Leo XIII), provide the best available Latin text. The Marietta editions, in several volumes that appeared throughout the twentieth century, reproduce the Leonine Latin text in a more convenient format with useful research aids. Nor have all Aquinas's works been translated into English. The *Summa Theologica* is available in a twenty-two-volume English edition by the Fathers of the English Dominican Province (1920–31). The *Summa Contra Gentiles* was translated by the English Dominican Fathers (1923–29). A selection of translations by various hands of Aquinas's biblical commentaries can be found in the Aquinas Scripture Series (1966–). *The Pocket Aquinas*, edited by Vernon O. Bourke (1968), offers selections from Aquinas's writings in readable translations. James A. Weisheipl's *Friar Thomas D'Aquino* (rev. ed., 1983), is the standard biography.

F. C. Copleston's *Aquinas* (1955) is a useful introduction to both Aquinas's philosophy and its historical background. M. D. Chenu's *Toward Understanding St. Thomas* (1964) offers a classic interpretation of Aquinas's thought. Umberto Eco's *Aesthetics of Thomas Aquinas* (1988) examines the difficulty of deriving an aesthetics from Aquinas's thought, making connections with issues in contemporary aesthetics. Norman Kretzmann and Eleanore Stump's *Cambridge Companion to Aquinas* (1993) provides ten studies designed to introduce all aspects of Aquinas's thought, including his work on biblical commentary. Richard Ingardia's *Thomas Aquinas: International Bibliography, 1977–1990* (1993), an indispensable and well-organized bibliography, gives synopses of many published items.

From Summa Theologica[1]

From *Question I*

NINTH ARTICLE

WHETHER HOLY SCRIPTURE SHOULD USE METAPHORS?

We proceed thus to the Ninth Article:—

Objection 1. It seems that the Holy Scripture should not use metaphors. For that which is proper to the lowest science seems not to befit this science, which holds the highest place of all. But to proceed by the aid of various similitudes and figures is proper to poetry, the least of all the sciences. Therefore it is not fitting that this science should make use of such similitudes.

Obj. 2. Further, this doctrine seems to be intended to make truth clear. Hence a reward is held out to those who manifest it: *They that explain me shall have life everlasting.*[2] But by such similitudes truth is obscured. Therefore to put forward divine truths by likening them to corporeal things does not befit this science.

Obj. 3. Further, the higher creatures are, the nearer they approach to the divine likeness. If therefore any creature be taken to represent God, this representation ought chiefly to be taken from the higher creatures, and not from the lower; yet this is often found in the Scriptures.

1. Translated by Fathers of the English Dominican Province.

2. Ecclesiasticus 24.31.

On the contrary, It is written: *I have multiplied visions, and I have used similitudes by the ministry of the prophets.*[3] But to put forward anything by means of similitudes is to use metaphors. Therefore this sacred science may use metaphors.

I answer that, It is befitting Holy Writ to put forward divine and spiritual truths by means of comparisons with material things. For God provides for everything according to the capacity of its nature. Now it is natural to man to attain to intellectual truths through sensible objects, because all our knowledge originates from sense. Hence in Holy Writ spiritual truths are fittingly taught under the likeness of material things. This is what Dionysius says: *We cannot be enlightened by the divine rays except they be hidden within the covering of many sacred veils.*[4] It is also befitting Holy Writ, which is proposed to all without distinction of persons—*To the wise and to the unwise I am a debtor*[5]—that spiritual truths be expounded by means of figures taken from corporeal things, in order that thereby even the simple who are unable by themselves to grasp intellectual things may be able to understand it.

Reply Obj. 1. Poetry makes use of metaphors to produce a representation, for it is natural to man to be pleased with representations. But sacred doctrine makes use of metaphors as both necessary and useful.

Reply Obj. 2. The ray of divine revelation is not extinguished by the sensible imagery wherewith it is veiled, as Dionysius says;[6] and its truth so far remains that it does not allow the minds of those to whom the revelation has been made, to rest in the metaphors, but raises them to the knowledge of truths; and through those to whom the revelation has been made others also may receive instruction in these matters. Hence those things that are taught metaphorically in one part of Scripture, in other parts are taught more openly. The very hiding of truth in figures in useful for the exercise of thoughtful minds, and as a defence against the ridicule of the impious, according to the words *Give not that which is holy to dogs.*[7]

Reply Obj. 3. As Dionysius says,[8] it is more fitting that divine truths should be expounded under the figure of less noble than of nobler bodies, and this for three reasons. Firstly, because thereby men's minds are the better preserved from error. For then it is clear that these things are not literal descriptions of divine truths, which might have been open to doubt had they been expressed under the figure of nobler bodies, especially for those who could think of nothing nobler than bodies. Secondly, because this is more befitting the knowledge of God that we have in this life. For what He is not is clearer to us than what He is. Therefore similitudes drawn from things farthest away from God form within us a truer estimate that God is above whatsoever we may say or think of Him. Thirdly, because thereby divine truths are the better hidden from the unworthy.[9]

3. Hosea 12.10.
4. From *The Celestial Hierarchy* 1 [translator's note]. Its author, Pseudo-Dionysius, was a Neoplatonic writer of late-5th-century Syria who successfully passed himself off as Dionysius the Areopagite, whose conversion by St. Paul is recorded in Acts 17.34. His writing was influenced by PLOTINUS.
5. Romans 1.14.
6. *Celestial Hierarchy* 1 [translator's note].
7. Matthew 7.6.
8. *Celestial Hierarchy* 1 [translator's note].
9. In his reply to objection 3, Aquinas expresses some traditional justifications for using figurative language when speaking of God. Some, including the argument that such language obscures divine truths from the unworthy, are repeated in BOCCACCIO'S defense of poetry in *Genealogy of the Gentile Gods* (1350–62; see below). There is a paradox involved in Aquinas's explanation that we know God better negatively through what he is *not* than through what he *is*, which we can never comprehend.

TENTH ARTICLE
WHETHER IN HOLY SCRIPTURE A WORD MAY HAVE SEVERAL SENSES?

We proceed thus to the Tenth Article:—

Objection 1. It seems that in Holy Writ a word cannot have several senses, historical or literal, allegorical, tropological or moral, and anagogical. For many different senses in one text produce confusion and deception and destroy all force of argument. Hence no argument, but only fallacies, can be deduced from a multiplicity of propositions. But Holy Writ ought to be able to state the truth without any fallacy. Therefore in it there cannot be several senses to a word.

Obj. 2. Further, Augustine says that *the Old Testament has a fourfold division as to history, etiology, analogy, and allegory.*[1] Now these four seem altogether different from the four divisions mentioned in the first objection. Therefore it does not seem fitting to explain the same word of Holy Writ according to the four different senses mentioned above.

Obj. 3. Further, besides these senses, there is the parabolical,[2] which is not one of these four.

On the contrary, Gregory says: *Holy Writ by the manner of its speech transcends every science, because in one and the same sentence, while it describes a fact, it reveals a mystery.*[3]

I answer that, The author of Holy Writ is God, in whose power it is to signify His meaning, not by words only (as man also can do), but also by things themselves. So, whereas in every other science things are signified by words, this science has the property, that the things signified by the words have themselves also a signification. Therefore that first signification whereby words signify things belongs to the first sense, the historical or literal. That signification whereby things signified by words have themselves also a signification is called the spiritual sense, which is based on the literal, and presupposes it. Now this spiritual sense has a threefold division. For as the Apostle says the Old Law is a figure of the New Law,[4] and Dionysius says *the New Law itself is a figure of future glory.*[5] Again, in the New Law, whatever our Head has done is a type of what we ought to do. Therefore, so far as the things of the Old Law signify the things of the New Law, there is the allegorical sense; so far as the things done in Christ, or so far as the things which signify Christ, are types of what we ought to do, there is the moral sense. But so far as they signify what relates to eternal glory, there is the anagogical sense. Since the literal sense is that which the author intends, and since the author of Holy Writ is God, Who by one act comprehends all things by His intellect, it is not unfitting, as Augustine says, if, even according to the literal sense, one word in Holy Writ should have several senses.[6]

Reply Obj. 1. The multiplicity of these senses does not produce equivocation or any other kind of multiplicity, seeing that these senses are not multiplied because one word signifies several things; but because the things signified by the words can be themselves types of other things. Thus in Holy Writ no con-

1. *On the Usefulness of Belief* 3 [translator's note]. AUGUSTINE (354–430), early Christian philosopher and theologian.
2. Expressed in a parable.
3. From *Moralia in Job* 20.1 [translator's note], by Pope Gregory I (540–604).
4. A rough paraphrase of Hebrews 10.1.
5. *Celestial Hierarchy* 1 [translator's note.]
6. *Confessions* 12.31.42 [translator's note].

fusion results, for all the senses are founded on one—the literal—from which alone can any argument be drawn, and not from those intended in allegory, as Augustine says.[7] Nevertheless, nothing of Holy Scripture perishes on account of this, since nothing necessary to faith is contained under the spiritual sense which is not elsewhere put forward by the Scripture in its literal sense.

Reply Obj. 2. These three—history, etiology, analogy—are grouped under the literal sense. For it is called history, as Augustine expounds,[8] whenever anything is simply related; it is called etiology when its cause is assigned, as when Our Lord gave the reason why Moses allowed the putting away of wives—namely, on account of the hardness of men's hearts; it is called analogy whenever the truth of one text of Scripture is shown not to contradict the truth of another. Of these four, allegory alone stands for the three spiritual senses. Thus Hugh of S. Victor[9] includes the anagogical under the allegorical sense, laying down three senses only—the historical, the allegorical, and the tropological.

Reply Obj. 3. The parabolical sense is contained in the literal, for by words things are signified properly and figuratively. Nor is the figure itself, but that which is figured, the literal sense. When Scripture speaks of God's arm, the literal sense is not that God has such a member, but only what is signified by this member, namely, operative power. Hence it is plain that nothing false can ever underlie the literal sense of Holy Writ.

1265–73

7. *Epistles* 93.8.42 (Augustine's letter against the Donatists, a heretical Christian sect of the 4th and 5th centuries).
8. *Epistles* 93.8.24.
9. *De Sacramentis*, 4.4, prologue [translator's note]. HUGH OF ST. VICTOR (ca. 1097–1141), educator and biblical commentator.

DANTE ALIGHIERI
1265–1321

The Divine Comedy (1307–21) secured Dante's reputation as the greatest poet of the Middle Ages; his literary criticism marks him as the first major theorist of European vernacular literature. Yet the relationship between Dante's masterpiece and his comments on poetics has vexed scholars throughout the modern period. How could a work as monumental and groundbreaking as *The Divine Comedy* be the product of as derivative and seemingly reductive a poetics as that described in his famous letter to Can Grande della Scala (1319)? Many have denied the authenticity of this letter, believing that the theologically driven allegory depicted there could not have been the basis for so great a poem. Such a position, however, neglects the subtleties of Dante's adaptation of the techniques of biblical exegesis to poetry. At the heart of these debates are questions about the nature and status of allegorical representation that have perennially engaged critics, including twentieth-century figures such as Erich Auerbach and PAUL DE MAN.

Much of Dante's literary criticism is derivative of the great twelfth- and thirteenth-century biblical scholars who preceded him—especially THOMAS AQUINAS, to whom he is most immediately indebted. But he is the first to make the intellectual achievements of medieval Latin culture accessible to those who did not know Latin and, just as significantly, to apply them to secular texts that could circulate among a growing audience of vernacular readers. In his *Eloquence in the Vernacular Tongue* (ca. 1304–08), Dante writes, "I see that such eloquence is unquestionably needed by almost everyone, for not only men, but even women and children (to the extent their nature allows) strive for it." His goal as a critic was to "enlighten the discernment of those who, like the blind, roam the streets thinking for the most part that what is really behind is in front." In fourteenth-century Europe, Dante's defense of Italian, his own vernacular, as an appropriate vehicle for poetry was innovative; indeed, the debate continued to rage long after—taken up, for example, by JOACHIM DU BELLAY in sixteenth-century France, JOHN DRYDEN in seventeenth-century England, and NGUGI WĂ THIONG'O in twentieth-century Kenya. In addition, Dante's remarks on the polysemous nature of poetic language continue to resound within present-day debates about allegory.

Dante Alighieri was born in Florence to a family that was neither wealthy nor especially prominent. His father, Alighiero di Bellincione d'Alighiero, was a member of the lesser nobility. Little is known about Dante's early education, though he probably received elementary instruction in grammar, language, and philosophy. Later he was a pupil of the Florentine encyclopedist, statesman, and poet Brunetto Latini, who, in the *The Divine Comedy*, is confined to the seventh circle of Hell for his sins against nature (sodomy). Under Latini's direction, Dante studied literature and rhetoric and associated himself with several respected Florentine poets, including Guido Cavalcanti. In 1283 he inherited a modest amount of money from his parents, and two years later he married Gemma Donati, who bore him four children. The death in 1290 of his childhood friend Beatrice Portinari proved to be a turning point in Dante's life, propelling him to begin an intense study of the philosophical works of Boethius (480–524 C.E.), Cicero (106–43 B.C.E.), and ARISTOTLE (384–322 B.C.E.). It also resulted in the appearance of his only work to be written in Florence. Dante's commemoration of Beatrice's death, *La Vita Nuova* (ca. 1295, *The New Life*), was a new, innovative approach to love poetry that equated love with mystical and spiritual revelation. His memorialization of Beatrice would continue in *The Divine Comedy*, where she serves as his guide to redemption in the third volume, *Paradiso*.

In the last decade of the thirteenth century, Dante became involved in Florence's increasingly violent politics. For much of the late thirteenth century Italy was engulfed in a civil war between the Ghibellines (a party favoring imperial rule for Italy) and the Guelphs (a party advocating control by the papacy). By the time of Dante's birth, Florence had become a Guelph stronghold; but the Guelph party itself had split into two factions, the White and the Black, divided more by competing family loyalties than by opposing political philosophies. In 1295 Dante, a supporter of the White Guelphs, got entangled in the city's politics by enrolling in the Guild of Doctors and Pharmacists. A year later he participated in a citizen's government known as the Council of the Hundred. He was elected for a term as one of the six priors, or magistrates, of Florence in 1300. By 1302, however, the Black Guelphs had begun to displace the Whites in Florentine politics, and Dante was exiled on pain of death if he returned to Florence. He spent the next few years wandering around Italy, during which time he produced both *De Vulgari Eloquentia* (*Eloquence in the Vernacular Tongue*), a theoretical and practical defense of the literary uses of the vernacular (written, ironically, in Latin), and *Il Convivio* (1306–09, *The Banquet*), an encyclopedic collection of *canzoni* (or short poems) followed by related prose commentaries on philosophy. Both projects were abandoned before they were completed, probably because as early as 1306 Dante became caught up in the plan of *The Divine Comedy*.

By 1312 Dante took up residence in Verona, where he sought the patronage of that city's imperial vicar, Can Grande della Scala, a member of the powerful Scaliger family. There he wrote most of his greatest work, *The Divine Comedy*, dedicating its final volume, the *Paradiso*, to his patron. *De Monarchia*, a political treatise, was most likely written around 1317. Dante spent the last three years of his life in Ravenna; he died without having ever returned to his native Florence.

In our selections, Dante confronts the problem of how to understand and construe textual meaning. Both his encyclopedic treatise *Il Convivio* and his famous letter dedicating the *Paradiso* to his patron, Can Grande della Scala, examine the relationship between general critical principles and the detailed interpretation of specific parts of a text. Dante is remarkably consistent in his descriptions of how poetry is to be read and interpreted. He extends to vernacular poetry the four senses of allegorical interpretation—the literal, the allegorical, the moral, and the anagogical—articulated in earlier medieval commentaries on biblical texts. In doing so, he effects a synthesis between the "allegory of the poets," or the allegories that Christian writers such as Bernardus Silvestris attributed to pagan poets such as Virgil, and the "allegory of the theologians," or the interpretations of Scriptures developed by exegetes such as HUGH OF ST. VICTOR and Aquinas. Although in classical rhetoric *allegory* involves one thing while meaning another, Dante insists that his allegories are not simple substitution codes (this is how Bernardus earlier understands Virgil's *Aeneid*). Instead, each of the four "senses" of the text inheres in and evokes the other three simultaneously. The text is polysemous: that is, it has many meanings—including the literal—that occur in a single imaginative act. Dante's commentaries demonstrate that textual exegesis (explication) was not expected to follow the theory of allegorical "senses" in any dogmatic or wooden way. That a poem could be interpreted literally and in three figurative senses (allegorical, moral, and anagogical) does not imply that every episode or every symbol must contain all four meanings. Dante offers a more subtle approach. Much of the richness of *The Divine Comedy*, for example, derives from the gap allegory opens up between the sign and what it might signify. The promise of stable signification seemingly held out by the allegorical method is offset by his claim that the text is polysemous, open to many meanings. This recurring paradox has also fascinated present-day critics of allegory, who are generally more interested than was Dante in the destabilization of meaning that accompanies the possibility of multiple meanings.

BIBLIOGRAPHY

Dante's literary criticism can be found in the Italian *Opere minori di Dante Alighieri* (1986). The standard Italian edition of *Il Convivio* was edited by Maria Simonelli (1966). Two recent English translations of *Il Convivio*, by Christopher Ryan (1989) and by Richard H. Lansing (1990), both based on the Simonelli edition, are superior to earlier translations. *The Letters of Dante* (1920), with Latin text, edited and with English translation by Paget Toynbee, is the standard edition of Dante's letters. The best translation of the "Letter to Can Grande" can be found in Robert S. Haller's *Literary Criticism of Dante Alighieri* (1973), which also contains *Eloquence in the Vernacular Tongue* and other critical statements. The best biography of Dante remains Michele Barbi's *Life of Dante* (1933; trans. 1954).

Dante has been the subject of commentaries by important poet-critics, the most prominent among them T. S. Eliot's *Dante* (1928). Erich Auerbach, in *Dante: Poet of the Secular World* (1929) and *Mimesis: The Representation of Reality in Western Literature* (1953), argues that Dante's comments on allegorical reading are central to an interpretation of *The Divine Comedy*. For important introductions to Dantean poetics, see Thomas Bergin, *An Approach to Dante* (1965), and Francis Fergusson, *Dante* (1966). Peter Dronke, in *Dante and the Medieval Latin Tradition* (1986), and Henry Ansgar Kelly, in *Tragedy and Comedy from Dante to Pseudo-Dante* (1989), have both questioned the authenticity of the letter to Can Grande, arguing that Auerbach's insistence on a figural reading of *The Divine Comedy* based on that letter is mistaken. J. F. Took's *Dante Lyric Poet and Philosopher: An Introduction to the Minor Works*

(1990) contains an important chapter on *Il Convivio*. In *Dante's Epistle to Cangrande* (1993), Robert Hollander summarizes the debate over the letter to Can Grande, while defending Dante's authorship and its relevance to the allegorical reading of *The Divine Comedy*. For a bibliography on Dante, consult the *American Dante Biography*, edited by Anthony L. Pelligrini and Christopher Kleinhenz (1993).

From Il Convivio[1]

From *Book Two*

CHAPTER 1

Now that by way of a preface my bread has been sufficiently prepared in the preceding book through my own assistance, time calls and requires my ship to leave port; thus, having set the sail of my reason to the breeze of my desire, I enter upon the open sea with the hope of a smooth voyage and a safe and praiseworthy port at the end of my feast. But so that this food of mine may be more profitable, I wish to show, before it appears, how the first course must be eaten.[2]

As I stated in the first chapter, this exposition must be both literal and allegorical. To convey what this means, it is necessary to know that writings can be understood and ought to be expounded principally in four senses. The first is called the literal, and this is the sense that does not go beyond the surface of the letter, as in the fables of the poets. The next is called the allegorical, and this is the one that is hidden beneath the cloak of these fables, and is a truth hidden beneath a beautiful fiction. Thus Ovid says that with his lyre Orpheus tamed wild beasts and made trees and rocks move toward him,[3] which is to say that the wise man with the instrument of his voice makes cruel hearts grow tender and humble and moves to his will those who do not devote their lives to knowledge and art; and those who have no rational life whatsoever are almost like stones. Why this kind of concealment was devised by the wise will be shown in the penultimate book. Indeed the theologians take this sense otherwise than do the poets; but since it is my intention here to follow the method of the poets, I shall take the allegorical sense according to the usage of the poets.[4]

The third sense is called moral, and this is the sense that teachers should intently seek to discover throughout the scriptures, for their own profit and that of their pupils; as, for example, in the Gospel we may discover that when

1. Translated by Richard H. Lansing.
2. In the allegorical framework of *Il Convivio*, Dante uses the conceit of a banquet to represent human knowledge. Like Boethius's *Consolation of Philosophy* (ca. 524 C.E.), *Il Convivio* employs a combination of verse and prose commentary called *prosimetrum*. In Dante's allegorical banquet, the "meat" is the *canzoni*, or verses, and the "bread" the commentaries on those verses.
3. Ovid (43 B.C.E.–17 C.E.), *Metamorphoses*, 11.1–2. In Greek mythology, Orpheus was the greatest of all mortal musicians.
4. What Dante means by distinguishing between the allegory of the poets and the allegory of the theologians is not entirely clear and has given rise to endless speculation. The theologians insist on the veracity of all four levels of meaning, and conceived of the allegorical levels (the typological, tropological, and anagogical) to depend on a literal level which was historically true. In the allegory of the poets, as exemplified by the allusion to the myth of Orpheus, the literal level is a "bella menzongna," a beautiful fiction having no basis in historical reality. In the allegory of the theologians, moreover, the second level always refers to some aspect of Christ's historical being, of which he is the ideal type, which is not the case with the poets. The third and fourth levels are shared in common by both modes of allegory [translator's note].

Christ ascended the mountain to be transfigured, of the twelve Apostles he took with him but three, the moral meaning of which is that in matters of great secrecy we should have few companions.[5]

The fourth sense is called anagogical, that is to say, beyond the senses; and this occurs when a scripture is expounded in a spiritual sense which, although it is true also in the literal sense, signifies by means of the things signified a part of the supernal things of eternal glory, as may be seen in the song of the Prophet which says that when the people of Israel went out of Egypt, Judea was made whole and free.[6] For although it is manifestly true according to the letter, that which is spiritually intended is no less true, namely, that when the soul departs from sin it is made whole and free in its power. In this kind of explication, the literal should always come first, as being the sense in whose meaning the others are enclosed, and without which it would be impossible and illogical to attend to the other senses, and especially the allegorical. It would be impossible because in everything that has an inside and an outside it is impossible to arrive at the inside without first arriving at the outside; consequently, since in what is written down the literal meaning is always the outside, it is impossible to arrive at the other senses, especially the allegorical, without first arriving at the literal.

Moreover, it would be impossible because in every natural or artificial thing it is impossible to proceed to the form unless the subject on which the form must be imposed is prepared first—just as it is impossible for a piece of jewelry to acquire its form if the material (that is, its subject) is not first arranged and prepared, or a chest to acquire its form if the material (that is, the wood) is not first arranged and prepared. Consequently, since the literal meaning is always the subject and material of the other senses, especially of the allegorical, it is impossible to come to an understanding of them before coming to an understanding of it. Moreover, it would be impossible because in every natural or artificial thing it is impossible to proceed unless the foundation is laid first, as in a house or in studying; consequently, since explication is the building up of knowledge, and the explication of the literal sense is the foundation of the others, especially of the allegorical, it is impossible to arrive at the other senses without first arriving at it.

Moreover, even supposing it were possible, it would be illogical, that is to say out of order, and would therefore be carried out with great labor and much confusion. Consequently as the Philosopher says in the first book of the *Physics*,[7] nature wills that we proceed in due order in our learning, that is, by proceeding from that which we know better to that which we know not so well; I say that nature wills it since this way of learning is by nature innate in us. Therefore if the senses other than the literal are less understood (which they are, as is quite apparent), it would be illogical to proceed to explain them if the literal had not been explicated first. For these reasons, therefore, I shall on each occasion discuss first the literal meaning concerning each canzone, and afterwards I shall discuss its allegory (that is, the hidden truth), at times touching on the other senses, when opportune, as time and place deem proper.

1306–09

5. The apostles Peter, James, and John; see Matthew 17.1–8, Mark 9.1–7, Luke 9.28–36 [translator's note].

6. Psalm 114; Dante refers to this same psalm in his "Letter to Can Grande" (below).

7. Aristotle, *Physics* 1.1, 184a17–21.

From The Letter to Can Grande[1]

* * *

[6] Therefore, if one should wish to present an introduction to a part of a work, it is necessary to present some conception of the whole work of which it is a part. For this reason I, who wish to present something in the form of an introduction to the above-mentioned part of the whole *Comedy*, have decided to preface it with some discussion of the whole work, in order to make the approach to the part easier and more complete.[2] There are six questions, then, which should be asked at the beginning about any doctrinal work: what is its subject, its form, its agent, its end, the title of the book, and its branch of philosophy. In three cases the answers to these questions will be different for the part of the work I propose to give you than for the whole, that is, in the cases of its subject, form, and title, while in the other three, as will be clear upon inspection, they will be the same. Thus these first three should be specifically asked in a discussion of the whole work, after which the way will be clear for an introduction to the part. Let us, then, ask the last three questions not only about the whole but also about the offered part itself.

[7] For the clarification of what I am going to say, then, it should be understood that there is not just a single sense in this work:[3] it might rather be called *polysemous*, that is, having several senses. For the first sense is that which is contained in the letter, while there is another which is contained in what is signified by the letter. The first is called literal, while the second is called allegorical, or moral or anagogical. And in order to make this manner of treatment clear, it can be applied to the following verses: "When Israel went out of Egypt, the house of Jacob from a barbarous people, Judea was made his sanctuary, Israel his dominion."[4] Now if we look at the letter alone, what is signified to us is the departure of the sons of Israel from Egypt during the time of Moses; if at the allegory, what is signified to us is our redemption through Christ; if at the moral sense, what is signified to us is the conversion of the soul from the sorrow and misery of sin to the state of grace; if at the anagogical, what is signified to us is the departure of the sanctified soul from bondage to the corruption of this world into the freedom of eternal glory. And although these mystical senses are called by various names, they may all be called allegorical, since they are all different from the literal or historical. For allegory is derived from the Greek *alleon*, which means in Latin *alienus* ("belonging to another") or *diversus* ("different").

[8] This being established, it is clear that the subject about which these two senses play must also be twofold. And thus it should first be noted what the subject of the work is when taken according to the letter, and then what its subject is when understood allegorically. The subject of the whole work, then, taken literally, is the state of souls after death, understood in a simple sense; for the movement of the whole work turns upon this and about this.

1. Translated by Robert Haller. Can Grande della Scala (1287–1329), the imperial vicar of Verona, was Dante's patron; his name means "Big Dog."
2. Dante dedicated the third volume of *The Divine Comedy*, the *Paradiso*, to Can Grande; the letter serves as an introduction to that part of the poem.
3. *The Divine Comedy*.
4. Psalm 114.1–2; Dante uses the same psalm to illustrate the anagogical level of meaning in *Il Convivio* (see above).

If on the other hand the work is taken allegorically, the subject is man, in the exercise of his free will, earning or becoming liable to the rewards or punishments of justice.

* * *

[10] The title of the work is, "Here begins the Comedy of Dante Alighieri, a Florentine by birth but not in character." To understand the title, it must be known that comedy is derived from *comos*, "a village," and from *oda*, "a song," so that a comedy is, so to speak, "a rustic song."[5] Comedy, then, is a certain genre of poetic narrative differing from all others. For it differs from tragedy in its matter, in that tragedy is tranquil and conducive to wonder at the beginning, but foul and conducive to horror at the end, or catastrophe, for which reason it is derived from *tragos*, meaning "goat," and *oda*, making it, as it were, a "goat song," that is, foul as a goat is foul. This is evident in Seneca's[6] tragedies. Comedy, on the other hand, introduces a situation of adversity, but ends its matter in prosperity, as is evident in Terence's[7] comedies. And for this reason some writers have the custom of saying in their salutations, by way of greeting, "a tragic beginning and a comic ending to you." And, as well, they differ in their manner of speaking. Tragedy uses an elevated and sublime, style, while comedy uses an unstudied and low style, which is what Horace implies in the *Art of Poetry* where he allows comic writers occasionally to speak like the tragic, and also the reverse of this:

> Yet sometimes even comedy elevates its voice,
> and angry Chremes rages in swelling tones;
> and in tragedy Telephus and Peleus often lament
> in prosaic speeches. . . .[8]

So from this it should be clear why the present work is called the *Comedy*. For, if we consider the matter, it is, at the beginning, that is, in Hell, foul and conducive to horror, but at the end, in Paradise, prosperous, conducive to pleasure, and welcome. And if we consider the manner of speaking, it is unstudied and low, since its speech is the vernacular, in which even women communicate. There are, besides these, other genres of poetic narrative, such as pastoral verse, elegy, satire, and the hymn of thanksgiving, as could also be gathered from Horace in his *Art of Poetry*. But there is no purpose to discussing these at this time.

* * *

1321

5. For a similar derivation of "comedy" (usually linked to the Greek *kōmos*, "revel," not *kōmē*, "village"), see ARISTOTLE, *Poetics* 3, 1447a (above).
6. Roman philosopher and author of several tragedies (ca. 4 B.C.E.–65 C.E.).
7. Roman comic dramatist (ca. 190–159 B.C.E.).
8. HORACE [65–8 B.C.E.], *Art of Poetry* 93–96 [translator's note]; reprinted above. Chremes: a character in Aristophanes' comedy *Ecclesiazusae* (ca. 392 B.C.E.). Telephus: in Greek mythology, a son of Heracles. Peleus: the father of the Greek hero Achilles.

GIOVANNI BOCCACCIO
1313–1375

Giovanni Boccaccio, author of the famous *Decameron* (1358), was, with DANTE and Petrarch, a pioneer of Italian vernacular literature and of the humanism that would become the philosophical basis of the Renaissance. Although Boccaccio's present-day reputation is based primarily on the bawdy tales of the *Decameron*, his romances and scholarly works were indispensible sources for poets throughout the Renaissance. His *Genealogia Deorum Gentilium* (1350–62, *Genealogy of the Gentile Gods*), an encyclopedic compendium in Latin of pagan mythology designed as a guide to the ancient poets, culminates in books 14 and 15 with a defense of poetry against the criticisms of it that reach back to PLATO's *Republic*. Like John of Salisbury in the twelfth century, Boccaccio defends poetry in terms that are unmistakably medieval. But he also stands in a long line of practicing poets who have written in defense of their art, ranging from HORACE (65–8 B.C.E.), JOACHIM DU BELLAY (ca. 1522–1560), and SIR PHILIP SIDNEY (1554–1586) to JOHN DRYDEN (1631–1700), ALEXANDER POPE (1688–1744), WILLIAM WORDSWORTH (1770–1850), and PERCY BYSSHE SHELLEY (1792–1822).

Boccaccio was born in Tuscany, the illegitimate son of a merchant, Boccaccino di Chelino, and raised in Florence. Having provided him with a grammatical and literary education, as well as practical business training, his father sent him in 1327 to serve an apprenticeship in Naples. Boccaccio, however, preferred the aristocratic intellectual circles of the court of Robert of Anjou to a life in commerce. He began to mingle in courtly society and to write stories in verse and prose. He fell in love with—and wrote about—an unattainable aristocratic woman he called Fiammetta, who has been identified as Maria d'Aquino, an illegitimate daughter of King Robert. His first literary works appeared during this period, including the allegorical poem *La caccia di Diana* (ca. 1334, *Diana's Hunt*) and two romances: *Filostrato* (ca. 1335)—a version of the story of Troilus and Criseida, later adapted by both Chaucer and Shakespeare—and *Teseida* (ca. 1339), a source of Chaucer's *Knight's Tale*. In 1341 Boccaccio returned to Florence, where he discovered a different kind of intellectual and artistic community, one that followed in the style of the recently deceased Dante. Under the influence of this literary tradition of allegorical didacticism that stressed the moral and symbolic dimensions of literature, he wrote the allegorical works *Comedy of the Florentine Nymphs* (1341–42) and *Fiammetta* (1343). By 1348, when the bubonic plague had reached Italy, Boccaccio began his greatest work, the hundred prose tales of the *Decameron* (1348–53). The plague provides their framework—ten young people retreat to the country to escape the disease and tell ten stories each as a means of entertaining themselves during their confinement.

About 1350, around the same time that he began the *Genealogy of the Gentile Gods*, Boccaccio became involved in Florentine politics, serving on various ambassadorial missions. He also met Petrarch, beginning a friendship that would last until Petrarch's death in 1374. He turned from literature to scholarship, especially to the study of classical history, literature, and mythology, translating the Roman historian Livy, searching for ancient manuscripts, learning Greek, and attempting to establish an academic chair in Greek in Florence. Between 1350 and 1362 he wrote in Latin most of the *Genealogy*, as well as such scholarly collections as his *Fates of Illustrious Men* (1356, *De Casibus Virorum Illustrium*) and *Concerning Famous Women* (1361, *De Mulieribus Claris*), which was an important source for CHRISTINE DE PIZAN's famous *City of Ladies* (1405). In 1362 Boccaccio underwent a spiritual crisis during which he considered burning his secular writing and taking holy orders; he was dissuaded from both by Petrarch. A year later he retired to his native town, Certaldo, where he remained active in Florentine politics. By 1373 he had completed a biography, *Life of Dante*. In the same year, he is said to have met the English poet Chaucer in Florence. He died at Certaldo two years later.

Boccaccio intended *Genealogy of the Gentile Gods* as a monumental work of scholarship, a mythological sourcebook that would introduce readers to the study of the ancient poets. His decision to write in Latin rather than Italian is a measure of its seriousness as a scholarly project. Books 1–13, mostly completed by 1360, contain Boccaccio's allegorical interpretations of Greek mythology. By the 1360s, however, he seemed to feel that some kind of defense of the ancient poets was necessary as well, to show that they were, as he writes in the first chapter of book 15, "really men of wisdom, . . . their compositions full of profit and pleasure to the reader." Boccaccio's defense of poetry in books 14 and 15 compiles and arranges in a single document a series of arguments both for and against poetry that had been in circulation for at least a thousand years. Together with Plato's writing on poetry and ARISTOTLE's *Poetics* (which was not recovered in Europe until the fifteenth century), it provides the substance of Renaissance literary theory. The influence of the *Genealogy*'s defense of poetry during the Renaissance is easily discernible, for instance, in Sir Philip Sidney's *Apology for Poetry* (see below), published in England over two centuries later.

In chapter 5 of book 14 Boccaccio neutralizes the arguments of poetry's detractors, especially the philosophers who, since Plato, had been chief among those denouncing poetry as a distraction from the pursuit of truth. In the Middle Ages, the theologians had inherited the philosopher's mantle. Both philosophy and theology enjoyed enormous prestige in this period, beside which all other forms of knowledge, including poetry, were dismissed as trivial—especially in Italy, where the study of theology was more isolated from the other liberal arts than in the rest of Europe. Boccaccio borrows a scene from Dante's *Il Convivio* (see above), ultimately derived from Boethius's *Consolation of Philosophy* (ca. 524), opening chapter 5 with a vision of Lady Philosophy. Unlike either Dante or Boethius, however, Boccaccio puts poets in "high places," as Lady Philosophy's counselors, and relegates philosophers and other critics of poetry to the "noisy crowd" surrounding her. In a neat reversal, the text's allegory makes the poets the true followers of philosophy, while poetry's detractors are exposed as impostors. Placing the criticisms of poetry into the mouths of this crowd of pretenders robs them of their force; at the same time, poetry is redefined as proceeding, like philosophy, from "the bosom of God." Later in the text, Boccaccio concedes that philosophy does arrive at truth, but only by slow reason; poets do so by leaps of imagination.

Chapter 7 contains Boccaccio's most important ideas about poetry, ideas that draw both on his own experience as a poet and on critics who preceded him, including Horace, AUGUSTINE (354–430 C.E.), MACROBIUS (b. ca. 360 C.E.), Dante, and his friend Petrarch. He defines poetry as "fervid and exquisite invention" combined with "fervid expression, in speech or writing," insisting that inspiration, education in the liberal arts, and craft are equally important in its creation. Following Aristotle and the Roman orator Cicero, Boccaccio carefully distinguishes poetry from rhetoric, countering a medieval tendency to subordinate poetry to both rhetoric and grammar. While the poet needs to master the rules and methods of rhetoric, poetry transcends it both in its "invention" and its "expression." Whereas rhetoricians are required to be "simple and clear," poets have license to invent wonders and to make language seem strange.

In chapter 12, Boccaccio takes on the charge that poets are often obscure, engaging in an argument that sounds remarkably similar to contemporary debates about theoretical jargon. If poets are obscure, so too, he argues, are philosophers such as Plato and Aristotle, who "abound in difficulties so tangled and involved that . . . they have yielded no clear nor consistent meaning." Holy Scriptures, he points out, are full of ambiguous and difficult passages, yet no critic would dare, for fear of blasphemy, accuse their author of deliberate obscurity for the sake of appearing clever. Obscurity, for Boccaccio, is both engaging and fruitful, as it is for MAIMONIDES (1135–1204). It protects poetry from vulgar people, while usefully prompting multiple interpretations from the learned.

True to his roots in medieval linguistics, which insists on a fundamental distinction between words used "properly" and those used "figuratively," Boccaccio never allows himself to question openly the notion of language as a transparent medium referring to an independent reality. For him, poetry is always subordinate to some higher reality—philosophy, theology, the divine. However, by insisting that poetry's "veil of fiction" "clothes" the naked truth, Boccaccio unwittingly challenges traditional assumptions about the referential nature of language and poetry, pointing toward the fundamentally figurative basis of all language.

BIBLIOGRAPHY

A modern Italian edition of the complete works of Giovanni Boccaccio is now in progress under the editorial direction of Vittore Branca, *Tutte le opera di Giovanni Boccaccio* (10 vols. to date, 1964–). For the Latin text of *Genealogy of the Gentile Gods*, consult the definitive edition by Vincenzo Romano (1951). An English translation of books 14 and 15 of *Genealogy of the Gentile Gods* is available in Charles G. Osgood, *Boccaccio on Poetry* (1930). Other of Boccaccio's critical works in English include his *Life of Dante*, translated by P. H. Wicksteed (1922); *De mulieribus claris: Concerning Famous Women*, translated by Guido A. Guarino (1963); and *De casibus: The Fates of Illustrious Men*, translated in an abridged version by Louis Brewer Hall (1965). For an intellectual biography of Boccaccio in English with important primary material translated, see Vittore Branca, *Boccaccio: The Man and His Works* (1976).

Much of the secondary criticism of Boccaccio focuses on the *Decameron*. The introduction to Charles Osgood's *Boccaccio on Poetry* is an indispensible guide to Boccaccio's literary criticism. Erich Auerbach's chapter on Boccaccio in *Mimesis* (1953) offers a fundamental discussion of realism in his writing. Herbert G. Wright traces Boccaccio's considerable influence on English poets in *Boccaccio in England: From Chaucer to Tennyson* (1957). For a general introduction to Boccaccio and his work, see Judith Powers Serafini-Sauli, *Giovanni Boccaccio* (1982). Thomas Hyde's essay "Boccaccio and the Genealogies of Myth," *PMLA* 100 (1985), offers a close analysis of the *Genealogy of the Gentile Gods*. Gregory Stone provides an advanced study of Boccaccio's literary criticism in *The Ethics of Nature in the Middle Ages: On Boccaccio's Poetaphysics* (1998). For a bibliography, consult Joseph P. Consoli, *Giovanni Boccaccio: An Annotated Bibliography* (1992).

From Genealogy of the Gentile Gods[1]

From *Book 14*

V. OTHER CAVILLERS AT THE POETS AND THEIR IMPUTATIONS

There is also, O most serene of rulers,[2] as you know far better than I, a kind of house established in this world by God's gift, in the image of a celestial council, and devoted only to sacred studies. Within, on a lofty throne, sits Philosophy,[3] messenger from the very bosom of God, mistress of all knowledge. Noble is her mien and radiant with godlike splendor. There she sits

1. Translated by Charles G. Osgood.
2. Boccaccio claims that his treatise was commissioned by King Hugh of Cypress, king of Cyprus and Jerusalem from 1324 to 1358. Hugh was dead by 1359; it is not clear why Boccaccio continues to address him.
3. The ultimate source for this image of Lady Philosophy is Boethius's *Consolation of Philosophy* (ca. 524 C.E.), Prose 1.3.

arrayed in royal robes and adorned with a golden crown, like the Empress of all the World. In her left hand she holds several books, with her right hand she wields a royal sceptre, and in clear and fluent discourse she shows forth to such as will listen the truly praiseworthy ideals of human character, the forces of our Mother Nature, the true good, and the secrets of heaven. If you enter you do not doubt that it is a sanctuary full worthy of all reverence; and if you look about, you will clearly see there every opportunity for the higher pursuits of the human mind, both speculation and knowledge, and will gaze with wonder till you regard it not merely as one all-inclusive household, but almost the very image of the divine mind. Among other objects of great veneration there, behind the mistress of the household, are certain men seated in high places, few in number, of gentle aspect and utterance, who are so distinguished by their seriousness, honesty, and true humility, that you take them for gods not mortals. These men abound in the faith and doctrine of their mistress, and give freely to others of the fullness of their knowledge.

But there is also another group—a noisy crowd—of all sorts and conditions. Some of these have resigned all pride, and live in watchful obedience to the injunctions of their superiors, in hopes that their obsequious zeal may gain them promotion. But others there are who grow so elated with what is virtually elementary knowledge, that they fall upon their great mistress' robes as it were with their talons, and in violent haste tear away a few shreds as samples; then don various titles which they often pick up for a price; and, as puffed up as if they knew the whole subject of divinity, they rush forth from the sacred house, setting such mischief afoot among ignorant people as only the wise can calculate. Yet these rascals are sworn conspirators against all high arts. First they try to counterfeit a good man; they exchange their natural expression for an anxious, careful one. They go about with downcast eye to appear inseparable from their thoughts. Their pace is slow to make the uneducated think that they stagger under an excessive weight of high speculation. They dress unpretentiously, not because they are really modest, but only to mask themselves with sanctity. Their talk is little and serious. If you ask them a question they heave a sigh, pause a moment, raise their eyes to heaven, and at length deign to answer. They hope the bystanders will infer from this that their words rise slowly to their lips, not from any lack of eloquence, but because they are fetched from the remote sanctuary of heavenly secrets. They profess piety, sanctity, and justice, and often, forsooth, utter the words of the prophet,[4] "The zeal of God's house hath eaten me up."

Then they proceed to display their wonderful knowledge, and whatever they don't know they damn—to good effect too. This they do to avoid inquiry about subjects of which they are ignorant, or else to affect scorn and indifference in such matters as cheap, trivial, and obvious, while they have devoted themselves to things of greater importance. When they have caught inexperienced minds in traps of this sort, they proceed boldly to range about town, dabble in business, give advice, arrange marriages, appear at big dinners, dictate wills, act as executors of estates, and otherwise display arrogance unbecoming to a philosopher. Thus they blow up a huge cloud of

4. David, Psalms 69.9; John 2.17 [translator's note].

popular reputation, and thereby so strut with vanity that, when they walk abroad, they want to have everybody's finger pointing them out, to overhear people saying that they are great masters of their subjects, and see how the grand folk rise to meet them in the squares of the city and call them "Rabbi,"[5] speak to them, invite them, give place and defer to them. Straightway they throw off all restraint and become bold enough for anything; they are not afraid to lay their own sickles to the harvest of another; and haply, while they are basely defiling other people's business, the talk may fall upon poetry and poets. At the sound of the word they blaze up in such a sudden fury that you would say their eyes were afire. They cannot stop; they go raging on by the very momentum of their wrath. Finally, like conspirators against a deadly enemy, in the schools, in public squares, in pulpits, with a lazy crowd, as a rule, for an audience, they break out into such mad denunciation of poets that the bystanders are afraid of the speakers themselves, let alone the harmless objects of attack.

They say poetry is absolutely of no account, and the making of poetry a useless and absurd craft; that poets are tale-mongers, or, in lower terms, liars; that they live in the country among the woods and mountains because they lack manners and polish. They say, besides, that their poems are false, obscure, lewd, and replete with absurd and silly tales of pagan gods, and that they make Jove,[6] who was, in point of fact, an obscene and adulterous man, now the father of gods, now king of heaven, now fire, or air, or man, or bull, or eagle, or similar irrelevant things; in like manner poets exalt to fame Juno[7] and infinite others under various names. Again and again they cry out that poets are seducers of the mind, prompters of crime, and, to make their foul charge, fouler, if possible, they say they are philosophers' apes, that it is a heinous crime to read or possess the books of poets; and then, without making any distinction, they prop themselves up, as they say, with Plato's authority[8] to the effect that poets ought to be turned out-of-doors—nay, out of town, and that the Muses,[9] their mumming mistresses, as Boethius[1] says, being sweet with deadly sweetness, are detestable, and should be driven out with them and utterly rejected. But it would take too long to cite everything that their irritable spite and deadly hatred prompt these madmen to say. It is also before judges like these—so eminent, forsooth, so fair, so merciful, so well-inclined—that my work will appear, O glorious Prince; and I know full well they will gather about it like famished lions,[2] to seek what they may devour. Since my book has entirely to do with poetic material, I cannot look for a milder sentence from them than in their rage they thunder down upon poets. I am well aware that I offer my breast to the same missiles that their hatred has already employed; but I shall endeavor to ward them off.

O merciful God, meet now this foolish and ill-considered clamor of mad men, and oppose their rage. And thou, O best of kings, as I advance upon their line, support me with the strength of thy noble soul, and help me in my fight for thee; for courage and a stout heart must now be mine. Sharp and poisonous are their weapons, but weak withal. Foolish judges though

5. Literally, "my master," "my teacher" (Hebrew).
6. Jupiter, the chief Roman god (identified with the Greek god Zeus).
7. Jupiter's wife and sister, the chief Roman goddess (identified with the Greek goddess Hera).
8. See PLATO, *Republic* 3.398a–b (above).
9. In Greek mythology, 9 daughters of Memory who preside over the arts and all intellectual pursuits.
1. Roman Christian philosopher (470–524).
2. Like the Devil: 1 Peter 5.8 [translator's note].

they be, they are strong in other ways, and I tremble with fear before them, unless God, who deserteth not them that trust in Him, and thou, also, favor me. Slender is my strength and my mind weak, but great is my expectation of help; borne up by such hope, I shall rush upon them with justice at my right hand.

VII. THE DEFINITION OF POETRY, ITS ORIGIN, AND FUNCTION

This poetry, which ignorant triflers cast aside, is a sort of fervid and exquisite invention, with fervid expression, in speech or writing, of that which the mind has invented. It proceeds from the bosom of God, and few, I find, are the souls in whom this gift is born; indeed so wonderful a gift it is that true poets have always been the rarest of men. This fervor of poesy is sublime in its effects: it impels the soul to a longing for utterance; it brings forth strange and unheard-of creations of the mind; it arranges these meditations in a fixed order, adorns the whole composition with unusual interweaving of words and thoughts; and thus it veils truth in a fair and fitting garment of fiction. Further, if in any case the invention so requires, it can arm kings, marshal them for war, launch whole fleets from their docks, nay, counterfeit sky, land, sea, adorn young maidens with flowery garlands, portray human character in its various phases, awake the idle, stimulate the dull, restrain the rash, subdue the criminal, and distinguish excellent men with their proper meed of praise: these, and many other such, are the effects of poetry. Yet if any man who has received the gift of poetic fervor shall imperfectly fulfil its function here described, he is not, in my opinion, a laudable poet. For, however deeply the poetic impulse stirs the mind to which it is granted, it very rarely accomplishes anything commendable if the instruments by which its concepts are to be wrought out are wanting—I mean, for example, the precepts of grammar and rhetoric, an abundant knowledge of which is opportune. I grant that many a man already writes his mother tongue admirably, and indeed has performed each of the various duties of poetry as such; yet over and above this, it is necessary to know at least the principles of the other Liberal Arts,[3] both moral and natural, to possess a strong and abundant vocabulary, to behold the monuments and relics of the Ancients, to have in one's memory the histories of the nations, and to be familiar with the geography of various lands, of seas, rivers and mountains.

Furthermore, places of retirement, the lovely handiwork of Nature herself, are favorable to poetry, as well as peace of mind and desire for worldly glory; the ardent period of life also has very often been of great advantage. If these conditions fail, the power of creative genius frequently grows dull and sluggish.

Now since nothing proceeds from this poetic fervor, which sharpens and illumines the powers of the mind, except what is wrought out by art,[4] poetry is generally called an art. Indeed the word poetry has not the origin that many carelessly suppose, namely *poio, pois*, which is but Latin *fingo, fingis*; rather it is derived from a very ancient Greek word *poetes*,[5] which means in

3. The liberal arts in the Middle Ages included the trivium (grammar, rhetoric, and logic) and the quadrivium (arithmetic, geometry, music, and astronomy).

4. Conscious skill, technique, indispensable to poetic creation [translator's note].

5. Boccaccio's limitations in Greek have allowed him to follow Isidore of Seville—bad etymology and all—in this whole passage, as did writers before him who knew no Greek [translator's note].

Latin exquisite discourse (*exquisita locutio*). For the first men who, thus inspired, began to employ an exquisite style of speech, such, for example, as song in an age hitherto unpolished, to render this unheard-of discourse sonorous to their hearers, let it fall in measured periods; and lest by its brevity it fail to please, or, on the other hand, become prolix and tedious, they applied to it the standard of fixed rules, and restrained it within a definite number of feet and syllables. Now the product of this studied method of speech they no longer called by the more general term poesy, but poem. Thus as I said above, the name of the art, as well as its artificial product, is derived from its effect.

Now though I allege that this science of poetry has ever streamed forth from the bosom of God upon souls while even yet in their tenderest years, these enlightened cavillers will perhaps say that they cannot trust my words. To any fair-minded man the fact is valid enough from its constant recurrence. But for these dullards I must cite witnesses to it. If, then, they will read what Cicero,[6] a philosopher rather than a poet, says in his oration delivered before the senate in behalf of Aulus Licinius Archias,[7] perhaps they will come more easily to believe me. He says: "And yet we have it on the highest and most learned authority, that while other arts are matters of science and formula and technique, poetry depends solely upon an inborn faculty, is evoked by a purely mental activity, and is infused with a strange supernal inspiration."

But not to protract this argument, it is now sufficiently clear to reverent men, that poetry is a practical art,[8] springing from God's bosom and deriving its name from its effect, and that it has to do with many high and noble matters that constantly occupy even those who deny its existence. If my opponents ask when and in what circumstances, the answer is plain: the poets would declare with their own lips under whose help and guidance they compose their inventions when, for example, they raise flights[9] of symbolic steps to heaven, or make thick-branching trees[1] spring aloft to the very stars, or go winding about mountains to their summits. Haply, to disparage this art of poetry now unrecognized by them, these men will say that it is rhetoric which the poets employ. Indeed, I will not deny it in part, for rhetoric has also its own inventions. Yet, in truth, among the disguises of fiction rhetoric has no part, for whatever is composed as under a veil, and thus exquisitely wrought, is poetry and poetry alone.[2]

Isidore of Seville (ca. 560–636), Spanish bishop and encyclopedist; see his *Etymologiarum* 8.7.2, "De poeta." The Greek *poieō* (which is, in fact, related to "poet") means "make, create"; the Latin *fingo* means "form, invent."

6. Roman statesman, orator, and author (106–43 B.C.E.).

7. A Greek poet of Antioch, whose claim of Roman citizenship was successfully defended by Cicero; the greater part of his oration is devoted to glorifying literature (the quotation is from *Pro Archia* 8.18).

8. *Facultas* (ability, power, capacity, skill [Latin]) [translator's note].

9. Dante's mountain of Purgatory, and perhaps the steps from circle to circle (*Purgatorio* 11.40; 13.1; 17.65, 77; 25.8; etc.); or the three steps in *Purgatorio* 9.76ff.; or the mystic stairway of the Seventh Heaven (*Paradiso* 21.8; 22.68) [translator's note]. For DANTE ALIGHIERI (1265–1321), see above.

1. Like Pandarus and Bitias in Virgil's *Aeneid* [19 B.C.E.], 9.677–82: "While they within stand at the right and left / Before the turrets, armed, their lofty heads / Flashing with plumes. So by some river's bank, / Whether the Po or pleasant Athesis, / Two breezy oaks lift up their unshorn heads, / And nod their lofty tops" [translator's note].

2. According to Aristotle (*Rhetoric* 3.2) poetry can create wonder by strange matter and expression, as rhetoric should not. Cicero (*De Oratore* 1.16) says that the poet is more restricted than the orator by "numbers" but less in choice of words. Augustine (*De Ordine* 2.14.40) finds the grammarians rather than the rhetoricians are poetry's proper judges. In the Middle Ages the academic conception of poetry became debased and subordinated to rhetoric and grammar. Boccaccio obviously is

XII. The Obscurity of Poetry Is Not Just Cause for Condemning It

These cavillers further object that poetry is often obscure, and that poets are to blame for it, since their end is to make an incomprehensible statement appear to be wrought with exquisite artistry; regardless of the old rule of the orators, that a speech must be simple and clear. Perverse notion! Who but a deceiver himself would have sunk low enough not merely to hate what he could not understand, but incriminate it, if he could? I admit that poets are at times obscure. At the same time will these accusers please answer me? Take those philosophers among whom they shamelessly intrude; do they always find their close reasoning as simple and clear as they say an oration should be? If they say yes, they lie; for the works of Plato and Aristotle, to go no further, abound in difficulties so tangled and involved that from their day to the present, though searched and pondered by many a man of keen insight, they have yielded no clear nor consistent meaning. But why do I talk of philosophers? There is the utterance of Holy Writ, of which they especially like to be thought expounders; though proceeding from the Holy Ghost, is it not full to overflowing with obscurities and ambiguities? It is indeed, and for all their denial, the truth will openly assert itself. Many are the witnesses, of whom let them be pleased to consult Augustine,[3] a man of great sanctity and learning, and of such intellectual power that, without a teacher, as he says himself, he learned many arts, besides all that the philosophers teach of the ten categories. Yet he did not blush to admit that he could not understand the beginning of Isaiah. It seems that obscurities are not confined to poetry. Why then do they not criticise philosophers as well as poets? Why do they not say that the Holy Spirit wove obscure sayings into his works, just to give them an appearance of clever artistry? As if He were not the sublime Artificer of the Universe![4] I have no doubt they are bold enough to say such things, if they were not aware that philosophers already had their defenders, and did not remember the punishment[5] prepared for them that blaspheme against the Holy Ghost. So they pounce upon the poets because they seem defenseless, with the added reason that, where no punishment is imminent, no guilt is involved. They should have realized that when things perfectly clear seem obscure, it is the beholder's fault. To a half-blind man, even when the sun is shining its brightest, the sky looks cloudy. Some things are naturally so profound that not without difficulty can the most exceptional keenness in intellect sound their depths; like the sun's globe, by which, before they can clearly discern it, strong eyes are sometimes repelled.[6] On the other hand, some things, though naturally clear perhaps, are so veiled by the artist's skill that scarcely anyone could by mental effort derive sense from them; as

protesting against the medieval opinion partly by appealing to the Ancients, but chiefly by consulting the fact of a poet's experience [translator's note]. For ARISTOTLE (384–322 B.C.E.) and the theologian AUGUSTINE (354–430 C.E.), see above.

3. Augustine, *Confessions* 4.16: "And what did it profit me that, when scarcely twenty years old, a book of Aristotle's entitled The Ten Predicaments [*Categories*] fell into my hands? . . . I read it alone and understood it . . . And what did it profit me that I . . . read unaided, and understood, all the books that I could get of the so-called liberal arts? . . . Whatever was written either on rhetoric or logic, geometry, music, or arithmetic, did I, without any great difficulty, and without the teaching of any man, understand." Cited by Petrarch, *Invectivae contra Medicum* [1355], 3, p. 1105 [translator's note].

4. Wisdom 7.21, 22 [translator's note].

5. Mark 3.29 [translator's note].

6. Perhaps a reminiscence of Dante, *Paradiso* 1.54ff. A favorite figure with Dante: cf. *Purgatorio* 32.11; *Paradiso* 25.118; etc. [translator's note].

the immense body of the sun when hidden in clouds cannot be exactly located by the eye of the most learned astronomer. That some of the prophetic poems are in this class, I do not deny.

Yet not by this token is it fair to condemn them; for surely it is not one of the poet's various functions to rip up and lay bare the meaning which lies hidden in his inventions. Rather where matters truly solemn and memorable are too much exposed, it is his office by every effort to protect as well as he can and remove them from the gaze of the irreverent, that they cheapen not by too common familiarity. So when he discharges this duty and does it ingeniously, the poet earns commendation, not anathema.

Wherefore I again grant that poets are at times obscure, but invariably explicable if approached by a sane mind; for these cavillers view them with owl eyes, not human. Surely no one can believe that poets invidiously veil the truth with fiction, either to deprive the reader of the hidden sense, or to appear the more clever; but rather to make truths which would otherwise cheapen by exposure the object of strong intellectual effort and various interpretation, that in ultimate discovery they shall be more precious. In a far higher degree is this the method of the Holy Spirit; nay, every right-minded man should be assured of it beyond any doubt. Besides it is established by Augustine in the *City of God*, Book Eleven, when he says:

"The obscurity of the divine word has certainly this advantage, that it causes many opinions about the truth to be started and discussed, each reader seeing some fresh meaning in it."

Elsewhere he says of Psalm 126:[7]

"For perhaps the words are rather obscurely expressed for this reason, that they may call forth many understandings, and that men may go away the richer, because they have found that closed which might be opened in many ways, than if they could open and discover it by one interpretation."

To make further use of Augustine's testimony (which so far is adverse to these recalcitrants), to show them how I apply to the obscurities of poetry his advice on the right attitude toward the obscurities of Holy Writ, I will quote his comment on Psalm 146:[8]

"There is nothing in it contradictory: somewhat there is which is obscure, not in order that it may be denied thee, but that it may exercise him that shall afterward receive it," etc.

But enough of the testimony of holy men on this point, I will not bore my opponents by again urging them to regard the obscurities of poetry as Augustine regards the obscurities of Holy Writ. Rather I wish that they would wrinkle their brows a bit, and consider fairly and squarely, how, if this is true of sacred literature addressed to all nations, in far greater measure is it true of poetry, which is addressed to the few.

If by chance in condemning the difficulty of the text, they really mean its figures of diction and oratorical colors and the beauty which they fail to recognize in alien words, if on this account they pronounce poetry obscure—my only advice is for them to go back to the grammar schools,[9]

7. Augustine, *Enarratio: Patrilogia. Latina* 37.1675. Boccaccio's quotation immediately precedes the passage on the obscurity of Isaiah cited above [translator's note].

8. *Enarratio: Patrilogia. Latina* 37.1907. The preceding words are "Honor God's Scripture, honor God's Word, though it be not plain; in reverence wait for understanding. Be not wanton to accuse either the obscurity or seeming contradiction of Scripture" (trans. Coke) [translator's note].

9. The study of poetry was subject either to grammar or to rhetoric in the medieval scheme. See

bow to the ferule, study, and learn what license ancient authority granted the poets in such matters, and give particular attention to such alien terms as are permissible beyond common and homely use. But why dwell so long upon the subject? I could have urged them in a sentence to put off the old mind,[1] and put on the new and noble; then will that which now seems to them obscure look familiar and open. Let them not trust to concealing their gross confusion of mind in the precepts of the old orators; for I am sure the poets were ever mindful of such. But let them observe that oratory is quite different, in arrangement of words, from fiction, and that fiction has been consigned to the discretion of the inventor as being the legitimate work of another art than oratory. "In poetic narrative above all, the poets maintain majesty of style and corresponding dignity." As saith Francis Petrarch[2] in the Third Book of his *Invectives*, contrary to my opponents' supposition, "Such majesty and dignity are not intended to hinder those who wish to understand, but rather propose a delightful task, and are designed to enhance the reader's pleasure and support his memory. What we acquire with difficulty and keep with care is always the dearer to us;" so continues Petrarch.[3] In fine, if their minds are dull, let them not blame the poets but their own sloth. Let them not keep up a silly howl against those whose lives and actions contrast most favorably with their own. Nay, at the very outset they have taken fright at mere appearances, and bid fair to spend themselves for nothing. Then let them retire in good time, sooner than exhaust their torpid minds with the onset and suffer a violent repulse.

But I repeat my advice to those who would appreciate poetry, and unwind its difficult involutions. You must read, you must persevere, you must sit up nights, you must inquire, and exert the utmost power of your mind. If one way does not lead to the desired meaning, take another; if obstacles arise, then still another; until, if your strength holds out, you will find that clear which at first looked dark. For we are forbidden by divine command[4] to give that which is holy to dogs, or to cast pearls before swine.

1350–62

book 14, chapter 7. Though Boccaccio does not mention rhetoric in this passage, it is, like 14.7, a stroke on behalf of the liberation of poetry from technical bondage [translator's note].

1. Ephesians 4.22; Colossians 3.9 [translator's note].

2. Italian poet and humanist (1304–1374).

3. *Invectivae contra Medicum*, p. 1105. Petrarch has just been comparing the obscurity of poets with that of Holy Writ, not citing the difference between oratory and poetry. Boccaccio's quotation, either through his carelessness or corruption of his text, differs slightly from Petrarch [translator's note].

4. Matthew 7.6 [translator's note].

CHRISTINE DE PIZAN
ca. 1365–ca. 1429

The most prolific woman writer of the Middle Ages, Christine de Pizan was the first European woman to earn a living as a writer and, as such, she was acutely aware of the difficulty of reconciling the demands of writing with the occupations of women. In *Christine's Vision* (1405), a lengthy complaint against Fortune in the tradition of Boethius's *Consolation of Philosophy* (ca. 524), she laments that "although I was naturally inclined to scholarship from my birth, my occupation with the tasks common to married women and the burden of frequent childbearing had deprived me of it." The sheer volume of her literary output is all the more remarkable for a woman who was married and bearing children at the age of fifteen.

Christine was born in Venice around 1365. Shortly after, her father, Tommasso di Benvenuto da Pizzano, an astrologer physician, received an offer of employment from Charles V of France—the age's greatest patron—and in 1368 he brought his family to Paris. Around 1380, at "the age when young girls are customarily assigned husbands" (according to *Christine's Vision*), Christine was married to Etienne de Castel. In the same year, the death of Charles V meant the loss of the royal patronage Tommasso had enjoyed; the family fortunes soon began to wane. In 1389 both Tommasso and Castel died, leaving Christine a twenty-five-year-old widow with three small children and a large household. Though her father and husband left her a small inheritance, they also left her with debts, which required many years of expensive litigation to settle. Fortunately, Christine's father had given her some education, so Christine turned to writing to support her family.

From 1399 until her death in 1429 she wrote more than twenty volumes of prose and verse, which she presented to members of the French court, relying on their uncertain patronage. In her earliest composition, *Epistle of the God of Love* (1399), she deplored the popularity of the *Romance of the Rose*, one of the central works of medieval French literature, for its negative representations of women. In 1402 she initiated France's first literary debate—what became known as the "Quarrel of the *Rose*"—over the merits of Jean de Meun's continuation of that poem. In the course of this debate, Christine disputed some of the most prominent fifteenth-century French intellectuals, including Jean Gerson, chancellor of the University of Paris, and Jeun de Montreuil, the provost of Lille and a royal secretary. But Christine did not limit herself only to women's concerns, to the so-called *querelle des femmes* for which we remember her today. In 1404 she won her first large commission from Philip the Bold of Burgundy to write a biography of his father, Charles V. During her career she wrote on subjects as diverse as good government (something sorely lacking in early-fifteenth-century France), military strategy, religion, morality, and ethics. She died shortly after completing the *Ditié de la pucelle* (1429), a poem about Joan of Arc.

The Book of the City of Ladies, the work for which Christine is best known, was completed in 1405. In it, Christine continues a critique of misogyny begun in the Quarrel of the *Rose*. Her criticisms reveal a typically medieval distrust of the excesses of poetic language cut loose from proper signification. Misogynist writing is untrue because its authors have not understood the proper use of language. Christine's distrust of false representation reveals her indebtedness to theories of language pioneered by ST. AUGUSTINE, while her interest in allegory links her with writers such as QUINTILIAN, HUGH OF ST. VICTOR, and DANTE, all of whom developed medieval notions of exegesis. Her attempt to counter the misogynist representations of the "philosophers and poets" with true representations of "good women" owes its largest debt to BOCCACCIO's *Concerning Famous Women* (1361), though she is far from being an uncritical reader of that text. While nearly three-quarters of the tales in the *City of Ladies* are found in Boccaccio's work, Christine's adaptations show her to be a resisting reader, her text a refutation of Boccaccio's often back-handed praise of women.

The opening of the *City of Ladies* illustrates some ways in which women read and write under the conditions of patriarchy. The predominance of "wicked insults" about women and their behavior in the books she reads prompts Christine to disregard everything she knows about women and to ask God why, if women were so evil, she could not have been born as a man. The process of building a "city of ladies" entails reeducating herself to read as a woman and to discern true from false representations of women. Christine's collection of stories about illustrious women might be read as an early attempt to counter what SANDRA M. GILBERT AND SUSAN GUBAR in the twentieth century call the "anxiety of authorship" suffered by the woman writer, the fear that "because she can never become a precursor, the act of creation will isolate and destroy her." To clear the ground for a "city of ladies," Reason, her guide, must unpack the logical errors in misogynist discourse, articulating the reasons that so many learned men would slander women. But that is only a first step. The woman writer overcomes her anxiety of authorship only by actively seeking female precursors, the task that Christine sets herself in the *City of Ladies*. Like so many female critics who would follow her—for example, MARY WOLLSTONECRAFT and VIRGINIA WOOLF—Christine recognizes that because women have been denied education and thus kept ignorant, they have been unable to counter male images of female wickedness. Despite this spirited defense of women, we would be wrong to claim Christine as a feminist precursor. Her social vision of women's proper sphere is ultimately quite conservative, even for its time. Nevertheless, the *City of Ladies* remains an important document, an early voice of female resistance to the tradition of male misogyny.

BIBLIOGRAPHY

Perhaps the surest sign of the critical neglect of Christine de Pizan is the lack of any editions or translations of her collected works. Maurice Roy edited *Oeuvres poétiques de Christine de Pisan* (1886–89), but it excludes the prose works for which Christine is best known. Charity Canon Willard edited a selection of Christine's works in translation, *The Writings of Christine de Pizan* (1992), which better captures the diversity of her writing. Generally, it is easier to find translations than editions of individual works. Eric Hicks edited the "Quarrel of the *Rose*" as *Le Débat sur le Roman de la Rose* (1977). The only edition of *The Book of the City of Ladies* in the original Old French is Maureen Curnow's 1975 Ph.D. dissertation, "The *Livre de la Cité des Dames*: A Critical Edition," which Earl Jeffrey Richards translated as *The Book of the City of Ladies* in 1982. Much of what we know about Christine's life comes to us from her own autobiographical writing, especially *Christine's Vision*, translated by Glenda K. McLeod (1993). Charity Canon Willard offers the best modern biography in *Christine de Pizan: Her Life and Works* (1984).

Critical interest in Christine and her writing increased exponentially in the 1980s and 1990s, largely because of the influence of feminist criticism. Sandra Hindman's *Christine de Pizan's "Epistre d'Othea": Painting and Politics at the Court of Charles VI* (1986) offers a richly detailed description of the social context of Christine's writing. Sheila Delany's controversial essay "Mothers to Think Back Through: Who Are They? The Ambiguous Example of Christine de Pizan," in *Medieval Texts, Contemporary Readers* (ed. Laurie A. Finke and Martin B. Shichtman, 1987) was instrumental in raising questions about feminist appropriations of Christine. Maureen Quilligan's *Allegory of Female Authority: Christine de Pizan's "Cité des Dames"* (1991) offers a sophisticated theoretical analysis of *The City of Ladies*. The variety of critical responses to Christine is usefully represented by collections of essays, of which the best are *Politics, Gender, and Genre: The Political Thought of Christine de Pizan*, edited by Margaret Brabant (1992), and *Christine de Pizan and the Categories of Difference*, edited by Marilyn Desmond (1998). Other resources include Angus J. Kennedy, *Christine de Pizan: A Bibliographic Guide* (1984; supplement 1994), and Edith Yenal, *Christine de Pizan: A Bibliography* (1989).

From The Book of the City of Ladies[1]

From *Part One*

1. HERE BEGINS THE BOOK OF THE CITY OF LADIES, WHOSE FIRST CHAPTER TELLS WHY AND FOR WHAT PURPOSE THIS BOOK WAS WRITTEN.

[1.1.1] One day as I was sitting alone in my study surrounded by books on all kinds of subjects, devoting myself to literary studies, my usual habit, my mind dwelt at length on the weighty opinions of various authors whom I had studied for a long time. I looked up from my book, having decided to leave such subtle questions in peace and to relax by reading some light poetry. With this in mind, I searched for some small book. By chance a strange volume came into my hands, not one of my own, but one which had been given to me along with some others. When I held it open and saw from its title page that it was by Mathéolus,[2] I smiled, for though I had never seen it before, I had often heard that like other books it discussed respect for women. I thought I would browse through it to amuse myself. I had not been reading for very long when my good mother called me to refresh myself with some supper, for it was evening. Intending to look at it the next day, I put it down. The next morning, again seated in my study as was my habit, I remembered wanting to examine this book by Mathéolus. I started to read it and went on for a little while. Because the subject seemed to me not very pleasant for people who do not enjoy lies, and of no use in developing virtue or manners, given its lack of integrity in diction and theme, and after browsing here and there and reading the end, I put it down in order to turn my attention to more elevated and useful study. But just the sight of this book, even though it was of no authority, made me wonder how it happened that so many different men—and learned men among them—have been and are so inclined to express both in speaking and in their treatises and writings so many wicked insults about women and their behavior. Not only one or two and not even just this Mathéolus (for this book had a bad name anyway and was intended as a satire) but, more generally, judging from the treaties of all philosophers and poets and from all the orators—it would take too long to mention their names—it seems that they all speak from one and the same mouth. They all concur in one conclusion: that the behavior of women is inclined to and full of every vice. Thinking deeply about these matters, I began to examine my character and conduct as a natural woman and, similarly, I considered other women whose company I frequently kept, princesses, great ladies, women of the middle and lower classes, who had graciously told me of their most private and intimate thoughts, hoping that I could judge impartially and in good conscience whether the testimony of so many notable men could be true. To the best of my knowledge, no matter how long I confronted or dissected the problem, I could not see or realize how their claims could be true when compared to the natural behavior and character of women. Yet I still argued vehemently against women, saying

1. Translated by Earl Jeffrey Richards.
2. The *Liber Lamentationum Matheoluli (The Book of the Lamentations of Mathéolus)*, composed around 1300, translated from Latin into French in the last decades of the 14th century.

that it would be impossible that so many famous men—such solemn scholars, possessed of such deep and great understanding, so clear-sighted in all things, as it seemed—could have spoken falsely on so many occasions that I could hardly find a book on morals where, even before I had read it in its entirety, I did not find several chapters or certain sections attacking women, no matter who the author was. This reason alone, in short, made me conclude that, although my intellect did not perceive my own great faults and, likewise, those of other women because of its simpleness and ignorance, it was however truly fitting that such was the case. And so I relied more on the judgment of others than on what I myself felt and knew. I was so transfixed in this line of thinking for such a long time that it seemed as if I were in a stupor. Like a gushing fountain, a series of authorities, whom I recalled one after another, came to mind, along with their opinions on this topic. And I finally decided that God formed a vile creature when He made woman, and I wondered how such a worthy artisan could have deigned to make such an abominable work which, from what they say, is the vessel as well as the refuge and abode of every evil and vice. As I was thinking this, a great unhappiness and sadness welled up in my heart, for I detested myself and the entire feminine sex, as though we were monstrosities in nature. And in my lament I spoke these words:

[1.1.2] "Oh, God, how can this be? For unless I stray from my faith, I must never doubt that Your infinite wisdom and most perfect goodness ever created anything which was not good. Did You yourself not create woman in a very special way and since that time did You not give her all those inclinations which it pleased You for her to have? And how could it be that You could go wrong in anything? Yet look at all these accusations which have been judged, decided, and concluded against women. I do not know how to understand this repugnance. If it is so, fair Lord God, that in fact so many abominations abound in the female sex, for You Yourself say that the testimony of two or three witnesses lends credence, why shall I not doubt that this is true? Alas, God, why did You not let me be born in the world as a man, so that all my inclinations would be to serve You better, and so that I would not stray in anything and would be as perfect as a man is said to be? But since Your kindness has not been extended to me, then forgive my negligence in Your service, most fair Lord God, and may it not displease You, for the servant who receives fewer gifts from his lord is less obliged in his service." I spoke these words to God in my lament and a great deal more for a very long time in sad reflection, and in my folly I considered myself most unfortunate because God had made me inhabit a female body in this world.[3]

4. HERE THE LADY EXPLAINS TO CHRISTINE THE CITY WHICH SHE HAS BEEN COMMISSIONED TO BUILD AND HOW SHE WAS CHARGED TO HELP CHRISTINE BUILD THE WALL AND ENCLOSURE, AND THEN GIVES HER NAME.

[1.4.1] "Thus, fair daughter, the prerogative among women has been bestowed on you to establish and build the City of Ladies. For the foundation

3. While she is engaged in this lamentation, three ladies appear to Christine, comforting her. The first speaks to her, telling her that with their help she will build a city of ladies, which would house "all ladies of fame and women worthy of praise."

and completion of this City you will draw fresh waters from us as from clear fountains, and we will bring you sufficient building stone, stronger and more durable than any marble with cement could be. Thus your City will be extremely beautiful, without equal, and of perpetual duration in the world.

[1.4.1] "Have you not read that King Tros founded the great city of Troy with the aid of Apollo, Minerva, and Neptune,[4] whom the people of that time considered gods, and also how Cadmus founded the city of Thebes with the admonition of the gods? And yet over time these cities fell and have fallen into ruin. But I prophesy to you, as a true sybil,[5] that this City, which you will found with our help, will never be destroyed, nor will it ever fall, but will remain prosperous forever, regardless of all its jealous enemies. Although it will be stormed by numerous assaults, it will never be taken or conquered.

[1.4.3] "Long ago the Amazon kingdom was begun through the arrangement and enterprise of several ladies of great courage who despised servitude, just as history books have testified. For a long time afterward they maintained it under the rule of several queens, very noble ladies whom they elected themselves, who governed them well and maintained their dominion with great strength. Yet, although they were strong and powerful and had conquered a large part of the entire Orient in the course of their rule and terrified all the neighboring lands (even the Greeks, who were then the flower of all countries in the world, feared them), nevertheless, after a time, the power of this kingdom declined, so that as with all earthly kingdoms, nothing but its name has survived to the present. But the edifice erected by you in this City which you must construct will be far stronger, and for its founding I was commissioned, in the course of our common deliberation, to supply you with durable and pure mortar to lay the sturdy foundations and to raise the lofty walls all around, high and thick, with mighty towers and strong bastions, surrounded by moats with firm blockhouses, just as is fitting for a city with a strong and lasting defense. Following our plan, you will set the foundations deep to last all the longer, and then you will raise the walls so high that they will not fear anyone. Daughter, now that I have told you the reason for our coming and so that you will more certainly believe my words, I want you to learn my name, by whose sound alone you will be able to learn and know that, if you wish to follow my commands, you have in me an administrator so that you may do your work flawlessly. I am called Lady Reason; you see that you are in good hands. For the time being then, I will say no more."[6]

8. HERE CHRISTINE TELLS HOW, UNDER REASON'S COMMAND AND ASSISTANCE, SHE BEGAN TO EXCAVATE THE EARTH AND LAY THE FOUNDATION.

[1.8.1] Then Lady Reason responded and said, "Get up, daughter! Without waiting any longer, let us go to the Field of Letters. There the City of Ladies will be founded on a flat and fertile plain, where all fruits and freshwater rivers are found and where the earth abounds in all good things. Take the pick of your understanding and dig and clear out a great ditch wherever you

4. Christine uses the Roman names of the Greek gods: Apollo, god of music and prophecy; Minerva (Athena), goddess of war and wisdom; and Neptune (Poseidon), god of the sea.

5. Prophetess.

6. The second and third ladies introduce themselves as Rectitude and Justice. Christine thanks the ladies for their comfort and promises to obey them in all things.

see the marks of my ruler, and I will help you carry away the earth on my own shoulders."

[1.8.2] I immediately stood up to obey her commands and, thanks to these three ladies, I felt stronger and lighter than before. She went ahead, and I followed behind, and after we had arrived at this field I began to excavate and dig, following her marks with the pick of cross-examination. And this was my first work:

[1.8.3] "Lady, I remember well what you told me before, dealing with the subject of how so many men have attacked and continue to attack the behavior of women, that gold becomes more refined the longer it stays in the furnace, which means the more women have been wrongfully attacked, the greater waxes the merit of their glory. But please tell me why and for what reason different authors have spoken against women in their books, since I already know from you that this is wrong; tell me if Nature makes man so inclined or whether they do it out of hatred and where does this behavior come from?"

Then she replied, "Daughter, to give you a way of entering into the question more deeply, I will carry away this first basketful of dirt. This behavior most certainly does not come from Nature, but rather is contrary to Nature, for no connection in the world is as great or as strong as the great love which, through the will of God, Nature places between a man and a woman. The causes which have moved and which still move men to attack women, even those authors in those books, are diverse and varied, just as you have discovered. For some have attacked women with good intentions, that is, in order to draw men who have gone astray away from the company of vicious and dissolute women, with whom they might be infatuated, or in order to keep these men from going mad on account of such women, and also so that every man might avoid an obscene and lustful life. They have attacked all women in general because they believe that women are made up of every abomination."

"My lady," I said then, "excuse me for interrupting you here, but have such authors acted well, since they were prompted by a laudable intention? For intention, the saying goes, judges the man."

"That is a misleading position, my good daughter," she said, "for such sweeping ignorance never provides an excuse. If someone killed you with good intention but out of foolishness, would this then be justified? Rather, those who did this, whoever they might be, would have invoked the wrong law; causing any damage or harm to one party in order to help another party is not justice, and likewise attacking all feminine conduct is contrary to the truth, just as I will show you with a hypothetical case. Let us suppose they did this intending to draw fools away from foolishness. It would be as if I attacked fire—a very good and necessary element nevertheless—because some people burnt themselves, or water because someone drowned. The same can be said of all good things which can be used well or used badly. But one must not attack them if fools abuse them, and you have yourself touched on this point quite well elsewhere in your writings.[7] But those who have spoken like this so abundantly—whatever their intentions might be—have formulated their arguments rather loosely only to make their point. Just

7. Reason may be referring to Christine's letters in the debate over the *Romance of the Rose* (1402).

like someone who has a long and wide robe cut from a very large piece of cloth when the material costs him nothing and when no one opposes him, they exploit the rights of others. But just as you have said elsewhere, if these writers had only looked for the ways in which men can be led away from foolishness and could have been kept from tiring themselves in attacking the life and behavior of immoral and dissolute women—for to tell the straight truth, there is nothing which should be avoided more than an evil, dissolute, and perverted woman, who is like a monster in nature, a counterfeit estranged from her natural condition, which must be simple, tranquil, and upright—then I would grant you that they would have built a supremely excellent work. But I can assure you that these attacks on all women—when in fact there are so many excellent women—have never originated with me, Reason, and that all who subscribe to them have failed totally and will continue to fail. So now throw aside these black, dirty, and uneven stones from your work, for they will never be fitted into the fair edifice of your City.

[1.8.4] "Other men have attacked women for other reasons: such reproach has occurred to some men because of their own vices and others have been moved by the defects of their own bodies, others through pure jealousy, still others by the pleasure they derive in their own personalities from slander. Others, in order to show they have read many authors, base their own writings on what they have found in books and repeat what other writers have said and cite different authors."

* * *

From *Part Two*

36. AGAINST THOSE MEN WHO CLAIM IT IS NOT GOOD FOR WOMEN TO BE EDUCATED.

[2.36.1] Following these remarks,[8] I, Christine, spoke, "My lady, I realize that women have accomplished many good things and that even if evil women have done evil, it seems to me, nevertheless, that the benefits accrued and still accruing because of good women—particularly the wise and literary ones and those educated in the natural sciences whom I mentioned above—outweigh the evil. Therefore, I am amazed by the opinion of some men who claim that they do not want their daughters, wives, or kinswomen to be educated because their mores would be ruined as a result."

She responded, "Here you can clearly see that not all opinions of men are based on reason and that these men are wrong. For it must not be presumed that mores necessarily grow worse from knowing the moral sciences, which teach the virtues, indeed, there is not the slightest doubt that moral education amends and ennobles them. How could anyone think or believe that whoever follows good teaching or doctrine is the worse for it? Such an opinion cannot be expressed or maintained. I do not mean that it would be good for a man or a woman to study the art of divination or those fields of learning which are forbidden—for the holy Church did not remove them from common use without good reason—but it should not be believed that women are the worse for knowing what is good.

[2.36.2] "Quintus Hortensius, a great rhetorician and consumately skilled

8. By Christine's second guide, Rectitude.

orator in Rome, did not share this opinion. He had a daughter, named Hortensia,[9] whom he greatly loved for the subtlety of her wit. He had her learn letters and study the science of rhetoric, which she mastered so thoroughly that she resembled her father Hortensius not only in wit and lively memory but also in her excellent delivery and order of speech—in fact, he surpassed her in nothing. As for the subject discussed above, concerning the good which comes about through women, the benefits realized by this woman and her learning were, among others, exceptionally remarkable. That is, during the time when Rome was governed by three men,[1] this Hortensia began to support the cause of women and to undertake what no man dared to undertake. There was a question whether certain taxes should be levied on women and on their jewelry during a needy period in Rome. This woman's eloquence was so compelling that she was listened to, no less readily than her father would have been, and she won her case.

[2.36.3] "Similarly, to speak of more recent times, without searching for examples in ancient history, Giovanni Andrea,[2] a solemn law professor in Bologna not quite sixty years ago, was not of the opinion that it was bad for women to be educated. He had a fair and good daughter, named Novella, who was educated in the law to such an advanced degree that when he was occupied by some task and not at leisure to present his lectures to his students, he would send Novella, his daughter, in his place to lecture to the students from his chair. And to prevent her beauty from distracting the concentration of her audience, she had a little curtain drawn in front of her. In this manner she could on occasion supplement and lighten her father's occupation. He loved her so much that, to commemorate her name, he wrote a book of remarkable lectures on the law which he entitled *Novella super Decretalium*,[3] after his daughter's name.

[2.36.4] "Thus, not all men (and especially the wisest) share the opinion that it is bad for women to be educated. But it is very true that many foolish men have claimed this because it displeased them that women knew more than they did. Your father, who was a great scientist and philosopher, did not believe that women were worth less by knowing science; rather, as you know, he took great pleasure from seeing your inclination to learning. The feminine opinion of your mother, however, who wished to keep you busy with spinning and silly girlishness, following the common custom of women, was the major obstacle to your being more involved in the sciences. But just as the proverb already mentioned above says, 'No one can take away what Nature has given,' your mother could not hinder in you the feeling for the sciences which you, through natural inclination, had nevertheless gathered together in little droplets. I am sure that, on account of these things, you do not think you are worth less but rather that you consider it a great treasure for yourself; and you doubtless have reason to."

And I, Christine, replied to all of this, "Indeed, my lady, what you say is as true as the Lord's Prayer."

1405

9. Hortensia appears in BOCCACCIO's *Concerning Famous Women* (1361), chap. 82. Quintus Hortensius: dictator (a temporary position of great power) appointed in 287 B.C.E.

1. Rome was usually governed by two men (consuls elected for two-year terms); the third here is the dictator.

2. Andrea (1275–1347) must have been known to Christine's father.

3. Literally, "new things about the decrees" (Latin).

GIAMBATTISTA GIRALDI
1504–1573

An Italian Renaissance dramatist, poet, and literary theorist who distinguished himself as an early advocate of innovative literary form, Giambattista Giraldi argued in favor of vernacular languages and national literatures—two contentious issues since at least the time of DANTE ALIGHIERI—and underscored how evolving social conditions inevitably determine the changing modes of literature and the values of criticism. Giraldi's work promoting the new Renaissance romantic epic ("romance") was especially controversial, eliciting criticism from many of his contemporaries who argued for the tried-and-true ideas of antiquity, particularly those of ARISTOTLE and HORACE, and for strict adherence to the rules of classical genres. As a learned scholar, Giraldi was not opposed in principle to the classical tradition. In fact, he was influenced by Aristotle's *Poetics*, whose authority grew steadily in Italy over the course of the sixteenth century. Unlike many of his fellow critics, however, Giraldi was willing to question and limit Aristotle's precepts. In the so-called debate between the "ancients" and the "moderns," which continued into the eighteenth century with ALEXANDER POPE and SAMUEL JOHNSON, Giraldi finally sided with the moderns, adding fuel to the growing controversy in the Renaissance over the legitimacy of emerging forms of literature.

Born in Ferrara, Giraldi taught rhetoric at the University of Ferrara from 1541 to 1562. Perhaps the most noteworthy biographical detail about his life is the controversy between him and a student, Giovambattista Pigna, over the originality of his ideas on the romance form. Pigna was the first to publish a defense of the new genre, titled *I romanzi* (1554), but Giraldi charged him with plagiarism, an accusation with which subsequent scholars have tended to agree. In literary matters, Giraldi is especially noted for writing an accomplished series of tragedies, including *Orbecche* (1541) and *Dido* (1543). Although influenced by the classical tradition of drama, Giraldi was the first tragic playwright to depict atrocities on stage rather than simply reporting them through a messenger, as Aristotle had advised in the *Poetics*; and he was among a growing number of writers who departed from the classical tradition in their use of the vernacular language. He enjoys the further distinction of having made the first reference in modern criticism to the doctrine of the unity of time in his *Discorso delle comedie et delle tragedie* (1554, *Discourse on Comedy and Tragedy*), anticipating, among others, the seventeenth-century French writer PIERRE CORNEILLE. He also composed an influential series of *novelle* called *Hecatomithi* (1565, *The Hundred Stories*), from which Shakespeare later derived the plots for *Othello* and *Measure for Measure*. In his poetry Giraldi referred to himself as "Cynthius," an epithet for the Greek god Apollo who was believed to be born atop Mount Cynthus on the Aegean island of Delos. As a result, he became known in Italy as "Giraldi Cinzio" or "Il Cinzio," and in England as "Cynthio" or "Cinthio."

Giraldi contributed most influentially to Renaissance poetics in the controversy over the genre of the new romance, whose groundbreaking example is *Orlando Furioso* (1516), composed by the major Italian poet Ludovico Ariosto (1474–1533), whom as a youth Giraldi befriended. Written in the vernacular tongue rather than in Latin, Renaissance romances are long narrative poems in metrical form on courtly subjects that combine some of the techniques of the classical epic with the methods and materials of the medieval romance; they are usually marked by an abundance of characters and plot lines. Edmund Spenser's *Faerie Queene* (1590) is the premier English example. Opponents of the form argued that romance violated not only Aristotle's preference for single unified actions but also time-tested conventions established by the epic poets Homer and Virgil. Intervening in the heated debate with his *Discorso intorno al comporre dei romanzi* (1554, *Discourse on the Composition of*

Romances), while also being prompted by Pigna, Giraldi mounted a spirited defense of the modern romance form, and of Ariosto in particular, writing in effect a manifesto on behalf of a new European hybrid genre.

In our excerpts from the *Discourse*, Giraldi first claims that the multiple plots of the romance genre possess an *organic* unity, much like a well-proportioned body. Such a modern organicist claim, even if unjustified by most Renaissance romances, is an interesting anticipation of Romantic theories of poetry (as exemplified, for instance, by SAMUEL TAYLOR COLERIDGE). Giraldi argues against strict imitation of classical modes, on the grounds that poetry, following the dictates of "decorum," ought to judiciously reflect the mores of specific places, times, and peoples. Moreover, he argues for a moral view of poetry, as SIR PHILIP SIDNEY does in England at the time, but against the values of classical literatures, which are not suitable for his own age, not least because of their pagan religions.

In many respects Giraldi shows himself to be a modern, a tendency that extends to his critical distaste for the excessive allegorizing of classical and medieval criticism, such as one finds in Bernadus Silvestris's *Commentary on the First Six Books of Virgil's "Aeneid"*. Giraldi's controversial modern view also turns a skeptical eye toward the secularized four-level model of interpretation that arose out of the medieval commentary tradition, passing from theological writings like those of THOMAS AQUINAS to the more secular writings of Dante and GIOVANNI BOCCACCIO. He is especially impatient with the oversubtle and lengthy commentaries on the Italian lyric poet Petrarch (1304–1374).

From a contemporary perspective, one jarring aspect of Giraldi's theory of decorum is his emphasis on "blood, position, dignity, and authority." It is clear that he takes a bold step in poetic theory with his attempt to historicize art; but reflecting the prevailing views of his time, he leaves the function of art subordinated to the service of an aristocratic status quo, inattentive to art's critical or oppositional possibilities. Yet Giraldi contributes to an important defense of the modern that parallels related arguments made during the Renaissance by GIACOPO MAZZONI in Italy, JOACHIM DU BELLAY in France, and George Puttenham in England. Furthermore, he sets the stage for the later theoretical discussions surrounding the great romances of the period, Torquato Tasso's *Gerusalemme Liberata* (1575) and Spenser's *Faerie Queene*. His work continues to shape scholarship on the romance form to this day.

BIBLIOGRAPHY

The authoritative edition of the Italian text of the *Discourse on the Composition of Romances* (1554) appears in Giraldi's *Scritti Estetici: De' Romanzi, delle Comedie, e delle Tragedie*, edited by Giulio Antimaco (1864), which also includes *Discorso delle comedie et delle tragedie* (1554) in Italian. These two discourses constitute Giraldi's principal works of criticism. *Giraldi Cinthio on Romances*, translated by Henry L. Snuggs (1968), presents an English translation of the complete *Discourse on the Composition of Romances*, plus a useful introduction and notes. *Literary Criticism: Plato to Dryden* (ed. Allan H. Gilbert, 1962) contains translated excerpts from the *Discourse* and a series of Giraldi's pieces defending his critical views of tragedy against Aristotelian precepts. A complete English translation of Giraldi's *Discourse on Comedy and Tragedy* is not available, nor is a biography.

Joel E. Spingarn's *History of Literary Criticism in the Renaissance* (2d ed., 1908) presents some valuable remarks on Giraldi's theories in relationship to both drama and romance, but Bernard Weinberg's *History of Literary Criticism in the Italian Renaissance* (2 vols., 1961) offers the most comprehensive and authoritative presentation in English of Giraldi's work, conveniently situated within a detailed overview of Italian Renaissance criticism. Baxter Hathaway's *Marvels and Commonplaces: Renaissance Literary Criticism* (1968) discusses Giraldi's position in the battle between realism and fantasy in Renaissance literary criticism. On Giraldi's dramatic theories and practices, see Philip Russell Horne's *Tragedies of Giambattista Cinthio Giraldi* (1962), Peggy Osborn's *G. B. Giraldi's Altile: The Birth of a New Dramatic Genre in Renaissance Ferrara* (1992), and Mary G. Morrison's *Tragedies of G. B. Giraldi Cinthio: The Transformation of Narrative Source into Stage Play* (1997). No bibliographies on Giraldi in English are available.

From Discourse on the Composition of Romances[1]

* * *

In setting out to write about the art of composing Romances, Messer Giovambattista,[2] I see I am undertaking a hard and fatiguing task, since, indeed, no one that I am aware of has written on this subject and since many authors have written variously in this form of poetry, not only in other nations and peoples but also among us Italians. My difficulty is increased by your ability and learning, which is such that I doubt my being able to write anything you have not already seen and considered, because, while my pupil, you studied poetry, diligently absorbed what I said, and wrote about poems of all kinds. Since then you have devoted yourself to study and writing and have continually read or written excellent works. But although my undertaking may be difficult and laborious, nevertheless the love I have had for you during the long time you were my pupil leads me to devote myself to the task.

* * *

Romances Not of One Action

Now in turning to the subject: It should be pointed out that subjects or materials of Romances are not in the manner of Vergil's and Homer's,[3] both of whom undertook imitating only one action of one man, whereas ours have imitated many actions not of one man only but of many, since they build the whole fabric of their work upon eight or ten persons, but they give to the work the name of that person or that action which is dominant in the whole work and on which all the others depend, or at least to that which reasonably binds them together. This kind of poem, moreover, came from neither the Greeks nor the Latins; indeed it came laudably from our own language, having given to the excellent writers of it the same authority which the two writers already named gave to their works.

* * *

Organic Interrelation of Parts

But, returning to our subject: When the writer has planned where he is to begin his work, he ought to exercise great diligence to see that the parts fit together as do the parts of the body. * * * In putting the framework together,

1. Translated by Henry L. Snuggs.
2. Giovambattista Pigna (1529–1575), an Italian writer, critic, and student of Giraldi. Giraldi accused Pigna of stealing his ideas for his book *I romanzi* (1554), which was published before the *Discourse*. Pigna had apparently solicited his teacher's ideas by letter and then published them in his work. Leaving this address to Pigna intact is part of Giraldi's strategy to explain the similarity of their work and to gain recognition for the originality of his work here.
3. Greek epic poet (ca. 842 c. B.C.E.); his *Iliad* focuses on Achilles and his *Odyssey* on Odysseus. Virgil (70–19 B.C.E.), Roman epic poet, his *Aeneid* centers on the Trojan Aeneas.

he will seek to fill up the hollows and to equalize the size of the members. This can be done by putting the filling matters in proper and necessary places, such as loves, hates, plaints, laughter, jests, grave matter, discords, peace-makings, ugly and beautiful things, descriptions of places, times, persons, fables feigned by himself and drawn from olden times, voyages, wanderings, shows, unforeseen events, deaths, funeral rites, lamentations, recognitions, things terrible and pitiable, nuptials, births, victories, triumphs, single combats, jousts, tournaments, catalogs, marshaling of troops, and other similar things which perhaps are such that it would be no small task to detail all one by one. There is nothing above or under the heavens or in the depths of the abyss that is not at the command and under the judgment of the prudent poet who can with varied ornaments embellish the body of his work and bring it not merely to an excellent but to a lovely figure. With these he gives the parts a just measure and decorous ornament, in such proportion that the result is a disciplined and well constituted body.[4]

The arrangement ought to be considered not only in the principal parts, which are the beginning, the middle, and the end, but in every bit of these parts. For this reason the poet ought to consider not only the whole body but each particular part, so that each may be set with beautiful order in its place, with admirable grace, and with the proper proportion and so that the whole, with that beauty and grace, will be to each of them proper and fitting. Just as the face takes on its own beauty and color and as the neck takes both in another form, and the breast, the arms, and the other parts of the body have their own forms, so the ornaments of each part of the poem are varied and diverse. Concerning this matter it is not possible to give laws other than to advise the writer that he discern in the light of his judgment what belongs to the form of the body on which he is about to create, advising him, however, not to become so preoccupied with one part that it makes the others, by not fitting in the whole, seem ugly or their beauty deformed. It is better that the whole be moderately beautiful than that two or three be so excellent that their excellence both to themselves and to the others be a cause of the deformity of the rest[.]

* * *

Undue Limitation by Ancient Poets

To speak now generally: I say that judicious authors gifted in composing ought not so to limit their freedom within the bounds set by those who wrote before them that they dare not set foot outside the tracks of others. Apart from being a bad use of the gifts that mother nature gave them, such restraint would prevent poetry from going beyond certain bounds which one writer has marked off and from moving a foot from the way the first fathers made it walk. The great Vergil, understanding that if architecture, military science, rhetoric, geometry, music, and the other arts worthy of the liberal mind are allowed to add, to increase, to diminish, to change, judged that this was much more fitting for the poet, to whom had been given the same power given by the consent of the world to the excellent painter, namely, the authority to vary the likenesses according to the artistic purpose. He showed therefore

4. Giraldi promotes symmetry, proportion, and variety, but not economy in literary form.

how in many places good writers, treading where the ancients trod, can turn aside somewhat from the beaten path, letting at times their own footprints go toward Helicon.[5] This is to be seen not only in the Latins but also in the Greeks, above all in Homer, and even more in our Tuscan poets, whose compositions are of no less value in their language than those of the Greek and Latin poets in theirs, although the Tuscans have not followed the ways of the Greek and Latin. To speak truly, our language has also its forms of poetry so properly its own that they are not those of any other language or nation. Indeed one ought not to try to hold the Tuscan poet within the confines that bind the Greek and Latin, as we have said sufficiently elsewhere.

Modern Poets as Models

One ought to walk along those roads which the better poets of our tongue have laid out, with the same authority that the Greek and Latin poets have had in their languages. For this reason I have laughed many times at some who have wished to proclaim the writers of the Romances to be completely under the laws of art as given by Aristotle and Horace,[6] not considering that neither of them knew this language or this manner of composing. Indeed these works are not to be put at all under such laws and rules, but ought to be left with the boundaries set by those who among us have given authority and reputation to this form of poetry. Just as the Greeks and Latins have drawn the art of their writing from their poets, so we also ought to draw from our poets and hold ourselves to that form which the better poets of the Romances have given us. We see that Ovid,[7] ingenious poet, laid aside in his *Metamorphoses* the laws of Vergil and Homer and did not follow the laws of Aristotle given us in his *Poetics*; nevertheless, he emerged as a beautifully artistic poet, with such benefit to the Latin language that he became a wonder. He was not reprehended nonetheless because he did not follow in the footsteps of the others. This happened because he devoted himself to the writings of matter for which rules and examples did not exist, just as there were no materials on our Romances. Just as he who would write a poem of one action would err if he ignored his models and the laws derived from all the works of like composition, so he who would write Romances of more than one action would err if he did not follow those who are now recognized as great and excellent; in the Romances of more than one action the writers to be followed will be those whose mode of composing will merit praise.

* * *

The Civil Function of the Poet

The function, then, of our poet, as regards the inducing of mores, is to praise virtuous actions and censure the vicious; and by means of the terrible and

5. A mountain sacred to Apollo and the Muses, who had a temple there.
6. Roman lyric poet and satirist (65–8 B.C.E.). ARISTOTLE (384–322 B.C.E.), Greek philosopher. They gave "the laws of art" in, respectively, *Ars Poetica* and *Poetics* (for both, see above).
7. Roman poet (43 B.C.E.–17 C.E.); his major epic-length *Metamorphoses* is a compendium of different mythological stories united not by a single character but by the common theme of metamorphosis.

the miserable to make the vicious actions odious to him who reads. In these two respects the writers of Romances in our language are much ampler than the heroic Greeks and Latins, who only hinted at such censures and praises, whereas ours go further, especially in praising or censuring things of their time. This custom (insofar as I can understand it) was first begun by Dante,[8] who also surpassed the times before him. This was then accepted most graciously by our judicious Petrarch[9] not only in his canzoni and sonnets, as in the canzone on Italy and the sonnets on Rome but also in his *Triumphs*, in which at many places he passes into digressions and then turns back skillfully to the subject he left. In this same manner our great and magnificent Ariosto[1] has also succeeded, as he did admirably in putting into his work things beyond the scope of his primary purpose, but which contribute a marvelous beauty to his work. And such things will contribute much to the works of others who will put them in judiciously and decorously.

* * *

Decorum

In these matters as in others, the poet ought always to have his eye on decorum, which is none other than what is fitting to places, times, and persons. Thus the ancient observers of nature said that decorum was that beauty, that grace, born from the forms of speaking when judgment and moderation were joined together and carried in themselves some manifestation of mores. These mores should be reflected in speech no less than the loveliness of color in a beautiful body; in other words, decorum is nothing other than grace and appropriateness. So the poet ought to be mindful not only of the actions but also of the speeches and responses which men carry on among themselves. For one would speak with a king in a different way than he would speak with a gentleman, and a king will answer another king as he would not answer one of his subjects or another lesser prince. He will speak to soldiers to urge them into battle otherwise than to quiet people who are in armed rebellion. In still a different way one captain will speak to another and one senator to another. So it happens with other kinds of persons, according to their blood, position, dignity, and authority, and according to places and times;[2] these things are left to the judgment of the writer, because estimation of this springs entirely from and rests in the writer's prudence.

* * *

Absurdity of Excessive Allegoresis

They become only frenetic who by the example of these authors make so many fantasies on the works of Petrarch and of other writers that, for every sonnet on which they choose to comment, they compose a whole volume.[3]

8. DANTE ALIGHIERI (1265–1321), Italian poet; his *Divine Comedy* (1321) is an epic Christian poem.
9. Italian writer and poet (1304–1374). Written at different times between 1340 and 1374, but never presented as a single poem, his *Triumphs* are six long poems covering the themes of love, chastity, death, fame, time, and eternity.
1. Ludovico Ariosto (1471–1533), Italian poet; author of the major romance *Orlando Furioso* (1516).
2. In introducing his persons, the poet ought to consider carefully what they are prone to do and to suffer. In doing so, he will find useful a knowledge of the differences in nations and in natures, the manners of life, usages, and customs; and the management of affairs and the power of those who he will bring in [Giraldi's note].
3. Giraldi is chastising critics who produce lengthy and fantastical allegorical interpretations of poems.

In the name of philosophers they would draw out not only the Platonic and Peripatetic[4] philosophies and all that is contained within the golden circle of all the disciplines—called by the better wits the study of humanity—but also the cabalistic[5] superstitions and all that is in divine and human laws, making chimeras and fantasies completely foreign to the meaning of the things on which they comment. Not to speak of others, there were and are today some who, departing from the true sense, make such fabrications on some of Petrarch's things that these appear spiritual; and call them marvels; and find therein the voice of love, or nature, or Jove, or Juno,[6] or desire, or beauty, or the sun, or the sky; and such other things they would derive which have never been written from the beginning of the world up to their age. Petrarch would no more have subscribed to these visionary things if he had seen them than he would to one who made him an ecclesiastic, vesting him as a minor friar, girding him with a cord, and putting wooden clogs on his feet. This is bad usage indeed and unworthy of acceptance by intelligent men! Although such exhibitions may show a man to be learned and versed in various disciplines, they show him to be without judgment in applying them without moderation. I do not know, Messer Giovambattista, what such men think they are doing. As for me, I think there is no writing in the world so inane about which such fabricated dreams cannot be made, whenever a learned and ingenious man wishes to waste his time on them.

You and I knew Mariano Buonincontro of Palermo, a man of incisive and lively intelligence, who at an early age was a recipient here in Ferrara of an honorary doctor of laws. To make fun of such geniuses, this man made (as you know) the most beautiful sonnets in the world, as to diction and rhythm, but which said nothing and were without sense. Then he allowed them to be issued under the name of some fine man; he himself moved among the others and let it be known that he wished to discuss them, saying that their sense was marvelous. He therefore induced everyone to make fantastic judgments about them. Among the others he issued one that seemed to be on the death of the illustrious Signora the Duchess of Urbino. Here it is.

I piu lievi, che Tigre, pensier miei
Scorgendo il cor, che tra doi petti intiero
Tiene un pensier, poi che gl'ingombra il vero
Et folle error, fuggono i casi rei.
Et benche da gli antichi Semidei
Biasmato fosse ovunque ogn'altro è fiero
Monte d'orgogli. Ahi lassa, io gia non spero
Gioir in quel disir, c'haver vorrei.
Onde dal crudo suon stancata l'alma
Germoglia in me l'ardir, poi che s'agghiaccia,
Et scalda hor quinci, hor quindi il caldo gelo.
Et io del verde fior perdo la traccia;
Me l'asconde lo sdegno in picciol velo
Tolta da i tronchi error la grave salma.
    Benche, chi tien la palma

4. Aristotelian.
5. Pertaining to a form of medieval Jewish mysticism.
6. Queen of the Roman gods. Jove: king of the Roman gods.

De gli inganni morta', brami con forza
Condur a l'empio fin l'amara scorza.[7]

He said that this was a work of rare genius. Spreading abroad about it some things to make it seem to be his, he induced a very learned but injudicious Sienese to make on it a commentary divided into four books, which is still read. So point by point, which made no sense and said nothing, that fellow spun out stuff such as he had never read in all his life.

* * *

[E]xpositions ought to be brief, since lengthy ones are an annoyance in this language as they were in Latin (if the subject did not merit, as, for example, Macrobius' commentary of Cicero's *Dream of Scipio* and Hierocles[8] on the verses of Pythagoras[9]). In this respect the Greeks were too verbose, especially those who commented on Homer. Some of these run into exceedingly long commentaries; others go into such fantastic matters that (like other Chrysippuses)[1] they would allegorize every story in Homer, reading meanings into the poem which he perhaps never imagined. Landino would do the same for Vergil,[2] but little success followed him, not because he did not show himself learned and intelligent but because the Italians have similar discourses in abundance, and it is not our intention to linger over these. They may leave this pretension to the Greeks, who in order to make their fable-writers and poets appear more than human are taken with these vanities.

* * *

1554

7. The sonnet is indeed nonsense, as the following "literal" translation will show: "Happier than a tiger my thoughts, discerning my heart, which among learned bosoms entirely holds a thought, since it loads on it the true and the foolish mistake, they flee the evil events. And although it should be blamed by the old demigods wherever all other is a fierce mountain of pride. Alas, already I do not hope to rejoice in that desire that I would like to have. Therefore, wearied by the harsh sound, the soul sprouts ardor in me when it is reaped to the ground and warms up, now here, now there, the hot frost, and I lose trace of a green flower; for me scorn hid it in a little veil taken by mutilated error from the grave corpse; though he who holds the palm of the mortal frauds may yearn with force to lead to the impious end the bitter rind" [translator's note].

8. Hierocles of Alexander [5th c. C.E.], the Latin title of his work is *Commentarius in Aurea Carmina Pythagoreorum* [translator's note]. MACROBIUS (b. ca. 360), Roman author; for his *Commentary*, see above.

9. Greek philosopher and mathematician (6th c. B.C.E.).

1. The Greek philosopher [ca. 280–207 B.C.E.]. A long catalog of his works is appended to his life in Diogenes Laertius, 7. Except for a few fragments, these are lost. Precisely where Giraldi derived what he says of Chrysippus as an allegorizer of Homer and to which of his works he refers is uncertain [translator's note].

2. Cristoforo Landino (1424–1492) was so embued with Neoplatonism that he conceived of poetry as allegorical and involving "arcani e divini sensi," as in his commentary on the *Aeneid* (1478) [translator's note].

JOACHIM DU BELLAY
ca. 1522–1560

Joachim du Bellay is known for having written one of the first theoretical defenses of a vernacular language against an imperial language. Contemporary postcolonial writers often attack the prestige of European languages, but those same European languages were once considered by Renaissance authors to be inferior to Latin and Greek. In *The Defence and Illustration of the French Language* (1549), Joachim du Bellay argued that with careful cultivation, French was capable of equaling Greek and Latin as a literary language. But du Bellay's defense of the vernacular was paradoxically also an attack on the vernacular: French poetry, in his view, had to abandon its own popular forms in order to acquire the dignity of the classics.

Born in Anjou (France), a younger son in a minor branch of an ancient and noble French family, Joachim du Bellay possessed, from the beginning, both nobility and resentment. Impoverished, in poor health, and abandoned, du Bellay was to dream of a future as noble as the past—a nobility obtained through the pen rather than the sword. He was a frail child, and one of his long illnesses later left him nearly deaf. Both his parents had died by the time he was ten, leaving him in the care of an older brother. In one of the few references to his early years, Joachim berates his brother for indifference and for neglecting his education. Still, he did learn Latin and ultimately left home to study law at Poitiers, where he appears to have concentrated more on studying rhetoric and entering poetry competitions. His time at Poitiers is described by scholars as setting the scene for his entrance into the world of scholarship, poetry, and the life of the mind, the world that would become his legacy.

By all accounts, the turning point of du Bellay's life was the day he met PIERRE DE RONSARD, a distant cousin encountered by chance, apparently at a country inn. They were about the same age, with a common passion for learning and a shared love of poetry. Ronsard was a student in Paris at the Collège de Coqueret, a small, run-down boardinghouse that was one of many colleges that then formed the University of Paris. Du Bellay moved to Paris and enrolled at Coqueret in 1547.

Jean Dorat, the master at Coqueret, was a young, enthusiastic scholar of Greek philology, the historical and comparative study of the language, literature, and culture of ancient Greece. As master, he transformed the college into a center of humanism and rigorous scholarship. The handful of young noblemen who lived there studied literally around the clock, sometimes working in shifts to make the most efficient use of candles. They learned Greek, Latin, and Italian poetry and argued about translations, rhetoric, and the use of language. They soon began to see themselves as a unified group destined to bring about revolutionary changes in poetry. The group first called itself the Brigade but later chose a more peaceful, and more grandiose, name: the *Pléiade*, or constellation of seven poets (Pierre de Ronsard, Joachim du Bellay, Jean-Antoine de Baïf, Etienne Jodelle, Pontus de Tyard, Rémy Belleau, and Jean Dorat himself). Believing in the divine inspiration of poetry, they looked to the future, intent on creating a rich language that would benefit French poets to come.

Two years after his arrival in Paris, du Bellay wrote and published *The Defence and Illustration of the French Language*. That same year he published a collection of love sonnets in French, *L'Olive* (the sonnet was one of the few vernacular forms approved by the Pléiade). In 1553 he accompanied Cardinal Jean du Bellay, his cousin, to Rome, where he served, grumblingly, as the cardinal's secretary. Two of his major works came out of his four-year stay in Italy: the sonnets in *Les Antiquitez de Rome* (1558) praise the glories of ancient Rome, while the poems in *Les Regrets* (1558) tell of the disillusionment he felt in the Rome of the present day. His failed love affair with a married Italian woman seems to have hastened his return to his newly appreciated homeland. Two years later, miserable, he died at the age of thirty-seven.

To understand du Bellay's argument in the *Defence*, we must recall the status of the French language during the sixteenth century. While Latin was the language of scholarship, legal documents, and poetry, the French vernacular suffered from an intellectual inferiority complex as the language of the masses, more frequently spoken than written. This two-language social order led to continual discord over the comparative value of languages, particularly French and Latin. During the 1530s and 1540s, scholars enthusiastically translated the texts of ancient Greece and Rome into the vernacular. However, because Latin was considered a richer, more poetic language, these same men composed their own poetry in Latin. The weighty presence of Latin in the church, in the academy, and in the poetry of French authors signified to some a linguistic enslavement. The question naturally arose as to what equips a language for eloquence. Was it the very nature of Greek and Latin that allowed a flourishing of scholarship? Or, rather, were all languages potentially equal?

The Defence and Illustration of the French Language was written with a specific goal: to justify the French vernacular by establishing a new poetics to elevate the status of French and, in turn, France itself. A 1548 pamphlet had set the popular forms of French poetry on a par with Greek and Latin works, but the students at the Collège de Coqueret saw this declaration of victory in the battle for French as premature. French poetry required the enrichment provided by a study of classical authors. The Pléiade needed to respond with a manifesto, and du Bellay was the man for the job. As the pamphlet that provoked his treatise indicates, vernacular forms were already enjoying a lively reception through the efforts of poets of lowly birth such as Clément Marot, a rival of du Bellay's. Du Bellay was thus engaging in a class struggle with other French poets while defending French against Latin.

The *Defence* begins with a distinction between the natural and the cultural. Claiming that all languages are potentially equal in value, du Bellay points out the fundamental difference between plants and languages. While languages may appear to be of the same order as plants, they are, in fact, cultural constructs and thus not subject to the same *natural* variations of strength and weakness. The relative weakness of the French language is only temporary. Du Bellay supports this claim by discussing the rise of Latin: the Romans borrowed extensively from Greek authors but wrote in Latin; through imitation, they transformed Latin from a rather rough and brutish tongue to a language of literature and philosophy. Even the Greeks, he will later claim, drew from the wisdom of Egypt and India.

Although du Bellay begins his treatise by distinguishing between languages and plants, he goes on to employ a wide array of agricultural metaphors to describe the kinds of cultivation needed to transform a feeble language into a fruitful one. The metaphor of grafting seems ideal, conveying a process neither natural nor artificial: the grafting of one language onto another makes possible the development of robust new forms.

To enrich the vernacular, du Bellay recommends translation as a way of incorporating the knowledge of the ancients; but for highly rhetorical writings, especially poetry, translation cannot capture stylistic invention, which is specific to each language. Therefore, for poetry, imitation rather than translation is needed. The word du Bellay uses for a properly cultivated language is *copious*, which can be read as both "abundant" and "copied." But imitation should not be slavish: imitation can improve a natural genius but not create one. Without imitation, genius remains "wild"; without genius, imitation remains "apelike." What is to be imitated is the *spirit* of the original, not its external form.

Nevertheless, classical forms are inherently richer than popular forms, and French poets should adopt them, swallowing their classical predecessors whole and cannibalistically incorporating their genius. French poetry should abandon the ballades, rondelets, and virelays of the medieval popular tradition in favor of more learned forms: the ode (soon to be cultivated by Ronsard), the elegy, the eclogue, the sonnet. Du Bellay thus exhorts French poets to imitate and reincarnate the poets of Greece and Rome in order to demonstrate that French poetry can be as noble as the classics.

By trying to become something it was not, French poetry began to become what it is. The struggle between classical and popular forms gave rise to a kind of poetry that could not have been derived from either alone. Du Bellay's defense of French, ambivalent though it was about the popular roots of the vernacular, launched a poetic movement destined to stand as one of the golden moments of French poetry.

BIBLIOGRAPHY

Little of du Bellay's work has been translated into English: the *Defence* is available in an English translation by Gladys M. Turquet (1939), as is *Regrets*, translated by C. H. Sisson (1984). *Joachim du Bellay* (1971) by L. Clark Keating includes a biography as well as a general introduction.

There are relatively few book-length studies of du Bellay in English; however, many books on Renaissance poetics contain chapters on him. Especially useful are the chapters in W. F. Patterson's *Three Centuries of French Poetic Theory: A Critical History of the Chief Arts of Poetry in France (1328–1630)* (1935) and in S. J. Holyoake's concise study, *An Introduction to French Sixteenth Century Poetic Theory* (1972). The chapter on du Bellay in Margaret Ferguson's *Trials of Desire: Renaissance Defenses of Poetry* (1983) examines the political and historical context of the *Defence*, as well as the implications of du Bellay's own "borrowing" from Italian treatises. For a theoretical discussion of the Pléiade poets as a whole, see Grahame Castor's *Pléiade Poetics: A Study in Sixteenth-Century Thought and Terminology* (1964). Other good general studies include Dorothy Coleman, *The Chaste Muse: A Study of Joachim Du Bellay's Poetry* (1980), and David Hartley, *Patriotism in the Work of Joachim Du Bellay: A Study of the Relationship between the Poet and France* (1993). Margaret Brady Wells has compiled an extensive unannotated bibliography: *Du Bellay, a Bibliography* (1974).

From The Defence and Illustration of the French Language[1]

From *Book I*

CHAPTER I.
THE ORIGIN OF LANGUAGES

If nature (of whom a personage of high renown has not without reason doubted whether we should call her mother or stepmother[2]) had given to men a common will and consent, besides the innumerable commodities which would have thereby resulted, human inconstancy would not have needed to forge for itself so many manners of speaking. Which diversity and confusion can rightly be called the Tower of Babel.[3] For languages are not born of themselves after the fashion of herbs, roots, or trees: some infirm and weak in their nature; the others healthy, robust, and more fitted to carry the burden of human conceptions; but all their virtue is born in the world of the desire and will of mortals. That (it seems to me) is a great reason why one should not thus praise one language and blame the other; since they all come from a single source and origin, that is from the caprice[4] of men, and have been formed from a single judgment for a single end, that is to signify amongst us the conceptions and understandings of the mind. It is true that

1. Translated by Gladys M. Turquet.
2. That is, kind or merciless; see *Natural History* 7.1, by the Roman writer Pliny the Elder (23–79 C.E.).
3. See Genesis 11, which describes how God responded to men's attempt to build this tower to heaven by confusing their language, thereby creating many different languages where there had been one for all people.
4. The original French is *fantaisie* (fantasy, imagination).

in the succession of time, some from having been more carefully regulated have become richer than others; but this should not be attributed to the felicity of the said languages, but to the sole artifice and industry of men. So then all the things which nature has created, all the arts and sciences in the four quarters of the globe, are each in their own way the same thing; but since men are of diverse wills, therefore do they speak and write diversely. In this connection I cannot sufficiently blame the foolish arrogance and temerity of some in our nation who, being in no wise Greek nor Latin, misprize and reject with a more than stoical haughtiness all things written in French; and I cannot sufficiently wonder at the strange opinion of some learned men who think that our vulgar tongue[5] is incapable of good letters and erudition: as if an invention for language alone should be judged good or bad. The former I do not[6] undertake to satisfy. The latter I desire (if it be possible for me) to bring to change their opinion by means of a few reasons which I hope to deduce: not that I feel myself more far-seeing in that, or in other things, than they, but because the affection they bear towards foreign languages does not allow them to make healthy and complete judgment of their vulgar tongue.

CHAPTER II.

THAT THE FRENCH LANGUAGE SHOULD NOT BE CALLED BARBAROUS

To begin, then, to enter the subject, concerning the meaning of this word barbarous: in ancient times they were called barbarous who spoke Greek incorrectly. For as strangers coming to Athens strove to speak Greek, they often fell into this absurd expression βάρβαρος.[7]

Afterwards the Greeks transported the name to brutal and cruel manners, calling all nations outside Greece, *Barbarians*. That should in no way diminish the excellence of our tongue; because this Greek arrogance, admiring only its own inventions, had neither law nor privilege to legitimize its own nation and bastardize all the others; as Anacharsis said: the Scythians[8] were barbarians among the Greeks, but the Athenians were also barbarians among the Scythians, and even had the barbarity of the customs of our ancestors moved them to call us Barbarians, I do not see that things are so that we should now be considered as such; seeing that in civility of manners, equity of laws, magnanimity of heart, in short, in all forms and ways of living no less praiseworthy than profitable, we are not anything less than they; and still further, seeing that they themselves are now such that we may justly call them by that name which they gave to others. Still less should this happen because the Romans called us Barbarians, seeing that in their ambition and insatiable hunger for glory, they sought not only to subjugate but to render other nations vile and abject beside them: principally the Gauls,[9] from whom they suffered more shame and hurt than from others.

In this connection, thinking many times, whence comes it that the deeds of the Roman people are so celebrated throughout the world, nay, so far

5. The vernacular (here, French).
6. "Do not": added by the editor to correct the translator's error.
7. Barbarous (Greek).
8. The Greek name for the nomadic peoples north of the Black Sea, in what is today Moldova, Ukraine, and western Russia. Anacharsis (6th c. B.C.E.), Scythian prince who traveled widely in Greece and was later credited with many pithy sayings.
9. Ancient Celtic peoples occupying the area that became modern France.

more highly preferred to those of all other nations taken together, I find no greater reason than this: that the Romans did have so great a multitude of writers that most of their deeds (to say no worse) through the space of so many years, ardour in battle, laying waste of Italy, invasions of foreigners, have been preserved entire until our times. On the contrary, the actions of other nations, especially of the Gauls, before they fell into the power of the French,[1] and the actions of the French themselves since they gave their name to the Gauls, have been so ill collected, that we have almost lost not only the glory of them, but even the memory of them. Thereto the envy of the Romans has aided, who, as if in a certain conspiracy conspiring against us, weakened, as far as they were able, our warlike glory, whose brilliance they could not endure, and not only have they done us wrong thereby, but, to render us still more contemptible, they have called us brutal, cruel, and barbarous. Someone will say: Why have they exempted the Greeks from this name? Because they would have done more harm to themselves than to the Greeks, from whom they borrowed all the good which they had, at least with regard to the sciences and the illustration of their language. These reasons seem to me sufficient to make any equitable adjudicator of things understand, that our language (though we have been called barbarians by our enemies and by those who had no right to give to us this name) should yet not be misprized, especially by those to whom it is proper and natural: and who are in nothing less than the Greeks or Romans.

CHAPTER III.
WHY THE FRENCH LANGUAGE IS NOT SO RICH AS THE GREEK AND LATIN

And if our language be not so copious and rich as the Greek or Latin, that must not be imputed to it as a fault, as if of itself it could never be other than poor or sterile: but rather must one attribute it to the ignorance of our ancestors, who having (as someone[2] says, speaking of the ancient Romans) in higher esteem well-doing than fair speaking, and liking to leave to posterity examples of virtue, rather than precepts, deprived themselves of the glory of their fine deeds, and us of the fruit of the imitation thereof: and by the same means have left us our language so poor and bare that it has need of the ornaments and (so to speak) the plumes[3] of other persons. But who would say that Greek and Latin were always in the state of excellence wherein they were seen in the time of Homer and of Demosthenes, of Virgil and of Cicero?[4] And if these authors had judged, that never, whatever diligence and culture were brought thereto, would these tongues have been able to produce greater fruit, would they have laboured so much to bring them to that point where we now see them? So can I say of our tongue, which now begins to flower without fructifying; or rather, like a plant and small shoot, has not yet flowered, still less borne all the fruit that it might well produce. That

1. That is, the Franks, German tribes that entered the Roman provinces in the 3d century C.E. and overthrew the last Roman governor in Gaul in 486.
2. The Roman historian Sallust (86–34 B.C.E.) in *Bellum Catalinae* 8.
3. The French *plumes* allows a pun here [translator's note]. *Plume* means both "pen" and "feather."
4. Du Bellay chooses conventional representatives of excellence in Greek and Latin: in epic poetry, Homer (ca. 8th c. B.C.E.) and Virgil (70–19 B.C.E.); and in oratory, the Athenian Demosthenes (384–322 B.C.E.) and Cicero (106–43 B.C.E.).

certainly, not by any defect in the nature thereof, as apt to engender as others, but by the fault of those who have had the care of it, and have not sufficiently cultivated it; but like a wild plant in that same desert where it had begun to live, without ever watering it, or pruning, or guarding from brambles and thorns which shaded it, have let it grow old and almost die. And if the ancient Romans had been as negligent of the culture of their language when first it began to bud, certainly it would never in so short a time have become so great. But they, in the manner of good agriculturals, did first transplant it from a wild to a domestic place; then that it might the earlier and the better fructify, cutting off all round the useless twigs, in exchange for these did restore free and domestic branches, drawn in masterly fashion from the Greek tongue, which quickly were so well grafted and made like unto their trunk that henceforward they appeared no longer adopted but natural. Thence were born in the Latin tongue those flowers and those fruits coloured with the great eloquence, the numbers,[5] and the artificial binding together of phrases, all which things, not so much by its own nature as by artifice, every language is accustomed to produce. Therefore if the Greeks and the Romans, more diligent in the cultivation of their languages than we in that of ours, were unable to find therein, except with great toil and industry, either grace or number or finally any eloquence, should we marvel if our vulgar tongue is not so rich as it well might be, and thereby take the opportunity to misprize it as a vile thing and of little price? The time will come (maybe), and I hope for it with the help of good French fortune, when this noble and puissant kingdom will in its turn obtain the reins of sovereignty, and when our language (if with Francis[6] the whole French language be not buried), which now begins to throw out its roots, will emerge from the ground, and rise to such height and greatness, that it can equal the Greeks themselves and the Romans, producing, even as they, Homers and Demosthenes, Virgils and Ciceros, just as France has sometimes produced her Pericles, Nicias, Alcibiades, Themistocles, Caesars, and Scipios.[7]

CHAPTER IV.
THAT THE FRENCH LANGUAGE IS NOT SO POOR AS MANY ESTEEM IT

I do not, however, consider our vulgar tongue, as it now is, to be so vile, so abject as do these ambitious admirers of the Greek and Latin tongues, who would not think, were they even Pitho,[8] goddess of persuasion, that they could say anything good, unless it were in a foreign tongue, not comprehended of the vulgar. And he who will look closely, will discover that our French tongue is not so poor that it cannot render faithfully what it borrows from others, not so unfertile that it cannot produce of itself some fruit of good invention by means of the industry and diligence of its cultivators, if some are found who are such good friends of their country and of themselves, that they will apply themselves thereto. But to whom, after God, shall we

5. Meters.
6. Francis I (1494–1547), king of France (1515–47) and patron of the arts.
7. Du Bellay names famous statesmen and generals. The Greeks, all Athenians, were active during the 5th century B.C.E.—Pericles (ca. 495–429), Nicias (ca. 470–413), Alcibiades (ca. 450–404), and Themistocles (ca. 528–462). Julius Caesar (100–44 B.C.E.) and Scipio Africanus (ca. 236–184/3 B.C.E.) were the most brilliant generals of Roman antiquity as well as statesmen.
8. That is, Peitho (literally, "persuasion": Greek), in Greek mythology the personification of persuasion and seduction.

render thanks for such a benefit if not to our late good king and father, Francis, the first of that name and first in all virtues? I say first, since he has in his noble kingdom first restored all the good arts and sciences in their ancient dignity: and our language, which before was harsh and ill-polished, he has thus rendered elegant, and if not so copious as it well might be, at least a faithful interpreter of all others. And it is in such wise that philosophers, historians, doctors, poets, orators, both Greek and Roman, have learned to speak in French. What shall I say of the Hebrews? The sacred writings give ample testimony of what I say. I leave aside here the superstitious reasonings of those who maintain that the mysteries of theology ought not to be laid bare and, as it were, profaned in the vulgar tongue,[9] and that which those in the opposite camp allege. For this discussion is proper only for that which I have undertaken, which is solely to show that our language had not at its birth the gods and the stars in such enmity, that it cannot one day attain to the height of excellence and perfection as well as the others, since all sciences can faithfully and copiously be treated in it, as may be seen in the very great number of books, Greek and Latin, nay, even Italian and Spanish and others, translated into French by many excellent pens of our day.

CHAPTER V.
THAT TRANSLATIONS ARE NOT SUFFICIENT TO GIVE PERFECTION TO THE FRENCH LANGUAGE

In any case this most praiseworthy labour of translation seems not to me the only means, nor sufficient, to raise our vulgar tongue to be the equal and paragon of the other tongues. Which I claim to prove so clearly that none (as I believe) will wish to contradict, unless he be a manifest calumniator of truth; and firstly: It is a thing agreed among all the best authors of rhetoric, that there are five parts of fair speaking: invention, elocution, arrangement, memory, and pronunciation.[1] Now since the two last are to be learned, not so much by the benefit of tongues as they are given to each of us according to the fertility of his nature, increased and maintained by studious exercise and continual diligence, since also arrangement lies rather in the discernment and good judgment of the orator than in definite rules and precepts—seeing that the events of time, the circumstances of place, the conditions of persons, and the diversity of occasions, are innumerable—I will content myself with speaking of the two first: that is of invention and of elocution. The office then of the orator is to speak elegantly and copiously of each thing proposed. Now this faculty of speaking thus of all things, can be acquired only by the perfect understanding of the sciences, which were first treated by the Greeks, and next by the Romans, imitators of them. It is therefore necessary that these two tongues be understood by him who would acquire this copiousness and richness of invention, the first and principal piece in the harness of the orator. And touching this point, faithful translators can greatly serve and aid those who have not the sole means of devoting themselves to foreign tongues. But as for elocution, certainly the most difficult part, and without which all other things are, as it were, useless, and like a

9. Many within the Catholic Church resisted the publication of the Bible in French.

1. These divisions are standard in Greek and Latin handbooks of rhetoric.

sword still covered with its sheath—elocution (say I) by which principally an orator is judged more excellent, and a manner of speaking better, than another—as for that elocution from which is derived the name of eloquence itself, and whose virtue lies in words which are proper to the common usage of speech used therein and not alienated therefrom; in the metaphors, allegories, comparisons, similitudes, energies,[2] and so many other figures and ornaments without which any oration or poem is bare, maimed, and weak, I shall never believe that this can be learned from translators, because it is impossible to render it with the same grace which the author used; since each language has a something proper to itself alone, of which if you strive to express the nativeness in another language, observing the law of translation, which is not to expatiate yourself beyond the limits of the author, your diction will be constrained, cold, and ungraceful. And to prove it be thus, read me a Demosthenes and a Homer in Latin, a Cicero and a Virgil in French, to see if they will engender such emotions, nay, if even as a Proteus,[3] they will transform you in diverse sorts, as you feel, reading these authors in their own languages. You will seem to pass from the burning mountain of Etna to the cold summit of Caucasus.[4] And that which I say of the Greek and Latin languages, should equally be said of all the vulgar tongues, of which I will cite as an example only a Petrarch,[5] of whom I dare to say that if Homer and Virgil, born again, had undertaken to translate him, they could not render him with the same grace and naturalness as lies in his own native Tuscan. In any case, some in our time have undertaken to make him speak in French.[6] These briefly are the reasons which have made me think that the diligent service of translators, in other ways most useful for instructing those ignorant of foreign tongues in the knowledge of things, is not sufficient to give to our own language that perfection, that final touch which painters give to their pictures, which we desire. And if the reasons which I have alleged seem not strong enough, I will produce for my guarantors and defenders the ancient Roman authors, poets principally and orators, who (as Cicero translated some books of Xenophon and Aratus,[7] and as Horace gives the precepts of good translating[8]) have devoted themselves to this part more for their study and particular profit than for the publication and amplification of their language, their glory, and the convenience of others. If any have seen some works of that time under the title of translations, I mean works of Cicero, of Virgil, and that most happy age of Augustus,[9] they can deny what I say.

2. Aristotle, *energeia* [translator's note]: a crucial term in the philosophy of ARISTOTLE that is usually translated "actuality." In *Rhetoric* 3.1,1411b, he declares that "vivid presentation" is achieved by "expressions that signify activity/actuality."

3. In Greek mythology a seer, son of Poseidon (god of the sea), who is able to assume different shapes at will.

4. Mountain range between the Black and Caspian Seas. Etna: a volcano on the eastern coast of Sicily.

5. Italian poet and scholar (1304–1374).

6. Beginning early in the 16th century, several French translations of Petrarch appeared, most notably by the French poet Clément Marot (ca. 1496–1544), du Bellay's rival.

7. Greek poet (ca. 315–ca. 240 B.C.E.); his best-known work, a poem on astronomy titled *Phaenomena*, was translated by Cicero. Xenophon (ca. 428/7–ca. 354 B.C.E.) Athenian historian and general, author of the *Anabasis*, which significantly influenced Latin literature.

8. Du Bellay may have in mind the advice of the Roman poet HORACE (65–8 B.C.E.) in *Ars Poetica*, lines 268–69, to "study Greek models night and day."

9. The first emperor of Rome (63 B.C.E.–14 C.E.; proclaimed emperor, 27). He was a great patron of letters, and, after decades of civil war, his rule was a time of peace and prosperity.

CHAPTER VI.
OF BAD TRANSLATORS, AND OF NOT TRANSLATING THE POETS

But what shall I say of some truly more worthy to be called traducers[1] than translators? For they traduce those whom they undertook to explain, robbing them of their glory, and by the same means seduce ignorant readers, showing them white for black; and, to acquire the name of savants, they translate on credit those languages of which they never understood the first elements, like Hebrew and Greek; and again, to make themselves the better known, tackle the poets—a race of authors certainly to which if I were able or wished to translate I would so little address myself, because of that excellence of invention which they have more than others, that grandeur of style, magnificence of words, gravity of sentences, audacity and variety of figures, and countless other lights of poetry: in short, that energy, and I know not what of spirit which is in their writings, which the Latins would call genius.[2] All which things can as much be expressed in translating, as a painter can represent the soul with the body of him whom he undertakes to draw from nature. What I say is not addressed to those who by the command of princes and great lords translate the most famous Greek and Latin poets, because the obedience one owes to such personages admits of no excuse in this place, but indeed I mean to speak to those who from blitheness of heart (as we say) undertake such things lightly and in the same way acquit themselves thereof. O Apollo! O muses![3] thus to profane the sacred relics of antiquity! But I will say no more thereof. He then who would make a work worthy of price in his own tongue, let him leave this labour of translating, principally the poets, to those who from a laborious and little profitable thing, I would even say useless, nay, harmful, to the enrichment of their language, rightly get more of vexation than of glory.

CHAPTER VII.
HOW THE ROMANS ENRICHED THEIR LANGUAGE

If the Romans (someone will say) did not devote themselves to this labour of translation, by what means then were they able to enrich their language, even to make it almost equal to the Greek? Imitating the best Greek authors, transforming themselves into them, devouring them; and, after having well digested them, converting them into blood and nourishment, taking for themselves, each according to his nature, and the argument he wished to choose, the best author of whom they observed diligently all the most rare and exquisite virtues, and these like shoots, as I have already said, they grafted and applied to their own tongue. By doing this (I say) the Romans did build those fine writings which we praise and admire so much, now equalling one of these writings with the Greeks and now excelling them.

And of what I say, give good proof Cicero and Virgil, whom willingly and for their honour I name always in the Latin tongue, of whom the one gave himself entirely to the imitation of the Greeks, counterfeited, and did express

1. The English cannot reproduce the neat Italian *traduttori, traditori*, nor du Bellay's *traditeurs . . . traducteurs* [translator's note].
2. The guardian spirit of a person or place.
3. In Greek mythology, 9 daughters of Memory who preside over the arts and all intellectual pursuits. Apollo: the Greek and Roman god of music and prophecy.

in so lively a fashion the fertility of Plato, the vehemence of Demosthenes, and the joyful sweetness of Isocrates, that Molo, the Rhodian,[4] once hearing him declaim, cried that he brought Greek eloquence to Rome. The other did so well imitate Homer, Hesiod, and Theocritus,[5] that it has since been said of him that of these three he surpassed the first, equalled the second, and approached so closely to the other, that if the felicity of the arguments he treated had been equal, it were doubtful to whom to give the palm. I therefore ask you who are busied only with translations, if these so famous authors had amused themselves with translating, would they have raised their language to the excellence and height wherein we now see it? Think not then by any diligence and industry that you may employ in this direction, to so do that our language, which still creeps along the ground, may lift its head and rise up on its feet.

From *Book II*

CHAPTER III.

THAT NATURAL TALENT IS NOT SUFFICIENT FOR HIM WHO IN POETRY WOULD MAKE A WORK WORTHY OF IMMORTALITY

But since that in all languages there are good and bad, I will not (reader) that without election and judgment you should take the first comer. It were far better to write without imitation than resemble a bad author, since it is a thing agreed among the most learned that natural talent can do more without doctrine than doctrine without natural talent. However, since the amplification of our language (which is whereof I treat) cannot be made without doctrine, and without erudition, I would fain warn those who aspire to this glory to imitate the good Greek and Roman authors, nay, even the Italian, Spanish, and others, or else not to write at all, except to oneself (as we say) and to one's muses. Let one not cite here some of ours, who without doctrine, and at most none other than mediocre, have acquired great reputation in our tongue.[6] Those who readily admire small things, and disdain that which exceeds their judgment, may attach to them what value they will, but I know well that the learned will put them in no other rank than those who speak French well, and who have (as Cicero said, of the ancient Roman authors) good wit but very little artifice. Let it not be alleged to me also that poets are born, for that applies to the ardour and alacrity of spirit, which naturally excites poets, and without which all doctrine would be imperfect and useless. Certainly it would be too easy a thing, and therein contemptible, to become eternal through renown, if the felicity of nature, given over to the most unlearned, were sufficient to make a thing worthy of immortality. Who would fly through the hands and mouths of men,[7] must long remain within his chamber; and who desires to live in the memory of posterity must, as though dead in himself, sweat and tremble many a time; and even as our

4. Apollonius Molon (1st c. B.C.E.), rhetorician who lectured at Rhodes and visited Rome; he taught Cicero and other Romans. PLATO (ca. 427–ca. 327 B.C.E.), Greek philosopher; like him, Cicero wrote philosophical dialogues, including *De Republica*. Isocrates (436–338 B.C.E), Athenian orator, rhetorician, and teacher.

5. Greek poet (ca. 300–260 B.C.E.), whose pastoral poetry Virgil imitated in his *Eclogues*. Hesiod (active ca. 700 B.C.E.), Greek didactic poet whom Virgil imitated in his *Georgics*.

6. The allusion is again to Clément Marot, who was a popular poet at the court of Francis I.

7. Here begins a passage lifted verbatim from one of du Bellay's Italian predecessors, Sperone Speroni (*Dialogo delle lingue*, 1542).

courtier poets drink, eat, and sleep at their ease, so must he endure hunger, thirst, and long vigils. These are the things whereon the writings of men fly to heaven. But in order that I may return to the beginning of this question, let our imitator first consider those whom he would imitate, and that which in them he can imitate and which should be imitated, in order not to do as those, who wishing to appear like unto some great lord, will imitate a petty gesture or vicious way of acting in him, rather than his virtues and good graces. Before all things must he have the judgment to know his own strength, and test how much his shoulders can carry; let him sound diligently his natural gifts, and compose himself for the imitation of him whom he feels he most nearly approaches. Otherwise his imitation will resemble that of the ape.

CHAPTER IV.

WHAT KINDS OF POEMS THE FRENCH POET SHOULD CHOOSE

Read, then, and read again (O future poet); with daily and with nightly hand, turn the leaves of your Greek and Latin exemplars, then leave aside all these old French poesies to the floral games of Toulouse, and the contest of Rouen,[8] the rondels, ballades, virelays, chants royal, songs, and other such spices[9] which do corrupt the taste of our tongue, and serve not, save to bear witness to our ignorance. Throw thyself upon these pleasant epigrams, not as do to-day a host of makers of new stories, who in ten lines are content to say nothing of worth in the first nine, provided that in the tenth is the little word to laugh at, but in imitation of a Martial,[1] or of some other well approved; if lasciviousness please thee not, mingle the profitable with the agreeable.[2] Distil with a flowing style, and not rugged, these touching elegies after the example of an Ovid, a Tibullus, and a Propertius,[3] mingling therein at times those ancient fables, no small ornament of poetry. Sing me those odes, unknown as yet of the French muse, on a lute well accorded to the sound of the Greek and Roman lyre, and let there be no line wherein appeareth not some vestige of rare and ancient erudition. And for this, matter will be furnished thee by the praises of the gods and virtuous men, the immutable order of earthly things, the solicitudes of young men such as love, flowing wine, and good cheer. Above all things see that this kind of poem be far removed from the vulgar, enriched and made illustrious with proper words and epithets by no means idle, adorned with grave sentences, and varied with all manner of poetical colours and ornaments: not like a *Laissez la verde couleur, Amour avecques Psyches, O combien est heureuse,*[4] and other such works, more worthy to be called vulgar songs than odes or lyrical verses. As for epistles, they are not a kind of poem which can greatly enrich our vulgar tongue, since they are readily of familiar and domestic things, unless thou

8. The oldest of several bourgeois fraternal societies established beginning in the 12th century to cultivate music and poetry. The Floral Games of Toulouse: an institution founded in 1323 by seven minstrel poets; during the 16th century, at the height of its glory, it was renamed the College of the Art and Science of Rhetoric.

9. Vernacular French medieval poetic genres.

1. Roman poet (ca. 10–ca. 104 C.E.) best known for his witty epigrams that depicted Roman society, high and low (sometimes in very coarse language).

2. Compare Horace, *Ars Poetica,* line 343: "The man who combines pleasure with usefulness wins every suffrage."

3. Roman poet (ca. 50–ca. 15. B.C.E.), one of the great masters of Latin love elegy (that is, a poem in elegiac couplets, a specific metrical form). Ovid (43 B.C.E.–17 C.E.) and Tibullus (ca. 50–19 B.C.E.) also wrote highly polished elegies.

4. Three 16th-century French *chansons* (songs): "Leave the Green Color," "Love [or Cupid] with Psyche," and "Oh How Happy."

didst wish to make them in imitation of elegies as Ovid did, or sententious and grave, as Horace.[5] As much, too, do I say of satires, which the French, I know not how, have called *coqs à l'âne,*[6] in which I advise thee to exercise thyself as little as possible, just as I desire thee to be removed from ill-speaking, unless thou didst wish, after the example of the ancients, in heroic verse (that is to say, lines of ten to eleven, and not only of eight to nine [syllables]), under the name of satire, and not with that inept title *coq à l'âne,* modestly to tax the vices of thine age, sparing the names of the vicious persons. Thou hast for this Horace, who, according to Quintilian,[7] holds the first place among the satirists. Ring me out those fine sonnets, a no less learned than pleasing Italian invention, conformable in name with the ode, and different from it only in that the sonnet has ambiguous lines, regulated and limited; and the ode may run through all manner of lines freely, nay, even invent them at pleasure, after the example of Horace, who did sing in nineteen sorts of lines, as the grammarians tell us. For the sonnet, then, thou hast Petrarch and some modern Italians. Sing me on well-resounding pipe, or on well-joined flute, those pleasant rustic eclogues,[8] after the example of Theocritus and Virgil: or marine eclogues, after the manner of Sannazaro,[9] the Neapolitan gentleman. Might it please the muses that in all these kinds of poetry which I have named we had many such imitations, as is this eclogue on the birth of the son of Monseigneur the Dauphin, to my taste one of the best little works that Marot[1] ever made. Adopt also into the French family those flowing and dainty hendecasyllables, following the example of a Catullus, a Pontanus, and a Secundus,[2] which thou shalt be able to do, if not in quantity at least in the number of syllables. As for comedies and tragedies, if kings and republics would restore them to their ancient dignity, which the farces and moralities have usurped, I should be of the opinion that thou shouldst busy thyself therewith, and if thou dost wish to do so, for the adorning of thy language, thou knowest where thou shouldst find their archetypes.

1549

5. Horace's epistles are conversational, not grave; but the long poems of *Epistles* 2 concern literature. Ovid's elegiac epistles are his *Heroides* (letters from legendary women to their absent lovers or husbands) and his *Tristia* and *Letters from Pontus* (describing the hardships of the poet's exile and pleading for leniency).

6. From the expression *sauter du coq à l'âne* (to jump from the cock to the donkey); stories characterized by absurd associations.

7. Roman rhetorician and teacher of oratory (ca. 30/35–ca. 100 C.E.; see above); he calls Horace the best satirist in *Institutio Oratoria* 10.1.94.

8. Short poems—often pastoral—in the form of a dialogue or soliloquy, particularly popular during the 15th and 16th centuries.

9. Jacopo Sannazaro (1458–1530), a poet born in Naples who was greatly admired by the poets of the Pléiade.

1. Clément Marot, official court poet. The Dauphin: Francis of Valois, the future King Francis II, born January 19, 1544.

2. Joannes Secundus (1511–1536), Latin name of the neo-Latin poet Jean Everaerts. Giovanni Pontano (1426–1503), neo-Latin prose writer and poet of the Italian Renaissance. Catullus (ca. 84–ca. 54 B.C.E.), Roman lyric poet who was the first to adopt Greek hendecasyllabics—11-syllable lines in a set pattern of "quantity" (i.e., syllable length)—to represent everyday Latin speech.

PIERRE DE RONSARD
1524–1585

Often referred to by his contemporaries in France as the "Prince of Poets," Pierre de Ronsard enjoyed considerable fame during his lifetime. His reputation went into eclipse a century later as a strict codification of French poetry accompanied the rise of the classical theater, of which Renaissance poetry—exemplified by Ronsard—was treated as a crude precursor. But he was brought out of the shadows again by the Romantics, who were eager to find a looser and more lyrical alternative to those same classic verse forms. His rescuers, however, were precisely those whose influence would make it difficult for readers to appreciate him on his own terms: the Romantics privileged originality, subjectivity, and marginality, which were not at all in Ronsard's mind or vocabulary. For him, the poet aspired to equal the ancients and to give public and universal voice to enduring truths.

Ronsard was born into a family with a long tradition of political connections and royal service. His grandfather, who had been in the employ of Louis XI, had fought in wars with the duke of Orléans (later Louix XII) and Francis I. Ronsard's father, a committed humanist, served Francis I as *maître d'hôtel du roi* and governor to the king's children, and spent four years in Madrid with them while they were held as hostages in place of their father. The loyal courtier was rewarded by the king with the refurbishing of his country manor, done in high Italian style by Italian workmen. The Ronsard family was Catholic, patriotic, and noble, and their manor in the Loire valley, like the court of Francis I, became a center of Renaissance values and learning. At the age of nine, Pierre was sent to the Collège de Navarre in Paris, where he did so badly that he withdrew after a term. He then left to take a series of positions as a young courtier. At age twelve, he became page to the king's children, chiefly to the fourteen-year-old Charles, duke of Orléans. Soon he accompanied the duke's sister to Scotland, and thereafter he made other diplomatic journeys to the Netherlands, London, and Alsace. During one of his journeys to Alsace, he contracted a serious illness and became partially deaf; this automatically precluded him from having a diplomatic or military career. Barred from a life of active service, he nevertheless went on to serve four monarchs with his poetic voice. In 1543 he received simple tonsure from Bishop René du Bellay (great-uncle of the poet JOACHIM DU BELLAY), a position that, while short of ordination as a priest, made him eligible to receive revenue from church properties and established him as a celibate churchman for the rest of his life.

At the age of twenty, after his father's death, Ronsard returned to Paris and undertook the study of Greek and Latin letters. He was invited to study with the twelve-year-old son of Lazare de Baïf, a diplomat with whom Ronsard had traveled when he was younger; both were instructed by France's foremost Hellenist, Jean Dorat. Eventually, the two followed Dorat to the Collège de Coqueret, a small boarding college that was part of the University of Paris system. The dedicated group of eager young scholars at Coqueret worked tirelessly to master a curriculum consisting almost exclusively of Greek and Latin poetry. They began to see themselves as a unified, select group with a mission that turned out to be nothing less than a revolution of French poetic language. First they called themselves the "Brigade," but soon they adopted the name *Pléiade*. The young men of the Pléiade (Ronsard, Joachim du Bellay, and five others) began publishing their poetry and entered the public discourse about poetic theory in 1549 with du Bellay's *Defence and Illustration of the French Language* (see above). They established themselves as an intellectual aristocracy, believing in the divine origin of poetry and their own position as poetic equals to their classical precursors.

Ronsard's first published poems served as illustrations of Pléiade poetic ideals. Written in French, they were closely modeled on classical and Italian forms. In 1550 the first four books of his *Odes* were published. Two years later he published his first sonnets, *Les Amours de Cassandre*, ostensibly inspired by his love for a Florentine banker's daughter, Cassandre de Salviati. His sonnets, like Petrarch's, exemplify that strange amalgam of Christianity and pagan philosophy that came to be known as Neoplatonism (see PLOTINUS), clearly marked out by the names of the women he addresses: Cassandra (who prophesied the Trojan War), Marie (who was the virgin mother of Christ), and Helen (whose abduction caused the Trojan War).

His most ambitious work was never completed. Wishing to rival the classical epic poems, Ronsard envisioned a French *Aeneid*, the *Franciade*, on which he began work in 1554, early in his poetic career. He finally published the first four books of it in 1572, but left both the court and the epic on the death of his patron, Charles IX, in 1574. He composed his most celebrated work—a series of poems called *Sonnets to Hélène* (1578)—after leaving the public arena of court poet. These poems were written near the end of his life, when he fell in love with the much younger Hélène de Sugères, a lady-in-waiting to Catherine de Medici; she ultimately refused his passion for her, but did not prevent his poetic consummation with her name.

Ronsard is remembered today mainly for his sonnets, but he wrote in at least twenty genres, and his voice and purpose ranged widely. In the early 1560s his writings responded to and participated in the rising tension between Catholics and Protestants. As a court poet and a churchman, he was a defender of Catholicism, but his stance was more practical and patriotic than theological. He wanted poetry to strengthen the state, not individual freedom. For him Protestants, even French Protestants (called Huguenots), were foreigners. They upset the genteel coexistence of the court, the church, and the classics on which his poetry was based. Strict Calvinists went so far as to express suspicions about the sensuality and paganness of any poetry that imitated the Greeks and the Romans. What had once seemed universal and eternal suddenly became partisan and historical. Ronsard's writing became more political and polemical during the first period of violent conflict; but when the Peace of Amboise ended the first war of religion in 1563, he began to withdraw from public rhetoric and tried to reestablish a more distant, oracular, ahistorical voice for poetry. It was at this point that he wrote "A Brief on the Art of French Poetry" (1565). The "Brief"'s seeming distance from any historical events is a response to, not a sign of detachment from, the trauma of civil war. It was part of a short-lived historical moment in which the French court attempted to achieve tolerance and cultural unity.

"A Brief on the Art of French Poetry," written at the very middle point of Ronsard's poetic career, holds a place in the tradition of letters addressed by established poets to young, aspiring poets. Like HORACE's *Ars Poetica* (see above) or Rainer Maria Rilke's *Letters to a Young Poet* (1929), Ronsard's "Brief" takes the form of advice on both the specifics of poetry and on how to live as a poet. It is a prose letter written to Alphonse Delbène (1540–1608), a young member of the noble Florentine Del-Bene family that had taken refuge in French courts in the early sixteenth century, fleeing Francis I's unsuccessful campaigns in Italy. In the "Brief" Ronsard is trying to accomplish several tasks: to combine classical poetics with Christian beliefs, to combine invention with imitation, to adjudicate the claims of competing languages and dialects, and to explore some of the techniques of a well-made poem in French.

He begins his counsel with the importance of divine inspiration. Divine power is transmitted to mortals through the medium of poetry: the poet is to men what God is to the poet. Ronsard's belief in poetic inspiration echos PLATO's *Ion* (see above), in which a chain of inspiration runs from the gods to the Muses to the inspired artist. Ronsard upholds the Pléiade's respect for classical models, echoing in his subtitles the *inventio, disposito,* and *elocutio* of traditional rhetoric. He teaches the young poet not only how to imitate classical poets, making sure to explain that their mythology is to be taken as an allegory of the powers of God, but also how to train his eye on contemporary crafts and skills, particularly metallurgy, so as to learn (and not just imitate) the craft of poetry. In one of the earliest arguments in favor of the poetry workshop, he encourages his addressee to share his poems widely with his fellows. He comments on the technical apparatus of French vernacular poetry, offering guidelines for rhythm, rhyme, and musicality; in this he resembles his contemporaries GIAMBATTISTA GIRALDI in Italy and George Puttenham in England.

Drawing, as does Homer, on the most vivid and concrete of figures, the poet, he argues, must nevertheless find what is most proper and harmonious to his subject. Individual imagination not tempered by the scrutiny of other poets and by the example of great predecessors risks becoming disordered, fantastic, "monstrous." But appropriate and healthy hybridization makes a language stronger. In an age in which France was in the process of being consolidated politically and linguistically, Ronsard recommends that the poet take his vocabulary not just from the court but from the rich dialects of the provinces. The true French poet should rise above history and write poetry for the ages.

Not until Victor Hugo in the nineteenth century would French poetry again achieve so classical and public a voice. But Hugo, writing ambitious epics while exiled by Napoleon III, saw the moral authority of poetry as a kind of alternative government, not as a handmaiden of the court. Nor was Hugo the only nineteenth-century poet to revive Ronsard's voice. The Romantic critic Sainte-Beuve resurrected the Renaissance to counteract the rigidity of post-Renaissance classical verse forms developed in the theater. Yet Ronsard's influence has been both anticlassic and classic: the classical pantheon itself underwent a revival in the mid–nineteeth century, spurred by the so-called Parnassian poets, to the point that CHARLES BAUDELAIRE lamented, "Who will deliver us from the Greeks and the Romans?" The virtuosity and freshness of Ronsard's manipulation of the classical past, of the sonnet form, of the oracular tone, and of the French language have continued to inspire poets four centuries after he wrote his letter to Alphonse Delbène. The serenity of his view of poetry has perhaps come to sound dated in the turbulence of modern times, but it is important to remember that his own century was no less turbulent. His advice to rise above petty polemics and historical contests is itself a contested, but often appealing, contribution to the history of poetics.

BIBLIOGRAPHY

The standard two-volume *Oeuvres Complètes* of Ronsard's work exists in the Pléiade edition (whose name harks back to the group of poets that he led); it was revised in 1994. Morris Bishop's *Ronsard, Prince of Poets* (1940) and D. B. Wyndham Lewis's *Ronsard* (1944) are somewhat dated biographical studies (a 1990 biography by Michel Simonin is available in French). *Pierre de Ronsard* (1970) by K. R. W. Jones provides a general introduction. Isidore Silver's work should be included in any serious Ronsard scholarship, most notably the three-volume study *The Intellectual Evolution of Ronsard* (1969–92) and *Three Ronsard Studies* (1978). A collection of essays edited by Terence Cave, *Ronsard the Poet* (1973), offers an excellent study of Ronsard's poetic vision, including both classical and Renaissance influences. It also contains a good bibliography. For a comparative approach, see Alfred W. Satterthwaite, *Spenser, Ronsard, and du Bellay: A Renaissance Comparison* (1960). There is an annotated bibliography on Ronsard in the *Critical Bibliography of French Literature*, vol. 2, *The Sixteenth Century* (rev. ed., 1985).

From A Brief on the Art of French Poetry[1]

Although the art of Poetry can be neither learned nor taught by precept, it being a thing more experiential than traditional, yet, in so far as human art, attainment, and labor will permit, I wish to lay down some rules by which one day you[2] may be able to reach the first order of skill in this happy calling, by my means, who confess myself reasonably learned in it. Always you will hold the Muses in reverence, in singular veneration, and not have them serve for any purpose dishonorable, ridiculous, or libelous; but you are to keep them beloved and sacramental, the daughters of Jupiter[3] which is to say, of God, who in his sacred grace, first through them made known to ignorant peoples the excellence of his majesty. For poetry was in the earliest time only an allegorical theology, to carry into men's coarse brains, by charming and prettily colored fables, the secret truths which they could not comprehend if openly declared. The Athenian Eumolpus, Linus the instructor of Hercules, Orpheus, Homer, Hesiod[4] invented this excellent profession. So poets were called divine, not so much for the god-like soul which made them wonderful above others, as for the communion which they had with oracles, prophets, diviners, sibyls, interpreters of dreams, for of what these knew the poets had learned the superior part: to what the oracles said in few words, these elevated persons gave expansion, color, commentary, being for the people what the sibyls and diviners were but for themselves. A long time afterward appeared in the same country the second school of poets, whom I call human, as being more filled with artifice and labor, than with divine inspiration. As an example of the latter, the Roman poets swarmed in abundance, with so many puffed out and artificial books that they brought to book-stores more burden than honor, except for five or six, whose understanding of their art, accompanied by perfect craftsmanship, has always held my admiration.

But since the Muses are not willing to reside in a soul unless it be kindly, saintly, virtuous, you should act always with kindness, never with meanness, sullenness, or chagrin; moved by a fine spirit, let nothing enter your soul which is not superhuman, divine. You are to bear in highest regard conceptions which are elevated, grand, beautiful—not those that lie round the earth. For the principal thing is invention, which comes as much from goodness of nature as from the lessons of the good ancient authors. If you attempt a great work, you should show yourself religious and God-fearing, beginning the poem either with his name or with another which will represent some effect of his majesty, as in the example of the Greek poets, "Sing, O Goddess,

1. Translated by James Harry Smith.
2. Alphonse Delbène (1540–1608), an aspiring young French poet whose Italian parents had come to France during Francis I's failed campaigns in Italy.
3. In Roman mythology, king of the gods. In Greek mythology, the 9 Muses (who preside over the arts and all intellectual pursuits) are the daughters of Zeus and Mnemosyne (literally, "Memory").
4. Ronsard names mythical and historical figures of classical Greece, all images of "divine poets" that can mediate between Muses and men: Eumolpus, raised in Thrace but linked to Athens through his mother, is said to have founded the mysteries at Eleusis and to have excelled in singing and in playing the flute and lyre; Linus, the son of Apollo, god of music, was said to have taught the lyre to Heracles (whom the Romans called "Hercules"), greatest of the legendary Greek heroes, and to Orpheus, a musician unrivaled among mortals; Homer is credited with composing the *Iliad* and *Odyssey* (ca. 8th c. B.C.E.); and Hesiod, a didactic poet (active ca. 700 B.C.E.), is often paired with Homer as the other main representative of early epic.

the wrath," "Tell me of the man, O Muse," "With Zeus let us begin," "Beginning from thee O Phoebus,"[5] and of the Latin, "Great Mother of Rome," "Muse, relate to me the causes."[6] For the Muses, Apollo, Mercury, Pallas, Venus,[7] and other such deities represent to us no other thing than powers of God, to which the earliest men gave various names, in accord with the different effects of his incomparable majesty. And it must also show you that nothing can be good or perfect, if the beginning not come of God. Then, you are to study the writings of the good poets, and learn by heart as many of them as you can. You are to take great pains to correct and file your verses, and are not to excuse faults in them any more than a good gardener neglects his poles when he sees them overburdened with branches useless or of little account. You are to hold sweet converse with the other poets of your time: you will honor the oldest among them as your fathers, those your age, as your brothers, the younger, as the children. And you will show to your fellow poets your writings, for you should let nothing see the light which has not first been viewed and reviewed by your friends whom you think the best qualified on the matter; to the end that by such relationships and familiarities of your minds, with the learning and the talent that you have, you will arrive with ease at the height of all honor, having for local example the virtues of your father,[8] who not only has surpassed in his, the Italian language, those in highest reputation in his time, but even has made the victory doubtful between himself and those who write today with most purity and learning the old language of the Romans.

But since you have denied recognition to Greek and Latin as mediums of composition, and only French remains, which ought to be the more readily commended to you, as it is your native language, I shall say a few things that seem expedient, and without losing you in a large and tedious forest, I shall conduct you straightway, and by the path which I have found shortest, so that you may easily overtake those who first set out on the road, and may find yourself not out-stripped to any extent at all.

In the manner in which Latin verse has its feet,[9] as you know, we have in our French poetry a certain measure of syllables, according to the kind of poem to be written; and this cannot be trespassed without offense to the law of our verse, the particular measures and numbers of which I treat more amply farther on. We have also a *cæsure*[1] on the vowel *e*, which is done away whenever it is encountered with another vowel or a diphthong, provided that the vowel which follows *e* not have the force of a consonant. In imitation of my precepts you will appoint the verses, masculine and feminine,[2] as well as it be possible for you to do, to approach nearest music and the harmony of instruments, in the favor of which poetry seems to have been born: for poetry without instruments, or without the grace of one or more voices, is in no

5. First lines from, respectively, Homer's *Iliad* and *Odyssey*, Theocritus's *Idyll* 17 (ca. 260 B.C.E.), and an unidentified work [based on translator's note].
6. Opening invocations from two Roman poems, Lucretius's *De Rerum Natura* (ca. 55 B.C.E.) and Virgil's *Aeneid* (17 B.C.E.) [based on translator's note].
7. In Roman mythology, goddess of love. Apollo: Greek and Roman god of music, healing, and prophecy. Mercury: Roman messenger-god. Pallas: Athena, Greek goddess of wisdom, the arts, and war.
8. Bartolomeo Del-Bene, Italian poet and historian.
9. The basic building blocks of Latin and Greek verse forms, consisting of various fixed patterns of long and short syllables.
1. A caesura, a pause in a line of verse; but here Ronsard means an elision, the omission of an unstressed vowel.
2. In French poetry, a feminine ending occurs when the last word in a line ends in a mute "e"; all other lines have masculine endings.

wise charming, any more than instruments unenlivened by a pleasing voice. If you happen to have composed the two first verses masculine in ending, make the next two feminine, and proceed in this manner for the remainder of your elegy or *chanson*,[3] that the musicians may the more easily harmonize with it. As to lyric verse, you will build the first couplet as you desire, but the others must follow the plan of the first. If you make use of Greek and Roman proper names, you will, in so far as your tongue permits, give them French terminations; there are many which cannot so be changed. You ought not to disdain our old Latin words, but to choose them with prudence.

You will frequent the practitioners of all trades, seamanship, hunting, falconry, and especially those that owe the perfection in their craft to the furnace: goldsmiths, foundrymen, blacksmiths, metallurgists; and from them you will store up many good and lively semblances, along with the very names of the instruments, to enrich and beautify your work. For just as one may not call a body fair, comely, or gifted, unless it be made up of blood, veins, arteries, and tendons, and, above all, have a purely natural color, so Poetry cannot be charming, alive, or perfect without excellent inventions, descriptions, comparisons, which are the nerve and the life of books, which can force the centuries to leave them, in universal remembrance, victorious over time.

You are to learn to choose dexterously, and to appropriate to your work the most significant words of the dialects of our France, when those of your nation are not sufficiently proper or significant, not troubling yourself whether they be of Gascony, Poitou, Normandy, Manche, Lyonnais, or another province, provided only that they be good, and that they properly express what you want to say; without affecting too much the speech of the court, which is many times quite mediocre to be the language of courtly ladies and of gentlemen, who pursue more the practice of arms than of well chosen speech. You will observe that the Greek language would never have been so scattered and so full of dialects and varieties of words as it is, had not the majority of the republics that flourished in that time selfishly desired that their learned citizens write in their own particular dialects. And because of that there has come down an infinity of dialects, phrases, and manners of speaking, which even today carry on their foreheads the marks of their native countries, which are held indifferently good by the learned pens that write of that time. For a country can never be so entirely perfect that it may not borrow some something from its neighbor. And I doubt not that if there remained in France the Dukes of Burgundy, Picardy, Normandy, Brittany, Champaign, Gascony, they would yet desire the extreme honor of their subjects' writing in a provincial dialect. For princes must be no less eager to widen the bounds of their realms than, on the example of the Romans, to extend the language of their countries through all nations. But today, France under one king, we are compelled, if we wish to come to any honor, to speak the courtier's language; or our labor, however learned it may be, is liable to be estimated of little value, or may be totally scorned. And since the goods and favors come in from this source, it is often necessary to yield to the opinion of some court lady or some young courtier, who will often have as little knowledge of good and true poetry as they have skill in arms and other of the more honorable exercises.

3. Song (French).

Of Invention[4]

Since I have mentioned invention before, it seems to me that it would be timely here to refresh your memory by a short notice of it. Invention is nothing other than the natural virtue of an imagination, conceiving the ideas and forms of all things that can be imagined, whether of heaven or of earth, living or inanimate, for the purpose of afterwards representing, describing, imitating: for just as the aim of the orator is to persuade, so that of the poet is to imitate, invent, and represent—things which are, or which may be—in a resemblance to truth. And it must not be doubted that after one has invented boldly and well, a "disposition" of verse which is effective will follow, for disposition follows invention, in all cases, just as the shadow does a body. When I bid you invent fair things and great, I do not mean inventions fantastic and melancholic; these do not more correspond to one another than do the broken dreams of one in a frenzy, or terribly tormented by a fever, to an imagination bruised or injured, in which a thousand monstrous forms, without order or connection, are represented. But your inventions, on which I cannot give you rules, as they are of the spirit, must be well ordered and appointed. And although they seem to pass those of the vulgar, they must nevertheless be such as can easily be conceived and understood by everyone.

Of Disposition

As invention depends upon the refined state of the mind, so disposition depends upon sound invention, consisting in an elegant and consummate placing and ordering of the things invented; it does not permit what appertains to one place to be put in another, but, operating by artifice, study, and application, it disposes and sets each matter to its proper point. For examples of it you may take the ancient authors and those of the moderns who have during the last fifteen years illuminated our literature, now justly proud in this glorious achievement. Happy demi-gods, they who cultivate their own earth, nor strive after another, from which they could only return thankless and unhappy, unrecompensed, unhonored. The first to dare abandon the ancient Greek and Roman languages for the greater glory of their own truly must be good sons, not ungrateful citizens; worthy to be signalized in a public statue, wherein from age to age men shall encounter a lasting memorial of them and of their greatness: not that other languages should be ignored; for I counsel you to know them perfectly, and from them, as from an old treasure found under the earth, enrich your own nation. For it is very difficult to write well in the vernacular if one be not perfectly, or at least fairly, learned in those more honored and more famous languages.

Of Elocution

Elocution is a propriety and splendor of words, properly chosen and adorned, in varying lengths of sentence, which make the verse glitter like precious stones on the fingers of some great lord. Under elocution I put choice of words, which Virgil and Horace[5] so conscientiously observed. For you ought

4. The traditional divisions of ancient rhetoric are invention, arrangement (disposition), diction (elocution), memory, and delivery; Ronsard omits the last two.

5. Roman poet (65–8 B.C.E.; see above), much studied in the early Renaissance. Virgil (70–19

to strive to be well supplied with words, and to call the most appropriate and significant that you can to serve as the sinew and force of your song, which will shine in proportion as the words be significant, and chosen with judgment. You are not to forget the comparisons, the descriptions of places, streams, forests, mountains, of night, and of sunrise, of mid-day, of the winds, the sea, of gods and goddesses, with their proper attributes, dress, cars, horses: guiding yourself in this by imitation of Homer, whom you are to observe as a divine example, from whom you are to draw, as from life, the most perfect lineaments for your picture.

Of Poetry in General

You are to know that great poems never begin at the first point of the action, nor are so completed as that the reader, taken with the delight of it, may not still wish the end farther off; but the good literary craftsmen begin in the middle, and knowing so well how to join the beginning to the middle, and the middle to the end, make of the pieces so produced a body entire and perfect. Never begin a poem on a large scale unless its subject stretch back before the memory of men; and invoke the Muse, who remembers everything, being a goddess, to sing to you things of which men can remember nothing. The others, little poems, may be begun abruptly, the lyric odes, for example, in the composition of which I advise you to train yourself first, taking care above all against being more the versifier than the poet: for fable and fictions have furnished the material for the good poets, those who have been recommended to posterity from as far back as memory goes; and mere verse is but the aim of the ignorant versifier, who thinks that he has made great headway in his work when he has composed a great many rhyming verses which so smell of prose that I am amazed how our French publishers can print such drugs, to the confusion of authors, and of our nation as a whole. I should inform you of the proper subjects for each particular kind of poem, if you had not already read the *arts of poetry* of Horace and of Aristotle,[6] in which I know you are fairly well versed.

I counsel you to avoid epithets[7] relating to objects of nature, as they do not advance at all the sense of what you want to say; for example, *the flowing river, the green bough,* and infinite others. You should seek out epithets which mean something, not merely fill up your verse form, or trifle with your sense. Take this verse for an example:

The vaulted sky encloses all the earth.

I have said "vaulted," and not "burning," "clear," "high," or "azure," because a vault appertains to the embracing and enclosing a thing. You may well say,

The small boat goes along the running wave,

because the course of the water makes the boat to run. The Romans have been very cautious observers of this rule, Virgil and Horace among the others. The Greeks, as in all things pertaining to verse, have been freer about it, and have not regarded it so closely. You are also to avoid the manner of

B.C.E.), Roman poet generally viewed as the greatest of the Augustans.

6. For the *Ars Poetica* of Horace and the *Poetics* of ARISTOTLE, see above.

7. Adjectives or adjectival phrases expressing a characteristic of the person or thing described.

composition of the Italians in your language, who commonly put four or five epithets one after the other in the same verse, as for example, "dear, comely, angelic, rich gifts." You can see that such epithets are more to puff up and paint the verse than to fill any need in it. Content yourself with one epithet, or at most, with two, unless some time for amusement you make five or six, but if you follow my advice in the matter, that will happen as infrequently as you can manage.

Of Rhyme

Rhyme is the correspondence and cadence of syllables, falling at the ends of the verses, which I wish you to observe as well for masculine as the feminine, in the two complete, perfect syllables, or at least in the masculine, provided that it be resonant, and of a sound perfect and entire. Examples of the feminine: *France, Esperance, despence, negligence, familiere, foumiliere, premiere, chere, mere*. Examples of the masculine: *surmonter, monter, donter, sauter, Juppiter*. Always you are to be more attentive to good invention and to the words, than to the rhyme, which comes easily enough of itself after some little practise and experience.

* * *

And you must not worry, as I've said so many times, about the opinions that people might have of your writing, keeping as a firm rule that it is better to be in the service of truth than in the service of opinion.[8] People only want to know what they see in front of their eyes, and, lending credence without proof, think that our forebears were wiser than we, and that we must follow them completely, without inventing anything new. In this they err greatly against bountiful nature, which they believe today to be sterile and barren of minds, and which they think bestowed at the beginning all the virtues upon the first men without saving any to offer—as a generous mother should—to those who would be born later, throughout the many centuries to come.

1565

8. The final paragraph of the treatise is translated by the editor.

GIACOPO MAZZONI
1548–1598

In his *On the Defense of the* Comedy *of Dante* (1587, *Della difesa della Comedia di Dante*), the Italian Renaissance philosopher and scholar Giacopo Mazzoni set out to defend DANTE ALIGHIERI's great medieval poem from a growing number of detractors. As was also the case with the new Renaissance romantic epic, a genre defended by Mazzoni's elder contemporary GIAMBATTISTA GIRALDI, Dante's extended dream allegory was widely criticized as unrealistic. Instead of subscribing to the general preference for what PLATO had called realistic ("icastic") imitation, Mazzoni chose to defend "phantastic" or purely imaginary imitation, claiming it to be the basis of Dante's *Divine Comedy*. In the process, Mazzoni developed an elaborate theory of the poetic "idol" (image or simulacrum), going well beyond the defense of a particular poem to formulate what many scholars believe to be the most fully developed system of literary aesthetics of the Renaissance.

Born in Cesena, Italy, Mazzoni as a young man was educated in Bologna, where he learned Hebrew, Greek, Latin, rhetoric, and poetics. In 1563 he entered the University of Padua to study philosophy and jurisprudence. Thereafter, he taught for brief periods at the universities in Rome, Pisa, and his native Cesena. He spent much of his time managing his family estates, but he often entered into public debates with many prominent public figures and made the acquaintance of such famous Italian writers as Sperone Speroni, Ludovico Castelvetro, and Torquato Tasso, among others. He was reputed to have an astoundingly good memory, able to recall at will any part of the works of Lucretius (ca. 94–55 B.C.E.), Virgil (70–19 B.C.E.), Dante, and Ludovico Ariosto (1474–1533), and he routinely defeated all opponents at public memory contests. He considered himself primarily a philosopher, an identification clearly reflected not only in the sophisticated argumentative structure of the *Defense* but also in his major work, *De Triplici Hominum Vita, Activa Nempe, Contemplativa, et Religiosa Methodi Tres* (1576, *On the Three Ways of Man's Life: the Active, the Contemplative, and the Religious*), a philosophical attempt in Latin to reconcile the views of PLATO and ARISTOTLE. In this work, as in the *Defense*, Mazzoni demonstrates a command of the history of philosophy and cites an impressive number of authorities and sources. His abiding concern with Dante scholarship is demonstrated by his having published before his *Defense* the polemical *Discorso in difesa della Commedia della divino poeta Dante* (1572, *The Discourse in Defense of the* Comedy *of the Divine Poet Dante*). Critics generally agree, however, that the earlier work is much less successful.

Taken from Mazzoni's book-length "Introduction and Summary" to his *Defense*, our selection has very few references to Dante, offering instead a straightforward presentation of Mazzoni's theory of poetry. Reflecting his celebrated memory, this text shows extensive reliance on a wide range of classical philosophers and rhetoricians, including Plato and Aristotle, as well as various Greek sophists and Neoplatonists, particularly Philostratus (active 3d c. C.E.) and Proclus (412–485 C.E.). Considered structurally, the "Introduction and Summary" presents three definitions of poetry one right after the other. Each definition views poetry from a different perspective, that of the poem, the audience, and social utility (or what the author calls the "civil faculty").

Mazzoni indicates, to begin with, that poetry is an imitative art that has as its object the idol (image or simulacrum), not classical literary models, as other Renaissance theorists, such as PIERRE DE RONSARD, argued. The concrete particulars that the image presents, however, are primarily *phantastic* (imaginary or marvelous) rather than *icastic* (realistic). As a result, poetry is a species of sophistic rhetoric in that it deals with what is credible and persuasive, not with what is necessarily true. Seen from the perspective of the audience, the goal of poetry is to move the reader to pleasure and delight in the perception of believable images (idols). Mazzoni argues, in addition, that the distinct pleasure of poetry should ultimately lead to its social utility or moral purpose. As an entertaining recreational game, poetry is a means of pleasantly interrupting the serious business of the world in order that business may be later resumed with freshness and vigor. It does instruct, but in a concealed way; consequently it may be regarded at its best as regulated by the civil faculty. Mazzoni's view here is summed up cryptically in his belief that Aristotle's "*Poetics* is the ninth book of [his] *Politics*."

A distinctive feature of Mazzoni's work is that it proceeds by continuous logical differentiation. Defining poetry for him requires making precise distinctions between similar but different phenomena. Perhaps the key distinction is the earliest, involving three types of objects: the idea, the work, and the idol, which conform to the observable, the fabricable, and the imitable. Here Mazzoni isolates the distinct traits of poetry by differentiating it from epistemology (the observable) and the practical arts (the fabricable). After subdividing the imitable into the phantastic and icastic, he goes on to assess these two forms of imitation in relation to ancient and "second" sophistic rhetoric. Since ancient sophistic used made-up names and second sophistic named real individuals, Mazzoni classifies the phantastic under the former and the icastic under the latter. In this differentiation he further emphasizes the autonomy and the imaginative or phantastic force of the image. Such complex sets of distinctions form the basis of Mazzoni's "Introduction and Summary," which tries to develop a complete and perfect definition of poetry.

Along the way Mazzoni distinguishes "poetics" from poetry, and he also develops a sociological theory of genre. Poetics examines a poem in relationship to the civil faculty, noting prescribed standards, rules, and laws, while poetry looks at a poem from the perspective of its making, attending to its form. As for genre, Mazzoni notes that there are three kinds of poetry: the comic, the heroic, and the tragic. Each of these is addressed to one of the three sorts of people whom Plato thought necessary for civil society: artisans, soldiers, and magistrates, respectively. (Artisans include lower-and middle-class citizens.) Mazzoni's point is that each genre regulates a particular social class, instilling civil obedience. The humor of comic poetry consoles artisans, resigning them to their low or modest estate, while the glorious battles of heroic poetry inspire soldiers to freely defend their country. Tragic poetry depicts the downfall of noble persons and, in so doing, encourages magistrates to take their duties seriously.

Some critics of Mazzoni have perceived contradictions in his definitions of poetry, particularly in his attempt to reconcile the pleasures of imitation with the lessons of the civil faculty. Moreover, some twentieth-century theory implicitly questioned his distinction between icastic and phantastic imitation, pointing out the artifice involved in even "realistic" modes of imitation. In spite of these criticisms, Mazzoni raises to a rigorous level of analysis the discussion of literary mimesis (imitation and representation) initiated by Plato and Aristotle. In emphasizing poetry's relationship to images and games, he also foreshadows later Romantic interest in theories of imagination and aesthetic play, as exemplified most influentially in the works, respectively, of SAMUEL TAYLOR COLERIDGE and FRIEDRICH VON SCHILLER.

BIBLIOGRAPHY

There is no complete English translation of *On the Defense of the* Comedy *of Dante.* A book-length English rendering of its "Introduction and Summary" can be found in *On the Defense of the Comedy of Dante: Introduction and Summary*, translated by Robert L. Montgomery (1983), who also provides detailed scholarly annotations plus a superb preface covering textual, historical, biographical, and critical matters. The standard modern Italian edition is *Introduzione della Difesa della "Commedia" di Dante*, edited by Enrico Musacchio and Gigino Pellegrini (1982). A generous selection of excerpted passages from other parts of *On the Defense of the Comedy of Dante* appears in *Literary Criticism: Plato to Dryden* (ed. and trans. Allan H. Gilbert, 1940). A dated biography in Italian exists, Pierantonio Serassi's *La Vita di Jacopo Mazzoni, Patrizio Cesenate* (1790). Illuminating biographical details can be found in Montgomery's preface.

A comprehensive and authoritative critical overview of Mazzoni's work appears in Bernard Weinberg's magisterial *History of Literary Criticism in the Italian Renaissance* (2 vols., 1961). Also useful are Baxter Hathaway's *Age of Criticism: The Late Renaissance in Italy* (1962) and his *Marvels and Commonplaces: Renaissance Literary Criticism* (1968): the former contextualizes Mazzoni's work in relationship to five leading issues of his time, while the latter narrows its context to the debates surrounding imitation. A formalist critique of how Mazzoni evades defining poetry can be found in Robin Louis McAllister's "Meaning, Language, and Conceptualization: Alternatives in Mazzoni and Dante," *Language and Style* 5 (1971). For a New Critical perspective on Mazzoni that accentuates the novelty of his treatment of the image, see Murray Krieger's "Jacopo Mazzoni, Repository of Diverse Critical Traditions or Source of a New One?" in his *Poetic Presence and Illusion: Essays in Critical History and Theory* (1979). A limited bibliography of criticism can be found in Montgomery's book; for a bibliography of primary texts, see Weinberg's history.

From On the Defense of the *Comedy* of Dante

From *Introduction and Summary*[1]

It seems to me that before we proceed to discuss matters belonging to this defense, it would be well to offer first in briefer form what may be termed a summary notion of the art of poetry and of the defense of Dante,[2] bringing together some considerations scattered through the present volume and adding some others, the whole of which will serve not only as an opportune introduction to what I am going to say, but also as a brief compendium of what has been said.

It is the common opinion of all schools of philosophy that the arts and sciences are distinguished and separated from one another by means of a proper and particular object or subject. (I do not at this point differentiate between these two names around which each school constructs its discourse.) But no matter how this subject is handled, there is no agreement at all in opinion within the same school. For some (and the Bishop of Caserta[3] in his *Monomachia* followed this opinion) prefer to think that the objects of the arts and sciences are distinct according to a distinction between things insofar as they are things. And on the basis of this condition they are forced to admit two quite extraordinary conclusions. The first is that metaphysics is a comprehensive science, that which concerns itself (so to speak) with universal being, and that the other arts and sciences are a part of it, considering each of these some part of universal being. The second conclusion (if the first is correct) is that each particular art and science has for its subject some thing that could not then be the subject of any other art or science. And since both of these conclusions are quite false, as is shown elsewhere (we will discuss it briefly later), it must therefore be judged that the above opinion is not in any way conformable to the truth. [7] Passing on then to a better and truer opinion and following the Peripatetics,[4] I say, as they believe, that the arts and sciences derive their true and real distinctions from objects, not insofar as they are things, but insofar as they are (forgive me, all you strictly Tuscan writers, the necessity of this word) knowable[5] and, if one can speak so, artificiable.

* * *

1. Translated by Robert L. Montgomery, who occasionally adds clarifying words in brackets. The bracketed section numbers correspond to those of the 1587 first edition, which is not paginated.
2. The Italian poet DANTE ALIGHIERI (1265–1321).
3. Antonio Bernardi (1503–1565), bishop of Caserta from 1552 to 1554.
4. Followers of the Greek philosopher ARISTOTLE (384–322 B.C.E.).
5. Mazzoni uses the word *scibili*, a borrowing from Latin.

[8] Since on this topic I find no doctrine more copious or sound than that of Plato[6] in the tenth book of the *Republic*, so, following in his footsteps, I say that there are three types of objects and that they have three ways in which they can be devised; as a consequence these constitute three species of arts in the first category. The objects are idea, work, and idol. The idea is the object of the ruling, or we might say, the governing arts. The work is the object of the fabricating arts, and the idol is the object of the imitating arts. Therefore the modes of the objects of the arts, insofar as they are capable of being differently treated by artifice will be three; that is, the observable, the fabricable, the imitable. The arts that only contemplate a thing pertinent to some object are the ruling arts, and they are founded in the idea. Such is the art of horsemanship when it deals with the bridle. For the art of horsemanship does not consist in making the bridle but is concerned only with the idea of how it has to work and prescribes to the bridle maker what he must hold to, to make it work. [9] The arts that make the bridle (which was first conceived by the ruling art) are those that have as object what is called the work. The arts that make what was first conceived by the ruling arts are the fabricating arts and have as object what is called the work, and such is bridlemaking, which makes the work of the bridle and nothing else. The imitating arts have been so named because they deal with the object only insofar as it is imitable; hence Plato said that it has an idol as object, which means the simulacrum or image of some other things.

Since, therefore, the same thing may be treated in different sciences under different modes of the knowable, so also the same thing can be submitted to different arts by different modes of artifice. And we have a clear example in the bridle: it belongs to the art of horsemanship when considered in its idea, to the art of bridlemaking when made as a work, and to painting when imitated as an idol.

But there may arise a doubt of some importance in thus distinguishing the imitative arts from other arts, for it would seem that the fabricating arts also deserve the name of imitation, since each one of these imitates in its work the model of the idea conceived by the ruling art. Thus, for example, the art of bridlemaking forms a bridle exactly in conformity to the idea conceived by horsemanship. Therefore it would seem that the fabricating arts are not very well distinguished from the imitating arts. I respond that (as has already been said) the distinction between arts derives from their objects insofar as they are capable of being devised variously and distinctly. [10] Now the artifice of the work is not only to represent the idea of the ruling art; it also has to serve other ends. And in this way we can say that bridlemaking forms the bridle in accordance with the idea conceived by horsemanship; still, this bridle is not made in order to represent the similitude of the idea, but rather so that it can be used in various ways in managing horses. Hence we see that the artifice of the fabricating arts aims at something other than just representing or resembling; therefore I say that the fabricating arts cannot be called imitative. But those arts that have the idol as object have an object that has no other end in its artifice but to represent and resemble; hence they are called imitative. And just as philosophers have come to call the logical faculty rational, not because it uses reason—for in this sense all the arts and all the faculties are rational—but because it has an object that takes

6. Greek philosopher (427–347 B.C.E.). For book 10 of *Republic*, see above.

all its being from reason and in reason; so we say that the imitative arts are so named, not because they use imitation—for in this sense all the arts involve more or less some kind of imitation—but because they have objects that have no other being or use except by reason of imitation or in imitation.

* * *

It can therefore be concluded that the imitative arts have been so named because they have as objects those things which are good for no other end or no other use than to represent or to resemble; and they are distinguished from the other arts that are not called imitative because their objects are good for other uses or other ends than representation or resemblance alone. In this way, then, the idol is the object of the imitative arts. [11] But in order to understand clearly what this idol, which is the true and sufficient object of the imitative arts, is, and in order to unravel all the complications that are wont to become involved in this subject, so that we may anticipate a perfect and settled account of it, it is necessary to begin at some distance.

* * *

[15] Coming now to our topic, I say that when we previously concluded that the idol is the object of the imitative arts, we did not mean that sort of idol that originates without human artifice, * * * but instead that which does have its origins in our artifice, arising only from our phantasy or our intellect by means of our choice and will, like the idols in painting, sculpture, and so on. I conclude therefore that this species of idol is that which is a suitable object of human imitation and that when Aristotle said at the beginning of the *Poetics* that all the kinds of poetry are imitation,[7] he meant that sort of imitation which has as its object the idol that arises from human artifice in the way we stated. Rather I will say further that all imitations that arise from human artifice insofar as they are imitations have the idol as object in this manner.

But it would seem that the words of Suidas[8] are contrary to this determination, for he shows himself believing that the idol that derives from human artifice is not an adequate object of the imitative arts, unless the idol is joined to some other different thing that he calls a similitude. Here are his words: "Idols are effigies of things that do not subsist, like tritons, sphinxes, or centaurs. But similitudes are the images of subsistent things, like beasts or men." [16] According to this statement of Suidas we see that there are two imitations. One of them represents the true, as a painter does when he represents with colors the effigy of a known man; and the other represents the caprice of the person who is doing the imitating, just as the painter does when he depicts according to the caprice of his phantasy. We see at the same time that the idol is the object of this second sort of imitation and at the same time that the similitude is the object of the first. Therefore, it is not true that the idol that is born of human artifice is an adequate object of every imitation.

7. "Epic poetry and tragedy, comedy also and dithyrambic poetry, and the music of the flute and the lyre in most of their forms, are all in their general conception modes of imitation," *Poetics* 1 (trans. S. H. Butcher). In emphasizing imitation as the production of man-made images, Mazzoni seems to make a silent comment on Plato's theory of daemonic inspiration in *Ion* [translator's note]. For the dialogue *Ion*, see above.

8. Greek lexicographer (late 10th c. C.E.).

We may respond that this statement of Suidas concerning the idol is too narrow and also in opposition to what other writers have said. Hesychius,[9] uttering other sentiments about the term "idol," speaks as follows: "The idol is similitude, image, and sign." He shows clearly then with these words that the idol is also taken as a similitude and as an image of something discovered. Ammonius in the *Etymology* and Favorinus[1] in the *Vocabulary* explaining the etymology of the idol have said that it derives "from the verb εἴδω, which means match or resemble," almost as if it meant that the idol is of things that are apparent but not found and of things that are found, of which it represents the likeness. Let us add to it what Plato left us in writing in the *Sophist* that imitation is of two species, one of which he names the icastic, and it is that which represents things that are really found or at least have been, and the other he called phantastic, of which we have examples in paintings made according to the caprice of the artist. And even he himself says the same thing in the tenth book of the *Republic*, namely that the idol is the object of every imitation. Therefore the idol must also be common to phantastic imitation. * * *

I believe, then, that everyone is able to understand up to this point what imitative art is and how it is distinguished from other arts that are not imitative, and what the idol is, which is the object of imitation. Now I add that poetry ought to be placed under this imitative art or imitation, as a species under its genus. Therefore, in beginning to define poetry one can say that it is imitation.

* * *

[29] Now let us sum up the discussion to this point concerning the nature of the imitative arts, their distinctiveness from the nonimitative arts, and the fact that poetry which is icastic or phantastic, dramatic or narrative, always has imitation for its genus, since it always forms idols and images in the ways mentioned.

The genus of poetry having been established, it remains for us to investigate the differences according to which it has come to be distinguished and separated from all the other imitative arts. And first of all it would seem that reason requires that we find the instrument proper to poetic imitation, and then its subject matter, and next its efficient cause, and then its final cause. In this fashion we will have established its definition completely and perfectly.

Now if we can find a genus that includes only three species, that is, harmony, number, and meter, we will by combining them with imitation have arrived at a proper instrument. But since such a genus is not to be found, we will compensate with rules taught by Aristotle at the beginning of the *Posterior Analytics*,[2] and instead of the general term we will take the names

9. Alexandrian grammarian (active 4th c. C.E.).
1. Rhetorician of Rome (ca. 80–ca. 150 C.E.). Ammonius (active 5th c. C.E.), Alexandrian philosopher, disciple of Proclus.
2. *Posterior Analytics* 1.2, 71b–72b. Aristotle here argues the case for syllogistically arriving at a general conclusion on the basis of premises that are certain and require no prior demonstration to establish their certainty. Moreover, the premises must be better known than the conclusion. Mazzoni will try to arrive at the distinctive generic description of poetry by using those attributes necessary to it, namely harmony, number, and meter. In other words, he will argue that poetry is a name given to a kind of imitation using these instruments, but as a genus its character is assumed rather than a previously given certainty [translator's note].

of all three species and say that poetry is an imitation made with harmony, with number, and with meter, singly or together.

* * *

[44] Now that we have found the genus, and the individuality of poetry—that is, its instrument[3]—we can be said to have discovered its entire form. Next it would appear that orderliness requires that we turn to inquire into its proper subject and material. In the opinion of many these are falsehood and lying, even though the verisimilar is a fitting subject of poetry. And they have let themselves be induced to believe this because they think that the true poet is one who by himself fabricates the invention of his poem, adding that he who takes it from a place other than his own invention does not deserve the name of a true poet. They suppose also that this is the opinion of Aristotle, who called Empedocles[4] more often a natural philosopher than a poet, because not his own invention but the truth of natural things was thought to exhibit itself in his verses.[5] And in another place he says that Herodotus's[6] history reduced to verse would still be history. And in this context I wish to mention that Euphronius in one of his comedies compared the poet to a cook in the following two lines cited by Athenaeus[7] in his *Banquet of the Wise Men*: "The cook is no different from the poet, since both use wit to make art." * * * On account of all these authorities and others besides, it would be very easy to fall into the view of those who maintain that poetry has no subject other than the fabulous and false, but is yet linked to the verisimilar, since verisimilitude, according to the rule of Aristotle, is to be sought in the poets' fables.

[45] On the contrary, I maintain that this opinion does not conform to the truth for many reasons. Among these I am going to choose those which I think are most to the point. Therefore I will note first that the verisimilar false comes into some other arts that are different from that of the poets, such as rhetoric, which Aristides in the oration against the *Gorgias* of Plato and Philostratus[8] in the Proem to the *Lives of the Sophists* calls "praise" [*adulante*], that which always and everywhere impresses the verisimilar false on the minds of judges to turn them from the straight way of justice. And on this topic I recall having read a most splendid dialogue by Signor Camillo Paleotti, a most erudite gentleman and also the most illustrious Maecenas[9] of letters in this century, in which with very effective arguments and lively reasons he shows that the verisimilar false is, though greatly abused by the corrupt world, virtually the universal subject of the arts, the sciences, and education. Therefore it cannot be concluded that it is the proper and sufficient subject of the poets' art. Moreover, if it were to be the true subject of poetry, then poetry could not in any way be capable of truth; yet Plato wrote, Aristotle agreed, and reason persuades us that just the contrary is the case.

3. Mazzoni has just argued that the instruments of poetry are taken from music because they produce delight and because they reduce to order the immoderate pleasures that poetic imitation can instill.
4. Greek philosopher, poet, orator, physician, scientist, and statesman (ca. 493–ca. 433 B.C.E.).
5. *Poetics* 1, 1447b.
6. Greek historian (ca. 484–ca. 425 B.C.E.). See Aristotle, *Poetics* 9, 1451b.
7. Greek scholar (active ca. 200 C.E.). Euphronius (active mid–3d c. B.C.E.), an obscure Greek comic poet.
8. Greek sophist (b. ca. 170 C.E.). Aristides (2d c. C.E.), celebrated Greek sophist.
9. That is, patron; the Roman statesman Maecenas (d. 8 B.C.E.) was a great patron of letters. Paleotti (1552–1597), Catholic cardinal who wrote on law, religious subjects, and morality.

Therefore Plato in the *Republic* and in the *Laws* having approved that kind of poetry which treats the Gods in conformity to the truth, has demonstrated that he believes that truth is not repugnant to poetry.[1] [46] Likewise Aristotle has confirmed this judgment in three places in the *Poetics*. The first is in these words: "And if it happens that anyone treats poetically of things that have actually happened, he would nevertheless be a poet. For nothing prevents anything that has actually happened from being such that it might happen and could happen in a verisimilar way, so that he who treats them is a poet." The second place is at the beginning of the defense of poets: "For either he represents things that have happened or are said to have happened or appear to have happened or ought to have happened." The third is a little after this where he writes: "And beyond this it will be objected that the things he has said are not true. But they are what ought to be true."[2] In all three places, and especially in the last two, we see manifestly that Aristotle has sometimes conceded that the poet may use the true as a subject and that from everything said before, the idol in icastic imitation is, in Aristotle's opinion, a poetic idol.

But in addition to the authority of Plato and Aristotle, there is also reason to prove that the poet sometimes utters what is true. For when he is recounting the wanderings of some hero, he can do no less many times than describe places in the countryside. In these he follows the facts of geography, so either it must be said that he occasionally loses his title of poet, which would be quite ridiculous, or we must confess that the true may sometimes be a poetic subject. And we have already shown that idols and images can also be made from the true, both in narrative and in representation [i.e., drama].

From all these considerations it seems to me that we ought to affirm two conclusions as correct. The first of them is that the false is not always necessarily the subject of poetry. The second is that since the subject of poetry is sometimes true and sometimes false, there is consequently a need to constitute a poetic subject that by itself can be sometimes true and sometimes false. * * *

[47] Now if we remove the false and in its place put the true, we do not therefore destroy poetry, since we have already said that it can stand together with the true. The same can be said of the possible, for if the impossible is substituted in poetry, it will not therefore come to be corrupted or spoiled, if the impossible is credible. But if we take away the credible and in its place put the incredible, the nature of poetry is totally destroyed. And on the other hand taking the credible and at the same time removing the possible, we still have the poetic subject, as Aristotle has clearly testified in the following words: "As to what belongs to poetry, the credible impossible is more often to be preferred to the incredible and possible."[3] Therefore it ought to be said that among all these there is no more appropriate subject of poetry than the credible. And even more to the point, how much the credible by its very nature includes both the true and the false, for often not only the true but also the false is credible.

* * *

1. Cf. *Republic* 2.377–79 [see above] and *Laws* 7.801 [translator's note].
2. *Poetics* 9, 1451b; 25, 1460b; and 25, 1460b.
3. *Poetics* 24, 1460a.

[51] Therefore, the credible is the object of that persuasion whose end is that which has now been demonstrated. And because it has already been decided on the authority of Aristotle that the credible is the subject of the art of the poets, it seems to me that we can draw three conclusions from what has been said. The first of them is that the poet being always concerned with the credible, he must as a necessary consequence treat everything in a fashion suitable to the credible, that is, always making use of singular and sensible means to represent the things he writes about whatever they may be. [52] And even if he treats things pertinent to contemplative doctrine, he must make every effort to represent them by idols and sensible simulacra, which Empedocles did not do. Hence, he was more often termed a physicist than a poet. In this matter Dante is really marvelous, as we will demonstrate more fully in the fifth book. For the present we must be content with this single example in which he speaks of the most holy and ineffable Trinity, writing:

Within the profound and clear substance
Of the exalted light three circles appeared to me,
Of three colors and one magnitude.
And one in the other, like a rainbow in a rainbow
Seemed reflected, and the third seemed like
Fire breathed forth equally from the one and the other.[4]

And for this reason it also happens that the poet uses such frequent comparisons and lengthy and specific parables. And whoever looks for the reasons why the poet is obligated at the very least in his storytelling to use this mode of the credible may rest content with the following reason: because the poet must speak to the people, among whom are many rude and uneducated men, and if he were to discuss knowable things in a mode appropriate to the sciences, they would not understand. And so he treats his subject in a credible mode, that is, instructing by means of comparisons and similitudes taken from sensible things, and the people, who understand that in sensible things truth resides in a way that is revealed by the poet, easily believe for this reason that the same is true of intelligible things.

From this we are able to conclude that it is not denied to the poet to treat things pertinent to the sciences and the speculative intellect, but he treats them in a credible manner, making idols and poetic images, as Dante, with most marvelous and noble artifice, has certainly done in representing all intellectual nature and the intelligible world itself with idols and images most beautifully to all eyes.

I recall that Plato in the *Phaedrus*, exalting his own invention, wrote just to this point: "But of that place that is beyond the heavens, I do not know that any of the poets has ever treated or is likely to treat it in a manner worthy of the way it is."[5] And so on. But if he had seen Dante's third canticle, he would without any doubt have recognized his own invention as inferior and given the palm to Dante, and consequently to poets for knowing how to make idols and images appropriate to giving to the popular understanding the quality of the supercelestial world. Concerning this I have written at length in the fifth book where I also show with what tact Dante has at times

4. *Paradiso* 33.115–20 [translator's note].

5. *Phaedrus* 247c.

introduced either a philosopher or a theologian to discuss matters pertinent to the contemplative sciences in an understandable fashion, never deviating from the credible. [53] The second conclusion is that, since the poet has the credible as his subject, he ought therefore to oppose credible things to the true and the false, the possible and the impossible, by which I mean that he ought to give more importance to the credible than to any of the others I have enumerated.

Therefore, if it should happen that two things should appear before the poet, one of them false but credible and the other true but incredible or at least not very credible, then the poet must leave the true and follow the credible. And if anyone wants an example, let him read what I have written in the seventy-third chapter of the third book, where it is shown that Ariosto[6] has described the mouths of the Ganges River according to credibility, departing totally from the truth. And if the Ganges were such that its mouths faced the south, as Ariosto has said, then it would also be necessary to say that Taprobana is New Zealand and not Sumatra.[7] And yet Ariosto, following the credible and leaving the true, has said that Sumatra is Taprobana. This is discussed in the thirtieth chapter of the third book.

The third and last conclusion, which is almost a corollary of the previous two, is that poetry, in order to give more importance to the credible than to the true, must be strictly categorized under the rational faculty named by the ancients "sophistic." [54] And for a complete understanding of this truth, which (unless I am mistaken) has until now remained mysterious, it must be understood that the poetic art may be taken in two modes, that is, either according as it is concerned with the laws of the poetic idol, or according as it is concerned with fashioning or forming the poetic idol.

The first mode ought to be called "poetics" and the second "poetry." In the first mode is the ruling art, which uses the idol and is part of the civil faculty, as we will show a little further on. In the second mode is the art that forms and fabricates the idol and is a species of the rational faculty. As I have said, it ought to be included under sophistic, since it does not care about the true. I am aware that I may have offended the sensibilities of poets by fastening upon an art considered until now virtually divine and the title of sophistic, which has come to be thought repellent and scandalous. Yet to console them a bit I wish to dwell a bit upon the art of the sophists to show where it has or does not have positive or negative meanings. And for an easier understanding of what we have to say, I will set down here the words of Philostratus at the beginning of his *Lives of the Sophists*, which will be seen to contain a summary knowledge of the sophistic art very different from that commonly understood. Here then are the words of Philostratus:

> Ancient sophistic must be called philosophical rhetoric, since it argues the same things treated by philosophers. Those who bring forward questions and doubts about each little item, have neglected to understand the ancient sophists about whom they speak with such assurance. Even so, their introductions say, "I understand this," "I know this," "It is just a portion that I have considered." Or, "Nothing is permanent for men." Either this mode of beginning adds luster to an oration or it makes

6. Ludovico Ariosto (1474–1533), Italian poet.
7. A glance at the atlas will confirm Ariosto's superior knowledge of geography and the points of the compass [translator's note].

plainer what is going to be treated. It was part of human prophecy, which the Egyptians and the Chaldeans studied, and before them the Indians prophesied by means of the stars. It belonged to the oracles, as the Pythian oracle[8] said,

"I know the number of grains of sand and how great the seas are."

And this:

"Of wood were the walls which Jove gave to Tritonia [Athena]." Also, both Orestes and Alcmeon[9] killing their mothers and many other things similarly fashioned were the subjects that the ancient sophists practised, and, drawing them out at length, they ornamented them everywhere with conceits, referring to the gods, heroes, justice, strength, and sometimes going even higher, they treated the creation of the world itself.

[55] In these words of Philostratus we have the proposition that sophistic is what treats everything rhetorically—that is, credibly—and reasons confidently with a certain vaunting of its propositions and takes feigned subjects like Orestes and Alcmeon, imitating the one or the other and representing them by idols. Now, that such representation by idols and images is proper to the sophistic art Plato has clearly shown in the *Sophist* where he names it 'Ειδωλοποιητίκην, that is, "The making of idols,"[1] that which represents apparent reality. This was also confirmed by Alexander Aphrodisias[2] in his *Commentary on the Elenches of Aristotle*. Philostratus in the place cited above, seeking to prove that Prodicus Chio[3] was also a sophist, shows that he wrote a book in which he dealt with a matter pertinent to moral philosophy, namely, the appetites for virtue and vice which are at war within young men, and made idols and images for them. [55] He then says, "And for this purpose Prodicus Chio wrote a pleasant speech in which virtue and vice in feminine guise stood around Hercules.[4] But he adorned and altered both of them as he saw fit and presented them to the young Hercules, here ease and softness and there discomfort and toil."

It seems to me therefore that one can reasonably say that poetry deserves to be placed under this ancient sophistic, since it also treats things credibly and speaks with such boldness as to profess to know all things by means of the Muses and Apollo.[5] Certainly Hesiod,[6] as a poet, became arrogant enough to pretend to know all things past, present, and future at once, and on this point I was pleased to see the opinion of a well-read commentator[7] on the *Poetics* who feels that it is not suitable to the poet in any way to use words or modes of speech which place in doubt the things he discusses, for, professing the credible more than others, he ought to utter things with great assurance and boldness. Thus on this condition also the poet deserves the name of sophist, and even more he deserves it as the maker of idols and as representing everything with images, as has been shown at sufficient length in the preceding discourse.

8. The most famous of Apollo's oracles, at Delphi; its priestess was the Pythia.
9. In Greek mythology, each avenged his father's death by killing his mother.
1. Plato's word is *eidōlopoiikē*; see especially *Sophist* 235b–236c, 268d.
2. Aristotelian commentator known as Exegetes (active 200 C.E.).
3. Prodicus of Chios (active 5th c. B.C.E.), a sophist concerned with precise diction and a friend of Socrates.
4. The Roman name for Heracles, the greatest hero of classical mythology.
5. The ancient Greeks considered the Muses and Apollo to be the sources of inspiration for the arts and sciences.
6. Greek didactic poet (active ca. 700 B.C.E.).
7. Ludovico Castelvetro (ca. 1505–1571), Italian critic and philologist.

Philostratus also says that the ancient sophists willingly talked of gods and heroes, which material is held to be appropriate to poets. And therefore in this respect also it can be concluded that poetry is a species of ancient sophistic. But in order to understand perfectly everything pertinent to this discourse, it will be well to disclose all the other species of sophistic and then to see which are convenient to poetry, and which are not. Therefore, having discussed ancient sophistic in the words quoted above, Philostratus then shows that there is another species that he calls second sophistic, about which he writes in the following way: "Following this was one which does not suit the term new, for it also was ancient. But more often than not it favors and takes as its subjects the poor, the rich, gentlemen, or tyrants, giving them names, as in history. The old sophistic of Gorgias Leontinus originated in Thessaly, and the second sophistic of Aeschines,[8] son of Astrometus, was already in decline in the Athenian republic."

[57] We know by these words of Philostratus that the old sophistic was not different from the second in any other way, except that the old used made-up names and the second used real names. Whence it can be said that icastic poetry is a species of the second sophistic and phantastic poetry is a species of the ancient sophistic. Now I think that everyone should know that Philostratus believed the sophistic art to be that which set the true aside to behold the credible, and that he considered it worthy and noble, not low and scandalous, as Boethius[9] preferred to depict it, and perhaps also Aristotle and Plato. But to reconcile those authors who have condemned sophistic with those who have praised it, we have to understand that sophistic was considered in some way to partake of the rectitude of true philosophy.

Now only true philosophy directs the intellect by means of the true and the will by means of the good. Therefore only the sophistic totally contrary to true philosophy misdirects the intellect by means of the false and the will by means of evil. It was this sort of sophistic which was condemned by Plato and Aristotle and all their followers, and apparently Plato wanted to gather under this species of sophistic the poetry of Homer[1] as that which misdirected the intellect by representing false things about the gods and heroes and that which misdirected the will with that variety of imitation and immoderate augmenting of our feelings which were discussed just previously.[2] [58] And therefore one could say that any other poetry like that of Homer would have to be placed under the sophistic condemned by that philosopher, and not only was it banished from Plato's *Republic* but also from that of the Athenians, as Philostratus has written in the following words: "The Athenians, perceiving the eloquence of the sophists, chased them from the courts, on the grounds that they dominated the courts with unjust utterance and had too great a power over the law." Therefore the species of sophistic condemned by the philosopher is that which misdirects the intellect with falsehood and the will with injustice. Under which he also places that sort of poetry which produces the same disorders and which does not really deserve the name of poetry, since it does not form its idols according to the laws of poetic practice or theory, as was plainly discussed a little before.

8. Famous Athenian orator (ca. 397–ca. 322 B.C.E.). GORGIAS (ca. 483–376 B.C.E), famous rhetor and sophist known for eloquence and skepticism.
9. Roman philosopher (ca. 480–524 C.E.).

1. Greek epic poet (8th c. B.C.E.); his *Iliad* and *Odyssey* were in effect the national poems of ancient Greece.
2. *Republic* 2.377–78 and *Protagoras* 316 [translator's note].

The second species of sophistic is that which Philostratus called the old sophistic, which indeed sets feigned things before the intellect, yet does not mislead the will, so that it claims in every way to make it conformable to what is just. And that kind of sophistic was never condemned by the ancients. And if, even so, it should appear to someone that it deserves condemnation for misleading the intellect by some falsehood, I say that he should know that the ancient pagan philosophers (being at variance in this matter with the truth of sacred theology) have praised this misleading of the intellect in certain things, when it is directed to a legitimate end. And in this respect Plato preferred that the magistrate should be able to tell lies to his citizens for the sake of some public good.[3] I pass over the fact that this species of sophistic almost always contains some truth under the skin of a first appearance.

Now I maintain that phantastic poetry regulated by the proper laws belongs to that ancient sophistic, since it also offers feigned things to our intellects in order to regulate the appetite. And often it contains under the outer covering of fiction the truth of many noble concepts.

The third species of sophistic is that which Philostratus called the second sophistic, which does not employ feigned names and events, but rather true names and real actions on which are based discussions appropriate to the rules of justice. [59] And this was also much praised by the ancients: thus Demosthenes[4] and Aeschines professed to be most worthy and excellent in this kind, as Philostratus makes evident in the following words: "In this way Aeschines and Demosthenes publicly traded insults, when they were trying a case before the courts." And this was also called a species of sophistic, because even though it made use of true things in the cause of justice, yet it did so in a credible manner. For which reason the sophists sometimes departed from the truth if the false were a more credible or effective instrument in persuading those of what they wished. There is no better example than the following warning by Valerius Harpocration[5] about an oration of Demosthenes: "Demosthenes affirmed in his oration on the fleet that the revenue of the Athenian republic was six thousand talents[6] (a sum of three million six hundred thousand escudos), writing thus: 'He will hear that our fields yield us a revenue of six million talents.' This was either an error on the part of the scribe, or the orator spoke cleverly to make it appear that the republic had a greater ability to make war than the king of Persia."

Under the third species of sophistic we ought in my judgment to place icastic poetry, which represents true actions and persons but always in a credible way. [60] Therefore, on the basis of this entire discussion of sophistic with the fundamentals we have provided, everyone can understand that poetry is a rational faculty and that, among other rational faculties, it ought not to be placed with those that teach the truth, avoiding all other matters, but with those that employ all their power to examine the apparent credible, avoiding the true, and that this was the reason the ancients called it sophistic. To all these reasons may be added the authority of two most excellent writers. The first is Plato, who, as we have said, called the sophist a maker of idols,

3. *Republic* 3.389b (see above).
4. Athenian orator and statesman (384–322 B.C.E.); his great rival was Aeschines.
5. Alexandrian lexicographer and scholar of oratory (active 2d c. C.E.).
6. About 340,000 lbs. (an Athenian talent was ca. 57 lbs.) of silver.

that is, a sophistic imitator. In the tenth book of the *Republic* where he discusses the imitator he calls him the "marvelous sophist," adding that he never represents the true, but always the apparent. "The painter," he says, "does not paint the real bed, only its appearance." And just after this he says clearly that an imitation is three stages removed from the truth, the first stage being the art of using, the second the art of making, and the third that of imitating. And then he concludes: "Therefore the imitator imitates at a distance from the truth, and, as we have seen, he is able to do all things because he touches only a small part of them, and that part is an image."[7] The second authority is Plutarch, who in the essay where he deals with how a young man ought to listen to poems, writes as follows: "But he who does not forget, but always keeps in mind the tricks of poetry in telling lies, will say to it at every turn, 'O clever device, whose hide is more varied than the lynx's, why when joking do you deceive with a serious brow, pretending to tell the truth?' "[8] And he has previously shown that poetry willingly accepts the lie in order better to please.

Therefore, I firmly conclude that poetry is a sophistic art and that through imitation, which is its proper genus, and the credible, which is its subject, and through delight, which is its end, when it is under that genus, and has that subject, and gains that end, it is many times forced to find room for the false. And although I have only cited Philostratus, Plato, and Plutarch on this point, a thousand others could be found whom I have left in the wings so as not to be too long.

And so the credible is the subject of poetry. But because it is also the subject of rhetoric we must necessarily see in what way it can be made to become proper to both poetry and rhetoric, since we will not fall into the error of those who accept the verisimilar false.

[61] I say therefore that the credible insofar as it is credible is the subject of rhetoric and the credible insofar as it is marvelous is the subject of poetry, for poetry must not only utter credible things but also marvelous things. And for this reason when it can do so credibly, it falsifies human and natural history and passes beyond them to impossible things, as I prove in the sixth chapter of the third book and in the others following, in which a full digression treats this material. So that, if two things equally credible were offered to the poet, one of them more marvelous than the other, though false, not just impossible, the poet ought to take it and refuse the other. And if anyone wants examples, let him read the abovementioned digression, in which, I am convinced, he will find many to the point in each of Aristotle's ten predicaments.[9]

But perhaps there is someone who might wonder why the credible marvelous is not found in company with the true. And he might also suppose that what was said before—that poetry sometimes admits the true—is wrong. I respond that sometimes true things are found in poetry which are often more marvelous than the false, not only in natural things, as Pliny the Younger[1] has shown in the eighth book of his *Letters* when he writes to

7. *Republic* 10.596d, 597e; 601d, 602c; 603a.
8. Plutarch, "How a Young Man Should Study Poetry," *Moralia*, Loeb ed., vol. 1, pp. 83–84 [translator's note]. Plutarch (ca. 50–ca. 120 C.E.), Greek biographer and moralist.
9. The "predicaments" or predicables make up Aristotle's *Categories*. They are substance, quantity, quality, relation, place, time, position, state, action, and affection [translator's note].
1. Roman rhetorician (ca. 61–ca. 112 C.E.), nephew of the natural historian Pliny the Elder. Among his correspondents on literary subjects was Caninius Rufus, of whom little else is known.

Caninius Rufus, but also in human history, as that same Pliny has shown in the ninth book, writing to the same Caninius. [62] In the latter he explains that the war made on Dacia by the Emperor Trajan,[2] although true, was nevertheless a worthy subject for a poem because it was marvelous. Here are his words: "I greatly approve your plan of writing a poem on the Dacian war, for where could you have found a subject so fresh, so eventful, so broad, and, in short, so poetical; a subject which, although most true, is also marvelous. You will write of rivers turned into new channels, of bridges thrust across rivers for the first time, of camps pitched on precipitous mountains."[3] See how well Pliny demonstrates that the true can sometimes reach the marvelous. Concerning this topic there only remains to discuss that authority by which it seems to be proven that the false, insofar as it is verisimilar, is a poetic subject. I mention first of all that it is the case that Aristotle calls Empedocles more a physicist than a poet, and this is confirmed by Plutarch in the essay on understanding poems cited above: "I do not know of poetry without fable or fiction. For the verses of Empedocles and of Parmenides, the *Theriaca* of Nicander, and the sayings of Theognis[4] are more often than not sermons, so that as a vehicle to cast off the baseness of prose, I prefer the grandeur and measure of poetry."[5] Now as for the authority of Aristotle, we can respond to it in two ways, the first of which is that he has said that Empedocles is more often a physicist than a poet, but he has not by that statement said absolutely that he is not a poet, so that affirming that he is more of a physicist than a poet, he has in some way said that he is a poet, since the grammarians tell us that the comparative assumes the positive.

The second way of answering Aristotle is that it could be said (as it was said above) that Empedocles did not merit the name of poet, not because he dealt with true things, for it has already been shown that poetry is able sometimes to treat the true; but because he dealt with things belonging to the sciences scientifically, when he was obligated as a poet to treat them credibly, that is, forming idols and images, matching his mode of instruction more often to the sensitive than to the intellectual powers. As for Plutarch, I say that either he is really speaking of the true and perfect poet, who (as it is said) ought more often to be placed under phantastic imitation, rather than icastic imitation, or his opinion is in opposition to that of Aristotle and Plato, that is, that poetry cannot in any fashion be made from the true. And this answer ought to suffice for the authority of Plutarch, which has been cited to the contrary. [63] To Aristotle's text where he writes that the history of Herodotus laid out in verse would still be history, and so not worthy of the name of poetry, I respond that it is true, but that it does not follow from this that one cannot in some way make a poem out of history, when it is represented as the credible marvelous in idols and particularized images. But if it were narrated in the mode appropriate to history, without making idols and images, even if it were laid out in verse, it would always remain history.

2. Roman emperor, 98–117 C.E. (b. 53); he successfully conquered Dacia (roughly equivalent to modern Romania) in 105.

3. Pliny the Younger, *Letters*, book 8, letter 4. The reference to a natural marvel is in book 9, letter 33 [translator's note].

4. A Greek elegiac poet of Megara (active ca. 540 B.C.E.), known for his large fragmentary collection of gnomic verses. Parmenides (b. ca. 515 B.C.E.) Greek didactic poet and philosopher known for his *On Nature*, which contains the earliest Greek discussion of philosophical method. Nicander (2d c. B.C.E.), Greek poet and grammarian.

5. Plutarch, "How a Young Man Should Study Poetry," *Moralia*, Loeb ed., vol. 1, pp. 83–85 [translator's note].

And this was what Aristotle meant at that place [in the *Poetics*]. To the authority of Euphron,[6] I respond that the true can also be sweetened by narrating it in conformity with the credible, using idols and images.

For this reason I believe that icastic poetry, which takes a true subject from history, may nevertheless combine some things of its own in order to render that history more particularized. This is no doubt even more clearly evident in the dramatic-icastic than in the narrative-icastic.

As for the authority of Plato in the *Phaedo*, I say that he discussed phantastic poetry which always takes a fabulous subject, either forming one totally feigned or falsifying a true story. And for this reason he says in that place [the *Phaedo*] that the poet deserves his name more often for his inventing of fables than for his inventing of verses.[7] Or one might say that he takes the fable in the sense of every invention that can be suitable to the poem and names it fable, because for him such subjects are false and fabulous. [64] But it should not for this reason be said that he did not believe that the true could be a poetic subject, since in an infinite number of other places he says just the contrary, as has already been shown.

Therefore let us summarize what has been said on the poetic subject, that it ought to be credible and at the same time marvelous, and then joining this subject to the form already disclosed above, we can now say that *poetry is an imitation made with harmony, rhythm, and verses, singly or together, of things credible and marvelous.*

There remains for the completion of this definition that we find the efficient and final causes of poetry. Now as for the efficient cause, we might dispatch it by saying that it is the human intellect. But this is a cause common to all the other arts, and we only wish to find one that is more appropriate to poetry and that, joined to its end, will reveal the proper origin and legitimate use of poetry.

Therefore in order to lay the foundation for this, I believe there is no surer way than to consider what that art is that discovers the use of poetry, because that, unless I deceive myself, will reveal the origin and the end of poetry. I think, then, that the civil faculty[8] is that which discovers not only the use of poetry but also explains the norm and the rules for the poetic idol. The following consideration presses me toward this belief, namely, that all the natural powers and the arts that are born of human reason are usually directed to contrary objects, as for example medicine, which not only deals with health and healthful potions but also with sickness and poisons. We can say also that the legal profession likewise not only professes to deal with justice but with injustice as well.

Now keeping this in mind, I say that the civil faculty not only professes to understand the justness of human actions but also the justness of the cessation of human actions, a justness that is opposed to the first justness as deprivation is opposed to habit. * * * [65] But the cessation of a process, as will be explained a little further on, must dispose and prepare men so that they are more apt and eager for the process. Therefore the same faculty will provide the rule for the activity and its cessation. [66] And note that I do not

6. Poet of Greek New Comedy (active 270 B.C.E.).

7. Apparently a somewhat inaccurate reference to *Phaedo* 61b.

8. By the civil faculty Mazzoni means, roughly speaking, ethics, or the mode of discourse that decides the social relevance of something [translator's note].

take cessation to be total privation or extinction or activity, but only cessation of serious and difficult activities, and so in the word *cessation* we include the activities of play and amusement which we do for recreation and entertainment. So it can be said that the contrariety of function and cessation is not only privation but (as was said above) also positive. It is privation insofar as the cessation indicates the absence of serious work. It is positive insofar as the cessation of serious work might contain some pleasant activity apt to restore the spirits fatigued by the more important function. This is clearly enough indicated by Aristotle in the tenth book of the *Ethics* and the eighth of the *Politics*, where discussing cessation (which he treats at length in the fifth chapter of the second book), the name is always ἀνάπαυσισ and not σχολή[9] to make it clear that he does not take the otium that is the father of all vices as entertainment or the cessation of serious things, but rather some peaceful and gentle activity.[1]

So it appears to me that one can firmly say that in order for cessation to be the opposite of the privative and positive activity, it must necessarily be the concern of one art and a single faculty. But the civil faculty is that which considers the rightness of an activity, so it should also consider the rightness of its cessation. Within it, as I have said, are contained all the activities of amusement, that is, those performed in games. Therefore the consideration of the rightness of pleasure will without any doubt be pertinent in some way to the civil faculty and to moral philosophy. But among all games none is found more worthy, more noble, and more central than what the poets' work has made. Therefore the civil faculty takes care to consider principally among the other pleasures the standard and rightness of poetry.

Now, that the ancients believed that poetry was a game is shown in the abovementioned chapter of the second book on the authority of Virgil, Horace, Timocles[2] the comic poet, Plato in the tenth book of the *Republic*, and in the fifth of the *Laws*, and Eusebius of Caesarea[3] in the twelfth book of the *Evangelical Preparations*. To these can be added the authority of Aristotle, who in the seventh book of the *Politics* calls games "the imitations of those things you do seriously." And there is the authority of Plato who in the second book of the *Laws* says of poetic imitation: "Again I call it amusement and play."[4] From all these considerations it seems to me that it can be reasonably said that the civil faculty ought to be divided into two principal parts, one of which is concerned with the laws of activities and is given the general name of politics, that is the civil law. [67] The other is concerned with the laws of cessation or the laws of recreational activities, and is called poetics. And on this basis I believe that the *Poetics* is the ninth book of the *Politics*, and my view seems to me all the more correct in that I find in the eighth book of the *Politics* and at the beginning of the first chapter of the *Poetics* he commences to deal with music, in order to proceed step by step to discuss the recreation of the civil faculty. And so I say that the first seven books of

9. Both Greek terms can denote rest and repose, but the first (*anapausis*) suggests leisure and relaxation while the second (*scholē*) implies idleness.

1. *Nicomachean Ethics* 10.3; *Politics* 8 generally concerns education and leisure. The sixth chapter of the second book would seem more to Mazzoni's point than the fifth, which deals with a number of topics ranging from the justice system to political innovation [translator's note].

2. Greek poet of Middle Comedy (active ca. 330 B.C.E.). Virgil (70–19 B.C.E.), Roman poet. HORACE (65–8 B.C.E.), Roman lyric poet and satirist.

3. Bishop of Caesarea and historian of the early Christian church (ca. 260–340 C.E.).

4. Aristotle, *Politics* 7.1334a; Plato, *Laws* 2.667e [translator's note].

the *Politics* speak of the civil faculty at work and the last two speak of the civil faculty (so to speak) at rest, a state we have just previously called poetics.[5]

Therefore poetics is part of the civil faculty and is what prescribes the standards, the rules, and the laws of the idol in poetry. So in a way it can be said that poetics deals with the idea of the idol and poetry with the making of it. Thus poetics will be in its genus the ruling art, using the idol made by poets to that end we have just previously mentioned. And in its genus poetry will be the fabricating art, the maker of the idol, which is then to be used by poetics and by the civil faculty.

[68] We can therefore add to the previous words concerning the definition of poetry its efficient cause and say: *Poetry is an imitation made with harmony, number, and verses, singly or together, of credible and marvelous things discovered by the civil faculty.*

Up to this point we have disclosed the form, the subject matter, and the making of poetry, so that it remains only to turn our hand to the discussion of its final cause. Ancient and modern writers have raised a great fuss about this, not knowing very well whether they should take usefulness or delight or both, or neither the one nor the other, as the end of poetry.

* * *

[70] Now for a complete solution to the present questions, it is necessary to understand that it is not inappropriate for the same thing when considered in diverse ways to have diverse and different ends. And because in this matter I desire to be understood by everyone, it will not perhaps weigh against me to discuss the abovementioned proposition by means of some examples taken from natural things. Therefore I maintain that nature (as is demonstrated at length in the fifty-fifth chapter of the third book) forms the tongues of animals for one principal end, that is for taste, in order that by means of the delight taken in the tasting of food animals will be almost violently impelled to keep themselves alive. And therefore it can be said definitely that nature has formed the tongue in order to serve as an instrument of the vital powers and the concupiscible appetite. However (as Aristotle has declared in many places cited in the abovementioned chapter), nature has sometimes directed that same tongue to an end other than taste, since in men it has made it also an instrument of speech, and consequently as such it is not just an instrument of the vital power or the concupiscible appetite, but, rather, of the rational power and appetite. And at other times it has also been formed as an instrument of the irascible power, having been placed among their weapons of defense, as is seen in bees and in certain other insects.

Thus it can be said that the adequate and principal end that nature proposes in the fashioning of the tongue is taste, since the tongue is not found fashioned by nature unless it is directed to this end. [71] But for all this it can also be added that sometimes nature forms that same tongue to serve another end and consequently it is an instrument of other powers than the

5. The latter part of book 7 and all of book 8 discuss liberal education, that is, the education appropriate to a free man. For Aristotle this means not just someone not a slave, but a citizen relieved from the compulsion to labor or earn a living by commerce. The civil faculty at rest or leisure thus concerns itself with contemplation and with the study and appreciation of certain kinds of elevated enjoyment such as music and poetry [translator's note].

concupiscible or vital, and this is clearly seen in the tongues of bees and men. The first of these is an instrument not only of the concupiscible appetite but also of the irascible, and in this second mode it is not made for taste but for defense. The second is an instrument of the vital power and of the rational, and in the latter mode its end is human speech. Therefore, the tongue can be considered in three different manners, that is, as an instrument of the concupiscible, of the irascible, or of the rational appetites, and in each one of these modes it always has a different end—when used by the concupiscible power, it has taste as its end; when used by the irascible, offense; when used by the rational, speech—yet in such a way that taste seems always to be the more suitable and essential end among all the others.

In like fashion I say that poetry can be considered in three different modes, that is, as an imitative art, either as enjoyment or amusement simply, or as enjoyment or amusement directed, ruled, and defined by the civil faculty. If it is considered as an imitative art, I say that it has no other end than to represent or resemble correctly. And this is what Plato, Proclus, and Maximus of Tyre[6] meant in the passages cited above. [72] Now it should be understood that (as Aristotle has written in the tenth book of the *Ethics*) delight is an accident proper to some functions, and among them is without doubt most proper to imitation, since it seems in a way joined to it so that no mode of imitation can be found that does not at the same time bring both delight and pleasure. * * *

Since, therefore, imitation is always linked to delight, so it happens that all those who have attempted to produce games and enjoyment have produced them with some kind of imitation, as I have shown in discussing the ancient game of chess in the sixth chapter of the second book, and I may add here (to provide an example different from those two) the game of primero,[7] in which is represented the image of ochlocracy, that is, that republic in which the common people have the most power. For since in this kind of republic the aristocrats are weak and the common people strong, so in the game the cards commonly given the noblest names are of lesser value than the other cards that have the vulgar name of waste paper because of their baseness. Now since imitation itself can be considered as part of the above-mentioned game, in this mode it has no other end than to represent the image of ochlocracy and can be deemed a game and amusement, and in such a mode we recognize no other end than delight and pleasure. So I say that poetry can in the same way be thought of as an imitative art and as a game and amusement.

In the first mode it has as its end the correctness of the idol, that is, whether the thing has been imitated in an appropriate way. But in the second mode it contemplates delight and pleasure as its end, and these are joined to a good and perfect imitation. [73] Therefore, I conclude that poetry as an imitative art has the correctness of the idol as its end, but as a thing that should be used for play and amusement and to interrupt some more serious and rigorous business, it here proposes as its end delight born of appropriate imitation. Now this delight that poetry brings us can be looked at in two ways: that is, either as free and independent of any law, or as subject to and

6. Sophist (ca. 125–185 C.E.). Proclus (412–485 C.E.), Neoplatonic philosopher and systematizer known for his commentaries on Plato's works.

7. A card game, often called "prime" in Renaissance England [translator's note].

regulated by the civil faculty. In the first mode it is the end of that poetry which was classified under the kind of sophistic worthy of blame, because it disordered the appetite with immoderate delight, producing complete rebellion against reason and bringing on damage and loss to a virtuous life.

That was the sort of poetry banished from his republic by Plato, concerning the reason for which Maximus of Tyre has written in his eighth sermon that just as Mithecus, the most excellent cook, was banished by the Spartans, despite the fact that he was greatly esteemed among the other peoples of Greece, only because his art had no other end than to please the taste, which was totally repugnant to the sobriety of the Lacedaemonians;[8] so also did Plato banish poets from his republic as having regard for nothing other than delighting too freely. [74] And Proclus in the *Poetic Questions*, having admitted that this sort of poetry is truly enjoyable, supplies the reasons why it is damaging and harmful to civil life: "I will therefore suggest two reasons why Plato did not accept tragedy and comedy in a proper republic as worthy of the education of the young. One was the variety (as it is called) of the imitations; the other was the unlimited moving of the passions, which he wished to moderate however he could. To this can be added as a third the case of saying any sort of wickedness in those same genres about gods and heroes." And so on.

If, therefore, one has to reason about the end of this poetry, it can be definitely said that as an imitative art its end is the correctness of the idol, but that as recreation its only end is pleasure.

But if delight is considered insofar as it is regulated and defined by the civil faculty, we will necessarily have to say that it is directed toward the useful and consequently is that species of poetry which was placed under praiseworthy sophistic, that is, under that which orders the appetite and submits it to the reason, and, considered as game, defined by the civil faculty to have usefulness as its end. It is nevertheless true that I do not ascertain that this species of poetry is as rough and austere as Proclus claims in the first poetic questions, where he distinguishes two species of poetry, the good and the evil, in the following words: "But it is especially the job of the laws concerning the instruction of youth to keep an eye on such poetry as that which is genuinely enjoyable, pleasing, but not useful for teaching virtue, and which the more it is enjoyable, so the more it is harmful. And to the same laws belongs the choice of an austere muse that guides us to virtue by the right way. For we do not find the wonder of medicine in what is pleasant but in that which heals." In these words of Proclus we see that he believes poetry has to be more a medicine than an enjoyment and that consequently by giving it the useful as its end he does not mind if he separates it from any sort of delight. [75] But it is beyond doubt that in this he disagrees with Plato, who has clearly admitted in many places that poetry is the bringer of the useful to our minds by means of the delight it offers us under the species of enjoyment and recreation.

And to understand fully this favorable opinion of Plato's one has to know that there are three sorts of men to whom he apparently believed the civil faculty—by which we mean moral philosophy—could bring some betterment. These three sorts are: those disposed and habituated to the good, those

8. Citizens of Sparta (also called "Lacedaemon").

who are wicked and habituated to evil, and those who are not disposed or in any way habituated either to good or evil. Among the first sort are the men who have learned to curb the disorderly movements of the appetites, and I think that these are the ones who practise moral philosophy well (as Plato himself writes in the *Protagoras* and the *Gorgias*) insofar as it is lawful, that is, insofar as it gives laws and precepts for living well and happily and free of passion. Of the second sort are impious men used to despising the decrees of the law, and for these he shows at length in the *Gorgias* that moral philosophy is useful, insofar as it is judicial, that is, insofar as evildoers are punished by penalties established in trials.[9] [76] Of the third sort are young girls and boys and all those who feel the tumult of passions, who, in addition, are not used to either good or evil, but who still can be taught the way of virtue and as well be instructed in the way of vice. And because these—as Aristotle has written at the beginning of the *Ethics*—are greatly agitated by their turbulent passions and violent affections, therefore, he believes, they are not apt listeners to the teaching of moral philosophy.[1] But Plato thinks that even these may be offered moral teachings seasoned with poetic sweetness. So it appears that Plato believes (according to what he writes in the second, third, and tenth books of the *Republic*, but even more plainly in the second book of the *Laws*) that the poetic faculty is the civil faculty, or moral philosophy, and it gives instruction to those who are unfit for naked instruction, either because of their age or the strength of their passions. And so I conclude with Proclus that Plato sometimes calls poetry a medicine, like that which aims to make souls healthy, and thus has usefulness as its end.

But I disagree with Proclus because he does not recognize any sort of delight in poetry. Even Plato allows that it introduces the useful by means of delight, for thus he praises it and calls it play and wants to be so understood: "Because the more tender minds do not accept serious studies, their studies are called games and songs and are performed as play; so when men are physically ill, those who care for them spread their nourishment with sweet condiments, but they make unhealthful food unpleasant, so that they learn to accept the one and reject the other."[2]

* * *

[78] Now without any doubt I think that as regards the end of poetry this is a correct opinion, that is, that perfect poetry regards delight as the cause of the useful. And as proof of my opinion, I am going to make the following discussion a little different from that of Plato.

Therefore I say that perfect poetry is game and is modified by the civil faculty; insofar as it is recreation it has delight as its end, but insofar as it is modified or, so to speak, characterized by moral philosophy, it puts delight first in order to provide a later benefit. And from this it seems to me that the civil faculty has decided that everyone may enjoy the delight that comes from poetry. And it has been so established by Plato in his *Laws* and by other legislators. I say further that the Athenian Republic so valued the delight brought to the people by poets that they were not ashamed to give each year many hundreds of coins to its citizens to buy themselves seats in the theatre

9. Cf. *Protagoras* 342–43 and *Gorgias* 476–77 [translator's note].
1. Aristotle, *Nicomachean Ethics* 1.4, 1095a [translator's note].
2. *Laws* 2.653–54 [translator's note]; the passage quoted does not appear in *Laws*, however.

where they could more easily hear the comedies and tragedies acted. * * * [79] And if it should seem to anyone that it is necessary to set forth more in detail the mode and type of this benefit, I am pressed, in order to satisfy this desire, to say something briefly.

[80] Plato wanted his republic to be composed of three sorts of persons: artisans, soldiers, and magistrates. Proclus added that under the category of artisans Plato included all the lower- and middle-class citizens, and that under the category of magistrates he included all those more powerful people who had the government of the republic in their hands. Now based upon this supposition I say that there are, deriving from the providence of the civil faculty in the city, three principal kinds of poetry—the heroic, the tragic, and the comic, each one of which makes use of delight to benefit all the people; each principally aimed at the benefit of one of those three parts that are, according to Plato, necessary to civil community. And so we say that the heroic poem was principally directed at soldiers, since by means of the virtuous actions of the heroes represented in such poems, they would be as if spurred on by glory driven to imitate it. Tragedy principally looks to the utility and benefit of princes, magistrates, and the powerful and, so as to keep them always under the justice of the laws, represents freely the dreadful and terrible downfall of great persons, which comes almost to be a bridle to restrain and moderate the size of their fortune. Comedy has as its principal intention the benefit of persons of low or moderate estate, and to console them for their modest fortune it usually presents actions that always end happily. And in this way, I think, the civil faculty inclines to the understanding that the humble and popular life is so much more enjoyable and filled with greater contentment than the grand or regal life.* * *

[82] Since the civil faculty seeks to implant in the minds of humble citizens obedience to their superiors, so that out of desire for novelties they should not be moved to disobedience or rebellion, and so that they should always remain content with their condition, it gave birth to comedy, in which the humble life is shown to be happy, fortunate, and capable of infinite solace. On the other hand, since the more powerful and all those raised to the mastery of others have not had to pay too much attention to their fortune, and consequently have become insupportable and insolent in their rule, the civil faculty wished to create tragedy, which would function as an adequate counterweight to the insolence of prosperous fortune. Hence all those who find themselves in such a condition will be able to extract useful instruction in moderating the pride characteristic of their state. [83] This usefulness of tragedy, I believe, is clearly enough indicated by Dio Chrysostum[3] in these words: "Nor is it anyone poor that the tragic situation deals with. On the contrary, all tragedies concern the Atreides, the Agamemnons, and the Oedipuses,[4] who possess a great abundance of gold, silver, fields, and cattle. So they say that the golden fleece was the greatest of all misfortunes." And so on.

Now it seems to me that from what has been said before concerning the utility to be derived from comedy and tragedy, we can conclude that those two kinds of poems are directed by the civil faculty to the extinguishing of

3. Rhetorician (ca. 40–ca.120 C.E.), an adherent of Cynic-Stoic philosophy.

4. The sons of Atreus (i.e., the Atreides), Menelaus and Agamemnon, like Oedipus, were kings of Greek city-states.

sedition and the preservation of peace. And because the civil faculty also has to keep military education in mind, in order that in times of war the republic may be capable of defending itself, it seems to me that it can probably be supposed that for this end the civil faculty created the heroic poem, in which is celebrated the highest strength of the heroes, and especially of those who generously disdain death for the sake of the country, to the end of reminding our soldiers of like examples so that they will consequently be more prone to despise the perils of death for the safety and increase of the public good. And in this way we see that these three species of poetry ruled by the civil faculty, in addition to delight, bring utility and benefit to the republic, instructing in an almost concealed way the three kinds of men, from which (according to Plato) the ideal order of citizens is made up. * * *

[84] Now to come to the end of this definition, I think it would be well to recapitulate in a brief epilogue what has been said before about the final cause of poetry. I say therefore that since language is always the instrument of the concupiscible power and has enjoyment as its end, but that, nevertheless considered as an instrument of the irascible power, it has as its end the defense of the sensitive soul; and if considered as an instrument of the rational power, its end is language. In the same way poetry is always an imitative art, and insofar as it is such, its end is always to represent the images of things correctly. Nevertheless, considered as a game, its end is delight; and considered as a game modified by the civil faculty, its immediate end is delight, but directed to profit.

On this premise, it seems to me that it can be concluded that poetry is capable of three definitions according as it is looked at in three different ways, that is, either as imitation, or purely as a game, or as a game modified by the civil faculty. In the first mode it can, perhaps, be defined this way: *Poetry is an art made with verse, number, and harmony, singly or together, imitative of the credible marvelous, and invented by the human intellect to represent the images of things suitably*. In the second mode this other definition would perhaps be appropriate: *Poetry is a game made with verse, number, and harmony, singly or together, imitating the credible marvelous, and invented by the human intellect in order to delight*. Now, since of poetry considered in the first mode we have come to understand all the authority that acknowledges correct imitation as the poetic end, so of poetry considered in the second mode we have expounded all the other authority that accepts only delight as poetic end[.] * * *

[85] In the third mode perhaps there is room for this last definition: *Poetry is a game made with verses, number, and harmony, singly or together, imitating the credible marvelous and invented by the civil faculty to delight the people in a useful way*. Of poetry considered in this mode, we have to understand fully all the authorities that attribute to it the end of usefulness by means of delight. [86] In this regard we should attend to the following words of Proclus, in which he talks of poetry more as a kind of learning than as imitation: "Now if it must be an imitation, as we have said, it also has to concern itself with worthy goodness. For I say that all its virtuous deeds, whether or not they are fashioned by imitation, have no more important end than the good."

From these three definitions there necessarily follow four corollaries. The first of these is that poetry taken in the first two modes is neither ruled nor governed by the civil faculty. The second is that only poetry in the third mode is that which is ruled and governed by moral philosophy or the civil faculty. The third is that the poetic that considers the idol in the first mode and that which likewise considers the idol in the second mode of poetry should not in any way be called a part of moral philosophy. The fourth and last corollary is that only the poetic that considers the idol in the third mode of poetry is that which really deserves to be called part of the civil faculty. And each good poet should put together his poems according to the rules of this mode of poetry, as Dante has done better than all the others.

* * *

1587

SIR PHILIP SIDNEY
1554–1586

Sir Philip Sidney embodied the aristocratic ideals of the Renaissance man: he was a courtier, soldier, statesman, amateur scholar, and poet—a legendary figure in his own lifetime. Author of the first English sonnet sequence, Sidney also wrote the first landmark of literary criticism in English. In 1579, a Puritan minister named Stephen Gosson published an attack on the theaters titled *The School of Abuse*, dedicating it, without permission, "to the right noble Gentleman, Master Philip Sidney, Esquire"; Sidney countered the following year with his defense, *An Apology for Poetry*, sometimes called *A Defence of Poetry* (1580–81). Though it responds to specific attacks, the *Apology* enjoys significance far beyond its occasion for its synthesis of the Renaissance understanding of classical literary theory, which set the terms of literary debate in England for the next two centuries, and for its formidable handling of its genre—the defense of poetry—which Sidney adapted from classical and medieval models.

Because Gosson's attack draws so heavily on PLATO's objections to poetry, Sidney's *Apology* reads like a reply to the *Republic*. Though his classicism is filtered through the Italian humanists of the fourteenth and fifteenth century (it echoes BOCCACCIO's defense of poetry in *Genealogy of the Gentile Gods*), Sidney relies particularly on ARISTOTLE's *Poetics* and HORACE's *Ars Poetica*. His remarks on the state of the English language and its poetry would define the significant literary issues for later English critics—including JOHN DRYDEN and APHRA BEHN in the seventeenth century and SAMUEL JOHNSON in the eighteenth—shaping the direction taken by post-Renaissance neoclassicism.

Sidney was born at Penshurst, the eldest son of Sir Henry Sidney and Mary Dudley, daughter of the duke of Northampton. His godfather, after whom he was named, was Philip II of Spain, husband of Queen Mary I. In 1564 he entered Shrewsbury school in Shropshire. By 1568 he was a student in Christ Church at Oxford University, though he left in 1571 without taking a degree, perhaps because of an outbreak of the plague. He departed England for the traditional "Grand Tour" of the Continent, arriving in Paris in 1572, in time to witness the infamous St. Bartholomew's Day Massacre of the Protestants.

In March 1575 Sidney returned to London, succeeding his father as Queen Elizabeth's cupbearer (a purely ceremonial position). The next year he traveled to Ireland with his father, the lord deputy, and the earl of Essex (Walter Devereux).

Negotiations began for a marriage between Sidney, then twenty-three, and Essex's fourteen-year-old daughter Penelope. Sidney began writing sonnets addressed to her, calling her Stella and himself Astrophil, a literary exercise inspired by the sonnets of the Italian poet Petrarch (1304–1374) to Laura. Though in 1581 Penelope married another, the sonnets continued for many years, even after Sidney's own marriage.

Sidney, who was greatly admired both in England and on the Continent for his sophistication and learning, was for several years unable to find employment at court; he belonged to the faction led by his uncle Robert Dudley, the earl of Leicester, one of Queen Elizabeth's favorites. He divided his time between visits with his illustrious friends, among them the poet Edmund Spenser, and his own writing. When he fell out of favor with the queen, he retreated to his sister's estate and began work on the *Old Arcadia*, also known as *The Countess of Pembroke's Arcadia* (after his sister), a pastoral romance alternating prose and poetry that was completed about 1581. Two sonnet sequences followed, *Certaine Sonets* (1581) and *Astrophil and Stella* (1581–82). He also began, but did not complete, a revision of the *Arcadia*. In keeping with his sense of the decorum required of a courtier, none of Sidney's works, including the *Apology*, was published during his lifetime; instead, they circulated privately among his friends in manuscript.

By 1583 Sidney's fortunes seemed to be changing. He was knighted and finally given a government appointment. In the fall he married Frances Walshingham, daughter of Queen Elizabeth's secretary of state, and his father-in-law paid off his considerable debts. In 1585 the queen appointed him governor of Flushing in the Netherlands, where she had sent troops to fight against Spain in support of the Protestant cause. There, in September 1586, in a raid on a Spanish convoy at Zutphen, Sidney was wounded by a bullet in the left thigh. The wound became infected, and he died at Arnhem on October 17 at the age of thirty-two. All Europe mourned his loss, and after a lavish state funeral he was buried in St. Paul's Cathedral in London.

An Apology for Poetry is a classic statement of Renaissance literary theory primarily because of its scope, its typicality, and its grace and clarity. Unlike his English contemporary George Puttenham, Sidney displays little interest in formulating the technical rules of poetry or rhetoric; he treats the subject of poetry much more broadly. At the same time, Sidney's debts are clear; he is a synthesizer, not a trailblazer. *An Apology* is a veritable encyclopedia of Renaissance humanism. Though structured as a classical oration with the standard seven parts (exordium, proposition, division, examination, refutation, digression, peroration), Sidney's text is more usefully understood as treating three major topics. The first part defends the dignity of poetry, demonstrating its superiority to philosophy and history because it combines the moral precepts of the one with the entertaining examples of the other, all the while cloaking its lessons with the pleasurable devices of art. Along the way, Sidney discusses the ethics of genres, ranging from pastoral, elegy, and satire to comedy, tragedy, and epic. The second part deals with the specific objections raised against poetry, in particular the charge that the poet is a liar. Sidney follows Boccaccio on this point, famously declaring: "Now for the poet, he nothing affirms, and therefore never lieth." Poets' imitations are not lies, as Plato charged, because poets make no truth claims. The third part of the essay examines the current state of English literature. Here Sidney, the practicing poet, offers some critical comments on diction, poetic figures, meter, rhyme, rhythm, and the English vernacular compared to other languages. Of particular interest is Sidney's pointed criticism of the English drama for failing to adhere to the unities of time and place sketched in Aristotle's *Poetics*. This issue would occupy neoclassical critics of the drama from PIERRE CORNEILLE through Samuel Johnson.

A fundamental aesthetic problem of the late sixteenth century concerns the object and purpose of poetry's representation. Sidney's definition of poetry sets an agenda for the discussion of poetry that brings together many of the learned commonplaces of Renaissance criticism: "an art of imitation, . . . that is to say, a representing, counterfeiting, or figuring forth—to speak metaphorically, a speaking picture—with this end, to teach and delight." This definition is less notable for its originality (it is drawn almost word for word from the Italian-born humanist Julius Caesar Scaliger's *Poetics* of 1561, which, in turn, was indebted to Aristotle's *Poetics* and Horace's *Ars Poetica*) than for the insights it gives into the critical controversies of the period. The definition, and Sidney's subsequent discussion of it, raises three issues—all derived from Plato's discussion of poetry in the *Republic*—that dominate literary criticism until the end of the eighteenth century: the nature of imitation, the problem of defining nature, and the injunction that poetry serve moral ends.

Although the principle of imitation reigned unchallenged in literary theory from the Renaissance to the end of the eighteenth century, not all critics meant the same thing by *imitation*, nor did they necessarily agree on what is imitated (compare GIACOPO MAZZONI's extremely elaborate contemporaneous views on the subject with Sidney's). At the center of the controversy over imitation was a debate about nature itself: what constituted nature and what was the status of representations of "reality"? Like the third-century C.E. philosopher PLOTINUS, Sidney uses the Platonic theory of Forms to refute Plato's criticism of poetry. The Neoplatonic mimesis espoused by Sidney held that the nature the poet imitated was the ideal, not the material, world. In the Renaissance, the ideal of nature was God's cosmological plan. Sidney perhaps best represents this viewpoint when he argues that "right poets" "imitate to teach and delight, and to imitate borrow nothing of what is, hath been, or shall be, but range only reined with learned discretion into the divine consideration of what may be and should be." This view of mimesis is based on a religious belief in providential design; because the universe is the product of divine wisdom, the purpose of the poet is ultimately to affirm the rule of justice and order. The ideal that Sidney invokes—what may be or should be—is more "real" than what is. In the next century this view of nature runs head on into the scientific revolution, and the debate is recast in Dryden's *Essay of Dramatic Poesy* (see below) and elsewhere.

Critics of the *Apology*, especially modern ones, have argued that it is derivative, that Sidney is simply not an original theorist, and that the rhetorical play and intertextual abundance of his Renaissance prose is tiring. Yet so long as contemporary literary theorists such as JACQUES DERRIDA, Richard Rorty, and DONNA HARAWAY are still debating the status of nature and the ideological stakes involved in representation, Sidney's essay, with its elegant variation on Platonic mimesis, will repay close scrutiny.

BIBLIOGRAPHY

The complete works of Sir Philip Sidney are available in *Complete Works*, edited by Albert Feuillerat (4 vols., 1922–26). The standard edition of *An Apology for Poetry* with copious endnotes may be found in *The Miscellaneous Prose of Sir Philip Sidney*, edited by Katherine Duncan-Jones and Jan Van Dorsten (1973). There are several other single-volume editions of the text, including Forrest G. Robinson's 1970 edition. For a seventeenth-century biography, consult *Sir Fulke Greville's Life of Sir Philip Sidney* (1652), available in *The Prose of Fulke Greville*, edited by Mark Caldwell (1987). For a recent biography, see Katherine Duncan-Jones, *Sir Philip Sidney: Courtier Poet* (1991).

Forrest G. Robinson, *The Shape of Things Known: Sidney's Apology in Its Philosophical Tradition* (1972), is an important book-length study of Sidney's famous essay. A. C. Hamilton provides a brief but important study of Sidney in *Sir Philip Sidney: A Study of His Life and Works* (1977). Andrew D. Weiner, in *Sir Philip Sidney and the Poetics of Protestantism: A Study of Contexts* (1978), places the poet and critic within the context of the religious controversies that dominated his life and times. For an introduction to Sidney, see Katherine Duncan-Jones's excellent contribution to the Oxford Authors series, *Sir Philip Sidney* (1989). Critical interest in Sidney's "self-fashioning," his creation of images of himself in both his poetry and criticism, is evidenced by such books as Alan Hager's *Dazzling Images: The Masks of Sir Philip Sidney* (1991) and Edward Berry's *Making of Sir Philip Sidney* (1998). Peter C. Herman's *Squitter-wits and Muse-haters: Sidney, Spenser, Milton, and Renaissance Antipoetic Sentiments* (1996) examines the sixteenth- and seventeenth-century debates about poetry with which Sidney's *Apology* engages. For a bibliography, consult *Sir Philip Sidney: An Annotated Bibliography of Texts and Criticism (1554–1984)*, edited by Donald V. Stump (1994).

An Apology for Poetry

When the right virtuous Edward Wotton[1] and I were at the Emperor's Court together, we gave ourselves to learn horsemanship of John Pietro Pugliano, one that with great commendation had the place of an esquire[2] in his stable. And he, according to the fertileness of the Italian wit, did not only afford us the demonstration of his practice, but sought to enrich our minds with the contemplations therein, which he thought most precious. But with none I remember mine ears were at any time more loaden, than when (either angered with slow payment, or moved with our learner-like admiration) he exercised his speech in the praise of his faculty. He said soldiers were the noblest estate of mankind, and horsemen the noblest of soldiers. He said they were the masters of war and ornaments of peace, speedy goers and strong abiders, triumphers both in camps and courts. Nay, to so unbelieved[3] a point he proceeded, as that no earthly thing bred such wonder to a prince as to be a good horseman. Skill of government was but a *pedanteria*[4] in comparison. Then would he add certain praises by telling what a peerless beast a horse was; the only serviceable courtier without flattery, the beast of most beauty, faithfulness, courage, and such more, that if I had not been a piece of a logician before I came to him, I think he would have persuaded me to have wished myself a horse. But thus much at least with his no few words he drave into me, that self-love is better than any gilding to make that seem gorgeous wherein ourselves are parties. Wherein, if Pugliano his strong affection and weak arguments will not satisfy you, I will give you a nearer example of myself, who (I know not by what mischance), in these my not old years and idlest times, having slipped into the title of a poet, am provoked to say something unto you in the defence of that my unelected vocation, which if I handle with more good will than good reasons, bear with me, sith the scholar is to be pardoned that followeth the steps of his master. And yet I must say that, as I have just cause to make a pitiful defence of poor poetry, which from almost the highest estimation of

1. Edward Wotton (1548–1626), first Baron Wotton, was an English courtier and statesman. During his Continental travels Sidney spent the winter of 1574–75 at the Imperial Court of Maximilian II in Vienna. In company with his mentor, Hubert Languet, Sidney engaged in a warm friendship with Wotton. At the end of May 1575, Wotton joined Sidney in Antwerp for the return voyage to England. A decade later Wotton was mentioned in Sidney's will and served as a pallbearer in the poet's funeral procession [Forrest G. Robinson's note].
2. An esquire, or equerry, was an officer in charge of the horses and stables of a noble personage [Robinson's note].
3. Unbelievable.
4. Pedantry, useless book learning (Italian).

learning is fallen to be the laughing-stock of children, so have I need to bring some more available[5] proofs, sith the former is by no man barred of his deserved credit, the silly[6] latter hath had even the names of philosophers used to the defacing of it, with great danger of civil war among the Muses.[7]

And first, truly, to all them that, professing learning, inveigh against poetry, may justly be objected that they go very near to ungratefulness to seek to deface that which, in the noblest nations and languages that are known, hath been the first light-giver to ignorance, and first nurse, whose milk by little and little enabled them to feed afterwards of tougher knowledges. And will they now play the hedgehog that, being received into the den, drave out his host? Or rather the vipers, that with their birth kill their parents? Let learned Greece, in any of her manifold sciences, be able to show me one book before Musaeus, Homer, and Hesiod,[8] all three nothing else but poets. Nay, let any history be brought that can say any writers were there before them, if they were not men of the same skill as Orpheus, Linus,[9] and some other are named, who, having been the first of that country that made pens deliverers of their knowledge to their posterity, may justly challenge to be called their fathers in learning: for not only in time they had this priority (although in itself antiquity be venerable), but went before them, as causes to draw with their charming sweetness the wild untamed wits to an admiration of knowledge. So as Amphion was said to move stones with his poetry to build Thebes,[1] and Orpheus to be listened to by beasts, indeed stony and beastly people, so among the Romans were Livius Andronicus and Ennius.[2] So in the Italian language, the first that made it aspire to be a treasure-house of science were the poets Dante, Boccaccio, and Petrarch.[3] So in our English were Gower and Chaucer,[4] after whom, encouraged and delighted with their excellent fore-going, others have followed to beautify our mother tongue, as well in the same kind as in other arts.

This did so notably show itself, that the philosophers of Greece durst not a long time appear to the world but under the masks of poets. So Thales, Empedocles, and Parmenides[5] sang their natural philosophy in verses; so did Pythagoras and Phocylides their moral counsels; so did Tyrtaeus in war matters and Solon[6] in matters of policy: or rather, they being poets, did exercise

5. Efficacious: that may avail.
6. Here used with an affectionate rather than pejorative connotation [Robinson's note].
7. In Greek mythology, 9 daughters of Memory who preside over the arts and all intellectual pursuits.
8. Greek didactic epic poet (active ca. 700 B.C.E.). Musaeus: mythical singer associated with Orpheus, mythical musician unrivaled among mortals. Homer (ca. 8th c. B.C.E.) Greek epic poet to whom the *Iliad* and the *Odyssey* are attributed.
9. Mythical singer; in some accounts, he taught Orpheus and Heracles.
1. Ancient Greek city whose mythical founders were Amphion and Zethus, twin sons of Zeus; by playing his lyre, Amphion built the city's walls.
2. Two of the earliest Roman poets: Livius Andronicus (d. ca. 205 B.C.E.) wrote tragedies, comedies, and an adaptation of Homer's *Odyssey*; Ennius (239–169 B.C.E.) wrote dramas, satires, and an epic history of Rome.
3. Scholar and humanist (1304–1374). DANTE ALIGHIERI (1265–1321), best known for the *Divine Comedy*. GIOVANNI BOCCACCIO (1313–1375), best known for *The Decameron*.
4. Author (ca. 1343–1400) of *The Canterbury Tales*. John Gower (1330–1408), poet who wrote in French and Latin as well as English.
5. Author (b. ca. 515 B.C.E.) of *On Nature*, in hexameter verse. Thales (6th c. B.C.E.), astronomer and geometer, who in fact left no writings. Empedocles (ca. 493–ca. 433 B.C.E.), scientist and statesman who wrote two philosophical poems, *On Nature* and *Purifications*.
6. Athenian poet and statesman (active early 6th c. B.C.E.). Pythagoras (6th c. B.C.E.), Greek philosopher and mathematician. Phocylides (active 544–591 B.C.E.), gnomic poet of Miletus. Tyrtaeus (7th c. B.C.E.), Spartan poet and general whose works include war songs.

their delightful vein in those points of highest knowledge which before them lay hid to the world. For that wise Solon was directly a poet, it is manifest, having written in verse the notable fable of the Atlantic Island, which was continued by Plato.[7]

And truly, even Plato, whosoever well considereth shall find that in the body of his work, though the inside and strength were philosophy, the skin as it were and beauty depended most of poetry, for all standeth upon dialogues, wherein he feigneth many honest burgesses of Athens to speak of such matters, that if they had been set on the rack they would never have confessed them; besides his poetical describing the circumstances of their meetings, as the well ordering of a banquet, the delicacy of a walk, with interlacing mere tales, as Gyges'[8] ring and others, which who knoweth not to be flowers of poetry did never walk into Apollo's[9] garden.

And even historiographers (although their lips sound of things done, and verity be written in their foreheads) have been glad to borrow both fashion and perchance weight of poets. So Herodotus[1] entitled his *History* by the name of the nine Muses, and both he and all the rest that followed him either stole or usurped of poetry their passionate describing of passions, the many particularities of battles, which no man could affirm; or, if that be denied me, long orations put in the mouths of great kings and captains, which it is certain they never pronounced. So that truly, neither philosopher nor historiographer could at the first have entered into the gates of popular judgments if they had not taken a great passport of poetry, which, in all nations at this day where learning flourisheth not, is plain to be seen; in all which they have some feeling of poetry.

In Turkey, besides their law-giving divines, they have no other writers but poets. In our neighbor country Ireland, where truly learning goeth very bare, yet are their poets held in a devout reverence. Even among the most barbarous and simple Indians where no writing is, yet have they their poets, who make and sing songs which they call *areytos*,[2] both of their ancestors' deeds and praises of their gods; a sufficient probability that, if ever learning come among them, it must be by having their hard dull wits softened and sharpened with the sweet delights of poetry. For until they find a pleasure in the exercises of the mind, great promises of much knowledge will little persuade them that know not the fruits of knowledge. In Wales, the true remnant of the ancient Britons, as there are good authorities to show the long time they had poets which they called *bards*, so through all the conquests of Romans, Saxons, Danes, and Normans, some of whom did seek to ruin all memory of learning from among them, yet do their poets even to this day last, so as it is not more notable in soon beginning than in long continuing.

But since the authors of most of our sciences were the Romans, and before them the Greeks, let us a little stand upon their authorities, but even so far as to see what names they have given unto this now scorned skill. Among

7. Greek philosopher (ca. 427–ca. 347 B.C.E.; see above), who writes of the lost continent of Atlantis in *Timaeus* 25 and *Critias*.

8. King of Lydia, ca. 685–657 B.C.E.; according to Plato (*Republic* 2.359d–360b), after the shepherd Gyges found a ring that enabled him to become invisible, he was able to assume the rule of the kingdom.

9. Greek and Roman god of poetry.

1. Greek historian (ca. 484–ca. 425 B.C.E.); his *History* was divided into 9 "Muses" by a later editor.

2. This was a ceremonial dance accompanied by songs, common among the Indians in the Americas [Robinson's note].

the Romans a poet was called *vates*, which is as much as a diviner, foreseer, or prophet, as by his conjoined words *vaticinium* and *vaticinari*,[3] is manifest; so heavenly a title did that excellent people bestow upon this heart-ravishing knowledge. And so far were they carried into the admiration thereof, that they thought in the chanceable hitting upon any such verses great foretokens of their following fortunes were placed. Whereupon grew the word of *Sortes Virgilianae*, when by sudden opening Virgil's[4] book they lighted upon any verse of his making, whereof the Histories of the Emperors' Lives are full: as of Albinus,[5] the governor of our island, who in his childhood met with this verse,

Arma amens capio nec sat rationis in armis,[6]

and in his age performed it; which, although it were a very vain and godless superstition, as also it was to think that spirits were commanded by such verses—whereupon this word charms, derived of *carmina*,[7] cometh—so yet serveth it to show the great reverence those wits were held in. And altogether not without ground, since both the oracles of Delphos and Sibylla's[8] prophecies were wholly delivered in verses. For that same exquisite observing of number and measure in words, and that high flying liberty of conceit proper to the poet, did seem to have some divine force in it.

And may not I presume a little further, to show the reasonableness of this word *vates*, and say that the holy David's Psalms are a divine poem?[9] If I do, I shall not do it without the testimony of great learned men, both ancient and modern. But even the name Psalms will speak for me, which being interpreted is nothing but songs; then, that it is fully written in meter, as all learned hebricians agree,[1] although the rules be not yet fully found; lastly and principally, his handling his prophecy, which is merely poetical. For what else is the awaking his musical instruments, the often and free changing of persons, his notable *prosopopoeias*,[2] when he maketh you, as it were, see God coming in His majesty, his telling of the beasts' joyfulness, and hills leaping, but a heavenly poesy,[3] wherein almost he showeth himself a passionate lover of that unspeakable and everlasting beauty to be seen by the eyes of the mind, only cleared by faith?[4] But truly, now having named him, I fear me I seem to profane that holy name, applying it to poetry, which is among us thrown down to so ridiculous an estimation. But they that with quiet judg-

3. To prophesy. *Vates*: poet-prophet. *Vaticinium*: a prophecy (all Latin).

4. Roman poet (70–19 B.C.E.). *Sortes Virgilianae*: literally, "Virgilian lots" (Latin)—the practice of using a randomly chosen line from Virgil's *Aeneid* to tell one's fortune.

5. Roman governor of Britain, hailed as emperor by his troops in 195 C.E.; defeated two years later, he committed suicide.

6. Out of my mind I seized my arms, although there was little reason in arms (or, "I had no plan for battle"); *Aeneid* 2.314.

7. Songs, poems (Latin); the Romans also used the word to mean "magic charms."

8. Originally a single prophetic female, the Sibyl was gradually pluralized into a number of local personages. The Sibylline prophecies, as described by Virgil (*Aeneid* 6.77–101), were ecstatic verse riddles like those delivered at Dephi. Delphos: in antiquity the location of the Delphic Oracle. The presiding deity was Apollo, at whose temple the woman Pythia delivered prophetic riddles [Robinson's note].

9. The biblical King David is traditionally credited with writing the Book of Psalms, thought to be divinely inspired.

1. Many Renaissance scholars who knew some Hebrew erroneously thought the psalms were written in verse forms approximating classical meters.

2. Personifications (Greek).

3. Sidney is generally careful to distinguish between "poetry," the finished product of the poet's art, and "poesy," the craft or technique of writing [Robinson's note].

4. The notion that faith serves to clarify inner vision was a commonplace in Christian thought [Robinson's note].

ments will look a little deeper into it, shall find the end and working of it such, as being rightly applied, deserveth not to be scourged out of the Church of God.

But now let us see how the Greeks named it and how they deemed of it. The Greeks called him a poet, which name hath, as the most excellent, gone through other languages. It cometh of this word *poiein*, which is, to make, wherein I know not whether by luck or wisdom we Englishmen have met with the Greeks in calling him a maker: which name, how high and incomparable a title it is, I had rather were known by marking the scope of other sciences than by my partial allegation.

There is no art delivered to mankind that hath not the works of nature for his[5] principal object, without which they could not consist, and on which they so depend, as they become actors and players, as it were, of what nature will have set forth. So doth the astronomer look upon the stars, and by that he seeth, setteth down what order nature hath taken therein. So do the geometrician and arithmetician in their diverse sorts of quantities. So doth the musician in times tell you which by nature agree, which not. The natural philosopher thereon hath his name, and the moral philosopher standeth upon the natural virtues, vices, and passions of man; and follow nature (saith he) therein, and thou shalt not err. The lawyer saith what men have determined; the historian what men have done. The grammarian speaketh only of the rules of speech, and the rhetorician and logician, considering what in nature will soonest prove and persuade, thereon give artificial[6] rules, which still are compassed within the circle of a question, according to the proposed matter. The physician weigheth the nature of a man's body, and the nature of things helpful or hurtful unto it. And the metaphysic, though it be in the second and abstract notions, and therefore be counted supernatural, yet doth he indeed build upon the depth of nature.[7] Only the poet, disdaining to be tied to any such subjection, lifted up with the vigor of his own invention, doth grow in effect another nature, in making things either better than nature bringeth forth, or quite anew, forms such as never were in nature, as the Heroes, Demigods, Cyclops, Chimeras, Furies,[8] and such like; so as he goeth hand in hand with nature, not enclosed within the narrow warrant of her gifts, but freely ranging only within the zodiac of his own wit.

Nature never set forth the earth in so rich tapestry as divers poets have done, neither with pleasant rivers, fruitful trees, sweet smelling flowers, nor whatsoever else may make the too much loved earth more lovely. Her world is brazen, the poets only deliver a golden.

But let those things alone and go to man, for whom as the other things are, so it seemeth in him her uttermost cunning is employed, and know

5. Its.

6. Part of an established discipline or art. The usage here bears none of the pejorative connotations ("fictitious," "unnatural") current today [Robinson's note].

7. The metaphysician ("metaphysic") is not concerned with specific sense impressions (first notions), but with universals which have been abstracted from sensory experience. Sidney's psychology is Aristotelian at this point, for his assurance that "second and abstract notions" are derived from "the depth of nature" implies that the forms conceived in the mind are immanent in the natural world [Robinson's note].

8. In Greek mythology, avenging deities who punish crimes both in this world and after death. Heroes: in the Greek sense, individuals who are part human, part divine. Demigods: offspring of a god and a mortal. Cyclops: one-eyed giants. Chimeras: fire-breathing female monsters with a lion's head, goat's body, and serpent's tail.

whether she have brought forth so true a lover as Theagenes, so constant a friend as Pylades, so valiant a man as Orlando, so right a prince as Xenophon's Cyrus,[9] so excellent a man every way as Virgil's Aeneas. Neither let this be jestingly conceived, because the works of the one be essential,[1] the other in imitation or fiction; for any understanding knoweth the skill of the artificer standeth in that *Idea* or fore-conceit of the work, and not in the work itself. And that the poet hath that *Idea* is manifest by delivering them forth in such excellency as he hath imagined them. Which delivering forth also is not wholly imaginative, as we are wont to say by them that build castles in the air, but so far substantially it worketh, not only to make a Cyrus, which had been but a particular excellency, as nature might have done, but to bestow a Cyrus upon the world to make many Cyruses, if they will learn aright why and how that maker made him.

Neither let it be deemed too saucy a comparison to balance the highest point of man's wit with the efficacy of nature, but rather give right honor to the heavenly Maker of that maker, who having made man to His own likeness, set him beyond and over all the works of that second nature, which in nothing he showeth so much as in poetry, when with the force of a divine breath he bringeth things forth far surpassing her doings, with no small argument to the incredulous of that first accursed fall of Adam: sith our erected wit maketh us know what perfection is, and yet our infected will keepeth us from reaching unto it. But these arguments will by few be understood, and by fewer granted. Thus much (I hope) will be given me, that the Greeks with some probability of reason gave him the name above all names of learning.

Now let us go to a more ordinary opening of him, that the truth may be more palpable: and so I hope, though we get not so unmatched a praise as the etymology of his names will grant, yet his very description, which no man will deny, shall not justly be barred from a principal commendation.

Poesy therefore is an art of imitation, for so Aristotle termeth it in this word *mimesis*, that is to say, a representing, counterfeiting, or figuring forth—to speak metaphorically, a speaking picture—with this end, to teach and delight.[2] Of this have been three several kinds.

The chief both in antiquity and excellency were they that did imitate the inconceivable excellencies of God. Such were David in his Psalms, Solomon in his Song of Songs, in his Ecclesiastes and Proverbs, Moses and Deborah[3] in their Hymns, and the writer of Job; which, beside other, the learned Emanuel Tremellius and Franciscus Junius[4] do entitle the poetical part of the Scripture. Against these none will speak that hath the Holy Ghost in due

9. Cyrus the Great of Persia, exemplary ruler in the *Cryopaedia*, a Greek prose romance by the Greek military commander and historian Xenophon (ca. 223/7–ca. 354 B.C.E.). Theagenes: hero of Heliodorus's Greek romance, *Aethiopica* (3d c. C.E.). Pylades: friend of Orestes (the son of Agamemnon and Clytemnestra). Orlando: hero of several Italian poems, including Ludovico Ariosto's *Orlando Furioso* (1532).

1. Actual or real, as opposed to something "in imitation or fiction" [Robinson's note].

2. Compare HORACE (65–8 B.C.E.), *Ars Poetica*, line 333: 'Poets aim either to do good or to give pleasure.' ARISTOTLE (384–322 B.C.E) begins the *Poetics* by discussing the nature of poetic *mimēsis* (see above).

3. A biblical prophet and judge of Israel who sings a famous song of triumph when the king of Canaan is defeated (Judges 5). Solomon: the biblical king of Israel was traditionally viewed as the author of the books named. Moses: after the Egyptians pursuing the Israelites perished in the Red Sea, Moses sang a triumphal song of praise to God (Exodus 1.1–15).

4. Emanuel Tremellius (1510–1580), a Jew converted to Protestantism, and Franciscus Junius (1545–1602), a French Protestant scholar, together produced a Latin translation of the Bible (1575–80) [Robinson's note].

holy reverence. In this kind, though in a full wrong divinity, were Orpheus, Amphion, Homer in his Hymns,[5] and many other, both Greeks and Romans. And this poesy must be used by whosoever will follow St. James his counsel in singing psalms when they are merry,[6] and I know is used with the fruit of comfort by some, when in sorrowful pangs of their death-bringing sins, they find the consolation of the never-leaving goodness.

The second kind is of them that deal with matters philosophical: either moral, as Tyrtaeus, Phocylides, and Cato;[7] or natural, as Lucretius, and Virgil's *Georgics*;[8] or astronomical, as Manilius and Pontanus; or historical, as Lucan:[9] which who mislike, the fault is in their judgments quite out of taste, and not in the sweet food of sweetly uttered knowledge.

But because this second sort is wrapped within the fold of the proposed subject, and takes not the course of his own invention, whether they properly be poets or no let grammarians dispute,[1] and go to the third, indeed right poets, of whom chiefly this question ariseth. Betwixt whom and these second is such a kind of difference as betwixt the meaner sort of painters (who counterfeit only such faces as are set before them), and the more excellent, who having no law but wit, bestow that in colors upon you which is fittest for the eye to see: as the constant though lamenting look of Lucretia when she punished in herself another's fault.[2] Wherein he painteth not Lucretia whom he never saw, but painteth the outward beauty of such a virtue. For these third be they which most properly do imitate to teach and delight, and to imitate borrow nothing of what is, hath been, or shall be, but range only reined with learned discretion into the divine consideration of what may be and should be. These be they that, as the first and most noble sort, may justly be termed *vates*, so these are waited on in the excellentest languages and best understandings with the fore-described name of poets. For these indeed do merely make to imitate, and imitate both to delight and teach, and delight to move men to take that goodness in hand which without delight they would fly as from a stranger, and teach, to make them know that goodness where-unto they are moved: which being the noblest scope to which ever any learning was directed, yet want there not idle tongues to bark at them.

These be subdivided into sundry more special denominations. The most notable be the Heroic, Lyric, Tragic, Comic, Satiric, Iambic, Elegiac, Pastoral, and certain others, some of these being termed according to the matter they deal with, some by the sorts of verses they liked best to write in. For indeed the greatest part of poets have apparelled their poetical inventions in that numbrous[3] kind of writing which is called verse; indeed but apparelled, verse being but an ornament and no cause to poetry, sith there have been

5. Poems (8th–6th c. B.C.E.) in epic style on mythic subjects, by various unknown authors. "Wrong divinity": inspired by false gods.

6. "Is any [among you] merry? Let him sing psalms" (James 5.13).

7. Dionysius Cato, the reputed author of the Latin *Disticha de Moribus* (3d c. C.E.), a popular elementary textbook on morality in medieval and Elizabethan schools.

8. A didactic poem about and celebrating agriculture. Lucretius (ca. 99–50 B.C.E.), Roman poet whose epic on Epicurean philosophy is titled *On the Nature of Things*.

9. Roman statesman and poet (39–65 C.E.), who wrote a historical epic, *The Civil War*. Manilius (active ca. 10–20 C.E.), author of the *Astronomica*, a didactic poem on astrology. [Pontanus: Latin name of Giovanni Pontano (1426–1503), whose poem on the stars, *Urania*, Sidney may have known.—Robinson's note.]

1. For Sidney and other Renaissance writers the study of grammar also encompassed writing, composition, spelling, speech, and "literature," including poetry and history.

2. In Roman legend, Lucretia was raped by the son of the king of Rome; after telling her husband, she committed suicide (the popular uprising that followed, led by Junius Brutus, resulted in the founding of the Roman Republic in 510 B.C.E.).

3. In poetic meters.

many most excellent poets that never versified, and now swarm many versifiers that need never answer to the name of poets. For Xenophon, who did imitate so excellently as to give us *effigiem justi imperii*, the portraiture of a just empire, under the name of Cyrus (as Cicero saith of him[4]), made therein an absolute heroical poem. So did Heliodorus in his sugared invention of that picture of love in Theagenes and Cariclea, and yet both these writ in prose: which I speak to show, that it is not rhyming and versing that maketh a poet, no more than a long gown maketh an advocate, who though he pleaded in armor should be an advocate and no soldier. But it is that feigning notable images of virtues, vices, or what else, with that delightful teaching, which must be the right describing note to know a poet by: although indeed the senate of poets hath chosen verse as their fittest raiments, meaning, as in matter they passed all in all, so in manner to go beyond them, not speaking (table talk fashion, or like men in a dream) words as they chanceably fall from the mouth, but peizing[5] each syllable of each word by just proportion according to the dignity of the subject.

Now therefore it shall not be amiss first to weigh this latter sort of poetry by his works, and then by his parts, and if in neither of these anatomies[6] he be condemnable, I hope we shall obtain a more favorable sentence. This purifying of wit, this enriching of memory, enabling of judgment, and enlarging of conceit,[7] which commonly we call learning, under what name soever it come forth, or to what immediate end soever it be directed, the final end is to lead and draw us to as high a perfection as our degenerate souls, made worse by their clayey lodgings, can be capable of. This, according to the inclination of the man, bred many formed impressions.[8] For some that thought this felicity principally to be gotten by knowledge and no knowledge to be so high and heavenly as acquaintance with the stars, gave themselves to astronomy; others, persuading themselves to be demi-gods if they knew the causes of things, became natural and supernatural philosophers; some an admirable delight drew to music; and some, the certainty of demonstration, to the mathematics. But all, one and other, having this scope, to know, and by knowledge to lift up the mind from the dungeon of the body to the enjoying his own divine essence. But when by the balance of experience it was found that the astronomer, looking to the stars, might fall into a ditch, that the inquiring philosopher might be blind in himself, and the mathematician might draw forth a straight line with a crooked heart, then lo did proof, the overruler of opinions, make manifest that all these are but serving sciences, which, as they have each a private end in themselves, so yet are they all directed to the highest end of the mistress knowledge, by the Greeks called *architectonike*,[9] which stands (as I think) in the knowledge of a man's self, in the ethic and politic consideration, with the end of well doing and not of well knowing only:[1] even as the saddler's next end is to make a good saddle, but his farther end, to serve a nobler faculty, which is horsemanship;

4. See Cicero's *Epistles to His Brother Quintus* 1.8.23 [Robinson's note]. Cicero (106–43 B.C.E.), Roman statesman and orator.
5. Weighing.
6. Analyses.
7. Concept.
8. Each man, according to the disposition of his faculties, is drawn to one or another of the arts and sciences [Robinson's note].
9. Literally, "of or for a master builder" (thus the art or science that governs all, just as a master builder directs workers).
1. Following Aristotle, Sidney argues that the arts and sciences culminate in a master science (*architectonike*) which comprehends the knowledge of the ultimate human good. But where Aristotle designates politics as the supreme discipline, Sidney selects that self-knowledge which results in "well doing" [Robinson's note].

so the horseman's to soldiery, and the soldier not only to have the skill, but to perform the practice of a soldier. So that, the ending end of all earthly learning, being virtuous action, those skills that most serve to bring forth that have a most just title to be princes over all the rest.

Wherein if we can show the poet's nobleness by setting him before his other competitors, among whom as principal challengers step forth the moral philosophers, whom, me thinketh, I see coming towards me with a sullen gravity, as though they could not abide vice by daylight, rudely clothed for to witness outwardly their contempt of outward things, with books in their hands against glory, whereto they set their names, sophistically speaking against subtlety, and angry with any man in whom they see the foul fault of anger. These men casting largesse as they go of definitions, divisions, and distinctions,[2] with a scornful interrogative do soberly ask whether it be possible to find any path so ready to lead a man to virtue as that which teacheth what virtue is; and teacheth it not only by delivering forth his very being, his causes and effects, but also by making known his enemy vice, which must be destroyed, and his cumbersome servant passion, which must be mastered, by showing the generalities that containeth it, and the specialities that are derived from it; lastly, by plain setting down, how it extendeth itself out of the limits of a man's own little world to the government of families, and maintaining of public societies.

The historian scarcely giveth leisure to the moralist to say so much, but that he, loaden with old mouse-eaten records, authorizing himself (for the most part) upon other histories, whose greatest authorities are built upon the notable foundation of hearsay, having much ado to accord differing writers, and to pick truth out of partiality, better acquainted with a thousand years ago than with the present age, and yet better knowing how this world goeth than how his own wit runneth, curious for antiquities and inquisitive of novelties, a wonder to young folks and a tyrant in table talk, denieth in a great chafe that any man, for teaching of virtue and virtuous actions, is comparable to him. I am *testis temporum, lux veritatis, vita memoriae, magistra vitae, nuncia vetustatis.*[3] The philosopher (saith he) teacheth a disputative virtue, but I do an active; his virtue is excellent in the dangerless Academy of Plato,[4] but mine showeth forth her honorable face in the battles of Marathon, Pharsalia, Poitiers, and Agincourt.[5] He teacheth virtue by certain abstract considerations, but I only bid you follow the footing of them that have gone before you. Old-aged experience goeth beyond the fine-witted philosopher, but I give the experience of many ages. Lastly, if he make the song-book, I put the learner's hand to the lute; and if he be the guide, I am the light.

Then would he allege you innumerable examples, confirming story by

2. Terms from medieval scholastic logic which survived in Renaissance handbooks. Definition is the most general statement about an object, stating its genus and specific difference (e.g., "man is a rational animal"). Division is a more specific classification into species, parts, or adjuncts, and distinction is the separation of a substance and its accidents [that is, properties or attributes that are nonessential; Robinson's note].

3. "I am the witness of the times, the light of truth, the life of memory, the teacher of life, and the messenger of antiquity"; from Cicero, *De Oratore* 2.9.36 (which has *nuntia*, not *nuncia*; the subject is "history").

4. Plato's school on the outskirts of Athens, founded about 385 B.C.E.

5. All sites of great victories: at Marathon, the Greeks defeated the Persians in 490 B.C.E.; at Pharsalia, Julius Caesar defeated Pompey in 48 B.C.E.; at Poitiers, the English defeated the French in 1356; and at Agincourt, Henry V defeated the French in 1415.

story, how much the wisest senators and princes have been directed by the credit of history, as Brutus, Alphonsus of Aragon,[6] and who not, if need be? At length the long line of their disputation maketh a point in this, that the one giveth the precept, and the other the example.[7]

Now whom shall we find (sith the question standeth for the highest form[8] in the school of learning) to be moderator? Truly, as me seemeth, the poet; and if not a moderator, even the man that ought to carry the title from them both, and much more from all other serving sciences. Therefore compare we the poet with the historian and with the moral philosopher, and if he go beyond them both, no other human skill can match him. For as for the divine, with all reverence it is ever to be excepted, not only for having his scope as far beyond any of these as eternity exceedeth a moment, but even for passing each of these in themselves. And for the lawyer, though *jus*[9] be the daughter of justice, and justice the chief of virtues, yet because he seeketh to make men good rather *formidine poenae* than *virtutis amore*,[1] or to say righter, doth not endeavor to make men good, but that their evil hurt not others; having no care so he be a good citizen, how bad a man he be; therefore as our wickedness maketh him necessary, and necessity maketh him honorable, so is he not in the deepest truth to stand in rank with these who all endeavor to take naughtiness away, and plant goodness even in the secretest cabinet of our souls. And these four are all that any way deal in that consideration of men's manners, which being the supreme knowledge, they that best breed it deserve the best commendation.

The philosopher therefore and the historian are they which would win the goal, the one by precept, the other by example. But both, not having both, do both halt. For the philosopher, setting down with thorny argument the bare rule, is so hard of utterance and so misty to be conceived, that one that hath no other guide but him shall wade in him till he be old before he shall find sufficient cause to be honest. For his knowledge standeth so upon the abstract and general that happy is that man who may understand him, and more happy that can apply what he doth understand.

On the other side, the historian, wanting the precept, is so tied, not to what should be but to what is, to the particular truth of things and not to the general reason of things, that his example draweth no necessary consequence, and therefore a less fruitful doctrine.

Now doth the peerless poet perform both: for whatsoever the philosopher saith should be done, he giveth a perfect picture of it in someone by whom he presupposeth it was done, so as he coupleth the general notion with the particular example. A perfect picture I say, for he yieldeth to the powers of the mind an image of that whereof the philosopher bestoweth but a wordish description, which doth neither strike, pierce, nor possess the sight of the soul so much as that other doth. For as in outward things, to a man that had never seen an elephant or a rhinoceros, who should tell him most exquisitely all their shapes, color, bigness, and particular marks; or of a gorgeous palace, the architecture, with declaring the full beauties, might well make the hearer

6. Alphonsus V of Aragon (1396–1458) carried the Roman histories written by Livy and Caesar into battle with him. Brutus: Marcus Brutus (85–42 B.C.E.) was inspired to rise up against Caesar by the thought of his great republican ancestor, Junius Brutus, who expelled the Tarquin kings.

7. "The one" is philosophy, "the other," history.

8. Grade level.

9. Law (Latin).

1. "From fear of punishment" and "by love of virtue"; from Horace, *Epistles* 1.16.52–53.

able to repeat, as it were by rote, all he had heard, yet should never satisfy his inward conceits with being witness to itself of a true lively knowledge. But the same man, as soon as he might see those beasts well painted, or the house well in model, should straightways grow without need of any description, to a judicial[2] comprehending of them. So no doubt the philosopher, with his learned definition, be it of virtue, vices, matters of public policy or private government, replenisheth the memory with many infallible grounds of wisdom, which, notwithstanding, lie dark before the imaginative and judging power if they be not illuminated or figured forth by the speaking picture of poesy.

Tully[3] taketh much pains and many times not without poetical helps to make us know the force love of our country hath in us. Let us but hear old Anchises[4] speaking in the midst of Troy's flames, or see Ulysses[5] in the fulness of all Calypso's delights bewail his absence from barren and beggarly Ithaca. Anger, the Stoics say, was a short madness: let but Sophocles bring you Ajax on a stage, killing and whipping sheep and oxen, thinking them the army of Greeks with their chieftains Agamemnon and Menelaus,[6] and tell me if you have not a more familiar insight into anger than finding in the schoolmen his genus and difference. See whether wisdom and temperance in Ulysses and Diomedes, valor in Achilles, friendship in Nisus and Euryalus,[7] even to an ignorant man, carry not an apparent shining; and contrarily, the remorse of conscience in Oedipus, the soon repenting pride in Agamemnon, the self-devouring cruelty in his father Atreus,[8] the violence of ambition in the two Theban brothers, the sour-sweetness of revenge in Medea;[9] and to fall lower, the Terentian Gnatho and our Chaucer's Pandar,[1] so expressed that we now use their names to signify their trades; and finally, all virtues, vices, and passions so in their own natural seats laid to the view that we seem not to hear of them, but clearly to see through them.

But even in the most excellent determination of goodness, what philosopher's counsel can so readily direct a prince as the feigned Cyrus in Xenophon, or a virtuous man in all fortunes, as Aeneas in Virgil, or a whole commonwealth, as the way of Sir Thomas More's[2] *Utopia*? I say the way, because where Sir Thomas More erred, it was the fault of the man and not

2. Judicious.
3. Cicero (his full name is Marcus Tullius Cicero).
4. The father of Aeneas: he resists when Aeneas comes to carry him out of Troy as it is being sacked (Virgil, *Aeneid* 2.634–49).
5. Odysseus, king of Ithaca, who on his way home from Troy was held for years against his will by Calypso, a sea nymph on an island in the Ionian Sea. For his lamentation, see *Odyssey* 5.151–58.
6. In the tragedy *Ajax*, by Sophocles (ca. 496–406 B.C.E.), after Achilles' arms have been given to Odysseus, Ajax is driven mad by Athena and slays the Greek herds, believing them to be the Greeks who have scorned his claim to the armor.
7. All figures in Homer's *Iliad* and Virgil's *Aeneid*: Ulysses is regularly characterized by such epithets as "inventive" and "wise"; Diomedes, a great fighter, demonstrates his temperance when he exchanges armor with rather than fighting Glaucus, a Trojan ally whose grandfather had been a guest of his own grandfather (*Iliad* 6.119–236); Nisus and Eurylus, Trojans who accompanied Aeneas to Italy, are inseparable friends, and Nisus dies avenging Eurylus's death (*Aeneid* 9.176–445).
8. All figures often treated in Greek tragedy: Oedipus unknowingly kills his father and marries his mother; Agamemnon regrets too late the pride that persuaded him to enter his home by walking on purple silks fit for a god (see Aeschylus, *Agamemnon*, 458 B.C.E., lines 918–49); and Atreus serves his brother Thyestes the flesh of Thyestes' sons as punishment for committing adultery with Atreus's wife.
9. Medea's revenge on her husband Jason, who has deserted her to marry a king's daughter, is to murder his—and her own—children. "The two Theban brothers": Polynices and Eteocles, the two sons of Oedipus, who kill one another fighting over the rule of Thebes.
1. Pandarus, the type of the pander, from Chaucer's *Troilus and Criseyde* (ca. 1385). Gnatho: a boastful parasite whose name through the 17th century was synonymous with parasite or sycophant; from the Roman comedy *Eunuchus* by Terence (ca. 190-159 B.C.E.).
2. English writer, humanist, and statesman (1477–1535); his *Utopia* (1516) described an ideal society.

of the poet, for that way of patterning a commonwealth was most absolute, though he perchance hath not so absolutely performed it. For the question is, whether the feigned image of poesy or the regular instruction of philosophy hath the more force in teaching: wherein if the philosophers have more rightly showed themselves philosophers than the poets have obtained to the high top of their profession, as in truth,

Mediocribus esse poetis,
Non dii, non homines, non concessere columnae;[3]

it is, I say again, not the fault of the art, but that by few men that art can be accomplished.

Certainly, even our Saviour Christ could as well have given the moral commonplaces of uncharitableness and humbleness as the divine narration of Dives and Lazarus; or of disobedience and mercy, as that heavenly discourse of the lost child and the gracious father;[4] but that His through-searching wisdom knew the estate of Dives burning in hell, and of Lazarus being in Abraham's bosom, would more constantly (as it were) inhabit both the memory and judgment. Truly, for myself, me seems I see before my eyes the lost child's disdainful prodigality, turned to envy a swine's dinner: which by the learned divines are thought not historical acts, but instructing parables. For conclusion, I say the philosopher teacheth, but he teacheth obscurely, so as the learned only can understand him; that is to say, he teacheth them that are already taught. But the poet is the food for the tenderest stomachs, the poet is indeed the right popular philosopher, whereof Aesop's[5] tales give good proof; whose pretty allegories, stealing under the formal tales of beasts, make many more beastly than beasts begin to hear the sound of virtue from these dumb speakers.

But now may it be alleged that if this imagining of matters be so fit for the imagination, then must the historian needs surpass, who bringeth you images of true matters, such as indeed were done, and not such as fantastically or falsely may be suggested to have been done. Truly, Aristotle himself, in his discourse of poesy, plainly determineth this question, saying that poetry is *philosophoteron* and *spoudaioteron*, that is to say, it is more philosophical and more studiously serious than history.[6] His reason is, because poesy dealeth with *katholou*, that is to say, with the universal consideration, and the history with *kathekaston*, the particular: now, saith he, the universal weighs what is fit to be said or done, either in likelihood or necessity (which the poesy considereth in his imposed names), and the particular only marks whether Alcibiades[7] did or suffered this or that. Thus far Aristotle, which reason of his (as all his) is most full of reason.

For indeed, if the question were whether it were better to have a particular act truly or falsely set down, there is no doubt which is to be chosen, no more than whether you had rather have Vespasian's[8] picture right as he was,

3. But neither men nor gods nor shop-fronts allow a poet to be mediocre (Latin); Horace, *Ars Poetica*, lines 372–73).
4. References to two biblical parables, that of the beggar Lazarus and the rich man (*dives* in Latin means "rich"; Luke 16. 19–25) and that of the prodigal son (Luke 15.11–32).
5. The supposed author of a collection of Greek fables. Like parables from the Bible, allegorical tales teach by vivid exemplification rather than bald definition. Aesop's *Fables* were very popular during the Renaissance, both for their "delightful teaching" and as an introduction to Greek [Robinson's note].
6. See *Poetics* 9, 1450a36–1451b11.
7. Athenian general and politician (ca. 450–404 B.C.E.).
8. Roman emperor (9–79 C.E.; ruled 69–79).

or at the painter's pleasure, nothing resembling. But if the question be for your own use and learning, whether it be better to have it set down as it should be or as it was, then certainly is more doctrinable the feigned Cyrus in Xenophon than the true Cyrus in Justin,[9] and the feigned Aeneas in Virgil than the right Aeneas in Dares Phrygius.[1] As to a lady that desired to fashion her countenance to the best grace, a painter should more benefit her to portrait a most sweet face, writing Canidia[2] upon it, than to paint Canidia as she was, who Horace sweareth was foul and ill favored.

If the poet do his part aright, he will show you in Tantalus,[3] Atreus, and such like, nothing that is not to be shunned; in Cyrus, Aeneas, Ulysses, each thing to be followed; where the historian, bound to tell things as things were, cannot be liberal (without he will be poetical) of a perfect pattern, but as in Alexander or Scipio[4] himself, show doings, some to be liked, some to be misliked. And then how will you discern what to follow but by your own discretion, which you had without reading Quintus Curtius?[5] And whereas a man may say, though in universal consideration of doctrine the poet prevaileth, yet that the history, in his saying such a thing was done, doth warrant a man more in that he shall follow. The answer is manifest, that if he stand upon that was, as if he should argue, because it rained yesterday, therefore it should rain today, then indeed it hath some advantage to a gross conceit.[6] But if he know an example only informs a conjectured likelihood, and so go by reason, the poet doth so far exceed him, as he is to frame his example to that which is most reasonable, be it in warlike, politic, or private matters; where the historian in his bare way hath many times that which we call fortune to overrule the best wisdom. Many times he must tell events whereof he can yield no cause; or if he do, it must be poetical.

For that a feigned example hath as much force to teach as a true example (for as for to move, it is clear, sith the feigned may be tuned to the highest key of passion), let us take one example wherein a poet and a historian do concur. Herodotus and Justin do both testify that Zopyrus, King Darius'[7] faithful servant, seeing his master long resisted by the rebellious Babylonians, feigned himself in extreme disgrace of his king, for verifying of which he caused his own nose and ears to be cut off: and so flying to the Babylonians, was received, and for his known valor so far credited that he did find means to deliver them over to Darius. Much like matter doth Livy record of Tarquinius[8] and his son. Xenophon excellently feigneth such

9. Justinus, who made a summary (3d c. C.E.) of the Augustan *Philippic Histories*; it was widely read in the Middle Ages.
1. A priest of Hephaestus at Troy (*Iliad* 5.9–10), supposed author of a pre-Homeric account of the Trojan War whose Latin prose "translation" was drawn on by medieval authors.
2. A sorceress whom Horace describes in *Epode* 7 as murdering a boy to make love charms (*Epode* 17 is a mock recantation, pretending fear of her powers).
3. Legendary king (grandfather of Atreus) who tested the gods by cooking and serving them his dismembered son Pelops; he suffers eternal hunger and thirst, standing in a pool and surrounded by fruit that remains always out of reach.
4. Roman general (ca. 236–184/3 B.C.E.), who defeated Hannibal and the Carthaginians. Alexander: Alexander the Great (356–323 B.C.E.), Macedonian king whose conquests reached to India and who was probably the greatest general of antiquity.
5. Quintus Curtius Rufus (active ca. mid–1st c. C.E.), rhetorician and historian who wrote a 10-book history of Alexander, portraying him as a fortunate tyrant.
6. Large-scale poetical image.
7. Persian king (ca. 550–486 B.C.E.) who had to quell numerous revolts during his reign; the most important was in Babylonia. Zopyrus: a Persian who ended the 20-month siege of Babylon by the trick Sidney describes.
8. Lucius Tarquinius Superbus, the last king of Rome (by tradition, reigned 534–510 B.C.E.), whose son, Lucius Tarquinius Priscus, pretended to desert to the enemy and then acted to his father's advantage. Livy (59 B.C.E.–17 C.E.), Roman historian.

another stratagem performed by Abradatas[9] in Cyrus' behalf. Now would I fain[1] know, if occasion be presented unto you to serve your prince by such an honest dissimulation, why you do not as well learn it of Xenophon's fiction as of the other's verity? And truly so much the better, as you shall save your nose by the bargain, for Abradatas did not counterfeit so far. So then the best of the historian is subject to the poet; for whatsoever action or faction, whatsoever counsel, policy, or war stratagem the historian is bound to recite, that may the poet (if he list[2]) with his imitation make his own, beautifying it both for further teaching and more delighting, as it pleaseth him: having all, from Dante his heaven to his hell, under the authority of his pen. Which if I be asked what poets have done so, as I might well name some, yet say I, and say again, I speak of the art and not of the artificer.

Now, to that which commonly is attributed to the praise of histories, in respect of the notable learning is gotten by marking the success, as though therein a man should see virtue exalted and vice punished; truly that commendation is peculiar to poetry, and far off from history. For indeed poetry ever setteth virtue so out in her best colors, making fortune her well-waiting handmaid, that one must needs be enamored of her. Well may you see Ulysses in a storm and in other hard plights, but they are but exercises of patience and magnanimity, to make them shine the more in the near-following prosperity. And of the contrary part, if evil men come to the stage, they ever go out (as the tragedy writer[3] answered to one that misliked the show of such persons) so manacled as they little animate folks to follow them. But the historian, being captived to the truth of a foolish world, is many times a terror from well doing, and an encouragement to unbridled wickedness. For see we not valiant Miltiades rot in his fetters; the just Phocion and the accomplished Socrates put to death like traitors; the cruel Severus live prosperously; the excellent Severus miserably murdered; Sylla and Marius dying in their beds; Pompey and Cicero[4] slain then, when they would have thought exile a happiness? See we not virtuous Cato driven to kill himself, and rebel Caesar[5] so advanced that his name yet after 1600 years lasteth in the highest honor? And mark but even Caesar's own words of the fore-named Sylla (who in that only did honestly, to put down his dishonest tyranny), *literas nescivit*,[6] as if want of learning caused him to do well. He meant it not by poetry,

9. A king of Susa (6th c. B.C.E.) and ally of the Assyrians against Cyrus who later joined Cyrus, according to Xenophon's *Cyropaedia*.
1. Willingly, gladly.
2. Wishes.
3. The Greek tragedian Euripides (ca. 483–ca. 406 B.C.E.), according to the *Moralia* of Plutarch (ca. 50–ca. 120 C.E.).
4. Killed at Antony's command as he was trying to escape from Rome (his orations defending the Republic and against Antony after Caesar's death had earned him a place on the list of proscribed enemies). Miltiades (ca. 550–489 B.C.E.), Athenian general and victor at Marathon later imprisoned by the Athenians. Phocian (4th c. B.C.E.), Athenian general and statesman unjustly executed for treason because he had opposed the will of the people. Socrates (469–399 B.C.E.), Greek philosopher immortalized in the writings of his pupil Plato and condemned to death on charges of impiety and corrupting youth. "Cruel Severus": Lucius Septimus Severus (145/6–211 C.E.), emperor of Rome (193–211), who is perhaps called cruel because he spent much of his time putting down rebellions and dealing with rivals. "Excellent Severus": Alexander Severus (208/9–235 C.E.), emperor of Rome (222–35), a peaceful and religious man slain by his troops. Sylla and Marius: Lucius Cornelius Sulla (ca. 138–78 B.C.E.) and Gaius Marius (157–86 B.C.E.), Roman generals whose struggle for military and political supremacy led to civil war (88–82 B.C.E.). Pompey: Pompey the Great (106–48 B.C.E.), Roman soldier and statesman defeated at Pharsalia by his former ally, Caesar, and murdered in Egypt.
5. Julius Caesar's rebellion against the Senate in 49 B.C.E. led to civil war and the end of the Roman Republic. Cato: Cato the Younger (95–46 B.C.E.), a defender of the Republic who committed suicide after Caesar's decisive victory at Thapsus.
6. He was ignorant of letters (Latin).

which not content with earthly plagues, deviseth new punishments in hell for tyrants, nor yet by philosophy, which teacheth *occidendos esse*;[7] but no doubt by skill in history, for that indeed can afford you Cypselus, Periander, Phalaris, Dionysius,[8] and I know not how many more of the same kennel, that speed well enough in their abominable unjustice or usurpation. I conclude therefore, that he excelleth history, not only in furnishing the mind with knowledge, but in setting it forward to that which deserveth to be called and accounted good: which setting forward and moving to well doing indeed setteth the laurel crown[9] upon the poet as victorious, not only of the historian, but over the philosopher, howsoever in teaching it may be questionable.

For suppose it be granted (that which I suppose with great reason may be denied) that the philosopher, in respect of his methodical proceeding, doth teach more perfectly than the poet: yet do I think that no man is so much *philophilosophos*[1] as to compare the philosopher in moving with the poet. And that moving is of a higher degree than teaching, it may by this appear: that it is well nigh the cause and the effect of teaching. For who will be taught if he be not moved with desire to be taught; and what so much good doth that teaching bring forth (I speak still of moral doctrine) as that it moveth one to do that which it doth teach? For as Aristotle saith, it is not *gnosis* but *praxis*[2] must be the fruit. And how *praxis* can be, without being moved to practice, is no hard matter to consider.

The philosopher showeth you the way, he informeth you of the particularities, as well of the tediousness of the way, as of the pleasant lodging you shall have when your journey is ended, as of the many by-turnings that may divert you from your way. But this is to no man but to him that will read him, and read him with attentive studious painfulness; which constant desire, whosoever hath in him, hath already passed half the hardness of the way, and therefore is beholding[3] to the philosopher but for the other half. Nay truly, learned men have learnedly thought that where once reason hath so much overmastered passion as that the mind hath a free desire to do well, the inward light each mind hath in itself is as good as a philosopher's book; seeing in nature we know it is well to do well, and what is well and what is evil, although not in the words of art which philosophers bestow upon us; for out of natural conceit[4] the philosophers drew it. But to be moved to do that which we know, or to be moved with desire to know, *hoc opus, hic labor est.*[5]

Now therein of all sciences (I speak still of human, and according to the human conceits) is our poet the monarch. For he doth not only show the way, but giveth so sweet a prospect into the way, as will entice any man to enter into it. Nay, he doth as if your journey should lie through a fair vineyard, at the first give you a cluster of grapes, that full of that taste, you may long to pass further. He beginneth not with obscure definitions which must

7. That they must be killed (Latin).
8. All Greek "tyrants" (that is, rulers): Cypselus, in Corinth, ca. 657–625 B.C.E.; Periander, son of Cypselos, in Corinth, 625–585 B.C.E.; Phalaris, whose rule in Acragas (Sicily), ca. 570–ca. 544 B.C.E, was notoriously cruel; and Dionysius, in Syracuse, 405–367 B.C.E.
9. Like the crowns (of various greens, including laurel) awarded to victors in the Greek athletic contests; laurel, because of its association with Apollo, is linked to poetry.
1. A lover of philosophers (Greek).
2. Action (Greek). *Gnosis*: knowledge (Greek). See *Nicomachean Ethics* 1.3, 1095a.
3. Beholden.
4. The distinction here is between concepts in their natural form, seen in the mind, and concepts artificially set forth in words [Robinson's note].
5. This is the work, this is the labor (Latin); Virgil, *Aeneid* 6.129.

blur the margent with interpretations and load the memory with doubtfulness, but he cometh to you with words set in delightful proportion, either accompanied with, or prepared for, the well enchanting skill of music; and with a tale forsooth he cometh unto you, with a tale which holdeth children from play and old men from the chimney corner. And pretending no more, doth intend the winning of the mind from wickedness to virtue, even as the child is often brought to take most wholesome things by hiding them in such other as have a pleasant taste: which, if one should begin to tell them the nature of aloes or rhubarb[6] they should receive, would sooner take their physic at their ears than at their mouth. So is it in men (most of which are childish in the best things till they be cradled in their graves), glad they will be to hear the tales of Hercules,[7] Achilles, Cyrus, and Aeneas; and hearing them, must needs hear the right description of wisdom, valor, and justice; which, if they had been barely, that is to say, philosophically set out, they would swear they be brought to school again.

That imitation whereof poetry is, hath the most conveniency to nature of all other, insomuch that, as Aristotle saith, those things which in themselves are horrible, as cruel battles, unnatural monsters, are made in poetical imitation delightful.[8] Truly, I have known men that, even with reading *Amadis de Gaule*[9] (which God knoweth wanteth much of a perfect poesy), have found their hearts moved to the exercise of courtesy, liberality, and especially courage. Who readeth Aeneas carrying old Anchises on his back that wisheth not it were his fortune to perform so excellent an act? Whom do not the words of Turnus move (the tale of Turnus having planted his image in the imagination)?

Fugientem haec terra videbit,
Usque adeone mori miserum est?[1]

Where the philosophers, as they scorn to delight, so must they be content little to move, saving wrangling whether virtue be the chief or the only good, whether the contemplative or the active life do excel: which Plato and Boethius[2] well knew, and therefore made mistress philosophy very often borrow the masking raiment of poesy. For even those hard-hearted evil men who think virtue a school name, and know no other good but *indulgere genio,*[3] and therefore despise the austere admonitions of the philosopher, and feel not the inward reason they stand upon, yet will be content to be delighted, which is all the good fellow poet seemeth to promise, and so steal to see the form of goodness (which seen they cannot but love) ere themselves be aware, as if they took a medicine of cherries.

Infinite proofs of the strange effects of this poetical invention might be alleged; only two shall serve, which are so often remembered as I think all men know them. The one of Menenius Agrippa,[4] who, when the whole peo-

6. Two bitter purgatives.
7. The Roman spelling of Heracles, greatest of the legendary Greek heroes.
8. See *Poetics* 4, 1448b. "Conveniency to": accordance with.
9. A Spanish prose romance (first published 1508, but the story dates at least to the 14th c.).
1. Will this land see Turnus fleeing? Is it so terrible to die? (Latin); Virgil, *Aeneid* 12.645–46. Turnus: legendary king in Italy who made war against the newly arrived Trojans and was defeated by Aeneas in single combat.
2. Neoplatonic Roman philosopher (ca. 480–524), author of *The Consolation of Philosophy.*
3. To indulge one's appetite (Latin); slightly misquoted from *Satire* 5.151 by the Roman poet Persius (34–62 C.E.).
4. Plebeian consul who reputedly used a fable from Aesop (retold by Sidney) in 494 B.C.E. to convince the plebes of the futility of secession.

ple of Rome had resolutely divided themselves from the Senate, with apparent show of utter ruin, though he were (for that time) an excellent orator, came not among them upon trust of figurative speeches or cunning insinuations, and much less with far fet[5] maxims of philosophy, which (especially if they were Platonic) they must have learned geometry before they could well have conceived; but forsooth he behaves himself like a homely[6] and familiar poet. He telleth them a tale, that there was a time when all the parts of the body made a mutinous conspiracy against the belly, which they thought devoured the fruits of each other's labor: they concluded they would let so unprofitable a spender starve. In the end, to be short (for the tale is notorious, and as notorious that it was a tale), with punishing the belly they plagued themselves. This applied by him wrought such effect in the people, as I never read that ever words brought forth but then so sudden and so good an alteration; for upon reasonable conditions a perfect reconcilement ensued. The other is of Nathan the prophet,[7] who when the holy David had so far forsaken God as to confirm adultery with murder, when he was to do the tenderest office of a friend, in laying his own shame before his eyes, sent by God to call again so chosen a servant, how doth he it but by telling of a man whose beloved lamb was ungratefully taken from his bosom?—the application most divinely true, but the discourse itself feigned; which made David (I speak of the second and instrumental cause[8]), as in a glass, to see his own filthiness, as that heavenly psalm of mercy[9] well testifieth.

By these therefore examples and reasons I think it may be manifest that the poet, with that same hand of delight, doth draw the mind more effectually than any other art doth. And so a conclusion not unfitly ensueth, that as virtue is the most excellent resting place for all worldly learning to make his end of, so poetry, being the most familiar to teach it, and most princely to move towards it, in the most excellent work is the most excellent workman.

But I am content not only to decipher him by his works (although works in commendation or dispraise must ever hold an high authority), but more narrowly will examine his parts, so that (as in a man), though all together may carry a presence full of majesty and beauty, perchance in some one defectious[1] piece we may find a blemish. Now in his parts, kinds, or species (as you list to term them), it is to be noted that some poesies have coupled together two or three kinds, as tragical and comical, whereupon is risen the tragi-comical. Some, in the like manner, have mingled prose and verse, as Sannazzaro[2] and Boethius. Some have mingled matters heroical and pastoral. But that cometh all to one in this question, for if severed they be good, the conjunction cannot be hurtful. Therefore, perchance forgetting some, and leaving some as needless to be remembered, it shall not be amiss in a word to cite the special kinds, to see what faults may be found in the right use of them.

Is it then the pastoral poem which is misliked (for perchance where the hedge is lowest they will soonest leap over)?[3] Is the poor pipe disdained which

5. Fetched.
6. Unsophisticated.
7. Told in 2 Samuel 12; after committing adultery with Bathsheba, King David contrived to have her husband, Uriah, killed in battle.
8. The second cause is the parable itself, while the first cause is David's acceptance of God's will [Robinson's note].
9. Psalm 51, in which David prays for the remission of his sins [Robinson's note]. Glass: mirror.
1. Defective.
2. Jacopo Sannazaro (1458–1530), whose pastoral romance *Arcadia* (1502) influenced Sidney's own *Arcadia*.
3. Like most Renaissance poets, Sidney thinks of the pastoral as the humblest of the poetic genres, designed for low subjects and to be executed in an equally low style [Robinson's note].

sometime out of Meliboeus' mouth can show the misery of people under hard lords or ravening soldiers? And again, by Tityrus,[4] what blessedness is derived to them that lie lowest from the goodness of them that sit highest? sometimes, under the pretty tales of wolves and sheep, can include the whole considerations of wrong doing and patience; sometimes show that contention for trifles can get but a trifling victory; where perchance a man may see that even Alexander and Darius,[5] when they strave who should be cock of this world's dunghill, the benefit they got was that the after-livers may say,

Haec memini et victum frustra contendere Thirsin:
Ex illo Corydon, Corydon est tempore nobis.[6]

Or is it the lamenting elegiac?[7] which in a kind heart would move rather pity than blame, who bewails with the great philosopher Heraclitus[8] the weakness of mankind and the wretchedness of the world; who surely is to be praised, either for compassionate accompanying just causes of lamentation, or for rightly painting out how weak be the passions of woefulness. Is it the bitter but wholesome iambic?[9] which rubs the galled mind in making shame the trumpet of villainy with bold and open crying out against naughtiness. Or the satiric? who

Omne vafer vitium, ridenti tangit amico,[1]

who sportingly never leaveth until he make a man laugh at folly, and at length ashamed to laugh at himself, which he cannot avoid, without avoiding the folly; who, while

Circum praecordia ludit,[2]

giveth us to feel how many head-aches a passionate life bringeth us to; how, when all is done,

Est Ulubris, animus si nos non deficit aequus[3]

No, perchance it is the comic, whom naughty play-makers and stage-keepers have justly made odious. To the argument of abuse I will answer after. Only thus much now is to be said, that the comedy is an imitation of the common errors of our life, which he representeth in the most ridiculous and scornful sort that may be, so as it is impossible that any beholder can be content to be such a one.

Now, as in geometry the oblique must be known as well as the right, and in arithmetic the odd as well as the even, so in the actions of our life who

4. A speaker in Virgil's *Eclogue* 1, as is Meliboeus; Meliboeus laments the seizure of his land, confiscated for the use of resettled ex-soldiers, while Tityrus rejoices that his lands were protected by a patron in Rome.

5. The invading Alexander twice defeated Darius, the king of Persia, before Darius was deposed and finally murdered in 330 B.C.E. by his own soldiers.

6. These things I remember, that the conquered Thyrsis contended in vain./From this time Corydon, Corydon is ours (Latin); Virgil, *Eclogues* 7.69–70. The victory of Alexander the Great over Darius of Persia comes to the same thing as Corydon's victory over Thyrsis in a singing contest.

7. In classical poetry, a poem in a specific metrical form; in English poetry, any serious poem on love or death.

8. Greek pre-Socratic (active ca. 500 B.C.E.), known as "the weeping philosopher" because of his gloomy views; Heraclitus emphasized that all things are in flux.

9. Metrical form that Aristotle associates with lampoons (*Poetics* 4, 1448b).

1. The rascal probes his friend's every fault while making him laugh (Latin); slightly misquoted from Persius, *Satire* 1.116–17, who is describing the satires of Horace.

2. He plays with his [friend's] heart (Latin); Persius 1.117.

3. Even in Ulubrae, if our equanimity doesn't fail us [what we seek (i.e., to live well) is here] (Latin); slightly adapted from Horace, *Epistles* 1.11.30. Ulubrae was an uninspiring town surrounded by marshes.

seeth not the filthiness of evil wanteth a great foil to perceive the beauty of virtue. This doth the comedy handle so in our private and domestical matters, as with hearing it we get as it were an experience what is to be looked for of a niggardly Demea, of a crafty Davus, of a flattering Gnatho, of a vainglorious Thraso;[4] and not only to know what effects are to be expected, but to know who be such by the signifying badge[5] given them by the comedian. And little reason hath any man to say that men learn evil by seeing it so set out, sith, as I said before, there is no man living but, by the force truth hath in nature, no sooner seeth these men play their parts, but wisheth them *in pistrinum;*[6] although perchance the sack of his own faults lie so behind his back that he seeth not himself dance the same measure; whereto yet nothing can more open his eyes than to find his own actions contemptibly set forth. So that the right use of comedy will (I think) by nobody be blamed, and much less of the high and excellent tragedy, that openeth the greatest wounds and showeth forth the ulcers that are covered with tissue; that maketh kings fear to be tyrants, and tyrants manifest their tyrannical humors; that with stirring the affects of admiration and commiseration teacheth the uncertainty of this world, and upon how weak foundations gilden roofs are builded; that maketh us know,

Qui sceptra saevus duro imperio regit,
Timet timentes, metus in auctorem redit.[7]

But how much it can move, Plutarch yieldeth a notable testimony of the abominable tyrant Alexander Pheraeus,[8] from whose eyes a tragedy well made and represented drew abundance of tears; who without all pity had murdered infinite numbers, and some of his own blood, so as he that was not ashamed to make matters for tragedies, yet could not resist the sweet violence of a tragedy. And if it wrought no further good in him, it was that he, in despite of himself, withdrew himself from hearkening to that which might mollify his hardened heart. But it is not the tragedy they do mislike; for it were too absurd to cast out so excellent a representation of whatsoever is most worthy to be learned.

Is it the lyric[9] that most displeaseth? who with his tuned lyre and well accorded voice giveth praise, the reward of virtue, to virtuous acts; who gives moral precepts and natural problems;[1] who sometimes raiseth up his voice to the height of the heavens in singing the lauds of the immortal God. Certainly, I must confess my own barbarousness, I never heard the old song of Percy and Douglas[2] that I found not my heart moved more than with a trumpet; and yet is it sung but by some blind crowder[3] with no rougher voice

4. Type characters in Terence: respectively, the overbearing father, clever servant, parasite, and braggart. Terence was the chief classical model for comedy during the Renaissance.
5. A character's "signifying badge" was his name, dress, manner, and other characteristics [Robinson's note].
6. To the mill (Latin); mills were worked usually by draft animals, but sometimes by Roman slaves being punished.
7. He who wields the scepter with harsh authority/Fears those who fear him; the fear returns to its author (Latin); slightly misquoted from *Oedipus*, lines 705–6, by the philosopher and playwright Seneca the Younger (ca. 4 B.C.E.–65 C.E.).
8. Ruler of Pherae, 369–358 B.C.E.; in his *Life of Pelopidas*, Plutarch (ca. 50–ca. 120 C.E.) records that Alexander, whose savagery he details, wept at the sufferings of Hecuba and Andromache in the Greek playwright Euripides' *Troades* (415 B.C.E.).
9. That is, a song accompanied by a musical instrument, usually the lyre.
1. "Problems" were questions posed for discussion [Robinson's note].
2. Antagonists in *The Battle of Chevy Chase*, a 15th-century poem commemorating the 1388 Battle of Otteburn.
3. Player of a crowd, an ancient Welsh stringed instrument; a fiddler.

than rude style; which, being so evil apparelled in the dust and cobwebs of that uncivil age, what would it work, trimmed in the gorgeous eloquence of Pindar?[4] In Hungary I have seen it the manner at all feasts, and other such meetings, to have songs of their ancestors' valor, which that right soldier-like nation think the chiefest kindlers of brave courage. The incomparable Lacedemonians[5] did not only carry that kind of music ever with them to the field, but even at home, as such songs were made, so were they all content to be the singers of them; when the lusty men were to tell what they did, the old men what they had done, and the young men what they would do. And where a man may say that Pindar many times praiseth highly victories of small moment, matters rather of sport than virtue; as it may be answered, it was the fault of the poet, and not of the poetry, so indeed the chief fault was in the time and custom of the Greeks, who set those toys at so high a price that Philip of Macedon reckoned a horse-race won at Olympus among his three fearful felicities.[6] But as the unimitable Pindar often did, so is that kind most capable and most fit to awake the thoughts from the sleep of idleness to embrace honorable enterprises.

There rests the heroical, whose very name (I think) should daunt all back-biters; for by what conceit can a tongue be directed to speak evil of that which draweth with it no less champions than Achilles, Cyrus, Aeneas, Turnus, Tydeus, and Rinaldo?[7] who doth not only teach and move to a truth, but teacheth and moveth to the most high and excellent truth; who maketh magnanimity and justice shine throughout all misty fearfulness and foggy desires; who, if the saying of Plato and Tully be true, that who could see virtue would be wonderfully ravished with the love of her beauty, this man sets out to make her more lovely in her holiday apparel, to the eye of any that will deign not to disdain until they understand. But if anything be already said in the defence of sweet poetry, all concurreth to the maintaining the heroical, which is not only a kind, but the best and most accomplished kind of poetry. For as the image of each action stirreth and instructeth the mind, so the lofty image of such worthies most inflameth the mind with desire to be worthy, and informs with counsel how to be worthy. Only let Aeneas be worn in the tablet of your memory, how he governeth himself in the ruin of his country; in the preserving his old father and carrying away his religious ceremonies;[8] in obeying the god's commandment to leave Dido,[9] though not only all passionate kindness, but even the human consideration of virtuous gratefulness, would have craved other of him; how in storms, how in sports, how in war, how in peace, how a fugitive, how victorious, how besieged, how besieging, how to strangers, how to allies, how to enemies, how to his own; lastly, how in his inward self, and how in his outward gov-

4. Greek lyric poet (ca. 518–438 B.C.E.), known for his elaborate odes honoring victors in athletic contests. "Uncivil age": the Middle Ages.

5. Spartans.

6. According to Plutarch (*Life of Alexander* 3), Philip of Macedon received news of a victory in battle, a winner at the race track in Olympia, and the birth of Alexander, all on the same day [Robinson's note].

7. A hero in Ariosto's *Orlando Furioso* and Torquato Tasso's *Gerusalemme Liberata* (1581). Tydeus: one of the "seven against Thebes," mythical heroes who aided Polynices' attempt to wrest rule of Thebes from his brother Eteocles, featured in the epic *Thebais* by Statius (ca. 46–96 C.E.).

8. Virgil, *Aeneid* 2.705–20. "Ceremonies": religious objects (here, the household gods).

9. The queen of Carthage, whom Jupiter orders Aeneas to leave so that he may fulfill his destiny in Italy. As he departs, she commits suicide. See *Aeneid* 4.

ernment. And, I think, in a mind not prejudiced with a prejudicating humor, he will be found in excellency fruitful; yea, even as Horace saith,

melius Chrysippo et Crantore.[1]

But truly I imagine it falleth out with these poet-whippers, as with some good women, who often are sick, but in faith they cannot tell where. So the name of poetry is odious to them, but neither his cause nor effects, neither the sum that contains him nor the particularities descending from him, give any fast handle to their carping dispraise.

Sith then poetry is of all human learning the most ancient and of most fatherly antiquity, as from whence other learnings have taken their beginnings; sith it is so universal that no learned nation doth despise it, nor no barbarous nation is without it; sith both Roman and Greek gave divine names unto it, the one of prophesying, the other of making, and that indeed, that name of making is fit for him, considering that whereas other arts retain themselves within their subject and receive, as it were, their being from it, the poet only bringeth his own stuff, and doth not learn a conceit out of a matter, but maketh matter for a conceit; sith neither his description nor his end containeth any evil, the thing described cannot be evil; sith his effects be so good as to teach goodness and to delight the learners; sith therein (namely in moral doctrine, the chief of all knowledges) he doth not only far pass the historian, but for instructing is well nigh comparable to the philosopher, and for moving, leaves him behind him; sith the Holy Scripture (wherein there is no uncleanness) hath whole parts in it poetical, and that even our Saviour Christ vouchsafed to use the flowers of it; sith all his kinds are not only in their united forms, but in their severed dissections, fully commendable; I think (and think I think rightly) the laurel crown appointed for triumphing captains doth worthily (of all other learnings) honor the poet's triumph.[2]

But because we have ears as well as tongues, and that the lightest reasons that may be will seem to weigh greatly if nothing be put in the counterbalance, let us hear, and, as well as we can, ponder, what objections may be made against this art, which may be worthy either of yielding or answering.

First, truly, I note not only in these *mysomousoi*, poet-haters, but in all that kind of people who seek a praise by dispraising others, that they do prodigally spend a great many wandering words in quips and scoffs, carping and taunting at each thing which, by stirring the spleen[3] may stay the brain from a thorough beholding the worthiness of the subject. Those kind of objections, as they are full of very idle easiness, sith there is nothing of so sacred a majesty but that an itching tongue may rub itself upon it, so deserve they no other answer, but instead of laughing at the jest, to laugh at the jester. We know a playing wit can praise the discretion of an ass, the comfortableness of being in debt, and the jolly commodity of being sick of the plague. So of the contrary side, if we will turn Ovid's verse,

1. A better [teacher] than Chrysippus and Crantor (Latin); Horace, *Epistles* 1.2.4, referring to Homer. Chrysippus (ca. 280–207 B.C.E.), Stoic philosopher. Crantor (ca. 335–ca. 275 B.C.E.), philosopher and commentator on Plato.
2. Sidney is perhaps thinking of the crowning of Petrarch as poet laureate at Rome in 1341. In ancient Rome the laurel crown was generally reserved for victorious generals [Robinson's note].
3. Thought in the Renaissance to be the source of melancholy and ill temper.

Ut lateat virtus proximitate mali,[4]

that good lie hid in nearness of the evil, Agrippa will be as merry in showing the vanity of science as Erasmus[5] was in commending of folly. Neither shall any man or matter escape some touch of these smiling railers. But for Erasmus and Agrippa, they had another foundation than the superficial part would promise. Marry, these other pleasant fault-finders, who will correct the verb before they understand the noun, and confute others' knowledge before they confirm their own, I would have them only remember that scoffing cometh not of wisdom. So as the best title in true English they get with their merriments is to be called good fools, for so have our grave forefathers ever termed that humorous kind of jesters.

But that which giveth greatest scope to their scorning humors is rhyming and versing. It is already said (and, as I think, truly said), it is not rhyming and versing that maketh poesy. One may be a poet without versing, and a versifier without poetry. But yet presuppose it were inseparable (as indeed it seemeth Scaliger[6] judgeth), truly it were an inseparable commendation. For if *oratio* next to *ratio*, speech next to reason, be the greatest gift bestowed upon mortality, that cannot be praiseless which doth most polish that blessing of speech, which considers each word not only (as a man may say) by his forcible quality, but by his best measured quantity,[7] carrying even in themselves a harmony (without (perchance) number, measure, order, proportion be in our time grown odious). But lay aside the just praise it hath, by being the only fit speech for music (music, I say, the most divine striker of the senses), thus much is undoubtedly true, that if reading be foolish without remembering, memory being the only treasurer of knowledge, those words which are fittest for memory are likewise most convenient for knowledge.

Now, that verse far exceedeth prose in the knitting up of the memory, the reason is manifest. The words (besides their delight, which hath a great affinity to memory) being so set as one word cannot be lost but the whole work fails; which accuseth itself, calleth the remembrance back to itself, and so most strongly confirmeth it. Besides, one word so, as it were, begetting another, as be it in rhyme or measured verse, by the former a man shall have a near guess to the follower. Lastly, even they that have taught the art of memory have showed nothing so apt for it as a certain room divided into many places, well and thoroughly known. Now that hath the verse in effect perfectly, every word having his natural seat, which seat must needs make the words remembered. But what needeth more in a thing so known to all men? Who is it that ever was a scholar that doth not carry away some verses

4. Adapted from the *Ars Amatoria (Art of Love)* 2.662 of the Roman poet Ovid (43 B.C.E.–17 C.E.); Sidney's translation follows.
5. Desiderius Erasmus (1466–1536), Dutch humanist scholar, author of *The Praise of Folly* (1509). Agrippa: Heinrich Cornelius Agrippa von Nettesheim (1486–1535), German doctor and occult philosopher; in *On the Uncertainty and Vanity of Arts and Sciences* (ca. 1530), he attacked the idea that knowledge is based in human reason.
6. Julius Caesar Scaliger (1484–1558), Italian-born French classical scholar; in his *Poetics* (1561), he claimed that the poet's product was verses (and not, with Aristotle, the imitation of human action).
7. In classical poetry the basic rhythmic unit is quantitative, based on the time required to pronounce a syllable. English poetry, on the other hand, derives its rhythm from the accent (long or short, stressed or unstressed) given to a syllable. For a short period during the Renaissance, however, there was a controversial and ultimately unsuccessful attempt (centering around Sidney and his associates) to compose English poetry in quantitative meters [Robinson's note].

of Virgil, Horace, or Cato, which in his youth he learned, and even to his old age serve him for hourly lessons? as

Percontatorem fugito, nam garrulus idem est.[8]

Dum sibi quisque placet, credula turba sumus.[9]

But the fitness it hath for memory is notably proved by all delivery of arts: wherein for the most part, from grammar to logic, mathematic, physic, and the rest, the rules chiefly necessary to be borne away are compiled in verses. So that verse, being in itself sweet and orderly, and being best for memory, the only handle of knowledge, it must be in jest that any man can speak against it.

Now then go we to the most important imputations laid to the poor poets. For aught I can *yet* learn, they are these. First, that there being many other more fruitful knowledges, a man might better spend his time in them than in this. Secondly, that it is the mother of lies. Thirdly, that it is the nurse of abuse, infecting us with many pestilent desires, with a siren's sweetness drawing the mind to the serpent's tail of sinful fancy. And herein especially comedies give the largest field to ear,[1] as Chaucer saith; how both in other nations and in ours, before poets did soften us, we were full of courage, given to martial exercises, the pillars of manlike liberty, and not lulled asleep in shady idleness with poets' pastimes. And lastly, and chiefly, they cry out with an open mouth, as if they had outshot Robin Hood, that Plato banished them out of his commonwealth.[2] Truly, this is much, if there be much truth in it.

First, to the first, that a man might better spend his time is a reason indeed; but it doth (as they say) but *petere principium:*[3] for if it be, as I affirm, that no learning is so good as that which teacheth and moveth to virtue, and that none can both teach and move thereto so much as poetry, then is the conclusion manifest that ink and paper cannot be to a more profitable purpose employed. And certainly, though a man should grant their first assumption, it should follow (methinks) very unwillingly, that good is not good because better is better. But I still and utterly deny that there is sprung out of earth a more fruitful knowledge.

To the second therefore, that they should be the principal liars, I answer paradoxically, but truly, I think truly, that of all writers under the sun the poet is the least liar, and, though he would, as a poet can scarcely be a liar. The astronomer, with his cousin the geometrician, can hardly escape, when they take upon them to measure the height of the stars. How often, think you, do the physicians lie when they aver things good for sickness, which afterwards send Charon[4] a great number of souls drowned in a potion before they come to his ferry? And no less of the rest, which take upon them to affirm. Now for the poet, he nothing affirms, and therefore never lieth. For, as I take it, to lie is to affirm that to be true which is false; so as the other artists,[5] and especially the historian, affirming many things, can, in the

8. Flee the inquirer, for he is talkative (Latin); Horace, *Epistles* 1.18.69.
9. While each pleases himself, we are a credulous crowd (Latin); Ovid, *Remedia Amoris* (*Remedy of Love*), 686.
1. To plow; Chaucer uses the phrase "a large feeld to ere" in *The Knight's Tale*, line 28.
2. See *Republic* 3.398a–b, 10.595a–608b (above).
3. Beg the question (Latin); that is, assume the truth of what is to be proved.
4. In classical mythology, the ferryman who takes the souls of the dead over the river Styx.
5. Practitioners of all the liberal arts, which include history and philosophy as well as poetry, painting, and sculpture.

cloudy knowledge of mankind, hardly escape from many lies. But the poet (as I said before) never affirmeth. The poet never maketh any circles about your imagination to conjure you to believe for true what he writes. He citeth not authorities of other histories, but even for his entry calleth the sweet Muses to inspire into him a good invention; in troth, not laboring to tell you what is or is not, but what should or should not be. And therefore, though he recount things not true, yet because he telleth them not for true, he lieth not, without we will say that Nathan lied in his speech before alleged to David; which, as a wicked man durst scarce say, so think I none so simple would say that Aesop lied in the tales of his beasts; for who thinks that Aesop writ it for actually true were well worthy to have his name chronicled among the beasts he writeth of. What child is there that, coming to a play, and seeing Thebes written in great letters upon an old door, doth believe that it is Thebes? If then a man can arrive at that child's age to know that the poet's persons and doings are but pictures what should be, and not stories what have been, they will never give the lie to things not affirmatively but allegorically and figuratively written. And therefore, as in history looking for truth, they go away full fraught with falsehood, so in poesy looking for fiction, they shall use the narration but as an imaginative ground-plot of a profitable invention.[6]

But hereto is replied that the poets give names to men they write of, which argueth a conceit of an actual truth, and so, not being true, proves a falsehood. And doth the lawyer lie then, when under the names of John a Stile and John a Noakes[7] he puts his case? But that is easily answered. Their naming of men is but to make their picture the more lively, and not to build any history: painting men, they cannot leave men nameless. We see we cannot play at chess but that we must give names to our chessmen; and yet, methinks, he were a very partial champion of truth that would say we lied for giving a piece of wood the reverend title of a Bishop. The poet nameth Cyrus or Aeneas no other way than to show what men of their fames, fortunes, and estates should do.

Their third is, how much it abuseth men's wit, training it to wanton sinfulness and lustful love: for indeed that is the principal, if not the only, abuse I can hear alleged. They say the comedies rather teach than reprehend amorous conceits. They say the lyric is larded with passionate sonnets, the elegiac weeps the want of his mistress, and that even to the heroical Cupid hath ambitiously climbed.[8] Alas, Love, I would thou couldst as well defend thyself as thou canst offend others. I would those on whom thou dost attend could either put thee away, or yield good reason why they keep thee. But grant love of beauty to be a beastly fault (although it be very hard, sith only man, and no beast, hath that gift to discern beauty); grant that lovely name of love to deserve all hateful reproaches (although even some of my masters the philosophers spent a good deal of their lamp-oil in setting forth the excellency of it); grant, I say, whatsoever they will have granted, that not only love, but lust, but vanity, but (if they list) scurrility, possesseth many leaves of the poet's books; yet think I, when this is granted, they will find their sentence

6. The "ground-plot" is a bare skeleton or frame upon which the reader is to work out ("invent") the full meaning of the poet's original "*Idea* or fore-conceit" [Robinson's note].

7. That is, hypothetical names (like "John Doe").

8. Cupid's invasion of the world of heroic action is one of the central themes in Sidney's *Arcadia* [Robinson's note]. Cupid: Roman god of love.

may with good manners put the last words foremost, and not say that poetry abuseth man's wit, but that man's wit abuseth poetry.

For I will not deny but that man's wit may make poesy (which should be *eikastike*, which some learned have defined, figuring forth good things) to be *phantastike,*[9] which doth contrariwise infect the fancy with unworthy objects; as the painter, that should give to the eye either some excellent perspective, or some fine picture fit for building or fortification, or containing in it some notable example, as Abraham sacrificing his son Isaac, Judith killing Holofernes, David fighting with Goliath,[1] may leave those, and please an ill-pleased eye with wanton shows of better hidden matters. But what, shall the abuse of a thing make the right use odious? Nay truly, though I yield that poesy may not only be abused, but that being abused, by the reason of his sweet charming force it can do more hurt than any other army of words, yet shall it be so far from concluding that the abuse should give reproach to the abused, that contrariwise it is a good reason that whatsoever being abused doth most harm, being rightly used (and upon the right use each thing conceiveth his title) doth most good.

Do we not see the skill of physic (the best rampire[2] to our often-assaulted bodies), being abused, teach poison the most violent destroyer? Doth not knowledge of law, whose end is to even and right all things, being abused, grow the crooked fosterer of horrible injuries? Doth not (to go to the highest) God's word abused breed heresy, and His name abused become blasphemy? Truly a needle cannot do much hurt, and as truly (with leave of ladies be it spoken) it cannot do much good. With a sword thou mayest kill thy father, and with a sword thou mayest defend thy prince and country. So that, as in their calling poets the fathers of lies they say nothing, so in this their argument of abuse they prove the commendation.

They allege herewith that before poets began to be in price[3] our nation hath set their hearts' delight upon action, and not upon imagination, rather doing things worthy to be written than writing things fit to be done. What that before time was, I think scarcely Sphinx[4] can tell, sith no memory is so ancient that hath the precedence of poetry. And certain it is that, in our plainest homeliness, yet never was the Albion[5] nation without poetry. Marry, this argument, though it be levelled against poetry, yet is it indeed a chain-shot[6] against all learning, or bookishness, as they commonly term it. Of such mind were certain Goths,[7] of whom it is written that, having in the spoil of a famous city taken a fair library, one hangman (belike fit to execute the fruits of their wits) who had murdered a great number of bodies, would have set fire on it. No, said another very gravely, take heed what you do, for while they are busy about these toys, we shall with more leisure conquer their countries. This indeed is the ordinary doctrine of ignorance, and many words

9. The art of producing appearances. *Eikastike*: the art of copying or portraying (both Greek). The terms are contrasted by Plato, *Sophist* 236d.
1. All biblical references: Abraham prepares to sacrifice Isaac in Genesis 22; Judith kills Holofernes, a general of Nebuchadnezzer who is besieging her city, after tricking him into a drunken stupor,in Judith 12 (a book of the Apocrypha); David fights and slays the Philistine giant Goliath in 1 Samuel 17.
2. Rampart, fortification. "Physic": medicine.
3. Highly esteemed.
4. In Greek mythology, the riddling monster (with a woman's face, lion's body, and bird's wings) bested by Oedipus.
5. Ancient name for Britain.
6. A kind of shot (mostly used in naval warfare, to destroy masts and rigging) formed by two balls connected by a chain.
7. A Germanic people who sacked Athens in 267 C.E.

sometimes I have heard spent in it; but because this reason is generally against all learning as well as poetry, or rather all learning but poetry; because it were too large a digression to handle, or at least too superfluous (sith it is manifest that all government of action is to be gotten by knowledge, and knowledge best by gathering many knowledges, which is reading), I only, with Horace, to him that is of that opinion,

Jubeo stultum esse libenter;[8]

for as for poetry itself, it is the freest from this objection.

For poetry is the companion of camps. I dare undertake *Orlando Furioso* or honest King Arthur,[9] will never displease a soldier: but the quiddity of *ens* and *prima materia* will hardly agree with a corselet.[1] And therefore, as I said in the beginning, even Turks and Tartars are delighted with poets. Homer, a Greek, flourished before Greece flourished. And if to a slight conjecture a conjecture may be opposed, truly it may seem that, as by him their learned men took almost their first light of knowledge, so their active men received their first motions of courage. Only Alexander's example may serve, who by Plutarch is accounted of such virtue that fortune was not his guide, but his foot-stool; whose acts speak for him, though Plutarch did not, indeed the phoenix of warlike princes. This Alexander left his schoolmaster, living Aristotle, behind him, but took dead Homer with him. He put the philosopher Callisthenes[2] to death for his seeming philosophical, indeed mutinous, stubbornness; but the chief thing he ever was heard to wish for was that Homer had been alive. He well found he received more bravery of mind by the pattern of Achilles than by hearing the definition of fortitude. And therefore, if Cato misliked Fulvius[3] for carrying Ennius with him to the field, it may be answered that if Cato misliked it, the noble Fulvius liked it, or else he had not done it: for it was not the excellent Cato Uticensis[4] (whose authority I would much more have reverenced), but it was the former, in truth a bitter punisher of faults, but else a man that had never well sacrificed to the Graces.[5] He misliked and cried out upon all Greek learning, and yet, being eighty years old, began to learn it, belike fearing that Pluto[6] understood not Latin. Indeed, the Roman laws allowed no person to be carried to the wars but he that was in the soldier's roll, and therefore, though Cato misliked his unmustered person, he misliked not his work. And if he had, Scipio Nasica,[7] judged by common consent the best Roman, loved him. Both the other Scipio brothers,[8] who had by their virtues no less surnames than of Asia and Afric, so loved him that they caused his body to be buried in their sepulcher. So

8. I gladly order that he be a fool (Latin); misquoted from Horace, *Satires* 1.1.63.
9. Legendary British king, famous for creating the Round Table.
1. A piece of armor that covers the torso. "The quiddity of *ens* and *prima materia*": the whatness of being and primal matter; Sidney is mocking the elaborate language of scholastic philosophy.
2. Aristotle's nephew, a historian who accompanied and wrote about Alexander. After a quarrel with Alexander, he was accused of conspiracy and executed (327 B.C.E.).
3. Marcus Fulvius Nobilior, patron of Ennius, who took the poet on his Aetolian campaign of 189 B.C.E. Cato: Cato the Elder (234–149 B.C.E.), a famously stern moralist.
4. Cato the Elder's great-grandson, an opponent of Caesar.
5. Three goddesses of beauty and charm, dear friends of the Muses.
6. Roman god of the underworld and the dead.
7. Roman consul in 191 B.C.E., of whom little is known; Livy's *Histories* (29.14) records that "the Senate judged him to be the best of good men in the whole community."
8. Two cousins of Scipio Nasica: Lucius Cornelius Scipio earned the name *Asiatius* by defeating Antiochus at Magnesia in 189 B.C.E. Publius Cornelius Scipio (ca. 236–184/3 B.C.E.) earned the name *Africanus* in 201 by defeating Hannibal and the Carthaginians in Africa.

as Cato, his authority being but against his person, and that answered with so far greater than himself, is herein of no validity.

But now indeed my burden is great; now Plato his name is laid upon me, whom I must confess, of all philosophers I have ever esteemed most worthy of reverence, and with great reason, sith of all philosophers he is the most poetical. Yet if he will defile the fountain out of which his flowing streams have proceeded, let us boldly examine with what reasons he did it. First, truly a man might maliciously object that Plato, being a philosopher, was a natural enemy of poets: for indeed, after the philosopher had picked out of the sweet mysteries of poetry the right discerning true points of knowledge, they forthwith putting it in method, and making a school-art of that which the poets did only teach by a divine delightfulness, beginning to spurn at their guides like ungrateful prentices, were not content to set up shops for themselves but sought by all means to discredit their masters; which, by the force of delight being barred them, the less they could overthrow them, the more they hated them. For indeed, they found for Homer seven cities, and strave who should have him for their citizen; where many cities banished philosophers as not fit members to live among them. For only repeating certain of Euripides' verses, many Athenians had their lives saved of the Syracusans, when the Athenians themselves thought many philosophers unworthy to live.[9] Certain poets, as Simonides and Pindar, had so prevailed with Hiero the First,[1] that of a tyrant they made him a just king, where Plato could do so little with Dionysius,[2] that he himself of a philosopher was made a slave. But who should do thus, I confess, should requite the objections made against poets with like cavillation[3] against philosophers; as likewise one should do that should bid one read *Phaedrus* or *Symposium* in Plato, or the discourse of love in Plutarch, and see whether any poet do authorize abominable filthiness,[4] as they do. Again, a man might ask out of what commonwealth Plato did banish them. In sooth, thence where he himself alloweth community of women. So as belike this banishment grew not for effeminate wantonness, sith little should poetical sonnets be hurtful when a man might have what woman he listed. But I honor philosophical instructions, and bless the wits which bred them, so as they be not abused, which is likewise stretched to poetry.

Saint Paul[5] himself (who yet for the credit of poets allegeth twice two poets, and one of them by the name of prophet) setteth a watchword upon philosophy, indeed upon the abuse; so doth Plato, upon the abuse, not upon poetry. Plato found fault that the poets of his time filled the world with wrong opinions of the gods, making light tales of that unspotted essence, and therefore would not have the youth depraved with such opinions.[6] Herein may much be said; let this suffice: the poets did not induce such opinions,

9. In 413 B.C.E. the Athenians, led by Nicias, were defeated by the Syracusans. Plutarch reports (*Life of Nicias* 29) that many of the Athenians were saved from bondage by their knowledge of Euripides, whose poetry was in great esteem among their captors; he also relates (23) the harsh fate of philosophers in Athens [Robinson's note].

1. Tyrant of Syracuse (478–467/6 B.C.E.), whose court was visited by Pindar in 476. Simonides (ca. 556–468 B.C.E.), Greek lyric and elegiac poet who visited the court of Hieron about 476.

2. Syracusan ruler (b. ca. 397 B.C.E.) who became tyrant of Syracuse in 367. Invited to Sicily by an influential Syracusan, Plato tried with little success to mold Dionysius into a philosopher-king. After Dionysius tricked Plato into returning in 361, he temporarily imprisoned the philosopher.

3. Frivolous objections.

4. That is, homosexuality.

5. Early Christian apostle (d. ca. 62 C.E.); see Acts 17.28: "For in him [the Lord] we live, and move, and have our being; as certain also of your own poets have said."

6. See *Republic* 2.377a–380c (above).

but did imitate those opinions already induced. For all the Greek stories can well testify that the very religion of that time stood upon many and many-fashioned gods, not taught so by the poets, but followed according to their nature of imitation. Who list may read in Plutarch the discourses of Isis and Osiris,[7] of the cause why oracles ceased, of the divine providence, and see whether the theology of that nation stood not upon such dreams, which the poets indeed superstitiously observed, and truly (sith they had not the light of Christ) did much better in it than the philosophers, who, shaking off superstition, brought in atheism. Plato therefore (whose authority I had much rather justly construe than unjustly resist) meant not in general of poets, in those words of which Julius Scaliger saith, *Qua authoritate barbari quidam atque hispidi abuti velint ad poetas e republica exigendos;*[8] but only meant to drive out those wrong opinions of the Deity (whereof now, without further law, Christianity hath taken away all the hurtful belief), perchance (as he thought) nourished by the then esteemed poets. And a man need go no further than to Plato himself to know his meaning: who, in his dialogue called *Ion*, giveth high and rightly divine commendation to poetry.[9] So as Plato, banishing the abuse, not the thing, not banishing it, but giving due honor unto it, shall be our patron and not our adversary. For indeed, I had much rather (sith truly I may do it) show their mistaking of Plato (under whose lion's skin they would make an ass-like braying against poesy) than go about to overthrow his authority; whom, the wiser a man is, the more just cause he shall find to have in admiration; especially sith he attributeth unto poesy more than myself do, namely, to be a very inspiring of a divine force, far above man's wit, as in the afore-named dialogue is apparent.

Of the other side, who would show the honors have been by the best sort of judgments granted them, a whole sea of examples would present themselves: Alexanders, Caesars, Scipios, all favorers of poets; Laelius,[1] called the Roman Socrates, himself a poet, so as part of *Heautontimorumenos*[2] in Terence was supposed to be made by him. And even the Greek Socrates, whom Apollo confirmed to be the only wise man, is said to have spent part of his old time in putting Aesop's fables into verses. And therefore full evil should it become his scholar Plato to put such words in his master's mouth against poets. But what need more? Aristotle writes the Art of Poesy; and why, if it should not be written? Plutarch teacheth the use to be gathered of them, and how if they should not be read? And who reads Plutarch's either history or philosophy, shall find he trimmeth both their garments with guards of poesy. But I list not to defend poesy with the help of her underling historiography. Let it suffice that it is a fit soil for praise to dwell upon; and what dispraise may set upon it, is either easily overcome, or transformed into just commendation.

So that, sith the excellencies of it may be so easily and so justly confirmed, and the low-creeping objections so soon trodden down, it not being an art

7. The topics that Sidney mentions derive from chapters in Plutarch's *Moralia*. The Egyptian deities Osiris and his wife Isis, for example, appear in *De Iside et Osiride* (*On Isis and Osiris*) [Robinson's note].

8. Whose authority some barbarous and insensitive men wish to misuse in order to expel poets from the state (Latin); Scaliger, *Poetics* 1.20 [Robinson's note].

9. In *Ion* (see esp. 533d–535a), Socrates argues that poets rely not on art but on divine inspiration (see above).

1. Gaius Laelius (b. ca. 186 B.C.E.), promoter of the study of literature and philosophy, nicknamed "Wise." Cicero compares him to Socrates in *De Officiis* 1.90.

2. *The Self-Tormentor* (163 B.C.E.).

of lies, but of true doctrine; not of effeminateness, but of notable stirring of courage; not of abusing man's wit, but of strengthening man's wit; not banished, but honored by Plato; let us rather plant more laurels for to engarland our poets' heads (which honor of being laureate, as besides them only triumphant captains wear, is a sufficient authority to show the price they ought to be had in), than suffer the ill-favoring breath of such wrong-speakers once to blow upon the clear springs of poesy.

But sith I have run so long a career in this matter, methinks before I give my pen a full stop it shall be but a little more lost time to inquire why England (the mother of excellent minds) should be grown so hard a step-mother to poets, who certainly in wit ought to pass all other, sith all only proceedeth from their wit, being indeed makers of themselves, not takers of others. How can I but exclaim

Musa, mihi causas memora, quo numine laeso?[3]

Sweet poesy, that hath anciently had kings, emperors, senators, great captains, such as, besides a thousand others, David, Adrian, Sophocles, Germanicus,[4] not only to favor poets, but to be poets. And of our nearer times can present for her patrons a Robert, king of Sicily, the great King Francis of France, King James of Scotland;[5] such cardinals as Bembus and Bibbiena;[6] such famous preachers and teachers as Beza and Melanchthon;[7] so learned philosophers as Fracastorius[8] and Scaliger; so great orators as Pontanus and Muretus; so piercing wits as George Buchanan;[9] so grave counselors as, besides many, but before all, that Hospital of France,[1] than whom (I think) that realm never brought forth a more accomplished judgment, more firmly builded upon virtue—I say these, with numbers of others, not only to read others' poesies, but to poetise for others' reading—that poesy, thus embraced in all other places, should only find in our time a hard welcome in England, I think the very earth lamenteth it, and therefore decketh our soil with fewer laurels than it was accustomed. For heretofore poets have in England also flourished, and, which is to be noted, even in those times when the trumpet of Mars[2] did sound loudest. And now that an overfaint quietness should seem to strew the house for poets, they are almost in as good reputation as the mountebanks[3] at Venice. Truly even that, as of the one side it giveth great praise to poesy, which like Venus[4] (but to better purpose) had rather be troubled in the net with Mars than enjoy the homely quiet of Vulcan;[5] so serves it for a piece of a reason why they are less grateful

3. O Muse, remind me of the causes, of the offense to [Juno's] divine power (Latin); Virgil, *Aeneid* 1.8.

4. The nephew and adopted son (15 B.C.E.–19 C.E.) of the emperor Tiberius. Adrian: Hadrian (76–138 C.E.), emperor of Rome (117–38), a noted patron of the arts.

5. Either King James I of England (who was James VI of Scotland, 1566–1625) or James I of Scotland (1394–1437). Robert: Robert of Anjou (1278–1343), who ruled Naples for 34 years (1309–43) and was a patron of Petrarch. King Francis (1494–1547),French king known as a patron of the arts.

6. Bernardo Dovizi (1470–1520), who wrote the first comedy in Italian, *Calandria* (with a plot derived from Plautus). Bembus: Pietro Bembo (1470–1547), Italian Renaissance grammarian and an editor and author of poetry.

7. Philip Melanchthon (1497–1560), German humanist, theologian, and Protestant reformer. Theodore Beza (1519–1605), French author, translator, and theologian who succeeded John Calvin as leader of the Protestant Reformation.

8. Girolamo Fracastoro (ca. 1484–1553), Italian physician, poet, astronomer, and geologist.

9. Scottish humanist and author (1506–1582), tutor to Mary, Queen of Scots, and James VI of Scotland. Muretus: Marc-Antoine de Muret (1526–1585), French humanist, classical scholar, and poet.

1. Michel de L'Hospital (ca. 1504–1573), lawyer, humanist, poet, and advocate of religious tolerance.

2. Roman god of war.

3. Showmen peddling quack medicine from a platform.

4. Roman goddess of love.

5. Roman god of fire and metalworking; Vulcan captured his wife Venus in adultery with Mars in a fine chain-link net and hauled them in it before

to idle England, which now can scarce endure the pain of a pen. Upon this necessarily followeth that base men with servile wits undertake it, who think it enough if they can be rewarded of the printer. And so as Epaminondas[6] is said, with the honor of his virtue to have made an office, by his exercising it which before was contemptible, to become highly respected; so these, no more but setting their names to it, by their own disgracefulness disgrace the most graceful poesy. For now, as if all the Muses were got with child to bring forth bastard poets, without any commission they do post over the banks of Helicon,[7] till they make the readers more weary than post-horses; while in the meantime they,

Queis meliore luto finxit praecordia Titan,[8]

are better content to suppress the out-flowing of their wit than, by publishing them, to be accounted knights of the same order.

But I, that before ever I durst aspire unto the dignity, am admitted into the company of the paper-blurrers, do find the very true cause of our wanting estimation is want of desert, taking upon us to be poets in despite of Pallas.[9] Now wherein we want desert were a thank-worthy labor to express; but if I knew, I should have mended myself. But I, as I never desired the title, so have I neglected the means to come by it. Only, over-mastered by some thoughts, I yielded an inky tribute unto them. Marry, they that delight in poesy itself should seek to know what they do, and how they do, and especially look themselves in an unflattering glass of reason, if they be inclinable unto it. For poesy must not be drawn by the ears; it must be gently led, or rather it must lead; which was partly the cause that made the ancient-learned affirm it was a divine gift, and no human skill; sith all other knowledges lie ready for any that hath strength of wit; a poet no industry can make, if his own genius be not carried unto it; and therefore is it an old proverb, *orator fit, poeta nascitur.*[1] Yet confess I always that as the fertilest ground must be manured, so must the highest flying wit have a Daedalus[2] to guide him. That Daedalus, they say, both in this and in other, hath three wings to bear itself up into the air of due commendation: that is, Art, Imitation, and Exercise. But these, neither artificial rules nor imitative patterns, we much cumber ourselves withal. Exercise indeed we do, but that very fore-backwardly: for where we should exercise to know, we exercise as having known; and so is our brain delivered of much matter which never was begotten by knowledge. For there being two principal parts, matter to be expressed by words, and words to express the matter; in neither we use Art or Imitation rightly. Our matter is *quodlibet* indeed, though wrongly performing Ovid's verse,

Quicquid conabor dicere, versus erit:[3]

never marshalling it into an assured rank, that almost the readers cannot tell where to find themselves.

---

the other gods. The story is told in Homer, *Odyssey* 8.266–366, and Ovid, *Metamorphosis* 4.169–89.

6. Theban statesman and general (ca. 410–362 B.C.E.), famous for defeating the Spartans at Leuctra in 371.

7. Boeotian mountain, home of the Muses. The "bank" properly belongs to the spring Hippocrene, a source of poetic inspiration.

8. Whose heart Titan fashioned with finer earth (Latin); adopted from *Satire* 14.35, by the Roman poet Juvenal (ca. 55–ca. 140 C.E.).

9. Without wisdom. Pallas Athena was thought to be the personification of wisdom [Robinson's note].

1. An orator is made, a poet is born (Latin).

2. In Greek mythology, a consummately skilled Athenian artisan; he escaped King Minos of Crete by fashioning wings of feathers and wax and flying to Greece.

3. Whatever I will try to say, it will be verse (Latin); Ovid, *Tristia* 4.10.26. *Quodlibet*: what you will (Latin).

Chaucer undoubtedly did excellently in his *Troilus and Criseyde,* of whom truly I know not whether to marvel more, either that he in that misty time could see so clearly, or that we in this clear age walk so stumblingly after him. Yet had he great wants, fit to be forgiven in so reverent antiquity. I account the *Mirror of Magistrates*[4] meetly furnished of beautiful parts, and in the Earl of Surrey's[5] lyrics many things tasting of a noble birth, and worthy of a noble mind. *The Shepherd's Calendar*[6] hath much poetry in his eclogues, indeed worthy the reading if I be not deceived. That same framing of his style to an old rustic language I dare not allow, sith neither Theocritus[7] in Greek, Virgil in Latin, nor Sannazzaro in Italian, did affect it. Besides these, do I not remember to have seen but few (to speak boldly) printed that have poetical sinews in them: for proof whereof, let but most of the verses but put in prose, and then ask the meaning, and it will be found that one verse did but beget another, without ordering at the first what should be at the last; which becomes a confused mass of words with a tingling sound of rhyme, barely accompanied with reason.

Our tragedies and comedies (not without cause cried out against), observing rules neither of honest civility nor of skillful poetry, excepting *Gorboduc*[8] (again I say, of those that I have seen), which notwithstanding, as it is full of stately speeches and well sounding phrases, climbing to the height of Seneca his style,[9] and as full of notable morality, which it doth most delightfully teach, and so obtain the very end of poesy; yet in troth it is very defective in the circumstances, which grieveth me, because it might not remain as an exact model of all tragedies. For it is faulty both in place and time, the two necessary companions of all corporal actions. For where the stage should always represent but one place, and the uttermost time presupposed in it should be, both by Aristotle's precept and common reason, but one day, there is both many days and many places inartificially[1] imagined.

But if it be so in *Gorboduc*, how much more in all the rest? where you shall have Asia of the one side, and Afric of the other, and so many other under-kingdoms, that the player, when he cometh in, must ever begin with telling where he is, or else the tale will not be conceived. Now ye shall have three ladies walk to gather flowers, and then we must believe the stage to be a garden. By and by we hear news of shipwreck in the same place, and then we are to blame if we accept it not for a rock. Upon the back of that comes out a hideous monster with fire and smoke, and then the miserable beholders are bound to take it for a cave. While in the meantime two armies fly in, represented with four swords and bucklers, and then what hard heart will not receive it for a pitched field?

Now of time they are much more liberal, for ordinary it is that two young princes[2] fall in love. After many traverses, she is got with child, delivered of a fair boy, he is lost, groweth a man, falls in love, and is ready to get another child, and all this in two hours' space: which, how absurd it is in sense, even

4. *A Mirror for Magistrates* (1559), a collection of Elizabethan poems on the fall of great men in English history (each told in the 1st person).
5. Henry Howard, earl of Surrey (1517–1547), English poet.
6. Work of 1579 by Edmund Spenser, author of *The Faerie Queen*, who dedicated it to Sidney.
7. Greek poet (ca. 300–ca. 260 B.C.E.), whose *Idylls* are the earliest models for pastoral poetry.
8. An English play (first performed 1562) written by Thomas Sackville and Thomas Norton.
9. The tragedies as well as the prose style of Seneca had great influence in the Renaissance.
1. Without artifice. For Aristotle's limit on the time of a tragedy, see *Poetics* 5, 1449b.
2. Sovereigns (of either sex).

sense may imagine, and art hath taught, and all ancient examples justified, and at this day, the ordinary players in Italy will not err in. Yet will some bring in an example of *Eunuchus* in Terence, that containeth matter of two days, yet far short of twenty years. True it is, and so was it to be played in two days, and so fitted to the time it set forth. And though Plautus[3] hath in one place done amiss, let us hit with him, and not miss with him. But they will say, how then shall we set forth a story which containeth both many places and many times? And do they not know that a tragedy is tied to the laws of poesy, and not of history, not bound to follow the story, but having liberty, either to feign a quite new matter, or to frame the history to the most tragical conveniency? Again, many things may be told which cannot be showed, if they know the difference betwixt reporting and representing. As for example, I may speak (though I am here) of Peru, and in speech digress from that to the description of Calicut; but in action I cannot represent it without Pacolet's horse.[4] And so was the manner the ancients took, by some *nuncius*[5] to recount things done in former time or other place.

Lastly, if they will represent an history, they must not (as Horace saith) begin *ab ovo,*[6] but they must come to the principal point of that one action which they will represent. By example this will be best expressed. I have a story of young Polydorus,[7] delivered for safety's sake, with great riches, by his father Priam, to Polymnestor, king of Thrace, in the Trojan war time. He, after some years, hearing the overthrow of Priam, for to make the treasure his own, murdereth the child. The body of the child is taken up by Hecuba. She, the same day, findeth a sleight to be revenged most cruelly of the tyrant. Where now would one of our tragedy writers begin, but with the delivery of the child? Then should he sail over into Thrace, and so spend I know not how many years, and travel numbers of places. But where doth Euripides? Even with the finding of the body, leaving the rest to be told by the spirit of Polydorus. This need no further to be enlarged; the dullest wit may conceive it.

But besides these gross absurdities, how all their plays be neither right tragedies, nor right comedies, mingling kings and clowns not because the matter so carrieth it, but thrust in clowns by head and shoulders, to play a part in majestical matters, with neither decency nor discretion, so as neither the admiration and commiseration, nor the right sportfulness, is by their mongrel tragi-comedy obtained. I know Apuleius[8] did somewhat so, but that is a thing recounted with space of time, not represented in one moment: and I know the ancients have one or two examples of tragi-comedies, as Plautus hath *Amphitrio*. But if we mark them well, we shall find that they never, or very daintily, match horn-pipes and funerals. So falleth it out, that having indeed no right comedy, in that comical part of our tragedy we have nothing but scurrility, unworthy of any chaste ears, or some extreme show of doltishness, indeed fit to lift up a loud laughter, and nothing else: where the whole tract of a comedy should be full of delight, as the tragedy should be still maintained in a well raised admiration.

3. Roman comic playwright (d. ca. 184 B.C.E.).
4. Flying horse owned by a dwarf in the French romance *Valentine and Orson* (1489). Calicut: port in southwest India.
5. Messenger (Latin).
6. From the beginning; literally, "from the egg" (Latin). See Horace, *Ars Poetica* 147.
7. Told in Euripides' *Hecuba* (ca. 424 B.C.E.).
8. Author (b. ca. 123 C.E.) of *The Golden Ass*, a Latin satirical romance.

But our comedians think there is no delight without laughter; which is very wrong, for though laughter may come with delight, yet cometh it not of delight, as though delight should be the cause of laughter; but well may one thing breed both together: nay, rather in themselves they have, as it were, a kind of contrariety; for delight we scarcely do, but in things that have a conveniency to ourselves, or to the general nature; laughter almost ever cometh of things most disproportioned to ourselves and nature. Delight hath a joy in it, either permanent or present. Laughter hath only a scornful tickling. For example, we are ravished with delight to see a fair woman, and yet are far from being moved to laughter. We laugh at deformed creatures, wherein certainly we cannot delight. We delight in good chances, we laugh at mischances; we delight to hear the happiness of our friends or country, at which he were worthy to be laughed at that would laugh; we shall contrarily laugh sometimes to find a matter quite mistaken and go down the hill against the bias,[9] in the mouth of some such men, as for the respect of them one shall be heartily sorry, yet he cannot choose but laugh; and so is rather pained than delighted with laughter. Yet deny I not but that they may go well together; for as in Alexander's picture[1] well set out, we delight without laughter, and in twenty mad antics we laugh without delight, so in Hercules, painted with his great beard and furious countenance, in a woman's attire, spinning at Omphale's[2] commandment, it breedeth both delight and laughter. For the representing of so strange a power in love procureth delight, and the scornfulness of the action stirreth laughter.

But I speak to this purpose, that all the end of the comical part be not upon such scornful matters as stirreth laughter only, but, mixed with it, that delightful teaching which is the end of poesy. And the great fault even in that point of laughter, and forbidden plainly by Aristotle,[3] is that they stir laughter in sinful things, which are rather execrable than ridiculous: or in miserable, which are rather to be pitied than scorned. For what is it to make folks gape at a wretched beggar or a beggarly clown; or against law of hospitality, to jest at strangers because they speak not English so well as we do? What do we learn? sith it is certain

Nil habet infelix paupertas durius in se,
Quam quod ridiculos homines facit.[4]

But rather a busy loving courtier; a heartless threatening Thraso, a self-wise-seeming schoolmaster; an awry-transformed traveler: these, if we saw walk in stage names, which we play naturally, therein were delightful laughter, and teaching delightfulness: as in the other, the tragedies of Buchanan do justly bring forth a divine admiration. But I have lavished out too many words of this play matter. I do it because, as they are excelling parts of poesy, so is there none so much used in England, and none can be more pitifully abused; which, like an unmannerly daughter, showing a bad education, causeth her mother poesy's honesty to be called in question.

9. Contrary to its expected course. The balls used in lawn bowling have a bias, a peculiarity in weight or shape that causes them to swerve.
1. Plutarch, in his *Life of Alexander* 4, discusses Apelles' (4th c. B.C.E.) famous painting of Alexander [Robinson's note].
2. Queen of Lydia, whom the legendary hero served for 3 years as a slave in order to be purified of a murder; during that time he fell in love with her.
3. See Aristotle, *Nicomachean Ethics* 4.8, 1128a.
4. Luckless poverty has nothing harsher in it than that it makes men ridiculous (Latin); Juvenal, *Satire* 3.152–53.

Other sorts of poetry almost have we none, but that lyrical kind of songs and sonnets: which, Lord, if He gave us so good minds, how well it might be employed, and with how heavenly fruit, both private and public, in singing the praises of the immortal beauty, the immortal goodness of that God who giveth us hands to write and wits to conceive; of which we might well want words, but never matter; of which we could turn out eyes to nothing but we should ever have new budding occasions. But truly many of such writings as come under the banner of unresistable love, if I were a mistress, would never persuade me they were in love; so coldly they apply fiery speeches, as men that had rather read lovers' writings, and so caught up certain swelling phrases, which hang together, like a man which once told me the wind was at north-west and by south, because he would be sure to name winds enough, than that in truth they feel these passions, which easily (as I think) may be bewrayed, by that same forcibleness or *energia*[5] (as the Greeks call it) of the writer. But let this be a sufficient though short note, that we miss the right use of the material point of poesy.

Now, for the outside of it, which is words, or (as I may term it) diction, it is even well worse. So is that honey-flowing matron eloquence apparelled, or rather disguised in a courtesan-like painted affectation: one time with so far fet words, that may seem monsters, but must seem strangers to any poor Englishman; another time, with coursing[6] of a letter, as if they were bound to follow the method of a dictionary; another time, with figures and flowers, extremely winter-starved. But I would this fault were only peculiar to versifiers, and had not as large possession among prose-printers; and (which is to be marvelled) among many scholars; and (which is to be pitied) among some preachers. Truly I could wish, if at least I might be so bold to wish in a thing beyond the reach of my capacity, the diligent imitators of Tully and Demosthenes[7] (most worthy to be imitated) did not so much keep Nizolian paperbooks[8] of their figures and phrases, as by attentive translation (as it were) devour them whole, and make them wholly theirs. For now they cast sugar and spice upon every dish that is served to the table, like those Indians, not content to wear earrings at the fit and natural place of the ears, but they will thrust jewels through their nose and lips because they will be sure to be fine.

Tully, when he was to drive out Catiline,[9] as it were with a thunderbolt of eloquence, often used that figure of repetition, *Vivit Vivit? Imo vero etiam in senatum venit,*[1] &c. Indeed, inflamed with a well-grounded rage, he would have his words (as it were) double out of his mouth, and so do that artificially which we see men do in choler naturally. And we, having noted the grace of those words, hale them in sometime to a familiar epistle, when it were too too much choler[2] to be choleric. How well store of *similiter cadences*[3] doth

5. A very specific kind of energy; Aristotle (*Rhetoric* 3.10–11, 1410b–12a) and Scaliger (*Poetics* 3.26) both emphasize that *energeia* is that quality in language which makes concepts or ideas clear [Robinson's note].
6. Pursuing (to create alliteration).
7. Athenian statesman (384–322 B.C.E.) considered the greatest Greek orator (as Cicero was thought the greatest Roman orator).
8. Commonplace books like those of the Italian lexicographer Marius Nizolius (16th c.).
9. Lucius Sergius Catalina (ca. 108–62 B.C.E.), Roman whose frustrated political ambitions (including a consular election lost to Cicero) led him to plan an uprising in Rome; Cicero denounced the conspiracy in a famous series of "Catalinarian" orations.
1. He lives. Does he live? Yes, and in fact he even comes into the Senate (Latin); Cicero, *In Catilinam* 1.1.2.
2. Anger.
3. Similar cadences (Latin; properly, *cadentia*); the effect achieved when consecutive sentences or phrases terminate with the same cadence [Robinson's note].

sound with the gravity of the pulpit, I would but invoke Demosthenes' soul to tell, who with a rare daintiness useth them. Truly they have made me think of the sophister[4] that with too much subtlety would prove two eggs three, and though he might be counted a sophister, had none for his labor. So these men, bringing in such a kind of eloquence, well may they obtain an opinion of a seeming fineness, but persuade few, which should be the end of their fineness.

Now for similitudes in certain printed discourses, I think all herbarists,[5] all stories of beasts, fowls, and fishes are rifled up, that they come in multitudes to wait upon any of our conceits; which certainly is as absurd a surfeit to the ears as is possible: for the force of a similitude not being to prove anything to a contrary disputer, but only to explain to a willing hearer; when that is done, the rest is a most tedious prattling, rather over-swaying the memory from the purpose whereto they were applied, than any whit informing the judgment, already either satisfied, or by similitudes not to be satisfied. For my part, I do not doubt, when Antonius and Crassus,[6] the great forefathers of Cicero in eloquence, the one (as Cicero testifieth of them) pretended not to know art, the other not to set by it, because with a plain sensibleness they might win credit of popular ears; which credit is the nearest step to persuasion; which persuasion is the chief mark of oratory; I do not doubt (I say) but that they used these knacks very sparingly; which, who doth generally use, any man may see doth dance to his own music, and so be noted by the audience more careful to speak curiously[7] than to speak truly.

Undoubtedly (at least to my opinion undoubtedly) I have found in divers smally[8] learned courtiers a more sound style than in some professors of learning; of which I can guess no other cause but that the courtier, following that which by practice he findeth fittest to nature, therein (though he know it not) doth according to art, though not by art: where the other, using art to show art, and not to hide art (as in these cases he should do), flieth from nature, and indeed abuseth art.

But what? methinks I deserve to be pounded[9] for straying from poetry to oratory: but both have such an affinity in this wordish consideration, that I think this digression will make my meaning receive the fuller understanding; which is not to take upon me to teach poets how they should do, but only, finding myself sick among the rest, to show some one or two spots of the common infection grown among the most part of writers; that, acknowledging ourselves somewhat awry, we may bend to the right use both of matter and manner; whereto our language giveth us great occasion, being indeed capable of any excellent exercising of it. I know some will say it is a mingled language. And why not so much the better, taking the best of both the other?[1] Another will say it wanteth grammar. Nay truly, it hath that praise, that it wanteth not grammar: for grammar it might have, but it needs it not; being so easy of itself, and so void of those cumbersome differences of cases, gen-

4. A sophist; one who relies on specious reasoning.
5. Those skilled in herbs; herbalists.
6. Lucius Licinius Crassus (140–ca. 90 B.C.E.), outstanding orator who is the chief speaker in Cicero's *De Oratore*. Antonius: Marcus Antonius (143–87 B.C.E.), Crassus's rival, portrayed with him in *De Oratore* and *Brutus* (also by Cicero).
7. Elaborately, artfully.
8. Slightly.
9. Impounded, like a trespassing animal.
1. Sidney refers to the use of other languages—Greek and Latin (or French)—to enhance the style of English.

ders, moods, and tenses, which I think was a piece of the Tower of Babylon's curse,[2] that a man should be put to school to learn his mother-tongue. But for the uttering sweetly and properly the conceits of the mind, which is the end of speech, that hath it equally with any other tongue in the world; and is particularly happy in compositions of two or three words together, near the Greek, far beyond the Latin, which is one of the greatest beauties can be in a language.

Now of versifying there are two sorts, the one ancient, the other modern: the ancient marked the quantity of each syllable, and according to that framed his verse; the modern, observing only number (with some regard of the accent), the chief life of it standeth in that like sounding of the words which we call rhyme. Whether of these be the more excellent would bear many speeches: the ancient (no doubt) more fit for music, both words and tune observing quantity, and more fit lively to express divers passions, by the low and lofty sound of the well-weighed syllable. The latter likewise, with his rhyme, striketh a certain music to the ear; and, in fine, sith it doth delight, though by another way, it obtains the same purpose: there being in either sweetness, and wanting in neither majesty. Truly the English, before any other vulgar language I know, is fit for both sorts: for, for the ancient, the Italian is so full of vowels that it must ever be cumbered with elisions; the Dutch,[3] so of the other side with consonants, that they cannot yield the sweet sliding fit for a verse; the French in his whole language hath not one word that hath his accent in the last syllable saving two, called *antepenultima*; and little more hath the Spanish, and therefore very gracelessly may they use dactyls.[4] The English is subject to none of these defects.

Now for the rhyme, though we do not observe quantity, yet we observe the accent very precisely, which other languages either cannot do, or will not do so absolutely. That *caesura*,[5] or breathing place in the midst of the verse, neither Italian nor Spanish have; the French and we never almost fail of. Lastly, even the very rhyme itself, the Italian cannot put in the last syllable, by the French named the masculine rhyme, but still in the next to the last, which the French call the female, or the next before that, which the Italians term *sdrucciola*.[6] The example of the former is *buono, suono*; of the *sdrucciola* is *femina, semina*. The French, of the other side, hath both the male, as *bon, son*, and the female, as *plaise, tasie*. But the *sdrucciola* he hath not: where the English hath all three, as *due, true; father, rather; motion, potion;* with much more which might be said, but that I find already the triflingness of this discourse is much too much enlarged.

So that sith the ever-praiseworthy poesy is full of virtue-breeding delightfulness, and void of no gift that ought to be in the noble name of learning; sith the blames laid against it are either false or feeble; sith the cause why it is not esteemed in England is the fault of poet-apes, not poets; sith, lastly,

2. That the one language of the people be confounded, so "that they may not understand one another's speech"; the story of the Tower of Babel is told in Genesis 11.

3. German.

4. A dactyl, composed of an accented and two unaccented syllables (e.g. fórmŭlăte is obviously easier to produce in languages abundant with words that have accented antepenultimate ["the last saving two"] syllables) [Robinson's note].

5. A pause in a line of poetry; English poetry is much more flexible in its use of the caesura than the poetry of many other European vernacular languages.

6. Literally, "slippery": that is, the easy sliding of rhymes of three or more syllables.

our tongue is most fit to honor poesy, and to be honored by poesy; I conjure you all that have had the evil luck to read this ink-wasting toy of mine, even in the name of the nine Muses, no more to scorn the sacred mysteries of poesy, no more to laugh at the name of poets, as though they were next inheritors to fools, no more to jest at the reverent title of a rhymer; but to believe with Aristotle that they were the ancient treasurers of the Grecians' divinity; to believe with Bembus that they were first bringers-in of all civility; to believe with Scaliger that no philosopher's precepts can sooner make you an honest man than the reading of Virgil; to believe with Clauserus, the translator of Cornutus,[7] that it pleased the heavenly Deity, by Hesiod and Homer, under the veil of fables, to give us all knowledge, logic, rhetoric, philosophy natural and moral, and *quid non?*[8] to believe with me that there are many mysteries contained in poetry, which of purpose were written darkly, lest by profane wits it should be abused, to believe with Landino[9] that they are so beloved of the gods, that whatsoever they write proceeds of a divine fury; lastly, to believe themselves when they tell you they will make you immortal by their verses.

Thus doing, your name shall flourish in the printers' shops; thus doing, you shall be of kin to many a poetical preface; thus doing, you shall be most fair, most rich, most wise, most all, you shall dwell upon superlatives. Thus doing, though you be *libertino patre natus*, you shall suddenly grow *Hurculea proles*,[1]

Si quid mea carmina possunt[2]

Thus doing, your soul shall be placed with Dante's Beatrix, or Virgil's Anchises.[3] But if (fie of such a but) you be born so near the dull-making cataract of Nilus that you cannot hear the planet-like music of poetry,[4] if you have so earth-creeping a mind that it cannot lift itself up to look to the sky of poetry, or rather, by a certain rustical disdain, will become such a mome as to be a Momus[5] of poetry; then, though I will not wish unto you the ass's ears of Midas,[6] nor to be driven by a poet's verses (as Bubonax[7] was) to hang himself, nor to be rhymed to death, as it is said to be done in Ireland;[8] yet thus much curse I must send you in the behalf of all poets, that while you live, you live in love, and never get favor for lacking skill of a sonnet; and when you die, your memory die from the earth for want of an epitaph.

1580–81 1595

7. Lucius Annaeus Cornutus (b. ca. 20 C.E.), teacher of rhetoric and Stoic philosophy at Rome. Clauserus: Conrad Clauser, a 16th-century German humanist.
8. What not (Latin).
9. Christoforo Landino (1424–1504), Florentine humanist who developed this argument in his edition of Dante's *Divine Comedy* (1481).
1. A descendant of Hercules (Latin). *Libertino patre natus*: born of an ex-slave father (Latin); Horace, *Satires* 1.6.6.
2. If my songs can do anything (Latin); Virgil, *Aeneid* 9.446.
3. That is, with the blessed dead; Dante meets Beatrice in heaven in the *Divine Comedy*, and Aeneas finds his father, Anchises, in the Elysian Fields during his journey to the underworld (*Aeneid* 6).
4. Resembling the music of the spheres, the most beautiful of all music. Nilus: Cicero compared the Nile River's cataracts, whose noise deafened those who lived nearby, to the music of the spheres, which deafened all people (*Scipio's Dream* 5).
5. Greek son of Night, a sleepy god always mocking and criticizing. "Mome": a stupid person, blockhead.
6. Legendary king of Phrygia; when Midas judged Pan the winner of a musical contest with Apollo, Apollo gave him ass's ears (this is the version told in Ovid, *Metamorphoses* 11.146–93).
7. Sidney fuses the names of the two involved: Bupalus, a sculptor who hanged himself, and Hipponax, the 6th-century B.C.E. poet who satirized him.
8. Irish bards were thought to be able to cause death with their rhymed charms.

PIERRE CORNEILLE
1606–1684

Pierre Corneille provoked literary quarrels, infuriated critics, and delighted audiences for the better part of the seventeenth century. Decidedly not a courtly *dramatist*, Corneille was a *playwright*. A member of the emerging bourgeoisie, he wrote plays for money and to please audiences, not to curry favor with the royal or the literary establishment. It is therefore ironic that he is often seen today as the spokesman and exemplar of French classical theater. His promotion of classical "rules" is in part a plea for the value of not taking them too literally.

Corneille was born in the Normandy town of Rouen, France, where his father was a minor administrative official. After undergoing a rigorous and regulated Jesuit education, in which he excelled in Latin, he began legal studies in 1622; two years later he enrolled at the bar of Rouen. He argued only one case, with disastrous results: he stumbled over his words and stuttered, and at the age of nineteen he abandoned a legal career that had just begun. His father then bought him two modest magisterial posts in Rouen, in the department of rivers and forests. In 1629 a troupe of actors passed through Rouen, and Corneille showed them the script for a five-act comedy, *Mélite*. No one quite knows when he composed the play, or what may have inspired him to launch himself suddenly into the world of theater. The troupe took the play to Paris, where it was performed that winter and was the hit of the 1629–30 season. For the next several years, he wrote a new play each season—mostly comedies, but also tragicomedies and tragedies.

In 1637 Corneille's most famous play, *Le Cid* (based on a Spanish original; its title derived from the Arab word for "lord"), appeared and incited a flurry of critical attention that became known as the "Quarrel of *The Cid*." The Quarrel originated in the tension between Corneille's two audiences: the public and the critics. The public loved *Le Cid*, whose success was demonstrated even at the level of language: a new expression, "beau comme *Le Cid*" (as fine as *Le Cid*), entered the Parisian vernacular. The critics, on the other hand, sought to demonstrate the moral threat posed by the play, and in a series of pamphlets they attacked it and its author. In *Le Cid* a young woman, torn between love and duty, seems about to marry the man who has just killed her father. Such behavior, the critics argued, offends both reason and moral values. Drawing on the classical authority of both ARISTOTLE and HORACE, they insisted on the didactic function of the theater. A play's moral instruction, they claimed, was achieved by strict adherence to the rules of classical theater; these included the unities of time, place, and action and—more important—the need for both verisimilitude (*vraisemblance*) and decorum (*bienséance*). The critics held that a play should not only please, but please according to the rules. Louis XIII's chief minister, Cardinal de Richelieu, considered the stage the site for enacting a universal public virtue. He had founded the Académie Française (the French Academy) just two years before the staging of *Le Cid*, and the Quarrel offered him the public forum to assert his public moral authority. After a year of literary skirmishes—pamphlets and protests on the subversive nature of art and the need for public virtue—Richelieu, who had once included Corneille among his privileged "Five Authors," stepped in: with the authority of absolutism and the Académie, he proclaimed *Le Cid* contrary to the rules of *vraisemblance*. Corneille retreated to Rouen and indirectly answered the attacks by composing two tragedies on Roman themes, *Horace* (1639) and *Cinna* (1642). Both works adhere to the classical rules of composition.

In his conformity to the very rules that had been invoked against him, Corneille was implicitly siding with his critics and using the controversy to rethink his own baroqueness. The term *baroque*, derived from the artistic extravagance originally associated with the architecture of Catholic Spain and Italy, refers to a recurrent stylistic tendency rather than simply to a period, art form, or culture. In France the baroque is seen as extending the exuberance of the Renaissance, while classicism is seen as taming it. The baroque is based on energy, antithesis, exaggeration, and the stretching and transgressing of boundaries; the classical is based on balance and on the intensity of restraint. To the French, paradoxically, Shakespeare is too "baroque"—mixed, impure, multileveled, imperfect. In French classical theater, the forces of the baroque are internalized and held in precarious equilibrium within the self. Corneille succeeded in finding within classical rules a framework more suitable for his dramas of subjective conflict than that offered by the more diffuse and extravagant spectacles of the baroque theater that had inspired his earlier works. In 1642 he also wrote *Polyeucte martyr*, treating a Christian subject in the style of a classical work. The four plays of this period (*Le Cid, Horace, Cinna*, and *Polyeucte*) constitute what was later termed Corneille's tetralogy.

The luxuriant growth of the French language called for a century earlier by the poets JOACHIM DU BELLAY and PIERRE DE RONSARD had undergone a severe pruning in the early seventeenth century by a strict legislator of classical verse forms, François de Malherbe, and the golden age of French classical theater (called "neoclassical" in England) had begun. Malherbe prescribed the decorum of verse, which was followed quite faithfully for the next two centuries, both in theater and in lyric poetry: the twelve-syllable line, called an "alexandrine," was expected to break in the middle and not run on to the next line without a grammatical justification; in addition, rhyme should alternate between "masculine" and "feminine" endings. Corneille continued to be an anomalous champion of this theatrical and poetic regulation.

By the mid-1640s, Corneille was clearly the master of the French stage; he continued to live in Rouen, while traveling frequently to Paris. Married in 1641, he led the life of a provincial Catholic bourgeois with his wife and, eventually, seven children. In 1644 his first collection of plays was published. Now under the new political regime, the regency of Anne of Austria and her prime minister, Cardinal Mazarin (both Richelieu and Louis XIII had died), Corneille continued in his fame. In 1647, when he was considered for the third time, Corneille was elected to the French Academy.

During the revolt (known as "La Fronde") of a group of powerful nobles against the monarchy, Corneille's plays waned somewhat in popularity, though he wrote several "machine plays" that delighted crowds with their spectacular special effects and settings. Whenever a play of his was not well received, Corneille tended to retreat from public life. During one of his retreats he translated and published Thomas à Kempis's fifteenth-century Latin treatise *The Imitation of Jesus Christ* (1656); while it was obviously a radical shift from theatrical comedies, the translation was a great popular success.

His plays of the 1660s—mostly tragedies—were less popular than his earlier works. Times had changed: Corneille was still respected, but two younger playwrights—Racine and Molière—were beginning to steal the hearts of audiences and the favor of the court of the "Sun King," Louis XIV. Racine began his career by attacking Corneille, and the rivalry reached a head when, in 1670, Corneille and Racine were each urged to write a tragedy on the same topic (the doomed love between a Roman emperor and the queen of Palestine), unaware of the other's intention. Racine's *Bérénice* was deemed superior to Corneille's *Tite et Bérénice*, and Racine subsequently went on to write his greatest plays. Corneille continued to write, too, but with diminishing success; his last play, *Suréna, général des Parthes*, was produced in 1675. He died in 1684; in the following year his younger brother, Thomas Corneille, also a playwright, was given his seat in the French Academy, with the blessing of the belatedly gracious Racine.

More than twenty years after the Quarrel of *Le Cid*, Corneille wrote and published a defense of his dramatic style. The defense took the form of *Trois Discours sur le poème dramatique* (1660, *Three Discourses on Dramatic Poetry*), which was published in the seventh edition of his theatrical works. His discourses had a double aim: on the one hand, he needed to uphold the authority of Aristotle and the "ancients" against the frenzy and formlessness of the baroque; on the other, he needed to defend his theatrical practices against the rigid interpretation of that same Aristotle, whose authority had underpinned the Academy's criticism of *Le Cid*. Although he is often seen as a rigid apologist for classical form, Corneille actually argues for flexibility, for a practical adaptation of the sometimes unclear statements made in the *Poetics*, suiting the spirit but not always the letter of Aristotle's description of a well-made tragedy.

Corneille's *Trois Discours* directly responded to the publication in 1657 of the Abbé d'Aubignac's *Pratique du théâtre (The Practice of Theater)*, but the essays were obviously part of a much larger critical dialogue that had been going on throughout Corneille's career—a dialogue that had in many ways begun the year *Le Cid* opened in Paris. In *An Essay of Dramatic Poesy* (1668; see below), the English dramatist JOHN DRYDEN took up the issues with equal intensity. In the *Discourses*, written to introduce the three volumes of Corneille's own plays (the play printed under the author's supervision being a relatively recent departure from ancient practice), Corneille cites only himself among living dramatists, referring often to the ancients. The three essays each endorse Aristotelian ideas but argue that the strict rules of French classical theater are based on an overly literal interpretation of the *Poetics*. Again and again, Corneille claims that everyone agrees with Aristotle—they just don't agree on what he means.

Corneille opens the first discourse by quoting Aristotle's declaration that the sole purpose of drama is to please the spectator, and he repeatedly demonstrates that this desire to please the spectator will serve as his first axiom, to which the other rules of classical theater will often, but not always, be subordinate. The moralists of the seventeenth century, citing Aristotle, argued that the classical conventions necessarily led to didactic theater. But Corneille makes the didactic function secondary to entertainment. Though citing the same sources—Aristotle and Horace—he interprets them to challenge received ideas and to serve his own aesthetic ends. For example, in the first *Discours*, on the matter of *bienséance*, he views Aristotle's statement that a character's morals must be "good" not as a call for "naive depiction of vices and virtues," but rather as an insistence on character development: each character must be true to his or her history. To support his claim, he lists many examples from classical Greek theater of heroes who are adulterers or killers; here, says Corneille, classical theater transcends the simplistic idea that audiences need moral heroes to be "good" and adulterers and killers to be "bad" and therefore punished. It is more important to portray human behavior as it is, in keeping with a character's birth, family, and social status, than to offer flawless paragons of moral behavior.

In the second *Discours*, Corneille discusses the Aristotelian ideas on the nature of tragedy, especially the ways in which the tragic hero elicits pity and fear from the audience, which in turn leads to a purging, or catharsis, of those passions. He argues that human emotions are complicated and that the oppositions inherent in human nature, such as the contradictory forces of love and duty, will evoke pity and empathy from the audience. While classical theory prescribes that all actions should be both probable and necessary, some of the most intense tragic effects are created by predicaments that are not, at least according to *bienséance*, probable. Yet these unlikely events can nevertheless reveal something fundamental about human nature.

"Of the Three Unities of Action, Time, and Place," our selection, continues in the tone of the first two discourses. Using many examples from his own plays and quoting liberally from Aristotle's *Poetics*, Corneille in the third *Discours* both justifies his own dramatic works and explains the theories behind them. Above all, he is a pragmatist—a successful playwright and seasoned craftsman who has refused to submit to the prescriptive dicta of theatrical critics of his time. He knows that a play must please, even dazzle the audience.

Here he shows how the three unities can, at times, assist in the overall aim of theater. He begins by discussing the unity of action, which, for Corneille, does not require only one action on stage. "One complete action" may contain several other less-developed actions, which may or may not take place on the stage. He allows for some action to take place offstage between acts, and he also allows for particular actions that do not necessarily bring about the principal action. He does advise the writer to avoid actions that have happened before the time of the play, since such narrations of prior events will burden the spectator's memory, and he criticizes the multiple subplots that characterize Shakespearean drama.

The unity of time is founded on Aristotle's statement that the action of a play should be contained "within a single circuit of the sun." Corneille dismisses the argument as to whether Aristotle's maxim referred to a twelve-hour day or a twenty-four-hour day, offering instead the principle of proportion. A portrait will "gain in excellence" as it closely resembles reality. Since a play lasts about two hours, the action represented should come as close to two hours as possible. Yet precision in this unity may make the spectator aware of an unnatural need to compress the action; therefore, as with most theatrical strictures, Corneille wishes to allow latitude, and above all to "leave the matter of duration to the imagination of the spectators."

Corneille similarily calls for a judicious approach to the unity of place. Baroque plays, which sometimes spanned continents, were clearly in violation of *vraisemblance*. But a confined space like that of the theater itself—royal apartments, for example—might turn out to be overly restrictive (Shakespeare could be said to have gotten around this by staging his plays in a theater called the Globe). The concentration provided by a spatial confinement approaching that of the theater itself should always make sense. One should seek unity as much as possible, but at the same time recognize that not every subject can be adapted to its demands.

Within the strictures derived from Aristotle, then, Corneille is arguing for a loosening, not a tightening, of classical rules. His discussion of the unities, often taken to be prescriptive, is really a defense of flexibility. True, he brandishes Aristotle's authority against the exuberance of baroque forms. But his Aristotle can be adapted to fit a wide range of theatrical practices. The point, he concludes, is "to make the ancient rules agree with modern pleasures." Corneille would have been surprised to find that for later playwrights, especially in Germany during the early eighteenth century, he had become the epitome of the cold nobility and rigid formalism of the same classical theater into which he had constantly attempted to breathe life.

BIBLIOGRAPHY

Corneille's third *Discours* is the one most often reprinted, in part because its title, "Of the Three Unities of Time, Place, and Action," is so closely associated with the theory of classical drama. The three *Discours* do not exist in a single English edition. The first, "On the Uses and Elements of Dramatic Poetry," is translated by Beatrice Stewart MacClintock in *European Theories of the Drama* (ed. Barrett H. Clark, 1965). The second, "Discourse on Tragedy and of the Methods of Treating it, according to Probability and Necessity," can be found in *Dramatic Essays of the Neoclassic Age* (ed. Henry Hitch Adams and Baxter Hathaway, 1950). The third, our selection, is found in *The Continental Model* (ed. Scott Elledge and Donald Schier, 1960). The three essays are published together in French, with a helpful introduction and notes in English, in *Pierre Corneille: Writings on the Theatre*, edited by H. T. Barnwell (1965).

Two notable introductory works are P. J. Yarrow, *Corneille* (1963), and Claire L. Carlin, *Pierre Corneille Revisited* (1998); the latter offers a biographical chapter. Mitchell Greenberg's *Corneille, Classicism, and the Ruses of Symmetry* (1986) is an invaluable study of Corneille's tragic universe. David R. Clarke, *Pierre Corneille: Poetics and Political Drama under Louis XIII* (1992), and John Lyons, *The Tragedy of Origins: Pierre Corneille and Historical Perspective* (1966), provide two different interpretations of the nature of "history" in Corneille's plays. Two comparative studies—Benedetto Croce's classic *Ariosto, Shakespeare, and Corneille* (1920) and

A. Donald Sellstrom's more speculative *Corneille, Tasso, and Modern Poetics* (1986)—are of interest. The best bibliography of Corneille studies is the Corneille chapter in *A Critical Bibliography of French Literature*, vol. 3A, *The Seventeenth Century* (ed. Mare Fumaroli and Gwyneth Castor, 1983).

Of the Three Unities of Action, Time, and Place[1]

The two preceding discourses and the critical examination of the plays which my first two volumes contain have furnished me so many opportunities to explain my thoughts on these matters[2] that there would be little left for me to say if I absolutely forbade myself to repeat.

I hold then, as I have already said, that in comedy, unity of action consists in the unity of plot or the obstacle to the plans of the principal actors, and in tragedy in the unity of peril, whether the hero falls victim to it or escapes. It is not that I claim that several perils cannot be allowed in the latter or several plots or obstacles in the former, provided that one passes necessarily from one to the other; for then escape from the first peril does not make the action complete since the escape leads to another danger; and the resolution of one plot does not put the actors at rest since they are confounded afresh in another. My memory does not furnish me any ancient examples of this multiplicity of perils linked each to each without the destruction of the unity of action; but I have noted independent double action as a defect in *Horace* and in *Théodore*,[3] for it is not necessary that the first kill his sister upon gaining his victory nor that the other give herself up to martyrdom after having escaped prostitution; and if the death of Polyxène and that of Astyanax in Seneca's[4] *Trojan Women* do not produce the same irregularity I am very much mistaken.

In the second place, the term unity of action does not mean that tragedy should show only one action on the stage. The one which the poet chooses for his subject must have a beginning, a middle, and an end;[5] and not only are these three parts separate actions which find their conclusion in the principal one, but, moreover, each of them may contain several others with the same subordination. There must be only one complete action, which leaves the mind of the spectator serene; but that action can become complete only through several others which are less perfect and which, by serving as preparation, keep the spectator in a pleasant suspense. This is what must be contrived at the end of each act in order to give continuity to the action. It is not necessary that we know exactly what the actors are doing in the intervals which separate the acts, nor even that they contribute to the action when they do not appear on the stage; but it is necessary that each act leave us in the expectation of something which is to take place in the following one.

If you asked me what Cléopâtre is doing in *Rodogune*[6] between the time

1. Translated by Donald Schier.
2. The principles Corneille had derived from ARISTOTLE's *Poetics* (see above). The first two discourses were "On the Uses and Elements of Dramatic Poetry" and "Discourse on Tragedy and of the Methods of Treating It, according to Probability and Necessity." Each play also had an *examen* (critical examination) appended by Corneille.
3. Two tragedies by Corneille, written respectively in 1640 and 1645.
4. Seneca the Younger (ca. 4 B.C.E.–65 C.E.), Roman philosopher, statesman, and tragedian.
5. See Aristotle, *Poetics* 7, 1450b.
6. *Rodogune, Princesse des Parthes* (1644), a tragedy by Corneille in which Cleopatra, queen of Syria, promises the throne to the one of her two sons, Antiochus and Seleucus, who will bring to her the head of Rodogune, with whom both are in

when she leaves her two sons in the second act until she rejoins Antiochus in the fourth, I should be unable to tell you, and I do not feel obliged to account for her; but the end of this second act prepares us to see an amicable effort by the two brothers to rule and to hide Rodogune from the venomous hatred of their mother. The effect of this is seen in the third act, whose ending prepares us again to see another effort by Antiochus to win back these two enemies one after the other and for what Séleucus does in the fourth, which compels that unnatural mother [Cléopâtre] to resolve upon what she tries to accomplish in the fifth, whose outcome we await with suspense.

In *Le Menteur*[7] the actors presumably make use of the whole interval between the third and fourth acts to sleep; their rest, however, does not impede the continuity of the action between those two acts because the third does not contain a complete event. Dorante ends it with his plan to seek ways to win back the trust of Lucrèce, and at the very beginning of the next he appears so as to be able to talk to one of her servants and to her, should she show herself.

When I say that it is not necessary to account for what the actors do when they are not on stage, I do not mean that it is not sometimes very useful to give such an accounting, but only that one is not forced to do it, and that one ought to take the trouble to do so only when what happens behind the scenes is necessary for the understanding of what is to take place before the spectators. Thus I say nothing of what Cléopâtre did between the second and the fourth acts, because during all that time she can have done nothing important as regards the principal action which I am preparing for; but I point out in the very first lines of the fifth act that she has used the interval between these latter two for the killing of Séleucus, because that death is part of the action. This is what leads me to state that the poet is not required to show all the particular actions which bring about the principal one; he must choose to show those which are the most advantageous, whether by the beauty of the spectacle or by the brilliance or violence of the passions they produce, or by some other attraction which is connected with them, and to hide the others behind the scenes while informing the spectator of them by a narration or by some other artistic device; above all, he must remember that they must all be so closely connected that the last are produced by the preceding and that all have their source in the protasis[8] which ought to conclude the first act. This rule, which I have established in my first *Discourse*, although it is new and contrary to the usage of the ancients, is founded on two passages of Aristotle. Here is the first of them: "There is a great difference," he says, "between events which succeed each other and those which occur because of others."[9] The Moors come into the Cid[1] after the death of the Count and not because of the death of the Count; and the fisherman comes into *Don Sanche*[2] after Charles is suspected of being the Prince of Aragon and not because he is suspected of it; thus both are to be criticized. The second passage is even more specific and says precisely "that

love. When Seleucus is killed, Cleopatra prepares to poison Antiochus and Rodogune, but ends up drinking the poison herself.

7. *The Liar* (1643), a comedy by Corneille in which a provincial fabulator, Dorante, seeks to impress two Parisian women, Lucrèce and Clarice.

8. The introductory act or exposition of classical Greek drama (literally, "that which is put forward"; Greek), a term of late antiquity.

9. Aristotle, *Poetics* 10, 1452a.

1. *Le Cid* (1637), a tragedy by Corneille.

2. *Don Sanche d'Aragon* (1649), a heroic comedy by Corneille.

everything that happens in tragedy must arise necessarily or probably from what has gone before."[3]

The linking of the scenes which unites all the individual actions of each act and of which I have spoken in criticizing *La Suivante*[4] is a great beauty in a poem and one which serves to shape continuity of action through continuity of presentation; but, in the end, it is only a beauty and not a rule. The ancients did not always abide by it although most of their acts have but two or three scenes. This made things much simpler for them than for us, who often put as many as nine or ten scenes into each act. I shall cite only two examples of the scorn with which they treated this principle: one is from Sophocles,[5] in *Ajax*, whose monologue before he kills himself has no connection with the preceding scene; the other is from the third act of Terence's[6] *The Eunuch*, where Antipho's soliloquy has no connection with Chremes and Pythias who leave the stage when he enters. The scholars of our century, who have taken the ancients for models in the tragedies they have left us, have even more neglected that linking than did the ancients, and one need only glance at the plays of Buchanan, Grotius, and Heinsius,[7] of which I spoke in the discussion of *Polyeucte*,[8] to agree on that point. We have so far accustomed our audiences to this careful linking of scenes that they cannot now witness a detached scene without considering it a defect; the eye and even the ear are outraged by it even before the mind has been able to reflect upon it. The fourth act of *Cinna*[9] falls below the others through this flaw; and what formerly was not a rule has become one now through the assiduousness of our practice.

I have spoken of three sorts of linkings in the discussion of *La Suivante*: I have shown myself averse to those of sound, indulgent to those of sight, favorable to those of presence and speech; but in these latter I have confused two things which ought to be separated. Links of presence and speech both have, no doubt, all the excellence imaginable; but there are links of speech without presence and of presence without speech which do not reach the same level of excellence. An actor who speaks to another from a hiding-place without showing himself forms a link of speech without presence which is always effective; but that rarely happens. A man who remains on stage merely to hear what will be said by those whom he sees making their entrance forms a link of presence without speech; this is often clumsy and falls into mere pretense, being contrived more to accede to this new convention which is becoming a precept than for any need dictated by the plot of the play. Thus, in the third act of *Pompée*,[1] Achorée, after having informed Charmion of the reception Caesar gave to the king when he presented to him the head of that

3. Aristotle, *Poetics* 10, 1452a.
4. *The Lady's Maid* (1633), a comedy by Corneille; his earlier criticism was in the *examen* to the play.
5. Greek tragic dramatist (ca. 496–406 B.C.E.). *Ajax* (ca. 441) is generally regarded as the earliest of his extant plays.
6. Roman comic dramatist (ca. 190–ca. 159 B.C.E.); *Eunuchus* was produced in 161.
7. Daniël Heinsius (1580–1655), Dutch poet and classical scholar; he published an edition of Aristotle's *Poetics* (1611), and his *De Tragoediae Constitutione* (1611) decisively influenced French classical theater. George Buchanan (1506–1582), Scottish humanist, educator, and man of letters who taught Latin in Paris and was known throughout Europe as a scholar and a Latin poet. Hugo Grotius (1583–1645), Dutch jurist whose writings also included a number of tragedies.
8. *Polyeucte martyr* (1640), a Christian tragedy by Corneille; this earlier discussion was in the *examen* to the play.
9. *Cinna, ou la clémence d'Auguste* (1641, *Cinna, or the Clemency of Augustus*), a tragedy by Corneille. In an effort to avenge her father, Emilie incites her beloved Cinna to overthrow the emperor, Augustus. He is betrayed by a fellow conspirator, Maxime, also in love with Emilie; the conspirators are, in the end, all pardoned by a merciful Augustus.
1. *La mort de Pompée* (1642, *The Death of Pompey*), a tragedy by Corneille.

hero, remains on the stage where he sees the two of them come together merely to hear what they will say and report it to Cléopâtre. Ammon does the same thing in the fourth act of *Andromède*[2] for the benefit of Phinée, who retires when he sees the king and all his court arriving. Characters who become mute connect rather badly scenes in which they play little part and in which they count for nothing. It is another matter when they hide in order to find out some important secret from those who are speaking and who think they are not overheard, for then the interest which they have in what is being said, added to a reasonable curiosity to find out what they cannot learn in any other way, gives them an important part in the action despite their silence; but in these two examples Ammon and Achorée lend so cold a presence to the scenes they overhear that, to be perfectly frank, whatever feigned reason I give them to serve as pretext for their action, they remain there only to connect the scenes with those that precede, so easily can both plays dispense with what they do.

Although the action of the dramatic poem must have its unity, one must consider both its parts: the complication and the resolution. "The complication is composed," according to Aristotle, "in part of what has happened off stage before the beginning of the action which is there described, and in part from what happens on stage; the rest belongs to the resolution. The change of fortune forms the separation of these two parts. Everything which precedes it is in the first part, and this change, with what follows it, concerns the other."[3] The complication depends entirely upon the choice and industrious imagination of the poet and no rule can be given for it, except that in it he ought to order all things according to probability or necessity, a point which I have discussed in the second *Discourse*; to this I add one piece of advice, which is that he involve himself as little as possible with things which have happened before the action he is presenting. Such narrations are annoying, usually because they are not expected, and they disturb the mind of the spectator, who is obliged to burden his memory with what has happened ten or twelve years before in order to understand what he is about to see; but narrations which describe things which happen and take place behind the scenes once the action has started always produce a better effect because they are awaited with some curiosity and are a part of the action which is being shown. One of the reasons why so many illustrious critics favor *Cinna* above anything else I have done is that it contains no narration of the past, the one Cinna makes in describing his plot to Emilie being rather an ornament which tickles the mind of the spectators than a necessary marshaling of the details they must know and impress upon their memories for the understanding of what is to come. Emilie informs them adequately in the first two scenes that he is conspiring against Augustus in her favor, and if Cinna merely told her that the plotters are ready for the following day he would advance the action just as much as by the hundred lines he uses to tell both what he said to them and the way in which they received his words. There are plots which begin at the very birth of the hero like that of *Héraclius*,[4] but these great efforts of the imagination demand an extraordinary

2. A successful "machine play" (extravagant spectacle) (1650) by Corneille.
3. Aristotle, *Poetics* 18, 1455b.
4. *Héraclius, empereur d'Orient* (1647), a tragedy by Corneille. In this complicated drama of near-incest and mistaken identity, the main characters are Héraclius, the legitimate prince; Phocas, the usurping ruler; Martian, son (unbeknownst to him) of Phocas; and Pulchérie, sister of Héraclius.

attention of the spectator and often keep him from taking a real pleasure in the first performances, so much do they weary him.

In the resolution I find two things to avoid: the mere change of intention and the machine.[5] Not much skill is required to finish a poem when he who has served as the obstacle to the plans of the principal actors for four acts desists in the fifth without being constrained to do so by any remarkable event; I have spoken of this in the first *Discourse* and I shall add nothing to that here. The machine requires no more skill when it is used only to bring down a god who straightens everything out when the actors are unable to do so. It is thus that Apollo functions in the *Orestes*:[6] this prince and his friend Pylades, accused by Tyndarus and Menelaus of the death of Clytemnestra and condemned after prosecution by them, seize Helen and Hermione; they kill, or think they kill the first, and threaten to do the same with the other if the sentence pronounced against them is not revoked. To smooth out these difficulties Euripides seeks nothing subtler than to bring Apollo down from heaven, and he, by absolute authority, orders that Orestes marry Hermione and Pylades Electra; and lest the death of Helen prove an obstacle to this, it being improbable that Hermione would marry Orestes since he had just killed her mother, Apollo informs them that she is not dead, that he has protected her from their blows and carried her off to heaven at the moment when they thought they were killing her. This use of the machine is entirely irrelevant, being founded in no way on the rest of the play, and makes a faulty resolution. But I find a little too harsh the opinion of Aristotle, who puts on the same level the chariot Medea uses to flee from Corinth after the vengeance she has taken on Creon.[7] It seems to me there is a sufficient basis for this in the fact that she has been made a magician and that actions of hers as far surpassing natural forces as that one have been mentioned in the play. After what she did for Jason at Colchis and after she had made his father Aeson young again following his return, and after she had attached invisible fire to the gift she gave to Creusa, the flying chariot is not improbable and the poem has no need of other preparation for that extraordinary effect. Seneca gives it preparation by this line which Medea speaks to her nurse:

> Tuum quoque ipsa corpus hinc mecum aveham;[8]

and I by this one which she speaks to Aegeus

> I shall follow you tomorrow by a new road.[9]

Thus the condemnation of Euripides, who took no precautions, may be just and yet not fall on Seneca or on me: and I have no need to contradict Aristotle in order to justify myself on this point.

5. That is, the *deus ex machina* (god from a machine; Latin); in some Greek tragedies, a sort of crane lowered a god from the sky to provide a quick resolution to an entangled plot.

6. A drama (408 B.C.E.) by Euripides (ca. 485–ca. 406 B.C.E.), the Greek playwright who used the *deus ex machina* most frequently. In the Greek myth, Orestes kills his mother, Clytemnestra, to avenge her murder of his father, Agamemnon. Tyndareus is the father of Clytemnestra and of Helen (of Troy), whose husband is Menelaus; Hermione is Helen's daughter, and Electra is Orestes' sister. Apollo is the Greek god of music and prophecy.

7. At the end of Euripides' *Medea* (431 B.C.E); see *Poetics* 15, 1453a–1454b. At Colchis, Medea, a sorceress, helps Jason steal the Golden Fleece, and later marries him; when he chooses to marry the daughter of Creon, king of Corinth (unnamed in Euripides' play, named Creusa in Seneca's), she sends Jason's new wife a robe covered in a deadly ointment and kills Jason's and her two children, escaping in the dragon-drawn chariot of Helios (the sun), her grandfather.

8. Seneca, *Medea*, line 975: "I'll also carry away your corpse from here with me" (Medea is addressing her dead child).

9. Corneille, *Médée* (1635); Aegeus is a legendary king of Athens, whom Medea marries after fleeing Corinth.

From the action I turn to the acts, each of which ought to contain a portion of it, but not so equal a portion that more is not reserved for the last than for the others and less given to the first than to the others. Indeed, in the first act one may do no more than depict the moral nature of the characters and mark off how far they have got in the story which is to be presented. Aristotle does not prescribe the number of the acts; Horace limits it to five;[1] and although he prohibits having fewer, the Spaniards are obstinate enough to stop at three and the Italians often do the same thing. The Greeks used to separate the acts by the chanting of the chorus, and since I think it reasonable to believe that in some of their poems they made it chant more than four times, I should not want to say they never exceeded five. This way of distinguishing the acts was less handy than ours, for either they paid attention to what the chorus was chanting or they did not; if they did, the mind of the spectators was too tense and had no time in which to rest; if they did not, attention was too much dissipated by the length of the chant, and when a new act began, an effort of memory was needed to recall to the imagination what had been witnessed and at what point the action had been interrupted. Our orchestra presents neither of these two inconveniences; the mind of the spectator relaxes while the music is playing and even reflects on what he has seen, to praise it or to find fault with it depending on whether he has been pleased or displeased; and the short time the orchestra is allowed to play leaves his impressions so fresh that when the actors return he does not need to make an effort to recall and resume his attention.

The number of scenes in each act has never been prescribed by rule, but since the whole act must have a certain number of lines which make its length proportionate to that of the others, one may include in it more or fewer scenes depending on whether they are long or short to fill up the time which the whole act is to consume. One ought, if possible, to account for the entrance and exit of each actor; I consider this rule indispensable, especially for the exit, and think there is nothing so clumsy as an actor who leaves the stage merely because he has no more lines to speak.

I should not be so rigorous for the entrances. The audience expects the actor, and although the setting represents the room or the study of whoever is speaking, yet he cannot make his appearance there unless he comes out from behind the tapestry, and it is not always easy to give a reason for what he has just done in town before returning home, since sometimes it is even probable that he has not gone out at all. I have never seen anybody take offense at seeing Emilie begin *Cinna* without saying why she has come to her room; she is presumed to be there before the play begins, and it is only stage necessity which makes her appear from behind the scenes to come there. Thus I should willingly dispense from the rigors of the rule the first scene of each act but not the others, because once an actor is on the stage anyone who enters must have a reason to speak to him or, at least, must profit from the opportunity to do so when it offers. Above all, when an actor enters twice in one act, in comedy or in tragedy, he must either lead one to expect that he will soon return when he leaves the first time, like Horace in the second act and Julie in the third act of *Horace*, or explain on returning why he has come back so soon.

1. The Roman poet HORACE (65–8 B.C.E.), *Ars Poetica*, lines 189–90 (see above).

Aristotle wishes the well-made tragedy to be beautiful and capable of pleasing without the aid of actors and quite aside from performance.[2] So that the reader may more easily experience that pleasure, his mind, like that of the spectator, must not be hindered, because the effort he is obliged to make to conceive and to imagine the play for himself lessens the satisfaction which he will get from it. Therefore, I should be of the opinion that the poet ought to take great care to indicate in the margin the less important actions which do not merit being included in the lines, and which might even mar the dignity of the verse if the author lowered himself to express them. The actor easily fills this need on the stage, but in a book one would often be reduced to guessing and sometimes one might even guess wrong, unless one were informed in this way of these little things. I admit that this is not the practice of the ancients; but you must also allow me that because they did not do it they have left us many obscurities in their poems which only masters of dramatic art can explain; even so, I am not sure they succeed as often as they think they do. If we forced ourselves to follow the method of the ancients completely, we should make no distinction between acts and scenes because the Greeks did not. This failure on their part is often the reason that I do not know how many acts there are in their plays, nor whether at the end of an act the player withdraws so as to allow the chorus to chant, or whether he remains on stage without any action while the chorus is chanting, because neither they nor their interpreters have deigned to give us a word of indication in the margin.

We have another special reason for not neglecting that helpful little device as they did: this is that printing puts our plays in the hands of actors who tour the provinces and whom we can thus inform of what they ought to do, for they would do some very odd things if we did not help them by these notes. They would find themselves in great difficulty at the fifth act of plays that end happily, where we bring together all the actors on the stage (a thing which the ancients did not do); they would often say to one what is meant for another, especially when the same actor must speak to three or four people one after the other. When there is a whispered command to make, like Cléopâtre's to Laonice which sends her to seek poison,[3] an aside would be necessary to express this in verse if we were to do without the marginal indications, and that seems to me much more intolerable than the notes, which give us the real and only way, following the opinion of Aristotle, of making the tragedy as beautiful in the reading as in performance, by making it easy for the reader to imagine what the stage presents to the view of the spectators.

The rule of the unity of time is founded on this statement of Aristotle "that the tragedy ought to enclose the duration of its action in one journey of the sun or try not to go much beyond it."[4] These words gave rise to a famous dispute as to whether they ought to be understood as meaning a natural day of twenty-four hours or an artificial day of twelve; each of the two opinions has important partisans, and, for myself, I find that there are subjects so difficult to limit to such a short time that not only should I grant the twenty-four full hours but I should make use of the license which the philosopher

2. Aristotle, *Poetics* 6, 1450b.
3. In *Rodogune*.
4. Aristotle, *Poetics* 5, 1449b.

gives to exceed them a little and should push the total without scruple as far as thirty. There is a legal maxim which says that we should broaden the mercies and narrow the rigors of the law, *odia restringenda, favores ampliandi*; and I find that an author is hampered enough by this constraint which forced some of the ancients to the very edge of the impossible. Euripides in *The Suppliants*[5] makes Theseus leave Athens with an army, fight a battle beneath the walls of Thebes, which was ten or twelve leagues away, and return victorious in the following act; and between his departure and the arrival of the messenger who comes to tell the story of his victory, the chorus has only thirty-six lines to speak. That makes good use of such a short time. Aeschylus[6] makes Agamemnon come back from Troy with even greater speed. He had agreed with Clytemnestra, his wife, that as soon as the city was taken he would inform her by signal fires built on the intervening mountains, of which the second would be lighted as soon as the first was seen, the third at the sight of the second, and so on; by this means she was to learn the great news the same night. However, scarcely had she learned it from the signal fires when Agamemnon arrives, whose ship, although battered by a storm, if memory serves, must have traveled as fast as the eye could see the lights. *The Cid* and *Pompée*, where the action is a little precipitate, are far from taking so much license; and if they force ordinary probability in some way, at least they do not go as far as such impossibilities.

Many argue against this rule, which they call tyrannical, and they would be right if it were founded only on the authority of Aristotle; but what should make it acceptable is the fact that common sense supports it. The dramatic poem is an imitation, or rather a portrait of human actions, and it is beyond doubt that portraits gain in excellence in proportion as they resemble the original more closely. A performance lasts two hours and would resemble reality perfectly if the action it presented required no more for its actual occurrence. Let us then not settle on twelve or twenty-four hours, but let us compress the action of the poem into the shortest possible period, so that the performance may more closely resemble reality and thus be more nearly perfect. Let us give, if that is possible, to the one no more than the two hours which the other fills. I do not think that *Rodogune* requires much more, and perhaps two hours would be enough for *Cinna*. It we cannot confine the action within the two hours, let us take four, six, or ten, but let us not go much beyond twenty-four for fear of falling into lawlessness and of so far reducing the scale of the portrait that it no longer has its proportionate dimensions and is nothing but imperfection.

Most of all, I should like to leave the matter of duration to the imagination of the spectators and never make definite the time the action requires unless the subject needs this precision, but especially not when probability is a little forced, as in the *Cid*, because precision serves only to make the crowded action obvious to the spectator. Even when no violence is done to a poem by the necessity of obeying this rule, why must one state at the beginning that the sun is rising, that it is noon at the third act, and that the sun is setting at the end of the last act? This is only an obtrusive affectation; it is enough to establish the possibility of the thing in the time one gives to it and

5. A tragedy first performed ca. 422 B.C.E.
6. Greek tragic dramatist (525–456 B.C.E.); Corneille describes the beginning of his *Agamemnon* (458).

that one be able to determine the time easily if one wishes to pay attention to it, but without being compelled to concern oneself with the matter. Even in those actions which take no longer than the performance it would be clumsy to point out that a half hour has elapsed between the beginning of one act and the beginning of the next.

I repeat what I have said elsewhere,[7] that when we take a longer time, as, for instance, ten hours, I should prefer that the eight extra be used up in the time between the acts and that each act should have as its share only as much time as performance requires especially when all scenes are closely linked together. I think, however, that the fifth act, by special privilege, has the right to accelerate time so that the part of the action which it presents may use up more time than is necessary for performance. The reason for this is that the spectator is by then impatient to see the end, and when the outcome depends on actors who are off stage, all the dialogue given to those who are on stage awaiting news of the others drags and action seems to halt. There is no doubt that from the point where Phocas exits in the fifth act of *Héraclius* until Amyntas enters to relate the manner of his death, more time is needed for what happens off stage than for the speaking of the lines in which Héraclius, Martian, and Pulchérie complain of their misfortune. Prusias and Flaminius, in the fifth act of *Nicomède*,[8] do not have the time they would need to meet at sea, take counsel with each other, and return to the defense of the queen; and the Cid has not enough time to fight a duel with Don Sanche during the conversations of the Infanta with Léonor and of Chimène with Elvire. I was aware of this and yet have had no scruples about this acceleration of which, perhaps, one might find several examples among the ancients, but the laziness of which I have spoken will force me to rest content with this one, which is from the *Andria*[9] of Terence. Simo slips his son Pamphilus into the house of Glycerium in order to get the old man, Crito, to come out and to clear up with him the question of the birth of his mistress, who happens to be the daughter of Chremes. Pamphilus enters the house, speaks to Crito, asks him for the favor and returns with him; and during this exit, this request, and this re-entry, Simo and Chremes, who remain on stage, speak only one line each, which could not possibly give Pamphilus more than time enough to ask where Crito is, certainly not enough to talk with him and to explain to him the reasons for which he should reveal what he knows about the birth of the unknown girl.

When the conclusion of the action depends on actors who have not left the stage and about whom no one is awaiting news, as in *Cinna* and *Rodogune*, the fifth act has no need of this privilege because then all the action takes place in plain sight, as does not happen when part of it occurs off stage after the beginning of the act. The other acts do not merit the same freedom. If there is not time enough to bring back an actor who has made his exit, or to indicate what he has done since that exit, the accounting can be postponed to the following act; and the music, which separates the two acts, may use up as much time as is necessary; but in the fifth act no postponement is possible: attention is exhausted and the end must come quickly.

7. In the *Examen de Mélite*, which precedes the present Discourse in the edition published by Corneille [translator's note].

8. A tragedy (1651) by Corneille.

9. *The Maid of Andros* (166 B.C.E.), Terence's first play.

I cannot forget that although we must reduce the whole tragic action to one day, we can nevertheless make known by a narration or in some other more artful way what the hero of the tragedy has been doing for several years, because there are plays in which the crux of the plot lies in an obscurity of birth which must be brought to light, as in *Oedipus*.[1] I shall not say again that the less one burdens oneself with past actions, the more favorable the spectator will be, because of the lesser degree of trouble he is given when everything takes place in the present and no demands are made on his memory except for what he has seen; but I cannot forget that the choice of a day both illustrious and long-awaited is a great ornament to a poem. The opportunity for this does not always present itself, and in all that I have written until now you will find only four of that kind: the day in *Horace* when two nations are to decide the question of supremacy of empire by a battle; and the ones in *Rodogune, Andromède*, and *Don Sanche*. In *Rodogune* it is a day chosen by two sovereigns for the signature of a treaty of peace between the hostile crowns, for a complete reconciliation of the two rival governments through a marriage, and for the elucidation of a more than twenty-year-old secret concerning the right of succession of one of the twin princes on which the fate of the kingdom depends, as does the outcome of both their loves. The days in *Andromède* and *Don Sanche* are not of lesser importance, but, as I have just said, such opportunities do not often present themselves, and in the rest of my works I have been able to choose days remarkable only for what chance makes happen on them and not by the use to which public arrangements destined them long ago.

As for the unity of place, I find no rule concerning it in either Aristotle or Horace. This is what leads many people to believe that this rule was established only as a consequence of the unity of one day, and leads them to imagine that one can stretch the unity of place to cover the points to which a man may go and return in twenty-four hours. This opinion is a little too free, and if one made an actor travel post-haste, the two sides of the theater might represent Paris and Rouen. I could wish, so that the spectator is not at all disturbed, that what is performed before him in two hours might actually be able to take place in two hours, and that what he is shown in a stage setting which does not change might be limited to a room or a hall depending on a choice made beforehand; but often that is so awkward, if not impossible, that one must necessarily find some way to enlarge the place as also the time of the action. I have shown exact unity of place in *Horace, Polyeucte*, and *Pompée*, but for that it was necessary to present either only one woman, as in *Polyeucte*; or to arrange that the two who are presented are such close friends and have such closely related interests that they can be always together, as in *Horace*; or that they may react as in *Pompée* where the stress of natural curiosity drives Cléopâtre from her apartments in the second act and Cornélie in the fifth; and both enter the great hall of the king's palace in anticipation of the news they are expecting. The same thing is not true of *Rodogune*: Cléopâtre and she have interests which are too divergent to permit them to express their most secret thoughts in the same place. I might say of that play what I have said of *Cinna*, where, in general, everything happens

1. The *Oedipus Rex* (ca. 430 B.C.E.) of Sophocles is the best-known treatment of the story (an *Oedipus* of Seneca is also extant); at the climax of the play Oedipus learns that he has unknowingly killed his father and married his mother. Corneille wrote his *Oedipe* in 1659.

in Rome and, in particular, half of the action takes place in the quarters of Auguste and half of it in Emilie's apartments. Following that arrangement, the first act of this tragedy would be laid in Rodogune's antechamber, the second, in Cléopâtre's apartments, the third, in Rodogune's; but if the fourth act can begin in Rodogune's apartments it cannot finish there, and what Cléopâtre says to her two sons one after the other would be badly out of place there. The fifth act needs a throne room where a great crowd can be gathered. The same problem is found in *Héraclius.* The first act could very well take place in Phocas's quarters, the second, in Léontine's apartments; but if the third begins in Pulchérie's rooms, it cannot end there, and it is outside the bounds of probability that Phocas should discuss the death of her brother in Pulchérie's apartments.

The ancients, who made their kings speak in a public square, easily kept a rigorous unity of place in their tragedies. Sophocles, however, did not observe it in his *Ajax*, when the hero leaves the stage to find a lonely place in which to kill himself and does so in full view of the people; this easily leads to the conclusion that the place where he kills himself is not the one he has been seen to leave, since he left it only to choose another.

We do not take the same liberty of drawing kings and princesses from their apartments, and since often the difference and the opposition on the part of those who are lodged in the same palace do not allow them to take others into their confidence or to disclose their secrets in the same room, we must seek some other compromise about unity of place if we want to keep it intact in our poems; otherwise we should have to decide against many plays which we see succeeding brilliantly.

I hold, then, that we ought to seek exact unity as much as possible, but as this unity does not suit every kind of subject, I should be very willing to concede that a whole city has unity of place. Not that I should want the stage to represent the whole city, that would be somewhat too large, but only two or three particular places enclosed within its walls. Thus the scene of *Cinna* does not leave Rome, passing from the apartments of Auguste to the house of Emilie. *Le Menteur* takes place in the Tuileries and in the Place Royale at Paris, and *La Suite*[2] shows us the prison and Mélisse's house at Lyons. *The Cid* increases even more the number of particular places without leaving Seville; and since the close linking of scenes is not observed in that play, the stage in the first act is supposed to represent Chimène's house, the Infante's apartments in the king's palace, and the public square; the second adds to these the king's chamber. No doubt there is some excess in this freedom. In order to rectify in some way this multiplication of places when it is inevitable, I should wish two things done: first, that the scene should never change in a given act but only between the acts, as is done in the first three acts of *Cinna*; the other, that these two places should not need different stage settings and that neither of the two should ever be named, but only the general place which includes them both, as Paris, Rome, Lyons, Constantinople, and so forth. This would help to deceive the spectator, who, seeing nothing that would indicate the difference in the places, would not notice the change, unless it was maliciously and critically pointed out, a thing which few are capable of doing,

2. *La Suite du Menteur* (1643, *Sequel to the Liar*), a comedy by Corneille.

most spectators being warmly intent upon the action which they see on the stage. The pleasure they take in it is the reason why they do not seek out its imperfections lest they lose their taste for it; and they admit such an imperfection only when forced, when it is too obvious, as in *Le Menteur* and *La Suite*, where the different settings force them to recognize the multiplicity of places in spite of themselves.

But since people of opposing interests cannot with verisimilitude unfold their secrets in the same place, and since they are sometimes introduced into the same act through the linking of scenes which the unity of place necessarily produces, one must find some means to make it compatible with the contradiction which rigorous probability finds in it, and consider how to preserve the fourth act of *Rodogune* and the third of *Héraclius*, in both of which I have already pointed out the contradiction which lies in having enemies speak in the same place. Jurists allow legal fictions, and I should like, following their example, to introduce theatrical fictions by which one could establish a theatrical place which would not be Cléopâtre's chamber nor Rodogune's, in the play of that name, nor that of Phocas, of Léontine or of Pulchérie in *Héraclius*, but a room contiguous to all these other apartments, to which I should attribute these two privileges: first, that each of those who speaks in it is presumed to enjoy the same secrecy there as if he were in his own room; and second, that whereas in the usual arrangement it is sometimes proper for those who are on stage to go off, in order to speak privately with others in their rooms, these latter might meet the former on stage without shocking convention, so as to preserve both the unity of place and the linking of scenes. Thus Rodogune, in the first act, encounters Laonice, whom she must send for so as to speak with her; and, in the fourth act, Cléopâtre encounters Antiochus on the very spot where he has just moved Rodogune to pity, even though in utter verisimilitude the prince ought to seek out his mother in her own room since she hates the princess too much to come to speak to him in Rodogune's, which, following the first scene, would be the locus of the whole act, if one did not introduce that compromise which I have mentioned into the rigorous unity of place.

Many of my plays will be at fault in the unity of place if this compromise is not accepted, for I shall abide by it always in the future when I am not able to satisfy the ultimate rigor of the rule. I have been able to reduce only three plays, *Horace, Polyeucte*, and *Pompée*, to the requirements of the rule. If I am too indulgent with myself as far as the others are concerned, I shall be even more so for those which may succeed on the stage through some appearance of regularity. It is easy for critics to be severe; but if they were to give ten or a dozen plays to the public, they might perhaps slacken the rules more than I do, as soon as they have recognized through experience what constraint their precision brings about and how many beautiful things it banishes from our stage. However that may be, these are my opinions, or if you prefer, my heresies concerning the principal points of the dramatic art, and I do not know how better to make the ancient rules agree with modern pleasures. I do not doubt that one might easily find better ways of doing that, and I shall be ready to accept them when they have been put into practice as successfully as, by common consent, mine have been.

1660

JOHN DRYDEN
1631–1700

John Dryden worked expertly in poetry, drama, criticism, and translation. He was a true literary professional, an eminent (if controversial) public writer who took pride in his craft. While his achievements are impressive and his influence significant, his writing is often too topical and occasional to give great pleasure to nonspecialist readers today. In poetry and criticism, Dryden prepared the way for later writers who built upon what he had done—ALEXANDER POPE and SAMUEL JOHNSON in particular.

Biographical evidence suggests that Dryden's middle-class parents supported the Puritan cause and Parliament. Dryden was educated at Westminster School and at Trinity College, Cambridge, receiving his degree in 1654.

His first important poem, *Heroic Stanzas* (1658, published 1659), eulogized Oliver Cromwell, the Puritan religious, military, and political leader and the lord protector of England (1653–58). Dryden was present at Cromwell's funeral, as were the Puritan poets John Milton and Andrew Marvell. In 1660, when Charles II assumed the throne eleven years after the execution of his father, Charles I, Dryden celebrated the event in his poem *Astrea Redux* ("justice restored"). This and later shifts in his political and religious positions led many critics to charge that he was an opportunist; but as SAMUEL JOHNSON noted in his *Life of Dryden*, "if he changed, he changed with the nation."

Annus Mirabilis ("year of wonders," 1667), a historical poem that describes two events of 1666, the English defeat of the Dutch naval fleet and the Great Fire in London that destroyed two-thirds of the city, helped win Dryden the poet laureateship in 1668. Other celebrated poems include the mock-heroic "Mac Flecknoe" (1682), a model for Pope's *Dunciad*; the political satires *Absalom and Achitophel* (1681) and *The Medal* (1682); and two religious poems, "Religio Laici" ("a layman's religion," 1682), which is a defense of Anglicanism, and *The Hind and the Panther* (1687), which criticizes the Anglican Church and reflects Dryden's conversion to Catholicism.

Dryden also was the major dramatist of his day. His best comedy is *Marriage à la Mode* (1671), and his most noteworthy tragedies are *Aureng-Zebe* (in rhymed couplets, 1675) and *All for Love, or The World Well Lost* (in blank verse, 1677). The last of these, influenced by French neoclassic theory, adapts Shakespeare's *Antony and Cleopatra* to the three unities of action, place, and time (see PIERRE CORNEILLE). In addition to plays and dramatic criticism, Dryden produced skillful translations of such classical authors as Persius, Juvenal, Plutarch, and Virgil; some scholars have judged his *Fables, Ancient and Modern* (1700), consisting of translations and paraphrases of Ovid, BOCCACCIO, and Chaucer, to be his finest achievement. Dryden's critical writings also form a significant and serious body of work. From his defenses, prefaces, dedications, prologues, and epilogues—and his poems on or to other writers and artists—we can piece together his literary and critical views.

Dryden occupies a central place in the history of English criticism and prose. His relaxed, conversational style, MATTHEW ARNOLD observed in the nineteenth century, is "such as we would all gladly use if we only knew how." Dryden examined the nature of comedy and tragedy, satire, poetry, and translation. He knew well, and was influenced by, Greek, Roman, and neoclassical French texts and theories; at the same time, he valued English writers from Chaucer to Ben Jonson and Shakespeare and sought to mediate among classical, modern, and national literary traditions.

Dryden's judgments are solid and sensible. "A man should have a reasonable, philosophical, and in some measure mathematical head to be a complete and excellent poet," he once observed, "and besides this should have experience in all sorts of humors and manners of men; should be thoroughly skilled in conversation and should have a great knowledge of mankind in general." His formulations are frequently witty and his advice cogent, as in his preface to the *Fables*: "An Author is not to write all he can, but only all he ought." Dryden respects authority and precedent without being weighed down by them: "If the plays of the Ancients are more correctly plotted, ours are more beautifully written. . . . 'Tis not enough that Aristotle has said so, for Aristotle drew his models of tragedy from Sophocles and Euripides; and if he had seen ours, might have changed his mind." His tone is urbane, cultured, and civilized; and like Arnold and T. S. ELIOT, his criticism benefits from his own wide range of experience in creative writing.

Dryden's strengths and limits as a critic are displayed in his best-known critical work, the lengthy conversation *An Essay of Dramatic Poesy* (1668; rev. 1684), from which we take our first selection. His stated purpose is "to vindicate the honor of our English writers from the censure of those who unjustly prefer the French before them." Through his four speakers, he treats the relationship between the ancients and the moderns, French dramatic theory and English practice, and the use of rhyme in drama, commenting along the way on Shakespeare, Jonson, and other authors. Samuel Johnson maintained of the *Essay* that "modern English prose begins here"; he identifies Dryden as "the father of English criticism." But while the *Essay* is confident, leisurely, graceful, exploratory, and spirited, it is nonetheless a little slow and sometimes pedantic. The tone is appealing up to a point: Dryden favors balance, counterpoint, argument; he uses the "essay" form to undertake a tentative inquiry. He seeks to break down and complicate distinctions, opening up such apparently fixed terms as *propriety* and *decorum*. But the *Essay* overall lacks the energy, boldness, and edge of Dryden's best satiric poems.

Dryden's criticism shines in excerpts, like those included here from the *Essay* (which set the terms of Shakespeare criticism for the next century) and the passages on tragedy from the preface to *Troilus and Cressida* and on translation from the preface to *Sylvae*. At his focused best, he is informed and judicious. Everyone interested in the history of criticism should know why he mattered and value his reflections on literary tradition, genre, and the theory and practice of translation. He is a leader in the distinguished line of England's poet-critics that begins with Sidney and includes Johnson, SAMUEL TAYLOR COLERIDGE, Arnold, and Eliot.

BIBLIOGRAPHY

For many years the standard edition of Dryden was the eighteen-volume collection first published in 1808 and revised in 1882–93. It has been replaced by the University of California Press edition, edited E. N. Hooker, H. T. Swedenberg Jr., et al. (14 vols. to date, 1956–). There are two well-annotated collections of Dryden's criticism, the first edited by W. P. Ker (2 vols., 1900), the second by George Watson (2 vols., 1962). Other helpful collections include John Aden, *Critical Opinions of John Dryden* (1963); *Literary Criticism of John Dryden*, edited by Arthur C. Kirsch (1966); and H. James Jensen, *A Glossary of John Dryden's Critical Terms* (1969).

The best biography is James Anderson Winn, *John Dryden and His World* (1987). Also valuable are James Marshall Osborn, *John Dryden: Some Biographical Facts and Problems* (rev. ed., 1965), and Winn, *"When Beauty Fires the Blood": Love and the Arts in the Age of Dryden* (1992). A good survey of the life and works is Paul Hammond, *John Dryden: A Literary Life* (1991).

Important modern studies of Dryden include T. S. Eliot, *Homage to John Dryden* (1924) and *John Dryden: The Poet, the Dramatist, the Critic* (1932); and Louis I. Bredvold, *The Intellectual Milieu of John Dryden* (1934). The best books on the criticism are Edward Pechter, *Dryden's Classical Theory of Literature* (1975), and James Engell, *Forming the Critical Mind: Dryden to Coleridge* (1989). Philip Harth, *Contexts of Dryden's Thought* (1968), is the standard work on Dryden's philosophical and religious views; Harth's *Pen for a Party: Dryden's Tory Propaganda in Its Contexts* (1993) is also valuable. Michael Werth Gelber, *The Just and the Lively: The Literary Criticism of John Dryden* (1999), analyzes the criticism as a full and coherent body of literary theory.

For bibliographic works, see Hugh Macdonald, *John Dryden: A Bibliography of Early Editions and Drydeniana* (1939); *John Dryden: The Critical Heritage*, edited by James Kinsley and Helen Kinsley (1971); *An Annotated Bibliography of John Dryden: Texts and Studies, 1949–1973*, edited by John A. Zamonski (1975); *John Dryden: A Survey and Bibliography of Critical Studies, 1895–1974*, edited by David J. Latt and Samuel Holt Monk (1976); and James M. Hall, *John Dryden: A Reference Guide* (1984).

From An Essay of Dramatic Poesy

* * *

"To begin, then, with Shakspeare.[1] He was the man who of all modern, and perhaps ancient poets, had the largest and most comprehensive soul. All the images of nature were still present to him, and he drew them, not laboriously, but luckily; when he describes anything, you more than see it, you feel it too. Those who accuse him to have wanted learning, give him the greater commendation: he was naturally learned; he needed not the spectacles of books to read nature; he looked inwards, and found her there. I cannot say he is everywhere alike; were he so, I should do him injury to compare him with the greatest of mankind. He is many times flat, insipid; his comic wit degenerating into clenches,[2] his serious swelling into bombast. But he is always great, when some great occasion is presented to him; no man can say he ever had a fit subject for his wit, and did not then raise himself as high as above the rest of poets,

Quantum lenta solent inter viburna cupressi.[3]

The consideration of this made Mr. Hales of Eaton[4] say, that there was no subject of which any poet ever writ, but he would produce it much better done in Shakspeare; and however others are now generally preferred before him, yet the age wherein he lived, which had contemporaries with him Fletcher and Jonson,[5] never equalled them to him in their esteem: and in the last king's court,[6] when Ben's reputation was at highest, Sir John Suckling,[7] and with him the greater part of the courtiers, set our Shakspeare far above him.

"Beaumont and Fletcher, of whom I am next to speak, had, with the advantage of Shakspeare's wit, which was their precedent, great natural gifts, improved by study: Beaumont especially being so accurate a judge of plays,

1. In this excerpt, Neander (the Dryden character) is speaking. William Shakespeare (1564–1616) wrote plays between about 1590 and 1612.
2. Puns, quibbles.
3. As do cypresses among the bending shrubs (Latin). From Virgil, *Eclogues* 1.125 (37 B.C.E.).
4. John Hales (1584–1656), a fellow of Eton, one of England's most famous endowed boarding schools (founded in 1440).
5. Ben Jonson (1572–1637), English dramatist and poet. John Fletcher (1579–1625), English dramatist who collaborated with Francis Beaumont (1584–1616) on a number of plays from 1606 to 1613 (each also wrote plays on his own).
6. Charles I (1600–1649, reigned 1625–49).
7. English poet and courtier (1609–1642).

that Ben Jonson, while he lived, submitted all his writings to his censure, and, 'tis thought, used his judgment in correcting, if not contriving, all his plots. What value he had for him, appears by the verses he writ to him;[8] and therefore I need speak no farther of it. The first play that brought Fletcher and him in esteem was their *Philaster:*[9] for before that, they had written two or three very unsuccessfully, as the like is reported of Ben Jonson, before he writ *Every Man in his Humour*.[1] Their plots were generally more regular than Shakspeare's, especially those which were made before Beaumont's death; and they understood and imitated the conversation of gentlemen much better; whose wild debaucheries, and quickness of wit in repartees, no poet before them could paint as they have done. Humour,[2] which Ben Jonson derived from particular persons, they made it not their business to describe: they represented all the passions very lively, but above all, love. I am apt to believe the English language in them arrived to its highest perfection: what words have since been taken in, are rather superfluous than ornamental. Their plays are now the most pleasant and frequent entertainments of the stage; two of theirs being acted through the year for one of Shakspeare's or Jonson's: the reason is, because there is a certain gaiety in their comedies, and pathos in their more serious plays, which suit generally with all men's humours. Shakspeare's language is likewise a little obsolete, and Ben Jonson's wit comes short of theirs.

"As for Jonson, to whose character I am now arrived, if we look upon him while he was himself (for his last plays were but his dotages),[3] I think him the most learned and judicious writer which any theatre ever had. He was a most severe judge of himself, as well as others. One cannot say he wanted wit, but rather that he was frugal of it. In his works you find little to retrench or alter. Wit, and language, and humour also in some measure, we had before him; but something of art was wanting to the drama till he came. He managed his strength to more advantage than any who preceded him. You seldom find him making love in any of his scenes, or endeavouring to move the passions; his genius was too sullen and saturnine[4] to do it gracefully, especially when he knew he came after those who had performed both to such an height. Humour was his proper sphere; and in that he delighted most to represent mechanic people.[5] He was deeply conversant in the ancients, both Greek and Latin, and he borrowed boldly from them: there is scarce a poet or historian among the Roman authors of those times whom he has not translated in *Sejanus* and *Catiline*.[6] But he has done his robberies so openly, that one may see he fears not to be taxed by any law. He invades authors like a monarch; and what would be theft in other poets is only victory in him. With the spoils of these writers he so represents old Rome to us, in its rites, ceremonies, and customs, that if one of their poets had written either of his tragedies, we had seen less of it than in him. If there was any fault in his language, 'twas that he weaved it too closely and laboriously, in his comedies[7] especially: perhaps, too, he did a little too much Romanise our tongue, leav-

8. The epigram "To Francis Beaumont" (1616).
9. Produced in 1608 or 1609.
1. Produced in 1598.
2. That is, a dominating passion or propensity; the phrase "comedy of humours" was applied to Jonson's comic dramas and characters.
3. Dryden is referring here to such late and mediocre plays as *The New Inn* (1629) and *A Tale of a Tub* (1633).
4. Heavy, melancholy, sullen.
5. Manual workers, artisans.
6. Jonson's two Roman plays, 1603 and 1611.
7. In the first edition of the *Essay*, Dryden wrote "in his serious plays."

ing the words which he translated almost as much Latin as he found them: wherein, though he learnedly followed their language, he did not enough comply with the idiom of ours. If I would compare him with Shakspeare, I must acknowledge him the more correct poet, but Shakspeare the greater wit. Shakspeare was the Homer, or father of our dramatic poets; Jonson was the Virgil, the pattern of elaborate writing; I admire him, but I love Shakspeare. To conclude of him; as he has given us the most correct plays, so in the precepts which he has laid down in his *Discoveries*,[8] we have as many and profitable rules for perfecting the stage, as any wherewith the French can furnish us."[9]

* * *

1668, 1684

From Preface to *Troilus and Cressida*

* * *

I hasten to the end or scope of Tragedy, which is, to rectify or purge our passions, fear, and pity.

To instruct delightfully is the general end of all poetry. Philosophy instructs, but it performs its work by precept; which is not delightful, or not so delightful as example. To purge the passions by example is therefore the particular instruction which belongs to Tragedy. Rapin,[1] a judicious critic, has observed from Aristotle, that pride and want of commiseration are the most predominant vices in mankind; therefore, to cure us of these two, the inventors of Tragedy have chosen to work upon two other passions, which are fear and pity. We are wrought to fear by their setting before our eyes some terrible example of misfortune, which happened to persons of the highest quality; for such an action demonstrates to us that no condition is privileged from the turns of fortune; this must of necessity cause terror in us, and consequently abate our pride. But when we see that the most virtuous, as well as the greatest, are not exempt from such misfortunes, that consideration moves pity in us, and insensibly works us to be helpful to, and tender over, the distressed; which is the noblest and most god-like of moral virtues. Here it is observable that it is absolutely necessary to make a man virtuous, if we desire he should be pitied: we lament not, but detest, a wicked man; we are glad when we behold his crimes are punished, and that poetical justice is done upon him. Euripides was censured by the critics of his time for making his chief characters too wicked; for example, Phædra,[2] though she loved her son-in-law with reluctancy, and that it was a curse upon her family for offending Venus,[3] yet was thought too ill a pattern for the stage. Shall we therefore banish all char-

8. Jonson's *Timber, or Discoveries Made upon Men and Matter* (1640) is a series of notes and extracts on writing and other subjects.
9. Most notably in PIERRE CORNEILLE'S *Of the Three Unities* (1660; see above).
1. René Rapin (1621–1687), French Jesuit priest, poet, and critic. He draws on the *Poetics* (see above) of the Greek philosopher ARISTOTLE (384–322 B.C.E.).
2. A character in the Greek tragedy *Hippolytus* (428 B.C.E.) by Euripides (ca. 485–406 B.C.E.).
3. The Roman name for Aphrodite, the Greek goddess of love.

acters of villainy? I confess I am not of that opinion; but it is necessary that the hero of the play be not a villain; that is, the characters, which should move our pity, ought to have virtuous inclinations, and degrees of moral goodness in them. As for a perfect character of virtue, it never was in Nature, and therefore there can be no imitation of it; but there are alloys of frailty to be allowed for the chief persons, yet so that the good which is in them shall outweigh the bad, and consequently leave room for punishment on the one side and pity on the other.

After all, if any one will ask me whether a tragedy cannot be made upon any other grounds than those of exciting pity and terror in us, Bossu,[4] the best of modern critics, answers thus in general: That all excellent arts, and particularly that of poetry, have been invented and brought to perfection by men of a transcendent genius; and that, therefore, they who practise afterwards the same arts are obliged to tread in their footsteps, and to search in their writings the foundation of them; for it is not just that new rules should destroy the authority of the old. But Rapin writes more particularly thus, that no passions in a story are so proper to move our concernment as fear and pity; and that it is from our concernment we receive our pleasure is undoubted; when the soul becomes agitated with fear for one character, or hope for another, then it is that we are pleased in Tragedy, by the interest which we take in their adventures.

Here, therefore, the general answer may be given to the first question, how far we ought to imitate Shakspeare and Fletcher[5] in their plots; namely, that we ought to follow them so far only as they have copied the excellencies of those who invented and brought to perfection Dramatic Poetry; those things only excepted which religion, custom of countries, idioms of languages, etc., have altered in the superstructures, but not in the foundation of the design.

How defective Shakspeare and Fletcher have been in all their plots Mr. Rymer[6] has discovered in his criticisms: neither can we, who follow them, be excused from the same or greater errors; which are the more unpardonable in us because we want their beauties to countervail our faults. The best of their designs, the most approaching to antiquity, and the most conducing to move pity, is the *King and no King*,[7] which, if the farce of Bessus[8] were thrown away, is of that inferior sort of tragedies which end with a prosperous event. It is probably derived from the story of Œdipus, with the character of Alexander the Great in his extravagances given to Arbaces. The taking of this play, amongst many others, I cannot wholly ascribe to the excellency of the action, for I find it moving when it is read: 'tis true the faults of the plot are so evidently proved that they can no longer be denied. The beauties of it must therefore lie either in the lively touches of the passion, or we must conclude, as I think we may, that even in imperfect plots there are less degrees of Nature, by which some faint emotions

4. René Le Bossu (1631–1680), a French critic whose discourse on epic poetry, published in 1675 and translated in English in 1695, was admired by English critics.

5. John Fletcher (1579–1625), English dramatist best known for his collaborations with Francis Beaumont (1584–1616). He is said to have collaborated with William Shakespeare (1564–1616) on *Henry VIII* and *The Two Noble Kinsman*.

6. Thomas Rymer (1641–1713), historian and critic; author of *The Tragedies of the Last Age Consider'd* (1678), which Dryden admired, and *A Short View of Tragedy* (1693), infamous for its attack on Shakespeare.

7. A tragicomedy by Beaumont and Fletcher (1611).

8. A cowardly braggart in *A King and No King*. Arbaces is another character in the play.

of pity and terror are raised in us; as a less engine will raise a less proportion of weight, though not so much as one of Archimedes's[9] making; for nothing can move our nature but by some natural reason which works upon passions. And since we acknowledge the effect there must be something in the cause.

* * *

1679

From Preface to *Sylvae*

* * *

For, after all, a translator is to make his author appear as charming as possibly he can, provided he maintains his character, and makes him not unlike himself. Translation is a kind of drawing after the life; where every one will acknowledge there is a double sort of likeness, a good one and a bad. 'Tis one thing to draw the outlines true, the features like, the proportions exact, the colouring itself perhaps tolerable; and another thing to make all these graceful, by the posture, the shadowings, and, chiefly, by the spirit which animates the whole. I cannot, without some indignation, look on an ill copy of an excellent original; much less can I behold with patience Virgil, Homer,[1] and some others, whose beauties I have been endeavouring all my life to imitate, so abused, as I may say, to their faces, by a botching interpreter. What English readers, unacquainted with Greek or Latin, will believe me, or any other man, when we commend those authors, and confess we derive all that is pardonable in us from their fountains, if they take those to be the same poets whom our Oglebys[2] have translated? But I dare assure them, that a good poet is no more like himself in a dull translation than his carcass would be to his living body. There are many who understand Greek and Latin, and yet are ignorant of their mother-tongue. The proprieties and delicacies of the English are known to few; 'tis impossible even for a good wit[3] to understand and practise them, without the help of a liberal education, long reading, and digesting of those few good authors we have amongst us, the knowledge of men and manners, the freedom of habitudes and conversation with the best company of both sexes; and, in short, without wearing off the rust which he contracted while he was laying in a stock of learning. Thus difficult it is to understand the purity of English, and critically to discern not only good writers from bad, and a proper style from a corrupt, but also to distinguish that which is pure in a good author from that which is vicious and corrupt in him. And for want of all these requisites, or the greatest part of them, most of our ingenious young men take up some cried-up English poet for their model, adore him, and imitate him, as they think, without knowing wherein he is defective, where he is boyish and trifling,

9. Greek mathematician, engineer, and physicist (3d c. B.C.E.). He famously remarked, "Give me a place to stand and I will move the earth."
1. Virgil (70–19 B.C.E.) and Homer (ca. 8th c. B.C.E.) are traditionally judged the greatest classical poets.
2. John Ogilby (1600–1676), a Scottish mapmaker, translated works by Virgil and Homer.
3. Intelligence.

wherein either his thoughts are improper to his subject, or his expressions unworthy of his thoughts, or the turn of both is unharmonious. Thus it appears necessary that a man should be a nice[4] critic in his mother-tongue before he attempts to translate a foreign language. Neither is it sufficient that he be able to judge of words and style, but he must be a master of them too; he must perfectly understand his author's tongue and absolutely command his own. So that to be a thorough translator he must be a thorough poet. Neither is it enough to give his author's sense in good English, in poetical expressions, and in musical numbers;[5] for though all these are exceeding difficult to perform, there yet remains an harder task; and 'tis a secret of which few translators have sufficiently thought. I have already hinted a word or two concerning it; that is, the maintaining the character of an author, which distinguishes him from all others, and makes him appear that individual poet whom you would interpret. For example, not only the thoughts, but the style and versification of Virgil and Ovid[6] are very different: yet I see, even in our best poets who have translated some parts of them, that they have confounded their several talents, and, by endeavouring only at the sweetness and harmony of numbers, have made them both so much alike that, if I did not know the originals, I should never be able to judge by the copies which was Virgil and which was Ovid. It was objected against a late noble painter[7] that he drew many graceful pictures, but few of them were like. And this happened to him because he always studied himself more than those who sat to him. In such translators I can easily distinguish the hand which performed the work, but I cannot distinguish their poet from another. Suppose two authors are equally sweet, yet there is a great distinction to be made in sweetness, as in that of sugar and that of honey. I can make the difference more plain by giving you (if it be worth knowing) my own method of proceeding in my translations out of four several poets in this volume; Virgil, Theocritus, Lucretius, and Horace.[8] In each of these, before I undertook them, I considered the genius and distinguishing character of my author. I looked on Virgil as a succinct and grave majestic writer; one who weighed not only every thought, but every word and syllable; who was still aiming to crowd his sense into as narrow a compass as possibly he could; for which reason he is so very figurative that he requires (I may almost say) a grammar apart to construe him. His verse is everywhere sounding the very thing in your ears whose sense it bears, yet the numbers are perpetually varied to increase the delight of the reader; so that the same sounds are never repeated twice together. On the contrary, Ovid and Claudian,[9] though they write in styles differing from each other, yet have each of them but one sort of music in their verses. All the versification and little variety of Claudian is included within the compass of four or five lines, and then he begins again in the same tenor; perpetually closing his sense at the end of a verse, and that verse commonly which they call golden, or two substantives and two adjectives, with a verb betwixt them to keep the peace. Ovid, with all his

4. Fastidious.
5. Harmonious verse.
6. Roman poet (43 B.C.E.–17 C.E.).
7. The Dutch-born British painter Sir Peter Lely (1618–1680).
8. Roman poet (65–8 B.C.E.; see above). Theocritus (ca. 300–ca. 260 B.C.E.), Greek pastoral poet. Lucretius (ca. 94–55 B.C.E.), Roman philosopher and poet.
9. A Greek-speaking Alexandrian (d. ca. 404 C.E.) who found great success in Rome writing Latin poetry.

sweetness, has as little variety of numbers and sound as he: he is always, as it were, upon the hand-gallop, and his verse runs upon carpet-ground.[1] He avoids, like the other, all synalœphas, or cutting off one vowel when it comes before another in the following word; so that, minding only smoothness, he wants[2] both variety and majesty. But to return to Virgil: though he is smooth where smoothness is required, yet he is so far from affecting it that he seems rather to disdain it; frequently makes use of synalœphas, and concludes his sense in the middle of his verse. He is everywhere above conceits of epigrammatic wit and gross hyperboles; he maintains majesty in the midst of plainness; he shines, but glares not; and is stately without ambition, which is the vice of Lucan.[3] I drew my definition of poetical wit from my particular consideration of him: for propriety of thoughts and words are only to be found in him; and where they are proper they will be delightful. Pleasure follows of necessity as the effect does the cause, and therefore is not to be put into the definition. This exact propriety of Virgil I particularly regarded as a great part of his character; but must confess, to my shame, that I have not been able to translate any part of him so well as to make him appear wholly like himself. For where the original is close no version can reach it in the same compass. Hannibal Caro's,[4] in the Italian, is the nearest, the most poetical, and the most sonorous of any translation of the *Æneids*; yet, though he takes the advantage of blank verse, he commonly allows two lines for one of Virgil, and does not always hit his sense. Tasso[5] tells us, in his letters, that Sperone Speroni, a great Italian wit, who was his contemporary, observed of Virgil and Tully,[6] that the Latin orator endeavoured to imitate the copiousness of Homer, the Greek poet; and that the Latin poet made it his business to reach the conciseness of Demosthenes,[7] the Greek orator. Virgil therefore, being so very sparing of his words, and leaving so much to be imagined by the reader, can never be translated as he ought in any modern tongue. To make him copious is to alter his character; and to translate him line for line is impossible, because the Latin is naturally a more succinct language[8] than either the Italian, Spanish, French, or even than the English, which, by reason of its monosyllables, is far the most compendious of them. Virgil is much the closest[9] of any Roman poet, and the Latin hexameter has more feet than the English heroic.[1]

Besides all this, an author has the choice of his own thoughts and words, which a translator has not; he is confined by the sense of the inventor to those expressions which are the nearest to it: so that Virgil, studying[2] brevity, and having the command of his own language, could bring those words into a narrow compass, which a translator cannot render without circumlocutions. In short, they who have called him the torture of grammarians, might

1. Smooth ground. "Hand-gallop": an easy gallop: (i.e., with the horse held well in hand).
2. Lacks.
3. Roman writer of prose and verse (39–65 C.E.). His unfinished epic poem on the Roman civil war, though overwritten, had many 17th-century admirers.
4. Annibale Caro (1507–1566), translator of the *Aeneid* (1581).
5. Torquato Tasso (1544–1595), Italian poet. Tasso makes this statement not in a letter but in his *Discourse on the Art of Poetry* (1587). Sperone Speroni of Padua (1500–1588) was considered one of Tasso's enemies.
6. Marcus Tullius Cicero (106–43 B.C.E.), Roman statesman and the greatest orator of the Republic.
7. The greatest Athenian orator (384–322 B.C.E.).
8. Latin lacks the words "a," "an," and "the."
9. Most condensed.
1. English heroic or epic couplets are in iambic pentameter and thus use a line one metrical foot shorter than the Latin dactylic hexameter.
2. Aiming at.

also have called him the plague of translators; for he seems to have studied not to be translated. I own that, endeavouring to turn his *Nisus and Euryalus*[3] as close as I was able, I have performed that episode too literally; that giving more scope to *Mezentius and Lausus*,[4] that version, which has more of the majesty of Virgil, has less of his conciseness; and all that I can promise for myself is only that I have done both better than Ogleby, and perhaps as well as Caro; so that, methinks, I come like a malefactor, to make a speech upon the gallows, and to warn all other poets, by my sad example, from the sacrilege of translating Virgil. Yet, by considering him so carefully as I did before my attempt, I have made some faint resemblance of him; and had I taken more time, might possibly have succeeded better; but never so well as to have satisfied myself.

* * *

1685

3. Devoted Trojan friends and companions who die together in a dramatic episode of the *Aeneid*, book 9.

4. Mezentius, cruel king of the Tyrrhenians, who was driven from his throne by his subjects; he and his son Lausus are killed by Aeneas at the close of book 10 of the *Aeneid*.

APHRA BEHN
1640–1689

In *A Room of One's Own* (1929), VIRGINIA WOOLF writes that "All women together ought to let flowers fall upon the tomb of Aphra Behn, . . . for it was she who earned them the right to speak their minds." Behn was the first Englishwoman to earn a living as a writer. As such, she became the model for the commercial woman writer operating outside the narrow circle of mainstream propriety while trying to gain a place within it. In her critical writing, she reveals the obstacles faced by a woman striving to earn a living in a profession dominated by men. She describes her exclusion from the polite society that would underwrite and support her plays, as well as the different standards applied to her as a woman. Perhaps because of her sex, her literary criticism tells us more about the everyday difficulties faced by practicing dramatists than do the writings of any literary critic of the time. The prefaces to her plays are peopled by theater managers and licensors who threaten to suppress her plays, critics who find them obscene, and audiences who shout them down; there are directors who rewrite her lines and actors who mangle them. Her critical writing, unburdened by the classical university education that was denied to her, undermines the commonplaces of seventeenth-century criticism by setting her practical experience as a playwright against the "rules" of neoclassical orthodoxy articulated by earlier critics such as SIR PHILIP SIDNEY, PIERRE CORNEILLE, and JOHN DRYDEN.

Although the circumstances of Behn's birth remain mired in controversy, she was most probably born Aphra Johnson, and may have been the daughter of Bartholomew Johnson and Elizabeth Denham baptized in Harbledown outside of Canterbury, England, on December 14, 1640. In her early twenties, Behn went with her family to Surinam (Dutch Guiana), then an English possession, where her father or a relative of her father was nominated to the post of lieutenant-governor. He died en route, but the family settled in Surinam anyway; they remained there until 1664, when England resigned the colony to the Dutch. She describes her life in Surinam in her famous novel *Oroonoko* (1688). On her return to England, she married a city merchant named Behn, a gentleman of Dutch extraction about whom little is known. Her married life was brief: by 1666 her husband was dead, perhaps one of the victims of the plague that swept London in 1665–66, and she was forced to earn a living on her own. In 1666 she was persuaded by Thomas Killegrew, then licensee of the King's Theater, to act as a spy in the second Anglo-Dutch War. But the English government failed to pay even Behn's living expenses while she was in Holland, and she had to borrow money to survive. When she returned to London in 1667, she was imprisoned for failure to pay her debts. Somehow she regained her freedom, and by 1670 she had begun her career as a dramatist with the successful production of *The Forced Marriage* at Lincoln's Inn Fields. She went on to become one of the most prolific writers of the late seventeenth century, surpassed in output only by John Dryden, England's poet laureate.

Behn wrote during the Restoration, which began in 1660 when Charles II returned from exile in France to take the throne after a twenty-year interregnum. The Puritans had closed the theaters at the beginning of the English Civil War, in the early 1640s; the two that now reopened were very different from those of Shakespeare's day, a generation earlier. The most revolutionary change was that women, not boys, played women's roles. The presence of actresses in the Restoration theater undoubtedly enabled Behn to make a successful living writing plays, though women playwrights, like actresses, were never considered quite respectable.

During her career Behn wrote at least eighteen plays, as well as many poems and prose works. In addition she is considered one of the "mothers" of the English novel. Her best and most successful plays were *The Rover* (1677) and *The Lucky Chance* (1687). Though her sex alone was enough to make her a controversial writer, she did not shy away from the political controversies of her day, remaining all her life a staunch royalist. In 1682 she was briefly arrested and charged with "abusive reflections upon persons of quality" for an epilogue she had written chastising the duke of Monmouth, the illegitimate son of Charles II, for his rebellion against his father. She also wrote the first antislavery novel, *Oroonoko*, which was later made into a play by Thomas Southern. On April 16, 1689, Aphra Behn died and was buried in Westminster Abbey—not among the poets in Poets' Corner, but in the cloister. Her epitaph is attributed to her former lover John Hoyle: "Here lies proof that wit can never be/ Defence enough against mortality."

Behn's work as a literary critic—which is limited primarily to the prefaces and dedicatory letters she wrote for her plays—falls into two periods, each marked by a sustained piece of critical writing: the "Epistle to the Reader" prefacing her third play, *The Dutch Lover* (1673), and the preface to *The Lucky Chance*, written toward the end of her career. In these two selections we can see the development of Behn's critical attitudes toward the fashionable literary debates of her day, especially those about propriety and decorum in the drama.

The "Epistle to the Reader" was written when Behn was trying to establish a name for herself in the extremely competitive world of the theater. With characteristic acerbic wit, her "Epistle" exposes the elitist underpinnings of late-seventeenth-century literary theory. She is the first English critic to reject outright HORACE's platitude that literature must instruct and delight. Most English writers responded to earlier Puritan attacks on the theater by arguing that plays were a means of inculcating morality, but Behn rejects this approach. She argues that poetry—and drama in particular—rarely if ever improves anyone's morality, nor indeed are plays written with such an end in mind. Their purpose is to entertain, and that is the sole measure of their success. Behn's "apology" for her art does not draw on the authority of the classical tradition embodied by venerable critics such as ARISTOTLE and Horace. Unlike Dryden, who in *An Essay of Dramatic Poesy* (1668) charts the evolution of the modern stage from classical antiquity, sprinkling his argument liberally with Latin and Greek quotations, Behn has everything to gain from separating her profession—playwriting—from literary activities that required a university education and knowledge of languages to which she was denied access because of her sex. Stripping away the "Academick frippery" that surrounded the debate over the "musty rules of Unity," she suggests that more important than the structural unity of a play's action, time, and plot is the competence of the actors who perform it. Not preoccupied by the classical defense of poetry, she is able to discuss with scathing honesty the realities of competing in the theatrical world of the late seventeenth century.

Behn's prose style is more difficult than is usual even for a seventeenth-century text. In "Epistle to the Reader," she mimics the philosophically dense and incomprehensible language of fashionable intellectual debate as well as the modish slang of the day. Unable to call on the shared intellectual tradition that shaped the literary criticism of contemporaries like Dryden, Behn's criticism is immersed in the day-to-day culture of the fashionable society she hoped would support her efforts as a writer, and these references sometimes seem obscure to all but historians of the period.

Moving from the bantering wit and dense style of the "Epistle" to the later preface to *The Lucky Chance*, a more orthodox statement about literature and a defense against charges of impropriety, one is struck by the difference in tone and content. Perhaps chastened by her imprisonment, or simply reflecting her position in 1687 as a more successful, less marginalized, dramatist, Behn expresses her desire to "tread in those successful Paths my Predecessors have so long thriv'd in, to take those Measures that both the Ancient and Modern Writers have set me," thus linking herself with the tradition she had rejected in her earlier essay. Nevertheless, Behn still eloquently and forthrightly defends her right to compete as a writer on equal terms with men. She attacks the overt sexual biases and double standards of the criticism of her day that condemned a play simply because of the sex of its author, exposing what the late-twentieth-century feminist Mary Ellmann, in *Thinking about Women* (1968), called criticism by sexual analogy. Such criticism treats books by women as if they *were* women, indulging in an "intellectual measuring of busts and hips." In pleading for "my Masculine Part the Poet in me," Behn anticipates the feminist analyses of critics such as SANDRA M. GILBERT AND SUSAN GUBAR, who argue that the Western tradition of literature has gendered authorship as a masculine activity, thereby creating, in women, an "anxiety of authorship."

It would be a mistake, however, to make too great a claim for Behn's feminism. Her libertine pose masked a conservative royalist politics and a desire for access to the elite society that excluded her. She saw herself as an exception to the rule of women's exclusion from the profession of writing rather than as a pathbreaker demonstrating the error of that rule. Her outspokenness and her refusal to conform politely to the dictates of modesty and propriety led later generations of critics, like Dr. John Doran, writing in his *Annals of the English Stage* (1864), to dismiss her as "a mere harlot who danced through uncleanness and dared them to follow," but these same qualities have made her a figure of great interest to feminist critics.

BIBLIOGRAPHY

The standard text of Behn's works is the seven-volume edition by Janet M. Todd, *The Works of Aphra Behn* (1992–96). For two valuable biographies of Behn, see Maureen Duffy, *The Passionate Shepherdess: Aphra Behn, 1640–1689* (1977), and Angeline Goreau, *Reconstructing Aphra: A Social Biography of Aphra Behn* (1980). Frederick M. Link's *Aphra Behn* (1968) offers a useful introduction to Behn's work. Tanya Claire Tenkarian describes Behn's contributions to the development of the novel in *Aphra Behn and the Rise of the English Novel: Gender and Genre* (1993). The two best anthologies of essays, with contributions by several prominent Behn scholars, are *Rereading Aphra Behn: History, Theory, and Criticism*, edited by Heidi Hutner

(1993), and *Aphra Behn Studies*, edited by Janet M. Todd (1996). Todd describes Behn's literary reputation in *The Critical Fortunes of Aphra Behn* (1998).

For bibliography, see Mary Ann O'Donnell, *Aphra Behn: An Annotated Bibliography of Primary and Secondary Sources* (1986). Consult the bibliography in Janet M. Todd's *Secret Life of Aphra Behn* (1996) for an update.

From The Dutch Lover

Epistle to the Reader

Good, Sweet, Honey, Sugar-candied
READER[1]

(Which I think is more than any one has call'd you yet.) I must have a word or two with you before you do advance into the Treatise; but 'tis not to beg your pardon for diverting you from your affairs, by such an idle Pamphlet as this is, for I presume you have not much to do, and therefore are to be obliged to me for keeping you from worse imployment, and if you have a better, you may get you gone about your business: but if you will mispend your time, pray lay the fault upon your self; for I have dealt pretty fairly in the matter, and told you in the Title Page what you are to expect within. Indeed, had I hung out a sign of the Immortality of the Soul, of the Mystery of Godliness, or of Ecclesiastical Policie, and then had treated you with Indiscerpibility, and Essential Spissitude (words,[2] which though I am no competent Judge of, for want of Languages, yet I fancy strongly ought to mean just nothing) with a company of Apocryphal midnight tales cull'd out of the choicest insignificant Authors; If I had only prov'd in Folio that *Apollonius*[3] was a naughty Knave, or had presented you with two or three of the worst principles transcrib'd out of the peremptory and ill natur'd, (though prettily ingenious) Doctor of *Malmsbury*[4] undigested, and ill manag'd by a silly, fancy, ignorant, impertinent,[5] ill educated Chaplain, I were then indeed sufficiently in fault; but having inscrib'd Comedy on the beginning of my Book, you may guess pretty near what peny-worths you are like to have, and ware[6] your money and your time accordingly.

I would not yet be understood to lessen the dignity of Playes, for surely they deserve a place among the middle, if not the better sort of Books, for I have heard that most of that which bears the name of Learning, and which has abused such quantities of Ink and Paper, and continually imploys so many ignorant, unhappy souls for ten, twelve, twenty years in the University[7]

1. In the prefaces to the printed texts of plays, the habit of mocking readers often complemented the mockery of audiences in prologues [except as indicated, all notes are Janet M. Todd's].
2. The habit of confounding the public with difficult words was much mocked.
3. Apollonius is probably Apollonius of Tyana, a Greek philosopher following Pythagoras (6th c. B.C.E.). He was born at the beginning of the Christian era, and to some skeptics such as Charles Blount (and later Voltaire [1694–1778]) he represented a coherent and admirable moral alternative to Christ and his teaching. "In Folio" indicated a full sized sheet of paper or parchment folded only once, therefore a volume of the largest size.
4. Thomas Hobbes (1588–1679), born in Wiltshire, was an influential materialist whose avoidance of Christian concepts provoked much abuse and argument. [Malmsbury: Malmesbury, a town in Wiltshire.—editor's note.]
5. Rude [editor's note].
6. Spend [editor's note].
7. The colleges at Oxford and Cambridge University followed a very traditional curriculum, which Behn more than once criticized [editor's note].

(who yet poor wretches think they are doing something all the while) as Logick, &c. and several other things (that shall be nameless, lest I should mispel them) are much more absolutely nothing than the errantest Play that e're was writ. Take notice, Reader, I do not assert this purely upon my own knowledge, but I think I have known it very fully prov'd, both sides being fairly heard, and seen some ingenious opposers of it most abominably baffled in the Argument: Some of which I have got so perfectly by rote, that if this were a proper place for it, I am apt to think myself could almost make it clear; and as I would not undervalue Poetry, so neither am I altogether of their judgement, who believe no wisdom in the world beyond it. I have often heard indeed (and read) how much the World was anciently oblig'd to it for most of that which they call'd Science, which my want of letters makes me less assur'd of than others happily may be: but I have heard some wise men say, that no considerable part of the useful knowledge was this way communicated, and on the other way, that it hath serv'd to propagate so many idle superstitions, as all the benefits it hath or can be guilty of, can never make sufficient amends for, which unaided by the unluckey charms of Poetry, could never have possest a thinking Creature such as man. However true this is, I am my self well able to affirm that none of all our English Poets, and least the Dramatique (so I think you call them) can be justly charg'd with too great reformation of mens minds or manners, and for that I may appeal to general experiment, if those who are the most assiduous Disciples of the Stage, do not make the fondest[8] and the lewdest crew about this Town; for if you should unhappily converse [with] them through the year, you will not find one dram of sence amongst a Club of them, unless you will allow for such a little Link-Boys[9] Ribaldry, thick larded with unseasonable oaths, & impudent defiance of God, and all things serious, and that at such a senceless damn'd unthinking rate, as, if 'twere well distributed, would spoil near half the Apothecaries trade, and save the sober people of the Town the charge of Vomits;[1] And it was smartly said, (how prudently I cannot tell) by a late learned Doctor, who, though himself no great asserter of a Deity, (as you'l believe by that which follows) yet was observed to be continually perswading of this sort of men (if I for once may call them so) of the necessity and truth of our Religion; and being ask'd how he came to bestir himself so much this way, made answer, that it was because their ignorance and indiscreet debauch made them a scandal to the profession of Atheism. And for their wisdom and design, I never knew it reach beyond the invention of some notable expedient, for the speedier ridding them of their estate, (a devilish clog to Wit and Parts) than other grouling[2] Mortals know, or battering half a dozen fair new Windows in a Morning after their debauch, whilst the dull unjantee[3] Rascal they belong to is fast asleep. But I'l proceed no farther in their character, because that miracle of Wit (in spight of Academick frippery) the mighty *Echard*[4] hath already done it to my satisfaction; and whoever undertakes a Suppliment to any thing he hath discourst, had better for their reputation be doing nothing.

Besides, this Theam is worn too thread-bare by the whiffling[5] would-be

8. Most foolish, most idiotic [editor's note].
9. Boys employed to carry torches to light people through the streets.
1. Purges [editor's note].
2. Growling [editor's note].
3. Dull, not showy [editor's note].
4. John Eachard mocked the university education of the clergy.
5. Moving inconstantly, "as if driven by a puff of wind," *Johnson's Dictionary* [published in 1755 by SAMUEL JOHNSON].

Wits of the Town, and of both the stone-blind-eyes of the Kingdom. And therefore to return to that which I before was speaking of, I will have leave to say that in my judgement the increasing number of our latter Plays have not done much more towards the amending of mens Morals, or their Wit, than hath the frequent Preaching, which this last age hath been pester'd with, (indeed without all Controversie they have done less harm) nor can I once imagine what temptation any one can have to expect it from them: for, sure I am, no Play was ever writ with that design.[6] If you consider Tragedy, you'l find their best of characters unlikely patterns for a wise man to pursue: For he that is the Knight of the Play, no sublunary feats must serve his Dulcinea;[7] for if he can't bestrid the Moon, he'l ne'er make good his business to the end, and if he chance to be offended, he must without considering right or wrong confound all things he meets, and put you half a score likely tall fellows into each pocket; and truly if he come not something near this pitch, I think the Tragedies not worth a farthing; for Playes were certainly intended for the exercising of mens passions, not their understandings, and he is infinitely far from wise, that will bestow one moments private meditation on such things: And as for Comedie, the finest folks you meet with there, are still unfitter for your imitation, for though within a leaf or two of the Prologue, you are told that they are people of Wit, good Humour, good Manners, and all that: yet if the Authors did not kindly add their proper names, you'd never know them by their characters; for whatsoe'er's the matter, it hath happen'd so spightfully in several Playes, which have been prettie well receiv'd of late, that even those persons that were meant to be the ingenious Censors of the Play, have either prov'd the most debauch'd, or most unwittie people in the Companie: nor is this error very lamentable, since as I take it Comedie was never meant, either for a converting or confirming Ordinance:[8] In short, I think a Play the best divertisement[9] that wise men have; but I do also think them nothing so, who do discourse as formallie about the rules of it, as if 'twere the grand affair of humane life. This being my opinion of Plays, I studied only to make this as entertaining as I could, which whether I have been successful in, my gentle Reader, you may for your shilling judge.[1] To tell you my thoughts of it, were to little purpose, for were they very ill, you may be sure I would not have expos'd it; nor did I so till I had first consulted most of those who have a reputation for judgement of this kind; who were at least so civil (if not kind) to it as did incourage me to venture it upon the Stage, and in the Press: Nor did I take their single word for it, but us'd their reasons as a confirmation of my own.

Indeed that day 'twas Acted first, there comes me into the Pit, a long, lither, phlegmatick, white, ill-favour'd, wretched Fop,[2] an officer in Masquerade newly transported with a Scarfe & Feather[3] out of *France*, a sorry

6. Throughout the century the stage had been attacked by Puritans as a pernicious influence on the morals of the spectators. Many playwrights including Dryden sought to counter this by urging the ethical and moral base of their work. [JOHN DRYDEN (1631–1700), English playwright, poet, and critic—editor's note.]

7. A reference to Cervantes' *Don Quixote* [1605, 1616], where the hero's beloved is called Dulcinea. Don Quixote was famous for his lofty but unrealisable ideals. ["Sublunary": terrestrial, of this world—editor's note.]

8. Authoritative direction.

9. Entertainment [editor's note].

1. Costs of seats in the theatre varied but on the whole the cheapest seats in the gallery went for a shilling. In the pit a seat was about half a crown and in the boxes four shillings.

2. Lither means lazy or sluggish according to Elisha Coles' *An English Dictionary* (1676); phlegmatic means "full of Phlegme, the cold and moist humour of the body"; a fop is a foolish dandy. [Coles (1640–1680), a schoolmaster who was among the earliest English lexicographers—editor's note.]

3. Military dandyism.

Animal that has nought else to shield it from the uttermost contempt of all mankind, but that respect which we afford to Rats and Toads, which though we do not well allow to live, yet when considered as a part of God's Creation, we make honourable mention of them. A thing, Reader——but no more of such a Smelt:[4] This thing, I tell ye, opening that which serves it for a mouth, out issued such a noise as this to those that sate about it, that they were to expect a woful Play, God damn him, for it was a womans. Now how this came about I am not sure, but I suppose he brought it piping hot from some, who had with him the reputation of a villanous Wit: for Creatures of his size of sence talk without all imagination, such scraps as they pick up from other folks. I would not for a world be taken arguing with such a propertie as this; but if I thought there were a man of any tolerable parts, who could upon mature deliberation distinguish well his right-hand from his left, and justly state the difference between the number of sixteen and two, yet had this prejudice upon him; I would take a little pains to make him know how much he errs. For waving the examination,[5] why women having equal education with men, were not as capable of knowledge, of whatever sort as well as they: I'l only say as I have touch'd before, that Plays have no great room for that which is mens great advantage over women, that is Learning: We all well know that the immortal *Shakespears* Playes (who was not guilty of much more of this than often falls to womens share)[6] have better pleas'd the World than *Johnsons* works, though by the way 'tis said that *Benjamin* was no such Rabbi neither, for I am inform'd his Learning was but Grammer high;[7] (sufficient indeed to rob poor *Salust*[8] of his best Orations) and it hath been observ'd, that they are apt to admire him most confoundedly, who have just such a scantling of it as he had; and I have seen a man the most severe of *Johnsons* Sect,[9] sit with his Hat remov'd less than a hairs breadth from one sullen posture for almost three hours at the Alchymist; who at that excellent Play of *Harry* the Fourth[1] (which yet I hope is far enough from Farce) hath very hardly kept his Doublet whole; but affectation hath always had a greater share both in the actions and discourse of men than truth and judgement have: and for our Modern ones, except our most unimitable Laureat,[2] I dare to say I know of none that write at such a formidable rate, but that a woman may well hope to reach their greatest hights. Then for their musty rules of Unity,[3] and God knows what besides, if they meant any thing, they are

4. A simpleton [editor's note].
5. Refraining from an investigation into [editor's note].
6. Much was made of Shakespeare's lack of university education which allowed him to be a useful predecessor for a female playwright. See Dryden's *An Essay of Dramatic Poesy* (1668): "He was naturally learn'd; he needed not the spectacles of books to read Nature. . . ."
7. In the Restoration Ben Jonson [1572–1637] was the most esteemed of the dramatists writing before the Interregnum. "Grammer high" indicated the level achieved at a grammar school, where learned languages were grammatically taught. ["The Interregnum": 1649–60, the period between Charles I's execution and the Restoration of the monarchy and the accession of Charles II—editor's note.]
8. Sallust (86–34 B.C.E.) was a Roman historian whose works on the Catiline conspiracy [in 63 B.C.E.] provided many plots for English playwrights. Jonson's *Catiline* was performed in 1611.
9. A reference to those believing in the rules of drama such as Thomas Shadwell [1643–1692] who had had success with *The Sullen Lovers* (1688) and *The Humourists* (1671). In his preface to the printed text of the former he praised the three unities and declared that all playwrights should imitate Jonson in the creation of humour characters, "though none are like to come near; he being the onely person that appears to me to have made perfect Representations of Humane Life."
1. *The Alchemist* by Jonson and *Henry IV* by Shakespeare. The line between proper comedy and farce was frequently drawn. For example in his preface to *An Evening's Love* (1671) Dryden wrote, "Comedy consists . . . of natural actions and characters; . . . Farce . . . of forced humours, and unnatural events."
2. John Dryden became poet laureate in 1668 [editor's note].
3. The three unities of time, place, and action; see above SIR PHILIP SIDNEY, PIERRE CORNEILLE, and Dryden [editor's note].

enough intelligible, and as practible by a woman; but really methinks they that disturb their heads with any other rules of Playes besides the making them pleasant, and avoiding of scurrility, might much better be imploy'd in studying how to improve mens too too imperfect knowledge of that ancient English Game, which hight long Laurence:[4] And if Comedy should be the Picture of ridiculous mankind, I wonder any one should think it such a sturdy task, whilst we are furnish'd with such precious Originals as him, I lately told you of; if at least that Character do not dwindle into Farce, and so become too mean an entertainment for those persons who are us'd to think. Reader, I have a complaint or two to make to you, and I have done; Know then this Play was hugely injur'd in the Acting, for 'twas done so imperfectly as never any was before, which did more harm to this than it could have done to any of another sort; the Plot being busie (though I think not intricate) and so requiring a continual attention, which being interrupted by the intolerable negligence of some that acted in it, must needs much spoil the beauty on't. My Dutch Lover[5] spoke but little of what I intended for him, but supply'd it with a deal of idle stuff, which I was wholly unacquainted with, till I had heard it first from him; so that Jack-pudding[6] ever us'd to do: which though I knew before, I gave him yet the part, because I knew him so acceptable to most o'th' lighter Periwigs about the Town, and he indeed did vex me so, I could almost be angry: Yet, but Reader, you remember, I suppose, a fusty piece of Latine that has past from hand to hand this thousand years they say (and how much longer I can't tell) in favour of the dead.[7] I intended him a habit much more notably ridiculous, which if it can ever be important was so here, for many of the Scenes in the three last Acts depended upon the mistakes of the Colonel for *Haunce*, which the ill-favour'd likeness of their Habits is suppos'd to cause. Lastly, my Epilogue was promis'd me by a Person[8] who had surely made it good, if any, but he failing of his word, deputed one, who has made it as you see, and to make out your penyworth you have it here. The Prologue is by misfortune lost. Now, Reader, I have eas'd my mind of all I had to say, and so sans farther complyment, Adieu.

1673

Preface to *The Lucky Chance*

The little Obligation I have to some of the witty Sparks[1] and Poets of the Town, has put me on a Vindication of this Comedy from those Censures that Malice, and ill Nature have thrown upon it, tho in vain: The Poets I

4. A Long Lawrence was an instrument marked with signs about three inches long like a short ruler or totem with eight sides. Each side had a different set of markings of strokes, zigzags and crosses. A game of chance was played especially at Christmas, each player rolling the Long Lawrence and losing or winning pins or tokens according to which side came up. The term "Lawrence" may have come from the marks, seeming like the bars of a gridiron on which St. Lawrence was martyred. See Alice Bertha Gomme, *The Traditional Games of England, Scotland, and Ireland* (London, 1894).

5. Behn may be referring to the famous comic actor Edward Angel when she blamed the actor playing Haunce [the Dutch Lover] for ad-libbing instead of following her lines.

6. Low-class buffoon [editor's note].

7. The proverb is *De mortuis nil nisi bonum*, Speak well of the dead.

8. Possibly a reference to Edward Ravenscroft with whom Behn was friendly at the time. His failure might have been due to a bout of venereal disease. Ravenscroft wrote the epilogue for Behn's *The Town-Fopp* (1676). [Ravenscroft (ca. 1654–1707), British playwright—editor's note.]

1. Fops, dandies [except as indicated, all subsequent notes are Janet M. Todd's].

heartily excuse, since there is a sort of Self-Interest in their Malice, which I shou'd rather call a witty Way they have in this Age, of Railing at every thing they find with pain successful, and never to shew good Nature and speak well of any thing; but when they are sure 'tis damn'd, then they afford it that worse Scandal, their Pity. And nothing makes them so through-stitcht an Enemy as a full Third Day,[2] that's Crime enough to load it with all manner of Infamy; and when they can no other way prevail with the Town, they charge it with the old never failing Scandal——That's 'tis not fit for the Ladys: As if (if it were as they falsly give it out) the Ladys were oblig'd to hear Indecencys only from their Pens and Plays; and some of them have ventur'd to treat 'em as Coursely as 'twas possible, without the least Reproach from them; and in some of their most Celebrated Plays have entertained 'em with things, that if I should here strip from their Wit and Occasion that conducts 'em in and makes them proper, their fair Cheeks would perhaps wear a natural Colour[3] at the reading them: yet are never taken Notice of, because a Man writ them, and they may hear that from them they blush at from a Woman——But I make a Challenge to any Person of common Sense and Reason——that is not wilfully bent on ill Nature, and will in spight of Sense wrest a double *Entendre* from every thing, lying upon the Catch for a Jest or a Quibble, like a Rook for a Cully;[4] but any unprejudic'd Person that knows not the Author, to read any of my Comedys and compare 'em with others of this Age, and if they find one Word that can offend the chastest Ear, I will submit to all their peevish Cavills; but Right or Wrong they must be Criminal because a Woman's; condemning them without having the Christian Charity, to examine whether it be guilty or not, with reading, comparing, or thinking; the Ladies taking up any Scandal on Trust from some conceited Sparks, who will in spight of Nature be Wits and *Beaus*; then scatter it for Authentick all over the Town and Court, poysoning of others Judgment with their false Notions, condemning it to worse than Death, Loss of Fame. And to fortifie their Detraction, charge me with all the Plays that have ever been offensive; though I wish with all their Faults I had been the Author of some of those they have honour'd me with.

For the farther Justification of this Play; it being a Comedy of Intrigue, Dr. *Davenant*[5] out of Respect to the Commands he had from Court, to take great Care that no Indecency should be in Plays, sent for it and nicely look't it over, putting out any thing he but imagin'd the Criticks would play with. After that, Sir *Roger L'Estrange*[6] read it and licens'd it, and found no such Faults as 'tis charg'd with: Then Mr. *Killigrew*,[7] who more severe than any, from the strict Order he had, perus'd it with great Circumspection; and lastly the Master Players, who you will I hope in some Measure esteem Judges of Decency and their own Interest, having been so many Years Prentice to the Trade of Judging.

2. Good payment from the third night's profits, the traditional recompense for the playwright; through-stitcht: complete, from a stitch that went right through the cloth.

3. A blush rather than cosmetic paint.

4. A card-sharper or a cheat for a victim. ["Quibble": a pun—editor's note.]

5. Charles Davenant (1656–1714), eldest son of Sir William Davenant, who received the patent for the Duke's Company after the Restoration. Charles was co-owner of the United Company, which put on *The Lucky Chance*; he was also an M.P. and helped in the licensing of plays.

6. Licenser of published works throughout most of the Restoration and a man much admired by Behn for his propagandist efforts for the royal government.

7. Charles Killigrew (1655–1725), co-owner of the United Company and Master of the Revels. He was responsible for the content of performed plays.

I say, after all these Supervisors the Ladys may be convinc'd, they left nothing that cou'd offend, and the Men of their unjust Reflections on so many Judges of Wit and Decencys. When it happens that I challenge any one, to point me out the least Expression of what some have made their Discourse, they cry, *That Mr.* Leigh[8] *opens his Night Gown, when he comes into the Bride-chamber*; if he do, which is a Jest of his own making, and which I never saw, I hope he has his Cloaths on underneath? And if so, where is the Indecency? I have seen in that admirable Play of *Oedipus*,[9] the Gown open'd wide, and the Man shown in his Drawers and Wastecoat, and never thought it an Offence before. Another crys, *Why we know not what they mean, when the Man takes a Woman off the Stage, and another is thereby cuckolded*; is that any more than you see in the most Celebrated of your Plays? as the *City Politicks*, the *Lady Mayoress*, and the *Old Lawyers Wife*,[1] who goes with a Man she never saw before, and comes out again the joyfull'st Woman alive, for having made her Husband a Cuckold with such Dexterity, and yet I see nothing unnatural nor obscene: 'tis proper for the Characters. So in that lucky Play of the *London Cuckolds*,[2] not to recite Particulars. And in that good Comedy of *Sir Courtly Nice*,[3] the *Taylor to the young Lady*——in the fam'd Sir *Fopling, Dorimont* and *Bellinda*,[4] see the very Words——In *Valentinian*,[5] see the Scene between the *Court Bawds*. And *Valentinian* all loose and rufl'd a Moment after the Rape, and all this you see without scandal, and a thousand others. The *Moor* of *Venice* in many places. The *Maids Tragedy*——see the Scene of undressing the Bride, and between the *King* and *Amintor*, and after between the *King* and *Evadne*[6]——All these I Name as some of the best Plays I know; If I should repeat the Words exprest in these Scenes I mention, I might justly be charg'd with coarse ill Manners, and very little Modesty, and yet they so naturally fall into the places they are design'd for, and so are proper for the Business, that there is not the least Fault to be found with them; though I say those things in any of mine wou'd damn the whole Peice, and alarm the Town. Had I a Day or two's time, as I have scarce so many Hours to write this in (the Play, being all printed off and the Press waiting,) I would sum up all your Beloved Plays, and all the things in them that are past with such Silence by; because written by Men: such Masculine Strokes in me, must not be allow'd. I must conclude those Women (if there be any such) greater Criticks in that sort of Conversation than my self, who find any of that sort of mine, or any thing that can justly

8. Anthony Leigh, the famous comic actor. The offending action is specified in the stage directions.
9. A play of 1678 by Nathaniel Lee and Dryden; in act 2, scene I, Oedipus enters sleepwalking in his shirt. [JOHN DRYDEN (1631–1700), English playwright, poet, and critic—editor's note.]
1. *City Politicks*: John Crowne's Tory play performed in the season of 1682–83. The Lady Mayoress and the Old Lawyers Wife are two characters who make their husbands cuckolds.
2. A popular play of Behn's friend, Edward Ravenscroft, performed in 1681. It has three cuckolds in it.
3. John Crowne's comedy from 1685, *The Taylor to the Young Lady*, uses double entendres in his talk with the young woman and her aunt in act 2, scene 2.
4. Etherege's *Man of Mode; or, Sir Fopling Flutter* (1676). The hero, Dorimant, sleeps with Belinda and then describes the pleasure. [George Etherege (1635–1692), English comic playwright—editor's note.]
5. Edward Hyde, Lord Rochester's 1684 revision of Francis Beaumont (ca. 1584–1616) and John Fletcher's (1579–1625) earliest play, which concerns the rape of Lucina by the emperor Valentinian. Beaumont and Fletcher were younger contemporaries of Shakespeare, known for their popular collaborations [editor's note].
6. *The Maid's Tragedy* was a popular play by Beaumont and Fletcher, revived in the Restoration; in it the King forces a marriage between Amintor and Evadne his mistress and indulges in bawdy remarks about the wedding night and the failure of consummation. The Moor of Venice: Shakespeare's *Othello* [1603–04], one of the first plays to be performed on the Restoration stage.

be reproach't. But 'tis in vain by dint of Reason or Comparison to convince the obstinate Criticks, whose Business is to find Fault, if not by a loose and gross Imagination to create them, for they must either find the Jest, or make it; and those of this sort fall to my share, they find Faults of another kind for the Men Writers. And this one thing I will venture to say, though against my Nature, because it has a Vanity in it: That had the Plays I have writ come forth under any Mans Name, and never known to have been mine; I appeal to all unbyast Judges of Sense, if they had not said that Person had made as many good Comedies, as any one Man that has writ in our Age; but a Devil on't the Woman damns the Poet.

Ladies, for its further Justification to you, be pleas'd to know, that the first Copy of this Play was read by several Ladys of very great Quality, and unquestioned Fame, and received their most favourable Opinion, not one charging it with the Crime, that some have been pleas'd to find in the Acting. Other Ladys who saw it more than once, whose Quality and Vertue can sufficiently justifie any thing they design to favour, were pleas'd to say, they found an Entertainment in it very far from scandalous; and for the Generality of the Town, I found by my Receipts it was not thought so Criminal. However, that shall not be an Incouragement to me to trouble the Criticks with new Occasion of affronting me, for endeavouring at least to divert; and at this rate, both the few Poets that are left, and the Players who toil in vain, will be weary of their Trade.

I cannot omit to tell you, that a Wit of the Town, a Friend of mine at *Wills* Coffee House,[7] the first Night of the Play, cry'd it down as much as in him lay, who before had read it and assured me he never saw a prettier Comedy. So complaisant one pestilent Wit will be to another, and in the full Cry make his Noise too; but since 'tis to the witty Few I speak, I hope the better Judges will take no Offence, to whom I am oblig'd for better Judgments; and those I hope will be so kind to me, knowing my Conversation not at all addicted to the Indecencys alledged, that I would much less practice it in a Play, that must stand the Test of the censuring World. And I must want common Sense, and all the Degrees of good Manners, renouncing my Fame, all Modesty and Interest for a silly Sawcy fruitless Jest, to make Fools laugh, and Women blush, and wise Men asham'd; My self all the while, if I had been guilty of this Crime charg'd to me, remaining the only stupid, insensible. Is this likely, is this reasonable to be believ'd by any body, but the wilfully blind? All I ask, is the Priviledge for my Masculine Part the Poet in me, (if any such you will allow me) to tread in those successful Paths my Predecessors have so long thriv'd in, to take those Measures that both the Ancient and Modern Writers have set me, and by which they have pleas'd the World so well. If I must not, because of my Sex, have this Freedom, but that you will usurp all to your selves; I lay down my Quill, and you shall hear no more of me, no not so much as to make Comparisons, because I will be kinder to my Brothers of the Pen, than they have been to a defenceless Woman; for I am not content to write for a Third day only. I value Fame as much as if I had been born a *Hero*; and if you rob me of that, I can retire from the ungrateful World, and scorn its fickle Favours.

1687

7. A famous London coffeehouse in Covent Garden kept by Will Unwin.

GIAMBATTISTA VICO
1668–1744

The Italian philosopher Giambattista Vico is noted for his original insights into the origins and development of language and culture. An advocate of a holistic approach, centered on language, to the study of society, he produced wide-ranging analyses that addressed issues not only in history and sociology but also in jurisprudence, philosophy, theology, politics, rhetoric, and poetics. His most celebrated accomplishment, from the perspective of the twenty-first century, is his monumental *Scienza nuova* (*New Science*), which he issued in three editions (1725, 1730, 1744). Anticipating the developmental theories of G. W. F. HEGEL and KARL MARX, this work presents the now-famous theory of the three periods of social development, which he termed the ages of the gods, heroes, and men. Among the distinctive features of each period are differences in language and literature as well as in government and law. The general sense, as in Hegel and Marx, is that human nature is not absolute but historical, a product of changing social institutions and material configurations. For literary theory, the most important claims of Vico's *New Science* are its arguments for the origin of human society in the prerational poetic nature of human beings and for the primordial status of four "master tropes" of rhetoric.

Born in Naples, Vico was the son of a bookseller. He received an education in Scholastic philosophy and in rhetoric from a series of Neapolitan clergymen, becoming proficient in Latin literature. By the age of seventeen, Vico was applying himself to the study of civil and canon (church) law, writing poetry on the side as a pleasant diversion. He became accomplished enough as a poet that for much of his life he was often called on by the aristocracy to write occasional verse for important public events, such as weddings or funerals. He briefly studied law at the University of Naples, but he relied mostly on local tutors and self-education. As a young man, he befriended a group of "modern" intellectuals, known as the Investigators, who critiqued or rejected the authority of the "ancients." Central to this controversial group was the new philosophy of Galileo Galilei (1564–1642), Francis Bacon (1561–1626), and René Descartes (1596–1650), as well as the "alternative" classical views of the Greek philosopher Epicurus (341–270 B.C.E.) and the Roman poet Lucretius (ca. 94–55 B.C.E.). Reflecting the widespread intellectual changes in Europe that have come to be known as the Enlightenment, the group was largely concerned with putting science and philosophy on a rational and empirical foundation.

In 1699 Vico became professor of rhetoric at the University of Naples, a position he held for more than forty years. His early annual orations, now available in *On Humanistic Education* (1993), address the proper methods and functions of education. During this time he joined the Palatine Academy, an eclectic group of modern intellectuals committed to the emerging values of the Enlightenment. As befitted his education and intellectual associations, Vico was interested in a wide variety of subjects, including the physical sciences and mathematics. In 1710 he published his first major work, *De antiquissima Italorum sapientia* (*On the Most Ancient Wisdom of the Italians*), which attempts to reconstruct the nonrationalistic philosophy of a pre-Roman civilization via the etymological study of Latin words. Here and in his other works, Vico strove to be a persuasive philologist, as he studied cultures and their histories through languages, especially etymologies; his philological work was not valued in his own time, but it was later admired by such leading twentieth-century critics as Erich Auerbach and EDWARD W. SAID. Vico's next important publication, *Il diritto universale* (1720–22, *Universal Law*), focused on the historical origin and development of jurisprudence. In chronological order, it traced the emergence of different types of society, identifying a particular form of law with each while also making important links to various linguistic, literary, and religious forms. Later, at the invitation of a nobleman, Vico also published his autobiography (1725–28), the first modern example of its kind.

In 1725 Vico published the first edition of his *New Science*. As a study of the nonrationalistic origins and historical development of "gentile" (pre-Christian, non-Jewish) societies, it strongly resembles the two major works that preceded it. He considered the *New Science* his most important work, which would reveal the underlying order in the diversity of the gentile nations just as Isaac Newton's *Principia Mathematica* (1687) had unveiled the eternal laws of nature. Vico was deeply disappointed by the book's reception, however, which tended to be unfavorable when not indifferent. Feeling misunderstood and unacknowledged, he described himself as "a foreigner in his own country." In 1735 he was appointed the official historian to Charles Bourbon, then king of Naples and Sicily, but he remained primarily concerned with revising his *New Science*. He published a second edition in 1730 and prepared a third, which appeared shortly after his death in 1744.

Our selections, taken from the third edition, begin with Vico's discussion of the historical stages that gentile nations have traversed. Comparing the various ancient histories of the Egyptians, Chaldeans, Scythians, Phoenicians, Greeks, and Romans, he reveals an underlying universal pattern—the expression of a divine providence working in the world, reducing multiplicity to order. The necessary course (*corso*) that the nations must run passes through the ages of the gods, heroes, and men. Each age is characterized by a particular kind of nature, custom, jurisprudence, government, and language. A distinctive feature of Vico's sequence of ages—unlike the classical movement from golden to iron age—is its susceptibility to what he calls a "recourse" (*ricorso*) or recurrence, which suggests that a nation may retraverse a previous stage or all three.

One of Vico's main concerns is the poetic nature of the first human beings in the age of the gods, the "master key" of his science. As he explains it, the first human beings apprehended the world in a "poetic" manner. With vigorous imaginations and robust senses, but feeble powers of reasoning, they responded to their unknown world with passionate fear and wonder, creating sublime images of nature. In this regard, Vico's portrait of the early poets suggests the influence of LONGINUS's classical theory of sublimity; a bit later, Jean-Jacques Rousseau (1712–1778) would make a similar argument about the origin of languages. The point, for Vico, is that the poetic nature of the first human beings inaugurated their world. In support of this view, he points out that the first poets anthropomorphized nature and accounted for the unknown in human and metaphorical terms. Vico's famous example is the "primitive" human response to the terror of lightning and thunder: namely, the imaginative creation of the angry sky god, Jove.

Vico suggests that the religions—as well as the logic, morals, economics, politics, physics, cosmography, astronomy, geography, and history—of the gentile nations are rooted in poetic and rhetorical responses to nature. In some sense the foundations of civil society can be said to reside in the modifications of the minds and institutions of human beings. But such modifications are not so much analytical or rational as they are poetic or, more precisely, rhetorical. Metaphor, synecdoche, metonymy, and irony, Vico's four master figures, shape human beings' apprehension of the world.

Perhaps the most pointed criticism of Vico's thinking is that he reduces the complexities of culture and society to a "universal history." One can also criticize Vico for displaying little concern for cultures and histories beyond those of Greece and Rome and for unfairly privileging Christianity by not treating it historically. Despite the limitations of his methodology and his cultural chauvinism, however, Vico's attention to poetic expression offers a corrective to the dominant rational thought of the Enlightenment, bearing comparison with MARTIN HEIDEGGER's later theories of poetry: both thinkers assign poetry a fundamental role in world building. His sense of a human nature as fundamentally historical, moreover, anticipates Karl Marx, who refers approvingly to Vico in a famous footnote to *Capital* (1867). Finally, Vico pioneers the concern with rhetorical tropes as foundational to human life developed by such twentieth-century thinkers as ROMAN JAKOBSON, HAYDEN WHITE, PAUL DE MAN, and HAROLD BLOOM, a great admirer of Vichian poetics.

BIBLIOGRAPHY

The standard Italian edition of Vico's works is edited by Benedetto Croce and Fausto Nicolini (8 vols. in 11, 1914–42). English translations include *On the Study Methods of Our Time* (1709; trans. 1990); *On the Most Ancient Wisdom of the Italians* (1710; trans. 1988); *The Autobiography of Giambattista Vico* (1725–28; trans. 1944); the third edition of *The New Science of Giambattista Vico* (1744; trans. 1968), to which has been added Vico's "Practic of the New Science"; and *On Humanistic Education* (trans. 1993) and *The Art of Rhetoric* (trans. 1996), both translated and edited by Giorgio A. Pinton and Arthur W. Shippee. *Vico: Selected Writings*, edited and translated by Leon Pompa (1982), includes selections from *On the Most Ancient Wisdom of the Italians*, the 1725 version of the *New Science*, and Vico's orations. For information on Vico's life, see his autobiography cited above; Robert Flint's *Vico* (1901; rpt. 1979); and H. P. Adam's *Life and Writings of Giambattista Vico* (1935). A valuable brief introduction to the life and work is Peter Burke's *Vico* (1985).

Benedetto Croce's *Philosophy of Giambattista Vico* (1911; trans. 1913) is an important critical study that put Vico's work on the map in the early twentieth century. For a sense of the wide range and multidisciplinary nature of Vico studies, see the following three collections: *Giambattista Vico: An International Symposium*, edited by Giorgio Tagliacozzo and Hayden White (1969); *Giambattista Vico's Science of Humanity*, edited by Tagliacozzo and Donald Phillip Verene (1976); and *Vico: Past and Present*, edited by Tagliacozzo (1981). Also helpful in this regard are Max Harold Fisch and Thomas Goddard Bergin's introduction to Vico's autobiography cited above and the annual volumes of *New Vico Studies* (1983–), published by the Institute for Vico Studies. Illuminating studies of the *New Science* include Verene's *Vico's Science of the Imagination* (1981), Leon Pompa's *Vico: A Study of the New Science* (2d ed., 1990), Ernesto Grassi's *Vico and Humanism: Essays on Vico, Heidegger, and Rhetoric* (1990), Joseph Mali's *Rehabilitation of Myth: Vico's "New Science"* (1992), and Giuseppe Mazzotta's *New Map of the World: The Poetic Philosophy of Giambattista Vico* (1999). A philosophical and historically informed study of Vico is available in Isaiah Berlin's *Vico and Herder: Two Studies in the History of Ideas* (1976). On the subject of Marx and Vico, see *Vico and Marx: Affinities and Contrasts*, edited by Giorgio Tagliacozzo (1983). For discussions of Vico in relationship to rhetoric, see Michael Mooney's *Vico in the Tradition of Rhetoric* (1985) and John D. Schaeffer's *Sensus Communis: Vico, Rhetoric, and the Limits of Relativism* (1990). Bibliographies of criticism and primary texts appear in Robert Crease's *Vico in English: A Bibliography of Writings by and about Giambattista Vico* (1978), Molly Black Verene's *Vico: A Bibliography of Works in English from 1884 to 1994* (1994), and the annual volumes of *New Vico Studies*.

From The New Science[1]

* * *

31 This New Science or metaphysic, studying the common nature of nations in the light of divine providence, discovers the origins of divine and human institutions among the gentile nations, and thereby establishes a sys-

1. Translated by Thomas Goddard Bergin and Max Harold Fisch, who occasionally supply clarifying words or references in brackets.

tem of the natural law of the gentes,[2] which proceeds with the greatest equality and constancy through the three ages which the Egyptians handed down to us as the three periods through which the world had passed up to their time. These are: (1) The age of the gods, in which the gentiles believed they lived under divine governments, and everything was commanded them by auspices[3] and oracles, which are the oldest institutions in profane history. (2) The age of the heroes, in which they reigned everywhere in aristocratic commonwealths, on account of a certain superiority of nature which they held themselves to have over the plebs. (3) The age of men, in which all men recognized themselves as equal in human nature, and therefore there were established first the popular commonwealths and then the monarchies, both of which are forms of human government.

32 In harmony with these three kinds of nature and government, three kinds of language were spoken which compose the vocabulary of this Science: (1) That of the time of the families when gentile men were newly received into humanity. This, we shall find, was a mute language of signs and physical objects having natural relations to the ideas they wished to express. (2) That spoken by means of heroic emblems, or similitudes, comparisons, images, metaphors, and natural descriptions, which make up the great body of the heroic language which was spoken at the time the heroes reigned. (3) Human language using words agreed upon by the people, a language of which they are absolute lords, and which is proper to the popular commonwealths and monarchical states; a language whereby the people may fix the meaning of the laws by which the nobles as well as the plebs are bound. Hence, among all nations, once the laws had been put into the vulgar[4] tongue, the science of laws passed from the control of the nobles. Hitherto, among all nations, the nobles, being also priests, had kept the laws in a secret language as a sacred thing. That is the natural reason for the secrecy of the laws among the Roman patricians until popular liberty arose.

Now these are the same three languages that the Egyptians claimed had been spoken before in their world, corresponding exactly both in number and in sequence to the three ages that had run their course before them. (1) The hieroglyphic or sacred or secret language, by means of mute acts. This is suited to the uses of religion, for which observance is more important than discussion. (2) The symbolic, by means of similitudes, such as we have just seen the heroic language to have been. (3) The epistolary or vulgar, which served the common uses of life. These three types of language are found among the Chaldeans, Scythians, Egyptians, Germans, and all the other ancient gentile nations; although hieroglyphic writing survived longest among the Egyptians, because for a longer time than the others they were closed to all foreign nations (as for the same reason it still survives among the Chinese), and hence we have a proof of the vanity of their imagined remote antiquity.

33 We here bring to light the beginnings not only of languages but also of letters, which philology[5] has hitherto despaired of finding. We shall give a specimen of the extravagant and monstrous opinions that have been held

2. Heathen peoples (ecclesiastical). "The gentile nations": pre-Christian non-Hebrew societies.
3. Those who prophesy from the flight of birds.
4. Ordinary, common.
5. The discipline that studies culture and its history through languages, especially through historical and comparative linguistics.

up to now. We shall observe that the unhappy cause of this effect is that philologists have believed that among the nations languages first came into being and then letters; whereas (to give here a brief indication of what will be fully proved in this volume) letters and languages were born twins and proceeded apace through all their three stages. These beginnings are precisely exhibited in the causes of the Latin language, as set forth in the first edition of the *New Science* (which is the second of the three passages on whose account we do not regret that book). By the reasoning out of these causes many discoveries have been made in ancient Roman history, government, and law, as you will observe a thousand times, O reader, in this volume. From this example, scholars of oriental languages, of Greek, and, among the modern languages, particularly of German, which is a mother language, will be enabled to make discoveries of antiquities far beyond their expectations and ours.

34 We find that the principle of these origins both of languages and of letters lies in the fact that the first gentile peoples, by a demonstrated necessity of nature, were poets who spoke in poetic characters. This discovery, which is the master key of this Science, has cost us the persistent research of almost all our literary life, because with our civilized natures we [moderns] cannot at all imagine and can understand only by great toil the poetic nature of these first men. The [poetic] characters of which we speak were certain imaginative genera (images for the most part of animate substances, of gods or heroes, formed by their imagination) to which they reduced all the species or all the particulars appertaining to each genus; exactly as the fables of human times, such as those of late comedy, are intelligible genera reasoned out by moral philosophy, from which the comic poets form imaginative genera (for the best ideas of the various human types are nothing but that) which are the persons of the comedies. These divine or heroic characters were true fables or myths, and their allegories are found to contain meanings not analogical but univocal, not philosophical but historical, of the peoples of Greece of those times.

Since these genera (for that is what the fables in essence are) were formed by most vigorous imaginations, as in men of the feeblest reasoning powers, we discover in them true poetic sentences, which must be sentiments clothed in the greatest passions and therefore full of sublimity and arousing wonder. Now the sources of all poetic locution are two: poverty of language and need to explain and be understood. Heroic speech followed immediately on the mute language of acts and objects that had natural relations to the ideas they were meant to signify, which was used in the divine times. Lastly, in the necessary natural course of human institutions, language among the Assyrians, Syrians, Phoenicians, Egyptians, Greeks, and Latins began with heroic verses, passed thence to iambics,[6] and finally settled into prose. This gives certainty to the history of the ancient poets and explains why in the German language, particularly in Silesia, a province of peasants, there are many natural versifiers, and in the Spanish, French and Italian languages the first authors wrote in verse.

35 From these three languages is formed the mental dictionary by which

6. Poetic metrical feet (a short plus a long syllable) that approximate the rhythm of conversation. "Heroic verses": the formal dactylic hexameter (a 6-foot line, based on the syllabic pattern long-short-short) of Greek and Latin epic.

to interpret properly all the various articulated languages, and we make use of it here wherever it is needed. In the first edition of the *New Science* we gave a detailed illustration of it, in which this idea of it was presented: that from the eternal properties of the fathers, which we in virtue of this Science considered them to have had in the state of the families and of the first heroic cities in the time when the languages were formed, we find proper meanings [of terms] in fifteen different languages, both dead and living, by which they were diversely called, sometimes from one property and sometimes from another. (This is the third passage in which we take satisfaction in that edition of our book.) Such a lexicon is necessary for learning the language spoken by the ideal eternal history traversed in time by the histories of all nations; and for scientifically adducing authorities to confirm what is discussed in the natural law of the gentes and hence in every particular jurisprudence.

36 Along with these three languages—proper to the three ages in which three forms of government prevailed, conforming to three types of civil natures, which succeed one another as the nations run their course—we find there went also in the same order a jurisprudence suited to each in its time.[7]

* * *

51 Premising such reflections on the vain opinion of their own antiquity held by these gentile nations and above all by the Egyptians, we should begin our study of gentile learning by scientifically ascertaining this important starting-point—where and when that learning had its first beginnings in the world—and by adducing human reasons thereby in support of Christian faith, which takes its start from the fact that the first people of the world were the Hebrews, whose prince was Adam, created by the true God at the time of the creation of the world. It follows that the first science to be learned should be mythology or the interpretation of fables; for, as we shall see, all the histories of the gentiles have their beginnings in fables, which were the first histories of the gentile nations. By such a method the beginnings of the sciences as well as of the nations are to be discovered, for they sprang from the nations and from no other source. It will be shown throughout this work that they had their beginnings in the public needs or utilities of the peoples and that they were later perfected as acute individuals applied their reflection to them. This is the proper starting-point for universal history, which all scholars say is defective in its beginnings.

* * *

331 But in the night of thick darkness enveloping the earliest antiquity, so remote from ourselves, there shines the eternal and never failing light of a truth beyond all question: that the world of civil society[8] has certainly been made by men, and that its principles are therefore to be found within the modifications of our own human mind. Whoever reflects on this cannot but marvel that the philosophers should have bent all their energies to the study of the world of nature, which, since God made it, He alone knows; and that they should have neglected the study of the world of nations, or civil world,

7. The three types of jurisprudence are mystic theology, civil equity (reason of state), and natural equity.

8. The totality of institutions constituting gentile human societies governed by law.

which, since men had made it, men could come to know. This aberration was a consequence of that infirmity of the human mind by which, immersed and buried in the body, it naturally inclines to take notice of bodily things, and finds the effort to attend to itself too laborious ; just as the bodily eye sees all objects outside itself but needs a mirror to see itself.

* * *

342 In one of its principal aspects, this Science must therefore be a rational civil theology of divine providence, which seems hitherto to have been lacking. For the philosophers have either been altogether ignorant of it, as the Stoics and the Epicureans[9] were, the latter asserting that human affairs are agitated by a blind concourse of atoms, the former that they are drawn by a deaf [inexorable] chain of cause and effect; or they have considered it solely in the order of natural things, giving the name of natural theology to the metaphysics in which they contemplate this attribute [i.e., the providence] of God, and in which they confirm it by the physical order observed in the motions of such bodies as the spheres and the elements and in the final cause observed in other and minor natural things. But they ought to have studied it in the economy of civil institutions, in keeping with the full meaning of applying to providence the term "divinity" [i.e., the power of divining], from *divinari*, to divine, which is to understand what is hidden *from* men—the future—or what is hidden *in* them—their consciousness. It is this [divinatory providence] that makes up the first and principal part of the subject matter of jurisprudence, namely the divine institutions [e.g., augury] on which depend the human institutions which make up its other and complementary part. Our new Science must therefore be a demonstration, so to speak, of what providence has wrought in history, for it must be a history of the institutions by which, without human discernment or counsel, and often against the designs of men, providence has ordered this great city of the human race. For though this world has been created in time and particular, the institutions established therein by providence are universal and eternal.

* * *

349 Our Science therefore comes to describe at the same time an ideal eternal history traversed in time by the history of every nation in its rise, development, maturity, decline, and fall. Indeed, we make bold to affirm that he who meditates this Science narrates to himself this ideal eternal history so far as he himself makes it for himself by that proof "it had, has, and will have to be." For the first indubitable principle posited above is that this world of nations has certainly been made by men, and its guise must therefore be found within the modifications of our own human mind. And history cannot be more certain than when he who creates the things also narrates them. Now, as geometry, when it constructs the world of quantity out of its elements, or contemplates that world, is creating it for itself, just so does our Science [create for itself the world of nations], but with a reality greater by just so much as the institutions having to do with human affairs are more

9. Followers of the Greek philosopher Epicurus (341–271 B.C.E.). Stoics: followers of the Greek philosopher Zeno (335–263 B.C.E.).

real than points, lines, surfaces, and figures are. And this very fact is an argument, O reader, that these proofs are of a kind divine and should give thee a divine pleasure, since in God knowledge and creation are one and the same thing.

* * *

361 We have said above in the Axioms that all the histories of the gentile nations have had fabulous beginnings, that among the Greeks (who have given us all we know of gentile antiquity) the first sages were the theological poets, and that the nature of everything born or made betrays the crudeness of its origin. It is thus and not otherwise that we must conceive the origins of poetic wisdom. And as for the great and sovereign esteem in which it has been handed down to us, this has its origin in the two conceits,[1] that of nations and that of scholars, and it springs even more from the latter than from the former. For just as Manetho,[2] the Egyptian high priest, translated all the fabulous history of Egypt into a sublime natural theology, so the Greek philosophers translated theirs into philosophy. And they did so not merely for the reason that the histories as they had come down to both alike were most unseemly, but for the following five reasons as well.

362 The first was reverence for religion, for the gentile nations were everywhere founded by fables on religion. The second was the grand effect thence derived, namely this civil world, so wisely ordered that it could only be the effect of a superhuman wisdom. The third was the occasions which, as we shall see, these fables, assisted by the veneration of religion and the credit of such great wisdom, gave the philosophers for instituting research and for meditating lofty things in philosophy. The fourth was the ease with which they were thus enabled, as we shall also show farther on, to explain their sublime philosophical meditations by means of the expressions happily left them by the poets. The fifth and last, which is the sum of them all, is the confirmation of their own meditations which the philosophers derived from the authority of religion and the wisdom of the poets. Of these five reasons, the first two and the last contain the praises of the divine wisdom which ordained this world of nations, and the witness the philosophers bore to it even in their errors. The third and fourth are deceptions permitted by divine providence, that thence there might arise philosophers to understand and recognize it for what it truly is, an attribute of the true God.

363 Throughout this book it will be shown that as much as the poets had first sensed in the way of vulgar wisdom, the philosophers later understood in the way of esoteric wisdom; so that the former may be said to have been the sense and the latter the intellect of the human race. What Aristotle[3] [*On the Soul* 432a7f] said of the individual man is therefore true of the race in general: *Nihil est in intellectu quin prius fuerit in sensu*. That is, the human mind does not understand anything of which it has had no previous impression (which our modern metaphysicians call "occasion") from the senses. Now the mind uses the intellect when, from something it senses, it gathers

1. Forms of excessively high regard for one's own worth or virtue. Among nations conceit is demonstrated by the claim of nearly every gentile nation to have been the origin of civilization; among scholars it is manifested in the attribution of one's own knowledge and wisdom to various kinds of ancient writings.
2. Egyptian priest and historian (active ca. 280 B.C.E.); his *History of Egypt*, which covered rulers from mythical times to 323, became the basis of our conventional numbering of dynasties.
3. Greek philosopher (384–322 B.C.E.; see above).

something which does not fall under the senses; and this is the proper meaning of the Latin verb *intelligere*.

364 Now, before discussing poetic wisdom, it is necessary for us to see what wisdom in general is. Wisdom is the faculty which commands all the disciplines by which we acquire all the sciences and arts that make up humanity. Plato[4] [in his *Alcibiades I*, 124eff?] defines wisdom as "the perfecter of man." Man, in his proper being as man, consists of mind and spirit, or, if we prefer, of intellect and will. It is the function of wisdom to fulfill both these parts in man, the second by way of the first, to the end that by a mind illuminated by knowledge of the highest institutions, the spirit may be led to choose the best. The highest institutions in this universe are those turned toward and conversant with God; the best are those which look to the good of all mankind. The former are called divine institutions, the latter human. True wisdom, then, should teach the knowledge of divine institutions in order to conduct human institutions to the highest good. We believe that this was the plan upon which Marcus Terentius Varro,[5] who earned the title "most learned of the Romans," erected his great work, [*The Antiquities*] of *Divine and Human Institutions*, of which the injustice of time has unhappily bereft us. We shall treat of these institutions in the present book so far as the weakness of our education and the meagerness of our erudition permit.

365 Wisdom among the gentiles began with the Muse, defined by Homer[6] in a golden passage of the *Odyssey* [8.63] as "knowledge of good and evil," and later called divination. It was on the natural prohibition of this practice, as something naturally denied to man, that God founded the true religion of the Hebrews, from which our Christian religion arose. The Muse must thus have been properly at first the science of divining by auspices, and this was the vulgar wisdom of all nations, of which we shall have more to say presently. It consisted in contemplating God under the attribute of his providence, so that from *divinari* his essence came to be called divinity. We shall see presently that the theological poets, who certainly founded the humanity of Greece, were versed in this wisdom, and this explains why the Latins called the judicial astrologers "professors of wisdom." Wisdom was later attributed to men renowned for useful counsels given to mankind, as in the case of the Seven Sages of Greece.[7] The attribution was then extended to men who for the good of peoples and nations wisely ordered and governed commonwealths. Still later the word "wisdom" came to mean knowledge of natural divine things; that is, metaphysics, called for that reason divine science, which, seeking knowledge of man's mind in God, and recognizing God as the source of all truth, must recognize him as the regulator of all good. So that metaphysics must essentially work for the good of the human race, whose preservation depends on the universal belief in a provident divinity. It is perhaps for having demonstrated this providence that Plato deserved to be called divine; and that which denies to God this great attribute must be

4. Greek philosopher (ca. 427–ca. 347 B.C.E); modern scholars believe that PLATO did not write the *Alcibiades*.
5. Roman scholar (116–27 B.C.E.).
6. Greek epic poet (ca. 8th c. B.C.E.). Homer's *Iliad* begins "Sing, Muse, . . ."
7. Seven statesman and thinkers of the early 5th century B.C.E., credited with formulating pithy aphorisms (e.g., "Know thyself"; "Avoid extremes"). Plato (*Protagoras* 343a) names them as Solon of Athens, Chilon of Sparta, Thales of Miletus, Bias of Priene, Cleobulus of Lindus, Pittacus of Mitylene, and Myson of Chen.

called stupidity rather than wisdom. Finally among the Hebrews, and thence among us Christians, wisdom was called the science of eternal things revealed by God; a science which, among the Tuscans, considered as knowledge of the true good and true evil, perhaps owed to that fact the first name they gave it, "science in divinity."

366 We must therefore distinguish more truly than Varro did the three kinds of theology. First, poetic theology, that of the theological poets, which was the civil theology of all the gentile nations. Second, natural theology, that of the metaphysicians. Third, our Christian theology, a mixture of civil and natural with the loftiest revealed theology; all three united in the contemplation of divine providence. (Our third kind takes the place of Varro's poetic theology, which among the gentiles was the same as civil theology, though he distinguished it from both civil and natural theology because, sharing the vulgar common error that the fables contained high mysteries of sublime philosophy, he believed it to be a mixture of the two.) Divine providence has so conducted human institutions that, starting from the poetic theology which regulated them by certain sensible signs believed to be divine counsels sent to man by the gods, and by means of the natural theology which demonstrates providence by eternal reasons which do not fall under the senses, the nations were disposed to receive revealed theology in virtue of a supernatural faith, superior not only to the senses but to human reason itself.

367 But because metaphysics is the sublime science which distributes their determinate subject matters to all the so-called subaltern sciences; and because the wisdom of the ancients was that of the theological poets, who without doubt were the first sages of the gentile world; and because the origins of all things must by nature have been crude: for all these reasons we must trace the beginnings of poetic wisdom to a crude metaphysics. From this, as from a trunk, there branch out from one limb logic, morals, economics, and politics, all poetic; and from another, physics, the mother of cosmography and astronomy, the latter of which gives their certainty to its two daughters, chronology and geography—all likewise poetic. We shall show clearly and distinctly how the founders of gentile humanity by means of their natural theology (or metaphysics) imagined the gods; how by means of their logic they invented languages; by morals, created heroes; by economics, founded families, and by politics, cities; by their physics, established the beginnings of things as all divine; by the particular physics of man, in a certain sense created themselves; by their cosmography, fashioned for themselves a universe entirely of gods; by astronomy, carried the planets and constellations from earth to heaven; by chronology, gave a beginning to [measured] times; and how by geography the Greeks, for example, described the [whole] world within their own Greece.

368 Thus our Science comes to be at once a history of the ideas, the customs, and the deeds of mankind. From these three we shall derive the principles of the history of human nature, which we shall show to be the principles of universal history, which principles it seems hitherto to have lacked.

* * *

374 From these first men, stupid, insensate, and horrible beasts, all the philosophers and philologians should have begun their investigations of the wisdom of the ancient gentiles; that is, from the giants in the proper sense in which we have just taken them. (Father Boulduc[8] in his *De ecclesia ante Legem* says the scriptural names of the giants signify "pious, venerable and illustrious men"; but this can be understood only of the noble giants who by divination founded the gentile religions and gave the age of giants its name.) And they should have begun with metaphysics, which seeks its proofs not in the external world but within the modifications of the mind of him who meditates it. For since this world of nations has certainly been made by men, it is within these modifications that its principles should have been sought. And human nature, so far as it is like that of animals, carries with it this property, that the senses are its sole way of knowing things.

375 Hence poetic wisdom, the first wisdom of the gentile world, must have begun with a metaphysics not rational and abstract like that of learned men now, but felt and imagined as that of these first men must have been, who, without power of ratiocination, were all robust sense and vigorous imagination. This metaphysics was their poetry, a faculty born with them (for they were furnished by nature with these senses and imaginations); born of their ignorance of causes, for ignorance, the mother of wonder, made everything wonderful to men who were ignorant of everything. Their poetry was at first divine, because, as we saw in the passage from Lactantius,[9] they imagined the causes of the things they felt and wondered at to be gods. (This is now confirmed by the American Indians, who call gods all the things that surpass their small understanding. We may add the ancient Germans dwelling about the Arctic Ocean, of whom Tacitus[1] tells that they spoke of hearing the sun pass at night from west to east through the sea, and affirmed that they saw the gods. These very rude and simple nations help us to a much better understanding of the founders of the gentile world with whom we are now concerned.) At the same time they gave the things they wondered at substantial being after their own ideas, just as children do, whom we see take inanimate things in their hands and play with them and talk to them as though they were living persons.

376 In such fashion the first men of the gentile nations, children of nascent mankind, created things according to their own ideas. But this creation was infinitely different from that of God. For God, in his purest intelligence, knows things, and, by knowing them, creates them; but they, in their robust ignorance, did it by virtue of a wholly corporeal imagination. And because it was quite corporeal, they did it with marvelous sublimity; a sublimity such and so great that it excessively perturbed the very persons who by imagining did the creating, for which they were called "poets," which is Greek for "creators." Now this is the threefold labor of great poetry: (1) to invent sublime fables suited to the popular understanding, (2) to perturb to excess, with a view to the end proposed: (3) to teach the vulgar to act virtuously, as the poets have taught themselves; as will presently be shown. Of this nature of human institutions it remained an eternal property, expressed in a noble phrase of Tacitus, that frightened men vainly "no sooner imagine than they believe" (*fingunt simul creduntque*).[2]

377 Of such natures must have been the first founders of gentile human-

8. Jacques Boulduc (d. 1646), French priest and author.
9. Firmianus Lactantius (ca. 240–ca. 320 C.E.), Roman Christian writer and rhetorician; Vico refers to *Divine Institutions* 1.15.
1. Cornelius Tacitus (ca. 55–ca. 120 C.E.), Roman historian; Vico refers to *Germania* 45.
2. Tacitus, *Annales* 6.5.10 [translators' note].

ity when at last the sky fearfully rolled with thunder and flashed with lightning, as could not but follow from the bursting upon the air for the first time of an impression so violent. As we have postulated, this occurred a hundred years after the flood in Mesopotamia[3] and two hundred years after it throughout the rest of the world; for it took that much time to reduce the earth to such a state that, dry of the moisture of the universal flood, it could send up dry exhalations or matter igniting in the air to produce lightning. Thereupon a few giants, who must have been the most robust, and who were dispersed through the forests on the mountain heights where the strongest beasts have their dens, were frightened and astonished by the great effect whose cause they did not know, and raised their eyes and became aware of the sky. And because in such a case the nature of the human mind leads it to attribute its own nature to the effect, and because in that state their nature was that of men all robust bodily strength, who expressed their very violent passions by shouting and grumbling, they pictured the sky to themselves as a great animated body, which in that aspect they called Jove, the first god of the so-called greater gentes, who meant to tell them something by the hiss of his bolts and the clap of his thunder. And thus they began to exercise that natural curiosity which is the daughter of ignorance and the mother of knowledge, and which, opening the mind of man, gives birth to wonder. This characteristic still persists in the vulgar, who, when they see a comet or sundog[4] or some other extraordinary thing in nature, and particularly in the countenance of the sky, at once turn curious and anxiously inquire what it means. When they wonder at the prodigious effects of the magnet on iron, even in this age of minds enlightened and instructed by philosophy, they come out with this: that the magnet has an occult sympathy for the iron; and so they make of all nature a vast animate body which feels passions and affections.

378 But the nature of our civilized minds is so detached from the senses, even in the vulgar, by abstractions corresponding to all the abstract terms our languages abound in, and so refined by the art of writing, and as it were spiritualized by the use of numbers, because even the vulgar know how to count and reckon, that it is naturally beyond our power to form the vast image of this mistress called "Sympathetic Nature." Men shape the phrase with their lips but have nothing in their minds; for what they have in mind is falsehood, which is nothing; and their imagination no longer avails to form a vast false image. It is equally beyond our power to enter into the vast imagination of those first men, whose minds were not in the least abstract, refined, or spiritualized, because they were entirely immersed in the senses, buffeted by the passions, buried in the body. That is why we said above that we can scarcely understand, still less imagine, how those first men thought who founded gentile humanity.

379 In this fashion the first theological poets created the first divine fable, the greatest they ever created: that of Jove, king and father of men and gods, in the act of hurling the lightning bolt; an image so popular, disturbing, and instructive that its creators themselves believed in it, and feared, revered, and worshiped it in frightful religions. And by that trait of the human mind

3. That is, Noah's Flood (Genesis 7).
4. A bright spot tinged with color that can appear on a parhelic circle (a luminous halo parallel to the horizon at the altitude of the sun).

noticed by Tacitus whatever these men saw, imagined, or even made or did themselves they believed to be Jove; and to all of the universe that came within their scope, and to all its parts, they gave the being of animate substance. This is the civil history of the expression "All things are full of Jove" (*Iovis omnia plena*)[5] by which Plato later understood the ether which penetrates and fills everything.[6] But for the theological poets Jove was no higher than the mountain peaks. The first men, who spoke by signs, naturally believed that lightning bolts and thunderclaps were signs made to them by Jove; whence from *nuo*, to make a sign, came *numen*, the divine will, by an idea more than sublime and worthy to express the divine majesty. They believed that Jove commanded by signs, that such signs were real words, and that nature was the language of Jove. The science of this language the gentiles universally believed to be divination, which by the Greeks was called theology, meaning the science of the language of the gods. Thus Jove acquired the fearful kingdom of the lightning and became the king of men and gods; and he acquired the two titles, that of best (*optimus*) in the sense of strongest (*fortissimus*) (as by a reverse process *fortis* meant in early Latin what *bonus*[7] did in late), and that of greatest (*maximus*) from his vast body, the sky itself. From the first great benefit he conferred on mankind by not destroying it with his bolts, he received the title *Soter*, or savior. (This is the first of the three principles we have taken for our Science.) And for having put an end to the feral wandering of these few giants, so that they became the princes of the gentes, he received the epithet *Stator*, stayer or establisher. The Latin philologians explain this epithet too narrowly from Jove, invoked by Romulus, having stopped the Romans in their flight from the battle with the Sabines.[8]

380 Thus the many Joves the philologians wonder at are so many physical histories preserved for us by the fables, which prove the universality of the flood. For every gentile nation had its Jove, and the Egyptians had the conceit to say that their Jove Ammon was the most ancient of them all.

381 Thus, in accordance with what has been said about the principles of the poetic characters, Jove was born naturally in poetry as a divine character or imaginative universal, to which everything having to do with the auspices was referred by all the ancient gentile nations, which must therefore all have been poetic by nature. Their poetic wisdom began with this poetic metaphysics, which contemplated God by the attribute of his providence; and they were called theological poets, or sages who understood the language of the gods expressed in the auspices of Jove; and were properly called divine in the sense of diviners, from *divinari*, to divine or predict. Their science was called Muse, defined by Homer as the knowledge of good and evil; that is, divination on the prohibition of which God ordained his true religion for Adam. Because they were versed in this mystic theology, the Greek poets, who explained the divine mysteries of the auspices and oracles, were called *mystae*, which Horace[9] learnedly renders "interpreters of the gods." Every gentile nation had its own sybil versed in this science, and we find mention

5. Virgil, *Eclogue* 3.60 [translators' note].
6. Plato, *Cratylus* 412d [translators' note].
7. Good (Latin); *optimus* is its superlative form.
8. Romulus, mythical founder of Rome, procured wives for his citizens by inviting the Sabines, a group of neighboring tribes, to a festival and seizing the women; this led to a series of wars (which ended with Romulus as king).
9. Roman poet and satirist (65–8 B.C.E.); Vico quotes *Ars Poetica*, line 391 (see above).

of twelve of them. Sybils and oracles are the most ancient institutions of the gentile world.

382 All the things here discussed agree with that golden passage of Eusebius[1] [i.e., Lactantius] on the origins of idolatry: that the first people, simple and rough, invented the gods "from terror of present power." Thus it was fear which created gods in the world; not fear awakened in men by other men, but fear awakened in men by themselves. Along with this origin of idolatry is demonstrated likewise the origin of divination, which was brought into the world at the same birth. The origins of these two were followed by that of the sacrifices made to procure or rightly understand the auspices.

383 That such was the origin of poetry is finally confirmed by this eternal property of it: that its proper material is the credible impossibility. It is impossible that bodies should be minds, yet it was believed that the thundering sky was Jove. And nothing is dearer to poets than singing the marvels wrought by sorceresses by means of incantations. All this is to be explained by a hidden sense the nations have of the omnipotence of God. From this sense springs another by which all peoples are naturally led to do infinite honors to divinity. In this manner the poets founded religions among the gentiles.

384 All that has been so far said here upsets all the theories of the origin of poetry from Plato and Aristotle down to Patrizzi, Scaliger, and Castelvetro.[2] For it has been shown that it was deficiency of human reasoning power that gave rise to poetry so sublime that the philosophies which came afterward, the arts of poetry and of criticism, have produced none equal or better, and have even prevented its production. Hence it is Homer's privilege to be, of all the sublime, that is, the heroic poets, the first in the order of merit as well as in that of age. This discovery of the origins of poetry does away with the opinion of the matchless wisdom of the ancients, so ardently sought after from Plato to Bacon's *De sapientia veterum*.[3] For the wisdom of the ancients was the vulgar wisdom of the lawgivers who founded the human race, not the esoteric wisdom of great and rare philosophers. Whence it will be found, as it has been in the case of Jove, that all the mystic meanings of lofty philosophy attributed by the learned to the Greek fables and the Egyptian hieroglyphics are as impertinent as the historical meanings they both must have had are natural.

* * *

400 That which is metaphysics insofar as it contemplates things in all the forms of their being, is logic insofar as it considers things in all the forms by which they may be signified. Accordingly, as poetry has been considered by us above as a poetic metaphysics in which the theological poets imagined bodies to be for the most part divine substances, so now that same poetry is considered as poetic logic, by which it signifies them.

401 "Logic" comes from *logos*, whose first and proper meaning was *fabula*, fable, carried over into Italian as *favella*, speech. In Greek the fable

1. Lactantius, *Divine Institutions* 1.15.
2. Vico names three Italian Renaissance philosophers noted for their critical engagement with classical literary theory, particularly Aristotle's *Poetics*: Francesco Patrizzi (1529–1597), Julius Caesar Scaliger (1484–1558), and Lodovico Castelvetro (1505–1571).
3. *On the Wisdom of the Ancients*, by Francis Bacon (1561–1626), an English philosopher, was published in 1609.

was also called *mythos*, myth, whence comes the Latin *mutus*, mute. For speech was born in mute times as mental [or sign] language, which Strabo[4] in a golden passage says existed before vocal or articulate [language]; whence *logos* means both word and idea. It was fitting that the matter should be so ordered by divine providence in religious times, for it is an eternal property of religions that they attach more importance to meditation than to speech. Thus the first language in the first mute times of the nations must have begun with signs, whether gestures or physical objects, which had natural relations to the ideas [to be expressed]. For this reason *logos*, or word, meant also deed to the Hebrews and thing to the Greeks, as Thomas Gataker[5] observes in his *De instrumenti stylo*. Similarly, *mythos* came to be defined for us as *vera narratio*, or true speech, the natural speech which first Plato and then Iamblichus[6] said had been spoken in the world at one time. But this was mere conjecture on their part, and Plato's effort to recover this speech in the *Cratylus* was therefore vain, and he was criticized for it by Aristotle and Galen.[7] For that first language, spoken by the theological poets, was not a language in accord with the nature of the things it dealt with (as must have been the sacred language invented by Adam, to whom God granted divine onomathesia, the giving of names to things according to the nature of each), but was a fantastic speech making use of physical substances endowed with life and most of them imagined to be divine.

402 This is the way in which the theological poets apprehended Jove, Cybele or Berecynthia, and Neptune,[8] for example, and, at first mutely pointing, explained them as substances of the sky, the earth, and the sea, which they imagined to be animate divinities and were therefore true to their senses in believing them to be gods. By means of these three divinities, in accordance with what we have said above concerning poetic characters, they explained everything appertaining to the sky, the earth, and the sea. And similarly by means of the other divinities they signified the other kinds of things appertaining to each, denoting all flowers, for instance, by Flora, and all fruits by Pomona. We nowadays reverse this practice in respect of spiritual things, such as the faculties of the human mind, the passions, virtues, vices, sciences, and arts; for the most part the ideas we form of them are so many feminine personifications, to which we refer all the causes, properties, and effects that severally appertain to them. For when we wish to give utterance to our understanding of spiritual things, we must seek aid from our imagination to explain them and, like painters, form human images of them. But these theological poets, unable to make use of the understanding, did the opposite and more sublime thing: they attributed senses and passions, as we saw not long since, to bodies, and to bodies as vast as sky, sea, and earth. Later, as these vast imaginations shrank and the power of abstraction grew, the personifications were reduced to diminutive signs. Metonymy[9] drew a cloak of learning over the prevailing ignorance of these origins of human

4. Greek geographer (ca. 64 B.C.E.—ca. 23 C.E.).
5. English Puritan churchman (1574–1654); he published *De Novi Instrumenti Stylo Dissertatio* in 1648.
6. Greek Neoplatonic philosopher (ca. 250–ca. 325 C.E.).
7. Greek physician and philosopher (129–ca. 199 C.E.).
8. Roman god of the sea. Berecynthia and Cybele: Roman goddesses associated with nature.
9. A rhetorical trope or figure of speech in which one word is substituted for another to which it is related in some way other than by resemblance (e.g., by contiguity, as in "crown" used for "king").

institutions, which have remained buried until now. Jove becomes so small and light that he is flown about by an eagle. Neptune rides the waves in a fragile chariot. And Cybele rides seated on a lion.

* * *

404 All the first tropes are corollaries of this poetic logic. The most luminous and therefore the most necessary and frequent is metaphor. It is most praised when it gives sense and passion to insensate things, in accordance with the metaphysics above discussed, by which the first poets attributed to bodies the being of animate substances, with capacities measured by their own, namely sense and passion, and in this way made fables of them. Thus every metaphor so formed is a fable in brief. This gives a basis for judging the time when metaphors made their appearance in the languages. All the metaphors conveyed by likeness taken from bodies to signify the operations of abstract minds must date from times when philosophies were taking shape. The proof of this is that in every language the terms needed for the refined arts and recondite sciences are of rustic origin.

405 It is noteworthy that in all languages the greater part of the expressions relating to inanimate things are formed by metaphor from the human body and its parts and from the human senses and passions. Thus, head for top or beginning; the brow and shoulders of a hill; the eyes of needles and of potatoes; mouth for any opening; the lip of a cup or pitcher; the teeth of a rake, a saw, a comb; the beard of wheat; the tongue of a shoe; the gorge of a river; a neck of land; an arm of the sea; the hands of a clock; heart for center (the Latins used *umbilicus*, navel, in this sense); the belly of a sail; foot for end or bottom; the flesh of fruits; a vein of rock or mineral; the blood of grapes for wine; the bowels of the earth.[1] Heaven or the sea smiles; the wind whistles; the waves murmur; a body groans under a great weight. The farmers of Latium used to say the fields were thirsty, bore fruit, were swollen with grain; and our rustics speak of plants making love, vines going mad, resinous trees weeping. Innumerable other examples could be collected from all languages. All of which is a consequence of our axiom that man in his ignorance makes himself the rule of the universe, for in the examples cited he has made of himself an entire world. So that, as rational metaphysics teaches that man becomes all things by understanding them (*homo intelligendo fit omnia*), this imaginative metaphysics shows that man becomes all things by *not* understanding them (*homo non intelligendo fit omnia*); and perhaps the latter proposition is truer than the former, for when man understands he extends his mind and takes in the things, but when he does not understand he makes the things out of himself and becomes them by transforming himself into them.

406 In such a logic, sprung from such a metaphysics, the first poets had to give names to things from the most particular and the most sensible ideas. Such ideas are the sources, respectively, of synecdoche[2] and metonymy. Metonymy of agent for act resulted from the fact that names for agents were commoner than names for acts. Metonymy of subject for form and accident

1. Several of Vico's examples for which there are no common English parallels are here omitted, and substitutions are made for several others [translators' note].

2. A rhetorical trope or figure of speech in which a part is substituted for a whole or vice versa, as in "all hands on deck."

was due to inability to abstract forms and qualities from subjects. Certainly metonymy of cause for effect produced in each case a little fable, in which the cause was imagined as a woman clothed with her effects: ugly Poverty, sad Old Age, pale Death.

407 Synecdoche developed into metaphor as particulars were elevated into universals or parts united with the other parts together with which they make up their wholes. Thus the term "mortals" was originally and properly applied only to men, as the only beings whose mortality there was any occasion to notice. The use of "head" for man or person, so frequent in vulgar Latin, was due to the fact that in the forest only the head of a man could be seen from a distance. The word "man" itself is abstract, comprehending as in a philosophic genus the body and all its parts, the mind and all its faculties, the spirit and all its dispositions. In the same way, *tignum* and *culmen*, log and top, came to be used with entire propriety when thatching was the practice for rafter and thatch; and later, with the adornment of cities, they signified all the materials and trim of a building. Again, *tectum*, roof, came to mean a whole house because in the first times a covering sufficed for a house. Similarly, *puppis*, poop, for a ship, because it was the highest part and therefore the first to be seen by those on shore; as in the returned barbarian times a ship was called a sail. Similarly, *mucro*, point, for sword, because the latter is an abstract word and as in a genus comprehends pummel, hilt, edge, and point; and it was the point they felt which aroused their fear. Similarly, the material for the formed whole, as iron for sword, because they did not know how to abstract the form from the material. That bit of synecdoche and metonymy, *Tertia messis erat* ("It was the third harvest"), was doubtless born of a natural necessity, for it took more than a thousand years for the astronomical term "year" to rise among the nations; and even now the Florentine peasantry say, "We have reaped so many times," when they mean "so many years." And that knot of two synecdoches and a metonymy, *Post aliquot, mea regna videns, mirabor, aristas*? ("After a few harvests shall I wonder at seeing my kingdoms?"),[3] betrays only too well the poverty of expression of the first rustic times, in which the phrase "so many ears of wheat"—even more particular than harvests—was used for "so many years." And because of the excessive poverty of the expression, the grammarians have assumed an excess of art behind it.

408 Irony certainly could not have begun until the period of reflection, because it is fashioned of falsehood by dint of a reflection which wears the mask of truth. Here emerges a great principle of human institutions, confirming the origin of poetry disclosed in this work: that since the first men of the gentile world had the simplicity of children, who are truthful by nature, the first fables could not feign anything false; they must therefore have been, as they have been defined above, true narrations.

409 From all this it follows that all the tropes (and they are all reducible to the four types above discussed), which have hitherto been considered ingenious inventions of writers, were necessary modes of expression of all the first poetic nations, and had originally their full native propriety. But these expressions of the first nations later became figurative when, with the further development of the human mind, words were invented which signi-

3. Virgil, *Eclogue* 1.69 [translators' note].

fied abstract forms or genera comprising their species or relating parts with their wholes. And here begins the overthrow of two common errors of the grammarians: that prose speech is proper speech, and poetic speech is improper; and that prose speech came first and afterward speech in verse.

* * *

779 We have shown that poetic wisdom justly deserves two great and sovereign tributes. The one, clearly and constantly accorded to it, is that of having founded gentile mankind, though the conceit of nations on the one hand and that of scholars on the other, the former with ideas of an empty magnificence and the latter with ideas of an impertinent philosophical wisdom, have in effect denied it this honor by their very efforts to affirm it. The other, concerning which a vulgar tradition has come down to us, is that the wisdom of the ancients made its wise men, by a single inspiration, equally great as philosophers, lawmakers, captains, historians, orators, and poets, on which account it has been so greatly sought after. But in fact it made or rather sketched them such as we have found them in the fables. For in these, as in embryos or matrices,[4] we have discovered the outlines of all esoteric wisdom. And it may be said that in the fables the nations have in a rough way and in the language of the human senses described the beginnings of this world of sciences, which the specialized studies of scholars have since clarified for us by reasoning and generalization. From all this we may conclude what we set out to show in this Book: that the theological poets were the sense and the philosophers the intellect of human wisdom.

1725, 1744

4. Wombs, places of origin.

JOSEPH ADDISON
1672–1719

The English poet, dramatist, and essayist Joseph Addison is best known as the co-author with Richard Steele of an influential series of periodical essays, published in *The Tatler* (April 12, 1709–January 2, 1711) and *The Spectator* (first series, March 1, 1711–December 6, 1712; second series, 1714). He is distinguished for his clear, orderly prose style, which did much to elevate the status of the essay as a literary form, and for his skillful descriptions of character, which helped prepare the way for later eighteenth-century pioneers in a new English genre, the novel. Addison was an important cultural and literary figure, particularly for middle-class readers. As he explained in *Spectator* No. 10: "It was said of Socrates that he brought philosophy down from heaven to inhabit among men; and I shall be ambitious to have it said of me that I have brought philosophy out of closets and libraries, schools and colleges, to dwell in clubs and assemblies, at tea-tables and in coffeehouses." Addison achieved this goal and became a model for generations of critics and essayists.

Addison was educated at Oxford, where he excelled in classical studies and composed Latin verse that JOHN DRYDEN admired. By his early twenties, Addison had already published poetry, but he was as intent on political advancement as on literary success. He used his literary talents to praise leading statesmen of the Whig political party, which sought to limit royal power. His career reached its height in 1713, when his neoclassical tragedy *Cato* was produced in London; it focuses on the Roman republican Cato (95–46 B.C.E.), who chose suicide rather than submit to the dictator Julius Caesar. SAMUEL JOHNSON judged *Cato* "rather a poem in dialogue than a drama," and modern scholars have found it tedious; but it was a popular success and was frequently performed, in part because many interpreted it as a commentary on the English political scene.

Successful in both literature and politics, Addison was appointed undersecretary of state (1706); secretary to Lord Wharton, the lord lieutenant in Ireland (1709); and chief secretary for Ireland (1715). Later he served as lord commissioner for trade (1716), and on retirement he was rewarded with a generous pension. He had entered Parliament as a Whig in 1708 and held his seat until his death in 1719.

Addison's partnership with the Irish writer and Whig supporter Steele—whom he had known since their school days together—began in 1709. He contributed 42 essays to Steele's *Tatler*, and collaborated with Steele on 36 others; he wrote even more—274 essays of a total of 555—for their joint venture *The Spectator. The Tatler* appeared three times a week, *The Spectator* every day except Sunday (both were later published in book form). These periodicals gave Addison a means to fulfill his cultural mission. He concurred with the ideal that Steele defined for *The Tatler*, which was "to enliven Morality with Wit, and to temper Wit with Morality," thereby offering men and women a guide to virtue. But together with urbane, witty sketches of fictional characters (notably the eccentric, kindly country gentleman Sir Roger de Coverley) and advice on conduct were essays devoted to the writings of John Locke, John Milton, and others. Addison claimed that each copy that was purchased was in turn passed on to twenty people or more, and he hoped that his lucid treatment of important topics in literature and philosophy would significantly influence the public's critical judgment and taste.

In our first selection, *Spectator* No. 62, Addison examines the nature of wit, one of the most complex, shifting terms in poetics. In a broad sense, it means the natural ability to perceive and understand, keen intelligence, quick and subtle perception; but it refers more specifically to the capacity of writers to perceive and express relationships between seemingly disparate or incongruous things in striking, paradoxical, surprising figures of speech. From the seventeenth through the eighteenth centuries, wit was a central topic in literary theory and criticism. ALEXANDER POPE defined it most memorably—"True wit is nature to advantage dressed, / What oft was thought, but ne'er so well expressed" (*An Essay on Criticism*, 1711; see below)—but Dryden and Johnson also discuss it in detail.

For the Romantics and Victorians, wit mattered less than imagination. Sometimes too, in this period and even earlier, wit was simultaneously praised and devalued, taken as a sign of quickness in repartee but not necessarily of serious or profound reflection. As Voltaire remarked in his *Philosophical Dictionary* (1764), "he who cannot shine by thought, seeks to bring himself into notice by a witticism." In this sense, it was frequently associated with satire, comedy, and humor. But in the modern period, T. S. ELIOT, F. R. Leavis, and CLEANTH BROOKS reinvigorated the serious meanings of wit and enriched critical understanding of the play of irony and paradox, linking it to the best in the English poetical tradition.

Addison begins by quoting John Locke's distinction between *wit*, which emphasizes congruity and resemblance, and *judgment*, which stresses distinction and difference. But he adds that true wit requires a verbal effect that delights and surprises the reader. The resemblance must not be unduly common or familiar, nor wholly verbal—ideas as well as words are involved. Most of Addison's discussion treats such "mixed wit," but he ends by moving outward from the writer's use of language to the responses of readers, anticipating the intricate issues of aesthetics probed later in the century by

DAVID HUME, IMMANUEL KANT, and other philosophers and theorists. Like Dryden and the French critic Jean Regnauld de Segrais (1624–1701), Addison aims to teach readers to value wit in its best forms and not to rest content with simpler uses, however appealing at first these might be; indeed, he connects wit with the quality of humanity.

In our second selection, from *Spectator* No. 412, Addison examines the imagination. He reiterates his point about the uncommon and the new, describing the pleasure that we receive when our sight is refreshed by a surprising and gratifying view of an object or scene that gives us a new idea of something that we thought we already understood. Addison's discussion of "greatness" reflects the interest in the sublime sparked by the French critic Nicolas Boileau's 1674 translation of *On Sublimity*, a Greek text attributed to LONGINUS (first century C.E.; see above). Like wit, *the sublime* is a complex term and literary category. It connotes majesty, awe, nobility, and spiritual, moral, and intellectual excellence. In some discussions, it chiefly refers to something *in* natural scenes and landscapes; at the same time, the term often evokes the response of viewers—their sensations and feelings that Nature creates—a topic that Kant later explored in his *Critique of Judgment* (1790; see below).

For his part, Addison appears especially interested in the viewer, audience, reader—in what one might call the psychology of the sublime. In other papers (e.g., *Spectator* No. 416), he extends his inquiry into the sublime and the beautiful by distinguishing between the primary and secondary pleasures of the imagination; in the first, the viewer responds directly to an object, whereas in the second, he or she is returned to that object through a work of literature or art. Addison suggests that the writer or artist can thus kindle pleasures that rival or exceed those that Nature itself provides.

Addison's brief critical and theoretical papers, while lucid, are rarely profound or deep. Dryden is the more pioneering critic and theorist, and Pope the more brilliantly adroit: Addison does not operate at their level. Nor does he show the sophistication and depth that later critics (including EDMUND BURKE, Johnson, and SAMUEL TAYLOR COLERIDGE) display in treating the same topics. But Addison remains significant for the influential cultural work—the work of the public intellectual—that he undertook. He read widely in literature and philosophy (both English and French), summarized well what he had discovered, and successfully brought it into the public sphere. In defining terms and making distinctions, Addison gave his readers the critical vocabulary that they needed to sort and categorize the relationship between words and ideas, between the world they inhabited and the literature they consumed. Though he is not as central to the tradition of theory and criticism as are Johnson and Coleridge, Addison is a key influence on both of them.

BIBLIOGRAPHY

Donald F. Bond prepared modern editions of *The Spectator* (5 vols., 1965) and *The Tatler* (3 vols., 1987). One-volume editions include *Addison and Steele: Selections from "The Tatler" and "The Spectator"*, edited by R. J. Allen (1957); *Selected Essays from "The Tatler," "The Spectator," and "The Guardian"*, edited by Daniel McDonald (1973); and *Selections from the "Tatler" and the "Spectator" of Steele and Addison*, edited by Angus Ross (1982). For Addison's correspondence, see *Letters*, edited by Walter Graham (1941).

A good biography is Peter Smithers, *The Life of Joseph Addison* (2d ed., 1968). For a cogent brief overview, consult Robert M. Otten, *Joseph Addison* (1982). Helpful critical studies include Lee Andrew Elioseff, *The Cultural Milieu of Addison's Literary Criticism* (1963); Edward A. Bloom and Lillian D. Bloom, *Joseph Addison's Sociable Animal: In the Market Place, on the Hustings, in the Pulpit* (1971); and Michael G. Ketcham, *Transparent Designs: Reading, Performance, and Form in the "Spectator" Papers* (1985). Other resources include *Addison and Steele: The Critical Heritage*, edited by Edward A. Bloom and Lillian D. Bloom (1980), and Charles A. Knight, *Joseph Addison and Richard Steele: A Reference Guide, 1730–1991* (1994).

The Spectator, No. 62

[*True and False Wit*]

Scribendi recte sapere est et principium et fons.[1]
—HOR., Ars Poet. 309.

Mr. Locke[2] has an admirable reflection upon the difference of wit and judgment, whereby he endeavours to show the reason why they are not always the talents of the same person. His words are as follow: 'And hence, perhaps, may be given some reason of that common observation, that men who have a great deal of wit and prompt memories, have not always the clearest judgment, or deepest reason. For wit lying most in the assemblage of ideas, and putting those together with quickness and variety, wherein can be found any resemblance or congruity, thereby to make up pleasant pictures and agreeable visions in the fancy; judgment, on the contrary, lies quite on the other side, in separating carefully one from another, ideas wherein can be found the least difference, thereby to avoid being misled by similitude, and by affinity to take one thing for another. This is a way of proceeding quite contrary to metaphor and allusion; wherein, for the most part, lies that entertainment and pleasantry of wit which strikes so lively on the fancy, and is therefore so acceptable to all people.'

This is, I think, the best and most philosophical account that I have ever met with of wit, which generally, though not always, consists in such a resemblance and congruity of ideas as this author mentions. I shall only add to it, by way of explanation, that every resemblance of ideas is not that which we call wit, unless it be such an one that gives delight and surprise to the reader. These two properties seem essential to wit, more particularly the last of them. In order therefore that the resemblance in the ideas be wit, it is necessary that the ideas should not lie too near one another in the nature of things; for where the likeness is obvious, it gives no surprise. To compare one man's singing to that of another, or to represent the whiteness of any object by that of milk and snow, or the variety of its colours by those of the rainbow, cannot be called wit, unless, besides this obvious resemblance, there be some further congruity discovered in the two ideas that is capable of giving the reader some surprise. Thus when a poet tells us, the bosom of his mistress is as white as snow, there is not wit in the comparison; but when he adds, with a sigh, that it is as cold too, it then grows into wit. Every reader's memory may supply him with innumerable instances of the same nature. For this reason, the similitudes in heroic poets, who endeavour rather to fill the mind with great conceptions, than to divert it with such as are new and surprising, have

1. Knowledge is the source and fount of writing correctly (Latin). From *Ars Poetica* (see above) by the Roman lyric poet HORACE (65–8 B.C.E.).

2. John Locke (1632–1704), English philosopher. The "reflection" is in his *Essay concerning Human Understanding* (1690), 2.11.2.

seldom anything in them that can be called wit. Mr. Locke's account of wit, with this short explanation, comprehends most of the species of wit, as metaphors, similitudes, allegories, enigmas, mottoes, parables, fables, dreams, visions, dramatic writings, burlesque, and all the methods of allusion: as there are many other pieces of wit (how remote soever they may appear at first sight from the foregoing description) which upon examination will be found to agree with it.

As true wit generally consists in this resemblance and congruity of ideas, false wit chiefly consists in the resemblance and congruity sometimes of single letters, as in anagrams, chronograms, lipograms,[3] and acrostics; sometimes of syllables, as in echoes and doggerel rhymes; sometimes of words, as in puns and quibbles; and sometimes of whole sentences or poems, cast into the figures of eggs, axes, or altars:[4] nay, some carry the notion of wit so far, as to ascribe it even to external mimicry; and to look upon a man as an ingenious person, that can resemble the tone, posture, or face of another.

As true wit consists in the resemblance of ideas, and false wit in the resemblance of words, according to the foregoing instances; there is another kind of wit which consists partly in the resemblance of ideas, and partly in the resemblance of words; which for distinction's sake I shall call mixed wit. This kind of wit is that which abounds in Cowley, more than in any author that ever wrote. Mr. Waller[5] has likewise a great deal of it. Mr. Dryden is very sparing in it. Milton had a genius much above it. Spenser[6] is in the same class with Milton. The Italians, even in their epic poetry, are full of it. Monsieur Boileau,[7] who formed himself upon the ancient poets, has everywhere rejected it with scorn. If we look after mixed wit among the Greek writers, we shall find it nowhere but in the epigrammatists. There are indeed some strokes of it in the little poem ascribed to Musæus,[8] which by that, as well as many other marks, betrays itself to be a modern composition. If we look into the Latin writers, we find none of this mixed wit in Virgil, Lucretius, or Catullus;[9] very little in Horace, but a great deal of it in Ovid, and scarce anything else in Martial.[1]

Out of the innumerable branches of mixed wit, I shall choose one instance which may be met with in all the writers of this class. The passion of love in its nature has been thought to resemble fire; for which reason the words fire and flame are made use of to signify love. The witty poets therefore have taken an advantage from the doubtful meaning of the word fire, to make an infinite number of witticisms. Cowley observing the cold regard of his mis-

3. Compositions in which all words containing a certain letter or letters are omitted. "Chronograms": phrases in which certain letters express a date (e.g., capitalized letters that stand for Roman numerals).

4. Famous example of such pattern or shaped poems include "The Altar" and "Easter Wings" by George Herbert (1593–1633).

5. Edmund Waller (1606–1687), English poet admired for his development of the heroic couplet. Abraham Cowley (1618–1667), English metaphysical poet. Unusual metaphor is characteristic of metaphysical poetry.

6. Edmund Spenser (ca. 1552–1599), English poet whose works include the epic *The Faerie Queene*. JOHN DRYDEN (1631–1700), English poet, dramatist, and critic. John Milton (1608–1674), English poet and prose writer; his masterpiece is the epic *Paradise Lost*.

7. Nicolas Boileau (1636–1711), French poet, dramatist, and critic; author of *The Art of Poetry*, a treatise in verse (1674).

8. Greek poet (probably late 5th c. C.E.). "The little poem": *Hero and Leander*, translated in 1635.

9. All poets of the Latin "Golden Age," writing in varied genres on a range of subjects: eclogues, georgics, and epic (Virgil, 70–19 B.C.E.); philosophy (Lucretius, ca. 94–55 B.C.E.); and love lyrics and elegy (Catullus, ca. 84–ca. 54 B.C.E.).

1. Roman poet (ca. 40–ca. 104 C.E.), known for his epigrams. Ovid (43 B.C.E.–17 C.E.), Roman poet of outstanding verbal brilliance, author of love poetry and a highly mannered epic, the *Metamorphoses*.

tress's eyes,[2] and at the same time their power of producing love in him, considers them as burning-glasses made of ice; and finding himself able to live in the greatest extremities of love, concludes the torrid zone to be habitable. When his mistress has read his letter written in juice of lemon by holding it to the fire, he desires her to read it over a second time by love's flames. When she weeps, he wishes it were inward heat that distilled those drops from the limbec.[3] When she is absent he is beyond eighty, that is, thirty degrees nearer the pole[4] than when she is with him. His ambitious love is a fire that naturally mounts upwards; his happy love is the beams of heaven, and his unhappy love flames of hell. When it does not let him sleep, it is a flame that sends up no smoke; when it is opposed by counsel and advice, it is a fire that rages the more by the wind's blowing upon it. Upon the dying of a tree in which he had cut his loves, he observes that his written flames had burned up and withered the tree. When he resolves to give over his passion, he tells us that one burnt like him for ever dreads the fire. His heart is an Ætna, that instead of Vulcan's shop encloses Cupid's forge in it.[5] His endeavouring to drown his love in wine, is throwing oil upon the fire. He would insinuate to his mistress, that the fire of love, like that of the sun (which produces so many living creatures) should not only warm but beget. Love is another place cooks pleasure at his fire. Sometimes the poet's heart is frozen in every breast, and sometimes scorched in every eye. Sometimes he is drowned in tears, and burnt in love, like a ship set on fire in the middle of the sea.

The reader may observe in every one of these instances, that the poet mixes the qualities of fire with those of love; and in the same sentence speaking of it both as a passion, and as real fire, surprises the reader with those seeming resemblances or contradictions that make up all the wit in this kind of writing. Mixed wit therefore is a composition of pun and true wit, and is more or less perfect as the resemblance lies in the ideas or in the words: its foundations are laid partly in falsehood and partly in truth: reason puts in her claim for one half of it, and extravagance for the other. The only province therefore for this kind of wit, is epigram, or those little occasional poems that in their own nature are nothing else but a tissue of epigrams. I cannot conclude this head of mixed wit, without owning that the admirable poet out of whom I have taken the examples of it, had as much true wit as any author that ever writ; and indeed all other talents of an extraordinary genius.

It may be expected, since I am upon this subject, that I should take notice of Mr. Dryden's definition of wit; which, with all the deference that is due to the judgment of so great a man, is not so properly a definition of wit, as of good writing in general. Wit, as he defines it, is 'a propriety of words and thoughts adapted to the subject.'[6] If this be a true definition of wit, I am apt to think that Euclid[7] was the greatest wit that ever set pen to paper: it is certain there never was a greater propriety of words and thoughts adapted

2. In "The Mistress, or Several Copies of Love-Verses" (1647).
3. Alembic: that is, an apparatus used in distillation.
4. That is, 30 degrees nearer than in England, which is roughly 50 degrees north of the equator.
5. Mt. Etna, a volcano in Sicily, was supposed to be the workshop of Vulcan, the Roman god of fire, who had a forge; Cupid, son of Vulcan and Venus, was the Roman boy-god of love.
6. Dryden, preface to *The State of Innocence* (1674, 1677): "The definition of wit . . . is only this: that it is a propriety of thoughts and words; or, in other terms, thoughts and words elegantly adapted to the subject."
7. Greek mathematician (active ca. 300 B.C.E.), author of a 13-volume treatise on mathematics, the *Elements*.

to the subject, than what that author has made use of in his elements. I shall only appeal to my reader, if this definition agrees with any notion he has of wit: if it be a true one, I am sure Mr. Dryden was not only a better poet, but a greater wit than Mr. Cowley; and Virgil a much more facetious man than either Ovid or Martial.

Bouhours,[8] whom I look upon to be the most penetrating of all the French critics, has taken pains to show that it is impossible for any thought to be beautiful which is not just, and has not its foundation in the nature of things; that the basis of all wit is truth; and that no thought can be valuable, of which good sense is not the ground-work. Boileau has endeavoured to inculcate the same notion in several parts of his writings, both in prose and verse. This is that natural way of writing, that beautiful simplicity, which we so much admire in the compositions of the ancients; and which nobody deviates from, but those who want strength of genius to make a thought shine in its own natural beauties. Poets who want this strength of genius to give that majestic simplicity to nature, which we so much admire in the works of the ancients, are forced to hunt after foreign ornaments, and not to let any piece of wit of what kind soever escape them. I look upon these writers as Goths[9] in poetry, who, like those in architecture, not being able to come up to the beautiful simplicity of the old Greeks and Romans, have endeavoured to supply its place with all the extravagances of an irregular fancy. Mr. Dryden makes a very handsome observation on Ovid's writing a letter from Dido to Æneas,[1] in the following words: 'Ovid (says he, speaking of Virgil's fiction of Dido and Æneas) takes it up after him, even in the same age, and makes an ancient heroine of Virgil's new-created Dido; dictates a letter for her just before her death to the ungrateful fugitive; and, very unluckily for himself, is for measuring a sword with a man so much superior in force to him, on the same subject. I think I may be judge of this, because I have translated both. The famous author of the art of love[2] has nothing of his own; he borrows all from a greater master in his own profession, and, which is worse, improves nothing which he finds: nature fails him, and being forced to his old shift, he has recourse to witticism. This passes indeed with his soft admirers, and gives him the preference to Virgil in their esteem.'

Were not I supported by so great an authority as that of Mr. Dryden, I should not venture to observe, that the taste of most of our English poets, as well as readers, is extremely Gothic. He quotes Monsieur Segrais[3] for a threefold distinction of the readers of poetry: in the first of which he comprehends the rabble of readers, whom he does not treat as such with regard to their quality, but to their numbers and the coarseness of their taste. His words are as follow: 'Segrais has distinguished the readers of poetry, according to their capacity of judging, into three classes. (He might have said the

8. Dominique Bouhours (1628–1702), Jesuit teacher and grammarian; one of his works was translated into English in 1705 as *The Art of Criticism*.

9. Germanic peoples who invaded the Roman Empire in the early centuries of the Christian era. "Gothic" at this time has several meanings: Germanic; medieval, not classical; barbarous, crude. It also refers to a medieval architectural style not derived from Greek or Roman models.

1. In one of Ovid's *Heroides*, which were verse letters between mythological lovers. Dryden's observation is from the dedication to his translation of Virgil's *Aeneid* (1697), Ovid's source for the story of Dido, the legendary founder and queen of Carthage, who killed herself when Aeneas, the legendary founder of Rome, deserted her.

2. *The Art of Love* is a didactic poem by Ovid.

3. Jean Regnauld de Segrais (1624–1701), French poet who translated Virgil's *Aeneid* and *Georgics*; Dryden quotes from an essay prefixed to that translation.

same of writers too, if he had pleased.) In the lowest form he places those whom he calls *les petits esprits*,[4] such things as are our upper-gallery audience in a play-house; who like nothing but the husk and rind of wit, prefer a quibble, a conceit, an epigram, before solid sense and elegant expression: these are mob-readers. If Virgil and Martial stood for parliament-men, we know already who would carry it.[5] But though they make the greatest appearance in the field, and cry the loudest, the best on't is they are but a sort of French Huguenots, or Dutch boors,[6] brought over in herds, but not naturalised; who have not lands of two pounds per annum in Parnassus,[7] and therefore are not privileged to poll.[8] Their authors are of the same level, fit to represent them on a mountebank's stage, or to be masters of the ceremonies in a bear-garden:[9] yet these are they who have the most admirers. But it often happens, to their mortification, that as their readers improve their stock of sense (as they may by reading better books, and by conversation with men of judgment) they soon forsake them.'

I must not dismiss this subject without observing, that as Mr. Locke in the passage above mentioned has discovered the most fruitful source of wit, so there is another of a quite contrary nature to it, which does likewise branch itself out into several kinds. For not only the resemblance but the opposition of ideas does very often produce wit; as I could show in several little points, turns, and antitheses, that I may possibly enlarge upon in some future speculation.

1711

The Spectator, No. 412

[*On the Sublime*]

—Divisum sic breve fiet opus.[1]
—MART., Epig. 4.83.

I shall first consider those pleasures of the imagination which arise from the actual view and survey of outward objects. And these, I think, all proceed from the sight of what is great, uncommon, or beautiful. There may, indeed, be something so terrible or offensive, that the horror or loathsomeness of an object may overbear the pleasure which results from its greatness, novelty, or beauty; but still there will be such a mixture of delight in the very disgust it gives us, as any of these three qualifications are most conspicuous and prevailing.

By greatness, I do not only mean the bulk of any single object, but the largeness of a whole view, considered as one entire piece. Such are the prospects of an open champian[2] country, a vast uncultivated desert, of huge

4. The small-minded (French).
5. That is, the witty Martial would defeat the solemn Virgil in an election.
6. Peasants. Addison here names the largest groups of immigrants in England.
7. Greek mountain sacred to Apollo and the Muses, and thus associated with poetry.
8. Vote. Only those who met certain property requirements could vote.
9. The site of bearbaiting (setting dogs on a chained bear for entertainment).
1. Divided thus, the work will be made brief (Latin). From the Roman poet Martial (ca. 40–ca. 104 C.E.), *Epigrams*.
2. Unbroken level plain.

heaps of mountains, high rocks and precipices, or a wide expanse of waters, where we are not struck with the novelty or beauty of the sight, but with that rude kind of magnificence which appears in many of these stupendous works of Nature. Our imagination loves to be filled with an object, or to grasp at anything that is too big for its capacity. We are flung into a pleasing astonishment at such unbounded views, and feel a delightful stillness and amazement in the soul at the apprehension of them. The mind of man naturally hates everything that looks like a restraint upon it, and is apt to fancy itself under a sort of confinement, when the sight is pent up in a narrow compass, and shortened on every side by the neighbourhood of walls or mountains. On the contrary, a spacious horizon is an image of liberty, where the eye has room to range abroad, to expatiate[3] at large on the immensity of its views, and to lose itself amidst the variety of objects that offer themselves to its observation. Such wide and undetermined[4] prospects are as pleasing to the fancy, as the speculations of eternity or infinitude are to the understanding. But if there be a beauty or uncommonness joined with this grandeur, as in a troubled ocean, a heaven adorned with stars and meteors, or a spacious landscape cut out into rivers, woods, rocks, and meadows, the pleasure still grows upon us, as it arises from more than a single principle.

Everything that is new or uncommon raises a pleasure in the imagination, because it fills the soul with an agreeable surprise, gratifies its curiosity, and gives it an idea of which it was not before possessed. We are, indeed, so often conversant with one set of objects, and tired out with so many repeated shows of the same things, that whatever is new or uncommon contributes a little to vary human life, and to divert our minds, for a while, with the strangeness of its appearance: it serves us for a kind of refreshment, and takes off from that satiety we are apt to complain of in our usual and ordinary entertainments. It is this that bestows charms on a monster, and makes even the imperfections of nature please us. It is this that recommends variety, where the mind is every instant called off to something new, and the attention not suffered to dwell too long, and waste itself on any particular object. It is this, likewise, that improves what is great or beautiful, and makes it afford the mind a double entertainment. Groves, fields, and meadows are at any season of the year pleasant to look upon, but never so much as in the opening of the spring, when they are all new and fresh with their first gloss upon them, and not yet too much accustomed and familiar to the eye. For this reason there is nothing that more enlivens a prospect than rivers, jetteaus,[5] or falls of water, where the scene is perpetually shifting, and entertaining the sight every moment with something that is new. We are quickly tired with looking upon hills and valleys, where everything continues fixed and settled in the same place and posture, but find our thoughts a little agitated and relieved at the sight of such objects as are ever in motion, and sliding away from beneath the eye of the beholder.

But there is nothing that makes its way more directly to the soul than beauty, which immediately diffuses a secret satisfaction and complacency through the imagination, and gives a finishing to anything that is great or uncommon. The very first discovery of it strikes the mind with an inward

3. Range freely.
4. Open.
5. Fountains or jets of water.

joy, and spreads a cheerfulness and delight through all its faculties. There is not, perhaps, any real beauty or deformity more in one piece of matter than another, because we might have been so made that whatsoever now appears loathsome to us might have shown itself agreeable; but we find by experience that there are several modifications of matter which the mind, without any previous consideration, pronounces at first sight beautiful or deformed. Thus we see that every different species of sensible[6] creatures has its different notions of beauty, and that each of them is most affected with the beauties of its own kind. This is nowhere more remarkable than in birds of the same shape and proportion, where we often see the male determined in his courtship by the single grain[7] or tincture of a feather, and never discovering any charms but in the colour of its species.[8]

* * *

There is a second kind of beauty that we find in the several products of art and nature which does not work in the imagination with that warmth and violence as the beauty that appears in our proper species, but is apt, however, to raise in us a secret delight, and a kind of fondness for the places or objects in which we discover it. This consists either in the gaiety or variety of colours, in the symmetry and proportion of parts, in the arrangement and disposition of bodies, or in a just mixture and concurrence of all together. Among these several kinds of beauty the eye takes most delight in colours. We nowhere meet with a more glorious or pleasing show in nature than what appears in the heavens at the rising and setting of the sun, which is wholly made up of those different stains of light that show themselves in clouds of a different situation. For this reason we find the poets, who are always addressing themselves to the imagination, borrowing more of their epithets from colours than from any other topic.

As the fancy delights in everything that is great, strange, or beautiful, and is still more pleased the more it finds of these perfections in the same object, so it is capable of receiving a new satisfaction by the assistance of another sense. Thus any continued sound, as the music of birds, or a fall of water, awakens every moment the mind of the beholder, and makes him more attentive to the several beauties of the place that lie before him. Thus if there arises a fragrancy of smells or perfumes, they heighten the pleasures of the imagination, and make even the colours and verdure of the landscape appear more agreeable; for the ideas of both senses recommend each other, and are pleasanter together than when they enter the mind separately. As the different colours of a picture, when they are well disposed, set off one another, and receive an additional beauty from the advantage of their situation.

1712

6. Endowed with sensation.
7. Hue.
8. We have omitted here 19 lines of Latin verse, probably by Addison himself, describing the courtship of birds.

EDWARD YOUNG
1683–1765

Edward Young's *Conjectures on Original Composition* (1759) is rarely included in anthologies of criticism and theory, and his poetry has not fared much better, though his once extremely popular poem *Night Thoughts* is often mentioned in literary histories and sometimes excerpted in anthologies. But *Conjectures*, like THOMAS LOVE PEACOCK's "Four Ages of Poetry" (1820), is a text that deserves to be better known. In part *Conjectures* is interesting simply as a revelation of Young's ambitious, competitive, and discontented literary personality; more broadly, it is significant as a vigorous mid-eighteenth-century statement of ideas about poetic originality and imagination that writers in the Romantic period, decades later, would richly develop in their criticism and would seek to embody in their poetry.

Young was born in the village of Upham, near Winchester, the county town of Hampshire in southern England, where his father was rector. He was educated at Winchester School and later at New College and Corpus Christi College of Oxford University, where he became a fellow of All Souls College in 1708. He received the degrees of bachelor of laws in 1714 and doctor of laws in 1719.

After failing to win patronage and preferment through a panegyric in heroic couplets, Young tried his hand at religious verse and blank-verse tragedies. Perhaps disappointment at the slow pace of his literary and political career led Young to make plans for the priesthood; he was ordained in 1724. In 1728 he became royal chaplain to King George II, but the office did not lead to the kind of position that Young had hoped for. In 1730 he became rector of Welwyn, a Hertfordshire village twenty miles from London, where he continued writing poetry.

In 1731 Young married Elizabeth Lee; she died in 1740, a blow from which he never recovered. It is believed by some scholars that *The Complaint, or Night Thoughts on Life, Death, and Immortality* (1742–46) was meant to commemorate his wife and other family members who had passed away. After *Night Thoughts*, Young wrote little. The only literary work of significant interest that Young composed in his final decades is the curiously spirited and life-affirming treatise *Conjectures on Original Composition*.

There is some difference of opinion among scholars about the sources for *Conjectures*, which is presented in the form of a letter "To the Author of *Sir Charles Grandison*"—Samuel Richardson, the writer of epistolary novels who was a friend of Young's and acted as a literary adviser to him. Some literary historians have suggested that Young's essay developed directly from his conversations with Richardson about the critic Joseph Warton's *Essay on the Genius and Writings of Pope* (1756), which Warton had dedicated to Young. Warton's text includes an account of the challenges faced by modern poets living in an unheroic age and outlines a theory of history purporting to show that the power of the poetic imagination has been shrinking. According to Warton, the present is a period of didactic verse closer to prose than to the sublime poetry that Shakespeare and Milton created, and Young may be taking aim at this somewhat dismaying view of the contemporary literary scene.

Other scholars have traced Young's arguments to his reading of the treatise *On Sublimity*, attributed to the Greek author LONGINUS, thereby situating Young near to EDMUND BURKE's *Philosophical Inquiry into the Origin of Our Ideas on the Sublime and the Beautiful* (1757; see below) and related texts on the sublime by JOSEPH ADDISON, DAVID HUME, and other critics and philosophers in the eighteenth century. Whatever its sources, Young's text—a potent half-polemic, half-meditation—is a puzzle. The dismal, dreary author of *Night Thoughts*, a man in his late seventies, here celebrates the imagination, extols human potential, and urges writers to reach for originality and genius. In discussing the merits of the "ancients and the moderns," and the relationship between native genius and the rules, Young takes part in a debate made familiar by the writings of many poets and critics in France and England in the seventeenth and eighteenth centuries. But key differences in Young's argument propel it toward the Romantic period rather than incline it backward toward the neoclassical era.

At one juncture, for example, Young uses biological and organic metaphors, stating that "an Original" is "of a vegetable nature; it rises spontaneously from the vital root of genius." Such organic terms for poetic composition would be invoked years later by German and English Romantic poets and critics, especially SAMUEL TAYLOR COLERIDGE. And when Young comments on the hazards of imitation and the perils of self-doubt, he almost appears to be preparing a path for RALPH WALDO EMERSON's exhortations to know and reverence ourselves, strive to be original, make contact with and affirm the power of the divinity within.

Young acknowledges the achievements of the ancients, but he stresses that the work of modern writers need not be inferior to them. Writers in the present day should not so much imitate the poems by the ancients as they should follow (that is, be inspired by) the ancients' spirit, the genius that these texts from the past exemplify. If we base our work on that by the ancient authors, then we risk denying our own potential for greatness and suppress the genius within us. At one point Young complains that "illustrious examples engross, prejudice and intimidate." Originality requires invention and innovation, leading to the discovery and discussion of new subjects. It is the progressive element or trait in persons that makes history new rather than a repetition of actions already done. It is also valuable because it foregrounds the individual and hence is in keeping with the Protestant tradition of personal freedom and independence.

BIBLIOGRAPHY

In the eighteenth and nineteenth centuries, there were a number of editions of Young's poetical works; a two-volume *Complete Works* was published in 1854. To date, the only modern text of *Conjectures on Original Composition* is that edited by Edith J. Morley in 1918 (reprinted in facsimile editions in 1966 and 1970). Henry Charles Shelley, *The Life and Letters of Edward Young* (1914), is outdated; see now *The Correspondence of Edward Young, 1683–1765,* edited by Henry Pettit (1971).

Cecil Vivian Wicker, *Edward Young and the Fear of Death: A Study in Romantic Melancholy* (1952), focuses on the poetry and says little about *Conjectures*. Isabel St. John Bliss, *Edward Young* (1969), offers a useful brief survey. Joel Weinsheimer's *Imitation* (1984) treats the theory of "imitation" in literature and comments on Young, John Locke, and Samuel Johnson. In "The Stranger within Young's *Conjectures*," *ELH* 53.3 (1986), Robert L. Chibka explores Young's theory of originality. For bibliography, see Francesco Cordasco, *Edward Young: A Handlist of Critical Notices and Studies* (1950), and James E. May, "A Bibliography of Secondary Materials for the Study of Edward Young, 1683–1765," *Bulletin of Bibliography* 46.4 (1989).

From Conjectures[1] on Original Composition

I begin with *Original* Composition; and the more willingly, as it seems an original subject to me, who have seen nothing hitherto written on it: But, first, a few thoughts on Composition in general. Some are of opinion, that its growth, at present, is too luxuriant; and that the Press is overcharged.

1. Interpretations of signs, forecasts, as well as guesses.

Overcharged, I think, it could never be, if none were admitted, but such as brought their Imprimatur from *sound Understanding*, and the *Public Good*. Wit, indeed, however brilliant, should not be permitted to gaze self-enamoured on its useless Charms, in that Fountain of Fame (if so I may call the Press), if beauty is all that it has to boast; but, like the first *Brutus*,[2] it should sacrifice its most darling offspring to the sacred interests of virtue, and real service of mankind.

This restriction allowed, the more composition the better. To men of letters, and leisure, it is not only a noble amusement, but a sweet refuge; it improves their parts, and promotes their peace: It opens a back-door out of the bustle of this busy, and idle world, into a delicious garden of moral and intellectual fruits and flowers; the key of which is denied to the rest of mankind. When stung with idle anxieties, or teazed with fruitless impertinence, or yawning over insipid diversions, then we perceive the blessing of a letter'd recess. With what a gust do we retire to our disinterested, and immortal friends in our closet,[3] and find our minds, when applied to some favourite theme, as naturally, and as easily quieted, and refreshed, as a peevish child (and peevish children are we all till we fall asleep) when laid to the breast? Our happiness no longer lives on charity; nor bids fair for a fall, by leaning on that most precarious, and thorny pillow, another's pleasure, for our repose. How independent of the world is he, who can daily find new acquaintance, that at once entertain, and improve him, in the little world, the minute but fruitful creation, of his own mind?

These advantages *Composition* affords us, whether we write ourselves, or in more humble amusement peruse the works of others. While we bustle thro' the thronged walks of public life, it gives us a respite, at least, from care; a pleasing pause of refreshing recollection. If the country is our choice, or fate, there it rescues us from *sloth* and *sensuality*, which, like obscene vermin, are apt gradually to creep unperceived into the delightful bowers of our retirement, and to poison all its sweets. Conscious guilt robs the rose of its scent, the lilly of its lustre; and makes an *Eden* a deflowered, and dismal scene.

Moreover, if we consider life's endless evils, what can be more prudent, than to provide for consolation under them? A consolation under them the wisest of men have found in the pleasures of the pen. Witness, among many more, *Thucydides, Xenophon, Tully, Ovid, Seneca, Pliny* the younger,[4] who says *In uxoris infirmitate, & amicorum periculo, aut morte turbatus, ad studia, unicum doloris levamentum, confugio*. And why not add to these their modern equals, *Chaucer, Rawleigh, Bacon, Milton, Clarendon*,[5] under the same shield, unwounded by misfortune, and nobly smiling in distress?

Composition was a cordial to these under the frowns of fortune; but evils

2. The traditional founder of the Roman Republic (6th c. B.C.E.); according to legend, he killed his two sons when he discovered that they were conspiring to restore the Tarquins, the Etruscan family whose members had ruled as kings.

3. "A small room of privacy and retirement" (Johnson's *Dictionary*, 1755).

4. Roman orator and statesman (62–113). Young inaccurately quotes his *Letters* 8.19: "Distracted by my wife's ill health, by the dangerous illness or death of my friends, I fly to my studies, the sole consolation of my sorrows." Thucydides (455–400 B.C.E.), Greek historian. Xenophon (ca. 428 / 7–ca. 354 B.C.E.), Greek historian and essayist. Tully: Marcus Tullius Cicero (106–43 B.C.E.), Roman writer, statesman, and orator. Ovid (43 B.C.E.–17 C.E.), Roman poet. Seneca the Younger (ca. 4 B.C.E.–65 C.E.), Roman philosopher, dramatist, and statesman.

5. Edward Hyde, earl of Clarendon (1609–1674), English politician and historian. Geoffrey Chaucer (ca. 1343–1400), English poet. Rawleigh: Sir Walter Ralegh (1552–1618), English courtier, navigator, colonizer, and writer. Francis Bacon (1561–1626), English philosopher and statesman. John Milton (1608–1674), English poet.

there are, which her smiles cannot prevent, or cure. Among these are the languors of old age. If those are held honourable, who in a hand benumbed by time have grasped the just sword in defence of their country; shall they be less esteemed, whose unsteady pen vibrates to the last in the cause of religion, of virtue, of learning? Both these are happy in *this*, that by fixing their attention on objects most important, they escape numberless little anxieties, and that *tedium vitae*[6] which often hangs so heavy on its evening hours. May not this insinuate some apology for my spilling ink, and spoiling paper, so late in life?

But there are, who write with vigor, and success, to the world's delight, and their own renown. These are the glorious fruits where genius prevails. The mind of a man of genius is a fertile and pleasant field, pleasant as *Elysium*, and fertile as *Tempe*;[7] it enjoys a perpetual spring. Of that spring, *Originals* are the fairest flowers: *Imitations* are of quicker growth, but fainter bloom. *Imitations* are of two kinds; one of nature, one of authors: The first we call *Originals*, and confine the term *Imitation* to the second. I shall not enter into the curious enquiry of what is, or is not, strictly speaking, *Original*, content with what all must allow, that some compositions are more so than others; and the more they are so, I say, the better. *Originals* are, and ought to be, great favourites, for they are great benefactors; they extend the republic of letters, and add a new province to its dominion: *Imitators* only give us a sort of duplicates of what we had, possibly much better, before; increasing the mere drug of books, while all that makes them valuable, *knowledge* and *genius*, are at a stand. The pen of an *original* writer, like *Armida's*[8] wand, out of a barren waste calls a blooming spring: Out of that blooming spring an *Imitator* is a transplanter of laurels, which sometimes die on removal, always languish in a foreign soil.

But suppose an *Imitator* to be most excellent (and such there are), yet still he but nobly builds on another's foundation; his debt is, at least, equal to his glory; which therefore, on the balance, cannot be very great. On the contrary, an *Original*, tho' but indifferent (its *Originality* being set aside), yet has something to boast; it is something to say with him in *Horace*,

Meo *sum Pauper in aere*;[9]

and to share ambition with no less than *Cæsar*,[1] who declared he had rather be the first in a village, than the second at *Rome*.

Still farther: An *Imitator* shares his crown, if he has one, with the chosen object of his imitation; an *Original* enjoys an undivided applause. An *Original* may be said to be of a *vegetable* nature; it rises spontaneously from the vital root of genius; it *grows*, it is not *made*: *Imitations* are often a sort of *manufacture* wrought up by those *mechanics*, *art*, and *labour*, out of pre-existent materials not their own.

Again: We read *Imitation* with somewhat of his languor, who listens to a twice-told tale: Our spirits rouze[2] at an *Original*; that is a perfect stranger, and all throng to learn what news from a foreign land: And tho' it comes,

6. Irksomeness of life (Latin).
7. A valley (sacred to Apollo) in northeast Greece between Mount Olympus and Mount Ossa. Elysium: in classical mythology, the dwelling place of the blessed dead.
8. The enchantress in the epic *Jerusalem Delivered* (1581), by the Italian poet Torquato Tasso.
9. I'm poor [but live] on my own money (Latin). *Epistles* 2.2.12, by the Roman poet HORACE (65–8 B.C.E.).
1. Julius Caesar (100–44 B.C.E.), Roman statesman and general whose dictatorship ended the Republic.
2. Rouse, awaken.

like an *Indian* prince, adorned with feathers only, having little of weight; yet of our attention it will rob the more solid, if not equally new: Thus every telescope is lifted at a new-discovered star; it makes a hundred astronomers in a moment, and denies equal notice to the sun. But if an *Original*, by being as excellent, as new, adds admiration to surprize, then are we at the writer's mercy; on the strong wing of his imagination, we are snatched from *Britain* to *Italy*, from climate to climate, from pleasure to pleasure; we have no home, no thought, of our own; till the magician drops his pen: And then falling down into ourselves, we awake to flat realities, lamenting the change, like the beggar who dreamt himself a prince.

It is with thoughts, as it is with words; and with both, as with men; they may grow old, and die. Words tarnished, by passing thro' the mouths of the vulgar, are laid aside as inelegant, and obsolete. So thoughts, when become too common, should lose their currency; and we should send new metal to the mint, that is, new meaning to the press. The division of tongues at *Babel*[3] did not more effectually debar men from *making themselves a name* (as the Scripture speaks,) than the too great concurrence, or union of tongues will do for ever. We may as well grow good by another's virtue, or fat by another's food, as famous by another's thought. The world will pay its debt of praise but once; and instead of applauding, explode a second demand, as a cheat.

If it is said, that most of the *Latin* classics, and all the *Greek*, except, perhaps, *Homer, Pindar*, and *Anacreon*,[4] are in the number of *Imitators*, yet receive our highest applause; our answer is, That they tho' not *real*, are *accidental Originals*; the works they imitated, few excepted, are lost: They, on their father's decease, enter as lawful heirs, on their estates in fame: The fathers of our copyists are still in possession; and secured in it, in spite of *Goths*,[5] and Flames, by the perpetuating power of the Press. Very late must a modern *Imitator's* fame arrive, if it waits for their decease.

An *Original* enters early on reputation: *Fame*, fond of new glories, sounds her trumpet in triumph at its birth; and yet how few are awaken'd by it into the noble ambition of like attempts? Ambition is sometimes no vice in life; it is always a virtue in Composition. High in the towering *Alps* is the fountain of the *Po*;[6] high in fame, and in antiquity, is the fountain of an *Imitator's* undertaking; but the river, and the imitation, humbly creep along the vale. So few are our *Originals*, that, if all other books were to be burnt, the letter'd world would resemble some metropolis in flames, where a few incombustible buildings, a fortress, temple, or tower, lift their heads, in melancholy grandeur, amid the mighty ruin. Compared with this conflagration, old *Omar*[7] lighted up but a small bonfire, when he heated the baths of the Barbarians, for eight months together, with the famed *Alexandrian* library's inestimable spoils, that no prophane book might obstruct the triumphant progress of his holy *Alcoran*[8] round the globe.

But why are *Originals* so few? not because the writer's harvest is over, the great reapers of antiquity having left nothing to be gleaned after them; nor

3. Where God—alarmed that the people, speaking a single tongue, were successfully building a tower to "make [them] a name"—is said to have "confound[ed] their language." See Genesis 11.1–9.
4. Greek lyric poet (b. ca. 570 B.C.E.). Homer (ca. 8th c. B.C.E.), earliest Greek epic poet. Pindar (518–438 B.C.E.), Greek lyric poet.
5. Germanic invaders of the Roman Empire in the early centuries of the Christian era.
6. A river in northern Italy; it rises near the border with France, on Monte Viso in the Alps.
7. A caliph (ca. 581–644), or leader of an Islamic polity. This story of the destruction of the great library at Alexandria, in northern Egypt, on the city's capture by the Arabs is now discounted (it had already burned several times, most recently in 391).
8. The Koran.

because the human mind's teeming time is past, or because it is incapable of putting forth unprecedented births; but because illustrious examples *engross*, *prejudice*, and *intimidate*. They *engross* our attention, and so prevent a due inspection of ourselves; they *prejudice* our judgment in favour of their abilities, and so lessen the sense of our own; and they *intimidate* us with the splendor of their renown, and thus under diffidence bury our strength. Nature's impossibilities, and those of diffidence lie wide asunder.

Let it not be suspected, that I would weakly insinuate any thing in favour of the moderns, as compared with antient authors; no, I am lamenting their great inferiority. But I think it is no *necessary* inferiority; that it is not from divine destination, but from some cause far beneath the moon:[9] I think that human souls, thro' all periods, are equal; that due care, and exertion, would set us nearer our immortal predecessors than we are at present; and he who questions and confutes this, will show abilities not a little tending toward a proof of that equality, which he denies.

After all, the first antients had no merit in being *Originals*: They could *not* be *Imitators*. Modern writers have a *choice* to make; and therefore have a merit in their power. They may soar in the regions of *liberty*, or move in the soft fetters of easy *imitation*; and *imitation* has as many plausible reasons to urge, as *Pleasure* had to offer to *Hercules*.[1] *Hercules* made the choice of an hero, and *so* became immortal.

Yet let not assertors of classic excellence imagine, that I deny the tribute it so well deserves. He that admires not antient authors, betrays a secret he would conceal, and tells the world, that he does not understand them. Let us be as far from neglecting, as from copying, their admirable compositions: Sacred be their rights, and inviolable their fame. Let our understanding feed on theirs; they afford the noblest nourishment; But let them nourish, not annihilate, our own. When we read, let our imagination kindle at their charms; when we write, let our judgment shut them out of our thoughts; treat even *Homer* himself as his royal admirer was treated by the cynic; bid him stand aside, nor shade our Composition from the beams of our own genius; for nothing *Original* can rise, nothing immortal, can ripen, in any other sun.[2]

Must we then, you say, not imitate antient authors? Imitate them, by all means; but imitate aright. He that imitates the divine *Iliad*, does not imitate *Homer*; but he who takes the same method, which *Homer* took, for arriving at a capacity of accomplishing a work so great. Tread in his steps to the sole fountain of immortality; drink where he drank, at the true *Helicon*,[3] that is, at the breast of nature: Imitate; but imitate not the *Composition*, but the *Man*. For may not this paradox pass into a maxim? *viz*. 'The less we copy the renowned antients, we shall resemble them the more.'

But possibly you may reply, that you must either imitate *Homer*, or depart

9. In *An Enquiry into the Life and Writings of Homer* (1735), the classical scholar Thomas Blackwell speculates that the planets may influence or even cause genius and originality.

1. According to tradition, two women appeared before the legendary hero Hercules (Heracles) when he was pondering which course of life to follow: Pleasure offered a life of enjoyment, while Virtue offered a life of labor and fame. Hercules chose the latter.

2. An allusion to an exchange said to have occurred between Alexander the Great (356–323 B.C.E.) and the Greek philosopher Diogenes (ca. 400–ca. 325 B.C.E.), founder of the Cynic school of philosophy, which emphasized self-sufficiency and the pursuit of virtue. When Alexander asked what he could do for Diogenes, the philosopher answered: "Just stand aside so you don't keep the sun off me."

3. Mountain in central Greece, sacred to Apollo; it was the home of the Muses, and the spring Hippocrene, struck from the rock by the foot of the flying horse Pegasus, provided inspiration to poets.

from nature. Not so: For suppose you was to change place, in time, with *Homer*; then, if you write naturally, you might as well charge *Homer* with an imitation of you. Can you be said to imitate *Homer* for writing *so*, as you would have written, if *Homer* had never been? As far as a regard to nature, and sound sense, will permit a departure from your great predecessors; so far, ambitiously, depart from them; the farther from them in *similitude*, the nearer are you to them in *excellence*; you rise by it into an *Original*; become a noble collateral, not an humble descendant from them. Let us build our Compositions with the spirit, and in the taste, of the antients; but not with their materials: Thus will they resemble the structures of *Pericles* at *Athens*, which *Plutarch*[4] commends for having had an air of antiquity as soon as they were built. All eminence, and distinction, lies out of the beaten road; excursion, and deviation, are necessary to find it; and the more remote your path from the highway, the more reputable; if, like poor *Gulliver*[5] (of whom anon) you fall not into a ditch, in your way to glory.

What glory to come near, what glory to reach, what glory (presumptuous thought!) to surpass, our predecessors? And is that then in nature absolutely impossible? Or is it not, rather, contrary to nature to fail in it? Nature herself sets the ladder, all wanting is our ambition to climb. For by the bounty of nature we are as strong as our predecessors; and by the favour of time (which is but another round in nature's scale) we stand on higher ground. As to the *first*, were *they* more than men? Or are we less? Are not our minds cast in the same mould with those before the flood?[6] The flood affected matter; mind escaped. As to the *second*; though we are moderns, the world is an antient; more antient far, than when they, whom we most admire, filled it with their fame. Have we not their beauties, as stars, to guide; their defects, as rocks, to be shunn'd; the judgment of ages on both, as a chart to conduct, and a sure helm to steer us in our passage to greater perfection than theirs? And shall we be stopt in our rival pretensions to fame by this just reproof?

> Stat contra, dicitque tibi tua pagina, fur *es*.
>
> MART.[7]

It is by a sort of noble contagion, from a general familiarity with their writings, and not by any particular sordid theft, that we can be the better for those who went before us. Hope we, from plagiarism, any dominion in literature; as that of *Rome* arose from a nest of thieves?

Rome was a powerful ally to many states; antient authors are our powerful allies; but we must take heed, that they do not succour, till they enslave, after the manner of *Rome*. Too formidable an idea of their superiority, like a spectre, would fright us out of a proper use of our wits; and dwarf our understanding, by making a giant of theirs. Too great awe for them lays genius under restraint, and denies it that free scope, that full elbow-room, which is requisite for striking its most masterly strokes. Genius is a master-workman, learning is but an instrument; and an instrument, tho' most val-

4. Greek essayist and biographer (ca. 50–ca. 120 C.E.). Under the leadership of Pericles (ca. 495–429 B.C.E.), Athens built many temples and structures (the most famous being the Parthenon on the Acropolis); see Plutarch, *Pericles* 13.

5. The hero of Jonathan Swift's satire *Gulliver's Travels* (1726).

6. That is, the biblical Flood (Genesis 6–9) that destroyed all humanity except for Noah and his family. Young may also have in mind JOHN DRYDEN's "Epistle to Congreve" (1694); Dryden refers to previous generations of poets, before the English Revolution and the Restoration (1660), as "the giant race, before the flood" (line 5).

7. The Roman poet Martial (ca. 40–ca. 104 C.E.), *Epigrams* 1.55. 12: "Your page confronts you and says to you, You are a thief."

uable, yet not always indispensable. Heaven will not admit of a partner in the accomplishment of some favourite spirits; but rejecting all human means, assumes the whole glory to itself. Have not some, tho' not famed for erudition, *so* written, as almost to persuade us, that they shone brighter, and soared higher, for escaping the boasted aid of that proud ally?

Nor is it strange; for what, for the most part, mean we by genius, but the power of accomplishing great things without the means generally reputed necessary to that end? A *genius* differs from a *good understanding*, as a magician from a good architect; *that* raises his structure by means invisible; *this* by the skilful use of common tools. Hence genius has ever been supposed to partake of something divine. *Nemo unquam vir magnus fuit, sine aliquo afflatu divino*.[8]

Learning, destitute of this superior aid, is fond, and proud, of what has cost it much pains; is a great lover of rules, and boaster of famed examples: As beauties less perfect, who owe half their charms to cautious art, learning inveighs against natural unstudied graces, and small harmless inaccuracies, and sets rigid bounds to that liberty, to which genius often owes its supreme glory; but the no-genius its frequent ruin. For unprescribed beauties, and unexampled excellence, which are characteristics of *genius*, lie without the pale of *learning's* authorities, and laws; which pale, genius must leap to come at them: But by that leap, if genius is wanting, we break our necks; we lose that little credit, which possibly we might have enjoyed before. For rules, like crutches, are a needful aid to the lame, tho' an impediment to the strong. A *Homer* casts them away; and, like his *Achilles*,

Jura negat sibi nata, nihil non arrogat,[9]

by native force of mind. There is something in poetry beyond prose-reason; there are mysteries in it not to be explained, but admired; which render mere prose-men infidels to their divinity. And here pardon a second paradox; *viz.* '*Genius* often then deserves most to be praised, when it is most sure to be condemned; that is, when its excellence, from mounting high, to weak eyes is quite out of sight.'

If I might speak farther of learning, and genius, I would compare genius to virtue, and learning to riches. As riches are most wanted where there is least virtue; so learning where there is least genius. As virtue without much riches can give happiness, so genius without much learning can give renown. As it is said in *Terence*,[1] *Pecuniam negligere interdum maximum est lucrum*; so to neglect of learning, genius sometimes owes its greater glory. Genius, therefore, leaves but the second place, among men of letters, to the learned. It is their merit, and ambition, to fling light on the works of genius, and point out its charms. We most justly reverence their informing radius for that favour; but we must much more admire the radiant stars pointed out by them.

A star of the first magnitude among the moderns was *Shakespeare* ; among the antients, *Pindar*; who (as *Vossius*[2] tells us) boasted of his no-learning,

8. No one was ever a great man without some divine inspiration (Latin). Inaccurately quoted from Cicero, *De Natura Deorum* (*On the Nature of the Gods*), 2.66.

9. He denies that the laws were made for him, and sets no limits to his claims (Latin). Slightly misquoted from Horace, *Ars Poetica*, line 122 (see above). Achilles: the greatest Greek warrior at Troy and the focus of Homer's *Iliad*.

1. Roman comic playwright (ca. 120–159 B.C.E.); the quotation is from *Adelphi* 2.216: "Sometimes the best way to make money is to disregard it."

2. G. J. Vossius (1577–1649), Dutch critic, rhetorician, and scholar.

calling himself the eagle, for his flight above it. And such genii as these may, indeed, have much reliance on their own native powers. For genius may be compared to the natural strength of the body; learning to the super-induced accoutrements of arms: if the first is equal to the proposed exploit, the latter rather encumbers, than assists; rather retards, than promotes, the victory. *Sacer nobis inest Deus*,[3] says *Seneca*. With regard to the moral world, *conscience*, with regard to the intellectual, *genius*, is that god within. Genius can set us right in Composition, without the rules of the learned; as conscience sets us right in life, without the laws of the land: *This*, singly, can make us good, as men: *that*, singly, as writers, can, sometimes, make us great.

I say, sometimes, because there is a genius, which stands in need of learning to make it shine. Of genius there are two species, an earlier, and a later; or call them *infantine*, and *adult*. An adult genius comes out of nature's hand, as *Pallas*[4] out of *Jove's* head, at full growth, and mature: *Shakespeare's* genius was of this kind; On the contrary, *Swift* stumbled at the threshold, and set out for distinction on feeble knees:[5] His was an infantine genius; a genius, which, like other infants, must be nursed, and educated, or it will come to nought: Learning is its nurse, and tutor; but this nurse may overlay with an indigested load, which smothers common sense; and this tutor may mislead, with pedantic prejudice, which vitiates the best understanding: As too great admirers of the fathers of the church[6] have sometimes set up their authority against the true sense of Scripture; so too great admirers of the classical fathers have sometimes set up their authority, or example, against reason.

* * *

Quite clear of the dispute concerning *antient and modern learning*, we speak not of performance, but powers. The modern powers are equal to those before them; modern performance in general is deplorably short. How great are the names just mentioned? Yet who will dare affirm, that as great may not rise up in some future, or even in the present age? Reasons there are why talents may not *appear*, none why they may not *exist*, as much in one period as another. An evocation of vegetable fruits depends on rain, air, and sun; an evocation of the fruits of genius no less depends on externals. What a marvellous crop bore it in *Greece*, and *Rome*? And what a marvellous sunshine did it there enjoy? What encouragement from the nature of their governments, and the spirit of their people? *Virgil* and *Horace* owed their divine talents to Heaven; their immortal works, to men; thank *Mæcenas* and *Augustus*[7] for them. Had it not been for these, the genius of those poets had lain buried in their ashes. *Athens* expended on her theatre, painting, sculpture, and architecture, a tax levied for the support of a war. *Cæsar* dropt his papers when *Tully* spoke; and *Philip* trembled at the voice of *Demosthenes*:[8] And has there arisen but one *Tully*, one *Demosthenes*, in so long a course of years?

3. Divinity dwells within us (Latin). Scholars have not found these exact words in Seneca's writings, but a similar statement can be found in his *Moral Epistles* 41.
4. Athena, Greek goddess of war and wisdom and patroness of the arts, said to have been born full-grown from the head of Zeus (whom the Romans identified with Jupiter, or Jove).
5. Swift began his literary career unsuccessfully, writing Pindaric odes.
6. Early Christian writers who established church doctrine before the 8th century (e.g., AUGUSTINE).
7. First emperor of Rome (63 B.C.E.–14 C.E.). Virgil (70–19 B.C.E.), Roman poet. Maecenas (d. 8 C.E.), trusted counselor of Augustus and a famous patron of the arts.
8. Greek orator (384–322 B.C.E.), who exhorted the citizens of Athens to resist Philip II (382–336 B.C.E.), the king of Macedon.

The powerful eloquence of them both in one stream, should never bear me down into the melancholy persuasion, that several have not been born, tho' they have not emerged. The sun as much exists in a cloudy day, as in a clear; it is outward, accidental circumstances that with regard to genius either in nation, or age,

Collectas fugat nubes, solemque reducit.

Virg.[9]

As great, perhaps, greater than those mentioned (presumptuous as it may sound) may, possibly, arise; for who hath fathomed the mind of man? Its bounds are as unknown, as those of the creation; since the birth of which, perhaps, not One has so far exerted, as not to leave his possibilities beyond his attainments, his powers beyond his exploits. Forming our judgments, altogether by what *has* been done, without knowing, or at all inquiring, what possibly *might* have been done, we naturally enough fall into too mean an opinion of the human mind. If a sketch of the divine Iliad before *Homer* wrote, had been given to mankind, by some superior being, or otherwise, its execution would, probably, have appeared beyond the power of man. Now, to surpass it, we think impossible. As the first of these opinions would evidently have been a mistake, why may not the second be so too? Both are founded on the same bottom; on our ignorance of the possible dimensions of the mind of man.

Nor are we only ignorant of the dimensions of the human mind in general, but even of our own. That a man may be scarce less ignorant of his own powers, than an oyster of its pearl, or a rock of its diamond; that he may possess dormant, unsuspected abilities, till awakened by loud calls, or stung up by striking emergencies, is evident from the sudden eruption of some men, out of perfect obscurity, into publick admiration, on the strong impulse of some animating occasion; not more to the world's great surprize, than their own. Few authors of distinction but have experienced something of this nature, at the first beamings of their yet unsuspected genius on their hitherto dark Composition: The writer starts at it, as at a lucid meteor in the night; is much surprized; can scarce believe it true. During his happy confusion, it may be said to him, as to Eve at the lake,

What there thou seest, fair creature, is thyself.

Milt.[1]

Genius, in this view, is like a dear friend in our company under disguise; who, while we are lamenting his absence, drops his mask, striking us, at once, with equal surprize and joy. This sensation, which I speak of in a writer, might favour, and so promote, the fable of poetic inspiration: A poet of a strong imagination, and stronger vanity, on feeling it, might naturally enough realize the world's mere compliment, and think himself truly inspired. Which is not improbable; for enthusiasts of all kinds do no less.

Since it is plain that men may be strangers to their own abilities; and by thinking meanly of them without just cause, may possibly lose a name, perhaps a name immortal; I would find some means to prevent these evils.

9. Virgil, *Aeneid* 1.143: "He puts to flight the gathered clouds, and he brings back the sun."

1. Milton, *Paradise Lost* (1667), 4.468.

Whatever promotes virtue, promotes something more, and carries its good influence beyond the *moral* man: To prevent these evils, I borrow two golden rules from *ethics*, which are no less golden in *Composition*, than in life. 1. *Know thyself*; 2dly, *Reverence thyself*: I design to repay ethics in a future letter,[2] by two rules from rhetoric for its service.

Ist. *Know thyself*. Of ourselves it may be said, as *Martial* says of a bad neighbour,

Nil tam prope, proculque nobis.[3]

Therefore dive deep into thy bosom; learn the depth, extent, bias, and full fort of thy mind; contract full intimacy with the stranger within thee; excite and cherish every spark of intellectual light and heat, however smothered under former negligence, or scattered through the dull, dark mass of common thoughts; and collecting them into a body, let thy genius rise (if a genius thou hast) as the sun from chaos; and if I should then say, like an *Indian*, *Worship it*, (though too bold) yet should I say little more than my second rule enjoins, (*viz.*) *Reverence thyself*.

That is, let not great examples, or authorities, browbeat thy reason into too great a diffidence of thyself: Thyself so reverence, as to prefer the native growth of thy own mind to the richest import from abroad; such borrowed riches make us poor. The man who thus reverences himself, will soon find the world's reverence to follow his own. His works will stand distinguished; his the sole property of them; which property alone can confer the noble title of an *author*; that is, of one who (to speak accurately) *thinks*, and *composes*; while other invaders of the press, how voluminous, and learned soever, (with due respect be it spoken) only *read*, and *write*.

This is the difference between those two luminaries in literature, the well-accomplished scholar, and the divinely-inspired enthusiast; the *first* is, as the bright morning star; the *second*, as the rising sun. The writer who neglects those two rules above will never stand alone; he makes one of a group, and thinks in wretched unanimity with the throng: Incumbered with the notions of others, and impoverished by their abundance, he conceives not the least embryo of new thought; opens not the least vista thro' the gloom of ordinary writers, into the bright walks of rare imagination, and singular design; while the true genius is crossing all publick roads into fresh untrodden ground; he, up to the knees in antiquity, is treading the sacred footsteps of great examples, with the blind veneration of a bigot saluting the papal toe;[4] comfortably hoping full absolution for the sins of his own understanding, from the powerful charm of touching his idol's infallibility.

* * *

Shakespeare mingled no water with his wine, lower'd his genius by no vapid imitation. *Shakespeare* gave us a *Shakespeare*, nor could the first in antient fame have given us more! *Shakespeare* is not their son, but brother; their equal; and that, in spite of all his faults. Think you this too bold? Consider, in those antients what is it the world admires? Not the fewness of their faults, but the number and brightness of their beauties; and if *Shakespeare* is their

2. Never written.
3. Nothing else is so near and yet so far from us (Latin); Martial, *Epigrams* 1.86.
4. English Protestants of the time held Catholics and Catholicism in low regard.

equal (as he doubtless is) in that, which in them is admired, then is *Shakespeare* as great as they; and not impotence, but some other cause, must be charged with his defects. When we are setting these great men in competition, what but the comparative size of their genius is the subject of our inquiry? And a giant loses nothing of his size, tho' he should chance to trip in his race. But it is a compliment to those heroes of antiquity to suppose *Shakespeare* their equal only in dramatic powers; therefore, though his faults had been greater, the scale would still turn in his favour. There is at least as much genius on the *British* as on the *Grecian* stage, tho' the former is not swept so clean; so clean from violations not only of the *dramatic*, but *moral* rule; for an honest heathen, on reading some of our celebrated scenes, might be seriously concerned to see, that our obligations to the religion of nature were cancel'd by Christianity.

Johnson,[5] in the serious drama, is as much an imitator, as *Shakespeare* is an original. He was very learned, as *Sampson*[6] was very strong, to his own hurt: Blind to the nature of tragedy, he pulled down all antiquity on his head, and buried himself under it; we see nothing of *Johnson*, nor indeed, of his admired (but also murdered) antients; for what shone in the historian is a cloud on the poet; and *Cataline*[7] might have been a good play, if *Salust* had never writ.

Who knows whether *Shakespeare* might not have thought less, if he had read more? Who knows if he might not have laboured under the load of *Johnson's* learning, as *Enceladus*[8] under *Ætna*? His mighty genius, indeed, through the most mountainous oppression would have breathed out some of his inextinguishable fire; yet, possibly, he might not have risen up into that giant, that much more than common man, at which we now gaze with amazement, and delight. Perhaps he was as learned as his dramatic province required; for whatever other learning he wanted, he was master of two books, unknown to many of the profoundly read, though books, which the last conflagration alone can destroy; the book of nature, and that of man. These he had by heart, and has transcribed many admirable pages of them, into his immortal works. These are the fountain-head, whence the *Castalian* streams[9] of *original* composition flow; and these are often mudded by other waters, tho' waters in their distinct chanel, most wholesome and pure: As two chymical liquors, separately clear as crystal, grow foul by mixture, and offend the sight. So that he had not only as much learning as his dramatic province required, but, perhaps, as it could safely bear. If *Milton* had spared some of his learning, his muse would have gained more glory, than he would have lost, by it.

* * *

1759

5. That is, Ben Jonson (1572–1637).
6. The biblical hero Samson, who pulled down the pillars of a building to kill his enemies and himself (Judges 16.23–30).
7. A Roman tragedy (1611) by Jonson, based on *The Conspiracy of Catiline*, by the Roman historian Sallust (ca. 86–35 B.C.E.)
8. In Greek mythology, the most powerful of the giants who warred against the gods; defeated, he was buried under Sicily's Mount Etna.
9. Waters flowing from a fountain on Mount Parnassus, sacred to Apollo and the Muses; those who drink them are inspired with the gift of poetry.

ALEXANDER POPE
1688–1744

Scholars have noted dozens of sources—the Roman writers HORACE and QUINTILIAN, the French poet-critic Nicolas Boileau (1636–1711), his English contemporary JOHN DRYDEN, and many more—for Alexander Pope's versified "art of poetry," *An Essay on Criticism* (1711); but their labors, while valuable, in a sense miss the central point. Pope advanced no claims for the originality of the views he presented, and in the final analysis his poem is memorable perhaps less for its doctrine than for the brilliance of its style, which revitalizes familiar teachings and makes them sparkle. It delightfully illustrates Pope's own view of literary "borrowing": that "poets, like merchants, should repay with something of their own what they take from others, not, like pirates, make prize of all they meet." The *Essay* is a sophisticated, witty poem, a compendium of critical principles, with much reading and reflection behind it—from an author who was astonishingly young when it was written.

Pope was born in London in 1688, the year of the Glorious Revolution, when the Catholic King James II was deposed in favor of Protestant William III and Mary II. He was the son of a linen merchant who was Roman Catholic, and thus suffered from the controls of England's anti-Catholic laws. Though not always strictly enforced, these laws were onerous. Catholics were prevented from practicing their religion freely; they could not legally reside within ten miles of London; they were not allowed to attend the universities, vote, or hold public offices or seats in Parliament. In 1711 Pope's family moved to Binfield in Windsor Forest, thirty miles outside London, a place that Pope described evocatively in one of his best early poems, "Windsor-Forest" (1713).

A local priest taught Greek and Latin to Pope, and he picked up French and Italian during a short term of study in London. Pope's father encouraged him to write verse, insisting that his son's rhymes be perfect, and Pope early on crafted "imitations" of Chaucer (ca. 1343–1400), Edmund Spenser (1552–1599), Edmund Waller (1606–1687), and Abraham Cowley (1618–1667). Limitations not simply legal but also physical encouraged him to focus on his literary efforts. Tuberculosis of the bones in childhood had curved Pope's spine and stunted his growth—he was only four and a half feet tall—and throughout his life he suffered from frequent and severe headaches.

In addition to *An Essay on Criticism* and "Windsor-Forest," Pope's major poems include "The Rape of the Lock" (1712; enlarged ed., 1714); *The Dunciad*, targeting Pope's literary enemies (first published anonymously in 1728; enlarged eds. 1742, 1743); *Moral Essays* (1731–35); *Imitations of Horace* (1733–38) and their prologue, "An Epistle to Dr. Arbuthnot" (1735); and *An Essay on Man* (1733–34), a philosophical poem designed to "vindicate the ways of God to Man" (1.16). Pope also produced a magnificent translation of the *Iliad* (1715–20), co-translated the *Odyssey* (1725–26), and edited the works of Shakespeare (1725). He had concerns outside literature; his keen interests in painting, sculpture, architecture, and horticulture were expressed in the garden and grotto that he built at Twickenham, a five-acre villa he rented on the Thames, where he moved with his mother after his father's death in 1718.

An Essay on Criticism was published anonymously on May 15, 1711, a week before the poet's twenty-third birthday. The manuscript we have is dated in Pope's hand, "Written in the year 1709," but elsewhere he put the date of composition as early as 1706. And though he claimed to have written the *Essay* quickly, the manuscript shows that he revised his poem carefully. For later editions, Pope provided a table of contents and divided the 750-line poem into three parts—the second starting at line 201 and the third at line 560.

Pope means his lively heroic couplets to remind readers of principles they already should know. Like many writers in the seventeenth and eighteenth centuries, he judges literature to be plagued by ill-informed, careless, proud, and pompous critics, whose mistaken evaluations of texts mislead authors as well as readers. John Dryden, in "The Author's Apology for Heroic Poetry" (1677), similarly laments that he and his fellow authors have "fallen into an age of illiterate, censorious, and detracting people, who, thus qualified, set up for critics." In the *Essay* Pope writes that the dismaying state of criticism reflects a broad historical decline from the Greek and Roman past—the golden age of art, when critics generously sought to advise authors and to instruct readers on how to appreciate them.

The best works of art, Pope maintains, derive from a deeply felt, well-reasoned study of Nature; and studying the great works of the past leads one to see their reliance on the stable principles of harmony and order that Nature itself teaches. This is Pope's and his age's neoclassicism—to imitate the ancient authors and adopt the critical precepts that these authors and their texts embody. Like Jonathan Swift, JOSEPH ADDISON, and other significant writers of the early to mid–eighteenth century, Pope particularly admired the authors, notably Virgil, Ovid, and Horace, who had flourished during the reign of the Roman emperor Augustus (27 B.C.E.–14 C.E.), and he sought through his writing to make his own era similarly "Augustan" in its literary production. Reading Homer and Virgil, Pope believed, sharpens taste and judgment and enables us to perceive the intimate relationship between art and Nature. The classic texts are, like Nature, a standard and a guide. Their balance, harmony, and good proportion are evident in their parts as well as demonstrated in the whole. In the prosody of a poem, for example, the sound and meter in a well-proportioned and well-regulated work enact the actions and the sense conveyed (see lines 364–73).

At moments, as when Pope rebukes pride and envy (e.g., lines 201–18), the *Essay* might strike some readers today as less about literature and criticism than about morality. But as Pope sees it, good authors or critics must truly know themselves and possess a finely developed moral sense and purpose. Such people know and abide by the limits of human aspiration, seek models for right aesthetic and moral conduct, and guard against the self-delusion and self-destructiveness of overweening pride.

Some critics contend that Pope uses his chief terms, such as *Nature, wit,* and *judgment*, too loosely, and they have claimed that the *Essay* lacks a coherent structure. It is, like Horace's *Ars Poetica*, more associative than logical; it offers encouragement and advice in a sequence of briskly paced observations on the nature of art, the value of the ancients, the importance of the rules, the need to observe decorum in word selection, the connection between artistic creation and criticism, and other topics. The key words are invoked in different passages to enliven the specific point at hand. Rather than using them "loosely," Pope deliberately draws on all of their senses.

For example, *wit* (from the Old English *witan*, "to know") is a complex, multivalent word, difficult to pin down, and Pope capitalizes adroitly on its range of meanings and implications. It means, first, the mind or the understanding, the faculty of reasoning and thinking. In his *Dictionary* (1755), SAMUEL JOHNSON gives as its "original signification" "the powers of the mind; the mental faculties; the intellects." But wit can also refer, he notes, to a poetic conceit, figure of speech, felicitous phrasing, common sense, inventiveness, astuteness of perception, the capacity to see resemblance in apparently unlike things, cleverness, fancy, genius; it can mean the imaginative power that judgment must temper and control (see, e.g., lines 82–83), even as it also implies judgment itself—wit curbing excessive wit. Pope offers his own definition in perhaps the best-known couplets of the *Essay*:

> *True Wit* is *Nature* to Advantage drest,
> What oft was *Thought*, but ne'er so well *Exprest*,
> *Something*, whose Truth convinc'd at Sight we find,
> That gives us back the Image of our Mind. (lines 297–300)

Wit *is* Nature; it instances something that we have all thought, but whose sheer truth the poet now makes compelling through his or her language. True wit is subtle, sharp, and, above all, surprising—a striking image, a vivid metaphor, a paradoxical figure of speech. Addison and Johnson also delve into the nature of wit, but it is Pope who exemplifies the meanings of this complex word and idea more inventively than any other writer in the canon of eighteenth-century English literature.

The most memorable assessment of the *Essay* remains Samuel Johnson's: "[The *Essay*] exhibits every mode of excellence that can embellish or dignify didactick composition, selection of matter, novelty of arrangement, justness of precept, splendour of illustration, and propriety of digression." It is a hopeful work, all the more affecting in light of the political quarrels and ferocious literary feuds in which Pope engaged later in his career. These climaxed in his gigantic satire of literary idiocy, *The Dunciad, in Four Books*, published in October 1743. In this great last text of his poetic career, Pope describes the sublime awfulness of hordes of pedants, false poets, and dunces. His dazzling punitive wit here takes on the grotesque grandeur of mock-epic, on a scale eclipsing that displayed in the elegant, highly cultivated early work. *The Dunciad* shows Pope's angry realization of the difficulty in winning wide acceptance for the neoclassical views that he had advocated and had described with both power and grace in *An Essay on Criticism*.

BIBLIOGRAPHY

The standard source for studying Pope is the *Twickenham Edition of the Works of Alexander Pope* (11 vols., 1939–69). Volume 1 (1961), edited by E. Audra and Aubrey Williams, includes a carefully annotated text of *An Essay on Criticism*. Also recommended is Robert M. Schmitz's *"Essay on Criticism," 1709; A Study of the Bodleian Manuscript Text with Facsimiles, Transcripts, and Variants* (1962), which examines the manuscript version of the *Essay*. A good one-volume selection is *Poetry and Prose of Alexander Pope*, edited by Aubrey Williams (1969), which uses the text established for the Twickenham edition. Other important primary sources include *The Correspondence of Alexander Pope*, edited by George Sherburn (5 vols., 1956); and two volumes of prose works, the first edited by Norman Ault, *The Prose Works of Alexander Pope* (1936), and the second by Rosemary Cowler, *The Prose Works of Alexander Pope*, vol. 2, *The Major Works, 1725–1744* (1986). For selections from Pope's critical writings, see *Literary Criticism of Alexander Pope*, edited by Bertrand A. Goldgar (1965).

There are two superb biographical treatments: George Sherburn, *The Early Career of Alexander Pope* (1934), which covers the period to 1727; and Maynard Mack, *Alexander Pope: A Life* (1985), which examines the life and the writings in depth and detail. Also recommended: Howard Erskine-Hill, *The Social Milieu of Alexander Pope: Lives, Example, and the Poetic Response* (1975); Maynard Mack, *The Garden and the City: Retirement and Politics in the Later Poetry of Pope, 1731–1743* (1969); and Reginald Berry, *A Pope Chronology* (1988).

Two older studies of Pope's verse remain valuable: Geoffrey Tillotson, *On The Poetry of Pope* (2d ed., 1950), and Reuben Brower, *Alexander Pope: The Poetry of Allusion* (1959). These should be supplemented by Laura Brown, *Alexander Pope* (1985), a Marxist study that relates Pope to the culture of empire and capitalism; Ellen Pollak, *The Poetics of Sexual Myth: Gender and Ideology in the Verse of Swift and Pope* (1985), a feminist analysis; G. Douglas Atkins, *Quests of Difference: Reading Pope's Poems* (1986), which draws on Jacques Derrida's and Paul de Man's deconstructive theories and practices; Leopold Damrosch Jr., *The Imaginative World of Alexander Pope* (1987), a keen exploration of Pope's literary career as the product of his feelings of isolation and sexual, artistic, political, and financial marginality; Valerie Rumbold, *Women's Place in Pope's World* (1989), a cogent treatment of Pope's relationships with women and his poetry about them; and Helen Deutsch, *Resemblance and Disgrace: Alexander Pope and the Deformation of Culture* (1996).

Much of the best critical work on Pope has been collected in *Essential Articles for the Study of Pope*, edited by Maynard Mack (1968); *Alexander Pope: A Critical Anthology*, edited by F. W. Bateson and N. A. Joukovsky (1971); *Alexander Pope: Writers and Their Backgrounds*, edited by Peter Dixon (1972); and *Pope: The Critical Heritage*, edited by James Barnard (1973). Recent collections include *The Enduring Legacy: Alexander Pope Tercentenary Essays*, edited by G. S. Rousseau and Pat Rogers (1988), and *Pope: New Contexts*, edited by David Fairer (1990). See also the special issue of *The New Orleans Review*, vol. 15 (1980), edited by Ronald Schleifer and titled *The Poststructuralist Pope*. Helpful bibliographical works are Reginald H. Griffith, *Alexander Pope: A Bibliography* (2 vols., 1922–27), and Wolfgang Kowalk, *Alexander Pope: An Annotated Bibliography of Twentieth-Century Criticism, 1900–1979* (1981).

An Essay on Criticism

———Si quid novisti rectius istis,
Candidus imperti; si non, his utere mecum.

—HORAT.[1]

'Tis hard to say, if greater Want of Skill
Appear in *Writing* or in *Judging* ill;
But, of the two, less dang'rous is th' Offence,
To tire our *Patience*, than mis-lead our *Sense*:
Some few in *that*, but Numbers err in *this*,
Ten Censure[2] wrong for one who Writes amiss;
A *Fool* might once *himself* alone expose,
Now *One* in *Verse* makes many more in *Prose*.
'Tis with our *Judgments* as our *Watches*, none
Go just *alike*, yet each believes his own.
In *Poets* as true *Genius* is but rare,
True *Taste* as seldom is the *Critick's* Share;
Both must alike from Heav'n derive their Light,
These *born* to Judge, as well as those to Write.
Let such teach others who themselves excell,
And *censure freely* who have *written well*.
Authors are partial to their *Wit*, 'tis true,
But are not *Criticks* to their *Judgment* too?
Yet if we look more closely, we shall find
Most have the *Seeds* of Judgment in their Mind;
Nature affords at least a *glimm'ring Light*;
The *Lines*, tho' touch'd but faintly, are drawn right.
But as the slightest Sketch, if justly trac'd,
Is by ill *Colouring* but the more disgrac'd,
So by *false Learning* is *good Sense* defac'd;
Some are bewilder'd in the Maze of Schools,
And some made *Coxcombs*[3] Nature meant but *Fools*.
In search of *Wit* these lose their *common Sense*,
And then turn Criticks in their own Defence.

1. HORACE (65–8 B.C.E.), *Epistles* 1.6.67–68: "If you know any maxims better than these, be so good as to let me know them; if not, use these as I do."

2. Judge.

3. Pretenders to learning, conceited asses.

Each burns alike, who can, or cannot write,
Or with a *Rival*'s, or an *Eunuch*'s spite.
All *Fools* have still an Itching to deride,
And fain *wou'd* be upon the *Laughing Side:*
If *Mævius* Scribble in *Apollo*'s[4] spight,
There are, who *judge* still *worse* than he can *write*.
Some have at first for *Wits*, then *Poets* past,
Turn'd *Criticks* next, and prov'd plain *Fools* at last;
Some neither can for *Wits* nor *Criticks* pass,
As heavy Mules are neither *Horse* nor *Ass*.
Those half-learn'd Witlings, num'rous in our Isle,
As half-form'd Insects on the Banks of *Nile;*[5]
Unfinish'd Things, one knows not what to call,
Their Generation's so *equivocal*:
To tell[6] 'em, wou'd a *hundred Tongues* require,
Or *one vain Wit's*, that might a hundred tire.
But *you* who seek to *give* and *merit* Fame,
And justly bear a Critick's noble Name,
Be sure *your self* and your own *Reach* to know,
How far your *Genius, Taste*, and *Learning* go;
Launch not beyond your Depth, but be discreet,
And mark *that Point* where Sense and Dulness *meet*.
Nature to all things fix'd the Limits fit,
And wisely curb'd proud Man's pretending Wit:
As on the *Land* while *here* the *Ocean* gains,
In *other Parts* it leaves wide sandy Plains;
Thus in the *Soul* while *Memory* prevails,
The solid Pow'r of *Understanding* fails;
Where Beams of warm *Imagination* play,
The *Memory*'s soft Figures melt away.
One *Science*[7] only will one *Genius* fit;
So *vast* is Art,[8] so *narrow* Human Wit:
Not only bounded to *peculiar Arts*,
But oft in *those*, confin'd to *single Parts*.
Like Kings we lose the Conquests gain'd before,
By vain Ambition still to make them more:
Each might his *sev'ral Province* well command,
Wou'd all but *stoop* to what they *understand*.
First follow NATURE,[9] and your Judgment frame
By her just Standard, which is still the same:[1]
Unerring Nature, still divinely bright,
One *clear, unchang'd*, and *Universal* Light,
Life, Force, and Beauty, must to all impart,
At once the *Source*, and *End*, and *Test* of *Art*.

4. Greek and Roman god of poetry. Maevius: a bad poet (1st c. B.C.E.), to whom both Virgil (*Eclogue* 3) and Horace (*Epode* 10) allude.
5. The ancients believed that forms of animal and insect life were spontaneously generated on the banks of the Nile River.
6. Count.
7. Branch of learning.
8. Pope alludes to a maxim attributed to Hippocrates (469–399 B.C.E.), celebrated Greek physician: "Life is short, but art [sometimes translated 'science'] is long, opportunity fleeting, experiment dangerous, judgment difficult."
9. The term encompasses the physical world, the sum of human experiences, and the principle of order and coherence in the universe.
1. Compare JOHN DRYDEN's claim in *Parallel betwixt Poetry and Painting* (1695): "For Nature is still the same in all ages, and can never be contrary to herself."

Art from that Fund each *just Supply* provides,
Works *without Show*,[2] and *without Pomp* presides:
In some fair Body thus th' informing Soul
With Spirits feeds, with Vigour fills the whole,
Each Motion guides, and ev'ry Nerve sustains;
It self unseen, but in th' *Effects*, remains.
Some, to whom Heav'n in Wit has been profuse,
Want as much more, to turn it to its use;
For *Wit*[3] and *Judgment* often are at strife,
Tho' meant each other's Aid, like *Man* and *Wife*.
'Tis more to *guide* than *spur* the Muse's Steed;[4]
Restrain his Fury, than provoke his Speed;
The winged Courser, like a gen'rous[5] Horse,
Shows most true Mettle when you *check* his Course.
  Those RULES of old *discover'd*, not *devis'd*,
Are *Nature* still, but *Nature Methodiz'd*;
Nature, like *Liberty*,[6] is but restrain'd
By the same Laws which first *herself* ordain'd.
  Hear how learn'd *Greece* her useful Rules indites,
When to repress, and when indulge our Flights:
High on *Parnassus'*[7] Top her Sons she show'd,
And pointed out those arduous Paths they trod,
Held from afar, aloft, th' Immortal Prize,
And urg'd the rest by equal Steps to rise;
Just *Precepts* thus from great *Examples* giv'n,
She drew from *them* what they deriv'd from *Heav'n*.
The gen'rous Critick *fann'd* the *Poet's Fire*,
And taught the World, *with Reason* to *Admire*.
Then Criticism the Muse's Handmaid prov'd,
To dress her Charms, and make her more belov'd;
But following Wits from that Intention stray'd;
Who cou'd not win the Mistress, woo'd the Maid;
Against the Poets *their own Arms* they turn'd,
Sure to hate most the Men from whom they *learn'd*.
So modern *Pothecaries*, taught the Art
By *Doctor's Bills*[8] to play the *Doctor's Part*,
Bold in the Practice of *mistaken Rules*,
Prescribe, apply, and call their *Masters Fools*.
Some on the Leaves[9] of ancient Authors prey,
Nor Time nor Moths e'er spoil'd so much as they:
Some dryly plain, without Invention's Aid,
Write dull *Receits*[1] how Poems may be made:
These leave the Sense, their Learning to display,
And those explain the Meaning quite away.

2. Pope here recalls the familiar Latin maxim *ars est celare artem* (the art is to conceal the art).
3. *Wit* has a range of meanings, including reasoning power, intelligence, mental soundness, sanity, astuteness of perception or judgment, and the ability to see relationships between seemingly disparate things. It also can refer to a person of sound judgment and perception.
4. Pegasus, the winged horse of classical mythology, identified with inspiration. Muse: one of the 9 daughters of Memory who preside over the arts and all intellectual pursuits.
5. High spirited, noble.
6. In the manuscript, Pope wrote "monarchy."
7. Mountain in central Greece, sacred to Apollo, the Muses, and Dionysus.
8. Medical prescriptions. "Pothecaries": druggists.
9. Pages.
1. Recipes, prescriptions.

You then whose Judgment the right Course wou'd steer,
Know well each ANCIENT's proper *Character*,
His *Fable, Subject, Scope* in ev'ry Page,
Religion, Country, Genius of his *Age*:
Without all these at once before your Eyes,
Cavil you may, but never *Criticize*.
Be *Homer*'s Works[2] your *Study*, and *Delight*,
Read them by Day, and meditate by Night,
Thence form your Judgment, thence your Maxims bring,
And trace the Muses *upward* to their *Spring*;[3]
Still with *It self compar'd*, his *Text* peruse;
And let your *Comment* be the *Mantuan Muse*.[4]
When first young *Maro* in his boundless Mind
A Work t'outlast Immortal *Rome* design'd,
Perhaps he seem'd *above* the Critick's Law,
And but from *Nature's Fountains* scorn'd to draw:
But when t'examine ev'ry Part he came,
Nature and *Homer* were, he found, the *same*:
Convinc'd, amaz'd, he checks the bold Design,
And Rules as strict his labour'd Work confine,
As if the *Stagyrite*[5] o'erlook'd each Line.
Learn hence for Ancient *Rules* a just Esteem;
To copy *Nature* is to copy *Them*.
Some Beauties yet, no Precepts can declare,
For there's a *Happiness*[6] as well as *Care*.
Musick resembles *Poetry*, in each
Are *nameless Graces* which no Methods teach,
And which a *Master-Hand* alone can reach.
If, where the *Rules* not far enough extend,
(Since Rules were made but to promote their End)
Some Lucky LICENSE answers to the full
Th' Intent propos'd, *that License* is a *Rule*.
Thus *Pegasus*, a nearer way to take,
May boldly deviate from the common Track.
Great Wits sometimes may *gloriously offend*,
And *rise* to *Faults* true Criticks *dare not mend*;
From *vulgar Bounds* with *brave Disorder* part,
And *snatch* a *Grace* beyond the Reach of Art,
Which, without passing thro' the *Judgment*, gains
The *Heart*, and all its End *at once* attains.
In *Prospects*, thus, some *Objects* please our Eyes,
Which *out of* Nature's *common Order* rise,
The shapeless *Rock*, or hanging *Precipice*.
But tho' the *Ancients* thus their *Rules* invade,
(As *Kings* dispense with *Laws* Themselves have made)
Moderns, beware! Or if you must offend

2. As the earliest Greek literature, Homer's *Iliad* and *Odyssey* (ca. 8th c. B.C.E.) were considered the source of all subsequent poetry.
3. Hippocrene, a spring sacred to the Muses on Mt. Helicon, in central Greece.
4. Virgil (70–19 B.C.E.), born near Mantua (his full name was Publius Vergilius Maro). As the author of the greatest Latin epic, the *Aeneid*, he is often linked with Homer.
5. ARISTOTLE (384–322 B.C.E.), born in Stagira (in Macedonia). Later critics derived the "rules" for tragedy and epic from his *Poetics* (see above).
6. Good luck; felicity.

Against the *Precept*, ne'er transgress its *End*,
Let it be *seldom*, and *compell'd by Need*,
And have, at least, *Their Precedent* to plead.
The Critick else proceeds without Remorse,
Seizes your Fame, and puts his Laws in force.
I know there are,[7] to whose presumptuous Thoughts
Those *Freer Beauties*, ev'n in *Them*, seem Faults:[8]
Some Figures *monstrous* and *mis-shap'd* appear,
Consider'd *singly*, or beheld too *near*,
Which, but *proportion'd* to their *Light*, or *Place*,
Due Distance *reconciles* to Form and Grace.
A prudent Chief not always must display
His Pow'rs in *equal Ranks*, and *fair Array*,
But with th' *Occasion* and the *Place* comply,
Conceal his Force, nay seem sometimes to *Fly*.
Those oft are *Stratagems* which *Errors* seem,
Nor is it *Homer Nods,*[9] but *We* that *Dream*.
Still green with Bays[1] each *ancient* Altar stands,
Above the reach of *Sacrilegious* Hands,
Secure from *Flames*, from *Envy's* fiercer Rage,
Destructive *War*, and all-involving *Age*.
See, from *each Clime* the Learn'd their Incense bring;
Hear, in *all Tongues* consenting[2] *Pæans* ring!
In Praise so just, let ev'ry Voice be join'd,[3]
And fill the *Gen'ral Chorus* of *Mankind*!
Hail *Bards Triumphant*! born in *happier Days*;
Immortal Heirs of *Universal* Praise!
Whose Honours with Increase of Ages *grow*,
As Streams roll down, *enlarging* as they flow!
Nations *unborn* your mighty Names shall sound,
And Worlds applaud that must not yet be *found*!
Oh may some Spark of *your* Cœlestial Fire
The last, the meanest of your Sons inspire,
(That on weak Wings, from far, pursues your Flights;
Glows while he *reads*, but *trembles* as he *writes*)
To teach vain Wits a Science *little known*,
T' *admire* Superior Sense, and *doubt* their own!

Of all the Causes which conspire to blind
Man's erring Judgment, and misguide the Mind,
What the weak Head with strongest Byass[4] rules,
Is *Pride*, the *never-failing Vice of Fools*.
Whatever Nature has in *Worth* deny'd,
She gives in large Recruits[5] of *needful Pride*;
For as in *Bodies*, thus in *Souls*, we find
What wants in *Blood* and *Spirits*, swell'd with *Wind*;
Pride, where Wit fails, steps in to our Defence,

7. That is, I know there are those.
8. Pronounced "fawts."
9. Compare Horace, *Ars Poetica*, lines 358–59: "even . . . good Homer goes to sleep" (often translated "nods").
1. Laurels, associated with Apollo and thus with poetry.
2. In harmony.
3. Pronounced "jined."
4. Bias, a term from lawn bowling: the irregularity in the shape of the ball that causes it to swerve.
5. Supplies, troops, reinforcements.

And fills up all the *mighty Void* of *Sense*!
If once right Reason drives *that Cloud* away,
Truth breaks upon us with *resistless Day*;
Trust not your self; but your Defects to know,
Make use of ev'ry *Friend*—and ev'ry *Foe*.
 A *little Learning* is a dang'rous Thing;
Drink deep, or taste not the *Pierian*[6] Spring:
There *shallow Draughts* intoxicate the Brain,
And drinking *largely* sobers us again.
Fir'd at first Sight with what the *Muse* imparts,
In *fearless Youth* we tempt[7] the Heights of Arts,
While from the bounded *Level* of our Mind,
Short Views we take, nor see the *Lengths behind*,
But *more advanc'd*, behold with strange Surprize
New, distant Scenes of *endless* Science rise!
So pleas'd at first, the towring *Alps* we try,
Mount o'er the Vales, and seem to tread the Sky;
Th' Eternal Snows appear already past,
And the first *Clouds* and *Mountains* seem the last:
But *those attain'd*, we tremble to survey
The growing Labours of the lengthen'd Way,
Th' *increasing* Prospect *tires* our wandring Eyes,
Hills peep o'er Hills, and *Alps* on *Alps* arise!
 A perfect Judge will *read* each Work of Wit
With the same Spirit that its Author *writ*,
Survey the *Whole*, nor seek slight Faults to find,
Where *Nature moves*, and *Rapture warms* the Mind;
Nor lose, for that malignant dull Delight,
The *gen'rous Pleasure* to be charm'd with Wit.
But in such Lays[8] as neither *ebb*, nor *flow*,
Correctly cold, and *regularly low*,
That shunning Faults, one quiet *Tenour* keep;
We cannot *blame* indeed—but we may *sleep*.
In Wit, as Nature, what affects our Hearts
Is not th' Exactness of peculiar Parts;
'Tis not a *Lip*, or *Eye*, we Beauty call,
But the joint Force and full *Result* of *all*.
Thus when we view some well-proportion'd Dome,[9]
(The *World's* just Wonder, and ev'n *thine* O *Rome*!)
No single Parts unequally surprize;
All comes *united* to th' admiring Eyes;
No monstrous Height, or Breadth, or Length appear;
The *Whole* at once is *Bold*, and *Regular*.
 Whoever thinks a faultless Piece to see,
Thinks what ne'er was, nor is, nor e'er shall be.
In ev'ry Work regard the *Writer's End*,
Since none can compass more than they *Intend*;
And if the *Means* be just, the *Conduct* true,

6. Belonging to the Pierides, another name for the Muses (the spring is Hippocrene).
7. Attempt, dare.
8. Songs; narrative poems or ballads.
9. Specifically, the dome of St. Peter's Basilica in Rome (16th c.).

Applause, in spite of trivial Faults, is due.[1]
As Men of Breeding, sometimes Men of Wit,
T' avoid *great Errors*, must the *less* commit,
Neglect the Rules each *Verbal Critick* lays,
For *not* to know some Trifles, is a Praise.
Most Criticks, fond of some subservient Art,
Still make the *Whole* depend upon a *Part*,
They talk of *Principles*, but Notions prize,
And All to one lov'd Folly Sacrifice.
Once on a time, *La Mancha*'s Knight,[2] they say,
A certain *Bard* encountring on the Way,
Discours'd in Terms as just, with Looks as Sage,
As e'er cou'd *Dennis*,[3] of the *Grecian* Stage;
Concluding all were desp'rate Sots and Fools,
Who durst depart from *Aristotle*'s Rules.
Our Author, happy in a Judge so nice,[4]
Produc'd his Play, and beg'd the Knight's Advice,
Made him observe the *Subject* and the *Plot*,
The *Manners, Passions, Unities*,[5] what not?
All which, exact to *Rule* were brought about,
Were but a *Combate in the Lists*[6] left out.
What! Leave the Combate out? Exclaims the Knight;
Yes, or we must renounce the *Stagyrite*.
Not so by Heav'n (he answers in a Rage)
Knights, Squires, and Steeds, must enter on the Stage.
So vast a Throng the Stage can ne'er contain.
Then build a New, or act it in a Plain.
Thus Criticks, of less *Judgment* than *Caprice*,
Curious,[7] not *Knowing*, not *exact*, but *nice*,
Form *short Ideas*; and offend in *Arts*
(As most in *Manners*) by a *Love to Parts*.
Some to *Conceit*[8] alone their Taste confine,
And glitt'ring Thoughts struck out[9] at ev'ry Line;
Pleas'd with a Work where nothing's just or fit;
One *glaring Chaos* and *wild Heap* of *Wit*:
Poets like Painters, thus, unskill'd to trace
The *naked Nature* and the *living Grace*,
With *Gold* and *Jewels* cover ev'ry Part,
And hide with *Ornaments* their *Want of Art*.
True Wit is *Nature* to Advantage drest,
What oft was *Thought*, but ne'er so well *Exprest*,
Something, whose Truth convinc'd at Sight we find,
That gives us back the Image of our Mind:
As Shades more sweetly recommend the Light,

1. Compare John Dryden, "The Author's Apology for Heroic Poetry" (1677): " 'Tis malicious and unmannerly to snarl at the little lapses of a pen, from which Virgil himself stands not exempted."
2. Don Quixote, title character of the work by Miguel de Cervantes (1605, 1615); but Pope's story is taken from a spurious sequel to *Don Quixote* written by Don Alonzo Fernandez de Avellaneda (trans. 1705).
3. John Dennis (1657–1734), English critic and playwright.
4. Precise, overrefined.
5. The neoclassical unities (of action, time, and place) thought to govern drama; see PIERRE CORNEILLE, *Of the Three Unities*. (1660; above).
6. Field for jousting.
7. Particular, difficult to satisfy.
8. The extravagant use of similes and metaphors.
9. Produced by a stroke of invention.

So modest Plainness sets off sprightly Wit:
For *Works* may have more *Wit* than does 'em good,
As *Bodies* perish through Excess of *Blood*.[1]
Others for *Language* all their Care express,
And value *Books*, as Women *Men*, for *Dress*:
Their Praise is still—*The Stile is excellent*:
The *Sense*, they humbly take upon Content.[2]
Words are like *Leaves*; and where they most abound,
Much *Fruit* of *Sense* beneath is rarely found.
False Eloquence, like the *Prismatic Glass*,
Its gawdy Colours spreads on *ev'ry place;*[3]
The Face of Nature we no more Survey,
All glares *alike*, without *Distinction* gay:
But true *Expression*, like th' unchanging *Sun*,
Clears, and *improves* whate'er it shines upon,
It *gilds* all Objects, but it *alters* none.
Expression is the *Dress* of *Thought*, and still
Appears more *decent* as more *suitable*;
A vile Conceit in pompous Words exprest,
Is like a Clown in regal Purple drest;
For diff'rent *Styles* with diff'rent *Subjects* sort,
As several Garbs with Country, Town, and Court.
Some by *Old Words* to Fame have made Pretence;
Ancients in *Phrase*, meer Moderns in their *Sense*!
Such *labour'd Nothings*, in so *strange* a Style,
Amaze th'unlearn'd, and make the Learned *Smile*.
Unlucky, as *Fungoso*[4] in the Play,
These Sparks with aukward Vanity display
What the Fine Gentleman wore *Yesterday*!
And but so mimick ancient Wits at best,
As Apes our Grandsires in their *Doublets drest*.
In *Words*, as *Fashions*, the same Rule will hold;
Alike Fantastick, if *too New*, or *Old*;
Be not the *first* by whom the *New* are try'd,
Nor yet the *last* to lay the *Old* aside.
But most by *Numbers*[5] judge a Poet's Song,
And *smooth* or *rough*, with them, is *right* or *wrong*;
In the bright *Muse* tho' thousand *Charms* conspire,
Her *Voice* is all these tuneful Fools admire,
Who haunt *Parnassus* but to please their Ear,
Not mend their Minds; as some to *Church* repair,
Not for the *Doctrine*, but the *Musick* there.
These *Equal Syllables* alone require,
Tho' oft the Ear the *open Vowels* tire,[6]
While *Expletives*[7] their feeble Aid *do* join,

1. Standard medical practice of Pope's time included bleeding patients to reduce their "excess of blood."
2. Accept on authority.
3. An allusion to Isaac Newton's *Optics* (1703), which discusses the prism and spectrum.
4. A poor student in Ben Jonson's play *Every Man out of His Humour* (1599), who tries without success to keep up with the fashions.
5. Meters.
6. That is, when a word ending in a vowel is followed by a word beginning with one (e.g., "the open"). Throughout this passage, Pope exemplifies in his verse the fault or virtue discussed.
7. Words used to complete the number of feet needed in a line of verse without adding to the sense.

And ten low Words oft creep in one dull Line,
While they ring round the same *unvary'd Chimes*,
With sure *Returns* of still *expected Rhymes*.
Where-e'er you find *the cooling Western Breeze*,
In the next Line, it *whispers thro' the Trees*;
If *Chrystal Streams with pleasing Murmurs creep*,
The Reader's threaten'd (not in vain) with *Sleep*.
Then, at the *last*, and *only* Couplet fraught
With some *unmeaning* Thing they call a *Thought*,
A *needless Alexandrine*[8] ends the Song,
That like a wounded Snake, drags its slow length along.
Leave such to tune their own dull Rhimes, and know
What's *roundly smooth*, or *languishingly slow*;
And praise the *Easie Vigor* of a Line,
Where *Denham*'s Strength, and *Waller*'s Sweetness join.[9]
True Ease in Writing comes from Art, not Chance,
As those move easiest who have learn'd to dance.
'Tis not enough no Harshness gives Offence,
The *Sound* must seem an *Eccho* to the *Sense*.
Soft is the Strain when *Zephyr*[1] gently blows,
And the *smooth Stream* in *smoother Numbers* flows;
But when loud Surges lash the sounding Shore,
The *hoarse, rough Verse* shou'd like the *Torrent* roar.
When *Ajax*[2] strives, some Rock's vast Weight to throw,
The Line too *labours*, and the Words move *slow*;
Not so, when swift *Camilla*[3] scours the Plain,
Flies o'er th'unbending Corn, and skims along the Main.
Hear how *Timotheus'*[4] vary'd Lays surprize,
And bid Alternate Passions fall and rise!
While, at each Change, the Son of *Lybian Jove*[5]
Now *burns* with Glory, and then *melts* with Love;
Now his *fierce Eyes* with *sparkling Fury* glow;
Now *Sighs* steal out, and *Tears begin to flow*:
Persians and *Greeks* like *Turns of Nature*[6] found,
And the *World's Victor* stood subdu'd by *Sound*!
The Pow'r of Musick all our Hearts allow;
And what *Timotheus* was, is *Dryden* now.
Avoid *Extreams*; and shun the Fault of such,
Who still are pleas'd *too little*, or *too much*.
At ev'ry Trifle scorn to take Offence,
That always shows *Great Pride*, or *Little Sense*;
Those *Heads* as *Stomachs* are not sure the best
Which nauseate all, and nothing can digest.

8. A line of 12 syllables (rather than the usual 10), like line 357.
9. Pope, like Dryden before him, admired the English poets John Denham (1615–1669) and, especially, Edmund Waller (1606–1687) for having improved English versification (in particular, the heroic couplet, the form used in this poem).
1. The west wind; a gentle breeze.
2. A Greek hero in the *Iliad*, known for his great strength.
3. A woman warrior who fought against the Trojans in Italy. In *Aeneid* 7.808–11, Virgil describes her ability to skim over ears of wheat (i.e., "corn") and over the sea.
4. Greek poet (ca. 450–ca. 360 B.C.E.).
5. Alexander the Great (356–323 B.C.E.), who liked to claim that Zeus (identified with the Roman Jupiter) was his father. Priests of the celebrated oracle of Zeus Ammon in Siwa, north of the Libyan desert, greeted Alexander as the son of Zeus.
6. Alternations of feelings.

Yet let not each gay *Turn* thy Rapture move,
For Fools *Admire*, but Men of Sense *Approve*;[7]
As things seem *large* which we thro' *Mists* descry,
Dulness is ever apt to *Magnify*.
Some *foreign* Writers, some our *own* despise;
The *Ancients* only, or the *Moderns* prize:
(Thus *Wit*, like *Faith*, by each Man is apply'd
To *one small Sect*, and All are *damn'd beside*.)
Meanly they seek the Blessing to confine,
And force *that Sun* but on a *Part* to Shine;
Which not alone the *Southern Wit* sublimes,[8]
But ripens Spirits in cold *Northern Climes*;
Which from the first has shone on *Ages past*,
Enlights the *present*, and shall warm the *last*:
(Tho' *each* may feel *Increases* and *Decays*,
And see now *clearer* and now *darker Days*)
Regard not then if Wit be *Old* or *New*,
But blame the *False*, and value still the *True*.
Some ne'er advance a Judgment of their own,
But *catch* the *spreading Notion* of the Town;
They reason and conclude by *Precedent*,
And own *stale Nonsense* which they ne'er invent.
Some judge of Authors' *Names*, not *Works*, and then
Nor praise nor blame the *Writings*, but the *Men*.
Of all this *Servile Herd* the worst is He
That in *proud Dulness* joins with *Quality*,[9]
A constant Critick at the Great-man's Board,
To *fetch and carry* Nonsense for my Lord.
What *woful stuff* this Madrigal wou'd be,
In some starv'd Hackny Sonneteer,[1] or me?
But let a *Lord* once own the *happy Lines*,
How the *Wit brightens*! How the *Style refines*!
Before *his* sacred Name flies ev'ry Fault,
And each *exalted* Stanza *teems* with *Thought*!
The *Vulgar* thus through *Imitation* err;
As oft the *Learn'd* by being *Singular*;
So much they scorn the Crowd, that if the Throng
By *Chance* go right, they *purposely* go wrong;
So Schismatics[2] the *plain Believers* quit,
And are but damn'd for having *too much Wit*.
Some praise at Morning what they blame at Night;
But always think the *last* Opinion *right*.
A Muse by these is like a Mistress us'd,
This hour she's *idoliz'd*, the next *abus'd*,
While their weak Heads, like Towns unfortify'd,
'Twixt Sense and Nonsense daily change their Side.
Ask them the Cause; *They're wiser still*, they say;
And still to Morrow's wiser than to Day.
We think our *Fathers* Fools, so *wise* we grow;

7. Judge with discrimination (vs. wonder at without comprehension).
8. Raises up.
9. People of high rank.
1. Hireling poet.
2. Sectarians in religion.

Our *wiser Sons*, no doubt, will think *us* so.
Once *School-Divines*[3] this zealous Isle o'erspread;
Who knew most *Sentences*[4] was *deepest read*;
Faith, Gospel, All, seem'd made to be *disputed*,
And none had *Sense enough to be Confuted*.
Scotists and *Thomists*,[5] now, in Peace remain,
Amidst their *kindred Cobwebs* in *Duck-Lane*.[6]
If *Faith* it self has *diff'rent Dresses* worn,
What wonder *Modes* in *Wit* shou'd take their Turn?
Oft, leaving what is Natural and fit,
The *current Folly* proves the *ready Wit*,[7]
And Authors think their Reputation safe,
Which lives as long as *Fools* are pleas'd to *Laugh*.
  Some valuing those of their own *Side*, or *Mind*,
Still make themselves the measure of Mankind;
Fondly[8] we think we honour Merit then,
When we but praise *Our selves* in *Other Men*.
Parties in *Wit* attend on those of *State*,
And publick Faction doubles private Hate.
Pride, Malice, Folly, against *Dryden* rose,
In various Shapes of *Parsons, Criticks, Beaus*;[9]
But *Sense* surviv'd, when *merry Jests* were past;
For rising Merit will *buoy up* at last.
Might he return, and bless once more our Eyes,
New *Blackmores* and new *Milbourns*[1] must arise;
Nay shou'd great *Homer* lift his awful[2] Head,
Zoilus[3] again would start up from the Dead.
Envy will *Merit* as its *Shade* pursue,
But like a Shadow, proves the *Substance* true;
For envy'd Wit, like *Sol* Eclips'd, makes known
Th' *opposing Body's* Grossness, not its *own*.
When first that Sun too powerful Beams displays,
It draws up Vapours which obscure its Rays;
But ev'n those Clouds at last adorn its Way,
Reflect new Glories, and augment the Day.
  Be thou the *first* true Merit to befriend;
His Praise is lost, who stays till *All* commend;
Short is the Date, alas, of *Modern Rhymes*;
And 'tis but just to let 'em live *betimes*.[4]
No longer now that Golden Age appears,

3. Medieval theologians.
4. A reference to Peter Lombard's *Four Books of Sentences* (ca. 1145–51), which in a long series of questions presents the views of the fathers and doctors of the church on complex doctrinal matters; it became the standard theological text of the Middle Ages.
5. The two main schcols of medieval philosophy were the followers of Duns Scotus (ca. 1270–1308) and of THOMAS AQUINAS (1225–1274).
6. A London street where old books were sold.
7. Facile, clever expression.
8. Foolishly.
9. John Wilmot (1647–1680)9 second earl of Rochester, and George Villiers (1627–1687), second duke of Buckingham. "Parsons": these included Jeremy Collier (1650–1726), whose *Short View of the Immorality and Profaneness of the English Stage* (1698) targeted Dryden. "Criticks": these included Thomas Shadwell (ca. 1642–1692), an English dramatist and poet who savagely attacked Dryden in the 1680s.
1. Luke Milbourne (1649–1720), a clergyman whose *Notes on Dryden's Virgil* (1698) criticized the translation. Sir Richard Blackmore (1654–1729), physician and poet who criticized Dryden in *Satire against Wit* (1700).
2. Awe-inspiring.
3. A 4th-century B.C.E. philosopher and grammarian notorious for his bitter attacks on the *Iliad* and the *Odyssey*.
4. Before it is too late.

When *Patriarch-Wits* surviv'd a *thousand Years*;
Now Length of *Fame* (our *second* Life) is lost,
And bare Threescore is all ev'n That can boast:
Our Sons their Fathers' *failing Language* see,
And such as *Chaucer* is, shall *Dryden* be.[5]
So when the faithful *Pencil* has design'd
Some *bright Idea* of the Master's Mind,
Where a *new World* leaps out at his command,
And ready Nature waits upon his Hand;
When the ripe Colours *soften* and *unite*,
And sweetly *melt* into just Shade and Light,
When mellowing Years their full Perfection give,
And each Bold Figure just begins to *Live*;
The *treach'rous Colours* the fair Art betray,
And all the bright Creation fades away!
  Unhappy *Wit*, like most mistaken Things,
Attones not for the *Envy* which it brings.
In *Youth* alone its empty Praise we boast,
But soon the Short-liv'd Vanity is lost!
Like some fair *Flow'r* the early *Spring* supplies,
That gaily Blooms, but ev'n in blooming *Dies*.
What is this *Wit* which must our Cares employ?
The *Owner's Wife*, that *other Men* enjoy,
Then most our *Trouble* still when most *admir'd*,
And still the more we *give*, the more *requir'd*;
Whose Fame with *Pains* we guard, but lose with *Ease*,
Sure *some* to *vex*, but never *all* to *please*;
'Tis what the *Vicious fear*, the *Virtuous shun*;
By *Fools* 'tis *hated*, and by *Knaves undone*!
  If *Wit* so much from *Ign'rance* undergo,
Ah let not *Learning* too commence its Foe!
Of old, those met *Rewards* who cou'd *excel*,
And such were *Prais'd* who but *endeavour'd well*:
Tho' *Triumphs* were to *Gen'rals* only due,
Crowns were reserv'd to grace the *Soldiers* too.[6]
Now, they who reach *Parnassus'* lofty Crown,
Employ their Pains to spurn some others down;
And while Self-Love each jealous Writer rules,
Contending Wits become the *Sport of Fools*:
But still the *Worst* with most Regret commend,
For each *Ill Author* is as bad a *Friend*.
To what base Ends, and by what abject Ways,
Are Mortals urg'd thro' *Sacred*[7] *Lust of Praise*!
Ah ne'er so *dire* a *Thirst of Glory* boast,
Nor in the *Critick* let the *Man* be lost!
Good-Nature and *Good-Sense* must ever join;
To Err is *Humane*;[8] to Forgive, *Divine*.

5. Like others of his day, Pope believed that changes in the English language would eventually make Dryden's verse seem as distant and strange as Chaucer's.
6. At the time of the Roman general's triumph—a formal procession celebrating an important victory—various crowns were awarded to those of his soldiers who had won distinction.
7. Accursed.
8. Human.

But if in Noble Minds some Dregs remain,
Not yet purg'd off, of Spleen and sow'r Disdain,
Discharge that Rage on more Provoking Crimes,
Nor fear a Dearth in these Flagitious[9] Times.
No Pardon vile *Obscenity* should find,
Tho' *Wit* and *Art* conspire to move your Mind;
But *Dulness* with *Obscenity* must prove
As Shameful sure as *Impotence* in *Love*.
In the fat Age of Pleasure, Wealth, and Ease,
Sprung the rank Weed, and thriv'd with large Increase;
When *Love* was all an easie Monarch's[1] Care;
Seldom at *Council*, never in a *War*:
Jilts rul'd the State, and Statesmen *Farces* writ;
Nay *Wits* had *Pensions*, and *young Lords*[2] had *Wit*:
The Fair state panting at a *Courtier's Play*,
And not a Mask[3] went *un-improv'd* away:
The modest Fan was lifted up no more,
And Virgins *smil'd* at what they *blush'd* before—
The following Licence of a Foreign Reign[4]
Did all the Dregs of bold *Socinus*[5] drain;
Then Unbelieving Priests reform'd the Nation,
And taught more *Pleasant* Methods of Salvation;
Where Heav'ns Free Subjects might their *Rights* dispute,
Lest God himself shou'd seem too *Absolute*.
Pulpits their *Sacred Satire* learn'd to spare,
And Vice *admir'd*[6] to find a *Flatt'rer there*!
Encourag'd thus, Witt's *Titans*[7] brav'd the Skies,
And the Press groan'd with Licenc'd *Blasphemies*—
These Monsters, Criticks! with your Darts engage,
Here point your Thunder, and exhaust your Rage!
Yet shun their Fault, who, *Scandalously nice*,
Will needs *mistake* an Author *into Vice*;
All seems Infected that th' Infected spy,
As all looks yellow to the Jaundic'd Eye.[8]

LEARN then what MORALS Criticks ought to show,
For 'tis but *half a Judge's Task*, to *Know*.
'Tis not enough, Taste, Judgment, Learning, join;
In all you speak, let Truth and Candor[9] shine:
That not alone what to your *Sense* is due,
All may allow; but seek your *Friendship* too.
Be *silent* always when you *doubt* your Sense;

9. Extremely wicked, heinous.
1. Charles II (1630–1685).
2. These include George Villiers, John Wilmot, and Charles Sackville, sixth earl of Dorset (1638–1706). "Jilts": harlots, here Charles's mistresses. "Farces": Villiers, *The Rehearsal* (1671); Sir Charles Sedley, *The Mulberry Garden* (1668); and Sir George Etherege, *The Man of Mode* (1676).
3. Fashionable women often wore masks to the theater.
4. England's William III (1650–1702), whose policies increased toleration toward religious Nonconformists, came from the Netherlands.
5. Faustus Socinus (1539–1604), who developed a doctrine rejecting the divinity of Christ that was first espoused by his uncle, the Italian theologian Laelius Socinus (1525–1562).
6. Was amazed.
7. Giants born of Earth and Heaven, whom Zeus and the Olympian gods defeated in battle.
8. The Romans believed that to those suffering from jaundice (a yellow discoloration of the skin and the whites of the eyes), everything takes on a yellow tinge.
9. Impartiality.

And *speak*, tho' *sure*, with *seeming Diffidence*:
Some positive persisting Fops we know,
Who, if *once wrong*, will needs be *always so*;
But you, with Pleasure own your Errors past,
And make each Day a *Critick*[1] on the last.
'Tis not enough your Counsel still be *true*,
Blunt Truths more Mischief than *nice Falshoods* do;
Men must be *taught* as if you taught them *not*;
And Things *unknown* propos'd as Things *forgot*:
Without *Good Breeding, Truth* is disapprov'd;
That only makes *Superior* Sense *belov'd*.
Be Niggards of Advice on no Pretence;
For the *worst Avarice* is that of *Sense*:
With mean Complacence[2] ne'er betray your Trust,
Nor be so *Civil* as to prove *Unjust*;
Fear not the Anger of the Wise to raise;
Those best can *bear Reproof*, who *merit Praise*.
'Twere well, might Criticks still this Freedom take;
But *Appius*[3] reddens at each Word you speak,
And *stares, Tremendous*! with a *threatning Eye*,
Like some *fierce Tyrant* in *Old Tapestry*!
Fear most to tax an *Honourable* Fool,
Whose Right it is, *uncensur'd* to be dull;
Such without *Wit* are Poets when they please,
As without *Learning* they can take *Degrees*.[4]
Leave dang'rous *Truths* to unsuccessful *Satyrs*,[5]
And *Flattery* to fulsome *Dedicators*,
Whom, when they *Praise*, the World believes no more,
Than when they promise to give *Scribling* o'er.
'Tis best sometimes your Censure to restrain,
And *charitably* let the Dull be *vain*:
Your Silence there is better than your *Spite*,
For who can *rail* so long as they can *write*?
Still humming on, their drowzy Course they keep,
And *lash'd* so long, like *Tops*, are lash'd *asleep*.[6]
False Steps but help them to renew the Race,
As after *Stumbling*, Jades[7] will *mend* their Pace.
What Crouds of these, impenitently bold,
In *Sounds* and jingling *Syllables* grown old,
Still *run on* Poets in a raging Vein,
Ev'n to the Dregs and *Squeezings* of the *Brain*;
Strain out the last, dull droppings of their Sense,
And Rhyme with all the *Rage* of *Impotence*!
Such shameless *Bards* we have; and yet 'tis true,
There are as mad, abandon'd *Criticks* too.
The Bookful Blockhead, ignorantly read,
With *Loads* of *Learned Lumber* in his Head,

1. Critique of, commentary on.
2. Desire to please.
3. John Dennis; Appius, in his tragedy *Appius and Virginia* (1709), was highly sensitive to criticism. Dennis frequently used the word "tremendous."
4. Those in certain positions (e.g., privy councillors) could receive university degrees without fulfilling any requirements.
5. Satires.
6. When tops spin rapidly they "sleep," seeming not to move.
7. Worn-out horses.

With his own Tongue still edifies his Ears,
And always *List'ning to Himself* appears.
All Books he reads, and all he reads assails,
From *Dryden's Fables* down to *Durfey's Tales*.[8]
With *him*, most Authors steal their Works, or buy;
Garth[9] did not write his own *Dispensary*.
Name a new *Play*, and *he's* the Poet's *Friend*,
Nay show'd his Faults—but when wou'd Poets mend?
No Place so Sacred from such Fops is barr'd,
Nor is *Paul's Church* more safe than *Paul's Church-yard*:[1]
Nay, fly to *Altars; there* they'll talk you dead;
For *Fools* rush in where *Angels* fear to tread.
Distrustful *Sense* with modest Caution speaks;
It still *looks home*, and *short Excursions* makes;
But *ratling Nonsense* in full *Vollies* breaks;
And never shock'd, and never turn'd aside,
Bursts out, resistless, with a thundring Tyde!
But where's the Man, who Counsel *can* bestow,
Still *pleas'd* to *teach*, and yet not *proud* to *know*?
Unbiass'd, or[2] by *Favour* or by *Spite*;
Not *dully prepossest*, nor *blindly right*;
Tho' Learn'd, well-bred; and tho' well-bred, sincere;
Modestly bold, and Humanly severe?
Who to a *Friend* his Faults can freely show,
And gladly praise the Merit of a *Foe*?
Blest with a *Taste* exact, yet unconfin'd;
A *Knowledge* both of *Books* and *Humankind*;
Gen'rous Converse;[3] a *Soul* exempt from *Pride*;
And *Love to Praise*, with *Reason* on his Side?
Such once were *Criticks*, such the Happy *Few*,
Athens and *Rome* in better Ages knew.
The mighty *Stagyrite* first left the Shore,
Spread all his Sails, and durst the Deeps explore;
He steer'd securely, and discover'd far,
Led by the Light of the *Mæonian*[4] *Star*.
Poets, a *Race* long unconfin'd and free,
Still fond and proud of *Savage Liberty*,
Receiv'd his Laws,[5] and stood convinc'd 'twas fit
Who conquer'd *Nature*, shou'd preside o'er *Wit*.
Horace still charms with graceful Negligence,
And without Method *talks* us into Sense,
Will like a *Friend* familiarly convey
The *truest Notions* in the *easiest way*.[6]
He, who Supream in Judgment, as in Wit,
Might boldly censure, as he boldly writ,

8. *Tales Tragical and Comical* (1704), by Thomas D'Urfey (1653–1723). Dryden's *Fables: Fables, Ancient and Modern* (1700), a set of verse translations.
9. Sir Samuel Garth (1661–1719), later a friend of Pope's, was (wrongly) accused of falsely claiming authorship of the mock-heroic *The Dispensary* (1699).
1. Where booksellers had stalls.
2. Either.
3. Well-bred conversation.
4. Of Maeonia (region of Asia Minor), where Homer was said to have been born.
5. Rules for literary composition.
6. Least formal, highly accessible.

Yet *judg'd* with *Coolness* tho' he sung with *Fire*;
His *Precepts* teach but what his *Works* inspire.
Our Criticks take a contrary Extream,
They *judge* with *Fury*, but they *write* with *Fle'me*:[7]
Nor suffers *Horace* more in wrong *Translations*
By *Wits* than *Criticks* in as wrong *Quotations*.
See *Dionysius*[8] *Homer's* Thoughts refine,
And call new Beauties forth from ev'ry Line!
Fancy and Art in gay *Petronius*[9] please,
The *Scholar's Learning*, with the *Courtier's Ease*.
In grave *Quintilian's*[1] copious Work we find
The justest *Rules*, and clearest *Method* join'd;
Thus *useful Arms* in Magazines[2] we place,
All rang'd in *Order*, and dispos'd with *Grace*,
But less to please the Eye, than arm the Hand,
Still fit for Use, and ready at Command.
Thee, bold *Longinus*![3] all the Nine[4] inspire,
And bless *their Critick* with a *Poet's Fire*.
An ardent *Judge*, who Zealous in his Trust,
With *Warmth* gives Sentence, yet is always *Just*;
Whose *own Example* strengthens all his Laws,
And *Is himself* that great *Sublime* he draws.
Thus long succeeding Criticks justly reign'd,
License repress'd, and *useful Laws* ordain'd;
Learning and *Rome* alike in Empire grew
And *Arts* still *follow'd* where her *Eagles*[5] *flew*;
From the same Foes, at last, both felt their Doom,
And the same Age saw *Learning* fall, and *Rome*.
With *Tyranny*, then *Superstition* join'd,
As that the *Body*, this enslav'd the *Mind*;
Much was *Believ'd*, but little *understood*,
And to be *dull* was constru'd to be *good*;
A *second* Deluge Learning thus o'er-run,
And the *Monks* finish'd what the *Goths* begun.[6]
At length, *Erasmus*,[7] that *great, injur'd* Name,
(The *Glory* of the Priesthood, and the *Shame*!)
Stemm'd the *wild Torrent* of a *barb'rous Age*,
And drove those *Holy Vandals* off the Stage.
But see! each *Muse*, in *Leo's*[8] Golden Days,
Starts from her Trance, and trims her wither'd Bays!

7. Phlegm, thought to cause sluggishness and indifference; it was one of the four humors in early physiology.
8. Dionysius of Halicarnassus, Greek rhetor and historian active in Rome ca. 30–7 B.C.E.
9. Petronius Arbiter, the author of the *Satyricon* (1st c. C.E.); he may have been the courtier Petronius who was the judge on questions of taste at the court of Nero (emperor 54–68).
1. Roman rhetorician (ca. 30/35–100 C.E.); his "copious work" is the 12-volume *Institutio Oratoria* (see above).
2. Storehouses.
3. Greek rhetorican (1st c. C.E.), to whom the treatise *On Sublimity* is attributed (see above).
4. The 9 Muses.
5. Emblems on the Roman army's banners.
6. That is, the medieval theologians put the finishing touches on the damage done to learning by the Goths and Vandals, the Germanic peoples who had earlier sacked Rome.
7. Dutch scholar and philosopher (1466–1536), author of *The Praise of Folly*, a humanist satire on the abuses of learning. He was "the glory of the priesthood" because of his erudition and goodness, and its "shame" in that he was persecuted.
8. Pope Leo X (1475–1521), a patron of learning and the arts during the Italian Renaissance.

Rome's ancient *Genius*,[9] o'er its *Ruins* spread,
Shakes off the *Dust*, and rears his rev'rend Head!
Then *Sculpture* and her *Sister-Arts* revive;
Stones leap'd to *Form*, and *Rocks* began to *live*;
With *sweeter Notes* each *rising Temple* rung;
A *Raphael* painted, and a *Vida*[1] sung!
Immortal *Vida*! on whose honour'd Brow
The Poet's *Bays* and Critick's *Ivy*[2] grow:
Cremona[3] now shall ever boast thy Name,
As next in Place to *Mantua*, next in Fame.
But soon by Impious Arms from *Latium*[4] chas'd,
Their *ancient Bounds* the banish'd Muses past;
Thence Arts o'er all the *Northern World* advance;
But *Critic Learning* flourish'd most in *France*.
The *Rules*, a Nation born to serve, obeys,
And *Boileau*[5] still in Right of *Horace* sways.
But *we*, brave *Britons, Foreign Laws* despis'd,
And kept *unconquer'd*, and *unciviliz'd*,
Fierce for the *Liberties of Wit*, and bold,
We still defy'd the *Romans*, as *of old*.
Yet *some* there were, among the *sounder Few*
Of those who *less presum'd*, and *better knew*,
Who durst assert the *juster Ancient Cause*,
And here *restor'd* Wit's *Fundamental Laws*.
Such was the Muse, whose Rules and Practice tell,
Nature's chief Master-piece is writing well.[6]
Such was *Roscomon*[7]—not more *learn'd* than *good*,
With Manners gen'rous as his Noble Blood;
To him the Wit of *Greece* and *Rome* was known,
And ev'ry Author's *Merit*, but his own.
Such late was *Walsh*,[8]—the Muse's Judge and Friend,
Who justly knew to blame or to commend;
To Failings *mild*, but *zealous* for Desert;
The *clearest Head*, and the *sincerest Heart*.
This humble Praise, lamented *Shade*! receive,
This Praise at least a grateful Muse may give!
The Muse, whose early Voice you taught to Sing,
Prescrib'd her Heights, and prun'd her tender Wing,
(Her Guide now lost) no more attempts to *rise*,
But in low Numbers short Excursions tries:
Content, if hence th' Unlearn'd their Wants may view,
The Learn'd reflect on what before they knew:
Careless of *Censure*, nor too fond of *Fame*,

9. Guardian or protective spirit of a place.
1. Marco Girolamo Vida (ca. 1480–1566), Italian poet who wrote in Latin. Raphael: Raffaello Santi (1483–1520), Italian painter.
2. Symbol of poetry and learning.
3. City in northern Italy.
4. Italy. Rome was sacked by Hapsburg mercenaries in 1527; Pope suggests that learning then fled to other parts of Europe, especially France.
5. Nicolas Boileau (1636–1711), French critic and poet; his works include the poem *L'Art poétique* (1674).
6. Quoted from the *Essay on Poetry* (1682), by Pope's friend and supporter John Sheffield (1648–1721).
7. Wentworth Dillon (ca. 1633–1685), fourth earl of Roscommon, poet and critic; author of the *Essay on Translated Verse* (1684).
8. William Walsh (1663–1708), whom Dryden praised as "the best critic of our nation"; he was Pope's friend and mentor.

Still pleas'd to *praise*, yet not afraid to *blame*,
Averse alike to *Flatter*, or *Offend*,
Not *free* from Faults, nor yet too vain to *mend*.

1711

SAMUEL JOHNSON
1709–1784

As countless anecdotes attest, Samuel Johnson was cantankerous and dogmatic. He inveighed against the philosopher George Berkeley's (1685–1753) apparent denial of the reality of the external world by kicking a stone and declaring, "I refute him *thus*." And he coined many mordant aphorisms, such as "The road to hell is paved with good intentions" and "Patriotism is the last refuge of a scoundrel." Theatrical, deliberately provocative, and beloved by many friends and admired by fellow writers, Johnson is one of the most influential critics in English literary history. "The best part of every author," Johnson affirmed, "is in general to be found in his book," and this is true in his own case. Though he often chastised himself for indolence, fearful that salvation would be denied to him because he was not fully using his great gifts, he was in fact astonishingly productive, and in many genres. His literary labors include a monumental *Dictionary of the English Language*, a comprehensive edition of Shakespeare, and the *Lives of the English Poets*, a set of insightful, vividly written biographical and literary portraits of seventeenth- and eighteenth-century authors.

Johnson was born at Lichfield, Staffordshire, a town about 100 miles northwest of London. His father was a bookseller, and his education consisted largely of the volumes in his father's bookshop and what was "whipped" into him by the master of the grammar school in Lichfield. He attended Pembroke College at Oxford for only a year, leaving in December 1729 because he lacked the funds to continue. At Oxford, he later recounted, "I was miserably poor, and I thought to fight my way by my literature and my wit"; the fight, continuing in later years, would leave him in poverty for most of his life.

Johnson was an intense, discerning reader; as the economist Adam Smith recalled, "Johnson knew more books than any man alive." While at Oxford, he pored over the popular devotional tract *A Serious Call to a Devout and Holy Life* (1729), by the schoolmaster and minister William Law. He termed Law's book "the finest piece of hortatory theology in any language," and it is the foundation for the prayers and meditations that he composed later in his life.

In July 1735 Johnson married Elizabeth Jervis Porter, a forty-six-year-old widow and mother of three children. With money from her, Johnson opened a school in Edial, near Lichfield, in 1736. One of his students was David Garrick, who became a poet, essayist, and acclaimed actor. While there, Johnson worked on an historical tragedy, *Irene*, which recounts the story of the love of Sultan Mahomet for the lovely Irene, a Christian slave captured in Constantinople. (The play was not performed until 1749, in a production that Garrick organized.) The school soon proved a failure, however, in part because Johnson lacked the credential of a university degree.

In 1737 Johnson and Garrick traveled to London; with a population between 650,000 and 700,000, it had become the largest city in Europe. Johnson found it captivating and later famously professed: "Why, Sir, you find no man, at all intellectual, who is willing to leave London. No, Sir, when a man is tired of London, he is tired of life; for there is in London all that life can afford." Once settled there, he began his association with the *Gentleman's Magazine*, contributing to it not only prose and poetry but also, from 1741 to 1744, a series of speeches purporting to represent debates in the House of Commons: he re-created them, relying solely on notes and reports.

Johnson was working on and planning larger projects as well. In 1745 he wrote "Miscellaneous Observations on the Tragedy of Macbeth," along with a proposal for an edition of Shakespeare; in the following year, he outlined his "Plan of a Dictionary of the English Language." His major prose publication of this period was *An Account of the Life of Mr. Richard Savage* (1744), a book that details the trials of a failed poet whom Johnson knew and the tribulations of Grub Street, the address of many literary hacks and desperate writers. In verse his central achievement was "The Vanity of Human Wishes," published in 1749. This solemn, disquieting rumination on the futility of worldly hopes and endeavors was the first composition that Johnson issued under his own name.

In the 1750s Johnson wrote many periodical essays. The best of this work appeared in *The Rambler*, which was published twice weekly from March 1750 to March 1752. The twentieth-century critic Walter Jackson Bate has described these pieces as "saturated with thought to an extent unexceeded by any other writer of English prose since Francis Bacon." Johnson's wife Elizabeth told him at the time: "I thought very well of you before this; but I did not imagine you could have written any thing equal to this." She died on March 17, 1752, three days after the publication of its last number. Johnson also contributed essays to his friend John Hawkesworth's periodical *The Adventurer*; and from 1758 to 1760, he wrote yet another series of essays, titled *The Idler*, which were published in a weekly newspaper, *The Universal Chronicle*. But Johnson's greatest accomplishment of the decade was *A Dictionary of the English Language*, published in two large folio volumes in April 1755. Nine years in the making, and compiled by Johnson and six assistants, it consists of 40,000 defined words and 114,000 quotations that illustrate the meanings.

In one week's time in January 1759, Johnson wrote his only long fictional work, *Rasselas*, so that he could pay for his mother's funeral and settle her debts. Three years later he received from King George III an annual pension of 300 pounds, winning at last a measure of economic security. Soon after, he met the Scotsman James Boswell, a twenty-two-year-old lawyer less interested in law than in literature and politics. Boswell cultivated Johnson's friendship; watched him in action at literary clubs with Adam Smith, the painter Joshua Reynolds, EDMUND BURKE, and other luminaries; sparred with him in conversation; and gathered facts and anecdotes about him. Boswell made Johnson the subject of what is often called the greatest biography in English, *The Life of Samuel Johnson, LL.D.* (1791).

Johnson's eight-volume edition of Shakespeare was published in October 1765. The much-delayed work was flawed: Johnson neither performed the complete collation of texts he had promised nor examined carefully the sources that Shakespeare had drawn on. And while he ignored the sonnets and poems, he (like the Romantic critics) treats the plays not as works for the stage but as texts to be read. Nonetheless, the preface—one of our selections—and the many interpretive notes amount to a compelling assessment. Johnson celebrates Shakespeare's gifts in portraying character and revealing truths about human nature and, more important, defends the playwright against charges of violating the dramatic unities of time and place and improperly mixing the genres of tragedy and comedy. Johnson was not the first to propose that authors be granted freedom to depart from classical rules and prescriptions for literary composition, but his authority and formidable style gave this position its irresistible legitimacy. SAMUEL TAYLOR COLERIDGE, William Hazlitt, and other critics in the early 1800s balked at (even as they oversimplified) Johnson's neoclassical principles and disputed his evaluations of authors, yet his support for rule-breaking innovation, in the preface to Shakespeare and elsewhere, helped prepare the literary and cultural ground for the Romantic revolution.

In 1777 Johnson, then sixty-seven, was approached by London booksellers to contribute brief prefaces to a multivolume edition of English poets. Though the original plan was scaled back (instead of including all reputable poets from Chaucer on, the survey began in the seventeenth century with Cowley), Johnson did much more than required, producing in all about 400,000 words of biographical and interpretive text on the fifty-two poets (all male). Each preface follows a three-part plan, as Johnson recounts the author's biography, summarizes the main features of his character, and critically examines the writings; the essays on Cowley, Milton, DRYDEN, POPE, and ADDISON expanded into panoramic studies of the writer's life and works.

The *Lives of the English Poets* (1783) is not a grand act of personal canon making. While Johnson proposed several additions, the choices generally were not his own. He believed in an English literary canon—one that surpassed the literatures of other nations—but that canon could not be determined by any single critic. Unlike such modern critics as T. S. ELIOT, F. R. Leavis, and HAROLD BLOOM, who seek through robust arguments to reorder literary rankings that they view as dated and objectionable, Johnson found the test of time decisive. As he explained in the preface to *Shakespeare*, "What has been longest known has been most considered, and what is most considered is best understood."

For Johnson, the best contemporary literature resembles the great literature of the past in its fidelity to the facts of unchanging human nature and in its concern for moral instruction—for guidance in how best to live (that is, how best to bear life's pain). "Nothing can please many," he wrote, "and please long, but just representations of general nature." Thus in our selection from *Rasselas* Johnson emphasizes that "the business of the poet . . . is to examine, not the individual, but the species; to remark general properties and large appearances." "Great thoughts," he observes in the *Life of Cowley* (our final selection), "are always general." Such an appeal to shared values does not entirely preclude literary originality. As "On Fiction," our selection from *The Rambler*, indicates, Johnson could accept the emerging genre of the novel as long as its practitioners stayed alert to their moral duty to readers. And often in his criticism he commends poets for their capacity to delight or surprise us, for their powers of verbal invention. But by originality, Johnson meant what was new and unexpected *and* deeply recognizable—the refreshed, reawakened expression of truths with which readers would already be familiar.

Johnson proposed writing a "History of Criticism as it relates to judging of authours, from Aristotle to the present age," but he never undertook this daunting project; his general attitude toward critics and criticism must be pieced together from essays, letters, and parts of the preface to Shakespeare and the *Lives of the English Poets*. In *Rambler* 92, Johnson comes as close as he does anywhere to defining the work of the critic, stressing "principles," "rational deduction," and "science" and concluding: "Criticism reduces those regions of literature under the dominion of science, which have hitherto known only the anarchy of ignorance, the caprices of fancy, and the tyranny of prescription." Yet on this topic, as so often in his writing, Johnson calls attention to facets of literary experience that undercut the very positions he elsewhere advocates: he is often his sharpest, most cogent critic. In the preface to *Shakespeare*, he readily acknowledges the limitations of "the rules of criticism": "there is always an appeal open from criticism to nature." Generic categories and literary conventions matter; critics must consider how well or badly an author abides by them. But historical context, Johnson realizes, must be considered as well; as he explains in his *Life of Dryden*, "That which is easy at one time was difficult at another." Thus even such a highly principled critic could contend, in his *Life of Pope*, that we err when we "judge by principles rather than perception."

Johnson possessed a strong sense of the power and responsibility of writers; as he emphasizes in *Rambler* 4, novelists must use their talents to correct error and teach good conduct: they should not describe persons and situations—however true-to-life these might be—that could corrupt the minds of readers, particularly the young and inexperienced. The poet has an equal burden. Offended by the mixture of sacred and profane elements in Milton's pastoral elegy "Lycidas," Johnson calls the poem vulgar and disgusting, indecent and impious. This assault on "Lycidas" is notorious, yet it is significant less for the stridency of Johnson's judgment than for the strength of his response, the intensity of his experience as a reader.

The motions of Johnson's mind are more supple, balanced (if precariously at times), and even contradictory than might be predicted of a voice that is so confident and proud. We should heed his performance as a writer—the behavior of his language, the turns and tones of his subtle and complex sentences and paragraphs—in order to appreciate him fully. The final two paragraphs of the *Life of Cowley*, in which Johnson sums up the achievements of the metaphysical poets after having criticized them, illustrate his flexibility of mind. For modern readers, Johnson's style and point of view may require some getting accustomed to. But as MATTHEW ARNOLD concluded ("Johnson's *Lives*," 1878) in a formulation still pertinent today: "The more we study Johnson, the higher will be our esteem for the power of his mind, the width of his interests, the largeness of his knowledge, the freshness, fearlessness, and strength of his judgments."

BIBLIOGRAPHY

The standard edition has been *The Works of Samuel Johnson* (11 vols., 1825; reprinted in 1970 as *Dr. Johnson's Works*). It is being superseded by *The Yale Edition of the Works of Samuel Johnson* (13 vols. to date, 1958–). Other valuable editions of Johnson's works include *The Lives of the English Poets*, edited by George Birkbeck Hill (3 vols., 1905); *Johnson's "Lives of the Poets": A Selection*, edited by J. P. Hardy (1971); and *The Life of Richard Savage*, edited by Clarence Tracy (1971). *The Letters of Samuel Johnson*, edited by Bruce Redford (5 vols., 1992–94), known as the Hyde Edition, is an indispensable resource. *The Complete English Poems*, edited by J. D. Fleeman (1971), is a well-edited collection. The best one-volume selection of Johnson's poetry and prose is *Samuel Johnson*, edited by Donald Greene (1984). On Johnson's critical outlook, see *The Critical Opinions of Samuel Johnson*, a topical anthology compiled by Joseph Epes Brown (1926).

The points of departure for biography are James Boswell, *The Journal of a Tour to the Hebrides* (1785) and *The Life of Samuel Johnson, LL.D.* (1791). Of the many editions of these works—often published together—the best, with detailed notes, is by George Birkbeck Hill, revised and enlarged by L. F. Powell (6 vols., 1934–50, 1964). There are a number of excellent modern biographies: James L. Clifford, *Young Sam* [or *Samuel*] *Johnson* (1955), and his *Dictionary Johnson: Samuel Johnson's Middle Years* (1979); Walter Jackson Bate, *Samuel Johnson* (1977), which includes expert commentary on Johnson's writings; Thomas Kaminski, *The Early Career of Samuel Johnson* (1987); John Wain, *Samuel Johnson* (rev. ed., 1988), a vivid portrait of Johnson as a literary professional; Robert DeMaria Jr., *The Life of Samuel Johnson: A Critical Biography* (1993), a first-rate survey of Johnson's literary career; Richard Holmes, *Dr. Johnson and Mr. Savage* (1993); and Lawrence I. Lipking, *Samuel Johnson: The Life of an Author* (1998). Donald Greene, *Samuel Johnson* (rev. ed., 1989), offers a fine briefer treatment. Also useful are Norman Page, *A Dr. Johnson Chronology* (1990), and Pat Rogers, *The Samuel Johnson Encyclopedia* (1996).

For a range of critical opinion, see Walter Jackson Bate, *The Achievement of Samuel Johnson* (1958); Paul Fussell, *Samuel Johnson and the Life of Writing* (1971), filled with sharp perceptions about Johnson's rhetoric and relation to his readers; and Thomas Reinert, *Regulating Confusion: Samuel Johnson and the Crowd* (1996), which explores Johnson's attitudes toward the crowd, the city, and urban culture. Early critical reception is collected in *Johnson: The Critical Heritage*, edited by James T.

Boulton (1971). Collections of criticism include *Samuel Johnson: New Critical Essays*, edited by Isobel Grundy (1984); *Johnson and His Age*, edited by James Engell (1984); and *Johnson after Two Hundred Years*, edited by Paul J. Korshin (1986).

On Johnson's literary criticism, see Jean H. Hagstrum, *Samuel Johnson's Literary Criticism* (1952), a good overview of Johnson's attitudes toward nature, the sublime, wit, and other key topics; Leopold Damrosch Jr., *The Uses of Johnson's Criticism* (1976); Morris R. Brownell, *Samuel Johnson's Attitude to the Arts* (1989), which astutely examines Johnson's positions on music, art, and architecture; Steven Lynn, *Samuel Johnson after Deconstruction: Rhetoric and "The Rambler"* (1992), with interesting comparisons between Johnson and Harold Bloom, Jacques Derrida, and other contemporary theorists; Charles Hinnant, *"Steel for the Mind": Samuel Johnson and Critical Discourse* (1994), which relates Johnson's work to recent debates in literary theory; and Robert DeMaria Jr., *Samuel Johnson and the Life of Reading* (1997). Examinations of Johnson's critical work on Shakespeare include G. F. Parker, *Johnson's Shakespeare* (1989), offering cogent analysis of responses to Johnson by Romantic poets and critics, and Edward Tomarken, *Samuel Johnson on Shakespeare: The Discipline of Criticism* (1991). On Johnson as biographer of poets, consult Robert Folkenflik, *Samuel Johnson, Biographer* (1978); Martin Maner, *The Philosophical Biographer: Doubt and Dialectic in Johnson's "Lives of the Poets"* (1988); and Catherine Neal Parke, *Samuel Johnson and Biographical Thinking* (1991).

The standard bibliography is William P. Courtney and David Nichol Smith, *A Bibliography of Samuel Johnson* (1915). It is supplemented by R. W. Chapman and Allen T. Hazen, "Johnsonian Bibliography: A Supplement to Courtney," in *Oxford Bibliographical Society, Proceedings and Papers*, vol. 5, pt. 3 (1938). James L. Clifford and Donald J. Greene, *Samuel Johnson: A Survey and Bibliography of Critical Studies* (1970), contains 4,000 items. See also Donald Greene and John A. Vance, *A Bibliography of Johnsonian Studies, 1970–1985* (1987).

The Rambler, No. 4

[*On Fiction*]

Simul et jucunda et idonea dicere vitae.[1]

—Horace, ARS POETICA, 1.334.

And join both profit and delight in one.

—Creech.[2]

The works of fiction, with which the present generation seems more particularly delighted,[3] are such as exhibit life in its true state, diversified only by accidents that daily happen in the world, and influenced by passions and qualities which are really to be found in conversing with mankind.

This kind of writing may be termed not improperly the comedy of romance,[4] and is to be conducted nearly by the rules of comic poetry. Its province is to bring about natural events by easy means, and to keep up curiosity without the help of wonder: it is therefore precluded from the

1. "To speak of life both agreeably and appropriately" (Latin). HORACE (65–8 B.C.E.), Roman poet; for the *Ars Poetica* (Art of Poetry), see above.
2. Thomas Creech (1659–1700), English classical scholar. Here he translates the epigraph above.
3. Possibly Tobias Smollett's *Roderick Random* (1748) and Henry Fielding's *Tom Jones* (1749).
4. An entertaining story of love and adventure, which includes elements of fantasy and myth.

machines and expedients of the heroic romance, and can neither employ giants to snatch away a lady from the nuptial rites, nor knights to bring her back from captivity; it can neither bewilder its personages in desarts,[5] nor lodge them in imaginary castles.

I remember a remark made by Scaliger upon Pontanus,[6] that all his writings are filled with the same images; and that if you take from him his lillies and his roses, his satyrs and his dryads,[7] he will have nothing left that can be called poetry. In like manner, almost all the fictions of the last age will vanish, if you deprive them of a hermit and a wood, a battle and a shipwreck.

Why this wild strain of imagination found reception so long, in polite and learned ages, it is not easy to conceive; but we cannot wonder that, while readers could be procured, the authors were willing to continue it: for when a man had by practice gained some fluency of language, he had no further care than to retire to his closet, let loose his invention, and heat his mind with incredibilities;[8] a book was thus produced without fear of criticism, without the toil of study, without knowledge of nature, or acquaintance with life.

The task of our present writers is very different; it requires, together with that learning which is to be gained from books, that experience which can never be attained by solitary diligence, but must arise from general converse, and accurate observation of the living world. Their performances have, as Horace expresses it, *plus oneris quantum veniae minus*,[9] little indulgence, and therefore more difficulty. They are engaged in portraits of which every one knows the original, and can detect any deviation from exactness of resemblance. Other writings are safe, except from the malice of learning, but these are in danger from every common reader; as the slipper ill executed was censured by a shoemaker who happened to stop in his way at the Venus of Apelles.[1]

But the fear of not being approved as just copyers of human manners, is not the most important concern that an author of this sort ought to have before him. These books are written chiefly to the young, the ignorant, and the idle, to whom they serve as lectures of conduct, and introductions into life. They are the entertainment of minds unfurnished with ideas, and therefore easily susceptible of impressions; not fixed by principles, and therefore easily following the current of fancy; not informed by experience, and consequently open to every false suggestion and partial account.

That the highest degree of reverence should be paid to youth, and that nothing indecent should be suffered to approach their eyes or ears; are precepts extorted by sense and virtue from an ancient writer,[2] by no means eminent for chastity of thought. The same kind, tho' not the same degree of caution, is required in every thing which is laid before them, to secure them from unjust prejudices, perverse opinions, and incongruous combinations of images.

5. Deserts.
6. Jovanius Pontanus (1426–1503), Italian poet. The remark was by Julius Caesar Scaliger, an Italian-born French scholar (1484–1558), in his *Poetics* 5.4.
7. In classical mythology, wood nymphs. "Satyrs": goatlike sylvan deities.
8. Things that cannot be believed. "Closet": "a small room of privacy and retirement" (Johnson's *Dictionary*).
9. Slightly misquoted from Horace, *Epistles* 2.1.170 (translated by Johnson).
1. Greek painter (4th c. B.C.E.). The story of the shoemaker correcting the artist's representation comes from the Roman writer Pliny the Elder (23/4–79 C.E.), *Natural History* 35.84.
2. Juvenal (ca. 55–ca. 140 C.E.), Roman poet; see *Satire* 14.

In the romances formerly written, every transaction and sentiment was so remote from all that passes among men, that the reader was in very little danger of making any applications to himself; the virtues and crimes were equally beyond his sphere of activity; and he amused himself with heroes and with traitors, deliverers and persecutors, as with beings of another species, whose actions were regulated upon motives of their own, and who had neither faults nor excellencies in common with himself.

But when an adventurer is levelled with the rest of the world, and acts in such scenes of the universal drama, as may be the lot of any other man; young spectators fix their eyes upon him with closer attention, and hope by observing his behavior and success to regulate their own practices, when they shall be engaged in the like part.

For this reason these familiar histories may perhaps be made of greater use than the solemnities of professed morality, and convey the knowledge of vice and virtue with more efficacy than axioms and definitions. But if the power of example is so great, as to take possession of the memory by a kind of violence, and produce effects almost without the intervention of the will, care ought to be taken that, when the choice is unrestrained, the best examples only should be exhibited; and that which is likely to operate so strongly, should not be mischievous or uncertain in its effects.

The chief advantage which these fictions have over real life is, that their authors are at liberty, tho' not to invent, yet to select objects, and to cull from the mass of mankind, those individuals upon which the attention ought most to be employ'd; as a diamond, though it cannot be made, may be polished by art, and placed in such a situation, as to display that lustre which before was buried among common stones.

It is justly considered as the greatest excellency of art, to imitate nature; but it is necessary to distinguish those parts of nature, which are most proper for imitation: greater care is still required in representing life, which is so often discoloured by passion, or deformed by wickedness. If the world be promiscuously[3] described, I cannot see of what use it can be to read the account; or why it may not be as safe to turn the eye immediately upon mankind, as upon a mirror which shows all that presents itself without discrimination.

It is therefore not a sufficient vindication of a character, that it is drawn as it appears, for many characters ought never to be drawn; nor of a narrative, that the train of events is agreeable to observation and experience, for that observation which is called knowledge of the world, will be found much more frequently to make men cunning than good. The purpose of these writings is surely not only to show mankind, but to provide that they may be seen hereafter with less hazard; to teach the means of avoiding the snares which are laid by Treachery for Innocence, without infusing any wish for that superiority with which the betrayer flatters his vanity; to give the power of counteracting fraud, without the temptation to practise it; to initiate youth by mock encounters in the art of necessary defence, and to increase prudence without impairing virtue.

Many writers, for the sake of following nature, so mingle good and bad qualities in their principal personages, that they are both equally conspicu-

3. In a mixed, disorderly fashion.

ous; and as we accompany them through their adventures with delight, and are led by degrees to interest ourselves in their favour, we lose the abhorrence of their faults, because they do not hinder our pleasure, or, perhaps, regard them with some kindness for being united with so much merit.

There have been men indeed splendidly wicked, whose endowments threw a brightness on their crimes, and whom scarce any villainy made perfectly detestable, because they never could be wholly divested of their excellencies; but such have been in all ages the great corrupters of the world, and their resemblance ought no more to be preserved, than the art of murdering without pain.

Some have advanced, without due attention to the consequences of this notion, that certain virtues have their correspondent faults, and therefore that to exhibit either apart is to deviate from probability. Thus men are observed by Swift to be "grateful in the same degree as they are resentful."[4] This principle, with others of the same kind, supposes man to act from a brute impulse, and persue a certain degree of inclination, without any choice of the object; for, otherwise, though it should be allowed that gratitude and resentment arise from the same constitution of the passions, it follows not that they will be equally indulged when reason is consulted; yet unless that consequence be admitted, this sagacious maxim becomes an empty sound, without any relation to practice or to life.

Nor is it evident, that even the first motions to these effects are always in the same proportion. For pride, which produces quickness of resentment, will obstruct gratitude, by unwillingness to admit that inferiority which obligation implies; and it is very unlikely, that he who cannot think he receives a favour will acknowledge or repay it.

It is of the utmost importance to mankind, that positions of this tendency should be laid open and confuted; for while men consider good and evil as springing from the same root, they will spare the one for the sake of the other, and in judging, if not of others at least of themselves, will be apt to estimate their virtues by their vices. To this fatal error all those will contribute, who confound the colours of right and wrong, and instead of helping to settle their boundaries, mix them with so much art, that no common mind is able to disunite them.

In narratives, where historical veracity has no place, I cannot discover why there should not be exhibited the most perfect idea of virtue; of virtue not angelical, nor above probability, for what we cannot credit we shall never imitate, but the highest and purest that humanity can reach, which, exercised in such trials as the various revolutions of things shall bring upon it, may, by conquering some calamities, and enduring others, teach us what we may hope, and what we can perform. Vice, for vice is necessary to be shewn, should always disgust; nor should the graces of gaiety, or the dignity of courage, be so united with it, as to reconcile it to the mind. Wherever it appears, it should raise hatred by the malignity of its practices, and contempt by the meanness of its stratagems; for while it is supported by either parts or spirit, it will be seldom heartily abhorred. The Roman tyrant[5] was content to be

4. These are the words of the English poet and critic ALEXANDER POPE (1688–1744), not the English satirist and poet Jonathan Swift (1667–1745). The contemporary source is the Swift-Pope *Miscellanies* 2 (1727): 354. "Grateful": pleasing, agreeable.

5. The emperor Gaius Julius Caesar Germanicus (12–41 C.E.), known as "Caligula."

hated, if he was but feared; and there are thousands of the readers of romances willing to be thought wicked, if they may be allowed to be wits. It is therefore to be steadily inculcated, that virtue is the highest proof of understanding, and the only solid basis of greatness; and that vice is the natural consequence of narrow thoughts, that it begins in mistake, and ends in ignominy.

1750

From The History of Rasselas, Prince of Abyssinia

Chapter X.

Imlac's History Continued. A Dissertation upon Poetry

"Wherever I[1] went, I found that Poetry was considered as the highest learning, and regarded with a veneration somewhat approaching to that which man would pay to the Angelick Nature. And it yet fills me with wonder, that, in almost all countries, the most ancient poets are considered as the best: whether it be that every other kind of knowledge is an acquisition gradually attained, and poetry is a gift conferred at once; or that the first poetry of every nation surprised them as a novelty, and retained the credit by consent which it received by accident at first: or whether, as the province of poetry is to describe. Nature and Passion, which are always the same, the first writers took possession of the most striking objects for description, and the most probable occurrences for fiction, and left nothing to those that followed them, but transcription of the same events, and new combinations of the same images. Whatever be the reason, it is commonly observed that the early writers are in possession of nature, and their followers of art: that the first excel in strength and invention, and the latter in elegance and refinement.[2]

"I was desirous to add my name to this illustrious fraternity. I read all the poets of Persia and Arabia, and was able to repeat by memory the volumes,[3] that are suspended in the mosque of Mecca. But I soon found that no man was ever great by imitation. My desire of excellence impelled me to transfer my attention to nature and to life. Nature was to be my subject, and men to be my auditors: I could never describe what I had not seen: I could not hope to move those with delight or terrour, whose interests and opinions I did not understand.

"Being now resolved to be a poet, I saw every thing with a new purpose; my sphere of attention was suddenly magnified: no kind of knowledge was to be overlooked. I ranged mountains and deserts for images and resemblances, and pictured upon my mind every tree of the forest and flower of the valley. I observed with equal care the crag of the rock and the pinnacles of the palace. Sometimes I wandered along the mazes of the rivulet, and sometimes watched the changes of the summer clouds. To a poet nothing

1. The speaker is the philosopher and poet Imlac, who is addressing Prince Rasselas, son of the emperor of Abyssinia.

2. Johnson's observations here are connected to debates in the period about what constituted poetic originality and whether modern authors could achieve it. See EDWARD YOUNG, *Conjectures on Original Composition* (1759; above).

3. Illuminated manuscripts of sacred texts, "suspended" or hung in mosques.

can be useless. Whatever is beautiful, and whatever is dreadful, must be familiar to his imagination: he must be conversant with all that is awfully vast or elegantly little.[4] The plants of the garden, the animals of the wood, the minerals of the earth, and meteors of the sky, must all concur to store his mind with inexhaustible variety: for every idea is useful for the inforcement or decoration of moral or religious truth;[5] and he, who knows most, will have most power of diversifying his scenes, and of gratifying his reader with remote allusions and unexpected instruction.

"All the appearances of nature I was therefore careful to study, and every country which I have surveyed has contributed something to my poetical powers.

"In so wide a survey, said the prince, you must surely have left much unobserved. I have lived, till now, within the circuit of those mountains, and yet cannot walk abroad without the sight of something which I had never beheld before, or never heeded.

"The business of a poet, said Imlac, is to examine, not the individual, but the species: to remark general properties and large appearances: he does not number the streaks of the tulip, or describe the different shades in the verdure of the forest. He is to exhibit in his portraits of nature such prominent and striking features, as recal the original to every mind; and must neglect the minuter discriminations, which one may have remarked, and another have neglected, for those characteristicks which are alike obvious to vigilance and carelessness.

"But the knowledge of nature is only half the task of a poet; he must be acquainted likewise with all the modes of life. His character requires that he estimate the happiness and misery of every condition; observe the power of all the passions in all their combinations, and trace the changes of the human mind as they are modified by various institutions and accidental influences of climate or custom, from the spriteliness of infancy to the despondence of decrepitude. He must divest himself of the prejudices of his age or country; he must consider right and wrong in their abstracted and invariable state; he must disregard present laws and opinions, and rise to general and transcendental[6] truths, which will always be the same: he must therefore content himself with the slow progress of his name; contemn the applause of his own time, and commit his claims to the justice of posterity. He must write as the interpreter of nature, and the legislator of mankind, and consider himself as presiding over the thoughts and manners of future generations; as a being superiour to time and place.

"His labour is not yet at an end: he must know many languages and many sciences; and, that his stile may be worthy of his thoughts, must, by incessant practice, familiarize to himself every delicacy of speech and grace of harmony."

1759

4. Johnson is drawing on EDMUND BURKE's account of the sublime in *A Philosophical Enquiry into the Origin of Our Ideas of the Sublime and Beautiful* (1757; see below).

5. In "A Defence of 'An Essay of Dramatic Poesy' " (1668), JOHN DRYDEN states: "moral truth is the mistress of the poet as much as of the philosopher; poesy must resemble natural truth, but it must *be* ethical."

6. "General; pervading many particulars" (Johnson's *Dictionary*).

From Preface to Shakespeare

That praises are without reason lavished on the dead, and that the honours due only to excellence are paid to antiquity, is a complaint likely to be always continued by those, who, being able to add nothing to truth, hope for eminence from the heresies of paradox; or those, who, being forced by disappointment upon consolatory expedients, are willing to hope from posterity what the present age refuses, and flatter themselves that the regard which is yet denied by envy, will be at last bestowed by time.

Antiquity, like every other quality that attracts the notice of mankind, has undoubtedly votaries that reverence it, not from reason, but from prejudice. Some seem to admire indiscriminately whatever has been long preserved, without considering that time has sometimes co-operated with chance; all perhaps are more willing to honour past than present excellence; and the mind contemplates genius through the shades of age, as the eye surveys the sun through artificial opacity. The great contention of criticism is to find the faults of the moderns, and the beauties of the ancients. While an authour is yet living we estimate his powers by his worst performance, and when he is dead we rate them by his best.

To works, however, of which the excellence is not absolute and definite, but, gradual and comparative; to works not raised upon principles demonstrative and scientifick, but appealing wholly to observation and experience, no other test can be applied than length of duration and continuance of esteem. What mankind have long possessed they have often examined and compared; and if they persist to value the possession, it is because frequent comparisons have confirmed opinion in its favour. As among the works of nature no man can properly call a river deep, or a mountain high, without the knowledge of many mountains, and many rivers; so in the productions of genius, nothing can be stiled excellent till it has been compared with other works of the same kind. Demonstration[1] immediately displays its power, and has nothing to hope or fear from the flux of years; but works tentative and experimental must be estimated by their proportion to the general and collective ability of man, as it is discovered in a long succession of endeavours. Of the first building that was raised, it might be with certainty determined that it was round or square; but whether it was spacious or lofty must have been referred to time. The Pythagorean scale of numbers[2] was at once discovered to be perfect; but the poems of *Homer* we yet know not to transcend the common limits of human intelligence, but by remarking, that nation after nation, and century after century, has been able to do little more than transpose his incidents, new-name his characters, and paraphrase his sentiments.

The reverence due to writings that have long subsisted arises therefore not from any credulous confidence in the superior wisdom of past ages, or gloomy persuasion of the degeneracy of mankind, but is the consequence of acknowledged and indubitable positions, that what has been longest known has been most considered, and what is most considered is best understood.

1. "The highest degree of deducible or argumental evidence" (Johnson's *Dictionary*).
2. The Greek philosopher and mathematician Pythagoras (6th c. B.C.E.) is thought to have discovered the musical ratios of the octave (2:1), the fifth (3:2), and the fourth (4:3).

The Poet, of whose works I have undertaken the revision,[3] may now begin to assume the dignity of an ancient, and claim the privilege of established fame and prescriptive veneration. He has long outlived his century, the term commonly fixed as the test of literary merit.[4] Whatever advantages he might once derive from personal allusions, local customs, or temporary opinions, have for many years been lost; and every topick of merriment, or motive of sorrow, which the modes of artificial life afforded him, now only obscure the scenes which they once illuminated. The effects of favour and competition are at an end; the tradition of his friendships and his enmities has perished; his works support no opinion with arguments, nor supply any faction with invectives; they can neither indulge vanity nor gratify malignity; but are read without any other reason than the desire of pleasure, and are therefore praised only as pleasure is obtained; yet, thus unassisted by interest or passion, they have past through variations of taste and changes of manners, and, as they devolved from one generation to another, have received new honours at every transmission.

But because human judgment, though it be gradually gaining upon certainty, never becomes infallible; and approbation, though long continued, may yet be only the approbation of prejudice or fashion; it is proper to inquire, by what peculiarities of excellence *Shakespeare* has gained and kept the favour of his countrymen.

Nothing can please many, and please long, but just representations of general nature. Particular manners can be known to few, and therefore few only can judge how nearly they are copied. The irregular combinations of fanciful invention may delight a-while, by that novelty of which the common satiety of life sends us all in quest; but the pleasures of sudden wonder are soon exhausted, and the mind can only repose on the stability of truth.

Shakespeare is above all writers, at least above all modern writers, the poet of nature; the poet that holds up to his readers a faithful mirrour of manners and of life.[5] His characters are not modified by the customs of particular places, unpractised by the rest of the world; by the peculiarities of studies or professions, which can operate but upon small numbers; or by the accidents of transient fashions or temporary opinions: they are the genuine progeny of common humanity, such as the world will always supply, and observation will always find. His persons act and speak by the influence of those general passions and principles by which all minds are agitated, and the whole system of life is continued in motion. In the writings of other poets a character is too often an individual; in those of *Shakespeare* it is commonly a species.

It is from this wide extension of design that so much instruction is derived. It is this which fills the plays of *Shakespeare* with practical axioms and domestick wisdom. It was said of *Euripides*,[6] that every verse was a precept; and it may be said of *Shakespeare*, that from his works may be collected a system of civil and oeconomical[7] prudence. Yet his real power is not shewn in the splendour of particular passages, but by the progress of his fable,[8] and the

3. That is, the process of editing.
4. See HORACE (65–8 B.C.E.), *Epistles* 2.1.39.
5. Hamlet counsels the players to remember that the purpose of acting "is to hold as 'twere the mirror up to nature"; *Hamlet* (ca. 1600), 3.2.20.
6. Greek tragedian (ca. 485–ca. 406 B.C.E.).
7. That is, pertaining to political economy.
8. "The series or contexture of events which constitute a poem epic or dramatic" (Johnson's *Dictionary*).

tenour of his dialogue; and he that tries to recommend him by select quotations, will succeed like the pedant in *Hierocles*,[9] who, when he offered his house to sale, carried a brick in his pocket as a specimen.

It will not easily be imagined how much *Shakespeare* excells in accommodating his sentiments to real life, but by comparing him with other authours. It was observed of the ancient schools of declamation, that the more diligently they were frequented, the more was the student disqualified for the world, because he found nothing there which he should ever meet in any other place. The same remark may be applied to every stage but that of *Shakespeare*. The theatre, when it is under any other direction, is peopled by such characters as were never seen, conversing in a language which was never heard, upon topicks which will never arise in the commerce of mankind. But the dialogue of this authour is often so evidently determined by the incident which produces it, and is pursued with so much ease and simplicity, that it seems scarcely to claim the merit of fiction, but to have been gleaned by diligent selection out of common conversation, and common occurrences.

Upon every other stage the universal agent is love, by whose power all good and evil is distributed, and every action quickened or retarded. To bring a lover, a lady and a rival into the fable; to entangle them in contradictory obligations, perplex them with oppositions of interest, and harrass them with violence of desires inconsistent with each other; to make them meet in rapture and part in agony; to fill their mouths with hyperbolical joy and outrageous sorrow; to distress them as nothing human ever was distressed; to deliver them as nothing human ever was delivered; is the business of a modern dramatist. For this probability is violated, life is misrepresented, and language is depraved. But love is only one of many passions; and as it has no great influence upon the sum of life, it has little operation in the dramas of a poet, who caught his ideas from the living world, and exhibited only what he saw before him. He knew, that any other passion, as it was regular or exorbitant, was a cause of happiness or calamity.

Characters thus ample and general were not easily discriminated and preserved, yet perhaps no poet ever kept his personages more distinct from each other. I will not say with *Pope*,[1] that every speech may be assigned to the proper speaker, because many speeches there are which have nothing characteristical; but perhaps, though some may be equally adapted to every person, it will be difficult to find, any that can be properly transferred from the present possessor to another claimant. The choice is right, when there is reason for choice.

Other dramatists can only gain attention by hyperbolical or aggravated characters, by fabulous and unexampled excellence or depravity, as the writers of barbarous romances invigorated the reader by a giant and a dwarf; and he that should form his expectations of human affairs from the play, or from the tale, would be equally deceived. *Shakespeare* has no heroes; his scenes are occupied only by men, who act and speak as the reader thinks that he should himself have spoken or acted on the same occasion: Even where the agency is supernatural the dialogue is level with life. Other writers disguise

9. Hierocles of Alexander (5th c. C.E.), Greek Neoplatonic philosopher and author of a book of humorous anecdotes that Johnson translated in 1741.

1. In *Preface to Shakespeare* (1725), by ALEXANDER POPE (1688–1744).

the most natural passions and most frequent incidents; so that he who contemplates them in the book will not know them in the world: *Shakespeare* approximates the remote, and familiarizes the wonderful; the event which he represents will not happen, but if it were possible, its effects would probably be such as he has assigned; and it may be said, that he has not only shewn human nature as it acts in real exigencies, but as it would be found in trials, to which it cannot be exposed.

This therefore is the praise of *Shakespeare*, that his drama is the mirrour of life; that he who has mazed[2] his imagination, in following the phantoms which other writers raise up before him, may here be cured of his delirious extasies, by reading human sentiments in human language, by scenes from which a hermit may estimate the transactions of the world, and a confessor predict the progress of the passions.

His adherence to general nature has exposed him to the censure of criticks, who form their judgments upon narrower principles. *Dennis* and *Rhymer* think his *Romans* not sufficiently *Roman*; and *Voltaire*[3] censures his kings as not completely royal. *Dennis* is offended, that *Menenius*,[4] a senator of *Rome*, should play the buffoon; and *Voltaire* perhaps thinks decency violated when the *Danish* Usurper[5] is represented as a drunkard. But *Shakespeare* always makes nature predominate over accident; and if he preserves the essential character, is not very careful of distinctions superinduced and adventitious. His story requires Romans or kings, but he thinks only on men. He knew that *Rome*, like every other city, had men of all dispositions; and wanting a buffoon, he went into the senate-house for that which the senate-house would certainly have afforded him. He was inclined to shew an usurper and a murderer not only odious but despicable, he therefore added drunkenness to his other qualities, knowing that kings love wine like other men, and that wine exerts its natural power upon kings. These are the petty cavils of petty minds; a poet overlooks the casual distinction of country and condition, as a painter, satisfied with the figure, neglects the drapery.

The censure which he has incurred[6] by mixing comick and tragick scenes, as it extends to all his works, deserves more consideration. Let the fact be first stated, and then examined.

Shakespeare's plays are not in the rigorous and critical sense either tragedies or comedies, but compositions of a distinct kind; exhibiting the real state of sublunary[7] nature, which partakes of good and evil, joy and sorrow, mingled with endless variety of proportion and innumerable modes of combination; and expressing the course of the world, in which the loss of one is the gain of another; in which, at the same time, the reveller is hasting to his wine, and the mourner burying his friend; in which the malignity of one is sometimes defeated by the frolick of another; and many mischiefs and many benefits are done and hindered without design.

Out of this chaos of mingled purposes and casualties the ancient poets, according to the laws which custom had prescribed, selected some the crimes

2. That is, followed the complex and winding paths.
3. The pen name of François Marie Arouet (1694–1778), French Enlightenment writer and critic, who assailed Shakespeare for breaking the classical rules of drama. John Dennis (1657–1734), English playwright and critic. Thomas Rymer (1641–1713), English critic and historian.
4. A character in Shakespeare's *Coriolanus* (1608).
5. Claudius, the murderer of Hamlet's father, the king.
6. From Voltaire.
7. Beneath the moon; of this world, earthly.

of men, and some their absurdities; some the momentous vicissitudes of life, and some the lighter occurrences; some the terrours of distress, and some the gayeties of prosperity. Thus rose the two modes of imitation, known by the names of *tragedy* and *comedy*, compositions intended to promote different ends by contrary means, and considered as so little allied, that I do not recollect among the *Greeks* or *Romans* a single writer who attempted both.

Shakespeare has united the powers of exciting laughter and sorrow not only in one mind, but in one composition. Almost all his plays are divided between serious and ludicrous characters, and, in the successive evolutions of the design, sometimes produce seriousness and sorrow, and sometimes levity and laughter.

That this is a practice contrary to the rules of criticism will be readily allowed; but there is always an appeal open from criticism to nature. The end of writing is to instruct; the end of the poetry is to instruct by pleasing.[8] That the mingled drama may convey all the instruction of tragedy or comedy cannot be denied, because it includes both in its alternations of exhibition and approaches nearer than either to the appearance of life, by shewing how great machinations and slender designs may promote or obviate one another, and the high and the low co-operate in the general system by unavoidable concatenation.

It is objected, that by this change of scenes the passions are interrupted in their progression, and that the principal event, being not advanced by a due gradation of preparatory incidents, wants at last the power to move, which constitutes the perfection of dramatick poetry. This reasoning is so specious, that it is received as true even by those who in daily experience feel it to be false. The interchanges of mingled scenes seldom fail to produce the intended vicissitudes of passion. Fiction cannot move so much, but that the attention may be easily transferred; and though it must be allowed that pleasing melancholy be sometimes interrupted by unwelcome levity, yet let it be considered likewise, that melancholy is often not pleasing, and that the disturbance of one man may be the relief of another; that different auditors have different habitudes; and that, upon the whole, all pleasure consists in variety.

The players,[9] who in their edition divided our authour's works into comedies, histories, and tragedies, seem not to have distinguished the three kinds by any very exact or definite ideas.

An action which ended happily to the principal persons, however serious or distressful through its intermediate incidents, in their opinion, constituted a comedy. This idea of a comedy continued long amongst us; and plays were written, which, by changing the catastrophe, were tragedies to-day, and comedies to-morrow.

Tragedy was not in those times poem of more general dignity or elevation than comedy; it required only a calamitous conclusion, with which the common criticism of that age was satisfied, whatever lighter pleasure it afforded in its progress.

History was a series of actions, with no other than chronological succession, independent on each other, and without any tendency to introduce or regulate the conclusion. It is not always very nicely distinguished from trag-

8. See Horace, *Ars Poetica*, lines 343–44 (above).
9. John Heminges (d. 1630) and Henry Condell (d. 1627), members of Shakespeare's acting company, edited the Shakespeare First Folio, published in 1623.

edy. There is not much nearer approach to unity of action in the tragedy of *Antony and Cleopatra*, than in the history of *Richard the Second*. But a history might be continued through many plays; as it had no plan, it had no limits.

Through all these denominations of the drama, *Shakespeare*'s mode of composition is the same; an interchange of seriousness and merriment, by which the mind is softened at one time, and exhilarated at another. But whatever be his purpose, whether to gladden or depress, or to conduct the story, without vehemence or emotion, through tracts of easy and familiar dialogue, he never fails to attain his purpose; as he commands us, we laugh or mourn, or sit silent with quiet expectation, in tranquillity without indifference.

When *Shakespeare*'s plan is understood, most of the criticisms of *Rhymer* and *Voltaire* vanish away. The play of *Hamlet* is opened, without impropriety, by two sentinels; *Iago*[1] bellows at *Brabantio*'s window, without injury to the scheme of the play, though in terms which a modern audience would not easily endure; the character of *Polonius*[2] is seasonable and useful; and the Grave-diggers themselves may be heard with applause.

Shakespeare engaged in dramatick poetry with the world open before him; the rules of the ancients were yet known to few; the publick judgment was unformed; he had no example of such fame as might force him upon imitation, nor criticks of such authority as might restrain his extravagance: He therefore indulged his natural disposition, and his disposition, as *Rhymer* has remarked, led him to comedy. In tragedy he often writes, with great appearance of toil and study, what is written at last with little felicity; but in his comick scenes, he seems to produce without labour, what no labour can improve. In tragedy he is always struggling after some occasion to be comick; but in comedy he seems to repose, or to luxuriate, as in a mode of thinking congenial to his nature. In his tragick scenes there is always something wanting, but his comedy often surpasses expectation or desire. His comedy pleases by the thoughts and the language, and his tragedy for the greater part by incident and action. His tragedy seems to be skill, his comedy to be instinct.

The force of his comick scenes has suffered little diminution from the changes made by a century and a half, in manners or in words. As his personages act upon principles arising from genuine passion, very little modified by particular forms, their pleasures and vexations are communicable to all times and to all places; they are natural, and therefore durable; the adventitious peculiarities of personal habits, are only superficial dies, bright and pleasing for a little while, yet soon fading to a dim tinct, without any remains of former lustre; but the discriminations of true passion are the colours of nature; they pervade the whole mass, and can only perish with the body that exhibits them. The accidental compositions of heterogeneous modes are dissolved by the chance which combined them; but the uniform simplicity of primitive qualities neither admits increase, nor suffers decay. The sand heaped by one flood is scattered by another, but the rock always continues in its place. The stream of time, which is continually washing the dissoluble fabricks of other poets, passes without injury by the adamant[3] of *Shakespeare*.

If there be, what I believe there is, in every nation, a style which never

1. In *Othello* (1603–04).
2. A meddling figure of comedy in *Hamlet*, as are the grave diggers.
3. An impregnable and surpassingly hard substance.

becomes obsolete, a certain mode of phraseology so consonant and congenial to the analogy and principles of its respective language as to remain settled and unaltered; this style is probably to be sought in the common intercourse of life, among those who speak only to be understood, without ambition of elegance. The polite are always catching modish innovations, and the learned depart from established forms of speech, in hope of finding or making better; those who wish for distinction forsake the vulgar, when the vulgar is right; but there is a conversation above grossness and below refinement, where propriety resides, and where this poet seems to have gathered his comick dialogue. He is therefore more agreeable to the ears of the present age than any other authour equally remote, and among his other excellencies deserves to be studied as one of the original masters of our language.

These observations are to be considered not as unexceptionably constant, but as containing general and predominant truth. *Shakespeare*'s familiar dialogue is affirmed to be smooth and clear, yet not wholly without ruggedness or difficulty; as a country may be eminently fruitful, though it has spots unfit for cultivation: His characters are praised as natural, though their sentiments are sometimes forced, and their actions improbable; as the earth upon the whole is spherical, though its surface is varied with protuberances and cavities.

Shakespeare with his excellencies has likewise faults, and faults sufficient to obscure and overwhelm any other merit. I shall shew them in the proportion in which they appear to me, without envious malignity or superstitious veneration. No question can be more innocently discussed than a dead poet's pretensions to renown; and little regard is due to that bigotry which sets candour higher than truth.

His first defect is that to which may be imputed most of the evil in books or in men. He sacrifices virtue to convenience, and is so much more careful to please than to instruct, that he seems to write without any moral purpose. From his writings indeed a system of social duty may be selected, for he that thinks reasonably must think morally; but his precepts and axioms drop casually from him; he makes no just distribution of good or evil, nor is always careful to shew in the virtuous a disapprobation of the wicked; he carries his persons indifferently through right and wrong, and at the close dismisses them without further care, and leaves their examples to operate by chance. This fault the barbarity of his age cannot extenuate; for it is always a writer's duty to make the world better, and justice is a virtue independant on[4] time or place.

The plots are often so loosely formed, that a very slight consideration may improve them, and so carelessly pursued, that he seems not always fully to comprehend his own design. He omits opportunities of instructing or delighting which the train of his story seems to force upon him, and apparently rejects those exhibitions which would be more affecting, for the sake of those which are more easy.

It may be observed, that in many of his plays the latter part is evidently neglected. When he found himself near the end of his work, and, in view of his reward, he shortened the labour to snatch the profit. He therefore remits his efforts where he should most vigorously exert them, and his catastrophe[5] is improbably produced or imperfectly represented.

4. Independent of.

5. The climax of a dramatic action.

He had no regard to distinction of time or place, but gives to one age or nation, without scruple, the customs, institutions, and opinions of another, at the expence not only of likelihood, but of possibility. These faults *Pope* has endeavoured, with more zeal than judgment, to transfer to his imagined interpolators.[6] We need not wonder to find *Hector* quoting *Aristotle*, when we see the loves of *Theseus* and *Hippolyta*[7] combined with the *Gothick* mythology of fairies. *Shakespeare*, indeed, was not the only violator of chronology, for in the same age *Sidney*, who wanted not the advantages of learning, has, in his *Arcadia*,[8] confounded the pastoral with the feudal times, the days of innocence, quiet and security, with those of turbulence, violence, and adventure.

In his comick scenes he is seldom very successful, when he engages his characters in reciprocations of smartness and contests of sarcasm; their jests are commonly gross, and their pleasantry licentious; neither his gentlemen nor his ladies have much delicacy, nor are sufficiently distinguished from his clowns by any appearance of refined manners. Whether he represented the real conversation of his time is not easy to determine; the reign of *Elizabeth*[9] is commonly supposed to have been a time of stateliness, formality and reserve; yet perhaps the relaxations of that severity were not very elegant. There must, however, have been always some modes of gayety preferable to others, and a writer ought to chuse the best.

In tragedy his performance seems constantly to be worse, as his labour is more. The effusions of passion which exigence forces out are for the most part striking and energetick; but whenever he solicits his invention, or strains his faculties, the offspring of his throes is tumour,[1] meanness, tediousness, and obscurity.

In narration he affects a disproportionate pomp of diction, and a wearisome train of circumlocution, and tells the incident imperfectly in many words, which might have been more plainly delivered in few. Narration in dramatick poetry is naturally tedious, as it is unanimated and inactive, and obstructs the progress of the action; it should therefore always be rapid, and enlivened by frequent interruption. *Shakespeare* found it an encumbrance, and instead of lightening it by brevity, endeavoured to recommend it by dignity and splendour.

His declamations or set speeches are commonly cold and weak, for his power was the power of nature; when he endeavoured, like other tragick writers, to catch opportunities of amplification, and instead of inquiring what the occasion demanded, to show how much his stores of knowledge could supply, he seldom escapes without the pity or resentment of his reader.

It is incident[2] to him to be now and then entangled with an unwieldy sentiment, which he cannot well express, and will not reject; he struggles with it a while, and if it continues stubborn, comprises it in words such as occur, and leaves it to be disentangled and evolved[3] by those who have more leisure to bestow upon it.

6. In his *Preface to Shakespeare*, Pope maintained that "the many blunders and illiteracies of the first publishers of [Shakespeare's] works" explain why the texts are marred by errors and anachronisms.
7. Figures from Greek mythology who are characters in *A Midsummer Night's Dream* (ca. 1595). Hector: a character in *Troilus and Cressida* (1601–02; see 2.2.165–66); the Greek philosopher ARISTOTLE (384–322 B.C.E.) lived centuries after the events in that play are presumed to have occurred.
8. A prose romance (1590) by SIR PHILIP SIDNEY (1554–1586).
9. Elizabeth I (1533–1603; reigned 1558–1603).
1. "Affected pomp; false magnificence; puffy grandeur" (Johnson's *Dictionary*).
2. Likely to happen.
3. Deduced, worked out. "Comprises": sums up.

Not that always where the language is intricate the thought is subtle, or the image always great where the line is bulky; the equality of words to things is very often neglected, and trivial sentiments and vulgar ideas disappoint the attention, to which they are recommended by sonorous epithets and swelling figures.[4]

But the admirers of this great poet have never less reason to indulge their hopes of supreme excellence, than when he seems fully resolved to sink them in dejection, and mollify them with tender emotions by the fall of greatness, the danger of innocence, or the crosses of love. He is not long soft and pathetick without some idle conceit, or contemptible equivocation. He no sooner begins to move, than he counteracts himself; and terrour and pity, as they are rising in the mind, are checked and blasted by sudden frigidity.

A quibble[5] is to *Shakespeare*, what luminous vapours are to the traveller; he follows it at all adventures; it is sure to lead him out of his way, and sure to engulf him in the mire. It has some malignant power over his mind, and its fascinations are irresistible. Whatever be the dignity or profundity of his disquisition, whether he be enlarging knowledge or exalting affection, whether he be amusing attention with incidents, or enchaining it in suspense, let but a quibble spring up before him, and he leaves his work unfinished. A quibble is the golden apple for which he will always turn aside from his career,[6] or stoop from his elevation. A quibble, poor and barren as it is, gave him such delight, that he was content to purchase it, by the sacrifice of reason, propriety and truth. A quibble was to him the fatal *Cleopatra* for which he lost the world, and was content to lose it.[7]

It will be thought strange, that, in enumerating the defects of this writer, I have not yet mentioned his neglect of the unities;[8] his violation of those laws which have been instituted and established by the joint authority of poets and of criticks.

For his other deviations from the art of writing I resign him to critical justice, without making any other demand in his favour, than that which must be indulged to all human excellence: that his virtues be rated with his failings: But, from the censure which this irregularity may bring upon him, I shall, with due reverence to that learning which I must oppose, adventure to try how I can defend him.

His histories, being neither tragedies nor comedies are not subject to any of their laws; nothing more is necessary to all the praise which they expect, than that the changes of action be so prepared as to be understood, that the incidents be various and affecting, and the characters consistent, natural, and distinct. No other unity is intended, and therefore none is to be sought.

In his other works he has well enough preserved the unity of action. He has not, indeed, an intrigue regularly perplexed and regularly unravelled: he does not endeavour to hide his design only to discover it, for this is seldom the order of real events, and *Shakespeare* is the poet of nature: But his plan has commonly what *Aristotle* requires, a beginning, a middle, and an end;[9]

4. Figures of speech.
5. "A low conceit depending on the sound of words; a pun" (Johnson's *Dictionary*).
6. Course. In Greek mythology, Atalanta lost a footrace to Hippomenes (who thereby won her in marriage) because she paused to pick up three golden apples that he dropped in her path.
7. In Shakespeare's tragedy *Antony and Cleopatra* (1606–07), the renowned soldier Mark Antony is willing to trade his eminent position for the love of the Egyptian queen Cleopatra.
8. That is, the neoclassical unities of time, place, and action.
9. Aristotle, *Poetics* 7 (see above).

one event is concatenated with another, and the conclusion follows by easy consequence. There are perhaps some incidents that might be spared, as in other poets there is much talk that only fills up time upon the stage; but the general system makes gradual advances, and the end of the play is the end of expectation.

To the unities of time and place he has shewn no regard; and perhaps a nearer view of the principles on which they stand will diminish their value, and withdraw from them the veneration which, from the time of *Corneille*,[1] they have very generally received, by discovering that they have given more trouble to the poet, than pleasure to the auditor.

The necessity of observing the unities of time and place arises from the supposed necessity of making the drama credible. The criticks hold it impossible, that an action of months or years can be possibly believed to pass in three hours; or that the spectator can suppose himself to sit in the theatre, while ambassadors go and return between distant kings, while armies are levied and towns besieged, while an exile wanders and returns, or till he whom they saw courting his mistress, shall lament the untimely fall of his son. The mind revolts from evident falsehood, and fiction loses its force when it departs from the resemblance of reality.

From the narrow limitation of time necessarily arises the contraction of place. The spectator, who knows that he saw the first act at *Alexandria*, cannot suppose that he sees the next at *Rome*, at a distance to which not the dragons of *Medea*[2] could, in so short a time, have transported him; he knows with certainty that he has not changed his place, and he knows that place cannot change itself; that what was a house cannot become a plain; that what was *Thebes* can never be *Persepolis*.

Such is the triumphant language with which a critick exults over the misery of an irregular poet, and exults commonly without resistance or reply. It is time therefore to tell him by the authority of *Shakespeare*, that he assumes, as an unquestionable principle, a position, which, while his breath is forming it into words, his understanding pronounces to be false. It is false, that any representation is mistaken for reality; that any dramatick fable in its materiality was ever credible, or, for a single moment, was ever credited.

The objection arising from the impossibility of passing the first hour at *Alexandria*, and the next at *Rome*, supposes, that when the play opens, the spectator really imagines himself at *Alexandria*, and believes that his walk to the theatre has been a voyage to *Egypt*, and that he lives in the days of *Antony* and *Cleopatra* Surely he that imagines this may imagine more. He that can take the stage at one time for the palace of the *Ptolemies*, may take it in half an hour for the promontory of *Actium*. Delusion, if delusion be admitted, has no certain limitation; if the spectator can be once persuaded, that his old acquaintance are *Alexander* and *Caesar*, that a room illuminated with candles is the plain of *Pharsalia*, or the bank of *Granicus*,[3] he is in a state of elevation above the reach of reason, or of truth, and from the heights of

1. PIERRE CORNEILLE (1606–1684), French tragic dramatist whose very popular play *Le Cid* was criticized for violating the three unities. See his *Of the Three Unities* (1660; above).
2. According to Greek mythology, after avenging herself on her unfaithful husband, Jason, by murdering their children, Medea departed in a chariot drawn by dragons.
3. A river in Asia Minor (near the site of Troy) that gave its name to a famous battle at which Alexander the Great routed the Persians (334 B.C.E.). Pharsalia: at Pharsalus, Julius Caesar defeated his Roman rival Pompey (48 B.C.E.).

empyrean poetry, may despise the circumscriptions of terrestrial nature. There is no reason why a mind thus wandering in extasy should count the clock, or why an hour should not be a century in that calenture[4] of the brains that can make the stage a field.

The truth is, that the spectators are always in their senses, and know, from the first act to the last, that the stage is only a stage, and that the players are only players. They came to hear a certain number of lines recited with just gesture and elegant modulation. The lines relate to some action, and an action must be in some place; but the different actions that compleat a story may be in places very remote from each other; and where is the absurdity of allowing that space to represent first *Athens*, and then *Sicily*, which was always known to be neither *Sicily* nor *Athens*, but a modern theatre?

By supposition, as place is introduced, time may be extended; the time required by the fable elapses for the most part between the acts; for, of so much of the action as is represented, the real and poetical duration is the same. If, in the first act, preparations for war against *Mithridates* are represented to be made in *Rome*, the event of the war may, without absurdity, be represented, in the catastrophe, as happening in *Pontus*; we know that there is neither war, nor preparation for war; we know that we are neither in *Rome* nor *Pontus*; that neither *Mithridates* nor *Lucullus* are before us. The drama exhibits successive imitations of successive actions; and why may not the second imitation represent an action that happened years after the first, if it be so connected with it, that nothing but time can be supposed to intervene? Time is, of all modes of existence, most obsequious to the imagination; a lapse of years is as easily conceived as a passage of hours. In contemplation we easily contract the time of real actions, and therefore willingly permit it to be contracted when we only see their imitation.

It will be asked, how the drama moves, if it is not credited. It is credited with all the credit due to a drama. It is credited, whenever it moves, as a just picture of a real original; as representing to the auditor what he would himself feel, if he were to do or suffer what is there feigned to be suffered or to be done. The reflection that strikes the heart is not, that the evils before us are real evils, but that they are evils to which we ourselves may be exposed. If there be any fallacy, it is not that we fancy the players, but that we fancy ourselves unhappy for a moment; but we rather lament the possibility than suppose the presence of misery, as a mother weeps over her babe, when she remembers that death may take it from her. The delight of tragedy proceeds from our consciousness of fiction; if we thought murders and treasons real, they would please no more.

Imitations produce pain or pleasure, not because they are mistaken for realities, but because they bring realities to mind. When the imagination is recreated by a painted landscape, the trees are not supposed capable to give us shade, or the fountains coolness; but we consider, how we should be pleased with such fountains playing beside us, and such woods waving over us. We are agitated in reading the history of *Henry* the Fifth, yet no man takes his book for the field of *Agencourt*.[5] A dramatick exhibition is a book recited with concomitants that encrease or diminish its effect. Familiar comedy is often more powerful on the theatre, than in the page; imperial tragedy

4. A delirium (specifically, a delusion suffered by sailors who imagine that the sea is a green field).

5. Agincourt, a village in France near which an English army under Henry V defeated a much larger French force in 1415.

is always less. The humour of *Petruchio* may be heightened by grimace; but what voice or what gesture can hope to add dignity or force to the soliloquy of *Cato*.[6]

A play read, affects the mind like a play acted. It is therefore evident, that the action is not supposed to be real; and it follows, that between the acts a longer or shorter time may be allowed to pass, and that no more account of space or duration is to be taken by the auditor of a drama, than by the reader of a narrative, before whom may pass in an hour the life of a hero, or the revolutions of an empire.

Whether *Shakespeare* knew the unities, and rejected them by design, or deviated from them by happy ignorance, it is, I think, impossible to decide, and useless to enquire. We may reasonably suppose, that, when he rose to notice, he did not want[7] the counsels and admonitions of scholars and criticks, and that he at last deliberately persisted in a practice, which he might have begun by chance. As nothing is essential to the fable, but unity of action, and as the unities of time and place arise evidently from false assumptions, and, by circumscribing the extent of the drama, lessen its variety, I cannot think it much to be lamented, that they were not known by him, or not observed: Nor, if such another poet could arise, should I very vehemently reproach him, that his first act passed at *Venice*, and his next in *Cyprus*.[8] Such violations of rules merely positive,[9] become the comprehensive genius of *Shakespeare*, and such censures are suitable to the minute and slender criticism of *Voltaire:*

Non usque adeo permiscuit imis
Longus summa dies, ut non, si voce Metelli
Serventur leges, malint a Caesare tolli.[1]

Yet when I speak thus slightly of dramatick rules, I cannot but recollect how much wit and learning may be produced against me; before such authorities I am afraid to stand, not that I think the present question one of those that are to be decided by mere authority, but because it is to be suspected, that these precepts have not been so easily received but for better reasons than I have yet been able to find. The result of my enquiries, in which it would be ludicrous to boast of impartiality, is, that the unities of time and place are not essential to a just drama, that though they may sometimes conduce to pleasure, they are always to be sacrificed to the nobler beauties of variety and instruction; and that a play, written with nice[2] observation of critical rules, is to be contemplated as an elaborate curiosity, as the product of superfluous and ostentatious art, by which is shewn, rather what is possible, than what is necessary.

He that, without diminution of any other excellence, shall preserve all the unities unbroken, deserves the like applause with the architect, who shall display all the orders of architecture[3] in a citadel, without any deduction

6. The title character of a tragedy by JOSEPH ADDISON (1713); his soliloquy on immortality (5.1.1–40), delivered just before he kills himself, was admired in the 18th century as an expression of noble sentiment. Petruchio: Petruccio, the hero in Shakespeare's comedy *The Taming of the Shrew* (ca. 1592).

7. Lack.

8. Places that figure in Shakespeare's tragedy *Othello*.

9. Arbitrary; not natural.

1. The course of time has not wrought such confusion that the laws would not rather be trampled on by Caesar than saved by Metellus (Latin; trans. J. D. Duff). From Lucan, *Civil War* (ca. 63 C.E.), 3.138–40.

2. Precise.

3. Building styles, characterized by the type of classical column used.

from its strength; but the principal beauty of a citadel is to exclude the enemy; and the greatest graces of a play, are to copy nature and instruct life.

Perhaps, what I have here not dogmatically but deliberately written, may recal the principles of the drama to a new examination. I am almost frighted at my own temerity; and when I estimate the fame and the strength of those that maintain the contrary opinion, am ready to sink down in reverential silence; as *Æneas* withdrew from the defence of *Troy*, when he saw *Neptune* shaking the wall, and *Juno* heading the besiegers.[4]

Those whom my arguments cannot persuade to give their approbation to the judgment of *Shakespeare*, will easily, if they consider the condition of his life, make some allowance for his ignorance.

Every man's performances, to be rightly estimated, must be compared with the state of the age in which he lived, and with his own particular opportunities; and though to the reader a book be not worse or better for the circumstances of the authour, yet as there is always a silent reference of human works to human abilities, and as the enquiry, how far man may extend his designs, or how high he may rate his native force, is of far greater dignity than in what rank we shall place any particular performance, curiosity is always busy to discover the instruments, as well as to survey the workmanship, to know how much is to be ascribed to original powers, and how much to casual and adventitious help. The palaces of *Peru* or *Mexico* were certainly mean and incommodious habitations, if compared to the houses of *European* monarchs; yet who could forbear to view them with astonishment, who remembered that they were built without the use of iron?

* * *

1765

From Lives of the English Poets

From *Cowley*[1]

* * *

[ON METAPHYSICAL WIT]

Cowley, like other poets who have written with narrow views and, instead of tracing intellectual pleasure to its natural sources in the mind of man, paid their court to temporary prejudices, has been at one time too much praised and too much neglected at another.

Wit, like all other things subject by their nature to the choice of man, has its changes and fashions, and at different times takes different forms. About the beginning of the seventeenth century appeared a race of writers that may be termed the metaphysical poets,[2] of whom in a criticism on the works of Cowley it is not improper to give some account.

4. See Virgil, *Aeneid* (19 B.C.E.) 2.610–14. Aeneas is a heroic warrior, but Neptune and Juno are gods.
1. The English poet and essayist Abraham Cowley (1618–1667).
2. A term probably taken from JOHN DRYDEN's complaint about the poetry of John Donne (1572–1631) in *A Discourse Concerning the Original and Progress of Satire* (1693): "He affects the metaphysics . . . and perplexes the minds of the fair sex with nice speculations of philosophy, when he

The metaphysical poets were men of learning, and to shew their learning was their whole endeavour; but, unluckily resolving to shew it in rhyme, instead of writing poetry they only wrote verses, and very often such verses as stood the trial of the finger better than of the ear; for the modulation was so imperfect that they were only found to be verses by counting the syllables.

If the father of criticism[3] has rightly denominated poetry τέχνη μιμητική, *an imitative art*, these writers will without great wrong lose their right to the name of poets, for they cannot be said to have imitated any thing: they neither copied nature nor life; neither painted the forms of matter nor represented the operations of intellect.

Those however who deny them to be poets allow them to be wits. Dryden confesses of himself and his contemporaries that they fall below Donne in wit, but maintains that they surpass him in poetry.

If Wit be well described by Pope as being 'that which has been often thought, but was never before so well expressed,'[4] they certainly never attained nor ever sought it, for they endeavoured to be singular in their thoughts, and were careless of their diction. But Pope's account of wit is undoubtedly erroneous; he depresses it below its natural dignity, and reduces it from strength of thought to happiness of language.

If by a more noble and more adequate conception that be considered as Wit which is at once natural and new, that which though not obvious is, upon its first production, acknowledged to be just; if it be that, which he that never found it, wonders how he missed; to wit of this kind the metaphysical poets have seldom risen. Their thoughts are often new, but seldom natural; they are not obvious, but neither are they just; and the reader, far from wondering that he missed them, wonders more frequently by what perverseness of industry they were ever found.

But Wit, abstracted from its effects upon the hearer, may be more rigorously and philosophically considered as a kind of *discordia concors*;[5] a combination of dissimilar images, or discovery of occult resemblances in things apparently unlike. Of wit, thus defined, they have more than enough. The most heterogeneous ideas are yoked by violence together; nature and art are ransacked for illustrations, comparisons, and allusions; their learning instructs, and their subtilty surprises; but the reader commonly thinks his improvement dearly bought, and, though he sometimes admires, is seldom pleased.

From this account of their compositions it will be readily inferred that they were not successful in representing or moving the affections. As they were wholly employed on something unexpected and surprising they had no regard to that uniformity of sentiment, which enables us to conceive and to excite the pains and the pleasure of other minds: they never enquired what on any occasion they should have said or done, but wrote rather as beholders than partakers of human nature; as beings looking upon good and evil, impassive and at leisure; as Epicurean[6] deities making remarks on the actions of men

should engage their hearts, and entertain them with the softness of love." See also T. S. ELIOT, "The Metaphysical Poets" (1921; below).

3. The Greek philosopher ARISTOTLE (387–322 B.C.E).

4. Slightly misquoted from *An Essay on Criticism* (1711), line 298, by ALEXANDER POPE (1688–1744; see above).

5. Harmonious disharmony (Latin).

6. That is, free from disturbance. The Greek philosopher Epicurus (341–270 B.C.E.) taught that personal happiness is the highest good, best attained through austere living and the study of philosophy.

and the vicissitudes of life, without interest and without emotion. Their courtship was void of fondness and their lamentation of sorrow. Their wish was only to say what they hoped had been never said before.

Nor was the sublime[7] more within their reach than the pathetick; for they never attempted that comprehension and expanse of thought which at once fills the whole mind, and of which the first effect is sudden astonishment, and the second rational admiration. Sublimity is produced by aggregation, and littleness by dispersion. Great thoughts are always general, and consist in positions not limited by exceptions, and in descriptions not descending to minuteness. It is with great propriety that subtlety, which in its original import means exility[8] of particles, is taken in its metaphorical meaning for nicety of distinction. Those writers who lay on the watch for novelty could have little hope of greatness; for great things cannot have escaped former observation. Their attempts were always analytick: they broke every image into fragments, and could no more represent by their slender conceits and laboured particularities the prospects of nature or the scenes of life, than he who dissects a sun-beam with a prism can exhibit the wide effulgence of a summer noon.

What they wanted however of the sublime they endeavoured to supply by hyperbole; their amplification had no limits: they left not only reason but fancy behind them, and produced combinations of confused magnificence that not only could not be credited, but could not be imagined.

Yet great labour directed by great abilities is never wholly lost: if they frequently threw away their wit upon false conceits, they likewise sometimes struck out unexpected truth: if their conceits were far-fetched, they were often worth the carriage.[9] To write on their plan it was at least necessary to read and think. No man could be born a metaphysical poet, nor assume the dignity of a writer by descriptions copied from descriptions, by imitations borrowed from imitations, by traditional imagery and hereditary similes, by readiness of rhyme and volubility of syllables.

In perusing the works of this race of authors the mind is exercised either by recollection or inquiry; either something already learned is to be retrieved, or something new is to be examined. If their greatness seldom elevates, their acuteness often surprises; if the imagination is not always gratified, at least the powers of reflection and comparison are employed; and in the mass of materials, which ingenious absurdity has thrown together, genuine wit and useful knowledge may be sometimes found, buried perhaps in grossness of expression, but useful to those who know their value, and such as, when they are expanded to perspicuity and polished to elegance, may give lustre to works which have more propriety though less copiousness of sentiment.

* * *

1783

7. On the sublime, see the writings of JOSEPH ADDISON (1672–1719; above) and EDMUND BURKE (1729–1797; below).

8. Smallness in number or size.

9. That is, worth the trouble of carrying them so far.

DAVID HUME
1711–1776

The Scottish philosopher and historian David Hume responded to and developed the empiricist work of his predecessors John Locke (1632–1704) and George Berkeley (1685–1753). He, too, opposed the rationalist belief in innate ideas and held that knowledge derives from experience. But he moved beyond them toward a position of radical skepticism, denying the possibility of certain knowledge and maintaining that the mind itself is a bundle of sensations. Indeed, Hume reached the conclusion that we cannot derive and prove a theory of reality at all; we can know only experience and must base our beliefs upon it.

Hume is one of the major figures of the Enlightenment. Many criticized his skeptical views as extremist and alarming, especially because they challenged religious orthodoxy; yet many others acclaimed him as one of Scotland's and Europe's foremost thinkers. In the words of the modern scholar Walter Jackson Bate, "in Hume's writings, human reason was dissected with such devastating effect that philosophy has never since quite recovered the traditional classical confidence in reason." This achievement is all the more fascinating from a man described by one friend, the Scottish economist Adam Smith, "as approaching as nearly to the idea of a perfectly wise and virtuous man, as perhaps the nature of human frailty will admit."

Hume's major philosophical and moral writings include *A Treatise of Human Nature* (1739–40), usually regarded as his masterpiece and an extraordinary achievement for an author in his mid-twenties; *Essays, On Moral and Political Subjects* (1741); *An Enquiry Concerning Human Understanding*—a simplified version of the *Treatise* (1748); and *An Enquiry Concerning the Principles of Morals* (1751, "of all my writings incomparably the best"). He also wrote *Political Discourses* (1752), *The Natural History of Religion* (1755), and the *History of England* (6 vols., 1754–62), which for decades was the standard work in the field. The extent of Hume's skepticism is reflected in his late writings on religion, where he disputes all claims for any rational or natural theology; knowing that these ideas would be controversial, he withheld the text of *The Dialogues Concerning Natural Religion* (1779) until after his death.

Born in Edinburgh, David Hume attended the university there. In 1734 he journeyed to Anjou, in northwest France, where he studied and wrote. In 1739 he returned to England to help prepare his *Treatise* for publication. Later in life, Hume professed that this book was ill-argued and philosophically immature, yet it remains perhaps his most widely read work (particularly the first section, on morals). The poor response to the *Treatise* deeply disappointed him—he remarked that it "fell dead-born from the press"—but the greater success of the later *Essays* led him to hope that he might be selected for the chair of moral philosophy at the University of Edinburgh in 1744. His critics, however, protested that his views were heretical and even atheistic. For example, Hume argued that "the idea of God, as meaning an infinitely intelligent, wise, and good Being, arises from reflecting on the operations of our own mind, and augmenting, without limit, those qualities of goodness and wisdom." Men and women, so it seems, make their Maker; and Hume's own calm in the face of such observations disturbed his detractors all the more.

Having failed to receive the academic position he sought, Hume then took leave of Edinburgh for a long period, traveling and serving in a number of educational, military, and diplomatic posts in Scotland, England, and Europe. In 1748 he published his *Enquiry Concerning Human Understanding*, which revised and popularized book 1 of his *Treatise*. Two new sections, "Of Miracles" and "Of a Particular Providence and of a Future State," show Hume's dissent from religious belief and doctrine, as does, less directly, the slightly later *Enquiry Concerning the Principles of Morals*. For Hume, sentiments and not the decrees of God are the basis for morality.

From the early 1750s to the mid-1760s, Hume spent most of his time in Edinburgh. In 1752 he was made keeper of the Advocates Library, a post that enabled him to concentrate on the historical research and writing that led to his *History*. In 1763 he took a diplomatic position in Paris, where—admired for his intellectual gifts and personality—he became friends with aristocrats and literary men. Hume spent his final years mostly in Edinburgh, revising and correcting his works. His friends Adam Smith, the writer and playwright S. J. Pratt, and Samuel Johnson's biographer James Boswell all described how Hume, without a belief in an afterlife, prepared for death—thereby sparking yet more charges of apostasy. The publication in 1779 of Hume's *Dialogues* and, in 1782, of two essays on suicide and immortality renewed these accusations and criticisms.

Hume is skeptical, but he is also intellectually curious, lucid in his prose, and cogent and complicated in his thought; he is sometimes perplexing and contradictory, but never obscure, in argument. We can gain some sense of the nature of his skepticism by pondering the connection, as he sees it, between one event and another. The *cause* of their connection, Hume argues, is something for which we have no impression and thus no idea; as a result, we ourselves infer this causal link. But while we cannot see or prove the connection, we can say we know that it exists, because of the cause-and-effect relationship that we draw from our experience, which leads us to expect that it will recur.

Our selection, "Of the Standard of Taste," is a celebrated literary performance, and it bears suggestively on modern and contemporary debates about standards in criticism, reader-response theory, interpretive communities, and canon formation. The essay itself has an unusual origin. In 1756 Hume had prepared a new book for publication, to be titled *Five Dissertations*; its five essays were "The Natural History of Religion," "Of the Passions," "Of Tragedy," "Of Suicide," and "Of the Immortality of the Soul." The antireligious thrust of the final two essays, however, made Hume's publisher fearful, and he was in fact threatened with prosecution should they appear in print. Hume replaced the two troublesome essays with "Of the Standard of Taste," and the book—retitled *Four Dissertations*—was published early in 1757.

Hume begins with the fact of critical disagreement, the wide variations in "taste" that testify both to the different observations that persons make and to the different terms—or differing meanings attached to the same terms—that they use to describe what they have experienced. In light of all this, he asks, can we ever hope to identify a "standard of taste"? The first answer seems to be that we cannot. As we ponder the idea of a standard, we find ourselves inclined to say that merit or value is always in the eye of the beholder—thus one person praises an object as beautiful that another, or most others, would say is ugly. How can that atypical view be disputed or, in Hume's word, "regulated"? We are left with differences in taste, and no standard for discriminating among them in any final sense.

But Hume then queries the position that he has just seemed to endorse. Does not common sense tell us all that in poetry John Milton is superior to John Ogilby, and in prose Joseph Addison is superior to John Bunyan? The epic poems of Homer, which gave pleasure to readers in classical times, continue to do the same for readers in England and France in the eighteenth century. His poetry has endured when that by many others (whose compositions once enjoyed a high reputation) has not. Hume therefore proposes that each person has the capacity for recognizing true beauty, which offers after all the prospect of a "true standard of taste and sentiment." Of course, not all capacities are realized; as Hume puts it, some people lack "*delicacy* of imagination" and are therefore unable to feel the "proper sentiment of beauty."

More experience: this is Hume's main remedy for the shortcomings in aesthetic response that afflict some persons. He recommends that they practice an art and reexamine its works, making their taste finer, more subtle and discriminating. Hume stresses the need for comparisons among a range of works only to insist, a moment later, that we examine the object at hand free from "prejudice." Here, as elsewhere,

Hume may appear to be contradicting himself on a point that he seemed to judge crucial. But such shifts are part of the open, flexible, and exploratory nature of his approach.

Hume's essay is flawed. His slighting reference to the Koran is unacceptable, and he takes for granted judgments (e.g., Addison's superiority to Bunyan) that many today would quarrel with—a point that exposes his reliance on the "common sense" of his time. Moreover, his argument has a circularity that is hard to overlook. Some persons, he says, have a finer taste than others. How do we know this? Because it is universally acknowledged to be so.

Though Hume's style marks him as a writer of the eighteenth century, in certain respects his views anticipate certain disquieting ironies of poststructuralist theory. The scholar James Engell has described Hume's position in this essay in terms that evoke JACQUES DERRIDA: "The standard of taste becomes a presence that is, in a sense, an absence. . . . Hume is saying that in matters of taste, although there is very definitely at any given time in history a center or a standard, we cannot define or find that center—at least we cannot precisely agree what it is. It is always, for us, decentered." As a philosopher Hume is close to us; we read him often with a shock of recognition.

BIBLIOGRAPHY

For Hume's writings, see *The Essays, Moral, Political, and Literary,* edited by T. H. Green and T. H. Grose (4 vols., 1874–75), and *The Philosophical Works of David Hume,* edited by T. H. Green and T. H. Grose (4 vols., 1882–86; rpt. 1964). Eugene F. Miller has prepared a good modern edition of Hume's essays (rev. ed., 1987). For a one-volume collection, see *The Essential David Hume*, edited by Robert Paul Wolff (1969). The correspondence is available in *The Letters of David Hume*, edited by J. Y. T. Greig (2 vols., 1932), and *New Letters of David Hume*, edited by Raymond Klibansky and Ernest C. Mossner (1954). The standard biography is Ernest C. Mossner, *The Life of David Hume* (2d ed., 1980).

Introductions to Hume's work include D. G. C. MacNabb, *David Hume: His Theory of Knowledge and Morality* (2d ed., 1966); Terence Penelhum, *Hume* (1975); Barry Stroud, *Hume* (1977); and A. J. Ayer, *Hume* (1980). For more detailed discussions, see Norman Kemp Smith, *The Philosophy of David Hume: A Critical Study of Its Origins and Central Doctrines* (1966); James Noxon, *Hume's Philosophical Development* (1973); John Passmore, *Hume's Intentions* (3d ed., 1980); Donald W. Livingston, *Hume's Philosophy of Common Life* (1984); and Anthony Flew, *David Hume, Philosopher of Moral Science* (1986). On the empiricist tradition, see Jonathan Francis Bennett, *Locke, Berkeley, Hume: Central Themes* (1971).

On Hume as a literary critic and theorist, see Teddy Brunius, *David Hume on Criticism* (1952), and Jan Wilbanks, *Hume's Theory of Imagination* (1968). Chapter 2 in Terry Eagleton, *The Ideology of the Aesthetic* (1990), examining Hume, Shaftesbury, and Burke, is illuminating. Hume has also received much attention as a literary artist in his own right; see Leo Braudy, *Narrative Form in History and Fiction: Hume, Fielding, and Gibbon* (1970); John J. Richetti, *Philosophical Writing: Locke, Berkeley, Hume* (1983); Jerome Christensen, *Practicing Enlightenment: Hume and the Formation of a Literary Career* (1987); Leopold Damrosch, *Fictions of Reality in the Age of Hume and Johnson* (1989); M. A. Box, *The Suasive Art of David Hume* (1990); Adam Potkay, *The Fate of Eloquence in the Age of Hume* (1994); and Adela Pinch, *Strange Fits of Passion: Epistemologies of Emotion, Hume to Austen* (1996).

An excellent resource is *The Cambridge Companion to Hume*, edited by David Norton (1993), which includes an essay by Peter Jones on Hume's literary and aesthetic theory. See also T. E. Jessop, *A Bibliography of David Hume and of Scottish Philosophy from Frances Hutcheson to Lord Balfour* (1938); Roland Hall, *A Hume Bibliography, from 1930* (1971); the bibliographical essay in *Hume and the Enlight-*

enment (ed. William B. Todd, 1974); and Roland Hall, *Fifty Years of Hume Scholarship: A Bibliographical Guide* (1978).

Of the Standard of Taste

The great variety of Taste, as well as of opinion, which prevails in the world, is too obvious not to have fallen under every one's observation. Men of the most confined knowledge are able to remark[1] a difference of taste in the narrow circle of their acquaintance, even where the persons have been educated under the same government, and have early imbibed the same prejudices. But those, who can enlarge their view to contemplate distant nations and remote ages, are still more surprized at the great inconsistence and contrariety. We are apt to call *barbarous* whatever departs widely from our own taste and apprehension: But soon find the epithet of reproach retorted on us. And the highest arrogance and self-conceit is at last startled, on observing an equal assurance on all sides, and scruples, amidst such a contest of sentiment, to pronounce positively in its own favour.

As this variety of taste is obvious to the most careless enquirer; so will it be found, on examination, to be still greater in reality than in appearance. The sentiments of men often differ with regard to beauty and deformity of all kinds, even while their general discourse is the same. There are certain terms in every language, which import blame, and others praise; and all men, who use the same tongue, must agree in their application of them. Every voice is united in applauding elegance, propriety, simplicity, spirit in writing; and in blaming fustian, affectation, coldness, and a false brilliancy: But when critics come to particulars, this seeming unanimity vanishes; and it is found, that they had affixed a very different meaning to their expressions. In all matters of opinion and science, the case is opposite: The difference among men is there oftener found to lie in generals than in particulars; and to be less in reality than in appearance. An explanation of the terms commonly ends the controversy; and the disputants are surprized to find, that they had been quarrelling, while at bottom they agreed in their judgment.

Those who found morality on sentiment, more than on reason, are inclined to comprehend ethics under the former observation, and to maintain, that, in all questions, which regard conduct and manners, the difference among men is really greater than at first sight it appears. It is indeed obvious, that writers of all nations and all ages concur in applauding justice, humanity, magnanimity, prudence, veracity; and in blaming the opposite qualities. Even poets and other authors, whose compositions are chiefly calculated to please the imagination, are yet found from HOMER down to FENELON,[2] to inculcate the same moral precepts, and to bestow their applause and blame on the same virtues and vices. This great unanimity is usually ascribed to the influence of plain reason; which, in all these cases, maintains similar sentiments

1. Observe, notice.
2. François Fénelon (1651–1715), French churchman and writer, author of a didactic romance of Homeric characters, *The Adventures of Telemachus* (1699). Telemachus is the son of Odysseus and Penelope. Homer: the epics the *Iliad* (whose central figure is Achilles) and the *Odyssey* (centered on Odysseus, or Ulysses) were often taken as the starting point of Western literature (ca. 8th c. B.C.E.).

in all men, and prevents those controversies, to which the abstract sciences are so much exposed. So far as the unanimity is real, this account may be admitted as satisfactory: But we must also allow that some part of the seeming harmony in morals may be accounted for from the very nature of language. The word *virtue*, with its equivalent in every tongue, implies praise; as that of *vice* does blame: And no one, without the most obvious and grossest impropriety, could affix reproach to a term, which in general acceptation is understood in a good sense; or bestow applause, where the idiom requires disapprobation. HOMER'S general precepts, where he delivers any such, will never be controverted; but it is obvious, that, when he draws particular pictures of manners, and represents heroism in ACHILLES and prudence in ULYSSES, he intermixes a much greater degree of ferocity in the former, and of cunning and fraud in the latter, than FENELON would admit of. The sage ULYSSES in the GREEK poet seems to delight in lies and fictions, and often employs them without any necessity or even advantage: But his more scrupulous son, in the FRENCH epic writer, exposes himself to the most imminent perils, rather than depart from the most exact line of truth and veracity.

The admirers and followers of the ALCORAN[3] insist on the excellent moral precepts interspersed throughout that wild and absurd performance. But it is to be supposed, that the ARABIC words, which correspond to the ENGLISH, equity, justice, temperance, meekness, charity, were such as, from the constant use of that tongue, must always be taken in a good sense; and it would have argued the greatest ignorance, not of morals, but of language, to have mentioned them with any epithets, besides those of applause and approbation. But would we know, whether the pretended prophet had really attained a just sentiment of morals? Let us attend to his narration; and we shall soon find, that he bestows praise on such instances of treachery, inhumanity, cruelty, revenge, bigotry, as are utterly incompatible with civilized society. No steady rule of right seems there to be attended to; and every action is blamed or praised, so far only as it is beneficial or hurtful to the true believers.

The merit of delivering true general precepts in ethics is indeed very small. Whoever recommends any moral virtues, really does no more than is implied in the terms themselves. That people, who invented the word *charity*, and used it in a good sense, inculcated more clearly and much more efficaciously, the precept, *be charitable*, than any pretended legislator or prophet, who should insert such a *maxim* in his writings. Of all expressions, those, which, together with their other meaning, imply a degree either of blame or approbation, are the least liable to be perverted or mistaken.

It is natural for us to seek a *Standard of Taste*; a rule, by which the various sentiments of men may be reconciled; at least, a decision, afforded, confirming one sentiment, and condemning another.

There is a species of philosophy, which cuts off all hopes of success in such an attempt, and represents the impossibility of ever attaining any standard of taste. The difference, it is said, is very wide between judgment and sentiment. All sentiment is right; because sentiment has a reference to nothing beyond itself, and is always real, wherever a man is conscious of it. But all determinations of the understanding are not right; because they have a

3. The Koran, which collects and records the revelations of the Prophet Muhammad.

reference to something beyond themselves, to wit, real matter of fact; and are not always conformable to that standard. Among a thousand different opinions which different men may entertain of the same subject, there is one, and but one, that is just and true; and the only difficulty is to fix and ascertain it. On the contrary, a thousand different sentiments, excited by the same object, are all right: Because no sentiment represents what is really in the object. It only marks a certain conformity or relation between the object and the organs or faculties of the mind; and if that conformity did not really exist, the sentiment could never possibly have being. Beauty is no quality in things themselves: It exists merely in the mind which contemplates them; and each mind perceives a different beauty. One person may even perceive deformity, where another is sensible of beauty; and every individual ought to acquiesce in his own sentiment, without pretending to regulate those of others. To seek the real beauty, or real deformity, is as fruitless an enquiry, as to pretend to ascertain the real sweet or real bitter. According to the disposition of the organs, the same object may be both sweet and bitter; and the proverb has justly determined it to be fruitless to dispute concerning tastes. It is very natural, and even quite necessary, to extend this axiom to mental, as well as bodily taste; and thus common sense, which is so often at variance with philosophy, especially with the sceptical kind, is found, in one instance at least, to agree in pronouncing the same decision.

But though this axiom, by passing into a proverb, seems to have attained the sanction of common sense; there is certainly a species of common sense which opposes it, at least serves to modify and restrain it. Whoever would assert an equality of genius and elegance between OGILBY and MILTON, or BUNYAN and ADDISON,[4] would be thought to defend no less an extravagance, than if he had maintained a mole-hill to be as high as TENERIFFE,[5] or a pond as extensive as the ocean. Though there may be found persons, who give the preference to the former authors; no one pays attention to such a taste; and we pronounce without scruple the sentiment of these pretended critics to be absurd and ridiculous. The principle of the natural equality of tastes is then totally forgot, and while we admit it on some occasions, where the objects seem near an equality, it appears an extravagant paradox, or rather a palpable absurdity, where objects so disproportioned are compared together.

It is evident that none of the rules of composition are fixed by reasonings *a priori*, or can be esteemed abstract conclusions of the understanding, from comparing those habitudes[6] and relations of ideas, which are eternal and immutable. Their foundation is the same with that of all the practical sciences, experience; nor are they any thing but general observations, concerning what has been universally found to please in all countries and in all ages. Many of the beauties of poetry and even of eloquence are founded on falsehood and fiction, on hyperboles, metaphors, and an abuse or perversion of terms from their natural meaning. To check the sallies of the imagination, and to reduce every expression to geometrical truth and exactness, would be the most contrary to the laws of criticism; because it would produce a work, which, by universal experience, has been found the most insipid and dis-

4. Hume pairs two poets, John Ogilby (1600–1676) and John Milton (1608–1674), and two prose writers, John Bunyan (1628–1688) and JOSEPH ADDISON (1672–1719).

5. Largest of the Canary Islands and site of a volcanic peak.

6. Habits.

agreeable. But though poetry can never submit to exact truth, it must be confined by rules of art, discovered to the author either by genius or observation. If some negligent or irregular writers have pleased, they have not pleased by their transgressions of rule or order, but in spite of these transgressions: They have possessed other beauties, which were conformable to just criticism; and the force of these beauties has been able to overpower censure, and give the mind a satisfaction superior to the disgust arising from the blemishes. ARIOSTO[7] pleases; but not by his monstrous and improbable fictions, by his bizarre mixture of the serious and comic styles, by the want of coherence in his stories, or by the continual interruptions of his narration. He charms by the force and clearness of his expression, by the readiness and variety of his inventions, and by his natural pictures of the passions, especially those of the gay and amorous kind: And however his faults may diminish our satisfaction, they are not able entirely to destroy it. Did our pleasure really arise from those parts of his poem, which we denominate faults, this would be no objection to criticism in general: It would only be an objection to those particular rules of criticism, which would establish such circumstances to be faults, and would represent them as universally blameable. If they are found to please, they cannot be faults; let the pleasure, which they produce, be ever so unexpected and unaccountable.

But though all the general rules of art are founded only on experience and on the observation of the common sentiments of human nature, we must not imagine, that, on every occasion, the feelings of men will be conformable to these rules. Those finer emotions of the mind are of a very tender and delicate nature, and require the concurrence of many favourable circumstances to make them play with facility and exactness, according to their general and established principles. The least exterior hindrance to such small springs, or the least internal disorder, disturbs their motion, and confounds the operation of the whole machine. When we would make an experiment of this nature, and would try the force of any beauty or deformity, we must choose with care a proper time and place, and bring the fancy to a suitable situation and disposition. A perfect serenity of mind, a recollection of thought, a due attention to the object; if any of these circumstances be wanting, our experiment will be fallacious, and we shall be unable to judge of the catholic and universal beauty. The relation, which nature has placed between the form and the sentiment, will at least be more obscure; and it will require greater accuracy to trace and discern it. We shall be able to ascertain its influence not so much from the operation of each particular beauty, as from the durable admiration, which attends those works, that have survived all the caprices of mode and fashion, all the mistakes of ignorance and envy.

The same HOMER, who pleased at ATHENS and ROME two thousand years ago, is still admired at PARIS and at LONDON. All the changes of climate, government, religion, and language, have not been able to obscure his glory. Authority or prejudice may give a temporary vogue to a bad poet or orator; but his reputation will never be durable or general. When his compositions are examined by posterity or by foreigners, the enchantment is dissipated,

7. Lodovico Ariosto (1474–1533), Italian poet; his masterpiece is the romantic epic *Orlando Furioso* (1516).

and his faults appear in their true colours. On the contrary, a real genius, the longer his works endure, and the more wide they are spread, the more sincere is the admiration which he meets with. Envy and jealousy have too much place in a narrow circle; and even familiar acquaintance with his person may diminish the applause due to his performances: But when these obstructions are removed, the beauties, which are naturally fitted to excite agreeable sentiments, immediately display their energy; and while the world endures, they maintain their authority over the minds of men.

It appears then, that, amidst all the variety and caprice of taste, there are certain general principles of approbation or blame, whose influence a careful eye may trace in all operations of the mind. Some particular forms or qualities, from the original structure of the internal fabric, are calculated to please, and others to displease; and if they fail of their effect in any particular instance, it is from some apparent defect or imperfection in the organ. A man in a fever would not insist on his palate as able to decide concerning flavours; nor would one, affected with the jaundice, pretend to give a verdict with regard to colours.[8] In each creature, there is a sound and a defective state; and the former alone can be supposed to afford us a true standard of taste and sentiment. If, in the sound state of the organ, there be an entire or a considerable uniformity of sentiment among men, we may thence derive an idea of the perfect beauty; in like manner as the appearance of objects in day-light, to the eye of a man in health, is denominated their true and real colour, even while colour is allowed to be merely a phantasm of the senses.

Many and frequent are the defects in the internal organs, which prevent or weaken the influence of those general principles, on which depends our sentiment of beauty or deformity. Though some objects, by the structure of the mind, be naturally calculated to give pleasure, it is not to be expected, that in every individual the pleasure will be equally felt. Particular incidents and situations occur, which either throw a false light on the objects, or hinder the true from conveying to the imagination the proper sentiment and perception.

One obvious cause, why many feel not the proper sentiment of beauty, is the want of that *delicacy* of imagination, which is requisite to convey a sensibility of those finer emotions. This delicacy every one pretends to: Every one talks of it; and would reduce every kind of taste or sentiment to its standard. But as our intention in this essay is to mingle some light of the understanding with the feelings of sentiment, it will be proper to give a more accurate definition of delicacy, than has hitherto been attempted. And not to draw our philosophy from too profound a source, we shall have recourse to a noted story in DON QUIXOTE.[9]

It is with good reason, says SANCHO to the squire with the great nose, that I pretend to have a judgment in wine: This is a quality hereditary in our family. Two of my kinsmen were once called to give their opinion of a hogshead, which was supposed to be excellent, being old and of a good vintage. One of them tastes it; considers it; and after mature reflection pronounces the wine to be good, were it not for a small taste of leather, which he per-

8. It was thought that to a person whose eye was discolored by jaundice, everything would look yellow; see ALEXANDER POPE, *An Essay on Criticism* (1711), lines 558–59.

9. The novel *Don Quixote* (1605, 1615), by Miguel de Cervantes; this story comes from part 2, chapter 13.

ceived in it. The other, after using the same precautions, gives also his verdict in favour of the wine; but with the reserve of a taste of iron, which he could easily distinguish. You cannot imagine how much they were both ridiculed for their judgment. But who laughed in the end? On emptying the hogshead, there was found at the bottom, an old key with a leathern thong tied to it.

The great resemblance between mental and bodily taste will easily teach us to apply this story. Though it be certain, that beauty and deformity, more than sweet and bitter, are not qualities in objects, but belong entirely to the sentiment, internal or external; it must be allowed, that there are certain qualities in objects, which are fitted by nature to produce those particular feelings. Now as these qualities may be found in a small degree, or may be mixed and confounded with each other, it often happens, that the taste is not affected with such minute qualities, or is not able to distinguish all the particular flavours, amidst the disorder, in which they are presented. Where the organs are so fine, as to allow nothing to escape them; and at the same time so exact as to perceive every ingredient in the composition: This we call delicacy of taste, whether we employ these terms in the literal or metaphorical sense. Here then the general rules of beauty are of use; being drawn from established models, and from the observation of what pleases or displeases, when presented singly and in a high degree: And if the same qualities, in a continued composition and in a smaller degree, affect not the organs with a sensible delight or uneasiness, we exclude the person from all pretensions to this delicacy. To produce these general rules or avowed patterns of composition is like finding the key with the leathern thong; which justified the verdict of SANCHO'S kinsmen, and confounded those pretended judges who had condemned them. Though the hogshead had never been emptied, the taste of the one was still equally delicate, and that of the other equally dull and languid: But it would have been more difficult to have proved the superiority of the former, to the conviction of every by-stander. In like manner, though the beauties of writing had never been methodized, or reduced to general principles; though no excellent models had ever been acknowledged; the different degrees of taste would still have subsisted, and the judgment of one man been preferable to that of another; but it would not have been so easy to silence the bad critic, who might always insist upon his particular sentiment, and refuse to submit to his antagonist. But when we show him an avowed principle of art; when we illustrate this principle by examples, whose operation, from his own particular taste, he acknowledges to be conformable to the principle; when we prove, that the same principle may be applied to the present case, where he did not perceive or feel its influence: He must conclude, upon the whole, that the fault lies in himself, and that he wants the delicacy, which is requisite to make him sensible of every beauty and every blemish, in any composition or discourse.

It is acknowledged to be the perfection of every sense or faculty, to perceive with exactness its most minute objects, and allow nothing to escape its notice and observation. The smaller the objects are, which become sensible to the eye, the finer is that organ, and the more elaborate its make and composition. A good palate is not tried by strong flavours; but by a mixture of small ingredients, where we are still sensible of each part, notwithstanding its minuteness and its confusion with the rest. In like manner, a quick and acute perception of beauty and deformity must be the perfection of our mental taste; nor can a man be satisfied with himself while he suspects, that any excellence or blemish in a discourse has passed him unobserved. In this case, the perfection of the man, and the perfection of the sense or feeling, are found to be united. A very delicate palate, on many occasions, may be a great inconvenience both to a man himself and to his friends: But a delicate taste of wit or beauty must always be a desirable quality; because it is the source of all the finest and most innocent enjoyments, of which human nature is susceptible. In this decision the sentiments of all mankind are agreed. Wherever you can ascertain a delicacy of taste, it is sure to meet with approbation; and the best way of ascertaining it is to appeal to those models and principles, which have been established by the uniform consent and experience of nations and ages.

But though there be naturally a wide difference in point of delicacy between one person and another, nothing tends further to encrease and improve this talent, than *practice* in a particular art, and the frequent survey or contemplation of a particular species of beauty. When objects of any kind are first presented to the eye or imagination, the sentiment, which attends them, is obscure and confused; and the mind is, in a great measure, incapable of pronouncing concerning their merits or defects. The taste cannot perceive the several excellencies of the performance; much less distinguish the particular character of each excellency, and ascertain its quality and degree. If it pronounce the whole in general to be beautiful or deformed, it is the utmost that can be expected; and even this judgment, a person, so unpractised, will be apt to deliver with great hesitation and reserve. But allow him to acquire experience in those objects, his feeling becomes more exact and nice:[1] He not only perceives the beauties and defects of each part, but marks the distinguishing species of each quality, and assigns it suitable praise or blame. A clear and distinct sentiment attends him through the whole survey of the objects; and he discerns that very degree and kind of approbation or displeasure, which each part is naturally fitted to produce. The mist dissipates, which seemed formerly to hang over the object: The organ acquires greater perfection in its operations; and can pronounce, without danger of mistake, concerning the merits of every performance. In a word, the same address and dexterity, which practice gives to the execution of any work, is also acquired by the same means, in the judging of it.

So advantageous is practice to the discernment of beauty, that, before we can give judgment on any work of importance, it will even be requisite, that that very individual performance be more than once perused by us, and be surveyed in different lights with attention and deliberation. There is a flutter or hurry of thought which attends the first perusal of any piece, and which confounds the genuine sentiment of beauty. The relation of the parts is not discerned: The true characters of style are little distinguished: The several perfections and defects seem wrapped up in a species of confusion, and present themselves indistinctly to the imagination. Not to mention, that there is a species of beauty, which, as it is florid and superficial, pleases at first; but being found incompatible with a just expression either of reason or passion, soon palls upon the taste, and is then rejected with disdain, at least rated at a much lower value.

1. Refined.

It is impossible to continue in the practice of contemplating any order of beauty, without being frequently obliged to form *comparisons* between the several species and degrees of excellence, and estimating their proportion to each other. A man, who has had no opportunity of comparing the different kinds of beauty, is indeed totally unqualified to pronounce an opinion with regard to any object presented to him. By comparison alone we fix the epithets of praise or blame, and learn how to assign the due degree of each. The coarsest daubing contains a certain lustre of colours and exactness of imitation, which are so far beauties, and would affect the mind of a peasant or Indian with the highest admiration. The most vulgar ballads are not entirely destitute of harmony or nature; and none but a person, familiarized to superior beauties, would pronounce their numbers[2] harsh, or narration uninteresting. A great inferiority of beauty gives pain to a person conversant in the highest excellence of the kind, and is for that reason pronounced a deformity: As the most finished object, with which we are acquainted, is naturally supposed to have reached the pinnacle of perfection, and to be entitled to the highest applause. One accustomed to see, and examine, and weigh the several performances, admired in different ages and nations, can alone rate the merits of a work exhibited to his view, and assign its proper rank among the productions of genius.

But to enable a critic the more fully to execute this undertaking, he must preserve his mind free from all *prejudice*,[3] and allow nothing to enter into his consideration, but the very object which is submitted to his examination. We may observe, that every work of art, in order to produce its due effect on the mind, must be surveyed in a certain point of view, and cannot be fully relished by persons, whose situation, real or imaginary, is not conformable to that which is required by the performance. An orator addresses himself to a particular audience, and must have a regard to their particular genius,[4] interests, opinions, passions, and prejudices; otherwise he hopes in vain to govern their resolutions, and inflame their affections. Should they even have entertained some prepossessions against him, however unreasonable, he must not overlook this disadvantage; but, before he enters upon the subject, must endeavour to conciliate their affection, and acquire their good graces. A critic of a different age or nation, who should peruse this discourse, must have all these circumstances in his eye, and must place himself in the same situation as the audience, in order to form a true judgment of the oration. In like manner, when any work is addressed to the public, though I should have a friendship or enmity with the author, I must depart from this situation; and considering myself as a man in general, forget, if possible, my individual being and my peculiar circumstances. A person influenced by prejudice, complies not with this condition; but obstinately maintains his natural position, without placing himself in that point of view, which the performance supposes. If the work be addressed to persons of a different age or nation, he makes no allowance for their peculiar views and prejudices; but, full of the manners of his own age and country, rashly condemns what seemed admirable in the eyes of those for whom alone the discourse was calculated. If the work be executed for the public, he never sufficiently

2. Metrical structure.
3. An unreasonable preconceived judgment or conviction.
4. Disposition.

enlarges his comprehension, or forgets his interest as a friend or enemy, as a rival or commentator. By this means, his sentiments are perverted; nor have the same beauties and blemishes the same influence upon him, as if he had imposed a proper violence on his imagination, and had forgotten himself for a moment. So far his taste evidently departs from the true standard; and of consequence loses all credit and authority.

It is well known, that in all questions, submitted to the understanding, prejudice is destructive of sound judgment, and perverts all operations of the intellectual faculties: It is no less contrary to good taste; nor has it less influence to corrupt our sentiment of beauty. It belongs to *good sense* to check its influence in both cases; and in this respect, as well as in many others, reason, if not an essential part of taste, is at least requisite to the operations of this latter faculty. In all the nobler productions of genius, there is a mutual relation and correspondence of parts; nor can either the beauties or blemishes be perceived by him, whose thought is not capacious enough to comprehend all those parts, and compare them with each other, in order to perceive the consistence and uniformity of the whole. Every work of art has also a certain end or purpose, for which it is calculated; and is to be deemed more or less perfect, as it is more or less fitted to attain this end. The object of eloquence is to persuade, of history to instruct, of poetry to please by means of the passions and the imagination. These ends we must carry constantly in our view, when we peruse any performance; and we must be able to judge how far the means employed are adapted to their respective purposes. Besides, every kind of composition, even the most poetical, is nothing but a chain of propositions and reasonings; not always, indeed, the justest and most exact, but still plausible and specious, however disguised by the colouring of the imagination. The persons introduced in tragedy and epic poetry, must be represented as reasoning, and thinking, and concluding, and acting, suitably to their character and circumstances; and without judgment, as well as taste and invention, a poet can never hope to succeed in so delicate an undertaking. Not to mention, that the same excellence of faculties which contributes to the improvement of reason, the same clearness of conception, the same exactness of distinction, the same vivacity of apprehension, are essential to the operations of true taste, and are its infallible concomitants. It seldom, or never happens, that a man of sense, who has experience in any art, cannot judge of its beauty; and it is no less rare to meet with a man who has a just taste without a sound understanding.

Thus, though the principles of taste be universal, and nearly, if not entirely the same in all men; yet few are qualified to give judgment on any work of art, or establish their own sentiment as the standard of beauty. The organs of internal sensation are seldom so perfect as to allow the general principles their full play, and produce a feeling correspondent to those principles. They either labour under some defect, or are vitiated by some disorder; and by that means, excite a sentiment, which may be pronounced erroneous. When the critic has no delicacy, he judges without any distinction, and is only affected by the grosser and more palpable qualities of the object: The finer touches pass unnoticed and disregarded. Where he is not aided by practice, his verdict is attended with confusion and hesitation. Where no comparison has been employed, the most frivolous beauties, such as rather merit the name of defects, are the object of his admiration. Where he lies under the influence of prejudice, all his natural sentiments are perverted. Where good sense is wanting, he is not qualified to discern the beauties of design and reasoning, which are the highest and most excellent. Under some or other of these imperfections, the generality of men labour; and hence a true judge in the finer arts is observed, even during the most polished ages, to be so rare a character: Strong sense, united to delicate sentiment, improved by practice, perfected by comparison, and cleared of all prejudice, can alone entitle critics to this valuable character; and the joint verdict of such, wherever they are to be found, is the true standard of taste and beauty.

But where are such critics to be found? By what marks are they to be known? How distinguish them from pretenders? These questions are embarrassing; and seem to throw us back into the same uncertainty, from which, during the course of this essay, we have endeavoured to extricate ourselves.

But if we consider the matter aright, these are questions of fact, not of sentiment. Whether any particular person be endowed with good sense and a delicate imagination, free from prejudice, may often be the subject of dispute, and be liable to great discussion and enquiry: But that such a character is valuable and estimable will be agreed in by all mankind. Where these doubts occur, men can do no more than in other disputable questions, which are submitted to the understanding: They must produce the best arguments, that their invention suggests to them; they must acknowledge a true and decisive standard to exist somewhere, to wit, real existence and matter of fact; and they must have indulgence to such as differ from them in their appeals to this standard. It is sufficient for our present purpose, if we have proved, that the taste of all individuals is not upon an equal footing, and that some men in general, however difficult to be particularly pitched upon, will be acknowledged by universal sentiment to have a preference above others.

But in reality the difficulty of finding, even in particulars, the standard of taste, is not so great as it is represented. Though in speculation, we may readily avow a certain criterion in science and deny it in sentiment, the matter is found in practice to be much more hard to ascertain in the former case than in the latter. Theories of abstract philosophy, systems of profound theology, have prevailed during one age: In a successive period, these have been universally exploded: Their absurdity has been detected: Other theories and systems have supplied their place, which again gave place to their successors: And nothing has been experienced more liable to the revolutions of chance and fashion than these pretended decisions of science. The case is not the same with the beauties of eloquence and poetry. Just expressions of passion and nature are sure, after a little time, to gain public applause, which they maintain for ever. ARISTOTLE, and PLATO, and EPICURUS, and DESCARTES,[5] may successively yield to each other: But TERENCE and VIRGIL[6] maintain an universal, undisputed empire over the minds of men. The abstract philosophy of CICERO[7] has lost its credit: The vehemence of his oratory is still the object of our admiration.

Though men of delicate taste be rare, they are easily to be distinguished in society, by the soundness of their understanding and the superiority of

5. Hume names four philosophers: the Greeks ARISTOTLE (384–322 B.C.E.), PLATO (ca. 427–ca. 347 B.C.E.), and Epicurus (341–270 B.C.E.), and the French René Descartes (1596–1650).

6. Roman poet (70–19 B.C.E.). Terence (ca. 190–159 B.C.E.), Roman comic playwright.

7. Roman statesman and orator (106–43 B.C.E.).

their faculties above the rest of mankind. The ascendant, which they acquire, gives a prevalence to that lively approbation, with which they receive any productions of genius, and renders it generally predominant. Many men, when left to themselves, have but a faint and dubious perception of beauty, who yet are capable of relishing any fine stroke, which is pointed out to them. Every convert to the admiration of the real poet or orator is the cause of some new conversion. And though prejudices may prevail for a time, they never unite in celebrating any rival to the true genius, but yield at last to the force of nature and just sentiment. Thus, though a civilized nation may easily be mistaken in the choice of their admired philosopher, they never have been found long to err, in their affection for a favourite epic or tragic author.

But notwithstanding all our endeavours to fix a standard of taste, and reconcile the discordant apprehensions of men, there still remain two sources of variation, which are not sufficient indeed to confound all the boundaries of beauty and deformity, but will often serve to produce a difference in the degrees of our approbation or blame. The one is the different humours of particular men; the other, the particular manners and opinions of our age and country. The general principles of taste are uniform in human nature: Where men vary in their judgments, some defect or perversion in the faculties may commonly be remarked; proceeding either from prejudice, from want of practice, or want of delicacy; and there is just reason for approving one taste, and condemning another. But where there is such a diversity in the internal frame or external situation as is entirely blameless on both sides, and leaves no room to give one the preference above the other; in that case a certain degree of diversity in judgment is unavoidable, and we seek in vain for a standard, by which we can reconcile the contrary sentiments.

A young man, whose passions are warm, will be more sensibly touched with amorous and tender images, than a man more advanced in years, who takes pleasure in wise, philosophical reflections concerning the conduct of life and moderation of the passions. At twenty, OVID may be the favourite author; HORACE at forty; and perhaps TACITUS[8] at fifty. Vainly would we, in such cases, endeavour to enter into the sentiments of others, and divest ourselves of those propensities, which are natural to us. We choose our favourite author as we do our friend, from a conformity of humour and disposition. Mirth or passion, sentiment or reflection; whichever of these most predominates in our temper, it gives us a peculiar sympathy with the writer who resembles us.

One person is more pleased with the sublime; another with the tender; a third with raillery. One has a strong sensibility to blemishes, and is extremely studious of correctness: Another has a more lively feeling of beauties, and pardons twenty absurdities and defects for one elevated or pathetic[9] stroke. The ear of this man is entirely turned towards conciseness and energy; that man is delighted with a copious, rich, and harmonious expression. Simplicity is affected by one; ornament by another. Comedy, tragedy, satire, odes, have each its partizans, who prefer that particular species of writing to all others. It is plainly an error in a critic, to confine his approbation to one species or style of writing, and condemn all the rest. But it is almost impossible not to

8. Roman public official and historian (ca. 55–ca. 120 C.E.). Ovid (43 B.C.E.–17 C.E.), Roman poet best known for his love poetry. HORACE (65–8 B.C.E.), Roman lyric poet and satirist whose works often reflected his own life.

9. That is, full of pathos or feeling.

feel a predilection for that which suits our particular turn and disposition. Such preferences are innocent and unavoidable, and can never reasonably be the object of dispute, because there is no standard, by which they can be decided.

For a like reason, we are more pleased, in the course of our reading, with pictures and characters, that resemble objects which are found in our own age or country, than with those which describe a different set of customs. It is not without some effort, that we reconcile ourselves to the simplicity of ancient manners, and behold princesses carrying water from the spring, and kings and heroes dressing their own victuals. We may allow in general, that the representation of such manners is no fault in the author, nor deformity in the piece; but we are not so sensibly touched with them. For this reason, comedy is not easily transferred from one age or nation to another. A FRENCHMAN or ENGLISHMAN is not pleased with the ANDRIA of TERENCE, or CLITIA of MACHIAVEL;[1] where the fine lady, upon whom all the play turns, never once appears to the spectators, but is always kept behind the scenes, suitably to the reserved humour of the ancient GREEKS and modern ITALIANS. A man of learning and reflection can make allowance for these peculiarities of manners; but a common audience can never divest themselves so far of their usual ideas and sentiments, as to relish pictures which no wise resemble them.

But here there occurs a reflection, which may, perhaps, be useful in examining the celebrated controversy concerning ancient and modern learning; where we often find the one side excusing any seeming absurdity in the ancients from the manners of the age, and the other refusing to admit this excuse, or at least, admitting it only as an apology for the author, not for the performance. In my opinion, the proper boundaries in this subject have seldom been fixed between the contending parties. Where any innocent peculiarities of manners are represented, such as those above mentioned, they ought certainly to be admitted; and a man, who is shocked with them, gives an evident proof of false delicacy and refinement. The poet's *monument more durable than brass*,[2] must fall to the ground like common brick or clay, were men to make no allowance for the continual revolutions of manners and customs, and would admit of nothing but what was suitable to the prevailing fashion. Must we throw aside the pictures of our ancestors, because of their ruffs and fardingales?[3] But where the ideas of morality and decency alter from one age to another, and where vicious manners are described, without being marked with the proper characters of blame and disapprobation; this must be allowed to disfigure the poem, and to be a real deformity. I cannot, nor is it proper I should, enter into such sentiments; and however I may excuse the poet, on account of the manners of his age, I never can relish the composition. The want of humanity and of decency, so conspicuous in the characters drawn by several of the ancient poets, even sometimes by HOMER and the GREEK tragedians, diminishes considerably the merit of their noble performances, and gives modern authors an advantage over them. We are not interested in the fortunes and sentiments of such rough heroes: We are

1. Niccolò Machiavelli (1469–1527), Italian political theorist; he wrote the play *Clizia* in 1525. In *Andria* (166 B.C.E.), the young woman at the center of the action never speaks a word.

2. Horace, *Odes* 3.30.1.

3. Farthingales: supports (such as hoops) that expanded skirts to extend them at the hip line. "Ruffs": stiff collars.

displeased to find the limits of vice and virtue so much confounded: And whatever indulgence we may give to the writer on account of his prejudices, we cannot prevail on ourselves to enter into his sentiments, or bear an affection to characters, which we plainly discover to be blameable.

The case is not the same with moral principles, as with speculative opinions of any kind. These are in continual flux and revolution. The son embraces a different system from the father. Nay, there scarcely is any man, who can boast of great constancy and uniformity in this particular. Whatever speculative errors may be found in the polite writings of any age or country, they detract but little from the value of those compositions. There needs but a certain turn of thought or imagination to make us enter into all the opinions, which then prevailed, and relish the sentiments or conclusions derived from them. But a very violent effort is requisite to change our judgment of manners, and excite sentiments of approbation or blame, love or hatred, different from those to which the mind from long custom has been familiarized. And where a man is confident of the rectitude of that moral standard, by which he judges, he is justly jealous of it, and will not pervert the sentiments of his heart for a moment, in complaisance to any writer whatsoever.

Of all speculative errors, those, which regard religion, are the most excusable in compositions of genius; nor is it ever permitted to judge of the civility or wisdom of any people, or even of single persons, by the grossness or refinement of their theological principles. The same good sense, that directs men in the ordinary occurrences of life, is not hearkened to in religious matters, which are supposed to be placed altogether above the cognizance of human reason. On this account, all the absurdities of the pagan system of theology must be overlooked by every critic, who would pretend to form a just notion of ancient poetry; and our posterity, in their turn, must have the same indulgence to their forefathers. No religious principles can ever be imputed as a fault to any poet, while they remain merely principles, and take not such strong possession of his heart, as to lay him under the imputation of *bigotry* or *superstition*. Where that happens, they confound the sentiments of morality, and alter the natural boundaries of vice and virtue. They are therefore eternal blemishes, according to the principle abovementioned: nor are the prejudices and false opinions of the age sufficient to justify them.

It is essential to the ROMAN catholic religion to inspire a violent hatred of every other worship, and to represent all pagans, mahometans,[4] and heretics as the objects of divine wrath and vengeance. Such sentiments, though they are in reality very blameable, are considered as virtues by the zealots of that communion, and are represented in their tragedies and epic poems as a kind of divine heroism. This bigotry has disfigured two very fine tragedies of the FRENCH theatre, POLIEUCTE and ATHALIA;[5] where an intemperate zeal for particular modes of worship is set off with all the pomp imaginable, and forms the predominant character of the heroes. "What is this," says the sublime JOAD to JOSABET, finding her in discourse with MATHAN, the priest of BAAL, "Does the daughter of DAVID speak to this traitor? Are you not afraid, lest the earth should open and pour forth flames to devour you both? Or lest these holy walls should fall and crush you together? What is his purpose? Why comes that enemy of God hither to poison the air, which we breathe,

4. Muslims.
5. *Athalie* (1691), by Jean Racine; Hume quotes from 3.5. *Polyeucte* (1641–42), play by PIERRE CORNEILLE.

with his horrid presence?" Such sentiments are received with great applause on the theatre of PARIS; but at LONDON the spectators would be full as much pleased to hear ACHILLES tell AGAMEMNON, that he was a dog in his forehead, and a deer in his heart, or JUPITER threaten JUNO with a sound drubbing, if she will not be quiet.[6]

RELIGIOUS principles are also a blemish in any polite composition, when they rise up to superstition, and intrude themselves into every sentiment, however remote from any connection with religion. It is no excuse for the poet, that the customs of his country had burthened[7] life with so many religious ceremonies and observances, that no part of it was exempt from that yoke. It must for ever be ridiculous in PETRARCH[8] to compare his mistress, LAURA, to JESUS CHRIST. Nor is it less ridiculous in that agreeable libertine, BOCCACE,[9] very seriously to give thanks to GOD ALMIGHTY and the ladies, for their assistance in defending him against his enemies.

1757

6. See Homer, *Iliad* 1.225, 565–67. Hume's point is that English audiences are unmoved by the tragedies' Catholic sentiments.
7. Burdened.
8. Francesco Petrarca (1304–1374), Italian poet, scholar, and humanist; Laura is the subject of a series of love lyrics titled *Canzoniere* or *Rima* (see, e.g., no. 3 for the comparison to Jesus).
9. GIOVANNI BOCCACCIO (1313–1375), Italian poet and writer. His most famous work, the *Decameron* (1351–53), is a collection of 100 tales supposedly told over 10 days; Hume refers here to the introduction to "The Fourth Day."

IMMANUEL KANT
1724–1804

Immanuel Kant's massive contributions to modern metaphysics, epistemology, and ethics aside, his *Critique of Judgment* (1790) ranks with Aristotle's *Poetics* among our most important philosophical treatises on art. Kant's book is a compendium of the beliefs about and ideals for art that have come to be called *aestheticism* (the separation of artistic concerns and values into their own sphere, which is seen as superior to all others). The branch of philosophy dealing with the nature of beauty, art, and taste first arose in the mid–eighteenth century in the work of Edmund Alexander Baumgarten, DAVID HUME, and EDMUND BURKE. Kant's *Critique of Judgment* responds to and augments their earlier work while giving art an exalted place within human existence, a place that justifies the new philosophical interest in art as a distinct sphere of human activity. The specifics of Kant's characterization of art resonate throughout the Romantic and modernist periods and have become a frequent target of post–World War II theorists and philosophers.

Kant was born in Königsberg, East Prussia, where he attended the university, became a professor at that same university, and died shortly after his retirement. He never married and he never traveled outside of East Prussia. His regular, uneventful life is summed up in the legend that Königsberg residents set their clocks by his appearance for his afternoon walk at precisely the same time each day. His early work was mostly in the natural sciences, with one excursion into aesthetics: *Observations on the Feeling of the Beautiful and Sublime* (1764). In this work, he argues that such feelings are purely subjective, precisely the position he sets himself against when later revisiting the same terrain in his *Critique of Judgment*.

Kant's major work begins with the *Critique of Pure Reason* (1781), in which he develops his "critical philosophy" to overcome David Hume's subjectivist skepticism. This "first critique" was followed by two others: the *Critique of Practical Reason* (1788) and the *Critique of Judgment*. The three books cover the true, the good, and the beautiful, respectively. By *critique* Kant meant a delineation of the fundamental or "transcendent" conditions necessary to any particular mental process. Thus the *Critique of Pure Reason* presents the mental forms (or categories) that must be in place within the perceiving subject for any successful apprehension of the external world. He insists that these universals (for example, cause and effect, or unity) are implanted within every human being and underwrite the very possibility of "understanding" (that is, the ability to process, organize, and comprehend the data given to our senses by the outside world). We can never directly know what he calls "things-in-themselves," because we process sensory data through preexisting mental categories.

The *Critique of Practical Reason* attempts to provide a universal foundation for morals, which concern nonphysical ideas, not material realities. Kant's basic claim is that practical reason in each individual dictates the same fundamental moral dictum: never do anything that you could not willingly endorse being done by everyone else in the world.

The first two critiques create a gap between the physical (sensible) and nonphysical (supersensible) worlds. Understanding deals with the physical world of cause and effect, where each occurrence has been determined by prior events. Because practical reason deals with ideas, it exists in a realm of freedom. The ability to think makes humans free, but they are also physical creatures subject to physical causality. The *Critique of Judgment* exists to bridge this gap between what Kant sees as two aspects of human nature. The very word *aesthetic*, whose Greek root means "of the senses," aids Kant's efforts to get from the sensory to the supersensible. Beauty is experienced through the senses, but points us beyond mere sensation.

That Kant fixes on the aesthetic experience of beauty to solve a pressing problem in his own large-scale system has been irrelevant to many of the artists and writers who subsequently adopted or adapted his characterization of art. The literature on the *Critique of Judgment* divides into two traditions, one focusing on Kant's overall philosophical project and the other focusing on the theory of art one can derive from Kant's work; our selection is slanted toward the latter, but to understand Kant's way of approaching the whole topic of art we must also take into account his broader philosophical goal.

Kant's primary aim is to establish the "subjective universality" of the judgment that something is beautiful or sublime. Judgment in general is the determination of whether a particular instance qualifies as one thing or another. For example, given the number "10," I judge it to be an even number because I recognize that it is divisible by 2. Or when I judge the object in front of me to be a table, I am (Kant says) simply "subsuming" a particular thing under the general concept of table, a concept I already possess. Such judgments are "determinative" and "objective." Since the concepts *even number* and *table* already exist and unambiguously provide the rule my judgment follows, there is little room for error or disagreement.

The statements "it's beautiful" and "it's a table" are identical in form, yet we are much more likely to disagree over the former. Why? Kant's answer has two parts. On the one hand, by saying "it's beautiful" rather than "I think it's beautiful," I am claiming that beauty resides in the object and I am thus making a claim to validity beyond my individual, subjective preferences. On the other hand, *beautiful* is not a determinative concept like *table* or *even number*: judgments about beauty are instead "reflective," occurring in the absence of a firm rule or standard, and hence are more likely to generate disagreement. The ability to judge well amid such uncertainties is called *taste*—and some people have better taste than others (though Kant would insist that everyone has the potential to achieve the highest possible taste).

In considering the notion of taste, Kant is (once again) engaging with David Hume. While accepting Hume's contention that taste is something learned, Kant believes that he failed in "Of the Standard of Taste" (1757; see above) to defend against the possible conclusion that it is culturally relative. Kant's solution is to distinguish between what is "agreeable," what is "good," and what is "beautiful." (As a rule of thumb, reading Kant becomes easier when one pays attention to what distinctions he attempts to draw and why.) The good is a matter of reason—and of what we *should* desire. The agreeable is a matter of the senses—and of what we physically desire. The beautiful mixes the sensible with the nonsensible—and involves no desire whatsoever: thus Kant calls judgments of beauty "disinterested." Perhaps nothing Kant advanced has been as influential as this severance of the beautiful from interest. His basic notion is that a sensory experience of pleasure can move from the subjective ("that is pleasing to me") to the objective ("that should please everyone") only if purged of its individual, interested elements.

Kant uses the example of the difference between taste in food and taste in flowers. My daughter and I can agree that cotton candy is sweet, but she likes and desires it while I dislike and do not desire it. There is no disputing taste in such matters precisely because it is tied to idiosyncratic, physiological appetites. But Kant believes that things change when we perceive a field of flowers—or a painting of flowers. The flowers have no purpose in relation to my life or my physical needs. I can contemplate them disinterestedly, and thus my judgment about their beauty is not connected to their gratifying my personal sensibility. My statement "they are beautiful" solicits, Kant says, the agreement of everyone else in a way that my statement "I like green beans" does not.

The understanding of art that follows from this analysis was widely adopted. MATTHEW ARNOLD's "Function of Criticism at the Present Time" (1864) is an important attempt to extend the ideal of disinterestedness to criticism; more recent critics have attempted to refute the notion (see our selections by PIERRE BOURDIEU, BARBARA HERRNSTEIN SMITH, and TERRY EAGLETON). Crucially, Kant's argument leads him to elevate artistic form over matter. Because he is trying to demote the physical appeal of the aesthetic, he claims that the formal properties of the observed object, not its physical and material properties, most influence judgments of beauty. Sensual responses are subjective (later writers also consider them vulgar), failing to rise above the level of the agreeable. This distinction is still used today by some to distinguish pornography from art with sexual content. In addition, the valorization of form over matter resurfaces in the various modernist versions of "abstract" and "nonrepresentational" art that emerge between 1850 (Flaubert's desire to write a novel about nothing) and 1950 (abstract expressionism).

Disinterestedness as an aesthetic ideal also entails distinguishing between the useful and the nonutilitarian work of art. At its most extreme, it generates the credo of aestheticism: "art for art's sake" (for example, see our selections from THÉOPHILE GAUTIER, WALTER PATER, and OSCAR WILDE). The beautiful object should not be tainted with any mundane purpose. The troubled relationship between art and commerce stems in part from this dream of an art that can transcend all petty worldly concerns. Kant expresses this aim in a famous formula: the beautiful object reveals "purposiveness without purpose." That is, the object is comprehensible only if we assume it was made by a purposive agent (an a priori condition of aesthetic judgment that Kant's "critique" reveals), even though it has no particular, determinative purpose. The formal coherence of flowers is incomprehensible apart from a general assumption of their "purposiveness," although we can ascribe no particular purpose to them. Art objects aspire to general purposiveness in the absence of any concrete purpose.

As we apprehend such objects, we respond with "free play" of the mind (a notion further developed by FRIEDRICH VON SCHILLER, among many others). The aesthetic therefore provides an experience of freedom within the physical world of causal determination. Aesthetic experience is crucial to Kant because it makes possible a "harmony" between our human freedom and our physical immersion in the world—the feeling that is the true foundation of our experiences of beauty. And because such harmony is available to all humans, I can solicit their agreement with my particular judgments of beauty. But in any particular case, I may not succeed in gaining others' agreement. Kant is careful to say that beauty is only an "ideal," not a "concept." The example is singular, but it carries a general significance. Each artwork, like every judgment about beauty, solicits its audience's approval both as a particular and as an example of a kind, a genre, or an act of criticism. For that reason, there is no rule of beauty: its validity for everyone will always be "exemplary."

For Kant, beauty intimates the harmony within our dual human nature as free and physical beings. Beauty ultimately refers to the subjective experience of this harmony rather than to any property in the object that promotes that experience. Hence aesthetic experience is "subjective"; but because all humans are susceptible to the experience of harmony, this response possesses a "universality" usually absent in subjective judgments. Kant goes even further when he calls beauty "the symbol of morality" (§59) and comes close to providing beauty a purpose and an interest. His own interests in writing the third critique certainly come to light in this statement: he wants the experience of the beautiful to signity that humans live in an "intelligible" universe, that the ideas and precepts generated by human reason are in tune with the nature of the universe itself. The experience of beauty tells us that mind and world fit.

The sublime, in contrast, shows us a misfit between mind and world. When we experience a hurricane or an earthquake, nature appears to dwarf human concerns and capabilities. The sublime, according to Kant, allows us to glimpse things beyond comprehension and to experience the limits of the sensible, physical world, generating feelings of awe and terror. This experience of the limits of the sensible, of its inability to encompass aspects of our mental world, reminds us of "the superiority of the rational vocation of our cognitive powers over the greatest power of sensibility." But even while performing this important function of pointing us away from the sensible toward the mysterious supersensible, the sublime remains disquieting because in doing so it indicates a split between the two. It is just this experience of disjunction that Kant needs to subsume within the grander overarching experience of harmony that comes with the beautiful. Thus "the concept of the sublime in nature is not nearly as important and rich in implications as that of the beautiful in nature."

Kant inherits the notion of the sublime as a central feature of the aesthetic from LONGINUS and Burke, but he addresses it primarily to contain it; his remarks, though suggestive, have had relatively little influence. He is not particularly sympathetic to the brand of Romantic melancholy that emphasizes the tragic gulf between human aspirations and what the world renders possible. Nor is he interested in the recurrent artistic experience of struggling to express the ineffable with the limited material resources (sound, paint, stone) afforded to the arts. The revival of interest in the sublime in poststructuralist writers such as PAUL DE MAN and JEAN-FRANÇOIS LYOTARD has informed recent critiques of the Kantian aesthetics of beauty.

In fact, attitudes toward Kant are something of a litmus test among post-1945 theorists. Section 40 encapsulates what we might call Kant's liberal optimism—his belief that disinterested judgments can enable "unprejudiced," "broadened" thinking and pave the way toward "enlightenment" and agreement. The *sensus communis*, an understanding shared by all humans, serves as both the guarantor (since everyone potentially possesses it) and the end result of the discussions surrounding varying judgments. Anti-Kantians (often proponents of the sublime) deny the possibility of such common ground for discussion and eventual agreement, arguing that the translation of different viewpoints into a common language always already erases or represses the very differences that constitute the disagreement.

It might seem surprising that the *Critique of Judgment* has been an extraordinarily influential text on art. After all, in some ways, the book is hardly about art at all. Most of Kant's examples come from nature, and *aesthetic* in his usage refers more to what is experienced through the senses than to something specifically artistic. Like Aristotle, he focuses on the spectator's response rather than on artistic production, but without Aristotle's interest in the elements or properties of the art object. Kant apparently believes that it makes no difference whether the object is natural or human-made. Even when he does distinguish art from nature in §43, Kant is more concerned with preserving art's freedom—aligning it with beauty against the determined world of science and the utilitarian concerns of craft—than with examining the consequences of art's being (by definition) artificial. He never considers why the beauties offered by nature do not suffice, or what art can do that nature cannot.

Not surprisingly, Kant's influential description of the genius (the creative artist) highlights freedom above all else. The genius has a natural gift for using the materials (words, paint, musical notes) of the various arts "to express what is ineffable," that is, nonmaterial ideas and emotions. In the greatest artworks, imagination's freedom harmonizes with understanding's lawfulness, a result achievable not "by any compliance with rules, . . . but . . . only by the subject's nature."

Although there were always dissenters, Kant's general account of the aesthetic as formal, free, nonutilitarian, disinterested, and nonsensory was the prevailing orthodoxy for almost two centuries. That so many post–World War II theorists have written against the *Critique of Judgment* testifies to the continuing importance of the understanding of art that it enshrines and that they have attempted to revise.

BIBLIOGRAPHY

The Cambridge edition of the works of Immanuel Kant (1992–) now in progress will offer the first complete scholarly edition in English of all of Kant's writing (in the list below, all translations published after 1991 belong to this edition). *Theoretical Philosophy, 1755–1770*, edited by David Walford (1992), contains much of Kant's early work (although not his 1764 book on aesthetics), while *Practical Philosophy*, edited by Mary J. Gregor (1996), collects the major works on morality (including *Groundwork of the Metaphysics of Morals*, 1785; *Critique of Practical Reason*, 1788; and *The Metaphysics of Morals*, 1797, along with the important essays "What Is Enlightenment?" 1784 and "Toward Perpetual Peace," 1795). Kant's major individual works are *Observations on the Feeling of the Beautiful and Sublime* (1764: trans. 1960); *Critique of Pure Reason* (1781; trans. 1998); *Prolegomena to Any Future Metaphysics* (1783; trans. 1950); *Metaphysical Foundations of Natural Science* (1786; trans. 1970); *Critique of Judgment* (1790; trans. 1987); *Religion within the Boundaries of Mere Reason* (1793; trans. 1998); *The Conflict of Faculties* (1798; trans. 1979); and *Anthropology from a Pragmatic Point of View* (1798; trans. 1974). Kant's essays, lectures, and letters can be found in *Kant: On History*, edited by Louis White Beck (1963); *Selected Pre-Critical Writings and Correspondence with Beck*, edited by G. B. Kerferd and D. E. Walford (1968); *Kant's Political Writings*, edited by Hans Reiss (1970); *Lectures on Philosophical Theology*, edited by Allen W. Wood and Gertrude M. Clark (1978); *Perpetual Peace and Other Essays on Politics, History, and Morals*, edited by Ted Humphrey (1983); *Lectures on Logic*, edited by J. Michael Young (1992); *Lectures on Ethics*, edited by Peter Heath and J. B. Schneewind (1997); *Lectures on Metaphysics*, edited by Karl Ameriks and Steve Naragon (1997); and *Correspondence*, edited by Arnulf Zweig (1999). The best biography is Ernst Cassirer's *Kant's Life and Thought* (1921; trans. 1981).

The secondary literature on Kant is immense. *The Cambridge Companion to Kant*, edited by Paul Guyer (1992), offers the best single-volume overview of Kant's career. The best introduction to standard philosophical responses to the *Critique of Judgment* is *Essays in Kant's Aesthetics*, edited by Ted Cohen and Paul Guyer (1982). See also

René Wellek's *Immanuel Kant in England* (1931). Of the many encounters with the third critique from within "theory," the following works have been especially important: Hannah Arendt, *Lectures on Kant's Political Philosophy* (1982); Pierre Bourdieu, *Distinction: A Social Critique of the Judgement of Taste* (1979; trans. 1984); Jacques Derrida, *The Truth in Painting* (1978; trans. 1987); Barbara Herrnstein Smith, *Contingencies of Value* (1988); Terry Eagleton, *The Ideology of the Aesthetic* (1990); J. M. Bernstein, *The Fate of Art* (1992); and Jean-François Lyotard, *Lessons on the Analytic of the Sublime* (1991; trans. 1994). Paul Guyer's *Kant and the Claims of Taste* (2d ed., 1997) is the most comprehensive treatment of the *Critique of Judgment* within Anglo-American philosophy. The most useful bibliography on Kant is found in *The Cambridge Companion; Essays in Kant's Aesthetics* offers an extensive, though now somewhat dated, bibliography on that topic.

From Critique of Judgment[1]

From *Introduction*

Judgment in general is the ability to think the particular as contained under the universal. If the universal (the rule, principle, law) is given, then judgment, which subsumes the particular under it, is *determinative* (even though [in its role] as transcendental judgment it states a priori the conditions that must be met for subsumption under that universal to be possible). But if only the particular is given and judgment has to find the universal for it, then this power is merely *reflective*.

* * *

ON THE AESTHETIC PRESENTATION OF THE PURPOSIVENESS[2] OF NATURE

What is merely subjective in the presentation of an object, i.e., what constitutes its reference to the subject and not to the object, is its aesthetic character; but whatever in it serves, or can be used, to determine the object (for cognition)[3] is its logical validity. In the cognition of an object of sense these two references [to the subject and to the object] occur together.

* * *

[T]hat subjective [feature] of a presentation *which cannot at all become an element of cognition* is the *pleasure* or *displeasure* connected with that presentation. For through this pleasure or displeasure I do not cognize anything in the object of the presentation, though it may certainly be the effect of some cognition. Now a thing's purposiveness, insofar as it is presented in the perception of the thing, is also not a characteristic of the object itself (for no such characteristic can be perceived), even though it can be inferred from a cognition of things. Therefore, the subjective [feature] of the pres-

1. Translated by Werner S. Pluhar, who occasionally retains the original German words or adds information in brackets in the text. Unless otherwise specified, parenthetical terms are in Latin and are translated in the text.
2. The general sense that a thing was formed by a purposive hand, although without a specific function or purpose (a key term in Kant's aesthetic theory).
3. The process in which sense data plus the categories of understanding ("pure reason") combine in our ability to apprehend and name objects in the external world. "Aesthetic": pertaining to an individual's sensory experiences.

entation which cannot at all become an element of cognition is the purposiveness that precedes the cognition of an object and that we connect directly with this presentation even if we are not seeking to use the presentation of the object for cognition. Therefore, in this case we call the object purposive only because its presentation is directly connected with the feeling of pleasure, and this presentation itself is an aesthetic presentation of purposiveness. The only question is whether there is such a presentation of purposiveness at all.

When pleasure is connected with mere apprehension (*apprehensio*) of the form of an object of intuition, and we do not refer the apprehension to a concept so as to give rise to determinate cognition, then we refer the presentation not to the object but solely to the subject; and the pleasure cannot express anything other than the object's being commensurate with the cognitive powers that are, and insofar as they are, brought into play when we judge reflectively, and hence [expresses] merely a subjective formal purposiveness of the object. For this apprehension of forms by the imagination could never occur if reflective judgment did not compare them, even if unintentionally, at least with its ability [in general] to refer intuitions to concepts. Now if in this comparison a given presentation unintentionally brings the imagination (the power of a priori intuitions) into harmony with the understanding (the power of concepts), and this harmony arouses a feeling of pleasure, then the object must thereupon be regarded as purposive for the reflective power of judgment. A judgment of this sort is an aesthetic judgment about the object's purposiveness; it is not based on any concept we have of the object, nor does it provide such a concept. When the form of an object (rather than what is material in its presentation, viz., in sensation) is judged in mere reflection on it (without regard to a concept that is to be acquired from it) to be the basis of a pleasure in such an object's presentation, then the presentation of this object is also judged to be connected necessarily with this pleasure, and hence connected with it not merely for the subject apprehending this form but in general for everyone who judges [it]. The object is then called beautiful, and our ability to judge by such a pleasure (and hence also with universal validity) is called taste.

* * *

From *Book I. Analytic of the Beautiful*

§1. A JUDGMENT OF TASTE IS AESTHETIC

If we wish to decide whether something is beautiful or not, we do not use understanding to refer the presentation to the object so as to give rise to cognition; rather, we use imagination[4] (perhaps in connection with understanding) to refer the presentation to the subject and his feeling of pleasure or displeasure. Hence a judgment of taste is not a cognitive judgment and so is not a logical judgment but an aesthetic one, by which we mean a judgment whose determining basis *cannot be other* than *subjective*. But any reference of presentations, even of sensations, can be objective (in which case it signifies what is real [rather than formal] in an empirical presentation);

4. The ability to represent in thought the features experienced in the sense perception of the external world.

excepted is a reference to the feeling of pleasure and displeasure—this reference designates nothing whatsoever in the object, but here the subject feels himself, [namely] how he is affected by the presentation.

To apprehend a regular, purposive building with one's cognitive power (whether the presentation is distinct or confused) is very different from being conscious of this presentation with a sensation of liking. Here the presentation is referred only to the subject, namely, to his feeling of life, under the name feeling of pleasure or displeasure, and this forms the basis of a very special power of discriminating and judging. This power does not contribute anything to cognition, but merely compares the given presentation in the subject with the entire presentational power, of which the mind becomes conscious when it feels its own state. The presentations given in a judgment may be empirical (and hence aesthetic), but if we refer them to the object, the judgment we make by means of them is logical. On the other hand, even if the given presentations were rational, they would still be aesthetic if, and to the extent that, the subject referred them, in his judgment, solely to himself (to his feeling).

§2. THE LIKING THAT DETERMINES A JUDGMENT OF TASTE IS DEVOID OF ALL INTEREST

Interest is what we call the liking we connect with the presentation of an object's existence. Hence such a liking always refers at once to our power of desire, either as the basis that determines it, or at any rate as necessarily connected with that determining basis. But if the question is whether something is beautiful, what we want to know is not whether we or anyone cares, or so much as might care, in any way, about the thing's existence, but rather how we judge it in our mere contemplation of it (intuition or reflection). Suppose someone asks me whether I consider the palace I see before me beautiful. I might reply that I am not fond of things of that sort, made merely to be gaped at. Or I might reply like that Iroquois *sachem* who said that he liked nothing better in Paris than the eating-houses.[5] I might even go on, as *Rousseau*[6] would, to rebuke the vanity of the great who spend the people's sweat on such superfluous things. I might, finally, quite easily convince myself that, if I were on some uninhabited island with no hope of ever again coming among people, and could conjure up such a splendid edifice by a mere wish, I would not even take that much trouble for it if I already had a sufficiently comfortable hut. The questioner may grant all this and approve of it; but it is not to the point. All he wants to know is whether my mere presentation of the object is accompanied by a liking, no matter how indifferent I may be about the existence of the object of this presentation. We can easily see that, in order for me to say that an object is *beautiful*, and to prove that I have taste, what matters is what I do with this presentation within myself, and not the [respect] in which I depend on the object's existence. Everyone has to admit that if a judgment about beauty is mingled with the least interest then it is very partial and not a pure judgment of taste. In

5. Kant's reference has been traced to Pierre François Xavier de Charlevoix, *History and General Description of New France* (Paris, 1744) [translator's note]. Charlevoix (1682–1761), French Jesuit explorer.

6. Jean-Jacques Rousseau (1712–1778), Swiss-born French political philosopher and novelist.

order to play the judge in matters of taste, we must not be in the least biased in favor of the thing's existence but must be wholly indifferent about it.

There is no better way to elucidate this proposition, which is of prime importance, than by contrasting the pure disinterested liking that occurs in a judgment of taste with a liking connected with interest, especially if we can also be certain that the kinds of interest I am about to mention are the only ones there are.

§3. A LIKING *FOR THE AGREEABLE* IS CONNECTED WITH INTEREST

AGREEABLE *is what the senses like in sensation.*

* * *

Now, that a judgment by which I declare an object to be agreeable expresses an interest in that object is already obvious from the fact that, by means of sensation, the judgment arouses a desire for objects of that kind, so that the liking presupposes something other than my mere judgment about the object: it presupposes that I have referred the existence of the object to my state insofar as that state is affected by such an object. This is why we say of the agreeable not merely that we *like* it but that it *gratifies* us. When I speak of the agreeable, I am not granting mere approval: the agreeable produces an inclination. Indeed, what is agreeable in the liveliest way requires no judgment at all about the character of the object, as we can see in people who aim at nothing but enjoyment (this is the word we use to mark the intensity of the gratification): they like to dispense with all judging.

§4. A LIKING *FOR THE GOOD* IS CONNECTED WITH INTEREST

Good is what, by means of reason, we like through its mere concept. We call something (viz., if it is something useful) *good for* [this or that] if we like it only as a means. But we call something *intrinsically good* if we like it for its own sake. In both senses of the term, the good always contains the concept of a purpose, consequently a relation of reason to a volition (that is at least possible), and hence a liking for the existence of an object or action. In other words, it contains some interest or other.

In order to consider something good, I must always know what sort of thing the object is [meant] to be, i.e., I must have a [determinate] concept of it. But I do not need this in order to find beauty in something. Flowers, free designs, lines aimlessly intertwined and called foliage: these have no significance, depend on no determinate concept, and yet we like [*gefallen*] them. A liking [*Wohlgefallen*] for the beautiful must depend on the reflection, regarding an object, that leads to some concept or other (but it is indeterminate which concept this is). This dependence on reflection also distinguishes the liking for the beautiful from [that for] the agreeable, which rests entirely on sensation.[7]

It is true that in many cases it seems as if the agreeable and the good are one and the same. Thus people commonly say that all gratification (especially if it lasts) is intrinsically good, which means roughly the same as to be (last-

7. That is, the pleasure derived from beauty is related to the indeterminate concept of purposiveness; thus judgments of beauty stand between the pure sensuousness of the agreeable and the pure rationality of the good.

ingly) agreeable and to be good are one and the same. Yet it is easy to see that in talking this way they are merely substituting one word for another by mistake, since the concepts that belong to these terms are in no way interchangeable. Insofar as we present an object as agreeable, we present it solely in relation to sense; but if we are to call the object good [as well], and hence an object of the will, we must first bring it under principles of reason, using the concept of a purpose. [So] if something that gratifies us is also called *good*, it has a very different relation to our liking. This is [also] evident from the fact that in the case of the good there is always the question whether it is good merely indirectly or good directly (i.e., useful, or intrinsically good), whereas in the case of the agreeable this question cannot even arise, since this word always signifies something that we like directly. (What we call beautiful is also liked directly.)

* * *

But despite all this difference between the agreeable and the good, they do agree in this: they are always connected with an interest in their object. This holds not only for the agreeable—see §3—and for what is good indirectly (useful), which we like as the means to something or other that is agreeable, but also for what is good absolutely and in every respect, i.e., the moral good, which carries with it the highest interest. For the good is the object of the will (a power of desire that is determined by reason). But to will something and to have a liking for its existence, i.e., to take an interest in it, are identical.

§5. COMPARISON OF THE THREE SORTS OF LIKING, WHICH DIFFER IN KIND

Both the agreeable and the good refer to our power of desire and hence carry a liking with them, the agreeable a liking that is conditioned pathologically by stimuli (*stimuli*), the good a pure practical liking that is determined not just by the presentation of the object but also by the presentation of the subject's connection with the existence of the object; i.e., what we like is not just the object but its existence as well. A judgment of taste, on the other hand, is merely *contemplative*, i.e., it is a judgment that is indifferent to the existence of the object: it [considers] the character of the object only by holding it up to our feeling of pleasure and displeasure. Nor is this contemplation, as such, directed to concepts, for a judgment of taste is not a cognitive judgment (whether theoretical or practical) and hence is neither *based* on concepts, nor directed to them as *purposes*.

Hence the agreeable, the beautiful, and the good designate three different relations that presentations have to the feeling of pleasure and displeasure, the feeling by reference to which we distinguish between objects or between ways of presenting them. The terms of approbation which are appropriate to each of these three are also different. We call *agreeable* what GRATIFIES us, *beautiful* what we just LIKE, good what we ESTEEM, or *endorse* [*billigen*], i.e., that to which we attribute [*setzen*] an objective value. Agreeableness holds for nonrational animals too; beauty only for human beings, i.e., beings who are animal and yet rational, though it is not enough that they be rational (e.g., spirits) but they must be animal as well; the good, however, holds for every rational being as such, though I cannot fully justify and explain this proposition until later. We may say that, of all these three kinds of liking, only the liking involved in taste for the beautiful is disinterested and *free*, since we are not compelled to give our approval by any interest, whether of sense or of reason. So we might say that [the term] liking, in the three cases mentioned, refers to *inclination*, or to *favor*, or to *respect*. For FAVOR is the only free liking. Neither an object of inclination, nor one that a law of reason enjoins on us as an object of desire, leaves us the freedom to make an object of pleasure for ourselves out of something or other. All interest either presupposes a need or gives rise to one; and, because interest is the basis that determines approval, it makes the judgment about the object unfree.

Consider, first, the interest of inclination, [which occurs] with the agreeable. Here everyone says: Hunger is the best sauce; and to people with a healthy appetite anything is tasty provided it is edible. Hence if people have a liking of this sort, that does not prove that they are selecting [*Wahl*] by taste. Only when their need has been satisfied can we tell who in a multitude of people has taste and who does not.

EXPLICATION OF THE BEAUTIFUL INFERRED FROM THE FIRST MOMENT[8]

Taste is the ability to judge an object, or a way of presenting it, by means of a liking or disliking *devoid of all interest*. The object of such a liking is called *beautiful*.

§6. THE BEAUTIFUL IS WHAT IS PRESENTED WITHOUT CONCEPTS AS THE OBJECT OF A *UNIVERSAL* LIKING

This explication of the beautiful can be inferred from the preceding explication of it as object of a liking devoid of all interest. For if someone likes something and is conscious that he himself does so without any interest, then he cannot help judging that it must contain a basis for being liked [that holds] for everyone. He must believe that he is justified in requiring a similar liking from everyone because he cannot discover, underlying this liking, any private conditions, on which only he might be dependent, so that he must regard it as based on what he can presuppose in everyone else as well. He cannot discover such private conditions because his liking is not based on any inclination he has (nor on any other considered interest whatever): rather, the judging person feels completely *free* as regards the liking he accords the object. Hence he will talk about the beautiful as if beauty were a characteristic of the object and the judgment were logical (namely, a cognition of the object through concepts of it), even though in fact the judgment is only aesthetic and refers the object's presentation merely to the subject. He will talk in this way because the judgment does resemble a logical judgment inasmuch as we may presuppose it to be valid for everyone. On the other hand, this universality cannot arise from concepts. For from concepts there is no transition to the feeling of pleasure or displeasure (except in pure practical laws; but these carry an interest with them, while none is connected with pure judgments of taste). It follows that,

8. The "analytic of the beautiful" of book 1 is divided into four "moments," which treat beauty in terms of quality, quantity, purposes, and liking for the object, respectively.

since a judgment of taste involves the consciousness that all interest is kept out of it, it must also involve a claim to being valid for everyone, but without having a universality based on concepts. In other words, a judgment of taste must involve a claim to subjective universality.

§7. COMPARISON OF THE BEAUTIFUL WITH THE AGREEABLE AND THE GOOD IN TERMS OF THE ABOVE CHARACTERISTIC

As regards the *agreeable* everyone acknowledges that his judgment, which he bases on a private feeling and by which he says that he likes some object, is by the same token confined to his own person. Hence, if he says that canary wine is agreeable he is quite content if someone else corrects his terms and reminds him to say instead: It is agreeable to *me*. This holds moreover not only for the taste of the tongue, palate, and throat, but also for what may be agreeable to any one's eyes and ears. To one person the color violet is gentle and lovely, to another lifeless and faded. One person loves the sound of wind instruments, another that of string instruments. It would be foolish if we disputed about such differences with the intention of censuring another's judgment as incorrect if it differs from ours, as if the two were opposed logically. Hence about the agreeable the following principle holds: *Everyone has his own taste* (of sense).

It is quite different (exactly the other way round) with the beautiful. It would be ridiculous if someone who prided himself on his taste tried to justify [it] by saying: This object (the building we are looking at, the garment that man is wearing, the concert we are listening to, the poem put up to be judged) is beautiful *for me*. For he must not call it *beautiful* if [he means] only [that] *he* likes it. Many things may be charming and agreeable to him; no one cares about that. But if he proclaims something to be beautiful, then he requires the same liking from others; he then judges not just for himself but for everyone, and speaks of beauty as if it were a property of things. That is why he says: The *thing* is beautiful, and does not count on other people to agree with his judgment of liking on the ground that he has repeatedly found them agreeing with him; rather, he *demands* that they agree. He reproaches them if they judge differently, and denies that they have taste, which he nevertheless demands of them, as something they ought to have. In view of this [*sofern*], we cannot say that everyone has his own particular taste. That would amount to saying that there is no such thing as taste at all, no aesthetic judgment that could rightfully lay claim to everyone's assent.

* * *

§8. IN A JUDGMENT OF TASTE THE UNIVERSALITY OF THE LIKING IS PRESENTED ONLY AS SUBJECTIVE

* * *

We must begin by fully convincing ourselves that in making a judgment of taste (about the beautiful) we require [*ansinnen*] *everyone* to like the object, yet without this liking's being based on a concept (since then it would be the good), and that this claim to universal validity belongs so essentially to a judgment by which we declare something to be *beautiful* that it would not occur to anyone to use this term without thinking of universal validity;

instead, everything we like without a concept would then be included with the agreeable. For as to the agreeable we allow everyone to be of a mind of his own, no one requiring [*zumuten*] others to agree with his judgment of taste. But in a judgment of taste about beauty we always require others to agree. Insofar as judgments about the agreeable are merely private, whereas judgments about the beautiful are put forward as having general validity (as being public), taste regarding the agreeable can be called taste of sense, and taste regarding the beautiful can be called taste of reflection, though the judgments of both are aesthetic (rather than practical) judgments about an object, [i.e.,] judgments merely about the relation that the presentation of the object has to the feeling of pleasure and displeasure. But surely there is something strange here. In the case of the taste of sense, not only does experience show that its judgment (of a pleasure or displeasure we take in something or other) does not hold universally, but people, of their own accord, are modest enough not even to require others to agree (even though there actually is, at times, very widespread agreement in these judgments too). Now, experience teaches us that the taste of reflection, with its claim that its judgment (about the beautiful) is universally valid for everyone, is also rejected often enough: What is strange is that the taste of reflection should nonetheless find itself able (as it actually does) to conceive of judgments that can demand such agreement, and that it does in fact require this agreement from everyone for each of its judgments. What the people who make these judgments dispute about is not whether such a claim is possible; they are merely unable to agree, in particular cases, on the correct way to apply this ability.

* * *

If we judge objects merely in terms of concepts, then we lose all presentation of beauty. This is why there can be no rule by which someone could be compelled to acknowledge that something is beautiful. No one can use reasons or principles to talk us into a judgment on whether some garment, house, or flower is beautiful. We want to submit the object to our own eyes, just as if our liking of it depended on that sensation. And yet, if we then call the object beautiful, we believe we have a universal voice, and lay claim to the agreement of everyone, whereas any private sensation would decide solely for the observer himself and his liking.

We can see, at this point, that nothing is postulated in a judgment of taste except such a *universal voice* about a liking unmediated by concepts. Hence all that is postulated is the *possibility* of a judgment that is aesthetic and yet can be considered valid for everyone. The judgment of taste itself does not *postulate* everyone's agreement (since only a logically universal judgment can do that, because it can adduce reasons); it merely *requires* this agreement from everyone, as an instance of the rule, an instance regarding which it expects confirmation not from concepts but from the agreement of others. Hence the universal voice is only an idea. (At this point we are not yet inquiring on what this idea rests.) Whether someone who believes he is making a judgment of taste is in fact judging in conformity with that idea may be uncertain; but by using the term beauty he indicates that he is at least referring his judging to that idea, and hence that he intends it to be a judgment of taste. For himself, however, he can attain certainty on this point, by merely being conscious that he is separating whatever belongs to the agreeable and the good from the liking that remains to him after that. It is only for this that he counts on everyone's assent, and he would under these conditions [always] be justified in this claim, if only he did not on occasion fail to observe these conditions and so make an erroneous judgment of taste.

§9. INVESTIGATION OF THE QUESTION WHETHER IN A JUDGMENT OF TASTE THE FEELING OF PLEASURE PRECEDES THE JUDGING OF THE OBJECT OR THE JUDGING PRECEDES THE PLEASURE

The solution of this problem is the key to the critique of taste and hence deserves full attention.

If the pleasure in the given object came first, and our judgment of taste were to attribute only the pleasure's universal communicability to the presentation of the object, then this procedure would be self-contradictory. For that kind of pleasure would be none other than mere agreeableness in the sensation, so that by its very nature it could have only private validity, because it would depend directly on the presentation by which the object *is given*.

Hence it must be the universal communicability of the mental state, in the given presentation, which underlies the judgment of taste as its subjective condition, and the pleasure in the object must be its consequence. Nothing, however, can be communicated universally except cognition, as well as presentation insofar as it pertains to cognition; for presentation is objective only insofar as it pertains to cognition, and only through this does it have a universal reference point with which everyone's presentational power is compelled to harmonize. If, then, we are to think that the judgment about this universal communicability of the presentation has a merely subjective determining basis, i.e., one that does not involve a concept of the object, then this basis can be nothing other than the mental state that we find in the relation between the presentational powers [imagination and understanding] insofar as they refer a given presentation to *cognition in general*.

When this happens, the cognitive powers brought into play by this presentation are in free play, because no determinate concept restricts them to a particular rule of cognition. Hence the mental state in this presentation must be a feeling, accompanying the given presentation, of a free play of the presentational powers directed to cognition in general. Now if a presentation by which an object is given is, in general, to become cognition, we need *imagination* to combine the manifold of intuition, and *understanding*[9] to provide the unity of the concept uniting the [component] presentations. This state of *free play* of the cognitive powers, accompanying a presentation by which an object is given, must be universally communicable; for cognition, the determination of the object with which given presentations are to harmonize (in any subject whatever) is the only way of presenting that holds for everyone.

But the way of presenting [which occurs] in a judgment of taste is to have subjective universal communicability without presupposing a determinate concept; hence this subjective universal communicability can be

9. The a priori mental categories. "The manifold of intuition": the sense data that we receive from the outside world.

nothing but [that of] the mental state in which we are when imagination and understanding are in free play (insofar as they harmonize with each other as required for *cognition in general*). For we are conscious that this subjective relation suitable for cognition in general must hold just as much for everyone, and hence be just as universally communicable, as any determinate cognition, since cognition always rests on that relation as its subjective condition.

Now this merely subjective (aesthetic) judging of the object, or of the presentation by which it is given, precedes the pleasure in the object and is the basis of this pleasure, [a pleasure] in the harmony of the cognitive powers. But the universal subjective validity of this liking, the liking we connect with the presentation of the object we call beautiful, is based solely on the mentioned universality of the subjective conditions for judging objects.

* * *

EXPLICATION OF THE BEAUTIFUL INFERRED FROM THE SECOND MOMENT

Beautiful is what, without a concept, is liked universally.

* * *

§11. A JUDGMENT OF TASTE IS BASED ON NOTHING BUT THE *FORM OF PURPOSIVENESS* OF AN OBJECT (OR OF THE WAY OF PRESENTING IT)

Whenever a purpose is regarded as the basis of a liking, it always carries with it an interest, as the basis that determines the judgment about the object of the pleasure. Hence a judgment of taste cannot be based on a subjective purpose. But a judgment of taste also cannot be determined by a presentation of an objective purpose, i.e., a presentation of the object itself as possible according to principles of connection in terms of purposes, and hence it cannot be determined by a concept of the good. For it is an aesthetic and not a cognitive judgment, and hence does not involve a *concept* of the character and internal or external possibility of the object through this or that cause; rather, it involves merely the relation of the presentational powers to each other, insofar as they are determined by a presentation.

Now this relation, [present] when [judgment] determines an object as beautiful, is connected with the feeling of a pleasure, a pleasure that the judgment of taste at the same time declares to be valid for everyone. Hence neither an agreeableness accompanying the presentation, nor a presentation of the object's perfection and the concept of the good, can contain the basis that determines [such a judgment]. Therefore the liking that, without a concept, we judge to be universally communicable and hence to be the basis that determines a judgment of taste, can be nothing but the subjective purposiveness in the presentation of an object, without any purpose (whether objective or subjective), and hence the mere form of purposiveness, insofar as we are conscious of it, in the presentation by which an object is *given* us.

* * *

§13. A PURE JUDGMENT OF TASTE IS INDEPENDENT OF CHARM AND EMOTION

All interest ruins a judgment of taste and deprives it of its impartiality, especially if, instead of making the purposiveness precede the feeling of pleasure as the interest of reason does, that interest bases the purposiveness on the feeling of pleasure; but this is what always happens in an aesthetic judgment that we make about something insofar as it gratifies or pains us. Hence judgments affected in this way can make either no claim at all to a universally valid liking, or a claim that is diminished to the extent that sensations of that kind are included among the bases determining the taste. Any taste remains barbaric if its liking requires that *charms* and *emotions* be mingled in, let alone if it makes these the standard of its approval.

And yet, (though beauty should actually concern only form), charms are frequently not only included with beauty, as a contribution toward a universal aesthetic liking, but are even themselves passed off as beauties, so that the matter of the liking is passed off as the form.[1] This is a misunderstanding that, like many others having yet some basis in truth, can be eliminated by carefully defining these concepts.

A *pure judgment of taste* is one that is not influenced by charm or emotion (though these may be connected with a liking for the beautiful), and whose determining basis is therefore merely the purposiveness of the form.

§14. ELUCIDATION BY EXAMPLES

Aesthetic judgments, just like theoretical (i.e., logical) ones, can be divided into empirical and pure. Aesthetic judgments are empirical if they assert that an object or a way of presenting it is agreeable or disagreeable; they are pure if they assert that it is beautiful. Empirical aesthetic judgments are judgments of sense (material aesthetic judgments); only pure aesthetic judgments (since they are formal) are properly judgments of taste.

Hence a judgment of taste is pure only insofar as no merely empirical liking is mingled in with the basis that determines it. But this is just what happens whenever charm or emotion have a share in a judgment by which something is to be declared beautiful.

Here again some will raise objections, trying to make out, not merely that charm is a necessary ingredient in beauty, but indeed that it is sufficient all by itself to [deserve] being called beautiful.

* * *

But the view that the beauty we attribute to an object on account of its form is actually capable of being heightened by charm is a vulgar error that is very prejudicial to genuine, uncorrupted, solid [*gründlich*] taste. It is true that charms may be added to beauty as a supplement: they may offer the mind more than that dry liking, by also making the presentation of the object interesting to it, and hence they may commend to us taste and its cultivation, above all if our taste is still crude and unpracticed. But charms do actually impair the judgment of taste if they draw attention to themselves as [if they were] bases for judging beauty. For the view that they contribute to beauty

1. That is, material embellishments are mistakenly thought to be the source of beauty.

is so far off the mark that it is in fact only as aliens that they must, indulgently, be granted admittance when taste is still weak and unpracticed, and only insofar as they do not interfere with the beautiful form.

In painting, in sculpture, indeed in all the visual arts, including architecture and horticulture insofar as they are fine arts, *design* is what is essential; in design the basis for any involvement of taste is not what gratifies us in sensation, but merely what we like because of its form. The colors that illuminate the outline belong to charm. Though they can indeed make the object itself vivid to sense, they cannot make it beautiful and worthy of being beheld. Rather, usually the requirement of beautiful form severely restricts [what] colors [may be used], and even where the charm [of colors] is admitted it is still only the form that refines the colors.

All form of objects of the senses (the outer senses or, indirectly, the inner sense as well) is either *shape* or *play*; if the latter, it is either play of shapes (in space, namely, mimetic art and dance), or mere play of sensations (in time). The *charm* of colors or of the agreeable tone of an instrument may be added, but it is the *design* in the first case and the *composition* in the second that constitute the proper object of a pure judgment of taste; that the purity of the colors and of the tones, or for that matter their variety and contrast, seem to contribute to the beauty, does not mean that, because they themselves are agreeable, they furnish us, as it were, with a supplement to, and one of the same kind as, our liking for the form. For all they do is to make the form intuitable more precisely, determinately, and completely, while they also enliven the presentation by means of their charm, by arousing and sustaining the attention we direct toward the object itself.

Even what we call *ornaments (parerga)*,[2] i.e., what does not belong to the whole presentation of the object as an intrinsic constituent, but [is] only an extrinsic addition, does indeed increase our taste's liking, and yet it too does so only by its form, as in the case of picture frames, or drapery on statues, or colonnades around magnificent buildings. On the other hand, if the ornament itself does not consist in beautiful form but is merely attached, as a gold frame is to a painting so that its charm may commend the painting for our approval, then it impairs genuine beauty and is called *finery*.

Emotion, a sensation where agreeableness is brought about only by means of a momentary inhibition of the vital force followed by a stronger outpouring of it, does not belong to beauty at all. But sublimity (with which the feeling of emotion is connected) requires a different standard of judging from the one that taste uses as a basis. Hence a pure judgment of taste has as its determining basis neither charm nor emotion, in other words, no sensation, which is [merely] the matter of an aesthetic judgment.

* * *

§16. A Judgment of Taste by Which We Declare an Object Beautiful under the Condition of a Determinate Concept Is Not Pure

There are two kinds of beauty, free beauty (*pulchritudo vaga*) and merely accessory beauty (*pulchritudo adhaerens*). Free beauty does not presuppose a concept of what the object is [meant] to be. Accessory beauty does pre-

2. By-works, subordinate things (Greek).

suppose such a concept, as well as the object's perfection in terms of that concept. The free kinds of beauty are called (self-subsistent) beauties of this or that thing. The other kind of beauty is accessory to a concept (i.e., it is conditioned beauty) and as such is attributed to objects that fall under the concept of a particular purpose.

Flowers are free natural beauties. Hardly anyone apart from the botanist knows what sort of thing a flower is [meant] to be; and even he, while recognizing it as the reproductive organ of a plant, pays no attention to this natural purpose when he judges the flower by taste. Hence the judgment is based on no perfection of any kind, no intrinsic purposiveness to which the combination of the manifold might refer. Many birds (the parrot, the humming-bird, the bird of paradise) and a lot of crustaceans in the sea are [free] beauties themselves [and] belong to no object determined by concepts as to its purpose, but we like them freely and on their own account. Thus designs *à la grecque*,[3] the foliage on borders or on wallpaper, etc., mean nothing on their own: they represent [*vorstellen*] nothing, no object under a determinate concept, and are free beauties. What we call fantasias in music (namely, music without a topic [*Thema*]), indeed all music not set to words, may also be included in the same class.

When we judge free beauty (according to mere form) then our judgment of taste is pure. Here we presuppose no concept of any purpose for which the manifold is to serve the given object, and hence no concept [as to] what the object is [meant] to represent; our imagination is playing, as it were, while it contemplates the shape, and such a concept would only restrict its freedom.

* * *

§17. ON THE IDEAL OF BEAUTY

There can be no objective rule of taste, no rule of taste that determines by concepts what is beautiful. For any judgment from this source [i.e., taste] is aesthetic, i.e., the basis determining it is the subject's feeling and not the concept of an object. If we search for a principle of taste that states the universal criterion of the beautiful by means of determinate concepts, then we engage in a fruitless endeavor, because we search for something that is impossible and intrinsically contradictory. The universal communicability of the sensation (of liking or disliking)—a universal communicability that is indeed not based on a concept—[I say that] the broadest possible agreement among all ages and peoples regarding this feeling that accompanies the presentation of certain objects is the empirical criterion [for what is beautiful]. This criterion, although weak and barely sufficient for a conjecture, [does suggest] that a taste so much confirmed by examples stems from [a] deeply hidden basis, common to all human beings, underlying their agreement in judging the forms under which objects are given them.

That is why we regard some products of taste as *exemplary*. This does not mean that taste can be acquired by imitating someone else's. For taste must be an ability one has oneself; and although someone who imitates a model

3. The phrase *à la grecque* [in the style of the Greeks; French] was apparently used in the eighteenth century—and is still used by some present-day French art historians—to characterize the classicism in what is now called the Louis XVI style [translator's note].

may manifest skill insofar as he succeeds in this, he manifests taste only insofar as he can judge that model himself. From this, however, it follows that the highest model, the archetype of taste, is a mere idea, an idea which everyone must generate within himself and by which he must judge any object of taste, any example of someone's judging by taste, and even the taste of everyone [else].

Idea properly means a rational concept, and *ideal* the presentation of an individual being as adequate to an idea. Hence that archetype of taste, which does indeed rest on reason's indeterminate idea of a maximum, but which still can be presented not through concepts but only in an individual exhibition, may more appropriately be called the ideal of the beautiful. Though we do not have such an ideal in our possession, we do strive to produce it within us. But it will be merely an ideal of the imagination, precisely because it does not rest on concepts but rests on an exhibition, and the power of exhibition is the imagination.

* * *

EXPLICATION OF THE BEAUTIFUL INFERRED FROM THE THIRD MOMENT

Beauty is an object's form of *purposiveness* insofar as it is perceived in the object *without the presentation of a purpose.*[4]

§18. WHAT THE MODALITY OF A JUDGMENT OF TASTE IS

About any presentation I can say at least that there is a *possibility* for it (as a cognition) to be connected with a pleasure. About that which I call *agreeable* I say that it *actually* gives rise to pleasure in me. But we think of the *beautiful* as having a *necessary* reference to liking. This necessity is of a special kind. It is not a theoretical objective necessity, allowing us to cognize a priori that everyone *will feel* this liking for the object I call beautiful. Nor is it a practical objective necessity, where, through concepts of a pure rational will that serves freely acting beings as a rule, this liking is the necessary consequence of an objective law and means nothing other than that one absolutely (without any further aim) ought to act in a certain way. Rather, as a necessity that is thought in an aesthetic judgment, it can only be called *exemplary*, i.e., a necessity of the assent of *everyone* to a judgment that is regarded as an example of a universal rule that we are unable to state. Since an aesthetic judgment is not an objective and cognitive one, this necessity cannot be derived from determinate concepts and hence is not apodeictic.[5] Still less can it be inferred from the universality of experience (from a thorough agreement among judgments about the beauty of a certain object). For

4. It might be adduced as a counterinstance to this explication that there are things in which we see a purposive form without recognizing a purpose in them [but which we nevertheless do not consider beautiful]. Examples are the stone utensils sometimes excavated from ancient burial mounds, which are provided with a hole as if for a handle. Although these clearly betray in their shape a purposiveness whose purpose is unknown, we do not declare them beautiful on that account. And yet, the very fact that we regard them as work[s] of art already forces us to admit that we are referring their shape to some intention or other and to some determinate purpose. That is also why we have no direct liking whatever for their intuition. A flower, on the other hand, e.g., a tulip, is considered beautiful, because in our perception of it we encounter a certain purposiveness that, given how we are judging the flower, we do not refer to any purpose whatever [Kant's note].

5. Absolutely certain.

not only would experience hardly furnish a sufficient amount of evidence for this, but a concept of the necessity of these judgments cannot be based on empirical judgments.

§19. THE SUBJECTIVE NECESSITY THAT WE ATTRIBUTE TO A JUDGMENT OF TASTE IS CONDITIONED

A judgment of taste requires everyone to assent; and whoever declares something to be beautiful holds that everyone *ought* to give his approval to the object at hand and that he too should declare it beautiful. Hence the *ought* in an aesthetic judgment, even once we have [*nach*] all the data needed for judging, is still uttered only conditionally. We solicit everyone else's assent because we have a basis for it that is common to all. Indeed, we could count on that assent, if only we could always be sure that the instance had been subsumed correctly under that basis, which is the rule for the approval.

* * *

§22. THE NECESSITY OF THE UNIVERSAL ASSENT THAT WE THINK IN A JUDGMENT OF TASTE IS A SUBJECTIVE NECESSITY THAT WE PRESENT AS OBJECTIVE BY PRESUPPOSING A COMMON SENSE

Whenever we make a judgment declaring something to be beautiful, we permit no one to hold a different opinion, even though we base our judgment only on our feeling rather than on concepts; hence we regard this underlying feeling as a common rather than as a private feeling. But if we are to use this common sense in such a way, we cannot base it on experience; for it seeks to justify us in making judgments that contain an ought: it does not say that everyone *will* agree with my judgment, but that he *ought* to. Hence the common sense, of whose judgment I am at that point offering my judgment of taste as an example, attributing to it *exemplary* validity on that account, is a mere ideal standard. With this standard presupposed, we could rightly turn a judgment that agreed with it, as well as the liking that is expressed in it for some object, into a rule for everyone. For although the principle is only subjective, it would still be assumed as subjectively universal (an idea necessary for everyone); and so it could, like an objective principle, demand universal assent insofar as agreement among different judging persons is concerned, provided only we were certain that we had subsumed under it correctly.

That we do actually presuppose this indeterminate standard of a common sense is proved by the fact that we presume to make judgments of taste. But is there in fact such a common sense, as a constitutive principle of the possibility of experience, or is there a still higher principle of reason that makes it only a regulative principle for us, [in order] to bring forth in us, for higher purposes, a common sense in the first place? In other words, is taste an original and natural ability, or is taste only the idea of an ability yet to be acquired and [therefore] artificial, so that a judgment of taste with its requirement for universal assent is in fact only a demand of reason to produce such agreement in the way we sense? In the latter case the *ought*, i.e., the objective necessity that everyone's feeling flow along with the particular feeling of each person, would signify only that there is a possibility of reaching such agreement; and the judgment of taste would only offer an example of the application of this principle. These questions we neither wish to nor can investigate at this point. For the present our task is only to analyze the power of taste into its elements, and to unite these ultimately in the idea of a common sense.

EXPLICATION OF THE BEAUTIFUL INFERRED FROM THE FOURTH MOMENT

Beautiful is what without a concept is cognized as the object of a *necessary* liking.

GENERAL COMMENT ON THE FIRST DIVISION[6] OF THE ANALYTIC

If we take stock of the above analyses, we find that everything comes down to the concept of taste, namely, that taste is an ability to judge an object in reference to the *free lawfulness* of the imagination. Therefore, in a judgment of taste the imagination must be considered in its freedom. This implies, first of all, that this power is here not taken as reproductive, where it is subject to the laws of association, but as productive and spontaneous (as the originator of chosen forms of possible intuitions). Moreover, [second,] although in apprehending a given object of sense the imagination is tied to a determinate form of this object and to that extent does not have free play (as it does [e.g.] in poetry), it is still conceivable that the object may offer it just the sort of form in the combination of its manifold as the imagination, if it were left to itself [and] free, would design in harmony with the *understanding's lawfulness* in general. And yet, to say that the *imagination* is *free* and yet *lawful of itself*, i.e., that it carries autonomy with it, is a contradiction. The understanding alone gives the law. But when the imagination is compelled to proceed according to a determinate law, then its product is determined by concepts (as far as its form is concerned); but in that case the liking, as was shown above, is a liking not for the beautiful but for the good (of perfection, at any rate, formal perfection), and the judgment is not a judgment made by taste. It seems, therefore, that only a lawfulness without a law, and a subjective harmony of the imagination with the understanding without an objective harmony—where the presentation is referred to a determinate concept of an object—is compatible with the free lawfulness of the understanding (which has also been called purposiveness without a purpose) and with the peculiarity of a judgment of taste.

From *Book II. Analytic of the Sublime*

§23. TRANSITION FROM THE POWER OF JUDGING THE BEAUTIFUL TO THAT OF JUDGING THE SUBLIME

The beautiful and the sublime are similar in some respects. We like both for their own sake, and both presuppose that we make a judgment of reflection rather than either a judgment of sense or a logically determinative one. Hence in neither of them does our liking depend on a sensation, such as that of the agreeable, nor on a determinate concept, as does our liking for

6. That is, the first book—the analytic of the beautiful.

the good; yet we do refer the liking to concepts, though it is indeterminate which concepts these are. Hence the liking is connected with the mere exhibition or power of exhibition, i.e., the imagination, with the result that we regard this power, when an intuition is given us, as harmonizing with the *power of concepts*, i.e., the understanding or reason, this harmony furthering [the aims of] these. That is also why both kinds of judgment are *singular* ones that nonetheless proclaim themselves universally valid for all subjects, though what they lay claim to is merely the feeling of pleasure, and not any cognition of the object.

But some significant differences between the beautiful and the sublime are also readily apparent. The beautiful in nature concerns the form of the object, which consists in [the object's] being bounded. But the sublime can also be found in a formless object, insofar as we present *unboundedness*, either [as] in the object or because the object prompts us to present it, while yet we add to this unboundedness the thought of its totality. So it seems that we regard the beautiful as the exhibition of an indeterminate concept of the understanding, and the sublime as the exhibition of an indeterminate concept of reason.[7] Hence in the case of the beautiful our liking is connected with the presentation of *quality*, but in the case of the sublime with the presentation of *quantity*. The two likings are also very different in kind. For the one liking ([that for] the beautiful) carries with it directly a feeling of life's being furthered, and hence is compatible with charms and with an imagination at play. But the other liking (the feeling of the sublime) is a pleasure that arises only indirectly: it is produced by the feeling of a momentary inhibition of the vital forces followed immediately by an outpouring of them that is all the stronger. Hence it is an emotion, and so it seems to be seriousness, rather than play, in the imagination's activity. Hence, too, this liking is incompatible with charms, and, since the mind is not just attracted by the object but is alternately always repelled as well, the liking for the sublime contains not so much a positive pleasure as rather admiration and respect, and so should be called a negative pleasure.

But the intrinsic and most important distinction between the sublime and the beautiful is presumably the following. If, as is permissible, we start here by considering only the sublime in natural objects (since the sublime in art is always confined to the conditions that [art] must meet to be in harmony with nature), then the distinction in question comes to this: (Independent) natural beauty carries with it a purposiveness in its form, by which the object seems as it were predetermined for our power of judgment, so that this beauty constitutes in itself an object of our liking. On the other hand, if something arouses in us, merely in apprehension and without any reasoning on our part, a feeling of the sublime, then it may indeed appear, in its form, contrapurposive for our power of judgment, incommensurate with our power of exhibition, and as it were violent to our imagination, and yet we judge it all the more sublime for that.

We see from this at once that we express ourselves entirely incorrectly when we call this or that *object of nature* sublime, even though we may quite correctly call a great many natural objects beautiful; for how can we call something by a term of approval if we apprehend it as in itself contrapur-

7. *Reason* refers to our mental work with nonphysical ideas; *understanding* refers to apprehension and cognition of the physical world.

posive? Instead, all we are entitled to say is that the object is suitable for exhibiting a sublimity that can be found in the mind. For what is sublime, in the proper meaning of the term, cannot be contained in any sensible form but concerns only ideas of reason, which, though they cannot be exhibited adequately, are aroused and called to mind by this very inadequacy, which can be exhibited in sensibility. Thus the vast ocean heaved up by storms cannot be called sublime. The sight of it is horrible; and one must already have filled one's mind with all sorts of ideas if such an intuition is to attune it to a feeling that is itself sublime, inasmuch as the mind is induced to abandon sensibility and occupy itself with ideas containing a higher purposiveness.

Independent natural beauty reveals to us a technic of nature that allows us to present nature as a system in terms of laws whose principle we do not find anywhere in our understanding: the principle of a purposiveness directed to our use of judgment as regards appearances. Under this principle, appearances must be judged as belonging not merely to nature as governed by its purposeless mechanism, but also to [nature considered by] analogy with art. Hence even though this beauty does not actually expand our cognition of natural objects, it does expand our concept of nature, namely, from nature as mere mechanism to the concept of that same nature as art, and that invites us to profound investigations about [how] such a form is possible. However, in what we usually call sublime in nature there is such an utter lack of anything leading to particular objective principles and to forms of nature conforming to them, that it is rather in its chaos that nature most arouses our ideas of the sublime, or in its wildest and most ruleless disarray and devastation, provided it displays magnitude and might. This shows that the concept of the sublime in nature is not nearly as important and rich in implications as that of the beautiful in nature, and that this concept indicates nothing purposive whatever in nature itself but only in what *use* we can make of our intuitions of nature so that we can feel a purposiveness within ourselves entirely independent of nature. For the beautiful in nature we must seek a basis outside ourselves, but for the sublime a basis merely within ourselves and in the way of thinking that introduces sublimity into our presentation of nature. This is a crucial preliminary remark, which separates our ideas of the sublime completely from the idea of a purposiveness of *nature*, and turns the theory of the sublime into a mere appendix to our aesthetic judging of the purposiveness of nature. For through these ideas we do not present a particular form in nature, but only develop [the] purposive use that the imagination makes of the presentation of nature.

* * *

§25. EXPLICATION OF THE TERM SUBLIME

We call *sublime* what is *absolutely [schlechthin] large*. To be large [*groß*] and to be a magnitude [*Größe*] are quite different concepts (*magnitudo* and *quantitas*). Also, *saying simply [schlechtweg] (simpliciter)* that something is large is quite different from saying that it is *absolutely large* (*absolute, non comparative magnum*).[8] The latter is *what is large beyond all comparison*.

* * *

8. Absolutely, not comparatively, large (Latin).

The above explication can also be put as follows: *That is sublime in comparison with which everything else is small.* We can easily see here that nothing in nature can be given, however large we may judge it, that could not, when considered in a different relation, be degraded all the way to the infinitely small, nor conversely anything so small that it could not, when compared with still smaller standards, be expanded for our imagination all the way to the magnitude of a world; telescopes have provided us with a wealth of material in support of the first point, microscopes in support of the second. Hence, considered on this basis, nothing that can be an object of the senses is to be called sublime. [What happens is that] our imagination strives to progress toward infinity, while our reason demands absolute totality as a real idea, and so [the imagination,] our power of estimating the magnitude of things in the world of sense, is inadequate to that idea. Yet this inadequacy itself is the arousal in us of the feeling that we have within us a supersensible power; and what is absolutely large is not an object of sense, but is the use that judgment makes naturally of certain objects so as to [arouse] this (feeling), and in contrast with that use any other use is small. Hence what is to be called sublime is not the object, but the attunement[9] that the intellect [gets] through a certain presentation that occupies reflective judgment.

Hence we may supplement the formulas already given to explicate the sublime by another one: *Sublime is what even to be able to think proves that the mind has a power surpassing any standard of sense.*

§26. ON ESTIMATING THE MAGNITUDE OF NATURAL THINGS, AS WE MUST FOR THE IDEA OF THE SUBLIME

* * *

In order for the imagination to take in a quantum intuitively, so that we can then use it as a measure or unity in estimating magnitude by numbers, the imagination must perform two acts: *apprehension (apprehensio)*, and *comprehension (comprehensio aesthetica)*. Apprehension involves no problem, for it may progress to infinity. But comprehension becomes more and more difficult the farther apprehension progresses, and it soon reaches its maximum, namely, the aesthetically largest basic measure for an estimation of magnitude. For when apprehension has reached the point where the partial presentations of sensible intuition that were first apprehended are already beginning to be extinguished in the imagination, as it proceeds to apprehend further ones, the imagination then loses as much on the one side as it gains on the other; and so there is a maximum in comprehension that it cannot exceed.

This serves to explain a comment made by *Savary* in his report on Egypt:[1] that in order to get the full emotional effect from the magnitude of the pyramids one must neither get too close to them nor stay too far away. For if one stays too far away, then the apprehended parts (the stones on top of one another) are presented only obscurely, and hence their presentation has no effect on the subject's aesthetic judgment; and if one gets too close, then the eye needs some time to complete the apprehension from the base

9. That is, the mental sensation that attends perceiving an object that exceeds the capacity of our senses.

1. *Lettres sur l'Égypte* (1785–86, *Letters on Egypt*), by Claude-Étienne Savary (1750–1788), French traveler.

to the peak, but during that time some of the earlier parts are invariably extinguished in the imagination before it has apprehended the later ones, and hence the comprehension is never complete. Perhaps the same observation can explain the bewilderment or kind of perplexity that is said to seize the spectator who for the first time enters St. Peter's Basilica in Rome. For he has the feeling that his imagination is inadequate for exhibiting the idea of a whole, [a feeling] in which imagination reaches its maximum, and as it strives to expand that maximum, it sinks back into itself, but consequently comes to feel a liking [that amounts to an] emotion [*rührendes Wohlgefallen*].

I shall say nothing for now regarding the basis of this liking, a liking connected with a presentation from which one would least expect it, namely, a presentation that makes us aware of its own inadequacy and hence also of its subjective unpurposiveness for the power of judgment in its estimation of magnitude. Here I shall only point out that if the aesthetic judgment in question is to be *pure* (*unmixed with any teleological* and hence rational judgment), and if we are to give an example of it that is fully appropriate for the critique of *aesthetic* judgment, then we must point to the sublime not in products of art (e.g., buildings, columns, etc.), where both the form and the magnitude are determined by a human purpose, nor in natural things *whose very concept carries with it a determinate purpose* (e.g., animals with a known determination in nature), but rather in crude nature (and even in it only insofar as it carries with it no charm, nor any emotion aroused by actual danger), that is, merely insofar as crude nature contains magnitude. For in such a presentation nature contains nothing monstrous (nor anything magnificent or horrid); it does not matter how far the apprehended magnitude has increased, just as long as our imagination can comprehend it within one whole. An object is *monstrous* if by its magnitude it nullifies the purpose that constitutes its concept. And *colossal* is what we call the mere exhibition of a concept if that concept is almost too large for any exhibition (i.e., if it borders on the relatively monstrous); for the purpose of exhibiting a concept is hampered if the intuition of the object is almost too large for our power of apprehension. A pure judgment about the sublime, on the other hand, must have no purpose whatsoever of the object as the basis determining it, if it is to be aesthetic and not mingled with some judgment of understanding or of reason.

Since the presentation of anything that our merely reflective power of judgment is to like without an interest must carry with it a purposiveness that is subjective and yet universally valid, but since in the sublime (unlike the beautiful) our judging is not based on a purposiveness of the *form* of the object, the following questions arise: What is this subjective purposiveness, and how does it come to be prescribed as a standard, thereby providing a basis for a universally valid liking accompanying the mere estimation of magnitude—an estimation that has been pushed to the point where the ability of our imagination is inadequate to exhibit the concept of magnitude?

When the imagination performs the combination [*Zusammensetzung*] that is required to present a magnitude, it encounters no obstacles and on its own progresses to infinity, while the understanding guides it by means of numerical concepts, for which the imagination must provide the schema; and in this procedure, which is involved in the logical estimation of magnitude, there is indeed something objectively purposive under the concept of a purpose (since any measuring is a purpose).

* * *

The infinite, however, is absolutely large (not merely large by comparison). Compared with it everything else (of the same kind of magnitudes) is small. But—and this is most important—to be able even to think the infinite as *a whole* indicates a mental power that surpasses any standard of sense. For [thinking the infinite as a whole while using a standard of sense] would require a comprehension yielding as a unity a standard that would have a determinate relation to the infinite, one that could be stated in numbers; and this is impossible. If the human mind is nonetheless to *be able even to think* the given infinite without contradiction, it must have within itself a power that is supersensible, whose idea of a noumenon[2] cannot be intuited but can yet be regarded as the substrate underlying what is mere appearance, namely, our intuition of the world. For only by means of this power and its idea do we, in a pure intellectual estimation of magnitude, comprehend the infinite in the world of sense *entirely under* a concept, even though in a mathematical estimation of magnitude by *means of numerical concepts* we can never think it in its entirety. Even a power that enables us to think the infinite of supersensible intuition as given (in our intelligible substrate) surpasses any standard of sensibility. It is large beyond any comparison even with the power of mathematical estimation—not, it is true, for [the pursuit of] a theoretical aim on behalf of our cognitive power, but still as an expansion of the mind that feels able to cross the barriers of sensibility with a different (a practical) aim.

Hence nature is sublime in those of its appearances whose intuition carries with it the idea of their infinity. But the only way for this to occur is through the inadequacy of even the greatest effort of our imagination to estimate an object's magnitude. In the mathematical estimation of magnitude, however, the imagination is equal to the task of providing, for any object, a measure that will suffice for this estimation, because the understanding's numerical concepts can be used in a progression and so can make any measure adequate to any given magnitude. Hence it must be the *aesthetic* estimation of magnitude where we feel that effort, our imagination's effort to perform a comprehension that surpasses its ability to encompass [*begreifen*] the progressive apprehension in a whole of intuition, and where at the same time we perceive the inadequacy of the imagination—unbounded though it is as far as progressing is concerned—for taking in and using, for the estimation of magnitude, a basic measure that is suitable for this with minimal expenditure on the part of the understanding. Now the proper unchangeable basic measure of nature is the absolute whole of nature, which, in the case of nature as appearance, is infinity comprehended. This basic measure, however, is a self-contradictory concept (because an absolute totality of an endless progression is impossible). Hence that magnitude of a natural object to which the imagination fruitlessly applies its entire ability to comprehend must lead the concept of nature to a supersensible substrate (which underlies both nature and

2. Something as it is in itself (which Kant sets against *phenomenon*, a "mere appearance" grasped through the senses).

our ability to think), a substrate that is large beyond any standard of sense and hence makes us judge as *sublime* not so much the object as the mental attunement in which we find ourselves when we estimate the object.

Therefore, just as the aesthetic power of judgment in judging the beautiful refers the imagination in its free play to the *understanding* so that it will harmonize with the understanding's *concepts* in general (which concepts they are is left indeterminate), so in judging a thing sublime it refers the imagination to *reason* so that it will harmonize subjectively with reason's *ideas* (which ideas they are is indeterminate), i.e., so that it will produce a mental attunement that conforms to and is compatible with the one that an influence by determinate (practical) ideas would produce on feeling.

This also shows that true sublimity must be sought only in the mind of the judging person, not in the natural object the judging of which prompts this mental attunement. Indeed, who would want to call sublime such things as shapeless mountain masses piled on one another in wild disarray, with their pyramids of ice, or the gloomy raging sea? But the mind feels elevated in its own judgment of itself when it contemplates these without concern for their form and abandons itself to the imagination and to a reason that has come to be connected with it—though quite without a determinate purpose, and merely expanding it—and finds all the might of the imagination still inadequate to reason's ideas.

* * *

§27. ON THE QUALITY OF LIKING IN OUR JUDGING OF THE SUBLIME

The feeling that it is beyond our ability to attain to an idea *that is a law for us* is RESPECT. Now the idea of comprehending every appearance that may be given us in the intuition of a whole is an idea enjoined on us by a law of reason, which knows no other determinate measure that is valid for everyone and unchanging than the absolute whole. But our imagination, even in its greatest effort to do what is demanded of it and comprehend a given object in a whole of intuition (and hence to exhibit the idea of reason), proves its own limits and inadequacy, and yet at the same time proves its vocation to [obey] a law, namely, to make itself adequate to that idea. Hence the feeling of the sublime in nature is respect for our own vocation. But by a certain subreption[3] (in which respect for the object is substituted for respect for the idea of humanity within our[selves, as] subject[s]) this respect is accorded an object of nature that, as it were, makes intuitable for us the superiority of the rational vocation of our cognitive powers over the greatest power of sensibility.

Hence the feeling of the sublime is a feeling of displeasure that arises from the imagination's inadequacy, in an aesthetic estimation of magnitude, for an estimation by reason, but is at the same time also a pleasure, aroused by the fact that this very judgment, namely, that even the greatest power of sensibility is inadequate, is [itself] in harmony with rational ideas, insofar as striving toward them is still a law for us. For it is a law (of reason) for us, and part of our vocation, to estimate any sense object in nature that is large for us as being small when compared with ideas of reason; and whatever

3. A misrepresentation; a misunderstanding derived from such a misrepresentation.

arouses in us the feeling of this supersensible vocation is in harmony with that law. Now the greatest effort of the imagination in exhibiting the unity [it needs] to estimate magnitude is [itself] a reference to something *large absolutely*, and hence also a reference to reason's law to adopt only this something as the supreme measure of magnitude. Hence our inner perception that every standard of sensibility is inadequate for an estimation of magnitude by reason is [itself] a harmony with laws of reason, as well as a displeasure that arouses in us the feeling of our supersensible vocation, according to which finding that every standard of sensibility is inadequate to the ideas of reason is purposive and hence pleasurable.

In presenting the sublime in nature the mind feels *agitated*, while in an aesthetic judgment about the beautiful in nature it is in *restful* contemplation. This agitation (above all at its inception) can be compared with a vibration, i.e., with a rapid alternation of repulsion from, and attraction to, one and the same object. If a [thing] is excessive for the imagination (and the imagination is driven to [such excess] as it apprehends [the thing] in intuition), then [the thing] is, as it were, an abyss in which the imagination is afraid to lose itself. Yet, at the same time, for reason's idea of the supersensible [this same thing] is not excessive but conforms to reason's law to give rise to such striving by the imagination. Hence [the thing] is now attractive to the same degree to which [formerly] it was repulsive to mere sensibility. The judgment itself, however, always remains only aesthetic here. For it is not based on a determinate concept of the object, and presents merely the subjective play of the mental powers themselves (imagination and reason) as harmonious by virtue of their contrast. For just as, when we judge the beautiful, imagination and *understanding* give rise to a subjective purposiveness of the mental powers by their *accordance*, so do imagination and *reason* here give rise to such a purposiveness by their *conflict*, namely, to a feeling that we have a pure and independent reason, or a power for estimating magnitude, whose superiority cannot be made intuitable by anything other than the inadequacy of that power which in exhibiting magnitudes (of sensible objects) is itself unbounded.

* * *

§28. ON NATURE AS A MIGHT

Might is an ability that is superior to great obstacles. It is called *dominance* [*Gewalt*] if it is superior even to the resistance of something that itself possesses might. When in an aesthetic judgment we consider nature as a might that has no dominance over us, then it is *dynamically sublime*.

If we are to judge nature as sublime dynamically, we must present it as arousing fear. (But the reverse does not hold: not every object that arouses fear is found sublime when we judge it aesthetically.) For when we judge [something] aesthetically (without a concept), the only way we can judge a superiority over obstacles is by the magnitude of the resistance. But whatever we strive to resist is an evil, and it is an object of fear if we find that our ability [to resist it] is no match for it. Hence nature can count as a might, and so as dynamically sublime, for aesthetic judgment only insofar as we consider it as an object of fear.

We can, however, consider an object *fearful* without being afraid *of* it, namely, if we judge it in such a way that we merely *think* of the case where we might possibly want to put up resistance against it, and that any resistance would in that case be utterly futile. Thus a virtuous person fears God without being afraid of him. For he does not think of wanting to resist God and his commandments as a possibility that should worry *him*. But for every such case, which he thinks of as not impossible intrinsically, he recognizes God as fearful.

Just as we cannot pass judgment on the beautiful if we are seized by inclination and appetite, so we cannot pass judgment at all on the sublime in nature if we are afraid. For we flee from the sight of an object that scares us, and it is impossible to like terror that we take seriously. That is why the agreeableness that arises from the cessation of a hardship is *gladness*. But since this gladness involves our liberation from a danger, it is accompanied by our resolve never to expose ourselves to that danger again. Indeed, we do not even like to think back on that sensation, let alone actively seek out an opportunity for it.

On the other hand, consider bold, overhanging and, as it were, threatening rocks, thunderclouds piling up in the sky and moving about accompanied by lightning and thunderclaps, volcanoes with all their destructive power, hurricanes with all the devastation they leave behind, the boundless ocean heaved up, the high waterfall of a mighty river, and so on. Compared to the might of any of these, our ability to resist becomes an insignificant trifle. Yet the sight of them becomes all the more attractive the more fearful it is, provided we are in a safe place. And we like to call these objects sublime because they raise the soul's fortitude above its usual middle range and allow us to discover in ourselves an ability to resist which is of a quite different kind, and which gives us the courage [to believe] that we could be a match for nature's seeming omnipotence.

For although we found our own limitation when we considered the immensity of nature and the inadequacy of our ability to adopt a standard proportionate to estimating aesthetically the magnitude of nature's *domain*, yet we also found, in our power of reason, a different and nonsensible standard that has this infinity itself under it as a unit; and since in contrast to this standard everything in nature is small, we found in our mind a superiority over nature itself in its immensity. In the same way, though the irresistibility of nature's might makes us, considered as natural beings, recognize our physical impotence, it reveals in us at the same time an ability to judge ourselves independent of nature, and reveals in us a superiority over nature that is the basis of a self-preservation quite different in kind from the one that can be assailed and endangered by nature outside us. This keeps the humanity in our person from being degraded, even though a human being would have to succumb to that dominance [of nature]. Hence if in judging nature aesthetically we call it sublime, we do so not because nature arouses fear, but because it calls forth our strength (which does not belong to nature [within us]), to regard as small the [objects] of our [natural] concerns: property, health, and life, and because of this we regard nature's might (to which we are indeed subjected in these [natural] concerns) as yet not having such dominance over us, as persons, that we should have to bow to it if our highest principles were at stake and we had to choose between upholding or abandoning them.

Hence nature is here called sublime [*erhaben*] merely because it elevates [*erhebt*] our imagination, [making] it exhibit those cases where the mind can come to feel its own sublimity, which lies in its vocation and elevates it even above nature.

This self-estimation loses nothing from the fact that we must find ourselves safe in order to feel this exciting liking, so that (as it might seem), since the danger is not genuine, the sublimity of our intellectual ability might also not be genuine. For here the liking concerns only our ability's *vocation*, revealed in such cases, insofar as the predisposition to this ability is part of our nature, whereas it remains up to us, as our obligation, to develop and exercise this ability. And there is truth in this, no matter how conscious of his actual present impotence man may be when he extends his reflection thus far.

I admit that this principle seems farfetched and the result of some subtle reasoning, and hence high-flown [*überschwenglich*] for an aesthetic judgment. And yet our observation of man proves the opposite, and proves that even the commonest judging can be based on this principle, even though we are not always conscious of it. For what is it that is an object of the highest admiration even to the savage? It is a person who is not terrified, not afraid, and hence does not yield to danger but promptly sets to work with vigor and full deliberation. Even in a fully civilized society there remains this superior esteem for the warrior, except that we demand more of him: that he also demonstrate all the virtues of peace—gentleness, sympathy, and even appropriate care for his own person—precisely because they reveal to us that his mind cannot be subdued by danger. Hence, no matter how much people may dispute, when they compare the statesman with the general, as to which one deserves the superior respect, an aesthetic judgment decides in favor of the general. Even war has something sublime about it if it is carried on in an orderly way and with respect for the sanctity of the citizens' rights. At the same time it makes the way of thinking of a people that carries it on in this way all the more sublime in proportion to the number of dangers in the face of which it courageously stood its ground. A prolonged peace, on the other hand, tends to make prevalent a mere[ly] commercial spirit, and along with it base selfishness, cowardice, and softness, and to debase the way of thinking of that people.

* * *

§29. ON THE MODALITY OF A JUDGMENT ABOUT THE SUBLIME IN NATURE

Beautiful nature contains innumerable things about which we do not hesitate to require everyone's judgment to agree with our own, and can in fact expect such agreement without being wrong very often. But we cannot with the same readiness count on others to accept our judgment about the sublime in nature. For it seems that, if we are to pass judgment on that superiority of [such] natural objects, not only must our aesthetic power of judgment be far more cultivated, but also so must the cognitive powers on which it is based.

In order for the mind to be attuned to the feeling of the sublime, it must be receptive to ideas. For it is precisely nature's inadequacy to the ideas—and this presupposes both that the mind is receptive to ideas and that the imagination strains to treat nature as a schema for them—that constitutes what both repels our sensibility and yet attracts us at the same time, because it is a dominance [*Gewalt*] that reason exerts over sensibility only for the sake of expanding it commensurately with reason's own domain (the practical one) and letting it look outward toward the infinite, which for sensibility is an abyss. It is a fact that what is called sublime by us, having been prepared through culture, comes across as merely repellent to a person who is uncultured and lacking in the development of moral ideas. In all the evidence of nature's destructive force [*Gewalt*], and in the large scale of its might, in contrast to which his own is nonexistent, he will see only the hardship, danger, and misery that would confront anyone forced to live in such a place. Thus (as Mr. de Saussure[4] relates) the good and otherwise sensible Savoyard peasant did not hesitate to call anyone a fool who fancies glaciered mountains. He might even have had a point, if Saussure had acted merely from fancy, as most travelers tend to, in exposing himself to the dangers involved in his observations, or in order that he might some day be able to describe them with pathos. In fact, however, his intention was to instruct mankind, and that excellent man got, in addition, the soul-stirring sensation and gave it into the bargain to the readers of his travels.

But the fact that a judgment about the sublime in nature requires culture (more so than a judgment about the beautiful) still in no way implies that it was initially produced by culture and then introduced to society by way of (say) mere convention. Rather, it has its foundation in human nature: in something that, along with common sense, we may require and demand of everyone, namely, the predisposition to the feeling for (practical) ideas, i.e., to moral feeling.

This is what underlies the necessity—which we include in our judgment about the sublime—of the assent of other people's judgment to our own. For just as we charge someone with a lack of *taste* if he is indifferent when he judges an object of nature that we find beautiful, so we say that someone has no *feeling* if he remains unmoved in the presence of something we judge sublime. But we demand both taste and feeling of every person, and, if he has any culture at all, we presuppose that he has them. But we do so with this difference: taste we demand unhesitatingly from everyone, because here judgment refers the imagination merely to the understanding, our power of concepts; in the case of feeling, on the other hand, judgment refers the imagination to reason, our power of ideas, and so we demand feeling only under a subjective presupposition (though we believe we are justified and permitted to require [fulfillment of] this presupposition in everyone): we presuppose moral feeling in man. And so we attribute necessity to this [kind of] aesthetic judgment as well.

* * *

§40. ON TASTE AS A KIND OF *SENSUS COMMUNIS*

We often call the power of judgment a sense, when what we notice is not so much its reflection as merely its result. We then speak of a sense of truth, a sense of decency, of justice, etc. We do this even though we know, or at least

4. Horace Bénédict de Saussure (1740–1799), Swiss geologist and botanist [translator's note].

properly ought to know, that a sense cannot contain these concepts, let alone have the slightest capacity to pronounce universal rules, but that a conception of truth, propriety, beauty, or justice could never enter our thoughts if we were not able to rise above the senses to higher cognitive powers. [This] *common human understanding*, which is merely man's sound ([but] not yet cultivated) understanding, is regarded as the very least that we are entitled to expect from anyone who lays claim to the name of human being; and this is also why it enjoys the unfortunate honor of being called common sense (*sensus communis*), and this, indeed, in such a way that the word common (not merely in our language, where it is actually ambiguous, but in various others as well) means the same as *vulgar*—i.e., something found everywhere, the possession of which involves no merit or superiority whatever.

Instead, we must [here] take *sensus communis* to mean the idea of a sense *shared* [by all of us], i.e., a power to judge that in reflecting takes account (a priori), in our thought, of everyone else's way of presenting [something], in order *as it were* to compare our own judgment with human reason in general and thus escape the illusion that arises from the ease of mistaking subjective and private conditions for objective ones, an illusion that would have a prejudicial influence on the judgment. Now we do this as follows: we compare our judgment not so much with the actual as rather with the merely possible judgments of others, and [thus] put ourselves in the position of everyone else, merely by abstracting from the limitations that [may] happen to attach to our own judging; and this in turn we accomplish by leaving out as much as possible whatever is matter, i.e., sensation, in the presentational state, and by paying attention solely to the formal features of our presentation or of our presentational state. Now perhaps this operation of reflection will seem rather too artful to be attributed to the ability we call *common* sense. But in fact it only looks this way when expressed in abstract formulas. Intrinsically nothing is more natural than abstracting from charm and emotion when we seek a judgment that is to serve as a universal rule.

[Let us compare with this *sensus communis*] the common human understanding, even though the latter is not being included here as a part of the critique of taste. The following maxims may serve to elucidate its principles: (1) to think for oneself; (2) to think from the standpoint of everyone else; and (3) to think always consistently. The first is the maxim of an *unprejudiced*, the second of a *broadened*, the third of a *consistent* way of thinking. The first is the maxim of a reason that is never *passive*. A propensity to a passive reason, and hence to a heteronomy of reason, is called *prejudice*; and the greatest prejudice of all is *superstition*, which consists in thinking of nature as not subject to rules which the understanding through its own essential law lays down as the basis of nature. Liberation from superstition is called *enlightenment*; for although liberation from prejudices generally may also be called enlightenment, still superstition deserves to be called a prejudice preeminently (*in sensu eminenti*),[5] since the blindness that superstition creates in a person, which indeed it even seems to demand as an obligation, reveals especially well the person's need to be guided by others, and hence his state of a passive reason. As for the second maxim concerning

5. In the prominent sense [of the term] (Latin).

[a person's] way of thinking, it seems that we usually [use a negative term and] call someone limited (of a *narrow* mind as opposed to a *broad* mind) if his talents are insufficient for a use of any magnitude (above all for intensive use). But we are talking here not about the power of cognition, but about the *way of thinking* [that involves] putting this power to a purposive use; and this, no matter how slight may be the range and the degree of a person's natural endowments, still indicates a man with a *broadened way of thinking* if he overrides the private subjective conditions of his judgment, into which so many others are locked, as it were, and reflects on his own judgment from a *universal standpoint* (which he can determine only by transferring himself to the standpoint of others). The third maxim, the one concerning a *consistent* way of thinking, is hardest to attain and can in fact be attained only after repeated compliance with a combination of the first two has become a skill. We may say that the first of these maxims is the maxim of the understanding, the second that of judgment, the third that of reason.

Resuming now the thread from which I just digressed, I maintain that taste can be called a *sensus communis* more legitimately than can sound understanding, and that the aesthetic power of judgment deserves to be called a shared sense more than does the intellectual one, if indeed we wish to use the word *sense* to stand for an effect that mere reflection has on the mind, even though we then mean by sense the feeling of pleasure. We could even define taste as the ability to judge something that makes our feeling in a given presentation *universally communicable* without mediation by a concept.

The aptitude that human beings have for communicating their thoughts to one another also requires that imagination and understanding be related in such a way that concepts can be provided with accompanying intuitions, and intuitions in turn with accompanying concepts, these intuitions and concepts joining to [form] cognition. But here the harmony of the two mental powers is *law-governed*, under the constraint of determinate concepts. Only where the imagination is free when it arouses the understanding, and the understanding, without using concepts, puts the imagination into a play that is regular [i.e., manifests regularity], does the presentation communicate itself not as a thought but as the inner feeling of a purposive state of mind.

Hence taste is our ability to judge a priori the communicability of the feelings that (without mediation by a concept) are connected with a given presentation.

* * *

§43. ON ART IN GENERAL

(1) *Art* is distinguished from *nature* as doing (*facere*) is from acting or operating in general (*agere*); and the product or result of art is distinguished from that of nature, the first being a work (*opus*), the second an effect (*effectus*).

By right we should not call anything art except a production through freedom, i.e., through a power of choice that bases its acts on reason. For though we like to call the product that bees make (the regularly constructed honeycombs) a work of art, we do so only by virtue of an analogy with art; for as soon as we recall that their labor is not based on any rational deliberation on their part, we say at once that the product is a product of their nature (namely, of instinct), and it is only to their creator that we ascribe it as art.

[It is true that] if, as sometimes happens when we search through a bog, we come across a piece of hewn wood, we say that it is a product of art, rather than of nature, i.e., that the cause which produced it was thinking of a purpose to which this object owes its form. Elsewhere too, I suppose, we see art in everything that is of such a character that before it became actual its cause must have had a presentation of it (as even in the case of bees), yet precisely without the cause's having [in fact] *thought* of that effect. But if we simply call something a work of art in order to distinguish it from a natural effect, then we always mean by that a work of man.

(2) *Art*, as human skill, is also distinguished from *science* ([i.e., we distinguish] *can* from *know*), as practical from theoretical ability, as technic from theory (e.g., the art of surveying from geometry). That is exactly why we refrain from calling anything art that we *can* do the moment we *know* what is to be done, i.e., the moment we are sufficiently acquainted with what the desired effect is. Only if something [is such that] even the most thorough acquaintance with it does not immediately provide us with the skill to make it, then to that extent it belongs to art. *Camper*[6] describes with great precision what the best shoe would have to be like, yet he was certainly unable to make one.

(3) *Art* is likewise distinguished from *craft*. The first is also called *free art*, the second could also be called *mercenary art*. We regard free art [as an art] that could only turn out purposive (i.e., succeed) if it is play, in other words, an occupation that is agreeable on its own account; mercenary art we regard as labor, i.e., as an occupation that on its own account is disagreeable (burdensome) and that attracts us only through its effect (e.g., pay), so that people can be coerced into it. To judge whether, in a ranking of the guilds, watchmakers should be counted as artists but smiths as craftsmen, we would have to take a viewpoint different from the one adopted here: we would have to compare [*Proportion*] the talents that each of these occupations presupposes. Whether even among the so-called seven free arts[7] a few may not have been included that should be numbered with the sciences, as well as some that are comparable to crafts, I do not here wish to discuss. It is advisable, however, to remind ourselves that in all the free arts there is yet a need for something in the order of a constraint, or, as it is called, a *mechanism*. (In poetry, for example, it is correctness and richness of language, as well as prosody and meter.) Without this the *spirit*, which in art must be *free* and which alone animates the work, would have no body at all and would evaporate completely. This reminder is needed because some of the more recent educators believe that they promote a free art best if they remove all constraint from it and convert it from labor into mere play.

* * *

6. Peter Camper (1722–1789), Dutch anatomist and naturalist [translator's note].

7. That is, the liberal arts of medieval education, made up of the trivium (grammar, logic, and rhetoric) and the more advanced quadrivium (music, arithmetic, geometry, and astronomy). *Liber* means "free" in Latin.

§49. ON THE POWERS OF THE MIND WHICH CONSTITUTE GENIUS

* * *

In a word, an aesthetic idea is a presentation of the imagination which is conjoined with a given concept and is connected, when we use imagination in its freedom, with such a multiplicity of partial presentations that no expression that stands for a determinate concept can be found for it. Hence it is a presentation that makes us add to a concept the thoughts of much that is ineffable, but the feeling of which quickens our cognitive powers and connects language, which otherwise would be mere letters, with spirit.

So the mental powers whose combination (in a certain relation) constitutes *genius* are imagination and understanding. One qualification is needed, however. When the imagination is used for cognition, then it is under the constraint of the understanding and is subject to the restriction of adequacy to the understanding's concept. But when the aim is aesthetic, then the imagination is free, so that, over and above that harmony with the concept, it may supply, in an unstudied way, a wealth of undeveloped material for the understanding which the latter disregarded in its concept. But the understanding employs this material not so much objectively, for cognition, as subjectively, namely, to quicken the cognitive powers, though indirectly this does serve cognition too. Hence genius actually consists in the happy relation—one that no science can teach and that cannot be learned by any diligence—allowing us, first, to discover ideas for a given concept, and, second, to hit upon a way of *expressing* these ideas that enables us to communicate to others, as accompanying a concept, the mental attunement that those ideas produce. The second talent is properly the one we call spirit. For in order to express what is ineffable in the mental state accompanying a certain presentation and to make it universally communicable—whether the expression consists in language or painting or plastic art—we need an ability [viz., spirit] to apprehend the imagination's rapidly passing play and to unite it in a concept that can be communicated without the constraint of rules (a concept that on that very account is original, while at the same time it reveals a new rule that could not have been inferred from any earlier principles or examples).

If, after this analysis, we look back to the above explication of what we call *genius*, we find: *First*, genius is a talent for art, not for science, where we must start from distinctly known rules that determine the procedure we must use in it. *Second*, since it is an artistic talent, it presupposes a determinate concept of the product, namely, its purpose; hence genius presupposes understanding, but also a presentation (though an indeterminate one) of the material, i.e., of the intuition, needed to exhibit this concept, and hence presupposes a relation of imagination to understanding. *Third*, it manifests itself not so much in the fact that the proposed purpose is achieved in exhibiting a determinate concept, as, rather, in the way *aesthetic ideas*, which contain a wealth of material [suitable] for that intention, are offered or expressed; and hence it presents the imagination in its freedom from any instruction by rules, but still as purposive for exhibiting the given concept. Finally, *fourth*, the unstudied, unintentional subjective purposiveness in the imagination's free harmony with the understanding's lawfulness presupposes such a proportion and attunement of these powers as cannot be brought about by any compliance with rules, whether of science or of mechanical imitation, but can be brought about only by the subject's nature.

These presuppositions being given, genius is the exemplary originality of a subject's natural endowment in the *free* use of his cognitive powers. Accordingly, the product of a genius (as regards what is attributable to genius in it rather than to possible learning or academic instruction) is an example that is meant not to be imitated, but to be followed by another genius. (For in mere imitation the element of genius in the work—what constitutes its spirit—would be lost.) The other genius, who follows the example, is aroused by it to a feeling of his own originality, which allows him to exercise in art his freedom from the constraint of rules, and to do so in such a way that art itself acquires a new rule by this, thus showing that the talent is exemplary. But since a genius is nature's favorite and so must be regarded as a rare phenomenon, his example gives rise to a school for other good minds, i.e., a methodical instruction by means of whatever rules could be extracted from those products of spirit and their peculiarity; and for these [followers] fine art is to that extent imitation, for which nature, through a genius, gave the rule.

But this imitation becomes *aping* if the pupil *copies* everything, including even the deformities that the genius had to permit only because it would have been difficult to eliminate them without diminishing the force of the idea. This courage [to retain deformities] has merit only in a genius. A certain *boldness* of expression, and in general some deviation from the common rule, is entirely fitting for a genius; it is however not at all worthy of imitation, but in itself always remains a defect that [any]one must try to eliminate, though the genius has, as it were, a privilege to allow the defect to remain [anyway], because the inimitable [element] in the momentum of his spirit would be impaired by timorous caution.

* * *

§59. ON BEAUTY AS THE SYMBOL OF MORALITY

* * *

Now I maintain that the beautiful is the symbol of the morally good; and only because we refer [*Rücksicht*] the beautiful to the morally good (we all do so [*Beziehung*] naturally and require all others also to do so, as a duty) does our liking for it include a claim to everyone else's assent, while the mind is also conscious of being ennobled, by this [reference], above a mere receptivity for pleasure derived from sense impressions, and it assesses the value of other people too on the basis of [their having] a similar maxim in their power of judgment. The morally good is the intelligible that taste has in view, as I indicated in the preceding section;[8] for it is with this intelligible that even our higher cognitive powers harmonize, and without this intelligible contradictions would continually arise from the contrast between the nature

8. Section 58, omitted from our selection.

of these powers and the claims that taste makes. In this ability [taste], judgment does not find itself subjected to a heteronomy from empirical laws, as it does elsewhere in empirical judging—concerning objects of such a pure liking it legislates to itself, just as reason does regarding the power of desire. And because the subject has this possibility within him, while outside [him] there is also the possibility that nature will harmonize with it, judgment finds itself referred to something that is both in the subject himself and outside him, something that is neither nature nor freedom and yet is linked with the basis of freedom, the supersensible, in which the theoretical and the practical power are in an unknown manner combined and joined into a unity. I shall now bring up a few points of this analogy [between the beautiful and the morally good], noting at the same time what difference there is between them.

(1) The beautiful we like *directly* (but only in intuition reflect[ed upon], not in its concept, as we do morality). (2) We like it *without any interest*. (Our liking for the morally good is connected necessarily with an interest, but with an interest that does not precede our judgment about the liking but is produced by this judgment in the first place.) (3) In judging the beautiful, we present the *freedom* of the imagination (and hence [of] our power [of] sensibility) as harmonizing with the lawfulness of the understanding. (In a moral judgment we think the freedom of the will as the will's harmony with itself according to universal laws of reasons.) (4) We present the subjective principle for judging the beautiful as *universal*, i.e., as valid for everyone, but as unknowable through any universal concept. (The objective principle of morality we also declare to be universal[ly valid], i.e., [valid] for all subjects, as well as for all acts of the same subject, but also declare to be knowable through a universal concept.) Hence not only is a moral judgment capable of [having] determinate constitutive principles, but its possibility *depends* on our basing the[se] maxims on those principles and their universality.

The common understanding also habitually bears this analogy in mind, and beautiful objects of nature or of art are often called by names that seem to presuppose that we are judging [these objects] morally. We call buildings or trees majestic and magnificent, or landscapes cheerful and gay; even colors are called innocent, humble, or tender, because they arouse sensations in us that are somehow analogous to the consciousness we have in a mental state produced by moral judgments. Taste enables us, as it were, to make the transition from sensible charm to a habitual moral interest without making too violent a leap; for taste presents the imagination as admitting, even in its freedom, of determination that is purposive for the understanding, and it teaches us to like even objects of sense freely, even apart from sensible charm.

1790

EDMUND BURKE
1729–1797

The sublime, which Edmund Burke examines in his major work *A Philosophical Enquiry into the Origins of Our Ideas of the Sublime and Beautiful* (1757), is one of the most intriguing terms in the history of literary criticism and theory. When invoked to name the defining quality of a great literary or artistic work, it usually suggests grandeur, vastness, awe, immense power. But the concept has a complex history, and critics and theorists have for centuries explored its meanings. It was first described in the treatise *On Sublimity*, written in the first century C.E. by a Greek rhetorian known (because of an early misattribution) as LONGINUS; in this text, the sublime is defined as "excellence in language" and as the "expression of a great spirit." It is associated as well with frightening, huge phenomena in nature—volcanoes, storms, the surging seas. Here already are signs of the tensions and ambiguities that Burke, and others in the eighteenth and nineteenth centuries, inquired into. Is the sublime a fact about nature or art, or both? Is the sublime a property of the work of literature itself? Or is it, instead, less in the work than in the soul, mind, or character of the genius who produces the work? Or—yet another variation—is it an extraordinary experience brought about by the power of the perceiver, and thus testimony not to the work or to the author but to something in the reader, something special in the intensity of the reader's response?

While Burke's contribution to aesthetics is significant, he is best known as a political theorist and statesman. He was born in Dublin, Ireland; his father, a lawyer, was a Protestant, and his mother was a Roman Catholic. He attended Trinity College in Dublin from 1743 to 1748 and then in 1750 began the study of law at the Middle Temple in London. His first publication, a satiric work titled *A Vindication of Natural Society*, was published anonymously in 1756. It was followed the next year by the *Enquiry*, also published anonymously, and this book won praise from scholars and critics in England and abroad. Burke soon became friends with a number of accomplished writers and artists, including Oliver Goldsmith, SAMUEL JOHNSON, and Joshua Reynolds; Johnson called Burke's work on the sublime "an example of true criticism." Beginning in 1758, Burke was also the editor (anonymously) of *The Annual Register*, a survey of world affairs; he held the position for three decades.

In 1765 Burke was appointed secretary to the Marquess of Rockingham, a notable Whig political leader, and he became a member of Parliament. He took an active role in debates over the relationship between Parliament and the king, as George III attempted to increase the power of the monarchy; the Whigs sought to limit royal authority. In his pamphlet *Thoughts on the Cause of the Present Discontents* (1770), Burke criticized George's choice of ministers and presented a new conception of political "party." Traditionally, political parties had been seen as inherently subversive and unpatriotic, as well as sources of factionalism; but Burke viewed parties as collectives brought together on the basis of shared public principles. Rightly conceived, "party" was a "constitutional link between king and parliament, providing consistency and strength in administration, or principled criticism in opposition."

In addition to his efforts to limit the power of the king, Burke was involved in the 1760s and 1770s in the disputes about how best to govern the American colonies, a question considered in *Thoughts*. He delivered a number of speeches on this issue, faulting the policies of the British government for being rigid, contradictory, and unworkable. He called for "conciliation"—not an end to imperial authority but a more pragmatic exercise of it that would take into serious account the reasons for the colonists' complaints about taxation and lack of representation.

Burke was also an angry, incisive critic of the French Revolution, which broke out in 1789 and which many British writers, including WILLIAM WORDSWORTH and SAMUEL TAYLOR COLERIDGE initially welcomed and supported. In his classic text *Reflections on the Revolution in France* (1790), Burke inveighed against unfettered democracy and dangerous appeals to the universal "rights of man" as he defended tradition, monarchy, and a hereditary aristocracy. He resisted abstract speculation and (as he defined them) systems and schemes for social and political change that ignored the long history and organic interrelatedness of sociopolitical life, culture, and institutions. Society, for Burke, means a "partnership" between "those who are living, those who are dead, and those who are yet to be born." It is dangerously wrong to interfere with this partnership, however alluring the ideals invoked as justification.

In the excerpt below, we see Burke writing as a literary theorist, taking up a subject that previous critics had discussed and that resonated in the verse of contemporary poets. He is indebted, for example, to JOSEPH ADDISON's essays on taste, the imagination, and the sublime (see above) and to DAVID HUME's "Of the Standard of Taste" (1757; see above). Like those writers, he operates within the empirical tradition that John Locke had established in *An Essay concerning Human Understanding* (1690)—that knowledge derives from sense experience and that simple ideas are combined into more complex ones. Burke has also absorbed the melancholy, reflective, sometimes ominous and disquieting poetry of EDWARD YOUNG ("Night Thoughts," 1742), Thomas Gray ("Elegy Written in a Country Churchyard," 1751), and others. He is interested in the psychological and physical nature of our response to the exalted and the fearful, the terrible and terrifying, both in art and in nature.

Burke begins with "On Taste," a long introduction (added for the second edition) covering aesthetic judgment. Like Hume, he aims to show that we can do better than simply conclude that "Taste cannot be disputed," as if there were no shared standards and principles for judgment. He says, for example, that while a man may come to prefer the taste of tobacco to that of sugar, neither he nor anyone else believes that tobacco is sweet. An "acquired" preference is not the same as a "natural" one, he explains. In their sense of pleasure and pain, Burke concludes, persons are the same: "Light is more pleasing than darkness. . . . No man thinks a goose to be more beautiful than a swan." This does not mean that everyone speaks with equal insight and accuracy about a work of art: some possess more knowledge than others and hence they see elements in the work that others do not. Thus some persons might seem not properly to value Virgil's epic poem, the *Aeneid* (19 B.C.E.), not because their taste is defective but primarily because they lack knowledge and experience. One can detect in this commentary on "taste" Burke's investment in the idea of consensus, the notion that persons of different social and cultural backgrounds can nonetheless reach agreement on principles and standards—a belief that decades later would fuel his furious response to the upheavals of the French Revolution.

Burke's stress on knowledge and experience is evident in his account of the relation between taste and judgment. "A wrong taste," he explains, is caused by "a defect of judgment" that reflects "a weakness of understanding" or, "more commonly," a "want of proper exercise." Burke emphasizes that differences in taste derive from prejudices and passions that mar judgment, rather than from any intrinsic gifts of imagination and insight that make some persons naturally better judges than others. "Sensibility" is important, he states, but he insists that experience and knowledge can develop and strengthen judgment, even as he adds that in the response to literature there is less difference in judgment than in the response to philosophy and abstract argument: "Men are far better agreed on the excellence of a description in Virgil, than on the truth or falsehood of a theory of Aristotle."

The later sections of Burke's book treat the sublime and its relationship to the beautiful. Used as an adjective, "sublime" (from the Latin *sublimis*, "on high, uplifted, raised up") in the sixteenth and seventeenth centuries meant grand, elevated, lofty. By the middle of the seventeenth century, it also suggested the highest moral, intellectual, or emotional level, as well as great nobility of character. Late in the century, it was used as both an adjective and a noun to refer, as it does today, to a sensation—overwhelming awe, astonishment, fear, terror—produced by great scenes in nature and powerful works of literature and art.

Though Burke read Longinus's text when he was a student at Trinity, he seems already to have been fascinated by the idea and experience of the sublime. For example, while in his teens he commented in a letter on a flood he saw in Dublin: "It gives me pleasure to see nature in these great though terrible scenes. It fills the mind with grand ideas, and turns the soul in upon itself." In his *Essay on Criticism* (1711; see above), ALEXANDER POPE had highlighted the order, harmony, and proportion that characterized Nature—and that writers should seek to embody in their work. But in this letter and in his book on the sublime, Burke is getting at an irrational element in both nature and art, something not captured by terms such as *reason, order, proportion*, and *balance*.

Burke also delves into the response of the reader or viewer to the sublime, and in his attention to the psychological nature of response he looks forward to the philosopher IMMANUEL KANT in his *Critique of Judgment* (1790), the German dramatist and critic G. E. LESSING, Coleridge, and RALPH WALDO EMERSON. Coleridge and Emerson, and, later, Walt Whitman, discover the sublime in the commonplace and everyday through the power of the perceiving mind—the capacity to recognize and voice, as Whitman does, the awe-inspiring infinite meaningfulness of a leaf of grass. Burke's influence on the understanding of the "terror" associated with the sublime is also apparent in the theory and practice of the Gothic novel; in *The Mysteries of Udolpho* (1794), Ann Radcliffe describes the impact of terror on the mind in Burkean terms: "A terror of this nature, as it occupies and expands the mind, and elevates it to a high expectation, is purely sublime, and leads us, by a kind of fascination, to seek even the object from which we appear to shrink."

Unlike some theorists of the era, though like Kant later in the century, Burke makes a distinction between the sublime and the beautiful. The sublime he connects to terror, obscurity, vastness, infinity; the beautiful he associates with smallness, brightness of color, the finite. His book stands roughly midway between the elegant neoclassicism of JOHN DRYDEN and Pope and the transcendence-seeking Romantic poetry and criticism of Wordsworth and Coleridge. Burke was one of the central figures in the challenge to the tradition that Dryden and Pope represented, and he helped prepare the way for the literary revolution of the 1790s—which coincided with the French Revolution that he so despised. In yet another irony, for the deconstructionists PAUL DE MAN, JACQUES DERRIDA, and their followers, the sublime has come to signify the plurality in language that keeps meaning from ever achieving a fixed form: dizzying, disorienting, and disorder-generating, it is dramatically at odds with the values that Burke in his political writing eloquently defended.

BIBLIOGRAPHY

For complete editions of Burke, see *Works* (9 vols., 1839) and *Works* (8 vols., 1868–80). A modern edition is in progress: *Writings and Speeches of Edmund Burke*, edited by Paul Langford (5 vols. to date, 1981–). An important source is the *Correspondence* (10 vols., 1958–78). A selection of the letters has been edited by Harvey C. Mansfield (1984). There are two annotated editions of *A Philosophical Enquiry into the Origin of Our Ideas of the Sublime and Beautiful*, the first by James T. Boulton (1958), the second by Adam Phillips (1990). For Burke's biography, consult Alice P. Miller, *Edmund Burke and His World* (1979), and Stanley Ayling, *Edmund Burke: His Life and Opinions* (1988). For a detailed, measured assessment, see F. P. Lock's study (in progress), *Edmund Burke* (1998–).

Literary critics have paid much attention recently to Burke as a thinker and writer. Good discussions can be found in David Bromwich, *A Choice of Inheritance: Self and*

Community from Edmund Burke to Robert Frost (1989); Terry Eagleton, *The Ideology of the Aesthetic* (1990); Frances Ferguson, *Solitude and the Sublime: Romanticism and the Aesthetics of Individuation* (1992), a study of Burke, Kant, and eighteenth- and nineteenth-century aesthetic theory; and Tom Furniss, *Edmund Burke's Aesthetic Ideology: Language, Gender, and Political Economy in Revolution* (1993). For background, see *The Sublime: A Reader in British Eighteenth-Century Aesthetic Theory*, edited by Andrew Ashfield and Peter de Bolla (1996). Bibliographical resources on Burke include William B. Todd, *A Bibliography of Edmund Burke* (1964); Clara I. Gandy, *Edmund Burke: A Bibliography of Secondary Studies to 1982* (1983); and Leonard W. Cowie, *Edmund Burke, 1729–1797: A Bibliography* (1994).

From A Philosophical Enquiry into the Origin of Our Ideas of the Sublime and Beautiful

Introduction on Taste

On a superficial view, we may seem to differ very widely from each other in our reasonings, and no less in our pleasures: but notwithstanding this difference, which I think to be rather apparent than real, it is probable that the standard both of reason and Taste is the same in all human creatures. For if there were not some principles of judgment as well as of sentiment common to all mankind, no hold could possibly be taken either on their reason or their passions, sufficient to maintain the ordinary correspondence of life. It appears indeed to be generally acknowledged, that with regard to truth and falsehood there is something fixed. We find people in their disputes continually appealing to certain tests and standards which are allowed on all sides, and are supposed to be established in our common nature. But there is not the same obvious concurrence in any uniform or settled principles which relate to Taste. It is even commonly supposed that this delicate and aerial[1] faculty, which seems too volatile to endure even the chains of a definition, cannot be properly tried by any test, nor regulated by any standard. There is so continual a call for the exercise of the reasoning faculty, and it is so much strengthened by perpetual contention, that certain maxims of right reason seem to be tacitly settled amongst the most ignorant. The learned have improved on this rude science, and reduced those maxims into a system. If Taste has not been so happily cultivated, it was not that the subject was barren, but that the labourers were few or negligent; for to say the truth, there are not the same interesting motives to impel us to fix the one, which urge us to ascertain the other. And after all, if men differ in their opinion concerning such matters, their difference is not attended with the same important consequences, else I make no doubt but that the logic of Taste, if I may be allowed the expression, might very possibly be as well digested, and we might come to discuss matters of this nature with as much certainty, as those which seem more immediately within the province of mere reason. And indeed it is very necessary at the entrance into such an enquiry, as our present, to make this point as clear as possible; for if Taste has no fixed principles, if the imagination is not affected according to some invariable and certain laws, our labour is like to be employed to very little purpose;

1. Reaching high into the air, lofty.

as it must be judged an useless, if not an absurd undertaking, to lay down rules for caprice, and to set up for a legislator of whims and fancies.

The term Taste, like all other figurative terms, is not extremely accurate: the thing which we understand by it, is far from a simple and determinate idea in the minds of most men, and it is therefore liable to uncertainty and confusion. I have no great opinion of a definition, the celebrated remedy for the cure of this disorder. For when we define, we seem in danger of circumscribing nature within the bounds of our own notions, which we often take up by hazard, or embrace on trust, or form out of a limited and partial consideration of the object before us, instead of extending our ideas to take in all that nature comprehends, according to her manner of combining. We are limited in our enquiry by the strict laws to which we have submitted at our setting out.

——Circa vilem patulumque morabimur orbem
Unde pudor proferre pedem vetat aut operis lex.[2]

A definition may be very exact, and yet go but a very little way towards informing us of the nature of the thing defined; but let the virtue of a definition be what it will, in the order of things, it seems rather to follow than to precede our enquiry, of which it ought to be considered as the result. It must be acknowledged that the methods of disquisition and teaching may be sometimes different, and on very good reason undoubtedly; but for my part, I am convinced that the method of teaching which approaches most nearly to the method of investigation, is incomparably the best; since not content with serving up a few barren and lifeless truths, it leads to the stock on which they grew; it tends to set the reader himself in the track of invention, and to direct him into those paths in which the author has made his own discoveries, if he should be so happy as to have made any that are valuable.

But to cut off all pretence for cavilling, I mean by the word Taste no more than that faculty, or those faculties of the mind which are affected with, or which form a judgment of the works of imagination and the elegant arts. This is, I think, the most general idea of that word, and what is the least connected with any particular theory. And my point in this enquiry is to find whether there are any principles, on which the imagination is affected, so common to all, so grounded and certain, as to supply the means of reasoning satisfactorily about them. And such principles of Taste, I fancy there are; however paradoxical it may seem to those, who on a superficial view imagine, that there is so great a diversity of Tastes both in kind and degree, that nothing can be more indeterminate.

All the natural powers in man, which I know, that are conversant about external objects, are the Senses; the Imagination; and the Judgment. And first with regard to the senses. We do and we must suppose, that as the conformation of their organs are nearly, or altogether the same in all men, so the manner of perceiving external objects is in all men the same, or with little difference. We are satisfied that what appears to be light to one eye, appears light to another; that what seems sweet to one palate, is sweet to

2. Misquoted from HORACE (65–8 B.C.E.), *Ars Poetica* (see above): "We shall linger with the low and open world, from which place modesty or the law of the work prevent our feet from moving" (lines 132, 135). Burke leaves out the word *non*: Horace is instructing the aspiring poet *not* to linger.

another; that what is dark and bitter to this man, is likewise dark and bitter to that; and we conclude in the same manner of great and little, hard and soft, hot and cold, rough and smooth; and indeed of all the natural qualities and affections of bodies. If we suffer ourselves to imagine, that their senses present to different men different images of things, this sceptical proceeding will make every sort of reasoning on every subject vain and frivolous, even that sceptical reasoning itself, which had persuaded us to entertain a doubt concerning the agreement of our perceptions. But as there will be very little doubt that bodies present similar images to the whole species, it must necessarily be allowed, that the pleasures and the pains which every object excites in one man, it must raise in all mankind, whilst it operates naturally, simply, and by its proper powers only; for if we deny this, we must imagine, that the same cause operating in the same manner, and on subjects of the same kind, will produce different effects, which would be highly absurd. Let us first consider this point in the sense of Taste, and the rather as the faculty in question has taken its name from that sense. All men are agreed to call vinegar sour, honey sweet, and aloes[3] bitter; and as they are all agreed in finding these qualities in those objects, they do not in the least differ concerning their effects with regard to pleasure and pain. They all concur in calling sweetness pleasant, and sourness and bitterness unpleasant. Here there is no diversity in their sentiments; and that there is not appears fully from the consent of all men in the metaphors which are taken from the sense of Taste. A sour temper, bitter expressions, bitter curses, a bitter fate, are terms well and strongly understood by all. And we are altogether as well understood when we say, a sweet disposition, a sweet person, a sweet condition, and the like. It is confessed, that custom, and some other causes, have made many deviations from the natural pleasures or pains which belong to these several Tastes; but then the power of distinguishing between the natural and the acquired relish remains to the very last. A man frequently comes to prefer the Taste of tobacco to that of sugar, and the flavour of vinegar to that of milk; but this makes no confusion in Tastes, whilst he is sensible that the tobacco and vinegar are not sweet, and whilst he knows that habit alone has reconciled his palate to these alien pleasures. Even with such a person we may speak, and with sufficient precision, concerning Tastes. But should any man be found who declares, that to him tobacco has a Taste like sugar, and that he cannot distinguish between milk and vinegar; or that tobacco and vinegar are sweet, milk bitter, and sugar sour, we immediately conclude that the organs of this man are out of order, and that his palate is utterly vitiated. We are as far from conferring with such a person upon Tastes, as from reasoning concerning the relations of quantity with one who should deny that all the parts together were equal to the whole. We do not call a man of this kind wrong in his notions, but absolutely mad. Exceptions of this sort in either way, do not at all impeach our general rule, nor make us conclude that men have various principles concerning the relations of quantity, or the Taste of things. So that when it is said, Taste cannot be disputed, it can only mean, that no one can strictly answer what pleasure or pain some particular man may find from the Taste of some particular thing. This indeed cannot be disputed; but we may dispute, and with sufficient

3. A purgative drug was derived from the juice of aloe plants.

clearness too, concerning the things which are naturally pleasing or disagreeable to the sense. But when we talk of any peculiar or acquired relish, then we must know the habits, the prejudices, or the distempers[4] of this particular man, and we must draw our conclusion from those.

This agreement of mankind is not confined to the Taste solely. The principle of pleasure derived from sight is the same in all. Light is more pleasing than darkness. Summer, when the earth is clad in green, when the heavens are serene and bright, is more agreeable than winter, when everything makes a different appearance. I never remember that any thing beautiful, whether a man, a beast, a bird, or a plant, was ever shewn, though it were to an hundred people, that they did not all immediately agree that it was beautiful, though some might have thought that it fell short of their expectation, or that other things were still finer. I believe no man thinks a goose to be more beautiful than a swan, or imagines that what they call a Friezland hen excels a peacock. It must be observed too, that the pleasures of the sight are not near so complicated, and confused, and altered by unnatural habits and associations, as the pleasures of the Taste are; because the pleasures of the sight more commonly acquiesce in themselves; and are not so often altered by considerations which are independent of the sight itself. But things do not spontaneously present themselves to the palate as they do to the sight; they are generally applied to it, either as food or as medicine; and from the qualities which they possess for nutritive or medicinal purposes, they often form the palate by degrees, and by force of these associations. Thus opium is pleasing to Turks, on account of the agreeable delirium it produces. Tobacco is the delight of Dutchmen, as it diffuses a torpor and pleasing stupefaction. Fermented spirits please our common people, because they banish care, and all consideration of future or present evils. All of these would lie absolutely neglected if their properties had originally gone no further than the Taste; but all these, together with tea and coffee, and some other things, have past from the apothecary's shop to our tables, and were taken for health long before they were thought of for pleasure. The effect of the drug has made us use it frequently; and frequent use, combined with the agreeable effect, has made the Taste itself at last agreeable. But this does not in the least perplex our reasoning; because we distinguish to the last the acquired from the natural relish. In describing the Taste of an unknown fruit, you would scarcely say, that it had a sweet and pleasant flavour like tobacco, opium, or garlic, although you spoke to those who were in the constant use of these drugs, and had great pleasure in them. There is in all men a sufficient remembrance of the original natural causes of pleasure, to enable them to bring all things offered to their senses to that standard, and to regulate their feelings and opinions by it. Suppose one who had so vitiated his palate as to take more pleasure in the Taste of opium than in that of butter or honey, to be presented with a bolus of squills; there is hardly any doubt but that he would prefer the butter or honey to this nauseous morsel, or to any other bitter drug to which he had not been accustomed; which proves that his palate was naturally like that of other men in all things, that it is still like the palate of other men in many things, and only vitiated in some particular points. For in judging of any new thing, even of a Taste similar to that which

4. Disturbances of the bodily "humors" or "tempers" once thought to govern human physiology.

he has been formed by habit to like, he finds his palate affected in the natural manner, and on the common principles. Thus the pleasure of all the senses, of the sight, and even of the Taste, that most ambiguous of the senses, is the same in all, high and low, learned and unlearned.

Besides the ideas, with their annexed pains and pleasures, which are presented by the sense; the mind of man possesses a sort of creative power of its own; either in representing at pleasure the images of things in the order and manner in which they were received by the senses, or in combining those images in a new manner, and according to a different order. This power is called Imagination; and to this belongs whatever is called wit, fancy, invention, and the like. But it must be observed, that this power of the imagination is incapable of producing any thing absolutely new; it can only vary the disposition of those ideas which it has received from the senses.[5] Now the imagination is the most extensive province of pleasure and pain, as it is the region of our fears and our hopes, and of all our passions that are connected with them; and whatever is calculated to affect the imagination with these commanding ideas, by force of any original natural impression, must have the same power pretty equally over all men. For since the imagination is only the representative of the senses, it can only be pleased or displeased with the images from the same principle on which the sense is pleased or displeased with the realities; and consequently there must be just as close an agreement in the imaginations as in the senses of men. A little attention will convince us that this must of necessity be the case.

But in the imagination, besides the pain or pleasure arising from the properties of the natural object, a pleasure is perceived from the resemblance, which the imitation has to the original; the imagination, I conceive, can have no pleasure but what results from one or other of these causes. And these causes operate pretty uniformly upon all men, because they operate by principles in nature, and which are not derived from any particular habits or advantages. Mr. Locke very justly and finely observes of wit, that it is chiefly conversant in tracing resemblances; he remarks at the same time, that the business of judgment is rather in finding differences.[6] It may perhaps appear, on this supposition, that there is no material distinction between the wit and the judgment, as they both seem to result from different operations of the same faculty of *comparing*. But in reality, whether they are or are not dependent on the same power of the mind, they differ so very materially in many respects, that a perfect union of wit and judgment is one of the rarest things in the world. When two distinct objects are unlike to each other, it is only what we expect; things are in their common way; and therefore they make no impression on the imagination: but when two distinct objects have a resemblance, we are struck, we attend to them, and we are pleased. The mind of man has naturally a far greater alacrity and satisfaction in tracing resemblances than in searching for differences; because by making resemblance we produce *new images*, we unite, we create, we enlarge our stock; but in making distinctions we offer no food at all to the imagination; the task itself is more severe and irksome, and what pleasure we derive from it is something of a negative and indirect nature. A piece of news is told me in

5. Compare *An Essay concerning Human Understanding* (1690), 2.2.2, 2.12.2, by the English empiricist philosopher John Locke (1632–1704).
6. Locke, *Essay*, 2.11.2. "Wit": intelligence.

the morning; this, merely as a piece of news, as a fact added to my stock, gives me some pleasure. In the evening I find there was nothing in it. What do I gain by this, but the dissatisfaction to find that I had been imposed upon? Hence it is, that men are much more naturally inclined to belief than to incredulity. And it is upon this principle, that the most ignorant and barbarous nations have frequently excelled in similitudes, comparisons, metaphors, and allegories, who have been weak and backward in distinguishing and sorting their ideas. And it is for a reason of this kind that Homer[7] and the oriental writers, though very fond of similitudes, and though they often strike out such as are truly admirable, they seldom take care to have them exact; that is, they are taken with the general resemblance, they paint it strongly, and they take no notice of the difference which may be found between the things compared.

Now as the pleasure of resemblance is that which principally flatters the imagination, all men are nearly equal in this point, as far as their knowledge of the things represented or compared extends. The principle of this knowledge is very much accidental, as it depends upon experience and observation, and not on the strength or weakness of any natural faculty; and it is from this difference in knowledge that what we commonly, though with no great exactness, call a difference in Taste proceeds. A man to whom sculpture is new, sees a barber's block,[8] or some ordinary piece of statuary; he is immediately struck and pleased, because he sees something like an human figure; and entirely taken up with this likeness, he does not at all attend to its defects. No person, I believe, at the first time of seeing a piece of imitation ever did. Some time after, we suppose that this novice lights upon a more artificial[9] work of the same nature; he now begins to look with contempt on what he admired at first; not that he admired it even then for its unlikeness to a man, but for that general though inaccurate resemblance which it bore to the human figure. What he admired at different times in these so different figures, is strictly the same; and though his knowledge is improved, his Taste is not altered. Hitherto his mistake was from a want of knowledge in art, and this arose from his inexperience; but he may be still deficient from a want of knowledge in nature. For it is possible that the man in question may stop here, and that the masterpiece of a great hand may please him no more than the middling performance of a vulgar artist; and this not for want of better or higher relish, but because all men do not observe with sufficient accuracy on the human figure to enable them to judge properly of an imitation of it. And that the critical Taste does not depend upon a superior principle in men, but upon superior knowledge, may appear from several instances. The story of the ancient painter and the shoemaker is very well known. The shoemaker set the painter right with regard to some mistakes he had made in the shoe of one of his figures, and which the painter, who had not made such accurate observations on shoes, and was content with a general resemblance, had never observed.[1] But this was no impeachment to the Taste of the painter, it only shewed some want of knowledge in the art of making

7. Greek poet (ca. 8th c. B.C.E.) to whom the earliest works of Greek literature, the *Iliad* and *Odyssey*, are attributed.

8. A wooden head for a wig.

9. Skillfully made.

1. In his *Natural History* 35.84, the Roman writer Pliny the Elder (23/4–79 C.E.) tells this story of the Greek painter Apelles. See also SAMUEL JOHNSON, *The Rambler*, No. 4 (1750; above).

shoes. Let us imagine, that an anatomist had come into the painter's working room. His piece is in general well done, the figure in question in a good attitude, and the parts well adjusted to their various movements; yet the anatomist, critical in his art, may observe the swell of some muscle not quite just in the peculiar action of the figure. Here the anatomist observes what the painter had not observed, and he passes by what the shoemaker had remarked. But a want of the last critical knowledge in anatomy no more reflected on the natural good Taste of the painter, or of any common observer of his piece, than the want of an exact knowledge in the formation of a shoe. A fine piece of a decollated[2] head of St. John the Baptist was shewn to a Turkish emperor; he praised many things, but he observed one defect; he observed that the skin did not shrink from the wounded part of the neck. The sultan on this occasion, though his observation was very just, discovered no more natural Taste than the painter who executed this piece, or than a thousand European connoisseurs who probably never would have made the same observation. His Turkish majesty had indeed been well acquainted with that terrible spectacle, which the others could only have represented in their imagination. On the subject of their dislike there is a difference between all these people, arising from the different kinds and degrees of their knowledge; but there is something in common to the painter, the shoemaker, the anatomist, and the Turkish emperor, the pleasure arising from a natural object, so far as each perceives it justly imitated; the satisfaction in seeing an agreeable figure; the sympathy proceeding from a striking and affecting incident. So far as Taste is natural, it is nearly common to all.

In poetry, and other pieces of imagination, the same parity may be observed. It is true, that one man is charmed with Don Bellianis,[3] and reads Virgil coldly; whilst another is transported with the Eneid,[4] and leaves Don Bellianis to children. These two men seem to have a Taste very different from each other; but in fact they differ very little. In both these pieces, which inspire such opposite sentiments, a tale exciting admiration is told; both are full of action, both are passionate, in both are voyages, battles, triumphs, and continual changes of fortune. The admirer of Don Bellianis perhaps does not understand the refined language of the Eneid, who if it was degraded into the style of the Pilgrim's Progress,[5] might feel it in all its energy, on the same principle which made him an admirer of Don Bellianis.

In his favorite author he is not shocked with the continual breaches of probability, the confusion of times, the offences against manners, the trampling upon geography; for he knows nothing of geography and chronology, and he had never examined the grounds of probability. He perhaps reads of a shipwreck on the coast of Bohemia;[6] wholly taken up with so interesting an event, and only solicitous for the fate of his hero, he is not in the least troubled at this extravagant blunder. For why should he be shocked at a shipwreck on the coast of Bohemia, who does not know but that Bohemia may be an island in the Atlantic ocean? and after all, what reflection is this on the natural good Taste of the person here supposed?

2. Beheaded.
3. Geronimo Fernández's chivalric romance *Historia del valeroso é invencible Principe don Belianis de Grecia* (1547–49), published in full and in translation as *The Famous and Delectable History of Don Bellienis of Greece* (1673).
4. Virgil's *Aeneid* (19 B.C.E.).
5. *The Pilgrim's Progress* (1678), popular religious allegory by John Bunyan.
6. A notorious geographical error in Shakespeare, *The Winter's Tale* (ca. 1611), 3.3.2: Bohemia has no seacoast.

So far then as Taste belongs to the imagination, its principle is the same in all men; there is no difference in the manner of their being affected, nor in the causes of the affection; but in the *degree* there is a difference, which arises from two causes principally; either from a greater degree of natural sensibility, or from a closer and longer attention to the object. To illustrate this by the procedure of the senses in which the same difference is found, let us suppose a very smooth marble table to be set before two men; they both perceive it to be smooth, and they are both pleased with it, because of this quality. So far they agree. But suppose another, and after that another table, the latter still smoother than the former, to be set before them. It is now very probable that these men, who are so agreed upon what is smooth, and in the pleasure from thence, will disagree when they come to settle which table has the advantage in point of polish. Here is indeed the great difference between Tastes, when men come to compare the excess or diminution of things which are judged by degree and not by measure. Nor is it easy, when such a difference arises, to settle the point, if the excess or diminution be not glaring. If we differ in opinion about two quantities, we can have resource to a common measure, which may decide the question with the utmost exactness; and this I take it is what gives mathematical knowledge a greater certainty than any other. But in things whose excess is not judged by greater or smaller, as smoothness and roughness, hardness and softness, darkness and light, the shades of colours, all these are very easily distinguished when the difference is any way considerable, but not when it is minute, for want of some common measures which perhaps may never come to be discovered. In these nice[7] cases, supposing the acuteness of the sense equal, the greater attention and habit in such things will have the advantage. In the question about the tables, the marble polisher will unquestionably determine the most accurately. But notwithstanding this want of a common measure for settling many disputes relative to the senses and their representative the imagination, we find that the principles are the same in all, and that there is no disagreement until we come to examine into the preeminence or difference of things, which brings us within the province of the judgment.

So long as we are conversant with the sensible qualities of things, hardly any more than the imagination seems concerned; little more also than the imagination seems concerned when the passions are represented, because by the force of natural sympathy they are felt in all men without any recourse to reasoning, and their justness recognized in every breast. Love, grief, fear, anger, joy, all these passions have in their turns affected every mind; and they do not affect it in an arbitrary or casual manner, but upon certain, natural and uniform principles. But as many of the works of imagination are not confined to the representation of sensible objects, nor to efforts upon the passions, but extend themselves to the manners, the characters, the actions, and designs of men, their relations, their virtues and vices, they come within the province of the judgment, which is improved by attention and by the habit of reasoning. All these make a very considerable part of what are considered as the objects of Taste; and Horace sends us to the schools of philosophy and the world for our instruction in them.[8] Whatever certainty is to be acquired in morality and the science of life; just the same degree of certainty have we in what relates to them in works of imitation. Indeed it is

7. Involving great precision.

8. Horace, *Ars Poetica* 309–18.

for the most part in our skill in manners, and in the observances of time and place, and of decency in general, which is only to be learned in those schools to which Horace recommends us, that what is called Taste by way of distinction, consists; and which is in reality no other than a more refined judgment. On the whole it appears to me, that what is called Taste, in its most general acceptation, is not a simple idea, but is partly made up of a perception of the primary pleasures of sense, of the secondary pleasures of the imagination, and of the conclusions of the reasoning faculty, concerning the various relations of these, and concerning the human passions, manners and actions. All this is requisite to form Taste, and the ground-work of all these is the same in the human mind; for as the senses are the great originals of all our ideas, and consequently of all our pleasures, if they are not uncertain and arbitrary, the whole ground-work of Taste is common to all, and therefore there is a sufficient foundation for a conclusive reasoning on these matters.

Whilst we consider Taste, merely according to its nature and species, we shall find its principles entirely uniform; but the degree in which these principles prevail in the several individuals of mankind, is altogether as different as the principles themselves are similar. For sensibility and judgment, which are the qualities that compose what we commonly call a *Taste,* vary exceedingly in various people. From a defect in the former of these qualities, arises a want of Taste; a weakness in the latter, constitutes a wrong or bad one. There are some men formed with feelings so blunt, with tempers so cold and phlegmatic, that they can hardly be said to be awake during the whole course of their lives. Upon such persons, the most striking objects make but a faint and obscure impression. There are others so continually in the agitation of gross and merely sensual pleasures, or so occupied in the low and drudgery of avarice, or so heated in the chace[9] of honours and distinction, that their minds, which had been used continually to the storms of these violent and tempestuous passions, can hardly be put in motion by the delicate and refined play of the imagination. These men, though from a different cause, become as stupid and insensible as the former; but whenever either of these happen to be struck with any natural elegance or greatness, or with these qualities in any work of art, they are moved upon the same principle.

The cause of a wrong Taste is a defect of judgment. And this may arise from a natural weakness of understanding (in whatever the strength of that faculty may consist) or, which is much more commonly the case, it may arise from a want of proper and well-directed exercise, which alone can make it strong and ready. Besides that ignorance, inattention, prejudice, rashness, levity, obstinacy, in short, all those passions, and all those vices which pervert the judgment in other matters, prejudice it no less in this its more refined and elegant province. These causes produce different opinions upon every thing which is an object of the understanding, without inducing us to suppose, that there are no settled principles of reason. And indeed on the whole one may observe, that there is rather less difference upon matters of Taste among mankind, than upon most of those which depend upon the naked reason; and that men are far better agreed on the excellence of a description in Virgil, than on the truth or falsehood of a theory of Aristotle.[1]

9. Chase.
1. On the Greek philosopher (384–322 B.C.E.), see above.

A rectitude of judgment in the arts which may be called a good Taste, does in a great measure depend upon sensibility; because if the mind has no bent to the pleasures of the imagination, it will never apply itself sufficiently to works of that species to acquire a competent knowledge in them. But, though a degree of sensibility is requisite to form a good judgment, yet a good judgment does not necessarily arise from a quick sensibility of pleasure; it frequently happens that a very poor judge, merely by force of a greater complexional[2] sensibility, is more affected by a very poor piece, than the best judge by the most perfect; for as every thing new, extraordinary, grand, or passionate is well calculated to affect such a person, and that the faults do not affect him, his pleasure is more pure and unmixed; and it is merely a pleasure of the imagination, it is much higher than any which is derived from a rectitude of the judgment; the judgment is for the greater part employed in throwing stumbling blocks in the way of the imagination, in dissipating the scenes of its enchantment, and in tying us down to the disagreeable yoke of our reason: for almost the only pleasure that men have in judging better than others, consists in a sort of conscious pride and superiority, which arises from thinking rightly; but then, this is an indirect pleasure, a pleasure which does not immediately result from the object which is under contemplation. In the morning of our days, when the senses are unworn and tender, when the whole man is awake in every part, and the gloss of novelty fresh upon all the objects that surround us, how lively at that time are our sensations, but how false and inaccurate the judgments we form of things? I despair of ever receiving the same degree of pleasure from the most excellent performances of genius which I felt at that age, from pieces which my present judgment regards as trifling and contemptible. Every trivial cause of pleasure is apt to affect the man of too sanguine a complexion: his appetite is too keen to suffer his Taste to be delicate; and he is in all respects what Ovid says of himself in love,

Molle meum levibus cor est violabile telis,
Et semper causa est, cur ego semper amem.[3]

One of this character can never be a refined judge; never what the comic poet calls *elegans formarum, spectator*.[4] The excellence and force of a composition must always be imperfectly estimated from its effect on the minds of any, except we know the temper and character of those minds. The most powerful effects of poetry and music have been displayed, and perhaps are still displayed, where these arts are but in a very low and imperfect state. The rude hearer is affected by the principles which operate in these arts even in their rudest condition; and he is not skilful enough to perceive the defects. But as the arts advance towards their perfection, the science of criticism advances with equal pace, and the pleasure of judges is frequently interrupted by the faults which are discovered in the most finished compositions.

Before I leave this subject I cannot help taking notice of an opinion which

2. Constitutional.
3. Slightly misquoted from the Roman poet Ovid, *Heroides* (ca. 5 C.E.): "My soft heart is vulnerable to light darts, and there is always a reason why I am always in love" (15.79–80).
4. From *Eunuchus* (161 B.C.E.), by the Roman comic playwright Terence: "a refined observer of forms" (line 566).

many persons entertain, as if the Taste were a separate faculty of the mind, and distinct from the judgment and imagination; a species of instinct by which we are struck naturally, and at the first glance, without any previous reasoning with the excellencies, or the defects of a composition. So far as the imagination and the passions are concerned, I believe it true, that the reason is little consulted; but where disposition, where decorum, where congruity are concerned, in short wherever the best Taste differs from the worst, I am convinced that the understanding operates and nothing else; and its operation is in reality far from being always sudden, or when it is sudden, it is often far from being right. Men of the best Taste by consideration, come frequently to change these early and precipitate judgments which the mind from its aversion to neutrality and doubt loves to form on the spot. It is known that the Taste (whatever it is) is improved exactly as we improve our judgment, by extending our knowledge, by a steady attention to our object, and by frequent exercise. They who have not taken these methods, if their Tastes decides quickly, it is always uncertainly; and their quickness is owing to their presumption and rashness, and not to any sudden irradiation that in a moment dispels all darkness from their minds. But they who have cultivated that species of knowledge which makes the object of Taste, by degrees and habitually attain not only a soundness, but a readiness of judgment, as men do by the same methods on all other occasions. At first they are obliged to spell, but at last they read with ease and with celerity: but this celerity of its operation is no proof, that the Taste is a distinct faculty. Nobody I believe has attended the course of a discussion, which turned upon matters within the sphere of mere naked reason, but must have observed the extreme readiness with which the whole process of the argument is carried on, the grounds discovered, the objections raised and answered, and the conclusions drawn from premises, with a quickness altogether as great as the Taste can be supposed to work with; and yet where nothing but plain reason either is or can be suspected to operate. To multiply principles for every different appearance, is useless, and unphilosophical too in a high degree.

This matter might be pursued much further; but it is not the extent of the subject which must prescribe our bounds, for what subject does not branch out to infinity? it is the nature of our particular scheme, and the single point of view in which we consider it, which ought to put a stop to our researches.

From *Part I*

SECTION VII. OF THE SUBLIME

Whatever is fitted in any sort to excite the ideas of pain, and danger, that is to say, whatever is in any sort terrible, or is conversant about terrible objects, or operates in a manner analogous to terror, is a source of the *sublime*; that is, it is productive of the strongest emotion which the mind is capable of feeling. I say the strongest emotion, because I am satisfied the ideas of pain are much more powerful than those which enter on the part of pleasure. Without all doubt, the torments which we may be made to suffer, are much greater in their effect on the body and mind, than any pleasures which the most learned voluptuary could suggest, or than the liveliest imagination, and the most sound and exquisitely sensible body could enjoy. Nay I am in great doubt, whether any man could be found who would earn a life of the most perfect satisfaction, at the price of ending it in the torments, which justice inflicted in a few hours on the late unfortunate regicide in France.[5] But as pain is stronger in its operation than pleasure, so death is in general a much more affecting idea than pain; because there are very few pains, however exquisite, which are not preferred to death; nay, what generally makes pain itself, if I may say so, more painful, is, that it is considered as an emissary of this king of terrors. When danger or pain press too nearly, they are incapable of giving any delight, and are simply terrible; but at certain distances, and with certain modifications, they may be, and they are delightful, as we every day experience. The cause of this I shall endeavour to investigate hereafter.

From *Part III*

SECTION XXVII. THE SUBLIME AND BEAUTIFUL COMPARED

On closing this general view of beauty, it naturally occurs, that we should compare it with the sublime; and in this comparison there appears a remarkable contrast. For sublime objects are vast in their dimensions, beautiful ones comparatively small; beauty should be smooth, and polished; the great, rugged and negligent; beauty should shun the right line, yet deviate from it insensibly; the great in many cases loves the right line, and when it deviates, it often makes a strong deviation; beauty should not be obscure; the great ought to be dark and gloomy; beauty should be'light and delicate; the great ought to be solid, and even massive. They are indeed ideas of a very different nature, one being founded on pain, the other on pleasure; and however they may vary afterwards from the direct nature of their causes, yet these causes keep up and eternal distinction between them, a distinction never to be forgotten by any whose business it is to affect the passions. In the infinite variety of natural combinations we must expect to find the qualities of things the most remote imaginable from each other united in the same object. We must expect also to find combinations of the same kind in the works of art. But when we consider the power of an object upon our passions, we must know that when any thing is intended to affect the mind by the force of some predominant property, the affection produced is like to be the more uniform and perfect, if all the other properties or qualities of the object be of the same nature, and tending to the same design as the principal;

If black, and white blend, soften, and unite,
A thousand ways, are there no black and white?[6]

If the qualities of the sublime and beautiful are sometimes found united, does this prove, that they are the same, does it prove, that they are any way

5. Robert-François Damiens (1715–1757), who attempted to kill Louis XV on January 5, 1757, was tortured to death on March 28.

6. Slightly misquoted from ALEXANDER POPE, *An Essay on Man* (1733–34), 2.213–14.

allied, does it prove even that they are not opposite and contradictory? Black and white may soften, may blend, but they are not therefore the same. Nor when they are so softened and blended with each other, or with different colours, is the power of black as black, or of white as white, so strong as when each stands uniform and distinguished.

1757, 1759

GOTTHOLD EPHRAIM LESSING
1729–1781

Gotthold Ephraim Lessing is known for having questioned one of the most famous statements never meant. In HORACE's *Ars Poetica*, the Latin phrase *ut pictura poesis* (as painting, so poetry) was taken by many generations of critics to be prescriptive ("poetry *should* be like painting") rather than analogical ("poetry, like painting, does the following . . ."). Regardless of Horace's intent, the prescription has been immensely productive for poetry; but in *Laocoön* (1766) Lessing attacks this presumption of equivalence between poetry and painting, spelling out the differences between the visual and the verbal arts.

Born in Kamenz, Saxony, to a country pastor, Lessing was the first of twelve children (five died in childhood). After acquiring a solid education in languages and sciences, he enrolled at the University of Leipzig and soon fell under the spell of a more worldly and freethinking friend. His parents, alarmed by this influence and by Lessing's familiarity with the theater, called him home. When he explained to them that the hostility between church and theater could be overcome by improving the theater, he was allowed to return to Leipzig, where he became actively involved with a theatrical company, writing and producing plays. Unfortunately, the company failed, leaving Lessing to cover the debts; he fled, first to Wittenberg, then to Berlin.

Once in Berlin, he declared financial independence; working as a translator, reviewer, and playwright, he became the first German author to live by his pen. He found intellectual companionship with several close friends, especially the philosopher Moses Mendelssohn, who was introduced to Lessing as a chess partner and who influenced many of Lessing's aesthetic ideas.

In Berlin Lessing developed his gifts for both drama and debate. To him, the recommendation that German theater imitate seventeenth-century French classical drama (an idea promoted by Johann Christoph Gottsched) seemed a terrible mistake. The French had literalized ARISTOTLE and tied the theater to an overly formal set of rules. In his play *Miss Sara Sampson* (1755), Lessing attempted something quite different from PIERRE CORNEILLE, the epitome of classicism. He wrote the first German bourgeois tragedy—that is, a tragedy involving not the court but a middle-class family. He also entered the first of several intense polemical exchanges on unlikely topics by writing *Vademecum* (1754), a critique of a translation of Horace written by a pastor who was, unfortunately for Lessing, a protégé of Frederick II of Prussia. Frederick later repaid him by not appointing him to the post of royal librarian in Berlin.

Though he was barely supporting himself, the next few years were very productive: he wrote fables and a treatise on fables, plays, and a life of Sophocles, and he collaborated on the *Letters Concerning the Most Recent Literature* (1759–81) with his friends Mendelssohn and Gotthold Samuel Nicolai. In these letters, Lessing continued his campaign to free drama from French classicism, arguing that it should take its inspiration from Shakespeare. He also became close friends with a poet and military man who later served as the model for the hero of his comedy of honor, *Minna von Barnhelm* (1767). In 1760 Lessing took up a post as secretary to a general in Breslau. His excellent salary enabled him to send money to his family and to buy books. It was during this period that he wrote *Laokoon, oder Über die Grenzen der Malerei und Poesie* (*Laocoön, or On the Limits of Painting and Poetry*), from which our selection is taken.

Thwarted in his hopes to become the royal librarian in Berlin, he became dramatist and consultant to a repertory theater in Hamburg. There he began publishing the periodical the *Hamburg Dramaturgy* (which contained views far more radical than any he could practice), invested in a publishing house, and engaged again in a polemic—this time with the antiquarian Christian Adolphe Klotz, who had attacked his *Laocoön*. In response, he wrote *Letters of Antiquarian Content* (1768–69) and *How the Ancients Portrayed Death* (1769). Finally, unable to extricate himself from the dispute, frustrated with the constraints of the theater, and unsuccessful in business, he took refuge in the post of librarian at the Ducal Library in Wolfenbüttel.

Lessing was well suited for the job, though the library was dilapidated and isolated. As he put it in order, he corresponded with scholars and, in 1773, began publishing some of the library's holdings. He also began a correspondence with the recently widowed Eva König (whose family he had known in Hamburg), whom he married in 1776; a year later Eva gave birth to a child, and both died within days.

Lessing continued his work in drama, completing *Emilia Galotti*, a political tragedy, in 1772. *Nathan the Wise*, a dramatic poem about religious tolerance, was performed at Easter 1778; it stirred controversy by putting its message of universal brotherhood in the mouth of a noble Jew. Lessing went on publishing his library discoveries as well, and the fragments from Heinrich Samuel Reimarus's thesis on natural religion embroiled him in his final, and most intense, polemical exchange. His main attacker was Johann Melchior Goeze, and Lessing's angry *Anti-Goeze* pamphlets of 1778 and other writings on religion led to his being censored: he had to to submit his later writings to the duke for approval. His provocative argument was that the truth of religion could never be captured in any fixed form; even the Bible was full of errors and contradictions It was the *search* for truth and not any one Truth that proved the value of humanity. Little wonder that Lessing fell so readily into polemic: for him, such exchanges did not lead to truth but enacted it. In his last work, *The Education of the Human Race* (1780), Lessing continued to analyze the relation between reason and faith, education and revelation. Furious with all existing religions, Lessing was equally furious with smug atheism or complacent freethinking. His health declined after 1778, and he died at Wolfenbüttel at the age of fifty-two.

In spite of the variety of his interests and writings, Lessing's importance for literary criticism in English rests almost exclusively on the impact of his 1766 *Laocoön*. He begins it by discussing the role of the critic, whose duty with respect to the work of art is to make distinctions and discern causes rather than simply to register effects. While endorsing the well-known saying of the early-fifth-century B.C.E. poet Simonides that painting is mute poetry and poetry a speaking picture, he argues that although the two arts are similar in *aim* (imitation) and in *effect* (pleasure), they differ greatly in *means* (visual versus verbal). Lessing goes on to analyze their differences.

In the course of his essay, Lessing takes on a veritable bookshelf of other writings, most notably Count Caylus's *Tableaux tirés de l'Iliade, de l'Odyssée d'Homère et de l'Enéide de Virgile, avec des observations générales sur le costume* (1757, *Scenes from Homer's Iliad and Odyssey and Virgil's Aeneid, with General Comments about Costume*); Joseph Spence's 1747 dialogues on visual and verbal art called *Polymetis*; and, most important, Johann Joachim Winckelmann's 1754 *Gedanken über die Nachahmung der greichischen Werke* (*Thoughts on the Imitation of Greek Works*). It is Winckelmann's concept of classical Greek "noble simplicity and quiet grandeur" that

Lessing wishes to combat, not in the visual arts (where, he argues, it belonged) but in the verbal arts: epic and (implicitly) tragedy. The cold formalism of classical French drama was too much like sculpture; Lessing wants to make sure that the art of imitation in drama draws on Aristotle (plot is the "imitation of an *action*") rather than PLATO (mimesis is the imitation of a *form*). Winckelmann's idealization of Greek beauty had a powerful appeal; indeed, it was still being attacked a century later by FRIEDRICH NIETZSCHE in *The Birth of Tragedy* (1872).

Laocoön stands as the first modern contribution to what we might call "media studies," in the sense that Lessing attempts to describe the limits and possibilities of the visual and verbal *media*. Our selection highlights the lines of the analysis and minimizes the polemical digressions and extended classical allusions, emphasizing the argument—which runs as follows. Painting is more similar to its subject than poetry is: in painting, both the medium and the thing imitated are visual, whereas poetry can use only words, arbitrary designations, to convey things that do not resemble words at all. In addition, visual art is static while verbal art unfolds through succession. Visual art is an art of *space;* verbal art is an art of *time*. Verbal art cannot equal the instant vividness of sculpture or painting, but it can depict things that visual art cannot capture: invisibility, negation, rhetoric. Visual art, in order to achieve maximum dynamism, has to choose the "pregnant moment," the moment most suggestive of the entire situation.

The word "pregnant" has come to have a life of its own in Lessing criticism in English; it was used by many translators (though not ours) to render the German *fruchtbar* ("fruitful"—here translated "effective") and *prägnant* (from the verb *prägen*, "to stamp, emboss, impress"; the adjective does mean "pregnant," but only figuratively, as "pregnant with meaning"—here translated "suggestive"). This phantom pregnancy is a good symbol of what Lessing is describing: the moment most likely to contain forces that can be continued in the imagination of the spectator. In visual art, therefore, a covert narrative force is always present. The same force exists in verbal descriptions of purely visual phenomena; even when poetry depicts an object rather than an action, it moves along the object in time as if from the standpoint of the object's maker rather than of its passive viewer.

Lessing's distinction between the arts has often been contested. In his 1957 essay on Lessing, the art historian E. H. Gombrich points out that visual art itself is conventional, not natural. In 1945 the literary critic Joseph Frank protested that a literary work of art exists not just in time but also in space. And many art historians have objected that a painting cannot be viewed all at once; it must be experienced through time. Taking an opposite tack, some theorists of ecphrasis (the depiction of a work of visual art in a poem) have felt that Lessing opens up possibilities he doesn't pursue. Far from being impossible in poetry, ecphrasis constitutes an interesting poetic challenge.

Because of his persistent fascination with what could *not* be visualized, Lessing is a particularly useful theorist of verbal art. In his discussion of fables, he points out that the test of a good fable is the impossibility of illustrating it. In his last writings about religion, he argues that even writing has too positive an existence to convey what escapes representation altogether. Perhaps this dissatisfaction with *every* medium is what makes his writings so suggestive for literary and aesthetic theory.

BIBLIOGRAPHY

Lessing's *Laokoon* (1766) has been translated into English many times. The most easily accessible edition was published in 1962 as *Laocoön: An Essay on the Limits of Painting and Poetry*, translated with an introduction and useful notes by Edward Allen McCormick. Many of Lessing's other theoretical works, however, are available only in German. The best recent selection of Lessing's works, heavily oriented toward theater, is *Nathan the Wise, Minna von Barnhelm, and Other Plays and Writings*, edited by Peter Demetz (1991). For Lessing's drama theory, see *Hamburg Dramaturgy*, edited by Victor Lange (1962). See also *Lessing's Theological Writings*, edited by Henry Chadwick (1956). A more complete English translation was undertaken by E. C. Beasley and Helen Zimmern, under the editorship of Edward Bell, more than a century ago: *Selected Prose Works of G. E. Lessing* (1890). Good general studies devoted to Lessing's life and works are H. B. Garland, *Lessing: The Founder of Modern German Literature* (1962), and Edward M. Batley, *Catalyst of Enlightenment: Gotthold Ephraim Lessing* (1990). Studies situating Lessing in a larger context include a very useful collective volume edited by Alexej Ugrinsky called *Lessing and the Enlightenment* (1986) and Robert S. Leventhal's *Disciplines of Interpretation: Lessing, Herder, Schlegel, and Hermeneutics in Germany, 1750–1800* (1994). Early in the twentieth century, Irving Babbitt's *New Laokoon: An Essay on the Confusion of the Arts* (1910) attempted to restore Lessing's sense of distinction to a world led astray by Romanticism's tendency to cross or blur boundaries. E. H. Gombrich's short *Lessing* (1957) paints a brilliant portrait of a man whose dialectical mind had no real use for visual art.

The publication in 1984 of David Wellbery's *Lessing's "Laocoön": Semiotics and Aesthetics in the Age of Reason* brought Lessing into post-Saussurian discussions of sign theory. Simon Richter's *Laocoön's Body and the Aesthetics of Pain: Winckelmann, Lessing, Herder, Moritz, Goethe* (1992) provides an interesting analysis of the relation between pain and beauty. Carol Jacobs offers a good analysis of the rhetoric of Lessing's polemics in "Fictional Histories: Lessing's *Laocoön*," in her *Telling Time* (1993). Susan Gustafson's *Absent Mothers and Orphaned Fathers: Narcissism and Abjection in Lessing's Aesthetic and Dramatic Production* (1995) combines a discussion of Lessing's plays with a reading of the *Laocoön* that uses Julia Kristeva's theory of maternal erasure or "abjection," in a daring feminist psychoanalysis. A special issue of *Poetics Today* on Lessing (20.2 [1999]) offers a very interesting collection of essays, particularly striking for the debates about gender as a category of analysis. The volume concludes with a long, energetic, polemical review of the literature on Lessing by Meir Sternberg. For debates about ecphrasis, see Murray Krieger's 1967 essay "*Ekphrasis* and the Still Movement of Poetry; or, *Laokoön* Revisited," later collected in Krieger's *Ekphrasis: The Illusion of the Natural Sign* (1992); W. J. T. Mitchell's 1984 essay "Space and Time: Lessing's *Laocoön* and the Politics of Genre," later collected in his *Iconology: Image, Text, Ideology* (1986); and James Heffernan's *Museum of Words* (1993). There is a bibliography in German on Lessing by Doris Kuhles, *Lessing-Bibliographie 1971–1985* (1988).

From Laocoön[1]

From *Preface*

The first person to compare painting with poetry was a man of fine feeling who observed that both arts produced a similar effect upon him. Both, he felt, represent absent things as being present and appearance as reality. Both create an illusion, and in both cases the illusion is pleasing.

A second observer, in attempting to get at the nature of this pleasure, discovered that both proceed from the same source. Beauty, a concept which we first derive from physical objects, has general rules applicable to a number of things: to actions and thoughts as well as to forms.

1. Translated by Edward Allen McCormick (who sometimes adds clarifying words or phrases in square brackets); the full title is *Laocoön, or On the Limits of Painting and Poetry*.

A third, who examined the value and distribution of these general rules, observed that some of them are more predominant in painting, others in poetry. Thus, in the one case poetry can help to explain and illustrate painting, and in the other painting can do the same for poetry.

The first was the amateur, the second the philosopher, and the third the critic.

The first two could not easily misuse their feelings or their conclusions. With the critic, however, the case was different. The principal value of his observations depends on their correct application to the individual case. And since for every one really discerning critic there have always been fifty clever ones, it would have been a miracle if this application had always been made with the caution necessary to maintain a proper balance between the two arts.

* * *

From *Chapter One*

The general and distinguishing characteristics of the Greek masterpieces of painting and sculpture are, according to Herr Winckelmann,[2] noble simplicity and quiet grandeur, both in posture and in expression. "As the depths of the sea always remain calm," he says "however much the surface may be agitated, so does the expression in the figures of the Greeks reveal a great and composed soul in the midst of passions."

> Such a soul is depicted in Laocoön's[3] face—and not only in his face—under the most violent suffering. The pain is revealed in every muscle and sinew of his body, and one can almost feel it oneself in the painful contraction of the abdomen without looking at the face or other parts of the body at all. However, this pain expresses itself without any sign of rage either in his face or in his posture. He does not raise his voice in a terrible scream, which Virgil describes his Laocoön as doing;[4] the way in which his mouth is open does not permit it. Rather he emits the anxious and subdued sigh described by Sadolet.[5] The pain of body and the nobility of soul are distributed and weighed out, as it were, over the entire figure with equal intensity. Laocoön suffers, but he suffers like the Philoctetes of Sophocles[6]; his anguish pierces our very soul, but at the same time we wish that we were able to endure our suffering as well as this great man does.
>
> Expressing so noble a soul goes far beyond the formation of a beautiful body. This artist must have felt within himself that strength of spirit

2. Johann Joachim Winckelmann (1717–1768), German classical scholar whose *Thoughts on the Imitation of Greek Works in Painting and Sculpture* (1754) prompted Lessing's response.
3. A Trojan priest. The best-known version of his story is found in the *Aeneid*, by the Roman poet Virgil (70–19 B.C.E.), who describes how when Laocoön unsuccessfully tries to warn his countrymen against the Greek "gift" of the Trojan horse, the goddess Athena sends two huge serpents to strangle him and his two sons (2.40–56, 199–227). The famous sculpture described by Winckelmann represents the three dying figures in the grip of the snakes; discovered in 1506, it is thought to be a collaborative work of the 2d century B.C.E. Laocoön is thus depicted in both sculpture and poetry, giving Lessing the pivot on which he will differentiate between the arts.
4. *Aeneid* 2.222.
5. Jacopo Sadoleto (1477–1547), Italian prelate and poet, who wrote a poem about the Laocoön group when it was discovered.
6. Greek tragedian (ca. 496–406 B.C.E.). The Greek hero Philoctetes used the bow and arrows of Heracles; he sailed for Troy but was left behind on an island because a wound on his foot, caused by snakebite, produced a horrible smell. He remained alone for 10 years, until on the advice of an oracle he and his bow were brought to Troy.

> which he imparted to his marble. In Greece artists and philosophers were united in one person, and there was more than one Metrodorus.[7] Philosophy extended its hand to art and breathed into its figures more than common souls. . . .[8]

The remark on which the foregoing comments are based, namely that the pain in Laocoön's face is not expressed with the same intensity that its violence would lead us to expect, is perfectly correct. It is also indisputable that this very point shows truly the wisdom of the artist. Only the ill-informed observer would judge that the artist had fallen short of nature and had not attained the true pathos of suffering.

But as to the reasons on which Herr Winckelmann bases this wisdom, and the universality of the rule which he derives from it, I venture to be of a different opinion.

* * *

[I]f, according to the ancient Greeks, crying aloud when in physical pain is compatible with nobility of soul, then the desire to express such nobility could not have prevented the artist from representing the scream in his marble. There must be another reason why he differs on this point from his rival the poet,[9] who expresses this scream with deliberate intention.

From *Chapter Two*

Whether it be fact or fiction that Love inspired the first artistic effort in the fine arts,[1] this much is certain: she never tired of guiding the hands of the old masters. Painting, as practiced today, comprises all representations of three-dimensional bodies on a plane. The wise Greek, however, confined it to far narrower limits by restricting it to the imitation of beautiful bodies only. The Greek artist represented only the beautiful, and ordinary beauty, the beauty of a lower order, was only his accidental subject, his exercise, his relaxation. The perfection of the object itself in his work had to give delight, and he was too great to demand of his audience that they be satisfied with the barren pleasure that comes from looking at a perfect resemblance, or from consideration of his skill as a craftsman. Nothing in his art was dearer to him or seemed nobler than its ultimate purpose.

"Who would want to paint you when no one even wants to look at you?" an old epigrammatist[2] asks of an exceedingly deformed man. Many an artist of our time would say, "Be as ugly as possible, I will paint you nevertheless. Even though no one likes to look at you, they will still be glad to look at my picture, not because it portrays you but because it is a proof of my art, which knows how to present such a monster so faithfully."

* * *

7. An Athenian (2d c. B.C.E.) who, according to Pliny the Elder (23/4–79 C.E.; see *Natural History* 35.135), was both a painter and a philosopher.
8. Winckelmann, *Thoughts on the Imitation of Greek Works*, pp. 21, 22 [Lessing's note]. Some of the author's notes have been edited, and some omitted.
9. That is, Virgil.

1. Lessing alludes to the story of a Corinthian maid who, saddened by her lover's impending departure drew his outline on a wall while he slept (see Pliny the Elder, *Natural History* 35.151); her father, a potter, filled in the outline with clay and thus invented bas relief.
2. Antiochus of Syracuse (5th c. B.C.E.).

The law of the Olympic judges sprang from the same idea of the beautiful. Every victor in the Olympic games received a statue, but only the three-time winner had a portrait-statue erected in his honor. This was to prevent the increase of mediocre portraits among works of art, for a portrait, although admitting idealization, is dominated by likeness. It is the ideal of one particular man and not of man in general.

We laugh when we hear that among the ancients even the arts were subject to the civil code. But we are not always right when we do so. Unquestionably, laws must not exercise any constraint on the sciences, for the ultimate goal of knowledge is truth. Truth is a necessity to the soul, and it is tyranny to impose the slightest constraint on the satisfaction of this essential need. But the ultimate goal of the arts is pleasure, and this pleasure is not indispensable. Hence it may be for the lawmaker to determine what kind of pleasure and how much of each kind he will permit.

The plastic arts in particular—aside from the inevitable influence they exert on the character of a nation—have an effect that demands close supervision by the law. If beautiful men created beautiful statues, these statues in turn affected the men, and thus the state owed thanks also to beautiful statues for beautiful men. (With us the highly susceptible imagination of mothers seems to express itself only in producing monsters.)

From this point of view I believe I can find some truth in some of the ancient tales which are generally rejected as outright lies. The mothers of Aristomenes, Aristodamas, Alexander the Great, Scipio, Augustus, and Galerius[3] all dreamed during pregnancy that they had relations with a serpent. The serpent was a symbol of divinity, and the beautiful statues and paintings depicting Bacchus, Apollo, Mercury, or Hercules[4] were seldom without one. Those honest mothers had feasted their eyes on the god during the day, and their confused dreams recalled the image of the reptile. Thus I save the dream and abandon the interpretation born of the pride of their sons and the impudence of the flatterer. For there must be some reason why the adulterous fantasy was always a serpent.

But I am digressing. I wanted simply to establish that among the ancients beauty was the supreme law of the visual arts. Once this has been established, it necessarily follows that whatever else these arts may include must give way completely if not compatible with beauty, and, if compatible, must at least be subordinate to it.

Let us consider expression. There are passions and degrees of passion which are expressed by the most hideous contortions of the face and which throw the whole body into such unnatural positions as to lose all the beautiful contours of its natural state. The ancient artists either refrained from depicting such emotions or reduced them to a degree where it is possible to show them with a certain measure of beauty.

* * *

3. This list mixes the legendary (the first 2 are Greek heroes) and the historical—the great general Alexander of Macedonia (356–323 B.C.E.), the Roman general Scipio Africanus (236–184/3 B.C.E.), and the Roman emperors Augustus (63 B.C.E.–14 C.E.) and Galerius (ca. 250–ca. 311 C.E.).

4. The Roman name for Heracles, the greatest of the Greek heroes. Bacchus: Greek and Roman god of wine and a name of Dionysus, whose cult was orgiastic. Apollo: Greek and Roman god of music, healing, and prophecy. Mercury: Roman messenger of the gods.

If we apply this now to the Laocoön, the principle which I am seeking becomes apparent. The master strove to attain the highest beauty possible under the given condition of physical pain. The demands of beauty could not be reconciled with the pain in all its disfiguring violence, so it had to be reduced. The scream had to be softened to a sigh, not because screaming betrays an ignoble soul, but because it distorts the features in a disgusting manner. Simply imagine Laocöon's mouth forced wide open, and then judge! Imagine him screaming, and then look! From a form which inspired pity because it possessed beauty and pain at the same time, it has now become an ugly, repulsive figure from which we gladly turn away. For the sight of pain provokes distress; however, the distress should be transformed, through beauty, into the tender feeling of pity.

The wide-open mouth, aside from the fact that the rest of the face is thereby twisted and distorted in an unnatural and loathsome manner, becomes in painting a mere spot and in sculpture a cavity, with most repulsive effect.

* * *

From *Chapter Three*

As I have already said, art has been given a far wider scope in modern times. It is claimed that representation in the arts covers all of visible nature, of which the beautiful is but a small part. Truth and expression are art's first law, and as nature herself is ever ready to sacrifice beauty for the sake of higher aims, so must the artist subordinate it to his general purpose and pursue it no farther than truth and expression permit. It is enough that truth and expression transform the ugliest aspects of nature into artistic beauty.

But even if we were willing to leave these ideas for the moment unchallenged as to their value, we would still have to consider, quite independently of these ideas, why the artist must nevertheless set certain restraints upon expression and never present an action at its climax.

The single moment of time to which art must confine itself by virtue of its material limitations will lead us, I believe, to such considerations.

If the artist can never make use of more than a single moment in ever-changing nature, and if the painter in particular can use this moment only with reference to a single vantage point, while the works of both painter and sculptor are created not merely to be given a glance but to be contemplated—contemplated repeatedly and at length—then it is evident that this single moment and the point from which it is viewed cannot be chosen with too great a regard for its effect. But only that which gives free rein to the imagination is effective.[5] The more we see, the more we must be able to imagine. And the more we add in our imaginations, the more we must think we see. In the full course of an emotion, no point is less suitable for this than its climax. There is nothing beyond this, and to present the utmost to the eye is to bind the wings of fancy and compel it, since it cannot soar above the impression made on the senses, to concern itself with weaker images, shunning the visible fullness already represented as a limit beyond which it cannot

5. In German, *fruchtbar*: "fruitful."

go. Thus, if Laocoön sighs, the imagination can hear him cry out; but if he cries out, it can neither go one step higher nor one step lower than this representation without seeing him in a more tolerable and hence less interesting condition. One either hears him merely moaning or else sees him dead.

Furthermore, this single moment, if it is to receive immutable permanence from art, must express nothing transitory. According to our notions, there are phenomena, which we conceive as being essentially sudden in their beginning and end and which can be what they are only for a brief moment. However, the prolongation of such phenomena in art, whether agreeable or otherwise, gives them such an unnatural appearance that they make a weaker impression the more often we look at them, until they finally fill us with disgust or horror. La Mettrie,[6] who had himself portrayed in painting and engraving as a second Democritus, seems to be laughing only the first few times we look at him. Look at him more often and the philosopher turns into a fop. His laugh becomes a grin. The same holds true for screaming. The violent pain which extorts the scream either soon subsides or else destroys the sufferer. When a man of firmness and endurance cries out he does not do so unceasingly, and it is only the seeming perpetuity of such cries when represented in art that turns them into effeminate helplessness or childish petulance. This, at least, the artist of the Laocoön had to avoid, even if screaming had not been detrimental to beauty, and if his art had been allowed to express suffering without beauty.

Among the ancient painters Timomachus[7] seems to have been the one most fond of subjects that display extreme passion. His raving Ajax and his infanticide Medea[8] were famous paintings, but from the descriptions we have of them it is clear that he thoroughly understood and was able to combine two things: that point or moment which the beholder not so much sees as adds in his imagination, and that appearance which does not seem so transitory as to become displeasing through its perpetuation in art. Timomachus did not represent Medea at the moment when she was actually murdering her children, but a few moments before, when a mother's love was still struggling with her vengefulness. We can foresee the outcome of this struggle; we tremble in anticipation of seeing Medea as simply cruel, and our imagination takes us far beyond what the painter could have shown us in this terrible moment. But for this very reason we are not offended at Medea's perpetual indecision, as it is represented in art, but wish it could have remained that way in reality. We wish that the duel of passions had never been decided, or at least had continued long enough for time and reflection to overcome rage and secure the victory for maternal feelings. This wisdom on the part of Timomachus has earned him lavish and frequent praise and

6. Julien Offroy de La Mettrie (1709–1751), French physician and philosopher, whose *L'Homme machine* (1747) made him the most notorious materialist of his day. The Greek Democritus (ca. 460–ca. 370 B.C.E.) was also a materialist (he argued that everything, including the soul, is composed of atoms); he was known as the "laughing philosopher," perhaps because he believed that individuals were responsible for their own well-being.

7. Byzantine painter (late 4th c. B.C.E.) mentioned by Pliny the Elder (35.11).

8. A sorceress from Colchis who took revenge on her husband Jason (for deserting her to marry a king's daughter) by killing his (and her) two children. Ajax: one of the greatest Greek warriors at Troy; driven mad by Athena, he killed animals believing that he was attacking the Greek leaders who had refused to give him the armor of the dead Achilles (when he regained his senses, he killed himself). Both figures were often treated in art and tragedies.

raised him far above another, unknown painter who was foolish enough to depict Medea at the height of her rage, thus endowing her brief instant of madness with a permanence that is an affront to all nature.

* * *

From *Chapter Nine*

If we wish to compare the painter and the poet in particular instances, we must first know whether they both enjoyed complete freedom; whether, that is to say, they could work toward producing the greatest possible effect in their respective arts without any external constraint.

Religion often represented just such an external constraint on the classical artist. His work, destined for worship and devotion, could not always be as perfect as it would have been if he had had as his sole aim the pleasure of his spectators. But superstition overloaded the gods with symbols, and the most beautiful gods were not always honored as such.

In the temple at Lemnos, from which the pious Hypsipyle[9] rescued her father in the disguise of the god, Bacchus was represented with horns. No doubt he appeared this way in all his temples since the horns were symbolic and one of his necessary attributes. Only the free artist, who did not have to create his Bacchus for some temple, omitted this symbol; and if we find none with horns among the extant statues of him, we may perhaps take this as proof that none of them belongs among the consecrated ones under which he was actually worshiped. Besides this, it is highly probable that the wrath of pious iconoclasts during the first centuries of Christianity fell in great part on these latter. Only seldom did they spare a work of art, because it had not been desecrated by adoration.

However, since pieces of both kinds are to be found among the excavated objects of antiquity, I should prefer that only those be called works of art in which the artist had occasion to show himself as such and in which beauty was his first and ultimate aim. None of the others, which betray too obvious traces of religious conventions, deserves this name because in their case the artist did not create for art's sake,[1] but his art was merely a handmaid of religion, which stressed meaning more than beauty in the material subjects it allotted to art for execution. By this I do not mean to say that religion has not also frequently sacrificed meaning for beauty, or, out of consideration for art and the more refined taste of the period, has ceased to emphasize it to such a degree that beauty alone would seem to be the sole object.

* * *

From *Chapter Ten*

I comment on an expression of astonishment in Spence[2] which clearly shows how little thought he must have given to the limits of poetry and painting.

9. Daughter of King Thaos, the son of Dionysus; the women of the island of Lemnos killed all the other men, who had left their wives for Thracian women.

1. Possibly the first use of the expression "art for art's sake."

2. Joseph Spence (1699–1768), an Oxford professor whose *Polymetis* (1747), written in dialogues, is one of the targets of Lessing's criticism.

"As to the muses in general," he says, "it is strange that the poets are so brief in describing them, far briefer in fact than might be expected for goddesses to whom they are so greatly indebted."[3]

What can this mean but that he is amazed that when poets speak of the muses they do not use the mute language of painters? To the poets Urania is the muse of astronomy; we recognize her office from her name and her functions. The artist, in order to make her recognizable, must show her pointing with a wand to a celestial globe. The wand, the globe, and the pointing position are his letters, from which he lets us spell out the name Urania. But when the poet wishes to say that Urania had foreseen his death long ago in the stars,

> Ipsa diu positis lethum praedixerat astris Uranie . . . [4]

why should he, out of respect for the painter, add: "Urania, her wand in hand, the celestial globe before her"? It is as though a man who can and may speak were at the same time using those signs which the mutes in the Turkish seraglio[5] invented among themselves for lack of a voice.

Spence again expresses the same astonishment when speaking of the moral beings, those divinities whom the ancients made preside over the virtues and the conduct of human life. "It should be remarked," he says, "that the Roman poets have far less to say about the best of these moral beings than one would expect. On this point the artists are much more complete, and whoever wants to know what appearance each of them made need only look at the coins of the Roman emperors. The poets, to be sure, often speak of these beings as persons, but of their attributes, their clothing and their appearance in general they have little to say."[6]

When the poet personifies abstractions, he characterizes them sufficiently by their names and the actions he has them perform.

The artist lacks these means and must therefore add to his personified abstractions symbols by which they may be recognized. But because these symbols are something different and mean something different, they make the figures allegorical.

The female figure with a bridle in her hand; another leaning against a pillar—these are, in art, allegorical figures. For the poet, however, Moderation and Constancy are not allegorical beings but simply personified abstractions.

Necessity invented these symbols for the artist, for only through them can he make it understood what this or that figure is supposed to represent. But why should the poet have forced upon him what the artist had to accept of necessity; a necessity which he himself has no part of?

The very thing which so surprised Spence should be prescribed to poets as a general law. They must not convert the necessities of painting into a part of their own wealth. Nor must they regard the means that art has invented in order to keep up with poetry as perfections which should give

3. *Polymetis*, Dialogue VIII, p. 91 [Lessing's note]. "Muses": in Greek mythology, the 9 daughters of memory who preside over the arts and all intellectual pursuits.

4. Statius, *Thebaid* 8.551 [Lessing's note]; the preceding clause translates the Latin. Statius (ca. 46–96 C.E.), Roman poet.

5. The harem, women's quarters overseen at courts by eunuchs and, in Lessing's account, mutes.

6. *Polymetis*, Dialogue X, pp. 137, 139 [Lessing's note].

them reason for envy. When the artist adorns a figure with symbols, he raises what was a mere figure to a higher being; but if the poet employs these artistic trimmings, he turns that higher being into a puppet.

* * *

Chapter Twelve

Homer[7] treats of two kinds of beings and actions, visible and invisible. This distinction cannot be made in painting, where everything is visible and visible in but one way. Hence, when Count Caylus[8] makes the pictures of invisible actions follow the visible ones in an unbroken sequence, and when in his paintings showing mixed actions, i.e., those in which both visible and invisible beings take part, he does not and perhaps cannot specify how the latter (which only we who look at the picture are supposed to discover in it) are to be introduced so that the figures in the painting do not see them (or at least appear not to see them)—when Count Caylus does this, I say, the series as a whole as well as a number of single pictures necessarily become extremely confused, incomprehensible, and self-contradictory.

Still, with the book before us it would be possible to remedy this fault. The worst of it is that when painting erases the distinction between visible and invisible beings it simultaneously destroys all those characteristic features by which this latter, higher order is raised above the lower one.

For example, when the gods, who are divided as to the fate of the Trojans, finally come to blows, the entire battle is represented in the poem as being invisible.[9] This invisibility gives the imagination free rein to enlarge the scene and envisage the persons and actions of the gods on a grander scale than the measure of ordinary man. But painting must adopt a visible scene, whose various indispensable parts become the scale for the figures participating in it—a scale which the eye has ready at hand and whose lack of proportion to the higher beings makes them appear monstrous on the artist's canvas.

Minerva, whom Mars[1] ventures to attack first in this battle, steps back and with her mighty hand seizes a large, black, rough stone which the united strength of men had rolled there for a landmark in times past:

> ἡ δ' ἀναχασσαμένη λίθον εἵλετο χειρὶ παχείῃ
> κείμενον ἐν πεδίῳ, μέλανα, τρηχύν τε μέγαν τε,
> τόν ῥ' ἄνδρες πρότεροι θέσαν ἔμμεναι οὖρον αρούρης·[2]

In order to form a proper estimate of the size of this stone we should remember that Homer makes his heroes twice as strong as the strongest men of his own time but tells us that these again were surpassed in strength by the men whom Nestor[3] knew in his youth. Now I ask, if Minerva hurls a stone which no one man, not even one from Nestor's youth, could set up as a landmark—if Minerva hurls such a stone at Mars, of what stature is the goddess sup-

7. Greek epic poet (ca. 8th c. B.C.E.) to whom the *Iliad* and the *Odyssey* are attributed.
8. Philippe de Tubières (1692–1765), French art critic; his *Scenes from Homer's Iliad and Odyssey and Virgil's Aeneid* (1757) is the third of Lessing's targets.
9. *Iliad* 21.385 [Lessing's note].
1. Ares, Greek god of war. Minerva: Athena, Greek goddess of war and wisdom.
2. But Athene giving back caught up in her heavy hand a stone / that lay in the plain, black and rugged and huge, one which men / of a former time had set there as boundary mark of the cornfield; *Iliad* 21.403–5 (trans. Richmond Lattimore) [translator's note].
3. The oldest of the Greek generals who fought at Troy.

posed to be? If her stature is in proportion to the size of the stone, then the element of the marvelous disappears. A man three times my size naturally ought to be able to hurl a stone three times as large as I can. But if the stature of the goddess is not in proportion to the size of the stone, an improbability for the eye arises in the painting whose offensiveness is not removed by the cold calculation that a goddess must possess superhuman strength. Wherever I see a greater effect, I also expect to see a greater cause.

And Mars, thrown to the ground by this mighty stone,

ἑπτὰ δ' ἐπέσχε πέλεθρα πεσών,[4]

covered seven acres of land. It is impossible for the painter to give the god this extraordinary size, and yet if he does not do so, it is no longer Mars—or at least not the Homeric Mars—who is lying on the ground, but a common warrior.

Longinus[5] says that it seemed to him now and then as though Homer raised his men to gods and reduced his gods to men. Painting carries out this reduction. In it everything which in the poem raises the gods above godlike human creatures vanishes altogether. Size, strength, and swiftness—qualities which Homer always has in store for his gods in a higher and more extraordinary degree than that bestowed on his finest heroes—must in the painting sink to the common level of humanity. Jupiter and Agamemnon, Apollo and Achilles, Ajax and Mars[6] all become exactly the same kind of beings, recognizable by nothing more than their outward conventional symbols.

The means which painting uses to convey to us that this or that object must be thought of as invisible is a thin cloud veiling the side of the object that is turned toward the other persons in the pictures. It appears that this cloud was borrowed from Homer, for when in the tumult of battle one of the more important heroes runs into great danger, from which only a divine power can save him, the poet has the protecting divinity envelop him in a thick cloud, or in darkness, and so carry him away, as Paris is carried off by Venus, or Idaeus by Neptune, or Hector by Apollo.[7] And Caylus never fails to recommend heartily this mist or cloud to the artist when he outlines for him a painting of such occurrences. And yet who can fail to see that concealment by cloud or night is, for the poet, nothing more than a poetic expression for rendering a thing invisible? For that reason it has always been a source of surprise to me to see this poetic expression actually used and a real cloud introduced in the painting, behind which the hero stands hidden from his enemy as behind a screen. That was not what the poet intended. It exceeds the limits of painting, for in this case the cloud is a true hieroglyphic, a mere symbol, which does not render the rescued hero invisible, but says to the spectators: you must imagine to yourselves that he is invisible. It is no

4. Falling, he covered seven *plethra*; *Iliad* 21.407. One *plethron* was 10,000 square feet.

5. The name given the 1st century C.E. author of *On Sublimity* (see above); the reference is to section 7.

6. Lessing pairs each god with an appropriate man. Jupiter: Zeus, king of the Gods. Agamemnon: king of Mycenae and leader of the Greeks at Troy. Achilles: the greatest Greek warrior at Troy and the focus of the *Iliad*.

7. All episodes from the *Iliad* (3.380–82, 5.23, 20.443–44). Paris: prince of Troy who was awarded the most beautiful woman in the world by Aphrodite (Venus), goddess of love, for naming her the most beautiful of 3 goddess. Idaeus: son of a Trojan priest of Hephaestus who is in fact saved by Hephaestus, the god of the forge. Hector: oldest prince of Troy and the greatest of the Trojan warriors (Apollo favored the Trojans).

better than the scrolls that issue from the mouths of figures in old Gothic paintings.

It is true that when Apollo rescues Hector from Achilles, Homer has the latter make three further thrusts with his spear into the thick mist (τρὶς δ' 'ηέρα τύψε βαθεῖαν).[8] But in the language of poetry this means only that Achilles was so enraged that he made the three additional thrusts before realizing that his enemy was no longer before him. Achilles did not see an actual mist, and the power of the gods to render invisible did not lie in any mist, but in their ability to bear the object away swiftly. It was only to show that this abduction took place too quickly for the human eye to follow the disappearing body that the poet first conceals it in a mist or cloud. And it was not because a cloud appeared in place of the abducted body, but because we think of that which is wrapped in mist as being invisible. Accordingly, Homer sometimes inverts the case, and instead of rendering the object invisible, causes the subject to be struck blind. For example, Neptune blinds Achilles when he rescues Aeneas from his murderous hands by suddenly snatching him out of the thick of the fight and placing him in the rear.[9] Actually, however, Achilles' eyes are no more blinded than, in the former example, the abducted heroes are wrapped in a cloud. The poet merely makes this or that addition in order to make more palpable to our senses that extreme rapidity of abduction which we call disappearance.

However, painters have appropriated the Homeric mist not only in those cases where Homer himself used it, or would have used it (namely, in rendering persons invisible or causing them to disappear), but in every instance where the spectator is supposed to see something in the painting which the characters themselves, or some of them, cannot see. Minerva became visible to Achilles alone when she prevented him from assaulting Agamemnon.[1] I know of no other way to express this, says Caylus, than by concealing her from the rest of the council by a cloud. But this is in complete violation of the spirit of the poet! Invisibility is the natural condition of his gods; no blindfolding, no interruption of the rays of light is needed to prevent them from being seen; but an enlightenment, an increased power of mortal vision is required, if they are intended to be seen. Thus it is not only that in painting the cloud is an arbitrary and not a natural sign; but this arbitrary sign does not even possess the definite distinctness which it could have as such, for it is used both to render the visible invisible and the invisible visible.

Chapter Fifteen

As experience shows, the poet can raise to this degree of illusion the representation of objects other than those that are visible. Consequently, whole categories of pictures which the poet claims as his own must necessarily be beyond the reach of the artist. Dryden's *Song for St. Cecelia's Day*[2] is full of musical pictures which leave the painter's brush idle. But I do not want to stray too far from my subject with such examples, from which in the final

8. *Iliad* 20.446 [Lessing's note].

9. *Iliad*, 20.321–29 [Lessing's note]. Neptune: Poseidon, god of the sea. Aeneas: Trojan ally, a son of Aphrodite and later the founder of the colony that became Rome.

1. *Iliad* 1.194–98.

2. Also called *Alexander's Feast*, this ode was written in 1687 and set to music by Handel in 1739 [translator's note]. John Dryden (1631–1700), English poet, dramatist, and critic.

analysis we learn little more than that colors are not sounds and ears not eyes.[3]

I will confine myself rather to the consideration of pictures of visible objects only, which are common to both poet and painter. Why is it that a number of poetic pictures of this kind are of no use to the painter and, conversely, many real pictures lose most of their effect when treated by the poet? Example may guide me here. I repeat: the picture of Pandarus[4] in the fourth book of the *Iliad* is one of the most elaborate and graphic in all of Homer. From the seizing of the bow to the flight of the arrow every moment is painted, and all these moments follow in such close succession and yet are so distinct, one from the other, that if we did not know how a bow should be handled, we would be able to learn it from this description alone. Pandarus takes out his bow, strings it, opens the quiver, chooses an unused, well-feathered arrow, adjusts the arrow's notch to the string and draws both back; the string is brought close to the breast, the metal point of the arrow comes close to the bow, the great round bow springs open again with a clang, the string vibrates, and the arrow has sped away, flying eagerly toward its mark.

Caylus cannot have overlooked this splendid picture. What, then, did he find there to make him consider it unable to afford material to his artists? And why was it that the council of deliberating and drinking gods seemed to him better suited for his purpose? The subjects are visible in both cases, and what more than visible subjects does the painter need to fill his canvas?

The difficulty must be this: although both subjects, being visible, are equally suitable for actual painting, there is still this essential difference between them: in the one case the action is visible and progressive, its different parts occurring one after the other in a sequence of time, and in the other the action is visible and stationary, its different parts developing in coexistence in space. But if painting, by virtue of its symbols or means of imitation, which it can combine in space only, must renounce the element of time entirely, progressive actions, by the very fact that they are progressive, cannot be considered to belong among its subjects. Painting must be content with coexistent actions or with mere bodies which, by their position, permit us to conjecture an action. Poetry, on the other hand. . . .

From *Chapter Sixteen*

But I shall attempt now to derive the matter from its first principles.

I reason thus: if it is true that in its imitations painting uses completely different means or signs than does poetry, namely figures and colors in space rather than articulated sounds in time, and if these signs must indisputably bear a suitable relation to the thing signified, then signs existing in space can express only objects whose wholes or parts coexist, while signs that follow one another can express only objects whose wholes or parts are consecutive.

Objects or parts of objects which exist in space are called bodies. Accordingly, bodies with their visible properties are the true subjects of painting.

Objects or parts of objects which follow one another are called actions. Accordingly, actions are the true subjects of poetry.

3. An allusion to a quotation in Caylus from Jean de la Fontaine (1621–1695), French author of fables.

4. An ally of the Trojans who broke the truce between the Greeks and Trojans in the passage described (*Iliad* 4.105–26).

However, bodies do not exist in space only, but also in time. They persist in time, and in each moment of their duration they may assume a different appearance or stand in a different combination. Each of these momentary appearances and combinations is the result of a preceding one and can be the cause of a subsequent one, which means that it can be, as it were, the center of an action. Consequently, painting too can imitate actions, but only by suggestion through bodies.

On the other hand, actions cannot exist independently, but must be joined to certain beings or things. Insofar as these beings or things are bodies, or are treated as such, poetry also depicts bodies, but only by suggestion through actions.

Painting can use only a single moment of an action in its coexisting compositions and must therefore choose the one which is most suggestive[5] and from which the preceding and succeeding actions are most easily comprehensible.

Similarly, poetry in its progressive imitations can use only one single property of a body. It must therefore choose that one which awakens the most vivid image of the body, looked at from the point of view under which poetry can best use it. From this comes the rule concerning the harmony of descriptive adjectives and economy in description of physical objects.

I should put little faith in this dry chain of reasoning did I not find it completely confirmed by the procedure of Homer, or rather if it had not been just this procedure that led me to my conclusions. Only on these principles can the grand style of the Greek be defined and explained, and only thus can the proper position be assigned to the opposite style of so many modern poets, who attempt to rival the painter at a point where they must necessarily be surpassed by him.

I find that Homer represents nothing but progressive actions. He depicts bodies and single objects only when they contribute toward these actions, and then only by a single trait. No wonder, then, that where Homer paints, the artist finds little or nothing to do himself; and no wonder that his harvest can be found only where the story assembles a number of beautiful bodies in beautiful positions and in a setting favorable to art, however sparingly the poet himself may paint these bodies, these positions, and this setting. If we go through the whole series of paintings as Caylus proposes them, one by one, we find that each is a proof of this remark.

* * *

From *Chapter Seventeen*

But the objection will be raised that the symbols of poetry are not only successive but are also arbitrary; and, as arbitrary symbols, they are of course able to represent bodies as they exist in space. Examples of this might be taken from Homer himself. We need only to recall his shield of Achilles[6] to have the most decisive instance of how discursively and yet at the same time poetically a single object may be described by presenting its coexistent parts.

I shall reply to this twofold objection. I call it twofold because a correct

5. In German, *den prägnantesten wählen*: "choose the most pregnant (with meaning)."
6. Forged by the god Hephaestus to replace the armor borrowed by his friend Patroclus, whom Hector killed; its intricate work is described at length (*Iliad* 18.478–608).

deduction must hold good even without examples; and, conversely, an example from Homer is of importance to me even when I am unable to justify it by means of deduction.

It is true that since the symbols of speech are arbitrary, the parts of a body may, through speech, be made to follow one another just as readily as they exist side by side in nature. But this is a peculiarity of speech and its signs in general and not as they serve the aims of poetry. The poet does not want merely to be intelligible, nor is he content—as is the prose writer—with simply presenting his image clearly and concisely. He wants rather to make the ideas he awakens in us so vivid that at that moment we believe that we feel the real impressions which the objects of these ideas would produce on us. In this moment of illusion we should cease to be conscious of the means which the poet uses for this purpose, that is, his words. This was the substance of the definition of a poetical painting given above. But the poet is always supposed to paint, and we shall now see how far bodies with their coexistent parts adapt themselves to this painting.

* * *

From *Chapter Eighteen*

And yet should Homer himself have lapsed into this lifeless description of material objects? I do hope that there are but few passages which one can find to support this; and I feel certain that these few passages are of such a nature as to confirm the rule to which they seem to be the exception.

It remains true that succession of time is the province of the poet just as space is that of the painter.

It is an intrusion of the painter into the domain of the poet, which good taste can never sanction, when the painter combines in one and the same picture two points necessarily separate in time, as does Fra Mazzuoli[7] when he introduces the rape of the Sabine women[8] and the reconciliation effected by them between their husbands and relations, or as Titian[9] does when he presents the entire history of the prodigal son, his dissolute life, his misery, and his repentance.

It is an intrusion of the poet into the domain of the painter and a squandering of much imagination to no purpose when, in order to give the reader an idea of the whole, the poet enumerates one by one several parts or things which I must necessarily survey at one glance in nature if they are to give the effect of a whole.

But as two equitable and friendly neighbors do not permit the one to take unbecoming liberties in the heart of the other's domain, yet on their extreme frontiers practice a mutual forbearance by which both sides make peaceful compensation for those slight aggressions which, in haste and from force of circumstance, the one finds himself compelled to make on the other's privilege: so also with painting and poetry.

To support this I will not cite the fact that in great historical paintings the

7. Francesco Mazzuoli (1503–1540), Italian painter.
8. A famous legend of early Rome. Romulus, its mythical founder, gained wives for the men he had gathered to his new city by inviting neighboring peoples to a festival and seizing the women. The war that followed between Romans and Sabines ended when the Sabine women thrust themselves onto the battlefield between their fathers and their new husbands, leading to peace and the union of the foes under a single government.
9. Tiziano Vecelli (ca. 1477–1576), Italian painter. For the story of the prodigal son, see Luke 15.11–32.

single moment is always somewhat extended, and that perhaps there is not a single work comprising a wealth of figures in which each one of them is in exactly that motion and position it should be in at the moment of the main action; some are represented in the attitude of a somewhat earlier, others in that of a somewhat later moment. This is a liberty which the master must justify by certain refinements in the arrangement—in the way he uses his figures and places them closer to or more distant from the main action—which permits them to take a more or less momentary part in what is going on. I shall merely make use of a remark made by Mengs concerning Raphael's[1] drapery. "In his paintings," he says, "there is a reason for every fold, whether it be because of its own weight or because of the movement of the limbs. Sometimes we can tell from them how they were before, and Raphael even tried to attach significance to this. We can see from the folds whether an arm or a leg was in a backward or forward position prior to its movement; whether the limb had moved or is moving from contraction to extension, or whether it had been extended and is now contracted."[2] It is indisputable that in this case the artist is combining two different moments into one. For since that part of the drapery which lies on the foot immediately follows it in its forward motion—unless the drapery be of very stiff material and hence entirely unsuitable for painting—there is no moment in which the garment can form any other fold whatsoever except that which the actual position of the limb requires. However, if it is permitted to form a different fold, then the drapery is represented at the moment preceding and the limb at the following. Nevertheless, who would be so particular with the artist who finds it advantageous to show us these two moments at the same time? Who would not praise him rather for having had the understanding and the courage to commit such a minor error for the sake of obtaining greater perfection of expression?

The poet deserves the same forbearance. His progressive imitation actually allows him to allude to only one side, only one characteristic of his material objects at one time. But when the happy structure of his language permits him to do this in a single word, why should he not be allowed to add a second word now and then? And why not even a third, if it is worth the trouble? Or even a fourth? I have already said that for Homer a ship is only a black ship, or a hollow ship, or a swift ship, or at the most a well-manned black ship. This is to be understood of his style in general. Here and there we find a passage in which he adds a third descriptive epithet. Καμπύλα κύκλα, χάλκεα, ὀκτάκνημα[3] round, bronze, eight-spoked wheels. And also a fourth: ἀσπίδα πάντοσ' ἐΐσην, καλὴν, χαλκείην, ἐξήλατον,[4] a uniformly smooth, beautiful, embossed bronze shield. Who would censure him for this? Who would not rather thank him for this little extravagance when he feels what a good effect it can have in some few suitable passages?

But I shall not allow the particular justification of either poet or painter to be based on the above-mentioned analogy of the two friendly neighbors. A mere analogy neither proves nor justifies anything. The following consideration must be their real justification: just as in the painter's art two differ-

1. Raffaello Santi (1483–1520), Italian painter. Anton Raphael Mengs (1728–1779), German painter and art critic; a close friend of Winckelmann.

2. *Thoughts about Beauty and Taste in Painting* [1771], p. 69 [Lessing's note].

3. *Iliad* 5.722–23.

4. *Iliad* 12.294–95.

ent moments border so closely on one another that we can, without hesitation, accept them as one, so in the poet's work do the several features representing the various parts and properties in space follow one another in such rapid succession that we believe we hear them all at once.

It is in this, I say, that the excellence of Homer's language aids him unusually well. It not only allows him the greatest possible freedom in the accumulation and combination of epithets, but it finds such a happy arrangement for these accumulated adjectives that the awkward suspension of their noun disappears. Modern languages are lacking entirely in one or more of these advantages. For example, the French must paraphrase the καμπυλα κυκλα, χάλκεα, ὀκτάκνημα with "the round wheels, which were of bronze and had eight spokes." They give the meaning but destroy the picture. Yet the picture is everything here and the meaning nothing; and without the former the latter turns the liveliest of poets into a tiresome bore, a fate which has often befallen our good Homer under the pen of the conscientious Madame Dacier.[5] The German language, on the other hand, can usually translate Homer's epithets with equally short equivalent adjectives, although it is unable to imitate the advantageous arrangement of Greek. We can say, to be sure, *die runden, ehernen, achtspeichigten* . . . [the round, brazen, eight-spoked], but *Räder* [wheels] drags behind. Who does not feel that three different predicates, before we learn the subject, can produce only an indistinct and confused picture? The Greek combines the subject and the first predicate, and leaves the others to follow. He says, "round wheels, brazen, eight-spoked." And so we know immediately what he is speaking of. In conformity with the natural order of thought, we first become acquainted with the thing itself and then with its accidents. Our [German] language does not enjoy this advantage. Or should I say, it does enjoy it but can seldom make use of it without ambiguity? Both amount to the same thing. For if we place the adjectives after the subject, they must stand *in statu absoluto*, i.e., in uninflected form. Hence, we must say *runde Räder, ehern und achtspeichigt* (round wheels, brazen and eight-spoked). However, in this *statu* the German adjectives are identical with the German adverbs, and if we take them as such with the next verb that is predicated of the subject, they not infrequently produce a completely false, and in any case a very uncertain meaning.

But I am lingering over trifles and it may appear as if I were going to forget the shield, the shield of Achilles, that is—the famous picture which more than anything else caused Homer to be considered by the ancients a master of painting.[6] A shield, it will be said, is a single material object which the poet cannot present by describing its coexistent parts. And yet Homer, in more than a hundred splendid verses, has described this shield, its material, its form, all the figures which filled its enormous surface, so exactly and in such detail that it was not difficult for modern artists to produce a drawing of it exact in every part.

My answer to this particular objection is that I have already answered it. Homer does not paint the shield as finished and complete, but as a shield that is being made. Thus, here too he has made use of that admirable artistic

5. Anne Lefèvre Dacier (ca. 1650–1720), well-known French translator of Greek and Latin works, including both the *Iliad* (1699) and the *Odyssey* (1708).

6. Dionysius Halicarnassus, *Vita Homeri*, in Thomas Gale, *Opuscula mythologica* [1671], p. 401 [Lessing's note].

device: transforming what is coexistent in his subject into what is consecutive, and thereby making the living picture of an action out of the tedious painting of an object. We do not see the shield, but the divine master as he is making it. He steps up to the anvil with hammer and tongs, and after he has forged the plates out of the rough, the pictures which he destines for the shield's ornamentation rise before our eyes out of the bronze, one after the other, beneath the finer blows of his hammer. We do not lose sight of him until all is finished. Now the shield is complete, and we marvel at the work. But it is the believing wonder of the eyewitness who has seen it forged.

* * *

From *Chapter Twenty-One*

We might ask whether poetry does not lose too much when we take from her all depictions of physical beauty? But who would do this? If we dissuade her from taking one particular way to attain such pictures, and from following confusedly the footsteps of a sister art without ever reaching the same goal, do we thereby exclude her from every other path where art in turn must see poetry take the lead?

The same Homer, who so assiduously refrains from detailed descriptions of physical beauties, and from whom we scarcely learn in passing that Helen had white arms and beautiful hair,[7] nevertheless knows how to convey to us an idea of her beauty which far surpasses anything art is able to accomplish toward that end. Let us recall the passage where Helen steps before an assembly of Trojan elders. The venerable old men see her, and one says to the other:

> Οὐ νέμεσις Τρῶας και ἐϋκνήμιδας Ἀχαιοὺς
> τοιῇδ' ἀμφὶ γυναικὶ πολὺν χρόνον ἄλγεα πάσχειν'
> αἰνῶς ἀθανάτῃσι θεῇς εἰς ὦπα ἔοικεν.[8]

What can convey a more vivid idea of beauty than to let cold old age acknowledge that she is indeed worth the war which had cost so much blood and so many tears?

What Homer could not describe in all its various parts he makes us recognize by its effect. Paint for us, you poets, the pleasure, the affection, the love and delight which beauty brings, and you have painted beauty itself.

* * *

1766

7. *Iliad* 3.329; "white arms" 121 [Lessing's note]. Helen: in Greek mythology, daughter of Zeus and Leda and wife of Menelaus; her abduction by Paris led to the Trojan War.

8. *Iliad* 3.156–58 [Lessing's note]. "Surely there is no blame on Trojans and strong-greaved Achaians / if for long time they suffer hardship for a woman like this one. Terrible is the likeness of her face to immortal goddesses" (trans. Lattimore).

FRIEDRICH VON SCHILLER
1759–1805

Friedrich von Schiller was one of the foremost German writers of the late eighteenth and early nineteenth centuries. Perhaps best known for his dramas, he was also an editor, a journalist, a writer of vivid letters (especially to Goethe and to the German philologist and diplomat Wilhelm von Humboldt), a historian, a translator (of Euripides, Shakespeare, and Racine), a poet, and a literary theorist.

Born in Marbach, Germany, Schiller became an army medical officer in Stuttgart in 1780. But soon he began seriously working on poetry and drama, choosing a literary career. He published *Die Räuber* (1781, *The Robbers*) at his own expense, and its performance in 1782 was a landmark in German theatrical history. Romantic writers in England, especially SAMUEL TAYLOR COLERIDGE and the critic William Hazlitt, admired *The Robbers* for its presentation of the themes of liberty, abuse of power, and authoritarianism.

On the recommendation of Goethe, Schiller was named professor of history at the University of Jena in 1789, and in 1797–98 they worked together on a collection of ballads (a collaboration contemporaneous with that of WILLIAM WORDSWORTH and Coleridge in England).

Many readers admire Schiller's lyrics and ballads, though his long didactic poems (e.g., *The Artists,* 1789, on the power of art to civilize and bring compassion to mankind) are more famous; best known to English-speaking audiences is his "Ode to Joy," which Beethoven set to music in his monumental Ninth Symphony.

In several influential texts on literary and dramatic theory, aesthetics, and the sublime, Schiller explored the relations between art, politics, and history. He himself looked primarily to IMMANUEL KANT's *Critique of Judgment* (1790; see above), and his development of and response to Kant's ideas later influenced the literary theory of the German Romantic writers and of Coleridge.

In *On the Aesthetic Education of Man* (1795), Schiller was writing in the immediate aftermath of the French regicide and Reign of Terror, during which thousands were executed. The sufferings and shocks of the French Revolution inform his inquiry into the role of art: how can humankind achieve freedom when the failure of political solutions is so graphically displayed? In this text, which grew from a series of actual letters to a benefactor (our selection contains three letters), Schiller explains that freedom can occur only through education, and the key to education is the experience of beauty—the elevation of mind and soul through art. Beauty allows persons to ennoble their nature; each of us can become a "beautiful soul" (*schöne Seele*) harmonizing duty and inclination through art, which Schiller associates with the "play impulse" or "play drive" that makes reconciliation and transcendence possible.

Schiller's *On Naive and Reflective Poetry* (1795–96), a companion piece, contrasts the ancients and the moderns, their different attitudes toward nature, and their performances in poetry. (Often the title's second adjective is given as "sentimental," but that term does not accurately translate *sentimentalisch.*) Modern poets, Schiller states, will never regain the naive—that is, the immediate and unconscious—relationship to nature that the ancients enjoyed. He focuses not on rules to be obeyed or ignored but rather on different types of consciousness. As in *On the Aesthetic Education of Man,* his primary concern is the author's conception of self and of the ideals and purposes of art—the motivating power that informs and imparts life to the text.

Schiller's broad sense of a break between a harmonious past and the divided or disrupted present in which artists perceive the difficulty, if not the impossibility, of embodying their hopes and desires in their actual work, is echoed in the poetry and criticism of MATTHEW ARNOLD, T. S. ELIOT, and many other nineteenth- and twentieth-century writers. They may disagree on the timing, but all emphasize that this shift in consciousness—a dissociation of sensibility—manifests itself in the operations of individual thought and feeling and in the style and structure of poetry.

In the selection below from *On the Aesthetic Education of Man*, Schiller touches on the sense of acute cultural crisis that impels his arguments about the priority of the aesthetic. He summons up an optimistic vision of the artist preparing "the shape of things to come," even as he testifies to the ordeal of being an artist in a hostile environment. Defy the world's opinion: this is Schiller's advice to those wondering whether they can endure in the midst of an unsympathetic and corrupt age. The artist should be true to the heart's "noble impulses": "Impart to the world you would influence a *Direction* towards the good, and the quiet rhythm of time will bring it to fulfilment." Through our inner potential, we revitalize ourselves and reinvigorate (and sometimes disturb and unsettle) others.

The weakness of this position is that Schiller separates "the rhythm of time" (which he trusts) from the very different rhythm of the world of Utility that, he concedes, now rules but that he believes can be transcended. Others grappled more directly with the comprehensive changes driven by the accelerating power of capitalism, described by the Scottish-born historian (and biographer of Schiller) Thomas Carlyle in "Signs of the Times" (1829): "Not the external and the physical alone is now managed by machinery, but the internal and spiritual also. . . . Men are grown mechanical in head and in heart, as well as in hand." Not just KARL MARX AND FRIEDRICH ENGELS but the Victorian critics and social reformers John Ruskin and William Morris responded to this alienation in ways that Schiller—whose aesthetic works are grounded less in historical reference and analysis than in idealization of the harmonious wholeness of the ancient Greeks—could not.

Yet Schiller, a prophet of the alienation that would pain many later authors, believed that this alienation could be overcome through the civilizing power of literature, enabling a higher Ideal to triumph over the degraded principles and practices to which persons were currently (and so mistakenly) loyal. A passionate advocate for individual and political freedom, Schiller gave everything to his art; "the Muses drained me dry," he wrote to Goethe (1795), and, after a long period of poor health, he died in his mid-forties.

BIBLIOGRAPHY

German editions of Schiller's writings include the *Säkular-Ausgabe*, edited by Eduard von der Hellen (16 vols., 1904–05), and the *Horenausgabe*, edited by C. Schüddekopf and C. Hofer (22 vols., 1910–26), which includes many of his letters. German scholars have noted that many English translations of Schiller's texts are unreliable. Coleridge's translation of *Wallenstein* (1800) is important. The translation and edition of *On the Aesthetic Education of Man* by E. M. Wilkinson and L. A. Willoughby (1967) is outstanding. A single-volume edition is *Friedrich Schiller: An Anthology for Our Times*, (trans. Jane Bannard Greene et al., 1959). For a selection of Schiller's writings on criticism and aesthetics, see *Essays*, edited by Walter Hinderer and Daniel O. Dahlstrom (1993).

A good biographical point of departure is William Witte, *Schiller* (1949). See also John Simon, *Friedrich Schiller* (1981), and T. J. Reed, *Schiller* (1991). For critical analysis, consult S. S. Kerry, *Schiller's Writings on Aesthetics* (1961); Charles E. Passage, *Friedrich Schiller* (1975); Juliet Sychrava, *Schiller to Derrida: Idealism in Aesthetics* (1989); and Lesley Sharpe, *Friedrich Schiller: Drama, Thought, and Politics* (1991), a well-contextualized treatment of Schiller's work as a dramatist, poet, and literary theorist. Patrick T. Murray, *The Development of German Aesthetic Theory from Kant to Schiller: A Philosophical Commentary on Schiller's "Aesthetic Education of Man," 1795* (1994), places Schiller's aesthetics in their literary and national contexts. See also Linda Marie Brooks, *The Menace of the Sublime to the Individual Self:*

Kant, Schiller, Coleridge, and the Disintegration of Romantic Identity (1996), and R. D. Miller, *Schiller and the Ideal of Freedom* (1970).

For a concise study of the critical writings, see René Wellek, "Kant and Schiller," in *A History of Modern Criticism, 1750–1950*, vol. 1, *The Later Eighteenth Century* (1955). A more detailed, challenging assessment can be found in Anthony Savile, *Aesthetic Reconstructions: The Seminal Writings of Lessing, Kant, and Schiller* (1987). T. J. Reed, *The Classical Centre: Goethe and Weimar, 1775–1832* (1980), is stimulating on the relationship between Goethe and Schiller. For bibliography, see Wolfgang Vulpius, *Schiller-Bibliographie, 1893–1958* (1959) and *Schiller-Bibliographie, 1959–63* (1967); and R. Pick, "Schiller in England, 1787–1960: A Bibliography," *Publications of the English Goethe Society* 30 (1961).

From On the Aesthetic Education of Man[1]

Second Letter

1. BUT should it not be possible to make better use of the freedom you accord me than by keeping your attention fixed upon the domain of the fine arts? Is it not, to say the least, untimely to be casting around for a code of laws for the aesthetic world at a moment when the affairs of the moral offer interest of so much more urgent concern, and when the spirit of philosophical inquiry is being expressly challenged by present circumstances to concern itself with that most perfect of all the works to be achieved by the art of man: the construction of true political freedom?

2. I would not wish to live in a century other than my own, or to have worked for any other. We are citizens of our own Age no less than of our own State. And if it is deemed unseemly, or even inadmissible, to exempt ourselves from the morals and customs of the circle in which we live, why should it be less of a duty to allow the needs and taste of our own epoch some voice in our choice of activity?

3. But the verdict of this epoch does not, by any means, seem to be going in favour of art, not at least of the kind of art to which alone my inquiry will be directed. The course of events has given the spirit of the age a direction which threatens to remove it ever further from the art of the Ideal. This kind of art must abandon actuality, and soar with becoming boldness above our wants and needs; for Art is a daughter of Freedom, and takes her orders from the necessity inherent in minds, not from the exigencies of matter. But at the present time material needs reign supreme and bend a degraded humanity beneath their tyrannical yoke. *Utility* is the great idol of our age, to which all powers are in thrall and to which all talent must pay homage. Weighed in this crude balance, the insubstantial merits of Art scarce tip the scale, and, bereft of all encouragement, she shuns the noisy market-place of our century. The spirit of philosophical inquiry[2] itself is wresting from the imag-

1. Translated by E. M. Wilkinson and L. A. Willoughby. These letters were originally addressed to Schiller's benefactor Friedrich Christian, duke of Augustenburg.

2. Pertaining not only to the study of fundamental principles but also to the empirical investigation into practical things.

ination one province after another, and the frontiers of art contract the more the boundaries of science expand.

4. Expectantly the gaze of philosopher and man of the world alike is fixed on the political scene, where now, so it is believed, the very fate of mankind is being debated. Does it not betray a culpable indifference to the common weal not to take part in this general debate? If this great action is, by reason of its cause and its consequences, of urgent concern to every one who calls himself man, it must, by virtue of its method of procedure, be of quite special interest to every one who has learnt to think for himself. For a question which has hitherto always been decided by the blind right of might, is now, so it seems, being brought before the tribunal of Pure Reason[3] itself, and anyone who is at all capable of putting himself at the centre of things, and of raising himself from an individual into a representative of the species, may consider himself at once a member of this tribunal, and at the same time, in his capacity of human being and citizen of the world, an interested party who finds himself more or less closely involved in the outcome of the case. It is, therefore, not merely his own cause which is being decided in this great action; judgement is to be passed according to laws which he, as a reasonable being, is himself competent and entitled to dictate.

5. How tempting it would be for me to investigate such a subject in company with one who is as acute a thinker as he is a liberal citizen of the world! And to leave the decision to a heart which has dedicated itself with such noble enthusiasm to the weal of humanity. What an agreeable surprise if, despite all difference in station, and the vast distance which the circumstances of the actual world make inevitable, I were, in the realm of ideas, to find my conclusions identical with those of a mind as unprejudiced as your own! That I resist this seductive temptation, and put Beauty before Freedom, can, I believe, not only be excused on the score of personal inclination, but also justified on principle. I hope to convince you that the theme I have chosen is far less alien to the needs of our age than to its taste. More than this: if man is ever to solve that problem of politics in practice he will have to approach it through the problem of the aesthetic, because it is only through Beauty that man makes his way to Freedom. But this cannot be demonstrated without my first reminding you of the principles by which Reason is in any case guided in matters of political legislation.

Sixth Letter

1. HAVE I not perhaps been too hard on our age in the picture I have just drawn? That is scarcely the reproach I anticipate. Rather a different one: that I have tried to make it prove too much. Such a portrait, you will tell me, does indeed resemble mankind as it is today; but does it not also resemble any people caught up in the process of civilization, since all of them, without exception, must fall away from Nature by the abuse of Reason before they can return to her by the use of Reason?

3. See IMMANUEL KANT, *The Critique of Pure Reason* (1781). In the preface Kant states that his goal is to "assure to reason its lawful claims, and dismiss all groundless pretensions, not by despotic decrees, but in accordance with its own eternal and unalterable laws."

2. Closer attention to the character of our age will, however, reveal an astonishing contrast between contemporary forms of humanity and earlier ones, especially the Greek. The reputation for culture and refinement, on which we otherwise rightly pride ourselves *vis-à-vis* humanity in its *merely* natural state, can avail us nothing against the natural humanity of the Greeks. For they were wedded to all the delights of art and all the dignity of wisdom, without however, like us, falling a prey to their seduction. The Greeks put us to shame not only by a simplicity to which our age is a stranger; they are at the same time our rivals, indeed often our models, in those very excellences with which we are wont to console ourselves for the unnaturalness of our manners. In fullness of form no less than of content, at once philosophic and creative, sensitive and energetic, the Greeks combined the first youth of imagination with the manhood of reason in a glorious manifestation of humanity.

3. At that first fair awakening of the powers of the mind, sense and intellect did not as yet rule over strictly separate domains; for no dissension had as yet provoked them into hostile partition and mutual demarcation of their frontiers. Poetry had not as yet coquetted with wit, nor speculation prostituted itself to sophistry. Both of them could, when need arose, exchange functions, since each in its own fashion paid honour to truth. However high the mind might soar, it always drew matter lovingly along with it; and however fine and sharp the distinctions it might make, it never proceeded to mutilate. It did indeed divide human nature into its several aspects, and project these in magnified form into the divinities of its glorious pantheon; but not by tearing it to pieces; rather by combining its aspects in different proportions, for in no single one of their deities was humanity in its entirety ever lacking. How different with us Moderns! With us too the image of the human species is projected in magnified form into separate individuals—but as fragments, not in different combinations, with the result that one has to go the rounds from one individual to another in order to be able to piece together a complete image of the species. With us, one might almost be tempted to assert, the various faculties appear as separate in practice as they are distinguished by the psychologist in theory, and we see not merely individuals, but whole classes of men, developing but one part of their potentialities, while of the rest, as in stunted growths, only vestigial traces remain.

4. I do not underrate the advantages which the human race today, considered as a whole and weighed in the balance of intellect, can boast in the face of what is best in the ancient world. But it has to take up the challenge in serried ranks, and let whole measure itself against whole. What individual Modern could sally forth and engage, man against man, with an individual Athenian for the prize of humanity?

5. Whence this disadvantage among individuals when the species as a whole is at such an advantage? Why was the individual Greek qualified to be the representative of his age, and why can no single Modern venture as much? Because it was from all-unifying Nature that the former, and from the all-dividing Intellect that the latter, received their respective forms.

6. It was civilization itself which inflicted this wound upon modern man. Once the increase of empirical knowledge, and more exact modes of thought, made sharper divisions between the sciences inevitable, and once the increasingly complex machinery of State necessitated a more rigorous separation of ranks and occupations, then the inner unity of human nature was severed too, and a disastrous conflict set its harmonious powers at variance. The intuitive and the speculative understanding now withdrew in hostility to take up positions in their respective fields, whose frontiers they now began to guard with jealous mistrust; and with this confining of our activity to a particular sphere we have given ourselves a master within, who not infrequently ends by suppressing the rest of our potentialities. While in the one a riotous imagination ravages the hard-won fruits of the intellect, in another the spirit of abstraction stifles the fire at which the heart should have warmed itself and the imagination been kindled.

7. This disorganization, which was first started within man by civilization and learning, was made complete and universal by the new spirit of government. It was scarcely to be expected that the simple organization of the early republics should have survived the simplicity of early manners and conditions; but instead of rising to a higher form of organic existence it degenerated into a crude and clumsy mechanism. That polypoid character of the Greek States, in which every individual enjoyed an independent existence but could, when need arose, grow into the whole organism, now made way for an ingenious clock-work, in which, out of the piecing together of innumerable but lifeless parts, a mechanical kind of collective life ensued. State and Church, laws and customs, were now torn asunder; enjoyment was divorced from labour, the means from the end, the effort from the reward. Everlastingly chained to a single little fragment of the Whole, man himself develops into nothing but a fragment; everlastingly in his ear the monotonous sound of the wheel that he turns, he never develops the harmony of his being, and instead of putting the stamp of humanity upon his own nature, he becomes nothing more than the imprint of his occupation or of his specialized knowledge. But even that meagre, fragmentary participation, by which individual members of the State are still linked to the Whole, does not depend upon forms which they spontaneously prescribe for themselves (for how could one entrust to their freedom of action a mechanism so intricate and so fearful of light and enlightenment?); it is dictated to them with meticulous exactitude by means of a formulary which inhibits all freedom of thought. The dead letter takes the place of living understanding, and a good memory is a safer guide than imagination and feeling.

8. When the community makes his office the measure of the man; when in one of its citizens it prizes nothing but memory, in another a mere tabularizing[4] intelligence, in a third only mechanical skill; when, in the one case, indifferent to character, it insists exclusively on knowledge, yet is, in another, ready to condone any amount of obscurantist thinking as long as it is accompanied by a spirit of order and law-abiding behaviour; when, moreover, it insists on special skills being developed with a degree of intensity which is

4. Making lists or tables.

only commensurate with its readiness to absolve the individual citizen from developing himself in extensity—can we wonder that the remaining aptitudes of the psyche are neglected in order to give undivided attention to the one which will bring honour and profit? True, we know that the outstanding individual will never let the limits of his occupation dictate the limits of his activity. But a mediocre talent will consume in the office assigned him the whole meagre sum of his powers, and a man has to have a mind above the ordinary if, without detriment to his calling, he is still to have time for the chosen pursuits of his leisure. Moreover, it is rarely a recommendation in the eyes of the State if a man's powers exceed the tasks he is set, or if the higher needs of the man of parts constitute a rival to the duties of his office. So jealously does the State insist on being the sole proprietor of its servants that it will more easily bring itself (and who can blame it?) to share its man with the Cytherean, than with the Uranian, Venus.[5]

9. Thus little by little the concrete life of the Individual is destroyed in order that the abstract idea of the Whole may drag out its sorry existence, and the State remains for ever a stranger to its citizens since at no point does it ever make contact with their feeling. Forced to resort to classification in order to cope with the variety of its citizens, and never to get an impression of humanity except through representation at second hand, the governing section ends up by losing sight of them altogether, confusing their concrete reality with a mere construct of the intellect; while the governed cannot but receive with indifference laws which are scarcely, if at all, directed to them as persons. Weary at last of sustaining bonds which the State does so little to facilitate, positive society begins (this has long been the fate of most European States) to disintegrate into a state of primitive morality, in which public authority has become but one party *more*, to be hated and circumvented by those who make authority necessary, and only obeyed by such as are capable of doing without it.

10. With this twofold pressure upon it, from within and from without, could humanity well have taken any other course than the one it actually took? In its striving after inalienable possessions in the realm of ideas, the spirit of speculation could do no other than become a stranger to the world of sense, and lose sight of matter for the sake of form. The practical spirit, by contrast, enclosed within a monotonous sphere of material objects, and within this uniformity still further confined by formulas, was bound to find the idea of an unconditioned Whole receding from sight, and to become just as impoverished as its own poor sphere of activity. If the former was tempted to model the actual world on a world conceivable by the mind, and to exalt the subjective conditions of its own perceptual and conceptual faculty into laws constitutive of the existence of things, the latter plunged into the opposite extreme of judging all experience whatsoever by one particular fragment of experience, and of wanting to make the rules of its *own* occupation apply indiscriminately to all others. The one was bound to become the victim of empty subtilities, the other of narrow pedantry; for the former stood too high to discern the particular, the latter too low to survey the Whole. But the

5. Uranian Venus presides over sacred love; Cytherean Venus presides over profane love.

damaging effects of the turn which mind thus took were not confined to knowledge and production; it affected feeling and action no less. We know that the sensibility of the psyche depends for its intensity upon the liveliness, for its scope upon the richness, of the imagination. The preponderance of the analytical faculty must, however, of necessity, deprive the imagination of its energy and warmth, while a more restricted sphere of objects must reduce its wealth. Hence the abstract thinker very often has a *cold* heart, since he dissects his impressions, and impressions can move the soul only as long as they remain whole; while the man of practical affairs often has a *narrow* heart, since his imagination, imprisoned within the unvarying confines of his own calling, is incapable of extending itself to appreciate other ways of seeing and knowing.

11. It was part of my procedure to uncover the disadvantageous trends in the character of our age and the reasons for them, not to point out the advantages which Nature offers by way of compensation. I readily concede that, little as individuals might benefit from this fragmentation of their being, there was no other way in which the species as a whole could have progressed. With the Greeks, humanity undoubtedly reached a maximum of excellence, which could neither be maintained at that level nor rise any higher. Not maintained, because the intellect was unavoidably compelled by the store of knowledge it already possessed to dissociate itself from feeling and intuition in an attempt to arrive at exact discursive understanding; not rise any higher, because only a specific degree of clarity is compatible with a specific fullness and warmth. This degree the Greeks had attained; and had they wished to proceed to a higher stage of development, they would, like us, have had to surrender their wholeness of being and pursue truth along separate paths.

12. If the manifold potentialities in man were ever to be developed, there was no other way but to pit them one against the other. This antagonism of faculties and functions is the great instrument of civilization—but it is only the instrument; for as long as it persists, we are only on the way to becoming civilized. Only through individual powers in man becoming isolated, and arrogating to themselves exclusive authority, do they come into conflict with the truth of things, and force the Common Sense, which is otherwise content to linger with indolent complacency on outward appearance, to penetrate phenomena in depth. By pure thought usurping authority in the world of sense, while empirical thought is concerned to subject the usurper to the conditions of experience, both these powers develop to their fullest potential, and exhaust the whole range of their proper sphere. And by the very boldness with which, in the one case, imagination allows her caprice to dissolve the existing world-order, she does, in the other, compel Reason to rise to the ultimate sources of knowing, and invoke the law of Necessity against her.

13. One-sidedness in the exercise of his powers must, it is true, inevitably lead the individual into error; but the species as a whole to truth. Only by concentrating the whole energy of our mind into a *single* focal point, contracting our whole being into a single power, do we, as it were, lend wings to this individual power and lead it, by artificial means, far beyond the limits

which Nature seems to have assigned to it. Even as it is certain that all individuals taken together would never, with the powers of vision granted them by Nature alone, have managed to detect a satellite of Jupiter which the telescope reveals to the astronomer, so it is beyond question that human powers of reflection would never have produced an analysis of the Infinite or a Critique of Pure Reason,[6] unless, in the individuals called to perform such feats, Reason had separated itself off, disentangled itself, as it were, from all matter, and by the most intense effort of abstraction armed their eyes with a glass for peering into the Absolute. But will such a mind, dissolved as it were into pure intellect and pure contemplation, ever be capable of exchanging the rigorous bonds of logic for the free movement of the poetic faculty, or of grasping the concrete individuality of things with a sense innocent of preconceptions and faithful to the object? At this point Nature sets limits even to the most universal genius, limits which he cannot transcend; and as long as philosophy has to make its prime business the provision of safeguards against error, truth will be bound to have its martyrs.

14. Thus, however much the world as a whole may benefit through this fragmentary specialization of human powers, it cannot be denied that the individuals affected by it suffer under the curse of this cosmic purpose. Athletic bodies can, it is true, be developed by gymnastic exercises; beauty only through the free and harmonious play of the limbs. In the same way the keying up of individual functions of the mind can indeed produce extraordinary human beings; but only the equal tempering of them all, happy and complete human beings. And in what kind of relation would we stand to either past or future ages, if the development of human nature were to make such sacrifice necessary? We would have been the serfs of mankind; for several millennia we would have done slaves' work for them, and our mutilated nature would bear impressed upon it the shameful marks of this servitude. And all this in order that a future generation might in blissful indolence attend to the care of its moral health, and foster the free growth of its humanity!

15. But can Man really be destined to miss himself for the sake of any purpose whatsoever? Should Nature, for the sake of her own purposes, be able to rob us of a completeness which Reason, for the sake of hers, enjoins upon us? It must, therefore, be wrong if the cultivation of individual powers involves the sacrifice of wholeness. Or rather, however much the law of Nature tends in that direction, it must be open to us to restore by means of a higher Art the totality of our nature which the arts themselves have destroyed.

Ninth Letter

1. BUT is this not, perhaps, to argue in a circle? Intellectual education is to bring about moral education, and yet moral education is to be the condition of intellectual education? All improvement in the political sphere is to proceed from the ennobling of character—but how under the influence of a

6. That is, Kant's *Critique of Pure Reason*.

barbarous constitution is character ever to become ennobled? To this end we should, presumably, have to seek out some instrument not provided by the State, and to open up living springs which, whatever the political corruption, would remain clear and pure.

2. I have now reached the point to which all my preceding reflections have been tending. This instrument is Fine Art; such living springs are opened up in its immortal exemplars.

3. Art, like Science, is absolved from all positive constraint and from all conventions introduced by man; both rejoice in absolute *immunity* from human arbitrariness. The political legislator may put their territory out of bounds; he cannot rule within it. He can proscribe the lover of truth; Truth itself will prevail. He can humiliate the artist; but Art he cannot falsify. True, nothing is more common than for both, science as well as art, to pay homage to the spirit of the age, or for creative minds to accept the critical standards of prevailing taste. In epochs where character becomes rigid and obdurate, we find science keeping a strict watch over its frontiers, and art moving in the heavy shackles of rules; in those where it becomes enervated and flabby, science will strive to please, and art to gratify. For whole centuries thinkers and artists will do their best to submerge truth and beauty in the depths of a degraded humanity; it is they themselves who are drowned there, while truth and beauty, with their own indestructible vitality, struggle triumphantly to the surface.

4. The artist is indeed the child of his age; but woe to him if he is at the same time its ward or, worse still, its minion! Let some beneficent deity snatch the suckling betimes from his mother's breast, nourish him with the milk of a better age, and suffer him to come to maturity under a distant Grecian sky. Then, when he has become a man, let him return, a stranger, to his own century; not, however, to gladden it by his appearance, but rather, terrible like Agamemnon's son,[7] to cleanse and to purify it. His theme he will, indeed, take from the present; but his form he will borrow from a nobler time, nay, from beyond time altogether, from the absolute, unchanging, unity of his being. Here, from the pure aether[8] of his genius, the living source of beauty flows down, untainted by the corruption of the generations and ages wallowing in the dark eddies below. The theme of his work may be degraded by vagaries of the public mood, even as this has been known to ennoble it; but its form, inviolate, will remain immune from such vicissitudes. The Roman of the first century had long been bowing the knee before his emperors when statues still portrayed him erect; temples continued to be sacred to the eye long after the gods had become objects of derision; and the infamous crimes of a *Nero* or a *Commodus*[9] were put to shame by the noble style of the building whose frame lent them cover. Humanity has lost its dignity; but Art has rescued it and preserved it in significant stone. Truth lives on in

7. Orestes, who "cleansed" his home on his return by killing his mother Clytemnestra and her lover Aegisthus, who had murdered Agamemnon (a myth often treated in Greek tragedy, most notably in Aeschylus's *Oresteia* trilogy, 458 B.C.E.).

8. For the Greeks, the clear air beyond the clouds; the element breathed by the gods.

9. Both were notoriously cruel emperors of Rome: Nero (37–68 C.E.), emperor 54–68; Commodus (161–192), emperor 180–92. Under the Republic, which ended in the 1st century B.C.E., Romans did not "bow the knee."

the illusion of Art, and it is from this copy, or after-image, that the original image will once again be restored. Just as the nobility of Art *survived* the nobility of Nature, so now Art goes before her, a voice rousing from slumber and preparing the shape of things to come. Even before Truth's triumphant light can penetrate the recesses of the human heart, the poet's imagination will intercept its rays, and the peaks of humanity will be radiant while the dews of night still linger in the valley.

5. But how is the artist to protect himself against the corruption of the age which besets him on all sides? By disdaining its opinion. Let him direct his gaze upwards, to the dignity of his calling and the universal Law, not downwards towards Fortune and the needs of daily life. Free alike from the futile busyness which would fain set its mark upon the fleeting moment, and from the impatient spirit of enthusiasm which applies the measure of the Absolute to the sorry products of Time, let him leave the sphere of the actual to the intellect, which is at home there, whilst he strives to produce the Ideal out of the union of what is possible with what is necessary. Let him express this ideal both in semblance and in truth, set the stamp of it upon the play of his imagination as upon the seriousness of his conduct, let him express it in all sensuous and spiritual forms, and silently project it into the infinity of time.

6. But not everyone whose soul glows with this ideal was granted either the creative tranquillity or the spirit of long patience required to imprint it upon the silent stone, or pour it into the sober mould of words, and so entrust it to the executory hands of time. Far too impetuous to proceed by such unobtrusive means, the divine impulse to form often hurls itself directly upon present-day reality and upon the life of action, and undertakes to fashion anew the formless material presented by the moral world. The misfortunes of the human race speak urgently to the man of feeling; its degradation more urgently still; enthusiasm is kindled, and in vigorous souls ardent longing drives impatiently on towards action. But did he ever ask himself whether those disorders in the moral world offend his reason, or whether they do not rather wound his self-love? If he does not yet know the answer, he will detect it by the zeal with which he insists upon specific and prompt results. The pure moral impulse is directed towards the Absolute. For such an impulse time does not exist, and the future turns into the present from the moment that it is seen to develop with inevitable Necessity out of the present. In the eyes of a Reason which knows no limits, the Direction is at once the Destination, and the Way[1] is completed from the moment it is trodden.

7. To the young friend of truth and beauty who would inquire of me how, despite all the opposition of his century, he is to satisfy the noble impulses of his heart, I would make answer: Impart to the world you would influence a *Direction* towards the good, and the quiet rhythm of time will bring it to fulfilment. You will have given it this direction if, by your teaching, you have elevated its thoughts to the Necessary and the Eternal, if, by your actions and your creations, you have transformed the Necessary and the Eternal into

1. See John 14.6: "Jesus saith unto him, I am the way, the truth, and the life: no man cometh unto the Father, but by me."

an object of the heart's desire. The edifice of error and caprice will fall—it must fall, indeed it has already fallen—from the moment you are certain that it is on the point of giving way. But it is in man's inner being that it must give way, not just in the externals he presents to the world. It is in the modest sanctuary of your heart that you must rear victorious truth, and project it out of yourself in the form of beauty, so that not only thought can pay it homage, but sense, too, lay loving hold on its appearance. And lest you should find yourself receiving from the world as it is the model you yourself should be providing, do not venture into its equivocal company without first being sure that you bear within your own heart an escort from the world of the ideal. Live with your century; but do not be its creature. Work for your contemporaries; but create what they need, not what they praise. Without sharing their guilt, yet share with noble resignation in their punishment, and bow your head freely beneath the yoke which they find as difficult to dispense with as to bear. By the steadfast courage with which you disdain their good fortune, you will show them that it is not through cowardice that you consent to share their sufferings. Think of them as they ought to be, when called upon to influence them; think of them as they are, when tempted to act on their behalf. In seeking their approval appeal to what is best in them, but in devising their happiness recall them as they are at their worst; then your own nobility will awaken theirs, and their unworthiness not defeat your purpose. The seriousness of your principles will frighten them away, but in the play of your semblance they will be prepared to tolerate them; for their taste is purer than their heart, and it is here that you must lay hold of the timorous fugitive. In vain will you assail their precepts, in vain condemn their practice; but on their leisure hours you can try your shaping hand. Banish from their pleasures caprice, frivolity, and coarseness, and imperceptibly you will banish these from their actions and, eventually, from their inclinations too. Surround them, wherever you meet them, with the great and noble forms of genius, and encompass them about with the symbols of perfection, until Semblance conquer Reality, and Art triumph over Nature.

1795

MARY WOLLSTONECRAFT

1759–1797

Mary Wollstonecraft wrote one of the first treatises of modern feminism. *A Vindication of the Rights of Woman* (1792) inserts an analysis of the relations between the sexes into a wholesale revolutionary attack on hereditary privilege of all sorts—birth, wealth, rank, *and* gender. Of course, not every revolutionary theorist in the 1790s would include male privilege on such a list: the French National Assembly's Declaration of the Rights of Man in 1789 said nothing about the rights of women. Yet Wollstonecraft's argument for rational education for both sexes was based on the promise of freedom enthusiastically greeted by many English writers in the early days of the French Revolution.

Wollstonecraft had previously written *A Vindication of the Rights of Men* (1790), one of the first polemical responses to EDMUND BURKE's conservative *Reflections on the Revolution in France* (1790). Months before Thomas Paine's perhaps better-known *Rights of Man* (1791–92), Wollstonecraft composed the first *Vindication* at white heat; it was printed anonymously. For Wollstonecraft, Burke's defense of the charms of existing arrangements was of a piece with the implicit gendering of his earlier aesthetic distinction between the beautiful and the sublime in his *Philosophical Enquiry into the Origin of Our Ideas of the Sublime and Beautiful* (1757; see above). Beauty was a property of weaker entities than man; sublimity, of stronger. Women's beauty was thus synonymous with women's inferiority. In both her *Vindications*, Wollstonecraft skillfully demystifies all arguments designed to justify inequality on the basis of existing arrangements, customs, or feelings alone.

As the second-born and first daughter of six children, she experienced firsthand the preference accorded men in both property and dignity. Her older brother was the only grandchild to inherit part of his grandfather's fortune (made in the silk industry), much of which was consumed by Mary's father as he attempted to lead the life of a gentleman farmer. As his finances worsened, he appropriated money that had been set aside for the other children and seems to have become increasingly brutal. At age nineteen Mary decided to strike out on her own.

In addition to trying her hand at several of the positions open to middle-class women without resources (lady's companion, governess, seamstress), Wollstonecraft opened a school at Newington Green with her two younger sisters and a dear friend, Fanny Blood. Although Mary's formal education had ended when she was fifteen, she was an avid reader and later taught herself French, German, Dutch, and Italian. The school failed, but the experience gave rise to Wollstonecraft's first publication, *Thoughts on the Education of Daughters* (1786), and to an acquaintance with anti-establishment thinkers, especially the Dissenter Dr. Richard Price (whose sermon on the anniversary of England's Glorious Revolution of 1688 was soon to provoke Burke's *Reflections*).

While working as a governess for the Kingsborough family in Ireland, Wollstonecraft wrote her first novel—*Mary, A Fiction* (1788); when dismissed by the Kingsboroughs (for reasons that are unclear), she returned to London, where her sympathetic publisher, Joseph Johnson, put her to work doing translations and reviews for his new *Analytical Review*. Around his table gathered some of the most interesting intellectuals of the day, including the radical thinker Thomas Paine, the painter Henry Fuseli, the political philosopher and novelist William Godwin, and the poet William Blake.

When the Bastille prison was stormed by a Paris mob in 1789, inaugurating the French Revolution, English radicals looked to France with great enthusiasm. As WILLIAM WORDSWORTH would later put it in his poem "French Revolution" (1809), "Bliss was it in that dawn to be alive[.] . . . What temper at the prospect did not wake / To happiness unthought of?" (also included in *The Prelude* [1805] 10.692–707). It was in this climate that Mary Wollstonecraft composed her *Vindications*. To the promise of liberty and equality for all men, Wollstonecraft added the simple but radical idea that women, too, had a right to develop their faculties freely, that the laws subjecting them to fathers or husbands could be changed, and that their existing defects (and indeed their charms) were largely a result of social conditioning, and could be modified. By comparing women to military men—both are fond of dress, trained in obedience, and not expected to think for themselves—she implies that education and socialization account for more differences than does gender alone.

At the time of writing *A Vindication of the Rights of Woman*, Wollstonecraft was just beginning to experience the additional complications that a life of passion could create for an independent woman attempting to live by her reason. She fell in love with Henry Fuseli and horrified his wife by suggesting that the three of them might live together. Soon thereafter, she went to Paris alone.

Once in France, she wrote about the French Revolution (her *Historical and Moral View of the Origin and Progress of the French Revolution, and the Effect It Has Produced in Europe* was published in 1794), observed the Reign of Terror with increasing recoil, and fell in love with a dashing American, Gilbert Imlay, who, when British citizens were being rounded up, registered her as his wife for her protection. She conceived a child with him, whom she named Fanny, after Fanny Blood. Though the birth was without complications, Wollstonecraft's life was not. Gilbert was often absent on "business," and on two occasions when Wollstonecraft was to join him in London, she discovered evidence of his infidelities. She twice attempted suicide; between attempts, she offered to journey to Scandinavia to investigate some business dealings for Imlay, and, traveling with a toddler and an attendant, wrote letters detailing her travels (later published as *Letters Written during a Short Residence in Norway, Denmark, and Sweden*, 1796). But the relationship with Imlay was over. As VIRGINIA WOOLF memorably surmised in her 1929 short essay on Wollstonecraft (reprinted in *The Second Common Reader*): "Tickling minnows he had hooked a dolphin, and the creature rushed him through the waters till he was dizzy and only wanted to escape."

Wollstonecraft reentered the circle of intellectuals around Joseph Johnson, and this time she found a great deal to discuss with the forty-year-old William Godwin, who was now at the peak of his career (having published *Political Justice* in 1793 and the novel *Caleb Williams* in 1794). Soon "it was friendship melting into love," as Godwin later described it. Both of them were opposed to marriage on principle—he felt that all formal commitments violate the feelings that inspire them, and she felt that marriage laws disadvantage women. Nevertheless, when Mary found herself pregnant again, they married at the beginning of 1797 so that the child would be legitimate. Ironically, many "respectable" acquaintances who had wanted to believe that Mary was married to Imlay broke off relations when this gesture of propriety revealed the earlier illegitimacy.

The author of *A Vindication of the Rights of Woman* was happily working on a novel titled *Maria, or the Wrongs of Woman* (the play—and lack of symmetry—between universal "rights" and gender-specific "wrongs" sums up the differences between Wollstonecraft's treatises and her novels) while she awaited the birth of "William." But she and Godwin had little chance to test their marital experiment. On September 10, 1797, she died of an infection contracted during unsuccessful attempts to remove her broken and unexpelled placenta, eleven days after giving birth to a daughter—the future Mary Shelley, author of a Gothic novel of education (*Frankenstein*) and wife of a passionate disciple of both Godwin and Wollstonecraft, PERCY BYSSHE SHELLEY.

Unlike other middle-class women, whose husbands, fathers, wealth, or connections veiled their legal powerlessness, Mary Wollstonecraft clearly saw the damage caused by sexual inequality. She was socialized for but she never experienced a life of respectable dependency. The first readers of *A Vindication of the Rights of Woman* applauded her apparent commitment to bourgeois respectability, but when Godwin published in his *Memoirs of Mary Wollstonecraft* (1798) a frank account of her subsequent sexual life, the increasingly conservative public reacted to her lack of deference (for which modern feminists applaud her) with horror. Her freedom and independence were seen as proof of licentiousness and immorality.

Mary Wollstonecraft was a cultural and not a literary critic, but as an acute reader of the contradictions inherent in the literary tradition she is a forerunner of "ideological" reading. Literature was central to her work in several fundamental ways. In her novels, she plumbs the conflicts between reason and emotion ("sensibility"), or within reason itself, neither of which are dealt with in her treatises. In her reply to Burke, she does not separate his aesthetic from his political theory. And she finds at the heart of the literary canon the same sexual inequality and incoherence she is arguing against in society at large.

In the extract printed below, for example, Wollstonecraft begins by pointing out two incompatible moments in Milton's *Paradise Lost:* Adam's plea to God for an equal and Eve's birth as an unequal. How are these to be reconciled? If God exists, she argues, and if humans are all characterized by their capacity for immortality, then one God fits all, and virtue must be the same in kind, if not in degree, for both sexes. The obedience and secondariness expected of women ("He for God only, she for God in him," as Milton put it) make a mockery of true companionship, giving women access only to a reflection of the light of reason that they should seek for themselves. In good Enlightenment fashion, Wollstonecraft comes close to taking the Serpent's role, arguing Eve out of blind obedience and into independent thinking.

Wollstonecraft is particularly concerned with the education of women, entering a larger discussion concerning education in general during the period. Jean-Jacques Rousseau's *Emile* (1762) had argued that men should have *less* rather than *more* education. Society needed to return to, preserve, and nurture man's natural goodness. Wollstonecraft agreed with much that Rousseau wrote about fresh air, exercise, and natural reason, but she vigorously criticized his differentiation between the educations of Emile and of Sophie. While Emile was expected to develop all his faculties, Sophie was expected to develop only in such a way as to remain "pleasing" to men. Wollstonecraft was not alone in calling for change—she had reviewed with approval Catharine Macauley Graham's *Letters on Education* (1790), and her treatise was dedicated to Charles-Maurice de Talleyrand-Périgord, who had promoted women's education in a 1791 report to the French National Assembly—but her logic was particularly incisive.

Today Wollstonecraft is celebrated for her early advocacy of women's equality and rationality and for arguing against the degradation and subjugation of women justified by "the arbitrary power of beauty." Her unblinking accounts of existing female defects in mind, body, and character—which sometimes sound misogynist themselves—were in the service of the new forms of freedom and education sought by proponents of Enlightenment reason and revolutionary change.

BIBLIOGRAPHY

Mary Wollstonecraft has been well served by modern editors. Her complete works have been edited in seven volumes by Janet Todd and Marilyn Butler (1989), and *A Vindication of the Rights of Woman* is available in several accessible editions. Her two novels *Mary* and *Maria* (along with *Matilda*, an early novel by Mary Wollstonecraft Shelley, her daughter) have been published in a single volume edited by Janet Todd (1991). An excellent edition of the two *Vindications*, with helpful notes and appendixes, has been prepared by D. L. Macdonald and Kathleen Scherf (1997). Following the first modern scholarly biography, Ralph Wardle's *Mary Wollstonecraft* (1951), numerous others have appeared; particularly noteworthy are Claire Tomalin's *Life and Death of Mary Wollstonecraft* (1974), Gary Kelly's *Revolutionary Feminism: The Mind and Career of Mary Wollstonecraft* (1992), and Janet Todd's *Mary Wollstonecraft: A Revolutionary Life* (2000). Many general studies of Wollstonecraft devote substantial space to the intertwining of her life and work: good basic introductions include Moira Ferguson and Janet Todd's *Mary Wollstonecraft* (1984), Jennifer Lorch's *Mary Wollstonecraft: The Making of a Radical Feminist* (1990), and Harriet Jump's *Mary Wollstonecraft: Writer* (1994). For a good selection of recent essays, see *Feminist Interpretations of Mary Wollstonecraft*, edited by Maria Falco (1996). To contextualize Wollstonecraft within the aesthetics and politics of her day, see Mary Poovey, *The Proper Lady and the Woman Writer: Ideology as Style in the Works of Mary Wollstonecraft, Mary Shelley, and Jane Austen* (1984); the debate about Enlightenment "reason" between Timothy Reiss and Frances Ferguson in *Gender and Theory* (ed. Linda Kauffman, 1989); Syndy Conger, *Mary Wollstonecraft and the Language of Sensibility* (1994); and Claudia Johnson's discussion of politics, gender, and sentimentality in *Equivocal Beings: Politics, Gender, and Sentimentality in the 1790s*

(1995). Susan Gubar's examination of current feminist criticism, *Critical Condition: Feminism at the Turn of the Century* (2000), contains an analysis of Wollstonecraft's own misogyny. Janet Todd's *Mary Wollstonecraft: An Annotated Bibliography* (1976) is helpful for the period before the flowering of contemporary feminist criticism, but it needs updating.

From A Vindication of the Rights of Woman

From *Chapter II.*
The Prevailing Opinion of a Sexual Character Discussed

To account for, and excuse the tyranny of man, many ingenious arguments have been brought forward to prove, that the two sexes, in the acquirement of virtue, ought to aim at attaining a very different character: or, to speak explicitly, women are not allowed to have sufficient strength of mind to acquire what really deserves the name of virtue. Yet it should seem, allowing them to have souls, that there is but one way appointed by Providence to lead *mankind* to either virtue or happiness.

If then women are not a swarm of ephemeron[1] triflers, why should they be kept in ignorance under the specious name of innocence? Men complain, and with reason, of the follies and caprices of our sex, when they do not keenly satirize our headstrong passions and groveling vices.—Behold, I should answer, the natural effect of ignorance! The mind will ever be unstable that has only prejudices to rest on, and the current will run with destructive fury when there are no barriers to break its force. Women are told from their infancy, and taught by the example of their mothers, that a little knowledge of human weakness, justly termed cunning, softness of temper, *outward* obedience, and a scrupulous attention to a puerile kind of propriety, will obtain for them the protection of man; and should they be beautiful, every thing else is needless, for, at least, twenty years of their lives.

Thus Milton[2] describes our first frail mother; though when he tells us that women are formed for softness and sweet attractive grace, I cannot comprehend his meaning, unless, in the true Mahometan[3] strain, he meant to deprive us of souls, and insinuate that we were beings only designed by sweet attractive grace, and docile blind obedience, to gratify the senses of man when he can no longer soar on the wing of contemplation.

How grossly do they insult us who thus advise us only to render ourselves gentle, domestic brutes! For instance, the winning softness so warmly, and frequently, recommended, that governs by obeying. What childish expressions, and how insignificant is the being—can it be an immortal one? who will condescend to govern by such sinister methods! "Certainly," says Lord Bacon, "man is of kin to the beasts by his body; and if he be not of kin to God by his spirit, he is a base and ignoble creature!"[4] Men, indeed, appear to me to act in a very unphilosophical manner when they try to secure the

1. Short-lived (literally, living only one day).
2. John Milton (1608–1674), English poet whose epic poem, *Paradise Lost* (1667), tells the biblical story of the fall of humankind; Wollstonecraft refers to book 4.298.
3. Muslim. Islam was thought to deny that women have souls.
4. Francis Bacon (1561–1626), *Essays or Counsels Civil and Moral* (1625), Essay 16, "Of Atheism" [D. L. Macdonald and Kathleen Scherf's note].

good conduct of women by attempting to keep them always in a state of childhood. Rousseau[5] was more consistent when he wished to stop the progress of reason in both sexes, for if men eat of the tree of knowledge, women will come in for a taste;[6] but, from the imperfect cultivation which their understandings now receive, they only attain a knowledge of evil.

Children, I grant, should be innocent; but when the epithet is applied to men, or women, it is but a civil term for weakness. For if it be allowed that women were destined by Providence to acquire human virtues, and by the exercise of their understandings, that stability of character which is the firmest ground to rest our future hopes upon, they must be permitted to turn to the fountain of light, and not forced to shape their course by the twinkling of a mere satellite.[7] Milton, I grant, was of a very different opinion; for he only bends to the indefeasible right of beauty, though it would be difficult to render two passages which I now mean to contrast, consistent. But into similar inconsistencies are great men often led by their senses.

> "To whom thus Eve with *perfect beauty* adorn'd.
> My Author and Disposer, what thou bidst
> *Unargued* I obey; so God ordains;
> God is *thy law, thou mine*: to know no more
> Is Woman's *happiest* knowledge and her *praise*."[8]

These are exactly the arguments that I have used to children; but I have added, your reason is now gaining strength, and, till it arrives at some degree of maturity, you must look up to me for advice—then you ought to *think*, and only rely on God.

Yet in the following lines Milton seems to coincide with me; when he makes Adam thus expostulate with his Maker.

> "Hast thou not made me here thy substitute,
> And these inferior far beneath me set?
> Among *unequals* what society
> Can sort, what harmony or true delight?
> Which must be mutual, in proportion due
> Giv'n and receiv'd; but in *disparity*
> The one intense, the other still remiss
> Cannot well suit with either, but soon prove
> Tedious alike: of *fellowship* I speak
> Such as I seek, fit to participate
> All rational delight—"[9]

In treating, therefore, of the manners of women, let us, disregarding sensual arguments, trace what we should endeavour to make them in order to co-operate, if the expression be not too bold, with the supreme Being.

By individual education, I mean, for the sense of the word is not precisely defined, such an attention to a child as will slowly sharpen the senses, form

5. Jean-Jacques Rousseau (1712–1778), Swiss-born French political philosopher; author of *Emile, or, On Education* (1762). All references to Rousseau in this selection are to book 5 of *Emile*, unless otherwise specified.

6. See Genesis 2–3. The story of "man's first disobedience" (1.1) in eating this fruit forms the center of Milton's *Paradise Lost*.

7. That is, women should turn to the sun, not the moon.

8. Milton, *Paradise Lost* 4.634–38 (Wollstonecraft's italics).

9. *Paradise Lost* 8.381–91 (Wollstonecraft's italics). "Participate": partake of.

the temper, regulate the passions as they begin to ferment, and set the understanding to work before the body arrives at maturity; so that the man may only have to proceed, not to begin, the important task of learning to think and reason.

To prevent any misconstruction, I must add, that I do not believe that a private education can work the wonders which some sanguine writers have attributed to it. Men and women must be educated, in a great degree, by the opinions and manners of the society they live in. In every age there has been a stream of popular opinion that has carried all before it, and given a family character, as it were, to the century. It may then fairly be inferred, that, till society be differently constituted, much cannot be expected from education. It is, however, sufficient for my present purpose to assert, that, whatever effect circumstances have on the abilities, every being may become virtuous by the exercise of its own reason; for if but one being was created with vicious inclinations, that is positively bad, what can save us from atheism? or if we worship a God, is not that God a devil?

Consequently, the most perfect education, in my opinion, is such an exercise of the understanding as is best calculated to strengthen the body and form the heart. Or, in other words, to enable the individual to attain such habits of virtue as will render it independent. In fact, it is a farce to call any being virtuous whose virtues do not result from the exercise of its own reason. This was Rousseau's opinion respecting men:[1] I extend it to women, and confidently assert that they have been drawn out of their sphere by false refinement, and not by an endeavour to acquire masculine qualities. Still the regal homage which they receive is so intoxicating, that till the manners of the times are changed, and formed on more reasonable principles, it may be impossible to convince them that the illegitimate power, which they obtain, by degrading themselves, is a curse, and that they must return to nature and equality, if they wish to secure the placid satisfaction that unsophisticated affections impart. But for this epoch we must wait—wait, perhaps, till kings and nobles, enlightened by reason, and, preferring the real dignity of man to childish state, throw off their gaudy hereditary trappings: and if then women do not resign the arbitrary power of beauty—they will prove that they have *less* mind than man.

I may be accused of arrogance; still I must declare what I firmly believe, that all the writers who have written on the subject of female education and manners from Rousseau to Dr. Gregory,[2] have contributed to render women more artificial, weak characters, than they would otherwise have been; and, consequently, more useless members of society. I might have expressed this conviction in a lower key; but I am afraid it would have been the whine of affection, and not the faithful expression of my feelings, of the clear result, which experience and reflection have led me to draw. When I come to that division of the subject, I shall advert to the passages that I more particularly disapprove of, in the works of the authors I have just alluded to; but it is first necessary to observe, that my objection extends to the whole purport of those books, which tend, in my opinion, to degrade one half of the human species, and render women pleasing at the expence of every solid virtue.

1. Expressed early in *Emile*.
2. John Gregory (1724–1773), *A Father's Legacy to His Daughters* (1774). Wollstonecraft included substantial excerpts from Gregory in *The Female Reader* ([compiled in] 1789) [Macdonald and Scherf's note].

Though, to reason on Rousseau's ground, if man did attain a degree of perfection of mind when his body arrived at maturity, it might be proper, in order to make a man and his wife *one*, that she should rely entirely on his understanding; and the graceful ivy, clasping the oak that supported it, would form a whole in which strength and beauty would be equally conspicuous. But, alas! husbands, as well as their helpmates, are often only overgrown children; nay, thanks to early debauchery, scarcely men in their outward form—and if the blind lead the blind, one need not come from heaven[3] to tell us the consequence.

Many are the causes that, in the present corrupt state of society, contribute to enslave women by cramping their understandings and sharpening their senses. One, perhaps, that silently does more mischief than all the rest, is their disregard of order.

To do every thing in an orderly manner, is a most important precept, which women, who, generally speaking, receive only a disorderly kind of education, seldom attend to with that degree of exactness that men, who from their infancy are broken into method, observe. This negligent kind of guess-work, for what other epithet can be used to point out the random exertions of a sort of instinctive common sense, never brought to the test of reason? prevents their generalizing matters of fact—so they do to-day, what they did yesterday, merely because they did it yesterday.

This contempt of the understanding in early life has more baneful consequences than is commonly supposed; for the little knowledge which women of strong minds attain, is, from various circumstances, of a more desultory kind than the knowledge of men, and it is acquired more by sheer observations on real life, than from comparing what has been individually observed with the results of experience generalized by speculation. Led by their dependent situation and domestic employments more into society, what they learn is rather by snatches; and as learning is with them, in general, only a secondary thing, they do not pursue any one branch with that persevering ardour necessary to give vigour to the faculties, and clearness to the judgment. In the present state of society, a little learning is required to support the character of a gentleman; and boys are obliged to submit to a few years of discipline. But in the education of women, the cultivation of the understanding is always subordinate to the acquirement of some corporeal accomplishment; even while enervated by confinement and false notions of modesty, the body is prevented from attaining that grace and beauty which relaxed half-formed limbs never exhibit. Besides, in youth their faculties are not brought forward by emulation; and having no serious scientific study, if they have natural sagacity it is turned too soon on life and manners. They dwell on effects, and modifications, without tracing them back to causes; and complicated rules to adjust behaviour are a weak substitute for simple principles.

As a proof that education gives this appearance of weakness to females, we may instance the example of military men, who are, like them, sent into the world before their minds have been stored with knowledge or fortified by principles. The consequences are similar; soldiers acquire a little super-

3. That is, be Jesus; in Matthew 15.14 he declares that "if the blind lead the blind, both shall fall into the ditch."

ficial knowledge, snatched from the muddy current of conversation, and, from continually mixing with society, they gain, what is termed a knowledge of the world; and this acquaintance with manners and customs has frequently been confounded with a knowledge of the human heart. But can the crude fruit of casual observation, never brought to the test of judgment, formed by comparing speculation and experience, deserve such a distinction? Soldiers, as well as women, practise the minor virtues with punctilious politeness. Where is then the sexual difference, when the education has been the same? All the difference that I can discern, arises from the superior advantage of liberty, which enables the former to see more of life.

It is wandering from my present subject, perhaps, to make a political remark; but, as it was produced naturally by the train of my reflections, I shall not pass it silently over.

Standing armies can never consist of resolute, robust men; they may be well disciplined machines, but they will seldom contain men under the influence of strong passions, or with very vigorous faculties. And as for any depth of understanding, I will venture to affirm, that it is as rarely to be found in the army as amongst women; and the cause, I maintain, is the same. It may be further observed, that officers are also particularly attentive to their persons, fond of dancing, crowded rooms, adventures, and ridicule.[4] Like the *fair* sex, the business of their lives is gallantry.—They were taught to please, and they only live to please. Yet they do not lose their rank in the distinction of sexes, for they are still reckoned superior to women, though in what their superiority consists, beyond what I have just mentioned, it is difficult to discover.

The great misfortune is this, that they both acquire manners before morals, and a knowledge of life before they have, from reflection, any acquaintance with the grand ideal outline of human nature. The consequence is natural; satisfied with common nature, they become a prey to prejudices, and taking all their opinions on credit, they blindly submit to authority. So that, if they have any sense, it is a kind of instinctive glance, that catches proportions, and decides with respect to manners; but fails when arguments are to be pursued below the surface, or opinions analyzed.

May not the same remark be applied to women? Nay, the argument may be carried still further, for they are both thrown out of a useful station by the unnatural distinctions established in civilized life. Riches and hereditary honours have made cyphers of women to give consequence to the numerical figure;[5] and idleness has produced a mixture of gallantry and despotism into society, which leads the very men who are the slaves of their mistresses to tyrannize over their sisters, wives, and daughters. This is only keeping them in rank and file, it is true. Strengthen the female mind by enlarging it, and there will be an end to blind obedience; but, as blind obedience is ever sought for by power, tyrants and sensualists are in the right when they endeavour to keep women in the dark, because the former only want slaves, and the latter a play-thing. The sensualist, indeed, has been the most dangerous of

4. Why should women be censured with petulant acrimony, because they seem to have a passion for a scarlet coat? Has not education placed them more on a level with soldiers than any other class of men? [Wollestonecraft's note]. "Ridicule": that which is ridiculous.

5. That is, women are merely zeroes ("ciphers") to add to the family name, inflating its value but being nothing in themselves.

tyrants, and women have been duped by their lovers, as princes by their ministers, whilst dreaming that they reigned over them.

I now principally allude to Rousseau, for his character of Sophia is, undoubtedly, a captivating one, though it appears to me grossly unnatural; however it is not the superstructure, but the foundation of her character, the principles on which her education was built, that I mean to attack; nay, warmly as I admire the genius of that able writer, whose opinions I shall often have occasion to cite, indignation always takes place of admiration, and the rigid frown of insulted virtue effaces the smile of complacency, which his eloquent periods[6] are wont to raise, when I read his voluptuous reveries. Is this the man, who, in his ardour for virtue, would banish all the soft arts of peace, and almost carry us back to Spartan discipline? Is this the man who delights to paint the useful struggles of passion, the triumphs of good dispositions, and the heroic flights which carry the glowing soul out of itself?—How are these mighty sentiments lowered when he describes the pretty foot and enticing airs of his little favourite! But, for the present, I wave[7] the subject, and, instead of severely reprehending the transient effusions of overweening sensibility, I shall only observe, that whoever has cast a benevolent eye on society, must often have been gratified by the sight of humble mutual love, not dignified by sentiment, or strengthened by a union in intellectual pursuits. The domestic trifles of the day have afforded matters for cheerful converse, and innocent caresses have softened toils which did not require great exercise of mind or stretch of thought: yet, had not the sight of this moderate felicity excited more tenderness than respect? An emotion similar to what we feel when children are playing, or animals sporting,[8] whilst the contemplation of the noble struggles of suffering merit has raised admiration, and carried our thoughts to that world where sensation will give place to reason.

Women are, therefore, to be considered either as moral beings, or so weak that they must be entirely subjected to the superior faculties of men.

Let us examine this question. Rousseau declares that a woman should never, for a moment, feel herself independent, that she should be governed by fear to exercise her *natural* cunning, and made a coquetish slave in order to render her a more alluring object of desire, a *sweeter* companion to man, whenever he chooses to relax himself. He carries the arguments, which he pretends to draw from the indications of nature, still further, and insinuates that truth and fortitude, the corner stones of all human virtue, should be cultivated with certain restrictions, because, with respect to the female character, obedience is the grand lesson which ought to be impressed with unrelenting rigour.

What nonsense! when will a great man arise with sufficient strength of mind to puff away the fumes which pride and sensuality have thus spread over the subject! If women are by nature inferior to men, their virtues must

6. Sentences.
7. Waive.
8. Similar feelings has Milton's pleasing picture of paradisiacal happiness ever raised in my mind; yet, instead of envying the lovely pair, I have, with conscious dignity, or Satanic pride, turned to hell for sublimer objects. In the same style, when viewing some noble monument of human art, I have traced the emanation of the Deity in the order I admired, till, descending from that giddy height, I have caught myself contemplating the grandest of all human sights;—for fancy quickly placed, in some solitary recess, an outcast of fortune, rising superior to passion and discontent [Wollestonecraft's note].

be the same in quality, if not in degree, or virtue is a relative idea; consequently, their conduct should be founded on the same principles, and have the same aim.[9]

Connected with man as daughters, wives, and mothers, their moral character may be estimated by their manner of fulfilling those simple duties; but the end, the grand end of their exertions should be to unfold their own faculties and acquire the dignity of conscious virtue. They may try to render their road pleasant; but ought never to forget, in common with man, that life yields not the felicity which can satisfy an immortal soul. I do not mean to insinuate, that either sex should be so lost in abstract reflections or distant views, as to forget the affections and duties that lie before them, and are, in truth, the means appointed to produce the fruit of life; on the contrary, I would warmly recommend them, even while I assert, that they afford most satisfaction when they are considered in their true, sober light.

Probably the prevailing opinion, that woman was created for man, may have taken its rise from Moses's poetical story;[1] yet, as very few, it is presumed, who have bestowed any serious thought on the subject, ever supposed that Eve was, literally speaking, one of Adam's ribs, the deduction must be allowed to fall to the ground; or, only be so far admitted as it proves that man, from the remotest antiquity, found it convenient to exert his strength to subjugate his companion, and his invention to shew that she ought to have her neck bent under the yoke, because the whole creation was only created for his convenience or pleasure.

Let it not be concluded that I wish to invert the order of things; I have already granted that, from the constitution of their bodies, men seem to be designed by Providence to attain a greater degree of virtue. I speak collectively of the whole sex; but I see not the shadow of a reason to conclude that their virtues should differ in respect to their nature. In fact, how can they, if virtue has only one eternal standard? I must therefore, if I reason consequentially, as strenuously maintain that they have the same simple direction, as that there is a God.

It follows then that cunning should not be opposed to wisdom, little cares to great exertions, or insipid softness, varnished over with the name of gentleness, to that fortitude which grand views alone can inspire.

I shall be told that woman would then lose many of her peculiar graces, and the opinion of a well known poet might be quoted to refute my unqualified assertion. For Pope has said, in the name of the whole male sex,

> "Yet ne'er so sure our passion to create,
> As when she touch'd the brink of all we hate."[2]

In what light this sally places men and women, I shall leave to the judicious to determine; meanwhile I shall content myself with observing, that I cannot discover why, unless they are mortal,[3] females should always be degraded by being made subservient to love or lust.

To speak disrespectfully of love is, I know, high treason against sentiment

9. Rousseau argues that men's and women's virtues are essentially different [Macdonald and Scherf's note].

1. Moses was traditionally credited with writing the first 5 books of the Bible; see Genesis 2.18–25.

2. ALEXANDER POPE (1688–1744), "Epistle II, To a Lady: Of the Characters of Women" (1735), 51–52.

3. That is, unless they are not as capable as men of immortal life.

and fine feelings; but I wish to speak the simple language of truth, and rather to address the head than the heart. To endeavour to reason love out of the world, would be to out Quixote[4] Cervantes, and equally offend against common sense; but an endeavour to restrain this tumultuous passion, and to prove that it should not be allowed to dethrone superior powers, or to usurp the sceptre which the understanding should ever coolly wield, appears less wild.

Youth is the season for love in both sexes; but in those days of thoughtless enjoyment provision should be made for the more important years of life, when reflection takes place of sensation. But Rousseau, and most of the male writers who have followed his steps, have warmly inculcated that the whole tendency of female education ought to be directed to one point:—to render them pleasing.

Let me reason with the supporters of this opinion who have any knowledge of human nature, do they imagine that marriage can eradicate the habitude of life? The woman who has only been taught to please will soon find that her charms are oblique sunbeams, and that they cannot have much effect on her husband's heart when they are seen every day, when the summer is passed and gone. Will she then have sufficient native energy to look into herself for comfort, and cultivate her dormant faculties? or, is it not more rational to expect that she will try to please other men; and, in the emotions raised by the expectation of new conquests, endeavour to forget the mortification her love or pride has received? When the husband ceases to be a lover—and the time will inevitably come, her desire of pleasing will then grow languid, or become a spring of bitterness; and love, perhaps, the most evanescent of all passions, gives place to jealousy or vanity.

I now speak of women who are restrained by principle or prejudice; such women, though they would shrink from an intrigue with real abhorrence, yet, nevertheless, wish to be convinced by the homage of gallantry that they are cruelly neglected by their husbands; or, days and weeks are spent in dreaming of the happiness enjoyed by congenial souls till their health is undermined and their spirits broken by discontent. How then can the great art of pleasing be such a necessary study? it is only useful to a mistress; the chaste wife, and serious mother, should only consider her power to please as the polish of her virtues, and the affection of her husband as one of the comforts that render her task less difficult and her life happier.—But, whether she be loved or neglected, her first wish should be to make herself respectable, and not to rely for all her happiness on a being subject to like infirmities with herself.

* * *

1792

4. That is, to be more foolishly impractical than Don Quixote, the overly idealistic title character of the novel (1605, 1615) by Miguel de Cervantes (1547–1616).

GERMAINE NECKER DE STAËL
1766–1817

Mme de Staël is one of the few women writers without whom the history of French literature cannot be told. Bridging the gap between the old regime and the Revolution, between national and comparative literatures, and between classical aesthetics and *littérature engagée*, her writings were an advance justification of both Romanticism and realism in France. Celebrated for her conversation, condemned for her sexuality, and alternately lauded and vilified for her politics, she embodied the kind of freedom that revolutionary theorists seldom imagined for women. She was a child of the Enlightenment and never abandoned the principles of self-realization it entailed. "The only reason to fear women's wit," she wrote in 1800, "would be some sort of scrupulous anxiety about their happiness. And indeed, by developing their rational minds one might well be enlightening them as to the misfortunes often connected with their fate; but the same reasoning would apply to the effect of the enlightenment on the happiness of the human race in general, a question which seems to me to have been decided once and for all."

Germaine de Staël was born in Paris to Swiss Protestant parents. Her father, Jacques Necker, had amassed a fortune in banking, thanks to French laws that prevented most Catholics from lending money at high interest. Her mother, Suzanne (née Curchod), maintained a celebrated salon. Germaine seems not to have inherited her mother's great beauty, but her childhood was spent in the company of famous Enlightenment figures such as Edward Gibbon, chronicler of the fall of the Roman Empire and former suitor of Suzanne Curchod; Denis Diderot and Jean d'Alembert, authors of the *Encyclopédie*; and many others. Her father, appointed to act as Louis XVI's finance minister in 1777, was lionized by both the king, whose treasury he restored, and the people, whom he fed. Indeed, it was his dismissal by the king in 1789 that led to the storming of the Bastille.

At age nineteen, Germaine Necker was one of the wealthiest heiresses in Europe. Her parents, seeking a son-in-law who was not Catholic, briefly considered William Pitt the Younger, but she was unwilling to move to England. In 1786 she settled on a young Swedish suitor very much in favor with the French and the Swedish courts. Erik Magnus de Staël-Holstein, a penniless nobleman, had had his eye on Germaine's fortune since she was twelve. King Gustavus III made him Swedish ambassador to France for life (in a complicated bargain in which France gave Sweden the Caribbean Island of St. Barthélémy), and Germaine was assured she would never have to live in Sweden.

Germaine de Staël supplemented this marriage of convenience through passionate involvements with some of the most interesting men of the century. Her lovers were numerous; among the best known were Charles-Maurice de Talleyrand, then bishop of Autun; Count Louis de Narbonne, whose ambivalence during the early revolutionary period led him to support both Lafayette and the royal family; Benjamin Constant, whose brilliant conversation matched her own and who fictionalized their affair in his novel *Adolphe* (1816); and Adolphe Ribbing, who masterminded the assassination of the same Swedish king who had brought about her marriage. August Wilhelm von Schlegel was central to her intellectual life and preceptor to her children (she gave birth to five, and only the first—who died in infancy—was conceived within marriage). Her last love was a younger man and a commoner, John Rocca, with whom at forty-five she bore a retarded son and whom she secretly married before she died (Erik having died in 1802). On reading Mme de Staël's first novel, *Delphine* (1802), and recognizing the autobiographical elements in it, Talleyrand quipped: "Mme de Staël has disguised both herself and me as women in her novel." De Staël's mother, influenced by Jean-Jacques Rousseau's theories of education in his *Emile* (1762) but switching the gender roles presented in that work, had brought her daughter up with the independence of an Emile, not the compliance of a Sophie.

Although she wanted nothing more than to live in Paris, Mme de Staël spent most of her adult life elsewhere—not just in France but also in England, Germany, Italy, Sweden, Russia, Austria, and, most important, Switzerland, where her parents, in and out of favor in France, had bought the château of Coppet in 1784. Her exile by Napoleon in 1803 to "forty leagues from Paris" was only the most official of her banishments by political forces on the left and on the right. Her defense of a constitutional monarchy was too royalist for the revolutionary Jacobins, and her defense of a republic was too revolutionary for the aristocratic *émigrés*. A moderate in favor of both liberty and property, she offended everyone. The authors of the French constitution frequented her Paris salon, but she wrote in defense of Queen Marie Antoinette. Napoleon, neither constitutional nor republican, was a worthy opponent for fourteen years. He not only exiled her from Paris but also planted spies in her entourage, had her correspondence read, took offense at all her writings, and stopped publication of her *On Germany* in 1810. Yet her opposition to Napoleon did not prevent a certain identification: in his final days, she informed him of a plot on his life. In 1815, when Napoleon was at last defeated, she hoped for a constitutional monarchy but rallied to the support of the restoration of Louis XVIII; she was reimbursed, in the process, for the two million francs her father had lent the royal treasury.

Wherever she lived, Mme de Staël configured a brilliant salon around her. Her passion for intellectual conversation both seduced and exhausted her guests, whom she received, in the manner of the old regime, from the moment she awoke to the moment she retired (a day whose length grew as her insomnia worsened). Conversations within the "Groupe de Coppet" (Coppet Group) revolved around liberal opposition to Napoleon and around Romantic ideals of literature and human progress. Leading figures such as Johann Wolfgang von Goethe, Wilhelm von Humboldt, Lord Byron, Simonde de Sismondi, and Juliette Récamier fueled Mme de Staël's changing sense of the possibilities. Her château at Coppet has remained a gathering place for scholars and writers; colloquia on her work regularly take place there, where she was laid to rest next to her parents.

De Staël's early "Essay on Fictions," published in 1795 (our first selection), makes the case, in her characteristic epigrammatic style, for what was eventually to become the nineteenth-century realist novel. Novels, she claims, should broaden their range to include every human predicament, not simply romantic love. Novels can give the creative intellect the space to explore every intractable problem facing postrevolutionary man and woman. Fictions in which "nothing is true and everything is likely" will challenge novel writers to represent what they take to be the real. Unlike philosophical allegories, which subordinate fiction to ideas, and historical fictions, which subordinate fiction to facts, the novel can re-create the world as it is and, in the process, change it. Useless if merely accurate or merely imaginary, literature has the power to move, to awaken, to inform, to distract, and to console. Far from being outside of history, the novel can come to grips with everything that *makes* history.

On Literature Considered in Its Relationship to Social Institutions (1800), from which our second selection is taken, is a fitting monument to the turn from the eighteenth to the nineteenth century. Deeply connected to the fate of the French Revolution, which had just passed through the Reign of Terror (during which Mme de Staël lost many friends and was almost executed herself), *On Literature* describes history as an ongoing process that, whatever its setbacks, ultimately heads toward human progress and perfectibility. As a domain in which the mind can stretch itself to the utmost, literature is an intimate part of the process. When, in later conversation, Mme de Staël was introduced to Goethe's views on art for art's sake, she found this Weimar aesthetic contrary to all she hoped for from literature, but so dialectical was her mind that she loved to find an idea she could resist. As Goethe later reported, "My obstinate contrariness often drove her to despair, but it was then that she was at her most amiable and that she displayed her mental and verbal agility most brilliantly."

Romanticism in France is rooted in the writings of Rousseau, another Swiss, but by all accounts the decisive turn was taken when Mme de Staël introduced German Romanticism to the French. In her book *On Germany* (1810), she offered Europe and particularly France an alternative to the empire of Napoleon with his taste for classicism and absolutism. Her division between northern literature (melancholy, medieval, Christian, emotional, misty—Romantic) and southern literature (sunny, rational, sensual, pagan—classical) was both cosmopolitan and nationalist in an age when modern nationalism was just taking shape. All of the categories were problematic, but despite the rhetorical force of Mme de Staël's oppositions, their thrust was less essential ("the German soul," "the French mind") than dialectical. Within the French tradition, the seeds of Romanticism already existed: all that was needed was to make them grow. And German thinkers would provide the nutrients.

In addition to her theoretical and political writings, de Staël is famous for two novels—*Delphine* (1802) and *Corinne, or Italy* (1807). The latter paints a portrait of a celebrated, independent woman artist; her art is deepened by her love for an Englishman who, initially attracted by her talent, eventually abandons her for a less complex partner. Corinne, who is half English and half Italian, combines the genius of the Mediterranean with the sensitivity of the North in her poetry, but she suffers, in the end, from culture's inability to incorporate superior and complex women. Mme de Staël had much to say about the plight of the woman intellectual, whether living in a monarchy or in a republic, a plight that is nowhere more cogently analyzed than in our selection from *On Literature*. The category of "exceptional woman," a term invented by French culture both to counteract and to appropriate women like Mme de Staël, continued to function well into the twentieth century, as SIMONE DE BEAUVOIR was to find out. By separating the exception from the condition of women in general, society recognizes and benefits from female talent without having to change its view—often shared by the exceptional woman herself—of women as such.

BIBLIOGRAPHY

In addition to the literary and cultural works mentioned above, Mme de Staël's writings include many stories and plays, a tribute to Rousseau (*Letters on Rousseau*, 1788), *Reflections on the Trial of the Queen* (1793), *Reflections on Peace* (1794), *The Influence of the Passions* (1796), *Reflections on Suicide* (1813), and "The Spirit of Translation" (1816). Posthumously published were the *Considerations on the Principal Events of the French Revolution* (1818), *Ten Years of Exile* (1820), the *Complete Works* (1820), and many volumes of correspondence, some of which is still being discovered. Mme de Staël's work is not all easy to obtain in English translation. A wide range of selections can be found in *Madame de Staël on Politics, Literature, and National Character*, edited and translated by Monroe Berger (1964), and in *An Extraordinary Woman*, edited and translated by Vivian Folkenflik (1987). The biography by J. Christopher Herold, *Mistress to an Age* (1958), is, while somewhat dated, informative and well written.

In France there is a very active de Staël industry, which publishes a journal, *Cahiers staëliens* (*Staël Notebooks*), and holds many conferences. The most important figure in this enterprise is Simone Ballayé, whose work has not been much translated into English, but who has contributed an essay to the excellent anthology *Germaine de Staël: Crossing the Borders*, edited by Madelyn Gutwirth, Avriel Goldberger, and Karyna Szmurlo (1991). Madelyn Gutwirth's own *Madame de Staël, Novelist: The Emergence of the Artist as Woman* (1978) is also good, especially in its account of the shift in de Staël studies opened up by feminist criticism. Two fine general studies of Mme de Staël's life and works are Charlotte Hogsett, *The Literary Existence of Germaine de Staël* (1987), and Gretchen Rous Besser, *Germaine de Staël Revisited*

(1994). For an analysis of the place of *On Germany* in the rise of Romanticism, see John Claiborne Isbell, *The Birth of European Romanticism: Truth and Propaganda in Staël's "De l'Allemagne," 1810–1813* (1994). And for a study of the complexity of gender roles and models in Rousseau and de Staël, see Lori Jo Marso's excellent *(Un)Manly Citizens* (1999). There is an extensive annotated bibliography of criticism on de Staël in French by Pierre H. Dubé, *Bibliographie de la Critique sur Madame de Staël, 1789–1994* (1998).

From Essay on Fictions[1]

Introduction

Man's most valuable faculty is his imagination. Human life seems so little designed for happiness that we need the help of a few creations, a few images, a lucky choice of memories to muster some sparse pleasure on this earth and struggle against the pain of all our destinies—not by philosophical force, but by the more efficient force of distraction. The dangers of imagination have been discussed a good deal, but there is no point in looking up what impotent mediocrity and strict reason have said on this topic over and over again. The human race is not about to give up being stimulated, and anyone who has the gift of appealing to people's emotions is even less likely to give up the success promised by such talent. The number of necessary and evident truths is limited; it will never be enough for the human mind or heart. The highest honor may well go to those who discover such truths, but the authors of books producing sweet emotions or illusions have also done useful work for humanity. Metaphysical precision cannot be applied to man's affections and remain compatible with his nature. Beginnings are all we have on this earth—there is no limit. Virtue is actual and real, but happiness floats in space; anyone who tries to examine happiness inappropriately will destroy it, as we dissolve the brilliant images of the mist if we walk straight through them. And yet the advantage of fictions is not the pleasure they bring. If fictions please nothing but the eye, they do nothing but amuse; but if they touch our hearts, they can have a great influence on all our moral ideas. This talent may be the most powerful way there is of controlling behavior and enlightening the mind. Man has only two distinct faculties: reason and imagination. All the others, even feeling, are simply results or combinations of these two. The realm of fiction, like that of imagination, is therefore vast. Fictions do not find obstacles in passions: they make use of them. Philosophy may be the invisible power in control of fictions, but if she is the first to show herself, she will destroy all their magic.

When I talk about fictions, I will therefore be considering them from two perspectives of content and charm: this kind of writing may contain pleasure without useful purpose, but never vice versa. Fictions are meant to attract us; the more moral or philosophical the result one is trying to achieve, the more they have to be decked out with things to move us, leading us to the goal without advance warning. In mythological fictions I will consider only the poet's talent; these fictions could well be examined in the light of their

1. Translated by Vivian Folkenflik.

religious influence, but such a point of view is absolutely foreign to my subject. I will be discussing the writings of the ancients according to the impression they create in our times, so my concern must be with their literary talent rather than their religious beliefs.

Fictions can be divided into three groups: (1) marvelous and allegorical fictions, (2) historical fictions, (3) fictions in which everything is both invented and imitated, where nothing is true and everything is likely.[2]

This topic should really be discussed in an extensive treatise including most existing literary works and involving thoughts on almost every topic, since the complete exposition of any one idea is connected to the whole chain of ideas. But I am only trying to prove that the most useful kind of fiction will be novels taking life as it is, with delicacy, eloquence, depth, and morality, and I have excluded everything irrelevant to that goal from this essay.

III

The third and last part of this essay must deal with the usefulness of natural fictions, as I call them, where everything is both invented and imitated, so that nothing is true but everything looks true to life. Tragedies with completely imaginary subjects will not be included here; they portray a more lofty nature, an extraordinary situation at an extraordinary level. The verisimilitude of such plays depends on events that are extremely rare, and morally applicable to very few people. Comedies and other dramas are in the theater what novels are to other fiction: their plots are taken from private life and natural circumstances. However, the conventions of the theater deprive us of the commentary which gives examples of reflections their individuality. Dramas are allowed to choose their characters among people other than kings and heroes, but they can show only broadly defined situations, because there is no time for nuance. And life is not concentrated like that—does not happen in contrasts—is not really theatrical in the way plays have to be written. Dramatic art has different effects, advantages, and means which might well be discussed separately, but I think only the modern novel is capable of achieving the constant, accurate usefulness we can get from the picture of our ordinary, habitual feelings. People usually make a separate case of what they call philosophical novels; all novels should be philosophical, as they should all have a moral goal. Perhaps, however, we are not guided so inevitably toward this moral goal when all the episodes narrated are focused on one principal idea, exempting the author from all probability in the way one situation follows another. Each chapter then becomes a kind of allegory—its events are only there to illustrate the maxim at the end. The novels *Candide, Zadig,* and *Memnon,*[3] while delightful in other respects, would be much more useful if they were not marvelous, if they offered an example instead of an emblem and if, as I say, the whole story did not have to relate to the same goal. Such novels are at the same disadvantage as teachers: children never believe them, because they make everything that happens relate to the lesson at hand. Children unconsciously know already

2. That is, realist novels, discussed under heading III.

3. Tales by Voltaire: *Zadig* was published in 1747; *Memnon* in 1749, *Candide* in 1759 [translator's note].

that there is less regularity than that in real life. Events are also invented in novels like Richardson's and Fielding's,[4] where the author is trying to keep close to life by following with great accuracy the stages, developments, and inconsistencies of human history, and the way the results of experience always come down to the morality of actions and the advantages of virtue, nonetheless. In these novels, however, the feelings are so natural that the reader often believes he is being spoken to directly, with no artifice but the tactfulness of changing the names.

The art of novel-writing does not have the reputation it deserves because of a throng of bad writers overwhelming us with their colorless productions; in this genre, perfection may require the greatest genius, but mediocrity is well within everyone's grasp. This infinite number of colorless novels has almost used up the passion portrayed in them; one is terrified of finding the slightest resemblance in one's own life to the situations they describe. It has taken the very greatest masters to bring this genre back again, despite the writers who have degraded it. And others have dragged it even lower by including disgusting scenes of vice. Despite the fact that fiction's main advantage is to gather around man everything in nature that might be useful to him as a lesson or model, some writers supposed we might have some kind of use for these detestable paintings of evil habits. As if such fictions could ever leave a heart that rejected them in the same state of purity as a heart that had never known them! The novel as we conceive of it, however—as we have a few examples of it—is one of the most beautiful creations of the human mind, and one of the most influential on individual morality, which is what ultimately determines the morality of the public.

There is a very good reason why public opinion does not have enough respect for the writing of good novels, however. This is because novels are considered to be exclusively devoted to the portrayal of love—the most violent, universal, and true passion of them all, but also the passion which inspires no interest at any other time of life than youth, since youth is all it influences. We may well believe that all deep and tender feelings belong to the nature of love, and that hearts which have neither known nor pardoned love cannot feel enthusiasm in friendship, devotion in misery, worship of one's parents, passion for one's children. One can feel respect for one's duties, but no delight or self-surrender in their accomplishment, if one has not loved with all the strength of one's soul, ceasing to be one's self to live entirely in another. The destiny of women and the happiness of men who are not called upon to govern empires often depend for the rest of their lives on the role they gave to the influence of love in their youth. Nevertheless, when people reach a certain age, they completely forget the impression love made on them. Their character changes; they devote themselves to other goals, other passions; and these new interests are what we should extend the subjects of novels to include. A new career would then be open to authors who have the talent to paint all the emotions of the human heart, and are able to use their intimate knowledge of it to involve us. Ambition, pride, greed, vanity could be the primary topic of novels which would have situations as varied as those arising from love, and fresher plots. Will people object that such a tableau of men's passions exists in history, and that we should

4. Samuel Richardson (1689–1761) and Henry Fielding (1707–1754), English novelists.

look for it there? History does not reach the lives of private men, feelings and characters that do not result in public events. History does not act on you with sustained moral interest. Reality often fails to make an effect; and the commentary needed to make a lasting impression would stop the essential quick narrative pace, and give dramatic form to a work that should have a very different sort of merit. And the moral of history can never be completely clear. This may be because one cannot always show with any degree of certainty the inner feelings that punish the wicked in their prosperity and reward the virtuous in their misery, or perhaps because man's destiny is not completed in this life. Practical morality is founded on the advantages of virtue, but the reading of history does not always put it in the limelight.

Great historians (especially Tacitus)[5] do try to attach some moral to every event they relate, making us envy the dying Germanicus, and hate Tiberius at the pinnacle of his grandeur. But they can still portray only those feelings certified by facts. What stays with us from a reading of history is more likely to be the influence of talent, the brilliance of glory, the advantages of power, than the quiet, subtle, gentle morality which is the basis of individual happiness and the relationship between individuals. Everyone would think me ridiculous if I said I set no value on history, and that I preferred fictions—as if fictions did not arise from experience, and as if the delicate nuances shown in novels did not come from the philosophical results and mother-ideas presented by the great panorama of public events! However, the morality of history only exists in bulk. History gives constant results by means of the recurrence of a certain number of chances: its lessons apply to nations, not individuals. Its examples always fit nations, because if one considers them in a general way they are invariable; but it never explains the exceptions. These exceptions can seduce each man as an individual; the exceptional circumstances consecrated by history leave vast empty spaces into which the miseries and wrongs that make up most private destinies could easily fall. On the other hand, novels can paint characters and feeling with such force and detail that they make more of an impression of hatred for vice and love for virtue than any other kind of reading. The morality of novels belongs more to the development of the internal emotions of the soul than to the events they relate. We do not draw a useful lesson from whatever arbitrary circumstance the author invents as punishment for the crime; what leaves its indelible mark on us comes from the truthful rendition of the scenes, the gradual process or sequence of wrongdoing, the enthusiasm for sacrifices, the sympathy for misfortune. Everything is so true to life in such novels that we have no trouble persuading ourselves that everything could happen just this way—not past history, but often, it seems, the history of the future.

Novels give a false idea of mankind, it has been said. This is true of bad novels, as it is true of paintings which imitate nature badly. When novels are good, however, nothing gives such an intimate knowledge of the human heart as these portrayals of the various circumstances of private life and the impressions they inspire. Nothing gives so much play to reflection, which

5. Roman historian (ca. 55–ca. 120 C.E.). In *Annales* 2, Tacitus recounts the strains between Tiberius (42 B.C.E.–37 C.E.; emperor, 14 C.E.–37 C.E.) and his nephew Germanicus (15 B.C.E.–19 C.E.), whom he adopted but whose popularity he perceived as a threat; given command of the eastern provinces, Germanicus died (probably poisoned) in Syria.

finds much more to discover in details than in generalities. Memoirs would be able to do this if their only subjects were not, as in history, famous men and public events. If most men had the wit and good faith to give a truthful, clear account of what they had experienced in the course of their lives, novels would be useless—but even these sincere narratives would not have all the advantages of novels. We would still have to add a kind of dramatic effect to the truth; not deforming it, but condensing it to set it off. This is the art of the painter: far from distorting objects, it represents them in a way that makes them more immediately apprehended. Nature sometimes shows us things all on the same level, eliminating any contrasts; if we copy her too slavishly we become incapable of portraying her. The most truthful account is always an imitative truth: as a tableau, it demands a harmony of its own. However remarkable a true story may be for its nuances, feelings, and characters, it cannot interest us without the talent necessary for the composition of fiction. But despite our admiration for the genius that lets us penetrate the recesses of the human heart, it is impossible to bear all those minute details with which even the most famous novels are burdened. The author thinks they add to the picture's verisimilitude, blind to the fact that anything that slows down the interest destroys the only truth fiction has: the impression it produces. To put everything that happens in a room onstage is to destroy theatrical illusion completely. Novels have dramatic conventions also: the only thing necessary in an invention is what adds to the effect one is creating. If a glance, a movement, or an unnoticed circumstance helps paint a character or develop our understanding of a feeling, the simpler the means, the greater the merit in catching it—but a scrupulously detailed account of an ordinary event diminishes verisimilitude instead of increasing it. Thrown back on a positive notion of what is true by the kind of details that belong only to truth, you soon break out of the illusion, weary of being unable to find either the instruction of history or the interest of a novel.

The greatest power of fiction is its talent to touch us; almost all moral truths can be made tangible if they are shown in action. Virtue has so much influence on human happiness or misery that one can make most of life's situations depend on it. Some severe philosophers condemn all emotions, wanting moral authority to rule by a simple statement of moral duty. Nothing is less suited to human nature. Virtue must be brought to life if she is to fight the passions with any chance of winning; a sort of exaltation must be aroused for us to find any charm in sacrifice; misfortune must be embellished for us to prefer it to the great charm of guilty enticement; and the touching fictions which incite the soul to generous feelings make it unconsciously engage itself in a promise that it would be ashamed to retract in similar circumstances. But the more real power there is in fiction's talent for touching us, the more important it becomes to widen its influence to the passions of all ages, and the duties of all situations. The primary subject of novels is love, and characters who have nothing to do with it are present only as accessories. It would be possible to find a host of new subjects if one followed a different plan. *Tom Jones*[6] has the most general moral of any novel: love appears in it as only one of many means of showing the philosophical result.

6. *The History of Tom Jones, a Foundling* (1749), a novel by Fielding.

The real aim of *Tom Jones* is to show the uncertainty of judgments founded on appearances, proving the superiority of natural and what we may call involuntary virtues over reputations based on mere respect for external etiquette. And this is one of the most useful, most deservedly famous of all novels. *Caleb Williams*, by Mr. Godwin,[7] is a recent novel which, despite some tedious passages and oversights, seems to give a good idea of this inexhaustible genre. Love plays no part in this fiction; the only motives for the action are the hero's unbridled passion for the world's respect and Caleb's overpowering curiosity, leading him to discover whether or not Falkland deserves the esteem he enjoys. We read this story with all the absorption inspired by romantic interest and the reflection commanded by the most philosophical tableau.

Some successful fictions do give pictures of life unrelated to love: several *Moral Tales* of Marmontel, a few chapters of *Sentimental Journey*, various anecdotes from the *Spectator*[8] and other books on morality, some pieces taken from German literature, whose superiority is growing every day. There is still, however, no new Richardson devoting himself to paint men's other passions in a novel completely exploring the progress and consequences of these passions. The success of such a work would come from the truth of its characters, the force of its contrasts and the energy of its situations, rather than from that feeling which is so easy to paint, so quick to arouse interest, pleasing women by what it makes them remember even if it cannot attract them by the greatness or novelty of the scenes it presents. What beautiful things we would find in the Lovelace[9] of ambition! What philosophical developments, if we were eager to explain and analyze all the passions, as novels have already done for love! Let no one object that books on morality are enough to teach us a knowledge of our duties; such books cannot possibly go into all the nuances of delicacy, or detail the myriad resources of the passions. We can glean a morality purer and higher from novels than from any didactic work on virtue; didactic works are so dry that they have to be too indulgent. Maxims have to be generally applicable, so they never achieve that heroic delicacy we may offer as a model but cannot reasonably impose as a duty. Where is the moralist who could say: "If your whole family wants you to marry a detestable man, and you are prompted by their persecution to give a few signs of the most innocent interest to the man you find attractive, you are going to bring death and dishonor upon yourself"? This, however, is the plot of *Clarissa*; this is what we read with admiration, without a word of protest to the author who touches us and holds us captive. What moralist would claim that it is better to abandon oneself to deep despair, the sort of despair that threatens life and disturbs the mind, rather than marry the most virtuous man in the world if his religion is different from your own? Well, we need not approve of the superstitious opinions of *Clementina*,[1] but love struggling against a scruple of conscience and duty winning out over

7. William Godwin (1756–1836), English novelist and political theorist, married to MARY WOLLSTONECRAFT; *Caleb Williams* was published in 1794.

8. A periodical (1711–12) written by JOSEPH ADDISON and Richard Steele. Jean-François Marmontel (1723–1799), French author whose *Moral Tales* (1761–86) appeared first in a journal. *Sentimental Journey through England and France:* a 1768 narrative by Laurence Sterne.

9. The villain-hero who seduces the title character in Richardson's *Clarissa, or, The History of a Young Lady* (1747–48).

1. The Italian woman who renounces the eponymous hero of Richardson's *History of Sir Charles Grandison* (1753–54) [shortened translator's note].

passion are a sight that moves and touches even loose-principled people who would have rejected such a conclusion disdainfully if it had been a maxim preceding the tableau instead of an effect that followed it. In novels of a less sublime genre, there are so many subtle rules for women's conduct! We could support this opinion by quoting from masterpieces like *The Princess of Clèves, The Count of Comminge, Paul and Virginia, Cecilia*, most of the writings of Madame Riccoboni, *Caroline*, whose charm is felt by everyone, the touching episode of Caliste, the letters of Camilla,[2] in which the mistakes of a woman and their miserable consequences give a more moral and severe picture than the spectacle of virtue itself, and many other French, English, and German works. Novels have the right to offer the severest morality without revolting our hearts; they have captured feeling, the only thing that can successfully plead for indulgence. Pity for misfortune or interest in passion often win the struggle against books of morality, but good novels have the art of putting this emotion itself on their side and using it for their own ends.

There is still one serious objection to love stories: that they paint love in such a way as to arouse it, and that there are moments in life when this danger wins out over every kind of advantage. This drawback could not exist in novels about any other human passion, however. By recognizing the most fleeting symptoms of a dangerous inclination from the very beginning, one could turn oneself as well as others away from it. Ambition, pride, and avarice often exist without the least consciousness on the part of those they rule. Love feeds on the portrait of its own feelings, but the best way to fight the other passions is to make them be recognized. If the features, tricks, means, and results of these passions were as fully shown and popularized by novels as the history of love, society would have more trustworthy rules and more scrupulous principles about all the transactions of life. Even if purely philosophical writings could predict and detail all the nuances of actions, as do novels, dramatic morality would still have the great advantage of arousing indignant impulses, and exaltation of soul, a sweet melancholy—the various effects of fictional situations, and a sort of supplement to existence. This impression resembles the one we have of real facts we might have witnessed, but it is less distracting for the mind than the incoherent panorama of events around us, because it is always directed toward a single goal. Finally, there are men over whom duty has no influence, and who could still be preserved from crime by developing within them the ability to be moved. Characters capable of adopting humanity only with the help of such a faculty of emotion, the physical pleasure of the soul, would naturally not deserve much respect; nevertheless, if the effect of these touching fictions became widespread enough among the people, it might give us some assurance that we would no longer have in our country those beings whose character poses the most incomprehensible moral problem that has ever existed. The gradual steps from the known to the unknown stop well before we reach any understanding of the emotions which rules the executioners of France. Neither events nor books can have developed in them the least trace of humanity, the memory

2. All these works are novels. *The Princess of Clèves* is by Mme de La Fayette (1678); *The Count of Comminge* (1735) is by Mme de Tencin; *Paul and Virginia* (1787) is by Jacques-Henri Bernadin de Saint-Pierre; *Cecilia* (1782) and *Camilla* (1796) are by Fanny Burney; Marie-Jeanne Riccoboni (1713–1792) wrote a number of novels in the mid–18th century. *Caroline* is probably *Caroline de Litchfield* (1785), by Isabelle de Montolieu. Isabelle de Charrière, later [Benjamin] Constant's intimate friend, wrote *Caliste* (1787) [translator's note].

of a single sensation of pity, any mobility within the mind itself for them to remain capable of that constant cruelty, so foreign to all the impulses of nature—a cruelty which has given mankind its first limitless concept, the complete idea of crime.

There are writings whose principal merit is the eloquence of passion, such as the "Epistle of Abelard" by Pope, *Werther*, the *Portuguese Letters*, and especially *The New Héloïse*.[3] The aim of such works is often moral, but what remains with us more than anything else is the absolute power of the heart. We cannot classify such novels. Every century has one soul and one genius capable of achieving this—it cannot be a genre, it cannot be a goal. Who would want to proscribe these miracles of the word, these deep impressions which satisfy all the emotions of the passionate? Readers enthusiastic about such talent are very few in number; these works always do their admirers good. Let ardent, sensitive souls admire them; they cannot make their language understood by anyone else. The feelings that disturb such beings are rarely understood; constantly condemned, they would believe themselves alone in the world, they would soon hate their own nature for isolating them, if a few passionate, melancholy works did not make them hear a voice in the desert of life, letting them find in solitude a few rays of the happiness that escapes them in the middle of society. The pleasure of retreat is refreshing after the vain attempts of disappointed hope; far from this unfortunate creature, the entire universe may be in motion, but such eloquent, tender writing stays near him as his most faithful friend, the one who understands him best. Yes, a book must be right if it offers even one day's distraction from pain; it helps the best of men. Of course there are also sorrows that come from one's own character flaws, but so many of them come from superiority of mind or sensitivity of heart! and there are so many that would be easier to bear if one had fewer good qualities! I respect the suffering heart, even when it is unknown to me; I take pleasure in fictions whose only effect might be to comfort this heart by capturing its interest. In this life, which we pass through rather than feel, the distributor of the only real happiness of which human nature is capable would be someone who distracts man from himself and others, suspending the action of the passions by substituting independent pleasures for them—if the influence of his talent could only last.

1795

From On Literature Considered in Its Relationship to Social Institutions[1]

On Women Writers (2.4)

> Unhappiness is like the black mountain of Bember, at the edge of the blazing kingdom of Lahor. As long as you are climbing it, you

3. *Julie, or the New Heloise* (1761), an epistolary novel by Jean-Jacques Rousseau. "Epistle of Abelard": "Eloisa to Abelard" (1717), by ALEXANDER POPE (1688–1744); Héloïse fell in love with and secretly married her tutor, the 11th-century theologian Pierre Abélard (on discovery, she was sent to a convent and he became a monk). *Werther: The Sorrows of Young Werther* (1774), by Johann Wolfgang von Goethe. *The Portuguese Letters*: letters (published 1699) said to have been written by a Portuguese nun to her lover, a French officer, but probably written by their French "translator," Gabriel Joseph de Lavergne, vicomte de Guilleragues.

1. Translated by Vivian Folkenflik.

> see nothing ahead of you but sterile rocks; but once you are at the peak, heaven is at your head, and at your feet the kingdom of Cashmere.
>
> —*The Indian Hut*, by Bernadin de Saint-Pierre[2]

The existence of women in society is still uncertain in many ways. A desire to please excites their minds; reason recommends obscurity; and their triumphs and failures and equally and completely arbitrary.

I believe a day will come when philosophical legislators will give serious attention to the education of women, to the laws protecting them, to the duties which should be imposed on them, to the happiness which can be guaranteed them. At present, however, most women belong neither to the natural nor to the social order. What succeeds for some women is the ruin of others; their good points may do them harm, their faults may prove useful. One minute they are everything, the next nothing. Their destiny resembles that of freedmen under the emperors: if they try to gain any influence, this unofficial power is called criminal, while if they remain slaves their destiny is crushed.

It would no doubt be generally preferable for women to devote themselves entirely to the domestic virtues, but the peculiar thing about men's judgments of women is that they are much likelier to forgive women for neglecting these duties than for attracting attention by unusual talent. Men are quite willing to tolerate women's degradation of the heart, so long as it is accompanied by mediocrity of mind. The best behavior in the world can scarcely obtain forgiveness for real superiority.

I am now going to discuss the various causes of this peculiar phenomenon, beginning with the condition of women writers in monarchies, then in republics. I am interested in the differences these political situations make in the destinies of women who set their minds upon literary celebrity; I will then consider more generally the sort of happiness fame can promise these women.

In monarchies, women have ridicule to fear; in republics, hatred.

In a monarchy, the sense of the right and proper is so acute that any unusual act or impulse to change one's situation looks ridiculous right away. Anything your rank or position forces you to do finds a thousand admirers; everything you invent spontaneously, with no obligation, is judged severely and in advance. The jealousy natural to all men calms down only if you can apologize for success under cover of some obligation. Unless you cover fame itself with the excuse of your situation and practical interests, if people think your only motive is a need to distinguish yourself, you will annoy those whom ambition is leading in the same direction as yourself.

Men can always hide their vanity or their craving for applause under the appearance or reality of stronger, nobler passions; but women who write are generally assumed to be primarily inspired by a wish to show off their wit. As a result, the public is very reluctant to grant its approval, and the public's sense that women cannot do without this approval is precisely what tempts it to deny it. In every walk of life, as soon as a man sees your obvious need of him, his feelings for you almost always cool down. A woman publishing a

2. French naturalist and author (1737–1814), heavily influenced by the writings of Jean-Jacques Rousseau (1712–1788); his novel *The Indian Hut* was published in 1791. "Lahor" and "Cashmere," now better known as Lahore and Kashmir, are regions of northern India (in 1947 Lahore was divided between India and Pakistan).

book makes herself so dependent on public opinion that those who mete it out make her harshly aware of their power.

These general causes, acting more or less uniformly in all countries, are reinforced by various circumstances peculiar to the French monarchy. The spirit of chivalry, still lingering on in France, was opposed in some respects to the overeager cultivation of letters even by men; it must have aroused all the more dislike for women concentrating on literary studies and turning their thoughts away from their primary concern, the sentiments of the heart. The niceties of the code of honor might well make men averse from submitting themselves to the motley criticism attracted by publicity. How much more must they have disliked seeing the creatures entrusted to their protection—their wives, sisters, daughters—running the gauntlet of public criticism, or even giving the public the right to make a habit of talking about them!

Great talent could triumph over all these considerations, but it was still hard for women to bear reputations as authors nobly, simultaneously combining them with the independence of high rank and keeping up the dignity, grace, ease, and unself-consciousness that were supposed to distinguish their habitual style and manners.

Women were certainly allowed to sacrifice household occupations to a love of society and its pleasures; serious study, however, was condemned as pedantic. If from the very first moment one did not rise above the teasing which went on from all sides, this teasing would end by discouraging talent and poisoning the well of confidence and exaltation.

Some of these disadvantages are not found in republics, especially if one of the goals of the republic is the encouragement of enlightenment. It might perhaps be natural for literature to become women's portion in such a state, and for men to devote themselves entirely to higher philosophy.

The education of women has always followed the spirit of the constitutions established in free countries. In Sparta, women were accustomed to the exercises of war; in Rome, they were expected to have austere and patriotic virtues. If we want the moving principle of the French Republic to be the emulation of enlightenment and philosophy, it is only reasonable to encourage women to cultivate their minds, so that men can talk with them about ideas that would hold their interest.

Nevertheless, ever since the Revolution men have deemed it politically and morally useful to reduce women to a state of the most absurd mediocrity. They have addressed women only in a wretched language with no more delicacy than wit. Women have no longer any motive to develop their minds. This has been no improvement in manners or morality. By limiting the scope of ideas we have not succeeded in bringing back the simplicity of primitive life: the only result of less wit has been less delicacy, less respect for public opinion, fewer ways to endure solitude. And this applies to everything else in the current intellectual climate too: people invariably think that enlightenment is the cause of whatever is going wrong, and they want to make up for it by making reason go backward. Either morality is a false concept, or the more enlightened we are the more attached to morality we become.

If Frenchmen could give their wives all the virtues of Englishwomen, including retiring habits and a taste for solitude, they would do very well to prefer such virtues to the gifts of brilliant wit. All the French will manage to do this way, however, is to make their women read nothing, know nothing, and become incapable of carrying on a conversation with an interesting idea, or an apt expression, or eloquent language. Far from being kept at home by this happy ignorance, Frenchwomen unable to direct their children's education would become less fond of them. Society would become more necessary to these women—and also more dangerous, because no one could talk to them of anything but love, and this love would not even have the delicacy that can stand in for morality.

If such an attempt to make women completely insipid and frivolous ever succeeded, there would be several important losses to national morality and happiness. Women would have fewer ways to calm men's furious passions. They would no longer have any useful influence over opinion—and women are the ones at the heart of everything relating to humanity, generosity, delicacy. Women are the only human beings outside the realm of political interest and the career of ambition, able to pour scorn on base actions, point out ingratitude, and honor even disgrace if that disgrace is caused by noble sentiments. The opinion of society would no longer have any power over men's actions at all if there were no women left in France enlightened enough to make their judgments count, and imposing enough to inspire genuine respect.

I firmly believe that under the ancien régime, when opinion exerted such wholesome authority, this authority was the work of women distinguished by character and wit. Their eloquence was often quoted when they were inspired by some generous scheme or defending the unfortunate; if the expression of some sentiment demanded courage because it would offend those in power.

These are the same women who gave the strongest possible proofs of devotion and energy during the course of the Revolution.

Men in France will never be republican enough to manage without the independence and pride that comes naturally to women. Women may indeed have had too much influence on public affairs under the ancien régime; but they are no less dangerous when bereft of enlightenment, and therefore of reason. Their influence then turns to an inordinate craving for luxury, undiscerning choices, indelicate recommendations. Such women debase the men they love, instead of exalting them. And is the state the better off for it? Should the very limited risk of meeting a woman whose superiority is out of line with the destiny of her sex deprive the republic of France's reputation for the art of pleasing and living in society? Without any women, society can be neither agreeable nor amusing; with women bereft of wit, or the kind of conversational grace which requires the best education, society is spoiled rather than embellished. Such women introduce a kind of idiotic chatter and cliquish gossip into the conversation, alienating all the superior men and reducing brilliant Parisian gatherings to young men with nothing to do and young women with nothing to say.

We can find disadvantages to everything in life. There are probably disadvantages to women's superiority—and to men's; to the vanity of clever people; to the ambition of heroes; to the imprudence of kind hearts, the irritability of independent minds, the recklessness of courage, and so forth. But does that mean we should use all our energy to fight natural gifts, and direct our social institutions toward humbling our abilities? It is hardly as if there were some guarantee that such degradation would promote familial or governmental authority. Women without the wit for conversation or writing are usually just that much more skillful at escaping their duties. Unenlightened countries may not understand how to be free, but they are able to change their masters with some frequency.

Enlightening, teaching, and perfecting women together with men on the national and individual level: this must be the secret for the achievement of every reasonable goal, as well as the establishment of any permanent social or political relationships.

The only reason to fear women's wit would be some sort of scrupulous anxiety about their happiness. And indeed, by developing their rational minds one might well be enlightening them as to the misfortunes often connected with their fate; but that same reasoning would apply to the effect of enlightenment on the happiness of the human race in general, a question which seems to me to have been decided once and for all.

If the situation of women in civil society is so imperfect, what we must work toward is the improvement of their lot, not the degradation of their minds. For women to pay attention to the development of mind and reason would promote both enlightenment and the happiness of society in general. The cultivated education they deserve could have only one really unfortunate result: if some few of them were to acquire abilities distinguished enough to make them hungry for glory. Even this risk, however, would do society no harm, and would only be unfortunate for the very limited number of women whom nature might dedicate to the torture of useless superiority.

And if there were to be some woman seduced by intellectual celebrity and insistent on achieving it! How easy it would be to divert her, if she were caught in time! She could be shown the dreadful destiny to which she was on the verge of committing herself. Examine the social order, she would be told; you will soon see it up in arms against any woman trying to raise herself to the height of masculine reputation.

As soon as any woman is pointed out as a person of distinction, the general public is prejudiced against her. The common people judge according to a few common rules which can be followed without taking any risks. Whatever goes beyond the habitual immediately offends people who consider daily routine the safeguard of mediocrity. A superior man is enough to startle them; a superior woman, straying even farther from the beaten track, must surprise and annoy them even more. A distinguished man almost always has some important career as his field of action, so his talents may turn out to be useful to the interests of even those who least value the delights of the mind. The man of genius may become a man of power, so envious and silly people humor him. But a clever woman is only called upon to offer them new ideas and lofty sentiments, about which they could not care less; her celebrity seems to them much ado about nothing.

Even glory can be a source of reproach to a woman, because it contrasts with her natural destiny. Strict virtue condemns the celebrity even of something which is good in itself, because it damages the perfection of modesty. Men of wit are so astounded by the existence of women rivals that they cannot judge them with either an adversary's generosity or a protector's indulgence. This is a new kind of combat, in which men follow the laws of neither kindness nor honor.

Suppose, as a crowning misfortune, a woman were to acquire celebrity in a time of political dissension. People would think her influence unbounded, even if she had no influence at all; accuse her of all her friends' actions; and hate her for everything she loved. It is far preferable to attack a defenseless target than a dangerous one.

Nothing lends itself more quickly to vague assumptions than the dubious life of a woman with a famous name and an obscure career. An empty-witted man may inspire ridicule, a man of bad character may drop under the weight of contempt, a mediocre man may be cast aside—but everyone would much rather attack the unknown power they call a woman. When the plans of the ancients did not work out, they used to convince themselves that fate had thwarted them. Our modern vanity also prefers to attribute its failures to secret causes instead of to itself; in time of need, what stands in for fatality is the supposed power of famous women.

Women have no way to show the truth, no way to throw light on their lives. The public hears the lie; only their intimate friends can judge the truth. What real way is there for a woman to disprove slanderous accusations? A man who had been slandered lets his actions answer the universe, saying, "My life is a witness: it too must be heard."[3] But where can a woman find any such witness? A few private virtues, hidden favors, feelings locked into the narrow circle of her situation, writings which may make her known in places where she does not live, in times when she will no longer exist.

A man can refute calumny in his work itself, but self-defense is an additional handicap for women. For a woman to justify herself is a new topic for gossip. Women feel there is something pure and delicate in their nature, quickly withered by the very gaze of the public. Wit, talent, passion in the soul may make them emerge from this mist which should always be surrounding them, but they will always yearn for it as their true refuge.

However distinguished women may be, the sight of ill will makes them tremble. Courageous in misfortune, they are cowards against dislike; thought uplifts them, but their character is still weak and sensitive. Most women whose superior abilities make them want renown are like Erminia dressed in armor.[4] Warriors see the helmet, the lance, the bright plume of feathers, and think they are up against strength, so they attack with violence; with the very first blows, they have struck at the heart.

Such injustices can not only spoil a woman's happiness and peace of mind, but also alienate even the most important objects of her affection. Who can be sure that a libelous portrayal will not strike at the truth of memory? Who knows whether or not slanderers, having wreaked havoc with life, will rob death itself of the tender, regretful feelings that should be associated with the memory of a beloved woman?

So far I have portrayed only the unfairness of men: but what about the threat of injustice from other women? Do not women secretly arouse the malevolence of men? Do women ever form an alliance with a famous woman, sustaining her, defending her, supporting her faltering steps?

And that is still not all. Public opinion seems to release men from every duty toward a recognizably superior woman. Men can be ungrateful to her, unfaithful, even wicked, without making public opinion responsible for

3. No source has been identified; but the quoted sentence is written in the French classical alexandrine (12-syllable) meter.

4. In Tasso's *Jerusalem Delivered* (1581), the princess Erminia wears borrowed armor to seek her love Tancred in the Christian camp [translator's note].

avenging her. "Is she not an extraordinary woman?" That says it all; she is abandoned to her own strength, and left to struggle with misery. She lacks both the sympathy inspired by a woman and the power protecting a man. Like the pariahs of India,[5] such a woman parades her peculiar existence among classes she cannot belong to, which consider her as destined to exist on her own, the object of curiosity and perhaps a little envy: what she deserves, in fact, is pity.

1800

5. Those who are at the bottom or outside of the traditional caste system of India (the words in the epigraph from *The Indian Hut* are spoken by a pariah).

FRIEDRICH SCHLEIERMACHER
1768–1834

German philosopher, classical philologist, and leading liberal Protestant theologian, Friedrich Schleiermacher is best known as a founder of modern general hermeneutics: that is, the art of understanding and interpreting discourse through systematic procedures. His most important contribution to the history of theory and criticism is arguably his "Outline of the 1819 Lectures," a fragmentary document produced in midcareer and published from handwritten notes after his death. In this pioneering depiction of the processes of textual understanding, Schleiermacher argued that to understand a text fully one must understand simultaneously the entire thought of a writer as well as the whole language he or she employs, keeping in mind that the language modifies the author's thought just as the author's thought modifies the language. The two major tasks of textual interpretation, according to Schleiermacher, are to comprehend the language and historical culture of a text (grammatical interpretation) and to reconstruct an author's purpose (psychological or "technical" interpretation). With these insights Schleiermacher laid the foundation of modern hermeneutics, preparing the way for such important yet widely divergent twentieth-century theorists of interpretation as MARTIN HEIDEGGER and E. D. HIRSCH JR.

Schleiermacher was born in Breslau, Prussia, and studied at two Moravian Brethren schools and at the University of Halle. During the late 1790s he began his celebrated translation into German of almost all of Plato's works (still in print); he was active in the Berlin circle of Romanticists, being a close associate and briefly roommate of Friedrich Schlegel, to whose vanguard journal, *Athenaeum*, he was an early contributor. He served as chaplain and professor of theology and philosophy at Halle between 1804 and 1806, later taking a position at the University of Berlin (1810–34), which he co-founded. Schleiermacher regularly preached at Trinity Church in Berlin, advocating the right of union for Reformed and Lutheran groups in Prussia, freedom of the church from the state, shorter working hours, social insurance, and women's rights.

Schleiermacher's theology reflects the influence of Romanticism and Moravian pietism, especially in his two most famous works, *On Religion: Speeches to Its Cultured Despisers* (1799) and *The Christian Faith* (1821–22), which argue that religion is an intuitive feeling for and dependence on the infinite realm, not a set of moral or metaphysical principles; religion needed no external justification. It was to convince his fellow German Romantics that they were not as far from religion as they believed that he undertook the first book, a confession of faith that gained him a national reputation overnight. Today he is often regarded as one of the most significant Protestant theologians since Luther. In his time his influence was wide, reaching such figures as RALPH WALDO EMERSON, who also devalued doctrine in favor of intuitive dependence on the infinite.

His interest in understanding the Bible led to Schleiermacher's concern with hermeneutics. In his "Outline of the 1819 Lectures," our selection, he expands on his basic distinction between grammatical and psychological interpretation, noting that the latter involves two distinct methods. Using the first, divinatory interpretation, one seeks to identify intuitively with the author; Schleiermacher sees this as representing a feminine dimension of our knowledge of human nature. (This mode of interpretation echoes his notions about religion as an intuitive feeling.) Using the second method, comparative interpretation, one works to understand a text as a type or historical genre; it is purportedly a masculine force.

Both psychological and grammatical interpretation primarily seek to isolate the text's central idea, procedure, or motivating principle in light of which all textual details can be gauged. Artful interpretation requires such centering and multiple rigorous readings. But problems do arise, some of which are avoidable and some not. Interpretation necessarily gets caught up in various circularities. Readers early in the process intuit the meaning of a text, which then predetermines the directions of meaning. This is one version of the celebrated "hermeneutic circle" of interpretation, identified by Schleiermacher and later explored by leading hermeneuticists, especially Heidegger and Hans-Georg Gadamer (b. 1900). To understand the whole text, Schleiermacher points out, one must understand each part; but to understand each part, one must understand the whole. He expands this circle by requiring that to understand an individual text, an interpreter must understand the complete historical context and vocabulary of a language—foreknowledge derived paradoxically from individual texts.

Schleiermacher catalogues several types of avoidable misunderstanding, which result from bias, mistaking a text's meaning, or misjudging the value of a segment of text. (Under the influence of FRIEDRICH NIETZSCHE and SIGMUND FREUD, contemporary critics such as HAROLD BLOOM and PAUL DE MAN, unlike Schleiermacher, have come to conceive "misunderstanding" as an ineradicable, productive element of all understanding.) Moreover, for Schleiermacher allegorical interpretation—that is, reading symbolically—risks erroneously discovering everything in everything, unless the text itself legitimates the approach with an allusion appropriate to both the contextual and the central textual ideas. Finally, historical interpretation can run into trouble by construing an ancient text in terms of modern conditions instead of uncovering its writer's relationship to his or her milieu and language.

Schleiermacher posits two broad categories of texts. "Objective texts" such as histories and epics require a minimum of psychological interpretation and a maximum of grammatical interpretation, whereas "subjective texts" such as personal letters and lyrics call for more psychological than grammatical interpretation. The goal of hermeneutics in either case is—as he famously declared—"to understand the discourse just as well and even better than its creator." We have no way of knowing the creator's purpose other than through reconstruction, but "No individual inspection of a work ever exhausts its meaning."

Helpfully, Schleiermacher outlines four types of positive hermeneutical reconstruction. There are two types of grammatical or objective reconstruction—historical and divinatory—and two types of psychological or subjective reconstruction—historical and divinatory. In brief, objective historical reconstruction examines how language shapes the text, objective divinatory reconstruction analyzes how the text itself developed that language, subjective historical reconstruction explores the text as the product of the author's soul, and subjective divinatory reconstruction attempts to determine how the process of writing affects the writer's inner thoughts. Interpretation for Schleiermacher is at once psychological and grammatical, intuitive and comparative. It is an art of understanding, not just explaining, the act of a living, intuiting person gifted with foreknowledge and experience of life as well as linguistic and cultural competence—an art that always requires a leap into the midst of textual complexities and circularities.

Earlier German hermeneutics, as practiced in the contexts of theology, law, and literature, focused narrowly on philology, particularly its penchant for interpretive procedures and rules of validation. Schleiermacher here broadens its scope toward a phenomenological philosophy attentive to the roles of intuition, understanding, and foreknowledge in the lived world of human beings. This shift was variously amplified by his greatest successors, Wilhelm Dilthey (1833–1911), Heidegger, and Gadamer. Schleiermacher is generally credited with grounding hermeneutics in human understanding, with according language a foundational role in interpretation, and with highlighting the interdependence of mind and medium, subject and object, divination and comparison.

However much successors and followers admire and build on Schleiermacher's work, they find problems with his hermeneutic theory. In the various editions of his *Truth and Method—Outline for a Philosophical Hermeneutics* (1960), Gadamer characterizes the principle of divination as hopelessly Romantic, and he faults Schleiermacher for not taking into account the historical context and prejudices of the interpreter, which, he shrewdly argues, are essential constituents of understanding. Intuition assumes uniform human experience; prejudices arise in a world of antagonistic standpoints. And the leading modern French hermeneuticist, Paul Ricoeur (b. 1913), contends that Schleiermacher does not sufficiently distinguish between the author and the ideas governing the work; Ricoeur sees the latter as the true object of interpretation. Schleiermacher vacillates, too, on what constitutes the "text" (or object of inquiry)—it is sometimes the author's oeuvre (complete works), sometimes a particular work, and sometimes a genre or cultural archive.

Various critics, moreover, have noted Schleiermacher's tendency, especially in his late works, to "psychologize": that is, to pass through language to the supposed prelinguistic mental processes and intentions of the author, forgetting that grammar and psychology are interdependent. When this happens, Schleiermacher's hermeneutics turns into psychological reconstruction, which is the direction taken by Dilthey. A similar path is staked out by E. D. Hirsch Jr., who, however, turns to interpretative reconstruction as a way to rectify the rampant critical subjectivism and relativism that he believes plague contemporary literary criticism, including much hermeneutics.

In spite of criticisms, Schleiermacher's contributions to hermeneutics should not be underestimated. His psychological notion of divination enabled him to explicitly correct and complement earlier Enlightenment concepts of rationality. He usefully jettisoned the old rigid separations of hermeneutics into specialized biblical, legal, and literary kinds, developing a self-conscious project for a general hermeneutics. Like his important contemporaries FRIEDRICH SCHILLER and SAMUEL TAYLOR COLERIDGE, he attempted to reconcile well-entrenched inherited philosophical oppositions, especially subject/object, finite/infinite, individual/social, and psychology/grammar. He construed understanding as an act of dialogue, not verification. Lastly, he pictured the act of interpretation as antiauthoritarian and nonhierarchical, in keeping with the radical social forces of his time (committed to toppling monarchical regimes and feudal class arrangements, manifested especially in the French Revolution) and with the dynamics of early democracy and capitalism. All these elements, which marked Schleiermacher historically as a Romantic, significantly influenced the work of later philosophical hermeneutics.

BIBLIOGRAPHY

Schleiermacher's collected works, *Sämtliche Werke* (1835–64), mainly lecture notes, were published after his death in thirty-one volumes, including theological writings, sermons, and philosophical and miscellaneous texts, plus four volumes of letters (1858–63). Starting in the early 1980s his collected writings and correspondence began to appear in a projected forty-volume German edition, *Kritische Gesamtausgabe*, with approximately a dozen volumes reaching print in the first two decades. His manuscripts on interpretation theory were published posthumously and first translated into English by James Duke and Jack Forstman as *Hermeneutics: The Handwritten Manuscripts* (1977), based on the German edition by Heinz Kimmerle (1959; 2d ed., 1974), and then more fully in a new translation, *Hermeneutics and Criticism and Other Writings*, edited and translated by Andrew Bowie (1998).

Biographical information is available in *The Life of Schleiermacher as Unfolded in His Autobiography and Letters* (2 vols., 1860), translated by Frederica Rowan; Wilhelm Dilthey's monumental but unfinished *Das Leben Schleiermachers* (1870); Friedrich Wilhelm Kantzenbach's *Friedrich Daniel Ernst Schleiermacher in Selbstzeugnissen und Bilddokumenten* (1967); and Martin Redeker's spiritually sympathetic intellectual biography, *Schleiermacher: Life and Thought* (1968; trans. 1973).

Informative texts about Schleiermacher's work include Richard B. Brandt's *Philosophy of Schleiermacher: The Development of His Theory of Scientific and Religious Knowledge* (1941); Richard E. Palmer's valuable introduction, *Hermeneutics: Interpretation Theory in Schleiermacher, Dilthey, Heidegger, and Gadamer* (1969); Manfred Frank's landmark reassessment of Schleiermacher's hermeneutics in *Das individuelle Allgemeine: Textstrukturierung und -interpretation nach Schleiermacher* (1977); Tilottama Rajan's contemporary contextualizing in *The Supplement of Reading: Figures of Understanding in Romantic Theory and Practice* (1990); Julie Ellison's innovative feminist exegesis and critique of Schleiermacher's hermeneutics in *Delicate Subjects: Romanticism, Gender, and the Ethics of Understanding* (1990); the cogent introduction in Jean Grondin's *Introduction to Philosophical Hermeneutics* (1994); and Andrew Bowie's chapter factoring in the groundbreaking recent work of Manfred Frank in *From Romanticism to Critical Theory: The Philosophy of German Literary Theory* (1997). Terrence Tice's *Schleiermacher Bibliography* (1966) contains almost 2,000 items with annotations, and another 1,250 were added to his *Schleiermacher Bibliography (1784–1984): Updating and Commentary* (1985).

From Hermeneutics

From *Outline of the 1819 Lectures*[1]

INTRODUCTION[2]

1. Hermeneutics as the art of understanding does not yet exist in general; rather, only various specialized hermeneutics exist.

1. [We speak of] only the art of understanding, not the exposition of the understanding. The latter would only be a specialized part of the art of

1. Edited and translated by Jan Wojcik and Roland Haas, who occasionally insert the original German or explanatory words or phrases in brackets.

2. The Outline consists of an "Introduction," "First Part: The Grammatical Exposition," and "Second Part: The Technical (or Psychological) Interpretation." The headings are somewhat misleading. The "Introduction" gives a systematic exposition of principles for analyzing the language and psychological manifestations of a literary text. The "First Part" elaborates the principles for the

speaking and writing that could only be dependent on the general principles of hermeneutics.

2. This refers as well to difficult points in foreign-language texts. In reading them, one more often presumes familiarity with the subject matter and the language. When one is familiar with both, the distinction between them becomes difficult to make because one has perhaps not understood properly the more apparent. Only an artistic understanding consistently grasps the discourse [*Reden*] of a text [*Schrift*].[3]

3. Usually one supposes that one could rely on a healthy knowledge of human nature for formulating the general principles of interpretation. But then there is the danger that one would also tend to rely on a healthy feeling about the exceptional qualities of a text in determining what they meant.

2. It is very difficult to determine the exact nature of a general hermeneutics.

1. For a long time it was handled as a supplement to logic, but as one had to give up all logical tenets in its practice, this had to cease. The philosopher has no inclination to establish a theory about hermeneutics because he believes that it is more important to be understood than to understand.

2. Philology[4] has made positive contributions throughout history. But its method of hermeneutics is simply to aggregate observations.

3. [Hermeneutics is] the art of relating discourse [*Reden*] and understanding [*Verstehen*] to each other; discourse, however, being on the outer sphere of thought, requires that one must think of hermeneutics as an art, and thus as philosophical.

1. Thus the art of exposition depends on their composition. They are mutually dependent to the point that where discourse is without art, so is the understanding of it.

4. Discourse is the mediation of shareable thought. As a result both rhetoric and hermeneutics share a common relationship to the dialectic.[5]

1. Discourse is of course also a mediation of thought among individuals. Thought becomes complete only through interior discourse, and in this respect discourse could be considered manifested thought. But where the thinker thinks original thoughts, he himself requires the art of discourse to transform them into expressions that afterwards require exposition [*Auslegung*].

2. The unity of hermeneutics and rhetoric results from the fact that every act of understanding is the obverse of an act of discourse, in that one must come to grasp the thought which was at the base of the discourse.

---

analysis of language; the "Second Part" extends the "Introduction" in describing how the two parts of interpretation work together in the "divination" of a text. We limit our translation to the "Introduction" and the "Second Part" which comprise the heart of Schleiermacher's hermeneutical principles. We have referred to the marginal notes Schleiermacher added to the manuscript in 1828 only when they clarified ambiguities in the text [translators' note].

3. Discourse (*Reden*) is Schleiermacher's term for the discursive sense of a text, shaped by the particular language the author uses to express his inner thoughts (see 4–6). Here he makes a distinction between the literal meaning of a text (*Schrift*) and the discursive meaning (*Reden*) that is most obvious when one reads a somewhat unfamiliar foreign language (see 14.2) [translators' note].

4. The scholarly discipline dedicated to the historical understanding of foreign cultures through linguistic and comparative analysis of texts.

5. That part of logic concerned with thinking, notably thinking embodied in discourse.

3. The dependence of both on the dialectic results from the fact that all development of knowledge is dependent on both discourse and understanding.

5. As every discourse has a two-part reference, to the whole language and to the entire thought of its creator, so all understanding of speech consists of two elements [*Momenten*]—understanding the speech as it derives from the language and as it derives from the mind of the thinker.

1. Every speech derives from a given language. One can also turn this around and say that originally and continuously language only comes into being through discourse; at any rate, communication presupposes the accessibility of the language; that is, a shared knowledge of the same. When something comes between unmediated discourse and communication, the art of discourse begins, for one must take into consideration the possibility that the listener might find something strange in someone else's use of language.

2. Every discourse depends on earlier thought. One can also turn this around, of course, but in relation to communication it remains true, since the art of understanding only has to do with progressive thinking.

3. It follows that every person is on one hand a locus in which a given language is formed after an individual fashion and, on the other, a speaker who is only able to be understood within the totality of the language. In the same way, he is also a constantly developing spirit, while his discourse remains an object within the context of other intellection.

6. Understanding is only an interaction of these two elements.

1. Discourse can only be understood as a fact of the spirit if it is understood as a characteristic of the language, because the innateness of the language modifies the spirit.

2. It can also only be understood as a modification of the language if it is understood as a fact of the spirit, because all influences of individuals on the language are manifested through discourse.

7. Both stand completely equal, and one could only with injustice claim that the grammatical interpretation is the inferior and the psychological the superior.

1. The psychological is the superior only if one views language as the means by which the individual communicates his thoughts; the grammatical is then merely a cleaning away of temporary difficulties.

2. The grammatical is the superior if one views language as stipulating the thinking of all individuals and the individual's discourse only as a locus at which the language manifests itself.

3. Only by means of such a reciprocity could one find both to be completely similar.

8. The essential hermeneutical task is to handle every part in such a way that the handling of the other parts will produce no change in the results, or, in other words, every part must be handled as a discrete unit with equal respect paid to all other parts.

1. This reciprocity is important even if one part predominates over the other according to what was said in paragraph six.

2. But each is only complete if it makes the other redundant and contributes to construing the other, because indeed language [*Sprache*] can only be learned inasmuch as its discourse [*Rede*] can be understood; and in the same way, the inner cohesion of humanity can only be understood as it manifests itself externally through its discourse.

9. Exposition [*Auslegung*] is an art.

1. Every part stands by itself. Every composition is a finite certainty out of the infinite uncertainty. Language is an infinite because every element can be determined in a specific manner only through the other elements. And this is also true for the psychological part because every perspective of an individual is infinite; and the outside influences on people extend into the disappearing horizon. A composition composed of such elements cannot be defined by rules, which carry with them the security of their application.

2. Should the grammatical part be considered by itself, one would need in some cases a complete knowledge of the language, or, in others, a complete knowledge of the person. As neither can ever be complete, one must go from one to the other, and it is not possible to give any rules as to how this should be done.

10. The successful performance of the art depends on a linguistic talent and a talent for assessing individual human nature.

1. By the first point we do not mean the facility for learning foreign languages—the difference between the mother tongue and a foreign language does not come into consideration here for the time being; rather, a sense for the contemporaneity of a language, for analogy, difference, etc. One could mean by this that rhetoric and hermeneutics must always be together. Just as hermeneutics requires other talents, so also does rhetoric, if not always the same ones. The linguistic talent, at any rate, is shared, even if the hermeneutical method develops it differently than the rhetorical method does.

2. The knowledge of human nature is here the superior of those subjective elements in the development of discourse. No less importantly, hermeneutics and artistic human presentation are always together. But a great number of hermeneutical mistakes are based on the deficiency of linguistic talent, or in its faulty application.

3. Inasmuch as these talents are generally given by nature, so hermeneutics is a commonsense endeavor. Inasmuch as a person is missing one talent, he is crippled, and the other talents can only serve to help him adjudicate about that which all together would have permitted him to know directly.

11. Not all discourse is on an equal footing for exposition. Certain discourses have no value for it, others an absolute value; the majority lie between these two points.

1. Something of no value might excite no interest as an entity, but would still be important in the language as a reiteration which language requires for the preservation of its continuity. But that which repeats only already available things is worth nothing in itself. Like talking about the

weather. Alone, this is not an absolute nothing, only minimal. For it developed itself in the same way as significant things.

2. When the grammatical aspect predominates in a work, even the most imaginative, we call it classical. When the psychological aspect predominates, we call it original. And, of course, one part could absolutely dominate the other only if the author was an absolute genius.

3. To be classical, a work must be more than transitory; it must determine subsequent production. No less so the original. And even the best work cannot be free from influence.

12. When both aspects of interpretation—the analysis of the grammatical and the psychological part of a text—are used equally throughout, they are nevertheless always used in different proportions.

1. This follows from the fact that something of grammatical insignificance does not necessarily have to be of psychological insignificance, and vice versa; and insignificancy in one does not imply insignificancy in the other.

2. A minimum of psychological interpretation is needed with a predominately objective subject. [To this belongs] pure history, especially of specific individuals, as comprehensive studies tend more to draw on subjective conclusions; also epics, commercial discussions which want to become history, and strictly didactic writings of every kind. The interpreter's subjectivity should not enter the exposition; rather, it should be affected by the exposition. A minimum of grammatical interpretation accompanies a maximum of psychological in the exposition of personal letters, especially when they transmit didactic advice or historical information. (Lyrics or polemics too?)

13. There is no other diversity in the methods of exposition aside from those cited above.

1. As an example, we can take the wonderful perspective which comes from the argument over the historical exposition of the New Testament, based on the question whether there are special modes of interpretation reserved for it alone. In this debate the assertion of the historical school is the only correct one, that the New Testament authors are products of their age. The only danger in their reasoning is their tendency to overlook the power of Christianity to create new concepts and forms of expression; they tend to explain everything in light of available concepts and forms. To correct the historical style of interpretation one has to resist this one-sidedness. Correct interpretation requires a relationship of the grammatical and psychological interpretation, since new concepts can arise out of new emotional experiences.

2. One would also err if one thought of a historical interpretation as simply a retrospective view of the textual events. One must keep in mind that what was written was often written in a different day and age from the one in which the interpreter lives; it is the primary task of interpretation not to understand an ancient text in view of modern thinking, but to rediscover the original relationship between the writer and his audience.

3. The Allegorical Interpretation. First of all, it is not an interpretation of an allegory, where the only purpose is to understand the figurative mean-

ing without reference to whether there is truth at the base of it or not. Examples of allegories would be the parable of the sower, or the story of the rich man.[6] Rather, allegorical interpretation begins with a presupposition that the meaning is lacking in the immediate context, and so one needs to supply a figurative one. With this supposition one is unsatisfied with the general principle that every speech can have only one grammatical meaning. The dissatisfaction arises, perhaps, from the correct assessment that an allusion in a text does point to a second meaning; one who does not comprehend it could completely follow the whole context, but would still be missing one meaning situated within the discourse. The danger is that one could find an allusion which is not situated within the discourse. Then one would dissect the discourse improperly. The test for a proper allusion is this: to see whether it seems entwined as one of the contextual ideas within the main line of thought, to assess whether the explicit thoughts inspire the implicit. But the contextual ideas are not therewith to be considered merely individual and insignificant. Rather, just as the whole world is made up of many men, each idea contributes to its whole sense, even if it appears only as its dark shadow.

There is, after all, a parallelism in many various lines of thought, so that something could inspire something else; for example, there is parallelism between the physical and ethical, and between the musical and the visual arts. One should be careful, however, to detect whether there are any indications for the figurative expressions one seems to detect. The allegorical interpretations which have been made without such indication, especially in traditional interpretations of Homer and the Bible, all depend on a special assumption. This is that the books of Homer[7] and the Old Testament are special compendiums, the Old Testament above all, which contains all wisdom in some form or another. Along with this, both of them have appeared to have a mystical content compounded of sententious philosophy on the one hand and history on the other.

With myths, however, no technical interpretation is possible, since one cannot focus on an individual text[8] and alternatively compare the literal and the figurative meaning. There is certainly a different situation regarding the New Testament which leads to two kinds of blunders. First, its association with the Old Testament encourages the use of the same methods often associated with the Old Testament interpretation. Second, the New Testament interpreters tend more than their Old Testament counterparts to view the Holy Spirit as the book's author. But the Holy Spirit cannot be thought of as a temporally contingent and characteristic consciousness. From this false view springs the inclination to find everything foreshadowed everywhere. Common sense, or precise instructions on how texts should be read, can protect texts from this inclination, but isolated passages which seem to be unmeaningful in themselves seem to encourage it.

4. Here the question occasionally intrudes upon us, whether the holy books of the Holy Spirit must be handled differently than others. We must not be concerned with dogmatic decisions about inspiration, since they themselves derive from interpretation. We must not distinguish between the

6. Both in the New Testament: for the sower, see Matthew 13.1–9, 18–23; for the rich man, see Luke 16.19–31.

7. The *Iliad* and the *Odyssey* (ca. 8th c. B.C.E.), each divided into 24 books.

8. Myths have no single author and no single established text; therefore technical (psychological) interpretation is impossible.

preaching and the writing of the apostles, since their future church had to be built on the preaching. And it follows from this that we must not believe that the whole of Christianity directly developed from the writings, since they are all aimed at specific communities and could also not have been understood by subsequent readers if they had not been understood by the original audience. Each community simply sought out the specific characteristics of the Jesus story according to its own given particular focus on the many details. Therefore, we must expose it to the same method and consider that even if the authors were no more than dead tools, still the Holy Spirit could only have spoken through them as they themselves would have spoken.

5. The most dangerous deviation from this principle is encouraged by the cabalistic[9] style of exposition which directs its endeavors to find everything in everything. Only their interpretive endeavors which respect the diversity which results from the various relationships of both constructed parts can rightfully be called exposition.

14. The difference between artful and crude exposition has nothing to do with whether the work is familiar or strange, or with the discourse or the text, but solely with whether one wants to understand certain things exactly or not.

1. If it were only foreign and old texts that needed the art, the original readers would not have needed it, and the art would then depend on the differences between them and us. This difference must first be resolved, of course, through a knowledge of language and history; the exposition begins only after a successful identification of the text's original meaning. The difference between interpreting an old foreign text and a local contemporary one is only that with the old text the process of discovering its relevance to its milieu cannot completely precede the identification of its meaning; rather, both must be integrated from the beginning.

2. The text [*Schrift*] is not always the focus of attention either. Otherwise the art would only become necessary through the difference between text and discourse; that is to say, by the absence of the living voice and by the inaccessibility of other personal influences. These things, however, require exposition themselves, while they always remain somewhat nebulous. A living voice can certainly facilitate understanding a great deal, but even the writer must take into consideration that writing is not the same as speaking. If it were, then the art of exposition would be superfluous, which is, of course, not the case. Consequently, the need for exposition depends on the difference between written and spoken discourse, when the latter does not accompany the former.

3. Thus, when discourse and text behave so that no other difference remains between them save the one indicated, it follows that the artfully correct exposition has no other goal than that which we have in hearing every common spoken discourse.

15. The careless practice of the art results from the fact that understanding is pursued in the light of a negative goal: that misunderstanding should be avoided.

9. Esoteric, mystical.

1. Careless interpretation tends to limit its understanding to obtaining certain easy-to-attain goals.

2. But even it must avail itself of the art in difficult cases; and thus hermeneutics can even arise from the artless practice. But since it only sees difficulties as isolated problems, it becomes an aggregate of observations. And for the same reason tends to consider itself a specialized hermeneutics because it brings special methods to the solving of difficult problems. This is how the theological, the juristic, and the philological methods originated, and what they consider to be their special purposes.

3. The basis for their view is the peculiarity of their special languages and the peculiar manner in which their speakers communicate to their hearers.

16. Strict interpretation begins with misunderstanding and searches out a precise understanding.

1. This results from its beginning with an assumption about what the meaning is that properly should only be discovered in the way the language and intention present it.

2. Careless interpretation distinguishes only the [predetermined] sense from the manner of expression, which in fact depend on each other for their mutual identity, the determination of which is the minimum requirement for avoiding artless practice.[1]

17. Two things should be avoided: qualitatively misunderstanding the content, and quantitatively misunderstanding nuance.

1. Examined objectively, qualitative misunderstanding is mistaking the place of a part of a discourse in the language with that of another one, as, for example, the confusion of the meaning of a word with that of another. The qualitative misunderstanding is subjective, the mistaking of the meaning of an expression, so that one gives the same thing a different meaning than the speaker gave to it in his sphere.

2. Quantitative misunderstanding arises from a subjective response to the value of the elaboration a speaker gives to a part of the text, or by analogy from an objective response to a part taken out of context.

3. The quantitative, which is normally taken little into account, always leads to the qualitative.

4. These negative expressions cover all interpretive operations. But one could not develop the rules from their negativity alone; rather, one must develop them positively, with a constant eye on the negative.

5. One must also distinguish the difference between passive and active misunderstanding. The latter is timidity which, however it might be the consequence of a bias that nothing can appear certain unless it is very obvious, can still entertain very false assumptions.

18. The art can only develop its rules from a positive formula, and this is the historical and the divinatory [prophetic], objective and subjective reconstruction [*Nachkonstruieren*] of the given discourse.

1. Paraphrase: artful interpretation begins with a hunch about a text's meaning which it continuously corrects and refines; careless interpretation begins with a prejudice about a text's meaning which it forces the text to support [translators' note].

1. Objective historical reconstruction considers how the discourse behaves in the totality of the language, and considers a text's self-contained knowledge as a product of the language. Objective divinatory reconstruction assesses how the discourse itself developed the language. Without both of these, one cannot avoid qualitative and quantitative misunderstanding.

2. Subjective historical reconstruction considers a discourse as a product of the soul; subjective divinatory assesses how the process of writing affects the writer's inner thoughts. Without both, just as was the case above, misunderstanding is once again unavoidable.

3. The task is this, to understand the discourse just as well and even better than its creator. Since we have no unmediated knowledge of that which is within him, we must first seek to become conscious of much which he could have remained unconscious of, unless he had become self-reflectingly his own reader. For objective reconstruction he has no more data than we do.

4. Posed in this manner, the task is an infinite one, because there is an infinity of the past and the future that we wish to see in the moment of discourse. Hence, this art is just as capable of inspiration as any other. In fact, a text has no meaning unless it can give rise to this inspiration. However, the decision on how far one wishes to pursue an approach must be, in any case, determined practically, and actually is a question for a specialized hermeneutics and not for a general one.

19. One must first equate oneself with the author by objective and subjective reconstruction before applying the art.

1. With objective reconstruction one proceeds through a knowledge of the language as the author used it. It must be more exact than even the original readers possessed, who themselves had to put themselves in the place of the author. With subjective reconstruction one proceeds through the knowledge of the author's inner and outer life.

2. But both can only be completely secured through a similarly complete exposition. For only from a reading of all of an author's works can one become familiar with his vocabulary, his character, and his circumstances.

20. The vocabulary and the history of the period in which an author works constitute the whole within which his texts must be understood with all their peculiarities.

1. This complete knowledge is contained within an apparent circle,[2] so that every extraordinary thing can only be understood in the context of the general of which it is a part, and vice versa. And all knowledge can only be scientific to the extent that it is complete.

2. This circle makes possible an identification with the author, and thus it follows that, first, the more complete knowledge we possess, the better bolstered we are for exposition, and, second, no material for exposition can be understood in isolation; rather, every reading makes us better suited for understanding by enriching our previous knowledge. We can only be satisfied with immediate understanding when dealing with the meaningless.

2. The troubling yet unavoidable "hermeneutic circle" of interpretation.

21. If the knowledge of the particular vocabulary can only be amassed during the exposition through lexical help and through individual observation, there can exist no self-sufficient exposition.

1. Only an independent knowledge of the actual life of a language gives one a source independent of the exposition for the knowledge of the vocabulary. For this reason we have only an incomplete understanding of what Greek and Latin words mean. Hence, the first lexical task in such cases is to consider the whole literature as a context for understanding the individual linguistic item. These complementary tasks balance each other through the exposition itself, contributing to an artful exposition.

2. Under the term *vocabulary* I subsume the dialect, period, and the mode—prose or poetry.

3. Even first impressions should be based on lexical meaning, for spontaneous interpretation can only rest on prior knowledge [*Vorkenntnisse*], but even all decisions about the language in dictionaries and in explanatory notes proceed from special and other perhaps unreliable expositions.

4. In the area of the New Testament, one can say with certainty that the unreliability and arbitrariness of the exposition rests largely on this fault. This is because contrasting analogies always develop from individual observations. For example, the development of New Testament vocabulary is rooted in classical antiquity and developed through Macedonian Greek through its use by the profane Jewish writers and by Josephus and Philo, by the deuterocanonical writers, and by the writers of the Septuagint,[3] who flavored their Greek with Hebrewisms.

22. Even if the necessary knowledge of history comes only from prolegomena, there can still exist no self-sufficient exposition.

1. Such prolegomena are the sort of critical helps it is the duty of a publisher who desires to be a mediator to use. But they must depend on a knowledge of the whole literary circle a work belongs to, and the whole development of an author himself. Thus they are themselves dependent on exposition, and so are all reckonings whose beginnings are not determined by a specific goal. The exact expositor must, however, gradually glean everything from the sources themselves, and it is because of this that his task can only progress from easy to more difficult. But the dependency becomes most injurious if one brings in such notes in the prolegomena that actually could only be derived from the interpreted work itself.

2. The New Testament has given birth to a special discipline: the writing of the introduction. This is not an actual organic component of the theological discipline; but it is a practical expedient, partly for the beginner, partly for the master, since it is easier to bring together all of the relevant examinations in one place. But the expositor should always contribute to it so as to augment and relate the great mass of evidence.

23. An individual element can only be understood in light of its place in the whole text; and therefore, a cursory reading for an overview of the whole must precede the exact exposition.

3. A Greek translation of the Hebrew Scriptures by Jewish scholars (ca. 3d c. B.C.E.). Flavius Josephus (b. 37/8 C.E.) and Philo Judaeus (ca. 20 B.C.E.–ca. 50 C.E.): secular Jewish writers of history and philosophy, respectively. "Deuterocanonical writers": authors of books of the Scriptures contained in the Septuagint but not in the Hebrew canon.

1. Understanding appears to go in endless circles, for a preliminary understanding of even the individuals themselves comes from a general knowledge of the language.

2. Synopses that the author gives himself are too dry to engage even the technical aspect of interpretation, and with summaries like those publishers authorize for prefaces one comes under the influence of their interpretations.

3. The aim is to find the main idea in light of which the others must be measured, and this goes as well for the technical aspect—to find the main procedure from which the others can more easily be found. It is similarly indispensable for grammatical interpretation, which is obvious from the various forms of misunderstanding it often raises.

4. One can omit it easier when dealing with the unmeaningful, and although with difficult works it appears to be less helpful, it is actually all the more indispensable. A general summary is characteristically the least help in understanding difficult writers.

Should the exposition be done partially, one would eventually have to connect both aspects in the execution of the interpretation, but in theory one must divide and handle each specially, even if afterwards one must endeavor to develop each so completely that the other becomes indispensable, or, what is more important, so that its result coincides with the first. The grammatical interpretation leads the way.

PART TWO
THE TECHNICAL INTERPRETATION

1. The common beginning for both the technical and the grammatical interpretation is the general overview which grasps the unity of the work and the main features of the composition. The unity of the work, the theme, will be viewed here as the writer's motivating principle, and the foundation of the composition as his peculiar nature as it is manifested in each motif.

The unity of the work derives from the manner in which the grammatical constructions available in the language are composed or connected. The author sets a verbal object in motion as communication. The difference between popular and scientific works is that the author of the former arranges the subject according to his peculiar style, which mirrors itself in his ordering. Because each author has minor conceptions each of which is determined by his peculiarities, one can recognize them from among analogous omissions and anomalous inclusions.

I perceive the author as he functions in the language: partly bringing forth new things by his use of language, partly retaining qualities of language which he repeats and transmits. In the same way, from a knowledge of an area of speech, I can perceive the author's language as its product and see how he operates under its aegis. Both methods are the same process begun from different starting points.

2. The ultimate goal of the psychological [technical] exposition is nothing other than to perceive the consequences of the beginning; that is to say, to consider the work as it is formed by its parts, and to perceive every part in light of the work's overall subject as its motivation; this is also to say that the form is seen to be shaped by the subject matter.

When I have looked at everything individually, there is nothing left over to understand. It is also obvious in itself that the apparent contrast between understanding the individual parts and understanding the whole disappears when every part receives the same treatment as the whole. But the goal [of good interpretation] is only achieved in the continuity of both perspectives. Even when much is only to be understood grammatically, it is not understood fully unless one can make an intrinsic analysis which never loses sight of the genesis of the work.

3. The goal of good interpretation is to understand the style completely.

We are accustomed to understanding style as the handling of language. We presume that thought and language intertwine throughout, and the specific manner with which one understands the subject requires an understanding of the arrangement of words: i.e., the handling of language.

The peculiarity of an individual conception results from what is missing or added to a conventional conception. Whatever peculiarity results from imitation or habit results in a bad style.

4. Good interpretation can only be approximated.

We are, considering all advances in hermeneutical theory, still far from making it a perfect art, as the perennial fights over the writings of Homer and over the comparative merits of the three tragic writers[4] show.

No individual inspection of a work ever exhausts its meaning; interpretation can always be rectified. Even the best is only an approximation of the meaning. Because interpretation so seldom succeeds, and because even the superior critic is open to criticism, we can see that we are still far from the goal of making hermeneutics a perfect art.

5. Before beginning the technical exposition, we must know the manner in which the subject occurred to the originator, and how he acquired his language, and anything else one can learn about his mannerisms.

First, one must consider the prior development of the genre of the work at the time when it was written; second, one must consider the use made of the genre typically in the place where the writer worked and in adjacent areas; finally, no exact understanding of the development and usage is possible without a knowledge of the related contemporary literature and especially the works the author might have used as a model. Such a cohesive study is indispensable.

The third goal raises very troublesome problems. We could say that the interpretive process as a whole is only as easy as this step is to take. But because even this step requires a judgment which can also be anticipated in the previous steps, it is possible that one might be able to omit it. Biographies of the author were originally annexed to their works for this purpose; nowadays this connection is overlooked. The best sort of prolegomena attends to the first two points.

With these contextualizations [*Vorkenntnissen*] in hand one can gain an

4. That is, the Greek tragedians Aeschylus, Sophocles, and Euripides (all active 5th c. B.C.E.). "Perennial fights": over whether the *Iliad* and *Odyssey* were by a single poet or were collections of short works put together from various sources.

excellent perception of the essential characteristic of a work upon a first reading.

6. The whole task requires the use of two methods, the divinatory and the comparative, which, however, as they constantly refer back to each other, must not be separated.

Using the divinatory, one seeks to understand the writer intimately [*unmittelbar*] to the point that one transforms oneself into the other. Using the comparative, one seeks to understand a work as a characteristic type, viewing the work, in other words, in light of others like it. The one is the feminine force in the knowledge of human nature; the other is the masculine.

Both refer back to each other. The first depends on the fact that every person has a susceptibility to intuiting others, in addition to his sharing many human characteristics. This itself appears to depend on the fact that everyone shares certain universal traits; divination consequently is inspired as the reader compares himself with the author.

But how does the comparative come to subsume the subject under a general type? Obviously, either by comparing, which could go on infinitely, or by divination.

Neither may be separated from the other, because divination receives its security first from an affirmative comparison, without which it might become outlandish. But the comparative of itself cannot yield a unity. The general and specific must permeate each other, and this can only happen by means of divination.

7. The idea of the work, by which the author's fundamental purpose [*Wille*] reveals itself, can only be understood in terms of the convergence of the basic material and its peculiarity of his developments.

The basic material by itself stipulates no set manner of execution. As a rule it is easy enough to determine, even if it is not exactly specified; but for all that, one can be mistaken. One finds the purpose of the work most precisely in its peculiar or characteristic development of its material. Often the characteristic motif has only a limited influence on certain sections of a work, but nonetheless shapes the character of the work by its influence on others. The interpretive knack is to somehow intuit the meaning while being cautiously aware of how the intuition in some ways predetermines the process of validating it.

1819, 1828 1959, 1974

GEORG WILHELM FRIEDRICH HEGEL
1770–1831

IMMANUEL KANT (1724–1804) and G. W. F. HEGEL are the ARISTOTLE and PLATO of modern Continental philosophy, the two dominant figures from whom everything else seems to flow. Hegel is a great synthesizer, a system builder who bequeaths to modern thought the conviction that an individual entity's meaning rests not in itself but in the relationship of that thing to other things within an all-encompassing, ever-changing whole. Where the part is *situated* is crucial. All modern criticism that stresses the historical and social context of utterances or intertextual connections is Hegelian to some degree.

Hegel was the son of a minor court official in the duchy of Württemburg, in what is now Germany. He studied theology at the University of Tübingen, where he became friends with the poet Friedrich Hölderlin and the philosopher Friedrich von Schelling. After graduating in 1793, Hegel worked as a private tutor until he began teaching at the University of Jena in 1801, the year he published his first book. In 1807 he published *Phenomenology of Spirit*, the first version of his grand philosophical vision and one of the great philosophical masterpieces of all time. A sexual scandal (he had a child with his landlord's wife) forced Hegel to leave Jena in 1807, and he would not teach in a university again until 1816. He reached the height of his fame and influence with his lectures at the University of Berlin, which he delivered regularly from 1818 until his death. Many of these series were published either by Hegel himself or from the notes taken by his students, as was *Lectures on Fine Art* (1835–38).

Hegel is usually associated with the *dialectic*, which entails the confrontation of any thesis with its opposite (antithesis), and the resultant synthesis of the two through a process of "overcoming" (*aufgehoben* in German). We might call the dialectic the motor of the Hegelian system, stressing movement and change over stasis. This system, which places individual elements in relation to one another, is in constant motion. Meaning and truth are never fixed because they are always in process. The world possesses not determinate being but only momentary resting places on the stages of becoming. Hegel does believe that there will be stasis and perfection at the end of history, and at times he appears to believe that his philosophy is that end, the moment when consciousness fully understands its own nature—its essential unity with all that exists. Spirit (*Geist*) is the name Hegel most often uses to designate this fundamental unity, and the goal of philosophy is to gain the "absolute knowledge" that would consist of Spirit recognizing the world as its own emanation. The changes of history, its dialectical path, would then come to an end. The dream of such completion has proven extraordinarily alluring yet often dangerous. Shorn of that dream, Hegel's philosophy gives us a dynamic world of interrelationships in which the various elements contend with one another through dialectical struggle. Hegel's most famous disciple, KARL MARX, adopts both the vision of struggle and the dream of an end to strife. But Hegelian themes also echo, in a different key, throughout the work of poststructuralists such as MICHEL FOUCAULT and JULIA KRISTEVA.

Our first selection presents the most famous instance of dialectical confrontation in Hegel, the so-called Master-Slave ("lord" and "bondsman" in our translation) dialectic. Although dense and abstract, this section of *Phenomenology of Spirit* has been very influential, especially in France, where, by way of Alexandre Kojève's celebrated *Introduction to the Reading of Hegel* (1947), it shaped the thought of JEAN-PAUL SARTRE, SIMONE DE BEAUVOIR, JACQUES LACAN, and JACQUES DERRIDA, among others. The question Hegel asks is this: how does a human being come to consciousness of itself as a self (a consciousness that animals lack)? Hegel assumes that humans are not born with the sense "I am John Smith, and this is what I believe and am like." How then do we acquire self-consciousness? Only in meeting with something that is not the self, according to Hegel. Confrontation with my limits, with the not-self, enables me to identify what is self, what belongs to me. The reality of this discovered self depends on two things: I must have the consciousness that I am a self (which Hegel calls "being-for-self"), and my existence must be acknowledged or recognized by other human beings ("being-for-others"). In Hegel's words, "Self-consciousness exists in and for itself when, and by the fact that, it so exists for another; that is, it exists only in being acknowledged."

Most interpreters have seen Hegel as demonstrating that selfhood is a social fact. The child develops a sense of self largely because others treat it as a self—and the self will be socially constructed in different ways, depending on how it is treated. Selves are not born but made, in a dialectical social process of interrelationships among selves. This ongoing process proceeds through "moments" that Hegel then identifies as stages on the way toward full self-consciousness. Just as the self develops consciousness over time, so the human species as a whole passes through moments in history on the path to absolute knowledge. *Phenomenology of Spirit* traces this movement of humans through time to the culminating moment of the full self-consciousness of Spirit.

In the Master-Slave dialectic, the counterposed selves who are coming to consciousness have so much at stake that their relationships are a constant source of strife, "such that they prove themselves and each other through a life-and-death struggle." Selves do not take their fundamental dependence on others kindly. Here power enters the discussion, as Hegel imagines that each individual would prefer to guarantee continued recognition from the other, while not extending that recognition in turn. Such imbalance, taken to its extreme, is figured by Hegel as the relationship between a master and a slave, which is established in a battle that ends when the Slave grants recognition and service to the Master in return for continued life. (Both the Master and Slave stake their life in the battle, but the loser becomes a slave by choosing a life of servitude over death at the hand of the victor.)

The Master, however, finds victory hollow. Recognition, like love, has value only when it is freely given, when it comes from someone who is like me in status. If the other acknowledges my existence only because forced to do so, how can that calm my lurking doubt about who I am? (Hegel not only anticipates the processes of self-formation described by SIGMUND FREUD but also describes the existential anxiety that haunts any attachment to "identity.") The Master's access to his own selfhood is mediated through his relationship to the Slave; and since that Slave is "not an independent consciousness, but a dependent one," the Master "is, therefore, not certain of *being-for-self* as the truth of himself." By obliterating the Slave's independence, the Master has removed the very "other" that must be encountered to achieve selfhood.

Meanwhile, the Slave moves from the "dread . . . it has experienced" in the face of "death, the absolute Lord [or Master]" to a fairly satisfactory self-consciousness achieved through work. (The Hegelian description of labor as redeeming greatly influenced Marx.) The Slave gains a sense of self because his labor has an effect on a material world of resistant objects. The Master has lost contact with the non-self (except with the Slave) because he has left all physical interaction with the world to the Slave. This ironic reversal of the Master-Slave relationship points toward the reciprocity of dependence that Hegel sees as characterizing human relationships: "They *recognize* themselves as *mutually recognizing* one another." Only if I am willing to acknowledge that the other is also a self, who has a need and a right to be a being-for-self, can I satisfactorily establish my own selfhood.

This account provides a memorable and persuasive model for understanding the complex dynamics of intersubjective relationships. Selfhood is a social product that individuals crave; identity has to be constructed through contentious interaction with and relation to others; this process makes us dependent on others, and thus inclined to resent and fear them; and such dependence involves forms of psychological and social power that are distinct from physical force or the power afforded by superior wealth. Whenever modern literary theorists and critics have been interested in questions of identity and of the self's confrontation with the other (however understood),

Hegel's famous account of the Master-Slave dialectic has hovered in the background.

Our second selection consists of excerpts from the introduction to *Lectures on Fine Art*—Hegel's contribution to philosophical aesthetics, the field that seeks to define the aims of the arts, the features of art objects, the activity of artists, and the effects of the arts on audiences. Aesthetics dates from the 1750s, but Hegel clearly echoes Plato on the arts. For Hegel, the fundamental goal of humanity is to come to full consciousness of the Idea (or Spirit), and philosophy is the golden road to that goal. Yet, unlike Plato, he wants to praise art, not condemn it. Because Hegel accepts the superiority of spirit over matter, truth over appearance, universal over particular, intellectual over sensual, and logic over feeling, he must argue that art, understood correctly, is not merely a sensuous, material, singular thing; instead, it contributes to human understanding of the Idea.

Hegel takes the line of argument suggested by his model of thinking. Just as the self in the Master-Slave dialectic can come to self-consciousness only through encountering an other, so thinking needs to encounter an object. The Spirit or Idea dwells within humans, but as "a *thinking* consciousness" a person "draws out of himself and puts *before himself* what . . . is." After art has given Spirit a concrete form, it can be apprehended. This account makes art part of the philosophical project of coming to full consciousness—and provides Hegel with firm answers to a number of problems that bedevil aesthetics.

In the first part of our selection, Hegel reviews previous notions of the arts, steering a middle path between accounts that emphasize rules and those that rely on pure inspiration. More important, Hegel asserts the superiority of human-made artistic objects to God-made natural ones by appealing to their spiritual purpose. Spirit dwells in nature as well as in humans, but only humans are conscious of reaching an awareness of spirit. A man needs art "to lift the inner and outer world into his spiritual consciousness as an object in which he recognizes again his own self." In Hegel's quasi-religious philosophy, human life reaches its highest form when we recognize that the spirit of the creator permeates all of the created world, including ourselves. To discover this true self, to align ourselves with spirit, is to attain "free rationality."

True to his historicist convictions, in the second part of our selection Hegel presents the movement to full self-consciousness as occurring in stages. Symbolic, classical, and romantic art form a dialectical triad. Symbolic art, tied to "perceived natural objects," attempts but fails to attach a spiritual significance to those objects. This failure has its uses, since at least "the foreignness of the Idea to natural phenomena" is made manifest. The gap here between the natural and the spiritual is, Hegel tells us, "sublime," a striking revision of a category invoked in antiquity by LONGINUS and in the eighteenth century by JOSEPH ADDISON, EDMUND BURKE, and Kant.

The failure of primitive symbolic art, associated with the ancient Near East, generates its antithesis, classical art; and what Hegel sees as the higher, Western tradition begins. By focusing on "the human form," the Greeks gave the Idea an adequate material embodiment. Since humans are a potent example of the union of spirit and body, Hegel finds ingenious the classical solution to the problem of "bring[ing] the spiritual before our eyes in a sensuous manner." But it too has a defect—the opposite of that of symbolic art, which could not give the Idea a local habitation and name. Classical art fails because it "determine[s]" spirit "as particular and human," thus obscuring its "absolute and eternal" essence.

This "defect . . . demands a transition to a higher form," the romantic. The threat of classical art lies in its sensuousness. Romantic art, even as it utilizes sensuous forms, must move both artist and audience (by irony and sublimity) toward "the *inwardness of self-consciousness*," toward the indwelling spirit. As a synthesis and overcoming of symbolic and classical art, romantic art dissociates the idea from the sensuous form (as does symbolic art) even as it presents the sensuous form (as does classical art). Romantic art stages the "inadequacy" of the material embodiment so that "the Idea . . . appear[s] *perfected* in itself as spirit and heart."

Thus Hegel is a champion of Romantic art. In the move from sensuous form to inwardness, he places the expression of "subjective inner depth" and "reflective emotion" at the center of the artistic enterprise. This notion of art as expression is the cornerstone of Romantic aesthetics—WILLIAM WORDSWORTH, PERCY BYSSHE SHELLEY, and RALPH WALDO EMERSON are among the nineteenth-century writers who espouse some version of an expressivist aesthetic—and it continues to dominate popular understandings of art, especially poetry. But Hegel's historicism also suggests a broader expressivist understanding of art, in which the artwork is viewed as an expression of an era, zeitgeist, culture, or nation rather than of the artist's self. In both cases, artistic representation is tied not to some visible thing imitated by the artist but to some invisible ideas, emotions, attitudes, values, or spirit.

While much contemporary critical practice, knowingly or not, is Hegelian, postmodern theory has self-consciously struggled (sometimes desperately) to slough off Hegelian habits. The great problem is Hegel's will to totality, the movement of his philosophy, through dialectical overcoming and synthesis, to include everything. Postmodern theorists resist this philosophical imperialism, this "totalizing impulse," insisting that inclusion through the dialectic always comes at the price of overcoming what is most singular and different in the incorporated other. The problem with subsuming everything into a totalizing system is the erasure of difference. Hence, in our selection Hegel makes art safe for philosophy by downplaying or explaining away everything that makes art different from and even antithetical to thinking.

By highlighting the different and the singular, postmodernists question Hegel's placing of everything into a relational, systematic whole. But since postmodern theory does accept that meaning is the product of systematic, though differential, relations, Hegel has been hard to negate. Because he can be neither banished nor embraced, Hegel remains a figure to whom much contemporary theory obsessively returns.

BIBLIOGRAPHY

Edited by Eva Moldenhauer and Karl Markus Michel, Hegel's *Werke* (22 vols., 1969–72) is a complete German edition of his writings. Most of his work has been translated into English, though there is no standard scholarly edition of the complete works. Of special relevance to students of literature are *Philosophy of Right*, translated by T. M. Knox (1942): *Hegel's Aesthetics: Lectures on Fine Art*, translated by T. M. Knox (2 vols., 1975); *Lectures on the Philosophy of World History*, edited by H. B. Nisbet (1975); *Phenomenology of Spirit*, translated by A. V. Miller (1977); and *Lectures on the History of Philosophy*, edited by Robert Brown (3 vols., 1990). *The Hegel Reader*, edited by Stephen Houlgate (1998), offers selections covering the breadth of Hegel's interests. The best biography is Terry Pinkard's *Hegel: A Biography* (2000).

The secondary literature on Hegel is immense; thus the following bibliography is extremely selective. Jean Hyppolite's *Genesis and Structure of Hegel's Phenomenology of Spirit* (1946; trans. 1974) and Alexandre Kojève's *Introduction to the Reading of Hegel* (1947; trans. 1969) are two French works that shaped the existentialist and poststructuralist understandings of Hegel. Herbert Marcuse's *Reason and Revolution: Hegel and the Rise of Social Theory* (1941) and György Lukács's *The Young Hegel* (1948; trans. 1975) are important documents in Western Marxism's appropriation of Hegel.

Jack Kaminsky's *Hegel on Art* (1962) provides a useful summary of Hegel's aesthetics, while G. R. G. Mure's *The Philosophy of Hegel* (1965) is a good overview of Hegel's whole philosophical system. The single best, and most influential, overview is Charles Taylor's *Hegel* (1975), which also comes in a slimmer version called *Hegel and Modern Society* (1979). Two other good overviews are Robert Solomon's *In the Spirit of Hegel* (1983), which focuses on *Phenomenology of Spirit*, and Peter Singer's *Hegel* (1983), which is especially fine on Hegel's politics.

Jacques Derrida's *Glas* (1974, trans. 1986) is the most important of many poststructuralist encounters with Hegel. For other reexaminations of Hegel through the lens of contemporary theory, see William Desmond, *Art and the Absolute: A Study of Hegel's Aesthetics* (1986); David Kolb, *The Critique of Pure Modernity: Hegel, Hei-*

degger, and After (1986); Stephen Houlgate, *Hegel, Nietzsche, and the Criticism of Metaphysics* (1986); Judith Butler, *Subjects of Desire: Hegelian Reflections in Twentieth-Century France* (1987); and John McGowan, *Postmodernism and Its Critics* (1991). The best places for those unfamiliar with Hegel to start are Stephen Houlgate's superb *Freedom, Truth, and History: An Introduction to Hegel's Philosophy* (1991) and *The Cambridge Companion to Hegel*, edited by Frederick C. Beiser (1993), which provides clear essays that summarize Hegel's work in areas ranging from metaphysics to ethics. Works that continue to analyze him in relation to current debates and themes in literary theory include Slavoj Žižek, *Tarrying with the Negative: Kant, Hegel, and the Critique of Ideology* (1993); Paul Redding, *Hegel's Hermeneutics* (1996); *Feminist Interpretations of Hegel*, edited by Patricia J. Mills, (1996); Jeffrey A. Gauthier, *Hegel and Feminist Social Criticism: Justice, Recognition, and the Feminine* (1997); Robert R. Williams, *Hegel's Ethics of Recognition* (1997); *Hegel, History, and Interpretation*, edited by Shaun Gallagher (1997); and *Hegel after Derrida*, edited by Stuart Barnett (1998).

Kurt Steinhauer's massive German/English *Hegel Bibliographie* (1980, with additional volumes in 1993) covers almost all the secondary literature from 1802 onward. A more manageable bibliography, helpfully arranged by topic, can be found in *The Cambridge Companion to Hegel* (cited above).

From Phenomenology of Spirit[1]

[*The Master-Slave Dialectic*]

178. Self-consciousness exists in and for itself when, and by the fact that, it so exists for another; that is, it exists only in being acknowledged [*als ein Anerkanntes*]. The Notion of this its unity in its duplication embraces many and varied meanings. Its moments, then, must on the one hand be held strictly apart, and on the other hand must in this differentiation at the same time also be taken and known as not distinct, or in their opposite significance. The twofold significance of the distinct moments has in the nature of self-consciousness to be infinite, or directly the opposite of the determinateness in which it is posited. The detailed exposition of the Notion of this spiritual unity in its duplication will present us with the process of Recognition [*Anerkennen*].

179. Self-consciousness is faced by another self-consciousness; it has come *out of itself*. This has a twofold significance: first, it has lost itself, for it finds itself as an *other* being; secondly, in doing so it has superseded the other, for it does not see the other as an essential being, but in the other sees its own self.

180. It must supersede this otherness of itself. This is the supersession of the first ambiguity, and is therefore itself a second ambiguity. First, it must proceed to supersede the *other* independent being in order thereby to become certain of *itself* as the essential being; secondly, in so doing it proceeds to supersede its *own* self, for this other is itself.

181. This ambiguous supersession of its ambiguous otherness is equally an ambiguous return *into itself*. For first, through the supersession, it receives back its own self, because, by superseding *its* otherness, it again becomes equal to itself; but secondly, it equally gives the other self-consciousness

1. Translated by A. V. Miller who sometimes retains the original German or adds clarifying words or phrases in brackets and has added the paragraph numbers.

back again to itself, for it saw itself in the other, but supersedes this being of itself in the other and thus lets the other again go free.

182. Now, this movement of self-consciousness in relation to another self-consciousness has in this way been represented as the action of *one* self-consciousness, but this action of the one has itself the double significance of being both its own action and the action of the other as well. For the other is equally independent and self-contained, and there is nothing in it of which it is not itself the origin. The first does not have the object before it merely as it exists primarily for desire, but as something that has an independent existence of its own, which, therefore, it cannot utilize for its own purposes, if that object does not of its own accord do what the first does to it. Thus the movement is simply the double movement of the two self-consciousnesses. Each sees the *other* do the same as it does; each does itself what it demands of the other, and therefore also does what it does only in so far as the other does the same. Action by one side only would be useless because what is to happen can only be brought about by both.

183. Thus the action has a double significance not only because it is directed against itself as well as against the other, but also because it is indivisibly the action of one as well as of the other.

184. In this movement we see repeated the process which presented itself as the play of Forces, but repeated now in consciousness. What in that process was *for us*, is true here of the extremes themselves. The middle term is self-consciousness which splits into the extremes; and each extreme is this exchanging of its own determinateness and an absolute transition into the opposite. Although, as consciousness, it does indeed come *out of itself*, yet, though out of itself, it is at the same time kept back within itself, is *for itself*, and the self outside it, is for *it*. It is aware that it at once is, and is not, another consciousness, and equally that this other is *for itself* only when it supersedes itself as being for itself, and is for itself only in the being-for-self of the other. Each is for the other the middle term, through which each mediates itself with itself and unites with itself; and each is for itself, and for the other, an immediate being to its own account, which at the same time is such only through this mediation.[2] They *recognize* themselves as *mutually recognizing* one another.

185. We have now to see how the process of this pure Notion of recognition, of the duplicating of self-consciousness in its oneness, appears to self-consciousness. At first, it will exhibit the side of the inequality of the two, or the splitting-up of the middle term into the extremes which, as extremes, are opposed to one another, one being only *recognized*, the other only *recognizing*.

186. Self-consciousness is, to begin with, simple being-for-self, self-equal through the exclusion from itself of everything else. For it, its essence and absolute object is 'I'; and in this immediacy, or in this [mere] being, of its being-for-self, it is an *individual*. What is 'other' for it is an unessential, negatively characterized object. But the 'other' is also a self-consciousness; one individual is confronted by another individual. Appearing thus immediately on the scene, they are for one another like ordinary objects, *independent* shapes, individuals submerged in the being [or immediacy] of *Life*—for the object in its immediacy is here determined as Life. They are, *for each*

2. That is, the encounter with the other is necessary for self-consciousness.

other, shapes of consciousness which have not yet accomplished the movement of absolute abstraction, of rooting-out all immediate being, and of being merely the purely negative being of self-identical consciousness; in other words, they have not as yet exposed themselves to each other in the form of pure being-for-self, or as self-consciousness. Each is indeed certain of its own self, but not of the other, and therefore its own self-certainty still has no truth. For it would have truth only if its own being-for-self had confronted it as an independent object, or, what is the same thing, if the object had presented itself as this pure self-certainty. But according to the Notion of recognition this is possible only when each is for the other what the other is for it, only when each in its own self through its own action, and again through the action of the other, achieves this pure abstraction of being-for-self.

187. The presentation of itself, however, as the pure abstraction of self-consciousness consists in showing itself as the pure negation of its objective mode, or in showing that it is not attached to any specific *existence*, not to the individuality common to existence as such, that it is not attached to life. This presentation is a twofold action: action on the part of the other, and action on its own part. In so far as it is the action of the *other*, each seeks the death of the other. But in doing so, the second kind of action, action on its own part, is also involved; for the former involves the staking of its own life. Thus the relation of the two self-conscious individuals is such that they prove themselves and each other through a life-and-death struggle. They must engage in this struggle, for they must raise their certainty of being *for themselves* to truth, both in the case of the other and in their own case. And it is only through staking one's life that freedom is won; only thus is it proved that for self-consciousness, its essential being is not [just] being, not the *immediate* form in which it appears, not its submergence in the expanse of life, but rather that there is nothing present in it which could not be regarded as a vanishing moment, that it is only pure *being-for-self*. The individual who has not risked his life may well be recognized as a *person*, but he has not attained to the truth of this recognition as an independent self-consciousness. Similarly, just as each stakes his own life, so each must seek the other's death, for it values the other no more than itself; its essential being is present to it in the form of an 'other', it is outside of itself and must rid itself of its self-externality. The other is an *immediate* consciousness entangled in a variety of relationships, and it must regard its otherness as a pure being-for-self or as an absolute negation.

188. This trial by death, however, does away with the truth which was supposed to issue from it, and so, too, with the certainty of self generally. For just as life is the *natural* setting of consciousness, independence without absolute negativity, so death is the *natural* negation of consciousness, negation without independence, which thus remains without the required significance of recognition. Death certainly shows that each staked his life and held it of no account, both in himself and in the other; but that is not for those who survived this struggle. They put an end to their consciousness in its alien setting of natural existence, that is to say, they put an end to themselves, and are done away with as *extremes* wanting to be *for themselves*, or to have an existence of their own. But with this there vanishes from their interplay the essential moment of splitting into extremes with opposite char-

acteristics; and the middle term collapses into a lifeless unity which is split into lifeless, merely immediate, unopposed extremes; and the two do not reciprocally give and receive one another back from each other consciously, but leave each other free only indifferently, like things. Their act is an abstract negation, not the negation coming from consciousness, which supersedes in such a way as to preserve and maintain what is superseded, and consequently survives its own supersession.[3]

189. In this experience, self-consciousness learns that life is as essential to it as pure self-consciousness. In immediate self-consciousness the simple 'I' is the absolute object which, however, for us or in itself is absolute mediation, and has as its essential moment lasting independence. The dissolution of that simple unity is the result of the first experience; through this there is posited a pure self-consciousness, and a consciousness which is not purely for itself but for another, i.e. is a merely *immediate* consciousness, or consciousness in the form of *thinghood*. Both moments are essential. Since to begin with they are unequal and opposed, and their reflection into a unity has not yet been achieved, they exist as two opposed shapes of consciousness; one is the independent consciousness whose essential nature is to be for itself, the other is the dependent consciousness whose essential nature is simply to live or to be for another. The former is lord [*Herr*], the other is bondsman [*Knecht*].[4]

190. The lord is the consciousness that exists *for itself*, but no longer merely the Notion of such a consciousness. Rather, it is a consciousness existing *for itself* which is mediated with itself through another consciousness, i.e. through a consciousness whose nature it is to be bound up with an existence that is independent, or thinghood in general. The lord puts himself into relation with both of these moments, to a *thing* as such, the object of desire, and to the consciousness for which thinghood is the essential characteristic. And since he is (a) *qua* the Notion of self-consciousness an immediate relation of *being-for-self*, but (b) is now at the same time mediation, or a being-for-self which is for itself only through another, he is related (a) immediately to both, and (b) mediately to each through the other. The lord relates himself mediately to the bondsman through a being [a thing] that is independent, for it is just this which holds the bondsman in bondage; it is his chain from which he could not break free in the struggle, thus proving himself to be dependent, to possess his independence in thinghood. But the lord is the power over this thing, for he proved in the struggle that it is something merely negative; since he is the power over this thing and this again is the power over the other [the bondsman], it follows that he holds the other in subjection. Equally, the lord relates himself mediately to the thing through the bondsman; the bondsman, *qua* self-consciousness in general, also relates himself negatively to the thing, and takes away its independence; but at the same time the thing is independent *vis-à-vis* the bondsman, whose negating of it, therefore, cannot go to the length of being altogether done with it to the point of annihilation; in other words, he only *works* on it. For the lord, on the other hand, the *immediate* relation becomes through this mediation the sheer negation of the thing, or the enjoyment of it. What

3. This description of "the negation coming from consciousness" encapsulates the dialectic.

4. *Herr* and *Knecht* have often been translated "Master" and "Slave."

desire failed to achieve, he succeeds in doing, viz. to have done with the thing altogether, and to achieve satisfaction in the enjoyment of it. Desire failed to do this because of the thing's independence; but the lord, who has interposed the bondsman between it and himself, takes to himself only the dependent aspect of the thing and has the pure enjoyment of it. The aspect of its independence he leaves to the bondsman, who works on it.

191. In both of these moments the lord achieves his recognition through another consciousness; for in them, that other consciousness is expressly something unessential, both by its working on the thing, and by its dependence on a specific existence. In neither case can it be lord over the being of the thing and achieve absolute negation of it. Here, therefore, is present this moment of recognition, viz. that the other consciousness sets aside its own being-for-self, and in so doing itself does what the first does to it. Similarly, the other moment too is present, that this action of the second is the first's own action; for what the bondsman does is really the action of the lord. The latter's essential nature is to exist only for himself; he is the sheer negative power for whom the thing is nothing. Thus he is the pure, essential action in this relationship, while the action of the bondsman is impure and unessential. But for recognition proper the moment is lacking, that what the lord does to the other he also does to himself, and what the bondsman does to himself he should also do to the other. The outcome is a recognition that is one-sided and unequal.

192. In this recognition the unessential consciousness is for the lord the object, which constitutes the *truth* of his certainty of himself. But it is clear that this object does not correspond to its Notion, but rather that the object in which the lord has achieved his lordship has in reality turned out to be something quite different from an independent consciousness. What now really confronts him is not an independent consciousness, but a dependent one. He is, therefore, not certain of *being-for-self* as the truth of himself. On the contrary, his truth is in reality the unessential consciousness and its unessential action.

193. The *truth* of the independent consciousness is accordingly the servile consciousness of the bondsman. This, it is true, appears at first *outside* of itself and not as the truth of self-consciousness. But just as lordship showed that its essential nature is the reverse of what it wants to be, so too servitude in its consummation will really turn into the opposite of what it immediately is; as a consciousness forced back into itself, it will withdraw into itself and be transformed into a truly independent consciousness.

194. We have seen what servitude is only in relation to lordship. But it is a self-consciousness, and we have now to consider what as such it is in and for itself. To begin with, servitude has the lord for its essential reality; hence the *truth* for it is the independent consciousness that it is *for itself*. However, servitude is not yet aware that this truth is implicit in it. But it does in fact contain within itself this truth of pure negativity and being-for-self, for it has experienced this its own essential nature. For this consciousness has been fearful, not of this or that particular thing or just at odd moments, but its whole being has been seized with dread; for it has experienced the fear of death, the absolute Lord. In that experience it has been quite unmanned, has trembled in every fibre of its being, and everything solid and stable has been shaken to its foundations. But this pure universal movement, the absolute melting-away of everything stable, is the simple, essential nature of self-

consciousness. absolute negativity, *pure being-for-self*, which consequently is *implicit* in this consciousness. This moment of pure being-for-self is also *explicit* for the bondsman, for in the lord it exists for him as his *object*. Furthermore, his consciousness is not this dissolution of everything stable merely in principle; in his service he *actually* brings this about. Through his service he rids himself of his attachment to natural existence in every single detail; and gets rid of it by working on it.

195. However, the feeling of absolute power both in general, and in the particular form of service, is only implicitly this dissolution, and although the fear of the lord is indeed the beginning of wisdom, consciousness is not therein aware that it is a being-for-self. Through work, however, the bondsman becomes conscious of what he truly is. In the moment which corresponds to desire in the lord's consciousness, it did seem that the aspect of unessential relation to the thing fell to the lot of the bondsman, since in that relation the thing retained its independence. Desire has reserved to itself the pure negating of the object and thereby its unalloyed feeling of self. But that is the reason why this satisfaction is itself only a fleeting one, for it lacks the side of objectivity and permanence. Work, on the other hand, is desire held in check, fleetingness staved off; in other words, work forms and shapes the thing. The negative relation to the object becomes its *form* and something *permanent*, because it is precisely for the worker that the object has independence. This *negative* middle term or the formative *activity* is at the same time the individuality or pure being-for-self of consciousness which now, in the work outside of it, acquires an element of permanence.[5] It is in this way, therefore, that consciousness, *qua* worker, comes to see in the independent being [of the object] its *own* independence.

196. But the formative activity has not only this positive significance that in it the pure being-for-self of the servile consciousness acquires an existence; it also has negative significance with respect to its first moment, *fear*. For, in fashioning the thing, the bondsman's own negativity, his being-for-self, becomes an object for him only through his setting at nought the existing *shape* confronting him. But this objective *negative* moment is none other than the alien being before which it has trembled. Now, however, he destroys this alien negative moment, posits *himself* as a negative in the permanent order of things, and thereby becomes *for himself*, someone existing on his own account. In the lord, the being-for-self is an 'other' for the bondsman, or is only *for* him [i.e. is not his own]; in fear, the being-for-self is present in the bondsman himself; in fashioning the thing, he becomes aware that being-for-self belongs to *him*, that he himself exists essentially and actually in his own right. The shape does not become something other than himself through being made external to him; for it is precisely this shape that is his pure being-for-self, which in this externality is seen by him to be the truth. Through this rediscovery of himself by himself, the bondsman realizes that it is precisely in his work wherein he seemed to have only an alienated existence that he acquires a mind of his own. For this reflection, the two moments of fear and service as such, as also that of formative activity, are necessary, both being at the same time in a universal mode. Without the discipline of service and obedience, fear remains at the formal stage, and

5. Work as "formative activity," according to Hegel, creates a stable object that comes to signify a similar stability for the consciousness that shapes that object.

does not extend to the known real world of existence. Without the formative activity, fear remains inward and mute, and consciousness does not become explicitly *for itself*. If consciousness fashions the thing without that initial absolute fear, it is only an empty self-centered attitude; for its form or negativity is not negativity *per se*, and therefore its formative activity cannot give it a consciousness of itself as essential being. If it has not experienced absolute fear but only some lesser dread, the negative being has remained for it something external, its substance has not been infected by it through and through. Since the entire contents of its natural consciousness have not been jeopardized, determinate being still *in principle* attaches to it; having a 'mind of one's own' is self-will, a freedom which is still enmeshed in servitude. Just as little as the pure form can become essential being for it, just as little is that form, regarded as extended to the particular, a universal formative activity, an absolute Notion; rather it is a skill which is master over some things, but not over the universal power and the whole of objective being.

1807

From Lectures on Fine Art[1]

From *Introduction*

* * *

THE WORK OF ART AS A PRODUCT OF HUMAN ACTIVITY

(*a*) As for the first point, that a work of art is a product of human activity, this view has given rise to the thought that this activity, being the *conscious* production of an external object, can also be *known* and expounded, and learnt and pursued by others. For what one man makes, another, it may seem, could make or imitate too, if only he were first acquainted with the manner of proceeding; so that, granted universal acquaintance with the rules of artistic production, it would only be a matter of everyone's pleasure to carry out the procedure in the same manner and produce works of art. It is in this way that the rule-providing theories, mentioned above, with their prescriptions calculated for practical application, have arisen. But what can be carried out on such directions can only be something formally regular and mechanical. For the mechanical alone is of so external a kind that only a purely empty exercise of will and dexterity is required for receiving it into our ideas and activating it; this exercise does not require to be supplemented by anything concrete, or by anything not prescribed in universal rules. This comes out most vividly when such prescriptions do not limit themselves to the purely external and mechanical, but extend to the significant and spiritual activity of the artist. In this sphere the rules contain only vague generalities, for example that 'the theme should be interesting, every character should speak according to his standing, age, sex, and situation'. But if rules are to satisfy here, then their prescriptions should have been drawn up at the same time with such precision that they could be observed just as they

1. Translated by T. M. Knox, who sometimes adds explanatory words or phrases in brackets.

are expressed, without any further spiritual activity of the artist's. Being abstract in content, however, such rules reveal themselves, in their pretence of adequacy to fill the consciousness of the artist, as wholly inadequate, since artistic production is not a formal activity in accordance with given specifications. On the contrary, as spiritual activity it is bound to work from its own resources and bring before the mind's eye a quite other and richer content and more comprehensive individual creations [than formulae can provide]. Therefore, in so far as such rules do actually contain something specific and therefore of practical utility, they may apply in case of need, but still can afford no more than specifications for purely external circumstances.

(*b*) Thus, as it turns out, the tendency just indicated has been altogether abandoned, and instead of it the opposite one has been adopted to the same extent. For the work of art was no longer regarded as a product of *general* human activity, but as a work of an entirely *specially gifted* spirit which now, however, is supposed to give free play simply and *only* to its own particular gift, as if to a specific natural force; it is to cut itself altogether loose from attention to universally valid laws and from a conscious reflection interfering with its own instinctive-like productive activity. Indeed it is supposed to be protected from such reflection, since its productions could only be contaminated and spoiled by such awareness. From this point of view the work of art has been claimed as a product of *talent* and *genius*, and the natural element in talent and genius has been especially emphasized. In a way, rightly, since talent is specific and genius universal capability, which man has not the power to give to himself purely and simply through his own self-conscious activity. On this topic we shall speak at greater length later.

Here we have only to mention the false aspect of this view, namely that in artistic production all consciousness of the artist's own activity is regarded as not merely superfluous but even deleterious. In that case production by talent and genius appears as only a *state* and, in particular, a state of *inspiration*. To such a state, it is said, genius is excited in part by an object, and in part can transpose itself into it by its own caprice, a process in which, after all, the good services of the champagne bottle are not forgotten. In Germany this notion became prominent at the time of the so-called *Period of Genius* which was introduced by Goethe's first poetical productions and then sustained by Schiller's.[2] In their earliest works these poets began afresh, setting aside all the rules then fabricated; they worked deliberately against these rules and thereby surpassed all other writers. However, I will not go further into the confusions which have been prevalent about the concept of inspiration and genius, and which prevail even today about the omnicompetence of inspiration as such. All that is essential is to state the view that, even if the talent and genius of the artist has in it a natural element, yet this element essentially requires development by thought, reflection on the mode of its productivity, and practice and skill in producing. For, apart from anything else, a main feature of artistic production is external workmanship, since the work of art has a purely technical side which extends into handicraft, especially in architecture and sculpture, less so in painting and music, least of all in poetry. Skill in technique is not helped by any inspiration, but

2. Johann Wolfgang von Goethe (1749–1832) and FRIEDRICH VON SCHILLER (1759–1805) were the two most important poets of the Romantic period in Germany.

only by reflection, industry, and practice. But such skill the artist is compelled to have in order to master his external material and not be thwarted by its intractability.

Now further, the higher the standing of the artist, the more profoundly should he display the depths of the heart and the spirit; these are not known directly but are to be fathomed only by the direction of the artist's own spirit on the inner and outer world. So, once again, it is study whereby the artist brings this content into his consciousness and wins the stuff and content of his conceptions.

* * *

(c) A third view concerning the idea of the work of art as a product of human activity refers to the placing of the work of art in relation to the external phenomena of nature. Here the ordinary way of looking at things took easily to the notion that the human art-product ranked below the product of nature; for the work of art has no feeling in itself and is not through and through enlivened, but, regarded as an external object, is dead; but we are accustomed to value the living higher than the dead. That the work of art has no life and movement in itself is readily granted. What is alive in nature is, within and without, an organism purposefully elaborated into all its tiniest parts, while the work of art attains the appearance of life only on its surface; inside it is ordinary stone, or wood and canvas, or, as in poetry, an idea expressed in speech and letters. But this aspect—external existence—is not what makes a work into a product of fine art; a work of art is such only because, originating from the spirit, it now belongs to the territory of the spirit; it has received the baptism of the spiritual and sets forth only what has been formed in harmony with the spirit. Human interest, the spiritual value possessed by an event, an individual character, an action in its complexity and outcome, is grasped in the work of art and blazoned more purely and more transparently than is possible on the ground of other non-artistic things. Therefore the work of art stands higher than any natural product which has not made this journey through the spirit. For example, owing to the feeling and insight whereby a landscape has been represented in a painting, this work of the spirit acquires a higher rank than the mere natural landscape. For everything spiritual is better than any product of nature. Besides, no natural being is able, as art is, to present the divine Ideal.

Now on what the spirit draws from its own inner resources in works of art it confers permanence in their external existence too; on the other hand, the individual living thing in nature is transient, vanishing, changeable in outward appearance, while the work of art persists, even if it is not mere permanence which constitutes its genuine pre-eminence over natural reality, but its having made spiritual inspiration conspicuous.

But nevertheless this higher standing of the work of art is questioned by another idea commonly entertained. For nature and its products, it is said, are a work of God, created by his goodness and wisdom, whereas the art-product is a purely human work, made by human hands according to human insight. In this contrast between natural production as a divine creation and human activity as something merely finite there lies directly the misunderstanding that God does not work in and through men at all, but restricts the sphere of his activity to nature alone. This false opinion must be completely rejected if we are to penetrate to the true nature of art. Indeed, over against this view we must cling to the opposite one, namely that God is more honoured by what the spirit makes than by the productions and formations of nature. For not only is there something divine in man, but it is active in him in a form appropriate to the being of God in a totally different and higher manner than it is in nature. God is spirit, and in man alone does the medium, through which the Divine passes, have the form of conscious and actively self-productive spirit; but in nature this medium is the unconscious, the sensuous, and the external, which stands far below consciousness in worth. Now in art-production God is just as operative as he is in the phenomena of nature; but the Divine, as it discloses itself in the work of art, has been generated out of the spirit, and thus has won a suitable thoroughfare for its existence, whereas just being *there* in the unconscious sensuousness of nature is not a mode of appearance appropriate to the Divine.

(*d*) Now granted that the work of art is made by man as the creation of his spirit, a final question arises, in order to derive a deeper result from the foregoing [discussion], namely, what is man's *need* to produce works of art? On the one hand, this production may be regarded as a mere play of chance and fancies which might just as well be left alone as pursued; for it might be held that there are other and even better means of achieving what art aims at and that man has still higher and more important interests than art has the ability to satisfy. On the other hand, however, art seems to proceed from a higher impulse and to satisfy higher needs,—at times the highest and absolute needs since it is bound up with the most universal views of life and the religious interests of whole epochs and peoples.—This question about the non-contingent but absolute need for art, we cannot yet answer completely, because it is more concrete than an answer could turn out to be at this stage. Therefore we must content ourselves in the meantime with making only the following points.

The universal and absolute need from which art (on its formal side) springs has its origin in the fact that man is a *thinking* consciousness, i.e. that man draws out of himself and puts *before himself* what he is and whatever else is. Things in nature are only *immediate* and *single*, while man as spirit *duplicates* himself, in that (i) he *is* as things in nature are, but (ii) he is just as much *for* himself; he sees himself, represents himself to himself, thinks, and only on the strength of this active placing himself before himself is he spirit. This consciousness of himself man acquires in a two-fold way: *first, theoretically*, in so far as inwardly he must bring himself into his own consciousness, along with whatever moves, stirs, and presses in the human breast; and in general he must see himself, represent himself to himself, fix before himself what thinking finds as his essence, and recognize himself alone alike in what is summoned out of himself and in what is accepted from without. *Secondly*, man brings himself before himself by *practical* activity, since he has the impulse, in whatever is directly given to him, in what is present to him externally, to produce himself and therein equally to recognize himself. This aim he achieves by altering external things whereon he impresses the seal of his inner being and in which he now finds again his own characteristics. Man does this in order, as a free subject, to strip the external world of its inflexible foreignness and to enjoy in the shape of things only an external realization of himself. Even a child's first impulse involves this practical alteration of external things; a boy throws stones into the river and now marvels at the circles drawn in the water as an effect in which he gains an intuition of something that is his own doing. This need runs through the most diversiform phenomena up to that mode of self-production in external things which is present in the work of art. And it is not only with external things that man proceeds in this way, but no less with himself, with his own natural figure which he does not leave as he finds it but deliberately alters. This is the cause of all dressing up and adornment, even if it be barbaric, tasteless, completely disfiguring, or even pernicious like crushing the feet of Chinese ladies, or slitting the ears and lips. For it is only among civilized people that alteration of figure, behaviour, and every sort and mode of external expression proceeds from spiritual development.

The universal need for art, that is to say, is man's rational need to lift the inner and outer world into his spiritual consciousness as an object in which he recognizes again his own self. The need for this spiritual freedom he satisfies, on the one hand, within by making what is within him explicit to himself, but correspondingly by giving outward reality to this his explicit self, and thus in this duplication of himself by bringing what is in him into sight and knowledge for himself and others. This is the free rationality of man in which all acting and knowing, as well as art too, have their basis and necessary origin.

* * *

DEVELOPMENT OF THE IDEAL INTO THE PARTICULAR FORMS OF THE BEAUTY OF ART

But because the Idea is in this way a concrete unity, this unity can enter the art-consciousness only through the unfolding and then the reconciliation of the particularizations of the Idea,[3] and, through this development, artistic beauty acquires a *totality of particular stages and forms*. Therefore, after studying artistic beauty in itself and on its own account, we must see how beauty as a whole decomposes into its particular determinations. This gives, as the *second* part of our study, the doctrine of the *forms of art*. These forms find their origin in the different ways of grasping the Idea as content, whereby a difference in the configuration in which the Idea appears is conditioned. Thus the forms of art are nothing but the different relations of meaning and shape, relations which proceed from the Idea itself and therefore provide the true basis for the division of this sphere. For division must always be implicit in the concept, the particularization and division of which is in question.

We have here to consider *three* relations of the Idea to its configuration.

(*a*) *First*, art begins when the Idea, still in its indeterminacy and obscurity, or in bad and untrue determinacy, is made the content of artistic shapes. Being indeterminate, it does not yet possess in itself that individuality which the Ideal demands; its abstraction and one-sidedness leave its shape externally defective and arbitrary. The first form of art is therefore rather a *mere search* for portrayal than a capacity for true presentation; the Idea has not found the form even in itself and therefore remains struggling and striving

3. That is, the different historical forms of art.

after it. We may call this form, in general terms, the *symbolic* form of art. In it the abstract Idea has its shape outside itself in the natural sensuous material from which the process of shaping starts[4] and with which, in its appearance, this process is linked. Perceived natural objects are, on the one hand, primarily left as they are, yet at the same time the substantial Idea is imposed on them as their meaning so that they now acquire a vocation to express it and so are to be interpreted as if the Idea itself were present in them. A corollary of this is the fact that natural objects have in them an aspect according to which they are capable of representing a universal meaning. But since a complete correspondence is not yet possible, this relation can concern only an *abstract* characteristic, as when, for example, in a lion strength is meant.

On the other hand, the abstractness of this relation brings home to consciousness even so the foreignness of the Idea to natural phenomena, and the Idea, which has no other reality to express it, launches out in all these shapes, seeks itself in them in their unrest and extravagance, but yet does not find them adequate to itself. So now the Idea exaggerates natural shapes and the phenomena of reality itself into indefiniteness and extravagance; it staggers round in them, it bubbles and ferments in them, does violence to them, distorts and stretches them unnaturally, and tries to elevate their phenomenal appearance to the Idea by the diffuseness, immensity, and splendour of the formations employed. For the Idea is here still more or less indeterminate and unshapable, while the natural objects are thoroughly determinate in their shape.

In the incompatibility of the two sides to one another, the relation of the Idea to the objective world therefore becomes a *negative* one, since the Idea, as something inward, is itself unsatisfied by such externality, and, as the inner universal substance thereof, it persists *sublime* above all this multiplicity of shapes which do not correspond with it. In the light of this sublimity, the natural phenomena and human forms and events are accepted, it is true, and left as they are, but yet they are recognized at the same time as incompatible with their meaning which is raised far above all mundane content.

These aspects constitute in general the character of the early artistic pantheism of the East, which on the one hand ascribes absolute meaning to even the most worthless objects, and, on the other, violently coerces the phenomena to express its view of the world whereby it becomes bizarre, grotesque, and tasteless, or turns the infinite but abstract freedom of the substance [i.e. the one Lord] disdainfully against all phenomena as being null and evanescent. By this means the meaning cannot be completely pictured in the expression and, despite all striving and endeavour, the incompatibility of Idea and shape still remains unconquered.—This may be taken to be the first form of art, the symbolic form with its quest, its fermentation, its mysteriousness, and its sublimity.

(*b*) In the *second* form of art which we will call the *classical*, the double defect of the symbolic form is extinguished. The symbolic shape is imperfect

4. An unknown block of stone may symbolize the Divine, but it does not represent it. Its natural shape has no connection with the Divine and is therefore external to it and not an embodiment of it. When shaping begins, the shapes produced are symbols, perhaps, but in themselves are fantastic and monstrous [Hegel's note].

because, (i) in it the Idea is presented to consciousness only as indeterminate or determined *abstractly*, and, (ii) for this reason the correspondence of meaning and shape is always defective and must itself remain purely abstract. The classical art-form clears up this double defect; it is the free and adequate embodiment of the Idea in the shape peculiarly appropriate to the Idea itself in its essential nature. With this shape, therefore, the Idea is able to come into free and complete harmony. Thus the classical art-form is the first to afford the production and vision of the completed Ideal and to present it as actualized in fact.

Nevertheless, the conformity of concept and reality in classical art must not be taken in the purely *formal* sense of a correspondence between a content and its external configuration, any more than this could be the case with the Idea itself. Otherwise every portrayal of nature, every cast of features, every neighbourhood, flower, scene, etc., which constitutes the end and content of the representation, would at once be classical on the strength of such congruity between content and form. On the contrary, in classical art the peculiarity of the content consists in its being itself the concrete Idea, and as such the concretely spiritual, for it is the spiritual alone which is the truly inner [self]. Consequently, to suit such a content we must try to find out what in nature belongs to the spiritual in and for itself. The *original* Concept itself it must be which *invented* the shape for concrete spirit, so that now the *subjective* Concept—here the spirit of art—has merely *found* this shape and made it, as a natural shaped existent, appropriate to free individual spirituality. This shape, which the Idea as spiritual—indeed as individually determinate spirituality—assumes when it is to proceed out into a temporal manifestation, is the human form. Of course personification and anthropomorphism have often been maligned as a degradation of the spiritual, but in so far as art's task is to bring the spiritual before our eyes in a sensuous manner, it must get involved in this anthropomorphism, since spirit appears sensuously in a satisfying way only in its body. The transmigration of souls[5] is in this respect an abstract idea, and physiology should have made it one of its chief propositions that life in its development had necessarily to proceed to the human form as the one and only sensuous appearance appropriate to spirit.

But the human body in its forms counts in classical art no longer as a merely sensuous existent, but only as the existence and natural shape of the spirit, and it must therefore be exempt from all the deficiency of the purely sensuous and from the contingent finitude of the phenomenal world. While in this way the shape is purified in order to express in itself a content adequate to itself, on the other hand, if the correspondence of meaning and shape is to be perfect, the spirituality, which is the content, must be of such a kind that it can express itself completely in the natural human form, without towering beyond and above this expression in sensuous and bodily terms. Therefore here the spirit is at once determined as particular and human, not as purely absolute and eternal, since in this latter sense it can proclaim and express itself only as spirituality.

This last point in its turn is the defect which brings about the dissolution

5. Reincarnation, belief in which was widespread in Greek antiquity; it began with Greek Orphic cults and followers of the pre-Socratic philosopher Pythagoras (6th c. B.C.E.).

of the classical art-form and demands a transition to a higher form, the *third*, namely the *romantic*.

(*c*) The romantic form of art cancels again the completed unification of the Idea and its reality, and reverts, even if in a higher way, to that difference and opposition of the two sides which in symbolic art remained unconquered. The classical form of art has attained the pinnacle of what illustration by art could achieve, and if there is something defective in it, the defect is just art itself and the restrictedness of the sphere of art. This restrictedness lies in the fact that art in general takes as its subject-matter the spirit (i.e. the *universal*, infinite and concrete in its nature) in a *sensuously* concrete form, and classical art presents the complete unification of spiritual and sensuous existence as the *correspondence* of the two. But in this blending of the two, spirit is not in fact represented in its *true nature*. For spirit is the infinite subjectivity of the Idea, which as absolute inwardness cannot freely and truly shape itself outwardly on condition of remaining moulded into a bodily existence as the one appropriate to it.[6]

Abandoning this [classical] principle, the romantic form of art cancels the undivided unity of classical art because it has won a content which goes beyond and above the classical form of art and its mode of expression. This content—to recall familiar ideas—coincides with what Christianity asserts of God as a spirit, in distinction from the Greek religion which is the essential and most appropriate content for classical art. In classical art the concrete content is *implicitly* the unity of the divine nature with the human, a unity which, just because it is only immediate and implicit, is adequately manifested also in an immediate and sensuous way. The Greek god is the object of naïve intuition and sensuous imagination, and therefore his shape is the bodily shape of man. The range of his power and his being is individual and particular. Contrasted with the individual he is a substance and power with which the individual's inner being is only implicitly at one but without itself possessing this oneness as inward subjective knowledge. Now the higher state is the *knowledge* of that *implicit* unity which is the content of the classical art-form and is capable of perfect presentation in bodily shape. But this elevation of the implicit into self-conscious knowledge introduces a tremendous difference. It is the infinite difference which, for example, separates man from animals. Man is an animal, but even in his animal functions, he is not confined to the implicit, as the animal is; he becomes conscious of them, recognizes them, and lifts them, as, for instance, the process of digestion, into self-conscious science. In this way man breaks the barrier of his implicit and immediate character, so that precisely because he *knows* that he is an animal, he ceases to be an animal and attains knowledge of himself as spirit.

Now if in this way what was implicit at the previous stage, the unity of divine and human nature, is raised from an *immediate* to a *known* unity, the *true* element for the realization of this content is no longer the sensuous immediate existence of the spiritual in the bodily form of man, but instead the *inwardness of self-consciousness*. Now Christianity brings God before our imagination as spirit, not as an individual, particular spirit, but as absolute

6. In other words, thought is "inwardness" in the sense that thoughts are not outside one another in the way that parts of a body are. That is why the spirit cannot find an adequate embodiment in things but only in thoughts, or at least only in the inner life [Hegel's note].

in spirit and in truth. For this reason it retreats from the sensuousness of imagination into spiritual inwardness and makes this, and not the body, the medium and the existence of truth's content. Thus the unity of divine and human nature is a known unity, one to be realized only by *spiritual* knowing and *in spirit*. The new content, thus won, is on this account not tied to sensuous presentation, as if that corresponded to it, but is freed from this immediate existence which must be set down as negative, overcome, and reflected into the spiritual unity. In this way romantic art is the self-transcendence of art but within its own sphere and in the form of art itself.

We may, therefore, in short, adhere to the view that at this third stage the subject-matter of art is *free concrete spirituality*, which is to be manifested as *spirituality* to the spirituality inward. In conformity with this subject-matter, art cannot work for sensuous intuition. Instead it must, on the one hand, work for the inwardness which coalesces with its object simply as if with itself, for subjective inner depth, for reflective emotion, for feeling which, as spiritual, strives for freedom in itself and seeks and finds its reconciliation only in the inner spirit. This *inner* world constitutes the content of the romantic sphere and must therefore be represented as this inwardness and in the pure appearance of this depth of feeling. Inwardness celebrates its triumph over the external and manifests its victory in and on the external itself, whereby what is apparent to the senses alone sinks into worthlessness.

On the other hand, however, this romantic form too, like all art, needs an external medium for its expression. Now since spirituality has withdrawn into itself out of the external world and immediate unity therewith, the sensuous externality of shape is for this reason accepted and represented, as in symbolic art, as something inessential and transient; and the same is true of the subjective finite spirit and will, right down to the particularity and caprice of individuality, character, action, etc., of incident, plot, etc. The aspect of external existence is consigned to contingency and abandoned to the adventures devised by an imagination whose caprice can mirror what is present to it, *exactly as it is*, just as readily as it can jumble the shapes of the external world and distort them grotesquely. For this external medium has its essence and meaning no longer, as in classical art, in itself and its own sphere, but in the heart which finds its manifestation in itself instead of in the external world and *its* form of reality, and this reconciliation with itself it can preserve or regain in every chance, in every accident that takes independent shape, in all misfortune and grief, and indeed even in crime.

Thereby the separation of Idea and shape, their indifference and inadequacy to each other, come to the fore again, as in symbolic art, but with this essential difference, that, in romantic art, the Idea, the deficiency of which in the symbol brought with it deficiency of shape, now has to appear *perfected* in itself as spirit and heart. Because of this higher perfection, it is not susceptible of an adequate union with the external, since its true reality and manifestation it can seek and achieve only within itself.

This we take to be the general character of the symbolic, classical, and romantic forms of art, as the three relations of the Idea to its shape in the sphere of art. They consist in the striving for, the attainment, and the transcendence of the Ideal as the true Idea of beauty.

1835–38

WILLIAM WORDSWORTH
1770–1850

"I am not a critic," William Wordsworth stated in 1830, "and set little value upon the art. The preface which I wrote long ago to my own Poems I was put upon to write by the urgent entreaties of a friend, and heartily regret I ever had anything to do with it; though I do not reckon the principles then advanced erroneous." Wordsworth defined himself as a poet above all, and he is less prolific and gifted as a literary theorist and critic than his friend SAMUEL TAYLOR COLERIDGE. Nevertheless, the preface that he wrote for the second edition of their book *Lyrical Ballads* (1800) is one of the most important documents in English criticism.

Wordsworth was born in Cockermouth, Cumberland, in the English Lake District. His mother died when he was eight; his father, an attorney, died less than six years later. Wordsworth was educated first at Hawkshead Grammar School, Westmorland, a boarding school noted for its training in mathematics and classics, and then at Cambridge University (1787–91), spending July–October 1790 on a walking tour of Europe. In France he was caught up in the excitement that followed the fall of the Bastille on July 14, 1789, and he became a fervent republican sympathizer.

Wordsworth's guardians wanted him to become an Anglican minister, but he persuaded them to support another twelve months of residence in France. When he was forced to return home in December 1792 by the threat of war between France and England, Wordsworth left behind the pregnant Annette Vallon; he supported her and their daughter in later years.

In 1793 Wordsworth's first works of poetry were published, *Descriptive Sketches* and *An Evening Walk*. In 1795 a legacy of £900 from a friend gave him the freedom to pursue a career as a poet. At this time he was living with his sister Dorothy; in 1797 they moved to Alfoxden in Somerset, with Coleridge (whom the poet had met in September 1795) a short distance away. There Wordsworth began to write the lyric and dramatic poems that many readers judge to be the central achievement of his career. The twentieth-century critic NORTHROP FRYE connects the poet's innovative descriptions to social and political critique: "In Wordsworth the existing social and educational structure is artificial, full of inert custom and hypocrisy. Nature is a better teacher than books, and one finds one's lost identity with nature in moments of feeling in which one is penetrated by the sense of nature's 'huge and mighty forms' " (quoting Wordsworth's *Prelude* 1.398).

Wordsworth's early compositions, and his creative partnership with Coleridge, resulted in September 1798 in the anonymous publication of *Lyrical Ballads*. The volume opened with Coleridge's "Ancient Mariner" and closed with Wordsworth's "Tintern Abbey"; all but three of the intervening poems were Wordsworth's. A new edition of *Lyrical Ballads*, incorporating Wordsworth's Preface and many new poems, was issued in 1800; this edition gave Wordsworth's name on the title page but not Coleridge's (whose "Ancient Mariner" was moved back to become the penultimate poem in the collection). In the Preface, Wordsworth declared that the book's object was "to choose incidents and situations from common life and to relate or describe them . . . in a selection of language really used by men, . . . tracing in them . . . the primary laws of our nature." Still another edition was published in 1802, and it was reprinted in 1805.

In later decades, Wordsworth not only wrote new poems but also revised (not always for the better) his earlier work. A collected edition, which includes many of his best poems and two critical essays, was published in 1815. His collections culminated in the six-volume edition of 1849–50. In these years the poet enjoyed both personal happiness—marrying Mary Hutchinson in 1802 and winning recognition as a national figure (he was named poet laureate in 1843)—and painful losses, including the death at sea of his favorite brother in 1805, a long and never wholly ended estrangement from Coleridge, the deaths of two of his children in 1812, and the physical and mental decline of his sister Dorothy that began in the 1830s. An even earlier loss was of his liberal ideals, much to the dismay of such younger poets as Byron, Keats, and SHELLEY. Wordsworth was horrified by the bloody aftermath of the French Revolution and alarmed by the rise of the French military leader and emperor Napoleon; he became increasingly orthodox in his political, social, and religious beliefs.

The critic HAROLD BLOOM has said that in dramatizing the movements of the individual consciousness, Wordsworth made "the poet's own subjectivity" the "prevalent subject" of poetry. Wordsworth spurred writers to break free from the authority of neoclassical rules and conventions and to find inspiration instead in the emotions, experiences, and speech of ordinary persons. In valuing naturalness and spontaneity, Wordsworth was proposing not that poets abandon literary craft but that poetry should begin with acts of self-expression and self-exploration. There is much truth in the familiar generalization that Romantic poets are visionary, evocative describers of nature—its scenes, settings, landscapes. But the movement outward into the natural world is really one dimension of an interior journey or quest into what Wordsworth called "the hiding-places of man's power." M. H. Abrams concisely explains this fundamental change, in his classic study *The Mirror and the Lamp: Romantic Theory and the Critical Tradition* (1953):

> The paramount cause of poetry is not, as in Aristotle, a formal cause, determined primarily by the human actions and qualities imitated; nor, as in neoclassic criticism a final cause, the effect intended upon the audience; but instead an efficient cause—the impulse within the poet of feelings and desires seeking expression, or the compulsion of the "creative" imagination which, like God the creator, has its internal source of motion.

A number of the formulations in the preface have become widely known and are permanently linked to Wordsworth's name—for example, that the modern poems included in *Lyrical Ballads* fit to "metrical arrangement a selection of the real language of men in a state of vivid sensation," and that "good poetry is the spontaneous overflow of powerful feelings," "tak[ing] its origin from emotion recollected in tranquillity." Yet, as W. J. B. Owen and other scholars have noted, Wordsworth is less original than his bold tone and manner suggest; much of what he says about figurative language, poetic diction, and the relationship between poetry and prose draws on an array of eighteenth-century English writings on emotion, knowledge, and aesthetic theory. That we remember Wordsworth's words, not those of his sources, testifies both to the eloquence of his prose and to its association with a magnificent series of poems.

In his criticism, and in the Preface especially, Wordsworth seeks to explain and defend his own literary practice; in this respect, he is akin to fellow poets JOHN DRYDEN and T. S. ELIOT and the novelist HENRY JAMES, whose criticism fabricates frameworks through which their creative endeavors should be understood and appreciated. Like them, Wordsworth possesses a sharp sense of literary history and tradition; where he differs is in his refusal or failure to make the interpretation and evaluation of writers and texts an integral part of his literary project and identity. Indeed, overall his criticism—found in prefaces for his books of poems, a few essays, sentences and paragraphs in letters, and tossed-off opinions and asides in conversations with friends and acquaintances—is not impressive, nor are his judgments compelling. He radically misunderstood and devalued ALEXANDER POPE, SAMUEL JOHNSON, Goethe, and Byron and failed to perceive the genius of Thomas Carlyle and RALPH WALDO EMERSON. As he admitted himself, he was not much interested in the writing of his contemporaries; he cared little for novels, despite living in a period when the novel as a genre was coming to a new, rich prominence. Instead, Wordsworth's mission is to return to basic, timeless truths—and thus he raises and confronts such questions as "What is a Poet?" and "To whom does he address himself?"

Like many important theoretical works by creative writers, Wordsworth's Preface is not always in accord with his actual practice. In the *Biographia Literaria* (1817), Coleridge makes exactly this point and states further that Wordsworth simply asserts without proof that the language of rural folk has a richer reality than that of city dwellers. There are other overemphases, ambiguities, and contradictions in Wordsworth's arguments as well. He stresses that poetry heals and restores the feelings of persons; but when one reviews his poetry and prose as a whole, particularly that of his later career, his point becomes hard to grasp: does Wordsworth mean that poetry will lead to a regenerated society or, instead, that it will accommodate readers to their society as it is? And despite Wordsworth's insistence that the poet engage and employ the language "really used by men," and that such language is best located among those living a "low and rustic life," two of his own greatest literary heroes, as the scholar René Wellek has pointed out, were Spenser and Milton—"the most learned, even bookish poets of the English tradition."

The Preface is to some extent a political text as well as a literary position paper. Wordsworth's desire to select "incidents and situations from common life" blends into poetry the democratic sentiments that the French Revolution had inspired in him in the early 1790s. By advocating "the real language of men," Wordsworth cuts against the neoclassical view that the language of poetry must be more elevated than everyday speech. The rebelliousness in this stance helps us understand why the Romantic critic and essayist William Hazlitt connected Wordsworth's verse with "the revolutionary movement of our age": "His Muse," Hazlitt said, "is a levelling one." By directing attention to ballads, folklore, and other materials usually deemed nonliterary or unpoetical, Wordsworth expands the range of subjects for poetry. He honors children and common men and women, and even criminals and idiots: his poetry does not bestow dignity on them but expresses the dignity they already possess.

Wordsworth was actively concerned about the pressures that impinge on the lives of those living in newly industrialized cities, the pressures that threaten to reduce the mind "to a state of almost savage torpor" and that lead individuals to immerse themselves in reports and stories of sensational incidents. Here he looks forward to the opposition between high and mass or popular cultures that modern critics such as RAYMOND WILLIAMS later explored. Insofar as the Preface establishes the writer as an adversary to popular culture and the always-accelerating trends in social and cultural life, Wordsworth anticipates themes articulated by writers ranging from Shelley to D. H. Lawrence. The poet, he maintains in an important appendix added in 1802, "is the rock of defense of human nature; an upholder and preserver, carrying every where with him relationship and love." Moreover, as he discusses in some detail, poets in the future will be obliged to defend the worth of their activity as against that of the scientists. This is a struggle to which MATTHEW ARNOLD, later in the nineteenth century, and I. A. Richards and the New Critics, in the twentieth century, return with even greater urgency.

BIBLIOGRAPHY

A new complete edition, under the general editorship of Stephen Parrish, is being published by Cornell (1975–). For the criticism and related prose writings, see *Prose Works*, edited by W. J. B. Owen and J. M. Smyser (3 vols., 1974). Collections of Wordsworth's critical prose include *The Critical Opinions of William Wordsworth*, edited by Markham L. Peacock (1950), which presents 450 pages of primary source quotations divided into three categories—subjects, authors, and works, and Wordsworth on his own works; *Literary Criticism of William Wordsworth*, edited by Paul M. Zall (1966); and *Wordsworth's Literary Criticism*, edited by W. J. B. Owen (1974). A good single-volume edition of the poetry and prose is *William Wordsworth*, in the Oxford Authors Series, edited by Stephen Gill (1984).

The standard biography, *William Wordsworth: A Biography*, is by Mary Moorman (2 vols., 1957–65), but Stephen Gill's *William Wordsworth: A Life* (1989) is also valuable. On the poet's early adulthood, see Kenneth R. Johnston, *The Hidden Wordsworth: Poet, Lover, Rebel, Spy* (1998). See also Mark L. Reed, *Wordsworth: The Chronology of the Early Years, 1770–1799* (1967) and *Wordsworth: The Chronology of the Middle Years, 1800–1815* (1975). For intellectual and literary contexts, consult Duncan Wu, *Wordsworth's Reading, 1770–1799* (1993) and *Wordsworth's Reading, 1800–1815* (1995).

For an excellent study of Wordsworth's Preface as well as an edition of the text, see *Wordsworth's Preface to "Lyrical Ballads,"* edited by W. J. B. Owen (1957). Also insightful is Owen's *Wordsworth as Critic* (1969). There is an extensive body of scholarship on the relationship between Wordsworth and Coleridge and its importance for literary theory and criticism. Among the best books on this topic are Lucy Newlyn, *Coleridge, Wordsworth, and the Language of Allusion* (1986); Theresa M. Kelley, *Wordsworth's Revisionary Aesthetics* (1988); Paul Magnuson, *Coleridge and Wordsworth: A Lyrical Dialogue* (1988); Nicholas Roe, *Wordsworth and Coleridge: The Radical Years* (1988); and Susan Eilenberg, *Strange Power of Speech: Wordsworth, Coleridge, and Literary Possession* (1992).

See also three collections of essays: *The Age of William Wordsworth*, edited by Kenneth R. Johnston and Gene W. Ruoff (1987); *Romantic Revolutions: Criticism and Theory*, edited by Kenneth R. Johnston (1990); and *Wordsworth in Context*, edited by Pauline Fletcher and John Murphy (1992). For further background and bibliography, see the relevant entries in *The English Romantic Poets: A Review of Research and Criticism* (ed. Frank Jordan, 1985), and *British Romantic Poets, 1789–1832*, first and second series (ed. John R. Greenfield, 1990).

Preface to *Lyrical Ballads, with Pastoral and Other Poems* (1802)[1]

The first Volume of these Poems has already been submitted to general perusal. It was published, as an experiment, which, I hoped, might be of some use to ascertain, how far, by fitting to metrical arrangement a selection of the real language of men in a state of vivid sensation, that sort of pleasure and that quantity of pleasure may be imparted, which a Poet may rationally endeavour to impart.

I had formed no very inaccurate estimate of the probable effect of those Poems: I flattered myself that they who should be pleased with them would read them with more than common pleasure: and, on the other hand, I was well aware, that by those who should dislike them they would be read with more than common dislike. The result has differed from my expectation in this only, that I have pleased a greater number, than I ventured to hope I should please.

For the sake of variety, and from a consciousness of my own weakness, I was induced to request the assistance of a Friend,[2] who furnished me with the Poems of the ANCIENT MARINER, the FOSTER-MOTHER'S TALE, the NIGHTINGALE, and the Poem entitled LOVE. I should not, however, have requested this assistance, had I not believed that the Poems of my Friend would in a

1. This preface first appeared in the second edition of *Lyrical Ballads*, expanded to two volumes and dated 1800. For an edition published in 1802, Wordsworth revised the preface (he made more revisions for subsequent editions) and added an appendix; the important additions to the 1800 text are here given in brackets.

2. SAMUEL TAYLOR COLERIDGE (1772–1834), English poet and critic.

great measure have the same tendency as my own, and that, though there would be found a difference, there would be found no discordance in the colours of our style; as our opinions on the subject of poetry do almost entirely coincide.

Several of my Friends are anxious for the success of these Poems from a belief, that, if the views with which they were composed were indeed realized, a class of Poetry would be produced, well adapted to interest mankind permanently, and not unimportant in the multiplicity, and in the quality of its moral relations: and on this account they have advised me to prefix a systematic defence of the theory, upon which the poems were written. But I was unwilling to undertake the task, because I knew that on this occasion the Reader would look coldly upon my arguments, since I might be suspected of having been principally influenced by the selfish and foolish hope of *reasoning* him into an approbation of these particular Poems: and I was still more unwilling to undertake the task, because, adequately to display my opinions, and fully to enforce my arguments, would require a space wholly disproportionate to the nature of a preface. For to treat the subject with the clearness and coherence of which I believe it susceptible, it would be necessary to give a full account of the present state of the public taste in this country, and to determine how far this taste is healthy or depraved; which, again, would not be determined, without pointing out, in what manner language and the human mind act and re-act on each other, and without retracing the revolutions, not of literature alone, but likewise of society itself. I have therefore altogether declined to enter regularly upon this defence; yet I am sensible, that there would be some impropriety in abruptly obtruding upon the Public, without a few words of introduction, Poems so materially different from those upon which general approbation is at present bestowed.

It is supposed, that by the act of writing in verse an Author makes a formal engagement that he will gratify certain known habits of association; that he not only thus apprizes the Reader that certain classes of ideas and expressions will be found in his book, but that others will be carefully excluded. This exponent or symbol held forth by metrical language must in different areas of literature have excited very different expectations: for example, in the age of Catullus, Terence and Lucretius, and that of Statius or Claudian;[3] and in our own country, in the age of Shakespeare and Beaumont and Fletcher, and that of Donne and Cowley, or Dryden, or Pope.[4] I will not take upon me to determine the exact import of the promise which by the act of writing in verse an Author, in the present day, makes to his Reader; but I am certain, it will appear to many persons that I have not fulfilled the terms of an engagement thus voluntarily contracted. [They who have been accustomed to the gaudiness and inane phraseology of many modern writers, if they persist in reading this book to its conclusion, will, no doubt, frequently have to struggle with feelings of strangeness and aukward-

3. Wordsworth names Roman poets in different genres, before and after the common era (and thus writing in "Golden" vs. "Silver" Latin): Catullus (84–54 B.C.E.), lyric poet; Terence (ca. 190–159 B.C.E.), comic dramatist; Lucretius (ca. 94–55 B.C.E.), didactic poet; Statius (45–96 C.E.), epic poet; and Claudian (d. ca. 404 C.E.), an Alexandrian whose Latin poetry represents the end of the classical tradition.

4. Wordsworth names three English dramatists—Shakespeare (1564–1616), Francis Beaumont (ca. 1584–1616), and John Fletcher (1579–1625); and four poets—John Donne (1572–1631), Abraham Cowley (1618–1667), JOHN DRYDEN (1631–1700), and ALEXANDER POPE (1688–1744). As their dates suggest, he focuses here less on chronology than on style.

ness: they will look round for poetry, and will be induced to inquire by what species of courtesy these attempts can be permitted to assume that title.] I hope therefore the Reader will not censure me, if I attempt to state what I have proposed to myself to perform; and also, (as far as the limits of a preface will permit) to explain some of the chief reasons which have determined me in the choice of my purpose: that at least he may be spared any unpleasant feeling of disappointment, and that I myself may be protected from the most dishonourable accusation which can be brought against an Author, namely, that of an indolence which prevents him from endeavouring to ascertain what is his duty, or, when his duty is ascertained, prevents him from performing it.

The principal object, then, which I proposed to myself in these Poems was to [chuse incidents and situations from common life, and to relate or describe them, throughout, as far as was possible, in a selection of language really used by men; and, at the same time, to throw over them a certain colouring of imagination, whereby ordinary things should be presented to the mind in an unusual way; and, further, and above all, to make these incidents and situations interesting] by tracing in them, truly though not ostentatiously, the primary laws of our nature: chiefly, as far as regards the manner in which we associate ideas in a state of excitement. Low and rustic life was generally chosen, because in that condition, the essential passions of the heart find a better soil in which they can attain their maturity, are less under restraint, and speak a plainer and more emphatic language; because in that condition of life our elementary feelings co-exist in a state of greater simplicity, and, consequently, may be more accurately contemplated, and more forcibly communicated; because the manners of rural life germinate from those elementary feelings; and, from the necessary character of rural occupations, are more easily comprehended; and are more durable; and lastly, because in that condition the passions of men are incorporated with the beautiful and permanent forms of nature. The language, too, of these men is adopted (purified indeed from what appear to be its real defects, from all lasting and rational causes of dislike or disgust) because such men hourly communicate with the best objects from which the best part of language is originally derived; and because, from their rank in society and the sameness and narrow circle of their intercourse, being less under the influence of social vanity they convey their feelings and notions in simple and unelaborated expressions. Accordingly, such a language, arising out of repeated experience and regular feelings, is a more permanent, and a far more philosophical language, than that which is frequently substituted for it by Poets, who think that they are conferring honour upon themselves and their art, in proportion as they separate themselves from the sympathies of men, and indulge in arbitrary and capricious habits of expression, in order to furnish food for fickle tastes, and fickle appetites, of their own creation.[5]

I cannot, however, be insensible of the present outcry against the triviality and meanness both of thought and language, which some of my contemporaries have occasionally introduced into their metrical compositions; and I acknowledge that this defect, where it exists, is more dishonourable to the

5. It is worth while here to observe that the affecting parts of Chaucer [ca. 1343–1400] are almost always expressed in language pure and universally intelligible even to this day [Wordsworth's note].

Writer's own character than false refinement or arbitrary innovation, though I should contend at the same time that it is far less pernicious in the sum of its consequences. From such verses the Poems in these volumes will be found distinguished at least by one mark of difference, that each of them has a worthy *purpose*. Not that I mean to say, that I always began to write with a distinct purpose formally conceived; but I believe that my habits of meditation have so formed my feelings, as that my descriptions of such objects as strongly excite those feelings, will be found to carry along with them a *purpose*. If in this opinion I am mistaken, I can have little right to the name of a Poet. For all good poetry is the spontaneous overflow of powerful feelings: but though this be true, Poems to which any value can be attached, were never produced on any variety of subjects but by a man, who being possessed of more than usual organic sensibility, had also thought long and deeply. For our continued influxes of feeling are modified and directed by our thoughts, which are indeed the representatives of all our past feelings; and, as by contemplating the relation of these general representatives to each other we discover what is really important to men, so, by the repetition and continuance of this act, our feelings will be connected with important subjects, till at length, if we be originally possessed of much sensibility, such habits of mind will be produced, that, by obeying blindly and mechanically the impulses of those habits, we shall describe objects, and utter sentiments, of such a nature and in such connection with each other, that the understanding of the being to whom we address ourselves, if he be in a healthful state of association, must necessarily be in some degree enlightened, and his affections ameliorated.

I have said that each of these poems has a purpose. I have also informed my Reader what this purpose will be found principally to be: namely, to illustrate the manner in which our feelings and ideas are associated in a state of excitement. But, speaking in language somewhat more appropriate, it is to follow the fluxes and refluxes of the mind when agitated by the great and simple affections of our nature. This object I have endeavoured in these short essays to attain by various means; by tracing the maternal passion through many of its more subtle windings, as in the poems of the IDIOT BOY and the MAD MOTHER; by accompanying the last struggles of a human being, at the approach of death, cleaving in solitude to life and society, as in the Poem of the FORSAKEN INDIAN; by showing, as in the Stanzas entitled WE ARE SEVEN, the perplexity and obscurity which in childhood attend our notion of death, or rather our utter inability to admit that notion; or by displaying the strength of fraternal, or to speak more philosophically, of moral attachment when early associated with the great and beautiful objects of nature, as in THE BROTHERS; or, as in the Incident of SIMON LEE, by placing my Reader in the way of receiving from ordinary moral sensations another and more salutary impression than we are accustomed to receive from them. It has also been part of my general purpose to attempt to sketch characters under the influence of less impassioned feelings, as in the TWO APRIL MORNINGS, THE FOUNTAIN, THE OLD MAN TRAVELLING, THE TWO THIEVES, &c. characters of which the elements are simple, belonging rather to nature than to manners, such as exist now, and will probably always exist, and which from their constitution may be distinctly and profitably contemplated. I will not abuse the indulgence of my Reader by dwelling longer upon this subject; but it is proper that I should mention one other circumstance which distinguishes these Poems from the popular Poetry of the day; it is this, that the feeling therein developed gives importance to the action and situation, and not the action and situation to the feeling. My meaning will be rendered perfectly intelligible by referring my Reader to the Poems entitled POOR SUSAN and the CHILDLESS FATHER, particularly to the last Stanza of the latter Poem.

I will not suffer a sense of false modesty to prevent me from asserting, that I point my Reader's attention to this mark of distinction, far less for the sake of these particular Poems than from the general importance of the subject. The subject is indeed important! For the human mind is capable of being excited without the application of gross and violent stimulants; and he must have a very faint perception of its beauty and dignity who does not know this, and who does not further know, that one being is elevated above another, in proportion as he possesses this capability. It has therefore appeared to me, that to endeavour to produce or enlarge this capability is one of the best services in which, at any period, a Writer can be engaged; but this service, excellent at all times, is especially so at the present day. For a multitude of causes, unknown to former times, are now acting with a combined force to blunt the discriminating powers of the mind, and unfitting it for all voluntary exertion to reduce it to a state of almost savage torpor. The most effective of these causes are the great national events which are daily taking place,[6] and the encreasing accumulation of men in cities, where the uniformity of their occupations produces a craving for extraordinary incident, which the rapid communication of intelligence[7] hourly gratifies. To this tendency of life and manners the literature and theatrical exhibitions of the country have conformed themselves. The invaluable works of our elder writers, I had almost said the works of Shakespeare and Milton, are driven into neglect by frantic novels, sickly and stupid German Tragedies,[8] and deluges of idle and extravagant stories in verse.—When I think upon this degrading thirst after outrageous stimulation, I am almost ashamed to have spoken of the feeble effort with which I have endeavoured to counteract it; and, reflecting upon the magnitude of the general evil, I should be oppressed with no dishonorable melancholy, had I not a deep impression of certain inherent and indestructible qualities of the human mind, and likewise of certain powers in the great and permanent objects that act upon it, which are equally inherent and indestructible; and did I not further add to this impression a belief, that the time is approaching when the evil will be systematically opposed, by men of greater powers, and with far more distinguished success.

Having dwelt thus long on the subjects and aim of these Poems, I shall request the Reader's permission to apprize him of a few circumstances relating to their *style*, in order, among other reasons, that I may not be censured for not having performed what I never attempted. [The Reader will find that personifications of abstract ideas rarely occur in these volumes; and, I hope, are utterly rejected as an ordinary device to elevate the style, and raise it

6. The French Revolution and the Napoleonic Wars, primarily between France and Great Britain (1799–1815), that grew out of it and out of the rise to power of the French general Napoléon Bonaparte (1769–1821), later emperor (1804–15).

7. Information, news (daily newspapers were spreading rapidly in England).

8. German melodramas by authors such as August von Kotzebue (1761–1819); in Jane Austen's novel *Mansfield Park* (1814), the Bertram family performs Elizabeth Inchbald's *Lovers' Vows*, which is based on von Kotzebue's *Das kind der Lieber*. "Frantic novels": Gothic novels, such as *The Mysteries of Udolpho* (1794) by Ann Radcliffe and *The Monk* (1796) by M. G. Lewis.

above prose. I have proposed to myself to imitate, and, as far as is possible, to adopt the very language of men; and assuredly such personifications do not make any natural or regular part of that language. They are, indeed, a figure of speech occasionally prompted by passion, and I have made use of them as such; but I have endeavoured utterly to reject them as a mechanical device of style, or as a family language which Writers in metre seem to lay claim to by prescription.] I have wished to keep my Reader in the company of flesh and blood, persuaded that by so doing I shall interest him. I am, however, well aware that others who pursue a different track may interest him likewise; I do not interfere with their claim, I only wish to prefer a different claim of my own. There will also be found in these volumes little of what is usually called poetic diction; I have taken as much pains to avoid it as others ordinarily take to produce it; this I have done for the reason already alleged, to bring my language near to the language of men, and further, because the pleasure which I have proposed to myself to impart is of a kind very different from that which is supposed by many persons to be the proper object of poetry. I do not know how, without being culpably particular, I can give my Reader a more exact notion of the style in which I wished these poems to be written than by informing him that I have at all times endeavoured to look steadily at my subject, consequently, I hope that there is in these Poems little falsehood of description, and that my ideas are expressed in language fitted to their respective importance. Something I must have gained by this practice, as it is friendly to one property of all good poetry, namely good sense; but it has necessarily cut me off from a large portion of phrases and figures of speech which from father to son have long been regarded as the common inheritance of Poets. I have also thought it expedient to restrict myself still further, having abstained from the use of many expressions, in themselves proper and beautiful, but which have been foolishly repeated by bad Poets, till such feelings of disgust are connected with them as it is scarcely possible by any art of association to overpower.

If in a Poem there should be found a series of lines, or even a single line, in which the language, though naturally arranged, and according to the strict laws of metre, does not differ from that of prose, there is a numerous class of critics, who, when they stumble upon these prosaisms, as they call them, imagine that they have made a notable discovery, and exult over the Poet as over a man ignorant of his own profession. Now these men would establish a canon of criticism which the Reader will conclude he must utterly reject, if he wishes to be pleased with these volumes. And it would be a most easy task to prove to him, that not only the language of a large portion of every good poem, even of the most elevated character, must necessarily, except with reference to the metre, in no respect differ from that of good prose, but likewise that some of the most interesting parts of the best poems will be found to be strictly the language of prose, when prose is well written. The truth of this assertion might be demonstrated by innumerable passages from almost all the poetical writings, even of Milton himself. I have not space for much quotation; but, to illustrate the subject in a general manner, I will here adduce a short composition of Gray,[9] who was at the head of those who, by

9. Thomas Gray (1716–1771); the poem quoted is "Sonnet on the Death of Richard West" (1775; West was a friend of Gray's at Eton). Gray, in a letter to West, had maintained that "the language of the age is never the language of poetry."

their reasonings, have attempted to widen the space of separation betwixt Prose and Metrical composition, and was more than any other man curiously elaborate in the structure of his own poetic diction.

In vain to me the smiling mornings shine,
And reddening Phoebus[1] lifts his golden fire:
The birds in vain their amorous descant join,
Or chearful fields resume their green attire.
These ears, alas! for other notes repine;
A different object do these eyes require;
My lonely anguish melts no heart but mine;
And in my breast the imperfect joys expire;
Yet morning smiles the busy race to cheer,
And new-born pleasure brings to happier men;
The fields to all their wonted tribute bear;
To warm their little loves the birds complain.
I fruitless mourn to him that cannot hear,
And weep the more because I weep in vain.

It will easily be perceived that the only part of this Sonnet which is of any value is the lines printed in Italics: it is equally obvious, that, except in the rhyme, and in the use of the single word 'fruitless' for fruitlessly, which is so far a defect, the language of these lines does in no respect differ from that of prose.

[By the foregoing quotation I have shewn that the language of Prose may yet be well adapted to Poetry; and I have previously asserted that a large portion of the language of every good poem can in no respect differ from that of good Prose. I will go further. I do not doubt that it may be safely affirmed, that there neither is, nor can be, any essential difference between the language of prose and metrical composition.] We are fond of tracing the resemblance between Poetry and Painting,[2] and, accordingly, we call them Sisters: but where shall we find bonds of connection sufficiently strict to typify the affinity betwixt metrical and prose composition? They both speak by and to the same organs; the bodies in which both of them are clothed may be said to be of the same substance, their affections are kindred, and almost identical, not necessarily differing even in degree; Poetry[3] sheds no tears 'such as Angels weep,'[4] but natural and human tears; she can boast of no celestial Ichor[5] that distinguishes her vital juices from those of prose; the same human blood circulates through the veins of them both.

If it be affirmed that rhyme and metrical arrangement of themselves constitute a distinction which overturns what I have been saying on the strict

1. Apollo, Roman and Greek god of the sun, here identified with the sun.
2. A topic examined, for example, by the poets and critics HORACE, *Ars Poetica* (ca. 10 B.C.E.); Dryden, *A Parallel of Poetry and Painting* (1695); SIR PHILIP SIDNEY, *An Apology for Poetry* (1595); Pope, *An Essay on Criticism* (1711); GOTTHOLD EPHRAIM LESSING, *Laocöon* (1766); and SAMUEL JOHNSON, *Idler*, no. 34 (1758).
3. I here use the word "Poetry" (though against my own judgment) as opposed to the word Prose, and synonymous with metrical composition. But much confusion has been introduced into criticism by this contradistinction of Poetry and Prose, instead of the more philosophical one of Poetry and Matter of Fact, or Science. The only strict antithesis to Prose is Metre; nor is this, in truth, a *strict* antithesis; because lines and passages of metre so naturally occur in writing prose, that it would be scarcely possible to avoid them, even if it were desirable [Wordsworth's note].
4. From John Milton, *Paradise Lost* (1667), 1.620.
5. In Greek mythology, the fluid that flows in the veins of the gods.

affinity of metrical language with that of prose, and paves the way for other artificial distinctions which the mind voluntarily admits,[6] [I answer that the language of such Poetry as I am recommending is, as far as is possible, a selection of the language really spoken by men; that this selection, wherever it is made with true taste and feeling, will of itself form a distinction far greater than would at first be imagined, and will entirely separate the composition from the vulgarity and meanness of ordinary life; and, if metre be superadded thereto, I believe that a dissimilitude will be produced altogether sufficient for the gratification of a rational mind. What other distinction would we have? Whence is it to come? And where is it to exist? Not, surely, where the Poet speaks through the mouths of his characters: it cannot be necessary here, either for elevation of style, or any of its supposed ornaments; for, if the Poet's subject be judiciously chosen, it will naturally, and upon fit occasion, lead him to passions the language of which, if selected truly and judiciously, must necessarily be dignified and variegated, and alive with metaphors and figures. I forbear to speak of an incongruity which would shock the intelligent Reader, should the Poet interweave any foreign splendour of his own with that which the passion naturally suggests: it is sufficient to say that such addition is unnecessary. And, surely, it is more probable that those passages, which with propriety abound with metaphors and figures, will have their due effect, if, upon other occasions where the passions are of a milder character, the style also be subdued and temperate.

But, as the pleasure which I hope to give by the Poems I now present to the Reader must depend entirely on just notions upon this subject, and, as it is in itself of the highest importance to our taste and moral feelings, I cannot content myself with these detached remarks. And if, in what I am about to say, it shall appear to some that my labour is unnecessary, and that I am like a man fighting a battle without enemies, I would remind such persons that, whatever may be the language outwardly holden[7] by men, a practical faith in the opinions which I am wishing to establish is almost unknown. If my conclusions are admitted, and carried as far as they must be carried if admitted at all, our judgments concerning the works of the greatest Poets both ancient and modern will be far different from what they are at present, both when we praise, and when we censure: and our moral feelings influencing, and influenced by these judgments will, I believe, be corrected and purified.

Taking up the subject, then, upon general grounds, I ask what is meant by the word Poet? What is a Poet? To whom does he address himself? And what language is to be expected from him? He is a man speaking to men: a man, it is true, endued with more lively sensibility, more enthusiasm and tenderness, who has a greater knowledge of human nature, and a more comprehensive soul, than are supposed to be common among mankind; a man pleased with his own passions and volitions, and who rejoices more than other men in the spirit of life that is in him; delighting to contemplate similar volitions and passions as manifested in the goings-on of the Universe, and habitually impelled to create them where he does not find them. To these

6. Here begins the longest and most important addition made in 1802; it contains 9 paragraphs.

7. Held.

qualities he has added a disposition to be affected more than other men by absent things as if they were present; an ability of conjuring up in himself passions, which are indeed far from being the same as those produced by real events, yet (especially in those parts of the general sympathy which are pleasing and delightful) do more nearly resemble the passions produced by real events, than any thing which, from the motions of their own minds merely, other men are accustomed to feel in themselves; whence, and from practice, he has acquired a greater readiness and power in expressing what he thinks and feels, and especially those thoughts and feelings which, by his own choice, or from the structure of his own mind, arise in him without immediate external excitement.

But, whatever portion of this faculty we may suppose even the greatest Poet to possess, there cannot be a doubt but that the language which it will suggest to him, must, in liveliness and truth, fall far short of that which is uttered by men in real life, under the actual pressure of those passions, certain shadows of which the Poet thus produces, or feels to be produced, in himself. However exalted a notion we would wish to cherish of the character of a Poet, it is obvious, that, while he describes and imitates passions, his situation is altogether slavish and mechanical, compared with the freedom and power of real and substantial action and suffering. So that it will be the wish of the Poet to bring his feelings near to those of the persons whose feelings he describes, nay, for short spaces of time perhaps, to let himself slip into an entire delusion, and even confound and identify his own feelings with theirs; modifying only the language which is thus suggested to him, by a consideration that he describes for a particular purpose, that of giving pleasure. Here, then, he will apply the principle on which I have so much insisted, namely, that of selection; on this he will depend for removing what would otherwise be painful or disgusting in the passion; he will feel that there is no necessity to trick out or elevate nature: and, the more industriously he applies this principle, the deeper will be his faith that no words, which his fancy or imagination can suggest, will be to be compared with those which are the emanations of reality and truth.

But it may be said by those who do not object to the general spirit of these remarks, that, as it is impossible for the Poet to produce upon all occasions language as exquisitely fitted for the passion as that which the real passion itself suggests, it is proper that he should consider himself as in the situation of a translator, who deems himself justified when he substitutes excellences of another kind for those which are unattainable by him; and endeavours occasionally to surpass his original, in order to make some amends for the general inferiority to which he feels that he must submit. But this would be to encourage idleness and unmanly despair. Further, it is the language of men who speak of what they do not understand; who talk of Poetry as of a matter of amusement and idle pleasure; who will converse with us as gravely about a *taste* for Poetry, as they express it, as if it were a thing as indifferent as a taste for Rope-dancing, or Frontiniac[8] or Sherry. Aristotle, I have been told, hath said, that Poetry is the most philosophic of all writing:[9] it is so: its object is truth, not individual and local, but general, and operative; not stand-

8. A sweet wine.
9. See ARISTOTLE, *Poetics* 9, 1451b: "poetry is at once more like philosophy and more worth while than history, since poetry tends to make general statements, while those of history are particular."

ing upon external testimony, but carried alive into the heart by passion; truth which is its own testimony, which gives strength and divinity to the tribunal to which it appeals, and receives them from the same tribunal. Poetry is the image of man and nature. The obstacles which stand in the way of the fidelity of the Biographer and Historian, and of their consequent utility, are incalculably greater than those which are to be encountered by the Poet who has an adequate notion of the dignity of his art. The Poet writes under one restriction only, namely, that of the necessity of giving immediate pleasure to a human Being possessed of that information which may be expected from him, not as a lawyer, a physician, a mariner, an astronomer or a natural philosopher, but as a Man. Except this one restriction, there is no object standing between the Poet and the image of things; between this, and the Biographer and Historian there are a thousand.

Nor let this necessity of producing immediate pleasure be considered as a degradation of the Poet's art. It is far otherwise. It is an acknowledgment of the beauty of the universe, an acknowledgment the more sincere, because it is not formal, but indirect; it is a task light and easy to him who looks at the world in the spirit of love: further, it is a homage paid to the native and naked dignity of man, to the grand elementary principle of pleasure, by which he knows, and feels, and lives, and moves.[1] We have no sympathy but what is propagated by pleasure: I would not be misunderstood; but wherever we sympathize with pain it will be found that the sympathy is produced and carried on by subtle combinations with pleasure. We have no knowledge, that is, no general principles drawn from the contemplation of particular facts, but what has been built up by pleasure, and exists in us by pleasure alone. The Man of Science,[2] the Chemist and Mathematician, whatever difficulties and disgusts they may have had to struggle with, know and feel this. However painful may be the objects with which the Anatomist's knowledge is connected, he feels that his knowledge is pleasure; and where he has no pleasure he has no knowledge. What then does the Poet? He considers man and the objects that surround him as acting and re-acting upon each other, so as to produce an infinite complexity of pain and pleasure; he considers man in his own nature and in his ordinary life as contemplating this with a certain quantity of immediate knowledge, with certain convictions, intuitions, and deductions which by habit become of the nature of intuitions; he considers him as looking upon this complex scene of ideas and sensations, and finding every where objects that immediately excite in him sympathies which, from the necessities of his nature, are accompanied by an overbalance of enjoyment.

To this knowledge which all men carry about with them, and to these sympathies in which without any other discipline than that of our daily life we are fitted to take delight, the Poet principally directs his attention. He considers man and nature as essentially adapted to each other, and the mind of man as naturally the mirror of the fairest and most interesting qualities of nature. And thus the Poet, prompted by this feeling of pleasure which accompanies him through the whole course of his studies, converses with general nature with affections akin to those, which, through labour and

1. Compare St. Paul's declaration that in God "we live, and move, and have our being" (Acts 17.28).
2. Wordsworth may have had in mind in particular the English chemist Humphrey Davy (1778–1829), who had lectured at the Royal Institution on January 21, 1802.

length of time, the Man of Science has raised up in himself, by conversing with those particular parts of nature which are the objects of his studies. The knowledge both of the Poet and the Man of Science is pleasure; but the knowledge of the one cleaves to us as a necessary part of our existence, our natural and unalienable inheritance; the other is a personal and individual acquisition, slow to come to us, and by no habitual and direct sympathy connecting us with our fellow-beings. The Man of Science seeks truth as a remote and unknown benefactor; he cherishes and loves it in his solitude: the Poet, singing a song in which all human beings join with him, rejoices in the presence of truth as our visible friend and hourly companion. Poetry is the breath and finer spirit of all knowledge; it is the impassioned expression which is in the countenance of all Science. Emphatically may it be said of the Poet, as Shakespeare hath said of man, 'that he looks before and after.'[3] He is the rock of defence of human nature; an upholder and preserver, carrying every where with him relationship and love. In spite of difference of soil and climate, of language and manners, of laws and customs, in spite of things silently gone out of mind and things violently destroyed, the Poet binds together by passion and knowledge the vast empire of human society, as it is spread over the whole earth, and over all time. The objects of the Poet's thoughts are every where; though the eyes and senses of man are, it is true, his favorite guides, yet he will follow wheresoever he can find an atmosphere of sensation in which to move his wings. Poetry is the first and last of all knowledge—it is as immortal as the heart of man. If the labours of Men of Science should ever create any material revolution, direct or indirect, in our condition, and in the impressions which we habitually receive, the Poet will sleep then no more than at present, but he will be ready to follow the steps of the Man of Science, not only in those general indirect effects, but he will be at his side, carrying sensation into the midst of the objects of the Science itself. The remotest discoveries of the Chemist, the Botanist, or Mineralogist, will be as proper objects of the Poet's art as any upon which it can be employed, if the time should ever come when these things shall be familiar to us, and the relations under which they are contemplated by the followers of these respective Sciences shall be manifestly and palpably material to us as enjoying and suffering beings. If the time should ever come when what is now called Science, thus familiarized to men, shall be ready to put on, as it were, a form of flesh and blood, the Poet will lend his divine spirit to aid the transfiguration, and will welcome the Being thus produced, as a dear and genuine inmate of the household of man.—It is not, then, to be supposed that any one, who holds that sublime notion of Poetry which I have attempted to convey, will break in upon the sanctity and truth of his pictures by transitory and accidental ornaments, and endeavour to excite admiration of himself by arts, the necessity of which must manifestly depend upon the assumed meanness of his subject.

What I have thus far said applies to Poetry in general; but especially to those parts of composition where the Poet speaks through the mouths of his characters; and upon this point it appears to have such weight that I will conclude, there are few persons of good sense, who would not allow that the dramatic parts of composition are defective, in proportion as they deviate

3. *Hamlet* (ca. 1600), 4.4.36 ("Looking before and after").

from the real language of nature, and are coloured by a diction of the Poet's own, either peculiar to him as an individual Poet, or belonging simply to Poets in general, to a body of men who, from the circumstance of their compositions being in metre, it is expected will employ a particular language.

It is not, then, in the dramatic parts of composition that we look for this distinction of language; but still it may be proper and necessary where the Poet speaks to us in his own person and character. To this I answer by referring my Reader to the description which I have before given of a Poet. Among the qualities which I have enumerated as principally conducing to form a Poet, is implied nothing differing in kind from other men, but only in degree. The sum of what I have there said is, that the Poet is chiefly distinguished from other men by a greater promptness to think and feel without immediate external excitement, and a greater power in expressing such thoughts and feelings as are produced in him in that manner. But these passions and thoughts and feelings are the general passions and thoughts and feelings of men. And with what are they connected? Undoubtedly with our moral sentiments and animal sensations, and with the causes which excite these; with the operations of the elements and the appearances of the visible universe; with storm and sun-shine, with the revolutions of the seasons, with cold and heat, with loss of friends and kindred, with injuries and resentments, gratitude and hope, with fear and sorrow. These, and the like, are the sensations and objects which the Poet describes, as they are the sensations of other men, and the objects which interest them. The Poet thinks and feels in the spirit of the passions of men. How, then, can his language differ in any material degree from that of all other men who feel vividly and see clearly? It might be *proved* that it is impossible. But supposing that this were not the case, the Poet might then be allowed to use a peculiar language when expressing his feelings for his own gratification, or that of men like himself. But Poets do not write for Poets alone, but for men. Unless therefore we are advocates for that admiration which depends upon ignorance, and that pleasure which arises from hearing what we do not understand, the Poet must descend from this supposed height, and, in order to excite rational sympathy, he must express himself as other men express themselves. To this it may be added, that while he is only selecting from the real language of men, or, which amounts to the same thing, composing accurately in the spirit of such selection, he is treading upon safe ground, and we know what we are to expect from him. Our feelings are the same with respect to metre; for, as it may be proper to remind the Reader,] the distinction of metre is regular and uniform, and not like that which is produced by what is usually called poetic diction, arbitrary, and subject to infinite caprices upon which no calculation whatever can be made. In the one case, the Reader is utterly at the mercy of the Poet respecting what imagery or diction he may choose to connect with the passion, whereas, in the other, the metre obeys certain laws, to which the Poet and Reader both willingly submit because they are certain, and because no interference is made by them with the passion but such as the concurring testimony of ages has shown to heighten and improve the pleasure which co-exists with it.

It will now be proper to answer an obvious question, namely, Why, professing these opinions, have I written in verse? To this, in addition to such answer as is included in what I have already said, I reply in the first place, because, however I may have restricted myself, there is still left open to me what confessedly constitutes the most valuable object of all writing, whether in prose or verse, the great and universal passions of men, the most general and interesting of their occupations, and the entire world of nature, from which I am at liberty to supply myself with endless combinations of forms and imagery. Now, supposing for a moment that whatever is interesting in these objects may be as vividly described in prose, why am I to be condemned, if to such description I have endeavoured to superadd the charm which, by the consent of all nations, is acknowledged to exist in metrical language? To this, by such as are unconvinced by what I have already said, it may be answered, that a very small part of the pleasure given by Poetry depends upon the metre, and that it is injudicious to write in metre, unless it be accompanied with the other artificial distinctions of style with which metre is usually accompanied, and that by such deviation more will be lost from the shock which will be thereby given to the Reader's associations, than will be counterbalanced by any pleasure which he can derive from the general power of numbers.[4] In answer to those who still contend for the necessity of accompanying metre with certain appropriate colours of style in order to the accomplishment of its appropriate end, and who also, in my opinion, greatly under-rate the power of metre in itself, it might perhaps, as far as relates to these Poems, have been almost sufficient to observe, that poems are extant, written upon more humble subjects, and in a more naked and simple style than I have aimed at, which poems have continued to give pleasure from generation to generation. Now, if nakedness and simplicity be a defect, the fact here mentioned affords a strong presumption that poems somewhat less naked and simple are capable of affording pleasure at the present day; and, what I wished *chiefly* to attempt, at present, was to justify myself for having written under the impression of this belief.

But I might point out various causes why, when the style is manly, and the subject of some importance, words metrically arranged will long continue to impart such a pleasure to mankind as he who is sensible of the extent of that pleasure will be desirous to impart. The end of Poetry is to produce excitement in co-existence with an over-balance of pleasure. Now, by the supposition, excitement is an unusual and irregular state of the mind; ideas and feelings do not in that state succeed each other in accustomed order. But, if the words by which this excitement is produced are in themselves powerful, or the images and feelings have an undue proportion of pain connected with them, there is some danger that the excitement may be carried beyond its proper bounds. Now the co-presence of something regular, something to which the mind has been accustomed in various moods and in a less excited state, cannot but have great efficacy in tempering and restraining the passion by an intertexture of ordinary feeling, [and of feeling not strictly and necessarily connected with the passion. This is unquestionably true, and hence, though the opinion will at first appear paradoxical, from the tendency of metre to divest language in a certain degree of its reality, and thus to throw a sort of half consciousness of unsubstantial existence over the whole composition, there can be little doubt but that more pathetic situations and sentiments, that is, those which have a greater proportion of pain connected

4. Metrical language.

with them, may be endured in metrical composition, especially in rhyme, than in prose. The metre of the old Ballads is very artless; yet they contain many passages which would illustrate this opinion, and, I hope, if the following Poems be attentively perused, similar instances will be found in them.] This opinion may be further illustrated by appealing to the Reader's own experience of the reluctance with which he comes to the re-perusal of the distressful parts of Clarissa Harlowe, or the Gamester.[5] While Shakespeare's writings, in the most pathetic scenes, never act upon us as pathetic beyond the bounds of pleasure—an effect which, in a much greater degree than might at first be imagined, is to be ascribed to small, but continual and regular impulses of pleasurable surprise from the metrical arrangement.—On the other hand (what it must be allowed will much more frequently happen) if the Poet's words should be incommensurate with the passion, and inadequate to raise the Reader to a height of desirable excitement, then, (unless the Poet's choice of his metre has been grossly injudicious) in the feelings of pleasure which the Reader has been accustomed to connect with metre in general, and in the feeling, whether chearful or melancholy, which he has been accustomed to connect with that particular movement of metre, there will be found something which will greatly contribute to impart passion to the words, and to effect the complex end which the Poet proposes to himself.

If I had undertaken a systematic defence of the theory upon which these poems are written, it would have been my duty to develope the various causes upon which the pleasure received from metrical language depends. Among the chief of these causes is to be reckoned a principle which must be well known to those who have made any of the Arts the object of accurate reflection; I mean the pleasure which the mind derives from the perception of similitude in dissimilitude. This principle is the great spring of the activity of our minds, and their chief feeder. From this principle the direction of the sexual appetite, and all the passions connected with it, take their origin: it is the life of our ordinary conversation; and upon the accuracy with which similitude in dissimilitude, and dissimilitude in similitude are perceived, depend our taste and our moral feelings. It would not have been a useless employment to have applied this principle to the consideration of metre, and to have shown that metre is hence enabled to afford much pleasure, and to have pointed out in what manner that pleasure is produced. But my limits will not permit me to enter upon this subject, and I must content myself with a general summary.

I have said that Poetry is the spontaneous overflow of powerful feelings: it takes its origin from emotion recollected in tranquillity: the emotion is contemplated till by a species of reaction the tranquillity disappears, and an emotion, kindred to that which was before the subject of contemplation, is gradually produced, and does itself actually exist in the mind. In this mood successful composition generally begins, and in a mood similar to this it is carried on; but the emotion, of whatever kind and in whatever degree, from various causes is qualified by various pleasures, so that in describing any passions whatsoever, which are voluntarily described, the mind will upon the

5. *The Gamester* (1753), a tragedy by Edward Moore, about gambling. *Clarissa Hardowe*: an epistolary novel (1747–48) by Samuel Richardson; the title character is abducted and raped, and she dies of grief.

whole be in a state of enjoyment. Now, if Nature be thus cautious in preserving in a state of enjoyment a being thus employed, the Poet ought to profit by the lesson thus held forth to him, and ought especially to take care, that whatever passions he communicates to his Reader, those passions, if his Reader's mind be sound and vigorous, should always be accompanied with an overbalance of pleasure. Now the music of harmonious metrical language, the sense of difficulty overcome, and the blind association of pleasure which has been previously received from works of rhyme or metre of the same or similar construction, an indistinct perception perpetually renewed of language closely resembling that of real life, and yet, in the circumstance of metre, differing from it so widely, all these imperceptibly make up a complex feeling of delight, which is of the most important use in tempering the painful feeling which will always be found intermingled with powerful descriptions of the deeper passions. This effect is always produced in pathetic and impassioned poetry; while, in lighter compositions, the ease and gracefulness with which the Poet manages his numbers are themselves confessedly a principal source of the gratification of the Reader. I might perhaps include all which it is *necessary* to say upon this subject by affirming, what few persons will deny, that, of two descriptions, either of passions, manners, or characters, each of them equally well executed, the one in prose and the other in verse, the verse will be read a hundred times where the prose is read once. We see that Pope, by the power of verse alone, has contrived to render the plainest common sense interesting, and even frequently to invest it with the appearance of passion. In consequence of these convictions I related in metre the Tale of GOODY BLAKE AND HARRY GILL, which is one of the rudest of this collection. I wished to draw attention to the truth, that the power of the human imagination is sufficient to produce such changes even in our physical nature as might almost appear miraculous. The truth is an important one; the fact (for it is a *fact*) is a valuable illustration of it. And I have the satisfaction of knowing that it has been communicated to many hundreds of people who would never have heard of it, had it not been narrated as a Ballad, and in a more impressive metre than is usual in Ballads.

Having thus explained a few of the reasons why I have written in verse, and why I have chosen subjects from common life, and endeavoured to bring my language near to the real language of men, if I have been too minute in pleading my own cause, I have at the same time been treating a subject of general interest; and it is for this reason that I request the Reader's permission to add a few words with reference solely to these particular poems, and to some defects which will probably be found in them. I am sensible that my associations must have sometimes been particular instead of general, and that, consequently, giving to things a false importance, sometimes from diseased impulses I may have written upon unworthy subjects; but I am less apprehensive on this account, than that my language may frequently have suffered from those arbitrary connections of feelings and ideas with particular words and phrases, from which no man can altogether protect himself. Hence I have no doubt, that, in some instances, feelings even of the ludicrous may be given to my Readers by expressions which appeared to me tender and pathetic. Such faulty expressions, were I convinced they were faulty at present, and that they must necessarily continue to be so, I would willingly take all reasonable pains to correct. But it is dangerous to make these alterations on the simple authority of a few individuals, or even of certain classes of men; for where the understanding of an Author is not convinced, or his feelings altered, this cannot be done without great injury to himself: for his own feelings are his stay and support, and, if he sets them aside in one instance, he may be induced to repeat this act till his mind loses all confidence in itself, and becomes utterly debilitated. To this it may be added, that the Reader ought never to forget that he is himself exposed to the same errors as the Poet, and perhaps in a much greater degree: for there can be no presumption in saying, that it is not probable he will be so well acquainted with the various stages of meaning through which words have passed, or with the fickleness or stability of the relations of particular ideas to each other; and above all, since he is so much less interested in the subject, he may decide lightly and carelessly.

Long as I have detained my Reader, I hope he will permit me to caution him against a mode of false criticism which has been applied to Poetry in which the language closely resembles that of life and nature. Such verses have been triumphed over in parodies of which Dr. Johnson's stanza is a fair specimen.

> 'I put my hat upon my head,
> And walk'd into the Strand,
> And there I met another man
> Whose hat was in his hand.'[6]

Immediately under these lines I will place one of the most justly admired stanzas of the '*Babes* in the Wood.'[7]

> 'These pretty Babes with hand in hand
> Went wandering up and down;
> But never more they saw the Man
> Approaching from the Town.'

In both these stanzas the words, and the order of the words, in no respect differ from the most unimpassioned conversation. There are words in both, for example, 'the Strand,' and 'the Town,' connected with none but the most familiar ideas; yet the one stanza we admit as admirable, and the other as a fair example of the superlatively contemptible. Whence arises this difference? Not from the metre, not from the language, not from the order of the words; but the *matter* expressed in Dr. Johnson's stanza is contemptible. The proper method of treating trivial and simple verses, to which Dr. Johnson's stanza would be a fair parallelism, is not to say, This is a bad kind of poetry, or This is not poetry; but This wants sense; it is neither interesting in itself, nor can *lead* to any thing interesting; the images neither originate in that sane state of feeling which arises out of thought, nor can excite thought or feeling in the Reader. This is the only sensible manner of dealing with such verses. Why trouble yourself about the species till you have previously decided upon the genus? Why take pains to prove that an ape is not a Newton,[8] when it is self-evident that he is not a man?

6. Printed in the *London Magazine*, April 1785, parodying the ballad *The Hermit of Warkworth* (1771), by Thomas Percy. The Strand: a business street in central London.

7. A popular name for the old ballad "The Children in the Wood," which tells of two children cruelly treated by a wicked uncle. It is included in Thomas Percy's collection *Reliques of Ancient English Poetry* (3 vols., 1765), which Wordsworth valued highly.

8. Sir Isaac Newton (1642–1727), English scientist and mathematician.

I have one request to make of my Reader, which is, that in judging these Poems he would decide by his own feelings genuinely, and not by reflection upon what will probably be the judgment of others. How common is it to hear a person say, 'I myself do not object to this style of composition, or this or that expression, but to such and such classes of people it will appear mean or ludicrous.' This mode of criticism, so destructive of all sound unadulterated judgment, is almost universal: I have therefore to request, that the Reader would abide independently by his own feelings, and that if he finds himself affected he would not suffer such conjectures to interfere with his pleasure.

If an Author by any single composition has impressed us with respect for his talents, it is useful to consider this as affording a presumption, that, on other occasions where we have been displeased, he nevertheless may not have written ill or absurdly; and, further, to give him so much credit for this one composition as may induce us to review what has displeased us with more care than we should otherwise have bestowed upon it. This is not only an act of justice, but, in our decisions upon poetry especially, may conduce in a high degree to the improvement of our own taste: for an *accurate* taste in poetry, and in all the other arts, as Sir Joshua Reynolds[9] has observed, is an *acquired* talent, which can only be produced by thought, and a long continued intercourse with the best models of composition. This is mentioned, not with so ridiculous a purpose as to prevent the most inexperienced Reader from judging for himself, (I have already said that I wish him to judge for himself;) but merely to temper the rashness of decision, and to suggest, that, if Poetry be a subject on which much time has not been bestowed, the judgment may be erroneous; and that in many cases it necessarily will be so.

I know that nothing would have so effectually contributed to further the end which I have in view, as to have shewn of what kind the pleasure is, and how that pleasure is produced, which is confessedly produced by metrical composition essentially different from that which I have here endeavoured to recommend: for the Reader will say that he has been pleased by such composition; and what can I do more for him? The power of any art is limited; and he will suspect, that, if I propose to furnish him with new friends, it is only upon condition of his abandoning his old friends. Besides, as I have said, the Reader is himself conscious of the pleasure which he has received from such composition, composition to which he has peculiarly attached the endearing name of Poetry; and all men feel an habitual gratitude, and something of an honorable bigotry for the objects which have long continued to please them; we not only wish to be pleased, but to be pleased in that particular way in which we have been accustomed to be pleased. There is a host of arguments in these feelings; and I should be the less able to combat them successfully, as I am willing to allow, that, in order entirely to enjoy the Poetry which I am recommending, it would be necessary to give up much of what is ordinarily enjoyed. But, would my limits have permitted me to point out how this pleasure is produced, I might have removed many obstacles, and assisted my Reader in perceiving that the powers of language are not so

9. Portrait painter, essayist, and lecturer (1723–1792), author of annual *Discourses* (1769–90) on the arts delivered to students at the Royal Academy. See *Discourse* XII: "The habit of contemplating and brooding over the ideas of great geniuses, till you find yourself warmed by the contact, is the true method of forming an artist-like mind."

limited as he may suppose; and that it is possible that poetry may give other enjoyments, of a purer, more lasting, and more exquisite nature. This part of my subject I have not altogether neglected; but it has been less my present aim to prove, that the interest excited by some other kinds of poetry is less vivid, and less worthy of the nobler powers of the mind, than to offer reasons for presuming, that, if the object which I have proposed to myself were adequately attained, a species of poetry would be produced, which is genuine poetry; in its nature well adapted to interest mankind permanently, and likewise important in the multiplicity and quality of its moral relations.

From what has been said, and from a perusal of the Poems, the Reader will be able clearly to perceive the object which I have proposed to myself: he will determine how far I have attained this object; and, what is a much more important question, whether it be worth attaining: and upon the decision of these two questions will rest my claim to the approbation of the public.

Appendix to the Preface (1802)

As perhaps I have no right to expect from a Reader of an Introduction to a volume of Poems that attentive perusal without which it is impossible, imperfectly as I have been compelled to express my meaning, that what I have said in the Preface should throughout be fully understood, I am the more anxious to give an exact notion of the sense in which I use the phrase *poetic diction*; and for this purpose I will here add a few words concerning the origin of the phraseology which I have condemned under that name.—The earliest Poets of all nations generally wrote from passion excited by real events; they wrote naturally, and as men: feeling powerfully as they did, their language was daring, and figurative. In succeeding times, Poets, and men ambitious of the fame of Poets, perceiving the influence of such language, and desirous of producing the same effect, without having the same animating passion, set themselves to a mechanical adoption of those figures of speech, and made use of them, sometimes with propriety, but much more frequently applied them to feelings and ideas with which they had no natural connection whatsoever. A language was thus insensibly produced, differing materially from the real language of men in *any situation*. The Reader or Hearer of this distorted language found himself in a perturbed and unusual state of mind: when affected by the genuine language of passion he had been in a perturbed and unusual state of mind also: in both cases he was willing that his common judgment and understanding should be laid asleep, and he had no instinctive and infallible perception of the true to make him reject the false; the one served as a passport for the other. The agitation and confusion of mind were in both cases delightful, and no wonder if he confounded the one with the other, and believed them both to be produced by the same, or similar causes. Besides, the Poet spake to him in the character of a man to be looked up to, a man of genius and authority. Thus, and from a variety of other causes, this distorted language was received with admiration; and Poets, it is probable, who had before contented themselves for the most part with misapplying only expressions which at first had been dictated by real passion, carried the abuse still further, and introduced phrases composed apparently in the spirit of the original figurative language of passion, yet altogether of their own invention, and distinguished by various degrees of wanton deviation from good sense and nature.

It is indeed true that the language of the earliest Poets was felt to differ materially from ordinary language, because it was the language of extraordinary occasions; but it was really spoken by men, language which the Poet himself had uttered when he had been affected by the events which he described, or which he had heard uttered by those around him. To this language it is probable that metre of some sort or other was early superadded. This separated the genuine language of Poetry still further from common life, so that whoever read or heard the poems of these earliest Poets felt himself moved in a way in which he had not been accustomed to be moved in real life, and by causes manifestly different from those which acted upon him in real life. This was the great temptation to all the corruptions which have followed: under the protection of this feeling succeeding Poets constructed a phraseology which had one thing, it is true, in common with the genuine language of poetry, namely, that it was not heard in ordinary conversation; that it was unusual. But the first Poets, as I have said, spake a language which, though unusual, was still the language of men. This circumstance, however, was disregarded by their successors; they found that they could please by easier means: they became proud of a language which they themselves had invented, and which was uttered only by themselves; and, with the spirit of a fraternity, they arrogated it to themselves as their own. In process of time metre became a symbol or promise of this unusual language, and whoever took upon him to write in metre, according as he possessed more or less of true poetic genius, introduced less or more of this adulterated phraseology into his compositions, and the true and the false became so inseparably interwoven that the taste of men was gradually perverted; and this language was received as a natural language; and at length, by the influence of books upon men, did to a certain degree really become so. Abuses of this kind were imported from one nation to another, and with the progress of refinement this diction became daily more and more corrupt, thrusting out of sight the plain humanities of nature by a motley masquerade of tricks, quaintnesses, hieroglyphics, and enigmas.

It would be highly interesting to point out the causes of the pleasure given by this extravagant and absurd language: but this is not the place; it depends upon a great variety of causes, but upon none perhaps more than its influence in impressing a notion of the peculiarity and exaltation of the Poet's character, and in flattering the Reader's self-love by bringing him nearer to a sympathy with that character; an effect which is accomplished by unsettling ordinary habits of thinking, and thus assisting the Reader to approach to that perturbed and dizzy state of mind in which if he does not find himself, he imagines that he is *balked* of a peculiar enjoyment which poetry can, and ought to bestow.

The sonnet which I have quoted from Gray, in the Preface, except the lines printed in Italics, consists of little else but this diction, though not of the worst kind; and indeed, if I may be permitted to say so, it is far too common in the best writers, both antient and modern. Perhaps I can in no way, by positive example, more easily give my Reader a notion of what I mean by the phrase *poetic diction* than by referring him to a comparison between the metrical paraphrases which we have of passages in the old and new

Testament, and those passages as they exist in our common Translation. See Pope's 'Messiah' throughout, Prior's 'Did sweeter sounds adorn my flowing tongue,'[1] &c. &c. 'Though I speak with the tongues of men and of angels,' &c. &c. See 1st Corinthians, chapter 13th. By way of immediate example, take the following of Dr. Johnson:[2]

'Turn on the prudent Ant thy heedless eyes,
Observe her labours, Sluggard, and be wise;
No stern command, no monitory voice,
Prescribes her duties, or directs her choice;
Yet, timely provident, she hastes away
To snatch the blessings of a plenteous day;
When fruitful Summer loads the teeming plain,
She crops the harvest and she stores the grain.
How long shall sloth usurp thy useless hours,
Unnerve thy vigour, and enchain thy powers?
While artful shades thy downy couch enclose,
And soft solicitation courts repose,
Amidst the drowsy charms of dull delight,
Year chases year with unremitted flight,
Till want now following, fraudulent and slow,
Shall spring to seize thee, like an ambushed foe.'

From this hubbub of words pass to the original. 'Go to the Ant, thou Sluggard, consider her ways, and be wise: which having no guide, overseer, or ruler, provideth her meat in the summer, and gathereth her food in the harvest. How long wilt thou sleep, O Sluggard? when wilt thou arise out of thy sleep? Yet a little sleep, a little slumber, a little folding of the hands to sleep. So shall thy poverty come as one that travaileth, and thy want as an armed man.' Proverbs, chap. 6th.

One more quotation and I have done. It is from Cowper's verses[3] supposed to be written by Alexander Selkirk:

'Religion! what treasure untold
Resides in that heavenly word!
More precious than silver and gold,
Or all that this earth can afford.
But the sound of the church-going bell
These valleys and rocks never heard,
Ne'er sighed at the sound of a knell,
Or smiled when a sabbath appear'd.

Ye winds, that have made me your sport,
Convey to this desolate shore
Some cordial endearing report
Of a land I must visit no more.
My Friends, do they now and then send

1. "Charity. A Paraphrase on the Thirteenth Chapter of the First Epistle to the Corinthians" (1703), by Matthew Prior (1664–1721). "Messiah": a "sacred eclogue" (1712), imitating Virgil's Latin *Eclogue* 4 (ca. 37 B.C.E.).
2. "The Ant" (1766).
3. "Verses Supposed to be Written by Alexander Selkirk" (1782), stanzas 4–5, by William Cowper (1731–1800). Selkirk (1676–1721), a Scottish sailor who lived from 1704 to 1709 on an uninhabited island off the coast of Chile.

A wish or a thought after me?
O tell me I yet have a friend,
Though a friend I am never to see.'

I have quoted this passage as an instance of three different styles of composition. The first four lines are poorly expressed; some Critics would call the language prosaic; the fact is, it would be bad prose, so bad, that it is scarcely worse in metre. The epithet 'church-going' applied to a bell, and that by so chaste[4] a writer as Cowper, is an instance of the strange abuses which Poets have introduced into their language till they and their Readers take them as matters of course, if they do not single them out expressly as objects of admiration. The two lines 'Ne'er sighed at the sound,' &c. are, in my opinion, an instance of the language of passion wrested from its proper use, and, from the mere circumstance of the composition being in metre, applied upon an occasion that does not justify such violent expressions; and I should condemn the passage, though perhaps few Readers will agree with me, as vicious poetic diction. The last stanza is throughout admirably expressed: it would be equally good whether in prose or verse, except that the Reader has an exquisite pleasure in seeing such natural language so naturally connected with metre. The beauty of this stanza tempts me here to add a sentiment which ought to be the pervading spirit of a system, detached parts of which have been imperfectly explained in the Preface,—namely, that in proportion as ideas and feelings are valuable, whether the composition be in prose or in verse, they require and exact one and the same language.

1800, 1802

4. Austere, ornament-free.

SAMUEL TAYLOR COLERIDGE
1772–1834

Samuel Taylor Coleridge has been praised as the premier English literary intellectual of his era and as the first modern critic, a writer who sought to integrate literary analysis with the insights of other disciplines and who labored (with less than complete success) to give literary criticism a philosophical foundation. But he has also been dismissed and derided in hostile tones rarely found in academic commentary. Was Coleridge a great original thinker? He drew on many eighteenth-century and contemporary authors, particularly German idealist and Romantic philosophers and critics, including IMMANUEL KANT, FRIEDRICH VON SCHILLER, Friedrich and A. W. Schlegel, and Friedrich von Schelling—and some scholars have commended him for introducing the best of German thought to an English readership. Less charitably, though with some reason, others have termed these literary debts, references, and borrowings to be nothing more than plagiarisms.

Coleridge has also been rebuked and mocked for the ambitious projects he proposed, launched, but left undone: an eight- to ten-volume history of literature, an epic poem on the origin of evil, and so on. He had extraordinary literary gifts, but was an undisciplined author who failed to make full use of his exceptional talents—as he himself knew well. Coleridge wrote in his copy of his book *The Statesman's Manual* (1816) that while he had produced a number of significant works, he stood in the world's eyes as "the wild eccentric Genius that has published nothing but fragments & splendid Tirades." With the possible exception of the *Biographia Literaria* (1817) and a handful of poems, none of his works holds together as an effective whole. Yet as a writer, and as a speaker (we have ample records of his conversations and lectures), he was, and still is, brilliantly impressive and stimulating.

Coleridge was born the son of the vicar of Ottery St. Mary, a small town in southwest England; but at age nine, following the death of his father, he was sent to school in London, attending Christ's Hospital as a charity student. In 1791 he enrolled in Jesus College, Cambridge University; two years later, plagued by debts, he enlisted in the Fifteenth Light Dragoons under the alias Silas Tomkyn Comberbache (S.T.C.). He was soon rescued from this mistake by his family and returned to the university, but he left in December 1794 without completing his degree.

In June 1794, while on a walking tour, Coleridge met the poet Robert Southey at Oxford, and the two concocted a plan for a "pantisocracy" (a society ruled by equals). They decided on a location (in Pennsylvania) and on the twelve men who, with their wives, would create this agricultural commune; but the only action taken was Coleridge's engagement (made necessary by the scheme) to Sara Fricker, the sister of Southey's fiancée. Though the plan collapsed, he married her in 1795.

In late 1794 Coleridge's first published poetry appeared (sonnets addressed to contemporary political radicals such as William Godwin and Joseph Priestley). In 1795 he worked as a journalist and lectured in Bristol on politics, religion, and history. Most scholars believe that he there first met WILLIAM WORDSWORTH, beginning an intense friendship that soon led to the most significant collaboration in English literary history. By May 1796 Coleridge was calling Wordsworth "a very dear friend of mine, who is in my opinion the best poet of the age," and his own first collection of poetry, *Poems on Various Subjects*, had just been published. In December, Coleridge and his wife Sara settled in Nether Stowey, and soon thereafter Wordsworth and his sister Dorothy moved nearby, to Alfoxden. Beginning in mid-1797 Coleridge and Wordsworth worked together on *Lyrical Ballads*, which they published anonymously in September 1798. Among the works of this period, Coleridge's high point as a poet, are "This Lime Tree Bower My Prison," "The Rime of the Ancient Mariner," "Frost at Midnight," "Fears in Solitude," "The Nightingale," part I of "Christabel," and probably the fragment "Kubla Khan" as well.

Leaving his wife and two children behind, Coleridge accompanied the Wordsworths to Germany in September 1798, where he read and absorbed the philosophical and literary speculations of Kant, Schelling, the Schlegels, and Schiller (whose work he later translated).

On his return to England in mid-1799, Coleridge wrote political articles and made plans (unrealized) for a biography of the German critic and dramatist GOTTHOLD EPHRAIM LESSING and for a major book on Romantic metaphysics. The Coleridges followed the Wordsworths to the Lake District in 1800; and although the second edition of *Lyrical Ballads* (1800) appeared with only Wordsworth's name on the title page and with a long preface by Wordsworth that ignored Coleridge's poems, the men remained close. But Coleridge's personal life was in disarray. Already indifferent to his wife, he had fallen in love with Sara Hutchinson, whose sister, Mary, Wordsworth would marry in 1802; even worse, he had become dependent on laudanum (opium dissolved in alcohol, widely used to treat a number of disorders). Leaving his family behind, Coleridge spent two years traveling the Mediterranean and working in Malta; but he returned to England in 1806 still an addict. He lived for some months with the Wordsworths, and the relationship grew strained; the men finally broke on bitter terms in 1810.

Under the circumstances, Coleridge was surprisingly productive. In 1809 and

1810, he wrote and published *The Friend*, a periodical that ran for twenty-eight issues; and between 1808 and 1819, he lectured frequently on politics, religion, education, philosophy, and literature, offering especially incisive commentaries on Shakespeare and Milton. During the period from June to September 1815, he focused on the *Biographia Literaria*, which he dictated rather than wrote. From spring 1816 until his death in 1834, Coleridge lived in Highgate, a northern suburb of London, with and under the care of Dr. James Gillman, who helped control his drug addiction.

By this time known as the "Sage of Highgate," Coleridge published *Christabel and Other Poems* (1816); the first volume of his collected poems, *Sibylline Leaves* (1817; expanded 1828, 1834); and his *Poetical Works* (3 vols., 1828; 2d ed., 1829; 3d ed., 1834). His major prose works are *Lay Sermons* (1816, 1817), essays on national education and the structure of an organic society; *Biographia Literaria* (1817); "Treatise on Method" (included in the three-volume edition of *The Friend*, 1818); *Aids to Reflection* (1825; 2d ed., 1831); and *On the Constitution of the Church and State* (1829; 2d ed., 1830), in which he proposed the establishment of teachers, scholars, and priests as an independent estate of the realm, "the clerisy." In addition, *Table Talk* (edited by his nephew Henry Coleridge, 1836), which displays his skills in conversation; *Literary Remains* (1836), which contains an account of his 1818–19 lectures on "the history of philosophy" and the "general course of literature"; and *Anima Poetae* (1895), selections from his notebooks, all appeared after his death.

Coleridge frequently professed a commitment to system, logic, and method, but his own practice time and again resists global theories and highly elaborated schemes and structures. It is the penetrating phrase or sentence, the powerful paragraph of speculation, and the shrewd, suggestive judgment that reveal Coleridge at his best. Still, for English and American critics in the early twentieth century, especially I. A. Richards, CLEANTH BROOKS, and other New Critics, the central Coleridge text is *Biographia Literaria*, where they found and built on Coleridge's famous theory of the imagination, his exposition of organic unity, and his treatment of poetry as the reconciliation of opposites.

Biographia Literaria, a hastily assembled work, mixes modes and genres. It includes autobiography, philosophy, literary theory, and analytical literary criticism, as well as a memoir of Wordsworth, a study of his poems, and a critique of his theory of poetic diction. At the center of Coleridge's project is his inquiry into and defense of the imagination. Coleridge's account, distinguishing between "fancy" and "imagination," lacks the splendor and breadth of PERCY BYSSHE SHELLEY's tribute to the imagination in the *Defence of Poetry* (written 1821; see below) as "the great instrument of moral good," but it has exercised a greater influence on later literary theory and criticism. Coleridge speaks first of the "primary" imagination: the "living power" of God, in the eternal act of creation, it is also the power of creation in each person. The "secondary" imagination echoes the primary; in conjunction with the will and understanding, it dissolves in order to re-create, making whole and harmonizing as a "synthetic and magical power." Fancy, in contrast, merely associates "fixities and definites."

This is an intriguing, if elusive, theory, over which commentators have puzzled. But the real importance of Coleridge's words is their departure from eighteenth-century neoclassical theory. SAMUEL JOHNSON, in his *Dictionary* (1765), offers "fancy" as one of the definitions of "imagination"; that Coleridge makes a distinction between the two has important implications for his conception of the poet and the poem. Neoclassical critics such as ALEXANDER POPE and Johnson could exempt only a great genius like Shakespeare from external rules of literary decorum, insisting that others rely on deliberate craft; but for Coleridge the creative work of every poet springs from an imaginative power at once available for analysis yet mysterious in its sources. He sees a poem as *organic*, true to itself, acquiring its shape like a plant from a seed and thereby growing according to its own internal law of development.

Coleridge's theory of the primary and secondary imagination honors the creative capacity of persons while remaining steadfast to the primacy of God; even more,

Coleridge implies that each re-creative act that a poet performs is an act of worship. As modern scholars have pointed out, Coleridge was the most devout of all the major Romantic writers; his Christian faith is central to all his work. He sees "a similar union of the universal and the individual" in religion and in the fine arts. Yet implicit in Coleridge's theory of the imagination are both difficulty and failure, which take on added bleakness in this context. When he sets the imagination in contrast to a world of "essentially fixed and dead objects," does he mean that God has made a world that is dead—at least until awakened or renewed by a creative act?

Coleridge makes a similar distinction in his commentaries on allegory and symbol (one of which, from *The Statesman's Manual*, is excerpted below). Allegory, he indicates, is mechanical and formulaic, part of the larger problem of our degenerate age of triumphant "mechanic" philosophy; but symbol is organically unified, fusing the particular and the general, the temporal and the eternal. This distinction is crucial for Coleridge, yet, as PAUL DE MAN argues in "The Rhetoric of Temporality" (1969), his arguments do not sustain it: the more that Coleridge explores the distinction, the more he complicates and blurs its terms. Indeed, some of his best-known poetry ("The Rime of the Ancient Mariner," "Kubla Khan," "Christabel") has invited allegorical interpretation.

Coleridge's emphasis on the power of the imagination is at odds with much contemporary theory and historical and cultural criticism, which is suspicious of claims that appear to give certain individuals the power to create new worlds out of nothing but their imagination. The New Historicist STEPHEN GREENBLATT speaks, for example, not of the imaginative power and prowess of the author but of "social energy"; and it is true that Coleridge pays too little attention to the powerful social networks of signification in which an author's work takes shape. But recent theorists, reacting perhaps too sweepingly against the idea of the author as a Romantic genius, have tended to undervalue the creative power of the individual author, the agent of the imagination who, as Coleridge says of Shakespeare, demonstrates his authority and skill "not only in the general construction, but in all the detail."

BIBLIOGRAPHY

Primary sources include *The Collected Works of Samuel Taylor Coleridge*, general editor Kathleen Coburn (13 vols. to date, 1969–), published by the Bollingen Foundation and Princeton University Press, superbly edited and with comprehensive introductions; *The Collected Letters*, edited by Earl Leslie Griggs (6 vols., 1956–71); and *Selected Letters*, edited by H. J. Jackson (1987). Also illuminating are *The Notebooks*, edited by Kathleen Coburn (4 vols. to date, 1957–). Collections of Coleridge's criticism include *Shakespearean Criticism* (2 vols., 1930) and *Miscellaneous Criticism* (1936), both edited by T. M. Raysor. See also *Coleridge on the Seventeenth Century*, edited by Roberta Florence Brinkley (1955), and *Writings on Shakespeare: A Selection of the Essays, Notes, and Lectures*, edited by Terence Hawkes (1959).

Walter Jackson Bate, *Coleridge* (1968), is a fine introduction to the life and works; two volumes by Richard Holmes, *Coleridge: Early Visions, 1772–1804* (1989) and *Coleridge: Darker Reflections, 1804–1834* (1999) constitute the best biography. Rosemary Ashton, *The Life of Samuel Taylor Coleridge: A Critical Biography* (1996), is astute. Norman Fruman, *Coleridge: The Damaged Archangel* (1971), assembles the evidence of Coleridge's plagiarisms.

The best point of departure for studying Coleridge's criticism is the *Biographia Literaria*. See especially the editions by James Engell and Walter Jackson Bate, vol. 7 of the Bollingen *Samuel Taylor Coleridge* (1983), and by John Shawcross (2 vols., 1907). Scholarly studies of *Biographia Literaria* include Kathleen M. Wheeler, *Sources, Processes, and Methods in Coleridge's "Biographia Literaria"* (1980); Catherine Miles Wallace, *The Design of "Biographia Literaria"* (1983); and *Coleridge's "Biographia Literaria": Text and Meaning*, edited by Frederick Burwick (1989), which presents fourteen essays on major themes of the text and on its style, sources, significance for the history of Romanticism, and connections to contemporary literary theory. For critical responses to Coleridge to the year 1900, consult *Coleridge: The Critical Heritage*, edited by J. R. de J. Jackson (2 vols., 1970–91).

There are many fine books on Coleridge's literary theory: J. A. Appleyard, *Coleridge's Philosophy of Literature: The Development of a Concept of Poetry, 1791–1819* (1965); Thomas McFarland, *Coleridge and the Pantheist Tradition* (1969), which includes cogent chapters on Coleridge's plagiarisms and pantheist beliefs; J. R. de J. Jackson, *Method and Imagination in Coleridge's Criticism* (1969); J. Robert Barth, *The Symbolic Imagination: Coleridge and the Romantic Tradition* (1977); and Jerome C. Christensen, *Coleridge's Blessed Machine of Language* (1981). On Coleridge's theories of literary language and poetic diction, see Emerson R. Marks, *Coleridge on the Language of Verse* (1981), a fine treatment of Coleridge's interest in language "as an artistic medium"; Timothy Corrigan, *Coleridge, Language, and Criticism* (1982); Paul Hamilton, *Coleridge's Poetics* (1983), an insightful study of Coleridge's significant influence on post-Romantic literary criticism; James C. McKusick, *Coleridge's Philosophy of Language* (1986); and A. C. Goodson, *Verbal Imagination: Coleridge and the Language of Modern Criticism* (1988), which relates Coleridge's theory of poetry to the development of modern literary criticism.

For bibliographies see *Samuel Taylor Coleridge: An Annotated Bibliography of Criticism and Scholarship*, edited by Richard and Josephine Haven and Maurianne Adams (2 vols., 1976–83), which covers work to 1939. See also Jefferson D. Caskey and Melinda M. Capper, *Samuel Taylor Coleridge: A Selective Bibliography of Criticism, 1935–1977* (1978).

From The Statesman's Manual[1]

* * *

But do you require some one or more particular passage from the Bible, that may at once illustrate and exemplify its applicability to the changes and fortunes of empires? Of the numerous chapters that relate to the Jewish tribes, their enemies and allies, before and after their division into two kingdoms, it would be more difficult to state a single one, from which some guiding light might *not* be struck. And in nothing is Scriptural history more strongly contrasted with the histories of highest note in the present age[2] than in its freedom from the hollowness of abstractions. While the latter present a shadow-fight of Things and Quantities, the former gives us the history of Men, and balances the important influence of individual Minds with the previous state of the national morals and manners, in which, as constituting a specific susceptibility, it presents to us the true cause both of the Influence itself, and of the Weal or Woe that were its Consequents. How should it be otherwise? The histories and political economy of the present and preceding century partake in the general contagion of its mechanic philosophy, and are the *product* of an unenlivened generalizing Understanding. In the Scriptures they are the living *educts*[3] of the Imagination; of that reconciling and medi-

1. The full title is *The Statesman's Manual; or The Bible the Best Guide to Political Skill and Foresight: A Lay Sermon, Addressed to the Higher Classes of Society, with an Appendix Containing Comments and Essays Connected with the Study of the Inspired Writings.*

2. Probably a reference to DAVID HUME, *History of England* (5 vols., 1754–62), and Edward Gibbon, *The History of the Decline and Fall of the Roman Empire* (6 vols., 1776–88).

3. Things drawn forth, developed.

atory power, which incorporating the Reason in Images of the Sense, and organizing (as it were) the flux of the Senses by the permanence and self-circling energies of the Reason, gives birth to a system of symbols, harmonious in themselves, and consubstantial with the truths, of which they are the *conductors*. These are the Wheels which Ezekiel[4] beheld, when the hand of the Lord was upon him, and he saw visions of God as he sate among the captives by the river of Chebar. *Whithersoever the Spirit was to go, the wheels went, and thither was their spirit to go: for the spirit of the living creature was in the wheels also*. The truths and the symbols that represent them move in conjunction and form the living chariot that bears up (for *us*) the throne of the Divine Humanity. Hence, by a derivative, indeed, but not a divided, influence, and though in a secondary yet in more than a metaphorical sense, the Sacred Book is worthily intitled *the* WORD OF GOD. Hence too, its contents present to us the stream of time continuous as Life and symbol of Eternity, inasmuch as the Past and the Future are virtually contained in the Present. According therefore to our relative position on its banks the Sacred History becomes prophetic, the Sacred Prophecies historical, while the power and substance of both inhere in its Laws, its Promises, and its Comminations.[5] In the Scriptures therefore both Facts and Persons must of necessity have a two-fold significance, a past and a future, a temporary and a perpetual, a particular and a universal application. They must be at once Portraits and Ideals.

Eheu! paupertina philosophia in paupertinam religionem ducit:[6]—A hunger-bitten and idea-less philosophy naturally produces a starveling and comfortless religion. It is among the miseries of the present age that it recognizes no medium between *Literal* and *Metaphorical*. Faith is either to be buried in the dead letter, or its name and honors usurped by a counterfeit product of the mechanical understanding, which in the blindness of self-complacency confounds SYMBOLS with ALLEGORIES. Now an Allegory is but a translation of abstract notions into a picture-language which is itself nothing but an abstraction from objects of the senses; the principal being more worthless even than its phantom proxy, both alike unsubstantial, and the former shapeless to boot. On the other hand a Symbol (ὃ ἔστιν ἄει ταυτηγόρικον)[7] is characterized by a translucence of the Special in the Individual or of the General in the Especial or of the Universal in the General. Above all by the translucence of the Eternal through and in the Temporal. It always partakes of the Reality which it renders intelligible;[8] and while it enunciates the whole, abides itself as a living part in that Unity, of which it is the representative. The other are but empty echoes which the fancy arbitrarily associates with apparitions of matter, less beautiful but not less shadowy than the sloping orchard or hill-side pasture-field seen in the transparent lake below. Alas! for the flocks that are to be

4. A Hebrew prophet (6th c. B.C.E.) during the Babylonian Exile, when thousands of Jews were deported from Palestine by King Nebuchadrezzar. For his vision of the wheels, see Ezekiel 1.1–21; Coleridge quotes verse 20.
5. Threats of divine vengeance.
6. Alas! An impoverished philosophy leads to an impoverished religion (Latin).
7. Which is always tautegorical (Greek). According to the *Oxford English Dictionary*, Coleridge invented this word (as well as its Greek "original"), which he said meant "expressing the *same* subject but with a difference."
8. The notion of partaking of a "Reality" that is known only through individual (imperfect) instantiations strongly echoes PLATO's theory of unchanging, eternal Forms or Ideas, in whose reality ordinary objects "participate" (see the selection from *Republic* 7 above; more generally on Forms, see *Parmenides*).

led forth to such pastures! *"It shall even be as when the hungry dreameth, and behold! he eateth; but he waketh and his soul is empty: or as when the thirsty dreameth, and behold he drinketh; but he awaketh and is faint!"* (ISAIAH XXIX. 8.) O! that we would seek for the bread which was given from heaven, that we should eat thereof and be strengthened! O that we would draw at the well at which the flocks of our forefathers had living water drawn for them, even that water which, instead of mocking the thirst of him to whom it is given, becomes a well within himself springing up to life everlasting![9]

* * *

From *Appendix C*

* * *

That, which we find in ourselves, is (gradu mutato)[1] the substance and the life of *all* our knowledge. Without this latent presence of the "I am,"[2] all modes of existence in the external world would flit before us as colored shadows, with no greater depth, root, or fixture, than the image of a rock hath in a gliding stream or the rain-bow on a fast-sailing rain-storm. The human mind is the compass, in which the laws and actuations of all outward essences are revealed as the dips and declinations. (The application of Geometry to the forces and movements of the material world is both proof and instance.) The fact therefore, that the mind of man in its own primary and constituent forms represents the laws of nature, is a mystery which of itself should suffice to make us religious: for it is a problem of which God is the only solution, God, the one before all, and of all, and through all!—True natural philosophy is comprized in the study of the science and language of *symbols*. The power delegated to nature is all in every part: and by a symbol I mean, not a metaphor or allegory or any other figure of speech or form of fancy, but an actual and essential part of that, the whole of which it represents. Thus our Lord speaks symbolically when he says that "the eye is the light of the body."[3]

* * *

1816

From Biographia Literaria[1]

From *Part I*

FROM CHAPTER 1

* * *

As the result of all my reading and meditation, I abstracted two critical aphorisms, deeming them to comprize the conditions and criteria of poetic style;

9. This sentence echoes and alludes to John 4.14.
1. On a different level (Latin).
2. See Exodus 3.14: "And God said unto Moses: I AM THAT I AM." Compare also Coleridge's *Biographia Literaria* (1817), chap. 12: "We begin with the I KNOW MYSELF, in order to end with the absolute I AM. We proceed from the SELF, in order to lose and find all self in GOD."
3. Matthew 6.22: "The light of the body is the eye."
1. The full title is *Biographia Literaria; Or, Biographical Sketches of My Literary Life and Opinions*. Footnotes by Coleridge have been omitted from this selection.

first, that not the poem which we have *read*, but that to which we *return*, with the greatest pleasure, possesses the genuine power, and claims the name of *essential poetry*. Second, that whatever lines can be translated into other words of the same language, without diminution of their significance, either in sense, or association, or in any worthy feeling, are so far vicious[2] in their diction. Be it however observed, that I excluded from the list of worthy feelings, the pleasure derived from mere novelty, in the reader, and the desire of exciting wonderment at his powers in the author. Oftentimes since then, in perusing French tragedies, I have fancied two marks of admiration at the end of each line, as hieroglyphics of the author's own admiration at his own cleverness. Our genuine admiration of a great poet is a continuous *under-current* of feeling; it is every where present, but seldom any where as a separate excitement. I was wont boldly to affirm, that it would be scarcely more difficult to push a stone out from the pyramids with the bare hand, than to alter a word, or the position of a word, in Milton or Shakspeare, (in their most important works at least) without making the author say something else, or something worse, than he does say. One great distinction, I appeared to myself to see plainly, between, even the characteristic faults of our elder poets, and the false beauty of the moderns. In the former, from DONNE to COWLEY,[3] we find the most fantastic out-of-the-way thoughts, but in the most pure and genuine mother English; in the latter, the most obvious thoughts, in language the most fantastic and arbitrary. Our faulty elder poets sacrificed the passion, and passionate flow of poetry, to the subtleties of intellect, and to the starts of wit; the moderns to the glare and glitter of a perpetual, yet broken and heterogeneous imagery, or rather to an amphibious something, made up, half of image, and half of abstract meaning. The one sacrificed the heart to the head; the other both heart and head to point and drapery.

* * *

FROM CHAPTER 4

* * *

This excellence,[4] which in all Mr. Wordsworth's writings is more or less predominant, and which constitutes the character of his mind, I no sooner felt, than I sought to understand. Repeated meditations led me first to suspect, (and a more intimate analysis of the human faculties, their appropriate marks, functions, and effects matured my conjecture into full conviction) that fancy and imagination were two distinct and widely different faculties, instead of being, according to the general belief, either two names with one meaning, or at furthest, the lower and higher degree of one and the same power. It is not, I own, easy to conceive a more apposite translation of the Greek *Phantasia*, than the Latin Imaginatio; but it is equally true that in all societies there exists an instinct of growth, a certain collective, unconscious good sense working progressively to desynonymize[5] those words originally of

2. Defective.
3. Abraham Cowley (1618–1667), English satirist, poet, and essayist. John Donne (1572–1631), English poet. Both wrote so-called metaphysical poetry, reliant on complex metaphors and images.
4. Coleridge has just claimed that it is the mark of genius "to represent familiar objects so as to awaken in the minds of others a kindred feeling concerning them." A considerable portion of the *Biographia Literaria* is devoted to a critical analysis of the English poet WILLIAM WORDSWORTH (1770–1850), Coleridge's friend and collaborator.
5. To differentiate in meaning words previously synonymous (so defined by the *Oxford English*

the same meaning, which the conflux of dialects had supplied to the more homogeneous languages, as the Greek and German: and which the same cause, joined with accidents of translation from original works of different countries, occasion in mixt languages like our own. The first and most important point to be proved is, that two conceptions perfectly distinct are confused under one and the same word, and (this done) to appropriate that word exclusively to one meaning, and the synonyme (should there be one) to the other. But if (as will be often the case in the arts and sciences) no synonyme exists, we must either invent or borrow a word. In the present instance the appropriation had already begun, and been legitimated in the derivative adjective: Milton[6] had a highly *imaginative*, Cowley a very *fanciful* mind. If therefore I should succeed in establishing the actual existences of two faculties generally different, the nomenclature would be at once determined. To the faculty by which I had characterized Milton, we should confine the term *imagination* while the other would be contra-distinguished as *fancy*. Now were it once fully ascertained, that this division is no less grounded in nature, than that of delirium from mania, or Otway's

> Lutes, lobsters, seas of milk, and ships of amber,[7]

from Shakespear's

> What! have his daughters brought him to this pass?[8]

or from the preceding apostrophe to the elements;[9] the theory of the fine arts, and of poetry in particular, could not, I thought, but derive some additional and important light. It would in its immediate effects furnish a torch of guidance to the philosophical critic; and ultimately to the poet himself. In energetic minds, truth soon changes by domestication into power; and from directing in the discrimination and appraisal of the product, becomes influencive in the production. To admire on principle, is the only way to imitate without loss of originality.

FROM CHAPTER 13

* * *

The IMAGINATION then I consider either as primary, or secondary. The primary IMAGINATION I hold to be the living Power and prime Agent of all human Perception and as a repetition in the finite mind of the eternal act of creation in the infinite I AM.[1] The secondary I consider as an echo of the former, co-existing with the conscious will, yet still as identical with the primary in the *kind* of its agency, and differing only in *degree*, and in the *mode* of its operation. It dissolves, diffuses, dissipates, in order to re-create; or where this process is rendered impossible, yet still at all events it struggles to idealize and to unify. It is essentially *vital*, even as all objects (*as* objects) are essentially fixed and dead.

Fancy, on the contrary, has no other counters to play with, but fixities and

Dictionary, which gives this as the first use of the word).

6. John Milton (1608–1674) was a contemporary of but far greater poet than Cowley.

7. *Venice Preserved* (1682), 5.2.151, by Thomas Otway (1652–1685). Coleridge uses the word "lobsters" where Otway had written "laurels."

8. *King Lear* (ca. 1604–05), 3.4.61 (Shakespeare begins the line "What, has").

9. That is, Lear's address to the storm, 3.2.1–9, 13–23.

1. See Exodus 3.14: "And God said unto Moses, I AM THAT I AM."

definites. The Fancy is indeed no other than a mode of Memory emancipated from the order of time and space; and blended with, and modified by that empirical phenomenon of the will, which we express by the word CHOICE. But equally with the ordinary memory it must receive all its materials ready made from the law of association.

* * *

From *Part II*

CHAPTER 14

During the first year that Mr. Wordsworth and I were neighbours,[2] our conversations turned frequently on the two cardinal points of poetry, the power of exciting the sympathy of the reader by a faithful adherence to the truth of nature, and the power of giving the interest of novelty by the modifying colours of imagination. The sudden charm, which accidents of light and shade, which moon-light or sun-set diffused over a known and familiar landscape, appeared to represent the practicability of combining both. These are the poetry of nature. The thought suggested itself (to which of us I do not recollect) that a series of poems might be composed of two sorts. In one, the incidents and agents were to be, in part at least, supernatural; and the excellence aimed at was to consist in the interesting of the affections by the dramatic truth of such emotions, as would naturally accompany such situations, supposing them real. And real in *this* sense they have been to every human being who, from whatever source of delusion, has at any time believed himself under supernatural agency. For the second class, subjects were to be chosen from ordinary life; the characters and incidents were to be such, as will be found in every village and its vicinity, where there is a meditative and feeling mind to seek after them, or to notice them, when they present themselves.

In this idea originated the plan of the "Lyrical Ballads;" in which it was agreed, that my endeavours should be directed to persons and characters supernatural, or at least romantic; yet so as to transfer from our inward nature a human interest and a semblance of truth sufficient to procure for these shadows of imagination that willing suspension of disbelief for the moment, which constitutes poetic faith. Mr. Wordsworth, on the other hand, was to propose to himself as his object, to give the charm of novelty to things of every day, and to excite a feeling analogous to the supernatural, by awakening the mind's attention from the lethargy of custom, and directing it to the loveliness and the wonders of the world before us; an inexhaustible treasure, but for which in consequence of the film of familiarity and selfish solicitude we have eyes, yet see not, ears that hear not, and hearts that neither feel nor understand.[3]

With this view I wrote the "Ancient Mariner," and was preparing among other poems, the "Dark Ladie," and the "Christabel," in which I should have more nearly realized my ideal, than I had done in my first attempt. But Mr. Wordsworth's industry had proved so much more successful, and the number of his poems so much greater,[4] that my compositions, instead of forming a

2. In 1797–98 Coleridge was living at Nether Stowey and Wordsworth was nearby at Alfoxden, in southwest England.

3. See Isaiah 6.9–10.

4. Wordsworth wrote 19 of the 23 poems in the first edition of *Lyrical Ballads* (1798).

balance, appeared rather an interpolation of heterogeneous matter. Mr. Wordsworth added two or three poems written in his own character, in the impassioned, lofty, and sustained diction, which is characteristic of his genius. In this form the "Lyrical Ballads" were published; and were presented by him, as an *experiment*,[5] whether subjects, which from their nature rejected the usual ornaments and extra-colloquial style of poems in general, might not be so managed in the language of ordinary life as to produce the pleasurable interest, which it is the peculiar business of poetry in impart. To the second edition he added a preface of considerable length; in which notwithstanding some passages of apparently a contrary import, he was understood to contend for the extension of this style to poetry of all kinds, and to reject as vicious and indefensible all phrases and forms of style that were not included in what he (unfortunately, I think, adopting an equivocal expression) called the language of *real* life. From this preface, prefixed to poems in which it was impossible to deny the presence of original genius, however mistaken its direction might be deemed, arose the whole long continued controversy.[6] For from the conjunction of perceived power with supposed heresy I explain the inveteracy and in some instances, I grieve to say, the acrimonious passions, with which the controversy has been conducted by the assailants.

Had Mr. Wordsworth's poems been the silly, the childish things, which they were for a long time described as being; had they been really distinguished from the compositions of other poets merely by meanness of language and inanity of thought; had they indeed contained nothing more than what is found in the parodies and pretended imitations of them; they must have sunk at once, a dead weight, into the slough[7] of oblivion, and have dragged the preface along with them. But year after year increased the number of Mr. Wordsworth's admirers. They were found too not in the lower classes of the reading public, but chiefly among young men of strong sensibility and meditative minds; and their admiration (inflamed perhaps in some degree by opposition) was distinguished by its intensity, I might almost say, by its *religious* fervour. These facts, and the intellectual energy of the author, which was more or less consciously felt, where it was outwardly and even boisterously denied, meeting with sentiments of aversion to his opinions, and of alarm at their consequences, produced an eddy of criticism, which would of itself have borne up the poems by the violence, with which it whirled them round and round. With many parts of this preface in the sense attributed to them and which the words undoubtedly seem to authorise, I never concurred; but on the contrary objected to them as erroneous in principle, and as contradictory (in appearance at least) both to other parts of the same preface, and to the author's own practice in the greater number of the poems themselves. Mr. Wordsworth in his recent collection has, I find, degraded this prefatory disquisition to the end of his second volume, to be

5. See the brief advertisement to the first edition of *Lyrical Ballads*: "The majority of the following poems are to be considered as experiments. They were written chiefly with a view to ascertain how far the language of conversation in the middle and lower classes of society is adapted to the purposes of poetic pleasure."

6. That is, the controversy that arose over Wordsworth's theory and practice of poetry, especially in hostile essays by the critic Francis Jeffrey in the *Edinburgh Review*. See Wordsworth, preface to *Lyrical Ballads* (1800; above).

7. Soft, muddy ground.

read or not at the reader's choice.[8] But he has not, as far as I can discover, announced any change in his poetic creed. At all events, considering it as the source of a controversy, in which I have been honored more, than I deserve, by the frequent conjunction of my name with his, I think it expedient to declare once for all, in what points I coincide with his opinions, and in what points I altogether differ. But in order to render myself intelligible I must previously, in as few words as possible, explain my ideas, first, of a POEM; and secondly, of POETRY itself, in *kind*, and in *essence*.

The office of philosophical *disquisition* consists in just *distinction*; while it is the privilege of the philosopher to preserve himself constantly aware, that distinction is not division. In order to obtain adequate notions of any truth, we must intellectually separate its distinguishable parts; and this is the technical *process* of philosophy. But having so done, we must then restore them in our conceptions to the unity, in which they actually co-exist; and this is the *result* of philosophy. A poem contains the same elements as a prose composition; the difference therefore must consist in a different combination of them, in consequence of a different object proposed. According to the difference of the object will be the difference of the combination. It is possible, that the object may be merely to facilitate the recollection of any given facts or observations by artificial arrangement; and the composition will be a poem, merely because it is distinguished from prose by metre, or by rhyme, or by both conjointly. In this, the lowest sense, a man might attribute the name of a poem to the well known enumeration of the days in the several months;

> Thirty days hath September,
> April, June, and November, &c.

and others of the same class and purpose. And as a particular pleasure is found in anticipating the recurrence of sounds and quantities, all compositions that have this charm superadded, whatever be their contents, *may* be entitled poems.

So much for the superficial *form*. A difference of object and contents supplies an additional ground of distinction. The immediate purpose may be the communication of truths; either of truth absolute and demonstrable, as in works of science; or of facts experienced and recorded, as in history. Pleasure, and that of the highest and most permanent kind, may *result* from the *attainment* of the end; but it is not itself the immediate end. In other works the communication of pleasure may be the immediate purpose; and though truth, either moral or intellectual, ought to be the *ultimate* end, yet this will distinguish the character of the author, not the class to which the work belongs. Blest indeed is that state of society, in which the immediate purpose would be baffled by the perversion of the proper ultimate end; in which no charm of diction or imagery could exempt the Bathyllus even of an Anacreon, or the Alexis of Virgil,[9] from disgust and aversion!

But the communication of pleasure may be the immediate object of a work

8. For *Poems* (2 vols., 1815), Wordsworth moved the preface for *Lyrical Ballads* to an appendix and wrote a new preface and "supplementary" essay.

9. The Roman poet (70–19 B.C.E.) whose *Eclogue* 2 (ca. 37 B.C.E.) is the shepherd Corydon's lovesick address to the male slave Alexis. Bathyllus: a beautiful boy of Samos to whom several odes of the Greek lyric poet Anacreon (b. ca. 570 B.C.E.) are addressed.

not metrically composed; and that object may have been in a high degree attained, as in novels and romances. Would then the mere superaddition of metre, with or without rhyme, entitle *these* to the name of poems? The answer is, that nothing can permanently please, which does not contain in itself the reason why it is so, and not otherwise.[1] If metre be superadded, all other parts must be made consonant with it. They must be such, as to justify the perpetual and distinct attention to each part, which an exact correspondent recurrence of accent and sound are calculated to excite. The final definition then, so deduced, may be thus worded. A poem is that species of composition, which is opposed to works of science, by proposing for its *immediate* object pleasure, not truth; and from all other species (having *this* object in common with it) it is discriminated by proposing to itself such delight from the *whole*, as is compatible with a distinct gratification from each component *part*.

Controversy is not seldom excited in consequence of the disputants attaching each a different meaning to the same word; and in few instances has this been more striking, than in disputes concerning the present subject. If a man chooses to call every composition a poem, which is rhyme, or measure, or both, I must leave his opinion uncontroverted. The distinction is at least competent to characterize the writer's intention. If it were subjoined, that the whole is likewise entertaining or affecting, as a tale, or as a series of interesting reflections, I of course admit this as another fit ingredient of a poem, and an additional merit. But if the definition sought for be that of a *legitimate* poem, I answer, it must be one, the parts of which mutually support and explain each other; all in their proportion harmonizing with, and supporting the purpose and known influences of metrical arrangement. The philosophic critics of all ages coincide with the ultimate judgement of all countries, in equally denying the praises of a just poem, on the one hand, to a series of striking lines or distichs,[2] each of which absorbing the whole attention of the reader to itself disjoins it from its context, and makes it a separate whole, instead of an harmonizing part; and on the other hand, to an unsustained composition, from which the reader collects rapidly the general result unattracted by the component parts. The reader should be carried forward, not merely or chiefly by the mechanical impulse of curiosity, or by a restless desire to arrive at the final solution; but by the pleasureable activity of mind excited by the attractions of the journey itself. Like the motion of a serpent, which the Egyptians made the emblem of intellectual power; or like the path of sound through the air; at every step he pauses and half recedes, and from the retrogressive movement collects the force which again carries him onward. Precipitandus est *liber* spiritus,[3] says Petronius Arbiter most happily. The epithet, *liber*, here balances the preceding verb; and it is not easy to conceive more meaning condensed in fewer words.

But if this should be admitted as a satisfactory character of a poem, we have still to seek for a definition of poetry. The writings of PLATO, and Bishop TAYLOR, and the Theoria Sacra of BURNET,[4] furnish undeniable proofs that

1. Coleridge's editors cite SAMUEL JOHNSON, *Rambler*, no. 154 (1751): "That which hopes to resist the blast of malignity, and stand firm against the attacks of time, must contain in itself some original principle of growth."
2. Paired lines (in Greek and Latin verse, such couplets do not rhyme).
3. The free spirit must be hurried onward (Latin); from *Satyricon* 118, a novel by the Roman writer Petronius Arbiter (1st c. C.E.). *Liber* means "free."
4. Thomas Burnet (1635–1735), an English clergyman who wrote *Telluris Theoria Sacra* (1681,

poetry of the highest kind may exist without metre, and even without the contradistinguishing objects of a poem. The first chapter of Isaiah (indeed a very large proportion of the whole book) is poetry in the most emphatic sense: yet it would be not less irrational than strange to assert, that pleasure, and not truth, was the immediate object of the prophet. In short, whatever *specific* import we attach to the word, poetry, there will be found involved in it, as a necessary consequence, that a poem of any length neither can be, or ought to be, all poetry. Yet if an harmonious whole is to be produced, the remaining parts must be preserved *in keeping* with the poetry; and this can be no otherwise effected than by such a studied selection and artificial arrangement, as will partake of *one*, though not a *peculiar*, property of poetry. And this again can be no other than the property of exciting a more continuous and equal attention, than the language of prose aims at, whether colloquial or written.

My own conclusions on the nature of poetry, in the strictest use of the word, have been in part anticipated in the preceding disquisition on the fancy and imagination.[5] What is poetry? is so nearly the same question with, what is a poet? that the answer to the one is involved in the solution of the other. For it is a distinction resulting from the poetic genius itself, which sustains and modifies the images, thoughts, and emotions of the poet's own mind. The poet, described in *ideal* perfection, brings the whole soul of man into activity, with the subordination of its faculties to each other, according to their relative worth and dignity. He diffuses a tone, and spirit of unity, that blends, and (as it were) *fuses*, each into each, by that synthetic and magical power, to which we have exclusively appropriated the name of imagination. This power, first put in action by the will and understanding, and retained under their irremissive,[6] though gentle and unnoticed, controul (*laxis effertur habenis*)[7] reveals itself in the balance or reconciliation of opposite or discordant qualities: of sameness, with difference; of the general, with the concrete; the idea, with the image; the individual, with the representative; the sense of novelty and freshness, with old and familiar objects; a more than usual state of emotion, with more than usual order; judgement ever awake and steady self-possession, with enthusiasm and feeling profound or vehement; and while it blends and harmonizes the natural and the artificial, still subordinates art to nature; the manner to the matter; and our admiration of the poet to our sympathy with the poetry. "Doubtless," as Sir John Davies[8] observes of the soul (and his words may with slight alteration be applied, and even more appropriately to the poetic IMAGINATION.)

> Doubtless this could not be, but that she turns
> Bodies to spirit by sublimation strange,
> As fire converts to fire the things it burns,
> As we our food into our nature change.

The Sacred Theory of the Earth). Jeremy Taylor (1613–1667), Anglican religious writer whose sermons Coleridge esteemed. On the Greek philosopher PLATO (ca. 427–ca. 347 B.C.E.), see above.

5. In chapter 4.

6. Unremitting.

7. It is exalted with loose reins (Latin).

8. English poet (1569–1626). Coleridge slightly misquotes his poem *Nosce Teipsum* (1599; the title means "know thyself"), which explores the theme of immortality and the nature of the soul.

From their gross matter she abstracts their forms,
And draws a kind of quintessence from things;
Which to her proper nature she transforms
To bear them light, on her celestial wings.

Thus does she, when from individual states
She doth abstract the universal kinds;
Which then re-clothed in divers names and fates
Steal access through our senses to our minds.

Finally, GOOD SENSE is the BODY of poetic genius, FANCY its DRAPERY, MOTION its LIFE, and IMAGINATION the SOUL that is every where, and in each; and forms all into one graceful and intelligent whole.

1817

THOMAS LOVE PEACOCK
1785–1866

Thomas Love Peacock's "Four Ages of Poetry" is less well-known than the text that it inspired—PERCY BYSSHE SHELLEY's *Defence of Poetry* (written 1821; see below). But Peacock's satiric attack on the value of poetry is a stimulating work that scornfully dismantles the ambitions and achievements of the Romantic authors who were Peacock's contemporaries and, in some cases, his friends. It is not always clear what Peacock's own position is; in part, he succeeds in making readers uncomfortable precisely because we feel it possible that he really believes what he is saying. Indeed, he suggests something about the marginal place of poetry in the modern period that the Romantic poets may have sensed all too keenly themselves—that their exalted claims for poetry could not be maintained in the midst of modern industry, science, and commerce; that few outside their circle were interested in what they had to say; and that poets had overlooked the plain truth of their marginality because of their own self-regard and self-absorption.

Peacock was born the son of a glass merchant, in Weymouth, Dorset, in southern England. His formal schooling ended when he was thirteen, but an inheritance from his father enabled him to embark on a career as a writer, first as a poet and later as a novelist and essayist. In 1812 he met Shelley, and the two became good friends. At first they supported each other's work; later they were friendly antagonists. Peacock became Shelley's literary executor after his death.

Peacock is a skillful satirist; in his novels he particularly delighted in witty dissections of the main figures of the Romantic movement, including WILLIAM WORDSWORTH, SAMUEL TAYLOR COLERIDGE, Byron, Robert Southey, and Shelley. Among these entertaining "comic romances" (Peacock's term) were *Headlong Hall* (1816), *Melincourt* (1817), and *Nightmare Abbey* (1818). Despite their sensitivity to the abuse and ridicule inflicted by reviewers and critics, the Romantic writers seem not to have minded Peacock's verbal play and caricature. They saw in his work—filled with conversation interspersed with lyric poems and drinking songs—evidence of genuine talent, and perhaps they sensed the complexity of his response to their literary innovations. Peacock's other works include an "Essay on Fashionable Literature" (a fragment written in 1818); reviews and articles written from the 1820s to the 1850s on literature, satire, and the theater; *Gryll Grange* (1860), a satire on the Victorian age that some scholars judge his most accomplished book; and *Memoirs of Shelley* (1858–60).

Peacock also had another, very different career. Beginning in 1818–19, he was the examiner of India correspondence for the East India Company, whose government-supported trading monopoly made it the major force in Great Britain's control of India's peoples, markets, and resources. His supervisor was James Mill, the Scottish utilitarian philosopher and economist, whose position Peacock took over after Mill's death in 1836. James Mill and his more famous son, John Stuart Mill, were intellectuals engaged in addressing social problems. They sought, as utilitarians, to ensure the greatest happiness of the greatest number; and there is a strong current of social and political interest and commitment in Peacock's "Four Ages of Poetry."

Peacock's own life contained much unhappiness. He married in 1820, but his wife suffered a breakdown after the death of their three-year-old daughter from which she never recovered. Two other daughters predeceased him. Peacock retired on a pension in March 1856 and devoted himself to his library, filled with fine editions of Greek, Latin, and Italian classics.

In "The Four Ages of Poetry," Peacock's writing is barbed and derisive but has a serious purpose. Poetry began, he notes, with the warrior's wish for acclaim, which a bard, inspired by strong liquor, came forward to provide: poetry was thus merely another commodity in the marketplace. Here and elsewhere, Peacock wants to make readers reexamine the poets' myths of their origins, the stories through which generations have been taught literary and cultural history; he proposes instead to tell the unadorned truth that the poets and their idealizing followers and critics have concealed or failed to perceive. This same puncturing of historical reputation and pretense is displayed in Peacock's ridicule of the Romantic "Lake Poets" Wordsworth and Coleridge as well as Southey, Sir Walter Scott, Byron, and others. His sallies are extreme and often unfair, but the satirist's point is to be provocative—to unsettle us with the kernel of accuracy lurking in overstatements and to shake our unexamined confidence in conventional opinions.

Peacock boldly asks an unnerving question: since there are already many good poems in existence, why are new ones needed? A new era of business and science has dawned, and Peacock claims that his contemporaries have not shown any originality in responding to it. The poets' pride in their rich self-expression is simply self-indulgence, an admission that poetry is too weak to engage social concerns or contribute to knowledge. At times Peacock seems to be playfully teasing, in effect signaling the poets that he does not really hold the position he presents so forcefully. Occasionally one suspects that Peacock is mimicking the voice of a utilitarian, an act of impersonation that the shrewdest members of his audience would recognize. But at other moments Peacock appears to be in deadly earnest, disgusted at the complacency of poets so immersed in their theories and texts that they have missed the glaring signs of their own irrelevance.

Peacock is hardly the first to attack contemporary poetry. Writers from Ben Jonson and JOHN DRYDEN in the seventeenth century to ALEXANDER POPE and SAMUEL JOHNSON in the eighteenth had severely criticized the poetry of their own day. But they were serious poets themselves, and their complaints and satiric thrusts were aimed not at poetry per se but at its degradation in the marketplace; too many so-called poets had compromised their integrity in overeager attempts to please patrons and all readers. Ultimately Jonson and the others argued that authentic poets and critics should be more rigorous in maintaining high standards. To Peacock, in contrast, standards are irrelevant: taking the side neither of the neoclassical nor of the Romantic writers, he drives home the point that gifted persons waste their energies when they pursue the vocation of a poet. No mature mind, he insists, should content itself with the trifles and toys of childhood.

At the same time, Peacock is not a booster of business and moneymaking but a liberal dissenter, making a provocative case. He accuses poets and writers of standing outside the society they think they are leading. Peacock said *No* to the literary theory and practice of many of the best minds of his era, without offering any substitutes. As he revealingly stated in a late essay on Greek literature: "it is in negation that Plato shines most,—in the exposure of the errors of others."

In reading "The Four Ages of Poetry," we see clearly why the radical poet Shelley felt compelled to answer it. Peacock's argument is brilliant and unrelenting, and the momentum of his prose as he moves to his conclusion shows that he knew he was constructing a case that would be difficult but crucial for poets to refute. Perhaps it is not surprising that today "The Four Ages of Poetry" is viewed primarily within the context of Shelley studies. The only readers able to take pleasure in this essay in its own right are those who are confident that they can advance an effective reply to it—and constructing such a reply now is an even more daunting task than it was in Peacock and Shelley's day.

BIBLIOGRAPHY

For the writings of Peacock, see *Works of T. L. Peacock*, edited by H. F. B. Brett-Smith and C. E. Jones (10 vols., 1924–34; rpt. 1967); *Novels*, edited by David Garnett (2 vols., 1948); and *Poems*, edited by Brimley Johnson (1906). For biographical context, see Howard Mills, *Peacock: His Circle and His Age* (1968), which highlights Peacock's friendship with Shelley; and Robert Forbes Felton, *Thomas Love Peacock* (1973). There are three enlightening studies of Peacock's literary work: Carl Dawson, *His Fine Wit: A Study of Thomas Love Peacock* (1970), treats Peacock as an "outspoken enemy of industrial might, a feminist, and a student of mythology"; James Mulvihill, *Thomas Love Peacock* (1987); and Marilyn Butler, *Peacock Displayed: A Satirist in His Context* (1979), which includes an examination of each of Peacock's novels and provides a separate account of his work as a social and cultural critic. For bibliography, consult J. P. Donovan, "Thomas Love Peacock," in *Literature of the Romantic Period: A Bibliographical Guide* (ed. Michael O'Neil, 1988).

The Four Ages of Poetry

> Qui inter haec nutriuntur non magis sapere possunt, quam bene olere qui in culinâ habitant.
>
> Petronius.[1]

Poetry, like the world, may be said to have four ages, but in a different order: the first age of poetry being the age of iron; the second, of gold; the third, of silver; and the fourth, of brass.[2]

The first, or iron age of poetry, is that in which rude bards celebrate in rough numbers the exploits of ruder chiefs, in days when every man is a warrior, and when the great practical maximum of every form of society, "to keep what we have and to catch what we can," is not yet disguised under names of justice and forms of law, but is the naked motto of the naked sword, which is the only judge and jury in every question of *meum* and *tuum*.[3] In

1. Those who are nourished among these things are no more able to taste than those who live in a kitchen are able to smell well (Latin). From *Satyricon* 2, by the Roman writer Petronius (1st c. C.E.).
2. The myth of 4 (or 5) ages goes back to the Greek poet Hesiod (active ca. 700 B.C.E.), *Works and Days*, lines 109–201; see also *Metamorphoses* (ca. 8 C.E.), 1.89–150, by the Roman poet Ovid. Traditionally, the first (and best) age is the golden age.
3. Mine and yours (Latin).

these days, the only three trades flourishing (besides that of priest which flourishes always) are those of king, thief, and beggar: the beggar being for the most part a king deject, and the thief a king expectant. The first question asked of a stranger is, whether he is a beggar or a thief:[4] the stranger, in reply, usually assumes the first, and awaits a convenient opportunity to prove his claim to the second appellation.

The natural desire of every man to engross to himself as much power and property as he can acquire by any of the means which might makes right, is accompanied by the no less natural desire of making known to as many people as possible the extent to which he has been a winner in this universal game. The successful warrior becomes a chief; the successful chief becomes a king: his next want is an organ to disseminate the fame of his achievements and the extent of his possessions; and this organ he finds in a bard, who is always ready to celebrate the strength of his arm, being first duly inspired by that of his liquor. This is the origin of poetry, which, like all other trades, takes its rise in the demand for the commodity, and flourishes in proportion to the extent of the market.

Poetry is thus in its origin panegyrical. The first rude songs of all nations appear to be a sort of brief historical notices, in a strain of tumid hyperbole, of the exploits and possessions of a few pre-eminent individuals. They tell us how many battles such an one has fought, how many helmets he has cleft, how many breastplates he has pierced, how many widows he has made, how much land he has appropriated, how many houses he has demolished for other people, what a large one he has built for himself, how much gold he has stowed away in it, and how liberally and plentifully he pays, feeds, and intoxicates the divine and immortal bards, the sons of Jupiter,[5] but for whose everlasting songs the names of heroes would perish.

This is the first stage of poetry before the invention of written letters. The numerical modulation is at once useful as a help to memory, and pleasant to the ears of uncultured men, who are easily caught by sound: and from the exceeding flexibility of the yet unformed language, the poet does no violence to his ideas in subjecting them to the fetters of number. The savage indeed lisps in numbers,[6] and all rude and uncivilized people express themselves in the manner which we all call poetical.

The scenery by which he is surrounded, and the superstitions which are the creed of his age, form the poet's mind. Rocks, mountains, seas, unsubdued forests, unnavigable rivers, surround him with forms of power and mystery, which ignorance and fear have peopled with spirits, under multifarious names of gods, goddesses, nymphs, genii,[7] and dæmons. Of all these personages marvellous tales are in existence: the nymphs are not indifferent to handsome young men, and the gentlemen-genii are much troubled and very troublesome with a propensity to be rude to pretty maidens: the bard therefore finds no difficulty in tracing the genealogy of his chief to any of the deities in his neighbourhood with whom the said chief may be most desirous of claiming relationship.

4. See the *Odyssey* (ca. 8th c. B.C.E.), passim: and Thucydides, 1.5 [Peacock's note]. Thucydides (ca. 455–ca. 400 B.C.E.) Athenian historian, author of an incomplete history of the Peloponnesian War between Sparta and Athens (431–404 B.C.E.).

5. The Roman king of the gods, identified with the Greek god Zeus.

6. See ALEXANDER POPE, "An Epistle to Dr. Arbuthnot" (1735): "I lisp'd in Numbers, for the Numbers came" (line 128). "Numbers": metrical verse.

7. Spirits of the place.

In this pursuit, as in all others, some of course will attain a very marked pre-eminence; and these will be held in high honour, like Demodocus in the Odyssey, and will be consequently inflated with boundless vanity, like Thamyris[8] in the Iliad. Poets are as yet the only historians and chroniclers of their time, and the sole depositories of all the knowledge of their age; and though this knowledge is rather a crude congeries of traditional phantasies than a collection of useful truths, yet, such as it is, they have it to themselves. They are observing and thinking, while others are robbing and fighting: and though their object be nothing more than to secure a share of the spoil, yet they accomplish this end by intellectual, not by physical, power: their success excites emulation to the attainment of intellectual eminence: thus they sharpen their own wits and awaken those of others, at the same time that they gratify vanity and amuse curiosity. A skilful display of the little knowledge they have gains them credit for the possession of much more which they have not. Their familiarity with the secret history of gods and genii obtains for them, without much difficulty, the reputation of inspiration; thus they are not only historians but theologians, moralists, and legislators: delivering their oracles *ex cathedrâ*, and being indeed often themselves (as Orpheus and Amphion[9]) regarded as portions and emanations of divinity: building cities with a song, and leading brutes with a symphony; which are only metaphors for the faculty of leading multitudes by the nose.

The golden age of poetry finds its materials in the age of iron. This age begins when poetry begins to be retrospective; when something like a more extended system of civil polity is established; when personal strength and courage avail less to the aggrandizing of their possessor and to the making and marring of kings and kingdoms, and are checked by organized bodies, social institutions, and hereditary successions. Men also live more in the light of truth and within the interchange of observation; and thus perceive that the agency of gods and genii is not so frequent among themselves as, to judge from the songs and legends of the past time, it was among their ancestors. From these two circumstances, really diminished personal power, and apparently diminished familiarity with gods and genii, they very easily and naturally deduce two conclusions: 1st, That men are degenerated, and 2nd, That they are less in favour with the gods. The people of the petty states and colonies, which have now acquired stability and form, which owed their origin and first prosperity to the talents and courage of a single chief, magnify their founder through the mists of distance and tradition, and perceive him achieving wonders with a god or goddess always at his elbow. They find his name and his exploits thus magnified and accompanied in their traditionary songs, which are their only memorials. All that is said of him is in this character. There is nothing to contradict it. The man and his exploits and his tutelary deities are mixed and blended in one invariable association. The marvellous too is very much like a snowball: it grows as it rolls downward, till the little nucleus of truth which began its descent from the summit is hidden in the accumulation of superinduced hyperbole.

When tradition, thus adorned and exaggerated, has surrounded the foun-

8. A legendary Thracian poet and musician whose boasting was punished by the Muses (see *Iliad* 2.594–600). Demodocus: a blind bard at the court of the Phaeacian king Alcinous (see *Odyssey* 8.43–92).

9. A son of Zeus and Antiope, who ruled Thebes with his twin brother Zethus; he built the city's walls by charming the stones into place with his lyre. Orpheus: legendary Greek musician whose playing could move trees and beasts (as well as persuade the lord of the underworld to conditionally release his dead wife).

ders of families and states with so much adventitious power and magnificence, there is no praise which a living poet can, without fear of being kicked for clumsy flattery, address to a living chief, that will not still leave the impression that the latter is not so great a man as his ancestors. The man must in this case be praised through his ancestors. Their greatness must be established, and he must be shown to be their worthy descendant. All the people of a state are interested in the founder of their state. All states that have harmonized into a common form of society, are interested in their respective founders. All men are interested in their ancestors. All men love to look back into the days that are past. In these circumstances traditional national poetry is reconstructed and brought like chaos into order and form. The interest is more universal: understanding is enlarged: passion still has scope and play: character is still various and strong: nature is still unsubdued and existing in all her beauty and magnificence, and men are not yet excluded from her observation by the magnitude of cities or the daily confinement of civic life: poetry is more an art: it requires greater skill in numbers, greater command of language, more extensive and various knowledge, and greater comprehensiveness of mind. It still exists without rivals in any other department of literature; and even the arts, painting and sculpture certainly, and music probably, are comparatively rude and imperfect. The whole field of intellect is its own. It has no rivals in history, nor in philosophy, nor in science. It is cultivated by the greatest intellects of the age, and listened to by all the rest. This is the age of Homer, the golden age of poetry. Poetry has now attained its perfection: it has attained the point which it cannot pass: genius therefore seeks new forms for the treatment of the same subjects: hence the lyric poetry of Pindar and Alcæus,[1] and the tragic poetry of Æschylus and Sophocles. The favour of kings, the honour of the Olympic crown,[2] the applause of present multitudes, all that can feed vanity and stimulate rivalry, await the successful cultivator of this art, till its forms become exhausted, and new rivals arise around it in new fields of literature, which gradually acquire more influence as, with the progress of reason and civilization, facts become more interesting than fiction: indeed the maturity of poetry may be considered the infancy of history. The transition from Homer to Herodotus is scarcely more remarkable than that from Herodotus[3] to Thucydides: in the gradual dereliction of fabulous incident and ornamented language, Herodotus is as much a poet in relation to Thucydides as Homer is in relation to Herodotus. The history of Herodotus is half a poem: it is written while the whole field of literature yet belonged to the Muses, and the nine books of which it was composed were therefore of right, as well as of courtesy, superinscribed with their nine names.

Speculations, too, and disputes, on the nature of man and of mind; on moral duties and on good and evil; on the animate and inanimate components of the visible world; begin to share attention with the eggs of Leda and the horns of Io,[4] and to draw off from poetry a portion of its once undivided audience.

1. Greek poet of Mytilene on Lesbos (b. ca. 620 B.C.E.). Pindar (518–438 B.C.E.), Greek poet from Boeotia. Both Aeschylus and Sophocles were active in the 5th century B.C.E.
2. Victors at the quadrennial games at Olympia (first held 776 B.C.E.) won a wreath of wild olive.
3. Greek historian (ca. 484–ca. 420 B.C.E.), author of a history of the Persian Wars (499–479 B.C.E.). A later editor divided the work into nine "Muses" (each Muse was thought to preside over a different branch of the arts or sciences).
4. In Greek mythology, daughter of the river-god Inachus (mythical founder of Argos); after seducing her, Zeus turned her into a cow to protect her

Then comes the silver age, or the poetry of civilized life. This poetry is of two kinds, imitative and original. The imitative consists in recasting, and giving an exquisite polish to, the poetry of the age of gold: of this Virgil is the most obvious and striking example.[5] The original is chiefly comic, didactic, or satiric: as in Menander, Aristophanes, Horace, and Juvenal.[6] The poetry of this age is characterized by an exquisite and fastidious selection of words, and a laboured and somewhat monotonous harmony of expression: but its monotony consists in this, that experience having exhausted all the varieties of modulation, the civilized poetry selects the most beautiful, and prefers the repetition of these to ranging through the variety of all. But the best expression being that into which the idea naturally falls, it requires the utmost labour and care so to reconcile the inflexibility of civilized language and the laboured polish of versification with the idea intended to be expressed, that sense may not appear to be sacrificed to sound. Hence numerous efforts and rare success.

This state of poetry is however a step towards its extinction. Feeling and passion are best painted in, and roused by, ornamental and figurative language; but the reason and the understanding are best addressed in the simplest and most unvarnished phrase. Pure reason and dispassionate truth would be perfectly ridiculous in verse, as we may judge by versifying one of Euclid's[7] demonstrations. This will be found true of all dispassionate reasoning whatever, and all reasoning that requires comprehensive views and enlarged combinations. It is only the more tangible points of morality, those which command assent at once, those which have a mirror in every mind, and in which the severity of reason is warmed and rendered palatable by being mixed up with feeling and imagination, that are applicable even to what is called moral poetry: and as the sciences of morals and of mind advance towards perfection, as they become more enlarged and comprehensive in their views, as reason gains the ascendancy in them over imagination and feeling, poetry can no longer accompany them in their progress, but drops into the back ground, and leaves them to advance alone.

Thus the empire of thought is withdrawn from poetry, as the empire of facts had been before. In respect of the latter, the poet of the age of iron celebrates the achievements of his contemporaries; the poet of the age of gold celebrates the heroes of the age of iron; the poet of the age of silver recasts the poems of the age of gold: we may here see how very slight a ray of historical truth is sufficient to dissipate all the illusions of poetry. We know no more of the men than of the gods of the Iliad; no more of Achilles than we do of Thetis; no more of Hector and Andromache than we do of Vulcan and Venus:[8] these belong altogether to poetry; history has no share in them:

from the jealousy of Hera. Leda: the wife of Tyndareus, mythical king of Sparta; Zeus took the form of a swan to seduce her. According to one account, she bore two eggs; one contained the half-divine Polydeuces (or Pollux) and Helen, the other Castor and Clytemnestra.

5. The Latin poetry of Virgil (70–19 B.C.E.) might be said to imitate Greek originals: his *Eclogues*, the *Idylls* of Theocritus (ca. 300–ca. 260 B.C.E.); his *Georgics*, the *Works and Days* of Hesiod and works by the Alexandrian didactic poets; and his *Aeneid*, the *Odyssey* and *Iliad* of Homer.

6. Peacock puts together writers usually placed in distinct "ages" of literature. The Greek comic dramatists Menander (ca. 342–ca. 292 B.C.E.) and Aristophanes (ca. 450–ca. 385 B.C.E.) exemplify New and Old Comedy, respectively; the Roman lyric and satiric poet HORACE (65–8 B.C.E.) is a writer of Augustan or "Golden" Latin, while Juvenal (ca. 55–ca. 140 C.E.), the last great Roman satirist, wrote "Silver" Latin.

7. Greek mathematician (active ca. 300 B.C.E.), famous for his 13-volume textbook, the *Elements*.

8. Peacock pairs human and divine characters of the *Iliad*: the mortal Achilles with his mother, the sea nymph Thetis; the Trojan prince Hector (slain

but Virgil knew better than to write an epic about Cæsar; he left him to Livy;[9] and travelled out of the confines of truth and history into the old regions of poetry and fiction.

Good sense and elegant learning, conveyed in polished and somewhat monotonous verse, are the perfection the original and imitative poetry of civilized life. Its range is limited, and when exhausted, nothing remains but the *crambe repetita*[1] of common-place, which at length becomes thoroughly wearisome, even to the most indefatigable readers of the newest new nothings.

It is now evident that poetry must either cease to be cultivated, or strike into a new path. The poets of the age of gold have been imitated and repeated till no new imitation will attract notice: the limited range of ethical and didactic poetry is exhausted: the associations of daily life in an advanced state of society are of very dry, methodical, unpoetical matters-of-fact: but there is always a multitude of listless idlers, yawning for amusement, and gaping for novelty: and the poet makes it his glory to be foremost among their purveyors.

Then comes the age of brass, which, by rejecting the polish and the learning of the age of silver, and taking a retrograde stride to the barbarisms and crude traditions of the age of iron, professes to return to nature and revive the age of gold. This is the second childhood of poetry. To the comprehensive energy of the Homeric Muse, which, by giving at once the grand outline of things, presented to the mind a vivid picture in one or two verses, inimitable alike in simplicity and magnificence, is substituted a verbose and minutely-detailed description of thoughts, passions, actions, persons, and things, in that loose rambling style of verse, which any one may write, *stans pede in uno*,[2] at the rate of two hundred lines in an hour. To this age may be referred all the poets who flourished in the decline of the Roman Empire. The best specimen of it, though not the most generally known, is the Dionysiaca of Nonnus,[3] which contains many passages of exceeding beauty in the midst of masses of amplification and repetition.

The iron age of classical poetry may be called the bardic; the golden, the Homeric; the silver, the Virgilian; and the brass, the Nonnic.

Modern poetry has also its four ages: but "it wears its rue with a difference."[4]

To the age of brass in the ancient world succeeded the dark ages, in which the light of the Gospel began to spread over Europe, and in which, by a mysterious and inscrutable dispensation, the darkness thickened with the progress of the light. The tribes that overran the Roman Empire brought back the days of barbarism, but with this difference, that there were many books in the world, many places in which they were preserved, and occasionally some one by whom they were read, who indeed (if he escaped being

by Achilles) and his wife, Andromache, with Vulcan (god of fire and metalworking) and his wife, Venus (goddess of love).

9. Roman historian (59 B.C.E–17 C.E.). Caesar: Julius Caesar (100–44 B.C.E.), whose assumption of power marked the end of the Roman Republic; the emperor Augustus (63 B.C.E–14 C.E.) was his grandnephew and heir.

1. Cabbage served a second time; same old story (Latin).

2. While standing on one foot (Latin).

3. Greek poet of Egypt (ca. 5th c. C.E.); his *Dionysiaca*, an epic in 48 books, treats Dionysus's conquest of India.

4. See *Hamlet* (ca. 1600), 4.5.179, where the mad Ophelia, bearing various herbs and flowers, says, "O, you must wear your rue with a difference." In heralding, a "difference" is the variation on a coat of arms that distinguishes a minor branch of the family.

burned *pour l'amour de Dieu*),[5] generally lived an object of mysterious fear, with the reputation of magician, alchymist,[6] and astrologer. The emerging of the nations of Europe from this superinduced barbarism, and their settling into new forms of polity, was accompanied, as the first ages of Greece had been, with a wild spirit of adventure, which, co-operating with new manners and new superstitions, raised up a fresh crop of chimæras,[7] not less fruitful, though far less beautiful, than those of Greece. The semi-deification of women by the maxims of the age of chivalry, combining with these new fables, produced the romance of the middle ages. The founders of the new line of heroes took the place of the demi-gods of Grecian poetry. Charlemagne and his Paladins,[8] Arthur and his knights of the round table, the heroes of the iron age of chivalrous poetry, were seen through the same magnifying mist of distance, and their exploits were celebrated with even more extravagant hyperbole. These legends, combined with the exaggerated love that pervades the songs of the troubadours, the reputation of magic that attached to learned men, the infant wonders of natural philosophy, the crazy fanaticism of the crusades, the power and privileges of the great feudal chiefs, and the holy mysteries of monks and nuns, formed a state of society in which no two laymen could meet without fighting, and in which the three staple ingredients of lover, prize-fighter, and fanatic, that composed the basis of the character of every true man, were mixed up and diversified, in different individuals and classes, with so many distinctive excellencies, and under such an infinite motley variety of costume, as gave the range of a most extensive and picturesque field to the two great constituents of poetry, love and battle.

From these ingredients of the iron age of modern poetry, dispersed in the rhymes of minstrels and the songs of the troubadours, arose the golden age, in which the scattered materials were harmonized and blended about the time of the revival of learning; but with this peculiar difference, that Greek and Roman literature pervaded all the poetry of the golden age of modern poetry, and hence resulted a heterogeneous compound of all ages and nations in one picture; an infinite licence, which gave to the poet the free range of the whole field of imagination and memory. This was carried very far by Ariosto,[9] but farthest of all by Shakespeare and his contemporaries, who used time and locality merely because they could not do without them, because every action must have its when and where: but they made no scruple of deposing a Roman Emperor by an Italian Count, and sending him off in the disguise of a French pilgrim to be shot with a blunderbuss by an English archer. This makes the old English drama very picturesque, at any rate, in the variety of costume, and very diversified in action and character; though it is a picture of nothing that ever was seen on earth except a Venetian carnival.

The greatest of English poets, Milton,[1] may be said to stand alone between

5. For the love of God (French). That is, as a heretic condemned to burn at the stake.
6. Alchemist.
7. Fire-breathing she-monsters of Greek mythology, usually represented as having a lion's head, a goat's body, and a serpent's tail.
8. Champions (here, noblemen of the court). Charlemagne: Charles the Great (742–814), king of the Franks, the founder of the first empire in western Europe after the fall of Rome.
9. Ludovico Ariosto (1474–1533), Italian poet, author of the romantic epic *Orlando Furioso* (1516).
1. John Milton (1608–1674), who wrote pastoral poems, lyric poems, and sonnets as well as epics.

the ages of gold and silver, combining the excellencies of both; for with all the energy, and power, and freshness of the first, he united all the studied and elaborate magnificence of the second.

The silver age succeeded; beginning with Dryden, coming to perfection with Pope, and ending with Goldsmith, Collins, and Gray.[2]

Cowper[3] divested verse of its exquisite polish; he thought in metre, but paid more attention to his thoughts than his verse. It would be difficult to draw the boundary of prose and blank verse between his letters and his poetry.

The silver age was the reign of authority; but authority now began to be shaken, not only in poetry but in the whole sphere of its dominion. The contemporaries of Gray and Cowper were deep and elaborate thinkers. The subtle scepticism of Hume, the solemn irony of Gibbon, the daring paradoxes of Rousseau, and the biting ridicule of Voltaire,[4] directed the energies of four extraordinary minds to shake every portion of the reign of authority. Enquiry was roused, the activity of intellect was excited, and poetry came in for its share of the general result. The changes had been rung on lovely maid and sylvan shade, summer heat and green retreat, waving trees and sighing breeze, gentle swains and amorous pains, by versifiers who took them on trust, as meaning something very soft and tender, without much caring what: but with this general activity of intellect came a necessity for even poets to appear to know something of what they professed to talk of. Thomson[5] and Cowper looked at the trees and hills which so many ingenious gentlemen had rhymed about so long without looking at them at all, and the effect of the operation on poetry was like the discovery of a new world. Painting shared the influence, and the principles of picturesque beauty were explored by adventurous essayists with indefatigable pertinacity.[6] The success which attended these experiments, and the pleasure which resulted from them, had the usual effect of all new enthusiasms, that of turning the heads of a few unfortunate persons, the patriarchs of the age of brass, who, mistaking the prominent novelty for the all-important totality, seem to have ratiocinated much in the following manner: "Poetical genius is the finest of all things, and we feel that we have more of it than any one ever had. The way to bring it to perfection is to cultivate poetical impressions exclusively. Poetical impressions can be received only among natural scenes: for all that is artificial is anti-poetical. Society is artificial, therefore we will live out of society. The mountains are natural, therefore we will live in the mountains. There we shall be shining models of purity and virtue, passing the whole day in the innocent and amiable occupation of going up and down hill, receiving poet-

2. Peacock lists the English poets JOHN DRYDEN (1631–1700), Oliver Goldsmith (1730–1774), William Collins (1721–1759), and Thomas Gray (1716–1771).
3. William Cowper (1731–1800), English poet.
4. Pen name of François Marie Arouet (1694–1778), French philosopher, dramatist, and poet. DAVID HUME (1711–1776), Scottish philosopher and historian. Edward Gibbon (1734–1794), English historian whose "solemn irony" is displayed in *The History of the Decline and Fall of the Roman Empire* (1776–88). Jean-Jacques Rousseau (1712–1778), Swiss-born French philosopher and writer.
5. James Thomson (1700–1748), Scottish-born English poet whose works include *The Seasons* (1726–30).
6. Peacock is referring to such books as William Gilpin's *On Picturesque Beauty* (1792), Uvedale Price's *Essays on the Picturesque* (1794), and Richard Payne Knight's *Analytical Inquiry into the Principles of Taste* (1805). "The picturesque" refers to rough or irregular forms of beauty, especially in a landscape or its representations, which are striking or interesting in an unusual way; some writers treated it as a midway point between the sublime and the beautiful.

ical impressions, and communicating them in immortal verse to admiring generations." To some such perversion of intellect we owe that egregious confraternity of rhymesters, known by the name of the Lake Poets;[7] who certainly did receive and communicate to the world some of the most extraordinary poetical impressions that ever were heard of, and ripened into models of public virtue, too splendid to need illustration. They wrote verses on a new principle; saw rocks and rivers in a new light; and remaining studiously ignorant of history, society, and human nature, cultivated the phantasy only at the expence of the memory and the reason; and contrived, though they had retreated from the world for the express purpose of seeing nature as she was, to see her only as she was not, converting the land they lived in into a sort of fairy-land, which they peopled with mysticisms and chimæras. This gave what is called a new tone to poetry, and conjured up a herd of desperate imitators, who have brought the age of brass prematurely to its dotage.

The descriptive poetry of the present day has been called by its cultivators a return to nature. Nothing is more impertinent than this pretension. Poetry cannot travel out of the regions of its birth, the uncultivated lands of semi-civilized men. Mr. Wordsworth, the great leader of the returners to nature, cannot describe a scene under his own eyes without putting into it the shadow of a Danish boy or the living ghost of Lucy Gray,[8] or some similar phantastical parturition of the moods of his own mind.

In the origin and perfection of poetry, all the associations of life were composed of poetical materials. With us it is decidedly the reverse. We know too that there are no Dryads in Hyde-park nor Naiads in the Regent's-canal.[9] But barbaric manners and supernatural interventions are essential to poetry. Either in the scene, or in the time, or in both, it must be remote from our ordinary perceptions. While the historian and the philosopher are advancing in, and accelerating, the progress of knowledge, the poet is wallowing in the rubbish of departed ignorance, and raking up the ashes of dead savages to find gewgaws and rattles for the grown babies of the age. Mr. Scott[1] digs up the poachers and cattle-stealers of the ancient border. Lord Byron[2] cruizes for thieves and pirates on the shores of the Morea and among the Greek Islands. Mr. Southey[3] wades through ponderous volumes of travels and old chronicles, from which he carefully selects all that is false, useless, and absurd, as being essentially poetical; and when he has a commonplace book full of monstrosities, strings them into an epic. Mr. Wordsworth picks up village legends from old women and sextons; and Mr. Coleridge,[4] to the valuable information acquired from similar sources, superadds the dreams of crazy theologians and the mysticisms of German metaphysics, and favours

7. Particularly, WILLIAM WORDSWORTH (1770–1850) and SAMUEL TAYLOR COLERIDGE (1772–1834).

8. Wordsworth's poems include "The Danish Boy" (1800) and "Lucy Gray" (1800); he used the heading "Moods of My Own Mind" for a section of his *Poems in Two Volumes* (1807).

9. In Regent's Park in north-central London. "Dryads": Greek nymphs associated with trees. Hyde Park: a large public park in west-central London. "Naiads": nymphs, associated with freshwater sources.

1. Sir Walter Scott (1771–1832), Scottish novelist and poet, whose works include *Minstrelsy of the Scottish Border* (1802–03).

2. George Gordon, Lord Byron (1788–1824), English Romantic poet; Peacock here refers to *The Giaour* (1813), a story of romantic passion and vengeance.

3. Robert Southey (1774–1843), English poet, biographer, and professional writer. The epic made of "monstrosities" may refer to his *Roderick: The Last of the Goths* (1814).

4. See Coleridge's "Rime of the Ancient Mariner" and "Christabel" in *Lyrical Ballads* (1798). For Wordsworth, see *The Excursion* (1814).

the world with visions in verse, in which the quadruple elements of sexton, old woman, Jeremy Taylor, and Emanuel Kant,[5] are harmonized into a delicious poetical compound. Mr. Moore presents us with a Persian, and Mr. Campbell[6] with a Pennsylvanian tale, both formed on the same principle as Mr. Southey's epics, by extracting from a perfunctory and desultory perusal of a collection of voyages and travels, all that useful investigation would not seek for and that common sense would reject.

These disjointed relics of tradition and fragments of second-hand observation, being woven into a tissue of verse, constructed on what Mr. Coleridge calls a new principle[7] (that is, no principle at all), compose a modern-antique compound of frippery and barbarism, in which the puling sentimentality of the present time is grafted on the misrepresented ruggedness of the past into a heterogeneous congeries of unamalgamating manners, sufficient to impose on the common readers of poetry, over whose understandings the poet of this class possesses that commanding advantage, which, in all circumstances and conditions of life, a man who knows something, however little, always possesses over one who knows nothing.

A poet in our times is a semi-barbarian in a civilized community. He lives in the days that are past. His ideas, thoughts, feelings, associations, are all with barbarous manners, obsolete customs, and exploded superstitions. The march of his intellect is like that of a crab, backward. The brighter the light diffused around him by the progress of reason, the thicker is the darkness of antiquated barbarism, in which he buries himself like a mole, to throw up the barren hillocks of his Cimmerian[8] labours. The philosophic mental tranquillity which looks round with an equal eye on all external things, collects a store of ideas, discriminates their relative value, assigns to all their proper place, and from the materials of useful knowledge thus collected, appreciated, and arranged, forms new combinations that impress the stamp of their power and utility on the real business of life, is diametrically the reverse of that frame of mind which poetry inspires, or from which poetry can emanate. The highest inspirations of poetry are resolvable into three ingredients: the rant of unregulated passion, the whining of exaggerated feeling, and the cant of factitious sentiment: and can therefore serve only to ripen a splendid lunatic like Alexander, a puling driveller like Werter,[9] or a morbid dreamer like Wordsworth. It can never make a philosopher, nor a statesman, nor in any class of life an useful or rational man. It cannot claim the slightest share in any one of the comforts and utilities of life of which we have witnessed so many and so rapid advances. But though not useful, it may be said it is highly ornamental, and deserves to be cultivated for the pleasure it yields. Even if this be granted, it does not

5. IMMANUEL KANT (1724–1804), German idealist philosopher. Taylor (1613–1667), English theologian, devotional writer, and bishop.

6. Thomas Campbell (1777–1844), Scottish poet and journalist; in his *Gertrude of Wyoming* (1809), "Wyoming" refers to a settlement in Pennsylvania. Thomas Moore (1779–1852), Irish poet; his "Persian tale" is the popular *Lalla Rookh* (1817), a series of four oriental tales in verse within a prose frame.

7. In the preface to "Christabel," Coleridge states that its meter is "founded on a new principle . . . of counting in each line the accents, not the syllables."

8. That is, done in gloom and darkness. According to Homer (*Odyssey* 11.14–19), the Cimmerians lived in a land where the sun never shone.

9. The protagonist of *The Sorrows of Young Werther* (1774) by Johann Wolfgang von Goethe. Alexander: usually identified as Alexander the Great (356–323 B.C.E.), one of greatest generals of the ancient world. Perhaps he is a "lunatic" for insisting that the Greek cities treat him like a god.

follow that a writer of poetry in the present state of society is not a waster of his own time, and a robber of that of others. Poetry is not one of those arts which, like painting, require repetition and multiplication, in order to be diffused among society. There are more good poems already existing than are sufficient to employ that portion of life which any mere reader and recipient of poetical impressions should devote to them, and these having been produced in poetical times, are far superior in all the characteristics of poetry to the artificial reconstructions of a few morbid ascetics in unpoetical times. To read the promiscuous rubbish of the present time to the exclusion of the select treasures of the past, is to substitute the worse for the better variety of the same mode of enjoyment.

But in whatever degree poetry is cultivated, it must necessarily be to the neglect of some branch of useful study: and it is a lamentable spectacle to see minds, capable of better things, running to seed in the specious indolence of these empty aimless mockeries of intellectual exertion. Poetry was the mental rattle that awakened the attention of intellect in the infancy of civil society: but for the maturity of mind to make a serious business of the playthings of its childhood, is as absurd as for a full-grown man to rub his gums with coral, and cry to be charmed to sleep by the jingle of silver bells.

As to that small portion of our contemporary poetry, which is neither descriptive, nor narrative, nor dramatic, and which, for want of a better name, may be called ethical, the most distinguished portion of it, consisting merely of querulous, egotistical rhapsodies, to express the writer's high dissatisfaction with the world and every thing in it, serves only to confirm what has been said of the semi-barbarous character of poets, who from singing dithyrambics and "Io Triumphe,"[1] while society was savage, grow rabid, and out of their element, as it becomes polished and enlightened.

Now when we consider that it is not the thinking and studious, and scientific and philosophical part of the community, not to those whose minds are bent on the pursuit and promotion of permanently useful ends and aims, that poets must address their minstrelsy, but to that much larger portion of the reading public, whose minds are not awakened to the desire of valuable knowledge, and who are indifferent to any thing beyond being charmed, moved, excited, affected, and exalted: charmed by harmony, moved by sentiment, excited by passion, affected by pathos, and exalted by sublimity: harmony, which is language on the rack of Procrustes;[2] sentiment, which is canting egotism in the mask of refined feeling; passion, which is the commotion of a weak and selfish mind; pathos, which is the whining of an unmanly spirit; and sublimity, which is the inflation of an empty head: when we consider that the great and permanent interests of human society become more and more the main spring of intellectual pursuit; that in proportion as they become so, the subordinacy of the ornamental to the useful will be more and more seen and acknowledged; and that therefore the progress of useful art and science, and of moral and political knowledge, will continue more and more to withdraw attention from frivolous and unconducive, to

1. The cry of Roman soldiers as they marched in their generals' triumphs through the streets of Rome. "Dithyrambics": Greek lyric poetry sung by a chorus and leader, in turn, in honor of Dionysus (Greek god of wine and fertility), usually telling the stories of heroes.

2. A legendary robber of Attica who forced travelers to fit his bed, cutting off or stretching limbs as necessary.

solid and conducive studies: that therefore the poetical audience will not only continually diminish in the proportion of its number to that of the rest of the reading public, but will also sink lower and lower in the comparison of intellectual acquirement: when we consider that the poet must still please his audience, and must therefore continue to sink to their level, while the rest of the community is rising above it: we may easily conceive that the day is not distant, when the degraded state of every species of poetry will be as generally recognized as that of dramatic poetry has long been: and this not from any decrease either of intellectual power, or intellectual acquisition, but because intellectual power and intellectual acquisition have turned themselves into other and better channels, and have abandoned the cultivation and the fate of poetry to the degenerate fry[3] of modern rhymesters, and their olympic judges, the magazine critics, who continue to debate and promulgate oracles about poetry, as if it were still what it was in the Homeric age, the all-in-all of intellectual progression, and as if there were no such things in existence as mathematicians, astronomers, chemists, moralists, metaphysicians, historians, politicians, and political economists, who have built into the upper air of intelligence a pyramid, from the summit of which they see the modern Parnassus[4] far beneath them, and, knowing how small a place it occupies in the comprehensiveness of their prospect, smile at the little ambition and the circumscribed perceptions with which the drivellers and mountebanks upon it are contending for the poetical palm and the critical chair.

1820

3. Offspring.
4. A mountain in Greece, sacred to Apollo and the Muses and to Dionysus.

PERCY BYSSHE SHELLEY
1792–1822

Like the American poet Walt Whitman, Percy Bysshe Shelley has been revered by many readers for his haunting lyrics and, even more, for the radical views he expresses in both his poetry and prose. But more than any other nineteenth-century poet, he came in for relentless and mean-spirited abuse at the hands of the major modernist poets and critics, including T. S. ELIOT, F. R. Leavis, JOHN CROWE RANSOM, and Allen Tate. For them, Shelley represented everything that modern poetry was seeking to move beyond, and they pummeled him time and again for (as they saw it) the intersecting weaknesses of his poetry and his character: dreaminess, arrogance, self-absorption, irresponsibility. They judged his personal conduct offensive and his verse marred by muddled imagery and confused symbolism. Writing in 1950, the critic Leslie Fiedler reflected: "The only way to find out if a poet is immortal is to kill him; Milton and Wordsworth slain have risen; Cowley and Shelley are rotting in their tombs." Shelley seemed no more likely to recover his prestige than did the third-tier metaphysical poet with whom he was paired.

This downgrading of Shelley was already under way in the nineteenth century. In *Essays in Criticism* (1865), MATTHEW ARNOLD slighted him: "The right sphere for Shelley's genius was the sphere of music, not of poetry . . . A beautiful and ineffectual angel, beating in the void his luminous wings in vain." And in *Literary Studies* (1884), the editor and essayist Walter Bagehot concluded: "He floats away into an imaginary Elysium or an expected Utopia; beautiful and excellent, of course, but having nothing in common with the absolute laws of the present world." This tone seemed to be justified by Shelley himself, who, for example, observed to his friend Edward Trelawny: "When my brain gets heated with thought it soon boils and throws off images and words faster than I can skim them off." But Shelley's words to Trelawny bear witness to his creative energy and exhilaration, to his yearning to break free from constraint. Shelley's commitment to personal and social freedom perhaps provides the best context for understanding and valuing his writing. His poetry and prose attacked social and political tyranny, assailing the ways in which law and religion functioned to support an oppressive state. In phrasing that anticipated RALPH WALDO EMERSON's in *Nature* (1836), "The American Scholar" (1837), and other seminal American Transcendentalist texts, Shelley declared: "Let us believe in a kind of optimism in which we are our own gods" (letter, 1819). As he once said, he sought to call attention to the "else unfelt oppressions of this earth" ("Julian and Maddalo," line 450), that is, to make readers feel the nature and depth of human oppression and lift them to a higher conception of possibility. In doing this, he was performing the special office of the poet.

Shelley was born the son of a wealthy squire (and member of Parliament) near Horsham in Sussex, England. He was educated first at Syon House Academy, in Brentford, a western suburb of London, and then at Eton, the largest and most famous of England's public (i.e., endowed boarding) schools, where he was dubbed "mad Shelley" for his antics and "Eton atheist" for his skeptical views on religion. Imaginative and rebellious, he was already writing prose and poems while in his teens. He entered University College, Oxford University, in 1810; there he read such radical authors as William Godwin, author of the *Enquiry concerning Political Justice* (1793), and Thomas Paine, author of *The Rights of Man* (1791–92) and *The Age of Reason* (1793).

In March 1811, because Shelley coauthored an empiricist pamphlet, *The Necessity of Atheism*, which he then mailed to the bishops and heads of the colleges at Oxford, he was expelled from the university. His life became even more scandalous when he eloped to Edinburgh, Scotland, with sixteen-year-old Harriet Westbrook. This action, together with his refusal to renounce the pamphlet, caused a breach with his family that cost Shelley his inheritance.

After their marriage in August 1811, the young couple spent the next three years in England and Ireland, moving often. Shelley corresponded with Godwin, wrote addresses and proposals on such topics as Catholic emancipation, and was kept under watch by the civil authorities. His first important poem, *Queen Mab*, which exhibits his radical views on both religion and conventional morality, was privately printed in 1831. He wrote and lectured on a host of other subjects as well, from freedom of the press to vegetarianism. During this time, Harriet bore two children; but she and Shelley grew estranged.

When Shelley fell in love with Mary Godwin, the sixteen-year-old daughter of William Godwin and the English writer and reformer MARY WOLLSTONECRAFT, he acted according to his views on the primacy of love. Leaving his family behind, in 1814 he traveled to France with Mary (and her fifteen-year-old half-sister, Jane "Claire" Clairmont). After travels in France, Switzerland, and Germany, they returned to London; in spring 1815 Mary gave birth to a daughter who died prematurely, and in 1816 she bore a son, William. In Switzerland, with the Romantic poet Lord Byron as their companion during the summer of 1816, Mary began her famous novel *Frankenstein* while Percy worked on such major philosophical poems as "Hymn to Intellectual Beauty" and "Mont Blanc." They married, despite their objections to the institution of marriage, after Harriet drowned herself in 1816. Harriet's parents quickly secured a decree declaring Shelley unfit to have custody of his and Harriet's children, who were placed in foster care at his expense. In spring 1818 he left England for Italy, where he spent the rest of his life with Mary, their three children (two of whom died, within a nine-month period in 1818–19), Claire Clairmont, and her daughter (whose father was Byron).

While in Pisa, Shelley lived amid a circle of writers and adventurers, including Byron and Edward Trelawny. In April 1822 he moved to the village of Lerici on the Gulf of Spezia, where he wrote a number of his best lyrics and vivid letters. Caught in a sudden storm while in a boat with his friend Edward Williams, he drowned in July 1822. Shelley left unfinished a political drama and "The Triumph of Life," a dream allegory that has figured significantly in contemporary criticism and theory (e.g., see the essays by HAROLD BLOOM, PAUL DE MAN, JACQUES DERRIDA, and others in *Deconstruction and Criticism*, 1997).

Shelley matters in literary history above all for his poetry, but his prose works are often powerful and remain undervalued. The best (and best-known) of them is *A Defence of Poetry*, which he wrote in response to his friend THOMAS LOVE PEACOCK's "Four Ages of Poetry" (1820; see above). Peacock presents a satiric, witty survey of the historical rise and decline of poetry that draws a parallel between the classical and modern periods. He traces English poetry's movement from the iron age of song, to the golden age of Shakespeare, then to the silver age of ALEXANDER POPE, and, finally, to the brass age of his Romantic contemporaries, whose work consists, he says, of "rant," "whining," and "cant." In reply, Shelley honors the activity of the poet and emphasizes that poetry has increased, rather than diminished, in importance in the modern era. Many of the ideas he presents are fairly familiar, deriving from PLATO and, especially, from SIR PHILIP SIDNEY's *Apology for Poetry* (1595, also known as *The Defence of Poesie*), which Shelley read as he prepared and planned his own work. But Shelley gives them a fervent Romantic cast, particularly in the glowing images and passionate rhythms of the *Defence's* final passages.

Peacock and Shelley had met in 1812, and they visited and corresponded with one another often. After Peacock's "Four Ages" appeared, Shelley wrote in a letter, January 1821, that he planned "an answer" to it: "It is very clever but, I think, very false." On March 21, he sent Peacock the first part of an essay meant to be its "antidote." In the original plan for the *Defence*, Shelley included a number of references to Peacock, but most of these were omitted when the text was prepared for publication after his death. Originally, too, the *Defence* was to have three parts: a general defense of poetry and its role in society, a survey of the development of English poetry, and a discussion of the literature of the day. Only the first part was completed.

Despite being an incomplete piece that draws on and adapts his own earlier writings—the prefaces to *The Revolt of Islam* and *Prometheus Unbound*, "Discourse on the Manners of the Ancient Greeks" (which prefaced his translation of Plato's *Symposium*), "Essay on Christianity," the first two chapters of *A Philosophical View of Reform*, and "Essay on the Devil"—the *Defence* is held together by the force of Shelley's personality and his literary and political convictions. Poetry, says Shelley, combines wisdom with delight; it is a source of pleasure; and it inculcates virtue, as readers seek to imitate the noble traits of character that Homer portrays in his heroes. Poetry kindles the sympathetic imagination, enabling us to locate ourselves "in the place of another"; it thereby unites individuals by breaking down the differences among them. It is so closely linked to the society from which it rises that its health serves as a barometer of society's health. It counterbalances the ascendant sciences of calculation and accumulation, which exacerbate inequality and selfishness. It is a universal spiritual force of evanescent inspiration, superseding logic and will and possessing prophetic power. At a memorable moment Shelley even envisions literature as one great poem that all poets have built up since time began.

There are tensions, even contradictions, in Shelley's text that his powerful prose cannot reconcile or explain. Thus on the one hand, he presents much historical commentary on ancient Greek and Roman literary genres and on the literature of later periods. But on the other hand, his highest flights of rhetoric pay tribute to the power of poetry to transcend history. There is a gap between the kind of historical particularity that Shelley provides in his running literary and cultural comments and the general function that he assigns to poetry as "something divine" that "enlarges the circumference of the imagination."

In addition, Shelley's claims for the special qualities of the poet are problematic in his own terms. In exalting poets as the "best and happiest minds," the "unacknowledged legislators of the World," he paradoxically reinvokes the social distinctions, the ranking of persons, the law-giving from on high, that his works so fiercely challenge. Indeed, there may be a darker dimension to the vital, vigorous rhetoric that Shelley mobilizes in defense of literature. As RAYMOND WILLIAMS remarks in *Culture and Society* (1958), Shelley means the word *unacknowledged* to imply poets' importance—their great (albeit almost invisible) sociopolitical work. But the term also carries "the felt helplessness of a generation" as "a culture now dominated by science and industry [fails] to bestow upon poets the 'acknowledgment' that they merit." Williams also points out the mixed implications of Shelley's language about poets: their special high status both distinguishes and marginalizes them, separating them from the community to which Shelley insists they contribute so much.

The poet, Shelley maintains, is a power working for social and moral transformation—the chief influence in civilizing the community. Yet the poet, he also says, is "a nightingale, who sits in darkness and sings to cheer its own solitude with sweet sounds." Shelley's forthright testimonies on behalf of poetry and the tensions and contradictions that his rhetoric attempts to surmount continue to fascinate the *Defence*'s readers.

BIBLIOGRAPHY

For Shelley's prose, primary sources include *The Prose Works*, edited by E. B. Murray (1 vol. to date, 1993–), and *The Letters*, edited by Frederick L. Jones (2 vols., 1964). For a single-volume collection that includes critical essays, see *Shelley's Poetry and Prose*, edited by Donald H. Reiman and Sharon B. Powers (1977). Other resources include *Shelley and His Circle, 1773–1822*, edited by Kenneth Neill Cameron (9 vols. to date, 1961–), which presents the manuscripts by Shelley, his family, friends, and literary acquaintances held in the New York Public Library; it contains important critical and contextual commentary. The standard biographical work is Newman Ivey White, *Shelley* (2 vols., 1940). Kenneth Neill Cameron, in *The Young Shelley* (1950) and *Shelley: The Golden Years* (1974), is informative on the poet's radical political views. Richard Holmes, *Shelley: The Pursuit* (1974), gives a good sense of the person behind the poetry and prose.

On Shelley's literary theory, consult Fanny Delisle, *A Study of Shelley's "A Defence of Poetry": A Textual and Critical Evaluation* (2 vols., 1974). Among the many studies of Shelley's poetic theory and practice are Harold Bloom, *Shelley's Mythmaking* (1959); Earl Wasserman, *Shelley: A Critical Reading* (1971); William Keach, *Shelley's Style* (1984), which deals well with Shelley's complex and contradictory attitudes toward language; and Jerrold E. Hogle, *Shelley's Process: Radical Transference and the Development of His Major Works* (1988). On the relationships between literature and politics in Shelley's life and works, see Timothy Clark, *Embodying Revolution: The Figure of the Poet in Shelley* (1989); Michael O'Neill, *The Human Mind's Imaginings: Conflict and Achievement in Shelley's Poetry* (1989); David Duff, *Romance and Revolution: Shelley and the Politics of a Genre* (1994); and Timothy Morton, *Shelley and the Revolution in Taste: The Body and the Natural World* (1994).

Helpful on trends in Shelley scholarship are *Shelley: The Critical Heritage*, edited by James E. Barcus (1975); *Decontruction and Criticism*, by Harold Bloom et al. (1979), which offers a series of exemplary deconstructive readings of "The Triumph of Life"; *Essays on Shelley*, edited by Miriam Allott (1982); *The New Shelley: Later Twentieth-Century Views*, edited by G. Kim Blank (1991); and *Shelley: Poet and Legislator of the World*, edited by Betty T. Bennett and Stuart Curran (1996). For bibliography, look to Clement Dunbar, *Bibliography of Shelley Studies: 1823–1950* (1976), and *Shelley Studies, 1950–1984: An Annotated Bibliography* (1986).

From A Defence of Poetry, or Remarks Suggested by an Essay Entitled "The Four Ages of Poetry"[1]

* * *

Poetry is ever accompanied with pleasure: all spirits on which it falls, open themselves to receive the wisdom which is mingled with its delight. In the infancy of the world, neither poets themselves nor their auditors are fully aware of the excellence of poetry: for it acts in a divine and unapprehended manner, beyond and above consciousness; and it is reserved for future generations to contemplate and measure the mighty cause and effect in all the strength and splendour of their union.[2] Even in modern times, no living poet ever arrived at the fulness of his fame; the jury which sits in judgement upon a poet, belonging as he does to all time, must be composed of his peers: it must be impanelled by Time from the selectest of the wise of many generations. A Poet is a nightingale, who sits in darkness and sings to cheer its own solitude with sweet sounds; his auditors are as men entranced by the melody of an unseen musician, who feel that they are moved and softened, yet know not whence or why. The poems of Homer and his contemporaries were the delight of infant Greece; they were the elements of that social system which is the column upon which all succeeding civilization has reposed. Homer embodied the ideal perfection of his age in human character; nor can we doubt that those who read his verses were awakened to an ambition of becoming like to Achilles, Hector and Ulysses:[3] the truth and beauty of friendship, patriotism and persevering devotion to an object, were unveiled to the depths in these immortal creations: the sentiments of the auditors must have been refined and enlarged by a sympathy with such great and lovely impersonations, until from admiring they imitated, and from imitation they identified themselves with the objects of their admiration. Nor let it be objected, that these characters are remote from moral perfection, and that they can by no means be considered as edifying patterns for general imitation. Every epoch under names more or less specious has deified its peculiar errors. Revenge is the naked Idol of the worship of a semi-barbarous age; and Self-deceit is the veiled Image of unknown evil before which luxury and satiety lie prostrate. But a poet considers the vices of his contemporaries as the temporary dress in which his creations must be arrayed, and which

1. "The Four Ages of Poetry" (1820), by THOMAS LOVE PEACOCK.
2. This emphasis on the pleasure given by poetry echoes SIR PHILIP SIDNEY's *Apology for Poetry* (1595). See also WILLIAM WORDSWORTH's preface to *Lyrical Ballads* (1800): "Nor let this necessity of producing immediate pleasure be considered as a degradation of the Poet's art. It is far otherwise."
3. Odysseus, the hero of the *Odyssey*. Achilles and Hector are the greatest warriors (Greek and Trojan, respectively) of the *Iliad*. These poems are the earliest Greek epics (ca. 8th c. B.C.E.)

cover without concealing the eternal proportions of their beauty. An epic or dramatic personage is understood to wear them around his soul, as he may the antient armour or the modern uniform around his body; whilst it is easy to conceive a dress more graceful than either. The beauty of the internal nature cannot be so far concealed by its accidental vesture, but that the spirit of its form shall communicate itself to the very disguise, and indicate the shape it hides from the manner in which it is worn. A majestic form and graceful motions will express themselves through the most barbarous and tasteless costume. Few poets of the highest class have chosen to exhibit the beauty of their conceptions in its naked truth and splendour; and it is doubtful whether the alloy of costume, habit, etc., be not necessary to temper this planetary music[4] for mortal ears.

The whole objection however of the immorality of poetry rests upon a misconception of the manner in which poetry acts to produce the moral improvement of man. Ethical science arranges the elements which poetry has created, and propounds schemes and proposes examples of civil and domestic life: nor is it for want of admirable doctrines that men hate, and despise, and censure, and deceive, and subjugate one another. But Poetry acts in another and diviner manner. It awakens and enlarges the mind itself by rendering it the receptable of a thousand unapprehended combinations of thought. Poetry lifts the veil from the hidden beauty of the world, and makes familiar objects be as if they were not familiar: it reproduces all that it represents, and the impersonations clothed in its Elysian[5] light stand thenceforward in the minds of those who have once contemplated them, as memorials of that gentle and exalted content which extends itself over all thoughts and actions with which it coexists. The great secret of morals is Love: or a going out of our own nature, and an identification of ourselves with the beautiful which exists in thought, action, or person, not our own.[6] A man, to be greatly good, must imagine intensely and comprehensively; he must put himself in the place of another and of many others; the pains and pleasures of his species must become his own. The great instrument of moral good is the imagination; and poetry administers to the effect by acting upon the cause. Poetry enlarges the circumference of the imagination by replenishing it with thoughts of ever new delight, which have the power of attracting and assimilating to their own nature all other thoughts, and which form new intervals and interstices whose void for ever craves fresh food. Poetry strengthens that faculty which is the organ of the moral nature of man, in the same manner as exercise strengthens a limb. A Poet therefore would do ill to embody his own conceptions of right and wrong, which are usually those of his place and time, in his poetical creations, which participate in neither. By this assumption of the inferior office of interpreting the effect, in which perhaps after all he might acquit himself but imperfectly, he would resign the glory in a participation in the cause. There was little danger that Homer, or any of the eternal poets, should have so far misunderstood themselves as to have abdicated this throne of their widest dominion. Those in

4. The music of the spheres: the beautiful sound said to be made by the movements of the planets.
5. Paradisiacal. According to classical mythology, after death the blessed dwell in the Elysian Fields.
6. Editors have noted the influence here of PLATO's *Symposium* (ca. 384 B.C.E.), which Shelley himself translated. He rendered one of its key sentences "Love, therefore, and every thing else that desires anything, desires that which is absent and beyond his reach, that which it has not, that which it not itself, that which it wants."

whom the poetical faculty, though great, is less intense, as Euripides, Lucan, Tasso, Spenser,[7] have frequently affected a moral aim, and the effect of their poetry is diminished in exact proportion to the degree in which they compel us to advert to this purpose.

Homer and the cyclic poets[8] were followed at a certain interval by the dramatic and lyrical Poets of Athens, who flourished contemporaneously with all that is most perfect in the kindred expressions of the poetical faculty; architecture, painting, music, the dance, sculpture, philosophy, and we may add the forms of civil life. For although the scheme of Athenian society was deformed by many imperfections[9] which the poetry existing in Chivalry and Christianity have erased from the habits and institutions of modern Europe; yet never at any other period has so much energy, beauty, and virtue, been developed: never was blind strength and stubborn form so disciplined and rendered subject to the will of man, or that will less repugnant to the dictates of the beautiful and the true, as during the century which preceded the death of Socrates.[1] Of no other epoch in the history of our species have we records and fragments stamped so visibly with the image of the divinity in man. But it is Poetry alone, in form, in action, or in language, which has rendered this epoch memorable above all others, and the storehouse of examples to everlasting time. For written poetry existed at the epoch simultaneously with the other arts, and it is an idle enquiry to demand which gave and which received the light, which all as from a common focus have scattered over the darkest periods of succeeding time. We know no more of cause and effect than a constant conjunction of events: Poetry is ever found to coexist with whatever other arts contribute to the happiness and perfection of man. I appeal to what has already been established to distinguish between the cause and the effect.

It was at the period here adverted to, that the Drama had its birth; and however a succeeding writer may have equalled or surpassed those few great specimens of the Athenian drama which have been preserved to us, it is indisputable that the art itself never was understood or practised according to the true philosophy of it, as at Athens. For the Athenians employed language, action, music, painting, the dance, and religious institutions, to produce a common effect in the representation of the highest idealisms of passion and of power; each division in the art was made perfect in its kind by artists of the most consummate skill, and was disciplined into a beautiful proportion and unity one towards another. On the modern stage a few only of the elements capable of expressing the image of the poet's conception are employed at once. We have tragedy without music and dancing; and music and dancing without the highest impersonations of which they are the fit accompaniment, and both without religion and solemnity. Religious institution has indeed been usually banished from the stage. Our system of divesting the actor's face of a mask, on which the many expressions appropriated to his dramatic character might be moulded into one permanent and unchanging expression, is favourable only to a partial and inharmonious

7. Edmund Spenser (1552–1599), English poet. Euripides (ca. 485–ca. 406 B.C.E.), Greek tragedian. Lucan (39–65 C.E.), Roman poet. Torquato Tasso (1544–1595), Italian poet.

8. Poets after Homer who filled out the story of the Trojan War.

9. That is, slavery and the second-class status of women (Shelley explicitly names these "imperfections" below).

1. That is, the 5th century B.C.E., the golden age of Athenian politics and art (the philosopher Socrates was put to death in 399 B.C.E.).

effect; it is fit for nothing but a monologue, where all the attention may be directed to some great master of ideal mimicry. The modern practice of blending comedy with tragedy, though liable to great abuse in point of practice, is undoubtedly an extension of the dramatic circle; but the comedy should be as in King Lear, universal, ideal, and sublime. It is perhaps the intervention of this principle which determines the balance in favour of King Lear against the Œdipus Tyrannus or the Agamemnon, or, if you will, the trilogies with which they are connected;[2] unless the intense power of the choral poetry, especially that of the latter, should be considered as restoring the equilibrium. King Lear, if it can sustain this comparison, may be judged to be the most perfect specimen of the dramatic art existing in the world; in spite of the narrow conditions to which the poet was subjected by the ignorance of the philosophy of the Drama which has prevailed in modern Europe. Calderon[3] in his religious Autos has attempted to fulfill some of the high conditions of dramatic representation neglected by Shakespeare; such as the establishing a relation between the drama and religion, and the accommodating them to music and dancing; but he omits the observation of conditions still more important, and more is lost than gained by a substitution of the rigidly-defined and ever-repeated idealisms of a distorted superstition for the living impersonations of the truth of human passion.

But we digress.—The Author of the Four Ages of Poetry has prudently omitted to dispute on the effect of the Drama upon life and manners. For, if I know the knight by the device of his shield, I have only to inscribe Philoctetes[4] or Agamemnon or Othello upon mine to put to flight the giant sophisms which have enchanted him, as the mirror of intolerable light, though on the arm of one of the weakest of the Paladins,[5] could blind and scatter whole armies of necromancers and pagans. The connexion of scenic exhibitions with the improvement or corruption of the manners of men, has been universally recognized: in other words, the presence or absence of poetry in its most perfect and universal form has been found to be connected with good and evil in conduct and habit. The corruption which has been imputed to the drama as an effect, begins, when the poetry employed in its constitution, ends: I appeal to the history of manners whether the periods of the growth of the one and the decline of the other have not corresponded with an exactness equal to any other example of moral cause and effect.

The drama at Athens, or wheresoever else it may have approached to its perfection, coexisted with the moral and intellectual greatness of the age. The tragedies of the Athenian poets are as mirrors in which the spectator beholds himself, under a thin disguise of circumstance, stript of all but that ideal perfection and energy which every one feels to be the internal type of all that he loves, admires, and would become. The imagination is enlarged by a sympathy with pains and passions so mighty, that they distend in their

2. Sophocles' "trilogy" (the plays were not performed together) is *Oedipus Tyrannus* (ca. 430 B.C.E.), *Oedipus Coloneus* (ca. 401), and *Antigone* (ca. 441); Aeschylus's Oresteian trilogy (458) comprises *Agamemnon, The Libation Bearers*, and *The Eumenides. King Lear* was first performed ca. 1605.

3. Pedro Calderón de la Barca (1600–1681), Spanish dramatist and poet; after he became a priest in 1651, he wrote only *autos sacramentales*, one-act religious dramas (usually allegorical).

4. Greek hero in the Trojan War and the subject of many tragedies; that by Sophocles (ca. 409 B.C.E.) survives.

5. The twelve peers of the court of Charlemagne (742–814), king of the Franks and founder of the first western European empire after the fall of Rome.

conception the capacity of that by which they are conceived; the good affections are strengthened by pity, indignation, terror and sorrow;[6] and an exalted calm is prolonged from the satiety of this high exercise of them into the tumult of familiar life; even crime is disarmed of half its horror and all its contagion by being represented as the fatal consequence of the unfathomable agencies of nature; error is thus divested of its wilfulness; men can no longer cherish it as the creation of their choice. In a drama of the highest order there is little food for censure or hatred; it teaches rather self-knowledge and self-respect. Neither the eye nor the mind can see itself, unless reflected upon that which it resembles. The drama, so long as it continues to express poetry, is as a prismatic and many-sided mirror, which collects the brightest rays of human nature and divides and reproduces them from the simplicity of these elementary forms, and touches them with majesty and beauty, and multiplies all that it reflects, and endows it with the power of propagating its like wherever it may fall.

But in periods of the decay of social life, the drama sympathizes with that decay. Tragedy becomes a cold imitation of the form of the great masterpieces of antiquity, divested of all harmonious accompaniment of the kindred arts; and often the very form misunderstood: or a weak attempt to teach certain doctrines, which the writer considers as moral truths; and which are usually no more than specious flatteries of some gross vice or weakness with which the author in common with his auditors are infected. Hence what has been called the classical and domestic drama. Addison's "Cato"[7] is a specimen of the one; and would it were not superfluous to cite examples of the other! To such purposes Poetry cannot be made subservient. Poetry is a sword of lightning, ever unsheathed, which consumes the scabbard that would contain it. And thus we observe that all dramatic writings of this nature are unimaginative in a singular degree; they affect sentiment and passion: which, divested of imagination, are other names for caprice and appetite. The period in our own history of the grossest degradation of the drama is the reign of Charles II[8] when all forms in which poetry had been accustomed to be expressed became hymns to the triumph of kingly power over liberty and virtue. Milton[9] stood alone illuminating an age unworthy of him. At such periods the calculating principle pervades all the forms of dramatic exhibition, and poetry ceases to be expressed upon them. Comedy loses its ideal universality: wit succeeds to humour; we laugh from self-complacency and triumph instead of pleasure; malignity, sarcasm and contempt, succeed to sympathetic merriment; we hardly laugh, but we smile. Obscenity, which is ever blasphemy against the divine beauty in life, becomes, from the very veil which it assumes, more active if less disgusting: it is a monster for which the corruption of society for ever brings forth new food, which it devours in secret.

The drama being that form under which a greater number of modes of expression of poetry are susceptible of being combined than any other, the

6. One interpretation of ARISTOTLE's idea of "catharsis" in tragedy, expressed in *Poetics* 6, 1449b (see above).
7. The popular neoclassical tragedy (1713) about the Roman statesman Cato by the English poet and essayist JOSEPH ADDISON (1672–1719).
8. King of England (1630–1685; reigned 1660–85) during the Restoration, a period with a reputation for dissoluteness and frivolity.
9. The poet John Milton (1608–1674) was a supporter of the Puritan Revolution and a defender of the execution of Charles I (king of England from 1625 to 1649).

connexion of poetry and social good is more observable in the drama than in whatever other form: and it is indisputable that the highest perfection of human society has ever corresponded with the highest dramatic excellence; and that the corruption or the extinction of the drama in a nation where it has once flourished, is a mark of a corruption of manners, and an extinction of the energies which sustain the soul of social life. But, as Machiavelli[1] says of political institutions, that life may be preserved and renewed, if men should arise capable of bringing back the drama to its principles. And this is true with respect to poetry in its most extended sense: all language, institution and form, require not only to be produced but to be sustained: the office and character of a poet participates in the divine nature as regards providence, no less than as regards creation.

Civil war, the spoils of Asia, and the fatal predominance first of the Macedonian,[2] and then of the Roman arms were so many symbols of the extinction or suspension of the creative faculty in Greece. The bucolic writers,[3] who found patronage under the lettered tyrants of Sicily and Egypt, were the latest representatives of its most glorious reign. Their poetry is intensely melodious: like the odour of the tuberose, it overcomes and sickens the spirit with excess of sweetness; whilst the poetry of the preceding age was as a meadow-gale of June which mingles the fragrance of all the flowers of the field, and adds a quickening and harmonizing spirit of its own which endows the sense with a power of sustaining its extreme delight. The bucolic and erotic delicacy in written poetry is correlative with that softness in statuary, music, and the kindred arts, and even in manners and institutions which distinguished the epoch to which we now refer. Nor is it the poetical faculty itself, or any misapplication of it, to which this want of harmony is to be imputed. An equal sensibility to the influence of the senses and the affections is to be found in the writings of Homer and Sophocles: the former especially has clothed sensual and pathetic images with irresistible attractions. Their superiority over these succeeding writers consists in the presence of those thoughts which belong to the inner faculties of our nature, not in the absence of those which are connected with the external; their incomparable perfection consists in an harmony of the union of all. It is not what the erotic writers have, but what they have not, in which their imperfection consists. It is not inasmuch as they were Poets, but inasmuch as they were not Poets, that they can be considered with any plausibility as connected with the corruption of their age. Had that corruption availed so as to extinguish in them the sensibility to pleasure, passion and natural scenery, which is imputed to them as an imperfection, the last triumph of evil would have been achieved. For the end of social corruption is to destroy all sensibility to pleasure; and therefore it is corruption. It begins at the imagination and the intellect as at the core, and distributes itself thence as a paralyzing venom, through the affections into the very appetites, until all become a torpid mass in which sense hardly survives. At the approach of such a period, Poetry ever addresses

1. Niccolò Machiavelli (1469–1527), Italian political philosopher; he discusses political institutions in *The Prince* (1513) and *The Discourses* (ca. 1518).

2. Alexander the Great (356–323 B.C.E.), king of Macedonia, whose conquests extended to Egypt and India.

3. Greek pastoral poets, who wrote of shepherds and country folk; the first was Theocritus (ca. 300–ca. 260 B.C.E.) followed by Moschus (active ca. 150 B.C.E.) and Bion (active ca. 100 B.C.E.).

itself to those faculties which are the last to be destroyed, and its voice is heard, like the footsteps of Astræa,[4] departing from the world. Poetry ever communicates all the pleasure which men are capable of receiving: it is ever still the light of life; the source of whatever of beautiful, or generous, or true can have place in an evil time. It will readily be confessed that those among the luxurious citizens of Syracuse and Alexandria who were delighted with the poems of Theocritus, were less cold, cruel and sensual than the remnant of their tribe. But corruption must have utterly destroyed the fabric of human society before Poetry can ever cease. The sacred links of that chain have never been entirely disjoined, which descending through the minds of many men is attached to those great minds, whence as from a magnet the invisible effluence is sent forth, which at once connects, animates and sustains the life of all. It is the faculty which contains within itself the seeds at once of its own and of social renovation. And let us not circumscribe the effects of the bucolic and erotic poetry within the limits of the sensibility of those to whom it was addressed. They may have perceived the beauty of those immortal compositions, simply as fragments and isolated portions: those who are more finely organized, or born in a happier age, may recognize them as episodes to that great poem, which all poets, like the co-operating thoughts of one great mind, have built up since the beginning of the world.

The same revolutions within a narrower sphere had place in antient Rome; but the actions and forms of its social life never seem to have been perfectly saturated with the poetical element. The Romans appear to have considered the Greeks as the selectest treasuries of the selectest forms of manners and of nature, and to have abstained from creating in measured language, sculpture, music or architecture, anything which might bear a particular relation to their own condition, whilst it should bear a general one to the universal constitution of the world. But we judge from partial evidence; and we judge perhaps partially. Ennius, Varro, Pacuvius, and Accius,[5] all great poets, have been lost. Lucretius is in the highest, and Virgil[6] in a very high sense, a creator. The chosen delicacy of the expressions of the latter is as a mist of light which conceals from us the intense and exceeding truth of his conceptions of nature. Livy[7] is instinct with poetry. Yet Horace, Catullus, Ovid,[8] and generally the other great writers of the Virgilian age, saw man and nature in the mirror of Greece. The institutions also and the religion of Rome were less poetical than those of Greece, as the shadow is less vivid than the substance. Hence poetry in Rome, seemed to follow rather than accompany the perfection of political and domestic society. The true Poetry of Rome lived

4. The goddess of justice. She dwelled on earth during the Golden Age but was driven into heaven during the Iron Age by humanity's evil ways. See Ovid, *Metamorphoses* (ca. 10 C.E.), 1.149–50; Juvenal, *Satire* 6.19–20 (ca. 116 C.E.).

5. All pre-Augustan writers, whose work survives only in fragments: Ennius (239–169 B.C.E.), author of tragedies, comedies, prose, and an epic on Roman history, *Annales*; Varro (116–27 B.C.E.), the greatest scholar among the Romans, who wrote or edited hundreds of books (one on the Latin language survives in part, together with a volume of a work on farm management); Pacuvius (220–ca. 130 B.C.E.), author of tragedies and satires; and Accius (170–ca. 90 B.C.E.), author of tragedies and a 9-book poem on the history of literature, *Didascalica*.

6. Author (70–19 B.C.E.) of the *Aeneid*, generally considered the greatest Latin epic. Lucretius (ca. 94–55 B.C.E.), philosopher and author of a didactic Epicurean poem, *On the Nature of Things*.

7. Roman historian (59 B.C.E.–17 C.E.).

8. Author (43 B.C.E.–17 C.E.) of love poetry, fictional love letters, and the mock-heroic *Metamorphoses*. HORACE (65–8 B.C.E.), author of odes, satires, epistles, and the *Ars Poetica* (see above). Catullus (ca. 84–ca. 54 B.C.E.), author of lyric love poetry and elegy.

in its institutions; for whatever of beautiful, true and majestic they contained could have sprung only from the faculty which creates the order in which they consist. The life of Camillus, the death of Regulus;[9] the expectation of the Senators, in their godlike state, of the victorious Gauls; the refusal of the Republic to make peace with Hannibal after the battle of Cannae,[1] were not the consequences of a refined calculation of the probable personal advantage to result from such a rhythm and order in the shews of life, to those who were at once the poets and the actors of the immortal dramas. The imagination beholding the beauty of this order, created it out of itself according to its own idea: the consequence was empire, and the reward ever-living fame. These things are not the less poetry, *quia carent vate sacro*.[2] They are the episodes of the cyclic poem written by Time upon the memories of men. The Past, like an inspired rhapsodist, fills the theatre of everlasting generations with their harmony.

At length the antient system of religion and manners had fulfilled the circle of its revolution. And the world would have fallen into utter anarchy and darkness, but that there were found poets among the authors of the Christian and Chivalric systems of manners and religion, who created forms of opinion and action never before conceived; which, copied into the imaginations of men, became as generals to the bewildered armies of their thoughts. It is foreign to the present purpose to touch upon the evil produced by these systems: except that we protest, on the ground of the principles already established, that no portion of it can be imputed to the poetry they contain.

It is probable that the astonishing poetry of Moses, Job, David, Solomon and Isaiah[3] had produced a great effect upon the mind of Jesus and his disciples. The scattered fragments preserved to us by the biographers of this extraordinary person, are all instinct with the most vivid poetry. But his doctrines seem to have been quickly distorted. At a certain period after the prevalence of a system of opinions founded upon those promulgated by him, the three forms into which Plato had distributed the faculties of mind[4] underwent a sort of apotheosis, and became the object of the worship of the civilized world. Here it is to be confessed that "Light seems to thicken," and

> The crow makes wing to the rooky wood,
> Good things of day begin to droop and drowze,
> And night's black agents to their preys do rouze.[5]

But mark how beautiful an order has sprung from the dust and blood of this fierce chaos! how the World, as from a resurrection, balancing itself on the golden wings of knowledge and of hope, has reassumed its yet unwearied

9. Marcus Atilius Regulus (d. ca. 249 B.C.E.): Roman general who, though himself held by the Carthaginians, persuaded the Roman Senate not to ransom him and the other soldiers; he returned to Carthage and died in captivity (perhaps tortured to death; see Horace, *Odes* 3.5). Marcus Furius Camillus (d. ca. 365 B.C.E.), the second founder of Rome, who managed the city's military and political recovery after the Gallic invasion of 387/6 B.C.E.

1. Village in Apulia where in 216 B.C.E. the Romans suffered a major defeat by Hannibal, the great Carthaginian general (247–183/2 B.C.E.); the Romans ultimately won the war, however.

2. Because they lack a sacred poet (Latin); from Horace, *Odes* 4.9.28.

3. Job and Isaiah were once regarded as the authors of the books of the Bible given their names; Moses is traditionally credited with writing the entire Torah (the first five books of the Bible); David was thought to have composed most of the Psalms; Ecclesiastes, Proverbs, and the Song of Solomon were ascribed to Solomon.

4. Plato divided the human soul into three parts: the desiring, the rational, and the spirited (see *Republic* 4.439d–444a).

5. *Macbeth* (ca. 1606), 3.2.51–54, slightly misquoted.

flight into the Heaven of time. Listen to the music, unheard by outward ears, which is as a ceaseless and invisible wind, nourishing its everlasting course with strength and swiftness.

The poetry in the doctrines of Jesus Christ, and the mythology and institutions of the Celtic conquerors of the Roman empire,[6] outlived the darkness and the convulsions connected with their growth and victory, and blended themselves into a new fabric of manners and opinion. It is an error to impute the ignorance of the dark ages to the Christian doctrines or the predominance of the Celtic nations. Whatever of evil their agencies may have contained sprung from the extinction of the poetical principle, connected with the progress of despotism and superstition. Men, from causes too intricate to be here discussed, had become insensible and selfish: their own will had become feeble, and yet they were its slaves, and thence the slaves of the will of others: lust, fear, avarice, cruelty and fraud, characterised a race amongst whom no one was to be found capable of *creating* in form, language, or institution. The moral anomalies of such a state of society are not justly to be charged upon any class of events immediately connected with them, and those events are most entitled to our approbation which could dissolve it most expeditiously. It is unfortunate for those who cannot distinguish words from thoughts, that many of these anomalies have been incorporated into our popular religion.

It was not until the eleventh century that the effects of the poetry of the Christian and Chivalric systems began to manifest themselves. The principle of equality had been discovered and applied by Plato in his Republic, as the theoretical rule of the mode in which the materials of pleasure and of power produced by the common skill and labour of human beings ought to be distributed among them. The limitations of this rule were asserted by him to be determined only by the sensibility of each, or the utility to result to all. Plato, following the doctrines of Timæus and Pythagoras,[7] taught also a moral and intellectual system of doctrine comprehending at once the past, the present, and the future condition of man. Jesus Christ divulged the sacred and eternal truths contained in these views to mankind, and Christianity, in its abstract purity, became the exoteric expression of the esoteric doctrines of the poetry and wisdom of antiquity. The incorporation of the Celtic nations with the exhausted population of the South, impressed upon it the figure of the poetry existing in their mythology and institutions. The result was a sum of the action and reaction of all the causes included in it; for it may be assumed as a maxim that no nation or religion can supersede any other without incorporating into itself a portion of that which it supersedes. The abolition of personal and domestic slavery, and the emancipation of women from a great part of the degrading restraints of antiquity were among the consequences of these events.

The abolition of personal slavery is the basis of the highest political hope that it can enter into the mind of man to conceive. The freedom of women produced the poetry of sexual love. Love became a religion, the idols of whose worship were ever present. It was as if the statues of Apollo and the Muses[8]

6. The Germanic tribes of northern Europe.
7. Greek philosopher and mathematician (ca. 6th B.C.E.). Timaeus: a Pythagorean, perhaps a fictional character, who is the key speaker in Plato's *Timaeus.*
8. In Greek mythology, 9 daughters of Memory who preside over the arts and all intellectual pursuits. Apollo: Greek and Roman god of poetry.

had been endowed with life and motion and had walked forth among their worshippers; so that earth became peopled by the inhabitants of a diviner world. The familiar appearance and proceedings of life became wonderful and heavenly; and a paradise was created as out of the wrecks of Eden. And as this creation itself is poetry, so its creators were poets; and language were the instrument of their art: "Galeotto fù il libro, e chi lo scrisse."[9] The Provençal Trouveurs, or inventors, preceded Petrarch,[1] whose verses are as spells, which unseal the inmost enchanted fountains of the delight which is in the grief of Love. It is impossible to feel them without becoming a portion of that beauty which we contemplate: it were superfluous to explain how the gentleness and the elevation of mind connected with these sacred emotions can render men more amiable, more generous, and wise, and lift them out of the dull vapours of the little world of self. Dante understood the secret things of love even more than Petrarch. His *Vita Nuova*[2] is an inexhaustible fountain of purity of sentiment and language: it is the idealized history of that period, and those intervals of his life which were dedicated to love. His apotheosis of Beatrice in Paradise and the gradations of his own love and her loveliness, by which as by steps he feigns himself to have ascended to the throne of the Supreme Cause, is the most glorious imagination of modern poetry. The acutest critics have justly reversed the judgement of the vulgar, and the order of the great acts of the "Divine Drama," in the measure of the admiration which they accord to the Hell, Purgatory and Paradise.[3] The latter is a perpetual hymn of everlasting love. Love, which found a worthy poet in Plato alone of all the antients, has been celebrated by a chorus of the greatest writers of the renovated world; and the music has penetrated the caverns of society, and its echoes still drown the dissonance of arms and superstition. At successive intervals, Ariosto, Tasso, Shakespeare, Spenser, Calderon, Rousseau,[4] and the great writers of our own age, have celebrated the dominion of love, planting as it were trophies in the human mind of that sublimest victory over sensuality and force. The true relation borne to each other by the sexes into which human kind is distributed has become less misunderstood; and if the error which confounded diversity with inequality of the powers of the two sexes has become partially recognized in the opinions and institutions of modern Europe, we owe this great benefit to the worship of which Chivalry was the law, and poets the prophets.

The poetry of Dante may be considered as the bridge thrown over the stream of time, which unites the modern and antient world. The distorted notions of invisible things which Dante and his rival Milton have idealized, are merely the mask and the mantle in which these great poets walk through eternity enveloped and disguised. It is a difficult question to determine how far they were conscious of the distinction which must have subsisted in their minds between their own creeds and that of the people. Dante at least appears to wish to mark the full extent of it by placing Riphæus, whom Virgil calls *justissimus unus*, in Paradise,[5] and observing a most heretical caprice

9. Gallehaut was the book and he who wrote it (Italian). From DANTE ALIGHIERI, *Inferno* (1321), 5.137.

1. Francesco Petrarca (1304–1374), Italian poet and scholar. "Provençal": the language of southern France. The troubadours of the south, 12th- and 13th-century poets, were the first to celebrate chivalric and courtly love.

2. *New Life* (ca. 1293), poetry and prose that tell of Dante's love for Beatrice.

3. The 3 books of Dante's *Divine Comedy*.

4. Jean-Jacques Rousseau (1712–1778), Swiss-born French philosopher and political theorist. Ludovico Ariosto (1474–1533), Italian epic poet.

5. Dante makes the Trojan warrior Riphaeus the only pagan in Paradise (see *Paradiso*, canto 20). *Justissimus unus*: the one most just [who was among the Trojans]; Virgil, *Aeneid* 2.426–27.

in his distribution of rewards and punishments. And Milton's poem contains within itself a philosophical refutation of that system of which, by a strange and natural antithesis, it has been a chief popular support. Nothing can exceed the energy and magnificence of the character of Satan as expressed in Paradise Lost.[6] It is a mistake to suppose that he could ever have been intended for the popular personification of evil. Implacable hate, patient cunning, and a sleepless refinement of device to inflict the extremest anguish on an enemy, these things are evil; and although venial in a slave are not to be forgiven in a tyrant; although redeemed by much that ennobles his defeat in one subdued, are marked by all that dishonours his conquest in the victor. Milton's Devil as a moral being is as far superior to his God as one who perseveres in some purpose which he has conceived to be excellent in spite of adversity and torture, is to one who in the cold security of undoubted triumph inflicts the most horrible revenge upon his enemy, not from any mistaken notion of inducing him to repent of a perseverance in enmity, but with the alleged design of exasperating him to deserve new torments. Milton has so far violated the popular creed (if this shall be judged to be a violation) as to have alleged no superiority of moral virtue to his God over his Devil. And this bold neglect of a direct moral purpose is the most decisive proof of the supremacy of Milton's genius. He mingled as it were the elements of human nature, as colours upon a single pallet, and arranged them into the composition of his great picture according to the laws of epic truth; that is, according to the laws of that principle by which a series of actions of the external universe and of intelligent and ethical beings is calculated to excite the sympathy of succeeding generations of mankind. The Divina Commedia and Paradise Lost have conferred upon modern mythology a systematic form; and when change and time shall have added one more superstition to the mass of those which have arisen and decayed upon the earth, commentators will be learnedly employed in elucidating the religion of ancestral Europe, only not utterly forgotten because it will have been stamped with the eternity of genius.

Homer was the first, and Dante the second epic poet: that is, the second poet the series of whose creations bore a defined and intelligible relation to the knowledge, and sentiment, and religion, and political conditions of the age in which he lived, and of the ages which followed it, developing itself in correspondence with their development. For Lucretius had limed the wings of his swift spirit in the dregs of the sensible world; and Virgil, with a modesty which ill became his genius, had affected the fame of an imitator even whilst he created anew all that he copied; and none among the flock of mock-birds, though their notes were sweet, Apollonius Rhodius, Quintus Calaber Smyrnaeus, Nonnus, Lucan, Statius, or Claudian,[7] have sought even to fulfil a single condition of epic truth. Milton was the third Epic Poet. For if the title of epic in its highest sense be refused to the Æneid, still less can it be

6. Shelley echoes the Romantic poet William Blake: "The reason Milton wrote in fetters when he wrote of Angels & God, and at liberty when of Devils & Hell, is because he was a true Poet and of the Devils party without knowing it," and "Energy is Eternal Delight" (*The Marriage of Heaven and Hell*, 1790). *Paradise Lost* was published in 1667.

7. Classical epic poets of varying quality, the first three writing in Greek and the others in Latin: Apollonius (3d c. B.C.E.), author of the *Argonautica*; Quintus Smyrnaeus (4th c. C.E.), author of a sequel to Homer's *Iliad*; Nonnus (5th c. C.E.), author of the 48-book *Dionysiaca*; Lucan, author of the *Civil War*; Statius (ca. 45–96 C.E.), author of the epic *Thebais*; and Claudian (d. 404 C.E.), a Greek-speaking Alexandrian whose poetry, including an unfinished epic, *The Rape of Proserpina*, marked the end of the classical tradition in Latin poetry.

conceded to the Orlando Furioso, the Gerusalemme Liberata, the Lusiad, or the Fairy Queen.[8]

Dante and Milton were both deeply penetrated with the antient religion of the civilized world; and its spirit exists in their poetry probably in the same proportion as its forms survived in the unreformed worship of modern Europe. The one preceded and the other followed the Reformation at almost equal intervals. Dante was the first religious reformer, and Luther[9] surpassed him rather in the rudeness and acrimony, than in the boldness of his censures of papal usurpation. Dante was the first awakener of entranced Europe: he created a language in itself music and persuasion out of a chaos of inharmonious barbarisms. He was the congregator of those great spirits who presided over the resurrection of learning; the Lucifer[1] of that starry flock which in the thirteenth century shone forth from republican Italy, as from a heaven, into the darkness of the benighted world. His very words are instinct with spirit; each is as a spark, a burning atom of inextinguishable thought; and many yet lie covered in the ashes of their birth, and pregnant with a lightning which has yet found no conductor. All high poetry is infinite; it is as the first acorn, which contained all oaks potentially. Veil after veil may be undrawn, and the inmost naked beauty of the meaning never exposed. A great Poem is a fountain for ever overflowing with the waters of wisdom and delight; and after one person and one age has exhausted all its divine effluence which their peculiar relations enable them to share, another and yet another succeeds, and new relations are ever developed, the source of an unforeseen and an unconceived delight.

The age immediately succeeding to that of Dante, Petrarch, and Boccaccio,[2] was characterized by a revival of painting, sculpture, music, and architecture. Chaucer caught the sacred inspiration, and the superstructure of English literature is based upon the materials of Italian invention.

But let us not be betrayed from a defence into a critical history of Poetry and its influence on Society. Be it enough to have pointed out the effects of poets, in the large and true sense of the word, upon their own and all succeeding times and to revert to the partial instances cited as illustrations of an opinion the reverse of that attempted to be established in the Four Ages of Poetry.

But poets have been challenged to resign the civic crown to reasoners and mechanists on another plea. It is admitted that the exercise of the imagination is most delightful, but it is alleged that that of reason is more useful. Let us examine as the grounds of this distinction, what is here meant by Utility.[3] Pleasure or good in a general sense, is that which the consciousness of a sensitive and intelligent being seeks, and in which when found it acquiesces. There are two kinds of pleasure, one durable, universal, and perma-

8. Shelley names epics by, respectively, Ariosto (1516, 1532), Tasso (1581), the Portuguese Luis Vaz de Camões (1572), and Spenser (1590, 1596).

9. Martin Luther (1483–1546), German theologian and reformer, founder of the Reformation.

1. Literally, "light bearer" (Latin), the morning star. In Milton's *Paradise Lost*, Lucifer is the leader of the revolt of the angels against God, and is called Satan after his fall.

2. GIOVANNI BOCCACCIO (1313–1375), Italian writer and poet.

3. Shelley replies here to the followers of Jeremy Bentham (1748–1832), English social reformer and philosopher, the founder of utilitarianism; he claimed that all conduct and legislation should aim at "the greatest happiness of the greatest number," and formulated a calculus of pleasure. Peacock argues in "The Four Ages of Poetry": "[Poetry] can never make a philosopher nor a statesman nor in any class of life a useful or rational man. It cannot claim the slightest share in any one of the comforts or utilities of life."

nent; the other transitory and particular. Utility may either express the means of producing the former or the latter. In the former sense, whatever strengthens and purifies the affections, enlarges the imagination, and adds spirit to sense, is useful. But the meaning in which the Author of the Four Ages of Poetry seems to have employed the word utility is the narrower one of banishing the importunity of the wants of our animal nature, the surrounding men with security of life, the dispersing the grosser delusions of superstition, and the conciliating such a degree of mutual forbearance among men as may consist with the motives of personal advantage.

Undoubtedly the promoters of utility in this limited sense, have their appointed office in society. They follow the footsteps of poets, and copy the sketches of their creations into the book of common life. They make space, and give time. Their exertions are of the highest value so long as they confine their administration of the concerns of the inferior powers of our nature within the limits due to the superior ones. But whilst the sceptic destroys gross superstitions, let him spare to deface, as some of the French writers have defaced, the eternal truths charactered upon the imaginations of men. Whilst the mechanist abridges, and the political œconomist combines, labour, let them beware that their speculations, for want of correspondence with those first principles which belong to the imagination, do not tend, as they have in modern England, to exasperate at once the extremes of luxury and want. They have exemplified the saying, "To him that hath, more shall be given; and from him that hath not, the little that he hath shall be taken away."[4] The rich have become richer, and the poor have become poorer; and the vessel of the state is driven between the Scylla and Charybdis[5] of anarchy and despotism. Such are the effects which must ever flow from an unmitigated exercise of the calculating faculty.

It is difficult to define pleasure in its highest sense; the definition involving a number of apparent paradoxes. For, from an inexplicable defect of harmony in the constitution of human nature, the pain of the inferior is frequently connected with the pleasures of the superior portions of our being. Sorrow, terror, anguish, despair itself are often the chosen expressions of an approximation to the highest good. Our sympathy in tragic fiction depends on this principle; tragedy delights by affording a shadow of the pleasure which exists in pain. This is the source also of the melancholy which is inseparable from the sweetest melody. The pleasure that is in sorrow is sweeter than the pleasure of pleasure itself. And hence the saying, "It is better to go to the house of mourning, than to the house of mirth."[6] Not that this highest species of pleasure is necessarily linked with pain. The delight of love and friendship, the extacy of the admiration of nature, the joy of the perception and still more of the creation of poetry is often wholly unalloyed.

The production and assurance of pleasure in this highest sense is true utility. Those who produce and preserve this pleasure are Poets or poetical philosophers.

The exertions of Locke, Hume, Gibbon, Voltaire, Rousseau,[7] and their

4. Mark 4.25.
5. That is, two equal dangers. In Greek mythology, Scylla and Charybdis are two monsters (who become a rock and whirlpool, respectively) that endanger sailors between Sicily and Italy.
6. Ecclesiastes 7.2.
7. I follow the classification adopted by the author of the Four Ages of Poetry. But Rousseau was essentially a poet. The others, even Voltaire, were mere reasoners [Shelley's note]. John Locke (1632–1704), English philosopher. DAVID HUME (1711–1776), Scottish empiricist philosopher,

disciples, in favour of oppressed and deluded humanity, are entitled to the gratitude of mankind. Yet it is easy to calculate the degree of moral and intellectual improvement which the world would have exhibited, had they never lived. A little more nonsense would have been talked for a century or two; and perhaps a few more men, women, and children, burnt as heretics. We might not at this moment have been congratulating each other on the abolition of the Inquisition in Spain.[8] But it exceeds all imagination to conceive what would have been the moral condition of the world if neither Dante, Petrarch, Boccaccio, Chaucer, Shakespeare, Calderon, Lord Bacon, nor Milton, had ever existed; if Raphael and Michael Angelo[9] had never been born; if the Hebrew poetry had never been translated; if a revival of the study of Greek literature had never taken place; if no monuments of antient sculpture had been handed down to us; and if the poetry of the religion of the antient world had been extinguished together with its belief. The human mind could never, except by the intervention of these excitements, have been awakened to the invention of the grosser sciences, and that application of analytical reasoning to the aberrations of society, which it is now attempted to exalt over the direct expression of the inventive and creative faculty itself.

We have more moral, political and historical wisdom, than we know how to reduce into practise; we have more scientific and œconomical knowledge than can be accommodated to the just distribution of the produce which it multiplies. The poetry in these systems of thought, is concealed by the accumulation of facts and calculating processes. There is no want of knowledge respecting what is wisest and best in morals, government, and political œconomy, or at least, what is wiser and better than what men now practise and endure. But we let "*I dare not* wait upon *I would*, like the poor cat i' the adage."[1] We want[2] the creative faculty to imagine that which we know; we want the generous impulse to act that which we imagine; we want the poetry of life: our calculations have outrun conception; we have eaten more than we can digest. The cultivation of those sciences which have enlarged the limits of the empire of man over the external world, has, for want of the poetical faculty, proportionally circumscribed those of the internal world; and man, having enslaved the elements, remains himself a slave. To what but a cultivation of the mechanical arts in a degree disproportioned to the presence of the creative faculty, which is the basis of all knowledge, is to be attributed the abuse of all invention for abridging and combining labour, to the exasperation of the inequality of mankind? From what other cause has it arisen that the discoveries which should have lightened, have added a weight to the curse imposed on Adam?[3] Poetry, and the principle of Self, of

historian, and economist Edward Gibbon (1737–1794), English historian best known as the author of *The History of the Decline and Fall of the Roman Empire* (6 vols., 1776–88). Voltaire: pen name of François-Marie Arouet (1694–1778), French writer and philosopher. These figures are apparently linked by their opposition, in different degrees, to Christianity.

8. The Spanish Inquisition, the harsh Roman Catholic tribunal for suppressing heresy, was established in 1478; it was not definitively abolished until the 1820 revolution led by reformist army officers.

9. Michelangelo [Buonarroti] (1475–1564), Italian Renaissance sculptor, painter, and architect. Francis Bacon (1561–1626), English philosopher and essayist. Raphael: Raffaello Sanzio (1483–1520), master painter of the Italian Renaissance.

1. *Macbeth*, 1.7.44–45.

2. Lack.

3. That is, the need to labor for a living; imposed on Adam because he and Eve ate the forbidden fruit of the tree of knowledge: "In the sweat of thy face shalt thou eat bread, till thou return unto the ground" (Genesis 3.19).

which money is the visible incarnation, are the God and the Mammon[4] of the world.

The functions of the poetical faculty are two-fold; by one it creates new materials of knowledge, and power and pleasure; by the other it engenders in the mind a desire to reproduce and arrange them according to a certain rhythm and order which may be called the beautiful and the good. The cultivation of poetry is never more to be desired than at periods when, from an excess of the selfish and calculating principle, the accumulation of the materials of external life exceed the quantity of the power of assimilating them to the internal laws of human nature. The body has then become too unwieldy for that which animates it.

Poetry is indeed something divine.[5] It is at once the centre and circumference of knowledge; it is that which comprehends all science, and that to which all science must be referred. It is at the same time the root and blossom of all other systems of thought; it is that from which all spring, and that which adorns all; and that which, if blighted, denies the fruit and the seed, and withholds from the barren world the nourishment and the succession of the scions of the tree of life. It is the perfect and consummate surface and bloom of things; it is as the odour and the colour of the rose to the texture of the elements which compose it, as the form and the splendour of unfaded beauty to the secrets of anatomy and corruption. What were Virtue, Love, Patriotism, Friendship &c.—what were the scenery of this beautiful Universe which we inhabit—what were our consolations on this side of the grave—and what were our aspirations beyond it—if Poetry did not ascend to bring light and fire from those eternal regions where the owl-winged faculty of calculation dare not ever soar? Poetry is not like reasoning, a power to be exerted according to the determination of the will. A man cannot say, "I will compose poetry." The greatest poet even cannot say it: for the mind in creation is as a fading coal which some invisible influence, like an inconstant wind, awakens to transitory brightness: this power arises from within, like the colour of a flower which fades and changes as it is developed, and the conscious portions of our natures are unprophetic either of its approach or its departure. Could this influence be durable in its original purity and force, it is impossible to predict the greatness of the results; but when composition begins, inspiration is already on the decline, and the most glorious poetry that has ever been communicated to the world is probably a feeble shadow of the original conception of the poet. I appeal to the greatest Poets of the present day, whether it be not an error to assert that the finest passages of poetry are produced by labour and study. The toil and the delay recommended by critics can be justly interpreted to mean no more than a careful observation of the inspired moments, and an artificial connexion of the spaces between their suggestions by the intertexture of conventional expressions; a necessity only imposed by a limitedness of the poetical faculty itself. For Milton conceived the Paradise Lost as a whole before he executed it in portions. We have his own authority also for the Muse having "dictated" to him the "unpremeditated song,"[6] and let this be an answer to those who would allege the fifty-six various readings of the first line of the Orlando

4. The personification of avarice and lust for worldly gain; according to Matthew 6.24 and Luke 16.13, it is impossible to serve both God and Mammon.

5. Compare Sidney's reference, in *An Apology for Poetry*, to poetry as "a divine gift."

6. *Paradise Lost* 9.20–24.

Furioso. Compositions so produced are to poetry what mosaic is to painting. This instinct and intuition of the poetical faculty is still more observable in the plastic and pictorial arts: a great statue or picture grows under the power of the artist as a child in the mother's womb, and the very mind which directs the hands in formation is incapable of accounting to itself for the origin, the gradations, or the media of the process.

Poetry is the record of the best and happiest moments of the happiest and best minds. We are aware of evanescent visitations of thought and feeling sometimes associated with place or person, sometimes regarding our own mind alone, and always arising unforeseen and departing unbidden, but elevating and delightful beyond all expression; so that even in the desire and the regret they leave, there cannot but be pleasure, participating as it does in the nature of its object. It is as it were the interpenetration of a diviner nature through our own; but its footsteps are like those of a wind over a sea, which the coming calm erases, and whose traces remain only as on the wrinkled sand which paves it. These and corresponding conditions of being are experienced principally by those of the most delicate sensibility and the most enlarged imagination; and the state of mind produced by them is at war with every base desire. The enthusiasm of virtue, love, patriotism, and friendship is essentially linked with these emotions; and whilst they last, self appears as what it is, an atom to a Universe. Poets are not only subject to these experiences as spirits of the most refined organization, but they can colour all that they combine with the evanescent hues of this etherial world; a word, a trait in the representation of a scene or a passion, will touch the enchanted chord, and reanimate, in those who have ever experienced these emotions, the sleeping, the cold, the buried image of the past. Poetry thus makes immortal all that is best and most beautiful in the world; it arrests the vanishing apparitions which haunt the interlunations[7] of life, and veiling them or in language or in form sends them forth among mankind, bearing sweet news of kindred joy to those with whom their sisters abide—abide, because there is no portal of expression from the caverns of the spirit which they inhabit into the universe of things. Poetry redeems from decay the visitations of the divinity in man.

Poetry turns all things to loveliness; it exalts the beauty of that which is most beautiful, and it adds beauty to that which is most deformed: it marries exultation and horror, grief and pleasure, eternity and change; it subdues to union under its light yoke all irreconcilable things. It transmutes all that it touches, and every form moving within the radiance of its presence is changed by wondrous sympathy to an incarnation of the spirit which it breathes; its secret alchemy turns to potable gold the poisonous waters which flow from death through life; it strips the veil of familiarity from the world, and lays bare the naked and sleeping beauty which is the spirit of its forms.

All things exist as they are perceived: at least in relation to the percipient. "The mind is its own place, and of itself can make a heaven of hell, a hell of heaven."[8] But poetry defeats the curse which binds us to be subjected to the accident of surrounding impressions. And whether it spreads its own figured curtain or withdraws life's dark veil from before the scene of things, it equally

7. Dark intervals.
8. Satan's defiant assertion in *Paradise Lost* 1.254–55, slightly misquoted.

creates for us a being within our being. It makes us the inhabitants of a world to which the familiar world is a chaos. It reproduces the common universe of which we are portions and percipients, and it purges from our inward sight the film of familiarity which obscures from us the wonder of our being.[9] It compels us to feel that which we perceive, and to imagine that which we know. It creates anew the universe after it has been annihilated in our minds by the recurrence of impressions blunted by reiteration. It justifies that bold and true word of Tasso—*Non merita nome di creatore, se non Iddio ed il Poeta.*[1]

A Poet, as he is the author to others of the highest wisdom, pleasure, virtue and glory, so he ought personally to be the happiest, the best, the wisest, and the most illustrious of men. As to his glory, let Time be challenged to declare whether the fame of any other institutor of human life be comparable to that of a poet. That he is the wisest, the happiest, and the best, inasmuch as he is a poet, is equally incontrovertible: the greatest poets have been men of the most spotless virtue, of the most consummate prudence, and, if we could look into the interior of their lives, the most fortunate of men: and the exceptions, as they regard those who possessed the poetic faculty in a high yet inferior degree, will be found on consideration to confirm rather than destroy the rule. Let us for a moment stoop to the arbitration of popular breath, and usurping and uniting in our own persons the incompatible characters of accuser, witness, judge and executioner, let us decide without trial, testimony, or form, that certain motives of those who are "there sitting where we dare not soar"[2] are reprehensible. Let us assume that Homer was a drunkard, that Virgil was a flatterer, that Horace was a coward, that Tasso was a madman, that Lord Bacon was a peculator,[3] that Raphael was a libertine, that Spenser was a poet laureate. It is inconsistent with this division of our subject to cite living poets, but Posterity has done ample justice to the great names now referred to. Their errors have been weighed and found to have been dust in the balance; if their sins "were as scarlet, they are now white as snow"; they have been washed in the blood of the mediator and the redeemer Time. Observe in what a ludicrous chaos the imputations of real or fictitious crime have been confused in the contemporary calumnies against poetry and poets; consider how little is, as it appears—or appears, as it is: look to your own motives, and judge not, lest ye be judged.[4]

Poetry, as has been said, in this respect differs from logic, that it is not subject to the controul of the active powers of the mind, and that its birth and recurrence has no necessary connexion with consciousness or will. It is presumptuous to determine that these are the necessary conditions of all mental causation, when mental effects are experienced insusceptible of being referred to them. The frequent recurrence of the poetical power, it is

9. Shelley echoes SAMUEL TAYLOR COLERIDGE in *Biographia Literaria* (1817), chap. 14, which describes Wordsworth's method as "awakening the mind's attention from the lethargy of custom, and directing it to the loveliness and the wonders of the world before us; an inexhaustible treasure, but for which in consequence of the film of familiarity and selfish solicitude we have eyes, yet see not, ears that hear not, and hearts that neither feel nor understand."

1. No one deserves the name of creator except God and the Poet (Italian). From Pierantonio Serassi's *Life of Torquato Tasso* (1785).

2. *Paradise Lost* 4.829, slightly misquoted.

3. Embezzler.

4. Shelley repeatedly echoes the Bible in this passage. Their errors have been weighed in the balance: Daniel 5.27; dust of the balance: Isaiah 40.15; were as scarlet: Isaiah 1.18; washed in the blood: Revelation 7.14; the mediator: Hebrews 9.15, 12.24; judge not: Matthew 7.1.

obvious to suppose, may produce in the mind an habit of order and harmony correlative with its own nature and with its effects upon other minds. But in the intervals of inspiration, and they may be frequent without being durable, a poet becomes a man, and is abandoned to the sudden reflux of the influences under which others habitually live. But as he is more delicately organized than other men, and sensible to pain and pleasure, both his own and that of others, in a degree unknown to them, he will avoid the one and pursue the other with an ardour proportioned to this difference. And he renders himself obnoxious to calumny, when he neglects to observe the circumstances under which these objects of universal pursuit and flight have disguised themselves in one another's garments.

But there is nothing necessarily evil in this error, and thus cruelty, envy, revenge, avarice, and the passions purely evil, have never formed any portion of the popular imputations on the lives of poets.

I have thought it most favourable to the cause of truth to set down these remarks according to the order in which they were suggested to my mind by a consideration of the subject itself, instead of following that of the treatise that excited me to make them public. Thus although devoid of the formality of a polemical reply; if the view they contain be just, they will be found to involve a refutation of the Four Ages of Poetry, so far at least as regards the first division of the subject. I can readily conjecture what should have moved the gall of the learned and intelligent author of that paper; I confess myself like him unwilling to be stunned by the Theseids of the hoarse Codri[5] of the day. Bavius and Mævius[6] undoubtedly are, as they ever were, insufferable persons. But it belongs to a philosophical critic to distinguish rather than confound.

The first part of these remarks has related to Poetry in its elements and principles; and it has been shewn, as well as the narrow limits assigned them would permit, that what is called poetry, in a restricted sense, has a common source with all other forms of order and of beauty according to which the materials of human life are susceptible of being arranged, and which is poetry in an universal sense.

The second part will have for its object an application of these principles to the present state of the cultivation of Poetry, and a defence of the attempt to idealize the modern forms of manners and opinion, and compel them into a subordination to the imaginative and creative faculty. For the literature of England, an energetic development of which has ever preceded or accompanied a great and free development of the national will, has arisen as it were from a new birth. In spite of the low-thoughted envy which would undervalue contemporary merit, our own will be a memorable age in intellectual achievements, and we live among such philosophers and poets as surpass beyond comparison any who have appeared since the last national struggle for civil and religious liberty.[7] The most unfailing herald, companion, and follower of the awakening of a great people to work a beneficial change in opinion or institution, is Poetry. At such periods there is an accumulation of the power

5. Juvenal begins *Satire* 1 by complaining about the Theseid (i.e., an epic poem on Theseus, the chief hero of Attica in ancient Greek legend) of "hoarse Codrus."

6. Mediocre Latin poets (1st c. B.C.E.) satirized by Virgil (*Eclogue* 3); Horace's *Epode* 10 is an attack on Maevius.

7. That is, the English Civil War (1642–46, 1648).

of communicating and receiving intense and impassioned conceptions respecting man and nature. The persons in whom this power resides, may often, as far as regards many portions of their nature, have little apparent correspondence with that spirit of good of which they are the ministers. But even whilst they deny and abjure, they are yet compelled to serve, the Power which is seated upon the throne of their own soul. It is impossible to read the compositions of the most celebrated writers of the present day without being startled with the electric life which burns within their words. They measure the circumference and sound the depths of human nature with a comprehensive and all-penetrating spirit, and they are themselves perhaps the most sincerely astonished at its manifestations, for it is less their spirit than the spirit of the age. Poets are the hierophants[8] of an unapprehended inspiration, the mirrors of the gigantic shadows which futurity casts upon the present, the words which express what they understand not; the trumpets which sing to battle, and feel not what they inspire: the influence which is moved not, but moves. Poets are the unacknowledged legislators of the World.

1821 — 1840

8. Interpreters of sacred mysteries.

RALPH WALDO EMERSON
1803–1882

"Emerson is God," declared the literary theorist HAROLD BLOOM in an interview in 1993, in perhaps the most extravagant testimony yet to Emerson's impact on American literature and culture. Lecturer, poet, and essayist, and the leading exponent of New England Transcendentalism, Emerson's advocacy of self-reliance and nonconformity inspired American writers of his own time—notably, Henry David Thoreau, Margaret Fuller, Emily Dickinson, and Walt Whitman—and later. Emerson was significant as well for English and European intellectuals and philosophers, including George Eliot (1819–1880) and FRIEDRICH NIETZSCHE (1844–1900), and for the American philosophers William James (1842–1910) and John Dewey (1859–1952). A radical thinker and a shaper of striking sentences and aphorisms, Emerson made claims for himself (and, by extension, for readers) as daring as Bloom makes for Emerson. "The simplest person who in his integrity worships God," Emerson affirms in his essay "The Over-Soul," "becomes God."

In *Nature* (1836), the lecture "The American Scholar" (1837), the Address before the Harvard Divinity School (1838), and two volumes of *Essays* (1841, 1844), Emerson announced and articulated nearly all of the central themes of Transcendentalism and, at the same time, subjected them to critique. He encouraged readers and audiences to feel the exaltation of their highest potential, to trust instinct and intuition (the signs of God's presence in persons), and to perceive Nature as a rich realm of truths more profound than any that human social orders made available. He expressed these themes in provocative, allusive prose, which proceeds with a rich if frequently discontinuous rhythm. At the same time, with regular self-questioning he maintained that there was no Transcendentalist party and no "pure" Transcendentalism at all.

Emerson attended the Boston Latin School and Harvard College (1817–21). While at Harvard, he began keeping a journal, and its stock of allusions, commentaries on his reading, and reflections on persons and events became the "Savings Bank"—annotated, cross-referenced, indexed—for his lectures, essays, and books. After graduation, Emerson taught school and then entered the Harvard Divinity School to prepare for the ministry, taking up a position at Boston's Second Unitarian Church in 1829. In September 1829 Emerson married the seventeen-year-old Ellen Louisa Tucker, but her health was poor, and she died from tuberculosis in February 1831.

Biographers have suggested that Emerson's grief led him to question his Unitarian faith, but his doubts about conventional Christian beliefs and his "antiquated" profession had been present in his journals and even sermons for years. Later, he remarked that if his teachers at the Harvard Divinity School had been aware of his true thoughts and feelings, they would not have allowed him to graduate. In October 1832, saying he could no longer administer the sacrament of the Lord's Supper, Emerson resigned as minister of his Boston church. He explained, "It is my desire to do nothing which I cannot do with my whole heart."

In December 1832, Emerson traveled to Europe, and during his nine months abroad he met WILLIAM WORDSWORTH, SAMUEL TAYLOR COLERIDGE, and the Scottish-born essayist and historian Thomas Carlyle, with whom he corresponded for half a century. After returning to the United States, he lectured on natural history, biography, and history settled in Concord, Massachusetts; remarried (Lydia Jackson in 1835); and worked on his first book, *Nature*, published anonymously (and at his own expense) in September 1836. Other important texts of this decade include "The American Scholar" and the Divinity School address, in which Emerson attacked religious tradition, doctrine, and the ministry for denying men and women the possibility for authentic self-discovery and religious fulfillment. "I think no man can go with his thoughts about him into one of our churches," he contended in the address, "without feeling that what hold the public worship had on men is gone, or going."

In the 1830s Emerson said, "I am a poet. . . . That is my nature & vocation," and he produced a number of difficult, gnomic poems that were collected in *Poems* (1847). But his real distinction lay in essays, journals, and books of cultural criticism and philosophy. Most scholars now agree that Emerson's best work is in the *Essays*, pointing especially to "History," "Self-Reliance," "The Over-Soul," "Circles," "The Poet," and "Experience." He followed the lectures and essays of the 1830s and 1840s with a series of powerful books: *Representative Men* (1850), which contains studies of PLATO, Goethe, and others; *English Traits* (1856), a shrewd work of social criticism in which Emerson examines English life, tradition, and culture; and *The Conduct of Life* (1860), based on lectures he had presented in 1851 and including three major philosophical pieces—"Fate," "Power," and "Illusions."

Emerson played an active role in the meetings of the Transcendental Club, which the Unitarian clergyman F. H. Hedge organized in 1836 for the "exchange of thought among those interested in the new views in philosophy, theology, and literature." Like the other Transcendentalists, Emerson believed that all of creation is one, that men and women are inherently good, that intuition is the source of truth, and that individual perception illuminates and structures the world. "Nothing is at last sacred but the integrity of your own mind," Emerson professed, and this view led him to criticize the traditions, beliefs, and practices of the past that restricted the intellectual and moral development of persons in the present. God dwells within, according to Emerson, and thus each person should, he said early and late, establish an "original relation to the universe."

In his *Essay Concerning Human Understanding* (1690), John Locke had argued that the senses produce a register of impressions of the physical world on the blank tablet (the *tabula rasa*) of the mind; the understanding transforms them into abstractions and complex ideas. Emerson disagreed. Drawing on the writings of IMMANUEL KANT and, even more, Coleridge (the *Biographia Literaria*, 1817, and the religious and philosophical treatise *Aids to Reflection*, 1825), Emerson made "understanding"—the process by which the mind gathers the evidence of the senses and converts it into knowledge of the external world—subordinate to "reason," which he defined as the intuitive perception of truth. In *Nature*, Emerson affirmed, "I become a transparent eyeball; I am nothing; the currents of the Universal Being circulate through me; I am part or particle of God."

Emerson's reference to "Universal Being" points to the American version of Neoplatonism that he espoused. Each person must seek to regain communion with "Universal Being" or (Emerson's terms vary) Nature or Spirit. When it is lost, human beings view themselves as (and behave as if they were) isolated, powerless, alienated, corrupt. When it is restored, they sense their wholeness and enjoy a thrilling power and independence. This ecstatic feeling, Emerson suggests, is precious and precarious, astonishing and invigorating yet difficult for human beings to sustain. His philosophy is one of constant striving, of working to perfect and empower the self. Those (including HENRY JAMES) who take it for easy optimism are mistaken. In "Fate," Emerson emphasizes that "Nature is no sentimentalist,—does not cosset or pamper us. We must see that the world is rough and surly, and will not mind drowning a man or a woman, but swallows your ship like a grain of dust." And in "The Poet," he pictures the imaginative seer as liberating us from ordinary life, which is characterized as miserable and prisonlike.

Our selections demonstrate Emerson's centrality for literary theory, philosophy (especially American pragmatism), and cultural criticism. The first, an excerpt from "The American Scholar," presents Emerson's mobile, and somewhat unnerving, account of the reading process. Truth, he suggests, does not lie in great books waiting for readers to extract it. "Creative reading," the right kind of reading, is instead the result of the truth that readers bring with them—a claim that would reemerge in the reader-response criticism of the 1970s and 1980s (without crediting Emerson). Reading should inspire us, Emerson states; but the genuine scholar, he implies, is occupied with reading only when there is nothing better to do. He is more concerned with writing, arguing that "each age must write its own books. . . . The books of an older period will not fit this." Emerson calls for truth-seekers—persons who look within themselves rather than in books for truth and who bear witness to their spiritual discoveries in books of their own.

As he makes clear in "The Poet" (1844), our second selection, the writer reports passionately on personal experiences that will stimulate readers embarked on their own spiritual and intellectual journeys. All experience is meaningful; no "sensual fact" (that is, nothing that is perceived by the senses) lacks spiritual significance. The special office of the "poet" (i.e., the imaginative writer) is to be alert to the meanings that saturate all of existence; all persons have the potential to be poets (which is one way in which the poet is "representative"), but those who actually become poet-geniuses are "sovereign": they are potentates, emperors, liberating gods. Though Emerson found PERCY BYSSHE SHELLEY "wholly unaffecting," his grand vision of the poet's powers is akin to Shelley's in "The Defence of Poetry" (written 1821; see above). In Emerson's view, the more faithful the poet is to Nature, to Nature's harmonies, the better will be his or her art. Overall, he pays little attention to craft, style, technique. For Emerson, a poem is defined by a thought that is "passionately alive," not by its pattern of rhyme or meter or structure; he explicitly puts content before form.

Through most of the essay, Emerson speaks in universal terms; but toward its end, his commitment to literary and cultural nationalism becomes clear. He beckons for American poets who will take as a basis for their verse the facts, the experiences, and the sweep of the land itself. Though he honors the great writers of the past and of other lands, he emphasizes that present-day citizens of the new nation cannot find inspiration in them. He admits, however, "I look in vain for the poet whom I describe."

Emerson appeals for a literature that is American and modern, and at moments he sounds akin to major twentieth-century theorists and practitioners of literary modernism. T. S. ELIOT and Ezra Pound, for example, would seem to share Emerson's belief that the poet makes things new: "The poet, by an ulterior intellectual perception, gives them a power which makes their old use forgotten, and puts eyes and a tongue into every dumb and inanimate object." But the Romantic cast of Emerson's arguments ultimately made him more a foe than a friend for the modernists, with important exceptions (such as Gertrude Stein and Robert Frost). Eliot, in particularly strong terms, rejected the concept of the poet as inspired sage or spiritual seer and reaffirmed the sobering significance of tradition (see "Tradition and the Individual Talent," 1919; below). The immersion in the literature of the past that Eliot believed necessary for poets to find the stimulus for literary work of their own would have struck Emerson as a postponement of the individual's direct endeavor to hearken to the voice within, to the inner light (a phrase that Eliot despised).

For Emerson, what counts is who the poet is, which perhaps suggests why as a reader he preferred biography and history to poetry and fiction. He valued books that recounted a gifted individual's quest for freedom, power, and great achievement. Writing in his journal on January 10, 1832, he noted: "The difficulty is that we do not make a world of our own but fall into institutions already made & have to accommodate ourselves to them to be useful at all." Harold Bloom no doubt exaggerated when he called Emerson "God," but some critics have proposed, without exaggeration, that there was no truly American writing before Emerson, and that his presence has influenced everything written since.

BIBLIOGRAPHY

The standard editions are *The Collected Works of Ralph Waldo Emerson*, edited by Robert Spiller et al. (4 vols. to date, 1971–); *The Early Lectures*, edited by Stephen Whicher, Robert Spiller, and Wallace E. Williams (3 vols., 1959–72); *Journals and Miscellaneous Notebooks*, edited by William H. Gilman et al. (16 vols., 1960–84); and *Letters*, edited by Ralph L. Rusk (6 vols., 1939). For excellent single-volume collections (which include annotations), consult *Emerson's Literary Criticism*, edited by Eric W. Carlson (1979), and *Ralph Waldo Emerson*, edited by Richard Poirier, in the Oxford Authors series (1990). For more wide-ranging selections, see the Emerson volumes in the Library of America series, especially *Essays and Lectures* (1983). For selections from the journals, refer to *Emerson in His Journals*, edited by Joel Porte (1982).

Ralph L. Rusk's *Life of Ralph Waldo Emerson* (1949) remains a basic starting point. Biographies have also been written by Gay Wilson Allen, *Waldo Emerson: A Biography* (1981), and John McAleer, *Ralph Waldo Emerson: Days of Encounter* (1984). Robert D. Richardson, *Emerson: The Mind on Fire* (1995), explores Emerson's career as an American scholar, reader, and writer. For an account of Emerson's friends and contemporaries, see Carlos Baker, *Emerson among the Eccentrics: A Group Portrait* (1996). For incisive commentaries on Emerson's style and strategies as a writer, turn to Warner Berthoff, introduction to his edition of *Nature* (1968); Alfred Kazin, *An American Procession* (1984); Richard Poirier, *The Renewal of Literature: Emersonian Reflections* (1984); and Poirier, *Poetry and Pragmatism* (1992).

Many books have been written on Emerson; particularly worthy of attention are Barbara L. Packer, *Emerson's Fall: A New Interpretation of the Major Essays* (1982), a keen analysis of Emerson's uses of language; Julie Ellison, *Emerson's Romantic Style* (1984); Irving Howe, *The American Newness: Culture and Politics in the Age of Emerson* (1986), a suggestive book that relates Emerson to his contemporaries; David Van Leer, *Emerson's Epistemology: The Argument of the Essays* (1986), a cogent investigation of Emerson's theory of knowledge; Richard A. Grusin, *Transcendentalist Her-*

meneutics: Institutional Authority and the Higher Criticism of the Bible (1991), which is helpful on religious contexts; Merton M. Sealts, *Emerson on the Scholar* (1992); George J. Stack, *Nietzsche and Emerson: An Elective Affinity* (1992), an argument for the German philosopher's deep indebtedness to Emerson's ideas; Christina Zwarg, *Feminist Conversations: Fuller, Emerson, and the Play of Reading* (1995); and Stanley Cavell, *Philosophical Passages: Wittgenstein, Emerson, Austin, Derrida* (1995), a rewarding meditation on Emerson's significance for twentieth-century philosophy. Also valuable are *Emerson and Thoreau: The Contemporary Reviews*, edited by Joel Myerson (1992); and *Critical Essays on Ralph Waldo Emerson*, edited by Robert E. Burkholder and Joel Myerson (1983).

Joel Myerson has prepared a bibliography of Emerson's writings, *Ralph Waldo Emerson: A Descriptive Bibliography* (1982), and, with Robert E. Burkholder, two bibliographies of secondary sources: *A Secondary Bibliography of Ralph Waldo Emerson* (1985) and *Ralph Waldo Emerson: An Annotated Bibliography of Criticism, 1980–1991* (1994). Albert J. Von Frank, *An Emerson Chronology* (1994), is an indispensable reference.

From The American Scholar[1]

* * *

The next great influence into the spirit of the scholar is the mind of the Past,—in whatever form, whether of literature, of art, of institutions, that mind is inscribed. Books are the best type of the influence of the past, and perhaps we shall get at the truth,—learn the amount of this influence more conveniently,—by considering their value alone.

The theory of books is noble. The scholar of the first age received into him the world around; brooded thereon; gave it the new arrangement of his own mind, and uttered it again. It came into him life; it went out from him truth. It came to him short-lived actions; it went out from him immortal thoughts. It came to him business; it went from him poetry. It was dead fact; now, it is quick thought. It can stand, and it can go. It now endures, it now flies, it now inspires. Precisely in proportion to the depth of mind from which it issued, so high does it soar, so long does it sing.

Or, I might say, it depends on how far the process had gone, of transmuting life into truth. In proportion to the completeness of the distillation, so will the purity and imperishableness of the product be. But none is quite perfect. As no air-pump can by any means make a perfect vacuum, so neither can any artist entirely exclude the conventional, the local, the perishable from his book, or write a book of pure thought, that shall be as efficient, in all respects, to a remote posterity, as to contemporaries, or rather to the second age. Each age, it is found, must write its own books; or rather, each generation for the next succeeding. The books of an older period will not fit this.

Yet hence arises a grave mischief. The sacredness which attaches to the act of creation, the act of thought, is transferred to the record. The poet chanting was felt to be a divine man: henceforth the chant is divine also.

1. First published as a pamphlet, with the title *An Oration, Delivered before the Phi Beta Society, at Cambridge, August 31, 1837*. Emerson chose the title "The American Scholar" when it was republished in *Nature, Addresses, and Lectures* (1849).

The writer was a just and wise spirit: henceforward it is settled the book is perfect; as love of the hero corrupts into worship of his statue. Instantly the book becomes noxious: the guide is a tyrant. The sluggish and perverted mind of the multitude, slow to open to the incursions of Reason, having once so opened, having once received this book, stands upon it, and makes an outcry if it is disparaged. Colleges are built on it. Books are written on it by thinkers, not by Man Thinking; by men of talent, that is, who start wrong, who set out from accepted dogmas, not from their own sight of principles. Meek young men grow up in libraries, believing it their duty to accept the views which Cicero, which Locke, which Bacon,[2] have given; forgetful that Cicero, Locke, and Bacon were only young men in libraries when they wrote these books.

Hence, instead of Man Thinking, we have the bookworm. Hence the book-learned class, who value books, as such; not as related to nature and the human constitution, but as making a sort of Third Estate[3] with the world and the soul. Hence the restorers of readings, the emendators,[4] the bibliomaniacs of all degrees.

Books are the best of things, well used; abused, among the worst. What is the right use? What is the one end which all means go to effect? They are for nothing but to inspire. I had better never see a book than to be warped by its attraction clean out of my own orbit, and made a satellite instead of a system. The one thing in the world, of value, is the active soul. This every man is entitled to; this every man contains within him, although in almost all men obstructed and as yet unborn. The soul active sees absolute truth and utters truth, or creates. In this action it is genius; not the privilege of here and there a favorite, but the sound estate of every man. In its essence it is progressive. The book, the college, the school of art, the institution of any kind, stop with some past utterance of genius. This is good, say they,—let us hold by this. They pin me down. They look backward and not forward. But genius looks forward: the eyes of man are set in his forehead, not in his hindhead: man hopes: genius creates. Whatever talents may be, if the man create not, the pure efflux of the Deity is not his;—cinders and smoke there may be, but not yet flame. There are creative manners, there are creative actions, and creative words; manners, actions, words, that is, indicative of no custom or authority, but springing spontaneous from the mind's own sense of good and fair.

On the other part, instead of being its own seer, let it receive from another mind its truth, though it were in torrents of light, without periods of solitude, inquest, and self-recovery, and a fatal disservice is done. Genius is always sufficiently the enemy of genius by over-influence. The literature of every nation bears me witness. The English dramatic poets have Shakspearized now for two hundred years.

Undoubtedly there is a right way of reading, so it be sternly subordinated. Man Thinking must not be subdued by his instruments. Books are for the scholar's idle times. When he can read God directly, the hour is too precious

2. Sir Francis Bacon (1561–1626), English statesman and writer, whose works include *The Advancement of Learning* (1605). Cicero (106–43 B.C.E.), Roman orator and statesman. John Locke (1632–1704), English philosopher, author of *An Essay Concerning Human Understanding* (1690).

3. In prerevolutionary France, the common people (the first estate or political order was the clergy, the second the nobility).

4. Editors of texts.

to be wasted in other men's transcripts of their readings. But when the intervals of darkness come, as come they must,—when the sun is hid and the stars withdraw their shining,—we repair to the lamps which were kindled by their ray, to guide our steps to the East again, where the dawn is. We hear, that we may speak. The Arabian proverb says, "A fig tree, looking on a fig tree, becometh fruitful."

It is remarkable, the character of the pleasure we derive from the best books. They impress us with the conviction that one nature wrote and the same reads. We read the verses of one of the great English poets, of Chaucer, of Marvell, of Dryden,[5] with the most modern joy,—with a pleasure, I mean, which is in great part caused by the abstraction of all *time* from their verses. There is some awe mixed with the joy of our surprise, when this poet, who lived in some past world, two or three hundred years ago, says that which lies close to my own soul, that which I also had well-nigh thought and said. But for the evidence thence afforded to the philosophical doctrine of the identity of all minds, we should suppose some preëstablished harmony, some foresight of souls that were to be, and some preparation of stores for their future wants, like the fact observed in insects, who lay up food before death for the young grub they shall never see.

I would not be hurried by any love of system, by any exaggeration of instincts, to underrate the Book. We all know, that as the human body can be nourished on any food, though it were boiled grass and the broth of shoes, so the human mind can be fed by any knowledge. And great and heroic men have existed who had almost no other information than by the printed page. I only would say that it needs a strong head to bear that diet. One must be an inventor to read well. As the proverb says, "He that would bring home the wealth of the Indies, must carry out the wealth of the Indies."[6] There is then creative reading as well as creative writing. When the mind is braced by labor and invention, the page of whatever book we read becomes luminous with manifold allusion. Every sentence is doubly significant, and the sense of our author is as broad as the world. We then see, what is always true, that as the seer's hour of vision is short and rare among heavy days and months, so is its record, perchance, the least part of his volume. The discerning will read, in his Plato[7] or Shakspeare, only that least part,—only the authentic utterances of the oracle;—all the rest he rejects, were it never so many times Plato's and Shakspeare's.

Of course there is a portion of reading quite indispensable to a wise man. History and exact science he must learn by laborious reading. Colleges, in like manner, have their indispensable office,—to teach elements. But they can only highly serve us when they aim not to drill, but to create; when they gather from far every ray of various genius to their hospitable halls, and by the concentrated fires, set the hearts of their youth on flame. Thought and knowledge are natures in which apparatus and pretension avail nothing. Gowns and pecuniary foundations, though of towns of gold, can never countervail the least sentence or syllable of wit. Forget this, and our American

5. JOHN DRYDEN (1631–1700), poet, dramatist, and critic. Geoffrey Chaucer (ca. 1343–1400), author of *The Canterbury Tales*. Andrew Marvell (1621–1678), poet and satirist.
6. Emerson likely found this proverb in James Boswell's *Life of Samuel Johnson, LL.D.* (1791), in the conversation for April 17, 1778.
7. On the Greek philosopher PLATO (ca. 427–ca. 347 B.C.E.), see above.

colleges will recede in their public importance, whilst they grow richer every year.

* * *

1837, 1849

The Poet

Those who are esteemed umpires of taste are often persons who have acquired some knowledge of admired pictures or sculptures, and have an inclination for whatever is elegant; but if you inquire whether they are beautiful souls, and whether their own acts are like fair pictures, you learn that they are selfish and sensual. Their cultivation is local, as if you should rub a log of dry wood in one spot to produce fire, all the rest remaining cold. Their knowledge of the fine arts is some study of rules and particulars, or some limited judgment of color or form, which is exercised for amusement or for show. It is a proof of the shallowness of the doctrine of beauty as it lies in the minds of our amateurs, that men seem to have lost the perception of the instant dependence of form upon soul. There is no doctrine of forms in our philosophy. We were put into our bodies, as fire is put into a pan to be carried about; but there is no accurate adjustment between the spirit and the organ, much less is the latter the germination of the former. So in regard to other forms, the intellectual men do not believe in any essential dependence of the material world on thought and volition. Theologians think it a pretty air-castle to talk of the spiritual meaning of a ship or a cloud, of a city or a contract, but they prefer to come again to the solid ground of historical evidence; and even the poets are contented with a civil and conformed manner of living, and to write poems from the fancy, at a safe distance from their own experience. But the highest minds of the world have never ceased to explore the double meaning, or shall I say the quadruple or the centuple or much more manifold meaning, of every sensuous fact; Orpheus, Empedocles, Heraclitus, Plato, Plutarch, Dante, Swedenborg,[1] and the masters of sculpture, picture and poetry. For we are not pans and barrows, nor even porters of the fire and torch-bearers, but children of the fire,[2] made of it, and only the same divinity transmuted and at two or three removes, when we know least about it. And this hidden truth, that the fountains whence all this river of Time and its creatures floweth are intrinsically ideal and beautiful, draws us to the consideration of the nature and functions of the Poet, or the man of Beauty; to the means and materials he uses, and to the general aspect of the art in the present time.

The breadth of the problem is great, for the poet is representative. He stands among partial men for the complete man, and apprises us not of his wealth, but of the common wealth. The young man reveres men of genius,

1. Emanuel Swedenborg (1688–1772), Swedish mystic and scientist. Orpheus: legendary Greek poet to whom hymns and fragments were attributed. Empedocles (ca. 493–ca. 433 B.C.E.), Heraclitus (active ca. 500 B.C.E.), and PLATO (ca. 427–ca. 347 B.C.E.): Greek philosophers. Plutarch (ca. 50–ca. 120 C.E.), Greek biographer and historian. DANTE ALIGHIERI (1265–1321), Italian poet, author of *The Divine Comedy*.

2. A phrase derived from Heraclitus, who used fire to symbolize the process of change.

because, to speak truly, they are more himself than he is. They receive of the soul as he also receives, but they more. Nature enhances her beauty, to the eye of loving men, from their belief that the poet is beholding her shows at the same time. He is isolated among his contemporaries by truth and by his art, but with this consolation in his pursuits, that they will draw all men sooner or later. For all men live by truth and stand in need of expression. In love, in art, in avarice, in politics, in labor, in games, we study to utter our painful secret. The man is only half himself, the other half is his expression.

Notwithstanding this necessity to be published, adequate expression is rare. I know not how it is that we need an interpreter, but the great majority of men seem to be minors, who have not yet come into possession of their own, or mutes, who cannot report the conversation they have had with nature. There is no man who does not anticipate a supersensual utility in the sun and stars, earth and water. These stand and wait[3] to render him a peculiar service. But there is some obstruction or some excess of phlegm[4] in our constitution, which does not suffer them to yield the due effect. Too feeble fall the impressions of nature on us to make us artists. Every touch should thrill. Every man should be so much an artist that he could report in conversation what had befallen him. Yet, in our experience, the rays or appulses[5] have sufficient force to arrive at the senses, but not enough to reach the quick and compel the reproduction of themselves in speech. The poet is the person in whom these powers are in balance, the man without impediment, who sees and handles that which others dream of, traverses the whole scale of experience, and is representative of man, in virtue of being the largest power to receive and to impart.

For the Universe has three children, born at one time, which reappear under different names in every system of thought, whether they be called cause, operation and effect; or, more poetically, Jove, Pluto, Neptune;[6] or, theologically, the Father, the Spirit and the Son; but which we will call here the Knower, the Doer and the Sayer. These stand respectively for the love of truth, for the love of good, and for the love of beauty. These three are equal. Each is that which he is, essentially, so that he cannot be surmounted or analyzed, and each of these three has the power of the others latent in him and his own, patent.

The poet is the sayer, the namer, and represents beauty. He is a sovereign, and stands on the centre. For the world is not painted or adorned, but is from the beginning beautiful; and God has not made some beautiful things, but Beauty is the creator of the universe. Therefore the poet is not any permissive potentate, but is emperor in his own right. Criticism is infested with a cant of materialism, which assumes that manual skill and activity is the first merit of all men, and disparages such as say and do not, overlooking the fact that some men, namely poets, are natural sayers, sent into the world to the end of expression, and confounds them with those whose province is action but who quit it to imitate the sayers. But Homer's words are as costly and admirable to Homer as Agamemnon's victories are to Agamemnon.[7] The

3. See John Milton, "When I Consider How My Light Is Spent" (1673): "They also serve who only stand and wait" (line 14).
4. One of the four "humors" of early physiology; said to cause sluggishness and lethargy.
5. Driving motions toward something.
6. Three Roman gods: king of the gods (Jove), god of the dead and ruler of the underworld (Pluto), and god of the sea (Neptune).
7. Commander of the Greek army in Homer's epic poem the *Iliad* (ca. 8th c. B.C.E.).

poet does not wait for the hero or the sage, but, as they act and think primarily, so he writes primarily what will and must be spoken, reckoning the others, though primaries also, yet, in respect to him, secondaries and servants; as sitters or models in the studio of a painter, or as assistants who bring building-materials to an architect.

For poetry was all written before time was, and whenever we are so finely organized that we can penetrate into that region where the air is music, we hear those primal warblings and attempt to write them down, but we lose ever and anon a word or a verse and substitute something of our own, and thus miswrite the poem. The men of more delicate ear write down these cadences more faithfully, and these transcripts, though imperfect, become the songs of the nations. For nature is as truly beautiful as it is good, or as it is reasonable, and must as much appear as it must be done, or be known. Words and deeds are quite indifferent modes of the divine energy. Words are also actions, and actions are a kind of words.

The sign and credentials of the poet are that he announces that which no man foretold. He is the true and only doctor;[8] he knows and tells; he is the only teller of news, for he was present and privy to the appearance which he describes. He is a beholder of ideas and an utterer of the necessary and causal. For we do not speak now of men of poetical talents, or of industry and skill in metre, but of the true poet. I took part in a conversation the other day concerning a recent writer of lyrics,[9] a man of subtle mind, whose head appeared to be a music-box of delicate tunes and rhythms, and whose skill and command of language we could not sufficiently praise. But when the question arose whether he was not only a lyrist but a poet, we were obliged to confess that he is plainly a contemporary, not an eternal man. He does not stand out of our low limitations, like a Chimborazo under the line,[1] running up from a torrid base through all the climates of the globe, with belts of the herbage of every latitude on its high and mottled sides; but this genius is the landscape-garden of a modern house, adorned with fountains and statues, with well-bred men and women standing and sitting in the walks and terraces. We hear, through all the varied music, the ground-tone of conventional life. Our poets are men of talents who sing, and not the children of music. The argument is secondary, the finish of the verses is primary.

For it is not metres, but a metre-making argument that makes a poem,—a thought so passionate and alive that like the spirit of a plant or an animal it has an architecture of its own, and adorns nature with a new thing. The thought and the form are equal in the order of time, but in the order of genesis the thought is prior to the form. The poet has a new thought; he has a whole new experience to unfold; he will tell us how it was with him, and all men will be the richer in his fortune. For the experience of each new age requires a new confession, and the world seems always waiting for its poet. I remember when I was young how much I was moved one morning by tidings that genius had appeared in a youth who sat near me at table. He had left his work and gone rambling none knew whither, and had written hundreds of lines, but could not tell whether that which was in him was therein told; he could tell nothing but that all was changed,—man, beast, heaven, earth

8. Teacher.
9. Perhaps the English poet Alfred, Lord Tennyson (1809–1892).
1. The equator. Chimborazo: a mountain in Ecuador, in the Andes range.

and sea. How gladly we listened! how credulous! Society seemed to be compromised. We sat in the aurora of a sunrise which was to put out all the stars. Boston seemed to be at twice the distance it had the night before, or was much farther than that. Rome,—what was Rome? Plutarch and Shakspeare were in the yellow leaf,[2] and Homer no more should be heard of. It is much to know that poetry has been written this very day, under this very roof, by your side. What! that wonderful spirit has not expired! These stony moments are still sparkling and animated! I had fancied that the oracles were all silent,[3] and nature had spent her fires; and behold! all night, from every pore, these fine auroras have been streaming. Every one has some interest in the advent of the poet, and no one knows how much it may concern him. We know that the secret of the world is profound, but who or what shall be our interpreter, we know not. A mountain ramble, a new style of face, a new person, may put the key into our hands. Of course the value of genius to us is in the veracity of its report. Talent may frolic and juggle; genius realizes and adds. Mankind in good earnest have availed so far in understanding themselves and their work, that the foremost watchman on the peak announces his news. It is the truest word ever spoken, and the phrase will be the fittest, most musical, and the unerring voice of the world for that time.

All that we call sacred history attests that the birth of a poet is the principal event in chronology. Man, never so often deceived, still watches for the arrival of a brother who can hold him steady to a truth until he has made it his own. With what joy I begin to read a poem which I confide in as an inspiration! And now my chains are to be broken; I shall mount above these clouds and opaque airs in which I live,—opaque, though they seem transparent,—and from the heaven of truth I shall see and comprehend my relations. That will reconcile me to life and renovate nature, to see trifles animated by a tendency, and to know what I am doing. Life will no more be a noise; now I shall see men and women, and know the signs by which they may be discerned from fools and satans. This day shall be better than my birthday: then I became an animal; now I am invited into the science of the real. Such is the hope, but the fruition is postponed. Oftener it falls that this winged man, who will carry me into the heaven, whirls me into mists, then leaps and frisks about with me as it were from cloud to cloud, still affirming that he is bound heavenward; and I, being myself a novice, am slow in perceiving that he does not know the way into the heavens, and is merely bent that I should admire his skill to rise like a fowl or a flying fish, a little way from the ground or the water; but the all-piercing, all-feeding and ocular air of heaven that man shall never inhabit. I tumble down again soon into my old nooks, and lead the life of exaggerations as before, and have lost my faith in the possibility of any guide who can lead me thither where I would be.

But, leaving these victims of vanity, let us, with new hope, observe how nature, by worthier impulses, has insured the poet's fidelity to his office of announcement and affirming, namely by the beauty of things, which becomes a new and higher beauty when expressed. Nature offers all her

2. See the words of Macbeth, in *Macbeth* (ca. 1606), 5.3.23–24; "My way of life / Is fall'n into the sere, the yellow leaf." See also George Gordon, Lord Byron, "On This Day I Complete My Thirty-sixth Year" (1824): "My days are in the yellow leaf" (line 5).

3. See John Milton, "On the Morning of Christ's Nativity" (1645): "The oracles are dumb" (line 173).

creatures to him as a picture-language. Being used as a type, a second wonderful value appears in the object, far better than its old value; as the carpenter's stretched cord, if you hold your ear close enough, is musical in the breeze. "Things more excellent than every image," says Jamblichus,[4] "are expressed through images." Things admit of being used as symbols because nature is a symbol, in the whole, and in every part. Every line we can draw in the sand has expression; and there is no body without its spirit or genius. All form is an effect of character; all condition, of the quality of the life; all harmony, of health; and for this reason a perception of beauty should be sympathetic, or proper only to the good. The beautiful rests on the foundations of the necessary.

The soul makes the body, as the wise Spenser teaches:—

"So every spirit, as it is more pure,
And hath in it the more of heavenly light,
So it the fairer body doth procure
To habit in, and it more fairly dight,
With cheerful grace and amiable sight.
For, of the soul, the body form doth take,
For soul is form, and doth the body make."[5]

Here we find ourselves suddenly not in a critical speculation but in a holy place, and should go very warily and reverently. We stand before the secret of the world, there where Being passes into Appearance and Unity into Variety.

The Universe is the externization of the soul. Wherever the life is, that bursts into appearance around it. Our science is sensual, and therefore superficial. The earth and the heavenly bodies, physics and chemistry, we sensually treat, as if they were self-existent; but these are the retinue of that Being we have. "The mighty heaven," said Proclus,[6] "exhibits, in its transfigurations, clear images of the splendor of intellectual perceptions; being moved in conjunction with the unapparent periods of intellectual natures." Therefore science always goes abreast with the just elevation of the man, keeping step with religion and metaphysics; or the state of science is an index of our self-knowledge. Since every thing in nature answers to a moral power, if any phenomenon remains brute and dark it is because the corresponding faculty in the observer is not yet active.

No wonder then, if these waters be so deep, that we hover over them with a religious regard. The beauty of the fable proves the importance of the sense; to the poet, and to all others; or, if you please, every man is so far a poet as to be susceptible of these enchantments of nature; for all men have the thoughts whereof the universe is the celebration. I find that the fascination resides in the symbol. Who loves nature? Who does not? Is it only poets, and men of leisure and cultivation, who live with her? No; but also hunters, farmers, grooms and butchers, though they express their affection in their choice of life and not in their choice of words. The writer wonders what the coachman or the hunter values in riding, in horses and dogs. It is not super-

4. Iamblichus (ca. 250–ca. 325 C.E.), Neoplatonic philosopher of Syria; Emerson read his *Life of Pythagoras*.
5. "An Hymne in Honour of Beautie" (1596), lines 127–33, by the English poet Edmund Spenser (1552–1599).
6. Greek Neoplatonic philosopher (412–485 C.E.).

ficial qualities. When you talk with him he holds these at as slight a rate as you. His worship is sympathetic; he has no definitions, but he is commanded in nature by the living power which he feels to be there present. No imitation or playing of these things would content him; he loves the earnest of the north wind, of rain, of stone and wood and iron. A beauty not explicable is dearer than a beauty which we can see to the end of. It is nature the symbol, nature certifying the supernatural, body overflowed by life which he worships with coarse but sincere rites.

The inwardness and mystery of this attachment drive men of every class to the use of emblems. The schools of poets and philosophers are not more intoxicated with their symbols than the populace with theirs. In our political parties, compute the power of badges and emblems. See the great ball which they roll from Baltimore to Bunker Hill![7] In the political processions, Lowell goes in a loom, and Lynn in a shoe, and Salem in a ship. Witness the cider-barrel, the log-cabin, the hickory-stick, the palmetto,[8] and all the cognizances of party. See the power of national emblems. Some stars, lilies, leopards, a crescent, a lion, an eagle, or other figure which came into credit God knows how, on an old rag of bunting, blowing in the wind on a fort at the ends of the earth, shall make the blood tingle under the rudest or the most conventional exterior. The people fancy they hate poetry, and they are all poets and mystics!

Beyond this universality of the symbolic language, we are apprised of the divineness of this superior use of things, whereby the world is a temple whose walls are covered with emblems, pictures and commandments of the Deity,—in this, that there is no fact in nature which does not carry the whole sense of nature; and the distinctions which we make in events and in affairs, of low and high, honest and base, disappear when nature is used as a symbol. Thought makes everything fit for use. The vocabulary of an omniscient man would embrace words and images excluded from polite conversation. What would be base, or even obscene, to the obscene, becomes illustrious, spoken in a new connection of thought. The piety of the Hebrew prophets purges their grossness.[9] The circumcision is an example of the power of poetry to raise the low and offensive. Small and mean things serve as well as great symbols. The meaner the type by which a law is expressed, the more pungent it is, and the more lasting in the memories of men; just as we choose the smallest box or case in which any needful utensil can be carried. Bare lists of words are found suggestive to an imaginative and excited mind as it is related of Lord Chatham that he was accustomed to read in Bailey's[1] Dictionary when he was preparing to speak in Parliament. The poorest experience is rich enough for all the purposes of expressing thought. Why covet a knowledge of new facts? Day and night, house and garden, a few books, a

7. In the Charlestown section of Boston. This stunt was undertaken by the Whig Party for their candidate William Henry Harrison during the presidential campaign in 1840 to illustrate that year's slogan, "Keep the ball a-rolling." Emerson then associates each Massachusetts town with its major product.

8. Emerson names symbols closely associated with politicians of the 1830s: the cider barrel and log cabin, with William Henry Harrison; the hickory stick, with "Old Hickory," Andrew Jackson (Democratic president, 1829–37); and the palmetto, with John C. Calhoun (Jackson's vice president), who was from South Carolina (the "palmetto state").

9. Emerson may have in mind such passages as Ezekiel's comparison of Jerusalem to a harlot (15) and his description of the city's sins (22).

1. Nathan (or Nathaniel) Bailey (d. 1742), lexicographer and philologist, author of *An Universal Etymological English Dictionary* (1721). Lord Chatham, William Pitt (1708–1778), English statesman and orator.

few actions, serve us as well as would all trades and all spectacles. We are far from having exhausted the significance of the few symbols we use. We can come to use them yet with a terrible simplicity. It does not need that a poem should be long. Every word was once a poem. Every new relation is a new word. Also we use defects and deformities to a sacred purpose, so expressing our sense that the evils of the world are such only to the evil eye. In the old mythology, mythologists observe, defects are ascribed to divine natures, as lameness to Vulcan, blindness to Cupid,[2] and the like,—to signify exuberances.

For as it is dislocation and detachment from the life of God that makes things ugly, the poet, who re-attaches things to nature and the Whole,—re-attaching even artificial things and violation of nature, to nature, by a deeper insight,—disposes very easily of the most disagreeable facts. Readers of poetry see the factory-village and the railway, and fancy that the poetry of the landscape is broken up by these; for these works of art are not yet consecrated in their reading; but the poet sees them fall within the great Order not less than the beehive or the spider's geometrical web. Nature adopts them very fast into her vital circles, and the gliding train of cars she loves like her own. Besides, in a centred mind, it signifies nothing how many mechanical inventions you exhibit. Though you add millions, and never so surprising, the fact of mechanics has not gained a grain's weight. The spiritual fact remains unalterable, by many or by few particulars; as no mountain is of any appreciable height to break the curve of the sphere. A shrewd country-boy goes to the city for the first time, and the complacent citizen is not satisfied with his little wonder. It is not that he does not see all the fine houses and know that he never saw such before, but he disposes of them as easily as the poet finds place for the railway. The chief value of the new fact is to enhance the great and constant fact of Life, which can dwarf any and every circumstance, and to which the belt of wampum and the commerce of America are alike.

The world being thus put under the mind for verb and noun, the poet is he who can articulate it. For though life is great, and fascinates and absorbs; and though all men are intelligent of[3] the symbols through which it is named; yet they cannot originally use them. We are symbols and inhabit symbols; workmen, work, and tools, words and things, birth and death, all are emblems; but we sympathize with the symbols, and being infatuated with the economical uses of things, we do not know that they are thoughts. The poet, by an ulterior intellectual perception, gives them a power which makes their old use forgotten, and puts eyes and a tongue into every dumb and inanimate object. He perceives the independence of the thought on the symbol, the stability of the thought, the accidency and fugacity[4] of the symbol. As the eyes of Lyncæus[5] were said to see through the earth, so the poet turns the world to glass, and shows us all things in their right series and procession. For through that better perception he stands one step nearer to things, and sees the flowing or metamorphosis; perceives that thought is multiform; that

2. The Roman god of love, son of Venus. Vulcan: the Roman god of fire and metalworking.
3. Acquainted with, versed in.
4. Transience, lack of enduring qualities. "Accidency": accidental or chance character.
5. In Greek mythology, the seaman with the keenest eyesight among those who sailed with Jason in quest of the Golden Fleece. See Apollonius of Rhodes, *Argonautica* 1.155.

within the form of every creature is a force impelling it to ascend into a higher form; and following with his eyes the life, uses the forms which express that life, and so his speech flows with the flowing of nature. All the facts of the animal economy, sex, nutriment, gestation, birth, growth, are symbols of the passage of the world into the soul of man, to suffer there a change and reappear a new and higher fact. He uses forms according to the life, and not according to the form. This is true science. The poet alone knows astronomy, chemistry, vegetation and animation, for he does not stop at these facts, but employs them as signs. He knows why the plain or meadow of space was strown with these flowers we call suns and moons and stars; why the great deep is adorned with animals, with men, and gods; for in every word he speaks he rides on them as the horses of thought.

By virtue of this science the poet is the Namer or Language-maker, naming things sometimes after their appearance, sometimes after their essence, and giving to every one its own name and not another's, thereby rejoicing the intellect, which delights in detachment or boundary. The poets made all the words, and therefore language is the archives of history, and, if we must say it, a sort of tomb of the muses. For though the origin of most of our words is forgotten, each word was at first a stroke of genius, and obtained currency because for the moment it symbolized the world to the first speaker and to the hearer. The etymologist finds the deadest word to have been once a brilliant picture. Language is fossil poetry. As the limestone of the continent consists of infinite masses of the shells of animalcules, so language is made up of images or tropes, which now, in their secondary use, have long ceased to remind us of their poetic origin. But the poet names the thing because he sees it, or comes one step nearer to it than any other. This expression or naming is not art, but a second nature, grown out of the first, as a leaf out of a tree. What we call nature is a certain self-regulated motion or change; and nature does all things by her own hands, and does not leave another to baptize her but baptizes herself; and this through the metamorphosis again. I remember that a certain poet[6] described it to me thus:—

Genius is the activity which repairs the decays of things, whether wholly or partly of a material and finite kind. Nature, through all her kingdoms, insures herself. Nobody cares for planting the poor fungus; so she shakes down from the gills of one agaric countless spores, any one of which, being preserved, transmits new billions of spores to-morrow or next day. The new agaric of this hour has a chance which the old one had not. This atom of seed is thrown into a new place, not subject to the accidents which destroyed its parent two rods off. She makes a man; and having brought him to ripe age, she will no longer run the risk of losing this wonder at a blow, but she detaches from him a new self, that the kind may be safe from accidents to which the individual is exposed. So when the soul of the poet has come to ripeness of thought, she detaches and sends away from it its poems or songs,—a fearless, sleepless, deathless progeny, which is not exposed to the accidents of the weary kingdom of time; a fearless, vivacious offspring, clad with wings (such was the virtue of the soul out of which they came) which carry them fast and far, and infix them irrecoverably into the hearts of men.

6. Emerson himself, in his journal, paraphrasing Plato.

These wings are the beauty of the poet's soul. The songs, thus flying immortal from their mortal parent, are pursued by clamorous flights of censures, which swarm in far greater numbers and threaten to devour them; but these last are not winged. At the end of a very short leap they fall plump down and rot, having received from the souls out of which they came no beautiful wings. But the melodies of the poet ascend and leap and pierce into the deeps of infinite time.

So far the bard taught me, using his freer speech. But nature has a higher end, in the production of new individuals, than security, namely *ascension*, or the passage of the soul into higher forms. I knew in my younger days the sculptor who made the statue of the youth which stands in the public garden. He was, as I remember, unable to tell directly what made him happy or unhappy, but by wonderful indirections he could tell. He rose one day, according to his habit, before the dawn, and saw the morning break, grand as the eternity out of which it came, and for many days after, he strove to express this tranquillity, and lo! his chisel had fashioned out of marble the form of a beautiful youth, Phosphorus,[7] whose aspect is such that it is said all persons who look on it become silent. The poet also resigns himself to his mood, and that thought which agitated him is expressed, but *alter idem*,[8] in a manner totally new. The expression is organic, or the new type which things themselves take when liberated. As, in the sun, objects paint their images on the retina of the eye, so they, sharing the aspiration of the whole universe, tend to paint a far more delicate copy of their essence in his mind. Like the metamorphosis of things into higher organic forms is their change into melodies. Over everything stands its dæmon or soul, and, as the form of the thing is reflected by the eye, so the soul of the thing is reflected by a melody. The sea, the mountain-ridge, Niagara, and every flower-bed, pre-exist, or super-exist, in pre-cantations,[9] which sail like odors in the air, and when any man goes by with an ear sufficiently fine, he overhears them and endeavors to write down the notes without diluting or depraving them.[1] And herein is the legitimation of criticism, in the mind's faith that the poems are a corrupt version of some text in nature with which they ought to be made to tally. A rhyme in one of our sonnets should not be less pleasing than the iterated nodes of a seashell, or the resembling difference of a group of flowers. The pairing of the birds is an idyl, not tedious as our idyls are; a tempest is a rough ode, without falsehood or rant; a summer, with its harvest sown, reaped and stored, is an epic song, subordinating how many admirably executed parts. Why should not the symmetry and truth that modulate these, glide into our spirits, and we participate the invention of nature?

This insight, which expresses itself by what is called Imagination, is a very high sort of seeing, which does not come by study, but by the intellect being where and what it sees; by sharing the path or circuit of things through forms, and so making them translucid to others. The path of things is silent. Will they suffer a speaker to go with them? A spy they will not suffer; a lover, a poet, is the transcendency of their own nature,—him they will suffer. The condition of true naming, on the poet's part, is his resigning himself to the divine *aura*[1] which breathes through forms, and accompanying that.

7. The Greek personification of the morning star (literally, "light-bearer"), sometimes represented as a youth bearing a torch.

8. A second self (Latin).

9. Enchantments, foretellings.

1. Gentle breeze; intangible quality, atmosphere.

It is a secret which every intellectual man quickly learns, that beyond the energy of his possessed and conscious intellect he is capable of a new energy (as of an intellect doubled on itself), by abandonment to the nature of things; that beside his privacy of power as an individual man, there is a great public power on which he can draw, by unlocking, at all risks, his human doors, and suffering the ethereal tides to roll and circulate through him; then he is caught up into the life of the Universe, his speech is thunder, his thought is law, and his words are universally intelligible as the plants and animals. The poet knows that he speaks adequately then only when he speaks somewhat wildly, or "with the flower of the mind;"[2] not with the intellect used as an organ, but with the intellect released from all service and suffered to take its direction from its celestial life; or as the ancients[3] were wont to express themselves, not with intellect alone but with the intellect inebriated by nectar. As the traveller who has lost his way throws his reins on his horse's neck and trusts to the instinct of the animal to find his road, so must we do with the divine animal who carries us through this world. For if in any manner we can stimulate this instinct, new passages are opened for us into nature; the mind flows into and through things hardest and highest, and the metamorphosis is possible.

This is the reason why bards love wine, mead, narcotics, coffee, tea, opium, the fumes of sandalwood and tobacco, or whatever other procurers of animal exhilaration. All men avail themselves of such means as they can, to add this extraordinary power to their normal powers; and to this end they prize conversation, music, pictures, sculpture, dancing, theatres, travelling, war, mobs, fires, gaming, politics, or love, or science, or animal intoxication,—which are several coarser or finer *quasi*-mechanical substitutes for the true nectar, which is the ravishment of the intellect by coming nearer to the fact. These are auxiliaries to the centrifugal tendency of a man, to his passage out into free space, and they help him to escape the custody of that body in which he is pent up, and of that jail-yard of individual relations in which he is enclosed. Hence a great number of such as were professionally expressers of Beauty, as painters, poets, musicians and actors, have been more than others wont to lead a life of pleasure and indulgence; all but the few who received the true nectar; and, as it was a spurious mode of attaining freedom, as it was an emancipation not into the heavens but into the freedom of baser places, they were punished for that advantage they won, by a dissipation and deterioration. But never can any advantage be taken of nature by a trick. The spirit of the world, the great calm presence of the Creator, comes not forth to the sorceries of opium or of wine. The sublime vision comes to the pure and simple soul in a clean and chaste body. That is not an inspiration, which we owe to narcotics, but some counterfeit excitement and fury. Milton says[4] that the lyric poet may drink wine and live generously, but the epic poet, he who shall sing of the gods and their descent unto men, must drink water out of a wooden bowl. For poetry is not 'Devil's wine,' but God's wine. It is with this as it is with toys. We fill the hands and nurseries of our children with all manner of dolls, drums and horses; withdrawing their eyes from the plain

2. A translation of a Greek phrase from the "Chaldean Oracles" (2d c. C.E., though attributed to the Persian religious leader and prophet Zoroaster, ca. 7th c. B.C.E.), selections from which appeared in the Transcendentalist journal, *The Dial*, in 1844. Others have noted as a source *The True Intellectual System of the Universe* (1678), by the English Neoplatonist Ralph Cudworth.

3. The Neoplatonists PLOTINUS (ca. 204/5–70 C.E.) and Proclus.

4. In *Elegy VI* (1629), lines 55–78.

face and sufficing objects of nature, the sun and moon, the animals, the water and stones, which should be their toys. So the poet's habit of living should be set on a key so low that the common influences should delight him. His cheerfulness should be the gift of the sunlight; the air should suffice for his inspiration, and he should be tipsy with water. That spirit which suffices quiet hearts, which seems to come forth to such from every dry knoll of sere grass, from every pine stump and half-imbedded stone on which the dull March sun shines, comes forth to the poor and hungry, and such as are of simple taste. If thou fill thy brain with Boston and New York, with fashion and covetousness, and wilt stimulate thy jaded senses with wine and French coffee, thou shalt find no radiance of wisdom in the lonely waste of the pine woods.

If the imagination intoxicates the poet, it is not inactive in other men. The metamorphosis excites in the beholder an emotion of joy. The use of symbols has a certain power of emancipation and exhilaration for all men. We seem to be touched by a wand which makes us dance and run about happily, like children. We are like persons who come out of a cave or cellar into the open air. This is the effect on us of tropes,[5] fables, oracles and all poetic forms. Poets are thus liberating gods. Men have really got a new sense, and found within their world another world, or nest of worlds; for, the metamorphosis once seen, we divine that it does not stop. I will not now consider how much this makes the charm of algebra and the mathematics, which also have their tropes, but it is felt in every definition; as when Aristotle defines *space* to be an immovable vessel in which things are contained;[6]—or when Plato defines a *line* to be a flowing point; or *figure* to be a bound of solid;[7] and many the like. What a joyful sense of freedom we have when Vitruvius[8] announces the old opinion of artists that no architect can build any house well who does not know something of anatomy. When Socrates, in Charmides, tells us that the soul is cured of its maladies by certain incantations, and that these incantations are beautiful reasons, from which temperance is generated in souls; when Plato calls the world an animal, and Timæus affirms that the plants also are animals; or affirms a man to be a heavenly tree, growing with his root, which is his head, upward; and, as George Chapman, following him, writes,

> "So in our tree of man, whose nervie root
> Springs in his top;"—

when Orpheus speaks of hoariness as "that white flower which marks extreme old age;" when Proclus calls the universe the statue of the intellect; when Chaucer, in his praise of 'Gentilesse,' compares good blood in mean condition to fire, which, though carried to the darkest house betwixt this and the mount of Caucasus, will yet hold its natural office and burn as bright as if twenty thousand men did it behold; when John saw, in the Apocalypse, the ruin of the world through evil, and the stars fall from heaven as the fig tree casteth her untimely fruit; when Æsop reports the whole catalogue of common daily relations through the masquerade of birds and beasts;[9]—we

5. Figures of speech.
6. ARISTOTLE (384–322 B.C.E.), *Physics* 4.
7. Plato, *Meno* 76.
8. Roman engineer and architect (1st c. B.C.E.), best known for his work *On Architecture*.
9. In the allusion-filled preceding lines, Emerson's references to calling the world "an animal" and to "plants also are animals" are taken from Plato's dialogues *Charmides* (157) and *Timaeus* (30, 77); George Chapman (1559–1634), an English poet and translator of Homer, wrote the lines quoted in the dedication to Prince Henry at the beginning of

take the cheerful hint of the immortality of our essence and its versatile habit and escapes, as when the gypsies say of themselves "it is in vain to hang them, they cannot die."[1]

The poets are thus liberating gods. The ancient British bards had for the title of their order, "Those who are free throughout the world." They are free, and they make free. An imaginative book renders us much more service at first, by stimulating us through its tropes, than afterward when we arrive at the precise sense of the author. I think nothing is of any value in books excepting the transcendental and extraordinary. If a man is inflamed and carried away by his thought, to that degree that he forgets the authors and the public and heeds only this one dream which holds him like an insanity, let me read his paper, and you may have all the arguments and histories and criticism. All the value which attaches to Pythagoras, Paracelsus, Cornelius Agrippa, Cardan, Kepler, Swedenborg, Schelling, Oken,[2] or any other who introduces questionable facts into his cosmogony, as angels, devils, magic, astrology, palmistry, mesmerism, and so on, is the certificate we have of departure from routine, and that here is a new witness. That also is the best success in conversation, the magic of liberty, which puts the world like a ball in our hands. How cheap even the liberty then seems; how mean to study, when an emotion communicates to the intellect the power to sap and upheave nature; how great the perspective! nations, times, systems, enter and disappear like threads in tapestry of large figure and many colors; dream delivers us to dream, and while the drunkenness lasts we will sell our bed, our philosophy, our religion, in our opulence.

There is good reason why we should prize this liberation. The fate of the poor shepherd, who, blinded and lost in the snow-storm, perishes in a drift within a few feet of his cottage door, is an emblem of the state of man. On the brink of the waters of life and truth, we are miserably dying. The inaccessibleness of every thought but that we are in, is wonderful. What if you come near to it; you are as remote when you are nearest as when you are farthest. Every thought is also a prison; every heaven is also a prison. Therefore we love the poet, the inventor, who in any form, whether in an ode or in an action or in looks and behavior, has yielded us a new thought. He unlocks our chains and admits us to a new scene.

This emancipation is dear to all men, and the power to impart it, as it must come from greater depth and scope of thought, is a measure of intellect. Therefore all books of the imagination endure, all which ascend to that truth that the writer sees nature beneath him, and uses it as his exponent.[3] Every verse or sentence possessing this virtue will take care of its own immortality. The religions of the world are the ejaculations of a few imaginative men.

But the quality of the imagination is to flow, and not to freeze. The poet did not stop at the color or the form, but read their meaning; neither may he rest in this meaning, but he makes the same objects exponents of his new

---

his translation; Chaucer's praise of "gentilesse" is in "The Wife of Bath's Tale" (ca. 1400), lines 1139–45; for John's vision, see Revelation 6.13; Aesop wrote his beast fables in the 6th century B.C.E.

1. George Borrow, *The Zincali; or, An Account of the Gypsies of Spain* (1842).

2. Lorenz Oken (1779–1851), German naturalist and mystic philosopher. Pythagoras (6th c. B.C.E.), Greek philosopher and mathematician. Paracelsus (1493–1541), German alchemist and writer on occult subjects. Henricus Cornelius Agrippa van Nettesheim (1486–1535), German physician and magician. Girolamo Cardano (1501–1576), Italian physician, astrologer, and mathematician. Johann Kepler (1571–1630), German astronomer. Friedrich Wilhelm Joseph von Schelling (1775–1854), German philosopher.

3. The means through which his beliefs are expounded.

thought. Here is the difference betwixt the poet and the mystic, that the last nails a symbol to one sense, which was a true sense for a moment, but soon becomes old and false. For all symbols are fluxional; all language is vehicular and transitive, and is good, as ferries and horses are, for conveyance, not as farms and houses are, for homestead. Mysticism consists in the mistake of an accidental and individual symbol for an universal one. The morning-redness happens to be the favorite meteor to the eyes of Jacob Behmen,[4] and comes to stand to him for truth and faith; and, he believes, should stand for the same realities to every reader. But the first reader prefers as naturally the symbol of a mother and child, or a gardener and his bulb, or a jeweller polishing a gem. Either of these, or of a myriad more, are equally good to the person to whom they are significant. Only they must be held lightly, and be very willingly translated into the equivalent terms which others use. And the mystic must be steadily told,—All that you say is just as true without the tedious use of that symbol as with it. Let us have a little algebra, instead of this trite rhetoric,—universal signs, instead of these village symbols,—and we shall both be gainers. The history of hierarchies seems to show that all religious error consisted in making the symbol too stark and solid, and was at last nothing but an excess of the organ of language.

Swedenborg, of all men in the recent ages, stands eminently for the translator of nature into thought. I do not know the man in history to whom things stood so uniformly for words. Before him the metamorphosis continually plays. Everything on which his eye rests, obeys the impulses of moral nature. The figs become grapes whilst he eats them. When some of his angels affirmed a truth, the laurel twig which they held blossomed in their hands. The noise which at a distance appeared like gnashing and thumping, on coming nearer was found to be the voice of disputants. The men in one of his visions, seen in heavenly light, appeared like dragons, and seemed in darkness; but to each other they appeared as men, and when the light from heaven shone into their cabin, they complained of the darkness, and were compelled to shut the window that they might see.

There was this perception in him which makes the poet or seer an object of awe and terror, namely that the same man or society of men may wear one aspect to themselves and their companions, and a different aspect to higher intelligences. Certain priests, whom he describes as conversing very learnedly together, appeared to the children who were at some distance, like dead horses; and many the like misappearances.[5] And instantly the mind inquires whether these fishes under the bridge, yonder oxen in the pasture, those dogs in the yard, are immutably fishes, oxen and dogs, or only so appear to me, and perchance to themselves appear upright men; and whether I appear as a man to all eyes. The Brahmins[6] and Pythagoras propounded the same question, and if any poet has witnessed the transformation he doubtless found it in harmony with various experiences. We have all seen changes as considerable in wheat and caterpillars. He is the poet and shall draw us with love and terror, who sees through the flowing vest the firm nature, and can declare it.

4. Jakob Böhme (1575–1624), German theosophist and mystic, author of *Aurora: The Day-Spring, or, Dawning of the Day in the East: or, Morning-Redness in the Rising of the Sun*.

5. Each chapter of Swedenborg's *Apocalypse Revealed* (1766) concludes with "Memorable Revelations."

6. Members of the highest Hindu caste, from which priests and religious teachers are drawn.

I look in vain for the poet whom I describe. We do not with sufficient plainness or sufficient profoundness address ourselves to life, nor dare we chaunt our own times and social circumstance. If we filled the day with bravery, we should not shrink from celebrating it. Time and nature yield us many gifts, but not yet the timely man, the new religion, the reconciler, whom all things await. Dante's praise is that he dared to write his autobiography in colossal cipher, or into universality.[7] We have yet had no genius in America, with tyrannous eye, which knew the value of our incomparable materials, and saw, in the barbarism and materialism of the times, another carnival of the same gods whose picture he so much admires in Homer; then in the Middle Age; then in Calvinism. Banks and tariffs, the newspaper and caucus, Methodism and Unitarianism, are flat and dull to dull people, but rest on the same foundations of wonder as the town of Troy and the temple of Delphi,[8] and are as swiftly passing away. Our log-rolling, our stumps and their politics, our fisheries, our Negroes and Indians, our boats and our repudiations,[9] the wrath of rogues and the pusillanimity of honest men, the northern trade, the southern planting, the western clearing, Oregon and Texas, are yet unsung. Yet America is a poem in our eyes; its ample geography dazzles the imagination, and it will not wait long for metres. If I have not found that excellent combination of gifts in my countrymen which I seek, neither could I aid myself to fix the idea of the poet by reading now and then in Chalmers's collection of five centuries of English poets.[1] These are wits more than poets, though there have been poets among them. But when we adhere to the ideal of the poet, we have our difficulties even with Milton and Homer. Milton is too literary, and Homer too literal and historical.

But I am not wise enough for a national criticism, and must use the old largeness a little longer, to discharge my errand from the muse to the poet concerning his art.

Art is the path of the creator to his work. The paths or methods are ideal and eternal, though few men ever see them; not the artist himself for years, or for a lifetime, unless he come into the conditions. The painter, the sculptor, the composer, the epic rhapsodist, the orator, all partake one desire, namely to express themselves symmetrically and abundantly, not dwarfishly and fragmentarily. They found or put themselves in certain conditions, as, the painter and sculptor before some impressive human figures; the orator into the assembly of the people; and the others in such scenes as each has found exciting to his intellect; and each presently feels the new desire. He hears a voice, he sees a beckoning. Then he is apprised, with wonder, what herds of dæmons hem him in. He can no more rest; he says, with the old painter, "By God it is in me and must go forth of me." He pursues a beauty, half seen, which flies before him. The poet pours out verses in every solitude. Most of the things he says are conventional, no doubt; but by and by he says something which is original and beautiful. That charms him. He would say nothing else but such things. In our way of talking we say 'That is yours, this is mine;' but the poet knows well that it is not his; that it is as strange and

7. In Dante's epic *Divine Comedy*, the poet himself plays a first-person role.
8. The site in Greece of the most important oracle of Apollo.
9. Refusals to pay debts. "Log-rolling": the exchange of political favors. "Stumps": speech platforms. "Boats": some editors print "boasts."
1. Alexander Chalmers (1759–1834), Scottish biographer and journalist, compiled *The Works of the English Poets, from Chaucer to Cowper* (21 vols., 1810).

beautiful to him as to you; he would fain hear the like eloquence at length. Once having tasted this immortal ichor,[2] he cannot have enough of it, and as an admirable creative power exists in these intellections, it is of the last importance that these things get spoken. What a little of all we know is said! What drops of all the sea of our science are baled[3] up! and by what accident it is that these are exposed, when so many secrets sleep in nature! Hence the necessity of speech and song; hence these throbs and heart-beatings in the orator, at the door of the assembly, to the end namely that thought may be ejaculated as Logos,[4] or Word.

Doubt not, O poet, but persist. Say 'It is in me, and shall out.' Stand there, balked and dumb, stuttering and stammering, hissed and hooted, stand and strive, until at last rage draw out of thee that *dream*-power which every night shows thee is thine own; a power transcending all limit and privacy, and by virtue of which a man is the conductor of the whole river of electricity. Nothing walks, or creeps, or grows, or exists, which must not in turn arise and walk before him as exponent of his meaning. Comes he to that power, his genius is no longer exhaustible. All the creatures by pairs and by tribes pour into his mind as into a Noah's ark, to come forth again to people a new world. This is like the stock of air for our respiration or for the combustion of our fireplace; not a measure of gallons, but the entire atmosphere if wanted. And therefore the rich poets, as Homer, Chaucer, Shakspeare, and Raphael,[5] have obviously no limits to their works except the limits of their lifetime, and resemble a mirror carried through the street, ready to render an image of every created thing.

O poet! a new nobility is conferred in groves and pastures, and not in castles or by the sword-blade any longer. The conditions are hard, but equal. Thou shalt leave the world, and know the muse only. Thou shalt not know any longer the times, customs, graces, politics, or opinions of men, but shalt take all from the muse. For the time of towns is tolled from the world by funereal chimes, but in nature the universal hours are counted by succeeding tribes of animals and plants, and by growth of joy on joy. God wills also that thou abdicate a manifold and duplex life, and that thou be content that others speak for thee. Others shall be thy gentlemen and shall represent all courtesy and worldly life for thee; others shall do the great and resounding actions also. Thou shalt lie close hid with nature, and canst not be afforded to the Capitol or the Exchange.[6] The world is full of renunciations and apprenticeships, and this is thine; thou must pass for a fool and a churl for a long season. This is the screen and sheath in which Pan[7] has protected his well-beloved flower, and thou shalt be known only to thine own, and they shall console thee with tenderest love. And thou shalt not be able to rehearse the names of thy friends in thy verse, for an old shame before the holy ideal. And this is the reward; that the ideal shall be real to thee, and the impressions of the actual world shall fall like summer rain, copious, but not troublesome to thy invulnerable essence. Thou shalt have the whole land for thy park and manor, the sea for thy bath and navigation, without tax and without envy; the woods and the rivers thou shalt own, and thou shalt possess

2. In Greek myth, the blood of the gods. Emerson may mean nectar, the drink of the gods.
3. Bailed.
4. Word (Greek), the term used in John 1.1: "In the beginning was the word."
5. Raffaello Santi (1483–1520), Italian painter.
6. The stock exchange.
7. Greek god of the woods and fields.

that wherein others are only tenants and boarders. Thou true land-lord! sea-lord! air-lord! Wherever snow falls or water flows or birds fly, wherever day and night meet in twilight, wherever the blue heaven is hung by clouds or sown with stars, wherever are forms with transparent boundaries, wherever are outlets into celestial space, wherever is danger, and awe, and love,—there is Beauty, plenteous as rain, shed for thee, and though thou shouldst walk the world over, thou shalt not be able to find a condition inopportune or ignoble.

1844

EDGAR ALLAN POE
1809–1849

Edgar Allan Poe is a writer most American critics love to hate—or hate to love. In France, on the other hand, Poe has been considered a writer of genius by admirers from CHARLES BAUDELAIRE to JACQUES LACAN. Is this discrepancy a sign that the French lack the finesse in English that the Americans possess? Or does it say something about two very different concepts of poetic language?

The American poet James Russell Lowell wrote in his *Fable for Critics* (1848):

> There comes Poe, with his Raven, like Barnaby Rudge,
> Three fifths of him genius and two fifths sheer fudge,
> Who talks like a book of iambs and pentameters,
> In a way to make people of common sense damn meters,
> Who has written some things quite the best of their kind,
> But the heart somehow seems all squeezed out by the mind.

For American readers, this view of Poe as excessively calculating exists side by side with a view of Poe as completely lacking control: he is seen as either sick (alcoholic, melancholic, necrophilic, impotent) or dissolute (alcoholic, immoral, untrustworthy, untruthful). Was it precisely this combination of craft and transgression that appealed to a poet like Baudelaire? Lowell was certainly right about one thing: genius or madman, visionary or drunk, seer or trickster, excessively in control or excessively out of control, Edgar Allan Poe was not made to please "people of common sense."

Born in Boston to the traveling actors David and Elizabeth Arnold Poe, Edgar lost both his father (who disappeared) and his mother (who died) by his third birthday. Edgar Poe was renamed "Edgar Allan" when he entered the home of the childless Frances and John Allan, although they never legally adopted him. As a self-made prosperous merchant in Richmond, Virginia, John Allan had little in common with his brilliant foster child, and the financial support he gave was always fraught and conditional. Edgar entered the University of Virginia in 1826 (a year after classes began at the college founded by Thomas Jefferson); but in an attempt to supplement his insufficient allowance, he gambled, lost money, and, when John Allan refused to make good the debt, left the university. Enlisting in the army in Boston under the name "Edgar A. Perry," he managed to pursue a double career: as a poet (his first book, *Tamerlane and Other Poems*, was signed "by a Bostonian") and as a military man. He asked for John Allan's financial help in attending the West Point military academy (grudgingly given) and in publishing his second book (denied); Edgar no sooner enrolled than deliberately got himself expelled in 1831 for disobeying orders.

Breaking with John Allan, Poe took up residence in Baltimore with the remnants of the Poe family: his father's mother, his older brother, his paternal aunt Maria Clemm, and her eight-year-old daughter, Virginia (whom he married in 1836, when she was not quite fourteen). He began submitting tales to writing contests and rose through the ranks of the *Southern Literary Messenger*, penning biting book reviews that increased the journal's circulation. His fierce originality and his desire for an American literary tradition not based on the "puffery" by which reviewers were expected to promote all American authors attracted both notice and misgivings: within two years he became the editor of the journal and then, in 1837, was fired. His would-be Southernness and his resentment of the Northern literary coteries through which writer's reputations were usually made gave him little tolerance for Northern ideals. He recoiled against literary didacticism in part out of irritation with the self-satisfactions of Northern abolitionist literature.

In 1838, still shy of his twentieth birthday, Poe wrote and published a novel, *The Narrative of Arthur Gordon Pym*, and collected his *Tales of the Grotesque and Arabesque* a year later. Moving to Philadelphia and then to New York, he was a prolific reviewer for *Graham's Magazine*, the *Broadway Review*, and other journals. He became a popular success for two of his most unlikely feats of writing: his hoax about a balloon journey across the Atlantic and his poem "The Raven." "The Raven" is based on a combination of absurdity and inevitability: a bereaved lover admits a black bird into his chamber on a stormy night and, receiving from the bird an unexpected answer to a question, asks it whether he will ever see his beloved again: the bird can only repeat the same word, "nevermore." The poem was written in 1842; Poe's wife Virginia had just burst a blood vessel while singing and was to die of tuberculosis in 1847. Critics have thus noted the biographical sources of the poem in Poe's anticipated mourning, but Poe tells a very different story about the poem's origins in our selection, "The Philosophy of Composition" (1846).

In demand as a writer and lecturer, Poe attempted to raise money to start a new journal called *The Stylus*, which had been a dream of his since 1843. But he often alienated even those close to him with his intermittent drinking, his nervous depression, his delusions of persecution, and his campaigns against plagiarism (his accusations against Henry Wadsworth Longfellow in particular lost him the friendship of Lowell, for whom Poe's "sheer fudge" probably included false accusations). He died of "congestion of the brain" at age forty.

Fated even beyond the grave to depend on the resources of those who lacked benevolence toward him, Poe owed his negative posthumous reputation to the editorial skills and moral perspectives of his literary executor, Rufus Griswold. Griswold told Poe's story as a cautionary tale fit for a temperance tract: it was a life full of promise, ruined by drink and the lack of a moral compass. With the pathological base of Poe's genius established, the diagnostic strain of American criticism later moved to psychoanalysis: now Poe was not morally bankrupt but mad, a patient etherized upon the table of necrophilia, repetition, and impotence. In 1926 Joseph Wood Krutch published *Edgar Allan Poe: A Study in Genius*, a psychoanalytical study typical of this early phase of Freudian criticism.

But in mid-nineteenth-century France, it was the poets who noticed him. Charles Baudelaire was immediately smitten by the image of a poet rejected and misunderstood in his own country. He translated many of Poe's tales and introduced Poe to a privileged audience quite inclined to find value in whatever the small-minded, puritanical, and mediocre Americans could not understand.

Baudelaire's young admirer, the French poet STÉPHANE MALLARMÉ, who claimed to have learned English only to read Poe, went on to translate the poems, which Baudelaire had largely left untranslated. Baudelaire and Mallarmé found in Poe a theory of poetry that privileged the aesthetic over the moral, the beautiful over the true, and artistic effect over authorial intention. "The Philosophy of Composition," published shortly after the success of "The Raven," is Poe's account of how he composed the poem "backwards" through sheer calculation. Often considered a mystification when read as a *record* of how Poe actually wrote "The Raven," the essay became for Baudelaire and Mallarmé (and later, for ROMAN JAKOBSON, who inherited Poe through the French symbolists) a superb *analysis* of its poetic language. In Poe's explanations, words and even letters—the signifier, not the signified—take the lead in creating the poetic effect. Like the intentionless repetition of a word by a bird made oracular only by the obsessed listener, the network of relations created by words alone is filled with meaning only by the reader. None of the essay's causal explanations can be taken at face value, but what Poe calls the "air of consequence" created by treating effects as causes situates the author's intention in the poem's design rather than in his own experience or sentiment. Which does not, of course, prevent readers from attributing a morbid state of mourning to the author, whose calculations are seen—perhaps rightly—as covering over raw feeling.

In the Freudian Marie Bonaparte's *Life and Works of Edgar Allan Poe* (1933; trans. 1949), the French poetic tradition met the psychoanalytic interpretation, and the status of Poe's poetry was lifted from symptom to dream. Later, in Jacques Lacan's celebrated "Seminar on 'The Purloined Letter' " (1966), Poe the patient was fully promoted to the position of analyst, ingeniously demonstrating, both in that story and in the mechanical repetitions depicted in "The Raven," an understanding of what FREUD would call the "repetition compulsion."

In a way, the two sides of Poe cannot be dissociated. Exploring the vast gap and tension between the unconscious and the intellect, Poe would never have gone so far if he had not known both madness and fabrication. What is seen as Poe's individual pathology, indeed, is often the revelation of aesthetic drives that are usually explained in another way. When Poe proclaims, in "The Philosophy of Composition," that "the death . . . of a beautiful woman is, unquestionably, the most poetical topic in the world," the generalization sounds pathological—until one remembers the many dead women in poetry whose authors cover up their attraction to the image by seeming only to lament it. In his stress on beauty, originality, and intense emotion, Poe is very much part of Romanticism; but in his emphasis on literary technique and construction; on details of meter, rhyme, and sound effects; and on fine calibration of scene, tone, and suspense, he is very much a forerunner of the modernism and its related formalism to come.

BIBLIOGRAPHY

Poe wrote in a surprising variety of literary genres: poems, fantastic tales designed to explore what Freud would call "the uncanny," detective stories (a genre he seems to have invented), novels, reviews, and literary theory. For a good collection of Poe's literary theory and criticism, see the interesting short collection edited by Leonard Cassuto, *Edgar Allan Poe: Literary Theory and Criticism* (1999). For more extensive collections, see the Library of America volume titled *Edgar Allan Poe: Essays and Reviews* (1984), with selections, notes, and a useful chronology by G. R. Thompson. *Literary Criticism of Edgar Allan Poe*, edited by Robert L. Hough (1965), and *Selections from the Critical Writings of Edgar Allan Poe*, edited by F. C. Prescott (1981), are also useful. The most recent full-length biography is Kenneth Silverman's *Edgar Allan Poe: Mournful and Never-Ending Remembrance* (1991). For an appreciation of broader biographical issues, the two essays on the history of Poe biography in *A Companion to Poe Studies* (ed. Eric W. Carlson, 1996) are indispensable, as is *A Poe Log: A Documentary Life of Edgar Allan Poe*, edited by Dwight Thomas and David K. Jackson, (1987).

For a book-length study of Poe's criticism, see Robert D. Jacobs's *Poe: Journalist and Critic* (1969). A good general collection of essays is *Critical Essays on Edgar Allan Poe*, edited by Eric W. Carlson (1987). Recent American work on poetic theory, race, gender, and historical context is found in *The American Face of Edgar Allan Poe*, edited by Shawn Rosenheim and Stephen Rachman (1995), which alludes to the earlier *The French Face of Edgar Allan Poe*, by Patrick Quinn (1954). The texts generated around Jacques Lacan's "Seminar on 'The Purloined Letter' "—authored by Lacan, Jacques Derrida, Barbara Johnson, and others—are collected in *The Purloined Poe* (ed. John P. Muller and William J. Richardson, 1988). And Roman Jakobson's essay on "The Raven" is in his *Language and Literature* (1987). For bibliographies, see J. Lasley Dameron and Irby B. Cauthen Jr., *Edgar Allan Poe: A Bibliography of Criticism, 1827–1967* (1974); Esther Hyneman, *Edgar Allan Poe: An Annotated Bibliography of Books and Articles in English* (1974); and Leona Rasmussen, *Edgar Allan Poe: An Annotated Bibliography* (1978).

The Philosophy of Composition

Charles Dickens, in a note now lying before me, alluding to an examination I once made of the mechanism of "Barnaby Rudge,"[1] says—"By the way, are you aware that Godwin wrote his 'Caleb Williams'[2] backwards? He first involved his hero in a web of difficulties, forming the second volume, and then, for the first, cast about him for some mode of accounting for what had been done."

I cannot think this the *precise* mode of procedure on the part of Godwin—and indeed what he himself acknowledges,[3] is not altogether in accordance with Mr. Dickens' idea—but the author of "Caleb Williams" was too good an artist not to perceive the advantage derivable from at least a somewhat similar process. Nothing is more clear than that every plot, worth the name, must be elaborated to its *dénouement* before any thing be attempted with the pen. It is only with the *dénouement* constantly in view that we can give a plot its indispensable air of consequence, or causation, by making the incidents, and especially the tone at all points, tend to the development of the intention.

There is a radical error, I think, in the usual mode of constructing a story. Either history affords a thesis—or one is suggested by an incident of the day—or, at best, the author sets himself to work in the combination of striking events to form merely the basis of his narrative—designing, generally, to fill in with description, dialogue, or autorial comment, whatever crevices of fact, or action, may, from page to page, render themselves apparent.

I prefer commencing with the consideration of an *effect*. Keeping originality *always* in view—for he is false to himself who ventures to dispense with so obvious and so easily attainable a source of interest—I say to myself, in the first place, "Of the innumerable effects, or impressions, of which the heart, the intellect, or (more generally) the soul is susceptible, what one shall I, on the present occasion, select?" Having chosen a novel, first, and secondly a vivid effect, I consider whether it can best be wrought by incident or tone—whether by ordinary incidents and peculiar tone, or the converse, or by peculiarity both of incident and tone—afterward looking about me (or rather within) for such combinations of event, or tone, as shall best aid me in the construction of the effect.

1. An 1841 novel by Dickens (1812–1870), the most popular English novelist of the 19th century. Published serially, it presents a murder mystery whose solution Poe tried to guess from the early installments.
2. A 1794 novel by the English political theorist William Godwin (1756–1836).
3. In his preface to the 1832 edition.

I have often thought how interesting a magazine paper might be written by any author who would—that is to say, who could—detail, step by step, the processes by which any one of his compositions attained its ultimate point of completion. Why such a paper has never been given to the world, I am much at a loss to say—but, perhaps, the autorial vanity has had more to do with the omission than any one other cause. Most writers—poets in especial—prefer having it understood that they compose by a species of fine frenzy—an ecstatic intuition[4]—and would positively shudder at letting the public take a peep behind the scenes, at the elaborate and vacillating crudities of thought—at the true purposes seized only at the last moment—at the innumerable glimpses of idea that arrived not at the maturity of full view—at the fully matured fancies discarded in despair as unmanageable—at the cautious selections and rejections—at the painful erasures and interpolations—in a word, at the wheels and pinions—the tackle for scene-shifting—the step-ladders and demon-traps—the cock's feathers, the red paint and the black patches, which, in ninety-nine cases out of the hundred, constitute the properties of the literary *histrio*.[5]

I am aware, on the other hand, that the case is by no means common, in which an author is at all in condition to retrace the steps by which his conclusions have been attained. In general, suggestions, having arisen pell-mell, are pursued and forgotten in a similar manner.

For my own part, I have neither sympathy with the repugnance alluded to, nor, at any time, the least difficulty in recalling to mind the progressive steps of any of my compositions; and, since the interest of an analysis, or reconstruction, such as I have considered a *desideratum*, is quite independent of any real or fancied interest in the thing analyzed, it will not be regarded as a breach of decorum on my part to show the *modus operandi* by which some one of my own works was put together. I select "The Raven,"[6] as the most generally known. It is my design to render it manifest that no one point in its composition is referrible either to accident or intuition—that the work proceeded, step by step, to its completion with the precision and rigid consequence of a mathematical problem.

Let us dismiss, as irrelevant to the poem *per se*, the circumstance—or say the necessity—which, in the first place, gave rise to the intention of composing a poem that should suit at once the popular and the critical taste.

We commence, then, with this intention.

The initial consideration was that of extent. If any literary work is too long to be read at one sitting, we must be content to dispense with the immensely important effect derivable from unity of impression—for, if two sittings be required, the affairs of the world interfere, and every thing like totality is at once destroyed. But since, *ceteris paribus*, no poet can afford to dispense with *any thing* that may advance his design, it but remains to be seen whether there is, in extent, any advantage to counterbalance the loss of unity which attends it. Here I say no, at once. What we term a long poem is, in fact, merely a succession of brief ones[7]—that is to say, of brief poetical effects. It is needless to demonstrate that a poem is such, only inasmuch as it intensely excites, by elevating, the soul; and all intense excitements are, through a

4. A critical allusion to RALPH WALDO EMERSON's essay "The Poet" (1844).
5. Actor (Latin).
6. Still Poe's best-known poem (1845).
7. Poe apparently has in mind the long, didactic poems of Henry Wadsworth Longfellow (1807–1882), an immensely popular American poet.

psychal necessity, brief. For this reason, at least one half of the "Paradise Lost"[8] is essentially prose—a succession of poetical excitements interspersed, *inevitably*, with corresponding depressions—the whole being deprived, through the extremeness of its length, of the vastly important artistic element, totality, or unity, of effect.

It appears evident, then, that there is a distinct limit, as regards length, to all works of literary art—the limit of a single sitting—and that, although in certain classes of prose composition, such as "Robinson Crusoe,"[9] (demanding no unity,) this limit may be advantageously overpassed, it can never properly be overpassed in a poem. Within this limit, the extent of a poem may be made to bear mathematical relation to its merit—in other words, to the excitement or elevation—again in other words, to the degree of the true poetical effect which it is capable of inducing; for it is clear that the brevity must be in direct ratio of the intensity of the intended effect:—this, with one proviso—that a certain degree of duration is absolutely requisite for the production of any effect at all.

Holding in view these considerations, as well as that degree of excitement which I deemed not above the popular, while not below the critical, taste, I reached at once what I conceived the proper *length* for my intended poem—a length of about one hundred lines. It is, in fact, a hundred and eight.

My next thought concerned the choice of an impression, or effect, to be conveyed: and here I may as well observe that, throughout the construction, I kept steadily in view the design of rendering the work *universally* appreciable. I should be carried too far out of my immediate topic were I to demonstrate a point upon which I have repeatedly insisted, and which, with the poetical, stands not in the slightest need of demonstration—the point, I mean, that Beauty is the sole legitimate province of the poem.[1] A few words, however, in elucidation of my real meaning, which some of my friends have evinced a disposition to misrepresent. That pleasure which is at once the most intense, the most elevating, and the most pure, is, I believe, found in the contemplation of the beautiful. When, indeed, men speak of Beauty, they mean, precisely, not a quality, as is supposed, but an effect—they refer, in short, just to that intense and pure elevation of *soul*—*not* of intellect, or of heart—upon which I have commented, and which is experienced in consequence of contemplating "the beautiful." Now I designate Beauty as the province of the poem, merely because it is an obvious rule of Art that effects should be made to spring from direct causes—that objects should be attained through means best adapted for their attainment—no one as yet having been weak enough to deny that the peculiar elevation alluded to, is *most readily* attained in the poem. Now the object, Truth, or the satisfaction of the intellect, and the object, Passion, or the excitement of the heart, are, although attainable, to a certain extent, in poetry, far more readily attainable in prose. Truth, in fact, demands a precision, and Passion, a *homeliness* (the truly passionate will comprehend me) which are absolutely antagonistic to that Beauty which, I maintain, is the excitement, or pleasurable elevation, of the

8. Long Christian epic (1667) by the English poet John Milton.
9. A 1719 novel by the English writer Daniel Defoe; because it is episodic, recounting the "Life and adventures" of the title character, it need not be unified.
1. Poe's view of Beauty as universally pleasing was loosely derived from the German philosopher IMMANUEL KANT (1724–1804), probably via the English poet and critic SAMUEL TAYLOR COLERIDGE (1772–1834).

soul. It by no means follows from any thing here said, that passion, or even truth, may not be introduced, and even profitably introduced, into a poem—for they may serve in elucidation, or aid the general effect, as do discords in music, by contrast—but the true artist will always contrive, first, to tone them into proper subservience to the predominant aim, and, secondly, to enveil them, as far as possible, in that Beauty which is the atmosphere and the essence of the poem.

Regarding, then, Beauty as my province, my next question referred to the *tone* of its highest manifestation—and all experience has shown that this tone is one of *sadness*. Beauty of whatever kind, in its supreme development, invariably excites the sensitive soul to tears. Melancholy is thus the most legitimate of all the poetical tones.

The length, the province, and the tone, being thus determined, I betook myself to ordinary induction, with the view of obtaining some artistic piquancy which might serve me as a key-note in the construction of the poem—some pivot upon which the whole structure might turn. In carefully thinking over all the usual artistic effects—or more properly *points*, in the theatrical sense—I did not fail to perceive immediately that no one had been so universally employed as that of the *refrain*. The universality of its employment sufficed to assure me of its intrinsic value, and spared me the necessity of submitting it to analysis. I considered it, however, with regard to its susceptibility of improvement, and soon saw it to be in a primitive condition. As commonly used, the *refrain*, or burden, not only is limited to lyric verse, but depends for its impression upon the force of monotone—both in sound and thought. The pleasure is deduced solely from the sense of identity—of repetition. I resolved to diversify, and so vastly heighten, the effect, by adhering, in general, to the monotone of sound, while I continually varied that of thought: that is to say, I determined to produce continuously novel effects, by the variation *of the application* of the *refrain*—the *refrain* itself remaining, for the most part, unvaried.

These points being settled, I next bethought me of the *nature* of my *refrain*. Since its application was to be repeatedly varied, it was clear that the *refrain* itself must be brief, for there would have been an insurmountable difficulty in frequent variations of application in any sentence of length. In proportion to the brevity of the sentence, would, of course, be the facility of the variation. This led me at once to a single word as the best *refrain*.

The question now arose as to the *character* of the word. Having made up my mind to a *refrain*, the division of the poem into stanzas was, of course, a corollary: the *refrain* forming the close to each stanza. That such a close, to have force, must be sonorous and susceptible of protracted emphasis, admitted no doubt: and these considerations inevitably led me to the long *o* as the most sonorous vowel, in connection with *r* as the most producible consonant.

The sound of the *refrain* being thus determined, it became necessary to select a word embodying this sound, and at the same time in the fullest possible keeping with that melancholy which I had predetermined as the tone of the poem. In such a search it would have been absolutely impossible to overlook the word "Nevermore." In fact, it was the very first which presented itself.

The next *desideratum* was a pretext for the continuous use of the one word "nevermore." In observing the difficulty which I at once found in inventing a sufficiently plausible reason for its continuous repetition, I did not fail to perceive that this difficulty arose solely from the pre-assumption that the word was to be so continuously or monotonously spoken by *a human* being—I did not fail to perceive, in short, that the difficulty lay in the reconciliation of this monotony with the exercise of reason on the part of the creature repeating the word. Here, then, immediately arose the idea of a *non*-reasoning creature capable of speech; and, very naturally, a parrot, in the first instance, suggested itself, but was superseded forthwith by a Raven, as equally capable of speech, and infinitely more in keeping with the intended *tone*.

I had now gone so far as the conception of a Raven—the bird of ill omen—monotonously repeating the one word, "Nevermore," at the conclusion of each stanza, in a poem of melancholy tone, and in length about one hundred lines. Now, never losing sight of the object *supremeness*, or perfection, at all points, I asked myself—"Of all melancholy topics, what, according to the *universal* understanding of mankind, is the *most* melancholy?" Death—was the obvious reply. "And when," I said, "is this most melancholy of topics most poetical?" From what I have already explained at some length, the answer, here also, is obvious—"When it most closely allies itself to *Beauty*: the death, then, of a beautiful woman is, unquestionably, the most poetical topic in the world—and equally is it beyond doubt that the lips best suited for such topic are those of a bereaved lover."

I had now to combine the two ideas; of a lover lamenting his deceased mistress and a Raven continuously repeating the word "Nevermore"—I had to combine these, bearing in mind my design of varying, at every turn, the *application* of the word repeated; but the only intelligible mode of such combination is that of imagining the Raven employing the word in answer to the queries of the lover. And here it was that I saw at once the opportunity afforded for the effect on which I had been depending—that is to say, the effect of the *variation of application*. I saw that I could make the first query propounded by the lover—the first query to which the Raven should reply "Nevermore"—that I could make this first query a commonplace one—the second less so—the third still less, and so on—until at length the lover, startled from his original *nonchalance* by the melancholy character of the word itself—by its frequent repetition—and by a consideration of the ominous reputation of the fowl that uttered it—is at length excited to superstition, and wildly propounds queries of a far different character—queries whose solution he has passionately at heart—propounds them half in superstition and half in that species of despair which delights in self-torture—propounds them not altogether because he believes in the prophetic or demoniac character of the bird (which, reason assures him, is merely repeating a lesson learned by rote) but because he experiences a phrenzied pleasure in so modeling his questions as to receive from the *expected* "Nevermore" the most delicious because the most intolerable of sorrow. Perceiving the opportunity thus afforded me—or, more strictly, thus forced upon me in the progress of the construction—I first established in mind the climax, or concluding query—that to which "Nevermore" should be in the last place an answer—that in reply to which this word "Nevermore" should involve the utmost conceivable amount of sorrow and despair.

Here then the poem may be said to have its beginning—at the end, where all works of art should begin—for it was here, at this point of my preconsiderations, that I first put pen to paper in the composition of the stanza:

"Prophet," said I, "thing of evil! prophet still if bird or devil!
By that heaven that bends above us—by that God we both adore,
Tell this soul with sorrow laden, if within the distant Aidenn.[2]
It shall clasp a sainted maiden whom the angels name Lenore—
Clasp a rare and radiant maiden whom the angels name Lenore."
Quoth the raven "Nevermore."

I composed this stanza, at this point, first that, by establishing the climax, I might the better vary and graduate, as regards seriousness and importance, the preceding queries of the lover—and, secondly, that I might definitely settle the rhythm, the metre, and the length and general arrangement of the stanza—as well as graduate the stanzas which were to precede, so that none of them might surpass this in rhythmical effect. Had I been able, in the subsequent composition, to construct more vigorous stanzas, I should, without scruple, have purposely enfeebled them, so as not to interfere with the climacteric effect.

And here I may as well say a few words of the versification. My first object (as usual) was originality. The extent to which this has been neglected, in versification, is one of the most unaccountable things in the world. Admitting that there is little possibility of variety in mere *rhythm*, it is still clear that the possible varieties of metre and stanza are absolutely infinite—and yet, *for centuries, no man, in verse, has ever done, or ever seemed to think of doing, an original thing*. The fact is, originality (unless in minds of very unusual force) is by no means a matter, as some suppose, of impulse or intuition. In general, to be found, it must be elaborately sought, and although a positive merit of the highest class, demands in its attainment less of invention than negation.

Of course, I pretend to no originality in either the rhythm or metre of the "Raven." The former is trochaic—the latter is octameter acatalectic, alternating with heptameter catalectic[3] repeated in the *refrain* of the fifth verse, and terminating with tetrameter catalectic. Less pedantically—the feet employed throughout (trochees) consist of a long syllable followed by a short: the first line of the stanza consists of eight of these feet—the second of seven and a half (in effect two-thirds)—the third of eight—the fourth of seven and a half—the fifth the same—the sixth three and a half. Now, each of these lines, taken individually, had been employed before, and what originality the "Raven" has, is in their *combination into stanza*; nothing even remotely approaching this combination has ever been attempted. The effect of this originality of combination is aided by other unusual, and some altogether novel effects, arising from an extension of the application of the principles of rhyme and alliteration.

The next point to be considered was the mode of bringing together the lover and the Raven—and the first branch of this consideration was the *locale*. For this the most natural suggestion might seem to be a forest, or the fields—but it has always appeared to me that a close *circumscription of space*

2. Arabic term for paradise, *Adn* (Eden)
3. Lacking a syllable in the last foot (thus a line of 7½ feet, as Poe explains). "Trochaic": based on a metrical foot of the pattern long-short, or stressed-unstressed. "Acatalectic": complete in its syllables (literally, "not catalectic").

is absolutely necessary to the effect of insulated incident:—it has the force of a frame to a picture. It has an indisputable moral power in keeping concentrated the attention, and, of course, must not be confounded with mere unity of place.

I determined, then, to place the lover in his chamber—in a chamber rendered sacred to him by memories of her who had frequented it. The room is represented as richly furnished—this in mere pursuance of the ideas I have already explained on the subject of Beauty, as the sole true poetical thesis.

The *locale* being thus determined, I had now to introduce the bird—and the thought of introducing him through the window, was inevitable. The idea of making the lover suppose, in the first instance, that the flapping of the wings of the bird against the shutter, is a "tapping" at the door, originated in a wish to increase, by prolonging, the reader's curiosity, and in a desire to admit the incidental effect arising from the lover's throwing open the door, finding all dark, and thence adopting the half-fancy that it was the spirit of his mistress that knocked.

I made the night tempestuous, first, to account for the Raven's seeking admission, and secondly, for the effect of contrast with the (physical) serenity within the chamber.

I made the bird alight on the bust of Pallas,[4] also for the effect of contrast between the marble and the plumage—it being understood that the bust was absolutely *suggested* by the bird—the bust of *Pallas* being chosen, first, as most in keeping with the scholarship of the lover, and, secondly, for the sonorousness of the word, Pallas, itself.

About the middle of the poem, also, I have availed myself of the force of contrast, with a view of deepening the ultimate impression. For example, an air of the fantastic—approaching as nearly to the ludicrous as was admissible—is given to the Raven's entrance. He comes in "with many a flirt and flutter."

Not the *least obeisance made he*—not a moment stopped or stayed he,
But with mien of lord or lady, perched above my chamber door.

In the two stanzas which follow, the design is more obviously carried out:—

Then this ebony bird beguiling my sad fancy into smiling
By the *grave and stern decorum of the countenance it wore*,
"Though thy *crest be shorn and shaven* thou," I said, "art sure no craven,
Ghastly grim and ancient Raven wandering from the nightly shore—
Tell me what thy lordly name is on the Night's Plutonian[5] shore!"
Quoth the Raven "Nevermore."

Much I marvelled *this ungainly fowl* to hear discourse so plainly,
Though its answer little meaning—little relevancy bore;
For we cannot help agreeing that no living human being
Ever yet was blessed with seeing bird above his chamber door—
Bird or beast upon the sculptured bust above his chamber door,
With such name as "Nevermore."

---

4. A title of Athena, the Greek goddess of wisdom, the arts, and war.

5. Of or pertaining to Pluto, Roman god of the underworld.

The effect of the *dénouement* being thus provided for, I immediately drop the fantastic for a tone of the most profound seriousness:—this tone commencing in the stanza directly following the one last quoted with the line,

But the Raven, sitting lonely on that placid bust, spoke only, etc.

From this epoch the lover no longer jests—no longer sees any thing even of the fantastic in the Raven's demeanor. He speaks of him as a "grim, ungainly, ghastly, gaunt, and ominous bird of yore," and feels the "fiery eyes" burning into his "bosom's core." This revolution of thought, or fancy, on the lover's part, is intended to induce a similar one on the part of the reader—to bring the mind into a proper frame for the *dénouement*—which is now brought about as rapidly and as *directly* as possible.

With the *dénouement* proper—with the Raven's reply, "Nevermore," to the lover's final demand if he shall meet his mistress in another world—the poem, in its obvious phase, that of a simple narrative, may be said to have its completion. So far, every thing is within the limits of the accountable—of the real. A raven, having learned by rote the single word "Nevermore," and having escaped from the custody of its owner, is driven, at midnight, through the violence of a storm, to seek admission at a window from which a light still gleams—the chamber-window of a student, occupied half in poring over a volume, half in dreaming of a beloved mistress deceased. The casement being thrown open at the fluttering of the bird's wings, the bird itself perches on the most convenient seat out of the immediate reach of the student, who, amused by the incident and the oddity of the visiter's demeanor, demands of it, in jest and without looking for a reply, its name. The raven addressed, answers with its customary word, "Nevermore"—a word which finds immediate echo in the melancholy heart of the student, who, giving utterance aloud to certain thoughts suggested by the occasion, is again startled by the fowl's repetition of "Nevermore." The student now guesses the state of the case, but is impelled, as I have before explained, by the human thirst for self-torture, and in part by superstition, to propound such queries to the bird as will bring him, the lover, the most of the luxury of sorrow, through the anticipated answer "Nevermore." With the indulgence, to the utmost extreme, of this self-torture, the narration, in what I have termed its first or obvious phase, has a natural termination, and so far there has been no overstepping of the limits of the real.

But in subjects so handled, however skilfully, or with however vivid an array of incident, there is always a certain hardness or nakedness, which repels the artistical eye. Two things are invariably required—first, some amount of complexity, or more properly, adaptation; and, secondly, some amount of suggestiveness—some under current, however indefinite of meaning. It is this latter, in especial, which imparts to a work of art so much of that *richness* (to borrow from colloquy a forcible term) which we are too fond of confounding with *the ideal*. It is the *excess* of the suggested meaning—it is the rendering this the upper instead of the under current of the theme—which turns into prose (and that of the very flattest kind) the so called poetry of the so called transcendentalists.[6]

6. A group of 19th-century writers and philosophers in New England; they viewed the individual soul as corresponding directly with the universe (thus eliminating language) and they located the truest source of knowledge in intuition, not experience. Emerson was one of the foremost Transcendentalists.

Holding these opinions, I added the two concluding stanzas of the poem—their suggestiveness being thus made to pervade all the narrative which has preceded them. The under current of meaning is rendered first apparent in the lines—

"Take thy beak from out *my heart*, and take thy form from off my door!"
Quoth the Raven "Nevermore!"

It will be observed that the words, "from out my heart," involve the first metaphorical expression in the poem. They, with the answer, "Nevermore," dispose the mind to seek a moral in all that has been previously narrated. The reader begins now to regard the Raven as emblematical—but it is not until the very last line of the very last stanza, that the intention of making him emblematical of *Mournful and Never-ending Remembrance* is permitted distinctly to be seen:

And the Raven, never flitting, still is sitting, still is sitting,
On the pallid bust of Pallas just above my chamber door;
And his eyes have all the seeming of a demon's that is dreaming,
And the lamplight o'er him streaming throws his shadow on the floor;
And my soul *from out that shadow* that lies floating on the floor
Shall be lifted—nevermore.

1846

THÉOPHILE GAUTIER
1811–1872

"Nothing is really beautiful unless it is useless," proclaims Théophile Gautier in our selection; "everything useful is ugly, for it expresses a need, and the needs of man are ignoble and disgusting, like his poor weak nature. The most useful place in a house is the lavatory."

In his celebrated manifesto of what came to be known as "art for art's sake," Gautier contrasts beauty and need, art and biological life. Art for art's sake had two origins in France. It was a consequence of the French assimilation of IMMANUEL KANT's theory, presented in the *Critique of Judgment* (1790), of the aesthetic as a disinterested, autonomous realm of pure beauty, and it was also a reaction against two very different ways of seeing art in the service of something else: while conservative moralists wanted artists to serve the cause of virtue, progressive liberals, including the Romantic writer Victor Hugo, wanted to enlist art in the cause of social justice. In England poetry was, similarly, dismissed as useless in THOMAS PEACOCK's satirical work "The Four Ages of Poetry" (1820), which PERCY BYSSHE SHELLEY answered in his *Defence of Poetry* (written 1821). Gautier spoke out, in the preface to his 1835 novel *Mademoiselle de Maupin*, against what he perceived as increasing pressure both from the right and from the left to judge art according to its moral or political functions. He brazenly defended the value not of the useful but of the useless, declaring, "I am among those to whom the superfluous is necessary."

Born in 1811 in the south of France, Gautier lived most of his life in Paris, where his father, a minor government official, moved the family in 1814. Remembered now more for his influence (BAUDELAIRE dedicated *Les Fleurs du mal* to him) than for his own works, Gautier nonetheless wrote in many genres—novels, poems, short stories, plays, ballets, literary histories, travel accounts. His fantastic tales (*contes fantastiques*) are still included in studies of that subgenre. He began his career as a member of the bohemian young Romantics and soon became famous for the flamboyant red vest he wore to the opening night of Victor Hugo's controversial play *Hernani* (1830). For almost twenty years he wrote a weekly literary column for the journal *La Presse*; then in 1855 he moved to *Le Moniteur Universel*, the semiofficial newspaper of the Second Empire. At the end of his life, he was no longer trying to "dumbfound the bourgeois" (*épater les bourgeois*) but rather attempting to entertain them with his wit and brilliance. He who had once taken pride in his extravagant nonconformity thus eventually became part of the establishment. He was a member of the salon of Princess Mathilda, Napoleon III's cousin; in 1868 she offered him a sinecure as her librarian. On the money he made from journalism, he supported his father, his two sisters, a son from an early liaison with Eugénie Fort, and his mistress Ernesta Grisi and their two daughters. When the Second Empire was brought to an end in 1871 by defeat in the Franco-Prussian War, Gautier was at a loss to know how to reinvent himself again. His death in 1872 was said to have been hastened by the near-destitution of his family during the Prussian siege of Paris, about which he published *Tableaux de siège* (1871). Thus the poet of sublime superfluity died, ultimately, of want.

Victor Hugo had earlier written a manifesto-by-preface to his unperformable play *Cromwell* (1827), and Gautier considered it to be "the tablets of the law" of Romanticism. The young would-be Romantic took to heart Hugo's call to rehabilitate the aesthetics of the grotesque in literature. In a series of articles he began to publish in 1834 in the journal *La France Littéraire* (later printed as *Les Grotesques*, 1844), he attempted to restore to literary prominence those authors who had been devalued by classical criteria. On the basis of his articles on the poets François Villon (1431–ca. 1463) and Théophile de Viau (1590–1626), he was attacked by an anonymous critic in the semiofficial newspaper of the bourgeois monarchy, *Le Constitutionnel*, for condoning immorality. A legal battle over literary censorship on moral grounds (prefiguring the more famous 1857 trials involving Baudelaire's *Les Fleurs de mal* and Flaubert's *Madame Bovary*) was settled in his favor, but Gautier's brush with the defenders of virtue led to some memorable moments in the preface he was writing to his current novel, *Mademoiselle de Maupin*.

The Romantic editor Eugène Renduel had suggested that Gautier write a novel, based on the life of the seventeeth-century cross-dressing singer and duellist Madeleine de Maupin, who had affairs with both men and women and died repentant at the age of thirty. Inspired by the recent success of historical novels by Sir Walter Scott and Victor Hugo, and expecting a swashbuckling adventure novel with a moral ending, Renduel was dismayed to find instead a lyrical tale of impossible love in the *Mademoiselle de Maupin* that Gautier presented to him.

It is a commonplace of Gautier criticism that the preface to *Mademoiselle de Maupin* has nothing to do with the novel, that it was tacked on simply to fill out the two volumes of the original publication. And indeed, the story of a cross-dressing woman who loves and leaves both the man and the woman who are in love with her appears, at first sight, to be a strange example of art for art's sake. This bisexual love story certainly further estranged Gautier from the defenders of virtue, but it did not immediately seem related to the vigorous defense of superfluity undertaken in his preface. Readers saw the depiction of impossible love as a symptom of Gautier's failed idealism rather than as a demonstration of art for art's sake. Yet the "double love" depicted in the novel is fundamentally, and not just circumstantially, unlivable. It is a love that can exist only in fantasy—or in literature. Thus in his novel as in his preface, Gautier critiques what he sees as a tendency to restrict the literary imagination either to remedies for material need or to moral instructions for living. A dimension of fantasy and play, justified neither by usefulness nor by goodness, is just as necessary to life: it lies in the realm of beauty. In this way, Gautier draws a relation between the superfluity of art and the fundamentally unsatisfiable dimension of desire.

In his later and most famous book of poems, *Emaux et camées* (1852, *Enamels and Cameos*; expanded ed., 1872), Gautier continues to equate poetry with decorative and superfluous luxuries, with craftmanship and intricate carving, with mastery of the difficulties of form. In the poem that stands as his "ars poetica" ("Art," written in 1857 and included in the later edition), he compares poetry to sculpture, exhorting the poet to "sculpt, chisel, and seal a dream into the resistant block." Already in the novel *Mademoiselle de Maupin*, he had claimed: "If there is something noble and fine about loving a statue, it is that your love is quite disinterested, that you need not fear the satiety or weariness of victory." "Disinterested," of course, was Kant's characterization of the nature of aesthetic pleasure. By 1857 Gautier's Romantic rebelliousness had congealed into the kind of "resistance" that material objects offer to artists. He and a number of other poets, calling themselves "Parnassians," turned to the classical world of myth and sculpture for inspiration.

For nineteenth-century French poets, the luxury and superfluity of form was often symbolized by "Oriental" figures: Moroccan arabesques, Chinese pots, Egyptian sphinxes. Gautier's *Enamels and Cameos* opened with the image of Goethe writing his own Orientalist work, the *West-östliche Divan* (1819, *The West-Eastern Divan*), while turning his back on the storm of history swirling around him. The splendid arabesques of Victor Hugo's book of Orientalist poetry, *Les Orientales* (1828), remained an inspiration for Gautier long after Hugo himself had gone on to more political writings.

Like other nineteenth-century French writers, then, Gautier used two privileged symbols of art for art's sake: lesbianism, equated with nonreproductive sexuality (Baudelaire's original title for *Les Fleurs du mal* was *Les Lesbiennes*), and Orientalism, equated with nonrepresentational art. In both cases, the symbol was chosen by European male writers to represent what was *not* bourgeois European patriarchy, and not to champion the rights of women or inhabitants of the East. The idealization of lesbians in art was accompanied by no perceptible diminution in misogyny in real life. And Romantic writers, who used the image of the Orient to highlight what they disliked about Europe, became very much Europeans when they set foot in the real Middle East, as EDWARD SAID makes clear in his critique of Orientalism (see below).

In recent years, Gautier has received a certain amount of attention, most of it negative, from critics who are working from contemporary versions of the very political and moral perspectives that Gautier was opposing. Marxist critics have seen art for art's sake as embodying the worst of formalism and mounting the most bourgeois of rebellions against bourgeois ideology; they assail its supposedly apolitical stance as instead confirming the status quo. Said, in analyzing European Orientalism, also attacks the aestheticizing conception of the Orient as apolitical. For feminists, queer theorists, and critics of sexuality, Gautier's importance is more ambiguous: he may have exploited rather than promoted women's sexual freedom, but whatever its intention, *Mademoiselle de Maupin* has always enjoyed a reputation among adolescents as an underground classic of liberating sexual ambiguity. The debates over the political, moral, and aesthetic function of literature that Gautier discussed in 1835 are still going on today.

BIBLIOGRAPHY

Because Gautier wrote a great deal—travel literature, literary history, art criticism, dance and music reviews, novels and short stories, plays and poetry—and because many of his works were published only in journals, there exists, even in French, no complete works. *Mademoiselle de Maupin*, however, translated by Joanna Richardson

(1981), is readily accessible. A critical edition of the preface in French, George Matoré's *La Préface de Mademoiselle de Maupin* (1946), contains helpful notes. A collection of Gautier's art criticism was translated in 1969 by Michael Clifford Spencer as *The Art Criticism of Théophile Gautier*. His *History of Romanticism* has been translated by Howard Fertig (1988). Joanna Richardson is also the author of the only full-length biography of Gautier (1958), which needs updating.

Enid Starkie's *From Gautier to Eliot: The Influence of France on English Literature, 1851–1939* (1960) was an influential study of Gautier as a proponent of "art for art's sake." There are no critical studies entirely devoted to his aesthetic theory, although many modern critical works contain a few pages of comment on Gautier; see the remarks on his poetry in Jean-Paul Sartre's *What Is Literature?* (1947), on Gautier's travels to the Orient in Edward Said's *Orientalism* (1978), on the French artistic image of the lesbian in Joan de Jean's *Fictions of Sappho, 1546–1937* (1989), and on cross-dressing in Marjorie Garber's *Vested Interests: Cross-Dressing and Cultural Anxiety* (1992). Two short general studies of Gautier deserve note: Richard Grant's *Théophile Gautier* (1975), the most complete general study in English but marred by dated and simplistic interpretations, and P. E. Tennant's *Théophile Gautier* (1975), a much crisper and better short study (with quotations left in French). The most complete bibliography, compiled by Andrew G. Gann and Peter J. Whyte, is published in *A Critical Bibliography of French Literature*, vol. 5 (ed. David Baguley, 1994).

From Preface to *Mademoiselle de Maupin*[1]

One of the most ridiculous things in the glorious epoch which we have the happiness to live in is undoubtedly the rehabilitation of virtue. It is undertaken by every paper, whatever its political hue, red, green, or tricolour.[2]

Virtue is certainly most respectable, and, heaven knows! we shouldn't want to show her disrespect, good and worthy woman that she is! Her eyes are shining through their spectacles, her stockings aren't put on too awry, she takes a pinch from her golden snuff-box with all imaginable grace, and her little dog makes its bow like a dancing-master. All this is true. We even agree that she isn't in too bad a shape for her age, and that she couldn't carry her years better than she does. She is a very agreeable grandmother—but a grandmother she is . . . It seems to me natural, especially when you're twenty, to prefer some immoral little thing who is very sprightly, flirtatious and obliging, with her hair somewhat ruffled, her skirt on the short side, her feet and eyes provocative, her cheeks slightly flushed, a laugh on her lips and her heart on her sleeve. The most monstrously virtuous journalists couldn't be of any other opinion; and, if they say the contrary, it's very probable that they don't think it. To think one thing and to write another happens every day, especially to virtuous people.

I remember the insults which were hurled before the Revolution (I'm talking of the July Revolution)[3] at the unfortunate and virginal Vicomte Sosthène de La Rochefoucauld,[4] who lengthened the dresses of the dancers at the

1. Translated by Joanna Richardson.
2. The red, white, and blue of the French flag (thus representing nationalism and anti-Bourbon sentiment). "Red": the revolutionary color. "Green": the color of a journal called *Vert-Vert* (Green-Green), which was favorable to Gautier.
3. The revolution of 1830 that ended the Bourbon restoration, replacing Charles X (1757–1836) with the "bourgeois king" Louis Philippe (1773–1850).
4. Ultraroyalist (1785–1864) who as director of fine arts in 1824 covered the genitals of statues with fig leaves.

Opéra, and with this patrician hands, stuck a modest plaster on the middle of every statue. M. le Vicomte Sosthène de La Rochefoucauld has been far surpassed. Modesty had been much improved since those days, and we achieve refinements which he wouldn't have imagined.

Personally I am not in the habit of looking at certain parts of statues. Like other people, I found the vine-leaf cut out by the Minister's scissors the most ridiculous thing in the world. Apparently I was wrong, and the vine-leaf is among the most praiseworthy of institutions.

* * *

In spite of all the respect we feel for the modern apostles, we think that the authors of these so-called immoral works,[5] though they aren't as married as the virtuous journalists, very frequently have a mother. Some of them have sisters, and they are provided with an abundant female family. But their mothers and sisters don't read novels, even immoral novels; they sew, embroider and busy themselves with housework. Their stockings, as M. Planard[6] would say, are—absolutely white; you can look at their legs—they are not *blue*, and the good Chrysale, who so hated learned women, would set them up as an example to the learned Philaminte.[7]

I come to the *wives*[8] of these gentlemen, since they have so many of them. However virginal their husbands may be, it seems to me that there are certain things which they ought to know. It may well be that their husbands haven't shown them anything. If so, I understand if they decide to keep them in this precious and blessed ignorance. God is great and Mahomet is his prophet![9] Women are curious; may heaven and morality grant that they satisfy their curiosity in a more legitimate manner than their grandmother, Eve, and not go and ask questions of the Serpent!

As for their daughters, if they have been to a boarding-school, I don't see what these books might teach them.

It is as ridiculous to say that a man is a drunkard because he describes an orgy, a rake because he describes debauchery, as to claim that a man is virtuous because he writes a moral book. Every day one sees the contrary. It is the character who speaks and not the author. His hero is an atheist, that doesn't mean that he himself is an atheist; he makes the brigands act and speak like brigands, he is not a brigand for that reason. At that rate, one would have to guillotine Shakespeare, Corneille, and all the authors of tragedies; they have committed more murders than Mandrin and Cartouche.[1] This has not been done, though, and in fact I don't believe it will be done for a long time, however virtuous and however moral the critics may become. It is one of the manias of these little scribblers with tiny minds, always to

5. That is, contemporary works. Gautier has been discussing the remarkable attentiveness of contemporary guardians of virtue to immorality in modern literature and their remarkable blindness to the immorality of the classical authors (especially Molière) whom they recommend.

6. Eugène de Planard (1783–1855), French dramatist and librettist.

7. Wife of Chrysale in Molière's play *The Learned Ladies* (1672). "Blue": that is, they are not bluestockings (female pedants).

8. In French, *épouses*; for Gautier the term (unlike the more traditional *femmes*) belongs to the hated bourgeois vocabulary of grocers, notaries, and so on.

9. Part of Islamic ritual prayer. Islam was thought to have especially restrictive practices toward women.

1. Louis Mandrin (1725–1755) and Louis-Domingue Cartouche (1693–1721), brigands and folk heroes. On PIERRE CORNEILLE (1606–1684), see above.

substitute the author for the work and to turn to the personality, to give some poor scandalous interest to their wretched rhapsodies. They know quite well that nobody would read them if they just contained their personal opinion.

We can hardly imagine the purpose of all this wrangling, the point of all this raging and baying. We can hardly imagine what pushes the nimble-footed Messrs Geoffroy to make themselves the Don Quixotes of morality,[2] to set themselves up as the policemen of literature, and to apprehend and cudgel, in the name of virtue, every idea which strolls through a book with its mob-cap a little askew or its skirt pulled up a little too high. It is very singular.

Whatever they say, the age is immoral (if that word means anything, which we very much doubt), and we need no proof except the quantity of immoral books that it produces and the success which they enjoy. Books follow manners and manners don't follow books. The Regency made Crébillon,[3] it wasn't Crébillon who made the Regency. The little shepherdesses of Boucher[4] were painted and bare-breasted because the little *marquises* were painted and bare-breasted. Pictures are done from models, and not models from pictures.[5] Someone or other said somewhere or other that literature and the arts had an influence on manners. Whoever it was, he was certainly a great fool. It is as if one said: green peas make the spring grow; green peas grow, on the contrary, because it is the spring, and cherries grow because it is the summer. Trees bear fruit, it is certainly not the fruit that bears the trees, and that is an eternal law, and unchanging in its variety; centuries follow one another, and each one bears its fruit, which is not the fruit of the previous century; books are the fruit of manners.

Beside the moral journalists, under this rain of homilies, as under a summer shower in a park, there has sprung up, between the planks of the Saint-Simonian[6] platform, a series of little mushrooms of a new and rather curious kind, whose natural history we are going to write.

These are the utilitarian critics. Poor people who had such short noses that they couldn't wear spectacles on them, and yet didn't see as far as their noses.

When an author tossed some or other book, novel or poetry, on to their desk—these gentlemen lay back nonchalantly in their armchairs, balanced them on their back legs, and, rocking to and fro with a knowing look, a superior air, they said:

'What is the use of this book? How can one apply it to moralization and to the wellbeing of the largest and poorest class? What! Not a word about the needs of society, nothing civilizing and progressive! How, instead of making the great synthesis of humanity, and following, through the events of history, the phases of regenerating and providential inspiration, how can one produce poems and novels which lead nowhere, and do not advance the present generation along the path to the future? How can one be concerned

2. That is, to act like the impractically idealistic title character of the novel (1605, 1615) by Miguel de Cervantes. Julien-Louis Geoffroy (1743–1814), traditionalist drama critic.

3. Prosper Crébillon (*fils*) (1707–1777), libertine novelist. The Regency: that is, the regency (1715–23) of Philippe II, duc d'Orléans.

4. François Boucher (1703–1770), French rococo painter.

5. Later, Gautier maintained the opposite, writing, "Nature is an invention of painters."

6. Following the philosophy of Claude Henri de Rouvroy, comte de Saint-Simon (1760–1825), a prominent French Utopian protosocialist theorist.

with style and rhyme in the presence of such grave matters? What do we care, ourselves, about style, and rhyme, and form? This is the real question (poor foxes, they are too green[7])! Society is suffering, it is suffering from great inner anguish (in other words, no one wants to subscribe to useful periodicals). It is for the poet to seek the cause of this uneasiness, and cure it. He will find the means by sympathizing, heart and soul, with humanity (philanthropic poets! That would be something rare and delightful). We await this poet and invoke him with all our prayers. When he appears, he will deserve the acclamations of the crowd, the palms, the wreaths, the prytaneum[8] . . . '

Well and good; but as we hope our reader will stay awake till the end of this happy preface, we shall not continue this very faithful imitation of the utilitarian style. By its nature, it is pretty soporific, and it might with advantage replace laudanum and academic speeches.

No, imbeciles, no, idiotic and goitrous creatures that you are, a book does not make jellied soup; a novel is not a pair of seamless boots; a sonnet, a syringe with a continuous spurt; a drama is not a railway, though all these things are essentially civilizing, and they advance humanity along the path of progress.

By the bowels of all the Popes, past, present and future, no, and two hundred thousand times no!

You don't make yourself a cotton cap out of a metonymy, you don't put on a comparison instead of a slipper; you can't use an antithesis as an umbrella; unfortunately you couldn't lay a few multicoloured rhymes on your stomach by way of a waistcoat. I have a deep conviction that an ode is too light an apparel for the winter, and that one wouldn't be better dressed with a strophe, an antistrophe and epode,[9] than the cynic's wife who contented herself with her virtue alone for shift, and went about stark naked, so the story goes.

However, the celebrated M. de La Calprenède[1] once had a coat, and, when someone asked him what it was made of, he answered: Silvandre. *Silvandre* was a play that he had just had successfully performed.

Such reasoning makes one shrug one's shoulders above one's head, and higher than the Duke of Gloucester.[2]

People who claim to be economists, and want to rebuild society from top to bottom, seriously suggest such nonsense.

A novel has two uses: one is material, the other spiritual, if you can use that expression about a novel. The material use is, for a start, the several thousand francs which go into the author's pocket, and ballast him so that the wind or the devil doesn't bear him away; for the publisher it is a fine thoroughbred horse which paws the ground and trots in front of his cabriolet of steel and ebony, as Figaro says.[3] For the paper-merchant, the material use is another factory on another stream, and often the means of spoiling a fine site; for the printers, it is a few barrels of logwood, to colour their gullets

7. A reference to Aesop's fable, retold by Jean de La Fontaine (1621–1695), in which the fox dismissed the ripe grapes that were out of reach as "too green."
8. Greek town hall.
9. The three stanza forms that make up a Pindaric ode.
1. Gauthier de Coste, sieur de La Calprenède (1610–1633), French playwright and novelist.
2. The future Richard III, portrayed in plays by Shakespeare and Casimir Delavigne (1793–1843) as a hunchback.
3. The newspaper *Figaro* had earlier printed this description of Eugène Renduel, the publisher of *Mademoiselle de Maupin*.

every week; for the reading-room, a heap of coppers, covered with very proletarian verdigris, and a quantity of grease which, if it were duly collected and used, would make whale-fishing superfluous. The spiritual use of novels is that, while people read them, they sleep, and don't read useful, virtuous and progressive periodicals, or other similar indigestible and stupefying drugs.

Let people say after this that novels don't contribute to civilization. I shan't talk about tobacconists, grocers, and sellers of fried potatoes; they have a very great interest in this branch of literature, since the paper it's printed on is generally of superior quality to that of the newspapers.[4]

It is really enough to make one laugh fit to burst, just to listen to the utilitarian republicans or Saint-Simonians. I should very much like, for a start, to know exactly what it means, this great gawky noun with which they stuff the emptiness of their columns every day, the noun which serves as a shibboleth[5] and a sacramental expression. Utility: what does the word mean, and what do we apply it to?

There are two kinds of utility, and the meaning of the term is always relative. What is useful for one is not useful for another. You are a cobbler, I am a poet. It is useful for me that my first line rhymes with my second. A rhyming dictionary is very useful to me; it is no use to you, except to cobble an old pair of boots, and it's fair to say that a shoemaker's knife wouldn't help me very much to make an ode. You will now object that a cobbler is much above a poet, and that people can more easily do without one than without the other. I have no wish to disparage the illustrious profession of cobbler, which I honour as much as the profession of constitutional monarch, but I humbly admit that I should rather have my shoe unsewn than my line ill-rhymed, and that I'd rather do without shoes than do without poetry. As I hardly ever go out, and walk more skilfully on my head than I do on my feet, I wear out fewer shoes than a virtuous republican who does nothing but run from one ministry to another to have some appointment thrown to him.

I know that there are those who prefer mills to churches, and the bread of the body to that of the soul. To them, I have nothing to say. They deserve to be economists in this world, and in the next.

Is there anything absolutely useful on this earth and in this life which we are living? To begin with, there is very little use in our being on earth and being alive. I defy the most learned of the company to say what purpose we serve, unless it is not to subscribe to *Le Constitutionnel*[6] or to any kind of paper whatever.

And then, if we admit *a priori* the usefulness of our existence, what do we really need to maintain it? Soup and a bit of meat twice a day is all we need to fill our stomachs, in the strict sense of the word. A coffin two feet wide and six feet long is more than enough for man after his death; he does not need a much larger space in his lifetime. A hollow cube seven or eight feet square, with a hole to breathe through, a single cell in the hive, that is all he needs for lodging and for shelter from the rain. A blanket, suitably rolled

4. Better-quality paper made better wrapping for their commodities.
5. Password. In Judges 12.5–6, the inability of Ephraimites to pronounce the word *shibboleth* betrayed them to their enemies, the Gileadites.
6. A journal (the semiofficial newspaper of the constitutional monarchy) that had attacked Gautier for promoting immorality.

round the body, will protect him as well as—and better than—the most elegant and the best-cut frock-coat from Straub's.[7]

With that, he will be able literally to subsist. They say in fact that one can live on twenty-five sous a day; but preventing oneself from dying is not living; and I don't see how a town which is planned for its usefulness would be pleasanter to live in than Père-Lachaise.[8]

Nothing beautiful is indispensable to life. If you suppressed the roses, the world would not materially suffer; yet who would wish there were an end of flowers? I would rather give up potatoes than roses, and I believe that there is only one utilitarian in the universe who could tear up a bed of tulips to plant cabbages.

What is the use of women's beauty? Provided that a woman is physically well formed, and that she is capable of bearing children, she will always be enough for economists.

What is the use of music? What is the use of painting? Who would be mad enough to prefer Mozart to M. Carrel, and Michelangelo to the inventor of white mustard?[9]

Nothing is really beautiful unless it is useless; everything useful is ugly, for it expresses a need, and the needs of man are ignoble and disgusting, like his poor weak nature. The most useful place in a house is the lavatory.

For myself—and I hope it does not displease these gentlemen—I am among those to whom the superfluous is necessary—and I prefer things and people in the inverse ratio to the services that they perform for me. I prefer to a certain useful pot a Chinese pot which is sprinkled with mandarins and dragons, a pot which is no use to me at all, and the talent of mine which I most esteem is guessing logogriphs and charades.[1] I should most joyfully renounce my rights as a Frenchman and as a citizen to see an authentic picture by Raphael, or a beautiful woman naked: Princess Borghese, for example, when she has posed for Canova, or Julia Grisi,[2] when she enters the bath. I should very readily agree, myself, to the return of that cannibal, Charles X, if he brought me back a hamper of Tokay or Johannisberg from his castle in Bohemia,[3] and I should find the electoral laws broad enough, if some streets were wider, and other things less wide. I was not born a dilettante, but I prefer the sound of screeching fiddles and tambourines to that of the President's little bell.[4] I should sell my trousers to have a ring, and my bread for jam. The most becoming occupation for a civilized man seems to me to be inactivity, or cogitating as one smokes one's pipe or cigar. I also have much esteem for those who play skittles, and those who write good verses. As you see, the utilitarian principles are far from being mine, and I shall never be editor of a virtuous paper, unless I am converted, which would be rather funny.

7. A celebrated society tailor.
8. A Parisian cemetery.
9. That is, to prefer great artists—the Austrian composer Wolfgang Amadeus Mozart (1756–1791) and the Italian painter and sculptor Michelangelo Buonarroti (1475–1564)—to purveyors of utility such as the Republican journalist Armand Carrel (1800–1836) and the inventor of white mustard (thought to have medicinal properties).
1. Two word games.
2. An opera singer (one of three musical sisters in Gautier's life; he idealized Julia and Carlotta, and later lived with the third, Ernesta). Raffaello Santi (1483–1520), Italian painter. Princess Pauline Borghese: Napoleon's sister, who modeled for the Italian sculptor Antonio Canova (1757–1822) in 1807.
3. Charles X fled first to Scotland and then to Prague. Tokay and Johannisberg are both wines from Central Europe.
4. Used to call a session of government to order.

Instead of creating a *prix Monthyon* as a reward for virtue, I should prefer, like Sardanapalus,[5] that great philosopher who has been so misunderstood, to give a handsome prize to the man who invented a pleasure—for enjoyment seems to me to be the end of life, and the only useful thing in the world. God has willed it so, He who created women, perfumes and light, lovely flowers, good wines, lively horses, greyhounds and angora cats: He who said not to His angels 'Be virtuous', but 'Be loving', He who has given us a mouth more responsive than the rest of our skin so that we may kiss women, eyes looking upwards that we may see the light, a subtle sense of smell to draw in the souls of flowers, strong thighs to grip the flanks of stallions and fly as swift as thought without railways or steam-boilers, sensitive hands to caress the long heads of greyhounds, the velvet backs of cats, and the satin shoulders of creatures of little virtue, and Who, in short, has given us alone the triple and glorious privilege of drinking without thirst, of striking light, and of making love in every season, which distinguishes us from the brute far more than the habit of reading papers and making charters.

My God! What a stupid thing it is, this so-called perfectibility[6] of the human race! I am sick and tired of hearing about it. You would really think that man was a machine which could be improved, and that a cog which was better engaged, a counterweight more appropriately placed, could make it work in an easier and more convenient way. When they come to giving a double stomach to man, so that he can ruminate like an ox, eyes on the other side of his head so that, like Janus,[7] he can see those who put out their tongues at him behind his back, and contemplate his *indignity* in a less uncomfortable position than that of the Callipygian Venus[8] in Athens when they fix wings on his shoulderblades so that he is not obliged to pay six sous to go by omnibus; when they have created a new organ for him, then well and good! The word *perfectibility* will begin to mean something.

* * *

1835

5. Legendary king of Assyria (by tradition, d. 817 B.C.E.), notorious for hedonism and luxury, who had recently been treated in Lord Byron's tragedy *Sardanapalus* (1821) and Eugène Delacroix's painting *The Death of Sardanapalus* (1827). *Prix Monthyon*: one in a series of annual prizes for virtue and public utility, distributed by the French Academy, that were founded in 1780 by the philanthropist Baron Monthyon (1733–1820).

6. A word made famous in political theories of human progress.

7. Roman god of doors and beginnings, represented with a double-faced head.

8. A statue depicting the goddess looking over her shoulder at her own buttocks (thus the name *callipygian*, "having beautiful buttocks"). A Roman copy of a Greek original, it was found not in Athens but Naples; there is a copy at Versailles.

KARL MARX 1818–1883 / FRIEDRICH ENGELS 1820–1895

Karl Marx and Friedrich Engels are central figures in the history of literary criticism and theory and in the development of cultural studies, though neither produced a body of literary-critical work. The young Marx wrote lyrics, attempted drama and fiction, and read deeply in eighteenth- and nineteenth-century German philosophy and aesthetics, and the writings of Marx and Engels often refer to and quote literature (ranging from classical Greek drama to the novels of Charles Dickens). But as economic historians, social theorists, and revolutionaries seeking to change the world, their main work lay elsewhere, and their direct contributions to literary criticism are scattered, uneven, and generally meager. Yet perhaps that incompleteness makes their comments and observations about literature and criticism all the more suggestive, giving a long line of twentieth-century writers—including GYÖRGY LUKÁCS, Bertolt Brecht, WALTER BENJAMIN, GAYATRI SPIVAK, and FREDRIC JAMESON—much speculative and interpretive leeway in developing their own Marxist theories of literature.

To many it may seem perverse to study Marxist theory today, given the collapse between 1989 and 1991 of Communist governments in the Soviet Union and in the nations of Eastern Europe. But we must clearly distinguish between Marx and Engels as social theorists, philosophers, historians, and cultural critics and as revolutionaries—or, more accurately, as revolutionaries under whose name Communist leaders and parties seized power. The fall of particular regimes, "Marxist" more in name than in ideas, does little to lessen the impact of Marx's relentless, fascinated, shocked (and shocking) examination of capitalism and its costs to the men and women caught in its grasp. In brilliant passages such as our selection from *Capital* (1867) on the working day, his skillfully modulated prose can be powerfully moving.

For literary and cultural criticism, the seminal passage by Marx appears in his preface to *A Contribution to the Critique of Political Economy* (1858–59, excerpted below). Here Marx emphasizes that he is concerned primarily with the "material conditions of life," the "economic structure of society." On this "foundation . . . rises a legal and political superstructure"; moreover, "The mode of production of material life conditions the social, political and intellectual life process in general. It is not the consciousness of men that determines their being, but, on the contrary, their social being that determines their consciousness." This formulation raises a number of questions: To what *degree* is consciousness socially and economically "determined"? What is the role of human agency? How closely connected are the base and the superstructure, and can the latter—which includes intellectual work and cultural institutions—affect the former?

The answers of Marx and Engels waver. As a famous passage (excerpted below) from the *Grundrisse* (1857–58, *Foundations* or *Outlines*) suggests, Marx found it difficult to explain the relationship between Greek art and the society within which it arose; his argument is hurried and unpersuasive. Engels, too, recognized the limitations of the base/superstructure model. In a letter to Joseph Bloch (our final selection), Engels maintains that "According to the materialist conception of history, the *ultimately* determining element in history is the production and reproduction of real life," insisting that economics is not the only determinant and leaving room for the influence of "human minds."

Marx was born in Trier, Prussia (a region now part of Germany), the son of a Jewish lawyer who had converted to Protestantism to protect his job. Marx studied at the universities of Bonn, Berlin, and Jena, receiving his doctorate in April 1841 for a thesis on the Greek philosophers Democritus and Epicurus. In 1842 he edited a radical newspaper in Cologne, but the German authorities, angered by his criticisms, forced him to resign in 1843. He then traveled to Paris, where he and Engels, whom he had met in Cologne, began their collaboration. Engels, born in Barmen, in western Germany, was the son of a wealthy textile manufacturer; in the 1840s, he managed a factory in England that his father owned, and his horror at the harsh economic and social conditions in Manchester led him to write *The Condition of the Working Class in England in 1844* (1845). Engels later said that as he and Marx worked together in Paris, their "agreement in all theoretical fields became obvious."

Marx and Engels's joint work in the 1840s includes *The Holy Family* (1845) and *The German Ideology* (not published until 1932). In these texts, and in Marx's polemical pamphlet *The Poverty of Philosophy* (1847), they sought to prove that economic and social forces shape human consciousness. This materialism was meant to displace the idealist view that human consciousness shapes economic and social forms. They based their interpretation of reality on *dialectical materialism*, believing that all change results from the constant conflict arising from the oppositions inherent in all ideas, movements, and events. They further argued that the internal tensions and contradictions in capitalism would lead inevitably to its demise.

Also important are Marx's writings collected in *Economic and Philosophic Manuscripts of 1844* (1932; trans. 1959), which contain much of his most passionate, incisive thinking about industrial conditions and the nature of consciousness under capitalism and present an excellent entry point into Marxist cultural analysis. Building on the work of the German philosopher Ludwig Feuerbach, author of *The Essence of Christianity* (1841), Marx is especially concerned here with the origin and impact of alienation. The industrial capitalist economy, says Marx, "alienates" individuals from the work that they do; unable to control their own labor, which they must "give" (sell) to another, they lack control and knowledge of themselves and never achieve their full human potential. However much they resent their situation, they believe—that is, they are conditioned to believe—that it cannot be changed, and that ultimately they have only themselves to blame for their discontent and failures.

Marx and Engels's most significant publication of the decade appeared in London in 1848: *Manifesto of the Communist Party* (soon known by and reprinted with the shorter title *The Communist Manifesto*). In this intense pamphlet Marx (who did the bulk of the writing) describes the triumphs of capitalism; the creation of a world market, world literature, and cosmopolitanism; the misery that capitalism imposes on the masses; the class struggle between the exploiters (owners) and the exploited (workers); the connection of people primarily via cash; the inevitability of revolution; and the dawn of a new, class-free society. Though specifically commissioned to state the principles and objectives of the Communist League (a secret organization composed primarily of German émigrés), it quickly became the position paper of militant working-class movements everywhere.

Because of his political writing and activity, Marx was expelled from both France and Germany in the late 1840s; in May 1849 he settled with his family in London. There, supported by Engels but nonetheless often in poverty, he resided for the remainder of his life. His major works during these decades are the *Grundrisse*, a manuscript of some 800 printed pages (1857–58, published 1939–41); the multivolume *Theories of Surplus Value* (1860s, published 1905–10); and above all *Das Kapital*, volume 1 of which appeared in 1867 (trans. 1886), with volumes 2 and 3, edited by Engels, published posthumously in 1885 and 1894 (trans. 1907, 1909). Marx also wrote many articles for newspapers in the United States and Europe. Engels's writings include *Herr Eugen Dühring's Revolution in Science* (1878, usually referred to as *Anti-Dühring*), parts of which later appeared as a summary of the basics of socialism titled *Socialism: Utopian and Scientific* (1892); *The Origin of the Family, Private Property, and the State* (1884); and *Dialectics of Nature* (1925).

The literary theorist and critic reading Marx and Engels may raise questions that the texts do not answer. What roles do writers, critics, and intellectuals play? Do they illuminate for workers the nature of capitalist exploitation, or instead act at the service of those who already and best understand their true circumstances? Should writers be free to state the social and political facts as they see them, or must the goal of working-class revolution always shape their work—and if so, who sets the limits?

Marx has one simple but powerful reply: the answers will come only when the contradictions within capitalism produce them. Capitalism has no remedy for the worst social and economic problems that it creates and that will eventually rend it asunder. Marx is certain that capitalism will end, and why: but no one can know exactly what the roles of intellectuals and critics will be, and what the new society will look like, until the force of historical necessity brings them into being.

Meanwhile, Marxist critics have work to perform, practicing a discipline linked to the goal of radical social change. Thus they must approach literature, literary education, criticism, and theory as integral parts of economic and social life. In *The German Ideology*, as our selection indicates, Marx and Engels emphasize that we must study *real* men and women and *real* processes, not what has typically been said or thought by and about them.

Marx thus promotes "ideology critique," that is, the demystifying exposure of how class interests really operate through cultural forms, whether political or legal, religious or philosophical, educational or literary. It is the nature of ideology to conceal the reality of class struggle from our perception and consciousness; and insofar as working-class people unconsciously absorb bourgeois values, they are unwitting carriers of "false consciousness."

The term *ideology* rarely appears in Marx's *Grundrisse* and *Capital*, but it is implicit in many of Marx's formulations of the difference between the surface and reality of capitalist society. Marxist critics are expected to investigate the systemic masking of the real methods and consequences of existing socioeconomic arrangements. Sometimes, however, Marx uses the term differently, as when he declares in *A Contribution to the Critique of Political Economy* that we grow aware of and fight the conflict between classes in "ideological forms."

Later Marxists have developed both the positive and negative senses of ideology. One dominant line of inquiry follows from the writings of ANTONIO GRAMSCI, who in his *Prison Notebooks* (published 1945–75) describes ideology as "the terrain on which men move, acquire consciousness of their position, struggle, etc."; he explores how a privileged social class can achieve cultural "hegemony," the manufactured assent to its beliefs and practices won peacefully through ideology. This concept of hegemony, developed by the British Marxist RAYMOND WILLIAMS (especially in *Marxism and Literature*, 1977) and by those he has influenced (notably STUART HALL and DICK HEBDIGE) has become fundamental to cultural studies. Critics use it in studying classic texts, the relationships and differences between canonical and noncanonical literature, popular culture, the media, education, and publishing—all outlets for ideology.

The power of ideology to mask and obscure is also at work in what Marx calls "the fetishism of commodities," which he discusses in our first selection from *Capital*. Under capitalism, human relations are increasingly characterized by more or less thoroughgoing alienation, monetization, and commodification. Relationships between workers and owners, buyers and sellers, are mediated through the things produced. These commodities become objects of fetishism—seeming to have an objective existence of their own that obscures the individual labor involved in their production. By being exchanged, they acquire a seemingly inherent value distinct from their use value or physical properties.

As a social and cultural theory, Marxism demands of its followers ongoing critical scrutiny and self-questioning of its own basic texts, which are richly suggestive but sometimes flawed and often incomplete. Marx and Engels underestimated, for example, the extraordinary power of capitalism to turn back and absorb opposition, and apparently they overlooked the damaging overstatements and reductiveness that mar their arguments. Moreover, though Marx was acutely responsive to the economic and political situation of workers, he appears incapable of actually seeing and making imaginative contact with them and their families, of conveying how they live, think, and feel. Even in his most illuminating work, Marx often mirrors the dehumanizing tendencies that his radical critiques of capitalism condemn. Individuals matter most to him as embodiments of ideas, as components of systems—a form of thinking that the best novelists of his time, such as Dickens and Balzac, brilliantly exposed and corrected.

On the "material conditions of life" and the "economic structure of society," Marx and Engels are sharp and compelling; on the subject of the creative and critical consciousness of persons and cultures, they falter. For foundational Marxist interpretations of cultural life, one must look instead to the work of such later theorists and critics as W. E. B. DU BOIS, EDMUND WILSON (in his writings of the 1930s), THEODOR ADORNO, C. L. R. James, and Raymond Williams. They built upon but went beyond the insights that Marx and Engels provide, and their critical projects drew directly from the literary texts and cultural traditions that Marx and Engels admired but never fully engaged.

BIBLIOGRAPHY

The fifty-volume English translation of the collected works of Marx and Engels, *Karl Marx, Frederick Engels: Collected Works* (1975–), is nearing completion. The best single-volume editions are David McLellan's *Karl Marx: Selected Writings* (1977) and Robert C. Tucker's *Marx-Engels Reader* (2d ed., 1978). For Marx's letters, see *Correspondence*, edited by Saul K. Padover (1979). Helpful introductions to Marx's life and writings include David McLellan, *Karl Marx: His Life and Thought* (1973); Isaiah Berlin, *Karl Marx: His Life and Environment* (4th ed., 1978); and Francis Wheen, *Karl Marx* (1999). On Engels, see Steven Marcus, *Engels, Manchester, and the Working Class* (1974), an excellent work of cultural history; W. O. Henderson, *The Life of Friedrich Engels* (1976); Terrell Carver, *Engels* (1981), a good overview; and Carver, *Marx and Engels: The Intellectual Relationship* (1983).

There is a vast secondary literature on Marx and Engels's views on literature and criticism and on the long line of theorists and critics who belong to the Marxist tradition. Essay collections provide a good starting point: see *Radical Perspectives in the Arts*, edited by Lee Baxandall (1972); *Marxism and Art: Writings in Aesthetics and Criticism*, edited by Berel Lang and Forrest Williams (1972); *Marxism and Art: Essays Classic and Contemporary*, edited by Maynard Solomon (1973); *Karl Marx and Frederick Engels on Literature and Art: A Selection of Writings*, edited by Lee Baxandall and Stefan Morawski (1974); and *Marxists on Literature: An Anthology*, edited by David Craig (1975). More up-to-date are *Contemporary Marxist Literary Criticism*, edited by Francis Mulhern (1992), and *Marxist Literary Theory: A Reader*, edited by Terry Eagleton and Drew Milne (1996). See also *Aesthetics and Politics*, edited by Ernst Bloch (1977), and *Marxism and the Interpretation of Culture*, edited by Cary Nelson and Lawrence Grossberg (1988).

On the history of Marx and Engels's interest in and response to literature, Peter Demetz's *Marx, Engels, and the Poets: Origins of Marxist Literary Criticism* (1967) and S. S. Prawer's *Karl Marx and World Literature* (1976) are informative. A concise and popular survey of Marxist literary criticism is Terry Eagleton, *Marxism and Literary Criticism* (1976). Tony Bennett, *Formalism and Marxism* (1979), deals well with Russian formalism and Marxist theory and criticism; and Fredric Jameson, *Marxism and Form: Twentieth-Century Dialectical Theories of Literature* (1971), examines several leading twentieth-century intellectuals influenced by Marx's writings. In *The Ideology of the Aesthetic* (1990) and *Ideology: An Introduction* (1991), Eagleton studies the meanings and implications of two key terms in Marxist criticism, *ideology* and *aesthetics*.

On the relationships between Marxism and recent theories of literature and criticism, consult Michael Ryan, *Marxism and Deconstruction: A Critical Articulation* (1982); John Frow, *Marxism and Literary History* (1986); and Scott Wilson, *Cultural Materialism: Theory and Practice* (1995). Dated but worth consulting are Lee Baxandall, *Marxism and Aesthetics: A Selective Annotated Bibliography* (1968), and Chris Bullock and David Peck, *Guide to Marxist Literary Criticism* (1980).

From Economic and Philosophic Manuscripts of 1844[1]

* * *

We have proceeded from the premises of political economy.[2] We have accepted its language and its laws. We presupposed private property, the separation of labour, capital and land, and of wages, profit of capital and rent of land—likewise division of labour, competition, the concept of exchange-value, etc. On the basis of political economy itself, in its own words, we have shown that the worker sinks to the level of a commodity and becomes indeed the most wretched of commodities;[3] that the wretchedness of the worker is in inverse proportion to the power and magnitude of his production; that the necessary result of competition is the accumulation of capital in a few hands, and thus the restoration of monopoly in a more terrible form; that finally the distinction between capitalist and land-rentier,[4] like that between the tiller of the soil and the factory-worker, disappears and that the whole of society must fall apart into the two classes—the property-*owners* and the propertyless *workers*.

Political economy proceeds from the fact of private property, but it does not explain it to us. It expresses in general, abstract formulae the *material* process through which private property actually passes, and these formulae it then takes for *laws*. It does not *comprehend* these laws—i.e., it does not demonstrate how they arise from the very nature of private property. Political economy does not disclose the source of the division between labour and capital, and between capital and land. When, for example, it defines the relationship of wages to profit, it takes the interest of the capitalists to be the ultimate cause; i.e., it takes for granted what it is supposed to evolve. Similarly, competition comes in everywhere. It is explained from external circumstances. As to how far these external and apparently fortuitous circumstances are but the expression of a necessary course of development, political economy teaches us nothing. We have seen how, to it, exchange itself appears to be a fortuitous fact. The only wheels which political economy sets in motion are *avarice* and the *war amongst the avaricious—competition*.

Precisely because political economy does not grasp the connections within the movement, it was possible to counterpose, for instance, the doctrine of competition to the doctrine of monopoly, the doctrine of craft-liberty to the doctrine of the corporation, the doctrine of the division of landed property to the doctrine of the big estate—for competition, craft-liberty and the division of landed property were explained and comprehended only as fortuitous, premeditated and violent consequences of monopoly, the corporation, and feudal property, not as their necessary, inevitable and natural consequences.

Now, therefore, we have to grasp the essential connection between private property, avarice, and the separation of labour, capital and landed property; between exchange and competition, value and the devaluation of men,

1. Translated by Martin Milligan.
2. The 19th-century social science concerned with the relations between political and economic processes (now often separated into political science and economics).
3. Because labor itself is sold to others, and at a very low price.
4. One who lives on income from land, stocks, or bonds.

monopoly and competition, etc.; the connection between this whole estrangement and the *money*-system.

Do not let us go back to a fictitious primordial condition as the political economist does, when he tries to explain. Such a primordial condition explains nothing. He merely pushes the question away into a grey nebulous distance. He assumes in the form of fact, of an event, what he is supposed to deduce—namely, the necessary relationship between two things—between, for example, division of labour and exchange. Theology in the same way explains the origin of evil by the fall of man: that is, it assumes as a fact, in historical form, what has to be explained.

We proceed from an *actual* economic fact.

The worker becomes all the poorer the more wealth he produces, the more his production increases in power and range. The worker becomes an ever cheaper commodity the more commodities he creates. With the *increasing value* of the world of things proceeds in direct proportion the *devaluation* of the world of men. Labour produces not only commodities; it produces itself and the worker as a *commodity*—and does so in the proportion in which it produces commodities generally.

This fact expresses merely that the object which labour produces—labour's product—confronts it as *something alien*, as a *power independent* of the producer. The product of labour is labour which has been congealed in an object, which has become material: it is the *objectification* of labour. Labour's realization is its objectification. In the conditions dealt with by political economy this realization of labour appears as *loss of reality* for the workers; objectification as *loss of the object* and *object-bondage*; appropriation as *estrangement*, as *alienation*.

So much does labour's realization appear as loss of reality that the worker loses reality to the point of starving to death. So much does objectification appear as loss of the object that the worker is robbed of the objects most necessary not only for his life but for his work. Indeed, labour itself becomes an object which he can get hold of only with the greatest effort and with the most irregular interruptions. So much does the appropriation of the object appear as estrangement that the more objects the worker produces the fewer can he possess and the more he falls under the dominion of his product, capital.

All these consequences are contained in the definition that the worker is related to the *product of his labour* as to an *alien* object. For on this premise it is clear that the more the worker spends himself, the more powerful the alien objective world becomes which he creates over-against himself, the poorer he himself—his inner world—becomes, the less belongs to him as his own. It is the same in religion. The more man puts into God, the less he retains in himself. The worker puts his life into the object; but now his life no longer belongs to him but to the object. Hence, the greater this activity, the greater is the worker's lack of objects. Whatever the product of his labour is, he is not. Therefore the greater this product, the less is he himself. The *alienation* of the worker in his product means not only that his labour becomes an object, an *external* existence, but that it exists *outside him*, independently, as something alien to him, and that it becomes a power of its own confronting him; it means that the life which he has conferred on the object confronts him as something hostile and alien.

Let us now look more closely at the *objectification*, at the production of the worker; and therein at the *estrangement*, the *loss* of the object, his product.

The worker can create nothing without *nature*, without the *sensuous external world*. It is the material on which his labor is manifested, in which it is active, from which and by means of which it produces.

But just as nature provides labor with the *means of life* in the sense that labour cannot *live* without objects on which to operate, on the other hand, it also provides the *means of life* in the more restricted sense—i.e., the means for the physical subsistence of the *worker* himself.

Thus the more the worker by his labour *appropriates* the external world, sensuous nature, the more he deprives himself of *means of life* in the double respect: first, that the sensuous external world more and more ceases to be an object belonging to his labour—to be his labour's *means of life*; and secondly, that it more and more ceases to be *means of life* in the immediate sense, means for the physical subsistence of the worker.

Thus in this double respect the worker becomes a slave of his object, first, in that he receives an *object of labour*, i.e., in that he receives *work*; and secondly, in that he receives *means of subsistence*. Therefore, it enables him to exist, first, as a *worker*; and, second, as a *physical subject*. The extremity of this bondage is that it is only as a *worker* that he continues to maintain himself as a *physical subject*, and that it is only as a *physical subject* that he is a *worker*.

(The laws of political economy express the estrangement of the worker in his object thus: the more the worker produces, the less he has to consume; the more values he creates, the more valueless, the more unworthy he becomes; the better formed his product, the more deformed becomes the worker; the more civilized his object, the more barbarous becomes the worker; the mightier labour becomes, the more powerless becomes the worker; the more ingenious labour becomes, the duller becomes the worker and the more he becomes nature's bondsman.)

Political economy conceals the estrangement inherent in the nature of labour by not considering the direct relationship between the worker (labour) *and production*. It is true that labour produces for the rich wonderful things—but for the worker it produces privation. It produces palaces—but for the worker, hovels. It produces beauty—but for the worker, deformity. It replaces labour by machines—but some of the workers it throws back to a barbarous type of labour, and the other workers it turns into machines. It produces intelligence—but for the worker idiocy, cretinism.

The direct relationship of labour to its produce is the relationship of the worker to the objects of his production. The relationship of the man of means to the objects of production and to production itself is only a *consequence* of this first relationship—and confirms it. We shall consider this other aspect later.

When we ask, then, what is the essential relationship of labour we are asking about the relationship of the *worker* to production.

Till now we have been considering the estrangement, the alienation of the worker only in one of its aspects, i.e., the worker's *relationship to the products of his labour*. But the estrangement is manifested not only in the result but in the *act of production*—within the *producing activity* itself. How would the worker come to face the product of his activity as a stranger, were it not that in the very act of production he was estranging himself from himself? The product is after all but the summary of the activity of production. If then the product of labour is alienation, production itself must be active alienation, the alienation of activity, the activity of alienation. In the estrangement of the object of labour is merely summarized the estrangement, the alienation, in the activity of labour itself.

What, then, constitutes the alienation of labour?

First, the fact that labour is *external* to the worker, i.e., it does not belong to his essential being; that in his work, therefore, he does not affirm himself but denies himself, does not feel content but unhappy, does not develop freely his physical and mental energy but mortifies his body and ruins his mind. The worker therefore only feels himself outside his work, and in his work feels outside himself. He is at home when he is not working, and when he is working he is not at home. His labour is therefore not voluntary, but coerced; it is *forced labour*. It is therefore not the satisfaction of a need; it is merely a *means* to satisfy needs external to it. Its alien character emerges clearly in the fact that as soon as no physical or other compulsion exists, labour is shunned like the plague. External labour, labour in which man alienates himself, is a labour of self-sacrifice, of mortification. Lastly, the external character of labour for the worker appears in the fact that it is not his own, but someone else's, that it does not belong to him, that in it he belongs, not to himself, but to another. Just as in religion the spontaneous activity of the human imagination, of the human brain and the human heart, operates independently of the individual—that is, operates on him as an alien, divine or diabolical activity—in the same way the worker's activity is not his spontaneous activity. It belongs to another; it is the loss of his self.

As a result, therefore, man (the worker) no longer feels himself to be freely active in any but his animal functions—eating, drinking, procreating, or at most in his dwelling and in dressing-up, etc.; and in his human functions he no longer feels himself to be anything but an animal. What is animal becomes human and what is human becomes animal.

* * *

1844 — 1932

From The German Ideology[1]

* * *

The fact is, therefore, that definite individuals who are productively active in a definite way enter into these definite social and political relations. Empirical observation must in each separate instance bring out empirically, and without any mystification and speculation, the connection of the social and political structure with production. The social structure and the State are continually evolving out of the life process of definite individuals, but of individuals, not as they may appear in their own or other people's imagina-

1. Translated by S. Ryazanskaya, based on an earlier translation by W. Lough.

tion, but as they *really* are; i.e., as they operate, produce materially, and hence as they work under definite material limits, presuppositions and conditions independent of their will.

The production of ideas, of conceptions, of consciousness, is at first directly interwoven with the material activity and the material intercourse of men, the language of real life. Conceiving, thinking, the mental intercourse of men, appear at this stage as the direct efflux of their material behaviour.[2] The same applies to mental production as expressed in the language of politics, laws, morality, religion, metaphysics, etc., of a people. Men are the producers of their conceptions, ideas, etc.—real, active men, as they are conditioned by a definite development of their productive forces and of the intercourse corresponding to these, up to its furthest forms. Consciousness can never be anything else than conscious existence, and the existence of men is their actual life-process. If in all ideology men and their circumstances appear upside-down as in a *camera obscura*,[3] this phenomenon arises just as much from their historical life-process as the inversion of objects on the retina does from their physical life-process.

In direct contrast to German philosophy[4] which descends from heaven to earth, here we ascend from earth to heaven. That is to say, we do not set out from what men say, imagine, conceive, nor from men as narrated, thought of, imagined, conceived, in order to arrive at men in the flesh. We set out from real, active men, and on the basis of their real life-process we demonstrate the development of the ideological reflexes and echoes of this life-process. The phantoms formed in the human brain are also, necessarily, sublimates of their material life-process, which is empirically verifiable and bound to material premises. Morality, religion, metaphysics, all the rest of ideology and their corresponding forms of consciousness, thus no longer retain the semblance of independence. They have no history, no development; but men, developing their material production and their material intercourse, alter, along with this their real existence, their thinking and the products of their thinking. Life is not determined by consciousness, but consciousness by life. In the first method of approach the starting-point is consciousness taken as the living individual; in the second method, which conforms to real life, it is the real living individuals themselves, and consciousness is considered solely as *their* consciousness.

This method of approach is not devoid of premises. It starts out from the real premises and does not abandon them for a moment. Its premises are men, not in any fantastic isolation and rigidity, but in their actual, empirically perceptible process of development under definite conditions. As soon as this active life-process is described, history ceases to be a collection of dead facts as it is with the empiricists[5] (themselves still abstract), or an imagined activity of imagined subjects, as with the idealists.

Where speculation ends—in real life—there real, positive science begins:

2. That is, the actions that human beings take in their relationship to the productive forces of their society.

3. Literally, "dark chamber" (Latin): an apparatus invented in the 17th century consisting of a darkened box with an aperture (usually a lens) through which an image is projected (inverted) on the opposite wall.

4. That is, idealism, which holds that reality and knowledge derive not from perceptions but from ideas or the workings of the human mind or spirit; idealists include IMMANUEL KANT (1724–1804) and GEORG WILHELM FRIEDRICH HEGEL (1770–1831).

5. Those who believe that experiences, especially of the senses, are the only sources of knowledge; for example, DAVID HUME (1711–1776).

the representation of the practical activity, of the practical process of development of men. Empty talk about consciousness ceases, and real knowledge has to take its place.

* * *

1845–46 1932

From The Communist Manifesto[1]

A spectre is haunting Europe—the spectre of Communism. All the Powers of old Europe have entered into a holy alliance to exorcise this spectre: Pope and Czar, Metternich and Guizot,[2] French Radicals and German police-spies.

Where is the party in opposition that has not been decried as Communistic by its opponents in power? Where the Opposition that has not hurled back the branding reproach of Communism, against the more advanced opposition parties, as well as against its reactionary adversaries?

Two things result from this fact.

I. Communism is already acknowledged by all European Powers to be itself a Power.

II. It is high time that Communists should openly, in the face of the whole world, publish their views, their aims, their tendencies, and meet this nursery tale of the Spectre of Communism with a Manifesto of the party itself.

To this end, Communists of various nationalities have assembled in London,[3] and sketched the following Manifesto, to be published in the English, French, German, Italian, Flemish and Danish languages.

I. *Bourgeois and Proletarians*[4]

The history of all hitherto existing society is the history of class struggles.

Freeman and slave, patrician and plebeian, lord and serf, guild-master[5] and journeyman,[6] in a word, oppressor and oppressed, stood in constant opposition to one another, carried on an uninterrupted, now hidden, now open fight, a fight that each time ended either in a revolutionary re-constitution of society at large, or in the common ruin of the contending classes.

In the earlier epochs of history, we find almost everywhere a complicated

1. Originally titled *Manifesto of the Communist Party*. This English text was edited by Engels.
2. François Pierre Guillaume Guizot (1787–1874), French statesman and historian who supported the idea of a constitutional monarchy. Metternich (1773–1859), Austrian statesman and foreign minister, who worked to suppress nationalist and popular constitutional movements.
3. Members of the Communist League (an international association made up mostly of German emigrés) met in November 1847; they commissioned the writing of the *Manifesto*.
4. By bourgeoisie is meant the class of modern Capitalists, owners of the means of social production and employers of wage-labour. By proletariat, the class of modern wage-labourers who, having no means of production of their own, are reduced to selling their labour-power in order to live [Engels's note].
5. Guild-master, that is, a full member of a guild, a master within, not a head of a guild [Engels's note].
6. A skilled artisan, not yet a full member of a guild, who works for master artisans rather than for himself.

arrangement of society into various orders, a manifold gradation of social rank. In ancient Rome we have patricians, knights, plebeians, slaves; in the Middle Ages, feudal lords, vassals, guild-masters, journeymen, apprentices, serfs; in almost all of these classes, again, subordinate gradations.

The modern bourgeois society that has sprouted from the ruins of feudal society has not done away with class antagonisms. It has but established new classes, new conditions of oppression, new forms of struggle in place of the old ones.

Our epoch, the epoch of the bourgeoisie, possesses, however, this distinctive feature: it has simplified the class antagonisms: Society as a whole is more and more splitting up into two great hostile camps, into two great classes directly facing each other: Bourgeoisie and Proletariat.

From the serfs of the Middle Ages sprang the chartered burghers[7] of the earliest towns. From these burgesses[8] the first elements of the bourgeoisie were developed.

The discovery of America, the rounding of the Cape,[9] opened up fresh ground for the rising bourgeoisie. The East-Indian and Chinese markets, the colonisation of America, trade with the colonies, the increase in the means of exchange and in commodities generally, gave to commerce, to navigation, to industry, an impulse never before known, and thereby, to the revolutionary element in the tottering feudal society, a rapid development.

The feudal system of industry, under which industrial production was monopolised by closed guilds, now no longer sufficed for the growing wants of the new markets. The manufacturing system took its place. The guild-masters were pushed on one side by the manufacturing middle class; division of labour between the different corporate guilds vanished in the face of division of labour in each single workshop.

Meantime the markets kept ever growing, the demand ever rising. Even manufacture no longer sufficed. Thereupon, steam and machinery revolutionised industrial production. The place of manufacture was taken by the giant, Modern Industry, the place of the industrial middle class, by industrial millionaires, the leaders of whole industrial armies, the modern bourgeois.

Modern industry has established the world-market, for which the discovery of America paved the way. This market has given an immense development to commerce, to navigation, to communication by land. This development has, in its turn, reacted on the extension of industry; and in proportion as industry, commerce, navigation, railways extended, in the same proportion the bourgeoisie developed, increased its capital, and pushed into the background every class handed down from the Middle Ages.

We see, therefore, how the modern bourgeoisie is itself the product of a long course of development, of a series of revolutions in the modes of production and of exchange.

Each step in the development of the bourgeoisie was accompanied by a corresponding political advance of that class. An oppressed class under the sway of the feudal nobility, an armed and self-governing association in the medieval commune;[1] here independent urban republic (as in Italy and Ger-

7. Privileged middle class.
8. Citizens.
9. The Cape of Good Hope, at the southern tip of Africa.

1. This was the name given their urban communities by the townsmen of Italy and France, after they had purchased or wrested their initial rights of self-government from their feudal lords [Engels's note].

many), there taxable "third estate"[2] of the monarchy (as in France), afterwards, in the period of manufacture proper, serving either the semi-feudal or the absolute monarchy as a counterpoise against the nobility, and, in fact, corner-stone of the great monarchies in general, the bourgeoisie has at last, since the establishment of Modern Industry and of the world-market, conquered for itself, in the modern representative State, exclusive political sway. The executive of the modern State is but a committee for managing the common affairs of the whole bourgeoisie.

The bourgeoisie, historically, has played a most revolutionary part.

The bourgeoisie, wherever it has got the upper hand, has put an end to all feudal, patriarchal, idyllic relations. It has pitilessly torn asunder the motley feudal ties that bound man to his "natural superiors," and has left remaining no other nexus between man and man than naked self-interest, than callous "cash payment." It has drowned the most heavenly ecstasies of religious fervour, of chivalrous enthusiasm, of philistine[3] sentimentalism, in the icy water of egotistical calculation. It has resolved personal worth into exchange value, and in place of the numberless indefeasible chartered freedoms, has set up that single, unconscionable freedom—Free Trade. In one word, for exploitation, veiled by religious and political illusions, it has substituted naked, shameless, direct, brutal exploitation.

The bourgeoisie has stripped of its halo every occupation hitherto honoured and looked up to with reverent awe. It has converted the physician, the lawyer, the priest, the poet, the man of science, into its paid wage-labourers.

The bourgeoisie has torn away from the family its sentimental veil, and has reduced the family relation to a mere money relation.

The bourgeoisie has disclosed how it came to pass that the brutal display of vigour in the Middle Ages, which Reactionists[4] so much admire, found its fitting complement in the most slothful indolence. It has been the first to show what man's activity can bring about. It has accomplished wonders far surpassing Egyptian pyramids, Roman aqueducts, and Gothic cathedrals; it has conducted expeditions that put in the shade all former Exoduses of nations and crusades.

The bourgeoisie cannot exist without constantly revolutionising the instruments of production, and thereby the relations of production, and with them the whole relations of society. Conservation of the old modes of production in unaltered form, was, on the contrary, the first condition of existence for all earlier industrial classes. Constant revolutionising of production, uninterrupted disturbance of all social conditions, everlasting uncertainty and agitation distinguish the bourgeois epoch from all earlier ones. All fixed, fast-frozen relations, with their train of ancient and venerable prejudices and opinions, are swept away, all new-formed ones become antiquated before they can ossify. All that is solid melts into air, all that is holy is profaned, and man is at last compelled to face with sober senses, his real conditions of life, and his relations with his kind.

The need of a constantly expanding market for its products chases the

2. The common people in France (the first estate or political order was the clergy, the second the nobility).

3. Materialist middle-class; a term borrowed from MATTHEW ARNOLD, "The Function of Criticism at the Present Time" (1864).

4. Reactionaries.

bourgeoisie over the whole surface of the globe. It must nestle everywhere, settle everywhere, establish connexions everywhere.

The bourgeoisie has through its exploitation of the world-market given a cosmopolitan character to production and consumption in every country. To the great chagrin of Reactionists, it has drawn from under the feet of industry the national ground on which it stood. All old-established national industries have been destroyed or are daily being destroyed. They are dislodged by new industries, whose introduction becomes a life and death question for all civilised nations, by industries that no longer work up indigenous raw material, but raw material drawn from the remotest zones; industries whose products are consumed, not only at home, but in every quarter of the globe. In place of the old wants, satisfied by the productions of the country, we find new wants, requiring for their satisfaction the products of distant lands and climes. In place of the old local and national seclusion and self-sufficiency, we have intercourse in every direction, universal inter-dependence of nations. And as in material, so also in intellectual production. The intellectual creations of individual nations become common property. National one-sidedness and narrow-mindedness become more and more impossible, and from the numerous national and local literatures, there arises a world literature.

The bourgeoisie, by the rapid improvement of all instruments of production, by the immensely facilitated means of communication, draws all, even the most barbarian, nations into civilisation. The cheap prices of its commodities are the heavy artillery with which it batters down all Chinese walls, with which it forces the barbarians' intensely obstinate hatred of foreigners to capitulate.[5] It compels all nations, on pain of extinction, to adopt the bourgeois mode of production; it compels them to introduce what it calls civilisation into their midst, i.e., to become bourgeois themselves. In one word, it creates a world after its own image.

The bourgeoisie has subjected the country to the rule of the towns. It has created enormous cities, has greatly increased the urban population as compared with the rural, and has thus rescued a considerable part of the population from the idiocy of rural life. Just as it has made the country dependent on the towns, so it has made barbarian and semi-barbarian countries dependent on the civilised ones, nations of peasants on nations of bourgeois, the East on the West.

The bourgeoisie keeps more and more doing away with the scattered state of the population, of the means of production, and of property. It has agglomerated population, centralised means of production, and has concentrated property in a few hands. The necessary consequence of this was political centralisation. Independent, or but loosely connected provinces, with separate interests, laws, governments and systems of taxation, became lumped together into one nation, with one government, one code of laws, one national class-interest, one frontier and one customs-tariff.

The bourgeoisie, during its rule of scarce one hundred years, has created more massive and more colossal productive forces than have all preceding generations together. Subjection of Nature's forces to man, machinery,

5. China unsuccessfully fought the Opium Wars (1839–42, 1856–60) to prevent the expansion of Western trade.

application of chemistry to industry and agriculture, steam-navigation, railways, electric telegraphs, clearing of whole continents for cultivation, canalisation of rivers, whole populations conjured out of the ground—what earlier century had even a presentiment that such productive forces slumbered in the lap of social labour?

* * *

1848, 1888

From Grundrisse[1]

* * *

In the case of the arts, it is well known that certain periods of their flowering are out of all proportion to the general development of society, hence also to the material foundation, the skeletal structure as it were, of its organization. For example, the Greeks compared to the moderns or also Shakespeare. It is even recognized that certain forms of art, e.g. the epic, can no longer be produced in their world epoch-making, classical stature as soon as the production of art, as such, begins; that is, that certain significant forms within the realm of the arts are possible only at an undeveloped stage of artistic development. If this is the case with the relation between different kinds of art within the realm of the arts, it is already less puzzling that it is the case in the relation of the entire realm to the general development of society. The difficulty consists only in the general formulation of these contradictions. As soon as they have been specified, they are already clarified.

Let us take e.g. the relation of Greek art and then of Shakespeare to the present time. It is well known that Greek mythology is not only the arsenal of Greek art but also its foundation. Is the view of nature and of social relations on which the Greek imagination and hence Greek [mythology] is based possible with self-acting mule spindles[2] and railways and locomotives and electrical telegraphs? What chance has Vulcan against Roberts & Co., Jupiter against the lightning rod and Hermes against the Credit Mobilier?[3] All mythology overcomes and dominates and shapes the forces of nature in the imagination and by the imagination; it therefore vanishes with the advent of real mastery over them. What becomes of Fama[4] alongside Printing House Square? Greek art presupposes Greek mythology, i.e. nature and the social forms already reworked in an unconsciously artistic way by the popular imagination. This is its material. Not any mythology whatever, i.e. not an arbitrarily chosen unconsciously artistic reworking of nature (here meaning everything objective, hence including society). Egyptian mythology could

1. Translated by Martin Nicolaus, who sometimes includes clarifying words in brackets: the title, usually left untranslated, means "outlines" or "foundations."
2. Machines used in spinning, invented in the late 18th century.
3. A major investment bank in France during the Second Empire (1852–70), against which Marx pits Hermes, Greek god of commerce and invention. The other two (Roman) gods are similarly paired: Vulcan, god of metalworking, with a commercial firm and Jupiter, supreme god and wielder of the thunderbolt, with a lightning rod.
4. Rumor (Latin), a Roman personification; she repeated whatever she heard until everyone knew it.

never have been the foundation or the womb of Greek art. But, in any case, a *mythology*. Hence, in no way a social development which excludes all mythological, all mythologizing relations to nature; which therefore demands of the artist an imagination not dependent on mythology.

From another side, is Achilles[5] possible with powder and lead? Or the *Iliad* with the printing press, not to mention the printing machine? Do not the song and the saga and the muse necessarily come to an end with the printer's bar,[6] hence do not the necessary conditions of epic poetry vanish?

But the difficulty lies not in understanding that the Greek arts and epic are bound up with certain forms of social development. The difficulty is that they still afford us artistic pleasure and that in a certain respect they count as a norm and as an unattainable model.

A man cannot become a child again, or he becomes childish. But does he not find joy in the child's naiveté, and must he himself not strive to reproduce its truth at a higher stage? Does not the true character of each epoch come alive in the nature of its children? Why should not the historic childhood of humanity, its most beautiful unfolding, as a stage never to return, exercise an eternal charm? There are unruly children and precocious children. Many of the old peoples belong in this category. The Greeks were normal children. The charm of their art for us is not in contradiction to the undeveloped stage of society on which it grew. [It] is its result, rather, and is inextricably bound up, rather, with the fact that the unripe social conditions under which it arose, and could alone arise, can never return.

1857–58 | 1939–42

From Preface to *A Contribution to the Critique of Political Economy*

* * *

The first work which I undertook for a solution of the doubts which assailed me was a critical review of the Hegelian philosophy of right, a work the introduction to which appeared in 1844 in the *Deutsch-Französische Jahrbücher*,[1] published in Paris. My investigation led to the result that legal relations as well as forms of state are to be grasped neither from themselves nor from the so-called general development of the human mind, but rather have their roots in the material conditions of life, the sum total of which Hegel, following the example of the Englishmen and Frenchmen of the eighteenth century, combines under the name of "civil society," that, however, the anatomy of civil society is to be sought in political economy. The investigation of the latter, which I began in Paris, I continued in Brussels, whither I had emigrated in consequence of an expulsion order of M. Guizot.[2] The

5. The greatest of the Greek warriors at Troy, and the focus of Homer's *Iliad* (ca. 8th c. B.C.E.).

6. Lever used to screw down the platen of a manual printing press (the German word used here, *Preßbengel*, can also mean printing in general). "The muse": goddess presiding over the arts and intellectual pursuits, traditionally invoked by epic poets as an aid to memory.

1. *German-French Yearbook*. The German philosopher GEORG WILHELM FRIEDRICH HEGEL (1770–1831) described his political philosophy in the *Philosophy of Right* (1821); Marx's essay was "Contribution to the Critique of Hegel's Philosophy of Right."

2. François Pierre Guillaume Guizot (1787–1874), French statesman and historian who supported the idea of a constitutional monarchy; he was the chief power in the government between 1840 and 1848.

general result at which I arrived and which, once won, served as a guiding thread for my studies, can be briefly formulated as follows: In the social production of their life, men enter into definite relations that are indispensable and independent of their will, relations of production which correspond to a definite stage of development of their material productive forces. The sum total of these relations of production constitutes the economic structure of society, the real foundation, on which rises a legal and political superstructure and to which correspond definite forms of social consciousness. The mode of production of material life conditions the social, political and intellectual life process in general. It is not the consciousness of men that determines their being, but, on the contrary, their social being that determines their consciousness. At a certain stage of their development, the material productive forces of society come in conflict with the existing relations of production, or—what is but a legal expression for the same thing—with the property relations within which they have been at work hitherto. From forms of development of the productive forces these relations turn into their fetters. Then begins an epoch of social revolution. With the change of the economic foundation the entire immense superstructure is more or less rapidly transformed. In considering such transformations a distinction should always be made between the material transformation of the economic conditions of production, which can be determined with the precision of natural science, and the legal, political, religious, aesthetic or philosophic—in short, ideological forms in which men become conscious of this conflict and fight it out. Just as our opinion of an individual is not based on what he thinks of himself, so can we not judge of such a period of transformation by its own consciousness; on the contrary, this consciousness must be explained rather from the contradictions of material life, from the existing conflict between the social productive forces and the relations of production. No social order ever perishes before all the productive forces for which there is room in it have developed; and new, higher relations of production never appear before the material conditions of their existence have matured in the womb of the old society itself. Therefore mankind always sets itself only such tasks as it can solve; since, looking at the matter more closely, it will always be found that the task itself arises only when the material conditions for its solution already exist or are at least in the process of formation. In broad outlines Asiatic, ancient, feudal, and modern bourgeois modes of production can be designated as progressive epochs in the economic formation of society. The bourgeois relations of production are the last antagonistic form of the social process of production—antagonistic not in the sense of individual antagonism, but of one arising from the social conditions of life of the individuals; at the same time the productive forces developing in the womb of bourgeois society create the material conditions for the solution of that antagonism.[3] This social formation brings, therefore, the prehistory of human society to a close.

* * *

1859

3. That is, socialism—the final "mode of production," which is in the process of emerging through the class struggle of the bourgeoisie and proletarians.

From Capital, Volume 1[1]

From *Chapter 1. Commodities*

SECTION 4. THE FETISHISM OF COMMODITIES AND THE SECRET THEREOF

A commodity appears, at first sight, a very trivial thing, and easily understood. Its analysis shows that it is, in reality, a very queer thing, abounding in metaphysical subtleties and theological niceties. So far as it is a value in use, there is nothing mysterious about it, whether we consider it from the point of view that by its properties it is capable of satisfying human wants, or from the point that those properties are the product of human labour. It is as clear as noon-day, that man, by his industry, changes the forms of the materials furnished by Nature, in such a way as to make them useful to him. The form of wood, for instance, is altered, by making a table out of it. Yet, for all that, the table continues to be that common, every-day thing, wood. But, so soon as it steps forth as a commodity, it is changed into something transcendent. It not only stands with its feet on the ground, but, in relation to all other commodities, it stands on its head, and evolves out of its wooden brain grotesque ideas, far more wonderful than "table-turning" ever was.

The mystical character of commodities does not originate, therefore, in their use-value. Just as little does it proceed from the nature of the determining factors of value. For, in the first place, however varied the useful kinds of labour, or productive activities, may be, it is a physiological fact, that they are functions of the human organism, and that each such function, whatever may be its nature or form, is essentially the expenditure of human brain, nerves, muscles, &c. Secondly, with regard to that which forms the ground-work for the quantitative determination of value, namely, the duration of that expenditure, or the quantity of labour, it is quite clear that there is a palpable difference between its quantity and quality. In all states of society, the labour-time that it costs to produce the means of subsistence, must necessarily be an object of interest to mankind, though not of equal interest in different stages of development. And lastly, from the moment that men in any way work for one another, their labour assumes a social form.

Whence, then, arises the enigmatical character of the product of labour, so soon as it assumes the form of commodities? Clearly from this form itself. The equality of all sorts of human labour is expressed objectively by their products all being equally values; the measure of the expenditure of labour-power by the duration of that expenditure, takes the form of the quantity of value of the products of labour; and finally, the mutual relations of the producers, within which the social character of their labour affirms itself, take the form of a social relation between the products.

A commodity is therefore a mysterious thing, simply because in it the social character of men's labour appears to them as an objective character stamped upon the product of that labour; because the relation of the producers to the sum total of their own labour is presented to them as a social

1. Translated by Samuel Moore and Edward Aveling, and edited by Engels.

relation, existing not between themselves, but between the products of their labour. This is the reason why the products of labour become commodities, social things whose qualities are at the same time perceptible and imperceptible by the senses. In the same way the light from an object is perceived by us not as the subjective excitation of our optic nerve, but as the objective form of something outside the eye itself. But, in the act of seeing, there is at all events, an actual passage of light from one thing to another, from the external object to the eye. There is a physical relation between physical things. But it is different with commodities. There, the existence of the things *quâ* commodities, and the value-relation between the products of labour which stamps them as commodities, have absolutely no connexion with their physical properties and with the material relations arising therefrom. There it is a definite social relation between men, that assumes, in their eyes, the fantastic form of a relation between things. In order, therefore, to find an analogy, we must have recourse to the mist-enveloped regions of the religious world. In that world the productions of the human brain appear as independent beings endowed with life, and entering into relation both with one another and the human race. So it is in the world of commodities with the products of men's hands. This I call the Fetishism which attaches itself to the products of labour,[2] so soon as they are produced as commodities, and which is therefore inseparable from the production of commodities.

This Fetishism of commodities has its origin, as the foregoing analysis has already shown, in the peculiar social character of the labour that produces them.

As a general rule, articles of utility become commodities, only because they are products of the labour of private individuals or groups of individuals who carry on their work independently of each other. The sum total of the labour of all these private individuals forms the aggregate labour of society. Since the producers do not come into social contact with each other until they exchange their products, the specific social character of each producer's labour does not show itself except in the act of exchange. In other words, the labour of the individual asserts itself as a part of the labour of society, only by means of the relations which the act of exchange establishes directly between the products, and indirectly, through them, between the producers. To the latter, therefore, the relations connecting the labour of one individual with that of the rest appear, not as direct social relations between individuals at work, but as what they really are, material relations between persons and social relations between things. It is only by being exchanged that the products of labour acquire, as values, one uniform social status, distinct from their varied forms of existence as objects of utility. This division of a product into a useful thing and a value becomes practically important, only when exchange has acquired such an extension that useful articles are produced for the purpose of being exchanged, and their character as values has therefore to be taken into account, beforehand, during production. From this moment the labour of the individual producer acquires socially a two-

2. By analogy with religious fetishism, the attribution of magical or divine power to objects. Similarly, according to Marx, we impute to commodities a life of their own (and a seemingly inherent value). We treat as relations between people what are in fact relations between commodities and people, thereby attributing human powers to things.

fold character. On the one hand, it must, as a definite useful kind of labour, satisfy a definite social want, and thus hold its place as part and parcel of the collective labour of all, as a branch of a social division of labour that has sprung up spontaneously. On the other hand, it can satisfy the manifold wants of the individual producer himself, only in so far as the mutual exchangeability of all kinds of useful private labour is an established social fact, and therefore the private useful labour of each producer ranks on an equality with that of all others. The equalisation of the most different kinds of labour can be the result only of an abstraction from their inequalities, or of reducing them to their common denominator, viz., expenditure of human labour-power or human labour in the abstract. The two-fold social character of the labour of the individual appears to him, when reflected in his brain, only under those forms which are impressed upon that labour in every-day practice by the exchange of products. In this way, the character that his own labour possesses of being socially useful takes the form of the condition, that the product must be not only useful, but useful for others, and the social character that his particular labour has of being the equal of all other particular kinds of labour, takes the form that all the physically different articles that are the products of labour, have one common quality, viz., that of having value.

Hence, when we bring the products of our labour into relation with each other as values, it is not because we see in these articles the material receptacles of homogeneous human labour. Quite the contrary: whenever, by an exchange, we equate as values our different products, by that very act, we also equate, as human labour, the different kinds of labour expended upon them. We are not aware of this, nevertheless we do it. Value, therefore, does not stalk about with a label describing what it is. It is value, rather, that converts every product into a social hieroglyphic. Later on, we try to decipher the hieroglyphic, to get behind the secret of our own social products; for to stamp an object of utility as a value, is just as much a social product as language. The recent scientific discovery, that the products of labour, so far as they are values, are but material expressions of the human labour spent in their production, marks, indeed, an epoch in the history of the development of the human race, but, by no means, dissipates the mist through which the social character of labour appears to us to be an objective character of the products themselves. The fact, that in the particular form of production with which we are dealing, viz., the production of commodities, the specific social character of private labour carried on independently, consists in the equality of every kind of that labour, by virtue of its being human labour, which character, therefore, assumes in the product the form of value—this fact appears to the producers, notwithstanding the discovery above referred to, to be just as real and final, as the fact, that, after the discovery by science of the component gases of air, the atmosphere itself remained unaltered.

What, first of all, practically concerns producers when they make in exchange, is the question, how much of some other product they get for their own? in what proportions the products are exchangeable? When these proportions have, by custom, attained a certain stability, they appear to result from the nature of the products, so that, for instance, one ton of iron and two ounces of gold appear as naturally to be of equal value as a pound of gold and a pound of iron in spite of their different physical and chemical qualities appear to be of equal weight. The character of having value, when once impressed upon products, obtains fixity only by reason of their acting and re-acting upon each other as quantities of value. These quantities vary continually, independently of the will, foresight and action of the producers. To them, their own social action takes the form of the action of objects, which rule the producers instead of being ruled by them. It requires a fully developed production of commodities before, from accumulated experience alone, the scientific conviction springs up, that all the different kinds of private labour, which are carried on independently of each other, and yet as spontaneously developed branches of the social division of labour, are continually being reduced to the quantitative proportions in which society requires them. And why? Because, in the midst of all the accidental and ever fluctuating exchange-relations between the products, the labour-time socially necessary for their production forcibly asserts itself like an over-riding law of Nature. The law of gravity thus asserts itself when a house falls about our ears. The determination of the magnitude of value by labour-time is therefore a secret, hidden under the apparent fluctuations in the relative values of commodities. Its discovery, while removing all appearance of mere accidentality from the determination of the magnitude of the values of products, yet in no way alters the mode in which that determination takes place.

Man's reflections on the forms of social life, and consequently, also, his scientific analysis of those forms, take a course directly opposite to that of their actual historical development. He begins, post festum,[3] with the results of the process of development ready to hand before him. The characters that stamp products as commodities, and whose establishment is a necessary preliminary to the circulation of commodities, have already acquired the stability of natural, self-understood forms of social life, before man seeks to decipher, not their historical character, for in his eyes they are immutable, but their meaning. Consequently it was the analysis of the prices of commodities that alone led to the determination of the magnitude of value, and it was the common expression of all commodities in money that alone led to the establishment of their characters as values. It is, however, just this ultimate money-form of the world of commodities that actually conceals, instead of disclosing, the social character of private labour, and the social relations between the individual producers. When I state that coats or boots stand in a relation to linen, because it is the universal incarnation of abstract human labour, the absurdity of the statement is self-evident. Nevertheless, when the producers of coats and boots compare those articles with linen, or, what is the same thing, with gold or silver, as the universal equivalent, they express the relation between their own private labour and the collective labour of society in the same absurd form.

The categories of bourgeois economy consist of such like forms. They are forms of thought expressing with social validity the conditions and relations of a definite, historically determined mode of production, viz., the production of commodities. The whole mystery of commodities, all the magic and necromancy that surrounds the products of labour as long as they take the form

3. After the feast (Latin); after the fact, too late.

of commodities, vanishes therefore, so soon as we come to other forms of production.

Since Robinson Crusoe's[4] experiences are a favourite theme with political economists, let us take a look at him on his island. Moderate though he be, yet some few wants he has to satisfy, and must therefore do a little useful work of various sorts, such as making tools and furniture, taming goats, fishing and hunting. Of his prayers and the like we take no account, since they are a source of pleasure to him, and he looks upon them as so much recreation. In spite of the variety of his work, he knows that his labour, whatever its form, is but the activity of one and the same Robinson, and consequently, that it consists of nothing but different modes of human labour. Necessity itself compels him to apportion his time accurately between his different kinds of work. Whether one kind occupies a greater space in his general activity than another, depends on the difficulties, greater or less as the case may be, to be overcome in attaining the useful effect aimed at. This our friend Robinson soon learns by experience, and having rescued a watch, ledger, and pen and ink from the wreck, commences, like a true-born Briton, to keep a set of books. His stock-book contains a list of the objects of utility that belong to him, of the operations necessary for their production; and lastly, of the labour-time that definite quantities of those objects have, on an average, cost him. All the relations between Robinson and the objects that form this wealth of his own creation, are here so simple and clear as to be intelligible without exertion, even to Mr. Sedley Taylor.[5] And yet those relations contain all that is essential to the determination of value.

Let us now transport ourselves from Robinson's island bathed in light to the European middle ages shrouded in darkness. Here, instead of the independent man, we find everyone dependent, serfs and lords, vassals and suzerains, laymen and clergy. Personal dependence here characterises the social relations of production just as much as it does the other spheres of life organised on the basis of that production. But for the very reason that personal dependence forms the ground-work of society, there is no necessity for labour and its products to assume a fantastic form different from their reality. They take the shape, in the transactions of society, of services in kind and payments in kind. Here the particular and natural form of labour, and not, as in a society based on production of commodities, its general abstract form is the immediate social form of labour. Compulsory labour is just as properly measured by time, as commodity-producing labour, but every serf knows that what he expends in the service of his lord, is a definite quantity of his own personal labour-power. The tithe to be rendered to the priest is more matter of fact than his blessing. No matter, then, what we may think of the parts played by the different classes of people themselves in this society, the social relations between individuals in the performance of their labour, appear at all events as their own mutual personal relations, and are not disguised under the shape of social relations between the products of labour.

4. The hero and title character of Daniel Defoe's 1719–20 novel, an English sailor shipwrecked for 24 years on a small tropical island. He is discussed by some political economists—including Adam Smith (1723–1790) and Jean-Jacques Rousseau (1712–1778)—who base their analyses of production on the solitary independent worker.

5. A Fellow of Trinity College, Cambridge (1834–1920), who wrote both about musical sounds and harmony and about the relationship between capital and labor.

For an example of labour in common or directly associated labour, we have no occasion to go back to that spontaneously developed form which we find on the threshold of the history of all civilised races. We have one close at hand in the patriarchal industries of a peasant family, that produces corn, cattle, yarn, linen, and clothing for home use. These different articles are, as regards the family, so many products of its labour, but as between themselves, they are not commodities. The different kinds of labour, such as tillage, cattle tending, spinning, weaving and making clothes, which result in the various products, are in themselves, and such as they are, direct social functions, because functions of the family, which, just as much as a society based on the production of commodities, possesses a spontaneously developed system of division of labour. The distribution of the work within the family, and the regulation of the labour-time of the several members, depend as well upon differences of age and sex as upon natural conditions varying with the seasons. The labour-power of each individual, by its very nature, operates in this case merely as a definite portion of the whole labour-power of the family, and therefore, the measure of the expenditure of individual labour-power by its duration, appears here by its very nature as a social character of their labour.

Let us now picture to ourselves, by way of change, a community of free individuals, carrying on their work with the means of production in common, in which the labour-power of all the different individuals is consciously applied as the combined labour-power of the community. All the characteristics of Robinson's labour are here repeated, but with this difference, that they are social, instead of individual. Everything produced by him was exclusively the result of his own personal labour, and therefore simply an object of use for himself. The total product of our community is a social product. One portion serves as fresh means of production and remains social. But another portion is consumed by the members as means of subsistence. A distribution of this portion amongst them is consequently necessary. The mode of this distribution will vary with the productive organisation of the community, and the degree of historical development attained by the producers. We will assume, but merely for the sake of a parallel with the production of commodities, that the share of each individual producer in the means of subsistence is determined by his labour-time. Labour-time would, in that case, play a double part. Its apportionment in accordance with a definite social plan maintains the proper proportion between the different kinds of work to be done and the various wants of the community. On the other hand, it also serves as a measure of the portion of the common labour borne by each individual, and of his share in the part of the total product destined for individual consumption. The social relations of the individual producers, with regard both to their labour and to its products, are in this case perfectly simple and intelligible, and that with regard not only to production but also to distribution.

The religious world is but the reflex of the real world. And for a society based upon the production of commodities, in which the producers in general enter into social relations with one another by treating their products as commodities and values, whereby they reduce their individual private labour to the standard of homogeneous human labour—for such a society,

Christianity with its *cultus*[6] of abstract man, more especially in its bourgeois developments, Protestantism, Deism,[7] &c., is the most fitting form of religion. In the ancient Asiatic and other ancient modes of production, we find that the conversion of products into commodities, and therefore the conversion of men into producers of commodities, holds a subordinate place, which, however, increases in importance as the primitive communities approach nearer and nearer to their dissolution. Trading nations, properly so called, exist in the ancient world only in its interstices, like the gods of Epicurus in the Intermundia,[8] or like Jews in the pores of Polish society. Those ancient social organisms of production are, as compared with bourgeois society, extremely simple and transparent. But they are founded either on the immature development of man individually, who has not yet severed the umbilical cord that unites him with his fellowmen in a primitive tribal community, or upon direct relations of subjection. They can arise and exist only when the development of the productive power of labour has not risen beyond a low stage, and when, therefore, the social relations within the sphere of material life, between man and man, and between man and Nature, are correspondingly narrow. This narrowness is reflected in the ancient worship of Nature, and in the other elements of the popular religions. The religious reflex of the real world can, in any case, only then finally vanish, when the practical relations of every-day life offer to man none but perfectly intelligible and reasonable relations with regard to his fellowmen and to Nature.

The life-process of society, which is based on the process of material production, does not strip off its mystical veil until it is treated as production by freely associated men, and is consciously regulated by them in accordance with a settled plan. This, however, demands for society a certain material ground-work or set of conditions of existence which in their turn are the spontaneous product of a long and painful process of development.

Political Economy has indeed analysed, however incompletely, value and its magnitude, and has discovered what lies beneath these forms. But it has never once asked the question why labour is represented by the value of its product and labour-time by the magnitude of that value. These formulæ, which bear it stamped upon them in unmistakeable letters that they belong to a state of society, in which the process of production has the mastery over man, instead of being controlled by him, such formulæ appear to the bourgeois intellect to be as much a self-evident necessity imposed by Nature as productive labour itself. Hence forms of social production that preceded the bourgeois form, are treated by the bourgeoisie in much the same way as the Fathers of the Church[9] treated pre-Christian religions.

To what extent some economists are misled by the Fetishism inherent in commodities, or by the objective appearance of the social characteristics of labour, is shown, amongst other ways, by the dull and tedious quarrel over the part played by Nature in the formation of exchange-value. Since exchange-value is a definite social manner of expressing the amount of labour

6. Care of; adoration, worship (Latin).

7. Belief in a supreme being as the source of existence that rejects the supernatural doctrines of Christianity and the influence or revelation of God in the universe, stressing instead the importance of reason and ethical conduct.

8. The spaces between the worlds (Latin). Epicurus: (341–270 B.C.E.), Greek philosopher who held that the gods had nothing to do with human affairs.

9. Early Christian writers who established Christian doctrine before the 8th century.

bestowed upon object, Nature has no more to do with it, than it has in fixing the course of exchange.

The mode of production in which the product takes the form of a commodity, or is produced directly for exchange, is the most general and most embryonic form of bourgeois production. It therefore makes its appearance at an early date in history, though not in the same predominating and characteristic manner as now-a-days. Hence its Fetish character is comparatively easy to be seen through. But when we come to more concrete forms, even this appearance of simplicity vanishes. Whence arose the illusions of the monetary system? To it gold and silver, when serving as money, did not represent a social relation between producers but were natural objects with strange social properties. And modern economy, which looks down with such disdain on the monetary system, does not its superstition come out as clear as noon-day, whenever it treats of capital? How long is it since economy discarded the physiocratic illusion, that rents grow out of the soil and not out of society?[1]

But not to anticipate, we will content ourselves with yet another example relating to the commodity-form. Could commodities themselves speak, they would say: Our use-value may be a thing that interests men. It is no part of us as objects. What, however, does belong to us as objects, is our value. Our natural intercourse as commodities proves it. In the eyes of each other we are nothing but exchange-values. Now listen how those commodities speak through the mouth of the economist. "Value"—(*i.e.*, exchange-value) "is a property of things, riches"—(*i.e.*, use-value) "of man. Value, in this sense, necessarily implies exchanges, riches do not." "Riches" (use-value) "are the attribute of men, value is the attribute of commodities. A man or a community is rich, a pearl or a diamond is valuable. . . . A pearl or a diamond is valuable" as a pearl or diamond. So far no chemist has ever discovered exchange-value either in a pearl or a diamond. The economic discoverers of this chemical element, who by-the-by lay special claim to critical acumen, find however that the use-value of objects belongs to them independently of their material properties, while their value, on the other hand, forms a part of them as objects. What confirms them in this view, is the peculiar circumstance that the use-value of objects is realised without exchange, by means of a direct relation between the objects and man, while, on the other hand, their value is realised only by exchange, that is, by means of a social process. Who fails here to call to mind our good friend, Dogberry, who informs neighbour Seacoal, that, "To be a well-favoured man is the gift of fortune; but reading and writing comes by Nature."[2]

From *Chapter 10. The Working-Day*

SECTION 5. THE STRUGGLE FOR A NORMAL WORKING-DAY. COMPULSORY LAWS FOR THE EXTENSION OF THE WORKING-DAY FROM THE MIDDLE OF THE 14TH TO THE END OF THE 17TH CENTURY

"What is a working-day? What is the length of time during which capital may consume the labour-power whose daily value it buys? How far may the work-

1. The Physiocrats, late-18th-century French economists who were proponents of free trade, believed that agriculture is the source of all wealth.
2. Shakespeare, *Much Ado about Nothing* (ca. 1598), 3.3.13–14 (slightly misquoted). Dogberry is a comic character, the commander of the watch; Seacoal is one of the watchman.

ing-day be extended beyond the working-time necessary for the reproduction of labour-power itself?" It has been seen that to these questions capital replies: the working-day contains the full 24 hours, with the deduction of the few hours of repose without which labour-power absolutely refuses its services again. Hence it is self-evident that the labourer is nothing else, his whole life through, than labour-power, that therefore all his disposable time is by nature and law labour-time, to be devoted to the self-expansion of capital. Time for education, for intellectual development, for the fulfilling of social functions and for social intercourse, for the free-play of his bodily and mental activity, even the rest time of Sunday (and that in a country of Sabbatarians!)—moonshine![3] But in its blind unrestrainable passion, its were-wolf hunger for surplus-labour, capital oversteps not only the moral, but even the merely physical maximum bounds of the working-day. It usurps the time for growth, development, and healthy maintenance of the body. It steals the time required for the consumption of fresh air and sunlight. It higgles[4] over a meal-time, incorporating it where possible with the process of production itself, so that food is given to the labourer as to a mere means of production, as coal is supplied to the boiler, grease and oil to the machinery. It reduces the sound sleep needed for the restoration, reparation, refreshment of the bodily powers to just so many hours of torpor as the revival of an organism, absolutely exhausted, renders essential. It is not the normal maintenance of the labour-power which is to determine the limits of the working-day; it is the greatest possible daily expenditure of labour-power, no matter how diseased, compulsory, and painful it may be, which is to determine the limits of the labourers' period of repose. Capital cares nothing for the length of life of labour-power. All that concerns it is simply and solely the maximum of labour-power, that can be rendered fluent in a working-day. It attains this end by shortening the extent of the labourer's life, as a greedy farmer snatches increased produce from the soil by robbing it of its fertility.

The capitalistic mode of production (essentially the production of surplus-value,[5] the absorption of surplus-labour), produces thus, with the extension of the working-day, not only the deterioration of human labour-power by robbing it of its normal, moral and physical, conditions of development and function. It produces also the premature exhaustion and death of this labour-power itself. It extends the labourer's time of production during a given period by shortening his actual life-time.

But the value of the labour-power includes the value of the commodities necessary for the reproduction of the worker, or for the keeping up of the working-class. If then the unnatural extension of the working-day, that capital necessarily strives after in its unmeasured passion for self-expansion, shortens the length of life of the individual labourer, and therefore the duration of his labour-power, the forces used up have to be replaced at a more rapid rate and the sum of the expenses for the reproduction of labour-power will be greater; just as in a machine the part of its value to be reproduced every day is greater the more rapidly the machine is worn out. It would seem

3. Nonsense, foolishness. Sabbatarians: those who favor strict observance of the Sabbath.
4. Haggles.
5. The difference between the amount of capital needed to produce something and the amount of capital that product is worth; it is created from labor power.

therefore that the interest of capital itself points in the direction of a normal working-day.

The slave-owner buys his labourer as he buys his horse. If he loses his slave, he loses capital that can only be restored by new outlay in the slave-mart. But "the rice-grounds of Georgia, or the swamps of the Mississippi may be fatally injurious to the human constitution; but the waste of human life which the cultivation of these districts necessitates, is not so great that it cannot be repaired from the teeming preserves of Virginia and Kentucky. Considerations of economy, moreover, which, under a natural system, afford some security for human treatment by identifying the master's interest with the slave's preservation, when once trading in slaves is practised, become reasons for racking to the uttermost the toil of the slave; for, when his place can at once be supplied from foreign preserves, the duration of his life becomes a matter of less moment than its productiveness while it lasts. It is accordingly a maxim of slave management, in slave-importing countries, that the most effective economy is that which takes out of the human chattel in the shortest space of time the utmost amount of exertion it is capable of putting forth. It is in tropical culture, where annual profits often equal the whole capital of plantations, that negro life is most recklessly sacrificed. It is the agriculture of the West Indies, which has been for centuries prolific of fabulous wealth, that has engulfed millions of the African race. It is in Cuba, at this day, whose revenues are reckoned by millions, and whose planters are princes, that we see in the servile class, the coarsest fare, the most exhausting and unremitting toil, and even the absolute destruction of a portion of its numbers every year."[6]

Mutato nomine de te fabula narratur.[7] For slave-trade read labour-market, for Kentucky and Virginia, Ireland and the agricultural districts of England, Scotland, and Wales, for Africa, Germany. We heard how over-work thinned the ranks of the bakers in London. Nevertheless, the London labour-market is always over-stocked with German and other candidates for death in the bakeries. Pottery, as we saw, is one of the shortest-lived industries. Is there any want therefore of potters? Josiah Wedgwood,[8] the inventor of modern pottery, himself originally a common workman, said in 1785 before the House of Commons that the whole trade employed from 15,000 to 20,000 people. In the year 1861 the population alone of the town centres of this industry in Great Britain numbered 101,302. "The cotton trade has existed for ninety years . . . It has existed for three generations of the English race, and I believe I may safely say that during that period it has destroyed nine generations of factory operatives."[9] * * *

What experience shows to the capitalist generally is a constant excess of population, *i.e.*, an excess in relation to the momentary requirements of surplus-labour-absorbing capital, although this excess is made up of generations of human beings stunted, short-lived, swiftly replacing each other, plucked, so to say, before maturity. And, indeed, experience shows to the intelligent observer with what swiftness and grip the capitalist mode of production,

6. Quoted from J. E. Cairnes, *The Slave Power* (London, 1862).

7. Once the name has been changed, the story is told about you (Latin); from HORACE (65–8 B.C.E.), *Satires* 1.1.69–70.

8. Noted English potter (1730–1795).

9. Quoted from a speech delivered in the House of Commons, April 27, 1863. The following ellipsis is the translators'.

dating, historically speaking, only from yesterday, has seized the vital power of the people by the very root—shows how the degeneration of the industrial population is only retarded by the constant absorption of primitive and physically uncorrupted elements from the country—shows how even the country labourers, in spite of fresh air and the principle of natural selection, that works so powerfully amongst them, and only permits the survival of the strongest, are already beginning to die off. Capital that has such good reasons for denying the sufferings of the legions of workers that surround it, is in practice moved as much and as little by the sight of the coming degradation and final depopulation of the human race, as by the probable fall of the earth into the sun. In every stock-jobbing swindle every one knows that some time or other the crash must come, but every one hopes that it may fall on the head of his neighbour, after he himself has caught the shower of gold and placed it in safety. *Après moi le déluge!*[1] is the watchword of every capitalist and of every capitalist nation. Hence Capital is reckless of the health or length of life of the labourer, unless under compulsion from society. To the out-cry as to the physical and mental degradation, the premature death, the torture of over-work, it answers: Ought these to trouble us since they increase our profits? But looking at things as a whole, all this does not, indeed, depend on the good or ill will of the individual capitalist. Free competition brings out the inherent laws of capitalist production, in the shape of external coercive laws having power over every individual capitalist.

The establishment of a normal working-day is the result of centuries of struggle between capitalist and labourer. The history of this struggle shows two opposed tendencies. Compare, *e.g.*, the English factory legislation of our time with the English Labour Statutes from the 14th century to well into the middle of the 18th. Whilst the modern Factory Acts[2] compulsorily shortened the working-day, the earlier statutes tried to lengthen it by compulsion. Of course the pretensions of capital in embryo—when, beginning to grow, it secures the right of absorbing a *quantum sufficit*[3] of surplus-labour, not merely by the force of economic relations, but by the help of the State—appear very modest when put face to face with the concessions that, growling and struggling, it has to make in its adult condition. It takes centuries ere the "free" labourer, thanks to the development of capitalistic production, agrees, *i.e.*, is compelled by social conditions, to sell the whole of his active life, his very capacity for work, for the price of the necessaries of life, his birthright for a mess of pottage.[4] Hence it is natural that the lengthening of the work-day, which capital, from the middle of the 14th to the end of the 17th century, tries to impose by State-measures on adult labourers, approximately coincides with the shortening of the working-day which, in the second half of the 19th century, has here and there been effected by the State to prevent the coining of children's blood into capital. That which to-day, *e.g.*, in the State of Massachusetts, until recently the freest State of the North-American Republic, has been proclaimed as the statutory limit of the labour of children under 12,[5] was

1. After me the flood (French); an old French proverb, often attributed to Louis XV or his mistress, Madame de Pompadour, after the 1757 defeat of the French and Austrian armies in the battle of Rossbach.
2. Series of measures, passed beginning in 1819, intended to improve working conditions (particularly for children and women workers).
3. Sufficient quantity (Latin).
4. As the hungry Esau sold his birthright to his brother Jacob; Genesis 25.29–34.
5. That is, a 10-hour day (the law passed in 1842).

in England, even in the middle of the 17th century, the normal working-day of able-bodied artisans, robust labourers, athletic blacksmiths.

* * *

1867

From Letter from Friedrich Engels to Joseph Bloch[1]

London, September 21–22, 1890

According to the materialist conception of history, the *ultimately* determining element in history is the production and reproduction of real life. More than this neither Marx nor I have ever asserted. Hence if somebody twists this into saying that the economic element is the *only* determining one, he transforms that proposition into a meaningless, abstract, senseless phrase. The economic situation is the basis, but the various elements of the superstructure: political forms of the class struggle and its results, to wit: constitutions established by the victorious class after a successful battle, etc., juridical forms, and then even the reflexes of all these actual struggles in the brains of the participants, political, juristic, philosophical theories, religious views and their further development into systems of dogmas, also exercise their influence upon the course of the historical struggles and in many cases preponderate in determining their *form*. There is an interaction of all these elements in which, amid all the endless host of accidents (that is, of things and events, whose inner connection is so remote or so impossible of proof that we can regard it as non-existent, as negligible) the economic movement finally asserts itself as necessary. Otherwise the application of the theory to any period of history one chose would be easier than the solution of a simple equation of the first degree.

We make our history ourselves, but, in the first place, under very definite assumptions and conditions. Among these the economic ones are ultimately decisive. But the political ones, etc., and indeed even the traditions which haunt human minds also play a part, although not the decisive one. The Prussian state also arose and developed from historical, ultimately economic causes. But it could scarcely be maintained without pedantry that among the many small states of North Germany, Brandenburg[2] was specifically determined by economic necessity to become the great power embodying the economic, linguistic and, after the Reformation, also the religious difference between North and South, and not by other elements as well (above all by its entanglement with Poland, owing to the possession of Prussia, and hence with international political relations—which were indeed also decisive in the formation of the Austrian dynastic power). Without making oneself ridiculous it would be a difficult thing to explain in terms of economics the existence of every small state in Germany, past and present, or the origin of the High German consonant shifts,[3] which widened the geographical wall of

1. A socialist (1871–1936), who in the 1890s was a student at the University of Berlin. The translator is not named.

2. Region that became the core of the kingdom of Prussia (1701–1871) and of the German Empire (1871–1918).

3. Linguistic changes (ca. 500–700 C.E.) that distinguish the German of central and southern Ger-

partition, formed by the mountains from the Sudetic range to the Taunus,[4] to the extent of a regular fissure across all Germany.

In the second place, however, history is made in such a way that the final result always arises from conflicts between many individual wills, of which each again has been made what it is by a host of particular conditions of life. Thus there are innumerable intersecting forces, an infinite series of parallelograms of forces which give rise to one resultant—the historical event. This may again itself be viewed as the product of a power which works as a whole, *unconsciously* and without volition. For what each individual wills is obstructed by everyone else, and what emerges is something that no one willed. Thus past history proceeds in the manner of a natural process and is essentially subject to the same laws of motion. But from the fact that individual wills—of which each desires what he is impelled to by his physical constitution and external, in the last resort economic, circumstances (either his own personal circumstances or those of society in general)—do not attain what they want, but are merged into a collective mean, a common resultant, it must not be concluded that their value is equal to zero. On the contrary, each contributes to the resultant and is to this degree involved in it.

I would furthermore ask you to study this theory from its original sources and not at second-hand; it is really much easier. Marx hardly wrote anything in which it did not play a part. But especially *The Eighteenth Brumaire of Louis Bonaparte* is a most excellent example of its application. There are also many allusions in *Capital*.[5] Then may I also direct you to my writings: *Herr Eugen Dühring's Revolution in Science* and *Ludwig Feuerbach and the End of Classical German Philosophy*,[6] in which I have given the most detailed account of historical materialism which, as far as I know, exists.

Marx and I are ourselves partly to blame for the fact that the younger people sometimes lay more stress on the economic side than is due to it. We had to emphasise the main principle *vis-à-vis* our adversaries, who denied it, and we had not always the time, the place or the opportunity to allow the other elements involved in the interaction to come into their rights. But when it was a case of presenting a section of history, that is, of a practical application, it was a different matter and there no error was possible. Unfortunately, however, it happens only too often that people think they have fully understood a new theory and can apply it without more ado from the moment they have mastered its main principles, and even those not always correctly. And I cannot exempt many of the more recent "Marxists" from this reproach, for the most amazing rubbish has been produced in this quarter, too.

* * *

1890

many (High German, the official dialect) from the speech of northern Germany (Low German); for example, *hopen* (to hope) becomes in High German *hoffen*, and *Plante* (plant) becomes *Pflanze*.

4. A mountain range in southwest central Germany. "The Sudetic range": the Sudetes, mountains between the Czech Republic and Poland.

5. Vol. 1 was published in 1867, vols. 2 and 3 in 1893 and 1894; *The Eighteenth Brumaire* first appeared in 1852.

6. Published in 1886; *Dühring's Revolution in Science*, now known as *Anti-Dühring*, was published in 1877–78.

CHARLES BAUDELAIRE
1821–1867

Charles Baudelaire, who wanted to include the right to contradict oneself among the Rights of Man, made self-contradiction into a quintessentially modern form of poetics. But his canonization as a major poet would have surprised both him and his contemporaries. Although his book *Les Fleurs du mal* (1857, *The Flowers of Evil*) is now considered a masterpiece, it had an inauspicious start. The volume explicitly addresses a "hypocritical reader" who will *not* want the self-image the poems depict. The book's notorious 1857 obscenity trial (which required Baudelaire to remove six poems and pay a fine) seemed to enact the rejection the poems predicted, but it also lent the author's celebrity an unseemly luster. Few of Baudelaire's friends could have foreseen a time when he would be hailed as a genius. And even *they* would not have guessed how many roles literary historians would assign to him.

Viewed by contemporaries as a late, decadent Romantic or as a Parnassian lover of art for art's sake, Baudelaire is often described as the founder of what would later be known as symbolism, especially in his theory of "universal analogy" and in his early sonnet "Correspondances." But what was peculiarly modern about Baudelaire was perhaps best described by one of his last editors, who called him "that strange classic of nonclassical things," or by the poet Paul Claudel (1868–1955), who said he combined "the style of Racine with the style of a journalist of the Second Empire." Theorists of Romanticism, Parnassianism, symbolism, modernism and even realism have all claimed him as a key figure, but in very different—sometimes antithetical—ways. It is hard to imagine a more fitting tribute to Baudelaire's practice of self-contradiction.

Baudelaire's father, François, was a sixty-year-old ex-priest and widower when he married Caroline Dufaÿs, a penniless orphan, who was twenty-six. When François died in 1827, he left Caroline with a twenty-two-year-old son, Alphonse, from his first marriage, along with her own five-year-old son, Charles. Charles later fondly remembered his mother as a beautiful widow whom he had all to himself during this period, but in 1828 she married a handsome army officer, Jacques Aupick, in some haste. It is not known when, or whether, Charles ever learned of the birth of his stillborn half-sister in December 1828.

Jacques Aupick's career in the military was remarkably successful; he was promoted to general on the same day that Charles passed the *baccalauréat* exam (despite having been expelled from his Parisian high school earlier in 1839 for swallowing rather than surrendering a note from a classmate). For the next two years, Baudelaire lived a bohemian life among artists and students, wrote poetry, contracted gonorrhea and sizable debts, and generally enjoyed life. His stepfather and half-brother, however, foreseeing only ruin from his failure to establish himself professionally, paid his debts, borrowed money from his patrimony, and sent him on what was planned as a yearlong voyage to India to separate him from "the slippery streets of Paris" (as Aupick put it) before he turned twenty-one. Baudelaire did indeed journey around Africa as far as Réunion Island, but caught a return ship there back to France. Though it failed to protect Charles's future bank account, the trip provided him with a different kind of capital: a store of poetic images and themes he was to draw on in his poetry.

Once back in Paris, Baudelaire fell in love with a beautiful mixed-race actress named Jeanne Duval. Along with his brief liaisons with other women, the poet maintained a complicated, tempestuous, sometimes domestic relationship with Jeanne for most of his life. When he turned twenty-one he came into the inheritance left him by his father—the interest from which would have given him an annual income of 2,400 francs (approximately the starting salary for a typical civil service job)—and quickly spent half of it. His mother, alarmed at the speed with which his funds were disappearing, imposed a legal mediator between him and what remained. For the next twenty years, Baudelaire's correspondence with editors and colleagues records his attempts to earn money through his writings, while the frequent letters he sent to his mother express both his desire to play on her maternal sympathies and his rage against the permanent infantilization his financial situation imposed. In March 1866 he suffered a stroke, undoubtedly caused by end-stage syphillis, while on an unsuccessful lecture tour in Belgium. The stroke left him partially paralyzed and aphasic, able to utter only the single word "crénom!" (from *sacré nom de Dieu!* or "holy name of God!"). He died in a Paris clinic seventeen months later, his mother by his side.

Baudelaire's first publications were *Salons*, reviews of the annual art exhibit at the Louvre museum. Unlike other rebels against society who were frequently supported by the same bourgeois world they scorned, Baudelaire was fully aware of the often perverse and hated interdependency between artists and patrons, beginning his *Salon of 1845* by describing the economic purpose of such annual shows: "One must please those on whose resources one wants to live." In 1847 he discovered the work of the American poet EDGAR ALLAN POE (1809–1849), whom he considered a fellow martyr to bourgeois values. Paradoxically, his translations of Poe would earn Baudelaire more money than all his other works put together; his introductions to the translations create a portrait of poetic genius that still shapes the French view of Poe to this day. He tried his hand at theater, wrote about drugs and addictions, published often contradictory theoretical essays in reviews, and started to publish his poetry; but *Les Fleurs du mal* did not appear until 1857, just months after the death of Jacques Aupick. When the volume drew legal charges of immorality, he removed the six "condemned" poems and published a new edition. The offending poems all dealt with female—particularly lesbian—sexuality (an early title of *Les Fleurs du mal* had been *Les Lesbiennes*). Baudelaire joined his contemporary THÉOPHILE GAUTIER and others in using lesbianism to get at the nature of art for art's sake. His descriptions of female sexuality were considered not only immoral but a sign of "realism," then a term of condemnation for works exposing frank, unidealized, and unpleasant realities. When, in 1949, the ban was finally lifted, the poems were defended on the grounds that they were symbolic, not realistic.

In everything he wrote (or sometimes in two equal and opposite texts), Baudelaire depicted a human nature profoundly at odds with itself. In the first section of *Les Fleurs du mal*, titled "Spleen et Idéal," the poet is torn between an aspiration toward an ideal ("Idéal") that can neither be realized nor renounced, and an attraction to degradation ("Spleen") that can neither be accepted nor denied. "Spleen," an English term used by eighteenth-century poets to mean "melancholy," here designates "depression," "boredom," "disgust," "abjection," "sin," and even "materiality." Baudelaire's poetic speaker becomes addicted to his torture, desiring what he flees and fleeing what he desires while remaining excruciatingly aware of his impossible position, which then becomes the subject of the poems.

In his later work, this metaphysical, aesthetic, or psychological self-division is subject to a further force of estrangement: the historical process. In the second edition of *Les Fleurs du mal* (1861), Baudelaire added a section called "Tableaux Parisiens" ("Parisian Scenes"). Responding to the reconstructions of Paris undertaken during the Second Empire, Baudelaire wrote (in his poem "Le Cygne"): "Paris is changing, but nothing in my melancholy has budged. . . . The form of a city changes faster, alas, than the heart of a man." The anachronistic relationship between man and his desires is exacerbated by the speed of modernization. Even alienation does not have a permanent form. It is this divided perception of modernity—not a simple process of change but something partly unchanging and partly fleeting, partly eternal and partly historical—that Baudelaire discusses in our selection, "The Painter of Modern Life" (1863).

"The Painter of Modern Life," first published in the widely circulated newspaper *Le Figaro*, sketches out an unprecedented theory of modern aesthetics. Many later critics have felt that the essay should have been about Édouard Manet, with whom Baudelaire was soon to become friends—and who they take to be the true "painter of modern life"—in preference to Constantin Guys, a minor nineteenth-century draftsman whom history has almost forgotten. But Baudelaire begins his essay with a plea for minor artists, indicating that what he appreciated in Guys was his *lack* of monumentality—the speed of his sketches, the almost photographic accuracy of his reportage (although Baudelaire scorned photography itself), and perhaps even his ephemerality. Guys captured for Baudelaire the aesthetics of the *flâneur*—an idler on the city streets, filled with curiosity but without goal or interest, made possible by the growth of modern commodity culture and display.

In his long essay, Baudelaire describes two complementary paradigms for the artist: the *flâneur*, who gives himself over to the crowd (Baudelaire calls it a "saintly prostitution of the soul" in his prose poem "Crowds"), and the dandy, who holds himself aloof and unmoved. While the *flâneur* is contextualized by new practices of shopping on the city streets, the dandy resists the promiscuity of buying and selling in general. In his recoil from vulgarity and commerce, the dandy personifies the stance of aristocracy, searching for *distinction* as opposed to the "leveling" that Baudelaire associates with democracy. Baudelaire's "modernity" is thus deeply opposed to the postrevolutionary economic modernization that also informs it.

Both the *flâneur* and the dandy contrast sharply with, but owe part of their appeal to, femininity. In section 11, "In Praise of Cosmetics," Baudelaire goes so far as to see makeup—a sign of theater as well as a sign of femininity—as a paradigm for art. In a violent put-down of the Romantic idealization of nature, he claims that nature can only counsel crime and self-interest, while everything good is a product of restraint and calculation. Hence cosmetics should not try to recover the artlessness of youth ("Nature"), but should frankly seek the beauty of artifice ("Art"). The implication for the modern artist is that everything of value comes through culture, not nature, and that to pretend otherwise leads to a distorted and distorting idealization of a nature that never existed.

Baudelaire thus forged "The Painter of Modern Life" out of a clash between nostalgia for lost aristocratic values and fascination with the contemporary street life of commodity culture. In his poetry and in his prose, he was able to distill from the shocks and chance encounters of the changing city a radically new poetics. Those "slippery streets of Paris" so feared by Jacques Aupick became, for Baudelaire and perhaps for modern art in general, the very substance of modernity.

BIBLIOGRAPHY

Baudelaire's prose works were collected after his death and published in two volumes, *Curiosités esthétiques* (1868) and *L'Art romantique* (1869). An excellent English edition of the main texts is available in two volumes, translated by Jonathan Mayne: *Art in Paris, 1845–1862* (1965) and *The Painter of Modern Life and Other Essays* (1965). Shorter selections can be found in *My Heart Laid Bare*, edited by Peter Quennell, translated by Norman Cameron (1950); *Baudelaire as a Literary Critic*, translated by Lois Boe Hyslop and Francis E. Hyslop Jr. (1964); and *Baudelaire: Writings on Art and Artists*, translated by P. E. Charvet (1972). *Baudelaire*, by Claude Pichois and Jean Ziegler (1987; trans. 1989), is a rich and meticulously researched biography.

Margaret Gilman's study, *Baudelaire the Critic* (1943), provides the classic introduction to Baudelaire's critical writings. Criticism of Baudelaire was for a long time influenced by Théophile Gautier's 1868 introduction to the third edition of *Les Fleurs du mal*. Gautier's Baudelaire was a lover of artifice, an adherent of art for art's sake. A good sampling of critical essays in this mode can be found in Henri Peyre's *Baudelaire: A Collection of Critical Essays* (1962). Early readers took Baudelaire at his word and lamented the bad luck that had given him such a mediocre mother, such a difficult financial situation, and such impossible desires. A study by Jean-Paul Sartre, *Baudelaire* (1946; trans. 1949), reversed this view: Sartre treated Baudelaire as a man who had gotten exactly what he wanted, including the appearance of having wanted something else. Another important critical perspective on Baudelaire's modernity took shape in the writings of Walter Benjamin, a number of which were published in English as *Charles Baudelaire: A Lyric Poet in the Era of High Capitalism* (1973). His study of Baudelaire was part of an immense project on the Paris Arcades, which was finally published as *Das Passagen-Werk* (1982; trans. 1999, *The Arcades Project*). This work by Benjamin is essential for an understanding of what is modern about Baudelaire.

T. J. Clark's *Painting of Modern Life: Paris in the Art of Manet and His Followers* (1984) takes its title, if little else, from Baudelaire and analyzes art in Paris as if Baudelaire *had* written about Manet. For more explicit discussions of Baudelaire and modern aesthetics, see David Carrier's *High Art: Charles Baudelaire and the Origins of Modernist Painting* (1996) and J. A. Hiddleston's *Baudelaire and the Art of Memory* (1999). Of the many recent critical studies, four focus on Baudelaire's modernity: essays by Paul de Man in *Blindness and Insight* (1971) and *The Rhetoric of Romanticism* (1984); Timothy Raser, *A Poetics of Art Criticism: The Case of Baudelaire* (1989); Richard Terdiman, *Present Past: Modernity and the Memory Crisis* (1993); and Susan Blood, *Baudelaire and the Aesthetics of Bad Faith* (1997). And finally, an excellent and wide-ranging collection of essays directly addressing Baudelaire's modernity can be found in *Baudelaire and the Poetics of Modernity*, edited by Patricia A. Ward (2001). The annotated bibliography in David Baguley's *Critical Bibliography of French Literature* (1994) is excellent, as are the annual bibliographical updates published by the W. T. Bandy Center for Baudelaire Studies at Vanderbilt University.

From The Painter of Modern Life[1]

From *I. Beauty, Fashion, and Happiness*

The world—and even the world of artists—is full of people who can go to the Louvre,[2] walk rapidly, without so much as a glance, past rows of very interesting, though secondary, pictures, to come to a rapturous halt in front of a Titian or a Raphael[3]—one of those that have been most popularized by the engraver's art; then they will go home happy, not a few saying to themselves, 'I know my Museum.' Just as there are people who, having once read Bossuet and Racine,[4] fancy that they have mastered the history of literature.

Fortunately from time to time there come forward righters of wrong, critics, amateurs, curious enquirers, to declare that Raphael, or Racine, does not contain the whole secret, and that the minor poets too have something good, solid and delightful to offer; and finally that however much we may love *general* beauty, as it is expressed by classical poets and artists, we are no less wrong to neglect *particular* beauty, the beauty of circumstance and the sketch of manners.

It must be admitted that for some years now the world has been mending its ways a little. The value which collectors today attach to the delightful coloured engravings of the last century proves that a reaction has set in in the direction where it was required; Debucourt, the Saint-Aubins[5] and many others have found their places in the dictionary of artists who are worthy of study. But these represent the past: my concern today is with the painting of manners of the present. The past is interesting not only by reason of the

1. Translated by Jonathan Mayne.
2. The national art museum of France, in Paris.
3. Two famous Italian Renaissance painters, Tiziano Vecellio (ca. 1488–1576) and Raffaello Santi (1483–1520).
4. Jean Racine (1639–1699), quintessential French neoclassical playwright. Jacques-Bénigne Bossuet (1627–1704), French bishop and neoclassical writer.
5. The brothers Charles (1721–1786) and Gabriel (1724–1780) de Saint-Aubin, along with Philibert-Louis Debucourt (1755–1832), were graphic artists and painters (as was Baudelaire's father).

beauty which could be distilled from it by those artists for whom it was the present, but also precisely because it is the past, for its historical value. It is the same with the present. The pleasure which we derive from the representation of the present is due not only to the beauty with which it can be invested, but also to its essential quality of being present.

* * *

This is in fact an excellent opportunity to establish a rational and historical theory of beauty, in contrast to the academic theory of an unique and absolute beauty; to show that beauty is always and inevitably of a double composition, although the impression that it produces is single—for the fact that it is difficult to discern the variable elements of beauty within the unity of the impression invalidates in no way the necessity of variety in its composition. Beauty is made up of an eternal, invariable element, whose quantity it is excessively difficult to determine, and of a relative, circumstantial element, which will be, if you like, whether severally or all at once, the age, its fashions, its morals, its emotions. Without this second element, which might be described as the amusing, enticing, appetizing icing on the divine cake, the first element would be beyond our powers of digestion or appreciation, neither adapted nor suitable to human nature. I defy anyone to point to a single scrap of beauty which does not contain these two elements.

Let me instance two opposite extremes in history. In religious art the duality is evident at the first glance; the ingredient of eternal beauty reveals itself only with the permission and under the discipline of the religion to which the artist belongs. In the most frivolous work of a sophisticated artist belonging to one of those ages which, in our vanity, we characterize as civilized, the duality is no less to be seen; at the same time the eternal part of beauty will be veiled and expressed if not by fashion, at least by the particular temperament of the artist. The duality of art is a fatal consequence of the duality of man. Consider, if you will, the eternally subsisting portion as the soul of art, and the variable element as its body. That is why Stendhal[6]—an impertinent, teasing, even a disagreeable critic, but one whose impertinences are often a useful spur to reflection—approached the truth more closely than many another when he said that 'Beauty is nothing else but a promise of happiness.' This definition doubtless overshoots the mark; it makes Beauty far too subject to the infinitely variable ideal of Happiness; it strips Beauty too neatly of its aristocratic quality: but it has the great merit of making a decided break with the academic error.

I have explained these things more than once before.[7] And these few lines will already have said enough on the subject for those who have a taste for the diversions of abstract thought. I know, however, that the majority of my own countrymen at least have but little inclination for these, and I myself am impatient to embark upon the positive and concrete part of my subject.

From *III. The Artist, Man of the World, Man of the Crowd, and Child*

Today I want to discourse to the public about a strange man, a man of so powerful and so decided an originality that it is sufficient unto itself and does

6. Pen name of Marie Henri Beyle (1783–1842), French novelist and critic; the quotation is from *De l'amour* (1822), chap. 17.

7. E.g. in the article on "Critical Method" on the occasion of the Exposition Universelle of 1855 [translator's note].

not even seek approval. Not a single one of his drawings is signed, if by signature you mean that string of easily forgeable characters which spell a name and which so many other artists affix ostentatiously at the foot of their least important trifles. Yet all his works are signed—with his dazzling *soul*; and art-lovers who have seen and appreciated them will readily recognize them from the description that I am about to give.

A passionate lover of crowds and incognitos, Monsieur C. G.[8] carries originality to the point of shyness. Mr. Thackeray,[9] who, as is well known, is deeply interested in matters of art, and who himself executes the illustrations to his novels, spoke one day of Monsieur G. in the columns of a London review.[1] The latter was furious, as though at an outrage to his virtue. Recently again, when he learnt that I had it in mind to write an appreciation of his mind and his talent, he begged me—very imperiously, I must admit—to suppress his name, and if I must speak of his works, to speak of them as if they were those of an anonymous artist. I will humbly comply with this singular request.

* * *

For ten years I had wanted to get to know Monsieur G., who is by nature a great traveller and cosmopolitan. I knew that for some time he had been on the staff of an English illustrated journal,[2] and that engravings after his travel-sketches, made in Spain, Turkey and the Crimea, had been published there. Since then I have seen a considerable quantity of those drawings, hastily sketched on the spot, and thus I have been able to *read*, so to speak, a detailed account of the Crimean campaign[3] which is much preferable to any other that I know. The same paper had also published, always without signature, a great number of his illustrations of new ballets and operas. When at last I ran him to earth, I saw at once that it was not precisely an *artist*, but rather a *man of the world* with whom I had to do.

* * *

And so, as a first step towards an understanding of Monsieur G., I would ask you to note at once that the mainspring of his genius is *curiosity*.

Do you remember a picture (it really is a picture!), painted—or rather written—by the most powerful pen of our age, and entitled *The Man of the Crowd?*[4] In the window of a coffee-house there sits a convalescent, pleasurably absorbed in gazing at the crowd, and mingling, through the medium of thought, in the turmoil of thought that surrounds him. But lately returned from the valley of the shadow of death, he is rapturously breathing in all the odours and essences of life; as he has been on the brink of total oblivion, he remembers, and fervently desires to remember, everything. Finally he hurls himself headlong into the midst of the throng, in pursuit of an unknown, half-glimpsed countenance that has, on an instant, bewitched him. Curiosity has become a fatal, irresistible passion!

8. Constantin Guys (1802–1892), prolific draftsman whose sketches of the Crimean War were forerunners of photojournalism.
9. William Makepeace Thackeray (1811–1863), English novelist and satirist.
1. The reference has not been traced [translator's note].
2. *The Illustrated London News* [translator's note].
3. War (1854–56) in which Britain, France, and Sardinia came to the aid of Turkey against Russia.
4. A story by EDGAR ALLAN POE, included among his *Tales* (1845) and translated by Baudelaire in the *Nouvelles Histoires Extraordinaires* [translator's note].

Imagine an artist who was always, spiritually, in the condition of that convalescent, and you will have the key to the nature of Monsieur G.

Now convalescence is like a return towards childhood. The convalescent, like the child, is possessed in the highest degree of the faculty of keenly interesting himself in things, be they apparently of the most trivial. Let us go back, if we can, by a retrospective effort of the imagination, towards our most youthful, our earliest, impressions, and we will recognize that they had a strange kinship with those brightly coloured impressions which we were later to receive in the aftermath of a physical illness, always provided that that illness had left our spiritual capacities pure and unharmed. The child sees everything in a state of newness; he is always *drunk*. Nothing more resembles what we call inspiration than the delight with which a child absorbs form and colour. I am prepared to go even further and assert that inspiration has something in common with a convulsion, and that every sublime thought is accompanied by a more or less violent nervous shock which has its repercussion in the very core of the brain. The man of genius has sound nerves, while those of the child are weak. With the one, Reason has taken up a considerable position; with the other, Sensibility is almost the whole being. But genius is nothing more nor less than *childhood recovered* at will—a childhood now equipped for self-expression with manhood's capacities and a power of analysis which enables it to order the mass of raw material which it has involuntarily accumulated.

* * *

The crowd is his element, as the air is that of birds and water of fishes. His passion and his profession are to become one flesh with the crowd. For the perfect *flâneur*,[5] for the passionate spectator, it is an immense joy to set up house in the heart of the multitude, amid the ebb and flow of movement, in the midst of the fugitive and the infinite. To be away from home and yet to feel oneself everywhere at home; to see the world, to be at the centre of the world, and yet to remain hidden from the world—such are a few of the slightest pleasures of those independent, passionate, impartial natures which the tongue can but clumsily define. The spectator is a *prince* who everywhere rejoices in his incognito. The lover of life makes the whole world his family, just like the lover of the fair sex who builds up his family from all the beautiful women that he has ever found, or that are—or are not—to be found; or the lover of pictures who lives in a magical society of dreams painted on canvas. Thus the lover of universal life enters into the crowd as though it were an immense reservoir of electrical energy. Or we might liken him to a mirror as vast as the crowd itself; or to a kaleidoscope gifted with consciousness, responding to each one of its movements and reproducing the multiplicity of life and the flickering grace of all the elements of life. He is an 'I' with an insatiable appetite for the 'non-I', at every instant rendering and explaining it in pictures more living than life itself, which is always unstable and fugitive.

* * *

Few men are gifted with the capacity of seeing; there are fewer still who possess the power of expression. So now, at a time when others are asleep,

5. Idler, man-about-town (French).

Monsieur G. is bending over his table, darting on to a sheet of paper the same glance that a moment ago he was directing towards external things, skirmishing with his pencil, his pen, his brush, splashing his glass of water up to the ceiling, wiping his pen on his shirt, in a ferment of violent activity, as though afraid that the image might escape him, cantankerous though alone, elbowing himself on. And the external world is reborn upon his paper, natural and more than natural, beautiful and more than beautiful, strange and endowed with an impulsive life like the soul of its creator. The phantasmagoria has been distilled from nature. All the raw materials with which the memory has loaded itself are put in order, ranged and harmonized, and undergo that forced idealization which is the result of a childlike perceptiveness—that is to say, a perceptiveness acute and magical by reason of its innocence!

IV. Modernity

And so away he goes, hurrying, searching. But searching for what? Be very sure that this man, such as I have depicted him—this solitary, gifted with an active imagination, ceaselessly journeying across the great human desert—has an aim loftier than that of a mere *flâneur*, an aim more general, something other than the fugitive pleasure of circumstance. He is looking for that quality which you must allow me to call 'modernity'; for I know of no better word to express the idea I have in mind. He makes it his business to extract from fashion whatever element it may contain of poetry within history, to distil the eternal from the transitory. Casting an eye over our exhibitions of modern pictures, we are struck by a general tendency among artists to dress all their subjects in the garments of the past. Almost all of them make use of the costumes and furnishings of the Renaissance, just as David[6] employed the costumes and furnishings of Rome. There is however this difference, that David, by choosing subjects which were specifically Greek or Roman, had no alternative but to dress them in antique garb, whereas the painters of today, though choosing subjects of a general nature and applicable to all ages, nevertheless persist in rigging them out in the costumes of the Middle Ages, the Renaissance or the Orient. This is clearly symptomatic of a great degree of laziness; for it is much easier to decide outright that everything about the garb of an age is absolutely ugly than to devote oneself to the task of distilling from it the mysterious element of beauty that it may contain, however slight or minimal that element may be. By 'modernity' I mean the ephemeral, the fugitive, the contingent, the half of art whose other half is the eternal and the immutable. Every old master has had his own modernity; the great majority of fine portraits that have come down to us from former generations are clothed in the costume of their own period. They are perfectly harmonious, because everything—from costume and coiffure down to gesture, glance and smile (for each age has a deportment, a glance and a smile of its own)—everything, I say, combines to form a completely viable whole. This transitory, fugitive element, whose metamorphoses are so rapid, must on no account be despised or dispensed

6. Jacques-Louis David (1748–1825), artist famous for his classical depictions of the French Revolution. Renaissance: in France, the 16th–17th centuries.

with. By neglecting it, you cannot fail to tumble into the abyss of an abstract and indeterminate beauty, like that of the first woman before the fall of man. If for the necessary and inevitable costume of the age you substitute another, you will be guilty of a mistranslation only to be excused in the case of a masquerade prescribed by fashion. (Thus, the goddesses, nymphs and sultanas of the eighteenth century are still convincing portraits, *morally* speaking.)

It is doubtless an excellent thing to study the old masters in order to learn how to paint; but it can be no more than a waste of labour if your aim is to understand the special nature of present-day beauty. The draperies of Rubens or Veronese[7] will in no way teach you how to depict *moire antique, satin à la reine*[8] or any other fabric of modern manufacture, which we see supported and hung over crinoline or starched muslin petticoat. In texture and weave these are quite different from the fabrics of ancient Venice or those worn at the court of Catherine.[9] Furthermore the cut of skirt and bodice is by no means similar; the pleats are arranged according to a new system. Finally the gesture and the bearing of the woman of today give to her dress a life and a special character which are not those of the woman of the past. In short, for any 'modernity' to be worthy of one day taking its place as 'antiquity', it is necessary for the mysterious beauty which human life accidentally puts into it to be distilled from it. And it is to this task that Monsieur G. particularly addresses himself.

I have remarked that every age had its own gait, glance and gesture. The easiest way to verify this proposition would be to betake oneself to some vast portrait-gallery, such as the one at Versailles.[1] But it has an even wider application. Within that unity which we call a Nation, the various professions and classes and the passing centuries all introduce variety, not only in manners and gesture, but even in the actual form of the face. Certain types of nose, mouth and brow will be found to dominate the scene for a period whose extent I have no intention of attempting to determine here, but which could certainly be subjected to a form of calculation. Considerations of this kind are not sufficiently familiar to our portrait-painters; the great failing of M. Ingres,[2] in particular, is that he seeks to impose upon every type of sitter a more or less complete, by which I mean a more or less despotic, form of perfection, borrowed from the repertory of classical ideas.

In a matter of this kind it would be easy, and indeed legitimate, to argue *a priori*. The perpetual correlation between what is called the 'soul' and what is called the 'body' explains quite clearly how everything that is 'material', or in other words an emanation of the 'spiritual', mirrors, and will always mirror, the spiritual reality from which it derives. If a painstaking, scrupulous, but feebly imaginative artist has to paint a courtesan of today and takes his 'inspiration' (that is the accepted word) from a courtesan by Titian or Raphael, it is only too likely that he will produce a work which is false, ambiguous and

7. Paolo Caliari (1528–1588), major painter of the 16th-century Venetian school (called "Veronese" because born in Verona). Peter Paul Rubens (1577–1640), Flemish baroque painter.

8. Literally "old-fashioned watered silk" and "satin for the queen" (French), two elegant modern fabrics.

9. Catherine de Medici (1519–1589), the queen consort of Henry II of France, and subsequently regent.

1. The royal palace at Versailles (near Paris), built (1676–1708) by Louis XIV; the seat of government for more than 100 years, it was designated a national museum in 1837.

2. Jean-August-Dominique Ingres (1780–1867), celebrated French painter and portraitist.

obscure. From the study of a masterpiece of that time and type he will learn nothing of the bearing, the glance, the smile or the living 'style' of one of those creatures whom the dictionary of fashion has successively classified under the coarse or playful titles of 'doxies', 'kept women', *lorettes*, or *biches*.[3]

The same criticism may be strictly applied to the study of the military man and the dandy, and even to that of animals, whether horses or dogs; in short, of everything that goes to make up the external life of this age. Woe to him who studies the antique for anything else but pure art, logic and general method! By steeping himself too thoroughly in it, he will lose all memory of the present; he will renounce the rights and privileges offered by circumstance—for almost all our originality comes from the seal which Time imprints on our sensations. I need hardly tell you that I could easily support my assertions with reference to many objects other than women. What would you say, for example, of a marine-painter (I am deliberately going to extremes) who, having to depict the sober and elegant beauty of a modern vessel, were to tire out his eyes by studying the overcharged, involved forms and the monumental poop of a galleon, or the complicated rigging of the sixteenth century? Again, what would you think if you had commissioned an artist to paint the portrait of a thoroughbred, famed in the annals of the turf, and he then proceeded to confine his researches to the Museums and contented himself with a study of the horse in the galleries of the past, in Van Dyck, Borgognone or Van der Meulen?[4]

Under the direction of nature and the tyranny of circumstance, Monsieur G. has pursued an altogether different path. He began by being an observer of life, and only later set himself the task of acquiring the means of expressing it. This has resulted in a thrilling originality in which any remaining vestiges of barbarousness or *naïveté* appear only as new proofs of his faithfulness to the impression received, or as a flattering compliment paid to truth. For most of us, and particularly for men of affairs, for whom nature has no existence save by reference to utility, the fantastic reality of life has become singularly diluted. Monsieur G. never ceases to drink it in; his eyes and his memory are full of it.

From *IX. The Dandy*

* * *

If I speak of love in connection with dandyism, this is because love is the natural occupation of the idle. The dandy does not, however, regard love as a special target to be aimed at. If I have spoken of money, this is because money is indispensable to those who make a cult of their emotions; but the dandy does not aspire to money as to something essential; this crude passion he leaves to vulgar mortals; he would be perfectly content with a limitless credit at the bank. Dandyism does not even consist, as many thoughtless people seem to believe, in an immoderate taste for the toilet and material elegance. For the perfect dandy these things are no more than symbols of

3. Affectionate terms for sexually free women of the demimonde.

4. The Flemish Anthony van Dyke (1599–1641), the French Jacques Courtois, il Borgognone (1620–1676), and the Flemish Adam Frans van der Meulen (1632–1690) all painted horses (in battle scenes, equestrian portraits, and murals).

his aristocratic superiority of mind. Furthermore to his eyes, which are in love with *distinction* above all things, the perfection of his toilet will consist in absolute simplicity, which is the best way, in fact, of achieving the desired quality. What then is this passion, which, becoming doctrine, has produced such a school of tyrants? what this unofficial institution which has formed so haughty and exclusive a sect? It is first and foremost the burning need to create for oneself a personal originality, bounded only by the limits of the proprieties. It is a kind of cult of the self which can nevertheless survive the pursuit of a happiness to be found in someone else—in woman, for example; which can even survive all that goes by in the name of illusions. It is the joy of astonishing others, and the proud satisfaction of never oneself being astonished. A dandy may be blasé, he may even suffer; but in this case, he will smile like the Spartan boy under the fox's tooth.[5]

* * *

Whether these men are nicknamed exquisites, *incroyables,*[6] beaux, lions or dandies, they all spring from the same womb; they all partake of the same characteristic quality of opposition and revolt; they are all representatives of what is finest in human pride, of that compelling need, alas only too rare today, of combating and destroying triviality. It is from this that the dandies obtain that haughty exclusiveness, provocative in its very coldness. Dandyism appears above all in periods of transition, when democracy is not yet all-powerful, and aristocracy is only just beginning to totter and fall. In the disorder of these times, certain men who are socially, politically and financially ill at ease, but are all rich in native energy, may conceive the idea of establishing a new kind of aristocracy, all the more difficult to shatter as it will be based on the most precious, the most enduring faculties, and on the divine gifts which work and money are unable to bestow. Dandyism is the last spark of heroism amid decadence; and the type of dandy discovered by our traveller in North America does nothing to invalidate this idea; for how can we be sure that those tribes which we call 'savage' may not in fact be the *disjecta membra*[7] of great extinct civilizations? Dandyism is a sunset; like the declining daystar, it is glorious, without heat and full of melancholy. But alas, the rising tide of democracy, which invades and levels everything, is daily overwhelming these last representatives of human pride and pouring floods of oblivion upon the footprints of these stupendous warriors. Dandies are becoming rarer and rarer in our country, whereas amongst our neighbours in England the social system and the constitution (the true constitution, I mean: the constitution which expresses itself through behaviour) will for a long time yet allow a place for the descendants of Sheridan, Brummel and Byron,[8] granted at least that men are born who are worthy of such a heritage.

What to the reader may have seemed a digression is not so in truth. The moral reflections and considerations provoked by an artist's drawings are in many cases the best translation of them that criticism can make; such sug-

5. According to legend, a Greek boy of Sparta who had stolen a fox hid it under his cloak and allowed the animal to devour his entrails rather than reveal the theft.
6. Incredibles (French): late-18th-century fops who called everything "incredible."
7. Scattered pieces (Latin).
8. The Irish-born dramatist Richard Brinsley Sheridan (1751–1816), George Bryan ("Beau") Brummell (1778–1840), and the poet George Gordon, Lord Byron (1788–1824) were all English dandies.

gestions form part of an underlying idea which begins to emerge as they are set out one after the other. It is hardly necessary to say that when Monsieur G. sketches one of his dandies on the paper, he never fails to give him his historical personality—his legendary personality, I would venture to say, if we were not speaking of the present time and of things generally considered as frivolous. Nothing is missed; his lightness of step, his social aplomb, the simplicity in his air of authority, his way of wearing a coat or riding a horse, his bodily attitudes which are always relaxed but betray an inner energy, so that when your eye lights upon one of those privileged beings in whom the graceful and the formidable are so mysteriously blended, you think: 'A rich man perhaps, but more likely an out-of-work Hercules!'[9]

The distinguishing characteristic of the dandy's beauty consists above all in an air of coldness which comes from an unshakeable determination not to be moved; you might call it a latent fire which hints at itself, and which could, but chooses not to burst into flame. It is this quality which these pictures express so perfectly.

XI. In Praise of Cosmetics

I remember a song, so worthless and silly that it seems hardly proper to quote from it in a work which has some pretensions to seriousness, but which nevertheless expresses very well, in its *vaudeville* manner, the aesthetic creed of people who do not think. 'Nature embellishes Beauty', it runs. It is of course to be presumed that, had he known how to write in French, the poet would rather have said 'Simplicity embellishes Beauty', which is equivalent to the following startling new truism: '*Nothing* embellishes *something*.'

The majority of errors in the field of aesthetics spring from the eighteenth century's false premiss in the field of ethics. At that time Nature was taken as ground, source and type of all possible Good and Beauty. The negation of original sin played no small part in the general blindness of that period. But if we are prepared to refer simply to the facts, which are manifest to the experience of all ages no less than to the readers of the Law Reports, we shall see that Nature teaches us nothing, or practically nothing. I admit that she *compels* man to sleep, to eat, to drink, and to arm himself as well as he may against the inclemencies of the weather: but it is she too who incites man to murder his brother, to eat him, to lock him up and to torture him; for no sooner do we take leave of the domain of needs and necessities to enter that of pleasures and luxury than we see that Nature can counsel nothing but crime. It is this infallible Mother Nature who has created parricide and cannibalism, and a thousand other abominations that both shame and modesty prevent us from naming. On the other hand it is philosophy (I speak of good philosophy) and religion which command us to look after our parents when they are poor and infirm. Nature, being none other than the voice of our own self-interest, would have us slaughter them. I ask you to review and scrutinize whatever is natural—all the actions and desires of the purely natural man: you will find nothing but frightfulness. Everything beau-

9. The Roman name of Heracles, the greatest of the legendary Greek heroes; among other feats, he performed 12 famous labors.

tiful and noble is the result of reason and calculation. Crime, of which the human animal has learned the taste in his mother's womb, is natural by origin. Virtue, on the other hand, is artificial, supernatural, since at all times and in all places gods and prophets have been needed to teach it to animalized humanity, man being powerless to discover it by himself. Evil happens without effort, naturally, fatally; Good is always the product of some art. All that I am saying about Nature as a bad counsellor in moral matters, and about Reason as true redeemer and reformer, can be applied to the realm of Beauty. I am thus led to regard external finery as one of the signs of the primitive nobility of the human soul. Those races which our confused and perverted civilization is pleased to treat as savage, with an altogether ludicrous pride and complacency, understand, just as the child understands, the lofty spiritual significance of the toilet. In their naif adoration of what is brilliant—many-coloured feathers, iridescent fabrics, the incomparable majesty of artificial forms—the baby and the savage bear witness to their disgust of the real, and thus give proof, without knowing it, of the immateriality of their soul. Woe to him who, like Louis XV[1] (the product not of a true civilization but of a recrudescence of barbarism), carries his degeneracy to the point of no longer having a taste for anything but nature unadorned.[2]

Fashion should thus be considered as a symptom of the taste for the ideal which floats on the surface of all the crude, terrestrial and loathsome bric-à-brac that the natural life accumulates in the human brain: as a sublime deformation of Nature, or rather a permanent and repeated attempt at her *reformation*. And so it has been sensibly pointed out (though the reason has not been discovered) that every fashion is charming, relatively speaking, each one being a new and more or less happy effort in the direction of Beauty, some kind of approximation to an ideal for which the restless human mind feels a constant, titillating hunger. But if one wants to appreciate them properly, fashions should never be considered as dead things; you might just as well admire the tattered old rags hung up, as slack and lifeless as the skin of St. Bartholomew,[3] in an old-clothes dealer's cupboard. Rather they should be thought of as vitalized and animated by the beautiful women who wore them. Only in this way can their sense and meaning be understood. If therefore the aphorism 'All fashions are charming' upsets you as being too absolute, say, if you prefer, 'All were once justifiably charming'. You can be sure of being right.

Woman is quite within her rights, indeed she is even accomplishing a kind of duty, when she devotes herself to appearing magical and supernatural; she has to astonish and charm us; as an idol, she is obliged to adorn herself in order to be adored. Thus she has to lay all the arts under contribution for the means of lifting herself above Nature, the better to conquer hearts and rivet attention. It matters but little that the artifice and trickery are known to all, so long as their success is assured and their effect always irresistible. By reflecting in this way the philosopher-artist will find it easy to justify all

1. King of France (1710–1774; reigned 1715–74).
2. We know that when she wished to avoid receiving the king, Mme Du Barry made a point of putting on rouge. It was quite enough; it was her way of closing the door. It was in fact by beautifying herself that she used to frighten away her royal disciple of nature [Baudelaire's note]. Marie Jeanne Bécu, comtesse du Barry (1743–1793), the mistress of Louis XV.
3. One of Jesus' disciples, said to have been martyred by being flayed alive.

the practices adopted by women at all times to consolidate and as it were to make divine their fragile beauty. To enumerate them would be an endless task: but to confine ourselves to what today is vulgarly called 'maquillage',[4] anyone can see that the use of rice-powder, so stupidly anathematized by our Arcadian philosophers,[5] is successfully designed to rid the complexion of those blemishes that Nature has outrageously strewn there, and thus to create an abstract unity in the colour and texture of the skin, a unity, which, like that produced by the tights of a dancer, immediately approximates the human being to the statue, that is to something superior and divine. As for the artificial black with which the eye is outlined, and the rouge with which the upper part of the cheek is painted, although their use derives from the same principle, the need to surpass Nature, the result is calculated to satisfy an absolutely opposite need. Red and black represent life, a supernatural and excessive life: its black frame renders the glance more penetrating and individual, and gives the eye a more decisive appearance of a window open upon the infinite; and the rouge which sets fire to the cheek-bone only goes to increase the brightness of the pupil and adds to the face of a beautiful woman the mysterious passion of the priestess.

Thus, if you will understand me aright, face-painting should not be used with the vulgar, unavowable object of imitating fair Nature and of entering into competition with youth. It has moreover been remarked that artifice cannot lend charm to ugliness and can only serve beauty. Who would dare to assign to art the sterile function of imitating Nature? Maquillage has no need to hide itself or to shrink from being suspected; on the contrary, let it display itself, at least if it does so with frankness and honesty.

I am perfectly happy for those whose owlish gravity prevents them from seeking Beauty in its most minute manifestations to laugh at these reflections of mine and to accuse them of a childish self-importance; their austere verdict leaves me quite unmoved; I content myself with appealing to true artists as well as to those women themselves who, having received at birth a spark of that sacred flame, would tend it so that their whole beings were on fire with it.

1863

4. Makeup (French).
5. Utopian lovers of nature; according to long-standing literary convention, Arcadia (a district of Greece) is the home of pastoral simplicity and happiness.

MATTHEW ARNOLD
1822–1888

In an assessment published in the 1970s, the New York Intellectual Lionel Trilling concluded that Matthew Arnold is "virtually the founding father of modern criticism in the English-speaking world." Citing our first selection, "The Function of Criticism at the Present Time" (1865), Trilling quoted Arnold's famous injunction that the critic should strive to "see the object as in itself it really is" and his celebrated definition of criticism as the "disinterested endeavour to learn and propagate the best that is known and thought in the world." These authoritative statements, Trilling maintained, gave later scholars and teachers their inspiration and interpretive mission.

Arnold provided literary criticism with an important social function and paved the way for its "institutionalization" in the academy. He regarded the writing and reading of literature as urgent activities in the world, insisting "that poetry is at bottom a criticism of life; that the greatness of a poet lies in his powerful and beautiful application of ideas to life,—to the question: How to live." Serious criticism, he believed, was responsible for generating and maintaining the context of ideas and high standards that the production of literature required. Even more: criticism, for Arnold, meant an engagement with history, education, politics, religion, philosophy and other subjects and concerns; literature is vitally connected to society and culture.

Arnold continues today to represent an ideal of literary and cultural humanism that many critics honor. But this same ideal is one that radical critics and contemporary literary theorists have sought to complicate or undermine. As the scholar Joseph Carroll has noted, Arnold's key term "disinterestedness" is "now the most violently disputed word in the Arnoldian lexicon," and many theorists from the 1970s to the present have launched their proposals by taking issue with Arnold's and his followers' account of the critic's role and procedures. For example, STANLEY FISH's reader-response criticism denies the possibility of "disinterested" objective perception, and the Marxist critic TERRY EAGLETON emphasizes Arnold's alignment with state power and the privileged classes in his stress on "timeless truths."

Arnold excelled as a critic and polemicist, and he frequently took delight in the public controversies that his books and articles kindled and in the charges hurled against him. But Arnold was also a poet, an educator, and an advocate for civility and moderation who followed in the footsteps of his eminent father—Thomas Arnold (1795–1842), a religious leader, historian, and, from 1828 to 1841, the influential, reform-minded headmaster of Rugby, a venerable boarding school for boys. At Rugby, Thomas Arnold added the study of French, German, and mathematics to the traditional classical curriculum and gave new emphasis to history and geography. He resolutely campaigned for Christianity, patriotism, self-reliance, loyalty, duty, and public service, and he won great renown for his commitment to them in education.

Educated at Rugby and Oxford University, Matthew Arnold seems at first to have concentrated more on his social life (he was something of a dandy) than on his studies. His poetry—most of which he wrote during the 1840s and 1850s—left him unsatisfied, yet it eloquently expresses the self-doubt, intellectual unease, and emotional hesitancy felt by midcentury intellectuals, when Charles Darwin's theories of evolution and the skeptical inquiry into the historical status and transmission of biblical texts (the "higher criticism") were calling the time-honored principles of Christian faith into question. Arnold's first two books were *The Strayed Reveller, and Other Poems* (1849) and *Empedocles on Etna, and Other Poems* (1852). In his preface to his 1853 collection—his first piece of published prose—Arnold articulated what he conceded was missing from his own verse: "the spirit of the great classical works," "their intense significance, their noble simplicity, and their calm pathos" that create "unity and profoundness of moral impression." He felt that this failure to evoke the best in European moral value was shared generally by modern literature.

In 1851 Arnold received an appointment as an inspector of schools, and this demanding work involved much tedious discussion with teachers and administrators and painstaking reviews of students' examinations and papers. It also required extensive travel in England and research trips abroad in 1859 and 1865, which led to three books on European (particularly French) systems of education. Though it was often wearying, Arnold took great pride in his work and did not retire until 1883; he viewed the schools as the crucial site for "civilising the next generation of the lower classes, who, as things are going, will have most of the political power of the country in their hands." Clearly, much more than literary interpretation was at stake. In his duties as an inspector, he saw the privations that workers and their families suffered, and he was dedicated to the task of social and cultural progress, identifying himself as a "Liberal of the future."

Arnold was named Professor of Poetry at Oxford University in 1857, a position he held until 1867. This appointment did not oblige him to teach or supervise students or to be in residence, and so he was able both to remain in his government post and to gain notice as a prolific social, cultural, and literary critic. His major prose works are *Essays in Criticism, First Series* (1865), *Essays in Criticism, Second Series* (1888), and *Culture and Anarchy* (1869), which examines the condition of England as represented by the three groups Arnold nicknamed the Barbarians (the aristocracy), the Philistines (the middle classes), and the Populace (the working classes). He also wrote extensively on religion, including *Literature and Dogma* (1873), which, he said, was the "most important" of all his prose works, the one most capable "of being useful." Examining the shaken doctrines and tenets of orthodox creeds and churches, it made a forthright case for a literary response and approach to the Scriptures that would treasure their enduring moral truths. *Literature and Dogma* sold 100,000 copies, far more than any of his other books.

Arnold stated in *Culture and Anarchy* that he wanted to heighten among the English "the impulse to the development of the whole man, to connecting and harmonizing all parts of him, perfecting all, leaving none to take their chance." Though these sentiments were presented as possessing a timeless validity, Arnold voiced them at a moment in English history when "anarchy"—social unrest and rioting—had erupted in the streets and revolution seemed a real possibility. The Reform Act of 1832 had increased the number of voters by 50 percent, but the working class and the poor remained without the vote. The defeat of an effort to extend eligibility to their ranks in 1866 brought down the Liberal government and spurred mass protests and violent demonstrations across the country. The Reform Act of 1867, passed in the midst of this social and political upheaval, added 938,000 voters and thereby doubled the size of the electorate.

Who shall inherit England? This question, which Trilling called central to one major tradition of English novelists from Charles Dickens (1812–1870) to E. M. Forster (1879–1970), was raised as well by intellectuals of the nineteenth century (such as Thomas Carlyle and John Ruskin) and twentieth century (such as T. S. ELIOT and D. H. Lawrence) in their works of cultural criticism. Not only *who* shall inherit England, but what kinds of power could they be trusted with? What forms of education should they receive? For Arnold in particular, the answers to these crucial, interconnected questions could be found in many literary sources—some in the distant past, others closer to his own era. He counseled moral betterment and spiritual renewal, achieved through the appreciative reading of the best literature. The best persons would be critics—poised, balanced, and reflective; they would be foes of fanaticism, zealotry, and political enthusiasm, and they would be aspirants to "perfection" (a term Arnold fastened on in both *Essays in Criticism* and *Culture and Anarchy*). Such arguments echo those of literary and philosophical precursors and contemporaries. In "An Apology for Poetry" (1595; see above), for example, SIR PHILIP SIDNEY had affirmed that "the final end" of learning "is to lead and draw us to as high a perfection as our degenerate souls, made worse by their clayey lodgings, can be capable of." And in "The Poet" (1844; see above), RALPH WALDO EMERSON, whose writings Arnold knew well, celebrated the poet as "representative of man, in virtue of being the largest power to receive and impart."

Arnold's limitations are not hard to identify. Because he is mainly interested in the personality and moral tone of the author, not in the resources of language or the unfolding meanings of literary works themselves, he does not devote much attention to specific texts (an exception is his series of lectures *On Translating Homer*, published in 1861). Lines that he does quote typically function for him as "touchstones," those "specimens of poetry of the high, the very highest quality" that "save us from fallacious estimates of value"—and that seem to beg the very question of "greatness" that they are meant to answer. Arnold assumed that his readers would know these authors and texts and their contexts, and that the "touchstones" would be recognized by all as profound and memorable. Yet he himself had little sympathy for (or understanding of) English writers of the eighteenth and nineteenth centuries. Moreover, Arnold mentioned fiction only briefly and not very perceptively. Unlike, for example, HENRY JAMES, he showed little interest in music, sculpture, painting, or the theater.

But even these serious faults do little to diminish the power with which Arnold defined the "function of criticism" for the Victorian and modern periods. Wholeheartedly defending literature against its enemies and detractors, whose emphasis on science, moneymaking, and commercial prosperity had led them to regard poetry as merely a pleasant pastime, he argued that it equipped men and women to perceive authentic value in the workings of the society and culture around them.

Criticism is not, ultimately, something one does; it gestures toward who one is. And the same is true of "culture," as Arnold presents it in *Culture and Anarchy* (excerpted below). Culture is "a study of perfection," an "*internal* condition"; it mandates a sharp yet supple movement of mind, a vigilant guard against an excess of commitment to a single point of view, and a refusal to accept the alluring power of extreme, polarizing judgments. Unlike later critics influenced by anthropology, Arnold does not view culture as designating the distinctive whole way of life of a people or a period. Nor would he agree with such critics as ANTONIO GRAMSCI, STUART HALL, and EDWARD SAID, who characterize culture as often an instrument of social and political control and conquest. For Arnold, culture is selective and harmonious, not conflictual. Criticism and culture loom large because of their beneficent effects on the individual, as they impel sustained acts of reflection and prevent persons from falling into complacency and "self-satisfaction."

Arnold defines criticism as involving flexibility, openness to new experiences, and curiosity (a word he explores in both "The Function of Criticism" and *Culture and Anarchy*). He insists, too, on the "free play" of mind—a phrase that poststructuralist theorists such as JACQUES DERRIDA would define far more radically and subversively, without Arnold's belief in a stable textual object that provides a center around which analysis and reflection occur. Arnold tethers criticism to a rigorous duty; criticism, he explains, "tends to *establish* an order of ideas" and seeks to "make the best ideas *prevail*." As his choice of verbs indicates, criticism is challenging work; the campaign must be waged, in a phrase used in "The Function of Criticism," with "inflexible honesty." Arnold firmly believes that some ideas are right and others wrong: he is no relativist. Nor is he a revolutionary, but rather a careful, cautious, deliberate reformer, wary of the ways in which the impulse for change can run wild and become destructive. A good literary critic is, inevitably for Arnold, a good critic in general: a person of culture embarked on a steady, steadfast inquiry into self and society. For all of his witty turns of phrase, topical references and allusions, and stylistic clarity and poise, Arnold is at heart a writer who realized, as he acknowledged in a letter in 1863, that his arguments would make "a good many people uncomfortable."

BIBLIOGRAPHY

The Complete Prose Works of Matthew Arnold, edited by R. H. Super (11 vols., 1960–77), offers a definitive text and excellent notes. P. J. Keating (1970) and Christopher Ricks (1972) have edited collections of Arnold's critical writings. For the poetry and prose, the editions by Lionel Trilling (1949) and A. Dwight Culler (1961) are useful, though thin in their annotations. For the correspondence, *Letters, 1848–1888*, edited by George W. E. Russell (2 vols., 1895) remains important. This edition, and other selections, will be superseded by the multivolume *Letters of Matthew Arnold*, edited by Cecil Y. Lang (1996–). Excellent biographies include Park Honan, *Matthew*

Arnold: A Life (1981); Nicholas Murray, *A Life of Matthew Arnold* (1995); and Ian Hamilton, *A Gift Imprisoned: The Poetic Life of Matthew Arnold* (1999).

For critical overviews, see Lionel Trilling, *Matthew Arnold* (1939); Douglas Bush, *Matthew Arnold: A Survey of His Poetry and Prose* (1971), an especially cogent and informative survey of Arnold's life and literary career; and Stefan Collini, *Arnold* (1988). Also helpful is a collection of essays, *Matthew Arnold*, edited by Kenneth Allott (1976).

Critical studies that focus on Arnold's prose include John Holloway, *The Victorian Sage: Studies in Argument* (1953), insightful on Arnold's style and rhetorical strategies; Raymond Williams, *Culture and Society: 1780–1950* (1958), a landmark history of British cultural criticism that includes a substantial discussion of Arnold; Vincent Buckley, *Poetry and Morality: Studies on the Criticism of Matthew Arnold, T. S. Eliot, and F. R. Leavis* (1959); Leon Gottfried, *Matthew Arnold and the Romantics* (1963); David J. DeLaura, *Hebrew and Hellene in Victorian England: Newman, Arnold, and Pater* (1969), which explicates keenly the affinities and differences between Arnold and his contemporaries and successors; Fred G. Walcott, *The Origins of Culture and Anarchy: Matthew Arnold and Popular Education in England* (1970); Sidney Coulling, *Matthew Arnold and His Critics: A Study of Arnold's Controversies* (1974), which provides historical context; Joseph Carroll, *The Cultural Theory of Matthew Arnold* (1982), an excellent study of Arnold's main themes and ideas; and Ruth apRoberts, *Arnold and God* (1983). For responses to Arnold by his contemporaries, see *Matthew Arnold—Prose Writings: The Critical Heritage*, edited by Carl Dawson and John Pfordresher (1979). Edward Said, in *The World, the Text, and the Critic* (1983), and Geoffrey H. Hartman, in *Criticism in the Wilderness: The Study of Literature Today* (1980), are among the important contemporary literary theorists who have assessed Arnold's impact on the academy. Additional commentaries can be found in an edition of *Culture and Anarchy* prepared by Samuel Lipman (1994).

Concentrating on Arnold's poetry but including pertinent commentary on the prose are A. Dwight Culler, *Imaginative Reason: The Poetry of Matthew Arnold* (1961); Alan Roper, *Arnold's Poetic Landscapes* (1969); and David G. Riede, *Matthew Arnold and the Betrayal of Language* (1988).

Thomas Burnett Smart has compiled *The Bibliography of Matthew Arnold* (1892); it should be supplemented by the listing in *The Works of Matthew Arnold*, vol. 15 (1903–04). See also Clinton Machann, *The Essential Matthew Arnold: An Annotated Bibliography of Major Modern Studies* (1993).

The Function of Criticism at the Present Time[1]

Many objections have been made to a proposition which, in some remarks of mine on translating Homer,[2] I ventured to put forth; a proposition about criticism, and its importance at the present day. I said: 'Of the literature of France and Germany, as of the intellect of Europe in general, the main effort, for now many years, has been a critical effort; the endeavour, in all branches of knowledge, theology, philosophy, history, art, science, to see the object as in itself it really is.' I added, that owing to the operation in English literature of certain causes, 'almost the last thing for which one would come to English

1. First delivered as a lecture at Oxford University, on October 29, 1864, and published in the *National Review* in November 1864, with the title given in the plural, "Functions." Arnold altered the title for the book version (1865) and added several footnotes. The text reprinted here is that of the 1875 third edition, the last one that Arnold prepared.

2. See Lecture II of *On Translating Homer* (1861). The Greek *Iliad* and *Odyssey* of Homer (ca. 8th c. B.C.E.) were a standard part of English elite education.

literature is just that very thing which now Europe most desires,—criticism'; and that the power and value of English literature was thereby impaired. More than one rejoinder declared that the importance I here assigned to criticism was excessive, and asserted the inherent superiority of the creative effort of the human spirit over its critical effort. And the other day, having been led by a Mr. Shairp's excellent notice of Wordsworth[3] to turn again to his biography, I found, in the words of this great man, whom I, for one, must always listen to with the profoundest respect, a sentence passed on the critic's business, which seems to justify every possible disparagement of it. Wordsworth says in one of his letters:—

'The writers in these publications' (the Reviews), 'while they prosecute their inglorious employment, can not be supposed to be in a state of mind very favourable for being affected by the finer influences of a thing so pure as genuine poetry.'

And a trustworthy reporter[4] of his conversation quotes a more elaborate judgment to the same effect:—

'Wordsworth holds the critical power very low, infinitely lower than the inventive; and he said to-day that if the quantity of time consumed in writing critiques on the works of others were given to original composition, of whatever kind it might be, it would be much better employed; it would make a man find out sooner his own level, and it would do infinitely less mischief. A false or malicious criticism may do much injury to the minds of others, a stupid invention, either in prose or verse, is quite harmless.'

It is almost too much to expect of poor human nature, that a man capable of producing some effect in one line of literature, should, for the greater good of society, voluntarily doom himself to impotence and obscurity in another. Still less is this to be expected from men addicted to the composition of the 'false or malicious criticism' of which Wordsworth speaks. However, everybody would admit that a false or malicious criticism had better never have been written. Everybody, too, would be willing to admit, as a general proposition, that the critical faculty is lower than the inventive. But is it true that criticism is really, in itself, a baneful and injurious employment; is it true that all time given to writing critiques on the works of others would be much better employed if it were given to original composition, of whatever kind this may be? Is it true that Johnson had better have gone on producing more *Irenes*[5] instead of writing his *Lives of the Poets*; nay, is it certain that Wordsworth himself was better employed in making his Ecclesiastical Sonnets than when he made his celebrated Preface,[6] so full of criticism, and

3. I cannot help thinking that a practice, common in England during the last century, and still followed in France, of printing a notice of this kind,—a notice by a competent critic,—to serve as an introduction to an eminent author's works, might be revived among us with advantage. To introduce all succeeding editions of Wordsworth, Mr. Shairp's notice might, it seems to me, excellently serve; it is written from the point of view of an admirer, nay, of a disciple, and that is right; but then the disciple must be also, as in this case he is, a critic, a man of letters, not, as too often happens, some relation or friend with no qualification for his task except affection for his author [Arnold's note]. John Campbell Shairp (1819–1885) was a friend of Arnold's at Balliol College, Oxford; the "notice" (in which Arnold is praised) is "Wordsworth: The Man and the Poet," *North British Review* 41 (August 1864): 1–54. WILLIAM WORDSWORTH (1770–1850) is the preeminent English Romantic poet.

4. Christopher Wordsworth, *Memoirs of William Wordsworth* (1851).

5. *Irene* (1749), an unsuccessful neoclassical tragedy by SAMUEL JOHNSON (1709–1784), whose *Lives of the Poets* (1779–81) were a considerable critical achievement.

6. The preface to *Lyrical Ballads* (1800, 1802; see above). The 132 "Ecclesiastical Sonnets" (1821–22), which recount the history of the Church of England, are not considered among Wordsworth's major works.

criticism of the works of others? Wordsworth was himself a great critic, and it is to be sincerely regretted that he has not left us more criticism; Goethe[7] was one of the greatest of critics, and we may sincerely congratulate ourselves that he has left us so much criticism. Without wasting time over the exaggeration which Wordsworth's judgment on criticism clearly contains, or over an attempt to trace the causes,—not difficult, I think, to be traced,[8]—which may have led Wordsworth to this exaggeration, a critic may with advantage seize an occasion for trying his own conscience, and for asking himself of what real service at any given moment the practice of criticism either is or may be made to his own mind and spirit, and to the minds and spirits of others.

The critical power is of lower rank than the creative. True; but in assenting to this proposition, one or two things are to be kept in mind. It is undeniable that the exercise of a creative power, that a free creative activity, is the highest function of man; it is proved to be so by man's finding in it his true happiness. But it is undeniable, also, that men may have the sense of exercising this free creative activity in other ways than in producing great works of literature or art; if it were not so, all but a very few men would be shut out from the true happiness of all men. They may have it in well-doing, they may have it in learning, they may have it in criticising. This is one thing to be kept in mind. Another is, that the exercise of the creative power in the production of great works of literature or art, however high this exercise of it may rank, is not at all epochs and under all conditions possible; and that therefore labour may be vainly spent in attempting it, which might with more fruit be used in preparing for it, in rendering it possible. This creative power works with elements, with materials; what if it has not those materials, those elements, ready for its use? In that case it must surely wait till they are ready. Now, in literature,—I will limit myself to literature, for it is about literature that the question arises,—the elements with which the creative power works are ideas; the best ideas on every matter which literature touches, current at the time. At any rate we may lay it down as certain that in modern literature no manifestation of the creative power not working with these can be very important or fruitful. And I say *current* at the time, not merely accessible at the time; for creative literary genius does not principally show itself in discovering new ideas, that is rather the business of the philosopher. The grand work of literary genius is a work of synthesis and exposition, not of analysis and discovery; its gift lies in the faculty of being happily inspired by a certain intellectual and spiritual atmosphere, by a certain order of ideas, when it finds itself in them; of dealing divinely with these ideas, presenting them in the most effective and attractive combinations,—making beautiful works with them, in short. But it must have the atmosphere, it must find itself amidst the order of ideas, in order to work freely; and these it is not so easy to command. This is why great creative epochs in literature are so rare, this is why there is so much that is unsatisfactory in the productions of many men of real genius; because, for the creation of a master-work of literature two powers must concur, the power of the man and the power of the moment, and the man is not enough without the moment;[9] the creative

7. Johann Wolfgang von Goethe (1749–1832), German poet, dramatist, novelist, and scientist.

8. That is, to hostile reviews of Wordsworth's poetry.

9. A reference to Hippolyte Taine's *History of English Literature* (3 vols., 1863); in the introduc-

power has, for its happy exercise, appointed elements, and those elements are not in its own control.

Nay, they are more within the control of the critical power. It is the business of the critical power, as I said in the words already quoted, 'in all branches of knowledge, theology, philosophy, history, art, science, to see the object as in itself it really is.' Thus it tends, at last, to make an intellectual situation of which the creative power can profitably avail itself. It tends to establish an order of ideas, if not absolutely true, yet true by comparison with that which it displaces; to make the best ideas prevail. Presently these new ideas reach society, the touch of truth is the touch of life, and there is a stir and growth everywhere; out of this stir and growth come the creative epochs of literature.

Or, to narrow our range, and quit these considerations of the general march of genius and of society,—considerations which are apt to become too abstract and impalpable,—every one can see that a poet, for instance, ought to know life and the world before dealing with them in poetry; and life and the world being in modern times very complex things, the creation of a modern poet, to be worth much, implies a great critical effort behind it; else it must be a comparatively poor, barren, and short-lived affair. This is why Byron's[1] poetry had so little endurance in it, and Goethe's so much; both Byron and Goethe had a great productive power, but Goethe's was nourished by a great critical effort providing the true materials for it, and Byron's was not; Goethe knew life and the world, the poet's necessary subjects, much more comprehensively and thoroughly than Byron. He knew a great deal more of them, and he knew them much more as they really are.

It has long seemed to me that the burst of creative activity in our literature, through the first quarter of this century, had about it in fact something premature; and that from this cause its productions are doomed, most of them, in spite of the sanguine hopes which accompanied and do still accompany them, to prove hardly more lasting than the productions of far less splendid epochs. And this prematureness comes from its having proceeded without having its proper data, without sufficient materials to work with. In other words, the English poetry of the first quarter of this century, with plenty of energy, plenty of creative force, did not know enough. This makes Byron so empty of matter, Shelley[2] so incoherent, Wordsworth even, profound as he is, yet so wanting in completeness and variety. Wordsworth cared little for books, and disparaged Goethe. I admire Wordsworth, as he is, so much that I cannot wish him different; and it is vain, no doubt, to imagine such a man different from what he is, to suppose that he *could* have been different. But surely the one thing wanting to make Wordsworth an even greater poet than he is,—his thought richer, and his influence of wider application,—was that he should have read more books, among them, no doubt, those of that Goethe whom he disparaged without reading him.

But to speak of books and reading may easily lead to a misunderstanding here. It was not really books and reading that lacked to our poetry at this

tion, the French critic and philosopher describes the impact of heredity, environment, and history ("la race, le milieu, le moment").

1. George Gordon, Lord Byron (1788–1824), English Romantic poet.

2. PERCY BYSSHE SHELLEY (1792–1822), English poet.

epoch; Shelley had plenty of reading, Coleridge[3] had immense reading. Pindar and Sophocles[4]—as we all say so glibly, and often with so little discernment of the real import of what we are saying—had not many books; Shakespeare was no deep reader. True; but in the Greece of Pindar and Sophocles, in the England of Shakspeare, the poet lived in a current of ideas in the highest degree animating and nourishing to the creative power; society was, in the fullest measure, permeated by fresh thought, intelligent and alive. And this state of things is the true basis for the creative power's exercise, in this it finds its data, its materials, truly ready for its hand; all the books and reading in the world are only valuable as they are helps to this. Even when this does not actually exist, books and reading may enable a man to construct a kind of semblance of it in his own mind, a world of knowledge and intelligence in which he may live and work. This is by no means an equivalent to the artist for the nationally diffused life and thought of the epochs of Sophocles or Shakspeare; but, besides that it may be a means of preparation for such epochs, it does really constitute, if many share in it, a quickening and sustaining atmosphere of great value. Such an atmosphere the many-sided learning and the long and widely-combined critical effort of Germany formed for Goethe, when he lived and worked. There was no national glow of life and thought there as in the Athens of Pericles or the England of Elizabeth.[5] That was the poet's weakness. But there was a sort of equivalent for it in the complete culture and unfettered thinking of a large body of Germans. That was his strength. In the England of the first quarter of this century there was neither a national glow of life and thought, such as we had in the age of Elizabeth, nor yet a culture and a force of learning and criticism such as were to be found in Germany. Therefore the creative power of poetry wanted, for success in the highest sense, materials and a basis; a thorough interpretation of the world was necessarily denied to it.

At first sight it seems strange that out of the immense stir of the French Revolution and its age should not have come a crop of works of genius equal to that which came out of the stir of the great productive time of Greece, or out of that of the Renascence, with its powerful episode the Reformation. But the truth is that the stir of the French Revolution took a character which essentially distinguished it from such movements as these. These were, in the main, disinterestedly intellectual and spiritual movements; movements in which the human spirit looked for its satisfaction in itself and in the increased play of its own activity. The French Revolution took a political, practical character. The movement which went on in France under the old *régime*, from 1700 to 1789, was far more really akin than that of the Revolution itself to the movement of the Renascence; the France of Voltaire and Rousseau[6] told far more powerfully upon the mind of Europe than the France of the Revolution. Goethe reproached this last expressly with having 'thrown quiet culture back.' Nay, and the true key to how much in our Byron, even

3. SAMUEL TAYLOR COLERIDGE (1772–1834), English poet and critic, whose wide reading in German Romantic philosophers led to his introducing many of their ideas to English readers.
4. Greek tragedian (ca. 496–406 B.C.E.). Pindar (ca. 518–438 B.C.E.), Greek lyric poet.
5. Elizabeth I (1553–1603; reigned 1558–1603). Pericles (ca. 495–429 B.C.E.), Athenian statesman, military leader, and supporter of the arts. He was the most influential man in Athens during the city's Golden Age.
6. Jean-Jacques Rousseau (1712–1778), Swiss-born French political theorist and philosopher. Voltaire: pen name of François Marie Arouet (1694–1778), French poet, dramatist, historian, and satirist.

in our Wordsworth, is this!—that they had their source in a great movement of feeling, not in a great movement of mind. The French Revolution, however,—that object of so much blind hatred,—found undoubtedly its motive-power in the intelligence of men, and not in their practical sense; this is what distinguishes it from the English Revolution of Charles the First's time. This is what makes it a more spiritual event than our Revolution, an event of much more powerful and worldwide interest, though practically less successful; it appeals to an order of ideas which are universal, certain, permanent. 1789 asked of a thing, Is it rational? 1642 asked of a thing, Is it legal? or, when it went furthest, Is it according to conscience? This is the English fashion, a fashion to be treated, within its own sphere, with the highest respect; for its success, within its own sphere, has been prodigious. But what is law in one place is not law in another; what is law here to-day is not law even here to-morrow; and as for conscience, what is binding on one man's conscience is not binding on another's. The old woman who threw her stool at the head of the surpliced minister in St. Giles's Church at Edinburgh[7] obeyed an impulse to which millions of the human race may be permitted to remain strangers. But the prescriptions of reason are absolute, unchanging, of universal validity; *to count by tens is the easiest way of counting*—that is a proposition of which every one, from here to the Antipodes, feels the force; at least I should say so if we did not live in a country where it is not impossible that any morning we may find a letter in the *Times* declaring that a decimal coinage is an absurdity.[8] That a whole nation should have been penetrated with an enthusiasm for pure reason, and with an ardent zeal for making its prescriptions triumph, is a very remarkable thing, when we consider how little of mind, or anything so worthy and quickening as mind, comes into the motives which alone, in general, impel great masses of men. In spite of the extravagant direction given to this enthusiasm, in spite of the crimes and follies in which it lost itself, the French Revolution derives from the force, truth, and universality of the ideas which it took for its law, and from the passion with which it could inspire a multitude for these ideas, a unique and still living power; it is—it will probably long remain—the greatest, the most animating event in history. And as no sincere passion for the things of the mind, even though it turn out in many respects an unfortunate passion, is ever quite thrown away and quite barren of good, France has reaped from hers one fruit—the natural and legitimate fruit, though not precisely the grand fruit she expected: she is the country in Europe where *the people* is most alive.

But the mania for giving an immediate political and practical application to all these fine ideas of the reason was fatal. Here an Englishman is in his element: on this theme we can all go on for hours. And all we are in the habit of saying on it has undoubtedly a great deal of truth. Ideas cannot be too much prized in and for themselves, cannot be too much lived with; but to transport them abruptly into the world of politics and practice, violently to revolutionise this world to their bidding,—that is quite another thing.

7. A riot broke out in July 1637 in St. Giles' Cathedral in protest against a new Anglican liturgy written by Archbishop Laud. It was said to have begun when a woman named Jenny Geddes threw her stool at the dean giving the service and accused him of saying Mass.

8. Letters in the London *Times* in 1863 debated whether England should change its system of weights and measures to the metric system (itself an outgrowth of the French Revolution).

There is the world of ideas and there is the world of practice; the French are often for suppressing the one and the English the other; but neither is to be suppressed. A member of the House of Commons said to me the other day: 'That a thing is an anomaly, I consider to be no objection to it whatever.' I venture to think he was wrong; that a thing is an anomaly *is* an objection to it, but absolutely and in the sphere of ideas: it is not necessarily, under such and such circumstances, or at such and such a moment, an objection to it in the sphere of politics and practice. Joubert[9] has said beautifully: 'C'est la force et le droit qui règlent toutes choses dans le monde; la force en attendant le droit.' (Force and right are the governors of this world; force till right is ready.) *Force till right is ready*; and till right is ready, force, the existing order of things, is justified, is the legitimate ruler. But right is something moral, and implies inward recognition, free assent of the will; we are not ready for right,—*right*, so far as we are concerned, *is not ready*,—until we have attained this sense of seeing it and willing it. The way in which for us it may change and transform force, the existing order of things, and become, in its turn, the legitimate ruler of the world, should depend on the way in which, when our times comes, we see it and will it. Therefore for other people enamoured of their own newly discerned right, to attempt to impose it upon us as ours, and violently to substitute their right for our force, is an act of tyranny, and to be resisted. It sets at nought the second great half of our maxim, *force till right is ready*. This was the grand error of the French Revolution; and its movement of ideas, by quitting the intellectual sphere and rushing furiously into the political sphere, ran, indeed, a prodigious and memorable course, but produced no such intellectual fruit as the movement of ideas of the Renascence, and created, in opposition to itself, what I may call an *epoch of concentration*. The great force of that epoch of concentration was England; and the great voice of the epoch of concentration was Burke.[1] It is the fashion to treat Burke's writings on the French Revolution as superannuated and conquered by the event; as the eloquent but unphilosophical tirades of bigotry and prejudice. I will not deny that they are often disfigured by the violence and passion of the moment, and that in some directions Burke's view was bounded, and his observation therefore at fault. But on the whole, and for those who can make the needful corrections, what distinguishes these writings is their profound, permanent, fruitful, philosophical truth. They contain the true philosophy of an epoch of concentration, dissipate the heavy atmosphere which its own nature is apt to engender round it, and make its resistance rational instead of mechanical.

But Burke is so great because, almost alone in England, he brings thought to bear upon politics, he saturates politics with thought. It is his accident[2] that his ideas were at the service of an epoch of concentration, not of an epoch of expansion; it is his characteristic that he so lived by ideas, and had such a source of them welling up within him, that he could float even an epoch of concentration and English Tory politics with them. It does not hurt him that Dr. Price[3] and the Liberals were enraged with him; it does not even

9. Joseph Joubert (1754–1824), French writer and moralist, known for his essays, maxims, and letters.

1. EDMUND BURKE (1729–1797), statesman and author of *Reflections on the French Revolution* (1790).

2. Fortune.

3. Richard Price (1723–1791), Welsh dissenting minister, moral philosopher, supporter of the American and French Revolutions, and one of Burke's opponents.

hurt him that George the Third and the Tories were enchanted with him. His greatness is that he lived in a world which neither English Liberalism nor English Toryism is apt to enter;—the world of ideas, not the world of catchwords and party habits. So far is it from being really true of him that he 'to party gave up what was meant for mankind,'[4] that at the very end of his fierce struggle with the French Revolution, after all his invectives against its false pretensions, hollowness, and madness, with his sincere conviction of its mischievousness, he can close a memorandum on the best means of combating it, some of the last pages he ever wrote,[5]—the *Thoughts on French Affairs*, in December 1791,—with these striking words:—

'The evil is stated, in my opinion, as it exists. The remedy must be where power, wisdom and information, I hope, are more united with good intentions than they can be with me. I have done with this subject, I believe, for ever. It has given me many anxious moments for the last two years. *If a great change is to be made in human affairs, the minds of men will be fitted to it; the general opinions and feelings will draw that way. Every fear, every hope will forward it; and then they who persist in opposing this mighty current in human affairs, will appear rather to resist the decrees of Providence itself, than the mere designs of men. They will not be resolute and firm, but perverse and obstinate*.'

That return of Burke upon himself has always seemed to me one of the finest things in English literature, or indeed in any literature. That is what I call living by ideas: when one side of a question has long had your earnest support, when all your feelings are engaged, when you hear all round you no language but one, when your party talks this language like a steam-engine and can imagine no other,—still to be able to think, still to be irresistibly carried, if so it be, by the current of thought to the opposite side of the question, and, like Balaam,[6] to be unable to speak anything *but what the Lord has put in your mouth*. I know nothing more striking, and I must add that I know nothing more un-English.

For the Englishman in general is like my friend the Member of Parliament, and believes, point-blank, that for a thing to be an anomaly is absolutely no objection to it whatever. He is like the Lord Auckland[7] of Burke's day, who, in a memorandum on the French Revolution, talks of 'certain miscreants, assuming the name of philosophers, who have presumed themselves capable of establishing a new system of society.' The Englishman has been called a political animal, and he values what is political and practical so much that ideas easily become objects of dislike in his eyes, and thinkers 'miscreants,' because ideas and thinkers have rashly meddled with politics and practice. This would be all very well if the dislike and neglect confined themselves to ideas transported out of their own sphere, and meddling rashly with practice; but they are inevitably extended to ideas as such, and to the whole life of intelligence; practice is everything, a free play of the mind is nothing. The notion of the free play of the mind upon all subjects being a pleasure in itself, being an object of desire, being an essential provider of elements without

4. An observation about "good Edmund" Burke in Oliver Goldsmith's poem "Retaliation" (1774), line 32.

5. R. H. Super, the modern editor of Arnold's prose works, notes that in fact Burke continued to write until his death in 1797.

6. Despite being sent by his king to curse the Israelites, Balaam blessed them, speaking "the word that God putteth in [his] mouth" (Numbers 22. 38).

7. William Eden, first Baron Auckland (1744–1814), statesman and diplomat.

which a nation's spirit, whatever compensations it may have for them, must, in the long run, die of inanition, hardly enters into an Englishman's thoughts. It is noticeable that the word *curiosity*, which in other languages is used in a good sense, to mean, as a high and fine quality of man's nature, just this disinterested love of a free play of the mind on all subjects, for its own sake,—it is noticeable, I say, that this word has in our language no sense of the kind, no sense but a rather bad and disparaging one. But criticism, real criticism, is essentially the exercise of this very quality. It obeys an instinct prompting it to try to know the best that is known and thought in the world, irrespectively of practice, politics, and everything of the kind; and to value knowledge and thought as they approach this best, without the intrusion of any other considerations whatever. This is an instinct for which there is, I think, little original sympathy in the practical English nature, and what there was of it has undergone a long benumbing period of blight and suppression in the epoch of concentration which followed the French Revolution.

But epochs of concentration cannot well endure for ever; epochs of expansion, in the due course of things, follow them. Such an epoch of expansion seems to be opening in this country. In the first place all danger of a hostile forcible pressure of foreign ideas upon our practice has long disappeared; like the traveller in the fable, therefore, we begin to wear our cloak a little more loosely.[8] Then, with a long peace, the ideas of Europe steal gradually and amicably in, and mingle, though in infinitesimally small quantities at a time, with our own notions. Then, too, in spite of all that is said about the absorbing and brutalising influence of our passionate material progress, it seems to me indisputable that this progress is likely, though not certain, to lead in the end to an apparition[9] of intellectual life; and that man, after he has made himself perfectly comfortable and has now to determine what to do with himself next, may begin to remember that he has a mind, and that the mind may be made the source of great pleasure. I grant it is mainly the privilege of faith, at present, to discern this end to our railways, our business, and our fortune-making; but we shall see if, here as elsewhere, faith is not in the end the true prophet. Our ease, our travelling, and our unbounded liberty to hold just as hard and securely as we please to the practice to which our notions have given birth, all tend to beget an inclination to deal a little more freely with these notions themselves, to canvass them a little, to penetrate a little into their real nature. Flutterings of curiosity, in the foreign sense of the word, appear amongst us, and it is in these that criticism must look to find its account. Criticism first; a time of true creative activity, perhaps,—which, as I have said, must inevitably be preceded amongst us by a time of criticism,—hereafter, when criticism has done its work.

It is of the last importance that English criticism should clearly discern what rule for its course, in order to avail itself of the field now opening to it, and to produce fruit for the future, it ought to take. The rule may be summed up in one word,—*disinterestedness*.[1] And how is criticism to show disinterestedness? By keeping aloof from what is called 'the practical view of things'; by resolutely following the law of its own nature, which is to be a free play of the mind on all subjects which it touches. By steadily refusing to lend

8. In Aesop's fable of the wind and the sun, the two have a contest (which the sun wins) to see which can first make a traveler remove his cloak.

9. An appearance before the world.

1. Objectivity, independence of judgment.

itself to any of those ulterior, political, practical considerations about ideas, which plenty of people will be sure to attach to them, which perhaps ought often to be attached to them, which in this country at any rate are certain to be attached to them quite sufficiently, but which criticism has really nothing to do with. Its business is, as I have said, simply to know the best that is known and thought in the world, and by in its turn making this known, to create a current of true and fresh ideas. Its business is to do this with inflexible honesty, with due ability; but its business is to do no more, and to leave alone all questions of practical consequences and applications, questions which will never fail to have due prominence given to them. Else criticism, besides being really false to its own nature, merely continues in the old rut which it has hitherto followed in this country, and will certainly miss the chance now given to it. For what is at present the bane of criticism in this country? It is that practical considerations cling to it and stifle it. It subserves interests not its own. Our organs of criticism are organs of men and parties having practical ends to serve, and with them those practical ends are the first thing and the play of mind the second; so much play of mind as is compatible with the prosecution of those practical ends is all that is wanted. An organ like the *Revue des Deux Mondes*,[2] having for its main function to understand and utter the best that is known and thought in the world, existing, it may be said, as just an organ for a free play of the mind, we have not. But we have the *Edinburgh Review*, existing as an organ of the old Whigs, and for as much play of the mind as may suit its being that; we have the *Quarterly Review*, existing as an organ of the Tories, and for as much play of mind as may suit its being that; we have the *British Quarterly Review*, existing as an organ of the political Dissenters, and for as much play of mind as may suit its being that; we have the *Times*, existing as an organ of the common, satisfied, well-to-do Englishman, and for as much play of mind as may suit its being that. And so on through all the various fractions, political and religious, of our society; every fraction has, as such, its organ of criticism, but the notion of combining all fractions in the common pleasure of a free disinterested play of mind meets with no favour. Directly this play of mind wants to have more scope, and to forget the pressure of practical considerations a little, it is checked, it is made to feel the chain. We saw this the other day in the extinction, so much to be regretted, of the *Home and Foreign Review*.[3] Perhaps in no organ of criticism in this country was there so much knowledge, so much play of mind; but these could not save it. The *Dublin Review* subordinates play of mind to the practical business of English and Irish Catholicism, and lives. It must needs be that men should act in sects and parties, that each of these sects and parties should have its organ, and should make this organ subserve the interests of its action; but it would be well, too, that there should be a criticism, not the minister of these interests, not their enemy, but absolutely and entirely independent of them. No other criticism will ever attain any real authority or make any real way towards its end,—the creating a current of true and fresh ideas.

It is because criticism has so little kept in the pure intellectual sphere, has so little detached itself from practice, has been so directly polemical and

2. A highly respected and widely read French bimonthly review of culture, the arts, politics, and economics.

3. Liberal Catholic quarterly in London (1862–64).

controversial, that it has so ill accomplished, in this country, its best spiritual work; which is to keep man from a self-satisfaction which is retarding and vulgarising, to lead him towards perfection, by making his mind dwell upon what is excellent in itself, and the absolute beauty and fitness of things. A polemical practical criticism makes men blind even to the ideal imperfection of their practice, makes them willingly assert its ideal perfection, in order the better to secure it against attack; and clearly this is narrowing and baneful for them. If they were reassured on the practical side, speculative considerations of ideal perfection they might be brought to entertain, and their spiritual horizon would thus gradually widen. Sir Charles Adderley[4] says to the Warwickshire farmers:—

'Talk of the improvement of breed! Why, the race we ourselves represent, the men and women, the old Anglo-Saxon race, are the best breed in the whole world. . . The absence of a too enervating climate, too unclouded skies, and a too luxurious nature, has produced so vigorous a race of people, and has rendered us so superior to all the world.'

Mr. Roebuck[5] to the Sheffield cutlers:—

'I look around me and ask what is the state of England? Is not property safe? Is not every man able to say what he likes? Can you not walk from one end of England to the other in perfect security? I ask you whether, the world over or in past history, there is anything like it? Nothing. I pray that our unrivalled happiness may last.'

Now obviously there is a peril for poor human nature in words and thoughts of such exuberant self-satisfaction, until we find ourselves safe in the streets of the Celestial City.

'Das wenige verschwindet leicht dem Blicke,
Der vorwärts sieht, wie viel noch übrig bleibt—'

says Goethe;[6] 'the little that is done seems nothing when we look forward and see how much we have yet to do.' Clearly this is a better line of reflection for weak humanity, so long as it remains on this earthly field of labour and trial.

But neither Sir Charles Adderley nor Mr. Roebuck is by nature inaccessible to considerations of this sort. They only lose sight of them owing to the controversial life we all lead, and the practical form which all speculation takes with us. They have in view opponents whose aim is not ideal, but practical; and in their zeal to uphold their own practice against these innovators, they go so far as even to attribute to this practice an ideal perfection. Somebody has been wanting to introduce a six-pound franchise, or to abolish church-rates,[7] or to collect agricultural statistics by force, or to diminish local self-government. How natural, in reply to such proposals, very likely improper or ill-timed, to go a little beyond the mark, and to say stoutly, 'Such a race of people as we stand, so superior to all the world! The old Anglo-Saxon race, the best breed in the whole world! I pray that our unrivalled happiness may last! I ask you whether, the world over or in past history, there is anything like it?' And so long as criticism answers this dithyramb by insist-

4. Conservative member of Parliament (1814–1905), wealthy holder of a large estate in Warwickshire.
5. John Arthur Roebuck (1801–1879), radical member of Parliament.
6. *Iphigenia in Tauris* (1787), 1.2.91–92.
7. Taxes legally imposed by the Church of England. "Six-pound franchise": a proposal by radicals to extend the vote to anyone who owned land or buildings worth £6 annual rent (not £10, as set in 1832).

ing that the old Anglo-Saxon race would be still more superior to all others if it had no church-rates, or that our unrivalled happiness would last yet longer with a six-pound franchise, so long will the strain, 'The best breed in the whole world.' swell louder and louder, everything ideal and refining will be lost out of sight, and both the assailed and their critics will remain in a sphere, to say the truth, perfectly unvital, a sphere in which spiritual progression is impossible. But let criticism leave church-rates and the franchise alone, and in the most candid spirit, without a single lurking thought of practical innovation, confront with our dithyramb this paragraph on which I stumbled in a newspaper immediately after reading Mr. Roebuck:—

'A shocking child murder has just been committed at Nottingham. A girl named Wragg[8] left the workhouse there on Saturday morning with her young illegitimate child. The child was soon afterwards found dead on Mapperly Hills, having been strangled. Wragg is in custody.'

Nothing but that; but, in juxtaposition with the absolute eulogies of Sir Charles Adderley and Mr. Roebuck, how eloquent, how suggestive are those few lines! 'Our old Anglo-Saxon breed, the best in the whole world!'—how much that is harsh and ill-favoured there is in this best! *Wragg!* If we are to talk of ideal perfection, of 'the best in the whole world,' has any one reflected what a touch of grossness in our race, what an original shortcoming in the more delicate spiritual perceptions, is shown by the natural growth amongst us of such hideous names,—Higginbottom, Stiggins, Bugg! In Ionia and Attica[9] they were luckier in this respect than 'the best race in the world'; by the Ilissus[1] there was no Wragg, poor thing! And 'our unrivalled happiness';—what an element of grimness, bareness, and hideousness mixes with it and blurs it; the workhouse, the dismal Mapperly Hills,—how dismal those who have seen them will remember;—the gloom, the smoke, the cold, the strangled illegitimate child! 'I ask you whether, the world over or in past history, there is anything like it?' Perhaps not, one is inclined to answer; but at any rate, in that case, the world is very much to be pitied. And the final touch,—short, bleak, and inhuman: *Wragg is in custody*. The sex lost in the confusion of our unrivalled happiness; or (shall I say?) the superfluous Christian name lopped off by the straightforward vigour of our old Anglo-Saxon breed! There is profit for the spirit in such contrasts as this; criticism serves the cause of perfection by establishing them. By eluding sterile conflict, by refusing to remain in the sphere where alone narrow and relative conceptions have any worth and validity, criticism may diminish its momentary importance, but only in this way has it a chance of gaining admittance for those wider and more perfect conceptions to which all its duty is really owed. Mr. Roebuck will have a poor opinion of an adversary who replies to his defiant songs of triumph only by murmuring under his breath, *Wragg is in custody*; but in no other way will these songs of triumph be induced gradually to moderate themselves, to get rid of what in them is excessive and offensive, and to fall into a softer and truer key.

It will be said that it is a very subtle and indirect action which I am thus prescribing for criticism, and that, by embracing in this manner the Indian virtue of detachment[2] and abandoning the sphere of practical life, it con-

8. Elizabeth Wragg; this crime was committed on September 10, 1864.

9. District of Greece that includes Athens. Ionia: area of the west coast of Asia Minor (where Homer is thought to have lived).

1. River south of Athens.

2. The ideal of detaching oneself from worldly activity, here associated with Hinduism.

demns itself to a slow and obscure work. Slow and obscure it may be, but it is the only proper work of criticism. The mass of mankind will never have any ardent zeal for seeing things as they are; very inadequate ideas will always satisfy them.[3] On these inadequate ideas reposes, and must repose, the general practice of the world. That is as much as saying that whoever sets himself to see things as they are will find himself one of a very small circle; but it is only by this small circle resolutely doing its own work that adequate ideas will ever get current at all. The rush and roar of practical life will always have a dizzying and attracting effect upon the most collected spectator, and tend to draw him into its vortex; most of all will this be the case where that life is so powerful as it is in England. But it is only by remaining collected, and refusing to lend himself to the point of view of the practical man, that the critic can do the practical man any service; and it is only by the greatest sincerity in pursuing his own course, and by at last convincing even the practical man of his sincerity, that he can escape misunderstandings which perpetually threaten him.

For the practical man is not apt for fine distinctions, and yet in these distinctions, truth and the highest culture greatly find their account. But it is not easy to lead a practical man,—unless you reassure him as to your practical intentions, you have no chance of leading him,—to see that a thing which he has always been used to look at from one side only, which he greatly values, and which, looked at from that side, quite deserves, perhaps, all the prizing and admiring which he bestows upon it,—that this thing, looked at from another side, may appear much less beneficent and beautiful, and yet retain all its claims to our practical allegiance. Where shall we find language innocent enough, how shall we make the spotless purity of our intentions evident enough, to enable us to say to the political Englishman that the British Constitution itself, which, seen from the practical side, looks such a magnificent organ of progress and virtue, seen from the speculative side,—with its compromises, its love of facts, its horror of theory, its studied avoidance of clear thoughts,—that, seen from this side, our august Constitution sometimes looks,—forgive me, shade of Lord Somers![4]—a colossal machine for the manufacture of Philistines?[5] How is Cobbett[6] to say this and not be misunderstood, blackened as he is with the smoke of a lifelong conflict in the field of political practice? how is Mr. Carlyle[7] to say it and not be misunderstood, after his furious raid into this field with his *Latter-day Pamphlets*? how is Mr. Ruskin,[8] after his pugnacious political economy? I say, the critic must keep out of the region of immediate practice in the political, social, humanitarian sphere, if he wants to make a beginning for that more free speculative treatment of things, which may perhaps one day make its benefits felt even in this sphere, but in a natural and thence irresistible manner.

Do what he will, however, the critic will still remain exposed to frequent

3. Arnold takes the terms "adequate" and "inadequate" from the *Ethics* (1677) of the Dutch philosopher Benedict de Spinoza.
4. John Somers (1651–1716), English constitutional lawyer and statesman.
5. The materialist middle classes (a name taken from a biblical people that waged war against the Israelites).
6. William Cobbett (1762–1835), English radical journalist and reformer.
7. Thomas Carlyle (1795–1881), Scottish-born essayist and historian; he expressed bitter antidemocratic views in *Latter-Day Pamphlets* (1850).
8. John Ruskin (1819–1900), art critic and social critic. In *Unto This Last* (1860–62), he challenged the business and industrial practices and materialism of the age.

misunderstandings, and nowhere so much as in this country. For here people are particularly indisposed even to comprehend that without this free disinterested treatment of things, truth and the highest culture are out of the question. So immersed are they in practical life, so accustomed to take all their notions from this life and its processes, that they are apt to think that truth and culture themselves can be reached by the process of this life, and that it is an impertinent singularity to think of reaching them in any other. 'We are all *terræ filii*,'[9] cries their eloquent advocate; 'all Philistines together. Away with the notion of proceeding by any other course than the course dear to the Philistines; let us have a social movement, let us organise and combine a party to pursue truth and new thought, let us call it *the liberal party*, and let us all stick to each other, and back each other up. Let us have no nonsense about independent criticism, and intellectual delicacy, and the few and the many. Don't let us trouble ourselves about foreign thought; we shall invent the whole thing for ourselves as we go along. If one of us speaks well, applaud him; if one of us speaks ill, applaud him too; we are all in the same movement, we are all liberals, we are all in pursuit of truth.' In this way the pursuit of truth becomes really a social, practical, pleasurable affair, almost requiring a chairman, a secretary, and advertisements; with the excitement of an occasional scandal, with a little resistance to give the happy sense of difficulty overcome; but, in general, plenty of bustle and very little thought. To act is so easy, as Goethe says; to think is so hard![1] It is true that the critic has many temptations to go with the stream, to make one of the party movement, one of these *terræ filii*; it seems ungracious to refuse to be a *terræ filius*, when so many excellent people are; but the critic's duty is to refuse, or, if resistance is vain, at least to cry with Obermann: *Périssons en résistant*.[2]

How serious a matter it is to try and resist, I had ample opportunity of experiencing when I ventured some time ago to criticise the celebrated first volume of Bishop Colenso.[3] The echoes of the storm which was then raised I still, from time to time, hear grumbling round me. That storm arose out of a misunderstanding almost inevitable. It is a result of no little culture to attain to a clear perception that science and religion are two wholly different things. The multitude will for ever confuse them, but happily that is of no great real importance, for while the multitude imagines itself to live by its false science, it does really live by its true religion. Dr. Colenso, however, in his first volume did all he could to strengthen the confusion,[4] and to make

9. Sons of the earth (Latin); that is, men of the soil.
1. A reference to Goethe's novel *Wilhelm Meister's Apprenticeship* (1795–96).
2. Let us die resisting (French). Quoted from *Obermann* (1804), a Romantic epistolary novel by Etienne de Sénancour.
3. So sincere is my dislike to all personal attack and controversy, that I abstain from reprinting, at this distance of time from the occasion which called them forth, the essays in which I criticised Dr. Colenso's book; I feel bound, however, after all that has passed, to make here a final declaration of my sincere impenitence for having published them. Nay, I cannot forbear repeating yet once more, for his benefit and that of his readers, this sentence from my original remarks upon him: *There is truth of science and truth of religion; truth of science does not become truth of religion till it is made religious.* And I will add: Let us have all the science there is from the men of science; from the men of religion let us have religion [Arnold's note]. John William Colenso (1814–1883), bishop of Natal in South Africa, whose controversial studies disputed orthodox theology and the historical accuracy of biblical texts. In "The Bishop and the Philosopher" (*Macmillan's Magazine*, January 1863), Arnold sharply criticized Colenso's scholarship and failure to address true spiritual needs.
4. It has been said I make it 'a crime against literary criticism and the higher culture to attempt to inform the ignorant.' Need I point out that the ignorant are not informed by being confirmed in a confusion? [Arnold's note]. Quoted from the jurist and essayist Fitzjames Stephen in "Mr. Matthew Arnold and His Countrymen," *Saturday Review*, December 3, 1864.

it dangerous. He did this with the best intentions, I freely admit, and with the most candid ignorance that this was the natural effect of what he was doing; but, says Joubert, 'Ignorance, which in matters of morals extenuates the crime, is itself, in intellectual matters, a crime of the first order.' I criticised Bishop Colenso's speculative confusion. Immediately there was a cry raised: 'What is this? here is a liberal attacking a liberal. Do not you belong to the movement? are not you a friend of truth? Is not Bishop Colenso in pursuit of truth? then speak with proper respect of his book. Dr. Stanley[5] is another friend of truth, and you speak with proper respect of his book; why make these invidious differences? both books are excellent, admirable, liberal; Bishop Colenso's perhaps the most so, because it is the boldest, and will have the best practical consequences for the liberal cause. Do you want to encourage to the attack of a brother liberal his, and your, and our implacable enemies, the *Church and State Review* or the *Record*,—the High Church rhinoceros and the Evangelical hyæna? Be silent, therefore; or rather speak, speak as loud as ever you can! and go into ecstasies over the eighty and odd pigeons.'[6]

But criticism cannot follow this coarse and indiscriminate method. It is unfortunately possible for a man in pursuit of truth to write a book which reposes upon a false conception. Even the practical consequences of a book are to genuine criticism no recommendation of it, if the book is, in the highest sense, blundering. I see that a lady[7] who herself, too, is in pursuit of truth, and who writes with great ability, but a little too much, perhaps, under the influence of the practical spirit of the English liberal movement, classes Bishop Colenso's book and M. Renan's[8] together, in her survey of the religious state of Europe, as facts of the same order, works, both of them, of 'great importance'; 'great ability, power, and skill'; Bishop Colenso's, perhaps, the most powerful; at least, Miss Cobbe gives special expression to her gratitude that to Bishop Colenso 'has been given the strength to grasp, and the courage to teach, truths of such deep import.' In the same way, more than one popular writer has compared him to Luther.[9] Now it is just this kind of false estimate which the critical spirit is, it seems to me, bound to resist. It is really the strongest possible proof of the low ebb at which, in England, the critical spirit is, that while the critical hit in the religious literature of Germany is Dr. Strauss's book,[1] in that of France M. Renan's book, the book of Bishop Colenso is the critical hit in the religious literature of England. Bishop Colenso's book reposes on a total misconception of the essential elements of the religious problem, as that problem is now presented for solution. To criticism, therefore, which seeks to have the best that is known and thought on this problem, it is, however well meant, of no importance whatever. M. Renan's book attempts a new synthesis of the elements furnished to us by the Four Gospels. It attempts, in my opinion, a synthesis, perhaps premature, perhaps impossible, certainly not successful. Up to the

5. Arthur Penrhyn Stanley (1815–1881), English biographer of Thomas Arnold, an ecclesiastical historian and advocate of religious toleration.
6. Colenso used mathematics to cast doubt on the historical validity of certain passages in Leviticus and Numbers.
7. Frances Power Cobbe (1822–1908), Irish social worker and author of books on reform, women's rights, and religion. Her "survey" is *Broken Lights* (1864).
8. Ernest Renan (1823–1892), French critic, historian, orientalist, and author of *The Life of Jesus* (1863).
9. Martin Luther (1483–1546), German religious reformer and founder of the Reformation.
1. David Friedrich Strauss (1808–1874), German theologian, author of *The Life of Jesus* (1835–36).

present time, at any rate, we must acquiesce in Fleury's sentence on such recastings of the Gospel-story: *Quiconque s'imagine la pouvoir mieux écrire, ne l'entend pas*.[2] M. Renan had himself passed by anticipation a like sentence on his own work, when he said: 'If a new presentation of the character of Jesus were offered to me, I would not have it; its very clearness would be, in my opinion, the best proof of its insufficiency.' His friends may with perfect justice rejoin that at the sight of the Holy Land, and of the actual scene of the Gospel-story, all the current of M. Renan's thoughts may have naturally changed, and a new casting of that story irresistibly suggested itself to him; and that this is just a case for applying Cicero's maxim: Change of mind is not inconsistency—*nemo doctus unquam mutationem consilii inconstantiam dixit esse*.[3] Nevertheless, for criticism, M. Renan's first thought must still be the truer one, as long as his new casting so fails more fully to commend itself, more fully (to use Coleridge's happy phrase about the Bible) to *find* us.[4] Still M. Renan's attempt is, for criticism, of the most real interest and importance, since, with all its difficulty, a fresh synthesis of the New Testament *data*,—not a making war on them, in Voltaire's fashion,[5] not a leaving them out of mind, in the world's fashion, but the putting a new construction upon them, the taking them from under the old, traditional, conventional point of view and placing them under a new one,—is the very essence of the religious problem, as now presented; and only by efforts in this direction can it receive a solution.

Again, in the same spirit in which she judges Bishop Colenso, Miss Cobbe, like so many earnest liberals of our practical race, both here and in America, herself sets vigorously about a positive reconstruction of religion, about making a religion of the future out of hand, or at least setting about making it. We must not rest, she and they are always thinking and saying, in negative criticism, we must be creative and constructive; hence we have such works as her recent *Religious Duty*,[6] and works still more considerable, perhaps by others, which will be in every one's mind. These works often have much ability; they often spring out of sincere convictions, and a sincere wish to do good; and they sometimes, perhaps, do good. Their fault is (if I may be permitted to say so) one which they have in common with the British College of Health, in the New Road. Every one knows the British College of Health; it is that building with the lion and the statue of the Goddess Hygeia before it; at least I am sure about the lion, though I am not absolutely certain about the Goddess Hygeia.[7] This building does credit, perhaps, to the resources of Dr. Morrison[8] and his disciples; but it falls a good deal short of one's idea of what a British College of Health ought to be. In England, where we hate public interference and love individual enterprise, we have a whole crop of places like the British College of Health; the grand name without the grand thing. Unluckily, creditable to individual enterprise as they are, they tend to

2. Whoever imagines he can write it better does not understand it (French). From the *Histoire ecclésiastique* (1691–1720), by the French historian and teacher Claude Fleury (1640–1723).
3. No educated man has ever said that a change of opinion is inconsistency (Latin). From *Letters to Atticus*, no. 16, by the Roman orator and statesman Cicero (106–43 B.C.E.).
4. See Coleridge's *Confessions of an Inquiring Spirit* (1840): "In the Bible there is more that *finds* me than I have experienced in all other books put together."
5. Voltaire's works include a number of attacks on Catholic doctrine and religious intolerance.
6. Published in 1864.
7. Greek deity personifying health.
8. James Morrison (1770–1840), merchant and vendor, described himself as "the Hygeist"; in 1828 he founded the British College of Health, from which he distributed his cure-all patent medicine.

impair our taste by making us forget what more grandiose, noble, or beautiful character properly belongs to a public institution. The same may be said of the religions of the future of Miss Cobbe and others. Creditable, like the British College of Health, to the resources of their authors, they yet tend to make us forget what more grandiose, noble, or beautiful character properly belongs to religious constructions. The historic religions, with all their faults, have had this; it certainly belongs to the religious sentiment, when it truly flowers, to have this; and we impoverish our spirit if we allow a religion of the future without it. What then is the duty of criticism here? To take the practical point of view, to applaud the liberal movement and all its works,—its New Road religions of the future into the bargain,—for their general utility's sake? By no means; but to be perpetually dissatisfied with these works, while they perpetually fall short of a high and perfect ideal.

For criticism, these are elementary laws; but they never can be popular, and in this country they have been very little followed, and one meets with immense obstacles in following them. That is a reason for asserting them again and again. Criticism must maintain its independence of the practical spirit and its aim. Even with well-meant efforts of the practical spirit it must express dissatisfaction, if in the sphere of the ideal they seem impoverishing and limiting. It must not hurry on to the goal because of its practical importance. It must be patient, and know how to wait; and flexible, and know how to attach itself to things and how to withdraw from them. It must be apt to study and praise elements that for the fulness of spiritual perfection are wanted, even though they belong to a power which in the practical sphere may be maleficent. It must be apt to discern the spiritual shortcomings or illusions of powers that in the practical sphere may be beneficent. And this without any notion of favouring or injuring, in the practical sphere, one power or the other; without any notion of playing off, in this sphere, one power against the other. When one looks, for instance, at the English Divorce Court,—an institution which perhaps has its practical conveniences, but which in the ideal sphere is so hideous; an institution which neither makes divorce impossible nor makes it decent, which allows a man to get rid of his wife, or a wife of her husband, but makes them drag one another first, for the public edification, through a mire of unutterable infamy,—when one looks at this charming institution, I say, with its crowded trails, its newspaper reports, and its money compensations, this institution in which the gross unregenerate British Philistine has indeed stamped an image of himself,—one may be permitted to find the marriage theory of Catholicism[9] refreshing and elevating. Or when Protestantism, in virtue of its supposed rational and intellectual origin, gives the law to criticism too magisterially, criticism may and must remind it that its pretensions, in this respect, are illusive and do it harm; that the Reformation was a moral rather than an intellectual event; that Luther's theory of grace no more exactly reflects the mind of the spirit than Bossuet's[1] philosophy of history reflects it; and that there is no more antecedent probability of the Bishop of Durham's stock of ideas being agreeable to perfect reason than of Pope Pius the Ninth's.[2] But criticism will not

9. That is, that in Christian marriage, once consummated, there can never be an absolute divorce.

1. Jacques Bénigne Bossuet (1627–1704), French bishop and moralist; he maintained that Providence guided history in order to establish Christianity and, especially, the Catholic Church.

2. Pius IX (1792–1878), pope from 1846 to 1878, was criticized for his conservative views. Bishop of Durham: Charles Thomas Baring (1807–1879).

on that account forget the achievements of Protestantism in the practical and moral sphere; nor that, even in the intellectual sphere, Protestantism, though in a blind and stumbling manner, carried forward the Renascence, while Catholicism threw itself violently across its path.

I lately heard a man of thought and energy contrasting the want of ardor and movement which he now found amongst young men in this country with what he remembered in his own youth, twenty years ago. 'What reformers we were then!' he exclaimed; 'what a zeal we had! how we canvassed every institution in Church and State, and were prepared to remodel them all on first principles!' He was inclined to regret, as a spiritual flagging, the lull which he saw. I am disposed rather to regard it as a pause in which the turn to a new mode of spiritual progress is being accomplished. Everything was long seen, by the young and ardent amongst us, in inseparable connection with politics and practical life. We have pretty well exhausted the benefits of seeing things in this connection, we have got all that can be got by so seeing them. Let us try a more disinterested mode of seeing them; let us betake ourselves more to the serener life of the mind and spirit. This life, too, may have its excesses and dangers; but they are not for us at present. Let us think of quietly enlarging our stock of true and fresh ideas, and not, as soon as we get an idea or half an idea, be running out with it into the street, and trying to make it rule there. Our ideas will, in the end, shape the world all the better for maturing a little. Perhaps in fifty years' time it will in the English House of Commons be an objection to an institution that it is an anomaly, and my friend the Member of Parliament will shudder in his grave. But let us in the meanwhile rather endeavour that in twenty years' time it may, in English literature, be an objection to a proposition that it is absurd. That will be a change so vast, that the imagination almost fails to grasp it. *Ab integro sæclorum nascitur ordo.*[3]

If I have insisted so much on the course which criticism must take where politics and religion are concerned, it is because, where these burning matters are in question, it is most likely to go astray. I have wished, above all, to insist on the attitude which criticism should adopt toward things in general; on its right tone and temper of mind. But then comes another question as to the subject-matter which literary criticism should most seek. Here, in general, its course is determined for it by the idea which is the law of its being; the idea of a disinterested endeavour to learn and propagate the best that is known and thought in the world, and thus to establish a current of fresh and true ideas. By the very nature of things, as England is not all the world, much of the best that is known and thought in the world cannot be of English growth, must be foreign; by the nature of things, again, it is just this that we are least likely to know, while English thought is streaming in upon us from all sides, and takes excellent care that we shall not be ignorant of its existence. The English critic of literature, therefore, must dwell much on foreign thought, and with particular heed on any part of it, which, while significant and fruitful in itself, is for any reason specially likely to escape him. Again, judging is often spoken of as the critic's one business, and so in some sense it is; but the judgment which almost insensibly forms itself in a

3. From the renewal of the generations a [great] order is born (Latin). From Virgil, *Eclogue* 4.5 (ca. 37 B.C.E.). This poem was sometimes interpreted by Christians as predicting the birth of the Messiah.

fair and clear mind, along with fresh knowledge, is the valuable one; and thus knowledge, and ever fresh knowledge, must be the critic's great concern for himself. And it is by communicating fresh knowledge, and letting his own judgment pass along with it,—but insensibly, and in the second place, not the first, as a sort of companion and clue, not as an abstract lawgiver,—that the critic will generally do most good to his readers. Sometimes, no doubt, for the sake of establishing an author's place in literature, and his relation to a central standard (and if this is not done, how are we to get at our *best in the world*?), criticism may have to deal with a subject-matter so familiar that fresh knowledge is out of the question, and then it must be all judgment; an enunciation and detailed application of principles. Here the great safeguard is never to let oneself become abstract, always to retain an intimate and lively consciousness of the truth of what one is saying, and, the moment this fails us, to be sure that something is wrong. Still, under all circumstances, this mere judgment and application of principles is, in itself, not the most satisfactory work to the critic; like mathematics, it is tautological, and cannot well give us, like fresh learning, the sense of creative activity.

But stop, some one will say; all this talk is of no practical use to us whatever; this criticism of yours is not what we have in our minds when we speak of criticism; when we speak of critics and criticism, we mean critics and criticism of the current English literature of the day; when you offer to tell criticism its function, it is to this criticism that we expect you to address yourself. I am sorry for it, for I am afraid I must disappoint these expectations. I am bound by my own definition of criticism: *a disinterested endeavour to learn and propagate the best that is known and thought in the world*. How much of current English literature comes into this 'best that is known and thought in the world'? Not very much, I fear; certainly less, at this moment, than of the current literature of France or Germany. Well, then, am I to alter my definition of criticism, in order to meet the requirements of a number of practising English critics, who, after all, are free in their choice of a business? That would be making criticism lend itself just to one of those alien practical considerations, which, I have said, are so fatal to it. One may say, indeed, to those who have to deal with the mass—so much better disregarded—of current English literature, that they may at all events endeavour, in dealing with this, to try it, so far as they can, by the standard of the best that is known and thought in the world; one may say, that to get anywhere near this standard, every critic should try and possess one great literature, at least, besides his own; and the more unlike his own, the better. But, after all, the criticism I am really concerned with,—the criticism which alone can much help us for the future, the criticism which, throughout Europe, is at the present day meant, when so much stress is laid on the importance of criticism and the critical spirit,—is a criticism which regards Europe as being, for intellectual and spiritual purposes, one great confederation, bound to a joint action and working to a common result; and whose members have, for their proper outfit, a knowledge of Greek, Roman, and Eastern antiquity, and of one another. Special, local, and temporary advantages being put out of account, that modern nation will in the intellectual and spiritual sphere make most progress, which most thoroughly carries out this programme. And what is that but saying that we too, all of us, as individuals, the more thoroughly we carry it out, shall make the more progress?

There is so much inviting us!—what are we to take? what will nourish us in growth towards perfection? That is the question which, with the immense field of life and of literature lying before him, the critic has to answer; for himself first, and afterwards for others. In this idea of the critic's business the essays brought together in the following pages[4] have had their origin; in this idea, widely different as are their subjects, they have, perhaps, their unity.

I conclude with what I said at the beginning: to have the sense of creative activity is the great happiness and the great proof of being alive, and it is not denied to criticism to have it; but then criticism must be sincere, simple, flexible, ardent, ever widening its knowledge. Then it may have, in no contemptible measure, a joyful sense of creative activity; a sense which a man of insight and conscience will prefer to what he might derive from a poor, starved, fragmentary, inadequate creation. And at some epochs no other creation is possible.

Still, in full measure, the sense of creative activity belongs only to genuine creation; in literature we must never forget that. But what true man of letters ever can forget it? It is no such common matter for a gifted nature to come into possession of a current of true and living ideas, and to produce amidst the inspiration of them, that we are likely to underrate it. The epochs of Æschylus[5] and Shakspeare make us feel their pre-eminence. In an epoch like those is, no doubt, the true life of literature; there is the promised land, towards which criticism can only beckon. That promised land it will not be ours to enter, and we shall die in the wilderness:[6] but to have desired to enter it, to have saluted it from afar, is already, perhaps, the best distinction among contemporaries; it will certainly be the best title to esteem with posterity.

1864, 1875

From Culture and Anarchy

From *Chapter 1.*
Sweetness and Light[1]

The disparagers of culture make its motive curiosity; sometimes, indeed, they make its motive mere exclusiveness and vanity. The culture which is supposed to plume itself on a smattering of Greek and Latin is a culture which is begotten by nothing so intellectual as curiosity; it is valued either out of sheer vanity and ignorance or else as an engine of social and class distinction, separating its holder, like a badge or title, from other people who have not got it. No serious man would call this *culture*, or attach any value to it, as culture, at all. To find the real ground for the very different estimate which serious people will set upon culture, we must find some motive for culture

4. In the book *Essays in Criticism*; this essay was the first in the volume.
5. Greek tragedian (525–456 B.C.E.).
6. Like Moses, who viewed the Promised Land but did not live to enter it. See Deuteronomy 32.48–52, 34.1–4.
1. First delivered, with the title "Culture and Its Enemies," as Arnold's final lecture as Professor of Poetry at Oxford University, June 7, 1867, and published in the *Cornhill Magazine* in July. It appeared as chapter 1 of *Culture and Anarchy* in 1869. The text reprinted here is that of the 1882 third edition, the last that Arnold himself prepared.

in the terms of which may lie a real ambiguity; and such a motive the word *curiosity* gives us.

I have before now pointed out[2] that we English do not, like the foreigners, use this word in a good sense as well as in a bad sense. With us the word is always used in a somewhat disapproving sense. A liberal and intelligent eagerness about the things of the mind may be meant by a foreigner when he speaks of curiosity, but with us the word always conveys a certain notion of frivolous and unedifying activity. In the *Quarterly Review*, some little time ago, was an estimate of the celebrated French critic, M. Sainte-Beuve,[3] and a very inadequate estimate it in my judgment was. And its inadequacy consisted chiefly in this: that in our English way it left out of sight the double sense really involved in the word *curiosity*, thinking enough was said to stamp M. Sainte-Beuve with blame if it was said that he was impelled in his operations as a critic by curiosity, and omitting either to perceive that M. Sainte-Beuve himself, and many other people with him, would consider that this was praiseworthy and not blameworthy, or to point out why it ought really to be accounted worthy of blame and not of praise. For as there is a curiosity about intellectual matters which is futile, and merely a disease, so there is certainly a curiosity,—a desire after the things of the mind simply for their own sakes and for the pleasure of seeing them as they are,—which is, in an intelligent being, natural and laudable. Nay, and the very desire to see things as they are implies a balance and regulation of mind which is not often attained without fruitful effort, and which is the very opposite of the blind and diseased impulse of mind which is what we mean to blame when we blame curiosity. Montesquieu[4] says: 'The first motive which ought to impel us to study is the desire to augment the excellence of our nature, and to render an intelligent being yet more intelligent.' This is the true ground to assign for the genuine scientific passion, however manifested, and for culture, viewed simply as a fruit of this passion; and it is a worthy ground, even though we let the term *curiosity* stand to describe it.

But there is of culture another view, in which not solely the scientific passion, the sheer desire to see things as they are, natural and proper in an intelligent being, appears as the ground of it. There is a view in which all the love of our neighbour, the impulses towards action, help, and beneficence, the desire for removing human error, clearing human confusion, and diminishing human misery, the noble aspiration to leave the world better and happier than we found it,—motives eminently such as are called social,—come in as part of the grounds of culture, and the main and pre-eminent part. Culture is then properly described not as having its origin in curiosity, but as having its origin in the love of perfection; it is *a study of perfection*. It moves by the force, not merely or primarily of the scientific passion for pure knowledge, but also of the moral and social passion for doing good. As, in the first view of it, we took for its worthy motto Montesquieu's words: 'To render an intelligent being yet more intelligent!' so, in the second view of

2. In "The Function of Criticism at the Present Time" (1864; see above).

3. Charles Augustin Sainte-Beuve (1804–1869), French literary critic. In the review mentioned (*Quarterly Review* 119 [January 1866]: 80–108), the author identifies Arnold as Sainte-Beuve's disciple and states that the *Essays in Criticism* are "graceful but perfectly unsatisfactory."

4. Charles de Secondat Montesquieu (1689–1755), French philosopher and legal and political theorist.

it, there is no better motto which it can have than these words of Bishop Wilson:[5] 'To make reason and the will of God prevail!'

Only, whereas the passion for doing good is apt to be overhasty in determining what reason and the will of God say, because its turn is for acting rather than thinking and it wants to be beginning to act; and whereas it is apt to take its own conceptions, which proceed from its own state of development and share in all the imperfections and immaturities of this, for a basis of action; what distinguishes culture is, that it is possessed by the scientific passion as well as by the passion of doing good; that it demands worthy notions of reason and the will of God, and does not readily suffer its own crude conceptions to substitute themselves for them. And knowing that no action or institution can be salutary and stable which is not based on reason and the will of God, it is not so bent on acting and instituting, even with the great aim of diminishing human error and misery ever before its thoughts, but that it can remember that acting and instituting are of little use, unless we know how and what we ought to act and to institute.

This culture is more interesting and more far-reaching than that other, which is founded solely on the scientific passion for knowing. But it needs times of faith and ardour, times when the intellectual horizon is opening and widening all round us, to flourish in. And is not the close and bounded intellectual horizon within which we have long lived and moved now lifting up, and are not new lights finding free passage to shine in upon us? For a long time there was no passage for them to make their way in upon us, and then it was of no use to think of adapting the world's action to them. Where was the hope of making reason and the will of God prevail among people who had a routine which they had christened reason and the will of God, in which they were inextricably bound, and beyond which they had no power of looking? But now the iron force of adhesion to the old routine,—social, political, religious,—has wonderfully yielded; the iron force of exclusion of all which is new has wonderfully yielded. The danger now is, not that people should obstinately refuse to allow anything but their old routine to pass for reason and the will of God, but either that they should allow some novelty or other to pass for these too easily, or else that they should underrate the importance of them altogether, and think it enough to follow action for its own sake, without troubling themselves to make reason and the will of God prevail therein. Now, then, is the moment for culture to be of service, culture which believes in making reason and the will of God prevail, believes in perfection, is the study and pursuit of perfection, and is no longer debarred, by a rigid invincible exclusion of whatever is new, from getting acceptance for its ideas, simply because they are new.

The moment this view of culture is seized, the moment it is regarded not solely as the endeavour to see things as they are, to draw towards a knowledge of the universal order which seems to be intended and aimed at in the world, and which it is a man's happiness to go along with or his misery to go counter to,—to learn, in short, the will of God,—the moment, I say, culture is considered not merely as the endeavour to *see* and *learn* this, but as the endeav-

5. Thomas Wilson (1663–1755), English churchman and author of devotional works. Arnold is condensing a passage from Wilson's *Maxims*.

our, also, to make it *prevail*, the moral, social, and beneficent character of culture becomes manifest. The mere endeavour to see and learn the truth for our own personal satisfaction is indeed a commencement for making it prevail, a preparing the way for this, which always serves this, and is wrongly, therefore, stamped with blame absolutely in itself and not only in its caricature and degeneration. But perhaps it has got stamped with blame, and disparaged with the dubious title of curiosity, because in comparison with this wider endeavour of such great and plain utility it looks selfish, petty, and unprofitable.

And religion, the greatest and most important of the efforts by which the human race has manifested its impulse to perfect itself,—religion, that voice of the deepest human experience,—does not only enjoin and sanction the aim which is the great aim of culture, the aim of setting ourselves to ascertain what perfection is and to make it prevail; but also, in determining generally in what human perfection consists, religion comes to a conclusion identical with that which culture,—culture seeking the determination of this question through *all* the voices of human experience which have been heard upon it, of art, science, poetry, philosophy, history, as well as of religion, in order to give a greater fulness and certainty to its solution,—likewise reaches. Religion says: *The kingdom of God is within you*;[6] and culture, in like manner, places human perfection in an *internal* condition, in the growth and predominance of our humanity proper, as distinguished from our animality. It places it in the ever-increasing efficacy and in the general harmonious expansion of those gifts of thought and feeling, which make the peculiar dignity, wealth, and happiness of human nature. As I have said on a former occasion:[7] 'It is in making endless additions to itself, in the endless expansion of its powers, in endless growth in wisdom and beauty, that the spirit of the human race finds its ideal. To reach this ideal, culture is an indispensable aid, and that is the true value of culture.' Not a having and a resting, but a growing and a becoming, is the character of perfection as culture conceives it; and here, too, it coincides with religion.

And because men are all members of one great whole, and the sympathy which is in human nature will not allow one member to be indifferent to the rest or to have a perfect welfare independent of the rest, the expansion of our humanity, to suit the idea of perfection which culture forms, must be a *general* expansion. Perfection, as culture conceives it, is not possible while the individual remains isolated. The individual is required, under pain of being stunted and enfeebled in his own development if he disobeys, to carry others along with him in his march towards perfection, to be continually doing all he can to enlarge and increase the volume of the human stream sweeping thitherward. And here, once more, culture lays on us the same obligation as religion, which says, as Bishop Wilson has admirably put it, that 'to promote the kingdom of God is to increase and hasten one's own happiness.'

But, finally, perfection,—as culture from a thorough disinterested study of human nature and human experience learns to conceive it,—is a harmonious expansion of *all* the powers which make the beauty and worth of human nature, and is not consistent with the over-development of any one

6. Luke 17.21.

7. In *A French Eton* (1864), chapter 3.

power at the expense of the rest. Here culture goes beyond religion, as religion is generally conceived by us.

If culture, then, is a study of perfection, and of harmonious perfection, general perfection, and perfection which consists in becoming something rather than in having something, in an inward condition of the mind and spirit, not in an outward set of circumstances,—it is clear that culture, instead of being the frivolous and useless thing which Mr. Bright, and Mr. Frederic Harrison,[8] and many other Liberals are apt to call it, has a very important function to fulfil for mankind. And this function is particularly important in our modern world, of which the whole civilisation is, to a much greater degree than the civilisation of Greece and Rome, mechanical and external, and tends constantly to become more so. But above all in our own country has culture a weighty part to perform, because here that mechanical character, which civilisation tends to take everywhere, is shown in the most eminent degree. Indeed nearly all the characters of perfection, as culture teaches us to fix them, meet in this country with some powerful tendency which thwarts them and sets them at defiance. The idea of perfection as an *inward* condition of the mind and spirit is at variance with the mechanical and material civilisation in esteem with us, and nowhere, as I have said, so much in esteem as with us. The idea of perfection as a *general* expansion of the human family is at variance with our strong individualism, our hatred of all limits to the unrestrained swing of the individual's personality, our maxim of 'every man for himself.' Above all, the idea of perfection as a *harmonious* expansion of human nature is at variance with our want of flexibility, with our inaptitude for seeing more than one side of a thing, with our intense energetic absorption in the particular pursuit we happen to be following. So culture has a rough task to achieve in this country. Its preachers have, and are likely long to have, a hard time of it, and they will much oftener be regarded, for a great while to come, as elegant or spurious Jeremiahs than as friends and benefactors. That, however, will not prevent their doing in the end good service if they persevere. And, meanwhile, the mode of action they have to pursue, and the sort of habits they must fight against, ought to be made quite clear for every one to see, who may be willing to look at the matter attentively and dispassionately.

Faith in machinery is, I said, our besetting danger; often in machinery most absurdly disproportioned to the end which this machinery, if it is to do any good at all, is to serve; but always in machinery, as if it had a value in and for itself.[9] What is freedom but machinery? what is population but machinery? what is coal but machinery? what are railroads but machinery? what is wealth but machinery? what are, even, religious organisations but machinery? Now almost every voice in England is accustomed to speak of these things as if they were precious ends in themselves, and therefore had some of the characters of perfection indisputably joined to them. I have before now noticed Mr. Roebuck's[1] stock argument for proving the greatness

8. English jurist and philosopher (1831–1923), and critic of Arnold's cultural views. John Bright (1811–1889), English political reformer, orator, and member of Parliament.

9. In "Signs of the Times" (1829), the Scottish-born author Thomas Carlyle had stated that it was now "the Mechanical Age. It is the Age of Machinery, in every outward and inward sense of that word."

1. John Arthur Roebuck (1801–1879), radical member of Parliament. "Before now": see "The Function of Criticism at the Present Time" (above).

and happiness of England as she is, and for quite stopping the mouths of all gainsayers. Mr. Roebuck is never weary of reiterating this argument of his, so I do not know why I should be weary of noticing it. 'May not every man in England say what he likes?'—Mr. Roebuck perpetually asks; and that, he thinks, is quite sufficient, and when every man may say what he likes, our aspirations ought to be satisfied. But the aspirations of culture, which is the study of perfection, are not satisfied, unless what men say, when they may say what they like, is worth saying,—has good in it, and more good than bad. In the same way the *Times*, replying to some foreign strictures on the dress, looks, and behaviour of the English abroad, urges that the English ideal is that every one should be free to do and to look just as he likes. But culture indefatigably tries, not to make what each raw person may like the rule by which he fashions himself; but to draw ever nearer to a sense of what is indeed beautiful, graceful, and becoming, and to get the raw person to like that.

And in the same way with respect to railroads and coal. Every one must have observed the strange language current during the late discussions as to the possible failure of our supplies of coal. Our coal, thousands of people were saying, is the real basis of our national greatness; if our coal runs short, there is an end of the greatness of England. But what *is* greatness?—culture makes us ask. Greatness is a spiritual condition worthy to excite love, interest, and admiration; and the outward proof of possessing greatness is that we excite love, interest, and admiration. If England were swallowed up by the sea to-morrow, which of the two, a hundred years hence, would most excite the love, interest, and admiration of mankind,—would most, therefore, show the evidences of having possessed greatness,—the England of the last twenty years, or the England of Elizabeth,[2] of a time of splendid spiritual effort, but when our coal, and our industrial operations depending on coal, were very little developed? Well, then, what an unsound habit of mind it must be which makes us talk of things like coal or iron as constituting the greatness of England, and how salutary a friend is culture, bent on seeing things as they are, and thus dissipating delusions of this kind and fixing standards of perfection that are real!

Wealth, again, that end to which our prodigious works for material advantage are directed,—the commonest of commonplaces tells us how men are always apt to regard wealth as a precious end in itself; and certainly they have never been so apt thus to regard it as they are in England at the present time. Never did people believe anything more firmly than nine Englishmen out of ten at the present day believe that our greatness and welfare are proved by our being so very rich. Now, the use of culture is that it helps us, by means of its spiritual standard of perfection, to regard wealth as but machinery, and not only to say as a matter of words that we regard wealth as but machinery, but really to perceive and feel that it is so. If it were not for this purging effect wrought upon our minds by culture, the whole world, the future as well as the present, would inevitably belong to the Philistines.[3] The people who believe most that most greatness and welfare are proved by our being very rich, and who most give their lives and thoughts to becoming rich, are

2. Elizabeth I (1533–1603; reigned 1558–1603).
3. The materialist middle classes (a name taken from a biblical people that waged war against the Israelites).

just the very people whom we call Philistines. Culture says: 'Consider these people, then, their way of life, their habits, their manners, the very tones of their voice; look at them attentively; observe the literature they read, the things which give them pleasure, the words which come forth out of their mouths, the thoughts which make the furniture of their minds: would any amount of wealth be worth having with the condition that one was to become just like these people by having it?' And thus culture begets a dissatisfaction which is of the highest possible value in stemming the common tide of men's thoughts in a wealthy and industrial community, and which saves the future, as one may hope, from being vulgarised, even if it cannot save the present.

Population, again, and bodily health and vigour, are things which are nowhere treated in such an unintelligent, misleading, exaggerated way as in England. Both are really machinery; yet how many people all around us do we see rest in them and fail to look beyond them! Why, one has heard people, fresh from reading certain articles of the *Times* on the Registrar-General's returns of marriages and births in this country,[4] who would talk of our large English families in quite a solemn strain, as if they had something in itself beautiful, elevating, and meritorious in them; as if the British Philistine would have only to present himself before the Great Judge with his twelve children, in order to be received among the sheep[5] as a matter of right!

But bodily health and vigour, it may be said, are not to be classed with wealth and population as mere machinery; they have a more real and essential value. True; but only as they are more intimately connected with a perfect spiritual condition than wealth or population are. The moment we disjoin them from the idea of a perfect spiritual condition, and pursue them, as we do pursue them, for their own sake and as ends in themselves, our worship of them becomes as mere worship of machinery, as our worship of wealth or population, and as unintelligent and vulgarising a worship as that is. Every one with anything like an adequate idea of human perfection has distinctly marked this subordination to higher and spiritual ends of the cultivation of bodily vigour and activity. 'Bodily exercise profiteth little; but godliness is profitable unto all things,' says the author of the Epistle to Timothy.[6] And the utilitarian Franklin[7] says as explicitly:—'Eat and drink such an exact quantity as suits the constitution of thy body, *in reference to the services of the mind*.' But the point of view of culture, keeping the mark of human perfection simply and broadly in view, and not assigning to this perfection, as religion or utilitarianism assigns to it, a special and limited character, this point of view, I say, of culture is best given by these words of Epictetus:[8]—'It is a sign of ἀφυΐα,' says he,—that is, of a nature not finely tempered,—'to give yourselves for instance, a great fuss about exercise, a great fuss about eating, a great fuss about drinking, a great fuss about walking, a great fuss about riding. All these things ought to be done merely by the way: the formation of the spirit and character must be our real concern.' This is admirable; and, indeed, the Greek word εὐφυΐα, a finely tempered nature, gives

4. "When Marriages are many and Deaths are few it is certain that the people are doing well" (London *Times*, February 3, 1866).
5. That is, the saved; see Matthew 25.31–46.
6. 1 Timothy 4.8.
7. Benjamin Franklin (1706–1790), American statesman, writer, and scientist. Arnold quotes Franklin's first recommendation in "Rules of Health," from *Poor Richard's Almanack* (1732–1757).
8. Greek Stoic philosopher (ca. 55–ca. 135 C.E.), who taught in Rome, in *Enchiridion* 41.

exactly the notion of perfection as culture brings us to conceive it: a harmonious perfection, a perfection in which the characters of beauty and intelligence are both present, which unites 'the two noblest of things,'—as Swift,[9] who of one of the two, at any rate, had himself all too little, most happily calls them in his *Battle of the Books,*—'the two noblest of things, *sweetness and light.*' The εὐφυής is the man who tends towards sweetness and light; the ἀφυής, on the other hand, is our Philistine. The immense spiritual significance of the Greeks is due to their having been inspired with this central and happy idea of the essential character of human perfection; and Mr. Bright's misconception of culture, as a smattering of Greek and Latin, comes itself, after all, from this wonderful significance of the Greeks having affected the very machinery of our education, and is in itself a kind of homage to it.

In thus making sweetness and light to be characters of perfection, culture is of like spirit with poetry, follows one law with poetry. Far more than on our freedom, our population, and our industrialism, many amongst us rely upon our religious organisations to save us. I have called religion a yet more important manifestation of human nature than poetry, because it has worked on a broader scale for perfection, and with greater masses of men. But the idea of beauty and of a human nature perfect on all its sides, which is the dominant idea of poetry, is a true and invaluable idea, though it has not yet had the success that the idea of conquering the obvious faults of our animality, and of a human nature perfect on the moral side,—which is the dominant idea of religion,—has been enabled to have; and it is destined, adding to itself the religious idea of a devout energy, to transform and govern the other.

The best art and poetry of the Greeks, in which religion and poetry are one, in which the idea of beauty and of a human nature perfect on all sides adds to itself a religious and devout energy, and works in the strength of that, is on this account of such surpassing interest and instructiveness for us, though it was,—as, having regard to the human race in general, and, indeed, having regard to the Greeks themselves, we must own,—a premature attempt, an attempt which for success needed the moral and religious fibre in humanity to be more braced and developed than it had yet been. But Greece did not err in having the idea of beauty, harmony, and complete human perfection, so present and paramount. It is impossible to have this idea too present and paramount; only, the moral fibre must be braced too. And we, because we have braced the moral fibre, are not on that account in the right way, if at the same time the idea of beauty, harmony, and complete human perfection, is wanting or misapprehended amongst us; and evidently it *is* wanting or misapprehended at present. And when we rely as we do on our religious organisations, which in themselves do not and cannot give us this idea, and think we have done enough if we make them spread and prevail, then, I say, we fall into our common fault of overvaluing machinery.

* * *

1867, 1882

9. Jonathan Swift (1667–1745), English satirist, poet, and clergyman. In *The Battle of the Books* (1704), he recounts why Aesop, judging a contest between the spider (here representing the moderns) and the bee (the ancients), decided in favor of the bee: "the difference is, that, instead of dirt and poison, we have rather chosen to fill our hives with honey and wax; thus furnishing mankind with the two noblest of things, which are sweetness and light." In the larger battle that Swift describes, the outcome is less certain.

WALTER PATER
1839–1894

Contemporary critics and theorists have returned to Walter Pater's books and essays, reexamined them in relation to current interests in figurative language, creativity in criticism, and historical study, and dramatically raised his critical stock. Literary histories had often described Pater as a "minor" Victorian overshadowed by MATTHEW ARNOLD. An impressionist critic who coined the English phrase "art for art's sake" (which he later amended to "art for its own sake"), he sketched, it was said, the adventures of his soul among masterpieces. Now, however, Pater's conception of art and exaltation of aesthetic experience have linked him with his contemporaries RALPH WALDO EMERSON and FRIEDRICH NIETZSCHE as a crucial writer for postmodern theory and criticism.

Pater's work has always been important for creative writers, including William Butler Yeats, who refashioned Pater's prose description of Leonardo da Vinci's *Mona Lisa* in *Studies in the History of the Renaissance* (1873) and made it the first "poem" in the *Oxford Book of Modern Verse* (1936). Pater has also inspired such twentieth-century theorists of literary and critical consciousness as GEORGES POULET and (in his early writings) PAUL DE MAN. HAROLD BLOOM and J. Hillis Miller point to Pater as having enriched and supplemented the Romantic tradition in criticism inaugurated by SAMUEL TAYLOR COLERIDGE and refined by John Ruskin (in *Modern Painters*, 1843–56, and *The Stones of Venice*, 1851–53).

Pater was born in the East End of London. His father, a surgeon, died in 1842, and he was raised in a household of women that included his mother, a grandmother, and an aunt. After attending King's School, Canterbury, he began his undergraduate career at Queen's College, Oxford University, where he wrote essays on Greek philosophy for the eminent scholar Benjamin Jowett. Pater received his degree in 1862 and the following year was elected to Old Mortality, a literary society at Oxford. He became a fellow of Oxford's Brasenose College in 1864, living first there and later in London as a teacher, scholar, and critic.

During the summer of 1865, Pater made his first trip to Italy, traveling in the company of his pupil and close friend C. L. Shadwell, to whom he would dedicate *Studies in the History of the Renaissance*. The paintings he saw in Florence and other cities deeply moved him, giving him "a richer, more daring sense of life than any to be seen in Oxford." For Pater, the Italian Renaissance was not merely a historical period but a tremor in the heart that marked the consciousness of the person attuned to its splendors. To know the glorious works of Renaissance art was intensely, indeed erotically, to *feel* them, and this feeling was Pater's means of countering the dulling of sensation, the termination of feeling, the inevitability of death.

Pater's first essays were published anonymously in the late 1860s. A study of Coleridge in the *Westminster Review* (1866) suggests that Pater found a central theme early on: "Modern thought is distinguished from ancient by its cultivation of the 'relative' spirit in place of the 'absolute.' . . . To the modern spirit nothing is, or can be rightly known, except relatively and under certain conditions." Pater's first publication under his name was "Notes on Leonardo da Vinci" (1869). *Studies in the History of the Renaissance*, a collection of essays on writers and Italian painters (including da Vinci and Sandro Botticelli), appeared four years later.

Pater's next book, the romance *Marius the Epicurean* (1885), describes the development of a young Roman in the time of Marcus Aurelius, the second-century C.E. Roman emperor and Stoic philosopher. He conceived it as the first of a three-part series—the second to be set in sixteenth-century France and the third in late-eighteenth-century England—but the other volumes remained unwritten. Pater's later books include *Imaginary Portraits* (1887), *Appreciations, with an Essay on Style* (1889), and *Plato and Platonism* (1893). *Greek Studies* (1895) and an unfinished romance, *Gaston de Latour* (1896), were published posthumously. The three-volume theological project that Pater planned for his later years, which he seems to have envisioned as a response to Arnold's writings on religion and culture, was left undone.

Studies in the History of the Renaissance was a momentous text for a number of Pater's younger contemporaries, including OSCAR WILDE. Pater states that his primary concern is with Italy in the fifteenth century, but he deliberately defines the term *Renaissance* much more widely, describing it as an "outbreak of the human spirit" from the "limits which the religious system of the middle ages imposed on the heart and the imagination." Throughout the book, Pater emphasizes the precious, fine textures of art, but always with the implication that only persons of rich receptiveness, of exquisite and accurate perception, can wholly sense and appreciate its singularities. The reliance on austere discipline to achieve liberation—the free life that art renders possible—helps explain Pater's great appeal. By making a religion of art, a sacred duty of artistic creation and perception, Pater built the foundation for modern aestheticist rapture as well as for impressionist criticism.

On publication, *Studies in the History of the Renaissance* received mixed reviews. Some concurred with Pater, against Ruskin, in his esteem for the Renaissance. But others attacked Pater for advocating pleasure as the highest good and self-gratification as the best rule for the conduct of life. George Eliot in a letter called the book "quite poisonous in its false principles of criticism and false conceptions of life." Some accused Pater of projecting nineteenth-century modes of thinking onto the Renaissance. To defend himself against these charges of hedonism and ahistoricism, Pater changed the title of the second edition (1877) to *The Renaissance: Studies in Art and Poetry* and omitted the conclusion, which declared that nothing mattered more than the experience of brilliant moments (he restored it, in a slightly modified form, for the third and fourth editions). The damage had been done, however; in later years, he failed to win Oxford appointments he might otherwise have received.

In the preface, Pater sounds a concrete, pragmatic note. Impatient with the notion that critics should seek broad, general definitions of key terms, he declares that "Beauty, like all other qualities presented to human experience, is relative." And referring to the pleasure that we receive from "a picture, a landscape, a fair personality in life or in a book," Pater intimates that on one level at least there is no difference between life and art, nature and culture: each matters only insofar as it gives pleasure.

Pater at first seems to directly challenge Arnold's dictum that the critic must see the object as in itself it really is by adding a necessary "first step": "to know one's own impression as it really is, to discriminate it, to realise it distinctly." Yet their goal is the same; knowing the impression is the means through which one perceives how and why one is "deeply moved by the presence of beautiful objects." This response to art matters, according to Pater, because it frees each mind from being "a solitary prisoner [in] its own dream of a world." Even more important, it frees individuals from their bondage to routine and particularly to death. The love of art for its own sake is what makes us, while the response lasts, more alive than dead. Like other late-nineteenth-century figures, Pater registers a heightened sense of fleeting beauty wherever it materializes, qualities also evident in so-called decadent literature and impressionist painting of the time.

Pater's view of criticism and art startled his contemporaries, because God is absent from it. Most of them saw death not as final but as the pathway to the highest form of life. Pater neither offers any religious consolation nor invokes the moral earnestness and high seriousness of earlier Victorian writers, including Thomas Carlyle, Arnold, and Eliot. Pater seems unconcerned as well about social and political change: there is no higher purpose than seizing, desperately, each moment for whatever intensities it might supply. This is obviously the main limitation of his position, for the responsibility of the critic is maximizing his or her *pleasure*, not contributing to knowledge or to change in a body politic that in Pater's view can no more withstand decay and death than anything or anyone else.

BIBLIOGRAPHY

Primary sources include *The Works of Walter Pater* (10 vols., 1910; rpt. 1967) and *Letters*, edited by Lawrence Evans (1970). See also *Walter Pater: Three Major Texts*, edited by William E. Buckler (1986), which includes *Studies in the History of the Renaissance, Appreciations*, and *Imaginary Portraits*. For a good selection, see *The Selected Writings of Walter Pater*, edited by Harold Bloom (1974). Thomas Wright's biography, *The Life of Walter Pater* (2 vols., 1907), is informative but not always reliable. Overviews of the life and work are provided by Ian Fletcher, *Walter Pater* (rev. ed., 1972), and Gerald Monsman, *Walter Pater* (1977).

For background and annotations for *Studies in the History of the Renaissance*, consult the editions by Adam Phillips (1986) and Donald L. Hill (1980). Context and analysis are offered by Paul Barolsky, *Walter Pater's Renaissance* (1987). Another useful resource is Billie Andrew Inman, *Walter Pater and His Reading, 1874–1877, with a Bibliography of His Library Borrowings, 1878–1894* (1990).

On Pater's criticism, see David J. DeLaura, *Hebrew and Hellene in Victorian England: Newman, Arnold, and Pater* (1969); William E. Buckler, *Walter Pater: The Critic as Artist of Ideas* (1987); and Jonathan Loesberg, *Aestheticism and Deconstruction: Pater, Derrida, and de Man* (1991), which argues for the philosophical and political force of Pater's aestheticist views in *Studies in the History of the Renaissance* and other works. Critical studies include Wolfgang Iser, *Walter Pater: The Aesthetic Moment* (1960; trans. 1987); Robert Keefe, *Walter Pater and the Gods of Disorder* (1988), on Pater's interest in Greek culture and mythology; Carolyn Williams, *Transfigured World: Walter Pater's Aesthetic Historicism* (1989), illuminating on Pater's narrative and rhetorical strategies in his criticism and fiction; Jay Fellows, *Tombs, Despoiled and Haunted: "Under-Textures" and "After-Thoughts" in Walter Pater* (1991); Denis Donoghue, *Walter Pater: Lover of Strange Souls* (1995), a suggestive study of Pater as a writer who sees criticism as "an opportunity for the exercise of self-consciousness"; and William Shuter, *Rereading Walter Pater* (1997), especially cogent on the influence of Heraclitus, Plato, and Hegel on Pater's thought.

Walter Pater: An Imaginative Sense of Fact, edited by Philip Dodd (1981), collects papers presented at the First International Pater Conference, held in Oxford in 1980. Another good collection is *Pater in the 1990s*, edited by Laurel Brake and Ian Small (1991). *Comparative Criticism*, vol. 17 (ed. E. S. Shaffer, 1995), includes excellent essays on Pater by Denis Donoghue, Richard Wollheim, and others. For his contemporaries' responses to Pater's writings, see *Walter Pater: The Critical Heritage*, edited R. M. Seiler (1980). See also *Walter Pater: An Annotated Bibliography of Writings about Him*, edited by Franklin Court (1979).

From Studies in the History of the Renaissance

Preface

Many attempts have been made by writers on art and poetry to define beauty in the abstract, to express it in the most general terms, to find some universal formula for it. The value of these attempts has most often been in the suggestive and penetrating things said by the way. Such discussions help us very little to enjoy what has been well done in art or poetry, to discriminate between what is more and what is less excellent in them, or to use words like beauty, excellence, art, poetry, with a more precise meaning than they would otherwise have. Beauty, like all other qualities presented to human experience, is relative; and the definition of it becomes unmeaning and useless in proportion to its abstractness. To define beauty, not in the most abstract but in the most concrete terms possible, to find, not its universal formula, but the formula which expresses most adequately this or that special manifestation of it, is the aim of the true student of æsthetics.

"To see the object as in itself it really is,"[1] has been justly said to be the aim of all true criticism whatever; and in æsthetic criticism the first step towards seeing one's object as it really is, is to know one's own impression as it really is, to discriminate it,[2] to realise it distinctly. The objects with which æsthetic criticism deals—music, poetry, artistic and accomplished forms of human life—are indeed receptacles of so many powers or forces: they possess, like the products of nature, so many virtues or qualities. What is this song or picture, this engaging personality presented in life or in a book, to *me*? What effect does it really produce on me? Does it give me pleasure? and if so, what sort or degree of pleasure? How is my nature modified by its presence, and under its influence? The answers to these questions are the original facts with which the æsthetic critic has to do; and, as in the study of light, of morals, of number, one must realise such primary data for one's self, or not at all. And he who experiences these impressions strongly, and drives directly at the discrimination and analysis of them, has no need to trouble himself with the abstract question what beauty is in itself, or what its exact relation to truth or experience—metaphysical questions, as unprofitable as metaphysical questions elsewhere. He may pass them all by as being, answerable or not, of no interest to him.

The æsthetic critic, then, regards all the objects with which he has to do, all works of art, and the fairer forms of nature and human life, as powers or forces producing pleasurable sensations, each of a more or less peculiar or unique kind. This influence he feels, and wishes to explain, by analysing and reducing it to its elements. To him, the picture, the landscape, the engaging personality in life or in a book, *La Gioconda*, the hills of Carrara, Pico of Mirandola,[3] are valuable for their virtues, as we say, in speaking of a herb, a wine, a gem; for the property each has of affecting one with a special, a unique, impression of pleasure. Our education becomes complete in proportion as our susceptibility to those impressions increases in depth and variety. And the function of the æsthetic critic is to distinguish, to analyse, and separate from its adjuncts, the virtue by which a picture, a landscape, a fair personality in life or in a book, produces this special impression of beauty or pleasure, to indicate what the source of that impression is, and under what conditions it is experienced. His end is reached when he has disengaged that virtue, and noted it, as a chemist notes some natural element, for himself and others; and the rule for those who would reach this end is stated with great exactness in the words of a recent critique of Sainte-Beuve:—*De se borner à connaître de près les belles choses, et à s'en nourrir en exquis amateurs, en humanistes accomplis.*[4]

1. MATTHEW ARNOLD's phrase, which he used first in "On Translating Homer" (1862) and then in the opening paragraph of a more widely read essay, "The Function of Criticism at the Present Time" (1864; see above).
2. To perceive its distinguishing features.
3. Giovanni Pico, count of Mirandola (1463–1494), an Italian humanist and Neoplatonist philosopher whom Pater examines in one of the chapters of *The Renaissance*. *La Gioconda*: Leonardo da Vinci's painting *Mona Lisa* (ca. 1504). Carrara: a region of Italy famous for its white marble.
4. One should limit oneself to knowing beautiful things intimately, and nourish oneself on them like exquisite amateurs, like accomplished humanists (French). Charles-Augustin Sainte-Beuve (1804–1869), an eminent French critic and journalist; he wrote this sentence in an 1867 essay on the French

What is important, then, is not that the critic should possess a correct abstract definition of beauty for the intellect, but a certain kind of temperament, the power of being deeply moved by the presence of beautiful objects. He will remember always that beauty exists in many forms. To him all periods, types, schools of taste, are in themselves equal. In all ages there have been some excellent workmen, and some excellent work done. The question he asks is always:—In whom did the stir, the genius, the sentiment of the period find itself? where was the receptacle of its refinement, its elevation, its taste? "The ages are all equal," says William Blake, "but genius is always above its age."[5]

Often it will require great nicety to disengage this virtue from the commoner elements with which it may be found in combination. Few artists, not Goethe or Byron[6] even, work quite cleanly, casting off all *débris*, and leaving us only what the heat of their imagination has wholly fused and transformed. Take, for instance, the writings of Wordsworth.[7] The heat of his genius, entering into the substance of his work, has crystallised a part, but only a part, of it; and in that great mass of verse there is much which might well be forgotten. But scattered up and down it, sometimes fusing and transforming entire compositions, like the Stanzas on *Resolution and Independence*, or the *Ode on the Recollections of Childhood*,[8] sometimes, as if at random, depositing a fine crystal here or there, in a matter it does not wholly search through and transmute, we trace the action of his unique, incommunicable faculty, that strange, mystical sense of a life in natural things, and of man's life as a part of nature, drawing strength and colour and character from local influences, from the hills and streams, and from natural sights and sounds. Well! that is the *virtue*, the active principle in Wordsworth's poetry; and then the function of the critic of Wordsworth is to follow up that active principle, to disengage it, to mark the degree in which it penetrates his verse.

The subjects of the following studies are taken from the history of the *Renaissance*, and touch what I think the chief points in that complex, many-sided movement. I have explained in the first of them what I understand by the word, giving it a much wider scope than was intended by those who originally used it to denote that revival of classical antiquity in the fifteenth century which was only one of many results of a general excitement and enlightening of the human mind, but of which the great aim and achievements of what, as Christian art, is often falsely opposed to the Renaissance, were another result. This outbreak of the human spirit may be traced far into the middle age itself, with its motives already clearly pronounced, the care for physical beauty, the worship of the body, the breaking down of those limits which the religious system of the middle age imposed on the heart and the imagination. I have taken as an example of this movement, this earlier Renaissance within the middle age itself, and as an expression of its qualities, two little compositions in early French; not because they constitute the best

poet and humanist JOACHIM DU BELLAY (1522–1560). Pater devotes a later chapter of *Studies in the Renaissance* to du Bellay.

5. From annotations to volume 1 of *The Works of Sir Joshua Reynolds* made by the Romantic poet Blake (1757–1827).

6. George Gordon, Lord Byron (1788–1824), English Romantic poet. Johann Wolfgang von Goethe (1749–1832), German poet, dramatist, and novelist.

7. WILLIAM WORDSWORTH (1770–1850), the greatest of the English Romantic poets.

8. That is, "Ode: Intimations of Immortality from Recollections of Early Childhood" (1807). "Resolution and Independence" was also published in 1807.

possible expression of them, but because they help the unity of my series, inasmuch as the Renaissance ends also in France, in French poetry, in a phase of which the writings of Joachim du Bellay are in many ways the most perfect illustration. The Renaissance, in truth, put forth in France an aftermath, a wonderful later growth, the products of which have to the full that subtle and delicate sweetness which belongs to a refined and comely decadence, as its earliest phases have the freshness which belongs to all periods of growth in art, the charm of *ascêsis*,[9] of the austere and serious girding of the loins in youth.

But it is in Italy, in the fifteenth century, that the interest of the Renaissance mainly lies,—in that solemn fifteenth century which can hardly be studied too much, not merely for its positive results in the things of the intellect and the imagination, its concrete works of art, its special and prominent personalities, with their profound æsthetic charm, but for its general spirit and character, for the ethical qualities of which it is a consummate type.

The various forms of intellectual activity which together make up the culture of an age, move for the most part from different starting-points, and by unconnected roads. As products of the same generation they partake indeed of a common character, and unconsciously illustrate each other; but of the producers themselves, each group is solitary, gaining what advantage or disadvantage there may be in intellectual isolation. Art and poetry, philosophy and the religious life, and that other life of refined pleasure and action in the conspicuous places of the world, are each of them confined to its own circle of ideas, and those who prosecute either of them are generally little curious of the thoughts of others. There come, however, from time to time, eras of more favourable conditions, in which the thoughts of men draw nearer together than is their wont, and the many interests of the intellectual world combine in one complete type of general culture. The fifteenth century in Italy is one of these happier eras, and what is sometimes said of the age of Pericles is true of that of Lorenzo:[1]—it is an age productive in personalities, many-sided, centralised, complete. Here, artists and philosophers and those whom the action of the world has elevated and made keen, do not live in isolation, but breathe a common air, and catch light and heat from each other's thoughts. There is a spirit of general elevation and enlightenment in which all alike communicate. The unity of this spirit gives unity to all the various products of the Renaissance; and it is to this intimate alliance with mind, this participation in the best thoughts which that age produced, that the art of Italy in the fifteenth century owes much of its grave dignity and influence.

I have added an essay on Winckelmann,[2] as not incongruous with the studies which precede it, because Winckelmann, coming in the eighteenth century, really belongs in spirit to an earlier age. By his enthusiasm for the things of the intellect and the imagination for their own sake, by his Hellenism, his life-long struggle to attain to the Greek spirit, he is in sympathy

9. Practice, training (Greek); but in his essay "Style," included in *Appreciations* (1889), Pater defines it as "self-restraint, a skillful economy of means."

1. Lorenzo de Medici (1449–1492), ruler of and patron of the arts in Florence, and himself a poet. Pericles (ca. 495–429 B.C.E.), Athenian statesman and patron of the arts and architecture.

2. Johann Joachim Winckelmann (1717–1768), German classical archaeologist and art historian.

with the humanists of a previous century. He is the last fruit of the Renaissance, and explains in a striking way its motive and tendencies.

Conclusion[3]

Λέγει που Ἡράκλειτος ὅτι πάντα χωρεῖ καὶ οὐδὲν μένει[4]

To regard all things and principles of things as inconstant modes or fashions has more and more become the tendency of modern thought. Let us begin with that which is without—our physical life. Fix upon it in one of its more exquisite intervals, the moment, for instance, of delicious recoil from the flood of water in summer heat. What is the whole physical life in that moment but a combination of natural elements to which science gives their names? But those elements, phosphorus and lime and delicate fibres, are present not in the human body alone: we detect them in places most remote from it. Our physical life is a perpetual motion of them—the passage of the blood, the waste and repairing of the lenses of the eye, the modification of the tissues of the brain under every ray of light and sound—processes which science reduces to simpler and more elementary forces. Like the elements of which we are composed, the action of these forces extends beyond us: it rusts iron and ripens corn. Far out on every side of us those elements are broadcast, driven in many currents; and birth and gesture and death and the springing of violets from the grave[5] are but a few out of ten thousand resultant combinations. That clear, perpetual outline of face and limb is but an image of ours, under which we group them—a design in a web, the actual threads of which pass out beyond it. This at least of flame-like our life has, that it is but the concurrence, renewed from moment to moment, of forces parting sooner or later on their ways.

Or if we begin with the inward world of thought and feeling, the whirlpool is still more rapid, the flame more eager and devouring. There it is no longer the gradual darkening of the eye, the gradual fading of colour from the wall—movements of the shore-side, where the water flows down indeed, though in apparent rest—but the race of the midstream, a drift of momentary acts of sight and passion and thought. At first sight experience seems to bury us under a flood of external objects, pressing upon us with a sharp and importunate, reality, calling us out of ourselves in a thousand forms of action. But when reflexion begins to play upon those objects they are dissipated under its influence; the cohesive force seems suspended like some trick of magic; each object is loosed into a group of impressions—colour, odour, texture—in the mind of the observer. And if we continue to dwell in thought on this world, not of objects in the solidity with which language invests them, but of impressions, unstable, flickering, inconsistent, which burn and are extin-

3. This brief "Conclusion" was omitted in the second edition of this book, as I conceived it might possibly mislead some of those young men into whose hands it might fall. On the whole, I have thought it best to reprint it here, with some slight changes which bring it closer to my original meaning. I have dealt more fully in *Marius the Epicurean* with the thoughts suggested by it [Pater's note]. *Marius the Epicurean* (1885), philosophical novel set in 2d-century C.E. Rome.

4. Somewhere Heraclitus says that all things are in motion and nothing is lasting (Greek); in *Plato and Platonism* (1893), Pater translated the end of the epigraph, "All things give way: nothing remaineth." Heraclitus (active ca. 500 B.C.E), pre-Socratic Greek philosopher.

5. An echo of Laertes' words at the grave of Ophelia, *Hamlet* (ca. 1600), 5.1.222–23: "And from her fair and unpolluted flesh / May violets spring."

guished with our consciousness of them, it contracts still further: the whole scope of observation is dwarfed into the narrow chamber of the individual mind. Experience, already reduced to a group of impressions, is ringed round for each one of us by that thick wall of personality through which no real voice has ever pierced on its way to us, or from us to that which we can only conjecture to be without. Every one of those impressions is the impression of the individual in his isolation, each mind keeping as a solitary prisoner its own dream of a world. Analysis goes a step further still, and assures us that those impressions of the individual mind to which, for each one of us, experience dwindles down, are in perpetual flight; that each of them is limited by time, and that as time is infinitely divisible, each of them is infinitely divisible also; all that is actual in it being a single moment, gone while we try to apprehend it, of which it may ever be more truly said that it has ceased to be than that it is. To such a tremulous wisp constantly re-forming itself on the stream, to a single sharp impression, with a sense in it, a relic more or less fleeting, of such moments gone by, what is real in our life fines itself down. It is with this movement, with the passage and dissolution of impressions, images, sensations, that analysis leaves off—that continual vanishing away, that strange, perpetual, weaving and unweaving of ourselves.

Philosophiren, says Novalis, *ist dephlegmatisiren, vivificiren*.[6] The service of philosophy, of speculative culture, towards the human spirit, is to rouse, to startle it to a life of constant and eager observation. Every moment some form grows perfect in hand or face; some tone on the hills or the sea is choicer than the rest; some mood of passion or insight or intellectual excitement is irresistibly real and attractive to us,—for that moment only. Not the fruit of experience, but experience itself, is the end. A counted number of pulses only is given to us of a variegated, dramatic life. How may we see in them all that is to be seen in them by the finest senses? How shall we pass most swiftly from point to point, and be present always at the focus where the greatest number of vital forces unite in their purest energy?

To burn always with this hard, gem-like flame, to maintain this ecstasy, is success in life. In a sense it might even be said that our failure is to form habits: for, after all, habit is relative to a stereotyped world, and meantime it is only the roughness of the eye that makes any two persons, things, situations, seem alike. While all melts under our feet, we may well grasp at any exquisite passion, or any contribution to knowledge that seems by a lifted horizon to set the spirit free for a moment, or any stirring of the senses, strange dyes, strange colours, and curious odours, or work of the artist's hands, or the face of one's friend. Not to discriminate every moment some passionate attitude in those about us, and in the very brilliancy of their gifts some tragic dividing of forces on their ways, is, on this short day of frost and sun, to sleep before evening. With this sense of the splendour of our experience and of its awful brevity, gathering all we are into one desperate effort to see and touch, we shall hardly have time to make theories about the things we see and touch. What we have to do is to be for ever curiously testing new opinions and courting new impressions, never acquiescing in a facile orthodoxy, of Comte, or of Hegel,[7] or of our own. Philosophical theories or ideas,

6. To philosophize is to cast away inertia, to bring oneself to life (German). Novalis: the pen name of Baron Friedrich von Hardenberg (1772–1801), German Romantic poet and novelist; "Fragmente II" from his *Hymns to the Night* (1800) is quoted here.

7. GEORG WILHELM FRIEDRICH HEGEL (1770–1831), German idealist philosopher. Auguste

as points of view, instruments of criticism, may help us to gather up what might otherwise pass unregarded by us. "Philosophy is the microscope of thought."[8] The theory or idea or system which requires of us the sacrifice of any part of this experience, in consideration of some interest into which we cannot enter, or some abstract theory we have not identified with ourselves, or of what is only conventional, has no real claim upon us.

One of the most beautiful passages of Rousseau[9] is that in the sixth book of the *Confessions*, where he describes the awakening in him of the literary sense. An undefinable taint of death had clung always about him, and now in early manhood he believed himself smitten by mortal disease. He asked himself how he might make as much as possible of the interval that remained; and he was not biassed by anything in his previous life when he decided that it must be by intellectual excitement, which he found just then in the clear, fresh writings of Voltaire.[1] Well! we are all *condamnés*, as Victor Hugo says: we are all under sentence of death but with a sort of indefinite reprieve—*les hommes sont tous condamnés à mort avec des sursis indéfinis*:[2] we have an interval, and then our place knows us no more. Some spend this interval in listlessness, some in high passions, the wisest, at least among "the children of this world,"[3] in art and song. For our one chance lies in expanding that interval, in getting as many pulsations as possible into the given time. Great passions may give us this quickened sense of life, ecstasy and sorrow of love, the various forms of enthusiastic activity, disinterested or otherwise, which come naturally to many of us. Only to be sure it is passion—that it does yield you this fruit of a quickened, multiplied consciousness. Of such wisdom, the poetic passion, the desire of beauty, the love of art for its own sake, has most. For art comes to you proposing frankly to give nothing but the highest quality to your moments as they pass, and simply for those moments' sake.

1873, 1893

Comte (1798–1857), French positivist philosopher.

8. From *Les Misérables* (1862), by Victor Hugo (1802–1885), the leader of the Romantic movement in France.

9. Jean-Jacques Rousseau (1712–1778), Swiss-born French philosopher and political theorist; his *Confessions* were published in 12 books (1781, 1788).

1. The editor Donald L. Hill has pointed out that Rousseau, in his *Confessions*, nowhere mentions reading the French Enlightenment philosopher and writer Voltaire (François-Marie Arouet, 1694–1778).

2. Men are all condemned to death with indefinite reprieves (French). From Hugo, *The Last Day of a Condemned Person* (1832).

3. Luke 16.8.

STÉPHANE MALLARMÉ

1842–1898

"Such is my life, devoid of anecdote," wrote Stéphane Mallarmé to Paul Verlaine, who had asked him to provide biographical information for a headnote in an anthology of contemporary poets. Mallarmé responded by describing a life entirely subordinate to writing: "I have always dreamed and attempted something else, with the patience of an alchemist, ready to sacrifice all vanity and satisfaction, as people once burned their furniture and their roof-beams, to stoke the fires of the Great Work. . . . The

Orphic explanation of the Earth, which is the sole duty of the poet and the literary game par excellence: the very rhythm of the book, coming alive impersonally all the way down to its pagination, would take its place alongside the equations of this dream, or Ode." Writing with a combination of grandiosity and modesty, Mallarmé spent a lifetime describing and exploring the tensions inherent not in personal life but in a poetry that aspires to the condition of music, mathematics, metaphysics, and myth.

Born in 1842 to a family of Parisian functionaries, Mallarmé spent his childhood in various boarding schools after the death of his mother in 1847. Married in 1863, he worked as a high school English teacher for the next thirty years, unhappily and unsuccessfully. (He claimed to have learned English in order to read EDGAR ALLAN POE.) To make ends meet, he undertook to write textbooks for language and literature instruction, cursing the amount of time these texts forced him to take away from what he saw as his true vocation, the invention of an entirely new kind of poetry. At his death in 1898, he considered his Great Work barely begun. Of the 1,659 pages included in the 1945 Pléiade edition of Mallarmé's works, fewer than 100 contain what he considered serious poems (a proportion still smaller in the updated edition), and even those he referred to as mere "calling cards."

How did a poet who wrote so little come to be known as the Master of French Symbolism? On the one hand, by holding weekly meetings at his Paris apartment, where he dazzled a whole generation of poets with opaque yet suggestive discourses no one could quite remember. On the other, by locating his writing *within* its own impossibility. The "vibratory near-disappearance," the "almost nothing," the "stilled ode, in the blanks" of his texts were paradoxes of writing, exploring while collapsing the differences between language and silence, presence and absence, verse and prose. And he always exaggerated his lack of accomplishment: his notoriously difficult poems exerted a tremendous fascination on his contemporaries, and even in his textbooks and in the fashion journal, *La Dernière Mode* (*The Latest Fashion*), which he wrote singlehandedly for four months, he worked out sustained, innovative aesthetic and linguistic theories.

In his later years, Mallarmé invented what he called the "critical poem," a genre of theoretical text as stylistically dense and complex as his verse. "Crisis in Poetry" (1896), our selection, belongs to that genre. In all of Mallarmé's writing, the distinction between "poetry" and "theory" breaks down: every text is a lesson in how language works, weaving and unweaving the poetic act that it itself is in the process of not quite accomplishing. The materiality of page, ink, paragraph, and spacing is often just as important as the logic of syntax, figure, and sense.

The crisis in poetry about which Mallarmé writes is in one sense peculiarly French. The classical French verse form, codified by François de Malherbe in the early seventeenth century and exemplified by PIERRE CORNEILLE, Jean Racine, and Jean-Baptiste Molière, was the alexandrine—a line of twelve syllables divided into two halves, or "hemistichs," by a pause called a *caesura*. For almost three centuries, the rules of prosody were strictly observed. Even the displacement of the caesura from its central position in the line caused an uproar when Victor Hugo dared to attempt it in 1830 (in his play *Hernani*). But as of 1886, just after the death of Hugo, the poetic line seemed to Mallarmé to be breaking up altogether. Poets were writing in "free verse." To a French ear, accustomed to counting syllables and evaluating rhyme, this was a revolution. Mallarmé even goes so far as to treat it as a kind of second French Revolution.

But in another sense, in Mallarmé's account of the "crisis," this "liberation" of verse is merely a way of rediscovering Language itself and is not, strictly speaking, confined to French: all languages mobilize sound and sense, rhythm and rhyme, deploying words as material, sensual objects with properties that go beyond their meanings, with connotations that create networks of effects, as well as with syntax and rhetoric that provide structure and suggestion. The sounds of words may be related to their meaning, but the very existence of multiple languages indicates that that relation is not one of perfect reflection. Mallarmé notes that unlike God, we do not speak words that are themselves the things they name. While God can say "Let there be light," and there is light, in French the spoken word *jour* (day) has a dark vowel sound while *nuit* (night) has a light sound. But our ability to notice this lack of attunement between sound and sense leads us to imagine a virtual language that would be perfectly in tune with itself. One might think that this perfect language would be pure poetry, but Mallarmé does not exactly say so. In fact, he claims that if this language existed, verse itself would not exist, because verse consists of compensating for the failings of language, creating a "total word, new, unknown to the language," suspending the multiple facets of an idea so that its fragments balance in a kind of "universal musicality."

Mallarmé was not the only symbolist whose highest ambitions for poetry were expressed in terms of music. Paul Verlaine (1844–1896) had already asked for "music above all things." And Richard Wagner, the German Romantic composer (1813–1883), had considerable influence on French poetry. That influence sprang less from his music than from his imperfectly understood but enthusiastically endorsed theory of the *Gesamtkunstwerk*, the total work of art, which would combine music, dance, theater, painting, and poetry. When Mallarmé speaks of Music, he refers simultaneously to two different things: a system of sounds that appeals directly to the senses and emotions, and a system of pure relations and intervals that has no referential but only a structural existence.

"Crisis in Poetry" offers a critique of two dominant aesthetic theories of the nineteenth century: namely, realism and Romanticism. About realism, Mallarmé suggests that a book can offer only "allusions," "suggestions"—effects—not any real object, "on which the pages would have difficulty closing." By describing realism as a book trying to enclose a palace, he is saying (somewhat humorously) that reality cannot be presented directly, that any realism is already an interpretation of the real. About Romanticism, Mallarmé critiques the notion that the "personal breath" or voice of the individual poet controls the meaning of the poem. Rather, he claims, in pure poetry the initiative is taken by words themselves in their clashes and rhymes. For Mallarmé, the poet is absent and anonymous. Intentionality and inspiration are eclipsed by the workings of language itself: the poet's voice is "stilled." Convinced that all poets are attempting to write the same Book, Mallarmé sees poetry as eternal, canonical, and unified rather than historically, culturally, and politically diverse. Mallarmé's concept of poetic anonymity is thus at the farthest remove from VIRGINIA WOOLF's. When Woolf claimed in 1929 that "anonymous was a woman," she was referring to the fact that creative women have often been deprived of a place in history and a proper name. For Mallarmé, poetic anonymity is a sign not of dispossession but of cultural authority—precisely the kind of cultural authority that has often deprived women of voice.

In Mallarmé's "Crisis in Poetry," the importance of the "liberation" of verse lies less in the actual accomplishments of writers in free verse than in the dissolution of the old distinction between verse and prose. In another essay, titled "Music and Letters" and first delivered as a lecture at Oxford and Cambridge in 1894, Mallarme goes so far as to say that "prose does not exist": there is "verse" as soon as there is style, as soon as there is any linguistic residue of effectiveness beyond pure instrumentality (what he calls the "journalistic" or "commercial" use of language). Ironically, Mallarmé himself never wrote in free verse. However difficult or "unknown to the language" his late poems may be, they observe classical forms of prosody. But he did undertake one experiment that was definitely not "classical," at least in its form. In *A Throw of the Dice Will Never Abolish Chance* (1897), Mallarmé positioned lines of varying lengths and sizes in different places on the page, letting a long conducting sentence be surrounded by subordinate clauses and typefaces, and sculpting the blanks as well as the writing. This stretching of the spacing of syntax to the breaking point, this exposure of the materiality of writing, and this recognition of the poetic line as an art of flows and interruptions have had a major impact on twentieth-century poetry and theory.

Indeed, French critics and theorists have been not only attentive to, but also influenced by, the writings of Mallarmé. It was largely by learning the lesson of Mallarmé that critics like ROLAND BARTHES came to speak of "the death of the author" in the making of literature. Rather than seeing the text as the emanation of an individual author's intentions, structuralists and deconstructors followed the paths and patterns of the linguistic signifier, paying new attention to syntax, spacing, intertextuality, sound, semantics, etymology, and even individual letters. The theoretical styles of JACQUES DERRIDA, JULIA KRISTEVA, and especially JACQUES LACAN also owe a great deal to Mallarmé's "critical poem."

BIBLIOGRAPHY

There are two authoritative French editions of Mallarmé's works: the Pléiade *Oeuvres complétes*, first edited by Henri Mondor and G. Jean-Aubry (1945) and updated by Bertrand Marchal (1998) and the Flammarion *Poésies*, edited by Carl-Paul Barbier and Charles Gordon Millan (1983). An excellent English translation by Henry Weinfield of Mallarmé's prose and verse poems, *Collected Poems*, has been published in a bilingual edition (1994), but there is no complete translation of the critical prose. Robert Greer Cohn, in *Mallarmé's Divagations: A Guide and Commentary* (1990), offers a useful blend of paraphrase and commentary. Bradford Cook translated a collection of poems, essays, and letters titled *Mallarmé: Selected Prose Poems, Essays, and Letters* (1956), and Mary Ann Caws edited his *Selected Poetry and Prose* (1982). Our selection is printed as an appendix to Rosemary Lloyd's *Mallarmé: The Poet and His Circle* (1999), a useful contextualization. Lloyd also translated *The Selected Letters of Stéphane Mallarmé* (1988), which contains many of Mallarmé's best-known statements about poetry. For a well-researched biography in English, see Gordon Millan, *Mallarmé: A Throw of the Dice* (1994).

The history of Mallarmé criticism reads like a history of twentieth-century developments in French criticism more generally. The first readers, including Mallarmé's first editor and biographer, Henri Mondor (a wealthy doctor who owned many of Mallarmé's papers), emphasized the metaphysical aspirations of Mallarmé's poetic project. An important example is Albert Thibaudet's *La Poésie de Stéphane Mallarmé* (1912). Reacting against Mallarmé's perceived other-worldly aestheticism, the existentialist Jean-Paul Sartre complained that literature had turned its back on life and separated the aesthetic from political engagement (*Mallarmé, or the Poet of Nothingness*, 1986; trans. 1988; also see our selection below from *What Is Literature?*). A good sampling of diverse approaches to Mallarmé can be found in *Stéphane Mallarmé*, edited by Harold Bloom (1987), and in *Literary Debate: Texts and Contexts*, edited by Denis Hollier and Jeffrey Mehlman (1999). Jacques Derrida, in *Dissemination* (1972; trans. 1981), analyzes Mallarmé's displacement of classical, Platonic concepts of mimesis; and Julia Kristeva, in *Revolution in Poetic Language* (1974; partial trans., 1984), uses the example of Mallarmé to define her concepts of "the semiotic" and "negativity" in poetry. Excellent studies by critics in English include Malcolm Bowie's *Mallarmé and the Art of Being Difficult* (1978) and Leo Bersani's *The Death of Stéphane Mallarmé* (1982). Other recent studies of Mallarmé's theory and practice of poetic language include Michael Temple, *The Name of the Poet* (1995); Graham Robb, *Unlocking Mallarmé* (1996); Roger Pearson, *Unfolding Mallarmé* (1996); and Richard Cándida Smith, *Mallarmé's Children* (1999). A collection of essays dealing with Mallarmé's legacy in France is *Meetings with Mallarmé*, edited by Michael Temple (1998). For a bibliographical overview of twentieth-century criticism, see D. Hampton Morris's *Stéphane Mallarmé: Twentieth-Century Criticism* (1989).

Crisis in Poetry[1]

Just now, abandoning any possibility of action, with the lassitude brought about by one afternoon after another of distressing bad weather,[2] I let fall, without any curiosity but with the feeling of having read it all twenty years ago, the thread of multicolored pearls that stud the rain, once more, in the glimmer of booklets in the bookshelves. Many a work under the bead-curtain will send out its own scintillation: as, in a mature sky against the window pane, I love to follow the lights of a storm.

Our phase, which is recent, is, if not closing, taking breath or perhaps stock: considering it attentively reveals the creative and fairly sure will power driving it.

Even the press, which usually needs twenty years to discover the news, is suddenly preoccupied with the subject, and on time.

Literature here is undergoing an exquisite crisis, a fundamental crisis.

Whoever grants that function a place, whether or not it be the first place, recognizes in this the substance of current affairs. We are observing, as a finale to the century not what last century observed,[3] not disruptions; but, outside the public arena, a trembling of the veil in the temple revealing significant folds, and to some extent, its tearing down.[4]

French readers, their habits disrupted by the death of Victor Hugo,[5] cannot fail to be disconcerted. Hugo, in his mysterious task, turned all prose, philosophy, eloquence, history, to verse, and as he was verse personified, he confiscated from any thinking person, anyone who talked or told stories, all but the right to speak. A monument in this desert, with silence far away; in a crypt, thus lies the godhead of a majestic and unconscious idea, to wit that the form we call verse is simply in itself literature; that there is verse as soon as diction is stressed, that there is rhythm as soon as style is emphasized. Poetry, I believe, waited respectfully until the giant who identified it with his tenacious hand, a hand stronger than that of a blacksmith, ceased to exist; waited until then before breaking up. The entire language, tailored to metrics, now recovered its vital rhythms and escaped, in a free disjunction of thousands of simple elements; and, as I'll show, it was not unlike the multiplicity of cries in an orchestra, but an orchestra remaining verbal.

The change dates from then: although it was surreptitiously and unexpectedly prepared beforehand by Verlaine,[6] who, fluid as he was, was called back to primitive forms.

A witness to this adventure, in which people have asked me to play a more efficacious role although such a role suits no one, I did at least take a fervent

1. "Crise de vers"; translated by Rosemary Lloyd.
2. *Le temps* in French means "weather" as well as "time." By describing an innocuous rainy day, Mallarmé is actually starting both his "news of the day" sequence and his "verse" sequence: the raindrops are like beads of glass (*verroterie* from *verre*, "glass," which sounds just like *vers* "verse"). The title of an earlier version of this essay brought the two sequences together by using the word *averse*, which means "shower" ("Averse ou critique," or "Shower or Criticism," 1895).
3. That is, the French Revolution of 1789.
4. An allusion to the veil in the temple separating off the Holy of Holies, which was said to be rent at the time of Christ's crucifixion to show that all men, not merely high priests, could have access to God (see Mark 15.38). In the same way, Mallarmé implies, the "veil" of prosody has been rent by the discovery of free verse.
5. Prolific French Romantic poet, novelist, and playwright (1802–1885).
6. Paul Verlaine (1844–1896), French poet known for the musicality of his verse.

interest in it and the time has come to talk about it, preferably from a distance, since what took place did so almost anonymously.

Let's grant that French poetry, because of the primary role played by rhyme in creating its enchantment, has, in its evolution up to our time, proved to be intermittent: for a time it gleams, then fades and waits. Extinct, or rather worn threadbare by repetition. Does the need to write poetry, in response to a variety of circumstances, now mean, after one of those periodical orgiastic excesses of almost a century comparable only to the Renaissance,[7] that the time has come for shadows and cooler temperatures? Not at all! It means that the gleam continues, though changed. The recasting, a process normally kept hidden, is taking place in public, by means of delicious approximations.

I think one can separate under a triple aspect the treatment given to the solemn canon of poetry, taking each in order.

That prosody, with its very brief rules, is nevertheless untouchable: it is what points to acts of prudence, such as the hemistich,[8] and what regulates the slightest effort at stimulating versification, like codes according to which abstention from flying is for instance a necessary condition for standing upright.[9] Exactly what one does not need to learn; because if you haven't guessed it yourself beforehand, then you've proved the uselessness of constraining yourself to it.

The faithful supporters of the alexandrine, our hexameter,[1] are loosening from within the rigid and puerile mechanism of its beat; the ear, set free from an artificial counter, discovers delight in discerning on its own all the possible combinations that twelve timbres can make amongst themselves.

It's a taste we should consider very modern.

Let's take an intermediate case, in no way the least curious:

The poet who possesses acute tact and who always considers this alexandrine as the definitive jewel, but one you bring out as you would a sword or a flower only rarely and only when there is some premeditated motive for doing so, touches it modestly and plays around it, lending it neighboring chords, before bringing it out superb and unadorned. On many occasions he lets his fingering falter on the eleventh syllable or continues it to the thirteenth. M. Henri de Régnier[2] excels in these accompaniments, of his own invention, I know, an invention as discrete and proud as the genius he instills into it, and revelatory of the fleeting disquiet felt by the performers faced with the instrument they have inherited. Something else, which could simply be the opposite, reveals itself as a deliberate rebellion in the absence of the old mold, grown weary, when Jules Laforgue,[3] from the outset, initiated us into the unquestionable charm of the incorrect line.

So far, in each of the models I've just mentioned, nothing apart from reserve and abandon, because of the lassitude caused by excessive recourse to our national rhythm; whose use, like that of the flag, ought to remain an exception. With this nevertheless amusing particularity that willful infrac-

7. That is, the Romantic period.
8. Half a verse line.
9. *Voler* means both "to fly" and "to steal"; *droiture* means "uprightness" in both the moral and the physical sense. The sentence can thus also mean "abstaining from stealing is (not) a necessary condition of honesty." In this way, the "laws" of verse are similar to the laws of gravity and honesty.
1. The meter of Greek and Latin epic poetry (based on 6 metrical feet). "The alexandrine": the meter of classical French verse, a 12-syllable line with a break (the caesura) in the middle, separating the two hemistichs. The English equivalent to both is iambic pentameter.
2. French poet and novelist (1864–1936), a faithful attender of Mallarmé's Tuesday gatherings.
3. French poet (1860–1887), born in Uruguay, known for his ironic, innovative verse.

tions or deliberate dissonances appeal to our delicacy, whereas, barely fifteen years ago, the pedant that we have remained would have felt as exasperated as if confronted with some ignorant sacrilege! I'll say that the memory of the strict line of poetry haunts these games on the side and confers on them a certain benefit.

The entire novelty, where free verse is concerned, resides not as the seventeenth century attributed verse to the fable or the opera (that was merely a non-strophic arrangement[4] of diverse famous meters) but in what it might be suitable to call its "polymorphous" nature: and we should now envisage the dissolution of the official number into whatever one wishes, as far as infinity, provided that it contains a renewed source of pleasure. Sometimes it's a euphony fragmented with the consent of an intuitive reader, someone with inborn and precious good taste—just now, M. Moréas; or a languishing gesture of dream, leaping up in passion and finding the right beat—that's M. Viélé-Griffin; beforehand it was M. Kahn with a very erudite notation of the tonal value of words. I'm giving names, for there are others who are typical, MM Charles Morice, Verhaeren, Dujardin, Mockel[5] and all, only as a proof of what I'm saying, so that you can consult their publications.

What's remarkable is that, for the first time in the course of any nation's literary history, concurrently with the great general and secular organs, in which, following an inborn keyboard, orthodoxy expresses its exaltation, whoever wishes to use his or her own techniques and individual hearing can create a personal instrument on which to breathe, to touch or stroke with skill; and it can be used on its own, and also be dedicated to the Language in general.

A high freedom has been acquired, the newest: I don't see, and this remains my own intensely felt opinion, that anything that has been beautiful in the past has been eliminated, and I remain convinced that on important occasions we will always conform to the solemn tradition, that owes its prevalence to the fact that it stems from the classical genius; only, when what's needed is a breath of sentiment or a story, there's no call to disturb the venerable echoes, so we'll look to do something else. Every soul is a melody, which needs only to be set in motion; and for that we each have our own flute or viola.

In my view this is the belated eruption of a real condition or of a possibility, that of not only expressing ourselves, but of bursting into song, as we see fit.

Languages, which are imperfect in so far as they are many, lack the supreme language: because thinking is like writing without instruments, not a whispering but still keeping silent, the immortal word, the diversity of idioms on earth, prevents anyone from proffering the words which otherwise would be at their disposal, each uniquely minted and in themselves revealing the material truth. This prohibition flourishes expressly in nature (you stumble upon it with a smile) so that there is no reason to consider yourself God; but, as soon as my mind turns to aesthetics, I regret that speech fails to express objects by marks that correspond to them in color and movement,

4. That is, not arranged in metrically complex stanzas (such as those characteristic of odes).

5. All poets writing in French and experimenting with free verse: Jean Moréas (1856–1910), born in Greece; Francis Viélé-Griffin (1864–1937), born in Virginia; Gustave Kahn (1859–1936); Charles Morice (1861–1919); Émile Verhaeren (1855–1916), born in Belgium; Édouard Dujardin (1861–1949), founder of *La Revue Wagnerienne*; and Albert Mockel (1866–1945), born in Belgium.

marks that exist in the instrument of the voice, among languages and sometimes in a single language. Compared to the word *ombre* (shadow) which is opaque, *ténèbres* (darkness) is not much blacker; how disappointing to discover the perversity that in contradictory fashion bestows on the word *jour* (day, light) sounds that are dark, while those of *nuit* (night) are bright.[6] We desire a word of brilliant splendor or conversely one that fades away; and as for simple, luminous alternatives. . . . *But,* we should note, *otherwise poetry would not exist:* philosophically, it is poetry that makes up for the failure of language, providing an extra extension.

Strange mystery; and from intentions no less strangely mysterious metrics burst forth in the days when everything was coming into being.

Let an average group of words, under the comprehension of the gaze, line up in definitive traits, surrounded by silence.

If, in the French case, no private invention were to surpass the prosody that we've inherited, there would be an outpouring of displeasure, as if a singer were unable, away from others or walking where he pleased among the infinite number of little flowers, wherever his voice met a notation, to pluck it. . . . This attempt took place just recently, and, leaving aside the erudite research in the same direction, accentuation[7] and so forth, that has been announced, I know that a seductive game leads, together with shreds of the old still recognizable line, to the possibility of eluding it or revealing it, rather than to a sudden discovery of something entirely alien. It just takes the time needed to loosen the constraints and whip up some zeal, where the school went astray. And it's very precious: but to go from that freedom to imagine more, or simply to think that each individual brings a new prosody arising from their own way of breathing—which is certainly how some people spell—well it's a joke to cause much laughter and to inspire the preface-writers to build their platforms. Similarity between lines of poetry and old proportions, this will provide the regularity that will last because the poetic act consists in suddenly seeing that an idea splits into a number of motives of equal value and in grouping them; they rhyme: and to place an external seal upon them we have their common metrics which the final beat binds together.

It is in the very interesting treatment meted out to versification in this age of recess and interregnum, no less than in our virginal mental circumstances, that lies the crisis.

To hear the unquestionable ray of light—as features gild or tear a meander of melodies: or Music rejoins Verse, to form, since Wagner,[8] Poetry.

It's not that one element or another moves away, advantageously, towards an integrity triumphing somewhere else, in the form of a concert that remains mute if it is not given voice, and the poem, enunciator: of their community or their new form, illuminating the instrumentation until it's obvious under the veil, as elocution descends from the sky of sounds. The

6. Harking back to theories of language discussed in PLATO's *Cratylus* (ca. 385 B.C.E.), Mallarmé describes words as though their sounds could imitate the things they name; here, vowel tones are expected to correspond to degrees of luminosity.

7. Unlike in English, syllables in French words bear no inherent accents: stress always falls on the last syllable of a word or group of words. French therefore lends itself to syllabic rather than accentual verse; but since stresses do occur before pauses, it is possible to shape their occurrence into patterns.

8. Richard Wagner (1813–1883), German composer, conductor, and author whose influence was pervasive among late-19th-century French poets even though his operas were largely banned in France after the Franco-Prussian War (1870–71).

modern meteor, the symphony, at the pleasure of the musicians or unbeknownst to them, draws closer to thought, but a thought which no longer draws on current expressions.

Some explosion of Mystery into all the skies of its impersonal magnificence, where the orchestra should not have failed to influence the ancient effort which has long sought to extract it from the mouth of the race.

A double indication arises from this—

Decadent or mystic,[9] the schools describe themselves or are given labels hastily by our news media,[1] and adopt, as meeting point, an Idealism[2] which (like fugues or sonatas) refuses the natural materials and brutally demands an exact thought to put them in order, so as to keep nothing but the mere suggestion. To create an exact relationship between the images, in such a way that a third aspect, fusible and light, and whose presence can be divined, will break free . . . We've abolished the pretension—an aesthetic error, although one that has commanded masterpieces[3]—of including on the subtle paper of the volume anything other than for instance the horror of the forest or the silent thunder scattered through the foliage, not the intrinsic and dense wood of the trees. A few bursts of the intimate pride truthfully trumpeted awaken the architecture of the palace, the only place where one can dwell; no stone, on which the pages would have difficulty closing.

"Monuments, the sea, the human face, in their plenitude, and as they are, preserving a virtue which is more attractive than if they were veiled by a description, call it *evocation*, or *allusion, suggestion:* that somewhat random terminology bears witness to the tendency, a very decisive tendency perhaps, that literary art has experienced, a tendency that limits it and dispenses it. Literature's witchery, if it is not to liberate from a fistful of dust or reality without enclosing it in the book, even as a text, that volatile dispersion which is the mind, which has nothing to do with anything but the musicality of everything."[4]

Speech has no connection with the reality of things except in matters commercial; where literature is concerned, speech is content merely to make allusions or to distill the quality contained in some idea.

On this condition the song burst forth, as a lighthearted joy.

This ambition, I call Transposition—Structure is something else.

The pure work of art implies the elocutionary disappearance of the poet who yields the initiative to words, set in motion by the clash of their inequalities; they illuminate each other with reciprocal lights like a virtual trail of fire on precious stones, replacing the perceptible breath of the old lyric or the individual enthusiastic direction of the sentence.

An order of the book of verse springs from it, innate or pervasive, and eliminates chance; such an order is essential, to omit the author: well, a subject, destined, implies amongst the elements of the whole, a certain accord as to the appropriate place for it within the volume. This is a possi-

9. Movements that were literary reactions against 19th-century bourgeois realism, positivism, and utilitarianism.

1. Despite his professed scorn for journalism, Mallarmé at this time often portrays himself as a purveyor of news. When asked to speak in England on the state of French poetry, he announced, "I do indeed bring news: verse has been tampered with."

2. A term (like *Spirit* and *Idea*) that in Mallarmé is often seen as having Platonic or Hegelian significance, referring to ultimate metaphysical realities.

3. That is, realist novels.

4. Mallarmé quotes his own "Music and Letters" (1894), originally delivered in England.

bility brought about by the fact that each cry has its echo—in the same way motifs balance each other, from a distance, producing neither the incoherent sublimity of the romantic pagination, nor that artificial unity of more recent times, measured out to the book en bloc. Everything becomes suspense, a fragmentary disposition with alternations and oppositions, all working towards the total rhythm of the white spaces, which would be the poem silenced; but it is translated to some extent by each pendant. I want to consider it as instinct, perceived in these publications and, if the supposed type does not remain separate from complementary types, youth, for once, in poetry where a dazzling and harmonious plenitude imposes itself, has stuttered the magic concept of the Work.[5] Some symmetry, in parallel fashion, which, from the situation of the lines in the poem that are linked to the authenticity of the poem within the volume, fly beyond it, several of them inscribing on the spiritual plane the amplified signature of the genius, anonymous and perfect as an artistic existence.

A chimera,[6] having thought of it proves, from the reflection of its scales, how much the current cycle or this last quarter century, is undergoing some absolute illumination—whose wild shower on my window panes wipes away the dripping murkiness sufficiently to illuminate those panes—that, more or less, all books contain the fusion of some counted repetitions: even if there were only one—the world's law—a bible of the kind nations simulate. The difference from one work to another offers as many lessons set forth in an immense competition for the true text, between the ages termed civilized or—lettered.

Certainly I never sit down on the terraces to hear a concert without glimpsing amidst the obscure sublimity some sketch of one or other of humanity's immanent poems or their original state, all the more comprehensible for not being spoken, and I see that to determine its vast line the composer experienced that easy suspension of even the temptation to express it. I imagine, through a no doubt ineradicable prejudice of writers, that nothing will remain if it is not given form; a form we have reached the stage, precisely, of seeking out, faced with a break in the great literary rhythms (I discussed this above) and their dispersal into shivers articulated in ways close to instrumentation. An art of achieving the transposition in the Book of the symphony or simply to take back our own: for there is no question that it is not the elementary sounds produced by the brass, strings, woods, but the intellectual word at its purest point that must lead, with plenitude and undeniably as the ensemble of links existing within everything, to Music.

An undeniable longing of my time has been to separate as if for different purposes the double state of the word, raw and immediate on the one hand, on the other, essential.

Telling, teaching, even describing, that's all very well and yet all that would be needed perhaps for each of us to exchange our thoughts as humans would be to take from or leave in the hand of another a coin, in silence, but the elementary use of speech serves the universal reporting in which all the contemporary written genres participate, with the exception of literature.

5. The (Great) Work, another name for the philosophers' stone, sought by the alchemists to turn base metals into gold. Mallarmé saw alchemy as an origin not only of aesthetics but also of political economy.

6. Literally, in Greek mythology a fire-breathing monster with a lion's head, a goat's body, and a serpent's tail; more generally, anything composed of incongruous parts, or an illusory mental fabrication.

What is the point of the marvel of transposing a fact of nature into its almost vibratory disappearance according to the action of the word, however, if it is not so that there emanates from it, without the predicament posed by a near or concrete reminder, the pure notion.

I say: a flower! And from the oblivion to which my voice relegates all contours, as something other than the unmentioned calyces, musically arises, the idea itself, and sweet, the flower absent from all bouquets.[7]

Contrary to the facile numerical and representative functions, as the crowd first treats it, speech which is above all dream and song, finds again in the Poet, by a necessity that is part of an art consecrated to fictions, its virtuality.

The line of several words which recreates a total word, new, unknown to the language and as if incantatory, achieves that isolation of speech: denying, in a sovereign gesture, the arbitrariness that clings to words despite the artifice of their being alternately plunged in meaning and sound, and causes you that surprise at not having heard before a certain ordinary fragment of speech, at the same time as the memory of the named object bathes in a new atmosphere.

1896

7. In the original, the sentence ends "l'absente de tous bouquets" (the absent of all bouquets). By omitting the word "flower,' the French thus demonstrates more forcefully that a name indicates the absence of the thing named.

HENRY JAMES
1843–1916

Born in New York City, Henry James typically is placed in anthologies of American literature, but he was in truth a cosmopolitan novelist and critic who sought to make his mark on the American, English, and European literary scenes. "We can deal freely with forms of civilization not our own," he affirmed in a letter in 1867, "can pick and choose and assimilate and in short (aesthetically) claim our property wherever we find it." He wished to bring about "a vast intellectual fusion and synthesis of the various National tendencies of the world"; his concern with the complex challenges and rewards of the "art of fiction" was general, not limited to American fiction alone.

Henry James Sr., a religious philosopher and visionary, believed that his five children should be educated with as few restrictions as possible; hence he had taken them to Europe in 1855 for a three-year acquisition of a "sensuous education." Theaters, art galleries, museums, monuments, and landscapes were his favored sites for learning. Among the gifted members of this family was William James, Henry's elder brother, a professor of philosophy and then psychology at Harvard whose influential books include *The Varieties of Religious Experience* (1902) and *Pragmatism* (1907). During the late 1860s and early 1870s, Henry James lived abroad much of the time; in 1876 he decided to reside in London and frequently visit the Continent, especially Rome and Paris.

James was an explorer of, and mediator between, cultures. One of his best early stories, "A Passionate Pilgrim" (1871), deals with the social and cultural challenges faced by an American visitor to Europe. He developed this theme of cultural interanimation and difference in travel writings, such as *Transatlantic Sketches* (1875), and in a series of novels and novellas that includes *Roderick Hudson* (1876), *The American* (1877), *The Europeans* (1878), *Daisy Miller* (1879), *An International Episode* (1879), and *The Portrait of a Lady* (1881). "I aspire to write in such a way," James declared, "that it would be impossible to an outsider to say whether I am at a given moment an American writing about England or an Englishman writing about America. . . . And so far from being ashamed of such an ambiguity I should be exceedingly proud of it, for it would be highly civilised."

As his work of the 1870s and early 1880s attests, James was already an accomplished author when our selection, "The Art of Fiction"—his credo as a novelist—was published in London in September 1884. A month after the essay appeared, James lamented in a letter to the critic and biographer T. S. Perry that "my poor article has not attracted the smallest attention here & I haven't heard, or seen, an allusion to it." But soon critics and reviewers, especially in England, began to refer and reply to the piece. In subsequent decades, as James's own reputation rose, "The Art of Fiction" gained prominence as an inquiry into, and defense of, the novelist's craft. A century later, the scholar James E. Miller Jr., judged it "perhaps the most popular and surely the most influential brief statement of fictional theory ever made."

British and American novelists before James, including Henry Fielding, Jane Austen, Sir Walter Scott, and Nathaniel Hawthorne, had commented on the nature of the novel and its relationship to the romance. Beginning in the mid–eighteenth century with SAMUEL JOHNSON, critics had considered the status and structure of "fiction" as a narrative form. Book-length studies included Clara Reeve's *Progress of Romance* (1785) and John Dunlop's massive two-volume survey, *The History of Fiction* (1816). And by 1884 countless essays and reviews in Victorian periodicals had debated plot, character, design and unity, morality in fiction, and many other topics in analyses written by such eminent novelists as George Eliot and by such noteworthy critics as G. H. Lewes and Leslie Stephen.

James added to his own rich experience as a writer the decades of development that the novel had undergone by the 1880s. He profited from extensive reading and close personal contact with the best writers of the day (among them William Dean Howells, Gustave Flaubert, Guy de Maupassant, Émile Zola, and Ivan Turgenev). As an active essayist and reviewer since the 1860s for the *Nation*, the *North American Review*, and the *Atlantic Monthly*, James was defining his own artistic identity and measuring himself alongside both national and international competition. His critical books of this period include *French Poets and Novelists* (1878) and *Hawthorne* (1879), and he examined fiction with a keen awareness of his own practice.

Taking as his point of departure an 1884 lecture by the popular novelist, historian, and philanthropist Walter Besant and borrowing its title, James insisted that the novelist be allowed to pursue artistic experiments freely. He told his friend Robert Louis Stevenson that "The Art of Fiction" was "simply a plea for liberty," which for him signified the writer's choice of subject and right both to experiment and to dissent from conventional standards and opinions. In one of the ironies that makes James so intriguing, he was a very *interested* critic, not an objective one. Even when he focuses on authors whom he genuinely admires, such as Honoré de Balzac, Turgenev, and George Eliot, he cannot quite bring himself to respond to (let alone accept) them on their own terms—though his theory implies that he should. Here, as elsewhere in his critical writings, his allegiance to his own artistic aims and methods prevented James from engaging writers with full understanding; his assessments of Charles Dickens, Walt Whitman, CHARLES BAUDELAIRE, and Fyodor Dostoyevsky, among others, suffer from his impatience with their often controversial subjects and innovations in form. James's criticisms thus sometimes tell us less about the shortcomings of the work discussed than about the tensions between his theory and practice.

Like MATTHEW ARNOLD in "The Function of Criticism at the Present Time" (1864; see above), James in "The Art of Fiction" maintains that criticism prepares and enhances the context for creative writing. And in an essay about Arnold published in the same year as "The Art of Fiction," James describes the good novel (it "emits its light and stimulates our desire for perfection") in a manner very close to Arnold's definition of "the pursuit of perfection" as "the pursuit of sweetness and light" in *Culture and Anarchy* (1869; see above). James's tone is forthright, optimistic, and celebratory of the power of the literary imagination. Indeed, "The Art of Fiction" is a controlled, resonant rearticulation of the tributes to the imagination voiced decades earlier by WILLIAM WORDSWORTH, SAMUEL TAYLOR COLERIDGE, PERCY BYSSHE SHELLEY, and RALPH WALDO EMERSON on behalf of the poet. James is often identified as a literary realist and early modernist—Ezra Pound and T. S. ELIOT esteemed him highly. But the roots of his creative and critical practice lie in Romanticism's organic conception of literary form, and in its exalted view of the literary vocation (the writer, James remarked, is an alchemist who "renews something like the old dream of the secret of life").

These connections are important to bear in mind when reading James's essay. "The Art of Fiction" often has been interpreted in isolation, with little note of its affinities to other critical and theoretical texts that preceded it. Sometimes it has been treated exclusively within the canon of James's own creative and critical writings, as a prelude both to his dense, difficult final three novels, *The Wings of the Dove* (1902), *The Ambassadors* (1903), and *The Golden Bowl* (1904), and to the later prefaces—a "comprehensive manual" for "aspirants" to the profession—that he composed for the twenty-six-volume New York Edition of his novels and stories (1907–09, 1917). Such intensively "Jamesian" readings value "The Art of Fiction" as a formative text in James's own career: it shows him, like Wordsworth and Coleridge, establishing the terms through which his own work should be understood and appraised. But if we locate the essay solely within James's corpus, we are prevented from understanding how this piece (and others he produced) contributes to his significance in the general history of narrative theory.

James's concern for taste, judgment, and discrimination glances backward to the eighteenth-century writers DAVID HUME and EDMUND BURKE. And when he hails the novel as "a personal, a direct impression of life," he more immediately echoes the heightened phrasing that WALTER PATER had employed in *Studies in the History of the Renaissance* (1873; see above). His account of the novel as an "organism" not only reinforces the account of "organic form" delineated by Coleridge in the *Biographia Literaria* but also anticipates the elaborations of this same idea in the writings of JOHN CROWE RANSOM, CLEANTH BROOKS, and other New Critics of the 1930s and 1940s.

"The Art of Fiction" is a subtle verbal performance; playful, witty, and ironic, it is both generous and tough-minded toward James's target-of-opportunity Walter Besant. Reading James profitably means paying close attention to his metaphors (e.g., the "huge spider-web" of experience) and analogies (e.g., between the novel and the picture). It means being alert as well to the illuminations provided by James's handling of specific words, as when he reiterates the "torment" of the writer. There are also key moments when James invites readers to reflect on the implications of his claims. In perhaps the most elusive of these, he asserts that "the deepest quality of a work of art will always be the quality of the mind of the producer." James realized the demands inherent in such a claim: How will we know, in the case of each novel, when we have made contact with the mind of its producer? How can we determine that mind's special quality? But his chosen criterion highlights the intimate relationship between writer and reader that the cosmopolitan James always looked for, and that he called on readers of "The Art of Fiction" to share.

BIBLIOGRAPHY

James's literary criticism has been collected by the Library of America in two volumes, titled *Essays, American and English Writers* and *European Writers and the Prefaces* (1984). This is an essential collection for the serious student of James's work. Selections can be found in *Literary Reviews and Essays on American, English, and French Literature*, edited by Albert Mordell (1957); *Henry James: Selected Literary Criticism*, edited by Morris Shapira (1963); *Theory of Fiction: Henry James*, edited by James E. Miller Jr. (1972), arranged according to topics and categories; *The House of Fiction: Essays on the Novel*, edited by Leon Edel (1973); *The Art of Criticism: Henry James on the Theory and the Practice of Fiction*, edited by William Veeder and Susan M. Griffin (1986), which includes excellent discussion of and detailed notes for each selection; and *The Critical Muse: Selected Literary Criticism of Henry James*, edited by Roger Gard (1988), which is the best selection for an overview of James's achievement in criticism and theory. Also important is *The Art of the Novel: Critical Prefaces by Henry James*, with an introduction by R. P. Blackmur (new ed., 1984), which gathers the prefaces that James wrote for the New York Edition. Additional primary sources include *Henry James: Autobiography*, edited by F. W. Dupee (1956), written in James's late labyrinthine, evocative manner; *The Complete Notebooks of Henry James*, edited by Leon Edel and Lyall H. Powers (1987); and *Letters*, edited by Leon Edel (4 vols., 1974–84).

The definitive biography is *Henry James*, variously subtitled, in five volumes by Leon Edel (1953–72); it is condensed and updated in the single volume *Henry James: A Life* (1985). Other excellent biographies include Fred Kaplan, *Henry James: The Imagination of Genius: A Biography* (1992), and Kenneth Graham, *Henry James: A Literary Life* (1995) Lyndall Gordon, *A Private Life of Henry James: Two Women and His Art* (1999), probes the impact on James's writing of two important relationships: one with his cousin Minnie Temple, the other with the author Constance Fenimore Woolson.

The best scholarly writings on James as a critic and theorist are Sarah B. Daugherty, *The Literary Criticism of Henry James* (1981), and Vivien Jones, *James the Critic* (1984). Also helpful are Adeline Tintner, *The Book World of Henry James: Appropriating the Classics* (1987); Jonathan Freedman, *Professions of Taste: Henry James, British Aestheticism, and Commodity Culture* (1990), which makes cogent connections among James, Walter Pater, and Oscar Wilde; Edwin S. Fussell, *The French Side of Henry James* (1990); Tony Tanner, *Henry James and the Art of Nonfiction* (1995), which includes a suggestive chapter on the criticism; and Pierre A. Walker, *Reading Henry James in French Cultural Contexts* (1995).

Among the many books on James's fiction, the most pertinent to his critical writings are Laurence Bedwell Holland, *The Expense of Vision: Essays on the Craft of Henry James* (1964), a brilliant analysis of the novels that relates them to the criticism, especially to the prefaces; John Carlos Rowe, *The Theoretical Dimensions of Henry James* (1984); Michael Anesko, *"Friction with the Market": Henry James and the Profession of Authorship* (1986), on the pressures that James faced in struggling to meet but not surrender to the demands of the literary marketplace; Sharon Cameron, *Thinking in Henry James* (1989); Ross Posnock, *The Trial of Curiosity: Henry James, William James, and the Challenge of Modernity* (1991), a wide-ranging comparison of the James brothers' attitudes toward the challenges of modernity; and Garry Hagberg, *Meaning and Interpretation: Wittgenstein, Henry James, and Literary Knowledge* (1994).

See also *A Bibliography of Henry James*, by Leon Edel and Dan H. Laurence, revised with the assistance of James Rambeau (3rd ed., 1982). Secondary sources are listed in Linda J. Taylor, *Henry James, 1866–1916: A Reference Guide* (1982); Kristin Pruitt McColgan, *Henry James, 1917–1959: A Reference Guide* (1979); Dorothy McInnis Scura, *Henry James, 1960–1974: A Reference Guide* (1979); and Judith E. Funston, *Henry James: A Reference Guide, 1975–1987* (1991).

The Art of Fiction

I should not have affixed so comprehensive a title to these few remarks, necessarily wanting in any completeness upon a subject the full consideration of which would carry us far, did I not seem to discover a pretext for my temerity in the interesting pamphlet lately published under this name by Mr. Walter Besant.[1] Mr. Besant's lecture at the Royal Institution—the original form of his pamphlet—appears to indicate that many persons are interested in the art of fiction, and are not indifferent to such remarks, as those who practise it may attempt to make about it. I am therefore anxious not to lose the benefit of this favourable association, and to edge in a few words under cover of the attention which Mr. Besant is sure to have excited. There is something very encouraging in his having put into form certain of his ideas on the mystery of story-telling.

It is a proof of life and curiosity—curiosity on the part of the brotherhood of novelists as well as on the part of their readers. Only a short time ago it might have been supposed that the English novel was not what the French call *discutable*.[2] It had no air of having a theory, a conviction, a consciousness of itself behind it—of being the expression of an artistic faith, the result of choice and comparison. I do not say it was necessarily the worse for that: it would take much more courage than I possess to intimate that the form of the novel as Dickens and Thackeray[3] (for instance) saw it had any taint of incompleteness. It was, however, *naïf* (if I may help myself out with another French word); and evidently if it be destined to suffer in any way for having lost its *naïveté* it has now an idea of making sure of the corresponding advantages. During the period I have alluded to there was a comfortable, good-humoured feeling abroad that a novel is a novel, as a pudding is a pudding, and that our only business with it could be to swallow it. But within a year or two, for some reason or other, there have been signs of returning animation—the era of discussion would appear to have been to a certain extent opened. Art lives upon discussion, upon experiment, upon curiosity, upon variety of attempt, upon the exchange of views and the comparison of standpoints; and there is a presumption that those times when no one has anything particular to say about it, and has no reason to give for practice or preference, though they may be times of honour, are not times of development—are times, possibly even, a little of dulness. The successful application of any art is a delightful spectacle, but the theory too is interesting; and though there is a great deal of the latter without the former I suspect there has never been a genuine success that has not had a latent core of conviction. Discussion, suggestion, formulation, these things are fertilising when they are frank and sincere. Mr. Besant has set an excellent example in saying what he thinks, for his part, about the way in which fiction should be written, as well as about the way in which it should be published; for his view of the "art," carried on into an appendix, covers that too. Other labourers in the same field will doubtless take up the argument, they will give it the light of their

1. English novelist, historian, and critic (1836–1901).
2. Discussable, debatable (French).
3. William Thackeray (1811–1863), English novelist and satirist. Charles Dickens (1812–1870), most popular 19th-century English novelist.

experience, and the effect will surely be to make our interest in the novel a little more what it had for some time threatened to fail to be—a serious, active, inquiring interest, under protection of which this delightful study may, in moments of confidence, venture to say a little more what it thinks of itself.

It must take itself seriously for the public to take it so. The old superstition about fiction being "wicked" had doubtless died out in England; but the spirit of it lingers in a certain oblique regard directed toward any story which does not more or less admit that it is only a joke. Even the most jocular novel feels in some degree the weight of the proscription that was formerly directed against literary levity: the jocularity does not always succeed in passing for orthodoxy. It is still expected, though perhaps people are ashamed to say it, that a production which is after all only a "make believe" (for what else is a "story"?) shall be in some degree apologetic—shall renounce the pretension of attempting really to represent life. This, of course, any sensible, wide-awake story declines to do, for it quickly perceives that the tolerance granted to it on such a condition is only an attempt to stifle it disguised in the form of generosity. The old evangelical hostility to the novel, which was as explicit as it was narrow, and which regarded it as little less favourable to our immortal part than a stage-play, was in reality far less insulting. The only reason for the existence of a novel is that it does attempt to represent life.[4] When it relinquishes this attempt, the same attempt that we see on the canvas of the painter, it will have arrived at a very strange pass. It is not expected of the picture that it will make itself humble in order to be forgiven; and the analogy between the art of the painter and the art of the novelist is, so far as I am able to see, complete. Their inspiration is the same, their process (allowing for the different quality of the vehicle), is the same, their success is the same. They may learn from each other, they may explain and sustain each other. Their cause is the same, and the honour of one is the honour of another. The Mahometans[5] think a picture an unholy thing, but it is a long time since any Christian did, and it is therefore the more odd that in the Christian mind the traces (dissimulated though they may be) of a suspicion of the sister art should linger to this day. The only effectual way to lay it to rest is to emphasise the analogy to which I just alluded—to insist on the fact that as the picture is reality, so the novel is history. That is the only general description (which does it justice) that we may give of the novel. But history also is allowed to represent life; it is not, any more than painting, expected to apologise. The subject-matter of fiction is stored up likewise in documents and records, and if it will not give itself away, as they say in California, it must speak with assurance, with the tone of the historian. Certain accomplished novelists have a habit of giving themselves away which must often bring tears to the eyes of people who take their fiction seriously. I was lately struck, in reading over many pages of Anthony Trollope,[6] with his want of discretion in this particular. In a digression, a parenthesis or an aside, he concedes to the reader that he and this trusting friend are only "making

4. In the first version of the essay, James wrote "*does* compete with life." Robert Louis Stevenson criticized the use of the word "compete" in his reply to James, "A Humble Remonstrance," in the December 1884 issue of *Longman's*.

5. Muslims (i.e., followers of Muhammad, or Mahomet). Islam generally prohibits representational art.

6. Prolific English novelist (1815–1882).

believe." He admits that the events he narrates have not really happened, and that he can give his narrative any turn the reader may like best. Such a betrayal of a sacred office seems to me, I confess, a terrible crime; it is what I mean by the attitude of apology, and it shocks me every whit as much in Trollope as it would have shocked me in Gibbon or Macaulay.[7] It implies that the novelist is less occupied in looking for the truth (the truth, of course I mean, that he assumes, the premises that we must grant him, whatever they may be), than the historian, and in doing so it deprives him at a stroke of all his standing-room. To represent and illustrate the past, the actions of men, is the task of either writer, and the only difference that I can see is, in proportion as he succeeds, to the honour of the novelist, consisting as it does in his having more difficulty in collecting his evidence, which is so far from being purely literary.[8] It seems to me to give him a great character, the fact that he has at once so much in common with the philosopher and the painter; this double analogy is a magnificent heritage.

It is of all this evidently that Mr. Besant is full when he insists upon the fact that fiction is one of the *fine* arts, deserving in its turn of all the honours and emoluments that have hitherto been reserved for the successful profession of music, poetry, painting, architecture. It is impossible to insist too much on so important a truth, and the place that Mr. Besant demands for the work of the novelist may be represented, a trifle less abstractly, by saying that he demands not only that it shall be reputed artistic, but that it shall be reputed very artistic indeed. It is excellent that he should have struck this note, for his doing so indicates that there was need of it, that his proposition may be to many people a novelty. One rubs one's eyes at the thought; but the rest of Mr. Besant's essay confirms the revelation. I suspect in truth that it would be possible to confirm it still further, and that one would not be far wrong in saying that in addition to the people to whom it has never occurred that a novel ought to be artistic, there are a great many others who, if this principle were urged upon them, would be filled with an indefinable mistrust. They would find it difficult to explain their repugnance, but it would operate strongly to put them on their guard. "Art," in our Protestant communities, where so many things have got so strangely twisted about, is supposed in certain circles to have some vaguely injurious effect upon those who make it an important consideration, who let it weigh in the balance. It is assumed to be opposed in some mysterious manner to morality, to amusement, to instruction. When it is embodied in the work of the painter (the sculptor is another affair!) you know what it is: it stands there before you, in the honesty of pink and green and a gilt frame; you can see the worst of it at a glance, and you can be on your guard. But when it is introduced into literature it becomes more insidious—there is danger of its hurting you before you know it. Literature should be either instructive or amusing, and there is in many minds an impression that these artistic preoccupations, the search for form, contribute to neither end, interfere indeed with both. They are too frivolous to be edifying, and too serious to be diverting; and they are moreover priggish and paradoxical and superfluous. That, I think, represents the manner in

7. Thomas Babington Macaulay (1800–1859), English historian, essayist and statesman. Edward Gibbon (1737–1794), English historian, author of *The History of the Decline and Fall of the Roman Empire* (6 vols., 1776–88).

8. On somewhat different grounds, ARISTOTLE argues in *Poetics* 9 (see above) that poetry is more philosophical and more worthwhile than history.

which the latent thought of many people who read novels as an exercise in skipping would explain itself if it were to become articulate. They would argue, of course, that a novel ought to be "good," but they would interpret this term in a fashion of their own, which indeed would vary considerably from one critic to another. One would say that being good means representing virtuous and aspiring characters, placed in prominent positions; another would say that it depends on a "happy ending," on a distribution at the last of prizes, pensions, husbands, wives, babies, millions, appended paragraphs, and cheerful remarks. Another still would say that it means being full of incident and movement, so that we shall wish to jump ahead, to see who was the mysterious stranger, and if the stolen will was ever found, and shall not be distracted from this pleasure by any tiresome analysis or "description." But they would all agree that the "artistic" idea would spoil some of their fun. One would hold it accountable for all the description, another would see it revealed in the absence of sympathy. Its hostility to a happy ending would be evident, and it might even in some cases render any ending at all impossible. The "ending" of a novel is, for many persons, like that of a good dinner, a course of dessert and ices, and the artist in fiction is regarded as a sort of meddlesome doctor who forbids agreeable aftertastes. It is therefore true that this conception of Mr. Besant's of the novel as a superior form encounters not only a negative but a positive indifference. It matters little that as a work of art it should really be as little or as much of its essence to supply happy endings, sympathetic characters, and an objective tone, as if it were a work of mechanics: the association of ideas, however incongruous, might easily be too much for it if an eloquent voice were not sometimes raised to call attention to the fact that it is at once as free and as serious a branch of literature as any other.

Certainly this might sometimes be doubted in presence of the enormous number of works of fiction that appeal to the credulity of our generation, for it might easily seem that there could be no great character in a commodity so quickly and easily produced. It must be admitted that good novels are much compromised by bad ones, and that the field at large suffers discredit from overcrowding. I think, however, that this injury is only superficial, and that the superabundance of written fiction proves nothing against the principle itself. It has been vulgarised, like all other kinds of literature, like everything else to-day, and it has proved more than some kinds accessible to vulgarisation. But there is as much difference as there ever was between a good novel and a bad one: the bad is swept with all the daubed canvases and spoiled marble into some unvisited limbo, or infinite rubbish-yard beneath the back-windows of the world, and the good subsists and emits its light and stimulates our desire for perfection. As I shall take the liberty of making but a single criticism of Mr. Besant, whose tone is so full of the love of his art, I may as well have done with it at once. He seems to me to mistake in attempting to say so definitely beforehand what sort of an affair the good novel will be. To indicate the danger of such an error as that has been the purpose of these few pages; to suggest that certain traditions on the subject, applied *a priori*, have already had much to answer for, and that the good health of an art which undertakes so immediately to reproduce life must demand that it be perfectly free. It lives upon exercise, and the very meaning of exercise is freedom. The only obligation to which in advance we may hold a novel, without incurring the accusation of being arbitrary, is that it be interesting. That general responsibility rests upon it, but it is the only one I can think of. The ways in which it is at liberty to accomplish this result (of interesting us) strike me as innumerable, and such as can only suffer from being marked out or fenced in by prescription. They are as various as the temperament of man, and they are successful in proportion as they reveal a particular mind, different from others. A novel is in its broadest definition a personal, a direct impression of life: that, to begin with, constitutes its value, which is greater or less according to the intensity of the impression. But there will be no intensity at all, and therefore no value, unless there is freedom to feel and say. The tracing of a line to be followed, of a tone to be taken, of a form to be filled out, is a limitation of that freedom and a suppression of the very thing that we are most curious about. The form, it seems to me, is to be appreciated after the fact: then the author's choice has been made, his standard has been indicated; then we can follow lines and directions and compare tones and resemblances. Then in a word we can enjoy one of the most charming of pleasures, we can estimate quality, we can apply the test of execution. The execution belongs to the author alone; it is what is most personal to him, and we measure him by that. The advantage, the luxury, as well as the torment and responsibility of the novelist, is that there is no limit to what he may attempt as an executant—no limit to his possible experiments, efforts, discoveries, successes. Here it is especially that he works, step by step, like his brother of the brush, of whom we may always say that he has painted his picture in a manner best known to himself. His manner is his secret, not necessarily a jealous one. He cannot disclose it as a general thing if he would; he would be at a loss to teach it to others. I say this with a due recollection of having insisted on the community of method of the artist who paints a picture and the artist who writes a novel. The painter *is* able to teach the rudiments of his practice, and it is possible, from the study of good work (granted the aptitude), both to learn how to paint and to learn how to write. Yet it remains true, without injury to the *rapprochement*,[9] that the literary artist would be obliged to say to his pupil much more than the other, "Ah, well, you must do it as you can.' " It is a question of degree, a matter of delicacy. If there are exact sciences, there are also exact arts, and the grammar of painting is so much more definite that it makes the difference.

I ought to add, however, that if Mr. Besant says at the beginning of his essay that the "laws of fiction may be laid down and taught with as much precision and exactness as the laws of harmony, perspective, and proportion," he mitigates what might appear to be an extravagance by applying his remark to "general" laws, and by expressing most of these rules in a manner with which it would certainly be unaccommodating to disagree. That the novelist must write from his experience, that his "characters must be real and such as might be met with in actual life;" that "a young lady brought up in a quiet country village should avoid descriptions of garrison life," and "a writer whose friends and personal experiences belong to the lower middle-class should carefully avoid introducing his characters into society;" that one should enter one's notes in a common-place book; that one's figures should be clear in

9. The bringing together (French); that is, of painting and novel writing.

outline; that making them clear by some trick of speech or of carriage is a bad method, and "describing them at length" is a worse one: that English Fiction should have a "conscious moral purpose;" that "it is almost impossible to estimate too highly the value of careful workmanship—that is, of style;" that "the most important point of all is the story," that "the story is everything": these are principles with most of which it is surely impossible not to sympathise. That remark about the lower middle-class writer and his knowing his place is perhaps rather chilling; but for the rest I should find it difficult to dissent from any one of these recommendations. At the same time, I should find it difficult positively to assent to them, with the exception, perhaps, of the injunction as to entering one's notes in a common-place book. They scarcely seem to me to have the quality that Mr. Besant attributes to the rules of the novelist—the "precision and exactness" of "the laws of harmony, perspective, and proportion." They are suggestive, they are even inspiring, but they are not exact, though they are doubtless as much so as the case admits of: which is a proof of that liberty of interpretation for which I just contended. For the value of these different injunctions—so beautiful and so vague—is wholly in the meaning one attaches to them. The characters, the situation, which strike one as real will be those that touch and interest one most, but the measure of reality is very difficult to fix. The reality of Don Quixote or of Mr. Micawber[1] is a very delicate shade; it is a reality so coloured by the author's vision that, vivid as it may be, one would hesitate to propose it as a model: one would expose one's self to some very embarrassing questions on the part of a pupil. It goes without saying that you will not write a good novel unless you possess the sense of reality; but it will be difficult to give you a recipe for calling that sense into being. Humanity is immense, and reality has a myriad forms; the most one can affirm is that some of the flowers of fiction have the odour of it, and others have not; as for telling you in advance how your nosegay should be composed, that is another affair. It is equally excellent and inconclusive to say that one must write from experience; to our supposititious aspirant such a declaration might savor of mockery. What kind of experience is intended, and where does it begin and end? Experience is never limited, and it is never complete; it is an immense sensibility, a kind of huge spider-web of the finest silken threads suspended in the chamber of consciousness, and catching every airborne particle in its tissue. It is the very atmosphere of the mind; and when the mind is imaginative—much more when it happens to be that of a man of genius—it takes to itself the faintest hints of life, it converts the very pulses of the air into revelations. The young lady living in a village has only to be a damsel upon whom nothing is lost to make it quite unfair (as it seems to me) to declare to her that she shall have nothing to say about the military. Greater miracles have been seen than that, imagination assisting, she should speak the truth about some of these gentlemen. I remember an English novelist, a woman of genius,[2] telling me that she was much commended for the impression she had managed to give in one of her tales of the nature and way of life of the French Protestant youth. She had been asked where she learned

1. Character in *David Copperfield* (1849–50), by Dickens. Don Quixote: title character of the novel (1605, 1615), by Miguel de Cervantes.
2. Identified by James's biographer Leon Edel as Anne Thackeray, Lady Ritchie (1837–1919), the daughter of William Thackeray and the author of *The Story of Elizabeth* (1862–63), to which James seems to be alluding.

so much about this recondite being, she had been congratulated on her peculiar opportunities. These opportunities consisted in her having once, in Paris, as she ascended a staircase, passed an open door where, in the household of a *pasteur*,[3] some of the young Protestants were seated at table round a finished meal. The glimpse made a picture; it lasted only a moment, but that moment was experience. She had got her direct personal impression, and she turned out her type. She knew what youth was, and what Protestantism; she also had the advantage of having seen what it was to be French, so that she converted these ideas into a concrete image and produced a reality. Above all, however, she was blessed with the faculty which when you give it an inch takes an ell, and which for the artist is a much greater source of strength than any accident of residence or of place in the social, scale. The power to guess the unseen from the seen, to trace the implication of things, to judge the whole piece by the pattern, the condition of feeling life in general so completely that you are well on your way to knowing any particular corner of it—this cluster of gifts may almost be said to constitute experience, and they occur in country and in town, and in the most differing stages of education. If experience consists of impressions, it may be said that impressions *are* experience, just as (have we not seen it?) they are the very air we breathe. Therefore, if I should certainly say to a novice, "Write from experience and experience only," I should feel that this was rather a tantalising monition if I were not careful immediately to add. "Try to be one of the people on whom nothing is lost!"

I am far from intending by this to minimise the importance of exactness—of truth of detail. One can speak best from one's own taste, and I may therefore venture to say that the air of reality (solidity of specification) seems to me to be the supreme virtue of a novel—the merit on which all its other merits (including that conscious moral purpose of which Mr. Besant speaks) helplessly and submissively depend. If it be not there they are all as nothing, and if these be there, they owe their effect to the success with which the author has produced the illusion of life. The cultivation of this success, the study of this exquisite process, form, to my taste, the beginning and the end of the art of the novelist. They are his inspiration, his despair, his reward, his torment, his delight. It is here in very truth that he competes with life; it is here that he competes with his brother the painter in *his* attempt to render the look of things, the look that conveys their meaning, to catch the colour, the relief, the expression, the surface, the substance of the human spectacle. It is in regard to this that Mr. Besant is well inspired when he bids him take notes. He cannot possibly take too many, he cannot possibly take enough. All life solicits him, and to "render" the simplest surface, to produce the most momentary illusion, is a very complicated business. His case would be easier, and the rule would be more exact, if Mr. Besant had been able to tell him what notes to take. But this, I fear, he can never learn in any manual; it is the business of his life. He has to take a great many in order to select a few, he has to work them up as he can, and even the guides and philosophers who might have most to say to him must leave him alone when it comes to the application of precepts, as we leave the painter in communion with his palette. That his characters "must be clear in outline," as Mr. Besant says—

3. Protestant minister, pastor (French).

he feels that down to his boots; but how he shall make them so is a secret between his good angel and himself. It would be absurdly simple if he could be taught that a great deal of "description" would make them so, or that on the contrary the absence of description and the cultivation of dialogue, or the absence of dialogue and the multiplication of "incident," would rescue him from his difficulties. Nothing, for instance, is more possible than that he be of a turn of mind for which this odd, literal opposition of description and dialogue, incident and description, has little meaning and light. People often talk of these things as if they had a kind of internecine distinctness, instead of melting into each other at every breath, and being intimately associated parts of one general effort of expression. I cannot imagine composition existing in a series of blocks, nor conceive, in any novel worth discussing at all, of a passage of description that is not in its intention narrative, a passage of dialogue that is not in its intention descriptive, a touch of truth of any sort that does not partake of the nature of incident, or an incident that derives its interest from any other source than the general and only source of the success of a work of art—that of being illustrative. A novel is a living thing, all one and continuous, like any other organism, and in proportion as it lives will it be found, I think, that in each of the parts there is something of each of the other parts. The critic who over the close texture of a finished work shall pretend to trace a geography of items will mark some frontiers as artificial, I fear, as any that have been known to history. There is an old-fashioned distinction between the novel of character and the novel of incident which must have cost many a smile to the intending fabulist who was keen about his work. It appears to me as little to the point as the equally celebrated distinction between the novel and the romance—to answer as little to any reality. There are bad novels and good novels, as there are bad pictures and good pictures; but that is the only distinction in which I see any meaning, and I can as little imagine speaking of a novel of character as I can imagine speaking of a picture of character. When one says picture one says of character, when one says novel one says of incident, and the terms may be transposed at will. What is character but the determination of incident? What is incident but the illustration of character? What is either a picture or a novel that is *not* of character? What else do we seek in it and find in it? It is an incident for a woman to stand up with her hand resting on a table and look out at you in a certain way; or if it be not an incident I think it will be hard to say what it is. At the same time it is an expression of character. If you say you don't see it (character in *that—allons donc!*),[4] this is exactly what the artist who has reasons of his own for thinking he *does* see it undertakes to show you. When a young man makes up his mind that he has not faith enough after all to enter the church as he intended, that is an incident, though you may not hurry to the end of the chapter to see whether perhaps he doesn't change once more. I do not say that these are extraordinary or startling incidents. I do not pretend to estimate the degree of interest proceeding from them, for this will depend upon the skill of the painter. It sounds almost puerile to say that some incidents are intrinsically much more important than others, and I need not take this precaution after having professed my sympathy for the major ones in remarking that the only classifi-

4. Come now, that's nonsense (French).

cation of the novel that I can understand is into that which has life and that which has it not.

The novel and the romance, the novel of incident and that of character—these clumsy separations appear to me to have been made by critics and readers for their own convenience, and to help them out of some of their occasional queer predicaments, but to have little reality or interest for the producer, from whose point of view it is of course that we are attempting to consider the art of fiction. The case is the same with another shadowy category which Mr. Besant apparently is disposed to set up—that of the "modern English novel"; unless indeed it be that in this matter he has fallen into an accidental confusion of stand-points. It is not quite clear whether he intends the remarks in which he alludes to it to be didactic or historical. It is as difficult to suppose a person intending to write a modern English as to suppose him writing an ancient English novel: that is a label which begs the question. One writes the novel, one paints the picture, of one's language and of one's time, and calling it modern English will not, alas! make the difficult task any easier. No more, unfortunately, will calling this or that work of one's fellow-artist a romance—unless it be, of course, simply for the pleasantness of the thing, as for instance when Hawthorne gave this heading to his story of *Blithedale*.[5] The French, who have brought the theory of fiction to remarkable completeness, have but one name for the novel, and have not attempted smaller things in it, that I can see, for that. I can think of no obligation to which the "romancer" would not be held equally with the novelist; the standard of execution is equally high for each. Of course it is of execution that we are talking—that being the only point of a novel that is open to contention. This is perhaps too often lost sight of, only to produce interminable confusions and cross-purposes. We must grant the artist his subject, his idea, his *donnée*:[6] our criticism is applied only to what he makes of it. Naturally I do not mean that we are bound to like it or find it interesting: in case we do not our course is perfectly simple—to let it alone. We may believe that of a certain idea even the most sincere novelist can make nothing at all, and the event may perfectly justify our belief; but the failure will have been a failure to execute, and it is in the execution that the fatal weakness is recorded. If we pretend to respect the artist at all, we must allow him his freedom of choice, in the face, in particular cases, of innumerable presumptions that the choice will not fructify. Art derives a considerable part of its beneficial exercise from flying in the face of presumptions, and some of the most interesting experiments of which it is capable are hidden in the bosom of common things. Gustave Flaubert has written a story about the devotion of a servant-girl to a parrot,[7] and the production, highly finished as it is, cannot on the whole be called a success. We are perfectly free to find it flat, but I think it might have been interesting; and I, for my part, am extremely glad he should have written it; it is a contribution to our knowledge of what can be done—or what cannot. Ivan Turgénieff has written a tale about a deaf and dumb serf and a lap-dog,[8] and the thing is touching, loving, a little masterpiece. He

5. *The Blithedale Romance* (1852), by Nathaniel Hawthorne (1804–1864). The American writer's clearest statement of the distinction he saw between novel and romance appears in his preface to *The House of Seven Gables* (1851).

6. That which is given, starting point (French).

7. "A Simple Soul" (1877), by the French author Flaubert (1821–1880).

8. "Mumu" (1856), by the Russian author Turgenev (1818–1883).

struck the note of life where Gustave Flaubert missed it—he flew in the face of a presumption and achieved a victory.

Nothing, of course, will ever take the place of the good old fashion of "liking" a work of art or not liking it: the most improved criticism will not abolish that primitive, that ultimate test. I mention this to guard myself from the accusation of intimating that the idea, the subject, of a novel or a picture, does not matter. It matters, to my sense, in the highest degree, and if I might put up a prayer it would be that artists should select none but the richest. Some, as I have already hastened to admit, are much more remunerative than others, and it would be a world happily arranged in which persons intending to treat them should be exempt from confusions and mistakes. This fortunate condition will arrive only, I fear, on the same day that critics become purged from error. Meanwhile, I repeat, we do not judge the artist with fairness unless we say to him, "Oh, I grant you your starting-point, because if I did not I should seem to prescribe to you, and heaven forbid I should take that responsibility. If I pretend to tell you what you must not take, you will call upon me to tell you then what you must take; in which case I shall be prettily caught. Moreover, it isn't till I have accepted your data that I can begin to measure you. I have the standard, the pitch; I have no right to tamper with your flute and then criticise your music. Of course I may not care for your idea at all; I may think it silly, or stale, or unclean; in which case I wash my hands of you altogether. I may content myself with believing that you will not have succeeded in being interesting, but I shall, of course, not attempt to demonstrate it, and you will be as indifferent to me as I am to you. I needn't remind you that there are all sorts of tastes: who can know it better? Some people, for excellent reasons, don't like to read about carpenters; others, for reasons even better, don't like to read about courtesans. Many object to Americans. Others (I believe they are mainly editors and publishers) won't look at Italians. Some readers don't like quiet subjects; others don't like bustling ones. Some enjoy a complete illusion, others the consciousness of large concessions. They choose their novels accordingly, and if they don't care about your idea they won't, *a fortiori*, care about your treatment."

So that it comes back very quickly, as I have said, to the liking: in spite of M. Zola,[9] who reasons less powerfully than he represents, and who will not reconcile himself to this absoluteness of taste, thinking that there are certain things that people ought to like, and that they can be made to like. I am quite at a loss to imagine anything (at any rate in this matter of fiction) that people *ought* to like or to dislike. Selection will be sure to take care of itself, for it has a constant motive behind it. That motive is simply experience. As people feel life, so they will feel the art that is most closely related to it. This closeness of relation is what we should never forget in talking of the effort of the novel. Many people speak of it as a factitious, artificial form, a product of ingenuity, the business of which is to alter and arrange the things that surround us, to translate them into conventional, traditional moulds. This, however, is a view of the matter which carries us but a very short way, condemns the art to an eternal repetition of a few familiar *clichés*, cuts short its

9. Émile Zola (1840–1902), French novelist, critic, and theorist of the naturalist movement in literature. James finds Zola's theory less impressive than his practice.

development, and leads us straight up to a dead wall. Catching the very note and trick, the strange irregular rhythm of life, that is the attempt whose strenuous force keeps Fiction upon her feet. In proportion as in what she offers us we see life *without* rearrangement do we feel that we are touching the truth; in proportion as we see it *with* rearrangement do we feel that we are being put off with a substitute, a compromise and convention. It is not uncommon to hear an extraordinary assurance of remark in regard to this matter of rearranging, which is often spoken of as if it were the last word of art. Mr. Besant seems to me in danger of falling into the great error with his rather unguarded talk about "selection." Art is essentially selection, but it is a selection whose main care is to be typical, to be inclusive. For many people art means rose-coloured window-panes, and selection means picking a bouquet for Mrs. Grundy.[1] They will tell you glibly that artistic considerations have nothing to do with the disagreeable, with the ugly; they will rattle off shallow commonplaces about the province of art and the limits of art till you are moved to some wonder in return as to the province and the limits of ignorance. It appears to me that no one can ever have made a seriously artistic attempt without becoming conscious of an immense increase—a kind of revelation—of freedom. One perceives in that case—by the light of a heavenly ray—that the province of art is all life, all feeling, all observation, all vision. As Mr. Besant so justly intimates, it is all experience. That is a sufficient answer to those who maintain that it must not touch the sad things of life, who stick into its divine unconscious bosom little prohibitory inscriptions on the end of sticks, such as we see in public gardens—"It is forbidden to walk on the grass; it is forbidden to touch the flowers; it is not allowed to introduce dogs or to remain after dark; it is requested to keep to the right." The young aspirant in the line of fiction whom we continue to imagine will do nothing without taste, for in that case his freedom would be of little use to him; but the first advantage of his taste will be to reveal to him the absurdity of the little sticks and tickets. If he have taste, I must add, of course he will have ingenuity, and my disrespectful reference to that quality just now was not meant to imply that it is useless in fiction. But it is only a secondary aid; the first is a capacity for receiving straight impressions.

Mr. Besant has some remarks on the question of "the story" which I shall not attempt to criticise, though they seem to me to contain a singular ambiguity, because I do not think I understand them. I cannot see what is meant by talking as if there were a part of a novel which is the story and part of it which for mystical reasons is not—unless indeed the distinction be made in a sense in which it is difficult to suppose that any one should attempt to convey anything. "The story," if it represents anything, represents the subject, the idea, the *donnée* of the novel; and there is surely no "school"—Mr. Besant speaks of a school—which urges that a novel should be all treatment and no subject. There must assuredly be something to treat; every school is intimately conscious of that. This sense of the story being the idea, the starting-point, of the novel, is the only one that I see in which it can be spoken of as something different from its organic whole; and since in proportion as the work is successful the idea permeates and penetrates it, informs and

1. The unseen arbiter of taste and morals in the play *Speed the Plough* (1798), by Thomas Morton; a symbol of moral rigidity.

animates it, so that every word and every punctuation-point contribute directly to the expression, in that proportion do we lose our sense of the story being a blade which may be drawn more or less out of its sheath. The story and the novel, the idea and the form, are the needle and thread, and I never heard of a guild of tailors who recommended the use of the thread without the needle, or the needle without the thread. Mr. Besant is not the only critic who may be observed to have spoken as if there were certain things in life which constitute stories, and certain others which do not. I find the same odd implication in an entertaining article[2] in the *Pall Mall Gazette*, devoted, as it happens, to Mr. Besant's lecture. "The story is the thing!" says this graceful writer, as if with a tone of opposition to some other idea. I should think it was, as every painter who, as the time for "sending in" his picture[3] looms in the distance, finds himself still in quest of a subject—as every belated artist not fixed about his theme will heartily agree. There are some subjects which speak to us and others which do not, but he would be a clever man who should undertake to give a rule—an index expurgatorius[4]—by which the story and the no-story should be known apart. It is impossible (to me at least) to imagine any such rule which shall not be altogether arbitrary. The writer in the *Pall Mall* opposes the delightful (as I suppose) novel of *Margot la Balafrée* to certain tales in which "Bostonian nymphs" appear to have "rejected English dukes for psychological reasons."[5] I am not acquainted with the romance just designated, and can scarcely forgive the *Pall Mall* critic for not mentioning the name of the author, but the title appears to refer to a lady who may have received a scar in some heroic adventure. I am inconsolable at not being acquainted with this episode, but am utterly at a loss to see why it is a story when the rejection (or acceptance) of a duke is not, and why a reason, psychological or other, is not a subject when a cicatrix is. They are all particles of the multitudinous life with which the novel deals, and surely no dogma which pretends to make it lawful to touch the one and unlawful to touch the other will stand for a moment on its feet. It is the special picture that must stand or fall, according as it seem to possess truth or to lack it. Mr. Besant does not, to my sense, light up the subject by intimating that a story must, under penalty of not being a story, consist of "adventures." Why of adventures more than of green spectacles?[6] He mentions a category of impossible things, and among them he places "fiction without adventure." Why without adventure, more than without matrimony, or celibacy, or parturition, or cholera, or hydropathy, or Jansenism?[7] This seems to me to bring the novel back to the hapless little *rôle* of being an artificial, ingenious thing—bring it down from its large, free character of an immense and exquisite correspondence with life. And what *is* adventure, when it comes to that, and by what sign is the listening pupil to recognise it? It is an adventure—an immense one—for me to write this little article;

2. "The Art of Fiction," *Pall Mall Gazette*, April 30, 1884, by the Scottish critic and journalist Andrew Lang.
3. That is, the time he sends it off to an exhibit at the Royal Academy.
4. Rule for justifying (James's Latin coinage).
5. In James's *International Episode* (1879) (the writer may also have had in mind *The Portrait of Lady*, 1881). *Margot: Margot the Scarred Woman* (1884), by the French romantic novelist Fortuné du Boisgobey.
6. An allusion to an episode in Oliver Goldsmith's *Vicar of Wakefield* (1766), in which a son spends the money from the sale of the family colt on a gross of green spectacles.
7. A Roman Catholic religious movement, condemned as heresy, that emphasized predestination and the importance of personal holiness; it grew out of the writings of the Dutch theologian Cornelis Jansen (1585–1638).

and for a Bostonian nymph to reject an English duke is an adventure only less stirring, I should say, than for an English duke to be rejected by a Bostonian nymph. I see dramas within dramas in that, and innumerable points of view. A psychological reason is, to my imagination, an object adorably pictorial; to catch the tint of its complexion—I feel as if that idea might inspire one to Titianesque[8] efforts. There are few things more exciting to me, in short, than a psychological reason, and yet, I protest, the novel seems to me the most magnificent form of art. I have just been reading, at the same time, the delightful story of *Treasure Island*, by Mr. Robert Louis Stevenson and, in a manner less consecutive, the last tale from M. Edmond de Goncourt, which is entitled *Chérie*.[9] One of these works treats of murders, mysteries, islands of dreadful renown, hairbreadth escapes, miraculous coincidences and buried doubloons. The other treats of a little French girl who lived in a fine house in Paris, and died of wounded sensibility because no one would marry her. I call *Treasure Island* delightful, because it appears to me to have succeeded wonderfully in what it attempts; and I venture to bestow no epithet upon *Chérie*, which strikes me as having failed deplorably in what it attempts—that is in tracing the development of the moral consciousness of a child. But one of these productions strikes me as exactly as much of a novel as the other, and as having a "story" quite as much. The moral consciousness of a child is as much a part of life as the islands of the Spanish Main, and the one sort of geography seems to me to have those "surprises" of which Mr. Besant speaks quite as much as the other. For myself (since it comes back in the last resort, as I say, to the preference of the individual), the picture of the child's experience has the advantage that I can at successive steps (an immense luxury, near to the "sensual pleasure" of which Mr. Besant's critic in the *Pall Mall* speaks) say Yes or No, as it may be, to what the artist puts before me. I have been a child in fact, but I have been on a quest for a buried treasure only in supposition, and it is a simple accident that with M. de Goncourt I should have for the most part to say No. With George Eliot,[1] when she painted that country with a far other intelligence, I always said Yes.

The most interesting part of Mr. Besant's lecture is unfortunately the briefest passage—his very cursory allusion to the "conscious moral purpose" of the novel. Here again it is not very clear whether he be recording a fact or laying down a principle; it is a great pity that in the latter case he should not have developed his idea. This branch of the subject is of immense importance, and Mr. Besant's few words point to considerations of the widest reach, not to be lightly disposed of. He will have treated the art of fiction but superficially who is not prepared to go every inch of the way that these considerations will carry him. It is for this reason that at the beginning of these remarks I was careful to notify the reader that my reflections on so large a theme have no pretension to be exhaustive. Like Mr. Besant, I have left the question of the morality of the novel till the last, and at the last I find I have used up my space. It is a question surrounded with difficulties,

8. That is, characteristic of the Venetian painter Titian (Tiziano Vecellio, ca. 1488–1576), especially famous for his use of color.

9. A psychological study of a young woman (1884), by Goncourt (1822–1896). *Treasure Island*, by Stevenson (1850–1894), was published in 1883.

1. English novelist (1819–1880). George Eliot depicted "that country" of a child's consciousness in *The Mill on the Floss* (1860) and *Silas Marner* (1861).

as witness the very first that meets us, in the form of a definite question, on the threshold. Vagueness, in such a discussion, is fatal, and what is the meaning of your morality and your conscious moral purpose? Will you not define your terms and explain how (a novel being a picture) a picture can be either moral or immoral? You wish to paint a moral picture or carve a moral statue: will you not tell us how you would set about it? We are discussing the Art of Fiction; questions of art are questions (in the widest sense) of execution; questions of morality are quite another affair, and will you not let us see how it is that you find it so easy to mix them up? These things are so clear to Mr. Besant that he has deduced from them a law which he sees embodied in English Fiction, and which is "a truly admirable thing and a great cause for congratulation." It is a great cause for congratulation indeed when such thorny problems become as smooth as silk. I may add that in so far as Mr. Besant perceives that in point of fact English Fiction has addressed itself preponderantly to these delicate questions he will appear to many people to have made a vain discovery. They will have been positively struck, on the contrary, with the moral timidity of the usual English novelist; with his (or with her) aversion to face the difficulties with which on every side the treatment of reality bristles. He is apt to be extremely shy (whereas the picture that Mr. Besant draws is a picture of boldness), and the sign of his work, for the most part, is a cautious silence on certain subjects. In the English novel (by which of course I mean the American as well), more than in any other, there is a traditional difference between that which people know and that which they agree to admit that they know, that which they see and that which they speak of, that which they feel to be a part of life and that which they allow to enter into literature. There is the great difference, in short, between what they talk of in conversation and what they talk of in print. The essence of moral energy is to survey the whole field, and I should directly reverse Mr. Besant's remark and say not that the English novel has a purpose, but that it has a diffidence. To what degree a purpose in a work of art is a source of corruption I shall not attempt to inquire; the one that seems to me least dangerous is the purpose of making a perfect work. As for our novel, I may say lastly on this score that as we find it in England to-day it strikes me as addressed in a large degree to "young people," and that this in itself constitutes a presumption that it will be rather shy. There are certain things which it is generally agreed not to discuss, not even to mention, before young people. That is very well, but the absence of discussion is not a symptom of the moral passion. The purpose of the English novel—"a truly admirable thing, and a great cause for congratulation"—strikes me therefore as rather negative.

There is one point at which the moral sense and the artistic sense lie very near together; that is in the light of the very obvious truth that the deepest quality of a work of art will always be the quality of the mind of the producer. In proportion as that intelligence is fine will the novel, the picture, the statue partake of the substance of beauty and truth. To be constituted of such elements is, to my vision, to have purpose enough. No good novel will ever proceed from a superficial mind; that seems to me an axiom which, for the artist in fiction, will cover all needful moral ground: if the youthful aspirant take it to heart it will illuminate for him many of the mysteries of "purpose." There are many other useful things that might be said to him, but I have come to the end of my article, and can only touch them as I pass. The critic in the *Pall Mall Gazette*, whom I have already quoted, draws attention to the danger, in speaking of the art of fiction, of generalising. The danger that he has in mind is rather, I imagine, that of particularising, for there are some comprehensive remarks which, in addition to those embodied in Mr. Besant's suggestive lecture, might without fear of misleading him be addressed to the ingenuous student. I should remind him first of the magnificence of the form that is open to him, which offers to sight so few restrictions and such innumerable opportunities. The other arts, in comparison, appear confined and hampered; the various conditions under which they are exercised are so rigid and definite. But the only condition that I can think of attaching to the composition of the novel is, as I have already said, that it be sincere. This freedom is a splendid privilege, and the first lesson of the young novelist is to learn to be worthy of it. "Enjoy it as it deserves," I should say to him; "take possession of it, explore it to its utmost extent, publish it, rejoice in it. All life belongs to you, and do not listen either to those who would shut you up into corners of it and tell you that it is only here and there that art inhabits, or to those who would persuade you that this heavenly messenger wings her way outside of life altogether, breathing a superfine air, and turning away her head from the truth of things. There is no impression of life, no manner of seeing it and feeling it, to which the plan of the novelist may not offer a place; you have only to remember that talents so dissimilar as those of Alexandre Dumas and Jane Austen,[2] Charles Dickens and Gustave Flaubert have worked in this field with equal glory. Do not think too much about optimism and pessimism; try and catch the colour of life itself. In France to-day we see a prodigious effort (that of Emile Zola, to whose solid and serious work no explorer of the capacity of the novel can allude without respect), we see an extraordinary effort vitiated by a spirit of pessimism on a narrow basis. M. Zola is magnificent, but he strikes an English reader as ignorant; he has an air of working in the dark; if he had as much light as energy, his results would be of the highest value. As for the aberrations of a shallow optimism, the ground (of English fiction especially) is strewn with their brittle particles as with broken glass. If you must indulge in conclusions, let them have the taste of a wide knowledge. Remember that your first duty is to be as complete as possible—to make as perfect a work. Be generous and delicate and pursue the prize."

1884, 1888

2. English novelist (1775–1817). Dumas (1802–1870), French dramatist and novelist whose works include *The Three Musketeers* (1844).

FRIEDRICH NIETZSCHE
1844–1900

Friedrich Nietzsche is the wild man, the self-proclaimed anti-Christ, of Western thought. A brilliant polemicist, he champions energy over reason and art over science while contemptuous of the quiet, "timid" virtues of domesticity, democracy, and peace. His extravagances not only remind us of modernism's persistent desire to shock the staid middle classes but also recall the many twentieth-century figures—from W. B. Yeats and Ezra Pound to MARTIN HEIDEGGER and PAUL DE MAN—whose genius is inextricably mixed with dubious political views. But Nietzsche, an inveterate foe of Christianity and of Platonic philosophy, is absolutely central to modern and postmodern attempts to rethink the Western tradition's most fundamental assumptions.

Nietzsche was born in Röcken, a small village in Prussian Saxony. He was the son and grandson (on both sides of the family) of Lutheran ministers. His father died when he was four and his younger brother died the next year, leaving him the only male in a household with five women. Nietzsche's subsequent infatuations with the work of German philosopher Arthur Schopenhauer (1788–1860) and with the work, theories, and wife of German composer Richard Wagner, followed by his equally violent rejections of the two men, are sometimes explained in terms of "surrogate father figures" and Oedipal rebellion. Certainly, Wagner and his wife Cosima dominated Nietzsche's life in the early 1870s. Having received his doctorate at the University of Leipzig, Nietzsche was appointed professor of philology at the University of Basel in Switzerland in 1869. He met Wagner and Cosima von Bülow in late 1868, and his first book, *The Birth of Tragedy* (1872), combines a new theory of Greek tragedy with an extended argument that Wagner's work constitutes a German rebirth of that ancient form. By 1876, however, Nietzsche had broken completely with Wagner, repelled by Wagner's turn to Christianity and his increasing anti-Semitism. That same year, ill health forced Nietzsche to stop teaching. In 1879 he officially resigned his university post, receiving a small disability pension. He spent the next ten years writing the books that present his ambitious attempt to overthrow Christianity and post-Socratic philosophy through a radical "revaluation of all values." The last ten years of Nietzsche's life were lost to incoherent madness. After a mental breakdown in 1889, he returned to Röcken to live with his mother; when she died, in 1897, he came under the care of his sister Elisabeth, which continued until his death.

Even before Nietzsche's death, his sister wrote a biography to publicize his work, and she published her own editions of his writings. She stressed those elements that accorded with her own anti-Semitic and pro-Aryan views and is often blamed for the Nazis' later appropriation of Nietzsche as a philosopher sympathetic to their policies. But blaming his sister does not absolve Nietzsche. Some aspects of his thought chime with National Socialism, while others contradict it. Those who read and interpret Nietzsche's challenging work must grapple with his relation to the Nazis, just as they must take into account his tremendous influence on modernism, existentialism, and poststructuralism.

Our first selection, the essay "On Truth and Lying in a Non-Moral Sense" (written 1873), was not published during Nietzsche's lifetime. It articulates a number of Nietzsche's major themes and became a favorite reference point for poststructuralists such as JACQUES DERRIDA and Paul de Man during the 1970s. Nietzsche's target here is nothing less than the epistemological foundations of Western philosophy. From PLATO on, Western philosophy has been committed (with a few exceptions) to ascertaining the fixed and solid truth that exists independently of human minds. Nietzsche simply denies that we can ever know anything except through the lens of human perception. We cannot put that lens aside in order to judge which perceptions accurately portray the world and which do not. Given this impossibility, why are humans committed to the search for "truth"? Because, Nietzsche answers, truth is a useful illusion, one that serves a fundamental drive to survive. Truth is a comfortable lie; it suggest that "the world [is] something which is similar in kind to humanity," and it boosts self-confidence, the untroubled conviction of being right. While Nietzsche is scornful of this smug "anthropomorphism," he does underline its utility.

The essay's account of language's role in human cognition has been especially influential among literary theorists. Nietzsche accepts that the outer world impinges on the human perceiver, but we translate that experience into human terms by naming it. This "first metaphor" introduces an unbridgeable gap, which leads Nietzsche to conclude that "subject and object" are "absolutely different spheres." Nor do the nonrepresentational additions ("supplements") supplied by language stop there. We also use the same name to designate separate experiences of nerve stimulation. We call today's "leaf" by the same word used to label yesterday's. This substitution of one "concept" in the place of multiple experiences is the "second metaphor" that Nietzsche identifies—and his account of how concepts erase awareness of differences would later echo throughout poststructuralism. "Every concept," he writes, "comes into being by making equivalent that which is non-equivalent[,] . . . by forgetting those features which differentiate one thing from another."

Once Nietzsche pulls the veil of illusion from our eyes and shows that truth is a "mobile army of metaphors, metonymies, anthropomorphisms," what next? One possible response is stoicism, described in the essay's last paragraph. Alone in an alien world, humans could just endure, preserving a "dignified equilibrium" in the face of everything to which life subjects them. More extreme is the "nihilistic" denial of this world as "fallen" or "evil," a position that Nietzsche associates with Christianity. Against stoicism and nihilism, Nietzsche calls on humans to forcefully and joyfully step into the vacuum created by the death of truth, of God, and of the other metaphysical guarantees on which the West has traditionally relied. We must learn not just to accept but to proudly affirm that "humanity" is a "mighty architectural genius who succeeds in erecting the infinitely complicated cathedral of concepts on moving foundations, or even, one might say, on flowing water." Nietzsche celebrates the creativity and the will that builds a world for humans to inhabit—and he takes the artist as his prime example of an individual responding joyfully to the challenge of shedding the illusion of truth.

Our selections from *The Birth of Tragedy* (1872) show how Nietzsche returns to Greek thought before Plato to discover the artistic form and worldview that he prefers to the Platonic and Christian traditions. (MATTHEW ARNOLD in the nineteenth century and MARTIN HEIDEGGER and Erich Auerbach in the twentieth also return to the pre-Socratic Greeks for principles to counter modernity.) Nietzsche's mantra in this text is that "only as an aesthetic phenomenon do existence and the world appear justified." This formula draws on the root meaning of *aesthetic* as "pertaining to sense perception." Nietzsche says that life is worthwhile only if we experience strong feelings or sensations. As WALTER PATER, who was writing at almost exactly the same time, would put it, the quality and intensity of our sensations indicates the quality of our lives. And for Nietzsche, as for Pater, the step from the "aesthetic" as sensation to the "aesthetic" as art is a short one. Art is the realm of heightened sensation. But whereas Pater stresses the experience of the spectator, Nietzsche focuses on the exuberant joy felt by the artist/creator in the struggle to bend recalcitrant materials to his or her will.

Nietzsche thus appears to promote heroic individualism and transcendent genius. He has often been read this way, not least by countless modernist artists, who also responded to his diatribes against the conformist "herds" that try to curb the strong, amoral artist. Much in Nietzsche celebrates the "will" of the "overman" (superman) and denigrates everything (from conventional morality to democracy) that would make the genius answerable to any authority outside of his self. "His" is used advisedly—Nietzsche often contrasts this individual's manly strength to the effeminate weakness of lesser souls.

Yet to read Nietzsche as a philosopher of heroic individualism is to miss much. Both our texts show that human suffering figures largely in Nietzsche's thought; the individual is subjected to a world that precedes and is more powerful than the self. Greek tragedy, in Nietzsche's view, grants us a glimpse of a "primordial unity" that predates individuation (which Nietzsche associates with comedy). He takes seriously the claim that Greek tragedy originated in choral songs performed at a festival of Dionysus and that Aeschylus introduced the first individualized characters.

Such individuation, Nietzsche argues in *The Birth of Tragedy*, is necessary for artistic expression, artistic form. (In his later work, he often claims that "the subject" is a grammatical form that we consistently mistake for a metaphysical entity.) The chaos of Dionysian nondifferentiation (intimated by music) can be rendered intelligible or expressible only by the "calm" Apollonian "semblance" (conveyed by words and images). But the glory of Greek tragedy is that it does not take Apollonian semblance for truth—or, at least, not for the entire truth. Prometheus becomes Nietzsche's primary example of the need to establish an existence apart from the primordial unity. But Prometheus "must suffer for the fact of [his] individuation." And Nietzsche insists that it is the sufferings of Dionysus himself, whose repeated deaths and rebirths enact the "end of individuation," that are represented in every tragedy. The "primal contradiction hidden within the things of this world" is that while humans can experience energy, will, and sensation only as individuals, the process of individuation separates them from the universe. Thus suffering is inevitable; the essence of the tragic view is to affirm that suffering, to glory in the active wrongdoing by which the hero offends the way things are, and to say, as Nietzsche imagines Aeschylus saying: "All that exists is just and unjust and is equally justified in both respects."

Tragedy can exist only so long as we recognize, accept, and affirm the irresolvable contradiction between our hopes and how the world is. Once we believe that suffering is not inevitable, tragedy dies: we begin to demand justice from our gods, and life is justified not as an aesthetic phenomenon but rather because justice is finally done. In the comic ending, the good are rewarded, the bad punished, and human desires and worldly facts are aligned. In *The Birth of Tragedy*, Nietzsche blames Euripides and Socrates for the death of the tragic worldview in ancient Athenian society. Euripides effects a reconciliation with the gods in many of his plays, thus assuring the audience that all can be made right in this world. Socrates, and then Plato, suggests that reason can lead humans to ascertain the truths of the universe to which they can conform.

Later in his career Nietzsche attacked Christianity for its essentially comic vision. We get hints of that critique here when he contrasts the Semitic notion of "sin" to the Aryan notion of "wrongdoing." This passage, with its oppositions of Aryan and Semite, masculine and feminine, highlights problematic features in Nietzsche's work (as does his lyric call for a rebirth of the German spirit). We admire the tragic hero, who often (as in Oedipus's case) could not have avoided wrongdoing. But the notion of "sin" indicates both that one is free to act and that acting differently would have been better, would (it is strongly implied) not have led to suffering. Nietzsche urges us to have the strength to love life even though suffering is inevitable. Indeed, he suggests that we are most alive when we suffer, because that is when we are feeling most intensely. The murdered and resurrected god whose myth embodies this worldview is the tragic Dionysus, not the comic Christ.

This mixture of nobility and masochism, of rebellion (against Plato and Christianity) and submission (to Dionysus), proved heady stuff to many modernists. Of course, other factors—ranging from SIGMUND FREUD's use of the Oedipal myth to the slaughter of a generation in World War I—also shaped the modernist fascination with tragedy and pre-Socratic Greece. But Nietzsche is central to attempts during the twentieth century to find imaginative and historical alternatives to both the Christian worldview and to the narrative of Western progress and enlightenment. That such attempts came from both the political left and the right indicates the complexity of the Western heritage and of Nietzsche's engagement with it.

For the modernists of the early twentieth century, Nietzsche was often more an attitude, a stance, than a philosopher. A few powerful phrases—"the death of God," "overman," "will to power," "herd morality," and "beyond good and evil"—suggested his blasphemous demystification of progressive, "enlightened" values. Nietzsche's aestheticism, his disdain of reason, and his lyrical style led many readers to see his work as existing somewhere between poetry and philosophy. But his work received much more extensive scholarly and philosophical analysis in the second half of the century. His critiques of truth, of substance, and of the self, along with his accounts of language and the formation of moral codes, have all been taken extremely seriously, despite their summary dismissal by some intellectuals. Perhaps debates about Nietzsche's politics have been especially fierce because his views have often been adopted—and not just by poststructuralists.

For literary critics, Nietzsche's methods may be as important as any view he holds. Famously described by the French philosopher Paul Ricoeur as, in company with KARL MARX and Freud, a founder of the "hermeneutics of suspicion," Nietzsche teaches us not to take any pronouncement at face value. If we want to understand the meaning of a term, we must discover its "genealogy"—the way the term has been deployed in specific circumstances to achieve specific results. (MICHEL FOUCAULT later explicitly adopted this Nietzschean method in his studies of the prison and of sexuality.) From the perspective of Nietzschean genealogy, terms are tools and weapons in the continual struggles and conflicts that characterize human interactions with the world and with each other. Nietzsche's own effort to alter our understanding of tragedy is concerned less with determining the "truth" of tragedy than with revising the dominant worldviews that his readers have inherited from Christianity and Western philosophy. The success of that attempt stands apart from whatever virtues his genealogical method possesses—but those to whom the method appeals have usually been sympathetic to the message.

BIBLIOGRAPHY

The standard German edition of Nietzsche's work is *Kritische Gesamtausgabe*, edited by Giorgio Colli and Mazzino Montinari (15 vols., 1967–77). Stanford University Press is in the process of publishing the Colli-Montinari edition in a twenty-volume English version edited by Bernd Magnus (3 vols. to date, 1995–). The major works are all available in English translation; the best translations follow, with the original German publication date given first: *The Birth of Tragedy*, translated by Ronald Speirs (1872; 1999); *Untimely Meditations*, translated by R. J. Hollingdale (1877; 1983); *On the Advantage and Disadvantage of History for Life*, translated by Peter Preuss (1877; 1980); *Human, All Too Human*, translated by R. J. Hollingdale (1878; 1986); *Daybreak: Thoughts on the Prejudices of Morality*, translated by R. J. Hollingdale (1881; 1982); *The Gay Science*, translated by Walter Kaufmann (1882; 1974); *Thus Spoke Zarathustra*, translated by R. J. Hollingdale (1885; 1973); *Beyond Good and Evil*, translated by Walter Kaufmann and R. J. Hollingdale (1886; 1966); *On the Genealogy of Morals*, translated by Walter Kaufmann and R. J. Hollingdale (1887; 1967); *The Case of Wagner*, translated by Walter Kaufmann (1888; 1966); *Twilight of the Idols*, translated by Walter Kaufmann (1889; 1954); *The Antichrist*, translated by Walter Kaufmann (1895; 1954); and *Ecce Homo*, translated by Walter Kaufmann (1908; 1967). *The Will to Power* (1901, 1910–11; 1967) is an important collection of entries from Nietzsche's notebooks, while *Nietzsche on Rhetoric and Language*, edited and translated by Sander L. Gilman, Carole Blair, and David J. Parent (1989), collects work of particular interest to literary critics. *Selected Letters of Friedrich Nietzsche*, edited and translated by Christopher Middleton (1969), is the most useful collection of letters. *Ecce Homo* is Nietzsche's half-mad and fascinating autobiography; the most readable biography is Ronald Hayman's *Nietzsche: A Critical Life* (1980).

Arthur Danto's *Nietzsche as Philosopher* (1965) remains a superb overview; it can be supplemented with Richard Schacht's *Nietzsche* (1983) and Alexander Nehamas's influential *Nietzsche: Life as Literature* (1985). *The Cambridge Companion to Nietzsche*, edited by Bernd Magnus and Kathleen M. Higgins (1996), collects essays that address a wide range of issues connected to Nietzsche's life, work, and influence. Martin Heidegger's *Nietzsche* (2 vols., 1961; trans. in 4 vols., 1979–87) is a major document of twentieth-century philosophy as well as a powerful, if idiosyncratic, interpretation of Nietzsche. Many poststructuralists have written extensively on Nietzsche. A partial list includes Michel Foucault, *Language, Counter-Memory, Practice* (1977); Paul de Man, *Allegories of Reading* (1979); Jacques Derrida, *Spurs: Nietzsche's Styles* (1978; trans. 1979); Gilles Deleuze, *Nietzsche and Philosophy* (1962; trans. 1983); and Sarah Kofman, *Nietzsche and Metaphor* (1972; trans. 1993). Four studies of particular relevance to literary critics are Alan D. Schrift, *Nietzsche and the Question of Interpretation* (1990); Henry Staten, *Nietzsche's Voice* (1990); Ernst Behler, *Confrontations: Derrida, Heidegger, Nietzsche* (1991); and John Sallis, *Crossings: Nietzsche and the Space of Tragedy* (1991). The reader who wants a sense of the ways that literary theorists (especially) have approached Nietzsche's work in recent decades can start with the many fine collections of essays on his work: *The New Nietzsche*, edited by David B. Allison (1977); *Why Nietzsche Now?*, edited by Daniel O'Hara (1985); *Friedrich Nietzsche*, edited by Harold Bloom (1987); *Nietzsche as Postmodernist: Essays Pro and Contra*, edited by Clayton Koelb (1990); *Feminist Interpretations of Friedrich Nietzsche*, edited by Kelly Oliver and Marilyn Pearsall (1998); and *Why Nietzsche Still?*, edited by Alan D. Schrift (2000). The most useful bibliography can be found in *The Cambridge Companion to Nietzsche* (cited above).

On Truth and Lying in a Non-Moral Sense[1]

1

In some remote corner of the universe, flickering in the light of the countless solar systems into which it had been poured, there was once a planet on which clever animals invented cognition. It was the most arrogant and most mendacious minute in the 'history of the world'; but a minute was all it was. After nature had drawn just a few more breaths the planet froze and the clever animals had to die. Someone could invent a fable like this and yet they would still not have given a satisfactory illustration of just how pitiful, how insubstantial and transitory, how purposeless and arbitrary the human intellect looks within nature; there were eternities during which it did not exist; and when it has disappeared again, nothing will have happened. For this intellect has no further mission that might extend beyond the bounds of human life. Rather, the intellect is human, and only its own possessor and progenitor regards it with such pathos, as if it housed the axis around which the entire world revolved. But if we could communicate with a midge we would hear that it too floats through the air with the very same pathos, feeling that it too contains within itself the flying centre of this world. There is nothing in nature so despicable and mean that would not immediately swell up like a balloon from just one little puff of that force of cognition; and just as every bearer of burdens wants to be admired,

1. Translated by Ronald Speirs. Except as indicated, all notes are the translator's.

so the proudest man of all, the philosopher, wants to see, on all sides, the eyes of the universe trained, as through telescopes, on his thoughts and deeds.

It is odd that the intellect can produce this effect, since it is nothing other than an aid supplied to the most unfortunate, most delicate and most transient of beings so as to detain them for a minute within existence; otherwise, without this supplement, they would have every reason to flee existence as quickly as did Lessing's infant son.[2] The arrogance inherent in cognition and feeling casts a blinding fog over the eyes and senses of human beings, and because it contains within itself the most flattering evaluation of cognition it deceives them about the value of existence. Its most general effect is deception—but each of its separate effects also has something of the same character.

As a means for the preservation of the individual, the intellect shows its greatest strengths in dissimulation, since this is the means to preserve those weaker, less robust individuals who, by nature, are denied horns or the sharp fangs of a beast of prey with which to wage the struggle for existence. This art of dissimulation reaches its peak in humankind, where deception, flattery, lying and cheating, speaking behind the backs of others, keeping up appearances,[3] living in borrowed finery, wearing masks, the drapery of convention, play-acting for the benefit of others and oneself—in short, the constant fluttering of human beings around the one flame of vanity is so much the rule and the law that there is virtually nothing which defies understanding so much as the fact that an honest and pure drive towards truth should ever have emerged in them. They are deeply immersed in illusions and dream-images; their eyes merely glide across the surface of things and see 'forms'; nowhere does their perception lead into truth; instead it is content to receive stimuli and, as it were, to play with its fingers on the back of things. What is more, human beings allow themselves to be lied to in dreams every night of their lives, without their moral sense ever seeking to prevent this happening, whereas it is said that some people have even eliminated snoring by will-power. What do human beings really know about themselves? Are they even capable of perceiving themselves in their entirety just once, stretched out as in an illuminated glass case? Does nature not remain silent about almost everything, even about our bodies, banishing and enclosing us within a proud, illusory consciousness, far away from the twists and turns of the bowels, the rapid flow of the blood stream and the complicated tremblings of the nerve-fibres? Nature has thrown away the key, and woe betide fateful curiosity should it ever succeed in peering through a crack in the chamber of consciousness, out and down into the depths, and thus gain an intimation of the fact that humanity, in the indifference of its ignorance, rests on the pitiless, the greedy, the insatiable, the murderous—clinging in dreams, as it were, to the back of a tiger. Given this constellation, where on earth can the drive to truth possibly have come from?

Insofar as the individual wishes to preserve himself in relation to other

2. Lessing's first and only son died immediately after birth, followed soon after by his mother. This drew from Lessing the comment "Was it good sense that they had to pull him into the world with iron tongs, or that he noticed the filth so quickly? Was it not good sense that he took the first opportunity to leave it again?" (Letter to Eschenburg, 10 January 1778). [GOTHOLD EPHRAIM LESSING (1729–1781), German dramatist and critic—editor's note.]

3. The verb Nietzsche uses is *repräsentieren*. This means keeping up a show in public, representing one's family, country, or social group before the eyes of the world.

individuals, in the state of nature he mostly used his intellect for concealment and dissimulation; however, because necessity and boredom also lead men to want to live in societies and herds, they need a peace treaty, and so they endeavour to eliminate from their world at least the crudest forms of the *bellum omnium contra omnes*.[4] In the wake of this peace treaty, however, comes something which looks like the first step towards the acquisition of that mysterious drive for truth. For that which is to count as 'truth' from this point onwards now becomes fixed, i.e. a way of designating things is invented which has the same validity and force everywhere, and the legislation of language also produces the first laws of truth, for the contrast between truth and lying comes into existence here for the first time: the liar uses the valid tokens of designation—words—to make the unreal appear to be real; he says, for example, 'I am rich', whereas the correct designation for this condition would be, precisely, 'poor'. He misuses the established conventions by arbitrarily switching or even inverting the names for things. If he does this in a manner that is selfish and otherwise harmful, society will no longer trust him and therefore exclude him from its ranks. Human beings do not so much flee from being tricked as from being harmed by being tricked. Even on this level they do not hate deception but rather the damaging, inimical consequences of certain species of deception. Truth, too, is only desired by human beings in a similarly limited sense. They desire the pleasant, life-preserving consequences of truth; they are indifferent to pure knowledge if it has no consequences, but they are actually hostile towards truths which may be harmful and destructive. And, besides, what is the status of those conventions of language? Are they perhaps products of knowledge, of the sense of truth? Is there a perfect match between things and their designations? Is language the full and adequate expression of all realities?

Only through forgetfulness could human beings ever entertain the illusion that they possess truth to the degree described above. If they will not content themselves with truth in the form of tautology, i.e. with empty husks, they will for ever exchange illusions for truth. What is a word? The copy of a nervous stimulation in sounds. To infer from the fact of the nervous stimulation that there exists a cause outside us is already the result of applying the principle of sufficient reason wrongly. If truth alone had been decisive in the genesis of language, if the viewpoint of certainty had been decisive in creating designations, how could we possibly be permitted to say, 'The stone is hard', as if 'hard' were something known to us in some other way, and not merely as an entirely subjective stimulus? We divide things up by gender, describing a tree as masculine and a plant as feminine[5]—how arbitrary these translations are! How far they have flown beyond the canon of certainty! We speak of a snake; the designation captures only its twisting movements and thus could equally well apply to a worm. How arbitrarily these borders are drawn, how one-sided the preference for this or that property of a thing! When different languages are set alongside one another it becomes clear that, where words are concerned, what matters is never truth, never the full

4. "War of all against all" [Latin]: phrase associated with Thomas Hobbes' description of the state of nature before the institution of political authority (*cf.* Hobbes, *De cive* I.12 and *Leviathan*, chapter XIII). [Hobbes (1588–1679), English political philosopher—editor's note.]

5. "Tree" is masculine in German (*der Baum*) and "plant" (*die Pflanze*) is feminine.

and adequate expression;[6] otherwise there would not be so many languages. The 'thing-in-itself'[7] (which would be, precisely, pure truth, truth without consequences) is impossible for even the creator of language to grasp, and indeed this is not at all desirable. He designates only the relations of things to human beings, and in order to express them he avails himself of the boldest metaphors. The stimulation of a nerve is first translated into an image: first metaphor! The image is then imitated by a sound: second metaphor! And each time there is a complete leap from one sphere into the heart of another, new sphere. One can conceive of a profoundly deaf human being who has never experienced sound or music; just as such a person will gaze in astonishment at the Chladnian sound-figures in sand,[8] find their cause in the vibration of a string, and swear that he must now know what men call sound—this is precisely what happens to all of us with language. We believe that when we speak of trees, colours, snow, and flowers, we have knowledge of the things themselves, and yet we possess only metaphors of things which in no way correspond to the original entities. Just as the musical sound appears as a figure in the sand, so the mysterious 'X' of the thing-in-itself appears first as a nervous stimulus, then as an image, and finally as an articulated sound. At all events, things do not proceed logically when language comes into being, and the entire material in and with which the man of truth, the researcher, the philosopher, works and builds, stems, if not from cloud-cuckoo land, then certainly not from the essence of things.

Let us consider in particular how concepts are formed; each word immediately becomes a concept, not by virtue of the fact that it is intended to serve as a memory (say) of the unique, utterly individualized, primary experience to which it owes its existence, but because at the same time it must fit countless other, more or less similar cases, i.e. cases which, strictly speaking, are never equivalent, and thus nothing other than non-equivalent cases. Every concept comes into being by making equivalent that which is non-equivalent. Just as it is certain that no leaf is ever exactly the same as any other leaf, it is equally certain that the concept 'leaf' is formed by dropping these individual differences arbitrarily, by forgetting those features which differentiate one thing from another, so that the concept then gives rise to the notion that something other than leaves exists in nature, something which would be 'leaf', a primal form, say, from which all leaves were woven, drawn, delineated, dyed, curled, painted—but by a clumsy pair of hands, so that no single example turned out to be a faithful, correct, and reliable copy of the primal form. We call a man honest; we ask, 'Why did he act so honestly today?' Our answer is usually: 'Because of his honesty.' Honesty!—yet again, this means that the leaf is the cause of the leaves. We have no knowledge of an essential quality which might be called honesty, but we do know of numerous individualized and hence non-equivalent actions which we equate with

6. Nietzsche uses the term *adäquat* which indicates that the meaning of something is fully conveyed by a word or expression; English "adequate" alone does not convey this sense completely.

7. Term used by the German philosopher IMMANUEL KANT (1724–1804) for the real object independent of our awareness of it. Kant argues that such categories as time and space, mentioned later by Nietzsche, are part of our own form of thought, not of what we observe [editor's note].

8. The vibration of a string can create figures in the sand (in an appropriately constructed sandbox) which give a visual representation of that which the human ear perceives as a tone. The term comes from the name of the physicist Ernst Chladni [1756–1827], whose experiments demonstrated the effect.

each other by omitting what is unlike, and which we now designate as honest actions; finally we formulate from them a *qualitas occulta*[9] with the name 'honesty'.

Like form, a concept is produced by overlooking what is individual and real, whereas nature knows neither forms nor concepts and hence no species, but only an 'X' which is inaccessible to us and indefinable by us. For the opposition we make between individual and species is also anthropomorphic and does not stem from the essence of things, although we equally do not dare to say that it does *not* correspond to the essence of things, since that would be a dogmatic assertion and, as such, just as incapable of being proved as its opposite.

What, then, is truth? A mobile army of metaphors, metonymies, anthropomorphisms, in short a sum of human relations which have been subjected to poetic and rhetorical intensification, translation, and decoration, and which, after they have been in use for a long time, strike a people as firmly established, canonical, and binding; truths are illusions of which we have forgotten that they are illusions, metaphors which have become worn by frequent use and have lost all sensuous vigour, coins which, having lost their stamp, are now regarded as metal and no longer as coins. Yet we still do not know where the drive to truth comes from, for so far we have only heard about the obligation to be truthful which society imposes in order to exist, i.e. the obligation to use the customary metaphors, or, to put it in moral terms, the obligation to lie in accordance with firmly established convention, to lie *en masse* and in a style that is binding for all. Now, it is true that human beings forget that this is how things are; thus they lie unconsciously in the way we have described, and in accordance with centuries-old habits—and precisely *because of this unconsciousness*, precisely because of this forgetting, they arrive at the feeling of truth. The feeling that one is obliged to describe one thing as red, another as cold, and a third as dumb, prompts a moral impulse which pertains to truth; from its opposite, the liar whom no one trusts and all exclude, human beings demonstrate to themselves just how honourable, confidence-inspiring and useful truth is. As creatures of *reason*, human beings now make their actions subject to the rule of abstractions; they no longer tolerate being swept away by sudden impressions and sensuous perceptions; they now generalize all these impressions first, turning them into cooler, less colourful concepts in order to harness the vehicle of their lives and actions to them. Everything which distinguishes human beings from animals depends on this ability to sublimate sensuous metaphors into a schema, in other words, to dissolve an image into a concept. This is because something becomes possible in the realm of these schemata which could never be achieved in the realm of those sensuous first impressions, namely the construction of a pyramidal order based on castes and degrees, the creation of a new world of laws, privileges, subordinations, definitions of borders, which now confronts the other, sensuously perceived world as something firmer, more general, more familiar, more human, and hence as something regulatory and imperative. Whereas every metaphor standing for a sensuous perception is individual and unique and is therefore always able to escape classification, the great edifice of concepts exhibits the rigid reg-

9. Hidden property (Latin).

ularity of a Roman *columbarium*,[1] while logic breathes out that air of severity and coolness which is peculiar to mathematics. Anyone who has been touched by that cool breath will scarcely believe that concepts too, which are as bony and eight-cornered as a dice and just as capable of being shifted around, are only the left-over *residue of a metaphor*, and that the illusion produced by the artistic translation of a nervous stimulus into images is, if not the mother, then at least the grandmother of each and every concept. Within this conceptual game of dice, however, 'truth' means using each die in accordance with its designation, counting its spots precisely, forming correct classifications, and never offending against the order of castes nor against the sequence of classes of rank. Just as the Romans and the Etruscans divided up the sky with rigid mathematical lines and confined a god in a space which they had thus delimited as in a *templum*,[2] all peoples have just such a mathematically divided firmament of concepts above them, and they understand the demand of truth to mean that the god of every concept is to be sought only in *his* sphere. Here one can certainly admire humanity as a mighty architectural genius who succeeds in erecting the infinitely complicated cathedral of concepts on moving foundations, or even, one might say, on flowing water; admittedly, in order to rest on such foundations, it has to be like a thing constructed from cobwebs, so delicate that it can be carried off on the waves and yet so firm as not to be blown apart by the wind. By these standards the human being is an architectural genius who is far superior to the bee; the latter builds with wax which she gathers from nature, whereas the human being builds with the far more delicate material of concepts which he must first manufacture from himself. In this he is to be much admired—but just not for his impulse to truth, to the pure cognition of things. If someone hides something behind a bush, looks for it in the same place and then finds it there, his seeking and finding is nothing much to boast about; but this is exactly how things are as far as the seeking and finding of 'truth' within the territory of reason is concerned. If I create the definition of a mammal and then, having inspected a camel, declare, 'Behold, a mammal', then a truth has certainly been brought to light, but it is of limited value, by which I mean that it is anthropomorphic through and through and contains not a single point which could be said to be 'true in itself', really and in a generally valid sense, regardless of mankind. Anyone who researches for truths of that kind is basically only seeking the metamorphosis of the world in human beings; he strives for an understanding of the world as something which is similar in kind to humanity, and what he gains by his efforts is at best a feeling of assimilation. Rather as the astrologer studies the stars in the service of human beings and in relation to humanity's happiness and suffering, this type of researcher regards the whole world as linked to humankind, as the infinitely refracted echo of an original sound, that of humanity, and as the multiple copy of a single, original image, that of humanity. His procedure is to measure all things against man, and in doing so he takes as his point of departure the erroneous belief that he has these things directly before him, as pure objects. Thus, forgetting that the original metaphors of perception were indeed metaphors, he takes them for the things themselves.

1. Originally a dovecote, then a catacomb with niches at regular intervals for urns containing the ashes of the dead.

2. Literally, a space marked out; the space of the heavens; sanctuary, temple (Latin) [editor's note].

Only by forgetting this primitive world of metaphor, only by virtue of the fact that a mass of images, which originally flowed in a hot, liquid stream from the primal power of the human imagination, has become hard and rigid, only because of the invincible faith that *this* sun, *this* window, this table is a truth in itself—in short only because man forgets himself as a subject, and indeed as *an artistically creative* subject, does he live with some degree of peace, security, and consistency; if he could escape for just a moment from the prison walls of this faith, it would mean the end of his 'consciousness of self'.[3] He even has to make an effort to admit to himself that insects or birds perceive a quite different world from that of human beings, and that the question as to which of these two perceptions of the world is the more correct is quite meaningless, since this would require them to be measured by the criterion of the *correct perception*, i.e. by a *non-existent* criterion. But generally it seems to me that the correct perception—which would mean the full and adequate expression of an object in the subject—is something contradictory and impossible; for between two absolutely different spheres, such as subject and object are, there is no causality, no correctness, no expression, but at most an *aesthetic* way of relating, by which I mean an allusive transference, a stammering translation into a quite different language. For which purpose a middle sphere and mediating force is certainly required which can freely invent and freely create poetry. The word appearance (*Erscheinung*) contains many seductions, and for this reason I avoid using it as far as possible; for it is not true that the essence of things appears in the empirical world. A painter who has no hands and who wished to express in song the image hovering before him will still reveal more through this substitution of one sphere for another than the empirical world betrays of the essence of things. Even the relation of a nervous stimulus to the image produced thereby is inherently not a necessary relationship; but when that same image has been produced millions of times and has been passed down through many generations of humanity, indeed eventually appears in the whole of humanity as a consequence of the same occasion, it finally acquires the same significance for all human beings, as if it were the only necessary image and as if that relation of the original nervous stimulus to the image produced were a relation of strict causality—in exactly the same way as a dream, if repeated eternally, would be felt and judged entirely as reality. But the fact that a metaphor becomes hard and rigid is absolutely no guarantee of the necessity and exclusive justification of that metaphor.

Anyone who is at home in such considerations will certainly have felt a deep mistrust of this kind of idealism when once he has become clearly convinced of the eternal consistency, ubiquitousness and infallibility of the laws of nature; he will then conclude that everything, as far as we can penetrate, whether to the heights of the telescopic world or the depths of the microscopic world, is so sure, so elaborated, so endless, so much in conformity to laws, and so free of lacunae, that science will be able to mine these shafts successfully for ever, and that everything found there will be in agreement and without self-contradiction. How little all of this resembles a product of the imagination, for if it were such a thing, the illusion and the unreality would be bound to be detectable somewhere. The first thing to be

3. The word Nietzsche uses here—*Selbstbewußtsein*—could also mean "self-confidence."

said against this view is this: if each of us still had a different kind of sensuous perception, if we ourselves could only perceive things as, variously, a bird, a worm, or a plant does, or if one of us were to see a stimulus as red, a second person were to see the same stimulus as blue, while a third were even to hear it as a sound, nobody would ever speak of nature as something conforming to laws; rather they would take it to be nothing other than a highly subjective formation. Consequently, what is a law of nature for us at all? It is not known to us in itself but only in its effects, i.e. in its relations to other laws of nature which are in turn known to us only as relations. Thus, all these relations refer only to one another, and they are utterly incomprehensible to us in their essential nature; the only things we really know about them are things which we bring to bear on them: time and space, in other words, relations of succession and number. But everything which is wonderful and which elicits our astonishment at precisely these laws of nature, everything which demands explanation of us and could seduce us into being suspicious of idealism, is attributable precisely and exclusively to the rigour and universal validity of the representations of time and space. But these we produce within ourselves and from ourselves with the same necessity as a spider spins; if we are forced to comprehend all things under these forms alone, then it is no longer wonderful that what we comprehend in all these things is actually nothing other than these very forms; for all of them must exhibit the laws of number, and number is precisely that which is most astonishing about things. All the conformity to laws which we find so imposing in the orbits of the stars and chemical processes is basically identical with those qualities which we ourselves bring to bear on things, so that what we find imposing is our own activity. Of course the consequence of this is that the artistic production of metaphor, with which every sensation begins within us, already presupposes those forms, and is thus executed in them; only from the stability of these original forms can one explain how it is possible for an edifice of concepts to be constituted in its turn from the metaphors themselves. For this conceptual edifice is an imitation of the relations of time, space, and number on the foundations of metaphor.

2

Originally, as we have seen, it is *language* which works on building the edifice of concepts; later it is *science*. Just as the bee simultaneously builds the cells of its comb and fills them with honey, so science works unceasingly at that great *columbarium* of concepts, the burial site of perceptions, builds ever-new, ever-higher tiers, supports, cleans, renews the old cells, and strives above all to fill that framework which towers up to vast heights, and to fit into it in an orderly way the whole empirical world, i.e. the anthropomorphic world. If even the man of action binds his life to reason and its concepts, so as not to be swept away and lose himself, the researcher builds his hut close by the tower of science so that he can lend a hand with the building and find protection for himself beneath its already existing bulwarks. And he has need of protection, for there exist fearful powers which constantly press in on him and which confront scientific truth with 'truths' of quite another kind, on shields emblazoned with the most multifarious emblems.

That drive to form metaphors, that fundamental human drive which cannot be left out of consideration for even a second without also leaving out human beings themselves, is in truth not defeated, indeed hardly even tamed, by the process whereby a regular and rigid new world is built from its own sublimated products—concepts—in order to imprison it in a fortress. The drive seeks out a channel and a new area for its activity, and finds it in myth and in art generally. It constantly confuses the cells and the classifications of concepts by setting up new translations, metaphors, metonymies; it constantly manifests the desire to shape the given world of the waking human being in ways which are just as multiform, irregular, inconsequential, incoherent, charming and ever-new, as things are in the world of dream. Actually the waking human being is only clear about the fact that he is awake thanks to the rigid and regular web of concepts, and for that reason he sometimes comes to believe that he is dreaming if once that web of concepts is torn apart by art. Pascal is right to maintain that if the same dream were to come to us every night we would occupy ourselves with it just as much as we do with the things we see every day: 'If an artisan could be sure to dream each night for a full twelve hours that he was a king,' says Pascal, 'I believe he would be just as happy as a king who dreamt for twelve hours each night that he was an artisan.'[4] Thanks to the constantly effective miracle assumed by myth, the waking day of a people who are stimulated by myth, as the ancient Greeks were, does indeed resemble dream more than it does the day of a thinker whose mind has been sobered by science. If, one day, any tree may speak as a nymph, or if a god can carry off virgins in the guise of a bull, if the goddess Athene herself is suddenly seen riding on a beautiful chariot in the company of Pisistratus through the market-places of Athens[5]—and that was what the honest Athenian believed—then anything is possible at any time, as it is in dream, and the whole of nature cavorts around men as if it were just a masquerade of the gods who are merely having fun by deceiving men in every shape and form.

But human beings themselves have an unconquerable urge to let themselves be deceived, and they are as if enchanted with happiness when the bard recites epic fairy-tales as if they were true, or when the actor in a play acts the king more regally than reality shows him to be. The intellect, that master of pretence, is free and absolved of its usual slavery for as long as it can deceive without *doing harm*, and it celebrates its Saturnalian festivals[6] when it does so; at no time is it richer, more luxuriant, more proud, skilful, and bold. Full of creative contentment, it jumbles up metaphors and shifts the boundary stones of abstraction, describing a river, for example, as a moving road that carries men to destinations to which they normally walk. The intellect has now cast off the mark of servitude; whereas it normally labours, with dull-spirited industry, to show to some poor individual who lusts after life the road and the tools he needs, and rides out in search of spoils and booty for its master, here the intellect has become the master itself and is

4. *Pensées* VI.386. [Blaise Pascal (1623–1662), French mathematician, theologian, and philosopher—editor's note.]
5. Herodotus 1.60. [The Greek historian (ca. 484–ca. 425 B.C.E.) describes in the passage cited a ruse of the Athenian ruler Pisistratus (d. 527 B.C.E.) after he was forced out of the city in 566: he dressed a tall, handsome woman in armor and led the people to believe that Athena, goddess of war and wisdom and the patron of Athens, was herself restoring him to power. "The guise of a bull": Zeus, the Greek king of the gods, took the form of a bull when he abducted Europa, a Phoenician princess—editor's note.]
6. Roman holidays at the winter solstice during which no business was conducted, slaves were temporarily freed, and the normal rules of propriety were suspended [editor's note].

permitted to wipe the expression of neediness from its face. Whatever the intellect now does, all of it, compared with what it did before, bears the mark of pretence, just as what it did before bore the mark of distortion. It copies human life, but it takes it to be something good and appears to be fairly content with it. That vast assembly of beams and boards to which needy man clings, thereby saving himself on his journey through life, is used by the liberated intellect as a mere climbing frame and plaything on which to perform its most reckless tricks; and when it smashes this framework, jumbles it up and ironically re-assembles it, pairing the most unlike things and dividing those things which are closest to one another, it reveals the fact that it does not require those makeshift aids of neediness, and that it is now guided, not by concepts but by intuitions. No regular way leads from these intuitions into the land of the ghostly schemata and abstractions; words are not made for them; man is struck dumb when he sees them, or he will speak only in forbidden metaphors and unheard-of combinations of concepts so that, by at least demolishing and deriding the old conceptual barriers, he may do creative justice to the impression made on him by the mighty, present intuition.

There are epochs in which the man of reason and the man of intuition stand side by side, the one fearful of intuition, the other filled with scorn for abstraction, the latter as unreasonable as the former is unartistic. They both desire to rule over life; the one by his knowledge of how to cope with the chief calamities of life by providing for the future, by prudence and regularity, the other by being an 'exuberant hero'[7] who does not see those calamities and who only acknowledges life as real when it is disguised as beauty and appearance. Where the man of intuition, as was once the case in ancient Greece, wields his weapons more mightily and victoriously than his contrary, a culture can take shape, given favourable conditions, and the rule of art over life can become established; all the expressions of a life lived thus are accompanied by pretence, by the denial of neediness, by the radiance of metaphorical visions, and indeed generally by the immediacy of deception. Neither the house, nor the gait, nor the clothing, nor the pitcher of clay gives any hint that these things were invented by neediness; it seems as if all of them were intended to express sublime happiness and Olympian[8] cloudlessness and, as it were, a playing with earnest things. Whereas the man who is guided by concepts and abstractions only succeeds thereby in warding off misfortune, is unable to compel the abstractions themselves to yield him happiness, and strives merely to be as free as possible of pain, the man of intuition, standing in the midst of a culture, reaps directly from his intuitions not just protection from harm but also a constant stream of brightness, a lightening of the spirit, redemption, and release. Of course, *when* he suffers, he suffers more severely; indeed he suffers more frequently because he does not know how to learn from experience and keeps on falling into the very same trap time after time. When he is suffering he is just as unreasonable as he is when happy, he shouts out loudly and knows no solace. How differ-

7. Phrase used to describe Siegfried in Wagner's *Götterdämmerung* (Act III). [Richard Wagner (1813–1883), German composer who was Nietzsche's friend and mentor until their falling out in 1876. *Götterdämmerung*, the conclusion of Wagner's *Ring* cycle, was first produced in 1876—editor's note.]

8. That is, characteristic of Mount Olympus, the home of the Greek gods [editor's note].

ently the same misfortune is endured by the stoic who has learned from experience and who governs himself by means of concepts! This man, who otherwise seeks only honesty, truth, freedom from illusions, and protection from the onslaughts of things which might distract him, now performs, in the midst of misfortune, a masterpiece of pretence, just as the other did in the midst of happiness: he does not wear a twitching, mobile, human face, but rather a mask, as it were, with its features in dignified equilibrium; he does not shout, nor does he even change his tone of voice. If a veritable storm-cloud empties itself on his head, he wraps himself in his cloak and slowly walks away from under it.

1873 1903

From The Birth of Tragedy[1]

1

We shall have gained much for the science of aesthetics when we have come to realize, not just through logical insight but also with the certainty of something directly apprehended (*Anschauung*), that the continuous evolution of art is bound up with the duality of the *Apolline* and the *Dionysiac* in much the same way as reproduction depends on there being two sexes which co-exist in a state of perpetual conflict interrupted only occasionally by periods of reconciliation. We have borrowed these names from the Greeks who reveal the profound mysteries of their view of art to those with insight, not in concepts, admittedly, but through the penetratingly vivid figures of their gods. Their two deities of art, Apollo and Dionysos,[2] provide the starting-point for our recognition that there exists in the world of the Greeks an enormous opposition, both in origin and goals, between the Apolline art of the image-maker or sculptor (*Bildner*) and the imageless art of music, which is that of Dionysos. These two very different drives (*Triebe*) exist side by side, mostly in open conflict, stimulating and provoking (*reizen*) one another to give birth to ever-new, more vigorous offspring in whom they perpetuate the conflict inherent in the opposition between them, an opposition only apparently bridged by the common term 'art'—until eventually, by a metaphysical miracle of the Hellenic 'Will', they appear paired and, in this pairing, finally engender a work of art which is Dionysiac and Apolline in equal measure: Attic tragedy.[3]

In order to gain a closer understanding of these two drives, let us think of them in the first place as the separate art-worlds of *dream* and *intoxication* (*Rausch*). Between these two physiological phenomena an opposition can be observed which corresponds to that between the Apolline and the Dionysiac. As Lucretius[4] envisages it, it was in dream that the magnificent figures of

1. Translated by Ronald Speirs. Except as indicated, all subsequent notes are the translator's; in the text, he occasionally retains the original German in parentheses. The full title is *The Birth of Tragedy from the Spirit of Music*.

2. Greek god of wine, the object of frenzied cult worship (somewhat muted in its official forms). Apollo: Greek god of music, prophecy, and medicine, associated with the higher developments of civilization; as Phoebus Apollo, he is god of light [editor's note].

3. Plays performed at the festival of Dionysus in Athens during the 5th century B.C.E. [editor's note].

4. Roman poet and philosopher (ca. 94–55 B.C.E.); see *De Rerum Natura* (*On the Nature of Things*) 5.1169–82 [editor's note].

the gods first appeared before the souls of men; in dream the great image-maker saw the delightfully proportioned bodies of super-human beings; and the Hellenic poet, if asked about the secrets of poetic procreation, would likewise have reminded us of dream and would have given an account much like that given by Hans Sachs in the *Meistersinger*:

> My friend, it is the poet's task
> To mark his dreams, their meaning ask.
> Trust me, the truest phantom man doth know
> Hath meaning only dreams may show:
> The arts of verse and poetry
> Tell nought but dreaming's prophecy.[5]

Every human being is fully an artist when creating the worlds of dream, and the lovely semblance of dream is the precondition of all the arts of image-making, including, as we shall see, an important half of poetry. We take pleasure in dreaming, understanding its figures without mediation; all forms speak to us; nothing is indifferent or unnecessary. Yet even while this dream-reality is most alive, we nevertheless retain a pervasive sense that it is *semblance*; at least this is my experience, and I could adduce a good deal of evidence and the statements of poets to attest to the frequency, indeed normality, of my experience. Philosophical natures even have a presentiment that hidden beneath the reality in which we live and have our being there also lies a second, quite different reality; in other words, this reality too is a semblance. Indeed Schopenhauer actually states that the mark of a person's capacity for philosophy is the gift for feeling occasionally as if people and all things were mere phantoms or dream-images.[6] A person with artistic sensibility relates to the reality of dream in the same way as a philosopher relates to the reality of existence: he attends to it closely and with pleasure, using these images to interpret life, and practising for life with the help of these events. Not that it is only the pleasant and friendly images which give him this feeling of complete intelligibility; he also sees passing before him things which are grave, gloomy, sad, dark, sudden blocks, teasings of chance, anxious expectations, in short the entire 'Divine Comedy'[7] of life, including the Inferno, but not like some mere shadow-play—for he, too, lives in these scenes and shares in the suffering—and yet never without that fleeting sense of its character as semblance. Perhaps others will recall, as I do, shouting out, sometimes successfully, words of encouragement in the midst of the perils and terrors of a dream: 'It is a dream! I will dream on!' I have even heard of people who were capable of continuing the causality of one and the same dream through three and more successive nights. All of these facts are clear evidence that our innermost being, the deep ground (*Untergrund*) common to all our lives, experiences the state of dreaming with profound pleasure (*Lust*) and joyous necessity.

The Greeks also expressed the joyous necessity of dream-experience in

5. Wagner, *Die Meistersinger*, Act III, sc. 2. [Richard Wagner (1813–1883), German composer whose music and aesthetic theories greatly influenced Nietzsche's argument in *The Birth of Tragedy*. Hans Sachs (1494–1576), German poet and dramatist who has a major role in Wagner's 1868 opera—editor's note.]

6. *Aus Schopenhauers handschriftlichem Nachlass*, ed. J. Frauenstädt (Leipzig 1874), p. 295. [Arthur Schopenhauer (1788–1860), German philosopher, a major influence on Nietzsche—editor's note.]

7. Epic poem by the Italian poet DANTE ALIGHIERI (1265–1321); in the first part of the *Inferno*, the poet narrates a passage through hell [editor's note].

their Apollo: as the god of all image-making energies, Apollo is also the god of prophecy. According to the etymological root of his name, he is 'the luminous one' (*der Scheinende*), the god of light; as such, he also governs the lovely semblance produced by the inner world of fantasy. The higher truth, the perfection of these dream-states in contrast to the only partially intelligible reality of the daylight world, together with the profound consciousness of the helping and healing powers of nature in sleep and dream, is simultaneously the symbolic analogue of the ability to prophesy and indeed of all the arts through which life is made possible and worth living. But the image of Apollo must also contain that delicate line which the dream-image may not overstep if its effect is not to become pathological, so that, in the worst case, the semblance would deceive us as if it were crude reality; his image (*Bild*) must include that measured limitation (*maßvolle Begrenzung*), that freedom from wilder impulses, that wise calm of the image-making god. In accordance with his origin, his eye must be 'sun-like'; even when its gaze is angry and shows displeasure, it exhibits the consecrated quality of lovely semblance. Thus, in an eccentric sense, one could apply to Apollo what Schopenhauer says about human beings trapped in the veil of maya:

> Just as the boatman sits in his small boat, trusting his frail craft in a stormy sea that is boundless in every direction, rising and falling with the howling, mountainous waves, so in the midst of a world full of suffering and misery the individual man calmly sits, supported by and trusting in the *principium individuationis*[8][. . .] (*World as Will and Representation*, I, p. 416)

Indeed one could say that Apollo is the most sublime expression of imperturbable trust in this principle and of the calm sitting-there of the person trapped within it; one might even describe Apollo as the magnificent divine image (*Götterbild*) of the *principium individuationis*, whose gestures and gaze speak to us of all the intense pleasure, wisdom and beauty of 'semblance'.

In the same passage Schopenhauer has described for us the enormous *horror* which seizes people when they suddenly become confused and lose faith in the cognitive forms of the phenomenal world because the principle of sufficient reason, in one or other of its modes, appears to sustain an exception. If we add to this horror the blissful ecstasy which arises from the innermost ground of man, indeed of nature itself, whenever this breakdown of the *principium individuationis* occurs, we catch a glimpse of the essence of the *Dionysiac*, which is best conveyed by the analogy of *intoxication*. These Dionysiac stirrings, which, as they grow in intensity, cause subjectivity to vanish to the point of complete self-forgetting, awaken either under the influence of narcotic drink, of which all human beings and peoples who are close to the origin of things speak in their hymns, or at the approach of spring when the whole of nature is pervaded by lust for life. In the German Middle Ages, too, ever-growing throngs roamed from place to place, impelled by the same Dionysiac power, singing and dancing as they went; in these St John's and St Vitus' dancers we recognize the Bacchic choruses of the Greeks, with

8. Principle of individuation (Latin). For Schopenhauer, the mind can apprehend the world only by dividing it up into individual things; this process produces an erroneous vision of reality, which he calls "the veil of maya" [editor's note].

their pre-history in Asia Minor, extending to Babylon and the orgiastic Sacaea.[9] There are those who, whether from lack of experience or from dullness of spirit, turn away in scorn or pity from such phenomena, regarding them as 'popular diseases' while believing in their own good health; of course, these poor creatures have not the slightest inkling of how spectral and deathly pale their 'health' seems when the glowing life of Dionysiac enthusiasts storms past them.

Not only is the bond between human beings renewed by the magic of the Dionysiac, but nature, alienated, inimical, or subjugated, celebrates once more her festival of reconciliation with her lost son, humankind. Freely the earth offers up her gifts, and the beasts of prey from mountain and desert approach in peace. The chariot of Dionysos is laden with flowers and wreaths; beneath its yoke stride panther and tiger. If one were to transform Beethoven's jubilant 'Hymn to Joy'[1] into a painting and place no constraints on one's imagination as the millions sink into the dust, shivering in awe, then one could begin to approach the Dionysiac. Now the slave is a freeman, now all the rigid, hostile barriers, which necessity, caprice, or 'impudent fashion'[2] have established between human beings, break asunder. Now, hearing this gospel of universal harmony, each person feels himself to be not simply united, reconciled or merged with his neighbour, but quite literally one with him, as if the veil of maya had been torn apart, so that mere shreds of it flutter before the mysterious primordial unity (*das Ur-Eine*). Singing and dancing, man expresses his sense of belonging to a higher community; he has forgotten how to walk and talk and is on the brink of flying and dancing, up and away into the air above. His gestures speak of his enchantment. Just as the animals now talk and the earth gives milk and honey,[3] there now sounds out from within man something supernatural: he feels himself to be a god, he himself now moves in such ecstasy and sublimity as once he saw the gods move in his dreams. Man is no longer an artist, he has become a work of art: all nature's artistic power reveals itself here, amidst shivers of intoxication, to the highest, most blissful satisfaction of the primordial unity. Here man, the noblest clay, the most precious marble, is kneaded and carved and, to the accompaniment of the chisel-blows of the Dionysiac world-artist, the call of the Eleusinian Mysteries rings out: 'Fall ye to the ground, ye millions? Feelst thou thy Creator, world?'[4]

* * *

9

Everything that rises to the surface in dialogue, the Apolline part of Greek tragedy, appears simple, transparent, beautiful. In this sense the dialogue is

9. A festival of the winter solstice. Nietzsche links together a number of ecstatic celebrations [editor's note].

1. Beethoven used a version of Schiller's ode *To Joy* for the choral finale of his Ninth Symphony. [Ludwig van Beethoven (1770–1827), German composer. FRIEDRICH VON SCHILLER (1759–1805), German poet and playwright—editor's note.]

2. Quotation from Schiller's *To Joy*.

3. Conflation of Euripides *Bacchae* lines 142 and 708–11 with Exodus 3.8.[Euripides (ca. 485–ca. 406 B.C.E.), the last of the three great Attic tragedians; Nietzsche associates him with the decline of tragedy. The Bacchae of the play are the frenzied women who follow Dionysus—editor's note.]

4. Schiller's *To Joy*, lines 33–34. [Eleusinian Mysteries: the most famous of the secret Greek cults, which were connected with Demeter (goddess of the fruits of the earth) and Dionysus. Eleusis was an important town in southwest Attica—editor's note.]

a copy of the Hellene, whose nature is expressed in dance, because in dance the greatest strength is still only potential, although it is betrayed by the suppleness and luxuriance of movement. Thus the language of Sophocles'[5] heroes surprises us by its Apolline definiteness and clarity, so that we feel as if we are looking straight into the innermost ground of its being, and are somewhat astonished that the road to this ground is so short. But if we once divert our gaze from the character of the hero as it rises to the surface and becomes visible—fundamentally, it is no more than an image of light (*Lichtbild*) projected on to a dark wall, i.e. appearance (*Erscheinung*) through and through—if, rather, we penetrate to the myth which projects itself in these bright reflections, we suddenly experience a phenomenon which inverts a familiar optical one. When we turn away blinded after a strenuous attempt to look directly at the sun, we have dark, coloured patches before our eyes, as if their purpose were to heal them; conversely, those appearances of the Sophoclean hero in images of light, in other words, the Apolline quality of the mask, are the necessary result of gazing into the inner, terrible depths of nature—radiant patches, as it were, to heal a gaze seared by gruesome night. Only in this sense may we believe that we have grasped the serious and significant concept of 'Greek serenity' (*Heiterkeit*) correctly; admittedly, wherever one looks at present one comes across a misunderstood notion of this as 'cheerfulness', something identified with a condition of unendangered ease and comfort.

The most suffering figure of the Greek stage, the unfortunate *Oedipus,*[6] was understood by Sophocles as the noble human being who is destined for error and misery despite his wisdom, but who in the end, through his enormous suffering, exerts on the world around him a magical, beneficent force which remains effective even after his death. The noble human being does not sin, so this profound poet wants to tell us; every law, all natural order, indeed the moral world, may be destroyed by his actions, yet by these very actions a higher, magical circle of effects is drawn which found a new world on the ruins of the old one that has been overthrown. This is what the poet, inasmuch as he is also a religious thinker, wishes to tell us; as a poet he first shows us a wonderfully tied trial-knot which the judge slowly undoes, strand by strand, to bring great harm upon himself; the genuinely Hellenic delight in this dialectical solution is so great that an air of sovereign serenity pervades the whole work, blunting all the sharp, horrifying preconditions of that trial. We encounter this same serenity in *Oedipus at Colonus*, but here it is elevated into infinite transfiguration; in this play the old man, stricken with an excess of suffering, and exposed, purely as a *suffering being*, to all that affects him, is contrasted with the unearthly serenity which comes down from the sphere of the gods as a sign to us that in his purely passive behaviour the hero achieves the highest form of activity, which has consequences reaching far beyond his own life, whereas all his conscious words and actions in his life hitherto have merely led to his passivity. Thus the trial-knot of the story

5. Greek tragedian (ca. 496–406 B.C.E.) [editor's note].

6. The hero of *Oedipus the King* (ca. 430 B.C.E.), who unknowing kills his father, the king of Thebes, and then marries his mother, becoming king in turn; when he discovers the truth, he blinds himself and is banished. In *Oedipus at Colonus* (produced posthumously), the ruler of Thebes unsuccessfully attempts to persuade Oedipus, now a dying old man, to return so that after his death he will benefit and not curse the city (Greek heroes were thought to exert power even when dead) [editor's note].

of Oedipus, which strikes the mortal eye as inextricably tangled, is slowly unravelled—and we are overcome by the most profound human delight at this matching piece of divine dialectic. If our explanation has done justice to the poet, the question remains whether the content of the myth has been exhausted thereby; at this point it becomes plain that the poet's whole interpretation of the story is nothing other than one of those images of light held out to us by healing nature after we have gazed into the abyss. Oedipus, murderer of his father, husband of his mother, Oedipus the solver of the Sphinx's riddle! What does this trinity of fateful deeds tell us? There is an ancient popular belief, particularly in Persia, that a wise magician can only be born out of incest; the riddle-solving Oedipus who woos his mother immediately leads us to interpret this as meaning that some enormous offence against nature (such as incest in this case) must first have occurred to supply the cause whenever prophetic and magical energies break the spell of present and future, the rigid law of individuation, and indeed the actual magic of nature. How else could nature be forced to reveal its secrets, other than by victorious resistance to her, i.e. by some unnatural event? I see this insight expressed in that terrible trinity of Oedipus' fates: the same man who solves the riddle of nature—that of the double-natured[7] sphinx—must also destroy the most sacred orders of nature by murdering his father and becoming his mother's husband. Wisdom, the myth seems to whisper to us, and Dionysiac wisdom in particular, is an unnatural abomination: whoever plunges nature into the abyss of destruction by what he knows must in turn experience the dissolution of nature in his own person. 'The sharp point of wisdom turns against the wise man; wisdom is an offence against nature': such are the terrible words the myth calls out to us. But, like a shaft of sunlight, the Hellenic poet touches the sublime and terrible Memnon's Column of myth[8] so that it suddenly begins to sound—in Sophoclean melodies!

I shall now contrast the glory of passivity with the glory of activity which shines around the *Prometheus* of Aeschylus.[9] What the thinker Aeschylus had to tell us here, but what his symbolic poetic image only hints at, has been revealed to us by the youthful Goethe in the reckless words of his Prometheus:

> Here I sit, forming men
> In my own image,
> A race to be like me,
> To suffer and to weep,
> To know delight and joy
> And heed you not,
> Like me![1]

Raising himself to Titanic heights, man fights for and achieves his own culture, and he compels the gods to ally themselves with him because, in his

7. Having the face of a woman and the body of a lion [editor's note].

8. The remnants of a monumental statue in Egypt were said to produce a musical tone when illuminated by the rays of the rising sun.

9. Greek tragedian (525–456 B.C.E.), generally credited with giving Attic drama its traditional form. *Prometheus Bound* depicts Prometheus, a Titan (pre-Olympian god) punished by Zeus, the supreme god who has overthrown the Titans, for giving fire to humans. Prometheus is chained to a rock in the mountains, where daily a vulture tears out his liver. According to some stories, Prometheus created humans out of mud [editor's note].

1. Goethe, *Prometheus*, lines 51 ff. [Johann Wolfgang von Goethe (1749–1832), German poet, playwright, and novelist; Nietzsche quotes the final stanza of his 1773 poem—editor's note.]

very own wisdom, he holds existence and its limits in his hands. But the most wonderful thing in that poem about Prometheus (which, in terms of its basic thought, is the true hymn of impiety) is its profound, Aeschylean tendency to *justice*: the limitless suffering of the bold 'individual' on the one hand, and the extreme plight of the gods, indeed a premonition of the twilight of the gods, on the other; the power of both these worlds of suffering to enforce reconciliation, metaphysical oneness—all this recalls in the strongest possible way the centre and principal tenet of the Aeschylean view of the world, which sees *moira*,[2] as eternal justice, throned above gods and men. If the boldness of Aeschylus in placing the world of the Olympians on his scales of justice seems astonishing, we must remember that the deep-thinking Greek had an unshakably firm foundation for metaphysical thought in his Mysteries, so that all attacks of scepticism could be discharged on the Olympians. The Greek artist in particular had an obscure feeling that he and these gods were mutually dependent, a feeling symbolized precisely in Aeschylus' Prometheus. The Titanic artist found within himself the defiant belief that he could create human beings and destroy the Olympian gods at least, and that his higher wisdom enabled him to do so, for which, admittedly, he was forced to do penance by suffering eternally. The magnificent 'ability' (*Können*) of the great genius, for which even eternal suffering is too small a price to pay, the bitter pride of the *artist*: this is the content and the soul of Aeschylus' play, whereas Sophocles, in his *Oedipus*, begins the prelude to the victory-hymn of the *saint*. But even Aeschylus's interpretation of the myth does not plumb its astonishing, terrible depths; rather, the artist's delight in Becoming, the serenity of artistic creation in defiance of all catastrophes, is merely a bright image of clouds and sky reflected in a dark sea of sadness. Originally, the legend of Prometheus belonged to the entire community of Aryan peoples[3] and documented their talent for the profound and the tragic; indeed, it is not unlikely that this myth is as significant for the Aryan character as the myth of the Fall is for the Semitic character, and that the relationship between the two myths is like that between brother and sister. The myth of Prometheus presupposes the unbounded value which naive humanity placed on *fire* as the true palladium[4] of every rising culture; but it struck those contemplative original men as a crime, a theft perpetrated on divine nature, to believe that man commanded fire freely, rather than receiving it as a gift from heaven, as a bolt of lightning which could start a blaze, or as the warming fire of the sun. Thus the very first philosophical problem presents a painful, irresolvable conflict between god and man, and pushes it like a mighty block of rock up against the threshold of every culture. Humanity achieves the best and highest of which it is capable by committing an offence and must in turn accept the consequences of this, namely the whole flood of suffering and tribulations which the offended heavenly powers *must* in turn visit upon the human race as it strives nobly towards higher things: a bitter thought, but one which, thanks to the *dignity* it accords to the offence, contrasts strangely with the Semitic myth of the Fall, where the

2. Fate or destiny (Greek) [editor's note].
3. Speakers of Indo-European, the prehistoric language whose descendents include Greek, German, English, and Hindi; here they are contrasted with speakers of Semitic languages, such as those who wrote Genesis in Hebrew [editor's note].
4. Here simply: "prized possession." [Specifically, in Greek mythology, the Palladium was a statue of the goddess Pallas Athena, whose presence at Troy supposedly kept the city safe—editor's note.]

origin of evil was seen to lie in curiosity, mendacious pretence, openness to seduction, lasciviousness, in short: in a whole series of predominantly feminine attributes. What distinguishes the Aryan conception is the sublime view that *active sin* is the true Promethean virtue; thereby we have also found the ethical foundation of pessimistic tragedy, its *justification* of the evil in human life, both in the sense of human guilt and in the sense of the suffering brought about by it. The curse in the nature of things, which the reflective Aryan is not inclined simply to explain away, the contradiction at the heart of the world, presents itself to him as a mixture of different worlds, e.g. a divine and a human one, each of which, taken individually, is in the right, but which, as one world existing alongside another, must suffer for the fact of its individuation. The heroic urge of the individual to reach out towards the general, the attempt to cross the fixed boundaries of individuation, and the desire to become the *one* world-being itself, all this leads him to suffer in his own person the primal contradiction hidden within the things of this world, i.e. he commits a great wrong and suffers. Thus great wrongdoing is understood as masculine by the Aryans, but as feminine by the Semites,[5] just as the original wrong was committed by a man and the original sin by a woman. These, incidentally, are the words of the warlocks' chorus:

> So what, if women on the whole
> Take many steps to reach the goal?
> Let them run as fast as they dare,
> With one good jump a man gets there.[6]

Anyone who understands the innermost kernel of the legend of Prometheus—namely that wrongdoing is of necessity imposed on the titanically striving individual—is bound also to sense the un-Apolline quality of this pessimistic view of things, for it is the will of Apollo to bring rest and calm to individual beings precisely by drawing boundaries between them, and by reminding them constantly, with his demands for self-knowledge and measure, that these are the most sacred laws in the world. But lest this Apolline tendency should cause form to freeze into Egyptian stiffness and coldness, lest the attempt to prescribe the course and extent of each individual wave should cause the movement of the whole lake to die away, the flood-tide of the Dionysiac would destroy periodically all the small circles in which the one-sidedly Apolline will attempted to confine Hellenic life. That sudden swell of the Dionysiac tide then lifts the separate little waves of individuals on to its back, just as the Titan Atlas,[7] brother of Prometheus, lifted up the earth. This Titanic urge to become, as it were, the Atlas of all single beings, and to carry them on a broad back higher and higher, further and further, is the common feature shared by the Promethean and the Dionysiac. In this respect the Prometheus of Aeschylus is a Dionysiac mask, whereas the aforementioned deep strain of justice in Aeschylus reveals to those with eyes to see his paternal descent from Apollo, the god of individuation and of the boundaries of justice. The double essence of Aeschylus' Prometheus, his simultaneously Apolline and Dionysiac nature, could therefore be expressed

5. The noun translated as "wrongdoing" (*der Frevel*) has masculine gender in German; "sin" (*die Sünde*) has feminine.
6. Goethe, *Faust* [1808], I, 3982 ff.
7. In Greek myth, punished for warring against the Olympian gods by having to bear the world upon his shoulders [editor's note].

like this: 'All that exists is just and unjust and is equally justified in both respects.'

That is your world. That you call a world.[8]

10

It is a matter of indisputable historical record that the only subject-matter of Greek tragedy, in its earliest form, was the sufferings of Dionysos, and that for a long time the only hero present on the stage was, accordingly, Dionysos. But one may also say with equal certainty that, right down to Euripides, Dionysos never ceased to be the tragic hero, and that all the famous figures of the Greek stage, Prometheus, Oedipus etc., are merely masks of that original hero, Dionysos. The fact that there is a deity behind all these masks is one of the essential reasons for the 'ideal' quality of those famous figures which has prompted so much astonishment. Someone or other (I do not know who) once remarked that all individuals, as individuals, are comic, and therefore un-tragic; from which one could conclude that the Greeks were quite *incapable* of tolerating any individuals on the tragic stage. And indeed this does appear to have been their feeling, just as the reason for the Platonic distinction between, and deprecation of, the 'idea' as opposed to the 'idol',[9] or copied image, lay deep within the Hellenic character. Using Plato's terminology, one would have to say something like this about the tragic figures of the Hellenic stage: the one, truly real Dionysos manifests himself in a multiplicity of figures, in the mask of a fighting hero and, as it were, entangled in the net of the individual will. In the way that he now speaks and acts, the god who appears resembles an erring, striving, suffering individual; and the fact that he *appears* at all with such epic definiteness and clarity, is the effect of Apollo, the interpreter of dreams, who interprets to the chorus its Dionysiac condition by means of this symbolic appearance. In truth, however, this hero is the suffering Dionysos of the Mysteries, the god who experiences the sufferings of individuation in his own person, of whom wonderful myths recount that he was torn to pieces by the Titans when he was a boy and is now venerated in this condition as Zagreus;[1] at the same time, it is indicated that his being torn into pieces, the genuinely Dionysiac *suffering*, is like a transformation into air, water, earth, and fire, so that we are to regard the state of individuation as the source and primal cause of all suffering, as something inherently to be rejected. From the smile of that Dionysos the Olympian gods were born, from his tears human beings. In this existence as a dismembered god, Dionysos has a double nature; he is both cruel, savage demon and mild, gentle ruler. But what the epopts[2] hoped for was the rebirth of Dionysos, which we must now understand, by premonition, as the end of individuation; the epopts' roaring song of jubilation rang out to greet this third Dionysos. Only in the hope of this

8. Goethe, *Faust*, I, 409.

9. That is, an *eikōn*, or "likeness," which PLATO (ca. 427–ca. 347 B.C.E.) sees as necessarily inferior to the Form or Idea (*idea*) of which it can be only an imperfect representation and through which it participates in what is truly real [editor's note].

1. A myth to the effect that Dionysos, under the name "Zagreus," is torn apart and then reassembled occurs in some late Hellenistic sources. Whether this is a survival of an older (perhaps secret) doctrine about Dionysos, as Nietzsche assumes, or a late innovative embellishment of earlier tradition is, given the state of our knowledge, undecidable. [This version of Dionysus is the son of Demeter; in most myths, he is said to be the son of a mortal woman, Semele, and Zeus—editor's note.]

2. Devoted followers who have "seen" their god.

is there a gleam of joy on the countenance of a world torn apart and shattered into individuals; myth symbolizes this in the image of Demeter, sunk in eternal mourning, who knows no *happiness* until she is told that she can give birth to Dionysos *again*. In the views described here we already have all the constituent elements of a profound and pessimistic way of looking at the world and thus at the same time, of *the doctrine of the Mysteries taught by tragedy*: the fundamental recognition that everything which exists is a unity; the view that individuation is the primal source of all evil; and art as the joyous hope that the spell of individuation can be broken, a premonition of unity restored.

* * *

24

* * *

At this point we need to take a bold run-up and vault into a metaphysics of art, as I repeat my earlier sentence that only as an aesthetic phenomenon do existence and the world appear justified; which means that tragic myth in particular must convince us that even the ugly and disharmonious is an artistic game which the Will, in the eternal fullness of its delight, plays with itself. Yet this difficult, primal phenomenon of Dionysiac art can be grasped in a uniquely intelligible and direct way in the wonderful significance of *musical dissonance*; as indeed music generally is the only thing which, when set alongside the world, can illustrate what is meant by the justification of the world as an aesthetic phenomenon. The pleasure engendered by the tragic myth comes from the same homeland as our pleasurable sensation of dissonance in music. The Dionysiac, with the primal pleasure it perceives even in pain, is the common womb from which both music and the tragic myth are born.

Could it not be that, with the assistance of musical dissonance, we have eased significantly the difficult problem of the effect of tragedy? After all, we do now understand the meaning of our desire to look, and yet to long to go beyond looking when we are watching tragedy; when applied to our response to the artistic use of dissonance, this state of mind would have to be described in similar terms we want to listen, but at the same time we long to go beyond listening. That striving towards infinity, that wing-beat of longing even as we feel supreme delight in a clearly perceived reality, these things indicate that in both these states of mind we are to recognize a Dionysiac phenomenon, one which reveals to us the playful construction and demolition of the world of individuality as an outpouring of primal pleasure and delight, a process quite similar to Heraclitus the Obscure's comparison of the force that shapes the world to a playing child who sets down stones here, there, and the next place, and who builds up piles of sand only to knock them down again.[3]

Thus, in order to judge the Dionysiac capacity of a people correctly, it is necessary for us to consider the evidence not simply of their music but also of their tragic myth. Given the intimate relationship between music and myth, one would expect that the atrophy of the one would be connected to

3. Heraclitus, fragment 52. [Heraclitus (active ca. 500 B.C.E), pre-Socratic Greek philosopher—editor's note.]

the degeneration and depravation of the other, if indeed it is true that any weakening of myth generally expresses a waning of the capacity for the Dionysiac. One only needs to glance at the development of the German character to be left in no doubt on both counts: we saw that the nature of Socratic optimism,[4] something which is as unartistic as it is parasitic on life, was revealed in equal measure both in opera and in the abstract character of our mythless existence, in an art which had sunk to the level of mere entertainment as much as in a life guided by concepts. We took some comfort, however, from certain signs that, despite all this, the German spirit has remained whole, in magnificent health, depth, and Dionysiac strength, resting and dreaming in an inaccessible abyss like a knight who has sunk into slumber; now the Dionysiac song rises from this abyss to tell us that, at this very moment, this German knight still dreams his ancient Dionysiac myth in blissfully grave visions. Let no one believe that the German spirit has lost its mythical home for ever, if it can still understand so clearly the voices of the birds which tell of its homeland. One day it will find itself awake, with all the morning freshness that comes from a vast sleep; then it will slay dragons, destroy the treacherous dwarfs, and awaken Brünnhilde—and not even Wotan's spear itself will be able to bar its path![5]

My friends, you who believe in the music of Dionysos, you also know what tragedy means for us. In it we have the tragic myth, reborn from music—and in this you may hope for all things and forget that which is most painful! But for all of us the most painful thing is that long period of indignity when the German genius lived in the service of treacherous dwarfs, estranged from hearth and home. You understand what my words mean—just as you will also understand, finally, my hopes.

25

Music and tragic myth both express, in the same way, the Dionysiac capacity of a people, and they cannot be separated from one another. Both originate in an artistic realm which lies beyond the Apolline; both transfigure a region where dissonance and the terrible image of the world fade away in chords of delight; both play with the goad of disinclination, trusting to their immeasurably powerful arts of magic; both justify by their play the existence of even the 'worst of all worlds'. Here the Dionysiac shows itself, in comparison with the Apolline, to be the eternal and original power of art which summons the entire world of appearances into existence, in the midst of which a new, transfiguring semblance is needed to hold fast within life the animated world of individuation. If you could imagine dissonance assuming human form—and what else is man?—this dissonance would need, to be able to live, a magnificent illusion which would spread a veil of beauty over its own nature. This is the true artistic aim of Apollo, in whose name we gather together all those countless illusions of beautiful semblance which, at every moment, make existence at all worth living at every moment and thereby urge us on to experience the next.

4. In sections that we have omitted, Nietzsche portrays the Greek philosopher Socrates (469–399 B.C.E.) as opposed to Dionysus and an ally of Euripides [editor's note].

5. In Wagner's opera *Siegfried* (1876) the hero slays a dragon (really the giant Fafner), kills the dwarf Mime, and awakens the heroine Brünnhilde despite the efforts of Wotan, chief of the gods, to block him [editor's note].

At the same time, only as much of that foundation of all existence, that Dionysiac underground of the world, can be permitted to enter an individual's consciousness as can be overcome, in its turn, by the Apolline power of transfiguration, so that both of these artistic drives are required to unfold their energies in strict, reciprocal proportion, according to the law of eternal justice. Where the Dionysiac powers rise up with such unbounded vigour as we are seeing at present, Apollo, too, must already have descended amongst us, concealed in a cloud, and his most abundant effects of beauty will surely be seen by a generation which comes after us.

That there is a need for this effect is a feeling which each of us would grasp intuitively, if he were ever to feel himself translated, even just in dream, back into the life of an ancient Hellene. As he wandered beneath rows of high, Ionic columns, gazing upwards to a horizon cut off by pure and noble lines, seeing beside him reflections of his own, transfigured form in luminous marble, surrounded by human beings who walk solemnly or move delicately, with harmonious sounds and a rhythmical language of gestures—would such a person, with all this beauty streaming in on him from all sides, not be bound to call out, as he raised a hand to Apollo: 'Blessed people of Hellas! How great must Dionysos be amongst you, if the God of Delos considers such acts of magic are needed to heal your dithyrambic[6] madness!' It is likely, however, that an aged Athenian would reply to a visitor in this mood, looking up at him with the sublime eye of Aeschylus: 'But say also this, curious stranger: how much did this people have to suffer in order that it might become so beautiful! But now follow me to the tragedy and sacrifice along with me in the temple of both deities!'

1872

6. Manifest in dithyrambs, choral poems originally sung in honor of Dionysus and later associated with highly excited music and impassioned language. Delos: Greek island in the Cyclades, site of an important oracle of Apollo [editor's note].

OSCAR WILDE
1854–1900

Oscar Wilde is known for his keen epigrammatic wit, dazzling skills in conversation, and scandalous homosexual behavior, which in 1895 led to his trial and imprisonment for sodomy. But Wilde was more than a brilliant—and tragic—cultural personality. He was a gifted, wonderfully entertaining, and disquieting writer, the author of an impressive body of work that includes the superb comedy *The Importance of Being Earnest*, the haunting novel *The Picture of Dorian Gray*, and sharp, suggestive critical essays.

Wilde was born in Dublin, Ireland. His father was a surgeon and respected author; his mother also wrote (both verse and prose). Educated in classics at Trinity College, Dublin, Wilde won a fellowship to Magdalen College, Oxford University. There he was influenced by the eminent art historian John Ruskin, WALTER PATER, and the Pre-Raphaelite brotherhood of English poets and painters. The young Wilde began to lead his life as if it were a work of art, to be crafted, cultivated, and made to sparkle. Defying orthodoxy and social convention, he was flamboyant and theatrical.

In 1881, at his own expense, Wilde published his first book, *Poems*, a promising but derivative volume that reflects the influence of Wilde's reading of John Keats (1795–1821), Algernon Swinburne (1837–1909), Pater, and the Pre-Raphaelites. In the following year, Wilde toured and lectured in the United States. It is said that on his arrival in New York City, when asked by customs officials if he had anything to declare, he replied, "Only my genius." Wilde was by now a leader of the aesthetic movement, which rallied around the dictum of "art for art's sake." His deliberate eccentricity and exuberant self-regard drew ridicule in the weekly comic periodical *Punch*, and he was parodied as Bunthorne in Gilbert and Sullivan's 1881 operetta *Patience*.

Though Wilde had (in the words of one recent scholar) "flirted" with homosexuality for a number of years, he married Constance Lloyd, daughter of a prominent Irish barrister, in 1884. For his two sons Wilde wrote stories—inspired by the Danish writer Hans Christian Andersen—included in *The Happy Prince and Other Tales* (1888) and *A House of Pomegranates* (1892). He also wrote reviews for the *Pall Mall Gazette* and, from 1887 to 1889, served as the editor of *Woman's World*, a popular periodical to which Constance also contributed articles on politics and women's issues.

In the early 1890s, Wilde hit his stride. *The Picture of Dorian Gray* appeared first in *Lippincott's Magazine* in 1890; the book, revised and expanded by six chapters, was published in 1891. It recounts the story of a beautiful young man who seems not to age but whose portrait becomes aged and ugly over time, the sign of his own corruption. In *Intentions* (1891), an important collection of essays, Wilde presented his keen and audacious views on literature, art, and criticism; and in *Collected Poems* (1892), he gathered his verse. Originally Wilde had hoped to center his literary career in poetry, but his greatest success was as a comic and satiric dramatist. His plays include *Lady Windemere's Fan* (1892); *A Woman of No Importance* (1893); *An Ideal Husband* (1895); and, above all, *The Importance of Being Earnest* (1895), which describes the courtships and betrothals of two young men-about-town who are leading double lives. Wilde also wrote the historical tragedies *The Duchess of Padua* (1892) and *Salomé* (1893); the latter, about the woman who danced before Herod and afterward demanded the head of John the Baptist, was written in French and then published in an English translation (1894) that included eerie, erotic illustrations by Aubrey Beardsley.

Wilde's pleasure in titillating and unnerving his audiences and readers resulted in many striking witticisms, such as Cecily's reproach in *The Importance of Being Earnest*: "I hope you have not been leading a double life, pretending to be wicked and being really good all the time. That would be hypocrisy." Yet in his own way, Wilde was deeply serious and morally earnest. A critic of middle-class Philistine smugness and moral complacency, he too wanted greater opportunity—though more than MATTHEW ARNOLD would have accepted—for freedom of expression and dissent, for the right to contest the status quo.

In one of his lectures in America, Wilde had declared, "To disagree with three fourths of all England on all points of view is one of the first elements of sanity." But in 1895 Wilde discovered that social and moral convention could be relentlessly punitive. When the marquess of Queensberry, the father of Wilde's lover, Lord Alfred Douglas, left a card at his club addressed "To Oscar Wilde, posing as a sodomite," Wilde unsuccessfully sued for libel—and then was himself arrested for violating the law forbidding "indecencies between grown-up men, in public or private." Wilde was found guilty and sentenced to two years' imprisonment at hard labor.

After his release in May 1897, Wilde—divorced, broken, bankrupt, and disgraced—left for France, calling himself "Sebastian Melmoth" ("Sebastian" after the Christian martyred by arrows in early-fourth-century Rome, and "Melmoth" after the doomed hero of Charles Maturin's 1820 Gothic novel *Melmoth the Wanderer*). Wilde spent the rest of his life as an exile in Europe, recovering enough focus as a writer to tell of his painful prison experiences in *The Ballad of Reading Gaol* (1898). He died in Paris in November 1900, having remarked, "If I were to survive into the twentieth century, it would be more than the English people could bear." *De Profundis* ("out of the depths," the first two words of the Latin version of Psalm 130), both a book-length letter of reproach to Lord Alfred and a personal testament, was published in 1905. His self-judgment in this text is unsparing, as he declares: "Terrible as was what the world did to me, what I did to myself was far more terrible still."

In the preface to *The Picture of Dorian Gray*, our first selection, Wilde sketches his position on art and morality in a sequence of aphorisms. Authentic artists, says Wilde, concern themselves with style and form, with the adroit handling of the artistic medium and the shaping of beautiful works. Morality, he explains, is not a matter of an artist's or writer's message; it instead rests in how well he or she has executed an aesthetic task. Wilde revises Arnold's statement that critics should be devoted to the best that has been thought and said by maintaining that the best is the most beautiful, whose nature is ultimately formal and stylistic rather than ethical. Wilde provokes us by concluding, "All art is quite useless."

In "The Critic as Artist" (1890, 1891), a brisk, pointed dialogue on the nature of, and relationship between, the arts and criticism, Wilde expands on and develops the claims he advanced in the preface. His mouthpiece Gilbert not only celebrates criticism in its own right but asserts and praises its superiority over so-called creative or primary literary and artistic work. Throughout, Wilde emphasizes and honors style, form, and self-conscious craft; in an anti-Romantic thrust, he devalues inspiration. He is antihistorical as well, opposed to history because of (and here he echoes RALPH WALDO EMERSON) the constraints that it imposes on individual expression.

"The details of history," according to Gilbert in part 1, "are always wearisome." Criticism "is more fascinating than history," for it "is concerned simply with oneself": it is a type of autobiography and impressionism. As Gilbert's comments on Ruskin and Pater indicate, for Wilde it does not matter whether the creative critic is faithful to the work of art: accurate statements about an aesthetic object or the artist's intentions count less than the critical essay's status as an independent work of art. In part 2, Wilde qualifies and complicates this position; for example, in his references to Shakespeare he concedes that historical study is important after all. But he continues to stress that "the highest Criticism, being the purest form of personal impression, is, in its way, more creative than creation."

Wilde is not an especially original thinker. He draws on nineteenth-century French and English authors, including the poet-critic THÉOPHILE GAUTIER, the novelist Joris-Karl Huysman, CHARLES BAUDELAIRE, and Pater. The concept of "art for art's sake" was in fact proposed by Gautier, in the preface to *Mademoiselle de Maupin* (1835), where he affirmed: "Les choses sont belles en proportion inverse de leur utilité" (Things are beautiful in inverse proportion to their usefulness). Sometimes, Wilde's cool, canny ironies can feel predictable, produced on cue and according to formula. There is a measure of truth to the complaint of the American cultural critic H. L. Mencken (1880–1956) that in his endless flaunting of paradoxes, Wilde can be as insufferable as an overpious preacher.

On the other hand, Wilde's epigrams and arguments at their best are compelling, and in recent years his life has drawn equal interest. Literary critics and theorists and scholars in gender and gay and lesbian studies have since the 1980s devoted countless books and essays to Wilde's writings and extraordinary and aggrieved life. Even earlier, critics including NORTHROP FRYE and HAROLD BLOOM praised him extravagantly; Frye, in *Creation and Recreation* (1980), portrayed Wilde as a theorist of the imagination equal in significance to the revolutionary painter and poet William Blake (1757–1827). Like Blake, and like the later Romantics PERCY BYSSHE SHELLEY and Emerson, Wilde contends that great writers and artists give structure to life through the power of their enlightened vision. Indeed, for him the terms and values of art themselves constitute life. Nature, Wilde maintained, "is our creation. . . . Things are because we see them." The result of critical inquiry is not truth, but an interpretation—or rather a series of misinterpretations, of misreadings, since we do not (and never will) possess an objectively known reality with which we could appraise and firmly decide among conflicting views.

This line of argument gives us a Wilde less akin to Pater than to the German philosopher FRIEDRICH NIETZSCHE, the Nietzsche of *The Will to Power* (1901) in particular: "It is our needs that interpret the world; our drives and their For and Against. Every drive is a kind of lust to rule; each one has its perspective that it would like to compel all the other drives to accept as a norm." Wilde lacks this tone of grim intensity, but his elegantly articulated ideas imply the consequences that Nietzsche and later authors have expressed.

BIBLIOGRAPHY

Wilde's *Complete Works* were published in twelve volumes in 1923. *The Complete Works of Oscar Wilde*, edited by Bobby Fong and Karl Beckson, is now being published by Oxford University Press; volume 1, *Poems and Poems in Prose*, appeared in 1999. There are a number of one-volume collections, including *Oscar Wilde: Selected Writings*, edited by Richard Ellmann (1961), and *Selected Writings of Oscar Wilde*, edited by Russell Fraser (1969). The best, because it is annotated, is *Oscar Wilde*, edited by Isobel Murray (1989). For the correspondence, see the volumes edited by Rupert Hart-Davis, *Letters* (1962) and *More Letters* (1985). For his literary criticism, consult *Literary Criticism of Oscar Wilde*, edited by Stanley Weintraub (1968), and *The Artist as Critic: Critical Writings of Oscar Wilde*, edited by Richard Ellmann (1969).

Biographies include Hesketh Pearson, *The Life of Oscar Wilde* (1946), a good overview of Wilde's career that deals well with his shift from poetry to fiction and drama, and Richard Ellmann, *Oscar Wilde* (1988), a major study, especially in its account of Wilde's early life and his response to John Ruskin, Walter Pater, Henry James, and contemporary French writers. Vyvyan Holland, *Oscar Wilde: A Pictorial Biography* (1960), is also valuable. H. Montgomery Hyde has edited *The Trials of Oscar Wilde* (1948); see also Hyde's *The Three Trials of Oscar Wilde* (1956) and *Oscar Wilde in Prison* (1956). Other resources include *Oscar Wilde: Interviews and Recollections*, edited by E. H. Mikhail (2 vols., 1979); *Oscar Wilde's Oxford Notebooks*, edited by Philip E. Smith II and Michael S. Helfand (1989); and Norman Page, *An Oscar Wilde Chronology* (1991).

Collections surveying the critical and scholarly response to Wilde include *Oscar Wilde: A Collection of Critical Essays*, edited by Richard Ellmann (1969); *Oscar Wilde: The Critical Heritage*, edited by Karl Beckson (1970); *Critical Essays on Oscar Wilde*, edited by Regenia Gagnier (1991); and *Oscar Wilde: A Collection of Critical Essays*, edited by Jonathan Freedman (1996).

Lawrence Danson, *Wilde's Intentions: The Artist in His Criticism* (1997), is an excellent treatment of Wilde's views on literature and criticism. A number of studies in the 1990s have focused on the social, sexual, and cultural issues that Wilde's life and, especially, his trial and imprisonment dramatize. Among these are Eve Kosofsky Sedgwick, *Epistemology of the Closet* (1990); Patricia Flanagan Behrendt, *Oscar Wilde: Eros and Aesthetics* (1991); Ed Cohen, *Talk on the Wilde Side: Toward a Genealogy of a Discourse on Male Sexualities* (1993); Melissa Knox, *Oscar Wilde: A Long and Lovely Suicide* (1994); Gary Schmidgall, *The Stranger Wilde: Interpreting Oscar* (1994); Alan Sinfield, *The Wilde Century: Effeminacy, Oscar Wilde, and the Queer Moment* (1994); and John Stokes, *Oscar Wilde: Myths, Miracles, and Imitations* (1996). Julia Prewitt Brown, *Cosmopolitan Criticism: Oscar Wilde's Philosophy of Art* (1997), deals succinctly with Wilde's aesthetic theory and its influence on later writers. Michael S. Foldy, *Trials of Oscar Wilde: Deviance, Morality, and Late-Victorian Society* (1998), describes the range of threats (including, but not limited to, deviant sexuality) that English society associated with Wilde. *Wilde the Irishman*, edited by Jerusha McCormack (1998), deals with the Irish dimension of Wilde's work and with the responses to Wilde by poets, playwrights, sculptors, and others. See also Bruce Bashford, *Oscar Wilde: The Critic as Humanist* (1999). Reference works include Stuart Mason, *Bibliography of Oscar Wilde* (1914); Thomas A. Mikolyzk, *Oscar Wilde: An Annotated Bibliography* (1993); Ian Small, *Oscar Wilde Revalued: An Essay on New Materials and Methods of Research* (1993); and Karl Beckson, *The Oscar Wilde Encyclopedia* (1998).

Preface to *The Picture of Dorian Gray*

The artist is the creator of beautiful things.

To reveal art and conceal the artist is art's aim. The critic is he who can translate into another manner or a new material his impression of beautiful things.

The highest as the lowest form of criticism is a mode of autobiography. Those who find ugly meanings in beautiful things are corrupt without being charming. This is a fault.

Those who find beautiful meanings in beautiful things are the cultivated. For these there is hope.

They are the elect to whom beautiful things mean only Beauty.

There is no such thing as a moral or an immoral book. Books are well written, or badly written. That is all.

The nineteenth century dislike of Realism is the rage of Caliban seeing his own face in a glass.[1]

The nineteenth century dislike of Romanticism is the rage of Caliban not seeing his own face in a glass.

The moral life of man forms part of the subject-matter of the artist, but the morality of art consists in the perfect use of an imperfect medium.

No artist desires to prove anything. Even things that are true can be proved.

No artist has ethical sympathies. An ethical sympathy in an artist is an unpardonable mannerism of style.

No artist is ever morbid. The artist can express everything.

Thought and language are to the artist instruments of an art.

Vice and virtue are to the artist materials for an art.

From the point of view of form, the type of all the arts is the art of the musician. From the point of view of feeling, the actor's craft is the type.

All art is at once surface and symbol.

Those who go beneath the surface do so at their peril.

Those who read the symbol do so at their peril.

It is the spectator, and not life, that art really mirrors.

Diversity of opinion about a work of art shows that the work is new, complex, and vital.

When critics disagree the artist is in accord with himself.

We can forgive a man for making a useful thing as long as he does not admire it. The only excuse for making a useless thing is that one admires it intensely.

All art is quite useless.

1891

1. Mirror. Caliban: half-human slave of Prospero in Shakespeare's play *The Tempest* (1611).

From The Critic as Artist[1]

From *Part 1*

* * *

Ernest. * * * I am quite ready to admit that I was wrong in what I said about the Greeks. They were, as you have pointed out, a nation of art critics. I acknowledge it, and I feel a little sorry for them. For the creative faculty is higher than the critical. There is really no comparison between them.

Gilbert. The antithesis between them is entirely arbitrary. Without the critical faculty, there is no artistic creation at all worthy of the name. You spoke a little while ago of that fine spirit of choice and delicate instinct of selection by which the artist realises life for us, and gives to it a momentary perfection. Well, that spirit of choice, that subtle tact of omission, is really the critical faculty in one of its most characteristic moods, and no one who does not possess this critical faculty can create anything at all in art. Arnold's definition of literature as a criticism of life,[2] was not very felicitous in form, but it showed how keenly he recognised the importance of the critical element in all creative work.

Ernest. I should have said that great artists worked unconsciously, that they were "wiser than they knew," as, I think, Emerson remarks somewhere.[3]

Gilbert. It is really not so, Ernest. All fine imaginative work is self-conscious and deliberate. No poet sings because he must sing. At least, no great poet does. A great poet sings because he chooses to sing. It is so now, and it has always been so. We are sometimes apt to think that the voices that sounded at the dawn of poetry were simpler, fresher, and more natural than ours, and that the world which the early poets looked at, and through which they walked, had a kind of poetical quality of its own, and almost without changing could pass into song. The snow lies thick now upon Olympus, and its steep, scarped sides are bleak and barren, but once, we fancy, the white feet of the Muses brushed the dew from the anemones in the morning, and at evening came Apollo[4] to sing to the shepherds in the vale. But in this we are merely lending to other ages what we desire, or think we desire, for our own. Our historical sense is at fault. Every century that produces poetry is, so far, an artificial century, and the work that seems to us to be the most natural and simple product of its time is always the result of the most self-conscious effort. Believe me, Ernest, there is no fine art without self-consciousness, and self-consciousness and the critical spirit are one.

Ernest. I see what you mean, and there is much in it. But surely you would admit that the great poems of the early world, the primitive, anonymous collective poems, were the result of the imagination of races, rather than of the imagination of individuals?

1. Originally titled "The True Function and Value of Criticism, with Some Remarks on the Importance of Doing Nothing." For his book *Intentions* (1891), Wilde retitled and revised the text.
2. Often in "The Critic as Artist," Wilde alludes or responds directly to MATTHEW ARNOLD's views on literature and criticism in *Essays in Criticism: First Series* (1865), in particular "The Function of Criticism at the Present Time" (see above).
3. See "The Over-Soul" and "Compensation," both in *Essays: First Series* (1841), by RALPH WALDO EMERSON (1803–1882).
4. The Greek god of prophecy, music, and poetry. Olympus: mountain range in northern Greece and home of the Greek gods. Muses: in Greek mythology, the 9 daughters of memory; they presided over the arts and sciences.

Gilbert. Not when they became poetry. Not when they received a beautiful form. For there is no art where there is no style, and no style where there is no unity, and unity is of the individual. No doubt Homer had old ballads and stories to deal with, as Shakespeare had chronicles and plays and novels from which to work, but they were merely his rough material. He took them and shaped them into song. They became his, because he made them lovely. They were built out of music,

> And so not built at all,
> And therefore built for ever.[5]

The longer one studies life and literature, the more strongly one feels that behind everything that is wonderful stands the individual, and that it is not the moment that makes the man, but the man who creates the age. Indeed, I am inclined to think that each myth and legend that seems to us to spring out of the wonder, or terror, or fancy of tribe and nation, was in its origin the invention of one single mind. The curiously limited number of the myths seems to me to point to this conclusion. But we must not go off into questions of comparative mythology. We must keep to criticism. And what I want to point out is this. An age that has no criticism is either an age in which art is immobile, hieratic, and confined to the reproduction of formal types, or an age that possesses no art at all. There have been critical ages that have not been creative, in the ordinary sense of the word, ages in which the spirit of man has sought to set in order the treasures of his treasure-house, to separate the gold from the silver, and the silver from the lead, to count over the jewels, and to give names to the pearls. But there has never been a creative age that has not been critical also. For it is the critical faculty that invents fresh forms. The tendency of creation is to repeat itself. It is to the critical instinct that we owe each new school that springs up, each new mould that art finds ready to its hand. There is really not a single form that art now uses that does not come to us from the critical spirit of Alexandria,[6] where these forms were either stereotyped, or invented, or made perfect. I say Alexandria, not merely because it was there that the Greek spirit became most self-conscious, and indeed ultimately expired in scepticism and theology, but because it was to that city, and not to Athens, that Rome turned for her models, and it was through the survival, such as it was, of the Latin language that culture lived at all. When, at the Renaissance, Greek literature dawned upon Europe, the soil had been in some measure prepared for it. But to get rid of the details of history, which are always wearisome, and usually inaccurate, let us say generally that the forms of art have been due to the Greek critical spirit. To it we owe the epic, the lyric, the entire drama in every one of its developments, including burlesque, the idyll, the romantic novel, the novel of adventure, the essay, the dialogue, the oration, the lecture, for which perhaps we should not forgive them, and the epigram, in all the wide meaning of that word. In fact, we owe it everything, except the sonnet, to which, however, some curious parallels of thought

5. Slightly misquoting Alfred, Lord Tennyson, *Idylls of the King* (1859–85), "Gareth and Lynette," lines 272–74.
6. City and major seaport in northern Egypt. Founded by Alexander the Great after he conquered Egypt in 331 B.C.E., it was the center of Hellenistic commerce and learning, with a great university and two royal libraries.

movement may be traced in the Anthology,[7] American journalism, to which no parallel can be found anywhere, and the ballad in sham Scotch dialect, which one of our most industrious writers[8] has recently proposed should be made the basis for a final and unanimous effort on the part of our second-rate poets to make themselves really romantic. Each new school, as it appears, cries out against criticism, but it is to the critical faculty in man that it owes its origin. The mere creative instinct does not innovate, but reproduces.

Ernest. You have been talking of criticism as an essential part of the creative spirit, and I now fully accept your theory. But what of criticism outside creation? I have a foolish habit of reading periodicals, and it seems to me that most modern criticism is perfectly valueless.

Gilbert. So is most modern creative work, also. Mediocrity weighing mediocrity in the balance, and incompetence applauding its brother—that is the spectacle which the artistic activity of England affords us from time to time. And yet, I feel I am a little unfair in this matter. As a rule, the critics—I speak, of course, of the higher class, of those, in fact, who write for the sixpenny papers—are far more cultured than the people whose work they are called upon to review. This is, indeed, only what one would expect, for criticism demands infinitely more cultivation than creation does.

Ernest. Really?

Gilbert. Certainly. Anybody can write a three-volumed novel.[9] It merely requires a complete ignorance of both life and literature. The difficulty that I should fancy the reviewer feels is the difficulty of sustaining any standard. Where there is no style a standard must be impossible. The poor reviewers are apparently reduced to be the reporters of the police court of literature, the chroniclers of the doings of the habitual criminals of art. It is sometimes said of them that they do not read all through the works they are called upon to criticise. They do not. Or at least they should not. If they did so, they would become confirmed misanthropes; or, if I may borrow a phrase from one of the pretty Newnham graduates, confirmed womanthropes[1] for the rest of their lives. Nor is it necessary. To know the vintage and quality of a wine one need not drink the whole cask. It must be perfectly easy in half an hour to say whether a book is worth anything or worth nothing. Ten minutes are really sufficient, if one has the instinct for form. Who wants to wade through a dull volume? One tastes it, and that is quite enough—more than enough, I should imagine. I am aware that there are many honest workers in painting as well as in literature who object to criticism entirely. They are quite right. Their work stands in no intellectual relation to their age. It brings us no new element of pleasure. It suggests no fresh departure of thought, or passion, or beauty. It should not be spoken of. It should be left to the oblivion that it deserves.

Ernest. But, my dear fellow—excuse me for interrupting you—you seem to me to be allowing your passion for criticism to lead you a great deal too

7. The Greek or Palatine Anthology, a collection of Greek epigrams (some from as early as the 7th c. B.C.E.) compiled ca. 980 C.E.

8. William Sharp (1855–1905), Scottish writer whose works (written under the name Fiona Macleod) include mystic Celtic tales and romances of peasant life.

9. Standard length of Victorian novels.

1. A nonsensical coinage meaning "woman-haters." Newnham College: the second of the colleges for women in Cambridge (founded in 1871; women initially did not follow the university curriculum and were not granted Cambridge degrees for another half century).

far. For, after all, even you must admit that it is much more difficult to do a thing than to talk about it.

Gilbert. More difficult to do a thing than to talk about it? Not at all. That is a gross popular error. It is very much more difficult to talk about a thing than to do it. In the sphere of actual life that is, of course, obvious. Anybody can make history. Only a great man can write it. There is no mode of action, no form of emotion, that we do not share with the lower animals. It is only by language that we rise above them, or above each other—by language, which is the parent, and not the child, of thought. Action, indeed, is always easy, and when presented to us in its most aggravated, because most continuous form, which I take to be that of real industry, becomes simply the refuge of people who have nothing whatsoever to do. No, Ernest, don't talk about action. It is a blind thing, dependent on external influences, and moved by an impulse of whose nature it is unconscious. It is a thing incomplete in its essence, because limited by accident, and ignorant of its direction, being always at variance with its aim. Its basis is the lack of imagination. It is the last resource of those who know not how to dream.

Ernest. Gilbert, you treat the world as if it were a crystal ball. You hold it in your hand, and reverse it to please a wilful fancy. You do nothing but rewrite history.

Gilbert. The one duty we owe to history is to rewrite it. That is not the least of the tasks in store for the critical spirit. When we have fully discovered the scientific laws that govern life we shall realise that the one person who has more illusions than the dreamer is the man of action. He, indeed, knows neither the origin of his deeds nor their results. From the field in which he thought that he had sown thorns we have gathered our vintage, and the fig-tree that he planted for our pleasure is as barren as the thistle, and more bitter.[2] It is because Humanity has never known where it was going that it has been able to find its way.

Ernest. You think, then, that in the sphere of action a conscious aim is a delusion?

Gilbert. It is worse than a delusion. If we lived long enough to see the results of our actions, it may be that those who call themselves good would be sickened with a dull remorse, and those whom the world calls evil stirred by a noble joy. Each little thing that we do passes into the great machine of life, which may grind our virtues to powder and make them worthless, or transform our sins into elements of a new civilisation, more marvellous and more splendid than any that has gone before. * * *

Ernest. * * * But surely, the higher you place the creative artist, the lower must the critic rank.

Gilbert. Why so?

Ernest. Because the best that he can give us will be but an echo of rich music, a dim shadow of clear-outlined form. It may, indeed, be that life is chaos, as you tell me that it is; that its martyrdoms are mean and its heroisms ignoble; and that it is the function of Literature to create, from the rough material of actual existence, a new world that will be more marvellous, more enduring, and more true than the world that common eyes look upon, and through which common natures seek to realise their perfection. But surely,

2. See Matthew 7.16: "Do men gather grapes of thorns, or figs of thistles?"

if this new world has been made by the spirit and touch of a great artist, it will be a thing so complete and perfect that there will be nothing left for the critic to do. I quite understand now, and indeed admit most readily, that it is far more difficult to talk about a thing than to do it. But it seems to me that this sound and sensible maxim, which is really extremely soothing to one's feelings, and should be adopted as its motto by every Academy of Literature all over the world, applies only to the relations that exist between Art and Life, and not to any relations that there may be between Art and Criticism.

Gilbert. But, surely, Criticism is itself an art. And just as artistic creation implies the working of the critical faculty, and, indeed, without it cannot be said to exist at all, so Criticism is really creative in the highest sense of the word. Criticism is, in fact, both creative and independent.

Ernest. Independent?

Gilbert. Yes; independent. Criticism is no more to be judged by any low standard of imitation or resemblance than is the work of poet or sculptor. The critic occupies the same relation to the work of art that he criticises as the artist does to the visible world of form and colour, or the unseen world of passion and of thought. He does not even require for the perfection of his art the finest materials. Anything will serve his purpose. And just as out of the sordid and sentimental amours of the silly wife of a small country doctor in the squalid village of Yonville-l'Abbaye, near Rouen, Gustave Flaubert[3] was able to create a classic, and make a masterpiece of style, so from subjects of little or of no importance, such as the pictures in this year's Royal Academy, or in any year's Royal Academy, for that matter, Mr. Lewis Morris's poems, M. Ohnet's novels, or the plays of Mr. Henry Arthur Jones,[4] the true critic can, if it be his pleasure so to direct or waste his faculty of contemplation, produce work that will be flawless in beauty and instinct with intellectual subtlety. Why not? Dulness is always an irresistible temptation for brilliancy, and stupidity is the permanent *Bestia Trionfans*[5] that calls wisdom from its cave. To an artist so creative as the critic, what does subject-matter signify? No more and no less than it does to the novelist and the painter. Like them, he can find his motives everywhere. Treatment is the test. There is nothing that has not in it suggestion or challenge.

Ernest. But is Criticism really a creative art?

Gilbert. Why should it not be? It works with materials, and puts them into a form that is at once new and delightful. What more can one say of poetry? Indeed, I would call criticism a creation within a creation. For just as the great artists, from Homer and Æschylus, down to Shakespeare and Keats,[6] did not go directly to life for their subject-matter, but sought for it in myth, and legend, and ancient tale, so the critic deals with materials that others have, as it were, purified for him, and to which imaginative form and colour have been already added. Nay, more, I would say that the highest Criticism,

3. French novelist (1821–1880); the "amours" are treated in *Madame Bovary* (1856).

4. English dramatist (1851–1929). Morris (1833–1907), Welsh poet, essayist, and barrister. Georges Ohnet (1848–1918), French novelist and dramatist.

5. Triumphant Beast (Italian); the reference is to *Spaccio della bestia Trionfante* (1584, *Expulsion of the Triumphant Beast*), a philosophical allegory by the Italian scientist and philosopher Giordano Bruno.

6. John Keats (1795–1821), English Romantic poet; roughly 2 centuries separated his works from those of Shakespeare, and the tragedies of Aeschylus (525–456 B.C.E.) from the epics of Homer.

being the purest form of personal impression, is, in its way, more creative than creation, as it has least reference to any standard external to itself, and is, in fact, its own reason for existing, and, as the Greeks would put it, in itself, and to itself, an end. Certainly, it is never trammelled by any shackles of verisimilitude. No ignoble considerations of probability, that cowardly concession to the tedious repetitions of domestic or public life, affect it ever. One may appeal from fiction unto fact. But from the soul there is no appeal.

Ernest. From the soul?

Gilbert. Yes, from the soul. That is what the highest Criticism really is, the record of one's own soul. It is more fascinating than history, as it is concerned simply with oneself. It is more delightful than philosophy, as its subject is concrete and not abstract, real and not vague. It is the only civilised form of autobiography, as it deals not with the events, but with the thoughts of one's life; not with life's physical accidents of deed or circumstance, but with the spiritual moods and imaginative passions of the mind. I am always amused by the silly vanity of those writers and artists of our day who seem to imagine that the primary function of the critic is to chatter about their second-rate work. The best that one can say of most modern creative art is that it is just a little less vulgar than reality, and so the critic, with his fine sense of distinction and sure instinct of delicate refinement, will prefer to look into the silver mirror or through the woven veil, and will turn his eyes away from the chaos and clamour of actual existence, though the mirror be tarnished and the veil be torn. His sole aim is to chronicle his own impressions. It is for him that pictures are painted, books written, and marble hewn into form.

Ernest. I seem to have heard another theory of Criticism.

Gilbert. Yes: it has been said by one whose gracious memory we all revere, and the music of whose pipe once lured Proserpina from her Sicilian fields, and made those white feet stir, and not in vain, the Cumnor cowslips, that the proper aim of Criticism is to see the object as in itself it really is.[7] But this is a very serious error, and takes no cognisance of Criticism's most perfect form, which is in its essence purely subjective, and seeks to reveal its own secret and not the secret of another. For the highest Criticism deals with art not as expressive, but as impressive, purely.

Ernest. But is that really so?

Gilbert. Of course it is. Who cares whether Mr. Ruskin's views on Turner[8] are sound or not? What does it matter? That mighty and majestic prose of his, so fervid and so fiery-coloured in its noble eloquence, so rich in its elaborate, symphonic music, so sure and certain, at its best, in subtle choice of word and epithet, is at least as great a work of art as any of those wonderful sunsets that bleach or rot on their corrupted canvases in England's Gallery;[9] greater, indeed, one is apt to think at times, not merely because its equal beauty is more enduring, but on account of the fuller variety of its appeal, soul speaking to soul in those long-cadenced lines, not through form and colour alone, though through these, indeed, completely and without loss,

7. Matthew Arnold defines the "aim of criticism" in "The Function of Criticism at the Present Time" (1864, 1865). In his poem "Thyrsis" (1866), Arnold says that he would supplicate Proserpina, the goddess of fertility and queen of the underworld, "in vain"; for while she knows Sicily well, she does not know the "Cumnor cowslips," near Oxford.

8. The painter J. M. W. Turner (1775–1851), passionately defended by the English writer, reformer, and art critic John Ruskin (1819–1900).

9. The National Gallery, in London.

but with intellectual and emotional utterance, with lofty passion and with loftier thought, with imaginative insight, and with poetic aim; greater, I always think, even as Literature is the greater art. Who, again, cares whether Mr. Pater has put into the portrait of Monna Lisa[1] something that Lionardo never dreamed of? The painter may have been merely the slave of an archaic smile, as some have fancied, but whenever I pass into the cool galleries of the Palace of the Louvre, and stand before that strange figure "set in its marble chair in that cirque of fantastic rocks, as in some faint light under sea," I murmur to myself, "She is older than the rocks among which she sits; like the vampire, she has been dead many times, and learned the secrets of the grave; and has been a diver in deep seas, and keeps their fallen day about her; and trafficked for strange webs with Eastern merchants; and, as Leda, was the mother of Helen of Troy, and, as St. Anne, the mother of Mary; and all this has been to her but as the sound of lyres and flutes, and lives only in the delicacy with which it has moulded the changing lineaments, and tinged the eyelids and the hands." And I say to my friend, "The presence that thus so strangely rose beside the waters is expressive of what in the ways of a thousand years man had come to desire"; and he answers me, "Hers is the head upon which all 'the ends of the world are come,' and the eyelids are a little weary."

And so the picture becomes more wonderful to us than it really is, and reveals to us a secret of which, in truth, it knows nothing, and the music of the mystical prose is as sweet in our ears as was that flute-player's music that lent to the lips of La Gioconda[2] those subtle and poisonous curves. Do you ask me what Lionardo would have said had any one told him of this picture that "all the thoughts and experience of the world had etched and moulded there in that which they had of power to refine and make expressive the outward form, the animalism of Greece, the lust of Rome, the reverie of the Middle Age with its spiritual ambition and imaginative loves, the return of the Pagan world, the sins of the Borgias?"[3] He would probably have answered that he had contemplated none of these things, but had concerned himself simply with certain arrangements of lines and masses, and with new and curious colour-harmonies of blue and green. And it is for this very reason that the criticism which I have quoted is criticism of the highest kind. It treats the work of art simply as a starting-point for a new creation. It does not confine itself—let us at least suppose so for the moment—to discovering the real intention of the artist and accepting that as final. And in this it is right, for the meaning of any beautiful created thing is, at least, as much in the soul of him who looks at it as it was in his soul who wrought it. Nay, it is rather the beholder who lends to the beautiful thing its myriad meanings, and makes it marvellous for us, and sets it in some new relation to the age, so that it becomes a vital portion of our lives, and a symbol of what we pray for, or perhaps of what, having prayed for, we fear that we may receive. The longer I study, Ernest, the more clearly I see that the beauty of the visible arts is, as the beauty of music, impressive primarily, and that it may be

1. In the essay on Leonardo da Vinci included in *Studies in the History of the Renaissance* (1873), by WALTER PATER (1839–1894); Gilbert then quotes Pater.

2. The subject of Leonardo's painting was the wife of Francesco del Gioconda; thus, the *Mona Lisa* is sometimes referred to as *La Gioconda*.

3. An Italian family, influential from the 14th to the 16th century, that included religious, military, and political leaders and patrons of the arts; they were notorious for their ruthlessness and greed.

marred, and indeed often is so, by any excess of intellectual intention on the part of the artist. For when the work is finished it has, as it were, an independent life of its own, and may deliver a message far other than that which was put into its lips to say. Sometimes, when I listen to the overture of *Tannhäuser*,[4] I seem indeed to see that comely knight treading delicately on the flower-strewn grass, and to hear the voice of Venus calling to him from the caverned hill. But at other times it speaks to me of a thousand different things, of myself, it may be, and my own life, or of the lives of others whom one has loved and grown weary of loving, or of the passions that man has known, or of the passions that man has not known, and so has sought for. To-night it may fill one with that *ΕΡΩΣ ΤΩΝ ΑΔΥΝΑΤΩΝ*, that *Amour de l'Impossible*,[5] which falls like a madness on many who think they live securely and out of reach of harm, so that they sicken suddenly with the poison of unlimited desire and, in the infinite pursuit of what they may not obtain, grow faint and swoon or stumble. To-morrow, like the music of which Aristotle and Plato tell us, the noble Dorian music[6] of the Greek, it may perform the office of a physician, and give us an anodyne against pain, and heal the spirit that is wounded, and "bring the soul into harmony with all right things." And what is true about music is true about all the arts. Beauty has as many meanings as man has moods. Beauty is the symbol of symbols. Beauty reveals everything, because it expresses nothing. When it shows us itself it shows us the whole fiery-coloured world.

Ernest. But is such work as you have talked about really criticism?

Gilbert. It is the highest Criticism, for it criticises not merely the individual work of art, but Beauty itself, and fills with wonder a form which the artist may have left void, or not understood, or understood incompletely.

Ernest. The highest Criticism, then, is more creative than creation, and the primary aim of the critic is to see the object as in itself it really is not; that is your theory, I believe?

Gilbert. Yes, that is my theory. To the critic the work of art is simply a suggestion for a new work of his own, that need not necessarily bear any obvious resemblance to the thing it criticises. The one characteristic of a beautiful form is that one can put into it whatever one wishes, and see in it whatever one chooses to see; and the Beauty, that gives to creation its universal and æsthetic element, makes the critic a creator in his turn, and whispers of a thousand different things which were not present in the mind of him who carved the statue or painted the panel or graved the gem.

It is sometimes said by those who understand neither the nature of the highest Criticism nor the charm of the highest Art, that the pictures that the critic loves most to write about are those that belong to the anecdotage of painting, and that deal with scenes taken out of literature or history. But this is not so. Indeed, pictures of this kind are far too intelligible. As a class, they rank with illustrations, and, even considered from this point of view, are failures, as they do not stir the imagination, but set definite bounds to it. For the domain of the painter is, as I suggested before, widely different from that

4. An 1845 opera by the German composer Richard Wagner, which describes the legendary relationship between the 14th-century German poet of the title and Venus, Roman goddess of love.
5. The Greek and French phrases both mean "love of the impossible."
6. Restrained and simple music associated with the Dorians, the last of the northern invaders of Greece (ca. 11th c. B.C.E.). On the Greek philosophers PLATO (ca. 427–347 B.C.E.) and ARISTOTLE (384–322 B.C.E.), see above.

of the poet. To the latter belongs life in its full and absolute entirety; not merely the beauty that men look at, but the beauty that men listen to also; not merely the momentary grace of form or the transient gladness of colour, but the whole sphere of feeling, the perfect cycle of thought. The painter is so far limited that it is only through the mask of the body that he can show us the mystery of the soul; only through conventional images that he can handle ideas; only through its physical equivalents that he can deal with psychology. And how inadequately does he do it then, asking us to accept the torn turban of the Moor for the noble rage of Othello, or a dotard in a storm for the wild madness of Lear! Yet it seems as if nothing could stop him. Most of our elderly English painters spend their wicked and wasted lives in poaching upon the domain of the poets, marring their motives by clumsy treatment, and striving to render, by visible form or colour, the marvel of what is invisible, the splendour of what is not seen. Their pictures are, as a natural consequence, insufferably tedious. They have degraded the visible arts into the obvious arts, and the one thing not worth looking at is the obvious. I do not say that poet and painter may not treat of the same subject. They have always done so, and will always do so. But while the poet can be pictorial or not, as he chooses, the painter must be pictorial always. For a painter is limited, not to what he sees in nature, but to what upon canvas may be seen.

And so, my dear Ernest, pictures of this kind will not really fascinate the critic. He will turn from them to such works as make him brood and dream and fancy, to works that possess the subtle quality of suggestion, and seem to tell one that even from them there is an escape into a wider world. It is sometimes said that the tragedy of an artist's life is that he cannot realise his ideal. But the true tragedy that dogs the steps of most artists is that they realise their ideal too absolutely. For, when the ideal is realised, it is robbed of its wonder and its mystery, and becomes simply a new starting point for an ideal that is other than itself. This is the reason why music is the perfect type of art. Music can never reveal its ultimate secret. This, also, is the explanation of the value of limitations in art. The sculptor gladly surrenders imitative colour, and the painter the actual dimensions of form, because by such renunciations they are able to avoid too definite a presentation of the Real, which would be mere imitation, and too definite a realisation of the Ideal, which would be too purely intellectual. It is through its very incompleteness that Art becomes complete in beauty, and so addresses itself, not to the faculty of recognition nor to the faculty of reason, but to the æsthetic sense alone, which, while accepting both reason and recognition as stages of apprehension, subordinates them both to a pure synthetic impression of the work of art as a whole, and, taking whatever alien emotional elements the work may possess, uses their very complexity as a means by which a richer unity may be added to the ultimate impression itself. You see, then, how it is that the æsthetic critic rejects those obvious modes of art that have but one message to deliver, and having delivered it becomes dumb and sterile, and seeks rather for such modes as suggest reverie and mood, and by their imaginative beauty make all interpretations true and no interpretation final. Some resemblance, no doubt, the creative work of the critic will have to the work that has stirred him to creation, but it will be such resemblance as exists, not between Nature and the mirror that the painter of landscape or figure may be supposed to hold up to her, but between Nature and the work of the decorative artist. Just as on the flowerless carpets of Persia, tulip and rose blossom indeed, and are lovely to look on, though they are not reproduced in visible shape or line; just as the pearl and purple of the sea-shell is echoed in the church of St. Mark at Venice; just as the vaulted ceiling of the wondrous chapel of Ravenna[7] is made gorgeous by the gold and green and sapphire of the peacock's tail, though the birds of Juno[8] fly not across it; so the critic reproduces the work that he criticises in a mode that is never imitative, and part of whose charm may really consist in the rejection of resemblance, and shows us in this way not merely the meaning but also the mystery of Beauty, and, by transforming each art into literature, solves once for all the problem of Art's unity.

* * *

From *Part 2*

* * *

Ernest. * * * You have told me that the highest criticism deals with art, not as expressive, but as impressive purely, and is, consequently, both creative and independent; is, in fact, an art by itself, occupying the same relation to creative work that creative work does to the visible world of form and colour, or the unseen world of passion and of thought. Well, now tell me, will not the critic be sometimes a real interpreter?

Gilbert. Yes; the critic will be an interpreter, if he chooses. He can pass from his sympathetic impression of the work of art as a whole, to an analysis or exposition of the work itself, and in this lower sphere, as I hold it to be, there are many delightful things to be said and done. Yet his object will not always be to explain the work of art. He may seek rather to deepen its mystery, to raise round it, and round its maker, that mist of wonder which is dear to both gods and worshippers alike. Ordinary people are "terribly at ease in Zion."[9] They propose to walk arm in arm with the poets, and have a glib, ignorant way of saying, "Why should we read what is written about Shakespeare and Milton? We can read the plays and the poems. That is enough." But an appreciation of Milton is, as the late Rector of Lincoln[1] remarked once, the reward of consummate scholarship. And he who desires to understand Shakespeare truly must understand the relations in which Shakespeare stood to the Renaissance and the Reformation, to the age of Elizabeth and the age of James;[2] he must be familiar with the history of the struggle for supremacy between the old classical forms and the new spirit of romance, between the school of Sidney, and Daniel, and Jonson, and the school of Marlowe[3] and Marlowe's greater son; he must know the materials that were

7. City in north central Italy, known for its Roman and Byzantine buildings, tombs (including that of the poet DANTE ALIGHIERI), and mosaics.
8. That is, peacocks (associated with Juno, the queen of the Roman gods).
9. In a passage in *Culture and Anarchy* (1868, 1869), Matthew Arnold quotes a remark by the Scottish-born essayist and historian Thomas Carlyle (1795–1881) on the difference between Hellenism and Hebraism: "Socrates is terribly at ease in Zion."
1. Mark Pattison (1813–1884), English scholar whose works include a book on John Milton (1879); he was elected rector of Lincoln College, Oxford University, in 1861.
2. James I (1566–1625) reigned 1603–25, after the death of Elizabeth I.
3. Christopher Marlowe (1564–1593), English poet and dramatist. SIR PHILIP SIDNEY (1554–1586), English poet, politician, and soldier. Sam-

at Shakespeare's disposal, and the method in which he used them, and the conditions of theatric presentation in the sixteenth and seventeenth centuries, their limitations and their opportunities for freedom, and the literary criticism of Shakespeare's day, its aims and modes and canons; he must study the English language in its progress, and blank or rhymed verse in its various developments; he must study the Greek drama, and the connection between the art of the creator of the Agamemnon[4] and the art of the creator of Macbeth; in a word, he must be able to bind Elizabethan London to the Athens of Pericles,[5] and to learn Shakespeare's true position in the history of European drama and the drama of the world. The critic will certainly be an interpreter, but he will not treat Art as a riddling Sphinx, whose shallow secret may be guessed and revealed by one whose feet are wounded and who knows not his name.[6] Rather, he will look upon Art as a goddess whose mystery it is his province to intensify, and whose majesty his privilege to make more marvellous in the eyes of men.

And here, Ernest, this strange thing happens. The critic will, indeed, be an interpreter, but he will not be an interpreter in the sense of one who simply repeats in another form a message that has been put into his lips to say. For, just as it is only by contact with the art of foreign nations that the art of a country gains that individual and separate life that we call nationality, so, by curious inversion, it is only by intensifying his own personality that the critic can interpret the personality and work of others, and the more strongly this personality enters into the interpretation the more real the interpretation becomes, the more satisfying, the more convincing, and the more true.

Ernest. I would have said that personality would have been a disturbing element.

Gilbert. No; it is an element of revelation. If you wish to understand others you must intensify your own individualism.

Ernest. What, then, is the result?

Gilbert. I will tell you, and perhaps I can tell you best by definite example. It seems to me that, while the literary critic stands, of course, first, as having the wider range, and larger vision, and nobler material, each of the arts has a critic, as it were, assigned to it. The actor is a critic of the drama. He shows the poet's work under new conditions, and by a method special to himself. He takes the written word, and action, gesture, and voice become the media of revelation. The singer, or the player on lute and viol, is the critic of music. The etcher of a picture robs the painting of its fair colours, but shows us by the use of a new material its true colour-quality, its tones and values, and the relations of its masses, and so is, in his way, a critic of it, for the critic is he who exhibits to us a work of art in a form different from that of the work itself, and the employment of a new material is a critical as well as a creative element. Sculpture, too, has its critic, who may be either the carver of a gem, as he was in Greek days, or some painter like Mantegna,[7] who

uel Daniel (1562–1619), English poet and historian. Ben Jonson (1572–1637), English poet and dramatist.

4. *Agamemnon* (458 B.C.E.) is the first play in the *Oresteia* trilogy of Aeschylus.

5. Great Athenian statesman, military leader, and famous patron of the arts (ca. 495–429 B.C.E.).

6. The parents of Oedipus (literally, "swollen foot") left their newborn son—his feet pierced and bound together—on a mountainside to die. He grew up to solve the Sphinx's riddle and fulfill the prophecy they had hoped to avert by his death (that he would kill his father). His story is told in the *Iliad* and in many Greek dramas, most notably Sophocles' *Oedipus Rex* (ca. 430 B.C.E.).

7. Andrea Mantegna (1431–1506), northern Italian painter and engraver, known for his mastery of perspective and compositional techniques.

sought to reproduce on canvas the beauty of plastic line and the symphonic dignity of processional bas-relief. And in the case of all these creative critics of art it is evident that personality is an absolute essential for any real interpretation. When Rubinstein plays to us the *Sonata Appassionata*[8] of Beethoven, he gives us not merely Beethoven, but also himself, and so gives us Beethoven absolutely—Beethoven reinterpreted through a rich artistic nature, and made vivid and wonderful to us by a new and intense personality. When a great actor plays Shakespeare we have the same experience. His own individuality becomes a vital part of the interpretation. People sometimes say that actors give us their own Hamlets, and not Shakespeare's; and this fallacy—for it is a fallacy—is, I regret to say, repeated by that charming and graceful writer who has lately deserted the turmoil of literature for the peace of the House of Commons—I mean the author of *Obiter Dicta*.[9] In point of fact, there is no such thing as Shakespeare's Hamlet. If Hamlet has something of the definiteness of a work of art, he has also all the obscurity that belongs to life. There are as many Hamlets as there are melancholies.

Ernest. As many Hamlets as there are melancholies?

Gilbert. Yes: and as art springs from personality, so it is only to personality that it can be revealed, and from the meeting of the two comes right interpretative criticism.

Ernest. The critic, then, considered as the interpreter, will give no less than he receives, and lend as much as he borrows?

Gilbert. He will be always showing us the work of art in some new relation to our age. He will always be reminding us that great works of art are living things—are, in fact, the only things that live. So much, indeed, will he feel this, that I am certain that, as civilisation progresses and we become more highly organised, the elect spirits of each age, the critical and cultured spirits, will grow less and less interested in actual life, and *will seek to gain their impressions almost entirely from what Art has touched*. For Life is terribly deficient in form. Its catastrophes happen in the wrong way and to the wrong people. There is a grotesque horror about its comedies, and its tragedies seem to culminate in farce. One is always wounded when one approaches it. Things last either too long, or not long enough.

* * *

Ernest. But where in this is the function of the critical spirit?

Gilbert. The culture that this transmission of racial experiences[1] makes possible can be made perfect by the critical spirit alone, and indeed may be said to be one with it. For who is the true critic but he who bears within himself the dreams, and ideas, and feelings of myriad generations, and to whom no form of thought is alien, no emotional impulse obscure? And who the true man of culture, if not he who by fine scholarship and fastidious rejection has made instinct self-conscious and intelligent, and can separate the work that has distinction from the work that has it not, and so by contact and comparison makes himself master of the secrets of style and school, and understands their meanings, and listens to their voices, and develops that

8. Piano Sonata in F Minor, opus 57 (1805), by Ludwig van Beethoven (1770–1827). Anton Rubinstein (1829–1894), famous Russian pianist.
9. Augustine Birrell (1850–1933), English writer and politician; *Obiter Dicta* was published in 3 vols. (1884, 1887, 1924).
1. That is, the experiences of a tribe, nation, or people, regarded as forming a distinct ethnic stock or group.

spirit of disinterested curiosity which is the real root, as it is the real flower, of the intellectual life, and thus attains to intellectual clarity; and, having learned "the best that is known and thought in the world," lives it—is not fanciful to say so—with those who are the Immortals?

Yes, Ernest: the contemplative life, the life that has for its aim not *doing* but *being*, and not *being* merely, but *becoming*—that is what the critical spirit can give us. The gods live thus: either brooding over their own perfection, as Aristotle tells us, or, as Epicurus[2] fancied, watching with the calm eyes of the spectator the tragi-comedy of the world that they have made. We, too, might live like them, and set ourselves to witness with appropriate emotions the varied scenes that man and nature afford. We might make ourselves spiritual by detaching ourselves from action, and become perfect by the rejection of energy. It has often seemed to me that Browning[3] felt something of this. Shakespeare hurls Hamlet into active life, and makes him realise his mission by effort. Browning might have given us a Hamlet who would have realised his mission by thought. Incident and event were to him unreal or unmeaning. He made the soul the protagonist of life's tragedy, and looked on action as the one undramatic element of a play. To us, at any rate, the *ΒΙΟΣ ΘΕΩΡΗΤΙΚΟΣ*[4] is the true ideal. From the high tower of Thought we can look out at the world. Calm, and self-centred, and complete, the æsthetic critic contemplates life, and no arrow drawn at a venture can pierce between the joints of his harness. He at least is safe. He has discovered how to live.

Is such a mode of life immoral? Yes: all the arts are immoral, except those baser forms of sensual or didactic art that seek to excite to action of evil or of good. For action of every kind belongs to the sphere of ethics. The aim of art is simply to create a mood. Is such a mode of life unpractical? Ah! it is not so easy to be unpractical as the ignorant Philistine[5] imagines. It were well for England if it were so. There is no country in the world so much in need of unpractical people as this country of ours. With us, Thought is degraded by its constant association with practice. Who that moves in the stress and turmoil of actual existence, noisy politician, or brawling social reformer, or poor, narrow-minded priest, blinded by the sufferings of that unimportant section of the community among whom he has cast his lot, can seriously claim to be able to form a disinterested intellectual judgment about any one thing? Each of the professions means a prejudice. The necessity for a career forces every one to take sides. We live in the age of the overworked, and the under-educated; the age in which people are so industrious that they become absolutely stupid. And, harsh though it may sound, I cannot help saying that such people deserve their doom. The sure way of knowing nothing about life is to try to make oneself useful.

Ernest. A charming doctrine, Gilbert.

Gilbert. I am not sure about that, but it has at least the minor merit of being true.

* * *

1890, 1891

2. Greek philosopher (341–270 B.C.E.) whose teachings emphasize gaining happiness through self-restraint, moderation, and detachment. Aristotle: see *Metaphysics* 12.7, 9.
3. Robert Browning (1812–1889), English poet.
4. *Bios theōrētikos*: contemplative life (Greek).
5. A member of a biblical people who waged war against the Israelites. Matthew Arnold applies the name in *Culture and Anarchy* to the complacent materialist middle classes, indifferent or antagonistic to artistic and cultural values.

SIGMUND FREUD
1856–1939

It is hard to imagine the twentieth century without Sigmund Freud. Along with Charles Darwin (1809–1882), KARL MARX (1818–1883), and Albert Einstein (1879–1955), he helped revolutionize the modern Western conception of human life and its place in the universe. For Freud, human reason was not master in its own house but a precarious defense mechanism struggling against, and often motivated by, unconscious desires and forces. His theory and practice of psychoanalysis have changed the way people think about themselves today, whether they are aware of it or not. At the same time, psychoanalysis has been controversial from the beginning because, unlike experimental science, it cannot be adequately tested, falsified, or objectified. It aims higher than—or falls short of—objective verifiability because it is a study of the very limits of objectivity itself. The impossibility of separating psychoanalysis from the biography of its founder has been used to discredit it, but in fact Freud's writings signal a significant change in the relation between autobiography and thought. They make visible in new ways the narrative challenges involved in telling the story of a life—one's own in particular. Freud's attention to language may help explain why his writings have grown in importance for literary scholars at the same time that they are increasingly criticized for diverging from the protocols of science. Yet perhaps it is also in large part because his writings exist at the limits of *both* literature and science that Freud continues to fascinate us.

Freud was born in Moravia (in what is now the Czech Republic), the first of seven children, to poor Jewish parents. His young mother, Amalia, was his father Jacob's third wife. The Freuds moved to Vienna in 1860, where Sigmund obtained all his education (with the exception of a few months in Paris). Although psychoanalysis today is associated with the "talking cure" and the theory of infantile sexuality, Freud began his career as a clinical neurologist, obtaining his medical degree in 1881. He entered the University of Vienna in 1873, at a time when Jews, who had moved to liberal Vienna in sizable numbers, were already being scapegoated for Austria's economic problems. Freud, in his *Autobiographical Study* (1925), attributed his independence of mind to his position just outside the "compact majority" (Henrik Ibsen's phrase) of German gentile culture, which he nevertheless also shared. When Nazi Germany annexed Austria in 1938, Freud left Vienna reluctantly and under duress. In his lifetime, social liberalism had given way to the most virulent anti-Semitism—a sad confirmation of his warning against taking any notion of the progress of civilization for granted.

While working to obtain his medical degree, Freud was distracted by his broad interests in research. Among other subjects, he became fascinated by the account given by the respected physician Josef Breuer of the treatment of a particularly intelligent hysterical patient. "Anna O." invented the term "talking cure"; she is often considered the first patient of psychoanalysis, although Freud himself never treated her. Fifteen years later, Freud and Breuer would write *Studies on Hysteria* (1895) about this and later cases. In the meantime Freud met Martha Bernays, the woman he hoped would become his wife, and went to Paris. Too poor to marry, he progressed in his profession by getting a small grant to work at the famous Salpêtrière mental hospital under the supervision of the medical showman and great specialist in hysteria Jean-Martin Charcot. In 1886 he returned to Vienna, opened his medical practice, and married Martha; they had six children (three girls and three boys). From 1891 onward, the Freuds lived at Berggasse 19, where Sigmund set up his famous consulting room.

In the years leading up to his groundbreaking *Interpretation of Dreams* (1900), Freud began a formative and intellectually wide-ranging correspondence with Wilhelm Fliess, an ear, nose, and throat specialist from Berlin. In his practice, Freud gradually abandoned the hypnotic treatments for hysteria recommended by Charcot, substituting instead a form of dialogue between patient and doctor. At first convinced that many of his patients had suffered sexual abuse (or "seduction") by their fathers in childhood, he later came to realize that some of his patients' tales of sexual events were fantasies. The death in 1896 of Freud's own father perhaps increased his unwillingness to believe in paternal guilt. What he called the "abandonment of the seduction theory" has become controversial in recent decades (largely because of Jeffrey Moussaieff Masson's 1984 book, *The Assault on Truth: Freud's Suppression of the Seduction Theory*), criticized as an abandonment of the realities of childhood sexual abuse. But the shift was not first and foremost a denial of the reality of incest; Freud saw in fantasies of incest a psychic reality, and an infantile sexuality, that had to be taken seriously in itself. In his move from realities of fact to realities of fantasy, however, Freud changed the sex of the representative subject: in his new theory of unconscious desire (the "Oedipus complex"), he substituted the desiring son for the abused daughter, the desirable mother for the guilty father. The father, in his account, was no longer a lawbreaker but a lawgiver: the enforcer of the law prohibiting incest between the son and the mother.

In order to gather evidence of the existence of unconscious forces at work in everyday life, Freud turned to psychological phenomena that were at once recognized and disregarded. His first three books—*The Interpretation of Dreams* (1900), *The Psychopathology of Everyday Life* (published in a journal in 1901 and as a book in 1904), and *Jokes and Their Relation to the Unconscious* (1905)—lay out the analytical strategies that would inform the better-known *Three Essays in the Theory of Sexuality* (1905). His theory would have been impossible without the meticulous study of the discredited forms of knowledge revealed by dreams, slips of the tongue, memory lapses, and jokes.

Freud continued seeing patients and published several extensive and now famous case studies—*Fragment of an Analysis of a Case of Hysteria* (better known as "Dora," 1905), "Analysis of a Phobia in a Five-Year-Old Boy" ("Little Hans," 1909), "Notes Upon a Case of Obsessional Neurosis" ("Rat Man," 1909), "Psycho-Analytic Notes on an Autobiographical Account of a Case of Paranoia" ("Schreber," 1911), and *From the History of an Infantile Neurosis* ("Wolf Man," written 1914 and published 1918). Each attempts to come to terms with a difficult psychoanalytic but also *narrative* challenge: for example, Dora left treatment before Freud was finished with her, and his later footnotes allude to oversights in his understanding; Wolf Man's childhood neurosis could be analyzed only through the screen of adult constructions; and Schreber was analyzed not as Freud's patient but as the author of an autobiography. Freud's case histories offer a fascinating hybrid of certainty, doubt, and inner debate.

In addition to his research and his practice, Freud, at the suggestion of a disciple, founded the Psychological Wednesday Society (later transformed into the Vienna Psychoanalytic Society) in 1902. He traveled to the United States in 1909 to lecture and receive an honorary degree from Clark University in Worcester, Massachusetts, accompanied by his younger colleagues CARL G. JUNG and Sandor Ferenczi (lectures subsequently published as *Five Lectures on Psychoanalysis*, 1910). The tensions—theoretical, personal, and institutional—between Freud and Jung were already growing; by the end of 1912, the two had essentially stopped speaking to each other. Freud took his revenge on his wayward disciples in his polemical "History of the Psycho-Analytic Movement" (1914). He also published a new series of lectures and a number of papers on psychoanalytic technique.

When World War I began Freud's three sons volunteered for the army, but he grew more and more critical of war as a solution to human problems. (Later, at the request of the League of Nations, Freud would collaborate with Albert Einstein in writing *Why War?* [1933].) The war deeply affected his thought, already in a new phase with the publication of his celebrated essay on narcissism in 1914. Traumatic neuroses seemed to put in question the dominance in psychic life of the "pleasure principle" that he had posited as the motive force of dreams. Even children's games sometimes seemed to give greater weight to the process of repetition itself than to the pleasurable thing repeated. It was at this time that Freud wrote his essay "The 'Uncanny' " (1919) and the longer *Beyond the Pleasure Principle* (1920). A sense of strangeness, of genuinely enigmatic forces, pervades his theory of the "death instinct" and the "repetition compulsion." But perhaps this strangeness was also a way of reconnecting with the strangeness of his original discoveries, which had grown quite familiar. The theoretical gains from this period are formulated in *The Ego and the Id* (1923). (The famous Latin names for the almost allegorical parts of the self—ego, id, superego—were bestowed by translators; Freud himself used German terms meaning "I," "it," and "over-I.")

In the 1920s Freud wrote about larger cultural forces and structures (*Group Psychology and the Analysis of the Ego*, 1921; *The Future of an Illusion*, 1927; and *Civilization and Its Discontents*, 1929), provided major reformulations of his theory, and turned his attention to the problem of sexual difference. His paper "Some Psychical Consequences of the Anatomical Distinction between the Sexes" (1925) began to explore the question of "castration" in a new way. When children observe that some people have penises and others do not, he asserted, they assume that everyone must at first have had one, and that in some people it had been cut off. This encounter with the fact of difference is more satisfying to the little boy than to the little girl. But the "psychic consequences" are far-reaching: the boy takes seriously the father's threat of castration as the punishment for incest, thus experiencing "castration anxiety," while the girl tries to deal with her "inferiority," thus feeling "penis envy." In later essays—especially "Female Sexuality" (1931) and "Femininity" (1932)—Freud attempted to make sense of the desires his theory allotted to women. Feminists have treated his theories with ambivalence: on the one hand, he had the merit of describing human sexuality as a *question*, not a *given*; on the other hand, his phrase "anatomy is destiny" seems in the final analysis to uphold the sexual certainties he himself questioned.

The lectures Freud wrote that include "Femininity" were never meant to be delivered; a series of operations for mouth cancer (beginning in 1923) had left him unable to perform in public. The political situation was also worrisome: Adolf Hitler had been appointed chancellor of Germany, and the Nazi Party was in control. Freud's books were among those burned in Berlin. His last book, *Moses and Monotheism*, was not completed until his own "exodus" to England in 1938. In London in 1939, his cancer worsening, Freud officially closed his practice; and, just after the Germans invaded Poland and after France and Britain declared war on Germany, Freud asked his physician to give him a lethal dose of morphine. He died in September of that year.

How did Freud practice interpretation, then, and how did his theory transform it? Although the details of each individual dream are particular to the dreamer, there are, says Freud, some dreams that occur widely and point to the existence of universal desires. Incest and its prohibition—the universal break between nature and culture, according to anthropologists—form the core of Freud's theory of unconscious desire. In our first selection from *The Interpretation of Dreams*, he turns to the same literary text as ARISTOTLE for a version of the fundamental human plot: Sophocles' *Oedipus Rex*. Warned by an oracle that he will kill his father and marry his mother, Oedipus leaves home in order to escape his fate, only to kill a man and marry a woman who turn out to be the very biological parents who had abandoned him as an infant in order to thwart the same oracle. Literature thus exists for Freud as a form of evidence: the play's centuries-long hold over the attention of viewers must correspond to its depiction of something universally fascinating and repressed. The truth told by the oracle corresponds to unconscious desire, fulfilling itself despite—or perhaps because of—every conscious effort to escape it. The plot of Sophocles' play also furnishes a parallel to the plot of an analysis: a patient's resistance to unconscious knowledge is like Oedipus's reluctance to learn his true identity. Freud goes on to discuss the relation between *Oedipus Rex* and Shakespeare's *Hamlet*—both in terms of the incest taboo. In answer to the question "Why does Hamlet delay his revenge for his father's death?" Freud replies, "Because his uncle has only carried out a murder that he himself wanted to accomplish." In a few short pages, Freud thus revolutionized the reading of two major canonical texts of Western culture and placed the world of the imagination at the center of human subjectivity.

Freud's attention to new modes of meaning has been immensely suggestive for literary studies. While the relation between literature and dreams has often been noted, as in the ancient work of MACROBIUS (b. ca. 360 C.E.), Freud pursues the connection beyond the realm of general symbolism to lay out a kind of rhetoric of everyday dreams. In our second selection, on the dream-work, he writes that dreams are not nonsensical but meaningful. They are composites made out of the residues of individual lives chosen by the unconscious to represent the fulfilment of a wish: no simple "key" can decode them. Only the dreamer can provide a set of associations to illuminate the "dream-thoughts" behind the dream. Beneath the composite surface, which functions like a puzzle, lies the wish, the puzzle's solution. The dream-thoughts function like a "latent content" behind the "manifest content" of the dream.

Distortion and disguise fill dreams—or literary texts—because the unconscious wish is in some way unacceptable and must evade censorship. Dreams have three main sources of unavoidable distortion, he argues: condensation, displacement, and the needs of representation. These unconscious "primary processes" are also subject to "secondary revision," the editing to which a dream is subject if the dreamer tries to remember it on awakening. Freud's description of the four rhetorical operations ("distortions") performed by dreams has been productively extended to literary texts: while the role of secondary revision there is stronger and more complex, literary texts may provide access to forces that are not directly accessible in other ways.

Freud often uses literary texts to illustrate or confirm his theory. His reading of a 1903 novella by Wilhelm Jensen (*Delusion and Dream in Wilhelm Jensen's "Gradiva,"* 1907) aims to ratify his theory of dreams; "Creative Writers and Daydreaming" (1908) expands on his description of fantasy life; in "The Theme of the Three Caskets" (1913), he turns again to Shakespeare; and in numerous other short essays and notes Freud focuses directly on literature or art. But some of the most explicit literary demonstrations function as "secondary revisions" of the theory itself, eliding the role of literature in *forming* central concepts (the Oedipus complex, narcissism, etc.). For Freud, it is always as if a bourgeois drama is playing on the conscious stage of the psyche, while a Greek tragedy is going on somewhere else.

Freud's celebrated essay on "The 'Uncanny,'" our third selection, offers both a literary application and a new theoretical direction. It contains an extensive analysis of E. T. A. Hoffmann's short story "The Sandman" (1816), in which a young man, Nathaniel, traumatized by the mysterious death of his father, falls in love with a wooden doll, Olympia, in preference to his flesh-and-blood sweetheart. Freud argues that what is uncanny about the story is related not to intellectual uncertainty about whether the doll is alive (as an article by Ernst Jentsch had speculated), but to anxiety about the cause of Nathaniel's father's death. When Nathaniel encounters Coppola, an optician, he thinks he recognizes Coppelius, a lawyer, whom he believes to have caused his father's death and who is conflated in his mind with the Sandman—a storybook figure who takes the eyes of little children who won't go to bed. These threats to the eyes are connected in Freud's mind to the castration complex (Oedipus had blinded himself on learning that he had fulfilled the prophecy). The uncanny return of these figures (the Sandman, Coppelius, Coppola) is also related to Freud's new sense of the "repetition compulsion." Dolls and inanimate objects, which for Freud are not uncanny in the story, nevertheless return to haunt the essay's discussion of "the omnipotence of thoughts" and of the supposedly surmounted childhood belief in animism.

Freud begins his discussion with the characteristics of the word *uncanny*, extensively documented through citations from a dictionary. The German *unheimlich* (unhomelike, uncanny) turns out to share a meaning with its apparent opposite. *Heimlich* (homey, familiar) can also mean "concealed, secret," and thus the opposite of the familiar and open. This process of estrangement of the familiar (of the "home") is exactly the same as the process of repression. The fear of being buried alive, for example, is a distorted desire to return to the mother's womb—the "home" of all humanity. The German term gives a clue to a process that psychoanalysis tries to understand more generally. Freud expresses astonishment that other languages lack the equivalent of what in German is such a handy word. But if all languages had the same process in the same place, that process would become a theme, a topic, and thus belong to conscious, rather than unconscious, knowledge.

The essay also addresses "aesthetics" more generally, as its first sentence announces. Indeed, it investigates what analyses of the "beautiful" and the "sublime" leave out: the disturbing, the unsettling, the uncomfortable. Freud's essay itself is far from beautiful: it wanders from topic to topic, it quotes others at great length, it places major points in footnotes, and, in general, it seems sewn together from mismatched parts. Yet this poorly sutured text offers the reader an opportunity to follow the *process*, and not just the *result*, of Freud's thinking. Indeed, that the essay lacks "organic" form, so that readers tend to get lost in it, contributes powerfully to its own uncanny effect. In recent years, partly as a result of Freud's essay, critics have devoted increasing attention to the Gothic in literature and to elements Freud associates with the uncanny—unexpected doubles, severed limbs, bodies buried alive, the return of the dead, magical thinking. Freud's reading of Hoffmann's story allows him to touch many theoretical bases that he, unlike many others, feels comfortable with—unacceptable authorial desires, castration anxieties, homosexual fantasies. But Freud's essay itself also makes readable the persistence of questions he dismisses, and it vividly reveals, in its wandering way, his fascination with what is escaping his grasp.

Freud's short essay titled "Fetishism" (1927), our final selection, builds on his analysis of the consequences of sexual difference. Certain men, he claims, cannot accept the evidence that the woman (the mother) doesn't have a penis. In order to fall in love with women and not become homosexual, they choose as a substitute some object that will continue to support the sexual interest they originally had in the missing maternal penis. The logic of fetishism thus involves both perceiving and denying the evidence of maternal "castration." In a very different way, the same logic of denial and displacement underlies Karl Marx's theory of "the fetishism of the commodity" (*Capital*, vol. 1, 1867; see above). There, the commodity itself appears to contain the value that is really produced by the processes of labor invisible behind it. Here, the substitute (foot, velvet, hair, etc.) appears to function like a sexual organ. In both cases there is a "gleam" around the fetish that attracts desire (sexual or commercial), as if the fetish actually contained the values that it represents.

Freud's analyses have had a fundamental impact on what we now understand as literary theory, influencing virtually every twentieth-century critic. On the one hand, Freud's radical new view of subjectivity has deeply affected the analysis of characters, authors, and readers, enabling a new understanding of split, hidden, or contradictory desires and intentions. On the other hand, for Freud literature is not just an illustration but also a source and authority for understanding those desires and intentions in the first place.

Perhaps more profoundly, Freud changed the nature of attentiveness itself. It was in listening to patients differently that Freud discovered the unconscious—a force of otherness as powerful as, but in no way equivalent to, a god. Inside every person, he said, there was *something* transmitting scrambled messages in a cryptic language, trying to break through the conscious surface of life. The "other" was in ourselves—indeed, it *was* ourselves. Despite the limitations of Freud's middle-class Viennese patriarchal assumptions, his conception of a human subjectivity fundamentally at odds with itself opened up possibilities he never dreamed of. Each person's life was documented in more than one way: official personal history (conscious remembrance and self-image) and unofficial personal history (the record of changes, traumas, desires, anxieties, and associations that might never have been conscious). Unconscious history contained impossible or forbidden wishes, repressed from the official record or simply outgrown—wishes that remained active in the unconscious and sought expression in dreams, mistakes, jokes, myths, and other discredited or discounted forms of communication. Psychoanalysis is the name for the theory and practice of their interpretation, and literary theory continues to derive inspiration from the psychoanalytic engagement with the most canonical as well as the most uncanonical of texts.

BIBLIOGRAPHY

The English translation of Freud's collected works, carried out under the direction of James Strachey for Leonard and Virginia Woolf's Hogarth Press, has become in many ways more authoritative than any collected works in German. This *Standard Edition of the Complete Psychological Works of Sigmund Freud* (24 vols., 1953–74) is thus the edition most often cited. A handy collection of Freud's literary and artistic essays was edited by Neil Hertz in 1997 under the title *Writings on Art and Literature*. For more general purposes, see Peter Gay's *Freud Reader* (1989) and Elisabeth Young-Bruehl's *Freud on Women* (1990). Many volumes of Freud's copious correspondence (he never left a letter unanswered) have also been published. A monumental three-volume biography, *The Life and Work of Sigmund Freud*, was published by Ernest Jones, who knew Freud well (1953–57; abridged into one volume, 1961). The more recent *Freud: A Life for Our Time* (1988) by Peter Gay is excellent; his invaluable bibliographical essays appended to each chapter delineate all the major debates.

Philip Rieff's *Freud: The Mind of the Moralist* (1959) and Peter Gay's *Reading Freud* (1990) are good introductions, the latter more literary. See also Paul Ricoeur's *Freud and Philosophy: An Essay on Interpretation* (1970) and Steven Marcus's *Freud and the Culture of Psychoanalysis: Studies in the Transition from Victorian Humanism to Modernity* (1984). For a recent collection of essays critical of Freud, see *Unauthorized Freud: Doubters Confront a Legend*, edited by Frederick C. Crews (1998).

For the centrality of Freud to contemporary critical theory, see the works of Jacques Lacan and Jacques Derrida. Related developments can be found in *The Literary Freud: Mechanisms of Defense and the Poetic Will* (1980), edited by Joseph H. Smith; Malcolm Bowie, *Psychoanalysis and the Future of Theory* (1993), speculates about Freud's continuing impact on discussions of art; while *Freud and Forbidden Knowledge*, edited by Peter L. Rudnytsky and Ellen Handler Spitz (1994), investigates the literary and religious sources of Freud's concepts. See also Graham Frankland's *Freud's Literary Culture* (2000).

For a good general approach to early feminist responses to Freud, see Juliet Mitchell's *Psychoanalysis and Feminism* (1974). A related work by Lisa Appignanesi and John Forrester, *Freud's Women* (1992), analyzes both the historical and the theoretical importance of femininity and of the many woman analysts and patients who surrounded Freud. Luce Irigaray, in *Speculum of the Other Woman* (1974; trans. 1985), and Sarah Kofman, in *The Enigma of Woman* (1980; trans. 1985), revisit Freud's writings on femininity from a French poststructuralist perspective. For a good overview of the intersection of Freud, feminism, and literary studies, see *In Dora's Case: Freud—Hysteria—Feminism*, edited by Charles Bernheimer and Claire Kahane (2d ed., 1990).

On Freud's *Interpretation of Dreams*, see Lawrence M. Porter, *The Interpretation of Dreams: Freud's Theories Revisited* (1987); Alexander Welsh, *Freud's Wishful Dream Book* (1994); Harvie Ferguson, *The Lure of Dreams: Sigmund Freud and the*

Construction of Modernity (1996); and the collection of interdisciplinary essays edited by Laura Marcus, *Sigmund Freud's "The Interpretation of Dreams": New Interdisciplinary Essays* (1999).

Two essays on Freud's "Uncanny" deserve special note: Hélène Cixous, "Fiction and Its Phantoms," *New Literary History* 7 (1976), and "Freud and the Sandman" by Neil Hertz, published in his study of the sublime, *The End of the Line: Essays on Psychoanalysis and the Sublime* (1985). Contemporary literary studies have been greatly affected by Freud's notion of the uncanny, from those focusing on the Renaissance (Marjorie Garber, *Shakespeare's Ghost Writers: Literature as Uncanny Causality*, 1984) to the Enlightenment (Terry Castle, *The Female Thermometer: Eighteenth-Century Culture and the Invention of the Uncanny*, 1995) to the posthuman Gothic (Judith Halberstam, *Skin Shows: Gothic Horror and the Technology of Monsters*, 1995). Julia Kristeva, in *Strangers to Ourselves* (1988; trans. 1991), applies the notion to political science, while Anthony Vidler, in *The Architectural Uncanny: Essays in the Modern Unhomely* (1994), explores it in architecture.

E. L. McCallum's *Object Lessons: How to Do Things with Fetishism* (1999) offers a full-scale analysis of Freud's notion. Two books attempt to combine the Freudian and the Marxian versions of fetishism: Slavoj Žižek's *The Sublime Object of Ideology* (1989) and Rachel Bowlby's *Shopping with Freud* (1993).

Much recent research deals with Freud's Jewishness: Marthe Robert's *From Oedipus to Moses: Freud's Jewish Identity* (1974; trans. 1976) and Susan Handelman's *Slayers of Moses: The Emergence of Rabbinic Interpretation in Modern Literary Theory* (1982) give two early versions of this analysis, later taken in other directions by Sander Gilman in both *Freud, Race, and Gender* (1993) and *The Case of Sigmund Freud: Medicine and Identity at the Fin de Siècle* (1993). Other recent new directions include Diana Fuss's *Identification Papers* (1995), which reads Freud through the lenses of queer and postcolonial theory.

The Cambridge Companion to Freud, edited by Jerome Neu (1991), is a useful resource. Among the bibliographies available in English, by far the best for the period up to 1988 is the bibliographical survey in Peter Gay's biography.

From The Interpretation of Dreams[1]

From *Chapter V. The Material and Sources of Dreams*

* * *

[THE OEDIPUS COMPLEX]

In my experience, which is already extensive, the chief part in the mental lives of all children who later become psychoneurotics is played by their parents. Being in love with the one parent and hating the other are among the essential constituents of the stock of psychical impulses which is formed at that time and which is of such importance in determining the symptoms of the later neurosis. It is not my belief, however, that psychoneurotics differ sharply in this respect from other human beings who remain normal—that they are able, that is, to create something absolutely new and peculiar to themselves. It is far more probable—and this is confirmed by occasional observations on normal children—that they are only distinguished by exhib-

1. Translated by James Strachey. This standard edition incorporates later revisions made by Freud.

iting on a magnified scale feelings of love and hatred to their parents which occur less obviously and less intensely in the minds of most children.

This discovery is confirmed by a legend that has come down to us from classical antiquity: a legend whose profound and universal power to move can only be understood if the hypothesis I have put forward in regard to the psychology of children has an equally universal validity. What I have in mind is the legend of King Oedipus and Sophocles'[2] drama which bears his name.

Oedipus, son of Laïus, King of Thebes, and of Jocasta, was exposed as an infant because an oracle had warned Laïus that the still unborn child would be his father's murderer. The child was rescued, and grew up as a prince in an alien court, until, in doubts as to his origin, he too questioned the oracle and was warned to avoid his home since he was destined to murder his father and take his mother in marriage. On the road leading away from what he believed was his home, he met King Laïus and slew him in a sudden quarrel. He came next to Thebes and solved the riddle set him by the Sphinx[3] who barred his way. Out of gratitude the Thebans made him their king and gave him Jocasta's hand in marriage. He reigned long in peace and honour, and she who, unknown to him, was his mother bore him two sons and two daughters. Then at last a plague broke out and the Thebans made enquiry once more of the oracle. It is at this point that Sophocles' tragedy opens. The messengers bring back the reply that the plague will cease when the murderer of Laïus has been driven from the land.

> But he, where is he? Where shall now be read
> The fading record of this ancient guilt?[4]

The action of the play consists in nothing other than the process of revealing, with cunning delays and ever-mounting excitement—a process that can be likened to the work of a psychoanalysis—that Oedipus himself is the murderer of Laïus, but further that he is the son of the murdered man and of Jocasta. Appalled at the abomination which he has unwittingly perpetrated, Oedipus blinds himself and forsakes his home. The oracle has been fulfilled.

Oedipus Rex is what is known as a tragedy of destiny. Its tragic effect is said to lie in the contrast between the supreme will of the gods and the vain attempts of mankind to escape the evil that threatens them. The lesson which, it is said, the deeply moved spectator should learn from the tragedy is submission to the divine will and realization of his own impotence. Modern dramatists have accordingly tried to achieve a similar tragic effect by weaving the same contrast into a plot invented by themselves. But the spectators have looked on unmoved while a curse or an oracle was fulfilled in spite of all the efforts of some innocent man: later tragedies of destiny have failed in their effect.

If *Oedipus Rex* moves a modern audience no less than it did the contemporary Greek one, the explanation can only be that its effect does not lie in the contrast between destiny and human will, but is to be looked for in the particular nature of the material on which that contrast is exemplified. There

2. Greek tragic dramatist (ca. 496–406 B.C.E.), author of *Oedipus the King* (ca. 430, better known by its Latin name, *Oedipus Rex*).

3. A monster with a woman's face, lion's body, and bird's wings who killed travelers who could not answer her riddle; when Oedipus solved it, she killed herself.

4. Lewis Campbell's translation (1883), lines 108–9 [translator's note].

must be something which makes a voice within us ready to recognize the compelling force of destiny in the *Oedipus*, while we can dismiss as merely arbitrary such dispositions as are laid down in [Grillparzer's] *Die Ahnfrau*[5] or other modern tragedies of destiny. And a factor of this kind is in fact involved in the story of King Oedipus. His destiny moves us only because it might have been ours—because the oracle laid the same curse upon us before our birth as upon him. It is the fate of all of us, perhaps, to direct our first sexual impulse towards our mother and our first hatred and our first murderous wish against our father. Our dreams convince us that that is so. King Oedipus, who slew his father Laïus and married his mother Jocasta, merely shows us the fulfilment of our own childhood wishes. But, more fortunate than he, we have meanwhile succeeded, in so far as we have not become psychoneurotics, in detaching our sexual impulses from our mothers and in forgetting our jealousy of our fathers. Here is one in whom these primaeval wishes of our childhood have been fulfilled, and we shrink back from him with the whole force of the repression by which those wishes have since that time been held down within us. While the poet, as he unravels the past, brings to light the guilt of Oedipus, he is at the same time compelling us to recognize our own inner minds, in which those same impulses, though suppressed, are still to be found. The contrast with which the closing Chorus leaves us confronted—

. . . Fix on Oedipus your eyes,
Who resolved the dark enigma, noblest champion and most wise.
Like a star his envied fortune mounted beaming far and wide:
Now he sinks in seas of anguish, whelmed beneath a raging tide . . . [6]

—strikes as a warning at ourselves and our pride, at us who since our childhood have grown so wise and so mighty in our own eyes. Like Oedipus, we live in ignorance of these wishes, repugnant to morality, which have been forced upon us by Nature, and after their revelation we may all of us well seek to close our eyes to the scenes of our childhood.[7]

There is an unmistakable indication in the text of Sophocles' tragedy itself that the legend of Oedipus sprang from some primaeval dream-material which had as its content the distressing disturbance of a child's relation to his parents owing to the first stirrings of sexuality. At a point when Oedipus, though he is not yet enlightened, has begun to feel troubled by his recollec-

5. *The Ancestress* (1817), by the Austrian dramatist Franz Grillparzer. The play's protagonist unknowingly falls in love with his sister and kills his father.

6. Campbell's translation, lines 1524–27 [translator's note].

7. [*Footnote added* 1914:] None of the findings of psycho-analytic research has provoked such embittered denials, such fierce opposition—or such amusing contortions—on the part of critics as this indication of the childhood impulses towards incest which persist in the unconscious. An attempt has even been made recently to make out, in the face of all experience, that the incest should only be taken as "symbolic."—Ferenczi ("The Symbolic Representation of the Pleasure and Reality Principles in the Oedipus Myth," 1912) has proposed an ingenious "over-interpretation" of the Oedipus myth, based on a passage in one of Schopenhauer's letters.—[*Added* 1919:] Later studies have shown that the "Oedipus complex," which was touched upon for the first time in the above paragraphs in the *Interpretation of Dreams*, throws a light of undreamt-of importance on the history of the human race and the evolution of religion and morality. (See my *Totem and Taboo*, 1912–13 [Essay IV].) [Freud's note].—[Actually the gist of this discussion of the Oedipus complex and of the *Oedipus Rex*, as well as of what follows on the subject of *Hamlet*, had already been put forward by Freud in a letter to Fliess as early as October 15, 1897. A still earlier hint at the discovery of the Oedipus complex was included in a letter of May 31, 1897.—The actual term "Oedipus complex" seems to have been first used by Freud in his published writings in the first of his "Contributions to the Psychology of Love" (1910)—translator's note.] Some of Freud's later footnotes are omitted.

tion of the oracle, Jocasta consoles him by referring to a dream which many people dream, though, as she thinks, it has no meaning:

> Many a man ere now in dreams hath lain
> With her who bare him. He hath least annoy
> Who with such omens troubleth not his mind.[8]

To-day, just as then, many men dream of having sexual relations with their mothers, and speak of the fact with indignation and astonishment. It is clearly the key to the tragedy and the complement to the dream of the dreamer's father being dead. The story of Oedipus is the reaction of the imagination to these two typical dreams. And just as these dreams, when dreamt by adults, are accompanied by feelings of repulsion, so too the legend must include horror and self-punishment. Its further modification originates once again in a misconceived secondary revision of the material, which has sought to exploit it for theological purposes. (Cf. the dream-material in dreams of exhibiting [discussed earlier].) The attempt to harmonize divine omnipotence with human responsibility must naturally fail in connection with this subject-matter just as with any other.

Another of the great creations of tragic poetry, Shakespeare's *Hamlet*, has its roots in the same soil as *Oedipus Rex*. But the changed treatment of the same material reveals the whole difference in the mental life of these two widely separated epochs of civilization: the secular advance of repression in the emotional life of mankind. In the *Oedipus* the child's wishful phantasy that underlies it is brought into the open and realized as it would be in a dream. In *Hamlet* it remains repressed; and—just as in the case of a neurosis—we only learn of its existence from its inhibiting consequences. Strangely enough, the overwhelming effect produced by the more modern tragedy has turned out to be compatible with the fact that people have remained completely in the dark as to the hero's character. The play is built up on Hamlet's hesitations over fulfilling the task of revenge that is assigned to him; but its text offers no reasons or motives for these hesitations and an immense variety of attempts at interpreting them have failed to produce a result. According to the view which was originated by Goethe[9] and is still the prevailing one to-day, Hamlet represents the type of man whose power of direct action is paralysed by an excessive development of his intellect. (He is 'sicklied o'er with the pale cast of thought'.)[1] According to another view, the dramatist has tried to portray a pathologically irresolute character which might be classed as neurasthenic. The plot of the drama shows us, however, that Hamlet is far from being represented as a person incapable of taking any action. We see him doing so on two occasions: first in a sudden outburst of temper, when he runs his sword through the eavesdropper behind the arras, and secondly in a premeditated and even crafty fashion, when, with all the callousness of a Renaissance prince, he sends the two courtiers to the death that had been planned for himself. What is it, then, that inhibits him in fulfilling the task set him by his father's ghost? The answer, once again, is that it is the peculiar nature of the task. Hamlet is able to do anything—

8. Campbell's translation, lines 982–84 [translator's note].
9. Johann Wolfgang von Goethe (1749–1832), German poet, playwright, and novelist.
1. *Hamlet* (ca. 1600), 3.1.87.

except take vengeance on the man who did away with his father and took that father's place with his mother, the man who shows him the repressed wishes of his own childhood realized. Thus the loathing which should drive him on to revenge is replaced in him by self-reproaches, by scruples of conscience, which remind him that he himself is literally no better than the sinner whom he is to punish. Here I have translated into conscious terms what was bound to remain unconscious in Hamlet's mind; and if anyone is inclined to call him a hysteric, I can only accept the fact as one that is implied by my interpretation. The distaste for sexuality expressed by Hamlet in his conversation with Ophelia fits in very well with this: the same distaste which was destined to take possession of the poet's mind more and more during the years that followed, and which reached its extreme expression in *Timon of Athens*. For it can of course only be the poet's own mind which confronts us in Hamlet. I observe in a book on Shakespeare by Georg Brandes[2] (1896) a statement that *Hamlet* was written immediately after the death of Shakespeare's father (in 1601), that is, under the immediate impact of his bereavement and, as we may well assume, while his childhood feelings about his father had been freshly revived. It is known, too, that Shakespeare's own son who died at an early age bore the name of 'Hamnet', which is identical with 'Hamlet'. Just as *Hamlet* deals with the relation of a son to his parents, so *Macbeth* (written at approximately the same period) is concerned with the subject of childlessness. But just as all neurotic symptoms, and, for that matter, dreams, are capable of being 'over-interpreted' and indeed need to be, if they are to be fully understood, so all genuinely creative writings are the product of more than a single motive and more than a single impulse in the poet's mind, and are open to more than a single interpretation. In what I have written I have only attempted to interpret the deepest layer of impulses in the mind of the creative writer.[3]

* * *

From *Chapter VI. The Dream-Work*

Every attempt that has hitherto been made to solve the problem of dreams has dealt directly with their *manifest* content as it is presented in our memory. All such attempts have endeavoured to arrive at an interpretation of dreams from their manifest content or (if no interpretation was attempted) to form a judgement as to their nature on the basis of that same manifest content. We are alone in taking something else into account. We have introduced a new class of psychical material between the manifest content of dreams and the conclusions of our enquiry: namely, their *latent* content, or (as we say) the 'dream-thoughts', arrived at by means of our procedure. It is from these dream-thoughts and not from a dream's manifest content that we disentangle its meaning. We are thus presented with a new task which had no previous existence: the task, that is, of investigating the relations

2. Danish critic and scholar (1842–1927); his *William Shakespeare* was translated into German in 1896.

3. [*Footnote added* 1919:] The above indications of a psycho-analytic explanation of *Hamlet* have since been amplified by Ernest Jones and defended against the alternative views put forward in the literature of the subject. (See Jones, *Hamlet and Oedipus*, 1910 [and, in a completer form, 1949].)—[*Added* 1930:] Incidentally, I have in the meantime ceased to believe that the author of Shakespeare's works was the man from Stratford [Freud's note].

between the manifest content of dreams and the latent dream-thoughts, and of tracing out the processes by which the latter have been changed into the former.

The dream-thoughts and the dream-content are presented to us like two versions of the same subject-matter in two different languages. Or, more properly, the dream-content seems like a transcript of the dream-thoughts into another mode of expression, whose characters and syntactic laws it is our business to discover by comparing the original and the translation. The dream-thoughts are immediately comprehensible, as soon as we have learnt them. The dream-content, on the other hand, is expressed as it were in a pictographic script, the characters of which have to be transposed individually into the language of the dream-thoughts. If we attempted to read these characters according to their pictorial value instead of according to their symbolic relation, we should clearly be led into error. Suppose I have a picture-puzzle, a rebus, in front of me. It depicts a house with a boat on its roof, a single letter of the alphabet, the figure of a running man whose head has been conjured away, and so on. Now I might be misled into raising objections and declaring that the picture as a whole and its component parts are nonsensical. A boat has no business to be on the roof of a house, and a headless man cannot run. Moreover, the man is bigger than the house; and if the whole picture is intended to represent a landscape, letters of the alphabet are out of place in it since such objects do not occur in nature. But obviously we can only form a proper judgement of the rebus if we put aside criticisms such as these of the whole composition and its parts and if, instead, we try to replace each separate element by a syllable or word that can be represented by that element in some way or other. The words which are put together in this way are no longer nonsensical but may form a poetical phrase of the greatest beauty and significance. A dream is a picture-puzzle of this sort and our predecessors in the field of dream-interpretation have made the mistake of treating the rebus as a pictorial composition: and as such it has seemed to them nonsensical and worthless.

(A).
THE WORK OF CONDENSATION

The first thing that becomes clear to anyone who compares the dream-content with the dream-thoughts is that a work of *condensation* on a large scale has been carried out. Dreams are brief, meagre and laconic in comparison with the range and wealth of the dream-thoughts. If a dream is written out it may perhaps fill half a page. The analysis setting out the dream-thoughts underlying it may occupy six, eight or a dozen times as much space. This relation varies with different dreams; but so far as my experience goes its direction never varies. As a rule one underestimates the amount of compression that has taken place, since one is inclined to regard the dream-thoughts that have been brought to light as the complete material, whereas if the work of interpretation is carried further it may reveal still more thoughts concealed behind the dream. I have already had occasion to point out that it is in fact never possible to be sure that a dream has been completely interpreted. Even if the solution seems satisfactory and without gaps, the possibility always remains that the dream may have yet another meaning.

Strictly speaking, then, it is impossible to determine the amount of condensation.

* * *

(B). THE WORK OF DISPLACEMENT

* * *

Among the thoughts that analysis brings to light are many which are relatively remote from the kernel of the dream and which look like artificial interpolations made for some particular purpose. That purpose is easy to divine. It is precisely *they* that constitute a connection, often a forced and far-fetched one, between the dream-content and the dream-thoughts; and if these elements were weeded out of the analysis the result would often be that the component parts of the dream-content would be left not only without overdetermination[4] but without any satisfactory determination at all. We shall be led to conclude that the multiple determination which decides what shall be included in a dream is not always a primary factor in dream-construction but is often the secondary product of a psychical force which is still unknown to us. Nevertheless multiple determination must be of importance in choosing what particular elements shall enter a dream, since we can see that a considerable expenditure of effort is used to bring it about in cases where it does not arise from the dream-material unassisted.

It thus seems plausible to suppose that in the dream-work a psychical force is operating which on the one hand strips the elements which have a high psychical value of their intensity, and on the other hand, *by means of overdetermination*, creates from elements of low psychical value new values, which afterwards find their way into the dream-content. If that is so, *a transference*[5] *and displacement of psychical intensities* occurs in the process of dream-formation, and it is as a result of these that the difference between the text of the dream-content and that of the dream-thoughts comes about. The process which we are here presuming is nothing less than the essential portion of the dream-work; and it deserves to be described as 'dream-displacement'. Dream-displacement and dream-condensation are the two governing factors to whose activity we may in essence ascribe the form assumed by dreams.

Nor do I think we shall have any difficulty in recognizing the psychical force which manifests itself in the facts of dream-displacement. The consequence of the displacement is that the dream-content no longer resembles the core of the dream-thoughts and that the dream gives no more than a distortion of the dream-wish which exists in the unconscious. But we are already familiar with dream-distortion. We traced it back to the censorship which is exercised by one psychical agency in the mind over another. Dream-displacement is one of the chief methods by which that distortion is achieved. *Is fecit cui profuit.*[6] We may assume, then, that dream-

4. That is, multiple causal factors (a model for causality implying a network rather than the simply linear).

5. A term that in psychoanalysis later comes to signify a displacement of psychical intensities from a person in the past to a person in the present (especially to the analyst, in the course of a treatment).

6. The old legal tag: "He did the deed who gained by it" [(Latin); translator's note].

displacement comes about through the influence of the same censorship—that is, the censorship of endopsychic defence.

The question of the interplay of these factors—of displacement, condensation and overdetermination—in the construction of dreams, and the question which is a dominant factor and which a subordinate one—all of this we shall leave aside for later investigation. But we can state provisionally a second condition which must be satisfied by those elements of the dream-thoughts which make their way into the dream: *they must escape the censorship imposed by resistance*. And henceforward in interpreting dreams we shall take dream-displacement into account as an undeniable fact.

(C).
THE MEANS OF REPRESENTATION IN DREAMS

In the process of transforming the latent thoughts into the manifest content of a dream we have found two factors at work: dream-condensation and dream-displacement. As we continue our investigation we shall, in addition to these, come across two further determinants which exercise an undoubted influence on the choice of the material which is to find access to the dream.

* * *

We are here interested only in the essential dream-thoughts. These usually emerge as a complex of thoughts and memories of the most intricate possible structure, with all the attributes of the trains of thought familiar to us in waking life. They are not infrequently trains of thought starting out from more than one centre, though having points of contact. Each train of thought is almost invariably accompanied by its contradictory counterpart, linked with it by antithetical association.

The different portions of this complicated structure stand, of course, in the most manifold logical relations to one another. They can represent foreground and background, digressions and illustrations, conditions, chains of evidence and counter-arguments. When the whole mass of these dream-thoughts is brought under the pressure of the dream-work, and its elements are turned about, broken into fragments and jammed together—almost like pack-ice—the question arises of what happens to the logical connections which have hitherto formed its framework. What representation do dreams provide for 'if', 'because', 'just as', 'although', 'either—or', and all the other conjunctions without which we cannot understand sentences or speeches?

In the first resort our answer must be that dreams have no means at their disposal for representing these logical relations between the dream-thoughts. For the most part dreams disregard all these conjunctions, and it is only the substantive content of the dream-thoughts that they take over and manipulate. The restoration of the connections which the dream-work has destroyed is a task which has to be performed by the interpretative process.

The incapacity of dreams to express these things must lie in the nature of the psychical material out of which dreams are made. The plastic arts of painting and sculpture labour, indeed, under a similar limitation as compared with poetry, which can make use of speech; and here once again the reason for their incapacity lies in the nature of the material which these two forms of art manipulate in their effort to express something. Before painting became acquainted with the laws of expression by which it is governed, it made attempts to get over this handicap. In ancient paintings small labels were hung from the mouths of the persons represented, containing in written characters the speeches which the artist despaired of representing pictorially.

At this point an objection may perhaps be raised in dispute of the idea that dreams are unable to represent logical relations. For there are dreams in which the most complicated intellectual operations take place, statements are contradicted or confirmed, ridiculed or compared, just as they are in waking thought. But here again appearances are deceitful. If we go into the interpretation of dreams such as these, we find that the whole of this *is part of the material of the dream-thoughts and is not a representation of intellectual work performed during the dream itself.* What is reproduced by the ostensible thinking in the dream is the *subject-matter* of the dream-thoughts and not the *mutual relations between them*, the assertion of which constitutes thinking. I shall bring forward some instances of this. But the easiest point to establish in this connection is that all spoken sentences which occur in dreams and are specifically described as such are unmodified or slightly modified reproductions of speeches which are also to be found among the recollections in the material of the dream-thoughts. A speech of this kind is often no more than an allusion to some event included among the dream-thoughts, and the meaning of the dream may be a totally different one.

* * *

What means does the dream-work possess for indicating these relations in the dream-thoughts which it is so hard to represent? I will attempt to enumerate them one by one.

In the first place, dreams take into account in a general way the connection which undeniably exists between all the portions of the dream-thoughts by combining the whole material into a single situation or event. They reproduce *logical connection* by *simultaneity in time*. Here they are acting like the painter who, in a picture of the School of Athens or of Parnassus,[7] represents in one group all the philosophers or all the poets. It is true that they were never in fact assembled in a single hall or on a single mountain-top; but they certainly form a group in the conceptual sense.

Dreams carry this method of reproduction down to details. Whenever they show us two elements close together, this guarantees that there is some specially intimate connection between what correspond to them among the dream-thoughts. In the same way, in our system of writing, '*ab*' means that the two letters are to be pronounced in a single syllable. If a gap is left between the '*a*' and the '*b*', it means that the '*a*' is the last letter of one word and the '*b*' is the first of the next one. So, too, collocations in dreams do not consist of any chance, disconnected portions of the dream-material, but of portions which are fairly closely connected in the dream-thoughts as well.

For representing *causal relations* dreams have two procedures which are in essence the same. Suppose the dream-thoughts run like this: 'Since this was so and so, such and such was bound to happen.' Then the commoner method of representation would be to introduce the dependent clause as an

7. A mountain in Greece sacred to Apollo and the Muses and hence the region of poetry. The School of Athens: Raphael's famous fresco of this title (1509–11) depicts philosophers of very different times as if they were contemporaries.

introductory dream and to add the principal clause as the main dream. If I have interpreted aright, the temporal sequence may be reversed. But the more extensive part of the dream always corresponds to the principal clause.

* * *

The alternative 'either—or' cannot be expressed in dreams in any way whatever. Both of the alternatives are usually inserted in the text of the dream as though they were equally valid. The dream of Irma's injection contains a classic instance of this.[8] Its latent thoughts clearly ran: 'I am not responsible for the persistence of Irma's pains; the responsibility lies *either* in her recalcitrance to accepting my solution, *or* in the unfavourable sexual conditions under which she lives and which I cannot alter, *or* in the fact that her pains are not hysterical at all but of an organic nature.' The dream, on the other hand, fulfilled *all* of these possibilities (which were almost mutually exclusive), and did not hesitate to add a fourth solution, based on the dream-wish. After interpreting the dream, I proceeded to insert the 'either—or' into the context of the dream-thoughts.

If, however, in reproducing a dream, its narrator feels inclined to make use of an 'either—or'—e.g. 'it was either a garden or a sitting-room'—what was present in the dream-thoughts was not an alternative but an 'and', a simple addition. An 'either—or' is mostly used to describe a dream-element that has a quality of vagueness—which, however, is capable of being resolved. In such cases the rule for interpretation is: treat the two apparent alternatives as of equal validity and link them together with an 'and'.

For instance, on one occasion a friend of mine was stopping in Italy and I had been without his address for a considerable time. I then had a dream of receiving a telegram containing this address. I saw it printed in blue on the telegraph form. The first word was vague:

'Via', perhaps
or *'Villa'*
or possibly even (*'Casa'*) } ; the second was clear: *'Secerno'*.

The second word sounded like some Italian name and reminded me of discussions I had had with my friend on the subject of etymology. It also expressed my anger with him for having kept his address *secret* from me for so long.[9] On the other hand, each of the three alternatives for the first word turned out on analysis to be an independent and equally valid starting-point for a chain of thoughts.[1]

During the night before my father's funeral I had a dream of a printed notice, placard or poster—rather like the notices forbidding one to smoke in railway waiting-rooms—on which appeared either

'You are requested to close the eyes'
or, 'You are requested to close an eye'.

8. Freud has previously described a dream in which he tells a patient, Irma, "If you still get pains, it's really only your fault"; it is that dream that Freud calls "the specimen dream of psychoanalysis."

9. The Italian word meaning "secret" is *segreto*; the verb *secernere* means "to secrete," in the sense of giving off a secretion.

1. This dream will be found described in greater detail in Freud's letter to [Wilhelm] Fliess (the friend in question) of April 28, 1897 [translator's note].

I usually write this in the form:

the
'You are requested to close eye(s).'
an

Each of these two versions had a meaning of its own and led in a different direction when the dream was interpreted. I had chosen the simplest possible ritual for the funeral, for I knew my father's own views on such ceremonies. But some other members of the family were not sympathetic to such puritanical simplicity and thought we should be disgraced in the eyes of those who attended the funeral. Hence one of the versions: 'You are requested to close an eye', i.e. to 'wink at' or 'overlook'. Here it is particularly easy to see the meaning of the vagueness expressed by the 'either—or'. The dream-work failed to establish a unified wording for the dream-thoughts which could at the same time be ambiguous, and the two main lines of thought consequently began to diverge even in the manifest content of the dream.[2]

In a few instances the difficulty of representing an alternative is got over by dividing the dream into two pieces of equal length.

The way in which dreams treat the category of contraries and contradictories is highly remarkable. It is simply disregarded. 'No' seems not to exist so far as dreams are concerned. They show a particular preference for combining contraries into a unity or for representing them as one and the same thing. Dreams feel themselves at liberty, moreover, to represent any element by its wishful contrary; so that there is no way of deciding at a first glance whether any element that admits of a contrary is present in the dream-thoughts as a positive or as a negative.[3]

* * *

1900, 1929

The "Uncanny"[1]

I

It is only rarely that a psycho-analyst feels impelled to investigate the subject of aesthetics, even when aesthetics is understood to mean not merely the theory of beauty but the theory of the qualities of feeling. He works in other strata of mental life and has little to do with the subdued emotional impulses which, inhibited in their aims and dependent on a host of concurrent factors,

2. This dream is reported by Freud in a letter to Fliess of November 2, 1896. It is there stated to have occurred during the night *after* the funeral. In its first wording the dream referred to closing the dead man's eyes as a filial duty [translator's note].

3. [*Footnote added* 1911:] I was astonished to learn from a pamphlet by K. Abel, *The Antithetical Meaning of Primal Words* (1884) (cf. my review of it, 1910)—and the fact has been confirmed by other philologists—that the most ancient languages behave exactly like dreams in this respect. In the first instance they have only a single word to describe the two contraries at the extreme ends of a series of qualities or activities (e.g., "strong-weak," "old-young," "far-near," "bind-sever"); they only form distinct terms for the two contraries by a secondary process of making small modifications in the common word. Abel demonstrates this particularly from Ancient Egyptian; but he shows that there are distinct traces of the same course of development in the Semitic and Indo-Germanic languages as well [Freud's note].

1. Translated by Alix Strachey, who sometimes adds a word or phrase in square brackets in the text for clarification.

usually furnish the material for the study of aesthetics. But it does occasionally happen that he has to interest himself in some particular province of that subject; and this province usually proves to be a rather remote one, and one which has been neglected in the specialist literature of aesthetics.

The subject of the 'uncanny'[2] is a province of this kind. It is undoubtedly related to what is frightening—to what arouses dread and horror; equally certainly, too, the word is not always used in a clearly definable sense, so that it tends to coincide with what excites fear in general. Yet we may expect that a special core of feeling is present which justifies the use of a special conceptual term. One is curious to know what this common core is which allows us to distinguish as 'uncanny' certain things which lie within the field of what is frightening.

As good as nothing is to be found upon this subject in comprehensive treatises on aesthetics, which in general prefer to concern themselves with what is beautiful, attractive and sublime—that is, with feelings of a positive nature—and with the circumstances and the objects that call them forth, rather than with the opposite feelings of repulsion and distress. I know of only one attempt in medico-psychological literature, a fertile but not exhaustive paper by Jentsch (1906).[3] But I must confess that I have not made a very thorough examination of the literature, especially the foreign literature, relating to this present modest contribution of mine, for reasons which, as may easily be guessed, lie in the times in which we live;[4] so that my paper is presented to the reader without any claim to priority.

In his study of the 'uncanny' Jentsch quite rightly lays stress on the obstacle presented by the fact that people vary so very greatly in their sensitivity to this quality of feeling. The writer of the present contribution, indeed, must himself plead guilty to a special obtuseness in the matter, where extreme delicacy of perception would be more in place. It is long since he has experienced or heard of anything which has given him an uncanny impression, and he must start by translating himself into that state of feeling, by awakening in himself the possibility of experiencing it. Still, such difficulties make themselves powerfully felt in many other branches of aesthetics; we need not on that account despair of finding instances in which the quality in question will be unhesitatingly recognized by most people.

Two courses are open to us at the outset. Either we can find out what meaning has come to be attached to the word 'uncanny' in the course of its history; or we can collect all those properties of persons, things, sense-impressions, experiences and situations which arouse in us the feeling of uncanniness, and then infer the unknown nature of the uncanny from what all these examples have in common. I will say at once that both courses lead to the same result: the uncanny is that class of the frightening which leads back to what is known of old and long familiar. How this is possible, in what circumstances the familiar can become uncanny and frightening, I shall show in what follows. Let me also add that my investigation was actually begun by collecting a number of individual cases, and was only later con-

2. The German word, translated throughout this paper by the English "uncanny," is *unheimlich*, literally "unhomely." The English term is not, of course, an exact equivalent of the German one [translator's note].

3. "On the Psychology of the Uncanny," by the German psychologist Ernst Jentsch (1867–1919).

4. An allusion to the First World War only just concluded [translator's note].

firmed by an examination of linguistic usage. In this discussion, however, I shall follow the reverse course.

The German word *'unheimlich'* is obviously the opposite of *'heimlich'* [homely], *'heimisch'* ['native']—the opposite of what is familiar; and we are tempted to conclude that what is 'uncanny' is frightening precisely because it is *not* known and familiar. Naturally not everything that is new and unfamiliar is frightening, however; the relation is not capable of inversion. We can only say that what is novel can easily become frightening and uncanny; some new things are frightening but not by any means all. Something has to be added to what is novel and unfamiliar in order to make it uncanny.

On the whole, Jentsch did not get beyond this relation of the uncanny to the novel and unfamiliar. He ascribes the essential factor in the production of the feeling of uncanniness to intellectual uncertainty; so that the uncanny would always, as it were, be something one does not know one's way about in. The better oriented in his environment a person is, the less readily will he get the impression of something uncanny in regard to the objects and events in it.

It is not difficult to see that this definition is incomplete, and we will therefore try to proceed beyond the equation 'uncanny' = 'unfamiliar'. We will first turn to other languages. But the dictionaries that we consult tell us nothing new, perhaps only because we ourselves speak a language that is foreign. Indeed, we get an impression that many languages are without a word for this particular shade of what is frightening.

I should like to express my indebtedness to Dr. Theodor Reik[5] for the following excerpts:—

LATIN: (K. E. Georges, *Deutschlateinisches Wörterbuch*, 1898). An uncanny place: *locus suspectus*; at an uncanny time of night: *intempesta nocte*.

GREEK: (Rost's and Schenkl's Lexikons). ξένος (i.e. strange, foreign).

ENGLISH: (from the dictionaries of Lucas, Bellows, Flügel and Muret-Sanders). Uncomfortable, uneasy, gloomy, dismal, uncanny, ghastly; (of a house) haunted; (of a man) a repulsive fellow.

FRENCH: (Sachs-Villatte). *Inquiétant, sinistre, lugubre, mal à son aise*.

SPANISH: (Tollhausen, 1889). *Sospechoso, de mal aguëro, lúgubre, siniestro*.

The Italian and Portuguese languages seem to content themselves with words which we should describe as circumlocutions. In Arabic and Hebrew 'uncanny' means the same as 'daemonic', 'gruesome'.

Let us therefore return to the German language. In Daniel Sanders's *Wörterbuch der Deutschen Sprache* (1860, 1:729), the following entry, which I here reproduce in full, is to be found under the word *'heimlich'*. I have laid stress on one or two passages by italicizing them.

Heimlich, adj., subst. *Heimlichkeit* (pl. *Heimlichkeiten*): I. Also *heimelich, heimelig*, belonging to the house, not strange, familiar, tame, intimate, friendly, etc.

(*a*) (Obsolete) belonging to the house or the family, or regarded as so

5. German psychologist (1888–1967).

belonging (cf. Latin *familiaris*, familiar): *Die Heimlichen*, the members of the household; *Der heimliche Rat* (Gen. xli, 45; 2 Sam. xxiii. 23; 1 Chron. xii. 25; Wisd. viii. 4), now more usually *Geheimer Rat* [Privy Councillor].

(*b*) Of animals: tame, companionable to man. As opposed to wild, e.g. 'Animals which are neither wild nor *heimlich*', etc. 'Wild animals . . . that are trained to be *heimlich* and accustomed to men.' 'If these young creatures are brought up from early days among men they become quite *heimlich*, friendly' etc.—So also: 'It (the lamb) is so *heimlich* and eats out of my hand.' 'Nevertheless, the stork is a beautiful, *heimelich* bird.'

(*c*) Intimate, friendly comfortable; the enjoyment of quiet content, etc., arousing a sense of agreeable restfulness and security as in one within the four walls of his house. 'Is it still *heimlich* to you in your country where strangers are felling your woods?' 'She did not feel too *heimlich* with him.' 'Along a high, *heimlich*, shady path . . . , beside a purling, gushing and babbling woodland brook.' 'To destroy the *Heimlichkeit* of the home.' 'I could not readily find another spot so intimate and *heimlich* as this.' 'We pictured it so comfortable, so nice, so cosy and *heimlich*.' 'In quiet *Heimlichkeit*, surrounded by close walls.' 'A careful housewife, who knows how to make a pleasing *Heimlichkeit* (*Häuslichkeit* [domesticity]) out of the smallest means.' 'The man who till recently had been so strange to him now seemed to him all the more *heimlich*.' 'The protestant land-owners do not feel . . . *heimlich* among their catholic inferiors.' 'When it grows *heimlich* and still, and the evening quiet alone watches over your cell.' 'Quiet, lovely and *heimlich*, no place more fitted for their rest.' 'He did not feel at all *heimlich* about it.'—Also, [in compounds] 'The place was so peaceful, so lonely, so shadily-*heimlich*.' 'The in- and outflowing waves of the current, dreamy and lullaby-*heimlich*.' Cf. in especial *Unheimlich* [see below]. Among Swabian Swiss authors in especial, often as a trisyllable: 'How *heimelich* it seemed to Ivo again of an evening, when he was at home.' 'It was so *heimelig* in the house.' 'The warm room and the *heimelig* afternoon.' 'When a man feels in his heart that he is so small and the Lord so great—that is what is truly *heimelig*.' 'Little by little they grew at ease and *heimelig* among themselves.' 'Friendly *Heimeligkeit*.' 'I shall be nowhere more *heimelich* than I am here.' 'That which comes from afar . . . assuredly does not live quite *heimelig* (*heimatlich* [at home], *freundnachbarlich* [in a neighbourly way]) among the people.' 'The cottage where he had once sat so often among his own people, so *heimelig*, so happy.' 'The sentinel's horn sounds so *heimelig* from the tower, and his voice invites so hospitably.' 'You go to sleep there so soft and warm, so wonderfully *heim'lig*.'—*This form of the word deserves to become general in order to protect this perfectly good sense of the word from becoming obsolete through an easy confusion with II* [see below]. Cf:' "*The Zecks* [a family name] *are all 'heimlich'.*" (in sense II) " *'Heimlich'? . . . What do you understand by 'heimlich'?" "Well, . . . they are like a buried spring or a dried-up pond. One cannot walk over it without always having the feeling that water might come up there again." "Oh, we call it 'unheimlich'; you call it 'heimlich'. Well, what makes you think that there is something secret and untrustworthy about this family?"* ' (Gutzkow).[6]

(*d*) Especially in Silesia: gay, cheerful; also of the weather.

6. Karl Gutzkow (1811–1878), German novelist and dramatist.

II. Concealed, kept from sight, so that others do not get to know of or about it, withheld from others. To do something *heimlich*, i.e. behind someone's back; to steal away *heimlich; heimlich* meetings and appointments; to look on with *heimlich* pleasure at someone's discomfiture; to sigh or weep *heimlich*; to behave *heimlich*, as though there was something to conceal; *heimlich* love-affair, love, sin; *heimlich* places (which good manners oblige us to conceal) (1 Sam. v. 6). 'The *heimlich* chamber' (privy) (2 Kings x. 27). Also, 'the *heimlich* chair'. 'To throw into pits or *Heimlichkeiten*'.—'Led the steeds *heimlich* before Laomedon.'—'As secretive, *heimlich*, deceitful and malicious towards cruel masters . . . as frank, open, sympathetic and helpful towards a friend in misfortune.' 'You have still to learn what is *heimlich* holiest to me.' 'The *heimlich* art' (magic). 'Where public ventilation has to stop, there *heimlich* machinations begin.' 'Freedom is the whispered watchword of *heimlich* conspirators and the loud battle-cry of professed revolutionaries.' 'A holy, *heimlich* effect.' 'I have roots that are most *heimlich*. I am grown in the deep earth.' 'My *heimlich* pranks.' 'If he is not given it openly and scrupulously he may seize it *heimlich* and unscrupulously.' 'He had achromatic telescopes constructed *heimlich* and secretly.' 'Henceforth I desire that there should be nothing *heimlich* any longer between us.'—To discover, disclose, betray someone's *Heimlichkeiten*; 'to concoct *Heimlichkeiten* behind my back'. 'In my time we studied *Heimlichkeit*.' 'The hand of understanding can alone undo the powerless spell of the *Heimlichkeit* (of hidden gold).' 'Say, where is the place of concealment . . . in what place of hidden *Heimlichkeit*?' 'Bees, who make the lock of *Heimlichkeiten*' (i.e. sealing-wax). 'Learned in strange *Heimlichkeiten*' (magic arts).

For compounds see above, Ic. Note especially the negative '*un-*': eerie, weird, arousing gruesome fear: 'Seeming quite *unheimlich* and ghostly to him.' 'The *unheimlich*, fearful hours of night.' 'I had already long since felt an *unheimlich*, even gruesome feeling.' 'Now I am beginning to have an *unheimlich* feeling.' . . . 'Feels an *unheimlich* horror.' '*Unheimlich* and motionless like a stone image.' 'The *unheimlich* mist called hill-fog.' 'These pale youths are *unheimlich* and are brewing heaven knows what mischief.' '*"Unheimlich" is the name for everything that ought to have remained . . . secret and hidden but has come to light*' (Schelling).[7]—'To veil the divine, to surround it with a certain *Unheimlichkeit*.'—*Unheimlich* is not often used as opposite to meaning II (above).

What interests us most in this long extract is to find that among its different shades of meaning the word '*heimlich*' exhibits one which is identical with its opposite, '*unheimlich*'. What is *heimlich* thus comes to be *unheimlich*. (Cf. the quotation from Gutzkow: 'We call it *"unheimlich"*; you call it *"heimlich"*.') In general we are reminded that the word '*heimlich*' is not unambiguous, but belongs to two sets of ideas, which, without being contradictory, are yet very different: on the one hand it means what is familiar and agreeable, and on the other, what is concealed and kept out of sight.[8] '*Unheimlich*' is customarily used, we are told, as the contrary only of the first signification of '*heimlich*', and not of the second. Sanders tells us nothing

7. Friedrich von Schelling (1775–1854), German philosopher.

8. According to the *Oxford English Dictionary*, a similar ambiguity attaches to the English "canny," which may mean not only "cosy" but also "endowed with occult or magical powers" [translator's note].

concerning a possible genetic connection between these two meanings of *heimlich*. On the other hand, we notice that Schelling says something which throws quite a new light on the concept of the *Unheimlich*, for which we were certainly not prepared. According to him, everything is *unheimlich* that ought to have remained secret and hidden but has come to light.

Some of the doubts that have thus arisen are removed if we consult Grimm's dictionary. (1877, 4.2:873ff.)

We read:

Heimlich; adj. and adv. *vernaculus, occultus*; MHG. heimelîch, heimlîch.

(P. 874.) In a slightly different sense: 'I feel *heimlich*, well, free from fear.' . . .

[3] (*b*) *Heimlich* is also used of a place free from ghostly influences . . . familiar, friendly, intimate.

(P. 875: *β*) Familiar, amicable, unreserved.

4. *From the idea of 'homelike', 'belonging to the house', the further idea is developed of something withdrawn from the eyes of strangers, something concealed, secret; and this idea is expanded in many ways* . . .

(P. 876.) 'On the left bank of the lake there lies a meadow *heimlich* in the wood.' (Schiller,[9] *Wilhelm Tell*, I. 4.) . . . Poetic license, rarely so used in modern speech . . . *Heimlich* is used in conjunction with a verb expressing the act of concealing: 'In the secret of his tabernacle he shall hide me *heimlich*.' (Ps. xxvii. 5.) . . . *Heimlich* parts of the human body, *pudenda* . . . 'the men that died not were smitten on their *heimlich* parts.' (1 Samuel v. 12.) . . .

(*c*) Officials who give important advice which has to be kept secret in matters of state are called *heimlich* councillors; the adjective, according to modern usage, has been replaced by *geheim* [secret] . . . 'Pharaoh called Joseph's name "him to whom secrets are revealed" ' (*heimlich* councillor). (Gen. xli. 45.)

(P. 878.) 6. *Heimlich*, as used of knowledge—mystic, allegorical: a *heimlich* meaning, *mysticus, divinus, occultus, figuratus*.

(P. 878.) *Heimlich* in a different sense, as withdrawn from knowledge, unconscious . . . *Heimlich* also has the meaning of that which is obscure, inaccessible to knowledge . . . 'Do you not see? They do not trust us; they fear the *heimlich* face of the Duke of Friedland.' (Schiller, *Wallensteins Lager*, Scene 2.)

9. *The notion of something hidden and dangerous, which is expressed in the last paragraph, is still further developed, so that 'heimlich' comes to have the meaning usually ascribed to 'unheimlich'*. Thus: 'At times I feel like a man who walks in the night and believes in ghosts; every corner is *heimlich* and full of terrors for him'. (Klinger,[1] *Theater*, 3:298.)

Thus *heimlich* is a word the meaning of which develops in the direction of ambivalence, until it finally coincides with its opposite, *unheimlich*. *Unheimlich* is in some way or other a sub-species of *heimlich*. Let us bear this discovery in mind, though we cannot yet rightly understand it, alongside of Schelling's definition of the *Unheimlich*. If we go on to examine individual instances of uncanniness, these hints will become intelligible to us.

9. FRIEDRICH VON SCHILLER (1759–1805), German dramatist, poet, and historian, whose plays include *Wilhelm Tell* (1804) and *Wallenstein's Camp* (1798).

1. Friedrich von Klinger (1752–1831), German dramatist and novelist.

II

When we proceed to review the things, persons, impressions, events and situations which are able to arouse in us a feeling of the uncanny in a particularly forcible and definite form, the first requirement is obviously to select a suitable example to start on. Jentsch has taken as a very good instance 'doubts whether an apparently animate being is really alive; or conversely, whether a lifeless object might not be in fact animate'; and he refers in this connection to the impression made by waxwork figures, ingeniously constructed dolls and automata. To these he adds the uncanny effect of epileptic fits, and of manifestations of insanity, because these excite in the spectator the impression of automatic, mechanical processes at work behind the ordinary appearance of mental activity. Without entirely accepting this author's view, we will take it as a starting-point for our own investigation because in what follows he reminds us of a writer who has succeeded in producing uncanny effects better than anyone else.

Jentsch writes: 'In telling a story, one of the most successful devices for easily creating uncanny effects is to leave the reader in uncertainty whether a particular figure in the story is a human being or an automaton, and to do it in such a way that his attention is not focused directly upon his uncertainty, so that he may not be led to go into the matter and clear it up immediately. That, as we have said, would quickly dissipate the peculiar emotional effect of the thing. E. T. A. Hoffmann[2] has repeatedly employed this psychological artifice with success in his fantastic narratives.'

This observation, undoubtedly a correct one, refers primarily to the story of 'The Sand-Man' in Hoffmann's *Nachtstücken,*[3] which contains the original of Olympia, the doll that appears in the first act of Offenbach's opera, *Tales of Hoffmann.*[4] But I cannot think—and I hope most readers of the story will agree with me—that the theme of the doll Olympia, who is to all appearances a living being, is by any means the only, or indeed the most important, element that must be held responsible for the quite unparalleled atmosphere of uncanniness evoked by the story. Nor is this atmosphere heightened by the fact that the author himself treats the episode of Olympia with a faint touch of satire and uses it to poke fun at the young man's idealization of his mistress. The main theme of the story is, on the contrary, something different, something which gives it its name, and which is always re-introduced at critical moments: it is the theme of the 'Sand-Man' who tears out children's eyes.

This fantastic tale opens with the childhood recollections of the student Nathaniel. In spite of his present happiness, he cannot banish the memories associated with the mysterious and terrifying death of his beloved father. On certain evenings his mother used to send the children to bed early, warning them that 'the Sand-Man was coming'; and, sure enough, Nathaniel would not fail to hear the heavy tread of a visitor, with whom his father would then be occupied for the evening. When questioned about the Sand-Man, his mother, it is true, denied that such a person existed except as a figure of

2. German author of fantastic and often humorous tales (1776–1822).
3. *Night Pieces* (1816–17); "The Sandman" was published in vol. 1 (1816).
4. An 1881 opera based on three tales by Hoffmann, by Jacques Offenbach (1819–1880), a German-born French composer of many light operas.

speech; but his nurse could give him more definite information: 'He's a wicked man who comes when children won't go to bed, and throws handfuls of sand in their eyes so that they jump out of their heads all bleeding. Then he puts the eyes in a sack and carries them off to the half-moon to feed his children. They sit up there in their nest, and their beaks are hooked like owls' beaks, and they use them to peck up naughty boys' and girls' eyes with.'

Although little Nathaniel was sensible and old enough not to credit the figure of the Sand-Man with such gruesome attributes, yet the dread of him became fixed in his heart. He determined to find out what the Sand-Man looked like; and one evening, when the Sand-Man was expected again, he hid in his father's study. He recognized the visitor as the lawyer Coppelius, a repulsive person whom the children were frightened of when he occasionally came to a meal; and he now identified this Coppelius with the dreaded Sand-Man. As regards the rest of the scene, Hoffmann already leaves us in doubt whether what we are witnessing is the first delirium of the panic-stricken boy, or a succession of events which are to be regarded in the story as being real. His father and the guest are at work at a brazier with glowing flames. The little eavesdropper hears Coppelius call out: 'Eyes here! Eyes here!' and betrays himself by screaming aloud. Coppelius seizes him and is on the point of dropping bits of red-hot coal from the fire into his eyes, and then of throwing them into the brazier, but his father begs him off and saves his eyes. After this the boy falls into a deep swoon; and a long illness brings his experience to an end. Those who decide in favour of the rationalistic interpretation of the Sand-Man will not fail to recognize in the child's phantasy the persisting influence of his nurse's story. The bits of sand that are to be thrown into the child's eyes turn into bits of red-hot coal from the flames; and in both cases they are intended to make his eyes jump out. In the course of another visit of the Sand-Man's, a year later, his father is killed in his study by an explosion. The lawyer Coppelius disappears from the place without leaving a trace behind.

Nathaniel, now a student, believes that he has recognized this phantom of horror from his childhood in an itinerant optician, an Italian called Giuseppe Coppola, who at his university town, offers him weather-glasses for sale. When Nathaniel refuses, the man goes on: 'Not weather-glasses? not weather-glasses? also got fine eyes, fine eyes!' The student's terror is allayed when he finds that the proffered eyes are only harmless spectacles, and he buys a pocket spy-glass from Coppola. With its aid he looks across into Professor Spalanzani's house opposite and there spies Spalanzani's beautiful, but strangely silent and motionless daughter, Olympia. He soon falls in love with her so violently that, because of her, he quite forgets the clever and sensible girl to whom he is betrothed. But Olympia is an automaton whose clock-work has been made by Spalanzani, and whose eyes have been put in by Coppola, the Sand-Man. The student surprises the two Masters quarrelling over their handiwork. The optician carries off the wooden eyeless doll; and the mechanician, Spalanzani, picks up Olympia's bleeding eyes from the ground and throws them at Nathaniel's breast, saying that Coppola had stolen them from the student. Nathaniel succumbs to a fresh attack of madness, and in his delirium his recollection of his father's death is mingled with this new experience. 'Hurry up! hurry up! ring of fire!' he cries. 'Spin about, ring of fire—Hurrah! Hurry up, wooden doll! lovely wooden doll, spin about—.'

He then falls upon the professor, Olympia's 'father', and tries to strangle him.

Rallying from a long and serious illness, Nathaniel seems at last to have recovered. He intends to marry his betrothed, with whom he has become reconciled. One day he and she are walking through the city market-place, over which the high tower of the Town Hall throws its huge shadow. On the girl's suggestion, they climb the tower, leaving her brother, who is walking with them, down below. From the top, Clara's attention is drawn to a curious object moving along the street. Nathaniel looks at this thing through Coppola's spy-glass, which he finds in his pocket, and falls into a new attack of madness. Shouting 'Spin about, wooden doll!' he tries to throw the girl into the gulf below. Her brother, brought to her side by her cries, rescues her and hastens down with her to safety. On the tower above, the madman rushes round, shrieking 'Ring of fire, spin about!'—and we know the origin of the words. Among the people who begin to gather below there comes forward the figure of the lawyer Coppelius, who has suddenly returned. We may suppose that it was his approach, seen through the spy-glass, which threw Nathaniel into his fit of madness. As the onlookers prepare to go up and overpower the madman, Coppelius laughs and says: 'Wait a bit; he'll come down of himself.' Nathaniel suddenly stands still, catches sight of Coppelius, and with a wild shriek 'Yes! "Fine eyes—fine eyes"!' flings himself over the parapet. While he lies on the paving-stones with a shattered skull the Sand-Man vanishes in the throng.

This short summary leaves no doubt, I think, that the feeling of something uncanny is directly attached to the figure of the Sand-Man, that is, to the idea of being robbed of one's eyes, and that Jentsch's point of an intellectual uncertainty has nothing to do with the effect. Uncertainty whether an object is living or inanimate, which admittedly applied to the doll Olympia, is quite irrelevant in connection with this other, more striking instance of uncanniness. It is true that the writer creates a kind of uncertainty in us in the beginning by not letting us know, no doubt purposely, whether he is taking us into the real world or into a purely fantastic one of his own creation. He has, of course, a right to do either; and if he chooses to stage his action in a world peopled with spirits, demons and ghosts, as Shakespeare does in *Hamlet*, in *Macbeth* and, in a different sense, in *The Tempest* and *A Midsummer-Night's Dream*, we must bow to his decision and treat his setting as though it were real for as long as we put ourselves into his hands. But this uncertainty disappears in the course of Hoffmann's story, and we perceive that he intends to make us, too, look through the demon optician's spectacles or spy-glass—perhaps, indeed, that the author in his very own person once peered through such an instrument. For the conclusion of the story makes it quite clear that Coppola the optician really *is* the lawyer Coppelius[5] and also, therefore, the Sand-Man.

There is no question therefore, of any intellectual uncertainty here: we know now that we are not supposed to be looking on at the products of a madman's imagination, behind which we, with the superiority of rational minds, are able to detect the sober truth; and yet this knowledge does not

5. Frau Dr. Rank has pointed out the association of the name with *coppella* = crucible, connecting it with the chemical operations that caused the father's death; and also with *coppo* = eye-socket [Freud's note].

lessen the impression of uncanniness in the least degree. The theory of intellectual uncertainty is thus incapable of explaining that impression.

We know from psycho-analytic experience, however, that the fear of damaging or losing one's eyes is a terrible one in children. Many adults retain their apprehensiveness in this respect, and no physical injury is so much dreaded by them as an injury to the eye. We are accustomed to say, too, that we will treasure a thing as the apple of our eye. A study of dreams, phantasies and myths has taught us that anxiety about one's eyes, the fear of going blind, is often enough a substitute for the dread of being castrated. The self-blinding of the mythical criminal, Oedipus,[6] was simply a mitigated form of the punishment of castration—the only punishment that was adequate for him by the *lex talionis*.[7] We may try on rationalistic grounds to deny that fears about the eye are derived from the fear of castration, and may argue that it is very natural that so precious an organ as the eye should be guarded by a proportionate dread. Indeed, we might go further and say that the fear of castration itself contains no other significance and no deeper secret than a justifiable dread of this rational kind. But this view does not account adequately for the substitutive relation between the eye and the male organ which is seen to exist in dreams and myths and phantasies; nor can it dispel the impression that the threat of being castrated in especial excites a peculiarly violent and obscure emotion, and that this emotion is what first gives the idea of losing other organs its intense colouring. All further doubts are removed when we learn the details of their 'castration complex' from the analysis of neurotic patients, and realize its immense importance in their mental life.

Moreover, I would not recommend any opponent of the psycho-analytic view to select this particular story of the Sand-Man with which to support his argument that anxiety about the eyes has nothing to do with the castration complex. For why does Hoffmann bring the anxiety about eyes into such intimate connection with the father's death? And why does the Sand-Man always appear as a disturber of love? He separates the unfortunate Nathaniel from his betrothed and from her brother, his best friend; he destroys the second object of his love, Olympia, the lovely doll; and he drives him into suicide at the moment when he has won back his Clara and is about to be happily united to her. Elements in the story like these, and many others, seem arbitrary and meaningless so long as we deny all connection between fears about the eye and castration; but they become intelligible as soon as we replace the Sand-Man by the dreaded father at whose hands castration is expected.[8]

6. Oedipus, a favorite subject of Greek tragedy and vase painting, was king of Thebes; he blinded himself when he realized that he had killed his father and married his mother.

7. Law of retaliation in kind (Latin).

8. In fact, Hoffmann's imaginative treatment of his material has not made such wild confusion of its elements that we cannot reconstruct their original arrangement. In the story of Nathaniel's childhood, the figures of his father and Coppelius represent the two opposites into which the father-imago is split by his ambivalence; whereas the one threatens to blind him—that is, to castrate him—, the other, the "good" father, intercedes for his sight. The part of the complex which is most strongly repressed, the death-wish against the "bad" father, finds expression in the death of the "good" father, and Coppelius is made answerable for it. This pair of fathers is represented later, in his student days, by Professor Spalanzani and Coppola the optician. The Professor is in himself a member of the father-series, and Coppola is recognized as identical with Coppelius the lawyer. Just as they used before to work together over the secret brazier, so now they have jointly created the doll Olympia; the Professor is even called the father of Olympia. This double occurrence of activity in common betrays them as divisions of the father-imago: both the mechanician and the optician were the father of Nathaniel (and of

We shall venture, therefore, to refer the uncanny effect of the Sand-Man to the anxiety belonging to the castration complex of childhood. But having reached the idea that we can make an infantile factor such as this responsible for feelings of uncanniness, we are encouraged to see whether we can apply it to other instances of the uncanny. We find in the story of the Sand-Man the other theme on which Jentsch lays stress, of a doll which appears to be alive. Jentsch believes that a particularly favourable condition for awakening uncanny feelings is created when there is intellectual uncertainty whether an object is alive or not, and when an inanimate object becomes too much like an animate one. Now, dolls are of course rather closely connected with childhood life. We remember that in their early games children do not distinguish at all sharply between living and inanimate objects, and that they are especially fond of treating their dolls like live people. In fact, I have occasionally heard a woman patient declare that even at the age of eight she had still been convinced that her dolls would be certain to come to life if she were to look at them in a particular, extremely concentrated, way. So that here, too, it is not difficult to discover a factor from childhood. But, curiously enough, while the Sand-Man story deals with the arousing of an early childhood fear, the idea of a 'living doll' excites no fear at all; children have no fear of their dolls coming to life, they may even desire it. The source of uncanny feelings would not, therefore, be an infantile fear in this case, but rather an infantile wish or even merely an infantile belief. There seems to be a contradiction here; but perhaps it is only a complication, which may be helpful to us later on.

Hoffmann is the unrivalled master of the uncanny in literature. His novel, *Die Elixiere des Teufels*,[9] contains a whole mass of themes to which one is tempted to ascribe the uncanny effect of the narrative; but it is too obscure and intricate a story for us to venture upon a summary of it. Towards the end of the book the reader is told the facts, hitherto concealed from him, from which the action springs; with the result, not that he is at last enlightened, but that he falls into a state of complete bewilderment. The author has piled up too much material of the same kind. In consequence one's grasp

Olympia as well). In the frightening scene in childhood, Coppelius, after sparing Nathaniel's eyes, had screwed off his arms and legs as an experiment; that is, he had worked on him as a mechanician would on a doll. This singular feature, which seems quite outside the picture of the Sand-Man, introduces a new castration equivalent; but it also points to the inner identity of Coppelius with his later counterpart, Spalanzani the mechanician, and prepares us for the interpretation of Olympia. This automatic doll can be nothing else than a materialization of Nathaniel's feminine attitude towards his father in his infancy. Her fathers, Spalanzani and Coppola, are, after all, nothing but new editions, reincarnations of Nathaniel's pair of fathers. Spalanzani's otherwise incomprehensible statement that the optician has stolen Nathaniel's eyes, so as to set them in the doll, now becomes significant as supplying evidence of the identity of Olympia and Nathaniel. Olympia is, as it were, a dissociated complex of Nathaniel's which confronts him as a person, and Nathaniel's enslavement to this complex is expressed in his senseless obsessive love for Olympia. We may with justice call love of this kind narcissistic, and we can understand why someone who has fallen victim to it should relinquish the real, external object of his love. The psychological truth of the situation in which the young man, fixated upon his father by his castration complex, becomes incapable of loving a woman, is amply proved by numerous analyses of patients whose story, though less fantastic, is hardly less tragic than that of the student Nathaniel.

Hoffmann was the child of an unhappy marriage. When he was three years old, his father left his small family, and was never united to them again. According to Grisebach, in his biographical introduction to Hoffmann's works, the writer's relation to his father was always a most sensitive subject with him [Freud's note]. Eduard Grisebach (1845–1906), German diplomat, editor, and literary historian; his edition of Hoffmann's *Complete Works* was published in 1905.

9. *The Devil's Elixirs* (1816).

of the story as a whole suffers, though not the impression it makes. We must content ourselves with selecting those themes of uncanniness which are most prominent, and with seeing whether they too can fairly be traced back to infantile sources. These themes are all concerned with the phenomenon of the 'double', which appears in every shape and in every degree of development. Thus we have characters who are to be considered identical because they look alike. This relation is accentuated by mental processes leaping from one of these characters to another—by what we should call telepathy—, so that the one possesses knowledge, feelings and experience in common with the other. Or it is marked by the fact that the subject identifies himself with someone else, so that he is in doubt as to which his self is, or substitutes the extraneous self for his own. In other words, there is a doubling, dividing and interchanging of the self. And finally there is the constant recurrence of the same thing[1]—the repetition of the same features or character-traits or vicissitudes, of the same crimes, or even the same names through several consecutive generations.

The theme of the 'double' has been very thoroughly treated by Otto Rank (1914).[2] He has gone into the connections which the 'double' has with reflections in mirrors, with shadows, with guardian spirits, with the belief in the soul and with the fear of death; but he also lets in a flood of light on the surprising evolution of the idea. For the 'double' was originally an insurance against the destruction of the ego, an 'energetic denial of the power of death', as Rank says; and probably the 'immortal' soul was the first 'double' of the body. This invention of doubling as a preservation against extinction has its counterpart in the language of dreams, which is fond of representing castration by a doubling or multiplication of a genital symbol. The same desire led the Ancient Egyptians to develop the art of making images of the dead in lasting materials. Such ideas, however, have sprung from the soil of unbounded self-love, from the primary narcissism which dominates the mind of the child and of primitive man. But when this stage has been surmounted, the 'double' reverses its aspect. From having been an assurance of immortality, it becomes the uncanny harbinger of death.

The idea of the 'double' does not necessarily disappear with the passing of primary narcissism, for it can receive fresh meaning from the later stages of the ego's development. A special agency is slowly formed there, which is able to stand over against the rest of the ego, which has the function of observing and criticizing the self and of exercising a censorship within the mind, and which we become aware of as our 'conscience'. In the pathological case of delusions of being watched, this mental agency becomes isolated, dissociated from the ego, and discernible to the physician's eye. The fact that an agency of this kind exists, which is able to treat the rest of the ego like an object—the fact, that is, that man is capable of self-observation—renders it possible to invest the old idea of a 'double' with a new meaning and to ascribe a number of things to it—above all, those things which seem to self-criticism to belong to the old surmounted narcissism of earliest times.[3]

1. This phrase seems to be an echo from Nietzsche (e.g., from the last part of *Also Sprach Zarathustra* [1883–92]). In chapter 3 of *Beyond the Pleasure Principle* (1920), Freud puts a similar phrase, "the perpetual recurrence of the same thing," into inverted commas [translator's note].

2. "Der Doppelgänger" ("The Double"), by Rank (1884–1939), Austrian psychotherapist and a colleague of Freud's.

3. I believe that when poets complain that two souls dwell in the human breast, and when popular psychologists talk of the splitting of people's egos,

But it is not only this latter material, offensive as it is to the criticism of the ego, which may be incorporated in the idea of a double. There are also all the unfulfilled but possible futures to which we still like to cling in phantasy, all the strivings of the ego which adverse external circumstances have crushed, and all our suppressed acts of volition which nourish in us the illusion of Free Will.[4]

But after having thus considered the *manifest* motivation of the figure of a 'double', we have to admit that none of this helps us to understand the extraordinarily strong feeling of something uncanny that pervades the conception; and our knowledge of pathological mental processes enables us to add that nothing in this more superficial material could account for the urge towards defence which has caused the ego to project that material outward as something foreign to itself. When all is said and done, the quality of uncanniness can only come from the fact of the 'double' being a creation dating back to a very early mental stage, long since surmounted—a stage, incidentally, at which it wore a more friendly aspect. The 'double' has become a thing of terror, just as, after the collapse of their religion, the gods turned into demons.[5]

The other forms of ego-disturbance exploited by Hoffmann can easily be estimated along the same lines as the theme of the 'double'. They are a harking-back to particular phases in the evolution of the self-regarding feeling, a regression to a time when the ego had not yet marked itself off sharply from the external world and from other people. I believe that these factors are partly responsible for the impression of uncanniness, although it is not easy to isolate and determine exactly their share of it.

The factor of the repetition of the same thing will perhaps not appeal to everyone as a source of uncanny feeling. From what I have observed, this phenomenon does undoubtedly, subject to certain conditions and combined with certain circumstances, arouse an uncanny feeling, which, furthermore, recalls the sense of helplessness experienced in some dream-states. As I was walking, one hot summer afternoon, through the deserted streets of a provincial town in Italy which was unknown to me, I found myself in a quarter of whose character I could not long remain in doubt. Nothing but painted women were to be seen at the windows of the small houses, and I hastened to leave the narrow street at the next turning. But after having wandered about for a time without enquiring my way, I suddenly found myself back in the same street, where my presence was now beginning to excite attention. I hurried away once more, only to arrive by another *détour* at the same place yet a third time. Now, however, a feeling overcame me which I can only describe as uncanny, and I was glad enough to find myself back at the piazza I had left a short while before, without any further voyages of discovery. Other situations which have in common with my adventure an unintended

what they are thinking of is this division (in the sphere of ego-psychology) between the critical agency and the rest of the ego, and not the antithesis discovered by psycho-analysis between the ego and what is unconscious and repressed. It is true that the distinction between these two antitheses is to some extent effaced by the circumstance that foremost among the things that are rejected by the criticism of the ego are derivatives of the repressed [Freud's note].

4. In [Hanns] Ewers's [1871–1943] *Der Student von Prag* [1912 film], which serves as the starting-point of Rank's study on the "double," the hero has promised his beloved not to kill his antagonist in a duel. But on his way to the duelling-ground he meets his "double," who has already killed his rival [Freud's note].

5. Heine, *Die Götter im Exil* [1854, "The Gods in Exile"; Freud's note]. Heinrich Heine (1797–1856), German poet and critic.

recurrence of the same situation, but which differ radically from it in other respects, also result in the same feeling of helplessness and of uncanniness. So, for instance, when, caught in a mist perhaps, one has lost one's way in a mountain forest, every attempt to find the marked or familiar path may bring one back again and again to one and the same spot, which one can identify by some particular landmark. Or one may wander about in a dark, strange room, looking for the door or the electric switch, and collide time after time with the same piece of furniture—though it is true that Mark Twain[6] succeeded by wild exaggeration in turning this latter situation into something irresistibly comic.

If we take another class of things, it is easy to see that there, too, it is only this factor of involuntary repetition which surrounds what would otherwise be innocent enough with an uncanny atmosphere, and forces upon us the idea of something fateful and inescapable when otherwise we should have spoken only of 'chance'. For instance, we naturally attach no importance to the event when we hand in an overcoat and get a cloakroom ticket with the number, let us say, 62; or when we find that our cabin on a ship bears that number. But the impression is altered if two such events, each in itself indifferent, happen close together—if we come across the number 62 several times in a single day, or if we begin to notice that everything which has a number—addresses, hotel rooms, compartments in railway trains—invariably has the same one, or at all events one which contains the same figures. We do feel this to be uncanny. And unless a man is utterly hardened and proof against the lure of superstition, he will be tempted to ascribe a secret meaning to this obstinate recurrence of a number; he will take it, perhaps, as an indication of the span of life allotted to him.[7] Or suppose one is engaged in reading the works of the famous physiologist, Hering,[8] and within the space of a few days receives two letters from two different countries, each from a person called Hering, though one has never before had any dealings with anyone of that name. Not long ago an ingenious scientist (Kammerer, 1919)[9] attempted to reduce coincidences of this kind to certain laws, and so deprive them of their uncanny effect. I will not venture to decide whether he has succeeded or not.

How exactly we can trace back to infantile psychology the uncanny effect of such similar recurrences is a question I can only lightly touch on in these pages; and I must refer the reader instead to another work,[1] already completed, in which this has been gone into in detail, but in a different connection. For it is possible to recognize the dominance in the unconscious mind of a 'compulsion to repeat' proceeding from the instinctual impulses and probably inherent in the very nature of the instincts—a compulsion powerful enough to overrule the pleasure principle, lending to certain aspects of the mind their daemonic character, and still very clearly expressed in the impulses of small children; a compulsion, too, which is responsible for a part

6. Pen name of Samuel L. Clemens (1835–1910), American writer. Freud refers to a passage in his 1880 work *A Tramp Abroad*.
7. Freud had himself reached the age of 62 a year earlier, in 1918 [translator's note].
8. Ewald Hering (1834–1918), German physiologist and psychologist.
9. *Das Gesetz der Serie* (*The Law of Series*), by the Austrian zoologist Paul Kammerer (1880–1926).

1. This was published a year later as *Beyond the Pleasure Principle* (1920). The various manifestations of the "compulsion to repeat" enumerated here are enlarged upon in chapters 2 and 3 of that work. The "compulsion to repeat" had already been described by Freud as a clinical phenomenon, in a technical paper published five years earlier [translator's note].

of the course taken by the analyses of neurotic patients. All these considerations prepare us for the discovery that whatever reminds us of this inner 'compulsion to repeat' is perceived as uncanny.

Now, however, it is time to turn from these aspects of the matter, which are in any case difficult to judge, and look for some undeniable instances of the uncanny, in the hope that an analysis of them will decide whether our hypothesis is a valid one.

In the story of 'The Ring of Polycrates',[2] the King of Egypt turns away in horror from his host, Polycrates, because he sees that his friend's every wish is at once fulfilled, his every care promptly removed by kindly fate. His host has become 'uncanny' to him. His own explanation, that the too fortunate man has to fear the envy of the gods, seems obscure to us; its meaning is veiled in mythological language. We will therefore turn to another example in a less grandiose setting. In the case history of an obsessional neurotic,[3] I have described how the patient once stayed in a hydropathic establishment and benefited greatly by it. He had the good sense, however, to attribute his improvement not to the therapeutic properties of the water, but to the situation of his room, which immediately adjoined that of a very accommodating nurse. So on his second visit to the establishment he asked for the same room, but was told that it was already occupied by an old gentleman, whereupon he gave vent to his annoyance in the words: 'I wish he may be struck dead for it.' A fortnight later the old gentleman really did have a stroke. My patient thought this an 'uncanny' experience. The impression of uncanniness would have been stronger still if less time had elapsed between his words and the untoward event, or if he had been able to report innumerable similar coincidences. As a matter of fact, he had no difficulty in producing coincidences of this sort; but then not only he but every obsessional neurotic I have observed has been able to relate analogous experiences. They are never surprised at their invariably running up against someone they have just been thinking of, perhaps for the first time for a long while. If they say one day 'I haven't had any news of so-and-so for a long time', they will be sure to get a letter from him the next morning, and an accident or a death will rarely take place without having passed through their mind a little while before. They are in the habit of referring to this state of affairs in the most modest manner, saying that they have 'presentiments' which 'usually' come true.

One of the most uncanny and wide-spread forms of superstition is the dread of the evil eye, which has been exhaustively studied by the Hamburg oculist Seligmann (1910–11).[4] There never seems to have been any doubt about the source of this dread. Whoever possesses something that is at once valuable and fragile is afraid of other people's envy, in so far as he projects on to them the envy he would have felt in their place. A feeling like this betrays itself by a look[5] even though it is not put into words; and when a man is prominent owing to noticeable, and particularly owing to unattractive,

2. A poem by Schiller, based on the story in the Greek historian Herodotus (ca. 484–ca. 425 B.C.E.), 3.40–43; it became in turn the basis of a 1-act opera by Erich Korngold (1913).

3. "Notes upon a Case of Obsessional Neurosis" (1909) [Freud's note].

4. *Der böse Blick und Verwandtes: Ein Beitrag zur Geschichte des Aberglaubens der aller Zeiten und Völker* (*The Evil Eye and Related Beliefs: An Investigation into the Superstitions of All Times and Peoples*), by Siegfried Seligmann (1870–1926).

5. "The evil eye" in German is *der böse Blick*, literally "the evil look" [translator's note].

attributes, other people are ready to believe that his envy is rising to a more than usual degree of intensity and that this intensity will convert it into effective action. What is feared is thus a secret intention of doing harm, and certain signs are taken to mean that that intention has the necessary power at its command.

These last examples of the uncanny are to be referred to the principle which I have called 'omnipotence of thoughts', taking the name from an expression used by one of my patients. And now we find ourselves on familiar ground. Our analysis of instances of the uncanny has led us back to the old, animistic conception of the universe. This was characterized by the idea that the world was peopled with the spirits of human beings; by the subject's narcissistic overvaluation of his own mental processes; by the belief in the omnipotence of thoughts and the technique of magic based on that belief; by the attribution to various outside persons and things of carefully graded magical powers, or *'mana'*;[6] as well as by all the other creations with the help of which man, in the unrestricted narcissism of that stage of development, strove to fend off the manifest prohibitions of reality. It seems as if each one of us has been through a phase of individual development corresponding to this animistic stage in primitive men, that none of us has passed through it without preserving certain residues and traces of it which are still capable of manifesting themselves, and that everything which now strikes us as 'uncanny' fulfils the condition of touching those residues of animistic mental activity within us and bringing them to expression.[7]

At this point I will put forward two considerations which, I think, contain the gist of this short study. In the first place, if psycho-analytic theory is correct in maintaining that every affect belonging to an emotional impulse, whatever its kind, is transformed, if it is repressed, into anxiety, then among instances of frightening things there must be one class in which the frightening element can be shown to be something repressed which *recurs*. This class of frightening things would then constitute the uncanny; and it must be a matter of indifference whether what is uncanny was itself originally frightening or whether it carried some *other* affect. In the second place, if this is indeed the secret nature of the uncanny, we can understand why linguistic usage has extended *das Heimliche* ['homely'] into its opposite, *das Unheimliche*; for this uncanny is in reality nothing new or alien, but something which is familiar and old-established in the mind and which has become alienated from it only through the process of repression. This reference to the factor of repression enables us, furthermore, to understand Schelling's definition of the uncanny as something which ought to have remained hidden but has come to light.

It only remains for us to test our new hypothesis on one or two more examples of the uncanny.

Many people experience the feeling in the highest degree in relation to death and dead bodies, to the return of the dead, and to spirits and ghosts. As we have seen some languages in use to-day can only render the German

6. Anthropological term used of "primitive" cultures.

7. Cf. my book *Totem and Taboo* (1912–13), Essay III, "Animism, Magic, and the Omnipotence of Thoughts," where the following footnote will be found: "We appear to attribute an 'uncanny' quality to impressions that seek to confirm the omnipotence of thoughts and the animistic mode of thinking in general, after we have reached a stage at which, in our *judgement*, we have abandoned such beliefs" [Freud's note].

expression 'an *unheimlich* house' by 'a *haunted* house'. We might indeed have begun our investigation with this example, perhaps the most striking of all, of something uncanny, but we refrained from doing so because the uncanny in it is too much intermixed with what is purely gruesome and is in part overlaid by it. There is scarcely any other matter, however, upon which our thoughts and feelings have changed so little since the very earliest times, and in which discarded forms have been so completely preserved under a thin disguise, as our relation to death. Two things account for our conservatism: the strength of our original emotional reaction to death and the insufficiency of our scientific knowledge about it. Biology has not yet been able to decide whether death is the inevitable fate of every living being or whether it is only a regular but yet perhaps avoidable event in life. It is true that the statement 'All men are mortal' is paraded in text-books of logic as an example of a general proposition; but no human being really grasps it, and our unconscious has as little use now as it ever had for the idea of its own mortality. Religions continue to dispute the importance of the undeniable fact of individual death and to postulate a life after death; civil governments still believe that they cannot maintain moral order among the living if they do not uphold the prospect of a better life hereafter as a recompense for mundane existence. In our great cities, placards announce lectures that undertake to tell us how to get into touch with the souls of the departed; and it cannot be denied that not a few of the most able and penetrating minds among our men of science have come to the conclusion, especially towards the close of their own lives, that a contact of this kind is not impossible. Since almost all of us still think as savages do on this topic, it is no matter for surprise that the primitive fear of the dead is still so strong within us and always ready to come to the surface on any provocation. Most likely our fear still implies the old belief that the dead man becomes the enemy of his survivor and seeks to carry him off to share his new life with him. Considering our unchanged attitude towards death, we might rather enquire what has become of the repression, which is the necessary condition of a primitive feeling recurring in the shape of something uncanny. But repression is there, too. All supposedly educated people have ceased to believe officially that the dead can become visible as spirits, and have made any such appearances dependent on improbable and remote conditions; their emotional attitude towards their dead, moreover, once a highly ambiguous and ambivalent one, has been toned down in the higher strata of the mind into an unambiguous feeling of piety.

We have now only a few remarks to add—for animism, magic and sorcery, the omnipotence of thoughts, man's attitude to death, involuntary repetition and the castration complex comprise practically all the factors which turn something frightening into something uncanny.

We can also speak of a living person as uncanny, and we do so when we ascribe evil intentions to him. But that is not all; in addition to this we must feel that his intentions to harm us are going to be carried out with the help of special powers. A good instance of this is the *'Gettatore'*,[8] that uncanny figure of Romanic superstition which Schaeffer,[9] with intuitive poetic feeling

8. Literally "thrower" (of bad luck), or "one who casts" (the evil eye) [translator's note].

9. Albrecht Schaeffer (1885–1950), who published the novel *Josef Montfort* in 1918.

and profound psycho-analytic understanding, has transformed into a sympathetic character in his *Josef Montfort*. But the question of these secret powers brings us back again to the realm of animism. It was the pious Gretchen's intuition that Mephistopheles possessed secret powers of this kind that made him so uncanny to her.

> Sie fühlt dass ich ganz sicher ein Genie,
> Vielleicht sogar der Teufel bin.[1]

The uncanny effect of epilepsy and of madness has the same origin. The layman sees in them the working of forces hitherto unsuspected in his fellow-men, but at the same time he is dimly aware of them in remote corners of his own being. The Middle Ages quite consistently ascribed all such maladies to the influence of demons, and in this their psychology was almost correct. Indeed, I should not be surprised to hear that psycho-analysis, which is concerned with laying bare these hidden forces, has itself become uncanny to many people for that very reason. In one case, after I had succeeded—though none too rapidly—in effecting a cure in a girl who had been an invalid for many years, I myself heard this view expressed by the patient's mother long after her recovery.

Dismembered limbs, a severed head, a hand cut off at the wrist, as in a fairy tale of Hauff's,[2] feet which dance by themselves, as in the book by Schaeffer which I mentioned above—all these have something peculiarly uncanny about them, especially when, as in the last instance, they prove capable of independent activity in addition. As we already know, this kind of uncanniness springs from its proximity to the castration complex. To some people the idea of being buried alive by mistake is the most uncanny thing of all. And yet psycho-analysis has taught us that this terrifying phantasy is only a transformation of another phantasy which had originally nothing terrifying about it at all, but was qualified by a certain lasciviousness—the phantasy, I mean, of intra-uterine existence.

There is one more point of general application which I should like to add, though, strictly speaking, it has been included in what has already been said about animism and modes of working of the mental apparatus that have been surmounted; for I think it deserves special emphasis. This is that an uncanny effect is often and easily produced when the distinction between imagination and reality is effaced, as when something that we have hitherto regarded as imaginary appears before us in reality, or when a symbol takes over the full functions of the thing it symbolizes, and so on. It is this factor which contributes not a little to the uncanny effect attaching to magical practices. The infantile element in this, which also dominates the minds of neurotics, is the over-accentuation of psychical reality in comparison with material reality—a feature closely allied to the belief in the omnipotence of thoughts. In the middle of the isolation of war-time a number of the English *Strand Magazine* fell into my hands; and, among other somewhat redundant matter, I

1. "She feels that surely I'm a genius now,—Perhaps the very Devil indeed!" Goethe, *Faust*, Part I [1808], scene 16; Bayard Taylor's translation [1870–71; translator's note]. Johann Wolfgang von Goethe (1749–1832), German poet, playwright, and dramatist. Mephistopheles is the spirit to whom the old Faust promises his soul; Gretchen is the young girl whom Faust, made young again, falls in love with and seduces.

2. *Die Geschichte von der abgehauenen Hand* (The Story of the Severed Hand) [translator's note]. Wilhelm Hauff (1802–1827), German novelist.

read a story about a young married couple who move into a furnished house in which there is a curiously shaped table with carvings of crocodiles on it. Towards evening an intolerable and very specific smell begins to pervade the house; they stumble over something in the dark; they seem to see a vague form gliding over the stairs—in short, we are given to understand that the presence of the table causes ghostly crocodiles to haunt the place, or that the wooden monsters come to life in the dark, or something of the sort. It was a naïve enough story, but the uncanny feeling it produced was quite remarkable.

To conclude this collection of examples, which is certainly not complete, I will relate an instance taken from psycho-analytic experience; if it does not rest upon mere coincidence, it furnishes a beautiful confirmation of our theory of the uncanny. It often happens that neurotic men declare that they feel there is something uncanny about the female genital organs. This *unheimlich* place, however, is the entrance to the former *Heim* [home] of all human beings, to the place where each one of us lived once upon a time and in the beginning. There is a joking saying that 'Love is home-sickness'; and whenever a man dreams of a place or a country and says to himself, while he is still dreaming: 'this place is familiar to me, I've been here before', we may interpret the place as being his mother's genitals or her body. In this case too, then, the *unheimlich* is what was once *heimisch*, familiar; the prefix '*un*' ['un-'] is the token of repression.

III

In the course of this discussion the reader will have felt certain doubts arising in his mind; and he must now have an opportunity of collecting them and bringing them forward.

It may be true that the uncanny [*unheimlich*] is something which is secretly familiar [*heimlich-heimisch*], which has undergone repression and then returned from it, and that everything that is uncanny fulfils this condition. But the selection of material on this basis does not enable us to solve the problem of the uncanny. For our proposition is clearly not convertible. Not everything that fulfils this condition—not everything that recalls repressed desires and surmounted modes of thinking belonging to the prehistory of the individual and of the race—is on that account uncanny.

Nor shall we conceal the fact that for almost every example adduced in support of our hypothesis one may be found which rebuts it. The story of the severed hand in Hauff's fairy tale certainly has an uncanny effect, and we have traced that effect back to the castration complex; but most readers will probably agree with me in judging that no trace of uncanniness is provoked by Herodotus's story of the treasure of Rhampsinitus,[3] in which the master-thief, whom the princess tries to hold fast by the hand, leaves his brother's severed hand behind with her instead. Again, the prompt fulfilment of the wishes of Polycrates undoubtedly affects us in the same uncanny way as it did the king of Egypt; yet our own fairy stories are crammed with instantaneous wish-fulfilments which produce no uncanny effect whatever. In the story of 'The Three Wishes', the woman is tempted by the savoury smell of

3. See Herodotus 2.121.

a sausage to wish that she might have one too, and in an instant it lies on a plate before her. In his annoyance at her hastiness her husband wishes it may hang on her nose. And there it is, dangling from her nose. All this is very striking but not in the least uncanny. Fairy tales quite frankly adopt the animistic standpoint of the omnipotence of thoughts and wishes, and yet I cannot think of any genuine fairy story which has anything uncanny about it. We have heard that it is in the highest degree uncanny when an inanimate object—a picture or a doll—comes to life; nevertheless in Hans Andersen's[4] stories the household utensils, furniture and tin soldiers are alive, yet nothing could well be more remote from the uncanny. And we should hardly call it uncanny when Pygmalion's beautiful statue comes to life.[5]

Apparent death and the re-animation of the dead have been represented as most uncanny themes. But things of this sort too are very common in fairy stories. Who would be so bold as to call it uncanny, for instance, when Snow-White opens her eyes once more?[6] And the resuscitation of the dead in accounts of miracles, as in the New Testament, elicits feelings quite unrelated to the uncanny. Then, too, the theme that achieves such an indubitably uncanny effect, the unintended recurrence of the same thing, serves other and quite different purposes in another class of cases. We have already come across one example in which it is employed to call up a feeling of the comic;[7] and we could multiply instances of this kind. Or again, it works as a means of emphasis, and so on. And once more: what is the origin of the uncanny effect of silence, darkness and solitude? Do not these factors point to the part played by danger in the genesis of what is uncanny, notwithstanding that in children these same factors are the most frequent determinants of the expression of fear [rather than of the uncanny]? And are we after all justified in entirely ignoring intellectual uncertainty as a factor, seeing that we have admitted its importance in relation to death?

It is evident therefore, that we must be prepared to admit that there are other elements besides those which we have so far laid down as determining the production of uncanny feelings. We might say that these preliminary results have satisfied *psycho-analytic* interest in the problem of the uncanny, and that what remains probably calls for an *aesthetic* enquiry. But that would be to open the door to doubts about what exactly is the value of our general contention that the uncanny proceeds from something familiar which has been repressed.

We have noticed one point which may help us to resolve these uncertainties: nearly all the instances that contradict our hypothesis are taken from the realm of fiction, of imaginative writing. This suggests that we should differentiate between the uncanny that we actually experience and the uncanny that we merely picture or read about.

What is *experienced* as uncanny is much more simply conditioned but comprises far fewer instances. We shall find, I think, that it fits in perfectly with our attempt at a solution, and can be traced back without exception to

4. Hans Christian Andersen (1805–1875), Danish writer best known for his fairy tales.

5. In *Metamorphoses* (ca. 10 C.E.), 10.243–97, the Roman poet Ovid tells the story of the sculptor Pygmalion, who fell in love with his own creation.

6. Snow White, believed dead, comes back to life when the poisoned apple is dislodged from her throat.

7. That is, in Mark Twain's *A Tramp Abroad*.

something familiar that has been repressed. But here, too, we must make a certain important and psychologically significant differentiation in our material, which is best illustrated by turning to suitable examples.

Let us take the uncanny associated with the omnipotence of thoughts, with the prompt fulfilment of wishes, with secret injurious powers and with the return of the dead. The condition under which the feeling of uncanniness arises here is unmistakable. We—or our primitive forefathers—once believed that these possibilities were realities, and were convinced that they actually happened. Nowadays we no longer believe in them, we have *surmounted* these modes of thought; but we do not feel quite sure of our new beliefs, and the old ones still exist within us ready to seize upon any confirmation. As soon as something *actually happens* in our lives which seems to confirm the old, discarded beliefs we get a feeling of the uncanny; it is as though we were making a judgement something like this: 'So, after all, it is *true* that one can kill a person by the mere wish!' or, 'So the dead *do* live on and appear on the scene of their former activities!' and so on. Conversely, anyone who has completely and finally rid himself of animistic beliefs will be insensible to this type of the uncanny. The most remarkable coincidences of wish and fulfilment, the most mysterious repetition of similar experiences in a particular place or on a particular date, the most deceptive sights and suspicious noises—none of these things will disconcert him or raise the kind of fear which can be described as 'a fear of something uncanny'. The whole thing is purely an affair of 'reality-testing', a question of the material reality of the phenomena.[8]

The state of affairs is different when the uncanny proceeds from repressed infantile complexes, from the castration complex, womb-phantasies, etc.; but experiences which arouse this kind of uncanny feeling are not of very frequent occurrence in real life. The uncanny which proceeds from actual experience belongs for the most part to the first group [the group dealt with in the previous paragraph]. Nevertheless the distinction between the two is theoretically very important. Where the uncanny comes from infantile complexes the question of material reality does not arise; its place is taken by psychical reality. What is involved is an actual repression of some content of thought and a return of this repressed content, not a cessation of *belief in the reality* of such a content. We might say that in the one case what had been repressed is a particular ideational content, and in the other the belief in its (material) reality. But this last phrase no doubt extends the term 'repres-

8. Since the uncanny effect of a "double" also belongs to this same group it is interesting to observe what the effect is of meeting one's own image unbidden and unexpected. Ernst Mach has related two such observations in his *Analyse der Empfindungen* (1900 [*Analysis of Sensations*]). On the first occasion he was not a little startled when he realized that the face before him was his own. The second time he formed a very unfavorable opinion about the supposed stranger who had entered the omnibus, and thought "What a shabby-looking school-master that man is who is getting in!"—I can report a similar adventure. I was sitting alone in my *wagon-lit* compartment when a more than usually violent jolt of the train swung back the door of the adjoining washing-cabinet, and an elderly gentleman in a dressing-gown and a travelling cap came in. I assumed that in leaving the washing-cabinet, which lay between the two compartments, he had taken the wrong direction and come into my cabinet by mistake. Jumping up with the intention of putting him right, I at once realized to my dismay that the intruder was nothing but my own reflection in the looking-glass on the open door. I can still recollect that I thoroughly disliked his appearance. Instead, therefore, of being *frightened* by our doubles, both Mach and I simply failed to recognize them as such. Is it not possible, though, that our dislike of them was a vestigial trace of the archaic reaction which feels the "double" to be something uncanny? [Freud's note]. Mach (1838–1916), Austrian physicist and philosopher.

sion' beyond its legitimate meaning. It would be more correct to take into account a psychological distinction which can be detected here, and to say that the animistic beliefs of civilized people are in a state of having been (to a greater or lesser extent) *surmounted* [rather than repressed]. Our conclusion could then be stated thus: an uncanny experience occurs either when infantile complexes which have been repressed are once more revived by some impression, or when primitive beliefs which have been surmounted seem once more to be confirmed. Finally, we must not let our predilection for smooth solutions and lucid exposition blind us to the fact that these two classes of uncanny experience are not always sharply distinguishable. When we consider that primitive beliefs are most intimately connected with infantile complexes, and are, in fact, based on them, we shall not be greatly astonished to find that the distinction is often a hazy one.

The uncanny as it is depicted in *literature*, in stories and imaginative productions, merits in truth a separate discussion. Above all, it is a much more fertile province than the uncanny in real life, for it contains the whole of the latter and something more besides, something that cannot be found in real life. The contrast between what has been repressed and what has been surmounted cannot be transposed on to the uncanny in fiction without profound modification; for the realm of phantasy depends for its effect on the fact that its content is not submitted to reality-testing. The somewhat paradoxical result is that *in the first place a great deal that is not uncanny in fiction would be so if it happened in real life; and in the second place that there are many more means of creating uncanny effects in fiction than there are in real life.*

The imaginative writer has this licence among many others, that he can select his world of representation so that it either coincides with the realities we are familiar with or departs from them in what particulars he pleases. We accept his ruling in every case. In fairy tales, for instance, the world of reality is left behind from the very start, and the animistic system of beliefs is frankly adopted. Wish-fulfilments, secret powers, omnipotence of thoughts, animation of inanimate objects, all the elements so common in fairy stories, can exert no uncanny influence here; for, as we have learnt, that feeling cannot arise unless there is a conflict of judgement as to whether things which have been 'surmounted' and are regarded as incredible may not, after all, be possible; and this problem is eliminated from the outset by the postulates of the world of fairy tales. Thus we see that fairy stories, which have furnished us with most of the contradictions to our hypothesis of the uncanny, confirm the first part of our proposition—that in the realm of fiction many things are not uncanny which would be so if they happened in real life. In the case of these stories there are other contributory factors, which we shall briefly touch upon later.

The creative writer can also choose a setting which though less imaginary than the world of fairy tales, does yet differ from the real world by admitting superior spiritual beings such as daemonic spirits or ghosts of the dead. So long as they remain within their setting of poetic reality, such figures lose any uncanniness which they might possess. The souls in Dante's *Inferno*, or the supernatural apparitions in Shakespeare's *Hamlet, Macbeth* or *Julius Caesar*, may be gloomy and terrible enough, but they are no more really uncanny than Homer's jovial world of gods.[9] We adapt our judgement to the imaginary reality imposed on us by the writer, and regard souls, spirits and ghosts as though their existence had the same validity as our own has in material reality. In this case too we avoid all trace of the uncanny.

The situation is altered as soon as the writer pretends to move in the world of common reality. In this case he accepts as well all the conditions operating to produce uncanny feelings in real life; and everything that would have an uncanny effect in reality has it in his story. But in this case he can even increase his effect and multiply it far beyond what could happen in reality, by bringing about events which never or very rarely happen in fact. In doing this he is in a sense betraying us to the superstitiousness which we have ostensibly surmounted; he deceives us by promising to give us the sober truth, and then after all overstepping it. We react to his inventions as we would have reacted to real experiences; by the time we have seen through his trick it is already too late and the author has achieved his object. But it must be added that his success is not unalloyed. We retain a feeling of dissatisfaction, a kind of grudge against the attempted deceit. I have noticed this particularly after reading Schnitzler's *Die Weissagung* [*The Prophecy*][1] and similar stories which flirt with the supernatural. However, the writer has one more means which he can use in order to avoid our recalcitrance and at the same time to improve his chances of success. He can keep us in the dark for a long time about the precise nature of the presuppositions on which the world he writes about is based, or he can cunningly and ingeniously avoid any definite information on the point to the last. Speaking generally, however, we find a confirmation of the second part of our proposition—that fiction presents more opportunities for creating uncanny feelings than are possible in real life.

Strictly speaking, all these complications relate only to that class of the uncanny which proceeds from forms of thought that have been surmounted. The class which proceeds from repressed complexes is more resistant and remains as powerful in fiction as in real experience, subject to one exception. The uncanny belonging to the first class—that proceeding from forms of thought that have been surmounted—retains its character not only in experience but in fiction as well, so long as the setting is one of material reality; but where it is given an arbitrary and artificial setting in fiction, it is apt to lose that character.

We have clearly not exhausted the possibilities of poetic licence and the privileges enjoyed by story-writers in evoking or in excluding an uncanny feeling. In the main we adopt an unvarying passive attitude towards real experience and are subject to the influence of our physical environment. But the story-teller has a *peculiarly* directive power over us; by means of the moods he can put us into, he is able to guide the current of our emotions, to dam it up in one direction and make it flow in another, and he often obtains a great variety of effects from the same material. All this is nothing

9. Freud names writers from a range of cultures and times: DANTE ALIGHIERI (1265–1321) visits the dead in hell in *Inferno*, the first volume of his *Divine Comedy*; in the tragedies of William Shakespeare (1564–1616) named here, ghosts appear; and in Homer's *Iliad* and *Odyssey* (ca. 8th c. B.C.E.), the gods play active roles.

1. A short story (1905) by the Austrian playwright and novelist Arthur Schnitzler (1862–1931).

new, and has doubtless long since been fully taken into account by students of aesthetics. We have drifted into this field of research half involuntarily, through the temptation to explain certain instances which contradicted our theory of the causes of the uncanny. Accordingly we will now return to the examination of a few of those instances.

We have already asked why it is that the severed hand in the story of the treasure of Rhampsinitus has no uncanny effect in the way that the severed hand has in Hauff's story. The question seems to have gained in importance now that we have recognized that the class of the uncanny which proceeds from repressed complexes is the more resistant of the two. The answer is easy. In the Herodotus story our thoughts are concentrated much more on the superior cunning of the master-thief than on the feelings of the princess. The princess may very well have had an uncanny feeling, indeed she very probably feel into a swoon; but *we* have no such sensations, for we put ourselves in the thief's place, not in hers. In Nestroy's farce, *Der Zerrissene* [*The Torn Man*],[2] another means is used to avoid any impression of the uncanny in the scene in which the fleeing man, convinced that he is a murderer, lifts up one trapdoor after another and each time sees what he takes to be the ghost of his victim rising up out of it. He calls out in despair, 'But I've only killed *one* man. Why this ghastly multiplication?' We know what went before this scene and do not share his error, so what must be uncanny to him has an irresistibly comic effect on us. Even a 'real' ghost, as in Oscar Wilde's *Canterville Ghost*,[3] loses all power of at least arousing *gruesome* feelings in us as soon as the author begins to amuse himself by being ironical about it and allows liberties to be taken with it. Thus we see how independent emotional effects can be of the actual subject-matter in the world of fiction. In fairy stories feelings of fear—including therefore uncanny feelings—are ruled out altogether. We understand this, and that is why we ignore any opportunities we find in them for developing such feelings.

Concerning the factors of silence, solitude and darkness, we can only say that they are actually elements in the production of the infantile anxiety from which the majority of human beings have never become quite free. This problem has been discussed from a psycho-analytic point of view elsewhere.

1919

Fetishism[1]

In the last few years I have had an opportunity of studying analytically a number of men whose object-choice was dominated by a fetish. There is no need to expect that these people came to analysis on account of their fetish. For though no doubt a fetish is recognized by its adherents as an abnormality, it is seldom felt by them as the symptom of an ailment accompanied by suffering. Usually they are quite satisfied with it, or even praise the way in

2. An 1845 production by the Austrian playwright Johann Nestroy (1801–1862).
3. A short story (1887) by the Irish-born writer WILDE (1854–1900).

1. Translated by Joan Rivière, who sometimes adds a word or phrase in square brackets in the text for clarification.

which it eases their erotic life. As a rule, therefore, the fetish made its appearance in analysis as a subsidiary finding.

For obvious reasons the details of these cases must be withheld from publication; I cannot, therefore, show in what way accidental circumstances have contributed to the choice of a fetish. The most extraordinary case seemed to me to be one in which a young man had exalted a certain sort of 'shine on the nose' into a fetishistic precondition. The surprising explanation of this was that the patient had been brought up in an English nursery but had later come to Germany, where he forgot his mother-tongue almost completely. The fetish, which originated from his earliest childhood, had to be understood in English, not German. The 'shine on the nose' [in German '*Glanz auf der Nase*']—was in reality a '*glance* at the nose'. The nose was thus the fetish, which, incidentally, he endowed at will with the luminous shine which was not perceptible to others.

In every instance, the meaning and the purpose of the fetish turned out, in analysis, to be the same. It revealed itself so naturally and seemed to me so compelling that I am prepared to expect the same solution in all cases of fetishism. When now I announce that the fetish is a substitute for the penis, I shall certainly create disappointment; so I hasten to add that it is not a substitute for any chance penis, but for a particular and quite special penis that had been extremely important in early childhood but had later been lost. That is to say, it should normally have been given up, but the fetish is precisely designed to preserve it from extinction. To put it more plainly: the fetish is a substitute for the woman's (the mother's) penis that the little boy once believed in and—for reasons familiar to us—does not want to give up.[2]

What happened, therefore, was that the boy refused to take cognizance of the fact of his having perceived that a woman does not possess a penis. No, that could not be true: for if a woman had been castrated, then his own possession of a penis was in danger; and against that there rose in rebellion the portion of his narcissism which Nature has, as a precaution, attached to that particular organ. In later life a grown man may perhaps experience a similar panic when the cry goes up that Throne and Altar are in danger, and similar illogical consequences will ensue. If I am not mistaken, Laforgue would say in this case that the boy 'scotomizes' his perception of the woman's lack of a penis.[3] A new technical term is justified when it describes a new fact or emphasizes it. This is not so here. The oldest word in our psychoanalytic terminology, 'repression', already relates to this pathological process. If we wanted to differentiate more sharply between the vicissitude of the *idea* as distinct from that of the *affect* and reserve the word '*Verdrängung*' ['repression'] for the affect, then the correct German word for the vicissitude of the idea would be '*Verleugnung*' ['disavowal']. 'Scotomization' seems to me particularly unsuitable, for it suggests that the perception is entirely wiped out,

2. This interpretation was made as early as 1910, in my study on Leonardo da Vinci [*Leonardo da Vinci and a Memory of His Childhood*], without any reasons being given for it [Freud's note].

3. I correct myself, however, by adding that I have the best reasons for supposing that Laforgue would not say anything of the sort. It is clear from his own remarks [in "Repression and Scotomization," 1926] that "scotomization" is a term which derives from descriptions of dementia praecox [schizophrenia], which does not arise from a carrying-over of psycho-analytic concepts to the psychoses and which has no application to developmental processes or to the formation of neuroses. In his exposition in the text of his paper, the author has been at pains to make this incompatibility clear [Freud's note]. René Laforgue (1894–1962), French psychoanalyst. "Scotomize": to form a mental blind spot about.

so that the result is the same as when a visual impression falls on the blind spot in the retina. In the situation we are considering, on the contrary, we see that the perception has persisted, and that a very energetic action has been undertaken to maintain the disavowal. It is not true that, after the child has made his observation of the woman, he has preserved unaltered his belief that women have a phallus. He has retained that belief, but he has also given it up. In the conflict between the weight of the unwelcome perception and the force of his counter-wish, a compromise has been reached, as is only possible under the dominance of the unconscious laws of thought—the primary processes. Yes, in his mind the woman *has* got a penis, in spite of everything; but this penis is no longer the same as it was before. Something else has taken its place, has been appointed its substitute, as it were, and now inherits the interest which was formerly directed to its predecessor. But this interest suffers an extraordinary increase as well, because the horror of castration has set up a memorial to itself in the creation of this substitute. Furthermore, an aversion, which is never absent in any fetishist, to the real female genitals remains a *stigma indelebile*[4] of the repression that has taken place. We can now see what the fetish achieves and what it is that maintains it. It remains a token of triumph over the threat of castration and a protection against it. It also saves the fetishist from becoming a homosexual, by endowing women with the characteristic which makes them tolerable as sexual objects. In later life, the fetishist feels that he enjoys yet another advantage from his substitute for a genital. The meaning of the fetish is not known to other people, so the fetish is not withheld from him: it is easily accessible and he can readily obtain the sexual satisfaction attached to it. What other men have to woo and make exertions for can be had by the fetishist with no trouble at all.

Probably no male human being is spared the fright of castration at the sight of a female genital. Why some people become homosexual as a consequence of that impression, while others fend it off by creating a fetish, and the great majority surmount it, we are frankly not able to explain. It is possible that, among all the factors at work, we do not yet know those which are decisive for the rare pathological results. We must be content if we can explain what has happened, and may for the present leave on one side the task of explaining why something has *not* happened.

One would expect that the organs or objects chosen as substitutes for the absent female phallus would be such as appear as symbols of the penis in other connections as well. This may happen often enough, but is certainly not a deciding factor. It seems rather that when the fetish is instituted some process occurs which reminds one of the stopping of memory in traumatic amnesia. As in this latter case, the subject's interest comes to a halt halfway, as it were; it is as though the last impression before the uncanny and traumatic one is retained as a fetish. Thus the foot or shoe owes its preference as a fetish—or a part of it—to the circumstance that the inquisitive boy peered at the woman's genitals from below, from her legs up; fur and velvet—as has long been suspected—are a fixation of the sight of the pubic hair, which should have been followed by the longed-for sight of the female member; pieces of underclothing, which are so often chosen as a fetish,

4. Indelible mark (Latin).

crystallize the moment of undressing, the last moment in which the woman could still be regarded as phallic. But I do not maintain that it is invariably possible to discover with certainty how the fetish was determined.

An investigation of fetishism is strongly recommended to anyone who still doubts the existence of the castration complex or who can still believe that fright at the sight of the female genital has some other ground—for instance, that it is derived from a supposed recollection of the trauma of birth.[5]

For me, the explanation of fetishism had another point of theoretical interest as well. Recently, along quite speculative lines, I arrived at the proposition that the essential difference between neurosis and psychosis was that in the former the ego, in the service of reality, suppresses a piece of the id,[6] whereas in a psychosis it lets itself be induced by the id to detach itself from a piece of reality. I returned to this theme once again later on.[7] But soon after this I had reason to regret that I had ventured so far. In the analysis of two young men I learned that each—one when he was two years old and the other when he was ten—had failed to take cognizance of the death of his beloved father—had 'scotomized' it—and yet neither of them had developed a psychosis. Thus a piece of reality which was undoubtedly important had been disavowed by the ego, just as the unwelcome fact of women's castration is disavowed in fetishists. I also began to suspect that similar occurrences in childhood are by no means rare, and I believed that I had been guilty of an error in my characterization of neurosis and psychosis. It is true that there was one way out of the difficulty. My formula needed only to hold good where there was a higher degree of differentiation in the psychical apparatus; things might be permissible to a child which would entail severe injury to an adult.

But further research led to another solution of the contradiction. It turned out that the two young men had no more 'scotomized' their father's death than a fetishist does the castration of women. It was only one current in their mental life that had not recognized their father's death; there was another current which took full account of that fact. The attitude which fitted in with the wish and the attitude which fitted in with reality existed side by side. In one of my two cases this split had formed the basis of a moderately severe obsessional neurosis. The patient oscillated in every situation in life between two assumptions: the one, that his father was still alive and was hindering his activities; the other, opposite one, that he was entitled to regard himself as his father's successor. I may thus keep to the expectation that in a psychosis the one current—that which fitted in with reality—would have in fact been absent.

Returning to my description of fetishism, I may say that there are many and weighty additional proofs of the divided attitude of fetishists to the question of the castration of women. In very subtle instances both the disavowal and the affirmation of the castration have found their way into the construction of the fetish itself. This was so in the case of a man whose fetish was an athletic support-belt which could also be worn as bathing drawers. This piece of clothing covered up the genitals entirely and concealed the distinc-

5. This argument was made by the Austrian psychotherapist Otto Rank in *The Trauma of Birth* (1924).

6. The unconscious (literally, "it"). In the Standard Edition, Freud's German terms *das Ich* ("the I," or "ego," referring to the conscious self) and *das Es* ("the it") are rendered in Latin, as is *das Uber-Ich* (the superego), the internalized voice of conscience and judgment directed toward the ego.

7. "Neurosis and Psychosis" (1924) and "The Loss of Reality in Neurosis and Psychosis" (1924) [Freud's note].

tion between them. Analysis showed that it signified that women were castrated and that they were not castrated; and it also allowed of the hypothesis that men were castrated, for all these possibilities could equally well be concealed under the belt—the earliest rudiment of which in his childhood had been the fig-leaf on a statue. A fetish of this sort, doubly derived from contrary ideas, is of course especially durable. In other instances the divided attitude shows itself in what the fetishist does with his fetish, whether in reality or in his imagination. To point out that he reveres his fetish is not the whole story; in many cases he treats it in a way which is obviously equivalent to a representation of castration. This happens particularly if he has developed a strong identification with his father and plays the part of the latter; for it is to him that as a child he ascribed the woman's castration. Affection and hostility in the treatment of the fetish—which run parallel with the disavowal and the acknowledgment of castration—are mixed in unequal proportions in different cases, so that the one or the other is more clearly recognizable. We seem here to approach an understanding, even if a distant one, of the behaviour of the *'coupeur de nattes'*.[8] In him the need to carry out the castration which he disavows has come to the front. His action contains in itself the two mutually incompatible assertions: 'the woman has still got a penis' and 'my father has castrated the woman'. Another variant, which is also a parallel to fetishism in social psychology, might be seen in the Chinese custom of mutilating the female foot and then revering it like a fetish after it has been mutilated. It seems as though the Chinese male wants to thank the woman for having submitted to being castrated.

In conclusion we may say that the normal prototype of fetishes is a man's penis, just as the normal prototype of inferior organs is a woman's real small penis, the clitoris.[9]

1927

8. A pervert who enjoys cutting off the hair of females [translator's note].

9. This is an allusion to Alfred Adler's insistence on "organ-inferiority" as the basis of all neuroses [translator's note]. Adler (1870–1937), Austrian psychiatrist who broke with Freud to form his own school of psychoanalysis in 1911.

FERDINAND DE SAUSSURE
1857–1913

Ferdinand de Saussure gave birth to structuralism by means of a book he never wrote. The *Course in General Linguistics*, based on student notes, was compiled by colleagues in 1916 after Saussure's death. Always described as being born into a "Swiss family distinguished for its intellectual achievements," Saussure, it seems, had no biography apart from the universities in which he studied or taught and the books he failed to write. In fact, Saussure's untimely death at age fifty-six is considered one of the few notable facts about him. Yet this man without a life came to be known as "the father of modern linguistics," and his intellectual progeny affected mid-twentieth-century thought in a wide variety of fields. After Saussure, the very idea of what it meant to study language was transformed.

In the late eighteenth century, the European study of languages had been revolutionized by the encounter with Sanskrit (brought about by the British colonization of India). Comparison among Sanskrit, Greek, and Latin suggested a common ancestor behind all three, which scholars dubbed Proto-Indo-European. Comparative philologists sought to map languages as comparative anatomists had mapped organisms. But the generation of Saussure's teachers, the Neogrammarians, had begun to explore the rules of affinity and transformation in a more truly historical way. Saussure studied historical linguistics with some of them at the University of Leipzig, where he published his only book, *Mémoire sur le système primitif des voyelles dans les langues indo-européennes* (*Memoir on the Primitive System of Vowels in Indo-European Languages*) in 1878, while he was still a graduate student. His precocity was recognized by scholars in the field, and his purely theoretical description of an unknown vowel was later confirmed by studies of the Hittite language.

After spending a year studying in Berlin and receiving his doctorate from the University of Leipzig in 1880, he became a senior lecturer at the École des Hautes Études (School for Advanced Study) in Paris, where he began by teaching Gothic and Old High German, later adding Sanskrit (which he had studied since 1874), Latin, Persian, and Lithuanian. In 1891 he accepted a professorship at the University of Geneva, teaching there for the rest of his life. It was in 1906 that, after the death of a colleague, he was asked to add "general linguistics" to his teaching in historical and comparative linguistics.

In a letter written in 1894 to fellow linguist Antoine Meillet, Saussure outlined his dissatisfaction with linguistic theory as he knew it:

> For a long time I have been above all preoccupied with the logical classification of linguistic facts and with the classification of the points of view from which we treat them; and I am more and more aware of the immense amount of work that would be required to show the linguist *what he is doing*. . . . The utter inadequacy of current terminology, the need to reform it and, in order to do that, to demonstrate what sort of object language is, continually spoil my pleasure in philology, though I have no dearer wish than not to be made to think about the nature of language in general.

Seldom has the condition for a real theoretical breakthrough been described so movingly. Saussure had taken "current terminology" to the point where it began to raise questions it could not answer. The need to study "the nature of language in general" was lived as a spoiled pleasure in philology.

As Saussure's originality increased, his scholarly productivity slowed. Searching for the best approach, he taught general linguistics in three different ways. Not only did he not write up his course, but he did not even keep his lecture notes, starting afresh each time. After his death, his young colleagues found themselves fabricating a synthesis of three fragmentary sets of student notes, with the result that the Saussure who is the author of the *Course in General Linguistics* is a function of the edited text, not its origin. Yet that was the Saussure who changed intellectual history.

What was Saussure's new theory of language? The diversity of languages, often thought to indicate a falling away from one original language (as in the story of Babel), indicated to Saussure not a story but a principle: the principle of the "arbitrary" (purely conventional) nature of the sign. Since there are thousands of human languages, the relation between words and things cannot be based on natural resemblances. For example, no inherent affinity or motivation leads people to call an avian creature *bird* or *oiseau*. Not only that, Saussure went on, but *language is not a nomenclature*. Rather than the world consisting of things that need names (the Adamic conception), each language brings into being, by describing, a world that it then knows as external. To be sure, the external world exists—but its reality remains quite nebulous until language articulates it. The way lines divide concepts and phrases, the way even concrete items are viewed, is specific to each language; each covers all that needs to be said, but in its different way.

Saussure's own theory illustrates this point: his terms *langage, langue*, and *parole* have never been satisfactorily translated into English. *Le langage* (in English, "language") is a general human faculty, that which enables us to speak of "body language" or "the language of fashion." *La langue*, which in English is also called "language," is the name for specific languages (*la langue anglaise*, the English language); but it is also the most general term for language itself, the term Saussure uses to name the object of linguistics. *La langue* in this sense does not exist: it is a theoretical object abstracted from the structures of specific languages. *La parole* (speech) is what Saussure calls "the executive side": the concrete utterances that constitute all acts of language. These individual utterances are excluded from his theory of language insofar as they only "execute" possibilities that exist in language already, or depart from it for creative purposes without fundamentally changing it. But where Saussure uses three terms for these distinctions, English only possesses two.

Language, for Saussure, is a structured system of conventional signs, studied in their internal complexity as if frozen in time (synchronically) rather than as changing over time (diachronically). Saussure saw the study of language as eventually forming part of a larger science of signs in culture, which he called *semiology*, a field that later scholars (see ROLAND BARTHES) went on to develop. The atom of language is the sign, which is functionally split into two parts: a *signifier* (sound-image) and a *signified* (concept), brought inseparably together like the two sides of a sheet of paper. The relation between the signifier and the signified is "arbitrary," not "motivated" (by natural resemblance), even in cases of onomatopoiea (words that sound like what they mean). The word *arbitrary* means not that individual speakers can just make language up, but precisely that they can't: the sign is a convention that has to be learned and is not subject to individual will. The point is not that languages do not change (they are changing all the time), but that the changes themselves follow paths that have more to do with the overall structure of the language than with any intentional intervention by its speakers.

Though the signifier and the signified seem to function together as a unit to produce signification, each has *value* only by virtue of the ways in which it differs from other terms. Here, the chain of signifiers and the chain of signifieds diverge. A signifier differs from other signifiers while its signified distinguishes itself from other signifieds, and the networks of connection and distinction are not parallel, as Saussure's misleading diagram of the two realms might suggest. Saussure's distinction between "signification" and "value" is similar to KARL MARX's distinction between "use value" and "exchange value": the first appears tied to the characteristics of the object or term, whereas the second is entirely a function of the system of exchange or of language. Saussure goes so far as to say that *everything* in language is relational: "in language there are only differences. Even more important: a difference generally implies positive terms between which the difference is set up; but in language there are only differences *without positive terms*" (Saussure's emphasis). In other words, neither ideas nor sounds exist prior to their combination. This description of a difference that does not depend on the prior existence of knowable entities is one of Saussure's most radical declarations.

Jokes often play on the purely differential aspect of language. A homeowner answering the phone and hearing that "The viper is coming" might feel fear, but when the voice on the line explains that "he's coming to vipe your vindows," what had initially been a serpent becomes a benign household maintenance worker. A foreign accent changes the sounds in a language without changing the system of differences. The sound *v* takes on the differential role of *w* in this joke as soon as it becomes clear *to what* it is being opposed.

Nevertheless, once combined, the signifier and signified do become a unit, an *articulus* in a system of articulations. The articulations are positive facts—the only kind of facts language possesses, since, as Saussure stresses, *language is a form and not a substance*. Once the differential structure has severed any natural connection between language and things, the sign becomes a building block of a system of oppositions: singular, plural; past, present, future; voiced, unvoiced; masculine, feminine. Saussure's favorite metaphor for the kind of structure he has in mind is chess: a rule-bound system of oppositions and differences that governs a closed but infinite set of operations.

In Saussure's conception of language, the sign is not only arbitrary but also linear (he thus uses a spatial term for what is in fact temporal, the succession of signs as they unfold in time during speech). Signs are combined like links in a chain to form the line of language according to two relations: the *syntagmatic* (all units present in their articulation) and the *associative* (all related units present in the mind but absent from the actual sequence). This distinction, later called *syntagmatic* and *paradigmatic*, would form an important part of ROMAN JAKOBSON's theory of metaphor and metonymy (see below). For Saussure, some syntagmatic relations beyond mere grammatical rules count as *language* rather than *speech*. Far from being freely chosen by each speaker, they constitute the "idioms" that a newcomer must master in order to "know" a language.

At the end of his life, Saussure was working on another project in which he had even less confidence than in his theory of general linguistics. According to notebooks published by Jean Starobinski starting in 1964 and eventually collected as *Les Mots sous les mots* (1971; trans. 1979, *Words upon Words*), Saussure was fascinated by the idea that within the verses written by certain Latin poets, deliberately concealed anagrams of proper names could be detected. Thus, a hidden poetics of names generated textual patterns that appeared to be dictated by the surface meanings of the words used as "carriers" for the letters. But Saussure could never be sure of what he found, and the notebooks remained hidden away. To compound the difficulty, the anagram project entailed a displacement of a major principle of the *Course*: while the *Course* treated the signifier-signified relation as a unit, the anagrams implied that signifiers and signifieds could function separately, that a signifier could serve more than one function, and that the signifier could take the lead in the organization of a text. These implications, which Saussure viewed with incredulity, had a profound impact on later textual theory.

Saussure's work provided the groundwork for both structuralism and poststructuralism. It was part of the larger "linguistic turn" in twentieth-century philosophy, history, anthropology, psychoanalysis, and literary studies. CLAUDE LÉVI-STRAUSS, for example, studied myths and kinship systems within different cultures as a system of signs to be interpreted. Roland Barthes explored the semiology of fashion, advertising, travel, and many other cultural phenomena. JACQUES DERRIDA, while critiquing Saussure's privileging of spoken language (Saussure called writing secondary, pathological, even monstrous with respect to the speech it records), nevertheless took up many aspects of Saussure's system of differences into what he called *différance*. LOUIS ALTHUSSER understood, on the basis of what Saussure says about language as a system, that economic and social structures, too, possess structural (rather than transitive) causality. And finally, JACQUES LACAN used Saussure to reformulate Freud in linguistic terms, while JULIA KRISTEVA developed a theory of the anagrammatical nature of literature.

Of course, the very things that made Saussure's thought so revealing and influential also led to the most serious objections. By focusing on the relation between signifier and signified, he gained insight into linguistic structure yet eliminated the world. "Bracketing the referent"—that is, leaving out the third dimension of the sign, that to which it refers—has been criticized by those, like TERRY EAGLETON, who find it impossible to speak of language without speaking of reference, things, history. After all, they argue, language is not chess. How can it be studied apart from the world to which it refers? How can reference not have a role in structure? In addition, language is neither unified nor closed, as deconstructors and poststructuralists were quick to point out. Even if it is frozen in time, conflict remains unresolved and essential within the system. And the later postmodern critique of the "universal subject" has emphasized that speakers are placed in very different positions within language by class, gender, race, geography, and so on. In our "viper" joke, for example, a small linguistic difference points to a whole system of class, property, ethnicity, and, varying with the gender of the homeowner, sexual politics—including an echo of the story of Adam, Eve, and the serpent.

Despite these criticisms, the *Course in General Linguistics* opened up as never before the question of the role of signs in culture and the role of language in the mind. As Jonathan Culler put it in *Ferdinand de Saussure* (1986), "What the study of language reveals about mind is not a set of primitive conceptions or natural ideas but the general structuring and differentiating operations by which things are made to signify."

BIBLIOGRAPHY

There are two existing English translations of the *Course in General Linguistics*, first edited by Charles Bally and Albert Sechehaye in 1916. The one that has become canonical is by Wade Baskin (1959). Roy Harris's more recent version (1983) solves certain problems but creates as many new ones. A critical edition comparing six different sources was published in French by Rudolf Engler (1967). Saussure's anagram project, edited by Jean Starobinski, has been translated as *Words upon Words* (1979). As one might expect, there are no biographies.

Several introductions to Saussure's work are excellent: Jonathan Culler's *Ferdinand de Saussure* (rev. ed., 1986) and David Holdcroft's *Saussure: Signs, System, and Arbitrariness* (1991) are accessible and clear. For a excellent exposition of the theories and limits of Saussure and the Russian formalists, see Fredric Jameson, *The Prison-House of Language: A Critical Account of Structuralism and Russian Formalism* (1972). Roy Harris's *Reading Saussure: A Critical Commentary of the "Cours de linguistique generale'* (1987) and Françoise Gadet's *Saussure and Contemporary Culture* (1987; trans. 1989) offer more information about Saussure in the context of linguistics. The even more detailed *Re-Reading Saussure: The Dynamics of Signs in Social Life* (1997) by Paul J. Thibault updates the discussion of many of the key concepts. For a confusing but detailed history of linguistics leading up to Saussure, see E. F. K. Koerner's *Ferdinand de Saussure: Origin and Development of His Linguistic Thought in Western Studies of Language* (1973). For a more theoretical discussion of Saussure's place in the history of linguistics, see Hans Aarsleff's insightful but not chronological *From Locke to Saussure: Essays on the Study of Language and Intellectual History* (1982). A bibliography, *Bibliographia Saussureana*, was compiled by E. F. K. Koerner (1972); more recent items can be found in the bibliographies of the Harris and Thibault volumes cited above.

From Course in General Linguistics[1]

From *Introduction*

CHAPTER III. THE OBJECT OF LINGUISTICS

2. *Place of Language in the Facts of Speech*

* * *

To summarize, these are the characteristics of language:

1) Language is a well-defined object in the heterogeneous mass of speech

1. Edited by Charles Bally and Albert Sechehaye in collaboration with Albert Riedlinger; translated by Wade Baskin, who occasionally includes the French in square brackets.

facts. It can be localized in the limited segment of the speaking-circuit where an auditory image becomes associated with a concept. It is the social side of speech, outside the individual who can never create nor modify it by himself; it exists only by virtue of a sort of contract signed by the members of a community. Moreover, the individual must always serve an apprenticeship in order to learn the functioning of language; a child assimilates it only gradually. It is such a distinct thing that a man deprived of the use of speaking retains it provided that he understands the vocal signs that he hears.

2) Language, unlike speaking, is something that we can study separately. Although dead languages are no longer spoken, we can easily assimilate their linguistic organisms. We can dispense with the other elements of speech; indeed, the science of language is possible only if the other elements are excluded.

3) Whereas speech is heterogeneous, language, as defined, is homogeneous. It is a system of signs in which the only essential thing is the union of meanings and sound-images, and in which both parts of the sign are psychological.

4) Language is concrete, no less so than speaking; and this is a help in our study of it. Linguistic signs, though basically psychological, are not abstractions; associations which bear the stamp of collective approval—and which added together constitute language—are realities that have their seat in the brain. Besides, linguistic signs are tangible; it is possible to reduce them to conventional written symbols, whereas it would be impossible to provide detailed photographs of acts of speaking [*actes de parole*]; the pronunciation of even the smallest word represents an infinite number of muscular movements that could be identified and put into graphic form only with great difficulty. In language, on the contrary, there is only the sound-image, and the latter can be translated into a fixed visual image. For if we disregard the vast number of movements necessary for the realization of sound-images in speaking, we see that each sound-image is nothing more than the sum of a limited number of elements or phonemes[2] that can in turn be called up by a corresponding number of written symbols. The very possibility of putting the things that relate to language into graphic form allows dictionaries and grammars to represent it accurately, for language is a storehouse of sound-images, and writing is the tangible form of those images.

3. *Place of Language in Human Facts: Semiology*

The foregoing characteristics of language reveal an even more important characteristic. Language, once its boundaries have been marked off within the speech data, can be classified among human phenomena, whereas speech cannot.

We have just seen that language is a social institution; but several features set it apart from other political, legal, etc. institutions. We must call in a new type of facts in order to illuminate the special nature of language.

Language is a system of signs that express ideas, and is therefore comparable to a system of writing, the alphabet of deaf-mutes, symbolic rites, polite formulas, military signals, etc. But it is the most important of all these systems.

2. The smallest distinctive unit of sound in a spoken language.

A science that studies the life of signs within society is conceivable; it would be a part of social psychology and consequently of general psychology; I shall call it *semiology* (from Greek *sēmeîon* 'sign'). Semiology would show what constitutes signs, what laws govern them. Since the science does not yet exist, no one can say what it would be; but it has a right to existence, a place staked out in advance. Linguistics is only a part of the general science of semiology; the laws discovered by semiology will be applicable to linguistics, and the latter will circumscribe a well-defined area within the mass of anthropological facts.

To determine the exact place of semiology is the task of the psychologist. The task of the linguist is to find out what makes language a special system within the mass of semiological data. This issue will be taken up again later; here I wish merely to call attention to one thing: if I have succeeded in assigning linguistics a place among the sciences, it is because I have related it to semiology.

Why has semiology not yet been recognized as an independent science with its own object like all the other sciences? Linguists have been going around in circles: language, better than anything else, offers a basis for understanding the semiological problem; but language must, to put it correctly, be studied in itself; heretofore language has almost always been studied in connection with something else, from other viewpoints.

There is first of all the superficial notion of the general public: people see nothing more than a name-giving system in language, thereby prohibiting any research into its true nature.

Then there is the viewpoint of the psychologist, who studies the sign-mechanism in the individual; this is the easiest method, but it does not lead beyond individual execution and does not reach the sign, which is social.

Or even when signs are studied from a social viewpoint, only the traits that attach language to the other social institutions—those that are more or less voluntary—are emphasized; as a result, the goal is by-passed and the specific characteristics of semiological systems in general and of language in particular are completely ignored. For the distinguishing characteristic of the sign—but the one that is least apparent at first sight—is that in some way it always eludes the individual or social will.

In short, the characteristic that distinguishes semiological systems from all other institutions shows up clearly only in language where it manifests itself in the things which are studied least, and the necessity or specific value of a semiological science is therefore not clearly recognized. But to me the language problem is mainly semiological, and all developments derive their significance from that important fact. If we are to discover the true nature of language we must learn what it has in common with all other semiological systems; linguistic forces that seem very important at first glance (e.g., the role of the vocal apparatus) will receive only secondary consideration if they serve only to set language apart from the other systems. This procedure will do more than to clarify the linguistic problem. By studying rites, customs, etc. as signs, I believe that we shall throw new light on the facts and point up the need for including them in a science of semiology and explaining them by its laws.

From *Part One. General Principles*

CHAPTER I. NATURE OF THE LINGUISTIC SIGN

1. *Sign, Signified, Signifier*

Some people regard language, when reduced to its elements, as a naming-process only—a list of words, each corresponding to the thing that it names. For example:

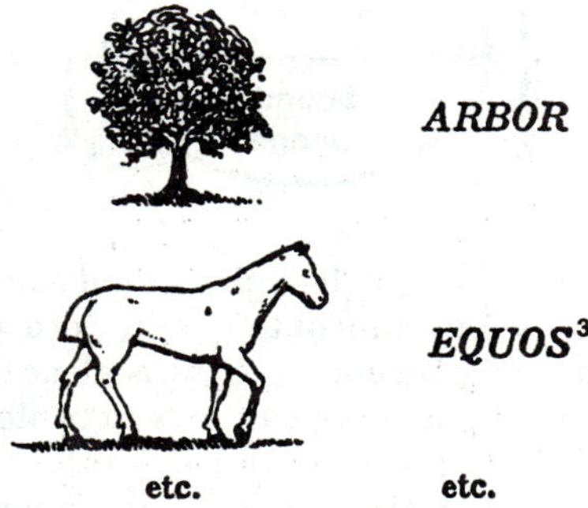

This conception is open to criticism at several points. It assumes that ready-made ideas exist before words (on this point, see below); it does not tell us whether a name is vocal or psychological in nature (*arbor*, for instance, can be considered from either viewpoint); finally, it lets us assume that the linking of a name and a thing is a very simple operation—an assumption that is anything but true. But this rather naive approach can bring us near the truth by showing us that the linguistic unit is a double entity, one formed by the associating of two terms.

We have seen in considering the speaking-circuit that both terms involved in the linguistic sign are psychological and are united in the brain by an associative bond. This point must be emphasized.

The linguistic sign unites, not a thing and a name, but a concept and a sound-image.[4] The latter is not the material sound, a purely physical thing, but the psychological imprint of the sound, the impression that it makes on our senses. The sound-image is sensory, and if I happen to call it "material," it is only in that sense, and by way of opposing it to the other term of the association, the concept, which is generally more abstract.

The psychological character of our sound-images becomes apparent when we observe our own speech. Without moving our lips or tongue, we can talk to ourselves or recite mentally a selection of verse. Because we regard the words of our language as sound-images, we must avoid speaking of the "phonemes" that make up the words. This term, which suggests vocal activity, is

3. Tree and horse (the more usual base form is *equus*), respectively (Latin).

4. The term sound-image may seem to be too restricted inasmuch as beside the representation of the sounds of a word there is also that of its articulation, the muscular image of the phonational act. But for F. de Saussure language is essentially a depository, a thing received from without. The sound-image is par excellence the natural representation of the word as a fact of potential language, outside any actual use of it in speaking. The motor side is thus implied or, in any event, occupies only a subordinate role with respect to the sound-image [Bally, Sechehaye, and Riedlinger's note].

applicable to the spoken word only, to the realization of the inner image in discourse. We can avoid that misunderstanding by speaking of the *sounds* and *syllables* of a word provided we remember that the names refer to the sound-image.

The linguistic sign is then a two-sided psychological entity that can be represented by the drawing:

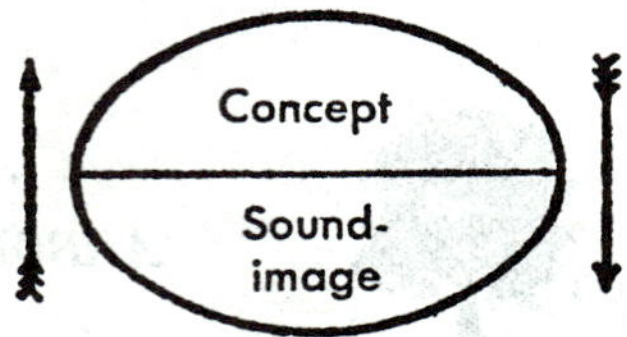

The two elements are intimately united, and each recalls the other. Whether we try to find the meaning of the Latin word *arbor* or the word that Latin uses to designate the concept "tree," it is clear that only the associations sanctioned by that language appear to us to conform to reality, and we disregard whatever others might be imagined.

Our definition of the linguistic sign poses an important question of terminology. I call the combination of a concept and a sound-image a *sign*, but in current usage the term generally designates only a sound-image, a word, for example (*arbor*, etc.). One tends to forget that *arbor* is called a sign only because it carries the concept "tree," with the result that the idea of the sensory part implies the idea of the whole.

Ambiguity would disappear if the three notions involved here were designated by three names, each suggesting and opposing the others. I propose to retain the word *sign* [*signe*] to designate the whole and to replace *concept* and *sound-image* respectively by *signified* [*signifié*] and *signifier* [*signifiant*]; the last two terms have the advantage of indicating the opposition that separates them from each other and from the whole of which they are parts. As regards *sign*, if I am satisfied with it, this is simply because I do not know of any word to replace it, the ordinary language suggesting no other.

The linguistic sign, as defined, has two primordial characteristics. In enunciating them I am also positing the basic principles of any study of this type.

2. *Principle I: The Arbitrary Nature of the Sign*

The bond between the signifier and the signified is arbitrary. Since I mean by sign the whole that results from the associating of the signifier with the signified, I can simply say: *the linguistic sign is arbitrary*.

The idea of "sister" is not linked by any inner relationship to the succession of sounds *s-ö-r* which serves as its signifier in French; that it could be represented equally by just any other sequence is proved by differences among languages and by the very existence of different languages: the signified "ox" has as its signifier *b-ö-f* on one side of the border and *o-k-s* (*Ochs*) on the other.[5]

No one disputes the principle of the arbitrary nature of the sign, but it is often easier to discover a truth than to assign to it its proper place. Principle I dominates all the linguistics of language; its consequences are numberless. It is true that not all of them are equally obvious at first glance; only after many detours does one discover them, and with them the primordial importance of the principle.

One remark in passing: when semiology becomes organized as a science, the question will arise whether or not it properly includes modes of expression based on completely natural signs, such as pantomime. Supposing that the new science welcomes them, its main concern will still be the whole group of systems grounded on the arbitrariness of the sign. In fact, every means of expression used in society is based, in principle, on collective behavior or—what amounts to the same thing—on convention. Polite formulas, for instance, though often imbued with a certain natural expressiveness (as in the case of a Chinese who greets his emperor by bowing down to the ground nine times), are nonetheless fixed by rule; it is this rule and not the intrinsic value of the gestures that obliges one to use them. Signs that are wholly arbitrary realize better than the others the ideal of the semiological process; that is why language, the most complex and universal of all systems of expression, is also the most characteristic; in this sense linguistics can become the master-pattern for all branches of semiology although language is only one particular semiological system.

The word *symbol* has been used to designate the linguistic sign, or more specifically, what is here called the signifier. Principle I in particular weighs against the use of this term. One characteristic of the symbol is that it is never wholly arbitrary; it is not empty, for there is the rudiment of a natural bond between the signifier and the signified. The symbol of justice, a pair of scales, could not be replaced by just any other symbol, such as a chariot.

The word *arbitrary* also calls for comment. The term should not imply that the choice of the signifier is left entirely to the speaker (we shall see below that the individual does not have the power to change a sign in any way once it has become established in the linguistic community); I mean that it is unmotivated, i.e. arbitrary in that it actually has no natural connection with the signified.

In concluding let us consider two objections that might be raised to the establishment of Principle I:

1) *Onomatopoeia* might be used to prove that the choice of the signifier is not always arbitrary. But onomatopoeic formations are never organic elements of a linguistic system. Besides, their number is much smaller than is generally supposed. Words like French *fouet* 'whip' or *glas* 'knell' may strike certain ears with suggestive sonority, but to see that they have not always had this property we need only examine their Latin forms (*fouet* is derived from *fāgus* 'beech-tree,' *glas* from *classicum* 'sound of a trumpet'). The quality of their present sounds, or rather the quality that is attributed to them, is a fortuitous result of phonetic evolution.

As for authentic onomatopoeic words (e.g. *glug-glug, tick-tock*, etc.), not

5. That is, in Germany.

only are they limited in number, but also they are chosen somewhat arbitrarily, for they are only approximate and more or less conventional imitations of certain sounds (cf. English *bow-wow* and French *ouaoua*). In addition, once these words have been introduced into the language, they are to a certain extent subjected to the same evolution—phonetic, morphological, etc.—that other words undergo (cf. *pigeon*, ultimately from Vulgar Latin *pīpiō*, derived in turn from an onomatopoeic formation): obvious proof that they lose something of their original character in order to assume that of the linguistic sign in general, which is unmotivated.

2) *Interjections*, closely related to onomatopoeia, can be attacked on the same grounds and come no closer to refuting our thesis. One is tempted to see in them spontaneous expressions of reality dictated, so to speak, by natural forces. But for most interjections we can show that there is no fixed bond between their signified and their signifier. We need only compare two languages on this point to see how much such expressions differ from one language to the next (e.g. the English equivalent of French *aïe!* is *ouch!*). We know, moreover, that many interjections were once words with specific meanings (cf. French *diable!* 'darn!' *mordieu!* 'golly!' from *mort Dieu* 'God's death,' etc.).

Onomatopoeic formations and interjections are of secondary importance, and their symbolic origin is in part open to dispute.

3. *Principle II: The Linear Nature of the Signifier*

The signifier, being auditory, is unfolded solely in time from which it gets the following characteristics: (a) it represents a span, and (b) the span is measurable in a single dimension; it is a line.

While Principle II is obvious, apparently linguists have always neglected to state it, doubtless because they found it too simple; nevertheless, it is fundamental, and its consequences are incalculable. Its importance equals that of Principle I; the whole mechanism of language depends upon it. In contrast to visual signifiers (nautical signals, etc.) which can offer simultaneous groupings in several dimensions, auditory signifiers have at their command only the dimension of time. Their elements are presented in succession; they form a chain. This feature becomes readily apparent when they are represented in writing and the spatial line of graphic marks is substituted for succession in time.

Sometimes the linear nature of the signifier is not obvious. When I accent a syllable, for instance, it seems that I am concentrating more than one significant element on the same point. But this is an illusion; the syllable and its accent constitute only one phonational act. There is no duality within the act but only different oppositions to what precedes and what follows.

From *Part Two. Synchronic Linguistics*

CHAPTER IV. LINGUISTIC VALUE

1. *Language as Organized Thought Coupled with Sound*

To prove that language is only a system of pure values, it is enough to consider the two elements involved in its functioning: ideas and sounds.

Psychologically our thought—apart from its expression in words—is only a shapeless and indistinct mass. Philosophers and linguists have always agreed in recognizing that without the help of signs we would be unable to make a clear-cut, consistent distinction between two ideas. Without language, thought is a vague, uncharted nebula. There are no pre-existing ideas, and nothing is distinct before the appearance of language.

Against the floating realm of thought, would sounds by themselves yield predelimited entities? No more so than ideas. Phonic substance is neither more fixed nor more rigid than thought; it is not a mold into which thought must of necessity fit but a plastic substance divided in turn into distinct parts to furnish the signifiers needed by thought. The linguistic fact can therefore be pictured in its totality—i.e. language—as a series of contiguous subdivisions marked off on both the indefinite plane of jumbled ideas (*A*) and the equally vague plane of sounds (*B*). The following diagram gives a rough idea of it:

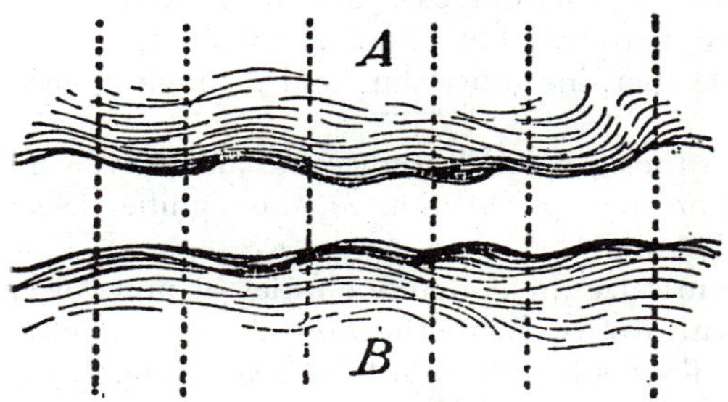

The characteristic role of language with respect to thought is not to create a material phonic means for expressing ideas but to serve as a link between thought and sound, under conditions that of necessity bring about the reciprocal delimitations of units. Thought, chaotic by nature, has to become ordered in the process of its decomposition. Neither are thoughts given material form nor are sounds transformed into mental entities; the somewhat mysterious fact is rather that "thought-sound" implies division, and that language works out its units while taking shape between two shapeless masses. Visualize the air in contact with a sheet of water; if the atmospheric pressure changes, the surface of the water will be broken up into a series of divisions, waves; the waves resemble the union or coupling of thought with phonic substance.

Language might be called the domain of articulations, using the word as it was defined earlier. Each linguistic term is a member, an *articulus* in which an idea is fixed in a sound and a sound becomes the sign of an idea.

Language can also be compared with a sheet of paper:[6] thought is the front and the sound the back; one cannot cut the front without cutting the back at the same time; likewise in language, one can neither divide sound from thought nor thought from sound; the division could be accomplished only abstractedly, and the result would be either pure psychology or pure phonology.

Linguistics then works in the borderland where the elements of sound and thought combine; *their combination produces a form, not a substance.*

These views give a better understanding of what was said before about the

6. The French expression *une feuille de papier* literally means "a *leaf* of paper."

arbitrariness of signs. Not only are the two domains that are linked by the linguistic fact shapeless and confused, but the choice of a given slice of sound to name a given idea is completely arbitrary. If this were not true, the notion of value would be compromised, for it would include an externally imposed element. But actually values remain entirely relative, and that is why the bond between the sound and the idea is radically arbitrary.

The arbitrary nature of the sign explains in turn why the social fact alone can create a linguistic system. The community is necessary if values that owe their existence solely to usage and general acceptance are to be set up; by himself the individual is incapable of fixing a single value.

In addition, the idea of value, as defined, shows that to consider a term as simply the union of a certain sound with a certain concept is grossly misleading. To define it in this way would isolate the term from its system; it would mean assuming that one can start from the terms and construct the system by adding them together when, on the contrary, it is from the interdependent whole that one must start and through analysis obtain its elements.

To develop this thesis, we shall study value successively from the viewpoint of the signified or concept (Section 2), the signifier (Section 3), and the complete sign (Section 4).

Being unable to seize the concrete entities or units of language directly, we shall work with words. While the word does not conform exactly to the definition of the linguistic unit, it at least bears a rough resemblance to the unit and has the advantage of being concrete; consequently, we shall use words as specimens equivalent to real terms in a synchronic system, and the principles that we evolve with respect to words will be valid for entities in general.

2. *Linguistic Value from a Conceptual Viewpoint*

When we speak of the value of a word, we generally think first of its property of standing for an idea, and this is in fact one side of linguistic value. But if this is true, how does *value* differ from *signification?* Might the two words be synonyms? I think not, although it is easy to confuse them, since the confusion results not so much from their similarity as from the subtlety of the distinction that they mark.

From a conceptual viewpoint, value is doubtless one element in signification, and it is difficult to see how signification can be dependent upon value and still be distinct from it. But we must clear up the issue or risk reducing language to a simple naming-process.

Let us first take signification as it is generally understood. As the arrows in the drawing show, it is only the counterpart of the sound-image. Everything that occurs concerns only the sound-image and the concept when we look upon the word as independent and self-contained.

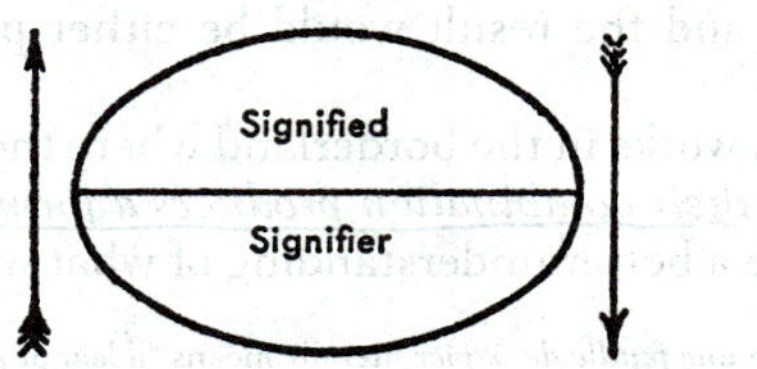

But here is the paradox: on the one hand the concept seems to be the counterpart of the sound-image, and on the other hand the sign itself is in turn the counterpart of the other signs of language.

Language is a system of interdependent terms in which the value of each term results solely from the simultaneous presence of the others, as in the diagram:

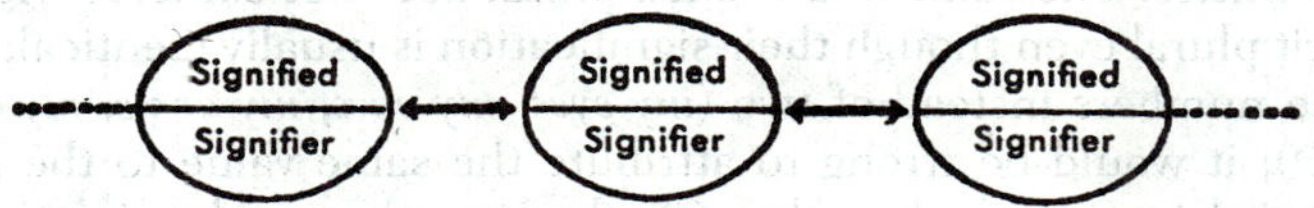

How, then, can value be confused with signification, i.e. the counterpart of the sound-image? It seems impossible to liken the relations represented here by horizontal arrows to those represented above by vertical arrows. Putting it another way—and again taking up the example of the sheet of paper that is cut in two—it is clear that the observable relation between the different pieces A, B, C, D, etc. is distinct from the relation between the front and back of the same piece as in A/A', B/B', etc.

To resolve the issue, let us observe from the outset that even outside language all values are apparently governed by the same paradoxical principle. They are always composed:

(1) of a *dissimilar* thing that can be *exchanged* for the thing of which the value is to be determined; and

(2) of *similar* things that can be *compared* with the thing of which the value is to be determined.

Both factors are necessary for the existence of a value. To determine what a five-franc piece is worth one must therefore know: (1) that it can be exchanged for a fixed quantity of a different thing, e.g. bread; and (2) that it can be compared with a similar value of the same system, e.g. a one-franc piece, or with coins of another system (a dollar, etc.). In the same way a word can be exchanged for something dissimilar, an idea; besides, it can be compared with something of the same nature, another word. Its value is therefore not fixed so long as one simply states that it can be "exchanged" for a given concept, i.e. that it has this or that signification: one must also compare it with similar values, with other words that stand in opposition to it. Its content is really fixed only by the concurrence of everything that exists outside it. Being part of a system, it is endowed not only with a signification but also and especially with a value, and this is something quite different.

A few examples will show clearly that this is true. Modern French *mouton* can have the same signification as English *sheep* but not the same value, and this for several reasons, particularly because in speaking of a piece of meat ready to be served on the table, English uses *mutton* and not *sheep*. The difference in value between *sheep* and *mouton* is due to the fact that *sheep* has beside it a second term while the French word does not.

Within the same language, all words used to express related ideas limit each other reciprocally; synonyms like French *redouter* 'dread,' *craindre* 'fear,' and *avoir peur* 'be afraid' have value only through their opposition: if *redouter* did not exist, all its content would go to its competitors. Conversely, some words are enriched through contact with others: e.g. the new element introduced in *décrépit* (un vieillard *décrépit*) results from the co-existence of *décrépi* (un mur *décrépi*).[7] The value of just any term is accordingly determined by its environment; it is impossible to fix even the value of the word signifying "sun" without first considering its surroundings: in some languages it is not possible to say "sit in the *sun*."

Everything said about words applies to any term of language, e.g. to grammatical entities. The value of a French plural does not coincide with that of a Sanskrit plural even though their signification is usually identical; Sanskrit has three numbers instead of two (*my eyes, my ears, my arms, my legs,* etc. are dual[8]); it would be wrong to attribute the same value to the plural in Sanskrit and in French; its value clearly depends on what is outside and around it.

If words stood for pre-existing concepts, they would all have exact equivalents in meaning from one language to the next; but this is not true. French uses *louer* (*une maison*) 'let (a house)' indifferently to mean both "pay for" and "receive payment for," whereas German uses two words, *mieten* and *vermieten*; there is obviously no exact correspondence of values. The German verbs *schätzen* and *urteilen*[9] share a number of significations, but that correspondence does not hold at several points.

Inflection offers some particularly striking examples. Distinctions of time, which are so familiar to us, are unknown in certain languages. Hebrew does not recognize even the fundamental distinctions between the past, present, and future. Proto-Germanic has no special form for the future; to say that the future is expressed by the present is wrong, for the value of the present is not the same in Germanic as in languages that have a future along with the present. The Slavic languages regularly single out two aspects of the verb: the perfective represents action as a point, complete in its totality; the imperfective represents it as taking place, and on the line of time. The categories are difficult for a Frenchman to understand, for they are unknown in French; if they were predetermined, this would not be true. Instead of pre-existing ideas then, we find in all the foregoing examples *values* emanating from the system. When they are said to correspond to concepts, it is understood that the concepts are purely differential and defined not by their positive content but negatively by their relations with the other terms of the system. Their most precise characteristic is in being what the others are not.

Now the real interpretation of the diagram of the signal becomes apparent. Thus

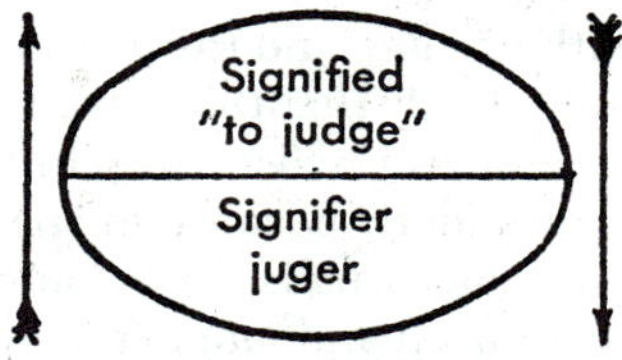

means that in French the concept "to judge" is linked to the sound-image *juger*; in short, it symbolizes signification. But it is quite clear that initially

7. The words translated as "decrepit" in "a decrepit old man" and "a decrepit wall" come from two different sources: *décrépit* is derived from the Latin *dēcrepitus, décrépi* from *crispus*.

8. A special form applied to 2 of something.

9. "To value, assess" and "to judge," respectively.

the concept is nothing, that is only a value determined by its relations with other similar values, and that without them the signification would not exist. If I state simply that a word signifies something when I have in mind the associating of a sound-image with a concept, I am making a statement that may suggest what actually happens, but by no means am I expressing the linguistic fact in its essence and fullness.

3. *Linguistic Value from a Material Viewpoint*

The conceptual side of value is made up solely of relations and differences with respect to the other terms of language, and the same can be said of its material side. The important thing in the word is not the sound alone but the phonic differences that make it possible to distinguish this word from all others, for differences carry signification.

This may seem surprising, but how indeed could the reverse be possible? Since one vocal image is no better suited than the next for what it is commissioned to express, it is evident, even *a priori,* that a segment of language can never in the final analysis be based on anything except its noncoincidence with the rest. *Arbitrary* and *differential* are two correlative qualities.

The alteration of linguistic signs clearly illustrates this. It is precisely because the terms *a* and *b* as such are radically incapable of reaching the level of consciousness—one is always conscious of only the *a*/*b* difference—that each term is free to change according to laws that are unrelated to its signifying function. No positive sign characterizes the genitive plural in Czech *žen;* still the two forms *žena: žen* function as well as the earlier forms *žena: ženb; žen* has value only because it is different.

Here is another example that shows even more clearly the systematic role of phonic differences: in Greek, *éphēn* is an imperfect and *éstēn* an aorist[1] although both words are formed in the same way; the first belongs to the system of the present indicative of *phēmī* 'I say,' whereas there is no present **stēmi*; now it is precisely the relation *phēmī: éphēn* that corresponds to the relation between the present and the imperfect (cf. *déiknūmi: edéiknūn,*[2] etc.). Signs function, then, not through their intrinsic value but through their relative position.

In addition, it is impossible for sound alone, a material element, to belong to language. It is only a secondary thing, substance to be put to use. All our conventional values have the characteristic of not being confused with the tangible element which supports them. For instance, it is not the metal in a piece of money that fixes its value. A coin nominally worth five francs may contain less than half its worth of silver. Its value will vary according to the amount stamped upon it and according to its use inside or outside a political boundary. This is even more true of the linguistic signifier, which is not phonic but incorporeal—constituted not by its material substance but by the differences that separate its sound-image from all others.

The foregoing principle is so basic that it applies to all the material elements of language, including phonemes. Every language forms its words on the basis of a system of sonorous elements, each element being a clearly delimited unit and one of a fixed number of units. Phonemes are character-

1. "Imperfect" and "aorist" are two past tenses of Greek verbs.
2. The present and imperfect, respectively, of the Greek verb "to show" (all the forms in this paragraph are 1st-person singular).

ized not, as one might think, by their own positive quality but simply by the fact that they are distinct. Phonemes are above all else opposing, relative, and negative entities.

Proof of this is the latitude that speakers have between points of convergence in the pronunciation of distinct sounds. In French, for instance, general use of a dorsal *r* does not prevent many speakers from using a tongue-tip trill; language is not in the least disturbed by it; language requires only that the sound be different and not, as one might imagine, that it have an invariable quality. I can even pronounce the French *r* like German *ch* in *Bach*, *doch*, etc., but in German I could not use *r* instead of *ch*, for German gives recognition to both elements and must keep them apart. Similarly, in Russian there is no latitude for *t* in the direction of *t'* (palatalized *t*), for the result would be the confusing of two sounds differentiated by the language (cf. *govorit'* 'speak' and *goverit* 'he speaks'), but more freedom may be taken with respect to *th* (aspirated *t*) since this sound does not figure in the Russian system of phonemes.

Since an identical state of affairs is observable in writing, another system of signs, we shall use writing to draw some comparisons that will clarify the whole issue. In fact:

1) The signs used in writing are arbitrary; there is no connection, for example, between the letter *t* and the sound that it designates.

2) The value of letters is purely negative and differential. The same person can write *t*, for instance, in different ways:

The only requirement is that the sign for *t* not be confused in his script with the signs used for *l*, *d*, etc.

3) Values in writing function only through reciprocal opposition within a fixed system that consists of a set number of letters. This third characteristic, though not identical to the second, is closely related to it, for both depend on the first. Since the graphic sign is arbitrary, its form matters little or rather matters only within the limitations imposed by the system.

4) The means by which the sign is produced is completely unimportant, for it does not affect the system (this also follows from characteristic 1). Whether I make the letters in white or black, raised or engraved, with pen or chisel—all this is of no importance with respect to their signification.

4. *The Sign Considered in Its Totality*

Everything that has been said up to this point boils down to this: in language there are only differences. Even more important: a difference generally implies positive terms between which the difference is set up; but in language there are only differences *without positive terms*. Whether we take the signified or the signifier, language has neither ideas nor sounds that existed before the linguistic system, but only conceptual and phonic differences that have issued from the system. The idea or phonic substance that a sign contains is of less importance than the other signs that surround it. Proof of this is that the value of a term may be modified without either its meaning or its sound being affected, solely because a neighboring term has been modified.

But the statement that everything in language is negative is true only if the signified and the signifier are considered separately; when we consider the sign in its totality, we have something that is positive in its own class. A linguistic system is a series of differences of sound combined with a series of differences of ideas; but the pairing of a certain number of acoustical signs with as many cuts made from the mass of thought engenders a system of values; and this system serves as the effective link between the phonic and psychological elements within each sign. Although both the signified and the signifier are purely differential and negative when considered separately, their combination is a positive fact; it is even the sole type of facts that language has, for maintaining the parallelism between the two classes of differences is the distinctive function of the linguistic institution.

Certain diachronic facts are typical in this respect. Take the countless instances where alteration of the signifier occasions a conceptual change and where it is obvious that the sum of the ideas distinguished corresponds in principle to the sum of the distinctive signs. When two words are confused through phonetic alteration (e.g. French *décrépit* from *dēcrepitus* and *décrépi* from *crispus*), the ideas that they express will also tend to become confused if only they have something in common. Or a word may have different forms (cf. *chaise* 'chair' and *chaire* 'desk'[3]). Any nascent difference will tend invariably to become significant but without always succeeding or being successful on the first trial. Conversely, any conceptual difference perceived by the mind seeks to find expression through a distinct signifier, and two ideas that are no longer distinct in the mind tend to merge into the same signifier.

When we compare signs—positive terms—with each other, we can no longer speak of difference; the expression would not be fitting, for it applies only to the comparing of two sound-images, e.g. *father* and *mother*, or two ideas, e.g. the idea "father" and the idea "mother"; two signs, each having a signified and signifier, are not different but only distinct. Between them there is only *opposition*. The entire mechanism of language, with which we shall be concerned later, is based on oppositions of this kind and on the phonic and conceptual differences that they imply.

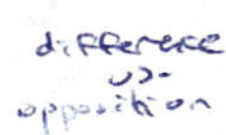

What is true of value is true also of the unit. A unit is a segment of the spoken chain that corresponds to a certain concept; both are by nature purely differential.

Applied to units, the principle of differentiation can be stated in this way: *the characteristics of the unit blend with the unit itself*. In language, as in any semiological system, whatever distinguishes one sign from the others constitutes it. Difference makes character just as it makes value and the unit.

Another rather paradoxical consequence of the same principle is this: in the last analysis what is commonly referred to as a "grammatical fact" fits the definition of the unit, for it always expresses an opposition of terms; it differs only in that the opposition is particularly significant (e.g. the formation of German plurals of the type *Nacht: Nächte*). Each term present in the grammatical fact (the singular without umlaut or final *e* in opposition to the plural with umlaut and *–e*) consists of the interplay of a number of opposi-

3. Both words derive from the Old French *chaiere*.

tions within the system. When isolated, neither *Nacht* nor *Nächte* is anything: thus everything is opposition. Putting it another way, the *Nacht: Nächte* relation can be expressed by an algebraic formula *a/b* in which *a* and *b* are not simple terms but result from a set of relations. Language, in a manner of speaking, is a type of algebra consisting solely of complex terms. Some of its oppositions are more significant than others; but units and grammatical facts are only different names for designating diverse aspects of the same general fact: the functioning of linguistic oppositions. This statement is so true that we might very well approach the problem of units by starting from grammatical facts. Taking an opposition like *Nacht: Nächte*, we might ask what are the units involved in it. Are they only the two words, the whole series of similar words, *a* and *ä*, or all singulars and plurals, etc.?

Units and grammatical facts would not be confused if linguistic signs were made up of something besides differences. But language being what it is, we shall find nothing simple in it regardless of our approach; everywhere and always there is the same complex equilibrium of terms that mutually condition each other. Putting it another way, *language is a form and not a substance*. This truth could not be overstressed, for all the mistakes in our terminology, all our incorrect ways of naming things that pertain to language, stem from the involuntary supposition that the linguistic phenomenon must have substance.

CHAPTER V. SYNTAGMATIC AND ASSOCIATIVE RELATIONS

1. *Definitions*

In a language-state everything is based on relations. How do they function?

Relations and differences between linguistic terms fall into two distinct groups, each of which generates a certain class of values. The opposition between the two classes gives a better understanding of the nature of each class. They correspond to two forms of our mental activity, both indispensable to the life of language.

In discourse, on the one hand, words acquire relations based on the linear nature of language because they are chained together. This rules out the possibility of pronouncing two elements simultaneously. The elements are arranged in sequence on the chain of speaking. Combinations supported by linearity are *syntagms*.[4] The syntagm is always composed of two or more consecutive units (e.g. French *re-lire* 're-read,' *contre tous* 'against everyone,' *la vie humaine* 'human life,' *Dieu est bon* 'God is good,' *s'il fait beau temps, nous sortirons* 'if the weather is nice, we'll go out,' etc.). In the syntagm a term acquires its value only because it stands in opposition to everything that precedes or follows it, or to both.

Outside discourse, on the other hand, words acquire relations of a different kind. Those that have something in common are associated in the memory, resulting in groups marked by diverse relations. For instance, the French word *enseignement* 'teaching' will unconsciously call to mind a host of other

4. It is scarcely necessary to point out that the study of *syntagms* is not to be confused with syntax. Syntax is only one part of the study of syntagms [Bally, Sechehaye, and Riedlinger's note].

words (*enseigner* 'teach,' *renseigner* 'acquaint,' etc.; or, *armement* 'armament,' *changement* 'amendment,' etc.; or *éducation* 'education,' *apprentissage* 'apprenticeship,' etc.). All those words are related in some way.

We see that the co-ordinations formed outside discourse differ strikingly from those formed inside discourse. Those formed outside discourse are not supported by linearity. Their seat is in the brain; they are a part of the inner storehouse that makes up the language of each speaker. They are *associative relations.*

The syntagmatic relation is *in praesentia.*[5] It is based on two or more terms that occur in an effective series. Against this, the associative relation unites terms *in absentia* in a potential mnemonic series.

From the associative and syntagmatic viewpoint a linguistic unit is like a fixed part of a building, e.g. a column. On the one hand, the column has a certain relation to the architrave that it supports; the arrangement of the two units in space suggests the syntagmatic relation. On the other hand, if the column is Doric, it suggests a mental comparison of this style with others (Ionic, Corinthian, etc.) although none of these elements is present in space: the relation is associative.

Each of the two classes of co-ordination calls for some specific remarks.

2. *Syntagmatic Relations*

The examples have already indicated that the notion of syntagm applies not only to words but to groups of words, to complex units of all lengths and types (compounds, derivatives, phrases, whole sentences).

It is not enough to consider the relation that ties together the different parts of syntagms (e.g. French *contre* 'against' and *tous* 'everyone' in *contre tous, contre* and *maître* 'master' in *contremaître* 'foreman'); one must also bear in mind the relation that links the whole to its parts (e.g. *contre tous* in opposition on the one hand to *contre* and on the other *tous*, or *contremaître* in opposition to *contre* and *maître*).

An objection might be raised at this point. The sentence is the ideal type of syntagm. But it belongs to speaking, not to language.[6] Does it not follow that the syntagm belongs to speaking? I do not think so. Speaking is characterized by freedom of combinations; one must therefore ask whether or not all syntagms are equally free.

It is obvious from the first that many expressions belong to language. These are the pat phrases in which any change is prohibited by usage, even if we can single out their meaningful elements (cf. *à quoi bon?* 'what's the use?' *allons donc!* 'nonsense!'). The same is true, though to a lesser degree, of expressions like *prendre la mouche*[7] 'take offense easily,' *forcer la main à quelqu'un* 'force someone's hand,' *rompre une lance* 'break a lance,' or even *avoir mal* (*à la tête*, etc.) 'have (a headache, etc.),' *à force de* (*soins*, etc.) 'by dint of (care, etc.),' *que vous en semble?* 'how do you feel about it?' *pas n'est besoin de* . . . 'there's no need for . . . ,' etc., which are characterized by peculiarities of signification or syntax. These idiomatic twists cannot be improvised; they are furnished by tradition. There are also words which, while

5. Present (Latin).
6. That is, it belongs to *la parole*, not to *la langue*, in Saussure's terms.
7. Literally, "lay hold of the fly."

lending themselves perfectly to analysis, are characterized by some morphological anomaly that is kept solely by dint of usage (cf. *difficulté* 'difficulty' beside *facilité* 'facility,' etc., and *mourrai* '[I] shall die' beside *dormirai* '[I] shall sleep').[8]

There are further proofs. To language rather than to speaking belong the syntagmatic types that are built upon regular forms. Indeed, since there is nothing abstract in language, the types exist only if language has registered a sufficient number of specimens. When a word like *indécorable*[9] arises in speaking, its appearance supposes a fixed type, and this type is in turn possible only through remembrance of a sufficient number of similar words belonging to language (*impardonable* 'unpardonable,' *intolérable* 'intolerable,' *infatigable* 'indefatigable,' etc.). Exactly the same is true of sentences and groups of words built upon regular patterns. Combinations like *la terre tourne* 'the world turns,' *que vous dit-il?* 'what does he say to you?' etc. correspond to general types that are in turn supported in the language by concrete remembrances.

But we must realize that in the syntagm there is no clear-cut boundary between the language fact, which is a sign of collective usage, and the fact that belongs to speaking and depends on individual freedom. In a great number of instances it is hard to class a combination of units because both forces have combined in producing it, and they have combined in indeterminable proportions.

3. *Associative Relations*

Mental association creates other groups besides those based on the comparing of terms that have something in common; through its grasp of the nature of the relations that bind the terms together, the mind creates as many associative series as there are diverse relations. For instance, in *enseignement* 'teaching,' *enseigner* 'teach,' *enseignons* '(we) teach,' etc., one element, the radical, is common to every term; the same word may occur in a different series formed around another common element, the suffix (cf. *enseignement, armement, changement*, etc.); or the association may spring from the analogy of the concepts signified (*enseignement, instruction, apprentissage, éducation*, etc.); or again, simply from the similarity of the sound-images (e.g. *enseignement* and *justement* 'precisely'). Thus there is at times a double similarity of meaning and form, at times similarity only of form or of meaning. A word can always evoke everything that can be associated with it in one way or another.

Whereas a syntagm immediately suggests an order of succession and a fixed number of elements, terms in an associative family occur neither in fixed numbers nor in a definite order. If we associate *painful, delightful, frightful*, etc. we are unable to predict the number of words that the memory will suggest or the order in which they will appear. A particular word is like the center of a constellation; it is the point of convergence of an indefinite number of co-ordinated terms.

8. The anomaly of the double *r* in the future forms of certain verbs in French may be compared to irregular plurals like *oxen* in English [translator's note].

9. That is, a word coined by analogy.

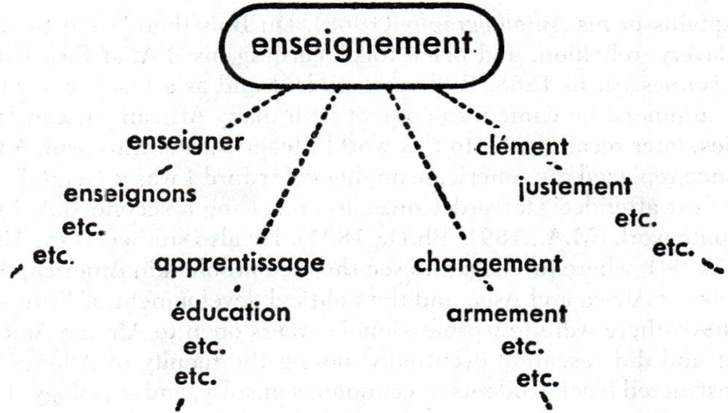

But of the two characteristics of the associative series—indeterminate order and indefinite number—only the first can always be verified; the second may fail to meet the test. This happens in the case of inflectional paradigms, which are typical of associative groupings. Latin *dominus, dominī, dominō*, etc. is obviously an associative group formed around a common element, the noun theme *domin-*, but the series is not indefinite as in the case of *enseignement, changement*, etc.; the number of cases is definite. Against this, the words have no fixed order of succession, and it is by a purely arbitrary act that the grammarian groups them in one way rather than in another; in the mind of speakers the nominative case is by no means the first one in the declension,[1] and the order in which terms are called depends on circumstances.

1906–13 1916

1. In standard grammars of inflected languages such as Greek and Latin, tables illustrating the case endings of each declension, or class of nouns or adjectives sharing the same forms, always begin with the nominative case (i.e., the form of the subject).

W. E. B. Du Bois
1868–1963

W. E. B. Du Bois excelled in many disciplines and creative endeavors, from sociology to social commentary to poetry. He was one of the most accomplished scholar-activists and public intellectuals in American history, and his extraordinary life spanned ninety-five years. Born, raised, and educated in the latter decades of the nineteenth century, Du Bois was a Romantic visionary and Victorian professional writer who decades later grappled with the political tensions of the cold war. But he was also an African American radical, a Pan-African leader, and eventually a defiant Marxist revolutionary.

William Edward Burghardt Du Bois was born in Great Barrington in western Massachusetts, a small town with few African American residents. Raised by his mother and her relatives, in his youth he became a lover of books, and he began writing early. Before even graduating from high school in 1885, Du Bois served as a correspondent for newspapers in Massachusetts and New York City.

As he explains in his *Autobiography* (1968), Du Bois then "went South," to "the South of slavery, rebellion, and black folk," earning his B.A. at Fisk University, in Nashville, Tennessee, in 1888. Both as a student and as a teacher in rural schools during the summers, he came into contact with many African African families and communities, later recalling: "Into this world I leapt with enthusiasm. A new loyalty and allegiance replaced my Americanism: henceforward I was a Negro."

Du Bois next attended Harvard University, receiving a second B.A. in 1890 and doing graduate work (M.A., 1891; Ph.D., 1895). He also studied at the University of Berlin (1892–94), where he "began to see the race problem in America, the problem of the peoples of Africa and Asia, and the political development of Europe as one."

In the 1890s there were few professional careers open to African Americans. Du Bois taught and did research, eventually joining the faculty of Atlanta University, where he instructed black students in economics, history, and sociology (1897–1910, 1933–44).

Du Bois's first book, based on his dissertation, was *The Suppression of the African Slave Trade to the United States of America, 1638–1870* (1896). He was a serious and well-trained scholar. But his belief in the transformative power of social scientific knowledge was shattered by the virulent racism of turn-of-the-century America, when segregation laws increased and anti-black terror and lynching intensified.

By 1900 Du Bois had already begun to project his vision of race relations outward from America's shores, becoming active in Pan-African organizations and congresses. In his major work *The Souls of Black Folk* (1903), he not only examines the history of slavery and segregation in the United States but also emphasizes, more generally, that "the problem of the Twentieth Century is the problem of the color line." Still, his focus is American; *The Souls of Black Folk* includes essays, sketches, and stories on African American politics, history, education, music, and culture. Du Bois speaks evocatively in it of "the veil" that separates blacks from whites, and he famously describes the "double consciousness" that defines African American identity: "One ever feels his twoness—an American, a Negro; two souls, two thoughts, two unreconciled strivings; two warring ideals in one dark body, whose dogged strength alone keeps it from being torn asunder."

Du Bois was perhaps best known at this time for his opposition to Booker T. Washington (1856–1915), the founder of Tuskegee Institute in Alabama and the leading spokesman on the national scene for African Americans—chosen for that position, Du Bois argued in *The Souls of Black Folk* and elsewhere, because he presented the accommodationist message that whites wanted to hear. Du Bois was far more militant; not satisfied with limited economic progress, he insisted on social and political rights, access to higher education, and the development of an elite African American intellectual and professional class (the "talented tenth").

Du Bois's opposition to Washington led him in 1905 to take a central role in the Niagara Movement for full rights for African Americans. He became editor of *Horizon: A Journal of the Color Line* (1907–10); he helped found the National Association for the Advancement of Colored People (NAACP) in 1909 and served as its director of publications and research; and he expanded his role in the international Pan-African movement. He was actively publishing books and articles, too, as a social critic and theorist, creative writer, and historian.

From 1910 to 1934 Du Bois was the editor of the NAACP's monthly magazine, *The Crisis*; by 1919 it reached an audience of 100,000 readers. He was an important influence on the writers and artists of the Harlem Renaissance and the "New Negro" movement of the 1920s. In the pages of *The Crisis*, he repeatedly urged readers to see "Beauty in Black," an imperative that a dazzling array of African American authors and artists sought to fulfill.

These diversely gifted men and women—LANGSTON HUGHES, Jean Toomer, ZORA NEALE HURSTON, Duke Ellington, and many others—were forming the intellectual vanguard for which Du Bois had called. But because their emphasis was cultural rather than political, he had a mixed response to them. Du Bois welcomed their innovative creative work, but he regretted the dependence of African American authors, artists, and musicians on white patrons and audiences. And while he called for greater openness and honesty about sexual themes, he was also quick to criticize some African American authors (for example, Claude McKay) for reinforcing white stereotypes of black sexual behavior.

The Depression of the 1930s hit African Americans hard and provoked Du Bois to call for "voluntary segregation," which, he maintained, would lead to economic self-sufficiency, solidarity, and self-advancement in a country that was not seeking to reach the goal of racial integration. Because of his separatist views, Du Bois was forced out of the NAACP in 1934.

From the 1930s until his death in 1963, Du Bois remained an activist and a prolific author. His books include the epic historical study *Black Reconstruction in America, 1860–1880* (1935); *Dusk of Dawn* (1940), which he described as "the autobiography of a concept of race"; and *Color and Democracy: Colonies and Peace* (1945), one of many writings of the 1940s and 1950s that challenged imperialism and made the case for African independence. Such pioneering, uncompromising work made him highly respected on the international scene. But together with his ever-deepening interest in Communism and admiration of the Soviet Union, it brought Du Bois under suspicion in the United States. In 1951 he was placed on trial for being an "unregistered foreign agent"; though he was acquitted, his passport was revoked from 1952 to 1958. Embittered by his treatment, in 1961 Du Bois joined the Communist Party, renounced his U.S. citizenship, and took up residence in Ghana. There, at work on a multivolume *Encyclopedia Africana*, he died in Accra, two years later.

Du Bois's writings in literary criticism and theory blend genteel Victorianism, literary realism and naturalism, and radical politics. As our selection, "Criteria of Negro Art" (1926), indicates, Du Bois believed that "all Art is propaganda and ever must be." In this address he tells African American writers and artists to strive for Truth and Beauty. But he also stresses the marketplace conditions, and the racism, that block and undercut African American literary and cultural achievement, and he insists on the need for art to function as agitation, protest, and racial propaganda. Underlying his argument is the problem that confronts all literary intellectuals who maintain strong political views: how to resolve the dual demands of art and politics. Du Bois affirms that the central duty of African American writers and artists is to advance the cause of the race; at the same time, he insists that they express the truth about African American life. But someone looking ahead several decades to reader-response theory (see, for example, STANLEY FISH and WOLFGANG ISER) might nonetheless propose that Du Bois's real concern is as much with a work's reception as with its production: How does the work of art affect the general American perception of African Americans? What will be the impact of the text on the social and political attitudes of readers?

The weakness in Du Bois's position lies precisely in his extreme demand that art must be used for propaganda and for nothing else. No doubt he believes that the needs of his people mandate this stark requirement. Yet in "Criteria of Negro Art" it clashes with his earlier evocation of the splendid beauty of Cologne's cathedral and the Venus de Milo, which he seems to value for their own sake rather than for any propagandistic service they did or might perform. Du Bois's vision is inclusive, and challengingly so: he links the cathedral and the famous Greek statue with a village in West Africa and a Negro song or spiritual. But he appears not to recognize the reductive nature of his fiery dismissal: "I do not care a damn for any art that is not used for propaganda."

Du Bois is only one voice in a complex, ongoing African American debate. His address can be profitably placed alongside and measured against the literary critical ideas that Zora Neale Hurston and Richard Wright articulate, and to which other twentieth-century authors—notably James Baldwin, Ralph Ellison, Amiri Baraka, and

Toni Morrison—have contributed. All, in their writings, have acknowledged Du Bois's majestic stature as an intellectual and cultural critic and historian. But all are also primarily creative writers—Du Bois was not—and they call for and exemplify forms of freedom in artistic expression that for political reasons he could not wholly share.

BIBLIOGRAPHY

The *Complete Published Works of W. E. B. Du Bois* has been edited by Herbert Aptheker (36 vols., 1973–86). It is supplemented by two other works edited by Aptheker: *The Correspondence of W. E. B. Du Bois* (3 vols., 1973–78) and *Against Racism: Unpublished Essays, Papers, Addresses, 1887–1961* (1985). The Du Bois volume in the Library of America series, edited by Nathan Irvin Huggins (1986), includes *The Suppression of the African Slave Trade, The Souls of Black Folk,* and *Dusk of Dawn,* as well as a number of essays. A range of selections is also available in *W. E. B. Du Bois: A Reader,* edited by David Levering Lewis (1995), and *The Oxford W. E. B. Du Bois Reader,* edited by Eric J. Sundquist (1996).

There are several excellent biographies: Manning Marable, *W. E. B. Du Bois, Black Radical Democrat* (1986), a cogently written survey by an author fully familiar with Du Bois's writings and the major issues in African American social and political history; Gerald Horne, *Black and Red: W. E. B. Du Bois and the Afro-American Response to the Cold War, 1944–1963* (1986), a detailed account of the final phase of Du Bois's career; and David L. Lewis, *W. E. B. Du Bois,* a comprehensive two-volume biography: *Biography of a Race, 1868–1919* (1993) and *The Fight for Equality and the American Century, 1919–1963* (2000).

The best study of Du Bois as a writer is Arnold Rampersad's *Art and Imagination of W. E. B. Du Bois* (1976), which explores all of Du Bois's major books. See also the extensive chapter on Du Bois in Eric J. Sundquist, *To Wake the Nations: Race in the Making of American Literature* (1993); Keith Eldon Byerman, *Seizing the Word: History, Art, and Self in the Work of W. E. B. Du Bois* (1994); Shamoon Zamir, *Dark Voices: W. E. B. Du Bois and American Thought, 1888–1903* (1995); and Adolph Reed Jr., *W. E. B. Du Bois and American Political Thought: Fabianism and the Color Line* (1997). Other helpful resources include two collections: *Critical Essays on W. E. B. Du Bois,* edited by William L. Andrews (1985), and *W. E. B. Du Bois on Race and Culture,* edited by Bernard W. Bell, Emily R. Grosholz, and James B. Stewart (1996), which sheds light on Du Bois's attitudes toward race, gender equality, and Pan-Africanism. Key bibliographic sources include Herbert Aptheker, *Annotated Bibliography of the Published Writings of W. E. B. Du Bois* (1973), and Paul G. Partington, *W. E. B. Du Bois: A Bibliography of His Published Writings* (1979).

Criteria of Negro Art

So many persons have asked for the complete text of the address delivered by Dr. Du Bois at the Chicago Conference of the National Association for the Advancement of Colored People that we are publishing the address here.[1]

I do not doubt but there are some in this audience who are a little disturbed at the subject of this meeting, and particularly at the subject I have chosen. Such people are thinking something like this: "How is it that an organization like this, a group of radicals trying to bring new things into the world, a fighting organization which has come up out of the blood and dust of battle, struggling for the right of black men to be ordinary human beings—how is

1. *The Crisis*; the address was delivered in 1926.

it that an organization of this kind can turn aside to talk about Art? After all, what have we who are slaves and black to do with Art?"

Or perhaps there are others who feel a certain relief and are saying, "After all it is rather satisfactory after all this talk about rights and fighting to sit and dream of something which leaves a nice taste in the mouth."

Let me tell you that neither of these groups is right. The thing we are talking about tonight is part of the great fight we are carrying on and it represents a forward and an upward look—a pushing onward. You and I have been breasting hills; we have been climbing upward; there has been progress and we can see it day by day looking back along blood-filled paths. But as you go through the valleys and over the foothills, so long as you are climbing, the direction,—north, south, east or west,—is of less importance. But when gradually the vista widens and you begin to see the world at your feet and the far horizon, then it is time to know more precisely whither you are going and what you really want.

What do we want? What is the thing we are after? As it was phrased last night it had a certain truth: We want to be Americans, full-fledged Americans, with all the rights of other American citizens. But is that all? Do we want simply to be Americans? Once in a while through all of us there flashes some clairvoyance, some clear idea, of what America really is. We who are dark can see America in a way that white Americans can not. And seeing our country thus, are we satisfied with its present goals and ideals?

In the high school where I studied we learned most of Scott's "Lady of the Lake"[2] by heart. In after life once it was my privilege to see the lake. It was Sunday. It was quiet. You could glimpse the deer wandering in unbroken forests; you could hear the soft ripple of romance on the waters. Around me fell the cadence of that poetry of my youth. I fell asleep full of the enchantment of the Scottish border. A new day broke and with it came a sudden rush of excursionists. They were mostly Americans and they were loud and strident. They poured upon the little pleasure boat,—men with their hats a little on one side and drooping cigars in the wet corners of their mouths; women who shared their conversation with the world. They all tried to get everywhere first. They pushed other people out of the way. They made all sorts of incoherent noises and gestures so that the quiet home folk and the visitors from other lands silently and half-wonderingly gave way before them. They struck a note not evil but wrong. They carried, perhaps, a sense of strength and accomplishment, but their hearts had no conception of the beauty which pervaded this holy place.

If you tonight suddenly should become full-fledged Americans; if your color faded, or the color line here in Chicago was miraculously forgotten; suppose, too, you became at the same time rich and powerful:—what is it that you would want? What would you immediately seek? Would you buy the most powerful of motor cars and outrace Cook County?[3] Would you buy the most elaborate estate on the North Shore? Would you be a Rotarian or a Lion or a What-not of the very last degree?[4] Would you wear the most striking clothes, give the richest dinners and buy the longest press notices?

Even as you visualize such ideals you know in your hearts that these are

2. A poem in six cantos about early-16th-century knights and ladies (1810), by Sir Walter Scott (1771–1832).

3. County in which Chicago is located.

4. The Rotary and Lions clubs are national service organizations; Freemasons are described as achieving certain degrees.

not the things you really want. You realize this sooner than the average white American because, pushed aside as we have been in America, there has come to us not only a certain distaste for the tawdry and flamboyant but a vision of what the world could be if it were really a beautiful world; if we had the true spirit; if we had the Seeing Eye, the Cunning Hand, the Feeling Heart; if we had, to be sure, not perfect happiness, but plenty of good hard work, the inevitable suffering that always comes with life; sacrifice and waiting, all that—but, nevertheless, lived in a world where men know, where men create, where they realize themselves and where they enjoy life. It is that sort of a world we want to create for ourselves and for all America.

After all, who shall describe Beauty? What is it? I remember tonight four beautiful things: The Cathedral at Cologne,[5] a forest in stone, set in light and changing shadow, echoing with sunlight and solemn song; a village of the Veys[6] in West Africa, a little thing of mauve and purple quiet, lying content and shining in the sun; a black and velvet room where on a throne rests, in old and yellowing marble; the broken curves of the Venus of Milo;[7] a single phrase of music in the Southern South—utter melody, haunting and appealing, suddenly arising out of night and eternity, beneath the moon.

Such is Beauty. Its variety is infinite, its possibility is endless. In normal life all may have it and have it yet again. The world is full of it; and yet today the mass of human beings are choked away from it, and their lives distorted and made ugly. This is not only wrong, it is silly. Who shall right this well-nigh universal failing? Who shall let this world be beautiful? Who shall restore to men the glory of sunsets and the peace of quiet sleep?

We black folk may help for we have within us as a race new stirrings, stirrings of the beginning of a new appreciation of joy, of a new desire to create, of a new will to be; as though in this morning of group life we had awakened from some sleep that at once dimly mourns the past and dreams a splendid future; and there has come the conviction that the Youth that is here today, the Negro Youth, is a different kind of Youth, because in some new way it bears this mighty prophecy on its breast, with a new realization of itself, with new determination for all mankind.

What has this Beauty to do with the world? What has Beauty to do with Truth and Goodness—with the facts of the world and the right actions of men? "Nothing," the artists rush to answer. They may be right. I am but an humble disciple of art and cannot presume to say. I am one who tells the truth and exposes evil and seeks with Beauty and for Beauty to set the world right. That somehow, somewhere eternal and perfect Beauty sits above Truth and Right I can conceive, but here and now and in the world in which I work they are for me unseparated and inseparable.

This is brought to us peculiarly when as artists we face our own past as a people. There has come to us—and it has come especially through the man we are going to honor tonight[8]—a realization of that past, of which for long years we have been ashamed, for which we have apologized. We thought nothing could come out of that past which we wanted to remember; which

5. Magnificent Gothic cathedral in Cologne, Germany, begun in 1248 and consecrated in 1322.
6. One of the Mandingo peoples of Senegal, West Africa.
7. Famous classical statue of Aphrodite, Greek goddess of love (2d c. B.C.E. copy of a 4th c. original), now armless.
8. Carter G. Woodson (1875–1950), to whom the NAACP in 1926 awarded the Spingarn Medal for African American achievement, was an African American educator and historian who in 1916 founded the *Journal of Negro History*.

we wanted to hand down to our children. Suddenly, this same past is taking on form, color and reality, and in a half shamefaced way we are beginning to be proud of it. We are remembering that the romance of the world did not die and lie forgotten in the Middle Age; that if you want romance to deal with you must have it here and now and in your own hands.

I once knew a man and woman. They had two children, a daughter who was white and a daughter who was brown; the daughter who was white married a white man; and when her wedding was preparing the daughter who was brown prepared to go and celebrate. But the mother said, "No!" and the brown daughter went into her room and turned on the gas and died. Do you want Greek tragedy swifter than that?

Or again, here is a little Southern Town and you are in the public square. On one side of the square is the office of a colored lawyer and on all the other sides are men who do not like colored lawyers. A white woman goes into the black man's office and points to the white-filled square and says, "I want five hundred dollars now and if I do not get it I am going to scream."

Have you heard the story of the conquest of German East Africa?[9] Listen to the untold tale: There were 40,000 black men and 4,000 white men who talked German. There were 20,000 black men and 12,000 white men who talked English. There were 10,000 black men and 400 white men who talked French. In Africa then where the Mountains of the Moon raised their white and snow-capped heads into the mouth of the tropic sun, where Nile and Congo rise and the Great Lakes swim, these men fought; they struggled on mountain, hill and valley, in river, lake and swamp, until in masses they sickened, crawled and died; until the 4,000 white Germans had become mostly bleached bones; until nearly all the 12,000 white Englishmen had returned to South Africa, and the 400 Frenchmen to Belgium and Heaven; all except a mere handful of the white men died; but thousands of black men from East, West and South Africa, from Nigeria and the Valley of the Nile, and from the West Indies still struggled, fought and died. For four years they fought and won and lost German East Africa; and all you hear about it is that England and Belgium conquered German Africa for the allies!

Such is the true and stirring stuff of which Romance is born and from this stuff come the stirrings of men who are beginning to remember that this kind of material is theirs; and this vital life of their own kind is beckoning them on.

The question comes next as to the interpretation of these new stirrings, of this new spirit: Of what is the colored artist capable? We have had on the part of both colored and white people singular unanimity of judgment in the past. Colored people have said: "This work must be inferior because it comes from colored people." White people have said: "It is inferior because it is done by colored people." But today there is coming to both the realization that the work of the black man is not always inferior. Interesting stories come to us. A professor in the University of Chicago read to a class that had studied literature a passage of poetry and asked them to guess the author. They guessed a goodly company from Shelley and Robert Browning down to Tennyson and Masefield. The author was Countée Cullen.[1] Or again the English

9. Du Bois reccunts events of World War I.

1. African American poet (1903–1946); his first book, *Color* (1925), used classical models such as the sonnet. Du Bois locates him in the company of the English poets Percy Bysshe Shelley (1792–1822), Robert Browning (1812–1889), Alfred,

critic John Drinkwater[2] went down to a Southern seminary, one of the sort which "finishes" young white women of the South. The students sat with their wooden faces while he tried to get some response out of them. Finally he said, "Name me some of your Southern poets." They hesitate. He said finally, "I'll start out with your best: Paul Laurence Dunbar"![3]

With the growing recognition of Negro artists in spite of the severe handicaps, one comforting thing is occurring to both white and black. They are whispering, "Here is a way out. Here is the real solution of the color problem. The recognition accorded Cullen, Hughes, Fauset, White[4] and others shows there is no real color line. Keep quiet! Don't complain! Work! All will be well!"

I will not say that already this chorus amounts to a conspiracy. Perhaps I am naturally too suspicious. But I will say that there are today a surprising number of white people who are getting great satisfaction out of these younger Negro writers because they think it is going to stop agitation of the Negro question. They say, "What is the use of your fighting and complaining; do the great thing and the reward is there." And many colored people are all too eager to follow this advice; especially those who are weary of the eternal struggle along the color line, who are afraid to fight and to whom the money of philanthropists and the alluring publicity are subtle and deadly bribes. They say, "What is the use of fighting? Why not show simply what we deserve and let the reward come to us?"

And it is right here that the National Association for the Advancement of Colored People comes upon the field, comes with its great call to a new battle, a new fight and new things to fight before the old things are wholly won; and to say that the Beauty of Truth and Freedom which shall some day be our heritage and the heritage of all civilized men is not in our hands yet and that we ourselves must not fail to realize.

There is in New York tonight a black woman molding clay by herself in a little bare room, because there is not a single school of sculpture in New York where she is welcome. Surely there are doors she might burst through, but when God makes a sculpture He does not always make the pushing sort of person who beats his way through doors thrust in his face. This girl is working her hands off to get out of this country so that she can get some sort of training.

There was Richard Brown.[5] If he had been white he would have been alive today instead of dead of neglect. Many helped him when he asked but he was not the kind of boy that always asks. He was simply one who made colors sing.

There is a colored woman in Chicago who is a great musician. She thought she would like to study at Fontainbleau this summer where Walter Damrosch[6] and a score of leaders of Art have an American school of music. But the application blank of this school says: "I am a white American and I apply for admission to the school."

We can go on the stage; we can be just as funny as white Americans wish

Lord Tennyson (1809–1892), and John Masefield (1878–1967).

2. English poet, dramatist, and critic (1882–1937).

3. African American short story writer and poet (1872–1906).

4. Walter White (1893–1955), NAACP leader and novelist. LANGSTON HUGHES (1902–1967), poet, fiction writer, and playwright. Jessie Redmon Fauset (ca. 1884–1961), novelist and editor.

5. An African American artist (d. 1917).

6. German American conductor and composer (1862–1950). Fontainbleau: Fontainebleau, a French resort.

us to be; we can play all the sordid parts that America likes to assign to Negroes; but for any thing else there is still small place for us.

And so I might go on. But let me sum up with this: Suppose the only Negro who survived some centuries hence was the Negro painted by white Americans in the novels and essays they have written. What would people in a hundred years say of black Americans? Now turn it around. Suppose you were to write a story and put in it the kind of people you know and like and imagine. You might get it published and you might not. And the "might not" is still far bigger than the "might." The white publishers catering to white folk would say, "It is not interesting"—to white folk, naturally not. They want Uncle Toms, Topsies,[7] good "darkies" and clowns. I have in my office a story with all the earmarks of truth. A young man says that he started out to write and had his stories accepted. Then he began to write about the things he knew best about, that is, about his own people. He submitted a story to a magazine which said, "We are sorry, but we cannot take it." "I sat down and revised my story, changing the color of the characters and the locale and sent it under an assumed name with a change of address and it was accepted by the same magazine that had refused it, the editor promising to take anything else I might send in providing it was good enough."

We have, to be sure, a few recognized and successful Negro artists; but they are not all those fit to survive or even a good minority. They are but the remnants of that ability and genius among us whom the accidents of education and opportunity have raised on the tidal waves of chance. We black folk are not altogether peculiar in this. After all, in the world at large, it is only the accident, the remnant, that gets the chance to make the most of itself; but if this is true of the white world it is infinitely more true of the colored world. It is not simply the great clear tenor of Roland Hayes[8] that opened the ears of America. We have had many voices of all kinds as fine as his and America was and is as deaf as she was for years to him. Then a foreign land heard Hayes and put its imprint on him and immediately America with all its imitative snobbery woke up. We approved Hayes because London, Paris and Berlin approved him and not simply because he was a great singer.

Thus it is the bounden duty of black America to begin this great work of the creation of Beauty, of the preservation of Beauty, of the realization of Beauty, and we must use in this work all the methods that men have used before. And what have been the tools of the artists in times gone by? First of all, he has used the Truth—not for the sake of truth, not as a scientist seeking truth, but as one upon whom Truth eternally thrusts itself as the highest handmaid of imagination, as the one great vehicle of universal understanding. Again artists have used Goodness—goodness in all its aspects of justice, honor and right—not for sake of an ethical sanction but as the one true method of gaining sympathy and human interest.

The apostle of Beauty thus becomes the apostle of Truth and Right not by choice but by inner and outer compulsion. Free he is but his freedom is ever bounded by Truth and Justice; and slavery only dogs him when he is denied the right to tell the Truth or recognize an ideal of Justice.

Thus all Art is propaganda and ever must be, despite the wailing of the

7. Uncle Tom and Topsy are African American characters, a saintly and an impish slave, respectively, in Harriet Beecher Stowe's novel *Uncle Tom's Cabin* (1852).

8. African American singer of classical works and spirituals (1887–1976), the son of former slaves.

purists. I stand in utter shamelessness and say that whatever art I have for writing has been used always for propaganda for gaining the right of black folk to love and enjoy. I do not care a damn for any art that is not used for propaganda. But I do care when propaganda is confined to one side while the other is stripped and silent.

In New York we have two plays: "White Cargo" and "Congo."[9] In "White Cargo" there is a fallen woman. She is black. In "Congo" the fallen woman is white. In "White Cargo" the black woman goes down further and further and in "Congo" the white woman begins with degradation but in the end is one of the angels of the Lord.

You know the current magazine story: A young white man goes down to Central America and the most beautiful colored woman there falls in love with him. She crawls across the whole isthmus to get to him. The white man says nobly, "No." He goes back to his white sweetheart in New York.

In such cases, it is not the positive propaganda of people who believe white blood divine, infallible and holy to which I object. It is the denial of a similar right of propaganda to those who believe black blood human, lovable and inspired with new ideals for the world. White artists themselves suffer from this narrowing of their field. They cry for freedom in dealing with Negroes because they have so little freedom in dealing with whites. DuBose Heyward writes "Porgy"[1] and writes beautifully of the black Charleston underworld. But why does he do this? Because he cannot do a similar thing for the white people of Charleston, or they would drum him out of town. The only chance he had to tell the truth of pitiful human degradation was to tell it of colored people. I should not be surprised if Octavus Roy Cohen[2] had approached the *Saturday Evening Post* and asked permission to write about a different kind of colored folk than the monstrosities he has created: but if he has, the *Post* has replied. "No. You are getting paid to write about the kind of colored people you are writing about."

In other words, the white public today demands from its artists, literary and pictorial, racial pre-judgment which deliberately distorts Truth and Justice, as far as colored races are concerned, and it will pay for no other.

On the other hand, the young and slowly growing black public still wants its prophets almost equally unfree. We are bound by all sorts of customs that have come down as second-hand soul clothes of white patrons. We are ashamed of sex and we lower our eyes when people will talk of it. Our religion holds us in superstition. Our worst side has been so shamelessly emphasized that we are denying we have or ever had a worst side. In all sorts of ways we are hemmed in and our new young artists have go to fight their way to freedom.

The ultimate judge has got to be you and you have got to build yourselves up into that wide judgment, that catholicity of temper[3] which is going to enable the artist to have his widest chance for freedom. We can afford the Truth. White folk today cannot. As it is now we are handing everything over to a white jury. If a colored man wants to publish a book, he has got to get a white publisher and a white newspaper to say it is great;

9. *Kongo* (1926), by Kilbourn Gordon and Chester DeVonde. *White Cargo*: *White Cargo: A Play of the Primitive* (1925), by Leon Gordon.
1. The 1925 novel by Heyward (1885–1940) that was the basis for the later opera *Porgy and Bess*.
2. South Carolina playwright, novelist, short story writer, and humorist (1891–1959).
3. Range of disposition.

and then you and I say so. We must come to the place where the work of art when it appears is reviewed and acclaimed by our own free and unfettered judgment. And we are going to have a real and valuable and eternal judgment only as we make ourselves free of mind, proud of body and just of soul to all men.

And then do you know what will be said? It is already saying. Just as soon as true Art emerges; just as soon as the black artist appears, someone touches the race on the shoulder and says, "He did that because he was an American, not because he was a Negro; he was born here; he was trained here; he is not a Negro—what is a Negro anyhow? He is just human; it is the kind of thing you ought to expect."

I do not doubt that the ultimate art coming from black folk is going to be just as beautiful, and beautiful largely in the same ways, as the art that comes from white folk, or yellow, or red; but the point today is that until the art of the black folk compels recognition they will not be rated as human. And when through art they compel recognition then let the world discover if it will that their art is as new as it is old and as old as new.

I had a classmate once who did three beautiful things and died. One of them was a story of a folk who found fire and then went wandering in the gloom of night seeking again the stars they had once known and lost; suddenly out of blackness they looked up and there loomed the heavens; and what was it that they said? They raised a mighty cry: "It is the stars, it is the ancient stars, it is the young and everlasting stars!"

1926

CARL GUSTAV JUNG
1875–1961

During the 1950s and 1960s, largely because of the attention paid to NORTHROP FRYE's writings on literary archetypes (see especially *Anatomy of Criticism*, 1957), the psychoanalyst Carl Gustav Jung became significant for the practice of literary criticism. Neither exactly a scientist nor a literary theorist, Jung is a gifted, original, interdisciplinary thinker, a mythographer of the conscious and unconscious mind, and a writer of dazzling erudition whose mystical blend of religion and spirituality with psychology may disturb some literary critics today but keeps him popular outside academic circles.

Jung was born in Switzerland to a German-speaking family. His father was a Protestant clergyman, and for brief a time Jung seemed headed toward the ministry himself. But he grew excited about philosophy and science and, choosing to embark on a career in medicine, he studied at the universities of Basel and Zurich, where he received his medical degree (1902). He became a staff member of the Burghölzli Asylum of the University of Zurich, working under the direction of Eugen Bleuler, a pioneer in the field of mental illness. Soon his research and studies of word association led him into a period of intense collaboration with SIGMUND FREUD (1907–12). But the two men fell out in 1912 over the publication of Jung's *Psychology of the Unconscious* (trans. 1916), in which he criticized as narrow and reductive Freud's conclusions about the sexual basis of neurosis. In 1914 he broke with Freud publicly by resigning from the International Psychoanalytic Society.

Jung made many contributions to psychology. In *Psychological Types* (1921; trans. 1923), for example, he developed and explored the terms *extroverted* (outward-looking) and *introverted* (inward-looking) to describe and differentiate between two personality types, and he examined as well the affinities between the conscious and the unconscious mind. Crucially, he distinguishes between the personal unconscious (repressed feelings and thoughts that an individual develops during his or her life) and the collective unconscious (the structure of inherited feelings, thoughts, and memories that all human beings possess). Within the collective unconscious are "archetypes," a word that combines the Greek *archē* (beginning) and *typos* (stamp or imprint). These are primordial images from the earliest stages of human existence; they are linked to such fundamental experiences and universal rites of passage as going on a journey, coming of age, or facing death. It is the presence of these archetypes, argues Jung, that connect and unify the major symbol systems of the world's myths, religions, and literatures.

Jung once defined archetypes as "*a priori*, inborn forms of 'intuition'"; elsewhere he referred to them as "complexes of experience that come upon us like fate," whose effects "are felt in our most personal life." As Jung concedes, "We must constantly bear in mind that what we mean by 'archetype' is in itself irrepresentable, but has effects which make visualizations of it possible, namely, the archetypal images and ideas. We meet with a similar situation in physics: there the smallest particles are themselves irrepresentable but have effects from the nature of which we can build up a model" (*Collected Works,* 8:133, 9:30). Jung emphasizes that "the archetypal representations (images and ideas) mediated to us by the unconscious should not be confused with the ['irrepresentable'] archetype as such," which "is characterized by certain formal elements and by certain fundamental meanings, although these can be grasped only approximately" (*Collected Works*, 8:417).

In their canny evasiveness and seductive manner of saying much but not quite enough, these passages illuminate Jung's style and strategy as a writer. He commands respect as an adroit, sometimes exasperating, and provocative verbal performer as well as the designer of a grand system or interpretive grid.

In our selection, "On the Relation of Analytical Psychology to Poetry" (first published in 1922), Jung remarks at the outset that he is concerned with the process of artistic creation, not with the nature of the work of art itself. Throughout his text, in sharply turned phrases and image-laden sentences, he exhibits his own creative powers. One dimension of the drama of Jung's essay is his effort to evoke a more vivid and persuasive account of literature and art than that achieved by Freud—himself a powerful, challenging writer.

Relying on terms familiar in his work, Jung contends that there are two types of artistic creation—"introverted" and "extraverted" (an alternate form with the same meaning as "extroverted"). Drawing on the German Romantic writer FRIEDRICH VON SCHILLER's argument in *On Naive and Sentimental Poetry* (1795–96), Jung defines introverted art as that which shows the artist contesting or contending against the object, whereas extraverted art shows the artist subordinating him- or herself to the object. Jung describes this second type in heightened language that achieves the kind of passionate sweep and exalted tone that we associate with Schiller, PERCY BYSSHE SHELLEY, and other Romantic writers. Indeed, to read and understand Jung it may be best to relate his work to that of Shelley or the visionary Romantic poet, artist, and engraver William Blake.

As Jung concludes this essay, he delves into the question of the source of symbols in works of art. They ultimately derive, he explains, not from the author's "personal unconscious" but from the "collective unconscious"—"a sphere of unconscious imagery," the "archetypes" whose "primordial images are the common heritage of mankind." Jung is interested not in a text's images but in the image that lies behind them. He gives the example of a work of art that expresses the ideal of the "mother country" or the "fatherland," which gains its power by evoking an archetype: the "participation mystique" of primitive man with the land on which he lived.

For literary critics and theorists, Jung functions as a master teacher whose learning and poetic insight equip his readers to recognize the foundational stories behind stories and grasp the core images whose content and form underlie the myths, tales, and legends of the world's diverse literary traditions. We should not simply read his work as if he were demonstrating an "approach"; it is in fact very difficult to extract a ready-made method of literary criticism from Jung's varied writings. They do, however, provide a rich resource for exploration, as he tests the boundaries of our thinking about the mind, creativity, and symbolism. Jung's best work is not in the systems he builds but in the process—when, in the midst of forming them, his writing attests to the power of the artistic imagination to resist containment and evade systematization.

BIBLIOGRAPHY

The standard English edition of Jung's writings is *The Collected Works of* C. G. *Jung*, edited by Herbert Read, Michael Fordham, and Gerhard Adler (14 vols. to date, 1966–; first published in 20 vols., 1953–83). It includes works originally published in English, revised versions of previously published texts, new translations, and translations of works formerly unavailable in English. Selections from his work can be found in *Psyche and Symbol*, edited by Violet S. de Laszlo (1958), and *The Essential Jung*, edited by Anthony Storr (1983). Another important source is the *Letters*, edited by Gerhard Adler (2 vols., 1973–75), and *The Freud/Jung Letters*, edited by William McGuire (1979). Biographies include Vincent Brome, *Jung* (1978); Gerhard Wehr, *Jung* (1985; trans. 1987); Richard Noll, *The Jung Cult: Origins of a Charismatic Movement* (1994); Noll, *The Aryan Christ: The Secret Life of Carl Jung* (1997); and Frank McLynn, *Carl Gustav Jung* (1997).

Perhaps the best place to begin studying Jung is with the sixteen essays in *The Cambridge Companion to Jung*, edited by Polly Young-Eisendrath and Terence Dawson (1997). Two good surveys are Anthony Storr, *C. G. Jung* (1973; rpt., 1991); and Anthony Stevens, *On Jung* (1990). *C. G. Jung and the Humanities: Toward a Hermeneutics of Culture*, edited by Karin Barnaby and Pellegrino D'Acierno (1990), includes essays on popular culture, gender, religion, and other topics. Also stimulating is Sonu Shamdasani, *Cult Fictions: C. G. Jung and the Founding of Analytical Psychology* (1998).

For Jung's impact on literary studies, consult Morris Philipson, *Outline of Jungian Aesthetics* (1963), and *Myth and Literature: Contemporary Theory and Practice*, edited by J. B. Vickery (1966). See also B. L. Knapp, *A Jungian Approach to Literature* (1984). The most comprehensive work in the field is *Jungian Literary Criticism*, edited by Richard Sugg (1992), which gives a full account of the history, theory, and practice of Jungian criticism of literature. Susan Rowland, *C. G. Jung and Literary Theory: The Challenge from Fiction* (1999), brings together Jung's theories with deconstruction and other forms of poststructuralism, and applies them to contemporary British writers. See Jos van Meurs, with John Kidd, *Jungian Literary Criticism, 1920–1980* (1988), an annotated bibliography. The *General Bibliography of C. G. Jung's Writings*, by Lisa Ress, William McGuire, Herbert Read, and Gerhard Adler (1992), updates and replaces the bibliography published as volume 19 of the *Collected Works of* C. G. *Jung* (1979).

On the Relation of Analytical Psychology to Poetry[1]

In spite of its difficulty, the task of discussing the relation of analytical psychology to poetry affords me a welcome opportunity to define my views on the much debated question of the relations between psychology and art in general. Although the two things cannot be compared, the close connections which undoubtedly exist between them call for investigation. These connections arise from the fact that the practice of art is a psychological activity and, as such, can be approached from a psychological angle. Considered in this light, art, like any other human activity deriving from psychic motives, is a proper subject for psychology. This statement, however, involves a very definite limitation of the psychological viewpoint when we come to apply it in practice. Only that aspect of art which consists in the process of artistic creation can be a subject for psychological study, but not that which constitutes its essential nature. The question of what art is in itself can never be answered by the psychologist, but must be approached from the side of aesthetics.

A similar distinction must be made in the realm of religion. A psychological approach is permissible only in regard to the emotions and symbols which constitute the phenomenology of religion, but which do not touch upon its essential nature. If the essence of religion and art could be explained, then both of them would become mere subdivisions of psychology. This is not to say that such violations of their nature have not been attempted. But those who are guilty of them obviously forget that a similar fate might easily befall psychology, since its intrinsic value and specific quality would be destroyed if it were regarded as a mere activity of the brain, and were relegated along with the endocrine functions to a subdivision of physiology. This too, as we know, has been attempted.

Art by its very nature is not science, and science by its very nature is not art; both these spheres of the mind have something in reserve that is peculiar to them and can be explained only in its own terms. Hence when we speak of the relation of psychology to art, we shall treat only of that aspect of art which can be submitted to psychological scrutiny without violating its nature. Whatever the psychologist has to say about art will be confined to the process of artistic creation and has nothing to do with its innermost essence. He can no more explain this than the intellect can describe or even understand the nature of feeling. Indeed, art and science would not exist as separate entities at all if the fundamental difference between them had not long since forced itself on the mind. The fact that artistic, scientific, and religious propensities still slumber peacefully together in the small child, or that with primitives the beginnings of art, science, and religion coalesce in the undifferentiated chaos of the magical mentality, or that no trace of "mind" can be found in the natural instincts of animals—all this does nothing to prove the existence of a unifying principle which alone would justify a reduction of the one to the other. For if we go so far back into the history of the mind that the distinctions between its various fields of activity become altogether invisible, we do not reach an underlying principle of their unity,

1. Translated by R. F. C. Hull.

but merely an earlier, undifferentiated state in which no separate activities yet exist. But the elementary state is not an explanatory principle that would allow us to draw conclusions as to the nature of later, more highly developed states, even though they must necessarily derive from it. A scientific attitude will always tend to overlook the peculiar nature of these more differentiated states in favour of their causal derivation, and will endeavour to subordinate them to a general but more elementary principle.

These theoretical reflections seem to me very much in place today, when we so often find that works of art, and particularly poetry, are interpreted precisely in this manner, by reducing them to more elementary states. Though the material he works with and its individual treatment can easily be traced back to the poet's personal relations with his parents, this does not enable us to understand his poetry. The same reduction can be made in all sorts of other fields, and not least in the case of pathological disturbances. Neuroses and psychoses are likewise reducible to infantile relations with the parents, and so are a man's good and bad habits, his beliefs, peculiarities, passions, interests, and so forth. It can hardly be supposed that all these very different things must have exactly the same explanation, for otherwise we would be driven to the conclusion that they actually are the same thing. If a work of art is explained in the same way as a neurosis, then either the work of art is a neurosis or a neurosis is a work of art. This explanation is all very well as a play on words, but sound common sense rebels against putting a work of art on the same level as a neurosis. An analyst might, in an extreme case, view a neurosis as a work of art through the lens of his professional bias, but it would never occur to an intelligent layman to mistake a pathological phenomenon for art, in spite of the undeniable fact that a work of art arises from much the same psychological conditions as a neurosis. This is only natural, because certain of these conditions are present in every individual and, owing to the relative constancy of the human environment, are constantly the same, whether in the case of a nervous intellectual, a poet, or a normal human being. All have had parents, all have a father- or a mother-complex, all know about sex and therefore have certain common and typical human difficulties. One poet may be influenced more by his relation to his father, another by the tie to his mother, while a third shows unmistakable traces of sexual repression in his poetry. Since all this can be said equally well not only of every neurotic but of every normal human being, nothing specific is gained for the judgment of a work of art. At most our knowledge of its psychological antecedents will have been broadened and deepened.

The school of medical psychology inaugurated by Freud[2] has undoubtedly encouraged the literary historian to bring certain peculiarities of a work of art into relation with the intimate, personal life of the poet. But this is nothing new in principle, for it has long been known that the scientific treatment of art will reveal the personal threads that the artist, intentionally or unintentionally, has woven into his work. The Freudian approach may, however, make possible a more exhaustive demonstration of the influences that reach back into earliest childhood and play their part in artistic creation. To this extent the psychoanalysis of art differs in no essential from the subtle psychological nuances of a penetrating literary analysis. The difference is at

2. SIGMUND FREUD (1856–1939), Austrian founder of psychoanalysis.

most a question of degree, though we may occasionally be surprised by indiscreet references to things which a rather more delicate touch might have passed over if only for reasons of tact. This lack of delicacy seems to be a professional peculiarity of the medical psychologist, and the temptation to draw daring conclusions easily leads to flagrant abuses. A slight whiff of scandal often lends spice to a biography, but a little more becomes a nasty inquisitiveness—bad taste masquerading as science. Our interest is insidiously deflected from the work of art and gets lost in the labyrinth of psychic determinants, the poet becomes a clinical case and, very likely, yet another addition to the curiosa of *psychopathia sexualis*.[3] But this means that the psychoanalysis of art has turned aside from its proper objective and strayed into a province that is as broad as mankind, that is not in the least specific of the artist and has even less relevance to his art.

This kind of analysis brings the work of art into the sphere of general human psychology, where many other things besides art have their origin. To explain art in these terms is just as great a platitude as the statement that "every artist is a narcissist." Every man who pursues his own goal is a "narcissist"—though one wonders how permissible it is to give such wide currency to a term specifically coined for the pathology of neurosis. The statement therefore amounts to nothing; it merely elicits the faint surprise of a *bon mot*. Since this kind of analysis is in no way concerned with the work of art itself, but strives like a mole to bury itself in the dirt as speedily as possible, it always ends up in the common earth that unites all mankind. Hence its explanations have the same tedious monotony as the recitals which one daily hears in the consulting-room.

The reductive method of Freud is a purely medical one, and the treatment is directed at a pathological or otherwise unsuitable formation which has taken the place of the normal functioning. It must therefore be broken down, and the way cleared for healthy adaptation. In this case, reduction to the common human foundation is altogether appropriate. But when applied to a work of art it leads to the results I have described. It strips the work of art of its shimmering robes and exposes the nakedness and drabness of *Homo sapiens*, to which species the poet and artist also belong. The golden gleam of artistic creation—the original object of discussion—is extinguished as soon as we apply to it the same corrosive method which we use in analysing the fantasies of hysteria. The results are no doubt very interesting and may perhaps have the same kind of scientific value as, for instance, a post-mortem examination of the brain of Nietzsche,[4] which might conceivably show us the particular atypical form of paralysis from which he died. But what would this have to do with *Zarathustra?* Whatever its subterranean background may have been, is it not a whole world in itself, beyond the human, all-too-human imperfections, beyond the world of migraine and cerebral atrophy?

I have spoken of Freud's reductive method but have not stated in what that method consists. It is essentially a medical technique for investigating morbid[5] psychic phenomena, and it is solely concerned with the ways and means of getting round or peering through the foreground of consciousness

3. The curiosities of sexual psychopathology (Latin).

4. FRIEDRICH NIETZSCHE (1844–1900), German philosopher, whose writings include *Thus Spake Zarathustra* (1883–92) and *Human, All Too Human* (1878).

5. Caused by disease.

in order to reach the psychic background, or the unconscious. It is based on the assumption that the neurotic patient represses certain psychic contents because they are morally incompatible with his conscious values. It follows that the repressed contents must have correspondingly negative traits—infantile-sexual, obscene, or even criminal—which make them unacceptable to consciousness. Since no man is perfect, everyone must possess such a background whether he admits it or not. Hence it can always be exposed if only one uses the technique of interpretation worked out by Freud.

In the short space of a lecture[6] I cannot, of course, enter into the details of the technique. A few hints must suffice. The unconscious background does not remain inactive, but betrays itself by its characteristic effects on the contents of consciousness. For example, it produces fantasies of a peculiar nature, which can easily be interpreted as sexual images. Or it produces characteristic disturbances of the conscious processes, which again can be reduced to repressed contents. A very important source for knowledge of the unconscious contents is provided by dreams, since these are direct products of the activity of the unconscious. The essential thing in Freud's reductive method is to collect all the clues pointing to the unconscious background, and then, through the analysis and interpretation of this material, to reconstruct the elementary instinctual processes. Those conscious contents which give us a clue to the unconscious background are incorrectly called *symbols* by Freud. They are not true symbols, however, since according to his theory they have merely the role of *signs* or *symptoms* of the subliminal processes. The true symbol differs essentially from this, and should be understood as an expression of an intuitive idea that cannot yet be formulated in any other or better way. When Plato, for instance, puts the whole problem of the theory of knowledge in his parable of the cave, or when Christ expresses the idea of the Kingdom of Heaven in parables,[7] these are genuine and true symbols, that is, attempts to express something for which no verbal concept yet exists. If we were to interpret Plato's metaphor in Freudian terms we would naturally arrive at the uterus, and would have proved that even a mind like Plato's was still struck on a primitive level of infantile sexuality. But we would have completely overlooked what Plato actually created out of the primitive determinants of his philosophical ideas; we would have missed the essential point and merely discovered that he had infantile-sexual fantasies like any other mortal. Such a discovery could be of value only for a man who regarded Plato as superhuman, and who can now state with satisfaction that Plato too was an ordinary human being. But who would want to regard Plato as a god? Surely only one who is dominated by infantile fantasies and therefore possesses a neurotic mentality. For him the reduction to common human truths is salutary on medical grounds, but this would have nothing whatever to do with the meaning of Plato's parable.

I have purposely dwelt on the application of medical psychoanalysis to works of art because I want to emphasize that the psychoanalytic method is at the same time an essential part of the Freudian doctrine. Freud himself

6. This essay was first delivered in May 1922 as a lecture to the Society for German Language and Literature in Zurich.

7. For example, see the parable of the Good Samaritan (Luke 10.30–37) and that of the Prodigal Son (Luke 15.11–32). "Parable of the cave": the allegory in PLATO's *Republic* (7.514–18) in which Socrates likens most of humanity to prisoners chained in a cave, seeing only the shadows of objects by firelight; the authentic seekers of knowledge are those who emerge from the cave to see the objects themselves in sunlight.

by his rigid dogmatism has ensured that the method and the doctrine—in themselves two very different things—are regarded by the public as identical. Yet the method may be employed with beneficial results in medical cases without at the same time exalting it into a doctrine. And against this doctrine we are bound to raise vigorous objections. The assumptions it rests on are quite arbitrary. For example, neuroses are by no means exclusively caused by sexual repression, and the same holds true for psychoses. There is no foundation for saying that dreams merely contain repressed wishes whose moral incompatibility requires them to be disguised by a hypothetical dream-censor. The Freudian technique of interpretation, so far as it remains under the influence of its own one-sided and therefore erroneous hypotheses, displays a quite obvious bias.

In order to do justice to a work of art, analytical psychology must rid itself entirely of medical prejudice; for a work of art is not a disease, and consequently requires a different approach from the medical one. A doctor naturally has to seek out the causes of a disease in order to pull it up by the roots, but just as naturally the psychologist must adopt exactly the opposite attitude towards a work of art. Instead of investigating its typically human determinants, he will inquire first of all into its meaning, and will concern himself with its determinants only in so far as they enable him to understand it more fully. Personal causes have as much or as little to do with a work of art as the soil with the plant that springs from it. We can certainly learn to understand some of the plant's peculiarities by getting to know its habitat, and for the botanist this is an important part of his equipment. But nobody will maintain that everything essential has then been discovered about the plant itself. The personal orientation which the doctor needs when confronted with the question of aetiology in medicine is quite out of place in dealing with a work of art, just because a work of art is not a human being, but is something supra-personal. It is a thing and not a personality; hence it cannot be judged by personal criteria. Indeed, the special significance of a true work of art resides in the fact that it has escaped from the limitations of the personal and has soared beyond the personal concerns of its creator.

I must confess from my own experience that it is not at all easy for a doctor to lay aside his professional bias when considering a work of art and look at it with a mind cleared of the current biological causality. But I have come to learn that although a psychology with a purely biological orientation can explain a good deal about man in general, it cannot be applied to a work of art and still less to man as creator. A purely causalistic psychology is only able to reduce every human individual to a member of the species *Homo sapiens*, since its range is limited to what is transmitted by heredity or derived from other sources. But a work of art is not transmitted or derived—it is a creative reorganization of those very conditions to which a causalistic psychology must always reduce it. The plant is not a mere product of the soil; it is a living, self-contained process which in essence has nothing to do with the character of the soil. In the same way, the meaning and individual quality of a work of art inhere within it and not in its extrinsic determinants. One might almost describe it as a living being that uses man only as a nutrient medium, employing his capacities according to its own laws and shaping itself to the fulfilment of its own creative purpose.

But here I am anticipating somewhat, for I have in mind a particular type of art which I still have to introduce. Not every work of art originates in the way I have just described. There are literary works, prose as well as poetry, that spring wholly from the author's intention to produce a particular result. He submits his material to a definite treatment with a definite aim in view; he adds to it and subtracts from it, emphasizing one effect, toning down another, laying on a touch of colour here, another there, all the time carefully considering the over-all result and paying strict attention to the laws of form and style. He exercises the keenest judgment and chooses his words with complete freedom. His material is entirely subordinated to his artistic purpose; he wants to express this and nothing else. He is wholly at one with the creative process, no matter whether he has deliberately made himself its spearhead, as it were, or whether it has made him its instrument so completely that he has lost all consciousness of this fact. In either case, the artist is so identified with his work that his intentions and his faculties are indistinguishable from the act of creation itself. There is no need, I think, to give examples of this from the history of literature or from the testimony of the artists themselves.

Nor need I cite examples of the other class of works which flow more or less complete and perfect from the author's pen. They come as it were fully arrayed into the world, as Pallas Athene[8] sprang from the head of Zeus. These works positively force themselves upon the author; his hand is seized, his pen writes things that his mind contemplates with amazement. The work brings with it its own form; anything he wants to add is rejected, and what he himself would like to reject is thrust back at him. While his conscious mind stands amazed and empty before this phenomenon, he is overwhelmed by a flood of thoughts and images which he never intended to create and which his own will could never have brought into being. Yet in spite of himself he is forced to admit that it is his own self speaking, his own inner nature revealing itself and uttering things which he would never have entrusted to his tongue. He can only obey the apparently alien impulse within him and follow where it leads, sensing that his work is greater than himself, and wields a power which is not his and which he cannot command. Here the artist is not identical with the process of creation; he is aware that he is subordinate to his work or stands outside it, as though he were a second person; or as though a person other than himself had fallen within the magic circle of an alien will.

So when we discuss the psychology of art, we must bear in mind these two entirely different modes of creation, for much that is of the greatest importance in judging a work of art depends on this distinction. It is one that had been sensed earlier by Schiller,[9] who as we know attempted to classify it in his concept of the *sentimental* and the *naïve*. The psychologist would call "sentimental" art *introverted* and the "naïve" kind *extraverted*. The introverted attitude is characterized by the subject's assertion of his conscious intentions and aims against the demands of the object, whereas the extraverted attitude is characterized by the subject's subordination to the demands which the

8. Greek goddess of war, the arts, and wisdom, who was born fully armed from the head of Zeus, king of the gods.

9. FRIEDRICH VON SCHILLER (1759–1805), German dramatist, lyric poet, and critic, whose works include *On Naive and Sentimental Poetry* (1795–96).

object makes upon him. In my view, Schiller's plays and most of his poems give one a good idea of the introverted attitude: the material is mastered by the conscious intentions of the poet. The extraverted attitude is illustrated by the second part of *Faust*:[1] here the material is distinguished by its refractoriness. A still more striking example is Nietzsche's *Zarathustra*, where the author himself observed how "one became two."

From what I have said, it will be apparent that a shift of psychological standpoint has taken place as soon as one speaks not of the poet as a person but of the creative process that moves him. When the focus of interest shifts to the latter, the poet comes into the picture only as a reacting subject. This is immediately evident in our second category of works, where the consciousness of the poet is not identical with the creative process. But in works of the first category the opposite appears to hold true. Here the poet appears to be the creative process itself, and to create of his own free will without the slightest feeling of compulsion. He may even be fully convinced of his freedom of action and refuse to admit that his work could be anything else than the expression of his will and ability.

Here we are faced with a question which we cannot answer from the testimony of the poets themselves. It is really a scientific problem that psychology alone can solve. As I hinted earlier, it might well be that the poet, while apparently creating out of himself and producing what he consciously intends, is nevertheless so carried away by the creative impulse that he is no longer aware of an "alien" will, just as the other type of poet is no longer aware of his own will speaking to him in the apparently "alien" inspiration, although this is manifestly the voice of his own self. The poet's conviction that he is creating in absolute freedom would then be an illusion: he fancies he is swimming, but in reality an unseen current sweeps him along.

This is not by any means an academic question, but is supported by the evidence of analytical psychology. Researchers have shown that there are all sorts of ways in which the conscious mind is not only influenced by the unconscious but actually guided by it. Yet is there any evidence for the supposition that a poet, despite his self-awareness, may be taken captive by his work? The proof may be of two kinds, direct or indirect. Direct proof would be afforded by a poet who thinks he knows what he is saying but actually says more than he is aware of. Such cases are not uncommon. Indirect proof would be found in cases where behind the apparent free will of the poet there stands a higher imperative that renews its peremptory demands as soon as the poet voluntarily gives up his creative activity, or that produces psychic complications whenever his work has to be broken off against his will.

Analysis of artists consistently shows not only the strength of the creative impulse arising from the unconscious, but also its capricious and wilful character. The biographies of great artists make it abundantly clear that the creative urge is often so imperious that it battens on their humanity and yokes everything to the service of the work, even at the cost of health and ordinary human happiness. The unborn work in the psyche of the artist is a force of nature that achieves its end either with tyrannical might or with the subtle cunning of nature herself, quite regardless of the personal fate of the man who is its vehicle. The creative urge lives and grows in him like a tree in the

1. Two-part verse drama (1808, 1832) by Johann Wolfgang von Goethe.

earth from which it draws its nourishment. We would do well, therefore, to think of the creative process as a living thing implanted in the human psyche. In the language of analytical psychology this living thing is an *autonomous complex*. It is a split-off portion of the psyche, which leads a life of its own outside the hierarchy of consciousness. Depending on its energy charge, it may appear either as a mere disturbance of conscious activities or as a supraordinate authority which can harness the ego to its purpose. Accordingly, the poet who identifies with the creative process would be one who acquiesces from the start when the unconscious imperative begins to function. But the other poet, who feels the creative force as something alien, is one who for various reasons cannot acquiesce and is thus caught unawares.

It might be expected that this difference in its origins would be perceptible in a work of art. For in the one case it is a conscious product shaped and designed to have the effect intended. But in the other we are dealing with an event originating in unconscious nature; with something that achieves its aim without the assistance of human consciousness, and often defies it by wilfully insisting on its own form and effect. We would therefore expect that works belonging to the first class would nowhere overstep the limits of comprehension, that their effect would be bounded by the author's intention and would not extend beyond it. But with works of the other class we would have to be prepared for something suprapersonal that transcends our understanding to the same degree that the author's consciousness was in abeyance during the process of creation. We would expect a strangeness of form and content, thoughts that can only be apprehended intuitively, a language pregnant with meanings, and images that are true symbols because they are the best possible expressions for something unknown—bridges thrown out towards an unseen shore.

These criteria are, by and large, corroborated in practice. Whenever we are confronted with a work that was consciously planned and with material that was consciously selected, we find that it agrees with the first class of qualities, and in the other case with the second. The example we gave of Schiller's plays, on the one hand, and *Faust II* on the other, or better still *Zarathustra*, is an illustration of this. But I would not undertake to place the work of an unknown poet in either of these categories without first having examined rather closely his personal relations with his work. It is not enough to know whether the poet belongs to the introverted or to the extraverted type, since it is possible for either type to work with an introverted attitude at one time, and an extraverted attitude at another. This is particularly noticeable in the difference between Schiller's plays and his philosophical writings, between Goethe's perfectly formed poems and the obvious struggle with his material in *Faust II*, and between Nietzsche's well-turned aphorisms and the rushing torrent of *Zarathustra*. The same poet can adopt different attitudes to his work at different times, and on this depends the standard we have to apply.

The question, as we now see, is exceedingly complicated, and the complication grows even worse when we consider the case of the poet who identifies with the creative process. For should it turn out that the apparently conscious and purposeful manner of composition is a subjective illusion of the poet, then his work would possess symbolic qualities that are outside the range of his consciousness. They would only be more difficult to detect, because the reader as well would be unable to get beyond the bounds of the poet's consciousness which are fixed by the spirit of the time. There is no Archimedean point[2] outside his world by which he could lift his time-bound consciousness off its hinges and recognize the symbols hidden in the poet's work. For a symbol is the intimation of a meaning beyond the level of our present powers of comprehension.

I raise this question only because I do not want my typological classification to limit the possible significance of works of art which apparently mean no more than what they say. But we have often found that a poet who has gone out of fashion is suddenly rediscovered. This happens when our conscious development has reached a higher level from which the poet can tell us something new. It was always present in his work but was hidden in a symbol, and only a renewal of the spirit of the time permits us to read its meaning. It needed to be looked at with fresher eyes, for the old ones could see in it only what they were accustomed to see. Experiences of this kind should make us cautious, as they bear out my earlier argument. But works that are openly symbolic do not require this subtle approach; their pregnant language cries out at us that they mean more than they say. We can put our finger on the symbol at once, even though we may not be able to unriddle its meaning to our entire satisfaction. A symbol remains a perpetual challenge to our thoughts and feelings. That probably explains why a symbolic work is so stimulating, why it grips us so intensely, but also why it seldom affords us a purely aesthetic enjoyment. A work that is manifestly not symbolic appeals much more to our aesthetic sensibility because it is complete in itself and fulfils its purpose.

What then, you may ask, can analytical psychology contribute to our fundamental problem, which is the mystery of artistic creation? All that we have said so far has to do only with the psychological phenomenology of art. Since nobody can penetrate to the heart of nature, you will not expect psychology to do the impossible and offer a valid explanation of the secret of creativity. Like every other science, psychology has only a modest contribution to make towards a deeper understanding of the phenomena of life, and is no nearer than its sister sciences to absolute knowledge.

We have talked so much about the meaning of works of art that one can hardly suppress a doubt as to whether art really "means" anything at all. Perhaps art has no "meaning," at least not as we understand meaning. Perhaps it is like nature, which simply *is* and "means" nothing beyond that. Is "meaning" necessarily more than mere interpretation—an interpretation secreted into something by an intellect hungry for meaning? Art, it has been said, is beauty, and "a thing of beauty is a joy for ever."[3] It needs no meaning, for meaning has nothing to do with art. Within the sphere of art, I must accept the truth of this statement. But when I speak of the relation of psychology to art we are outside its sphere, and it is impossible for us not to speculate. We must interpret, we must find meanings in things, otherwise we would be quite unable to think about them. We have to break down life and events, which are self-contained processes, into meanings, images, concepts, well knowing that in doing so we are getting further away from the

2. That is, no point at which to apply leverage. The Greek inventor and mathematician Archimedes (ca. 287–212 B.C.E.) is said to have declared, "Give me a place to stand and I will move the earth."

3. John Keats, "Endymion" (1818), 1.1.

living mystery. As long as we ourselves are caught up in the process of creation, we neither see nor understand; indeed we ought not to understand, for nothing is more injurious to immediate experience than cognition. But for the purpose of cognitive understanding we must detach ourselves from the creative process and look at it from the outside; only then does it become an image that expresses what we are bound to call "meaning." What was a mere phenomenon before becomes something that in association with other phenomena has meaning, that has a definite role to play, serves certain ends, and exerts meaningful effects. And when we have seen all this we get the feeling of having understood and explained something. In this way we meet the demands of science.

When, a little earlier, we spoke of a work of art as a tree growing out of the nourishing soil, we might equally well have compared it to a child growing in the womb. But as all comparisons are lame, let us stick to the more precise terminology of science. You will remember that I described the nascent work in the psyche of the artist as an autonomous complex. By this we mean a psychic formation that remains subliminal until its energy-charge is sufficient to carry it over the threshold into consciousness. Its association with consciousness does not mean that it is assimilated, only that it is perceived; but it is not subject to conscious control, and can be neither inhibited nor voluntarily reproduced. Therein lies the autonomy of the complex: it appears and disappears in accordance with its own inherent tendencies, independently of the conscious will. The creative complex shares this peculiarity with every other autonomous complex. In this respect it offers an analogy with pathological processes, since these too are characterized by the presence of autonomous complexes, particularly in the case of mental disturbances. The divine frenzy of the artist comes perilously close to a pathological state, though the two things are not identical. The *tertium comparationis*[4] is the autonomous complex. But the presence of autonomous complexes is not in itself pathological, since normal people, too, fall temporarily or permanently under their domination. This fact is simply one of the normal peculiarities of the psyche, and for a man to be unaware of the existence of an autonomous complex merely betrays a high degree of unconsciousness. Every typical attitude that is to some extent differentiated shows a tendency to become an autonomous complex, and in most cases it actually does. Again, every instinct has more or less the character of an autonomous complex. In itself, therefore, an autonomous complex has nothing morbid about it; only when its manifestations are frequent and disturbing is it a symptom of illness.

How does an autonomous complex arise? For reasons which we cannot go into here, a hitherto unconscious portion of the psyche is thrown into activity, and gains ground by activating the adjacent areas of association. The energy needed for this is naturally drawn from consciousness—unless the latter happens to identify with the complex. But where this does not occur, the drain of energy produces what Janet calls an *abaissement du niveau mental*.[5] The intensity of conscious interests and activities gradually diminishes, leading either to apathy—a condition very common with artists—or to a regressive development of the conscious functions, that is, they revert to an

4. Third [point] of comparison (Latin); that is, the common factor between two different things.
5. Lowering of the mental level (French). Pierre Janet (1859–1947), French psychologist and neurologist, best known for his theory of hysteria.

infantile and archaic level and undergo something like a degeneration. The "inferior parts of the functions," as Janet calls them, push to the fore; the instinctual side of the personality prevails over the ethical, the infantile over the mature, and the unadapted over the adapted. This too is something we see in the lives of many artists. The autonomous complex thus develops by using the energy that has been withdrawn from the conscious control of the personality.

But in what does an autonomous *creative* complex consist? Of this we can know next to nothing so long as the artist's work affords us no insight into its foundations. The work presents us with a finished picture, and this picture is amenable to analysis only to the extent that we can recognize it as a symbol. But if we are unable to discover any symbolic value in it, we have merely established that, so far as we are concerned, it means no more than what it says, or to put it another way, that it *is* no more than what it *seems* to be. I use the word "seems" because our own bias may prevent a deeper appreciation of it. At any rate we can find no incentive and no starting-point for an analysis. But in the case of a symbolic work we should remember the dictum of Gerhard Hauptmann:[6] "Poetry evokes out of words the resonance of the primordial word." The question we should ask, therefore, is: "What primordial image lies behind the imagery of art?"

This question needs a little elucidation. I am assuming that the work of art we propose to analyse, as well as being symbolic, has its source not in the *personal unconscious* of the poet, but in a sphere of unconscious mythology whose primordial images are the common heritage of mankind. I have called this sphere the *collective unconscious,* to distinguish it from the personal unconscious. The latter I regard as the sum total of all those psychic processes and contents which are capable of becoming conscious and often do, but are then suppressed because of their incompatibility and kept subliminal. Art receives tributaries from this sphere too, but muddy ones; and their predominance, far from making a work of art a symbol, merely turns it into a symptom. We can leave this kind of art without injury and without regret to the purgative methods employed by Freud.

In contrast to the personal unconscious, which is a relatively thin layer immediately below the threshold of consciousness, the collective unconscious shows no tendency to become conscious under normal conditions, nor can it be brought back to recollection by any analytical technique, since it was never repressed or forgotten. The collective unconscious is not to be thought of as a self-subsistent entity; it is no more than a potentiality handed down to us from primordial times in the specific form of mnemonic images or inherited in the anatomical structure of the brain. There are no inborn ideas, but there are inborn possibilities of ideas that set bounds to even the boldest fantasy and keep our fantasy activity within certain categories: *a priori* ideas, as it were, the existence of which cannot be ascertained except from their effects. They appear only in the shaped material of art as the regulative principles that shape it; that is to say, only by inferences drawn from the finished work can we reconstruct the age-old original of the primordial image.

The primordial image, or archetype, is a figure—be it a daemon,[7] a human

6. German dramatist and novelist (1862–1946).
7. For example, the *theios daimōn* (divine guide) of Socrates (Plato, *Apology* 31c–d).

being, or a process—that constantly recurs in the course of history and appears wherever creative fantasy is freely expressed. Essentially, therefore, it is a mythological figure. When we examine these images more closely, we find that they give form to countless typical experiences of our ancestors. They are, so to speak, the psychic residua of innumerable experiences of the same type. They present a picture of psychic life in the average, divided up and projected into the manifold figures of the mythological pantheon. But the mythological figures are themselves products of creative fantasy and still have to be translated into conceptual language. Only the beginnings of such a language exist, but once the necessary concepts are created they could give us an abstract, scientific understanding of the unconscious processes that lie at the roots of the primordial images. In each of these images there is a little piece of human psychology and human fate, a remnant of the joys and sorrows that have been repeated countless times in our ancestral history, and on the average follow ever the same course. It is like a deeply graven river-bed in the psyche, in which the waters of life, instead of flowing along as before in a broad but shallow stream, suddenly swell into a mighty river. This happens whenever that particular set of circumstances is encountered which over long periods of time has helped to lay down the primordial image.

The moment when this mythological situation reappears is always characterized by a peculiar emotional intensity; it is as though chords in us were struck that had never resounded before, or as though forces whose existence we never suspected were unloosed. What makes the struggle for adaptation so laborious is the fact that we have constantly to be dealing with individual and atypical situations. So it is not surprising that when an archetypal situation occurs we suddenly feel an extraordinary sense of release, as though transported, or caught up by an overwhelming power. At such moments we are no longer individuals, but the race; the voice of all mankind resounds in us. The individual man cannot use his powers to the full unless he is aided by one of those collective representations we call ideals, which releases all the hidden forces of instinct that are inaccessible to his conscious will. The most effective ideals are always fairly obvious variants of an archetype, as is evident from the fact that they lend themselves to allegory. The ideal of the "mother country," for instance, is an obvious allegory of the mother, as is the "fatherland" of the father. Its power to stir us does not derive from the allegory, but from the symbolical value of our native land. The archetype here is the *participation mystique* of primitive man with the soil on which he dwells, and which contains the spirits of his ancestors.

The impact of an archetype, whether it takes the form of immediate experience or is expressed through the spoken word, stirs us because it summons up a voice that is stronger than our own. Whoever speaks in primordial images speaks with a thousand voices; he enthrals and overpowers, while at the same time he lifts the idea he is seeking to express out of the occasional and the transitory into the realm of the ever-enduring. He transmutes our personal destiny into the destiny of mankind, and evokes in us all those beneficent forces that ever and anon have enabled humanity to find a refuge from every peril and to outlive the longest night.

That is the secret of great art, and of its effect upon us. The creative process, so far as we are able to follow it at all, consists in the unconscious activation of an archetypal image, and in elaborating and shaping this image into the finished work. By giving it shape, the artist translates it into the language of the present, and so makes it possible for us to find our way back to the deepest springs of life. Therein lies the social significance of art: it is constantly at work educating the spirit of the age, conjuring up the forms in which the age is most lacking. The unsatisfied yearning of the artist reaches back to the primordial image in the unconscious which is best fitted to compensate the inadequacy and one-sidedness of the present. The artist seizes on this image, and in raising it from deepest unconsciousness he brings it into relation with conscious values, thereby transforming it until it can be accepted by the minds of his contemporaries according to their powers.

Peoples and times, like individuals, have their own characteristic tendencies and attitudes. The very word "attitude" betrays the necessary bias that every marked tendency entails. Direction implies exclusion, and exclusion means that very many psychic elements that could play their part in life are denied the right to exist because they are incompatible with the general attitude. The normal man can follow the general trend without injury to himself; but the man who takes to the back streets and alleys because he cannot endure the broad highway will be the first to discover the psychic elements that are waiting to play their part in the life of the collective. Here the artist's relative lack of adaptation turns out to his advantage; it enables him to follow his own yearnings far from the beaten path, and to discover what it is that would meet the unconscious needs of his age. Thus, just as the one-sidedness of the individual's conscious attitude is corrected by reactions from the unconscious, so art represents a process of self-regulation in the life of nations and epochs.

I am aware that in this lecture I have only been able to sketch out my views in the barest outline. But I hope that what I have been obliged to omit, that is to say their practical application to poetic works of art, has been furnished by your own thoughts, thus giving flesh and blood to my abstract intellectual frame.

1922

LEON TROTSKY
1879–1940

Dedicated to the international workers' revolution and to Marxist theory, Leon Trotsky wrote little in the way of literary criticism, but his *Literature and Revolution* is an important text in the Marxist tradition. In it Trotsky argues cogently against formalist critical approaches even as he seeks to prevent literary study from being overtaken by the ideological imperatives of the communist state.

Born in November 1879, the son of a Jewish farm owner in Ukraine, Trotsky's name at birth was Lev Davidovich Bronstein. In his youth he was quickly recognized as a brilliant student with a promising future. He was also sympathetic to the plight of the farmers and peasants around him, and in the mid-1890s he turned to Marxism. His political activities led him to be exiled to Siberia in 1900; he escaped—with a forged passport that used the name of a jailer in Odessa's prison, Trotsky—and journeyed to London, where he, Vladimir Lenin, and others edited a journal, *The Spark*. In December 1905, having returned to Russia, Trotsky (as he was now named) was imprisoned again. Once again he escaped, and for the next few years, he worked as a journalist in Vienna, Paris, and New York City, where he was living when in 1917 the Russian Revolution began.

Trotsky returned to Russia, supported Lenin, joined the Bolshevik Party (the name derives from the Russian word for "majority"), and won election to its Central Committee. A superb orator, writer, and agitator, Trotsky first was appointed foreign minister and then commissar of war. He commanded the Red Army during the civil war that followed the Bolshevik seizure of power in 1917, and he believed that he would be Lenin's successor. But Joseph Stalin was a shrewder, more vicious politician; after Lenin's death in 1924, Stalin outmaneuvered Trotsky, who was eventually expelled from the Communist Party (1927) and deported (1929). He lived in Turkey (1929–33), France (1933–35), Norway (1935–36), and finally Mexico (1935–40). In August 1940, in Mexico City, a Spanish communist named Ramón Mercader assassinated him.

During the late 1920s and, especially, in the 1930s, a number of prominent communists in America rallied behind Trotsky's criticisms of official Communism and Soviet policy. These Trotskyists, including James P. Cannon and Max Shachtman, argued that the Soviet Union under Stalin had become undemocratic and bureaucratized; they saw it as no longer committed to the goal of international revolution. American Trotskyism enjoyed the support of influential critics and intellectuals, including Philip Rahv, William Phillips, and others associated in the mid- to late 1930s with the literary and political journal the *Partisan Review*. The critic IRVING HOWE was a Trotskyist student leader at City College in New York City, and later in his career he edited a selection of Trotsky's political writings (1963) and wrote a book about Trotsky (1978).

Trotsky's main contribution to Marxist theory is his concept of "permanent revolution." KARL MARX and FRIEDRICH ENGELS had predicted that the proletarian (that is, industrial workers') revolution would occur first in the industrialized nations of western Europe, but it had taken place instead in unmodernized, industrially undeveloped Russia. Trotsky argued that countries could follow different paths—developing "unevenly"—in the transition from feudalism to capitalism to socialism and communism. But the crucial point, for him, was that a revolution within one nation must lead to revolution internationally. For the revolution in Russia to succeed, it would need the reinforcement, Trotsky maintained, of revolutionary movements elsewhere, in particular in the advanced European societies. As he explains in his book *The Permanent Revolution* (1930):

> This struggle, under the conditions of an overwhelming predominance of capitalist relationships on the world arena, must inevitably lead to explosions, that is, internally to civil wars and externally to revolutionary wars. Therein lies the permanent character of the socialist revolution as such. . . . The socialist revolution begins on the national arena, it unfolds on the international arena, and is completed on the world arena.

Stalin for his part declared that "socialism in one country" was possible, that the revolution in the Soviet Union must be defended without qualification, and that Trotsky's commitment to world revolution thus was a form of betrayal, a failure to believe in and fight for the revolution in Russia. Stalin branded Trotsky the enemy of the Russian people, and it is generally believed that he ordered Trotsky's murder.

Trotsky produced his best literary and historical work—much of it directed against Stalinism—during his years in exile in the 1930s. His books of this period include an autobiography, *My Life* (1930; trans. 1930); the *History of the Russian Revolution* (3 vols., 1931–33; trans. 1932–33); the powerful anti-Stalinist polemic *The Revolution Betrayed* (1937); and many essays on events in Russia, Hitler's rise to power, fascism, and the Spanish Civil War. The greatest of these texts is his massive, vividly conceived and written *History*. This stunning, panoramic work is relentless in its momentum, immensely confident in its tone, and breathtaking in its visionary power. As a narrative informed by a grand conception of how each agent and incident form part of an epic whole, it has never been equaled—and because of Trotsky's unique position in the story and his literary gifts, it never will be. It is, of course, Trotsky's version of the revolution, his account of the creation of a near-paradise that Stalin corrupted. It is a brilliant and essentially literary work.

In our selection from *Literature and Revolution* (1924), Trotsky begins by saying that art is neither self-contained, separate from politics, nor political, a matter solely of ideology. He pays tribute to art ("it brings thought and feeling closer. . . . It enriches the spiritual experience"), and, while defining a "Marxist point of view," he stresses that Marxism does not require that we "dominate art by means of decrees and orders" or mandate that we esteem only those works of art that celebrate workers. We cannot, says Trotsky, prescribe to the literary artist how he or she should write.

At the same time, Trotsky by no means favors allowing art to exist independently of political judgments, as his adverse commentary on formalism and futurism indicates. Formalism was an early-twentieth-century movement in literary criticism that emphasized the analysis of literary language, its formal properties and strategies. (On Slavic formalism, see especially BORIS EICHENBAUM, MIKHAIL BAKHTIN, and ROMAN JAKOBSON.) It sought to align literary study with the methods of the sciences, moving away from biography, impressionism, and historical content and toward the disciplines of rhetoric and structuralist linguistics. Futurism, which overlapped formalism in time and to some extent in adherents (e.g., Jakobson and Shkolvsky were involved with both), was a major movement in Russian poetry and Italian art; it included disparate groups with the common belief that poetry is an autonomous and experimental art. Futurist poets sought to direct the language of poetry toward the language of the modern city, and they attacked the classic authors of the past, such as Aleksandr Pushkin (1799–1837) and Leo Tolstoy (1828–1910), whose work was, they claimed, outdated and irrelevant.

Trotsky displays a measure of respect for formalism; he appreciates its search for precise methods of analysis and evaluation. But he criticizes formalists, Shklovsky in particular, for being narrow and superficial—disconnected, like the futurists, from social process. Trotsky contends that new cultural movements cannot, and must not, reject the culture of the past; culture must absorb and grow within tradition. In the 1920s, when he stated these views, the Bolshevik regime was granting some leeway for experimentation and debate in literature and the arts; the only condition (soon to be made more strict and comprehensive) was that new art not criticize the revolution or party leaders and the state. In keeping with this time of relative openness, Trotsky is flexible and nondogmatic in professing that each work of art must be judged *as* art, though he insists that history shapes artistic production and that innovation in art arises from the pressures of historical context. "Artistic creation," he states, "is always a complicated turning inside out of old forms, under the influence of new stimuli which originate outside of art. . . . The effort to set art free from life, to declare it a craft self-sufficient unto itself, devitalizes and kills art."

Marxism alone, Trotsky believes, can explain the origins of a trend or development in the arts. In a later chapter of *Literature and Revolution*, while discussing the "formation of folklore," he declares that because Marxism emphasizes "the all-determining significance of natural and economic conditions," it is the only proper basis for description and judgment. Thus he endorses censorship and repression: "Our standard is, clearly, political, imperative and intolerant." Truth is not to emerge from debate in which positions are articulated and free to compete; it is known in advance, and hence the leadership should prescribe what is and is not to be tolerated.

The Marxist critic TERRY EAGLETON has observed: "In its blend of principled yet flexible Marxism and perceptive practical criticism, *Literature and Revolution* is a disquieting text for non-Marxist critics." But that disquiet results less from Trotsky's showing a laudable respect for artistic autonomy than from the conflict one senses between Trotsky's humanist conception of literature and art and his tendency toward dogmatism. As EDMUND WILSON notes in "Marxism and Literature" (1937; see below), "even in combatting" the party's tendency to use politics to appraise art, Trotsky himself "cannot avoid passing censure and pinning ribbons."

Trotsky would be impatient with such criticisms. Attacking liberal self-righteousness, he stated repeatedly that democracies claiming in theory to honor freedom of speech were always ready to repudiate it in practice. But this deflection of the argument does not remove the problem embedded in his own position.

BIBLIOGRAPHY

For students of literary criticism, the essential text by Trotsky is *Literature and Revolution* (1924). Selections from his voluminous writings can be found in *The Basic Writings of Trotsky*, edited by Irving Howe (1963); *The Age of Permanent Revolution: A Trotsky Anthology*, edited by Isaac Deutscher (1964); and *Leon Trotsky on Literature and Art*, edited by Paul N. Siegel (1970). *The Trotsky Papers, 1917–1922*, edited by Jan M. Meijer (2 vols., 1964–71) contains documents from the Trotsky Archive, including the Lenin-Trotsky correspondence. But many other sources are now becoming available, and studies undertaken in the future will make use of archival materials in the former Soviet Union that were inaccessible in the past.

The classic scholarly biography of Trotsky is the three-volume study by Isaac Deutscher: *The Prophet Armed, 1879–1921* (1954), *The Prophet Unarmed, 1921–1929* (1959), and *The Prophet Outcast, 1929–1940* (1963). A more recent treatment is offered by Ronald Segal, *Leon Trotsky: A Biography* (1979). See also Trotsky's *My Life* (1930).

A cogent survey is Irving Howe, *Leon Trotsky* (1978). Also important is Dmitri Antonovich Volkogonov, *Trotsky: The Eternal Revolutionary* (1992; trans. 1996). For discussions of Trotsky's political thought (which intersects with his ideas about literature and culture), see Baruch Knei-Paz, *The Social and Political Thought of Leon Trotsky* (1978); Ernest Mandel, *Trotsky: A Study in the Dynamic of His Thought* (1979); Robert S. Wistrich, *Trotsky: Fate of a Revolutionary* (1982); and Alex Callinicos, *Trotskyism* (1990). A dated but still useful resource is Louis Sinclair, *Leon Trotsky: A Bibliography* (1972).

From Literature and Revolution[1]

The Formalist School of Poetry and Marxism

Leaving out of account the weak echoes of pre-revolutionary ideologic systems, the only theory which has opposed Marxism in Soviet Russia these years is the Formalist theory of Art. The paradox consists in the fact that Russian Formalism connected itself closely with Russian Futurism,[2] and that while the latter was capitulating politically before Communism, Formalism opposed Marxism with all its might theoretically.

Victor Shklovsky[3] is the theorist of Futurism, and at the same time the head of the Formalist school. According to his theory, art has always been

1. Translated by Rose Strunsky.
2. A revolutionary movement in art and literature begun in Italy in 1909, stressing speed, modernity, machinery, and rebellion; it quickly found adherents in Russia.
3. An important Russian formalist critic (1893–1984).

the work of self-sufficient pure forms, and it has been recognized by Futurism for the first time. Futurism is thus the first conscious art in history, and the Formalist school is the first scientific school of art. Owing to the efforts of Shklovsky—and this is not an insignificant virtue!—the theory of art, and partly art itself, have at last been raised from a state of alchemy to the position of chemistry. The herald of the Formalist school, the first chemist of art, gives a few friendly slaps in passing to those Futurist "conciliators" who seek a bridge to the Revolution, and who try to find this bridge in the materialistic conception of history. Such a bridge is unnecessary; Futurism is entirely sufficient unto itself.

There are two reasons why it is necessary to pause a little before this Formalist school. One is for its own sake; in spite of the superficiality and reactionary character of the Formalist theory of art, a certain part of the research work of the Formalists is useful. The other reason is Futurism itself; however unfounded the claims of the Futurists to a monopolistic representation of the new art may be, one cannot thrust Futurism out of that process which is preparing the art of the future.

What is the Formalist school?

As it is represented at present by Shklovsky, Zhirmunsky, Jacobson[4] and others, it is extremely arrogant and immature. Having declared form to be the essence of poetry, this school reduces its task to an analysis (essentially descriptive and semi-statistical) of the etymology and syntax of poems, to the counting of repetitive vowels and consonants, of syllables and epithets. This analysis which the Formalists regard as the essence of poetry, or poetics, is undoubtedly necessary and useful, but one must understand its partial, scrappy, subsidiary and preparatory character. It can become an essential element of poetic technique and of the rules of the craft. Just as it is useful for a poet or a writer to make lists of synonyms for himself and increase their number so as to expand his verbal keyboard, so it is useful, and quite necessary for a poet, to estimate a word not only in accord with its inner meaning, but also in accord with its acoustics, because a word is passed on from man to man, first of all by acoustics. The methods of Formalism, confined within legitimate limits, may help to clarify the artistic and psychologic peculiarities of form (its economy, its movement, its contrasts, its hyperbolism,[5] etc.). This, in turn, may open a path—one of the paths—to the artist's feeling for the world, and may facilitate the discovery of the relations of an individual artist, or of a whole artistic school, to the social environment. In so far as we are dealing with a contemporary and living school which is still developing, there is an immediate significance in our transitional stage in probing it by means of a social probe and in clarifying its class roots, so that not only the reader, but the school itself could orientate itself, that is, know itself, purify and direct itself.

But the Formalists are not content to ascribe to their methods a merely subsidiary, serviceable and technical significance—similar to that which statistics has for social science, or the microscope for the biological sciences. No, they go much further. To them verbal art ends finally and fully with the word, and depictive art with color. A poem is a combination of sounds, a

4. ROMAN JAKOBSON (1896–1982), literary critic, theorist, and founder of the Moscow Linguistic Circle. Victor Maksimovich Zhirmunsky (1881–1971), Russian literary scholar.

5. Use of exaggeration (hyperbole).

painting is a combination of color spots and the laws of art are the laws of verbal combinations and of combinations of color spots. The social and psychologic approach which, to us, gives a meaning to the microscopic and statistical work done in connection with verbal material, is, for the Formalists, only alchemy.

"Art was always free of life, and its color never reflected the color of the flag which waved over the fortress of the City." (Shklovsky.) "Adjustment to the expression, the verbal mass, is the one essential element of poetry." (R. Jacobson, in his "Recent Russian Poetry".) "With a new form comes a new content. Form thus determines content." (Kruchenikh.)[6] "Poetry means the giving of form to the word, which is valuable in itself" (Jacobson), or, as Khlebnikov[7] says, "The word which is something in itself", etc.

True, the Italian Futurists have sought in the word a means of expressing the locomotive, the propeller, electricity, the radio, etc., for their own age. In other words, they sought a new form for the new content of life. But it turned out that "this was a reform in the field of reporting, and not in the field of poetic language". (Jacobson.) It is quite different with Russian Futurism; it carries to the end "the adjustment to verbal mass". For Russian Futurism, form determines content.

True, Jacobson is compelled to admit that "a series of new poetic methods finds application (?) for itself in urbanism" (in the culture of the city). But this is his conclusion: "Hence the urban poems of Mayakovsky[8] and Khlebnikov." In other words: not city culture, which has struck the eye and the ear of the poet and which has reeducated them, has inspired him with new form, with new images, new epithets, new rhythm, but, on the contrary, the new form, originating arbitrarily, forced the poet to seek appropriate material and so pushed him in the direction of the city! The development of the "verbal mass" went on arbitrarily from the "Odyssey" to "A Cloud in Trousers";[9] the torch, the wax candle, the electric lamp, had nothing to do with it! One has only to formulate this point of view clearly to have its childish inadequacy strike the eye. But Jacobson tries to insist; he replies in advance that the same Mayakovsky has such lines as these: "Leave the cities, you silly people." And the theorist of the Formalist school reasons profoundly: "What is this, a logical contradiction? But let others fasten on the poet's thoughts expressed in his works. To incriminate a poet with ideas and feelings is just as absurd as the behavior of the medieval public which beat the actor who played Judas." And so on.

It is quite evident that all this was written by a very capable high-school boy who had a very evident and quite "self-significant" intention to "stick the pen into our teacher of literature, a notable pedant". At sticking the pen, our bold innovators are masters, but they do not know how to use their pen theoretically or grammatically. This is not hard to prove.

Of course Futurism felt the suggestions of the city—of the tram-car, of electricity, of the telegraph, of the automobile, of the propeller, of the night cabaret (especially of the night cabaret) much before it found its new form.

6. Aleksei Eliseevich Kruchenykh (1886–1969), Russian poet and literary theorist.
7. Velimir (originally Viktor Vladimirovich) Khlebnikov (1885–1922), poet, poetic theorist, and founder of Russian futurism.
8. Vladimir Vladimirovich Mayakovsky (1893–1930), the leading poet of the Russian Revolution of 1917 and of the early Soviet period.
9. A major work (1915) by the Russian poet Mayakovsky. The *Odyssey* is one of the earliest epics of Western literature (ca. 8th c. B.C.E.).

Urbanism (city culture) sits deep in the subconsciousness of Futurism, and the epithets, the etymology, the syntax and the rhythm of Futurism are only an attempt to give artistic form to the new spirit of the cities which has conquered consciousness. And when Mayakovsky exclaims: "Leave the cities, you silly people", it is the cry of a man citified to the very marrow of his bones, who shows himself strikingly and clearly a city person, especially when he is outside the city, that is, when he "leaves the city" and becomes an inhabitant of a summer resort. It is not at all a question of "incriminating" (this word misses something!) a poet with the ideas and feelings which he expresses. Of course the way he expresses them makes the poet. But after all, a poet uses the language of the school which he has accepted or which he has created to fulfill tasks which lie outside of him. And this is even true also when he limits himself to lyricism, to personal love and personal death. Though individual shadings of poetic form correspond to individual makeup, they do go hand in hand with imitation and routine, in the feeling itself, as well as in the method of its expression. A new artistic form, taken in a large historic way, is born in reply to new needs. To take an example from intimate lyric poetry, one may say that between the physiology of sex and a poem about love there lies a complex system of psychological transmitting mechanisms in which there are individual, racial and social elements. The racial foundation, that is, the sexual basis of man, changes slowly. The social forms of love change more rapidly. They affect the psychologic superstructure of love, they produce new shadings and intonations, new spiritual demands, a need of a new vocabulary, and so they present new demands on poetry. The poet can find material for his art only in his social environment and transmits the new impulses of life through his own artistic consciousness. Language, changed and complicated by urban conditions, gives the poet a new verbal material, and suggests or facilitates new word combinations for the poetic formulation of new thoughts or of new feelings, which strive to break through the dark shell of the subconscious. If there were no changes in psychology produced by changes in the social environment, there would be no movement in art; people would continue from generation to generation to be content with the poetry of the Bible, or of the old Greeks.

But the philosopher of Formalism jumps on us, and says it is merely a question of a new form "in the field of reporting and not in the field of poetic language". There he struck us! If you will, poetry is reporting, only in a peculiar, grand style.

The quarrels about "pure art" and about art with a tendency took place between the liberals and the "populists". They do not become us. Materialistic dialectics[1] are above this; from the point of view of an objective historical process, art is always a social servant and historically utilitarian. It finds the necessary rhythm of words for dark and vague moods, it brings thought and feeling closer or contrasts them with one another, it enriches the spiritual experience of the individual and of the community, it refines feeling, makes it more flexible, more responsive, it enlarges the volume of thought in advance and not through the personal method of accumulated experience,

1. The Marxist theory that maintains the priority of matter over mind, stressing the material basis of reality as a changing dialectical process (or reciprocal interaction) of matter and mind.

it educates the individual, the social group, the class and the nation. And this it does quite independently of whether it appears in a given case under the flag of a "pure" or of a frankly tendencious[2] art. In our Russian social development tendenciousness was the banner of the intelligentsia which sought contact with the people. The helpless intelligentsia, crushed by Tsarism[3] and deprived of a cultural environment, sought support in the lower strata of society and tried to prove to the "people" that it was thinking only of them, living only for them and that it loved them "terribly". And just as the "populists" who went to the people were ready to do without clean linen and without a comb and without a toothbrush, so the intelligentsia was ready to sacrifice the "subtleties" of form in its art, in order to give the most direct and spontaneous expression to the sufferings and hopes of the oppressed. On the other hand, "pure" art was the banner of the rising bourgeoisie, which could not openly declare its bourgeois character, and which at the same time tried to keep the intelligentsia in its service. The Marxist point of view is far removed from these tendencies, which were historically necessary, but which have become historically *passé*. Keeping on the plane of scientific investigation, Marxism seeks with the same assurance the social roots of the "pure" as well as of the tendencious art. It does not at all "incriminate" a poet with the thoughts and feelings which he expresses, but raises questions of a much more profound significance, namely, to which order of feelings does a given artistic work correspond in all its peculiarities? What are the social conditions of these thoughts and feelings? What place do they occupy in the historic development of a society and of a class? And, further, what literary heritage has entered into the elaboration of the new form? Under the influence of what historic impulse have the new complexes of feelings and thoughts broken through the shell which divides them from the sphere of poetic consciousness? The investigation may become complicated, detailed or individualized, but its fundamental idea will be that of the subsidiary rôle which art plays in the social process.

Each class has its own policy in art, that is, a system of presenting demands on art, which changes with time; for instance, the Macænas-like protection[4] of court and grand seigneur, the automatic relationship of supply and demand which is supplemented by complex methods of influencing the individual, and so forth, and so on. The social and even the personal dependence of art was not concealed, but was openly announced as long as art retained its court character. The wider, more popular, anonymous character of the rising bourgeoisie led, on the whole, to the theory of "pure art", though there were many deviations from this theory. As indicated above, the tendencious literature of the "populist" intelligentsia was imbued with a class interest; the intelligentsia could not strengthen itself and could not conquer for itself a right to play a part in history without the support of the people. But in the revolutionary struggle, the class egotism of the intelligentsia was turned inside out, and in its left wing, it assumed the form of highest self-sacrifice.

2. Tendentious.
3. The autocratic government of Russia under the czars (tsars). Along with his family, the last of the czars, Nicholas II (1868–1918), was executed by the Bolsheviks in July 1918.
4. That is, patronage. Maecenas (d. 8 B.C.E.), trusted friend and counselor of Augustus Caesar, was a great patron of Roman poets (including HORACE and Virgil).

That is why the intelligentsia not only did not conceal art with a tendency, but proclaimed it, thus sacrificing art, just as it sacrificed many other things.

Our Marxist conception of the objective social dependence and social utility of art, when translated into the language of politics, does not at all mean a desire to dominate art by means of decrees and orders. It is not true that we regard only that art as new and revolutionary which speaks of the worker, and it is nonsense to say that we demand that the poets should describe inevitably a factory chimney, or the uprising against capital! Of course the new art cannot but place the struggle of the proletariat[5] in the center of its attention. But the plough of the new art is not limited to numbered strips. On the contrary, it must plow the entire field in all directions. Personal lyrics of the very smallest scope have an absolute right to exist within the new art. Moreover, the new man cannot be formed without a new lyric poetry. But to create it, the poet himself must feel the world in a new way. If Christ alone or Sabaoth[6] himself bends over the poet's embraces (as in the case of Akhmatova, Tsvetaeva, Shkapskaya[7] and others), then this only goes to prove how much behind the times his lyrics are and how socially and æsthetically inadequate they are for the new man. Even where such terminology is not a survival of experience so much as of words, it shows psychologic inertia and therefore stands in contradiction to the consciousness of the new man. No one is going to prescribe themes to a poet or intends to prescribe them. Please write about anything you can think of! But allow the new class which considers itself, and with reason, called upon to build a new world, to say to you in any given case: It does not make new poets of you to translate the philosophy of life of the Seventeenth Century into the language of the Acméists.[8] The form of art is, to a certain and very large degree, independent, but the artist who creates this form, and the spectator who is enjoying it, are not empty machines, one for creating form and the other for appreciating it. They are living people, with a crystallized psychology representing a certain unity, even if not entirely harmonious. This psychology is the result of social conditions. The creation and perception of art forms is one of the functions of this psychology. And no matter how wise the Formalists try to be, their whole conception is simply based upon the fact that they ignore the psychological unity of the social man, who creates and who consumes what has been created.

The proletariat has to have in art the expression of the new spiritual point of view which is just beginning to be formulated within him, and to which art must help him give form. This is not a state order, but an historic demand. Its strength lies in the objectivity of historic necessity. You cannot pass this by, nor escape its force.

The Formalist school seems to try to be objective. It is disgusted, and not without reason, with the literary and critical arbitrariness which operates only with tastes and moods. It seeks precise criteria for classification and valuation. But owing to its narrow outlook and superficial methods, it is constantly falling into superstitions, such as graphology and phrenology.

5. That is, the laboring class; more specifically, the class of industrial workers who lack their own means of production and who thus must sell their labor in order to live.
6. The Lord of Hosts.
7. Trotsky names major 20th-century Russian poets: Anna Akhmatova (Anna Andreyevna Gorenko, 1888–1966), Marina Tsvetaeva (1892–1941), and Mariya Shkapskaya (1891–1952).
8. Members of a small group of 20th-century vanguard Russian poets.

These two "schools" have also the task of establishing purely objective tests for determining human character; such as the number of the flourishes of one's pen and their roundness, and the peculiarities of the bumps on the back of one's head. One may assume that pen-flourishes and bumps do have some relation to character; but this relation is not direct, and human character is not at all exhausted by them. An apparent objectivism based on accidental, secondary and inadequate characteristics leads inevitably to the worst subjectivism. In the case of the Formalist school it leads to the superstition of the word. Having counted the adjectives, and weighed the lines, and measured the rhythms, a Formalist either stops silent with the expression of a man who does not know what to do with himself, or throws out an unexpected generalization which contains five per cent of Formalism and ninety-five per cent of the most uncritical intuition.

In fact, the Formalists do not carry their idea of art to its logical conclusion. If one is to regard the process of poetic creation only as a combination of sounds or words, and to seek along these lines the solution of all the problems of poetry, then the only perfect formula of "poetics" will be this: Arm yourself with a dictionary and create by means of algebraic combinations and permutations of words, all the poetic works of the world which have been created and which have not yet been created. Reasoning "formally" one may produce "Eugene Onegin"[9] in two ways: either by subordinating the selection of words to a preconceived artistic idea (as Pushkin himself did) or by solving the problem algebraically. From the "Formal" point of view, the second method is more correct, because it does not depend upon mood, inspiration, or other unsteady things, and has besides the advantage that while leading to "Eugene Onegin" it may bring one to an incalculable number of other great works. All that one needs is infinity in time, called eternity. But as neither mankind nor the individual poet have eternity at their disposal, the fundamental source of poetic words will remain, as before, the preconceived artistic idea understood in the broadest sense, as an accurate thought and as a clearly expressed personal or social feeling and as a vague mood. In its striving towards artistic materialization, this subjective idea will be stimulated and jolted by form and may be sometimes pushed on to a path which was entirely unforeseen. This simply means that verbal form is not a passive reflection of a preconceived artistic idea, but an active element which influences the idea itself. But such an active mutual relationship—in which form influences and at times entirely transforms content—is known to us in all fields of social and even biologic life. This is no reason at all for rejecting Darwinism[1] and Marxism and for the creation of a Formalist school either in biology or sociology.

Victor Shklovsky, who flits lightly from verbal Formalism to the most subjective valuations, assumes a very uncompromising attitude towards the historico-materialistic theory of art. In a booklet which he published in Berlin, under the title of "The March of the Horse", he formulates in the course of three small pages—brevity is a fundamental and, at any rate, an undoubted merit of Shklovsky—five (not four and not six, but five) exhaustive

9. Verse novel (1833) by the Russian writer Aleksandr Pushkin (1799–1837).

1. The biological process of development (through natural selection), theorized by Charles Darwin (1802–1882); here presented as parallel to the economic and political theories of KARL MARX (1818–1883).

arguments against the materialist conception of art. Let us examine these arguments, because it won't harm us to take a look and see what kind of chaff is handed out as the last word in scientific thought (with the greatest variety of scientific references on these same three microscopic pages).

"If the environment and the relations of production," says Shklovsky, "influenced art, then would not the themes of art be tied to the places which would correspond to these relations? But themes are homeless." Well, and how about butterflies? According to Darwin, they also "correspond" to definite relations, and yet they flit from place to place, just like an unweighted litterateur.

It is not easy to understand why Marxism should be supposed to condemn themes to a condition of serfdom. The fact that different peoples and different classes of the same people make use of the same themes, merely shows how limited the human imagination is, and how man tries to maintain an economy of energy in every kind of creation, even in the artistic. Every class tries to utilize, to the greatest possible degree, the material and spiritual heritage of another class. Shklovsky's argument could be easily transferred into the field of productive technique. From ancient times on, the wagon has been based on one and the same theme, namely, axles, wheels, and a shaft. However, the chariot of the Roman patrician was just as well adapted to his tastes and needs as was the carriage of Count Orlov, fitted out with inner comforts, to the tastes of this favorite of Catherine the Great.[2] The wagon of the Russian peasant is adapted to the needs of his household, to the strength of his little horse, and to the peculiarities of the country road. The automobile, which is undoubtedly a product of the new technique, shows, nevertheless, the same "theme", namely, four wheels on two axles. Yet every time a peasant's horse shies in terror before the blinding lights of an automobile on the Russian road at night, a conflict of two cultures is reflected in the episode.

"If environment expressed itself in novels," so runs the second argument, "European science would not be breaking its head over the question of where the stories of 'A Thousand and One Nights'[3] were made, whether in Egypt, India, or Persia." To say that man's environment, including the artist's, that is, the conditions of his education and life, find expression in his art also, does not mean to say that such expression has a precise geographic, ethnographic and statistical character. It is not at all surprising that it is difficult to decide whether certain novels were made in Egypt, India or Persia, because the social conditions of these countries have much in common. But the very fact that European science is "breaking its head" trying to solve this question from these novels themselves, shows that these novels reflect an environment, even though unevenly. No one can jump beyond himself. Even the ravings of an insane person contain nothing that the sick man had not received before from the outside world. But it would be an insanity of another order to regard his ravings as the accurate reflection of an external world. Only an experienced and thoughtful psychiatrist, who knows the past of the patient, will be able to find the reflected and distorted bits of reality in the contents of his ravings. Artistic creation, of course, is not a raving, though

2. Empress of Russia (1729–1796; reigned 1762–96). Gregory Orlov (1734–1783) was one of her court favorites.

3. A series of anonymous ancient tales in Arabic (also titled *The Arabian Nights*), codified in its present form ca. 1450.

it is also a deflection, a changing and a transformation of reality, in accordance with the peculiar laws of art. However fantastic art may be, it cannot have at its disposal any other material except that which is given to it by the world of three dimensions and by the narrower world of class society. Even when the artist creates heaven and hell, he merely transforms the experience of his own life into his phantasmagorias, almost to the point of his landlady's unpaid bill.

"If the features of class and caste are deposited in art," continues Shklovsky, "then how does it come that the various tales of the Great Russians about their nobleman are the same as their fairy tales about their priest?"

In essence, this is merely a paraphrase of the first argument. Why cannot the fairy tales about the nobleman and about the priest be the same, and how does this contradict Marxism? The proclamations which are written by well-known Marxists not infrequently speak of landlords, capitalists, priests, generals and other exploiters. The landlord undoubtedly differs from the capitalist, but there are cases when they are considered under one head. Why, then, cannot folk-art in certain cases treat the nobleman and the priest together, as the representatives of the classes which stand above the people and which plunder them? In the cartoons of Moor and of Deni,[4] the priest often stands side by side with the landlord, without any damage to Marxism.

"If ethnographic traits were reflected in art," Shklovsky goes on, "the folklore about the peoples beyond the border would not be interchangeable and could not be told by any one folk about another."

As you see, there is no letting up here. Marxism does not maintain at all that ethnographic traits have an independent character. On the contrary, it emphasizes the all-determining significance of natural and economic conditions in the formation of folk-lore. The similarity of conditions in the development of the herding and agricultural and primarily peasant peoples, and the similarity in the character of their mutual influence upon one another, cannot but lead to the creation of a similar folk-lore. And from the point of view of the question that interests us here, it makes absolutely no difference whether these homogeneous themes arose independently among different peoples, as the reflection of a life-experience which was homogeneous in its fundamental traits and which was reflected through the homogeneous prism of a peasant imagination, or whether the seeds of these fairy tales were carried by a favorable wind from place to place, striking root wherever the ground turned out to be favorable. It is very likely that, in reality, these methods were combined.

And finally, as a separate argument—"The reason (*i.e.*, Marxism) is incorrect in the fifth place"—Shklovsky points to the theme of abduction which goes through Greek comedy and reaches Ostrovsky.[5] In other words, our critic repeats, in a special form, his very first argument (as we see, even in so far as formal logic is concerned, all is not well with our Formalist). Yes, themes migrate from people to people, from class to class, and even from author to author. This means only that the human imagination is economi-

4. D. S. Moor (1883–1946) and V. N. Deni (1893–1946) were political cartoonists and satirists, known in particular for their agitational poster art in the decade after the Bolshevik Revolution. Posters mocking the Bolsheviks' enemies frequently grouped together landlords and priests (caricatured as fat and ugly).

5. Aleksandr Ostrovsky (1823–1886), Russian dramatist.

cal. A new class does not begin to create all of culture from the beginning, but enters into possession of the past, assorts it, touches it up, rearranges it, and builds on it further. If there were no such utilization of the "second-hand" wardrobe of the ages, historic processes would have no progress at all. If the theme of Ostrovsky's drama came to him through the Egyptians and through Greece, then the paper on which Ostrovsky developed his theme came to him as a development of the Egyptian papyrus through the Greek parchment. Let us take another and closer analogy: the fact that the critical methods of the Greek Sophists,[6] who were the pure Formalists of their day, have penetrated the theoretic consciousness of Shklovsky, does not in the least change the fact that Shklovsky himself is a very picturesque product of a definite social environment and of a definite age.

Shklovsky's destruction of Marxism in five points reminds us very much of those articles which were published against Darwinism in the magazine "The Orthodox Review" in the good old days. If the doctrine of the origin of man from the monkey were true, wrote the learned Bishop Nikanor of Odessa[7] thirty or forty years ago, then our grandfathers would have had distinct signs of a tail, or would have noticed such a characteristic in their grandfathers and grandmothers. Second, as everybody knows, monkeys can only give birth to monkeys. . . . Fifth, Darwinism is incorrect, because it contradicts Formalism—I beg your pardon, I meant to say the formal decisions of the universal church conferences. The advantage of the learned monk consisted, however, in the fact that he was a frank *passéist*[8] and took his cue from the Apostle Paul and not from physics, chemistry or mathematics, as the Futurist, Shklovsky, does.

It is unquestionably true that the need for art is not created by economic conditions. But neither is the need for food created by economics. On the contrary, the need for food and warmth creates economics. It is very true that one cannot always go by the principles of Marxism in deciding whether to reject or to accept a work of art. A work of art should, in the first place, be judged by its own law, that is, by the law of art. But Marxism alone can explain why and how a given tendency in art has originated in a given period of history; in other words, who it was who made a demand for such an artistic form and not for another, and why.

It would be childish to think that every class can entirely and fully create its own art from within itself, and, particularly, that the proletariat is capable of creating a new art by means of closed art guilds or circles, or by the Organization for Proletarian Culture, etc. Generally speaking, the artistic work of man is continuous. Each new rising class places itself on the shoulders of its preceding one. But this continuity is dialectic, that is, it finds itself by means of internal repulsions and breaks. New artistic needs or demands for new literary and artistic points of view are stimulated by economics, through the development of a new class, and minor stimuli are supplied by changes in the position of the class, under the influence of the growth of its wealth and cultural power. Artistic creation is always a complicated turning inside out of old forms, under the influence of new stimuli which originate

6. A group of 5th-century B.C.E. Greek philosophers who specialized in logic, argumentation, and rhetoric and who were known for their elaborate and sometimes specious arguments (see GORGIAS).

7. The Russian Orthodox archbishop of Kherson and Odessa (1827–1890).

8. Traditionalist.

outside of art. In this large sense of the word, art is a handmaiden. It is not a disembodied element feeding on itself, but a function of social man indissolubly tied to his life and environment. And how characteristic it is—if one were to reduce every social superstition to its absurdity—that Shklovsky has come to the idea of art's absolute independence from the social environment at a period of Russian history when art has revealed with such utter frankness its spiritual, environmental and material dependence upon definite social classes, subclasses and groups!

Materialism does not deny the significance of the element of form, either in logic, jurisprudence, or art. Just as a system of jurisprudence can and must be judged by its internal logic and consistency, so art can and must be judged from the point of view of its achievements in form, because there can be no art without them. However, a juridical theory which attempted to establish the independence of law from social conditions would be defective at its very base. Its moving force lies in economics—in class contradictions. The law gives only a formal and an internally harmonized expression of these phenomena, not of their individual peculiarities, but of their general character, that is, of the elements that are repetitive and permanent in them. We can see now with a clarity which is rare in history how new law is made. It is not done by logical deduction, but by empirical measurement and by adjustment to the economic needs of the new ruling class. Literature, whose methods and processes have their roots far back in the most distant past and represent the accumulated experience of verbal craftsmanship, expresses the thoughts, feelings, moods, points of view and hopes of the new epoch and of its new class. One cannot jump beyond this. And there is no need of making the jump, at least, for those who are not serving an epoch already past nor a class which has already outlived itself.

The methods of formal analysis are necessary, but insufficient. You may count up the alliterations in popular proverbs, classify metaphors, count up the number of vowels and consonants in a wedding song. It will undoubtedly enrich our knowledge of folk art, in one way or another; but if you don't know the peasant system of sowing, and the life that is based on it, if you don't know the part the scythe plays, and if you have not mastered the meaning of the church calendar to the peasant, of the time when the peasant marries, or when the peasant women give birth, you will have only understood the outer shell of folk art, but the kernel will not have been reached. The architectural scheme of the Cologne cathedral[9] can be established by measuring the base and the height of its arches, by determining the three dimensions of its naves, the dimensions and the placement of the columns, etc. But without knowing what a mediæval city was like, what a guild was, or what was the Catholic Church of the Middle Ages, the Cologne cathedral will never be understood. The effort to set art free from life, to declare it a craft self-sufficient unto itself, devitalizes and kills art. The very need of such an operation is an unmistakable symptom of intellectual decline.

The analogy with the theological arguments against Darwinism which was made above may appear to the reader external and anecdotal. That may be true, to some extent. But a much deeper connection exists. The Formalist theory inevitably reminds a Marxist who has done any reading at all of the

9. The largest gothic church in northern Europe (begun in the 13th c.).

familiar tunes of a very old philosophic melody. The jurists and the moralists (to recall at random the German Stammler, and our own subjectivist Mikhailovsky)[1] tried to prove that morality and law could not be determined by economics, because economic life was unthinkable outside of juridical and ethical norms. True, the formalists of law and morals did not go so far as to assert the complete independence of law and ethics from economics. They recognized a certain complex mutual relationship of "factors", and these "factors", while influencing one another, retained the qualities of independent substances, coming no one knew whence. The assertion of complete independence of the æsthetic "factor" from the influence of social conditions, as is made by Shklovsky, is an instance of specific hyperbole whose roots, by the way, lie in social conditions too; it is the megalomania of æsthetic turning our hard reality on its head. Apart from this peculiarity, the constructions of the Formalists have the same kind of defective methodology that every other kind of idealism has. To a materialist, religion, law, morals and art represent separate aspects of one and the same process of social development. Though they differentiate themselves from their industrial basis, become complex, strengthen and develop their special characteristics in detail, politics, religion, law, ethics and æsthetics remain, none the less, functions of social man and obey the laws of his social organization. The idealist, on the other hand, does not see a unified process of historic development which evolves the necessary organs and functions from within itself, but a crossing or combining and interacting of certain independent principles—the religious, political, juridical, æsthetic and ethical substances, which find their origin and explanation in themselves. The (dialectic) idealism of Hegel[2] arranges these substances (which are the eternal categories) in some sequence by reducing them to a genetic unity. Regardless of the fact that this unity with Hegel is the absolute spirit, which divides itself in the process of its dialectic manifestation into various "factors", Hegel's system, because of its dialectic character, not because of its idealism, gives an idea of historic reality which is just as good as the idea of a man's hand that a glove gives when turned inside out. But the Formalists (and their greatest genius was Kant)[3] do not look at the dynamics of development, but at a cross-section of it, on the day and at the hour of their own philosophic revelation. At the crossing of the line they reveal the complexity and multiplicity of the object (not of the process, because they do not think of processes). This complexity they analyze and classify. They give names to the elements, which are at once transformed into essences, into sub-absolutes, without father or mother; to wit, religion, politics, morals, law, art. Here we no longer have a glove of history turned inside out, but the skin torn from the separate fingers, dried out to a degree of complete abstraction, and this hand of history turns out to be the product of the "inter-action" of the thumb, the index, the middle finger, and all the other "factors". The æsthetic "factor" is the little finger, the smallest, but not the least beloved.

1. Nikolai Mikhailovsky (1842–1904), literary critic best known for his essays on Tolstoy and other Russian novelists; a leader of the liberal populists, he engaged in debates with Lenin and other Russian Marxists. Rudolf Stammler (1856–1938), German jurist and legal philosopher.

2. GEORG WILHELM FRIEDRICH HEGEL (1770–1831), German philosopher.

3. IMMANUEL KANT (1724–1804), German philosopher.

In biology, vitalism[4] is a variation of the same fetish of presenting the separate aspects of the world-process, without understanding its inner relation. A creator is all that is lacking for a super-social, absolute morality or æsthetics, or for a super-physical absolute "vital force". The multiplicity of independent factors, "factors" without beginning or end, is nothing but a masked polytheism. Just as Kantian idealism represents historically a translation of Christianity into the language of rationalistic philosophy, so all the varieties of idealistic formalization, either openly or secretly, lead to a God, as the Cause of all causes. In comparison with the oligarchy of a dozen sub-absolutes of the idealistic philosophy, a single personal Creator is already an element of order. Herein lies the deeper connection between the Formalist refutations of Marxism and the theological refutations of Darwinism.

The Formalist school represents an abortive idealism applied to the questions of art. The Formalists show a fast ripening religiousness. They are followers of St John. They believe that "In the beginning was the Word".[5] But we believe that in the beginning was the deed. The word followed, as its phonetic shadow.

1924

4. The theory or doctrine that life processes arise from or contain a nonmaterial vital principle and cannot be explained entirely as physical and chemical phenomena.

5. John 1.1.

VIRGINIA WOOLF

1882–1941

Invited to address the topic of "women and fiction" at Cambridge University's Newnham and Girton Colleges in October of 1928, Virginia Woolf presented two lectures that would later become, after considerable expansion and revision, her celebrated book *A Room of One's Own* (1929). Working at the intersection of modernism and feminism, both of which she stood for, Woolf analyzed the differences between women as *objects* of representation and women as *authors* of representation, and invited her audience to think about "the books that are not there." In the process, she opened up the entire territory of modern feminist criticism.

Woolf was a member of a highly literate and artistic family. Born Adeline Virginia Stephen, she was the daughter of Leslie Stephen, a distinguished Victorian literary figure, and Julia Jackson Duckworth Stephen, a beauty who had once frequented pre-Raphaelite circles. It was the second marriage for each. The resultant blended family included three Duckworths (George, Stella, and Gerald), one Stephen from the first marriage (Laura, later institutionalized because of mental retardation), and four new Stephens (Vanessa, Thoby, Virginia, and Adrian). Leslie Stephen lived in a world of letters: his first wife was the daughter of novelist William Makepeace Thackeray; he possessed a large library (in which Virginia got her education); he published several books of philosophy and literary history; and he became, partly for financial reasons, the first editor of the multivolume *Dictionary of National Biography* in 1882, the year of Virginia's birth. The Stephen family was organized in a typically Victorian way, the father occupying himself with money and intellectual matters and the mother attending to the emotional and social needs of her husband and eight children.

Her mother's death in 1895 was for thirteen-year-old Virginia a terrible loss. When Sir Leslie died nine years later, twenty-two-year-old Virginia felt an intense though ambivalent liberation, and began to write. The Stephen children moved across London to Gordon Square, Bloomsbury, where they were surrounded by Thoby's Cambridge friends, many of whom had been members of a college group known as the Apostles, and who later would become well known: Lytton Strachey, a biographer and historian; John Maynard Keynes, an economist; Clive Bell, a critic of art and literature; and Leonard Woolf, a writer of novels and political science.

In 1906, however, the circle was devastated by the unexpected loss of its connecting link: Thoby Stephen died of typhoid fever. Two days after Thoby's death, Vanessa agreed to marry Clive Bell. Virginia and her remaining brother, Adrian, moved to 29 Fitzroy Square (London), where Virginia began working on a novel. She had also begun to publish reviews for money and do some (unpaid) teaching in a working-class college. When she inherited £2,500 from an aunt, she acquired an important economic safety net.

In 1912 Virginia married Leonard Woolf, who had just returned from serving as an administrator in Ceylon (now Sri Lanka). They shared many intellectual interests and both felt themselves to be outsiders within their social circle. In response to Virginia's periodic nervous breakdowns, Leonard was both attentive and controlling: she relied on, and raged against, his prescriptions. In the 1920s, Virginia had an affair with Victoria ("Vita") Sackville-West, a fellow writer, who was married to Harold Nicolson, a diplomat. The relationship coincided with a period of great productivity and originality in Woolf's writing.

In 1917 Leonard had had the inspired idea of buying a printing press, originally to provide a therapeutic hobby. The Hogarth Press, born of a machine small enough to fit on a kitchen table, soon became an important disseminator of modernist texts. It published brightly covered books, often designed by Vanessa Bell or Roger Fry, and launched T. S. Eliot's *Waste Land* (1922); fiction by Maksim Gorky, E. M. Forster, and Katherine Mansfield; all the works of Virginia Woolf, beginning with *Jacob's Room* (1922); and the complete twenty-four-volume translation of the works of SIGMUND FREUD. The "Woolves," as their friends called them, had found their outlet.

Starting with *The Voyage Out*, her first novel (1915), Woolf wrote a great deal. Her novels experiment increasingly with form and style: *Mrs. Dalloway* (1925), her fourth, is set, like James Joyce's *Ulysses* in Dublin, in a single day in London, pairing the war and the drawing room; *To the Lighthouse* (1927) is a radical rethinking of what a novel can do, a fictional biography of her parents relying on a stream of consciousness narrative. Her later novels take diverse approaches to expanding the form, and she published three very different "biographies," including *Orlando* (1928, a novel celebrating her relationship with Vita), whose three-hundred-year-old protagonist changes sex in midlife, and *Flush* (1933), about the life of Elizabeth Barrett Browning's spaniel. Woolf also wrote more than four volumes' worth of essays and short fiction and two groundbreaking feminist works: *A Room of One's Own* and *Three Guineas* (1938).

Her productivity was all the more remarkable in that it was often punctuated by nervous illnesses and by treatments, of dubious effectiveness, that required her to stop writing. In 1941, with the voices in her head becoming more insistent and the war in Europe ever more threatening (she and Leonard, who was Jewish, had made provisions to kill themselves in the event of a Nazi invasion), she drowned herself.

People attempting to explain the sources of Woolf's creativity have written a great deal on several topics: her sexuality, her class position, and her madness. Much has been said about her sexuality: she had too much of it or too little; her androgyny obscured her bisexuality, or vice versa; she idealized motherhood, or feared it, or resented Leonard, who was afraid of inherited insanity, for deciding that they shouldn't have children; and so on. Evidence for these arguments comes, of course, from her writing itself; their contradictions indicate her success in finding textual forms—in her diaries and letters, her fiction and essays—that would allow all these forces to do battle.

Both of her feminist treatises link women and money. As one of the "daughters of educated men" (as she puts it in *Three Guineas*), she belonged to a culturally, if not economically, privileged class. In *A Room of One's Own* she argues that women need £500 a year (an amount somewhere between subsistence and comfort), and in *Three Guineas*—a meditation on the ties between war and patriarchal values—she responds to a solicitation to sign a petition and contribute money to a society for the prevention of war. On the one hand, the link she makes between freedom and property can be critiqued from a Marxist perspective; on the other, society's denial of women's independent rights over property marks a resistance to women's freedom. It is clear that Woolf is breaking a gender taboo, rather than merely claiming a class privilege, by going into the economic details of women's lives.

Woolf has also been seen as a representative of the sexual sea change that came after, and out of, the Victorian era. She grew up, like many others, in a world of exaggerated gender roles, secret transgressions, and repressive silence about sexual matters (she was apparently abused in childhood by her two stepbrothers). The Bloomsbury group, in contrast, broke gender taboos spectacularly—almost all of them had relations with both sexes, and they sometimes lived with the people they were *not* sleeping with. Nevertheless, even in liberated Bloomsbury, female creativity could still be categorized as "madness" whenever it became too hard to handle (this is the premise behind *The Madwoman in the Attic*, the influential 1979 study by SANDRA M. GILBERT AND SUSAN GUBAR). The line between psychopathology and impeded gifts is very hard to draw, as Woolf makes clear in her parable of Shakespeare's sister.

Our selection contains three celebrated moments from *A Room of One's Own*, which we have labeled "Shakespeare's Sister," "Chloe Liked Olivia," and "Androgyny." What would have happened, Woolf asks in the first, if Shakespeare had had a sister as gifted as himself? She would have lacked even the education *he* had, she answers. Shakespeare's sister would have been excluded from the Renaissance stage (on which all the parts were played by males); she would probably have found herself with child by some man who had taken pity on her; and, crazed by her gifts and her prospects, she would probably have ended up committing suicide. Judith Shakespeare thus represents one kind of "book that isn't there."

A second kind of missing book may be lurking behind the cover of the fictitious novel Woolf is about to open in our second section, Mary Carmichael's *Life's Adventure*. "Chloe liked Olivia," she reads, and looks about her to make sure the room contains only women. By wondering whether "that red curtain over there" conceals the figure of Sir Chartres Biron—the magistrate presiding at that very moment over the censorship trial of Radclyffe Hall's lesbian novel *The Well of Loneliness* (1928)—Woolf implies that one of the things that keeps women unfree is the law's policing of the relations women can have with women. Women in literature have almost always been imagined as *only* sexual, she argues, and usually only in their relations or nonrelations to men, leaving no dealings with each other but as rivals ("Cleopatra did not like Octavia"). But, Woolf exclaims, how small a part of any woman's life is the part seen by the other sex and in relation to the other sex! Women as authors now have the opportunity to depict "that vast chamber where nobody has yet been."

Woolf's idealization of authorial "androgyny" in our third passage would seem to fly in the face of her descriptions earlier in the essay of male and female sentences or male and female plots. How can she argue both that the exclusion of women from the canon has made a difference and that great authors are androgynous? Two clarifications need to be made. First, the "woman" in Shakespeare's brain is not the same as the "women" who did not write in history. But second, the women entering literature do more than fill up an absence. If the greatest authors used both "sides" of their brain, the new authors must do so as well. Her warning that "consciousness of sex" destroys literature can be interpreted as both feminist and antifeminist. Writing with "unconsciousness of sex" may very well be taken as "indifference to sex"—often seen as a modernist privileging of style over politics. Yet this unconsciousness does not preclude gender difference, mandating simply that the gender differences that inform good writing not become *conscious*. If women were free to write, would they not open a window on a world of experiences that have remained invisible, even to themselves? a world too quickly dismissed or devalued, a world that would *require* different sentences? Woolf presents *men*, not women, as having become overly conscious of their sex as a result of feminism. In arguing for a new writerly androgyny, Woolf comes close to what HÉLÈNE CIXOUS later calls "the other bisexuality."

A Room of One's Own is one of the most imitated titles ever devised. Written during the trial of Radclyffe Hall's lesbian novel and published during the same month as the stock market crash of 1929, *A Room of One's Own* marks an upheaval more subtle, yet in some ways as profound, as these. The time was right for it: the book was so successful that the proceeds enabled Virginia Woolf to add a room of her own onto her house in Sussex.

BIBLIOGRAPHY

Most of Woolf's works are available in easily accessible editions. *A Room of One's Own* and *Three Guineas*, edited by Hermione Lee, were published together in 1984. Woolf's other essays on women's writing, edited by Michèle Barrett, were published as *Women and Fiction* (1979). In addition to her novels and her feminist essays, Woolf collected some of her articles in two volumes called *The Common Reader* (1925, 1932). Before he died in 1969, Leonard Woolf edited her *Collected Essays* (4 vols., 1967); he also edited *A Writer's Diary* (1953), now superseded by *The Diary of Virginia Woolf*, edited by Anne Olivier Bell (5 vols., 1977–84), and *A Passionate Apprentice: The Early Journals, 1897–1909*, edited by Mitchell Leaska (1990). See also *The Letters of Virginia Woolf*, edited by Nigel Nicolson and Joanne Trautmann (6 vols., 1975–80).

There are at least a dozen biographies of Woolf. The first, *Virginia Woolf*, was written by her nephew, Quentin Bell, in 1973. The most even-handed and well-researched recent biography is Hermione Lee's monumental *Virginia Woolf* (1996). The flavor of the many "diagnostic" biographical studies can be gleaned from Alma Halbert Bond's *Who Killed Virginia Woolf? A Psychobiography* (1989), the kind of Freudian reading that has given Freudian readings a bad name; Louise de Salvo's *Virginia Woolf: The Impact of Childhood Sexual Abuse on Her Life and Work* (1989); and Mitchell Leaska's *Granite and Rainbow* (1998), which attributes all Woolf's creativity to her repressed relationship with her father.

The history of Woolf criticism mirrors the larger changes in twentieth-century criticism. An invaluable collection of contemporary reviews was published as *Virginia Woolf: The Critical Heritage*, edited by Robin Majumdar and Allen McLaurin (1975), which includes acerbic reviews in the journal *Scrutiny* (the most memorable may be Q. D. Leavis's review of *Three Guineas*). Woolf's canonization as a modernist is perhaps best illustrated by her inclusion in Erich Auerbach's monumental *Mimesis: The Representation of Reality in Western Literature* (1946). Early feminist criticism was often critical of Woolf: Elaine Showalter's *A Literature of Their Own* (1977), despite its title, dismisses Woolf's experience of femininity. But Jane Marcus's edited collections—*New Feminist Essays on Virginia Woolf* (1981) and *Virginia Woolf: A Feminist Slant* (1983)—began revising that picture; and when, in her groundbreaking *Textual/Sexual Politics* (1985), Toril Moi contrasted Anglo-American feminism's desire for realism with French feminism's interest in textuality, she called for a rereading of Woolf's style that has continued to this day. See, particularly, *Virginia Woolf: A Collection of Critical Essays*, edited by Margaret Homans (1993); Ellen Bayuk Rosenman, *A Room of One's Own: Women Writers and the Politics of Creativity* (1995); and Jane Goldman, *The Feminist Aesthetics of Virginia Woolf: Modernism, Post-Impressionism, and the Politics of the Visual* (1998). The emergence of gay and lesbian studies has focused new attention on the relationship between Virginia Woolf and Vita Sackville-West. Suzanne Raitt's *Vita and Virginia* (1993) gives a good overview of the relationship of the two writers, whose letters were dramatized in 1994 by Eileen Atkins in her play *Vita and Virginia* (starring Atkins and Vanessa Redgrave). Other valuable studies include Elizabeth Abel, *Virginia Woolf and the Fictions of Psychoanalysis* (1989); Pamela Caughie, *Virginia Woolf and Postmodernism* (1991); Gillian Beer, *Virginia Woolf: The Common Ground* (1996); and Rachel Bowlby, *Feminist Destinations and Further Essays on Virginia Woolf* (1997).

There are also two useful resources for Woolf studies: Edward Bishop's day-to-day chronicle of Woolf's activities, *A Virginia Woolf Chronology* (1989), and Mark Hussey's dictionary of Woolf information, *Virginia Woolf A to Z* (1995). The proceedings of the annual Virginia Woolf conference are published by Pace University Press (1992–). B. J. Kirkpatrick and Stuart N. Clarke compiled *A Bibliography of Virginia Woolf* (1997); a bibliographic update, *The Virginia Woolf Miscellany*, is published by Sonoma State University.

From A Room of One's Own

* * *

[SHAKESPEARE'S SISTER]

Let me imagine, since facts are so hard to come by, what would have happened had Shakespeare had a wonderfully gifted sister, called Judith, let us say. Shakespeare himself went, very probably—his mother was an heiress—to the grammar school, where he may have learnt Latin—Ovid, Virgil and Horace[1]—and the elements of grammar and logic. He was, it is well known, a wild boy who poached rabbits, perhaps shot a deer, and had, rather sooner than he should have done, to marry a woman in the neighborhood, who bore him a child rather quicker than was right. That escapade sent him to seek his fortune in London. He had, it seemed, a taste for the theatre; he began by holding horses at the stage door. Very soon he got work in the theatre, became a successful actor, and lived at the hub of the universe, meeting everybody, knowing everybody, practising his art on the boards, exercising his wits in the streets, and even getting access to the palace of the queen. Meanwhile his extraordinarily gifted sister, let us suppose, remained at home. She was as adventurous, as imaginative, as agog to see the world as he was. But she was not sent to school. She had no chance of learning grammar and logic, let alone of reading Horace and Virgil. She picked up a book now and then, one of her brother's perhaps, and read a few pages. But then her parents came in and told her to mend the stockings or mind the stew and not moon about with books and papers. They would have spoken sharply but kindly, for they were substantial people who knew the conditions of life for a woman and loved their daughter—indeed, more likely than not she was the apple of her father's eye. Perhaps she scribbled some pages up in an apple loft on the sly, but was careful to hide them or set fire to them. Soon, however, before she was out of her teens, she was to be betrothed to the son of a neighboring wool-stapler. She cried out that marriage was hateful to her, and for that she was severely beaten by her father. Then he ceased to scold her. He begged her instead not to hurt him, not to shame him in this matter of her marriage. He would give her a chain of beads or a fine

1. The 3 Roman poets—Ovid (43 B.C.E.–17 C.E.), Virgil (70–19 B.C.E.), and HORACE (65–8 B.C.E.)—were standard authors studied by boys in schools from the Renaissance on.

petticoat, he said; and there were tears in his eyes. How could she disobey him? How could she break his heart? The force of her own gift alone drove her to it. She made up a small parcel of her belongings, let herself down by a rope one summer's night and took the road to London. She was not seventeen. The birds that sang in the hedge were not more musical than she was. She had the quickest fancy, a gift like her brother's, for the tune of words. Like him, she had a taste for the theatre. She stood at the stage door; she wanted to act, she said. Men laughed in her face. The manager—a fat, loose-lipped man—guffawed. He bellowed something about poodles dancing and women acting—no woman, he said, could possibly be an actress.[2] He hinted—you can imagine what. She could get no training in her craft. Could she even seek her dinner in a tavern or roam the streets at midnight? Yet her genius was for fiction and lusted to feed abundantly upon the lives of men and women and the study of their ways. At last—for she was very young, oddly like Shakespeare the poet in her face, with the same grey eyes and rounded brows—at last Nick Greene[3] the actor-manager took pity on her; she found herself with child by that gentleman and so—who shall measure the heat and violence of the poet's heart when caught and tangled in a woman's body?—killed herself one winter's night and lies buried at some cross-roads where the omnibuses now stop outside the Elephant and Castle.[4]

That, more or less, is how the story would run, I think, if a woman in Shakespeare's day had had Shakespeare's genius. But for my part, I agree with the deceased bishop,[5] if such he was—it is unthinkable that any woman in Shakespeare's day should have had Shakespeare's genius. For genius like Shakespeare's is not born among labouring, uneducated, servile people. It was not born in England among the Saxons and the Britons. It is not born today among the working classes. How, then, could it have been born among women whose work began, according to Professor Trevelyan,[6] almost before they were out of the nursery, who were forced to it by their parents and held to it by all the power of law and custom? Yet genius of a sort must have existed among women as it must have existed among the working classes. Now and again an Emily Brontë or a Robert Burns[7] blazes out and proves its presence. But certainly it never got itself on to paper. When, however, one reads of a witch being ducked, of a woman possessed by devils, of a wise woman selling herbs, or even of a very remarkable man who had a mother, then I think we are on the track of a lost novelist, a suppressed poet, of some mute and inglorious Jane Austen,[8] some Emily Brontë who dashed her brains out on the moor or mopped and mowed about the highways crazed with the torture that her gift had put her to. Indeed, I would venture to guess that

2. In the Elizabethan theater, women's roles were played by boys.

3. Possibly modeled on Robert Greene (1558–1592), a dramatist whose 1592 pamphlet contains the first literary reference to Shakespeare (an attack).

4. Suicides were often buried at crossroads to prevent their spirits from returning. The Elephant and Castle was a famous tavern, bombed during World War II, that stood at one of the busiest intersections in London.

5. An "old gentleman" who earlier in the essay is said to have "declared that it was impossible for any woman past, present, or to come, to have the genius of Shakespeare."

6. George Macaulay Trevelyan (1876–1962), English historian; Woolf has already referred to his *History of England* (1926).

7. Scottish poet (1759–1796). Brontë (1818–1848), English novelist and poet.

8. Probably the most canonical of English women novelists (1775–1817); the phrase "some mute and inglorious Jane Austen" echoes "some mute inglorious Milton," in Thomas Gray's "Elegy Written in a Country Churchyard" (1751).

Anon, who wrote so many poems without signing them, was often a woman. It was a woman Edward Fitzgerald,[9] I think, suggested who made the ballads and the folk-songs, crooning them to her children, beguiling her spinning with them, or the length of the winter's night.

This may be true or it may be false—who can say?—but what is true in it, so it seemed to me, reviewing the story of Shakespeare's sister as I had made it, is that any woman born with a great gift in the sixteenth century would certainly have gone crazed, shot herself, or ended her days in some lonely cottage outside the village, half witch, half wizard, feared and mocked at. For it needs little skill in psychology to be sure that a highly gifted girl who had tried to use her gift for poetry would have been so thwarted and hindered by other people, so tortured and pulled asunder by her own contrary instincts, that she must have lost her health and sanity to a certainty.

* * *

[CHLOE LIKED OLIVIA]

I am almost sure, I said to myself, that Mary Carmichael[1] is playing a trick on us. For I feel as one feels on a switchback railway when the car, instead of sinking, as one has been led to expect, swerves up again. Mary is tampering with the expected sequence. First she broke the sentence; now she has broken the sequence. Very well, she has every right to do both these things if she does them not for the sake of breaking, but for the sake of creating. Which of the two it is I cannot be sure until she has faced herself with a situation. I will give her every liberty, I said, to choose what that situation shall be; she shall make it of tin cans and old kettles if she likes; but she must convince me that she believes it to be a situation; and then when she has made it she must face it. She must jump. And, determined to do my duty by her as reader if she would do her duty by me as writer, I turned the page and read . . . I am sorry to break off so abruptly. Are there no men present? Do you promise me that behind that red curtain over there the figure of Sir Chartres Biron[2] is not concealed? We are all women, you assure me? Then I may tell you that the very next words I read were these—"Chloe liked Olivia . . ." Do not start. Do not blush. Let us admit in the privacy of our own society that these things sometimes happen. Sometimes women do like women.

"Chloe liked Olivia," I read. And then it struck me how immense a change was there. Chloe liked Olivia perhaps for the first time in literature. Cleopatra did not like Octavia.[3] And how completely *Antony and Cleopatra* would have been altered had she done so! As it is, I thought, letting my mind, I am afraid, wander a little from *Life's Adventure*, the whole thing is simplified, conventionalised, if one dared say it, absurdly. Cleopatra's only feeling about Octavia is one of jealousy. Is she taller than I am? How does she do her hair?

9. English scholar and poet (1809–1883), who anonymously translated *The Rubáiyát of Omar Khayyam* (1859).

1. Woolf's name for a fictitious contemporary author of a novel, *Life's Adventure*, which bears a resemblance to the novel published by Mary Stopes (under the name Mary Carmichael) titled *Love's Creation* (1928).

2. The magistrate presiding over the trial that was to ban Radcliffe Hall's *Well of Loneliness* (1928) for depicting lesbianism.

3. In Shakespeare's *Antony and Cleopatra* (1606–07), Antony loves Cleopatra but marries Octavia to cement a political alliance; Cleopatra interrogates a messenger about Octavia's height, voice, gait, and hair color (3.3).

The play, perhaps, required no more. But how interesting it would have been if the relationship between the two women had been more complicated. All these relationships between women, I thought, rapidly recalling the splendid gallery of fictitious women, are too simple. So much has been left out, unattempted. And I tried to remember any case in the course of my reading where two women are represented as friends. There is an attempt at it in *Diana of the Crossways.*[4] They are confidantes, of course, in Racine[5] and the Greek tragedies. They are now and then mothers and daughters. But almost without exception they are shown in their relation to men. It was strange to think that all the great women of fiction were, until Jane Austen's day, not only seen by the other sex, but seen only in relation to the other sex. And how small a part of a woman's life is that; and how little can a man know even of that when he observes it through the black or rosy spectacles which sex puts upon his nose. Hence, perhaps, the peculiar nature of woman in fiction; the astonishing extremes of her beauty and horror; her alternations between heavenly goodness and hellish depravity—for so a lover would see her as his love rose or sank, was prosperous or unhappy. This is not so true of the nineteenth-century novelists, of course. Woman becomes much more various and complicated there. Indeed it was the desire to write about women perhaps that led men by degrees to abandon the poetic drama which, with its violence, could make so little use of them, and to devise the novel as a more fitting receptacle. Even so it remains obvious, even in the writing of Proust,[6] that a man is terribly hampered and partial in his knowledge of women, as a woman in her knowledge of men.

Also, I continued, looking down at the page again, it is becoming evident that women, like men, have other interests besides the perennial interests of domesticity. "Chloe liked Olivia. They shared a laboratory together. . . ." I read on and discovered that these two young women were engaged in mincing liver, which is, it seems, a cure for pernicious anaemia: although one of them was married and had—I think I am right in stating—two small children. Now all that, of course, has had to be left out, and thus the splendid portrait of the fictitious woman is much too simple and much too monotonous. Suppose, for instance, that men were only represented in literature as the lovers of women, and were never the friends of men, soldiers, thinkers, dreamers; how few parts in the plays of Shakespeare could be allotted to them; how literature would suffer! We might perhaps have most of Othello; and a good deal of Antony; but no Caesar, no Brutus, no Hamlet, no Lear, no Jaques[7]—literature would be incredibly impoverished, as indeed literature is impoverished beyond our counting by the doors that have been shut upon women. Married against their will, kept in one room, and to one occupation, how could a dramatist give a full or interesting or truthful account of them? Love was the only possible interpreter. The poet was forced to be passionate or bitter, unless indeed he chose to "hate women," which meant more often than not that he was unattractive to them.

Now if Chloe likes Olivia and they share a laboratory, which of itself will

4. An 1885 novel by George Meredith, who had been a friend of Woolf's father.
5. Jean Racine (1639–1699), French dramatist.
6. Marcel Proust (1871–1922), French novelist, whose multivolume *À la recherche du temps perdu* (1913–27, *Remembrance of Things Past*) Woolf read with great appreciation.
7. All characters in Shakespeare's plays, from *Othello, Antony and Cleopatra, Julius Caesar, Hamlet, King Lear*, and *As You Like It*.

make their friendship more varied and lasting because it will be less personal; if Mary Carmichael knows how to write, and I was beginning to enjoy some quality in her style; if she has a room to herself, of which I am not quite sure; if she has five hundred a year of her own—but that remains to be proved—then I think that something of great importance has happened.

For if Chloe likes Olivia and Mary Carmichael knows how to express it she will light a torch in that vast chamber where nobody has yet been. It is all half lights and profound shadows like those serpentine caves where one goes with a candle peering up and down, not knowing where one is stepping. And I began to read the book again, and read how Chloe watched Olivia put a jar on a shelf and say how it was time to go home to her children. That is a sight that has never been seen since the world began, I exclaimed. And I watched too, very curiously. For I wanted to see how Mary Carmichael set to work to catch those unrecorded gestures, those unsaid or half-said words, which form themselves, no more palpably than the shadows of moths on the ceiling, when women are alone, unlit by the capricious and coloured light of the other sex. She will need to hold her breath, I said, reading on, if she is to do it; for women are so suspicious of any interest that has not some obvious motive behind it, so terribly accustomed to concealment and suppression, that they are off at the flicker of an eye turned observingly in their direction. The only way for you to do it, I thought, addressing Mary Carmichael as if she were there, would be to talk of something else, looking steadily out of the window, and thus note, not with a pencil in a notebook, but in the shortest of shorthand, in words that are hardly syllabled yet, what happens when Olivia—this organism that has been under the shadow of the rock these million years—feels the light fall on it, and sees coming her way a piece of strange food—knowledge, adventure, art. And she reaches out for it, I thought, again raising my eyes from the page, and has to devise some entirely new combination of her resources, so highly developed for other purposes, so as to absorb the new into the old without disturbing the infinitely intricate and elaborate balance of the whole.

* * *

[ANDROGYNY]

But the sight of the two people getting into the taxi and the satisfaction it gave me made me also ask whether there are two sexes in the mind corresponding to the two sexes in the body, and whether they also require to be united in order to get complete satisfaction and happiness. And I went on amateurishly to sketch a plan of the soul so that in each of us two powers preside, one male, one female; and in the man's brain, the man predominates over the woman, and in the woman's brain, the woman predominates over the man. The normal and comfortable state of being is that when the two live in harmony together, spiritually cooperating. If one is a man, still the woman part of the brain must have effect; and a woman also must have intercourse with the man in her. Coleridge[8] perhaps meant this when he said that a great mind is androgynous. It is when this fusion takes place that the mind is fully fertilised and uses all its faculties. Perhaps a mind that is purely

8. SAMUEL TAYLOR COLERIDGE (1772–1834), English Romantic poet and critic; see *Table Talk*, September 1, 1832.

masculine cannot create, any more than a mind that is purely feminine, I thought. But it would be well to test what one meant by man-womanly, and conversely by woman-manly, by pausing and looking at a book or two.

Coleridge certainly did not mean, when he said that a great mind is androgynous, that it is a mind that has any special sympathy with women; a mind that takes up their cause or devotes itself to their interpretation. Perhaps the androgynous mind is less apt to make these distinctions than the single-sexed mind. He meant, perhaps, that the androgynous mind is resonant and porous; that it transmits emotion without impediment; that it is naturally creative, incandescent and undivided. In fact one goes back to Shakespeare's mind as the type of the androgynous, of the man-womanly mind, though it would be impossible to say what Shakespeare thought of women. And if it be true that it is one of the tokens of the fully developed mind that it does not think specially or separately of sex, how much harder it is to attain that condition now than ever before. Here I came to the books by living writers, and there paused and wondered if this fact were not at the root of something that had long puzzled me. No age can ever have been as stridently sex-conscious as our own; those innumerable books by men about women in the British Museum[9] are a proof of it. The Suffrage campaign[1] was no doubt to blame. It must have roused in men an extraordinary desire for self-assertion; it must have made them lay an emphasis upon their own sex and its characteristics which they would not have troubled to think about had they not been challenged. And when one is challenged, even by a few women in black bonnets, one retaliates, if one has never been challenged before, rather excessively. That perhaps accounts for some of the characteristics that I remember to have found here, I thought, taking down a new novel by Mr. A, who is in the prime of life and very well thought of, apparently, by the reviewers. I opened it. Indeed, it was delightful to read a man's writing again. It was so direct, so straightforward after the writing of women. It indicated such freedom of mind, such liberty of person, such confidence in himself. One had a sense of physical well-being in the presence of this well-nourished, well-educated, free mind, which had never been thwarted or opposed, but had had full liberty from birth to stretch itself in whatever way it liked. All this was admirable. But after reading a chapter or two a shadow seemed to lie across the page. It was a straight dark bar, a shadow shaped something like the letter "I." One began dodging this way and that to catch a glimpse of the landscape behind it. Whether that was indeed a tree or a woman walking[2] I was not quite sure. Back one was always hailed to the letter "I." One began to be tired of "I." Not but what this "I" was a most respectable "I"; honest and logical; as hard as a nut, and polished for centuries by good teaching and good feeding. I respect and admire that "I" from the bottom of my heart. But—here I turned a page or two, looking for something or other—the worst of it is that in the shadow of the letter "I" all is shapeless as mist. Is that a tree? No, it is a woman. But . . . she has not a bone in her body, I thought, watching Phoebe, for that was her name, coming across the beach. Then Alan got up and the shadow of Alan at once obliterated Phoebe. For Alan had views and Phoebe was quenched in the flood of his views. And

9. That is, in the Reading Room of the British Museum (in Bloomsbury), where Woolf did her research.

1. The movement to obtain the vote for women succeeded in England in 1918.

2. Possibly an allusion to Mark 8.24: "I see men as trees, walking."

then Alan, I thought, has passions; and here I turned page after page very fast, feeling that the crisis was approaching, and so it was. It took place on the beach under the sun. It was done very openly. It was done very vigorously. Nothing could have been more indecent. But . . . I had said "but" too often.[3] One cannot go on saying "but." One must finish the sentence somehow, I rebuked myself. Shall I finish it, "But—I am bored!" But why was I bored? Partly because of the dominance of the letter "I" and the aridity, which, like the giant beech tree, it casts within its shade. Nothing will grow there. And partly for some more obscure reason. There seemed to be some obstacle, some impediment of Mr. A's mind which blocked the fountain of creative energy and shored it within narrow limits. And remembering the lunch party at Oxbridge, and the cigarette ash and the Manx cat and Tennyson and Christina Rossetti[4] all in a bunch, it seemed possible that the impediment lay there. As he no longer hums under his breath, "There has fallen a splendid tear from the passion-flower at the gate," when Phoebe crosses the beach, and she no longer replies, "My heart is like a singing bird whose nest is in a water'd shoot," when Alan approaches what can he do? Being honest as the day and logical as the sun, there is only one thing he can do. And that he does, to do him justice, over and over (I said, turning the pages) and over again. And that, I added, aware of the awful nature of the confession, seems somehow dull. Shakespeare's indecency uproots a thousand other things in one's mind, and is far from being dull. But Shakespeare does it for pleasure; Mr. A, as the nurses say, does it on purpose. He does it in protest. He is protesting against the equality of the other sex by asserting his own superiority. He is therefore impeded and inhibited and self-conscious as Shakespeare might have been if he too had known Miss Clough and Miss Davies.[5] Doubtless Elizabethan literature would have been very different from what it is if the woman's movement had begun in the sixteenth century and not in the nineteenth.

What, then, it amounts to, if this theory of the two sides of the mind holds good, is that virility has now become self-conscious—men, that is to say, are now writing only with the male side of their brains. It is a mistake for a woman to read them, for she will inevitably look for something that she will not find. It is the power of suggestion that one most misses, I thought, taking Mr. B the critic in my hand and reading, very carefully and very dutifully, his remarks upon the art of poetry. Very able they were, acute and full of learning; but the trouble was, that his feelings no longer communicated; his mind seemed separated into different chambers; not a sound carried from one to the other. Thus, when one takes a sentence of Mr. B into the mind it falls plump to the ground—dead; but when one takes a sentence of Coleridge into the mind, it explodes and gives birth to all kinds of other ideas, and that is the only sort of writing of which one can say that it has the secret of perpetual life.

But whatever the reason may be, it is a fact that one must deplore. For it

3. The first word of *A Room of One's Own* is "But."

4. In the book's first chapter, Woolf discusses the missing tails of Manx cats along with the poems (quoted here) "Maud" (1855) by Alfred, Lord Tennyson (1809–1892), and "A Birthday" (1862), by Christina Rossetti (1830–1894), which represent what men and women, respectively, hummed at garden parties before the war. "Oxbridge": an invented place, blending Oxford and Cambridge Universities.

5. Anne Jemima Clough (1820–1892) and Emily Davies (1830–1921), leaders in the movement to promote women's education. Clough was the first principal of Newnham Hall, the first institution for women at Cambridge University; Davies helped found and was the first mistress of Girton College, the second such institution at Cambridge.

means—here I had come to rows of books by Mr. Galsworthy and Mr. Kipling[6]—that some of the finest works of our greatest living writers fall upon deaf ears. Do what she will a woman cannot find in them that fountain of perpetual life which the critics assure her is there. It is not only that they celebrate male virtues, enforce male values and describe the world of men; it is that the emotion with which these books are permeated is to a woman incomprehensible. It is coming, it is gathering, it is about to burst on one's head, one begins saying long before the end. That picture will fall on old Jolyon's head; he will die of the shock; the old clerk will speak over him two or three obituary words; and all the swans on the Thames will simultaneously burst out singing. But one will rush away before that happens and hide in the gooseberry bushes, for the emotion which is so deep, so subtle, so symbolical to a man moves a woman to wonder. So with Mr. Kipling's officers who turn their backs; and his Sowers who sow the Seed; and his Men who are alone with their Works; and the Flag—one blushes at all these capital letters as if one had been caught eavesdropping at some purely masculine orgy. The fact is that neither Mr. Galsworthy nor Mr. Kipling has a spark of the woman in him. Thus all their qualities seem to a woman, if one may generalise, crude and immature. They lack suggestive power. And when a book lacks suggestive power, however hard it hits the surface of the mind it cannot penetrate within.

And in that restless mood in which one takes books out and puts them back again without looking at them I began to envisage an age to come of pure, of self-assertive virility, such as the letters of professors (take Sir Walter Raleigh's[7] letters, for instance) seem to forebode, and the rulers of Italy have already brought into being. For one can hardly fail to be impressed in Rome by the sense of unmitigated masculinity; and whatever the value of unmitigated masculinity upon the state, one may question the effect of it upon the art of poetry. At any rate, according to the newspapers, there is a certain anxiety about fiction in Italy. There has been a meeting of academicians whose object it is "to develop the Italian novel." "Men famous by birth, or in finance, industry or the Fascist corporations" came together the other day and discussed the matter, and a telegram was sent to the Duce[8] expressing the hope "that the Fascist era would soon give birth to a poet worthy of it." We may all join in that pious hope, but it is doubtful whether poetry can come out of an incubator. Poetry ought to have a mother as well as a father. The Fascist poem, one may fear, will be a horrid little abortion such as one sees in a glass jar in the museum of some county town. Such monsters never live long, it is said; one has never seen a prodigy of that sort cropping grass in a field. Two heads on one body do not make for length of life.

However, the blame for all this, if one is anxious to lay blame, rests no more upon one sex than upon the other. All seducers and reformers are responsible, Lady Bessborough when she lied to Lord Granville; Miss Davies when she told the truth to Mr. Greg.[9] All who have brought about a state of

6. Rudyard Kipling (1865–1936), English poet and novelist. John Galsworthy (1867–1933), English novelist and playwright. Jolyon is a character in his *Forsyte Saga* (1906–22).
7. English essayist and critic (1861–1922), the first professor of English Literature at Oxford; his letters were published in 1926.
8. Benito Mussolini (1883–1945), Italian dictator.
9. Probably the English essayist William Rathbone Greg (1809–1891), who in a text of 1862 asked, "Why Are Women Redundant?" Lady Bessborough (1761–1821) is Henrietta, countess of Bessborough, the lover of Lord Granville Leveson-Gower (1773–1846).

sex-consciousness are to blame, and it is they who drive me, when I want to stretch my faculties on a book, to seek it in that happy age, before Miss Davies and Miss Clough were born, when the writer used both sides of his mind equally. One must turn back to Shakespeare then, for Shakespeare was androgynous; and so was Keats and Sterne and Cowper and Lamb and Coleridge. Shelley perhaps was sexless. Milton and Ben Jonson had a dash too much of the male in them. So had Wordsworth and Tolstoi.[1] In our time Proust was wholly androgynous, if not perhaps a little too much of a woman. But that failing is too rare for one to complain of it, since without some mixture of the kind the intellect seems to predominate and the other faculties of the mind harden and become barren. However, I consoled myself with the reflection that this is perhaps a passing phase; much of what I have said in obedience to my promise to give you the course of my thoughts will seem out of date; much of what flames in my eyes will seem dubious to you who have not yet come of age.

Even so, the very first sentence that I would write here, I said, crossing over to the writing-table and taking up the page headed Women and Fiction, is that it is fatal for any one who writes to think of their sex. It is fatal to be a man or woman pure and simple; one must be woman-manly or man-womanly. It is fatal for a woman to lay the least stress on any grievance; to plead even with justice any cause; in any way to speak consciously as a woman. And fatal is no figure of speech; for anything written with that conscious bias is doomed to death. It ceases to be fertilised. Brilliant and effective, powerful and masterly, as it may appear for a day or two, it must wither at nightfall; it cannot grow in the minds of others. Some collaboration has to take place in the mind between the woman and the man before the act of creation can be accomplished. Some marriage of opposites has to be consummated. The whole of the mind must lie wide open if we are to get the sense that the writer is communicating his experience with perfect fullness. There must be freedom and there must be peace. Not a wheel must grate, not a light glimmer. The curtains must be close drawn. The writer, I thought, once his experience is over, must lie back and let his mind celebrate its nuptials in darkness. He must not look or question what is being done. Rather, he must pluck the petals from a rose or watch the swans float calmly down the river. And I saw again the current which took the boat and the undergraduate and the dead leaves; and the taxi took the man and the woman,[2] I thought, seeing them come together across the street, and the current swept them away, I thought, hearing far off the roar of London's traffic, into that tremendous stream.

* * *

1929

1. All canonical authors, in varying degrees: John Keats (1795–1821), English poet; Laurence Sterne (1713–1768), English novelist; William Cowper (1731–1800), English poet; Charles Lamb (1775–1834), English essayist and critic; PERCY BYSSHE SHELLEY (1792–1822), English poet; John Milton (1608–1674), English poet; Ben Jonson (1572–1637), English poet and playwright; WILLIAM WORDSWORTH (1770–1850), English poet; and Leo Tolstoy (1828–1910), Russian novelist and moral philosopher.

2. Scenes described earlier in the book.

GYÖRGY LUKÁCS
1885–1971

The Marxist philosopher and aesthetician György Lukács played a fundamental role in the early development of Marxist literary and cultural theory. His original analysis of the commodity form in *History and Class Consciousness* (1923) continues to influence Marxist cultural theory, especially in the wide-ranging work of FREDRIC JAMESON. In the area of aesthetics, Lukács remains influential as well, not only because of his sophisticated historical approach to literature, best exemplified in *The Historical Novel* (1937), but also because of his participation in the so-called realism debate of the 1930s, which involved such Marxist luminaries as THEODOR ADORNO, WALTER BENJAMIN, and Bertolt Brecht. On the controversial question of representation in literature, Lukács was a staunch advocate of the realist position. He opposed the experimental aesthetics of high modernism, arguing that its obscure and fragmentary literary forms were symptomatic of the alienation characteristic of life under capitalism. For Lukács, realist literature was a salutary corrective to the disorienting conditions of modernity: at its best it presented an expansive picture (the concrete totality) of society, including the historical forces shaping it. Lukács contended that if realist literature were reenergized in the modern world, it would not only counter the decadence of bourgeois modernist experimentation but also "play the leading part, hitherto always denied it, in the democratic rebirth of nations." To this political and aesthetic cause, Lukács devoted much of his professional life, securing his reputation as realism's most passionate defender in the mid–twentieth century.

Born to an affluent Jewish family in Budapest, György Lukács displayed at an early age a repugnance for his parents' middle-class values. His father, József Lowinger, was the director of the Hungarian General Credit Bank, a leading financial institution of Austria-Hungary; Lowinger changed his last name to Lukács in 1890 to reflect his assimilation to Hungarian culture. Lukács's mother, Adél Wertheimer, derived her ancestry from one of the oldest and wealthiest Jewish families in Eastern Europe. In his youth Lukács embraced the fin de siècle attitudes inspired by the nineteenth-century writers Søren Kierkegaard, FRIEDRICH NIETZSCHE, and Fyodor Dostoyevski, among others. His intellectual interests eventually took him to Germany, where he studied under the sociologists Georg Simmel and Max Weber. Characterized by an anguished Romanticism, this initial phase of Lukács's career is reflected in his two early works, *Soul and Form* (1911) and *The Theory of the Novel* (1916), both published in German under the German version of his name, Georg Lukács. With its typology of forms indebted to G. W. F. HEGEL, the latter work became influential in large part because it interestingly historicized the novel; but Lukács later renounced it for developing a bleak view of the novel as fragmentary and ironic.

The barbarism of World War I, the promise of the Russian Revolution of 1917, and the subsequent demise of the Austro-Hungarian Empire precipitated Lukács's conversion to Marxism in 1918. He was a deeply committed communist, but he often ran into trouble with the Communist Party. He found his *History and Class Consciousness*, for example, censured by the Comintern Congress in Moscow. In this crucial work, which later became an important text for the student uprisings of the 1960s, Lukács addressed the widespread sense of fragmentation and alienation under capitalism, out of which emerged his conception of "reification"—the sense of objectification experienced by individuals who are subordinated to the rationalizing processes of commodity production and reduced to the status of things. He achieved an original synthesis of MARX's theory of commodity fetishism, Weber's concept of rationalization, and Hegel's philosophy of the dialectic. However, the Comintern objected to the unorthodox Hegelian (idealist) emphasis on the consciousness of the proletariat, thus setting the stage for Lukács's "autocriticisms," or public recantations of his own published writings.

From the 1930s onward, Lukács directed considerable effort toward the construction and defense of a Marxist realist aesthetic conceived in materialist terms and opposed to the idealist tradition from FRIEDRICH VON SCHILLER (1759–1805) to Arthur Schopenhauer (1788–1860). However, during Joseph Stalin's consolidation of power in the 1930s and up to the "thaw" of the 1950s, Lukács sometimes employed a coded language to express his unorthodox opinions on realism, because the theory and practice of literature in the Soviet Union had been increasingly regulated by the policy of Proletkult, the Bolshevik Party Central Committee, and the All Russian Association of Proletarian Writers (RAPP)—all of which endorsed the view that writers must serve the interests of the party. The result was a growing intolerance that prompted the exile of such figures as the revolutionary and cultural theorist LEON TROTSKY and the noted Russian formalist ROMAN JAKOBSON. Intellectual constraints were also imposed on BORIS EICHENBAUM, another formalist. At issue was the theory of "socialist realism," which was devised by Maxim Gorky in consultation with Stalin, promulgated by A. A. Zhdanov, and sanctioned by the Congress of Soviet Writers in 1934. In theory, socialist realism insisted that realistic novels must be overtly didactic, serving the interests of socialism and the working class. Trotsky thought such a definition of realism was too narrow, and Lukács himself would have nothing to do with it because he opposed overt didacticism and admired such European novelists as Walter Scott (1771–1832), Honoré de Balzac (1799–1850), and Thomas Mann (1875–1955), classifying them as "critical realists." After Stalin's death in 1953, Lukács was able to work more openly, summing up his views in *Die Eigenart des Ästhetischen* (1963, *The Specificity of the Aesthetic*).

Published originally in the German literary journal *Das Wort* (*The Word*), Lukács's "Realism in the Balance" (1938), our selection, is a classic Marxist essay from the realism debate that critiques German expressionism in particular and modernism in general, promoting instead realist literature. As its introduction indicates, the essay is a response to the major Marxist philosopher Ernst Bloch's defense of expressionism in "Discussing Realism" (1938). Lukács faults expressionism for being content merely to depict immediate sense impressions and fragmentary subjective states, as demonstrated by its practitioners' preference for montage. In "juxtaposing heterogeneous, unrelated pieces of reality torn from their context," expressionism attends only to the uncomprehended surfaces and appearances of things, producing opaque, chaotic, and random works. It thus abandons the goal of mirroring objective reality and its underlying socioeconomic laws, becoming instead a passive depiction of the alienation of people under capitalism. More important, by universalizing alienation (rather than seeing it as an effect of capitalism), the movement provides no basis for progressive politics. Looking at expressionism from the perspective of late 1930s politics, Lukács associated it with the undermining of the socialist revolution in Germany after World War I and the rise of fascism just before World War II.

Modern progressive art, Lukács explains, should not further alienate an already alienated audience: it should work toward revealing the underlying objective totality of the economic system responsible for reducing human beings to things. Realist literature performs just such a task. Demonstrating, like Marx, that the "relations of production of every society form a whole," great realist literature represents reality as it is—namely, as a totality, Lukács's key concept. At its best, the realist novel reflects the totality of social relationships by creating "types" or representative characters. Rather than abandoning plot for a chaotic montage or a disconnected stream of consciousness, it devises prophetic narratives that reveal the historical "tendencies" of development within society. Lukács thus argues that realism and not modernism constitutes the true avant-garde: an avant-garde not of self-identified leaders but of works whose portrayals anticipate where social developments are headed.

For Lukács, realism is distinguished from expressionism and other modernist artistic movements such as symbolism and surrealism, all of which regressively emphasize subjectivity, alienation, and fragmentation. He also distinguishes realism from other ostensibly realistic movements such as naturalism and impressionism, both of which focus on immediate and random sense perceptions. In his opinion, the entire historical progression of literary periods—naturalism, impressionism, symbolism, expressionism, and surrealism—marks an increasing dissolution of the objectivity of classic early-nineteenth-century realism, as represented most notably by Balzac's fiction, which occupies the opposite end of the spectrum from James Joyce's decadent modernist fiction. (The historical basis for this undermining of classic realism is fully developed in Lukács's *Historical Novel*.) Lukács's great hope is that twentieth-century realists like Thomas Mann can stem the tide of this reactionary process by providing the basis for a truly accessible "popular" literature attuned to objectivity and adaptable to leftist political coalitions and popular fronts.

Lukács's advocacy of realism came under immediate and persistent criticism. Perhaps best known is that of Bertolt Brecht, who accuses Lukács of inadvertently lapsing into formalism by privileging the form of an outdated nineteenth-century genre above all others. More severe are the criticisms directed at Lukács's central conceptions of totality and typicality. With the advent of postmodernism, totalizing theories in general have come under attack; for instance, the leading philosopher of the postmodern, JEAN-FRANÇOIS LYOTARD, famously urged his readers to "wage a war on totality" and to critique "grand narratives" that purport to explain everything. In spite of all this, Lukács's work has made important contributions to contemporary debates; his influence is clear in the roles that reification, realism, and periodization play in the work of Fredric Jameson, the most important American theorist of postmodernism.

BIBLIOGRAPHY

The standard edition of Lukács's writings is the German *Georg Lukács Werke* (17 vols., 1926–86). A number of scholarly edited texts are also available in Hungarian. English translations to date are *Soul and Form* (1910; trans. 1974), *The Theory of the Novel* (1916, trans. 1971), *History and Class Consciousness* (1923; trans. 1971), *Lenin: A Study on the Unity of His Thought* (1924; trans. 1971), *The Historical Novel* (1937; trans. 1962), *Studies in European Realism: A Sociological Survey of the Writings of Balzac, Stendhal, Zola, Tolstoy, Gorki, and Others* (1945; trans. 1950), *Goethe and His Age* (1947; trans. 1978), *Essays on Thomas Mann* (1947; trans. 1965), *The Young Hegel: Studies in the Relations between Dialectics and Economics* (1948; trans. 1976), *Essays on Realism* (1948; trans. 1981), *German Realists in the Nineteenth Century* (1951; trans. 1993), *The Destruction of Reason* (1954; trans. 1981), *The Meaning of Contemporary Realism* (1958; trans. 1963), *Conversations with Lukács* (1967; trans. 1975), *Tactics and Ethics: Political Writings, 1919–1929* (1968; trans. 1972), *Solzhenitsyn* (1969; trans. 1971), *Writer and Critic and Other Essays* (trans. 1970), *The Ontology of Social Being* (2 vols., 1976; trans. 1978), *Record of a Life: An Autobiographical Sketch* (1981; trans. 1983), *The Process of Democratization* (trans. 1991), and *In Defense of History and Class Consciousness* (trans. 1999). A sampling of essays is available in *The Lukács Reader*, edited by Arpad Kadarkay (1995). For a detailed biography, see Kadarkay's *Georg Lukács: Life, Thought, and Politics* (1991).

For critical responses to Lukács's involvement in the realism debate, see the essays by Theodor Adorno, Walter Benjamin, Bertolt Brecht, and Ernst Bloch in the often-cited *Aesthetics and Politics*, edited by the *New Left Review* (1977). Also helpful in this regard is Eugene Lunn's *Marxism and Modernism: An Historical Study of Lukács, Brecht, Benjamin, and Adorno* (1982). On Lukács's theory of the novel, see Lucien Goldmann, *Towards a Sociology of the Novel* (1964; trans. 1975), and J. M. Bernstein, *The Philosophy of the Novel: Lukács, Marxism, and the Dialectic of Form* (1984). Fredric Jameson's most developed account of Lukács's work appears in his *Marxism and Form* (1971). Béla Királyfalvi's *Aesthetics of György Lukács* (1975) offers a systematic examination of Lukács's aesthetic theories, while Terry Eagleton's introductory *Marxism and Literary Criticism* (1976) and his *Ideology of the Aesthetic* (1990) present some suggestive critical remarks on Lukács. Andrew Arato and Paul Breines's *The Young Lukács and the Origins of Western Marxism* (1979) and Martin Jay's *Marxism and Totality: The Adventures of a Concept from Lukács to Habermas* (1984) situate Lukács's work within the tradition of Western Marxism. For a survey of contemporary Marxist critics' assessments of Lukács, see the interviews gathered in *Lukács After Communism*, edited by Eva L. Corredor (1997). Bibliographies of Lukács's writing and criticism of it can be found in Peter Murphy's *Writings by and about Georg Lukács: A Bibliography* (1976), François Lapointe's *Georg Lukács and His Critics (1910–1982)* (1983), and Kadarkay's reader and biography mentioned above.

Realism in the Balance[1]

> In its day the revolutionary bourgeoisie conducted a violent struggle in the interests of its own class; it made use of every means at its disposal, including those of imaginative literature. What was it that made the vestiges of chivalry the object of universal ridicule? Cervantes' *Don Quixote*.[2] Don Quixote was the most powerful weapon in the arsenal of the bourgeoisie in its war against feudalism and aristocracy. The revolutionary proletariat could do with at least one little Cervantes (*laughter*) to arm it with a similar weapon. (Laughter and applause.)
>
> Georgi Dimitrov,[3] Speech given during an anti-Fascist evening in the Writers' Club in Moscow.

Anyone intervening at this late stage in the debate on Expressionism in *Das Wort* finds himself faced with certain difficulties.[4] Many voices have been raised in passionate defence of Expressionism. But as soon as we reach the point when it becomes imperative to specify *whom* we are to regard as the exemplary Expressionist writer, or even to include in the category of Expressionism, we find that opinions diverge so sharply that no single name can count on general agreement. One sometimes has the feeling, particularly when reading the most impassioned apologias, that perhaps there was no such thing as an Expressionist writer.

Since our present dispute is concerned not with the evaluation of individual writers but with general literary principles, it is not of paramount importance for us to resolve this problem. Literary history undoubtedly recognizes a trend known as Expressionism, a trend with its poets and its critics. In the discussion which follows I shall confine myself to questions of principle.

1. Translated by Rodney Livingstone; he occasionally inserts the original German words in brackets.
2. Novel (1605–1615) by Miguel de Cervantes (1547–1616).
3. Bulgarian Communist leader (1882–1949).
4. Inspired by Lukács's earlier essay "Expressionism: Its Significance and Decline" (1934), the debate on expressionism in the literary journal *Das Wort* (*The Word*) began in 1937 with an attack on the expressionist poet Gottfried Benn (1886–1956) by the German writer Alfred Kurella (1895–1975), who, following Lukács, argued that the subjective experimental art forms of expressionism were not only irrational but responsible for the rise of fascism in Germany. There followed a series of rejoinders by supporters of expressionism, including Herwarth Walden (1878–1941), editor of a key expressionist journal; Bela Balazs (1884–1949); Gustav von Wangenheim (1895–1975); and, most notably, the German Marxist philosopher Ernst Bloch (1885–1977), whose essay "Discussing Expressionism" (1938) prompted Lukács to write "Realism in the Balance."

1.

First, a preliminary question about the nature of the central issue: is it really a conflict between modern and classical (or even neo-classical) literature, as has been implied by a number of writers who have concentrated their attack on my critical activities? I submit that this way of posing the question is fundamentally wrong. Its implicit assumption is that modern art is identical with the development of specific literary trends leading from Naturalism and Impressionism via Expressionism to Surrealism. In the article by Ernst Bloch and Hanns Eisler in the *Neue Weltbühne*, to which Peter Fischer refers,[5] this theory is formulated in a particularly explicit and apodictic way. When these writers talk of modern art, its representative figures are taken *exclusively* from the ranks of the movements just referred to.

Let us not pass judgement at this stage. Let us rather enquire: can this theory provide an adequate foundation for the history of literature in our age?

At the very least, it must be pointed out that a quite different view is tenable. The development of literature, particularly in capitalist society, and particularly at capitalism's moment of crisis, is extraordinarily complex. Nevertheless, to offer a crude over-simplification, we may still distinguish three main currents in the literature of our age; these currents are not of course entirely distinct but often overlap in the development of individual writers:
1) Openly anti-realist or pseudo-realist literature which is concerned to provide an apologia for, and a defence of, the existing system. Of this group we shall say nothing here.
2) So-called avant-garde literature (we shall come to authentic modern literature in due course) from Naturalism to Surrealism. What is its general thrust? We may briefly anticipate our findings here by saying that its main trend is its growing distance from, and progressive dissolution of, realism.
3) The literature of the major realists of the day. For the most part these writers do not belong to any literary set; they are swimming against the mainstream of literary development, in fact, against the two currents noted above. As a general pointer to the complexion of this contemporary form of realism, we need only mention the names of Gorky, Thomas and Heinrich Mann and Romain Rolland.[6]

In the articles which leap so passionately to the defence of the rights of modern art against the presumptuous claims of the so-called neo-classicists, these leading figures of contemporary literature are not even mentioned. They simply do not exist in the eyes of modernist literature and its chroniclers. In Ernst Bloch's interesting work *Erbschaft dieser Zeit*,[7] a book rich both in information and in ideas, the name of Thomas Mann occurs only once, unless my memory deceives me; the author refers to Mann's (and Wassermann's[8]) 'bourgeois refinement' [*soignierte Bürgerlichkeit*] and with that he dismisses the matter.

5. E. Bloch and H. Eisler, 'Die Kunst zu erben," in *Die Neue Weltbühne*, 1938 [Lukács's note]. Eisler (1898–1962), German composer. Ernst Peter Fischer (1899–1972), German poet, philosopher, and aesthetician.
6. French novelist, playwright, and scholar (1866–1944). Maxim Gorki or Gorky (pseudonym of Aleksey Peshkov, 1868–1936), Russian author, considered the founder of Soviet socialist realism. Thomas Mann (1875–1955), German novelist and Nobel laureate for literature in 1929. Heinrich Mann (1871–1950), German novelist, brother of Thomas .
7. *Heritage of Our Times* (1934).
8. Jakob Wassermann (1873–1934), German novelist.

Views such as these turn the entire discussion on its head. It is high time to put it back on its feet and take up cudgels on behalf of the best modern literature, against its ignorant detractors. So the terms of the debate are not classics versus modernists; discussion must focus instead on the question: which are the progressive trends in the literature of today? It is the fate of realism that hangs in the balance.

2.

One of Ernst Bloch's criticisms of my old essay on Expressionism[9] is that I devoted too much attention to the theoreticians of the movement. Perhaps he will forgive me if I repeat this 'mistake' here and this time make his critical remarks on modern literature the focal point of my analysis. For I do not accept the view that the theoretical descriptions of artistic movements are unimportant—even when they make statements that are theoretically false. It is at such moments that they let the cat out of the bag and reveal the otherwise carefully concealed 'secrets' of the movement. Since, as a theoretician, Bloch is of quite a different stature than Picard and Pinthus[1] were in their day, it is not unreasonable for me to examine his theories in somewhat greater depth.

Bloch directs his attack at my view of 'totality'. (We may leave out of account the extent to which he interprets my position correctly. What is at issue is not whether I am right or whether he has understood me correctly, but the actual problem under discussion.) The principle to be refuted, he believes, is 'the undiluted objective realism which characterized Classicism'. According to Bloch my thought is premissed throughout 'on the idea of a closed and integrated reality . . . Whether such a totality in fact constitutes reality is open to question. If it is, then Expressionist experiments with disruptive and interpolative techniques are but an empty *jeu d'esprit*, as are the more recent experiments with montage and other devices making for discontinuity.'

Bloch regards my insistence on a unified reality as a mere hangover from the systems of classical idealism, and he goes on to formulate his own position as follows: 'What if authentic reality is also discontinuity? Since Lukács operates with a closed, objectivistic conception of reality, when he comes to examine Expressionism, he resolutely sets his face against any attempt on the part of artists to shatter any image of the world, even that of capitalism. Any art which strives to exploit the real fissures in surface inter-relations and to discover the new in their crevices, appears in his eyes merely as a wilful act of destruction. He thereby equates experiments in demolition with a condition of decadence.'

Here we have a coherent theoretical justification of the development of modern art, one which goes right to the heart of the ideological issues at stake. Bloch is absolutely right: a fundamental theoretical discussion of these questions 'would raise all the problems of the dialectical-materialist theory of reflection [*Abbildlehre*].' Needless to say, we cannot embark on such a discussion here, although I personally would greatly welcome the opportu-

9. "Expressionism: Its Significance and Decline" (1934).

1. Kurt Pinthus (1886–1975), German critic, known for editing *Menschheitsdämmerung* (1920, *Dawn of Humanity*), an influential anthology of expressionist poetry. Jacob Picard (1883–1967), German expressionist poet.

nity to do so. In the present debate we are concerned with a much simpler question, namely, does the 'closed integration', the 'totality' of the capitalist system, of bourgeois society, with its unity of economics and ideology, really form an objective whole, independent of consciousness?

Among Marxists—and in his latest book Bloch has stoutly proclaimed his commitment to Marxism—there should be no dispute on this point. Marx[2] says: 'The relations of production of every society form a whole.' We must underscore the word 'every' here, since Bloch's position essentially denies that this 'totality' applies to the capitalism of our age. So although the difference between our views seems to be immediate, formal and non-philosophical, one which revolves instead round a disagreement about the socio-economic interpretation of capitalism, nevertheless, since philosophy is a mental reflection of reality, important philosophical disagreements must be implicit in it.

It goes without saying that our quotation from Marx has to be understood historically—in other words, economic reality as a totality is itself subject to historical change. But these changes consist largely in the way in which all the various aspects of the economy are expanded and intensified, so that the 'totality' becomes ever more closely-knit and substantial. After all, according to Marx, the decisive progressive role of the bourgeoisie in history is to develop the world market, thanks to which the economy of the whole world becomes an objectively unified totality. Primitive economies create the superficial appearance of great unity; primitive-communist villages or towns in the early Middle Ages are obvious examples. But in such a 'unity' the economic unit is linked to its environment, and to human society as a whole, only by a very few threads. Under capitalism, on the other hand, the different strands of the economy achieve a quite unprecedented autonomy, as we can see from the examples of trade and money—an autonomy so extensive that financial crises can arise directly from the circulation of money. As a result of the objective structure of this economic system, the surface of capitalism appears to 'disintegrate' into a series of elements all driven towards independence. Obviously this must be reflected in the consciousness of the men who live in this society, and hence too in the consciousness of poets and thinkers.

Consequently the movement of its individual components towards autonomy is an objective fact of the capitalist economic system. Nevertheless this autonomy constitutes only one part of the overall process. The underlying unity, the totality, all of whose parts are objectively interrelated, manifests itself most strikingly in the fact of crisis. Marx gives the following analysis of the process in which the constituent elements necessarily achieve independence: 'Since they do in fact belong together, the process by means of which the complementary parts become independent must inevitably appear violent and destructive. The phenomenon in which their unity, the unity of discrete objects, makes itself felt, is the phenomenon of crisis. The independence assumed by processes which belong together and complement each other is violently destroyed. The crisis thus makes manifest the unity of processes which had become individually independent.'[3]

These, then, are the fundamental objective components of the 'totality' of

2. KARL MARX (1818–1883), German revolutionary, economist, and philosopher.

3. See *Capital*, vol. 1, p. 209, London 1976 (Penguin/NLR edition) [translator's note].

capitalist society. Every Marxist knows that the basic economic categories of capitalism are always reflected in the minds of men, directly, but always back to front. Applied to our present argument this means that in periods when capitalism functions in a so-called normal manner, and its various processes appear autonomous, people living within capitalist society think and experience it as unitary, whereas in periods of crisis, when the autonomous elements are drawn together into unity, they experience it as disintegration. With the general crisis of the capitalist system, the experience of disintegration becomes firmly entrenched over long periods of time in broad sectors of the population which normally experience the various manifestations of capitalism in a very immediate way.

3.

What has all this to do with literature?

Nothing at all for any theory—like those of Expressionism or Surrealism—which denies that literature has any reference to objective reality. It means a great deal, however, for a Marxist theory of literature. If literature is a particular form by means of which objective reality is reflected, then it becomes of crucial importance for it to grasp that reality as it truly is, and not merely to confine itself to reproducing whatever manifests itself immediately and on the surface. If a writer strives to represent reality as it truly is, i.e. if he is an authentic realist, then the question of totality plays a decisive role, no matter how the writer actually conceives the problem intellectually. Lenin repeatedly insisted on the practical importance of the category of totality: 'In order to know an object thoroughly, it is essential to discover and comprehend all of its aspects, its relationships and its "mediations". We shall never achieve this fully, but *insistence on all-round knowledge* will protect us from errors and inflexibility.'[4]

The literary practice of every true realist demonstrates the importance of the overall objective social context and the 'insistence on all-round knowledge' required to do it justice. The profundity of the great realist, the extent and the endurance of his success, depends in great measure on how clearly he perceives—as a creative writer—the true significance of whatever phenomenon he depicts. This will not prevent him from recognizing, as Bloch imagines, that the surface of social reality may exhibit 'subversive tendencies', which are correspondingly reflected in the minds of men. The motto to my old essay on Expressionism underscores the fact that I was anything but unaware of this factor. That motto, a quotation from Lenin, begins with these words: 'The inessential, the apparent, the surface phenomenon, vanishes more frequently, is less "solid", less "firm" than the "essence".'[5]

However, what is at issue here above all is not the mere recognition that such a factor actually exists in the context of the totality. It is even more important to see it as a factor in this totality, and not magnify it into the sole emotional and intellectual reality. So the crux of the matter is to understand the correct dialectical unity of appearance and essence. What matters is that

4. Lenin, *Collected Works*, vol. 32, p. 94. G.L.'s italics [translator's note]. Vladimir Lenin (1870–1924), leader of the 1917 Russian Revolution and first leader of the new Soviet state. The edition cited is published by Lawrence and Wishart (London).

5. Lenin, *Collected Works*, vol. 38, p. 130 [translator's note].

the slice of life shaped and depicted by the artist and re-experienced by the reader should reveal the relations between appearance and essence without the need for any external commentary. We emphasize the importance of shaping [*gestalten*] this relation, because, unlike Bloch, we do not regard the practice of left-wing Surrealists as an acceptable solution to the problem. We reject their method of 'inserting' [*Einmontierung*] theses into scraps of reality with which they have no organic connection.

By way of illustration, just compare the 'bourgeois refinement' of Thomas Mann with the Surrealism of Joyce.[6] In the minds of the heroes of both writers we find a vivid evocation of the disintegration, the discontinuities, the ruptures and the 'crevices' which Bloch very rightly thinks typical of the state of mind of many people living in the age of imperialism. Bloch's mistake lies merely in the fact that he identifies this state of mind directly and unreservedly with reality itself. He equates the highly distorted image created in this state of mind with the thing itself, instead of objectively unravelling the essence, the origins and the mediations of the distortion by comparing it with reality.

In this way Bloch does as a theorist exactly what the Expressionists and Surrealists do as artists. Let us take a look at Joyce's narrative method. Lest my hostile assessment put the matter in a false light, I shall quote Bloch's own analysis: 'Here, in and even beneath the flowing stream we find a mouth without Ego, drinking, babbling, pouring it out. The language mimes every aspect of this collapse, it is not a fully developed, finished product, let alone normative, but open-ended and confused. The sort of speech with puns and slips of the tongue that you normally find at moments of fatigue, in pauses in the conversation, and in dreamy or slovenly people—it is all here, only completely out of control. The words have become unemployed, they have been expelled from their context of meaning. The language moves along, sometimes a worm cut in pieces, sometimes foreshortened like an optical illusion, while at yet other times, it hangs down into the action like a piece of rigging.'

That is his account. Here is his final evaluation: 'An empty shell and the most fantastic sellout; a random collection of notes on crumpled scraps of paper, gobbledygook, a tangle of slippery eels, fragments of nonsense, and at the same time the attempt to found a scholastic system on chaos; . . . confidence tricks in all shapes and sizes, the jokes of a man who has lost his roots; blind alleys but paths everywhere—no aims but destinations everywhere. Montage[7] can now work wonders; in the old days it was only thoughts that could dwell side by side,[8] but now things can do the same, at least in these floodplains, these fantastic jungles of the void.'

We found it necessary to quote this lengthy passage because of the highly important, even crucial role given to Surrealist montage in Bloch's historical assessment of Expressionism. Earlier on in the book we find him, like all apologists of Expressionism, making a distinction between its genuine and its merely superficial exponents. According to him, the genuine aspirations

6. James Joyce (1882–1941), Irish modernist writer, author of *Ulysses* (1922).
7. The technique of juxtaposing heterogeneous elements removed from their contexts.
8. An allusion to celebrated lines in [FRIEDRICH VON] SCHILLER's *Wallensteins Tod* ([1799, *Wallenstein's Death*] 2.2): "The world is narrow, broad the mind—/Thoughts dwell easily side by side/Things collide violently in space" [translator's note].

of Expressionism live on. He writes: 'But even today there is no artist of great talent around without an Expressionist past, or at least without its highly variegated, highly storm-laden after-effects. The ultimate form of "Expressionism" was created by the so-called Surrealists; just a small group, but once again that is where the avant-garde is, and furthermore, Surrealism is nothing if not montage . . . it is an account of the chaos of reality as actually experienced, with all its caesuras and dismantled structures of the past.' The reader can see here very clearly, in Bloch's advocacy of Expressionism, just what he regards as the literary mainstream of our age. It is no less clear that his exclusion of every realist of importance from that literature is perfectly conscious.

I hope that Thomas Mann will pardon me for making use of him here as a counter-illustration. Let us call to mind his Tonio Kröger, or his Christian Buddenbrook, or the chief characters from *The Magic Mountain*.[9] Let us further suppose that they had been constructed, as Bloch requires, directly in terms of their own consciousness, and not by contrasting that consciousness with a reality independent of them. It is obvious that if we were confronted merely by the stream of associations in their minds, the resulting 'disruption of the surface' of life would be no less complete than in Joyce. We should find just as many 'crevices' as in Joyce. It would be a mistake to protest that these works were produced *before* the crisis of modernity—the objective crisis in Christian Buddenbrook, for example, leads to a more profound spiritual disturbance than in Joyce's heroes. *The Magic Mountain* is contemporary with Expressionism. So if Thomas Mann had contented himself with the direct photographic record of the ideas and scraps of experience of these characters, and with using them to construct a montage, he might easily have produced a portrait as 'artistically progressive' as the Joyce whom Bloch admires so hugely.

Given his modern themes, why does Thomas Mann remain so 'old-fashioned', so 'traditional'; why does he choose not to clamber on to the bandwagon of modernism? Precisely because he is a *true realist*, a term which in this case signifies primarily that, as a creative artist, he knows exactly who Christian Buddenbrook, who Tonio Kröger and who Hans Castorp, Settembrini and Naphta[1] are. He does not have to know it in the abstract way that a social scientist would know it; in that sense he may easily make mistakes, as Balzac, Dickens and Tolstoy[2] did before him. He knows it after the manner of a creative realist: he knows how thoughts and feelings grow out of the life of society and how experiences and emotions are parts of the total complex of reality. As a realist he assigns these parts to their rightful place within the total life context. He shows what area of society they arise from and where they are going to.

So when, for example, Thomas Mann refers to Tonio Kröger as a 'bourgeois who has lost his way', he does not rest content with that: he shows how and why he still is a bourgeois, for all his hostility to the bourgeoisie, his homelessness within bourgeois society, and his exclusion from the life of the bourgeois. Because he does all this, Mann towers as a creative artist and in

9. One of Mann's most celebrated novels (1924). The two characters mentioned are from Mann's novels *Tonio Kröger* (1903) and *Buddenbrooks* (1901).

1. Three characters in *The Magic Mountain*.

2. Leo Tolstoy (1828–1910), Russian novelist. Honoré de Balzac (1799–1850), French novelist. Charles Dickens (1812–1870), English novelist.

his grasp of the nature of society, above all those 'ultra-radicals' who imagine that their anti-bourgeois moods, their—often purely aesthetic—rejection of the stifling nature of petty-bourgeois existence, their contempt for plush armchairs or a pseudo-Renaissance cult in architecture, have transformed them into inexorable foes of bourgeois society.

4.

The modern literary schools of the imperialist era, from Naturalism to Surrealism, which have followed each other in such swift succession, all have one feature in common. They all take reality exactly as it manifests itself to the writer and the characters he creates. The form of this immediate manifestation changes as society changes. These changes, moreover, are both subjective and objective, depending on modifications in the reality of capitalism and also on the ways in which class struggle and changes in class structure produce different reflections on the surface of that reality. It is these changes above all that bring about the swift succession of literary schools together with the embittered internecine quarrels that flare up between them.

But both emotionally and intellectually they all remain frozen in their own immediacy; they fail to pierce the surface to discover the underlying essence, i.e. the real factors that relate their experiences to the hidden social forces that produce them. On the contrary, they all develop their own artistic style—more or less consciously—as a spontaneous expression of their immediate experience.

The hostility of all modern schools towards the very meagre vestiges of the older traditions of literature and literary history at this time culminates in a passionate protest against the arrogance of critics who would like to forbid writers, so it is alleged, to write as and how they wish. In so doing, the advocates of such movements overlook the fact that authentic freedom, i.e. freedom from the reactionary prejudices of the imperialist era (not merely in the sphere of art), cannot possibly be attained through mere spontaneity or by persons unable to break through the confines of their own immediate experience. For as capitalism develops, the continuous production and reproduction of these reactionary prejudices is intensified and accelerated, not to say consciously promoted by the imperialist bourgeoisie. So if we are ever going to be able to understand the way in which reactionary ideas infiltrate our minds, and if we are ever going to achieve a critical distance from such prejudices, this can only be accomplished by hard work, by abandoning and transcending the limits of immediacy, by scrutinizing all subjective experiences and measuring them against social reality. In short it can only be achieved by a deeper probing of the real world.

Artistically, as well as intellectually and politically, the major realists of our age have consistently shown their ability to undertake this arduous task. They have not shirked it in the past, nor do they today. The careers of Romain Rolland and of Thomas and Heinrich Mann are relevant here. Different though their development has been in other respects, this feature is common to them all.

Even though we have emphasized the failure of the various modern literary schools to progress beyond the level of immediate experience, we should not wish it to be thought that we decry the artistic achievements of serious writers from Naturalism to Surrealism. Writing from their own experience, they have often succeeded in developing a consistent and interesting mode of expression, a style of their own, in fact. But when we look at their work in the context of social reality, we see that it never rises above the level of immediacy, either intellectually or artistically.

Hence the art they create remains abstract and one-dimensional. (In this context it is immaterial whether the aesthetic theory espoused by a given school favours 'abstraction' in art or not. Ever since Expressionism the importance attached to abstraction has been consistently on the increase, in theory as well as in practice.) At this point the reader may well believe that he detects a contradiction in our argument: surely immediacy and abstraction are mutually exclusive? However, one of the greatest achievements of the dialectical method—already found in Hegel[3]—was its discovery and demonstration that immediacy and abstraction are closely akin, and, more particularly, that thought which begins in immediacy can only lead to abstraction.

In this context, too, Marx put Hegelian philosophy back on its feet, and in his analysis of economic relationships he repeatedly showed, in concrete terms, just how the kinship between immediacy and abstraction finds expression in the reflection of economic realities. We must confine ourselves to one brief illustration. Marx shows that the relationship between the circulation of money and its agent, mercantile capital, involves the obliteration of all mediations and so represents the most extreme form of abstraction in the entire process of capitalist production. If they are considered as they manifest themselves, i.e. in apparent independence of the overall process, the form they assume is that of the purely automatic, fetishized abstraction: 'money begets money'. This is why the vulgar economists who never advance beyond the immediate epiphenomena of capitalism feel confirmed in their beliefs by the abstract, fetishized world that surrounds them. They feel at home here like fish in water and hence give vent to passionate protests about the 'presumption' of a Marxist critique that requires them to look at the entire process of social reproduction. Their 'profundity, here as everywhere else, consists in perceiving the clouds of dust on the surface and then having the presumption to assert that all this dust is really very important and mysterious', as Marx comments à propos of Adam Müller.[4] It is from considerations such as these that I described Expressionism in my old essay on the subject as an 'abstraction away from reality'.

It goes without saying that without abstraction there can be no art—for otherwise how could anything in art have representative value? But like every movement, abstraction must have a direction, and it is on this that everything depends. Every major realist fashions the material given in his own experience, and in so doing makes use of techniques of abstraction, among others. But his goal is to penetrate the laws governing objective reality and to uncover the deeper, hidden, mediated, not immediately perceptible network of relationships that go to make up society. Since these relationships do not lie on the surface, since the underlying laws only make themselves felt in

3. GEORG WILHELM FRIEDRICH HEGEL (1770–1831), German philosopher.

4. German political philosopher (1779–1829).

very complex ways and are realized only unevenly, as trends, the labour of the realist is extraordinarily arduous, since it has both an artistic and an intellectual dimension. Firstly, he has to discover these relationships intellectually and give them artistic shape. Secondly, although in practice the two processes are indivisible, he must artistically conceal the relationships he has just discovered through the process of abstraction—i.e. he has to transcend the process of abstraction. This twofold labour creates a new immediacy, one that is artistically mediated; in it, even though the surface of life is sufficiently transparent to allow the underlying essence to shine through (something which is not true of immediate experience in real life), it nevertheless manifests itself as immediacy, as life as it actually appears. Moreover, in the works of such writers we observe the whole surface of life in all its essential determinants, and not just a subjectively perceived moment isolated from the totality in an abstract and over-intense manner.

This, then, is the artistic dialectic of appearance and essence. The richer, the more diverse, complex and 'cunning' (Lenin) this dialectic is, the more firmly it grasps hold of the living contradictions of life and society, then the greater and the more profound the realism will be.

In contrast to this, what does it mean to talk of an abstraction away from 'reality'? When the surface of life is only experienced immediately, it remains opaque, fragmentary, chaotic and uncomprehended. Since the objective mediations are more or less consciously ignored or passed over, what lies on the surface is frozen and any attempt to see it from a higher intellectual vantage-point has to be abandoned.

There is no state of inertia in reality. Intellectual and artistic activity must move either towards reality or away from it. It might seem paradoxical to claim that Naturalism has already provided us with an instance of the latter. The milieu theory, a view of inherited characteristics fetishized to the point of mythology, a mode of expression which abstractly pinpointed the immediate externals of life, along with a number of other factors, all those things thwarted any real artistic breakthrough to a living dialectic of appearance and essence. Or, more precisely, it was the absence of such a breakthrough that led to the Naturalist style. The two things were functions of each other.

This is why the photographically and phonographically exact imitations of life which we find in Naturalism could never come alive; this is why they remained static and devoid of inner tension. This is why the plays and novels of Naturalism seem to be almost interchangeable—for all their apparent diversity in externals. (This would be the place to discuss one of the major artistic tragedies of our time: the reasons why Gerhart Hauptmann[5] failed to become a great realist writer after such dazzling beginnings. But we have no space to explore this here. We would merely observe in passing that Naturalism inhibited rather than stimulated the development of the author of *The Weavers* and *The Beaver Coat*, and that even when he left Naturalism behind him he was still unable to discard its ideological assumptions.)

The artistic limitations of Naturalism quickly became obvious. But they were never subjected to fundamental criticism. Instead, the preferred method was always to confront one abstract form with another, apparently

5. German dramatist, poet, and novelist (1862–1946), the Nobel laureate for literature in 1912, known for founding German naturalism. *The Weavers* (1892), a tragic play, is considered his most successful work; *The Beaver Coat* (1893), a comedy, is less well-known.

contrary, but no less abstract form. It is symptomatic of the entire process that each movement in the past confined its attention entirely to the movement immediately preceding it; thus Impressionism concerned itself exclusively with Naturalism, and so on. Hence neither theory nor practice ever advanced beyond the stage of abstract confrontation. This remains true right up to the present discussion. Rudolf Leonhard,[6] for example, argues the historical inevitability of Expressionism in just this way: 'One of the foundations of Expressionism was the antagonism felt towards an Impressionism which had become unbearable, even impossible.' He develops this idea quite logically, but fails to say anything about the other foundations. It looks as if Expressionism were utterly opposed to, and incompatible with, the literary trends that preceded it. After all, what Expressionism emphasizes is its focus on essences; this is what Leonhard refers to as the 'non-nihilistic' feature of Expressionism.

But these essences are not the objective essence of reality, of the total process. They are purely subjective. I will refrain from quoting the old and now discredited theoreticians of Expressionism. But Ernst Bloch himself, when he comes to distinguish the true Expressionism from the false, puts the emphasis on subjectivity: 'In its original form Expressionism meant the shattering of images, it meant breaking up the surface from an original, i.e. subjective, perspective, one which wrenched things apart and dislocated them.'

This very definition made it inevitable that essences had to be torn from their context in a conscious, stylized and abstract way, and each essence taken in isolation. When followed through logically, Expressionism repudiated any connection with reality and declared a subjectivist war on reality and all its works. I would not wish to intervene here in the debate about whether, and to what extent, Gottfried Benn[7] can be thought of as a typical Expressionist. But I find that the sense of life which Bloch describes so picturesquely and fascinatingly in his account of Expressionism and Surrealism, finds its most direct, candid and vivid expression in Benn's book *Kunst und Macht*:[8] 'Between 1910 and 1925 the anti-naturalist style reigned supreme in Europe to the exclusion of almost everything else. For the fact is that there was no such thing as reality, at best there were only travesties of reality. Reality—that was a capitalist concept. . . . Mind [*Geist*] had no reality.' Wangenheim,[9] too in his highly eclectic apologia for Expressionism, arrives at similar conclusions, although by a less analytical, more descriptive route: 'Successful works could not be expected in any quantity, since there was no reality corresponding to it [i.e. to Expressionism.—G.L.] . . . Many an Expressionist longed to discover a new world by abandoning terra firma, leaping into the air and clinging to the clouds.'

We can find a perfectly clear and unambiguous formulation of this situation and its implications in Heinrich Vogeler.[1] His accurate assessment of abstraction in Expressionism leads him to the correct conclusion: 'It [i.e. Expressionism—G.L.] was the Dance of Death of bourgeois art . . . The Expressionists thought they were conveying the "essence of things" [*Wesen*], whereas in fact they revealed their decomposition [*Verwesung*].'

6. German socialist, pacifist, writer, and poet associated with expressionism (1889–1953).
7. German expressionist poet and essayist.
8. *Art and Power* (1934).
9. German author, actor, and stage producer.
1. German painter (1872–1942).

One inescapable consequence of an attitude alien or hostile to reality makes itself increasingly evident in the art of the 'avant-garde': a growing paucity of content, extended to a point where absence of content or hostility towards it is upheld on principle. Once again Gottfried Benn has put the situation in a nutshell: 'The very concept of content, too, has become problematic. Content—what's the point of it nowadays, it's all washed up, worn out, mere sham—self-indulgence of emotions, rigidity of feelings, clusters of discredited elements, lies, amorphous shapes. . . . '

As the reader can see for himself, this account closely parallels Bloch's own description of the world of Expressionism and Surrealism. Needless to say, their respective analyses lead Bloch and Benn to entirely opposite conclusions. At a number of points in his book, Bloch clearly sees the problematic nature of modern art as something arising from the attitude he himself describes: 'Hence major writers no longer make their home in their own subject-matter, for all substances crumble at their touch. The dominant world no longer presents them with a coherent image to depict, or to take as the starting-point for their imagination. All that remains is emptiness, shards for them to piece together.' Bloch goes on to explore the revolutionary period of the bourgeoisie down to Goethe.[2] He then continues: 'Goethe was succeeded not by a further development of the novel of education, but by the French novel of disillusionment, so that today in the perfected non-world, anti-world or ruined world of the grand bourgeois vacuum, "reconciliation" is neither a danger nor an option for the writer. Only a dialectical approach [?!—G.L.] is possible here: either as material for a dialectical montage or as an experiment in it. In the hands of Joyce even the world of Odysseus[3] became a kaleidoscopic gallery of the disintegrating and disintegrated world of today in microscopic cross-section—no more than a cross-section, because people today lack something, namely the most important thing of all . . .'

We have no desire to quibble with Bloch over trifles, such as his purely idiosyncratic use of the word 'dialectics', or the mistaken logic which allows him to suggest that the novel of disillusionment follows directly upon Goethe. (My early work, *The Theory of the Novel,*[4] is partly to blame for Bloch's *non-sequitur* here.) We are concerned with more vital issues. In particular, with the fact that Bloch—although his evaluation is the reverse of ours—expresses the notion that the subject-matter and the composition of works of literature depend on man's relationship to objective reality. So far so good. But when Bloch comes to demonstrate the historical legitimacy of Expressionism and Surrealism, he ceases to concern himself with the objective relations between society and the active men of our time, relations which, as we can see from *Jean Christophe,*[5] even permit a novel of education to be written. Instead, taking the isolated state of mind of a specific class of intellectuals as his starting-point, he constructs a sort of home-made model of the contemporary world, which logically enough appears to him as a 'non-world'—a conception which, regrettably enough, turns out to be very similar

2. Johann Wolfgang von Goethe (1749–1832), German poet, novelist, and dramatist.
3. That is, the adaptation of Homer's *Odyssey* (ca. 8th c. B.C.E.) in Joyce's *Ulysses*.
4. A pre-Marxist work (written in 1914 and 1915) that Lukács renounced after 1918 when he became a member of the Communist Party.
5. The major work of Romain Rolland, a novel in 10 volumes [1904–12] whose theme is Franco-German relations as reflected in the life of a German musician [translator's note].

to that of Benn. For writers who adopt this kind of stance towards reality there obviously cannot be any action, structure, content or composition in the 'traditional sense'. For people who experience the world like this it is in fact perfectly true that Expressionism and Surrealism are the only modes of self-expression still available. This philosophical justification of Expressionism and Surrealism suffers 'merely' from the fact that Bloch fails to make reality his touchstone and instead uncritically takes over the Expressionist and Surrealist attitude towards reality, and translates it into his own richly imaginative language.

Despite my sharp disagreement with all of Bloch's judgements, I find his formulation of certain facts both correct and valuable. In particular, he is the most consistent of all defenders of modernism in his demonstration that Expressionism necessarily leads to Surrealism. In this context he also deserves praise for having recognized that montage is the inevitable mode of expression in this phase of development. Moreover, his achievement here is all the greater because he shows that montage is important not only in modernist art, but also in the bourgeois philosophy of our time.

However, one consequence of this is that he brings out the anti-realistic one-dimensionality of the entire trend much more starkly than other theoreticians who think along these lines. This one-dimensionality—about which, incidentally, Bloch has nothing to say—was already a feature of Naturalism. In contrast to the Naturalist, the artistic 'refinement' introduced by Impressionism 'purifies' art even more completely of the complex mediations, the tortuous paths of objective reality, and the objective dialectics of Being and Consciousness. The symbolist movement is clearly and consciously one-dimensional from the outset, for the gulf between the sensuous incarnation of a symbol and its symbolic meaning arises from the narrow, single-tracked process of subjective association which yokes them together.

Montage represents the pinnacle of this movement and for this reason we are grateful to Bloch for his decision to set it so firmly in the centre of modernist literature and thought. In its original form, as photomontage, it is capable of striking effects, and on occasion it can even become a powerful political weapon. Such effects arise from its technique of juxtaposing heterogeneous, unrelated pieces of reality torn from their context. A good photomontage has the same sort of effect as a good joke. However, as soon as this one-dimensional technique—however legitimate and successful it may be in a joke—claims to give shape to reality (even when this reality is viewed as unreal), to a world of relationships (even when these relationships are held to be specious), or of totality (even when this totality is regarded as chaos), then the final effect must be one of profound monotony. The details may be dazzlingly colourful in their diversity, but the whole will never be more than an unrelieved grey on grey. After all, a puddle can never be more than dirty water, even though it may contain rainbow tints.

This monotony proceeds inexorably from the decision to abandon any attempt to mirror objective reality, to give up the artistic struggle to shape the highly complex mediations in all their unity and diversity and to synthesize them as characters in a work of literature. For this approach permits no creative composition, no rise and fall, no growth from within to emerge from the true nature of the subject-matter.

Whenever these artistic trends are dismissed as decadent, there is a cry of indignation against 'pedantic hectoring by eclectic academics'. Perhaps I shall be permitted, therefore, to appeal to Friedrich Nietzsche,[6] an expert on decadence whom my opponents hold in high regard in other matters too: 'What is the mark of every form of literary decadence?' he enquires. He replies: 'It is that life no longer dwells in the totality. The word becomes sovereign and escapes from the confines of the sentence; the sentence encroaches on the page, obscuring its meaning; the page gains in vitality at the cost of the whole—the whole ceases to be a whole. But that is the equation of every decadent style: always the same anarchy of the atoms, disintegration of the will. . . . Life, the same vitality, the vibrance and exuberance of life is compressed into the most minute structures, while the rest is impoverished. Paralysis, misery, petrifaction or hostility and chaos everywhere: in either case the consequences are the more striking, the higher one rises in the hierarchy of organizations. The whole as such no longer lives at all; it is composite, artificial, a piece of cerebration, an artefact.'[7] This passage from Nietzsche is just as truthful an account of the artistic implications of these literary trends as that of Bloch or Benn. I would invite Herwarth Walden,[8] who dismisses every critical interpretation of Expressionism as a vulgarization and who regards every example used to illustrate the theory and practice of Expressionism as an instance of 'vulgar-Expressionism' which proves nothing, to comment on the following adaptation of Nietzsche's theory of decadence to the theory of literary language in general: 'Why should only the sentence be comprehensible and not the word? . . . Since the poets like to dominate, they go ahead and make sentences, ignoring the rights of words. But it is the word that rules. The word shatters the sentence and the work of art is a mosaic. Only words can bind. Sentences are always just picked up out of nowhere.' This 'vulgar-Expressionist' theory of language comes in fact from Herwarth Walden himself.

It goes without saying that such principles are never applied with absolute consistency, even by Joyce. For 100 per cent chaos can only exist in the minds of the deranged, in the same way that Schopenhauer[9] had already observed that a 100 per cent solipsism is only to be found in a lunatic asylum. But since chaos constitutes the intellectual cornerstone of modernist art, any cohesive principles it contains must stem from a subject-matter alien to it. Hence the superimposed commentaries, the theory of simultaneity,[1] and so on. But none of this can be any more than a surrogate, it can only intensify the one-dimensionality, of this form of art.

5.

The emergence of all these literary schools can be explained in terms of the economy, the social structure and the class struggles of the age of imperi-

6. German philosopher (1844–1900; see above).
7. The words significantly omitted by Lukács after "disintegration of the will" are "freedom of the individual, in oral terms—generalized into a political theory: 'equal rights for all.' " Nietzsche, *Der Fall Wagner* [1888, *The Case of Wagner*] [translator's note].
8. German critic and editor of *Der Sturm* (1910–23), a prominent expressionist journal.
9. Arthur Schopenhauer (1788–1860), German philosopher.

1. Theory developed by Robert Delaunay [1885–1941], who together with [Wassily] Kandinsky [1866–1944] was one of the pioneers of abstraction in art. In his great series of "Window" paintings starting in 1912, he sought to put it into practice. Taking the transparent interpenetrating colours of [Paul] Cézanne's [1839–1906] later period, he fused them with the forms of analytical Cubism, and claimed that the result, a simultaneous impact of two or more colours, gave the picture a dynamic force [translator's note].

alism. So Rudolf Leonhard is absolutely right when he claims that Expressionism is a necessary historical phenomenon. But it is at best a half-truth when he goes on to assert, echoing Hegel's celebrated dictum, that 'Expressionism was real; so if it was real it was rational.' Even in Hegel the 'rationality of history' was never as straightforward as this, although he occasionally contrived to smuggle an apologia for the actual into his concept of reason. For a Marxist, 'rationality' (historical necessity) is unquestionably a more complex business. For Marxism the acknowledgment of a historical necessity neither implies a justification of what actually exists (not even during the period when it exists), nor does it express a fatalistic belief in the necessity of historical events. Once again we can illustrate this best with an example from economics. There can be no doubt that primitive accumulation, the separation of the small producers from their means of production, the creation of the proletariat, was—with all its inhumanities—a historical necessity. Nevertheless, no Marxist would dream of glorifying the English bourgeoisie of the period as the embodiment of the principle of reason in Hegel's sense. Even less would it occur to a Marxist to see thereby any fatalistic necessity in the development from capitalism to socialism. Marx repeatedly protested against the way in which people fatalistically insisted that the only possible development for the Russia of his day was from primitive accumulation to capitalism. Today, in view of the fact that socialism has been established in the Soviet Union, the idea that undeveloped countries can only achieve socialism via the route of primitive accumulation and capitalism is a recipe for counter-revolution. So if we concur with Leonhard, and agree that the emergence of Expressionism was historically necessary, this is not to say that we find it artistically valid, i.e. that it is a necessary constituent of the art of the future.

For this reason we must demur when Leonhard discerns in Expressionism 'the definition of man and the consolidation of things as a stepping-stone towards a new realism'. Bloch is absolutely in the right here when, unlike Leonhard, he looks to Surrealism and the dominance of montage as the necessary and logical heir to Expressionism. Our dear old Wangenheim inevitably arrives at completely eclectic conclusions when he tries to use the debate on Expressionism for his own purposes, i.e. to salvage and preserve the formalistic tendencies of his early work—tendencies which so often inhibited and even suppressed his native realism—by bringing them under the umbrella of a broad and undogmatic conception of realism. His aim in defending Expressionism is to rescue for socialist realism[2] a priceless heritage of permanent value. He attempts to defend his position in this way: 'Fundamentally, the theatre of Expressionism, even when its effects were powerful, reflected a world in tatters. The theatre of socialist realism reflects uniformity amidst all the diversity of its forms.' Is this why Expressionism has to become an essential component of socialist realism? Wangenheim has not got a single aesthetic or logical argument in reply, merely a biographical one: a reluctance to jettison his own earlier formalism.

Taking as his starting-point the historical assessment of Expressionism clearly stated in my old essay, Bloch goes on to make the following criticism

2. The Soviet-approved artistic and literary doctrine developed by Maxim Gorky, A. A. Zhdanov (1896–1948), and Joseph Stalin (1879–1953); officially adopted in 1934, it requires the optimistic depiction of socialism and the clear presentation of party doctrine, using conventional literary techniques.

of me: 'The result is that there can be no such thing as an avant-garde within late capitalist society; anticipatory movements in the superstructure[3] are disqualified from possessing any truth.' This accusation arises from the circumstance that Bloch regards the road that leads to Surrealism and montage as the only one open to modern art. If the role of the avant-garde is disputed, the inescapable conclusion in his eyes is that any ideological anticipation of social tendencies must be called in question.

But this is quite simply untrue. Marxism has always recognized the anticipatory function of ideology. To remain within the sphere of literature, we need only remind ourselves of what Paul Lafargue[4] has to say about Marx's evaluation of Balzac: 'Balzac was not just the chronicler of his own society, he was also the creator of prophetic figures who were still embryonic under Louis Philippe and who only emerged fully grown after his death, under Napoleon III.' But is this Marxian view still valid in the present? Of course it is. Such 'prophetic figures', however, are to be found exclusively in the works of the important realists. In the novels, stories and plays of Maxim Gorky such figures abound. Anyone who has been following recent events in the Soviet Union attentively and dispassionately will have realized that in his *Karamora*, his *Klim Samgin*, his *Dostigayev*,[5] etc., Gorky has created a series of typical figures which have only now revealed their real nature and who were 'prophetic' anticipations in Marx's sense. We might point with equal justice to the earlier works of Heinrich Mann, novels such as *Der Untertan* and *Professor Unrat*.[6] Who could deny that a large number of the repellent, mean and bestial features of the German bourgeoisie, and of a petty bourgeoisie seduced by demagogues, were 'prophetically' portrayed here and that they only blossomed completely later under Fascism? Nor should we overlook the character of Henri IV in this context.[7] On the one hand, he is a historically authentic figure, true to life; on the other hand he anticipates those humanist qualities which will only emerge fully in the struggles leading to the defeat of Fascism, in the fighters of the anti-Fascist Front.

Let us consider a counter-illustration, likewise from our own time. The ideological struggle against war was one of the principal themes of the best Expressionists. But what did they do or say to anticipate the new imperialist war raging all around us and threatening to engulf the whole civilized world? I hardly imagine that anyone today will deny that these works are completely obsolete and irrelevant to the problems of the present. On the other hand the realist writer Arnold Zweig[8] anticipated a whole series of essential features of the new war in his novels *Sergeant Grischa* and *Education before Verdun*. What he did there was to depict the relationship between the war

3. A term from Marxist social theory that refers to the realm of culture and ideology built atop society's socioeconomic base. "As in the base, so in the superstructure" is a Marxist rule of thumb.
4. Son-in-law of Karl Marx (1842–1911), founder in 1882 of the French Marxist Party. Louis Philippe (1773–1850) was France's constitutional monarch (1830–48); Louis-Napoléon (1808–1873) was elected president in 1848 and then became emperor (1850–70).
5. Varied works by Gorky: "Karamora" (1923) is a short story, *The Life of Klim Samgin* (1927–31) a multivolume novel, and *Dostigayev and Others* (1934) a play.
6. Translated into English as *Man of Straw* [1918] and *The Blue Angel* [1904] respectively [translator's note].
7. The eponymous hero of two novels Heinrich Mann published in the 1930s: *Die Jugend des Königs Henri Quatre* [1935, *Young Henry of Navarre*] and *Die Vollenkung des Königs Henri Quatre* [1938, *Henry, King of France*] [translator's note].
8. German Jewish writer (1887–1968); the novels mentioned were published in 1927 and 1935, respectively.

at the front and what went on behind the lines, and to show how the war represented the individual and social continuation and intensification of 'normal' capitalist barbarity.

There is nothing mysterious or paradoxical about any of this—it is the very essence of all authentic realism of any importance. Since such realism must be concerned with the creation of types (this has always been the case, from *Don Quixote* down to *Oblomov*[9] and the realists of our own time), the realist must seek out the lasting features in people, in their relations with each other and in the situations in which they have to act; he must focus on those elements which endure over long periods and which constitute the objective human tendencies of society and indeed of mankind as a whole.

Such writers form the authentic ideological avant-garde since they depict the vital, but not immediately obvious forces at work in objective reality. They do so with such profundity and truth that the products of their imagination receive confirmation from subsequent events—not merely in the simple sense in which a successful photograph mirrors the original, but because they express the wealth and diversity of reality, reflecting forces as yet submerged beneath the surface, which only blossom forth visibly to all at a later stage. Great realism, therefore, does not portray an immediately obvious aspect of reality but one which is permanent and objectively more significant, namely man in the whole range of his relations to the real world, above all those which outlast mere fashion. Over and above that, it captures tendencies of development that only exist incipiently and so have not yet had the opportunity to unfold their entire human and social potential. To discern and give shape to such underground trends is the great historical mission of the true literary avant-garde. Whether a writer really belongs to the ranks of the avant-garde is something that only history can reveal, for only after the passage of time will it become apparent whether he has perceived significant qualities, trends, and the social functions of individual human types, and has given them effective and lasting form. After what has been said already, I hope that no further argument is required to prove that only the major realists are capable of forming a genuine avant-garde.

So what really matters is not the subjective belief, however sincere, that one belongs to the avant-garde and is eager to march in the forefront of literary developments. Nor is it essential to have been the first to discover some technical innovation, however dazzling. What counts is the social and human content of the avant-garde, the breadth, the profundity and the truth of the ideas that have been 'prophetically' anticipated.

In short, what is at issue here is not whether or not we deny the possibility of anticipatory movements in the superstructure. The vital questions are: *what* was anticipated, in what manner and by whom?

We have already given a number of illustrations, and we could easily multiply them, to show what the major realists of our time have anticipated in their art, by their creation of types. So let us now turn the question round and enquire what Expressionism anticipated? The only answer we can possibly receive, even from Bloch, is: Surrealism, i.e. yet another literary school whose fundamental failure to anticipate social trends in its art has emerged with crystal clarity, and nowhere more clearly than from the description of

9. An 1859 novel by Ivan Goncharov, a Russian writer noted for illuminating class conditions in Russia.

it given by its greatest admirers. Modernism has not, nor has it ever had, anything to do with the creation of 'prophetic figures' or with the genuine anticipation of future developments.

If we have been successful in clarifying the criterion by which the literary avant-garde is to be distinguished, then it is no great problem to answer certain concrete questions. Who in our literature belongs to the avant-garde? 'Prophetic' writers of the stamp of Gorky, or writers like the late Hermann Bahr[1] who, like a drum-major, marched proudly at the head of every new movement from Naturalism to Surrealism, and then promptly dismissed each phase a year before it went out of fashion? Granted, Hermann Bahr is a caricature, and nothing could be further from my mind than to put him on the same footing as the sincere defenders of Expressionism. But he is the caricature of something real, namely of a formalist modernism, bereft of content, cut off from the mainstream of society.

It is an old truth of Marxism that every human activity should be judged according to its objective meaning in the total context, and not according to what the agent believes the importance of his activity to be. So, on the one hand, it is not essential to be a conscious 'modernist' at all costs (Balzac, we recall, was a royalist); and, on the other hand, even the most passionate determination, the most intense sense of conviction that one has revolutionized art and created something 'radically new', will not suffice to turn a writer into someone who can truly anticipate future trends, if determination and conviction are his sole qualifications.

6.

This ancient truth can also be expressed as a commonplace: the road to hell is paved with good intentions. The validity of this proverb may on occasion appear with the force of a home-truth to anyone who takes his own development seriously and is therefore prepared to criticize himself objectively and without pulling any punches. I am quite willing to start with myself. In the winter of 1914–15: subjectively, a passionate protest against the War, its futility and inhumanity, its destruction of culture and civilization. A general mood that was pessimistic to the point of despair. The contemporary world of capitalism appeared to be the consummation of Fichte's[2] 'age of absolute sinfulness'. My subjective determination was a protest of a progressive sort. The objective product, *The Theory of the Novel*, was a reactionary work in every respect, full of idealistic mysticism and false in all its assessments of the historical process. Then 1922: a mood of excitement, full of revolutionary impatience. I can still hear the bullets of the Red War against the imperialists whistling around my head, the excitement of being an outlaw in Hungary still reverberates within me.[3] Everything in me rebelled against the notion that the first great revolutionary wave was past and that the resolution of the Communist vanguard was insufficient to bring about the overthrow of capitalism. Thus the subjective foundation was revolutionary

1. Austrian novelist, critic, and playwright (1863–1934).
2. Johann Gottlieb Fichte (1762–1814), German philosopher. The quoted phrase is from *Characteristics of the Present Age* (1806), a work on the philosophy of history.
3. After serving in the short-lived Hungarian Soviet Republic in 1919, Lukács was exiled to Vienna; there he worked for the emigré Hungarian Communist Party until 1929, when he dropped out of active politics.

impatience. The objective product was *History and Class Consciousness*[4]—which was reactionary because of its idealism, because of its faulty grasp of the theory of reflection and because of its denial of a dialectics in nature. It goes without saying that I am not alone in having had such experiences at this time. On the contrary, it also happened to countless others. The opinion expressed in my old essay on Expressionism which has aroused so many dissenting voices, namely the assertion that ideologically Expressionism was closely related to the Independent Socialists,[5] is based on the aforementioned ancient truth.

In our debate on Expressionism, revolution (Expressionism) and Noske[6] have been put in opposing camps—in the good old Expressionist manner. But could Noske have managed to emerge the victor without the Independent Socialists, without their vacillation and hesitation, which prevented the Workers' Councils from seizing power while tolerating the organization and arming of reactionary forces? The Independent Socialists were, in party terms, the organized expression of the fact that even those German workers who were radical at the level of their feelings, were not yet equipped ideologically for revolution. The Spartacus League was too slow in detaching itself from the Independent Socialists and it did not criticize them incisively enough; both failures are an important index of the weakness and backwardness of the subjective side of the German revolution, the very factors that Lenin singled out right from the start in his critique of the Spartacus League.

Of course, the whole situation was anything but straightforward. In my original essay, for instance, I drew a very sharp distinction between leaders and masses within the Independent Socialists. The masses were instinctively revolutionary. They showed that they were also objectively revolutionary by going on strike in munitions factories, by undermining efforts at the front and by a revolutionary enthusiasm which culminated in the January strike. For all that, they remained confused and hesitant; they let themselves be ensnared by the demagogy of their leaders. The latter were in part consciously counter-revolutionary (Kautsky, Bernstein and Hilferding)[7] and worked objectively and expressly to preserve bourgeois rule, in collaboration with the old SPD leadership. Other leaders were subjectively sincere; but when it came to the crisis, they were unable to offer effective resistance to this sabotage of the revolution. Notwithstanding their sincerity and their reluctance, they slipped into the wake of the right-wing leadership until their misgivings finally led to a split within the Independent Socialists and so to their destruction. The really revolutionary elements in the Independent Socialist Party were those who, after Halle,[8] pressed for the Party's dissolution and the repudiation of its ideology.

What then of the Expressionists? They were ideologues. They stood

4. This 1923 work remains Lukács's most influential.

5. The Independent Social Democratic Party of Germany (USPD), one of several socialist parties (the Spartacus League was another) that emerged in opposition to the Social Democratic Party of Germany (SPD) which decided to collaborate with the bourgeois German government for the duration of World War I. Lukács's point is that in a time of ideological confusion, the expressionists—despite being socialists opposed to the war—played into the hands of the SPD with their antirealistic artworks.

6. Gustav Noske (1868–1946), right-wing leader of SPD; known as the "bloodhound of the revolution" for his military efforts to suppress the socialist revolution in Germany.

7. All three—Karl Kautsky (1854–1938), Eduard Bernstein (1850–1932), and Rudolf Hilferding (1877–1941)—were members of the SPD; Kautsky had been a founder of the USPD.

8. At its Congress in Halle in 1920, the USPD voted by a majority to merge with the KPD [Communist Democratic Party] [translator's note].

between leaders and masses. For the most part their convictions were sincerely held, though they were also mostly very immature and confused. They were deeply affected by the same uncertainties to which the immature revolutionary masses were also subject. In addition they were profoundly influenced by every conceivable reactionary prejudice of the age, and this made them more than susceptible to the widest possible range of anti-revolutionary slogans—abstract pacifism, ideology of non-violence, abstract critiques of the bourgeoisie, or all sorts of crazy anarchist notions. As ideologists, they stabilized both intellectually and artistically what was essentially a merely transitional ideological phase. From a revolutionary point of view, this phase was much more retrograde in many respects than the one in which the vacillating masses of Independent Socialists supporters found themselves. But the revolutionary significance of such phases of ideological transition lies precisely in their fluidity, in their forward movement, in the fact that they do not yield a crystallization. In this case stabilization meant that the Expressionists and those who were influenced by them were prevented from making further progress of a revolutionary kind. This negative effect, typical of every attempt to systematize ideological states of flux, received an especially reactionary colouring in the case of the Expressionists: firstly, because of the highflown pretensions to leadership, the sense of mission, which led them to proclaim eternal truths, particularly during the revolutionary years; secondly, because of the specifically anti-realist bias in Expressionism, which meant that they had no firm artistic hold on reality which might have corrected or neutralized their misconceptions. As we have seen, Expressionism insisted on the primacy of immediacy, and by conferring a pseudo-profundity and pseudo-perfection on immediate experience both in art and thought, it intensified the dangers which inevitably accompany all such attempts to stabilize an essentially transitional ideology.

Thus, to the extent that Expressionism really had any ideological influence, its effect was to discourage rather than to promote the process of revolutionary clarification among its followers. Here, too, there is a parallel with the ideology of the Independent Socialists. It is no coincidence that both came to grief on the same reality. It is an over-simplification for the Expressionists to claim that Expressionism was destroyed by Noske's victory. Expressionism collapsed, on the one hand, with the passing of the first wave of revolution, for the failure of which the ideology of the Independent Socialists must carry a heavy burden of responsibility. On the other hand, it suffered a loss of prestige from the growing clarity of the revolutionary consciousness of the masses who were beginning to advance with increasing confidence beyond the revolutionary catchwords from which they had started.

But Expressionism was not dethroned by the defeat of the first wave of revolution in Germany alone. The consolidation of the victory of the proletariat in the Soviet Union played an equally important role. As the proletariat gained a firmer control of the situation, as Socialism began to permeate more and more aspects of the Soviet economy, and as the cultural revolution gained wider and wider acceptance among the masses of the workers, so the art of the 'avant-garde' in the Soviet Union found itself gradually but inexorably forced back on to the defensive by an increasingly confident school of realism. So in the last analysis the defeat of Expressionism was a product of the maturity of the revolutionary masses. The careers of Soviet poets like Mayakovsky, or of Germans such as Becher,[9] make it clear that this is where the true reasons for the demise of Expressionism have to be sought and found.

7.

Is our discussion purely literary? I think not. I do not believe that any conflict between literary trends and their theoretical justification would have had such reverberations or provoked such discussion were it not for the fact that, in its ultimate consequences, it was felt to involve a political problem that concerns us all and influences us all in equal measure: the problem of the Popular Front.[1]

Bernhard Ziegler[2] raised the issue of popular art in a very pointed manner. The excitement generated by this question is evident on all sides and such a vigorous interest is surely to be welcomed. Bloch, too, is concerned to salvage the popular element in Expressionism. He says: 'It is untrue that Expressionists were estranged from ordinary people by their overweening arrogance. Again, the opposite is the case. The *Blue Rider*[3] imitated the stained glass at Murnau, and in fact was the first to open people's eyes to this moving and uncanny folk art. In the same way, it focused attention on the drawings of children and prisoners, on the disturbing works of the mentally sick, and on primitive art.' Such a view of popular art succeeds in confusing all the issues. Popular art does not imply an ideologically indiscriminate, 'arty' appreciation of 'primitive' products by connoisseurs. Truly popular art has nothing in common with any of that. For if it did, any swank who collects stained glass or negro sculpture, any snob who celebrates insanity as the emancipation of mankind from the fetters of the mechanistic mind, could claim to be a champion of popular art.

Today, of course, it is no easy matter to form a proper conception of popular art. The older ways of life of the people have been eroded economically by capitalism, and this has introduced a feeling of uncertainty into the world-view, the cultural aspirations, the taste and moral judgement of the people; it has created a situation in which people are exposed to the perversions of demagogy. Thus it is by no means always progressive simply to collect old folk products indiscriminately. Nor does such a rescue operation necessarily imply an appeal to the vital instincts of the people, which do remain progressive against all obstacles. Similarly, the fact that a literary work or a literary trend is greatly in vogue does not in itself guarantee that it is genuinely popular. Retrograde traditionalisms, such as regional art [*Heimatkunst*], and bad modern works, such as thrillers, have achieved mass circulation without being popular in any true sense of the word.

With all these reservations, however, it is still not unimportant to ask how

9. Johannes Becher (1891–1958), German expressionist poet. Vladimir Mayakovsky (1893–1930), Russian futurist poet.

1. All the different socialist groups that, along with the Communists, attempted in the 1930s to present a united front against the rise of fascism, especially against Adolf Hitler. The Popular Front became official Communist policy at the Seventh Comintern Congress of 1935.

2. Pseudonym of Alfred Kurella (1895–1975), an associate of Lukács who began the critique of expressionism in *Das Wort*.

3. Kandinsky's 1903 painting, widely associated with expressionism; it appeared on the cover of the groundbreaking expressionist publication *Blue Rider Almanac* (1912), issued by a group that took its name.

much of the real literature of our time has reached the masses, and how deeply it has penetrated. But what 'modernist' writer of the last few decades can even begin to compare with Gorky, with Anatole France,[4] Romain Rolland or Thomas Mann? That a work of such uncompromising artistic excellence as *Buddenbrooks* could be printed in millions of copies must give all of us food for thought. The whole problem of popular art would, as old Briest in Fontane's[5] novel used to say, 'lead us too far afield' for us to discuss it here. We shall confine ourselves therefore to two points, without pretending to an exhaustive treatment of either.

In the first place, there is the question of the cultural heritage. Wherever the cultural heritage has a living relationship to the real life of the people it is characterized by a dynamic, progressive movement in which the active creative forces of popular tradition, of the sufferings and joys of the people, of revolutionary legacies, are buoyed up, preserved, transcended and further developed. For a writer to possess a living relationship to the cultural heritage means being a son of the people, borne along by the current of the people's development. In this sense Maxim Gorky is a son of the Russian people, Romain Rolland a son of the French and Thomas Mann a son of the German people. For all their individuality and originality, for all their remoteness from an artiness which artificially collects and aestheticizes about the primitive, the tone and content of their writings grow out of the life and history of their people, they are an organic product of the development of their nation. That is why it is possible for them to create art of the highest quality while at the same time striking a chord which can and does evoke a response in the broad masses of the people.

The attitude of the modernists to the cultural heritage stands in sharp contrast to this. They regard the history of the people as a great jumble sale. If one leafs through the writings of Bloch, one will find him mentioning the topic only in expressions like 'useful legacies', 'plunder', and so on. Bloch is much too conscious a thinker and stylist for these to be mere slips of the pen. On the contrary, they are an index of his general attitude towards the cultural heritage. In his eyes it is a heap of lifeless objects in which one can rummage around at will, picking out whatever one happens to need at the moment. It is something to be taken apart and stuck together again in accordance with the exigencies of the moment.

Hanns Eisler has expressed the same attitude very clearly in an article he and Bloch wrote together. He was—rightly—highly enthusiastic about the *Don Carlos* demonstration in Berlin.[6] But instead of pondering what Schiller really represented, where his achievement and his limitations actually lay, what he has meant for the German people in the past and still means today, and what mountain of reactionary prejudices would have to be cleared away in order to forge the popular and progressive aspects of Schiller into a usable weapon for the Popular Front and for the emancipation of the German people—instead of all that, he merely puts forward the following programme for the benefit of writers in exile: 'What must our task be outside Germany? It is evident that it can only be for us all to help select and prepare classical

4. French novelist (1844–1924).

5. Theodor Fontane (1819–1898), the first master of the realistic novel in Germany; *Effi Briest* (1895) is his greatest work.

6. Hanns Eisler/Ernst Bloch: *Die Kunst zu erben* [translator's note]. *Don Carlos* (1787), a historical drama by Schiller, caused controversy with its confusing story and its deviation from historical fact.

material that is suitable for such a struggle.' Thus what Eisler proposes is to reduce the classics to an anthology and then to reassemble whatever 'material is suitable'. It would be impossible to conceive of a more alien, arrogant or negative attitude towards the glorious literary past of the German people.

Objectively, however, the life of the people is a continuum. A theory like that of the modernists which sees revolutions only as ruptures and catastrophes that destroy all that is past and shatter all connection with the great and glorious past, is akin to the ideas of Cuvier,[7] not those of Marx and Lenin. It forms an anarchistic pendant to the evolutionary theories of reformism. The latter sees nothing but continuity, the former sees nothing but ruptures, fissures and catastrophes. History, however, is the living dialectical unity of continuity and discontinuity, of evolution and revolution.

Thus here, as everywhere, everything depends on a correct appreciation of content. Lenin puts the Marxist view of the cultural heritage in this way: 'Marxism attained its world-historical importance as the ideology of the revolutionary proletariat by virtue of its refusal to reject the most valuable achievements of the bourgeois era. Instead, it appropriated and assimilated all that was valuable in a tradition of human thought and human culture stretching back over 2000 years.' So everything depends on recognizing clearly where to look for what is truly of value.

If the question is correctly formulated, in the context of the life and the progressive tendencies of the people, then it will lead us organically to our second point the question of realism. Modern theories of popular art, strongly influenced by avant-garde ideas, have pushed the sturdy realism of folk art very much into the background. On this issue, too, we cannot possibly discuss the entire problem in all its ramifications, so we shall confine our observations to one single, crucial point.

We are talking here to writers about literature. We must remind ourselves that owing to the tragic course of German history, the popular and realistic element in our literature is nothing like as powerful as in England, France or Russia. That very fact should spur us to attend all the more closely to the popular, realistic literature of the German past and to keep its vital, productive traditions alive. If we do so, we shall see that despite the whole 'German *misère*',[8] popular, realistic literature produced such major masterpieces as the *Simplizissimus* of Grimmelshausen.[9] It may be left to the Eislers of this world to take the book to pieces and estimate their montage value; for the living tradition of German literature it will continue to survive intact in all its greatness, and with all its limitations.[1]

7. Georges Cuvier (1769–1832). According to his theory every geological era terminated in a catastrophe and every new one was brought about by an immigration and a re-creation. He rejected theories of evolution [translator's note].
8. Trouble (French).
9. H. J. Christoffel Von Grimmelshausen (ca. 1621–1676). His picaresque novel *The Adventures of a Simpleton* (1669), set in the Thirty Years' War, is the major German literary work of the 17th century [translator's note].
1. The plural formulation "It may be left to the Eislers . . ." provoked Brecht to write the following *Minor Correction*: "In the debate on Expressionism in *Das Wort* something has happened in the heat of battle that stands in need of a minor correction. Lukács has been wiping the floor, so to speak, with my friend Eisler, who, incidentally, is hardly anyone's idea of a pale aesthete. It appears that Eisler has failed to exhibit the pious reverence towards the cultural heritage expected from the executors of a will. Instead he just rummaged around in it and declined to take everything into his possession. Well, it may be that, as an exile, he is not in a position to lug so much stuff around with him. However, perhaps I may be allowed a few comments on the formal aspects of the incident. Reference was made to 'the Eislers,' who were alleged to be doing, or not doing, something or other. In my opinion, the Lukácses ought to refrain from using such plurals when in fact there is only one Eisler among our musicians. The millions of white,

Only when the masterpieces of realism past and present are appreciated as *wholes*, will their topical, cultural and political value fully emerge. This value resides in their inexhaustible diversity, in contrast to the one-dimensionality of modernism. Cervantes and Shakespeare, Balzac and Tolstoy, Grimmelshausen and Gottfried Keller,[2] Gorky, Thomas and Heinrich Mann—all these can appeal to readers drawn from a broad cross-section of the people because their works permit access from so many different angles. The large-scale, enduring resonance of the great works of realism is in fact due to this accessibility, to the infinite multitude of doors through which entry is possible. The wealth of the characterization, the profound and accurate grasp of constant and typical manifestations of human life is what produces the great progressive reverberation of these works. The process of appropriation enables readers to clarify their own experiences and understanding of life and to broaden their own horizons. A living form of humanism prepares them to endorse the political slogans of the Popular Front and to comprehend its political humanism. Through the mediation of realist literature the soul of the masses is made receptive for an understanding of the great, progressive and democratic epochs of human history. This will prepare it for the new type of revolutionary democracy that is represented by the Popular Front. The more deeply anti-Fascist literature is embedded in this soil, the better able it will be to create contrasting types of good and evil, models of what should be admired and what hated—and the greater will be its resonance among the people.

In contrast to this, it is but a very narrow doorway which leads to Joyce or the other representatives of avant-garde literature: one needs a certain 'knack' to see just what their game is. Whereas in the case of the major realists, easier access produces a richly complex yield in human terms, the broad mass of the people can learn nothing from avant-garde literature. Precisely because the latter is devoid of reality and life, it foists on to its readers a narrow and subjectivist attitude to life (analogous to a sectarian point of view in political terms). In realism, the wealth of created life provides answers to the questions put by the readers themselves—life supplies the answers to the questions put by life itself! The taxing struggle to understand the art of the 'avant-garde', on the other hand, yields such subjectivist distortions and travesties that ordinary people who try to translate these atmospheric echoes of reality back into the language of their own experience, find the task quite beyond them.

A vital relationship to the life of the people, a progressive development of the masses' own experiences—this is the great social mission of literature. In his early works Thomas Mann found much to criticize in the literature of Western Europe. It is no accident that his objections to the problematic

yellow and black workers who have inherited the songs Eisler wrote for the masses will undoubtedly share my opinion here. But in addition there are all sorts of experts on music who think highly of Eisler's works, in which, so they tell me, he magnificently builds on and extends the cultural heritage of German music, and they would be very confused if the German émigrés should seek to outdo the seven cities of Greece, who quarreled about which of them had produced a single Homer, by allowing themselves to start boasting that they had seven Eislers." When the essay was revised for republication in book-form (Aufbau, Berlin 1948), Lukács rewrote the sentence to read "It may be left to Eisler and Bloch . . . ," while in vol. 4 *Probleme des Realismus*, Luchterhand 1971, we find: "It may be left to Eisler . . ." [translator's note]. Bertolt Brecht (1898–1956), German dramatist and Marxist.

2. Swiss writer known for realistic works (1819–1890).

nature and remoteness from life of many modern works were counterbalanced by his indication of an alternative creative ideal, in his description of the Russian literature of the nineteenth century as 'sacred'.[3] What he had in mind was this very same life-creating, popular progressiveness.

The Popular Front means a struggle for a genuine popular culture, a manifold relationship to every aspect of the life of one's own people as it has developed in its own individual way in the course of history. It means finding the guidelines and slogans which can emerge out of this life of the people and rouse progressive forces to new, politically effective activity. To understand the historical identity of the people does not, of course, imply an uncritical attitude towards one's own history—on the contrary, such criticism is the necessary consequence of real insight into one's own history. For no people, and the Germans least of all, has succeeded in establishing progressive democratic forces in a perfect form and without any setbacks. Criticism must be based, however, on an accurate and profound understanding of the realities of history. Since it was the age of imperialism which created the most serious obstacles to progress and democracy in the spheres of both politics and culture, a trenchant analysis of the decadent manifestations of this period—political, cultural and artistic—is an essential prerequisite for any breakthrough to a genuinely popular culture. A campaign against realism, whether conscious or not, and a resultant impoverishment and isolation of literature and art is one of the crucial manifestations of decadence in the realm of art.

In the course of our remarks we have seen that we should not simply accept this decline fatalistically. Vital forces which combat this decadence not just politically and theoretically, but also with all the instruments at the disposal of art, have made and continue to make themselves felt. The task that faces us is to lend them our support. They are to be found in a realism which has true depth and significance.

Writers in exile, together with the struggles of the Popular Front in Germany and other countries, have inevitably strengthened these positive forces. It might be thought sufficient to point to Heinrich and Thomas Mann,[4] who, starting from different assumptions, have steadily grown in stature in recent years both as writers and thinkers. But we are concerned here with a broad trend in anti-Fascist literature. We need only compare Feuchtwanger's[5] *Sons* with his *History of the Jewish Wars* to see the strenuous efforts he is making to overcome the subjectivist tendencies which distanced him from the masses, and to assimilate and formulate the real problems of ordinary people. Just a short while ago Alfred Döblin gave a talk in the Paris SDS[6] in which he declared his commitment to the historical and political relevance of literature and in which he saw a realism of the kind practised by Gorky as exemplary—an event of no little importance for the future course of our

3. Lukács is evidently referring to the celebrated discussion on the value of literature in *Tonio Kröger* [translator's note].

4. In 1933 both Manns were forced into exile by the Nazi government.

5. Lion Feuchtwanger (1884–1958), German writer, one of three editors of *Das Wort*; *The Jewish War* (1932; trans. as *Josephus*) and *The Sons* (1935) are the initial novels in a 3-volume trilogy on the Jewish historian and soldier Flavius Josephus (b. 37/8 C.E.), who both fought against and admired the Romans (and thus the trilogy was also on assimilation vs. Jewishness).

6. SDS—*Der Schutzvergand deutscher Schriftsteller* (Association for the Protection of the Rights of German Authors) where Döblin gave an important lecture *Die deutsche Literatur (im Ausland seit 1933)* in January 1938 [translator's note]. Döblin (1878–1957), German writer and early adherent of expressionism.

literature. In the third number of *Das Wort*, Brecht published a one-act playlet (*The Informer*)[7] in which he turns to what is for him a novel, highly differentiated and subtle form of realism as a weapon in the struggle against the inhumanity of Fascism. By depicting the fates of actual human beings, he provides a vivid image of the horrors of the Fascist reign of terror in Germany. He shows how Fascism destroys the entire foundations of the human community, how it destroys the trust between husbands, wives and children, and how in its inhumanity it actually undermines and annihilates the family, the very institution it claims to protect. Along with Feuchtwanger, Döblin and Brecht one could name a whole series of writers—the most important and the most talented we have—who have adopted a similar strategy, or are beginning to do so.

But this does not mean that the struggle to overcome the anti-realist traditions of the era of imperialism is over. Our present debate shows, on the contrary, that these traditions are still deeply rooted in important and loyal supporters of the Popular Front whose political views are unquestionably progressive. This is why such a forthright but comradely discussion was of such vital importance. For it is not just the masses who learn through their own experiences in the class-struggle; ideologists, writers and critics, have to learn too. It would be a grave error to overlook that growing trend towards realism which has emerged from the experiences of fighters in the Popular Front and which has even affected writers who favoured a very different approach before their emigration.

To make this very point, to reveal some of the intimate, varied and complex bonds which link the Popular Front, popular literature and authentic realism, is the task I have set out to accomplish in these pages.

1938

7. A scene from *Furcht und Elend des dritten Reichs* [1945], trans. by Eric Bentley as *The Private Life of the Master Race*. Brecht's reaction to Lukács's praise has been recorded in his *Arbeitsjournal* (vol. 1, p. 22): "Lukács has welcomed *The Informer* as if I were a sinner returning to the bosom of the Salvation Army. At last something taken from life itself! He has overlooked the montage of 27 scenes and the fact that it is really no more than a catalogue of gestures, such as the gesture of falling silent, of looking over one's shoulder, of terror, etc.; in short, the gestures of life under a dictatorship" [translator's note]. Brecht's early work was inspired by expressionism.

BORIS EICHENBAUM
1886–1959

The literary critics and theorists known as the Russian formalists flourished during a remarkable period in modern history, one which witnessed the Russian Revolution of 1917 and the first large-scale institution of a socialist state, the Union of Soviet Socialist Republics (U.S.S.R.). This was also an extraordinarily fertile time for experiment and innovation in the arts, as avant-garde modernist literary movements such as symbolism, futurism, and acmeism flourished. Although their movement ended in the late 1920s with the rise of Joseph Stalin and the suppression of ideas perceived to be noncommunist, the Russian formalists constitute the first group of theorists whom many contemporary literary scholars recognize as modern in their theoretical investigations of literary language, innovation, and history. Boris Eichenbaum was a leading figure among the Russian formalists, and his famous "Theory of the 'Formal Method'" (1926) surveys their history and their central theoretical concepts.

At St. Petersburg University, Eichenbaum initially planned to become a medical doctor but switched his studies to language and literature; he graduated in 1912. After teaching at a private secondary school, in 1918 he returned to the university—in 1924 renamed, with the city, Leningrad University in honor of the revolution's leader, V. I. Lenin—as a professor. In 1949 he was dismissed for "eclecticism and cosmopolitanism," but he was reinstated in 1956 at the Institute of Russian Literature at the university, where he taught until his death. Eichenbaum's involvement with the formalist movement represents only one phase, dating from the mid-1910s to 1928, in a long career as a critic and scholar. After 1928 his work shifted from the analytical approach of formalism to a series of biographical studies of the great Russian novelist Leo Tolstoy (1828–1910).

Like all of his colleagues who continued to work in the Stalinist era, Eichenbaum knew that if he wished to continue writing criticism, he would have to support socialist realism. He, like many ex-formalists, chose instead to turn to scholarly research; but unlike them, he faced continued persecution even after abandoning his theoretical work. The reason given was always his early record as a formalist, but probably the real motive, never directly stated, was anti-Semitism. Although Eichenbaum sustained a career on the margins of Soviet academic literary studies, he completed relatively little work after 1930. The final volume of his Tolstoy project appeared only posthumously, and the draft of another volume was lost during the German army's siege of Leningrad during World War II.

In "The Theory of the 'Formal Method,'" Eichenbaum takes stock of the first decade of work of the formalist movement. By using scare quotes around "formal method," he signals that he has adopted for convenience a label coined not by those within the movement but by opponents who criticized their focus on literary language and formal innovations. Most notably, the formalists were attacked in a famous analysis by the Marxist LEON TROTSKY (see above), an early leader of the Russian Revolution as well as a powerful writer on history and literature, who castigated them for their lack of attention to the social significance of literary works. In actuality, those joined under the mantle of formalism were not a tightly unified school but a heterogeneous movement. Although Eichenbaum is careful to say that his essay is not a "dogmatic codification" of formalism, it has regularly been construed as such.

Originally there were two different Russian formalist groups, which later came in close contact. The first was the Moscow Linguistic Circle, which initially gathered in 1914 and was led by ROMAN JAKOBSON until his departure for Prague in 1920. Primarily a group of researchers, the circle applied new scientific developments in linguistics to the study of literature. Other important members of the Moscow group were Osip Brik and Boris Tomashevsky. Meanwhile, in 1916 the Society for the Study of Poetic Language (known by the Russian acronym *Opoyaz*) first gathered in St. Petersburg (then called Petrograd), led by Victor Shklovsky, Eichenbaum, and Yury Tynyanov. Trained as literary scholars, they were less interested in linguistics and more concerned with literary history, although they rebelled against traditional biographical approaches. Both groups were influenced by the heady climate of the Russian Revolution and avant-garde art and literature in Russia, a context that promoted sweeping new ideas in all areas of life and culture. (Another group that flourished in Leningrad simultaneously with *Opoyaz* was the so-called Bakhtin Circle, organized around the philosopher-turned-critic MIKHAIL BAKHTIN). Other linguists and critics sympathetic to but independent of the formalist movement included Leo Jakubinsky, Victor Vinogradov, and Victor Zhirmunsky. Vladimir Propp, a folklorist who worked apart from both groups, is frequently associated with Russian formalism by present-day critics.

The first five of nine main sections of "The Theory of the 'Formal Method'" survey the themes and issues addressed by formalists during what Eichenbaum calls the movement's initial "years of struggle and polemics," 1916 to 1921. The remaining four sections cover the years 1922 to 1926. Overall, there is a heady as well as combative tone to the essay, recounting in sometimes heightened rhetoric the formalists' accomplishments and struggles against their antagonists ("We had to demolish the academic tradition"), who ranged from academic literary historians, biographers, and cultural critics to Russian symbolist poets and theoreticians, aestheticians, and dogmatic Marxists. Eichenbaum singles out several key opponents, especially Aleksandr Potebnya and Aleksandr Veselovsky, prominent literary scholars who represented the status quo of traditional criticism and thus served as foils. At one point Eichenbaum admits that "the basic passion for our historical-literary work had to be a passion for destruction and negation, and such was the original tone of our theoretical attacks."

"The Theory of the 'Formal Method'" provides a comprehensive review of the preoccupations of the formalists: the desire for a science or "poetics" of literature (hence Eichenbaum cites a biologist in the epigraph to the essay); the linguistic basis of literature and especially of poetry (drawing on Jakobson and others); the distinctive attributes of literature, its "literariness" and its autonomous history; the stress on literary devices; the view of literary history as an evolutionary accretion of innovative devices; the concept of the "dominant" (the focusing element of each literary structure, to which other elements are subordinate); the insistence on form and technique as part of content; and the nature of narrative (notably the key distinction between "story" or *fabula*, the raw chronological events of a narrative, and "plot" or *syuzhet*, the artistic arrangement of events, frequently out of chronological order).

Eichenbaum emphasizes Victor Shklovsky's role as the intellectual leader of the formalist movement, the first to identify and tackle its major concerns. While this stress has perhaps led later critics to overestimate Shklovsky's importance, his contributions were significant. Most influential is his concept of "defamiliarization" (*ostraneniye* in Russian), both as a goal of art and as a category of critical analysis. Using the example of a walk down a familiar street, Shklovsky points out that one's perceptions become automatic, so that one notices only what is out of the ordinary. But, he observes, literary artists take this tendency into account and show things out of the ordinary, thereby freshening and renewing readers' perceptions. This process of defamiliarization becomes a formalist measure of aesthetic value, privileging literary works that make the familiar strange and break the "automatism" of normal expectation; for Shklovsky, literary history builds on such aesthetic innovations.

The Russian formalists' theoretical focus, stress on the functional role of literary devices, and conception of the evolution of literary history distinguish them from other early- and mid-twentieth-century schools of criticism concerned with form, such as the American New Critics. The New Critics largely provided readings of individual literary works, focusing on what WILLIAM K. WIMSATT JR. called "the verbal icon," whereas the Russian formalists were more interested in making theoretical generalizations about the nature of literature and in defining the range of technical linguistic devices common to literary works. Moreover, the Russian formalists proposed an original model of literary history, combining the scientific schematization of devices with an account of historical change.

Although the formalist movement was suppressed, it has continued to wield broad influence. It was a progenitor of the Prague school of structuralism that flourished from the mid-1920s to 1948, especially through the mediation of Jakobson after his arrival there and through the work of Jan Mukařovský. After TZVETAN TODOROV recovered and translated key formalist texts, they provided an important model of analysis for the literary wing of French structuralism in the 1960s and 1970s—notably for the structuralist narratology of Todorov, ROLAND BARTHES, and Gérard Genette, which in turn influenced later Anglo-American theorists of narrative. Contemporary narrative theory continues to look back to the work of Shklovsky, Eichenbaum, and Propp. The formalist theory of literary history has been foundational for contemporary reception theory, particularly for the work of HANS ROBERT JAUSS, whose central concept of the "horizon of expectation" draws on formalist notions of defamiliarization. The evolutionary theory of literary history has also influenced Marxist accounts of aesthetics, despite Marxist reservations about the formalist view of the autonomy of literature. While in recent years interest in formal approaches to literature has declined—largely giving way to a social consciousness in a sense akin to what Trotsky had demanded—the Russian formalists remain foundational for contemporary theory in their emphases on making theoretical generalizations about the nature of literary works; their use of linguistics and their desire for a more exact, scientific study of literature; and their account of literary history and aesthetic innovation.

BIBLIOGRAPHY

"The Theory of the 'Formal Method' " originally appeared in 1926 (in Ukrainian; the Russian text translated here dates from 1927). Our selection, the best translation in English, is taken from *Russian Formalist Criticism: Four Essays*, translated and edited by Lee T. Lemon and Marion J. Reis (1965), which offers a good place to start investigating Russian formalism. Though uncollected, a number of other key essays from Eichenbaum's formalist period are available in English in diverse sources, among them his important "How Gogol's 'Overcoat' Is Made" (1919), in *Gogol from the Twentieth Century: Eleven Essays* (trans. and ed. Robert A. Maguire, 1974); and "O. Henry and the Theory of the Short Story" (1925), "Literary Environment" (1927), and a different translation of "The Theory of the 'Formal Method,' " all in *Readings in Russian Poetics: Formalist and Structuralist Views*, edited by Ladislav Matejka and Krystyna Pomorska (1971), which is the most comprehensive anthology of formalist writings in English. Additionally, Eichenbaum's monographs include *The Young Tolstoy* (1922; trans. 1972), *Lermontov* (1924; trans. 1977), *Tolstoy in the Fifties* (1928; trans. 1982), *Tolstoy in the Sixties* (1931; trans. 1982) and *Tolstoy in the Seventies* (1960; trans. 1982). The early Tolstoy volume is an analytical study of literary conventions, but its sequels replace formalist method with a biographical orientation. An exemplary biographical study, Carol Any's *Boris Eichenbaum: Voices of a Russian Formalist* (1994), traces several phases of Eichenbaum's career.

The standard critical account in English of Russian formalism as a whole, Victor Erlich's *Russian Formalism: History—Doctrine* (3d ed., 1981) devotes substantial attention to Eichenbaum's role in it. For a retrospective assessment from a colleague, see Roman Jakobson, "Boris Mikhailovich Eikhenbaum," *International Journal of Slavic Linguistics and Poetics* 6 (1963). Perhaps the most influential critical introduction of Russian formalism to contemporary American theory, Fredric Jameson's *Prison-House of Language: A Critical Account of Structuralism and Russian Formalism* (1972) credits Eichenbaum with being "the most pugnacious and combative of the group." In "The Changing Focus of Eikhenbaum's Tolstoi Criticism," *Russian Review* 37 (1978), Harold K. Schefski discusses Eichenbaum's shift away from formalism. See also Peter Steiner's *Russian Formalism: A Metapoetics* (1984) and Juri Streidter's *Literary Structure, Evolution, and Value: Russian Formalism and Czech Structuralism* (1989), which offer significant commentary on Eichenbaum. For comprehensive bibliographies, consult the entries on Eichenbaum in David Gorman's "Bibliography of Russian Formalism in English," *Style* 26 (1992), and his "Supplement to a Bibliography of Russian Formalism in English," *Style* 29 (1995).

From The Theory of the "Formal Method"[1]

> The worst, in my opinion, are those who describe science as if it were settled.
>
> [*Le pire, à mon avis, est celui qui représente la science comme faite.*]—
>
> A. de Candolle[2]

The so-called "formal method" grew out of a struggle for a science of literature that would be both independent and factual; it is not the outgrowth of a particular methodology. The notion of a "method" has been so exaggerated that it now suggests too much. In principle the question for the Formalist[3] is not how to study literature, but what the subject matter of literary study actually is. We neither discuss methodology nor quarrel about it. We speak and may speak only about theoretical principles suggested to us not by this or that ready-made methodology, but by the examination of specific material in its specific context. The Formalists' works in literary theory and literary history show this clearly enough, but during the past ten years so many new questions and old misunderstandings have accumulated that I feel it advisable to try to summarize some of our work—not as a dogmatic system but as a historical summation. I wish to show how the work of the Formalists began, how it evolved, and what it evolved into.

The evolutionary character of the development of the formal method is important to an understanding of its history; our opponents and many of our followers overlook it. We are surrounded by eclectics and late-comers who would turn the formal method into some kind of inflexible "formalistic" system in order to provide themselves with a working vocabulary, a program, and a name. A program is a very handy thing for critics, but not at all characteristic of our method. Our scientific approach has had no such prefabricated program or doctrine, and has none. In our studies we value a theory only as a working hypothesis to help us discover and interpret facts; that is, we determine the validity of the facts and use them as the material of our research. We are not concerned with definitions, for which the late-comers thirst; nor do we build general theories, which so delight eclectics. We posit specific principles and adhere to them insofar as the material justifies them. If the material demands their refinement or change, we change or refine them. In this sense we are quite free from our own theories—as science must be free to the extent that theory and conviction are distinct. There is no ready-made science; science lives not by settling on truth, but by overcoming error.

This essay is not intended to argue our position. The initial period of sci-

1. Translated by Lee T. Lemon and Marion J. Reis, who trimmed the text slightly and added the headings to the section numbers in the original; they sometimes include clarifying words or phrases in brackets in the text.
2. Alphonse de Candolle (1806–1893), Swiss botanist.
3. By "Formalists" I mean in this essay only that group of theoreticians who made up the Society for the Study of Poetic Language (the *Opoyaz*) and who began to publish their studies in 1916 [Eichenbaum's note]. Some of the author's notes have been edited and some omitted. Led by Victor Shklovsky (1893–1984), Eichenbaum, and Yury Tynyanov (1894–1943), *Opoyaz* was centered in St. Petersburg, but Eichenbaum also includes members of the Moscow Linguistic Circle in his account. Arising independently in 1914 but soon coming into contact with the Petersburg group, the circle was led by ROMAN JAKOBSON (1896–1982), Osip Brik (1888–1945), and Boris Tomashevsky (1890–1957).

entific struggle and journalistic polemics is past. Such attacks as that in *The Press and the Revolution*[4] (with which I was honored) can be answered only by new scientific works. My chief purpose here is to show how the formal method, by gradually evolving and broadening its field of research, spread beyond the usual "methodological" limits and became a special science of literature, a specific ordering of facts. Within the limits of this science, the most diverse methods may develop, if only because we focus on the empirical study of the material. Such study was, essentially, the aim of the Formalists from the very beginning, and precisely that was the significance of our quarrel with the old traditions. The name "formal method," bestowed upon the movement and now firmly attached to it, may be tentatively understood as a historical term; it should not be taken as an accurate description of our work. Neither "Formalism" as an aesthetic theory nor "methodology" as a finished scientific system characterizes us; we are characterized only by the attempt to create an independent science of literature which studies specifically literary material. We ask only for recognition of the theoretical and historical facts of literary art as such.

1. *The Origins of Formalism*

Representatives of the formal method were frequently reproached by various groups for their lack of clarity or for the inadequacy of their principles—for indifference to general questions of aesthetics, sociology, psychology, and so on. These reproofs, despite their varying merit, are alike in that they correctly grasp that the chief characteristic of the Formalists is indeed their deliberate isolation both from "aesthetics from above" and from all ready-made or self-styled general theories. This isolation (particularly from aesthetics) is more or less typical of all contemporary studies of art. Dismissing a whole group of general problems (problems of beauty, the aims of art, etc.), the contemporary study of art concentrates on the concrete problems of aesthetics. Without reference to socio-aesthetic premises, it raises questions about the idea of artistic "form" and its evolution. It thereby raises a series of more specific theoretical and historical questions. Such familiar slogans as Wölfflin's[5] "history of art without names" characterized experiments in the empirical analysis of style and technique (like Voll's[6] "experiment in the comparative study of paintings"). In Germany especially the study of the theory and history of the visual arts, which had had there an extremely rich history of tradition and experiment, occupied a central position in art studies and began to influence the general theory of art and its separate disciplines—in particular, the study of literature. In Russia, apparently for local historical reasons, literary studies occupied a place analogous to that of the visual arts in Germany.

The formal method has attracted general attention and become controversial not, of course, because of its distinctive methodology, but rather because of its characteristic attitude toward the understanding and the study of technique. The Formalists advocated principles which violated solidly entrenched traditional notions, notions which had appeared to be "axio-

4. A literary and intellectual journal of the period following the Russian Revolution of 1917; the attack on Eichenbaum occurred in 1924.

5. Heinrich Wölfflin (1864–1945), German art historian.

6. Karl Voll (1867–1917), German art historian.

matic" not only in the study of literature, but in the study of art generally. Because they adhered to their principles so strictly, they narrowed the distance between particular problems of literary theory and general problems of aesthetics. The ideas and principles of the Formalists, for all their concreteness, were pointedly directed towards a general theory of aesthetics. Our creation of a radically unconventional poetics,[7] therefore, implied more than a simple reassessment of particular problems; it had an impact on the study of art generally. It had its impact because of a series of historical developments, the most important of which were the crisis in philosophical aesthetics and the startling innovations in art (in Russia most abrupt and most clearly defined in poetry). Aesthetics seemed barren and art deliberately denuded—in an entirely primitive condition. Hence, Formalism and Futurism[8] seemed bound together by history.

But the general historical significance of the appearance of Formalism comprises a special theme; I must speak of something else here because I intend to show how the principles and problems of the formal method evolved and how the Formalists came to their present position.

Before the appearance of the Formalists, academic research, quite ignorant of theoretical problems, made use of antiquated aesthetic, psychological, and historical "axioms" and had so lost sight of its proper subject that its very existence as a science had become illusory. There was almost no struggle between the Formalists and the Academicians,[9] not because the Formalists had broken in the door (there were no doors), but because we found an open passageway instead of a fortress. The theoretical heritage which Potebnya and Veselovsky[1] left to their disciples seemed to lay like dead capital—a treasure which they were afraid to touch, the brilliance of which they had allowed to fade. In fact, authority and influence had gradually passed from academic scholarship to the "scholarship" of the journals, to the work of the Symbolist[2] critics and theoreticians. Actually, between 1907 and 1912 the books and essays of Vyacheslav Ivanov, Bryusov, Merezhkovsky, Chukovsky,[3] and others, were much more influential than the scholarly studies and dissertations of the university professors. This journalistic "scholarship," with all its subjectivity and tendentiousness, was supported by the theoretical principles and slogans of the new artistic movements and their propagandists. Such books as Bely's *Simvolizm*[4] (1910) naturally meant much more to the younger generation than the monographs on the history of literature which sprang up from no set of principles and which showed that the authors completely lacked both a scientific temperament and a scientific point of view.

The historical battle between the two generations [the Symbolists and the Formalists]—a battle which was fought over principles and was extraordi-

7. That is, a scientific theory of literature.
8. A revolutionary movement in art and literature begun in Italy in 1909, stressing speed, modernity, and rebellion; it quickly found adherents in Russia.
9. The established university-based literary scholars against whom the formalists rebelled.
1. Aleksandr Potebnya (1835–1891) and Aleksandr Veselovsky (1838–1906), Russian literary scholars.
2. A movement (with origins in 1870s France) that aimed at renovating Russian poetry at the beginning of the 20th century; it emphasized mysticism and aestheticism, in an impressionistic style.
3. All Russian literary figures associated with symbolism: Ivanov (1866–1949), Valery Bryusov (1873–1924), Dmitri Merezhkovsky (1865–1941), and Korney Chukovsky (1882–1969).
4. *Symbolism* (Russian). Andrey Bely: the pseudonym of Boris Bugayev (1880–1934), a Russian novelist, poet, and critic.

narily intense—was therefore resolved in the journals, and the battle line was drawn over Symbolist theory and Impressionistic criticism[5] rather than over any work being done by the Academicians. We entered the fight against the Symbolists in order to wrest poetics from their hands—to free it from its ties with their subjective philosophical and aesthetic theories and to direct it toward the scientific investigation of facts. We were raised on their works, and we saw their errors with the greatest clarity. At this time, the struggle became even more urgent because the Futurists (Khlebnikov, Kruchenykh, and Mayakovsky),[6] who were on the rise, opposed the Symbolist poetics and supported the Formalists.

The original group of Formalists was united by the idea of liberating poetic diction from the fetters of the intellectualism and moralism which more and more obsessed the Symbolists. The dissension among the Symbolist theoreticians (1910–1911) and the appearance of the Acmeists[7] prepared the way for our decisive rebellion. We knew that all compromises would have to be avoided, that history demanded of us a really revolutionary attitude—a categorical thesis, merciless irony, and bold rejections of whatever could not be reconciled with our position. We had to oppose the subjective aesthetic principles espoused by the Symbolists with an objective consideration of the facts. Hence our Formalist movement was characterized by a new passion for scientific positivism[8]—a rejection of philosophical assumptions, of psychological and aesthetic interpretations, etc. Art, considered apart from philosophical aesthetics and ideological theories, dictated its own position on things. We had to turn to facts and, abandoning general systems and problems, to begin "in the middle," with the facts which art forced upon us. Art demanded that we approach it closely; science, that we deal with the specific.

2. The Science of Literature: The Independent Value of Poetic Sound

The establishment of a specific and factual literary science was basic to the organization of the formal method. All of our efforts were directed toward disposing of the earlier position which, according to Alexander Veselovsky, made of literature an abandoned thing [a *res nullius*]. This is why the position of the Formalists could not be reconciled with other approaches and was so unacceptable to the eclectics. In rejecting these other approaches, the Formalists actually rejected and still reject not the methods, but rather the irresponsible mixing of various disciplines and their problems. The basis of our position was and is that the object of literary science, as such, must be the study of those specifics which distinguish it from any other material. (The secondary, incidental features of such material, however, may reasonably

5. Unsystematic, subjective criticism; elsewhere Eichenbaum calls it "journalistic" criticism.
6. Three Russian poets and critics: Velimir Khlebnikov (1885–1922), Alexey Kruchenykh (1886–1968), and Vladimir Mayakovsky (1893–1930).
7. The Acmeists, like the Futurists, rebelled against the principles and practices of the Symbolists. But unlike the Futurists, they attempted a highly controlled, polished style of poetry. The best-known Acmeists were Anna Akhmatova [1889–1966] and Osip Mandelstam [1891–1938]. The movement did not survive World War I [translators' note].
8. The view that knowledge and meaning derive solely from what can be empirically observed.

and rightly be used in a subordinate way by other scientific disciplines.) Roman Jakobson formulated this view with perfect clarity:

> The object of the science of literature is not literature, but literariness—that is, that which makes a given work a work of literature. Until now literary historians have preferred to act like the policeman who, intending to arrest a certain person, would, at any opportunity, seize any and all persons who chanced into the apartment, as well as those who passed along the street. The literary historians used everything—anthropology, psychology, politics, philosophy. Instead of a science of literature, they created a conglomeration of homespun disciplines. They seemed to have forgotten that their essays strayed into related disciplines—the history of philosophy, the history of culture, of psychology, etc.—and that these could rightly use literary masterpieces only as defective, secondary documents.[9]

To apply and strengthen this principle of specificity and to avoid speculative aesthetics, we had to compare literary facts with other kinds of facts, extracting from a limitless number of important orders of fact that order which would pertain to literature and would distinguish it from the others by its function. This was the method Leo Jakubinsky[1] followed in his essays in the first *Opoyaz* collection, in which he worked out the contrast between poetic and practical language that served as the basic principle of the Formalists' work on key problems of poetics. As a result, the Formalists did not look, as literary students usually had, toward history, culture, sociology, psychology, or aesthetics, etc., but toward linguistics, a science bordering on poetics and sharing material with it, but approaching it from a different perspective and with different problems. Linguistics, for its part, was also interested in the formal method in that what was discovered by comparing poetic and practical language could be studied as a purely linguistic problem, as part of the general phenomena of language. The relationship between linguistics and the formal method was somewhat analogous to that relation of mutual use and delimitation that exists, for example, between physics and chemistry. Against this background, the problems posed earlier by Potebnya and taken for granted by his followers were reviewed and reinterpreted.

Leo Jakubinsky's first essay, "On the Sounds of Poetic Language,"[2] compared practical and poetic language and formulated the difference between them:

> The phenomena of language must be classified from the point of view of the speaker's particular purpose as he forms his own linguistic pattern. If the pattern is formed for the purely practical purpose of communication, then we are dealing with a system of *practical language* (the language of thought) in which the linguistic pattern (sounds, morphological features, etc.) have no independent value and are merely a *means* of communication. But other linguistic systems, systems in which the

9. Roman Jakobson, *Noveyshaya russkaya poeziya* [*Modern Russian Poetry*] (Prague, 1921), p. 11 [Eichenbaum's note].
1. Russian linguist and critic (1892–1945), associated with *Opoyaz* but not a member.
2. Leo Jakubinsky, "O zvukakh poeticheskovo yazyka," *Sborniki* 1 (1916) [Eichenbaum's note].

> practical purpose is in the background (although perhaps not entirely hidden) are conceivable; they exist, and their linguistic patterns acquire *independent value*.

The establishment of this distinction was important both for the construction of a poetics and for understanding the Futurist's preference for "nonsense language"[3] as revealing the furthest extension of the sheer "independent" value of words, the kind of value partially observed in the language of children, in the glossolalia of religious sects,[4] and so on. The Futurist experiments in nonsense language were of prime significance as a demonstration against Symbolism which, in its theories, went no further than to use the idea of "instrumentation" to indicate the accompaniment of meaning by sound and so to de-emphasize the role of sound in poetic language. The problem of sound in verse was especially crucial because it was on this point that the Formalists and Futurists united to confront the theorists of Symbolism. Naturally, the Formalists gave battle at first on just that issue; the question of sound had to be disposed of first if we were to oppose the aesthetic and philosophical tendencies of the Symbolists with a system of precise observations and to reach the underlying scientific conclusions. This accounts for the content of the first volume of *Opoyaz*, a content devoted entirely to the problem of sound and nonsense language.

Victor Shklovsky, along with Jakubinsky, in "On Poetry and Nonsense Language,"[5] cited a variety of examples which showed that "even words without meaning are necessary." He showed such meaninglessness to be both a widespread linguistic fact and a phenomenon characteristic of poetry. "The poet does not decide to use the meaningless word; usually 'nonsense' is disguised as some kind of frequently delusive, deceptive content. Poets are forced to acknowledge that they themselves do not understand the content of their own verses." Shklovsky's essay, moreover, transfers the question from the area of pure sound, from the acoustical level (which provided the basis for impressionistic interpretations of the relation between sound and the description of objects or the emotion represented), to the level of pronunciation and articulation. "In the enjoyment of a meaningless 'nonsense word,' the articulatory aspect of speech is undoubtedly important. Perhaps generally a great part of the delight of poetry consists in pronunciation, in the independent dance of the organs of speech." The question of meaningless language thus became a serious scientific concern, the solution of which would help to clarify many problems of poetic language in general. Shklovsky also formulated the general question:

> If we add to our demand of the word as such that it serve to clarify understanding, that it be generally meaningful, then of course "meaningless" language, as a relatively superficial language, falls by the wayside. But it does not fall alone; a consideration of the facts forces one to wonder whether words always have a meaning, not only in meaningless speech, but also in simple poetic speech—or whether this notion is only a fiction resulting from our inattention.

3. Language used solely for its sound, ignoring its sense.
4. That is, speaking in tongues: ecstatic language-like utterances.
5. Victor Shklovsky, "O poezii i zaumnom yazyke," *Sborniki* 1 (1916) [Eichenbaum's note].

The natural conclusion of these observations and principles was that poetic language is not only a language of images, that sounds in verse are not at all merely elements of a superficial euphony, and that they do not play a mere "accompaniment" to meaning, but rather that they have an independent significance. The purpose of this work was to force a revision of Potebnya's general theory, which had been built on the conviction that poetry is "thought in images." Potebnya's analysis of poetry, the analysis which the Symbolists had adopted, treated the sound of verse as "expressive" of something behind it. Sound was merely onomatopoetic, merely "aural description." The works of Andrey Bely (who discovered the complete sound picture that champagne makes when poured from a bottle into a glass in two lines from Pushkin, and who also discovered the "noisomeness of a hangover" in Blok's[6] repetition of the consonantal cluster *rdt*) were quite typical. Such attempts to "explain" alliteration, bordering on parody, required a rebuff and an attempt to produce concrete evidence showing that sounds in verse exist apart from any connection with imagery, that they have an independent oral function.

Leo Jakubinsky, in his essays, provided linguistic support for [our arguments in favor of] the independent value of sound in verse. Osip Brik's essay on "Sound Repetitions"[7] illustrated the same point with quotations from Pushkin and Lermontov[8] arranged to present a variety of models. Brik doubted the correctness of the common opinion that poetic language is a language of "images":

> No matter how one looks at the interrelationship of image and sound, there is undoubtedly only one conclusion possible—the sounds, the harmonies, are not only euphonious accessories to meaning; they are also the result of an independent poetic purpose. The superficial devices of euphony do not completely account for the instrumentation of poetic speech. Such instrumentation represents on the whole an intricate product of the interaction of the general laws of harmony. Rhyme, alliteration, etc., are only obvious manifestations, particular cases, of the basic laws of euphony.

In opposing the work of Bely, Brik, in the same essay, made no comment at all on the meaning of this or that use of alliteration, but merely affirmed that repetition in verse is analogous to tautology in folklore—that is, that repetition itself plays something of an aesthetic role: "Obviously we have here diverse forms of one general principle, the principle of simple combination, by which either the sounds of the words or their meanings, or now one and now the other, serve as the material of the combination." Such an extension of one device to cover the various forms of poetic material is quite characteristic of the work of the Formalists during their initial period. After the presentation of Brik's essay the question of sound in verse lost something of its urgency, and the Formalists turned to questions of poetics in general.

6. Aleksandr Blok (1880–1921), Russian poet associated with symbolism. Aleksandr Pushkin (1799–1837), great Russian writer of fiction, plays, and especially poetry.

7. Osip Brik, "Zvukovye povtory," *Sborniki* 2 (1917) [Eichenbaum's note].

8. Mikhail Lermontov (1814–1841), Russian poet and novelist.

3. *Content and Correspondent Form Versus Technique as Content*

The Formalists began their work with the question of the sounds of verse—at that time the most controversial and most basic question. Behind this particular question of poetics stood more general theses which had to be formulated. The distinction between systems of poetic and practical language, which defined the work of the Formalists from the very beginning, was bound to result in the formulation of a whole group of basic questions. The idea of poetry as "thought by means of images" and the resulting formula, "Poetry = Imagery," clearly did not coincide with our observations and contradicted our tentative general principles. Rhythm, sound, syntax—all of these seemed secondary from such a point of view; they seemed uncharacteristic of poetry and necessarily extraneous to it. The Symbolists accepted Potebnya's general theory because it justified the supremacy of the image-symbol; yet they could not rid themselves of the notorious theory of the "harmony of form and content" even though it clearly contradicted their bent for formal experimentation and discredited it by making it seem mere "aestheticism." The Formalists, when they abandoned Potebnya's point of view, also freed themselves from the traditional correlation of "form and content" and from the traditional idea of form as an envelope, a vessel into which one pours a liquid (the content). The facts of art demonstrate that art's uniqueness consists not in the "parts" which enter into it but in their original *use*. Thus the notion of form was changed; the new notion of form required no companion idea, no correlative.

Even before the formation of the *Opoyaz* in 1914, at the time of the public performances of the Futurists, Shklovsky had published a monograph, *The Resurrection of the Word*,[9] in which he took exception partly to the concepts set forth by Potebnya and partly to those of Veselovsky (the question of imagery was not then of major significance) to advance the principle of perceptible form as the specific sign of artistic awareness:

> We do not experience the commonplace, we do not see it; rather, we recognize it. We do not see the walls of our room; and it is very difficult for us to see errors in proofreading, especially if the material is written in a language we know well, because we cannot force ourselves to see, to read, and not to "recognize" the familiar word. If we have to define specifically "poetic" perception and artistic perception in general, then we suggest this definition: "Artistic" perception is that perception in which we experience form—perhaps not form alone, but certainly form.

Perception here is clearly not to be understood as a simple psychological concept (the perception peculiar to this or that person), but, since art does not exist outside of perception, as an element in art itself. The notion of "form" here acquires new meaning; it is no longer an envelope, but a complete thing, something concrete, dynamic, self-contained, and without a correlative of any kind. Here we made a decisive break with the Symbolist principle that some sort of "content" is to shine through the "form." And we

9. Victor Shklovsky, *Voskresheniye slova* (Petersburg, 1914) [Eichenbaum's note].

broke with "aestheticism"—the preference for certain elements of form consciously isolated from "content."

But these general acknowledgements that there are differences between poetic and practical language and that the specific quality of art is shown in its particular use of the material were not adequate when we tried to deal with specific works. We had to find more specific formulations of the principle of perceptible form so that they could make possible the analysis of form itself—the analysis of form understood as content. We had to show that the perception of form results from special artistic techniques which force the reader to experience the form. Shklovsky's "Art as Technique," presenting its own manifesto of the Formalist method, offered a perspective for the concrete analysis of form. Here was a really clear departure from Potebnya and Potebnyaism and, at the same time, from the theoretical principles of Symbolism. The essay began with objections to Potebnya's basic view of imagery and its relation to content. Shklovsky indicates, among other things, that images are almost always static:

> The more you understand an age, the more convinced you become that the images a given poet used and which you thought his own were taken almost unchanged from another poet. The works of poets are classified or grouped according to the new techniques they discover and share, and according to their arrangement and development of the resources of language; poets are much more concerned with arranging images than creating them. Images are given to poets; the ability to remember them is far more important than the ability to create them. Imagistic thought does not, in any case, include all aspects of art or even all aspects of verbal art. A change in imagery is not essential to the development of poetry.[1]

He further pointed out the difference between poetic and nonpoetic images. The poetic image is defined as one of the devices of poetic language—as a device which, depending upon the problem, is as important as such other devices of poetic language as simple and negative parallelism, comparison, repetition, symmetry, hyperbole, etc., but no more important. Thus imagery becomes a part of a system of poetic devices and loses its theoretical dominance.

Shklovsky likewise repudiated the principle of artistic economy, a principle which had been strongly asserted in aesthetic theory, and opposed it with the device of "defamiliarization"[2] and the notion of "roughened form." That is, he saw art as increasing the difficulty and span of perception "because the process of perception is an aesthetic end in itself and must be prolonged";[3] he saw art as a means of destroying the automatism of perception; the purpose of the image is not to present the approximate meaning of its object to our understanding, but to create a special perception of the object—the creation of its "vision," and not the "recognition" of its meaning. Hence the image is usually connected with the process of defamiliarization.

1. Victor Shklovsky, "Art as Technique" (1917), in *Russian Formalist Criticism: Four Essays*, trans. and ed. Lee T. Lemon and Marion J. Reis (Lincoln: University of Nebraska Press, 1965), p. 7.
2. A formalist technical term (*ostraneniye* in Russian, also translated as "making strange") for making a familiar word, image, or event seem strange, thus countering habituated perception or "automatism" and provoking renewed aesthetic response. A related concept is that of "roughened" (*zatrudyonny*) form.
3. Shklovsky, "Art as Technique," p. 12.

The break with Potebnya was formulated definitely in Shklovsky's essay "Potebnya."[4] He repeats once more that imagery—symbolization—does not constitute the specific difference between poetic and prosaic (practical) language:

> Poetic language is distinguished from practical language by the perception of its structure. The acoustical, articulatory, or semantic aspects of poetic language may be felt. Sometimes one feels the verbal structure, the arrangement of the words, rather than their texture. The poetic image is one of the ways, but only one of the ways, of creating a perceptible structure designed to be experienced within its very own fabric. . . . The creation of a scientific poetics must begin inductively with a hypothesis built on an accumulation of evidence. That hypothesis is that poetic and prosaic languages exist, that the laws which distinguish them exist, and, finally, that these differences are to be analyzed.

These essays are to be read as the summation of the first phase of the Formalists' work. The main achievement of this period consisted in our establishment of a series of theoretical principles which provided working hypotheses for a further investigation of the data for the defeat of the current theories based on Potebnyaism. The chief strength of the Formalists, as these essays show, was neither the direction of their study of so-called "forms" nor the construction of a special "method"; their strength was founded securely on the fact that the specific features of the verbal arts had to be studied and that to do so it was first necessary to sort out the differing uses of poetic and practical language. Concerning form, the Formalists thought it important to change the meaning of this muddled term. It was important to destroy these traditional correlatives and so to enrich the idea of form with new significance. *The notion of "technique,"*[5] because it has to do directly with the distinguishing features of poetic and practical speech, *is much more significant in the long-range evolution of formalism than is the notion of "form."*

4. *Applications of Theory: Questions of Plot and Literary Evolution*

The preliminary stage of our theoretical work had passed. We had proposed general principles bearing directly upon factual material. We now had to move closer to the material and to make the problems themselves specific. At the center stood those questions of theoretical poetics that had previously been outlined only in general form. We had to move from questions about the sound of verse to a general theory of verse. The questions about the sound of verse, when originally posed, were meant only as illustrations of the difference between poetic and practical language. We had to move from questions about "technique-in-general" to the study of the specific devices of composition, to inquiry about plot, and so on. Our interest in opposing Veselovsky's general view and, specifically, in opposing his theory of plot, developed side by side with our interest in opposing Potebnya's.

At this time, the Formalists quite naturally used literary works only as material for supporting and testing their theoretical hypothesis; we had put

4. Victor Shklovsky, "Potebnya," *Poetika* (1919) [Eichenbaum's note].

5. A formalist technical term (*priyom* in Russian, also translated as "device") for any of the basic elements that have a function in an artistic composition.

aside questions of convention, literary evolution, etc. Now we felt it important to widen the scope of our study, to make a preliminary survey of the data, and to allow it to establish its own kind of "laws." In this way we freed ourselves from the necessity of resorting to abstract premises and at the same time mastered the materials without losing ourselves in details.

Shklovsky, with his theory of plot and fiction, was especially important during this period. He demonstrated the presence of special devices of "plot construction" and their relation to general stylistic devices in such diverse materials as the *skaz*, Oriental tales,[6] Cervantes' *Don Quixote*, Tolstoy's works, Sterne's *Tristram Shandy*,[7] and so on. I do not wish to go into details—those should be treated in specialized works and not in a general essay such as this on the Formalist method—but I do wish to cover those ideas in Shklovsky's treatment of plot which have a theoretical significance beyond any relationship they might have to particular problems of plots as such. Traces of those ideas can be found in the most advanced pieces of Formalist criticism.

The first of Shklovsky's works on plot, "The Relation of Devices of Plot Construction to General Devices of Style,"[8] raised a whole series of such ideas. In the first place, the proof that special devices of plot arrangement exist, a proof supported by the citation of great numbers of devices, changed the traditional notion of plot as a combination of a group of motifs[9] and made plot a compositional rather than a thematic concept. Thus the very concept of plot was changed; *plot* was no longer synonymous with *story*.[1] Plot construction became the natural subject of Formalist study, since plot constitutes the specific peculiarity of narrative *art*. The idea of form had been enriched, and as it lost its former abstractness, it also lost its controversial meaning. Our idea of form had begun to coincide with our idea of literature as such, with the idea of the literary fact.

Furthermore, the analogies which we established between the devices of plot construction and the devices of style had theoretical significance, for the step-by-step structure usually found in the epic was found to be analogous to sound repetition, tautology, tautological parallelism, and so on. All illustrated a general principle of verbal art based on parceling out and impending the action.

For instance, Roland's three blows on the stone in the *Song of Roland*[2] and the similar triple repetition common in tales may be compared, as a single type of phenomenon, with Gogol's[3] use of synonyms and with such linguistic structures as "hoity-toity," "a diller, a dollar," etc.[4] "These varia-

6. Folktales with exotic settings in India, Persia, and Arabic countries, like those collected in the *Arabian Nights*, written in Arabic but first translated and published in Europe in the eighteenth century. *Skaz*: a Russian literary form; perhaps best translated "yarn."

7. The works of three novelists working in different languages and periods: in Spanish, Miguel de Cervantes (1567–1616), also a poet and playwright, best-known for *Don Quixote* (1606, 1616); in Russian, Leo Tolstoy (1828–1910), who wrote plays and moral philosophy as well as novels, including *War and Peace* (1863–69); and in English, Laurence Sterne (1713–1768), whose *Tristram Shandy* (1759–67) is a deliberately eccentric "life" of its hero.

8. First published in Russian in 1919; translated in Viktor Shklovsky, *Theory of Prose*, trans. Benjamin Sher (Elmwood Park, Ill.: Dalkey Archive Press, 1990), pp. 15–51.

9. The smallest isolatable units of narrative (a term from folklore study).

1. A seminal formalist distinction in narrative theory: "story" (*fabula*, Latin) designates the events in their chronological sequence; "plot" (*syuzhet*, Russian) refers to the events in the order they are arranged by the author.

2. An 11th-century French epic; Roland, one of Charlemagne's paladins, attempts three times to break his sword against a stone to keep it from his enemies' hands.

3. Nikolay Gogol (1809–1852), Russian novelist and dramatist.

4. Eichenbaum gives two nonsense phrases here, *kudy-mudy* and *plyushki-mlyushki*. The point is that repetition of sound alone may keep alive cer-

tions of step-by-step construction usually do not all occur together, and attempts have been made to give each case a special explanation." Shklovsky shows how we attempt to demonstrate that the same device may reappear in diverse materials. Here we clashed with Veselovsky, who in such cases usually avoided theory and resorted to historical-genetic hypotheses. For instance, he explained epic repetition as a mechanism for the original performance (as embryonic song). But an explanation of the genetics of such a phenomenon, even if true, does not clarify the phenomenon as a fact of literature. Veselovsky and other members of the ethnographic school[5] used to explain the peculiar motifs and plots of the *skaz* by relating literature and custom; Shklovsky did not object to making the relationship but challenged it only as an explanation of the peculiarities of the *skaz*—he challenged it as an explanation of a specifically literary fact. The study of literary genetics can clarify only the origin of a device, nothing more; poetics must explain its literary function. The genetic point of view fails to consider the device as a self-determined use of material; it does not consider how conventional materials are selected by an author, how conventional devices are transformed, or how they are made to play a structural role. The genetic point of view does not explain how a convention may disappear and its literary function remain. The literary function remains not as a simple experience but as a literary device retaining a significance over and beyond its connection with the convention. Characteristically, Veselovsky had contradicted himself by considering the adventures of the Greek romance[6] as purely stylistic devices.

The Formalists naturally opposed Veselovsky's "ethnographism" because it ignored the special characteristic of the literary device and because it replaced the theoretical and evolutionary point of view with a genetic point of view.

Veselovsky saw "syncretism"[7] as a phenomenon of primitive poetry, a result of custom, and he later was censured for this in B. Kazansky's "The Concept of Historical Poetics."[8] Kazansky repudiated the ethnographic point of view by affirming the presence of syncretic tendencies in the very nature of each art, a presence especially obvious in some periods. The Formalists naturally could not agree with Veselovsky when he touched upon general questions of literary evolution. If the clash with the Potebnyaists clarified basic principles of poetics, the clash with Veselovsky's general view and with that of his followers clarified the Formalists' views on literary evolution and, thereby, on the structure of literary history.

Shklovsky began to deal with the subject of literary evolution in the essay I cited previously, "The Relation of Devices of Plot Construction to General Devices of Style." He had encountered Veselovsky's formula, a formula broadly based on the ethnographic principle that "the purpose of new form is to express new content," and he decided to advance a completely different point of view:

> The work of art arises from a background of other works and through association with them. The form of a work of art is defined by its relation

tain otherwise meaningless expressions [translators' note].

5. That is, those explaining literary material in terms of cultural background; ethnography is a field of anthropology.

6. Prose narratives introduced in the 1st century B.C.E., characterized by complicated adventures, terrifying dangers, and eroticism.

7. The combination of forms and beliefs.

8. Published in Russian in 1926 by Boris Kazansky (1891–1973), associated with the *Opoyaz* group.

> to other works of art, to forms existing prior to it. . . . Not only parody, but also any kind of work of art is created parallel to and opposed to some kind of form. *The purpose of the new form is not to express new content, but to change an old form which has lost its aesthetic quality.*[9]

Shklovsky supported this thesis with B[roder] Christiansen's[1] demonstration of "differentiated perceptions" or "perceptions of difference." He sees that the dynamism characteristic of art is based on this and is manifested in repeated violations of established rules. At the close of his essay, he quotes F[erdinand] Brunetière's[2] statements that "of all the influences active in the history of literature, the chief is the influence of *work on work*," and that "one should not, without good cause, increase the number of influences upon literature, under the assumption that literature is the expression of society, nor should one confuse the history of literature with the history of morals and manners. These are entirely different things."

Shklovsky's essay marked the changeover from our study of theoretical poetics to our study of the history of literature. Our original assumptions about form had been complicated by our observation of new features of evolutionary dynamics and their continuous variability. Our moving into the area of the history of literature was no simple expansion of our study; it resulted from the evolution of our concept of form. We found that we could not see the literary work in isolation, that we had to see its form against a background of other works rather than by itself. Thus the Formalists definitely went beyond "Formalism," if by "Formalism" one means (as some poorly informed critics usually did) some fabricated system which permitted us to be "classified," some system which zealously adapted itself to logic-chopping, or some system which joyously welcomed any dogma. Such scholastic "Formalism" was neither historical nor essentially connected with the work of the *Opoyaz*. We were not responsible for it; on the contrary, we were irreconcilably its enemies on principle.

5. *Prose Fiction: "Motivation" and Exposed Structure*

Later I shall return to the historical-literary work of the Formalists, but now I wish to conclude the survey of those theoretical principles and problems contained in the early work of the *Opoyaz*. The Shklovsky essay I referred to above contains still another idea which figured prominently in the subsequent study of the novel—the idea of "motivation."[3] The discovery of various techniques of plot construction (step-by-step structure, parallelism, framing, the weaving of motifs, etc.) clarified the difference between the elements used in the construction of a work and the elements comprising its material (its story, the choice of motifs, the characters, the themes, etc.). Shklovsky stressed this difference at that time because the basic problem was to show the identity of individual structural devices in the most diverse materials imaginable. The old scholarship worked exclusively with the material, taking it as the "content" and treating the remainder as an "external

9. See Shklovsky, *Theory of Prose*, p. 20.
1. German aesthetician (1869–1942).
2. French literary historian (1846–1906).
3. A formalist technical term for the functional reason governing the use of a particular device, ranging from a way to shock readers to the insertion of specific props required to further events in the action.

form" either totally without interest or of interest only to the dilettante. Hence the naive and pathetic aesthetics of our older literary critics and historians, who found "neglect of form" in Tyutchev's[4] poetry and simply "bad form" in Nekrasov and Dostoevsky.[5] The literary reputations of these authors were saved because their intensity of thought and mood excused their formlessness. Naturally, during the years of struggle and polemics against such a position, the Formalists directed all their forces to showing the significance of such compositional devices as motivation and ignored all other considerations. In speaking of the formal method and its evolution, we must constantly remember that many of the principles advanced by the Formalists in the years of tense struggle were significant not only as scientific principles, but also as slogans, as paradoxes sharpened for propaganda and controversy. To ignore this fact and to treat the work of the *Opoyaz* (between 1916 and 1921) in the same way as one would treat the academic scholarship is to ignore history.

The concept of motivation permitted the Formalists to approach literary works (in particular, novels and short stories) more closely and to observe the details of their structure, which Shklovsky did in two later works, *Plot Development* and *Sterne's* Tristram Shandy *and the Theory of the Novel.*[6] In these works, he studied the relationship between technique and motivation in Cervantes' *Don Quixote* and Sterne's *Tristram Shandy*. He uses *Tristram Shandy* as material for the study of the structure of the short story and the novel apart from literary history, and he studies *Don Quixote* as an instance of the transition from collections of tales (like the *Decameron*[7]) to the novel with a single hero whose travels justify or "motivate" its episodic structure. *Don Quixote* was chosen because the devices it contains and their motivation are not fully integrated into the entire context of the novel. Material is often simply inserted, not welded in; devices of plot construction and methods of using material to further the plot structure stand out sharply, whereas later structures tend "more and more to integrate the material tightly into the very body of the novel." While analyzing "how Don Quixote was made," Shklovsky also showed the instability of the hero and concluded that his "type" appeared "as the result of the business of constructing the novel." Thus the dominance of structure, of plot over material, was emphasized.

Neither a work fully "motivated" nor an art which deliberately does away with motivation and exposes the structure provides the most suitable material for the illumination of such theoretical problems. But the very existence of a work such as *Don Quixote*, with a deliberately exposed structure, confirms the relevance of these problems, confirms the fact that the problems need to be stated as problems, and confirms the fact that they are *significant* literary problems. Moreover, we were able to explain works of literature entirely in the light of these theoretical problems and principles, as Shklovsky did with *Tristram Shandy*. Shklovsky not only used the book to illustrate our theoretical position, he gave it new significance and once more attracted

4. Fyodor Tyutchev (1803–1873), Russian poet.
5. Fyodor Dostoyevsky (1821–1881), major Russian novelist. Nikolay Nekrasov (1821–1878), Russian poet and editor.
6. Both essays were first published in Russian in 1921, and are translated in Shklovsky, *Theory of Prose*. The latter, translated as "Sterne's *Tristram Shandy*: Stylistic Commentary," also appears in Lemon and Reis, *Russian Formalist Criticism*, pp. 25–57.
7. A collection of 100 tales in a frame story (1351–53), the most famous work of the Italian prose writer and poet GIOVANNI BOCCACCIO.

attention to it. Studied against the background of an interest in the *structure* of the novel, Sterne became a contemporary; people spoke about him, people who previously had found in his novel only boring chatter or eccentricities, or who had prejudged it from the point of view of its notorious "sentimentalism," a characteristic for which Sterne is as little to blame as Gogol for "realism."

Shklovsky pointed out Sterne's deliberate laying bare[8] of his methods of constructing *Tristram Shandy* and asserted that Sterne had "exaggerated" the structure of the novel. He had shown his awareness of form by his manner of violating it and by his manner of assembling the novel's contents. In his conclusion to the essay, Shklovsky formulated the difference between plot and story:

> The idea of plot is too often confused with the description of events—with what I propose provisionally to call the *story*. The story is, in fact, only material for plot formulation. The plot of *Eugeny Onegin*[9] is, therefore, not the romance of the hero with Tatyana, but the fashioning of the subject of this story as produced by the introduction of interrupting digressions. . . .
>
> The forms of art are explainable by the laws of art; they are not justified, by their realism. Slowing the action of a novel is not accomplished by introducing rivals, for example, but by simply *transposing* parts. In so doing the artist makes us aware of the aesthetic laws which underlie both the transposition and the slowing down of the action.[1]

My essay "How Gogol's 'Greatcoat' Was Made,"[2] also considers the structure of the novel, comparing the problem of plot with the problem of the *skaz*—the problem of structure based upon the narrator's manner of telling what had happened. I tried to show that Gogol's text "was made up of living speech patterns and vocalized emotions," that words and sentences are selected and joined by Gogol as they are in the oral *skaz*, in which articulation, mimicry, sound gestures, and so on, play a special role. From this point of view I showed how the structure of "The Greatcoat" imparts a grotesque tone to the tale by replacing the usual humor of the *skaz* (with its anecdotes, puns, etc.) with sentimental-melodramatic declamation. I discussed, in this connection, the end of "The Greatcoat" as the apotheosis of the grotesque—not unlike the mute scene in *The Inspector General*.[3] The traditional line of argument about Gogol's "romanticism" and "realism" proved unnecessary and unilluminating.

Thus we began to make some progress with the problem of the study of prose. The line between the idea of plot as structure and the idea of the story as material was drawn; this explanation of the typical techniques of plot construction opened the door for work on the history and theory of the novel; and furthermore, the *skaz* was treated as the structural basis of the plotless short story. These works have influenced a whole series of recent studies by persons not directly connected with the *Opoyaz*.

8. A formalist technical term (*obnazheniye*, Russian) for introducing an element in a composition without any artistic justification, thereby signaling that element's functional role (e.g., presenting a meeting as pure coincidence rather than trying to explain it).
9. An 1833 novel in verse by Pushkin (the title is usually translated *Eugene Onegin*); Tatyana is its heroine.
1. Shklovsky, "Sterne's *Tristram Shandy*," p. 57.
2. First published in Russian in 1919. "The Greatcoat" (1842) is Gogol's best-known story.
3. An 1836 play by Gogol; it ends with a minute and a half of silence as the curtain falls.

6. *Poetry: Meter versus a Complete Linguistic Prosody: Syntax, Intonation, Phonemics*

As our theoretical work broadened and deepened it naturally became specialized—the more so because persons who were only beginning their work or who had been working independently joined the *Opoyaz* group. Some of them specialized in the problems of poetry, others in the problems of prose. The Formalists insisted upon keeping clear the demarcation between poetry and prose in order to counterbalance the Symbolists, who were then attempting to erase the boundary line both in theory and in practice by painstakingly attempting to discover meter in prose.

The earlier sections of this essay show the intensity of our work on prose. We were pioneers in the area. Several Western works resembled ours (in particular, such observations on story material as Wilhelm Dibelius' *Englische Romankunst,*[4] 1910), but they had little relevance to our theoretical problems and principles. In our work on prose we felt almost free from tradition, but in dealing with verse the situation was different. The great number of works by Western and Russian literary theorists, the numerous practical and theoretical experiments of the Symbolists, and the special literature of the controversies over the concepts of rhythm and meter (produced between 1910 and 1917) complicated our study of poetry. The Futurists, in that same period, were creating new verse forms, and this complicated things still more. Given such conditions, it was difficult for us to pose the right problems. Many persons, instead of returning to basic questions, were concerned with special problems of metrics or with trying to put the accumulation of systems and opinions in good order. Meanwhile, we had no general theory of poetry: no theoretical elucidations of verse rhythm, of the connection of rhythm and syntax, of the sounds of verse (the Formalists had indicated only a few linguistic premises), of poetic diction and semantics, and so on. In other words, the nature of verse as such remained essentially obscure. We had to draw away from particular problems of metrics and to approach verse from some more disciplined perspective. We had, first of all, to pose the problem of rhythm so that it did not rest on metrics and would include a more substantial part of poetic speech.

Here, as in the previous section, I shall dwell upon the problem of verse only insofar as its exploration led to a new theoretical view of verbal art or a new view of the nature of poetic speech. Our position was stated first in Osip Brik's "On Rhythmic-Syntactic Figures" [1920], an unpublished lecture delivered before the *Opoyaz* group and, apparently, not even written out.[5] Brik demonstrated that verse contained stable syntactical figures indissolubly connected with rhythm. Thus rhythm was no longer thought of as an abstraction; it was made relevant to the very linguistic fabric of verse—the phrase. Metrics became a kind of background, significant, like the alphabet, for the reading and writing of verse. Brik's step was as important for the study of verse as the discovery of the relation of plot to structure was for the study of prose. The discovery that rhythmic patterns are related to the grammatical patterns of sentences destroyed the notion that rhythm is a superficial appendage, something floating on the surface of speech. Our theory of verse

4. *Art of the English Novel* (German). Dibelius (1876–1931), German literary scholar.

5. Brik's lecture was published in 1927 in *New Left* [translators' note].

was founded on the analysis of rhythm as the structural basis of verse, a basis which of itself determined all of its parts—both acoustical and nonacoustical. A superior theory of verse, which would make metrics but a kindergarten preparation, was in sight. The Symbolists and the group led by Bely, despite their attempts, could not travel our road because they still saw the central problem as metrics in isolation.

But Brik's work merely hinted at the possibility of a new way; like his first essay, "Sound Repetitions,"[6] it was limited to showing examples and arranging them into groups. From Brik's lecture one could move either into new problems or into the simple classification and cataloging, or systematizing, of the material. The lecture was not necessarily an expression of the formal method. V[ictor] Zhirmunsky continued the work of classification, in *The Composition of Lyric Verse.*[7] Zhirmunsky, who did not share the theoretical principles of the *Opoyaz*, was interested in the formal method as only one of the possible scientific approaches to the division of materials into various groups and headings. Given his understanding of the formal method, he could do nothing else; he accepted any superficial feature as a basis for the grouping of materials. Hence the unvarying cataloging and the pedantic tone of all of Zhirmunsky's theoretical work. Such works were not a major influence in the general evolution of the formal method; in themselves they merely emphasized the tendency (evidently historically inevitable) to give the formal method an academic quality. It is not surprising, therefore, that Zhirmunsky later completely withdrew from the *Opoyaz* over a difference of opinion about the principles he stated repeatedly in his last works (especially in his introduction to the translation of O[skar] Walzel's[8] *The Problem of Form in Poetry* [1923]).

My book, *Verse Melody,*[9] which was prepared as a study of the phonetics of verse and so was related to a whole group of Western works (by Sievers, Saran,[1] etc.), was relevant to Brik's work on rhythmic-syntactic figures. I maintained that stylistic differences were usually chiefly lexical:

> With that we drop the idea of versification as such, and take up poetic language in general. . . . We have to find something related to the *poetic phrase* that does not also lead us away from the *poetry* itself, something bordering on both phonetics and semantics. This "something" is syntax.

I did not examine the rhythmic-syntactic phenomena in isolation, but as part of an examination of the structural significance of metrical and vocal intonation. I felt it especially important both to assert the idea of a *dominant,*[2] upon which a given poetic style is organized, and to isolate the idea of "melody" as a system of intonations from the idea of the general "musicality" of verse. On this basis, I proposed to distinguish three fundamental styles of lyric poetry: declamatory (oratorical), melodic, and conversational. My entire book is devoted to the peculiarities of the melodic style—to peculiarities in the material of the lyrics of Zhukovsky, Tyutchev, Lermontov, and Fet.[3]

6. Published in Russian in 1919.
7. Published in Russian in 1921. Zhirmunsky (1891–1971), Russian critic specializing in poetry; associated with but not a member of the formalist movement.
8. German literary historian (1864–1944).
9. Boris Eichenbaum, *Melodika russkovo liricheskovo stikha* (Petrograd, 1922) [Eichenbaum's note].
1. Franz Saran (1866–1931), German verse theorist. Eduard Sievers (1850–1932), German linguist.
2. A formalist technical term for the element in a composition to which other elements are subordinate; for the formalists, a composition is not merely a set of elements but a hierarchy of them.
3. Afanasy Fet (1820–1892), Russian lyric poet. Vasily Zhukovsky (1783–1852), Russian poet and translator.

Avoiding ready-made schematizations, I ended the book with the conviction that "in scientific work, I consider the ability to see facts far more important than the construction of a system. Theories are necessary to clarify facts; in reality, theories are made of facts. Theories perish and change, but the facts they help discover and support remain."

The tradition of specialized metrical studies still continued among the Symbolist theoreticians (Bely, Bryusov, Bobrov,[4] Chudovsky, and others), but it gradually turned into precise statistical enumeration and lost what had been its dominant characteristic. Here the metrical studies of Boris Tomashevsky, concluded in his text *Russian Versification*,[5] played the most significant role. Thus, as the study of metrics became secondary, a subsidiary discipline with a very limited range of problems, the general theory of verse entered its first stage.

Tomashevsky's "Pushkin's Iambic Pentameter"[6] outlined the entire previous course of developments within the formal method, including its attempt to broaden and enrich the notion of poetic rhythm and to relate it to the structure of poetic language. The essay also attempted to go beyond the idea of meter in language. Hence the basic charge against Bely and his school: "The problem of rhythm is not conformity to imaginary meters; it is rather the distribution of expiratory energy within a single wave—the line itself."[7] In "The Problems of Poetic Rhythm" Tomashevsky expressed this with perfect clarity of principle. Here the earlier conflict between meter and rhythm is resolved by applying the idea of rhythm in verse to all of the elements of speech that play a part in the structure of verse. The rhythms of phrasal intonation and euphony (alliterations, etc.) are placed side by side with the rhythm of word accent. Thus we came to see the line as *a special form of speech* which functions as a single unit in the creation of poetry. We no longer saw the line as something which could create a "rhythmic variation" by resisting or adjusting to the metrical form (a view which Zhirmunsky continued to defend in his new work, *Introduction to Metrics*[8]). Tomashevsky wrote that:

> Poetic speech is *organized* in terms of its sounds. Taken singly, any phonetic element is subject to rules and regulations, but sound is a *complex* phenomenon. Thus classical metrics singles out accent and normalizes it by its rules. . . . But it takes little effort to shake the authority of traditional forms, because the notion persisted that the nature of verse is not fully explained by a single distinguishing feature, that poetry exists in "secondary" features, that a recognizable rhythm exists alongside meter, that poetry can be created by imposing a pattern on only these secondary features, and *that speech without meter may sound like poetry*.

The important idea of a "rhythmic impulse" (which had figured earlier in Brik's work) with a general rhythmic function is maintained here:

> Rhythmic devices may participate in various degrees in the creation of an artistic-rhythmic effect; this or that device may dominate various

4. Sergei Bobrov (1889–1971), Russian poet, critic, and novelist.
5. Published in Russian in 1923.
6. Boris Tomashevsky, "Pyatistopny iamb Pushkina," *Ocherki po poetike Pushkina* [*Essays on the Poetics of Pushkin*] (Berlin, 1923) [Eichenbaum's note].
7. Boris Tomashevsky, "Problema stikhotvornovo ritma," *Literaturnaya mysl* [*Literary Thought*] 2 (1922) [Eichenbaum's note].
8. Published in Russian in 1925.

> works—this or that means may be the *dominant*. The use of a given rhythmic device determines the character of the particular rhythm of the work. On this basis poetry may be classified as accented-metrical poetry (e.g., the description of the Battle of Poltava[9]), intoned-melodic poetry (the verses of Zhukovsky), or harmonic poetry (common during the recent years of Russian Symbolism).

Poetic form, so understood, is not contrasted with anything outside itself—with a "content" which has been laboriously set inside this "form"—but is understood as the genuine content of poetic speech. Thus the very idea of form, as it had been understood in earlier works, emerged with a new and more adequate meaning.

7. *Toward a More Complete Prosody*

In his essay "On Czech Versification" Roman Jakobson pointed out new problems in the general theory of poetic rhythm.[1] He opposed the [earlier] theory that "verse adapts itself completely to the spirit of the language," that is, that "form does not resist the material [it shapes]" with the theory that "poetic form is the organized coercion of language." He applied this refinement of the more orthodox view—a refinement in keeping with the formalist method—to the question of the difference between the phonetic qualities of practical language and those of poetic language. Although Jakubinsky had noted that the dissimilation of liquid consonants[2] is relatively infrequent in poetry, Jakobson showed that it existed in both poetic and practical language but that in practical language it is "accidental"; in poetic language it is, "so to speak, contrived; these are two distinct phenomena."

In the same essay Jakobson also clarified the principle distinction between emotional and poetic language (a distinction he had previously considered in his first book, *Modern Russian Poetry*):

> Although poetry may use the methods of emotive language, it uses them only for *its own* purposes. The similarities between the two kinds of language and the use of poetic language in the way that emotive language is used frequently leads to the assumption that the two are identical. The assumption is mistaken because it fails to consider the radical difference of *function* between the two kinds of language.

In this connection Jakobson refuted the attempts of [Maurice] Grammont[3] and other prosodists to explain the phonetic structure of poetry in terms either of onomatopoeia or of the emotional connection between sounds and images. "Phonetic structure," he wrote, "is not always a structure of audible images, nor is a structure of audible images always a method of emotional language." Jakobson's book was typical because it constantly went beyond the limits of its particular, special theme (the prosody of Czech verse) and shed light on general questions about the theory of poetic language and

9. In Pushkin's epic *Poltava* (1829); in 1709 Russian forces led by Peter I defeated the troops of Charles VII of Sweden at Poltava, in Ukraine.
1. Roman Jakobson, *O cheshskom stikhe preimuschestvenno v sopostavlenii s russkim* (Berlin, 1923) [Eichenbaum's note].
2. Consonants, such as English *l* and *r*, that are articulated without friction and can be sustained indefinitely.
3. French linguist (1865–1946).

verse. Thus his book ends with a whole essay on Mayakovsky, an essay complemented by his earlier piece on Khlebnikov.

In my own work on Anna Akhmatova[4] I also attempted to raise basic theoretical questions about the theory of verse—questions of the relation of rhythm to syntax and intonation, the relation of the sound of verse to its articulation, and lastly, the relation of poetic diction to semantics. Referring to a book which Yury Tynyanov was then preparing, I pointed out that "as words get into verse they are, as it were, taken out of ordinary speech. They are surrounded by a new aura of meaning and perceived not against the background of speech in general but against the background of poetic speech." I also indicated that the formation of collateral meanings, which disrupts ordinary verbal associations, is the chief peculiarity of the semantics of poetry.

Until then, the original connection between the formal method and linguistics had been growing considerably weaker. The difference that had developed between our problems was so great that we no longer needed the special support of the linguists, especially the support of those who were psychologically oriented. In fact, some of the work of the linguists was objectionable in principle. Tynyanov's *The Problem of Poetic Language*,[5] which had appeared just then, emphasized the difference between the study of psychological linguistics and the study of poetic language and style. This book showed the intimate relation that exists between the meanings of words and the poetic structure itself; it added new meaning to the idea of poetic rhythm and initiated the Formalists' investigation not only of acoustics and syntax, but also of the shades of meaning peculiar to poetic speech. In the introduction Tynyanov says:

> The study of poetry has of late been quite rewarding. Undoubtedly the prospect in the near future is for development in the whole field, although we all remember the systematic beginning of the study. But the study of poetry has been kept isolated from questions of poetic language and style; the study of the latter is kept isolated from the study of the former. The impression is given that neither the poetic language itself nor the poetic style itself has any connection with poetry, that the one does not depend upon the other. The idea of "poetic language," which was advanced not so long ago and is now changing, undoubtedly invited a certain looseness by its breadth and by the vagueness of its content, a content based on psychological linguistics.

Among the general questions of poetics revived and illuminated by this book, that of the idea of the "material" is most fundamental. The generally accepted view saw an opposition between form and content; when the distinction was made purely verbal, it lost its meaning. In fact, as I have already mentioned, our view gave form the significance of a thing complete in itself and strengthened it by considering the work of art in relation to its purpose. Our concept of form required no complement—except that other, artistically insignificant, kind of form. Tynyanov showed that the materials of verbal art were neither all alike nor all equally important, that "one feature may be

4. Boris Eichenbaum, *Anna Akhmatova* (Petrograd, 1923) [Eichenbaum's note].

5. Yury Tynyanov, *Problema stikhotvornovo yazyka* (Leningrad, 1924) [Eichenbaum's note].

prominent at the expense of the rest, so that the remainder is deformed and sometimes degraded to the level of a neutral prop." Hence the conclusion that "the idea of 'material' does not lie beyond the limits of form; the material itself is a formal element. To confuse it with external structural features is a mistake." After this, Tynyanov could make the notion of form more complex by showing that form is dynamic:

> The unity of the work is not a closed, symmetrical whole, but an unfolding, dynamic whole. Its elements are not static indications of equality and complexity, but always dynamic indications of correlation and integration. The form of literary works must be thought of as dynamic.

Rhythm is here presented as the fundamental specific factor which permeates all the elements of poetry. The objective sign of poetic rhythm is the establishment of a *rhythmic group* whose *unity* and *richness* exist side by side with each other. And again, Tynyanov affirms the principal distinction between prose and poetry:

> Poetry, as opposed to prose, tends toward unity and richness ranged around an uncommon object. This very "uncommonness" prevents the main point of the poem from being smoothed over. Indeed, it asserts the object with a new force. . . . Any element of prose brought into the poetic pattern is transformed into verse by that feature of it which asserts its function and which thus has two aspects: the emphasis of the structure—the versification—and the deformation of the uncommon object.

Tynyanov also raises the question of semantics: "In verse are not the ordinary semantic meanings of the words so distorted (a fact which makes complete paraphrase impossible) that the usual principles governing their arrangement no longer apply?" The entire second part of Tynyanov's book answers this question by defining the precise relation between rhythm and semantics. The facts show clearly that oral presentations are unified in part by rhythm. "This is shown in a more forceful and more compact integration of connectives than occurs in ordinary speech; words are made correlative by their positions"; prose lacks this feature.

Thus the Formalists abandoned Potebnya's theory and accepted the conclusions connected with it on a new basis, and a new perspective opened on to the theory of verse. Tynyanov's work permitted us to grasp even the remotest implications of these new problems. It became clear even to those only casually acquainted with the *Opoyaz* that the essence of our work consisted not in some kind of static "formal method," but in a study of the specific peculiarities of verbal art—we were not advocates of a method, but students of an object. Again, Tynyanov stated this:

> The object of a study claiming to be a study of art ought to be so specific that it is distinguished from other areas of intellectual activity and uses them for its own materials and tools. Each work of art represents a complex interaction of many factors; consequently, the job of the student is the definition of the specific character of this interaction.

8. *Style, Genre, and Historical Criticism*

Earlier I noted that the problem of the diffusion and change of form—the problem of literary evolution—is raised naturally along with theoretical problems. The problem of literary evolution arises in connection with a reconsideration of Veselovsky's view of *skaz* motifs and devices; the answer ("new form is not to express new content, but to replace old form") led to a new understanding of form. If form is understood as the very content, constantly changing according to its dependence upon previous "images," then we naturally had to approach it without abstract, ready-made, unalterable, classical schemes; and we had to consider specifically its historical sense and significance. The approach developed its own kind of dual perspective: the perspective of theoretical study (like Shklovsky's "Development of Plot" and my "Verse Melody"), which centered on a given theoretical problem and its applicability to the most diverse materials, and the perspective of historical studies—studies of literary evolution as such. The combination of these two perspectives, both organic to the subsequent development of the formal school, raised a series of new and very complex problems, many of which are still unsolved and even undefined.

Actually, the original attempt of the Formalists to take a particular structural device and to establish its identity in diverse materials became an attempt to differentiate, to understand, the *function* of a device in each given case. This notion of functional significance was gradually pushed toward the foreground and the original idea of the device pushed into the background. This kind of sorting out of its own general ideas and principles has been characteristic of our work throughout the evolution of the formal method. We have no dogmatic position to bind us and shut us off from facts. We do not answer for our schematizations; they may require change, refinement, or correction when we try to apply them to previously unknown facts. Work on specific materials compelled us to speak of functions and thus to revise our idea of the device. The theory itself demanded that we turn to history.

Here again we were confronted with the traditional academic sciences and the preferences of critics. In our student days the academic history of literature was limited chiefly to biographical and psychological studies of various writers—only the "greats," of course. Critics no longer made attempts to construct a history of Russian literature as a whole, attempts which evidenced the intention of bringing the great historical materials into a system; nevertheless, the traditions established by earlier histories (like A. N. Pypin's[6] *History of Russian Literature*) retained their scholarly authority, the more so because the following generation had decided not to pursue such broad themes. Meanwhile, the chief role was played by such general and somewhat vague notions as "realism" and "romanticism" (realism was said to be better than romanticism); evolution was understood as gradual perfection, as progress (from romanticism to realism); succession [of literary schools] as the peaceful transfer of the inheritance from father to son. But generally, there was no notion of literature as such; material taken from the history of social movements, from biography, etc. had replaced it entirely.

This primitive historicism, which led away from literature, naturally provoked the Symbolist theoreticians and critics into a denial of any kind of historicism. Their own discussions of literature, consequently, developed into impressionistic "études"[7] and "silhouettes," and they indulged in a widespread "modernization" of old writers, transforming them into "eternal com-

6. Aleksandr N. Pypin (1833–1904), Russian literary historian; his *History* was published in Russian in 1898–99.

7. Studies (French).

panions." The history of literature was silently (and sometimes aloud) declared unnecessary.

We had to demolish the academic tradition and to eliminate the bias of the journalists.[8] We had to advance against the first a new understanding of literary evolution and of literature itself—without the idea of progress and peaceful succession, without the ideas of realism and romanticism, without materials foreign to literature—as a specific order of phenomena, a specific order of material. We had to act against the second by pointing out concrete historical facts, fluctuating and changing forms, by pointing to the necessity of taking into account the specific functions of this or that device—in a word, we had to draw the line between the literary work as a definite historical fact and a free interpretation of it from the standpoint of contemporary literary needs, tastes, or interests. Thus the basic passion for our historical-literary work had to be a passion for destruction and negation, and such was the original tone of our theoretical attacks; our work later assumed a calmer note when we went on to solutions of particular problems.

That is why the first of our historical-literary pronouncements came in the form of theses expressed almost against our will in connection with some specific material. A particular question would unexpectedly lead to the formulation of a general problem, a problem that inextricably mixed theoretical and historical considerations. In this sense Tynyanov's *Dostoevsky and Gogol* and Shklovsky's *Rozanov*[9] were typical.

Tynyanov's basic problem was to show that Dostoevsky's *The Village of Stepanchikovo* is a parody, that behind its first level is hidden a second—it is a parody of Gogol's *Correspondence with Friends.*[1] But his treatment of this particular question was overshadowed by a whole theory of parody, a theory of parody as a stylistic device (stylized parody) and as one of the manifestations (having great historical-literary significance) of the dialectical development of literary groups. With this arose the problem of "succession" and "tradition" and, hence, the basic problems of literary evolution were posed:

> When one speaks of "literary tradition" or "succession" . . . usually one implies a certain kind of direct line uniting the younger and older representatives of a known literary branch. Yet the matter is much more complicated. There is no continuing direct line; there is rather a departure, a pushing away from the known point—a struggle. . . . Any literary succession is first of all a struggle, a destruction of old values and a reconstruction of old elements.

"Literary evolution" was complicated by the notion of struggle, of periodic uprisings, and so lost its old suggestion of peaceful and gradual development. Against this background, the literary relationship between Dostoevsky and Gogol was shown to be that of a complicated struggle.

In his *Rozanov*, Shklovsky showed, almost in the absence of basic themes, a whole theory of literary evolution which even then reflected the current discussion of such problems in *Opoyaz*. Shklovsky showed that literature moves forward in a broken line:

8. A derogatory reference to impressionist and symbolist critics.

9. Yury Tynyanov, *Dostoevsky i Gogol* (Petrograd, 1921); Victor Shklovsky, *Rozanov* (Petrograd, 1921) [Eichenbaum's note].

1. An 1847 collection of real and fictitious letters; Dostoyevsky's short novel was published in 1859.

> In each literary epoch there is not one literary school, but several. They exist simultaneously, with one of them representing the high point of the current orthodoxy. The others exist uncanonized, mutely; in Pushkin's time, for example, the courtly tradition of [Wilhelm] Kuchelbecker and [Alexander] Greboyedov[2] existed simultaneously with the tradition of Russian vaudeville verse and with such other traditions as that of the pure adventure novel of Bulgarin.[3]

The moment the old art is canonized, new forms are created on a lower level. A "young line" is created which

> grows up to replace the old, as the vaudevillist Belopyatkin is transformed into a Nekrasov (see Brik's discussion of the relationship); a direct descendent of the eighteenth century, Tolstoy, creates a new novel (see the work of Boris Eichenbaum); Blok makes the themes and times of the gypsy ballad acceptable, and Chekhov[4] introduces the "alarm clock" into Russian literature. Dostoevsky introduced the devices of the dime novel into the mainstream of literature. Each new literary school heralds a revolution, something like the appearance of a new class. But, of course, this is only an analogy. The vanquished line is not obliterated, it does not cease to exist. It is only knocked from the crest; it lies dormant and may again arise as a perennial pretender to the throne. Moreover, in reality the matter is complicated by the fact that the new hegemony is usually not a pure revival of previous forms but is made more complex by the presence of features of the younger schools and with features, now secondary, inherited from its predecessors on the throne.

Shklovsky is discussing the dynamism of genres, and he interprets Rozanov's books as embodiments of a new genre, as a new type of novel in which the parts are unconnected by motivation. "Thematically, Rozanov's books are characterized by the elevation of new themes; compositionally, by the revealed device." As part of this general theory, we introduced the notion of the "dialectical self-creation[5] of new forms," that is, hidden in the new form we saw both analogies with other kinds of cultural development and proof of the independence of the phenomena of literary evolution. In a simplified form, this theory quickly changed hands and, as always happens, became a simple and fixed scheme—very handy for critics. Actually, we have here only a general outline of evolution surrounded by a whole series of complicated conditions. From this general outline the Formalists moved on to a more consistent solution of historical-literary problems and facts, specifying and refining their original theoretical premises.

9. *Literary History and Literary Evolution*

Given our understanding of literary evolution as the dialectical change of forms, we did not go back to the study of those materials which had held the central position in the old-fashioned historical-literary work. We studied literary evolution insofar as it bore a distinctive character and only to the extent

2. Kuchelbecker (1797–1846) and Greboyedov (1795–1829), Russian writers.
3. Faddey Bulgarin (1789–1859), Polish-born Russian popular novelist, journalist, and critic.
4. Anton Chekhov (1860–1904), Russian dramatist and short story writer; the reference is to *The Alarm Clock*, a comic newspaper.
5. That is, creation through reciprocal interaction of a thing and its opposite.

that it stood alone, quite independent of other aspects of culture. In other words, we stuck exclusively to facts in order not to pass into an endless number of indefinite "connections" and "correspondences" which would do nothing at all to explain literary evolution. We did not take up questions of the biography and psychology of the artist because we assumed that these questions, in themselves serious and complex, must take their places in other sciences. We felt it important to find indications of historical regularity in evolution—that is why we ignored all that seemed, from this point of view, "circumstantial," not concerned with [literary] history. We were interested in the very process of evolution, in the very *dynamics* of literary form, insofar as it was possible to observe them in the facts of the past. For us, the central problem of the history of literature is the problem of evolution without personality—the study of literature as a *self-formed social phenomenon*. As a result, we found extremely significant both the question of the formation and changes of genres and the question of how "second-rate" and "popular" literature contributed to the formation of genres. Here we had only to distinguish that popular literature which prepared the way for the formation of new genres from that which arose out of their decay and which offered material for the study of historical inertia.

On the other hand, we were not interested in the past, in isolated historical facts, as such; we did not busy ourselves with the "restoration" of this or that epoch because we happened to like it. History gave us what the present could not—a stable body of material. But, precisely for this reason, we approached it with a stock of theoretical problems and principles suggested in part by the facts of contemporary literature. The Formalists, then, characteristically had a close interest in contemporary literature and also reconciled criticism and scholarship. The earlier literary historians had, to a great extent, kept themselves aloof from contemporary literature; the Symbolists had subordinated scholarship to criticism. We saw in the history of literature not so much a special theoretical *subject* as a special *approach*, a special cross section of literature. The character of our historical-literary work involved our being drawn not only to historical conclusions, but also to theoretical conclusions—to the posing of new theoretical problems and to the testing of old.

From 1922 to 1924 a whole series of Formalist studies of literary history was written, many of which, because of contemporary market conditions, remain unpublished and are known only as reports. * * *[6] There is, of course, not space enough here to speak of such works in detail. They usually took up "secondary" writers (those who form the background of literature) and carefully explained the traditions of their work, noting changes in genres, styles, and so on. As a result, many forgotten names and facts came to light, current estimates were shown to be inaccurate, traditional ideas changed, and, chiefly, the very process of literary evolution became clearer. The working out of this material has only begun. A new series of problems is before us: further differentiation of theoretical and historical literary ideas, introduction of new material, posing new questions, and so on.

I shall conclude with a general summary. The evolution of the formal method, which I have tried to present, has the look of a sequential development of theoretical principles—apart from the individual roles each of us

6. This deletion by the translators contains a long list of various formalist works.

played. Actually, the work of the *Opoyaz* group was genuinely collective. It was this way, obviously, because from the very beginning we understood the historical nature of our task; we did not see it as the personal affair of this or that individual. This was our chief connection with the times. Science itself is still evolving, and we are evolving with it. I shall indicate briefly the evolution of the formal method during these ten years:

1. From the original outline of the conflict of poetic language with practical we proceeded to differentiate the idea of practical language by its various functions (Jakubinsky) and to delimit the methods of poetic and emotional languages (Jakobson). Along with this we became interested in studying oratorical speech because it was close to practical speech but distinguished from it by function, and we spoke about the necessity of a revival of the poetic of rhetoric.

2. From the general idea of form, in its new sense, we proceeded to the idea of technique, and from here, to the idea of function.

3. From the idea of poetic rhythm as opposed to meter we proceeded to the idea of rhythm as a constructive element in the total poem and thus to an understanding of verse as a special form of speech having special linguistic (syntactical, lexical, and semantic) features.

4. From the idea of plot as structure we proceeded to an understanding of material in terms of its motivation, and from here to an understanding of material as an element participating in the construction but subordinate to the character of the dominant formal idea.

5. From the ascertainment of a single device applicable to various materials we proceeded to differentiate techniques according to function and from here to the question of the evolution of form—that is, to the problem of historical-literary study.

A whole new series of problems faces us, as Tynyanov's latest essay, "Literary Fact," shows.[7] Here the question of the relation between life and literature is posed, a question which many persons "answer" on the basis of a simple-minded dilettantism. Examples of how life becomes literature are shown and, conversely, of how literature passes into life:

> During the period of its deterioration a given genre is shoved from the center toward the periphery, but in its place, from the trivia of literature, from literature's backyard, and from life itself, new phenomena flow into the center.

Although I deliberately called this essay "The Theory of the 'Formal Method,'" I gave, obviously, a sketch of its evolution. We have no theory that can be laid out as a fixed, ready-made system. For us theory and history merge not only in words, but in fact. We are too well trained by history itself to think that it can be avoided. When we feel that we have a theory that explains everything, a ready-made theory explaining all past and future events and therefore needing neither evolution nor anything like it—then we must recognize that the formal method has come to an end, that the spirit of scientific investigation has departed from it. As yet, that has not happened.

1926, 1927

7. *Lef* [*Left*] 2.6 (1925) [Eichenbaum's note].

T. S. ELIOT
1888–1965

T. S. Eliot is the central Anglo-American poet and critic of the twentieth century. He is the author of the most influential poem, *The Waste Land* (1922), and the most authoritative literary essays and reviews. In the history of modern literary theory and criticism, Eliot belongs—with SAMUEL JOHNSON, SAMUEL TAYLOR COLERIDGE, and MATTHEW ARNOLD—among the poet-critics who have defined the critical standards of an era, recast the literary tradition, and established key terms for analysis and evaluation. So immense was Eliot's authority that the poet Dylan Thomas referred to him as "the Pope" and the critic Delmore Schwartz dubbed him a "literary dictator."

Thomas Stearns Eliot was born in St. Louis, Missouri, the seventh and youngest child of Henry Ware Eliot, a businessman, and Charlotte Stearns Eliot, an amateur poet and volunteer social worker. From 1898 to 1905, Eliot attended Smith Academy, a preparatory school where his studies included Greek and Latin, rhetoric, French, and German, and during 1905–06 he was a student at Milton Academy, in Milton, Massachusetts. In 1906 he entered Harvard University, receiving his bachelor's degree in 1909 and his master's in 1910.

At Harvard, Eliot became keenly interested in philosophy and comparative literature—DANTE's *Divine Comedy* was a sublime discovery for him. Important influences on his intellectual development include the philosopher, poet, and humanist George Santayana, from whom Eliot took a course on modern philosophy, and the literary scholar Irving Babbitt, a relentless foe of Romanticism, with whom Eliot studied nineteenth-century French literary criticism. A strong influence on his early verse was the theory of the dynamic flux and movement of consciousness propounded by the French philosopher Henri Bergson (1859–1941). But for Eliot's poetry and criticism, the crucial experience of his Harvard years was his reading in December 1908 of Arthur Symons's *Symbolist Movement in Literature* (1899), which introduced French symbolist poetry to English and American readers. Eliot was busy writing verse himself, publishing some of it in *The Harvard Advocate*; between 1909 and 1911, he worked on two of his best poems, "Portrait of a Lady" and "The Love Song of J. Alfred Prufrock," drawing on the style of irony and symbolism he had encountered in the nineteenth-century French poets—especially CHARLES BAUDELAIRE, Arthur Rimbaud, and Jules Laforgue—whom Symons quoted and discussed.

Eliot was a self-made modernist; as his friend Ezra Pound later said, Eliot had "trained himself *and* modernized himself *on his own*." In his introduction to Pound's *Selected Poems* (1928), Eliot made much the same point: "the form in which I began to write, in 1908 or 1909, was directly drawn from the study of Laforgue together with the later Elizabethan drama; and I do not know anyone who started from exactly that point." He read widely, modifying (and sometimes parodying) the verbal techniques of other poets.

After studying a year at the Sorbonne in Paris, Eliot returned to Harvard to pursue graduate work and serve as a teaching assistant. For his dissertation topic, he focused on the writings of the British idealist philosopher F. H. Bradley, the author of *Appearance and Reality* (1893). His research led him to the University of Marburg in Germany, in the summer of 1914; but as the threat of world war loomed, he relocated to Merton College, Oxford. He was to settle in England permanently.

In September 1914 Eliot met Pound, who quickly became his adviser, editor, and literary agent. "The Love Song of J. Alfred Prufrock" was published in *Poetry* magazine in June 1915; in the following month, Eliot married Vivien (sometimes Vivienne) Haigh-Wood. The marriage proved unhappy and, as Vivien's mental and physical illnesses deepened in the 1920s and 1930s, harrowing for both of them. His despair is reflected in the torment, bitterness, and isolation expressed in much of his poetry.

"No artist produces great art," Eliot claimed, "by a deliberate attempt to express his personality. He expresses his personality indirectly through concentrating upon a task which is a task in the same sense as the making of an efficient engine or the turning of a jug or a table-leg" (*Selected Essays, 1917–1932*). From one angle, Eliot's work is itself impersonal and objective; it is filled—especially the poetry—with masks, role-playing, and multiple voices. Yet it is saturated everywhere, too, with displaced personal pain, regret, sexual desire, and emotional and spiritual yearning.

For two years Eliot taught in grammar schools, gave lectures on literature, and wrote dense, technical articles and reviews on philosophy. In March 1917, tired of makeshift teaching, he took a job at Lloyd's Bank. He held this position for the next eight years, while laboring on his poetry—his first volume, *Prufrock and Other Observations*, appeared in 1917—and on literary criticism, publishing striking essays and book reviews in the *Times Literary Supplement* and other leading periodicals. A number are included in *The Sacred Wood* (1920), a landmark collection of criticism and theory.

Work and worry brought Eliot near a nervous breakdown, and to recuperate he went first to Margate, in southeast England, and then to a sanatorium in Lausanne, Switzerland, where he worked on the draft of a long poem he had started years earlier. In Paris, on his way back to London, he showed the draft to Ezra Pound, who edited it skillfully and turned it (in Eliot's words) from "a jumble of good and bad passages into a poem"—*The Waste Land*. Allusive, experimental, and technically daring, showily learned and archly witty, *The Waste Land* is a primary text of literary modernism. The poem was published in *The Criterion*—a new literary and cultural quarterly edited by Eliot—in October 1922. For many writers, critics, intellectuals, and general readers, *The Waste Land* evoked the waste and sterility of a Western world ravaged by the horrors of World War I, which had brought carnage on an unprecedented scale: more than 8.5 million soldiers and perhaps 13 million civilians had died. *The Waste Land* is not a poem "about" the war, but the war's trauma informs it from beginning to end.

Eliot was a literary and cultural force throughout the 1920s and 1930s. As editor of the quarterly *The Criterion* until the journal's demise in 1939, he published leading English modernists (including VIRGINIA WOOLF and James Joyce) and was the first to publish in English such significant European writers as Jean Cocteau and Marcel Proust. In 1925 Eliot accepted a position in the firm of Faber and Gwyer (later, Faber and Faber), which became a leading publisher of poets from Ezra Pound to Sylvia Plath. He began writing plays in the 1930s, with *Murder in the Cathedral* (1935), and he enjoyed considerable popular success with his dramas of the 1950s (including *The Cocktail Party*, 1950).

In 1927 Eliot became a British citizen and joined the Church of England; in the following year, he announced in *For Lancelot Andrewes*, a collection of critical essays, that he was "classicist in literature, royalist in politics, and Anglo-Catholic in religion." Eliot was conservative, even reactionary, and sometimes he drifted close to fascism and into racism and anti-Semitism. In his social and cultural writings and in much of his literary criticism of the 1930s and 1940s, Eliot is austere and sometimes censorious in attitude and pontificating in tone. From 1932 to 1933, he held the Charles Eliot Norton Professorship of Poetry at Harvard, where he delivered the lectures that became *The Use of Poetry and the Use of Criticism* (1933). Much of his late cultural criticism, gloomily resentful and hectoring, is today unread, but it does not diminish the force and influence of the best of Eliot's poetry and literary criticism. In 1948 he was awarded the Order of Merit by King George VI and the Nobel Prize in literature.

Our first selection, "Tradition and the Individual Talent" (1919), begins: "In English writing we seldom speak of tradition." The poise and authority of Eliot's critical voice, backed up by his masterful performances as a poet, soon made "tradition" a key topic for poets, critics, intellectuals, and teachers of literature in the academy. Two of the canonical texts of modern Anglo-American literary criticism,

F. R. Leavis's *Revaluation: Tradition and Development in English Poetry* (1936) and CLEANTH BROOKS's *Modern Poetry and the Tradition* (1939), were expansions of Eliot's ideas about tradition, and many other books (and countless syllabi) were similarly based on the terms that he had articulated.

For Eliot, each poem exists within the tradition from which it takes shape and which it, in turn, redefines. Thus tradition is both something to which the poet must be "faithful" and something that he or she actively makes: novelty emerges out of being steeped in tradition. Some later critics, such as HAROLD BLOOM, have characterized Eliot as a "weak" poet-critic because of the priority that he assigns to tradition, but in doing so they overlook the extent to which the poet challenges and revises the tradition to which he or she defers: "What happens when a new work of art is created," he stresses, "is something that happens simultaneously to all the works of art that preceded it." Eliot has also been criticized for picturing tradition as variously a "simultaneous order," a "living whole," an "ideal order," and the "mind of Europe," thereby idealizing its conflicts, contradictions, and omissions.

"The Metaphysical Poets" (1921) is another central work in the history of modern criticism. Almost as soon as it appeared, the difficult seventeenth-century metaphysical poets—John Donne, Andrew Marvell, and their contemporaries, whom Eliot described as "more often named than read, and more often read than profitably studied"—became models of good poetry. Eliot's essay is condensed in its argument, highly suggestive, and extraordinarily ambitious. In it he deploys the evaluative terms that in the eighteenth century Samuel Johnson had used against the metaphysical poets ("the most heterogeneous ideas are yoked by violence together") to elevate the very poets whom his eminent precursor had assailed, insisting that modern poetry *must* be difficult. He packs "The Metaphysical Poets" with unelaborated argument and assertion, stressing in particular the seventeenth century's disastrous "dissociation of sensibility" into "thought" and "feeling." In the process, he illustrates how "tradition" is made, is *forced*, into the form that later generations of writers require. Many of Eliot's readers took his generalizations as literal truths, and even skeptics, such as the English critic Frank Kermode (see *The Romantic Image*, 1957), judged that refuting Eliot demanded full-scale scholarly and critical demonstration.

Eliot liked being a bit of a troublemaker, saying outrageous things from on high and often not quite clarifying whether he meant them seriously. In "Hamlet and His Problems" (1920), for instance, Eliot presents his brilliant theory of the "objective correlative": "The only way of expressing emotion in the form of art is by finding an 'objective correlative'; in other words, a set of objects, a situation, a chain of events which shall be the formula for that particular emotion; such that, when the external facts, which must terminate in sensory experience, are given, the emotion is immediately evoked." Eliot uses *Hamlet* as a test case, surprisingly labeling the play an "artistic failure" precisely because in it the "emotions" that Shakespeare evokes are "in excess" of the facts of the story, the dramatic action. It is an absurd judgment, in which Eliot may not have believed, but which he uttered with such assurance that it is still cited and debated.

Eliot was adept at formulating the nature and function of literary criticism, and the New Critics (such as JOHN CROWE RANSOM and Brooks) invoked his critical practice as a model. He described criticism as "the disinterested exercise of intelligence . . . the elucidation of works of art and the correction of taste . . . the common pursuit of true judgment," and the New Critics followed his injunction to center arguments in analysis of specific passages and poems. "Comparison and analysis," Eliot said, "are the chief tools of the critic," enabling a precise perception of literary effects, relationships, and values. By the 1950s, Eliot was lamenting the rise of copiously detailed interpretation of texts—which he called "lemon-squeezing"—but perhaps more than anyone else he had launched the new movement. "Honest criticism and sensitive appreciation are directed not upon the poet but upon the poetry," Eliot states in section 2 of "Tradition and the Individual Talent." In such sentences, we can see the origins of the New Criticism, with its abiding concern for the words on the page—in R. P. Blackmur's formulation, "the words and the motions of the words . . . all the technical devices of literature."

For many critics in the 1970s and after, Eliot—Anglican, conservative, New Critical formalist—has been the archenemy. Bloom, for example, has derided Eliot's poetry and criticism and sought to revitalize the Romantic tradition that Eliot had shunned. Explicitly or implicitly, many others arguing for the inclusion of women and minority writers within the literary canon have attacked his judgments about literary and cultural tradition. Eliot's and the New Critics' "tradition," they maintain, is narrow and elitist, enshrining a limited range of authors and presenting to students a partial, misleading literary history.

While these critics have exposed Eliot's failings, they have not lessened his importance. Now that the critical sifting has been done, it may be possible to return to Eliot in order to see anew, and appreciate again, the scale of his accomplishments in poetry and prose. Literary modernism is unimaginable without Eliot; and the best of his work has remained extraordinarily influential.

BIBLIOGRAPHY

Among Eliot's books of criticism, the key texts are *The Sacred Wood* (1920), *Selected Essays* (3d ed., 1972), and *On Poetry and Poets* (1957). Other important publications include *Homage to John Dryden* (1924), in which appear the brilliant essays "John Dryden," "The Metaphysical Poets," and "Andrew Marvell." A good selection is *Selected Prose of T. S. Eliot*, edited by Frank Kermode (1975). There are hundreds of reviews, introductions to books, essays, and other critical pieces that have not yet been collected. For further insight into Eliot's development as a critic, one should also consult the posthumous book *The Varieties of Metaphysical Poetry*, edited by Ronald Schuchard (1993).

The Letters of T. S. Eliot, vol. 1 (covering 1898 to 1922), expertly edited by his second wife, Valerie Eliot (1988), is an essential source. Eliot did not want to be made the subject of a biography, and his estate has so far been true to his wishes: much source material is either sealed or is unavailable for citation. Despite these limitations, Peter Ackroyd's *T. S. Eliot* (1984) is a valuable, crisply written book. Also useful are Lyndall Gordon, *Eliot's Early Years* (1977) and *Eliot's New Life* (1988); she presents Eliot's life as a spiritual journey and is perceptive on the poetry, but pays little attention to the criticism. Tony Sharpe, *T. S. Eliot: A Literary Life* (1991), is also recommended.

A good place to begin study of Eliot is *T. S. Eliot: Critical Assessments*, edited by Graham Clarke (4 vols., 1990). The fourth volume includes commentaries on Eliot's critical writings. A number of older studies, which include discussion of Eliot's criticism, remain useful: F. O. Matthiessen, *The Achievement of T. S. Eliot: An Essay on the Nature of Poetry* (3d ed., 1958); Hugh Kenner, *The Invisible Poet: T. S. Eliot* (1959); Northrop Frye, *T. S. Eliot* (1967); and Bernard Bergonzi, *T. S. Eliot* (1972).

On Eliot and the modernist movement in literature, see John D. Margolis, *T. S. Eliot's Intellectual Development, 1922–1939* (1972); Piers Gray, *T. S. Eliot's Intellectual and Poetic Development, 1909–1922* (1982); Sanford Schwartz, *The Matrix of Modernism: Pound, Eliot, and Early Twentieth-Century Thought* (1985); Louis Menand, *Discovering Modernism: T. S. Eliot and His Context* (1987); *T. S. Eliot: The Modernist in History*, edited by Ronald Bush (1991), which includes a good essay by Michael North on Eliot and György Lukács; Gail McDonald, *Learning to Be Modern: Pound, Eliot, and the American University* (1993); and Jewel Spears Brooker, *Mastery and Escape: T. S. Eliot and the Dialectic of Modernism* (1994). Though somewhat dated in approach, C. K. Stead's *New Poetic: Yeats to Eliot* (rev. ed., 1987) and *Pound, Yeats, Eliot, and the Modernist Movement* (1986) are informative and acute in judgment. Of the many collections of essays on Eliot, the best is the special issue of the *Southern Review* 21.4 (autumn 1985).

The studies of Eliot's criticism are disappointing, but some good work can be found in *The Literary Criticism of T. S. Eliot: New Essays*, edited by David Newton-Molina (1977). In *T. S. Eliot and the Philosophy of Criticism* (1988), Richard Shusterman describes Eliot as a postmodernist and relates his work to that of Theodor Adorno, Richard Rorty, Jacques Derrida, and other philosophers and theorists. The social, cultural, and economic contexts for Eliot's poetry and criticism and the modernist movement are described in Lawrence Rainey, *Institutions of Modernism: Literary Elites and Public Culture* (1998).

Other resources include *The Cambridge Companion to T. S. Eliot*, edited by A. D. Moody (1994); Caroline Behr, *T. S. Eliot: A Chronology of His Life and Works* (1983); and *T. S. Eliot: The Critical Heritage*, edited by Michael Grant (1982). For bibliography, see Donald Gallup, *T. S. Eliot: A Bibliography* (rev. ed., 1969); Mildred Martin, *A Half-Century of Eliot Criticism: An Annotated Bibliography of Books and Articles in English, 1916–1965* (1972); and Beatrice Ricks, *T. S. Eliot: A Bibliography of Secondary Works* (1980).

Tradition and the Individual Talent

I

In English writing we seldom speak of tradition, though we occasionally apply its name in deploring its absence. We cannot refer to 'the tradition' or to 'a tradition'; at most, we employ the adjective in saying that the poetry of So-and-so is 'traditional' or even 'too traditional'. Seldom, perhaps, does the word appear except in a phrase of censure. If otherwise, it is vaguely approbative, with the implication, as to the work approved, of some pleasing archaeological reconstruction. You can hardly make the word agreeable to English ears without this comfortable reference to the reassuring science of archaeology.

Certainly the word is not likely to appear in our appreciations of living or dead writers. Every nation, every race, has not only its own creative, but its own critical turn of mind; and is even more oblivious of the shortcomings and limitations of its critical habits than of those of its creative genius. We know, or think we know, from the enormous mass of critical writing that has appeared in the French language the critical method or habit of the French; we only conclude (we are such unconscious people) that the French are 'more critical' than we, and sometimes even plume ourselves a little with the fact, as if the French were the less spontaneous. Perhaps they are; but we might remind ourselves that criticism is as inevitable as breathing, and that we should be none the worse for articulating what passes in our minds when we read a book and feel an emotion about it, for criticizing our own minds in their work of criticism. One of the facts that might come to light in this process is our tendency to insist, when we praise a poet, upon those aspects of his work in which he least resembles anyone else. In these aspects or parts of his work we pretend to find what is individual, what is the peculiar essence of the man. We dwell with satisfaction upon the poet's difference from his predecessors, especially his immediate predecessors; we endeavour to find something that can be isolated in order to be enjoyed. Whereas if we approach a poet without this prejudice we shall often find that not only the best, but the most individual parts of his work may be those in which the dead poets, his ancestors, assert their immortality most vigorously. And I do not mean the impressionable period of adolescence, but the period of full maturity.

Yet if the only form of tradition, of handing down, consisted in following the ways of the immediate generation before us in a blind or timid adherence to its successes, 'tradition' should positively be discouraged. We have seen many such simple currents soon lost in the sand; and novelty is better than repetition. Tradition is a matter of much wider significance. It cannot be inherited, and if you want it you must obtain it by great labour. It involves, in the first place, the historical sense, which we may call nearly indispensable to anyone who would continue to be a poet beyond his twenty-fifth year; and the historical sense involves a perception, not only of the pastness of the past, but of its presence; the historical sense compels a man to write not merely with his own generation in his bones, but with a feeling that the whole of the literature of Europe from Homer and within it the whole of the literature of his own country has a simultaneous existence and composes a simultaneous order. This historical sense, which is a sense of the timeless as well as of the temporal and of the timeless and of the temporal together, is what makes a writer traditional. And it is at the same time what makes a writer most acutely conscious of his place in time, of his own contemporaneity.

No poet, no artist of any art, has his complete meaning alone. His significance, his appreciation is the appreciation of his relation to the dead poets and artists. You cannot value him alone; you must set him, for contrast and comparison, among the dead. I mean this as a principle of aesthetic, not merely historical, criticism. The necessity that he shall conform, that he shall cohere, is not onesided; what happens when a new work of art is created is something that happens simultaneously to all the works of art which preceded it. The existing monuments form an ideal order among themselves, which is modified by the introduction of the new (the really new) work of art among them. The existing order is complete before the new work arrives; for order to persist after the supervention of novelty, the *whole* existing order must be, if ever so slightly, altered; and so the relations, proportions, values of each work of art toward the whole are readjusted; and this is conformity between the old and the new. Whoever has approved this idea of order, of the form of European, of English literature will not find it preposterous that the past should be altered by the present as much as the present is directed by the past. And the poet who is aware of this will be aware of great difficulties and responsibilities.

In a peculiar sense he will be aware also that he must inevitably be judged by the standards of the past. I say judged, not amputated, by them; not judged to be as good as, or worse or better than, the dead; and certainly not judged by the canons of dead critics. It is a judgment, a comparison, in which two things are measured by each other. To conform merely would be for the new work not really to conform at all; it would not be new, and would therefore not be a work of art. And we do not quite say that the new is more valuable because it fits in; but its fitting in is a test of its value—a test, it is true, which can only be slowly and cautiously applied, for we are none of us infallible judges of conformity. We say: it appears to conform, and is perhaps individual, or it appears individual, and may conform; but we are hardly likely to find that it is one and not the other.

To proceed to a more intelligible exposition of the relation of the poet to the past: he can neither take the past as a lump, an indiscriminate bolus, nor can he form himself wholly on one or two private admirations, nor can he form himself wholly upon one preferred period. The first course is inadmissible, the second is an important experience of youth, and the third is a pleasant and highly desirable supplement. The poet must be very conscious of the main current, which does not at all flow invariably through the most distinguished reputations. He must be quite aware of the obvious fact that art never improves, but that the material of art is never quite the same. He must be aware that the mind of Europe—the mind of his own country—a mind which he learns in time to be much more important than his own private mind—is a mind which changes, and that this change is a development which abandons nothing *en route*, which does not superannuate either Shakespeare, or Homer, or the rock drawing of the Magdalenian draughtsmen.[1] That this development, refinement perhaps, complication certainly, is not, from the point of view of the artist, any improvement. Perhaps not even an improvement from the point of view of the psychologist or not to the extent which we imagine; perhaps only in the end based upon a complication in economics and machinery. But the difference between the present and the past is that the conscious present is an awareness of the past in a way and to an extent which the past's awareness of itself cannot show.

Someone said: 'The dead writers are remote from us because we *know* so much more than they did'. Precisely, and they are that which we know.

I am alive to a usual objection to what is clearly part of my programme for the *métier* of poetry. The objection is that the doctrine requires a ridiculous amount of erudition (pedantry), a claim which can be rejected by appeal to the lives of poets in any pantheon. It will even be affirmed that much learning deadens or perverts poetic sensibility. While, however, we persist in believing that a poet ought to know as much as will not encroach upon his necessary receptivity and necessary laziness, it is not desirable to confine knowledge to whatever can be put into a useful shape for examinations, drawing-rooms, or the still more pretentious modes of publicity. Some can absorb knowledge, the more tardy must sweat for it. Shakespeare acquired more essential history from Plutarch[2] than most men could from the whole British Museum. What is to be insisted upon is that the poet must develop or procure the consciousness of the past and that he should continue to develop this consciousness throughout his career.

What happens is a continual surrender of himself as he is at the moment to something which is more valuable. The progress of an artist is a continual self-sacrifice, a continual extinction of personality.

There remains to define this process of depersonalization and its relation to the sense of tradition. It is in this depersonalization that art may be said to approach the condition of science. I therefore invite you to consider, as a

1. Artists of the late Paleolithic period who created the cave paintings discovered at La Madeleine, France.

2. Greek philosopher and biographer (ca. 50–ca. 120 C.E.); his *Lives* of important Greeks and Romans provided Shakespeare with source material for his Roman plays.

suggestive analogy, the action which takes place when a bit of finely filiated platinum is introduced into a chamber containing oxygen and sulphur dioxide.

II

Honest criticism and sensitive appreciation is directed not upon the poet but upon the poetry. If we attend to the confused cries of the newspaper critics and the susurrus of popular repetition that follows, we shall hear the names of poets in great numbers; if we seek not Blue-book knowledge[3] but the enjoyment of poetry, and ask for a poem, we shall seldom find it. I have tried to point out the importance of the relation of the poem to other poems by other authors, and suggested the conception of poetry as a living whole of all the poetry that has ever been written. The other aspect of this Impersonal theory of poetry is the relation of the poem to its author. And I hinted, by an analogy, that the mind of the mature poet differs from that of the immature one not precisely in any valuation of 'personality', not being necessarily more interesting, or having 'more to say', but rather by being a more finely perfected medium in which special, or very varied, feelings are at liberty to enter into new combinations.

The analogy was that of the catalyst. When the two gases previously mentioned are mixed in the presence of a filament of platinum, they form sulphurous acid. This combination takes place only if the platinum is present; nevertheless the newly formed acid contains no trace of platinum, and the platinum itself is apparently unaffected: has remained inert, neutral, and unchanged.[4] The mind of the poet is the shred of platinum. It may partly or exclusively operate upon the experience of the man himself; but, *the more perfect the artist, the more completely separate in him will be the man who suffers and the mind which creates*; the more perfectly will the mind digest and transmute the passions which are its material.

The experience, you will notice, the elements which enter the presence of the transforming catalyst, are of two kinds: emotions and feelings. The effect of a work of art upon the person who enjoys it is an experience different in kind from any experience not of art. It may be formed out of one emotion, or may be a combination of several; and various feelings, inhering for the writer in particular words or phrases or images, may be added to compose the final result. Or great poetry may be made without the direct use of any emotion whatever: composed out of feelings solely. Canto XV of the *Inferno* (Brunetto Latini)[5] is a working up of the emotion evident in the situation; but the effect, though single as that of any work of art, is obtained by considerable complexity of detail. The last quatrain gives an image, a feeling attaching to an image, which 'came',[6] which did not develop simply out of what precedes, but which was probably in suspension in the poet's mind

3. That is, the ability to name-drop, gleaned from the social register (or "blue book").
4. In *The Use of Poetry and the Use of Criticism* (1933), Eliot cited with approval an observation in an 1817 letter by the Romantic poet John Keats: "Men of Genius are great as certain etherial Chemicals operating on the Mass of neutral intellect—but they have not any individuality, any determined Character."
5. During his journey through Hell in the *Inferno* (1321), DANTE ALIGHIERI meets his former master Brunetto Latini, whom he still admires, confined in the seventh circle (for committing sodomy).
6. Dante likens Latini to the winner of the annual footrace in Verona.

until the proper combination arrived for it to add itself to. The poet's mind is in fact a receptacle for seizing and storing up numberless feelings, phrases, images, which remain there until all the particles which can unite to form a new compound are present together.

If you compare several representative passages of the greatest poetry you see how great is the variety of types of combination, and also how completely any semi-ethical criterion of 'sublimity' misses the mark.[7] For it is not the 'greatness', the intensity, of the emotions, the components, but the intensity of the artistic process, the pressure, so to speak, under which the fusion takes place, that counts. The episode of Paolo and Francesca[8] employs a definite emotion, but the intensity of the poetry is something quite different from whatever intensity in the supposed experience it may give the impression of. It is no more intense, furthermore, than Canto XXVI, the voyage of Ulysses,[9] which has not the direct dependence upon an emotion. Great variety is possible in the process of transmutation of emotion: the murder of Agamemnon,[1] or the agony of Othello, gives an artistic effect apparently closer to a possible original than the scenes from Dante. In the *Agamemnon*, the artistic emotion approximates to the emotion of an actual spectator; in *Othello* to the emotion of the protagonist himself. But the difference between art and the event is always absolute; the combination which is the murder of Agamemnon is probably as complex as that which is the voyage of Ulysses. In either case there has been a fusion of elements. The ode of Keats[2] contains a number of feelings which have nothing particular to do with the nightingale, but which the nightingale, partly perhaps because of its attractive name, and partly because of its reputation, served to bring together.

The point of view which I am struggling to attack is perhaps related to the metaphysical theory of the substantial unity of the soul: for my meaning is, that the poet has, not a 'personality' to express, but a particular medium, which is only a medium and not a personality, in which impressions and experiences combine in peculiar and unexpected ways. Impressions and experiences which are important for the man may take no place in the poetry, and those which become important in the poetry may play quite a negligible part in the man, the personality.

I will quote a passage which is unfamiliar enough to be regarded with fresh attention in the light—or darkness—of these observations:

And now methinks I could e'en chide myself
For doating on her beauty, though her death
Shall be revenged after no common action.
Does the silkworm expend her yellow labours
For thee? For thee does she undo herself?
Are lordships sold to maintain ladyships
For the poor benefit of a bewildering minute?

7. Eliot is seeking to distinguish his notion of the sublime not only from that of LONGINUS and EDMUND BURKE, who stressed "greatness," but also from that of MATTHEW ARNOLD, who had argued that the sublime effects of the highest poetry could and should function as a form of (or even a substitute for) religion.
8. Illicit lovers, who were murdered by Francesca's husband; Dante meets them in the second circle of Hell (*Inferno* 6.38–142).
9. Ulysses, suffering in Hell for his false counsel, describes to Dante the voyage—after his return to Ithaca—that ended in his death.
1. The story of the Greek warrior king Agamemnon, murdered by his wife Clytemnestra, is told by the tragedian Aeschylus in *Agamemnon* (458 B.C.E.). Shakespeare's *Othello* was written in 1603–04.
2. "Ode to a Nightingale" (1819), by John Keats (1795–1821).

Why does yon fellow falsify highways,
And put his life between the judge's lips,
To refine such a thing—keeps horse and men
To beat their valours for her? . . .[3]

In this passage (as is evident if it is taken in its context) there is a combination of positive and negative emotions: an intensely strong attraction toward beauty and an equally intense fascination by the ugliness which is contrasted with it and which destroys it. This balance of contrasted emotion is in the dramatic situation to which the speech is pertinent, but that situation alone is inadequate to it. This is, so to speak, the structural emotion, provided by the drama. But the whole effect, the dominant tone, is due to the fact that a number of floating feelings, having an affinity to this emotion by no means superficially evident, have combined with it to give us a new art emotion.

It is not in his personal emotions, the emotions provoked by particular events in his life, that the poet is in any way remarkable or interesting. His particular emotions may be simple, or crude, or flat. The emotion in his poetry will be a very complex thing, but not with the complexity of the emotions of people who have very complex or unusual emotions in life. One error, in fact, of eccentricity in poetry is to seek for new human emotions to express; and in this search for novelty in the wrong place it discovers the perverse. The business of the poet is not to find new emotions, but to use the ordinary ones and, in working them up into poetry, to express feelings which are not in actual emotions at all. And emotions which he has never experienced will serve his turn as well as those familiar to him. Consequently, we must believe that 'emotion recollected in tranquillity'[4] is an inexact formula. For it is neither emotion, nor recollection, nor, without distortion of meaning, tranquillity. It is a concentration, and a new thing resulting from the concentration, of a very great number of experiences which to the practical and active person would not seem to be experiences at all; it is a concentration which does not happen consciously or of deliberation. These experiences are not 'recollected', and they finally unite in an atmosphere which is 'tranquil' only in that it is a passive attending upon the event. Of course this is not quite the whole story. There is a great deal, in the writing of poetry, which must be conscious and deliberate. In fact, the bad poet is usually unconscious where he ought to be conscious, and conscious where he ought to be unconscious. Both errors tend to make him 'personal'. Poetry is not a turning loose of emotion, but an escape from emotion; it is not the expression of personality, but an escape from personality. But, of course, only those who have personality and emotions know what it means to want to escape from these things.

III

ὁ δὲ νοῦς ἴσως θειότερόν τι καὶ ἀπαθές ἐστιν.[5]

This essay proposes to halt at the frontier of metaphysics or mysticism, and confine itself to such practical conclusions as can be applied by the

3. Cyril Tourneur, *The Revenger's Tragedy* (1607), 3.5.67–78. Some scholars now credit this play, in whole or in part, to Thomas Middleton.
4. Quoted from WILLIAM WORDSWORTH, preface to *Lyrical Ballads* (1800; see above).
5. The mind is doubtless something more divine and unaffected (Greek). From ARISTOTLE, *De Anima* (*On the Soul*), 1.4, 408b.

responsible person interested in poetry. To divert interest from the poet to the poetry is a laudable aim: for it would conduce to a juster estimation of actual poetry, good and bad. There are many people who appreciate the expression of sincere emotion in verse, and there is a smaller number of people who can appreciate technical excellence. But very few know when there is an expression of *significant* emotion, emotion which has its life in the poem and not in the history of the poet. The emotion of art is impersonal. And the poet cannot reach this impersonality without surrendering himself wholly to the work to be done. And he is not likely to know what is to be done unless he lives in what is not merely the present, but the present moment of the past, unless he is conscious, not of what is dead, but of what is already living.

1919

The Metaphysical Poets

By collecting these poems from the work of a generation more often named than read, and more often read than profitably studied, Professor Grierson has rendered a service of some importance.[1] Certainly the reader will meet with many poems already preserved in other anthologies, at the same time that he discovers poems such as those of Aurelian Townshend or Lord Herbert of Cherbury here included. But the function of such an anthology as this is neither that of Professor Saintsbury's admirable edition of Caroline poets[2] nor that of the *Oxford Book of English Verse*. Mr. Grierson's book is in itself a piece of criticism, and a provocation of criticism; and we think that he was right in including so many poems of Donne, elsewhere (though not in many editions) accessible, as documents in the case of 'metaphysical poetry'.[3] The phrase has long done duty as a term of abuse, or as the label of a quaint and pleasant taste. The question is to what extent the so-called metaphysicals formed a school (in our own time we should say a 'movement'), and how far this so-called school or movement is a digression from the main current.

Not only is it extremely difficult to define metaphysical poetry, but difficult to decide what poets practise it and in which of their verses. The poetry of Donne (to whom Marvell and Bishop King[4] are sometimes nearer than any of the other authors) is late Elizabethan, its feeling often very close to that of Chapman. The 'courtly' poetry is derivative from Jonson, who borrowed liberally from the Latin; it expires in the next century with the sentiment and witticism of Prior.[5] There is finally the devotional verse of Herbert, Vaughan,

1. Eliot is reviewing the groundbreaking collection *Metaphysical Lyrics and Poems of the Seventeenth Century: Donne to Butler* (1921), edited by Herbert J. C. Grierson (1866–1960).
2. *Minor Poets of the Caroline Period* (1905–21), edited by George Saintsbury (1845–1933).
3. For the term, see SAMUEL JOHNSON, *Life of Cowley* (1783; above). John Donne (1572–1631), English poet, prose writer, and clergyman.
4. Henry King (1592–1669), English poet and Anglican bishop. Andrew Marvell (1621–1678), English poet and satirist.
5. Matthew Prior (1664–1721), English poet, epigrammatist, and diplomat. George Chapman (ca. 1559–1634), English poet, scholar, and playwright. Ben Jonson (1572–1637), English poet and playwright.

and Crashaw (echoed long after by Christina Rossetti and Francis Thompson);[6] Crashaw, sometimes more profound and less sectarian than the others, has a quality which returns through the Elizabethan period to the early Italians. It is difficult to find any precise use of metaphor, simile, or other conceit, which is common to all the poets and at the same time important enough as an element of style to isolate these poets as a group. Donne, and often Cowley,[7] employ a device which is sometimes considered characteristically 'metaphysical'; the elaboration (contrasted with the condensation) of a figure of speech to the furthest stage to which ingenuity can carry it. Thus Cowley develops the commonplace comparison of the world to a chess-board through long stanzas (*To Destiny*), and Donne, with more grace, in *A Valediction*,[8] the comparison of two lovers to a pair of compasses. But elsewhere we find, instead of the mere explication of the content of a comparison, a development by rapid association of thought which requires considerable agility on the part of the reader.

> *On a round ball*
> *A workeman that hath copies by, can lay*
> *An Europe, Afrique, and an Asia,*
> *And quickly make that, which was nothing,* All,
> *So doth each teare,*
> *Which thee doth weare,*
> *A globe, yea world by that impression grow,*
> *Till thy tears mixt with mine doe overflow*
> *This world, by waters sent from thee, my heaven dissolved so.*[9]

Here we find at least two connexions which are not implicit in the first figure, but are forced upon it by the poet: from the geographer's globe to the tear, and the tear to the deluge. On the other hand, some of Donne's most successful and characteristic effects are secured by brief words and sudden contrasts:

> *A bracelet of bright hair about the bone,*[1]

where the most powerful effect is produced by the sudden contrast of associations of 'bright hair' and of 'bone'. This telescoping of images and multiplied associations is characteristic of the phrase of some of the dramatists of the period which Donne knew: not to mention Shakespeare, it is frequent in Middleton, Webster, and Tourneur,[2] and is one of the sources of the vitality of their language.

Johnson, who employed the term 'metaphysical poets', apparently having Donne, Cleveland, and Cowley chiefly in mind, remarks of them that 'the most heterogeneous ideas are yoked by violence together'.[3] The force of this impeachment lies in the failure of the conjunction, the fact that often the

6. English poet (1859–1907), as are all those named here: George Herbert (1593–1633), the Welsh-born Henry Vaughan (1622–1695), Richard Crashaw (1612–1649), and Rossetti (1830–1894).

7. Abraham Cowley (1618–1667), English poet and essayist.

8. Donne, "A Valediction: Forbidding Mourning" (1633). Grierson gives the title of Cowley's poem as "Destinie."

9. Donne, "A Valediction: Of Weeping" (1633), lines 10–18.

1. Donne, "The Relic" (1633), line 6.

2. All English dramatists: Thomas Middleton (1580–1627), John Webster (ca. 1580–ca. 1625), and Cyril Tourneur (ca. 1575–1626).

3. Johnson, *Life of Cowley*. John Cleveland (1613–1658), poet and satirist.

ideas are yoked but not united; and if we are to judge of styles of poetry by their abuse, enough examples may be found in Cleveland to justify Johnson's condemnation. But a degree of heterogeneity of material compelled into unity by the operation of the poet's mind is omnipresent in poetry. We need not select for illustration such a line as:

Notre âme est un trois-mâts cherchant son Icarie;[4]

we may find it in some of the best lines of Johnson himself (*The Vanity of Human Wishes*):

His fate was destined to a barren strand,
A petty fortress, and a dubious hand;
He left a name at which the world grew pale,
To point a moral, or adorn a tale.[5]

where the effect is due to a contrast of ideas, different in degree but the same in principle, as that which Johnson mildly reprehended. And in one of the finest poems of the age (a poem which could not have been written in any other age), the *Exequy* of Bishop King, the extended comparison is used with perfect success: the idea and the simile become one, in the passage in which the Bishop illustrates his impatience to see his dead wife, under the figure of a journey:

Stay for me there; I will not faile
To meet thee in that hollow Vale.
And think not much of my delay;
I am already on the way,
And follow thee with all the speed
Desire can make, or sorrows breed.
Each minute is a short degree,
And ev'ry houre a step towards thee.
At night when I betake to rest,
Next morn I rise nearer my West
Of life, almost by eight houres sail,
Than when sleep breath'd his drowsy gale. . . .
But heark! My Pulse, like as a soft Drum
Beats my approach, tells Thee *I come;*
And slow howere my marches be,
I shall at last sit down by Thee.[6]

(In the last few lines there is that effect of terror which is several times attained by one of Bishop King's admirers, Edgar Poe.[7]) Again, we may justly take these quatrains from Lord Herbert's Ode,[8] stanzas which would, we think, be immediately pronounced to be of the metaphysical school:

So when from hence we shall be gone,
And be no more, nor you, nor I,

4. Our soul is a three-masted ship searching for her Icarie (French). From CHARLES BAUDELAIRE, "Le Voyage" (1861). Icarie: a utopia described in the French socialist Etienne Cabet's novel *Voyage en Icarie* (1840).
5. Johnson, "The Vanity of Human Wishes" (1749), lines 219–22, slightly misquoted ("fate" should be "fall").
6. King, "The Exequy" (1657), lines 89–114.
7. EDGAR ALLAN POE (1809–1849), American poet, critic, and short story writer.
8. "An Ode upon a Question Moved, Whether Love Should Continue Forever?" by Lord Herbert of Cherbury (1583–1648). Eliot quotes lines 129–40.

As one another's mystery,
Each shall be both, yet both but one.

This said, in her up-lifted face,
Her eyes, which did that beauty crown,
Were like two starrs, that having faln down,
Look up again to find their place:

While such a moveless silent peace
Did seize on their becalmed sense,
One would have thought some influence
Their ravished spirits did possess.

There is nothing in these lines (with the possible exception of the stars, a simile not at once grasped, but lovely and justified) which fits Johnson's general observations on the metaphysical poets in his essay on Cowley. A good deal resides in the richness of association which is at the same time borrowed from and given to the word 'becalmed'; but the meaning is clear, the language simple and elegant. It is to be observed that the language of these poets is as a rule simple and pure; in the verse of George Herbert this simplicity is carried as far as it can go—a simplicity emulated without success by numerous modern poets. The *structure* of the sentences, on the other hand, is sometimes far from simple, but this is not a vice; it is a fidelity to thought and feeling. The effect, at its best, is far less artificial than that of an ode by Gray.[9] And as this fidelity induces variety of thought and feeling, so it induces variety of music. We doubt whether, in the eighteenth century, could be found two poems in nominally the same metre, so dissimilar as Marvell's *Coy Mistress* and Crashaw's *Saint Teresa*;[1] the one producing an effect of great speed by the use of short syllables, and the other an ecclesiastical solemnity by the use of long ones:

Love, thou art absolute sole lord
Of life and death.

If so shrewd and sensitive (though so limited) a critic as Johnson failed to define metaphysical poetry by its faults, it is worth while to inquire whether we may not have more success by adopting the opposite method: by assuming that the poets of the seventeenth century (up to the Revolution)[2] were the direct and normal development of the precedent age; and, without prejudicing their case by the adjective 'metaphysical', consider whether their virtue was not something permanently valuable, which subsequently disappeared, but ought not to have disappeared. Johnson has hit, perhaps by accident, on one of their peculiarities, when he observes that 'their attempts were always analytic'; he would not agree that, after the dissociation, they put the material together again in a new unity.

It is certain that the dramatic verse of the later Elizabethan and early Jacobean poets expresses a degree of development of sensibility which is not found in any of the prose, good as it often is. If we except Marlowe, a man

9. Thomas Gray (1716–1771), "Elegy Written in a Country Churchyard" (1751), a poem of mourning and reflection.
1. Crashaw, "A Hymn to the Name and Honor of the Admirable Saint Teresa" (1652); Eliot quotes its opening lines. Marvell, "To His Coy Mistress" (1681).
2. Either the Glorious Revolution of 1688, when James II was replaced by William and Mary, or the English Civil War, which climaxed in the execution of Charles I in 1649; scholars disagree on Eliot's reference.

of prodigious intelligence, these dramatists were directly or indirectly (it is at least a tenable theory) affected by Montaigne.[3] Even if we except also Jonson and Chapman, these two were notably erudite, and were notably men who incorporated their erudition into their sensibility: their mode of feeling was directly and freshly altered by their reading and thought. In Chapman especially there is a direct sensuous apprehension of thought, or a recreation of thought into feeling, which is exactly what we find in Donne:

> *in this one thing, all the discipline*
> *Of manners and of manhood is contained;*
> *A man to join himself with th' Universe*
> *In his main sway, and make in all things fit*
> *One with that All, and go on, round as it;*
> *Not plucking from the whole his wretched part,*
> *And into straits, or into nought revert,*
> *Wishing the complete Universe might be*
> *Subject to such a rag of it as he;*
> *But to consider great Necessity.*[4]

We compare this with some modern passage:

> *No, when the fight begins within himself,*
> *A man's worth something. God stoops o'er his head,*
> *Satan looks up between his feet—both tug—*
> *He's left, himself, i' the middle; the soul wakes*
> *And grows. Prolong that battle through his life!*[5]

It is perhaps somewhat less fair, though very tempting (as both poets are concerned with the perpetuation of love by offspring), to compare with the stanzas already quoted from Lord Herbert's Ode the following from Tennyson:

> *One walked between his wife and child,*
> *With measured footfall firm and mild,*
> *And now and then he gravely smiled.*
> *The prudent partner of his blood*
> *Leaned on him, faithful, gentle, good,*
> *Wearing the rose of womanhood.*
> *And in their double love secure,*
> *The little maiden walked demure,*
> *Pacing with downward eyelids pure.*
> *These three made unity so sweet,*
> *My frozen heart began to beat,*
> *Remembering its ancient heat.*[6]

The difference is not a simple difference of degree between poets. It is something which had happened to the mind of England between the time of Donne or Lord Herbert of Cherbury and the time of Tennyson and Browning; it is the difference between the intellectual poet and the reflec-

3. Michel de Montaigne (1533–1592), French moralist and essayist. Christopher Marlowe (1564–1593), English dramatist and poet.
4. Chapman, *The Revenge of Bussy d'Ambois* (ca. 1610), 4.1.137–46.
5. "Bishop Blougram's Apology" (1855), lines 693–97, by Robert Browning (1812–1889).
6. "The Two Voices" (1832), lines 412–23, by Alfred, Lord Tennyson (1809–1892).

tive poet. Tennyson and Browning are poets, and they think; but they do not feel their thought as immediately as the odour of a rose. A thought to Donne was an experience; it modified his sensibility. When a poet's mind is perfectly equipped for its work, it is constantly amalgamating disparate experience; the ordinary man's experience is chaotic, irregular, fragmentary. The latter falls in love, or reads Spinoza,[7] and these two experiences have nothing to do with each other, or with the noise of the typewriter or the smell of cooking; in the mind of the poet these experiences are always forming new wholes.[8]

We may express the difference by the following theory: The poets of the seventeenth century, the successors of the dramatists of the sixteenth, possessed a mechanism of sensibility which could devour any kind of experience. They are simple, artificial, difficult, or fantastic, as their predecessors were; no less nor more than Dante, Guido Cavalcanti, Guinicelli, or Cino.[9] In the seventeenth century a dissociation of sensibility set in, from which we have never recovered; and this dissociation, as is natural, was aggravated by the influence of the two most powerful poets of the century, Milton and Dryden.[1] Each of these men performed certain poetic functions so magnificently well that the magnitude of the effect concealed the absence of others. The language went on and in some respects improved; the best verse of Collins, Gray, Johnson, and even Goldsmith[2] satisfies some of our fastidious demands better than that of Donne or Marvell or King. But while the language became more refined, the feeling became more crude. The feeling, the sensibility, expressed in the *Country Churchyard* (to say nothing of Tennyson and Browning) is cruder than that in the *Coy Mistress*.

The second effect of the influence of Milton and Dryden followed from the first, and was therefore slow in manifestation. The sentimental age began early in the eighteenth century, and continued. The poets revolted against the ratiocinative, the descriptive; they thought and felt by fits, unbalanced; they reflected. In one or two passages of Shelley's *Triumph of Life*, in the second *Hyperion*,[3] there are traces of a struggle toward unification of sensibility. But Keats and Shelley died, and Tennyson and Browning ruminated.

After this brief exposition of a theory—too brief, perhaps, to carry conviction—we may ask, what would have been the fate of the 'metaphysical' had the current of poetry descended in a direct line from them, as it descended in a direct line to them? They would not, certainly, be classified as metaphysical. The possible interests of a poet are unlimited; the more intelligent he is the better; the more intelligent he is the more likely that he will have interests: our only condition is that he turn them into poetry, and not merely meditate on them poetically. A philosophical theory which has entered into

7. Benedict de Spinoza (1632–1677), Dutch philosopher and theologian, whose major work is *Ethics* (1677).

8. Compare SAMUEL TAYLOR COLERIDGE, *Biographia Literaria* (1817; see above), chap. 14: "[The poet] diffuses a tone and spirit of unity, that blends, and (as it were) *fuses*, each into each, by that synthetic and magical power, to which we have exclusively appropriated the name of imagination."

9. Italian poets (roughly contemporary) all known for their *dolce stil nuovo* (sweet new style): DANTE ALIGHIERI (1265–1321), Guido Cavalcanti (1250–1300), Guido Guinicelli (1220–1276), and Cino da Pistoia (1270–1336).

1. JOHN DRYDEN (1631–1700), English poet, dramatist, and critic. John Milton (1608–1674), English writer of poetry and prose.

2. Oliver Goldsmith (1731–1774), Irish-born English poet, playwright, and novelist. William Collins (1721–1759), English poet.

3. "Hyperion, a fragment" and "The Fall of Hyperion" (written 1818–19), fragments of epic poems by John Keats (1795–1821). "The Triumph of Life" (written in 1822), an unfinished visionary poem by PERCY BYSSHE SHELLEY (1792–1822).

poetry is established, for its truth or falsity in one sense ceases to matter, and its truth in another sense is proved. The poets in question have, like other poets, various faults. But they were, at best, engaged in the task of trying to find the verbal equivalent for states of mind and feeling. And this means both that they are more mature, and that they wear better, than later poets of certainly not less literary ability.

It is not a permanent necessity that poets should be interested in philosophy, or in any other subject. We can only say that it appears likely that poets in our civilization, as it exists at present, must be *difficult*. Our civilization comprehends great variety and complexity, and this variety and complexity, playing upon a refined sensibility, must produce various and complex results. The poet must become more and more comprehensive, more allusive, more indirect, in order to force, to dislocate if necessary, language into his meaning. (A brilliant and extreme statement of this view, with which it is not requisite to associate oneself, is that of M. Jean Epstein, *La Poésie d' aujourd-hui.*)[4] Hence we get something which looks very much like the conceit—we get, in fact, a method curiously similar to that of the 'metaphysical poets', similar also in its use of obscure words and of simple phrasing.

O géraniums diaphanes, guerroyeurs sortilèges,
Sacrilèges monomanes!
Emballages, dévergondages, douches! O pressoirs
Des vendanges des grands soirs!
Layettes aux abois,
Thyrses au fond des bois!
Transfusions, représailles,
Relevailles, compresses et l' éternal potion,
Angélus! n' en pouvoir plus
De débâcles nuptiales! de débâles nuptiales![5]

The same poet could write also simply:

Elle est bien loin, elle pleure,
Le grand vent se lamente aussi . . . [6]

Jules Laforgue, and Tristan Corbière[7] in many of his poems, are nearer to the 'school of Donne' than any modern English poet. But poets more classical than they have the same essential quality of transmuting ideas into sensations, of transforming an observation into a state of mind.

Pour l' enfant, amoureux de cartes et d' estampes,
L' univers est égal à son vaste appétit.
Ah, que le monde est grand à la clarté des lampes!
Aux yeux du souvenir que le monde est petit![8]

4. *The Poetry of Today* (French), published in 1921.
5. O translucent geraniums, warring wizardry, / Monomaniac impieties! / Enwrappings, licentiousness, showers! O winepresses / Of grape harvestings on great evenings! / Layettes at bay, / Thrysis deep in the woods! / Transfusion, repayings, / Churchings, compresses and the eternal potion, / *Angelus*! can't bear any more / Those bursting nuptials! Bursting nuptials! (French; trans. June Guicharnaud). From *Derniers vers X* (1890, *Last Poems*), by the French symbolist poet Jules Laforgue (1860–1887).
6. She is far away, she weeps / The great wind also mourns (French). From Laforgue, *Derniers vers XI*, "Sur une défunte" ("On a Dead Woman").
7. French symbolist poet (1845–1875).
8. For the child in love with maps and prints, the universe matches his vast appetite. Ah, how big the world is, in the lamplight; but how small, viewed through the eyes of memory (French; trans. Francis Scarfe). From Baudelaire, "Le Voyage."

In French literature the great master of the seventeenth century—Racine[9]—and the great master of the nineteenth—Baudelaire—are in some ways more like each other than they are like anyone else. The greatest two masters of diction are also the greatest two psychologists, the most curious explorers of the soul. It is interesting to speculate whether it is not a misfortune that two of the greatest masters of diction in our language, Milton and Dryden, triumph with a dazzling disregard of the soul. If we continued to produce Miltons and Drydens it might not so much matter, but as things are it is a pity that English poetry has remained so incomplete. Those who object to the 'artificiality' of Milton or Dryden sometimes tell us to 'look into our hearts and write'.[1] But that is not looking deep enough; Racine or Donne looked into a good deal more than the heart. One must look into the cerebral cortex, the nervous system, and the digestive tracts.

May we not conclude, then, that Donne, Crashaw, Vaughan, Herbert and Lord Herbert, Marvell, King, Cowley at his best, are in the direct current of English poetry, and that their faults should be reprimanded by this standard rather than coddled by antiquarian affection? They have been enough praised in terms which are implicit limitations because they are 'metaphysical' or 'witty', 'quaint' or 'obscure,' though at their best they have not these attributes more than other serious poets. On the other hand, we must not reject the criticism of Johnson (a dangerous person to disagree with) without having mastered it, without having assimilated the Johnsonian canons of taste. In reading the celebrated passage in his essay on Cowley we must remember that by wit he clearly means something more serious than we usually mean to-day; in his criticism of their versification we must remember in what a narrow discipline he was trained, but also how well trained; we must remember that Johnson tortures chiefly the chief offenders, Cowley and Cleveland. It would be a fruitful work, and one requiring a substantial book, to break up the classification of Johnson (for there has been none since) and exhibit these poets in all their difference of kind and of degree, from the massive music of Donne to the faint, pleasing tinkle of Aurelian Townshend[2]—whose *Dialogue between a Pilgrim and Time* is one of the few regrettable omissions from the excellent anthology of Professor Grierson.

1921

9. Jean Racine (1639–1699), French playwright.
1. A slight recasting of the final words of the first sonnet in the sonnet sequence *Astrophil and Stella* (1591), by SIR PHILIP SIDNEY.
2. Poet and writer of court masques (ca. 1583–1643).

JOHN CROWE RANSOM
1888–1974

The poet, critic, and editor John Crowe Ransom is perhaps the central figure in the institutionalization of the New Criticism, the formalist theory and practice that dominated U.S. teaching and literary criticism in the mid–twentieth century. Through his essays on literary theory, his important work as an editor of the prestigious journal the *Kenyon Review*, and his friendships with many noteworthy authors and critics, Ransom was able to gain a wide and respectful hearing for his and the other New Critics' literary views and values. By the 1950s or perhaps even earlier, the New Critical focus on "the text itself" had become the basic method of literary criticism and of college and university pedagogy.

Ransom was born in Pulaski, Tennessee, the son of a Methodist minister. He was a brilliant student at Bowen School (a private academy) and then at Vanderbilt University in Nashville, where he received rigorous training in the classics. He studied Greek and Roman literature and history at Christ Church, Oxford University, on a Rhodes Scholarship from 1910 to 1913, and in 1914 joined the faculty of Vanderbilt's English Department. He became the central figure in Nashville's literary and cultural community, which in the 1920s and 1930s included the poets Allen Tate and Donald Davidson, the poet, novelist, and critic Robert Penn Warren, and the critic CLEANTH BROOKS.

In the early 1920s Ransom was one of the Fugitive poets, a group that came together in Nashville as "fugitives" both from preachy, sentimental nineteenth-century verse and from contemporary verse that struck them as far removed from the Southern regionalist values they embraced. They focused on the language, forms, and techniques of poetry and published in the bimonthly the *Fugitive* (1922–25); many of Ransom's best poems as well as a number of critical essays appeared in this journal. Later in the decade, Ransom played a prominent role in the Agrarian movement; he contributed both the introduction and a chapter to the Agrarian manifesto *I'll Take My Stand* (1930), a spirited attack on science and industrialization and a defense of Southern tradition and an agricultural economy.

During the Agrarian phase of his career, Ransom wrote many essays on social and cultural criticism, including "The South—Old or New?" (1928), "The Aesthetics of Regionalism" (1934), and "What Does the South Want?" (1936). But the Agrarian cause never won widespread support among Southerners, and by the late 1930s, Ransom was himself shifting away from sociocultural commentary. In 1937 he left Vanderbilt for a position in the English Department at Kenyon College in Ohio, a move that coincided with his sharp turn toward literary criticism and the reforms needed to give it precision and clarity as an autonomous academic discipline. In a 1937 letter to Allen Tate, Ransom noted that the new journal he hoped to launch at Kenyon should "stick to literature entirely. . . . In the severe field of letters there is vocation enough for us: in criticism, in poetry, in fiction."

For two decades, beginning in 1939, Ransom edited the *Kenyon Review*; this journal, which became one of the best U.S. literary quarterlies, was among his greatest achievements. Moreover, his distinguished reputation as an editor as well as a poet and critic enabled him to gain much institutional support for his ideas and programs. During the late 1940s, the Rockefeller Foundation provided funds for a series of *Kenyon Review* Fellows (scholars) and for the Kenyon School of English, which had on its faculty important intellectuals, creative writers, and critics—among the first (in 1948) were Eric Bentley, Cleanth Brooks, and William Empson. The *Kenyon Review* also offered fellowships each year to a poet, a writer of fiction, and a critic; prominent recipients included Flannery O'Connor, Howard Nemerov, and IRVING HOWE. The New Criticism was not simply a body of theory and practice but a network of programs, journals, and institutions, and Ransom was involved in nearly all of them.

Our selection from *The World's Body*, "Criticism, Inc." (1938), is, as its title suggests, Ransom's attempt to define the business of criticism—what it is not and what it should be. He lists a number of false or misleading types of current criticism—including the "ethical" approach of the New Humanism and Marxism—but he focuses primarily on the teaching of literature in universities by literary historians and scholars who stress backgrounds, sources, and influences rather than the poems themselves. Historical study, he contends, dominates at the expense of a truly "critical" approach, preventing students from acquiring the skills needed for them to understand the "technical effects" of literary works. As a result, they cannot respond in a direct, rigorous way to contemporary literature or, for that matter, to any poem placed before them.

Ransom instead urges teachers and students to concentrate on "technical studies of poetry." By this, he means studies of imagery, metaphor, and meter—the stylistic devices through which the poet differentiates the language of his or her text from that of prose. Ransom calls for a revitalized department of English that will make literary history, scholarship, and linguistics secondary to rigorous criticism. In his view, criticism must be rescued from book reviewers and amateurs who focus on feelings, not the artistic object itself, and reduce texts to paraphrases with a moral message. Advocating disciplinary coherence and integrity, Ransom is a harbinger of the professionalization of literary analysis that characterized mid- and late-twentieth-century U.S. literary culture.

These arguments had great appeal to many teachers and students, and Ransom's approach was so helpful for readers grappling with exacting modern poets that its limits were overlooked at first. By defining the work of literary studies, he supplied a clear procedure: the teacher-critic should concentrate on the text itself and not be distracted by nonliterary contexts and issues. But Ransom and the other New Critics, opponents pointed out, excluded too much; in giving literary studies a disciplinary identity, they failed to clarify how it could engage with social, cultural, and historical issues in a meaningful way. In a sense Ransom allowed the opposition to dictate the terms of his own approach—literary criticism is defined against, not in *relation* to, other fields, subjects, and disciplines. But why should the analysis of specific literary texts require the exclusion of other kinds of analytical work? Ransom defined the enterprise of "Criticism, Inc." with brilliant precision but too narrowly, as though the forms of social and cultural critique he had embarked on in his Agrarian writing were wholly incompatible with literary criticism.

To be sure, in stressing that critics should explore how the poem "removes itself from history" Ransom had a specific target: the practice of making history rather than the poem the object of attention in the classroom. Neither he nor the other New Critics asserted that history was irrelevant, or that teachers and students ignore everything except "the words on the page"; they assumed that teachers would be well-trained and knowledgeable about much more (as they were themselves). Indeed, those in the first generation of New Critics were later dismayed at the reductive, mechanical criticism and teaching practiced in their name.

As the New Criticism came under widespread attack in the 1960s and 1970s, it lost the authority it had enjoyed when Ransom, I. A. Richards, and Brooks first promoted it. Its emphasis on the text in and for itself seemed far removed from the crises and social movements—civil rights, antiwar, and women's—that were tearing American society apart. The New Critical canon was too limited (male and white) to prove acceptable to feminists, African American critics, and other theorists. In addition, by the 1970s poststructuralists were arguing that the New Critical distinction between what was inside and outside the text could not be maintained: thus the discrete poetic text that was to be the basis of literary studies seemed no longer to exist. Soon, from another direction, New Historicist scholars began to recuperate and renovate historical analysis; by demonstrating that close reading could be extended to all kinds of texts and documents, they made possible a richer, more diverse approach to history than that found in the earlier literary historians whom Ransom, Brooks, and the others had displaced.

Yet one crucial tenet of the New Critical program remains: the emphasis on "close reading," the central focus of the new business for literary studies that Ransom advocates in "Criticism, Inc." In this respect, the New Criticism has not so much faded as become the foundation that all modern approaches build upon.

BIBLIOGRAPHY

Ransom's books include *The World's Body* (1938), *The New Criticism* (1941), *Poems and Essays* (1955), and *Beating the Bushes* (1971). See also Ransom's *Selected Essays*, edited by Thomas Daniel Young and John Hindle (1984), and *Selected Letters*, edited by Young and George Core (1985). He also edited *The Kenyon Critics: Studies in Modern Literature from "The Kenyon Review"* (1951). Thomas Daniel Young has written an excellent biography: *Gentleman in a Dustcoat: A Biography of John Crowe Ransom* (1976). See also *John Crowe Ransom: Critical Essays and a Bibliography*, edited by Young (1968).

On the Agrarian movement and its relationship to the New Criticism, see John Lincoln Stewart, *The Burden of Time: The Fugitives and Agrarians* (1965); Alexander Karanikas, *Tillers of a Myth: Southern Agrarians as Social and Literary Critics* (1966); and Mark Jancovich, *The Cultural Politics of the New Criticism* (1993). Detailed information about Ransom and the New Critics can also be found in Marian Janssen, *The Kenyon Review, 1939–1970: A Critical History* (1990). *The New Criticism and Contemporary Literary Theory: Connections and Continuities*, edited by William J. Spurlin and Michael Fischer (1995), examines the history of modern criticism from the New Critics to later poststructuralist theorists. For bibliography of primary and secondary sources, consult Thomas Daniel Young, *John Crowe Ransom: An Annotated Bibliography* (1982).

Criticism, Inc.

It is strange, but nobody seems to have told us what exactly is the proper business of criticism. There are many critics who might tell us, but for the most part they are amateurs. So have the critics nearly always been amateurs; including the best ones. They have not been trained to criticism so much as they have simply undertaken a job for which no specific qualifications were required. It is far too likely that what they call criticism when they produce it is not the real thing.

There are three sorts of trained performers who would appear to have some of the competence that the critic needs. The first is the artist himself. He should know good art when he sees it; but his understanding is intuitive rather than dialectical—he cannot very well explain his theory of the thing. It is true that literary artists, with their command of language, are better critics of their own art than are other artists; probably the best critics of poetry we can now have are the poets. But one can well imagine that any artist's commentary on the art-work is valuable in the degree that he sticks to its technical effects, which he knows minutely, and about which he can certainly talk if he will.

The second is the philosopher, who should know all about the function of the fine arts. But the philosopher is apt to see a lot of wood and no trees, for his theory is very general and his acquaintance with the particular works of art is not persistent and intimate, especially his acquaintance with their technical effects. Or at least I suppose so, for philosophers have not proved that they can write close criticism by writing it; and I have the feeling that even their handsome generalizations are open to suspicion as being grounded more on other generalizations, those which form their prior philosophical stock, than on acute study of particulars.

The third is the university teacher of literature, who is styled professor, and who should be the very professional we need to take charge of the critical activity. He is hardly inferior as critic to the philosopher, and perhaps not on the whole to the poet, but he is a greater disappointment because we have the right to expect more of him. Professors of literature are learned but not critical men. The professional morale of this part of the university staff is evidently low. It is as if, with conscious or unconscious cunning, they had appropriated every avenue of escape from their responsibility which was decent and official; so that it is easy for one of them without public reproach to spend a lifetime in compiling the data of literature and yet rarely or never commit himself to a literary judgment.

Nevertheless it is from the professors of literature, in this country the professors of English for the most part, that I should hope eventually for the erection of intelligent standards of criticism. It is their business.

Criticism must become more scientific, or precise and systematic, and this means that it must be developed by the collective and sustained effort of learned persons—which means that its proper seat is in the universities.

Scientific: but I do not think we need be afraid that criticism, trying to be a sort of science, will inevitably fail and give up in despair, or else fail without realizing it and enjoy some hollow and pretentious career. It will never be a very exact science, or even a nearly exact one. But neither will psychology, if that term continues to refer to psychic rather than physical phenomena; nor will sociology, as Pareto,[1] quite contrary to his intention, appears to have furnished us with evidence for believing; nor even will economics. It does not matter whether we call them sciences or just systematic studies; the total effort of each to be effective must be consolidated and kept going. The studies which I have mentioned have immeasurably improved in understanding since they were taken over by the universities, and the same career looks possible for criticism.

Rather than occasional criticism by amateurs, I should think the whole enterprise might be seriously taken in hand by professionals. Perhaps I use a distasteful figure, but I have the idea that what we need is Criticism, Inc., or Criticism, Ltd.

The principal resistance to such an idea will come from the present incumbents of the professorial chairs. But its adoption must come from them too. The idea of course is not a private one of my own. If it should be adopted before long, the credit would probably belong to Professor Ronald S. Crane,[2] of the University of Chicago, more than to any other man. He is the first of the great professors to have advocated it as a major policy for departments of English. It is possible that he will have made some important academic history.

2

Professor Crane published recently a paper of great note in academic circles, on the reform of the courses in English. It appeared in *The English Journal*, under the title: "History Versus Criticism in the University Study of Litera-

1. Vilfredo Pareto (1848–1923), French-born Italian economist and sociologist.
2. The leader (1886–1967) of the Chicago School of neo-Aristotelian criticism, whose views were influenced by the restructuring of the undergraduate curriculum of the University of Chicago in the 1930s, to a focus on interdisciplinary studies and "Great Books." He published "History Versus Criticism" (discussed below) in 1935.

ture." He argues there that historical scholarship has been overplayed heavily in English studies, in disregard of the law of diminishing returns, and that the emphasis must now be shifted to the critical.

To me this means, simply: the students of the future must be permitted to study literature, and not merely about literature. But I think this is what the good students have always wanted to do. The wonder is that they have allowed themselves so long to be denied. But they have not always been amiable about it, and the whole affair presents much comic history.

At the University of Chicago, I believe that Professor Crane, with some others, is putting the revolution into effect in his own teaching, though for the time being perhaps with a limited programme, mainly the application of Aristotle's critical views. (My information is not at all exact.) The university is an opulent one, not too old to experience waves of reformational zeal, uninhibited as yet by bad traditions. Its department of English has sponsored plenty of old-line scholarship, but this is not the first time it has gone in for criticism. If the department should now systematically and intelligently build up a general school of literary criticism, I believe it would score a triumph that would be, by academic standards, spectacular. I mean that the alive and brilliant young English scholars all over the country would be saying they wanted to go there to do their work. That would place a new distinction upon the university, and it would eventually and profoundly modify the practices of many other institutions. It would be worth even more than Professor Crane's careful presentation of the theory.

This is not the first time that English professors have tilted against the historians, or "scholars," in the dull sense which that word has acquired. They did not score heavily, at those other times. Probably they were themselves not too well versed in the historical studies, so that it could be said with honest concern that they scarcely had the credentials to judge of such matters. At the same time they may have been too unproductive critically to offer a glowing alternative.

The most important recent diversion from the orthodox course of literary studies was that undertaken by the New Humanists.[3] I regret to think that it was not the kind of diversion which I am advocating; nor the kind approved by Professor Crane, who comments briefly against it. Unquestionably the Humanists did divert, and the refreshment was grateful to anybody who felt resentful for having his literary predilections ignored under the schedule of historical learning. But in the long run the diversion proved to be nearly as unliterary as the round of studies from which it took off at a tangent. No picnic ideas were behind it.

The New Humanists were, and are, moralists; more accurately, historians and advocates of a certain moral system. Criticism is the attempt to define and enjoy the æsthetic or characteristic values of literature, but I suppose the Humanists would shudder at "æsthetic" as hard as ordinary historical scholars do. Did an official Humanist ever make any official play with the term? I do not remember it. The term "art" is slightly more ambiguous, and

3. Members of an early-20th-century critical movement in the United States that attacked the decadence of modern life and the immorality of contemporary literature, condemning the influence of Romanticism and appealing for classical values. The leaders of New Humanism were Paul Elmer More (1864–1937), a critic, editor, and lecturer at Princeton University, and Irving Babbitt (1865–1933), professor of Romance languages at Harvard University.

they have availed themselves of that; with centuries of loose usage behind it, art connotes, for those who like, high seriousness, and high seriousness connotes moral self-consciousness, and an inner check, and finally either Plato or Aristotle.

Mr. Babbitt consistently played on the terms classical and romantic. They mean any of several things each, so that unquestionably Mr. Babbitt could make war on romanticism for purely moral reasons; and his preoccupation was ethical, not æsthetic. It is perfectly legitimate for the moralist to attack romantic literature if he can make out his case; for example, on the ground that it deals with emotions rather than principles, or the ground that its author discloses himself as flabby, intemperate, escapist, unphilosophical, or simply adolescent. The moral objection is probably valid; a romantic period testifies to a large-scale failure of adaptation, and defense of that failure to adapt, to the social and political environment; unless, if the Humanists will consent, it sometimes testifies to the failure of society and state to sympathize with the needs of the individual. But this is certainly not the charge that Mr. T. S. Eliot, a literary critic, brings against romanticism.[4] His, if I am not mistaken, is æsthetic, though he may not ever care to define it very sharply. In other words, the literary critic also has something to say about romanticism, and it might come to something like this: that romantic literature is imperfect in objectivity, or "æsthetic distance," and that out of this imperfection comes its weakness of structure; that the romantic poet does not quite realize the æsthetic attitude, and is not the pure artist. Or it might come to something else. It would be quite premature to say that when a moralist is obliged to disapprove a work the literary critic must disapprove it too.

Following the excitement produced by the Humanist diversion, there is now one due to the Leftists, or Proletarians,[5] who are also diversionists. Their diversion is likewise moral. It is just as proper for them to ferret out class-consciousness in literature, and to make literature serve the cause of loving-comradeship, as it is for the Humanists to censure romanticism and to use the topic, and the literary exhibit, as the occasion of reviving the Aristotelian moral canon. I mean that these are procedures of the same sort. Debate could never occur between a Humanist and a Leftist on æsthetic grounds, for they are equally intent on ethical values. But the debate on ethical grounds would be very spirited, and it might create such a stir in a department conducting English studies that the conventional scholars there would find themselves slipping, and their pupils deriving from literature new and seductive excitements which would entice them away from their scheduled English exercises.

On the whole, however, the moralists, distinguished as they may be, are like those who have quarrelled with the ordinary historical studies on purer or more aesthetic grounds: they have not occupied in English studies the positions of professional importance. In a department of English, as in any other going business, the proprietary interest becomes vested, and in old and reputable departments the vestees have uniformly been gentlemen who have gone through the historical mill. Their laborious Ph.D.'s and historical

4. At Harvard, ELIOT (1888–1965) was taught by Babbitt, who reinforced Eliot's own anti-Romantic tendencies

5. Marxist critics who emphasized the class struggle between workers (proletarians) and owners, and the problems of poverty and racism.

publications are their patents. Naturally, quite spontaneously, they would tend to perpetuate a system in which the power and the glory belonged to them. But English scholars in this country can rarely have better credentials than those which Professor Crane has earned in his extensive field, the eighteenth century. It is this which makes his disaffection significant.

It is really atrocious policy for a department to abdicate its own self-respecting identity. The department of English is charged with the understanding and the communication of literature, an art, yet it has usually forgotten to inquire into the peculiar constitution and structure of its product. English might almost as well announce that it does not regard itself as entirely autonomous, but as a branch of the department of history, with the option of declaring itself occasionally a branch of the department of ethics. It is true that the historical and the ethical studies will cluster round objects which for some reason are called artistic objects. But the thing itself the professors do not have to contemplate; and only last spring the head of English studies in a graduate school fabulously equipped made the following impromptu disclaimer to a victim who felt aggrieved at having his own studies forced in the usual direction: "This is a place for exact scholarship, and you want to do criticism. Well, we don't allow criticism here, because that is something which anybody can do."

But one should never speak impromptu in one's professional capacity. This speech may have betrayed a fluttery private apprehension which should not have been made public: that you can never be critical and be exact at the same time, that history is firmer ground than æsthetics, and that, to tell the truth, criticism is a painful job for the sort of mind that wants to be very sure about things. Not in that temper did Aristotle labor towards a critique in at least one branch of letters;[6] nor in that temper are strong young minds everywhere trying to sharpen their critical apparatus into precision tools, in this decade as never before.

It is not anybody who can do criticism. And for an example, the more eminent (as historical scholar) the professor of English, the less apt he is to be able to write decent criticism, unless it is about another professor's work of historical scholarship, in which case it is not literary criticism. The professor may not be without æsthetic judgments respecting an old work, especially if it is "in his period," since it must often have been judged by authorities whom he respects. Confronted with a new work, I am afraid it is very rare that he finds anything particular to say. Contemporary criticism is not at all in the hands of those who direct the English studies. Contemporary literature, which is almost obliged to receive critical study if it receives any at all, since it is hardly capable of the usual historical commentary, is barely officialized as a proper field for serious study.

Here is contemporary literature, waiting for its criticism; where are the professors of literature? They are watering their own gardens; elucidating the literary histories of their respective periods. So are their favorite pupils. The persons who save the occasion, and rescue contemporary literature from the humiliation of having to go without a criticism, are the men who had to leave the university before their time because they felt themselves being warped into mere historians; or those who finished the courses and took

6. In the *Poetics* (see above).

their punishment but were tough, and did not let it engross them and spoil them. They are home-made critics. Naturally they are not too wise, these amateurs who furnish our reviews and critical studies. But when they distinguish themselves, the universities which they attended can hardly claim more than a trifling share of the honor.

It is not so in economics, chemistry, sociology, theology, and architecture. In these branches it is taken for granted that criticism of the performance is the prerogative of the men who have had formal training in its theory and technique. The historical method is useful, and may be applied readily to any human performance whatever. But the exercise does not become an obsession with the university men working in the other branches; only the literary scholars wish to convert themselves into pure historians. This has gone far to nullify the usefulness of a departmental personnel larger, possibly, than any other, and of the lavish endowment behind it.

3

Presumably the departments of English exist in order to communicate the understanding of the literary art. That will include both criticism and also whatever may be meant by "appreciation." This latter term seems to stand for the kind of understanding that is had intuitively, without benefit of instruction, by merely being constrained to spend time in the presence of the literary product. It is true that some of the best work now being done in departments is by the men who do little more than read well aloud, enforcing a private act of appreciation upon the students. One remembers how good a service that may be, thinking perhaps of Professor Copeland of Harvard,[7] or Dean Cross at Greeley Teachers College. And there are men who try to get at the same thing in another way, which they would claim is surer: by requiring a great deal of memory work, in order to enforce familiarity with fine poetry. These might defend their strategy by saying that at any rate the work they required was not as vain as the historical rigmarole which the scholars made their pupils recite, if the objective was really literary understanding and not external information. But it would be a misuse of terms to employ the word instruction for the offices either of the professors who read aloud or of those who require the memory work. The professors so engaged are properly curators, and the museum of which they have the care is furnished with the cherished literary masterpieces, just as another museum might be filled with paintings. They conduct their squads from one work to another, making appropriate pauses or reverent gestures, but their own obvious regard for the masterpieces is somewhat contagious, and contemplation is induced. Naturally they are grateful to the efficient staff of colleagues in the background who have framed the masterpieces, hung them in the proper schools and in the chronological order, and prepared the booklet of information about the artists and the occasions. The colleagues in their turn probably feel quite happy over this division of labor, thinking that they have done the really productive work, and that it is appropriate now if less able men should undertake a little salesmanship.

7. Charles Townsend Copeland (1860–1952), member of the English department at Harvard. "Dean Cross" is Neal Cross, who served as chair of the English department at Greeley Teachers College (now the University of Northern Colorado).

Behind appreciation, which is private, and criticism, which is public and negotiable, and represents the last stage of English studies, is historical scholarship. It is indispensable. But it is instrumental and cannot be the end itself. In this respect historical studies have the same standing as linguistic studies: language and history are aids.

On behalf of the historical studies. Without them what could we make of Chaucer, for instance? I cite the familiar locus of the "hard" scholarship, the center of any program of advanced studies in English which intends to initiate the student heroically, and once for all, into the historical discipline. Chaucer writes allegories for historians to decipher, he looks out upon institutions and customs unfamiliar to us.[8] Behind him are many writers in various tongues from whom he borrows both forms and materials. His thought bears constant reference to classical and mediæval philosophies and sciences which have passed from our effective knowledge. An immense labor of historical adaptation is necessary before our minds are ready to make the æsthetic approach to Chaucer.

Or to any author out of our own age. The mind with which we enter into an old work is not the mind with which we make our living, or enter into a contemporary work. It is under sharp restraints, and it is quite differently furnished. Out of our actual contemporary mind we have to cancel a great deal that has come there under modern conditions but was not in the earlier mind at all. This is a technique on the negative side, a technique of suspension; difficult for practical persons, literal scientists, and aggressive moderns who take pride in the "truth" or the "progress" which enlightened man, so well represented in their own instance, has won. Then, on the positive side, we must supply the mind with the precise beliefs and ways of thought it had in that former age, with the specific content in which history instructs us; this is a technique of make-believe. The whole act of historical adaptation, through such techniques, is a marvellous feat of flexibility. Certainly it is a thing hard enough to justify university instruction. But it is not sufficient for an English program.

The achievement of modern historical scholarship in the field of English literature has been, in the aggregate, prodigious; it should be very proud. A good impression of the volume of historical learning now available for the students of English may be quickly had from inspecting a few chapters of the Cambridge History,[9] with the bibliographies. Or, better, from inspecting one of a large number of works which have come in since the Cambridge History: the handbooks, which tell all about the authors, such as Chaucer, Shakespeare, Milton, and carry voluminous bibliographies; or the period books, which tell a good deal about whole periods of literature.

There is one sense in which it may be justly said that we can never have too much scholarship. We cannot have too much of it if the critical intelligence functions, and has the authority to direct it. There is hardly a critical problem which does not require some arduous exercises in fact-finding, but each problem is quite specific about the kind of facts it wants. Mountains of facts may have been found already, but often they have been found for no purpose at all except the purpose of piling up into a big exhibit, to offer intoxicating delights to the academic population.

8. Chaucer's allegories include the dream-poems *The Book of the Duchess* (1369) and *The House of Fame* (ca. 1374–85).

9. *The Cambridge History of English Literature* (14 vols., 1907–17); and *The Cambridge History of American Literature* (4 vols., 1917–21).

To those who are æsthetically minded among students, the rewards of many a historical labor will have to be disproportionately slight. The official Chaucer course is probably over ninety-five per cent historical and linguistic, and less than five per cent aesthetic or critical. A thing of beauty is a joy forever.[1] But it is not improved because the student has had to tie his tongue before it. It is an artistic object, with a heroic human labor behind it, and on these terms it calls for public discussion. The dialectical possibilities are limitless, and when we begin to realize them we are engaged in criticism.

4

What is criticism? Easier to ask, What is criticism not? It is an act now notoriously arbitrary and undefined. We feel certain that the critical act is not one of those which the professors of literature habitually perform, and cause their students to perform. And it is our melancholy impression that it is not often cleanly performed in those loose compositions, by writers of perfectly indeterminate qualifications, that appear in print as reviews of books.

Professor Crane excludes from criticism works of historical scholarship and of Neo-Humanism, but more exclusions are possible than that. I should wish to exclude:

1. Personal registrations, which are declarations of the effect of the art-work upon the critic as reader. The first law to be prescribed to criticism, if we may assume such authority, is that it shall be objective, shall cite the nature of the object rather than its effects upon the subject. Therefore it is hardly criticism to assert that the proper literary work is one that we can read twice; or one that causes in us some remarkable physiological effect, such as oblivion of the outer world, the flowing of tears, visceral or laryngeal sensations, and such like; or one that induces perfect illusion, or brings us into a spiritual ecstasy; or even one that produces a catharsis of our emotions. Aristotle concerned himself with this last in making up his definition of tragedy[2]—though he did not fail to make some acute analyses of the objective features of the work also. I have read that some modern Broadway producers of comedy require a reliable person to seat himself in a trial audience and count the laughs; their method of testing is not so subtle as Aristotle's, but both are concerned with the effects. Such concern seems to reflect the view that art comes into being because the artist, or the employer behind him, has designs upon the public, whether high moral designs or box-office ones. It is an odious view in either case, because it denies the autonomy of the artist as one who interests himself in the artistic object in his own right, and likewise the autonomy of the work itself as existing for its own sake. (We may define a chemical as something which can effect a certain cure, but that is not its meaning to the chemist; and we may define toys, if we are weary parents, as things which keep our children quiet, but that is not what they are to engineers.) Furthermore, we must regard as uncritical the use of an extensive vocabulary which ascribes to the object properties really discovered in the subject, as: *moving, exciting, entertaining, pitiful; great*, if I am not mistaken, and *admirable*, on a slightly different ground; and, in strictness, *beautiful* itself.

1. John Keats, *Endymion* (1818), 1.1.

2. ARISTOTLE, *Poetics* 6, 1449b.

2. Synopsis and paraphrase. The high-school classes and the women's clubs delight in these procedures, which are easiest of all the systematic exercises possible in the discussion of literary objects. I do not mean that the critic never uses them in his analysis of fiction and poetry, but he does not consider plot or story as identical with the real content. Plot is an abstract from content.

3. Historical studies. These have a very wide range, and include studies of the general literary background; author's biography, of course with special reference to autobiographical evidences in the work itself; bibliographical items; the citation of literary originals and analogues, and therefore what, in general, is called comparative literature. Nothing can be more stimulating to critical analysis than comparative literature. But it may be conducted only superficially, if the comparisons are perfunctory and mechanical, or if the scholar is content with merely making the parallel citations.

4. Linguistic studies. Under this head come those studies which define the meaning of unusual words and idioms, including the foreign and archaic ones, and identify the allusions. The total benefit of linguistics for criticism would be the assurance that the latter was based on perfect logical understanding of the content, or "interpretation." Acquaintance with all the languages and literatures in the world would not necessarily produce a critic, though it might save one from damaging errors.

5. Moral studies. The moral standard applied is the one appropriate to the reviewer; it may be the Christian ethic, or the Aristotelian one, or the new proletarian gospel. But the moral content is not the whole content, which should never be relinquished.

6. Any other special studies which deal with some abstract or prose content taken out of the work. Nearly all departments of knowledge may conceivably find their own materials in literature, and take them out. Studies have been made of Chaucer's command of mediæval sciences, of Spenser's view of the Irish question, of Shakespeare's understanding of the law, of Milton's geography, of Hardy's place-names.[3] The critic may well inform himself of these materials as possessed by the artist, but his business as critic is to discuss the literary assimilation of them.

5

With or without such useful exercises as these, probably assuming that the intelligent reader has made them for himself, comes the critical act itself.

Mr. Austin Warren,[4] whose writings I admire, is evidently devoted to the academic development of the critical project. Yet he must be a fair representative of what a good deal of academic opinion would be when he sees no reason why criticism should set up its own house, and try to dissociate itself from historical and other scholarly studies; why not let all sorts of studies, including the critical ones, flourish together in the same act of sustained attention, or the same scheduled "course"? But so they are supposed to do at present; and I would only ask him whether he considers that criticism

3. Much of the fiction of Thomas Hardy (1840–1928) is set in "Wessex," a thinly fictionalized version of his native Dorsetshire. "The Irish question": The status of the Irish within the British Empire. The poet Edmund Spenser (1552–1599) wrote a defense of the current repressive policy, *A View of the Present State of Ireland* (pub. 1633).

4. American teacher and critic (1899–1986).

prospers under this arrangement. It has always had the chance to go ahead in the hands of the professors of literature, and it has not gone ahead. A change of policy suggests itself. Strategy requires now, I should think, that criticism receive its own charter of rights and function independently. If he fears for its foundations in scholarship, the scholars will always be on hand to reprove it when it tries to function on an unsound scholarship.

I do not suppose the reviewing of books can be reformed in the sense of being turned into pure criticism. The motives of the reviewers are as much mixed as the performance, and indeed they condition the mixed performance. The reviewer has a job of presentation and interpretation as well as criticism. The most we can ask of him is that he know when the criticism begins, and that he make it as clean and definitive as his business permits. To what authority may he turn?

I know of no authority. For the present each critic must be his own authority. But I know of one large class of studies which is certainly critical, and necessary, and I can suggest another sort of study for the critic's consideration if he is really ambitious.

Studies in the technique of the art belong to criticism certainly. They cannot belong anywhere else, because the technique is not peculiar to any prose materials discoverable in the work of art, nor to anything else but the unique form of that art. A very large volume of studies is indicated by this classification. They would be technical studies of poetry, for instance, the art I am specifically discussing, if they treated its metric; its inversions, solecisms, lapses from the prose norm of language, and from close prose logic; its tropes; its fictions, or inventions, by which it secures "æsthetic distance" and removes itself from history; or any other devices, on the general understanding that any systematic usage which does not hold good for prose is a poetic device.

A device with a purpose: the superior critic is not content with the compilation of the separate devices; they suggest to him a much more general question. The critic speculates on why poetry, through its devices, is at such pains to dissociate itself from prose at all, and what it is trying to represent that cannot be represented by prose.

I intrude here with an idea of my own, which may serve as a starting point of discussion. Poetry distinguishes itself from prose on the technical side by the devices which are, precisely, its means of escaping from prose. Something is continually being killed by prose which the poet wants to preserve. But this must be put philosophically. (Philosophy sounds hard, but it deals with natural and fundamental forms of experience.)

The critic should regard the poem as nothing short of a desperate ontological or metaphysical manœuvre. The poet himself, in the agony of composition, has something like this sense of his labors. The poet perpetuates in his poem an order of existence which in actual life is constantly crumbling beneath his touch. His poem celebrates the object which is real, individual, and qualitatively infinite. He knows that his practical interests will reduce this living object to a mere utility, and that his sciences will disintegrate it for their convenience into their respective abstracts. The poet wishes to defend his object's existence against its enemies, and the critic wishes to know what he is doing, and how. The critic should find in the poem a total poetic or individual object which tends to be universalized, but is not permitted to suffer this fate. His identification of the poetic object is in terms of the universal or commonplace object to which it tends, and of the tissue, or totality of connotation, which holds it secure. How does he make out the universal object? It is the prose object, which any forthright prosy reader can discover to him by an immediate paraphrase; it is a kind of story, character, thing, scene, or moral principle. And where is the tissue that keeps it from coming out of the poetic object? That is, for the laws of the prose logic, its superfluity; and I think I would even say, its irrelevance.

A poet is said to be distinguishable in terms of his style. It is a comprehensive word, and probably means: the general character of his irrelevances, or tissues. All his technical devices contribute to it, elaborating or individualizing the universal, the core-object; likewise all his material detail. For each poem even, ideally, there is distinguishable a logical object or universal, but at the same time a tissue of irrelevance from which it does not really emerge. The critic has to take the poem apart, or analyze it, for the sake of uncovering these features. With all the finesse possible, it is rude and patchy business by comparison with the living integrity of the poem. But without it there could hardly be much understanding of the value of poetry, or of the natural history behind any adult poem.

The language I have used may sound too formidable, but I seem to find that a profound criticism generally works by some such considerations. However the critic may spell them, the two terms are in his mind: the prose core to which he can violently reduce the total object, and the differentia, residue, or tissue, which keeps the object poetical or entire. The character of the poem resides for the good critic in its way of exhibiting the residuary quality. The character of the poet is defined by the kind of prose object to which his interest evidently attaches, plus his way of involving it firmly in the residuary tissue. And doubtless, incidentally, the wise critic can often read behind the poet's public character his private history as a man with a weakness for lapsing into some special form of prosy or scientific bondage.

Similar considerations hold, I think, for the critique of fiction, or of the non-literary arts. I remark this for the benefit of philosophers who believe, with propriety, that the arts are fundamentally one. But I would prefer to leave the documentation to those who are better qualified.

1938

MARTIN HEIDEGGER
1889–1976

One of the most influential philosophers of the twentieth century, Martin Heidegger spent much of his long career preoccupied by the age-old philosophical question of the meaning of "Being." He made his reputation with the publication of his magnum opus, *Being and Time* (1927, *Sein und Zeit*), a groundbreaking amalgam and extension of the phenomenology of Edmund Husserl (1859–1938) and the hermeneutics of Wilhelm Dilthey (1833–1911) that analyzes "what we really mean by the word 'being.' " His later philosophical reflections on Being, the writings that are most relevant for literary theorists and critics, are bound up inextricably with the experience and the analysis of poetry and language. For the later Heidegger, language and poetry are not simply devices employed to describe an already-existing world. Instead, "language is the house of Being," and poetry is the means by which humankind creates new worlds, new varieties of being.

Heidegger was born to a poor Catholic family in the small town of Messkirch, Germany. His education at the high schools in Konstanz and Freiburg was largely a preparation for the priesthood. While at Freiburg, he first became interested in philosophy following his reading of Franz Brentano's *On the Various Meanings of Being according to Aristotle* (1862) and Carl Braig's *On Being: An Outline of Ontology* (1896). He left high school in 1909 to become a Jesuit novice, but he was discharged within a month, most likely because he felt a lack of vocation for the priesthood. He instead entered Freiburg University, where he studied theology and scholastic philosophy. In 1911 a spiritual crisis prompted Heidegger to discontinue his training in theology and concentrate on philosophy. He was particularly influenced by Edmund Husserl's *Logical Investigations* (1900), a treatise that attempted a systematic inquiry into consciousness (what its author called "phenomenology"). In timely fashion, Heidegger completed his dissertation, *The Theory of the Judgment in Psychologism* (1913), and his habilitation thesis, *Duns Scotus's Theory of Categories and Meaning* (1915).

In 1919 Heidegger further distanced himself from Catholicism by officially announcing his breach with its theological system. Following World War I, he became a lecturer at Freiburg and an assistant to Husserl. He soon began to acquire a reputation as a brilliant teacher for his lectures on ARISTOTLE, St. Paul, St. AUGUSTINE, and phenomenology. In 1923 he became an associate professor at Marburg University, where he lectured on Greek, medieval, and German idealist philosophy. The year after the publication of his celebrated *Being and Time*, he succeeded Husserl at Freiburg.

In the early 1930s Heidegger developed sympathy for the Nazi cause, joining the National Socialist German Workers' Party in 1933, shortly after he was elected rector of Freiburg University. Understandably, this aspect of his career is extremely controversial. It is complicated by Heidegger's refusal following World War II to discuss his involvement with the Nazis. He did permit an interview on the subject in the 1960s, subsequently titled "Only a God Can Save Us Now," but only on the condition that it not appear during his lifetime; it was published in 1976.

Heidegger's early work significantly broadened the field of hermeneutics, the theory and art of interpretation. Whereas FRIEDRICH SCHLEIERMACHER (1768–1834) and Dilthey conceived of hermeneutics as the objective exegesis of a specific text or utterance, Heidegger proposed that hermeneutics was central to understanding in general, linking traditional modes of textual interpretation to phenomenology's focus on the contents of consciousness. In effect, he connected the apprehension of Being and the dynamics of language as co-constituents.

Through the 1930s Heidegger turned his attention more and more to the subject of art: one central outcome was his long lecture "The Origin of the Work of Art" (1935)—a main text for the later Heidegger. This development is commonly referred to as the "turn" (*Kehre*), because Heidegger became less concerned with the everyday human existence discussed in his *Being and Time* and increasingly preoccupied with the examination of language and poetry. Another distinguishing trait of the turn is that Heidegger changed his analytical discourse to a poetic prose style attentive to the multiple meanings of words. His late prose became performative: it followed the paths of thinking, including its false twists and turns, and broke down the traditional distinction between poetry and philosophy. Some of the major poets who figure prominently in his late lectures are the Germans Friedrich Hölderlin (1770–1843), Stefan George (1868–1933), and Rainer Maria Rilke (1875–1926) and the Austrian Georg Trakl (1887–1914).

Our selection, "Language" (1950), is a work of Heidegger's later years. In it he propounds his celebrated view that language speaks man. Language brings man and his world into conscious existence; it is inaugural speaking in that it grants an abode or a dwelling for the being of mortals in the larger context of what Heidegger cryptically calls the "fourfold world" (comprising earth, sky, divinities, and mortals). In this account, language is neither mimetic nor expressive: it does not represent an external reality, nor does it express a preexisting feeling or thought. Language shapes consciousness and perception, calling things into being; it does not merely designate or label objects. In poetry, Heidegger argues, the essence of language is manifested with particular clarity, since poetry is less concerned with communication and expression than with imaginative creation.

In our selection, Heidegger presents a now famous explication of Georg Trakl's poem "A Winter Evening." As a poetic or imaginative act, Trakl's poem, he argues, founds and fashions a world. It bids things to appear *as* things; things as things are constituted in language and thus revealed and made near. But for Heidegger, as he notes while discussing the last stanza of the poem, a "dif-ference" between thing and world subsists. This dif-ference is a fundamental threshold where the gathering of things and world in stillness happens. Poetry allows for meditation on the dif-ference, and thus it distinguishes itself from the worn-out instrumental language of everyday speech. This phenomenological account of language as inaugural and performative prefigures later poststructuralist accounts of textuality and discourse developed by PAUL DE MAN, JACQUES DERRIDA, and other admirers of Heidegger.

Heidegger has often been criticized for his views, especially for his mysticism and his quietism, both of which suggest that he never abandoned his youthful religious sensibilities. His late poetic style, moreover, has been criticized as repetitive and obscure, a form of smoke and mirrors. His focus on poetry as pure speech ignores the sociological or "dialogical" dimensions of discourse depicted, most famously, by his contemporary MIKHAIL BAKHTIN. But the major criticism of Heidegger is that he involved himself with the Nazi Party and remained publicly silent about it for the remainder of his life, raising the issue of whether his vast corpus of writings reflects Nazi ideology or sensibility. Some critics separate his philosophy from his politics, while others see the two as fundamentally related. While it is unlikely that this debate will be resolved to everyone's satisfaction, all acknowledge that Heidegger has had a tremendous influence on philosophy, particularly in Europe, as exemplified powerfully in the existentialism of JEAN-PAUL SARTRE, the phenomenological hermeneutics of Hans Georg Gadamer, and the deconstructive philosophy of Jacques Derrida. In this context, Heidegger is widely believed to be the most important Continental philosopher of the twentieth century.

BIBLIOGRAPHY

The standard edition of Heidegger's collected works in German is the *Gesamtausgabe* (1976–), which is projected to reach approximately one hundred volumes. An introductory collection of texts in English is available in *Basic Writings*, translated by various hands and edited by David Farrell Krell (rev. and expanded, 1992). English versions of Heidegger's writings bearing directly on his understanding of poetry and language are available in *Existence and Being*, edited by Werner Brock and translated by Douglas Scott (1949); *Poetry, Language, Thought*, edited and translated by Albert Hofstadter (1971); and *On the Way to Language*, translated by Peter D. Hertz and Joan Stambaugh (1971). Philosophical texts translated into English (with the date of German publication given first) include *What Is Philosophy?* (1956; 1956); *An Introduction to Metaphysics* (1953; 1959); *Being and Time*, translated first by John Macquarrie and Edward Robinson (1927; 1962), and then by Joan Stambaugh (1996); *What Is a Thing?* (1962; 1967); *Identity and Difference* (1957; 1969); *On Time and Being* (1969; 1972); *The Question Concerning Technology and Other Essays*, translated by William Lovitt (1977); *Nietzsche* (2 vols., 1961; 4 vols., 1979–87); *History of the Concept of Time: Prolegomena* (1979; 1985); *Hegel's Phenomenology of Spirit* (1980; 1988); *Kant and the Problem of Metaphysics*, translated by Richard Taft (1929; 1990); *The Concept of Time* (1992; 1992); *Basic Concepts* (1981; 1993); and *The Fundamental Concepts of Metaphysics: World, Finitude, Solitude* (1983; 1995). A translation of Heidegger's interview on his Nazi past, "Only a God Can Save Us Now," can be found in the journal *Philosophy Today* 20 (winter 1976). For noted biographies, see Hugo Ott's *Martin Heidegger: A Political Life* (1993) and Rüdiger Safranski's *Martin Heidegger: Between Good and Evil* (1994, trans. 1998).

For general introductions, see George Steiner's *Martin Heidegger* (2d ed., 1991); *The Cambridge Companion to Heidegger*, edited by Charles Guignon (1993); and Michael Inwood's *Heidegger* (1997). Among the important studies of Heidegger's views on language and poetry are *On Heidegger and Language*, edited by Joseph J. Kockelmans (1972); David A. White, *Heidegger and the Language of Poetry* (1978); *Martin Heidegger and the Question of Literature: Toward a Postmodern Literary Hermeneutics*, edited by William V. Spanos (1979); Paul A. Bové, *Destructive Poetics: Heidegger and Modern American Poetry* (1980); David Halliburton, *Poetic Thinking: An Approach to Heidegger* (1981); Joseph Kockelmans, *Heidegger on Art and Art Works* (1985); Gerald L. Bruns, *Heidegger's Estrangements: Language, Truth, and Poetry in the Later Writings* (1989); Hans Georg Gadamer, *Heidegger's Ways* (1983; trans. 1994); and Marc Froment-Meurice, *That Is to Say: Heidegger's Poetics* (1996; trans. 1998). On Heidegger and the Nazi question, see Pierre Bourdieu, *The Political Ontology of Martin Heidegger* (1975; trans. 1991); Victor Farias, *Heidegger and Nazism* (1987; trans. 1990); Jacques Derrida, *Of Spirit: Heidegger and the Question* (1987; trans. 1990); Jean-François Lyotard, *Heidegger and "the Jews"* (1988; trans. 1990); *The Heidegger Controversy: A Critical Reader*, edited by Richard Wolin (1992); and Fred Dallmayr, *The Other Heidegger* (1993). For bibliographies, see Hans-Martin Sass, *Martin Heidegger: Bibliography and Glossary* (1982); Joan Nordquist, *Martin Heidegger: A Bibliography* (1990) and *Martin Heidegger (II): A Bibliography* (1996); and *The Cambridge Companion to Heidegger*, cited above.

Language[1]

Man speaks. We speak when we are awake and we speak in our dreams. We are always speaking, even when we do not utter a single word aloud, but merely listen or read, and even when we are not particularly listening or speaking but are attending to some work or taking a rest. We are continually speaking in one way or another. We speak because speaking is natural to us. It does not first arise out of some special volition. Man is said to have language by nature. It is held that man, in distinction from plant and animal, is the living being capable of speech. This statement does not mean only that, along with other faculties, man also possesses the faculty of speech. It means to say that only speech enables man to be the living being he is as man. It is as one who speaks that man is—man. These are Wilhelm von Humboldt's[2] words. Yet it remains to consider what it is to be called—man.

In any case, language belongs to the closest neighborhood of man's being. We encounter language everywhere. Hence it cannot surprise us that as soon as man looks thoughtfully about himself at what is, he quickly hits upon

1. Translated by Albert Hofstadter.

2. German philologist and diplomat (1767–1835).

language too, so as to define it by a standard reference to its overt aspects. Reflection tries to obtain an idea of what language is universally. The universal that holds for each thing is called its essence or nature. To represent universally what holds universally is, according to prevalent views, the basic feature of thought. To deal with language thoughtfully would thus mean to give an idea of the nature of language and to distinguish this idea properly from other ideas. This lecture,[3] too, seems to attempt something of that kind. However, the title of the lecture is not "On the Nature of Language." It is only "Language." "Only," we say, and yet we are clearly placing a far more presumptuous title at the head of our project than if we were to rest content with just making a few remarks about language. Still, to talk about language is presumably even worse than to write about silence. We do not wish to assault language in order to force it into the grip of ideas already fixed beforehand. We do not wish to reduce the nature of language to a concept, so that this concept may provide a generally useful view of language that will lay to rest all further notions about it.

To discuss language, to place it, means to bring to its place of being not so much language as ourselves: our own gathering into the appropriation.[4]

We would reflect on language itself, and on language only. Language itself is—language and nothing else besides. Language itself is language. The understanding that is schooled in logic, thinking of everything in terms of calculation and hence usually overbearing, calls this proposition an empty tautology. Merely to say the identical thing twice—language is language—how is that supposed to get us anywhere? But we do not want to get anywhere. We would like only, for once, to get to just where we are already.

This is why we ponder the question, "What about language itself?" This is why we ask, "In what way does language occur as language?" We answer: *Language speaks*. Is this, seriously, an answer? Presumably—that is, when it becomes clear what speaking is.

To reflect on language thus demands that we enter into the speaking of language in order to take up our stay with language, i.e., within *its* speaking, not within our own. Only in that way do we arrive at the region within which it may happen—or also fail to happen—that language will call to us from there and grant us its nature. We leave the speaking to language. We do not wish to ground language in something else that is not language itself, nor do we wish to explain other things by means of language.

On the tenth of August, 1784 Hamann wrote to Herder[5] (*Hamanns Schriften*, ed. Roth, VII, pp. 151 f.):

> If I were as eloquent as Demosthenes[6] I would yet have to do nothing more than repeat a single word three times: reason is language, *logos*.[7]

3. "Language" is a revised version of Heidegger's lecture notes.
4. A complicated and elusive term in Heidegger's thought: the "appropriation" (*Ereignis*) refers to the original appearance and nature of being in language. The perceptible traits or qualities proper to the various things of the world are manifested, made present, and brought into their own being solely through the inaugural granting of language. Human beings dwell in this appropriation, perceiving only what language founds; thus, they do not speak language but are spoken by it.
5. Johann Gottfried von Herder (1744–1803), German philosopher, theologian, and critic. Johann Georg Hamann (1730–1788), German philosopher and theologian. [From Johann Georg Hamann, *Schriften*, edited by F. Roth and G. A. Wiener, 8 Parts (Berlin: G. Reimer, 1821)—Translator's note.]
6. Athenian orator and statesman (384–322 B.C.E.), generally held to be the greatest Greek orator.
7. Word, speech; discourse, reason (Greek).

> I gnaw at this marrow-bone and will gnaw myself to death over it. There still remains a darkness, always, over this depth for me; I am still waiting for an apocalyptic angel with a key to this abyss.

For Hamann, this abyss consists in the fact that reason is language. Hamann returns to language in his attempt to say what reason is. His glance, aimed at reason, falls into the depths of an abyss. Does this abyss consist only in the fact that reason resides in language, or is language itself the abyss? We speak of an abyss where the ground falls away and a ground is lacking to us, where we seek the ground and set out to arrive at a ground, to get to the bottom of something. But we do not ask now what reason may be; here we reflect immediately on language and take as our main clue the curious statement, "Language is language." This statement does not lead us to something else in which language is grounded. Nor does it say anything about whether language itself may be a ground for something else. The sentence, "Language is language," leaves us to hover over an abyss as long as we endure what it says.

Language is—language, speech. Language speaks. If we let ourselves fall into the abyss denoted by this sentence, we do not go tumbling into emptiness. We fall upward, to a height. Its loftiness opens up a depth. The two span a realm in which we would like to become at home, so as to find a residence, a dwelling place for the life of man.

To reflect on language means—to reach the speaking of language in such a way that this speaking takes place as that which grants an abode for the being of mortals.

What does it mean to speak? The current view declares that speech is the activation of the organs for sounding and hearing. Speech is the audible expression and communication of human feelings. These feelings are accompanied by thoughts. In such a characterization of language three points are taken for granted:

First and foremost, speaking is expression. The idea of speech as an utterance is the most common. It already presupposes the idea of something internal that utters or externalizes itself. If we take language to be utterance, we give an external, surface notion of it at the very moment when we explain it by recourse to something internal.

Secondly, speech is regarded as an activity of man. Accordingly we have to say that man speaks, and that he always speaks some language. Hence we cannot say, "Language speaks." For this would be to say: "It is language that first brings man about, brings him into existence." Understood in this way, man would be bespoken by language.

Finally, human expression is always a presentation and representation of the real and the unreal.

It has long been known that the characteristics we have advanced do not suffice to circumscribe the nature of language. But when we understand the nature of language in terms of expression, we give it a more comprehensive definition by incorporating expression, as one among many activities into the total economy of those achievements by which man makes himself.

As against the identification of speech as a merely human performance, others stress that the word of language is of divine origin. According to the opening of the Prologue of the Gospel of St. John, in the beginning the Word was with God.[8] The attempt is made not only to free the question of origin from the fetters of a rational-logical explanation, but also to set aside the limits of a merely logical description of language. In opposition to the exclusive characterization of word-meanings as concepts, the figurative and symbolical character of language is pushed into the foreground. Biology and philosophical anthropology, sociology and psychopathology, theology and poetics are all then called upon to describe and explain linguistic phenomena more comprehensively.

In the meantime, all statements are referred in advance to the traditionally standard way in which language appears. The already fixed view of the whole nature of language is thus consolidated. This is how the idea of language in grammar and logic, philosophy of language and linguistics, has remained the same for two and a half millennia, although knowledge about language has progressively increased and changed. This fact could even be adduced as evidence for the unshakable correctness of the leading ideas about language. No one would dare to declare incorrect, let alone reject as useless, the identification of language as audible utterance of inner emotions, as human activity, as a representation by image and by concept. The view of language thus put forth is correct, for it conforms to what an investigation of linguistic phenomena can make out in them at any time. And all *questions* associated with the description and explanation of linguistic phenomena also move within the precincts of this correctness.

We still give too little consideration, however, to the singular role of these correct ideas about language. They hold sway, as if unshakable, over the whole field of the varied scientific perspectives on language. They have their roots in an ancient tradition. Yet they ignore completely the oldest natural cast of language. Thus, despite their antiquity and despite their comprehensibility, they never bring us to language as language.

Language speaks. What about its speaking? Where do we encounter such speaking? Most likely, to be sure, in what is spoken. For here speech has come to completion in what is spoken. The speaking does not cease in what is spoken. Speaking is kept safe in what is spoken. In what is spoken, speaking gathers the ways in which it persists as well as that which persists by it—its persistence, its presencing. But most often, and too often, we encounter what is spoken only as the residue of a speaking long past.

If we must, therefore, seek the speaking of language in what is spoken, we shall do well to find something that is spoken purely rather than to pick just any spoken material at random. What is spoken purely is that in which the completion of the speaking that is proper to what is spoken is, in its turn, an original. What is spoken purely is the poem. For the moment, we must let this statement stand as a bare assertion. We may do so, if we succeed in hearing in a poem something that is spoken purely. But what poem shall speak to us? Here we have only one choice, but one that is secured against mere caprice. By what? By what is already told us as the presencing element in language, if we follow in thought the speaking *of language*. Because of this bond between what we think and what we are told by language we choose, as something spoken purely, a poem which more readily than others

8. John 1.1: "In the beginning was the Word, and the Word was with God, and the Word was God."

can help us in our first steps to discover what is binding in that bond. We listen to what is spoken. The poem bears the title:

A Winter Evening

Window with falling snow is arrayed,
Long tolls the vesper bell,
The house is provided well,
The table is for many laid.

Wandering ones, more than a few,
Come to the door on darksome courses.
Golden blooms the tree of graces
Drawing up the earth's cool dew.

Wanderer quietly steps within;
Pain has turned the threshold to stone.
There lie, in limpid brightness shown,
Upon the table bread and wine.

The two last verses of the second stanza and the third stanza read in the first version (Letter to Karl Kraus,[9] December 13, 1913):

Love's tender power, full of graces,
Binds up his wounds anew.

O! man's naked hurt condign.
Wrestler with angels mutely held,
Craves, by holy pain compelled,
Silently God's bread and wine.

(Cf. the new Swiss edition of the poems of G. Trakl edited by Kurt Horwitz, 1946.)[1]

The poem was written by Georg Trakl. Who the author is remains unimportant here, as with every other masterful poem. The mastery consists precisely in this, that the poem can deny the poet's person and name.

The poem is made up of three stanzas. Their meter and rhyme pattern can be defined accurately according to the schemes of metrics and poetics. The poem's content is comprehensible. There is not a single word which, taken by itself, would be unfamiliar or unclear. To be sure, a few of the verses sound strange, like the third and fourth in the second stanza:

Golden blooms the tree of graces
Drawing up the earth's cool dew.

Similarly, the second verse of the third stanza is startling:

Pain has turned the threshold to stone.

9. Austrian poet, critic, and journalist (1874–1936).

1. Georg Trakl, *Die Dichtungen. Gesamtausgabe mit einem Anhang: Zeugnisse und Erinnerungen*, ed. Kurt Horwitz (Zurich: Arche Verlag, 1946). This poem, "Ein Winterabend," may also be found in *Die Dichtungen*, 11th ed. (Salzburg: Otto Müller, 1938), p. 124. The letter to Karl Kraus may be found in *Erinnerung an Georg Trakl: Zeugnisse und Briefe* (Salzburg: Otto Müller, 1959), pp. 172–73 [translator's note]. Trakl (1887–1914), Austrian expressionist poet.

But the verses here singled out also manifest a particular beauty of imagery. This beauty heightens the charm of the poem and strengthens its aesthetic perfection as an artistic structure.

The poem describes a winter evening. The first stanza describes what is happening outside: snowfall, and the ringing of the vesper bell. The things outside touch the things inside the human homestead. The snow falls on the window. The ringing of the bell enters into every house. Within, everything is well provided and the table set.

The second stanza raises a contrast. While many are at home within the house and at the table, not a few wander homeless on darksome paths. And yet such—possibly evil—roads sometimes lead to the door of the sheltering house. To be sure, this fact is not presented expressly. Instead, the poem names the tree of graces.

The third stanza bids the wanderer enter from the dark outdoors into the brightness within. The houses of the many and the tables of their daily meals have become house of God and altar.

The content of the poem might be dissected even more distinctly, its form outlined even more precisely, but in such operations we would still remain confined by the notion of language that has prevailed for thousands of years. According to this idea language is the expression, produced by men, of their feelings and the world view that guides them. Can the spell this idea has cast over language be broken? Why should it be broken? In its essence, language is neither expression nor an activity of man. Language speaks. We are now seeking the speaking of language in the poem. Accordingly, what we seek lies in the poetry of the spoken word.

The poem's title is "A Winter Evening." We expect from it the description of a winter evening as it actually is. But the poem does not picture a winter evening occurring somewhere, sometime. It neither merely describes a winter evening that is already there, nor does it attempt to produce the semblance, leave the impression, of a winter evening's presence where there is no such winter evening. Naturally not, it will be replied. Everyone knows that a poem is an invention. It is imaginative even where it seems to be descriptive. In his fictive act the poet pictures to himself something that could be present in its presence. The poem, as composed, images what is thus fashioned for our own act of imaging. In the poem's speaking the poetic imagination gives itself utterance. What is spoken in the poem is what the poet enunciates out of himself. What is thus spoken out, speaks by enunciating its content. The language of the poem is a manifold enunciating. Language proves incontestably to be expression. But this conclusion is in conflict with the proposition "Language speaks," assuming that speaking, in its essential nature, is not an expressing.

Even when we understand what is spoken in the poem in terms of poetic composition, it seems to us, as if under some compulsion, always and only to be an expressed utterance. Language is expression. Why do we not reconcile ourselves to this fact? Because the correctness and currency of this view of language are insufficient to serve as a basis for an account of the nature of language. How shall we gauge this inadequacy? Must we not be bound by a different standard before we can gauge anything in that manner? Of course. That standard reveals itself in the proposition, "Language speaks." Up to this point this guiding proposition has had merely the function of warding off the ingrained habit of disposing of speech by throwing it at once among the phenomena of expression instead of thinking it in its own terms. The poem cited has been chosen because, in a way not further explicable, it demonstrates a peculiar fitness to provide some fruitful hints for our attempt to discuss language.

Language *speaks*. This means at the same time and before all else: *language* speaks. Language? And not man? What our guiding proposition demands of us now—is it not even worse than before? Are we, in addition to everything else, also going to deny now that man is the being who speaks? Not at all. We deny this no more than we deny the possibility of classifying linguistic phenomena under the heading of "expression." But we ask, "How does man speak?" We ask, "What is it to speak?"

Window with falling snow is arrayed
Long tolls the vesper bell.

This speaking names the snow that soundlessly strikes the window late in the waning day, while the vesper bell rings. In such a snowfall, everything lasting lasts longer. Therefore the vesper bell, which daily rings for a strictly fixed time, tolls long. The speaking names the winter evening time. What is this naming? Does it merely deck out the imaginable familiar objects and events—snow, bell, window, falling, ringing—with words of a language? No. This naming does not hand out titles, it does not apply terms, but it calls into the word. The naming calls. Calling brings closer what it calls. However this bringing closer does not fetch what is called only in order to set it down in closest proximity to what is present, to find a place for it there. The call does indeed call. Thus it brings the presence of what was previously uncalled into a nearness. But the call, in calling it here, has already called out to what it calls. Where to? Into the distance in which what is called remains, still absent.

The calling here calls into a nearness. But even so the call does not wrest what it calls away from the remoteness, in which it is kept by the calling there. The calling calls into itself and therefore always here and there—here into presence, there into absence. Snowfall and tolling of vesper bell are spoken to us here and now in the poem. They are present in the call. Yet they in no way fall among the things present here and now in this lecture hall. Which presence is higher, that of these present things or the presence of what is called?

The house is provided well,
The table is for many laid.

The two verses speak like plain statements, as though they were noting something present. The emphatic "is" sounds that way. Nevertheless it speaks in the mode of calling. The verses bring the well-provided house and the ready table into that presence that is turned toward something absent.

What does the first stanza call? It calls things, bids them come. Where? Not to be present among things present; it does not bid the table named in the poem to be present here among the rows of seats where you are sitting. The place of arrival which is also called in the calling is a presence sheltered in absence. The naming call bids things to come into such an arrival. Bidding is inviting. It invites things in, so that they may bear upon men as things.

The snowfall brings men under the sky that is darkening into night. The tolling of the evening bell brings them, as mortals, before the divine. House and table join mortals to the earth. The things that were named, thus called, gather to themselves sky and earth, mortals and divinities. The four are united primally in being toward one another, a fourfold. The things let the fourfold of the four stay with them. This gathering, assembling, letting-stay is the thinging of things. The unitary fourfold of sky and earth, mortals and divinities, which is stayed in the thinging of things, we call—the world. In the naming, the things named are called into their thinging. Thinging, they unfold world, in which things abide and so are the abiding ones. By thinging, things carry out world. Our old language calls such carrying *bern, bären*—Old High German *beran*—to bear; hence the words *gebaren*, to carry, gestate, give birth, and *Gebärde*, bearing, gesture. Thinging, things are things. Thinging, they gesture—gestate—world.

The first stanza calls things into their thinging, bids them come. The bidding that calls things calls them here, invites them, and at the same time calls out to the things, commending them to the world out of which they appear. Hence the first stanza names not only things. It simultaneously names world. It calls the "many" who belong as mortals to the world's fourfold. Things be-thing—i.e., condition—mortals. This now means: things, each in its time, literally visit mortals with a world. The first stanza speaks by bidding the things to come.

The second stanza speaks in a different way. To be sure, it too bids to come. But its calling begins as it calls and names mortals:

Wandering ones, more than a few . . .

Not all mortals are called, not the many of the first stanza, but only "more than a few"—those who wander on dark courses. These mortals are capable of dying as the wandering toward death. In death the supreme concealedness of Being crystallizes. Death has already overtaken every dying. Those "wayfarers" must first wander their way to house and table through the darkness of their courses; they must do so not only and not even primarily for themselves, but for the many, because the many think that if they only install themselves in houses and sit at tables, they are already bethinged, conditioned, by things and have arrived at dwelling.

The second stanza begins by calling more than a few of the mortals. Although mortals belong to the world's fourfold along with the divinities, with earth and sky, the first two verses of the second stanza do not expressly call the world. Rather, very much like the first stanza but in a different sequence, they at the same time name things—the door, the dark paths. It is the two remaining verses that expressly name the world. Suddenly they name something wholly different:

Golden blooms the tree of graces
Drawing up the earth's cool dew.

The tree roots soundly in the earth. Thus it is sound and flourishes into a blooming that opens itself to heaven's blessing. The tree's towering has been called. It spans both the ecstasy of flowering and the soberness of the nourishing sap. The earth's abated growth and the sky's open bounty belong together. The poem names the tree of graces. Its sound blossoming harbors the fruit that falls to us unearned—holy, saving, loving toward mortals. In the golden-blossoming tree there prevail earth and sky, divinities and mortals. Their unitary fourfold is the world. The word "world" is now no longer used in the metaphysical sense. It designates neither the universe of nature and history in its secular representation nor the theologically conceived creation (*mundus*), nor does it mean simply the whole of entities present (*kosmos*).[2]

The third and fourth lines of the second stanza call the tree of graces. They expressly bid the world to come. They call the world-fourfold here, and thus call world to the things.

The two lines start with the word "golden." So that we may hear more clearly this word and what it calls, let us recollect a poem of Pindar's:[3] *Isthmians* V. At the beginning of this ode the poet calls gold *periosion panton*, that which above all shines through everything, *panta*, shines through each thing present all around. The splendor of gold keeps and holds everything present in the unconcealedness of its appearing.

As the calling that names things calls here and there, so the saying that names the world calls into itself, calling here and there. It entrusts world to the things and simultaneously keeps the things in the splendor of world. The world grants to things their presence. Things bear world. World grants things.

The speaking of the first two stanzas speaks by bidding things to come to world, and world to things. The two modes of bidding are different but not separated. But neither are they merely coupled together. For world and things do not subsist alongside one another. They penetrate each other. Thus the two traverse a middle. In it, they are at one. Thus at one they are intimate. The middle of the two is intimacy—in Latin, *inter*. The corresponding German word is *unter*, the English *inter-*. The intimacy of world and thing is not a fusion. Intimacy obtains only where the intimate—world and thing—divides itself cleanly and remains separated. In the midst of the two, in the between of world and thing, in their *inter*, division prevails: a *dif-ference*.

The intimacy of world and thing is present in the separation of the between; it is present in the dif-ference. The word dif-ference is now removed from its usual and customary usage. What it now names is not a generic concept for various kinds of differences. It exists only as this single difference. It is unique. Of itself, it holds apart the middle in and through which world and things are at one with each other. The intimacy of the dif-ference is the unifying element of the *diaphora*, the carrying out that carries through. The dif-ference carries out world in its worlding, carries out things in their thinging. Thus carrying them out, it carries them toward one another. The dif-ference does not mediate after the fact by connecting world and things through a middle added on to them. Being the middle, it first determines world and things in their presence, i.e., in their being toward one another, whose unity it carries out.

The word consequently no longer means a distinction established between objects only by our representations. Nor is it merely a relation obtaining

2. Both *mundus* (Latin) and *kosmos* (Greek) mean "world," in the different senses that Heidegger gives.

3. Greek lyric poet (ca. 518–438 B.C.E.), known for his elaborate victory odes. In fact, the word *panton* is not used at the beginning of the poem cited.

between world and thing, so that a representation coming upon it can establish it. The dif-ference is not abstracted from world and thing as their relationship after the fact. The dif-ference for world and thing *disclosingly appropriates* things into bearing a world; it *disclosingly appropriates* world into the granting of things.

The dif-ference is neither distinction nor relation. The dif-ference is, at most, dimension for world and thing. But in this case "dimension" also no longer means a precinct already present independently in which this or that comes to settle. The dif-ference is *the* dimension, insofar as it measures out, apportions, world and thing, each to its own. Its allotment of them first opens up the separateness and towardness of world and thing. Such an opening up is the way in which the dif-ference here spans the two. The dif-ference, as the middle for world and things, metes out the measure of their presence. In the bidding that calls thing and world, what is really called is: the dif-ference.

The first stanza of the poem bids the things to come which, thinging, bear world. The second stanza bids that world to come which, worlding, grants things. The third stanza bids the middle for world and things to come: the carrying out of the intimacy. On this account the third stanza begins with an emphatic calling:

Wanderer quietly steps within.

Where to? The verse does not say. Instead, it calls the entering wanderer into the stillness. This stillness ministers over the doorway. Suddenly and strangely the call sounds:

Pain has turned the threshold to stone.

This verse speaks all by itself in what is spoken in the whole poem. It names pain. What pain? The verse says merely "pain." Whence and in what way is pain called?

Pain has turned the threshold to stone.

"Turned . . . to stone"—these are the only words in the poem that speak in the past tense. Even so, they do not name something gone by, something no longer present. They name something that persists and that has already persisted. It is only in turning to stone that the threshold presences at all.

The threshold is the ground-beam that bears the doorway as a whole. It sustains the middle in which the two, the outside and the inside, penetrate each other. The threshold bears the between. What goes out and goes in, in the between, is joined in the between's dependability. The dependability of the middle must never yield either way. The settling of the between needs something that can endure, and is in this sense hard. The threshold, as the settlement of the between, is hard because pain has petrified it. But the pain that became appropriated to stone did not harden into the threshold in order to congeal there. The pain presences unflagging in the threshold, as pain.

But what is pain? Pain rends. It is the rift. But it does not tear apart into dispersive fragments. Pain indeed tears asunder, it separates, yet so that at the same time it draws everything to itself, gathers it to itself. Its rending, as a separating that gathers, is at the same time that drawing which, like the pen-drawing of a plan or sketch, draws and joins together what is held apart in separation. Pain is the joining agent in the rending that divides and gathers. Pain is the joining of the rift. The joining is the threshold. It settles the between, the middle of the two that are separated in it. Pain joins the rift of the dif-ference. Pain is the dif-ference itself.

Pain has turned the threshold to stone.

The verse calls the dif-ference, but it neither thinks it specifically nor does it call its nature by this name. The verse calls the separation of the between, the gathering middle, in whose intimacy the bearing of things and the granting of world pervade one another.

Then would the intimacy of the dif-ference for world and thing be pain? Certainly. But we should not imagine pain anthropologically as a sensation that makes us feel afflicted. We should not think of the intimacy psychologically as the sort in which sentimentality makes a nest for itself.

Pain has turned the threshold to stone.

Pain has already fitted the threshold into its bearing. The dif-ference presences already as the collected presence, from which the carrying out of world and thing appropriatingly takes place. How so?

There lie, in limpid brightness shown,
Upon the table bread and wine.

Where does the pure brightness shine? On the threshold, in the settling of the pain. The rift of the dif-ference makes the limpid brightness shine. Its luminous joining decides the brightening of the world into its own. The rift of the dif-ference expropriates the world into its worlding, which grants things. By the brightening of the world in their golden gleam, bread and wine at the same time attain to their own gleaming. The nobly named things are lustrous in the simplicity of their thinging. Bread and wine are the fruits of heaven and earth, gifts from the divinities to mortals. Bread and wine gather these four to themselves from the simple unity of their fourfoldness. The things that are called bread and wine are simple things because their bearing of world is fulfilled, without intermediary, by the favor of the world. Such things have their sufficiency in letting the world's fourfold stay with them. The pure limpid brightness of world and the simple gleaming of things go through their between, the dif-ference.

The third stanza calls world and things into the middle of their intimacy. The seam that binds their being toward one another is pain.

Only the third stanza gathers the bidding of things and the bidding of world. For the third stanza calls primally out of the simplicity of the intimate bidding which calls the dif-ference by leaving it unspoken. The primal calling, which bids the intimacy of world and thing to come, is the authentic bidding. This bidding is the nature of speaking. Speaking occurs in what is spoken in the poem. It is the speaking of language. Language speaks. It speaks by bidding the bidden, thing-world and world-thing, to come to the between of the dif-ference. What is so bidden is commanded to arrive from out of the dif-ference into the dif-ference. Here we are thinking of the old sense of command, which we recognize still in the phrase, "Commit thy way unto the Lord."[4] The bidding of language commits the bidden thus to the

4. Psalm 37.5.

bidding of the dif-ference. The dif-ference lets the thinging of the thing rest in the worlding of the world. The dif-ference expropriates the thing into the repose of the fourfold. Such expropriation does not diminish the thing. Only so is the thing exalted into its own, so that it stays world. To keep in repose is to still. The dif-ference stills the thing, as thing, into the world.

Such stilling, however, takes place only in such a way that at the same time the world's fourfold fulfills the bearing of the thing, in that the stilling grants to the thing the sufficiency of staying world. The dif-ference stills in a twofold manner. It stills by letting things rest in the world's favor. It stills by letting the world suffice itself in the thing. In the double stilling of the dif-ference there takes place: stillness.

What is stillness? It is in no way merely the soundless. In soundlessness there persists merely a lack of the motion of entoning, sounding. But the motionless is neither limited to sounding by being its suspension, nor is it itself already something genuinely tranquil. The motionless always remains, as it were, merely the other side of that which rests. The motionless itself still rests on rest. But rest has its being in the fact that it stills. As the stilling of stillness, rest, conceived strictly, is always more in motion than all motion and always more restlessly active than any agitation.

The dif-ference stills particularly in two ways: it stills the things in thinging and the world in worlding. Thus stilled, thing and world never escape from the dif-ference. Rather, they rescue it in the stilling, where the dif-ference is itself the stillness.

In stilling things and world into their own, the dif-ference calls world and thing into the middle of their intimacy. The dif-ference is the bidder. The dif-ference gathers the two out of itself as it calls them into the rift that is the dif-ference itself. This gathering calling is the pealing. In it there occurs something different from a mere excitation and spreading of sound.

When the dif-ference gathers world and things into the simple onefold of the pain of intimacy, it bids the two to come into their very nature. The dif-ference is the command out of which every bidding itself is first called, so that each may follow the command. The command of the dif-ference has ever already gathered all bidding within itself. The calling, gathered together with itself, which gathers to itself in the calling, is the pealing as the peal.

The calling of the dif-ference is the double stilling. The gathered bidding, the command, in the form of which the dif-ference calls world and things, is the peal of stillness. Language speaks in that the command of the dif-ference calls world and things into the simple onefold of their intimacy.

Language speaks as the peal of stillness. Stillness stills by the carrying out, the bearing and enduring, of world and things in their presence. The carrying out of world and thing in the manner of stilling is the appropriative taking place of the dif-ference. Language, the peal of stillness, is, inasmuch as the dif-ference takes place. Language goes on as the taking place or occurring of the dif-ference for world and things.

The peal of stillness is not anything human. But on the contrary, the human is indeed in its nature given to speech—it is linguistic. The word "linguistic" as it is here used means: having taken place out of the speaking of language. What has thus taken place, human being, has been brought into its own by language, so that it remains given over or appropriated to the nature of language, the peal of stillness. Such an appropriating takes place in that the very *nature*, the *presencing*, of language *needs and uses* the speaking of mortals in order to sound as the peal of stillness for the hearing of mortals. Only as men belong within the peal of stillness are mortals able to speak in *their own* way in sounds.

Mortal speech is a calling that names, a bidding which, out of the simple onefold of the difference, bids thing and world to come. What is purely bidden in mortal speech is what is spoken in the poem. Poetry proper is never merely a higher mode (*melos*)[5] of everyday language. It is rather the reverse: everyday language is a forgotten and therefore used-up poem, from which there hardly resounds a call any longer.

The opposite of what is purely spoken, the opposite of the poem, is not prose. Pure prose is never "prosaic." It is as poetic and hence as rare as poetry.

If attention is fastened exclusively on human speech, if human speech is taken simply to be the voicing of the inner man, if speech so conceived is regarded as language itself, then the nature of language can never appear as anything but an expression and an activity of man. But human speech, as the speech of mortals, is not self-subsistent. The speech of mortals rests in its relation to the speaking of language.

At the proper time it becomes unavoidable to think of how mortal speech and its utterance take place in the speaking of language as the peal of the stillness of the dif-ference. Any uttering, whether in speech or writing, breaks the stillness. On what does the peal of stillness break? How does the broken stillness come to sound in words? How does the broken stillness shape the mortal speech that sounds in verses and sentences?

Assuming that thinking will succeed one day in answering these questions, it must be careful not to regard utterance, let alone expression, as the decisive element of human speech.

The structure of human speech can only be the manner (*melos*) in which the speaking of language, the peal of the stillness of the dif-ference, appropriates mortals by the command of the dif-ference.

The way in which mortals, called out of the dif-ference into the dif-ference, speak on their own part, is: by responding. Mortal speech must first of all have listened to the command, in the form of which the stillness of the dif-ference calls world and things into the rift of its onefold simplicity. Every word of mortal speech speaks out of such a listening, and as such a listening.

Mortals speak insofar as they listen. They heed the bidding call of the stillness of the dif-ference even when they do not know that call. Their listening draws from the command of the dif-ference what it brings out as sounding word. This speaking that listens and accepts is responding.

Nevertheless by receiving what it says from the command of the dif-ference, mortal speech has already, in its own way, followed the call. Response, as receptive listening, is at the same time a recognition that makes due acknowledgment. Mortals speak by responding to language in a twofold way, receiving and replying. The mortal word speaks by cor-responding in a multiple sense.

Every authentic hearing holds back with its own saying. For hearing keeps to itself in the listening by which it remains appropriated to the peal of

5. A song, tune, or melody considered apart from rhythm (Greek).

stillness. All responding is attuned to this restraint that reserves itself. For this reason such reserve must be concerned to be ready, in the mode of listening, for the command of the dif-ference. But the reserve must take care not just to hear the peal of stillness afterward, but to hear it even beforehand, and thus as it were to anticipate its command.

This anticipating while holding back determines the manner in which mortals respond to the dif-ference. In this way mortals live in the speaking of language.

Language speaks. Its speaking bids the dif-ference to come which expropriates world and things into the simple onefold of their intimacy.

Language speaks.

Man speaks in that he responds to language. This responding is a hearing. It hears because it listens to the command of stillness.

It is not a matter here of stating a new view of language. What is important is learning to live in the speaking of language. To do so, we need to examine constantly whether and to what extent we are capable of what genuinely belongs to responding: anticipation in reserve. For:

> Man speaks only as he responds to language.
> Language speaks.
> Its speaking speaks for us in what has been spoken:

A Winter Evening

Window with falling snow is arrayed.
Long tolls the vesper bell,
The house is provided well,
The table is for many laid.

Wandering ones, more than a few,
Come to the door on darksome courses.
Golden blooms the tree of graces
Drawing up the earth's cool dew.

Wanderer quietly steps within;
Pain has turned the threshold to stone.
There lie, in limpid brightness shown,
Upon the table bread and wine.

1950

ANTONIO GRAMSCI
1891–1937

A Marxist martyr, determined to balance "pessimism of the intellect" with "optimism of the will," Antonio Gramsci is central to cultural studies and to all attempts to locate the roles that literature and culture play in the establishment, maintenance, and contestation of political power. Caught between the Russian Revolution, which he hoped to see reenacted in Italy, and the rise to power instead of the Fascist Party led by Benito Mussolini, Gramsci's failed political efforts motivated his revisionist Marxism, which emphasized the way cultural activities interact with both the economy and the state to forge the "manufactured consent" he calls "hegemony."

Gramsci was born on the impoverished and marginalized island of Sardinia into the family of a minor government official. His schooling was interrupted at age twelve, when he was forced to begin working sixty-hour weeks to help support his family after his father's imprisonment following what may have been a politically motivated conviction for fraud. An early childhood bout with tuberculosis left Gramsci deformed (he described himself as a hunchback) and stunted (four feet, ten inches tall). Having won a modest scholarship, he left Sardinia in 1911 to attend the University of Turin. The site of Fiat's factories, Turin was a major industrial city of Italy and home to a strong socialist movement among the factory workers. By 1914 Gramsci was a committed socialist, and in December 1916 he became an editor of the official Socialist Party newspaper. For the next six years, he worked as a political journalist and editor for various leftist publications.

An enthusiastic champion of the Russian Revolution, Gramsci had reason to believe that Italy's socialist revolution would not be far behind. In response to a company lockout, Fiat workers occupied the factories and produced cars on their own in September 1920, while the Socialist Party's various trade unions had over two million members that same year. But membership quickly declined as Mussolini's Fascist movement grew. Fascism's nationalist trumpeting of the glories of empire and of Italy's Roman past swept away concerns about its use of a militaristic state to keep workers and other potential dissidents under strict control. As popular support for Fascism mounted, leftist groups fought among themselves over how to respond. In 1921 Gramsci was one of the leading figures in the formation of the Communist Party of Italy.

Like other European Communist parties, the Italian one looked to Moscow for financial and intellectual sustenance. While Gramsci spent the bulk of 1922 and 1923 in Russia, the newly installed Fascist government in Italy issued a warrant for his arrest. Elected to Parliament on the Communist ticket in 1924, Gramsci returned to take his seat, protected from prosecution by parliamentary immunity. Mussolini announced a one-party state the following year, and Gramsci was placed under police surveillance. The leaders of the Communist Party, including Gramsci, were arrested in November 1926 and were tried together in June 1928. Gramsci was sentenced to twenty years in prison. Released from prison because of ill health in April 1937, he died less than two weeks after gaining his freedom.

For four years (1929–33) in prison, before his health collapsed, Gramsci was allowed to write. The result was the four volumes of the *Quaderni del carcere* (*The Prison Notebooks*), on which most of Gramsci's reputation as a social and cultural theorist is based and from which "The Formation of the Intellectuals" is taken.

Gramsci is one of the major figures of Western Marxism, a term that covers the work of twentieth-century German, French, British, and Italian leftist intellectuals. One abiding concern of these theorists is why the working-class revolution predicted by KARL MARX did not occur in Western Europe. The orthodox reading of Marx, promulgated and enforced by the Russian Bolsheviks, claimed that both political action and intellectual beliefs derive from economic interest. Since capitalism is against the economic interest of the workers, and since the workers are much more numerous than their employers, a proletariat revolution should be both inevitable and successful. But Western Marxists recognized that many workers were indifferent or even hostile to workers' movements and socialism, and that many workers supported fascist parties, even when they seemed obvious enemies of workers' interests. Significantly, Western Marxists proposed that economic interests are only part of the story when one considers the beliefs, values, commitments, and aspirations that motivate action; cultural factors are also crucial. It is this attention to how culture influences attitudes and actions that has made Western Marxism important for literary and cultural studies.

Gramsci's immediate concern was the Left's failure to win the hearts and minds of the Italian people, who supported the Fascists instead. Vladimir Lenin had already theorized that the workers' revolution could not happen spontaneously; revolution could succeed only if a dedicated cadre of revolutionaries stirred the workers to action and organized those actions once they occurred. This vanguard is the "party" for Lenin; its necessity justified the leadership role taken by the Bolsheviks in a supposedly egalitarian revolution. Subsequent writers have seen Lenin's justification of "the dictatorship of the party" as the first step toward the betrayal of Marxism that led to the tyranny in Soviet Russia between 1919 and 1989.

Gramsci's meditations on intellectuals subtly contest Lenin's writings on the role of the party. He wants to consider how the intellectual can be effective, especially in moving people to action. (Similar worries still bedevil literary intellectuals who espouse political causes.) Gramsci identifies two types of intellectuals. Traditional intellectuals are the administrators and apologists for existing social and cultural institutions, such as schools, various religious denominations, corporations, the military, the press, political bureaucracies, and the judicial system. Writers, artists, and philosophers are traditional intellectuals insofar as they work within formal institutions. In contrast, organic intellectuals rise out of membership in social groups (or classes) that have an antagonistic relationship to established institutions and official power. They "articulate" those groups' needs and aspirations, which have frequently gone unexpressed. The organic intellectual does not simply parrot preexisting group beliefs or demands but brings to the level of public speech what has not been officially recognized. While a given group does have certain tendencies, the process of articulation itself will shape it, giving it new identities and commitments—new ways of understanding itself and its desires.

For Gramsci, the traditional Marxist notion of "class" is too inert if it leads us to believe that workers, by virtue of their social position, always belong to the same class and possess the same attitudes and interests. The phrase "historic bloc"—Gramsci's own coinage—expresses his sense that social groups are dynamically created in specific historical moments, or so-called conjunctures. Any bloc's ability to intervene effectively in social arrangements depends on the relative strength of other "blocs" in a social field marked by conflict and continual jockeying for advantage. Intellectuals play a key role in the ongoing formation and re-formation of historical blocs.

The emphasis on intellectuals, articulation, and the formation of a historic bloc culminates in the concept of "hegemony," which substantially revises standard Marxist theories of "ideology." There are two notions of ideology found in Marx's *German Ideology* (written 1845–46; see above): the first holds that a person's beliefs and values are a reflection of that person's economic interests (though often not recognized as such); the second maintains that the leading ideas of the ruling class will be the ruling ideas of the age. In both cases, ideology mirrors economic interest, though in complex ways. Hegemony, like the historic bloc, aims to make this static Marxist concept dynamic. Gramsci argues elsewhere that a stable state never rules by force alone but relies on a combination of coercion and consent. Dominance is secure only if a majority voluntarily complies with the law. Any group that aspires to rule must work to gain the people's consent, and this work must be done before any directly revolutionary effort to seize and hold on to "material force." The effort to win consent—an effort that is ongoing and never entirely successful (force will be needed against some recalcitrant citizens)—is the attempt to gain hegemony, the dominant position in a given society. Hegemony is "manufactured consent," created through the articulation of intellectuals in a public sphere in which contending articulations are also voiced.

Gramsci's dynamic model has been especially crucial for later British Marxists and for the version of cultural studies that comes from Britain. Leading figures in cultural studies such as STUART HALL and DICK HEBDIGE use the concept of hegemony to move away from the class-based politics of the Labour Party; they embrace instead a cultural politics that emphasizes the need of intellectuals to contest power in multiple ways and to engage issues of race, gender, and identity. The most frequent criticisms of Gramsci also resurface in evaluations of British cultural studies. Orthodox Marxists worry that concentrating on cultural influences on behavior will cause material and economic factors to slide from view. For those outside the Marxist tradition, the focus on intellectuals seems potentially antidemocratic, while the stress on gaining power within a conflicted social field often moves issues of ethics and justice to the margins. Despite such criticisms, Gramsci's focus on the cultural work that intellectuals do, joined with his revision of key Marxist concepts, ensures his continuing influence within cultural studies.

BIBLIOGRAPHY

Selections from the Prison Notebooks, edited by Quintin Hoare and Geoffrey Nowell Smith (1971), is the most accessible English text. Columbia University Press is issuing a new translation of the complete *Prison Notebooks*, by Joseph Buttigieg and Antonio Callari (2 vols to date, 1992–). *Letters from Prison*, edited by Frank Rosengarten (2 vols., 1994), is an informative supplement to the *Prison Notebooks*. Parts of Gramsci's work before the prison years have been translated, including *Selections from Political Writings*, edited by Quintin Hoare (2 vols., 1977–78); *Selections from Cultural Writings*, edited by David Forgacs and Geoffrey Nowell Smith (1991); and *Pre-Prison Writings*, edited by Richard Bellamy (1994). There are two biographies: Arnold Davidson's *Antonio Gramsci: Toward an Intellectual Biography* (1977) focuses on Gramsci's intellectual development, while Giuseppe Fiori's *Antonio Gramsci: Life of a Revolutionary* (1990) uses new sources to offer the most comprehensive account of Gramsci's life.

Of the various introductions to Gramsci's thought, James Joll's *Antonio Gramsci* (1977) is best for understanding him within the Marxist tradition; Renate Holub's *Antonio Gramsci: Beyond Marxism and Postmodernism* (1992) connects his work to contemporary theoretical debates; Paul Ransome's *Antonio Gramsci: A New Introduction* (1992) is especially good on his impact on British leftist intellectuals. Walter Adamson's *Hegemony and Revolution* (1980) is an extended study of Gramsci's political and cultural theory, while Robert Bocock's *Hegemony* (1986) provides an introductory overview of the title concept. Perry Anderson's *Considerations on Western Marxism* (1976), a key place to begin looking into Western Marxism, discusses Gramsci at some length. Ernesto Laclau and Chantal Mouffe's *Hegemony and Socialist Strategy* (1985) joins Gramsci with poststructuralist thought to provide a fundamental rethinking of Marxist theory. The selections by Stuart Hall and Dick Hebdige in this anthology record the influence of Gramsci on cultural studies; David Harris's *From Class Struggle to the Politics of Pleasure: The Effects of Gramscianism on Cultural Studies* (1993) and *Stuart Hall: Critical Dialogues in Cultural Studies*, edited by David Morley and Kuan-Hsing Chen (1996), explore this connection further. Joan Nordquist's *Antonio Gramsci: A Bibliography* (1987) offers an excellent bibliography both of English-language commentary on Gramsci and of Gramsci's own work in Italian and in English translation.

The Formation of the Intellectuals[1]

Are intellectuals an autonomous and independent social group, or does every social group have its own particular specialised category of intellectuals? The problem is a complex one, because of the variety of forms assumed to date by the real historical process of formation of the different categories of intellectuals.

The most important of these forms are two:

1. Every social group, coming into existence on the original terrain of an essential function in the world of economic production, creates together with itself, organically, one or more strata of intellectuals which give it homogeneity and an awareness of its own function not only in the economic but also in the social and political fields. The capitalist entrepreneur creates alongside himself the industrial technician, the specialist in political economy, the organisers of a new culture, of a new legal system, etc. It should be noted that the entrepreneur himself represents a higher level of social elaboration, already characterised by a certain directive [*dirigente*] and technical (i.e. intellectual) capacity: he must have a certain technical capacity, not only in the limited sphere of his activity and initiative but in other spheres as well, at least in those which are closest to economic production. He must be an organiser of masses of men; he must be an organiser of the "confidence" of investors in his business, of the customers for his product, etc.

If not all entrepreneurs, at least an *élite* amongst them must have the capacity to be an organiser of society in general, including all its complex organism of services, right up to the state organism, because of the need to create the conditions most favourable to the expansion of their own class; or at the least they must possess the capacity to choose the deputies (specialised employees) to whom to entrust this activity of organising the general system of relationships external to the business itself. It can be observed that the "organic" intellectuals which every new class creates alongside itself and elaborates in the course of its development, are for the most part "specialisations" of partial aspects of the primitive activity of the new social type which the new class has brought into prominence.[2]

Even feudal lords were possessors of a particular technical capacity, military capacity, and it is precisely from the moment at which the aristocracy loses its monopoly of technico-military capacity that the crisis of feudalism begins. But the formation of intellectuals in the feudal world and in the preceding classical world is a question to be examined separately: this formation and elaboration follows ways and means which must be studied concretely. Thus it is to be noted that the mass of the peasantry, although it performs an essential function in the world of production, does not elaborate its own "organic" intellectuals, nor does it "assimilate" any stratum of "tra-

1. Translated by Quintin Hoare and Geoffrey Nowell Smith, who occasionally retain the original Italian in brackets.

2. [Gaetano] Mosca's *Elementi di Scienza Politica* [*Elements of Political Science*] (new expanded edition, 1923) is worth looking at in this connection. Mosca's so-called "political class" is nothing other than the intellectual category of the dominant social group. Mosca's concept of "political class" can be connected with Pareto's concept of the *élite*, which is another attempt to interpret the historical phenomena of the intellectuals and their function in the life of the state and of society [Gramsci's note]. Vilfredo Pareto, (1848–1923), Italian economist and sociologist.

ditional" intellectuals, although it is from the peasantry that other social groups draw many of their intellectuals and a high proportion of traditional intellectuals are of peasant origin.

2. However, every "essential" social group which emerges into history out of the preceding economic structure, and as an expression of a development of this structure, has found (at least in all of history up to the present) categories of intellectuals already in existence and which seemed indeed to represent an historical continuity uninterrupted even by the most complicated and radical changes in political and social forms.

The most typical of these categories of intellectuals is that of the ecclesiastics, who for a long time (for a whole phase of history, which is partly characterised by this very monopoly) held a monopoly of a number of important services: religious ideology, that is the philosophy and science of the age, together with schools, education, morality, justice, charity, good works, etc. The category of ecclesiastics can be considered the category of intellectuals organically bound to the landed aristocracy. It had equal status juridically with the aristocracy, with which it shared the exercise of feudal ownership of land, and the use of state privileges connected with property.[3] But the monopoly held by the ecclesiastics in the superstructural field[4] was not exercised without a struggle or without limitations, and hence there took place the birth, in various forms (to be gone into and studied concretely), of other categories, favoured and enabled to expand by the growing strength of the central power of the monarch, right up to absolutism. Thus we find the formation of the *noblesse de robe*,[5] with its own privileges, a stratum of administrators, etc., scholars and scientists, theorists, non-ecclesiastical philosophers, etc.

Since these various categories of traditional intellectuals experience through an "*esprit de corps*" their uninterrupted historical continuity and their special qualification, they thus put themselves forward as autonomous and independent of the dominant social group. This self-assessment is not without consequences in the ideological and political field, consequences of wide-ranging import. The whole of idealist philosophy[6] can easily be connected with this position assumed by the social complex of intellectuals and can be defined as the expression of that social utopia by which the intellectuals think of themselves as "independent", autonomous, endowed with a character of their own, etc.

One should note however that if the Pope and the leading hierarchy of the Church consider themselves more linked to Christ and to the apostles

3. For one category of these intellectuals, possibly the most important after the ecclesiastical for its prestige and the social function it performed in primitive societies, the category of *medical men* in the wide sense, that is all those who "struggle" or seem to struggle against death and disease, compare the *Storia della medicina* [1927, *A History of Medicine*] of Arturo Castiglioni. Note that there has been a connection between religion and medicine, and in certain areas there still is: hospitals in the hands of religious orders for certain organisational functions, apart from the fact that wherever the doctor appears, so does the priest (exorcism, various forms of assistance, etc.). Many great religious figures were and are conceived of as great "healers": the idea of miracles, up to the resurrection of the dead. Even in the case of kings the belief long survived that they could heal with the laying on of hands, etc. [Gramsci's note].

4. From this has come the general sense of "intellectual" or "specialist" of the word *chierico* (clerk, cleric) in many languages of romance origin or heavily influenced, through church Latin, by the romance languages, together with its correlative *laico* (lay, layman) in the sense of profane, non-specialist [Gramsci's note].

5. Nobility of the robe or gown (French); Gramsci refers to judges and lawyers.

6. A philosophy that posits the existence of ideas, motives, and actions separate from their material, economic origins and consequences.

than they are to senators Agnelli and Benni, the same does not hold for Gentile and Croce,[7] for example: Croce in particular feels himself closely linked to Aristotle and Plato, but he does not conceal, on the other hand, his links with senators Agnelli and Benni, and it is precisely here that one can discern the most significant character of Croce's philosophy.

What are the "maximum" limits of acceptance of the term "intellectual"? Can one find a unitary criterion to characterise equally all the diverse and disparate activities of intellectuals and to distinguish these at the same time and in an essential way from the activities of other social groupings? The most widespread error of method seems to me that of having looked for this criterion of distinction in the intrinsic nature of intellectual activities, rather than in the ensemble of the system of relations in which these activities (and therefore the intellectual groups who personify them) have their place within the general complex of social relations. Indeed the worker or proletarian, for example, is not specifically characterised by his manual or instrumental work, but by performing this work in specific conditions and in specific social relations (apart from the consideration that purely physical labour does not exist and that even Taylor's[8] phrase of "trained gorilla" is a metaphor to indicate a limit in a certain direction: in any physical work, even the most degraded and mechanical, there exists a minimum of technical qualification, that is, a minimum of creative intellectual activity). And we have already observed that the entrepreneur, by virtue of his very function, must have to some degree a certain number of qualifications of an intellectual nature although his part in society is determined not by these, but by the general social relations which specifically characterise the position of the entrepreneur within industry.

All men are intellectuals, one could therefore say: but not all men have in society the function of intellectuals.[9]

When one distinguishes between intellectuals and non-intellectuals, one is referring in reality only to the immediate social function of the professional category of the intellectuals, that is, one has in mind the direction in which their specific professional activity is weighted, whether towards intellectual elaboration or towards muscular-nervous effort. This means that, although one can speak of intellectuals, one cannot speak of non-intellectuals, because non-intellectuals do not exist. But even the relationship between efforts of intellectual-cerebral elaboration and muscular-nervous effort is not always the same, so that there are varying degrees of specific intellectual activity. There is no human activity from which every form of intellectual participation can be excluded: *homo faber* cannot be separated from *homo sapiens*.[1] Each man, finally, outside his professional activity, carries on some form of intellectual activity, that is, he is a "philosopher", an artist, a man of taste, he participates in a particular conception of the world, has a conscious

7. Benedetto Croce (1866–1952) the major liberal, idealist philosopher of Italy; a staunch opponent of fascism, his international fame protected him. Giovanni Agnelli (1866–1945), founder of Fiat and an Italian senator. Antonio Benni (1880–1945), industrialist turned politician, later a Fascist minister. Giovanni Gentile (1874–1944), Sicilian philosopher, early ally of Croce, and later Fascist minister of education. Gramsci's point is that Croce, despite his idealism and antifascism, understands the realities of political and economic power, taking care to maintain good relations with his friends in high places.

8. Frederick Taylor (1856–1915), American efficiency expert who greatly influenced the organization of factory work.

9. Thus, because it can happen that everyone at some time fries a couple of eggs or sews up a tear in a jacket, we do not necessarily say that everyone is a cook or a tailor [Gramsci's note].

1. Literally, "man the thinker" (Latin). *Homo faber*: man the maker (Latin).

line of moral conduct, and therefore contributes to sustain a conception of the world or to modify it, that is, to bring into being new modes of thought.

The problem of creating a new stratum of intellectuals consists therefore in the critical elaboration of the intellectual activity that exists in everyone at a certain degree of development, modifying its relationship with the muscular-nervous effort towards a new equilibrium, and ensuring that the muscular-nervous effort itself, in so far as it is an element of a general practical activity, which is perpetually innovating the physical and social world, becomes the foundation of a new and integral conception of the world. The traditional and vulgarised type of the intellectual is given by the man of letters, the philosopher, the artist. Therefore journalists, who claim to be men of letters, philosophers, artists, also regard themselves as the "true" intellectuals. In the modern world, technical education, closely bound to industrial labour even at the most primitive and unqualified level, must form the basis of the new type of intellectual.

On this basis the weekly *Ordine Nuovo*[2] worked to develop certain forms of new intellectualism and to determine its new concepts, and this was not the least of the reasons for its success, since such a conception corresponded to latent aspirations and conformed to the development of the real forms of life. The mode of being of the new intellectual can no longer consist in eloquence, which is an exterior and momentary mover of feelings and passions, but in active participation in practical life, as constructor, organiser, "permanent persuader" and not just a simple orator (but superior at the same time to the abstract mathematical spirit); from technique-as-work one proceeds to technique-as-science and to the humanistic conception of history, without which one remains "specialised" and does not become "directive" (specialised and political).

Thus there are historically formed specialised categories for the exercise of the intellectual function. They are formed in connection with all social groups, but especially in connection with the more important, and they undergo more extensive and complex elaboration in connection with the dominant social group. One of the most important characteristics of any group that is developing towards dominance is its struggle to assimilate and to conquer "ideologically" the traditional intellectuals, but this assimilation and conquest is made quicker and more efficacious the more the group in question succeeds in simultaneously elaborating its own organic intellectuals.

The enormous development of activity and organisation of education in the broad sense in the societies that emerged from the medieval world is an index of the importance assumed in the modern world by intellectual functions and categories. Parallel with the attempt to deepen and to broaden the "intellectuality" of each individual, there has also been an attempt to multiply and narrow the various specialisations. This can be seen from educational institutions at all levels, up to and including the organisms that exist to promote so-called "high culture" in all fields of science and technology.

School is the instrument through which intellectuals of various levels are elaborated. The complexity of the intellectual function in different states can be measured objectively by the number and gradation of specialised schools: the more extensive the "area" covered by education and the more numerous

2. *New Order*, a socialist magazine edited by Gramsci in 1919–20.

the "vertical" "levels" of schooling, the more complex is the cultural world, the civilisation, of a particular state. A point of comparison can be found in the sphere of industrial technology: the industrialisation of a country can be measured by how well equipped it is in the production of machines with which to produce machines, and in the manufacture of ever more accurate instruments for making both machines and further instruments for making machines, etc. The country which is best equipped in the construction of instruments for experimental scientific laboratories and in the construction of instruments with which to test the first instruments, can be regarded as the most complex in the technical-industrial field, with the highest level of civilisation, etc. The same applies to the preparation of intellectuals and to the schools dedicated to this preparation; schools and institutes of high culture can be assimilated to each other. In this field also, quantity cannot be separated from quality. To the most refined technical-cultural specialisation there cannot but correspond the maximum possible diffusion of primary education and the maximum care taken to expand the middle grades numerically as much as possible. Naturally this need to provide the widest base possible for the selection and elaboration of the top intellectual qualifications—i.e. to give a democratic structure to high culture and top-level technology—is not without its disadvantages: it creates the possibility of vast crises of unemployment for the middle intellectual strata, and in all modern societies this actually takes place.

It is worth noting that the elaboration of intellectual strata in concrete reality does not take place on the terrain of abstract democracy but in accordance with very concrete traditional historical processes. Strata have grown up which traditionally "produce" intellectuals and these strata coincide with those which have specialised in "saving", i.e. the petty and middle landed bourgeoisie and certain strata of the petty and middle urban bourgeoisie. The varying distribution of different types of school (classical and professional) over the "economic" territory and the varying aspirations of different categories within these strata determine, or give form to, the production of various branches of intellectual specialisation. Thus in Italy the rural bourgeoisie produces in particular state functionaries and professional people, whereas the urban bourgeoisie produces technicians for industry. Consequently it is largely northern Italy which produces technicians and the South which produces functionaries and professional men.

The relationship between the intellectuals and the world of production is not as direct as it is with the fundamental social groups but is, in varying degrees, "mediated" by the whole fabric of society and by the complex of superstructures, of which the intellectuals are, precisely, the "functionaries". It should be possible both to measure the "organic quality" [*organicità*] of the various intellectual strata and their degree of connection with a fundamental social group, and to establish a gradation of their functions and of the superstructures from the bottom to the top (from the structural base upwards). What we can do, for the moment, is to fix two major superstructural "levels": the one that can be called "civil society", that is the ensemble of organisms commonly called "private", and that of "political society" or "the State". These two levels correspond on the one hand to the function of "hegemony" which the dominant group exercises throughout society and on the other hand to that of "direct domination" or command exercised through the State and "juridical" government. The functions in question are precisely organisational and connective. The intellectuals are the dominant group's "deputies" exercising the subaltern functions of social hegemony and political government. These comprise:

1. The "spontaneous" consent given by the great masses of the population to the general direction imposed on social life by the dominant fundamental group; this consent is "historically" caused by the prestige (and consequent confidence) which the dominant group enjoys because of its position and function in the world of production.

2. The apparatus of state coercive power which "legally" enforces discipline on those groups who do not "consent" either actively or passively. This apparatus is, however, constituted for the whole of society in anticipation of moments of crisis of command and direction when spontaneous consent has failed.

This way of posing the problem has as a result a considerable extension of the concept of intellectual, but it is the only way which enables one to reach a concrete approximation of reality. It also clashes with preconceptions of caste. The function of organising social hegemony and state domination certainly gives rise to a particular division of labour and therefore to a whole hierarchy of qualifications in some of which there is no apparent attribution of directive or organisational functions. For example, in the apparatus of social and state direction there exist a whole series of jobs of a manual and instrumental character (non-executive work, agents rather than officials or functionaries). It is obvious that such a distinction has to be made just as it is obvious that other distinctions have to be made as well. Indeed, intellectual activity must also be distinguished in terms of its intrinsic characteristics, according to levels which in moments of extreme opposition represent a real qualitative difference—at the highest level would be the creators of the various sciences, philosophy, art, etc., at the lowest the most humble "administrators" and divulgators of pre-existing, traditional, accumulated intellectual wealth.[3]

In the modern world the category of intellectuals, understood in this sense, has undergone an unprecedented expansion. The democratic-bureaucratic system has given rise to a great mass of functions which are not all justified by the social necessities of production, though they are justified by the political necessities of the dominant fundamental group. Hence Loria's[4] conception of the unproductive "worker" (but unproductive in relation to whom and to what mode of production?), a conception which could in part be justified if one takes account of the fact that these masses exploit their position to take for themselves a large cut out of the national income. Mass formation has standardised individuals both psychologically and in terms of individual qualification and has produced the same phenomena as with other standardised masses: competition which makes necessary organisations for the defence of professions, unemployment, over-production in the schools, emigration, etc.

1929–33 1948–51

3. Here again military organisation offers a model of complex gradations between subaltern officers, senior officers and general staff, not to mention the NCO's, whose importance is greater than is generally admitted. It is worth observing that all these parts feel a solidarity and indeed it is the lower strata that display the most blatant *esprit de corps*, from which they derive a certain "conceit" which is apt to lay them open to jokes and witticisms [Gramsci's note].

4. Achille Loria (1857–1943), Italian economic theorist.

ZORA NEALE HURSTON
1891–1960

Zora Neale Hurston's *Their Eyes Were Watching God* (1937) is said to be the most frequently taught text in U.S. colleges and universities, but few readers have paid attention to the rich body of her work—including other novels, stories, and cultural criticism. Hurston identified herself as a "literary anthropologist," a phrase that reflects her training in anthropology at Columbia University, her deep and abiding interest in folklore, and her commitment to the creative power of the literary imagination.

Born near Tuskegee, Alabama, Hurston grew up in Eatonville, Florida, the first incorporated, self-governing black township in the United States, where her father, a Baptist minister, served three terms as mayor. Her childhood experiences played a central role in the development of the characters and themes of her literary work. As Hurston's novels and her autobiography *Dust Tracks on a Road* (1942) attest, she felt an intimate bond to the customs, beliefs, and forms of speech of the African American community. Hurston studied between 1918 and 1924 at Howard University in Washington, D.C. Encouraged by Alain Locke, one of her teachers and a distinguished African American intellectual, she first submitted a story to the journal *Opportunity*, where it was published in December 1924. Hurston also contributed the story "Spunk" to Locke's groundbreaking collection *The New Negro* (1925).

In 1925 Hurston traveled to New York City, where she soon became one of the leading lights of the Harlem Renaissance, known both for her plays and stories and for her oral performances of black folklore and folktales. Helped by white patrons, she was able to attend Barnard College, studying with the eminent anthropologist Franz Boas, a professor at Columbia; she graduated in 1928. Her research in the South and in the Caribbean formed the basis of her landmark collection of African American folklore, *Mules and Men* (1935), which was followed by a second compilation, *Tell My Horse* (1938).

While undertaking ethnographic study in Haiti, Hurston completed *Their Eyes Were Watching God*. She had published one novel already—*Jonah's Gourd Vine* (1934), which focuses on a Baptist minister—and other novels would follow, including *Moses, Man of the Mountain* (1939), her retelling of the Exodus story. But *Their Eyes Were Watching God* is her masterpiece, an evocative, often painful, but ultimately celebratory account of its black heroine's quest for emotional and sexual fulfillment and personal freedom.

Hurston's defense of the language she uses in *Their Eyes Were Watching God* had appeared three years earlier, "Characteristics of Negro Expression" (1934). In that essay, our first selection, she describes the rich, flexible resources of African American dialect and folk expression. Her subject is language in the broadest sense—including gestures and forms of music and dance—but she dwells particularly on African American speech, which had so often been mocked and ridiculed, misinterpreted and devalued. "Negro dialect" was suppressed by schools and attacked by contemporary critics of language and culture such as H. L. Mencken. Hurston praises and celebrates the linguistic prowess and cultural greatness of her people, even as she also points to (and calls attention to the flaws in) efforts by white artists to adapt distinctively African American styles and expressions in language and, especially, in music and dance.

Hurston's career peaked in the 1930s. Her later novels were less successful, and other writings were left unfinished. She had come under attack by some black writers, such as Richard Wright and Ralph Ellison, who blasted *Their Eyes Were Watching God* as a "minstrel novel" and her writing as "calculated burlesque"; moreover, the benefits she saw in a black-run community like Eatonville made her suspicious of demands for integration, a view that set her outside the African American intellectual mainstream in the 1950s. During the final decade of her life, she worked as a cleaning woman and at other menial jobs. She died in poverty, forgotten, with none of her books in print. In the early 1970s, the African American novelist Alice Walker wrote movingly of locating the approximate site of Hurston's unmarked grave; Walker's essays, particularly her comments on *Their Eyes Were Watching God*, were instrumental in reviving Hurston's reputation.

In her last novel, *Seraph on the Suwanee* (1948), Hurston focused on a white woman, a shift implying a view of artistic freedom that our second selection, "What White Publishers Won't Print" (1950), makes explicit. Though her emphasis is on the need for publishers, theater producers, editors, and audiences to accept a more honest and nuanced treatment of black and other minority characters, she argues here against any restrictions on subject matter. For Hurston, it is crucial that writers and readers strive to break through racial and ethnic stereotypes, even when readers find the new kinds of characters and themes unfamiliar and disorienting. She stresses, on the one hand, that the consciousness of black people is different (and not captured by the reductive, distorted versions in popular thought and in past and present literature). But on the other hand, she contends that all individuals have much in common: "Minorities," she explains, are "just like everybody else."

Though set in a specific political context, when cold war tensions seemed to make imperative a national unity that appeared to be unattainable without better understanding of racial and ethnic minorities, "What White Publishers Won't Print" is in large part a lively adaptation of an oft-repeated (and historically very important) argument. In the nineteenth century, Frederick Douglass and other African American abolitionists argued that black men and women, slave and free alike, must be portrayed and understood as authentic individuals; many twentieth-century black writers and critics, including Wright, Ellison, W. E. B. DU BOIS, LANGSTON HUGHES, and James Baldwin, similarly attacked stereotyping and argued for artistic freedom. Hurston's call for literary works about average and well-to-do African Americans is both a plea for realism and a criticism of the typical depiction of "Negro" characters as quaint or exceptional.

But Hurston's essay also bears witness to her ongoing literary, critical, and cultural disputes with her peers. In her judgment, because of their emphasis on politics they misleadingly represent black experience as primarily defined by white racism, from which there is no escape. Hurston stresses that the search for freedom is profoundly personal and cannot be captured by the category of race alone. As "What White Publishers Won't Print" reveals, Hurston insists that the independence to explore the inner lives of her characters, white as well as black, is essential both sociopolitically and artistically.

BIBLIOGRAPHY

Hurston's novels, stories, folklore, memoirs, and other writings are available from the Library of America in two volumes edited by Cheryl A. Wall, *Novels and Stories* and *Folklore, Memoirs, and Other Writings* (1995). See also *I Love Myself: A Zora Neale Hurston Reader*, edited by Alice Walker (1979).

Robert Hemenway's *Zora Neale Hurston* (1977) is an indispensable biography that has done much to spark interest in Hurston's work. Lillie P. Howard's *Zora Neale Hurston* (1980) is a concise survey of Hurston's life and writings. The best studies of Hurston are Karla F. C. Holloway, *The Character of the Word: The Texts of Zora Neale Hurston* (1987); Lynda Marion Hill, *Social Rituals and the Verbal Art of Zora Neale Hurston* (1996); and Susan Edwards Meisenhelder, *Hitting a Straight Lick with a Crooked Stick: Race and Gender in the Work of Zora Neale Hurston* (1999).

Cheryl A. Wall's *Women of the Harlem Renaissance* (1995) places Hurston within a wider cultural and literary context. On the relation of Hurston's work to contemporary literary theory and African American cultural and literary studies, see Barbara

Johnson, *A World of Difference* (1987), and Henry Louis Gates Jr., *The Signifying Monkey: A Theory of Afro-American Literary Criticism* (1988). A helpful collection of essays is *Zora Neale Hurston: Perspectives Past and Present*, edited by Henry Louis Gates Jr. and K. A. Appiah (1993). For bibliography, see Adele S. Newson, *Zora Neale Hurston: A Reference Guide* (1987), and Rose Parkman Davis, *Zora Neale Hurston: An Annotated Bibliography and Reference Guide* (1997).

Characteristics of Negro Expression

Drama

The Negro's universal mimicry is not so much a thing in itself as an evidence of something that permeates his entire self. And that thing is drama.

His very words are action words. His interpretation of the English language is in terms of pictures. One act described in terms of another. Hence the rich metaphor and simile.

The metaphor is of course very primitive. It is easier to illustrate than it is to explain because action came before speech. Let us make a parallel. Language is like money. In primitive communities actual goods, however bulky, are bartered for what one wants. This finally evolves into coin, the coin being not real wealth but a symbol of wealth. Still later even coin is abandoned for legal tender, and still later for checks in certain usages.

Every phase of Negro life is highly dramatized. No matter how joyful or how sad the case there is sufficient poise for drama. Everything is acted out. Unconsciously for the most part of course. There is an impromptu ceremony always ready for every hour of life. No little moment passes unadorned.

Now the people with highly developed languages have words for detached ideas. That is legal tender. "That-which-we-squat-on" has become "chair." "Groan-causer" has evolved into "spear," and so on. Some individuals even conceive of the equivalent of check words, like "ideation" and "pleonastic." Perhaps we might say that *Paradise Lost* and *Sartor Resartus*[1] are written in check words.

The primitive man exchanges descriptive words. His terms are all close-fitting. Frequently the Negro, even with detached words in his vocabulary—not evolved in him but transplanted on his tongue by contact—must add action to it to make it do. So we have "chop-axe," "sitting-chair," "cook-pot" and the like because the speaker has in his mind the picture of the object in use. Action. Everything illustrated. So we can say the white man thinks in a written language and the Negro thinks in hieroglyphics.

A bit of Negro drama familiar to all is the frequent meeting of two opponents who threaten to do atrocious murder one upon the other.

Who has not observed a robust young Negro chap posing upon a street corner, possessed of nothing but his clothing, his strength and his youth? Does he bear himself like a pauper? No, Louis XIV[2] could be no more insolent in his assurance. His eyes say plainly "Female, halt!" His posture exults "Ah, female, I am the eternal male, the giver of life. Behold in my hot flesh

1. A dense philosophical satire (1833) by the Scottish-born historian and essayist Thomas Carlyle. *Paradise Lost* (1667), epic poem by John Milton.

2. King of France (1638–1715); his reign (1673–1715) was a flowering of French art, literature, and extravagant style.

all the delights of this world. Salute me, I am strength." All this with a languid posture, there is no mistaking his meaning.

A Negro girl strolls past the corner lounger. Her whole body panging and posing. A slight shoulder movement that calls attention to her bust, that is all of a dare. A hippy undulation below the waist that is a sheaf of promises tied with conscious power. She is acting out "I'm a darned sweet woman and you know it."

These little plays by strolling players are acted out daily in a dozen streets in a thousand cities, and no one ever mistakes the meaning.

Will to Adorn

The will to adorn is the second most notable characteristic in Negro expression. Perhaps his idea of ornament does not attempt to meet conventional standards, but it satisfies the soul of its creator.

In this respect the American Negro has done wonders to the English language. It has often been stated by etymologists that the Negro has introduced no African words to the language. This is true, but it is equally true that he has made over a great part of the tongue to his liking and has had his revision accepted by the ruling class. No one listening to a Southern white man talk could deny this. Not only has he softened and toned down strongly consonanted words like "aren't" to "aint" and the like, he has made new force words out of old feeble elements. Examples of this are "ham-shanked," "battle-hammed," "double-teen," "bodaciously," "muffle-jawed."

But the Negro's greatest contribution to the language is: (1) the use of metaphor and simile; (2) the use of the double descriptive; (3) the use of verbal nouns.

1. Metaphor and Simile
One at a time, like lawyers going to heaven.
You sho is propaganda.
Sobbing hearted.
I'll beat you till: (*a*) rope like okra, (*b*) slack like lime, (*c*) smell like onions.
Fatal for naked.
Kyting[3] along.
That's a lynch.
That's a rope.
Cloakers—deceivers.
Regular as pig-tracks.
Mule blood—black molasses.
Syndicating—gossiping.
Flambeaux—cheap café (lighted by flambeaux).
To put yo'self on de ladder.

2. The Double Descriptive
High-tall.

3. Hurrying.

Little-tee-ninchy (tiny).
Low-down.
Top-superior.
Sham-polish.
Lady-people.
Kill-dead.
Hot-boiling.
Chop-axe.
Sitting-chairs.
De watch wall.
Speedy-hurry.
More great and more better.

3. Verbal Nouns
She features somebody I know.
Funeralize.
Sense me into it.
Puts the shamery on him.
'Taint everybody you kin confidence.
I wouldn't friend with her.
Jooking—playing piano or guitar as it is done in Jook-houses (houses of ill-fame).
Uglying away.
I wouldn't scorn my name all up on you.
Bookooing (beaucoup) around—showing off.

Nouns from Verbs
Won't stand a broke.
She won't take a listen.
He won't stand straightening.
That is such a complement.
That's a lynch.

The stark, trimmed phrases of the Occident seem too bare for the voluptuous child of the sun, hence the adornment. It arises out of the same impulse as the wearing of jewelry and the making of sculpture—the urge to adorn.

On the walls of the homes of the average Negro one always finds a glut of gaudy calendars, wall pockets and advertising lithographs. The sophisticated white man or Negro would tolerate none of these, even if they bore a likeness to the Mona Lisa.[4] No commercial art for decoration. Nor the calendar nor the advertisement spoils the picture for this lowly man. He sees the beauty in spite of the declaration of the Portland Cement Works or the butcher's announcement. I saw in Mobile a room in which there was an overstuffed mohair living-room suite, an imitation mahogany bed and chifforobe, a console victrola.[5] The walls were gaily papered with Sunday supplements of the *Mobile Register*. There were seven calendars and three wall pockets. One of them was decorated with a lace doily. The mantel-shelf was covered with a

4. Painting (ca. 1504) by Leonardo da Vinci.

5. Brand of phonograph.

scarf of deep homemade lace, looped up with a huge bow of pink crepe paper. Over the door was a huge lithograph showing the Treaty of Versailles[6] being signed with a Waterman fountain pen.

It was grotesque, yes. But it indicated the desire for beauty. And decorating a decoration, as in the case of the doily on the gaudy wall pocket, did not seem out of place to the hostess. The feeling back of such an act is that there can never be enough of beauty, let alone too much. Perhaps she is right. We each have our standards of art, and thus are we all interested parties and so unfit to pass judgment upon the art concepts of others.

Whatever the Negro does of his own volition he embellishes. His religious service is for the greater part excellent prose poetry. Both prayers and sermons are tooled and polished until they are true works of art. The supplication is forgotten in the frenzy of creation. The prayer of the white man is considered humorous in its bleakness. The beauty of the Old Testament does not exceed that of a Negro prayer.

Angularity

After adornment the next most striking manifestation of the Negro is Angularity. Everything that he touches becomes angular. In all African sculpture and doctrine of any sort we find the same thing.

Anyone watching Negro dancers will be struck by the same phenomenon. Every posture is another angle. Pleasing, yes. But an effect achieved by the very means which an European strives to avoid.

The pictures on the walls are hung at deep angles. Furniture is always set at an angle. I have instances of a piece of furniture in the *middle* of a wall being set with one end nearer the wall than the other to avoid the simple straight line.

Asymmetry

Asymmetry is a definite feature of Negro art. I have no samples of true Negro painting unless we count the African shields, but the sculpture and carvings are full of this beauty and lack of symmetry.

It is present in the literature, both prose and verse. I offer an example of this quality in verse from Langston Hughes:[7]

> I ain't gonna mistreat ma good gal any more,
> I'm just gonna kill her next time she makes me sore.
>
> I treats her kind but she don't do me right,
> She fights and quarrels most ever' night.
>
> I can't have no woman's got such low-down ways
> Cause de blue gum woman aint de style now'days.
>
> I brought her from the South and she's goin on back,
> Else I'll use her head for a carpet track.

6. Peace treaty of 1919 that formally ended World War I.

7. African American poet (1902–1967; see below); the poem is "Evil Woman" (1927).

It is the lack of symmetry which makes Negro dancing so difficult for white dancers to learn. The abrupt and unexpected changes. The frequent change of key and time are evidences of this quality in music. (Note the St. Louis Blues.)[8]

The dancing of the justly famous Bo-Jangles and Snake Hips[9] are excellent examples.

The presence of rhythm and lack of symmetry are paradoxical, but there they are. Both are present to a marked degree. There is always rhythm, but it is the rhythm of segments. Each unit has a rhythm of its own, but when the whole is assembled it is lacking in symmetry. But easily workable to a Negro who is accustomed to the break in going from one part to another, so that he adjusts himself to the new tempo.

Dancing

Negro dancing is dynamic suggestion. No matter how violent it may appear to the beholder, every posture gives the impression that the dancer will do much more. For example, the performer flexes one knee sharply, assumes a ferocious face mask, thrusts the upper part of the body forward with clenched fists, elbows taut as in hard running or grasping a thrusting blade. That is all. But the spectator himself adds the picture of ferocious assault, hears the drums and finds himself keeping time with the music and tensing himself for the struggle. It is compelling insinuation. That is the very reason the spectator is held so rapt. He is participating in the performance himself—carrying out the suggestions of the performer.

The difference in the two arts is: the white dancer attempts to express fully; the Negro is restrained, but succeeds in gripping the beholder by forcing him to finish the action the performer suggests. Since no art ever can express all the variations conceivable, the Negro must be considered the greater artist, his dancing is realistic suggestion, and that is about all a great artist can do.

Negro Folklore

Negro folklore is not a thing of the past. It is still in the making. Its great variety shows the adaptability of the black man: nothing is too old or too new, domestic or foreign, high or low, for his use. God and the Devil are paired, and are treated no more reverently than Rockefeller and Ford.[1] Both of these men are prominent in folklore, Ford being particularly strong, and they talk and act like good-natured stevedores or mill-hands. Ole Massa is sometimes a smart man and often a fool. The automobile is ranged alongside of the oxcart. The angels and the apostles walk and talk like section hands. And through it all walks Jack, the greatest culture hero of the South; Jack beats them all—even the Devil, who is often smarter than God.

8. Song written in 1914 by W. C. Handy, performed most notably by the blues singer Bessie Smith, and often called the most popular blues song ever written.

9. Nicknames of, respectively, the African American dancers Bill Robinson (1878–1949) and Earl Tucker (1905–1937).

1. Henry Ford (1863–1947), American automobile manufacturer and pioneer of the assembly line. John D. Rockefeller (1839–1937), U.S. oil magnate and philanthropist of enormous wealth.

Culture Heroes

The Devil is next after Jack as a culture hero. He can outsmart everyone but Jack. God is absolutely no match for him. He is good-natured and full of humor. The sort of person one may count on to help out in any difficulty.

Peter the Apostle is the third in importance. One need not look far for the explanation. The Negro is not a Christian really. The primitive gods are not deities of too subtle inner reflection; they are hardworking bodies who serve their devotees just as laboriously as the suppliant serves them. Gods of physical violence, stopping at nothing to serve their followers. Now of all the apostles Peter is the most active. When the other ten fell back trembling in the garden, Peter wielded the blade on the posse.[2] Peter first and foremost in all action. The gods of no peoples have been philosophic until the people themselves have approached that state.

The rabbit, the bear, the lion, the buzzard, the fox are culture heroes from the animal world. The rabbit is far in the lead of all the others and is blood brother to Jack. In short, the trickster-hero of West Africa has been transplanted to America.

John Henry[3] is a culture hero in song, but no more so than Stacker Lee, Smokey Joe or Bad Lazarus. There are many, many Negroes who have never heard of any of the song heroes, but none who do not know John (Jack) and the rabbit.

EXAMPLES OF FOLKLORE AND THE MODERN CULTURE HERO

Why de Porpoise's Tail Is On Crosswise

Now, I want to tell you 'bout de porpoise. God had done made de world and everything. He set de moon and de stars in de sky. He got de fishes of de sea, and de fowls of de air completed.

He made de sun and hung it up. Then He made a nice gold track for it to run on. Then He said, "Now, Sun, I got everything made but Time. That's up to you. I want you to start out and go round de world on dis track just as fast as you kin make it. And de time it takes you to go and come, I'm going to call day and night." De Sun went zoonin' on cross de elements. Now, de porpoise was hanging round there and heard God what he tole de Sun, so he decided he'd take dat trip round de world hisself. He looked up and saw de Sun kytin' along, so he lit out too, him and dat Sun!

So de porpoise beat de Sun round de world by one hour and three minutes. So God said, "Aw naw, this aint gointer do! I didn't mean for nothin' to be faster than de Sun!" So God run dat porpoise for three days before he run him down and caught him, and took his tail off and put it on crossways to slow him up. Still he's de fastest thing in de water. And dat's why de porpoise got his tail on crossways.

2. See John 18.10–11: Peter draws a sword and cuts off the ear of a servant who is among those coming to seize Jesus.

3. Legendary and prodigiously strong black hero of American tall tales and ballads, and by far the best known of the "song heroes" named here (though in the 1930s the black bandleader Cab Calloway recorded songs featuring Stacker Lee and Smokey Joe).

Rockefeller and Ford

Once John D. Rockefeller and Henry Ford was woofing at each other. Rockefeller told Henry Ford he could build a solid gold road round the world. Henry Ford told him if he would he would look at it and see if he liked it, and if he did he would buy it and put one of his tin lizzies[4] on it.

Originality

It has been said so often that the Negro is lacking in originality that it has almost become a gospel. Outward signs seem to bear this out. But if one looks closely its falsity is immediately evident.

It is obvious that to get back to original sources is much too difficult for any group to claim very much as a certainty. What we really mean by originality is the modification of ideas. The most ardent admirer of the great Shakespeare cannot claim first source even for him. It is his treatment of the borrowed material.

So if we look at it squarely, the Negro is a very original being. While he lives and moves in the midst of a white civilization, everything that he touches is reinterpreted for his own use. He has modified the language, mode of food preparation, practice of medicine, and most certainly the religion of his new country, just as he adapted to suit himself the Sheik haircut made famous by Rudolph Valentino.[5]

Everyone is familiar with the Negro's modification of the whites' musical instruments, so that his interpretation has been adopted by the white man himself and then reinterpreted. In so many words, Paul Whiteman[6] is giving an imitation of a Negro orchestra making use of white-invented musical instruments in a Negro way. Thus has arisen a new art in the civilized world, and thus has our so-called civilization come. The exchange and re-exchange of ideas between groups.

Imitation

The Negro, the world over, is famous as a mimic. But this in no way damages his standing as an original. Mimicry is an art in itself. If it is not, then all art must fall by the same blow that strikes it down. When sculpture, painting, acting, dancing, literature neither reflect nor suggest anything in nature or human experience we turn away with a dull wonder in our hearts at why the thing was done. Moreover, the contention that the Negro imitates from a feeling of inferiority is incorrect. He mimics for the love of it. The group of Negroes who slavishly imitate is small. The average Negro glories in his ways. The highly educated Negro the same. The self-despisement lies in a middle class who scorns to do or be anything Negro. "That's just like a Nigger" is the most terrible rebuke one can lay upon this kind. He wears drab clothing, sits through a boresome church service, pretends to have no interest in the community, holds beauty contests, and otherwise apes all the mediocrities

4. Model T Fords (the first mass-produced car).
5. Italian-born American actor (1895–1926), a star of silent films, including *The Sheik* (1921).
6. American conductor (1890–1967).

of the white brother. The truly cultured Negro scorns him, and the Negro "farthest down" is too busy "spreading his junk" in his own way to see or care. He likes his own things best. Even the group who are not Negroes but belong to the "sixth race,"[7] buy such records as "Shake dat thing" and "Tight lak dat." They really enjoy hearing a good bible-beater preach, but wild horses could drag no such admission from them. Their ready-made expression is: "We done got away from all that now." Some refuse to countenance Negro music on the grounds that it is niggerism, and for that reason should be done away with. Roland Hayes[8] was thoroughly denounced for singing spirituals until he was accepted by white audiences. Langston Hughes is not considered a poet by this group because he writes of the man in the ditch, who is more numerous and real among us than any other.

But, this group aside, let us say that the art of mimicry is better developed in the Negro than in other racial groups. He does it as the mockingbird does it, for the love of it, and not because he wishes to be like the one imitated. I saw a group of small Negro boys imitating a cat defecating and the subsequent toilet of the cat. It was very realistic, and they enjoyed it as much as if they had been imitating a coronation ceremony. The dances are full of imitations of various animals. The buzzard lope, walking the dog, the pig's hind legs, holding the mule, elephant squat, pigeon's wing, falling off the log, seabord (imitation of an engine starting), and the like.

It is said that Negroes keep nothing secret, that they have no reserve. This ought not to seem strange when one considers that we are an outdoor people accustomed to communal life. Add this to all-permeating drama and you have the explanation.

There is no privacy in an African village. Loves, fights, possessions are, to misquote Woodrow Wilson, "Open disagreements openly arrived at."[9] The community is given the benefit of a good fight as well as a good wedding. An audience is a necessary part of any drama. We merely go with nature rather than against it.

Discord is more natural than accord. If we accept the doctrine of the survival of the fittest there are more fighting honors than there are honors for other achievements. Humanity places premiums on all things necessary to its well-being, and a valiant and good fighter is valuable in any community. So why hide the light under a bushel? Moreover, intimidation is a recognized part of warfare the world over, and threats certainly must be listed under that head. So that a great threatener must certainly be considered an aid to the fighting machine. So then if a man or woman is a facile hurler of threats why should he or she not show their wares to the community? Hence the holding of all quarrels and fights in the open. One relieves one's pent-up anger and at the same time earns laurels in intimidation. Besides, one does the community a service. There is nothing so exhilarating as watching well-matched opponents go into action. The entire world likes action, for that matter. Hence prize-fighters become millionaires.

7. A new and higher race that will evolve in the Americas from a great amalgamation of all the current races of the earth, according to the teachings of theosophy, a system of mystic and occult speculation popular in the late 19th and early 20th century.

8. American tenor (1887–1977).

9. In an address to Congress on January 8, 1918, President Wilson (1856–1924; 28th U.S. president, 1913–21) spoke of "Open covenants of peace, openly arrived at."

Likewise lovemaking is a biological necessity the world over and an art among Negroes. So that a man or woman who is proficient sees no reason why the fact should not be moot.[1] He swaggers. She struts hippily about. Songs are built on the power to charm beneath the bedclothes. Here again we have individuals striving to excel in what the community considers an art. Then if all of his world is seeking a great lover, why should he not speak right out loud?

It is all in a viewpoint. Lovemaking and fighting in all their branches are high arts, other things are arts among other groups where they brag about their proficiency just as brazenly as we do about these things that others consider matters for conversation behind closed doors. At any rate, the white man is despised by Negroes as a very poor fighter individually, and a very poor lover. One Negro, speaking of white men, said, "White folks is alright when dey gits in de bank and on de law bench, but dey sho' kin lie about wimmen folks."

I pressed him to explain. "Well you see, white mens makes out they marries wimmen to look at they eyes, and they know they gits em for just what us gits em for. 'Nother thing, white mens say they goes clear round de world and wins all de wimmen folks way from they men folks. Dat's a lie too. They don't win nothin, they buys em. Now de way I figgers it, if a woman don't want me enough to be wid me, 'thout[2] I got to pay her, she kin rock right on, but these here white men don't know what to do wid a woman when they gits her—dat's how come they gives they wimmen so much. They got to. Us wimmen works jus as hard as us does an come home an sleep wid us every night. They own wouldn't do it and its de mens fault. Dese white men done fooled theyself bout dese wimmen.

"Now me, I keeps me some wimmens all de time. Dat's whut dey wuz put here for—us mens to use. Dat's right now, Miss. Y'all wuz put here so us mens could have some pleasure. Course I don't run round like heap uh men folks. But if my ole lady go way from me and stay more'n two weeks, I got to git me somebody, aint I?"

The Jook

Jook is the word for a Negro pleasure house. It may mean a bawdy house. It may mean the house set apart on public works where the men and women dance, drink and gamble. Often it is a combination of all these.

In past generations the music was furnished by "boxes," another word for guitars. One guitar was enough for a dance; to have two was considered excellent. Where two were playing one man played the lead and the other seconded him. The first player was "picking" and the second was "framming," that is, playing chords while the lead carried the melody by dexterous finger work. Sometimes a third player was added, and he played a tom-tom effect on the low strings. Believe it or not, this is excellent dance music.

Pianos soon came to take the place of the boxes, and now player-pianos and victrolas are in all of the Jooks.

Musically speaking, the Jook is the most important place in America. For

1. Brought up.

2. Without, unless.

in its smelly, shoddy confines has been born the secular music known as blues, and on blues has been founded jazz. The singing and playing in the true Negro style is called "jooking."

The songs grow by incremental repetition as they travel from mouth to mouth and from Jook to Jook for years before they reach outside ears. Hence the great variety of subject-matter in each song.

The Negro dances circulated over the world were also conceived inside the Jooks. They too make the round of Jooks and public works before going into the outside world.

In this respect it is interesting to mention the Black Bottom. I have read several false accounts of its origin and name. One writer claimed that it got its name from the black sticky mud on the bottom of the Mississippi river. Other equally absurd statements gummed the press. Now the dance really originated in the Jook section of Nashville, Tennessee, around Fourth Avenue. This is a tough neighborhood known as Black Bottom—hence the name.

The Charleston is perhaps forty years old, and was danced up and down the Atlantic seaboard from North Carolina to Key West, Florida.

The Negro social dance is slow and sensuous. The idea in the Jook is to gain sensation, and not so much exercise. So that just enough foot movement is added to keep the dancers on the floor. A tremendous sex stimulation is gained from this. But who is trying to avoid it? The man, the woman, the time and the place have met. Rather, little intimate names are indulged in to heap fire on fire.

These too have spread to all the world.

The Negro theatre, as built up by the Negro, is based on Jook situations, with women, gambling, fighting, drinking. Shows like "Dixie to Broadway"[3] are only Negro in cast, and could just as well have come from pre-Soviet Russia.

Another interesting thing—Negro shows before being tampered with did not specialize in octoroon chorus girls. The girl who could hoist a Jook song from her belly and lam it against the front door of the theatre was the lead, even if she were as black as the hinges of hell. The question was "Can she jook?" She must also have a good belly wobble, and her hips must, to quote a popular work song, "Shake like jelly all over and be so broad, Lawd, Lawd, and be so broad." So that the bleached chorus is the result of a white demand and not the Negro's.

The woman in the Jook may be nappy headed and black, but if she is a good lover she gets there just the same. A favorite Jook song of the past has this to say:

Singer: It aint good looks dat takes you through dis world.
Audience: What is it, good mama?
Singer: Elgin movements[4] in your hips
Twenty years guarantee.

And it always brought down the house too.

3. A revue that opened on Broadway in 1924 featuring black performers, with music written by the black composer Will Vodery.

4. That is, the movements of an Elgin watch.

Oh de white gal rides in a Cadillac,
De yaller[5] gal rides de same,
Black gal rides in a rusty Ford
But she gits dere just de same.

The sort of woman her men idealize is the type that is put forth in the theatre. The art-creating Negro prefers a not too thin woman who can shake like jelly all over as she dances and sings, and that is the type he put forth on the stage. She has been banished by the white producer and the Negro who takes his cue from the white.

Of course a black woman is never the wife of the upper class Negro in the North. This state of affairs does not obtain in the South, however. I have noted numerous cases where the wife was considerably darker than the husband. People of some substance, too.

This scornful attitude towards black women receives mouth sanction by the mud-sills.[6]

Even on the works and in the Jooks the black man sings disparagingly of black women. They say that she is evil. That she sleeps with her fists doubled up and ready for action. All over they are making a little drama of waking up a yaller wife and a black one.

A man is lying beside his yaller wife and wakes her up. She says to him, "Darling, do you know what I was dreaming when you woke me up?" He says, "No honey, what was you dreaming?" She says, "I dreamt I had done cooked you a big, fine dinner and we was setting down to eat out de same plate and I was setting on yo' lap jus huggin you and kissin you and you was so sweet."

Wake up a black woman, and before you kin git any sense into her she be done up and lammed you over the head four or five times. When you git her quiet she'll say, "Nigger, know whut I was dreamin when you woke me up?"

You say, "No honey, what was you dreamin?" She says, "I dreamt you shook yo' rusty fist under my nose and I split yo' head open wid a axe."

But in spite of disparaging fictitious drama, in real life the black girl is drawing on his account at the commissary. Down in the Cypress Swamp[7] as he swings his axe he chants:

Dat ole black gal, she keep on grumblin,
New pair shoes, new pair shoes,
I'm goint to buy her shoes and stockings
Slippers too, slippers too.

Then adds aside: "Blacker de berry, sweeter de juice."

To be sure the black gal is still in power, men are still cutting and shooting their way to her pillow. To the queen of the Jook!

Speaking of the influence of the Jook, I noted that Mae West[8] in "Sex" had much more flavor of the turpentine quarters[9] than she did of the white bawd. I know that the piece she played on the piano is a very old Jook com-

5. Yellow (that is, mulatto).
6. Those at the bottom of the social scale.
7. In southern Florida.
8. American actress (1892–1980), who began in burlesque and continued to specialize in double entendre in films; she wrote as well as starred in the 1926 play *Sex*.
9. The housing (usually shanties) for black workers who collected tree sap to be processed into turpentine.

position. "Honey let yo' drawers hang low" had been played and sung in every Jook in the South for at least thirty-five years. It has always puzzled me why she thought it likely to be played in a Canadian bawdy house.

Speaking of the use of Negro material by white performers, it is astonishing that so many are trying it, and I have never seen one yet entirely realistic. They often have all the elements of the song, dance, or expression, but they are misplaced or distorted by the accent falling on the wrong element. Every one seems to think that the Negro is easily imitated when nothing is further from the truth. Without exception I wonder why the blackface comedians *are* blackface; it is a puzzle—good comedians, but darn poor niggers. Gershwin[1] and the other "Negro" rhapsodists come under this same axe. Just about as Negro as caviar or Ann Pennington's[2] athletic Black Bottom. When the Negroes who knew the Black Bottom in its cradle saw the Broadway version they asked each other, "Is you learnt dat new Black Bottom yet?" Proof that it was not *their* dance.

And God only knows what the world has suffered from the white damsels who try to sing Blues.

The Negroes themselves have sinned also in this respect. In spite of the goings up and down on the earth, from the original Fisk Jubilee Singers[3] down to the present, there has been no genuine presentation of Negro songs to white audiences. The spirituals that have been sung around the world are Negroid to be sure, but so full of musicians' tricks that Negro congregations are highly entertained when they hear their old songs so changed. They never use the new style songs, and these are never heard unless perchance some daughter or son has been off to college and returns with one of the old songs with its face lifted, so to speak.

I am of the opinion that this trick style of delivery was originated by the Fisk Singers; Tuskegee and Hampton[4] followed suit and have helped spread this misconception of Negro spirituals. This Glee Club style has gone on so long and become so fixed among concert singers that it is considered quite authentic. But I say again, that not one concert singer in the world is singing the songs as the Negro song-makers sing them.

If anyone wishes to prove the truth of this let him step into some unfashionable Negro church and hear for himself.

To those who want to institute the Negro theatre, let me say it is already established. It is lacking in wealth, so it is not seen in the high places. A creature with a white head and Negro feet struts the Metropolitan boards. The real Negro theatre is in the Jooks and the cabarets. Self-conscious individuals may turn away the eye and say, "Let us search elsewhere for our dramatic art." Let 'em search. They certainly won't find it. Butter Beans and Susie,[5] Bo-Jangles and Snake Hips are the only performers of the real Negro school it has ever been my pleasure to behold in New York.

1. George Gershwin (1898–1937), American composer who wrote both Broadway musicals and concert works that incorporated jazz elements, including *Rhapsody in Blue* (1924).

2. American dancer and actress (1893–1971).

3. An ensemble formed in 1871 at Fisk University, a historically black institution that opened in 1866 in Nashville, Tennessee; it that toured the United States and Europe to raise money for the school (the ensemble still exists).

4. Two schools begun as industrial training institutes, in Tuskegee, Alabama (founded 1881), and in Hampton, Virginia (founded 1868), respectively; both are now universities.

5. Married African American vaudeville entertainers, Jodie "Butterbeans" Edwards (1895–1967) and Susie Hawthorne (ca. 1896–1963), who toured together for almost 50 years.

Dialect

If we are to believe the majority of writers of Negro dialect and the burnt-cork artists,[6] Negro speech is a weird thing, full of "ams" and "Ises." Fortunately we don't have to believe them. We may go directly to the Negro and let him speak for himself.

I know that I run the risk of being damned as an infidel for declaring that nowhere can be found the Negro who asks "am it?" nor yet his brother who announces "Ise uh gwinter." He exists only for a certain type of writers and performers.

Very few Negroes, educated or not, use a clear clipped "I." It verges more or less upon "Ah." I think the lip form is responsible for this to a great extent. By experiment the reader will find that a sharp "I" is very much easier with a thin taut lip than with a full soft lip. Like tightening violin strings.

If one listens closely one will note too that a word is slurred in one position in the sentence but clearly pronounced in another. This is particularly true of the pronouns. A pronoun as a subject is likely to be clearly enunciated, but slurred as an object. For example: "You better not let me ketch yuh."

There is a tendency in some localities to add the "h" to "it" and pronounce it "hit." Probably a vestige of old English. In some localities "if" is "ef."

In storytelling "so" is universally the connective. It is used even as an introductory word, at the very beginning of a story. In religious expression "and" is used. The trend in stories is to state conclusions; in religion, to enumerate.

I am mentioning only the most general rules in dialect because there are so many quirks that belong only to certain localities that nothing less than a volume would be adequate.

> Now He told me, He said: "You got the three witnesses. One is water, one is spirit, and one is blood. And these three correspond with the three in heben—Father, Son, and Holy Ghost."
>
> Now I ast Him about this lyin in sin and He give me a handful of seeds and He tole me to sow 'em in a bed and He tole me: "I want you to watch them seeds." The seeds come up about in places and He said: "Those seeds that come up, they died in the heart of the earth and quickened and come up and brought forth fruit. But those seeds that didn't come up, they died in the heart of the earth and rottened.
>
> "And a soul that dies and quickens through my spirit they will live forever, but those that dont never pray, they are lost forever."

(Rev. JESSIE JEFFERSON.)[7]

1934

6. That is, white performers who act in blackface, a form popularized in the 19th century that lasted into the 1950s.

7. A local minister whom Hurston had observed.

What White Publishers Won't Print

I have been amazed by the Anglo-Saxon's lack of curiosity about the internal lives and emotions of the Negroes, and for that matter, any non-Anglo-Saxon peoples within our borders, above the class of unskilled labor.

This lack of interest is much more important than it seems at first glance. It is even more important at this time than it was in the past. The internal affairs of the nation have bearings on the international stress and strain,[1] and this gap in the national literature now has tremendous weight in world affairs. National coherence and solidarity is implicit in a thorough understanding of the various groups within a nation, and this lack of knowledge about the internal emotions and behavior of the minorities cannot fail to bar our understanding. Man, like all the other animals fears, and is repelled by that which he does not understand, and mere difference is apt to connote something malign.

The fact that there is no demand for incisive and full-dress stories around Negroes above the servant class is indicative of something of vast importance to this nation. This blank is NOT filled by the fiction built around upperclass Negroes exploiting the race problem. Rather, it tends to point it up. A college-bred Negro still is not a person like other folks, but an interesting problem, more or less. It calls to mind a story of slavery time. In this story, a master with more intellectual curiosity than usual, set out to see how much he could teach a particularly bright slave of his. When he had gotten him up to higher mathematics and to be a fluent reader of Latin, he called in a neighbor to show off his brilliant slave, and to argue that Negroes had brains just like the slave-owners had, and given the same opportunities, would turn out the same.

The visiting master of slaves looked and listened, tried to trap the literate slave in Algebra and Latin, and failing to do so in both, turned to his neighbor and said:

"Yes, he certainly knows his higher mathematics, and he can read Latin better than many white men I know, but I cannot bring myself to believe that he understands a thing that he is doing. It is all an aping of our culture. All on the outside. You are crazy if you think that it has changed him inside in the least. Turn him loose, and he will revert at once to the jungle. He is still a savage, and no amount of translating Virgil and Ovid[2] is going to change him. In fact, all you have done is to turn a useful savage into a dangerous beast."

That was in slavery time, yes, and we have come a long, long way since then, but the troubling thing is that there are still too many who refuse to believe in the ingestion and digestion of western culture as yet. Hence the lack of literature about the higher emotions and love life of upperclass Negroes and the minorities in general.

Publishers and producers are cool to the idea. Now, do not leap to the conclusion that editors and producers constitute a special class of unbeliev-

1. The cold war—the post–World War II rivalry between the United States and the Soviet Union.
2. Roman poets: the *Aeneid* of Virgil (70–19 B.C.) and stories from the *Metamorphoses* of Ovid (43 B.C.E.–17 C.E.) were staples of the schoolroom for centuries.

ers. That is far from true. Publishing houses and theatrical promoters are in business to make money. They will sponsor anything that they believe will sell. They shy away from romantic stories about Negroes and Jews because they feel that they know the public indifference to such works, unless the story or play involves racial tension. It can then be offered as a study in Sociology, with the romantic side subdued. They know the skepticism in general about the complicated emotions in the minorities. The average American just cannot conceive of it, and would be apt to reject the notion, and publishers and producers take the stand that they are not in business to educate, but to make money. Sympathetic as they might be, they cannot afford to be crusaders.

In proof of this, you can note various publishers and producers edging forward a little, and ready to go even further when the trial balloons show that the public is ready for it. This public lack of interest is the nut of the matter.

The question naturally arises as to the why of this indifference, not to say skepticism, to the internal life of educated minorities.

The answer lies in what we may call THE AMERICAN MUSEUM OF UNNATURAL HISTORY.[3] This is an intangible built on folk belief. It is assumed that all non-Anglo-Saxons are uncomplicated stereotypes. Everybody knows all about them. They are lay figures mounted in the museum where all may take them in at a glance. They are made of bent wires without insides at all. So how could anybody write a book about the nonexistent?

The American Indian is a contraption of copper wires in an eternal warbonnet, with no equipment for laughter, expressionless face and that says "How" when spoken to. His only activity is treachery leading to massacres. Who is so dumb as not to know all about Indians, even if they have never seen one, nor talked with anyone who ever knew one?

The American Negro exhibit is a group of two. Both of these mechanical toys are built so that their feet eternally shuffle, and their eyes pop and roll. Shuffling feet and those popping, rolling eyes denote the Negro, and no characterization is genuine without this monotony. One is seated on a stump picking away on his banjo and singing and laughing. The other is a most amoral character before a sharecropper's shack mumbling about injustice. Doing this makes him out to be a Negro "intellectual." It is as simple as all that.

The whole museum is dedicated to the convenient "typical." In there is the "typical" Oriental, Jew, Yankee, Westerner, Southerner, Latin, and even out-of-favor Nordics like the German. The Englishman "I say old chappie," and the gesticulating Frenchman. The least observant American can know them all at a glance. However, the public willingly accepts the untypical in Nordics, but feels cheated if the untypical is portrayed in others. The author of *Scarlet Sister Mary*[4] complained to me that her neighbors objected to her book on the grounds that she had the characters thinking, "and everybody know that Nigras don't think."

But for the national welfare, it is urgent to realize that the minorities do

3. New York City's American Museum of Natural History opened in 1877; among its exhibits were dioramas of "primitive" life similar to those mockingly suggested by Hurston.

4. The Southern writer Julia Peterkin (1880–1961), whose fiction focused on the Gullahs of coastal South Carolina; this novel was published in 1928.

think, and think about something other than the race problem. That they are very human and internally, according to natural endowment, are just like everybody else. So long as this is not conceived, there must remain that feeling of unsurmountable difference, and difference to the average man means something bad. If people were made right, they would be just like him.

The trouble with the purely problem arguments is that they leave too much unknown. Argue all you will or may about injustice, but as long as the majority cannot conceive of a Negro or a Jew feeling and reacting inside just as they do, the majority will keep right on believing that people who do not look like them cannot possibly feel as they do, and conform to the established pattern. It is well known that there must be a body of waived matter, let us say, things accepted and taken for granted by all in a community before there can be that commonality of feeling. The usual phrase is having things in common. Until this is thoroughly established in respect to Negroes in America, as well as of other minorities, it will remain impossible for the majority to conceive of a Negro experiencing a deep and abiding love and not just the passion of sex. That a great mass of Negroes can be stirred by the pageants of Spring and Fall; the extravaganza of summer, and the majesty of winter. That they can and do experience discovery of the numerous subtle faces as a foundation for a great and selfless love, and the diverse nuances that go to destroy that love as with others. As it is now, this capacity, this evidence of high and complicated emotions, is ruled out. Hence the lack of interest in a romance uncomplicated by the race struggle has so little appeal.

This insistence on defeat in a story where upperclass Negroes are portrayed perhaps says something from the subconscious of the majority. Involved in western culture, the hero or the heroine, or both, must appear frustrated and go down to defeat, somehow. Our literature reeks with it. Is it the same as saying, "You can translate Virgil, and fumble with the differential calculus, but can you really comprehend it? Can you cope with our subtleties?"

That brings us to the folklore of "reversion to type." This curious doctrine has such wide acceptance that it is tragic. One has only to examine the huge literature on it to be convinced. No matter how high we may *seem* to climb, put us under strain and we revert to type, that is, to the bush. Under a superficial layer of western culture, the jungle drums throb in our veins.

This ridiculous notion makes it possible for that majority who accept it to conceive of even a man like the suave and scholarly Dr. Charles S. Johnson[5] to hide a black cat's bone on his person, and indulge in a midnight voodoo ceremony, complete with leopard skin and drums, if threatened with the loss of the presidency of Fisk University, or the love of his wife. "Under the skin . . . better to deal with them in business, etc., but otherwise keep them at a safe distance and under control. I tell you, Carl Van Vechten,[6] think as you like, but they are just not like us."

The extent and extravagance of this notion reaches the ultimate in nonsense in the widespread belief that the Chinese have bizarre genitals, because of that eye-fold that makes their eyes seem to slant. In spite of the fact that

5. African American sociologist and educator (1893–1956) president of Fisk University from 1946 to 1956.

6. White American critic and novelist (1880–1964), whose works include *Nigger Heaven* (1926), a novel about Harlem life.

no biology has ever mentioned any such difference in reproductive organs makes no matter. Millions of people believe it. "Did you know that a Chinese has. . . ." Consequently, their quiet contemplative manner is interpreted as a sign of slyness and a treacherous inclination.

But the opening wedge for better understanding has been thrust into the crack. Though many Negroes denounced Carl Van Vechten's *Nigger Heaven* because of the title, and without ever reading it, the book, written in the deepest sincerity, revealed Negroes of wealth and culture to the white public. It created curiosity even when it aroused skepticism. It made folks want to know. Worth Tuttle Hedden's *The Other Room*[7] has definitely widened the opening. Neither of these well-written works take a romance of upperclass Negro life as the central theme, but the atmosphere and the background is there. These works should be followed up by some incisive and intimate stories from the inside.

The realistic story around a Negro insurance official, dentist, general practitioner, undertaker and the like would be most revealing. Thinly disguised fiction around the well known Negro names is not the answer, either. The "exceptional" as well as the Ol' Man Rivers[8] has been exploited all out of context already. Everybody is already resigned to the "exceptional" Negro, and willing to be entertained by the "quaint." To grasp the penetration of western civilization in a minority, it is necessary to know how the average behaves and lives. Books that deal with people like in Sinclair Lewis' *Main Street*[9] is the necessary metier. For various reasons, the average, struggling, nonmorbid Negro is the best-kept secret in America. His revelation to the public is the thing needed to do away with that feeling of difference which inspires fear, and which ever expresses itself in dislike.

It is inevitable that this knowledge will destroy many illusions and romantic traditions which America probably likes to have around. But then, we have no record of anybody sinking into a lingering death on finding out that there was no Santa Claus. The old world will take it in its stride. The realization that Negroes are no better nor no worse, and at times just as boring as everybody else, will hardly kill off the population of the nation.

Outside of racial attitudes, there is still another reason why this literature should exist. Literature and other arts are supposed to hold up the mirror to nature.[1] With only the fractional "exceptional" and the "quaint" portrayed, a true picture of Negro life in America cannot be. A great principle of national art has been violated.

These are the things that publishers and producers, as the accredited representatives of the American people, have not as yet taken into consideration sufficiently. Let there be light![2]

1950

7. Prize-winning novel published in 1947; Hedden (1896–1985), a white woman, was a champion of rights for blacks and women.

8. "Ol' Man River" is the title of a song sung by a black dockworker in the American musical *Show Boat* (1927), written by Jerome Kern and Oscar Hammerstein II.

9. Satiric 1920 novel about small-town America by Lewis (1885–1961).

1. In Shakespeare's *Hamlet* (ca. 1600), Hamlet urges the players "to hold as 'twere the mirror up to nature" (3.2.20).

2. Genesis 1.3.

WALTER BENJAMIN
1892–1940

"One of the foremost tasks of art has always been the creation of a demand which could be fully satisfied only later," remarks Walter Benjamin in his celebrated essay "The Work of Art in the Age of Mechanical Reproduction" (1936). The same could be said of Benjamin's criticism itself. During his lifetime, he was considered, by a small coterie of admirers such as the philosopher THEODOR ADORNO, one of the most original and promising writers on literature, language, and aesthetics of his generation; but at the time of his premature death fleeing the Nazis in 1940, his name had passed into obscurity both within and outside Germany. The publication in 1955 of a collection of his works in a German edition sponsored by Adorno spurred renewed attention, and since the 1970s Benjamin has become one of the most highly esteemed critics of the twentieth century; he is seen as an innovator in diverse fields, including Marxist literary criticism, deconstruction, historiography, and media studies. A broad speculative account of the interaction of industrial production and modern aesthetics, "The Work of Art in the Age of Mechanical Reproduction" has had particular influence in contemporary film and visual studies and is considered a fundamental work of cultural studies.

Born in Berlin into a wealthy Jewish family, Benjamin was first educated by private tutors, later attending boarding school and the University of Freiburg. He continued his studies in Berlin and Munich, but settled in Berne, Switzerland, in 1917 to avoid being drafted into the German army in World War I. In 1919 he received his doctorate from the university there; his thesis, *The Concept of Criticism in German Romanticism*, was published the following year. Returning to Berlin in 1920, he wrote essays and newspaper articles as he worked on a translation of the important nineteenth-century French poet CHARLES BAUDELAIRE, building a significant reputation as a cultural critic. Under financial pressure from his father, who wanted him to take a position in a bank, Benjamin considered starting a used book business but finally decided to pursue an academic career. To complete an additional requirement for a teaching post in the German university system, he wrote a second dissertation in 1925, *The Origins of German Tragic Drama* (1928; trans. 1977); however, it was rejected because of its density and difficulty. One examiner commented that it was an "incomprehensible morass" (another examiner who criticized the submission was MAX HORKHEIMER, later an associate of Benjamin's).

Thus thwarted, Benjamin became an independent scholar, writing articles for leading German periodicals, translating, and conducting research for an ambitious but never-completed historical work on nineteenth-century Paris later known as the *Arcades Project* (trans. 1999). During the twenties and thirties, he traveled across Europe; in a visit to Moscow (1926–27), he observed firsthand the achievements and limitations of the Bolshevik Revolution. Though his friend Gershom Scholem, the Jewish mystical thinker, urged him to emigrate to Palestine, Benjamin remained in Germany, participating in the German Communist Party (as his brother had done). Initially attracted to Marxism in the 1920s on reading GYÖRGY LUKÁCS's *History and Class Consciousness* (1923) and influenced by his friendship during the 1930s with the German Marxist writer Bertolt Brecht, Benjamin adopted increasingly left-wing political positions and showed the influence of Marxism in his writings on culture.

Exiled in Paris after the Nazi takeover in Germany in 1933, Benjamin lived a lonely and, as the threat of war approached, increasingly desperate existence. He struggled to support himself by writing while pursuing research for his *Arcades Project*, one small section of which, "On Some Motifs in Baudelaire" (1939), appeared in the journal of the Institute for Social Research at the University of Frankfurt. But Benjamin's methods and political orientation were increasingly at loggerheads with those of the institute—members of the Frankfurt School were turning away from the traditional paths of Marxism—and he became distant from his friend Adorno, as correspondence from the 1930s reveals. After the German invasion of France in 1940, Benjamin attempted to escape to Spain, intending to emigrate from there to the United States. Stopped at the border in the Pyrenees and fearful that he would be sent back to France to face internment in a concentration camp, Benjamin committed suicide.

Though many of his larger projects remained unfinished at the time of his death, and his essays were often composed under financial and emotional duress, Benjamin's work encompasses a rich and heterogeneous range: autobiographical writings and familiar essays on topics including his travels to Moscow, his experiments with hashish, and his love of book collecting; dense theoretical considerations of allegory and language, such as *Origins of German Tragic Drama* and "The Task of the Translator" (1923), which speculates on how translation offers fragments of a "pure language"; translations into German of Baudelaire and the modern French novelist Marcel Proust; literary criticism introducing contemporary authors such as Franz Kafka to general audiences; aphoristic considerations of the philosophy of history; and avowedly Marxist examinations of the role of art in modern society, such as "The Author as Producer" (1934) and "The Work of Art in the Age of Mechanical Reproduction." Academically trained but denied an academic career, Benjamin represents a crossover figure in literary theory, resembling the mid-twentieth-century American literary and social critic EDMUND WILSON in the range of his writing and cultural concerns, as well as the more academic Adorno in his philosophical sophistication.

Among the texts that Benjamin published under the auspices of the Frankfurt Institute, none has become more famous than "The Work of Art in the Age of Mechanical Reproduction." It introduces his seminal concept of "aura"—the unique quality traditionally attributed to an artwork, giving it a special status equivalent to that of a sacred object in religious ritual. Investigating the perennial theoretical problem of the relation of aesthetics to social history, Benjamin argues that the status of the artwork is not timeless: it changed with the advent of capitalist mass production, which dispelled its unique aura and revered standing by devaluing the concept of the "original." Taking photography and film as his prime examples, he speculates that social transformations induced by technological changes in production alter aesthetic perception itself. He contrasts painting—a topic of comparison made familiar in aesthetics by GOTTHOLD EPHRAIM LESSING (1729–1781)—with film, noting that the stream of images in film promotes a "deepening of apperception" and that the close-up, among other techniques, "extends our comprehension of the necessities which rule our lives." These are benefits of the mechanical reproduction of art.

Though many view Benjamin as a mystical thinker, he does not express nostalgia for a time when the artwork possessed an "aura"; indeed, he denounces theories that assert an auratic or ritualistic power of film, branding them politically and aesthetically regressive. In contrast to painting or orchestral music, film has revolutionary potential because it abolishes authenticity and aura and enjoins the participation of the audience. Echoing Brecht on the "alienation effects" achieved by actors and staging in experimental theater, Benjamin maintains that the very process through which a movie is constructed—shot by shot, as the editor sutures together sequences filmed at different times—prevents audience members from unconsciously empathizing or identifying with any actor, thereby provoking them to thought and perhaps to action.

Nonetheless, Benjamin recognizes that any art form can be turned to reactionary purposes, and that the apparatus or technology of film does not guarantee a singular political outcome. He thus dispels the utopian belief that technology necessarily generates beneficial changes (a belief sometimes expressed today in rhapsodic pronouncements on the World Wide Web, discussed by STUART MOULTHROP among others). Mindful of the uses that fascists had made of film—notably Leni Riefenstahl's *Triumph of the Will* (1934), an infamous celebration of Nazi ideology—Benjamin sternly rebukes the aestheticization of politics, by which sheer technical brilliance and beauty mask the representation of a pernicious political program. Instead of offering a fascination with aesthetic qualities, communism positively "politicizes art" by foregrounding political action in the work and compelling the audience to reflect on the problems it raises. As is often the case with Benjamin, "The Work of Art in the Age of Mechanical Reproduction" is less an authoritative statement of general aesthetic principles than a sequence of striking observations and an injunction for future work.

Some critics have stressed Benjamin's trajectory from the philosophical idealism of his early writings on language, aesthetics, and philosophy to his more explicitly Marxist later writings, but the very range of his work—on language, allegory, translation theory, historiography, aesthetics, film, and the philosophy of technology—has sometimes led commentators to shape Benjamin's work according to their own tastes. Beginning with his lifelong friend, Gershom Scholem, one prominent strand of readings foregrounds Benjamin's more philosophical works, seeing them as an expression of Jewish mysticism. Such readings downplay his mature works of the 1930s, viewing them as a misguided infatuation with the Marxist Brecht. Contemporary deconstructive critics, notably PAUL DE MAN and Geoffrey Hartman, draw on Benjamin's writings on allegory and language, claiming him as a precursor of deconstruction in his focus on the problematics of language. Marxists like TERRY EAGLETON have stressed his exemplary role as a revolutionary critic, though one with messianic leanings. Despite the legendary obscurity of his prose style and his use of idioms derived from mysticism and German idealist philosophy (especially in his earlier writings), Benjamin persistently calls attention in his later work to the influence of the means of production on culture; he commands the revolutionary intellectual to assume an attitude that would transform him "from a supplier of the productive apparatus into an engineer who sees it as his task to adapt this apparatus to the purposes of proletarian revolution" ("The Author as Producer").

BIBLIOGRAPHY

Not until decades after his death did Benjamin's diverse work become readily available in German and, increasingly, in English. In addition to his two dissertations, *The Concept of Criticism in German Romanticism* (1920) and *The Origin of German Tragic Drama* (1928; trans. 1977), he published many essays and articles and left several unfinished book manuscripts. The first collected edition in German, the two-volume *Schriften* (*Writings*), edited by Theodor Adorno and Gershom Scholem (1955), brought renewed attention to Benjamin's work. The standard scholarly edition of the complete writings in German is *Gesammelte Schriften*, edited by Rolf Tiedemann and Hermann Schweppenhäuser (7 vols., 1972–89). The first selection of essays in English, *Illuminations*, was edited by Hannah Arendt (1969); it includes the standard translation of "The Work of Art in the Age of Mechanical Reproduction" used in our anthology. A string of English collections followed, sometimes overlapping in material: *Charles Baudelaire: A Lyric Poet in the Era of High Capitalism* (1973); *Understanding Brecht* (1973); *Reflections: Essays, Aphorisms, Autobiographical Writings*, edited by Peter Demetz (1978); *One-Way Street and Other Writings* (1979); and *Moscow Diary*, edited by Gary Smith (1986). Harvard University Press has begun publishing a standard edition, including *Selected Writings, 1913–1926*, edited by Marcus Bullock and Michael W. Jennings (1996); *Selected Writings, 1927–1934*, edited by Michael W. Jennings, Howard Eiland, and Gary Smith (1999); a projected third volume of selected writings from 1935 to 1940; and the massive *Arcades Project* (1999). The series is seriously flawed, however: the volumes are incomplete (as the titles indicate), rely on earlier translations, and have sparse scholarly apparatus, omitting the extremely useful introductions and notes provided by Benjamin's more scrupulous German editors. Among several collections of letters, the most comprehensive is *The Correspondence of Walter Benjamin, 1910–1940*, edited by Scholem and Adorno (1966; trans. 1994).

The standard biography is Momme Brodersen's *Walter Benjamin: A Biography* (1990; trans. 1996), which replaces Bernd Witte's earlier *Walter Benjamin: An Intellectual Biography* (1985; trans. 1991). Gershom Scholem's *Walter Benjamin: The Story of a Friendship* (1975; trans. 1981) offers a firsthand personal account.

The secondary literature on Benjamin in English is extensive. Fredric Jameson provided an influential introduction of Benjamin to contemporary American literary theorists in *Marxism and Form: Twentieth-Century Dialectical Theories of Literature* (1971). Susan Buck-Morss's *The Origin of Negative Dialectics: Theodor W. Adorno, Walter Benjamin, and the Frankfurt School* (1977) roots Benjamin's work in the context of the Frankfurt School. A spirited attempt to recapture Benjamin for the Left was undertaken by Terry Eagleton in *Walter Benjamin, or Towards a Revolutionary Criticism* (1981). Much of the criticism on Benjamin, such as Richard Wolin, *Walter Benjamin: An Aesthetic of Redemption* (1982; 2d ed., 1994), follows the mystical interpretation inaugurated by Scholem. Michael Jennings's *Dialectical Images: Walter Benjamin's Theory of Literary Criticism* (1987) is a useful examination of Benjamin's critical methodology. Perhaps the best collection of criticism in English is *On Walter Benjamin: Critical Essays and Recollections*, edited by Gary Smith (1988); it contains important texts by Benjamin's contemporaries Adorno, Scholem, and Ernst Bloch and a well-informed assessment by the philosopher Jürgen Habermas. See also the companion volume edited by Smith, *Benjamin: Philosophy, History, Aesthetics* (1989). A synoptic account, Rainer Rochlitz's *Disenchantment of Art: The Philosophy of Walter Benjamin* (1992; trans. 1996), considers Benjamin's reflections on language, on art and modernity, and on politics and history.

Many critical studies of Benjamin focus on a single facet of his work. One prominent line of commentary comes from deconstruction; see Carol Jacobs's *In the Language of Walter Benjamin* (1999), which includes an influential essay originally published in 1975 on Benjamin's "The Task of the Translator," and Paul de Man's " 'Conclusion': On Walter Benjamin's 'The Task of the Translator' " (1981), which builds on Jacobs, finding that Benjamin suggests the deconstructive lesson of the unreliability of language. Benjamin is a touchstone for film critics; see, for example, the leading film scholar Miriam Hansen's "Benjamin, Cinema, and Experience," *New German Critique* 40 (1987).

The standard bibliography in German is *Walter Benjamin: Eine kommentierte Bibliographie*, compiled by Momme Brodersen et al. (1996), which includes a section on Benjamin's work in English. Gary Smith's *Benjamin* (cited above) includes a bibliography of Benjamin's work and selected secondary material up to 1988, and Rochlitz's *Disenchantment of Art* also includes a useful selective bibliography of primary and secondary sources.

The Work of Art in the Age of Mechanical Reproduction[1]

> "Our fine arts were developed, their types and uses were established, in times very different from the present, by men whose power of action upon things was insignificant in comparison with ours. But the amazing growth of our techniques, the adaptability and precision they have attained, the ideas and habits they are creating, make it a certainty that profound changes are impending in the ancient craft of the Beautiful. In all the arts there is a physical component which can no longer be considered or treated as it used to be, which cannot remain unaffected by our modern knowledge and power. For the last twenty years neither matter nor space nor

1. Translated by Harry Zohn.

> time has been what it was from time immemorial. We must expect great innovations to transform the entire technique of the arts, thereby affecting artistic invention itself and perhaps even bringing about an amazing change in our very notion of art."
>
> —Paul Valéry, PIÈCES SUR L'ART, "La Conquète de l'ubiquité," Paris.[2]

Preface

When Marx undertook his critique of the capitalistic mode of production,[3] this mode was in its infancy. Marx directed his efforts in such a way as to give them prognostic value. He went back to the basic conditions underlying capitalistic production and through his presentation showed what could be expected of capitalism in the future. The result was that one could expect it not only to exploit the proletariat with increasing intensity, but ultimately to create conditions which would make it possible to abolish capitalism itself.

The transformation of the superstructure, which takes place far more slowly than that of the substructure, has taken more than half a century to manifest in all areas of culture the change in the conditions of production. Only today can it be indicated what form this has taken. Certain prognostic requirements should be met by these statements. However, theses about the art of the proletariat after its assumption of power or about the art of a classless society would have less bearing on these demands than theses about the developmental tendencies of art under present conditions of production. Their dialectic[4] is no less noticeable in the superstructure than in the economy. It would therefore be wrong to underestimate the value of such theses as a weapon. They brush aside a number of outmoded concepts, such as creativity and genius, eternal value and mystery—concepts whose uncontrolled (and at present almost uncontrollable) application would lead to a processing of data in the Fascist sense. The concepts which are introduced into the theory of art in what follows differ from the more familiar terms in that they are completely useless for the purposes of Fascism. They are, on the other hand, useful for the formulation of revolutionary demands in the politics of art.

I

In principle a work of art has always been reproducible. Man-made artifacts could always be imitated by men. Replicas were made by pupils in practice of their craft, by masters for diffusing their works, and, finally, by third parties in the pursuit of gain. Mechanical reproduction of a work of art, however, represents something new. Historically, it advanced intermittently and in leaps at long intervals, but with accelerated intensity. The Greeks knew only two procedures of technically reproducing works of art: founding and stamping. Bronzes, terra cottas, and coins were the only art

2. Quoted from Paul Valéry, "The Conquest of Ubiquity," in *Aesthetics*, trans. Ralph Manheim (New York: Pantheon, 1964), p. 225 [translator's note]. Valéry (1871–1945), modernist French poet and essayist.

3. In the influential theory of the German social philosopher KARL MARX (1818–1883), capitalism's economic base (the mode of production, or "substructure") determines all noneconomic aspects of life ("superstructure"), including a society's legal, political, educational, religious, and cultural systems.

4. Reciprocal interaction.

works which they could produce in quantity. All others were unique and could not be mechanically reproduced. With the woodcut graphic art became mechanically reproducible for the first time, long before script became reproducible by print. The enormous changes which printing, the mechanical reproduction of writing, has brought about in literature are a familiar story. However, within the phenomenon which we are here examining from the perspective of world history, print is merely a special, though particularly important, case. During the Middle Ages engraving and etching were added to the woodcut; at the beginning of the nineteenth century lithography made its appearance.

With lithography the technique of reproduction reached an essentially new stage. This much more direct process was distinguished by the tracing of the design on a stone rather than its incision on a block of wood or its etching on a copperplate and permitted graphic art for the first time to put its products on the market, not only in large numbers as hitherto, but also in daily changing forms. Lithography enabled graphic art to illustrate everyday life, and it began to keep pace with printing. But only a few decades after its invention, lithography was surpassed by photography. For the first time in the process of pictorial reproduction, photography freed the hand of the most important artistic functions which henceforth devolved only upon the eye looking into a lens. Since the eye perceives more swiftly than the hand can draw, the process of pictorial reproduction was accelerated so enormously that it could keep pace with speech. A film operator shooting a scene in the studio captures the images at the speed of an actor's speech. Just as lithography virtually implied the illustrated newspaper, so did photography foreshadow the sound film. The technical reproduction of sound was tackled at the end of the last century. These convergent endeavors made predictable a situation which Paul Valéry pointed up in this sentence: "Just as water, gas, and electricity are brought into our houses from far off to satisfy our needs in response to a minimal effort, so we shall be supplied with visual or auditory images, which will appear and disappear at a simple movement of the hand, hardly more than a sign."[5] Around 1900 technical reproduction had reached a standard that not only permitted it to reproduce all transmitted works of art and thus to cause the most profound change in their impact upon the public; it also had captured a place of its own among the artistic processes. For the study of this standard nothing is more revealing than the nature of the repercussions that these two different manifestations—the reproduction of works of art and the art of the film—have had on art in its traditional form.

II

Even the most perfect reproduction of a work of art is lacking in one element: its presence in time and space, its unique existence at the place where it happens to be. This unique existence of the work of art determined the history to which it was subject throughout the time of its existence. This includes the changes which it may have suffered in physical condition over the years as well as the various changes in its ownership.[6] The traces of the

5. Valéry, p. 226 [translator's note].

6. Of course, the history of a work of art encompasses more than this. The history of the "Mona Lisa," for instance, encompasses the kind and

first can be revealed only by chemical or physical analyses which it is impossible to perform on a reproduction; changes of ownership are subject to a tradition which must be traced from the situation of the original.

The presence of the original is the prerequisite to the concept of authenticity. Chemical analyses of the patina of a bronze can help to establish this, as does the proof that a given manuscript of the Middle Ages stems from an archive of the fifteenth century. The whole sphere of authenticity is outside technical—and, of course, not only technical—reproducibility.[7] Confronted with its manual reproduction, which was usually branded as a forgery, the original preserved all its authority; not so *vis à vis* technical reproduction. The reason is twofold. First, process reproduction is more independent of the original than manual reproduction. For example, in photography, process reproduction can bring out those aspects of the original that are unattainable to the naked eye yet accessible to the lens, which is adjustable and chooses its angle at will. And photographic reproduction, with the aid of certain processes, such as enlargement or slow motion, can capture images which escape natural vision. Secondly, technical reproduction can put the copy of the original into situations which would be out of reach for the original itself. Above all, it enables the original to meet the beholder halfway, be it in the form of a photograph or a phonograph record. The cathedral leaves its locale to be received in the studio of a lover of art; the choral production, performed in an auditorium or in the open air, resounds in the drawing room.

The situations into which the product of mechanical reproduction can be brought may not touch the actual work of art, yet the quality of its presence is always depreciated. This holds not only for the art work but also, for instance, for a landscape which passes in review before the spectator in a movie. In the case of the art object, a most sensitive nucleus—namely, its authenticity—is interfered with whereas no natural object is vulnerable on that score. The authenticity of a thing is the essence of all that is transmissible from its beginning, ranging from its substantive duration to its testimony to the history which it has experienced. Since the historical testimony rests on the authenticity, the former, too, is jeopardized by reproduction when substantive duration ceases to matter. And what is really jeopardized when the historical testimony is affected is the authority of the object.[8]

One might subsume the eliminated element in the term "aura" and go on to say: that which withers in the age of mechanical reproduction is the aura of the work of art. This is a symptomatic process whose significance points beyond the realm of art. One might generalize by saying: the technique of reproduction detaches the reproduced object from the domain of tradition. By making many reproductions it substitutes a plurality of copies for a unique existence. And in permitting the reproduction to meet the beholder or listener in his own particular situation, it reactivates the object reproduced.

number of its copies made in the 17th, 18th, and 19th centuries [Benjamin's note]. Some of the author's notes have been edited, and some omitted.

7. Precisely because authenticity is not reproducible, the intensive penetration of certain (mechanical) processes of reproduction was instrumental in differentiating and grading authenticity. To develop such differentiations was an important function of the trade in works of art. The invention of the woodcut may be said to have struck at the root of the quality of authenticity even before its late flowering. To be sure, at the time of its origin a medieval picture of the Madonna could not yet be said to be "authentic." It became "authentic" only during the succeeding centuries and perhaps most strikingly so during the last one [Benjamin's note].

8. The poorest provincial staging of *Faust* is superior to a Faust film in that, ideally, it competes with the first performance at Weimar [Benjamin's note]. *Faust* (1808, 1832), a drama by the German Romantic poet, novelist, and playwright Johann Wolfgang von Goethe, who lived for most of his life in Weimar.

These two processes lead to a tremendous shattering of tradition which is the obverse of the contemporary crisis and renewal of mankind. Both processes are intimately connected with the contemporary mass movements. Their most powerful agent is the film. Its social significance, particularly in its most positive form, is inconceivable without its destructive, cathartic[9] aspect, that is, the liquidation of the traditional value of the cultural heritage. This phenomenon is most palpable in the great historical films. It extends to ever new positions. In 1927 Abel Gance exclaimed enthusiastically: "Shakespeare, Rembrandt, Beethoven will make films . . . all legends, all mythologies and all myths, all founders of religion, and the very religions . . . await their exposed resurrection, and the heroes crowd each other at the gate."[1] Presumably without intending it, he issued an invitation to a far-reaching liquidation.

III

During long periods of history, the mode of human sense perception changes with humanity's entire mode of existence. The manner in which human sense perception is organized, the medium in which it is accomplished, is determined not only by nature but by historical circumstances as well. The fifth century, with its great shifts of population, saw the birth of the late Roman art industry and the Vienna Genesis, and there developed not only an art different from that of antiquity but also a new kind of perception. The scholars of the Viennese school, Riegl and Wickhoff,[2] who resisted the weight of classical tradition under which these later art forms had been buried, were the first to draw conclusions from them concerning the organization of perception at the time. However far-reaching their insight, these scholars limited themselves to showing the significant, formal hallmark which characterized perception in late Roman times. They did not attempt—and, perhaps, saw no way—to show the social transformations expressed by these changes of perception. The conditions for an analogous insight are more favorable in the present. And if changes in the medium of contemporary perception can be comprehended as decay of the aura, it is possible to show its social causes.

The concept of aura which was proposed above with reference to historical objects may usefully be illustrated with reference to the aura of natural ones. We define the aura of the latter as the unique phenomenon of a distance, however close it may be. If, while resting on a summer afternoon, you follow with your eyes a mountain range on the horizon or a branch which casts its shadow over you, you experience the aura of those mountains, of that branch. This image makes it easy to comprehend the social bases of the contemporary decay of the aura. It rests on two circumstances, both of which are related to the increasing significance of the masses in contemporary life. Namely,

9. Purgative. Benjamin here invokes a sense different from the traditional literary meaning of catharsis, a term applied by ARISTOTLE (384–322 B.C.E.) in the *Poetics* (see above) to the emotional release experienced by an audience watching a drama.

1. Abel Gance, "Le Temps de l'image est venu" ["The Time of the Image Has Arrived" (French)], *L'Art cinématographique* 2 (1927): 94–95 [translator's note]. Gance (1889–1981), French silent film director. Rembrandt van Rijnn (1606–1669), Dutch painter. Ludwig van Beethoven (1770–1827), German composer.

2. Alois Riegl (1858–1905) and Franz Wickhoff (1853–1909), German art historians who studied the inception (hence "genesis") of European art in Vienna in the Middle Ages, an inception influenced by earlier Roman art.

the desire of contemporary masses to bring things "closer" spatially and humanly, which is just as ardent as their bent toward overcoming the uniqueness of every reality by accepting its reproduction.[3] Every day the urge grows stronger to get hold of an object at very close range by way of its likeness, its reproduction. Unmistakably, reproduction as offered by picture magazines and newsreels differs from the image seen by the unarmed eye. Uniqueness and permanence are as closely linked in the latter as are transitoriness and reproducibility in the former. To pry an object from its shell, to destroy its aura, is the mark of a perception whose "sense of the universal equality of things" has increased to such a degree that it extracts it even from a unique object by means of reproduction. Thus is manifested in the field of perception what in the theoretical sphere is noticeable in the increasing importance of statistics. The adjustment of reality to the masses and of the masses to reality is a process of unlimited scope, as much for thinking as for perception.

IV

The uniqueness of a work of art is inseparable from its being imbedded in the fabric of tradition. This tradition itself is thoroughly alive and extremely changeable. An ancient statue of Venus,[4] for example, stood in a different traditional context with the Greeks, who made it an object of veneration, than with the clerics of the Middle Ages, who viewed it as an ominous idol. Both of them, however, were equally confronted with its uniqueness, that is, its aura. Originally the contextual integration of art in tradition found its expression in the cult. We know that the earliest art works originated in the service of a ritual—first the magical, then the religious kind. It is significant that the existence of the work of art with reference to its aura is never entirely separated from its ritual function.[5] In other words, the unique value of the "authentic" work of art has its basis in ritual, the location of its original use value. This ritualistic basis, however remote, is still recognizable as secularized ritual even in the most profane forms of the cult of beauty.[6] The secular cult of beauty, developed during the Renaissance and prevailing for three centuries, clearly showed that ritualistic basis in its decline and the first deep crisis which befell it. With the advent of the first truly revolutionary means of reproduction, photography, simultaneously with the rise of socialism, art

3. To satisfy the human interest of the masses may mean to have one's social function removed from the field of vision. Nothing guarantees that a portraitist of today, when painting a famous surgeon at the breakfast table in the midst of his family, depicts his social function more precisely than a painter of the 17th century who portrayed his medical doctors as representing this profession, like Rembrandt in his "Anatomy Lesson" [Benjamin's note].

4. Roman name of Aphrodite, the goddess of love in Greek mythology.

5. The definition of the aura as a "unique phenomenon of a distance however close it may be" represents nothing but the formulation of the cult value of the work of art in categories of space and time perception. Distance is the opposite of closeness. The essentially distant object is the unapproachable one. Unapproachability is indeed a major quality of the cult image. True to its nature, it remains "distant, however close it may be." The closeness which one may gain from its subject matter does not impair the distance which it retains in its appearance [Benjamin's note].

6. To the extent to which the cult value of the painting is secularized the ideas of its fundamental uniqueness lose distinctness. In the imagination of the beholder the uniqueness of the phenomena which hold sway in the cult image is more and more displaced by the empirical uniqueness of the creator or of his creative achievement. To be sure, never completely so; the concept of authenticity always transcends mere genuineness. (This is particularly apparent in the collector who always retains some traces of the fetishist and who, by owning the work of art, shares in its ritual power.) Nevertheless, the function of the concept of authenticity remains determinate in the evaluation of art; with the secularization of art, authenticity displaces the cult value of the work [Benjamin's note].

sensed the approaching crisis which has become evident a century later. At the time, art reacted with the doctrine of *l'art pour l'art*,[7] that is, with a theology of art. This gave rise to what might be called a negative theology in the form of the idea of "pure" art, which not only denied any social function of art but also any categorizing by subject matter. (In poetry, Mallarmé[8] was the first to take this position.)

An analysis of art in the age of mechanical reproduction must do justice to these relationships, for they lead us to an all-important insight: for the first time in world history, mechanical reproduction emancipates the work of art from its parasitical dependence on ritual. To an ever greater degree the work of art reproduced becomes the work of art designed for reproducibility.[9] From a photographic negative, for example, one can make any number of prints; to ask for the "authentic" print makes no sense. But the instant the criterion of authenticity ceases to be applicable to artistic production, the total function of art is reversed. Instead of being based on ritual, it begins to be based on another practice—politics.

V

Works of art are received and valued on different planes. Two polar types stand out: with one, the accent is on the cult value; with the other, on the exhibition value of the work. Artistic production begins with ceremonial objects destined to serve in a cult. One may assume that what mattered was their existence, not their being on view. The elk portrayed by the man of the Stone Age on the walls of his cave was an instrument of magic. He did expose it to his fellow men, but in the main it was meant for the spirits. Today the cult value would seem to demand that the work of art remain hidden. Certain statues of gods are accessible only to the priest in the cella;[1] certain Madonnas remain covered nearly all year round; certain sculptures on medieval cathedrals are invisible to the spectator on ground level. With the emancipation of the various art practices from ritual go increasing opportunities for the exhibition of their products. It is easier to exhibit a portrait bust that can be sent here and there than to exhibit the statue of a divinity that has its fixed place in the interior of a temple. The same holds for the painting as against the mosaic or fresco that preceded it. And even though the public presentability of a mass originally may have been just as great as that of a

7. Art for art's sake (French), a 19th-century aesthetic doctrine; see WALTER PATER, above.

8. STÉPHANE MALLARMÉ (1842–1898), French poet.

9. In the case of films, mechanical reproduction is not, as with literature and painting, an external condition for mass distribution. Mechanical reproduction is inherent in the very technique of film production. This technique not only permits in the most direct way but virtually causes mass distribution. It enforces distribution because the production of a film is so expensive that an individual who, for instance, might afford to buy a painting no longer can afford to buy a film. In 1927 it was calculated that a major film, in order to pay its way, had to reach an audience of nine million. With the sound film, to be sure, a setback in its international distribution occurred at first: audiences became limited by language barriers. This coincided with the Fascist emphasis on national interests. It is more important to focus on this connection with Fascism than on this setback, which was soon minimized by synchronization. The simultaneity of both phenomena is attributable to the depression. The same disturbances which, on a larger scale, led to an attempt to maintain the existing property structure by sheer force led the endangered film capital to speed up the development of the sound film. The introduction of the sound film brought about a temporary relief, not only because it again brought the masses into the theaters but also because it merged new capital from the electrical industry with that of the film industry. Thus, viewed from the outside, the sound film promoted national interests, but seen from the inside it helped to internationalize film production even more than previously [Benjamin's note].

1. Small room (Latin); specifically, a priest's cell.

symphony, the latter originated at the moment when its public presentability promised to surpass that of the mass.

With the different methods of technical reproduction of a work of art, its fitness for exhibition increased to such an extent that the quantitative shift between its two poles turned into a qualitative transformation of its nature. This is comparable to the situation of the work of art in prehistoric times when, by the absolute emphasis on its cult value, it was, first and foremost, an instrument of magic. Only later did it come to be recognized as a work of art. In the same way today, by the absolute emphasis on its exhibition value the work of art becomes a creation with entirely new functions, among which the one we are conscious of, the artistic function, later may be recognized as incidental.[2] This much is certain: today photography and the film are the most serviceable exemplifications of this new function.

VI

In photography, exhibition value begins to displace cult value all along the line. But cult value does not give way without resistance. It retires into an ultimate retrenchment: the human countenance. It is no accident that the portrait was the focal point of early photography. The cult of remembrance of loved ones, absent or dead, offers a last refuge for the cult value of the picture. For the last time the aura emanates from the early photographs in the fleeting expression of a human face. This is what constitutes their melancholy, incomparable beauty. But as man withdraws from the photographic image, the exhibition value for the first time shows its superiority to the ritual value. To have pinpointed this new stage constitutes the incomparable significance of Atget,[3] who, around 1900, took photographs of deserted Paris streets. It has quite justly been said of him that he photographed them like scenes of crime. The scene of a crime, too, is deserted; it is photographed for the purpose of establishing evidence. With Atget, photographs become standard evidence for historical occurrences, and acquire a hidden political significance. They demand a specific kind of approach; free-floating contemplation is not appropriate to them. They stir the viewer; he feels challenged by them in a new way. At the same time picture magazines begin to put up signposts for him, right ones or wrong ones, no matter. For the first time, captions have become obligatory. And it is clear that they have an altogether different character than the title of a painting. The directives which the captions give to those looking at pictures in illustrated magazines soon become even more explicit and more imperative in the film where the meaning of each single picture appears to be prescribed by the sequence of all preceding ones.

2. Bertolt Brecht, on a different level, engaged in analogous reflections: "If the concept of 'work of art' can no longer be applied to the thing that emerges once the work is transformed into a commodity, we have to eliminate this concept with cautious care but without fear, lest we liquidate the function of the very thing as well. For it has to go through this phase without mental reservation, and not as noncommittal deviation from the straight path; rather, what happens here with the work of art will change it fundamentally and erase its past to such an extent that should the old concept be taken up again—and it will, why not?—it will no longer stir any memory of the thing it once designated" [Benjamin's note]. Brecht (1898–1956), Marxist German playwright and influential friend of Benjamin.

3. Eugène Atget (1856–1927), French photographer.

VII

The nineteenth-century dispute as to the artistic value of painting versus photography today seems devious and confused. This does not diminish its importance, however; if anything, it underlines it. The dispute was in fact the symptom of a historical transformation the universal impact of which was not realized by either of the rivals. When the age of mechanical reproduction separated art from its basis in cult, the semblance of its autonomy disappeared forever. The resulting change in the function of art transcended the perspective of the century; for a long time it even escaped that of the twentieth century, which experienced the development of the film.

Earlier much futile thought had been devoted to the question of whether photography is an art. The primary question—whether the very invention of photography had not transformed the entire nature of art—was not raised. Soon the film theoreticians asked the same ill-considered question with regard to the film. But the difficulties which photography caused traditional aesthetics were mere child's play as compared to those raised by the film. Whence the insensitive and forced character of early theories of the film. Abel Gance, for instance, compares the film with hieroglyphs: "Here, by a remarkable regression, we have come back to the level of expression of the Egyptians. . . . Pictorial language has not yet matured because our eyes have not yet adjusted to it. There is as yet insufficient respect for, insufficient cult of, what it expresses."[4] Or, in the words of Séverin-Mars: "What art has been granted a dream more poetical and more real at the same time! Approached in this fashion the film might represent an incomparable means of expression. Only the most high-minded persons, in the most perfect and mysterious moments of their lives, should be allowed to enter its ambience."[5] Alexandre Arnoux concludes his fantasy about the silent film with the question: "Do not all the bold descriptions we have given amount to the definition of prayer?"[6] It is instructive to note how their desire to class the film among the "arts" forces these theoreticians to read ritual elements into it—with a striking lack of discretion. Yet when these speculations were published, films like *L'Opinion publique* and *The Gold Rush*[7] had already appeared. This, however, did not keep Abel Gance from adducing hieroglyphs for purposes of comparison, nor Séverin-Mars from speaking of the film as one might speak of paintings by Fra Angelico.[8] Characteristically, even today ultrareactionary authors give the film a similar contextual significance—if not an outright sacred one, then at least a supernatural one. Commenting on Max Reinhardt's film version of *A Midsummer Night's Dream*, Werfel[9] states that undoubtedly it was the sterile copying of the exterior world with its streets, interiors, railroad stations, restaurants, motorcars, and beaches which until now had obstructed the elevation of the film to the realm of art. "The film

4. Gance, pp. 100–101 [translator's note].
5. Quoted in Gance, p. 100 [translator's note]. Séverin-Mars (Armand Jean de Malasayade, 1873–1921), French actor, author, and film director.
6. Alexandre Arnoux, *Cinéma* (Paris, 1929), p. 28 [translator's note]. Arnoux (1884–1978), French playwright.
7. Two American silent films written and directed by the English actor and filmmaker Charlie Chaplin (1889–1977), *L'Opinion publique* (*Public Opinion* [French], better known as *A Woman of Paris*, 1923) and *The Gold Rush* (1925).
8. Florentine painter (Giovanni da Fiesole, ca. 1400–1455), a monk whose works generally had religious subjects.
9. Franz Werfel (1890–1945), Austrian poet, playwright, and novelist. Reinhardt (1873–1943), Austrian-born actor and producer of theater and film; his version of *A Midsummer Night's Dream* was released in 1935.

has not yet realized its true meaning, its real possibilities . . . these consist in its unique faculty to express by natural means and with incomparable persuasiveness all that is fairylike, marvelous, supernatural."[1]

VIII

The artistic performance of a stage actor is definitely presented to the public by the actor in person; that of the screen actor, however, is presented by a camera, with a twofold consequence. The camera that presents the performance of the film actor to the public need not respect the performance as an integral whole. Guided by the cameraman, the camera continually changes its position with respect to the performance. The sequence of positional views which the editor composes from the material supplied him constitutes the completed film. It comprises certain factors of movement which are in reality those of the camera, not to mention special camera angles, close-ups, etc. Hence, the performance of the actor is subjected to a series of optical tests. This is the first consequence of the fact that the actor's performance is presented by means of a camera. Also, the film actor lacks the opportunity of the stage actor to adjust to the audience during his performance, since he does not present his performance to the audience in person. This permits the audience to take the position of a critic, without experiencing any personal contact with the actor. The audience's identification with the actor is really an identification with the camera. Consequently the audience takes the position of the camera; its approach is that of testing.[2] This is not the approach to which cult values may be exposed.

IX

For the film, what matters primarily is that the actor represents himself to the public before the camera, rather than representing someone else. One of the first to sense the actor's metamorphosis by this form of testing was Pirandello.[3] Though his remarks on the subject in his novel *Si Gira* were limited to the negative aspects of the question and the silent film only, this hardly impairs their validity. For in this respect, the sound film did not change anything essential. What matters is that the part is acted not for an audience but for a mechanical contrivance—in the case of the sound film, for two of them. "The film actor," wrote Pirandello, "feels as if in exile—exiled not only from the stage but also from himself. With a vague sense of discomfort he feels inexplicable emptiness: his body loses its corporeality, it evaporates, it is deprived of reality, life, voice, and the noises caused by his moving about, in order to be changed into a mute image, flickering an instant on the screen, then vanishing into silence. . . . The projector will play with

1. Franz Werfel, "Ein Summernachtstraum, Ein Film von Shakespeare und Reinhardt" ["*A Midsummer Night's Dream*, A Film by Shakespeare and Reinhardt"], *Neues Wiener Journal*, cited in *Lu* 15, November 1935 [translator's note].

2. The expansion of the field of the testable which mechanical equipment brings about for the actor corresponds to the extraordinary expansion of the field of the testable brought about for the individual through economic conditions. Thus, vocational aptitude tests become constantly more important. What matters in these tests are segmental performances of the individual. The film shot and the vocational aptitude test are taken before a committee of experts. The camera director in the studio occupies a place identical with that of the examiner during aptitude tests [Benjamin's note].

3. Luigi Pirandello (1867–1936), Italian dramatist and novelist; his novel *Si Gira* (1915) was translated as *Shoot!* in 1926.

his shadow before the public and he himself must be content to play before the camera." This situation might also be characterized as follows: for the first time—and this is the effect of the film—man has to operate with his whole living person, yet forgoing its aura. For aura is tied to his presence; there can be no replica of it. The aura which, on the stage, emanates from Macbeth, cannot be separated for the spectators from that of the actor. However, the singularity of the shot in the studio is that the camera is substituted for the public. Consequently, the aura that envelops the actor vanishes, and with it the aura of the figure he portrays.

It is not surprising that it should be a dramatist such as Pirandello who, in characterizing the film, inadvertently touches on the very crisis in which we see the theater. Any thorough study proves that there is indeed no greater contrast than that of the stage play to a work of art that is completely subject to or, like the film, founded in, mechanical reproduction. Experts have long recognized that in the film "the greatest effects are almost always obtained by 'acting' as little as possible. . . ." In 1932 Rudolf Arnheim saw "the latest trend . . . in treating the actor as a stage prop chosen for its characteristics and . . . inserted at the proper place."[4] With this idea something else is closely connected. The stage actor identifies himself with the character of his role. The film actor very often is denied this opportunity. His creation is by no means all of a piece; it is composed of many separate performances. Besides certain fortuitous considerations, such as cost of studio, availability of fellow players, décor, etc., there are elementary necessities of equipment that split the actor's work into a series of mountable episodes. In particular, lighting and its installation require the presentation of an event that, on the screen, unfolds as a rapid and unified scene, in a sequence of separate shootings which may take hours at the studio; not to mention more obvious montage. Thus a jump from the window can be shot in the studio as a jump from a scaffold, and the ensuing flight, if need be, can be shot weeks later when outdoor scenes are taken. Far more paradoxical cases can easily be construed. Let us assume that an actor is supposed to be startled by a knock at the door. If his reaction is not satisfactory, the director can resort to an expedient: when the actor happens to be at the studio again he has a shot fired behind him without his being forewarned of it. The frightened reaction can be shot now and be cut into the screen version. Nothing more strikingly shows that art has left the realm of the "beautiful semblance" which, so far, had been taken to be the only sphere where art could thrive.

X

The feeling of strangeness that overcomes the actor before the camera, as Pirandello describes it, is basically of the same kind as the estrangement felt

4. Rudolf Arnheim, *Film as Art* (Berkeley: University of California Press, 1957), pp. 138–39. If the actor thus becomes a stage property, this latter, on the other hand, frequently functions as actor. At least it is not unusual for the film to assign a role to the stage property. [For example,] a clock that is working will always be a disturbance on the stage. There it cannot be permitted its function of measuring time. Even in a naturalistic play, astronomical time would clash with theatrical time. Under these circumstances it is highly revealing that the film can, whenever appropriate, use time as measured by a clock. From this more than from many other touches it may clearly be recognized that under certain circumstances each and every prop in a film may assume important functions [Benjamin's note]. Arnheim (b. 1904), German-born writer on art and visual thinkings; *Film als Kunst* was originally published in 1932.

before one's own image in the mirror. But now the reflected image has become separable, transportable. And where is it transported? Before the public.[5] Never for a moment does the screen actor cease to be conscious of this fact. While facing the camera he knows that ultimately he will face the public, the consumers who constitute the market. This market, where he offers not only his labor but also his whole self, his heart and soul, is beyond his reach. During the shooting he has as little contact with it as any article made in a factory. This may contribute to that oppression, that new anxiety which, according to Pirandello, grips the actor before the camera. The film responds to the shriveling of the aura with an artificial build-up of the "personality" outside the studio. The cult of the movie star, fostered by the money of the film industry, preserves not the unique aura of the person but the "spell of the personality," the phony spell of a commodity. So long as the movie-makers' capital sets the fashion, as a rule no other revolutionary merit can be accredited to today's film than the promotion of a revolutionary criticism of traditional concepts of art. We do not deny that in some cases today's films can also promote revolutionary criticism of social conditions, even of the distribution of property. However, our present study is no more specifically concerned with this than is the film production of Western Europe.

It is inherent in the technique of the film as well as that of sports that everybody who witnesses its accomplishments is somewhat of an expert. This is obvious to anyone listening to a group of newspaper boys leaning on their bicycles and discussing the outcome of a bicycle race. It is not for nothing that newspaper publishers arrange races for their delivery boys. These arouse great interest among the participants, for the victor has an opportunity to rise from delivery boy to professional racer. Similarly, the newsreel offers everyone the opportunity to rise from passer-by to movie extra. In this way any man might even find himself part of a work of art, as witness Vertoff's *Three Songs About Lenin* or Ivens' *Borinage*.[6] Any man today can lay claim to being filmed. This claim can best be elucidated by a comparative look at the historical situation of contemporary literature.

For centuries a small number of writers were confronted by many thousands of readers. This changed toward the end of the last century. With the increasing extension of the press, which kept placing new political, religious, scientific, professional, and local organs before the readers, an increasing number of readers became writers—at first, occasional ones. It began with the daily press opening to its readers space for "letters to the editor." And today there is hardly a gainfully employed European who could not, in principle, find an opportunity to publish somewhere or other comments on

5. The change noted here in the method of exhibition caused by mechanical reproduction applies to politics as well. The present crisis of the bourgeois democracies comprises a crisis of the conditions which determine the public presentation of the rulers. Democracies exhibit a member of government directly and personally before the nation's representatives. Parliament is his public. Since the innovations of camera and recording equipment make it possible for the orator to become audible and visible to an unlimited number of persons, the presentation of the man of politics before camera and recording equipment becomes paramount. Parliaments, as much as theaters, are deserted. Radio and film not only affect the function of the professional actor but likewise the function of those who also exhibit themselves before this mechanical equipment, those who govern. Though their tasks may be different, the change affects equally the actor and the ruler. The trend is toward establishing controllable and transferrable skills under certain social conditions. This results in a new selection, a selection before the equipment from which the star and the dictator emerge victorious [Benjamin's note].

6. A 1933 film directed by Dutch director Joris Ivens (1898–1989). Dziga Vertoff (1896–1959), early Russian film director; *Three Songs about Lenin* appeared in 1934.

his work, grievances, documentary reports, or that sort of thing. Thus, the distinction between author and public is about to lose its basic character. The difference becomes merely functional; it may vary from case to case. At any moment the reader is ready to turn into a writer. As expert, which he had to become willy-nilly in an extremely specialized work process, even if only in some minor respect, the reader gains access to authorship. In the Soviet Union work itself is given a voice. To present it verbally is part of a man's ability to perform the work. Literary license is now founded on polytechnic rather than specialized training and thus becomes common property.[7]

All this can easily be applied to the film, where transitions that in literature took centuries have come about in a decade. In cinematic practice, particularly in Russia, this change-over has partially become established reality. Some of the players whom we meet in Russian films are not actors in our sense but people who portray *themselves*—and primarily in their own work process. In Western Europe the capitalistic exploitation of the film denies consideration to modern man's legitimate claim to being reproduced. Under these circumstances the film industry is trying hard to spur the interest of the masses through illusion-promoting spectacles and dubious speculations.

XI

The shooting of a film, especially of a sound film, affords a spectacle unimaginable anywhere at any time before this. It presents a process in which it is impossible to assign to a spectator a viewpoint which would exclude from the actual scene such extraneous accessories as camera equipment, lighting machinery, staff assistants, etc.—unless his eye were on a line parallel with the lens. This circumstance, more than any other, renders super-

7. The privileged character of the respective techniques is lost. Aldous Huxley writes: "Advances in technology have led . . . to vulgarity. . . . Process reproduction and the rotary press have made possible the indefinite multiplication of writing and pictures. Universal education and relatively high wages have created an enormous public who know how to read and can afford to buy reading and pictorial matter. A great industry has been called into existence in order to supply these commodities. Now, artistic talent is a very rare phenomenon; whence it follows . . . that, at every epoch and in all countries, most art has been bad. But the proportion of trash in the total artistic output is greater now than at any other period. That it must be so is a matter of simple arithmetic. The population of Western Europe has a little more than doubled during the last century. But the amount of reading—and seeing—matter has increased, I should imagine, at least twenty and possibly fifty or even a hundred times. If there were n men of talent in a population of x millions, there will presumably be 2n men of talent among 2x millions. The situation may be summed up thus. For every page of print and pictures published a century ago, twenty or perhaps even a hundred pages are published today. But for every man of talent then living, there are now only two men of talent. It may be of course that, thanks to universal education, many potential talents which in the past would have been stillborn are now enabled to realize themselves. Let us assume, then, that there are now three or even four men of talent to every one of earlier times. It still remains true to say that the consumption of reading—and seeing—matter has far outstripped the natural production of gifted writers and draughtsmen. It is the same with hearing-matter. Prosperity, the gramophone and the radio have created an audience of hearers who consume an amount of hearing-matter that has increased out of all proportion to the increase of population and the consequent natural increase of talented musicians. It follows from all this that in all the arts the output of trash is both absolutely and relatively greater than it was in the past; and that it must remain greater for just so long as the world continues to consume the present inordinate quantities of reading-matter, seeing-matter, and hearing-matter." Aldous Huxley, *Beyond the Mexique Bay: A Traveller's Journal* (1934; reprint, London, 1949), pp. 274ff. The mode of observation is obviously not progressive [Benjamin's note]. Huxley (1894–1963), English novelist and essayist.

ficial and insignificant any possible similarity between a scene in the studio and one on the stage. In the theater one is well aware of the place from which the play cannot immediately be detected as illusionary. There is no such place for the movie scene that is being shot. Its illusionary nature is that of the second degree, the result of cutting. That is to say, in the studio the mechanical equipment has penetrated so deeply into reality that its pure aspect freed from the foreign substance of equipment is the result of a special procedure, namely, the shooting by the specially adjusted camera and the mounting of the shot together with other similar ones. The equipment-free aspect of reality here has become the height of artifice; the sight of immediate reality has become an orchid in the land of technology.

Even more revealing is the comparison of these circumstances, which differ so much from those of the theater, with the situation in painting. Here the question is: How does the cameraman compare with the painter? To answer this we take recourse to an analogy with a surgical operation. The surgeon represents the polar opposite of the magician. The magician heals a sick person by the laying on of hands; the surgeon cuts into the patient's body. The magician maintains the natural distance between the patient and himself; though he reduces it very slightly by the laying on of hands, he greatly increases it by virtue of his authority. The surgeon does exactly the reverse; he greatly diminishes the distance between himself and the patient by penetrating into the patient's body, and increases it but little by the caution with which his hand moves among the organs. In short, in contrast to the magician—who is still hidden in the medical practitioner—the surgeon at the decisive moment abstains from facing the patient man to man; rather, it is through the operation that he penetrates into him.

Magician and surgeon compare to painter and cameraman. The painter maintains in his work a natural distance from reality, the cameraman penetrates deeply into its web. There is a tremendous difference between the pictures they obtain. That of the painter is a total one, that of the cameraman consists of multiple fragments which are assembled under a new law. Thus, for contemporary man the representation of reality by the film is incomparably more significant than that of the painter, since it offers, precisely because of the thoroughgoing permeation of reality with mechanical equipment, an aspect of reality which is free of all equipment. And that is what one is entitled to ask from a work of art.

reactionary vs progressive response.

XII

Mechanical reproduction of art changes the reaction of the masses toward art. The reactionary attitude toward a Picasso[8] painting changes into the progressive reaction toward a Chaplin movie. The progressive reaction is characterized by the direct, intimate fusion of visual and emotional enjoyment with the orientation of the expert. Such fusion is of great social significance. The greater the decrease in the social significance of an art form, the sharper the distinction between criticism and enjoyment by the public. The conventional is uncritically enjoyed, and the truly new is criticized with aversion. With regard to the screen, the critical and the receptive attitudes

8. Pablo Picasso (1881–1973), Spanish-born painter who was a pioneer of modern art.

of the public coincide. The decisive reason for this is that individual reactions are predetermined by the mass audience response they are about to produce, and this is nowhere more pronounced than in the film. The moment these responses become manifest they control each other. Again, the comparison with painting is fruitful. A painting has always had an excellent chance to be viewed by one person or by a few. The simultaneous contemplation of paintings by a large public, such as developed in the nineteenth century, is an early symptom of the crisis of painting, a crisis which was by no means occasioned exclusively by photography but rather in a relatively independent manner by the appeal of art works to the masses.

Painting simply is in no position to present an object for simultaneous collective experience, as it was possible for architecture at all times, for the epic poem in the past, and for the movie today. Although this circumstance in itself should not lead one to conclusions about the social role of painting, it does constitute a serious threat as soon as painting, under special conditions and, as it were, against its nature, is confronted directly by the masses. In the churches and monasteries of the Middle Ages and at the princely courts up to the end of the eighteenth century, a collective reception of paintings did not occur simultaneously, but by graduated and hierarchized mediation. The change that has come about is an expression of the particular conflict in which painting was implicated by the mechanical reproducibility of paintings. Although paintings began to be publicly exhibited in galleries and salons, there was no way for the masses to organize and control themselves in their reception. Thus the same public which responds in a progressive manner toward a grotesque film is bound to respond in a reactionary manner to surrealism.

XIII

The characteristics of the film lie not only in the manner in which man presents himself to mechanical equipment but also in the manner in which, by means of this apparatus, man can represent his environment. A glance at occupational psychology illustrates the testing capacity of the equipment. Psychoanalysis illustrates it in a different perspective. The film has enriched our field of perception with methods which can be illustrated by those of Freudian theory. Fifty years ago, a slip of the tongue passed more or less unnoticed. Only exceptionally may such a slip have revealed dimensions of depth in a conversation which had seemed to be taking its course on the surface. Since the *Psychopathology of Everyday Life*[9] things have changed. This book isolated and made analyzable things which had heretofore floated along unnoticed in the broad stream of perception. For the entire spectrum of optical, and now also acoustical, perception the film has brought about a similar deepening of apperception. It is only an obverse of this fact that behavior items shown in a movie can be analyzed much more precisely and from more points of view than those presented on paintings or on the stage. As compared with painting, filmed behavior lends itself more readily to analysis because of its incomparably more precise statements of the situation. In

9. An early work (1904) of SIGMUND FREUD (1856–1939), the Austrian founder of psychoanalysis; it discusses how what has come to be called a "Freudian slip" reveals unconscious feelings.

comparison with the stage scene, the filmed behavior item lends itself more readily to analysis because it can be isolated more easily. This circumstance derives its chief importance from its tendency to promote the mutual penetration of art and science. Actually, of a screened behavior item which is neatly brought out in a certain situation, like a muscle of a body, it is difficult to say which is more fascinating, its artistic value or its value for science. To demonstrate the identity of the artistic and scientific uses of photography which heretofore usually were separated will be one of the revolutionary functions of the film.

By close-ups of the things around us, by focusing on hidden details of familiar objects, by exploring commonplace milieus under the ingenious guidance of the camera, the film, on the one hand, extends our comprehension of the necessities which rule our lives; on the other hand, it manages to assure us of an immense and unexpected field of action. Our taverns and our metropolitan streets, our offices and furnished rooms, our railroad stations and our factories appeared to have us locked up hopelessly. Then came the film and burst this prison-world asunder by the dynamite of the tenth of a second,[1] so that now, in the midst of its far-flung ruins and debris, we calmly and adventurously go traveling. With the close-up, space expands; with slow motion, movement is extended. The enlargement of a snapshot does not simply render more precise what in any case was visible, though unclear: it reveals entirely new structural formations of the subject. So, too, slow motion not only presents familiar qualities of movement but reveals in them entirely unknown ones "which, far from looking like retarded rapid movements, give the effect of singularly gliding, floating, supernatural motions."[2] Evidently a different nature opens itself to the camera than opens to the naked eye—if only because an unconsciously penetrated space is substituted for a space consciously explored by man. Even if one has a general knowledge of the way people walk, one knows nothing of a person's posture during the fractional second of a stride. The act of reaching for a lighter or a spoon is familiar routine, yet we hardly know what really goes on between hand and metal, not to mention how this fluctuates with our moods. Here the camera intervenes with the resources of its lowerings and liftings, its interruptions and isolations, its extensions and accelerations, its enlargements and reductions. The camera introduces us to unconscious optics as does psychoanalysis to unconscious impulses.

XIV

One of the foremost tasks of art has always been the creation of a demand which could be fully satisfied only later.[3] The history of every art form shows

1. That is, the viewing time of the individual frames of a film.
2. Arnheim, pp. 116–17 [translator's note].
3. "The work of Art," says André Breton, "is valuable only in so far as it is vibrated by the reflexes of the future." Indeed, every developed art form intersects three lines of development. Technology works toward a certain form of art. Before the advent of the film there were photo booklets with pictures which flitted by the onlooker upon pressure of the thumb, thus portraying a boxing bout or a tennis match. Then there were the slot machines in bazaars; their picture sequences were produced by the turning of a crank.

Secondly, the traditional art forms in certain phases of their development strenuously work toward effects which later are effortlessly attained by the new ones. Before the rise of the movie the Dadaists' performances tried to create an audience reaction which Chaplin later evoked in a more natural way.

Thirdly, unspectacular social changes often promote a change in receptivity which will benefit the new art form. Before the movie had begun to cre-

critical epochs in which a certain art form aspires to effects which could be fully obtained only with a changed technical standard, that is to say, in a new art form. The extravagances and crudities of art which thus appear, particularly in the so-called decadent epochs, actually arise from the nucleus of its richest historical energies. In recent years, such barbarisms were abundant in Dadaism. It is only now that its impulse becomes discernible: Dadaism attempted to create by pictorial—and literary—means the effects which the public today seeks in the film.

Every fundamentally new, pioneering creation of demands will carry beyond its goal. Dadaism did so to the extent that it sacrificed the market values which are so characteristic of the film in favor of higher ambitions—though of course it was not conscious of such intentions as here described. The Dadaists attached much less importance to the sales value of their work than to its uselessness for contemplative immersion. The studied degradation of their material was not the least of their means to achieve this uselessness. Their poems are "word salad"[4] containing obscenities and every imaginable waste product of language. The same is true of their paintings, on which they mounted buttons and tickets. What they intended and achieved was a relentless destruction of the aura of their creations, which they branded as reproductions with the very means of production. Before a painting of Arp's or a poem by August Stramm it is impossible to take time for contemplation and evaluation as one would before a canvas of Derain's or a poem by Rilke.[5] In the decline of middle-class society, contemplation became a school for asocial behavior; it was countered by distraction as a variant of social conduct. Dadaistic activities actually assured a rather vehement distraction by making works of art the center of scandal. One requirement was foremost: to outrage the public.

From an alluring appearance or persuasive structure of sound the work of art of the Dadaists became an instrument of ballistics. It hit the spectator like a bullet, it happened to him, thus acquiring a tactile quality. It promoted a demand for the film, the distracting element of which is also primarily tactile, being based on changes of place and focus which periodically assail the spectator. Let us compare the screen on which a film unfolds with the canvas of a painting. The painting invites the spectator to contemplation; before it the spectator can abandon himself to his associations. Before the

---

ate its public, pictures that were no longer immobile captivated an assembled audience in the so-called *Kaiserpanorama*. Here the public assembled before a screen into which stereoscopes were mounted, one to each beholder. By a mechanical process individual pictures appeared briefly before the stereoscopes, then made way for others. Edison still had to use similar devices in presenting the first movie strip before the film screen and projection were known. This strip was presented to a small public which stared into the apparatus in which the succession of pictures was reeling off. Incidentally, the institution of the *Kaiserpanorama* shows very clearly a dialectic of the development. Shortly before the movie turned the reception of pictures into a collective one, the individual viewing of pictures in these swiftly outmoded establishments came into play once more with an intensity comparable to that of the ancient priest beholding the statue of a divinity in the cella [Benjamin's note]. Dadaists: members of a literary and artistic movement, founded in 1916, that stressed irrationality and anarchy and mocked normal aesthetic conventions. Breton (1896–1966), French artist and writer who broke with dadaism in 1921 and founded surrealism in 1924. Thomas Alva Edison (1847–1931), American inventor, holder of patents for the microphone (1877), the phonograph (1878), the incandescent lamp (1879), and the Kinetoscope (1889), the single-view machine described by Benjamin; he also experimented with synchronizing motion pictures and sound.

4. Incoherent speech or writing made up of real and invented words.

5. Rainer Maria Rilke (1875–1926), German poet. Jean Arp (1887–1966), French sculptor, one of the founders of dadaism. Stramm (1874–1915), German poet. André Derain (1880–1954), French painter.

movie frame he cannot do so. No sooner has his eye grasped a scene than it is already changed. It cannot be arrested. Duhamel, who detests the film and knows nothing of its significance, though something of its structure, notes this circumstance as follows: "I can no longer think what I want to think. My thoughts have been replaced by moving images."[6] The spectator's process of association in view of these images is indeed interrupted by their constant, sudden change. This constitutes the shock effect of the film, which, like all shocks, should be cushioned by heightened presence of mind.[7] By means of its technical structure, the film has taken the physical shock effect out of the wrappers in which Dadaism had, as it were, kept it inside the moral shock effect.[8]

XV

The mass is a matrix from which all traditional behavior toward works of art issues today in a new form. Quantity has been transmuted into quality. The greatly increased mass of participants has produced a change in the mode of participation. The fact that the new mode of participation first appeared in a disreputable form must not confuse the spectator. Yet some people have launched spirited attacks against precisely this superficial aspect. Among these, Duhamel has expressed himself in the most radical manner. What he objects to most is the kind of participation which the movie elicits from the masses. Duhamel calls the movie "a pastime for helots, a diversion for uneducated, wretched, worn-out creatures who are consumed by their worries . . . , a spectacle which requires no concentration and presupposes no intelligence . . . , which kindles no light in the heart and awakens no hope other than the ridiculous one of someday becoming a 'star' in Los Angeles."[9] Clearly, this is at bottom the same ancient lament that the masses seek distraction whereas art demands concentration from the spectator. That is a commonplace. The question remains whether it provides a platform for the analysis of the film. A closer look is needed here. Distraction and concentration form polar opposites which may be stated as follows: A man who concentrates before a work of art is absorbed by it. He enters into this work of art the way legend tells of the Chinese painter when he viewed his finished painting. In contrast, the distracted mass absorbs the work of art. This is most obvious with regard to buildings. Architecture has always represented the prototype of a work of art the reception of which is consum-

6. Georges Duhamel, *Scènes de la vie future* [*Scenes from the Future Life*] (Paris, 1930), p. 52 [translator's note]. Duhamel (1884–1966), French novelist and poet.

7. The film is the art form that is in keeping with the increased threat to his life which modern man has to face. Man's need to expose himself to shock effects is his adjustment to the dangers threatening him. The film corresponds to profound changes in the apperceptive apparatus—changes that are experienced on an individual scale by the man in the street in big-city traffic, on a historical scale by every present-day citizen [Benjamin's note].

8. As for Dadaism, insights important for Cubism and Futurism are to be gained from the movie. Both appear as deficient attempts of art to accommodate the pervasion of reality by the apparatus. In contrast to the film, these schools did not try to use the apparatus as such for the artistic presentation of reality, but aimed at some sort of alloy in the joint presentation of reality and apparatus. In Cubism, the premonition that this apparatus will be structurally based on optics plays a dominant part; in Futurism, it is the premonition of the effects of this apparatus which are brought out by the rapid sequence of the film strip [Benjamin's note]. Cubism and futurism are movements that both began before World War I: cubism, a reaction against sentimental and realistic painting, was concerned mainly with abstract forms; futurism, a radical movement in art and literature, glorified speed, war, and machinery and advocated rebellion.

9. Duhamel, p. 58 [translator's note].

mated by a collectivity in a state of distraction. The laws of its reception are most instructive.

Buildings have been man's companions since primeval times. Many art forms have developed and perished. Tragedy begins with the Greeks, is extinguished with them, and after centuries its "rules" only are revived.[1] The epic poem, which had its origin in the youth of nations, expires in Europe at the end of the Renaissance. Panel painting is a creation of the Middle Ages, and nothing guarantees its uninterrupted existence. But the human need for shelter is lasting. Architecture has never been idle. Its history is more ancient than that of any other art, and its claim to being a living force has significance in every attempt to comprehend the relationship of the masses to art. Buildings are appropriated in a twofold manner: by use and by perception—or rather, by touch and sight. Such appropriation cannot be understood in terms of the attentive concentration of a tourist before a famous building. On the tactile side there is no counterpart to contemplation on the optical side. Tactile appropriation is accomplished not so much by attention as by habit. As regards architecture, habit determines to a large extent even optical reception. The latter, too, occurs much less through rapt attention than by noticing the object in incidental fashion. This mode of appropriation, developed with reference to architecture, in certain circumstances acquires canonical value. For the tasks which face the human apparatus of perception at the turning points of history cannot be solved by optical means, that is, by contemplation, alone. They are mastered gradually by habit, under the guidance of tactile appropriation.

The distracted person, too, can form habits. More, the ability to master certain tasks in a state of distraction proves that their solution has become a matter of habit. Distraction as provided by art presents a covert control of the extent to which new tasks have become soluble by apperception. Since, moreover, individuals are tempted to avoid such tasks, art will tackle the most difficult and most important ones where it is able to mobilize the masses. Today it does so in the film. Reception in a state of distraction, which is increasing noticeably in all fields of art and is symptomatic of profound changes in apperception, finds in the film its true means of exercise. The film with its shock effect meets this mode of reception halfway. The film makes the cult value recede into the background not only by putting the public in the position of the critic, but also by the fact that at the movies this position requires no attention. The public is an examiner, but an absent-minded one.

Epilogue

The growing proletarianization of modern man and the increasing formation of masses are two aspects of the same process. Fascism attempts to organize the newly created proletarian masses without affecting the property structure which the masses strive to eliminate. Fascism sees its salvation in giving these masses not their right, but instead a chance to express themselves.[2] The masses have a right to change property relations; Fascism seeks

1. Tragedy developed from Greek religious festivals of Dionysus; Aristotle described the genre in his *Poetics*, but its "rules" were laid down by neoclassical critics and playwrights of the 17th and 18th century (e.g., see PIERRE CORNEILLE, above).

2. One technical feature is significant here, especially with regard to newsreels, the propagandist importance of which can hardly be overestimated. Mass reproduction is aided especially by the reproduction of masses. In big parades and monster ral-

to give them an expression while preserving property. The logical result of Fascism is the introduction of aesthetics into political life. The violation of the masses, whom Fascism, with its *Führer* cult, forces to their knees, has its counterpart in the violation of an apparatus which is pressed into the production of ritual values.

All efforts to render politics aesthetic culminate in one thing: war. War and war only can set a goal for mass movements on the largest scale while respecting the traditional property system. This is the political formula for the situation. The technological formula may be stated as follows: Only war makes it possible to mobilize all of today's technical resources while maintaining the property system. It goes without saying that the Fascist apotheosis of war does not employ such arguments. Still, Marinetti[3] says in his manifesto on the Ethiopian colonial war: "For twenty-seven years we Futurists have rebelled against the branding of war as antiaesthetic. . . . Accordingly we state: . . . War is beautiful because it establishes man's dominion over the subjugated machinery by means of gas masks, terrifying megaphones, flame throwers, and small tanks. War is beautiful because it initiates the dreamt-of metalization of the human body. War is beautiful because it enriches a flowering meadow with the fiery orchids of machine guns. War is beautiful because it combines the gunfire, the cannonades, the cease-fire, the scents, and the stench of putrefaction into a symphony. War is beautiful because it creates new architecture, like that of the big tanks, the geometrical formation flights, the smoke spirals from burning villages, and many others . . . Poets and artists of Futurism! . . . remember these principles of an aesthetics of war so that your struggle for a new literature and a new graphic art . . . may be illumined by them!"

This manifesto has the virtue of clarity. Its formulations deserve to be accepted by dialecticians. To the latter, the aesthetics of today's war appears as follows: If the natural utilization of productive forces is impeded by the property system, the increase in technical devices, in speed, and in the sources of energy will press for an unnatural utilization, and this is found in war. The destructiveness of war furnishes proof that society has not been mature enough to incorporate technology as its organ, that technology has not been sufficiently developed to cope with the elemental forces of society. The horrible features of imperialistic warfare are attributable to the discrepancy between the tremendous means of production and their inadequate utilization in the process of production—in other words, to unemployment and the lack of markets. Imperialistic war is a rebellion of technology which collects, in the form of "human material," the claims to which society has denied its natural material. Instead of draining rivers, society directs a human stream into a bed of trenches; instead of dropping seeds from airplanes, it

lies, in sports events, and in war, all of which nowadays are captured by camera and sound recording, the masses are brought face to face with themselves. This process, whose significance need not be stressed, is intimately connected with the development of the techniques of reproduction and photography. Mass movements are usually discerned more clearly by a camera than by the naked eye. A bird's-eye view best captures gatherings of hundreds of thousands. And even though such a view may be as accessible to the human eye as it is to the camera, the image received by the eye cannot be enlarged the way a negative is enlarged. This means that mass movements, including war, constitute a form of human behavior which particularly favors mechanical equipment [Benjamin's note].

3. Filippo Tommaso Marinetti (1876–1944), Italian poet and novelist who in 1909 founded futurism; for a time, the movement was endorsed by Italian Fascists. "The Ethiopian colonial war": an ambiguously worded 1889 treaty led Italy to claim Ethiopia as its protectorate; the war of 1895–96 forced Italy to recognize Ethiopia's independence, but in 1935 Italy invaded the country.

drops incendiary bombs over cities; and through gas warfare the aura is abolished in a new way.

"Fiat ars—pereat mundus,"[4] says Fascism, and as Marinetti admits, expects war to supply the artistic gratification of a sense perception that has been changed by technology. This is evidently the consummation of *"l'art pour l'art."* Mankind, which in Homer's time was an object of contemplation for the Olympian gods, now is one for itself. Its self-alienation has reached such a degree that it can experience its own destruction as an aesthetic pleasure of the first order. This is the situation of politics which Fascism is rendering aesthetic. Communism responds by politicizing art.

1936

4. Let art be made, let the world perish (Latin).

MIKHAIL M. BAKHTIN
1895–1975

Proclaimed by TZVETAN TODOROV as perhaps the greatest twentieth-century theorist of literature, M. M. Bakhtin, since his discovery in the 1970s, has been acclaimed by literary critics across a wide theoretical and political spectrum. He has been called a formalist, a Marxist, a Christian humanist, a conservative, and a radical; because his work intersects in eccentric ways with so many of the critical orthodoxies of twentieth-century literary criticism, it resists easy classification.

Almost everything about Bakhtin's life and writing is colored by the fact that his greatest period of productivity coincided with the Russian Revolution, the ensuing civil war (1918–21), and the repressive Soviet regime under Joseph Stalin. Lacking Communist Party credentials, he labored most of his adult life in obscurity, a circumstance that probably saved his life at a time when his close—and better connected—friends were disappearing into death camps. The circumstances of Bakhtin's life make it sometimes difficult to verify the authorship and chronology of his writings. Certain works written during his youth in the 1920s were not published until late in his life or after his death, and controversies continue over three disputed books from the 1920s that appeared under the names of his colleagues Valentin Vološinov and Pavel Medvedev, held by some to be the works of Bakhtin himself. Yet these difficulties in separating Bakhtin's voice from those of others are of a piece with his own philosophical beliefs about the dialogic nature of language. As he wrote in a note that was later published in his *Speech Genres and Other Late Essays*, "Quests for my own words are quests for a word that is not my own."

Born in the Russian town of Orel, Bakhtin grew up in Vilnius and later Odessa. He earned a degree in classics and philology from the University of Petrograd in 1918. Working as a schoolteacher in Nevel in western Russia during the civil war between the Red Army and the anti-Bolshevist White armies, he first met the group of intellectuals who would become part of his circle and within whose wide-ranging discussions Bakhtin would formulate the critical concepts that were to dominate his thinking for the rest of his life. In 1920 Bakhtin settled in Vitebsk, where his circle, which by now included Vološinov and Medvedev, continued to meet. In 1924 Bakhtin moved back to Petrograd (or St. Petersburg), now renamed Leningrad; there in January 1929 he was arrested and imprisoned for alleged antigovernment activity and the Socratic crime of "corrupting the young." In prison he suffered from health problems caused by chronic osteomyelitis, a painful inflammation of the bone marrow. He was sentenced to ten years in a labor camp, but on the intervention of friends, the sentence was commuted to six years' internal exile in Kazakhstan. In 1936, his exile over, he taught at Mordovia Pedagogical Institute in Saransk until new purges forced him to resign. He moved to a small town outside of Moscow where his worsening osteomyelitis led to the amputation of his right leg. After that surgery, Bakhtin had difficulty finding permanent employment, though he occasionally delivered lectures at the Gorky Institute of World Literature.

In the 1930s and 1940s Bakhtin began to write a dissertation on the French writer François Rabelais (1490–1553), as well as a book on novels that chronicle the main character's maturation and education (the Bildungsroman). World War II interrupted his work on the dissertation, and a shortage of cigarette paper led Bakhtin to sacrifice pages from the book on the Bildungsroman to his nicotine habit; only fragments of this book survive. Following the war, Bakhtin was allowed to return to his university position in Saransk, and to his unfinished dissertation on Rabelais. Although he was finally granted the doctoral degree, he could not publish his dissertation; it remained unread until it was discovered in the Gorky Institute's archives by graduate students in the early 1960s. After Stalin's death in 1953, Bakhtin's scholarly fortunes began to rise even as his health began to decline. In addition to osteomyelitis, he also suffered from emphysema caused by his heavy smoking. By the time of his death from complications of emphysema, he had become something of a cult figure in Russia. In the 1970s his reputation spread to Paris through the work of Eastern European émigrés such as JULIA KRISTEVA and Tzvetan Todorov; from there in the 1980s it reached North America and England, where his work had significant impact.

Bakhtin's earliest writings, in such essays as "Towards a Philosophy of the Act" (1919, published 1986) and "Author and Hero in Aesthetic Activity" (1919, published 1975), are densely philosophical and heavily indebted to IMMANUEL KANT (1724–1804). Although these lengthy essays exhibit a keen interest in phenomenology and the intersubjective nature of language, the publications of the Bakhtin Circle from the late 1920s defined the problems of language that would occupy Bakhtin for the rest of his life. In 1926 Vološinov published *Freudianism: A Marxist Critique*, and Medvedev followed in 1928 with *The Formal Method in Literary Scholarship*. In 1929 Vološinov's *Marxism and the Philosophy of Language* appeared and also Bakhtin's *Problems of Dostoevsky's Poetics*, the only book to be published under his own name before Stalin's death. Critics wary of Marxism have attempted to distance Bakhtin from the work of his circle, arguing that he did not share the Communist sympathies of Vološinov and Medvedev (both members of the Communist Party; both disappeared during the political purges of the 1930s). But regardless of whether Bakhtin actually wrote the books ascribed to his two colleagues, as some have claimed, the influences among the members of the circle were undoubtedly strong and indelible. Bakhtin's words became inextricably and dialogically intertwined with those of his collaborators, whose thought influenced the key concepts he later developed in his celebrated writings on the novel.

Bakhtin's theory of the novel relies on three key concepts. The *carnivalesque*—an idea first introduced in *Rabelais and His World* (written in the 1930s and 1940s, published 1965)—is Bakhtin's term for those forms of unofficial culture (the early novel among them) that resist official culture, political oppression, and totalitarian order through laughter, parody, and "grotesque realism." In "Forms of Time and Chronotope in the Novel" (1937–38), he develops the influential term *chronotope* to describe the intrinsic connectedness of time and space and their central role in constituting literary genres. Finally and most significantly, the *dialogism* of language, the "intense interanimation and struggle between one's own and another's word," would come to dominate Bakhtin's thinking about language after 1926. This concept of the multivoiced nature of discourse received its fullest treatment in "Discourse in the

Novel" (1934–35), a key text for narrative, linguistic, and literary theory, from which we have taken our selection.

Bakhtin here addresses the limitations for literary studies of the abstract and formal analyses of literary technique widespread among critics during the interwar period. Traditional linguistics, stylistics, and literary theory—including the theory of the Russian formalists, represented by critics like BORIS EICHENBAUM—as well as contemporary Marxist philosophy of language (see LEON TROTSKY) and the new structural linguistics indebted to FERDINAND DE SAUSSURE, all fail to articulate an adequate account of the novel because they have not pursued a properly "sociological stylistics." The philosophy of language on which these inadequate critical methods are based posits, on the one hand, a unitary system of language—a system of more or less absolute norms that govern speech—and, on the other hand, an individual who is seen as the controlling "author" of discourse. Bakhtin calls such a view of language "monologic," and he argues that it is alien to the dynamics of the novel because it describes not real, living language but an abstraction created through self-conscious deliberation about language and cut off from the daily ideological activities of social life. Living language exhibits *heteroglossia,* the term Bakhtin famously uses to describe the "internal stratification" of language: the interplay among its social dialects, class dialects, professional jargons, languages of generations and age groups and of passing fads, "languages that serve the specific sociopolitical purposes of the day, even of the hour." Heteroglossia, which Bakhtin hails as the characteristic stylistic feature of the novel, celebrates not, as structuralism does, the systematic nature of language but the multiplicity of all those "centrifugal" forces at work in language, the variety of social speech types, and the diversity of voices interacting with one another.

Central to Bakhtin's theory of the novel is his belief that language is fundamentally dialogic. "Discourse in the Novel" offers his most elaborate analysis of "dialogism" and its relationship to style in the novel. Between any word and its object, between any word and its speaking subject, between any word and its active respondent(s), Bakhtin argues, there exists "an elastic environment of other, alien words about the same object"; and this "dialogically agitated and tension-filled environment of alien words, value judgments and accents" that weaves in and out of discourse in complex patterns finds its most artistic expression in the novel. Bakhtin celebrates the dialogics of the novel while criticizing the monologism of poetry, which characteristically aims for a unified and pure discourse. Although conflict, contradiction, and doubt may be present in the subject matter of poetry, they do not, according to Bakhtin, enter into the language of the poem itself, as they consistently do in the novel.

Bakhtin's theories can sometimes appear confusing and vague because his critical terminology often seems at once evaluative and descriptive; he regularly establishes his critical vocabulary by defining certain terms positively against related terms given negative valences. Thus the novel is opposed to poetry, the carnivalesque to official discourse, the dialogic to the monologic. These judgments have posed problems for critics who value those genres that Bakhtin most frequently derogates as monologic, especially poetry, the epic, and drama. Other critics object that it is not clear to what degree Bakhtin espouses a mimetic theory of literature, insofar as language for him seems less to represent or reflect reality than to refract and rework it.

Nevertheless, Bakhtin's work has been much admired and extended by scholars in many fields. Those in cultural studies have found two major contributions particularly useful. First, Bakhtin focuses on "language" as the utterances of speaking subjects: that is, as spoken "discourse" and not the impersonal, prevocal signifiers or rhetorical tropes posited by the influential structuralist and poststructuralist traditions. Second, he insists that discourse unfolds in a heteroglot, dialogic force field of conflicting interests and ideologies—with literary language being only one of many discursive strata and itself divided by generic, stylistic, professional, and other special features.

These Bakhtinian views, widely advocated by cultural studies scholars, promote a complex sociopoetics suited to a contemporary globalized world of diverse peoples, languages, and cultural forms.

BIBLIOGRAPHY

The standard Russian-language edition of Bakhtin's works, *Sobranie sochinenii*, edited by S. G. Bocharov and L. A. Gogotishvill (1996–), is projected to include seven volumes. The earliest works survive only in fragments, collected and translated into English by Vadim Liapunov as *Art and Answerability* (1990) and *Toward a Philosophy of the Act* (1993). *Problems of Dostoevsky's Poetics*, first published in 1929, was revised and reissued in Russian in 1963; Caryl Emerson translated it into English in 1984. Bakhtin's dissertation of the 1930s and 1940s, finally published in 1965, was translated by Hélène Iswolsky as *Rabelais and His World* (1968). The important group of lengthy essays Bakhtin wrote between 1934 and 1941—including "Discourse in the Novel"—was not published in Russia until 1973; they were translated by Caryl Emerson and Michael Holquist as *The Dialogic Imagination* (1981). Fragments of Bakhtin's late—and largely unfinished—works were collected in a Russian volume and translated into English as *Speech Genres and Other Late Essays* (1986). Works attributed to Bakhtin by some scholars though their title pages list other authors include V. N. Vološinov, *Freudianism: A Marxist Critique* (1926; trans. 1976); P. N. Medvedev, *The Formal Method in Literary Scholarship* (1928; trans. 1978); and Vološinov, *Marxism and the Philosophy of Language* (1929; trans. 1973).

The standard biography is Katerina Clark and Michael Holquist, *Mikhail Bakhtin* (1984). Gary Saul Morson edited one of the first English collections of essays, *Bakhtin: Essays and Dialogues on His Work* (1981), still valuable for its critical readings. Tzvetan Todorov, who, with Julia Kristeva, was instrumental in bringing Bakhtin's work to the attention of the West, provides a useful brief introduction to Bakhtinian dialogics in *Mikhail Bakhtin: The Dialogic Principle* (1984). Two collections of essays—*Bakhtin and Cultural Theory*, edited by Ken Hirschkop and David Shepherd (1989), and *Rethinking Bakhtin: Extensions and Challenges*, edited by Gary Saul Morson and Caryl Emerson (1989)—offer readings of Bakhtin across a range of theoretical and political positions. For the feminist reception of Bakhtin, see Dale Bauer and Susan McKinstry, *Feminism, Bakhtin, and the Dialogic* (1991). Michael Holquist's *Dialogism: Bakhtin and His World* (1991) provides a comprehensive overview of Bakhtin's work. Gary Saul Morson and Caryl Emerson's *Mikhail Bakhtin: Creation of a Prosaics* (1990) is the single most thorough and authoritative book-length study of Bakhtin's writing and should be the starting point for more advanced study of his work. Michael F. Bernard-Donals, in *Mikhail Bakhtin: Between Phenomenology and Marxism* (1994), examines Bakhtin in relation to these two influential schools of twentieth-century theory. With the end of the cold war in 1989, the work of Russian scholars on Bakhtin has become available for the first time, notably in *Face to Face: Bakhtin in Russia and the West*, edited by Carol Adlam (1997), which collects essays from a 1995 Bakhtin conference in Moscow. Sue Vice's *Introducing Bakhtin* (1997) may be a more accessible introduction than Todorov's for students new to Bakhtin's thought. For a retrospective on Bakhtin's works that places him in the context of twentieth-century Russian thought, see Caryl Emerson, *The First One Hundred Years of Mikhail Bakhtin* (1997), as well as *Critical Essays of Bakhtin*, edited by Emerson (1999). Joan Nordquist has compiled two useful bibliographies, *Mikhail Bakhtin* (1988) and *Mikhail Bakhtin II: A Bibliography* (1993).

From Discourse in the Novel[1]

The principal idea of this essay is that the study of verbal art can and must overcome the divorce between an abstract "formal" approach and an equally abstract "ideological" approach. Form and content in discourse are one, once we understand that verbal discourse is a social phenomenon—social throughout its entire range and in each and every of its factors, from the sound image to the furthest reaches of abstract meaning.

It is this idea that has motivated our emphasis on "the stylistics of genre." The separation of style and language from the question of genre has been largely responsible for a situation in which only individual and period-bound overtones of a style are the privileged subjects of study, while its basic social tone is ignored. The great historical destinies of genres are overshadowed by the petty vicissitudes of stylistic modifications, which in their turn are linked with individual artists and artistic movements. For this reason, stylistics has been deprived of an authentic philosophical and sociological approach to its problems; it has become bogged down in stylistic trivia; it is not able to sense behind the individual and period-bound shifts the great and anonymous destinies of artistic discourse itself. More often than not, stylistics defines itself as a stylistics of "private craftsmanship" and ignores the social life of discourse outside the artist's study, discourse in the open spaces of public squares, streets, cities and villages, of social groups, generations and epochs. Stylistics is concerned not with living discourse but with a histological specimen made from it, with abstract linguistic discourse in the service of an artist's individual creative powers. But these individual and tendentious overtones of style, cut off from the fundamentally social modes in which discourse lives, inevitably come across as flat and abstract in such a formulation and cannot therefore be studied in organic unity with a work's semantic components.

Modern Stylistics & the Novel

Before the twentieth century, problems associated with a stylistics of the novel had not been precisely formulated—such a formulation could only have resulted from a recognition of the stylistic uniqueness of novelistic (artistic-prose) discourse.

For a long time treatment of the novel was limited to little more than abstract ideological examination and publicistic commentary. Concrete questions of stylistics were either not treated at all or treated in passing and in an arbitrary way: the discourse of artistic prose was either understood as being poetic in the narrow sense, and had the categories of traditional stylistics (based on the study of tropes) uncritically applied to it, or else such questions were limited to empty, evaluative terms for the characterization of language, such as "expressiveness," "imagery," "force," "clarity" and so on—without providing these concepts with any stylistic significance, however vague and tentative.

1. Translated by Caryl Emerson and Michael Holquist, who occasionally retain the original Russian words or add information in brackets.

Toward the end of the last century, as a counterweight to this abstract ideological way of viewing things, interest began to grow in the concrete problems of artistic craftsmanship in prose, in the problems of novel and short-story technique. However, in questions of stylistics the situation did not change in the slightest; attention was concentrated almost exclusively on problems of composition (in the broad sense of the word). But, as before, the peculiarities of the stylistic life of discourse in the novel (and in the short story as well) lacked an approach that was both principled and at the same time concrete (one is impossible without the other); the same arbitrary judgmental observations about language—in the spirit of traditional stylistics—continued to reign supreme, and they totally overlooked the authentic nature of artistic prose.

There is a highly characteristic and widespread point of view that sees novelistic discourse as an extra-artistic medium, a discourse that is not worked into any special or unique style. After failure to find in novelistic discourse a purely poetic formulation ("poetic" in the narrow sense) as was expected, prose discourse is denied any artistic value at all; it is the same as practical speech for everyday life, or speech for scientific purposes, an artistically neutral means of communication.[2]

Such a point of view frees one from the necessity of undertaking stylistic analyses of the novel; it in fact gets rid of the very problem of a stylistics of the novel, permitting one to limit oneself to purely thematic analyses of it.

It was, however, precisely in the 1920s that this situation changed: the novelistic prose word began to win a place for itself in stylistics. On the one hand there appeared a series of concrete stylistic analyses of novelistic prose; on the other hand, systematic attempts were made to recognize and define the stylistic uniqueness of artistic prose as distinct from poetry.

But it was precisely these concrete analyses and these attempts at a principled approach that made patently obvious the fact that all the categories of traditional stylistics—in fact the very concept of a *poetic* artistic discourse, which lies at the heart of such categories—were not applicable to novelistic discourse. Novelistic discourse proved to be the acid test for this whole way of conceiving style, exposing the narrowness of this type of thinking and its inadequacy in all areas of discourse's artistic life.

All attempts at concrete stylistic analysis of novelistic prose either strayed into linguistic descriptions of the language of a given novelist or else limited themselves to those separate, isolated stylistic elements of the novel that were includable (or gave the appearance of being includable) in the traditional categories of stylistics. In both instances the stylistic whole of the novel and of novelistic discourse eluded the investigator.

The novel as a whole is a phenomenon multiform in style and variform in

2. As recently as the 1920s, V. M. Žirmunskij [important fellow traveler of the Formalists (translators' note)] was writing: "When lyrical poetry appears to be authentically a work of *verbal art*, due to its choice and combination of words (on semantic as well as sound levels) all of which are completely subordinated to the aesthetic project, Tolstoy's novel, by contrast, which is free in its verbal composition, does not use words as an artistically significant element of interaction but as a neutral medium or as a system of significations subordinated (as happens in practical speech) to the communicative function, directing our attention to thematic aspects quite abstracted from purely verbal considerations. We cannot call such a *literary work* a work of *verbal art* or, in any case, not in the sense that the term is used for lyrical poetry" ["On the Problem of the Formal Method," in an anthology of his articles, *Problems of a Theory of Literature* (Leningrad, 1928, p. 173); Russian edition: "K voprosu o 'formal' nom metode'," in *Voprosy teorii literatury* (L., 1928) (trans.) Bakhtin's note]. Leo Tolstoy (1828–1910), Russian novelist and moral philosopher.

speech and voice. In it the investigator is confronted with several heterogeneous stylistic unities, often located on different linguistic levels and subject to different stylistic controls.

We list below the basic types of compositional-stylistic unities into which the novelistic whole usually breaks down:

(1) Direct authorial literary-artistic narration (in all its diverse variants);
(2) Stylization of the various forms of oral everyday narration (*skaz*);[3]
(3) Stylization of the various forms of semiliterary (written) everyday narration (the letter, the diary, etc.);
(4) Various forms of literary but extra-artistic authorial speech (moral, philosophical or scientific statements, oratory, ethnographic descriptions, memoranda and so forth);
(5) The stylistically individualized speech of characters.

These heterogeneous stylistic unities, upon entering the novel, combine to form a structured artistic system, and are subordinated to the higher stylistic unity of the work as a whole, a unity that cannot be identified with any single one of the unities subordinated to it.

The stylistic uniqueness of the novel as a genre consists precisely in the combination of these subordinated, yet still relatively autonomous, unities (even at times comprised of different languages) into the higher unity of the work as a whole: the style of a novel is to be found in the combination of its styles; the language of a novel is the system of its "languages." Each separate element of a novel's language is determined first of all by one such subordinated stylistic unity into which it enters directly—be it the stylistically individualized speech of a character, the down-to-earth voice of a narrator in *skaz*, a letter or whatever. The linguistic and stylistic profile of a given element (lexical, semantic, syntactic) is shaped by that subordinated unity to which it is most immediately proximate. At the same time this element, together with its most immediate unity, figures into the style of the whole, itself supports the accent of the whole and participates in the process whereby the unified meaning of the whole is structured and revealed.

The novel can be defined as a diversity of social speech types (sometimes even diversity of languages) and a diversity of individual voices, artistically organized. The internal stratification of any single national language into social dialects, characteristic group behavior, professional jargons, generic languages, languages of generations and age groups, tendentious languages, languages of the authorities, of various circles and of passing fashions, languages that serve the specific sociopolitical purposes of the day, even of the hour (each day has its own slogan, its own vocabulary, its own emphases)—this internal stratification present in every language at any given moment of its historical existence is the indispensable prerequisite for the novel as a genre. The novel orchestrates all its themes, the totality of the world of objects and ideas depicted and expressed in it, by means of the social diversity of speech types [*raznorečie*] and by the differing individual voices that flourish under such conditions. Authorial speech, the speeches of narrators,

3. This term has no precise equivalent in English; *skaz* is a technique or mode of narration that imitates the oral speech or "yarn" of an individualized narrator, as in Mark Twain's "Celebrated Jumping Frog of Calaveras County" (1865). *Skaz* was the subject of much Russian formalist criticism.

inserted genres, the speech of characters are merely those fundamental compositional unities with whose help heteroglossia [*raznorečie*] can enter the novel; each of them permits a multiplicity of social voices and a wide variety of their links and interrelationships (always more or less dialogized). These distinctive links and interrelationships between utterances and languages, this movement of the theme through different languages and speech types, its dispersion into the rivulets and droplets of social heteroglossia, its dialogization—this is the basic distinguishing feature of the stylistics of the novel.

Such a combining of languages and styles into a higher unity is unknown to traditional stylistics; it has no method for approaching the distinctive social dialogue among languages that is present in the novel. Thus stylistic analysis is not oriented toward the novel as a whole, but only toward one or another of its subordinated stylistic unities. The traditional scholar bypasses the basic distinctive feature of the novel as a genre; he substitutes for it another object of study, and instead of novelistic style he actually analyzes something completely different. He transposes a symphonic (orchestrated) theme on to the piano keyboard.

We notice two such types of substitutions: in the first type, an analysis of novelistic style is replaced by a description of the language of a given novelist (or at best of the "languages" of a given novel); in the second type, one of the subordinated styles is isolated and analyzed as if it were the style of the whole.

In the first type, style is cut off from considerations of genre, and from the work as such, and regarded as a phenomenon of language itself: the unity of style in a given work is transformed either into the unity of an individual language ("individual dialect"), or into the unity of an individual speech (*parole*). It is precisely the individuality of the speaking subject that is recognized to be that style-generating factor transforming a phenomenon of language and linguistics into a stylistic unity.

We have no need to follow where such an analysis of novelistic style leads, whether to a disclosing of the novelist's individual dialect (that is, his vocabulary, his syntax) or to a disclosing of the distinctive features of the work taken as a "complete speech act," an "utterance." Equally in both cases, style is understood in the spirit of Saussure:[4] as an individualization of the general language (in the sense of a system of general language norms). Stylistics is transformed either into a curious kind of linguistics treating individual languages, or into a linguistics of the utterance.

In accordance with the point of view selected, the unity of a style thus presupposes on the one hand a unity of language (in the sense of a system of general normative forms) and on the other hand the unity of an individual person realizing himself in this language.

Both these conditions are in fact obligatory in the majority of verse-based poetic genres, but even in these genres they far from exhaust or define the style of the work. The most precise and complete description of the individual language and speech of a poet—even if this description does choose to treat the expressiveness of language and speech elements—does not add up to a

4. Specifically, the emphasis by the French linguist FERDINAND DE SAUSSURE (1857–1913) on *langue* (a language system) and *parole* (individual speech).

stylistic analysis of the work, inasmuch as these elements relate to a system of language or to a system of speech, that is, to various linguistic unities and not to the system of the artistic work, which is governed by a completely different system of rules than those that govern the linguistic systems of language and of speech.

But—we repeat—in the majority of poetic genres, the unity of the language system and the unity (and uniqueness) of the poet's individuality as reflected in his language and speech, which is directly realized in this unity, are indispensable prerequisites of poetic style. The novel, however, not only does not require these conditions but (as we have said) even makes of the internal stratification of language, of its social heteroglossia and the variety of individual voices in it, the prerequisite for authentic novelistic prose.

Thus the substitution of the individualized language of the novelist (to the extent that one can recover this language from the "speech" and "language" systems of the novel) for the style of the novel itself is doubly imprecise: it distorts the very essence of a stylistics of the novel. Such substitution inevitably leads to the selection from the novel of only those elements that can be fitted within the frame of a single language system and that express, directly and without mediation, an authorial individuality in language. The whole of the novel and the specific tasks involved in constructing this whole out of heteroglot, multi-voiced, multi-styled and often multi-languaged elements remain outside the boundaries of such a study.

Such is the first type of substitution for the proper object of study in the stylistic analysis of the novel. We will not delve further into the diverse variations of this type, which are determined by the different ways in which such concepts as "the speech whole," "the system of language," "the individuality of the author's language and speech" are understood, and by a difference in the very way in which the relationship between style and language is conceived (and also the relationship between stylistics and linguistics). In all possible variants on this type of analysis, which acknowledge only one single language and a single authorial individuality expressing itself directly in that language, the stylistic nature of the novel slips hopelessly away from the investigator.

The second type of substitution is characterized not by an orientation toward the language of the author, but rather toward the style of the novel itself—although style thus understood is narrowed down to mean the style of merely one out of the several subordinated unities (which are relatively autonomous) within the novel.

In the majority of cases the style of the novel is subsumed under the concept of "epic style," and the appropriate categories of traditional stylistics are applied to it. In such circumstances only those elements of epic representation (those occurring predominantly in direct authorial speech) are isolated from the novel for consideration. The profound difference between novelistic and purely epic modes of expression is ignored. Differences between the novel and the epic are usually perceived on the level of composition and thematics alone.

In other instances, different aspects of novelistic style are selected out as most characteristic of one or another concrete literary work. Thus the narrational aspect can be considered from the point of view not of its objective descriptive mode, but of its subjective expression mode (expressiveness). One might select elements of vernacular extraliterary narration (*skaz*) or those aspects that provide the information necessary to further the plot (as one might do, for example, in analyzing an adventure novel).[5] And it is possible, finally, to select those purely dramatic elements of the novel that lower the narrational aspect to the level of a commentary on the dialogues of the novel's characters. But the system of languages in drama is organized on completely different principles, and therefore its languages sound utterly different than do the languages of the novel. In drama there is no all-encompassing language that addresses itself dialogically to separate languages, there is no second all-encompassing plotless (nondramatic) dialogue outside that of the (nondramatic) plot.

All these types of analysis are inadequate to the style not only of the novelistic whole but even of that element isolated as fundamental for a given novel—inasmuch as that element, removed from its interaction with others, changes its stylistic meaning and ceases to be that which it in fact had been in the novel.

The current state of questions posed by a stylistics of the novel reveals, fully and clearly, that all the categories and methods of traditional stylistics remain incapable of dealing effectively with the artistic uniqueness of discourse in the novel, or with the specific life that discourse leads in the novel. "Poetic language," "individuality of language," "image," "symbol," "epic style" and other general categories worked out and applied by stylistics, as well as the entire set of concrete stylistic devices subsumed by these categories (no matter how differently understood by individual critics), are all equally oriented toward the single-languaged and single-styled genres, toward the poetic genres in the narrow sense of the word. Their connection with this exclusive orientation explains a number of the particular features and limitations of traditional stylistic categories. All these categories, and the very philosophical conception of poetic discourse in which they are grounded, are too narrow and cramped, and cannot accommodate the artistic prose of novelistic discourse.

Thus stylistics and the philosophy of discourse indeed confront a dilemma: either to acknowledge the novel (and consequently all artistic prose tending in that direction) an unartistic or quasi-artistic genre, or to radically reconsider that conception of poetic discourse in which traditional stylistics is grounded and which determines all its categories.

This dilemma, however, is by no means universally recognized. Most scholars are not inclined to undertake a radical revision of the fundamental philosophical conception of poetic discourse. Many do not even see or recognize the philosophical roots of the stylistics (and linguistics) in which they work, and shy away from any fundamental philosophical issues. They utterly fail to see behind their isolated and fragmented stylistic observations and linguistic descriptions any theoretical problems posed by novelistic discourse. Others—more principled—make a case for consistent individualism in their understanding of language and style. First and foremost they seek in the stylistic phenomenon a direct and unmediated expression of authorial indi-

5. Artistic prose style has been studied in Russia by the Formalists largely on these two last levels, that is, either *skaz* (Eichenbaum) or plot-informational aspects (Shklovsky) were studied as most characteristic of literary prose [Bakhtin's note]. BORIS EICHENBAUM (1886–1959), Russian formalist critic. Viktor Shklovsky (1893–1984), Russian formalist writer and critic.

viduality, and such an understanding of the problem is least likely of all to encourage a reconsideration of basic stylistic categories in the proper direction.

However, there is another solution of our dilemma that does take basic concepts into account: one need only consider oft-neglected rhetoric, which for centuries has included artistic prose in its purview. Once we have restored rhetoric to all its ancient rights, we may adhere to the old concept of poetic discourse, relegating to "rhetorical forms" everything in novelistic prose that does not fit the Procrustean bed of traditional stylistic categories.[6]

Gustav Shpet,[7] in his time, proposed such a solution to the dilemma, with all due rigorousness and consistency. He utterly excluded artistic prose and its ultimate realization—the novel—from the realm of poetry, and assigned it to the category of purely rhetorical forms.[8]

Here is what Shpet says about the novel: "The recognition that contemporary forms of moral propaganda—i.e., the *novel*—do not spring from *poetic creativity* but are purely rhetorical compositions, is an admission, and a conception, that apparently cannot arise without immediately confronting a formidable obstacle in the form of the universal recognition, despite everything, that the novel *does* have a certain aesthetic value."[9]

Shpet utterly denies the novel any aesthetic significance. The novel is an extra-artistic rhetorical genre, "the contemporary form of moral propaganda"; artistic discourse is exclusively poetic discourse (in the sense we have indicated above).

Viktor Vinogradov[1] adopted an analogous point of view in his book *On Artistic Prose*, assigning the problem of artistic prose to rhetoric. While agreeing with Shpet's basic philosophical definitions of the "poetic" and the "rhetorical," Vinogradov was, however, not so paradoxically consistent: he considered the novel a syncretic, mixed form ("a hybrid formation") and admitted that it contained, along with rhetorical elements, some purely poetic ones.[2]

The point of view that completely excludes novelistic prose, as a rhetorical formation, from the realm of poetry—a point of view that is basically false—does nevertheless have a certain indisputable merit. There resides in it an acknowledgment in principle and in substance of the inadequacy of all contemporary stylistics, along with its philosophical and linguistic base, when it comes to defining the specific distinctive features of novelistic prose. And what is more, the very reliance on rhetorical forms has a great heuristic

6. Such a solution to the problem was especially tempting to adherents of the formal method in poetics: in fact, the re-establishment of rhetoric, with all its rights, greatly strengthens the Formalist position. Formalist rhetoric is a necessary addition to Formalist poetics. Our Formalists were being completely consistent when they spoke of the necessity of reviving rhetoric alongside poetics (on this, see B. M. Eichenbaum, *Literature* [*Literatura*; Leningrad, 1927], pp. 147–48) [Bakhtin's note].

7. Gustav Shpet (1879–1937), outstanding representative of the neo-Kantian and (especially) Husserlian traditions in Russia; as professor at the University of Moscow for many years he influenced many (among others, the young Roman Jakobson) [translators' note.] IMMANUEL KANT (1724–1804), German idealist philosopher. Edmund Husserl (1859–1938), German phenomenologist. JAKOBSON (1896–1982), Russian-born literary theorist and linguist.

8. Originally in his *Aesthetic Fragments* [*Estetičeskie fragmenty*]; in a more complete aspect in the book *The Inner Form of the Word* [*Vnutrennjaja forma slova*] (M., 1927) [Bakhtin's note].

9. *Vnutrennjaja forma slova*, p. 215 [Bakhtin's note].

1. Viktor Vinogradov (1895–1969), outstanding linguist and student of style in literature, a friendly critic of the Formalists, and an important theorist in his own right (especially his work on *skaz* technique) [translators' note].

2. V. V. Vinogradov, *On Artistic Prose* [*O xudožestvennom proze*], Moscow-Leningrad, 1930, pp. 75–106 [Bakhtin's note].

significance. Once rhetorical discourse is brought into the study with all its living diversity, it cannot fail to have a deeply revolutionizing influence on linguistics and on the philosophy of language. It is precisely those aspects of any discourse (the internally dialogic quality of discourse, and the phenomena related to it), not yet sufficiently taken into account and fathomed in all the enormous weight they carry in the life of language, that are revealed with great external precision in rhetorical forms, provided a correct and unprejudiced approach to those forms is used. Such is the general methodological and heuristic significance of rhetorical forms for linguistics and for the philosophy of language.

The special significance of rhetorical forms for understanding the novel is equally great. The novel, and artistic prose in general, has the closest genetic, family relationship to rhetorical forms. And throughout the entire development of the novel, its intimate interaction (both peaceful and hostile) with living rhetorical genres (journalistic, moral, philosophical and others) has never ceased; this interaction was perhaps no less intense than was the novel's interaction with the artistic genres (epic, dramatic, lyric). But in this uninterrupted interrelationship, novelistic discourse preserved its own qualitative uniqueness and was never reducible to rhetorical discourse.

The novel is an artistic genre. Novelistic discourse is poetic discourse, but one that does not fit within the frame provided by the concept of poetic discourse as it now exists. This concept has certain underlying presuppositions that limit it. The very concept—in the course of its historical formulation from Aristotle[3] to the present day—has been oriented toward the specific "official" genres and connected with specific historical tendencies in verbal ideological life. Thus a whole series of phenomena remained beyond its conceptual horizon.

Philosophy of language, linguistics and stylistics [i.e., such as they have come down to us] have all postulated a simple and unmediated relation of speaker to his unitary and singular "own" language, and have postulated as well a simple realization of this language in the monologic utterance of the individual. Such disciplines actually know only two poles in the life of language, between which are located all the linguistic and stylistic phenomena they know: on the one hand, the system of a *unitary language,* and on the other the *individual* speaking in this language.

Various schools of thought in the philosophy of language, in linguistics and in stylistics have, in different periods (and always in close connection with the diverse concrete poetic and ideological styles of a given epoch), introduced into such concepts as "system of language," "monologic utterance," "the speaking *individuum,*" various differing nuances of meaning, but their basic content remains unchanged. This basic content is conditioned by the specific sociohistorical destinies of European languages and by the destinies of ideological discourse, and by those particular historical tasks that ideological discourse has fulfilled in specific social spheres and at specific stages in its own historical development.

These tasks and destinies of discourse conditioned specific verbal-ideological movements, as well as various specific genres of ideological discourse, and ultimately the specific philosophical concept of discourse itself—

3. The Greek philosopher (384–322 B.C.E.) discusses poetic discourse in his *Poetics* (see above).

in particular, the concept of poetic discourse, which had been at the heart of all concepts of style.

The strength and at the same time the limitations of such basic stylistic categories become apparent when such categories are seen as conditioned by specific historical destinies and by the task that an ideological discourse assumes. These categories arose from and were shaped by the historically *aktuell*[4] forces at work in the verbal-ideological evolution of specific social groups; they comprised the theoretical expression of actualizing forces that were in the process of creating a life for language.

These forces are *the forces that serve to unify and centralize the verbal-ideological world.*

Unitary language constitutes the theoretical expression of the historical processes of linguistic unification and centralization, an expression of the centripetal forces of language. A unitary language is not something given [*dan*] but is always in essence posited [*zadan*]—and at every moment of its linguistic life it is opposed to the realities of heteroglossia. But at the same time it makes its real presence felt as a force for overcoming this heteroglossia, imposing specific limits to it, guaranteeing a certain maximum of mutual understanding and crystalizing into a real, although still relative, unity—the unity of the reigning conversational (everyday) and literary language, "correct language."

A common unitary language is a system of linguistic norms. But these norms do not constitute an abstract imperative; they are rather the generative forces of linguistic life, forces that struggle to overcome the heteroglossia of language, forces that unite and centralize verbal-ideological thought, creating within a heteroglot national language the firm, stable linguistic nucleus of an officially recognized literary language, or else defending an already formed language from the pressure of growing heteroglossia.

What we have in mind here is not an abstract linguistic minimum of a common language, in the sense of a system of elementary forms (linguistic symbols) guaranteeing a *minimum* level of comprehension in practical communication. We are taking language not as a system of abstract grammatical categories, but rather language conceived as ideologically saturated, language as a world view, even as a concrete opinion, insuring a *maximum* of mutual understanding in all spheres of ideological life. Thus a unitary language gives expression to forces working toward concrete verbal and ideological unification and centralization, which develop in vital connection with the processes of sociopolitical and cultural centralization.

Aristotelian poetics, the poetics of Augustine, the poetics of the medieval church, of "the one language of truth," the Cartesian poetics of neoclassicism, the abstract grammatical universalism of Leibniz (the idea of a "universal grammar"), Humboldt's[5] insistence on the concrete—all these, whatever their differences in nuance, give expression to the same centripetal forces in sociolinguistic and ideological life; they serve one and the same

4. Topical, of pressing current importance (German).

5. Wilhelm Freiherr von Humboldt (1767–1835), German humanist writer and philologist. AUGUSTINE (354–430), early Christian philosopher and theologian; on his poetics, see above. "The poetics of the medieval church": see HUGH OF ST. VICTOR (ca. 1097–1141). "The Cartesian poetics of neoclassicism": on these dualistic (from the French philosopher René Descartes, 1596–1650) poetics, see PIERRE CORNEILLE (1606–1684). Gottfried Wilhelm von Leibniz (1646–1716), German philosopher and mathematician.

project of centralizing and unifying the European languages. The victory of one reigning language (dialect) over the others, the supplanting of languages, their enslavement, the process of illuminating them with the True Word, the incorporation of barbarians and lower social strata into a unitary language of culture and truth, the canonization of ideological systems, philology with its methods of studying and teaching dead languages, languages that were by that very fact "unities," Indo-European linguistics with its focus of attention, directed away from language plurality to a single proto-language—all this determined the content and power of the category of "unitary language" in linguistic and stylistic thought, and determined its creative, style-shaping role in the majority of the poetic genres that coalesced in the channel formed by those same centripetal forces of verbal-ideological life.

But the centripetal forces of the life of language, embodied in a "unitary language," operate in the midst of heteroglossia. At any given moment of its evolution, language is stratified not only into linguistic dialects in the strict sense of the word (according to formal linguistic markers, especially phonetic), but also—and for us this is the essential point—into languages that are socio-ideological: languages of social groups, "professional" and "genetic" languages, languages of generations and so forth. From this point of view, literary language itself is only one of these heteroglot languages—and in its turn is also stratified into languages (generic, period-bound and others). And this stratification and heteroglossia, once realized, is not only a static invariant of linguistic life, but also what insures its dynamics: stratification and heteroglossia widen and deepen as long as language is alive and developing. Alongside the centripetal forces, the centrifugal forces of language carry on their uninterrupted work; alongside verbal-ideological centralization and unification, the uninterrupted processes of decentralization and disunification go forward.

Every concrete utterance of a speaking subject serves as a point where centrifugal as well as centripetal forces are brought to bear. The processes of centralization and decentralization, of unification and disunification, intersect in the utterance; the utterance not only answers the requirements of its own language as an individualized embodiment of a speech act, but it answers the requirements of heteroglossia as well; it is in fact an active participant in such speech diversity. And this active participation of every utterance in living heteroglossia determines the linguistic profile and style of the utterance to no less a degree than its inclusion in any normative-centralizing system of a unitary language.

Every utterance participates in the "unitary language" (in its centripetal forces and tendencies) and at the same time partakes of social and historical heteroglossia (the centrifugal, stratifying forces).

Such is the fleeting language of a day, of an epoch, a social group, a genre, a school and so forth. It is possible to give a concrete and detailed analysis of any utterance, once having exposed it as a contradiction-ridden, tension-filled unity of two embattled tendencies in the life of language.

The authentic environment of an utterance, the environment in which it lives and takes shape, is dialogized heteroglossia, anonymous and social as language, but simultaneously concrete, filled with specific content and accented as an individual utterance.

At the time when major divisions of the poetic genres were developing under the influence of the unifying, centralizing, centripetal forces of verbal-ideological life, the novel—and those artistic-prose genres that gravitate toward it—was being historically shaped by the current of decentralizing, centrifugal forces. At the time when poetry was accomplishing the task of cultural, national and political centralization of the verbal-ideological world in the higher official socio-ideological levels, on the lower levels, on the stages of local fairs and at buffoon spectacles, the heteroglossia of the clown sounded forth, ridiculing all "languages" and dialects; there developed the literature of the *fabliaux* and *Schwänke*[6] of street songs, folksayings, anecdotes, where there was no language-center at all, where there was to be found a lively play with the "languages" of poets, scholars, monks, knights and others, where all "languages" were masks and where no language could claim to be an authentic, incontestable face.

Heteroglossia, as organized in these low genres, was not merely heteroglossia vis-à-vis the accepted literary language (in all its various generic expressions), that is, vis-à-vis the linguistic center of the verbal-ideological life of the nation and the epoch, but was a heteroglossia consciously opposed to this literary language. It was parodic, and aimed sharply and polemically against the official languages of its given time. It was heteroglossia that had been dialogized.

Linguistics, stylistics and the philosophy of language that were born and shaped by the current of centralizing tendencies in the life of language have ignored this dialogized heteroglossia, in which is embodied the centrifugal forces in the life of language. For this very reason they could make no provision for the dialogic nature of language, which was a struggle among socio-linguistic points of view, not an intra-language struggle between individual wills or logical contradictions. Moreover, even intra-language dialogue (dramatic, rhetorical, cognitive or merely casual) has hardly been studied linguistically or stylistically up to the present day. One might even say outright that the dialogic aspect of discourse and all the phenomena connected with it have remained to the present moment beyond the ken of linguistics.

Stylistics has been likewise completely deaf to dialogue. A literary work has been conceived by stylistics as if it were a hermetic and self-sufficient whole, one whose elements constitute a closed system presuming nothing beyond themselves, no other utterances. The system comprising an artistic work was thought to be analogous with the system of a language, a system that could not stand in a dialogic interrelationship with other languages. From the point of view of stylistics, the artistic work as a whole—whatever that whole might be—is a self-sufficient and closed authorial monologue, one that presumes only passive listeners beyond its own boundaries. Should we imagine the work as a rejoinder in a given dialogue, whose style is determined by its interrelationship with other rejoinders in the same dialogue (in the totality of the conversation)—then traditional stylistics does not offer an adequate means for approaching such a dialogized style. The sharpest and externally most marked manifestations of this stylistic category—the polemical style, the parodic, the ironic—are usually classified as rhetorical and not as poetic phenomena. Stylistics locks every stylistic phenomenon into the monologic context of a given self-sufficient and hermetic utterance, imprisoning it, as it were, in the dungeon of a single context; it is not able to

6. Medieval comic folktales (German). *Fabliaux*: medieval short tales in verse (French).

exchange messages with other utterances; it is not able to realize its own stylistic implications in a relationship with them; it is obliged to exhaust itself in its own single hermetic context.

Linguistics, stylistics and the philosophy of language—as forces in the service of the great centralizing tendencies of European verbal-ideological life—have sought first and foremost for *unity* in diversity. This exclusive "orientation toward unity" in the present and past life of languages has concentrated the attention of philosophical and linguistic thought on the firmest, most stable, least changeable and most mono-semic aspects of discourse—on the *phonetic* aspects first of all—that are furthest removed from the changing socio-semantic spheres of discourse. Real ideologically saturated "language consciousness," one that participates in actual heteroglossia and multi-languagedness, has remained outside its field of vision. It is precisely this orientation toward unity that has compelled scholars to ignore all the verbal genres (quotidian, rhetorical, artistic-prose) that were the carriers of the decentralizing tendencies in the life of language, or that were in any case too fundamentally implicated in heteroglossia. The expression of this hetero- as well as polyglot consciousness in the specific forms and phenomena of verbal life remained utterly without determinative influence on linguistics and stylistic thought.

Therefore proper theoretical recognition and illumination could not be found for the specific feel for language and discourse that one gets in stylizations, in *skaz*, in parodies and in various forms of verbal masquerade, "not talking straight," and in the more complex artistic forms for the organization of contradiction, forms that orchestrate their themes by means of languages—in all characteristic and profound models of novelistic prose, in Grimmelshausen, Cervantes, Rabelais, Fielding, Smollett, Sterne[7] and others.

The problem of stylistics for the novel inevitably leads to the necessity of engaging a series of fundamental questions concerning the philosophy of discourse, questions connected with those aspects in the life of discourse that have had no light cast on them by linguistic and stylistic thought—that is, we must deal with the life and behavior of discourse in a contradictory and multi-languaged world.

Discourse in Poetry and Discourse in the Novel

For the philosophy of language, for linguistics and for stylistics structured on their base, a whole series of phenomena have therefore remained almost entirely beyond the realm of consideration: these include the specific phenomena that are present in discourse and that are determined by its dialogic orientation, first, amid others' utterances inside a *single* language (the primordial dialogism of discourse), amid other "social languages" within a single *national* language and finally amid different national languages within the same *culture*, that is, the same socio-ideological conceptual horizon.[8]

7. All important early novelists—German: Hans Jakob Christoffel von Grimmelshausen (ca. 1621–1676); Spanish: Miguel de Cervantes (1547–1616); French: François Rabelais (ca. 1490–ca. 1533); and English: Henry Fielding (1707–1754), (Scottish-born) Tobias Smollett (1721–1771), and Laurence Sterne (1713–1768).

8. Linguistics acknowledges only a mechanical reciprocal influencing and intermixing of languages (that is, one that is unconscious and determined by social conditions) which is reflected in abstract linguistic elements (phonetic and morphological) [Bakhtin's note].

In recent decades, it is true, these phenomena have begun to attract the attention of scholars in language and stylistics, but their fundamental and wide-ranging significance in all spheres of the life of discourse is still far from acknowledged.

The dialogic orientation of a word among other words (of all kinds and degrees of otherness) creates new and significant artistic potential in discourse, creates the potential for a distinctive art of prose, which has found its fullest and deepest expression in the novel.

We will focus our attention here on various forms and degrees of dialogic orientation in discourse, and on the special potential for a distinctive prose-art.

As treated by traditional stylistic thought, the word acknowledges only itself (that is, only its own context), its own object, its own direct expression and its own unitary and singular language. It acknowledges another word, one lying outside its own context, only as the neutral word of language, as the word of no one in particular, as simply the potential for speech. The direct word, as traditional stylistics understands it, encounters in its orientation toward the object only the resistance of the object itself (the impossibility of its being exhausted by a word, the impossibility of saying it all), but it does not encounter in its path toward the object the fundamental and richly varied opposition of another's word. No one hinders this word, no one argues with it.

But no living word relates to its object in a *singular* way: between the word and its object, between the word and the speaking subject, there exists an elastic environment of other, alien words about the same object, the same theme, and this is an environment that it is often difficult to penetrate. It is precisely in the process of living interaction with this specific environment that the word may be individualized and given stylistic shape.

Indeed, any concrete discourse (utterance) finds the object at which it was directed already as it were overlain with qualifications, open to dispute, charged with value, already enveloped in an obscuring mist—or, on the contrary, by the "light" of alien words that have already been spoken about it. It is entangled, shot through with shared thoughts, points of view, alien value judgments and accents. The word, directed toward its object, enters a dialogically agitated and tension-filled environment of alien words, value judgments and accents, weaves in and out of complex interrelationships, merges with some, recoils from others, intersects with yet a third group: and all this may crucially shape discourse, may leave a trace in all its semantic layers, may complicate its expression and influence its entire stylistic profile.

The living utterance, having taken meaning and shape at a particular historical moment in a socially specific environment, cannot fail to brush up against thousands of living dialogic threads, woven by socio-ideological consciousness around the given object of an utterance; it cannot fail to become an active participant in social dialogue. After all, the utterance arises out of this dialogue as a continuation of it and as a rejoinder to it—it does not approach the object from the sidelines.

The way in which the word conceptualizes its object is a complex act—all objects, open to dispute and overlain as they are with qualifications, are from one side highlighted while from the other side dimmed by heteroglot social opinion, by an alien word about them.[9] And into this complex play of light and shadow the word enters—it becomes saturated with this play, and must determine within it the boundaries of its own semantic and stylistic contours. The way in which the word conceives its object is complicated by a dialogic interaction within the object between various aspects of its socio-verbal intelligibility. And an artistic representation, an "image" of the object, may be penetrated by this dialogic play of verbal intentions that meet and are interwoven in it; such an image need not stifle these forces, but on the contrary may activate and organize them. If we imagine the *intention* of such a word, that is, its *directionality toward the object*, in the form of a ray of light, then the living and unrepealable play of colors and light on the facets of the image that it constructs can be explained as the spectral dispersion of the ray-word, not within the object itself (as would be the case in the play of an image-as-trope, in poetic speech taken in the narrow sense, in an "autotelic word"), but rather as its spectral dispersion in an atmosphere filled with the alien words, value judgments and accents through which the ray passes on its way toward the object; the social atmosphere of the word, the atmosphere that surrounds the object, makes the facets of the image sparkle.

The word, breaking through to its own meaning and its own expression across an environment full of alien words and variously evaluating accents, harmonizing with some of the elements in this environment and striking a dissonance with others, is able, in this dialogized process, to shape its own stylistic profile and tone.

Such is the *image in artistic prose* and the image of *novelistic prose* in particular. In the atmosphere of the novel, the direct and unmediated intention of a word presents itself as something impermissably naive, something in fact impossible, for naiveté itself, under authentic novelistic conditions, takes on the nature of an internal polemic and is consequently dialogized (in, for example, the work of the Sentimentalists, in Chateaubriand[1] and in Tostoy). Such a dialogized image can occur in all the poetic genres as well, even in the lyric (to be sure, without setting the tone).[2] But such an image can fully unfold, achieve full complexity and depth and at the same time artistic closure, only under the conditions present in the genre of the novel.

In the poetic image narrowly conceived (in the image-as-trope), all activity—the dynamics of the image-as-word—is completely exhausted by the play between the word (with all its aspects) and the object (in all its aspects). The word plunges into the inexhaustible wealth and contradictory multiplicity of the object itself, with its "virginal," still "unuttered" nature; therefore it presumes nothing beyond the borders of its own context (except, of course, what can be found in the treasure-house of language itself). The word forgets that its object has its own history of contradictory acts of verbal recognition, as well as that heteroglossia that is always present in such acts of recognition.

9. Highly significant in this respect is the struggle that must be undertaken in such movements as Rousseauism, Naturalism, Impressionism, Acmeism, Dadaism, Surrealism and analogous schools with the "qualified" nature of the object (a struggle occasioned by the idea of a return to primordial consciousness, to original consciousness, to the object itself in itself, to pure perception and so forth) [Bakhtin's note].

1. François-Auguste-René, vicomte de Chateaubriand (1768–1848), French novelist.

2. The Horatian lyric, Villon, Heine, Laforgue, Annenskij and others—despite the fact that these are extremely varied instances [Bakhtin's note]. All lyric poets: HORACE (65–8 B.C.E.), Roman; François Villon (1431–ca.1463), French; Heinrich Heine (1797–1856), German; Jules Laforgue (1860–1887), French; and Innokenty Annenskij (1855–1909), Russian.

For the writer of artistic prose, on the contrary, the object reveals first of all precisely the socially heteroglot multiplicity of its names, definitions and value judgments. Instead of the virginal fullness and inexhaustibility of the object itself, the prose writer confronts a multitude of routes, roads and paths that have been laid down in the object by social consciousness. Along with the internal contradictions inside the object itself, the prose writer witnesses as well the unfolding of social heteroglossia *surrounding* the object, the Tower-of-Babel mixing of languages[3] that goes on around any object; the dialectics of the object are interwoven with the social dialogue surrounding it. For the prose writer, the object is a focal point for heteroglot voices among which his own voice must also sound; these voices create the background necessary for his own voice, outside of which his artistic prose nuances cannot be perceived, and without which they "do not sound."

The prose artist elevates the social heteroglossia surrounding objects into an image that has finished contours, an image completely shot through with dialogized overtones; he creates artistically calculated nuances on all the fundamental voices and tones of this heteroglossia. But as we have already said, every extra-artistic prose discourse—in any of its forms, quotidian, rhetorical, scholarly—cannot fail to be oriented toward the "already uttered," the "already known," the "common opinion" and so forth. The dialogic orientation of discourse is a phenomenon that is, of course, a property of *any* discourse. It is the natural orientation of any living discourse. On all its various routes toward the object, in all its directions, the word encounters an alien word and cannot help encountering it in a living, tension-filled interaction. Only the mythical Adam, who approached a virginal and as yet verbally unqualified world with the first word, could really have escaped from start to finish this dialogic inter-orientation with the alien word that occurs in the object. Concrete historical human discourse does not have this privilege: it can deviate from such inter-orientation only on a conditional basis and only to a certain degree.

It is all the more remarkable that linguistics and the philosophy of discourse have been primarily oriented precisely toward this artificial, preconditioned status of the word, a word excised from dialogue and taken for the norm (although the primacy of dialogue over monologue is frequently proclaimed). Dialogue is studied merely as a compositional form in the structuring of speech, but the internal dialogism of the word (which occurs in a monologic utterance as well as in a rejoinder), the dialogism that penetrates its entire structure, all its semantic and expressive layers, is almost entirely ignored. But it is precisely this internal dialogism of the word, which does not assume any external compositional forms of dialogue, that cannot be isolated as an independent act, separate from the word's ability to form a concept [*koncipirovanie*] of its object—it is precisely this internal dialogism that has such enormous power to shape style. The internal dialogism of the word finds expression in a series of peculiar features in semantics, syntax and stylistics that have remained up to the present time completely unstudied by linguistics and stylistics (nor, what is more, have the peculiar semantic features of ordinary dialogue been studied).

The word is born in a dialogue as a living rejoinder within it; the word is

3. See Genesis 11.1–9.

shaped in dialogic interaction with an alien word that is already in the object. A word forms a concept of its own object in a dialogic way.

But this does not exhaust the internal dialogism of the word. It encounters an alien word not only in the object itself: every word is directed toward an *answer* and cannot escape the profound influence of the answering word that it anticipates.

The word in living conversation is directly, blatantly, oriented toward a future answer-word: it provokes an answer, anticipates it and structures itself in the answer's direction. Forming itself in an atmosphere of the already spoken, the word is at the same time determined by that which has not yet been said but which is needed and in fact anticipated by the answering word. Such is the situation in any living dialogue.

All rhetorical forms, monologic in their compositional structure, are oriented toward the listener and his answer. This orientation toward the listener is usually considered the basic constitutive feature of rhetorical discourse.[4] It is highly significant for rhetoric that this relationship toward the concrete listener, taking him into account, is a relationship that enters into the very internal construction of rhetorical discourse. This orientation toward an answer is open, blatant and concrete.

This open orientation toward the listener and his answer in everyday dialogue and in rhetorical forms has attracted the attention of linguists. But even where this has been the case, linguists have by and large gotten no further than the compositional forms by which the listener is taken into account; they have not sought influence springing from more profound meaning and style. They have taken into consideration only those aspects of style determined by demands for comprehensibility and clarity—that is, precisely those aspects that are deprived of any internal dialogism, that take the listener for a person who passively understands but not for one who actively answers and reacts.

The listener and his response are regularly taken into account when it comes to everyday dialogue and rhetoric, but every other sort of discourse as well is oriented toward an understanding that is "responsive"—although this orientation is not particularized in an independent act and is not compositionally marked. Responsive understanding is a fundamental force, one that participates in the formulation of discourse, and it is moreover an *active* understanding, one that discourse senses as resistance or support enriching the discourse.

Linguistics and the philosophy of language acknowledge only a passive understanding of discourse, and moreover this takes place by and large on the level of common language, that is, it is an understanding of an utterance's *neutral signification* and not its *actual meaning.*

The linguistic significance of a given utterance is understood against the background of language, while its actual meaning is understood against the background of other concrete utterances on the same theme, a background made up of contradictory opinions, points of view and value judgments—that is, precisely that background that, as we see, complicates the path of any word toward its object. Only now this contradictory environment of alien

4. Cf. V. Vinogradov's book *On Artistic Prose*, the chapter "Rhetoric and Poetics," pp. 75ff., where definitions taken from the older rhetorics are introduced [Bahktin's note].

words is present to the speaker not in the object, but rather in the consciousness of the listener, as his apperceptive background, pregnant with responses and objections. And every utterance is oriented toward this apperceptive background of understanding, which is not a linguistic background but rather one composed of specific objects and emotional expressions. There occurs a new encounter between the utterance and an alien word, which makes itself felt as a new and unique influence on its style.

A passive understanding of linguistic meaning is no understanding at all, it is only the abstract aspect of meaning. But even a more concrete *passive* understanding of the meaning of the utterance, an understanding of the speaker's intention insofar as that understanding remains purely passive, purely receptive contributes nothing new to the word under consideration, only mirroring it, seeking, at its most ambitious, merely the full reproduction of that which is already given in the word—even such an understanding never goes beyond the boundaries of the word's context and in no way enriches the word. Therefore, insofar as the speaker operates with such a passive understanding, nothing new can be introduced into his discourse; there can be no new aspects in his discourse relating to concrete objects and emotional expressions. Indeed the purely negative demands, such as could only emerge from a passive understanding (for instance, a need for greater clarity, more persuasiveness, more vividness and so forth), leave the speaker in his own personal context, within his own boundaries; such negative demands are completely immanent in the speaker's own discourse and do not go beyond his semantic or expressive self-sufficiency.

In the actual life of speech, every concrete act of understanding is active: it assimilates the word to be understood into its own conceptual system filled with specific objects and emotional expressions, and is indissolubly merged with the response, with a motivated agreement or disagreement. To some extent, primacy belongs to the response, as the activating principle: it creates the ground for understanding, it prepares the ground for an active and engaged understanding. Understanding comes to fruition only in the response. Understanding and response are dialectically merged and mutually condition each other; one is impossible without the other.

Thus an active understanding, one that assimilates the word under consideration into a new conceptual system, that of the one striving to understand, establishes a series of complex interrelationships, consonances and dissonances with the word and enriches it with new elements. It is precisely such an understanding that the speaker counts on. Therefore his orientation toward the listener is an orientation toward a specific conceptual horizon, toward the specific world of the listener; it introduces totally new elements into his discourse; it is in this way, after all, that various different points of view, conceptual horizons, systems for providing expressive accents, various social "languages" come to interact with one another. The speaker strives to get a reading on his own word, and on his own conceptual system that determines this word, within the alien conceptual system of the understanding receiver; he enters into dialogical relationships with certain aspects of this system. The speaker breaks through the alien conceptual horizon of the listener, constructs his own utterance on alien territory, against his, the listener's, apperceptive background.

This new form of internal dialogism of the word is different from that form determined by an encounter with an alien word within the object itself: here it is not the object that serves as the arena for the encounter, but rather the subjective belief system of the listener. Thus this dialogism bears a more subjective, psychological and (frequently) random character, sometimes crassly accommodating, sometimes provocatively polemical. Very often, especially in the rhetorical forms, this orientation toward the listener and the related internal dialogism of the word may simply overshadow the object: the strong point of any concrete listener becomes a self-sufficient focus of attention, and one that interferes with the word's creative work on its referent.

Although they differ in their essentials and give rise to varying stylistic effects in discourse, the dialogic relationship toward an alien word within the object and the relationship toward an alien word in the anticipated answer of the listener can, nevertheless, be very tightly interwoven with each other, becoming almost indistinguishable during stylistic analysis.

Thus, discourse in Tolstoy is characterized by a sharp internal dialogism, and this discourse is moreover dialogized in the belief system of the reader—whose peculiar semantic and expressive characteristics Tolstoy acutely senses—as well as in the object. These two lines of dialogization (having in most cases polemical overtones) are tightly interwoven in his style: even in the most "lyrical" expressions and the most "epic" descriptions, Tolstoy's discourse harmonizes and disharmonizes (more often disharmonizes) with various aspects of the heteroglot socio-verbal consciousness ensnaring the object, while at the same time polemically invading the reader's belief and evaluative system, striving to stun and destroy the apperceptive background of the reader's active understanding. In this respect Tolstoy is an heir of the eighteenth century, especially of Rousseau.[5] This propagandizing impulse sometimes leads to a narrowing-down of heteroglot social consciousness (against which Tolstoy polemicizes) to the consciousness of his immediate contemporary, a contemporary of the day and not of the epoch; what follows from this is a radical concretization of dialogization (almost always undertaken in the service of a polemic). For this reason Tolstoy's dialogization, no matter how acutely we sense it in the expressive profile of his style, sometimes requires special historical or literary commentary: we are not sure with *what* precisely a given tone is in harmony or disharmony, for this dissonance or consonance has entered into the positive project of creating a style.[6] It is true that such extreme concreteness (which approaches at time the feuilleton)[7] is present only in those secondary aspects, the overtones of internal dialogization in Tolstoy's discourse.

In those examples of the internal dialogization of discourse that we have chosen (the internal, as contrasted with the external, compositionally marked, dialogue) the relationship to the alien word, to an alien utterance enters into the positing of the style. Style organically contains within itself indices that reach outside itself, a correspondence of its own elements and the elements of an alien context. The internal politics of style (how the ele-

5. Jean-Jacques Rousseau (1712–1778), Swiss-born French philosopher and author.
6. Cf. B. M. Eichenbaum's book *Lev Tolstoj*, book I (Leningrad, 1928), which contains much relevant material; for example, an explication of the topical context of "Family Happiness" [Bakhtin's note]. Tolstoy famously observed in *Anna Karenina* (1875–77) that "Happy families are all alike; every unhappy family is unhappy in its own way."
7. Light, popular piece of newspaper writing.

ments are put together) is determined by its external politics (its relationship to alien discourse). Discourse lives, as it were, on the boundary between its own context and another, alien, context.

In any actual dialogue the rejoinder also leads such a double life: it is structured and conceptualized in the context of the dialogue as a whole, which consists of its own utterances ("own" from the point of view of the speaker) and of alien utterances (those of the partner). One cannot excise the rejoinder from this combined context made up of one's own words and the words of another without losing its sense and tone. It is an organic part of a heteroglot unity.

The phenomenon of internal dialogization, as we have said, is present to a greater or lesser extent in all realms of the life of the word. But if in extra-artistic prose (everyday, rhetorical, scholarly) dialogization usually stands apart, crystallizes into a special kind of act of its own and runs its course in ordinary dialogue or in other, compositionally clearly marked forms for mixing and polemicizing with the discourse of another—then in *artistic* prose, and especially in the novel, this dialogization penetrates from within the very way in which the word conceives its object and its means for expressing itself, reformulating the semantics and syntactical structure of discourse. Here dialogic inter-orientation becomes, as it were, an event of discourse itself, animating from within and dramatizing discourse in all aspects.

In the majority of poetic genres (poetic in the narrow sense), as we have said, the internal dialogization of discourse is not put to artistic use, it does not enter into the work's "aesthetic object," and is artificially extinguished in poetic discourse. In the novel, however, this internal dialogization becomes one of the most fundamental aspects of prose style and undergoes a specific artistic elaboration.

But internal dialogization can become such a crucial force for creating form only where individual differences and contradictions are enriched by social heteroglossia, where dialogic reverberations do not sound in the semantic heights of discourse (as happens in the rhetorical genres) but penetrate the deep strata of discourse, dialogize language itself and the world view a particular language has (the internal form of discourse)—where the dialogue of voices arises directly out of a social dialogue of "languages," where an alien utterance begins to sound like a socially alien language, where the orientation of the word among alien utterances changes into an orientation of a word among socially alien languages within the boundaries of one and the same national language.

In genres that are poetic in the narrow sense, the natural dialogization of the word is not put to artistic use, the word is sufficient unto itself and does not presume alien utterances beyond its own boundaries. Poetic style is by convention suspended from any mutual interaction with alien discourse, any allusion to alien discourse.

Any way whatever of alluding to alien languages, to the possibility of another vocabulary, another semantics, other syntactic forms and so forth, to the possibility of other linguistic points of view, is equally foreign to poetic style. It follows that any sense of the boundedness, the historicity, the social determination and specificity of one's own language is alien to poetic style, and therefore a critical qualified relationship to one's own language (as merely one of many languages in a heteroglot world) is foreign to poetic style—as is a related phenomenon, the incomplete commitment of oneself, of one's full meaning, to a given language.

Of course this relationship and the relationship to his own language (in greater or lesser degree) could never be foreign to a historically existent poet, as a human being surrounded by living hetero- and polyglossia; but this relationship could not find a place in the *poetic style* of his work without destroying that style, without transposing it into a prosaic key and in the process turning the poet into a writer of prose.

In poetic genres, artistic consciousness—understood as a unity of all the author's semantic and expressive intentions—fully realizes itself within its own language; in them alone is such consciousness fully immanent, expressing itself in it directly and without mediation, without conditions and without distance. The language of the poet is *his* language, he is utterly immersed in it, inseparable from it, he makes use of each form, each word, each expression according to its unmediated power to assign meaning (as it were, "without quotation marks"), that is, as a pure and direct expression of his own intention. No matter what "agonies of the word" the poet endured in the process of creation, in the finished work language is an obedient organ, fully adequate to the author's intention.

The language in a poetic work realizes itself as something about which there can be no doubt, something that cannot be disputed, something all-encompassing. Everything that the poet sees, understands and thinks, he does through the eyes of a given language, in its inner forms, and there is nothing that might require, for its expression, the help of any other or alien language. The language of the poetic genre is a unitary and singular Ptolemaic world[8] outside of which nothing else exists and nothing else is needed. The concept of many worlds of language, all equal in their ability to conceptualize and to be expressive, is organically denied to poetic style.

The world of poetry, no matter how many contradictions and insoluble conflicts the poet develops within it, is always illumined by one unitary and indisputable discourse. Contradictions, conflicts and doubts remain in the object, in thoughts, in living experiences—in short, in the subject matter—but they do not enter into the language itself. In poetry, even discourse about doubts must be cast in a discourse that cannot be doubted.

To take responsibility for the language of the work as a whole at all of its points as *its* language, to assume a full solidarity with each of the work's aspects, tones, nuances—such is the fundamental prerequisite for poetic style; style so conceived is fully adequate to a single language and a single linguistic consciousness. The poet is not able to oppose his own poetic consciousness, his own intentions to the language that he uses, for he is completely within it and therefore cannot turn it into an object to be perceived, reflected upon or related to. Language is present to him only from inside, in the work it does to effect its intention, and not from outside, in its objective specificity and boundedness. Within the limits of poetic style, direct unconditional intentionality, language at its full weight and the objective display of language (as a socially and historically limited linguistic reality) are all

8. That is, the stationary center of the universe. In the system of the universe postulated by Ptolemy (active 127–148 C.E.), the Alexandrian astronomer, mathematician, and geographer, the sun, planets, and stars revolve around the earth.

simultaneous, but incompatible. The unity and singularity of language are the indispensable prerequisites for a realization of the direct (but not objectively typifying) intentional individuality of poetic style and of its monologic steadfastness.

This does not mean, of course, that heteroglossia or even a foreign language is completely shut out of a poetic work. To be sure, such possibilities are limited: a certain latitude for heteroglossia exists only in the "low" poetic genres—in the satiric and comic genres and others. Nevertheless, heteroglossia (other socio-ideological languages) can be introduced into purely poetic genres, primarily in the speeches of characters. But in such a context it is objective. It appears, in essence, as a *thing*, it does not lie on the *same* plane with the real language of the work: it is the depicted gesture of one of the characters and does not appear as an aspect of the word doing the depicting. Elements of heteroglossia enter here not in the capacity of another language carrying its own particular points of view, about which one can say things not expressible in one's own language, but rather in the capacity of a depicted thing. Even when speaking of alien things, the poet speaks in his own language. To shed light on an alien world, he never resorts to an alien language, even though it might in fact be more adequate to that world. Whereas the writer of prose, by contrast—as we shall see—attempts to talk about even his *own* world in an alien language (for example, in the nonliterary language of the teller of tales, or the representative of a specific socio-ideological group); he often measures his own world by alien linguistic standards.

As a consequence of the prerequisites mentioned above, the language of poetic genres, when they approach their stylistic limit,[9] often becomes authoritarian, dogmatic and conservative, sealing itself off from the influence of extraliterary social dialects. Therefore such ideas as a special "poetic language," a "language of the gods," a "priestly language of poetry" and so forth could flourish on poetic soil. It is noteworthy that the poet, should he not accept the given literary language, will sooner resort to the artificial creation of a new language specifically for poetry than he will to the exploitation of actual available social dialects. Social languages are filled with specific objects, typical, socially localized and limited, while the artificially created language of poetry must be a directly intentional language, unitary and singular. Thus, when Russian prose writers at the beginning of the twentieth century began to show a profound interest in dialects and *skaz*, the Symbolists (Bal'mont, V. Ivanov) and later the Futurists dreamed of creating a special "language of poetry," and even made experiments directed toward creating such a language (those of V. Khlebnikov).[1]

The idea of a special unitary and singular language of poetry is a typical utopian philosopheme[2] of poetic discourse: it is grounded in the actual con-

9. It goes without saying that we continually advance as typical the extreme to which poetic genres aspire; in concrete examples of poetic works it is possible to find features fundamental to prose, and numerous hybrids of various generic types exist. These are especially widespread in periods of shift in literary poetic languages [Bahktin's note].

1. Velimir Khlebnikov (1885–1922), Russian experimental poet and playwright. Konstantin Balmont (1867–1943), Russian symbolist poet. Vyacheslav Ivanov (1866–1949), Russian poet and philologist. Symbolism, a poetic movement that began in France in the last third of the 19th century, emphasized the evocation of subjective emotion, via symbol and metaphor, rather than objective description. Futurism, a revolutionary movement in art and literature begun in Italy in 1909, stressed speed, modernity, and rebellion; it quickly found adherents in Russia.

2. In an argument, an inference or assumption.

ditions and demands of poetic style, which is always a style adequately serviced by one directly intentional language from whose point of view other languages (conversational, business and prose languages, among others) are perceived as objects that are in no way its equal.[3] The idea of a "poetic language" is yet another expression of that same Ptolemaic conception of the linguistic and stylistic world.

Language—like the living concrete environment in which the consciousness of the verbal artist lives—is never unitary. It is unitary only as an abstract grammatical system of normative forms, taken in isolation from the concrete, ideological conceptualizations that fill it, and in isolation from the uninterrupted process of historical becoming that is a characteristic of all living language. Actual social life and historical becoming create within an abstractly unitary national language a multitude of concrete worlds, a multitude of bounded verbal-ideological and social belief systems; within these various systems (identical in the abstract) are elements of language filled with various semantic and axiological content and each with its own different sound.

Literary language—both spoken and written—although it is unitary not only in its shared, abstract, linguistic markers but also in its forms for conceptualizing these abstract markers, is itself stratified and heteroglot in its aspect as an expressive system, that is, in the forms that carry its meanings.

This stratification is accomplished first of all by the specific organisms called *genres*. Certain features of language (lexicological, semantic, syntactic) will knit together with the intentional aim, and with the overall accentual system inherent in one or another genre: oratorical, publicistic, newspaper and journalistic genres, the genres of low literature (penny dreadfuls, for instance) or, finally, the various genres of high literature. Certain features of language take on the specific flavor of a given genre: they knit together with specific points of view, specific approaches, forms of thinking, nuances and accents characteristic of the given genre.

In addition, there is interwoven with this generic stratification of language a *professional* stratification of language, in the broad sense of the term "professional": the language of the lawyer, the doctor, the businessman, the politician, the public education teacher and so forth, and these sometimes coincide with, and sometimes depart from, the stratification into genres. It goes without saying that these languages differ from each other not only in their vocabularies; they involve specific forms for manifesting intentions, forms for making conceptualization and evaluation concrete. And even the very language of the writer (the poet or novelist) can be taken as a professional jargon on a par with professional jargons.

What is important to us here is the intentional dimensions, that is, the denotative and expressive dimension of the "shared" language's stratification. It is in fact not the neutral linguistic components of language being stratified and differentiated, but rather a situation in which the intentional possibilities of language are being expropriated: these possibilities are realized in specific directions, filled with specific content, they are made concrete, particular,

3. Such was the point of view taken by Latin toward national languages in the Middle Ages [Bakhtin's note].

and are permeated with concrete value judgments; they knit together with specific objects and with the belief systems of certain genres of expression and points of view peculiar to particular professions. Within these points of view, that is, for the speakers of the language themselves, these generic languages and professional jargons are directly intentional—they denote and express directly and fully, and are capable of expressing themselves without mediation; but outside, that is, for those not participating in the given purview, these languages may be treated as objects, as typifactions, as local color. For such outsiders, the intentions permeating these languages become *things*, limited in their meaning and expression; they attract to, or excise from, such language a particular word—making it difficult for the word to be utilized in a directly intentional way, without any qualifications.

But the situation is far from exhausted by the generic and professional stratification of the common literary language. Although at its very core literary language is frequently socially homogeneous, as the oral and written language of a dominant social group, there is nevertheless always present, even here, a certain degree of social differentiation, a social stratification, that in other eras can become extremely acute. Social stratification may here and there coincide with generic and professional stratification, but in essence it is, of course, a thing completely autonomous and peculiar to itself.

Social stratification is also and primarily determined by differences between the forms used to convey meaning and between the expressive planes of various belief systems—that is, stratification expresses itself in typical differences in ways used to conceptualize and accentuate elements of language, and stratification may not violate the abstractly linguistic dialectological unity of the shared literary language.

What is more, all socially significant world views have the capacity to exploit the intentional possibilities of language through the medium of their specific concrete instancing. Various tendencies (artistic and otherwise), circles, journals, particular newspapers, even particular significant artistic works and individual persons are all capable of stratifying language, in proportion to their social significance; they are capable of attracting its words and forms into their orbit by means of their own characteristic intentions and accents, and in so doing to a certain extent alienating these words and forms from other tendencies, parties, artistic works and persons.

Every socially significant verbal performance has the ability—sometimes for a long period of time, and for a wide circle of persons—to infect with its own intention certain aspects of language that had been affected by its semantic and expressive impulse, imposing on them specific semantic nuances and specific axiological overtones; thus, it can create slogan-words, curse-words, praise-words and so forth.

In any given historical moment of verbal-ideological life, each generation at each social level has its own language; moreover, every age group has as a matter of fact its own language, its own vocabulary, its own particular accentual system that, in their turn, vary depending on social level, academic institution (the language of the cadet, the high school student, the trade school student are all different languages) and other stratifying factors. All this is brought about by socially typifying languages, no matter how narrow the social circle in which they are spoken. It is even possible to have a family jargon define the societal limits of a language, as, for instance, the jargon of the Irtenevs[4] in Tolstoy, with its special vocabulary and unique accentual system.

And finally, at any given moment, languages of various epochs and periods of socio-ideological life cohabit with one another. Even languages of the day exist: one could say that today's and yesterday's socio-ideological and political "day" do not, in a certain sense, share the same language; every day represents another socio-ideological semantic "state of affairs," another vocabulary, another accentual system, with its own slogans, its own ways of assigning blame and praise. Poetry depersonalizes "days" in language, while prose, as we shall see, often deliberately intensifies difference between them, gives them embodied representation and dialogically opposes them to one another in unresolvable dialogues.

Thus at any given moment of its historical existence, language is heteroglot from top to bottom: it represents the co-existence of socio-ideological contradictions between the present and the past, between differing epochs of the past, between different socio-ideological groups in the present, between tendencies, schools, circles and so forth, all given a bodily form. These "languages" of heteroglossia intersect each other in a variety of ways, forming new socially typifying "languages."

Each of these "languages" of heteroglossia requires a methodology very different from the others; each is grounded in a completely different principle for marking differences and for establishing units (for some this principle is functional, in others it is the principle of theme and content, in yet others it is, properly speaking, a socio-dialectological principle). Therefore languages do not *exclude* each other, but rather intersect with each other in many different ways (the Ukrainian language, the language of the epic poem, of early Symbolism, of the student, of a particular generation of children, of the run-of-the-mill intellectual, of the Nietzschean[5] and so on). It might even seem that the very word "language" loses all meaning in this process—for apparently there is no single plane on which all these "languages" might be juxtaposed to one another.

In actual fact, however, there does exist a common plane that methodologically justifies our juxtaposing them: all languages of heteroglossia, whatever the principle underlying them and making each unique, are specific points of view on the world, forms for conceptualizing the world in words, specific world views, each characterized by its own objects, meanings and values. As such they all may be juxtaposed to one another, mutually supplement one another, contradict one another and be interrelated dialogically. As such they encounter one another and co-exist in the consciousness of real people—first and foremost, in the creative consciousness of people who write novels. As such, these languages live a real life, they struggle and evolve in an environment of social heteroglossia. Therefore they are all able to enter into the unitary plane of the novel, which can unite in itself parodic stylizations of generic languages, various forms of stylizations and illustrations of professional and period-bound languages, the languages of particular generations, of social dialects and others (as occurs, for example, in the English comic novel). They may all be drawn in by the novelist for the orchestration

4. Family in Tolstoy's short story "The Devil" (1911).

5. Follower of FRIEDRICH NIETZSCHE (1844–1900), German philologist and philosopher.

of his themes and for the refracted (indirect) expression of his intentions and values.

This is why we constantly put forward the referential and expressive—that is, intentional—factors as the force that stratifies and differentiates the common literary language, and not the linguistic markers (lexical coloration, semantic overtones, etc.) of generic languages, professional jargons and so forth—markers that are, so to speak, the sclerotic deposits of an intentional process, signs left behind on the path of the real living project of an intention, of the particular way it imparts meaning to general linguistic norms. These external markers, linguistically observable and fixable, cannot in themselves be understood or studied without understanding the specific conceptualization they have been given by an intention.

Discourse lives, as it were, beyond itself, in a living impulse [*napravlennost'*] toward the object; if we detach ourselves completely from this impulse all we have left is the naked corpse of the word, from which we can learn nothing at all about the social situation or the fate of a given word in life. *To study the word as such, ignoring the impulse that reaches out beyond it, is just as senseless as to study psychological experience outside the context of that real life toward which it was directed and by which it is determined.*

By stressing the intentional dimension of stratification in literary language, we are able, as has been said, to locate in a single series such methodologically heterogeneous phenomena as professional and social dialects, world views and individual artistic works, for in their intentional dimension one finds that common plane on which they can all be juxtaposed, and juxtaposed dialogically. The whole matter consists in the fact that there may be, between "languages," highly specific dialogic relations; no matter how these languages are conceived, they may all be taken as particular points of view on the world. However varied the social forces doing the work of stratification—a profession, a genre, a particular tendency, an individual personality—the work itself everywhere comes down to the (relatively) protracted and socially meaningful (collective) saturation of language with specific (and consequently limiting) intentions and accents. The longer this stratifying saturation goes on, the broader the social circle encompassed by it and consequently the more substantial the social force bringing about such a stratification of language, then the more sharply focused and stable will be those traces, the linguistic changes in the language markers (linguistic symbols), that are left behind in language as a result of this social force's activity—from stable (and consequently social) semantic nuances to authentic dialectological markers (phonetic, morphological and others), which permit us to speak of particular social dialects.

As a result of the work done by all these stratifying forces in language, there are no "neutral" words and forms—words and forms that can belong to "no one"; language has been completely taken over, shot through with intentions and accents. For any individual consciousness living in it, language is not an abstract system of normative forms but rather a concrete heteroglot conception of the world. All words have the "taste" of a profession, a genre, a tendency, a party, a particular work, a particular person, a generation, an age group, the day and hour. Each word tastes of the context and contexts in which it has lived its socially charged life; all words and forms are populated by intentions. Contextual overtones (generic, tendentious, individualistic) are inevitable in the word.

As a living, socio-ideological concrete thing, as heteroglot opinion, language, for the individual consciousness, lies on the borderline between oneself and the other. The word in language is half someone else's. It becomes "one's own" only when the speaker populates it with his own intention, his own accent, when he appropriates the word, adapting it to his own semantic and expressive intention. Prior to this moment of appropriation, the word does not exist in a neutral and impersonal language (it is not, after all, out of a dictionary that the speaker gets his words!), but rather it exists in other people's mouths, in other people's contexts, serving other people's intentions: it is from there that one must take the word, and make it one's own. And not all words for just anyone submit equally easily to this appropriation, to this seizure and transformation into private property: many words stubbornly resist, others remain alien, sound foreign in the mouth of the one who appropriated them and who now speaks them; they cannot be assimilated into his context and fall out of it; it is as if they put themselves in quotation marks against the will of the speaker. Language is not a neutral medium that passes freely and easily into the private property of the speaker's intentions; it is populated—overpopulated—with the intentions of others. Expropriating it, forcing it to submit to one's own intentions and accents, is a difficult and complicated process.

We have so far proceeded on the assumption of the abstract-linguistic (dialectological) unity of literary language. But even a literary language is anything but a closed dialect. Within the scope of literary language itself there is already a more or less sharply defined boundary between everyday-conversational language and written language. Distinctions between genres frequently coincide with dialectological distinctions (for example, the high—Church Slavonic[6]—and the low—conversational—genres of the eighteenth century); finally, certain dialects may be legitimized in literature and thus to a certain extent be appropriated by literary language.

As they enter literature and are appropriated to literary language, dialects in this new context lose, of course, the quality of closed socio-linguistic systems; they are deformed and in fact cease to be that which they had been simply as dialects. On the other hand, these dialects, on entering the literary language and preserving within it their own dialectological elasticity, their other-languagedness, have the effect of deforming the literary language; it, too, ceases to be that which it had been, a closed socio-linguistic system. Literary language is a highly distinctive phenomenon, as is the linguistic consciousness of the educated person who is its agent; within it, intentional diversity of speech [*raznorečivost'*] (which is present in every living dialect as a closed system) is transformed into diversity of language [*raznojazyčie*]; what results is not a single language but a dialogue of languages.

The national literary language of a people with a highly developed art of prose, especially if it is novelistic prose with a rich and tension-filled verbal-ideological history, is in fact an organized microcosm that reflects the macrocosm not only of national heteroglossia, but of European heteroglossia as well. The unity of a literary language is not a unity of a single, closed language system, but is rather a highly specific unity of several "languages" that have established contact and mutual recognition with each other (merely one of

6. The South Slavic language used in the standard 9th century translation of the Bible done by the brothers Sts. Cyril (827–869) and Methodius (826–885) and still used as a liturgical language by all Slavic Orthodox Christian Churches.

which is poetic language in the narrow sense). Precisely this constitutes the peculiar nature of the methodological problem in literary language.

Concrete socio-ideological language consciousness, as it becomes creative—that is, as it becomes active as literature—discovers itself already surrounded by heteroglossia and not at all a single, unitary language, inviolable and indisputable. The actively literary linguistic consciousness at all times and everywhere (that is, in all epochs of literature historically available to us) comes upon "languages," and not language. Consciousness finds itself inevitably facing the necessity of *having to choose a language*. With each literary-verbal performance, consciousness must actively orient itself amidst heteroglossia, it must move in and occupy a position for itself within it, it chooses, in other words, a "language." Only by remaining in a closed environment, one without writing or thought, completely off the maps of socio-ideological becoming, could a man fail to sense this activity of selecting a language and rest assured in the inviolability of his own language, the conviction that his language is predetermined.

Even such a man, however, deals not in fact with a single language, but with languages—except that the place occupied by each of these languages is fixed and indisputable, the movement from one to the other is predetermined and not a thought process; it is as if these languages were in different chambers. They do not collide with each other in his consciousness, there is no attempt to coordinate them, to look at one of these languages through the eyes of another language.

Thus an illiterate peasant, miles away from any urban center, naively immersed in an unmoving and for him unshakable everyday world, nevertheless lived in several language systems: he prayed to God in one language (Church Slavonic), sang songs in another, spoke to his family in a third and, when he began to dictate petitions to the local authorities through a scribe, he tried speaking yet a fourth language (the official-literate language, "paper" language). All these are *different languages*, even from the point of view of abstract socio-dialectological markers. But these languages were not dialogically coordinated in the linguistic consciousness of the peasant; he passed from one to the other without thinking, automatically: each was indisputably in its own place, and the place of each was indisputable. He was not yet able to regard one language (and the verbal world corresponding to it) through the eyes of another language (that is, the language of everyday life and the everyday world with the language of prayer or song, or vice versa).[7]

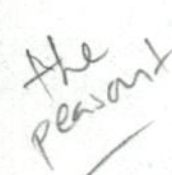

As soon as a critical interanimation of languages began to occur in the consciousness of our peasant, as soon as it became clear that these were not only various different languages but even internally variegated languages, that the ideological systems and approaches to the world that were indissolubly connected with these languages contradicted each other and in no way could live in peace and quiet with one another—then the inviolability and predetermined quality of these languages came to an end, and the necessity of actively choosing one's orientation among them began.

The language and world of prayer, the language and world of song, the language and world of labor and everyday life, the specific language and

7. We are of course deliberately simplifying: the real-life peasant could and did do this to a certain extent [Bakhtin's note].

world of local authorities, the new language and world of the workers freshly immigrated to the city—all these languages and worlds sooner or later emerged from a state of peaceful and moribund equilibrium and revealed the speech diversity in each.

Of course the actively literary linguistic consciousness comes upon an even more varied and profound heteroglossia within literary language itself, as well as outside it. Any fundamental study of the stylistic life of the word must begin with this basic fact. The nature of the heteroglossia encountered and the means by which one orients oneself in it determine the concrete stylistic life that the word will lead.

The poet is a poet insofar as he accepts the idea of a unitary and singular language and a unitary, monologically sealed-off utterance. These ideas are immanent in the poetic genres with which he works. In a condition of actual contradiction, these are what determine the means of orientation open to the poet. The poet must assume a complete single-personed hegemony over his own language, he must assume equal responsibility for each one of its aspects and subordinate them to his own, and only his own, intentions. Each word must express the poet's *meaning* directly and without mediation; there must be no distance between the poet and his word. The meaning must emerge from language as a single intentional whole: none of its stratification, its speech diversity, to say nothing of its language diversity, may be reflected in any fundamental way in his poetic work.

To achieve this, the poet strips the word of others' intentions, he uses only such words and forms (and only in such a way) that they lose their link with concrete intentional levels of language and their connection with specific contexts. Behind the words of a poetic work one should not sense any typical or reified images of genres (except for the given poetic genre), nor professions, tendencies, directions (except the direction chosen by the poet himself), nor world views (except for the unitary and singular world view of the poet himself), nor typical and individual images of speaking persons, their speech mannerisms or typical intonations. *Everything that enters the work must immerse itself in Lethe,*[8] *and forget its previous life in any other contexts: language may remember only its life in poetic contexts (in such contexts, however, even concrete reminiscences are possible).*

Of course there always exists a limited sphere of more or less concrete contexts, and a connection with them must be deliberately evidenced in poetic discourse. But these contexts are purely semantic and, so to speak, accented in the abstract; in their linguistic dimension they are impersonal or at least no particularly concrete linguistic specificity is sensed behind them, no particular manner of speech and so forth, no socially typical linguistic face (the possible personality of the narrator) need peek out from behind them. Everywhere there is only one face—the linguistic face of the author, answering for every word as if it were his own. No matter how multiple and varied these semantic and accentual threads, associations, pointers, hints, correlations that emerge from every poetic word, one language, one conceptual horizon, is sufficient to them all; there is no need of heteroglot social contexts. What is more, the very movement of the poetic symbol (for

8. A mythological river through Hades (literally, "forgetfulness"; Greek). All who drink from it lose their memory.

example, the unfolding of a metaphor) presumes precisely this unity of language, an unmediated correspondence with its object. Social diversity of speech, were it to arise in the work and stratify its language, would make impossible both the normal development and the activity of symbols within it.

The very rhythm of poetic genres does not promote any appreciable degree of stratification. *Rhythm, by creating an unmediated involvement between every aspect of the accentual system of the whole* (via the most immediate rhythmic unities), destroys in embryo those social worlds of speech and of persons that are potentially embedded in the word: in any case, rhythm puts definite limits on them, does not let them unfold or materialize. Rhythm serves to strengthen and concentrate even further the unity and hermetic quality of the surface of poetic style, and of the unitary language that this style posits.

As a result of this work—stripping all aspects of language of the intentions and accents of other people, destroying all traces of social heteroglossia and diversity of language—a tension-filled unity of language is achieved in the poetic work. This unity may be naive, and present only in those extremely rare epochs of poetry, when poetry had not yet exceeded the limits of a closed, unitary, undifferentiated social circle whose language and ideology were not yet stratified. More often than not, we experience a profound and conscious tension through which the unitary poetic language of a work rises from the heteroglot and language-diverse chaos of the literary language contemporary to it.

This is how the poet proceeds. The novelist working in prose (and almost any prose writer) takes a completely different path. He welcomes the heteroglossia and language diversity of the literary and extraliterary language into his own work not only not weakening them but even intensifying them (for he interacts with their particular self-consciousness). It is in fact out of this stratification of language, its speech diversity and even language diversity, that he constructs his style, while at the same time he maintains the unity of his own creative personality and the unity (although it is, to be sure, unity of another order) of his own style.

The prose writer does not purge words of intentions and tones that are alien to him, he does not destroy the seeds of social heteroglossia embedded in words, he does not eliminate those language characterizations and speech mannerisms (potential narrator-personalities) glimmering behind the words and forms, each at a different distance from the ultimate semantic nucleus of his work, that is, the center of his own personal intentions.

The language of the prose writer deploys itself according to degrees of greater or lesser proximity to the author and to his ultimate semantic instantiation: certain aspects of language directly and unmediatedly express (as in poetry) the semantic and expressive intentions of the author, others refract these intentions; the writer of prose does not meld completely with any of these words, but rather accents each of them in a particular way—humorously, ironically, parodically and so forth;[9] yet another group may stand even further from the author's ultimate semantic instantiation, still more thoroughly refracting his intentions; and there are, finally, those words that are

9. That is to say, the words are not his if we understand them as direct words, but they are his as things that are being transmitted ironically, exhibited and so forth, that is, as words that are understood from the distances appropriate to humor, irony, parody, etc. [Bakhtin's note].

completely denied any authorial intentions: the author does not express *himself* in them (as the author of the word)—rather, he *exhibits* them as a unique speech-thing, they function for him as something completely reified. Therefore the stratification of language—generic, professional, social in the narrow sense, that of particular world views, particular tendencies, particular individuals, the social speech diversity and language-diversity (dialects) of language—upon entering the novel establishs its own special order within it, and becomes a unique artistic system, which orchestrates the intentional theme of the author.

Thus a prose writer can distance himself from the language of his own work, while at the same time distancing himself, in varying degrees, from the different layers and aspects of the work. He can make use of language without wholly giving himself up to it, he may treat it as semi-alien or completely alien to himself, while compelling language ultimately to serve all his own intentions. The author does not speak in a given language (from which he distances himself to a greater or lesser degree), but he speaks, as it were, *through* language, a language that has somehow more or less materialized, become objectivized, that he merely ventriloquates.

The prose writer as a novelist does not strip away the intentions of others from the heteroglot language of his works, he does not violate those socio-ideological cultural horizons (big and little worlds) that open up behind heteroglot languages—rather, he welcomes them into his work. The prose writer makes use of words that are already populated with the social intentions of others and compels them to serve his own new intentions, to serve a second master. Therefore the intentions of the prose writer are refracted, and refracted at *different angles*, depending on the degree to which the refracted, heteroglot languages he deals with are socio-ideologically alien, already embodied and already objectivized.

The orientation of the word amid the utterances and languages of others, and all the specific phenomena connected with this orientation, takes on *artistic* significance in novel style. Diversity of voices and heteroglossia enter the novel and organize themselves within it into a structured artistic system. This constitutes the distinguishing feature of the novel as a genre.

Any stylistics capable of dealing with the distinctiveness of the novel as a genre must be a *sociological stylistics*. The internal social dialogism of novelistic discourse requires the concrete social context of discourse to be exposed, to be revealed as the force that determines its entire stylistic structure, its "form" and its "content," determining it not from without, but from within; for indeed, social dialogue reverberates in all aspects of discourse, in those relating to "content" as well as the "formal" aspects themselves.

The development of the novel is a function of the deepening of dialogic essence, its increased scope and greater precision. Fewer and fewer neutral, hard elements ("rock bottom truths") remain that are not drawn into dialogue. Dialogue moves into the deepest molecular and, ultimately, subatomic levels.

Of course, even the poetic word is social, but poetic forms reflect lengthier social processes, i.e., those tendencies in social life requiring centuries to unfold. The novelistic word, however, registers with extreme subtlety the tiniest shifts and oscillations of the social atmosphere; it does so, moreover, while registering it as a whole, in all of its aspects.

When heteroglossia enters the novel it becomes subject to an artistic reworking. The social and historical voices populating language, all its words and all its forms, which provide language with its particular concrete conceptualizations, are organized in the novel into a structured stylistic system that expresses the differentiated socio-ideological position of the author amid the heteroglossia of his epoch.

* * *

1934–35

MAX HORKHEIMER 1895–1973 THEODOR W. ADORNO 1903–1969

In a celebrated aphorism, the German philosopher and social critic Theodor Wiesengrund Adorno proclaimed that "To write poetry after Auschwitz is barbaric." This terse and austere statement encapsulates Adorno's bitterly melancholic understanding of modern art and society, which he often expressed in his highly influential writings on music, sociology, and aesthetics. For Adorno, as for some other members of the celebrated Institute for Social Research, the production of consumable, stylized mass art is complicit with a disinterested view of society that permits social atrocities such as Nazi concentration camps and genocide to go unchecked. The production of such art is also complicit with what Adorno and his fellow German social critic Max Horkheimer called the "culture industry," meaning the constellation of entertainment businesses that produce film, television, radio, magazines, and popular music—all phenomena created by mass technology in which the lines between art, advertising, and propaganda blur. In this world of manipulation and carefree amusement, mass art serves the status quo. As Adorno would assert on many occasions, the only legitimate form of art that can do some justice to the immense suffering in the world is the autonomous art of modernism, which, through its apparent detachment from reality, critiques the world as it is, holding up the promise of a better future.

Adorno was born in Frankfurt am Main to a wealthy and assimilated Jewish wine merchant, Oskar Wiesengrund, and his Catholic wife, Maria Calvelli-Adorno, whose last name Adorno may have assumed because he flirted with embracing his mother's faith. An important influence on Adorno's intellectual development was his training in music, particularly because in the 1920s it enabled him to meet and study with famous Viennese expressionist composers, such as Arnold Schoenberg and his disciples Alban Berg and Anton Webern. The atonal compositions of Schoenberg inspired Adorno, providing him with models for the unsystematic methodology of his critical work in philosophy, sociology, and aesthetics and for what art in the modern world should be. Another formative contemporary influence on Adorno was the noted film critic and social theorist Siegfried Kracauer, who introduced him to earlier German philosophy. As an anti-idealist who would become well-known for his groundbreaking sociological analyses of popular culture, Kracauer taught Adorno how to read the works of IMMANUEL KANT as symptomatic historical and social documents, which is how Adorno would later read mass art and the autonomous artworks of modernism.

At the University of Frankfurt in the 1920s, Kracauer introduced Adorno to WALTER BENJAMIN, who was also interested in sociological analyses of contemporary culture.

Adorno was particularly taken with Benjamin's *Origin of German Tragic Drama* (1928), whose reflections on antisystematic philosophy helped Adorno develop his "atonal" philosophy, which, as he would explain in his *Negative Dialectics* (1966), avoids fixed concepts, much as modernist autonomous art shuns any kind of didactic or affirmative statements. With the help of Benjamin and Kracauer, Adorno's circle of associates later widened to include Ernst Bloch, whom Adorno regarded as the leading philosopher of expressionism, and Bertolt Brecht, the foremost Marxist dramatist. During this time Adorno began studying various materialist approaches to culture, falling under the influence of unorthodox Marxian texts such as Bloch's *Spirit of Utopia* (1918) and GYÖRGY LUKÁCS's *History and Class Consciousness* (1922). Bloch's utopian notion of art influenced Adorno's understanding of autonomous art, and Lukács's conception of reification informed his theory of the "mass deception" wrought by the modern culture industry.

At the University of Frankfurt, Adorno also met Max Horkheimer, a member of the now famous interdisciplinary Institute for Social Research (the so-called Frankfurt School), which was founded in 1924 and concerned initially with Marxist political economy, labor-movement history, and Marx-Engels scholarship. Born near Stuttgart to an upwardly mobile Jewish family, Horkheimer as a young man resisted his father's plans for him to run the family textile business because he could not accept the exploitation of labor on which it was based. After World War I, Horkheimer began his studies in Munich and then moved to the University of Frankfurt, which offered an exciting environment for those interested in social philosophy. He studied with the neo-Kantian philosopher Hans Cornelius, submitted his *Habilitationsschrift* (dissertation) in 1925, and became a regular lecturer in the history of philosophy. Like Adorno, Horkheimer moved away from idealist philosophy and its unhistorical approaches to Marxist materialist views. When Horkheimer assumed the directorship of the institute in 1930, he shifted its focus to cultural studies and so-called Critical Theory, a term he coined for the emerging mode of theoretical and empirical social analyses of modern culture typical of Adorno, Herbert Marcuse, and other members of the Frankfurt School.

Through his relationship with Horkheimer, Adorno would publish in the institute's journal, become a member in 1938, and ultimately succeed Horkheimer as director in 1964. Even more important, in the mid-1930s Horkheimer invited Adorno to America to do sociological work for the institute, which had been forced to relocate after being closed by the Nazis in 1933. Adorno himself had been denied the right to teach at the university level because he was Jewish. Consequently, in 1938 Adorno accepted Horkheimer's invitation and moved to New York and then, in 1941, to Los Angeles. There Adorno and Horkheimer collaborated on *Dialectic of Enlightenment* (1947), their major critique of modern culture, in which they interrogate the notion that the Western world has been progressing since the Enlightenment. In this dense polemical work, they claim that the modern West has not fulfilled the utopian promise of the Enlightenment, becoming instead a rationalized, administered world that dominates individuals through instrumental reason, monopoly capitalism, and political totalitarianism.

Appearing as a long chapter in Adorno and Horkheimer's *Dialectic of Enlightenment*, "The Culture Industry: Enlightenment as Mass Deception" argues that the administered modern world is sustained in part by technologically reproduced mass art. In contrast to Benjamin, who on occasion was optimistic about the emancipatory potential of mass art, Adorno and Horkheimer contend that the culture industry serves the totalitarian impulses of modern capitalist society, not least because the interests of leading broadcasting firms, publishing companies, and motion picture studios are economically interwoven with those of all other capitalist industries. In its attempt to produce and reproduce the social relations of a homogenized society, the culture industry contributes to the liquidation of the individual and the maintenance of the status quo. It transforms art into commodities and people into complacent consumers, depicting a "realistic" world that is really no more than a combination of stereotypes, advertising, and propaganda.

The culture industry, moreover, helps create a state of mind in which people's desires for pleasure and happiness are activated but deferred in endless entertainment. It inculcates resignation, habituating consumers to the everyday drudgery of the modern world. It does not "sublimate" the desire for happiness by providing compensatory entertainment for the life of regimentation but instead "represses" the desire for happiness, depicting the modern world in a degraded tragedy of "realistic" characters who accept the inexorable order of things. In this way the culture industry manages the psyche of its consumers, a line of thought that weds Marxian and Freudian insights—a combination often first credited to the Frankfurt School.

After World War II, Adorno and Horkheimer returned to Germany and reestablished the Institute for Social Research at the University of Frankfurt, where they also assumed professorships. Horkheimer eventually became rector of the university, serving from 1951 to 1953. During the 1960s, as he completed *Negative Dialectics* and addressed timely sociological issues, Adorno worked on a monumental and never-completed study, *Aesthetic Theory*, which was posthumously published in 1970. In numerous published writings before his death, Adorno propounded his views on the autonomous art of modernism, praising such writers as Samuel Beckett and Franz Kafka, whose difficult works he viewed as specific responses to the historical and social conditions of modernity. For Adorno, modern art resists the self-evidence of empirical reality, lends suffering a voice, and acknowledges a better future to come. In the 1960s Adorno saw his Marxist utopian position on art and his melancholic "mandarin" view of mass culture criticized by German student activists who demonstrated against him, questioned his Marxist credentials, and charged him with political quietism. While his work on the culture industry accurately portrays tendencies present in mid-twentieth-century Western societies, many theorists would later find it losing some of its point toward the close of the century, when social disaggregation and niche marketing came to characterize mass societies. But even so, Adorno still serves as a forerunner for critics concerned with the politics of popular culture and the prospects for cultural studies.

BIBLIOGRAPHY

The authoritative German edition of Adorno's collected works is the projected twenty-three-volume *Gesammelte Schriften*, edited by Rolf Tiedemann (1970–). English translations of Adorno's writings on music theory, history, and criticism (with their original publication date given first) include *Philosophy of Modern Music* (1949; 1973), *Introduction to the Sociology of Music* (1962; 1976), *In Search of Wagner* (1952; 1981), *Alban Berg: Master of the Smallest Link* (1968; 1991), *Mahler: A Musical Physiognomy* (1960; 1992), *Quasi Una Fantasia: Essays on Modern Music* (1963; 1992), *Composing for the Films* (1994), *Sound Figures* (1959; 1998), and *Beethoven: The Philosophy of Music* (1993; 1998). A substantial number of English translations of Adorno's sociological writings are readily available, including *Prisms* (1955; 1967), *Dialectic of Enlightenment* (1947; 1972), *Aspects of Sociology* (1956; 1972), *Minima Moralia: Reflections from a Damaged Life* (1951; 1974), *The Positivist Dispute in German Sociology* (1976), *Culture Industry: Selected Essays on Mass Culture* (1991), and *Stars Come Down to Earth and Other Essays on the Irrational* (1994). Translations into English of works focusing on philosophy, aesthetics, and literature include *The Jargon of Authenticity* (1964; 1973), *Negative Dialectics* (1966; 1973), *Against Epistemology* (1956; 1982), *Kierkegaard: Construction of the Aesthetic* (1933; 1989), *Notes to Literature* (4 vols., 1958–74; 2 vols., 1991), *Hegel: Three Studies* (1963; 1993), and *Aesthetic Theory* (1970; two trans. published, 1984, 1997). For a biography of Adorno, see Martin Jay's *Adorno* (1984).

The projected eighteen-volume *Gesammelte Schriften* of Horkheimer, edited by

Alfred Schmidt and Gunzelin Schmid Noerr (1985–), is the definitive German edition of his work. The major English translations of his writings are *Eclipse of Reason* (1947), *Critical Theory: Selected Essays* (1972), *Critique of Instrumental Reason: Lectures and Essays Since the End of World War II* (1974), *Dawn and Decline: Notes 1926–1931 and 1950–1969* (1974), and *Between Philosophy and Social Science: Selected Early Writings* (1993). Representative essays by Horkheimer, Adorno, and other members of the Institute for Social Research, along with a helpful bibliography, can be found in *The Essential Frankfurt School Reader*, edited by Andrew Arato and Eike Gebhardt (1982).

For a discussion of Adorno and Horkheimer's early involvement with the Frankfurt School, see Martin Jay's *Dialectical Imagination: A History of the Frankfurt School and the Institute of Social Research, 1923–1950* (1973). Susan Buck-Morss's *Origin of Negative Dialectics: Theodor W. Adorno, Walter Benjamin, and the Frankfurt Institute* (1977) provides a historical account of the beginnings of Critical Theory. For useful studies of Adorno, Horkheimer, Critical Theory, and the work of the Frankfurt School as a whole, see David Held's *Introduction to Critical Theory: Horkheimer to Habermas* (1980) and *Foundations of the Frankfurt School of Social Research*, edited by Judith Marcus and Zoltán Tar (1984). Gillian Rose's *Melancholy Science: An Introduction to the Thought of Theodor W. Adorno* (1978) offers a wide-ranging study of Adorno's work. Fredric Jameson's controversial *Late Marxism: Adorno, or, the Persistence of the Dialectic* (1990) demonstrates the relevance of Adorno to postmodern times. Peter Uwe Hohendahl's *Prismatic Thought: Theodor W. Adorno* (1995) offers a general overview, while Deborah Cook's *The Culture Industry Revisited: Theodor W. Adorno on Mass Culture* (1996) gives a comprehensive study of Adorno's writings on the culture industry. For a critical overview of Horkheimer's work, along with a bibliography, see *On Max Horkheimer*, edited by Seyla Benhabib et al. (1993). Bibliographical information on Adorno is available in Jay's biography, mentioned above.

From Dialectic of Enlightenment[1]

From *The Culture Industry: Enlightenment as Mass Deception*

The sociological theory that the loss of the support of objectively established religion, the dissolution of the last remnants of precapitalism, together with technological and social differentiation or specialization, have led to cultural chaos is disproved every day; for culture now impresses the same stamp on everything. Films, radio and magazines make up a system which is uniform as a whole and in every part. Even the aesthetic activities of political opposites are one in their enthusiastic obedience to the rhythm of the iron system. The decorative industrial management buildings and exhibition centers in authoritarian countries are much the same as anywhere else. The huge gleaming towers that shoot up everywhere are outward signs of the ingenious planning of international concerns, toward which the unleashed entrepreneurial system (whose monuments are a mass of gloomy houses and business premises in grimy, spiritless cities) was already hastening. Even now the older houses just outside the concrete city centers look like slums, and the new bungalows on the outskirts are at one with the flimsy structures of world fairs in their praise of technical progress and their built-in demand to be

1. Translated by John Cumming.

discarded after a short while like empty food cans. Yet the city housing projects designed to perpetuate the individual as a supposedly independent unit in a small hygienic dwelling make him all the more subservient to his adversary—the absolute power of capitalism. Because the inhabitants, as producers and as consumers, are drawn into the center in search of work and pleasure, all the living units crystallize into well-organized complexes. The striking unity of microcosm and macrocosm presents men with a model of their culture: the false identity of the general and the particular. Under monopoly all mass culture is identical, and the lines of its artificial framework begin to show through. The people at the top are no longer so interested in concealing monopoly: as its violence becomes more open, so its power grows. Movies and radio need no longer pretend to be art. The truth that they are just business is made into an ideology in order to justify the rubbish they deliberately produce. They call themselves industries; and when their directors' incomes are published, any doubt about the social utility of the finished products is removed.

Interested parties explain the culture industry in technological terms. It is alleged that because millions participate in it, certain reproduction processes are necessary that inevitably require identical needs in innumerable places to be satisfied with identical goods. The technical contrast between the few production centers and the large number of widely dispersed consumption points is said to demand organization and planning by management. Furthermore, it is claimed that standards were based in the first place on consumers' needs, and for that reason were accepted with so little resistance. The result is the circle of manipulation and retroactive need in which the unity of the system grows ever stronger. No mention is made of the fact that the basis on which technology acquires power over society is the power of those whose economic hold over society is greatest. A technological rationale is the rationale of domination itself. It is the coercive nature of society alienated from itself. Automobiles, bombs, and movies keep the whole thing together until their leveling element shows its strength in the very wrong which it furthered. It has made the technology of the culture industry no more than the achievement of standardization and mass production, sacrificing whatever involved a distinction between the logic of the work and that of the social system. This is the result not of a law of movement in technology as such but of its function in today's economy. The need which might resist central control has already been suppressed by the control of the individual consciousness. The step from the telephone to the radio has clearly distinguished the roles. The former still allowed the subscriber to play the role of subject, and was liberal. The latter is democratic: it turns all participants into listeners and authoritatively subjects them to broadcast programs which are all exactly the same. No machinery of rejoinder has been devised, and private broadcasters are denied any freedom. They are confined to the apocryphal field of the "amateur," and also have to accept organization from above. But any trace of spontaneity from the public in official broadcasting is controlled and absorbed by talent scouts, studio competitions and official programs of every kind selected by professionals. Talented performers belong to the industry long before it displays them; otherwise they would not be so eager to fit in. The attitude of the public, which ostensibly and actually favors the system of the culture industry, is a part of the system and not an excuse for it. If one branch of art follows the same formula as one with a very different medium and content; if the dramatic intrigue of broadcast soap operas becomes no more than useful material for showing how to master technical problems at both ends of the scale of musical experience—real jazz or a cheap imitation; or if a movement from a Beethoven symphony is crudely "adapted" for a film sound-track in the same way as a Tolstoy novel is garbled in a film script: then the claim that this is done to satisfy the spontaneous wishes of the public is no more than hot air. We are closer to the facts if we explain these phenomena as inherent in the technical and personnel apparatus which, down to its last cog, itself forms part of the economic mechanism of selection. In addition there is the agreement—or at least the determination—of all executive authorities not to produce or sanction anything that in any way differs from their own rules, their own ideas about consumers, or above all themselves.

In our age the objective social tendency is incarnate in the hidden subjective purposes of company directors, the foremost among whom are in the most powerful sectors of industry—steel, petroleum, electricity, and chemicals. Culture monopolies are weak and dependent in comparison. They cannot afford to neglect their appeasement of the real holders of power if their sphere of activity in mass society (a sphere producing a specific type of commodity which anyhow is still too closely bound up with easygoing liberalism and Jewish intellectuals) is not to undergo a series of purges. The dependence of the most powerful broadcasting company on the electrical industry, or of the motion picture industry on the banks, is characteristic of the whole sphere, whose individual branches are themselves economically interwoven. All are in such close contact that the extreme concentration of mental forces allows demarcation lines between different firms and technical branches to be ignored. The ruthless unity in the culture industry is evidence of what will happen in politics. Marked differentiations such as those of A and B films, or of stories in magazines in different price ranges, depend not so much on subject matter as on classifying, organizing, and labeling consumers. Something is provided for all so that none may escape; the distinctions are emphasized and extended. The public is catered for with a hierarchical range of mass-produced products of varying quality, thus advancing the rule of complete quantification. Everybody must behave (as if spontaneously) in accordance with his previously determined and indexed level, and choose the category of mass product turned out for his type. Consumers appear as statistics on research organization charts, and are divided by income groups into red, green, and blue areas; the technique is that used for any type of propaganda.

How formalized the procedure is can be seen when the mechanically differentiated products prove to be all alike in the end. That the difference between the Chrysler range and General Motors products is basically illusory strikes every child with a keen interest in varieties. What connoisseurs discuss as good or bad points serve only to perpetuate the semblance of competition and range of choice. The same applies to the Warner Brothers and Metro Goldwyn Mayer productions. But even the differences between the more expensive and cheaper models put out by the same firm steadily diminish: for automobiles, there are such differences as the number of cylinders, cubic capacity, details of patented gadgets; and for films there are the number of stars, the extravagant use of technology, labor, and equipment, and the introduction of the latest psychological formulas. The universal criterion of merit is the amount of "conspicuous production," of blatant cash investment. The varying budgets in the culture industry do not bear the slightest relation to factual values, to the meaning of the products themselves. Even the technical media are relentlessly forced into uniformity. Television aims at a synthesis of radio and film, and is held up only because the interested parties have not yet reached agreement, but its consequences will be quite enormous and promise to intensify the impoverishment of aesthetic matter so drastically, that by tomorrow the thinly veiled identity of all industrial culture products can come triumphantly out into the open, derisively fulfilling the Wagnerian[2] dream of the *Gesamtkunstwerk*—the fusion of all the arts in one work. The alliance of word, image, and music is all the more perfect than in *Tristan* because the sensuous elements which all approvingly reflect the surface of social reality are in principle embodied in the same technical process, the unity of which becomes its distinctive content. This process integrates all the elements of the production, from the novel (shaped with an eye to the film) to the last sound effect. It is the triumph of invested capital, whose title as absolute master is etched deep into the hearts of the dispossessed in the employment line; it is the meaningful content of every film, whatever plot the production team may have selected.

* * *

The whole world is made to pass through the filter of the culture industry. The old experience of the movie-goer, who sees the world outside as an extension of the film he has just left (because the latter is intent upon reproducing the world of everyday perceptions), is now the producer's guideline. The more intensely and flawlessly his techniques duplicate empirical objects, the easier it is today for the illusion to prevail that the outside world is the straightforward continuation of that presented on the screen. This purpose has been furthered by mechanical reproduction since the lightning takeover by the sound film.

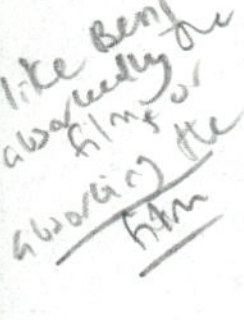

Real life is becoming indistinguishable from the movies. The sound film, far surpassing the theater of illusion, leaves no room for imagination or reflection on the part of the audience, who is unable to respond within the structure of the film, yet deviate from its precise detail without losing the thread of the story; hence the film forces its victims to equate it directly with reality. The stunting of the mass-media consumer's powers of imagination and spontaneity does not have to be traced back to any psychological mechanisms; he must ascribe the loss of those attributes to the objective nature of the products themselves, especially to the most characteristic of them, the sound film. They are so designed that quickness, powers of observation, and experience are undeniably needed to apprehend them at all; yet sustained thought is out of the question if the spectator is not to miss the relentless rush of facts. Even though the effort required for his response is semiautomatic, no scope is left for the imagination. Those who are so absorbed by the world of the movie—by its images, gestures, and words—that they are unable to supply what really makes it a world, do not have to dwell on

2. Richard Wagner (1813–1883), German composer. His operas include *Tristan und Isolde* (1859).

particular points of its mechanics during a screening. All the other films and products of the entertainment industry which they have seen have taught them what to expect; they react automatically. The might of industrial society is lodged in men's minds. The entertainments manufacturers know that their products will be consumed with alertness even when the customer is distraught, for each of them is a model of the huge economic machinery which has always sustained the masses, whether at work or at leisure—which is akin to work. From every sound film and every broadcast program the social effect can be inferred which is exclusive to none but is shared by all alike. The culture industry as a whole has molded men as a type unfailingly reproduced in every product. All the agents of this process, from the producer to the women's clubs, take good care that the simple reproduction of this mental state is not nuanced or extended in any way.

The art historians and guardians of culture who complain of the extinction in the West of a basic style-determining power are wrong. The stereotyped appropriation of everything, even the inchoate, for the purposes of mechanical reproduction surpasses the rigor and general currency of any "real style," in the sense in which cultural *cognoscenti* celebrate the organic precapitalist past. No Palestrina[3] could be more of a purist in eliminating every unprepared and unresolved discord than the jazz arranger in suppressing any development which does not conform to the jargon. When jazzing up Mozart he changes him not only when he is too serious or too difficult but when he harmonizes the melody in a different way, perhaps more simply, than is customary now. No medieval builder can have scrutinized the subjects for church windows and sculptures more suspiciously than the studio hierarchy scrutinizes a work by Balzac or Hugo[4] before finally approving it. No medieval theologian could have determined the degree of the torment to be suffered by the damned in accordance with the *ordo*[5] of divine love more meticulously than the producers of shoddy epics calculate the torture to be undergone by the hero or the exact point to which the leading lady's hemline shall be raised. The explicit and implicit, exoteric and esoteric catalog of the forbidden and tolerated is so extensive that it not only defines the area of freedom but is all-powerful inside it. Everything down to the last detail is shaped accordingly. Like its counterpart, avant-garde art, the entertainment industry determines its own language, down to its very syntax and vocabulary, by the use of anathema.[6] The constant pressure to produce new effects (which must conform to the old pattern) serves merely as another rule to increase the power of the conventions when any single effect threatens to slip through the net. Every detail is so firmly stamped with sameness that nothing can appear which is not marked at birth, or does not meet with approval at first sight.

* * *

In the culture industry the notion of genuine style is seen to be the aesthetic equivalent of domination. Style considered as mere aesthetic regularity is a romantic dream of the past. The unity of style not only of the Christian

3. Giovanni Pierluigi da Palestrina (1525–1594), Italian composer.
4. Victor Hugo (1802–1885), French poet and novelist. Honoré de Balzac (1799–1850), French novelist.
5. Order (Latin).
6. A vigorous curse or denunciation, usually by an ecclesiastical authority.

Middle Ages but of the Renaissance expresses in each case the different structure of social power, and not the obscure experience of the oppressed in which the general was enclosed. The great artists were never those who embodied a wholly flawless and perfect style, but those who used style as a way of hardening themselves against the chaotic expression of suffering, as a negative truth. The style of their works gave what was expressed that force without which life flows away unheard. Those very art forms which are known as classical, such as Mozart's music, contain objective trends which represent something different to the style which they incarnate. As late as Schönberg and Picasso,[7] the great artists have retained a mistrust of style, and at crucial points have subordinated it to the logic of the matter. What Dadaists and Expressionists[8] called the untruth of style as such triumphs today in the sung jargon of a crooner, in the carefully contrived elegance of a film star, and even in the admirable expertise of a photograph of a peasant's squalid hut. Style represents a promise in every work of art. That which is expressed is subsumed through style into the dominant forms of generality, into the language of music, painting, or words, in the hope that it will be reconciled thus with the idea of true generality. This promise held out by the work of art that it will create truth by lending new shape to the conventional social forms is as necessary as it is hypocritical. It unconditionally posits the real forms of life as it is by suggesting that fulfillment lies in their aesthetic derivatives. To this extent the claim of art is always ideology too. However, only in this confrontation with tradition of which style is the record can art express suffering. That factor in a work of art which enables it to transcend reality certainly cannot be detached from style; but it does not consist of the harmony actually realized, of any doubtful unity of form and content, within and without, of individual and society; it is to be found in those features in which discrepancy appears: in the necessary failure of the passionate striving for identity. Instead of exposing itself to this failure in which the style of the great work of art has always achieved self-negation, the inferior work has always relied on its similarity with others—on a surrogate identity.

In the culture industry this imitation finally becomes absolute. Having ceased to be anything but style, it reveals the latter's secret: obedience to the social hierarchy. Today aesthetic barbarity completes what has threatened the creations of the spirit since they were gathered together as culture and neutralized. To speak of culture was always contrary to culture. Culture as a common denominator already contains in embryo that schematization and process of cataloging and classification which bring culture within the sphere of administration. And it is precisely the industrialized, the consequent, subsumption which entirely accords with this notion of culture. By subordinating in the same way and to the same end all areas of intellectual creation, by occupying men's senses from the time they leave the factory in the evening to the time they clock in again the next morning with matter that bears the impress of the labor process they themselves have to sustain throughout the day, this subsumption mockingly satisfies the concept of a

7. Pablo Picasso (1881–1975), Spanish Cubist painter. Arnold Schoenberg (1874–1951), Austrian composer known for his expressionistic atonal or serial compositions (see following note).

8. Expressionism is an artistic movement that went beyond impressionism by magnifying dark inner experiences. Dadaism, a precursor to surrealism, is an artistic movement that protested the insanity of World War I by demolishing the tenets of art, philosophy, and logic.

unified culture which the philosophers of personality contrasted with mass culture.

* * *

Nevertheless the culture industry remains the entertainment business. Its influence over the consumers is established by entertainment; that will ultimately be broken not by an outright decree, but by the hostility inherent in the principle of entertainment to what is greater than itself. Since all the trends of the culture industry are profoundly embedded in the public by the whole social process, they are encouraged by the survival of the market in this area. Demand has not yet been replaced by simple obedience. As is well known, the major reorganization of the film industry shortly before World War I, the material prerequisite of its expansion, was precisely its deliberate acceptance of the public's needs as recorded at the box-office—a procedure which was hardly thought necessary in the pioneering days of the screen. The same opinion is held today by the captains of the film industry, who take as their criterion the more or less phenomenal song hits but wisely never have recourse to the judgment of truth, the opposite criterion. Business is their ideology. It is quite correct that the power of the culture industry resides in its identification with a manufactured need, and not in simple contrast to it, even if this contrast were one of complete power and complete powerlessness. Amusement under late capitalism is the prolongation of work. It is sought after as an escape from the mechanized work process, and to recruit strength in order to be able to cope with it again. But at the same time mechanization has such power over a man's leisure and happiness, and so profoundly determines the manufacture of amusement goods, that his experiences are inevitably after-images of the work process itself. The ostensible content is merely a faded foreground; what sinks in is the automatic succession of standardized operations. What happens at work, in the factory, or in the office can only be escaped from by approximation to it in one's leisure time. All amusement suffers from this incurable malady. Pleasure hardens into boredom because, if it is to remain pleasure, it must not demand any effort and therefore moves rigorously in the worn grooves of association. No independent thinking must be expected from the audience: the product prescribes every reaction: not by its natural structure (which collapses under reflection), but by signals. Any logical connection calling for mental effort is painstakingly avoided. As far as possible, developments must follow from the immediately preceding situation and never from the idea of the whole. For the attentive movie-goer any individual scene will give him the whole thing. Even the set pattern itself still seems dangerous, offering some meaning—wretched as it might be—where only meaninglessness is acceptable. Often the plot is maliciously deprived of the development demanded by characters and matter according to the old pattern. Instead, the next step is what the script writer takes to be the most striking effect in the particular situation. Banal though elaborate surprise interrupts the story-line. The tendency mischievously to fall back on pure nonsense, which was a legitimate part of popular art, farce and clowning, right up to Chaplin and the Marx Brothers,[9]

9. American comic actors: Chico (Leonard) (1887–1961), Harpo (Adolph) (1888–1964), Groucho (Julius Henry) (1890–1977), Gummo (Milton) (1893–1977), and Zeppo (Herbert) (1901–1979). Charlie (Sir Charles Spencer) Chaplin (1889–1977), English comic actor and producer.

is most obvious in the unpretentious kinds. This tendency has completely asserted itself in the text of the novelty song, in the thriller movie, and in cartoons, although in films starring Greer Garson and Bette Davis[1] the unity of the socio-psychological case study provides something approximating a claim to a consistent plot. The idea itself, together with the objects of comedy and terror, is massacred and fragmented. Novelty songs have always existed on a contempt for meaning which, as predecessors and successors of psychoanalysis, they reduce to the monotony of sexual symbolism. Today detective and adventure films no longer give the audience the opportunity to experience the resolution. In the non-ironic varieties of the genre, it has also to rest content with the simple horror of situations which have almost ceased to be linked in any way.

* * *

This raises the question whether the culture industry fulfills the function of diverting minds which it boasts about so loudly. If most of the radio stations and movie theaters were closed down, the consumers would probably not lose so very much. To walk from the street into the movie theater is no longer to enter a world of dream; as soon as the very existence of these institutions no longer made it obligatory to use them, there would be no great urge to do so. Such closures would not be reactionary machine wrecking. The disappointment would be felt not so much by the enthusiasts as by the slow-witted, who are the ones who suffer for everything anyhow. In spite of the films which are intended to complete her integration, the housewife finds in the darkness of the movie theater a place of refuge where she can sit for a few hours with nobody watching, just as she used to look out of the window when there were still homes and rest in the evening. The unemployed in the great cities find coolness in summer and warmth in winter in these temperature-controlled locations. Otherwise, despite its size, this bloated pleasure apparatus adds no dignity to man's lives. The idea of "fully exploiting" available technical resources and the facilities for aesthetic mass consumption is part of the economic system which refuses to exploit resources to abolish hunger.

The culture industry perpetually cheats its consumers of what it perpetually promises. The promissory note which, with its plots and staging, it draws on pleasure is endlessly prolonged; the promise, which is actually all the spectacle consists of, is illusory: all it actually confirms is that the real point will never be reached, that the diner must be satisfied with the menu. In front of the appetite stimulated by all those brilliant names and images there is finally set no more than a commendation of the depressing everyday world it sought to escape. Of course works of art were not sexual exhibitions either. However, by representing deprivation as negative, they retracted, as it were, the prostitution of the impulse and rescued by mediation what was denied. The secret of aesthetic sublimation is its representation of fulfillment as a broken promise. The culture industry does not sublimate; it represses. By repeatedly exposing the objects of desire, breasts in a clinging sweater or the naked torso of the athletic hero, it only stimulates the unsublimated forepleasure which habitual deprivation has long since reduced to a maso-

1. American actor (1908–1989). Garson (1904–1996), English actor.

chistic semblance. There is no erotic situation which, while insinuating and exciting, does not fail to indicate unmistakably that things can never go that far. The Hays Office merely confirms the ritual of Tantalus[2] that the culture industry has established anyway. Works of art are ascetic and unashamed; the culture industry is pornographic and prudish. Love is downgraded to romance. And, after the descent, much is permitted; even license as a marketable speciality has its quota bearing the trade description "daring." The mass production of the sexual automatically achieves its repression. Because of his ubiquity, the film star with whom one is meant to fall in love is from the outset a copy of himself. Every tenor voice comes to sound like a Caruso[3] record, and the "natural" faces of Texas girls are like the successful models by whom Hollywood has typecast them. The mechanical reproduction of beauty, which reactionary cultural fanaticism wholeheartedly serves in its methodical idolization of individuality, leaves no room for that unconscious idolatry which was once essential to beauty. The triumph over beauty is celebrated by humor—the *Schadenfreude*[4] that every successful deprivation calls forth. There is laughter because there is nothing to laugh at. Laughter, whether conciliatory or terrible, always occurs when some fear passes. It indicates liberation either from physical danger or from the grip of logic. Conciliatory laughter is heard as the echo of an escape from power; the wrong kind overcomes fear by capitulating to the forces which are to be feared. It is the echo of power as something inescapable. Fun is a medicinal bath. The pleasure industry never fails to prescribe it. It makes laughter the instrument of the fraud practised on happiness. Moments of happiness are without laughter only operettas and films portray sex to the accompaniment of resounding laughter. But Baudelaire is as devoid of humour as Hölderlin.[5] In the false society laughter is a disease which has attacked happiness and is drawing it into its worthless totality. To laugh at something is always to deride it, and the life which, according to Bergson,[6] in laughter breaks through the barrier, is actually an invading barbaric life, self-assertion prepared to parade its liberation from any scruple when the social occasion arises. Such a laughing audience is a parody of humanity. Its members are monads, all dedicated to the pleasure of being ready for anything at the expense of everyone else. Their harmony is a caricature of solidarity. What is fiendish about this false laughter is that it is a compelling parody of the best, which is conciliatory. Delight is austere: *res severa verum gaudium*.[7] The monastic theory that not asceticism but the sexual act denotes the renunciation of attainable bliss receives negative confirmation in the gravity of the lover who with foreboding commits his life to the fleeting moment. In the culture industry, jovial denial takes the place of the pain found in ecstasy and in asceticism The supreme law is that they shall not satisfy their desires at any price; they must laugh and be content with laughter. In every product of the culture industry, the permanent denial imposed by civilization is once

2. A Greek mythological figure whose punishment in Hades is always to have food and drink just out of his reach. "Hays Office": unofficial name of the Motion Picture Producers and Distributors of America, founded in 1922 by Will Hays to monitor the film industry (precursor to the Production Code Administration, founded in 1934).

3. Enrico Caruso (1873–1921), popular Italian opera tenor.

4. Grim joy (i.e., joy at others' troubles) (German).

5. Friedrich Hölderlin (1770–1843), German poet and translator. CHARLES BAUDELAIRE (1821–1867), French poet, critic, and forerunner of modernism.

6. Henri Bergson (1859–1941), French philosopher, author of *Laughter: An Essay on the Meaning of the Comic* (1911).

7. True joy is a serious thing (Latin).

again unmistakably demonstrated and inflicted on its victims. To offer and to deprive them of something is one and the same. This is what happens in erotic films. Precisely because it must never take place, everything centers upon copulation. In films it is more strictly forbidden for an illegitimate relationship to be admitted without the parties being punished than for a millionaire's future son-in-law to be active in the labor movement. In contrast to the liberal era, industrialized as well as popular culture may wax indignant at capitalism, but it cannot renounce the threat of castration. This is fundamental. It outlasts the organized acceptance of the uniformed seen in the films which are produced to that end, and in reality. What is decisive today is no longer puritanism, although it still asserts itself in the form of women's organizations, but the necessity inherent in the system not to leave the customer alone, not for a moment to allow him any suspicion that resistance is possible. The principle dictates that he should be shown all his needs as capable of fulfillment, but that those needs should be so predetermined that he feels himself to be the eternal consumer, the object of the culture industry. Not only does it make him believe that the deception it practices is satisfaction, but it goes further and implies that, whatever the state of affairs, he must put up with what is offered. The escape from everyday drudgery which the whole culture industry promises may be compared to the daughter's abduction in the cartoon: the father is holding the ladder in the dark. The paradise offered by the culture industry is the same old drudgery. Both escape and elopement are predesigned to lead back to the starting point. Pleasure promotes the resignation which it ought to help to forget.

* * *

The stronger the positions of the culture industry become, the more summarily it can deal with consumers' needs, producing them, controlling them, disciplining them, and even withdrawing amusement: no limits are set to cultural progress of this kind. But the tendency is immanent in the principle of amusement itself, which is enlightened in a bourgeois sense. If the need for amusement was in large measure the creation of industry, which used the subject as a means of recommending the work to the masses—the oleograph[8] by the dainty morsel it depicted, or the cake mix by a picture of a cake—amusement always reveals the influence of business, the sales talk, the quack's spiel. But the original affinity of business and amusement is shown in the latter's specific significance: to defend society. To be pleased means to say Yes. It is possible only by insulation from the totality of the social process, by desensitization and, from the first, by senselessly sacrificing the inescapable claim of every work, however inane, within its limits to reflect the whole. Pleasure always means not to think about anything, to forget suffering even where it is shown. Basically it is helplessness. It is flight; not, as is asserted, flight from a wretched reality, but from the last remaining thought of resistance. The liberation which amusement promises is freedom from thought and from negation. The effrontery of the rhetorical question. "What do people want?" lies in the fact that it is addressed—as if to reflective individuals—to those very people who are deliberately to be deprived of this individuality. Even when the public does—exceptionally—rebel against the

8. A chromolithograph printed on cloth to imitate an oil painting.

pleasure industry, all it can muster is that feeble resistance which that very industry has inculcated in it. Nevertheless, it has become increasingly difficult to keep people in this condition. The rate at which they are reduced to stupidity must not fall behind the rate at which their intelligence is increasing. In this age of statistics the masses are too sharp to identify themselves with the millionaire on the screen, and too slow-witted to ignore the law of the largest number. Ideology conceals itself in the calculation of probabilities. Not everyone will be lucky one day—but the person who draws the winning ticket, or rather the one who is marked out to do so by a higher power—usually by the pleasure industry itself, which is represented as unceasingly in search of talent. Those discovered by talent scouts and then publicized on a vast scale by the studio are ideal types of the new dependent average. Of course, the starlet is meant to symbolize the typist in such a way that the splendid evening dress seems meant for the actress as distinct from the real girl. The girls in the audience not only feel that they could be on the screen, but realize the great gulf separating them from it. Only one girl can draw the lucky ticket, only one man can win the prize, and if, mathematically, all have the same chance, yet this is so infinitesimal for each one that he or she will do best to write it off and rejoice in the other's success, which might just as well have been his or hers, and somehow never is. Whenever the culture industry still issues an invitation naïvely to identify, it is immediately withdrawn. No one can escape from himself any more. Once a member of the audience could see his own wedding in the one shown in the film. Now the lucky actors on the screen are copies of the same category as every member of the public, but such equality only demonstrates the insurmountable separation of the human elements. The perfect similarity is the absolute difference. The identity of the category forbids that of the individual cases. Ironically, man as a member of a species has been made a reality by the culture industry. Now any person signifies only those attributes by which he can replace everybody else: he is interchangeable, a copy. As an individual he is completely expendable and utterly insignificant, and this is just what he finds out when time deprives him of this similarity. This changes the inner structure of the religion of success—otherwise strictly maintained. Increasing emphasis is laid not on the path *per aspera ad astra*[9] (which presupposes hardship and effort), but on winning a prize. The element of blind chance in the routine decision about which song deserves to be a hit and which extra a heroine is stressed by the ideology. Movies emphasize chance. By stopping at nothing to ensure that all the characters are essentially alike, with the exception of the villain, and by excluding non-conforming faces (for example, those which, like Garbo's,[1] do not look as if you could say "Hello sister!" to them), life is made easier for movie-goers at first. They are assured that they are all right as they are, that they could do just as well and that nothing beyond their powers will be asked of them. But at the same time they are given a hint that any effort would be useless because even bourgeois luck no longer has any connection with the calculable effect of their own work. They take the hint. Fundamentally they all recognize chance (by which one occasionally makes his fortune) as the other side of planning. Precisely because

9. Through adversities to the stars (Latin).
1. Greta Garbo (born Greta Gustafsson, 1905–1990), famously reclusive Swedish-born American film star.

the forces of society are so deployed in the direction of rationality that anyone might become an engineer or manager, it has ceased entirely to be a rational matter who the one will be in whom society will invest training or confidence for such functions. Chance and planning become one and the same thing, because, given men's equality, individual success and failure—right up to the top—lose any economic meaning. Chance itself is planned, not because it affects any particular individual but precisely because it is believed to play a vital part. It serves the planners as an alibi, and makes it seem that the complex of transactions and measures into which life has been transformed leaves scope for spontaneous and direct relations between man. This freedom is symbolized in the various media of the culture industry by the arbitrary selection of average individuals. In a magazine's detailed accounts of the modestly magnificent pleasure-trips it has arranged for the lucky person, preferably a stenotypist (who has probably won the competition because of her contacts with local bigwigs), the powerlessness of all is reflected. They are mere matter—so much so that those in control can take someone up into their heaven and throw him out again: his rights and his work count for nothing. Industry is interested in people merely as customers and employees, and has in fact reduced mankind as a whole and each of its elements to this all-embracing formula. According to the ruling aspect at the time, ideology emphasizes plan or chance, technology or life, civilization or nature. As employees, men are reminded of the rational organization and urged to fit in like sensible people. As customers, the freedom of choice, the charm of novelty, is demonstrated to them on the screen or in the press by means of the human and personal anecdote. In either case they remain objects.

The less the culture industry has to promise, the less it can offer a meaningful explanation of life, and the emptier is the ideology it disseminates. Even the abstract ideals of the harmony and beneficence of society are too concrete in this age of universal publicity. We have even learned how to identify abstract concepts as sales propaganda. Language based entirely on truth simply arouses impatience to get on with the business deal it is probably advancing. The words that are not means appear senseless; the others seem to be fiction, untrue. Value judgments are taken either as advertising or as empty talk. Accordingly ideology has been made vague and noncommittal, and thus neither clearer nor weaker. Its very vagueness, its almost scientific aversion from committing itself to anything which cannot be verified, acts as an instrument of domination. It becomes a vigorous and prearranged promulgation of the status quo. The culture industry tends to make itself the embodiment of authoritative pronouncements, and thus the irrefutable prophet of the prevailing order.

* * *

By emphasizing the "heart of gold," society admits the suffering it has created: everyone knows that he is now helpless in the system, and ideology has to take this into account. Far from concealing suffering under the cloak of improvised fellowship, the culture industry takes pride in looking it in the face like a man, however great the strain on self-control. The pathos of composure justifies the world which makes it necessary. That is life—very hard, but just because of that so wonderful and so healthy. This lie does not shrink from tragedy. Mass culture deals with it, in the same way as centralized society does not abolish the suffering of its members but records and plans it. That it is why it borrows so persistently from art. This provides the tragic substance which pure amusement cannot itself supply, but which it needs if it is somehow to remain faithful to the principle of the exact reproduction of phenomena. Tragedy made into a carefully calculated and accepted aspect of the world is a blessing. It is a safeguard against the reproach that truth is not respected, whereas it is really being adopted with cynical regret. To the consumer who—culturally—has seen better days it offers a substitute for long-discarded profundities. It provides the regular movie-goer with the scraps of culture he must have for prestige. It comforts all with the thought that a tough, genuine human fate is still possible, and that it must at all costs be represented uncompromisingly. Life in all the aspects which ideology today sets out to duplicate shows up all the more gloriously, powerfully and magnificently, the more it is redolent of necessary suffering. It begins to resemble fate. Tragedy is reduced to the threat to destroy anyone who does not cooperate, whereas its paradoxical significance once lay in a hopeless resistance to mythic destiny. Tragic fate becomes just punishment, which is what bourgeois aesthetics always tried to turn it into. The morality of mass culture is the cheap form of yesterday's children's books. In a first-class production, for example, the villainous character appears as a hysterical woman who (with presumed clinical accuracy) tries to ruin the happiness of her opposite number, who is truer to reality, and herself suffers a quite untheatrical death. So much learning is of course found only at the top. Lower down less trouble is taken. Tragedy is made harmless without recourse to social psychology. Just as every Viennese operetta worthy of the name had to have its tragic finale in the second act, which left nothing for the third except to clear up misunderstandings, the culture industry assigns tragedy a fixed place in the routine. The well-known existence of the recipe is enough to allay any fear that there is no restraint on tragedy. The description of the dramatic formula by the housewife as "getting into trouble and out again" embraces the whole of mass culture from the idiotic women's serial to the top production. Even the worst ending which began with good intentions confirms the order of things and corrupts the tragic force, either because the woman whose love runs counter to the laws of the game plays with her death for a brief spell of happiness, or because the sad ending in the film all the more clearly stresses the indestructibility of actual life. The tragic film becomes an institution for moral improvement. The masses, demoralized by their life under the pressure of the system, and who show signs of civilization only in modes of behavior which have been forced on them and through which fury and recalcitrance show everywhere, are to be kept in order by the sight of an inexorable life and exemplary behavior. Culture has always played its part in taming revolutionary and barbaric instincts. Industrial culture adds its contribution. It shows the condition under which this merciless life can be lived at all. The individual who is thoroughly weary must use his weariness as energy for his surrender to the collective power which wears him out. In films, those permanently desperate situations which crush the spectator in ordinary life somehow become a promise that one can go on living. One has only to become aware of one's own nothingness, only to recognize defeat and one is one with it all. Society is full of desperate people and therefore a prey to rackets. In some of the most significant German novels of the pre-Fascist

era such as Döblin's *Berlin Alexanderplatz* and Fallada's[2] *Kleiner Mann, Was Nun*, this trend was as obvious as in the average film and in the devices of jazz. What all these things have in common is the self-derision of man. The possibility of becoming a subject in the economy, an entrepreneur or a proprietor, has been completely liquidated. Right down to the humblest shop, the independent enterprise, on the management and inheritance of which the bourgeois family and the position of its head had rested, became hopelessly dependent. Everybody became an employee; and in this civilization of employees the dignity of the father (questionable anyhow) vanishes. The attitude of the individual to the racket, business, profession or party, before or after admission, the Führer's gesticulations before the masses, or the suitor's before his sweetheart, assume specifically masochistic traits. The attitude into which everybody is forced in order to give repeated proof of his moral suitability for this society reminds one of the boys who, during tribal initiation, go round in a circle with a stereotyped smile on their faces while the priest strikes them. Life in the late capitalist era is a constant initiation rite. Everyone must show that he wholly identifies himself with the power which is belaboring him. This occurs in the principle of jazz syncopation, which simultaneously derides stumbling and makes it a rule. The eunuch-like voice of the crooner on the radio, the heiress's smooth suitor, who falls into the swimming pool in his dinner jacket, are models for those who must become whatever the system wants. Everyone can be like this omnipotent society; everyone can be happy, if only he will capitulate fully and sacrifice his claim to happiness. In his weakness society recognizes its strength, and gives him some of it. His defenselessness makes him reliable. Hence tragedy is discarded. Once the opposition of the individual to society was its substance. It glorified "the bravery and freedom of emotion before a powerful enemy, an exalted affliction, a dreadful problem."[3] Today tragedy has melted away into the nothingness of that false identity of society and individual, whose terror still shows for a moment in the empty semblance of the tragic. But the miracle of integration, the permanent act of grace by the authority who receives the defenseless person—once he has swallowed his rebelliousness—signifies Fascism. This can be seen in the humanitarianism which Döblin uses to let his Biberkopf[4] find refuge, and again in socially-slanted films. The capacity to find refuge, to survive one's own ruin, by which tragedy is defeated, is found in the new generation; they can do any work because the work process does not let them become attached to any. This is reminiscent of the sad lack of conviction of the homecoming soldier with no interest in the war, or of the casual laborer who ends up by joining a paramilitary organization. This liquidation of tragedy confirms the abolition of the individual.

In the culture industry the individual is an illusion not merely because of the standardization of the means of production. He is tolerated only so long as his complete identification with the generality is unquestioned. Pseudo

2. Hans Fallada (pseudonym of Rudolf Ditzen, 1893–1947); *Little Man, What Now?* was published in 1932. Alfred Döblin (1878–1957) published *Berlin Alexanderplatz* in 1929.

3. Nietzsche, *Götzendämmerung* [1888, *Twilight of the Idols*], *Werke*, vol. VIII, p. 136 [Horkheimer and Adorno's note]. FRIEDRICH NIETZSCHE (1844–1900), German philosopher.

4. Hero of *Berlin Alexanderplatz*.

individuality is rife: from the standardized jazz improvisation to the exceptional film star whose hair curls over her eye to demonstrate her originality. What is individual is no more than the generality's power to stamp the accidental detail so firmly that it is accepted as such. The defiant reserve or elegant appearance of the individual on show is mass-produced like Yale locks, whose only difference can be measured in fractions of millimeters. The peculiarity of the self is a monopoly commodity determined by society; it is falsely represented as natural. It is no more than the moustache, the French accent, the deep voice of the woman of the world, the Lubitsch[5] touch: finger prints on identity cards which are otherwise exactly the same, and into which the lives and faces of every single person are transformed by the power of the generality. Pseudo individuality is the prerequisite for comprehending tragedy and removing its poison: only because individuals have ceased to be themselves and are now merely centers where the general tendencies meet, is it possible to receive them again, whole and entire, into the generality. In this way mass culture discloses the fictitious character of the "individual" in the bourgeois era, and is merely unjust in boasting on account of this dreary harmony of general and particular. The principle of individuality was always full of contradiction. Individuation has never really been achieved. Self-preservation in the shape of class has kept everyone at the stage of a mere species being. Every bourgeois characteristic, in spite of its deviation and indeed because of it, expressed the same thing: the harshness of the competitive society. The individual who supported society bore its disfiguring mark; seemingly free, he was actually the product of its economic and social apparatus. Power based itself on the prevailing conditions of power when it sought the approval of persons affected by it. As it progressed, bourgeois society did also develop the individual. Against the will of its leaders, technology has changed human beings from children into persons. However, every advance in individuation of this kind took place at the expense of the individuality in whose name it occurred, so that nothing was left but the resolve to pursue one's own particular purpose. The bourgeois whose existence is split into a business and a private life, whose private life is split into keeping up his public image and intimacy, whose intimacy is split into the surly partnership of marriage and the bitter comfort of being quite alone, at odds with himself and everybody else, is already virtually a Nazi, replete both with enthusiasm and abuse; or a modern city-dweller who can now only imagine friendship as a "social contact": that is, as being in social contact with others with whom he has no inward contact. The only reason why the culture industry can deal so successfully with individuality is that the latter has always reproduced the fragility of society. On the faces of private individuals and movie heroes put together according to the patterns on magazine covers vanishes a pretense in which no one now believes; the popularity of the hero models comes partly from a secret satisfaction that the effort to achieve individuation has at last been replaced by the effort to imitate, which is admittedly more breathless. It is idle to hope that this self-contradictory, disintegrating "person" will not last for generations, that the system must collapse because of such a psychological split, or that the deceitful substi-

5. Ernst Lubitsch (1892–1947), German-American film director whose widely imitated style ("the Lubitsch touch") brought European elegance and irony to Hollywood cinema from the 1920s to the 1940s.

tution of the stereotype for the individual will of itself become unbearable for mankind. Since Shakespeare's *Hamlet*, the unity of the personality has been seen through as a pretense. Synthetically produced physiognomies show that the people of today have already forgotten that there was ever a notion of what human life was. For centuries society has been preparing for Victor Mature and Mickey Rooney.[6] By destroying they come to fulfill.

The idolization of the cheap involves making the average the heroic. The highest-paid stars resemble pictures advertising unspecified proprietary articles. Not without good purpose are they often selected from the host of commercial models. The prevailing taste takes its ideal from advertising, the beauty in consumption. Hence the Socratic saying that the beautiful is the useful[7] has now been fulfilled—ironically. The cinema makes propaganda for the culture combine as a whole; on radio, goods for whose sake the cultural commodity exists are also recommended individually. For a few coins one can see the film which cost millions, for even less one can buy the chewing gum whose manufacture involved immense riches—a hoard increased still further by sales. *In absentia*, but by universal suffrage, the treasure of armies is revealed, but prostitution is not allowed inside the country. The best orchestras in the world—clearly not so—are brought into your living room free of charge. It is all a parody of the never-never land, just as the national society is a parody of the human society. You name it, we supply it. A man up from the country remarked at the old Berlin Metropol theater that it was astonishing what they could do for the money; his comment has long since been adopted by the culture industry and made the very substance of production. This is always coupled with the triumph that it is possible; but this, in large measure, is the very triumph. Putting on a show means showing everybody what there is, and what can be achieved. Even today it is still a fair, but incurably sick with culture. Just as the people who had been attracted by the fairground barkers overcame their disappointment in the booths with a brave smile, because they really knew in advance what would happen, so the movie-goer sticks knowingly to the institution. With the cheapness of mass-produce luxury goods and its complement, the universal swindle, a change in the character of the art commodity itself is coming about. What is new is not that it is a commodity, but that today it deliberately admits it is one; that art renounces its own autonomy and proudly takes its place among consumption goods constitutes the charm of novelty. Art as a separate sphere was always possible only in a bourgeois society. Even as a negation of that social purposiveness which is spreading through the market, its freedom remains essentially bound up with the premise of a commodity economy. Pure works of art which deny the commodity society by the very fact that they obey their own law were always wares all the same. In so far as, until the eighteenth century, the buyer's patronage shielded the artist from the market, they were dependent on the buyer and his objectives. The purposelessness of the great modern work of art depends on the anonymity of the market. Its demands pass through so many intermediaries that the artist is exempt from any definite requirements—though admittedly only to a certain degree, for throughout the whole history of the bourgeoisie his

6. Mature (1913–1999) and Rooney (b. 1920), American actors.

7. See PLATO, *Hippias Major* 295c–e; as usual in Plato's dialogues, the Greek philosopher Socrates (469–399 B.C.E.) is the primary speaker.

autonomy was only tolerated, and thus contained an element of untruth which ultimately led to the social liquidation of art. When mortally sick, Beethoven hurled away a novel by Sir Walter Scott[8] with the cry: "Why, the fellow writes for money," and yet proved a most experienced and stubborn businessman in disposing of the last quartets, which were a most extreme renunciation of the market; he is the most outstanding example of the unity of those opposites, market and independence, in bourgeois art. Those who succumb to the ideology are precisely those who cover up the contradiction instead of taking it into the consciousness of their own production as Beethoven did: he went on to express in music his anger at losing a few pence, and derived the metaphysical *Es Muss Sein*[9] (which attempts an aesthetic banishment of the pressure of the world by taking it into itself) from the housekeeper's demand for her monthly wages. The principle of idealistic aesthetics—purposefulness without a purpose[1]—reverses the scheme of things to which bourgeois art conforms socially: purposelessness for the purposes declared by the market. At last, in the demand for entertainment and relaxation, purpose has absorbed the realm of purposelessness. But as the insistence that art should be disposable in terms of money becomes absolute, a shift in the internal structure of cultural commodities begins to show itself. The use which men in this antagonistic society promise themselves from the work of art is itself, to a great extent, that very existence of the useless which is abolished by compete inclusion under use. The work of art, by completely assimilating itself to need, deceitfully deprives men of precisely that liberation from the principle of utility which it should inaugurate. What might be called use value in the reception of cultural commodities is replaced by exchange value; in place of enjoyment there are gallery-visiting and factual knowledge: the prestige seeker replaces the connoisseur. The consumer becomes the ideology of the pleasure industry, whose institutions he cannot escape. One simply "has to" have seen *Mrs. Miniver*,[2] just as one "has to" subscribe to *Life* and *Time*. Everything is looked at from only one aspect: that it can be used for something else, however vague the notion of this use may be. No object has an inherent value; it is valuable only to the extent that it can be exchanged. The use value of art, its mode of being, is treated as a fetish; and the fetish, the work's social rating (misinterpreted as its artistic status) becomes its use value—the only quality which is enjoyed. The commodity function of art disappears only to be wholly realized when art becomes a species of commodity instead, marketable and interchangeable like an industrial product. But art as a type of product which existed to be sold and yet to be unsaleable is wholly and hypocritically converted into "unsaleability" as soon as the transaction ceases to be the mere intention and becomes its sole principle. No tickets could be bought when Toscanini conducted over the radio;[3] he was heard without charge, and every sound of the symphony was accompanied, as it were, by the sublime puff that the symphony was not interrupted by any advertising: "This concert is brought to you as a public service." The illusion was made possible by the profits of

8. Scottish poet and novelist (1771–1832), forced by financial difficulties late in his life to undertake much hack work.
9. It must be (German).
1. IMMANUEL KANT's terminology in his *Critique of Judgment* (1790; see above).
2. Movie (1942) with Greer Garson in the title role.
3. Arturo Toscanini conducted the National Broadcasting Company Symphony Orchestra, which was organized specifically for him in 1937, in a notable series of radio broadcasts.

the united automobile and soap manufacturers, whose payments keep the radio stations going—and, of course, by the increased sales of the electrical industry, which manufactures the radio sets.

* * *

1947

EDMUND WILSON
1895–1972

Intellectually curious and prolific, Edmund Wilson contributed to many journals and magazines, and for diverse audiences—writers, intellectuals, academics, and non-academics—he served as a potent source of informed taste and judgment. He seemed, as fellow critic Alfred Kazin noted, to have "the whole tradition of literature in his bones," and he became the foremost American literary journalist of the twentieth century.

Born in Red Bank, New Jersey, Wilson was the only child of prosperous but emotionally distant parents. He was educated in the classics at the Hill School in Pottstown, Pennsylvania, where, he later said, he was taught the virtues of "lucidity, force, and ease" in written expression, and at Princeton (1912–16), where his friends included F. Scott Fitzgerald (who called Wilson his "intellectual conscience").

After graduation, Wilson worked briefly as a reporter for the New York *Evening Sun*. Like the novelists John Dos Passos and Ernest Hemingway, who became his friends, he served in a hospital unit during World War I; he then was reassigned to the intelligence corps. When the war ended, he freelanced as a writer and worked as an editor of *Vanity Fair* (1920–21) and the *New Republic* (1926–31); later he became the main book reviewer for the *New Yorker* (1944–48).

Wilson's first important book was *Axel's Castle: A Study in the Imaginative Literature of 1870–1930* (1931), a pioneering study of modernism's relation to French symbolism, with chapters on William Butler Yeats, Marcel Proust, James Joyce, T. S. ELIOT, Gertrude Stein, and Paul Valéry. Yet even as he revealed his passionate interest in the literary innovations of modernism, he voiced his ambivalence in *Axel's Castle* itself and in his correspondence. He told his editor, Maxwell Perkins, "I believe that any literary movement which tends so to paralyze the will, to discourage literature from entering into action, has a very serious weakness, and I think that the time has now come for a reaction against it."

Part of Wilson's reaction was *To the Finland Station* (1940), a panoramic study of the origins of socialism, the careers and main ideas of KARL MARX and FRIEDRICH ENGELS, and the intellectual and historical contexts of the Russian Revolution. Linking political utopianism with aesthetic activity, Wilson portrayed Marx, Engels, and Vladimir Lenin as "poets themselves in their political vision"; their "genius," he added, "lay in the intensity of their imaginations and in the skill with which through the written and spoken word they were able to arouse others to see human life and history as they did."

This sharp feeling for individuals as agents of grand historical change makes Wilson, at his best, thrilling to read: he tells captivating, dramatic stories. It also makes him hard to categorize as a critic. Rather than interpreting texts, Wilson sought to "spotlight" (one of his favorite terms) particular writers in the contexts of their eras; thus he turned to biography, psychology, economics, politics, and history at roughly the same moment when JOHN CROWE RANSOM, CLEANTH BROOKS, and the other New Critics were calling for an "intrinsic" literary criticism based on close reading. For them, the focus was on the text itself and on a method transferable to others. Wilson, in contrast, refused to narrow his approach, praising those critics of the past—such as the nineteenth-century French writers Ernest Renan and Hippolyte Taine—who had used criticism as "the vehicle of all sorts of ideas about the purpose and destiny of human life in general."

Wilson's work ranges from fiction (e.g., a novel, *I Thought of Daisy*, 1929; rev. ed., 1967) to collections of literary essays (e.g., *The Wound and the Bow*, 1941) to travel writings (e.g., *The Scrolls from the Dead Sea*, 1955; rev. ed., 1969) to an 800-page study of the literature of the American Civil War, *Patriotic Gore* (1962), and a polemical pamphlet, *The Fruits of the MLA* (1969), criticizing academic scholars for their pedantic editorial practices and failure to help make the writings of American authors widely available. Wilson also assembled many collections of his essays and reviews—the best is *The Shores of Light: A Literary Chronicle of the Twenties and Thirties* (1952).

With the publication of *Axel's Castle* at one end and *To the Finland Station* at the other, the 1930s is the most interesting phase of Wilson's career. Our selection, "Marxism and Literature" (1938), bears witness to Wilson's indebtedness to Marxist thought and to his determination to correct mistaken notions about it. Even more, it shows his regard for the act of literary creation, for the separateness and specialness of the work of art, which, he insists, should not be judged on political grounds alone.

Politics and economics were pressing concerns of writers and intellectuals during the 1930s, as the stock market crash in October 1929 precipitated a total collapse in the American economy. Banks, farms, and businesses failed in unprecedented numbers, unemployment skyrocketed, and personal income was cut in half. President Herbert Hoover's efforts had no effect on this seemingly systemic failure, which was evident in markets around the world. For Wilson and others, Marxism explained what had happened: capitalism was breaking apart because of its internal conflicts and contradictions. Moreover, the Soviet Union of the 1920s appeared to many as a hopeful counterexample that confirmed the rightness of their faith in revolutionary transformation.

By 1930, as he studied events here and abroad, Wilson had moved toward the political left. He explained in *The American Jitters: A Year of the Slump* (1932; rev. ed., 1958), a book of social reportage on his cross-country travels in America during the early years of the Depression: "My present feeling is that my satisfaction in seeing the whole world fairly and sensibly run as Russia is now run, instead of by shabby politicians in the interests of acquisitive manufacturers, business men and bankers, would more than compensate me for any losses that I might incur in the process." In 1931, Wilson wrote an "Appeal" to progressives to "take Communism away from the Communists" and plant its principles in authentically American soil. He visited the Soviet Union in 1935 and reported on his experiences in *Travels in Two Democracies* (1936).

Despite his enthusiasm for the Soviet system, Wilson remained critical and independent. He was suspicious of Joseph Stalin's cult of personality, distrusted the ever-expanding Soviet bureaucracy, balked at the Communists' tendency to evaluate literature and criticism only in narrowly political terms, and saw the purge trials of the mid- to late 1930s—used by Stalin to kill off or imprison rivals and those deemed disloyal—as a monstrous sham. To borrow a phrase he applied to the novelist Theodore Dreiser, Wilson was an "unrussianizable American." He was drawn toward Marxism by its apparently accurate diagnosis of capitalism and by the sheer sweep and scale of its historical vision. But he was an undogmatic Marxist, not a Communist. For him, as for the African American novelist Richard Wright, Marxism was only a "starting point" ("Blueprint for Negro Writing," 1937).

In his essay "Marxism and Literature," first published in his collection *The Triple Thinkers* (1938; rev. ed., 1948), Wilson is both sympathetic and resistant to critics' attempts to connect Marxism and literature. Such connections were being made vigorously in the United States in *New Masses* and other radical magazines and journals, in collections of "proletarian" literature that depicted the struggles of the working class, and in books such as Granville Hicks's *The Great Tradition: An Interpretation of American Literature Since the Civil War* (1933). In this tightly constructed piece, Wilson musters evidence to demonstrate that the views of Marx and Engels on literature have been misinterpreted, sets them against those of Lenin and LEON TROTSKY, and condemns the repressiveness of Stalin's dictatorship. He emphasizes the folly of presuming that good literature can be made from ideological formulas, explores the prospects for literature and criticism in periods of political revolution, and sketches the differences between sociocultural conditions in the United States and the Soviet Union.

At the center of "Marxism and Literature" is Wilson's depoliticizing of Marxism—he defines its value as "throw[ing] a great deal of light on the origins and social significance of works of art"—and his high regard for "literary appreciation." One of the fascinations of the essay is the way it displays Wilson in the process of at once responding positively to and yet critiquing Marxism, while ensuring that he preserves the fundamental duties that must be performed by the critic of literature as an art.

BIBLIOGRAPHY

Wilson's major works of literary criticism include *Axel's Castle* (1931), *The Triple Thinkers* (1938; rev. ed., 1948), *The Wound and the Bow* (1941), and *Patriotic Gore* (1962). A wide-ranging selection of Wilson's writings is given in *The Portable Edmund Wilson*, edited by Lewis M. Dabney (1983), later revised and republished as *The Edmund Wilson Reader* (1997). See also *Edmund Wilson: Letters on Literature and Politics, 1912–1972*, edited by Elena Wilson (1977), and *The Nabokov-Wilson Letters: Correspondence between Vladimir Nabokov and Edmund Wilson, 1940–1971*, edited by Simon Karlinsky (1979). Wilson's journals and diaries—gathered and titled by decade, starting with *The Twenties*—have been edited by Leon Edel and (the final volume) Lewis Dabney (5 vols., 1975–93). Jeffrey Meyers has written a comprehensive biography, *Edmund Wilson* (1995), that includes cogent coverage of Wilson's literary and political writings of the 1920s and 1930s. For an overview that combines biography with critical analysis, see David Castronovo, *Edmund Wilson Revisited* (1999).

Critical studies include Sherman Paul, *Edmund Wilson: A Study of Literary Vocation in Our Time* (1965), especially good on Wilson's response to the Great Depression and his interest in Marxism; Warner Berthoff, *Edmund Wilson* (1968), a compelling, often critical assessment; Leonard Kriegel, *Edmund Wilson* (1971); George Douglas, *Edmund Wilson's America* (1983), which surveys Wilson's writings on American literature, politics, and culture; and Janet Groth, *Edmund Wilson: A Critic for Our Time* (1990). For commentaries and recollections by Alfred Kazin, Angus Wilson, John Updike, and others, consult *Edmund Wilson: The Man and His Work*, edited by John Wain (1978). Grant Webster, *The Republic of Letters: A History of Postwar American Literary Opinion* (1979), studies Wilson in relation to the New Critics and the New York Intellectuals. For an excellent collection of recent essays, see *Edmund Wilson: Centennial Reflections*, edited by Lewis M. Dabney (1997). Richard David Ramsey's *Edmund Wilson: A Bibliography* (1971) needs updating but remains valuable.

Marxism and Literature

1. LET us begin with Marx and Engels.[1] What was the role assigned to literature and art in the system of Dialectical Materialism?[2] This role was much less cut-and-dried than is nowadays often supposed. Marx and Engels conceived the forms of human society in any given country and epoch as growing out of the methods of production which prevailed at that place and time; and out of the relations involved in the social forms arose a 'superstructure' of higher activities such as politics, law, religion, philosophy, literature and art. These activities were not, as is sometimes assumed, wholly explicable in terms of economics. They showed the mold, in ways direct or indirect, of the social configuration below them, but each was working to get away from its roots in the social classes and to constitute a professional group, with its own discipline and its own standards of value, which cut across class lines. These departments 'all react upon one another and upon the economic base. It is not the case that the economic situation is the sole active cause and everything else only a passive effect. But there is a reciprocal interaction within a fundamental economic necessity, which in the last instance always asserts itself' (Engels to Hans Starkenburg,[3] January 25, 1894). So that the art of a great artistic period may reach a point of vitality and vision where it can influence the life of the period down to its very economic foundations. Simply, it must cease to flourish with the social system which made it possible by providing the artist with training and leisure, even though the artist himself may have been working for the destruction of that system.

2. Marx and Engels, unlike some of their followers, never attempted to furnish social-economic formulas by which the validity of works of art might be tested. They had grown up in the sunset of Goethe[4] before the great age of German literature was over, and they had both set out in their youth to be poets; they responded to imaginative work, first of all, on its artistic merits. They could ridicule a trashy writer like Eugène Sue[5] for what they regarded as his *petit bourgeois* remedies for the miseries of contemporary society (*The Holy Family*);[6] they could become bitter about Ferdinand Freiligrath,[7] who had deserted the Communist League and turned nationalist in 1870 (Marx to Engels, August 22, 1870). And Marx could even make similar jibes at Heine[8] when he thought that the latter had stooped to truckling to the authorities or when he read the expressions of piety in his will (Marx to Engels, December 21, 1866 and May 8, 1856). But Marx's daughter tells us that her father loved Heine 'as much as his work and was very indulgent of his political shortcomings. He used to say that the poets were originals, who must be allowed to go their own way, and that one shouldn't apply to them

1. For the aesthetic writings of the German socialists and theorists KARL MARX (1818–1883) and FRIEDRICH ENGELS (1820–1895), see above.
2. The Marxist theory that maintains the priority of matter over mind, stressing the material basis of reality as a changing dialectical process (or reciprocal interaction) of matter and mind.
3. Heinz Starkenburg, a German Social Democrat and editor, published this letter (actually sent to a law student named Walter Borgius).
4. Johann Wolfgang von Goethe (1749–1832), German poet, dramatist, and novelist.
5. Pseudonym of Marie-Joseph Sue (1804–1857), French author of sensational novels about urban life.
6. A work by Marx and Engels (1845). *Petit bourgeois*: lower-middle-class (French).
7. German political poet (1810–1876).
8. Heinrich Heine (1797–1856), German poet and essayist.

the same standards as to ordinary people.' It was not characteristic of Marx and Engels to judge literature—that is, literature of power and distinction—in terms of its purely political tendencies. In fact, Engels always warned the socialist novelists against the dangers of *Tendenz-Literatur* (Engels to Minna Kautsky, November 26, 1885; and to Margaret Harkness,[9] April 1888). In writing to Minna Kautsky about one of her novels, he tells her that the personalities of her hero and heroine have been dissolved in the principles they represent. 'You evidently,' he says, 'felt the need of publicly taking sides in this book, of proclaiming your opinions to the world . . . But I believe that the tendency should arise from the situation and the action themselves without being explicitly formulated, and that the poet is not under the obligation to furnish the reader with a ready-made historical solution for the future of the conflict which he describes.' When Ferdinand Lassalle[1] sent Marx and Engels his poetic tragedy, *Franz von Sickingen*, and invited them to criticize it, Marx replied that, 'setting aside any purely critical attitude toward the work,' it had on a first reading affected him powerfully—characteristically adding that upon persons of a more emotional nature it would doubtless produce an even stronger effect; and Engels wrote that he had read it twice and had been moved by it so profoundly that he had been obliged to lay it aside in order to arrive at any critical perspective. It was only after pulling themselves together and making some purely literary observations that they were able to proceed to discuss, from their special historical point of view, the period with which the drama dealt and to show how Lassalle's own political position had led him to mistake the role of his hero. Aeschylus[2] Marx loved for his grandeur and for the defiance of Zeus by Prometheus; Goethe they both immensely admired: Engels wrote of him as a 'colossal' and 'universal' genius whose career had been marred by an admixture in his character of the philistine and the courtier (*German Socialism in Verse and Prose*); Shakespeare Marx knew by heart and was extremely fond of quoting, but never—despite the long, learned and ridiculous essays which have appeared in the Soviet magazine, *International Literature*—attempted to draw from his plays any general social moral. So far, indeed, was Marx from having worked out a systematic explanation of the relation of art to social arrangements that he could assert, apropos of Greek art, in his *Introduction to the Critique of Political Economy*, that 'certain periods of highest development of art stand in no direct connection with the general development of society, nor with the material basis and the skeleton structure of its organization.'

3. With Marx and Engels there is not yet any tendency to specialize art as a 'weapon.' They were both too much under the influence of the ideal of the many-sided man of the Renaissance, of the 'complete' man, who, like Leonardo, had been painter, mathematician and engineer, or, like Machiavelli, poet, historian and strategist, before the division of labor had had the effect of splitting up human nature and limiting everyone to some single function (Engels' preface to his *Dialectic and Nature*). But with Lenin[3] we come to a

9. English novelist and socialist writer (1825–1897). *Tendenz-Literatur*: tendency literature (German); that is, literature written with a specific political slant and content. Kautsky (1837–1912), Austrian novelist.

1. Founder of the German Social Democratic Party (1825–1864).

2. Greek tragic dramatist (525–456 B.C.E.); in his *Prometheus Bound*, the Titan Prometheus continues to defy Zeus even as he is punished for stealing fire from the gods and giving it to mortals.

3. Vladimir Ilyich Lenin (born Ulyanov, 1870–1924), a founder of the Russian Communist Party; he led the Bolshevik faction of the party into power

Marxist who is specialized himself as an organizer and fighter. Like most Russians, Lenin was sensitive to music; but Gorky[4] tells us that on one occasion, after listening to Beethoven's Appassionata Sonata and exclaiming that he 'would like to listen to it every day: it is marvelous superhuman music—I always think with pride . . . what marvelous things human beings can do,' he screwed up his eyes and smiled sadly and added: 'But I can't listen to music too often. It affects your nerves, makes you want to say stupid, nice things, and stroke the heads of people who could create such beauty while living in this vile hell. And now you mustn't stroke anyone's head—you might get your hand bitten off.' Yet he was fond of fiction, poetry and the theater, and by no means doctrinaire in his tastes. Krupskaya[5] tells how, on a visit to a Youth Commune, he asked the young people, 'What do you read? Do you read Pushkin?' ' "Oh, no!" someone blurted out. "He was a bourgeois. Mayakovsky[6] for us." Ilyitch smiled. "I think Pushkin is better." ' Gorky says that one day he found Lenin with *War and Peace* lying on the table: ' "Yes, Tolstoy.[7] I wanted to read over the scene of the hunt, then remembered that I had to write a comrade. Absolutely no time for reading." . . . Smiling and screwing up his eyes, he stretched himself deliciously in his armchair and, lowering his voice, added quickly, "What a colossus, eh? What a marvelously developed brain! Here's an artist for you, sir. And do you know something still more amazing? You couldn't find a genuine *muzhik*[8] in literature till this count came upon the scene." ' In his very acute essays on Tolstoy, he deals with him much as Engels deals with Goethe—with tremendous admiration for Tolstoy's genius, but with an analysis of his non-resistance and mysticism in terms not, it is interesting to note, of the psychology of the landed nobility, but of the patriarchal peasantry with whom Tolstoy had identified himself. And Lenin's attitude toward Gorky was much like that of Marx toward Heine. He suggests in one of his letters that Gorky would be helpful as a journalist on the side of the Bolsheviks, but adds that he mustn't be bothered if he is busy writing a book.

4. Trotsky[9] is a literary man as Lenin never was, and he published in 1924 a most remarkable little study called *Literature and Revolution*. In this book he tried to illuminate the problems which were arising for Russian writers with the new society of the Revolution. And he was obliged to come to grips with a question with which Marx and Engels had not been much concerned—the question of what Mr. James T. Farrell[1] in his book, *A Note on Literary Criticism*, one of the few sensible recent writings on this subject, calls 'the carry-over value' of literature. Marx had assumed the value of Shakespeare and the Greeks and more or less left it at that. But what, the writers in Russia were now asking, was to be the value of the literature and art of the ages of barbarism and oppression in the dawn of socialist freedom?

in the October Revolution of 1917 and became the first head of the Soviet state. Engels's work is *The Dialectics of Nature* (1883).

4. Maxim Gorky (pseudonym of Aleksey Maksimovich Peshkov, 1868–1936), Russian short story writer and novelist.

5. Nadezhda Krupskaya (1869–1939) met Lenin in 1894, and they married four years later.

6. Vladimir Vladimirovich Mayakovsky (1893–1930), Russian futurist poet. Aleksandr Sergeyevich Pushkin (1799–1837), Russian novelist, playwright, and poet.

7. Count Leo Tolstoy (1828–1910), Russian novelist; *War and Peace* was published 1864–69.

8. A peasant in czarist Russia (Russian).

9. LEON TROTSKY (1879–1940), Russian Marxist theorist and revolutionary whose opposition to Stalin led to his expulsion from Russia in 1924. On *Literature and Revolution*, see above.

1. American novelist and critic (1904–1979); in *A Note on Literary Criticism* (1936), he discusses Marxist-influenced literature and criticism.

What in particular was to be the status of the culture of that bourgeois society from which socialism had just emerged and of which it still bore the unforgotten scars? Would there be a new proletarian literature, with new language, new style, new form, to give expression to the emotions and ideas of the new proletarian dictatorship? There had been in Russia a group called the Prolet-cult, which aimed at monopolizing the control of Soviet literature; but Lenin had discouraged and opposed it, insisting that proletarian culture was not something which could be produced synthetically and by official dictation of policy, but only by natural evolution as a 'development of those reserves of knowledge which society worked for under the oppression of capitalism, of the landlords, of the officials.' Now, in *Literature and Revolution*, Trotsky asserted that 'such terms as "proletarian literature" and "proletarian culture" are dangerous, because they erroneously compress the culture of the future into the narrow limits of the present day.' In a position to observe from his Marxist point of view the effects on a national literature of the dispossession of a dominant class, he was able to see the unexpected ways in which the presentments of life of the novelists, the feelings and images of the poets, the standards themselves of the critics, were turning out to be determined by their attitudes toward the social-economic crisis. But he did not believe in a proletarian culture which would displace the bourgeois one. The bourgeois literature of the French Revolution had ripened under the old regime; but the illiterate proletariat and peasantry of Russia had had no chance to produce a culture, nor would there be time for them to do so in the future, because the proletarian dictatorship was not to last: it was to be only a transition phase and to lead the way to 'a culture which is above classes and which will be the first truly human culture.' In the meantime, the new socialist literature would grow directly out of that which had already been produced during the domination of the bourgeoisie. Communism, Trotsky said, had as yet no artistic culture; it had only a political culture.

5. All this seems to us reasonable enough. But, reasonable and cultured as Trotsky is, ready as he is to admit that 'one cannot always go by the principles of Marxism in deciding whether to accept or reject a work of art,' that such a work 'should be judged in the first place by its own law—that is, by the law of art,' there is none the less in the whole situation something which is alien to us. We are not accustomed, in our quarter of the world, either to having the government attempt to control literature and art or to having literary and artistic movements try to identify themselves with the government. Yet Russia, since the Revolution, has had a whole series of cultural groups which have attempted to dominate literature either with or without the authority of the government; and Trotsky himself, in his official position, even in combating these tendencies, cannot avoid passing censure and pinning ribbons. Sympathizers with the Soviet regime used to assume that this state of affairs was inseparable from the realization of socialism: that its evils would be easily outgrown and that in any case it was a great thing to have the government take so lively an interest in culture. I believe that this view was mistaken. Under the Tsar, imaginative literature in Russia played a role which was probably different from any role it had ever played in the life of any other nation. Political and social criticism, pursued and driven underground by the censorship, was forced to incorporate itself in the dramatic imagery of fic-

tion. This was certainly one of the principal reasons for the greatness during the nineteenth century of the Russian theater and novel, for the mastery by the Russian writers—from Pushkin's time to Tolstoy's—of the art of implication. In the fifties and sixties, the stories of Turgenev,[2] which seem mild enough to us today, were capable of exciting the most passionate controversies—and even, in the case of *A Sportsman's Sketches*, causing the dismissal of the censor who had passed it—because each was regarded as a political message. Ever since the Revolution, literature and politics in Russia have remained inextricable. But after the Revolution the intelligentsia themselves were in power; and it became plain that in the altered situation the identification of literature with politics was liable to terrible abuses. Lenin and Trotsky, Lunacharsky[3] and Gorky, worked sincerely to keep literature free; but they had at the same time, from the years of the Tsardom, a keen sense of the possibility of art as an instrument of propaganda. Lenin took a special interest in the moving pictures from the propaganda point of view; and the first Soviet films by Eisenstein and Pudovkin,[4] were masterpieces of implication, as the old novels and plays had been. But Lenin died; Trotsky was exiled; Lunacharsky died. The administration of Stalin,[5] unliterary and uncultivated himself, slipped into depending more and more on literature as a means of manipulating a people of whom, before the Revolution, 70 or 80 per cent had been illiterate and who could hardly be expected to be critical of what they read. Gorky seems to have exerted what influence he could in the direction of liberalism: to him was due, no doubt, the liquidation of RAPP,[6] the latest device for the monopoly of culture, and the opening of the Soviet canon to the best contemporary foreign writing and the classics. But though this made possible more freedom of form and a wider range of reading, it could not, under the dictatorship of Stalin, either stimulate or release a living literature. Where no political opposition was possible, there was possible no political criticism; and in Russia political questions involve vitally the fate of society. What reality can there be for the Russians, the most socially-minded writers on earth, in a freedom purely 'esthetic'? Even the fine melodramatic themes of the post-revolutionary cinema and theater, with their real emotion and moral conviction, have been replaced by simple trash not very far removed from Hollywood, or by dramatized exemplifications of the latest 'directive' of Stalin which open the night after the speech that has announced the directive. The recent damning of the music of Shostakovich[7] on the ground that the commissars were unable to hum it seems a withdrawal from the liberal position. And it is probable that the death of Gorky, as well as the imprisonment of Bukharin and Radek,[8] have removed the last brakes from a precipitate descent, in the artistic as well as the political field, into a

2. Ivan Sergeyevich Turgenev (1818–1883), Russian novelist whose works include *A Sportsman's Sketches* (1852).
3. Alexander Lunacharsky (1875–1933), Russian writer and Soviet minister of education.
4. Vsevolod Pudovkin (1893–1953), Russian actor and film director. Sergei Eisenstein (1898–1948), generally acknowledged as one of the world's greatest film directors.
5. Joseph Stalin (1879–1953), Russian revolutionary and leader of the Soviet Union (1924–53); he forced Trotsky into internal exile in 1927 and banished him from the USSR in 1929.
6. The Russian Association of Proletarian Writers.
7. Dmitri Shostakovich (1906–1975), leading Russian composer of the mid-20th century, who was forced to reform his musical style by official attacks in the 1930s and again in 1948.
8. Karl Radek (ca. 1885–1939), Communist propagandist and early leader of the Communist International (Comintern); he died in a labor camp while serving a sentence for treason. Nikolai Ivanovich Bukharin (1888–1938), Bolshevik revolutionary and Soviet political figure, executed for treason during the purges of the 1930s.

nightmare of informing and repression. The practice of deliberate falsification of social and political history which began at the time of the Stalin-Trotsky crisis and which has now attained proportions so fantastic that the government does not seem to hesitate to pass the sponge every month or so over everything that the people have previously been told and to present them with a new and contradictory version of their history, their duty, and the characters and careers of their leaders—this practice cannot fail in the end to corrupt every department of intellectual life, till the serious, the humane, the clear-seeing must simply, if they can, remain silent.

6. Thus Marxism in Russia for the moment has run itself into a blind alley—or rather, it has been put down a well. The Soviets seem hardly at the present time to have retained even the Marxist political culture, even in its cruder forms—so that we are relieved from the authority of Russia as we are deprived of her inspiration. To what conclusions shall we come, then, at this time of day about Marxism and literature—basing our views not even necessarily upon texts from the Marxist Fathers, but upon ordinary commonsense? Well, first of all, that we can go even further than Trotsky in one of the dicta I have quoted above and declare that Marxism by itself can tell us nothing whatever about the goodness or badness of a work of art. A man may be an excellent Marxist, but if he lacks imagination and taste he will be unable to make the choice between a good and an inferior book both of which are ideologically unexceptionable. What Marxism *can* do, however, is throw a great deal of light on the origins and social significance of works of art. The study of literature in its relation to society is as old as Herder—and even Vico.[9] Coleridge[1] had flashes of insight into the connection between literary and social phenomena, as when he saw the Greek state in the Greek sentence and the individualism of the English in the short separate statements of Chaucer's Prologue. But the great bourgeois master of this kind of criticism was Taine,[2] with his *race* and *moment* and *milieu*; yet Taine, for all his scientific professions, responded artistically to literary art, and responded so vividly that his summings-up of writers and re-creations of periods sometimes rival or surpass their subjects. Marx and Engels further deepened this study of literature in relation to its social background by demonstrating for the first time inescapably the importance of economic systems. But if Marx and Engels and Lenin and Trotsky are worth listening to on the subject of books, it is not merely because they created Marxism, but also because they were capable of literary appreciation.

7. Yet the man who tries to apply Marxist principles without real understanding of literature is liable to go horribly wrong. For one thing, it is usually true in works of the highest order that the purport is not a simple message, but a complex vision of things, which itself is not explicit but implicit; and the reader who does not grasp them artistically, but is merely looking for

9. GIAMBATTISTA VICO (1668–1744), Italian philosopher of history. Johann Gottfried Herder (1744–1803), German philosopher, historian, and critic.

1. SAMUEL TAYLOR COLERIDGE (1772–1834), English Romantic poet and theorist.

2. Hippolyte Taine (1828–1893), French critic and philosopher, who describes the impact of heredity, environment, and history ("la race, le milieu, le moment") in the introduction to his *History of English Literature* (3 vols., 1863).

simple social morals, is certain to be hopelessly confused. Especially will he be confused if the author *does* draw an explicit moral which is the opposite of or has nothing to do with his real purport. Friedrich Engels, in the letter to Margaret Harkness already referred to above, in warning her that the more the novelist allows his political ideas to 'remain hidden, the better it is for the work of art,' says that Balzac, with his reactionary opinions, is worth a thousand of Zola,[3] with all his democratic ones. (Balzac was one of the great literary admirations of both Engels and Marx, the latter of whom had planned to write a book on him.) Engels points out that Balzac himself was, or believed himself to be, a legitimist engaged in deploring the decline of high society; but that actually 'his irony is never more bitter, his satire never more trenchant, than when he is showing us these aristocrats . . . for whom he felt so profound a sympathy,' and that 'the only men of whom he speaks with undissimulated admiration are his most determined political adversaries, the republican heroes of the Cloître-Saint-Merri,[4] the men who at that period (1830–1836) truly represented the popular masses.' Nor does it matter necessarily in a work of art whether the characters are shown engaged in a conflict which illustrates the larger conflicts of society or in one which from that point of view is trivial. In art—it is quite obvious in music, but it is also true in literature—a sort of law of moral interchangeability prevails: we may transpose the actions and the sentiments that move us into terms of whatever we do or are ourselves. Real genius of moral insight is a motor which will start any engine When Proust,[5] in his wonderful chapter on the death of the novelist Bergotte, speaks of those moral obligations which impose themselves in spite of everything and which seem to come through to humanity from some source outside its wretched self (obligations 'invisible only to fools—and are they really to them?'), he is describing a kind of duty which he felt only in connection with the literary work which he performed in his dark and fetid room; yet he speaks for every moral, esthetic or intellectual passion which holds the expediencies of the world in contempt. And the hero of Thornton Wilder's *Heaven's My Destination*,[6] the traveling salesman who tries to save souls in the smoking car and writes Bible texts on hotel blotters, is something more than a symptom of Thornton Wilder's religious tendencies: he is the type of all saints who begin absurdly; and Wilder's story would be as true of the socialist Upton Sinclair as of the Christian George Brush.[7] Nor does it necessarily matter, for the moral effect of a work of literature, whether the forces of bravery or virtue with which we identify ourselves are victorious or vanquished in the end. In Hemingway's story *The Undefeated*,[8] the old bull-fighter who figures as the hero is actually humiliated and killed, but his courage has itself been a victory. It is true, as I. Kashkin, the Soviet

3. Émile Zola (1840–1902), French novelist who formulated the principles of naturalism. Honoré de Balzac: French writer of realist novels (1799–1850).
4. Barricades called "the Cloister of Saint-Merri," raised in 1832 by radicals and workers who challenged the French constitutional monarch Louis-Philippe, where many were killed.
5. Marcel Proust (1871–1922), French novelist; he writes of the death of Bergotte in *The Captive*, vol. 6 of *Remembrance of Things Past*.
6. A 1934 novel by the American playwright and novelist Wilder (1897–1975).
7. The central character of Wilder's novel. Sinclair (1878–1968), prolific American writer of novels and nonfiction, many concerned with social and political problems; he was narrowly defeated in 1934 as the Democratic candidate for governor of California on the "End Poverty in California" platform.
8. In *Men without Women* (1927), by the American writer Ernest Hemingway (1899–1961).

critic, has said, that Hemingway has written much about decadence, but in order to write tellingly about death you have to have the principle of life, and those that have it will make it felt in spite of everything.

8. The Leftist critic with no literary competence is always trying to measure works of literature by tests which have no validity in that field. And one of his favorite occupations is giving specific directions and working out diagrams for the construction of ideal Marxist books. Such formulas are of course perfectly futile. The rules observed in any given school of art become apparent, not before but after, the actual works of art have been produced. As we were reminded by Burton Rascoe[9] at the time of the Humanist controversy, the esthetic laws involved in Greek tragedy were not formulated by Aristotle until at least half a century after Euripides and Sophocles were dead.[1] And the behavior of the Marxist critics has been precisely like that of the Humanists. The Humanists knew down to the last comma what they wanted a work of literature to be, but they never—with the possible exception, when pressed, of *The Bridge of San Luis Rey*,[2] about which they had, however, hesitations—were able to find any contemporary work which fitted their specifications. The Marxists did just the same thing. In an article called *The Crisis in Criticism* in the *New Masses* of February 1933, Granville Hicks[3] drew up a list of requirements which the ideal Marxist work of literature must meet. The primary function of such a work, he asserted, must be to 'lead the proletarian reader to recognize his role in the class struggle'—and it must therefore (1) 'directly or indirectly show the effects of the class struggle'; (2) 'the author must be able to make the reader feel that he is participating in the lives described'; and, finally, (3) the author's point of view must 'be that of the vanguard of the proletariat; he should be, or should try to make himself, a member of the proletariat.' This formula, he says, 'gives us . . . a standard by which to recognize the perfect Marxian novel'—and adds 'no novel as yet written perfectly conforms to our demands.' But the doctrine of 'socialist realism' promulgated at the Soviet Writers' Congress of August 1934 was only an attempt on a larger scale to legislate masterpieces into existence—a kind of attempt which always indicates sterility on the part of those who engage in it, and which always actually works, if it has any effect at all, to legislate existing good literature *out of* existence and to discourage the production of any more. The prescribers for the literature of the future usually cherish some great figure of the past whom they regard as having fulfilled their conditions and whom they are always bringing forward to demonstrate the inferiority of the literature of the present. As there has never existed a great writer who really had anything in common with these critics' conception of literature, they are obliged to provide imaginary versions of what their ideal great writers are like. The Humanists had Sophocles and Shakespeare; the socialist realists had Tolstoy. Yet it is certain that if Tolstoy had had to live up to the objectives and prohibitions which the socialist

9. Editor and critic (1892–1957), author of "Pupils of Polonius," an essay in *The Critique of Humanism: A Symposium* (1930). The Humanist critics in the United States, staunch foes of modern literature, included Irving Babbitt (1865–1933) and Paul Elmer More (1864–1937).

1. Both Greek tragedians died in 406 B.C.E.; ARISTOTLE, who formulated these "esthetic laws" in the *Poetics* (see above), was not born until 384 B.C.E.

2. A 1927 novel by Thornton Wilder.

3. A leading communist critic of the 1930s (1901–1982) and editor of the Marxist journal the *New Masses*.

realists proposed he could never have written a chapter; and that if Babbitt and More had been able to enforce against Shakespeare their moral and esthetic injunctions he would never have written a line. The misrepresentation of Sophocles, which has involved even a tampering with his text in the interests not merely of Humanism but of academic classicism in general, has been one of the scandalous absurdities of scholarship. The Communist critical movement in America, which had for its chief spokesman Mr. Hicks, tended to identify their ideal with the work of John Dos Passos.[4] In order to make this possible, it was necessary to invent an imaginary Dos Passos. This ideal Dos Passos was a Communist, who wrote stories about the proletariat, at a time when the real Dos Passos was engaged in bringing out a long novel about the effects of the capitalist system on the American middle class and had announced himself—in the *New Republic* in 1930—politically a 'middle-class liberal.' The ideal Dos Passos was something like Gorky without the mustache—Gorky, in the meantime, having himself undergone some transmogrification at the hands of Soviet publicity—and this myth was maintained until the Communist critics were finally compelled to repudiate it, not because they had acquired new light on Dos Passos, the novelist and dramatist, but because of his attitude toward events in Russia.

9. The object of these formulas for the future, as may be seen from the above quotations from Mr. Hicks, is to make of art an effective instrument in the class struggle. And we must deal with the dogma that 'art is a weapon.' It is true that art may be a weapon; but in the case of some of the greatest works of art, some of those which have the longest carry-over value, it is difficult to see that any important part of this value is due to their direct functioning as weapons. The *Divine Comedy*, in its political aspect, is a weapon for Henry of Luxemburg,[5] whom Dante—with his medieval internationalism and his lack of sympathy for the nationalistic instincts which were impelling the Italians of his time to get away from their Austrian emperors—was so passionately eager to impose on his countrymen. Today we may say with Carducci[6] that we would as soon see the crown of his 'good Frederick' rolling in Olona vale: 'Jove perishes; the poet's hymn remains.' And, though Shakespeare's *Henry IV* and *Henry V* are weapons for Elizabethan imperialism, their real center is not Prince Hal but Falstaff; and Falstaff is the father of *Hamlet* and of all Shakespeare's tragic heroes, who, if they illustrate any social moral—the moral, perhaps, that Renaissance princes, supreme in their little worlds, may go to pieces in all kinds of terrible ways for lack of a larger social organism to restrain them—do so evidently without Shakespeare's being aware of it. If these works may be spoken of as weapons at all, they are weapons in the more general struggle of modern European man emerging from the Middle Ages and striving to understand his world and himself—a function for which 'weapon' is hardly the right word. The truth is that there is short-range and long-range literature. Long-range literature attempts to sum up wide areas and long periods of human experience,

4. American novelist (1896–1970), whose writings of the 1930s—especially the panoramic *U.S.A.* trilogy (collected in 1938)—reflect left-wing views. He became increasingly conservative in later years.

5. Henry VII (ca.1275–1313), emperor and king of Germany (1308–13), originally count of Luxembourg. DANTE ALIGHIERI (1265–1321), who was deeply engaged in politics, hoped that reuniting Germany and Italy would put an end to the division within Florence.

6. Giosuè Carducci (1835–1907), Italian poet.

or to extract from them general laws; short-range literature preaches and pamphleteers with the view to an immediate effect. A good deal of the recent confusion of our writers in the Leftist camp has been due to their not understanding, or being unable to make up their minds, whether they are aiming at long-range or short-range writing.

10. This brings us to the question of what sort of periods are most favorable for works of art. One finds an assumption on the Left that revolutionary or pre-revolutionary periods are apt to produce new and vital forms of literature. This, of course, is very far from the truth in the case of periods of actual revolution. The more highly developed forms of literature require leisure and a certain amount of stability; and during a period of revolution the writer is usually deprived of both. The literature of the French Revolution consisted of the orations of Danton, the journalism of Camille Desmoulins and the few political poems that André Chenier[7] had a chance to write before he was guillotined. The literature of the Russian Revolution was the political writing of Lenin and Trotsky, and Alexander Blok's[8] poem, *The Twelve*, almost the last fruit of his genius before it was nipped by the wind of the storm. As for pre-revolutionary periods in which the new forces are fermenting, they *may* be great periods for literature—as the eighteenth century was in France and the nineteenth century in Russia (though here there was a decadence after 1905). But the conditions that make possible the masterpieces are apparently not produced by the impending revolutions, but by the phenomenon of literary technique, already highly developed, in the hands of a writer who has had the support of long-enduring institutions. He may reflect an age of transition, but it will not necessarily be true that his face is set squarely in the direction of the future. The germs of the Renaissance are in Dante and the longing for a better world in Virgil,[9] but neither Dante nor Virgil can in any real sense be described as a revolutionary writer: they sum up or write elegies for ages that are passing. The social organisms that give structure to their thought—the Roman Empire and the Catholic Church—are already showing signs of decay. It is impossible, therefore, to identify the highest creative work in art with the most active moments of creative social change. The writer who is seriously intent on producing long-range works of literature should, from the point of view of his own special personal interests, thank his stars if there is no violent revolution going on in his own country in his time. He may disapprove of the society he is writing about, but if it were disrupted by an actual upheaval he would probably not be able to write.

11. But what about 'proletarian literature' as an accompaniment of the social revolution? In the earlier days of the Communist regime in Russia, one used to hear about Russian authors who, in the effort to eliminate from their writings any vestige of the bourgeois point of view, had reduced their vocabulary and syntax to what they regarded as an A B C of essentials—with the result of becoming more unintelligible to the proletarian audience at whom they were aiming than if they had been Symbolist poets. (Indeed, the

7. André de Chénier (1762–1794), French poet and political journalist. Georges Jacques Danton (1759–1794), French revolutionary leader. Desmoulins (1760–1794), French journalist and revolutionary.

8. Aleksandr Aleksandrovich Blok (1880–1921), Russian critic, playwright, and symbolist poet; *The Twelve* was published in 1918.

9. Roman poet (70–19 B.C.E.), author of the great epic of Rome's foundation, the *Aeneid*; he lived through the end of the Roman Republic.

futurist poet Mayakovsky has since that time become a part of the Soviet canon.) Later on, as I have said, Soviet culture followed the road that Trotsky recommended: it began building again on the classics and on the bourgeois culture of other countries and on able revolutionary Russian writers who had learned their trade before the Revolution. 'Soviet publishers'—I quote from the Russian edition of *International Literature*, issue 2 of 1936—'are bringing out Hemingway and Proust not merely in order to demonstrate "bourgeois decay." Every genuine work of art—and such are the productions of Hemingway and Proust—enriches the writer's knowledge of life and heightens his esthetic sensibility and his emotional culture—in a word, it figures, in the broad sense, as a factor of educational value. Liberated socialist humanity inherits all that is beautiful, elevating and sustaining in the culture of previous ages.' The truth is that the talk in Soviet Russia about proletarian literature and art has resulted from the persistence of the same situation which led Tolstoy under the old regime to put on the muzhik's blouse and to go in for carpentry, cobbling and plowing: the difficulty experienced by an educated minority, who were only about 20 percent of the people, in getting in touch with the illiterate majority. In America the situation is quite different. The percentage of illiterates in this country is only something like 4 per cent; and there is relatively little difficulty of communication between different social groups. Our development away from England, and from the old world generally, in this respect—in the direction of the democratization of our idiom—is demonstrated clearly in H. L. Mencken's *The American Language*;[1] and if it is a question of either the use for high literature of the language of the people or the expression of the dignity and importance of the ordinary man, the country which has produced *Leaves of Grass* and *Huckleberry Finn*[2] has certainly nothing to learn from Russia. We had created during our pioneering period a literature of the common man's escape, not only from feudal Europe, but also from bourgeois society, many years before the Russian masses were beginning to write their names. There has been a section of our recent American literature of the last fifteen years or so—the period of the boom and the depression—which has dealt with our industrial and rural life from the point of view of the factory hand and the poor farmer under conditions which were forcing him to fight for his life, and this has been called proletarian literature; but it has been accompanied by books on the white-collar worker, the storekeeper, the well-to-do merchant, the scientist and the millionaire in situations equally disastrous or degrading. And this whole movement of critical and imaginative writing—though with some stimulus, certainly, from Russia—had come quite naturally out of our literature of the past. It is curious to observe that one of the best of the recent strike novels, *The Land of Plenty* by Robert Cantwell,[3] himself a Westerner and a former mill worker, owes a good deal to Henry James.

12. Yet when all these things have been said, all the questions have not been answered. All that has been said has been said of the past; and Marxism is something new in the world: it is a philosophical system which leads directly

1. First published in 1919 by Mencken (1880–1956), American newspaperman, critic, and editor; by 1938, it was in its 4th edition.

2. Both Walt Whitman's book of poetry (1855) and Mark Twain's novel (1884), in very different ways, are concerned with the dignity of the common people and with the spirit of the United States.

3. American proletarian writer (1908–1978); *The Land of Plenty* (1934) deals with labor troubles at a plywood factory in the Northwest. On the American writer HENRY JAMES (1843–1916), see above.

to programs of action. Has there ever appeared before in literature such a phenomenon as M. André Malraux,[4] who alternates between attempts, sometimes brilliant, to write long-range fiction on revolutionary themes, and exploits of aviation for the cause of revolution in Spain? Here creative political action and the more complex kind of imaginative writing have united at least to the extent that they have arisen from the same vision of history and have been included in the career of one man. The Marxist vision of Lenin—Vincent Sheean[5] has said it first—has in its completeness and its compelling force a good deal in common with the vision of Dante; but, partly realized by Lenin during his lifetime and still potent for some years after his death, it was a creation, not of literary art, but of actual social engineering. It is society itself, says Trotsky, which under communism becomes the work of art. The first attempts at this art will be inexpert and they will have refractory material to work with; and the philosophy of the Marxist dialectic involves idealistic and mythological elements which have led too often to social religion rather than to social art. Yet the human imagination has already come to conceive the possibility of re-creating human society; and how can we doubt that, as it acquires the power, it must emerge from what will seem by comparison the revolutionary 'underground' of art as we have always known it up to now and deal with the materials of actual life in ways which we cannot now even foresee? This is to speak in terms of centuries, of ages; but, in practicing and prizing literature, we must not be unaware of the first efforts of the human spirit to transcend literature itself.

1938, 1948

4. French novelist and critic (1901–1976). He commanded a squadron in the Republican air force in the Spanish Civil War.

5. Socialist journalist (1899–1975), and European correspondent for a number of American newspapers.

ROMAN JAKOBSON
1896–1982

Roman Jakobson's role in literary theory arises out of his use of two highly suggestive sets of paired terms: "linguistics and poetics" and "metaphor and metonymy." These terms, and the thoughts behind them, profoundly shaped the structuralist movement in anthropology, philosophy, and psychoanalysis as well as literary studies, especially in France after World War II. But this groundbreaking theorist chose to characterize himself as a "Russian philologist," the phrase inscribed on his tombstone. He was a linguist who could lecture in six languages ("unfortunately, all of them Russian," joked his colleagues, referring to his pronounced accent). A large proportion of his many publications addressed minute topics in phonology, Slavic languages and literatures, and folklore. Yet that technical linguistic work grounded bold speculations about human linguistic behavior that opened up new channels for research in a number of different fields.

Born in Moscow, Jakobson entered the Lazarev Institute of Oriental Languages there in his early teens; he went on to study linguistics, literature, and folklore at Moscow University, where in 1915 he co-founded the Moscow Linguistic Circle. In this period of ferment just before the Russian Revolution, he wrote poetry and moved in avant-garde circles; like his friend the poet Vladimir Mayakovsky and others, he thought that a social revolution should include a revolution in artistic forms. At St. Petersburg University, where he studied in 1917, he worked with Victor Schlovsky and BORIS EICHENBAUM in the Society for the Study of Poetic Language, a group that has come to be known as the "Russian formalists."

In 1920 Jakobson moved to Prague, where he studied linguistics and Old Czech literature; in 1926 he co-founded the Prague Linguistic Circle, which included Jan Mukařovský. The work of FERDINAND DE SAUSSURE (1857–1913) was central to the group, though Jakobson moved beyond the Swiss linguist in 1927 when he realized that the Saussurean dichotomy between linguistic synchrony (a cross section of language at a given time) and diachrony (a transverse section *through* time) was too absolute: languages could be studied structurally as they changed over time. His work on poetic language also questioned the two founding Saussurean principles of language, the arbitrariness and the linearity of the sign. Nevertheless, his disagreements with Saussure helped shape his thought.

In 1938, when the Nazis invaded Czechoslovakia, Jakobson fled to Denmark, then Norway, then Sweden, before settling in the United States in 1941. He taught at the École Libre des Hautes Études (Free School of Advanced Study) in New York, where in 1942 he met CLAUDE LÉVI-STRAUSS, who had fled France; the two began attending each other's lectures. In 1943 Jakobson co-founded the Linguistic Circle of New York; he taught at Columbia University until 1949, then moved to Harvard University, where he taught first Slavic languages and literatures and then linguistics. From 1957 onward, he held a concurrent professorship at the Massachusetts Institute of Technology. He became emeritus in 1967 but never retired; he was writing letters from his hospital bed as he lay dying.

As a linguist, Jakobson clarified many important concepts. Phonemes or morphemes, for example, were once thought to be the smallest units of language, but Jakobson showed them to comprise bundles of "distinctive features" that themselves were formed by binary oppositions: voiced/unvoiced, consonant/vowel, singular/plural, and so on. Furthermore, his analysis of the tendency of binary oppositions to fall into "marked/unmarked" pairs prepared the way for later ideological analyses of structures and norms—where the "unmarked" (often the male, white, Christian, heterosexual point of view) goes unexamined, functioning as the standard against which "differences" are defined.

As a reader of poetry, Jakobson pursued two kinds of analysis that are not often found together. By studying "the poetry of grammar and the grammar of poetry," he scrutinized linguistic patterns that contribute to the overall poetic effect but normally escape the notice of readers—leading many critics to protest that those patterns could not have been intended by the poet. At the same time, he was fascinated by the difficulty of separating a poet's life and work, not because the life explained the work but because the life was largely structured like another work. Jakobson was similar to but profoundly different from his contemporaries, the American New Critics, in several ways. Both opposed "vulgar biographism" and the "intentional fallacy" (see WILLIAM K. WIMSATT JR. AND MONROE C. BEARDSLEY, below), but Jakobson analyzed the myth of the poet as a function of cultural history, whereas the New Critics tuned their readings to a sense of the individual. Both Jakobson and the New Critics read texts closely, but the New Critics tended to frame interpretation within a working sense of imagination and mind, whereas Jakobson subjected the largest and the smallest patterns to linguistic and cultural analysis, without regard for individual craft. It was not that Jakobson did not believe in the unity of the human imagination, but precisely that he believed in it so much that he thought he was in no danger of departing from it. Jakobson welcomed the contributions of science to the work of literary studies, while the New Critics were trying to defend "humanistic" values *against* the spread of scientific "professionalism."

In his broad position paper "Linguistics and Poetics" (our first selection)—his concluding statement to a 1958 conference on style, published as *Style in Language* (ed. Thomas Sebeok, 1960)—Jakobson argues that what he calls the "poetic function" is at work in all verbal communication. The other five major functions of language are the *emotive* (focused on the speaker), the *conative* (focused on the addressee), the *phatic* (focused on the channel of communication), the *metalingual* (focused on explanations of the code itself), and the *referential* (focused on the context).

In defining the poetic function, Jakobson cites approvingly the French poet Paul Valéry (1871–1945), who called poetry a "sustained hesitation between the sound and the sense." He connects verbal art to the palpability (sound, sight) of signs. The poetic function consists of making connections *within the utterance* among the properties of the words, images, and sounds in a message, using those connections ("equivalences") to generate the linguistic sequence itself. Meter, rhyme, imagery, and generic conventions are not *subsequent* to the poetic function: they *are* the poetic function. Drawing on a mathematical sense of mapping ("projecting") one function upon another, he declares that "the poetic function projects the principle of equivalence from the axis of selection into the axis of combination." What does this formula mean? While ordinary speakers select one of the terms they perceive as equivalent in order to convey a message, the poet combines what is perceived as equivalent. Poetry seeks to *maximize* redundancy; ordinary communication seeks to *minimize* it.

Careful to distinguish between evaluation and analytical description, Jakobson discusses *the poetic function* rather than *poetry*. His remarks about the self-reflections and sounds in the 1950s political slogan "I like Ike" is a classic analysis of the poetic function without claiming to be an analysis of poetry. In showing how the slogan verbally embodies "the loving subject enveloped by the beloved object," he suggests the multiple uses to which the poetic function is put in everyday life, while noting that poetry employs all the "everyday" functions, too.

Literary scholars unwilling to separate function from evaluation have protested that Jakobson's definition fails to do justice to poetry, which depends on values of meaning and creativity. Jakobson claimed that the extent to which effects of meaning and creativity could be subject to linguistic analysis could not be known in advance. This did not keep critics from charging Jakobson with annexing poetics to linguistics. It was sometimes pointed out that the poets who best illustrate Jakobson's definition are not always those most esteemed in literary history. Here, as so often, EDGAR ALLAN POE—loved by the French, often dismissed by the Americans—stands as a test case, perhaps suggesting a parallel to Jakobson's impact on literary studies in France and in the United States. But in the final analysis, Jakobson does not, after all, claim to define poetry. He is more interested in how the poetic function accounts for broad linguistic behavior and effectiveness both within and outside any poetic canon. For this reason, he writes about Baudelaire, Shakespeare, Pushkin, Yeats, Blake, and Hopkins with the same curiosity he applies to the linguistic mechanisms of slogans, folklore, and everyday speech.

Jakobson's distinction between metaphor and metonymy in "Two Aspects of Language and Two Types of Aphasic Disturbances" (1956; our second selection) became for him—and many others following him—a key to language itself. Derived from studies of aphasia (inability to speak), Jakobson detected two primordial principles of language use: similarity and contiguity (i.e., resemblance and nearness). In the vast array of normal verbal behavior, both operate at once. But in the early stages of language learning by children, in the late stages of language loss by aphasics (who can either provide a synonym for a word or construct a sentence around it, but not both), and to some extent in literary forms like Romanticism or realism, the outline of the two distinct principles becomes visible. Jakobson chooses to call these *metaphor* and *metonymy*, using the names of two rhetorical figures that had not previously been set in opposition.

Metaphor, which has often stood as the general name for all figures and has long been the object of philosophical and rhetorical analyses, stands in Jakobson's essay as the name for any two terms related by similarity (synonymy, analogy, comparison, even antithesis, with or without the word *like*). The opposing term, *metonymy*, has historically generated far less commentary. It is usually defined as the substitution of symbol for thing symbolized ("the throne is in danger" for "the king is in danger"), maker for thing made ("I drive a Ford" or "I read Shakespeare"), container for contained ("drink the whole glass"), part for whole ("all hands on deck"), and so on. In each case, the association is *not* based on similarity; thus all are relations of contiguity. Contiguity is observed not just in the connections among the meanings of terms but also in the very fact of sequence, syntactically relating all terms that are present in a sentence. In Jakobson's scheme there are ultimately not two principles but four: similarity, contiguity, substitution, and combination. And all verbal behavior can be analyzed along these lines. JACQUES LACAN, building on SIGMUND FREUD's opposition between "condensation" and "displacement" in the rhetoric of dreams, sees in the relation between metaphor and metonymy the general psychoanalytic laws governing symptom and desire.

Jakobson was criticized for the same reasons he was praised. He was less interested in where to stop than in where to go, and his bold and painstaking writings opened up many domains of study in linguistics, poetics, folklore, and in the relations among them; but the gap between his microanalyses and his broad generalizations left much room for quibbles. He was fond of loosely paraphrasing the Roman playwright Terence: "Linguista sum; linguistici nihil a me alienum esse puto"—"I am a linguist; I consider nothing linguistic to be alien to me." (Terence's original formulation was "Homo [a human] sum; humani nil a me alienum puto.") In Jakobson's work, "linguistic" often became synonymous with Terence's "human."

BIBLIOGRAPHY

The best single collection of Jakobson's writings on literature is *Language in Literature*, edited by Krystyna Pomorska and Stephen Rudy (1987). A more complete selection is available in *Selected Writings* (7 vols., 1971–84), each volume of which is introduced with a "retrospective" by Jakobson himself. Biographical information is both plentiful and scant. The closest thing to a biography is a volume of conversations between Jakobson and Krystyna Pomorska, his third wife, titled *Dialogues* (1983); it perfectly illustrates Jakobson's "mythic" concept of autobiography: both participants are focused on displaying the charisma of Jakobson's intellectual, not personal, life.

Good introductions to Jakobson's work are Elmar Holenstein's *Roman Jakobson's Approach to Language: Phenomenological Structuralism* (1974; trans. 1976) and Richard Bradford's *Roman Jakobson: Life, Language, Art* (1994). For two excellent and different accounts of Russian formalism in context, see Victor Erlich, *Russian Formalism: History—Doctrine* (1955; 3d ed., 1981) and Fredric Jameson, *The Prison-House of Language: A Critical Account of Structuralism and Russian Formalism* (1972). *Roman Jakobson: Echoes of His Scholarship*, edited by Daniel Armstrong and C. H. Van Schooneveld (1977) gives a good general sense of the many directions Jakobson's interests have taken. Svetlana Boym's *Death in Quotation Marks: Cultural Myths of the Modern Poet* (1991) furthers Jakobson's analysis of mythic biography. For a bibliography of works by Jakobson, see Stephen Rudy, *Roman Jakobson: A Complete Bibliography of His Writings, 1912–1982* (1985); for critical writings about Jakobson, see the annotated overview by Bradford (mentioned above) along with bibliographies in the book by Holenstein and in *Language, Poetry, and Poetics: The Generation of the 1890s—Jakobson, Trubetszkoy, Majakovskij*, edited by Krystyna Pomorska, Elzbieta Chodakowska, Hugh McLean, and Brent Vine (1987).

From Linguistics and Poetics

* * *

I have been asked for summary remarks about poetics in its relation to linguistics. Poetics deals primarily with the question, "What makes a verbal message a work of art?" Because the main subject of poetics is the *differentia specifica*[1] of verbal art in relation to other arts and in relation to other kinds of verbal behavior, poetics is entitled to the leading place in literary studies.

Poetics deals with problems of verbal structure, just as the analysis of painting is concerned with pictorial structure. Since linguistics is the global science of verbal structure, poetics may be regarded as an integral part of linguistics.

Arguments against such a claim must be thoroughly discussed. It is evident that many devices studied by poetics are not confined to verbal art. We can refer to the possibility of transporting *Wuthering Heights*[2] into a motion picture, medieval legends into frescoes and miniatures, or *L'Aprés-midi d'un faune*[3] into music, ballet, and graphic art. However ludicrous the idea of the *Iliad* and *Odyssey* in comics may seem,[4] certain structural features of their plot are preserved despite the disappearance of their verbal shape. The question of whether W. B. Yeats was right in affirming that William Blake was "the one perfectly fit illustrator for the *Inferno* and the *Purgatorio*"[5] is a proof that different arts are comparable. The problems of the baroque or any other historical style transgress the frame of a single art. When handling the surrealistic metaphor, we could hardly pass by Max Ernst's pictures or Luis Buñuel's films, *The Andalusian Dog* and *The Golden Age*.[6] In short, many poetic features belong not only to the science of language but to the whole theory of signs, that is, to general semiotics.[7] This statement, however, is valid not only for verbal art but also for all varieties of language, since language shares many properties with certain other systems of signs or even with all of them (pansemiotic features).

Likewise, a second objection contains nothing that would be specific for literature: the question of relations between the word and the world concerns not only verbal art but actually all kinds of discourse. Linguistics is likely to explore all possible problems of relation between discourse and the "universe of discourse": what of this universe is verbalized by a given discourse and how it is verbalized. The truth values, however, as far as they are—to say with the logicians—"extra-linguistic entities," obviously exceed the bounds of poetics and of linguistics in general.

1. Specific difference (Latin).
2. An 1847 novel by Emily Brontë; the best-known film version was directed by William Wyler (1939).
3. *The Afternoon of a Faun* (1876), a poem by STÉPHANE MALLARMÉ it was set to music by Claude Debussy (1894), and choreographed and danced by Vaslav Nijinsky for Sergei Diaghilev's Ballets Russes (1912). Its original edition was illustrated by Édouard Manet.
4. Homer's epic poems (ca. 8th c. B.C.E.) were among the many literary works presented as comics in the American "Classics Illustrated" series (1940s–60s).
5. *Inferno* and *Purgatorio* are two of the three books of DANTE ALIGHIERI's *Divine Comedy* (1321). Yeats (1865–1939), Irish poet and dramatist. Blake (1757–1827), English poet and engraver.
6. Films (1928 and 1930, respectively), on which the Spanish-born filmmaker Buñuel (1900–1983) collaborated with the surrealist painter Salvador Dali (1904–1989). Ernst (1891–1976), German-born French painter.
7. *Semiotics*, a term derived from the work of the American philosopher C. S. Peirce (1839–1914), and *semiology*, from that of the Swiss linguist FERDINAND DE SAUSSURE (1857–1913), both name the general theory of signs. In practice, *semiotics* refers specifically to the science of the interpretation of signs (the study of whose meaning is called *semantics*).

Sometimes we hear that poetics in contradistinction to linguistics, is concerned with evaluation. This separation of the two fields from each other is based on a current but erroneous interpretation of the contrast between the structure of poetry and other types of verbal structure: the latter are said to be opposed by their "casual," designless nature to the "noncasual," purposeful character of poetic language. In point of fact, any verbal behavior is goal-directed, but the aims are different and the conformity of the means used to the effect aimed at is a problem that evermore preoccupies inquirers into the diverse kinds of verbal communication. There is a close correspondence, much closer than critics believe, between the question of linguistic phenomena expanding in space and time and the spatial and temporal spread of literary models. Even such discontinuous expansion as the resurrection of neglected or forgotten poets—for instance, the posthumous discovery and subsequent canonization of Emily Dickinson (d. 1886) and Gerard Manley Hopkins (d. 1889), the tardy fame of Lautréamont (d. 1870) among surrealist poets, and the salient influence of the hitherto ignored Cyprian Norwid (d. 1883) on Polish modern poetry—finds a parallel in the history of standard languages that tend to revive outdated models, sometimes long forgotten, as was the case in literary Czech, which toward the beginning of the nineteenth century leaned toward sixteenth-century models.

Unfortunately, the terminological confusion of "literary studies" with "criticism" tempts the student of literature to replace the description of the intrinsic values of a literary work with a subjective, censorious verdict. The label "literary critic" applied to an investigator of literature is as erroneous as "grammatical (or lexical) critic" would be applied to a linguist. Syntactic and morphologic[8] research cannot be supplanted by a normative grammar, and likewise no manifesto, foisting a critic's own tastes and opinions on creative literature, can serve as a substitute for an objective scholarly analysis of verbal art. This statement should not be mistaken for the quietist principle of laissez faire; any verbal culture involves programmatic, planning, normative endeavors. Yet why is a clear-cut discrimination made between pure and applied linguistics or between phonetics and orthoepy,[9] but not between literary studies and criticism?

Literary studies, with poetics as their focal point, consist like linguistics of two sets of problems: synchrony and diachrony.[1] The synchronic description envisages not only the literary production of any given stage but also that part of the literary tradition which for the stage in question has remained vital or has been revived. Thus, for instance, Shakespeare, on the one hand, and Donne, Marvell, Keats, and Emily Dickinson, on the other, are experienced by the present English poetic world, whereas the works of James Thomson and Longfellow,[2] for the time being, do not belong to viable artistic values. The selection of classics and their reinterpretation by a novel trend is a substantial problem of synchronic literary studies. Synchronic poetics, like synchronic linguistics, is not to be confused with statics; any stage dis-

8. Pertaining to the forms taken by words in usage (conjugations, tenses, declensions, etc.). "Syntactic": pertaining to the structure of phrases and sentences.
9. The study of correct pronunciation. "Phonetics": the study of the sounds of language.
1. Change in a system over time. "Synchrony": the relations of parts within a system arrested in time.
2. Jakobson contrasts the now highly regarded English poets John Donne (1562–1631), Andrew Marvell (1621–1678), John Keats (1795–1821), and the American Dickinson (who all, unlike Shakespeare, received relatively little attention in their lifetimes) to the once popular but now critically scorned Scottish-born English poet Thomson (1700–1748) and American poet Henry Wadsworth Longfellow (1807–1882).

criminates between more conservative and more innovative forms. Any contemporary stage is experienced in its temporal dynamics, and, on the other hand, the historical approach both in poetics and in linguistics is concerned not only with changes but also with continuous, enduring, static factors. A thoroughly comprehensive historical poetics or history of language is a superstructure to be built on a series of successive synchronic descriptions.

Insistence on keeping poetics apart from linguistics is warranted only when the field of linguistics appears to be illicitly restricted, for example, when the sentence is viewed by some linguists as the highest analyzable construction, or when the scope of linguistics is confined to grammar alone or uniquely to nonsemantic questions of external form or to the inventory of denotative devices with no reference to free variations. Voegelin has clearly pointed out the two most important and related problems that face structural linguistics, namely, a revision of "the monolithic hypothesis about language" and a concern with "the interdependence of diverse structures within one language."[3] No doubt, for any speech community, for any speaker, there exists a unity of language, but this over-all code represents a system of interconnected subcodes; every language encompasses several concurrent patterns, each characterized by different functions.

Obviously we must agree with Sapir that, on the whole, "ideation reigns supreme in language,"[4] but this supremacy does not authorize linguistics to disregard the "secondary factors." The emotive elements of speech, which, as Joos is prone to believe, cannot be described "with a finite number of absolute categories," are classified by him "as nonlinguistic elements of the real world." Hence, "for us they remain vague, protean, fluctuating phenomena," he concludes, "which we refuse to tolerate in our science."[5] Joos is indeed a brilliant expert in reduction experiments, and his emphatic demand for the "expulsion" of emotive elements "from linguistic science" is a radical experiment in reduction—*reductio ad absurdum*.

Language must be investigated in all the variety of its functions. Before discussing the poetic function we must define its place among the other functions of language. An outline of these functions demands a concise survey of the constitutive factors in any speech event, in any act of verbal communication. The ADDRESSER sends a MESSAGE to the ADDRESSEE. To be operative the message requires a CONTEXT referred to (the "referent" in another, somewhat ambiguous, nomenclature), graspable by the addressee, and either verbal or capable of being verbalized; a CODE fully, or at least partially, common to the addresser and addressee (or in other words, to the encoder and decoder of the message); and, finally, a CONTACT, a physical channel and psychological connection between the addresser and the addressee, enabling both of them to enter and stay in communication. All these factors inalienably involved in verbal communication may be schematized as follows:

3. Charles F. Voegelin, "Casual and Noncasual Utterances within Unified Structures," in *Style in Language*, ed. Thomas Sebeok (Cambridge, Mass., 1960), p. 57 [Jakobson's note].

4. Edward Sapir, *Language* (New York, 1921), p. 40 [Jakobson's note]. Sapir (1884–1939), German-born American linguist.

5. Martin Joos, "Description of Language Design," *Journal of the Acoustical Society of America* 22 (1950): 701–8 [Jakobson's note]. Joos (b. 1907), American linguist.

CONTEXT
ADDRESSER MESSAGE ADDRESSEE
CONTACT
CODE

Each of these six factors determines a different function of language. Although we distinguish six basic aspects of language, we could, however, hardly find verbal messages that would fulfill only one function. The diversity lies not in a monopoly of some one of these several functions but in a different hierarchical order of functions. The verbal structure of a message depends primarily on the predominant function. But even though a set (*Einstellung*) toward the referent, an orientation toward the context—briefly, the so-called REFERENTIAL, "denotative," "cognitive" function—is the leading task of numerous messages, the accessory participation of the other functions in such messages must be taken into account by the observant linguist.

The so-called EMOTIVE or "expressive" function, focused on the addresser, aims a direct expression of the speaker's attitude toward what he is speaking about. It tends to produce an impression of a certain emotion, whether true or feigned; therefore, the term "emotive," launched and advocated by Marty,[6] has proved to be preferable to "emotional." The purely emotive stratum in language is presented by the interjections. They differ from the means of referential language both by their sound pattern (peculiar sound sequences or even sounds elsewhere unusual) and by their syntactic role (they are not components but equivalents of sentences). "*Tut! Tut!* said McGinty": the complete utterance of Conan Doyle's[7] character consists of two suction clicks. The emotive function, laid bare in the interjections, flavors to some extent all our utterances, on their phonic, grammatical, and lexical level. If we analyze language from the standpoint of the information it carries, we cannot restrict the notion of information to the cognitive aspect of language. A man, using expressive features to indicate his angry or ironic attitude, conveys ostensible information, and evidently this verbal behavior cannot be likened to such nonsemiotic, nutritive activities as "eating grapefruit" (despite Chatman's bold simile).[8] The difference between [bɪg] and the emphatic prolongation of the vowel [bɪ:g] is a conventional, coded linguistic feature like the difference between the short and long vowel in such Czech pairs as [vi] "you" and [vi:] "knows," but in the latter pair the differential information is phonemic and in the former emotive. As long as we are interested in phonemic invariants, the English /i/ and /i:/ appear to be mere variants of one and the same phoneme, but if we are concerned with emotive units, the relation between the invariants and variants is reversed: length and shortness are invariants implemented by variable phonemes. Saporta's surmise that emotive difference is a nonlinguistic feature, "attributable to the

6. Anton Marty, *Untersuchungen zur Grundlegung der allgemeinen Grammatik und Sprachphilosophie*, I (Halle, 1908) [Jakobson's note]. Marty (1847–1914), Austrian linguist.

7. Sir Arthur Conan Doyle (1859–1930), English novelist, best known for his tales featuring Sherlock Holmes; the quotation is from *The Valley of Fear* (1915).

8. Seymour Chatman (b. 1928) was another American participant in the *Style* conference. No reference to grapefruit occurs in his paper, which discusses the metrical contrasts between the poets John Donne and ALEXANDER POPE. Perhaps there was some connection between "segmental sound" and grapefruit segments.

delivery of the message and not to the message,"[9] arbitrarily reduces the informational capacity of messages.

A former actor of Stanislavskij's[1] Moscow Theater told me how at his audition he was asked by the famous director to make forty different messages from the phrase *Segodnja večerom* (This evening), by diversifying its expressive tint. He made a list of some forty emotional situations, then emitted the given phrase in accordance with each of these situations, which his audience had to recognize only from the changes in the sound shape of the same two words. For our research work in the description and analysis of contemporary Standard Russian (under the auspices of the Rockefeller Foundation) this actor was asked to repeat Stanislavskij's test. He wrote down some fifty situations framing the same elliptic sentence and made of it fifty corresponding messages for a tape recording. Most of the messages were correctly and circumstantially decoded by Moscovite listeners. May I add that all such emotive cues easily undergo linguistic analysis.

Orientation toward the addressee, the CONATIVE function, finds its purest grammatical expression in the vocative and imperative, which syntactically, morphologically, and often even phonemically deviate from other nominal and verbal categories. The imperative sentences cardinally differ from declarative sentences: the latter are and the former are not liable to a truth test. When in O'Neill's[2] play *The Fountain*, Nano "(in a fierce tone of command)" says "Drink!"—the imperative cannot be challenged by the question "is it true or not?" which may be, however, perfectly well asked after such sentences as "one drank," "one will drink," "one would drink." In contradistinction to the imperative sentences, the declarative sentences are convertible into interrogative sentences: "did one drink?," "will one drink?," "would one drink?"

The traditional model of language as elucidated particularly by Bühler[3] was confined to these three functions—emotive, conative, and referential—and the three apexes of this model—the first person of the addresser, the second person of the addressee, and the "third person" properly (someone or something spoken of). Certain additional verbal functions can be easily inferred from this triadic model. Thus the magic, incantatory function is chiefly some kind of conversion of an absent or inanimate "third person" into an addressee of a conative message. "May this sty dry up, *tfu, tfu, tfu, tfu*" (Lithuanian spell).[4] "Water, queen river, daybreak! Send grief beyond the blue sea, to the sea bottom, like a gray stone never to rise from the sea bottom, may grief never come to burden the light heart of God's servant, may grief be removed and sink away" (North Russian incantation).[5] "Sun, stand thou still upon Gibeon; and thou, Moon, in the valley of Aj-a-lon. And the sun stood still, and the moon stayed" (Joshua 10.12). We observe, how-

9. Sol Saporta, "The Application of Linguistics to the Study of Poetic Language," in *Style in Language*, p. 88 [Jakobson's note]. Saporta (b. 1925), American linguist.

1. Konstantin Stanislavsky (1863–1938), Russian actor and director of the Moscow Art Theater, developed what became known in the United States as "method acting."

2. Eugene O'Neill (1888–1953), American playwright; *The Fountain* was staged in 1925.

3. Karl Bühler, "Die Axiomatik der Sprachwissenschaft," *Kant-Studien* (Berlin) 38 (1933): 19–20 [Jakobson's note]. Bühler (1879–1963): German psychologist.

4. V. J. Mansikka, *Litauische Zaubersprüche* (*Folklore Fellows Communications*) 87 (1929): 69 [Jakobson's note].

5. P. N. Rybnikov, *Pesni* (Moscow, 1910), III, 217–18 [Jakobson's note].

ever, three further constitutive factors of verbal communication and three corresponding functions of language.

There are messages primarily serving to establish, to prolong, or to discontinue communication, to check whether the channel works ("Hello, do you hear me?"), to attract the attention of the interlocutor or to confirm his continued attention ("Are you listening?" or in Shakespearean diction, "Lend me your ears!"—and on the other end of the wire "Um-hum!"). This set for contact, or in Malinowski's terms PHATIC function,[6] may be displayed by a profuse exchange of ritualized formulas, by entire dialogues with the mere purport of prolonging communication. Dorothy Parker[7] caught eloquent examples: " 'Well!' the young man said. 'Well!' she said. 'Well, here we are,' he said. 'Here we are,' she said, 'Aren't we?' 'I should say we were,' he said, 'Eeyop! Here we are.' 'Well!' she said. 'Well!' he said, 'well.' " The endeavor to start and sustain communication is typical of talking birds; thus the phatic function of language is the only one they share with human beings. It is also the first verbal function acquired by infants; they are prone to communicate before being able to send or receive informative communication.

A distinction has been made in modern logic between two levels of language: "object language" speaking of objects and "metalanguage" speaking of language.[8] But metalanguage is not only a necessary scientific tool utilized by logicians and linguists; it plays also an important role in our everyday language. Like Molière's Jourdain[9] who used prose without knowing it, we practice metalanguage without realizing the metalingual character of our operations. Whenever the addresser and/or the addressee need to check up whether they use the same code, speech is focused on the code: it performs a METALINGUAL (i.e., glossing) function. "I don't follow you—what do you mean?" asks the addressee, or in Shakespearean diction, "What is't thou say'st?" And the addresser in anticipation of such recapturing question inquires: "Do you know what I mean?" Imagine such an exasperating dialogue: "The sophomore was plucked." "But what is *plucked?*" "*Plucked* means the same as *flunked*." "And *flunked?*" "*To be flunked is to fail an exam.*" "And what is *sophomore?*" persists the interrogator innocent of school vocabulary. "*A sophomore* is (or means) a *second-year student*." All these equational sentences convey information merely about the lexical code of English; their function is strictly metalingual. Any process of language learning, in particular child acquisition of the mother tongue, makes wide use of such metalingual operations; and aphasia may often be defined as a loss of ability for metalingual operations.

I have brought up all the six factors involved in verbal communication except the message itself. The set (*Einstellung*) toward the message as such, focus on the message for its own sake, is the POETIC function of language. This function cannot be productively studied out of touch with the general

6. Bronislaw Malinowski, "The Problem of Meaning in Primitive Languages," in *The Meaning of Meaning*, ed. C. K. Ogden and I. A. Richards, 9th ed. (New York, 1953), pp. 296–336 [Jakobson's note]. Malinowski (1884–1942), Polish-born American anthropologist.

7. American writer of light verse and short stories (1893–1967); the quoted dialogue is from the story "Here We Are" (1931).

8. Term introduced by Alfred Tarski, *Pojęcie prawdy w jezykach nauk dedukcyjnych* (Warsaw, 1933), and "Der Wahrheitsbegriff in den formalisierten Sprachen," *Studia Philosophica* I (1936) [Jakobson's note].

9. M. Jourdain is the protagonist of *Le Bourgeois gentilhomme* (1670, *The Would-be Gentleman*), a play by Molière (pen name of Jean-Baptiste Poquelin, 1622–1673); he is surprised to learn that he has been speaking prose all his life without knowing it.

problems of language, and, on the other hand, the scrutiny of language requires a thorough consideration of its poetic function. Any attempt to reduce the sphere of the poetic function to poetry or to confine poetry to the poetic function would be a delusive oversimplification. The poetic function is not the sole function of verbal art but only its dominant, determining function, whereas in all other verbal activities it acts as a subsidiary, accessory constituent. This function, by promoting the palpability of signs, deepens the fundamental dichotomy of signs and objects. Hence, when dealing with the poetic function, linguistics cannot limit itself to the field of poetry.

"Why do you always say *Joan and Margery*, yet never *Margery and Joan*? Do you prefer Joan to her twin sister?" "Not at all, it just sounds smoother." In a sequence of two coordinate names, so far as no problems of rank interfere, the precedence of the shorter name suits the speaker, unaccountably for him, as a well-ordered shape for the message.

A girl used to talk about "the horrible Harry." "Why horrible?" "Because I hate him." "But why not *dreadful, terrible, frightful, disgusting?*" "I don't know why, but *horrible* fits him better." Without realizing it, she clung to the poetic device of paronomasia.[1]

The political slogan "I like Ike" /ay layk ayk/, succinctly structured, consists of three monosyllables and counts three diphthongs /ay/, each of them symmetrically followed by one consonantal phoneme, /..l..k..k/. The makeup of the three words presents a variation: no consonantal phonemes in the first word, two around the diphthong in the second, and one final consonant in the third. A similar dominant nucleus /ay/ was noticed by Hymes in some of the sonnets of Keats.[2] Both cola[3] of the trisyllabic formula "I like/Ike" rhyme with each other, and the second of the two rhyming words is fully included in the first one (echo rhyme), /layk/—/ayk/, a paronomastic image of a feeling which totally envelops its object. Both cola alliterate with each other, and the first of the two alliterating words is included in the second: /ay/—/ayk/, a paronomastic image of the loving subject enveloped by the beloved object. The secondary, poetic function of this campaign slogan reinforces its impressiveness and efficacy.

As I said, the linguistic study of the poetic function must overstep the limits of poetry, and, on the other hand, the linguistic scrutiny of poetry cannot limit itself to the poetic function. The particularities of diverse poetic genres imply a differently ranked participation of the other verbal functions along with the dominant poetic function. Epic poetry, focused on the third person, strongly involves the referential function of language; the lyric, oriented toward the first person, is intimately linked with the emotive function; poetry of the second person is imbued with the conative function and is either supplicatory or exhortative, depending on whether the first person is subordinated to the second one or the second to the first.

Now that our cursory description of the six basic functions of verbal communication is more or less complete, we may complement our scheme of the fundamental factors with a corresponding scheme of the functions:

1. A play on words that sound alike.
2. Dell H. Hymes, "Phonological Aspects of Style: Some English Sonnets," in *Style in Language*, pp. 123–26 [Jakobson's note]. Hymes (b. 1927), American anthropologist and linguist.
3. Sections of a sentence or rhythmical period (the plural of *colon*).

REFERENTIAL

EMOTIVE POETIC CONATIVE

PHATIC

METALINGUAL

What is the empirical linguistic criterion of the poetic function? In particular, what is the indispensable feature inherent in any piece of poetry? To answer this question we must recall the two basic modes of arrangement used in verbal behavior, *selection* and *combination*. If "child" is the topic of the message, the speaker selects one among the extant, more or less similar nouns like child, kid, youngster, tot, all of them equivalent in a certain respect, and then, to comment on this topic, he may select one of the semantically cognate verbs—sleeps, dozes, nods, naps. Both chosen words combine in the speech chain. The selection is produced on the basis of equivalence, similarity and dissimilarity, synonymy and antonymy, while the combination, the build-up of the sequence, is based on contiguity. *The poetic function projects the principle of equivalence from the axis of selection into the axis of combination*. Equivalence is promoted to the constitutive device of the sequence. In poetry one syllable is equalized with any other syllable of the same sequence; word stress is assumed to equal word stress, as unstress equals unstress; prosodic long is matched with long, and short with short; word boundary equals word boundary, no boundary equals no boundary; syntactic pause equals syntactic pause, no pause equals no pause. Syllables are converted into units of measure, and so are morae[4] or stresses.

It may be objected that metalanguage also makes a sequential use of equivalent units when combining synonymic expressions into an equational sentence: A = A ("*Mare is the female of the horse*"). Poetry and metalanguage, however, are in diametrical opposition to each other: in metalanguage the sequence is used to build an equation, whereas in poetry the equation is used to build a sequence.

* * *

1960

From Two Aspects of Language and Two Types of Aphasic Disturbances

V. The Metaphoric and Metonymic Poles

The varieties of aphasia[1] are numerous and diverse, but all of them lie between the two polar types just described. Every form of aphasic disturbance consists in some impairment, more or less severe, of the faculty either for selection and substitution or for combination and contexture. The former affliction involves a deterioration of metalinguistic operations, while the latter damages the capacity for maintaining the hierarchy of linguistic units. The relation of similarity is suppressed in the former, the relation of conti-

4. Short (unstressed) syllables.

1. Loss of the ability to use or understand speech.

guity in the latter type of aphasia. Metaphor is alien to the similarity disorder, and metonymy to the contiguity disorder.

The development of a discourse may take place along two different semantic lines: one topic may lead to another either through their similarity or through their contiguity. The metaphoric way would be the most appropriate term for the first case and the metonymic way for the second, since they find their most condensed expression in metaphor and metonymy respectively. In aphasia one or the other of these two processes is restricted or totally blocked—an effect which makes the study of aphasia particularly illuminating for the linguist. In normal verbal behavior both processes are continually operative, but careful observation will reveal that under the influence of a cultural pattern, personality, and verbal style, preference is given to one of the two processes over the other.

In a well-known psychological test, children are confronted with some noun and told to utter the first verbal response that comes into their heads. In this experiment two opposite linguistic predilections are invariably exhibited: the response is intended either as a substitute for or as a complement to the stimulus. In the latter case the stimulus and the response together form a proper syntactic construction, most usually a sentence. These two types of reaction have been labeled *substitutive* and *predicative*.

To the stimulus *hut* one response was *burnt out*; another *is a poor little house*. Both reactions are predicative; but the first creates a purely narrative context, while in the second there is a double connection with the subject *hut*: on the one hand, a positional (namely, syntactic) contiguity and, on the other, a semantic similarity.

The same stimulus produced the following substitutive reactions: the tautology *hut*; the synonyms *cabin* and *hovel*; the antonym *palace*; and the metaphors *den* and *burrow*. The capacity of two words to replace one another is an instance of positional similarity, and, in addition, all these responses are linked to the stimulus by semantic similarity (or contrast). Metonymical responses to the same stimulus, such as *thatch, litter,* or *poverty*, combine and contrast the positional similarity with semantic contiguity.

In manipulating these two kinds of connection (similarity and contiguity) in both their aspects (positional and semantic)—selecting, combining, and ranking them—an individual exhibits his personal style, his verbal predilections and preferences.

In verbal art the interaction of these two elements is especially pronounced. Rich material for the study of this relationship is to be found in verse patterns which require a compulsory *parallelism* between adjacent lines, for example in biblical poetry or in the Finnic and, to some extent, the Russian oral traditions. This provides an objective criterion of what in the given speech community acts as a correspondence. Since on any verbal level—morphemic, lexical, syntactic, and phraseological[2]—either of these two relations (similarity and contiguity) can appear—and each in either of two aspects, an impressive range of possible configurations is created. Either of the two gravitational poles may prevail. In Russian lyrical songs, for example, metaphoric constructions predominate, while in the heroic epics the metonymic way is preponderant.

In poetry there are various motives which determine the choice between

2. That is, pertaining respectively to the smallest meaningful sound, to individual words, to the structure of phrases and sentences, and to the organization of phrases into larger elements.

these alternants. The primacy of the metaphoric process in the literary schools of Romanticism and Symbolism has been repeatedly acknowledged, but it is still insufficiently realized that it is the predominance of metonymy which underlies and actually predetermines the so-called Realist trend, which belongs to an intermediary stage between the decline of Romanticism and the rise of Symbolism and is opposed to both. Following the path of contiguous relationships, the Realist author metonymically digresses from the plot to the atmosphere and from the characters to the setting in space and time. He is fond of synecdochic details. In the scene of Anna Karenina's suicide Tolstoj's[3] artistic attention is focused on the heroine's handbag; and in *War and Peace* the synecdoches "hair on the upper lip" and "bare shoulders" are used by the same writer to stand for the female characters to whom these features belong.

The alternative predominance of one or the other of these two processes is by no means confined to verbal art. The same oscillation occurs in sign systems other than language. A salient example from the history of painting is the manifestly metonymical orientation of Cubism, where the object is transformed into a set of synecdoches; the Surrealist painters[4] responded with a patently metaphorical attitude. Ever since the productions of D. W. Griffith,[5] the art of the cinema, with its highly developed capacity for changing the angle, perspective, and focus of shots, has broken with the tradition of the theater and ranged an unprecedented variety of synecdochic close-ups and metonymic set-ups in general. In such motion pictures as those of Charlie Chaplin and Eisenstein,[6] these devices in turn were overlaid by a novel, metaphoric montage with its lap dissolves—the filmic similes.

The bipolar structure of language (or other semiotic systems) and, in aphasia, the fixation on one of these poles to the exclusion of the other require systematic comparative study. The retention of either of these alternatives in the two types of aphasia must be confronted with the predominance of the same pole in certain styles, personal habits, current fashions, etc. A careful analysis and comparison of these phenomena with the whole syndrome of the corresponding type of aphasia is an imperative task for joint research by experts in psychopathology, psychology, linguistics, poetics, and semiotics, the general science of signs. The dichotomy discussed here appears to be of primal significance and consequence for all verbal behavior and for human behavior in general.[7]

To indicate the possibilities of the projected comparative research, I choose an example from a Russian folktale which employs parallelism as a comic device: "Thomas is a bachelor; Jeremiah is unmarried" (*Fomá xólost; Erjóma neženát*). Here the predicates in the two parallel clauses are associ-

3. Leo Tolstoy (1828–1910), Russian novelist and moral philosopher; his works include *Anna Karenina* (1873–76) and *War and Peace* (1864–69).
4. Members of an experimental literary and artistic movement founded in France in 1924; inspired in part by SIGMUND FREUD (1856–1939), Surrealists sought to express subconscious thought and feeling. Cubism: early-20th-century art movement that attempted to present objects from all points of view.
5. American film director and producer (1875–1948), a pioneer in motion pictures.
6. Cf. his striking essay "Dickens, Griffith, and We": Sergej Eisenstein, *Izbrannye stat'i* [*Selected Articles*] (Moscow, 1950) [Jakobson's note]. Chaplin (1889–1977), English actor and film director. Eisenstein (1898–1948), Russian film director, an early innovator in cinematic technique.
7. For the psychological and sociological aspects of this dichotomy, see Gregory Bateson's views on progressional and selective integration and Talcott Parsons on the conjunction-disjunction dichotomy in child development: J. Ruesch and G. Bateson, *Communication, the Social Matrix of Psychiatry* (New York, 1951); T. Parsons and R. F. Bales, *Family Socialization and Interaction Process* (Glencoe, Ill., 1955) [Jakobson's note].

ated by similarity: they are in fact synonymous. The subjects of both clauses are masculine proper names and hence morphologically similar, while on the other hand they denote two contiguous heroes of the same tale, created to perform identical actions and thus to justify the use of synonymous pairs of predicates. A somewhat modified version of the same construction occurs in a familiar wedding song in which each of the wedding guests is addressed in turn by his first name and patronymic: "Gleb is a bachelor; Ivanovič is unmarried." While both predicates here are again synonyms, the relationship between the two subjects is changed: both are proper names denoting the same man and are normally used contiguously as a mode of polite address.

In the quotation from the folktale, the two parallel clauses refer to two separate facts, the marital status of Thomas and the similar status of Jeremiah. In the verse from the wedding song, however, the two clauses are synonymous: they redundantly reiterate the celibacy of the same hero, splitting him into two verbal hypostases.[8]

The Russian novelist Gleb Ivanovič Uspenskij (1840–1902) in the last years of his life suffered from a mental illness involving a speech disorder. His first name and patronymic, *Gleb Ivanovič,* traditionally combined in polite intercourse, for him split into two distinct names designating two separate beings: Gleb was endowed with all his virtues, while Ivanovič, the name relating a son to his father, became the incarnation of all Uspenskij's vices. The linguistic aspect of this split personality is the patient's inability to use two symbols for the same thing, and it is thus a similarity disorder. Since the similarity disorder is bound up with the metonymical bent, an examination of the literary manner Uspenskij had employed as a young writer takes on particular interest. And the study of Anatolij Kamegulov, who analyzed Uspenskij's style, bears out our theoretical expectations. He shows that Uspenskij had a particular penchant for metonymy, and especially for synecdoche, and that he carried it so far that "the reader is crushed by the multiplicity of detail unloaded on him in a limited verbal space, and is physically unable to grasp the whole, so that the portrait is often lost."[9]

To be sure, the metonymical style in Uspenskij is obviously prompted by the prevailing literary canon of his time, late nineteenth-century "realism"; but the personal stamp of Gleb Invanovič made his pen particularly suitable for this artistic trend in its extreme manifestations and finally left its mark upon the verbal aspect of his mental illness.

A competition between both devices, metonymic and metaphoric, is manifest in any symbolic process, be it intrapersonal or social. Thus in an inquiry into the structure of dreams, the decisive question is whether the symbols and the temporal sequences used are based on contiguity (Freud's metonymic "displacement" and synecdochic "condensation")[1] or on similarity (Freud's "identification and symbolism"). The principles underlying magic rites have been resolved by Frazer[2] into two types: charms based on the law

8. Concepts to which real identity is attributed.

9. A. Kamegulov, *Stil' Gleba Uspenskogo* (Leningrad, 1930), pp. 65, 145. One of such disintegrated portraits cited in the monograph: "From underneath an ancient straw cap, with a black spot on its visor, peeked two braids resembling the tusks of a wild boar; a chin, grown fat and pendulous, had spread definitively over the greasy collar of the calico dicky and lay in a thick layer on the coarse collar of the canvas coat, firmly buttoned at the neck. From underneath this coat to the eyes of the observer protruded massive hands with a ring which had eaten into the fat finger, a cane with a copper top, a significant bulge of the stomach, and the presence of very broad pants, almost of a muslin quality, in the wide bottoms of which hid the toes of the boots" [Jakobson's note].

1. Sigmund Freud uses these terms in his analysis of the dream-work in *Interpretation of Dreams* (1900; see above).

2. James George Frazer (1854–1941), Scottish anthropologist and folklorist.

of similarity and those founded on association by contiguity. The first of these two great branches of sympathetic magic has been called "homoeopathic" or "imitative," and the second, "contagious" magic.[3] This bipartition is indeed illuminating. Nonetheless, for the most part, the question of the two poles is still neglected despite its wide scope and importance for the study of any symbolic behavior, especially verbal, and of its impairments. What is the main reason for this neglect?

Similarity in meaning connects the symbols of a metalanguage with the symbols of the language referred to. Similarity connects a metaphorical term with the term for which it is substituted. Consequently, when constructing a metalanguage to interpret tropes, the researcher possesses more homogeneous means to handle metaphor, whereas metonymy, based on a different principle, easily defies interpretation. Therefore nothing comparable to the rich literature on metaphor can be cited for the theory of metonymy. For the same reason, it is generally realized that Romanticism is closely linked with metaphor, whereas the equally intimate ties of Realism with metonymy usually remain unnoticed. Not only the tool of the observer but also the object of observation are responsible for the preponderance of metaphor over metonymy in scholarship. Since poetry is focused upon the sign, and pragmatical prose primarily upon the referent, tropes and figures were studied mainly as poetic devices. The principle of similarity underlies poetry; the metrical parallelism of lines or the phonic equivalence of rhyming words prompts the question of semantic similarity and contrast; there exist, for instance, grammatical and antigrammatical but never agrammatical rhymes. Prose, on the contrary, is forwarded essentially by contiguity. Thus for poetry, metaphor—and for prose, metonymy—is the line of least resistance and consequently the study of poetical tropes is directed chiefly toward metaphor. The actual bipolarity has been artificially replaced in these studies by an amputated, unipolar scheme which, strikingly enough, coincides with one of the two aphasic patterns, namely with the contiguity disorder.

1956

3. James G. Frazer, *The Golden Bough: A Study in Magic and Religion*, 3d ed. (Vienna, 1950), part I, chap. 3 [Jakobson's note].

KENNETH BURKE

1897–1993

A wild and wooly autodidact with a vision as expansive and eccentric as Walt Whitman's, Kenneth Burke stands as an American original among mid-twentieth-century literary critics. Although there is no Burkean school per se and many readers are not charmed by Burke's sprawling and (despite his best efforts) nonsystematic work, writers in numerous fields—especially literary criticism, sociology, anthropology, and communication and performance studies—find it richly suggestive. With the boom in literary theory in the 1970s and 1980s, his stock rose in literature departments. The range of his interdisciplinary interests, his rejection of modernist aestheticism and the belletristic close reading associated with Anglo-American New Criticism, his abiding political concerns, and his connection of issues in criticism to those in the Western philosophical tradition all link his work with post–New Critical theory.

Born and raised in Pittsburgh, Burke formed a lifelong friendship in high school with the critic and poet Malcolm Cowley. After short stints at Ohio State University and Columbia University, Burke quit school for good in 1918 and moved to New York City's Greenwich Village to become a writer. He was an active member of the downtown literary scene, working for the *Dial* (an influential "little magazine") and becoming friends with the poets William Carlos Williams and Hart Crane. Burke married in 1919 and had three daughters with his first wife, whom he divorced in the early 1930s. (He later had two sons with his first wife's sister, whom he married in 1933.) In the mid-1920s he moved out of Manhattan to a New Jersey farm, where he and his family lived in considerable poverty. Burke's short stories, poetry, reviews, and translations generated little income. In 1931 he published his first work of literary criticism, *Counter-Statement*, and in 1932 his first (and only) novel, *Towards a Better Life*. The disappointing reception of his novel apparently led Burke to conclude that his talents lay elsewhere. The rest of the decade was devoted to the broadly philosophical *Permanence and Change* (1935) and his work on genre, *Attitudes toward History* (1937). In 1943 Burke began teaching at Bennington College in Vermont, where he stayed until 1961.

Our selection, "Kinds of Criticism" (1946), calls for a criticism as capacious as the object it criticizes. All kinds of criticism, Burke tells us, serve useful purposes—and will be even more useful if the critic is as explicit as possible about his goals. But each kind of criticism must scrupulously avoid the temptation to champion one critical practice exclusively while denouncing others as illegitimate.

Burke here draws a basic distinction between "intrinsic" and "extrinsic" criticism. Intrinsic criticism attempts to focus its attention solely on the literary text. This approach, often called formalism or "close reading," is usually associated with mid-twentieth-century Anglo-American New Criticism. Its hallmarks are the tracking of intricate symbolic or semantic patterns in a text and an interest in formal literary and rhetorical structures. Extrinsic criticism, Burke tells us, is concerned instead "with the relation between the poem and its non-poetic or extra-poetic ground." Issues of biography, of social and historical context, and of audience reactions are just some examples of extratextual matters that the extrinsic critic might consider. Against a New Criticism that tried to limit literary critics to intrinsic interpretations, Burke insists: " 'In principle,' I can see no legitimate objection to such [extrinsic] inquiries." Burke, in fact, believes that intrinsic criticism is too narrow and severs the connection of literature to the world. Elsewhere, he famously calls literature "equipment for living." Poems and novels project "attitudes" toward existence in the world, displaying possible ways of living. Only if we locate the poem in terms of the world it addresses can we fully appreciate the possibilities it offers.

Poetry is so important to Burke precisely because it is a discourse of the whole in a modern age fragmented by specialists. Different types of criticism are more partial than the poem being studied. Close reading ("textual analysis," in Burke's essay), for example, can be extremely useful, but it does not exhaust the poem: it does not replicate or surpass the poem's complex interweaving of elements. Each kind of criticism, we might say, addresses only some facets of the poem's multifaceted reality. Burke hints at one kind of criticism—"a criticism of criticism"—that may achieve a holism comparable to that which he ascribes to poetry. This criticism of criticism looks very similar to standard definitions of theory: it will provide "systematic statements involving discrimination, classification, methodology, . . . and the like." Burke, however, resists having theory trump all other kinds of criticism. He points out theory's limits, the way its generalizations can occlude attention to the singularities of particular objects. Theory, too, is just one critical practice among others. And if criticism is to move toward holism, it must do as poetry does—not expecting any one critical essay or any one poem to contain everything, but accepting that all topics and methods are open for exploration by the writer (whether poet or critic).

In the 1940s Burke attempted to provide "the logical and procedural grounds" for a holistic criticism through a theoretical paradigm he christened Dramatism. Although he upheld the tenets of Dramatism throughout the rest of his long life, it is telling that Burke finished only two of the projected three volumes on the subject, *A Grammar of Motives* (1945) and *A Rhetoric of Motives* (1950); *A Symbolic of Motives* was never written. Here Burke attempts to lay out the essential components of human action and the ways in which these components can combine and interact. The five elements are act, scene, agent, agency, and purpose. (Later, Burke came to believe that "attitude" should be added to this list.) "Kinds of Criticism" suggests what can be accomplished with this list. Different critical practices can be characterized by their emphasis on different relations existing among the five basic elements. Biographical or psychological criticism, for example, focuses on the relation of act (writing a poem) to agent (the author). Historical and sociological criticisms explore the connections between scene (the social and cultural conditions of its writing) and act. If we take all the different possible permutations of the basic components, we would presumably have an exhaustive table of the possible forms of criticism.

Burke himself practiced a "rhetorical" criticism that starts from the fact of the poem's existence and tries to project the changes it will effect in its audience. His emphasis is on what the poem can and will do—to the author, to the audience, to the society. This rhetorical focus casts the poem as a social and cultural event, thereby anticipating more recent ideological and "cultural studies" approaches to literature as well as reader-response criticism. Burke's attention to the social networks in which poems are implicated and through which the poem's purposes are forwarded or thwarted explains his appeal to sociologists and anthropologist as well as literary critics.

The widespread return to rhetoric in the work of critics such as STANLEY FISH and PAUL DE MAN follows from an interest in how linguistic utterances aim to shape the numerous responses they generate. Burke's description of linguistic utterances as "symbolic actions" dovetails in many respects with rhetorical criticism and with J. L. AUSTIN's notion of "speech acts." Like Austin and the earlier American pragmatist philosophers William James (1842–1910) and John Dewey (1859–1952), Burke is committed to an agent who has some control over motives and actions even while embedded in social relations and language.

Burke's acts of practical criticism (including famous reading of poems by the Romantic poets John Keats and SAMUEL TAYLOR COLERIDGE), his examination of the grammar of action, and his emphasis on the rhetorical, consequential dimension of linguistic utterances provide useful models and powerful insights for today's critic. Because he is almost always used as a treasure trove of insights rather than as the source of a unified theory, Burke has been criticized for being incoherent (notably by René Wellek) but is rarely attacked directly. He is ignored by those who can't fathom his appeal, while employed and reread joyously by those who find pleasure and use in his associative style, his encyclopedic knowledge, and his Whitmanesque embrace of everything.

BIBLIOGRAPHY

The University of California Press keeps almost all of Burke's work in print. The major works are *The Complete White Oxen: Collected Short Fiction* (1924), *Counter-Statement* (1931), *Permanence and Change* (1935), *Attitudes toward History* (1937), *The Philosophy of Literary Form* (1941), *A Grammar of Motives* (1945), *A Rhetoric of Motives* (1950), *The Rhetoric of Religion* (1961), *Language as Symbolic Action* (1966), *Collected Poems, 1915–1967* (1968), and *The Selected Correspondence of Kenneth*

Burke and Malcolm Cowley: 1915–1981, edited by Paul Jay (1988). The closest thing to a biography is Jack Selzer's *Kenneth Burke in Greenwich Village* (1996), which covers the years up to 1932.

Critical Responses to Kenneth Burke, edited by William H. Rueckert (1969), collects reviews and early critical essays on Burke, while Rueckert's *Kenneth Burke and the Drama of Human Relations* (2d ed., 1982) remains the most comprehensive overview of Burke's Dramatism. The essays collected in *Representing Kenneth Burke*, edited by Hayden White and Margaret Brose (1982), especially the important contributions by White and Fredric Jameson, mark the revival of interest in Burke among literary theorists, as does Frank Lentricchia's influential *Criticism and Social Change* (1983). *The Legacy of Kenneth Burke*, edited by Herbert Simons and Trevor Melia (1989), offers more standard, but still substantial, engagements with Burke's work. Robert Wess's *Kenneth Burke: Rhetoric, Subjectivity, Postmodernism* (1996) provides the best comprehensive overview of Burke's whole career. *Kenneth Burke and the 21st Century*, edited by Bernard L. Brock (1998), contains essays that consider Burke's work in relation to various intellectuals developments of the 1980s and 1990s. Rueckert's *Critical Responses* has a superb bibliography of Burke's work and work on Burke up to 1968, and Simons and Melia's *Legacy* provides coverage for the period from 1968 to 1988.

Kinds of Criticism

In here surveying briefly the kinds of criticism, we don't hope to tell anybody anything he didn't already know. We merely hope for whatever clarification may come of a general survey. And we are more concerned to look over the field than to argue for any one method.

The critic can justify his choice of method in three ways: (1) by theoretical arguments defining its nature and the grounds of his choice; (2) by practical demonstrations of the method in operation; (3) by claims for it as a moral contribution over and above its value as a specialty (that is, he may argue for it as cultural amenity, equipment for living, means of political betterment, etc.). Often the third class of justifications is nondescript, deriving vitality from true or false promises of individual reward (social, occupational, financial, sexual, etc.), interests which are not recognized formally. When the critic is not challenged, these nondescript motives may be indicated by subtleties of tone suggesting that persons in the know take such-and-such for granted; when he is challenged, he will show an acrimony greater than the point at issue seems to call for. This third class of motives, which usually protects itself either by the magic of suggestion or by the bulldozing of vehemence, and which adds resonance to a writer's work, is as legitimate as the other two, in so far as it is explicitly stated. The greater the range and depth of considerations about which a critic can be explicit, the more he is fulfilling his task as a critic.

II

EXTRINSIC CRITICISM

Genetic:

Concern with the relation between the poem and its non-poetic or extra-poetic ground. The poem being the act of a human agent in a temporal scene, there is good reason for considering either the relations between act and scene (environmentalist, historical criticism) or the relations between act and agent (psychological criticism). Another step can be introduced here: The critic can ask first how the scene affects the consciousness of the agents, and next how the given emphases of consciousness attain their corresponding poetic expression.

"In principle," I can see no legitimate objection to such inquiries. The art that arises under primitive conditions, for instance, is obviously different from the art that arises under highly sophisticated conditions, and this goes also for sophisticated cults of "neo-primitivism." Similarly, the poet's physique, temperament and beliefs must figure as motives in his work, however far we may have to depart from a mere one-to-one correspondence between the character of the poet as a citizen and the characters of his work as poet

However, such criticism has often been quite naïve in its choice of terms, and in its failure to recognize the ways in which these terms both guide and restrict its inquiries. Often a choice among such terminologies is best justified by our third kind of argument: appeal to extrinsic interests (as when the ills of capitalism are cited as grounds for the special relevance of Marxist criticism *now*, or the secularization of cures for the sick soul is taken as ground for the favoring of a psychoanalytic approach to literature). Also, historical and psychological correlations are justifiable today on the grounds that new precisions in these fields offer new possibilities of development.

Implicational:

The Genetic is concerned with the possible extra-literary causes of the poem. The Implicational is concerned with extra-literary effects. It deals with an act-agent relation, or if you will, an act-patient relation: the response which the poem arouses in its audience. A possible complication would be a study of the effect which the writing of the poem has upon the poet himself. For in its role as a perfecting of his own thought, it may serve as incarnation designed to solve personal problems by symbolic, or ritualistic means. Psychoanalytic criticism is Genetic in inquiring about the psychological origins of poetry, but Implicational in viewing the poem as a symbolic device for solving problems of the personality. Here would belong concerns with the respects in which poetry may overtly or covertly serve as ritual of initiation, purification, farewell, rebirth, exorcism, commemoration, "flight and return" (with the object to which one returns having been transfigured by the journey); though such a list suggests that the Implicational is much nearer to Intrinsic criticism than the Genetic is.

The classical example of Implicational criticism is in the *Republic*, where Socrates asks what kind of art would best help form the ideal citizens of his ideal State.[1] Humanism of the Babbitt-Foerster[2] sort is typically Implicational. Michael Gold's attack on Thornton Wilder[3] (as "Prophet of the Genteel Christ") clearly illustrates the Implicational aspect of Marxist criticism: It suggests that Wilder's art helps form in readers an attitude which Gold

1. See PLATO, *Republic* (ca. 360 B.C.E.), 3.386–410e and 10.595a–608b.
2. Irving Babbitt (1865–1933) and Norman Foerster (1887–1972), American literary critics and champions in the 1920s of "new humanism," which insisted that literature embodied universal human values.
3. Three-time Pulitzer Prize–winning novelist and playwright (1897–1975). Gold (ca. 1893–1967), a Marxist Jewish American writer and critic; his "Wilder: Prophet of the Genteel Christ" appeared in the *New Republic*, October 22, 1930.

considers morally (politically) suspect. At the same time, it draws upon both psychological and environmentalist aspects of the Genetic; for it derives the quality of consciousness in Wilder's work from the nature of his character as member of a social class, and it derives the nature of this social class from the nature of the economic background.

Other words for Implicational might be "moral" or "futuristic." For the critic asks what effects upon future conduct are most likely to be implicit in the poem itself or in the values it embodies. But it is the kind of prognosticating that can prophesy after the event; as the critic might ask how readers of some past era were influenced by a given work or literary movement.

Concerns with the receptivity and resistance of audiences, with the extra-literary situations influencing such responses, and with the extra-literary *uses* to which the pure poetic medium may be applied, could be grouped under the head of Rhetoric. That is, when we ask, "What is Rhetoric?" it is enough to answer, "Rhetoric is the art of persuasion," and to expatiate upon this definition. But when we ask, "What all is Rhetoric?" we must inquire at length into the extra-literary factors involved in expression and its uses. The individual, competitive motives which we have called "nondescript" would also figure here.

III

INTRINSIC CRITICISM

Poetics:

Poetic in the strictest sense (as with the *Poetics* of Aristotle[4]) deals with the poem as a member of a class. If the poem is a ballad, for instance, the critic formulates the principles of balladry, and treats of individual ballads in terms of these principles. Casuistry can be employed for considering the unique respects in which the poem embodies (in variation) the principles common to its kind.

Such concern with a class of poems is Intrinsic because the principles reside in the *genre* only by residing in individuals that compose the *genre*. Each work has its way of embodying the given principles: hence, a discussion of class attributes, as so conceived, is at the same time a discussion of principles intrinsic to the individual work.

In our strongly individualistic, nominalistic[5] era, with its turn away from the substantiality of the familial, Poetic in the strict sense is not often written. Also, there is a way (somewhat analogous in literary theory to the step from Aquinas to Scotus[6] in theology) whereby we may conceive of the *genre* in a more individualized sense. Thus, we may speak of some one writer's *ars poetica,*[7] the principles characteristic of his own particular kind of writing. For not only would there be the principles of "the novel" in general; there would, more narrowly, be the principles of the "historical novel," of the "psychological novel," or the *roman expérimental*[8] etc. And, finally, the principles

4. Greek philosopher (384–322 B.C.E.); for the *Poetics*, see above.
5. Belonging to a philosophical view that holds universals (such as liberty or even the category "tree") to be only linguistic and not real things existing independent of language or thought.
6. Both THOMAS AQUINAS (1225–1274) and John Duns Scotus (ca. 1270–1308) were medieval philosophers. Aquinas was committed to the truth of universals, while Duns Scotus located truth in particulars.
7. Art (technique) of poetry (Latin).
8. Experimental novel (French).

of the "Flaubert novel," or "the Joycean[9] novel," etc. Thus one would eventually reduce the concept of class to the point where each work is in a class by itself, going its own unique way, its special principles of generation requiring it to be considered *sui generis*. The line is shifted farther and farther along until the individual poem is treated as a "family," with its parts all participating, each according to its nature, in the family identity. Poetic, as thus ultimately narrowed, fulfils in terms of principles and casuistry the ideals of individual portraiture which the Impressionist embodies in terms of character or personality.[1]

We should also include, under Poetic, books designed to teach the principles of some particular craft, "how to" books on playwriting, versification, the short story, etc.

The field may be extended to include discussion of any element that contributes to a work's effectiveness. Aristotle's *Poetics*, for instance, touches upon the cathartic aspect of tragedy; and by the same token, psychoanalysis may be said to contribute to Poetic in so far as it adds new precisions to the treatment of this matter. Here is an area where the Implicational impinges upon Poetic.

Reviewing:

The "news" about a book. Ideally, it is information given by an expert who has read the book, to a layman who has not read the book and wants to know whether he should read it. Advice to customers, like a market tip: "This is a good buy for such-and-such kind of literary investor."

The review aims at characterization by naming a work's salient traits. It has three main ways of summing up the work under discussion: (1) summarizing the contents; (2) quoting characteristic passages; (3) using "conclusive" adjectives that specify and evaluate the book's effects. Though reviewing does not, like Poetic, study the laws of a *genre*, it must at least indicate the *genre* in which a work belongs.

In its primary function, reviewing is really "previewing." Secondarily, it is general coverage of the field, for the reader who would learn about the "gist" of a book precisely because he does *not* intend to read it, but wants to know of it for topical reasons.

Reviewing in a more generalized form can lead into the *historical survey*, got by putting many reviews together and by seeking for characterizations that apply to the lot. Usually, in a more or less haphazard way, the reviewer of a particular book is affected by this wider logic of placement, hence in passing may assign the work a place in some larger curve of literary or cultural development.

In so far as a review is scholarly, the evaluative kind of summarization will get more attention than the purely informative kind. Hence, the "conclusive adjectives" may be substantiated by much reasoning and citation, to demonstrate the grounds for the critic's judgments, rather than leaving them, as so often with the purely informational kind of review, as assertions by the critic to be taken by the reader on faith. Ideally, the evaluative review should

9. Of James Joyce (1882–1941), Irish writer whose novels display extraordinary technical innovations. Gustave Flaubert (1821–1880), French novelist famous for his emphasis on the technique and craft of writing.

1. Impressionist criticism focuses on the critic's personal response to or impression of individual art works.

follow much the procedure of Coleridge[2] when discussing Wordsworth's poetry (in *Biographia Literaria*). That is, it should enumerate the essential vices and virtues of the work, and demonstrate each by adequate reporting or citing of relevant material. And it might round out the pattern, where practicable, by showing wherein virtues and vices derive from the same basic character.

Textual Analysis:

Art of the gloss; running commentary; line-by-line exegesis. Particularized appreciation, got by sustained and minute contemplation of a work. The critical commentator, as guide, calls attention to anything that he considers noteworthy: a sound effect here, an image there, a biographical or historical allusion, the comparison of a line in one place with a line somewhere else, appreciation of a felicity, interpretation of an ambiguous passage, etc.

At its worst, it is a mere reflex of the fact that, for courses in literary appreciation, the instructor is obliged by contract to fill an appointed number of hours with observations on prescribed texts. At its best, it sustains the intense contemplation of an object to the point where one begins to see not only more deeply into the object but beyond it, in the direction of generalizations about the kinds of art and artistic excellence, and even the principles of human thought and experience universally.

There must always be a large measure of elasticity in textual analysis; for the text is imperious and sets the demands. Hence there is a temptation for the analyst to become "unprincipled," living from one appreciative moment to the next, with little thought of the generalized critical morrow. And since it is no trick at all for a practised commentator to convert ten words of text into ten pages of appreciation, textual analysis threatens to become a mere feat of improvisation whereby the critic makes a free translation of firm poetry into loose critickese.

Reviewing and textual analysis move in opposite directions, the one towards superficial summary, the other towards a clutter of tiny insights whose worth is impaired by the law of diminishing returns. Yet skill in both these kinds is of great use in all the other kinds of criticism.

IV

MERGING OF EXTRINSIC AND INTRINSIC

Criticism of Criticism:

All the kinds of criticism we have been considering lead back to an ultimate kind, the Criticism of Criticism, which should provide the logical and procedural grounds for them. Here belong all systematic statements involving discrimination, classification, methodology, possibility and standards of evaluation, and the like. And ideally, here should be a terminology whose logic could be carried systematically into the most minute observations of Poetic and Textual Analysis.

However, there must always be a discrepancy between the object of our observation and the medium by which we observe, even though, as in this

2. The Romantic poet and critic SAMUEL TAYLOR COLERIDGE (1772–1834), whose *Biographia Literaria* (1817; see above) devotes much attention to describing and evaluating the poetry of his friend WILLIAM WORDSWORTH (1770–1850).

case, the object (the poem) and the medium (the critique) are both verbal. The relation between poetry and criticism is here somewhat analogous to the relation between "revelation" and "reason" in theology. The poem, as the given, is something extra, something by nature beyond the reach of a purely critical rationale: hence, in the intuiting of it, there is always something which the critical treatment cannot equal (just as there is, in a physical object, something which a poem about it could not equal). The poem, as the object of the critic's intuition, thus forever sets an obligation, that can never be wholly met, to bring the facts of the poem wholly within the orbit of the critic's terms. A criticism of the poem is not the poem (though at times a critic does seem to be asking of other critics that they do somehow contrive to write the poem over again, giving exactly the same quality of experience as the poem itself gives, in an idiom that simultaneously both is and is not a replica of the original).

Though the Criticism of Criticism should, in its ideal perfection, provide the events out of which all other kinds of criticism could be drawn, often the discrepancy between the poem and the critique is widened to the point where the Criticism of Criticism becomes *antithetical* to specific analysis. It is then given to kinds of analysis that serve as "statements of policy" about literature, and provide no leads at all into the areas of the intrinsic.

In so far as the Criticism of Criticism can provide terms that can be extended integrally (not by sheer addition) into all areas of criticism, it brings both Extrinsic and Intrinsic criticism under a single focus. The motive for seeking to attain this focus resides in the fact that no critic in the actual practice of his craft exemplifies any one of these kinds in its purity. Critics borrow in some measure from all the kinds. Hence there is always the logical pull towards the Criticism of Criticism as the ultimate methodizing of any criticism.

Esthetic:

Here also there is a merging of Extrinsic and Intrinsic, though by somewhat dubious means. Esthetic criticism at first view seems wholly Intrinsic. For it treats of poetry exclusively, and as poetry. Yet it identifies the Intrinsic principle of poetry with an Extrinsic principle, thus bringing the two realms together by the *estheticizing* of a non-esthetic term. Sensibility, Intuition, Imagination, for instance, are all terms that prevail outside the poetic orbit; as such, they would ordinarily be looked upon as Extrinsic; but by identifying them with the essence of the poetic, the Esthetic critic gives the Extrinsic an Intrinsic title. To my way of thinking, the resulting merger of the two realms is more apparent than real. But even if the reader disagrees with me as to the genuineness of the merger, I think he will agree as to the particular dialectical operation involved (most systematically embodied, perhaps, in the "Identity" philosophy of Schelling[3] for merging "Subject" and "Object").

Esthetic criticism is likely to stress a strict dialectical opposition between the Esthetic and Practical, Art of Utility, Play and Work, whereby the "amorality" of art may be affirmed in contrast with the moral factor necessarily prominent in real life. Or Art (as the realm of ends) may be pitted against the Scientific and the Practical (as the realm of means). The Esthetic thus

3. Friedrich von Schelling (1775–1854), German idealist philosopher and aesthetician.

by definition rules out Didactic, Propagandistic, Moralistic motives. No matter how strongly such motives may pervade actual poems, the Esthetic rules them out, as an element alien to its modes of measurement. Often, accordingly, Esthetic criticism allows critical issues to get turned backwards: It proposes to rule out of poetry ingredients which are not alien to poetry as it actually is, but are alien to the definition of what belongs in the ideal category of "the esthetic."

Such exclusion seems to be based upon a fallacy. For instance, if you distinguish between the good, the true, the expedient, and the beautiful, you have a convenience of discourse whereby you might take up these topics one by one. But it would be a fallacy to assume that such realms must *exist* in the same isolation with which they can be ideally treated as realms of *being*.

The Esthetic is often linked with the stress upon "Nature" or "Tradition," since both of these terms can be considered inherently poetic. Hence, the scene out of which the poem arises is thought to be pervaded with the same poetic spirit as the poem arising out of it. The Esthetic leads into Impressionism by a similar route, though in this case the source of the poem is situated in poetic agent rather than in poetic scene. That is, the poem is derived from the character of the poet as *poet*. Secondarily, the poem itself may be considered as a personality, and the Impressionist critic seeks to do its portrait.

The Esthetic approaches poetry not through the analysis of poems at one extreme, nor through general dialectical and philosophical considerations at the other, but through a *philosophy of poetry*, which it expands into a *philosophy of everything*.

1946

JACQUES LACAN

1901–1981

Difficult, polemical, and ironic, organized in sometimes baffling ways, and dotted with strange syntax, foreign words, wordplay, obscure allusions, personality, and mathematical formulas, Jacques Lacan's writings genuinely stretch the reader's resources. He writes psychoanalytic theory as if it were poetry, philosophy, and symbolic logic. In writing, Lacan says that he tries "to leave the reader no other way out than the way in, which I prefer to be difficult." The reader cannot simply pick up a "meaning" and carry it away. And that is the point. It is not the fact of difficulty, but the experience and path of difficulty that are significant. Lacan demystifies as a fantasy of omniscience the objective, impersonal, external position often associated with science and theory. But to analyze the consequences of *wanting it anyway* is at the heart of Lacanian psychoanalysis. Insofar as most psychoanalytic theory is today Lacanian or post-Lacanian, there is no way around Jacques Lacan, the French Freud.

Lacan is known for his larger-than-life persona, but his description of his career sounds distinctly unrevolutionary: it consists of a return to the discoveries of his predecessor. For more than thirty years, Lacan analyzed a single case: the writings of SIGMUND FREUD. Thus, what was revolutionary in his work was a reading—a reading that, he claimed, returned to what was radical about "the Freudian discovery" (which he always refers to in the singular). Lacan's return and its radicality were made possible by the development in his lifetime of modern linguistics: Lacan read Freud through the theories of FERDINAND DE SAUSSURE and ROMAN JAKOBSON, and, in the process, they all were changed. Like CLAUDE LÉVI-STRAUSS (by whose work he was also influenced), he found that the structuralist models opened up by Saussure made possible a sea change in theoretical thinking.

Born to middle-class Parisian Catholic parents who named him Jacques-Marie, he was the first of four children (the second child did not survive). His father worked for a soap and oil manufacturer. While Jacques renounced religion and dropped the "-Marie" from his name, his brother Marc-François entered a monastery. Though the celibacy of one brother was more than counterbalanced by the active sexual life of the other, it can be argued that both remained profoundly marked by the church.

In the 1920s Lacan studied medicine in Paris, beginning clinical training in psychiatry (which requires a medical degree) in 1927. Interested in paranoia (delusions of persecution) and erotomania (delusions of love), he connected his work with surrealism, particularly with that of the Spanish painter Salvador Dali, a contemporary whose theory of "paranoid criticism" resonated strongly with Lacan's research. In 1932 Lacan published his doctoral dissertation, *On Paranoiac Psychosis in Its Relations with the Personality*, and sent a copy to Freud. Although Freud lived another seven years and passed through Paris when escaping Nazi-occupied Austria in 1938, the two men never met. Freud acknowledged receipt of the thesis by postcard.

Lacan married Marie-Louise Blondin in 1934 (one month before the birth of their child) and pursued his training analysis with Rudolph Loewenstein, who later became, after emigrating to the United States, one of the founders of American "ego psychology," which was often a target of Lacan's critique. Like others of his generation, he was deeply affected by a famous series of lectures given on G. W. F. HEGEL by Alexandre Kojève in the 1930s. Lacan was particularly inspired by Kojève's interpretation of the Master-Slave dialectic and of the dynamics of recognition. But he was also struck by Kojève's ability to revolutionize a text by reading it against its critical reception. His reading of Freud would do nothing less. And for twenty years Lacan's weekly seminars played, for the next generation of French intellectuals, the role that Kojève's lectures had played for his.

In 1938 Lacan became a member of the Société Psychanalytique de Paris (SPP), the official French branch of the International Psycho-Analytical Society (IPA) founded by Freud in 1910. During the war, the SPP was forced to suspend its operations. Lacan's personal life was also in flux; the birth in 1941 of Judith Bataille, Lacan's daughter with Sylvia Bataille (the estranged wife of the celebrated critic and novelist Georges Bataille; their separation was not made public until the end of the war), led Marie-Louise to seek a divorce. In 1953 Lacan became president of the SPP and married Sylvia.

Relations between the Freudian establishment and Lacan were always fraught. The prominent psychoanalyst Marie Bonaparte, who had apparently had an affair with Lacan's analyst, was particularly suspicious of him. His practice of seeing patients for variable lengths of time (the so-called short sessions) rather than for the prescribed fifty minutes led the commission on instruction to demand that he regularize his practice. He never did so. His intuitive brilliance as a clinician was often incompatible with institutional rules and safeguards, yet his charismatic personality seemed to call for new institutions. He resigned from the SPP and joined the newer Société Française de Psychanalyse (SFP)—which, upon being told in 1963 that it could join the IPA if Lacan were not included, tried to ban his teaching and his practice. This episode is what Lacan called his "excommunication." Unwilling to conform to the existing rules and excluded from the official organizations, Lacan decided to set up on his own. He founded L'École Freudienne de Paris (the Freudian School of Paris), and with the support of LOUIS ALTHUSSER he moved his weekly seminar, which had been held at the Sainte-Anne hospital, to the prestigious École Normale.

In 1966 Lacan published a legendary 900-page collection of his essays and conference papers titled *Écrits* (*Writings*). Despite its difficulty, the book was a sensation. Crowds began filling his weekly seminar. Along with other French thinkers, Lacan spoke that same year at Johns Hopkins University at a conference—"The Languages of Criticism and the Sciences of Man"—that launched structuralism and poststructuralism in the United States. And together with Althusser, JACQUES DERRIDA, JULIA KRISTEVA, HÉLÈNE CIXOUS, and many others, Lacan became very closely associated with the intellectual ferment that helped lead to the student demonstrations in May 1968 in Paris. Indeed, some of his students became so disruptive that the director of the École Normale made it known to Lacan that he would have to seek another venue. In 1969 he began holding his seminars at the Faculté de Droit (Law School). Meanwhile, at the just-opened branch of the University of Paris at Vincennes, the first university department of psychoanalysis in France was created by people sympathetic to Lacan. Among them was Jacques-Alain Miller, a student of Althusser who later became important as Lacan's editor and son-in-law.

In 1975 Lacan visited the United States again, lecturing at Yale University and MIT. But controversy raged at the École Freudienne de Paris over two developments: the influence of Miller (who was not a medical doctor and preferred Lacan-the-logician to Lacan-the-clinician) and the new pedagogical procedure (called "la passe") that Lacan had introduced into his school to certify those who would receive the title "Analyste de l'École" (Analyst of the Freudian School). The controversy became so fierce that in 1980, the aging Lacan announced the closing of the school he had founded (and, in effect, his own impending death), saying, "Je dissous . . ." (I dissolve). But many members of the Freudian School felt the school was not his to dissolve. As he created a new school ("La Cause Freudienne"), they fought the legality of his dissolution of the old one, but lost. He died of cancer a little more than a year later.

Lacan published only one "book"—his 1932 dissertation; *Écrits* was a collection of assorted papers. But his name is attached to the many articles he published in the numerous journals of the Freudian School, and transcripts of all twenty-six of his annual book-length seminars were and still are being edited and published by Jacques-Alain Miller. His speaking style resembled writing in its "poetic" richness and its need for active listening but he did not consider his *Écrits* to be quite worthy of their name ("writings"). He jokingly referred to publication as poubellication (*poubelle* means "wastebasket").

The most influential seminar from the literary point of view is his 1955 seminar on EDGAR ALLAN POE's "Purloined Letter" (1845); parts were published as the opening texts in the French *Écrits*, but they are not included in the much shorter English translation of the book. (The entire seminar was published in English in 1988 as *The Ego in Freud's Theory and in the Technique of Psychoanalysis*.) In his "Seminar on 'The Purloined Letter' " Lacan shows how a text can be read even when a major piece of information is not disclosed, a lesson important for psychoanalysis. The *path* of the desired or feared letter in Poe's story does not depend on knowledge of its contents; and the behavior of those who seek it creates a story around their presumptions about the contents, whether or not the letter is ever opened. In this seminar, Lacan is commenting on Freud's concept of the "repetition compulsion," which he translates as "repetition automatism." The story is composed of two different scenes in which the same letter is stolen: the two scenes are repetitions of each other with the set roles being played by different characters. Like the lights on a news strip showing streaming headlines (the analogy is Lacan's), the individual characters are like the light bulbs that go on and off according to the structure being repeated, and not according to their individual volition or characteristics. The repetition is *unconscious*. For Lacan, in other words, Poe's story illustrates the fact that the letter's position among the characters, and not the psychology of the individuals, determines what each will do: "Their displacement is determined by the place which a pure signifier—the purloined letter—comes to occupy." Lacan calls this mechanism "symbolic determination." Like a "free cell" in the solitaire of that name (included in the software of many computers) that allows the other cards to be moved, the "pure" signifier functions as the point of articulation whether or not anything is known about it. Although the story's reader never gains access to the text of the letter, the story's characters do read it; like the analyst, the reader has to understand the functioning of the repetition without necessarily knowing its content.

For Lacan, there are three "orders" or "dimensions" in the psyche: the "Symbolic," the "Imaginary," and the "Real." They are all equally important to the formation of subjectivity. The Real is the easiest to define and the hardest to talk about. In fact, it *can't* be talked about; any such discussion is "impossible." The moment it becomes an object of discourse, it ceases to be the "Real" because it becomes real *for someone* and becomes the "truth." "We are used to the real. The truth we repress," writes Lacan late in his essay "The Agency of the Letter in the Unconscious." "The truth is always disturbing." The "Real" is also defined by Lacan as "that to which the fact that I'm thinking about it doesn't matter." But what is disturbing can be disturbing only *for someone*. The Real can thus only be studied in its effects on the other two dimensions, the Imaginary and the Symbolic.

The Imaginary originates in the human being's fascination with form. The fundamental role of form for the human being is described in Lacan's essay "The Mirror Stage as Formative of the Function of the I" (1949; the concept was introduced in a 1936 lecture), our first selection. The essay describes the founding moment of the Imaginary: the infant's recognition of its image in the mirror. The baby forgets how weak it is and identifies jubilantly with the wholeness of a reflected form. The human self thus comes into being through a fundamentally *aesthetic* recognition. The self-image that causes identification and recognition is a *fiction* "over there," dictating the efforts of the subject ("I") toward a totality and autonomy it can never attain. Through an external medium (a mirror), the child's fragmented body is made whole: the newly fashioned specular 'I" precedes the social "I."

The relation between the self and its image constitutes the "Imaginary" dimension—so named not because it is unreal, but because it involves an image. The Symbolic, in contrast, is the dimension of symbolization into which the human being's body, to the extent that he or she begins to *speak*, must translate itself. The Symbolic is the dimension of articulation, not equivalent to pointing or naming. Like algebra, the "Symbolic" is a structure of *relations* rather than *things*. (These terms can be confusing; for example, so-called phallic symbols would belong in the Imaginary, not the Symbolic dimension.)

"The Agency of the Letter in the Unconscious" (1957), from which our second selection is drawn, develops some aspects of the "symbolic" structure of the psyche. It is one of Lacan's most explicit structuralist attempts to bring Freud and Saussure together. The unconscious, for Lacan, is not a hidden reservoir of repressed desires but rather a form of rhetorical energy designed both to disguise and to express those desires, which exist for psychoanalysis only in their effects. "The unconscious is structured like a language," he famously claims. This means not that the unconscious *is* language, but that the unconscious is *like* a language—a foreign language. In other words, the unconscious is *structured*, not amorphous, and it *speaks* rhetorically through the dreams, mistakes, and symptoms of the subject. In the case of psychoanalytic symptoms, it is the body itself that provides the raw material that the unconscious uses to express itself and that the analyst, like a literary critic, must "read."

Saussure's influential model of the linguistic sign has two parts: the sign is composed of a *signifier* and a *signified*. In his example, a drawing of a tree functions as the signified (concept-image), while the spoken word "tree" functions as the signifier (sound-image). By playing with the notion of the tree in Western theory and poetry, Lacan makes it clear that even this representative of "nature" is really a form of "culture." Saussure's model of the sign has three implications that Lacan wants to challenge: that a sign is the representation of a thing, that signs function individually, and that the line that separates signifier from signified is only an abstract function of the diagram (see chapter 1 of Saussure's *Course in General Linguistics*, above). Lacan's countermodel of the sign—or rather, of the signifying chain—consists of two doors; one is labeled "ladies" and the other "gentlemen." The sign can no longer be considered a picture of a thing (since the doors are identical, except for their labels, and resemble neither men nor women). Rather, the sign is a structure into which the reader has to fit his or her body. The signs tell the reader where to "go": they instate the law of sexual difference but do not explain it. They also create a difference where none existed before; the doors are the same, but "ladies" and "gentlemen" are henceforth different. The line in the diagram plays the role of censor merely by dividing one sex from the other. Lacan rewrites Saussure's model of the sign as S/*s*. The "signifier" (S) marks the spot where the "signified" (*s*) has been struck by the bar of repression, which is indistinguishable from the structuring function of civilization. Signs thus systematically and unconsciously constitute all social codes, conventions, and prohibitions. We are constituted and acculturated by signs. Even before we begin to speak, we are already being spoken.

Language, in Lacan's analysis, operates on us as much as we operate on it. We follow the signs. Language speaks us. But in the process, we become split between a conscious self and an unconscious self that we repress, deny, and repeat. Given the power of the unconscious, Lacan rewrites the celebrated self-identity of Descartes's "I think, therefore I am" as enigmatic self-estrangement: "I think where I am not, therefore I am where I do not think." In attempting to describe the rhetoric of this self-estrangement, Lacan aligns Roman Jakobson's linguistic studies of metaphor and metonymy with Freud's distinction (in *The Interpretation of Dreams*, 1900) between condensation and displacement in the dream-work of the unconscious. Because an unconscious wish is, in Freud's model, unacceptable or forbidden, it must get around the censorship of consciousness if it is to express itself. It does so either by choosing a stand-in ("one word for another" = metaphor) or by sliding along and selecting adjacent signifiers ("word-to-word" = metonymy). In "The Agency of the Letter," Lacan thus extends the theories of Saussure and Jakobson in the direction of Freud's implicit rhetoric of unconscious processes, while at the same time drawing on modern linguistics to precisely formulate that which, in Freud, remains largely intuitive.

"The Signification of the Phallus" (1958), our final selection, is one of the most condensed, contested, suggestive, and misunderstood of Lacan's essays. It is about castration—a concept that never fails to be considered scandalous. Why, he asks, did Freud need the concept of castration at all? Women are not castrated men, are they? Little boys don't really believe their fathers will castrate them, do they? It's ridiculous to think that Mommy once had a penis and lost it, isn't it? How could a theory so manifestly absurd and disprovable have been taken seriously? The outrageousness of these infantile sexual theories is of course the point. The human being comes into sexuality epistemologically unprepared. But why did Freud imagine that *these* were the theories that came most readily to mind to stanch the wound created by the discovery that not everyone resembles me, and that *that* has something to do with sexuality?

Lacan tackles these questions in several ways. His originality lies in the connections he makes between the functioning of language and the functioning of desire. As soon as man begins to speak (there is no getting away from the masculine universal in Lacan), he must launder everything important or even routine about his bodily life through linguistic structures that don't exactly correspond to biological requirements. Lacan defines desire as what is left of absolute demand when all possible satisfaction of needs has been subtracted from it. In other words, desire is what by definition remains unsatisfiable.

Linguistic structures preexist the subject and are not created by him. Lacan calls "the Other" "the very locus evoked by the recourse to speech." (The *other* designates a mirror image, a counterpart or competitor, another person; the *Other*, capitalized, designates the Symbolic dimension itself insofar as the subject has to relate to it.) The very fact of speaking routes everything through the Other. The intuition that somehow one has lost direct connection with the body—that something about the body is missing—is itself a first definition of the concept of castration. This lost object that is defined retrospectively is also called, in Lacan's terms, *objet petit a* (a phrase that should be translated "object little o," since the *a* is from *autre*, "other"). The lost object is one that the subject never had, the loss brought into being by symbolization itself.

But if that were all, then everyone would be in exactly the same position with respect to the unattainability of naturalness. There would be no sexual asymmetry. Sexual difference would disappear. Thus, what Lacan has to add to this "universal" castration is a *specific* castration caused by the encounter with sexual difference. The castration that counts is the symbolic castration of the mother—the mother as not-all (not all there is for the child, not a total body form, not entirely focused on the child without other relationships). At this point, in other writings, Lacan describes the function of the father as both the instatement of language ("le nom du père"—the name of the father) and the prohibition of incest ("le non du père"—the "no" of the father).

The phallus that is determining in the phallic stage of human development is thus the one that has never existed. The "something missing" cannot be anything real: it can be generated only by the fact of structure itself. It is missing without ever having been there. It is an interpretation, a theory, a comparison, not a thing. The linguistic counterpart of the missing thing is an extra signifier whose only function is to be the name of the missing thing. There is no signified, but the signifier names the fact of signification—the fact that sexual difference is an interpretation—as such. For Lacan, the phallus is the name for that signifier.

In his seminar *Feminine Sexuality* (1972–73), Lacan goes so far as to claim that "there is no sexual relation." If there were a sexual relation, that would imply that the sexes are complementary, that they fit together to make a whole. But (according to Lacan and, he claims, all of literature), they don't. Women's pleasure is supplementary, not complementary, to a sexual universe that revolves around the position of the one, the phallus, the center. The wholeness and completion that is desired in the sexual relation is precisely what would make it impossible, deadly. When Lacan says that woman does not exist, he is referring to "woman" as a fantasy of complementarity. If "woman" existed, women could not. To account for the existence of women as something that does not merely confirm the preeminence of the phallic signifier, Lacan adds "God" to the couple. God is the third who keeps "two" from collapsing into "one." The point is not that Lacan "believes" in God, but that the position God occupies in the structure (that of the Other) cannot disappear. For that reason, Lacan focuses on the writings of mystics: Saint John of the Cross, Hadewijch d'Anvers, Saint Teresa—and Jacques Lacan.

It is easy to see why Lacan has been both useful for and anathema to feminists. On the one hand his theory is useful because it is not in any simple way essentialist: "men" and "women" are not essences or biological givens but rather positions in a structure. On the other hand, his theory is "phallocentric" in the very terms he uses to displace phallocentrism. He writes as if the ménage à trois implied in every relationship consisted of the phallus, the not-all, and God. Like Freud's theory, Lacan's theory takes patriarchy as a given. Whether his writing constitutes a defense or simply an analysis of that given is open to interpretation. The writings of the French feminists Luce Irigaray and Hélène Cixous, in particular, are attempts to give voice, figure, and flesh to alternative versions of sexuality starting from the feminine, not the phallic, perspective without falling into essentialist thinking themselves.

Any analysis, whether clinical or scholarly, implies what Lacan memorably calls "the subject presumed to know." The knowledge sought is presumed to exist somewhere. That fantasy of a knower "out there" is what we have to be cured of. But it is therefore ironic that no one performs the role of that knower better than Lacan. One can only conclude that the demystifier of the "subject presumed to know" is the most powerful of its incarnations. This is an observation with which PLATO's Socrates, who "knew nothing but the fact that he was ignorant," would agree.

BIBLIOGRAPHY

The literature on Lacan illustrates the axiom that the more difficult the text, the more extensive the bibliography. In addition to his thesis, *De la psychose paranoïaque dans ses rapports avec la personnalité* (1932, *On Paranoiac Psychosis in Its Relations with the Personality*; not yet translated), Lacan published *Écrits* (1966), a small selection of which appeared in English as *Ecrits: A Selection*, translated by Alan Sheridan (1977). The "Seminar on 'The Purloined Letter' " as it appears in the French *Écrits* can be found, translated by Jeffrey Mehlman, in *The Purloined Poe*, edited by John Muller and William Richardson (1988), an excellent casebook containing essays by Jacques Derrida, Barbara Johnson, and many others. Another notable early translation of and commentary on one of Lacan's essays is Anthony Wilden, *The Language of the Self* (1968), which treats Lacan's "Rome discourse," "Fonction et champ de la parole et du langage en psychanalyse" (1953, "The Function of Language in Psychoanalysis"). A selection of Lacan's writings on female sexuality with two substantial introductions was published as *Feminine Sexuality*, edited by Juliet Mitchell and Jacqueline Rose (1982). To date, the annual seminars of Lacan that have been translated into English are book 1, *Freud's Papers on Technique, 1953–54* (1988); book 2, *The Ego in Freud's Theory and in the Technique of Psychoanalysis, 1954–55* (1988); book 3, *The Psychoses, 1955–56* (1993); book 7, *The Ethics of Psychoanalysis, 1959–60* (1992); *The Four Fundamental Concepts of Psycho-Analysis* (1977), a series of lectures given in 1964; and book 20, *On Feminine Sexuality: The Limits of Love and Knowledge, 1972–73* (1998). Several others have appeared in French.

For an information-packed, fascinating biography, see the work of Elisabeth Roudinesco; volume 2 of her two-volume history of psychoanalysis in France (*La Bataille de cent ans*, 1982–86), devoted to Lacan, has been translated as *Jacques Lacan & Co.* (1990), and a separate work, *Jacques Lacan*, has also been translated (1993; trans. 1997). For a shorter but equally zesty account of psychoanalysis in France centered around Lacan's life and works, see Sherry Turkle, *Psychoanalytic Politics* (1978; rev. ed., 1992).

There are many introductions to Lacan's thought. The most useful for the nonspecialist are Elizabeth Grosz, *Jacques Lacan: A Feminist Introduction* (1990); Malcolm Bowie, *Lacan* (1991), a book that focuses particularly on Lacan's style; *Lacan and the Subject of Language*, edited by Ellie Ragland-Sullivan and Mark Bracher (1991); Madan Sarup, *Jacques Lacan* (1992), an introduction to Lacan in cultural context; Michael Payne, *Reading Theory: An Introduction to Lacan, Derrida, and Kristeva* (1993); Bruce Fink, *The Lacanian Subject* (1995); and *Lacan for Beginners*, written by Philip Hill and illustrated by David Leach (1997, 1999), which is unusually good as well as funny. For advanced engagements with the process of reading Lacan, see Jane Gallop's *Reading Lacan* (1985) and Shoshana Felman's *Jacques Lacan and the Adventure of Insight* (1987). For a good explanation of the differences between Lacanian and American psychoanalysis, see *The Subject and the Self: Lacan and American Psychoanalysis*, edited by Judith Feher Gurewich and Michel Tort (1996). On Lacan's importance for cultural and historical studies, see Juliet Flower MacCannell's *Figuring Lacan* (1986) and Teresa Brennan's *History after Lacan* (1993).

There are many critical and polemical books about Lacan. Some of the most interesting are Philippe Lacoue-Labarthe and Jean-Luc Nancy, *The Title of the Letter* (1973; trans. 1992), which continues the famous critique Jacques Derrida had begun in his reading of Lacan's seminar on "The Purloined Letter" (see "The Purveyor of Truth" in *The Purloined Poe*); François Roustang, *Dire Mastery* (1976; trans. 1982), which considers the combination of the religionlike nature of psychoanalysis and the tyrannical power of Jacques Lacan; and Mikkel Borch-Jacobsen, *Lacan: The Absolute Master* (1990; trans. 1991), a more restrained but still thoroughgoing critique of the effects of power in Lacan's theory. A theorist whose work is an ongoing reinterpretation of the work of Lacan is Slavoj Žižek; see his 1992 *Everything You've Ever Wanted to Know about Lacan (But Were Afraid to Ask Hitchcock)* and other works.

For a dated but annotated bibliography, see Michael Clark, *Jacques Lacan: An Annotated Bibliography* (1988). Dylan Evans has published *An Introductory Dictionary of Lacanian Psychoanalysis* (1996), which is extremely useful and contains a good bibliography.

The Mirror Stage as Formative of the Function of the I as Revealed in Psychoanalytic Experience[1]

The conception of the mirror stage that I introduced at our last congress, thirteen years ago, has since become more or less established in the practice of the French group.[2] However, I think it worthwhile to bring it again to your attention, especially today, for the light it sheds on the formation of the *I* as we experience it in psychoanalysis. It is an experience that leads us to oppose any philosophy directly issuing from the *Cogito*.[3]

Some of you may recall that this conception originated in a feature of human behaviour illuminated by a fact of comparative psychology. The child, at an age when he is for a time, however short, outdone by the chimpanzee in instrumental intelligence, can nevertheless already recognize as such his own image in a mirror. This recognition is indicated in the illuminative mimicry of the *Aha-Erlebnis*, which Köhler[4] sees as the expression of situational apperception, an essential stage of the act of intelligence.

This act, far from exhausting itself, as in the case of the monkey, once the image has been mastered and found empty, immediately rebounds in the case of the child in a series of gestures in which he experiences in play the relation between the movements assumed in the image and the reflected environment, and between this virtual complex and the reality it reduplicates—the child's own body, and the persons and things, around him.

This event can take place, as we have known since Baldwin,[5] from the age of six months, and its repetition has often made me reflect upon the startling spectacle of the infant in front of the mirror. Unable as yet to walk, or even to stand up, and held tightly as he is by some support, human or artificial (what, in France, we call a *'trotte-bébé'*[6]), he nevertheless overcomes, in a

1. Translated by Alan Sheridan, who occasionally includes the original French in parentheses.
2. That is, the Psychoanalytic Society of Paris, the official French branch of the International Psycho-Analytic Society.
3. I think (Latin), a reference to the philosophy of René Descartes (1596–1650), which was founded on the statement "I think, therefore I am" (*cogito ergo sum*)—that is, the occurrence of thought guarantees the existence of the thinker. Here, it implies that thinking can perfectly coincide with being and is the basis for human reality.
4. Wolfgang Köhler (1887–1967), German co-founder of Gestalt psychology. *Aha-Erlebnis*: aha experience (German).
5. James Baldwin (1861–1934), American developmental psychologist.
6. Baby trotter (French); that is, a walker.

flutter of jubilant activity, the obstructions of his support and, fixing his attitude in a slightly leaning-forward position, in order to hold it in his gaze, brings back an instantaneous aspect of the image.

For me, this activity retains the meaning I have given it up to the age of eighteen months. This meaning discloses a libidinal dynamism, which has hitherto remained problematic, as well as an ontological structure of the human world that accords with my reflections on paranoiac knowledge.[7]

We have only to understand the mirror stage *as an identification*, in the full sense that analysis gives to the term: namely, the transformation that takes place in the subject when he assumes an image—whose predestination to this phase-effect is sufficiently indicated by the use, in analytic theory, of the ancient term *imago*.[8]

This jubilant assumption of his specular image by the child at the *infans*[9] stage, still sunk in his motor incapacity and nursling dependence, would seem to exhibit in an exemplary situation the symbolic matrix in which the *I* is precipitated in a primordial form, before it is objectified in the dialectic of identification with the other, and before language restores to it, in the universal, its function as subject.

This form would have to be called the Ideal-I,[1] if we wished to incorporate it into our usual register, in the sense that it will also be the source of secondary identifications, under which term I would place the functions of libidinal normalization. But the important point is that this form situates the agency of the ego, before its social determination, in a fictional direction, which will always remain irreducible for the individual alone, or rather, which will only rejoin the coming-into-being (*le devenir*) of the subject asymptotically,[2] whatever the success of the dialectical syntheses by which he must resolve as *I* his discordance with his own reality.

The fact is that the total form of the body by which the subject anticipates in a mirage the maturation of his power is given to him only as *Gestalt*,[3] that is to say, in an exteriority in which this form is certainly more constituent than constituted, but in which it appears to him above all in a contrasting size (*un relief de stature*) that fixes it and in a symmetry that inverts it, in contrast with the turbulent movements that the subject feels are animating him. Thus, this *Gestalt*—whose pregnancy should be regarded as bound up with the species, though its motor style remains scarcely recognizable—by these two aspects of its appearance, symbolizes the mental permanence of the *I*, at the same time as it prefigures its alienating destination; it is still pregnant with the correspondences that unite the *I* with the statue in which man projects himself, with the phantoms that dominate him, or with the automaton in which, in an ambiguous relation, the world of his own making tends to find completion.

Indeed, for the *imagos*—whose veiled faces it is our privilege to see in outline in our daily experience and in the penumbra of symbolic efficacity[4]—the mirror-image would seem to be the threshold of the visible world, if we go by the mirror disposition that the *imago of one's own body* presents in

7. According to Lacan, knowledge itself is structured like paranoia, in that it projects a coherence onto the world that may not be there.
8. Likeness, statue (Latin).
9. Incapable of speech (Latin).
1. Throughout this article I leave in its peculiarity the translation I have adopted for Freud's *Ideal-Ich* [i.e., "je-idéal"] without further comment, other than to say that I have not maintained it since [Lacan's note].
2. Coming ever closer but never reaching.
3. Form, pattern, whole (German).
4. Cf. Claude Lévi-Strauss [b. 1908], *Structural Anthropology* [1958], chapter 10 [Lacan's note].

hallucinations or dreams, whether it concerns its individual features, or even its infirmities, or its object-projections; or if we observe the role of the mirror apparatus in the appearances of the *double*, in which psychical realities, however heterogeneous, are manifested.

That a *Gestalt* should be capable of formative effects in the organism is attested by a piece of biological experimentation that is itself so alien to the idea of psychical causality that it cannot bring itself to formulate its results in these terms. It nevertheless recognizes that it is a necessary condition for the maturation of the gonad of the female pigeon that it should see another member of its species, of either sex; so sufficient in itself is this condition that the desired effect may be obtained merely by placing the individual within reach of the field of reflection of a mirror. Similarly, in the case of the migratory locust, the transition within a generation from the solitary to the gregarious form can be obtained by exposing the individual, at a certain stage, to the exclusively visual action of a similar image, provided it is animated by movements of a style sufficiently close to that characteristic of the species. Such facts are inscribed in an order of homeomorphic identification that would itself fall within the larger question of the meaning of beauty as both formative and erogenic.[5]

But the facts of mimicry are no less instructive when conceived as cases of heteromorphic identification, in as much as they raise the problem of the signification of space for the living organism—psychological concepts hardly seem less appropriate for shedding light on these matters than ridiculous attempts to reduce them to the supposedly supreme law of adaptation. We have only to recall how Roger Caillois[6] (who was then very young, and still fresh from his breach with the sociological school in which he was trained) illuminated the subject by using the term *'legendary psychasthenia'*[7] to classify morphological mimicry as an obsession with space in its derealizing effect.

I have myself shown in the social dialectic that structures human knowledge as paranoiac[8] why human knowledge has greater autonomy than animal knowledge in relation to the field of force of desire, but also why human knowledge is determined in that 'little reality' (*ce peu de réalité*), which the Surrealists,[9] in their restless way, saw as its limitation. These reflections lead me to recognize in the spatial captation manifested in the mirror-stage, even before the social dialectic, the effect in man of an organic insufficiency in his natural reality—in so far as any meaning can be given to the word 'nature'.

I am led, therefore, to regard the function of the mirror-stage as a particular case of the function of the *imago*, which is to establish a relation between the organism and its reality—or, as they say, between the *Innenwelt* and the *Umwelt*.[1]

In man, however, this relation to nature is altered by a certain dehiscence at the heart of the organism, a primordial Discord betrayed by the signs of uneasiness and motor unco-ordination of the neo-natal months. The objective notion of the anatomical incompleteness of the pyramidal system[2] and

5. Giving rise to sexual desire. "Homeomorphic": having the same form (as opposed to "heteromorphic," differing from the usual form).
6. French philosopher and critic (1913–1978), who when young was a surrealist.
7. A term once used for general neuroses.
8. Cf. "Aggressivity in Psychoanalysis," in *Écrits* [Lacan's note]. "The social dialectic": human interactions.
9. Members of an experimental literary and artistic movement founded in France in 1924; inspired in part by SIGMUND FREUD, surrealists sought to express subconscious thought and feeling.
1. The inner world and the outer world (German).
2. Part of the central nervous system that links the brain and spinal cord and controls voluntary movement.

likewise the presence of certain humoral residues of the maternal organism confirm the view I have formulated as the fact of a real *specific prematurity of birth* in man.

It is worth noting, incidentally, that this is a fact recognized as such by embryologists, by the term *foetalization*, which determines the prevalence of the so-called superior apparatus of the neurax,[3] and especially of the cortex, which psycho-surgical operations lead us to regard as the intra-organic mirror.

This development is experienced as a temporal dialectic that decisively projects the formation of the individual into history. The *mirror stage* is a drama whose internal thrust is precipitated from insufficiency to anticipation—and which manufactures for the subject, caught up in the lure of spatial identification, the succession of phantasies that extends from a fragmented body-image to a form of its totality that I shall call orthopaedic[4]—and, lastly, to the assumption of the armour of an alienating identity, which will mark with its rigid structure the subject's entire mental development. Thus, to break out of the circle of the *Innenwelt* into the *Umwelt* generates the inexhaustible quadrature[5] of the ego's verifications.

This fragmented body—which term I have also introduced into our system of theoretical references—usually manifests itself in dreams when the movement of the analysis encounters a certain level of aggressive disintegration in the individual. It then appears in the form of disjointed limbs, or of those organs represented in exoscopy, growing wings and taking up arms for intestinal persecutions—the very same that the visionary Hieronymus Bosch[6] has fixed, for all time, in painting, in their ascent from the fifteenth century to the imaginary zenith of modern man. But this form is even tangibly revealed at the organic level, in the lines of 'fragilization' that define the anatomy of phantasy, as exhibited in the schizoid and spasmodic symptoms of hysteria.

Correlatively, the formation of the *I* is symbolized in dreams by a fortress, or a stadium—its inner arena and enclosure, surrounded by marshes and rubbish-tips,[7] dividing it into two opposed fields of contest where the subject flounders in quest of the lofty, remote inner castle whose form (sometimes juxtaposed in the same scenario) symbolizes the id in a quite startling way. Similarly, on the mental plane, we find realized the structures of fortified works, the metaphor of which arises spontaneously, as if issuing from the symptoms themselves, to designate the mechanisms of obsessional neurosis—inversion, isolation, reduplication, cancellation and displacement.

But if we were to build on these subjective givens alone—however little we free them from the condition of experience that makes us see them as partaking of the nature of a linguistic technique—our theoretical attempts would remain exposed to the charge of projecting themselves into the unthinkable of an absolute subject. This is why I have sought in the present hypothesis, grounded in a conjunction of objective data, the guiding grid for a *method of symbolic reduction*.[8]

3. Neuraxis, or central nervous system.
4. Relating to correct child rearing (Lacan is drawing on the core meanings of the word's Greek roots).
5. An allusion to "squaring the circle," or constructing a square whose area is equal to that of a given circle (an impossible task if, following the dictates of classical geometry, one uses only a straightedge and a compass).
6. Dutch painter (ca. 1450–1516), best known for his detailed depictions of grotesque, fantastic creatures. "Exoscopy": a view from outside.
7. Garbage dumps.
8. A method derived from the phenomenologists' practice of "bracketing" or isolating the experience being described.

It establishes in the *defences of the ego* a genetic order, in accordance with the wish formulated by Miss Anna Freud,[9] in the first part of her great work, and situates (as against a frequently expressed prejudice) hysterical repression and its returns at a more archaic stage than obsessional inversion and its isolating processes, and the latter in turn as preliminary to paranoic alienation, which dates from the deflection of the specular *I* into the social *I*.

This moment in which the mirror-stage comes to an end inaugurates, by the identification with the *imago* of the counterpart and the drama of primordial jealousy (so well brought out by the school of Charlotte Bühler in the phenomenon of infantile *transitivism*[1]), the dialectic that will henceforth link the *I* to socially elaborated situations.

It is this moment that decisively tips the whole of human knowledge into mediatization through the desire of the other, constitutes its objects in an abstract equivalence by the co-operation of others, and turns the I into that apparatus for which every instinctual thrust constitutes a danger, even though it should correspond to a natural maturation—the very normalization of this maturation being henceforth dependent, in man, on a cultural mediation as exemplified, in the case of the sexual object, by the Oedipus complex.[2]

In the light of this conception, the term primary narcissism,[3] by which analytic doctrine designates the libidinal investment characteristic of that moment, reveals in those who invented it the most profound awareness of semantic latencies. But it also throws light on the dynamic opposition between this libido[4] and the sexual libido, which the first analysts tried to define when they invoked destructive and, indeed, death instincts, in order to explain the evident connection between the narcissistic libido and the alienating function of the *I*, the aggressivity it releases in any relation to the other, even in a relation involving the most Samaritan of aid.[5]

In fact, they were encountering that *existential negativity* whose reality is so vigorously proclaimed by the contemporary philosophy of being and nothingness.[6]

But unfortunately that philosophy grasps negativity only within the limits of a self-sufficiency of consciousness, which, as one of its premises links to the *méconnaissances*[7] that constitute the ego, the illusion of autonomy to which it entrusts itself. This flight of fancy, for all that it draws, to an unusual extent, on borrowings from psychoanalytic experience culminates in the pretention of providing an existential psychoanalysis.

At the culmination of the historical effort of a society to refuse to recognize that it has any function other than the utilitarian one and if the anxiety of the individual confronting the 'concentrational'[8] form of the social bond that

9. Austrian-born English psychoanalyst (1895–1982), Freud's daughter; her "great work" is *The Ego and the Mechanisms of Defense* (1936).
1. Aggressive mimicry. Bühler (1893–1974), German child psychologist.
2. The universal internalization of the prohibited desire for one's mother and the love-hate relation to one's father posited by Freud. Lacan's point is that human desire is not natural: it is shaped by fictions and prohibitions.
3. Self-preservation.
4. Desire (Latin), a Freudian term.
5. That is, generous and altruistic help; for the parable of the good Samaritan, see Luke 10.30–37.
6. That is, by JEAN-PAUL SARTRE (1905–1980), author of *Being and Nothingness* (1943); the French philosopher argued that humans have no essence before they act and thus shape themselves through their autonomous choices.
7. Misrecognitions (French).
8. "*Concentrationnaire*," an adjective coined after World War II (this article was written in 1949) to describe the life of the concentration camp. In the hands of certain writers it became, by extension, applicable to many aspects of "modern" life [translator's note].

seems to arise to crown this effort, existentialism must be judged by the explanations it gives of the subjective impasses that have indeed resulted from it; a freedom that is never more authentic than when it is within the walls of a prison; a demand for commitment, expressing the impotence of a pure consciousness to master any situation; a voyeuristic-sadistic idealization of the sexual relation; a personality that realizes itself only in suicide; a consciousness of the other than can be satisfied only by Hegelian murder.[9]

These propositions are opposed by all our experience, in so far as it teaches us not to regard the ego as centred on the *perception-consciousness system*, or as organized by the 'reality principle'—a principle that is the expression of a scientific prejudice most hostile to the dialectic of knowledge. Our experience shows that we should start instead from the *function of méconnaissance* that characterizes the ego in all its structures, so markedly articulated by Miss Anna Freud. For, if the *Verneinung*[1] represents the patent form of that function, its effects will, for the most part, remain latent, so long as they are not illuminated by some light reflected on to the level of fatality, which is where the id manifests itself.

We can thus understand the inertia characteristic of the formations of the *I*, and find there the most extensive definition of neurosis—just as the captation of the subject by the situation gives us the most general formula for madness, not only the madness that lies behind the walls of asylums, but also the madness that deafens the world with its sound and fury.

The sufferings of neurosis and psychosis are for us a schooling in the passions of the soul, just as the beam of the psychoanalytic scales, when we calculate the tilt of its threat to entire communities, provides us with an indication of the deadening of the passions in society.

At this junction of nature and culture, so persistently examined by modern anthropology, psychoanalysis alone recognizes this knot of imaginary servitude that love must always undo again, or sever.

For such a task, we place no trust in altruistic feeling, we who lay bare the aggressivity that underlies the activity of the philanthropist, the idealist, the pedagogue, and even the reformer.

In the recourse of subject to subject that we preserve, psychoanalysis may accompany the patient to the ecstatic limit of the *'Thou art that,'* in which is revealed to him the cipher of his mortal destiny, but it is not in our mere power as practitioners to bring him to that point where the real journey begins.

1949

From The Agency of the Letter in the Unconscious[1]

* * *

As my title suggests, beyond this 'speech', what the psychoanalytic experience discovers in the unconscious is the whole structure of language. Thus from the outset I have alerted informed minds to the extent to which the notion

9. An allusion to the Master-Slave dialectic (see above) described by GEORG WILHELM FRIEDRICH HEGEL (1770–1831), German idealist philosopher.

1. Denial (German).

1. Translated by Alan Sheridan, who occasionally includes the original French in parentheses.

that the unconscious is merely the seat of the instincts will have to be rethought.

But how are we to take this 'letter' here? Quite simply, literally.[2]

By 'letter' I designate that material support that concrete discourse borrows from language.

This simple definition assumes that language is not to be confused with the various psychical and somatic functions that serve it in the speaking subject—primarily because language and its structure exist prior to the moment at which each subject at a certain point in his mental development makes his entry into it.

Let us note, then, that aphasias,[3] although caused by purely anatomical lesions in the cerebral apparatus that supplies the mental centre for these functions, prove, on the whole, to distribute their deficits between the two sides of the signifying effect of what we call here 'the letter' in the creation of signification.[4] A point that will be clarified later.

Thus the subject, too, if he can appear to be the slave of language is all the more so of a discourse in the universal movement in which his place is already inscribed at birth, if only by virtue of his proper name.

Reference to the experience of the community, or to the substance of this discourse, settles nothing. For this experience assumes its essential dimension in the tradition that this discourse itself establishes. This tradition, long before the drama of history is inscribed in it, lays down the elementary structures of culture. And these very structures reveal an ordering of possible exchanges which, even if unconscious, is inconceivable outside the permutations authorized by language.

With the result that the ethnographic duality of nature and culture is giving way to a ternary conception of the human condition—nature, society, and culture—the last term of which could well be reduced to language, or that which essentially distinguishes human society from natural societies.

But I shall not make of this distinction either a point or a point of departure, leaving to its own obscurity the question of the original relations between the signifier and labour. I shall be content, for my little jab at the general function of *praxis* in the genesis of history, to point out that the very society that wished to restore, along with the privileges of the producer, the causal hierarchy of the relations between production and the ideological superstructure to their full political rights, has none the less failed to give birth to an esperanto in which the relations of language to socialist realities would have rendered any literary formalism radically impossible.[5]

For my part, I shall trust only those assumptions that have already proven their value by virtue of the fact that language through them has attained the status of an object of scientific investigation.

2. "*À la lettre*" [translator's note].

3. Speech losses.

4. This aspect of aphasia, so useful in overthrowing the concept of "psychological function," which only obscures every aspect of the question, becomes quite clear in the purely linguistic analysis of the two major forms of aphasia worked out by one of the leaders of modern linguistics, ROMAN JAKOBSON [1896–1982]. See the most accessible of his works, the *Fundamentals of Language* (with Morris Halle, Gravenhage: Mouton, 1956), part II, chapters 1 to 4 [Lacan s note].

5. We may recall that the discussion of the need for a new language in communist society did in fact take place, and Stalin, much to the relief of those who adhered to his philosophy, put an end to it with the following formulation: language is not a superstructure [Lacan's note]. "Superstructure": the term used by KARL MARX (1818–1883) to designate the political, legal, social, and cultural forms of a society, which are based on its economic structure. Joseph Stalin (1879–1953), leader of the U.S.S.R. (1924–53).

For it is by virtue of this fact that linguistics[6] is seen to occupy the key position in this domain, and the reclassification of the sciences and a regrouping of them around it signals, as is usually the case, a revolution in knowledge; only the necessities of communication made me inscribe it at the head of this volume under the title 'the sciences of man'[7]—despite the confusion that is thereby covered over.

To pinpoint the emergence of linguistic science we may say that, as in the case of all sciences in the modern sense, it is contained in the constitutive moment of an algorithm that is its foundation. This algorithm is the following:

$$\frac{S}{s}$$

which is read as: the signifier over the signified, 'over' corresponding to the bar separating the two stages.

This sign should be attributed to Ferdinand de Saussure,[8] although it is not found in exactly this form in any of the numerous schemas, which none the less express it, to be found in the printed version of his lectures of the years 1906–7, 1908–9, and 1910–11, which the piety of a group of his disciples caused to be published under the title, *Cours de linguistique générale*, a work of prime importance for the transmission of a teaching worthy of the name, that is, that one can come to terms with only in its own terms.

That is why it is legitimate for us to give him credit for the formulation S/*s* by which, in spite of the differences among schools, the beginning of modern linguistics can be recognized.

The thematics of this science is henceforth suspended, in effect, at the primordial position of the signifier and the signified as being distinct orders separated initially by a barrier resisting signification. And that is what was to make possible an exact study of the connections proper to the signifier, and of the extent of their function in the genesis of the signified.

For this primordial distinction goes well beyond the discussion concerning the arbitrariness of the sign, as it has been elaborated since the earliest reflections of the ancients, and even beyond the impasse which, through the same period, has been encountered in every discussion of the bi-univocal correspondence between the word and the thing, if only in the mere act of naming. All this, of course, is quite contrary to the appearances suggested by the importance often imputed to the role of the index finger pointing to an object in the learning process of the *infans*[9] subject learning his mother tongue, or the use in foreign language teaching of so-called 'concrete' methods.

One cannot go further along this line of thought than to demonstrate that

6. By "linguistics" I mean the study of existing languages (*langues*) in their structure and in the laws revealed therein; this excludes any theory of abstract codes sometimes included under the heading of communication theory, as well as the theory, originating in the physical sciences, called information theory, or any semiology more or less hypothetically generalized [Lacan's note]. *Langue*, language in its totality is distinct from *parole*, language as actually spoken by an individual.

7. *Psychanalyse et sciences de l'homme* [Lacan's note]. Lacan is stressing the changes that the scientific study of language has brought about in the very notion of a "human science."

8. Swiss linguist (1857–1913; see above); he described and named the two parts of a linguistic sign, the *signified* (the concept or meaning) and the *signifier* (the sound that conveys the concept or meaning). His *Course in General Linguistics* was published in 1916.

9. Incapable of speech (Latin).

no signification can be sustained other than by reference to another signification:[1] in its extreme form this amounts to the proposition that there is no language (*langue*) in existence for which there is any question of its inability to cover the whole field of the signified, it being an effect of its existence as a language (*langue*) that it necessarily answers all needs. If we try to grasp in language the constitution of the object, we cannot fail to notice that this constitution is to be found only at the level of concept, a very different thing from a simple nominative, and that the thing, when reduced to the noun, breaks up into the double, divergent beam of the 'cause' (*causa*)[2] in which it has taken shelter in the French word *chose*, and the nothing (*rien*) to which it has abandoned its Latin dress (*rem*).

These considerations, important as their existence is for the philosopher, turn us away from the locus in which language questions us as to its very nature. And we will fail to pursue the question further as long as we cling to the illusion that the signifier answers to the function of representing the signified, or better, that the signifier has to answer for its existence in the name of any signification whatever.

For even reduced to this latter formulation, the heresy is the same—the heresy that leads logical positivism in search of the 'meaning of meaning',[3] as its objective is called in the language of its devotees. As a result, we can observe that even a text highly charged with meaning can be reduced, through this sort of analysis, to insignificant bagatelles, all that survives being mathematical algorithms that are, of course, without any meaning.[4]

To return to our formula S/*s*: if we could infer nothing from it but the notion of the parallelism of its upper and lower terms, each one taken in its globality, it would remain the enigmatic sign of a total mystery. Which of course is not the case.

In order to grasp its function I shall begin by reproducing the classic, yet faulty illustration (see below) by which its usage is normally introduced, and one can see how it opens the way to the kind of error referred to above.

TREE

1. Cf. the *De Magistro* of St. Augustine, especially the chapter "De significatione locutionis" which I analyzed in my seminar of June 23, 1954 [Lacan's note]. AUGUSTINE (354–430), early Christian philosopher and theologian.
2. Latin, as is *rem* (thing), below.
3. English in the original [translator's note]. *The Meaning of Meaning* was a 1923 work by Charles K. Ogden and I. A. Richards, English linguists who viewed the study of literature as an objective, scientific discipline.
4. So Mr. I. A. Richards, author of a work precisely in accord with such an objective, has in another work shown us its application. He took for his purposes a page from Mong-tse (Mencius, to the Jesuits) and called the piece, *Mencius on the Mind* [1932]. The guarantees of the purity of the experiment are nothing to the luxury of the approaches. And our expert on the traditional Canon that contains the text is found right on the spot in Peking where our demonstration-model mangle has been transported regardless of cost.

But we shall be no less transported, if less expensively, to see a bronze that gives out bell-tones at the slightest contact with thought, transformed into a rag to wipe the blackboard of the most dismaying British psychologism. And not without eventually being identified with the meninx of the author himself—all that remains of him or his object after having exhausted the meaning of the latter and the good sense of the former [Lacan's note]. "Meninx": a membrane around the brain.

In my lecture, I replaced this illustration with another, which has no greater claim to correctness than that it has been transplanted into that incongruous dimension that the psychoanalyst has not yet altogether renounced because of his quite justified feeling that his conformism takes its value entirely from it. Here is the other diagram:

LADIES GENTLEMEN

where we see that, without greatly extending the scope of the signifier concerned in the experiment, that is, by doubling a noun through the mere juxtaposition of two terms whose complementary meanings ought apparently to reinforce each other, a surprise is produced by an unexpected precipitation of an unexpected meaning: the image of twin doors symbolizing, through the solitary confinement offered Western Man for the satisfaction of his natural needs away from home, the imperative that he seems to share with the great majority of primitive communities by which his public life is subjected to the laws of urinary segregation.[5]

It is not only with the idea of silencing the nominalist debate[6] with a low blow that I use this example, but rather to show how in fact the signifier enters the signified, namely, in a form which, not being immaterial, raises the question of its place in reality. For the blinking gaze of a short sighted person might be justified in wondering whether this was indeed the signifier as he peered closely at the little enamel signs that bore it, a signifier whose signified would in this call receive its final honours from the double and solemn procession from the upper nave.

But no contrived example can be as telling as the actual experience of truth. So I am happy to have invented the above, since it awoke in the person whose word I most trust a memory of childhood, which having thus happily come to my attention is best placed here.

A train arrives at a station. A little boy and a little girl, brother and sister, are seated in a compartment face to face next to the window through which the buildings along the station platform can be seen passing as the train pulls to a stop. 'Look' says the brother, 'we're at Ladies!'; 'Idiot!' replies his sister, 'Can't you see we're at Gentlemen'.

Besides the fact that the rails in this story materialize the bar in the Saussurian algorithm (and in a form designed to suggest that its resistance may be other than dialectical), we should add that only someone who didn't have his eyes in front of the holes (it's the appropriate image here) could possibly

5. Lacan has transformed Saussure's model of the sign (in which the signified can still be understood to be a representation of a tree; see *Course in General Linguistics*, above) into a structure in which the representative function of the sign is less important than its law-giving function. In Saussure, the reader's body is not implicated; in Lacan, the sign exists to tell the reader where to "go." The two doors are identical, but the subject confronting them must conform to the law of "urinary segregation" (i.e., sexual difference) if he or she wishes to find bodily relief.

6. The debate that tries to determine which came first, words or things.

confuse the place of the signifier and the signified in this story, or not see from what radiating centre the signifier sends forth its light into the shadow of incomplete significations.

For this signifier will now carry a purely animal Dissension, destined for the usual oblivion of natural mists, to the unbridled power of ideological warfare, relentless for families, a torment to the Gods. For these children, Ladies and Gentlemen will be henceforth two countries towards which each of their souls will strive on divergent wings, and between which a truce will be the more impossible since they are actually the same country and neither can compromise on its own superiority without detracting from the glory of the other.

But enough. It is beginning to sound like the history of France. Which it is more human, as it ought to be, to evoke here than that of England, destined to tumble from the Large to the Small End of Dean Swift's egg.[7]

It remains to be conceived what steps, what corridor, the S of the signifier, visible here in the plurals[8] in which it focuses its welcome beyond the window, must take in order to rest its elbows on the ventilators through which, like warm and cold air, indignation and scorn come hissing out below.

One thing is certain: if the algorithm S/*s* with its bar is appropriate, access from one to the other cannot in any case have a signification. For in so far as it is itself only pure function of the signifier, the algorithm can reveal only the structure of a signifier in this transfer.

Now the structure of the signifier is, as it is commonly said of language itself, that it should be articulated.

This means that no matter where one starts to designate their reciprocal encroachments and increasing inclusions, these units are subjected to the double condition of being reducible to ultimate differential elements and of combining them according to the laws of a closed order.[9]

These elements, one of the decisive discoveries of linguistics, are *phonemes*; but we must not expect to find any *phonetic* constancy in the modulatory variability to which this term applies, but rather the synchronic[1] system of differential couplings necessary for the discernment of sounds in a given language. Through this, one sees that an essential element of the spoken word itself was predestined to flow into the mobile characters which, in a jumble of lower-case Didots or Garamonds,[2] render validly present what we call the 'letter', namely, the essentially localized structure of the signifier.

With the second property of the signifier, that of combining according to the laws of a closed order, is affirmed the necessity of the topological substratum of which the term I ordinarily use, namely, the signifying chain, gives an approximate idea: rings of a necklace that is a ring in another necklace made of rings.

Such are the structural conditions that define grammar as the order of

7. In *Gulliver's Travels* (1726), by the Irish-born English satirist and clergyman Jonathan Swift (1667–1745), the narrator visits an empire convulsed by civil war over the question of which end of an egg to eat from.

8. Not, unfortunately, the case in the English here—the plural of "gentleman" being indicated other than by the addition of an "s" [translator's note].

9. In structural linguistics these conditions are often termed the paradigmatic relationship, which obtains between items that can be substituted for one another in a given context (e.g., two adverbs) and the syntagmatic relationship, which obtains between linguistic items that combine to form a meaningful whole (e.g., the words in a given sentence).

1. At a single point in time (as opposed to the *diachronic*, which pertains to the development of a phenomenon over time).

2. Names of different type-faces [translator's note].

constitutive encroachments of the signifier up to the level of the unit immediately superior to the sentence, and lexicology as the order of constitutive inclusions of the signifier to the level of the verbal locution.

In examining the limits by which these two exercises in the understanding of linguistic usage are determined, it is easy to see that only the correlations between signifier and signifier provide the standard for all research into signification, as is indicated by the notion of 'usage' of a taxeme or semanteme,[3] which in fact refers to the context just above that of the units concerned.

But it is not because the undertakings of grammar and lexicology are exhausted within certain limits that we must think that beyond those limits signification reigns supreme. That would be an error.

For the signifier, by its very nature, always anticipates meaning by unfolding its dimension before it. As is seen at the level of the sentence when it is interrupted before the significant term: 'I shall never . . .', 'All the same it is . . .', 'And yet there may be . . .'. Such sentences are not without meaning, a meaning all the more oppressive in that it is content to make us wait for it.[4]

But the phenomenon is no different which by the mere recoil of a 'but' brings to the light, comely as the Shulamite, honest as the dew, the negress adorned for the wedding and the poor woman ready for the auction-block.[5]

From which we can say that it is in the chain of the signifier that the meaning 'insists'[6] but that none of its elements 'consists' in the signification of which it is at the moment capable.

We are forced, then, to accept the notion of an incessant sliding of the signified under the signifier—which Ferdinand de Saussure illustrates with an image resembling the wavy lines of the upper and lower Waters in miniatures from manuscripts of *Genesis*; a double flux marked by fine streaks of rain, vertical dotted lines supposedly confining segments of correspondence.

All our experience runs counter to this linearity, which made me speak once, in one of my seminars on psychosis, of something more like 'anchoring points' ('*points de capiton*')[7] as a schema for taking into account the dominance of the letter in the dramatic transformation that dialogue can effect in the subject.

The linearity that Saussure holds to be constitutive of the chain of discourse, in conformity with its emission by a single voice and with its horizontal position in our writing—if this linearity is necessary, in fact, it is not sufficient. It applies to the chain of discourse only in the direction in which it is orientated in time, being taken as a signifying factor in all languages in which 'Peter hits Paul' reverses its time when the terms are inverted.

But one has only to listen to poetry, which Saussure was no doubt in the habit of doing,[8] for a polyphony to be heard, for it to become clear that all discourse is aligned along the several staves of a score.

3. An irreducible unit of meaning. "Taxeme": a minimal linguistic feature (pitch, order, etc.) that differentiates two otherwise identical utterances.

4. To which verbal hallucination, when it takes this form, opens a communicating door with the Freudian structure of psychosis—a door until now unnoticed (cf. "On a Question Preliminary to Any Possible Treatment of Psychosis," *Écrits*) [Lacan's note].

5. The allusions are to the "I am black, but comely . . ." of the *Song of Solomon* [1.5], and to the 19th-century cliché of the "poor, but honest" woman [translator's note].

6. The word "insists"—like the French word *instance* (translated as "agency") in the title of the essay—emphasizes location ("in-") and law ("legal instance") rather than content, stressing the links in articulation rather than the meaning of any one term.

7. The image is that of an upholster's button.

8. The publication by Jean Starobinski, in *Le Mercure de France* (February 1964) of Saussure's notes on anagrams and their hypogrammatical use, from the Saturnine verses to the writings of Cicero,

There is in effect no signifying chain that does not have, as if attached to the punctuation of each of its units, a whole articulation of relevant contexts suspended 'vertically', as it were, from that point.

Let us take our word 'tree' again, this time not as an isolated noun, but at the point of one of these punctuations, and see how it crosses the bar of the Saussurian algorithm. (The anagram of '*arbre*' and '*barre*'[9] should be noted.)

For even broken down into the double spectre of its vowels and consonants, it can still call up with the robur[1] and the plane tree the significations it takes on, in the context of our flora, of strength and majesty. Drawing on all the symbolic contexts suggested in the Hebrew of the Bible, it erects on a barren hill the shadow of the cross. Then reduces to the capital Y, the sign of dichotomy which, except for the illustration used by heraldry, would owe nothing to the tree however genealogical we may think it. Circulatory tree, tree of life of the cerebellum, tree of Saturn, tree of Diana,[2] crystals formed in a tree struck by lightning, is it your figure that traces our destiny for us in the tortoise-shell cracked by the fire, or your lightning that causes that slow shift in the axis of being to surge up from an unnamable night into the *῞Εν πάντα*[3] of language:

No! says the Tree, it says No! in the shower of sparks
Of its superb head

lines that require the harmonics of the tree just as much as their continuation:

Which the storm treats as universally
As it does a blade of grass.[4]

For this modern verse is ordered according to the same law of the parallelism of the signifier that creates the harmony governing the primitive Slavic epic or the most refined Chinese poetry.

As is seen in the fact that the tree and the blade of grass are chosen from the same mode of the existent in order for the signs of contradiction—saying 'No!' and 'treat as'—to affect them, and also so as to bring about, through the categorical contrast of the particularity of 'superb' with the 'universally' that reduces it, in the condensation of the 'head' (*tête*) and the 'storm' (*tempête*), the indiscernible shower of sparks of the eternal instant.

But this whole signifier can only operate, it may be said, if it is present in the subject. It is this objection that I answer by supposing that it has passed over to the level of the signified.

For what is important is not that the subject know anything whatsoever. (If LADIES and GENTLEMEN were written in a language unknown to the little boy and girl, their quarrel would simply be the more exclusively a quarrel over words, but no less ready to take on signification.)

provides the corroboration that I then lacked [Lacan's note, added 1966]. "Saturnine verses": poetry in the Saturnian meter used by some early Latin writers (3d c. B.C.E.). Cicero (106–43 B.C.E.), Roman orator, philosopher, and undistinguished poet.

9. Tree and bar (French). Lacan goes on to explore the ways in which the "tree" has been fundamental to Western thought.

1. Oak (Latin).

2. Diana, Roman goddess of the hunt, and Saturn, the Roman god of agriculture, both had tree cults associated with them. In addition, the "tree" shape of a stag's antlers might also be associated with Diana.

3. All one (Greek).

4. *Non! dit l'Arbre, il dit: Non! dans l'étincellement / De sa tête superbe / Que la tempête traite universellement / Comme elle fait une herbe.* (Paul Valéry, "Au Platane," *Les Charmes* [1922]) [Lacan's note].

What this structure of the signifying chain discloses is the possibility I have, precisely in so far as I have this language in common with other subjects, that is to say, in so far as it exists as a language, to use it in order to signify *something quite other* than what it says. This function of speech is more worth pointing out than that of 'disguising the thought' (more often than not indefinable) of the subject; it is no less than the function of indicating the place of this subject in the search for the true.

I have only to plant my tree in a locution; climb the tree, even project on to it the cunning illumination a descriptive context gives to a word; raise it (*arborer*) so as not to let myself be imprisoned in some sort of *communiqué* of the facts, however official, and if I know the truth, make it heard, in spite of all the *between-the-lines* censures by the only signifier my acrobatics through the branches of the tree can constitute, provocative to the point of burlesque, or perceptible only to the practised eye, according to whether I wish to be heard by the mob or by the few.

The properly signifying function thus depicted in language has a name. We learned this name in some grammar of our childhood, on the last page, where the shade of Quintilian,[5] relegated to some phantom chapter concerning 'final considerations on style', seemed suddenly to speed up his voice in an attempt to get in all he had to say before the end.

It is among the figures of style, or tropes—from which the verb 'to find' (*trouver*) comes to us—that this name is found. This name is *metonymy*.[6]

I shall refer only to the example given there: 'thirty sails'. For the disquietude I felt over the fact that the word 'ship', concealed in this expression, seemed, by taking on its figurative sense, through the endless repetition of the same old example, only to increase its presence, obscured (*voilait*) not so much those illustrious sails (*voiles*)[7] as the definition they were supposed to illustrate.

The part taken for the whole, we said to ourselves, and if the thing is to be taken seriously, we are left with very little idea of the importance of this fleet, which 'thirty sails' is precisely supposed to give us: for each ship to have just one sail is in fact the least likely possibility.

By which we see that the connexion between ship and sail is nowhere but in the signifier, and that it is in the *word-to-word* connexion that metonymy is based.[8]

I shall designate as metonymy, then, the one side (*versant*) of the effective field constituted by the signifier, so that meaning can emerge there.

The other side is *metaphor*.[9] Let us immediately find an illustration; Quillet's[1] dictionary seemed an appropriate place to find a sample that would not

5. Roman rhetorician (ca. 30/35–ca. 100 C.E.; see above).

6. The substitution of one word for another dissociated with it in any way *except* resemblance (i.e., except as metaphor): part for whole ("thirty sails"), material for thing made ("a glass"), author's name for text ("Lacan"), and so on.

7. The French word *voile* has two meanings and two genders: *la voile* is a veil, while *le voile* is a sail. Playing on this ambiguity, Lacan shows that if "thirty sails" is a metonym for "thirty ships," that connection exists by linguistic convention rather than in reality.

8. I pay homage here to the works of Roman Jakobson—to which I owe much of this formulation; works to which a psychoanalyst can constantly refer in order to structure his own experience, and which render superfluous the "personal communications" of which I could boast as much as the next fellow [Lacan's note].

9. The substitution of one word for another associated by resemblance ("my love is a rose"). In "Two Aspects of Language and Two Types of Aphasic Disturbances" (1956; see above), Jakobson contrasts the two figures.

1. Aristide Quillet (1880–1955), publisher of a French dictionary.

seem to be chosen for my own purposes, and I didn't have to go any further than the well known line of Victor Hugo:

His sheaf was neither miserly nor spiteful . . .[2]

under which aspect I presented metaphor in my seminar on the psychoses.

It should be said that modern poetry and especially the Surrealist school[3] have taken us a long way in this direction by showing that any conjunction of two signifiers would be equally sufficient to constitute a metaphor, except for the additional requirement of the greatest possible disparity of the images signified, needed for the production of the poetic spark, or in other words for metaphoric creation to take place.

* * *

For in the analysis of dreams, Freud intends only to give us the laws of the unconscious in their most general extension.[4] One of the reasons why dreams were most propitious for this demonstration is exactly, Freud tells us, that they reveal the same laws whether in the normal person or in the neurotic.

But in either case, the efficacy of the unconscious does not cease in the waking state. The psychoanalytic experience does nothing other than establish that the unconscious leaves none of our actions outside its field. The presence of the unconscious in the psychological order, in other words in the relation-functions of the individual, should, however, be more precisely defined: it is not coextensive with that order, for we know that if unconscious motivation is manifest in conscious psychical effects, as well as in unconscious ones, conversely it is only elementary to recall to mind that a large number of psychical effects that are quite legitimately designated as unconscious, in the sense of excluding the characteristic of consciousness, are nonetheless without any relation whatever to the unconscious in the Freudian sense. So it is only by an abuse of the term that unconscious in that sense is confused with psychical, and that one may thus designate as psychical what is in fact an effect of the unconscious, as on the somatic for instance.

It is a matter, therefore, of defining the topography of this unconscious. I say that it is the very topography defined by the algorithm:

$$\frac{S}{s}$$

What we have been able to develop concerning the effects of the signifier on the signified suggests its transformation into:[5]

$$f(S)\frac{I}{s}$$

2. "Sa gerbe n'était pas avare ni haineuse," a line from "Booz endormi" [translator's note], by Hugo (1802–1885), French Romantic poet, playwright, and novelist. "Booz endormi," from Hugo's *La Légende des siècles* (1859), is a retelling of the Book of Ruth.

3. An experimental literary and artistic movement founded in France in 1924; surrealists sought to express subconscious thought and feeling, and believed that the incongruous juxtapositions created by automatic writing and painting revealed inner truths.

4. On SIGMUND FREUD (1856–1939), the Austrian founder of psychoanalysis, see above; *The Interpretation of Dreams* (1900) was his seminal work.

5. According to the equation, the function of the signifier is in inverse relation to (depends on the repression of) the signified.

We have shown the effects not only of the elements of the horizontal signifying chain, but also of its vertical dependencies in the signified, divided into two fundamental structures called metonymy and metaphor. We can symbolize them by, first:[6]

$$f(S \ldots S')S \cong S(-)s$$

that is to say, the metonymic structure, indicating that it is the connexion between signifier and signifier that permits the elision in which the signifier installs the lack-of-being in the object relation, using the value of 'reference back' possessed by signification in order to invest it with the desire aimed at the very lack it supports. The sign − placed between ( ) represents here the maintenance of the bar − which, in the original algorithm, marked the irreducibility in which, in the relations between signifier and signified, the resistance of signification is constituted.[7]

Secondly,[8]

$$f\left(\frac{S'}{S}\right)S \cong S(+)s$$

the metaphoric structure indicating that it is in the substitution of signifier for signifier that an effect of signification is produced that is creative or poetic, in other words, which is the advent of the signification in question.[9] The sign + between () represents here the crossing of the bar − and the constitutive value of this crossing for the emergence of signification.

This crossing expresses the condition of passage of the signifier into the signified that I pointed out above, although provisionally confusing it with the place of the subject.

It is the function of the subject, thus introduced, that we must now turn to since it lies at the crucial point of our problem.

'I think, therefore I am' (*cogito ergo sum*)[1] is not merely the formula in which is constituted, with the historical high point of reflection on the conditions of science, the link between the transparency of the transcendental subject and his existential affirmation.

Perhaps I am only object and mechanism (and so nothing more than phenomenon), but assuredly in so far as I think so, I am—absolutely. No doubt philosophers have brought important corrections to this formulation, notably that in that which thinks (*cogitans*), I can never constitute myself as anything but object (*cogitatum*). Nonetheless it remains true that by way of this extreme purification of the transcendental subject,[2] my existential link to its

6. According to the equation, the metonymic connection ("signifying chain") among signifiers depends on maintaining the bar of repression.

7. The sign ≅ here designates congruence [Lacan's note].

8. According to the equation, the metaphoric connection "crosses over"—it breaks through the bar between the unconscious signified and the signifying chain.

9. S' designating here the term productive of the signifying effect (or significance); one can see that the term is latent in metonymy, patent in metaphor [Lacan's note].

1. The Latin is the foundational statement of the French philosopher René Descartes (1596–1650), who relied on this certainty of existence to deduce other truths. Lacan will subtly critique American "ego psychology" for modeling the psyche on this attempt to make "thinking" coincide with "being," or to make the unconscious more like consciousness.

2. That is, the subject abstractly considered, outside of any experience.

project seems irrefutable, at least in its present form, and that: '*cogito ergo sum' ubi cogito, ibi sum,*[3] overcomes this objection.

Of course, this limits me to being there in my being only in so far as I think that I am in my thought; just how far I actually think this concerns only myself and if I say it, interests no one.[4]

Yet to elude this problem on the pretext of its philosophical pretensions is simply to admit one's inhibition. For the notion of subject is indispensable even to the operation of a science such as strategy (in the modern sense) whose calculations exclude all 'subjectivism'.

It is also to deny oneself access to what might be called the Freudian universe—in the way that we speak of the Copernican universe.[5] It was in fact the so-called Copernican revolution to which Freud himself compared his discovery, emphasizing that it was once again a question of the place man assigns to himself at the centre of a universe.

Is the place that I occupy as the subject of a signifier concentric or excentric, in relation to the place I occupy as subject of the signified?—that is the question.

It is not a question of knowing whether I speak of myself in a way that conforms to what I am, but rather of knowing whether I am the same as that of which I speak. And it is not at all inappropriate to use the word 'thought' here. For Freud uses the term to designate the elements involved in the unconscious, that is the signifying mechanisms that we now recognize as being there.

It is nonetheless true that the philosophical *cogito* is at the centre of the mirage that renders modern man so sure of being himself even in his uncertainties about himself, and even in the mistrust he has learned to practise against the traps of self-love.

Furthermore, if, turning the weapon of metonymy against the nostalgia that it serves, I refuse to seek any meaning beyond tautology, if in the name of 'war is war' and 'a penny's a penny' I decide to be only what I am, how even here can I elude the obvious fact that I am in that very act?

And it is no less true if I take myself to the other, metaphoric pole of the signifying quest, and if I dedicate myself to becoming what I am, to coming into being, I cannot doubt that even if I lose myself in the process, I am in that process.

Now it is on these very points, where evidence will be subverted by the empirical, that the trick of the Freudian conversion lies.

This signifying game between metonymy and metaphor, up to and including the active edge that splits my desire between a refusal of the signifier and a lack of being, and links my fate to the question of my destiny, this game, in all its inexorable subtlety, is played until the match is called,[6] there where I am not, because I cannot situate myself there.

That is to say, what is needed is more than these words with which, for a

3. Where I think, there I am (Latin).

4. It is quite otherwise if by posing a question such as "Why philosophers?" I become more candid than nature, for then I am asking not only the question that philosophers have been asking themselves for all time, but also the one in which they are perhaps most interested [Lacan's note].

5. That is, the universe at whose center was the sun, as the Polish astronomer Nicolaus Copernicus (1473–1543) suggested, and not the earth, as the Egyptian astronomer Ptolemy (active 127–148 C.E.) had believed. Freud compares his discoveries to a Copernican revolution in his *Introductory Lectures on Psychoanalysis* (1917).

6. That is, until I die.

brief moment I disconcerted my audience: I think where I am not, therefore I am where I do not think. Words that render sensible to an ear properly attuned with what elusive ambiguity[7] the ring of meaning flees from our grasp along the verbal thread.

What one ought to say is: I am not wherever I am the plaything of my thought; I think of what I am where I do not think to think.

This two-sided mystery is linked to the fact that the truth can be evoked only in that dimension of alibi in which all 'realism' in creative works takes its virtue from metonymy; it is likewise linked to this other fact that we accede to meaning only through the double twist of metaphor when we have the one and only key: the S and the *s* of the Saussurian algorithm are not on the same level, and man only deludes himself when he believes his true place is at their axis, which is nowhere.

Was nowhere, that is, until Freud discovered it; for if what Freud discovered isn't that, it isn't anything.

* * *

1957

The Signification of the Phallus[1]

The following is the original, unaltered text of a lecture that I delivered in German on 9 May, 1958, at the Max-Planck Institute, Munich, where Professor Paul Matussek had invited me to speak.

If one has any notion of the state of mind then prevalent in even the least unaware circles, one will appreciate the effect that my use of such terms as, for example, 'the other scene', which I was the first to extract from Freud's work, must have had.

If 'deferred action' (*Nachtrag*), to rescue another of these terms from the facility into which they have since fallen, renders this effort impracticable, it should be known that they were unheard of at that time.

We know that the unconscious castration complex[2] has the function of a knot:

(1) in the dynamic structuring of symptoms in the analytic sense of the term, that is to say, in that which is analysable in the neuroses, perversions, and psychoses;

(2) in a regulation of the development that gives its *ratio* to this first role: namely, the installation in the subject of an unconscious position without which he would be unable to identify himself with the ideal type of his sex, or to respond without grave risk to the needs of his partner in

7. "*Ambiguité de furet*"—literally, "ferret-like ambiguity." This is one of a number of references in Lacan to the game "hunt-the-slipper" (*jeu du furet*) [translator's note]. The wordplay depends on the name of the game (literally, "game of the ferret"), not the animal. "Hunt-the-slipper" is also known as "button, button, who's got the button."

1. Translated by Alan Sheridan, who occasionally includes the original French or German in parentheses.

2. A more general understanding of the castration complex theorized by SIGMUND FREUD. For Freud, "castration anxiety" was the fear of every male child that his desire to sleep with his mother would lead to his castration by his father (see *Three Essays on the Theory of Sexuality*, 1905).

the sexual relation, or even to accept in a satisfactory way the needs of the child who may be produced by this relation.

There is an antinomy, here, that is internal to the assumption by man (*Mensch*)[3] of his sex: why must he assume the attributes of that sex only through a threat—the threat, indeed, of their privation? In 'Civilization and its Discontents' Freud, as we know, went so far as to suggest a disturbance of human sexuality, not of a contingent, but of an essential kind, and one of his last articles concerns the irreducibility in any finite (*endliche*) analysis of the sequellae[4] resulting from the castration complex in the masculine unconscious and from *penisneid*[5] in the unconscious of women.

This is not the only aporia,[6] but it is the first that the Freudian experience and the metapsychology that resulted from it introduced into our experience of man. It is insoluble by any reduction to biological givens: the very necessity of the myth subjacent to the structuring of the Oedipus complex[7] demonstrates this sufficiently.

It would be mere trickery to invoke in this case some hereditary amnesic trait, not only because such a trait is in itself debatable, but because it leaves the problem unsolved: namely, what is the link between the murder of the father and the pact of the primordial law, if it is included in that law that castration should be the punishment for incest?

It is only on the basis of the clinical facts that any discussion can be fruitful. These facts reveal a relation of the subject to the phallus that is established without regard to the anatomical difference of the sexes, and which, by this very fact, makes any interpretation of this relation especially difficult in the case of women. This problem may be treated under the following four headings:

(1) from this 'why', the little girl considers herself, if only momentarily, as castrated, in the sense of deprived of the phallus, by someone, in the first instance by her mother, an important point, and then by her father, but in such a way that one must recognize in it a transference in the analytic sense of the term;
(2) from this 'why', in a more primordial sense, the mother is considered, by both sexes, as possessing the phallus, as the phallic mother;
(3) from this 'why', correlatively, the signification of castration in fact takes on its (clinically manifest) full weight as far as the formation of symptoms is concerned, only on the basis of its discovery as castration of the mother;
(4) these three problems lead, finally, to the question of the reason, in development, for the phallic stage.[8] We know that in this term Freud specifies the first genital maturation: on the one hand, it would seem to be characterized by the imaginary dominance of the phallic attribute and by masturbatory *jouissance*[9] and, on the other, it localizes this *jouissance* for the woman in the clitoris, which is thus raised to the function of the phallus. It therefore seems to exclude in both sexes, until the end of this

3. A human being of either sex (German).
4. Secondary consequences. "Civilization and Its Discontents" was published in 1930.
5. Penis envy (German).
6. Difficulty, logical impasse (a term often used in deconstructive criticism to indicate the point in a text where inherent contradictions render interpretation undecidable).
7. The universal internalization by the male child of the prohibited desire for his mother and the love-hate relation to his father, as posited by Freud.
8. According to Freud, the stages through which the child passes are the oral, anal, phallic, and (if the Oedipal complex is successfully resolved) genital (i.e., mature sexuality).
9. Orgasm (French).

stage, that is, to the decline of the Oedipal stage, all instinctual mapping of the vagina as locus of genital penetration.

This ignorance is suspiciously like *méconnaissance*[1] in the technical sense of the term—all the more so in that it is sometimes quite false. Does this not bear out the fable in which Longus[2] shows us the initiation of Daphnis and Chloe subordinated to the explanations of an old woman?

Thus certain authors have been led to regard the phallic stage as the effect of a repression, and the function assumed in it by the phallic object as a symptom. The difficulty begins when one asks, *what* symptom? Phobia, says one, perversion, says another, both, says a third. It seems in the last case that nothing more can be said: not that interesting transmutations of the object of a phobia into a fetish do not occur, but if they are interesting it is precisely on account of the difference of their place in the structure. It would be pointless to demand of these authors that they formulate this difference from the perspectives currently in favour, that is to say, in terms of the object relation. Indeed, there is no other reference on the subject than the approximate notion of part-object, which—unfortunately, in view of the convenient uses to which it is being put in our time, has never been subjected to criticism since Karl Abraham[3] introduced it.

The fact remains that the now abandoned discussion of the phallic stage, to be found in the surviving texts of the years 1928–32, is refreshing for the example it sets us of a *devotion to doctrine*—to which the degradation of psychoanalysis consequent on its *American transplantation* adds a note of nostalgia.

Merely to summarize the debate would be to distort the authentic diversity of the positions taken up by a Helene Deutsch, a Karen Horney, and an Ernest Jones,[4] to mention only the most eminent.

The series of three articles devoted by Jones to the subject are especially fruitful—if only for the development of the notion of *aphanisis* a term that he himself had coined.[5] For, in positing so correctly the problem of the relation between castration and desire, he demonstrates his inability to recognize what he nevertheless grasped so clearly that the term that earlier provided us with the key to it seems to emerge from his very failure.

Particularly amusing is the way in which he manages to extract from a letter by Freud himself a position that is strictly contrary to it: an excellent model in a difficult *genre*.

Yet the matter refuses to rest there, Jones appearing to contradict his own case for a re-establishment of the equality of natural rights (does he not win the day with the Biblical 'God created them man and woman' with which

1. Misrecognition; misprision (French).
2. Greek author (dates highly uncertain; 2d–6th c. C.E.) credited with writing the first pastoral prose romance, *Daphnis and Chloë*, which tells of two foundlings brought up by shepherds who meet in childhood and gradually fall in love.
3. German psychoanalyst (1877–1925), who focused on child sexual development. "Part-object": the tendency of a child to relate to parts rather than to complete objects (e.g., to the breast rather than the mother).
4. All early psychoanalysts: Deutsch (1884–1982), a Polish-born American who wrote on the psychology of women; Horney (1885–1952), a German-born American who rejected the notion of penis envy; and Jones (1879–1958), a British champion of psychoanalysis who wrote the first definitive biography of Freud (3 vols., 1953–57).
5. *Aphanisis*, the disappearance of sexual desire. This Greek term was introduced into psychoanalysis by Jones in "Early Development of Female Sexuality" (1927), in *Papers on Psycho-analysis*, 5th ed. (London, 1950). For Jones, the fear of aphanisis exists, in both boys and girls, at a deeper level than the castration complex [translator's note].

his plea concludes?). In fact, what has he gained in normalizing the function of the phallus as a part-object if he has to invoke its presence in the mother's body as an internal object, which term is a function of the phantasies revealed by Melanie Klein,[6] and if he cannot separate himself from Klein's view that these phantasies originate as far back as in early childhood, during Oedipal formation?

It might be a good idea to re-examine the question by asking what could have necessitated for Freud the evident paradox of his position. For one has to admit that he was better guided than anyone in his recognition of the order of unconscious phenomena, of which he was the inventor, and that, failing an adequate articulation of the nature of these phenomena, his followers were doomed to lose their way to a greater or lesser degree.

It is on the basis of the following bet—which I lay down as the principle of a commentary of Freud's work that I have pursued during the past seven years—that I have been led to certain results: essentially, to promulgate as necessary to any articulation of analytic phenomena the notion of the signifier, as opposed to that of the signified, in modern linguistic analysis.[7] Freud could not take this notion, which postdates him, into account, but I would claim that Freud's discovery stands out precisely because, although it set out from a domain in which one could not expect to recognize its reign, it could not fail to anticipate its formulas. Conversely, it is Freud's discovery that gives to the signifier/signified opposition the full extent of its implications: namely, that the signifier has an active function in determining certain effects in which the signifiable appears as submitting to its mark, by becoming through that passion the signified.

This passion of the signifier now becomes a new dimension of the human condition in that it is not only man who speaks, but that in man and through man *it* speaks (*ça parle*), that his nature is woven by effects in which is to be found the structure of language, of which he becomes the material, and that therefore there resounds in him, beyond what could be conceived of by a psychology of ideas, the relation of speech.

In this sense one can say that the consequences of the discovery of the unconscious have not yet been so much as glimpsed in theory, although its effects have been felt in praxis to a greater degree than perhaps we are aware of, if only in the form of effects of retreat.

It should be made clear that this advocacy of man's relation to the signifier as such has nothing to do with a 'culturalist' position in the ordinary sense of the term, the position in which Karen Horney, for example, was anticipated in the dispute concerning the phallus by a position described by Freud himself as a feminist one. It is not a question of the relation between man and language as a social phenomenon, there being no question even of something resembling the ideological psychogenesis with which we are familiar, and which is not superseded by peremptory recourse to the quite metaphysical notion, which lurks beneath its question-begging appeal to the concrete, conveyed so pitifully by the term 'affect'.

It is a question of rediscovering in the laws that govern that other scene

6. Austrian-born English psychoanalyst (1882–1960), particularly interested in early mother-child relations.

7. The sign was divided into *signified* (the meaning conveyed) and *signifier* (the symbol or sound that conveys that meaning) by the Swiss linguist FERDINAND DE SAUSSURE (1857–1913).

(*ein andere Schauplatz*),[8] which Freud, on the subject of dreams, designates as being that of the unconscious, the effects that are discovered at the level of the chain of materially unstable elements that constitutes language: effects determined by the double play of combination and substitution in the signifier, according to the two aspects that generate the signified, metonymy and metaphor; determining effects for the institution of the subject. From this test, a *topology*, in the mathematical sense of the term,[9] appears, without which one soon realizes that is impossible simply to note the structure of a symptom in the analytic sense of the term.

It speaks in the Other, I say, designating by the Other the very locus evoked by the recourse to speech in any relation in which the Other intervenes. If *it* speaks in the Other, whether or not the subject hears it with his ear, it is because it is there that the subject, by means of a logic anterior to any awakening of the signified, finds its signifying place. The discovery of what it articulates in that place, that is to say, in the unconscious, enables us to grasp at the price of what splitting (*Spaltung*) it has thus been constituted.[1]

The phallus reveals its function here. In Freudian doctrine, the phallus is not a phantasy, if by that we mean an imaginary effect. Nor is it as such an object (part-, internal, good, bad, etc.) in the sense that this term tends to accentuate the reality pertaining in a relation. It is even less the organ, penis or clitoris, that it symbolizes. And it is not without reason that Freud used the reference to the simulacrum that it represented for the Ancients.

For the phallus is a signifier, a signifier whose function, in the intrasubjective economy of the analysis, lifts the veil perhaps from the function it performed in the mysteries. For it is the signifier intended to designate as a whole the effects of the signified,[2] in that the signifier conditions them by its presence as a signifier.

Let us now examine the effects of this presence. In the first instance, they proceed from a deviation of man's needs from the fact that he speaks, in the sense that in so far as his needs are subjected to demand, they return to him alienated. This is not the effect of his real dependence (one should not expect to find here the parasitic conception represented by the notion of dependence in the theory of neurosis), but rather the turning into signifying form as such, from the fact that it is from the locus of the Other that its message is emitted.

That which is thus alienated in needs constitutes an *Urverdrängung* (primal repression), an inability, it is supposed, to be articulated in demand, but it re-appears in something it gives rise to that presents itself in man as desire (*das Begehren*). The phenomenology that emerges from analytic experience is certainly of a kind to demonstrate in desire the paradoxical, deviant, erratic, eccentric, even scandalous character by which it is distinguished from need. This fact has been too often affirmed not to have been always

8. Another theater (German). Freud, in *The Interpretation of Dreams*, uses this metaphor to refer to conscious and unconscious processes. Lacan extends this "topological" model of psychic location, suggesting that while a bourgeois drama may be playing on the main stage, a Greek tragedy is being performed somewhere else.

9. That is, the study of a figure's properties that are unchanged by such deformations as stretching.

1. In other words, the subject is "split" by language: even the most nonverbal of needs are formulated through the "elsewhere" that the system of language constitutes.

2. Lacan writes that the phallic signifier designates as a whole "les effets DE signifié" ("signified-effects," like "sound effects" or "special effects"), not "les effets DU signifié," which would imply that the signified functions as a knowable cause.

obvious to moralists worthy of the name. The Freudianism of earlier days seemed to owe its status to this fact. Paradoxically, however, psychoanalysis is to be found at the head of an ever-present obscurantism that is still more boring when it denies the fact in an ideal of theoretical and practical reduction of desire to need.

This is why we must articulate this status here, beginning with *demand*, whose proper characteristics are eluded in the notion of frustration (which Freud never used).

Demand in itself bears on something other than the satisfactions it calls for. It is demand of a presence or of an absence—which is what is manifested in the primordial relation to the mother, pregnant with that Other to be situated *within* the needs that it can satisfy. Demand constitutes the Other as already possessing the 'privilege' of satisfying needs, that it is to say, the power of depriving them of that alone by which they are satisfied. This privilege of the Other thus outlines the radical form of the gift of that which the Other does not have, namely, its love.

In this way, demand annuls (*aufhebt*) the particularity of everything that can be granted by transmuting it into a proof of love, and the very satisfactions that it obtains for need are reduced (*sich erniedrigt*) to the level of being no more than the crushing of the demand for love (all of which is perfectly apparent in the psychology of child-rearing, to which our analyst-nurses are so attached).

It is necessary, then, that the particularity thus abolished should reappear *beyond* demand. It does, in fact, reappear there, but preserving the structure contained in the unconditional element of the demand for love. By a reversal that is not simply a negation of the negation, the power of pure loss emerges from the residue of an obliteration. For the unconditional element of demand, desire substitutes the 'absolute' condition: this condition unties the knot of that element in the proof of love that is resistant to the satisfaction of a need. Thus desire is neither the appetite for satisfaction, nor the demand for love, but the difference that results from the subtraction of the first from the second, the phenomenon of their splitting (*Spaltung*).

One can see how the sexual relation occupies this closed field of desire, in which it will play out its fate. This is because it is the field made for the production of the enigma that this relation arouses in the subject by doubly 'signifying' it to him: the return of the demand that it gives rise to, as a demand on the subject of the need—an ambiguity made present on to the Other in question in the proof of love demanded. The gap in this enigma betrays what determines it, namely, to put it in the simplest possible way, that for both partners in the relation, both the subject and the Other, it is not enough to be subjects of need, or objects of love, but that they must stand for the cause of desire.

This truth lies at the heart of all the distortions that have appeared in the field of psychoanalysis on the subject of the sexual life. It also constitutes the condition of the happiness of the subject: and to disguise the gap it creates by leaving it to the virtue of the 'genital' to resolve it through the maturation of tenderness (that is to say, solely by recourse to the Other as reality), however well intentioned, is fraudulent nonetheless. It has to be said here that the French analysts, with their hypocritical notion of genital oblativity,[3] opened the way to the moralizing tendency, which, to the accompaniment of its Salvationist choirs, is now to be found everywhere.

In any case, man cannot aim at being whole (the 'total personality' is another of the deviant premises of modern psychotherapy), while ever the play of displacement and condensation to which he is doomed in the exercise of his functions marks his relation as a subject to the signifier.

The phallus is the privileged signifier of that mark in which the role of the logos[4] is joined with the advent of desire.

It can be said that this signifier is chosen because it is the most tangible element in the real of sexual copulation, and also the most symbolic in the literal (typographical) sense of the term, since it is equivalent there to the (logical) copula. It might also be said that, by virtue of its turgidity, it is the image of the vital flow as it is transmitted in generation.

All these propositions merely conceal the fact that it can play its role only when veiled, that is to say, as itself a sign of the latency with which any signifiable is struck, when it is raised (*aufgehoben*) to the function of signifier.

The phallus is the signifier of this *Aufhebung*[5] itself, which it inaugurates (initiates) by its disappearance. That is why the demon of *Αἰδως* (*Scham*, shame) arises at the very moment when, in the ancient mysteries, the phallus is unveiled (cf. the famous painting in the Villa di Pompei[6]).

It then becomes the bar which, at the hands of this demon, strikes the signified,[7] marking it as the bastard offspring of this signifying concatenation.

Thus a condition of complementarity is produced in the establishment of the subject by the signifier—which explains the *Spaltung* in the subject and the movement of intervention in which that 'splitting' is completed.

Namely:

(1) that the subject designates his being only by barring everything he signifies, as it appears in the fact that he wants to be loved for himself, a mirage that cannot be dismissed as merely grammatical (since it abolishes discourse);

(2) that the living part of that being in the *urverdrängt* (primally repressed) finds its signifier by receiving the mark of the *Verdrängung* (repression) of the phallus (by virtue of which the unconscious is language).

The phallus as signifier gives the ratio of desire (in the sense in which the term is used in music in the 'mean and extreme ratio' of harmonic division).

I shall also be using the phallus as an algorithm, so if I am to help you to grasp this use of the term I shall have to rely on the echoes of the experience that we share—otherwise, my account of the problem could go on indefinitely.

The fact that the phallus is a signifier means that it is in the place of the Other that the subject has access to it. But since this signifier is only veiled, as ratio of the Other's desire, it is this desire of the Other as such that the

3. A mature form of love in which it is the person as a whole, and not what he or she can give, that is loved.

4. Word, speech (Greek).

5. Raising, abolition (German), a term taken from the German philosopher GEORG WILHELM FRIEDRICH HEGEL (1770–1831). The verb *aufheben*, which means "to annul," "to preserve," and "to raise," is often translated "to sublate."

6. In the entrance hall of Pompeii's House of the Vettii is a fresco of the fertility god Priapus weighing his enormous phallus.

7. On this "bar," see Lacan's "Agency of the Letter in the Unconscious" (1957; above).

subject must recognize, that is to say, the other in so far as he is himself a subject divided by the signifying *Spaltung*.

The emergences that appear in psychological genesis confirm this signifying function of the phallus.

Thus, to begin with, the Kleinian fact that the child apprehends from the outset that the mother 'contains' the phallus may be formulated more correctly.

But it is in the dialectic[8] of the demand for love and the test of desire that development is ordered.

The demand for love can only suffer from a desire whose signifier is alien to it. If the desire of the mother *is* the phallus, the child wishes to be the phallus in order to satisfy that desire. Thus the division immanent in desire is already felt to be experienced in the desire of the Other, in that it is already opposed to the fact that the subject is content to present to the Other what in reality he may *have* that corresponds to this phallus, for what he has is worth no more than what he does not have, as far as his demand for love is concerned because that demand requires that he be the phallus.

Clinical experience has shown us that this test of the desire of the Other is decisive not in the sense that the subject learns by it whether or not he has a real phallus, but in the sense that he learns that the mother does not have it. This is the moment of the experience without which no symptomatic consequence (phobia) or structural consequence (*Penisneid*) relating to the castration complex can take effect. Here is signed the conjunction of desire, in that the phallic signifier is its mark, with the threat or nostalgia of lacking it.

Of course, its future depends on the law introduced by the father into this sequence.

But one may, simply by reference to the function of the phallus, indicate the structures that will govern the relations between the sexes.

Let us say that these relations will turn around a 'to be' and a 'to have', which, by referring to a signifier, the phallus, have the opposed effect, on the one hand, of giving reality to the subject in this signifier, and, on the other, of derealizing the relations to be signified.

This is brought about by the intervention of a 'to seem' that replaces the 'to have', in order to protect it on the one side, and to mask its lack in the other, and which has the effect of projecting in their entirety the ideal or typical manifestations of the behaviour of each sex, including the act of copulation itself, into the comedy.

These ideals take on new vigour from the demand that they are capable of satisfying, which is always a demand for love, with its complement of the reduction of desire to demand.

Paradoxical as this formulation may seem, I am saying that it is in order to be the phallus, that is to say, the signifier of the desire of the Other, that a woman will reject an essential part of femininity, namely, all her attributes in the masquerade.[9] It is for that which she is not that she wishes to be desired as well as loved. But she finds the signifier of her own desire in the

8. Reciprocal interaction.
9. An allusion to Joan Rivière's famous 1929 essay, "Womanliness as a Masquerade."

body of him to whom she addresses her demand for love. Perhaps it should not be forgotten that the organ that assumes this signifying function takes on the value of a fetish. But the result for the woman remains that an experience of love, which, as such (cf. above), deprives her ideally of that which the object gives, and a desire which finds its signifier in this object, converge on the same object. That is why one can observe that a lack in the satisfaction proper to sexual need, in other words, frigidity, is relatively well tolerated in women, whereas the *Verdrängung* (repression) inherent in desire is less present in women than in men.

In the case of men, on the other hand, the dialectic of demand and desire engenders the effects—and one must once more admire the sureness with which Freud situated them at the precise articulations on which they depended—of a specific depreciation (*Erniedrigung*) of love.

If, in effect, the man finds satisfaction for his demand for love in the relation with the woman, in as much as the signifier of the phallus constitutes her as giving in love what she does not have—conversely, his own desire for the phallus will make its signifier emerge in its persistent divergence towards 'another woman' who may signify this phallus in various ways, either as a virgin or as a prostitute. There results from this a centrifugal tendency of the genital drive in love life, which makes impotence much more difficult to bear for him, while the *Verdrängung* inherent in desire is more important.

Yet it should not be thought that the sort of infidelity that would appear to be constitutive of the male function is proper to it. For if one looks more closely, the same redoubling is to be found in the woman, except that the Other of Love as such, that is to say, in so far as he is deprived of what he gives, finds it difficult to see himself in the retreat in which he is substituted for the being of the very man whose attributes she cherishes.

One might add here that male homosexuality, in accordance with the phallic mark that constitutes desire, is constituted on the side of desire, while female homosexuality, on the other hand, as observation shows, is orientated on a disappointment that reinforces the side of the demand for love. These remarks should really be examined in greater detail, from the point of view of a return to the function of the mask in so far as it dominates the identifications in which refusals of demand are resolved.

The fact that femininity finds its refuge in this mask, by virtue of the fact of the *Verdrängung* inherent in the phallic mark of desire, has the curious consequence of making virile display in the human being itself seem feminine.

Correlatively, one can glimpse the reason for a characteristic that had never before been elucidated, and which shows once again the depth of Freud's intuition: namely, why he advances the view that there is only one *libido*,[1] his text showing that he conceives it as masculine in nature. The function of the phallic signifier touches here on its most profound relation: that in which the Ancients embodied the Νοῦς and the Λογὸς.[2]

1958

1. Desire (Latin).

2. "Mind" and "Word" (Greek).

LANGSTON HUGHES
1902–1967

The most celebrated African American writer of the first half of the twentieth century, Langston Hughes was a poet, playwright, and fiction writer who also worked tirelessly to promote black literature and, more generally, the status of black people in American society. Associated with the Harlem Renaissance, Hughes was interested in the relation of literature to the other arts; but he was particularly concerned with bridging the gap between "high" culture and the life of his people.

Hughes was born in Missouri and spent an impoverished childhood living with various relatives after his father, discouraged by American racism, moved to Mexico shortly after his birth. His mother was a Langston, born of a family that had played a prominent role in the fight against slavery. Among Hughes's Langston relatives were a veteran of John Brown's famous raid on Harper's Ferry in 1859 and a congressman from Virginia during the Reconstruction years. Hughes's life stabilized on joining his remarried mother in Cleveland when he was thirteen. After a successful four years at an integrated high school, he went to Columbia University for a year (1921–22) but dropped out.

Over the next four years, Hughes traveled widely, held a number of menial jobs, and published poetry in the journals that constituted the literary portion of the Harlem Renaissance—the outpouring of work in all the arts by young blacks during the 1920s and early 1930s. Hughes's work was included in Alain Locke's famous anthology *The New Negro* (1925), which announced the movement, and Hughes knew—and collaborated with—almost all the major figures of the Harlem Renaissance, though he did not himself spend much time in New York during the 1920s. His first book of poems, *Weary Blues*, was published in 1926, the same year he wrote the essay "The Negro Artist and the Racial Mountain" and enrolled in Lincoln University, the all-male black college in Southeastern Pennsylvania from which he received his B.A.

During the 1930s Hughes was desperately poor, living on funds provided by patrons or the earnings he could garner from poetry readings. Increasingly involved in radical causes, he wrote plays in support of the Scottsboro Boys (nine young black men from Alabama accused of raping two white women), spent almost a year in Russia, and served as a war correspondent during the Spanish Civil War. After World War II he taught at various universities, was called before the House Un-American Activities Committee as a suspected Communist, and lived to champion some of the young writers of the 1960s Black Arts Movement. His poetry has been his claim to fame, but increasing interest and attention have been paid to his fiction (both novels and short stories) and plays.

His biographer Arnold Rampersad calls our selection, "The Negro Artist and the Racial Mountain" (1926), the "finest essay of Hughes's life." It was written for the *Nation* as a solicited response to an essay by George Schuyler called "The Negro-Art Hokum," which argued that the idea of a separate black American culture and aesthetic was untenable. Hughes's reply succinctly captures the varied pressures under which the African American artist labors. First and foremost, perhaps, is the problem of a heterogeneous audience. The Negro (to use Hughes's term) poet knows that both black and white people are potential readers of his work. Yet those two audiences have very different expectations and demands. To complicate matters even further, Hughes's ever-present sensitivity to class deprives him of any simple image of the black audience. "High-toned" blacks are mostly terrified by the artist, afraid that he will endanger their desperate hold on respectability. "O, be respectable, write about nice people, show how good we are," Hughes imagines them saying. The "low-down folks," on the other hand, "are not ashamed of [the artist]—if they know he exists at all." Whereas "the better class Negro would tell the artist what to do, the people at least let him alone." But it's hardly a happy situation for the writer caught between an anxious and an unaware black audience.

Meanwhile, " 'Be stereotyped, don't go too far, don't shatter our illusions about you, don't amuse us too seriously. We will pay you,' say the whites." The Negro writer can win acclaim and fortune in the white world so long as he does nothing to disturb the whites' comfort, their conviction that they are good, enlightened people. The temptations created by these constraints are obvious. Just as the modernist artist often set out deliberately to shock and outrage the bourgeoisie, so the black artist will be tempted merely to shake the patronizing white audience out of its complacency.

Hughes intimates, without quite saying it directly, that the best work will please neither the black nor the white audience. (His example is Jean Toomer's *Cane*.) And like many modernists, he believes that such problems are best solved by developing an indifference to all audiences—by cultivating an art that is true to itself: "We younger Negro artists who create now intend to express our individual dark-skinned selves without fear or shame." Bravely and defiantly, Hughes proclaims that it "doesn't matter" if neither white nor colored audiences "are pleased" by this work. "Free within ourselves" and building "our temples for tomorrow," the younger artists are already creating "an honest American Negro literature."

Out of what material is that literature created? Here Hughes raises another recurring problem for African American writers. Despite his line about expressing "our individual dark-skinned selves," Hughes actually looks toward the collective experience of the black folk as the "great field of unused material ready for his art." Anticipating the black power movement of the 1960s, Hughes responds to America's persistent racism by insisting that " 'I am a Negro—and beautiful.' " The black artist should "interest himself in interpreting the beauty of his own people." Hence the essay's essential move: the repudiation of a black middle and upper class that has alienated itself from the black folk; Hughes will celebrate the common people. The problem, of course, is that Hughes himself is not of the folk, and to "interpret" their "beauty" is not identical with "expressing" his own "dark-skinned" individuality. There is a sizable gap between the "they" who "furnish a wealth of colorful, distinctive material for any artist" and the artist who belongs more obviously with the classes Hughes wishes to repudiate.

Hughes strives to find a meeting place in African American music, especially jazz (but also the blues): "Jazz to me is one of the inherent expressions of Negro life in America." Music provides an entry point to the "Negro soul," offering themes to which "the Negro artist can give his racial individuality." Hughes hopes that jazz's merger of the folk and the artist can be reproduced in the other arts: theater, painting, dance. He believes that a "racial art" is already evident in the literature of the Harlem Renaissance.

Writing in 1926, Hughes is uneasy about "the present vogue in things Negro," and he is scathing in his 1940 autobiography about the whites who poured into Harlem in the 1920s to listen to black music in clubs (like the famous Cotton Club) that excluded black patrons and black employees (with the sole exception of the musicians). He knows that black artists want their voices to be heard and that they are, like all artists, hungry for acclaim as well as for an audience. But he worries about the price paid for gaining the attention of whites. The perils facing the black artist are so many—from self-loathing to currying the favor of whites to providing a safe window on the exotic world of the racial other—that success depends on an honesty and fearlessness that are almost too much to ask. But these very difficulties point to another source of material for the African American artist, for "when he chooses to touch on the relations between Negroes and whites in this country with their innumerable overtones and undertones, . . . there is an inexhaustible supply of themes at hand." In calling on the African American artist to affirm his race, to cut loose from white standards and white ideals of high culture, and to explore the experience of the black folk and the realities of racism, Hughes enunciates a program for and vision of black literature that is taken up again during the civil rights and black power movements of the mid-1950s to the early 1970s.

BIBLIOGRAPHY

Hughes published ten books of poetry, eight of fiction, and twenty of nonfictional prose (several coauthored). His social and literary criticism appeared in *A New Song* (1938), *Freedom's Plow* (1943), *Jim Crow's Last Stand* (1943), *Laughing to Keep from Crying* (1952), *Black Misery* (1969), and *Good Morning Revolution: Uncollected Social Protest Writings by Langston Hughes*, edited by Faith Berry (1973). His correspondence with the influential black writer and editor Arna Bontemps has been published in *Arna Bontemps–Langston Hughes Letters, 1925–1967*, edited by Charles H. Nichols (1980). A selection from all his work is available in *The Langston Hughes Reader* (1958). Hughes also edited many works, among them the important literary anthologies *The Poetry of the Negro* (1949), with Arna Bontemps; *The Book of Negro Folklore* (1958), with Arna Bontemps; *New Negro Poets: USA* (1964); and *The Best Short Stories by Negro Writers* (1967).

Hughes wrote two autobiographies, *The Big Sea* (1940) and *I Wonder as I Wander* (1956). Two biographies are Faith Berry's *Langston Hughes: Before and Beyond Harlem* (1983) and Arnold Rampersad's authoritative two-volume *Life of Langston Hughes* (1986–88). Critical studies have focused almost entirely on the poetry, with some attention to the fiction and virtually none to the nonfictional work. R. Baxter Miller's *Art and Imagination of Langston Hughes* (1989) provides an informative overview. For a sense of Hughes's place in American letters and the range of responses to his work, the reader will be best served by consulting *Langston Hughes*, edited by Harold Bloom (1989), and *Langston Hughes: Critical Perspectives Past and Present*, edited by Henry Louis Gates Jr. and K. A. Appiah (1993). A full annotated bibliography of Hughes's own work and of critical commentary on the work can be found in Thomas A. Mikolyzk's *Langston Hughes: A Bio-Bibliography* (1990).

The Negro Artist and the Racial Mountain

One of the most promising of the young Negro poets[1] said to me once, "I want to be a poet—not a Negro poet," meaning, I believe, "I want to write like a white poet"; meaning subconsciously, "I would like to be a white poet"; meaning behind that, "I would like to be white." And I was sorry the young man said that, for no great poet has ever been afraid of being himself. And I doubted then that, with his desire to run away spiritually from his race, this boy would ever be a great poet. But this is the mountain standing in the way of any true Negro art in America—this urge within the race toward whiteness, the desire to pour racial individuality into the mold of American standardization, and to be as little Negro and as much American as possible.

But let us look at the immediate background of this young poet. His family is of what I suppose one would call the Negro middle class: people who are by no means rich yet never uncomfortable nor hungry—smug, contented, respectable folk, members of the Baptist church. The father goes to work every morning. He is a chief steward at a large white club. The mother sometimes does fancy sewing or supervises parties for the rich families of

1. According to Hughes's biographer Arnold Rampersad, this is almost certainly Countee Cullen (1903–1946), one of the African American poets associated with the Harlem Renaissance.

the town. The children go to a mixed school. In the home they read white papers and magazines. And the mother often says "Don't be like niggers" when the children are bad. A frequent phrase from the father is, "Look how well a white man does things." And so the word white comes to be unconsciously a symbol of all the virtues. It holds for the children beauty, morality, and money. The whisper of "I want to be white" runs silently through their minds. This young poet's home is, I believe, a fairly typical home of the colored middle class. One sees immediately how difficult it would be for an artist born in such a home to interest himself in interpreting the beauty of his own people. He is never taught to see that beauty. He is taught rather not to see it, or if he does, to be ashamed of it when it is not according to Caucasian patterns.

For racial culture the home of a self-styled "high-class" Negro has nothing better to offer. Instead there will perhaps be more aping of things white than in a less cultured or less wealthy home. The father is perhaps a doctor, lawyer, landowner, or politician. The mother may be a social worker, or a teacher, or she may do nothing and have a maid. Father is often dark but he has usually married the lightest woman he could find. The family attend a fashionable church where few really colored faces are to be found. And they themselves draw a color line. In the North they go to white theaters and white movies. And in the South they have at least two cars and a house "like white folks." Nordic manners, Nordic faces, Nordic hair, Nordic art (if any), and an Episcopal heaven. A very high mountain indeed for the would-be racial artist to climb in order to discover himself and his people.

But then there are the low-down folks, the so-called common element, and they are the majority—may the Lord be praised! The people who have their nip of gin on Saturday nights and are not too important to themselves or the community, or too well fed, or too learned to watch the lazy world go round. They live on Seventh Street in Washington or State Street in Chicago and they do not particularly care whether they are like white folks or anybody else. Their joy runs, bang! into ecstasy. Their religion soars to a shout. Work maybe a little today, rest a little tomorrow. Play awhile. Sing awhile. O, let's dance! These common people are not afraid of spirituals, as for a long time their more intellectual brethren were, and jazz is their child. They furnish a wealth of colorful, distinctive material for any artist because they still hold their own individuality in the face of American standardizations. And perhaps these common people will give to the world its truly great Negro artist, the one who is not afraid to be himself. Whereas the better-class Negro would tell the artist what to do, the people at least let him alone when he does appear. And they are not ashamed of him—if they know he exists at all. And they accept what beauty is their own without question.

Certainly there is, for the American Negro artist who can escape the restrictions the more advanced among his own group would put upon him, a great field of unused material ready for his art. Without going outside his race, and even among the better classes with their "white" culture and conscious American manners, but still Negro enough to be different, there is sufficient matter to furnish a black artist with a lifetime of creative work. And when he chooses to touch on the relations between Negroes and whites in this country with their innumerable overtones and undertones, surely, and especially for literature and the drama, there is an inexaustible supply of themes at hand. To these the Negro artist can give his racial individuality, his heritage of rhythm and warmth, and his incongruous humor that so often, as in the Blues, becomes ironic laughter mixed with tears. But let us look again at the mountain.

A prominent Negro clubwoman in Philadelphia paid eleven dollars to hear Raquel Meller[2] sing Andalusian popular songs. But she told me a few weeks before she would not think of going to hear "that woman," Clara Smith,[3] a great black artist, sing Negro folksongs. And many an upper-class Negro church, even now, would not dream of employing a spiritual in its services. The drab melodies in white folks' hymnbooks are much to be preferred. "We want to worship the Lord correctly and quietly. We don't believe in 'shouting.' Let's be dull like the Nordics," they say, in effect.

The road for the serious black artist, then, who would produce a racial art is most certainly rocky and the mountain is high. Until recently he received almost no encouragement for his work from either white or colored people. The fine novels of Chestnutt[4] go out of print with neither race noticing their passing. The quaint charm and humor of Dunbar's[5] dialect verse brought to him, in his day, largely the same kind of encouragement one would give a side-show freak (A colored man writing poetry! How odd!) or a clown (How amusing!).

The present vogue in things Negro, although it may do as much harm as good for the budding colored artist, has at least done this: it has brought him forcibly to the attention of his own people among whom for so long, unless the other race had noticed him beforehand, he was a prophet with little honor. I understand that Charles Gilpin[6] acted for years in Negro theaters without any special acclaim from his own, but when Broadway gave him eight curtain calls, Negroes, too, began to beat a tin pan in his honor. I know a young colored writer, a manual worker by day, who had been writing well for the colored magazines for some years, but it was not until he recently broke into the white publications and his first book was accepted by a prominent New York publisher that the "best" Negroes in his city took the trouble to discover that he lived there. Then almost immediately they decided to give a grand dinner for him. But the society ladies were careful to whisper to his mother that perhaps she'd better not come. They were not sure she would have an evening gown.

The Negro artist works against an undertow of sharp criticism and misunderstanding from his own group and unintentional bribes from the whites. "O, be respectable, write about nice people, show how good we are," say the Negroes. "Be stereotyped, don't go too far, don't shatter our illusions about you, don't amuse us too seriously. We will pay you," say the whites. Both would have told Jean Toomer[7] not to write "Cane." The colored people did

2. Spanish singer (1888–1962) who made her highly successful New York debut in the spring of 1926 (with the New York Philharmonic). Andalusia is a region of Spain; Meller would introduce her Spanish songs by telling little stories about the folkways of the different regions from which they came.

3. African American blues singer (1894–1935) who performed regularly in Harlem throughout the 1920s.

4. Charles Chesnutt (1858–1932), African American novelist who lived in Cleveland and published most of his work between 1890 and 1910.

5. Paul Laurence Dunbar (1872–1906), African American poet who died young of tuberculosis. He was a major influence on Hughes.

6. African American actor and theater manager (1878–1930). He played the title role in Eugene O'Neill's *Emperor Jones* in 1920, the first black actor to play the lead in a Broadway production. His all-black Lafayette stock company was based in Harlem.

7. African American writer (1894–1967). His book *Cane* (1923), a formally experimental mixture of poetry and prose, was a major landmark in the Harlem Renaissance.

not praise it. The white people did not buy it. Most of the colored people who did read "Cane" hate it. They are afraid of it. Although the critics gave it good reviews the public remained indifferent. Yet (excepting the work of DuBois)[8] "Cane" contains the finest prose written by a Negro in America. And like the singing of Robeson,[9] it is truly racial.

But in spite of the Nordicized Negro intelligentsia and the desires of some white editors we have an honest American Negro literature already with us. Now I await the rise of the Negro theater. Our folk music, having achieved world-wide fame, offers itself to the genius of the great individual American Negro composer who is to come. And within the next decade I expect to see the work of a growing school of colored artists who paint and model the beauty of dark faces and create with new technique the expressions of their own soul-world. And the Negro dancers who will dance like flame and the singers who will continue to carry our songs to all who listen—they will be with us in even greater numbers tomorrow.

Most of my own poems are racial in theme and treatment, derived from the life I know. In many of them I try to grasp and hold some of the meanings and rhythms of jazz. I am sincere as I know how to be in these poems and yet after every reading I answer questions like these from my own people: Do you think Negroes should always write about Negroes? I wish you wouldn't read some of your poems to white folks. How do you find anything interesting in a place like a cabaret? Why do you write about black people? You aren't black. What makes you do so many jazz poems?

But jazz to me is one of the inherent expressions of Negro life in America: the eternal tom-tom beating in the Negro soul—the tom-tom of revolt against weariness in a white world, a world of subway trains, and work, work, work; the tom-tom of joy and laughter, and pain swallowed in a smile. Yet the Philadelphia clubwoman is ashamed to say that her race created it and she does not like me to write about it. The old subconscious "white is best" runs through her mind. Years of study under white teachers, a lifetime of white books, pictures, and papers, and white manners, morals, and Puritan standards made her dislike the spirituals. And now she turns up her nose at jazz and all its manifestations—likewise almost everything else distinctly racial. She doesn't care for the Winold Reiss[1] portraits of Negroes because they are "too Negro." She does not want a true picture of herself from anybody. She wants the artist to flatter her, to make the white world believe that all Negroes are as smug and as near white in soul as she wants to be. But, to my mind, it is the duty of the younger Negro artist, if he accepts any duties at all from outsiders, to change through the force of his art that old whispering "I want to be white," hidden in the aspirations of his people, to "Why should I want to be white? I am a Negro—and beautiful!"

So I am ashamed for the black poet who says, "I want to be a poet, not a Negro poet," as though his own racial world were not as interesting as any other world. I am ashamed, too, for the colored artist who runs from the painting of Negro faces to the painting of sunsets after the manner of the

8. W. E. B. Du Bois (1868–1963), African American historian, sociologist, political activist, and author; the foremost black intellectual and academic of the first half of the twentieth century.

9. Paul Robeson (1898–1976), African American stage actor, singer, and political activist.

1. German-born painter (1886–1953), best known for his portraits of Native Americans and African Americans. He contributed most of the illustrations to Alain Locke's pathbreaking anthology *The New Negro* (1925).

academicians because he fears the strange un-whiteness of his own features. An artist must be free to choose what he does, certainly, but he must also never be afraid to do what he might choose.

Let the blare of Negro jazz bands and the bellowing voice of Bessie Smith[2] singing Blues penetrate the closed ears of the colored near-intellectuals until they listen and perhaps understand. Let Paul Robeson singing Water Boy, and Rudolph Fisher[3] writing about the streets of Harlem, and Jean Toomer holding the heart of Georgia in his hands, and Aaron Douglas[4] drawing strange black fantasies cause the smug Negro middle class to turn from their white, respectable, ordinary books and papers to catch a glimmer of their own beauty. We younger Negro artists who create now intend to express our individual dark-skinned selves without fear or shame. If white people are pleased we are glad. If they are not, it doesn't matter. We know we are beautiful. And ugly too. The tom-tom cries and the tom-tom laughs. If colored people are pleased we are glad. If they are not, their displeasure doesn't matter either. We build our temples for tomorrow, strong as we know how, and we stand on top of the mountain, free within ourselves.

1926

2. African American singer (ca. 1894–1937), known as "the Empress of the Blues."
3. African American short story writer and physician (1897–1934), associated with the Harlem Renaissance.
4. African American artist and educator (1899–1979), the most significant visual artist of the Harlem Renaissance. Douglas studied with Winold Reiss, and his work was included in Locke's *New Negro*.

GEORGES POULET
1902–1991

Throughout much of his long and distinguished career, the phenomenological literary critic Georges Poulet devoted himself to patient and reverential study of the various forms of human consciousness manifested in the history of French literature. For Poulet, whose criticism has been variously termed "criticism of identification," "consciousness of consciousness," and "genetic criticism," any given work of literature is not primarily a verbal medium, as it is for formalist critics like CLEANTH BROOKS, but an expression of a distinct form of human consciousness. Following in the footsteps of French rationalism, Poulet labels this form the *cogito*, which he characterizes as the transcendent living source of literature and the spiritual center of an author's entire body of writings. As a result, reading for Poulet becomes an intimate, meditative communion with the *cogito*. The reader selflessly and passively relives the mental universe of the author, achieving a coincidence of minds that mingles traditionally separated subject and object; their interanimation is a main feature of modern phenomenological philosophy.

Born in Chênée, Belgium, Poulet studied at the University of Liège, where he received his doctorate in 1927. He first drew international attention after World War II as a prominent member of the so-called Geneva School, a respected group of phenomenological literary critics that included such notable figures as Marcel Raymond, Albert Béguin, Jean Rousset, Jean Starobinski, and Jean-Pierre Richard. Poulet began his teaching career at the University of Edinburgh; he later became a professor in 1952 at Johns Hopkins University, a base from which his books subsequently influenced U.S. theory and criticism—especially the work of his younger colleague J. Hillis Miller, an ardent disciple of Poulet's during the 1950s and 1960s whose groundbreaking texts *The Disappearance of God* (1963) and *Poets of Reality* (1965) extended Poulet's approach. It was Hillis Miller who famously characterized the program of Geneva School criticism as the "consciousness of the consciousness of another, the transposition of the mental universe of an author into the interior space of the critic's mind." In 1958 Poulet returned to Europe, teaching first at the University of Zurich and completing his career in France at the University of Nice; he earned numerous honorary degrees, awards, and prizes for his work.

Poulet's most highly regarded achievement is the four-volume work of literary criticism *Studies in Human Time* (1949–68), which explores the distinctive expressions of consciousness and selfhood in the various writings of selected French authors, spanning the Renaissance to the modern period. Throughout this magisterial work Poulet attempts to examine all available examples of a particular author's writings, whether published or not; he thus considers letters, marginalia, journal entries, essays, and fragmentary or aborted texts, as well as literary works in major genres. Poulet believed that a critic may find a page of a discarded notebook to be as valuable as a finished poem in expressing or revealing an author's consciousness, for either text can reveal deep-seated psychic patterns, constants, or preoccupations. Such an inclusive approach, which ambitiously embraces the totality of an author's oeuvre, sharply distinguished the mid-twentieth-century work of Poulet from his American contemporaries, the New Critics, who concentrated on individual texts. Since these formalists, such as JOHN CROWE RANSOM and Cleanth Brooks, were primarily occupied with analyzing single, isolated poems and discovering the unique properties of poetic language, Poulet's focus on the oeuvre struck some U.S. critics as a breath of fresh air. It both broadened the scope and the field of opportunities available to literary studies and implicitly questioned the formalist conception of text and its distinction between literary and nonliterary texts.

Published in the first issue of the journal *New Literary History* in 1969, Poulet's "Phenomenology of Reading," our selection, offers a succinct programmatic statement of his critical approach. In the key first section of the essay, Poulet describes the peculiar nature of books, distinguishing them from other objects, such as sewing machines, vases, and statues, by applying one main criterion: the degree to which the object in question allows the reader to access or encounter the consciousness of the object's maker. As he sees it, an object such as a sewing machine does not elicit or induce subjective interest, for it presents merely an opaque, flat, lifeless surface. In contrast, objects such as a statue or a vase suggest an intriguing, mysterious interior with which one might have a relationship, prompting one to look closely and critically for a possible entrance to its secret chamber; but, in the end, no such entrance can be found. Thus they remain isolated and closed, preserving the distinction between object and subject, inside and outside, and barring any kind of deep, personal contemplative engagement with the consciousness of its artificer.

A book, however, is not a closed object like the others. During the process of reading, the reader becomes aware of a rational being emerging out of the book. Ideally, the barriers between the reader and the book fall away, eroding the opposition between subject and object and permitting an astonishing communion between the consciousness of the reader and that of the author. Poulet sees the reader as identifying with a pure form of the author's consciousness that can manifest itself only in an author's works (he discourages standard biographical criticism). Such identification can take different forms and possess different intensities, as Poulet makes clear in the second section of his essay, where he offers case studies. In this regard, Poulet was an unacknowledged pioneer of reader-response criticism. For him, the reader becomes a passive intuitive receptacle for the consciousness of the author and embodies an interior universe of mental entities (i.e., images, ideas, and words). These mental entities are objects, Poulet agrees, but they are subjectified objects, for they depend on the mind of the reader for their continued existence. The process of reading thus momentarily replaces the lifeless external objects and forms of books with the living internal objects of the author. Consequently the reader, dispossessed, "becomes" the thoughts of the author, enacting a wondrous merging with the presence of someone wholly other and unique. At the same time, the style of the critic engaged in this fashion veers away from analytical impartiality toward literary lyricism, which is why Hillis Miller labeled this criticism "literature about literature."

Poulet's theories of reading and criticism, as might be expected, have drawn a number of criticisms. In the 1950s some formalists charged Poulet with blurring the boundaries between various written artifacts and undermining the generic conventions and unique internal designs that are key elements in determining the value of a literary work. More pointed attacks appeared in the 1960s and 1970s, prompted by the rise of structuralism, poststructuralism, and deconstruction, which defined themselves in opposition to phenomenology: they explicitly forsook consciousness and authorial intention for textuality and intertextuality. One charge common at this time was that Poulet neglected the rhetorical and self-constitutive nature of "language," viewing it merely as an unproblematic transparent and disposable medium that allows access to some kind of prelinguistic, subjective sense of immediacy and plenitude (a fault often branded as "psychologism"). Many faulted Poulet for tending to view reading as a passive process, giving up on critical judgment and ideological critique as well as neglecting the extent to which the reader actively constructs the message of a work and fills in significant textual gaps and blanks.

In the United States, the signs of this changing attitude toward Poulet and phenomenological criticism became apparent in 1966 at the celebrated Johns Hopkins University conference "Languages of Criticism and Sciences of Man." Poulet presented an early version of "Phenomenology of Reading" titled "Criticism and the Experience of Interiority," but the rising stars of the conference were TZVETAN TODOROV, ROLAND BARTHES, JACQUES LACAN, and JACQUES DERRIDA, all variously associated with structuralism and poststructuralism; indeed, the conference is credited with introducing these schools of thought to the American academy. Poulet appeared anomalous next to such theorists, an incongruity made more obvious when the conference proceedings were later published under the title *The Structuralist Controversy* (1970). But for nearly a quarter of a century, Poulet inspired French and American literary critics, creating unforgettable portraits of his authors' souls. Still today his account of the experience of reading is one of the most moving ever penned.

BIBLIOGRAPHY

No collected edition of Poulet's works exists. English translations of individual books (with original dates of publication given first) include *Studies in Human Time* (1949; 1956), the first volume of Poulet's magnum opus (which also provides the multivolume work with its overall title); *The Interior Distance* (1952; 1959), the second volume of *Studies in Human Time; Metamorphoses of the Circle* (1961; 1966); *Proustian Space* (1977); *Who Was Baudelaire?* (1969; 1969); *Exploding Poetry: Baudelaire / Rimbaud* (1980; 1984). Major French works unavailable in English are *Le Point de départ* (1964), the third volume of *Studies in Human Time; Trois essais de mythologie romantique* (1966); *Les Chemins actuels de la critique* (1967); *Mesure de l'instant* (1968), the fourth volume of *Studies in Human Time; La Conscience critique* (1969); *Entre moi et moi: Essais critiques sur la conscience de soi* (1977); and *La Pensée indéterminée* (3 vols., 1985–90). A revealing collection of letters between Poulet and Marcel Raymond exists in French, titled *Correspondence: 1950–1977*, edited by Pierre Grotzer (1981).

J. Hillis Miller has published two influential assessments of Poulet's work, "The Geneva School: The Criticism of Marcel Raymond, Albert Béguin, Georges Poulet,

Jean Rousset, Jean-Pierre Richard, and Jean Starobinski" (1966) and "Geneva or Paris: The Recent Work of Georges Poulet" (1970), which adds several important theoretical sections to an earlier essay, "The Literary Criticism of Georges Poulet" (1963). (Miller's essays have been conveniently collected in his *Theory Now and Then*, 1991.) Sarah N. Lawall's *Critics of Consciousness: The Existential Structures of Literature* (1968) offers an overview of the Geneva School, providing individual chapters on each of its major figures, including Poulet, while Paul de Man's *Blindness and Insight: Essays in the Rhetoric of Contemporary Criticism* (1971) includes an often-cited critique of Poulet from the perspective of deconstruction. Robert R. Magliola's *Phenomenology and Literature: An Introduction* (1977) presents a critical account of the Geneva School as a whole, helpfully locating it within the larger context of phenomenological theory and criticism. An influential leftist critique of Poulet is propounded in Frank Lentricchia's *After the New Criticism* (1980). For tributes to Poulet by de Man, Miller, and others, see "Hommage à Georges Poulet," *Modern Language Notes* 97.5 (1982). A bibliography of Poulet's work can be found in *Correspondence* (listed above).

Phenomenology of Reading

At the beginning of Mallarmé's[1] unfinished story, *Igitur*, there is the description of an empty room, in the middle of which, on a table there is an open book. This seems to me the situation of every book, until someone comes and begins to read it. Books are objects. On a table, on bookshelves, in store windows, they wait for someone to come and deliver them from their materiality, from their immobility. When I see them on display, I look at them as I would at animals for sale, kept in little cages, and so obviously hoping for a buyer. For—there is no doubting it—animals do know that their fate depends on a human intervention, thanks to which they will be delivered from the shame of being treated as objects. Isn't the same true of books? Made of paper and ink, they lie where they are put, until the moment some one shows an interest in them. They wait. Are they aware that an act of man might suddenly transform their existence? They appear to be lit up with that hope. Read me, they seem to say. I find it hard to resist their appeal. No, books are not just objects among others.

This feeling they give me—I sometimes have it with other objects. I have it, for example, with vases and statues. It would never occur to me to walk around a sewing machine or to look at the under side of a plate. I am quite satisfied with the face they present to me. But statues make me want to circle around them, vases make me want to turn them in my hands. I wonder why. Isn't it because they give me the illusion that there is something in them which, from a different angle, I might be able to see? Neither vase nor statue seems fully revealed by the unbroken perimeter of its surfaces. In addition to its surfaces it must have an interior. What this interior might be, that is what intrigues me and makes me circle around them, as though looking for the entrance to a secret chamber. But there is no such entrance (save for the mouth of the vase, which is not a true entrance since it gives only access to a little space to put flowers in). So the vase and the statue are

1. STÉPHANE MALLARMÉ (1842–1898), French poet.

closed. They oblige me to remain outside. We can have no true rapport—whence my sense of uneasiness.

So much for statues and vases. I hope books are not like them. Buy a vase, take it home, put it on your table or your mantel, and, after a while, it will allow itself to be made a part of your household. But it will be no less a vase, for that. On the other hand, take a book, and you will find it offering, opening itself. It is this openness of the book which I find so moving. A book is not shut in by its contours, is not walled-up as in a fortress. It asks nothing better than to exist outside itself, or to let you exist in it. In short, the extraordinary fact in the case of a book is the falling away of the barriers between you and it. You are inside it; it is inside you; there is no longer either outside or inside.

Such is the initial phenomenon produced whenever I take up a book, and begin to read it. At the precise moment that I see, surging out of the object I hold open before me, a quantity of significations which my mind grasps, I realize that what I hold in my hands is no longer just an object, or even simply a living thing. I am aware of a rational being, of a consciousness; the consciousness of another, no different from the one I automatically assume in every human being I encounter, except that in this case the consciousness is open to me, welcomes me, lets me look deep inside itself, and even allows me, with unheard-of license, to think what it thinks and feel what it feels.

Unheard-of, I say. Unheard-of, first, is the disappearance of the "object." Where is the book I held in my hands? It is still there, and at the same time it is there no longer, it is nowhere. That object wholly object, that thing made of paper, as there are things made of metal or porcelaine, that object is no more, or at least it is as if it no longer existed, as long as I read the book. For the book is no longer a material reality. It has become a series of words, of images, of ideas which in their turn begin to exist. And where is this new existence? Surely not in the paper object. Nor, surely, in external space. There is only one place left for this new existence: my innermost self.

How has this come about? By what means, through whose intercession? How can I have opened my own mind so completely to what is usually shut out of it? I do not know. I know only that, while reading, I perceive in my mind a number of significations which have made themselves at home there. Doubtless they are still objects: images, ideas, words, objects of my thought. And yet, from this point of view, there is an enormous difference. For the book, like the vase, or like the statue, was an object among others, residing in the external world: the world which objects ordinarily inhabit exclusively in their own society or each on its own, in no need of being thought by my thought; whereas in this interior world where, like fish in an aquarium, words, images and ideas disport themselves, these mental entities, in order to exist, need the shelter which I provide: they are dependent on my consciousness.

This dependence is at once a disadvantage and an advantage. As I have just observed, it is the privilege of exterior objects to dispense with any interference from the mind. All they ask is to be let alone. They manage by themselves. But the same is surely not true of interior objects. By definition they are condemned to change their very nature, condemned to lose their materiality. They become images, ideas, words, that is to say purely mental entities. In sum, in order to exist as mental objects, they must relinquish their existence as real objects.

On the one hand, this is cause for regret. As soon as I replace my direct perception of reality by the words of a book, I deliver myself, bound hand and foot to the omnipotence of fiction. I say farewell to what is, in order to feign belief in what is not. I surround myself with fictitious beings; I become the prey of language. There is no escaping this take-over. Language surrounds me with its unreality.

On the other hand, the transmutation through language of reality into a fictional equivalent has undeniable advantages. The universe of fiction is infinitely more elastic than the world of objective reality. It lends itself to any use; it yields with little resistance to the importunities of the mind. Moreover—and of all its benefits I find this the most appealing—this interior universe constituted by language does not seem radically opposed to the *me* who thinks it. Doubtless what I glimpse through the words are mental forms not divested of an appearance of objectivity. But they do not seem to be of a nature other than my mind which thinks them. They are objects, but subjectified objects. In short, since everything has become part of my mind, thanks to the intervention of language, the opposition between the subject and its objects has been considerably attenuated. And thus the greatest advantage of literature is that I am persuaded by it that I am freed from my usual sense of incompatibility between my consciousness and its objects.

This is the remarkable transformation wrought in me through the act of reading. Not only does it cause the physical objects around me to disappear, including the very book I am reading, but it replaces those external objects with a congeries of mental objects in close *rapport* with my own consciousness. And yet the very intimacy in which I now live with my objects is going to present me with new problems. The most curious of these is the following: I am someone who happens to have as objects of his own thought, thoughts which are part of a book I am reading, and which are therefore the cogitations of another. They are the thoughts of another, and yet it is I who am their subject. The situation is even more astonishing than the one noted above. I am thinking the thoughts of another. Of course, there would be no cause for astonishment if I were thinking it as the thought of another. But I think it as my very own. Ordinarily there is the *I* which thinks, which recognizes itself (when it takes its bearings) in thoughts which may have come from elsewhere but which it takes upon itself as its own in the moment it thinks them. This is how we must take Diderot's[2] declaration "Mes pensées sont *mes* catins" ("My thoughts are *my* whores"). That is, they sleep with everybody without ceasing to belong to their author. Now, in the present case things are quite different. Because of the strange invasion of my person by the thoughts of another, I am a self who is granted the experience of thinking thoughts foreign to him. I am the subject of thoughts other than my own. My consciousness behaves as though it were the consciousness of another.

This merits reflection. In a certain sense I must recognize that no idea really belongs to me. Ideas belong to no one. They pass from one mind to another as coins pass from hand to hand. Consequently, nothing could be more misleading than the attempt to define a consciousness by the ideas which it utters or entertains. But whatever these ideas may be, however strong the tie which binds them to their source, however transitory may be

2. Denis Diderot (1713–1784), French author and encyclopedist.

their sojourn in my own mind, so long as I entertain them I assert myself as subject of these ideas; I am the subjective principle for whom the ideas serve for the time being as the predications. Furthermore, this subjective principle can in no wise be conceived as a predication, as something which is discussed, referred to. It is I who think, who contemplate, who am engaged in speaking. In short, it is never a *HE* but an *I*.

Now what happens when I read a book? Am I then the subject of a series of predications which are not *my* predications? That is impossible, perhaps even a contradiction in terms. I feel sure that as soon as I think something, that something becomes in some indefinable way my own. Whatever I think is a part of *my* mental world. And yet here I am thinking a thought which manifestly belongs to another mental world, which is being thought in me just as though I did not exist. Already the notion is inconceivable and seems even more so if I reflect that, since every thought must have a subject to think it, this *thought* which is alien to me and yet in me, must also have in me a *subject* which is alien to me. It all happens, then, as though reading were the act by which a thought managed to bestow itself within me with a subject not myself. Whenever I read, I mentally pronounce an *I*, and yet the *I* which I pronounce is not myself. This is true even when the hero of a novel is presented in the third person, and even when there is no hero and nothing but reflections or propositions: for as soon as something is presented as *thought*, there has to be a thinking subject with whom, at least for the time being, I identify, forgetting myself, alienated from myself. "JE est un autre." said Rimbaud.[3] Another *I*, who has replaced my own, and who will continue to do so as long as I read. Reading is just that: a way of giving way not only to a host of alien words, images, ideas, but also to the very alien principle which utters them and shelters them.

The phenomenon is indeed hard to explain, even to conceive, and yet, once admitted, it explains to me what might otherwise seem even more inexplicable. For how could I explain, without such take-over of my innermost subjective being, the astonishing facility with which I not only understand but even *feel* what I read. When I read as I ought, i.e., without mental reservation, without any desire to preserve my independence of judgment, and with the total commitment required of any reader, my comprehension becomes intuitive and any feeling proposed to me is immediately assumed by me. In other words, the kind of comprehension in question here is not a movement from the unknown to the known, from the strange to the familiar, from outside to inside. It might rather be called a phenomenon by which mental objects rise up from the depths of consciousness into the light of recognition. On the other hand—and without contradiction—reading implies something resembling the apperception I have of myself, the action by which I grasp straightway what I think as being thought by a subject (who, in this case, is not I). Whatever sort of alienation I may endure, reading does not interpret my activity as subject.

Reading, then, is the act in which the subjective principle which I call *I*, is modified in such a way that I no longer have the right, strictly speaking, to consider it as my *I*. I am on loan to another, and this other thinks, feels, suffers, and acts within me. The phenomenon appears in its most obvious

3. Arthur Rimbaud (1854–1891), French poet. "JE est un autre": *I* is an other (French).

and even naivest form in the sort of spell brought about by certain cheap kinds of reading, such as thrillers, of which I say "It gripped me." Now it is important to note that this possession of myself by another takes place not only on the level of objective thought, that is with regard to images, sensations, ideas which reading affords me, but also on the level of my very subjectivity. When I am absorbed in reading, a second self takes over, a self which thinks and feels for me. Withdrawn in some recess of myself, do I then silently witness this dispossession? Do I derive from it some comfort or, on the contrary, a kind of anguish? However that may be, someone else holds the center of the stage, and the question which imposes itself, which I am absolutely obliged to ask myself, is this: "Who is the usurper who occupies the forefront? What is this mind who all alone by himself fills my consciousness and who, when I say *I*, is indeed that *I*?"

There is an immediate answer to this question, perhaps too easy an answer. This *I* who thinks in me when I read a book, is the *I* of the one who writes the book. When I read Baudelaire or Racine,[4] it is really Baudelaire or Racine who thinks, feels, allows himself to be read within me. Thus a book is not only a book, it is the means by which an author actually preserves his ideas, his feelings, his modes of dreaming and living. It is his means of saving his identity from death. Such an interpretation of reading is not false. It seems to justify what is commonly called the biographical explication of literary texts. Indeed every word of literature is impregnated with the mind of the one who wrote it. As he makes us read it, he awakens in us the analogue of what he thought or felt. To understand a literary work, then, is to let the individual who wrote it reveal himself to us *in* us. It is not the biography which explicates the work, but rather the work which sometimes enables us to understand the biography.

But biographical interpretation is in part false and misleading. It is true that there is an analogy between the works of an author and the experiences of his life. The works may be seen as an incomplete translation of the life. And further, there is an even more significant analogy among all the works of a single author. Each of the works, however, while I am reading it, lives in me its own life. The subject who is revealed to me through my reading of it is not the author, either in the disordered totality of his outer experiences, or in the aggregate, better organized and concentrated totality, which is the one of his writings. Yet the subject which presides over the work can exist only in the work. To be sure, nothing is unimportant for understanding the work, and a mass of biographical, bibliographical, textual, and general critical information is indispensable to me. And yet this knowledge does not coincide with the internal knowledge of the work. Whatever may be the sum of the information I acquire on Baudelaire or Racine, in whatever degree of intimacy I may live with their genius, I am aware that this contribution (*apport*) does not suffice to illuminate for me in its own inner meaning, in its formal perfection, and in the subjective principle which animates it, the particular work of Baudelaire or Racine the reading of which now absorbs me. At this moment what matters to me is to live, from the inside, in a certain identity with the work and the work alone. It could hardly be otherwise. Nothing external to the work could possibly share the extraordinary claim which the work now exerts on me. It is there within me, not to send me back, outside

4. Jean Racine (1639–1699), French dramatist. CHARLES BAUDELAIRE (1821–1867), French poet.

itself, to its author, nor to his other writings, but on the contrary to keep my attention rivetted on itself. It is the work which traces in me the very boundaries within which this consciousness will define itself. It is the work which forces on me a series of mental objects and creates in me a network of words, beyond which, for the time being, there will be no room for other mental objects or for other words. And it is the work, finally, which, not satisfied thus with defining the content of my consciousness, takes hold of it, appropriates it, and makes of it that *I* which, from one end of my reading to the other, presides over the unfolding of the work, of the single work which I am reading.

And so the work forms the temporary mental substance which fills my consciousness; and it is moreover that consciousness, the *I*-subject, the continued consciousness of what is, revealing itself within the interior of the work. Such is the characteristic condition of every work which I summon back into existence by placing my consciousness at its disposal. I give it not only existence, but awareness of existence. And so I ought not to hesitate to recognize that so long as it is animated by this vital inbreathing inspired by the act of reading, a work of literature becomes (at the expense of the reader whose own life it suspends) a sort of human being, that it is a mind conscious of itself and constituting itself in me as the subject of its own objects.

II

The work lives its own life within me; in a certain sense, it thinks itself, and it even gives itself a meaning within me.

This strange displacement of myself by the work deserves to be examined even more closely.

If the work thinks itself in me, does this mean that, during a complete loss of consciousness on my part, another thinking entity invades me, taking advantage of my unconsciousness in order to think itself without my being able to think it? Obviously not. The annexation of my consciousness by another (the other which is the work) in no way implies that I am the victim of any deprivation of consciousness. Everything happens, on the contrary, as though, from the moment I become a prey to what I read, I begin to share the use of my consciousness with this being whom I have tried to define and who is the conscious subject ensconced at the heart of the work. He and I, we start having a common consciousness. Doubtless, within this community of feeling, the parts played by each of us are not of equal importance. The consciousness inherent in the work is active and potent; it occupies the foreground; it is clearly related to its *own* world, to objects which are *its* objects. In opposition, I myself, although conscious of whatever it may be conscious of, I play a much more humble role, content to record passively all that is going in me. A lag takes place, a sort of schizoid distinction between what I feel and what the other feels; a confused awareness of delay, so that the work seems first to think by itself, and then to inform me what it has thought. Thus I often have the impression, while reading, of simply witnessing an action which at the same time concerns and yet does not concern me. This provokes a certain feeling of surprise within me. I am a consciousness astonished by an existence which is not mine, but which I experience as though it were mine.

This astonished consciousness is in fact the consciousness of the critic:

the consciousness of a being who is allowed to apprehend as its own what is happening in the consciousness of another being. Aware of a certain gap, disclosing a feeling of identity, but of identity within difference, critical consciousness does not necessarily imply the total disappearance of the critic's mind in the mind to be criticized. From the partial and hesitant approximation of Jacques Rivière[5] to the exalted, digressive and triumphant approximation of Charles Du Bos,[6] criticism can pass through a whole series of nuances which we would be well advised to study. That is what I now propose to do. By discovering the various forms of identification and non-identification to be found in recent critical writing in French literature, I shall be able perhaps to give a better account of the variations of which this relationship—between criticizing subject and criticized object—is capable.

Let me take a first example. In the case of the first critic I shall speak of, this fusion of two consciousnesses is barely suggested. It is an uncertain movement of the mind toward an object which remains hidden. Whereas in the perfect identification of two consciousnesses, each sees itself reflected in the other, in this instance the critical consciousness can, at best, attempt but to draw closer to a reality which must remain forever veiled. In this attempt it uses the only mediators available to it in this quest, that is the senses. And since sight, the most intellectual of the five senses, seems in this particular case to come up against a basic opacity, the critical mind must approach its goal blindly, through the tactile exploration of surfaces, through a groping exploration of the material world which separates the critical mind from its object. Thus, despite the immense effort on the part of the sympathetic intelligence to lower itself to a level where it can, however lamely, make some progress in its quest toward the consciousness of the other, this enterprise is destined to failure. One senses that the unfortunate critic is condemned never to fulfill adequately his role as reader. He stumbles, he puzzles, he questions awkwardly a language which he is condemned never to read with ease; or rather, in trying to read the language, he uses a key which enables him to translate but a fraction of the text.

This critic is Jacques Rivière.

And yet it is from this failure that a much later critic will derive a more successful method of approaching a text. With this later critic, as with Rivière, the whole project begins with an attempt at identification on the most basic level. But this most primitive level is the one in which there flows, from mind to mind, a current which has only to be followed. To identify with the work means here, for the critic, to undergo the same experiences, beginning with the most elementary. On the level of indistinct thought, of sensations, emotions, images, and obsessions of preconscious life, it is possible for the critic to repeat, within himself, that life of which the work affords a first version, inexhaustibly revealing and suggestive. And yet such an imitation could not take place, in a domain so hard to define, without the aid of a powerful auxiliary. This auxiliary is language. There is no critical identification which is not prepared, realized, and incarnated through the agency of language. The deepest sentient life, hidden in the recesses of another's thoughts, could never be truly transposed, save for the mediation of words

5. French critic (1886–1925), editor of the influential journal *La Nouvelle Revue Française*.

6. French critic (1882–1939), associated with the journal *La Nouvelle Revue Française*.

which allow a whole series of equivalences to arise. To describe this phenomenon as it takes place in the criticism I am speaking of now, I can no longer be content with the usual distinctions between the signifier (*signifiant*) and the signified (*signifié*)[7] for what would it mean here to say that the language of the critic *signifies* the language of the literary work? There is not just equation, similitude. Words have attained a veritable power of recreation; they are a sort of material entity, solid and three-dimensional, thanks to which a certain life of the senses is reborn, finding in a network of verbal connotations the very conditions necessary for its replication. In other words, the language of criticism here dedicates itself to the business of mimicking physically the apperceptual world of the author. Strangely enough, the language of this sort of mimetic criticism becomes even more tangible, more tactile than the author's own; the poetry of the critic becomes more "poetic" than the poet's. This verbal *mimesis*, consciously exaggerated, is in no way servile, nor does it tend at all toward the pastiche. And yet it can reach its object only insofar as that object is deeply enmeshed in, almost confounded with, physical matter. This form of criticism is thus able to provide an admirable equivalent of the vital substratum which underlies all thought, and yet it seems incapable of attaining and expressing thought itself. This criticism is both helped and hindered by the language which it employs; helped, insofar as this language allows it to express the sensuous life in its original state, where it is still almost impossible to distinguish between subject and object; and yet hindered, too, because this language, too congealed and opaque, does not lend itself to analysis, and because the subjectivity which it evokes and describes is as though forever mired in its objects. And so the activity of criticism in this case is somehow incomplete, in spite of its remarkable successes. Identification relative to objects is accomplished almost too well: relative to subjectivity it is barely sketched.

This, then, is the criticism of Jean-Pierre Richard.[8]

In its extreme form, in the abolition of any subject whatsoever, this criticism seems to extract from a literary work a certain condensed matter, a material essence.

But what, then, would be a criticism which would be the reverse which would abolish the object and extract from the texts their most *subjective* elements?

To conceive such a criticism, I must leap to the opposite extreme. I imagine a critical language which would attempt deliberately to strip the literary language of anything concrete. In such a criticism it would be the artful aim of every line, of every sentence, of every metaphor, of every word, to reduce to the near nothingness of abstraction the images of the real world reflected by literature. If literature, by definition, is already a transportation of the real into the unreality of verbal conception, then the critical act in this case will constitute a transposition of this transposition, thus raising to the second power the "de-realization" of being through language. In this way, the mind puts the maximum distance between its thought and what *is*. Thanks to this withdrawal, and to the consequent dematerialization of every object thus

7. A distinction owed to the Swiss linguist FERDINAND DE SAUSSURE (1857–1913), who divided the sign into *signified* (the meaning conveyed) and *signifier* (the sound or symbol that conveys that meaning).

8. French critic (b. 1922), a member of the Geneva School.

pushed to the vanishing point, the universe represented in this criticism seems not so much the equivalent of the perceivable world, or of its literary representation, as rather its image crystallized through a process of rigorous intellectualization. Here criticism is no longer mimesis; it is the reduction of all literary forms to the same level of insignificance. In short, what survives this attempted annihilation of literature by the critical act? Nothing perhaps save a consciousness ceaselessly confronting the hollowness of mental objects, which yield without resistance, and an absolutely transparent language, which, by coating all objects with the same clear glaze, makes them ("like leaves seen far beneath the ice") appear to be infinitely far away. Thus, the language of this criticism plays a role exactly opposite to the function it has in Jean-Pierre Richard's criticism. It does indeed bring about the unification of critical thought with the mental world revealed by the literary work; but it brings it about at the expense of the work. Everything is finally annexed by the dominion of a consciousness detached from any object, a *hyper*-critical consciousness, functioning all alone, somewhere in the void.

Is there any need to say that this hyper-criticism is the critical thought of Maurice Blanchot?[9]

I have found it useful to compare the criticism of Richard to the criticism of Blanchot. I learn from this confrontation that the critic's linguistic apparatus can, just as he chooses, bring him closer to the work under consideration, or can remove him from it indefinitely. If he so wishes, he can approximate very closely the work in question, thanks to a verbal mimesis which transposes into the critic's language the sensuous themes of the work. Or else he can make language a pure crystallizing agent, an absolute translucence, which suffering no opacity to exist between subject and object, promotes the exercise of the cognitive power on the part of the subject, while at the same time accentuating in the object those characteristics which emphasize its infinite distance from the subject. In the first of the two cases, criticism achieves a remarkable *complicity*, but at the risk of losing its minimum lucidity; in the second case, it results in the most complete dissociation; the maximum lucidity thereby achieved only confirms a separation instead of a union.

Thus criticism seems to oscillate between two possibilities: a union without comprehension, and a comprehension without union. I may identify so completely with what I am reading that I lose consciousness not only of myself, but also of that other consciousness which lives within the work. Its proximity blinds me by blocking my prospect. But I may, on the other hand, separate myself so completely from what I am contemplating that the thought thus removed to a distance assumes the aspect of a being with whom I may never establish any relationship whatsoever. In either case, the act of reading has delivered me from egocentricity: another's thought inhabits me or haunts me, but in the first case I lose myself in that alien world, and in the other we keep our distance and refuse to identify. Extreme closeness and extreme detachment have then the same regrettable effect of making me fall short of the total critical act: that is to say, the exploration of that mysterious interrelationship which, through the mediation of reading and of language, is established to our mutual satisfaction between the work read and myself.

9. French writer and critic (b. 1907), associated with postwar phenomenological criticism.

Thus extreme proximity and extreme separation each have grave disadvantages. And yet they have their privileges as well. Sensuous thought is privileged to move at once to the heart of the work and to share its own life; clear thought is privileged to confer on its objects the highest degree of intelligibility. Two sorts of insight are here distinguishable and mutually exclusive: there is penetration by the senses and penetration by the reflective consciousness. Now rather than contrasting these two forms of critical activity, would there not be some way, I wonder, not of practicing them simultaneously, which would be impossible, but at least of combining them through a kind of reciprocation and alternation?

Is not this perhaps the method used today by Jean Starobinski?[1] For instance, it would not be difficult to find in his work a number of texts which relate him to Maurice Blanchot. Like Blanchot he displays exceptional lucidity and an acute awareness of distance. And yet he does not quite abandon himself to Blanchot's habitual pessimism. On the contrary, he seems inclined to optimism, even at times to a pleasant utopianism. Starobinski's intellect in this respect is analogous to that of Rousseau,[2] yearning for an immediate transparence of all beings to each other which would enable them to understand each other in an ecstatic happiness. From this point of view, is not the ideal of criticism precisely represented by the *fête citadine* (street celebration) of *fête champêtre* (rustic feast)? There is a milieu or a moment in the feast in which everyone communicates with everyone else, in which hearts are open like books. On a more modest scale, doesn't the same phenomenon occur in reading? Does not one being open its innermost self? Is not the other being enchanted by this opening? In the criticism of Starobinski we often find that crystalline tempo of music, that pure delight in understanding, that perfect sympathy between an intelligence which enters and that intelligence which welcomes it.

In such moments of harmony, there is no longer any exclusion, no inside or outside. Contrary to Blanchot's belief, perfect translucence does not result in separation. On the contrary, with Starobinski, all is perfect agreement, joy shared, the pleasure of understanding and of being understood. Moreover, such pleasure, however intellectual it may be, is not here exclusively a pleasure of the mind. For the relationship established on this level between author and critic is not a relationship between pure minds. It is rather between incarnate beings, and the particularities of their physical existence constitute not obstacles to understanding, but rather a complex of supplementary signs, a veritable language which must be deciphered and which enhances mutual comprehension. Thus for Starobinski, as much physician as critic, there is a reading of *bodies* which is likened to the reading of *minds*. It is not of the same nature, nor does it bring the intelligence to bear on the same area of human knowledge. But for the critic who practices it, this criticism provides the opportunity for a reciprocating exchange between different types of learning which have, perhaps, different degrees of transparency.

Starobinski's criticism, then, displays great flexibility. Rising at times to the heights of metaphysics, it does not disdain the farthest reaches of the

1. Swiss critic (b. 1920), psychiatrist, historian of science, and member of the Geneva School.

2. Jean-Jacques Rousseau (1712–1778), Swiss-born French philosopher and author.

subconscious. It is sometimes intimate, sometimes detached; it assumes all the degrees of identification and non-identification. But its final movement seems to consist in a sort of withdrawal, contradistinction with its earlier accord. After an initial intimacy with the object under study, this criticism has finally to detach itself, to move on, but this time in solitude. Let us not see this withdrawal as a failure of sympathy but rather as a way of avoiding the encumbrances of too prolonged a life in common. Above all we discern an acute need to establish bearings, to adopt the judicious perspective, to assess the fruits of proximity by examining them at a distance. Thus, Starobinski's criticism always ends with a view from afar, or rather from above, for while moving away it has also moved imperceptibly toward a dominating (*surplombante*) position. Does this mean that Starobinski's criticism like Blanchot's is doomed to end in a philosophy of separation? This, in a way, must be conceded, and it is no coincidence that Starobinski treats with special care the themes of melancholy and nostalgia. His criticism always concludes with a double farewell. But this farewell is exchanged by two beings who have begun by living together; and the one left behind continues to be illuminated by that critical intellect which moves on.

The sole fault with which I might reproach such criticism is the excessive ease with which it penetrates what it illuminates.

By dint of seeing in literary works only the thoughts which inhabit them, Starobinski's criticism somehow passes through their forms, not neglecting them, it is true, but without pausing on the way. Under its action literary works lose their opacity, their solidity, their objective dimension; like those palace walls which become transparent in certain fairy tales. And if it is true that the ideal act of criticism must seize (and reproduce) that certain relationship between an object and a mind which is the work itself, how could the act of criticism succeed when it suppresses one of the (polar) terms of this relationship?

My search must continue, then, for a criticism in which this relationship subsists. Could it perhaps be the criticism of Marcel Raymond and Jean Rousset?[3] Raymond's criticism always recognizes the presence of a double reality, both mental and formal. It strives to comprehend almost simultaneously an inner experience and a perfected form. On the one hand, no one allows himself to be absorbed with such complete self-forgetfulness into the thought of another. But the other's thought is grasped not at its highest, but at its most obscure, at its cloudiest point, at the point at which it is reduced to being a mere self-awareness scarcely perceived by the being which entertains it, and which yet to the eyes of the critic seems the sole means of access by which he can penetrate within the precincts of the alien mind.

But Raymond's criticism presents another aspect which is precisely the reverse of this confused identification of the critic's thought with the thought criticized. It is then the reflective contemplation of a formal reality which is the work itself. The work stands *before* the critical intelligence as a perfected object, which is in fact an enigma, an external thing existing in itself and with which there is no possibility of identification nor of inner knowledge.

Thus Raymond perceives sometimes a subject, sometimes an object. The subject is pure mind: it is a sheer indefinable presence, an almost inchoate

3. Raymond (1897–1981) and Rousset (b. 1910), both Swiss critics and members of the Geneva School.

entity, into which, by very virtue of its absence of form, it becomes possible for the critic's mind to penetrate. The work, on the contrary, exists only within a definite form, but this definition limits it, encloses it within its own contours, at the same time constraining the mind which studies it to remain on the outside. So that, if on the one hand the critical thought of Raymond tends to lose itself within an undefined subjectivity, on the other it tends to come to a stop before an impenetrable objectivity.

Admirably gifted to submit his own subjectivity to that of another, and thus to immerse itself in the obscurest depths of every mental entity, the mind of Raymond is less well equipped to penetrate the obstacle presented by the objective surface of the works. He then finds himself marking time, or moving in circles around the work, as around the vase or the statue mentioned before. Does Raymond then establish an insurmountable partition between the two realities—subjective, objective—unified though they may be in the work? No, indeed, at least not in his best essays, since in them, by careful intuitive apprehension of the text and participation by the critic in the powers active in the poet's use of language, there appears some kind of link between the objective aspects of the work and the undefined subjectivity which sustains it. A link not to be confused with a pure relation of identity. The perception of the formal aspects of the work becomes somehow an analogical language by means of which it becomes possible for the critic to go, within the work, beyond the formal aspects it presents. Nevertheless this association is never presented by Raymond as a dialectical process. The usual state described by his method of criticism is one of plenitude, and even of a double plenitude. A certain fulness of experience detected in the poet and re-lived in the mind of the critic, is connected by the latter with a certain perfection of form; but why this is so, and how it does become so, is never clearly explained.

Now is it then possible to go one step further? This is what is attempted by Jean Rousset, a former student of Raymond and perhaps his closest friend. He also dedicates himself to the task of discerning the structure of a work as well as the depth of an experience. Only what essentially matters to him is to establish a connection between the objective reality of the work and the organizing power which gives it shape. A work is not explained for him, as for the structuralists, by the exclusive interdependence of the objective elements which compose it. He does not see in it a fortuitous combination, interpreted *a posteriori* as if it were an *a priori* organization. There is not in his eyes any system of the work without a principle of systematization which operates in correlation with that work and which is even included in it. In short, there is no spider-web without a center which is the spider. On the other hand, it is not a question of going from the work to the psychology of the author, but of going back, within the sphere of the work, from the objective elements systematically arranged, to a certain power of organization, inherent in the work itself, as if the latter showed itself to be an intentional consciousness determining its arrangements and solving its problems. So that it would scarcely be an abuse of terms to say that it speaks, by means of its structural elements, an authentic language, thanks to which it discloses itself and means nothing but itself. Such then is the critical enterprise of Jean Rousset. It sets itself to use the objective elements of the work in order to attain, beyond them, a reality not formal, nor objective, written down however in forms and expressing itself by means of them. Thus the understanding of forms must not limit itself merely to the recording of their objective aspects. As Focillon[4] demonstrated from the point of view of art history, there is a "life of forms" perceptible not only in the historic development which they display from epoch to epoch, but within each single work, in the movement by which forms tend therein sometimes to stabilize and become static, and sometimes to change into one another. Thus the two contradictory forces which are always at work in any literary writing, the will to stability and the protean impulse, help us to perceive by their interplay how much forms are dependent on what Coleridge[5] called a shaping power which determines them, replaces them and transcends them. The teaching of Raymond finds then its most satisfying success in the critical method of Jean Rousset, a method which leads the seeker from the continuously changing frontiers of form to what is beyond form.

It is fitting then to conclude this inquiry here, since it has achieved its goal, namely to describe, relying on a series of more or less adequate examples, a critical method having as guiding principle the relation between subject and object. Yet there remains one last difficulty. In order to establish the interrelationship between subject and object, which is the principle of all creative work and of the understanding of it, two ways, at least theoretically, are opened, one leading from the objects to the subject, the other from the subject to the objects. Thus we have seen Raymond and Rousset, through perception of the objective structures of a literary work, strive to attain the subjective principle which upholds it. But, in so doing, they seem to recognize the precedence of the subject over its objects. What Raymond and Rousset are searching for in the objective and formal aspects of the work, is something which is previous to the work and on which the work depends for its very existence. So that the method which leads from the object to the subject does not differ radically at bottom from the one which leads from subject to object, since it does really consist in going from subject to subject through the object. Yet there is the risk of overlooking an important point. The aim of criticism is not achieved merely by the understanding of the part played by the subject in its interrelation with objects. When reading a literary work, there is a moment when it seems to me that the subject *present* in this work disengages itself from all that surrounds it, and stands alone. Had I not once the intuition of this, when visiting the Scuola de San Rocco in Venice, one of the highest summits of art, where there are assembled so many paintings of the same painter, Tintoretto?[6] When looking at all these masterpieces brought there together and revealing so manifestly their unity of inspiration, I had suddenly the impression of having reached the common essence present in all the works of a great master, an essence which I was not able to perceive, except when emptying my mind of all the particular images created by the artist. I became aware of a subjective power at work in all these pictures, and yet never so clearly understood by my mind as when I had forgotten all their particular figurations.

One may ask oneself: What is this subject left standing in isolation after all examination of a literary work? Is it the individual genius of the artist,

4. Henri Focillon (1881–1943), French art and cultural historian; he theorized the evolution of art forms in *Vie des formes* (*Life of Forms*, 1934).

5. SAMUEL TAYLOR COLERIDGE (1772–1834), English Romantic poet and critic; the reference here is to his theory of imagination.

6. Jacopo Robusti (1518–1594), Italian painter known as Tintoretto.

visibly present in his work, yet having an invisible life independent of the work? Or is it, as Valéry[7] thinks, an anonymous and abstract consciousness presiding, in its aloofness, over the operations of all more concrete consciousness? Whatever it may be, I am constrained to acknowledge that all subjective activity present in a literary work is not entirely explained by its relationship with forms and objects within the work. There is in the work a mental activity profoundly engaged in objective forms; and there is, at another level, forsaking all forms, a subject which reveals itself to itself (and to me) in its transcendence over all which is reflected in it. At this point, no object can any longer express it, no structure can any longer define it; it is exposed in its ineffability and in its fundamental indeterminacy. Such is perhaps the reason why the critic, in his elucidation of works, is haunted by this transcendence of mind. It seems then that criticism, in order to accompany the mind in this effort of detachment from itself, needs to annihilate, or at least momentarily to forget, the objective elements of the work, and to elevate itself to the apprehension of a subjectivity without objectivity.

1969

7. Paul Valéry (1871–1945), French poet, critic, and essayist.

JEAN-PAUL SARTRE
1905–1980

Jean-Paul Sartre was an eminent French philosopher, novelist, and dramatist who wrote much literary criticism and biography, including books on the nineteenth- and twentieth-century French writers CHARLES BAUDELAIRE, Gustave Flaubert, STÉPHANE MALLARMÉ, and Jean Genet. During his lifetime, he became known worldwide for his distinct brand of existentialism, which focused on the human experience of freedom and responsibility in a godless universe. For Sartre, "existence is prior to essence": because the world and human nature possess no fixed meaning, human beings are responsible for their own choices and actions. The experience of literature, Sartre argues, is precisely the experience of this freedom, an experience that draws together author and reader into the collaborative, future-oriented project of human existence, which is always in a state of becoming.

Born in Paris, Sartre was raised by his mother and his grandfather, his father having died a year after his birth. As a young man, he was educated at the elite Louis-le-Grand preparatory school and the Lycée Henri IV. Later he trained in philosophy at the prestigious École Normale Supérieure, receiving his postgraduate degree in 1929. At that time he met his famous intellectual associate and lifelong companion, the feminist existential philosopher SIMONE DE BEAUVOIR. Until the outbreak of World War II in 1939, Sartre taught philosophy at various secondary schools. From 1940 to 1941 he was a prisoner of war in Germany, and after being released he joined the French Resistance; until 1944 he worked as a journalist for the liberation of France, writing subversive underground publications. Philosophically, Sartre's experience of the war led him to a deeper appreciation of human freedom and responsibility. Politically, it led him to a Marxist position. Soon after the war Sartre and Beauvoir founded the prestigious journal *Les Temps Modernes*, which continues to be an important literary periodical in France.

Sartre's major philosophical work during the war was his *L'Être et le néant* (1943, *Being and Nothingness*), a magisterial book influenced by the phenomenological philosophies of MARTIN HEIDEGGER (1889–1976) and Edmund Husserl (1859–1938), whom Sartre began to study during the 1930s. Here Sartre makes his famous distinction between things that exist in themselves (*en-soi*) and human beings who exist for themselves (*pour-soi*), terms meant to distinguish between worldly objects and human consciousness. As a phenomenologist, Sartre links the two realms, observing that while human beings can apprehend the appearances of phenomena, they cannot grasp any kind of metaphysical reality, including God. All they can know is existence, which is contingent and unfixed. Conscious of the limits of knowledge and of mortality, human beings live with existential dread, facing the nothingness to come. And they live with the burden of the freedom to choose, to make of themselves what they will—but always in relation to the particular situations at hand. To the extent that they allow bureaucracies and entertainments to define and distract them, they live inauthentic lives.

Through Sartre's various literary works—novels such as *La Nausée* (1938, *Nausea*) and *Les Chemins de la liberté* (1945–49, *The Roads to Freedom*) and plays such as *Les Mouches* (1943, *The Flies*) and *Huis clos* (1945, *No Exit*)—his evolving philosophical views became accessible to a general audience. In 1964 he was awarded the Nobel Prize for literature; he refused it, mainly because he did not want his views to be compromised by association with the European status quo. Sartre's goal was to remain a radical political figure: to the end of his life, he agitated on behalf of social and political causes.

Our selection, "Pourquoi écrire?" ("Why Write?"), is a key chapter in Sartre's well-known *Qu'est-ce que la littérature?* (1948, *What Is Literature?*), which was originally published in six installments in *Les Temps Modernes* (February–July 1947). It begins with the existentialist assumption that "man is the means by which things are manifested." Much like Heidegger, Sartre indicates that the individual discloses or reveals being; by introducing relationships and order, by imposing unity on the diversity of the world, he or she directs being. In the same way, Sartre argues, the reader brings to life the literary object, which can exist only in the concrete act of reading. As he oddly but memorably puts it, "the literary object is a peculiar top which exists only in movement."

He is quick to point out, however, that the literary object imposes its own structures, so that the reader must work within set parameters. The reader completes what the writer has begun. In contrast to GEORGES POULET, a contemporaneous phenomenological critic who sees the reader as a submissive receptacle for the author's consciousness, Sartre views the relationship between writer and reader as a collaboration of equals in freedom. "For the reader, all is to do and all is already done"; the result is a "directed creation."

Not surprisingly, Sartre argues that the literary work makes an appeal to the freedom of the reader, who, while reading, foresees, waits, hypothesizes, dreams, hopes, and is deceived. The reader, in Sartre's portrait, is decidedly not a blank tablet; he possesses feelings, prejudices, values, and predispositions; she is credulous, generous, creative, critical. Authors need the reader's freedom for their work to exist authentically. Without it, they will cease to function as authors and their work will fall into obscurity, unread. In the larger social and political scheme of things, writers cannot endorse fascism or totalitarianism or any form of government that limits readers' freedoms, especially the freedom of expression.

The goal of art, Sartre asserts, is "to recover this world by giving it to be seen as it is, but as if it had its source in human freedom." Such a recovery leads to joy but also to responsibility. Reading creates a pact between freedoms, between authors and readers. In disclosing or revealing the world, it calls forth from the reader examination, admiration, and indignation. It engages our support, consent, critique, or opposition, for "at the heart of the aesthetic imperative we discern the moral imperative."

In "Why Write?" Sartre is suggestive and bold, but sometimes cryptic and shortsighted. He quarrels with IMMANUEL KANT's *Critique of Judgment* (1790; see above), but the outcome leaves his own aesthetic theory uncertain. He depicts writing as a recovery and readaptation of the "totality of being," yet he is unclear about the nature of this totality. And he remains obscure when criticizing the writer's arousal of emotions and when praising the intriguing inexhaustibility of reading. He is perhaps most often criticized for failing to pay sufficient attention to the nature of language. Consider, for example, his distinction between poetry and prose: poetry is a use of language that treats words as things, whereas prose is a more utilitarian, transparent medium. In this he differs from his famous predecessors Stéphane Mallarmé and Paul Valéry. Sartre's moral and political concerns lead him to value prose more—and in doing so he not only discounts poetry but also overlooks the ways in which language determines consciousness (a determination on which Heidegger focuses). Like Poulet, Sartre is more concerned with consciousness in itself than with its linguistic medium. For this and other reasons, when linguistically inspired structuralism and poststructuralism emerged in the 1960s, Sartre's work fell largely out of favor.

But the gradual turn toward the political in literary studies during recent decades has put Sartre's work in a different light. The ethical and political dimensions of his existentialist thought and activism; his dramatic, interactive accounts of writing and reading; and his portrait of the reader as a complex human being with specific interests and values serve as models for those writers and theorists critically engaged not just with the institution of literary studies but with the world at large.

BIBLIOGRAPHY

Qu'est-ce que la littérature? (1948) was translated by Bernard Frechtman in 1949 and is available in several editions, most recently in *"What Is Literature?" and Other Essays* (1988). Other works by Sartre bearing directly on literary and artistic matters are *The Imagination* (1936; trans. 1962); *The Psychology of the Imagination* (1940; trans. 1948); *Literary and Philosophical Essays* (1947; trans. 1962); *Baudelaire* (1947; trans. 1950); *Black Orpheus* (1949; trans. 1963); *Saint-Genet: Actor and Martyr* (1952; trans. 1964); *Essays in Aesthetics*, selected and translated by Wade Baskin (1963); *Situations* (1964; trans. 1965); *The Family Idiot: Gustave Flaubert, 1821–1857* (3 vols., 1971–72, trans. 5 vols., 1981–93); *Politics and Literature*, edited and translated by J. A. Underwood and John Calder (1973); and the posthumously published *Mallarmé, or, the Poet of Nothingness* (1986; trans. 1988). Sartre's major philosophical studies are *Transcendence of the Ego* (1936; trans. 1957), *The Emotions: Outline of a Theory* (1939; trans. 1948), *Existential Psychoanalysis* (1943; trans. 1953), *Being and Nothingness* (1943; trans. 1956), *Existentialism* (1946; trans. 1947), *Search for a Method* (1960; trans. 1963), and *Critique of Dialectical Reason* (2 vols., 1960–85; trans. 1976–90). See also Sartre's literary autobiography *The Words* (1964; trans. 1964), as well as the posthumously published *War Diaries of Jean-Paul Sartre: November 1939 to March 1940* (1984; trans. 1984) and *Witness to My Life: The Letters of Jean-Paul Sartre to Simone de Beauvoir* (1992; trans. 1992). Authoritative biographies are Annie Cohen-Solal's *Sartre: A Life* (1985; trans. 1987), Ronald Hayman's *Sartre: A Biography* (1991), and Philip Thody's *Jean-Paul Sartre* (1992).

For introductions to Sartre's work as a whole, see Arthur C. Danto's *Sartre* (1975), Catharine Savage Brosman's *Jean-Paul Sartre* (1983), and *The Cambridge Companion to Sartre*, edited by Christina Howells (1992). On Sartre's literary criticism, see Eugene F. Kaelin, *An Existentialist Aesthetic: The Theories of Sartre and Merleau-Ponty* (1962); Benjamin Suhl, *Jean-Paul Sartre: The Philosopher as a Literary Critic* (1970); J. H. Bauer, *Sartre and the Artist* (1970); Fredric Jameson, *Marxism and Form: Twentieth-Century Dialectical Theories of Literature* (1971), and "Three Methods in Sartre's Literary Criticism," in *Modern French Criticism* (ed. John K. Simon, 1972);

Joseph Halpern, *Critical Fictions: The Literary Criticism of Jean-Paul Sartre* (1976); and Christina Howells, *Sartre's Theory of Literature* (1979). For studies of the influential journal *Les Temps Modernes,* see Alain D. Ranwez, *Jean-Paul Sartre's "Les Temps Modernes": A Literary History, 1945–1952* (1981); Anna Boschetti, *The Intellectual Enterprise: Sartre and "Les Temps Modernes"* (1985; trans. 1988); and Howard Davies, *Sartre and "Les Temps Modernes"* (1987). For broader studies addressing historical context and comparative analysis, see Tony Judt, *Past Imperfect: French Intellectuals, 1944–1956* (1992); *Situating Sartre in Twentieth-Century Thought and Culture*, edited by Jean-François Fourny and Charles D. Minahen (1997); Michael Scriven, *Jean-Paul Sartre: Politics and Culture in Postwar France* (1999); and Ann Fulton, *Apostles of Sartre: Existentialism in America, 1945–1963* (1999). For bibliographies of Sartre's works and criticism, see Michel Contat and Michel Rybalka, *The Writings of Jean-Paul Sartre* (2 vols., 1974); Robert Wilcocks, *Jean-Paul Sartre: A Bibliography of International Criticism* (1975); and Joan Nordquist, *Jean-Paul Sartre: A Bibliography* (1993).

From What Is Literature?[1]

Why Write?

Each has his reasons: for one, art is a flight; for another a means of conquering. But one can flee into a hermitage, into madness, into death. One can conquer by arms. Why does it have to be *writing*, why does one have to manage one's escapes and conquests by *writing*? Because, behind the various aims of authors, there is a deeper and more immediate choice which is common to all of us. We shall try to elucidate this choice, and we shall see whether it is not in the name of this very choice of writing that the self-commitment of writers must be required.

Each of our perceptions is accompanied by the consciousness that human reality is a 'revealer', that is, it is through human reality that 'there is' being, or, to put it differently, that man is the means by which things are manifested. It is our presence in the world which multiplies relations. It is we who set up a relationship between this tree and that bit of sky. Thanks to us, that star which has been dead for millennia, that quarter moon, and that dark river are disclosed in the unity of a landscape. It is the speed of our car and our aeroplane which organizes the great masses of the earth. With each of our acts, the world reveals to us a new face. But, if we know that we are directors of being, we also know that we are not its producers. If we turn away from this landscape, it will sink back into its dark permanence. At least, it will sink back; there is no one mad enough to think that it is going to be annihilated. It is we who shall be annihilated, and the earth will remain in its lethargy until another consciousness comes along to awaken it. Thus, to our inner certainty of being 'revealers' is added that of being inessential in relation to the thing revealed.

One of the chief motives of artistic creation is certainly the need of feeling that we are essential in relationship to the world. If I fix on canvas or in writing a certain aspect of the fields or the sea or a look on someone's face which I have disclosed, I am conscious of having produced them by con-

1. Translated by Bernard Frechtman.

densing relationships, by introducing order where there was none, by imposing the unity of mind on the diversity of things. That is, I feel myself essential in relation to my creation. But this time it is the created object which escapes me; I cannot reveal and produce at the same time. The creation becomes inessential in relation to the creative activity. First of all, even if it appears finished to others, the created object always seems to us in a state of suspension; we can always change this line, that shade, that word. Thus, it never *forces itself*. A novice painter asked his teacher, 'When should I consider my painting finished?' And the teacher answered, 'When you can look at it in amazement and say to yourself "*I'm* the one who did *that*!" '

Which amounts to saying 'never'. For that would be virtually to consider one's work with someone else's eyes and to reveal what one has created. But it is self-evident that we are proportionally less conscious of the thing produced and more conscious of our productive activity. When it is a matter of pottery or carpentry, we work according to traditional patterns, with tools whose usage is codified; it is Heidegger's[2] famous 'they' who are working with our hands. In this case, the result can seem to us sufficiently strange to preserve its objectivity in our eyes. But if we ourselves produce the rules of production, the measures, the criteria, and if our creative drive comes from the very depths of our heart, then we never find anything but ourselves in our work. It is we who have invented the laws by which we judge it. It is our history, our love, our gaiety that we recognize in it. Even if we should look at it without touching it any further, we never *receive* from it that gaiety of love. We put them into it. The results which we have obtained on canvas or paper never seem to us *objective*. We are too familiar with the processes of which they are the effects. These processes remain a subjective discovery; they are ourselves, our inspiration, our trick, and when we seek to *perceive* our work, we create it again, we repeat mentally the operations which produced it; each of its aspects appears as a result. Thus, in the perception, the object is given as the essential thing and the subject as the inessential. The latter seeks essentiality in the creation and obtains it, but then it is the object which becomes the inessential.

This dialectic[3] is nowhere more apparent than in the art of writing, for the literary object is a peculiar top which exists only in movement. To make it come into view a concrete act called reading is necessary, and it lasts only as long as this act can last. Beyond that, there are only black marks on paper. Now, the writer cannot read what he writes, whereas the shoemaker can put on the shoes he has just made if they are his size, and the architect can live in the house he has built. In reading, one foresees; one waits. One foresees the end of the sentence, the following sentence, the next page. One waits for them to confirm or disappoint one's foresights. The reading is composed of a host of hypotheses, of dreams followed by awakenings, of hopes and deceptions. Readers are always ahead of the sentence they are reading in a merely probable future which partly collapses and partly comes together in proportion as they progress, which withdraws from one page to the next and forms the moving horizon of the literary object. Without waiting, without a future, without ignorance, there is no objectivity.

2. MARTIN HEIDEGGER (1889–1976), German philosopher; author of *Being and Time* (1927), to which Sartre refers.

3. Reciprocal interaction.

Now the operation of writing involves an implicit quasi-reading which makes real reading impossible. When the words form under his pen, the author doubtless sees them, but he does not see them as the reader does, since he knows them before writing them down. The function of his gaze is not to reveal, by brushing against them, the sleeping words which are waiting to be read, but to control the sketching of the signs. In short, it is a purely regulating mission, and the view before him reveals nothing except for slight slips of the pen. The writer neither foresees nor conjectures; he *projects*. It often happens that he awaits, as they say, the inspiration. But one does not wait for oneself the way one waits for others. If he hesitates, he knows that the future is not made, that he himself is going to make it, and if he still does not know what is going to happen to his hero, that simply means that he has not thought about it, that he has not decided upon anything. The future is then a blank page, whereas the future of the reader is two hundred pages filled with words which separate him from the end. Thus, the writer meets everywhere only *his* knowledge, *his* will, *his* plans, in short, himself. He touches only his own subjectivity; the object he creates is out of reach; he does not create it *for himself*. If he re-reads himself, it is already too late. The sentence will never quite be a thing in his eyes. He goes to the very limits of the subjective but without crossing it. He appreciates the effect of a touch, of an epigram, of a well-placed adjective, but it is the effect they will have on others. He can judge it, not feel it. Proust[4] never discovered the homosexuality of Charlus, since he had decided upon it even before starting on his book. And if a day comes when the book takes on for its author a semblance of objectivity, it is because years have passed, because he has forgotten it, because its spirit is quite foreign to him, and doubtless he is no longer capable of writing it. This was the case with Rousseau[5] when he re-read the *Social Contract* at the end of his life.

Thus, it is not true that one writes for oneself. That would be the worst blow. In projecting one's emotions on paper, one barely manages to give them a languid extension. The creative act is only an incomplete and abstract moment in the production of a work. If the author existed alone he would be able to write as much as he liked; the work as *object* would never see the light of day and he would either have to put down his pen or despair. But the operation of writing implies that of reading as its dialectical correlative and these two connected acts necessitate two distinct agents. It is the joint effort of author and reader which brings upon the scene that concrete and imaginary object which is the work of the mind. There is no art except for and by others.

Reading seems, in fact, to be the synthesis of perception and creation.[6] It posits the essentiality of both the subject and the object. The object is essential because it is strictly transcendent, because it imposes its own structures, and because one must wait for it and observe it; but the subject is also essential because it is required not only to disclose the object (that is, to make it possible for there to *be* an object) but also so that this object might

4. Marcel Proust (1871–1922), French novelist; Charlus is a character in Proust's *Remembrance of Things Past* (1913–27).

5. Jean-Jacques Rousseau (1712–1778), Swiss-born French philosopher and writer; the *Social Contract* was published in 1762.

6. The same is true in different degrees regarding the spectator's attitude before other works of art (paintings, symphonies, statues, etc.) [Sartre's note].

exist absolutely (that is, to produce it). In a word, the reader is conscious of disclosing in creating, of creating by disclosing. In reality, it is not necessary to believe that reading is a mechanical operation and that signs make an impression upon him as light does on a photographic plate. If he is inattentive, tired, stupid, or thoughtless, most of the relations will escape him. The object will never 'catch' with him (in the sense in which we say that fire 'catches' or 'doesn't catch'). He will draw some phrases out of the shadow, but they will seem to have appeared at random. If he is at his best, he will project beyond the words a synthetic form, each phrase of which will be no more than a partial function: the 'theme', the 'subject', or the 'meaning'. Thus, from the very beginning, the meaning is no longer contained in the words, since it is he, on the contrary, who allows the significance of each of them to be understood; and the literary object, though realized *through* language, is never given *in* language. On the contrary, it is by nature a silence and an opponent of the word. In addition, the hundred thousand words aligned in a book can be read one by one so that the meaning of the work does not emerge. Nothing is accomplished if the reader does not put himself from the very beginning and almost without a guide at the height of this silence; if, in short, he does not invent it and does not then place there, and hold on to, the words and sentences which he awakens. And if I am told that it would be more fitting to call this operation a re-invention or a discovery, I shall answer that, first, such a re-invention would be as new and as original an act as the first invention. And, especially, when an object has never existed before, there can be no question of re-inventing it or discovering it. For if the silence about which I am speaking is really the goal at which the author is aiming, he has, at least, never been familiar with it; his silence is subjective and anterior to language. It is the absence of words, the undifferentiated and lived silence of inspiration, which the word will then particularize, whereas the silence produced by the reader is an object. And at the very interior of this object there are more silences—which the author does not mention. It is a question of silences which are so particular that they could not retain any meaning outside the object which the reading causes to appear. However, it is these which give it its density and its particular face.

To say that they are unexpressed is hardly the word; for they are precisely the inexpressible. And that is why one does not come upon them at any definite moment in the reading; they are everywhere and nowhere. The quality of the marvellous in *Le Grand Meaulnes*, the grandioseness of *Armance*, the degree of realism and truth of Kafka's[7] mythology, these are never given. The reader must invent them all in a continual exceeding of the written thing. To be sure, the author guides him, but all he does is guide him. The landmarks he sets up are separated by the void. The reader must unite them; he must go beyond them. In short, reading is directed creation.

On the one hand, the literary object has no other substance than the reader's subjectivity; Raskolnikov's[8] waiting is *my* waiting which I lend him. Without this impatience of the reader he would remain only a collection of signs. His hatred of the police magistrate who questions him is my hatred

7. Franz Kafka (1883–1924), Austrian writer who was born and lived most of his life in Prague; his fictions often matter-of-factly present the unreal. *Le Grand Meaulnes* (1913), a novel by Henri Alain-Fournier. *Armance* (1827), a novel by Stendhal.

8. The central character in *Crime and Punishment* (1866), a novel by Fyodor Dostoyevsky.

which has been solicited and wheedled out of me by signs, and the police magistrate himself would not exist without the hatred I have for him via Raskolnikov. That is what animates him, it is his very flesh.

But on the other hand, the words are there like traps to arouse our feelings and to reflect them towards us. Each word is a path of transcendence; it shapes our feelings, names them, and attributes them to an imaginary personage who takes it upon himself to live them for us and who has no other substance than these borrowed passions; he confers objects, perspectives, and a horizon upon them.

Thus, for the reader, all is to do and all is already done; the work exists only at the exact level of his capacities; while he reads and creates, he knows that he can always go further in his reading, can always create more profoundly, and thus the work seems to him as inexhaustible and opaque as things. We would readily reconcile that 'rational intuition' which Kant[9] reserved to divine Reason with this absolute production of qualities, which, to the extent that they emanate from our subjectivity, congeal before our eyes into impenetrable objectivities.

Since the creation can find its fulfilment only in reading, since the artist must entrust to another the job of carrying out what he has begun, since it is only through the consciousness of the reader that he can regard himself as essential to his work, all literary work is an appeal. To write is to make an appeal to the reader that he lead into objective existence the revelation which I have undertaken by means of language. And if it should be asked *to what* the writer is appealing, the answer is simple. As the sufficient reason for the appearance of the aesthetic object is never found either in the book (where we find merely solicitations to produce the object) or in the author's mind, and as his subjectivity, which he cannot get away from, cannot give a reason for the act of leading into objectivity, the appearance of the work of art is a new event which cannot *be explained* by anterior data. And since this directed creation is an absolute beginning, it is therefore brought about by the freedom of the reader, and by what is purest in that freedom. Thus, the writer appeals to the reader's freedom to collaborate in the production of his work.

It will doubtless be said that all tools address themselves to our freedom since they are the instruments of a possible action, and that the work of art is not unique in that. And it is true that the tool is the congealed outline of an operation. But it remains on the level of the hypothetical imperative.[1] I may use a hammer to nail up a case or to hit my neighbour over the head. In so far as I consider it in itself, it is not an appeal to my freedom; it does not put me face to face with it; rather, it aims at using it by substituting a set succession of traditional procedures for the free invention of means. The book does not serve my freedom; it requires it. Indeed, one cannot address oneself to freedom as such by means of constraint, fascination, or entreaties. There is only one way of attaining it: first, by recognizing it, then, by having confidence in it, and finally, by requiring of it an act, an act in its own name—that is, in the name of the confidence that one brings to it.

9. IMMANUEL KANT (1724–1804), German philosopher. Kant's rational or pure intuitions work as a priori conditions that determine how we process sensations.

1. A term from Kant's moral philosophy; hypothetical imperatives depend on a preference for a particular end (e.g., "If I want to play the piano better, then I should practice"). Because they are subjective, they are not moral imperatives.

Thus, the book is not, like the tool, a means for any end whatever; the end to which it offers itself is the reader's freedom. And the Kantian expression 'finality without end'[2] seems to me quite inappropriate for designating the work of art. In fact, it implies that the aesthetic object presents only the appearance of a finality and is limited to soliciting the free and ordered play of the imagination. It forgets that the imagination of the spectator has not only a regulating function, but a constitutive one. It does not play; it is called upon to recompose the beautiful object beyond the traces left by the artist. The imagination cannot revel in itself any more than can the other functions of the mind; it is always on the outside, always engaged in an enterprise. There would be finality without end if some object offered such a well-arranged composition that it would lead us to suppose that it has an end even though we cannot ascribe one to it. By defining the beautiful in this way one can—and this is Kant's aim—liken the beauty of art to natural beauty, since a flower, for example, presents so much symmetry, such harmonious colours, and such regular curves, that one is immediately tempted to seek a finalist explanation for all these properties and to see them as just so many means at the disposal of an unknown end. But that is exactly the error. The beauty of nature is in no way comparable to that of art. The work of art *does not have* an end; there we agree with Kant. But the reason is that it *is* an end. The Kantian formula does not account for the appeal which resounds at the basis of each painting, each statue, each book. Kant believes that the work of art first exists as fact and that it is then seen. Whereas it exists only if one *looks* at it and if it is first pure appeal, pure exigence to exist. It is not an instrument whose existence is manifest and whose end is undetermined. It presents itself as a task to be discharged; from the very beginning it places itself on the level of the categorical imperative.[3] You are perfectly free to leave that book on the table. But if you open it, you assume responsibility for it. For freedom is experienced not in the enjoyment of free subjective functioning, but in a creative act required by an imperative. The absolute end, this imperative which is transcendent yet acquiesced in, which freedom itself adopts as its own, is what we call a value. The work of art is a value because it is an appeal.

If I appeal to my reader so that we may carry to a successful conclusion the enterprise which I have begun, it is self-evident that I consider him as a pure freedom, as an unconditioned activity; thus, in no case can I address myself to his passiveness, that is, try to *affect* him, to communicate to him, from the very first, emotions of fear, desire, or anger. There are, doubtless, authors who concern themselves solely with arousing these emotions because they are foreseeable, manageable, and because they have at their disposal sure-fire means for provoking them. But it is also true that they are reproached for this kind of thing, as Euripides[4] has been since antiquity because he had children appear on the stage. Freedom is alienated in the state of passion; it is abruptly engaged in partial enterprises; it loses sight of its task, which is to produce an absolute end. And the book is no longer anything but a means for feeding hate or desire. The writer should not seek

2. That is, "purposiveness without purpose," a key term in Kant's *Critique of Judgment* (1790; see above).

3. A term from Kant's moral philosophy; categorical imperatives are absolute and universal (e.g., "Treat people with respect"). They are moral principles: they do not rely on individual, subjective preferences.

4. Greek tragedian (ca. 485–ca. 406 B.C.E.).

to *overwhelm*; otherwise he is in contradiction with himself; if he wishes to *make demands* he must propose only the task to be fulfilled. Hence, the character of pure presentation which appears essential to the work of art. The reader must be able to make a certain aesthetic withdrawal. This is what Gautier[5] foolishly confused with 'art for art's sake' and the Parnassians[6] with the imperturbability of the artist. It is simply a matter of precaution, and Genet[7] more justly calls it the author's politeness towards the reader. But that does not mean that the writer makes an appeal to some sort of abstract and conceptual freedom. One certainly creates the aesthetic object with feelings; if it is touching, it appears through our tears; if it is comic, it will be recognized by laughter. However, these feelings are of a particular kind. They have their origin in freedom; they are loaned. The belief which I accord the tale is freely assented to. It is a Passion, in the Christian sense of the word, that is, a freedom which resolutely puts itself into a state of passiveness to obtain a certain transcendent effect by this sacrifice. The reader renders himself credulous; he descends into credulity which, though it ends by enclosing him like a dream, is at every moment conscious of being free. An effort is sometimes made to force the writer into this dilemma: 'Either one believes in your story, and it is intolerable, or one does not believe in it, and it is ridiculous'. But the argument is absurd because the characteristic of aesthetic consciousness is to be a belief by means of commitment, by oath, a belief sustained by fidelity to one's self and to the author, a perpetually renewed choice to believe. I can awaken at every moment, and I know it; but I do not want to; reading is a free dream. So that all feelings which are exacted on the basis of this imaginary belief are like particular modulations of my freedom. Far from absorbing or masking it, they are so many different ways it has chosen to reveal itself to itself. Raskolnikov, as I have said, would only be a shadow, without the mixture of repulsion and friendship which I feel for him and which makes him live. But, by a reversal which is the characteristic of the imaginary object, it is not his behaviour which excites my indignation or esteem, but my indignation and esteem which give consistency and objectivity to his behaviour. Thus, the reader's feelings are never dominated by the object, and as no external reality can condition them, they have their permanent source in freedom; that is, they are all generous—for I call a feeling generous which has its origin and its end in freedom. Thus, reading is an exercise in generosity, and what the writer requires of the reader is not the application of an abstract freedom but the gift of his whole person, with his passions, his prepossessions, his sympathies, his sexual temperament, and his scale of values. Only this person will give himself generously; freedom goes through and through him and comes to transform the darkest masses of his sensibility. And just as activity has rendered itself passive in order for it better to create the object, conversely, passiveness becomes an act; the man who is reading has raised himself to the highest degree. That is why we see people who are known for their toughness shed tears at the recital of imaginary misfortunes; for the moment, they have become what

5. THÉOPHILE GAUTIER (1811–1872), French poet and novelist. On "art for art's sake" and 19th-century aestheticism, see also WALTER PATER, above.

6. A varied group of mid-19th-century French poets who gravitated around Charles Leconte de Lisle (1818–1894) and became known for their impersonal approach to poetry.

7. Jean Genet (1910–1986), French dramatist and novelist.

they would have been if they had not spent their lives hiding their freedom from themselves.

Thus, the author writes in order to address himself to the freedom of readers, and he requires it in order to make his work exist. But he does not stop there; he also requires that they return this confidence which he has given them, that they recognize his creative freedom, and that they in turn solicit it by a symmetrical and inverse appeal. Here there appears the other dialectical paradox of reading; the more we experience our freedom, the more we recognize that of the other; the more he demands of us, the more we demand of him.

When I am enchanted with a landscape, I know very well that it is not I who create it, but I also know that without me the relations which are established before my eyes among the trees, the foliage, the earth, and the grass would not exist at all. I know that I can give no reason for the appearance of finality which I discover in the assortment of hues and in the harmony of the forms and movements created by the wind. Yet, it exists; there it is before my eyes, and I can make something more out of what is already there. But even if I believe in God, I cannot establish any passage, unless it be purely verbal, between the divine, universal solicitude and the particular spectacle which I am considering. To say that He made the landscape in order to charm me or that He made me the kind of person who is pleased by it is to take a question for an answer. Is the marriage of this blue and that green deliberate? How can I know? The idea of a universal providence is no guarantee of any particular intention, especially in the case under consideration, since the green of the grass is explained by biological laws, specific constants, and geographical determinism, while the reason for the blue of the water is accounted for by the depth of the river, the nature of the soil and the swiftness of the current. The assorting of the shades, if it is willed, can only be something *thrown into the bargain*;[8] it is the meeting of two causal series, that is to say, at first sight, a fact of chance. At best, the finality remains problematic. All the relations we establish remain hypotheses; no end is proposed to us in the manner of an imperative, since none is expressly revealed as having been willed by a creator. Thus, our freedom is never *called forth* by natural beauty. Or rather, there is an appearance of order in the whole which includes the foliage, the forms, and the movements, hence, the illusion of a calling forth which seems to solicit this freedom and which disappears immediately when one looks at it. Hardly have we begun to run our eyes over this arrangement, than the appeal disappears; we remain alone, free to tie one colour with another or with a third, to set up a relationship between the tree and the water, or between the tree and the sky, or between the tree, the water, and the sky. My freedom becomes caprice. To the extent that I establish new relationships, I remove myself further from the illusory objectivity which solicits me. I *muse* about certain motifs which are vaguely outlined by the things; the natural reality is no longer anything but a pretext for musing. Or, in that case, because I have deeply regretted that this arrangement which was momentarily perceived was not offered to me by somebody and consequently is not *real*, the result is that I fix my dream, that I transpose it to canvas or in writing. Thus, I interpose myself between the

8. In the original French, *par-dessus le marché*: "supplement," "extra."

finality without end which appears in the natural spectacles and the gaze of other men. I transmit it to them. It becomes human by this transmission. Art here is a ceremony of the *gift*, and the gift alone brings about the metamorphosis. It is something like the transmission of titles and powers in the matriarchate, where the mother does not possess the names but is the indispensable intermediary between uncle and nephew. Since I have captured this illusion in flight, since I lay it out for other men and have disentangled it and rethought it for them, they can consider it with confidence. It has become intentional. As for me, I remain, to be sure, at the border of the subjective and the objective without ever being able to contemplate the objective arrangement which I transmit.

The reader, on the contrary, progresses in security. However far he may go, the author has gone further. Whatever connections he may establish among the different parts of the book—among the chapters or the words—he has a guarantee, namely, that they have been expressly willed. As Descartes[9] says, he can even pretend that there is a secret order among parts which seem to have no connection. The creator has preceded him along the way, and the most beautiful disorders are effects of art, that is, again order. Reading is induction, interpolation, extrapolation, and the basis of these activities rests on the reader's will, as for a long time it was believed that that of scientific induction rested on the divine will. A gentle force accompanies us and supports us from the first page to the last. That does not mean that we fathom the artist's intentions easily. They constitute, as we have said, the object of conjectures, and there is an *experience* of the reader; but these conjectures are supported by the great certainty we have that the beauties which appear in the book are never accidental. In nature, the tree and the sky harmonize only by chance; if, on the contrary, in the novel, the protagonists find themselves in a *certain* tower, in a *certain* prison, if they stroll in a *certain* garden, it is a matter both of the restitution of independent causal series (the character had a certain state of mind which was due to a succession of psychological and social events; on the other hand, he betook himself to a determined place and the layout of the city required him to cross a certain park) and of the expression of a deeper finality, for the park came into existence only *in order to* harmonize with a certain state of mind, to express it by means of things or to put it into relief by a vivid contrast, and the state of mind itself was conceived in connection with the landscape. Here it is causality which is appearance and which might be called 'causality without cause', and it is the finality which is the profound reality. But if I can thus in all confidence put the order of ends under the order of causes, it is because by opening the book I am asserting that the object has its source in human freedom.

If I were to suspect the artist of having written out of passion and in passion, my confidence would immediately vanish, for it would serve no purpose to have supported the order of causes by the order of ends. The latter would be supported in its turn by a psychic causality and the work of art would end by re-entering the chain of determinism. Certainly I do not deny when I am reading that the author may be impassioned, nor even that he might have conceived the first plan of his work under the sway of passion.

9. René Descartes (1596–1650), French mathematician and philosopher.

But his decision to write supposes that he withdraws somewhat from his feelings, in short, that he has transformed his emotions into free emotions as I do mine while reading him, that is, that he is in an attitude of generosity.

Thus, reading is a pact of generosity between author and reader. Each one trusts the other; each one counts on the other, demands of the other as much as he demands of himself. For this confidence is itself generosity. Nothing can force the author to believe that his reader will use his freedom; nothing can force the reader to believe that the author has used his. Both of them make a free decision. There is then established a dialectical going-and-coming; when I read, I make demands; if my demands are met, what I am then reading provokes me to demand more of the author, which means to demand of the author that he demand more of me. And, vice versa, the author's demand is that I carry my demands to the highest pitch. Thus, my freedom, by revealing itself, reveals the freedom of the other.

It matters little whether the aesthetic object is the product of 'realistic' art (or supposedly such) or 'formal' art. At any rate, the natural relations are inverted; that tree in the foreground of the Cézanne[1] painting appears initially as the product of a causal chain. But the causality is an illusion; it will doubtless remain as a proposition as long as we look at the painting, but it will be supported by a deep finality; if the tree is placed in such a way it is because the rest of the painting *requires* that this form and those colours be placed in the foreground. Thus, through the phenomenal causality, our gaze attains finality as the deep structure of the object, and, beyond finality, it attains human freedom as its source and original basis. Vermeer's[2] realism is carried so far that at first it might be thought to be photographic. But if one considers the splendour of his texture, the pink and velvety glory of his little brick walls, the blue thickness of a branch of woodbine, the glazed darkness of his vestibules, the orange-coloured flesh of his faces, which are as polished as the stone of holy-water basins, one suddenly feels, in the pleasure that he experiences, that the finality is not so much in the forms or colours as in his material imagination. It is the very substance and temper of the things which here give the forms their reason for being. With this realist we are perhaps closest to absolute creation, since it is in the very passiveness of the matter that we meet the unfathomable freedom of man.

The work is never limited to the painted, sculpted, or narrated object. Just as one perceives things only against the background of the world, so the objects represented by art appear against the background of the universe. In the background of Fabrice's adventures are the Italy of 1820, Austria, France, the sky and stars which the Abbé Blanis[3] consults, and finally the whole earth. If the painter presents us with a field or a vase of flowers, his paintings are windows that open onto the whole world. We follow the red path which is buried among the wheat much farther than Van Gogh[4] has painted it, among other wheat fields, under other clouds, to the river which empties into the sea, and we extend to infinity, to the other end of the world, the deep finality which supports the existence of the field and the earth. So that, through the various objects which it produces or reproduces, the cre-

1. Paul Cézanne (1839–1906), French painter.
2. Jan Vermeer (1632–1675), Dutch painter.
3. Character in Stendhal's historical novel *The Charterhouse of Parma* (1839), which chronicles the exploits of Fabrizio del Dongo.
4. Vincent van Gogh (1853–1890), Dutch painter.

ative act aims at a total renewal of the world. Each painting, each book, is a recovery of the totality of being. Each of them presents this totality to the freedom of the spectator. For this is quite the final goal of art: to recover this world by giving it to be seen as it is, but as if it had its source in human freedom. But, since what the author creates takes on objective reality only in the eyes of the spectator, this recovery is consecrated by the ceremony of the spectacle—and particularly of reading. We are already in a better position to answer the question we raised a while ago: the writer chooses to appeal to the freedom of other men so that, by the reciprocal implications of their demands, they may re-adapt the totality of being to man and may again enclose the universe within man.

If we wish to go still further, we must bear in mind that the writer, like all other artists, aims at giving his reader a certain feeling that is customarily called aesthetic pleasure, and which I would very much rather call aesthetic joy, and that this feeling, when it appears, is a sign that the work is achieved. It is therefore fitting to examine it in the light of the preceding considerations. In effect, this joy, which is denied to the creator, in so far as he creates, becomes one with the aesthetic consciousness of the spectator, that is, in the case under consideration, of the reader. It is a complex feeling but one whose structures and condition are inseparable from one another. It is identical, at first, with the recognition of a transcendent and absolute end which, for a moment, suspends the utilitarian round of ends-means and means-ends,[5] that is, of an appeal or, what amounts to the same thing, of a value. And the positional consciousness which I take of this value is necessarily accompanied by the non-positional consciousness of my freedom, since my freedom is manifested to itself by a transcendent exigency. The recognition of freedom by itself is joy, but this structure of non-thetical[6] consciousness implies another: since, in effect, reading is creation, my freedom does not only appear to itself as pure autonomy but as creative activity, that is, it is not limited to giving itself its own law but perceives itself as being constitutive of the object. It is on this level that the phenomenon specifically is manifested, that is, a creation wherein the created object is given *as object* to its creator. It is the sole case in which the creator gets any enjoyment out of the object he creates. And the word enjoyment which is applied to the positional consciousness of the work read indicates sufficiently that we are in the presence of an essential structure of aesthetic joy. This positional enjoyment is accompanied by the non-positional consciousness of being essential in relation to an object perceived as essential. I shall call this aspect of aesthetic consciousness the feeling of security; it is this which stamps the strongest aesthetic emotions with a sovereign calm. It has its origin in the authentication of a strict harmony between subjectivity and objectivity. As, on the other hand, the aesthetic object is properly the world in so far as it is aimed at through the imaginary, aesthetic joy accompanies the positional consciousness that the world is a value, that is, a task proposed to human freedom. I shall call this the aesthetic modification of the human project, for, as usual, the world appears as the horizon of our situation, as the infinite dis-

5. In *practical life* a means may be taken for an end as soon as one searches for it, and each end is revealed as a means of attaining another end [Sartre's note].

6. Nondogmatic.

tance which separates us from ourselves, as the synthetic totality of the given, as the undifferentiated whole of obstacles and implements—but never as a demand addressed to our freedom. Thus, aesthetic joy proceeds to this level of the consciousness which I take of recovering and internalizing that which is non-ego *par excellence*, since I transform the given into an imperative and the fact into a value. The world is *my task*, that is, the essential and freely accepted function of my freedom is to make that unique and absolute object which is the universe come into being in an unconditioned movement. And, thirdly, the preceding structures imply a pact between human freedoms, for, on the one hand, reading is a confident and exacting recognition of the freedom of the writer, and, on the other hand, aesthetic pleasure, as it is itself experienced in the form of a value, involves an absolute exigence in regard to others; every man, in so far as he is a freedom, feels the same pleasure in reading the same work. Thus, all mankind is present in its highest freedom; it sustains the being of a world which is both *its* world and the 'external' world. In aesthetic joy the positional consciousness is an *image-making* consciousness of the world in its totality both as being and having to be, both as totally ours and totally foreign, and the more ours as it is the more foreign. The non-positional consciousness *really* envelops the harmonious totality of human freedoms in so far as it makes the object of a universal confidence and exigency.

To write is thus both to disclose the world and to offer it as a task to the generosity of the reader. It is to have recourse to the consciousness of others in order to make one's self be recognized as *essential* to the totality of being; it is to wish to live this essentiality by means of interposed persons; but, on the other hand, as the real world is revealed only by action, as one can feel oneself in it only by exceeding it in order to change it, the novelist's universe would lack depth if it were not discovered in a movement to transcend it. It has often been observed that an object in a story does not derive its density of existence from the number and length of the descriptions devoted to it, but from the complexity of its connections with the different characters. The more often the characters handle it, take it up, and put it down, in short, go beyond it towards their own ends, the more real will it appear. Thus, of the world of the novel, that is, the totality of men and things, we may say that in order for it to offer its maximum density the disclosure-creation by which the reader discovers it must also be an imaginary participation in the action; in other words, the more disposed one is to change it, the more alive it will be. The error of realism has been to believe that the real reveals itself to contemplation, and that consequently one could draw an impartial picture of it. How could that be possible, since the very perception is partial, since by itself the naming is already a modification of the object? And how could the writer, who wants himself to be essential to this universe, want to be essential to the injustice which this universe comprehends? Yet, he must be; but if he accepts being the creator of injustices, it is in a movement which goes beyond them towards their abolition. As for me who read, if I create and keep alive an unjust world, I cannot help making myself responsible for it. And the author's whole art is bent on obliging me to *create* what he *discloses*, therefore to compromise myself. So both of us bear the responsibility for the universe. And precisely because this universe is supported by the joint effort of our two freedoms, and because the author, with me as medium, has attempted to integrate it into the human, it must appear truly *in itself*, in its very marrow, as being shot through and through with a freedom which has taken human freedom as its end, and if it is not really the city of ends that it ought to be, it must at least be a stage along the way; in a word, it must be a becoming and it must always be considered and presented not as a crushing mass which weighs us down, but from the point of view of its going beyond towards that city of ends. However bad and hopeless the humanity which it paints may be, the work must have an air of generosity. Not, of course, that this generosity is to be expressed by means of edifying discourses and virtuous characters; it must not even be premeditated, and it is quite true that fine sentiments do not make fine books. But it must be the very warp and woof of the book, the stuff out of which the people and things are cut; whatever the subject, a sort of essential lightness must appear everywhere and remind us that the work is never a natural datum, but an *exigence* and a *gift*. And if I am given this world with its injustices, it is not so that I may contemplate them coldly, but that I may animate them with my indignation, that I may disclose them and create them with their nature as injustices, that is, as abuses to be suppressed. Thus, the writer's universe will only reveal itself in all its depth to the examination, the admiration, and the indignation of the reader; and the generous love is a promise to maintain, and the generous indignation is a promise to change, and the admiration a promise to imitate; although literature is one thing and morality a quite different one, at the heart of the aesthetic imperative we discern the moral imperative. For, since the one who writes recognizes, by the very fact that he takes the trouble to write, the freedom of his readers, and since the one who reads, by the mere fact of his opening the book, recognizes the freedom of the writer, the work of art, from whichever side you approach it, is an act of confidence in the freedom of men. And since readers, like the author, recognize this freedom only to demand that it manifest itself, the work can be defined as an imaginary presentation of the world in so far as it demands human freedom. The result of which is that there is no 'gloomy literature', since, however dark may be the colours in which one paints the world, one paints it only so that free men may feel their freedom as they face it. Thus, there are only good and bad novels. The bad novel aims to please by flattering, whereas the good one is an exigence and an act of faith. But above all, the unique point of view from which the author can present the world to those freedoms whose concurrence he wishes to bring about is that of a world to be impregnated always with more freedom. It would be inconceivable that this unleashing of generosity provoked by the writer could be used to authorize an injustice, and that the reader could enjoy his freedom while reading a work which approves or accepts or simply abstains from condemning the subjection of man by man. One can imagine a good novel being written by an American negro even if hatred of the whites were spread all over it, because it is the freedom of his race that he demands through this hatred. And, as he invites me to assume the attitude of generosity, the moment I feel myself a pure freedom I cannot bear to identify myself with a race of oppressors. Thus, I require of all freedoms that they demand the liberation of coloured people against the white race and against myself in so far as I am a part of it, but nobody can suppose for a moment that it is possible to write a good novel in praise of anti-Semitism.[7] For, the moment I feel that my freedom is indissolubly linked with that of all other men, it cannot be demanded of me that I use it to approve the enslavement of a part of these men. Thus, whether he is an essayist, a pamphleteer, a satirist, or a novelist, whether he speaks only of individual passions or whether he attacks the social order, the writer, a free man addressing free men, has only one subject—freedom.

Hence, any attempt to enslave his readers threatens him in his very art. A blacksmith can be affected by fascism in his life as a man, but not necessarily in his craft; a writer will be affected in both, and even more in his craft than in his life. I have seen writers, who before the war called for fascism with all their hearts, smitten with sterility at the very moment when the Nazis were loading them with honours. I am thinking of Drieu la Rochelle[8] in particular; he was mistaken, but he was sincere. He proved it. He had agreed to direct a Nazi-inspired review. The first few months he reprimanded, rebuked, and lectured his countrymen. No one answered him because no one was free to do so. He became irritated; he no longer *felt* his readers. He became more insistent, but no sign appeared to prove that he had been understood. No sign of hatred, nor of anger either; nothing. He seemed to have lost his bearings, the victim of a growing distress. He complained bitterly to the Germans. His articles had been superb; they became shrill. The moment arrived when he struck his breast; no echo, except among the bought journalists whom he despised. He handed in his resignation, withdrew it, again spoke, still in the desert. Finally, he said nothing, gagged by the silence of others. He had demanded the enslavement of others, but in his crazy mind he must have imagined that it was voluntary, that it was still free. It came; the man in him congratulated himself mightily, but the writer could not bear it. While this was going on, others, who, happily, were in the majority, understood that the freedom of writing implies the freedom of the citizen. One does not write for slaves. The art of prose is bound up with the only régime in which prose has meaning, democracy. When one is threatened, the other is too. And it is not enough to defend them with the pen. A day comes when the pen is forced to stop, and the writer must then take up arms. Thus, however you might have come to it, whatever the opinions you might have professed, literature throws you into battle. Writing is a certain way of wanting freedom; once you have begun, you are committed, willy-nilly.

Committed to what? Defending freedom? That's easy to say. Is it a matter of acting as a guardian of ideal values like Benda's 'clerk' before the betrayal,[9] or is it concrete everyday freedom which must be protected by our taking sides in political and social struggles? The question is tied up with another one, one very simple in appearance but which nobody ever asks himself: 'For whom does one write?'

1947, 1948

7. This last remark may arouse some readers. If so, I'd like to know a single good novel whose express purpose was to serve oppression, a single good novel which has been written against Jews, negroes, workers, or colonial people. "But if there isn't any, that's no reason why someone may not write one some day." But you then admit that you are an abstract theoretician. You, not I. For it is in the name of your abstract conception of art that you assert the possibility of a fact which has never come into being, whereas I limit myself to proposing an explanation for a recognized fact [Sartre's note].

8. Pierre Drieu la Rochelle (1893–1945), French novelist and essayist.

9. The reference here is to Julien Benda's *La Trahison des clercs* [1927, *The Treason of the Intellectuals*], translated into English as *The Great Betrayal* [translator's note]. Benda (1867–1956), French philosopher and novelist.

CLEANTH BROOKS

1906–1994

The reputation of Cleanth Brooks suffered during the 1970s and 1980s when his books and essays were repeatedly cited to illustrate the flaws of the American New Criticism. Brooks, it was said, isolated literary criticism by limiting it to intensive analysis of the text itself, ignored history, discounted readers, failed to consider writings by women and minorities, and disabled any and all attempts to relate literary study to political, social, and cultural issues and debates. But while there are shortcomings to Brooks's work, his criticism is more interesting and complex than the standard accounts suggest. He is a subtle, incisive interpreter of literary texts and an adept theorist whose turns and twists of argument anticipated the theories later deployed against him.

Brooks was born in Murray, Kentucky, one of six children of a Methodist minister. He attended McTyeire School, a private classical academy in Tennessee, and received his B.A. from Vanderbilt in 1928 and his M.A. from Tulane University in 1929. He next studied as a Rhodes scholar at Exeter College at Oxford, returning to the United States in 1932 to begin his teaching career at Louisiana State University in Baton Rouge.

While at Oxford, Brooks became good friends with Robert Penn Warren, another Vanderbilt graduate and Rhodes scholar; when Warren joined LSU's English department in 1934, the two of them started to work together on criticism and pedagogy. Disturbed by the inability of their students to interpret literary works, Brooks and Warren prepared a booklet designed to teach the skills of close reading by providing examples. Their desire to improve literary study in the classroom led to Brooks and Warren's influential, best-selling textbooks: *An Approach to Literature* (1936), *Understanding Poetry* (1938), *Understanding Fiction* (1943), *Modern Rhetoric* (1949), and, with Robert Heilman, *Understanding Drama* (1945).

From 1935 to 1942, Brooks and Warren co-edited the *Southern Review*, making it one of the foremost journals of its era. They published not only critical essays but also creative writing by Eudora Welty, Katherine Anne Porter, and others. In the first year alone, the authors appearing in the *Southern Review* included JOHN CROWE RANSOM, Allen Tate, Wallace Stevens, KENNETH BURKE, R. P. Blackmur, Randall Jarrell, Ford Madox Ford, and Yvor Winters—leading poets and critics of the time.

Brooks's two most important critical books, *Modern Poetry and the Tradition* (1939) and *The Well Wrought Urn: Studies in the Structure of Poetry* (1947), focus on poetry, and he extended and reinforced their arguments in essays, reviews, and lectures. For example, with J. E. Hardy, he edited and wrote detailed commentary for *Poems of Mr. John Milton* (1951), showing that Milton's verse, which T. S. ELIOT had attacked as numbing and monolithic, could be appreciated as subtle and complex. In 1947 Brooks left LSU for a professorship at Yale University (Warren later followed), where he taught until retiring in 1975. He researched, wrote, and published many essays and books on modern fiction and literary criticism, as well as editing textbooks.

In a retrospective 1989 essay on his teacher and friend John Crowe Ransom, Brooks said that as a Vanderbilt student he had read the Southern Agrarian manifesto of 1930, *I'll Take My Stand*, "over and over": "I tried my best to assimilate the whole position, philosophical and political. I learned a great deal from my intensive study." But in his own work he never argued on behalf of conservative Southern traditions, values, and beliefs as specifically and as forcefully as did Ransom, Warren, and Tate. For him the lesson put forward by the Agrarians was a general and unobjectionable one: "They asked that we consider what the good life is or ought to be."

Brooks was above all a literary critic and theorist. He said that his interest in "close reading" was kindled in his school days when he studied the classical languages—"my prep school discipline in reading Latin and Greek." He noted too that he was affected by the approach to literature and criticism taken by his teachers and friends at Vanderbilt, especially the poets, "who were talking about the making of poems." Like many young literary critics in the 1930s, Brooks rebelled against the emphasis in graduate studies on "historical and biographical" information and protested the lack of attention to "the interior life of the poem." At Oxford he encountered I. A. Richards's books *The Principles of Literary Criticism* (1924) and *Practical Criticism* (1929). Brooks did not accept everything he found in Richards's work—in particular, he disapproved of its "psychological terminology" and "confident positivism"—but as he read and reread *Principles* ("perhaps a dozen times" the first year he encountered it) and *Practical Criticism*, he borrowed terms (such as *tone*, *irony*, and *attitude*) and developed Richards's guidelines for examining the poem itself into his own intrinsic (or formalist) criticism.

For Brooks, criticism means scrutinizing technical elements, textual patterns, and incongruities in texts; as he indicates at the outset of *The Well Wrought Urn*, the critic should always begin "by making the closest examination of what the poem says as a poem." Genuine literary criticism is neither biographical nor historical, a matter of sources-and-influences and background information. Nor is it subjective, the record of a reader's impressions as he or she reacts to a literary work. In one sense Brooks seeks to make literary criticism more like a science—rigorous, precise, intensive, analytical. But like other formalist critics, he insists that literature and science use language in very different ways. Science is referential, abstract, and denotative, whereas literature is nonreferential, concrete, and connotative. "The tendency of science," he states in *The Well Wrought Urn*, "is necessarily to stabilize terms, to freeze them into strict denotations; the poet's tendency is by contrast disruptive. The terms are continually modifying each other, and thus violating their dictionary meanings."

In the chapter we reprint below, "The Heresy of Paraphrase," Brooks emphasizes that it is not the purpose of a poem to produce a statement, a proposition, a didactic lesson or message. Through irony, paradox, ambiguity, and other rhetorical and poetic devices of his or her art, the poet works constantly to resist any reduction of the poem to a paraphrasable core, favoring the presentation of conflicting facets of theme and patterns of resolved stresses. For Brooks, all poetry exhibits "irony," by which he means pervasive incongruity.

Brooks reiterates this point in our second selection, "The Formalist Critics" (1951): "in a successful work, form and content cannot be separated." Echoing the conclusions that WILLIAM K. WIMSATT JR. and MONROE BEARDSLEY presented in "The Intentional Fallacy" (1946; see below) and "The Affective Fallacy" (1949; see below), Brooks states that literary study deals not with the author, the reader, or the historical context but instead with the specific text at hand: "the formalist critic is concerned primarily with the work itself."

His focus on the text has led Brooks's critics to say that he misguidedly narrowed the field of literary criticism and pedagogy by brushing aside biographical and historical contexts. Many later theorists, including EDWARD SAID and STEPHEN GREENBLATT, have called attention to the antihistorical thrust of the New Criticism and sought to connect literary criticism with new forms of ideological critique and historical inquiry. But this complaint about Brooks and the New Critics is in fact an old one: it was made from the beginning of the New Critical movement, both by traditional literary scholars and by public intellectuals and writers. Because Brooks did more than anyone else to articulate and codify the principles of Anglo-American New Criticism and demonstrate how they applied to a wide range of texts, he became a prime target for opponents of the approach.

Already in 1942, Alfred Kazin was attacking the New Critics for making "a fetish of form." Philip Rahv, like Kazin a New York Intellectual, also objected to the restricted nature of the New Critical approach: "Their attachment to the text is what is appealing about the 'new critics'; what is unappealing is their neglect of context." Rahv indicted the New Critics for "a narrow textual-formalistic approach which cannot account for change and movement in literature and which systematically eliminates ideas from criticism." Throughout his career, Brooks insisted that these charges were inaccurate and unfair. He claimed that he was not ignoring biography and history, but that as a *literary* critic he was intent on exploring the attitudes toward history that an author expressed in the language of the text itself. For Brooks the text possesses organic unity. A poem by Donne or Marvell does not depend for its success on outside knowledge that we bring to it; it is richly ambiguous yet harmoniously orchestrated, coherent in its own special aesthetic terms.

Brooks's close readings, while illuminating, do run the risk of always coming to more or less the same conclusion. Each poem that he examines, from whatever period, receives the same kind of inspection of its images, metaphors, tones of voice; each is valued or reproved for its handling of irony and paradox in the labor of controlling incongruities. In a 1948 essay, the scholar-theorist R. S. Crane faulted Brooks for "critical monism," remarking that all of the texts from the Renaissance through the modern period treated in *The Well Wrought Urn* end up seeming like seventeenth-century lyrics. But Brooks from the outset pretty much conceded this point; as he notes in "The Heresy of Paraphrase," he is undertaking in his book an analytical experiment—reading eighteenth- and nineteenth-century poems "as one has learned to read Donne and the moderns." While acknowledging the historical differences among the poems, he intends to show that there are common elements in their use and organization of language.

Yet the terms and emphases that shape Brooks's argument about how poetry operates are an uneasy mix. On the one hand, he refers to the warping, resisting, and violating of meaning (for example, "the resistance which any good poem sets up against all attempts to paraphrase it"). On the other hand, taking his cue from SAMUEL TAYLOR COLERIDGE and I. A. Richards, he speaks of harmony, balance, order, unity. Perhaps these impulses are not contradictory; Brooks would likely say that the poem can contain a "tension" among its paradoxical meanings while maintaining its coherence. But later theorists here saw and exploited an opening in Brooks's position. If there is a warping or resisting of meaning, how intense and deep is it? Can one claim that irony empowers the poem to achieve unity, or is irony the dimension of literary language that undermines and forestalls unity?

In the work of poststructuralists such as PAUL DE MAN and BARBARA JOHNSON, it is precisely the competing, conflicting, indeed warring relationship among the words in the text that keeps it from the self-contained equilibrium that Brooks celebrates. Where he sees in the poem's "essential structure" a "pattern of resolutions and balances and harmonizations," the deconstructionist critic, in the words of his younger Yale colleague J. Hillis Miller, seeks "the thread in the text in question which will unravel it all."

Such an approach, in Brooks's mind, was gravely mistaken, and in his final years he sharply criticized Miller, STANLEY FISH, HAROLD BLOOM and other advocates of deconstruction and reader-response theory. In Brooks's view, poststructuralist theory denied the authority of the work of art and invited subjectivism and relativism, as each critic played with the text's language unmindful of aesthetic relevance and formal design. The irony, however, is that all of the newer critics had been trained as New Critics themselves: they seized on and reframed the insights and arguments that Brooks in particular had advanced, and were closer to him in their conception of literature and criticism than perhaps they realized. In 1975 another Yale professor, Paul de Man, affirmed in "Semiology and Rhetoric" (see below): "A literary text simultaneously asserts and denies the authority of its own rhetorical mode." He found radical instability where Brooks perceived harmony and balance, but the special sense of the paradoxical workings of literary language is one that these critics share. Brooks and de Man, New Criticism and deconstruction, are very different from one another, yet perhaps not so different after all.

BIBLIOGRAPHY

Brooks's most noteworthy books are *Modern Poetry and the Tradition* (1939), *The Well Wrought Urn: Studies in the Structure of Poetry* (1947), and the textbook on poetry he co-edited with Robert Penn Warren, *Understanding Poetry* (1938). See also his *William Faulkner: The Yoknapatawpha Country* (1963) and *William Faulkner: Toward Yoknapatawpha and Beyond* (1978). He also coauthored, with William K. Wimsatt Jr., *Literary Criticism: A Short History* (1957); with Warren and R. W. B. Lewis, he co-edited *American Literature: The Makers and the Making* (1973), a two-volume, 3,000-page anthology. Collections of his essays include *The Hidden God: Studies in Hemingway, Faulkner, Yeats, Eliot, and Warren* (1963), *A Shaping Joy: Studies in the Writer's Craft* (1971), *Historical Evidence and the Reading of Seventeenth-Century Poetry* (1991), and *Community, Religion, and Literature: Essays* (1995). Another important source is *Cleanth Brooks and Robert Penn Warren: A Literary Correspondence,* edited by James A. Grimshaw (1998). For an excellent biography, consult Mark Royden Winchell, *Cleanth Brooks and the Rise of Modern Criticism* (1996).

The Possibilities of Order: Cleanth Brooks and His Work, edited by Lewis P. Simpson (1976), is a valuable collection of critical essays that includes an interview with Brooks conducted by Robert Penn Warren. For cogent discussions of Brooks in the context of Anglo-American New Criticism, see Grant Webster, *The Republic of Letters: A History of Postwar American Literary Opinion* (1979), and James J. Sosnoski, *Token Professionals and Master Critics: A Critique of Orthodoxy in Literary Studies* (1994). See also Thomas W. Cutrer, *Parnassus on the Mississippi: "The Southern Review" and the Baton Rouge Literary Community, 1935–1942* (1984), and John Michael Walsh, *Cleanth Brooks: An Annotated Bibliography* (1990).

From The Well Wrought Urn

Chapter 11
The Heresy of Paraphrase

The ten poems[1] that have been discussed were not selected because they happened to express a common theme or to display some particular style or to share a special set of symbols. It has proved, as a matter of fact, somewhat surprising to see how many items they do have in common: the light symbolism as used in "L'Allegro-Il Penseroso" and in the "Intimations" ode, for example; or, death as a sexual metaphor in "The Canonization" and in *The Rape of the Lock*; or the similarity of problem and theme in the "Intimations" ode and "Among School Children."

On reflection, however, it would probably warrant more surprise if these ten poems did not have much in common. For they are all poems which most of us will feel are close to the central stream of the tradition. Indeed, if there

1. *The Well Wrought Urn* includes sequential analyses of ten works: John Donne, "The Canonization" (1633); William Shakespeare, *Macbeth* (ca. 1606); John Milton, "L'Allegro" and "Il Penseroso" (1632); Robert Herrick, "Corinna's Going A-Maying" (1648); ALEXANDER POPE, *The Rape of the Lock* (1714); Thomas Gray, "Elegy Written in a Country Churchyard" (1751); WILLIAM WORDSWORTH, "Ode: Intimations of Immortality from Recollections of Early Childhood" (1807); John Keats, "Ode on a Grecian Urn" (1819); Alfred, Lord Tennyson, "Tears, Idle Tears" (1847); and William Butler Yeats, "Among School Children" (1927).

is any doubt on this point, it will have to do with only the first and last members of the series[2]—poems whose relation to the tradition I shall, for reasons to be given a little later, be glad to waive. The others, it will be granted, are surely in the main stream of the tradition.

As a matter of fact, a number of the poems discussed in this book were not chosen by me but were chosen for me. But having written on these, I found that by adding a few poems I could construct a chronological series which (though it makes no pretension to being exhaustive of periods or types) would not leave seriously unrepresented any important period since Shakespeare. In filling the gaps I tried to select poems which had been held in favor in their own day and which most critics still admire. There were, for example, to be no "metaphysical" poems[3] beyond the first exhibit and no "modern" ones other than the last. But the intervening poems were to be read as one has learned to read Donne and the moderns. One was to attempt to see, in terms of this approach, what the masterpieces had in common rather than to see how the poems of different historical periods differed—and in particular to see whether they had anything in common with the "metaphysicals" and with the moderns.

The reader will by this time have made up his mind as to whether the readings are adequate. (I use the word advisedly, for the readings do not pretend to be exhaustive, and certainly it is highly unlikely that they are not in error in one detail or another.) If the reader feels that they are seriously inadequate, then the case has been judged; for the generalizations that follow will be thoroughly vitiated by the inept handling of the particular cases on which they depend.

If, however, the reader does feel them to be adequate, it ought to be readily apparent that the common goodness which the poems share will have to be stated, not in terms of "content" or "subject matter" in the usual sense in which we use these terms, but rather in terms of structure. The "content" of the poems is various, and if we attempt to find one *quality* of content which is shared by all the poems—a "poetic" subject matter or diction or imagery—we shall find that we have merely confused the issues. For what is it to be poetic? Is the schoolroom of Yeats's poem poetic or unpoetic? Is Shakespeare's "new-borne babe / Striding the blast" poetic whereas the idiot of his "Life is a tale tolde by an idiot"[4] is unpoetic? If Herrick's "budding boy or girl" is poetic, then why is not that monstrosity of the newspaper's society page, the "society bud,"[5] poetic too?

To say this is not, of course, to say that all materials have precisely the same potentialities (as if the various pigments on the palette had the same potentialities, any one of them suiting the given picture as well as another). But what has been said, on the other hand, requires to be said: for, if we are to proceed at all, we must draw a sharp distinction between the attractiveness or beauty of any particular item taken as such and the "beauty" of the poem considered as a whole. The latter is the effect of a total pattern, and of a kind of pattern which can incorporate within itself items intrinsically beau-

2. That is, the poems by Donne and Yeats.
3. The metaphysical poetry of the early 17th century (including that of Donne) is characterized by complex extended metaphors, unusual imagery, irregular meter, and highly condensed meanings.
4. *Macbeth* 1.7.21–22 and (slightly misquoted) 5.5.25–26.
5. A facetious term for a young, unmarried woman.

tiful or ugly, attractive or repulsive. Unless one asserts the primacy of the pattern, a poem becomes merely a bouquet of intrinsically beautiful items.

But though it is in terms of structure that we must describe poetry, the term "structure" is certainly not altogether satisfactory as a term. One means by it something far more internal than the metrical pattern, say, or than the sequence of images. The structure meant is certainly not "form" in the conventional sense in which we think of form as a kind of envelope which "contains" the "content." The structure obviously is everywhere conditioned by the nature of the material which goes into the poem. The nature of the material sets the problem to be solved, and the solution is the ordering of the material.

Pope's *Rape of the Lock* will illustrate: the structure is not the heroic couplet[6] as such, or the canto arrangement; for, important as is Pope's use of the couplet as one means by which he secures the total effect, the heroic couplet can be used—has been used many times—as an instrument in securing very different effects. The structure of the poem, furthermore, is not that of the mock-epic convention, though here, since the term "mock-epic" has implications of attitude, we approach a little nearer to the kind of structure of which we speak.

The structure meant is a structure of meanings, evaluations, and interpretations; and the principle of unity which informs it seems to be one of balancing and harmonizing connotations, attitudes, and meanings. But even here one needs to make important qualifications: the principle is not one which involves the arrangement of the various elements into homogeneous groupings, pairing like with like. It unites the like with the unlike. It does not unite them, however, by the simple process of allowing one connotation to cancel out another nor does it reduce the contradictory attitudes to harmony by a process of subtraction. The unity is not a unity of the sort to be achieved by the reduction and simplification appropriate to an algebraic formula. It is a positive unity, not a negative; it represents not a residue but an achieved harmony.

The attempt to deal with a structure such as this may account for the frequent occurrence in the preceding chapters of such terms as "ambiguity," "paradox," "complex of attitudes," and—most frequent of all, and perhaps most annoying to the reader—"irony." I hasten to add that I hold no brief for these terms as such. Perhaps they are inadequate. Perhaps they are misleading. It is to be hoped in that case that we can eventually improve upon them. But adequate terms—whatever those terms may turn out to be—will certainly have to be terms which do justice to the special kind of structure which seems to emerge as the common structure of poems so diverse on other counts as are *The Rape of the Lock* and "Tears, Idle Tears."

The conventional terms are much worse than inadequate: they are positively misleading in their implication that the poem constitutes a "statement" of some sort, the statement being true or false, and expressed more or less clearly or eloquently or beautifully; for it is from this formula that most of the common heresies about poetry derive. The formula begins by introducing a dualism which thenceforward is rarely overcome, and which at best can be overcome only by the most elaborate and clumsy qualifications. Where it is

6. A rhymed couplet in iambic pentameter (called "heroic" because of its use in English epic poetry).

not overcome, it leaves the critic lodged upon one or the other of the horns of a dilemma: the critic is forced to judge the poem by its political or scientific or philosophical truth; or, he is forced to judge the poem by its form as conceived externally and detached from human experience. Mr. Alfred Kazin,[7] for example, to take an instance from a recent and popular book, accuses the "new formalists"—his choice of that epithet is revealing—of accepting the latter horn of the dilemma because he notices that they have refused the former. In other words, since they refuse to rank poems by their messages, he assumes that they are compelled to rank them by their formal embellishments.

The omnipresence of this dilemma, a false dilemma, I believe, will also account for the fact that so much has been made in the preceding chapters of the resistance which any good poem sets up against all attempts to paraphrase it. The point is surely not that we cannot describe adequately enough for many purposes what the poem in general is "about" and what the general effect of the poem is: *The Rape of the Lock* is about the foibles of an eighteenth-century belle. The effect of "Corinna's going a-Maying" is one of gaiety tempered by the poignance of the fleetingness of youth. We can very properly use paraphrases as pointers and as shorthand references provided that we know what we are doing. But it is highly important that we know what we are doing and that we see plainly that the paraphrase is not the real core of meaning which constitutes the essence of the poem.

For the imagery and the rhythm are not merely the instruments by which this fancied core-of-meaning-which-can-be-expressed-in-a-paraphrase is directly rendered. Even in the simplest poem their mediation is not positive and direct. Indeed, whatever statement we may seize upon as incorporating the "meaning" of the poem, immediately the imagery and the rhythm seem to set up tensions with it, warping and twisting it, qualifying and revising it. This is true of Wordsworth's "Ode" no less than of Donne's "Canonization." To illustrate: if we say that the "Ode" celebrates the spontaneous "naturalness" of the child, there is the poem itself to indicate that Nature has a more sinister aspect—that the process by which the poetic lamb becomes the dirty old sheep or the child racing over the meadows becomes the balding philosopher is a process that is thoroughly "natural." Or, if we say that the thesis of the "Ode" is that the child brings into the natural world a supernatural glory which acquaintance with the world eventually and inevitably quenches in the light of common day, there is the last stanza and the drastic qualifications which it asserts: it is significant that the thoughts that lie too deep for tears are mentioned in this sunset stanza of the "Ode" and that they are thoughts, not of the child, but of the man.

We have precisely the same problem if we make our example *The Rape of the Lock*. Does the poet assert that Belinda is a goddess? Or does he say that she is a brainless chit? Whichever alternative we take, there are elaborate qualifications to be made. Moreover, if the simple propositions offered seem in their forthright simplicity to make too easy the victory of the poem over any possible statement of its meaning, then let the reader try to formulate a proposition that will say what the poem "says." As his proposition approaches adequacy, he will

7. American critic (1915–1998); his book is *On Native Grounds: An Interpretation of Modern American Prose Literature* (1942).

find, not only that it has increased greatly in length, but that it has begun to fill itself up with reservations and qualifications—and most significant of all—the formulator will find that he has himself begun to fall back upon metaphors of his own in his attempt to indicate what the poem "says." In sum, his proposition, as it approaches adequacy, ceases to be a proposition.

Consider one more case, "Corinna's going a-Maying." Is the doctrine preached to Corinna throughout the first four stanzas true? Or is it damnably false? Or is it a "harmlesse follie"? Here perhaps we shall be tempted to take the last option as the saving mean—what the poem really *says*—and my account of the poem at the end of the third chapter is perhaps susceptible of this interpretation—or misinterpretation. If so, it is high time to clear the matter up. For we mistake matters grossly if we take the poem to be playing with opposed extremes, only to point the golden mean in a doctrine which, at the end, will correct the falsehood of extremes. The reconcilement of opposites which the poet characteristically makes is not that of a prudent splitting of the difference between antithetical overemphases.

It is not so in Wordsworth's poem nor in Keats's nor in Pope's. It is not so even in this poem of Herrick's. For though the poem reflects, if we read it carefully, the primacy of the Christian mores, the pressure exerted throughout the poem is upon the pagan appeal; and the poem ends, significantly, with a reiteration of the appeal to Corinna to go a-Maying, an appeal which, if qualified by the Christian view, still, in a sense, has been deepened and made more urgent by that very qualification. The imagery of loss and decay, it must be remembered, comes in this last stanza after the admission that the May-day rites[8] are not a real religion but a "harmless follie."

If we are to get all these qualifications into our formulation of what the poem says—and they are relevant—then, our formulation of the "statement" made by Herrick's poem will turn out to be quite as difficult as that of Pope's mock-epic. The truth of the matter is that all such formulations lead away from the center of the poem—not toward it; that the "prose-sense" of the poem is not a rack on which the stuff of the poem is hung; that it does not represent the "inner" structure or the "essential" structure or the "real" structure of the poem. We may use—and in many connections must use—such formulations as more or less convenient ways of referring to parts of the poem. But such formulations are scaffoldings which we may properly for certain purposes throw about the building: we must not mistake them for the internal and essential structure of the building itself.

Indeed, one may sum up by saying that most of the distempers of criticism come about from yielding to the temptation to the take certain remarks which we make *about* the poem—statements about what it says or about what truth it gives or about what formulations it illustrates—for the essential core of the poem itself. As W. M. Urban puts it in his *Language and Reality*:[9] "The general principle of the inseparability of intuition and expression holds with special force for the aesthetic intuition. Here it means that form and content, or content and medium, are inseparable. The artist does not first intuit his object and then find the appropriate medium. It is rather in and

8. The traditional celebration of spring on May 1 including setting up and dancing around a maypole, crowning a May queen, and other amusements.

9. Wilbur Marshall Urban, *Language and Reality: The Philosophy of Language and the Principles of Symbolism* (1939).

through his medium that he intuits the object." So much for the process of composition. As for the critical process: "To pass from the intuitible to the nonintuitible is to negate the function and meaning of the symbol." For it "is precisely because the more universal and ideal relations cannot be adequately expressed directly that they are indirectly expressed by means of the more intuitible." The most obvious examples of such error (and for that reason those which are really least dangerous) are those theories which frankly treat the poem as propaganda. The most subtle (and the most stubbornly rooted in the ambiguities of language) are those which, beginning with the "paraphrasable" elements of the poem, refer the other elements of the poem finally to some role subordinate to the paraphrasable elements. (The relation between all the elements must surely be an organic one—there can be no question about that. There is, however, a very serious question as to whether the paraphrasable elements have primacy.)

Mr. Winters'[1] position will furnish perhaps the most respectable example of the paraphrastic heresy. He assigns primacy to the "rational meaning" of the poem. "The relationship, in the poem, between rational statement and feeling," he remarks in his latest book, "is thus seen to be that of motive to emotion." He goes on to illustrate his point by a brief and excellent analysis of the following lines from Browning:

So wore night; the East was gray,
White the broad-faced hemlock flowers. . . . [2]

"The verb *wore*," he continues, "means literally that the night passed, but it carries with it connotations of exhaustion and attrition which belong to the condition of the protagonist; and grayness is a color which we associate with such a condition. If we change the phrase to read: 'Thus night passed,' we shall have the same rational meaning, and a meter quite as respectable, but no trace of the power of the line: the connotation of *wore* will be lost, and the connotation of *gray* will remain in a state of ineffective potentiality."

But the word *wore* does not mean *literally* "that the night passed," it means literally "that the night *wore*"—whatever *wore* may mean, and as Winters' own admirable analysis indicates, *wore* "means," whether *rationally* or *irrationally*, a great deal. Furthermore, "So wore night" and "Thus night passed" can be said to have "the same rational meaning" only if we equate "rational meaning" with the meaning of a loose paraphrase. And can a loose paraphrase be said to be the "motive to emotion"? Can it be said to "generate" the feelings in question? (Or, would Mr. Winters not have us equate "rational statement" and "rational meaning"?)

Much more is at stake here than any quibble. In view of the store which Winters sets by rationality and of his penchant for poems which make their evaluations overtly, and in view of his frequent blindness to those poems which do not—in view of these considerations, it is important to see that what "So wore night" and "Thus night passed" have in common as their "rational meaning" is not the "rational meaning" of each but the lowest common denominator of both. To refer the structure of the poem to what is finally a paraphrase of the poem is to refer it to something outside the poem.

To repeat, most of our difficulties in criticism are rooted in the heresy of

1. The American poet and critic Yvor Winters (1900–1968).

2. "A Serenade at the Villa" (1855), by the English poet Robert Browning (1812–1889).

paraphrase. If we allow ourselves to be misled by it, we distort the relation of the poem to its "truth," we raise the problem of belief in a vicious and crippling form, we split the poem between its "form" and its "content"—we bring the statement to be conveyed into an unreal competition with science or philosophy or theology. In short, we put our questions about the poem in a form calculated to produce the battles of the last twenty-five years over the "use of poetry."[3]

If we allow ourselves to be misled by the heresy of paraphrase, we run the risk of doing even more violence to the internal order of the poem itself. By taking the paraphrase as our point of stance, we misconceive the function of metaphor and meter. We demand logical coherences where they are sometimes irrelevant, and we fail frequently to see imaginative coherences on levels where they are highly relevant. Some of the implications of the paraphrastic heresy are so stubborn and so involved that I have thought best to relegate them to an appendix.[4] There the reader who is interested may find further discussion of the problem and, I could hope, answers to certain misapprehensions of the positive theory to be adumbrated here.

But what would be a positive theory? We tend to embrace the doctrine of a logical structure the more readily because, to many of us, the failure to do so seems to leave the meaning of the poem hopelessly up in the air. The alternative position will appear to us to lack even the relative stability of an Ivory Tower: it is rather commitment to a free balloon. For, to deny the possibility of pinning down what the poem "says" to some "statement" will seem to assert that the poem really says nothing. And to point out what has been suggested in earlier chapters and brought to a head in this one, namely, that one can never measure a poem against the scientific or philosophical yardstick for the reason that the poem, when laid along the yardstick, is never the "full poem" but an abstraction from the poem—such an argument will seem to such readers a piece of barren logic-chopping—a transparent dodge.

Considerations of strategy then, if nothing more, dictate some positive account of what a poem is and does. And some positive account can be given, though I cannot promise to do more than suggest what a poem is, nor will my terms turn out to be anything more than metaphors.[5]

The essential structure of a poem (as distinguished from the rational or logical structure of the "statement" which we abstract from it) resembles that of architecture or painting: it is a pattern of resolved stresses. Or, to move closer still to poetry by considering the temporal arts, the structure of a poem resembles that of a ballet or musical composition. It is a pattern of resolutions and balances and harmonizations, developed through a temporal scheme.[6]

3. I do not, of course, intend to minimize the fact that some of these battles have been highly profitable, or to imply that the foregoing paragraphs could have been written except for the illumination shed by the discussions of the last 25 years. [Brooks's note].

4. In an appendix, Brooks discusses literary history, value judgments, and critical relativism.

5. For those who cannot be content with metaphors (or with the particular metaphors which I can give) I recommend René Wellek's excellent "The Mode of Existence of a Literary Work of Art" (*Southern Review*, spring, 1942). I shall not try to reproduce here as a handy, thumb-nail definition his account of a poem as "a stratified system of norms," for the definition would be relatively meaningless without the further definitions which he assigns to the individual terms which he uses. I have made no special use of his terms in this chapter, but I believe that the generalizations about poetry outlined here can be thoroughly accommodated to the position which his essay sets forth [Brooks's note]. Wellek (1903–1995), Austrian-born New Critic and historian of criticism.

6. In recent numbers of *Accent*, two critics for whose work I have high regard have emphasized the dynamic character of poetry. Kenneth Burke argues that if we are to consider a poem as a poem, we must consider it as a "mode of action." R. P. Blackmur asks us to think of it as gesture, "the

Or, to move still closer to poetry, the structure of a poem resembles that of a play. This last example, of course, risks introducing once more the distracting element, since drama, like poetry, makes use of words. Yet, on the whole, most of us are less inclined to force the concept of "statement" on drama than on a lyric poem; for the very nature of drama is that of something "acted out"—something which arrives at its conclusion through conflict—something which builds conflict into its very being. The dynamic nature of drama, in short, allows us to regard it as *an action* rather than as a formula for action or as a statement about action. For this reason, therefore, perhaps the most helpful analogy by which to suggest the structure of poetry is that of the drama, and for many readers at least, the least confusing way in which to approach a poem is to think of it as a drama.

The general point, of course, is not that either poetry or drama makes no use of ideas, or that either is "merely emotional"—whatever *that* is—or that there is not the closest and most important relationship between the intellectual materials which they absorb into their structure and other elements in the structure. The relationship between the intellectual and the nonintellectual elements in a poem is actually far more intimate than the conventional accounts would represent it to be: the relationship is not that of an idea "wrapped in emotion" or a "prose-sense decorated by sensuous imagery."

The dimension in which the poem moves is not one which excludes ideas, but one which does include attitudes. The dimension includes ideas, to be sure; we can always abstract an "idea" from a poem—even from the simplest poem—even from a lyric so simple and unintellectual as

Western wind, when wilt thou blow
That the small rain down can rain?
Christ, that my love were in my arms
And I in my bed again![7]

But the idea which we abstract—assuming that we can all agree on what that idea is—will always be *abstracted*: it will always be the projection of a plane along a line or the projection of a cone upon a plane.

If this last analogy proves to be more confusing than illuminating, let us return to the analogy with drama. We have argued that any proposition asserted in a poem is not to be taken in abstraction but is justified, in terms of the poem, if it is justified at all, not by virtue of its scientific or historical or philosophical truth, but is justified in terms of a principle analogous to that of dramatic propriety. Thus, the proposition that "Beauty is truth, truth beauty"[8] is given its precise meaning and significance by its relation to the total context of the poem.

---

outward and dramatic play of inward and imagined meaning." I do not mean to commit either of these critics to my own interpretation of dramatic or symbolic action; and I have, on my own part, several rather important reservations with respect to Mr. Burke's position. But there are certainly large areas of agreement among our positions. The reader might also compare the account of poetic structure given in this chapter with the following passage from Susanne Langer's *Philosophy in a New Key*: ". . . though the *material* of poetry is verbal, its import is not the literal assertion made in the words, but *the way the assertion is made*, and this involves the sound, the tempo, the aura of associations of the words, the long or short sequences of ideas, the wealth or poverty of transient imagery that contains them, the sudden arrest of fantasy by pure fact, or of familiar fact by sudden fantasy, the suspense of literal meaning by a sustained ambiguity resolved in a long-awaited key-word, and the unifying, all-embracing artifice of rhythm" [Brooks's note]. BURKE (1897–1993), American critic and philosopher. Blackmur (1904–1965), American critic and poet. Langer (1895–1985), American philosopher and aesthetician.

7. Anonymous 15th-century lyric.

8. From the next-to-last line of Keats's "Ode on a Grecian Urn."

This principle is easy enough to see when the proposition is asserted overtly in the poem—that is, when it constitutes a specific detail of the poem. But the reader may well ask: is it not possible to frame a proposition, a statement, which will adequately represent the total meaning of the poem; that is, is it not possible to elaborate a summarizing proposition which will "say," briefly and in the form of a proposition, what the poem "says" as a poem, a proposition which will say it fully and will say it exactly, no more and no less? Could not the poet, if he had chosen, have framed such a proposition? Cannot we as readers and critics frame such a proposition?

The answer must be that the poet himself obviously did not—else he would not have had to write his poem. We as readers can attempt to frame such a proposition in our effort to understand the poem; it may well help toward an understanding. Certainly, the efforts to arrive at such propositions can do no harm *if we do not mistake them for the inner core of the poem*—if we do not mistake them for "what the poem *really* says." For, if we take one of them to represent the essential poem, we have to disregard the qualifications exerted by the total context as of no account, or else we have assumed that we can reproduce the effect of the total context in a condensed prose statement.[9]

But to deny that the coherence of a poem is reflected in a logical paraphrase of its "real meaning" is not, of course, to deny coherence to poetry; it is rather to assert that its coherence is to be sought elsewhere. The characteristic unity of a poem (even of those poems which may accidentally possess a logical unity as well as this poetic unity) lies in the unification of attitudes into a hierarchy subordinated to a total and governing attitude. In the unified poem, the poet has "come to terms" with his experience. The poem does not merely eventuate in a logical conclusion. The conclusion of the poem is the working out of the various tensions—set up by whatever means—by propositions, metaphors, symbols. The unity is achieved by a dramatic process, not a logical; it represents an equilibrium of forces, not a formula. It is "proved" as a dramatic conclusion is proved: by its ability to resolve the conflicts which have been accepted as the *données* of the drama.

Thus, it is easy to see why the relation of each item to the whole context is crucial, and why the effective and essential structure of the poem has to do with the complex of attitudes achieved. A scientific proposition can stand alone. If it is true, it is true. But the expression of an attitude, apart from the occasion which generates it and the situation which it encompasses, is meaningless. For example, the last two lines of the "Intimations" ode,

> *To me the meanest flower that blows can give*
> *Thoughts that do often lie too deep for tears,*

9. We may, it is true, be able to adumbrate what the poem says if we allow ourselves enough words, and if we make enough reservations and qualifications, thus attempting to come nearer to the meaning of the poem by successive approximations and refinements, gradually encompassing the meaning and pointing to the area in which it lies rather than realizing it. The earlier chapters of this book, if they are successful, are obviously illustrations of this process. But such adumbrations will lack, not only the tension—the dramatic force—of the poem; they will be at best crude approximations of the poem. Moreover—and this is the crucial point—they will be compelled to resort to the methods of the poem—analogy, metaphor, symbol, etc.—in order to secure even this near an approximation.

Urban's comment upon this problem is interesting: he says that if we expand the symbol, "we lose the 'sense' or value of the symbol *as symbol*. The solution . . . seems to me to lie in an adequate theory of interpretation of the symbol. It does not consist in substituting *literal* for symbol sentences, in other words substituting 'blunt' truth for symbolic truth, but rather in deepening and enriching the meaning of the symbol" [Brooks's note].

when taken in isolation—I do not mean quoted in isolation by one who is even vaguely acquainted with the context—makes a statement which is sentimental if taken in reference to the speaker, and one which is patent nonsense if taken with a general reference. The man in the street (of whom the average college freshman is a good enough replica) knows that the meanest flower that grows does not give *him* thoughts that lie too deep for tears: and, if he thinks about the matter at all, he is inclined to feel that the person who can make such an assertion is a very fuzzy sentimentalist.

We have already seen the ease with which the statement "Beauty is truth, truth beauty" becomes detached from its context, even in the hands of able critics; and we have seen the misconceptions that ensue when this detachment occurs. To take one more instance: the last stanza of Herrick's "Corinna," taken in isolation, would probably not impress the average reader as sentimental nonsense. Yet it would suffer quite as much by isolation from its context as would the lines from Keats's "Ode." For, as mere statement, it would become something flat and obvious—of course our lives are short! And the conclusion from the fact would turn into an obvious truism for the convinced pagan, and, for the convinced Christian, equally obvious, though damnable, nonsense.

Perhaps this is why the poet, to people interested in hard-and-fast generalizations, must always seem to be continually engaged in blurring out distinctions, effecting compromises, or, at the best, coming to his conclusions only after provoking and unnecessary delays. But this last position is merely another variant of the paraphrastic heresy: to assume it is to misconceive the end of poetry—to take its meanderings as negative, or to excuse them (with the comfortable assurance that the curved line is the line of beauty) because we can conceive the purpose of a poem to be only the production, in the end, of a proposition—of a statement.

But the meanderings of a good poem (they are meanderings only from the standpoint of the prose paraphrase of the poem) are not negative, and they do not have to be excused; and most of all, we need to see what their positive function is; for unless we can assign them a positive function, we shall find it difficult to explain why one divergence from "the prose line of the argument" is not as good as another. The truth is that the apparent irrelevancies which metrical pattern and metaphor introduce do become relevant when we realize that they function in a good poem to modify, qualify, and develop the total attitude which we are to take in coming to terms with the total situation.

If the last sentence seems to take a dangerous turn toward some special "use of poetry"—some therapeutic value for the sake of which poetry is to be cultivated—I can only say that I have in mind no special ills which poetry is to cure. Uses for poetry are always to be found, and doubtless will continue to be found. But my discussion of the structure of poetry is not being conditioned at this point by some new and special role which I expect poetry to assume in the future or some new function to which I would assign it. The structure described—a structure of "gestures" or attitudes—seems to me to describe the essential structure of both the *Odyssey* and *The Waste Land*.[1] It

1. The modernist poem (1922) by T. S. ELIOT, usually not seen as structured like Homer's Greek epic (8th c. B.C.E.).

seems to be the kind of structure which the ten poems considered in this book possess in common.

If the structure of poetry is a structure of the order described, that fact may explain (if not justify) the frequency with which I have had to have recourse, in the foregoing chapters, to terms like "irony" and "paradox." By using the term irony, one risks, of course, making the poem seem arch and self-conscious, since irony, for most readers of poetry, is associated with satire, *vers de société*,[2] and other "intellectual" poetries. Yet, the necessity for some such term ought to be apparent; and irony is the most general term that we have for the kind of qualification which the various elements in a context receive from the context. This kind of qualification, as we have seen, is of tremendous importance in any poem. Moreover, irony is our most general term for indicating that recognition of incongruities—which, again, pervades all poetry to a degree far beyond what our conventional criticism has been heretofore willing to allow.

Irony in this general sense, then, is to be found in Tennyson's "Tears, Idle Tears" as well as in Donne's "Canonization." We have, of course, been taught to expect to find irony in Pope's *Rape of the Lock*, but there is a profound irony in Keats's "Ode on a Grecian Urn"; and there is irony of a very powerful sort in Wordsworth's "Intimations" ode. For the thrusts and pressures exerted by the various symbols in this poem are not avoided by the poet: they are taken into account and played, one against the other. Indeed, the symbols—from a scientific point of view—are used perversely: it is the child who is the best philosopher; it is from a kind of darkness—from something that is "shadowy"—that the light proceeds; growth into manhood is viewed, not as an extrication from, but as an incarceration within, a prison.

There should be no mystery as to why this must be so. The terms of science are abstract symbols which do not change under the pressure of the context. They are pure (or aspire to be pure) denotations; they are defined in advance. They are not to be warped into new meanings. But where is the dictionary which contains the terms of a poem? It is a truism that the poet is continually forced to remake language. As Eliot has put it, his task is to "dislocate language into meaning."[3] And, from the standpoint of a scientific vocabulary, this is precisely what he performs: for, rationally considered, the ideal language would contain one term for each meaning, and the relation between term and meaning would be constant. But the word, as the poet uses it, has to be conceived of, not as a discrete particle of meaning, but as a potential of meaning, a nexus or cluster of meanings.

What is true of the poet's language in detail is true of the larger wholes of poetry. And therefore, if we persist in approaching the poem as primarily a rational statement, we ought not to be surprised if the statement seems to be presented to us always in the ironic mode. When we consider the statement immersed in the poem, it presents itself to us, like the stick immersed in the pool of water, warped and bent. Indeed, whatever the statement, it will always show itself as deflected away from a positive, straightforward formulation.

It may seem perverse, however, to maintain, in the face of our revived

2. Verse of society (French); that is, verse that wittily treats topics favored by polite society.

3. From T. S. Eliot's essay "The Metaphysical Poets" (1921; see above).

interest in Donne, that the essential structure of poetry is not logical. For Donne has been appealed to of late as the great master of metaphor who imposes a clean logic on his images beside which the ordering of the images in Shakespeare's sonnets is fumbling and loose. It is perfectly true that Donne makes a great show of logic; but two matters need to be observed. In the first place, the elaborated and "logical" figure is not Donne's only figure or even his staple one. "Telescoped" figures like "Made one anothers hermitage" are to be found much more frequently than the celebrated comparison of the souls of the lovers to the legs of a pair of compasses. In the second place, where Donne uses "logic," he regularly uses it to justify illogical positions. He employs it to overthrow a conventional position or to "prove" an essentially illogical one.

Logic, as Donne uses it, is nearly always an ironic logic to state the claims of an idea or attitude which we have agreed, with our everyday logic, is false. This is not to say, certainly, that Donne is not justified in using his logic so, or that the best of his poems are not "proved" in the only senses in which poems can be proved.

But the proof is not a logical proof. "The Canonization" will scarcely prove to the hard-boiled naturalist that the lovers, by giving up the world, actually attain a better world. Nor will the argument advanced in the poem convince the dogmatic Christian that Donne's lovers are really saints.

In using logic, Donne as a poet is fighting the devil with fire. To adopt Robert Penn Warren's[4] metaphor (which, though I lift it somewhat scandalously out of another context, will apply to this one): "The poet, somewhat less spectacularly [than the saint], proves his vision by submitting it to the fires of irony—to the drama of the structure—in the hope that the fires will refine it. In other words, the poet wishes to indicate that his vision has been earned, that it can survive reference to the complexities and contradictions of experience."

The same principle that inspires the presence of irony in so many of our great poems also accounts for the fact that so many of them seem to be built around paradoxes. Here again the conventional associations of the term may prejudice the reader just as the mention of Donne may prejudice him. For Donne, as one type of reader knows all too well, was of that group of poets who wished to impress their audience with their cleverness. All of us are familiar with the censure passed upon Donne and his followers by Dr. Johnson,[5] and a great many of us still retain it as our own, softening only the rigor of it and the thoroughness of its application, but not giving it up as a principle.

Yet there are better reasons than that of rhetorical vain-glory that have induced poet after poet to choose ambiguity and paradox rather than plain, discursive simplicity. It is not enough for the poet to analyse his experience as the scientist does, breaking it up into parts, distinguishing part from part, classifying the various parts. His task is finally to unify experience. He must return to us the unity of the experience itself as man knows it in his own experience. The poem, if it be a true poem, is a simulacrum of reality—in this

4. Poet, novelist, and critic (1905–1989); co-editor with Brooks of *Understanding Poetry* (1938). The quotation is from Warren's essay "Pure and Impure Poetry" (1943).

5. SAMUEL JOHNSON (1709–1784), English critic, lexicographer, and poet. See his comments on metaphysical poetry in *Life of Cowley* (1783; above).

sense, at least, it is an "imitation"—by *being* an experience rather than any mere statement about experience or any mere abstraction from experience.

Tennyson cannot be content with *saying* that in memory the poet seems both dead *and* alive; he must dramatize its life-in-death for us, and his dramatization involves, necessarily, ironic shock and wonder. The dramatization demands that the antithetical aspects of memory be coalesced into one entity which—if we take it on the level of statement—is a paradox, the assertion of the union of opposites. Keats's Urn must express a life which is above life and its vicissitudes, but it must also bear witness to the fact that its life is not life at all but is a kind of death. To put it in other terms, the Urn must, in its role as historian, assert that myth is truer than history. Donne's lovers must reject the world in order to possess the world.

Or, to take one further instance: Wordsworth's light must serve as the common symbol for aspects of man's vision which seem mutually incompatible—intuition and analytic reason. Wordsworth's poem, as a matter of fact, typifies beautifully the poet's characteristic problem itself. For even this poem, which testifies so heavily to the way in which the world is split up and parceled out under the growing light of reason, cannot rest in this fact as its own mode of perception, and still be a poem. Even after the worst has been said about man's multiple vision, the poet must somehow prove that the child is father to the man, that the dawn light is still somehow the same light as the evening light.

If the poet, then, must perforce dramatize the oneness of the experience, even though paying tribute to its diversity, then his use of paradox and ambiguity is seen as necessary. He is not simply trying to spice up, with a superficially exciting or mystifying rhetoric, the old stale stockpot (though doubtless this will be what the inferior poet does generally and what the real poet does in his lapses). He is rather giving us an insight which preserves the unity of experience and which, at its higher and more serious levels, triumphs over the apparently contradictory and conflicting elements of experience by unifying them into a new pattern.

Wordsworth's "Intimations" ode, then, is not only a poem, but, among other things, a parable about poetry. Keats's "Ode on a Grecian Urn" is quite obviously such a parable. And, indeed, most of the poems which we have discussed in this study may be taken as such parables.

In one sense, Pope's treatment of Belinda raises all the characteristic problems of poetry. For Pope, in dealing with his "goddess," must face the claims of naturalism and of common sense which would deny divinity to her. Unless he faces them, he is merely a sentimentalist. He must do an even harder thing: he must transcend the conventional and polite attributions of divinity which would be made to her as an acknowledged belle. Otherwise, he is merely trivial and obvious. He must "prove" her divinity against the common-sense denial (the brutal denial) and against the conventional assertion (the polite denial). The poetry must be wrested from the context: Belinda's lock, which is what the rude young man wants and which Belinda rather prudishly defends and which the naturalist asserts is only animal and which displays in its curled care the style of a particular era of history, must be given a place of permanence among the stars.

1947

The Formalist Critics[1]

Here are some articles of faith I could subscribe to: *That literary criticism is a description and an evaluation of its object.*

That the primary concern of criticism is with the problem of unity—the kind of whole which the literary work forms or fails to form, and the relation of the various parts to each other in building up this whole.

That the formal relations in a work of literature may include, but certainly exceed, those of logic.

That in a successful work, form and content cannot be separated.

That form is meaning.

That literature is ultimately metaphorical and symbolic.

That the general and the universal are not seized upon by abstraction, but got at through the concrete and the particular.

That literature is not a surrogate for religion.

That, as Allen Tate[2] says, "specific moral problems" are the subject matter of literature, but that the purpose of literature is not to point a moral.

That the principles of criticism define the area relevant to literary criticism; they do not constitute a method for carrying out the criticism.

Such statements as these would not, however, even though greatly elaborated, serve any useful purpose here. The interested reader already knows the general nature of the critical position adumbrated—or, if he does not, he can find it set forth in writings of mine or of other critics of like sympathy. Moreover, a condensed restatement of the position here would probably beget as many misunderstandings as have past attempts to set it forth. It seems much more profitable to use the present occasion for dealing with some persistent misunderstandings and objections.

In the first place, to make the poem or the novel the central concern of criticism has appeared to mean cutting it loose from its author and from his life as a man, with his own particular hopes, fears, interests, conflicts, etc. A criticism so limited may seem bloodless and hollow. It will seem so to the typical professor of literature in the graduate school, where the study of literature is still primarily a study of the ideas and personality of the author as revealed in his letters, his diaries, and the recorded conversations of his friends. It will certainly seem so to literary gossip columnists who purvey literary chitchat. It may also seem so to the young poet or novelist, beset with his own problems of composition and with his struggles to find a subject and a style and to get a hearing for himself.

In the second place, to emphasize the work seems to involve severing it from those who actually read it, and this severance may seem drastic and therefore disastrous. After all, literature is written to be read. Wordsworth's poet was a man speaking to men.[3] In each Sunday *Times*, Mr. J. Donald Adams[4] points out that the hungry sheep look up and are not fed; and less

1. Originally published in the *Kenyon Review* in a series titled "My Credo."
2. American editor, poet, novelist, and critic (1899–1979).
3. See WILLIAM WORDSWORTH (1770–1850), preface to *Lyrical Ballads* (1800; above).
4. James Donald Adams (1891–1968), author and editor, best known for his weekly column (which began in 1943) in the *New York Times Book Review*. "The hungry sheep look up and are not fed" echoes line 125 of John Milton's "Lycidas" (1637), a pastoral elegy for the poet Edward King.

strenuous moralists than Mr. Adams are bound to feel a proper revulsion against "mere aestheticism." Moreover, if we neglect the audience which reads the work, including that for which it was presumably written, the literary historian is prompt to point out that the kind of audience that Pope[5] had did condition the kind of poetry that he wrote. The poem has its roots in history, past or present. Its place in the historical context simply cannot be ignored.

I have stated these objections as sharply as I can because I am sympathetic with the state of mind which is prone to voice them. Man's experience is indeed a seamless garment, no part of which can be separated from the rest. Yet if we urge this fact of inseparability against the drawing of distinctions, then there is no point in talking about criticism at all. I am assuming that distinctions are necessary and useful and indeed inevitable.

The formalist critic knows as well as anyone that poems and plays and novels are written by men—that they do not somehow happen—and that they are written as expressions of particular personalities and are written from all sorts of motives—for money, from a desire to express oneself, for the sake of a cause, etc. Moreover, the formalist critic knows as well as anyone that literary works are merely potential until they are read—that is, that they are re-created in the minds of actual readers, who vary enormously in their capabilities, their interests, their prejudices, their ideas. But the formalist critic is concerned primarily with the work itself. Speculation on the mental processes of the author takes the critic away from the work into biography and psychology. There is no reason, of course, why he should not turn away into biography and psychology. Such explorations are very much worth making. But they should not be confused with an account of the work. Such studies describe the process of composition, not the structure of the thing composed, and they may be performed quite as validly for the poor work as for the good one. They may be validly performed for any kind of expression—non-literary as well as literary.

On the other hand, exploration of the various readings which the work has received also takes the critic away from the work into psychology and the history of taste. The various imports of a given work may well be worth studying. I. A. Richards has put us all in his debt by demonstrating what different experiences may be derived from the same poem by an apparently homogeneous group of readers;[6] and the scholars have pointed out, all along, how different Shakespeare appeared to an 18th Century as compared with a 19th Century audience; or how sharply divergent are the estimates of John Donne's[7] lyrics from historical period to historical period. But such work, valuable and necessary as it may be, is to be distinguished from a criticism of the work itself. The formalist critic, because he wants to criticize the work itself, makes two assumptions: (1) he assumes that the relevant part of the author's intention is what he got actually into his work; that is, he assumes that the author's intention *as realized* is the "intention" that counts, not necessarily what he was conscious of trying to do, or what he now remembers he was then trying to do. And (2) the formalist critic assumes an ideal reader: that is, instead of focusing on the varying spectrum of possible readings, he

5. ALEXANDER POPE (1688–1744), English poet and satirist.

6. Brooks refers here to *Practical Criticism: A Study of Literary Judgment* (1929), by the English critic and theorist Richards (1893–1979).

7. English poet (1576–1631).

attempts to find a central point of reference from which he can focus upon the structure of the poem or novel.

But there *is* no ideal reader, someone is prompt to point out, and he will probably add that it is sheer arrogance that allows the critic, with his own blindsides and prejudices, to put himself in the position of that ideal reader. There is no ideal reader, of course, and I suppose that the practising critic can never be too often reminded of the gap between his reading and the "true" reading of the poem. But for the purpose of focusing upon the poem rather than upon his own reactions, it is a defensible strategy. Finally, of course, it is the strategy that all critics of whatever persuasion are forced to adopt. (The alternatives are desperate: either we say that one person's readings is as good as another's and equate those readings on a basis of absolute equality and thus deny the possibility of any standard reading. Or else we take a lowest common denominator of the various readings that have been made; that is, we frankly move from literary criticism into socio-psychology. To propose taking a consensus of the opinions of "qualified" readers is simply to split the ideal reader into a group of ideal readers.) As consequences of the distinction just referred to, the formalist critic rejects two popular tests for literary value. The first proves the value of the work from the author's "sincerity" (or the intensity of the author's feelings as he composed it). If we heard that Mr. Guest[8] testified that he put his heart and soul into his poems, we would not be very much impressed, though I should see no reason to doubt such a statement from Mr. Guest. It would simply be critically irrelevant. Ernest Hemingway's statement in a recent issue of *Time* magazine that he counts his last novel his best is of interest for Hemingway's biography, but most readers of *Across the River and Into the Trees*[9] would agree that it proves nothing at all about the value of the novel—that in this case the judgment is simply pathetically inept. We discount also such tests for poetry as that proposed by A. E. Housman[1]—the bristling of his beard at the reading of a good poem. The intensity of his reaction has critical significance only in proportion as we have already learned to trust him as a reader. Even so, what it tells us is something about Housman—nothing decisive about the poem.

It is unfortunate if this playing down of such responses seems to deny humanity to either writer or reader. The critic may enjoy certain works very much and may be indeed intensely moved by them. I am, and I have no embarrassment in admitting the fact; but a detailed description of my emotional state on reading certain works has little to do with indicating to an interested reader what the work is and how the parts of it are related.

Should all criticism, then, be self-effacing and analytic? I hope that the answer is implicit in what I have already written, but I shall go on to spell it out. Of course not. That will depend upon the occasion and the audience. In practice, the critic's job is rarely a purely critical one. He is much more

8. Edgar A. Guest (1881–1959), popular author whose sentimental poems were published daily in the *Detroit Free Press*.

9. *Across the River and into the Trees* received harsh reviews when it was published in 1950. Hemingway (1899–1961), American writer of fiction.

1. Classical scholar and poet (1859–1936). Housman stated in "The Name and Nature of Poetry" (1933): "Experience has taught me, when I am shaving of a morning, to keep watch over my thoughts, because, if a line of poetry strays into my memory, my skin bristles so that the razor ceases to act."

likely to be involved in dozens of more or less related tasks, some of them trivial, some of them important. He may be trying to get a hearing for a new author, or to get the attention of the freshman sitting in the back row. He may be comparing two authors, or editing a text; writing a brief newspaper review or reading a paper before the Modern Language Association.[2] He may even be simply talking with a friend, talking about literature for the hell of it. Parable, anecdote, epigram, metaphor—these and a hundred other devices may be thoroughly legitimate for his varying purposes. He is certainly not to be asked to suppress his personal enthusiasms or his interest in social history or in politics. Least of all is he being asked to *present* his criticisms as the close reading of a text. Tact, common sense, and uncommon sense if he has it, are all requisite if the practising critic is to do his various jobs well.

But it will do the critic no harm to have a clear idea of what his specific job as a critic is. I can sympathize with writers who are tired of reading rather drab "critical analyses," and who recommend brighter, more amateur, and more "human" criticism. As ideals, these are excellent; as recipes for improving criticism, I have my doubts. Appropriate vulgarizations of these ideals are already flourishing, and have long flourished—in the class room presided over by the college lecturer of infectious enthusiasm, in the gossipy Book-of-the-Month Club bulletins, and in the columns of the *Saturday Review of Literature*.

I have assigned the critic a modest, though I think an important, role. With reference to the help which the critic can give to the practising artist, the role is even more modest. As critic, he can give only negative help. Literature is not written by formula: he can have no formula to offer. Perhaps he can do little more than indicate whether in his opinion the work has succeeded or failed. Healthy criticism and healthy creation do tend to go hand in hand. Everything else being equal, the creative artist is better off for being in touch with a vigorous criticism. But the other considerations are never equal, the case is always special, and in a given case the proper advice *could* be: quit reading criticism altogether, or read political science or history or philosophy—or join the army, or join the church.

There is certainly no doubt that the kind of specific and positive help that someone like Ezra Pound[3] was able to give to several writers of our time is in one sense the most important kind of criticism that there can be. I think that it is not unrelated to the kind of criticism that I have described: there is the same intense concern with the text which is being built up, the same concern with "technical problems." But many other things are involved—matters which lie outside the specific ambit of criticism altogether, among them a knowledge of the personality of the particular writer, the ability to stimulate, to make positive suggestions.

A literary work is a document and as a document can be analysed in terms of the forces that have produced it, or it may be manipulated as a force in its own right. It mirrors the past, it may influence the future. These facts it would be futile to deny, and I know of no critic who does deny them. But the reduction of a work of literature to its causes does not constitute literary

2. The primary North American professional organization for scholars in English and foreign languages and literatures.

3. American poet and critic (1885–1972). Pound worked vigorously to promote T. S. ELIOT (1888–1965), Robert Frost (1874–1963), James Joyce (1882–1941), and other writers.

criticism; nor does an estimate of its effects. Good literature is more than effective rhetoric applied to true ideas—even if we could agree upon a philosophical yardstick for measuring the truth of ideas and even if we could find some way that transcended nose-counting for determining the effectiveness of the rhetoric.

A recent essay by Lionel Trilling bears very emphatically upon this point.[4] (I refer to him the more readily because Trilling has registered some of his objections to the critical position that I maintain.) In the essay entitled "The Meaning of a Literary Idea," Trilling discusses the debt to Freud and Spengler of four American writers, O'Neill, Dos Passos, Wolfe, and Faulkner. Very justly, as it seems to me, he choose Faulkner as the contemporary writer who, along with Ernest Hemingway, best illustrates the power and importance of ideas in literature. Trilling is thoroughly aware that his choice will seem shocking and perhaps perverse, "because," as he writes, "Hemingway and Faulkner have insisted on their indifference to the conscious intellectual tradition of our time and have acquired the reputation of achieving their effects by means that have the least possible connection with any sort of intellectuality or even with intelligence."

Here Trilling shows not only acute discernment but an admirable honesty in electing to deal with the hard cases—with the writers who do not clearly and easily make the case for the importance of ideas. I applaud the discernment and the honesty, but I wonder whether the whole discussion in his essay does not indicate that Trilling is really much closer to the so-called "new critics" than perhaps he is aware. For Trilling, one notices, rejects any simple one-to-one relation between the truth of the idea and the value of the literary work in which it is embodied. Moreover, he does not claim that "recognizable ideas of a force or weight are 'used' in the work," or "new ideas of a certain force and weight are 'produced' by the work." He praises rather the fact that we feel that Hemingway and Faulkner are "intensely at work upon the recalcitrant stuff of life." The last point is made the matter of real importance. Whereas Dos Passos, O'Neill, and Wolfe make us "feel that *they* feel that they have said the last word," "we seldom have the sense that [Hemingway and Faulkner] . . . have misrepresented to themselves the nature and the difficulty of the matter they work on."

Trilling has chosen to state the situation in terms of the writer's activity (Faulkner is intensely at work, etc.). But this judgment is plainly an inference from the quality of Faulkner's novels—Trilling has not simply heard Faulkner say that he has had to struggle with his work. (I take it Mr. Hemingway's declaration about the effort he put into the last novel impresses Trilling as little as it impresses the rest of us.)

Suppose, then, that we tried to state Mr. Trilling's point, not in terms of the effort of the artist, but in terms of the structure of the work itself. Should we not get something very like the terms used by the formalist critics? A description in terms of "tensions," of symbolic development, of ironies and their resolution? In short, is not the formalist critic trying to describe in terms

4. The essay referred to is included in *The Liberal Imagination: Essays on Literature and Society* (1950). The American critic Trilling (1905–1975) discusses in it the influence of the Austrian founder of psychoanalysis SIGMUND FREUD (1856–1939) and the German philosopher of history Oswald Spengler (1880–1936), author of *The Decline of the West* (1918–22), on the playwright Eugene O'Neill (1888–1953) and the novelists John Dos Passos (1896–1970), Thomas Wolfe (1900–1938), and William Faulkner (1897–1962).

of the dynamic form of the work itself how the recalcitrancy of the material is acknowledged and dealt with?

Trilling's definition of "ideas" makes it still easier to accommodate my position to his. I have already quoted a passage in which he repudiates the notion that one has to show how recognizable ideas are "used" in the work, or new ideas are "produced" by the work. He goes on to write: "All that we need to do is account for a certain aesthetic effect as being in some important part achieved by a mental process which is not different from the process by which discursive ideas are conceived, and which is to be judged by some of the criteria by which an idea is judged." One would have to look far to find a critic "formal" enough to object to this. What some of us have been at pains to insist upon is that literature does not simply "exemplify" ideas or "produce" ideas—as Trilling acknowledges. But no one claims that the writer is an inspired idiot. He uses his mind and his reader ought to use his, in processes "not different from the process by which discursive ideas are conceived." Literature is not inimical to ideas. It thrives upon ideas, but it does not present ideas patly and neatly. It involves them with the "recalcitrant stuff of life." The literary critic's job is to deal with that involvement.

The mention of Faulkner invites a closing comment upon the critic's specific job. As I have described it, it may seem so modest that one could take its performance for granted. But consider the misreadings of Faulkner now current, some of them the work of the most brilliant critics that we have, some of them quite wrong-headed, and demonstrably so. What is true of Faulkner is only less true of many another author, including many writers of the past. Literature has many "uses"—and critics propose new uses, some of them exciting and spectacular. But all the multiform uses to which literature can be put rest finally upon our knowing what a given work "means." That knowledge is basic.

1951

WILLIAM K. WIMSATT JR. 1907–1975

MONROE C. BEARDSLEY 1915–1985

"The Intentional Fallacy" (1946) and "The Affective Fallacy" (1949), coauthored by William Kurtz Wimsatt Jr. and Monroe C. Beardsley, are two of the most important position papers in the history of twentieth-century criticism. Neither presents an argument that is wholly original, but each codifies a crucial tenet of New Critical formalist orthodoxy. In "The Intentional Fallacy," Wimsatt and Beardsley argue that we cannot use the author's intention, even when we possess information about it, to judge a literary work; the work is a public utterance, not a private one that depends for its meaning on the intent or design of its author. In the later piece, "The Affective Fallacy," Wimsatt and Beardsley emphasize that the meaning of a literary work is not equivalent to its effects, especially its emotional impact, on the reader. Both of these positions are connected to Wimsatt and Beardsley's formalist view that analysis must center on the text itself: the critic's task is to examine its linguistic structure and its aesthetic unity as an autonomous object.

Wimsatt, born in Washington, D.C., attended Georgetown University and Yale University, where he received his Ph.D. In 1939 he became a member of Yale's English department, and he soon won wide acclaim for his work in eighteenth-century studies; his books in that field include *The Prose Style of Samuel Johnson* (1941) and *Philosophic Words: A Study of Style and Meaning in the "Rambler" and "Dictionary" of Samuel Johnson* (1948). But he is best known for his literary theory and criticism, notably *The Verbal Icon: Studies in the Meaning of Poetry* (1954), *Hateful Contraries: Studies in Literature and Criticism* (1965), *Day of the Leopards: Essays in Defense of the Poem* (1976), and, with CLEANTH BROOKS, *Literary Criticism: A Short History* (1957). Beardsley, a native of Connecticut, received his B.A. and Ph.D. from Yale University, and held a position in the Philosophy department there before moving on to Mount Holyoke College in 1944. He later taught at Swarthmore College and at Temple University, focusing on literary criticism and aesthetics; his books include *Aesthetics: Problems in the Philosophy of Criticism* (1958) and *Aesthetics from Classical Greece to the Present* (1966).

In their critique of intention, Wimsatt and Beardsley take aim at the Romantic idea of poetry as the expression of a writer's soul or personality. Influenced by T. S. ELIOT, as well as by JOHN CROWE RANSOM, Brooks, and other New Critics, Wimsatt and Beardsley define poetry as an impersonal art: what matters is the text itself. They also challenge literary historians who, according to Wimsatt and Beardsley, mistakenly believe that when evaluating a poem, one must know its biographical and historical origins. For Wimsatt and Beardsley, one must attend only to the organization of the words on the page and the coherence that the words do or do not possess. As they affirm near the beginning of the essay, "the poem itself shows what [the poet] is trying to do. And if the poet did not succeed, then the poem is not adequate evidence, and the critic must go outside the poem—for evidence of an intention that did not become effective in the poem."

"The Intentional Fallacy" is a powerful polemic, but somewhat confused, as critics have pointed out. How convincing, for example, is the distinction that its authors draw between the inside and the outside of a text? They insist a poem is a public utterance and hence cannot depend for its success on personal or private knowledge about the author, whether deliberately revealed or unearthed by literary historians and biographers. But one could reply that what an author says and the information that a scholar brings forward are public as well. It is precisely the idea that a text has discrete inside and outside meanings that clearly separate into the private and public that KENNETH BURKE, E. D. HIRSCH JR., HAROLD BLOOM, and SANDRA M. GILBERT AND SUSAN GUBAR, among many others, have in their different ways disputed. For the purposes of their polemic, Wimsatt and Beardsley's distinction is effective, but it has not held up under attack.

As with many key New Critical precepts, one of the appeals of "the intentional fallacy" is pedagogical. A teacher and class can concentrate on the text at hand without feeling that the students' interpretive work needs the support of information about the author and the historical period when the text was composed. Wimsatt and Beardsley have a convenient rule of thumb: if information about the author or period is relevant, it will be *in* the poem; if it is not realized in the poem already, then it is not relevant. Thus they regard as extraneous all reference to psychology, social history, and anthropology, disciplines focused on *extrinsic* rather than *intrinsic* matters—a key distinction for New Critics. Yet their claim creates pedagogical problems of its own, as E. D. Hirsch noted in *Validity in Interpretation* (1967; see below) and *The Aims of Interpretation* (1976). Once we set aside the author's intention, Hirsch maintains, we have no way to determine which reading of a poem is correct. The words on the page, he argues, can sustain interpretations that in fact conflict with one another, and the only principled way to resolve such disagreements is by recourse to the author's "original meaning."

Such foregrounding of authorial intention might seem to be common sense, but poets and novelists as well as critics have denied that the author is the best authority on the meaning of his or her work. T. S. Eliot, the most influential poet-critic of the twentieth century, remarks in *The Use of Poetry and the Use of Criticism* (1933) that "What a poem means is as much what it means to others as what it means to the author; and indeed, in the course of time a poet may become merely a reader in respect to his own works, forgetting his original meaning—or without forgetting, merely changing." Earlier, in *Studies in Classic American Literature* (1923), D. H. Lawrence set out this maxim: "Never trust the artist. Trust the tale. The proper function of a critic is to save the tale from the artist who created it." Wimsatt and Beardsley would accept these claims only insofar as they reaffirm the primacy of the text. For them, the text shapes and controls what we say about it. Meaning is in the text, not in the intention of the author and, as "The Affective Fallacy" suggests, not in the reader, either.

In "The Affective Fallacy," Wimsatt and Beardsley contend that what the poem *is* is one thing (and the important thing), and what it *does* is another: it should be judged on the basis of itself, not according to its effects. While not forbidding discussion of emotion or feeling, they seek instead to keep all lines of inquiry connected to the "text": that is, to the elements of the poem that account for the effects that it creates. They distinguish sharply between "classical objectivity" and "romantic reader psychology," and of course accent the former.

For Wimsatt and Beardsley, the authority is the poem. Only by keeping our focus on the text can we guard against the dangers of impressionism, subjectivism, and relativism—a vital concern for scholars and teachers intent on giving legitimacy to "English" as an academic field of study and source of scientific knowledge. This position reaches back at least as far as MATTHEW ARNOLD, who in "The Study of Poetry" (1880) warned against the "personal fallacy," by which we judge poetry "on grounds personal to ourselves." Paradoxically, however, many of the same critics who in the nineteenth and twentieth centuries highlighted the priority of the text also spoke about the creative or constructive role played by the reader. I. A. Richards, for example, in "The Interactions of Words" (1942) maintained: "Understanding is not a preparation for reading the poem. It is itself the poem. And it is a constructive, hazardous, free creative process, a process of conception through which a new being is growing in the mind."

During the late 1960s and 1970s, a new movement in criticism, reader-response theory, drew on the insights about the reading process that Richards and others had advanced or implied in formulating their text-centered approaches. One of its most important members, STANLEY FISH, explicitly invoked Wimsatt and Beardsley's arguments in his essay "Literature in the Reader" (1970). For Fish, criticism should be concerned with the "analysis of the developing responses of the reader in relation to the words as they succeed one another in time."

Other critics and theorists during this same period challenged and complicated Wimsatt and Beardsley's conception—in effect, a diminution—of the author. For example, MICHEL FOUCAULT and STEPHEN GREENBLATT are as much opposed to the Romantic conception of the author as were Wimsatt and Beardsley. But for them the author, reimagined and reconfigured, is nonetheless a focal point for literary investigation and analysis. Thus in "What Is an Author?" (1969; see below), Foucault considers not the author as such but rather the historical "author-function," a "mode of existence, circulation, and functioning of certain discourses within a society." For Wimsatt and Beardsley, and for those they influenced, this position, and reader-response criticism as well, takes us too far afield from the specific text, the self-contained poem. Studying literature in a disciplined way means directly examining literary artifacts, not authors or readers or social contexts.

"The Intentional Fallacy" and "The Affective Fallacy" are very important historically as key documents in the theory and practice of New Criticism, the dominant mode of American academic criticism during the mid–twentieth century. They remain sharply pertinent to debates today about interpretation and judgment, as WALTER BENN MICHAELS AND STEVEN KNAPP's essay "Against Theory" (1982; see below) and the many responses to its favorable account of "intention" suggest. Where do we locate the authority or control for textual meaning? in the poem itself? in the author? or in the reader? How do we define these terms, and what is their relationship to one another? Can we make a distinction between the inside and the outside of a text, between intrinsic and extrinsic criticism? What is the nature of the knowledge that literary study gives us? These are permanent questions in the field of literary theory and criticism, and Wimsatt and Beardsley raised and vitalized them as vividly as anyone has done.

BIBLIOGRAPHY

The major works of Wimsatt and of Beardsley are listed in the second paragraph of this headnote. Secondary sources on Wimsatt include Eliseo Vivas, "Mr. Wimsatt on the Theory of Literature," in *The Artistic Transaction and Essays on Theory of Literature* (1963); *Literary Theory and Structure: Essays in Honor of W. K. Wimsatt*, edited by Frank Brady, John Palmer, and Martin Price (1973); and René Wellek, "The Literary Theory of William K. Wimsatt," *Yale Review* 66 (1977). See also the overview by Robert Moynihan, in *Dictionary of Literary Biography*, vol. 63, *Modern American Critics, 1920–1955* (ed. Gregory S. Jay, 1988), which contains biographical and bibliographical information. Other than the two classic essays he coauthored with Wimsatt, Beardsley's work in philosophical aesthetics has had little impact in the field of literary criticism.

The Intentional Fallacy

> He owns with toil he wrote the following scenes;
> But, if they're naught, ne'er spare him for his pains:
> Damn him the more; have no commiseration
> For dullness on mature deliberation.
>
> William Congreve, Prologue to *The Way of the World*[1]

The claim of the author's "intention" upon the critic's judgment has been challenged in a number of recent discussions, notably in the debate entitled *The Personal Heresy*, between Professors Lewis and Tillyard,[2] and at least implicitly in periodical essays like those in the "Symposiums" of 1940 in the *Southern* and *Kenyon Reviews*.[3] But it seems doubtful if this claim and most of its romantic corollaries are as yet subject to any widespread questioning. The present writers, in a short article entitled "Intention" for a *Dictionary*[4] of literary criticism, raised the issue but were unable to pursue its implications at any length. We argued that the design or intention of the author is

1. Restoration comedy (1700) by the English dramatist and poet Congreve (1670–1729).
2. *The Personal Heresy: A Controversy by E. M. W. Tillyard and C. S. Lewis* (1939). Tillyard (1889–1962) was an English literary scholar, Lewis (1898–1963) an Irish-born literary scholar and novelist.
3. Cf. Louis Teeter, 'Scholarship and the Art of Criticism," *ELH* 5 (Sept. 1938), 173–94; René Wellek, review of Geoffrey Tillotson's *Essays in Criticism and Research, Modern Philology* 41 (May 1944), 262; G. Wilson Knight, *Shakespeare and Tolstoy*, English Association Pamphlet no. 88 (April 1934), p. 10; Bernard C. Heyl, *New Bearings in Esthetics and Art Criticism* (New Haven, 1943), pp. 66, 113, 149 [Wimsatt and Beardsley's note].
4. *Dictionary of World Literature*, ed. Joseph T. Shipley (New York, 1943), pp. 326–39 [Wimsatt and Beardsley's note].

neither available nor desirable as a standard for judging the success of a work of literary art, and it seems to us that this is a principle which goes deep into some differences in the history of critical attitudes. It is a principle which accepted or rejected points to the polar opposites of classical "imitation" and romantic expression. It entails many specific truths about inspiration, authenticity, biography, literary history and scholarship, and about some trends of contemporary poetry, especially its allusiveness. There is hardly a problem of literary criticism in which the critic's approach will not be qualified by his view of "intention."

"Intention," as we shall use the term, corresponds to *what he intended* in a formula which more or less explicitly has had wide acceptance. "In order to judge the poet's performance, we must know *what he intended.*" Intention is design or plan in the author's mind. Intention has obvious affinities for the author's attitude toward his work, the way he felt, what made him write.

We begin our discussion with a series of propositions summarized and abstracted to a degree where they seem to us axiomatic, if not truistic.

1. A poem does not come into existence by accident. The words of a poem, as Professor Stoll[5] has remarked, come out of a head, not out of a hat. Yet to insist on the designing intellect as a *cause* of a poem is not to grant the design or intention as a *standard*.

2. One must ask how a critic expects to get an answer to the question about intention. How is he to find out what the poet tried to do? If the poet succeeded in doing it, then the poem itself shows what he was trying to do. And if the poet did not succeed, then the poem is not adequate evidence, and the critic must go outside the poem—for evidence of an intention that did not become effective in the poem. "Only one *caveat* must be borne in mind," says an eminent intentionalist[6] in a moment when his theory repudiates itself; "the poet's aim must be judged at the moment of the creative act, that is to say, by the art of the poem itself."

3. Judging a poem is like judging a pudding or a machine. One demands that it work. It is only because an artifact works that we infer the intention of an artificer. "A poem should not mean but be."[7] A poem can *be* only through its *meaning*—since its medium is words—yet it *is*, simply *is*, in the sense that we have no excuse for inquiring what part is intended or meant.[8] Poetry is a feat of style by which a complex of meaning is handled all at once. Poetry succeeds because all or most of what is said or implied is relevant; what is irrelevant has been excluded, like lumps from pudding and "bugs" from machinery. In this respect poetry differs from practical messages, which are successful if and only if we correctly infer the intention. They are more abstract than poetry.

4. The meaning of a poem may certainly be a personal one, in the sense that a poem expresses a personality or state of soul rather than a physical

5. Elmer Edgar Stoll (1874–1959), literary critic whose works focused primarily on drama (especially Shakespeare).

6. J. E. Spingarn, "The New Criticism," in *Criticism in America* (New York, 1924), pp. 24–25 [Wimsatt and Beardsley's note].

7. From "Ars Poetica" (1926), by the American poet Archibald MacLeish.

8. As critics and teachers constantly do. "We have here a deliberate blurring. . . ." "Should this be regarded as ironic or unplanned?" ". . . is the literal meaning intended . . . ?" ". . . a paradox of religious faith which is intended to exult. . . ." "It seems to me that Herbert intends. . . ." These examples are chosen from three pages of an issue of *The Explicator* (Fredericksburg, Va.), 2, no. 1 (Oct. 1943). Authors often judge their own works in the same way. See *This Is My Best*, ed. Whit Burnett (New York, 1942), e.g., pp. 539–40 [Wimsatt and Beardsley's note].

object like an apple. But even a short lyric poem is dramatic, the response of a speaker (no matter how abstractly conceived) to a situation (no matter how universalized). We ought to impute the thoughts and attitudes of the poem immediately to the dramatic *speaker*, and if to the author at all, only by a biographical act of inference.

5. If there is any sense in which an author, by revision, has better achieved his original intention, it is only the very abstract, tautological, sense that he intended to write a better work and now has done it. (In this sense every author's intention is the same.) His former specific intention was not his intention. "He's the man we were in search of, that's true"; says Hardy's rustic constable, "and yet he's not the man we were in search of. For the man we were in search of was not the man we wanted."[9]

"Is not a critic," asks Professor Stoll, ". . . a judge, who does not explore his own consciousness, but determines the author's meaning or intention, as if the poem were a will, a contract, or the constitution? The poem is not the critic's own."[1] He has diagnosed very accurately two forms of irresponsibility, one which he prefers. Our view is yet different. The poem is not the critic's own and not the author's (it is detached from the author at birth and goes about the world beyond his power to intend about it or control it). The poem belongs to the public. It is embodied in language, the peculiar possession of the public, and it is about the human being, an object of public knowledge. What is said about the poem is subject to the same scrutiny as any statement in linguistics or in the general science of psychology or morals. Mr. Richards[2] has aptly called the poem a *class*—"a class of experiences which do not differ in any character more than a certain amount . . . from a standard experience." And he adds, "We may take as this standard experience the relevant experience of the poet when contemplating the completed composition." Professor Wellek[3] in a fine essay on the problem has preferred to call the poem "a system of norms," "extracted from every individual experience," and he objects to Mr. Richards' deference to the poet as reader. We side with Professor Wellek in not wishing to make the poet (outside the poem) an authority.

A critic of our *Dictionary* article, Mr. Ananda K. Coomaraswamy, has argued[4] that there are two kinds of enquiry about a work of art: (1) whether the artist achieved his intentions; (2) whether the work of art "ought ever to have been undertaken at all" and so "whether it is worth preserving." Number (2), Mr. Coomaraswamy maintains, is not "criticism of any work of art *qua* work of art," but is rather moral criticism; number (1) is artistic criticism. But we maintain that (2) need not be moral criticism: that there is another way of deciding whether works of art are worth preserving and whether, in a sense, they "ought" to have been undertaken, and this is the way of objec-

9. A close relative of the intentional fallacy is that of talking about "means" and "end" in poetry instead of "part" and "whole." We have treated this relation concisely in our dictionary article [Wimsatt and Beardsley's note]. The quotation is from "The Three Strangers" (1883), by the English writer Thomas Hardy (1840–1928).

1. E. E. Stoll, "The Tempest," *PMLA* 44 (Sept. 1932), 703 [Wimsatt and Beardsley's note].

2. I. A. Richards (1893–1979), English literary theorist. For his fullest statement of the view discussed, see *Principles of Literary Criticism* (1925).

3. René Wellek (1903–1995), Austrian-born American literary theorist and scholar; the "fine essay" is "The Mode of Existence of a Literary Work of Art," *Southern Review*, spring 1942.

4. Ananda K. Coomaraswamy, "Intention," *American Bookman* 1 (winter 1944), 41–48 [Wimsatt and Beardsley's note].

tive criticism of works of art as such, the way which enables us to distinguish between a skilful murder and a skilful poem. A skilful murder is an example which Mr. Coomaraswamy uses, and in his system the difference between the murder and the poem is simply a "moral" one, not an "artistic" one, since each if carried out according to plan is "artistically" successful. We maintain that (2) is an enquiry of more worth than (1), and since (2), and not (1), is capable of distinguishing poetry from murder, the name "artistic criticism" is properly given to (2).

II

It is not so much an empirical as an analytic judgment, not a historical statement, but a definition, to say that the intentional fallacy is a romantic one. When a rhetorician, presumably of the first century A.D., writes: "Sublimity is the echo of a great soul," or tells us that "Homer enters into the sublime actions of his heroes" and "shares the full inspiration of the combat," we shall not be surprised to find this rhetorician considered as a distant harbinger of romanticism and greeted in the warmest terms by so romantic a critic as Saintsbury.[5] One may wish to argue whether Longinus should be called romantic,[6] but there can hardly be a doubt that in one important way he is.

Goethe's[7] three questions for "constructive criticism" are "What did the author set out to do? Was his plan reasonable and sensible, and how far did he succeed in carrying it out?" If one leaves out the middle question, one has in effect the system of Croce[8]—the culmination and crowning philosophic expression of romanticism. The beautiful is the successful intuition-expression, and the ugly is the unsuccessful; the intuition or private part of art is *the* aesthetic fact, and the medium or public part is not the subject of aesthetic at all. Yet aesthetic reproduction takes place only "if all the other conditions remain equal."

> Oil-paintings grow dark, frescoes fade, statues lose noses . . . the text of a poem is corrupted by bad copyists or bad printing.

> The Madonna of Cimabue is still in the Church of Santa Maria Novella; but does she speak to the visitor of to-day as to the Florentines of the thirteenth century?

> *Historical interpretation* labours . . . to reintegrate in us the psychological conditions which have changed in the course of history. It . . . enables us to see a work of art (a physical object) as its *author saw it* in the moment of production.[9]

5. George Saintsbury (1845–1933), English scholar and critic, whose works include *A History of Criticism and Literary Taste in Europe from the Earliest Texts to the Present Day* (3 vols., 1900–05).
6. For the relation of Longinus to modern romanticism, see R. S. Crane, review of Samuel Monk's *The Sublime, Philological Quarterly* 15 (April 1936), 165–66 [Wimsatt and Beardsley's note]. On the Greek rhetorician LONGINUS, see above.
7. Johann Wolfgang Von Goethe (1749–1832), German poet, playwright, and novelist.
8. Benedetto Croce (1866–1952), Italian literary critic, and philosopher; Wimsatt and Beardsley quote his *Aesthetics as Science of Expression and General Linguistic* (1909).
9. It is true that Croce himself in his *Ariosto, Shakespeare, and Corneille*, trans. Douglas Ainslie (London, 1920), chap. 7, "The Practical Personality and the Poetical Personality," and in his *Defence of Poetry*, trans. E. F. Carritt (Oxford, 1933), p. 24, has delivered a telling attack on intentionalism, but the prevailing drift of such passages in the *Aesthetics* as we quote is in the opposite direction [Wimsatt and Beardsley's note].

The first italics are Croce's, the second ours. The upshot of Croce's system is an ambiguous emphasis on history. With such passages as a point of departure a critic may write a close analysis of the meaning or "spirit" of a play of Shakespeare or Corneille[1]—a process that involves close historical study but remains aesthetic criticism—or he may write sociology, biography, or other kinds of non-aesthetic history. The Crocean system seems to have given more of a boost to the latter way of writing.

"What has the poet tried to do," asks Spingarn in his 1910 Columbia Lecture from which we have already quoted, "and how has he fulfilled his intention?" The place to look for "insuperable" ugliness, says Bosanquet, in his third *Lecture* of 1914, is the "region of insincere and affected art."[2] The seepage of the theory into a non-philosophic place may be seen in such a book as Marguerite Wilkinson's inspirational *New Voices*,[3] about the poetry of 1919 to 1931—where symbols "as old as the ages . . . retain their strength and freshness" through "Realization." We close this section with two examples from quarters where one might least expect a taint of the Crocean. Mr. I. A. Richards' fourfold distinction of meaning into "sense," "feeling," "tone," "intention" has been probably the most influential statement of intentionalism in the past fifteen years, though it contains a hint of self-repudiation: "This function [intention]," says Mr. Richards, "is not on all fours with the others."[4] In an essay on "Three Types of Poetry" Mr. Allen Tate[5] writes as follows:

> We must understand that the lines
>
> Life like a dome of many-colored glass
> Stains the white radiance of eternity
>
> are not poetry; they express the *frustrated will* trying to compete with science. The *will* asserts a rhetorical proposition about the whole of life, but the *imagination* has not seized upon the materials of the poem and made them into a whole. Shelley's simile is imposed upon the material from above; it does not grow out of the material.

The last sentence contains a promise of objective analysis which is not fulfilled. The reason why the essay relies so heavily throughout on the terms "will" and "imagination" is that Mr. Tate is accusing the romantic poets of a kind of insincerity (romanticism in reverse) and at the same time is trying to describe something mysterious and perhaps indescribable, an "imaginative whole of life," a "wholeness of vision at a particular moment of experience," something which "yields us the quality of the experience." If a poet had a toothache at the moment of conceiving a poem, that would be part of the experience, but Mr. Tate of course does not mean anything like that. He is thinking about some kind of "whole" which in this essay at least he does not describe, but which doubtless it is the prime need of criticism to describe—in terms that may be publicly tested.

1. PIERRE CORNEILLE (1606–1684), French dramatist.
2. From *Three Lectures on Aesthetic* (1915) by the English philosopher Bernard Bosanquet (1848–1923).
3. *New Voices: An Introduction to Contemporary Poetry* (1919; rev. ed., 1923), by Wilkinson (1883–1928).
4. Richards, *Practical Criticism* (1929), part 3, chapter 1.
5. American poet and critic (1899–1979). In the passage that follows, Tate quotes from PERCY BYSSHE SHELLEY's pastoral elegy "Adonais" (1821).

III

> I went to the poets; tragic, dithyrambic, and all sorts. . . . I took them some of the most elaborate passages in their own writings, and asked what was the meaning of them. . . . Will you believe me? . . . there is hardly a person present who would not have talked better about their poetry than they did themselves. Then I knew that not by wisdom do poets write poetry, but by a sort of genius and inspiration.[6]

That reiterated mistrust of the poets which we hear from Socrates may have been part of a rigorously ascetic view in which we hardly wish to participate, yet Plato's Socrates saw a truth about the poetic mind which the world no longer commonly sees—so much criticism, and that the most inspirational and most affectionately remembered, has proceeded from the poets themselves.

Certainly the poets have had something to say that the analyst and professor could not say; their message has been more exciting: that poetry should come as naturally as leaves to a tree, that poetry is the lava of the imagination, or that it is emotion recollected in tranquillity.[7] But it is necessary that we realize the character and authority of such testimony. There is only a fine shade between those romantic expressions and a kind of earnest advice that authors often give. Thus Edward Young, Carlyle, Walter Pater:[8]

> I know two golden rules from *ethics*, which are no less golden in *Composition*, than in life. 1. *Know thyself*; 2dly, *Reverence thyself.*

> This is the grand secret for finding readers and retaining them: let him who would move and convince others, be first moved and convinced himself. Horace's rule, *Si vis me flere*,[9] is applicable in a wider sense than the literal one. To every poet, to every writer, we might say: Be true, if you would be believed.

> Truth! there can be no merit, no craft at all, without that. And further, all beauty is in the long run only *fineness* of truth, or what we call expression, the finer accommodation of speech to that vision within.

And Housman's little handbook[1] to the poetic mind yields the following illustration:

> Having drunk a pint of beer at luncheon—beer is a sedative to the brain, and my afternoons are the least intellectual portion of my life—I would go out for a walk of two or three hours. As I went along, thinking of nothing in particular, only looking at things around me and following the progress of the seasons, there would flow into my mind, with sudden and unaccountable emotion, sometimes a line or two of verse, sometimes a whole stanza at once. . . .

6. From PLATO (ca. 427–ca. 347 B.C.E.), *Apology* 22a–c.
7. The conceptions of poetry articulated by the Romantic poets John Keats (1795–1821), George Gordon, Lord Byron (1784–1824), and WILLIAM WORDSWORTH (1780–1850), respectively.
8. English critic and essayist (1839–1894; see above); his quotation is from "Style" (1888). YOUNG (1683–1765), English poet; his quotation is from *Conjectures on Original Composition* (1759). Thomas Carlyle (1795–1881), Scottish-born historian and essayist.
9. If you want me to cry [mourn first yourself] (Latin). From HORACE (65–8 B.C.E.), *Ars Poetica*, line 102.
1. *The Name and Nature of Poetry* (1933), by the English poet and classical scholar A. E. Housman (1859–1936).

This is the logical terminus of the series already quoted. Here is a confession of how poems were written which would do as a definition of poetry just as well as "emotion recollected in tranquility"—and which the young poet might equally well take to heart as a practical rule. Drink a pint of beer, relax, go walking, think on nothing in particular, look at things, surrender yourself to yourself, search for the truth in your own soul, listen to the sound of your own inside voice, discover and express the *vraie vérité*.[2]

It is probably true that all this is excellent advice for poets. The young imagination fired by Wordsworth and Carlyle is probably closer to the verge of producing a poem than the mind of the student who has been sobered by Aristotle[3] or Richards. The art of inspiring poets, or at least of inciting something like poetry in young persons, has probably gone further in our day than ever before. Books of creative writing such as those issued from the Lincoln School are interesting evidence of what a child can do if taught how to manage himself honestly.[4] All this, however, would appear to belong to an art separate from criticism, or to a discipline which one might call the psychology of composition, valid and useful, an individual and private culture, yoga, or system of self-development which the young poet would do well to notice, but different from the public science of evaluating poems.

Coleridge and Arnold[5] were better critics than most poets have been, and if the critical tendency dried up the poetry in Arnold and perhaps in Coleridge, it is not inconsistent with our argument, which is that judgment of poems is different from the art of producing them. Coleridge has given us the classic "anodyne" story, and tells what he can about the genesis of a poem[6] which he calls a "psychological curiosity," but his definitions of poetry and of the poetic quality "imagination" are to be found elsewhere and in quite other terms.

The day may arrive when the psychology of composition is unified with the science of objective evaluation, but so far they are separate. It would be convenient if the passwords of the intentional school, "sincerity," "fidelity," "spontaneity," "authenticity," "genuineness," "originality," could be equated with terms of analysis such as "integrity," "relevance," "unity," "function"; with "maturity," "subtlety," and "adequacy," and other more precise axiological terms—in short, if "expression" always meant aesthetic communication. But this is not so.

"Aesthetic" art, says Professor Curt Ducasse, an ingenious theorist of expression, is the conscious objectification of feelings, in which an intrinsic part is the critical moment. The artist corrects the objectification when it is not adequate, but this may mean that the earlier attempt was not successful in objectifying the self, or "it may also mean that it was a successful objectification of a self which, when it confronted us clearly, we disowned and repudiated in favor of another."[7] What is the standard by which we disown

2. True truth (French).
3. That is, by the *Poetics* (see above) of Aristotle (384–322 B.C.E.).
4. See Hugh Mearns, *Creative Youth* (Garden City, 1925), esp. pp. 10, 27–29. The technique of inspiring poems keeps pace today with a parallel analysis of the process of inspiration in successful artists. See Rosamond E. M. Harding, *An Anatomy of Inspiration* (Cambridge, 1940); Julius Portnoy, *A Psychology of Art Creation* (Philadelphia, 1942) [Wimsatt and Beardsley's note]. Lincoln School: an experimental school affiliated with Teachers College of Columbia University.
5. MATTHEW ARNOLD (1822–1888), English critic and poet. SAMUEL TAYLOR COLERIDGE (1772–1834), English poet and critic.
6. "Kubla Khan" (written 1797; pub. 1816); Coleridge's general account of poetry and the imagination is found in *Biographia Literaria* (1817; see above).
7. Curt Ducasse, *The Philosophy of Art* (New York, 1929), p. 116 [Wimsatt and Beardsley's note].

or accept the self? Professor Ducasse does not say. Whatever it may be, however, this standard is an element in the definition of art which will not reduce to terms of objectification. The evaluation of the work of art remains public; the work is measured against something outside the author.

IV

There is criticism of poetry and there is, as we have seen, author psychology, which when applied to the present or future takes the form of inspirational promotion; but author psychology can be historical too, and then we have literary biography, a legitimate and attractive study in itself, one approach, as Mr. Tillyard would argue, to personality, the poem being only a parallel approach. Certainly it need not be with a derogatory purpose that one points out personal studies, as distinct from poetic studies, in the realm of literary scholarship. Yet there is danger of confusing personal and poetic studies; and there is the fault of writing the personal as if it were poetic.

There is a difference between internal and external evidence for the meaning of a poem. And the paradox is only verbal and superficial that what is (1) internal is also public: it is discovered through the semantics and syntax of a poem, through our habitual knowledge of the language, through grammars, dictionaries, and all the literature which is the source of dictionaries, in general through all that makes a language and culture; while what is (2) external is private or idiosyncratic; not a part of the work as a linguistic fact: it consists of revelations (in journals, for example, or letters or reported conversations) about how or why the poet wrote the poem—to what lady, while sitting on what lawn, or at the death of what friend or brother. There is (3) an intermediate kind of evidence about the character of the author or about private or semi-private meanings attached to words or topics by an author or by a coterie of which he is a member. The meaning of words is the history of words, and the biography of an author, his use of a word, and the associations which the word had for *him*, are part of the word's history and meaning.[8] But the three types of evidence, especially (2) and (3), shade into one another so subtly that it is not always easy to draw a line between examples, and hence arises the difficulty for criticism. The use of biographical evidence need not involve intentionalism, because while it may be evidence of what the author intended, it may also be evidence of the meaning of his words and the dramatic character of his utterance. On the other hand, it may not be all this. And a critic who is concerned with evidence of type (1) and moderately with that of type (3) will in the long run produce a different sort of comment from that of the critic who is concerned with type (2) and with (3) where it shades into (2).

The whole glittering parade of Professor Lowes' *Road to Xanadu*,[9] for instance, runs along the border between types (2) and (3) or boldly traverses the romantic region of (2). " 'Kubla Khan'," says Professor Lowes, "is the fabric of a vision, but every image that rose up in its weaving had passed that

8. And the history of words *after* a poem is written may contribute meanings which if relevant to the original pattern should not be ruled out by a scruple about intention. Cf. C. S. Lewis and E. M. W. Tillyard, *The Personal Heresy* (Oxford, 1939), p. 16; Teeter, loc cit., pp. 183, 192; review of Tillotson's *Essays*, *TLS* 41 (April 1942), 174 [Wimsatt and Beardsley's note].

9. An exhaustive examination (1927; rev. ed., 1930) of the sources of Coleridge's poems "The Rime of the Ancient Mariner" and "Kubla Khan," by the literary historian John Livingston Lowes (1867–1945).

way before. And it would seem that there is nothing haphazard or fortuitous in their return." This is not quite clear—not even when Professor Lowes explains that there were clusters of associations, like hooked atoms, which were drawn into complex relation with other clusters in the deep well of Coleridge's memory, and which then coalesced and issued forth as poems. If there was nothing "haphazard or fortuitous" in the way the images returned to the surface, that may mean (1) that Coleridge could not produce what he did not have, that he was limited in his creation by what he had read or otherwise experienced, or (2) that having received certain clusters of associations, he was bound to return them in just the way he did, and that the value of the poem may be described in terms of the experiences on which he had to draw. The latter pair of propositions (a sort of Hartleyan associationism[1] which Coleridge himself repudiated in the *Biographia*) may not be assented to. There were certainly other combinations, other poems, worse or better, that might have been written by men who had read Bartram and Purchas and Bruce and Milton.[2] And this will be true no matter how many times we are able to add to the brilliant complex of Coleridge's reading. In certain flourishes (such as the sentence we have quoted) and in chapter headings like "The Shaping Spirit," "The Magical Synthesis," "Imagination Creatrix," it may be that Professor Lowes pretends to say more about the actual poems than he does. There is a certain deceptive variation in these fancy chapter titles; one expects to pass on to a new stage in the argument, and one finds—more and more sources, more about "the streamy nature of association."[3]

"Wohin der Weg?" quotes Professor Lowes for the motto of his book. "Kein Weg! Ins Unbetretene."[4] Precisely because the way is *unbetreten*, we should say, it leads away from the poem. Bartram's *Travels* contains a good deal of the history of certain words and romantic Floridan conceptions that appear in "Kubla Khan." And a good deal of that history has passed and was then passing into the very stuff of our language. Perhaps a person who has read Bartram appreciates the poem more than one who has not. Or, by looking up the vocabulary of "Kubla Khan" in the *Oxford English Dictionary*, or by reading some of the other books there quoted, a person may know the poem better. But it would seem to pertain little to the poem to know that *Coleridge* had read Bartram. There is a gross body of life, of sensory and mental experience, which lies behind and in some sense causes every poem, but can never be and need not be known in the verbal and hence intellectual composition which is the poem. For all the objects of our manifold experience, especially for the intellectual objects, for every unity, there is an action of the mind which cuts off roots, melts away context—or indeed we should never have objects or ideas or anything to talk about.

1. Characteristic of David Hartley (1705–1757), English philosopher and physician; his *Observations on Man: His Frame, His Duty, and His Expectations* (1749) links mental phenomena to the associations of simple sensation.

2. The English poet John Milton (1608–1674) is an anomaly in this list, whose other members are the American naturalist and traveler William Bartram (1739–1823), author of *Travels through North and South Carolina* (1791); the English compiler of travel books Samuel Purchas (ca. 1577–1626); and the Scottish traveler and author James Bruce (1730–1794).

3. Chapters 8, "The Pattern," and 16, "The Known and Familiar Landscape," will be found of most help to the student of the poem. For an extreme example of intentionalist criticism, see Kenneth Burke's analysis of *The Ancient Mariner* in *The Philosophy of Literary Form* (Baton Rouge, 1941), pp. 22–23, 93–102. Mr. Burke must be credited with realizing very clearly what he is up to [Wimsatt and Beardsley's note]. On the American critic BURKE (1897–1993), see above.

4. Where is the way? No way! It is untrodden (German). From Goethe's *Faust* (1808, 1832).

It is probable that there is nothing in Professor Lowes' vast book which could detract from anyone's appreciation of either *The Ancient Mariner* or *Kubla Khan*. We next present a case where preoccupation with evidence of type (3) has gone so far as to distort a critic's view of a poem (yet a case not so obvious as those that abound in our critical journals).

In a well-known poem by John Donne appears the following quatrain:

> Moving of th' earth brings harmes and feares,
> Men reckon what it did and meant,
> But trepidation of the spheares,
> Though greater farre, is innocent.[5]

A recent critic in an elaborate treatment of Donne's learning has written of this quatrain as follows:

> . . . he touches the emotional pulse of the situation by a skillful allusion to the new and the old astronomy. . . . Of the new astronomy, the "moving of the earth" is the most radical principle; of the old, the "trepidation of the spheres" is the motion of the greatest complexity. . . . As the poem is a valediction forbidding mourning, the poet must exhort his love to quietness and calm upon his departure; and for this purpose the figure based upon the latter motion (trepidation), long absorbed into the traditional astronomy, fittingly suggests the tension of the moment without arousing the "harmes and feares" implicit in the figure of the moving earth.[6]

The argument is plausible and rests on a well-substantiated thesis that Donne was deeply interested in the new astronomy and its repercussions in the theological realm. In various works Donne shows his familiarity with Kepler's *De Stella Nova*, with Galileo's *Siderius Nuncius*, with William Gilbert's *De Magnete*, and with Clavius's commentary on the *De Sphaera* of Sacrobosco.[7] He refers to the new science in his Sermon at Paul's Cross and in a letter to Sir Henry Goodyer.[8] In *The First Anniversary* he says the "new philosophy calls all in doubt." In the *Elegy on Prince Henry* he says that the "least moving of the center" makes "the world to shake."

It is difficult to answer argument like this, and impossible to answer it with evidence of like nature. There is no reason why Donne might not have written a stanza in which the two kinds of celestial motion stood for two sorts of emotion at parting. And if we become full of astronomical ideas and see Donne only against the background of the new science, we may believe that he did. But the text itself remains to be dealt with, the analyzable vehicle of a complicated metaphor. And one may observe: (1) that the movement of the earth according to the Copernican theory is a celestial motion, smooth and regular, and while it might cause religious or philosophic fears, it could not be associated with the crudity and earthiness of the kind of commotion which the speaker in the poem wishes to discourage; (2) that there is another

5. "A Valediction: Forbidding Mourning" (1633), lines 9–12, by the English poet Donne (1572–1631).
6. Charles M. Coffin, *John Donne and the New Philosophy* (New York, 1927), pp. 97–98 [Wimsatt and Beardsley's note].
7. All works of science, by Johannes Kepler (1571–1630), German astronomer and mathematician; Galileo (1564–1642), Italian astronomer and physicist; Gilbert (1544–1603), English court physician who studied electricity and magnetism; and Johannes de Sacrobosco (or John Holywood or Halifax), English mathematician (mid-13th c.), whose commentators include the Italian mathematician Christopher Clavius (16th c.).
8. A friend of Donne's and an occasional poet himself.

moving of the earth, an earthquake, which has just these qualities and is to be associated with the tear-floods and sigh-tempests of the second stanza of the poem; (3) that "trepidation" is an appropriate opposite of earthquake, because each is a shaking or vibratory motion; and "trepidation of the spheres" is "greater far" than an earthquake, but not much greater (if two such motions can be compared as to greatness) than the annual motion of the earth; (4) that reckoning what it "did and meant" shows that the event has passed, like an earthquake, not like the incessant celestial movement of the earth. Perhaps a knowledge of Donne's interest in the new science may add another shade of meaning, an overtone to the stanza in question, though to say even this runs against the words. To make the geo-centric and helio-centric antithesis the core of the metaphor is to disregard the English language, to prefer private evidence to public, external to internal.

V

If the distinction between kinds of evidence has implications for the historical critic, it has them no less for the contemporary poet and his critic. Or, since every rule for a poet is but another side of a judgment by a critic, and since the past is the realm of the scholar and critic, and the future and present that of the poet and the critical leaders of taste, we may say that the problems arising in literary scholarship from the intentional fallacy are matched by others which arise in the world of progressive experiment.

The question of "allusiveness," for example, as acutely posed by the poetry of Eliot, is certainly one where a false judgment is likely to involve the intentional fallacy. The frequency and depth of literary allusion in the poetry of Eliot and others has driven so many in pursuit of full meanings to the *Golden Bough*[9] and the Elizabethan drama that it has become a kind of commonplace to suppose that we do not know what a poet means unless we have traced him in his reading—a supposition redolent with intentional implications. The stand taken by Mr. F. O. Matthiessen[1] is a sound one and partially forestalls the difficulty.

> If one reads these lines with an attentive ear and is sensitive to their sudden shifts in movement, the contrast between the actual Thames and the idealized vision of it during an age before it flowed through a megalopolis is sharply conveyed by that movement itself, whether or not one recognizes the refrain to be from Spenser.

Eliot's allusions work when we know them—and to a great extent even when we do not know them, through their suggestive power.

But sometimes we find allusions supported by notes, and it is a very nice question whether the notes function more as guides to send us where we may be educated, or more as indications in themselves about the character of the allusions. "Nearly everything of importance . . . that is apposite to an appreciation of 'The Waste Land'," writes Mr. Matthiessen of Miss Weston's book,[2] "has been incorporated into the structure of the poem itself, or into

9. *The Golden Bough: A Study in Magic and Religion* (12 vols., 1890–1915), by J. G. Frazer; alluded to in *The Waste Land* (1922) by T. S. Eliot (1888–1965).

1. American literary critic (1902–1950); the quotation is from *The Achievement of T. S. Eliot: An Essay on the Nature of Poetry* (1935).

2. *From Ritual to Romance* (1920), by Jessie Weston (1850–1928).

Eliot's Notes." And with such an admission it may begin to appear that it would not much matter if Eliot invented his sources (as Sir Walter Scott[3] invented chapter epigraphs from "old plays" and "anonymous" authors, or as Coleridge wrote marginal glosses for "The Ancient Mariner"). Allusions to Dante, Webster, Marvell, or Baudelaire,[4] doubtless gain something because these writers existed, but it is doubtful whether the same can be said for an allusion to an obscure Elizabethan:

> The sound of horns and motors, which shall bring
> Sweeney to Mrs. Porter in the spring.[5]

"Cf. Day, *Parliament of Bees*:" says Eliot,

> When of a sudden, listening, you shall hear,
> A noise of horns and hunting, which shall bring
> Actaeon to Diana[6] in the spring,
> Where all shall see her naked skin. . . .

The irony is completed by the quotation itself; had Eliot, as is quite conceivable, composed these lines to furnish his own background, there would be no loss of validity. The conviction may grow as one reads Eliot's next note: "I do not know the origin of the ballad from which these lines are taken: it was reported to me from Sydney, Australia." The important word in this note—on Mrs. Porter and her daughter who washed their feet in soda water—is "ballad." And if one should feel from the lines themselves their "ballad" quality, there would be little need for the note. Ultimately, the inquiry must focus on the integrity of such notes as part of the poem, for where they constitute special information about the meaning of phrases in the poem, they ought to be subject to the same scrutiny as any of the other words in which it is written. Mr. Matthiessen believes the notes were the price Eliot "had to pay in order to avoid what he would have considered muffling the energy of his poem by extended connecting links in the text itself." But it may be questioned whether the notes and the need for them are not equally muffling. The omission from poems of the explanatory stratum on which is built the dramatic or poetic stuff is a dangerous responsibility. Mr. F. W. Bateson has plausibly argued[7] that Tennyson's "The Sailor Boy" would be better if half the stanzas were omitted, and the best versions of ballads like "Sir Patrick Spens"[8] owe their power to the very audacity with which the minstrel has taken for granted the story upon which he comments. What then if a poet finds he cannot take so much for granted in a more recondite context and rather than write informatively, supplies notes? It can be said in favor of this plan that at least the notes do not pretend to be dramatic, as they would if written in verse. On the other hand, the notes may look like unassimilated material lying loose beside the poem, necessary for

3. Scottish poet and novelist (1771–1832).
4. CHARLES BAUDELAIRE (1821–1867), French writer, translator, and critic. DANTE ALIGHIERI (1265–1321), Italian poet. John Webster (ca. 1580–ca. 1625), English playwright. Andrew Marvell (1621–1678), English metaphysical poet.
5. From "The Fire Sermon," part 3 of *The Waste Land*. The "obscure Elizabethan" is John Day (1574–ca. 1640), whose *Parliament of Bees* is an allegorical masque.
6. The Roman name of Artemis, the Greek goddess of the hunt; after the hunter Actaeon by chance saw her bathing, she turned him into a stag and he was torn apart by his own dogs.
7. In *English Poetry and the English Language: An Experiment in Literary History* (1934), by the English academic Bateson (1901–1978).
8. An early Scottish ballad. "The Sailor Boy" (1861), a 6-stanza poem by Alfred, Lord Tennyson (1809–1892).

the meaning of the verbal symbol, but not integrated, so that the symbol stands incomplete.

We mean to suggest by the above analysis that whereas notes tend to seem to justify themselves as external indexes to the author's *intention*, yet they ought to be judged like any other parts of a composition (verbal arrangement special to a particular context), and when so judged their reality as parts of the poem or their imaginative integration with the rest of the poem, may come into question. Mr. Matthiessen, for instance, sees that Eliot's titles for poems and his epigraphs are informative apparatus, like the notes. But while he is worried by some of the notes and thinks that Eliot "appears to be mocking himself for writing the note at the same time that he wants to convey something by it," Mr. Matthiessen believes that the "device" of epigraphs "is not at all open to the objection of not being sufficiently structural." "The *intention*," he says, "is to enable the poet to secure a condensed expression in the poem itself." "In each case the epigraph is *designed* to form an integral part of the effect of the poem." And Eliot himself, in his notes, has justified his poetic practice in terms of intention.

> The Hanged Man, a member of the traditional pack, fits my purpose in two ways: because he is associated in my mind with the Hanged God of Frazer, and because I associate him with the hooded figure in the passage of the disciples to Emmaus in Part V. . . . The man with Three Staves (an authentic member of the Tarot pack) I associate, quite arbitrarily, with the Fisher King himself.

And perhaps he is to be taken more seriously here, when off guard in a note, than when in his Norton Lectures[9] he comments on the difficulty of saying what a poem means and adds playfully that he thinks of prefixing to a second edition of *Ash Wednesday* some lines from *Don Juan*:[1]

> I don't pretend that I quite understand
> My own meaning when I would be *very* fine;
> But the fact is that I have nothing planned
> Unless it were to be a moment merry.

If Eliot and other contemporary poets have any characteristic fault, it may be in *planning* too much.[2]

Allusiveness in poetry is one of several critical issues by which we have illustrated the more abstract issue of intentionalism, but it may be for today the most important illustration. As a poetic practice allusiveness would appear to be in some recent poems an extreme corollary of the romantic intentionalist assumption, and as a critical issue it challenges and brings to light in a special way the basic premise of intentionalism. The following instance from the poetry of Eliot may serve to epitomize the practical implications of what we have been saying. In Eliot's "Love Song of J. Alfred Pruf-

9. Delivered at Harvard University in the winter of 1932–33; Eliot later published them as *The Use of Poetry and the Use of Criticism* (1933).

1. A mock epic (1819–24) by Byron; the lines quoted are from canto 4, stanza 5. Eliot published *Ash Wednesday* in 1930.

2. In his critical writings Eliot has expressed the right view of author psychology. See *The Use of Poetry and the Use of Criticism* (Cambridge, 1933), p. 139, and "Tradition and the Individual Talent" in *Selected Essays* (New York, 1932), though his record is not entirely consistent. See *A Choice of Kipling's Verse* (London, 1941), pp. 10–11, 20–21 [Wimsatt and Beardsley's note].

rock," towards the end, occurs the line: "I have heard the mermaids singing, each to each," and this bears a certain resemblance to a line in a Song[3] by John Donne, "Teach me to heare Mermaides singing," so that for the reader acquainted to a certain degree with Donne's poetry, the critical question arises: Is Eliot's line an allusion to Donne's? Is Prufrock thinking about Donne? Is Eliot thinking about Donne? We suggest that there are two radically different ways of looking for an answer to this question. There is (1) the way of poetic analysis and exegesis, which inquires whether it makes any sense if Eliot-Prufrock *is* thinking about Donne. In an earlier part of the poem, when Prufrock asks, "Would it have been worth while, . . . To have squeezed the universe into a ball," his words take half their sadness and irony from certain energetic and passionate lines of Marvell's "To His Coy Mistress."[4] But the exegetical inquirer may wonder whether mermaids considered as "strange sights" (to hear them is in Donne's poem analogous to getting with child a mandrake root) have much to do with Prufrock's mermaids, which seem to be symbols of romance and dynamism, and which incidentally have literary authentication, if they need it, in a line of a sonnet by Gérard de Nerval.[5] This method of inquiry may lead to the conclusion that the given resemblance between Eliot and Donne is without significance and is better not thought of, or the method may have the disadvantage of providing no certain conclusion. Nevertheless, we submit that this is the true and objective way of criticism, as contrasted to what the very uncertainty of exegesis might tempt a second kind of critic to undertake: (2) the way of biographical or genetic inquiry, in which, taking advantage of the fact that Eliot is still alive, and in the spirit of a man who would settle a bet, the critic writes to Eliot and asks what he meant, or if he had Donne in mind. We shall not here weigh the probabilities—whether Eliot would answer that he meant nothing at all, had nothing at all in mind—a sufficiently good answer to such a question—or in an unguarded moment might furnish a clear and, within its limit, irrefutable answer. Our point is that such an answer to such an inquiry would have nothing to do with the poem "Prufrock;" it would not be a critical inquiry. Critical inquiries, unlike bets, are not settled in this way. Critical inquiries are not settled by consulting the oracle.

1946

The Affective Fallacy

We might as well study the properties of wine by getting drunk
—Edward Hanslick, *The Beautiful in Music*.[1]

As the title of this essay invites comparison with that of an earlier and parallel essay of ours, "The Intentional Fallacy" (THE SEWANEE REVIEW, Summer,

3. "Go and catch a falling star" (1633). "Prufrock" was published in 1915.
4. "To His Coy Mistress" (1651), lines 41–42: "Let us roll our strength and all / Our sweetness up into one ball."
5. French symbolist poet (1808–1855); the sonnet is in *The Chimeras* (1854).
1. An 1854 work most recently translated as *On the Musically Beautiful: A Contribution towards the Revision of the Aesthetics of Music*. Hanslick (1825–1904), Austrian music critic.

1946), it may be relevant to assert at this point that we believe ourselves to be exploring two roads which have seemed to offer convenient detours around the acknowledged and usually feared obstacles to objective criticism, both of which, however, have actually led away from criticism and from poetry. The Intentional Fallacy is a confusion between the poem and its origins, a special case of what is known to philosophers as the Genetic Fallacy. It begins by trying to derive the standard of criticism from the psychological *causes* of the poem and ends in biography and relativism. The Affective Fallacy is a confusion between the poem and its *results* (what it *is* and what it *does*), a special case of epistemological skepticism, though usually advanced as if it had far stronger claims than the overall forms of skepticism. It begins by trying to derive the standard of criticism from the psychological effects of the poem and ends in impressionism and relativism. The outcome of either Fallacy, the Intentional or the Affective, is that the poem itself, as an object of specifically critical judgment, tends to disappear.

"Most of our criticism in literature and the arts," complains Mr. René Wellek in one of his English Institute essays, "is still purely emotive: it judges works of art in terms of their emotional effect . . . and describes this effect by exclamations, suggested moods."[2] We are perhaps not so pessimistic as Mr. Wellek about the pervasiveness of the critical method which he describes, but we believe there can be no doubt that his mistrust of the method is well-founded. Mr. C. S. Lewis in three lectures entitled *The Abolition of Man*[3] has recently turned what we should judge to be a discomforting scrutiny on the doctrine of emotive relativism as it appears in textbooks of English composition for use in schools. Mr. John Crowe Ransom in a chapter of his *New Criticism*,[4] "I. A. Richards: the Psychological Critic," has done the like for some of the more sophisticated claims of neuro-psychological poetics. In the present essay, we would discuss briefly the history and fruits of affective criticism, some of its correlatives in cognitive criticism, and hence certain cognitive characteristics of poetry which have made affective criticism plausible. We would observe also the premises of affective criticism, as they appear today, in certain philosophic and pseudo-philosophic disciplines of wide influence. And first and mainly that of "semantics."

I

The separation of emotive from referential meaning was urged very persuasively, it will be remembered, about twenty years ago in the earlier works of Mr. I. A. Richards.[5] The types of meaning which were defined in his *Practical Criticism* and in the *Meaning of Meaning* of Messrs. Ogden and Richards created, partly by suggestion, partly with the aid of direct statement, a clean "antithesis" between "symbolic and emotive use of language." In his *Practical Criticism* Mr. Richards spoke of "aesthetic" or "projectile" words—

2. "The Parallelism between Literature and the Arts," *English Institute Annual*, 1941 (New York, 1942), p. 50 [Wimsatt and Beardsley's note]. Wellek (1903–1995), Austrian-born American literary theorist and scholar.

3. *The Abolition of Man: or, Reflections on Education with Special Reference to the Teaching of English in the Upper Forms of Schools* (1947). Lewis (1898–1963), Irish-born literary scholar and novelist.

4. A 1941 book by Ransom (1888–1974), American poet and critic.

5. English literary theorist (1893–1979), who published *Practical Criticism* in 1929 and *Science and Poetry* in 1925. With the English linguist Charles Kay Ogden (1889–1957), he published *The Meaning of Meaning* in 1923.

adjectives by which we project feelings at objects themselves altogether innocent of these feelings or of any qualities corresponding to them. And in his succinct *Science and Poetry*, science is statement, poetry is pseudo-statement which plays the important role of making us feel better about things than statements would. After Mr. Richards—and under the influence too of Count Korzybski's non-Aristotelian *Science and Sanity*—came the semantic school of Messrs. Chase, Hayakawa, Walpole, and Lee.[6] Most recently Mr. C. L. Stevenson[7] in his *Ethics and Language* has given an account which, as it is more careful and explicit than the others, may be taken as most clearly pleading their cause—and best revealing its weakness.

One of the most emphatic points in Mr. Stevenson's system is the distinction between what a word *means* and what it *suggests*. To make the distinction in a given case, one applies what the semiotician calls a "linguistic rule" ("definition" in traditional terminology), the role of which is to stabilize responses to a word. The word "athlete" may be said to *mean* one interested in sports, among other things, but merely to *suggest* a tall young man. The linguistic rule is that "athletes are necessarily interested in sports, but may or may not be tall." All this is on the side of what may be called the *descriptive* (or *cognitive*) function of words. For a second and separate main function of words—that is, the *emotive*—there is no linguistic rule to stabilize responses and, therefore, in Mr. Stevenson's system, no parallel distinction between meaning and suggestion. Although the term "quasi-dependent emotive meaning" is recommended by Mr. Stevenson for a kind of emotive "meaning" which is "conditional to the cognitive *suggestiveness* of a sign," the main drift of his argument is that emotive "meaning" is something noncorrelative to and independent of descriptive (or cognitive) meaning. Thus, emotive "meaning" is said to survive sharp changes in descriptive meaning. And words with the same descriptive meaning are said to have very different emotive "meanings." "License" and "liberty," for example, Mr. Stevenson believes to have in some contexts the same descriptive meaning, but opposite emotive "meanings." Finally, there are words which he believes to have no descriptive meaning, yet a decided emotive "meaning": these are expletives of various sorts.

But a certain further distinction, and an important one, which does not appear in Mr. Stevenson's system—nor in those of his forerunners—is invited by his persistent use of the word "meaning" for both cognitive and emotive language functions and by the absence from the emotive of his careful distinction between "meaning" and "suggestion." It is a fact worth insisting upon that the term "emotive meaning," as used by Mr. Stevenson, and the more cautious term "feeling," as used by Mr. Richards to refer to one of his four types of "meaning," do not refer to any such cognitive meaning as that conveyed by the name of an emotion—"anger" or "love." Rather, these key terms refer to the *expression* of emotive states which Messrs. Ste-

6. Irving J. Lee (1909–1955), author of studies in the philosophy of language, including *Language Habits in Human Affairs: An Introduction to General Semantics* (1941). Count Alfred Korzybski (1879–1950), Polish-born American scholar and philosopher of language, author of *Science and Sanity: An Introduction to Non-Aristotelian Systems and General Semantics* (1933). Stuart Chase (1888–1985), American economist and social scientist S. I. Hayakawa (1906–1992), Canadian linguist and later U.S. senator. Hugh R. Walpole (1905–1997), American academic.

7. Charles L. Stevenson (ca. 1908–1979), American philosopher; *Ethics and Language* was published in 1944.

venson and Richards believe to be effected by certain words—for instance, "license," "liberty," "pleasant," "beautiful," "ugly"—and hence also to the emotive *response* which these words may evoke in a hearer. As the term "meaning" has been traditionally and usefully assigned to the cognitive, or descriptive, functions of language, it would have been well if these writers had employed, in such contexts, some less pre-empted term. "Import" might have been a happy choice. Such differentiation in vocabulary would have had the merit of reflecting a profound difference in linguistic function—all the difference between grounds of emotion and emotions themselves, between what is immediately meant by words and what is evoked by the meaning of words, or what more briefly might be said to be the "import" of the words themselves.

Without pausing to examine Mr. Stevenson's belief that expletives have no descriptive meaning, we are content to observe in passing that these words at any rate have only the vaguest emotive *import*, something raw, unarticulated, imprecise. "Oh!" (surprise and related feelings), "Ah!" (regret), "Ugh!" (distaste). It takes a more descriptive reference to specify the feeling. "In quiet she reposes. Ah! would that I did too." But a more central re-emphasis for Mr. Stevenson's position—and for that of his forerunners including Mr. Richards—seems required by a fact scarcely mentioned in semantic writings: namely, that a large and obvious area of emotive *import* depends directly upon descriptive meaning (either with or without words of explicit ethical valuation)—as when a person says and is believed: "General X ordered the execution of 50,000 civilian hostages," or "General X is guilty of the murder of 50,000 civilian hostages." And secondly, by the fact that a great deal of emotive *import* which does not depend thus directly on descriptive *meaning* does depend on descriptive *suggestion*. Here we have the "quasi-dependent emotive meaning" of Mr. Stevenson's system—a "meaning" to which surely he assigns too slight a role. This is the kind of emotive import, we should say, which appears when words change in descriptive *meaning* yet preserve a similar emotive "meaning"—when the Communists take over the term "democracy" and apply it to something else, preserving, however, the old descriptive *suggestion*, a government of, by, and for the people. It appears in pairs of words like "liberty" and "license," which even if they have the same descriptive meaning (as one may doubt), certainly carry very different descriptive suggestions. Or one might cite the word series in Bentham's[8] classic "Catalogue of Motives":—"humanity, good-will, partiality," "frugality, pecuniary interest, avarice." Or the other standard examples of emotive insinuation: "Animals sweat, men perspire, women glow." "I am firm, thou art obstinate, he is pigheaded." Or the sentence, "There should be a revolution every twenty years," to which the experimenter in emotive responses attaches now the name Karl Marx (and arouses suspicion), now that of Thomas Jefferson (and provokes applause).[9]

The principle applies conspicuously to the numerous examples offered by

8. Jeremy Bentham (1748–1832), English writer, reformer, and utilitarian philosopher; the "Catalogue" is in his *Introduction to the Principles of Morals and Legislation* (1789), chap. 10.

9. In letters to James Madison (1789) and Samuel Kercheval (1816), Jefferson (1743–1826) argued that each generation should act independently, choosing its own form of government at regular intervals of about 20 years. At the beginning of the cold war, the contrast between the Founding Father Jefferson and the German political and economic theorist MARX (1818–1883) had particular pointedness.

the school of Messrs. Hayakawa, Walpole, and Lee. In the interest of brevity, though in what may seem a quixotic defiance of the warnings of this school against unindexed generalization—according to which semanticist (1) is not semanticist (2) is not semanticist (3), and so forth—we call attention to Mr. Irving Lee's *Language Habits in Human Affairs*, particularly Chapters VII and VIII. According to Mr. Lee, every mistake that anyone ever makes in acting, since in some direct or remote sense it involves language or thought (which is related to language), may be ascribed to "bad language habits," a kind of magic misuse of words. No distinctions are permitted. Basil Rathbone,[1] handed a scenario entitled *The Monster*, returns it unread, but accepts it later under a different title. The Ephraimite says "Sibboleth" instead of "Shibboleth" and is slain.[2] A man says he is offended by four-letter words describing events in a novel, but not by the events. Another man receives an erroneously worded telegram which says that his son is dead. The shock is fatal. One would have thought that with this example Lee's simplifying prejudice might have broken down—that a man who is misinformed that his son is dead may have leave himself to drop dead without being thought a victim of emotive incantation. Or that the title of a scenario is some ground for the inference that it is a Grade-B horror movie; that the use of phonetic principles in choosing a password is reason rather than magic—as "lollapalooza" and "lullabye" were used against infiltration tactics on Guadalcanal;[3] that four-letter words may ascribe to events certain qualities which a reader himself finds it distasteful to contemplate and would rather not ascribe to them. None of these examples (except the utterly anomalous "Sibboleth") offers any evidence, in short, that what a word *does* to a person is to be ascribed to anything except what it *means*, or if this connection is not apparent, at the most and with a little reflection, by what it *suggests*.

A question about the relation of language to objects of emotion is a shadow and index of another question, about the cognitive status of emotions themselves. It is an entirely consistent cultural phenomenon that within the same period as the *floruit* of semantics one kind of anthropology has delivered a parallel attack upon the relation of the objects themselves to emotions, or more specifically, upon the constancy of their relations through the times and places of human societies. In the classic treatise of Westermarck[4] on *Ethical Relativity* we learn, for example, that the custom of eliminating the aged and unproductive has been practiced among certain primitive tribes and nomadic races. Other customs, that of exposing babies, that of suicide, that of showing hospitality to strangers—or the contrary custom of eating them, the reception of the Cyclops rather than that of Alcinous[5]—seem to have enjoyed in some cultures a degree of approval unknown or at least unusual in our own. But even Westermarck[6] has noticed that difference of

1. English actor (1892–1967).
2. The Gileadites used their enemies' inability to say *sh-* to detect them; see Judges 12.4–6.
3. That is, the Americans attempting to occupy the island in World War II believed that native speakers of Japanese would be unable to pronounce *l*-laden words.
4. Edward Alexander Westermarck (1862–1939), Finnish anthropologist; *Ethical Relativity* was published in 1932.
5. In Homer's *Odyssey* (ca. 8th c. B.C.E.), Odysseus was aided in his journey home to Ithaca by Alcinous, king of Phaeacia; the Cyclops planned to eat Odysseus and his companions.
6. More recent researches and more precise analysis have tended to reveal a greater universality in the emotive experience of cultures than Westermarck admits. As an example of this trend, see C. S. Ford, "Society, Culture, and the Human Organism," *Journal of General Psychology* 20 (1939), pp. 135–79 [Wimsatt and Beardsley's note].

emotion "largely originates in different measures of knowledge, based on experience of the consequences of conduct, and in different beliefs." That is to say, the different emotions, even though they are responses to similar objects or actions, may yet be responses to different qualities or functions—to the edibility of Odysseus rather than to his comeliness or manliness. A converse of this is the fact that for different objects in different cultures there may be on cognitive grounds emotions of similar quality—for the cunning of Odysseus and for the strategy of Montgomery at El Alamein.[7] There may be a functional analogy for any alien object of emotion. Were it otherwise, indeed, there would be no way of understanding and describing alien emotions, no basis on which the science of the cultural relativist might proceed.

We shall not pretend to frame any formal discourse upon affective psychology, the laws of emotion. At this point, nevertheless, we venture to rehearse some generalities about objects, emotions, and words. Emotion, it is true, has a well-known capacity to fortify opinion, to inflame cognition, and to grow upon itself in surprising proportions to grains of reason. We have mob-psychology, psychosis, and neurosis. We have "free-floating anxiety" and all the vaguely understood and inchoate states of apprehension, depression, or elation, the prevailing complexions of melancholy or cheer. But it is well to remember that these states are indeed inchoate or vague and by that fact may even verge upon the unconscious.[8] They are the correlatives of very generalized objects, of general patterns of conception or misconception. At a less intensely affective level, we have "sensitivity" and on the other hand what has been called "affective stupidity." There is the well-known saying of Pascal: "Le coeur a ses raisons que la raison ne connaît pas."[9] But to consider these sensitivities and "raisons" as special areas of knowing and response makes better sense than to refer them to a special faculty of knowing. "Moral sentiments," we take it, are a part of eighteenth-century history. We have, again, the popular and self-vindicatory forms of confessing emotion. "He makes me boil." "It burns me up." Or in the novels of Evelyn Waugh[1] a social event or a person is "sick-making." But these locutions involve an extension of the strict operational meaning of *make* or *effect*. A food or a poison causes pain or death, but for an emotion we have a reason or an object, not a cause. We have, as Mr. Ransom points out, not unspecified fear, but fear of something fearful, men with machine guns or the day of doom. If objects are ever connected by "emotional congruity," as in the association psychology of J. S. Mill,[2] this can mean only that similar emotions attach to various objects because of similarity in the objects or in their relations. What makes one angry is something painful, insulting, or unjust. One does not call it an angry thing. The feeling and its correlative, far from being the same, are almost opposites. And the distinction holds even when the name of the correlative quality is verbally cognate with that of the emotion,—

7. A town of northern Egypt on the Mediterranean Sea, where, in late 1942, British forces under General Bernard Montgomery decisively defeated Field Marshal Erwin Rommel's German troops and won a crucial Allied victory in World War II.

8. "If feeling be regarded as conscious, it is unquestionable that it involves in some measure an intellectual process." F. Paulhan, *The Laws of Feeling*, trans. C. K. Ogden (London, 1930), p. 153 [Wimsatt and Beardsley's note].

9. The heart has its reasons that reason knows nothing of (French). From the French moralist Blaise Pascal (1623–1662), *Pensées* (1670).

1. English writer (1903–1966), many of whose novels are satirical.

2. John Stuart Mill (1806–1873), English philosopher, economist, and social reformer.

as *lovable* to *loving*. Love, as Plato is at pains to make clear, loves that which it has not.[3]

The tourist who said a waterfall was pretty provoked the silent disgust of Coleridge, while the other who said it was sublime won his approval. This, as Mr. C. S. Lewis so well observes,[4] was not the same as if the tourist had said, "I feel sick," and Coleridge had thought, "No, I feel quite well."

The doctrine of emotive meaning propounded recently by the semanticists has seemed to offer a scientific basis for one kind of affective relativism in poetics—the personal. That is, if a person can correctly say either "liberty" or "license" in a given context independently of the cognitive quality of the context, merely at will or from emotion, it follows that a reader may likely feel either "hot" or "cold" and report either "bad" or "good" on reading either "liberty" or "license"—either an ode by Keats or a limerick. The sequence of licenses is endless. Similarly, the doctrines of one school of anthropology have gone far to fortify another kind of affective relativism, the cultural or historical, the measurement of poetic value by the degree of feeling felt by the readers of a given era. A different psychological criticism, that by author's intention, as we noted in our earlier essay, is consistent both with piety for the poet and with antiquarian curiosity and has been heavily supported by the historical scholar and biographer. So affective criticism, though in its personal or impressionistic form it meets with strong dislike from scholars, yet in its theoretical or scientific form finds strong support from the same quarter. The historical scholar, if not much interested in his own personal responses or in those of his students, is intensely interested in whatever can be discovered about those of any member of Shakespeare's audience.

II

Plato's feeding and watering of the passions[5] was an early example of affective theory, and Aristotle's counter-theory of catharsis was another (with modern intentionalistic analogues in theories of "relief" and "sublimation"). There was also the "transport" of the audience in the *Peri Hupsous*[6] (matching the great soul of the poet), and this had echoes of passion or enthusiasm among eighteenth-century Longinians. We have had more recently the contagion theory of Tolstoy (with its intentionalistic analogue in the emotive expressionism of Veron), the *Einfühlung* or empathy of Lipps and related pleasure theories, either more or less tending to the "objectification" of Santayana: "Beauty is pleasure regarded as the quality of a thing." An affinity for these theories is seen in certain theories of the comic during the same

3. In *Symposium* 189c–193d, PLATO (ca. 427–ca. 347 B.C.E.) presents a myth that explains love as a search for one's missing half; the original humans (2-headed and 8-limbed) were split by the gods.

4. The anecdote as cited by Mr. Lewis (*Abolition of Man*, Oxford, 1944, pp. 3, 9) differs, though not in a way relevant to our argument, from the version known to us in the *Journals of Dorothy Wordsworth*, ed. E. de Selincourt (London, 1941), 1: 223–24. Cf. E. de Selincourt, *Wordsworthian and Other Studies* (Oxford, 1947), p. 185 [Wimsatt and Beardsley's note]. Dorothy Wordsworth (1771–1855), younger sister of the poet WILLIAM WORDSWORTH; she spent much time in the company of her brother and his friend the poet and critic SAMUEL TAYLOR COLERIDGE.

5. Strictly, a theory not of poetry, but of morals, as, to take a curious modern instance, Lucie Guillet's *La Poéticothérapie, Efficacités du Fluide Poétique* (Paris, 1946), is a theory not of poetry but of healing. Aristotle's catharsis is a true theory of poetry, i.e., part of a definition of poetry [Wimsatt and Beardsley's note]. For ARISTOTLE'S (384–322 B.C.E.) *Poetics*, see above. Plato's account of the proper balance of the human soul is found in *Republic* 3–4.

6. *On Sublimity* (Greek), a 1st-century C.E. treatise attributed to LONGINUS (see above).

era, the relaxation theory of Penjon, the laughter theory of Mr. Max Eastman.[7] In their *Foundations of Aesthetics* Messrs. Ogden, Richards, and Wood listed sixteen types of aesthetic theory, of which at least seven may be described as affective. Among these the theory of Synaesthesis[8] (Beauty is what produces an equilibrium of appetencies) was the one they themselves espoused. This was developed at length by Mr. Richards in his *Principles of Literary Criticism*.[9]

The theories just mentioned may be considered as belonging to one branch of affective criticism, and that the main one, the emotive—unless the theory of empathy, with its transport of the self into the object, its vital meaning and enrichment of experience, belongs rather with a parallel and equally ancient affective theory, the imaginative. This is represented by the figure of vividness so often mentioned in the rhetorics—*efficacia, enargeia,* or the *phantasiai* in Chapter XV of *Peri Hupsous*. This if we mistake not is the imagination the "Pleasures" of which are celebrated by Addison[1] in his series of *Spectators*. It is an imagination implicit in the theories of Leibniz and Baumgarten,[2] that beauty lies in clear but confused, or sensuous, ideas; in the statement of Warton in his *Essay on Pope*[3] that the selection of "lively pictures . . . chiefly constitutes true poetry." In our time, as the emotive form of psychologistic or affective theory has found its most impressive champion in Mr. I. A. Richards, so the imaginative form has in Mr. Max Eastman, whose *Literary Mind* and *Enjoyment of Poetry* have much to say about vivid realizations or heightened consciousness.

But an important distinction can be made between those who have coolly investigated what poetry does to others and those who have testified what it does to themselves. The theory of intention or author-psychology, as we noted in our earlier essay, has been the intense conviction of poets themselves, Wordsworth, Keats, Housman,[4] and since the Romantic era, of young persons interested in poetry, the introspective amateurs and soul-cultivators. In a parallel way, affective theory has often been less a scientific view of literature than a prerogative—that of the soul adventuring among masterpieces, the contagious teacher, the poetic radiator—a magnetic rhapsodic Ion, a Saintsbury, a Quiller-Couch, a William Lyon Phelps.[5] Criticism on this theory has approximated the tone of the Buchmanite[6] confession, the

7. American writer and prominent radical (1883–1969), whose books *Enjoyment of Poetry* (1931) and *The Literary Mind: Its Place in an Age of Science* (1931) are mentioned later. Leo Tolstoy (1828–1910), Russian novelist and moral philosopher. Eugène Véron (1825–1889), French aesthetician. Theodor Lipps (1851–1914), German aesthetician. George Santayana (1863–1952), Spanish-born American moral and aesthetic philosopher. Auguste Penjon (1843–1919), French philosopher.

8. The harmony of different or opposing impulses produced by a work of art; a theory developed by C. K. Ogden, I. A. Richards, and James Wood in *The Foundations of Aesthetics* (1925).

9. Published in 1924.

1. JOSEPH ADDISON (1672–1719), English essayist and critic; many of his essays appeared in the periodical *The Spectator*.

2. Alexander Gottlieb Baumgarten (1714–1762), German philosopher and aesthetician. Baron Gottfried Wilhelm von Leibnitz (1646–1716), German philosopher and mathematician.

3. *An Essay on the Genius and Writings of Pope* (2 vols.; 1756, 1782), by the English poet and critic Joseph Warton (1722–1800).

4. A. E. Housman (1859–1936), English classicist and poet.

5. American educator and critic (1865–1943). Ion: a rhapsode featured in an early dialogue of that name by Plato; it focuses on the power of poetry and the concept of inspiration. George Saintsbury (1845–1933), English scholar and critic; his *History of Criticism and Literary Taste in Europe from the Earliest Texts to the Present Day*, 3 vols. (1900–05), is later quoted. Arthur Quiller-Couch (1863–1944), English poet and editor.

6. Characteristic of the American evangelist Frank Nathan Daniel Buchman (1878–1961).

revival meeting. "To be quite frank," says Anatole France, "the critic ought to say: 'Gentlemen, I am going to speak about myself apropos of Shakespeare, apropos of Racine. . . .' "[7] The sincerity of the critic becomes an issue, as for the intentionalist the sincerity of the poet.

"The mysterious entity called the Grand Style," says Saintsbury. . . . "My definition . . . [of it] would . . . come nearer to the Longinian Sublime."

> Whenever this perfection of expression acquires such force that it transmutes the subject and transports the hearer or reader, then and there the Grand Style exists, for so long, and in such degree, as the transmutation of the one and the transportation of the other lasts.

And if we follow him further in his three essays on the subject (the Grand Style in Shakespeare, in Milton, in Dante), we discover that "It is nearly as impossible to describe, meticulously, the constituents of its grandeur as to describe that of the majesty of the sun itself."

> The fact is . . . that this Grand Style is not easily tracked or discovered by observation, unless you give yourself up primarily to the *feeling* of it.

With Dante, "It is pure magic: the white magic of style and of grand style." This is the grand style, the emotive style, of nineteenth-century affective criticism. A somewhat less resonant style which has been heard in our columns of Saturday and Sunday reviewing and from our literary explorers is more closely connected with imagism and the kind of vividness sponsored by Mr. Eastman. In the *Book-of-the-Month Club News* Dorothy Canfield testifies to the power of a new novel: "To read this book is like living through an experience rather than just reading about it."[8] "And so a poem," says Hans Zinsser,

> means nothing to me unless it can carry me away with the gentle or passionate pace of its emotion, over obstacles of reality into meadows and covers of illusion . . . The sole criterion for me is whether it can sweep me with it into emotion or illusion of beauty, terror, tranquillity, or even disgust.[9]

It is but a short step to what we may call the physiological form of affective criticism. Beauty, said Burke[1] in the Eighteenth Century, is small and curved and smooth, clean and fair and mild; it "acts by relaxing the solids of the whole system." More recently, on the side of personal testimony, we have the oft-quoted goose-flesh experience in a letter of Emily Dickinson,[2] and the top of her head taken off; the bristling of the skin while Housman was

7. *On Life and Letters*, First Series, trans. A. W. Evans (London, 1911), preface, p. viii [Wimsatt and Beardsley's note]. France (1844–1924), French writer and critic. Jean Racine (1639–1699), French playwright.

8. *New York Times Book Review*, April 13, 1947, p. 29 [Wimsatt and Beardsley's note]. Canfield (1879–1958), American novelist and short story writer.

9. *As I Remember Him*, quoted by J. Donald Adams, "Speaking of Books," *New York Times Book Review*, April 20, 1947, p. 2. Mr. Adams's weekly department has been a happy hunting ground for such specimens [Wimsatt and Beardsley's note]. Zinsser (1878–1940), American bacteriologist and immunologist; *As I Remember Him* (1940) is his 3d-person autobiography.

1. EDMUND BURKE (1729–1797), English writer and statesman; his *Philosophical Inquiry into the Origins of Our Idea of the Sublime and Beautiful* (1757; see above) is quoted.

2. The American poet (1830–1886) made these comments to her editor, Thomas Wentworth Higginson, when they met in 1870 after a long correspondence.

shaving, the "shiver down the spine," the sensation in "the pit of the stomach."[3] And if poetry has been discerned by these tests, truth also. "All scientists," said D. H. Lawrence to Aldous Huxley, "are liars. . . . I don't care about evidence. Evidence doesn't mean anything to me. I don't feel it *here*." And, reports Huxley, "he pressed his two hands on his solar plexus."[4]

An even more advanced grade of affective theory, that of hallucination, would seem to have played some part in the neo-classic conviction about the unities of time and place, was given a modified continuation of existence in phrases of Coleridge[5] about a "willing suspension of disbelief" and a "temporary half faith," and may be found today in some textbooks. The hypnotic hypothesis of E. D. Snyder[6] might doubtless be invoked in its support. As this form of affective theory is the least theoretical in detail, has the least content, and makes the least claim on critical intelligence, so it is in its most concrete instances not a theory but a fiction or a fact—of no critical significance. In the Eighteenth Century Fielding conveys a right view of the hallucinative power of drama in his comic description of Partridge[7] seeing Garrick act the ghost scene in Hamlet. "O la! sir. . . . If I was frightened, I am not the only person. . . . You may call me coward if you will; but if that little man there upon the stage is not frightened, I never saw any man frightened in my life." Partridge is today found perhaps less often among the sophisticates at the theater than among the myriad audience of movie and radio. It is said, and no doubt reliably, that during the war Stefan Schnabel played Nazi roles in radio dramas so convincingly that he received numerous letters of complaint, and in particular one from a lady who said that she had reported him to General MacArthur.[8]

III

As the systematic affective critic professes to deal not merely, if at all, with his own experiences, but with those of persons in general, his most resolute search for evidence will lead him into the dreary and antiseptic laboratory, to testing with Fechner the effects of triangles and rectangles, to inquiring what kinds of colors are suggested by a line of Keats, or to measuring the motor discharges attendant upon reading it.[9] If animals could read poetry, the affective critic might make discoveries analogous to those of W. B. Cannon about *Bodily Changes in Pain, Hunger, Fear and Rage*[1]—the increased liberation of sugar from the liver, the secretion of adrenin from the adrenal gland. The affective critic is today actually able, if he wishes, to measure the

3. From Housman, *The Name and Nature of Poetry* (1933).

4. *The Olive Tree* (New York, 1937), p. 212 [Wimsatt and Beardsley's note]. Lawrence (1885–1930) and Huxley (1894–1963), English novelists.

5. See *Biographia Literaria* (1817; above) and Coleridge's lectures on Shakespeare.

6. See *Hypnotic Poetry: A Study of Trance Inducing Technique in Certain Poems and Its Literary Significance* (1930), by Edward Douglas Snyder.

7. A worthy but unworldly schoolmaster in *Tom Jones* (1749), by Henry Fielding (1707–1754). David Garrick (1717–1779), English actor and theater manager.

8. *New Yorker*, December 11, 1943, p. 28 [Wimsatt and Beardsley's note]. Schnabel (1912–1999), German actor. Douglas MacArthur (1880–1964), American commander of the Allied forces in the South Pacific during World War II.

9. "The final averages showed that the combined finger movements for the Byron experiments were eighteen metres longer than they were for Keats." R. C. Givler, *The Psycho-Physiological Effect of the Elements of Speech in Relation to Poetry* (Princeton, 1915), p. 62, quoted by Thomas C. Pollock, *The Nature of Literature* (Princeton, 1942), p. 110 [Wimsatt and Beardsley's note]. Gustav Theodor Fechner (1801–1887), German psychologist and physicist who studied the relationship between strength of stimulus and intensity of sensation.

1. Published in 1915 (2d ed., 1929).

"psycho-galvanic reflex" of persons subjected to a given moving picture.[2] But, as a recent writer on *Science and Criticism* points out: "Students have sincerely reported an 'emotion' at the mention of the word 'mother,' although a galvanometer indicated no bodily change whatever. They have also reported no emotion at the mention of 'prostitute,' although the galvanometer gave a definite kick."[3] Thomas Mann and a friend came out of a movie weeping copiously—but Mann narrates the incident in support of his view that movies are not Art. "Art is a *cold* sphere."[4] The gap between various levels of physiological experience and the perception of value remains wide, whether in the laboratory or not.

In a similar way, general affective theory at the literary level has, by the very implications of its program, produced very little actual criticism. The author of the ancient *Peri Hupsous* is weakest at the points where he explains that passion and sublimity are the palliatives or excuses (*alexipharmaka*) of bold metaphors, and that passions which verge on transport are the lenitives or remedies (*panakeia*) of such audacities in speech as hyperbole. The literature of catharsis has dealt with the historical and theoretical question whether Aristotle meant a medical or a lustratory[5] metaphor, whether the genitive which follows *katharsis* is of the thing purged or of the object purified. Even the early critical practice of Mr. I. A. Richards had little to do with his theory of synaesthesis. His *Practical Criticism* depended mainly on two important constructive principles of criticism which Mr. Richards has realized and insisted upon—(1) that rhythm (the vague, if direct, expression of emotion) and poetic form in general are intimately connected with and interpreted by other and more precise parts of poetic meaning, (2) that poetic meaning is inclusive or multiple and hence sophisticated. The latter quality of poetry may perhaps be the objective correlative of the affective state synaesthesis, but in applied criticism there would seem to be not much room for synaesthesis or for the touchy little attitudes of which it is composed.

The report of some readers, on the other hand, that a poem or story induces in them vivid images, intense feelings, or heightened consciousness, is neither anything which can be refuted nor anything which it is possible for the objective critic to take into account. The purely affective report is either too physiological or it is too vague. Feelings, as Hegel[6] has conveniently put it, "remain purely subjective affections of myself, in which the concrete matter vanishes, as though narrowed into a circle of the utmost abstraction." And the only constant or predictable thing about the vivid images which more eidetic readers experience is precisely their vividness—as may be seen by requiring a class of average pupils to draw illustrations of a short story or by consulting the newest Christmas edition of a childhood classic which one knew with the illustrations of Howard Pyle or N. C. Wyeth.[7] Vividness is not the thing in the work by which the work may be identified, but the result of a cognitive structure, which *is* the thing. "The

2. Wendell S. Dysinger and Christian A. Ruckmick, *The Emotional Response of Children to the Motion Picture Situation* (New York, 1933) [Wimsatt and Beardsley's note].
3. Herbert J. Muller, *Science and Criticism* (New Haven, 1943), p. 137 [Wimsatt and Beardsley's note].
4. "Ueber den Film," in *Die Forderung des Tages* (Berlin, 1930), p. 387 [Wimsatt and Beardsley's note]. Mann (1875–1955), German novelist and essayist.
5. Ritually purifying.
6. GEORG WILHELM FRIEDRICH HEGEL (1770–1831), German philosopher.
7. Pyle (1853–1911) and Wyeth (1882–1945), both prolific American book illustrators.

story is good," as the student so often says in his papers, "because it leaves so much to the imagination." The opaque accumulation of physical detail in some realistic novels has been an absurd reduction of plastic or graphic theory aptly dubbed by Mr. Middleton Murry "the pictorial fallacy."[8]

Certain theorists, notably Mr. Richards, have anticipated some difficulties of affective criticism by saying that it is not intensity of emotion that characterizes poetry (murder, robbery, fornication, horse-racing, war—perhaps even chess—take care of that better), but the subtle quality of patterned emotions which play at the subdued level of disposition or attitude. We have psychological theories of aesthetic distance, detachment, or disinterestedness. A criticism on these principles has already taken important steps toward objectivity. If Mr. Eastman's theory of imaginative vividness appears today chiefly in the excited puffs of the newspaper Book Sections, the campaign of the semanticists and the balanced emotions of Mr. Richards, instead of producing their own school of affective criticism, have contributed much to recent schools of cognitive analysis, of paradox, ambiguity, irony, and symbol. It is not always true that the emotive and cognitive forms of criticism will sound far different. If the affective critic (avoiding both the physiological and the abstractly psychological form of report) ventures to state with any precision what a line of poetry *does*—as "it fills us with a mixture of melancholy and reverence for antiquity"—either the statement will be patently abnormal or false, or it will be a description of what the meaning of the line *is*: "the spectacle of massive antiquity in ruins." Tennyson's "Tears, idle tears,"[9] as it deals with an emotion which the speaker at first seems not to understand, might be thought to be a specially emotive poem. "The last stanza," says Mr. Brooks in his recent analysis,[1] "evokes an intense emotional response from the reader." But this statement is not really a part of Mr. Brooks's criticism of the poem—rather a witness of his fondness for it. "The second stanza,"—Mr. Brooks might have said at an earlier point in his analysis—"gives us a momentary vivid realization of past happy experiences, then makes us sad at their loss." But he says actually: "The conjunction of the qualities of sadness and freshness is reinforced by the fact that the same basic symbol—the light on the sails of a ship hull down—has been employed to suggest both qualities." The distinction between these formulations may seem trivial, and in the first example which we furnished may be practically unimportant. Yet the difference between translatable emotive formulas and more physiological and psychologically vague ones—cognitively untranslatable—is theoretically of the greatest import. The distinction even when it is a very faint one is at the dividing point between paths which lead to polar opposites in criticism, to classical objectivity and to romantic reader psychology.

The critic whose formulations lean to the emotive and the critic whose formulations lean to the cognitive will in the long run produce a vastly different sort of criticism.

The more specific the account of the emotion induced by a poem, the more nearly it will be an account of the reasons for emotion, the poem itself, and the more reliable it will be as an account of what the poem is likely to

8. In *The Problem of Style* (1936). John Middleton Murry (1889–1957), English critic and editor.

9. An 1847 poem by Alfred, Lord Tennyson (1809–1892).

1. In *The Well Wrought Urn* (1947). CLEANTH BROOKS (1906–1994), American New Critic.

induce in other—sufficiently informed—readers. It will in fact supply the kind of information which will enable readers to respond to the poem. It will talk not of tears, prickles, or other physiological symptoms, of feeling angry, joyful, hot, cold, or intense, or of vaguer states of emotional disturbance, but of shades of distinction and relation between objects of emotion. It is precisely here that the discerning literary critic has his insuperable advantage over the subject of the laboratory experiment and over the tabulator of the subject's responses. The critic is not a contributor to statistically countable reports about the poem, but a teacher or explicator of meanings. His readers, if they are alert, will not be content to take what he says as testimony, but will scrutinize it as teaching. The critic's report will speak of emotions which are not only complex and dependent upon a precise object but also, and for these reasons, stable. This paradox, if it is one, is the analogue in emotive terms of the antique formula of the metaphysical critic, that poetry is both individual and universal—a concrete universal. It may well be that the contemplation of this object, or pattern of emotive knowledge, which is the poem, is the ground for some ultimate emotional state which may be termed the aesthetic (some empathy, some synaesthesis, some objectified feeling of pleasure). It may well be. The belief is attractive; it may exalt our view of poetry. But it is no concern of criticism, no part of criteria.

IV

Poetry, as Matthew Arnold believed, "attaches the emotion to the idea; the idea *is* the fact."[2] The objective critic, however, must admit that it is not easy to explain how this is done, how poetry makes ideas thick and complicated enough to attach emotions. In his essay on "Hamlet and His Problems"[3] Mr. T. S. Eliot finds Hamlet's state of emotion unsatisfactory because it lacks an "objective correlative," a "chain of events" which are the "formula of that *particular* emotion." The emotion is "in *excess* of the facts as they appear." It is "inexpressible." Yet Hamlet's emotion must be expressible, we submit, and actually expressed too (by something) in the play; otherwise Mr. Eliot would not know it is there—in excess of the facts. That Hamlet himself or Shakespeare may be baffled by the emotion is beside the point. The second chapter of Mr. Yvor Winters' *Primitivism and Decadence*[4] has gone much further in clarifying a distinction adumbrated by Mr. Eliot. Without embracing the extreme doctrine of Mr. Winters, that if a poem cannot be paraphrased it is a poor poem, we may yet with profit reiterate his main thesis: that there is a difference between the motive, as he calls it, or logic of an emotion, and the surface or texture of a poem constructed to describe the emotion, and that both are important to a poem. Mr. Winters has shown, we think, how there can be in effect "fine poems" about nothing. There is rational progression and there is "qualitative progression,"[5] the latter, with several subtly related modes, a characteristic of decadent poetry. Qualitative progression is the succession, the dream float, of images, not substantiated

2. From "The Study of Poetry" (1888), by the English poet and critic ARNOLD (1822–1888).
3. A 1919 essay included in *The Sacred Wood* (1920), by ELIOT (1888–1965).
4. *Primitivism and Decadence: A Study of American Experimental Poetry* (1937). Winters (1900–1968), American poet and critic.
5. The term, as Mr. Winters indicates, is borrowed from Mr. Kenneth Burke's *Counter-Statement* [Wimsatt and Beardsley's note]. On the American critic BURKE (1897–1993), see above.

by a plot. "Moister than an oyster in its clammy cloister, I'm bluer than a wooer who has slipped in a sewer," says Mr. Morris Bishop in a recent comic poem:

> Chiller than a killer in a cinema thriller,
> Queerer than a leerer at his leer in a mirror,
> Madder than an adder with a stone in the bladder.
> If you want to know why, I cannot but reply:
> It is really no affair of yours.[6]

The term "pseudo-statement" was for Mr. Richards a patronizing term by which he indicated the attractive nullity of poems. For Mr. Winters, the kindred term "pseudo-reference" is a name for the more disguised kinds of qualitative progression and is a term of reproach. It seems to us highly significant that for another psychological critic, Mr. Max Eastman, so important a part of poetry as metaphor is in effect too pseudo-statement. The vivid realization of metaphor comes from its being in some way an obstruction to practical knowledge (like a torn coat sleeve to the act of dressing). Metaphor operates by being abnormal or inept, the wrong way of saying something.[7] Without pressing the point, we should say that an uncomfortable resemblance to this doctrine appears in Mr. Ransom's logical structure and local texture of irrelevance.[8]

What Mr. Winters has said seems basic. To venture both a slight elaboration of this and a return to the problem of emotive semantics surveyed in our first section: it is a well-known but nonetheless important truth that there are two kinds of real objects which have emotive quality, the objects which are the literal reasons for human emotion, and those which by some kind of association suggest either the reasons or the resulting emotion:—the thief, the enemy, or the insult that makes us angry, and the hornet that sounds and stings somewhat like ourselves when angry; the murderer or felon, and the crow that kills small birds and animals or feeds on carrion and is black like the night when crimes are committed by men. The arrangement by which these two kinds of emotive meaning are brought together in a juncture characteristic of poetry is, roughly speaking, the simile, the metaphor, and the various less clearly defined forms of association. We offer the following crude example as a kind of skeleton figure to which we believe all the issues can be attached.

> I. X feels as angry as a hornet.
> II. X whose lunch has been stolen feels as angry as a hornet.

No. I is, we take it, the qualitative poem, the vehicle of a metaphor, an objective correlative—for nothing. No. II adds the tenor of the metaphor, the motive for feeling angry, and hence makes the feeling itself more specific. The total statement has a more complex and testable structure. The element

6. *New Yorker*, May 31, 1947, p. 33 [Wimsatt and Beardsley's note]. Bishop (1893–1973), scholar and author of many volumes of light verse.

7. On pp. 183–84 of his *Literary Mind*, Mr. Eastman notices the possibility of inapt metaphor and seems about to explain why this would not be, on his hypothesis, even better than apt metaphor. But he never does. On p. 188, "Poetic metaphor is the employment of words to suggest impractical identifications." On p. 185 he alludes to the value of synecdoche as focussing attention on qualities of objects. It would seem to escape his attention that metaphor does the same [Wimsatt and Beardsley's note].

8. See Ransom's essay "Criticism as Pure Speculation" (1941).

of aptitude, or ineptitude, is more susceptible of discussion. "Light thickens, and the crow makes wing to the rocky wood" might be a line from a poem about nothing, but initially owed much of its power, and we daresay still does, to the fact that it is spoken by a tormented murderer who, as night draws on, has sent his agents out to perform a further "deed of dreadful note."[9]

These distinctions bear a close relation to the difference between historical statement which may be a reason for emotion because it is believed (Macbeth has killed the king) and fictitious or poetic statement, where a large component of suggestion (and hence metaphor) has usually appeared. The first of course seldom occurs pure, at least not for the public eye. The coroner or the intelligence officer may content himself with it. Not the chronicler, the bard, or the newspaper man. To these we owe more or less direct words of value and emotion (the murder, the atrocity, the wholesale butchery) and all the repertoire of suggestive meanings which here and there in history—with somewhat to start upon—an Achilles, a Beowulf,[1] a Macbeth—have created out of a mere case of factual reason for intense emotion a specified, figuratively fortified, and permanent object of less intense but far richer emotion. With the decline of heroes and of faith in objects as important, we have had within the last century a great flowering of poetry which has tried the utmost to do without any hero or action or fiction of these—the qualitative poetry of Mr. Winters' analysis. It is true that any hero and action when they become fictitious take the first step toward the simply qualitative, and all poetry, so far as separate from history, tends to be formula of emotion. The hero and action are taken as symbolic. A graded series from fact to quality might include: (1) the historic Macbeth, (2) Macbeth as Renaissance tragic protagonist, (3) a *Macbeth* written by Mr. Eliot, (4) a *Macbeth* written by Mr. Pound.[2] As Mr. Winters has explained, "the prince is briefly introduced in the footnotes" of *The Waste Land*; "it is to be doubted that Mr. Pound could manage such an introduction." Yet in no one of these four stages has anything like a pure emotive poetry been produced. The semantic analysis which we have offered in our first section would say that even in the last stages a poetry of pure emotion is an illusion. What we have is a poetry where kings are only symbols or even a poetry of hornets and crows, rather than of human deeds. Yet a poetry about things. How these things are joined in patterns and with what names of emotion, remains always the critical question. "*The Romance of the Rose* could not, without loss," observes Mr. Lewis, "be rewritten as the *Romance of the Onion*."[3]

Poetry is characteristically a discourse about both emotions and objects, or about the emotive quality of objects, and this through its preoccupation with symbol and metaphor. An emotion felt for one object is identified by reference to its analogue felt for another—a fact which is the basis for the expressionist doctrine of "objectification" or the giving to emotion a solid and outside objectivity of its own. The emotions correlative to the objects of poetry become a part of the matter dealt with—not communicated to the

9. That is, the murder of Banquo by Macbeth's agents, plotted in Shakespeare's *Macbeth* (ca. 1606), 3.1; the lines quoted are 3.2.44, 51–52.

1. Hero of the Old English poem that bears his name. Achilles: hero of Homer's *Iliad* (ca. 8th c. B.C.E.).

2. Ezra Pound (1885–1972), American poet and critic.

3. From *The Personal Heresy: A Controversy by E. M. W. Tillyard and C. S. Lewis* (1939), chap. 5. *Romance of the Rose*: a 13th-century French allegorical romance.

reader like an infection or disease, not inflicted mechanically like a bullet or knife wound, not administered like a poison, not simply expressed as by expletives or grimaces or rhythms, but presented in their objects and contemplated as a pattern of knowledge. Poetry is a way of fixing emotions or making them more permanently perceptible when objects have undergone a functional change from culture to culture, or when as simple facts of history they have lost emotive value with loss of immediacy. Though the reasons for emotion in poetry may not be so simple as Ruskin's "noble grounds for the noble emotions,"[4] yet a great deal of constancy for poetic objects of emotion—if we will look for constancy—may be traced through the drift of human history. The murder of Duncan by Macbeth, whether as history of the Eleventh Century or chronicle of the Sixteenth, has not tended to become the subject of a Christmas carol. In Shakespeare's play it is an act difficult to duplicate in all its immediate adjuncts of treachery, deliberation, and horror of conscience. Set in its galaxy of symbols—the hoarse raven, the thickening light, and the crow making wing, the babe plucked from the breast, the dagger in the air, the ghost, the bloody hands—this ancient murder has become an object of strongly fixed emotive value. The corpse of Polynices, a far more ancient object and partially concealed from us by the difficulties of the Greek, shows a similar pertinacity in remaining among the understandable motives of higher duty.[5] Funeral customs have changed, but not the web of issues, religious, political, and private, woven about the corpse "unburied, unhonoured, all unhallowed." Again, certain objects partly obscured in one age wax into appreciation in another, and partly through the efforts of the poet. It is not true that they suddenly arrive out of nothing. The pathos of Shylock,[6] for example, is not a creation of our time, though a smugly modern humanitarianism, because it has slogans, may suppose that this was not felt by Shakespeare or Southampton[7]—and may not perceive its own debt to Shakespeare. "Poets," says Shelley, "are the unacknowledged legislators of the world."[8] And it may be granted at least that poets have been leading expositors of the laws of feeling.[9]

To the relativist historian of literature falls the uncomfortable task of establishing as discrete cultural moments the past when the poem was written and first appreciated, and the present into which the poem with its clear and nicely interrelated meanings, its completeness, balance, and tension has survived. A structure of emotive objects so complex and so reliable as to have been taken for great poetry by any past age will never, it seems safe to say, so wane with the waning of human culture as not to be recoverable at least by a willing student. And on the same grounds a confidence seems indicated for the objective discrimination of all future poetic phenomena, though the premises or materials of which such poems will be constructed cannot be prescribed or foreseen. If the exegesis of some poems depends upon the understanding of obsolete or exotic customs, the poems themselves are the

4. Quoted from vol. 3 of *Modern Painters* (1856), by the English art and social critic John Ruskin (1819–1900).
5. That is, the duty of a sister to give her brother, though a rebel, proper burial rites, even when the king has ordered that he be left unburied as an example. The story is told in Sophocles' *Antigone* (ca. 441 B.C.E.).
6. The ruthless moneylender in Shakespeare's *Merchant of Venice* (1598).
7. Henry Wriothesley, third earl of Southampton (1573–1624), English politician, soldier, and patron of Shakespeare.
8. See *A Defence of Poetry* (written 1821; above).
9. Cf. Paulhan, *The Laws of Feeling*, pp. 105, 110 [Wimsatt and Beardsley's note].

most precise emotive evaluation of the customs. In the poet's finely contrived objects of emotion and in other works of art the historian finds his most reliable evidence about the emotions of antiquity—and the anthropologist, about those of contemporary primitivism. To appreciate courtly love we turn to Chrétien de Troyes and Marie de France.[1] Certain attitudes of late fourteenth-century England, toward knighthood, toward monasticism, toward the bourgeoisie, are nowhere more precisely illustrated than in the prologue to *The Canterbury Tales*. The field worker among the Zunis or the Navahos finds no informant so informative as the poet or the member of the tribe who can quote its myths.[2] In short, though cultures have changed and will change, poems remain and explain; and there is no legitimate reason why criticism, losing sight of its durable and peculiar objects, poems themselves, should become a dependent of social history or of anthropology.

1949

1. French poet (12th c.), who wrote narratives of courtly romance based on Celtic stories. Chrétien (active 1160–1190), French court poet who wrote important early literary treatments of the Arthurian legends.
2. See, for example, Clyde Kluckhohn and Dorothea Leighton, *The Navaho* (Cambridge, 1946), pp. 134–38; Ruth Benedict, *Zuni Mythology* (New York, 1935), introduction. The emphasis of Bronislaw Malinowski's *Myth in Primitive Psychology* (New York, 1926) is upon the need of cultural context to interpret myth. Nevertheless the myth is the main point of the book. "The anthropologist," says Malinowski, "has the myth-maker at his elbow" (p. 17) [Wimsatt and Beardsley's note].

SIMONE DE BEAUVOIR
1908–1986

Written in the absence of any organized feminist movement, Simone de Beauvoir's classic manifesto, *The Second Sex* (1949), provided the theoretical basis for the emergence in the 1960s and 1970s of feminist activism in both Europe and North America. Though her significant contributions to existentialist philosophy have often been overshadowed by the fame of her lifelong associate and lover, the philosopher JEAN-PAUL SARTRE, Beauvoir's importance for feminist theory is indisputable. With her famous remark that "One is not born, but rather becomes, a woman," which opens the second volume of *The Second Sex* (the original French text was published separately in two volumes issued months apart), Beauvoir inaugurated the social constructionist critique of essentialism that occupied feminist literary theory in the 1980s and 1990s. While her uncompromising rejection of any notion of a female nature or essence finds echoes in the writing of later feminist theorists such as JULIA KRISTEVA, MONIQUE WITTIG, and JUDITH BUTLER, *The Second Sex* has left its mark on virtually every aspect of the late-twentieth-century women's movement.

Born Simone Lucie Ernestine Marie Bertrande de Beauvoir in Paris, Beauvoir grew up the elder of two daughters in a comfortable middle-class family. Educated in a conservative Catholic girls' preparatory school, she attended various institutions of higher learning, successfully pursuing *licenses* (equivalent to a master's degree) in literature, philosophy, and mathematics. Among the first generation of women to be educated in the elite universities that had once been all-male preserves, Beauvoir graduated in 1929 from the Sorbonne with a degree in philosophy, having written a thesis on Leibniz. While a student she met Sartre, who was studying philosophy at the École Normale Supérieure, and began a friendship with the philosopher most closely associated with existentialism; other fellow students included the phenomenologist Maurice Merleau-Ponty, the anthropologist CLAUDE LÉVI-STRAUSS, and the Jewish theologian and mystic Simone Weil. Beauvoir was only the ninth woman and the youngest student ever to pass the rigorous *agrégation* in philosophy (a competitive national exam for students who want to become tenured *lycée* professors), taking second place to Sartre (who had failed the first time). After completing her degree, she taught at various *lycées* in Marseilles, Rouen, and Paris from 1931 to 1943, when her contract was suspended after she was accused of sleeping with a student. Although she was reinstated after the war, she never taught again; for the rest of her life she supported herself by her writing.

The variety of Beauvoir's writing over the next half century is impressive. In 1945 she and Sartre, along with Merleau-Ponty, founded *Les Temps Modernes*, a monthly magazine devoted to politics and literature. Between 1943 and 1968, Beauvoir wrote six novels, winning the Prix Goncourt in 1954 for *Les Mandarins* (1954), a fictionalized account of postwar leftist intellectuals and their attempts to give up their "mandarin" (educated elite) status and engage in political activism. This novel includes characters who resemble Beauvoir, Sartre, the French writer Albert Camus, and the American novelist Nelson Algren, with whom Beauvoir had a relationship for nearly fifteen years. During this time, she also wrote four books on philosophy—including *The Ethics of Ambiguity* (1947), which importantly articulates an ethics for Sartrean existentialism—and a number of essays, some of them book-length, the best known of which is *The Second Sex*. In addition to novels, philosophy, and feminist critique, Beauvoir wrote at least six volumes of autobiography between 1958 and 1972, creating a detailed portrait of French intellectual life from the 1930s to the 1970s. Beauvoir addressed the issue of aging in *A Very Easy Death* (1964, *Une Mort très douce*), on her mother's death in a hospital; *Old Age* (1970, *La Viellesse*), a reflection on society's indifference to the elderly; and, in 1981, in *Adieux: A Farewell to Sartre*, a account of Sartre's last years. During the 1970s, Beauvoir was very active in feminist politics, in 1979 joining the editorial collective Questions Féministes.

The Second Sex is a wide-ranging, multidisciplinary essay that draws on and critiques history, biology, anthropology, literature, psychoanalysis, Marxism, and existentialist philosophy as means of understanding the lived experiences of women. Beauvoir argues that throughout history, women have been reduced to objects for men. Because men have imagined women as the "Other," women have been denied subjectivity. In this claim, Beauvoir echoes VIRGINIA WOOLF's statement in *A Room of One's Own* (1929) that women serve "as looking-glasses possessing the magic and delicious power of reflecting the figure of man at twice its natural size." While Beauvoir's argument that in patriarchal cultures man is the norm and woman the deviation has become a commonplace of feminist theory, in 1948 it was revolutionary. *The Second Sex* shows how these fundamental assumptions dominate social, political, and cultural life and how women have internalized this ideology, so that they live in a constant state of "inauthenticity." In existentialist terms, patriarchy constructs woman as immanence (as stagnation and immersion in nature) and man as transcendence (as continually striving for freedom and authenticity), thereby impeding women's struggle to achieve existential freedom and autonomous subjectivity.

To illustrate her theoretical insights, *The Second Sex* employs a number of different perspectives. In the first part Beauvoir examines woman "objectively"—that is, as object of analysis—through a series of cultural lenses, including biology, psychoanalysis, Marxism, history, literature, and myth. At the same time she critiques each of these cultural lenses. In the second part she examines women "subjectively" from the perspective of their own lived experience, showing the processes through which women internalize the ideologies of otherness that relegate them to immanence and to the position of being man's Other.

Our selection is the last in a series of three chapters on myths about women, asking what significance they have in "daily life." What is the relationship between the myth of the Eternal Feminine and the lived experience of actual women? True to her roots in existentialism, Beauvoir argues that "essence does not precede existence"; that is, a human being is neither more nor less than the sum total of her or his acts. The myth of the Eternal Feminine, however, takes the values, beliefs, practices, and institutions that constitute women's experience and projects them into the realm of Platonic Forms as timeless and unchanging essences. The myth becomes the only reality; against it, "the contrary facts of experience are impotent." Woman is defined as the absolute Other of man and denied any subjectivity.

Moreover, the various and invariably partial myths about femininity—each claiming to be a totalizing explanation—are contradictory, leading to the biggest myth of all: that women are mysterious, beyond the comprehension of men, an explanation that Beauvoir argues "flatters laziness and vanity at once." In fact, Beauvoir contends, in recognizing that all human beings have within them the potential for both transcendence and immanence, men would lose an attractive relationship that benefits them. Patriarchy relies on the myth of woman's essential immanence and her otherness in constructing male subjectivity.

As this summary suggests, the primary influence on *The Second Sex* is Sartrean existentialism. However, the extent of Beauvoir's debt to Sartre has been somewhat exaggerated and her own philosophical contributions to existentialism obscured. In particular, she rejects Sartre's alienating view of freedom, preferring instead to see authentic relationships as involving reciprocity between subjects, "the mutual recognition of free beings who confirm one another's freedom." In addition, she more quickly understood and developed the notion that the body is situated in culture and history, an idea that makes possible a more nuanced analysis of oppression and political activism. Because of her close association with Sartre, readers have also tended to overlook the other influences on *The Second Sex*, including phenomenology, Marxism, and psychoanalysis.

Our selection, which heavily influenced Kate Millett's 1970 feminist classic, *Sexual Politics*, illustrates what feminists in the 1960s and 1970s found most appealing in *The Second Sex*: its complete blurring of fictional and autobiographical ways of knowing the world and gaining a voice as a woman. Throughout *The Second Sex*, Beauvoir refuses to distinguish between literary accounts, anecdotes, and what might be taken as more "expert" discourses about women such as psychoanalysis and biology, a technique central to her project of tearing down (de-essentializing) patriarchal myths. This strategy empowered second-wave feminists to construct new discourses about women to counter those from which women's voices had largely been excluded.

Although *The Second Sex* has been an enormously influential text for feminist literary theory (even if its influence has often been tacit rather than explicit), it has not been without its critics, most of whom point to a masculinist bias in the text (seen as a result of Sartre's influence). Beauvoir, critics argue, tends to define what men do as transcendent and what women do—childbearing, motherhood, housework—as necessarily immanent. Economic independence is seen as the cornerstone of women's liberation, while both marriage and motherhood are disparaged as inauthentic choices. As Kristeva points out in "Women's Time" (1979), Beauvoir is unable to imagine that motherhood might be an active and authentic choice—even a form of transcendence. Beauvoir also tends to generalize from her specific observations of white, middle-class, and well-educated European women to universal claims about all women. Despite these criticisms, *The Second Sex*, revolutionary in its own time, offers a powerful analysis of the status of women and remains a foundational text for feminist theory.

BIBLIOGRAPHY

First published in France as *Le Deuxième Sexe* (1949), *The Second Sex* (1952) was published in the United States in an incomplete and notoriously inaccurate translation by a zoologist, H. M. Parshley, whose enthusiasm far exceeded his grasp of either philosophy or feminism. It remains to date the only translation of Beauvoir's most famous work. Besides her six novels, short stories, and play, Beauvoir wrote several books of philosophy and cultural criticism, including *Pyrrhus et Cinéas* (1944); *The Ethics of Ambiguity* (1947; trans. 1948); *L'Existentialisme et la sagesse des nations* (1948, *Existentialism and the Wisdom of Nations); America Day by Day* (1948; trans. 1948); *Must We Burn Sade?* (1951–52; trans. 1953); *The Long March* (1957; trans. 1958); *Brigitte Bardot and the Lolita Syndrome* (1959; trans. 1960); *Djamila Boupacha: The Story of a Young Algerian Girl Which Shocked Liberal French Opinion*, with Gisele Halimi (1962; trans. 1962); and *Old Age* (1970; trans. 1972). Although Beauvoir's extensive autobiographical writing—*Memories of a Dutiful Daughter* (1958; trans. 1959), *The Prime of Life* (1960; trans. 1962), *Force of Circumstances* (1963; trans. 1964), *A Very Easy Death* (1972; trans. 1973), *All Said and Done* (1972; trans. 1974), and *Adieux: A Farewell to Sartre* (1981; trans. 1984)—have supplied most of the information for her biographers, readers might wish to consult Deirdre Bair's biography *Simone de Beauvoir* (1990).

One of the earliest critical assessments of Beauvoir is Elaine Mark's *Simone de Beauvoir: Encounters with Death* (1973). Anne Whitmarsh's *Simone de Beauvoir and the Limits of Commitment* (1981) provides a meticulous study of Beauvoir's writing. Alice Schwarzer, in *After the Second Sex: Conversations with Simone de Beauvoir* (1984), collects a series of interviews. One of the most astute French writers on Beauvoir is Michèle le Doeuff; her *Hipparchia's Choice: An Essay Concerning Women, Philosophy, etc.* (1989; trans. 1991), which discusses Beauvoir in the context of women's relationship to philosophy, will appeal to more advanced students. Toril Moi's *Feminist Literary Theory and Simone de Beauvoir* (1990) explores the critical response of feminist theorists to *The Second Sex*, while her *Simone de Beauvoir: The Making of an Intellectual Woman* (1994) examines Beauvoir as the emblematic intellectual woman of the twentieth century. One of the best collections of criticism is *Feminist Interpretations of Simone de Beauvoir*, edited by Margaret A. Simons (1995). Both Karen Vintges's *Philosophy as Passion: The Thinking of Simone de Beauvoir* (1996) and Debra B. Bergoffen's *Philosophy of Simone de Beauvoir: Gendered Phenomenologies, Erotic Generosities* (1997) examine Beauvoir's writing from the perspective of philosophy. Margaret A. Simons's *Beauvoir and "The Second Sex": Feminism, Race, and the Origins of Existentialism* (1999) contains important essays that explore the continuing relevance of *The Second Sex* for key issues in feminist theory. For bibliography consult *Simone de Beauvoir: A Bibliography* (1991), by Joan Nordquist.

From The Second Sex[1]

Chapter XI. Myth and Reality

The myth of woman plays a considerable part in literature; but what is its importance in daily life? To what extent does it affect the customs and conduct of individuals? In replying to this question it will be necessary to state precisely the relations this myth bears to reality.

There are different kinds of myths. This one, the myth of woman, subli-

1. Translated by H. M. Parshley.

mating an immutable aspect of the human condition—namely, the "division" of humanity into two classes of individuals—is a static myth. It projects into the realm of Platonic ideas[2] a reality that is directly experienced or is conceptualized on a basis of experience; in place of fact, value, significance, knowledge, empirical law, it substitutes a transcendental Idea, timeless, unchangeable, necessary. This idea is indisputable because it is beyond the given: it is endowed with absolute truth. Thus, as against the dispersed, contingent, and multiple existences of actual women, mythical thought opposes the Eternal Feminine, unique and changeless. If the definition provided for this concept is contradicted by the behavior of flesh-and-blood women, it is the latter who are wrong: we are told not that Femininity is a false entity, but that the women concerned are not feminine. The contrary facts of experience are impotent against the myth. In a way, however, its source is in experience. Thus it is quite true that woman is other than man, and this alterity is directly felt in desire, the embrace, love; but the real relation is one of reciprocity; as such it gives rise to authentic drama. Through eroticism, love, friendship, and their alternatives, deception, hate, rivalry, the relation is a struggle between conscious beings each of whom wishes to be essential, it is the mutual recognition of free beings who confirm one another's freedom, it is the vague transition from aversion to participation. To pose Woman is to pose the absolute Other, without reciprocity, denying against all experience that she is a subject, a fellow human being.

In actuality, of course, women appear under various aspects; but each of the myths built up around the subject of woman is intended to sum her up *in toto*; each aspires to be unique. In consequence, a number of incompatible myths exist, and men tarry musing before the strange incoherencies manifested by the idea of Femininity. As every woman has a share in a majority of these archetypes—each of which lays claim to containing the sole Truth of woman—men of today also are moved again in the presence of their female companions to an astonishment like that of the old sophists[3] who failed to understand how man could be blond and dark at the same time! Transition toward the absolute was indicated long ago in social phenomena: relations are easily congealed in classes, functions in types, just as relations, to the childish mentality, are fixed in things. Patriarchal society, for example, being centered upon the conservation of the patrimony, implies necessarily, along with those who own and transmit wealth, the existence of men and women who take property away from its owners and put it into circulation. The men—adventurers, swindlers, thieves, speculators—are generally repudiated by the group; the women, employing their erotic attraction, can induce young men and even fathers of families to scatter their patrimonies, without ceasing to be within the law. Some of these women appropriate their victims' fortunes or obtain legacies by using undue influence; this role being regarded as evil, those who play it are called "bad women." But the fact is that quite to the contrary they are able to appear in some other setting—at home with their fathers, brothers, husbands, or lovers—as guardian angels; and the courtesan who "plucks" rich financiers is, for painters and writers,

2. Transcendent entities in whose reality existing things (their imperfect representations) participate; on the Greek philosopher PLATO (ca. 427–ca. 347 B.C.E.), see above.

3. Itinerant professional teachers of philosophy and especially rhetoric in 5th century B.C.E. Greece (see GORGIAS, above).

a generous patroness. It is easy to understand in actual experience the ambiguous personality of Aspasia or Mme de Pompadour.[4] But if woman is depicted as the Praying Mantis, the Mandrake, the Demon, then it is most confusing to find in woman also the Muse, the Goddess Mother, Beatrice.[5]

As group symbols and social types are generally defined by means of antonyms in pairs, ambivalence will seem to be an intrinsic quality of the Eternal Feminine. The saintly mother has for correlative the cruel stepmother, the angelic young girl has the perverse virgin: thus it will be said sometimes that Mother equals Life, sometimes that Mother equals Death, that every virgin is pure spirit or flesh dedicated to the devil.

Evidently it is not reality that dictates to society or to individuals their choice between the two opposed basic categories; in every period, in each case, society and the individual decide in accordance with their needs. Very often they project into the myth adopted the institutions and values to which they adhere. Thus the paternalism that claims woman for hearth and home defines her as sentiment, inwardness, immanence. In fact every existent is at once immanence and transcendence;[6] when one offers the existent no aim, or prevents him from attaining any, or robs him of his victory, then his transcendence falls vainly into the past—that is to say, falls back into immanence. This is the lot assigned to woman in the patriarchate; but it is in no way a vocation, any more than slavery is the vocation of the slave. The development of this mythology is to be clearly seen in Auguste Comte.[7] To identify Woman with Altruism is to guarantee to man absolute rights in her devotion, it is to impose on women a categorical imperative.

The myth must not be confused with the recognition of significance; significance is immanent in the object; it is revealed to the mind through a living experience; whereas the myth is a transcendent Idea that escapes the mental grasp entirely. When in *L'Âge d'homme* Michel Leiris[8] describes his vision of the feminine organs, he tells us things of significance and elaborates no myth. Wonder at the feminine body, dislike for menstrual blood, come from perceptions of a concrete reality. There is nothing mythical in the experience that reveals the voluptuous qualities of feminine flesh, and it is not an excursion into myth if one attempts to describe them through comparisons with flowers or pebbles. But to say that Woman is Flesh, to say that the Flesh is Night and Death, or that it is the splendor of the Cosmos, is to abandon terrestrial truth and soar into an empty sky. For man also is flesh

4. Jeanne-Antoinette Poisson, marquise de Pompadour (1721–1764), influential mistress (from 1745) of the French king Louis XV and a notable patron of literature and the arts. Aspasia: mistress of the 5th-century B.C.E. Athenian statesman Pericles, a woman of considerable learning.

5. Beatrice Portinari, the daughter of a noble Florentine family, who died at the age of 24 in 1290; she provided the inspiration for much of DANTE's poetry, especially his masterpiece, *The Divine Comedy* (1321). Praying Mantis: in the first paragraph of *The Second Sex*, Beauvoir writes of "the female praying mantis and the spider, [who,] satiated with love, crush and devour their partners." Mandrake: a plant long used as both a narcotic and an aphrodisiac. Muse: in Greek mythology, one of the 9 daughters of Memory who preside over the arts and all intellectual pursuits. Goddess Mother: any of a variety of feminine deities and maternal symbols of creativity, birth, fertility, sexual union, nurturing, and the cycle of growth. The term also has been applied to figures as diverse as the so-called Stone Age Venuses and the Virgin Mary.

6. All terms associated with existential philosophy. The *existent* is the subject of existentialism, the human actor whose subjectivity is shaped through human activity. Such activity that achieves liberty is a mode of *transcendence*; without it, there is only *immanence*, stagnation and subjugation to given conditions.

7. French philosopher (1798–1857), known as the founder of sociology and of positivism; he idealized the role of women in society.

8. French writer (1901–1990), a pioneer in modern confessional literature and a noted anthropologist, poet, and art critic. His *L'Âge d'homme* (1939, *Manhood: A Journey from Childhood into the Fierce Order of Virility*) was autobiographical.

for woman; and woman is not merely a carnal object; and the flesh is clothed in special significance for each person and in each experience. And likewise it is quite true that woman—like man—is a being rooted in nature; she is more enslaved to the species than is the male, her animality is more manifest; but in her as in him the given traits are taken on through the fact of existence, she belongs also to the human realm. To assimilate her to Nature is simply to act from prejudice.

Few myths have been more advantageous to the ruling caste than the myth of woman: it justifies all privileges and even authorizes their abuse. Men need not bother themselves with alleviating the pains and the burdens that physiologically are women's lot, since these are "intended by Nature"; men use them as a pretext for increasing the misery of the feminine lot still further, for instance by refusing to grant to woman any right to sexual pleasure, by making her work like a beast of burden.[9]

Of all these myths, none is more firmly anchored in masculine hearts than that of the feminine "mystery." It has numerous advantages. And first of all it permits an easy explanation of all that appears inexplicable; the man who "does not understand" a woman is happy to substitute an objective resistance for a subjective deficiency of mind; instead of admitting his ignorance, he perceives the presence of a "mystery" outside himself: an alibi, indeed, that flatters laziness and vanity at once. A heart smitten with love thus avoids many disappointments: if the loved one's behavior is capricious, her remarks stupid, then the mystery serves to excuse it all. And finally, thanks again to the mystery, that negative relation is perpetuated which seemed to Kierkegaard[1] infinitely preferable to positive possession; in the company of a living enigma man remains alone—alone with his dreams, his hopes, his fears, his love, his vanity. This subjective game, which can go all the way from vice to mystical ecstasy, is for many a more attractive experience than an authentic relation with a human being. What foundations exist for such a profitable illusion?

Surely woman is, in a sense, mysterious, "mysterious as is all the world," according to Maeterlinck.[2] Each is *subject* only for himself; each can grasp in immanence only himself, alone: from this point of view the *other* is always a mystery. To men's eyes the opacity of the self-knowing self, of the *pour-soi*,[3] is denser in the *other* who is feminine; men are unable to penetrate her special experience through any working of sympathy: they are condemned to ignorance of the quality of woman's erotic pleasure, the discomfort of menstruation, and the pains of childbirth. The truth is that there is mystery on both sides: as the *other* who is of masculine sex, every man, also, has within him a presence, an inner self impenetrable to woman; she in turn is in ignorance of the male's erotic feeling. But in accordance with the universal rule

9. Cf. Balzac: *Physiology of Marriage* [1830]: "Pay no attention to her murmurs, her cries, her pains; *nature has made her for our use* and for bearing everything: children, sorrows, blows and pains inflicted by man. Do not accuse yourself of hardness. In all the codes of so-called civilized nations, man has written the laws that ranged woman's destiny under this bloody epigraph: '*Vae victis*! Woe to the Weak!' " [Beauvoir's note]. Honoré de Balzac (1799–1850), French novelist renowned for fictions of French middle-class society.

1. Søren Kierkegaard (1813–1855), Danish philosopher and religious thinker, a forerunner of existentialism.

2. Maurice Maeterlinck (1862–1949), Belgian poet, dramatist, and essayist, whose antinaturalist plays were precursors of theater of the absurd.

3. Parshley translates the existentialist concept *pour-soi* as "the self-knowing self"; others prefer "being-for-itself," contrasting human consciousness with the being-in-itself (*en-soi*) of those creatures that lack consciousness.

I have stated, the categories in which men think of the world are established *from their point of view, as absolute*: they misconceive reciprocity, here as everywhere. A mystery for man, woman is considered to be mysterious in essence.

To tell the truth, her situation makes woman very liable to such a view. Her physiological nature is very complex; she herself submits to it as to some rigmarole from outside; her body does not seem to her to be a clear expression of herself; within it she feels herself a stranger. Indeed, the bond that in every individual connects the physiological life and the psychic life—or better the relation existing between the contingence of an individual and the free spirit that assumes it—is the deepest enigma implied in the condition of being human, and this enigma is presented in its most disturbing form in woman.

But what is commonly referred to as the mystery is not the subjective solitude of the conscious self, nor the secret organic life. It is on the level of communication that the word has its true meaning: it is not a reduction to pure silence, to darkness, to absence; it implies a stammering presence that fails to make itself manifest and clear. To say that woman is mystery is to say, not that she is silent, but that her language is not understood; she is there, but hidden behind veils; she exists beyond these uncertain appearances. What is she? Angel, demon, one inspired, an actress? It may be supposed either that there are answers to these questions which are impossible to discover, or, rather, that no answer is adequate because a fundamental ambiguity marks the feminine being; and perhaps in her heart she is even for herself quite indefinable: a sphinx.[4]

The fact is that she would be quite embarrassed to decide *what* she *is*; but this not because the hidden truth is too vague to be discerned: it is because in this domain there is no truth. An existent *is* nothing other than what he does; the possible does not extend beyond the real, essence does not precede existence: in pure subjectivity, the human being *is not anything*. He is to be measured by his acts. Of a peasant woman one can say that she is a good or a bad worker, of an actress that she has or does not have talent; but if one considers a woman in her immanent presence, her inward self, one can say absolutely nothing about her, she falls short of having any qualifications. Now, in amorous or conjugal relations, in all relations where the woman is the vassal, the other, she is being dealt with in her immanence. It is noteworthy that the feminine comrade, colleague, and associate are without mystery; on the other hand, if the vassal is male, if, in the eyes of a man or a woman who is older, or richer, a young fellow, for example, plays the role of the inessential object, then he too becomes shrouded in mystery. And this uncovers for us a substructure under the feminine mystery which is economic in nature.

A sentiment cannot be supposed to *be* anything. "In the domain of sentiments," writes Gide,[5] "the real is not distinguished from the imaginary. And if to imagine one loves is enough to be in love, then also to tell oneself that one imagines oneself to be in love when one is in love is enough to make one forthwith love a little less." Discrimination between the imaginary and

4. That is, an enigma; in Greek mythology, the sphinx was a monster with a woman's face, a lion's body, and a bird's wings whose riddle was finally answered by Oedipus.

5. André Gide (1869–1951), major French literary figure of the first half of the 20th century.

the real can be made only through behavior. Since man occupies a privileged situation in this world, he is in a position to show his love actively; very often he supports the woman or at least helps her; in marrying her he gives her social standing; he makes her presents; his independent economic and social position allows him to take the initiative and think up contrivances: it was M. de Norpois who, when separated from Mme de Villeparisis,[6] made twenty-four-hour trips to visit her. Very often the man is busy, the woman idle: he *gives* her the time he passes with her; she takes it: is it with pleasure, passionately, or only for amusement? Does she accept these benefits through love or through self-interest? Does she love her husband or her marriage? Of course, even the man's evidence is ambiguous: is such and such a gift granted through love or out of pity? But while normally a woman finds numerous advantages in her relations with a man, his relations with a woman are profitable to a man only in so far as he loves her. And so one can almost judge the degree of his affection by the total picture of his attitude.

But a woman hardly has means for sounding her own heart; according to her moods she will view her own sentiments in different lights, and as she submits to them passively, one interpretation will be no truer than another. In those rare instances in which she holds the position of economic and social privilege, the mystery is reversed, showing that it does not pertain to *one* sex rather than the other, but to the situation. For a great many women the roads to transcendence are blocked: because they *do* nothing, they fail to *make themselves* anything. They wonder indefinitely what they *could have* become, which sets them to asking about what they are. It is a vain question. If man fails to discover that secret essence of femininity, it is simply because it does not exist. Kept on the fringe of the world, woman cannot be objectively defined through this world, and her mystery conceals nothing but emptiness.

Furthermore, like all the oppressed, woman deliberately dissembles her objective actuality; the slave, the servant, the indigent, all who depend upon the caprices of a master,[7] have learned to turn toward him a changeless smile or an enigmatic impassivity; their real sentiments, their actual behavior, are carefully hidden. And moreover woman is taught from adolescence to lie to men, to scheme, to be wily. In speaking to them she wears an artificial expression on her face; she is cautious, hypocritical, play-acting.

But the Feminine Mystery as recognized in mythical thought is a more profound matter. In fact, it is immediately implied in the mythology of the absolute Other. If it be admitted that the inessential conscious being, too, is a clear subjectivity, capable of performing the *Cogito,*[8] then it is also admitted that this being is in truth sovereign and returns to being essential; in order that all reciprocity may appear quite impossible, it is necessary for the Other to be for itself an other, for its very subjectivity to be affected by its otherness; this consciousness which would be alienated as a consciousness, in its pure immanent presence, would evidently be Mystery. It would be Mystery in itself from the fact that it would be Mystery for itself; it would be absolute Mystery.

6. Two characters in Marcel Proust's multivolume novel, *À la recherche du temps perdu* (1913–27, *Remembrance of Things Past*).
7. An allusion to the famous Master-Slave dialectic of GEORG WILHELM FRIEDRICH HEGEL (1770–1831), described in his *Phenomenology of Spirit* (1807; see above).
8. I think (Latin); an allusion to the French philosopher René Descartes (1596–1650), whose most fundamental proposition was "cogito, ergo sum" (I think, therefore I am).

In the same way it is true that, beyond the secrecy created by their dissembling, there is mystery in the Black, the Yellow, in so far as they are considered absolutely as the inessential Other. It should be noted that the American citizen, who profoundly baffles the average European, is not, however, considered as being "mysterious": one states more modestly that one does not understand him. And similarly woman does not always "understand" man; but there is no such thing as a masculine mystery. The point is that rich America, and the male, are on the Master side and that Mystery belongs to the slave.

To be sure, we can only muse in the twilight byways of bad faith[9] upon the positive reality of the Mystery; like certain marginal hallucinations, it dissolves under the attempt to view it fixedly. Literature always fails in attempting to portray "mysterious" women; they can appear only at the beginning of a novel as strange, enigmatic figures; but unless the story remains unfinished they give up their secret in the end and they are then simply consistent and transparent persons. The heroes in Peter Cheyney's[1] books, for example, never cease to be astonished at the unpredictable caprices of women: no one can ever guess how they will act, they upset all calculations. The fact is that once the springs of their action are revealed to the reader, they are seen to be very simple mechanisms: this woman was a spy, that one a thief; however clever the plot, there is always a key; and it could not be otherwise, had the author all the talent and imagination in the world. Mystery is never more than a mirage that vanishes as we draw near to look at it.

We can see now that the myth is in large part explained by its usefulness to man. The myth of woman is a luxury. It can appear only if man escapes from the urgent demands of his needs; the more relationships are concretely lived, the less they are idealized. The fellah of ancient Egypt, the Bedouin[2] peasant, the artisan of the Middle Ages, the worker of today has in the requirements of work and poverty relations with his particular woman companion which are too definite for her to be embellished with an aura either auspicious or inauspicious. The epochs and the social classes that have been marked by the leisure to dream have been the ones to set up the images, black and white, of femininity. But along with luxury there was utility; these dreams were irresistibly guided by interests. Surely most of the myths had roots in the spontaneous attitude of man toward his own existence and toward the world around him. But going beyond experience toward the transcendent Idea was deliberately used by patriarchal society for purposes of self-justification; through the myths this society imposed its laws and customs upon individuals in a picturesque, effective manner; it is under a mythical form that the group-imperative is indoctrinated into each conscience. Through such intermediaries as religions, traditions, language, tales, songs, movies, the myths penetrate even into such existences as are most harshly enslaved to material realities. Here everyone can find sublimation of his drab experiences: deceived by the woman he loves, one declares that she is a Crazy Womb; another, obsessed by his impotence, calls her a Praying Mantis; still another enjoys his wife's company: behold, she is Harmony,

9. An existentialist term referring to the effort to avoid the responsibility of one's own freedom by denying its full extent.

1. English writer of detective fiction (1896–1951).

2. Arabic-speaking pastoral nomad of the Middle East and North Africa. "Fellah": agricultural laborer (Arabic), as opposed to a nomadic desert dweller.

Rest, the Good Earth! The taste for eternity at a bargain, for a pocket-sized absolute, which is shared by a majority of men, is satisfied by myths. The smallest emotion, a slight annoyance, becomes the reflection of a timeless Idea—an illusion agreeably flattering to the vanity.

The myth is one of those snares of false objectivity into which the man who depends on ready-made valuations rushes headlong. Here again we have to do with the substitution of a set idol for actual experience and the free judgments it requires. For an authentic relation with an autonomous existent, the myth of Woman substitutes the fixed contemplation of a mirage. "Mirage! Mirage!" cries Laforgue.[3] "We should kill them since we cannot comprehend them; or better tranquilize them, instruct them make them give up their taste for jewels, make them our genuinely equal comrades, our intimate friends, real associates here below, dress them differently, cut their hair short, say anything and everything to them." Man would have nothing to lose, quite the contrary, if he gave up disguising woman as a symbol. When dreams are official community affairs, clichés, they are poor and monotonous indeed beside the living reality; for the true dreamer, for the poet, woman is a more generous fount than is any down-at-heel marvel. The times that have most sincerely treasured women are not the period of feudal chivalry nor yet the gallant nineteenth century. They are the times—like the eighteenth century—when men have regarded women as fellow creatures; then it is that women seem truly romantic, as the reading of *Liaisons dangereuses, Le Rouge et le noir, Farewell to Arms*, is sufficient to show. The heroines of Laclos, Stendhal, Hemingway[4] are without mystery, and they are not the less engaging for that. To recognize in woman a human being is not to impoverish man's experience: this would lose none of its diversity, its richness, or its intensity if it were to occur between two subjectivities. To discard the myths is not to destroy all dramatic relation between the sexes, it is not to deny the significance authentically revealed to man through feminine reality; it is not to do away with poetry, love, adventure, happiness, dreaming. It is simply to ask that behavior, sentiment, passion be founded upon the truth.[5]

"Woman is lost. Where are the women? The women of today are not women at all!" We have seen what these mysterious slogans mean. In men's eyes—and for the legion of women who see through men's eyes—it is not enough to have a woman's body nor to assume the female function as mistress or mother in order to be a "true woman." In sexuality and maternity woman as subject can claim autonomy; but to be a "true woman" she must accept herself as the Other. The men of today show a certain duplicity of attitude which is painfully lacerating to women; they are willing on the whole to accept woman as a fellow being, an equal; but they still require her to remain the inessential. For her these two destinies are incompatible; she hesitates between one and the other without being exactly adapted to either, and from this comes her lack of equilibrium. With man there is no break

3. Jules Laforgue (1860–1887), French symbolist poet.

4. The authors of the three novels named: the French Pierre Choderlos de Laclos (1741–1803) wrote *Dangerous Liaisons* (1782); the French Stendhal, pen name of Henri-Marie Beyle (1783–1842), wrote *The Red and the Black* (1830); and the American Ernest Hemingway (1899–1961) wrote *A Farewell to Arms* (1929).

5. Laforgue goes on to say regarding woman: "Since she has been left in slavery, idleness, without occupation or weapon other than her sex, she has overdeveloped this aspect and has become the Feminine. . . . We have permitted this hypertrophy; she is here in the world for our benefit. . . . Well! that is all wrong. . . . Up to now we have played with woman as if she were a doll. This has lasted altogether too long! . . ." [Beauvoir's note].

between public and private life: the more he confirms his grasp on the world in action and in work, the more virile he seems to be; human and vital values are combined in him. Whereas woman's independent successes are in contradiction with her femininity, since the "true woman" is required to make herself object, to be the Other.

It is quite possible that in this matter man's sensibility and sexuality are being modified. A new æsthetics has already been born. If the fashion of flat chests and narrow hips—the boyish form—has had its brief season, at least the overopulent ideal of past centuries has not returned. The feminine body is asked to be flesh, but with discretion; it is to be slender and not loaded with fat; muscular, supple, strong, it is bound to suggest transcendence; it must not be pale like a too shaded hothouse plant, but preferably tanned like a workman's torso from being bared to the open sun. Woman's dress in becoming practical need not make her appear sexless: on the contrary, short skirts made the most of legs and thighs as never before. There is no reason why working should take away woman's sex appeal.[6] It may be disturbing to contemplate woman as at once a social personage and carnal prey: in a recent series of drawings by Peynet[7] (1948), we see a young man break his engagement because he was seduced by the pretty mayoress who was getting ready to officiate at his marriage. For a woman to hold some "man's position" and be desirable at the same time has long been a subject for more or less ribald joking; but gradually the impropriety and the irony have become blunted, and it would seem that a new form of eroticism is coming into being—perhaps it will give rise to new myths.

What is certain is that today it is very difficult for women to accept at the same time their status as autonomous individuals and their womanly destiny; this is the source of the blundering and restlessness which sometimes cause them to be considered a "lost sex." And no doubt it is more comfortable to submit to a blind enslavement than to work for liberation: the dead, for that matter, are better adapted to the earth than are the living. In all respects a return to the past is no more possible than it is desirable. What must be hoped for is that the men for their part will unreservedly accept the situation that is coming into existence; only then will women be able to live in that situation without anguish. Then Laforgue's prayer will be answered: "Ah, young women, when will you be our brothers, our brothers in intimacy without ulterior thought of exploitation? When shall we clasp hands truly?" Then Breton's[8] "Mélusine, no longer under the weight of the calamity let loose upon her by man alone, Mélusine set free . . ." will regain "her place in humanity." Then she will be a full human being, "when," to quote a letter of Rimbaud,[9] "the infinite bondage of woman is broken, when she will live in and for herself, man—hitherto detestable—having let her go free."

1949

6. A point that hardly needs to be made in America, where even cursory acquaintance with any well-staffed business office will afford confirmatory evidence [translator's note].

7. Raymond Peynet (1908–1999), French artist and designer.

8. André Breton (1896–1966), French surrealist poet, essayist, critic, and editor. In the legends of Brittany, Mélusine was part sea serpent and part woman.

9. Arthur Rimbaud (1854–1891), French symbolist poet.

CLAUDE LÉVI-STRAUSS
b. 1908

The French anthropologist Claude Lévi-Strauss is most famous for his role in the cross-disciplinary phenomenon known as "structuralism" that came to prominence in the late 1950s and reached its peak of popularity in the late 1960s. Taking inspiration from FERDINAND DE SAUSSURE (1857–1913), who had defined language as a system of signs and linguistics as a branch of semiology (the larger science of all signs), Lévi-Strauss argued that the objects of social anthropology—cultural phenomena such as kinship systems and rituals—consist of communications, not just functions. Focusing both on the role of unconscious structures in Western European cultural practices and on the meaningful order informing what had appeared to earlier Western observers as the purely irrational or instinct-driven customs of so-called primitive peoples, he simultaneously proclaimed the death of the Enlightenment concept of "Man" and posited a kind of universal mind. Reframing anthropology as a study of Culture rather than cultures, Lévi-Strauss underscored the discipline's implications for history, politics, art, literature, economics, and philosophy, dramatically transforming anthropology's profile in the academy. Within the discipline many scholars have contested the empirical validity of his analyses of kinship, totemism, and myth and have accused Lévi-Strauss of engaging in a kind of metaphysical colonization. Nevertheless, his adoption of linguistic metaphors and methods and his acute self-consciousness about the role of the ethnographer have had a lasting impact on the practice of anthropology proper and on the humanities and social sciences more generally. Though the structuralist method that Lévi-Strauss pioneered has been superseded, the analogy he proposed—that cultural phenomena constitute exchanges of messages and that cultural codes may be analyzed as languages—remains a tacit working assumption of many forms of cultural theory.

While Lévi-Strauss may be the best-known and most broadly influential anthropologist of the twentieth century, he never received formal academic training in the study of other cultures (ethnology). Born in Brussels, son of a painter and grandson of a rabbi, he grew up primarily in Paris. Having pursued studies in philosophy and law and passed the prestigious *agrégation* exam in philosophy in 1931 (along with fellow students Maurice Merleau-Ponty and SIMONE DE BEAUVOIR), he went on to spend a couple of years teaching philosophy in provincial secondary schools; but he soon became disaffected with that discipline. Evincing a bias that JACQUES DERRIDA was later to remark on, he complains of philosophy that "the signifier did not relate to any signified; there was no referent" (*Tristes Tropiques*, 1955). Yet more empirically oriented anthropologists have reproached Lévi-Strauss for failing to leave philosophy far enough behind. While his criticisms of philosophy seem implicitly to extol the virtues of firsthand observation, Lévi-Strauss later claimed to have "realized early on that [he] was a library man, not a fieldworker" and he suggested that "fieldwork is a kind of 'women's work' " for which he had "neither the interest nor the patience" (Eribon, *Conversations*, 1988). Indeed, he was to spend relatively little time among the people whose cultures he studied, instead drawing heavily on others' ethnographic data.

Lévi-Strauss conducted the fieldwork on which much of his later work was based between 1935 and 1938, during breaks from teaching sociology at the newly created University of São Paulo in Brazil. *Tristes Tropiques*, from which our selection is taken, was written almost twenty years later; it is among other things an autobiographical account of his expeditions into the Brazilian interior, where he sojourned among the Bororo, Caduveo, Nambikwara, and Tupi-Kawahib peoples. Lévi-Strauss returned to France in 1939 but the following year was dismissed from his teaching post: the racial laws of the Vichy government of occupied France decreed him ineligible to teach because he was a Jew. In 1941, with the help of an aunt living in the United States and a Rockefeller Foundation program to assist European scientists and scholars threatened by World War II, he was able to obtain an exit visa to travel to New York, where he was offered a position at the New School for Social Research.

In New York Lévi-Strauss met the Russian ROMAN JAKOBSON and attended his lectures on linguistics. This encounter affected him as a "revelation": "Jakobson revealed to me the existence of a body of doctrine that had already been formed within a discipline, linguistics, with which I was unacquainted" (Eribon, *Conversations*). Jakobson was elaborating Saussurean linguistics, with its proposition that language does not consist of positive terms with meaning in and of themselves, but instead is a system of relations in which each term is defined by its difference from other terms. Suggesting that "the kinship system is a language," Lévi-Strauss proposed adapting the methods of structural linguistics to the analysis of kinship and other cultural phenomena. He pursued this semiological project in his doctoral thesis at the Sorbonne, published as *The Elementary Structures of Kinship* (1949). In his view, the prohibition of incest, which seems to be a universal rule in human society, is designed not to ward off biological or psychological damage but to make women available for "trade" by men of their group with men of other groups. Extending the argument of Marcel Mauss, who in *The Gift* (1925) had emphasized the symbolic rather than the economic value of gifts exchanged, Lévi-Strauss suggests that gift giving in general and wife trafficking in particular are above all modes of communication. In other words, women and other gifts are traded as words are exchanged in conversation; the fact that in matrimonial exchange "the mediating factor . . . should be the *women of the group*, who are *circulated* between clans, lineages, or families, in place of the *words of the group*, which are *circulated* between individuals, does not at all change the fact that the essential aspect of the phenomenon is identical in both cases" (*Structural Anthropology*, 1958).

As the feminist theorists Teresa de Lauretis and Gayle Rubin have observed, this way of reading kinship systems excludes women from the role of cultural *agents*, treating them only as cultural *objects*. In addition, Lévi-Strauss's account of the origin of culture through the exchange of female "valuables *par excellence*" puts the symbolization and subordination of women at the root of culture. Theorists of gender and sexuality have found the critique of Lévi-Strauss's blind spot a useful starting point in challenging the naturalization of gender hierarchy.

The interest of literary theorists was initially attracted by Lévi-Strauss's work in mythology. His writings about myth were first published in book form in the manifesto-like *Structural Anthropology* and later in a four-volume collection, *Mythologiques* (1964–71). These and later writings focus not on what myths *mean*, but on what they *do*. What they do, he argues, is to make a story out of fundamental and irresolvable human contradictions or enigmas (for example, the differences between humans and animals, life and death, one and two). They layer many different versions of the same contradiction on top of each other, so that in essence a myth is "three-dimensional," not linear. It might be useful here to compare the structural analysis of myth by Lévi-Strauss to the "morphological" study of folktales by the Russian formalist Vladimir Propp (1895–1970), since both kinds of analysis influenced structuralism. Propp studied a large number of Russian folktales and found that, despite their differences, they all made use of a small number of functions (hero, helper, villain, test, prohibition, etc.) arranged in a predictable order. Narrative order was a function of unfolding linear time: the narrative had a beginning, a middle, and an end. For Lévi-Strauss, in contrast, the linear (or diachronic) ordering of a myth is less important than the systematic (or synchronic) pattern of repetitions, which can exist in different versions or different arrangements without disturbing the mythic system (he foresaw how useful computer analysis would be to this kind of study). In a famous essay, first published in English in 1955, titled "The Structural Study of Myth," Lévi-Strauss applied his method to the myth of Oedipus. Myths make order out of the simultaneity of conflicting theories: they narrate over, without resolving, a cultural contradiction.

The essay was published in the same year as his influential book *Tristes Tropiques*, a year that marked a turning point for Lévi-Strauss. After two failed attempts to be appointed to France's prestigious Collège de France, in 1959 he was appointed to the first chair in social anthropology; in 1973 he was elected to the French Academy. Lévi-Strauss, who had always considered himself an outsider, had become the consummate insider.

Written twenty years after the fieldwork on which it is based, *Tristes Tropiques* was an instant sensation and Lévi-Strauss became a best-selling author. It was first published in English in 1961 as *A World on the Wane* (with several chapters omitted); the book appeared in a more complete translation that dates from 1973 and leaves the title in French (literally, "sad tropics"). *Tristes Tropiques* began as a novel, became an autobiography, and ended up an account of an exoticized journey just like those Lévi-Strauss feared it would resemble. The book's first sentence is "I hate travelling and explorers." Praised as a masterpiece by such leading critics as Susan Sontag and George Steiner, loved and hated by a generation of anthropologists, and made into an opera in 1996 with libretto by the French feminist Catherine Clément and music by Georges Aperghis, *Tristes Tropiques* is a unique and symptomatic book. The sadness of its title comes from the unbearable loss of all societies previously uncontaminated by Western intrusions. But the desire to find and document such societies is a form of the very same evil that has already violated them: "Not content with having eliminated savage life, and unaware even of having done so, it [the Western public] feels the need feverishly to appease the nostalgic cannibalism of history with the shadows of those that history has already destroyed." Lamenting the blindness of the West, Lévi-Strauss also personifies it—an irony he recognizes.

Our selection from the work, "A Writing Lesson," shows Lévi-Strauss in all of his dimensions. Constantly baffled, lost, and nervous, yet confident in the intuitions of his own mind, he narrates a succession of encounters with the Nambikwara societies he tries to understand. His skill as a narrator is to make the reader feel that a great deal is not being understood and, at the same time, that all of human life is at stake. Something of the fictional power of writing is unmasked when Lévi-Strauss's wife contracts an eye disease and has to be evacuated. This is the only mention of her presence. The "eye disease" affects Lévi-Strauss's own narrative eye, previously so solitary and single: it reveals that Lévi-Strauss is not a lone fieldworker but part of a group of Westerners that had remained invisible. The chapter thus illustrates the manipulations of writing that it discusses in its central passages.

When an unpopular chief pretends to his people that he knows how to write, Lévi-Strauss launches into a famous meditation on the role of writing in world history. His theory of writing (discussed by Derrida in his poststructuralist *Of Grammatology*) can be usefully compared to PLATO's censorious myth of writing in the *Phaedrus* (see above; see also Derrida's comments on Plato in *Dissemination*). Writing, concludes Lévi-Strauss, is a technology for mass exploitation, a point MICHEL FOUCAULT would develop in his *Discipline and Punish* (1975). But the apparent anti-Western animus in Lévi-Strauss's remarks depends on a concept of societies without writing, an idealization of innocence lost, that is tied to an entirely Western fantasy he both attacks and prolongs: the fantasy of the noble savage.

It is tempting to apply Lévi-Strauss's theory of myths to his own multilayered writing in *Tristes Tropiques*, as Clifford Geertz (in *Works and Lives*, 1988) and Cleo McNelly (in "Natives, Women, and Claude Lévi-Strauss," 1975), in different ways, have done. What is the contradiction that Lévi-Strauss himself is covering over? One answer is suggested by his publication of "The Structural Study of Myth" at the same time as *Tristes Tropiques*. While *Tristes Tropiques* expresses the pain and mourns the destructive impact of Western civilization on non-Western people, the study of myth sees the different moments of human history as structurally simultaneous. On the one hand, this allows for a cultural relativism that enables Lévi-Strauss to contest any narrative of "progress," with its concomitant belief in the superiority of the modern. But on the other hand, it makes the destruction of "primitive" societies *total* so as to internalize the lost object. In seeing "neolithic" structures as located *within* modern civilization, he is papering over loss (and also survival) through incorporation. It is no longer necessary to mourn, because in a sense nothing is lost: the "savage" is internalized in the deep structures of "all" thought. Yet such structural consolation remains haunted by the history and remainders it represses. In *Tristes Tropiques*, Lévi-Strauss gives voice to that haunting.

BIBLIOGRAPHY

In addition to the works discussed above, Lévi-Strauss's notable publications include *The Savage Mind* (1962; trans. 1966); *Totemism* (1962; trans. 1963); "The Scope of Anthropology" (his 1960 inaugural lecture at the Collège de France; trans. 1967); *Mythologiques* (4 vols., 1964–71; trans. 1969–81 as *Introduction to the Science of Mythology*, with the individual volumes titled *The Raw and the Cooked, From Honey to Ashes, The Origin of Table Manners*, and *The Naked Man*); *Myth and Meaning* (1978), a short and very accessible introduction to the structural analysis of myth; *Anthropology and Myth* (1984; trans. 1986); and several additional volumes on myth. Besides the autobiographical *Tristes Tropiques*, the best sources of biographical information available in English are two books of interviews, the first set with Georges Charbonnier (1961; trans. 1969), the second with Didier Eribon (1988; trans. 1991), each published under the title *Conversations with Claude Lévi-Strauss*.

Good introductions to Lévi-Strauss's work include Edmund Leach's respectfully critical *Claude Lévi-Strauss* (1970), which is particularly useful for situating Lévi-Strauss in relation to the discipline of anthropology; David Pace, *Claude Lévi-Strauss: The Bearer of Ashes* (1983); Roland Champagne, *Claude Lévi-Strauss* (1987); and Marcel Hénaff, *Claude Lévi-Strauss and the Making of Structural Anthropology* (1991; trans. 1998).

Theoretically crucial readings of Lévi-Strauss's structuralism in general and *Tristes Tropiques* in particular have been published by Jacques Derrida in *Of Grammatology* (1967; trans. 1976) and *Writing and Difference* (1967; trans. 1978) and by Clifford Geertz in *The Interpretation of Cultures* (1973) and *Works and Lives: The Anthropologist as Author* (1988). Also noteworthy are several highly influential essays analyzing the sexual politics of Lévi-Strauss's kinship theory: Gayle Rubin, "The Traffic in Women: Notes on the 'Political Economy' of Sex," in *Toward an Anthropology of Women* (ed. Rayna Reiter, 1975); Hélène Cixous and Catherine Clément, *The Newly Born Woman* (1975; trans. 1986); and Luce Irigaray, *This Sex Which Is Not One* (1977; trans. 1985). Cleo McNelly's "Natives, Women, and Claude Lévi-Strauss," *Massachusetts Review* 16 (1975), addresses questions of race and gender in *Tristes Tropiques*, drawing comparisons with Charles Baudelaire and Joseph Conrad; other aspects of Lévi-Strauss's participation in literary trends are explored by James Boon's *From Symbolism to Structuralism: Lévi-Strauss in a Literary Tradition* (1972). In "The Ethnic Ethnographer: Judaism in *Tristes Tropiques*," *Representations*, no. 15 (1995), David Damrosch discusses the specter of Nazi terror and Lévi-Strauss's ambivalent treatment of his own ethnicity in *Tristes Tropiques*. In "Lévi-Strauss: The Writing Lesson Revisited," *Modern Language Review* 92 (1997), Christopher Johnson reexamines Lévi-Strauss's framing of the writing lesson episode and proposes a recontextualized interpretation of it. For bibliographies, see Joan Nordquist's *Claude Lévi-Strauss: A Bibliography* (1987), which covers publications in English, and Marcel Hénaff's book (cited above), which provides a selective but nevertheless extensive bibliography.

From Tristes Tropiques[1]

Chapter 28. A Writing Lesson

I was keen to find out, at least indirectly, the approximate size of the Nambikwara[2] population. In 1915, Rondon[3] had suggested a figure of twenty thousand, which was probably too high an estimate; but at that time, each group comprised several hundred members, and, according to information I had picked up along the line, there had since been a rapid decline. Thirty years ago, the known fraction of the Sabané[4] group comprised more than a thousand individuals; when the group visited the telegraph station at Campos Novos[5] in 1928, a hundred and twenty-seven men were counted in addition to women and children. However, in 1929 an influenza epidemic broke out when the group was camping in a locality known as Espirro. The illness developed into a form of pulmonary oedema[6] and, within forty-eight hours, three hundred natives had died. The group broke up, leaving the sick and the dying behind. Of the thousand Sabané who were once known to exist, there remained in 1938 only nineteen men with their women and children. These figures are perhaps to be explained, not only by the epidemic, but also by the fact that, a few years before, the Sabané had started a war against some of their eastern neighbours. But a large group, which had settled not far from Tres Buritis,[7] was wiped out by a flu epidemic in 1927, with the exception of six or seven individuals, of whom only three were still alive in 1938. The Tarundé[8] group, which was once one of the largest, numbered only twelve men (plus the women and children) in 1936; of these twelve men four survived in 1939.

Now, there were perhaps no more than two thousand natives scattered across the area. A systematic census was out of the question, because of the permanent hostility shown by certain groups and the fact that all groups were on the move during the nomadic period. But I tried to persuade my Utiarity[9] friends to take me to their village, after organizing some kind of meeting there with other groups to whom they were related either by kinship or marriage; in this way I would be able to gauge the size of a contemporary gathering and compare it in this respect with those previously observed. I promised to bring presents and to engage in barter. The chief of the group was rather reluctant to comply with my request: he was not sure of his guests, and if my companions and myself were to disappear in an area where no white men had set foot since the murder of the seven telegraph employees in 1925, the precarious peace which had prevailed since then might well be endangered for some time to come.

He finally agreed on condition that we reduced the size of our expedition,

1. Translated by John and Doreen Weightman.
2. A tribe of hunter-gatherers who live scattered in villages, primarily in Amazon rain forests in central Brazil.
3. Cândido Mariano da Silva Rondon (1865–1958), a Brazilian army engineer who "discovered" the Nambikwara in 1907 when he entered their territory to supervise construction of a telegraph line.
4. A language of the Nambikwara linguistic family; also, the subgroup of Nambikwara who speak this dialect.
5. A Brazilian settlement that was established on the telegraph line built through the Nambikwara territory.
6. That is, edema: accumulation of fluids.
7. Another Brazilian settlement built on the telegraph line.
8. A subgroup of the Nambikwara tribe (later anthropologists found no trace of this name).
9. The site of another telegraph station in Nambikwara territory.

taking only four oxen to carry the presents. Even so, it would be impossible to follow the usual tracks along the valley bottoms where the vegetation was too dense for the animals to get through. We would have to go across the plateaux following a route specially worked out for the occasion.

In retrospect, this journey, which was an extremely hazardous one, seems to me now to have been like some grotesque interlude. We had hardly left Juruena[1] when my Brazilian companion noticed that the women and children were not with us: we were accompanied only by the men, armed with bows and arrows. In travel books, such circumstances mean that an attack is imminent. So we moved ahead with mixed feelings, checking the position of our Smith-and-Wesson revolvers (our men pronounced the name as 'Cemite Vechetone') and our rifles from time to time. Our fears proved groundless: about midday we caught up with the rest of the group, whom the chief had taken the precaution of sending off the previous evening, knowing that our mules would advance more quickly than the basket-carrying women, whose pace was further slowed down by the children.

A little later, however, the Indians lost their way: the new route was not as straightforward as they had imagined. Towards evening we had to stop in the bush; we had been told that there would be game to shoot; the natives were relying on our rifles and had brought nothing with them; we only had emergency provisions, which could not possibly be shared out among everybody. A herd of deer grazing around a water-hole fled at our approach. The next morning, there was widespread discontent, openly directed against the chief who was held responsible for a plan he and I had devised together. Instead of setting out on a hunting or collecting expedition, all the natives decided to lie down under the shelters, leaving the chief to discover the solution to the problem. He disappeared along with one of his wives; towards evening we saw them both return, their heavy baskets full of the grasshoppers they had spent the entire day collecting. Although crushed grasshopper is considered rather poor fare, the natives all ate heartily and recovered their spirits. We set off again the following morning.

At last we reached the appointed meeting-place. It was a sandy terrace overlooking a stream lined with trees, between which lay half-hidden native gardens. Groups arrived intermittently. Towards evening, there were seventy-five persons representing seventeen families, all grouped together under thirteen shelters hardly more substantial than those to be found in native camps. It was explained to me that, during the rainy season, all these people would be housed in five round huts built to last for some months. Several of the natives appeared never to have seen a white man before and their surly attitude and the chief's edginess suggested that he had persuaded them to come rather against their will. We did not feel safe, nor did the Indians. The night promised to be cold, and as there were no trees on the terrace, we had to lie down like the Nambikwara on the bare earth. Nobody slept: the hours were spent keeping a close but polite watch on each other.

It would have been unwise to prolong such a dangerous situation, so I urged the chief to proceed without further delay to the exchange of gifts. It was at this point that there occurred an extraordinary incident that I can only explain by going back a little. It is unnecessary to point out that the

1. The site of a telegraph station on the edge of Nambikwara territory.

Nambikwara have no written language, but they do not know how to draw either, apart from making a few dotted lines or zigzags on their gourds. Nevertheless, as I had done among the Caduveo[2] I handed out sheets of paper and pencils. At first they did nothing with them, then one day I saw that they were all busy drawing wavy, horizontal lines. I wondered what they were trying to do, then it was suddenly borne upon me that they were writing or, to be more accurate, were trying to use their pencils in the same way as I did mine, which was the only way they could conceive of, because I had not yet tried to amuse them with my drawings. The majority did this and no more, but the chief had further ambitions. No doubt he was the only one who had grasped the purpose of writing. So he asked me for a writing-pad, and when we both had one, and were working together, if I asked for information on a given point, he did not supply it verbally but drew wavy lines on his paper and presented them to me, as if I could read his reply. He was half taken in by his own make-believe; each time he completed a line, he examined it anxiously as if expecting the meaning to leap from the page, and the same look of disappointment came over his face. But he never admitted this, and there was a tacit understanding between us to the effect that his unintelligible scribbling had a meaning which I pretended to decipher; his verbal commentary followed almost at once, relieving me of the need to ask for explanations.

As soon as he had got the company together, he took from a basket a piece of paper covered with wavy lines and made a show of reading it, pretending to hesitate as he checked on it the list of objects I was to give in exchange for the presents offered me: so-and-so was to have a chopper in exchange for a bow and arrows, someone else beads in exchange for his necklaces . . . This farce went on for two hours. Was he perhaps hoping to delude himself? More probably he wanted to astonish his companions, to convince them that he was acting as an intermediary agent for the exchange of the goods, that he was in alliance with the white man and shared his secrets. We were eager to be off, since the most dangerous point would obviously be reached when all the marvels I had brought had been transferred to native hands. So I did not try to explore the matter further, and we began the return journey with the Indians still acting as our guides.

The abortive meeting and the piece of humbug of which I had unwittingly been the cause had created an atmosphere of irritation; to make matters worse, my mule had ulcers in its mouth which were causing it pain. It either rushed impatiently ahead or came to a sudden stop; the two of us fell out. Suddenly, before I realized what was happening, I found myself alone in the bush, with no idea which way to go.

Travel books tell us that the thing to do is attract the attention of the main party by firing a shot. I got down from my mount and fired. No response. At the second shot I seemed to hear a reply. I fired a third, the only effect of which was to frighten the mule; it trotted off and stopped some distance away.

I systematically divested myself of my weapons and photographic equipment and laid them all at the foot of a tree, carefully noting its position. Then I ran off to recapture my mule, which I had glimpsed in the distance,

2. Another tribe living in Brazil.

seemingly in docile mood. It waited till I got near, then fled just as I was about to seize the reins, repeating this little game several times and leading me further and further on. In despair I took a leap and hung on to its tail with both hands. Surprised at this unwonted procedure, it made no further attempt to escape from me. I climbed back into the saddle and tried to return to collect my equipment, but we had wandered round so much that I was unable to find it.

Disheartened by the loss, I then decided to try and rejoin the caravan. Neither the mule nor I knew which way it had gone. Either I would decide on one direction which the mule was reluctant to follow, or I would let it have its head, and it would start going round in circles. The sun was sinking towards the horizon, I had lost my weapons and at any moment I expected to be pierced by a shower of arrows. I might not be the first person to have entered that hostile area, but my predecessors had not returned, and, irrespective of myself, my mule would be a most desirable prey for people whose food supplies were scanty. While turning these sombre thoughts over and over in my mind, I waited for the sun to set, my plan being to start a bush fire, since at least I had some matches. Just when I was about to do this, I heard voices: two Nambikwara had turned back as soon as my absence was noticed and had been following my trail since midday; for them, finding my equipment was child's play. They led me back through the darkness to the encampment, where the others were waiting.

Being still perturbed by this stupid incident, I slept badly and whiled away the sleepless hours by thinking over the episode of the exchange of gifts. Writing had, on that occasion, made its appearance among the Nambikwara but not, as one might have imagined, as a result of long and laborious training. It had been borrowed as a symbol, and for a sociological rather than an intellectual purpose, while its reality remained unknown. It had not been a question of acquiring knowledge, of remembering or understanding, but rather of increasing the authority and prestige of one individual—or function—at the expense of others. A native still living in the Stone Age had guessed that this great means towards understanding, even if he was unable to understand it, could be made to serve other purposes. After all, for thousands of years, writing has existed as an institution—and such is still the case today in a large part of the world—in societies the majority of whose members have never learnt to handle it. The inhabitants of the villages I stayed in in the Chittagong hills in eastern Pakistan were illiterate, but each village had its scribe who acted on behalf of individuals or of the community as a whole. All the villagers know about writing, and make use of it if the need arises, but they do so from the outside, as if it were a foreign mediatory agent that they communicate with by oral methods. The scribe is rarely a functionary or employee of the group: his knowledge is accompanied by power, with the result that the same individual is often both scribe and money-lender; not just because he needs to be able to read and write to carry on his business, but because he thus happens to be, on two different counts, someone who *has a hold* over others.

Writing is a strange invention. One might suppose that its emergence could not fail to bring about profound changes in the conditions of human existence, and that these transformations must of necessity be of an intellectual nature. The possession of writing vastly increases man's ability to preserve knowledge. It can be thought of as an artificial memory, the development of which ought to lead to a clearer awareness of the past, and hence to a greater ability to organize both the present and the future. After eliminating all other criteria which have been put forward to distinguish between barbarism and civilization, it is tempting to retain this one at least: there are peoples with, or without, writing; the former are able to store up their past achievements and to move with ever-increasing rapidity towards the goal they have set themselves, whereas the latter, being incapable of remembering the past beyond the narrow margin of individual memory, seem bound to remain imprisoned in a fluctuating history which will always lack both a beginning and any lasting awareness of an aim.

Yet nothing we know about writing and the part it has played in man's evolution justifies this view. One of the most creative periods in the history of mankind occurred during the early stages of the neolithic age, which was responsible for agriculture, the domestication of animals and various arts and crafts. This stage could only have been reached if, for thousands of years, small communities had been observing, experimenting and handing on their findings. This great development was carried out with an accuracy and a continuity which are proved by its success, although writing was still unknown at the time. If writing was invented between 4000 and 3000 B.C., it must be looked upon as an already remote (and no doubt indirect) result of the neolithic revolution, but certainly not as the necessary precondition for it. If we ask ourselves what great innovation writing was linked to, there is little we can suggest on the technical level, apart from architecture. But Egyptian and Sumerian architecture was not superior to the achievements of certain American peoples who knew nothing of writing in the pre-Columbian period. Conversely, from the invention of writing right up to the birth of modern science, the world lived through some five thousand years when knowledge fluctuated more than it increased. It has often been pointed out that the way of life of a Greek or Roman citizen was not so very different from that of an eighteenth-century middle-class European. During the neolithic age, mankind made gigantic strides without the help of writing; with writing, the historic civilizations of the West stagnated for a long time. It would no doubt be difficult to imagine the expansion of science in the nineteenth and twentieth centuries without writing. But, although a necessary precondition, it is certainly not enough to explain the expansion.

To establish a correlation between the emergence of writing and certain characteristic features of civilization, we must look in a quite different direction. The only phenomenon with which writing has always been concomitant is the creation of cities and empires, that is, the integration of large numbers of individuals into a political system, and their grading into castes or classes. Such, at any rate, is the typical pattern of development to be observed from Egypt to China, at the time when writing first emerged: it seems to have favoured the exploitation of human beings rather than their enlightenment. This exploitation, which made it possible to assemble thousands of workers and force them to carry our exhausting tasks, is a much more likely explanation of the birth of architecture than the direct link referred to above. My hypothesis, if correct, would oblige us to recognize the fact that the primary function of written communication is to facilitate slavery. The use of writing for disinterested purposes, and as a source of intellectual and aesthetic pleasure, is a secondary result, and more often than not it may even be turned into a means of strengthening, justifying or concealing the other.

There are, nevertheless, exceptions to the rule: there were native empires in Africa which grouped together several hundreds of thousands of subjects; millions lived under the Inca empire in pre-Columbian America. But in both continents such attempts at empire building did not produce lasting results. We know that the Inca empire was established around the twelfth century: Pizarro's's[3] soldiers would not have conquered it so easily, three centuries later, had they not found it in a state of advanced decay. Although we know little about ancient African history, we can sense that the situation must have been similar: great political groupings came into being and then vanished again within the space of a few decades. It is possible, then, that these examples confirm the hypothesis, instead of contradicting it. Although writing may not have been enough to consolidate knowledge, it was perhaps indispensable for the strengthening of dominion. If we look at the situation nearer home, we see that the systematic development of compulsory education in the European countries goes hand in hand with the extension of military service and proletarianization. The fight against illiteracy is therefore connected with an increase in governmental authority over the citizens. Everyone must be able to read, so that the government can say: Ignorance of the law is no excuse.

The process has moved from the national to the international level, thanks to a kind of complicity that has grown up between newly created states—which find themselves facing problems which we had to cope with a hundred or two hundred years ago—and an international society of privileged countries worried by the possibility of its stability being threatened by the reactions of peoples insufficiently trained in the use of the written word to think in slogans that can be modified at will or to be an easy prey to suggestion. Through gaining access to the knowledge stored in libraries, these peoples have also become vulnerable to the still greater proportion of lies propagated in printed documents. No doubt, there can be no turning back now. But in my Nambikwara village, the insubordinate characters were the most sensible. The villagers who withdrew their allegiance to their chief after he had tried to exploit a feature of civilization (after my visit he was abandoned by most of his people) felt in some obscure way that writing and deceit had penetrated simultaneously into their midst. They went off into a more remote area of the bush to allow themselves a period of respite. Yet at the same time I could not help admiring their chief's genius in instantly recognizing that writing could increase his authority, thus grasping the basis of the institution without knowing how to use it. At the same time, the episode drew my attention to another aspect of Nambikwara life: the political relationships between individuals and groups. I was soon to be able to observe them more directly.

While we were still at Utiarity, an epidemic of putrid ophthalmia had broken out among the natives. The infection, which was gonorrheal in origin, spread to the whole community, causing terrible pain and temporary blindness which could become permanent. For several days the group was completely paralysed. The natives treated the infection with water in which a

3. Francisco Pizzaro (ca. 1478–1541), a Spanish explorer and colonizer who conquered the Inca empire in western South America.

certain kind of bark had been allowed to soak and which they injected into the eye by means of a leaf rolled into a cornet shape. The disease spread to our group: the first person to catch it was my wife who had taken part in all my expeditions so far, her speciality being the study of material culture and skills; the infection was so serious that she had to be evacuated. Then it affected most of the men, as well as my Brazilian companion. Soon the expedition was brought to a halt; I left the main body to rest, with our doctor to give them such treatment as they needed, and with two men and a few beasts I headed for Campos Novos, near which post several bands of natives had been reported. I spent a fortnight there in semi-idleness, gathering barely ripe fruit in an orchard which had reverted to the wild state: there were guavas, the bitter taste and gritty texture of which always fall far short of their aroma, and caju, as brilliantly coloured as parrots, which contain an acid and strongly flavoured juice in the spongy cells of their coarse pulp. To get meat for our meals we had only to go a few hundred metres from the camp at dawn to a copse regularly visited by wood-pigeons, which were easy to shoot. It was at Campos Novos that I met with two groups, whom the expectation of my presents had lured down from the north.

These two groups were as ill-disposed towards each other as they both were towards me. From the start, they did not so much ask for my presents as demand to be given them. During the first few days, only one group was present, as well as a native from Utiarity who had gone on ahead of me. I think perhaps he was showing too great an interest in a young woman belonging to his hosts' group, since relations between the strangers and their visitor became strained almost at once and he started coming to my encampment in search of a more friendly atmosphere; he also shared my meals. This fact was noticed and one day while he was out hunting I received a visit from four natives forming a kind of delegation. In threatening tones, they urged me to put poison in my guest's food; they had, in fact, brought the necessary preparation along with them, a grey powder packed in four little tubes tied together with thread. It was a very awkward situation: if I refused outright, I might well be attacked by the group, whose hostile intentions called for a prudent response. I therefore thought it better to exaggerate my ignorance of the language, and I pretended to understand nothing at all. After several attempts, during which I was told over and over again that my protégé was *kakoré*, that is, very wicked, and should be got rid of as soon as possible, the delegation withdrew with many expressions of displeasure. I warned the interested party, who at once disappeared; I did not see him again until I returned to the area several months later.

Fortunately, the second group arrived the next day, thus providing the first with a different object on which to vent their animosity. The meeting took place at my encampment which was both neutral territory and the goal of these various journeyings. Consequently, I had a good view of the proceedings. The men had come alone; and almost immediately a lengthy conversation began between their respective chiefs. It might be more accurately termed a series of alternating monologues, uttered in plaintive, nasal tones which I had never heard before. 'We are extremely annoyed. You are our enemies!' moaned one group, whereupon the others replied more or less, 'We are not annoyed. We are your brothers. We are friends—friends! We can get along together! etc'. Once this exchange of provocations and protestations was over, a communal camp was set up next to mine. After a few songs and dances, during which each group ran down its own performance by comparing it with that of its opponents ('The Taimaindé are good singers! We are poor singers!'), the quarrel was resumed, and before long the tension heightened. The night had only just begun when the mixture of songs and arguments produced a most extraordinary din, the meaning of which I failed to grasp. Threatening gestures were made, and sometimes scuffles broke out, and other natives intervened as peacemakers. All the threatening gestures centred round the sexual organs. A Nambikwara Indian expresses dislike by grasping his penis in both hands and pointing it towards his opponent. This gesture is followed by an assault on that person, the aim being to pull off the tuft of *buriti* straw attached to the front of the belt above the genitals. These 'are hidden by the straw', and 'the object of the fight is to pull off the straw.' The action is purely symbolical, because the genital covering of the male is made of such flimsy material and is so insubstantial that it neither affords protection nor conceals the organs. Attempts are also made to seize the opponent's bow and arrows and to put them beyond his reach. Throughout these actions, the natives remain extremely tense, as if they were in a state of violent and pent-up anger. The scuffles may sometimes degenerate into a free-for-all, but on this occasion the fighting subsided at dawn. Still in the same stare of visible irritation and with gestures that were anything but gentle, the two sets of opponents then set about examining each other, fingering their ear-pendants, cotton bracelets and little feather ornaments, and muttering a series of rapid comments, such as 'Give it . . . give it . . . see, that's pretty,' while the owner would protest, 'It's ugly . . . old, . . . damaged!'

This 'reconciliatory inspection' marked the end of the quarrel, and initiated another kind of relationship between the groups: commercial exchanges. Rudimentary the material culture of the Nambikwara may be, but the crafts and produce of each group are highly prized by the others. The eastern Nambikwara need pottery and seeds; those from the north consider that their more southerly neighbours make particularly delicate necklaces. It follows that when a meeting between two groups is conducted peacefully, it leads to a reciprocal exchange of gifts; strife is replaced by barter.

Actually, it was difficult to believe that an exchange of gifts was in progress; the morning after the quarrel, each man went about his usual business and the objects or produce were passed from one to another without the giver calling attention to the fact that he was handing over a gift, and without the receiver paying any heed to his new acquisition. The items thus exchanged included raw cotton and balls of thread; lumps of wax or resin; urucu[4] paste; shells, ear-drops, bracelets and necklaces; tobacco and seeds, feathers and bamboo laths to be made into arrow heads; bundles of palm fibres, porcupine quills; whole pots or fragments of pottery and gourds. This mysterious exchange of goods went on for half a day, after which the groups took leave of each other and went their separate ways.

The Nambikwara rely, then, on the generosity of the other side. It simply does not occur to them to evaluate, argue, bargain, demand or take back. I offered a native a machete as payment for taking a message to a neighbouring group. On his return, I omitted to hand over the agreed reward immediately,

4. A tropical shrub (*Bixa orellana*), from whose seeds a red dye can be extracted.

thinking that he would come to fetch it. He did not do so, and the next day I could not find him; he had departed in a rage, so his companions told me, and I never saw him again. I had to ask another native to accept the present on his behalf. This being so, it is hardly surprising that, when the exchanges are over, one group should go off dissatisfied with its share, and (taking stock of its acquisitions and remembering its own gifts) should build up feelings of resentment which become increasingly aggressive. Very often these feelings are enough to start a war; of course, there are other causes, such as the need to commit, or avenge, a murder or the kidnapping of a woman; however, it does not seem that a group feels collectively bound to exact reprisals for some injury done to one of its members. Nevertheless, because of the hostility between the groups, such pretexts are often willingly accepted, especially if a particular group feels itself to be strong. The proposal is presented by a warrior who expounds his grievances in the same tone and style as is used for the inter-group speeches: 'Hallo! Come here! Come along! I am angry! very angry! arrows! big arrows!'

Clad in special finery, consisting of tufts of *buriti* straw daubed with red and helmets made from jaguar hides, the men assemble under the leadership of their chief and dance. A divinatory rite has to be performed: the chief, or the shaman in those groups which have one, hides an arrow somewhere in the bush. A search is made for it the following day. If it is stained with blood, war is decided upon; if not, the idea is dropped. Many expeditions begun in this way come to an end after a few kilometres' march. The excitement and enthusiasm abate, and the warriors return home. But some expeditions are carried through and may result in bloodshed. The Nambikwara attack at dawn and arrange their ambush by posting themselves at intervals in the bush. The signal for the attack is passed from man to man by means of the whistle which each carries slung around his neck. This consists of two bamboo tubes bound together with thread, and its sound approximates to the cricket's chirp; no doubt this is why its name is the same as that of the insect. The war arrows are identical to those normally used for hunting large animals, except that their spear-shaped tip is given a serrated edge. Arrows dipped in curare poison, which are commonly employed for hunting, are never used, because an opponent hit by one would be able to remove it before the poison had time to spread through his body.

1955

J. L. AUSTIN
1911–1960

The work of Oxford University philosopher John Langshaw Austin (along with that of Cambridge-based Ludwig Wittgenstein) broke the stranglehold of logical positivism on Anglo-American philosophy in the 1950s. Championing the virtues of "ordinary language" against the idealized and purified language that logical positivism tried to create, Austin stressed varieties of linguistic utterance that do not simply use names to refer to existing objects. His account of "performatives"—that is, words that are used to do things—has been especially influential for the understanding of literary language and, more recently, of the social processes through which identity is created and cultural values transmitted.

Although he published only seven essays during his lifetime, Austin was a legendary figure at Oxford University and in the philosophy departments of Harvard University and the University of California at Berkeley, where he lectured in the late 1950s. Austin was born in Lancaster, England, but spent his childhood in Scotland, where his father was a schoolmaster. After studying at Oxford, he joined the faculty there, briefly at All Soul's College, then from 1935 on at Magdalen College. He worked for the British Intelligence Corps during World War II and played a large role in coordinating intelligence for the Allied invasion of France on D day (June 6, 1944). He ended the war a lieutenant colonel, decorated by both France and the United States, as well as receiving the Order of the British Empire from the British government. Returning to Oxford in 1948, Austin presided over a generation of philosophers noted for their fierce intelligence and even fiercer subjection of one another's work to careful scrutiny. Austin's ability to find the holes in others' arguments made him feared as well as admired, while his own lectures and (few) published essays were models of clarity and logic. His was not a style of work likely to lead to prolific publication, but philosophers on both sides of the Atlantic came to believe something must be right if Austin could be convinced of its validity. Austin's early death in 1960 left his major projects unfinished, but two books—*Sense and Sensibilia* and *How to Do Things with Words*—were assembled posthumously from his lecture notes.

The logical positivism of Bertrand Russell, the early Wittgenstein, and the "Vienna Circle" (many of whom, notably Rudolph Carnap and Otto Neurath, joined American university faculties after fleeing the Nazis) reigned supreme in Anglo-American philosophy from the 1930s into the 1970s. But as early as 1937, Wittgenstein was radically rethinking his earlier position (in work not published until after his death in 1951), and Austin was leading a parallel attack at Oxford.

The three cornerstones of logical positivism were an epistemology based on sense data as the only source of certain knowledge, an account of linguistic meaning that tied a word's meaning to its reference to (or correspondence with) a perceivable fact in the world, and an insistence that knowledge claims and linguistic uses that did not meet these stringent criteria were "nonsense." Thus, famously, the positivists saw ethical judgments of right and wrong as emotive statements that presented personal preferences or recommendations for action in the guise of statements of fact. A. J. Ayer codified the positivist position in his widely read *Language, Truth, and Logic* (1936). Significantly, positivists recognized that everyday language was full of uses they deemed "nonsense." Their interest was directed, therefore, toward creating a rigorous language that, once purified of nonsense, would be adequate for the needs (as they understood them) of an epistemologically sound modern science. But, as critics soon pointed out, the positivists' own account of what was nonsense and what was certain knowledge was based not on sense data but on a normative understanding of what counts as true.

In *Sense and Sensibilia*, Austin dismantles the logical positivists' account of perception in order to undermine their model of knowledge. When he turns his attention to language, Austin champions "ordinary language" against the purified language the positivists try to create. He starts from a faith in the usages and distinctions found in the languages we already possess. His working principle is that such usages and distinctions probably make sense precisely because people have maintained them. We would not continue to use an expression like "saving for a rainy day" or make a distinction between "an accident" and "a mistake" unless such expressions and distinctions fit our experiences and served to clarify them. The philosopher should work from ordinary language, striving to make explicit the claims about the world and the social relations that such language already contains.

Austin is sometimes castigated as conservative, as accepting the world as given. And, certainly, he is suspicious of an intellectual arrogance that regards common sense and daily practice as most likely faulty. But the clarity that philosophy can bring to prevailing habits of speech and daily practice does not necessarily reinforce such habits and practices; it may stir efforts at reform.

Austin is a pluralist. In examining ordinary language, he sees that we use words for many different purposes. The logical positivists were fixated on reference—the use of words to pick out and designate some thing in the world. They believed that meaning resided in correspondence between word and world. Where such correspondence was absent, so was meaning. Austin recognizes referential utterances ("statements, reports or descriptions") as one kind of meaningful speech but chastises logical positivism for failing to notice, or for denigrating when noticing, other kinds including greetings, apologies, imperatives, pleas, curses, exclamations, and counter-conditionals ("if I were king, I would . . .").

In considering this range, Austin attempts in our selection, "Performative Utterances," to make a basic distinction. There are "statements," which refer to an already existing state of affairs "out there" and are "true" or "false" depending on whether the words fit the facts. And there are "performatives," which do not refer to an existing state of affairs but which, instead, bring a state of affairs into existence by being uttered. Performatives are speech acts, cases in which saying something counts as an action: they serve to alter the world, to bring something new into existence, or to modify, create, or establish a certain relationship between people. "[P]erformative utterances are not true or false, then"; rather, Austin deems them "felicitous" when they succeed in establishing the state of affairs they strive to create. He is interested in outlining the conditions that must be fulfilled for a performative to be felicitous.

For starters, Austin realizes (as did FERDINAND DE SAUSSURE and Wittgenstein) that individual utterances rely heavily on "background conditions" in order to make sense. Among these conditions are a whole set of "conventions," as well as the context in which an utterance is made. Austin points out that many conventions are, in fact, institutional, understanding "institutions" as formal organizations of authority. Performative speech acts such as a judge's sentencing of a criminal or a minister's "I now pronounce you man and wife" succeed only when uttered by a person with the appropriate authority.

Austin also considers noninstitutional causes of infelicity—insincerity, misunderstanding, and nonseriousness. When discussing these sources of "unhappy" utterances and returning to questions of truth and falsehood, Austin finds himself increasingly unable to sort out the different uses of language into separate bins. He cannot maintain the firm line between statements and performatives. If I say "with a stern look, he opened the debate," am I being merely descriptive, or does my use of the adjective "stern" create a view of events for my auditors? In addition, the verb "opened" is a "dead metaphor"; that is, a word designating physical action ("opening") is used to describe a different action. In other words, Austin runs into the kinds of difficulties FRIEDRICH NIETZSCHE describes in the essay "On Truth and Lying in a Non-Moral Sense" (1873; see above), difficulties that led Nietzsche eventually to claim that "there are no facts, only interpretations."

Austin does not phrase the problem in Nietzschean terms. But he does recognize that we seldom speak purely descriptively; we are always doing other things—even when we say "the chair is blue." We have a reason to say "the chair is blue," and that reason is almost always a desire to sway our auditor in some way or another. Austin's essay on performatives thus leads him to recognize the *rhetorical* element in most utterances. We say things in particular contexts to certain others with the aim of influencing their opinions, attitudes, beliefs, and so on. For this reason, Austin concludes the essay with the suggestion that utterances have "force" as well as "meaning"; he uses "force" to designate their impact on listeners, an impact that the speaker can try but cannot always manage to control. And he also concludes that we need to "loosen up" the dichotomy "true / false" so we can more subtly appraise the complex relation between facts and utterances.

Austin's notion of performatives entered literary theory through the JACQUES DERRIDA–John Searle debate of the 1970s. Derrida found Austin's work suggestive but castigated the British philosopher for trying to exclude "non-serious" utterances (a category that included statements made in poems) from consideration. The American philosopher Searle had studied under Austin at Oxford and he defended Austin against what he saw as Derrida's misunderstandings. The pyrotechnics of the debate—which cemented the hostility between Anglo-American philosophers and "French theory"—obscured the fact that Derrida found Austin's emphasis on how language produces things as well as simply reports them very important. JUDITH BUTLER and EVE KOSOFSKY SEDGWICK in the 1990s recuperated the notion of the performative for literary and cultural theorists by stressing the extent to which gender (and other) identities are produced through performances of the ritualized practices of daily life. Joining Derrida's emphasis on "iteration" (repetition) with Austin's insistence that language is productive, Butler and Sedgwick show how prevailing social scripts (ideology) acquire reality for individuals through being performed.

BIBLIOGRAPHY

Austin's two posthumously published sets of lectures are *How to Do Things with Words* (1962) and *Sense and Sensibilia* (1962). His essays are collected in *Philosophical Papers* (3d. ed., 1979). G. J. Warnock's "John Langshaw Austin, A Biographical Sketch," in *Symposium on J. L. Austin* (ed. K. T. Fann, 1969), is the most useful biographical source. The Fann volume, along with John Searle, *Speech Acts* (1969); Isaiah Berlin et al., *Essays on J. L. Austin* (1973); and *Speech Act Theory and Pragmatics,* edited by John Searle, Ferenc Kiefer, and Manfred Bierwisch (1980), provides good overviews of Austin's reception within Anglo-American philosophy. G. J. Warnock's *J. L. Austin* (1989) is an excellent, concise introductory text. Mary Louise Pratt's *Toward a Speech Act Theory of Literary Discourse* (1977), Charles Altieri's *Act and Quality* (1981), Shoshana Felman's *The Literary Speech Act* (1983), and Sandy Petrey's *Speech Acts and Literary Theory* (1990) are the most influential uses of Austin to account for the capacities of literary texts. Jacques Derrida's essay on Austin and his side in the debate with Searle is collected in *Limited INC* (1988); for Searle's side, one must go to the journal *Glyph* 1.1 (1977). The most original American disciple of Austin is Stanley Cavell, a philosopher who is also a major literary and film critic. He has revisited the Derrida-Searle debate in his *Philosophical Passages: Wittgenstein, Emerson, Austin, Derrida* (1995). The best available bibliography of responses to Austin can be found in Joseph J. DiGiovanna's *Linguistic Phenomenology: Philosophical Method in J. L. Austin* (1989), but it is incomplete and limited to work in Anglo-American philosophy.

Performative Utterances

I

You are more than entitled not to know what the word 'performative' means. It is a new word and an ugly word, and perhaps it does not mean anything very much. But at any rate there is one thing in its favour, it is not a profound word. I remember once when I had been talking on this subject that somebody afterwards said: 'You know, I haven't the least idea what he means, unless it could be that he simply means what he says'. Well, that is what I should like to mean.

Let us consider first how this affair arises. We have not got to go very far back in the history of philosophy to find philosophers assuming more or less as a matter of course that the sole business, the sole interesting business, of any utterance—that is, of anything we say—is to be true or at least false. Of course they had always known that there are other kinds of things which we say—things like imperatives, the expressions of wishes, and exclamations—some of which had even been classified by grammarians, though it wasn't perhaps too easy to tell always which was which. But still philosophers have assumed that the only things that they are interested in are utterances which report facts or which describe situations truly or falsely. In recent times this kind of approach has been questioned—in two stages, I think. First of all people began to say: 'Well, if these things are true or false it ought to be possible to decide which they are, and if we can't decide which they are they aren't any good but are, in short, nonsense'. And this new approach did a great deal of good; a great many things which probably are nonsense were found to be such. It is not the case, I think, that all kinds of nonsense have been adequately classified yet, and perhaps some things have been dismissed as nonsense which really are not; but still this movement, the verification movement, was, in its way, excellent.

However, we then come to the second stage. After all, we set some limits to the amount of nonsense that we talk, or at least the amount of nonsense that we are prepared to admit we talk; and so people began to ask whether after all some of those things which, treated as statements, were in danger of being dismissed as nonsense did after all really set out to be statements at all. Mightn't they perhaps be intended not to report facts but to influence people in this way or that, or to let off steam in this way or that? Or perhaps at any rate some elements in these utterances performed such functions, or, for example, drew attention in some way (without actually reporting it) to some important feature of the circumstances in which the utterance was being made. On these lines people have now adopted a new slogan, the slogan of the 'different uses of language'. The old approach, the old statemental approach, is sometimes called even a fallacy, the descriptive fallacy.

Certainly there are a great many uses of language. It's rather a pity that people are apt to invoke a new use of language whenever they feel so inclined, to help them out of this, that, or the other well-known philosophical tangle; we need more of a framework in which to discuss these uses of language; and also I think we should not despair too easily and talk, as people are apt to do, about the *infinite* uses of language. Philosophers will do this when they have listed as many, let us say, as seventeen; but even if there were something like ten thousand uses of language, surely we could list them all in time. This, after all, is no larger than the number of species of beetle that entomologists have taken the pains to list. But whatever the defects of either of these movements—the 'verification' movement or the 'use of language' movement—at any rate they have effected, nobody could deny, a great revolution in philosophy and, many would say, the most salutary in its history. (Not, if you come to think of it, a very immodest claim.)

Now it is one such sort of use of language that I want to examine here. I want to discuss a kind of utterance which looks like a statement and grammatically, I suppose, would be classed as a statement, which is not nonsensical, and yet is not true or false. These are not going to be utterances which contain curious verbs like 'could' or 'might', or curious words like 'good', which many philosophers regard nowadays simply as danger signals. They will be perfectly straightforward utterances, with ordinary verbs in the first person singular present indicative active, and yet we shall see at once that they couldn't possibly be true or false. Furthermore, if a person makes an utterance of this sort we should say that he is *doing* something rather than merely *saying* something. This may sound a little odd, but the examples I shall give will in fact not be odd at all, and may even seem decidedly dull. Here are three or four. Suppose, for example, that in the course of a marriage ceremony I say, as people will, 'I do'—(sc.[1] take this woman to be my lawful wedded wife). Or again, suppose that I tread on your toe and say 'I apologize'. Or again, suppose that I have the bottle of champagne in my hand and say 'I name this ship the *Queen Elizabeth*'. Or suppose I say 'I bet you sixpence it will rain tomorrow'. In all these cases it would be absurd to regard the thing that I say as a report of the performance of the action which is undoubtedly done—the action of betting, or christening, or apologizing. We should say rather that, in saying what I do, I actually perform that action. When I say 'I name this ship the *Queen Elizabeth*' I do not describe the christening ceremony, I actually perform the christening; and when I say 'I do' (sc. take this woman to be my lawful wedded wife), I am not reporting on a marriage, I am indulging in it.

Now these kinds of utterance are the ones that we call *performative* utterances. This is rather an ugly word, and a new word, but there seems to be no word already in existence to do the job. The nearest approach that I can think of is the word 'operative', as used by lawyers. Lawyers when talking about legal instruments will distinguish between the preamble, which recites the circumstances in which a transaction is effected, and on the other hand the operative part—the part of it which actually performs the legal act which it is the purpose of the instrument to perform. So the word 'operative' is very near to what we want. 'I give and bequeath my watch to my brother' would be an operative clause and is a performative utterance. However, the word 'operative' has other uses, and it seems preferable to have a word specially designed for the use we want.

Now at this point one might protest, perhaps even with some alarm, that I seem to be suggesting that marrying is simply saying a few words, that just saying a few words *is* marrying. Well, that certainly is not the case. The words have to be said in the appropriate circumstances, and this is a matter that will come up again later. But the one thing we must not suppose is that what is needed in addition to the saying of the words in such cases is the performance of some internal spiritual act, of which the words then are to be the report. It's very easy to slip into this view at least in difficult, portentous cases, though perhaps not so easy in simple cases like apologizing. In the case of promising—for example, 'I promise to be there tomorrow'—it's very easy to think that the utterance is simply the outward and visible (that is, verbal) sign of the performance of some inward spiritual act of promising, and this view has certainly been expressed in many classic places. There is the case of Euripides' Hippolytus,[2] who said 'My tongue swore to, but my

1. Scilicet; namely.
2. Euripides, *Hippolytus* (428 B.C.E.), line 612. The Greek word here translated "heart" is *phrēn*, which can also mean "mind" or "understanding."

heart did not'—perhaps it should be 'mind' or 'spirit' rather than 'heart', but at any rate some kind of backstage artiste. Now it is clear from this sort of example that, if we slip into thinking that such utterances are reports, true or false, of the performance of inward and spiritual acts, we open a loophole to perjurers and welshers and bigamists and so on, so that there are disadvantages in being excessively solemn in this way. It is better, perhaps, to stick to the old saying that our word is our bond.

However, although these utterances do not themselves report facts and are not themselves true or false, saying these things does very often *imply* that certain things are true and not false, in some sense at least of that rather woolly word 'imply'. For example, when I say 'I do take this woman to be my lawful wedded wife', or some other formula in the marriage ceremony, I do imply that I'm not already married, with wife living, sane, undivorced, and the rest of it. But still it is very important to realize that to imply that something or other is true, is not at all the same as saying something which is true itself.

These performative utterances are not true or false, then. But they do suffer from certain disabilities of their own. They can fail to come off in special ways, and that is what I want to consider next. The various ways in which a performative utterance may be unsatisfactory we call, for the sake of a name, the infelicities; and an infelicity arises—that is to say, the utterance is unhappy—if certain rules, transparently simple rules, are broken. I will mention some of these rules and then give examples of some infringements.

First of all, it is obvious that the conventional procedure which by our utterance we are purporting to use must actually exist. In the examples given here this procedure will be a verbal one, a verbal procedure for marrying or giving or whatever it may be; but it should be borne in mind that there are many non-verbal procedures by which we can perform exactly the same acts as we perform by these verbal means. It's worth remembering too that a great many of the things we do are at least in part of this conventional kind. Philosophers at least are too apt to assume that an action is always in the last resort the making of a physical movement, whereas it's usually, at least in part, a matter of convention.

The first rule is, then, that the convention invoked must exist and be accepted. And the second rule, also a very obvious one, is that the circumstances in which we purport to invoke this procedure must be appropriate for its invocation. If this is not observed, then the act that we purport to perform would not come off—it will be, one might say, a misfire. This will also be the case if, for example, we do not carry through the procedure—whatever it may be—correctly and completely, without a flaw and without a hitch. If any of these rules are not observed, we say that the act which we purported to perform is void, without effect. If, for example, the purported act was an act of marrying, then we should say that we 'went through a form' of marriage, but we did not actually succeed in marrying.

Here are some examples of this kind of misfire. Suppose that, living in a country like our own, we wish to divorce our wife. We may try standing her in front of us squarely in the room and saying, in a voice loud enough for all to hear, 'I divorce you'. Now this procedure is not accepted. We shall not thereby have succeeded in divorcing our wife, at least in this country and others like it. This is a case where the convention, we should say, does not exist or is not accepted. Again, suppose that, picking sides at a children's party, I say 'I pick George'. But George turns red in the face and says 'Not playing'. In that case I plainly, for some reason or another, have not picked George—whether because there is no convention that you can pick people who aren't playing, or because George in the circumstances is an inappropriate object for the procedure of picking. Or consider the case in which I say 'I appoint you Consul', and it turns out that you have been appointed already—or perhaps it may even transpire that you are a horse;[3] here again we have the infelicity of inappropriate circumstances, inappropriate objects, or what not. Examples of flaws and hitches are perhaps scarcely necessary—one party in the marriage ceremony says 'I will', the other says 'I won't'; I say 'I bet sixpence', but nobody says 'Done', nobody takes up the offer. In all these and other such cases, the act which we purport to perform, or set out to perform, is not achieved.

But there is another and a rather different way in which this kind of utterance may go wrong. A good many of these verbal procedures are designed for use by people who hold certain beliefs or have certain feelings or intentions. And if you use one of these formulae when you do not have the requisite thoughts or feelings or intentions then there is an abuse of the procedure, there is insincerity. Take, for example, the expression, 'I congratulate you'. This is designed for use by people who are glad that the person addressed has achieved a certain feat, believe that he was personally responsible for the success, and so on. If I say 'I congratulate you' when I'm not pleased or when I don't believe that the credit was yours, then there is insincerity. Likewise if I say I promise to do something, without having the least intention of doing it or without believing it feasible. In these cases there is something wrong certainly, but it is not like a misfire. We should not say that I didn't in fact promise, but rather that I did promise but promised insincerely; I did congratulate you but the congratulations were hollow. And there may be an infelicity of a somewhat similar kind when the performative utterance commits the speaker to future conduct of a certain description and then in the future he does not in fact behave in the expected way. This is very obvious, of course, if I promise to do something and then break my promise, but there are many kinds of commitment of a rather less tangible form than that in the case of promising. For instance, I may say 'I welcome you', bidding you welcome to my home or wherever it may be, but then I proceed to treat you as though you were exceedingly unwelcome. In this case the procedure of saying 'I welcome you' has been abused in a way rather different from that of simple insincerity.

Now we might ask whether this list of infelicities is complete, whether the kinds of infelicity are mutually exclusive, and so forth. Well, it is not complete, and they are not mutually exclusive; they never are. Suppose that you are just about to name the ship, you have been appointed to name it, and you are just about to bang the bottle against the stem; but at that very moment some low type comes up, snatches the bottle out of your hand, breaks it on the stem, shouts out 'I name this ship the *Generalissimo Stalin*',

3. A reference to an anecdote about the Roman emperor known as Caligula (Gaius Caesar Germanicus, 12–41 C.E.), who was said to have wished to make his favorite horse consul.

and then for good measure kicks away the chocks. Well, we agree of course on several things We agree that the ship certainly isn't now named the *Generalissimo Stalin*, and we agree that it's an infernal shame and so on and so forth. But we may not agree as to how we should classify the particular infelicity in this case. We might say that here is a case of a perfectly legitimate and agreed procedure which, however, has been invoked in the wrong circumstances, namely by the wrong person, this low type instead of the person appointed to do it. But on the other hand we might look at it differently and say that this is a case where the procedure has not as a whole been gone through correctly, because part of the procedure for naming a ship is that you should first of all get yourself appointed as the person to do the naming and that's what this fellow did not do. Thus the way we should classify infelicities in different cases will be perhaps rather a difficult matter, and may even in the last resort be a bit arbitrary. But of course lawyers, who have to deal very much with this kind of thing, have invented all kinds of technical terms and have made numerous rules about different kinds of cases, which enable them to classify fairly rapidly what in particular is wrong in any given case.

As for whether this list is complete, it certainly is not. One further way in which things may go wrong is, for example, through what in general may be called misunderstanding. You may not hear what I say, or you may understand me to refer to something different from what I intended to refer to, and so on. And apart from further additions which we might make to the list, there is the general over-riding consideration that, as we are performing an act when we issue these performative utterances, we may of course be doing so under duress or in some other circumstances which make us not entirely responsible for doing what we are doing. That would certainly be an unhappiness of a kind—any kind of non-responsibility might be called an unhappiness; but of course it is a quite different kind of thing from what we have been talking about. And I might mention that, quite differently again, we could be issuing any of these utterances, as we can issue an utterance of any kind whatsoever, in the course, for example, of acting a play or making a joke or writing a poem—in which case of course it would not be seriously meant and we shall not be able to say that we seriously performed the act concerned. If the poet says 'Go and catch a falling star'[4] or whatever it may be, he doesn't seriously issue an order. Considerations of this kind apply to any utterance at all, not merely to performatives.

That, then, is perhaps enough to be going on with. We have discussed the performative utterance and its infelicities. That equips us, we may suppose, with two shining new tools to crack the crib of reality maybe. It also equips us—it always does—with two shining new skids under our metaphysical feet. The question is how we use them.

II

So far we have been going firmly ahead, feeling the firm ground of prejudice glide away beneath our feet which is always rather exhilarating, but what next? You will be waiting for the bit when we bog down, the bit where we

4. The first line of an untitled poem (1633) by John Donne.

take it all back, and sure enough that's going to come but it will take time. First of all let us ask a rather simple question. How can we be sure, how can we tell, whether any utterance is to be classed as a performative or not? Surely, we feel, we ought to be able to do that. And we should obviously very much like to be able to say that there is a grammatical criterion for this, some grammatical means of deciding whether an utterance is performative. All the examples I have given hitherto do in fact have the same grammatical form; they all of them begin with the verb in the first person singular present indicative active—not just any kind of verb of course, but still they all are in fact of that form. Furthermore, with these verbs that I have used there is a typical asymmetry between the use of this person and tense of the verb and the use of the same verb in other persons and other tenses, and this asymmetry is rather an important clue.

For example, when we say 'I promise that . . . ', the case is very different from when we say 'He promises that . . . ', or in the past tense 'I promised that . . . '. For when we say 'I promise that . . . ' we do perform an act of promising—we give a promise. What we do *not* do is to report on somebody's performing an act of promising—in particular, we do not report on somebody's use of the expression 'I promise'. We actually do use it and do the promising. But if I say 'He promises', or in the past tense 'I promised', I precisely do report on an act of promising, that is to say an act of using this formula 'I promise'—I report on a present act of promising by him, or on a past act of my own. There is thus a clear difference between our first person singular present indicative active, and other persons and tenses. This is brought out by the typical incident of little Willie whose uncle says he'll give him half-a-crown[5] if he promises never to smoke till he's 55. Little Willie's anxious parent will say 'Of course he promises, don't you, Willie?' giving him a nudge, and little Willie just doesn't vouchsafe. The point here is that he must do the promising himself by saying 'I promise', and his parent is going too fast in saying he promises.

That, then, is a bit of a test for whether an utterance is performative or not, but it would not do to suppose that every performative utterance has to take this standard form. There is at least one other standard form, every bit as common as this one, where the verb is in the passive voice and in the second or third person, not in the first. The sort of case I mean is that of a notice inscribed 'Passengers are warned to cross the line by the bridge only', or of a document reading 'You are hereby authorized' to do so-and-so. These are undoubtedly performative, and in fact a signature is often required in order to show who it is that is doing the act of warning, or authorizing, or whatever it may be. Very typical of this kind of performative—especially liable to occur in written documents of course—is that the little word 'hereby' either actually occurs or might naturally be inserted.

Unfortunately, however, we still can't possibly suggest that every utterance which is to be classed as a performative has to take one or another of these two, as we might call them, standard forms. After all it would be a very typical performative utterance to say 'I order you to shut the door'. This satisfies all the criteria. It is performing the act of ordering you to shut the door, and it

5. Under the old U.K. system of money, a crown was worth 5 shillings; little Willie is given the equivalent of about a half-dollar.

is not true or false. But in the appropriate circumstances surely we could perform exactly the same act by simply saying 'Shut the door', in the imperative. Or again, suppose that somebody sticks up a notice 'This bull is dangerous', or simply 'Dangerous bull', or simply 'Bull'. Does this necessarily differ from sticking up a notice, appropriately signed, saying 'You are hereby warned that this bull is dangerous'? It seems that the simple notice 'Bull' can do just the same job as the more elaborate formula. Of course the difference is that if we just stick up 'Bull' it would not be quite clear that it is a warning; it might be there just for interest or information, like 'Wallaby' on the cage at the zoo, or 'Ancient Monument'. No doubt we should know from the nature of the case that it was a warning, but it would not be explicit.

Well, in view of this break-down of grammatical criteria, what we should like to suppose—and there is a good deal in this—is that any utterance which is performative could be reduced or expanded or analysed into one of these two standard forms beginning 'I . . . ' so and so or beginning 'You (or he) hereby . . . ' so and so. If there was any justification for this hope, as to some extent there is, then we might hope to make a list of all the verbs which can appear in these standard forms, and then we might classify the kinds of acts that can be performed by performative utterances. We might do this with the aid of a dictionary, using such a test as that already mentioned—whether there is the characteristic asymmetry between the first person singular present indicative active and the other persons and tenses—in order to decide whether a verb is to go into our list or not. Now if we make such a list of verbs we do in fact find that they fall into certain fairly well-marked classes. There is the class of cases where we deliver verdicts and make estimates and appraisals of various kinds. There is the class where we give undertakings, commit ourselves in various ways by saying something. There is the class where by saying something we exercise various rights and powers, such as appointing and voting and so on. And there are one or two other fairly well-marked classes.

Suppose this task accomplished. Then we could call these verbs in our list explicit performative verbs, and any utterance that was reduced to one or the other of our standard forms we could call an explicit performative utterance. 'I order you to shut the door' would be an explicit performative utterance, whereas 'Shut the door' would not—that is simply a 'primary' performative utterance or whatever we like to call it. In using the imperative we may be ordering you to shut the door, but it just isn't made clear whether we are ordering you or entreating you or imploring you or beseeching you or inciting you or tempting you, or one or another of many other subtly different acts which, in an unsophisticated primitive language, are very likely not yet discriminated. But we need not over-estimate the unsophistication of primitive languages. There are a great many devices that can be used for making clear, even at the primitive level, what act it is we are performing when we say something—the tone of voice, cadence, gesture—and above all we can rely upon the nature of the circumstances, the context in which the utterance is issued. This very often makes it quite unmistakable whether it is an order that is being given or whether, say, I am simply urging you or entreating you. We may, for instance, say something like this: 'Coming from him I was bound to take it as an order'. Still, in spite of all these devices, there is an unfortunate amount of ambiguity and lack of discrimination in default of our explicit performative verbs. If I say something like 'I shall be there', it may not be certain whether it is a promise, or an expression of intention, or perhaps even a forecast of my future behaviour, of what is going to happen to me; and it may matter a good deal, at least in developed societies, precisely which of these things it is. And that is why the explicit performative verb is evolved—to make clear exactly which it is, how far it commits me and in what way, and so forth.

This is just one way in which language develops in tune with the society of which it is the language. The social habits of the society may considerably affect the question of which performative verbs are evolved and which, sometimes for rather irrelevant reasons, are not. For example, if I say 'You are a poltroon', it might be that I am censuring you or it might be that I am insulting you. Now since apparently society approves of censuring or reprimanding, we have here evolved a formula 'I reprimand you', or 'I censure you', which enables us expeditiously to get this desirable business over. But on the other hand, since apparently we don't approve of insulting, we have not evolved a simple formula 'I insult you', which might have done just as well.

By means of these explicit performative verbs and some other devices, then, we make explicit what precise act it is that we are performing when we issue our utterance. But here I would like to put in a word of warning. We must distinguish between the function of making explicit what act it is we are performing, and the quite different matter of *stating* what act it is we are performing. In issuing an explicit performative utterance we are not stating what act it is, we are showing or making explicit what act it is. We can draw a helpful parallel here with another case in which the act, the conventional act that we perform, is not a speech-act but a physical performance. Suppose I appear before you one day and bow deeply from the waist. Well, this is ambiguous. I may be simply observing the local flora, tying my shoelace, something of that kind; on the other hand, conceivably I might be doing obeisance to you. Well, to clear up this ambiguity we have some device such as raising the hat, saying 'Salaam',[6] or something of that kind, to make it quite plain that the act being performed is the conventional one of doing obeisance rather than some other act. Now nobody would want to say that lifting your hat was stating that you were performing an act of obeisance; it certainly is not, but it does make it quite plain that you are. And so in the same way to say 'I warn you that . . .' or 'I order you to . . .' or 'I promise that . . .' is not to state that you are doing something, but makes it plain that you are—it does constitute your verbal performance, a performance of a particular kind.

So far we have been going along as though there was a quite clear difference between our performative utterances and what we have contrasted them with, statements or reports or descriptions. But now we begin to find that this distinction is not as clear as it might be. It's now that we begin to sink in a little. In the first place, of course, we may feel doubts as to how widely our performatives extend. If we think up some odd kinds of expression we use in odd cases, we might very well wonder whether or not they satisfy our rather vague criteria for being performative utterances. Suppose, for

6. Literally, "peace" (Arabic); a greeting sometimes spoken while making a ceremonial bow.

example, somebody says 'Hurrah'. Well, not true or false; he is performing the act of cheering. Does that make it a performative utterance in our sense or not? Or suppose he says 'Damn'; he is performing the act of swearing, and it is not true or false. Does that make it performative? We feel that in a way it does and yet it's rather different. Again, consider cases of 'suiting the action to the words'; these too may make us wonder whether perhaps the utterance should be classed as performative. Or sometimes, if somebody says 'I am sorry', we wonder whether this is just the same as 'I apologize'—in which case of course we have said it's a performative utterance—or whether perhaps it's to be taken as a description, true or false, of the state of his feelings. If he had said 'I feel perfectly awful about it', then we should think it must be meant to be a description of the state of his feelings. If he had said 'I apologize', we should feel this was clearly a performative utterance, going through the ritual of apologizing. But if he says 'I am sorry' there is an unfortunate hovering between the two. This phenomenon is quite common. We often find cases in which there is an obvious pure performative utterance and obvious other utterances connected with it which are not performative but descriptive, but on the other hand a good many in between where we're not quite sure which they are. On some occasions of course they are obviously used the one way, on some occasions the other way, but on some occasions they seem positively to revel in ambiguity.

Again, consider the case of the umpire when he says 'Out' or 'Over',[7] or the jury's utterance when they say that they find the prisoner guilty. Of course, we say, these are cases of giving verdicts, performing the act of appraising and so forth, but still in a way they have some connexion with the facts. They seem to have something like the duty to be true or false, and seem not to be so very remote from statements. If the umpire says 'Over', this surely has at least something to do with six balls in fact having been delivered rather than seven, and so on. In fact in general we may remind ourselves that 'I state that . . . ' does not look so very different from 'I warn you that . . . ' or 'I promise to . . . '. It makes clear surely that the act that we are performing is an act of stating, and so functions just like 'I warn' or 'I order'. So isn't 'I state that . . . ' a performative utterance? But then one may feel that utterances beginning 'I state that . . . ' do have to be true or false, that they *are* statements.

Considerations of this sort, then, may well make us feel pretty unhappy. If we look back for a moment at our contrast between statements and performative utterances, we realize that we were taking statements very much on trust from, as we said, the traditional treatment. Statements, we had it, were to be true or false; performative utterances on the other hand were to be felicitous or infelicitous. They were the doing of something, whereas for all we said making statements was not doing something. Now this contrast surely, if we look back at it, is unsatisfactory. Of course statements are liable to be assessed in this matter of their correspondence or failure to correspond with the facts, that is, being true or false. But they are also liable to infelicity every bit as much as are performative utterances. In fact some troubles that have arisen in the study of statements recently can be shown to be simply troubles of infelicity. For example, it has been pointed out that there is some-

7. Umpire's calls in cricket.

thing very odd about saying something like this: 'The cat is on the mat but I don't believe it is'. Now this is an outrageous thing to say, but it is not self-contradictory. There is no reason why the cat shouldn't be on the mat without my believing that it is. So how are we to classify what's wrong with this peculiar statement? If we remember now the doctrine of infelicity we shall see that the person who makes this remark about the cat is in much the same position as somebody who says something like this: 'I promise that I shall be there, but I haven't the least intention of being there'. Once again you can of course perfectly well promise to be there without having the least intention of being there, but there is something outrageous about saying it, about actually avowing the insincerity of the promise you give. In the same way there is insincerity in the case of the person who says 'The cat is on the mat but I don't believe it is', and he is actually avowing that insincerity—which makes a peculiar kind of nonsense.

A second case that has come to light is the one about John's children—the case where somebody is supposed to say 'All John's children are bald but John hasn't got any children'.[8] Or perhaps somebody says 'All John's children are bald', when as a matter of fact—he doesn't say so—John has no children. Now those who study statements have worried about this; ought they to say that the statement 'All John's children are bald' is meaningless in this case? Well, if it is, it is not a bit like a great many other more standard kinds of meaninglessness; and we see, if we look back at our list of infelicities, that what is going wrong here is much the same as what goes wrong in, say, the case of a contract for the sale of a piece of land when the piece of land referred to does not exist. Now what we say in the case of this sale of land, which of course would be effected by a performative utterance, is that the sale is void—void for lack of reference or ambiguity of reference; and so we can see that the statement about all John's children is likewise void for lack of reference. And if the man actually says that John has no children in the same breath as saying they're all bald, he is making the same kind of outrageous utterance as the man who says 'The cat is on the mat and I don't believe it is', or the man who says 'I promise to but I don't intend to'.

In this way, then, ills that have been found to afflict statements can be precisely paralleled with ills that are characteristic of performative utterances. And after all when we state something or describe something or report something, we do perform an act which is every bit as much an act as an act of ordering or warning. There seems no good reason why stating should be given a specially unique position. Of course philosophers have been wont to talk as though you or I or anybody could just go round stating anything about anything and that would be perfectly in order, only there's just a little question: is it true or false? But besides the little question, is it true or false, there is surely the question: *is* it in order? Can you go round just making statements about anything? Suppose for example you say to me 'I'm feeling pretty mouldy this morning'. Well, I say to you 'You're not'; and you say 'What the devil do you mean, I'm not?' I say 'Oh nothing—I'm just stating you're not, is it true or false?' And you say 'Wait a bit about whether it's true or false, the question is what did you mean by making statements about somebody

8. A reference to a famous example in "On Denoting" (1905) by Bertrand Russell, one of the earliest of the logical positivists: "The present king of France is bald."

else's feelings? I told you I'm feeling pretty mouldy. You're just not in a position to say, to state that I'm not'. This brings out that you can't just make statements about other people's feelings (though you can make guesses if you like); and there are very many things which, having no knowledge of, not being in a position to pronounce about, you just can't state. What we need to do for the case of stating, and by the same token describing and reporting, is to take them a bit off their pedestal, to realize that they are speech-acts no less than all these other speech-acts that we have been mentioning and talking about as performative.

Then let us look for a moment at our original contrast between the performative and the statement from the other side. In handling performatives we have been putting it all the time as though the only thing that a performative utterance had to do was to be felicitous, to come off, not to be a misfire, not to be an abuse. Yes, but that's not the end of the matter. At least in the case of many utterances which, on what we have said, we should have to class as performative—cases where we say 'I warn you to . . . ', 'I advise you to . . . ' and so on—there will be other questions besides simply: was it in order, was it all right, as a piece of advice or a warning, did it come off? After that surely there will be the question: was it good or sound advice? Was it a justified warning? Or in the case, let us say, of a verdict or an estimate: was it a good estimate, or a sound verdict? And these are questions that can only be decided by considering how the content of the verdict or estimate is related in some way to fact, or to evidence available about the facts. This is to say that we do require to assess at least a great many performative utterances in a general dimension of correspondence with fact. It may still be said, of course, that this does not make them *very* like statements because still they are not true or false, and that's a little black and white speciality that distinguishes statements as a class apart. But actually—though it would take too long to go on about this—the more you think about truth and falsity the more you find that very few statements that we ever utter are just true or just false. Usually there is the question are they fair or are they not fair, are they adequate or not adequate, are they exaggerated or not exaggerated? Are they too rough, or are they perfectly precise, accurate, and so on? 'True' and 'false' are just general labels for a whole dimension of different appraisals which have something or other to do with the relation between what we say and the facts. If, then, we loosen up our ideas of truth and falsity we shall see that statements, when assessed in relation to the facts, are not so very different after all from pieces of advice, warnings, verdicts, and so on.

We see then that stating something is performing an act just as much as is giving an order or giving a warning; and we see, on the other hand, that, when we give an order or a warning or a piece of advice, there is a question about how this is related to fact which is not perhaps so very different from the kind of question that arises when we discuss how a statement is related to fact. Well, this seems to mean that in its original form our distinction between the performative and the statement is considerably weakened, and indeed breaks down. I will just make a suggestion as to how to handle this matter. We need to go very much farther back, to consider all the ways and senses in which saying anything at all is doing this or that—because of course it is always doing a good many different things. And one thing that emerges when we do do this is that, besides the question that has been very much studied in the past as to what a certain utterance *means*, there is a further question distinct from this as to what was the *force*, as we may call it, of the utterance. We may be quite clear what 'Shut the door' means, but not yet at all clear on the further point as to whether as uttered at a certain time it was an order, an entreaty or whatnot. What we need besides the old doctrine about meanings is a new doctrine about all the possible forces of utterances, towards the discovery of which our proposed list of explicit performative verbs would be a very great help; and then, going on from there, an investigation of the various terms of appraisal that we use in discussing speech-acts of this, that, or the other precise kind—orders, warnings, and the like.

The notions that we have considered then, are the performative, the infelicity, the explicit performative, and lastly, rather hurriedly, the notion of the forces of utterances. I dare say that all this seems a little unremunerative, a little complicated. Well, I suppose in some ways it is unremunerative, and I suppose it ought to be remunerative. At least, though, I think that if we pay attention to these matters we can clear up some mistakes in philosophy; and after all philosophy is used as a scapegoat, it parades mistakes which are really the mistakes of everybody. We might even clear up some mistakes in grammar, which perhaps is a little more respectable.

And is it complicated? Well, it is complicated a bit; but life and truth and things do tend to be complicated. It's not things, it's philosophers that are simple. You will have heard it said, I expect, that over-simplification is the occupational disease of philosophers, and in a way one might agree with that. But for a sneaking suspicion that it's their occupation.

1956 1961

NORTHROP FRYE
1912–1991

By the mid-1950s, the New Critical "close reading" of texts had become the dominant theory and practice of literary criticism in the North American academy. Its reign was not uncontested; some scholars argued that this critical approach (see JOHN CROWE RANSOM and CLEANTH BROOKS) failed to consider historical and biographical contexts, and the "Chicago School" led by R. S. Crane maintained that the New Criticism emphasized irony and metaphor in all texts at the expense of crucial distinctions among the literary genres. But it was not until the late 1950s, with the publication of Northrop Frye's *Anatomy of Criticism* (1957), that the New Criticism was comprehensively challenged by a fully defined alternative.

In the *Anatomy of Criticism*, Frye pointedly contrasted his archetypal or myth criticism with the "rhetorical analysis of the new critics":

> The further back we go, the more conscious we are of the organizing design. At a great distance from, say, a Madonna, we can see nothing but the archetype of the Madonna, a large centripetal blue mass with a contrasting point of interest at its center. In the criticism of literature, too, we often have to "stand back" from the poem to see its archetypal organization.

Frye thus took issue with the critical orthodoxy of his own day, even as his approach looked forward to the structuralist poetics and analysis of narrative that theorists such as TVEZTAN TODOROV, ROLAND BARTHES, and HAYDEN WHITE would articulate in the 1960s and 1970s.

A Canadian born in southern Quebec province, Frye attended the University of Toronto, studied theology at Emmanuel College in Toronto, was ordained in the United Church of Canada in 1936, and then did postgraduate work at Merton College, Oxford University. He began his academic career at Victoria College, University of Toronto, in 1939, and later held administrative positions both in the English department and in the college. He was keenly interested in Canadian literature, culture, and education, but his influence as a literary critic, theorist, and educator extended worldwide. He lectured and taught at many colleges and universities in the United States, England, and elsewhere, winning numerous awards and prizes for his scholarship and criticism.

Frye's first book was *Fearful Symmetry: A Study of William Blake* (1947), an influential examination of Blake's symbolism. Here, Frye describes the imagination as the "creative force in the mind" from which "everything that we call culture and civilization" derives: "it is the power of transforming a sub-human physical world into a world with a human shape and meaning." The next important work, *Anatomy of Criticism*, articulated the role of archetypal symbols, myths, and generic conventions in creating literary meaning.

The word "archetype" derives from the Greek *archetypon*, which means "beginning pattern"; as developed by Frye within the field of literary criticism, it refers to a recurrent image, character, plot, or pattern that, through its repetitions in many works across the centuries, takes on a universal quality. Frye drew from many sources, including the Bible, Blake's prophetic books, and (from the early twentieth century) the German historicist writer Oswald Spengler, SIGMUND FREUD, the Scottish folklorist and anthropologist J. G. Frazer, and the classical historian Gilbert Murray. But perhaps the main source for Frye was the psychologist CARL JUNG, particularly Jung's account of the "collective unconscious." Part of what makes us human, according to Jung, is an "unconscious" inhabited by shared memories, desires, impulses, images, ideas—in a word, archetypes—distinct from the personal unconscious that each of us acquires from our individual experiences.

But Frye objected to being called a "Jungian critic." As he explains in *Anatomy of Criticism*, the literary critic should be "concerned only with ritual or dream patterns which are actually in what he is studying, however they got there." Throughout his career, he continued to focus on and define the repeating images that are structural "building blocks" of literature. It was, he later observed, "a vision of literature as forming a total schematic order" (*Spiritus Mundi*, 1976).

This conception of literature as constituting a total order or universe explains why Frye's work has intrigued and inspired theorists interested in intertextuality—the ways in which one text leads to, evokes, is made from, and is intersected by others. The French feminist theorist JULIA KRISTEVA, for example, described reading *Fearful Symmetry* in the late 1960s as a "revelation" in its insertion of the poetic text into Western literary tradition. Through *Anatomy of Criticism*, she adds, we can begin to grasp the "extraordinary polysemy of literary art and take up the challenge it permanently poses."

Frye's work has been widely discussed and admired but also sharply criticized. Often, in reply, Frye embraces the charge made against him. For example, he cheerfully admits his refusal to judge differences between good and bad literary works, even though this position puts him at odds with many of the major critics of the English and American traditions, as well as more recent theorists such as BARBARA HERRNSTEIN SMITH (see "Contingencies of Value," 1988, below). Marxist and leftist critics have stated that Frye strips away the historical and political meanings from texts; in the words of TERRY EAGLETON, Frye's "formalism" is "even more full-blooded than that of New Criticism. The New Critic allowed that literature was in some significant sense cognitive, yielding a sort of knowledge of the world; Frye insists that literature is an 'autonomous verbal structure' quite cut off from any reference beyond itself." But for Frye this is hardly a failing, for he is determined to understand literature in its own terms, "opposed to any construct—Marxist, Freudian, Thomist, or whatever—that is going to annex literature and simply explain literature in its own terminology" ("Freedom and Concern," 1985).

In our selection, "The Archetypes of Literature" (1951), Frye sketches an early version of his approach. He argues that literature teachers must not confuse literature with criticism: we cannot in our classrooms "teach literature"; rather, we teach the criticism of literature. If teachers aim as they should to make criticism a "systematic structure of knowledge," then they will need to shed their mistaken ideas and habitual practices. For Frye, a common mistake is assuming that criticism is the making of value judgments; these, he says, amount to no more than exercises in the history of taste. Other mistakes include the intensive analysis of specific texts (disconnected "close readings" do not lead us toward the goal of a unified and coherent field of scientific study) and a focus on conventional literary history (periods such as Gothic and baroque are cultural rather than truly literary categories).

In defining genuine criticism, Frye shows how it is connected to but different from philosophy, theology, history, and the social sciences, meriting autonomy as a rigorous and comprehensive professional university discipline. He finds the work of cultural anthropologists particularly valuable in his search for a "co-ordinating principle," and from Frazer, Jung, and others he develops his theory of "archetypes," such as the quest of the hero. Knowledge of the archetypes enables us to perceive the shared myths that literary works rely on and explore: through that awareness we can glimpse the underlying *structure* of the structures of all works.

Like Jung, Frye uses terms with a looseness that can make his writing both suggestive and exasperating. Sometimes he refers to the archetype; sometimes he states that the archetype is itself a myth, like the quest. And while his theory, supported by a rich and wide range of reading, allows him to make connections between many texts, he rarely if ever attends to the text's language. One could also point out that Frye's canon, while capacious, is not capacious enough: few women and minorities figure in it. In this respect Frye is no different from most other critics and theorists of his generation, and his theory could be said to have a built-in answer to the charge: the nature of archetypes ensures that they also structure the literature he himself fails to discuss, and thus in a sense he has included it after all.

Frye is an extraordinary synthesizer, whose system building is matched in twentieth-century literary criticism and theory only by the very different system building of I. A. Richards and KENNETH BURKE. At a certain point, however, the categories, patterns, classifications, lists, and charts in Frye's major theoretical works threaten to become formulaic, as perhaps happens at the close of the selection below. Many texts are briefly touched on and connections among them made, but none of them is really brought into sharp focus. Curiously enough, Frye now often seems most rewarding less for his bold vision of literature as a whole than for the essays on specific texts that he did produce. When he writes about Milton's elegy "Lycidas" (in *Fables of Identity*) or *Hamlet* (in *Northrop Frye on Shakespeare*), he demonstrates a subtle, sensitive, compelling feeling for the text in its own right—the text as related to countless other texts but a discrete literary experience nonetheless. Frye's work as a practical critic sometimes departs from the tenets of his theory, and is arguably the better for it.

BIBLIOGRAPHY

Frye's major books include *Fearful Symmetry* (1947), *Anatomy of Criticism* (1957), *T. S. Eliot* (1963), *The Return of Eden: Five Essays on Milton's Epics* (1965), and *A*

Study of English Romanticism (1968). He also wrote a number of books on Shakespeare, including *Fools of Time: Studies in Shakespearean Tragedy* (1967) and *Northrop Frye on Shakespeare* (1986). Among his collections of essays on diverse topics are *Fables of Identity: Studies in Poetic Mythology* (1963), *The Stubborn Structure: Essays on Criticism and Society* (1970), and *Spiritus Mundi: Essays on Literature, Myth, and Society* (1976). See also *Reading the World: Selected Writings, 1935–1976*, edited by Robert D. Denham (1990). In addition, Frye has been a significant force in turning the attention of literary scholars to the narratives and structural patterns of the Bible; his books on this subject include *The Great Code: The Bible and Literature* (1982) and *Words with Power: Being a Second Study of the Bible and Literature* (1990).

The University of Toronto Press has begun publication of *The Collected Works of Northrop Frye*, under the general editorship of Alvin A. Lee. Along with new editions of Frye's books, it will include his diaries, letters, student essays, speeches, fiction, and notebooks and other unpublished material. Three volumes have appeared to date: *The Correspondence of Northrop Frye and Helen Kemp, 1932–1939* (2 vols., 1996) and *Northrop Frye's Student Essays, 1932–1938*, edited by Robert D. Denham (1997). Frye gave many interviews about his life, work, and career; see, for example, the collection *Northrop Frye in Conversation*, edited by David Cayley (1996). Also valuable is John Ayre's *Northrop Frye: A Biography* (1989).

Good brief overviews include Robert D. Denham, *Northrop Frye and Critical Method* (1974); David Cook, *Northrop Frye: A Vision of the New World* (1986); Ian Balfour, *Northrop Frye* (1988); and Joseph Adamson, *Northrop Frye: A Visionary Life* (1993). The most comprehensive studies are A. C. Hamilton, *Northrop Frye: An Anatomy of His Criticism* (1990), and Jonathan Locke Hart, *Northrop Frye: The Theoretical Imagination* (1994).

There are a number of helpful collections: *Northrop Frye in Modern Criticism*, edited by Murray Krieger (1966), which includes essays by Krieger, Angus Fletcher, William K. Wimsatt Jr., and Geoffrey H. Hartman, comments by Frye, and a checklist of his writings; *Centre and Labyrinth: Essays in Honour of Northrop Frye*, edited by Eleanor Cook et al. (1983); *Northrop Frye and Eighteenth-Century Studies*, edited by Howard D. Weinbrot—a special issue of *Eighteenth-Century Studies* 24 (winter 1990–91); *Visionary Poetics: Essays on Northrop Frye's Criticism*, edited by Robert D. Denham and Thomas Willard (1991); *Northrop Frye*, edited by Harold Bloom (1992); and *The Legacy of Northrop Frye*, edited by Alvin A. Lee and Robert D. Denham (1994), which is especially useful in describing Frye's contributions to Canadian culture and his work on Romanticism, modernism, and religion. Another excellent collection is *Rereading Frye*, edited by David Boyd and Imre Salusinsky (1999).

See also Robert D. Denham, *Northrop Frye: An Annotated Bibliography of Primary and Secondary Sources* (1987), and the essays and bibliographies in the *Northrop Frye Newsletter*. The Northrop Frye Centre was established in 1988 at the University of Toronto.

The Archetypes of Literature[1]

Every organized body of knowledge can be learned progressively; and experience shows that there is also something progressive about the learning of literature. Our opening sentence has already got us into a semantic difficulty. Physics is an organized body of knowledge about nature, and a student of it says that he is learning physics, not that he is learning nature. Art, like

1. First published in the *Kenyon Review* series "My Credo."

nature, is the subject of a systematic study, and has to be distinguished from the study itself, which is criticism. It is therefore impossible to "learn literature": one learns about it in a certain way, but what one learns, transitively, is the criticism of literature. Similarly, the difficulty often felt in "teaching literature" arises from the fact that it cannot be done: the criticism of literature is all that can be directly taught. So while no one expects literature itself to behave like a science, there is surely no reason why criticism, as a systematic and organized study, should not be, at least partly, a science. Not a "pure" or "exact" science, perhaps, but these phrases form part of a 19th Century cosmology which is no longer with us. Criticism deals with the arts and may well be something of an art itself, but it does not follow that it must be unsystematic. If it is to be related to the sciences too, it does not follow that it must be deprived of the graces of culture.

Certainly criticism as we find it in learned journals and scholarly monographs has every characteristic of a science. Evidence is examined scientifically; previous authorities are used scientifically; fields are investigated scientifically; texts are edited scientifically. Prosody is scientific in structure; so is phonetics; so is philology. And yet in studying this kind of critical science the student becomes aware of a centrifugal movement carrying him away from literature. He finds that literature is the central division of the "humanities," flanked on one side by history and on the other by philosophy. Criticism so far ranks only as a subdivision of literature; and hence, for the systematic mental organization of the subject, the student has to turn to the conceptual framework of the historian for events, and to that of the philosopher for ideas. Even the more centrally placed critical sciences, such as textual editing, seem to be part of a "background" that recedes into history or some other non-literary field. The thought suggests itself that the ancillary critical disciplines may be related to a central expanding pattern of systematic comprehension which has not yet been established, but which, if it were established, would prevent them from being centrifugal. If such a pattern exists, then criticism would be to art what philosophy is to wisdom and history to action.

Most of the central area of criticism is at present, and doubtless always will be, the area of commentary. But the commentators have little sense, unlike the researchers, of being contained within some sort of scientific discipline: they are chiefly engaged, in the words of the gospel hymn, in brightening the corner where they are. If we attempt to get a more comprehensive idea of what criticism is about, we find ourselves wandering over quaking bogs of generalities, judicious pronouncements of value, reflective comments, perorations to works of research, and other consequences of taking the large view. But this part of the critical field is so full of pseudo-propositions, sonorous nonsense that contains no truth and no falsehood, that it obviously exists only because criticism, like nature, prefers a waste space to an empty one.

The term "pseudo-proposition" may imply some sort of logical positivist[2] attitude on my own part. But I would not confuse the significant proposition with the factual one; nor should I consider it advisable to muddle the study

2. Characteristic of the philosophy that views all knowledge as deriving from empirical experience and logical reasoning; any statement that cannot be proved true or false is nonsense (i.e., a "pseudo-proposition").

of literature with a schizophrenic dichotomy between subjective-emotional and objective-descriptive aspects of meaning, considering that in order to produce any literary meaning at all one has to ignore this dichotomy. I say only that the principles by which one can distinguish a significant from a meaningless statement in criticism are not clearly defined. Our first step, therefore, is to recognize and get rid of meaningless criticism: that is, talking about literature in a way that cannot help to build up a systematic structure of knowledge. Casual value-judgments belong not to criticism but to the history of taste, and reflect, at best, only the social and psychological compulsions which prompted their utterance. All judgments in which the values are not based on literary experience but are sentimental or derived from religious or political prejudice may be regarded as casual. Sentimental judgments are usually based either on non-existent categories or antitheses ("Shakespeare studied life, Milton books") or on a visceral reaction to the writer's personality. The literary chit-chat which makes the reputations of poets boom and crash in an imaginary stock exchange is pseudo-criticism. That wealthy investor Mr. Eliot, after dumping Milton on the market, is now buying him again; Donne has probably reached his peak and will begin to taper off; Tennyson may be in for a slight flutter but the Shelley stocks are still bearish.[3] This sort of thing cannot be part of any systematic study, for a systematic study can only progress: whatever dithers or vacillates or reacts is merely leisure-class conversation.

We next meet a more serious group of critics who say: the foreground of criticism is the impact of literature on the reader. Let us, then, keep the study of literature centripetal, and base the learning process on a structural analysis of the literary work itself. The texture of any great work of art is complex and ambiguous, and in unravelling the complexities we may take in as much history and philosophy as we please, if the subject of our study remains at the center. If it does not, we may find that in our anxiety to write about literature we have forgotten how to read it.

The only weakness in this approach is that it is conceived primarily as the antithesis of centrifugal or "background" criticism, and so lands us in a somewhat unreal dilemma, like the conflict of internal and external relations in philosophy. Antitheses are usually resolved, not by picking one side and refuting the other, or by making eclectic choices between them, but by trying to get past the antithetical way of stating the problem. It is right that the first effort of critical apprehension should take the form of a rhetorical or structural analysis of a work of art. But a purely structural approach has the same limitation in criticism that it has in biology. In itself it is simply a discrete series of analyses based on the mere existence of the literary structure, without developing any explanation of how the structure came to be what it was and what its nearest relatives are. Structural analysis brings rhetoric back to criticism, but we need a new poetics as well, and the attempt to construct a new poetics out of rhetoric alone can hardly avoid a mere complication of rhetorical terms into a sterile jargon. I suggest that what is at present missing from literary criticism is a co-ordinating principle, a central hypothesis which, like the theory of evolution in biology, will see the

3. Frye is referring to the evaluations of poets that the poet and critic T. S. ELIOT (1888–1965) made, and that others—for example, the English critic F. R. Leavis and the American Yvor Winters—subsequently reinforced, modified, or disputed.

phenomena it deals with as parts of a whole. Such a principle, though it would retain the centripetal perspective of structural analysis, would try to give the same perspective to other kinds of criticism too.

The first postulate of this hypothesis is the same as that of any science: the assumption of total coherence. The assumption refers to the science, not to what it deals with. A belief in an order of nature is an inference from the intelligibility of the natural sciences; and if the natural sciences ever completely demonstrated the order of nature they would presumably exhaust their subject. Criticism, as a science, is totally intelligible; literature, as the subject of a science, is, so far as we know, an inexhaustible source of new critical discoveries, and would be even if new works of literature ceased to be written. If so, then the search for a limiting principle in literature in order to discourage the development of criticism is mistaken. The assertion that the critic should not look for more in a poem than the poet may safely be assumed to have been conscious of putting there is a common form of what may be called the fallacy of premature teleology. It corresponds to the assertion that a natural phenomenon is as it is because Providence in its inscrutable wisdom made it so.

Simple as the assumption appears, it takes a long time for a science to discover that it is in fact a totally intelligible body of knowledge. Until it makes this discovery it has not been born as an individual science, but remains an embryo within the body of some other subject. The birth of physics from "natural philosophy" and of sociology from "moral philosophy" will illustrate the process. It is also very approximately true that the modern sciences have developed in the order of their closeness to mathematics. Thus physics and astronomy assumed their modern form in the Renaissance, chemistry in the 18th Century, biology in the 19th, and the social sciences in the 20th. If systematic criticism, then, is developing only in our day, the fact is at least not an anachronism.

We are now looking for classifying principles lying in an area between two points that we have fixed. The first of these is the preliminary effort of criticism, the structural analysis of the work of art. The second is the assumption that there is such a subject as criticism, and that it makes, or could make, complete sense. We may next proceed inductively from structural analysis, associating the data we collect and trying to see larger patterns in them. Or we may proceed deductively, with the consequences that follow from postulating the unity of criticism. It is clear, of course, that neither procedure will work indefinitely without correction from the other. Pure induction will get us lost in haphazard guessing; pure deduction will lead to inflexible and over-simplified pigeon-holing. Let us now attempt a few tentative steps in each direction, beginning with the inductive one.

II

The unity of a work of art, the basis of structural analysis, has not been produced solely by the unconditioned will of the artist, for the artist is only its efficient cause: it has form, and consequently a formal cause. The fact that revision is possible, that the poet makes changes not because he likes them better but because they are better, means that poems, like poets, are born and not made. The poet's task is to deliver the poem in as uninjured a state as possible, and if the poem is alive, it is equally anxious to be rid of him, and screams to be cut loose from his private memories and associations, his desire for self-expression, and all the other navel-strings and feeding tubes of his ego. The critic takes over where the poet leaves off, and criticism can hardly do without a kind of literary psychology connecting the poet with the poem. Part of this may be a psychological study of the poet, though this is useful chiefly in analysing the failures in his expression, the things in him which are still attached to his work. More important is the fact that every poet has his private mythology, his own spectroscopic band or peculiar formation of symbols, of much of which he is quite unconscious. In works with characters of their own, such as dramas and novels, the same psychological analysis may be extended to the interplay of characters, though of course literary psychology would analyse the behavior of such characters only in relation to literary convention.

There is still before us the problem of the formal cause of the poem, a problem deeply involved with the question of genres. We cannot say much about genres, for criticism does not know much about them. A good many critical efforts to grapple with such words as "novel" or "epic" are chiefly interesting as examples of the psychology of rumor. Two conceptions of the genre, however, are obviously fallacious, and as they are opposite extremes, the truth must lie somewhere between them. One is the pseudo-Platonic conception of genres as existing prior to and independently of creation, which confuses them with mere conventions of form like the sonnet. The other is that pseudo-biological conception of them as evolving species which turns up in so many surveys of the "development" of this or that form.

We next inquire for the origin of the genre, and turn first of all to the social conditions and cultural demands which produced it—in other words to the material cause of the work of art. This leads us into literary history, which differs from ordinary history in that its containing categories, "Gothic," "Baroque," "Romantic," and the like are cultural categories, of little use to the ordinary historian. Most literary history does not get as far as these categories, but even so we know more about it than about most kinds of critical scholarship. The historian treats literature and philosophy historically; the philosopher treats history and literature philosophically; and the so-called "history of ideas" approach marks the beginning of an attempt to treat history and philosophy from the point of view of an autonomous criticism.

But still we feel that there is something missing. We say that every poet has his own peculiar formation of images. But when so many poets use so many of the same images, surely there are much bigger critical problems involved than biographical ones. As Mr. Auden's brilliant essay *The Enchafèd Flood*[4] shows, an important symbol like the sea cannot remain within the poetry of Shelley or Keats or Coleridge:[5] it is bound to expand over many poets into an archetypal symbol of literature. And if the genre has a historical origin, why does the genre of drama emerge from medieval religion in a way so strikingly similar to the way it emerged from Greek religion centuries before? This is a problem of structure rather than origin, and suggests that there may be archetypes of genres as well as of images.

It is clear that criticism cannot be systematic unless there is a quality in

4. A set of lectures published by the poet and critic W. H. Auden (1907–1973) in 1950.
5. All English Romantic poets: PERCY BYSSHE SHELLEY (1792–1822), John Keats (1795–1821), and SAMUEL TAYLOR COLERIDGE (1772–1834).

literature which enables it to be so, an order of words corresponding to the order of nature in the natural sciences. An archetype should be not only a unifying category of criticism, but itself a part of a total form, and it leads us at once to the question of what sort of total form criticism can see in literature. Our survey of critical techniques has taken us as far as literary history. Total literary history moves from the primitive to the sophisticated, and here we glimpse the possibility of seeing literature as a complication of a relatively restricted and simple group of formulas that can be studied in primitive culture. If so, then the search for archetypes is a kind of literary anthropology, concerned with the way that literature is informed by preliterary categories such as ritual, myth and folk tale. We next realize that the relation between these categories and literature is by no means purely one of descent, as we find them reappearing in the greatest classics—in fact there seems to be a general tendency on the part of great classics to revert to them. This coincides with a feeling that we have all had: that the study of mediocre works of art, however energetic, obstinately remains a random and peripheral form of critical experience, whereas the profound masterpiece seems to draw us to a point at which we can see an enormous number of converging patterns of significance. Here we begin to wonder if we cannot see literature, not only as complicating itself in time, but as spread out in conceptual space from some unseen center.

This inductive movement towards the archetype is a process of backing up, as it were, from structural analysis, as we back up from a painting if we want to see composition instead of brushwork. In the foreground of the grave-digger scene in *Hamlet*, for instance, is an intricate verbal texture, ranging from the puns of the first clown to the *danse macabre*[6] of the Yorick soliloquy, which we study in the printed text. One step back, and we are in the Wilson Knight and Spurgeon group of critics,[7] listening to the steady rain of images of corruption and decay. Here too, as the sense of the place of this scene in the whole play begins to dawn on us, we are in the network of psychological relationships which were the main interest of Bradley.[8] But after all, we say, we are forgetting the genre: *Hamlet* is a play, and an Elizabethan play. So we take another step back into the Stoll and Shaw[9] group and see the scene conventionally as part of its dramatic context. One step more, and we can begin to glimpse the archetype of the scene, as the hero's *Liebestod*[1] and first unequivocal declaration of his love, his struggle with Laertes and the sealing of his own fate, and the sudden sobering of his mood that marks the transition to the final scene, all take shape around a leap into and return from the grave that has so weirdly yawned open on the stage.

At each stage of understanding this scene we are dependent on a certain kind of scholarly organization. We need first an editor to clean up the text for us, then the rhetorician and philologist, then the literary psychologist. We cannot study the genre without the help of the literary social historian,

6. Dance of death (French). See *Hamlet* (ca. 1600), 5.1.
7. Critics who call attention to Shakespeare's patterns of imagery and symbolism, led by Caroline Spurgeon (1869–1941) and G. Wilson Knight (1897–1985).
8. A. C. Bradley (1851–1935); his *Shakespearean Tragedy* (1904) provided a detailed study of "character."
9. The playwright and critic George Bernard Shaw (1856–1950). E. E. Stoll (1874–1959), critic who focused in his scholarship on the relationship of Shakespeare's plays to the dramatic conventions of the Elizabethan and Jacobean age.
1. Literally, "death of love" (German); the *Liebestod* is specifically an operatic aria or duet on the suicide of lovers and, more generally, the thematic linking of love and death.

the literary philosopher and the student of the "history of ideas," and for the archetype we need a literary anthropologist. But now that we have got our central pattern of criticism established, all these interests are seen as converging on literary criticism instead of receding from it into psychology and history and the rest. In particular, the literary anthropologist who chases the source of the Hamlet legend from the pre-Shakespeare play to Saxo,[2] and from Saxo to nature-myths, is not running away from Shakespeare: he is drawing closer to the archetypal form which Shakespeare recreated. A minor result of our new perspective is that contradictions among critics, and assertions that this and not that critical approach is the right one, show a remarkable tendency to dissolve into unreality. Let us now see what we can get from the deductive end.

III

Some arts move in time, like music; others are presented in space, like painting. In both cases the organizing principle is recurrence, which is called rhythm when it is temporal and pattern when it is spatial. Thus we speak of the rhythm of music and the pattern of painting; but later, to show off our sophistication, we may begin to speak of the rhythm of painting and the pattern of music. In other words, all arts may be conceived both temporally and spatially. The score of a musical composition may be studied all at once; a picture may be seen as the track of an intricate dance of the eye. Literature seems to be intermediate between music and painting: its words form rhythms which approach a musical sequence of sounds at one of its boundaries, and form patterns which approach the hieroglyphic or pictorial image at the other. The attempts to get as near to these boundaries as possible form the main body of what is called experimental writing. We may call the rhythm of literature the narrative, and the pattern, the simultaneous mental grasp of the verbal structure, the meaning or significance. We hear or listen to a narrative, but when we grasp a writer's total pattern we "see" what he means.

The criticism of literature is much more hampered by the representational fallacy than even the criticism of painting. That is why we are apt to think of narrative as a sequential representation of events in an outside "life," and of meaning as a reflection of some external "idea." Properly used as critical terms, an author's narrative is his linear movement; his meaning is the integrity of his completed form. Similarly an image is not merely a verbal replica of an external object, but any unit of a verbal structure seen as part of a total pattern or rhythm. Even the letters an author spells his words with form part of his imagery, though only in special cases (such as alliteration) would they call for critical notice. Narrative and meaning thus become respectively, to borrow musical terms, the melodic and harmonic contexts of the imagery.

Rhythm, or recurrent movement, is deeply founded on the natural cycle, and everything in nature that we think of as having some analogy with works of art, like the flower or the bird's song, grows out of a profound synchronization between an organism and the rhythms of its environment, especially that of the solar year. With animals some expressions of synchronization, like the mating dances of birds, could almost be called rituals. But in human

2. Saxo Grammaticus (13th c.), Danish historian whose *Gesta Danorum* includes the Hamlet story.

life a ritual seems to be something of a voluntary effort (hence the magical element in it) to recapture a lost rapport with the natural cycle. A farmer must harvest his crop at a certain time of year, but because this is involuntary, harvesting itself is not precisely a ritual. It is the deliberate expression of a will to synchronize human and natural energies at that time which produces the harvest songs, harvest sacrifices and harvest folk customs that we call rituals. In ritual, then, we may find the origin of narrative, a ritual being a temporal sequence of acts in which the conscious meaning or significance is latent: it can be seen by an observer, but is largely concealed from the participators themselves. The pull of ritual is toward pure narrative, which, if there could be such a thing, would be automatic and unconscious repetition. We should notice too the regular tendency of ritual to become encyclopedic. All the important recurrences in nature, the day, the phases of the moon, the seasons and solstices of the year, the crises of existence from birth to death, get rituals attached to them, and most of the higher religions are equipped with a definitive total body of rituals suggestive, if we may put it so, of the entire range of potentially significant actions in human life.

Patterns of imagery, on the other hand, or fragments of significance, are oracular in origin, and derive from the epiphanic moment, the flash of instantaneous comprehension with no direct reference to time, the importance of which is indicated by Cassirer in *Myth and Language*.[3] By the time we get them, in the form of proverbs, riddles, commandments and etiological folk tales, there is already a considerable element of narrative in them. They too are encyclopedic in tendency, building up a total structure of significance, or doctrine, from random and empiric fragments. And just as pure narrative would be unconscious act, so pure significance would be an incommunicable state of consciousness, for communication begins by constructing narrative.

The myth is the central informing power that gives archetypal significance to the ritual and archetypal narrative to the oracle. Hence the myth *is* the archetype, though it might be convenient to say myth only when referring to narrative, and archetype when speaking of significance. In the solar cycle of the day, the seasonal cycle of the year, and the organic cycle of human life, there is a single pattern of significance, out of which myth constructs a central narrative around a figure who is partly the sun, partly vegetative fertility and partly a god or archetypal human being. The crucial importance of this myth has been forced on literary critics by Jung and Frazer[4] in particular, but the several books now available on it are not always systematic in their approach, for which reason I supply the following table of its phases:

1.

The dawn, spring and birth phase. Myths of the birth of the hero, of revival and resurrection, of creation and (because the four phases are a cycle) of the defeat of the powers of darkness, winter and death. Subordinate characters: the father and the mother. The archetype of romance and of most dithyrambic and rhapsodic poetry.

3. Properly, *Language and Myth* (1925), by the German philosopher and historian of ideas Ernst Cassirer (1874–1945).

4. Sir James George Frazer (1854–1941), Scottish anthropologist and folklorist, whose *Golden Bough* (12 vols., 1890–1915) is largely concerned with the fertility figure. CARL GUSTAV JUNG (1875–1961), Swiss psychiatrist and theorist of archetypes.

2.

The zenith, summer, and marriage or triumph phase. Myths of apotheosis, of the sacred marriage, and of entering into Paradise. Subordinate characters: the companion and the bride. The archetype of comedy, pastoral and idyll.

3.

The sunset, autumn and death phase. Myths of fall, of the dying god, of violent death and sacrifice and of the isolation of the hero. Subordinate characters: the traitor and that siren. The archetype of tragedy and elegy.

4.

The darkness, winter and dissolution phase. Myths of the triumph of these powers; myths of floods and the return of chaos, of the defeat of the hero, and Götterdämmerung[5] myths. Subordinate characters: the ogre and the witch. The archetype of satire (see, for instance, the conclusion of *The Dunciad*).[6]

The quest of the hero also tends to assimilate the oracular and random verbal structures, as we can see when we watch the chaos of local legends that results from prophetic epiphanies consolidating into a narrative mythology of departmental gods. In most of the higher religions this in turn has become the same central quest-myth that emerges from ritual, as the Messiah myth became the narrative structure of the oracles of Judaism. A local flood may beget a folk tale by accident, but a comparison of flood stories will show how quickly such tales become examples of the myth of dissolution. Finally, the tendency of both ritual and epiphany to become encyclopedic is realized in the definitive body of myth which constitutes the sacred scriptures of religions. These sacred scriptures are consequently the first documents that the literary critic has to study to gain a comprehensive view of his subject. After he has understood their structure, then he can descend from archetypes to genres, and see how the drama emerges from the ritual side of myth and lyric from the epiphanic or fragmented side, while the epic carries on the central encyclopedic structure.

Some words of caution and encouragement are necessary before literary criticism has clearly staked out its boundaries in these fields. It is part of the critic's business to show how all literary genres are derived from the quest-myth, but the derivation is a logical one within the science of criticism: the quest-myth will constitute the first chapter of whatever future handbooks of criticism may be written that will be based on enough organized critical knowledge to call themselves "introductions" or "outlines" and still be able to live up to their titles. It is only when we try to expound the derivation chronologically that we find ourselves writing pseudo-prehistorical fictions and theories of mythological contract. Again, because psychology and

5. Literally, "the twilight of the gods" (German), and the title of an opera (1876) by the German composer Richard Wagner. More generally, the term refers to catastrophic collapse into violence and disorder.

6. Mock-heroic satire (1728–43) by ALEXANDER POPE.

anthropology are more highly developed sciences, the critic who deals with this kind of material is bound to appear, for some time, a dilettante of those subjects. These two phases of criticism are largely undeveloped in comparison with literary history and rhetoric, the reason being the later development of the sciences they are related to. But the fascination which *The Golden Bough* and Jung's book on libido symbols[7] have for literary critics is not based on dilettantism, but on the fact that these books are primarily studies in literary criticism, and very important ones.

In any case the critic who is studying the principles of literary form has a quite different interest from the psychologist's concern with states of mind or the anthropologist's with social institutions. For instance: the mental response to narrative is mainly passive; to significance mainly active. From this fact Ruth Benedict's[8] *Patterns of Culture* develops a distinction between "Apollonian" cultures based on obedience to ritual and "Dionysiac" ones based on a tense exposure of the prophetic mind to epiphany. The critic would tend rather to note how popular literature which appeals to the inertia of the untrained mind puts a heavy emphasis on narrative values, whereas a sophisticated attempt to disrupt the connection between the poet and his environment produces the Rimbaud type of *illumination*, Joyce's solitary epiphanies, and Baudelaire's[9] conception of nature as a source of oracles. Also how literature, as it develops from the primitive to the self-conscious, shows a gradual shift of the poet's attention from narrative to significant values, this shift of attention being the basis of Schiller's distinction between naive and sentimental poetry.[1]

The relation of criticism to religion, when they deal with the same documents, is more complicated. In criticism, as in history, the divine is always treated as a human artifact. God for the critic, whether he finds him in *Paradise Lost*[2] or the Bible, is a character in a human story; and for the critic all epiphanies are explained, not in terms of the riddle of a possessing god or devil, but as mental phenomena closely associated in their origin with dreams. This once established, it is then necessary to say that nothing in criticism or art compels the critic to take the attitude of ordinary waking consciousness towards the dream or the god. Art deals not with the real but with the conceivable; and criticism, though it will eventually have to have some theory of conceivability, can never be justified in trying to develop, much less assume, any theory of actuality. It is necessary to understand this before our next and final point can be made.

We have identified the central myth of literature, in its narrative aspect, with the quest-myth. Now if we wish to see this central myth as a pattern of meaning also, we have to start with the workings of the subconscious where the epiphany originates, in other words in the dream. The human cycle of waking and dreaming corresponds closely to the natural cycle of light and darkness, and it is perhaps in this correspondence that all imaginative life begins. The correspondence is largely an antithesis: it is in daylight that man

7. *Transformations and Symbols of the Libido* (1912; trans. first as *Psychology of the Unconscious* and then as *Symbols of Transformation*).

8. American anthropologist (1887–1948); *Patterns of Culture* was published in 1934.

9. CHARLES BAUDELAIRE (1821–1867), French symbolist poet. Arthur Rimbaud (1854–1891), French symbolist poet. James Joyce (1882–1941), Irish novelist who extended the term "epiphany" to refer to peak moments recorded in literature.

1. See *On Naive and Sentimental Poetry* (1795–96) by FRIEDRICH VON SCHILLER (1759–1805), German dramatist, poet, and historian.

2. Epic poem (1667) by John Milton.

is really in the power of darkness, a prey to frustration and weakness; it is in the darkness of nature that the "libido" or conquering heroic self awakes. Hence art, which Plato called a dream for awakened minds,[3] seems to have as its final cause the resolution of the antithesis, the mingling of the sun and the hero, the realizing of a world in which the inner desire and the outward circumstance coincide. This is the same goal, of course, that the attempt to combine human and natural power in ritual has. The social function of the arts, therefore, seems to be closely connected with visualizing the goal of work in human life. So in terms of significance, the central myth of art must be the vision of the end of social effort, the innocent world of fulfilled desires, the free human society. Once this is understood, the integral place of criticism among the other social sciences, in interpreting and systematizing the vision of the artist, will be easier to see. It is at this point that we can see how religious conceptions of the final cause of human effort are as relevant as any others to criticism.

The importance of the god or hero in the myth lies in the fact that such characters, who are conceived in human likeness and yet have more power over nature, gradually build up the vision of an omnipotent personal community beyond an indifferent nature. It is this community which the hero regularly enters in his apotheosis. The world of this apotheosis thus begins to pull away from the rotary cycle of the quest in which all triumph is temporary. Hence if we look at the quest-myth as a pattern of imagery, we see the hero's quest first of all in terms of its fulfillment. This gives us our central pattern of archetypal images, the vision of innocence which sees the world in terms of total human intelligibility. It corresponds to, and is usually found in the form of, the vision of the unfallen world or heaven in religion. We may call it the comic vision of life, in contrast to the tragic vision, which sees the quest only in the form of its ordained cycle.

We conclude with a second table of contents, in which we shall attempt to set forth the central pattern of the comic and tragic visions. One essential principle of archetypal criticism is that the individual and the universal forms of an image are identical, the reasons being too complicated for us just now. We proceed according to the general plan of the game of Twenty Questions, or, if we prefer, of the Great Chain of Being:[4]

1.

In the comic vision the *human* world is a community, or a hero who represents the wish-fulfillment of the reader. The archetype of images of symposium, communion, order, friendship and love. In the tragic vision the human world is a tyranny or anarchy, or an individual or isolated man, the leader with his back to his followers, the bullying giant of romance, the deserted or betrayed hero. Marriage or some equivalent consummation belongs to the comic vision; the harlot, witch and other varieties of Jung's "terrible mother" belong to the tragic one. All divine, heroic, angelic or other superhuman communities follow the human pattern.

3. See *Sophist* 266c, by the Greek philosopher PLATO (ca. 427–ca. 347 B.C.E.).
4. The notion of the universe as a hierarchical order consisting of an enormous (or even infinite) number of links; Frye probably has in mind Arthur O. Lovejoy's *Great Chain of Being* (1936).

2.

In the comic vision the *animal* world is a community of domesticated animals, usually a flock of sheep, or a lamb, or one of the gentler birds, usually a dove. The archetype of pastoral images. In the tragic vision the animal world is seen in terms of beasts and birds of prey, wolves, vultures, serpents, dragons and the like.

3.

In the comic vision the *vegetable* world is a garden, grove or park, or a tree of life, or a rose or lotus. The archetype of Arcadian images, such as that of Marvell's green world or of Shakespeare's forest comedies.[5] In the tragic vision it is a sinister forest like the one in *Comus* or at the opening of the *Inferno*,[6] or a heath or wilderness, or a tree of death.

4.

In the comic vision the *mineral* world is a city, or one building or temple, or one stone, normally a glowing precious stone—in fact the whole comic series, especially the tree, can be conceived as luminous or fiery. The archetype of geometrical images: the "starlit dome"[7] belongs here. In the tragic vision the mineral world is seen in terms of deserts, rocks and ruins, or of sinister geometrical images like the cross.

5.

In the comic vision the *unformed* world is a river, traditionally fourfold, which influenced the Renaissance image of the temperate body with its four humors.[8] In the tragic vision this world usually becomes the sea, as the narrative myth of dissolution is so often a flood myth. The combination of the sea and beast images gives us the leviathan and similar water-monsters.

Obvious as this table looks, a great variety of poetic images and forms will be found to fit it. Yeats's "Sailing to Byzantium,"[9] to take a famous example of the comic vision at random, has the city, the tree, the bird, the community of sages, the geometrical gyre and the detachment from the cyclic world. It is, of course, only the general comic or tragic context that determines the interpretation of any symbol: this is obvious with relatively neutral archetypes like the island, which may be Prospero's island or Circe's.[1]

Our tables are, of course, not only elementary but grossly over-simplified, just as our inductive approach to the archetype was a mere hunch. The important point is not the deficiencies of either procedure, taken by itself,

5. Shakespeare's forest (that is, pastoral) comedies include *As You Like It* (ca. 1599). For the "green world" of Andrew Marvell (1621–1678), English metaphysical poet, see especially "The Garden" (1681).

6. The first book of DANTE ALIGHIERI'S *Divine Comedy* (1321). *Comus* (1634), a religious masque by Milton.

7. See, for example, Coleridge's poem "Kubla Khan" (written 1797; pub. 1816), which refers to Kubla Khan's "stately pleasure-dome."

8. The four fluids of the body—blood, phlegm, choler, and black bile—whose relative proportions were thought to determine a person's disposition and general health.

9. Poem (1927) by the Irish poet William Butler Yeats (1865–1939).

1. In Greek mythology, a sorceress who lived on the island of Acaea (where Odysseus and his men land in Homer's *Odyssey*). Prospero's island: the setting of Shakespeare's play *The Tempest* (1611).

but the fact that, somewhere and somehow, the two are clearly going to meet in the middle. And if they do meet, the ground plan of a systematic and comprehensive development of criticism has been established.

1951

ROLAND BARTHES
1915–1980

Generally considered one of the leading figures in French structuralism, Roland Barthes is, as Jonathan Culler puts it, "famous for contradictory reasons." On the one hand, there is the scientific Barthes: the one who sought a universal grammar of narrative in his influential essay "Introduction to the Structural Study of Narrative" (1966), or who explored FERDINAND DE SAUSSURE's notion of semiology—a broad science of signs in human culture, of which linguistics would provide a model—in such works as *Elements of Semiology* (1965) and *The Fashion System* (1967). But on the other hand, there is the hedonist and connoisseur: the Barthes who wrote playfully and allusively about pleasure in *The Pleasure of the Text* (1973) and in *A Lover's Discourse* (1977). Even his literary tastes seemed contradictory: he promoted avant-garde writers (Robbe-Grillet, Brecht, Sollers), but he also loved and wrote about the most traditional of French authors (La Bruyère, Racine, Chateaubriand, Balzac, Proust). And he who questioned the importance of the author was himself preeminently an author—indeed, the only author to have written his own volume in a series of "perennial masters" (*Roland Barthes by Roland Barthes*, 1975). A quintessential "man of letters" in the traditional sense, he was also a man of letters in an idiosyncratic, literal sense, organizing three of his books alphabetically so as to avoid thematic or logical organization, and highlighting the material form of letters in one of his book titles, *S/Z* (1970). He was less a path breaker than a habit breaker, resolutely committed to unlearning the routines of intelligibility, even those he himself had helped promote.

Roland Barthes was born in Cherbourg. His father, a naval officer, was killed a year later, and Barthes's mother moved to the paternal family home in Bayonne in southern France. The theorist of the death of the author thus grew up without a father, living with or near his mother until her death in 1977, three years before his own. In 1924 mother and son moved to Paris, where Barthes progressed to the *baccalauréat* in the Parisian schools and began studying for entrance into the prestigious École Normale, until his promising academic trajectory was interrupted by the first of several attacks of tuberculosis. Meanwhile, his mother's already strained relations with her Parisian family worsened in 1927 when she gave birth to an illegitimate child—Roland's half-brother, Michel Salzado. Although Barthes's grandparents were well-off, they refused Henriette Binger Barthes and her two sons any financial support, with the result that Henriette had to scrape by on what she earned as a bookbinder.

From 1934 to 1950 Barthes's life alternated between tuberculosis sanitoria (he was exempted from military duty and spent the years of the Occupation in a sanatorium in the Isère), academic institutions where he studied, and, when his health permitted, teaching jobs in Biarritz and abroad in Bucharest and Alexandria. Despite—or perhaps because of—his forced convalescences, he read avidly, founded a theatrical troupe, and began to write. From the first Barthes's writings reflect both his idiosyncratic creativity and his attunement to the intellectual milieu in which he found himself. His first book, *Writing Degree Zero* (1953), initially published as articles in Albert Camus's journal, *Combat*, analyzes the history of literary styles in terms derived from Marx and from Sartre. In this book Barthes looks at the relations between Literature with a capital *L* and the various modern forms of its demystification, from STÉPHANE MALLARMÉ's "vibratory near-disappearance" to Camus's "blank" style (the "zero degree" of the title).

A second, quite different, project Barthes undertook at the same time was an extensive study of the imagery used by the nineteenth-century historian Jules Michelet. Scribbling passages on index cards, Barthes organized Michelet's "imagination" in ways that did not correspond to the explicit intentions of his writing. Like the work of the phenomenological critics Jean-Pierre Richard and GEORGES POULET, Barthes's analysis was a way of structuring Michelet's writing around its unconscious "obsessions." This research was published as a book titled *Michelet* (1954) in the same writers' series in which Barthes himself later appeared.

Barthes's third project in the mid-1950s, different yet again, was a series of short occasional pieces later published as *Mythologies* (1957). In this work, of which we give three examples, Barthes does a kind of Marxian semiology of mass culture and everyday life. His object is to show how mass culture is saturated with ideological propositions ("myths") presented as if they were natural and self-evident; the result in many ways anticipates what is today called "cultural studies." Barthes combines a sharp eye for the social life of signs with a subtle critique of the naturalizations of the ethnocentric, patriarchal, petit-bourgeois French worldview. Critical of the covert functions of *what-goes-without-saying*, Barthes nevertheless enjoys the exhibitions, advertisements, photographs, articles, films, wrestling matches, and commodities that provide the occasion for his little feats of writing. In the essay on soap powders, for example, he both ends up revealing that the competing products are owned by the same company and—in his descriptions of these products in terms of foam and fire, the depth of linen and the triumph of cleanliness—enjoys the process of "frothing" rhetorically himself. In fact, in a perfect illustration of how capitalism devours its critics, an executive at France's largest advertising firm found Barthes's work on advertising so compelling that he began studying with Barthes and persuaded him to work briefly as a consultant for the automaker Renault. Barthes was critical of the myth-making operations of petit-bourgeois culture, but he was also intrigued by the meaning-making functions of cultural objects themselves.

As a researcher in Paris for ten years at the CNRS (National Center for Scientific Research), Barthes—like many others in Paris at that time, including CLAUDE LÉVI-STRAUSS in anthropology, JACQUES LACAN in psychoanalysis, and TZVETAN TODOROV and Gérard Genette in literary studies—continued his exploration of the possibilities of extending Saussure's synchronic linguistic analysis to larger cultural structures. In 1962 Barthes was appointed to a tenured post in "the sociology of signs, symbols, and representations" at the École des Hautes Études (School for Advanced Study), where his seminar became legendary. His book *On Racine* (1963) raised hackles in the traditional academic community for its concentration on the structures of Racine's *textual* world rather than his biographical or historical world. Raymond Picard, a Racine scholar at the Sorbonne, countered with *New Criticism or New Fraud?* (1965). Barthes responded to Picard by arguing that traditional critics' recourse to the values of clarity, nobility, and humanity, which they treat as neutral and self-evident, actually exerts a coercive, censoring force on other interpretive possibilities.

The Picard affair is the backdrop for one of Barthes's most notorious essays, "The Death of the Author." Written at the height of the antiestablishment uprisings of May 1968, it assails academic criticism's typical focus on "the man and his work" (which is in many ways the organizing principle of the present anthology). Indeed, Barthes was surprised to find himself caught in 1968 between generations: while he was attacking the generation of Picard, the students—brandishing the antistructuralist slogan "Structures don't take to the streets!"—were rebelling against the generation of Barthes himself.

"The Death of the Author" begins with an example taken from Balzac's novella *Sarrasine*—the tale of a sculptor who falls in love with an Italian diva subsequently revealed to be not a woman but a castrato (*Sarrasine* was the text analyzed that year in his seminar, and Barthes went on to publish a full-length study of it in his book *S/Z*). Barthes focuses on a sentence in the text in which a series of exclamations about femininity cannot be clearly attributed to the conscious intentions of any one person, whether that be the author, the narrator, a character, or even "universal wisdom." Barthes argues that the effective, productive, and engaged reading of a text depends on the suspension of preconceived ideas about the character of the particular author—or even about human psychology in general. The text itself is feigning a set of assumptions it will subsequently reveal to be misguided. From the moment that writing detaches itself from an immediate context, "It is language which speaks, not the author." The author, the text, and the reader are each composed of a universe of quotations without origin or end. In its celebration of the birth of the reader, "The Death of the Author" explores the consequences of freeing the reading process from the constraints of fidelity to an origin, a unified meaning, an identity, or any other pregiven exterior or interior reality.

The publication of *S/Z* marks a turning point in Barthes's relation to structuralism. It is a multilevel analysis that refuses to structure the text otherwise than by cutting it into hundreds of little pieces of varying lengths (called *lexias*) and also by identifying five broad functions (called *codes*) at work in the text. Written as if it were meant to constitute a methodological examplar, it exaggerates the performance of methodology to such an extent that it becomes inimitable and perhaps parodic. When commentators look for a break between structuralism and poststructuralism, *S/Z* stands as a revealing hinge. In it Barthes pursues not so much a *critique* of structuralism (as does JACQUES DERRIDA, for example) as an *explosion* of it. The hints of larger structures at work are fragmentary and multiple, not sustained, and the theoretical comments are printed as digressions, numbering almost a hundred. Boredom with the structuralist project of reducing all narratives to a common grammar combines with delight in the foretaste of a multitude of grammars and rhetorics hinted at but not developed in *S/Z*.

Barthes's subsequent essay reprinted here, "From Work to Text" (1971), is one of the clearest available summaries (including the obligatory disavowal of such a summary) of the poststructuralist theory of the "text" as it was developed not only by Barthes but by all the writers associated with the vanguard journal *Tel Quel*, including Philippe Sollers, JULIA KRISTEVA, Derrida, and others. This description of "textuality" can be seen as one way of marking the transition between structuralism and poststructuralism. Whereas culture and language for Lévi-Strauss and Saussure were structured like a game (chess is the favorite example), the text is structured like *play*—children's play, musical performance, or the excess motion in a machine. But both structuralists and poststructuralists would contrast their analyses to the classical study of literary and other cultural objects ("work"). The *text* is a process; the *work* is a product. *Works* can be found on library shelves; *texts* are signifying fields into which one enters. (The development of the Internet has perhaps made this distinction seem less radical than it did in the 1970s.) Their point is not that literature can be divided into works and texts but that the reader can activate either the closure of the signified (the coherence of a meaning) or the "play" of the signifier (the dissemination and disruption of meanings). The text deserves no vital "respect"—it is not alive and can thus be "broken" or "manhandled" in ways that would violate organic forms. The death of the author turns out to be based not on a murder but on an elimination of the metaphor of life in the first place. The work is "consumed"; the text is "produced" (in *S/Z*, Barthes called these the *readerly* and the *writerly* aspects of a text). Barthes ends the essay by opening onto pleasure, a topic that would engage him more and more from then on.

In later writings (*The Empire of Signs*, 1970; *The Pleasure of the Text*, 1973; *Roland Barthes by Roland Barthes, 1975; Camera Lucida*, 1980; and the posthumously published *Incidents*, 1987), Roland Barthes seems to resurrect precisely the author he had killed off. But the contradiction is more apparent than real. While the disembodied, abstract author of the network of signs does indeed become an embodied and particular author the body and biography are both seen as historical, and both are structured like a text. The author is still not an extratextual *identity* determining meaning. The body can be read like a text, just as the text can be read like a body. Gaps in meaning, like the gaps in a garment, are equivalent sites of pleasure. *Roland Barthes by Roland Barthes* does not create a person retrospectively but gives an alphabetically arranged mosaic of the preoccupations of someone who is just like a character in a novel. Indeed, in an interview Barthes called autobiography a "novel that dares not speak its name." He thus subtly alludes to Wildean homosexuality ("The Love That Dares Not Speak Its Name") in a context in which Barthes's own homosexuality is being, by that very expression, *detached* from any real person. This sophisticated relation to homosexuality (neither hidden nor claimed) is readable throughout Barthes's work.

In 1976 this critic of academic criticism was elected to the Chair in Literary Semiology at France's most prestigious institution, the Collège de France. In his inaugural lecture, published as *Leçon* (1978), he explains why he is an unlikely choice for such a post and then goes on to recapitulate many of his thoughts about semiology and literature. Barthes thus ended up as one of the most established of antiestablishment academics.

Barthes's last book published during his lifetime, *Camera Lucida*, is both a meditation on photography and an act of mourning for his mother. Whereas in *Mythologies* he had revealed the contrived nature of the "reality" inherent in the campaign photograph, in *Camera Lucida*, on the contrary, he finds something in a photograph, particularly a snapshot, that is real. Neither a rhetorical sleight-of-hand nor an arbitrary contrivance, the photograph has a way of telling us "This has been." Although Barthes was only sixty-four years old at the time of its publication, the book reads in many ways like a voice from beyond the grave. That same year Roland Barthes was hit by a laundry truck in the street; his injuries proved fatal.

Writing on the cusp of structuralism and poststructuralism, Barthes was a master of the provocative essay, weaving together science and pleasure, critique and eloquence, and never simply choosing between them. For him, specialized vocabularies were delicious in themselves, and ordinary language already multidimensional.

BIBLIOGRAPHY

In addition to the thirteen book titles cited above, there are several volumes of Barthes's essays available in English. Barthes published four collections of essays in French, which have all been translated by Richard Howard (*Critical Essays*, 1972; *New Critical Essays*, 1980; *The Responsibility of Forms*, 1986; and *The Rustle of Language*, 1986). *A Barthes Reader*, edited by Susan Sontag (1982), has a good selection but does not include some of the best-known essays. The collection edited by Stephen Heath, *Image, Music, Text* (1977), is perhaps the best short selection available. A collection of interviews, *The Grain of the Voice: Interviews, 1962–1980*, was translated by Linda Coverdale (1985), and an additional informative interview published in *Tel Quel* has been translated in *The "Tel Quel" Reader* (ed. Patrick ffrench and Roland-François Lack, 1998).

There are numerous studies of Barthes's life and work. The biography by Louis-Jean Calvet, *Roland Barthes: A Biography* (trans. Sarah Wykes, 1995), is excellent. Of the general introductions to Barthes's work as a whole, the essay on Barthes by John Sturrock in *Structuralism and Since* (ed. John Sturrock, 1979) and the short *Roland Barthes* by Jonathan Culler (1983) are brief and meaty. Longer studies include books—all called *Roland Barthes*—by Philip Thody (1977, rev. 1983; an early conservative reading), Annette Lavers (1982; an early admirer and expositor), and Steven Ungar (1983; focusing on Barthes as "professor of desire"). More recent studies—still called *Roland Barthes*—include those by Michael Moriarty (1991; closely argued and extensive) and Rick Rylance (1994; readable and useful, organized in terms of Barthes's "hot" and "cold" writing). Among the numerous critical studies, *The Barthes Effect: The Essay as Reflective Text* by Réda Bensmaïa (1986; trans. 1987) deserves mention as an interesting study of the essay in Barthes and Montaigne. And, published together with Barthes's posthumous *Incidents* (1992), there is D. A. Miller's *Bringing Out Roland Barthes*, an analysis of the movement of gay desire through Barthes's texts. The annotated bibliography published by Sandford Freedman and Carole Anne Taylor, *Roland Barthes: A Bibliographical Reader's Guide* (1983), is useful but dated.

From Mythologies[1]

Soap-powders and Detergents

The first World Detergent Congress (Paris, September 1954) had the effect of authorizing the world to yield to *Omo* euphoria: not only do detergents have no harmful effect on the skin, but they can even perhaps save miners from silicosis. These products have been in the last few years the object of such massive advertising that they now belong to a region of French daily life which the various types of psycho-analysis would do well to pay some attention to if they wish to keep up to date. One could then usefully contrast the psycho-analysis of purifying fluids (chlorinated, for example) with that of soap-powders (*Lux, Persil*) or that of detergents (*Omo*). The relations between the evil and the cure, between dirt and a given product, are very different in each case.

Chlorinated fluids, for instance, have always been experienced as a sort of liquid fire, the action of which must be carefully estimated, otherwise the object itself would be affected, 'burnt'. The implicit legend of this type of product rests on the idea of a violent, abrasive modification of matter: the connotations are of a chemical or mutilating type: the product 'kills' the dirt. Powders, on the contrary, are separating agents: their ideal role is to liberate the object from its circumstantial imperfection: dirt is 'forced out' and no longer killed; in the *Omo* imagery, dirt is a diminutive enemy, stunted and black, which takes to its heels from the fine immaculate linen at the sole threat of the judgment of *Omo*. Products based on chlorine and ammonia are without doubt the representatives of a kind of absolute fire, a saviour but a blind one. Powders, on the contrary, are selective, they push, they drive dirt through the texture of the object, their function is keeping public order not making war. This distinction has ethnographic correlatives: the chemical fluid is an extension of the washerwoman's movements when she beats the clothes, while powders rather replace those of the housewife pressing and rolling the washing against a sloping board.

But even in the category of powders, one must in addition oppose against advertisements based on psychology those based on psycho-analysis (I use

1. Translated by Annette Lavers.

this word without reference to any specific school). *'Persil Whiteness'* for instance, bases its prestige on the evidence of a result; it calls into play vanity, a social concern with appearances, by offering for comparison two objects, one of which is *whiter than* the other. Advertisements for *Omo* also indicate the effect of the product (and in superlative fashion, incidentally), but they chiefly reveal its mode of action; in doing so, they involve the consumer in a kind of direct experience of the substance, make him the accomplice of a liberation rather than the mere beneficiary of a result; matter here is endowed with value-bearing states.

Omo uses two of these, which are rather novel in the category of detergents: the deep and the foamy. To say that *Omo* cleans in depth (see the Cinéma-Publicité advertisement)[2] is to assume that linen is deep, which no one had previously thought, and this unquestionably results in exalting it, by establishing it as an object favourable to those obscure tendencies to enfold and caress which are found in every human body. As for foam, it is well known that it signifies luxury. To begin with, it appears to lack any usefulness; then, its abundant, easy, almost infinite proliferation allows one to suppose there is in the substance from which it issues a vigorous germ, a healthy and powerful essence, a great wealth of active elements in a small original volume. Finally, it gratifies in the consumer a tendency to imagine matter as something airy, with which contact is effected in a mode both light and vertical, which is sought after like that of happiness either in the gustatory category (foie gras, entremets, wines), in that of clothing (muslin, tulle), or that of soaps (film-star in her bath). Foam can even be the sign of a certain spirituality, inasmuch as the spirit has the reputation of being able to make something out of nothing, a large surface of effects out of a small volume of causes (creams have a very different 'psycho-analytical' meaning, of a soothing kind: they suppress wrinkles, pain, smarting, etc.). What matters is the art of having disguised the abrasive function of the detergent under the delicious image of a substance at once deep and airy which can govern the molecular order of the material without damaging it. A euphoria, incidentally, which must not make us forget that there is one plane on which *Persil* and *Omo* are one and the same: the plane of the Anglo-Dutch trust *Unilever*.[3]

The Brain of Einstein[4]

Einstein's brain is a mythical object: paradoxically, the greatest intelligence of all provides an image of the most up-to-date machine, the man who is too powerful is removed from psychology, and introduced into a world of robots; as is well known, the supermen of science-fiction always have something reified about them. So has Einstein: he is commonly signified by his brain, which is like an object for anthologies, a true museum exhibit. Perhaps because of his mathematical specialization, superman is here divested of every magical character; no diffuse power in him, no mystery other than

2. French movie houses began their shows with a series of advertisements, which, like commercials on network television in the United States, helped provide revenue.
3. In other words, the two competing products are manufactured by the same company, Unilever.
4. Albert Einstein (1879–1955), celebrated physicist whose theory of relativity revolutionized theoretical physics and spurred interest in the exploitation of atomic energy.

mechanical: he is a superior, a prodigious organ, but a real, even a physiological one. Mythologically, Einstein is matter, his power does not spontaneously draw one towards the spiritual, it needs the help of an independent morality, a reminder about the scientist's 'conscience' (*Science without conscience,*[5] they said . . .).

Einstein himself has to some extent been a party to the legend by bequeathing his brain, for the possession of which two hospitals are still fighting as if it were an unusual piece of machinery which it will at last be possible to dismantle. A photograph shows him lying down, his head bristling with electric wires: the waves of his brain are being recorded, while he is requested to 'think of relativity'. (But for that matter, what does 'to think of' mean, exactly?) What this is meant to convey is probably that the seismograms will be all the more violent since 'relativity' is an arduous subject. Thought itself is thus represented as an energetic material, the measurable product of a complex (quasi-electrical) apparatus which transforms cerebral substance into power. The mythology of Einstein shows him as a genius so lacking in magic that one speaks about his thought as of a functional labour analogous to the mechanical making of sausages, the grinding of corn or the crushing of ore: he used to produce thought, continuously, as a mill makes flour, and death was above all, for him, the cessation of a localized function: '*the most powerful brain of all has stopped thinking*'.

What this machine of genius was supposed to produce was equations. Through the mythology of Einstein, the world blissfully regained the image of knowledge reduced to a formula. Paradoxically, the more the genius of the man was materialized under the guise of his brain, the more the product of his inventiveness came to acquire a magical dimension, and gave a new incarnation to the old esoteric image of a science entirely contained in a few letters. There is a single secret to the world, and this secret is held in one word; the universe is a safe of which humanity seeks the combination: Einstein almost found it, this is the myth of Einstein. In it, we find all the Gnostic[6] themes: the unity of nature, the ideal possibility of a fundamental reduction of the world, the unfastening power of the word, the age-old struggle between a secret and an utterance, the idea that total knowledge can only be discovered all at once, like a lock which suddenly opens after a thousand unsuccessful attempts. The historic equation[7] $E = mc^2$, by its unexpected simplicity, almost embodies the pure idea of the key, bare, linear, made of one metal, opening with a wholly magical ease a door which had resisted the desperate efforts of centuries. Popular imagery faithfully expresses this: *photographs* of Einstein show him standing next to a blackboard covered with mathematical signs of obvious complexity; but *cartoons* of Einstein (the sign that he has become a legend) show him chalk still in hand, and having just written on an empty blackboard, as if without preparation, the magic formula of the world. In this way mythology shows an awareness of the nature of the various tasks: research proper brings into play clockwork-like mechanisms and has its seat in a wholly material organ which

5. "Science without conscience is but the ruin of the Soul" (Rabelais, *Pantagruel* [1532], II, ch. 8) [Barthes's note].

6. Pertaining to Gnosticism, the doctrines of certain late Hellenistic and early Christian sects that promised salvation through esoteric knowledge of spiritual truths.

7. Einstein's famous formula showing that the energy (E) available in matter is equal to its mass (m) multiplied by the speed of light (c) squared.

is monstrous only by its cybernetic complication; discovery, on the contrary, has a magical essence, it is simple like a basic element, a principal substance, like the philosophers' stone of hermetists, tar-water for Berkeley, or oxygen for Schelling.[8]

But since the world is still going on, since research is proliferating, and on the other hand since God's share must be preserved, some failure on the part of Einstein is necessary: Einstein died, it is said, without having been able to verify '*the equation in which the secret of the world was enclosed*'. So in the end the world resisted; hardly opened, the secret closed again, the code was incomplete. In this way Einstein fulfills all the conditions of myth, which could not care less about contradictions so long as it establishes a euphoric security: at once magician and machine, eternal researcher and unfulfilled discoverer, unleashing the best and the worst, brain and conscience, Einstein embodies the most contradictory dreams, and mythically reconciles the infinite power of man over nature with the 'fatality' of the sacrosanct, which man cannot yet do without.

Photography and Electoral Appeal

Some candidates for Parliament adorn their electoral prospectus with a portrait. This presupposes that photography has a power to convert which must be analysed. To start with, the effigy of a candidate establishes a personal link between him and the voters; the candidate does not only offer a programme for judgment, he suggests a physical climate, a set of daily choices expressed in a morphology, a way of dressing, a posture. Photography thus tends to restore the paternalistic nature of elections, whose elitist essence has been disrupted by proportional representation and the rule of parties (the Right seems to use it more than the Left). Inasmuch as photography is an ellipse[9] of language and a condensation of an 'ineffable' social whole, it constitutes an anti-intellectual weapon and tends to spirit away 'politics' (that is to say a body of problems and solutions) to the advantage of a 'manner of being', a socio-moral status. It is well known that this antithesis is one of the major myths of Poujadism (Poujade[1] on television saying: '*Look at me: I am like you*').

Electoral photography is therefore above all the acknowledgment of something deep and irrational co-extensive with politics. What is transmitted through the photograph of the candidate are not his plans, but his deep motives, all his family, mental, even erotic circumstances, all this style of life of which he is at once the product, the example and the bait. It is obvious that what most of our candidates offer us through their likeness is a type of social setting, the spectacular comfort of family, legal and religious norms, the suggestion of innately owning such items of bourgeois property as Sunday Mass, xenophobia, steak and chips, cuckold jokes, in short, what we call an ideology. Needless to say the use of electoral photography presupposes a

8. Friedrich von Schelling (1775–1854), German idealist philosopher; he argued that the atmosphere displays a natural equilibrium between two opposed forces, one of which is oxygen. "The philosophers' stone": the imaginary substance sought by alchemists ("hermetists") to turn base metals into gold. George Berkeley (1685–1753), Anglo-Irish philosopher of empiricism, who wrote about the medicinal virtues of tar-water.

9. Ellipsis

1. Pierre-Marie Poujade (b. 1920), French politician; leader of a right-wing movement during the 1950s.

kind of complicity: a photograph is a mirror, what we are asked to read is the familiar, the known; it offers to the voter his own likeness, but clarified, exalted, superbly elevated into a type. This glorification is in fact the very definition of the photogenic: the voter is at once expressed and heroized, he is invited to elect himself, to weigh the mandate which he is about to give with a veritable physical transference: he is delegating his 'race'.

The types which are thus delegated are not very varied. First there is that which stands for social status, respectability, whether sanguine and well-fed (lists of 'National' parties), or genteel and insipid (lists of the M.R.P.[2]—the Christian Democrats). Then, the type of the intellectual (let it be repeated that we are dealing here with 'signified' types, not actual ones): whether sanctimonious like the candidate of centre right parties like the Rassemblement National, or 'searching' like that of the Communists. In the last two cases, the iconography is meant to signify the exceptional conjunction of thought and will, reflection and action: the slightly narrowed eyes allow a sharp look to filter through, which seems to find its strength in a beautiful inner dream without however ceasing to alight on real obstacles, as if the ideal candidate had in this case magnificently to unite social idealism with bourgeois empiricism. The last type is quite simply that of the 'good-looking chap', whose obvious credentials are his health and virility. Some candidates, incidentally, beautifully manage to win on both counts, appearing for instance as a handsome hero (in uniform) on one side of the handout, and as a mature and virile citizen on the other, displaying his little family. For in most cases, the morphological type is assisted by very obvious attributes: one candidate is surrounded by his kids (curled and dolled-up like all children photographed in France), another is a young parachutist with rolled-up sleeves, or an officer with his chest covered with decorations. Photography constitutes here a veritable blackmail by means of moral values: country, army, family, honour, reckless heroism.

The conventions of photography, moreover, are themselves replete with signs. A full-face photograph underlines the realistic outlook of the candidate, especially if he is provided with scrutinizing glasses. Everything there expresses penetration, gravity, frankness: the future deputy is looking squarely at the enemy, the obstacle, the 'problem'. A three-quarter face photograph, which is more common, suggests the tyranny of an ideal: the gaze is lost nobly in the future, it does not confront, it soars, and fertilizes some other domain, which is chastely left undefined. Almost all three-quarter face photos are ascensional, the face is lifted towards a supernatural light which draws it up and elevates it to the realm of a higher humanity; the candidate reaches the Olympus of elevated feelings, where all political contradictions are solved: peace and war in Algeria,[3] social progress and employers' profits, so-called 'free' religious schools and subsidies from the sugar-beet lobby, the Right and the Left (an opposition always 'superseded'!): all these coexist peacefully in this thoughtful gaze, nobly fixed on the hidden interests of Order.

1957

2. Mouvement Républicain Populaire (Republican Popular Movement; French).

3. The Algerian struggle for independence from France (1954–62).

The Death of the Author[1]

In his story *Sarrasine*[2] Balzac, describing a castrato disguised as a woman, writes the following sentence: '*This was woman herself, with her sudden fears, her irrational whims, her instinctive worries, her impetuous boldness, her fussings, and her delicious sensibility.*' Who is speaking thus? Is it the hero of the story bent on remaining ignorant of the castrato hidden beneath the woman? Is it Balzac the individual, furnished by his personal experience with a philosophy of Woman? Is it Balzac the author professing 'literary' ideas on femininity? Is it universal wisdom? Romantic psychology? We shall never know, for the good reason that writing is the destruction of every voice, of every point of origin. Writing is that neutral, composite, oblique space where our subject slips away, the negative where all identity is lost, starting with the very identity of the body writing.

No doubt it has always been that way. As soon as a fact is *narrated* no longer with a view to acting directly on reality but intransitively, that is to say, finally outside of any function other than that of the very practice of the symbol itself, this disconnection occurs, the voice loses its origin, the author enters into his own death, writing begins. The sense of this phenomenon, however, has varied; in ethnographic societies the responsibility for a narrative is never assumed by a person but by a mediator, shaman or relator whose 'performance'—the mastery of the narrative code—may possibly be admired but never his 'genius'. The author is a modern figure, a product of our society insofar as, emerging from the Middle Ages with English empiricism, French rationalism and the personal faith of the Reformation, it discovered the prestige of the individual, of, as it is more nobly put, the 'human person'. It is thus logical that in literature it should be this positivism, the epitome and culmination of capitalist ideology, which has attached the greatest importance to the 'person' of the author. The *author* still reigns in histories of literature, biographies of writers, interviews, magazines, as in the very consciousness of men of letters anxious to unite their person and their work through diaries and memoirs. The image of literature to be found in ordinary culture is tyrannically centred on the author, his person, his life, his tastes, his passions, while criticism still consists for the most part in saying that Baudelaire's work is the failure of Baudelaire the man, Van Gogh's his madness, Tchaikovsky's his vice.[3] The *explanation* of a work is always sought in the man or woman who produced it, as if it were always in the end, through the more or less transparent allegory of the fiction, the voice of a single person, the *author* 'confiding' in us.

Though the sway of the Author remains powerful (the new criticism[4] has often done no more than consolidate it), it goes without saying that certain writers have long since attempted to loosen it. In France, Mallarmé[5] was

1. Translated by Stephen Heath.
2. Short novel (1830) by Honoré de Balzac (1799–1850), about which Barthes was in the process of writing (see *S/Z*, 1970).
3. Pyotr Tchaikovsky (1840–1893), Russian composer; his "vice" is presumably homosexuality. CHARLES BAUDELAIRE (1821–1867), French poet. Vincent van Gogh (1853–1890), Dutch painter.
4. The "new criticism" in France at that time included structuralist, thematic, phenomenological, sociological, Marxist, and psychoanalytic criticism.
5. STÉPHANE MALLARMÉ (1842–1898), French poet.

doubtless the first to see and to foresee in its full extent the necessity to substitute language itself for the person who until then had been supposed to be its owner. For him, for us too, it is language which speaks, not the author; to write is, through a prerequisite impersonality (not at all to be confused with the castrating objectivity of the realist novelist), to reach that point where only language acts, 'performs', and not 'me'. Mallarmé's entire poetics consists in suppressing the author in the interests of writing (which is, as will be seen, to restore the place of the reader). Valéry,[6] encumbered by a psychology of the Ego, considerably diluted Mallarmé's theory but, his taste for classicism leading him to turn to the lessons of rhetoric, he never stopped calling into question and deriding the Author; he stressed the linguistic and, as it were, 'hazardous' nature of his activity, and throughout his prose works he militated in favour of the essentially verbal condition of literature, in the face of which all recourse to the writer's interiority seemed to him pure superstition. Proust[7] himself, despite the apparently psychological character of what are called his *analyses*, was visibly concerned with the task of inexorably blurring, by an extreme subtilization, the relation between the writer and his characters; by making of the narrator not he who has seen and felt nor even he who is writing, but he who *is going to write* (the young man in the novel—but, in fact, how old is he and who is he?—wants to write but cannot; the novel ends when writing at last becomes possible), Proust gave modern writing its epic. By a radical reversal, instead of putting his life into his novel, as is so often maintained, he made of his very life a work for which his own book was the model; so that it is clear to us that Charlus[8] does not imitate Montesquiou but that Montesquiou—in his anecdotal, historical reality—is no more than a secondary fragment, derived from Charlus. Lastly, to go no further than this prehistory of modernity, Surrealism, though unable to accord language a supreme place (language being system and the aim of the movement being, romantically, a direct subversion of codes—itself moreover illusory: a code cannot be destroyed, only 'played off'), contributed to the desacralization of the image of the Author by ceaselessly recommending the abrupt disappointment of expectations of meaning (the famous surrealist 'jolt'), by entrusting the hand with the task of writing as quickly as possible what the head itself is unaware of (automatic writing), by accepting the principle and the experience of several people writing together. Leaving aside literature itself (such distinctions really becoming invalid), linguistics has recently provided the destruction of the Author with a valuable analytical tool by showing that the whole of the enunciation is an empty process, functioning perfectly without there being any need for it to be filled with the person of the interlocutors. Linguistically, the author is never more than the instance writing, just as *I* is nothing other than the instance saying *I*: language knows a 'subject', not a 'person', and this subject, empty outside of the very enunciation which defines it, suffices to make language 'hold together', suffices, that is to say, to exhaust it.

The removal of the Author (one could talk here with Brecht[9] of a veritable 'distancing', the Author diminishing like a figurine at the far end of the lit-

6. Paul Valéry (1871–1945), French poet and critic.
7. Marcel Proust (1871–1922), French novelist.
8. Le baron de Charlus, a character in Proust's *Remembrance of Things Past* (1913–27), said to have been modeled on the aesthete Robert, comte de Montesquiou-Fezensac (1855–1921).
9. Bertolt Brecht (1898–1956), German poet and dramatist, whose "epic theater" was intended to distance and alienate the audience from traditional theatrical illusion.

erary stage) is not merely an historical fact or an act of writing; it utterly transforms the modern text (or—which is the same thing—the text is henceforth made and read in such a way that at all its levels the author is absent). The temporality is different. The Author, when believed in, is always conceived of as the past of his own book: book and author stand automatically on a single line divided into a *before* and an *after*. The Author is thought to *nourish* the book, which is to say that he exists before it, thinks, suffers, lives for it, is in the same relation of antecedence to his work as a father to his child. In complete contrast, the modern scriptor is born simultaneously with the text, is in no way equipped with a being preceding or exceeding the writing, is not the subject with the book as predicate; there is no other time than that of the enunciation and every text is eternally written *here* and *now*. The fact is (or, it follows) that *writing* can no longer designate an operation of recording, notation, representation, 'depiction' (as the Classics would say); rather, it designates exactly what linguists, referring to Oxford philosophy,[1] call a performative, a rare verbal form (exclusively given in the first person and in the present tense) in which the enunciation has no other content (contains no other proposition) than the act by which it is uttered—something like the *I declare* of kings or the *I sing* of very ancient poets. Having buried the Author, the modern scriptor can thus no longer believe, as according to the pathetic view of his predecessors, that this hand is too slow for his thought or passion and that consequently, making a law of necessity, he must emphasize this delay and indefinitely 'polish' his form. For him, on the contrary, the hand, cut off from any voice, borne by a pure gesture of inscription (and not of expression), traces a field without origin—or which, at least, has no other origin than language itself, language which ceaselessly calls into question all origins.

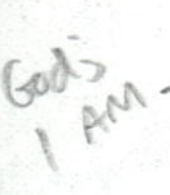

We know now that a text is not a line of words releasing a single 'theological' meaning (the 'message' of the Author-God) but a multi-dimensional space in which a variety of writings, none of them original, blend and clash. The text is a tissue of quotations drawn from the innumerable centres of culture. Similar to Bouvard and Pécuchet,[2] those eternal copyists, at once sublime and comic and whose profound ridiculousness indicates precisely the truth of writing, the writer can only imitate a gesture that is always anterior, never original. His only power is to mix writings, to counter the ones with the others, in such a way as never to rest on any one of them. Did he wish to *express himself*, he ought at least to know that the inner 'thing' he thinks to 'translate' is itself only a ready-formed dictionary, its words only explainable through other words, and so on indefinitely; something experienced in exemplary fashion by the young Thomas de Quincey,[3] he who was so good at Greek that in order to translate absolutely modern ideas and images into that dead language, he had, so Baudelaire tells us (in *Paradis Artificiels*),[4] 'created for himself an unfailing dictionary, vastly more extensive and complex than those resulting from the ordinary patience of purely literary themes'. Succeeding the Author, the scriptor no longer bears within him passions, humours, feelings, impressions, but rather this immense

1. That is, philosophy of language; see especially J. L. Austin, *How to Do Things with Words* (1962).
2. The title characters in Gustave Flaubert's unfinished novel *Bouvard and Pécuchet* (1881), who leave their jobs as copyists and unsuccessfully attempt to master all knowledge.
3. English essayist and critic (1785–1859).
4. *Artificial Paradises* (1869).

dictionary from which he draws a writing that can know no halt: life never does more than imitate the book, and the book itself is only a tissue of signs, an imitation that is lost, infinitely deferred.

Once the Author is removed, the claim to decipher a text becomes quite futile. To give a text an Author is to impose a limit on that text, to furnish it with a final signified, to close the writing. Such a conception suits criticism very well, the latter then allotting itself the important task of discovering the Author (or its hypostases:[5] society, history, psyche, liberty) beneath the work: when the Author has been found, the text is 'explained'—victory to the critic. Hence there is no surprise in the fact that, historically, the reign of the Author has also been that of the Critic, nor again in the fact that criticism (be it new) is today undermined along with the Author. In the multiplicity of writing, everything is to be *disentangled*, nothing *deciphered*; the structure can be followed, 'run' (like the thread of a stocking) at every point and at every level, but there is nothing beneath: the space of writing is to be ranged over, not pierced; writing ceaselessly posits meaning ceaselessly to evaporate it, carrying out a systematic exemption of meaning. In precisely this way literature (it would be better from now on to say *writing*), by refusing to assign a 'secret', an ultimate meaning, to the text (and to the world as text), liberates what may be called an anti-theological activity, an activity that is truly revolutionary since to refuse to fix meaning is, in the end, to refuse God and his hypostases—reason, science, law.

Let us come back to the Balzac sentence. No one, no 'person', says it: its source, its voice, is not the true place of the writing, which is reading. Another—very precise—example will help to make this clear: recent research (J.-P. Vernant)[6] has demonstrated the constitutively ambiguous nature of Greek tragedy, its texts being woven from words with double meanings that each character understands unilaterally (this perpetual misunderstanding is exactly the 'tragic'); there is, however, someone who understands each word in its duplicity and who, in addition, hears the very deafness of the characters speaking in front of him—this someone being precisely the reader (or here, the listener). Thus is revealed the total existence of writing: a text is made of multiple writings, drawn from many cultures and entering into mutual relations of dialogue, parody, contestation, but there is one place where this multiplicity is focused and that place is the reader, not, as was hitherto said, the author. The reader is the space on which all the quotations that make up a writing are inscribed without any of them being lost; a text's unity lies not in its origin but in its destination. Yet this destination cannot any longer be personal: the reader is without history, biography, psychology; he is simply that *someone* who holds together in a single field all the traces by which the written text is constituted. Which is why it is derisory to condemn the new writing in the name of a humanism hypocritically turned champion of the reader's rights. Classic criticism has never paid any attention to the reader; for it, the writer is the only person in literature. We are now beginning to let ourselves be fooled no longer by the arrogant antiphrastical[7] recriminations

5. Stand-ins (the concrete forms of abstractions).
6. Cf. Jean-Pierre Vernant (with Pierre Vidal-Naquet), *Mythe et tragédie en Grèce ancienne* (Paris, 1972), esp. pp. 19–40, 99–131 [translator's note]. Vernant (b. 1914), French scholar of ancient Greece.
7. Characterized by using a word to intend its opposite.

of good society in favour of the very thing it sets aside, ignores, smothers, or destroys; we know that to give writing its future, it is necessary to overthrow the myth: the birth of the reader must be at the cost of the death of the Author.

1968

From Work to Text[1]

It is a fact that over the last few years a certain change has taken place (or is taking place) in our conception of language and, consequently, of the literary work which owes at least its phenomenal existence to this same language. The change is clearly connected with the current development of (amongst other disciplines) linguistics, anthropology, Marxism and psychoanalysis (the term 'connection' is used here in a deliberately neutral way: one does not decide a determination, be it multiple and dialectical). What is new and which affects the idea of the work comes not necessarily from the internal recasting of each of these disciplines, but rather from their encounter in relation to an object which traditionally is the province of none of them. It is indeed as though the *interdisciplinarity* which is today held up as a prime value in research cannot be accomplished by the simple confrontation of specialist branches of knowledge. Interdisciplinarity is not the calm of an easy security; it begins *effectively* (as opposed to the mere expression of a pious wish) when the solidarity of the old disciplines breaks down—perhaps even violently, via the jolts of fashion—in the interests of a new object and a new language neither of which has a place in the field of the sciences that were to be brought peacefully together, this unease in classification being precisely the point from which it is possible to diagnose a certain mutation. The mutation in which the idea of work seems to be gripped must not, however, be over-estimated: it is more in the nature of an epistemological slide than of a real break. The break, as is frequently stressed, is seen to have taken place in the last century with the appearance of Marxism and Freudianism;[2] since then there has been no further break, so that in a way it can be said that for the last hundred years we have been living in repetition. What History, our History, allows us today is merely to slide, to vary, to exceed, to repudiate. Just as Einsteinian science[3] demands that *the relativity of the frames of reference* be included in the object studied, so the combined action of Marxism, Freudianism and structuralism demands, in literature, the relativization of the relations of writer, reader and observer (critic). Over against the traditional notion of the *work*, for long—and still—conceived of in a, so to speak, Newtonian way, there is now the requirement of a new object, obtained by the sliding or overturning of former categories. That object is the *Text*. I know the word is fashionable (I am myself often led to use it) and therefore regarded by some with suspicion, but that is exactly

1. Translated by Stephen Heath.
2. On the economic and political theorist KARL MARX (1818–1883) and the founder of psychoanalysis SIGMUND FREUD (1856–1939), see above.
3. That is, the theory of special relativity developed by Albert Einstein (1879–1955), which explains what the mechanical worldview associated with Sir Isaac Newton (1642–1727) could not: the interactions of radiation and matter viewed from different inertial frames of reference.

why I should like to remind myself of the principal propositions at the intersection of which I see the Text as standing. The word 'proposition' is to be understood more in a grammatical than in a logical sense: the following are not argumentations but enunciations, 'touches', approaches that consent to remain metaphorical. Here then are these propositions; they concern method, genres, signs, plurality, filiation, reading and pleasure.

1. The Text is not to be thought of as an object that can be computed. It would be futile to try to separate out materially works from texts. In particular, the tendency must be avoided to say that the work is classic, the text avant-garde; it is not a question of drawing up a crude honours list in the name of modernity and declaring certain literary productions 'in' and others 'out' by virtue of their chronological situation: there may be 'text' in a very ancient work, while many products of contemporary literature are in no way texts. The difference is this: the work is a fragment of substance, occupying a part of the space of books (in a library for example), the Text is a methodological field. The opposition may recall (without at all reproducing term for term) Lacan's[4] distinction between 'reality' and 'the real': the one is displayed, the other demonstrated; likewise, the work can be seen (in bookshops, in catalogues, in exam syllabuses), the text is a process of demonstration, speaks according to certain rules (or against certain rules); the work can be held in the hand, the text is held in language, only exists in the movement of a discourse (or rather, it is Text for the very reason that it knows itself as text); the Text is not the decomposition of the work, it is the work that is the imaginary tail of the Text; or again, *the Text is experienced only in an activity of production*. It follows that the Text cannot stop (for example on a library shelf); its constitutive movement is that of cutting across (in particular, it can cut across the work, several works).

2. In the same way, the Text does not stop at (good) Literature; it cannot be contained in a hierarchy, even in a simple division of genres. What constitutes the Text is, on the contrary (or precisely), its subversive force in respect of the old classifications. How do you classify a writer like Georges Bataille?[5] Novelist, poet, essayist, economist, philosopher, mystic? The answer is so difficult that the literary manuals generally prefer to forget about Bataille who, in fact, wrote texts, perhaps continuously one single text. If the Text poses problems of classification (which is furthermore one of its 'social' functions), this is because it always involves a certain experience of limits (to take up an expression from Philippe Sollers). Thibaudet[6] used already to talk—but in a very restricted sense—of limit-works (such as Chateaubriand's[7] *Vie de Rancé*, which does indeed come through to us today as a 'text'); the Text is that which goes to the limit of the rules of enunciation (rationality, readability, etc.). Nor is this a rhetorical idea, resorted to for some 'heroic' effect: the Text tries to place itself very exactly *behind* the limit of the *doxa*[8] (is not general opinion—constitutive of our democratic societies and powerfully aided by mass communications—defined by its limits, the energy with

4. JACQUES LACAN (1901–1981), French psychoanalyst.
5. French writer (1897–1962).
6. Albert Thibaudet (1874–1936), French critic. Sollers (b. 1936), French writer.
7. François-René, vicomte de Chateaubriand (1768–1848), French writer and statesman. In 1980 a new edition of his *Life of Rancé* (1844) was published with a preface by Barthes.
8. Received opinion (Greek).

which it excludes, its *censorship?*). Taking the word literally, it may be said that the Text is always *paradoxical*.

3. The Text can be approached, experienced, in reaction to the sign. The work closes on a signified.[9] There are two modes of signification which can be attributed to this signified: either it is claimed to be evident and the work is then the object of a literal science, of philology, or else it is considered to be secret, ultimate, something to be sought out, and the work then falls under the scope of a hermeneutics, of an interpretation (Marxist, psychoanalytic, thematic, etc.); in short, the work itself functions as a general sign and it is normal that it should represent an institutional category of the civilization of the Sign. The Text, on the contrary, practises the infinite deferment of the signified, is dilatory; its field is that of the signifier and the signifier must not be conceived of as 'the first stage of meaning', its material vestibule, but, in complete opposition to this, as its *deferred action*. Similarly, the *infinity* of the signifier refers not to some idea of the ineffable (the unnameable signified) but to that of a *playing*; the generation of the perpetual signifier (after the fashion of a perpetual calendar) in the field of the text (better, of which the text is the field) is realized not according to an organic progress of maturation or a hermeneutic course of deepening investigation, but, rather, according to a serial movement of disconnections, overlappings, variations. The logic regulating the Text is not comprehensive (define 'what the work means') but metonymic; the activity of associations, contiguities, carryings-over coincides with a liberation of symbolic energy (lacking it, man would die); the work—in the best of cases—is *moderately* symbolic (its symbolic runs out, comes to a halt); the Text is *radically* symbolic: *a work conceived, perceived and received in its integrally symbolic nature is a text*. Thus is the Text restored to language; like language, it is structured but off-centred, without closure (note, in reply to the contemptuous suspicion of the 'fashionable' sometimes directed at structuralism, that the epistemological privilege currently accorded to language stems precisely from the discovery there of a paradoxical idea of structure: a system with neither close nor centre).

4. The Text is plural. Which is not simply to say that it has several meanings, but that it accomplishes the very plural of meaning: an *irreducible* (and not merely an acceptable) plural. The Text is not a co-existence of meanings but a passage, an overcrossing; thus it answers not to an interpretation, even a liberal one, but to an explosion, a dissemination. The plural of the Text depends, that is, not on the ambiguity of its contents but on what might be called the *stereographic plurality* of its weave of signifiers (etymologically, the text is a tissue, a woven fabric). The reader of the Text may be compared to someone at a loose end (someone slackened off from any imaginary); this passably empty subject strolls—it is what happened to the author of these lines, then it was that he had a vivid idea of the Text—on the side of a valley, a *oued*[1] flowing down below (*oued* is there to bear witness to a certain feeling of unfamiliarity); what he perceives is multiple, irreducible, coming from a disconnected, heterogeneous variety of substances and perspectives: lights, colours, vegetation, heat, air, slender explosions of noises, scant cries of

9. The sign was divided into *signified* (the meaning conveyed) and *signifier* (the symbol or sound that conveys that meaning) by the Swiss linguist FERDINAND DE SAUSSURE (1857–1913).

1. Wadi (Arabic); a streambed that is usually dry, except during the rainy season.

birds, children's voices from over on the other side, passages, gestures, clothes of inhabitants near or far away. All these *incidents* are half-identifiable: they come from codes which are known but their combination is unique, founds the stroll in a difference repeatable only as difference. So the Text: it can be it only in its difference (which does not mean its individuality), its reading is semelfactive[2] (this rendering illusory any inductive-deductive science of texts—no 'grammar' of the text) and nevertheless woven entirely with citations, references, echoes, cultural languages (what language is not?), antecedent or contemporary, which cut across it through and through in a vast stereophony. The intertextual in which every text is held, it itself being the text-between of another text, is not to be confused with some origin of the text: to try to find the 'sources', the 'influences' of a work, is to fall in with the myth of filiation; the citations which go to make up a text are anonymous, untraceable, and yet *already read*: they are quotations without inverted commas. The work has nothing disturbing for any monistic philosophy (we know that there are opposing examples of these); for such a philosophy, plural is the Evil. Against the work, therefore, the text could well take as its motto the words of the man possessed by demons (*Mark* 5: 9): 'My name is Legion: for we are many.' The plural of demoniacal texture which opposes text to work can bring with it fundamental changes in reading, and precisely in areas where monologism appears to be the Law: certain of the 'texts' of Holy Scripture traditionally recuperated by theological monism (historical or anagogical) will perhaps offer themselves to a diffraction of meanings (finally, that is to say, to a materialist reading), while the Marxist interpretation of works, so far resolutely monistic, will be able to materialize itself more by pluralizing itself (if, however, the Marxist 'institutions' allow it).

5. The work is caught up in a process of filiation. Are postulated: a *determination* of the work by the world (by race, then by History), a *consecution* of works amongst themselves, and a *conformity* of the work to the author. The author is reputed the father and the owner of his work: literary science therefore teaches *respect* for the manuscript and the author's declared intentions, while society asserts the legality of the relation of author to work (the '*droit d'auteur*'[3] or 'copyright', in fact of recent date since it was only really legalized at the time of the French Revolution). As for the Text, it reads without the inscription of the Father. Here again, the metaphor of the Text separates from that of the work: the latter refers to the image of an *organism* which grows by vital expansion, by 'development' (a word which is significantly ambiguous, at once biological and rhetorical); the metaphor of the Text is that of the *network*; if the Text extends itself, it is as a result of a combinatory systematic (an image, moreover, close to current biological conceptions of the living being). Hence no vital 'respect' is due to the Text: it can be *broken* (which is just what the Middle Ages did with two nevertheless authoritative texts—Holy Scripture and Aristotle); it can be read without the guarantee of its father, the restitution of the inter-text paradoxically abolishing any legacy. It is not that the Author may not 'come back' in the Text, in his text, but he then does so as a 'guest'. If he is a novelist, he is inscribed

2. A neologism—*sema* (Greek) = sign; *semi* (Latin) = half; *factio* (Latin) = making—suggesting that the reading of "text" is largely sign production.

3. Right of the author (French).

in the novel like one of his characters, figured in the carpet; no longer privileged, paternal, aletheological,[4] his inscription is ludic. He becomes, as it were, a paper-author: his life is no longer the origin of his fictions but a fiction contributing to his work; there is a reversion of the work on to the life (and no longer the contrary); it is the work of Proust, of Genet[5] which allows their lives to be read as a text. The word 'bio-graphy' re-acquires a strong, etymological sense, at the same time as the sincerity of the enunciation—veritable 'cross' borne by literary morality—becomes a false problem: the *I* which writes the text, it too, is never more than a paper-*I*.

6. The work is normally the object of a consumption; no demagogy is intended here in referring to the so-called consumer culture but it has to be recognized that today it is the 'quality' of the work (which supposes finally an appreciation of 'taste') and not the operation of reading itself which can differentiate between books: structurally, there is no difference between 'cultured' reading and casual reading in trains. The Text (if only by its frequent 'unreadability') decants the work (the work permitting) from its consumption and gathers it up as play, activity, production, practice. This means that the Text requires that one try to abolish (or at the very least to diminish) the distance between writing and reading, in no way by intensifying the projection of the reader into the work but by joining them in a single signifying practice. The distance separating reading from writing is historical. In the times of the greatest social division (before the setting up of democratic cultures), reading and writing were equally privileges of class. Rhetoric, the great literary code of those times, taught one to *write* (even if what was then normally produced were speeches, not texts). Significantly, the coming of democracy reversed the word of command: what the (secondary) School prides itself on is teaching to *read* (well) and no longer to write (consciousness of the deficiency is becoming fashionable again today: the teacher is called upon to teach pupils to 'express themselves', which is a little like replacing a form of repression by a misconception). In fact, *reading*, in the sense of consuming, is far from *playing* with the text. 'Playing' must be understood here in all its polysemy: the text itself *plays* (like a door, like a machine with 'play') and the reader plays twice over, playing the Text as one plays a game, looking for a practice which re-produces it, but, in order that that practice not be reduced to a passive, inner *mimesis*[6] (the Text is precisely that which resists such a reduction), also playing the Text in the musical sense of the term. The history of music (as a practice, not as an 'art') does indeed parallel that of the Text fairly closely: there was a period when practising amateurs[7] were numerous (at least within the confines of a certain class) and 'playing' and 'listening' formed a scarcely differentiated activity; then two roles appeared in succession, first that of the performer, the interpreter to whom the bourgeois public (though still itself able to play a little—the whole history of the piano) delegated its playing, then that of the (passive) amateur, who listens to music without being able to play (the gramophone record takes the place of the piano). We know that today post-serial music[8]

4. A neologism—*alētheia* (Greek) = the self-presentation of Truth; *theological* = relating to the study of religious faith—meaning that the author's writing no longer operates in a theological realm of truth.
5. Jean Genet (1910–1986), French dramatist. Marcel Proust (1871–1922), French novelist.
6. Representation, imitation (Greek).
7. Barthes was an avid amateur pianist.
8. Music that was a reaction against serialism, the total mathematization of all musical variables in the atonal compositions of Pierre Boulez (b. 1925)

has radically altered the role of the 'interpreter', who is called on to be in some sort the co-author of the score, completing it rather than giving it 'expression'. The Text is very much a score of this new kind: it asks of the reader a practical collaboration. Which is an important change, for who executes the work? (Mallarmé[9] posed the question, wanting the audience to *produce* the book). Nowadays only the critic executes the work (accepting the play on words). The reduction of reading to a consumption is clearly responsible for the 'boredom' experienced by many in the face of the modern ('unreadable') text, the avant-garde film or painting: to be bored means that one cannot produce the text, open it out, *set it going*.

7. This leads us to pose (to propose) a final approach to the Text, that of pleasure. I do not know whether there has ever been a hedonistic aesthetics (eudæmonist philosophies are themselves rare). Certainly there exists a pleasure of the work (of certain works); I can delight in reading and re-reading Proust, Flaubert, Balzac, even—why not?—Alexandre Dumas.[1] But this pleasure, no matter how keen and even when free from all prejudice, remains in part (unless by some exceptional critical effort) a pleasure of consumption; for if I can read these authors, I also know that I cannot *re-write* them (that it is impossible today to write 'like that') and this knowledge, depressing enough, suffices to cut me off from the production of these works, in the very moment their remoteness establishes my modernity (is not to be modern to know clearly what cannot be started over again?). As for the Text, it is bound to *jouissance*,[2] that is to a pleasure without separation. Order of the signifier, the Text participates in its own way in a social utopia; before History (supposing the latter does not opt for barbarism), the Text achieves, if not the transparence of social relations, that at least of language relations: the Text is that space where no language has a hold over any other, where languages circulate (keeping the circular sense of the term).

These few propositions, inevitably, do not constitute the articulations of a Theory of the Text and this is not simply the result of the failings of the person here presenting them (who in many respects has anyway done no more than pick up what is being developed round about him). It stems from the fact that a Theory of the Text cannot be satisfied by a metalinguistic exposition: the destruction of meta-language, or at least (since it may be necessary provisionally to resort to meta-language) its calling into doubt, is part of the theory itself: the discourse on the Text should itself be nothing other than text, research, textual activity, since the Text is that *social* space which leaves no language safe, outside, nor any subject of the enunciation in position as judge, master, analyst, confessor, decoder. The theory of the Text can coincide only with a practice of writing.

1971

and others; in some cases the interpreter shapes a deliberately "open" work, still viewed as a network of variables.

9. STÉPHANE MALLARMÉ (1842–1898), French poet.

1. French novelist and dramatist (1802–1870). Gustave Flaubert (1821–1880) and Honoré de Balzac (1799–1850), French novelists.

2. In French, *jouissance* (the surprise of orgasm, bliss, ecstasy) is distinguished from *plaisir* (pleasure).

LOUIS ALTHUSSER
1918–1990

One of the most influential and distinctive Marxist thinkers of the second half of the twentieth century, Louis Althusser came to prominence in the volatile 1960s. His work combined the new, scientifically oriented methods of structuralism developed by CLAUDE LÉVI-STRAUSS, JACQUES LACAN, and others with a commitment to political engagement and social transformation, laying the groundwork for a revolution in theory that affected fields ranging from literary criticism and cultural studies to history and politics. "Ideology and Ideological State Apparatuses (Notes towards an Investigation)" (1970), his most influential essay and our second selection, analyzes how dominant social systems enforce their control—subtly molding human subjects through ideology—and how they reproduce themselves. "A Letter on Art in Reply to André Daspre" (1966), though less widely known, succinctly explores the relation of art to ideology.

Born in French-held Algeria, Louis Althusser was educated in Marseilles and at the Lycée du Parc in Lyons. In 1939 he was admitted to the prestigious École Normale Supérieure in Paris, but his academic career was delayed when he was drafted into the military during the early days of World War II. Captured in 1940 and held for five years in a German prisoner-of-war camp, he returned to the École Normale after the war, completing a master's thesis on the philosopher G. W. F. HEGEL (1770–1831) in 1948. He then joined the faculty at the school, also doing doctoral work under the supervision of the celebrated Hegelian philosopher Jean Hyppolite. His membership in the French Communist Party from 1948 on was also decisive for his future work. His relations with the Party hierarchy were never easy, and his writings were often attacked by official Communist philosophers—he was almost expelled in 1966 in a dispute over China's Cultural Revolution—but Althusser remained a lifelong member. In *For Marx* (1965; trans. 1969), he encapsulates his intellectual career and how he became, in a famous phrase, "a Marxist in philosophy," noting three coordinates: the underdevelopment of Marxist theory within French communism, the impoverishment of French philosophy since the Enlightenment, and the political situation of the international communist movement in the post-Stalin era. Also formative were the political events in France during his lifetime, which he called "the terrible education of deeds"; these included the Spanish Civil War, World War II, and the cold war that followed.

Publishing little before the 1960s, Althusser undertook during the 1950s a long march through both the Marxist classics and KARL MARX'S influences (notably Hegel and Ludwig Feuerbach, 1804–1872). His research culminated in a series of important texts, gathered in *For Marx* and *Reading Capital* (the latter coauthored with his student Étienne Balibar, 1965; trans. 1970), both of which quickly captured the attention of French and later British intellectuals. Althusser's interventions changed the face of Western Marxist theory, shattering the pieties of Stalinist dogmatism and the newer Marxist humanism, which, influenced by Hegel and the twentieth-century philosophers GYÖRGY LUKÁCS and JEAN-PAUL SARTRE, saw Marxism as an effort to recover an alienated humanity. Elevating the individual as its center of concern, humanism generally stresses human freedom and self-determination; in contrast, many structuralist thinkers argue that freedom of thought and action is limited by linguistic, psychological, or socioeconomic systems. Propounding an "antihumanism," Althusser emphasizes the scientific aspects of Marxism, in particular its investigation of how societal structures determine lived experience. His critique of humanism continues to help shape postmodern and poststructuralist theory.

Following Marx and FRIEDRICH ENGELS's central claim in *The Communist Manifesto* (1848; see above) that "the history of all hitherto existing society is the history of class struggles,' Althusser held that philosophy was bound by political obligations and that the task of the philosopher was to "represent the class struggle in theory," taking the side of the oppressed in ongoing ideological struggles with representatives of the ruling class. His injunction inspired the participants in the May 1968 student and worker uprising in France; but Althusser himself was absent during the turbulent events of May, recuperating in a sanatorium from a recurrence of the clinical depression that had plagued him following his experiences in World War II. After recovering he embarked on an ambitious new theoretical project addressing two questions: how a society achieves stability over time by reproducing its dominant relations of production and what conditions make social revolution possible. "Ideology and Ideological State Apparatuses" stems from this larger project, which was never completed. Althusser would continue to teach and to write throughout the 1970s, but his illness worsened, and in 1980 he murdered his wife in a manic fit of rage. Declared mentally incompetent, he was sentenced to house arrest under psychiatric care and isolated from all but a few friends. At the time of his death a decade later, Althusser's reputation had reached a low point.

Althusser's major concepts—"ideological state apparatuses," "interpellation," "imaginary relations," and "overdetermination"—permeate the discourse of contemporary literary and cultural theory, and his theory of ideology has influenced virtually all subsequent serious work on the topic. The problem that Althusser sets out to solve in "Ideology and Ideological State Apparatuses"—to determine how a society reproduces its basic social relations, thereby ensuring its continuing existence—is a perennial one in social theory, raised as early as PLATO's *Republic* (ca. 373 B.C.E.). Plato thought that the key to sustaining a just state was controlling the education of its citizens, particularly its ruling class. Althusser concurs, while emphasizing that the dominant values in a society are for the most part endorsed by the majority of its members. Winning their endorsement is the work of ideology, and Althusser employs a structuralist account of the societal mechanisms that inculcate such consent, as well as a psychoanalytic account of how ideology makes individuals "subjects" of the dominant social order. Contrary to its colloquial sense, which suggests a set of ideas or beliefs that one chooses to espouse or reject, ideology for Althusser is not voluntary but the result of structural factors in society; he thus dispenses with the standard humanist notion of free will.

Althusser famously terms the societal mechanisms for creating pliant, obedient citizens who practice dominant values "ideological state apparatuses" (ISAs). Complex, numerous, and differing from one society to another, they are civil institutions that have legal standing (hence their designation as "state" apparatuses), including churches, schools, the family, courts, political parties, unions, the media, sports, and the arts. ISAs differ from "repressive state apparatuses" (RSAs), such as the police, the military, the prison system, and government, in several key ways: they are not unified, they operate primarily in the private sphere, and they attain their power not by means of explicit coercion or force but through implicit consent realized in accepted "practices." One tacitly learns the practice of obedience to authority, for example, in church, in school, at home, or on sports teams. As Althusser notes, a dominant social order would not survive if it relied only on force, and he traces the rising influence of schools as the dominant ISA in modern society. Schools have supplanted the church in this role, instilling in students the habits that will make them productive workers in modern capitalist societies, so that they show up at the factory or office day after day without question.

Althusser's theory revises the standard Marxist definition of ideology as "false consciousness," the explanation of why people willingly participate in the capitalist exploitation seen to undergird modern society. Many Marxists argue that we simply misunderstand what is really going on: believing that the economic system is fair and offers equal opportunity, rather than favoring those who control the means of production and capital, we identify with and emulate the owners and capitalists. Althusser retains the classical Marxist stress on economic causes, which he says are decisive "in the last instance," but his concept of the ISAs presents a fuller explanation of the diverse societal processes of ideology. It also allows for more complexity: ISAs operate with "relative autonomy," sometimes for different and contradictory ends (they are "overdetermined"). His theory thus has affinities with the thought a generation earlier of the Italian Marxist ANTONIO GRAMSCI, whose concept of hegemony explains the flexibility of social dominance and its operation through cultural institutions.

Althusser defines ideology as "the imaginary relationship of individuals to their real conditions of existence." It is here that he turns to a subtle psychoanalytic account, adopting Jacques Lacan's concepts of the imaginary, mirroring, and subject formation. Revising SIGMUND FREUD's concepts of the unconscious, ego, and superego, Lacan posits a three-part structure—the Imaginary, the Real, and the Symbolic—that forms the individual subject. The Imaginary constitutes the preverbal realm in which human beings exist from earliest years; it is not a false but a primordial structure of consciousness. For Althusser, ideology takes the place of the Imaginary, which one is "born into" and which, like the Freudian unconscious, deeply influences how one acts. But unlike Lacan, he sees an individual's subjectivity as generated through social forces. Using Lacan's ideas of mirroring and recognition, Althusser describes how ISAs "interpellate or hail individuals as subjects." A pivotal stage in character development for Lacan is "the mirror stage," when an infant recognizes him- or herself in a mirror. For Althusser, ideology works through our tacit recognition of being hailed, as when we turn around to answer the call, "Hey, you there!"

Though Althusser focused largely on political theory, and his writings on art and literature were unsystematic and occasional, "A Letter on Art" briefly investigates the effect of ideology on artworks. In keeping with the Marxist "reflection" theory of art, held by LEON TROTSKY and to some extent Lukács, Althusser observes that art is formed out of and pictures ideological raw materials; but he also reasons that it maintains a certain distance from the ideologies "to which it alludes." He thus grants "authentic" art a special critical status in "mak[ing] us *see*" the ideologies "from which it detaches itself," exposing ideology "in some sense *from the inside*." Other twentieth-century ideas lurking in the background are *defamiliarization*, as defined by the Russian formalists BORIS EICHENBAUM and Victor Shklovsky, and especially *estrangement*, as described by the German Marxist playwright Bertolt Brecht. Although Althusser allows art itself a special value, he also recognizes that the arts are embedded in institutions (museums, publishing houses, media, recording companies, Hollywood studios, and so forth) that function as ISAs, shoring up the ideas and values of the ruling class through imaginative representations.

Provoking sharp reaction as well as a devoted following, Althusser's work has had wide-ranging influence. Some have found his reliance on a structural account of society too deterministic; others, most notably E. P. Thompson, the English historian usually considered a founding father of cultural studies, have criticized his lack of attention to empirical history. Despite Thompson's disavowal, Althusser's concept of ideology has been crucial to cultural studies, as recounted in STUART HALL's "Cultural Studies and Its Theoretical Legacies" (1992; see below) and as evidenced in DICK HEBDIGE's *Subculture: The Meaning of Style* (1979; see below). Althusser's concept of ideology has also been foundational for the leading contemporary Marxist literary critics in Britain and in America, TERRY EAGLETON and FREDRIC JAMESON. Eagleton's *Criticism and Ideology* (1976), for instance, draws heavily on Althusser, though focusing on how art produces ideology rather than how ideology informs art. Jameson's *The Political Unconscious: Narrative as a Socially Symbolic Act* (1981; see below), perhaps the most sustained consideration of the ideological implications of the modern novel, both elaborates on and critiques Althusser. Less faithfully, the French sociologist PIERRE BOURDIEU shows the influence of Althusser in his focus on education and its formative effect in producing "distinction" and creating "cultural capital"; Bourdieu swerves, however, from traditional Marxist analyses by stressing the cultural over the economic. Although the breadth of his influence has dissipated some of the Marxist political charge of his social critique, Althusser's theory of ideology remains a touchstone in contemporary criticism.

BIBLIOGRAPHY

Althusser's major essays are collected in three influential books: *For Marx* (1965; trans. 1969); *Lenin and Philosophy and Other Essays* (1969; trans. 1971), which contains "Ideology and Ideological State Apparatuses"; and *Reading Capital*, a reconsideration of Marx's masterwork written with his student Étienne Balibar (1968; trans. 1970). Subsequent collections in English, gathering his many essays, are *Politics and History: Montesquieu, Rousseau, Hegel, and Marx* (1972), which includes the long essay published as his first book, *Montesquieu: Politics and History* (1959); *Essays in Self-Criticism* (1974; trans. 1976); *Philosophy and the Spontaneous Philosophy of the Scientists, and Other Essays* (1974; trans. 1990); *Essays on Ideology* (1984); *Writings on Psychoanalysis: Freud and Lacan* (1993; trans. 1996); *The Spectre of Hegel: Early Writings* (1977); and *Machiavelli and Us* (1999). *Journal de captivité: Stalag XA 1940–1945* (1992, *Journal of Captivity*) records Althusser's experiences as a prisoner of war. Written during the mid-1980s, the autobiographical texts collected in *The Future Lasts Forever*, edited by Olivier Corpet and Yann Moulier Boutang (1992; trans. 1993), should be approached with caution, since many passages bear witness to Althusser's mental decline. The definitive biography is Yann Moulier Boutang, *Louis Althusser: Une Biographie (Louis Althusser: A Biography)*; only the first volume, *La Formation du mythe (1918–1956)* (1992, *The Formation of the Myth*) has appeared to date.

For early applications of Althusserian theory to literature, see *A Theory of Literary Production* (1966; trans. 1978), by his student Pierre Macherey; Terry Eagleton, *Criticism and Ideology* (1976); and Fredric Jameson, *The Political Unconscious: Narrative as a Socially Symbolic Act* (1981). The famous critique by the English historian E. P. Thompson, "The Poverty of Theory or an Orrery of Errors" (1978), declared Althusserian theory to be Stalinist. Perry Anderson recuperates Althusser against Thompson's charges in *Arguments within English Marxism* (1980). Of the many accounts of Althusser's use of structuralism, the best is Ted Benton's *Rise and Fall of Structural Marxism* (1984). For a central document in feminist debates over Althusserian Marxism, see Juliet Mitchell, *Women: The Longest Revolution* (1984). In *Althusser: The Detour of Theory* (1987), the best single critical account, Gregory Elliott helpfully traces the political background that shaped Althusser's work. *Imaginary Relations: Aesthetics and Ideology in the Theory of Historical Materialism* (1987) by Michael Sprinker is an influential treatment of the relation of Althusserian theory to poststructuralist aesthetics. See also Eagleton's overview *Ideology: An Introduction* (1991).

Gregory Elliott also edited an excellent collection of critical essays from a range of political and theoretical perspectives, *Althusser: A Critical Reader* (1994); see especially the essay by Francis Mulhern considering Althusser's impact on literary studies. *The Althusserian Legacy*, edited by E. Ann Kaplan and Michael Sprinker (1994), contains several important essays on Althusser's impact across the disciplines, together with a revealing interview with his onetime student Jacques Derrida. Elliot's *Althusser: A Critical Reader* includes a comprehensive bibliography of all Althusser's publications up to 1993.

A Letter on Art in Reply to André Daspre[1]

La Nouvelle Critique has sent me your letter.[2] I hope you will permit me, if not to reply to all the questions it poses, at least to add a few comments to yours in the line of your own reflections.

First of all, you should know that I am perfectly conscious of the *very schematic* character of my article on Humanism. As you have noticed, it has the disadvantage that it gives a 'broad' idea of ideology without going into the analysis of details. As it does not mention art, I realize that it is possible to wonder whether art should or should not be ranked as such among ideologies, to be precise, whether art and ideology are one and the same thing. That, I feel, is how you have been tempted to *interpret* my silence.

The problem of the relations between art and ideology is a very complicated and difficult one. However, I can tell you in what directions our investigations tend. *I do not rank real art among the ideologies*, although art does have a quite particular and specific relationship with ideology. If you would like some idea of the initial elements of this thesis and the very complicated developments it promises, I advise you to read carefully the article Pierre Macherey has written on 'Lenin as a critic of Tolstoy.'[3] Of course, that article is only a beginning, but it does pose the problem of the relations between art and ideology and of the specificity of art. This is the direction in which we are working, and we hope to publish important studies on this subject in a few months' time.

The article will also give you a first idea of the relationship between art and knowledge. Art (I mean authentic art, not works of an average or mediocre level) does not give us a *knowledge* in the *strict sense*, it therefore does not replace knowledge (in the modern sense: scientific knowledge), but what it gives us does nevertheless maintain a certain *specific relationship* with knowledge. This relationship is not one of identity but one of difference. Let me explain. I believe that the peculiarity of art is to 'make us see' (*nous donner à voir*), 'make us perceive', 'make us feel' something which *alludes* to reality. If we take the case of the novel, Balzac or Solzhenitsyn,[4] as you refer to them, they make us *see, perceive* (but not *know*) something which *alludes* to reality.

It is essential to take the words which make up this first provisional definition literally if we are to avoid lapsing into an identification of what art gives us and what science gives us. What art makes us *see*, and therefore gives to us in the form of *'seeing'*, *'perceiving'* and *'feeling'* (which is not the form of *knowing*), is the *ideology* from which it is born, in which it bathes, from which it detaches itself as art, and to which it *alludes*. Macherey has shown this very clearly in the case of Tolstoy, by extending Lenin's analyses.

1. Translated by Ben Brewster. Daspre: a minor figure in the French Communist Party.

2. Daspre's response to an excerpt from Althusser's essay "Marxism and Humanism" published in the French journal *La Nouvelle Critique* (*New Critique*) in March 1965; the full text was published in Althusser's *For Marx* (1965; trans. 1969). Dapre's letter appeared in the April 1966 issue.

3. Reprinted as a chapter in *A Theory of Literary Production* (1966; trans. 1978) by Macherey (b. 1938), French Marxist literary theorist and student of Althusser's. V. I. Lenin (1870–1924), political theorist and leader of the Russian Revolution of 1917, who wrote several pieces on the Russian novelist Leo Tolstoy (1828–1910).

4. Aleksandr Solzhenitsyn (b. 1918), Nobel Prize–winning Russian novelist, many of whose writings focus on the repressions of Joseph Stalin's regime (1927–53). Honoré de Balzac (1799–1850), French novelist whose works faithfully depict everyday life.

Balzac and Solzhenitsyn give us a 'view' of the ideology to which their work alludes and with which it is constantly fed, a view which presupposes a *retreat*, an *internal distantiation* from the very ideology from which their novels emerged. They make us 'perceive' (but not know) in some sense *from the inside*, by an *internal distance*, the very ideology in which they are held.

These distinctions, which are not just shades of meaning but specific differences, should *in principle* enable us to resolve a number of problems.

First the problem of the 'relations' between art and science. Neither Balzac nor Solzhenitsyn gives us any *knowledge* of the world they describe, they only make us 'see', 'perceive' or 'feel' the reality of the ideology of that world. When we speak of ideology we should know that ideology slides into all human activity, that it is identical with the 'lived' experience of human existence itself: that is why the form in which we are 'made to see' ideology in great novels has as its content the 'lived' experience of individuals. This 'lived' experience is not a *given*, given by a pure 'reality', but the spontaneous 'lived experience' of ideology in its peculiar relationship to the real. This is an important comment, for it enables us to understand that art does not deal with a reality *peculiar to itself*, with a *peculiar domain* of reality in which it has a monopoly (as you tend to imply when you write that 'with art, knowledge becomes human', that the object of art is 'the individual'), whereas science deals with a *different domain* of reality (say, in opposition to 'lived experience' and the 'individual', the abstraction of structures). Ideology is also an object of science, the 'lived experience' is also an object of science, the 'individual' is also an object of science. The real difference between art and science lies in the *specific form* in which they give us the same object in quite different ways: art in the form of 'seeing' and 'perceiving' or 'feeling', science in the form of *knowledge* (in the strict sense, by concepts).

The same thing can be said in other terms. If Solzhenitsyn does 'make us see' the 'lived experience' (in the sense defined earlier) of the 'cult of personality'[5] and its effects, in no way does he give us a *knowledge* of them: this knowledge is the conceptual knowledge of the complex mechanisms which eventually produce the 'lived experience' that Solzhenitsyn's novel discusses. If I wanted to use Spinoza's[6] language again here, I could say that art makes us 'see' 'conclusions without premisses', whereas knowledge makes us penetrate into the mechanism which produces the 'conclusions' out of the 'premisses'. This is an important distinction, for it enables us to understand that a novel on the 'cult', however profound, may draw attention to its 'lived' effects, but *cannot give an understanding of it*; it may put the question of the 'cult' on the agenda, but it cannot *define the means* which will make it possible to remedy these effects.

In the same way, these few elementary principles perhaps enable us to point the direction from which we can hope for an answer to another question you pose: how is it that Balzac, despite his personal political options, 'makes us see' the 'lived experience' of capitalist society in a critical form? I do not believe one can say, as you do, that he *'was forced by the logic of his art to abandon certain of his political conceptions in his work as a novelist'*.

5. A phrase from the German philosophers MAX HORKHEIMER (1895–1973) and THEODOR ADORNO (1903–1969), who critiqued the focus in bourgeois mass culture on celebrity figures; it refers here to Stalin.

6. Benedict de Spinoza (1632–1677), Dutch philosopher.

On the contrary, we know that Balzac *never abandoned* his political positions. We know even more: his peculiar, reactionary political positions played a decisive part in the production of the content of his work. This is certainly a paradox, but it is the case, and history provides us with a number of examples to which Marx[7] drew our attention (on Balzac, I refer you to the article by R. Fayolle[8] in the special 1965 number of *Europe*). These are examples of a deformation of sense very commonly found in the dialectic of ideologies. See what Lenin says about Tolstoy (cf. Macherey's article): Tolstoy's personal ideological position is one component of the deep-lying causes of the *content* of his work. The fact that the content of the work of Balzac and Tolstoy is 'detached' from their political ideology and in some way makes us 'see' it from the *outside*, makes us 'perceive' it by a distantiation inside that ideology, *presupposes that ideology itself*. It is certainly possible to say that it is an 'effect' of *their art* as novelists that it produces this distance inside their ideology, which makes us 'perceive' it, but it is not possible to say, as you do, that art *'has its own logic'* which *'made Balzac abandon his political conceptions'*. On the contrary, *only because he retained them could he produce his work*, only because he stuck to his political ideology could he produce *in it* this internal 'distance' which gives us a critical 'view' of it.

As you see, in order to answer most of the questions posed for us by the existence and specific nature of art, we are forced to produce an adequate (scientific) *knowledge* of the processes which produce the 'aesthetic effect' of a work of art. In other words, in order to answer the question of the relationship between art and knowledge we must produce a *knowledge of art*.

You are conscious of this necessity. But you ought also to know that in this issue we still have a long way to go. The *recognition* (even the political recognition) of the existence and importance of art does not constitute *a knowledge of art*. I do not even think that it is possible to take as the beginnings of knowledge the texts you refer to, or even Joliot-Curie quoted by Marcenac.[9] To say a few words about the sentence attributed to Joliot-Curie, it contains a terminology—'aesthetic *creation*, scientific *creation*'—a terminology which is certainly quite common, but one which in my opinion must be *abandoned* and replaced by another, in order to be able to pose the problem of the knowledge of art in the proper way. I know that the artist, and the art lover, *spontaneously* express themselves in terms of 'creation', etc. It is a 'spontaneous' language, but we know from Marx and Lenin that every 'spontaneous' language is an *ideological* language, the vehicle of an ideology, here the ideology of art and of the activity productive of aesthetic effects. Like all knowledge, the knowledge of art presupposes a preliminary *rupture* with the language of *ideological spontaneity* and the constitution of a body of scientific concepts to replace it. It is essential to be conscious of the necessity for this rupture with ideology to be able to undertake the constitution of the edifice of a knowledge of art.

Here perhaps, is where I must express a sharp reservation about what you

7. KARL MARX (1818–1883), German social, political, and economic theorist.

8. Roger Fayolle (b. 1928), French literary critic.

9. Jean Marcenac [1913–1984], *Les Lettres françaises*, 1966. "I have always regretted the fact that F. Joliot-Curie never pursued the project he suggested to me at the time of Eluard's death, the project of a comparative study of poetic creation and scientific creation, which he thought might eventually prove an identity in their procedures" [translator's note]. Jean-Frédéric Joliot-Curie (1900–1958), Nobel Prize–winning French physicist and also member of the French Communist Party. Paul Éluard (1895–1952), French surrealist and lyric poet.

say. I am not perhaps speaking about exactly what you *want* or *would like* to say, but about what you *actually* do say. When you counterpose *'rigorous reflection on the concepts of Marxism'* to *'something else'*, in particular to what art gives us, I believe you are establishing a comparison which is either incomplete or illegitimate. Since art in fact provides us with *something else* other than science, there is not an opposition between them, but a difference. On the contrary, if it is a matter of *knowing* art, it is absolutely essential to begin with *'rigorous reflection on the basic concepts of Marxism'*: there is no other way. And when I say, *'it is essential to begin . . .'*, it is not enough to *say* it, it is essential to *do* it. If not, it is easy to extricate oneself with a passing acknowledgement, like *'Althusser proposes to return to a rigorous study of Marxist theory. I agree that this is indispensable. But I do not believe that it is enough.'* My response to this is the only real criticism: there is a way of declaring an exigency 'indispensable' which consists precisely of *dispensing with it*, dispensing with a careful consideration of all its implications and consequences—by the acknowledgement accorded it in order to move quickly on to 'something else'. Now I believe that the only way we can hope to reach a real knowledge of art, to go deeper into the specificity of the work of art, to know the mechanisms which produce the 'aesthetic effect', is precisely to spend a long time and pay the greatest attention to the *'basic principles of Marxism'* and not to be in a hurry to 'move on to something else', for if we move on too quickly to 'something else' we shall arrive not at a *knowledge* of art, but at an *ideology* of art: e.g., at the latent humanist ideology which may be induced by what you say about the relations between art and the 'human', and about artistic 'creation', etc.

If we must turn (and this demands slow and arduous work) to the 'basic principles of Marxism' in order to be able to pose correctly, in concepts which are not the *ideological* concepts of aesthetic spontaneity, but *scientific* concepts adequate to their object, and thus necessarily *new* concepts, it is not in order to pass art silently by or to sacrifice it to science: it is quite simply in order to *know* it, and to give it its due.

1966

From Ideology and Ideological State Apparatuses (Notes towards an Investigation)[1]

From *On the Reproduction of the Conditions of Production*

* * *

As Marx said, every child knows that a social formation which did not reproduce the conditions of production at the same time as it produced would not last a year.[2] The ultimate condition of production is therefore the reproduction of the conditions of production. This may be 'simple' (reproducing exactly the previous conditions of production) or 'on an extended scale' (expanding them). Let us ignore this last distinction for the moment.

What, then, is *the reproduction of the conditions of production?*

1. Translated by Ben Brewster, who sometimes retains the French word or phrase in parentheses.
2. Marx to Kugelmann, July 11, 1868, *Selected Correspondence* (Moscow, 1955), p. 209 [Althusser's note]. KARL MARX (1881–1883), German social, economic, and political theorist. Some of the author's notes have been edited, and some omitted.

* * *

To simplify my exposition, and assuming that every social formation arises from a dominant mode of production,[3] I can say that the process of production sets to work the existing productive forces in and under definite relations of production.

It follows that, in order to exist, every social formation must reproduce the conditions of its production at the same time as it produces, and in order to be able to produce. It must therefore reproduce:

1. the productive forces,
2. the existing relations of production.

* * *

Reproduction of Labour-Power

* * *

How is the reproduction of labour power ensured?

It is ensured by giving labour power the material means with which to reproduce itself: by wages. Wages feature in the accounting of each enterprise, but as 'wage capital', not at all as a condition of the material reproduction of labour power.

However, that is in fact how it 'works', since wages represent only that part of the value produced by the expenditure of labour power which is indispensable for its reproduction: sc. indispensable to the reconstitution of the labour power of the wage-earner (the wherewithal to pay for housing, food and clothing, in short to enable the wage-earner to present himself again at the factory gate the next day—and every further day God grants him); and we should add: indispensable for raising and educating the children in whom the proletarian reproduces himself (in n models where n = 0, 1, 2, etc. . . .) as labour power.

Remember that this quantity of value (wages) necessary for the reproduction of labour power is determined not by the needs of a 'biological' Guaranteed Minimum Wage (*Salaire Minimum Interprofessionnel Garanti*) alone, but by the needs of a historical minimum (Marx noted that English workers need beer while French proletarians need wine)—i.e. a historically variable minimum.

I should also like to point out that this minimum is doubly historical in that it is not defined by the historical needs of the working class 'recognized' by the capitalist class, but by the historical needs imposed by the proletarian class struggle (a double class struggle: against the lengthening of the working day and against the reduction of wages).

However, it is not enough to ensure for labour power the material conditions of its reproduction if it is to be reproduced as labour power. I have said that the available labour power must be 'competent', i.e. suitable to be set to work in the complex system of the process of production. The development of the productive forces and the type of unity historically constitutive of the productive forces at a given moment produce the result that the labour power

3. Now capitalism, which superseded the feudal mode of production of the medieval period, and which will be supplanted, according to Marx, by socialism.

has to be (diversely) skilled and therefore reproduced as such. Diversely: according to the requirements of the socio-technical division of labour, its different 'jobs' and 'posts'.

How is this reproduction of the (diversified) skills of labour power provided for in a capitalist regime? Here, unlike social formations characterized by slavery or serfdom, this reproduction of the skills of labour power tends (this is a tendential law) decreasingly to be provided for 'on the spot' (apprenticeship within production itself), but is achieved more and more outside production: by the capitalist education system, and by other instances and institutions.

What do children learn at school? They go varying distances in their studies, but at any rate they learn to read, to write and to add—i.e. a number of techniques, and a number of other things as well, including elements (which may be rudimentary or on the contrary thoroughgoing) of 'scientific' or 'literary culture', which are directly useful in the different jobs in production (one instruction for manual workers, another for technicians, a third for engineers, a final one for higher management, etc.). Thus they learn 'know-how'.

But besides these techniques and knowledges, and in learning them, children at school also learn the 'rules' of good behaviour, i.e. the attitude that should be observed by every agent in the division of labour, according to the job he is 'destined' for: rules of morality, civic and professional conscience, which actually means rules of respect for the socio-technical division of labour and ultimately the rules of the order established by class domination. They also learn to 'speak proper French', to 'handle' the workers correctly, i.e. actually (for the future capitalists and their servants) to 'order them about' properly, i.e. (ideally) to 'speak to them' in the right way, etc.

To put this more scientifically, I shall say that the reproduction of labour power requires not only a reproduction of its skills, but also, at the same time, a reproduction of its submission to the rules of the established order, i.e. a reproduction of submission to the ruling ideology for the workers, and a reproduction of the ability to manipulate the ruling ideology correctly for the agents of exploitation and repression, so that they, too, will provide for the domination of the ruling class 'in words'.

In other words, the school (but also other State institutions like the Church, or other apparatuses like the Army) teaches 'know-how', but in forms which ensure *subjection to the ruling ideology* or the mastery of its 'practice'. All the agents of production, exploitation and repression, not to speak of the 'professionals of ideology' (Marx), must in one way or another be 'steeped' in this ideology in order to perform their tasks 'conscientiously'—the tasks of the exploited (the proletarians), of the exploiters (the capitalists), of the exploiters' auxiliaries (the managers), or of the high priests of the ruling ideology (its 'functionaries'), etc.

The reproduction of labour power thus reveals as its *sine qua non* not only the reproduction of its 'skills' but also the reproduction of its subjection to the ruling ideology or of the 'practice' of that ideology, with the proviso that it is not enough to say 'not only but also', for it is clear that *it is in the forms and under the forms of ideological subjection that provision is made for the reproduction of the skills of labour power.*

But this is to recognize the effective presence of a new reality: *ideology*.

* * *

From *Infrastructure and Superstructure*

On a number of occasions I have insisted on the revolutionary character of the Marxist conception of the 'social whole' insofar as it is distinct from the Hegelian[4] 'totality'. I said (and this thesis only repeats famous propositions of historical materialism) that Marx conceived the structure of every society as constituted by 'levels' or 'instances' articulated by a specific determination: the *infrastructure*, or economic base (the 'unity' of the productive forces and the relations of production) and the *superstructure*, which itself contains two 'levels' or 'instances': the politico-legal (law and the State) and ideology (the different ideologies, religious, ethical, legal, political, etc.).

Besides its theoretico-didactic interest (it reveals the difference between Marx and Hegel), this representation has the following crucial theoretical advantage: it makes it possible to inscribe in the theoretical apparatus of its essential concepts what I have called their *respective indices of effectivity*. What does this mean?

It is easy to see that this representation of the structure of every society as an edifice containing a base (infrastructure) on which are erected the two 'floors' of the superstructure, is a metaphor, to be quite precise, a spatial metaphor: the metaphor of a topography (*topique*).[5] Like every metaphor, this metaphor suggests something, makes something visible. What? Precisely this: that the upper floors could not 'stay up' (in the air) alone, if they did not rest precisely on their base.

Thus the object of the metaphor of the edifice is to represent above all the 'determination in the last instance' by the economic base. The effect of this spatial metaphor is to endow the base with an index of effectivity known by the famous terms: the determination in the last instance of what happens in the upper 'floors' (of the superstructure) by what happens in the economic base.

Given this index of effectivity 'in the last instance', the 'floors' of the superstructure are clearly endowed with different indices of effectivity. What kind of indices?

It is possible to say that the floors of the superstructure are not determinant in the last instance, but that they are determined by the effectivity of the base; that if they are determinant in their own (as yet undefined) ways, this is true only insofar as they are determined by the base.

Their index of effectivity (or determination), as determined by the determination in the last instance of the base, is thought by the Marxist tradition in two ways: (1) there is a 'relative autonomy' of the superstructure with respect to the base; (2) there is a 'reciprocal action' of the superstructure on the base.

We can therefore say that the great theoretical advantage of the Marxist topography, i.e. of the spatial metaphor of the edifice (base and superstructure) is simultaneously that it reveals that questions of determination (or of

4. Of GEORG FRIEDRICH WILHELM HEGEL (1770–1831), German idealist philosopher.

5. *Topography* from the Greek *topos*: place. A topography represents in a definite space the respective *sites* occupied by several realities: thus the economic is *at the bottom* (the base), the superstructure *above it* [Althusser's note].

index of effectivity) are crucial; that it reveals that it is the base which in the last instance determines the whole edifice; and that, as a consequence, it obliges us to pose the theoretical problem of the types of 'derivatory' effectivity peculiar to the superstructure, i.e. it obliges us to think what the Marxist tradition calls conjointly the relative autonomy of the superstructure and the reciprocal action of the superstructure on the base.

* * *

I shall give a short analysis of Law, the State and Ideology *from this point of view*. And I shall reveal what happens both from the point of view of practice and production on the one hand, and from that of reproduction on the other.

From *The State*

The Marxist tradition is strict, here: in the *Communist Manifesto* and the *Eighteenth Brumaire* (and in all the later classical texts, above all in Marx's writings on the Paris Commune and Lenin's[6] on *State and Revolution*), the State is explicitly conceived as a repressive apparatus. The State is a 'machine' of repression, which enables the ruling classes (in the nineteenth century the bourgeois class and the 'class' of big landowners) to ensure their domination over the working class, thus enabling the former to subject the latter to the process of surplus-value extortion (i.e. to capitalist exploitation).

The State is thus first of all what the Marxist classics have called *the State apparatus*. This term means: not only the specialized apparatus (in the narrow sense) whose existence and necessity I have recognized in relation to the requirements of legal practice, i.e. the police, the courts, the prisons; but also the army, which (the proletariat has paid for this experience with its blood) intervenes directly as a supplementary repressive force in the last instance, when the police and its specialized auxiliary corps are 'outrun by events'; and above this ensemble, the head of State, the government and the administration.

Presented in this form, the Marxist-Leninist 'theory' of the State has its finger on the essential point, and not for one moment can there be any question of rejecting the fact that this really is the essential point. The State apparatus, which defines the State as a force of repressive execution and intervention 'in the interests of the ruling classes' in the class struggle conducted by the bourgeoisie and its allies against the proletariat, is quite certainly the State, and quite certainly defines its basic 'function'.

* * *

The Essentials of the Marxist Theory of the State

Let me first clarify one important point: the State (and its existence in its apparatus) has no meaning except as a function of *State power*. The whole

6. V. I. Lenin (1870–1924), leader of the Russian Revolution of 1917 and author of many works on revolutionary politics, including *The State and Revolution: The Marxist Theory of the State and the Tasks of the Proletariat in the Revolution* (1917). Marx's famous *Communist Manifesto* (co-written with FRIEDRICH ENGELS) dates from 1848, and his *Eighteenth Brumaire of Louis Bonaparte* from 1852. The latter, along with his *Class Stuggles in France, 1848–1850* (1850) and *The Civil War in France* (1871), deals with political struggles in France; the Paris Commune was a revolutionary government briefly established in Paris in the spring of 1871.

of the political class struggle revolves around the State. By which I mean around the possession, i.e. the seizure and conservation of State power by a certain class or by an alliance between classes or class fractions. This first clarification obliges me to distinguish between State power (conservation of State power or seizure of State power), the objective of the political class struggle on the one hand, and the State apparatus on the other.

We know that the State apparatus may survive, as is proved by bourgeois 'revolutions' in nineteenth-century France (1830, 1848), by *coups d'état* (2 December, May 1958), by collapses of the State (the fall of the Empire in 1870, of the Third Republic in 1940), or by the political rise of the petty bourgeoisie (1890–95 in France), etc., without the State apparatus being affected or modified:[7] it may survive political events which affect the possession of State power.

Even after a social revolution like that of 1917,[8] a large part of the State apparatus survived after the seizure of State power by the alliance of the proletariat and the small peasantry: Lenin repeated the fact again and again.

It is possible to describe the distinction between State power and State apparatus as part of the 'Marxist theory' of the State, explicitly present since Marx's *Eighteenth Brumaire* and *Class Struggles in France*.

To summarize the 'Marxist theory of the State' on this point, it can be said that the Marxist classics have always claimed that (1) the State is the repressive State apparatus, (2) State power and State apparatus must be distinguished, (3) the objective of the class struggle concerns State power, and in consequence the use of the State apparatus by the classes (or alliance of classes or of fractions of classes) holding State power as a function of their class objectives, and (4) the proletariat must seize State power in order to destroy the existing bourgeois State apparatus and, in a first phase, replace it with a quite different, proletarian, State apparatus, then in later phases set in motion a radical process, that of the destruction of the State (the end of State power, the end of every State apparatus).

In this perspective, therefore, what I would propose to add to the 'Marxist theory' of the State is already there in so many words. But it seems to me that even with this supplement, this theory is still in part descriptive, although it does now contain complex and differential elements whose functioning and action cannot be understood without recourse to further supplementary theoretical development.

The State Ideological Apparatuses

* * *

In order to advance the theory of the State it is indispensable to take into account not only the distinction between *State power* and *State apparatus*, but also another reality which is clearly on the side of the (repressive) State

7. After the French Revolution (1789–92) and through the 19th century, France became a modern bureaucratic state dominated by the bourgeoisie (rather than a feudal aristocracy). Althusser refers to the overthrow of the restored Bourbon monarchy in 1830; the "February Revolution" of 1848 after which Napoleon III became president and in 1852 emperor, establishing the Second Empire, which fell in 1870; and the Paris Commune and the establishment of the Third Republic, which ended with the German occupation of France in 1940. In 1958, during a political crisis caused by France's colonial war in Algeria, Charles de Gaulle (1890–1970), the leader of the French Resistance during World War II, became premier with broad powers and then president (1959–69) of the Fifth Republic.

8. That is, in Russia.

apparatus, but must not be confused with it. I shall call this reality by its concept: *the ideological State apparatuses.*[9]

What are the ideological State apparatuses (ISAs)?

They must not be confused with the (repressive) State apparatus. Remember that in Marxist theory, the State Apparatus (SA) contains: the Government, the Administration, the Army, the Police, the Courts, the Prisons, etc., which constitute what I shall in future call the Repressive State Apparatus. Repressive suggests that the State Apparatus in question 'functions by violence'—at least ultimately (since repression, e.g. administrative repression, may take non-physical forms).

I shall call Ideological State Apparatuses a certain number of realities which present themselves to the immediate observer in the form of distinct and specialized institutions. I propose an empirical list of these which will obviously have to be examined in detail, tested, corrected and reorganized. With all the reservations implied by this requirement, we can for the moment regard the following institutions as Ideological State Apparatuses (the order in which I have listed them has no particular significance):

—the religious ISA (the system of the different Churches),
—the educational ISA (the system of the different public and private 'Schools'),
—the family ISA,[1]
—the legal ISA,[2]
—the political ISA (the political system, including the different Parties),
—the trade-union ISA,
—the communications ISA (press, radio and television, etc.),
—the cultural ISA (Literature, the Arts, sports, etc.).

I have said that the ISAs must not be confused with the (Repressive) State Apparatus. What constitutes the difference?

As a first moment, it is clear that while there is *one* (Repressive) State Apparatus, there is a *plurality* of Ideological State Apparatuses. Even presupposing that it exists, the unity that constitutes this plurality of ISAs as a body is not immediately visible.

As a second moment, it is clear that whereas the—unified—(Repressive) State Apparatus belongs entirely to the *public* domain, much the larger part of the Ideological State Apparatuses (in their apparent dispersion) are part, on the contrary, of the *private* domain. Churches, Parties, Trade Unions, families, some schools, most newspapers, cultural ventures, etc., etc., are private.

We can ignore the first observation for the moment. But someone is bound to question the second, asking me by what right I regard as Ideological *State*

9. To my knowledge, Gramsci is the only one who went any distance in the road I am taking. He had the "remarkable" idea that the State could not be reduced to the (Repressive) State Apparatus, but included, as he put it, a certain number of institutions from "*civil society*": the Church, the Schools, the trade unions, etc. Unfortunately, Gramsci did not systematize his institutions, which remained in the state of acute but fragmentary notes (cf. Gramsci, *Selections from the Prison Notebooks* [International Publishers, 1971], pp. 12, 259, 260–63) [Althusser's note]. ANTONIO GRAMSCI (1891–1937), Italian Marxist philosopher.

1. The family obviously has other "functions" than that of an ISA. It intervenes in the reproduction of labour power. In different modes of production it is the unit of production and/or the unit of consumption [Althusser's note].

2. The "Law" belongs both to the (Repressive) State Apparatus and to the system of the ISAs [Althusser's note].

Apparatuses, institutions which for the most part do not possess public status, but are quite simply *private* institutions. As a conscious Marxist, Gramsci already forestalled this objection in one sentence. The distinction between the public and the private is a distinction internal to bourgeois law, and valid in the (subordinate) domains in which bourgeois law exercises its 'authority'. The domain of the State escapes it because the latter is 'above the law': the State, which is the State *of* the ruling class, is neither public nor private; on the contrary, it is the precondition for any distinction between public and private. The same thing can be said from the starting-point of our State Ideological Apparatuses. It is unimportant whether the institutions in which they are realized are 'public' or 'private'. What matters is how they function. Private institutions can perfectly well 'function' as Ideological State Apparatuses. A reasonably thorough analysis of any one of the ISAs proves it.

But now for what is essential. What distinguishes the ISAs from the (Repressive) State Apparatus is the following basic difference: the Repressive State Apparatus functions 'by violence', whereas the Ideological State Apparatuses *function 'by ideology*.'

I can clarify matters by correcting this distinction. I shall say rather that every State Apparatus, whether Repressive or Ideological, 'functions' both by violence and ideology, but with one very important distinction which makes it imperative not to confuse the Ideological State Apparatus with the (Repressive) State Apparatus.

This is the fact that the (Repressive) State Apparatus functions massively and predominantly *by repression* (including physical repression), while functioning secondarily by ideology. (There is no such thing as a purely repressive apparatus.) For example, the Army and the Police also function by ideology both to ensure their own cohesion and reproduction, and in the 'values' they propound externally.

In the same way, but inversely, it is essential to say that for their part the Ideological State Apparatuses function massively and predominantly *by ideology*, but they also function secondarily by repression, even if ultimately, but only ultimately, this is very attenuated and concealed, even symbolic. (There is no such thing as a purely ideological apparatus.) Thus Schools and Churches use suitable methods of punishment, expulsion, selection, etc., to 'discipline' not only their shepherds, but also their flocks. The same is true of the Family. . . . The same is true of the cultural IS Apparatus (censorship, among other things), etc.

Is it necessary to add that this determination of the double 'functioning' (predominantly, secondarily) by repression and by ideology, according to whether it is a matter of the (Repressive) State Apparatus or the Ideological State Apparatus, makes it clear that very subtle explicit or tacit combinations may be woven from the interplay of the (Repressive) State Apparatus and the Ideological State Apparatuses? Everyday life provides us with innumerable examples of this, but they must be studied in detail if we are to go further than this mere observation.

Nevertheless, this remark leads us towards an understanding of what constitutes the unity of the apparently disparate body of the ISAs. If the ISAs 'function' massively and predominantly by ideology, what unifies their diversity is precisely this functioning, insofar as the ideology by which they function is always in fact unified, despite its diversity and its contradictions, *beneath the ruling ideology*, which is the ideology of 'the ruling class'. Given the fact that the 'ruling class' in principle holds State power (openly or more often by means of alliances between classes or class fractions), and therefore has its disposal the (Repressive) State Apparatus, we can accept the fact that this same ruling class is active in the Ideological State Apparatuses insofar as it is ultimately the ruling ideology which is realized in the Ideological State Apparatuses, precisely in its contradictions. Of course, it is a quite different thing to act by laws and decrees in the (Repressive) State Apparatus and to 'act' through the intermediary of the ruling ideology in the Ideological State Apparatuses. We must go into the details of this difference—but it cannot mask the reality of a profound identity. To my knowledge, *no class can hold State power over a long period without at the same time exercising its hegemony over and in the State Ideological Apparatuses.* I only need one example and proof of this: Lenin's anguished concern to revolutionize the educational Ideological State Apparatus (among others), simply to make it possible for the Soviet proletariat, who had seized State power, to secure the future of the dictatorship of the proletariat and the transition of socialism.

This last comment puts us in a position to understand that the Ideological State Apparatuses may be not only the *stake*, but also the *site* of class struggle, and often of bitter forms of class struggle. The class (or class alliance) in power cannot lay down the law in the ISAs as easily as it can in the (repressive) State apparatus, not only because the former ruling classes are able to retain strong positions there for a long time, but also because the resistance of the exploited classes is able to find means and occasions to express itself there, either by the utilization of their contradictions, or by conquering combat positions in them in struggle.[3]

* * *

From *On the Reproduction of the Relations of Production*

I can now answer the central question which I have left in suspense for many long pages: *how is the reproduction of the relations of production secured?*

In the topographical language (Infrastructure, Superstructure), I can say: for the most part, it is secured by the legal-political and ideological superstructure.

But as I have argued that it is essential to go beyond this still descriptive language, I shall say: for the most part, it is secured by the exercise of State

3. What I have said in these few brief words about the class struggle in the ISAs is obviously far from exhausting the question of the class struggle.

To approach this question, two principles must be borne in mind:

The first principle was formulated by Marx in the preface to *A Contribution to the Critique of Political Economy* [1859]: "In considering such transformations [a social revolution] a distinction should always be made between the material transformation of the economic conditions of production, which can be determined with the precision of natural science, and the legal, political, religious, aesthetic or philosophic—in short, ideological forms in which men become conscious of this conflict and fight it out." The class struggle is thus expressed and exercised in ideological forms, thus also in the ideological forms of the ISAs. But the class struggle *extends far beyond* these forms, and it is because it extends beyond them that the struggle of the exploited classes may also be exercised in the forms of the ISAs, and thus turn the weapon of ideology against the classes in power.

This is by virtue of the *second principle*: the class struggle extends beyond the ISAs because it is rooted elsewhere than in ideology, in the Infrastructure, in the relations of production, which are relations of exploitation and constitute the base for class relations [Althusser's note].

power in the State Apparatuses, on the one hand the (Repressive) State Apparatus, on the other the Ideological State Apparatuses.

What I have just said must also be taken into account, and it can be assembled in the form of the following three features:

1. All the State Apparatuses function both by repression and by ideology, with the difference that the (Repressive) State Apparatus functions massively and predominantly by repression, whereas the Ideological State Apparatuses function massively and predominantly by ideology.

2. Whereas the (Repressive) State Apparatus constitutes an organized whole whose different parts are centralized beneath a commanding unity, that of the politics of class struggle applied by the political representatives of the ruling classes in possession of State power, the Ideological State Apparatuses are multiple, distinct, 'relatively autonomous' and capable of providing an objective field to contradictions which express, in forms which may be limited or extreme, the effects of the clashes between the capitalist class struggle and the proletarian class struggle, as well as their subordinate forms.

3. Whereas the unity of the (Repressive) State Apparatus is secured by its unified and centralized organization under the leadership of the representatives of the classes in power executing the politics of the class struggle of the classes in power, the unity of the different Ideological State Apparatuses is secured, usually in contradictory forms, by the ruling ideology, the ideology of the ruling class.

Taking these features into account, it is possible to represent the reproduction of the relations of production in the following way, according to a kind of 'division of labour'.

The role of the repressive State apparatus, insofar as it is a repressive apparatus, consists essentially in securing by force (physical or otherwise) the political conditions of the reproduction of relations of production which are in the last resort *relations of exploitation*. Not only does the State apparatus contribute generously to its own reproduction (the capitalist State contains political dynasties, military dynasties, etc.), but also and above all, the State apparatus secures by repression (from the most brutal physical force, via mere administrative commands and interdictions, to open and tacit censorship) the political conditions for the action of the Ideological State Apparatuses.

In fact, it is the latter which largely secure the reproduction specifically of the relations of production, behind a 'shield' provided by the repressive State apparatus. It is here that the role of the ruling ideology is heavily concentrated, the ideology of the ruling class, which holds State power. It is the intermediation of the ruling ideology that ensures a (sometimes teeth-gritting) 'harmony' between the repressive State apparatus and the Ideological State Apparatuses, and between the different State Ideological Apparatuses.

We are thus led to envisage the following hypothesis, as a function precisely of the diversity of ideological State Apparatuses in their single, because shared, role of the reproduction of the relations of production.

Indeed we have listed a relatively large number of ideological State apparatuses in contemporary capitalist social formations: the educational apparatus, the religious apparatus, the family apparatus, the political apparatus, the trade-union apparatus, the communications apparatus, the 'cultural' apparatus, etc.

But in the social formations of that mode of production characterized by 'serfdom' (usually called the feudal mode of production), we observe that although there is a single repressive State apparatus which, since the earliest known Ancient States, let alone the Absolute Monarchies, has been formally very similar to the one we know today, the number of Ideological State Apparatuses is smaller and their individual types are different. For example, we observe that during the Middle Ages, the Church (the religious ideological State apparatus) accumulated a number of functions which have today devolved on to several distinct ideological State apparatuses, new ones in relation to the past I am invoking, in particular educational and cultural functions. Alongside the Church there was the family Ideological State Apparatus, which played a considerable part, incommensurable with its role in capitalist social formations. Despite appearances, the Church and the Family were not the only Ideological State Apparatuses. There was also a political Ideological State Apparatus (the Estates General, the *Parlement*, the different political factions and Leagues, the ancestors of the modern political parties, and the whole political system of the free Communes and then of the *Villes*[4]). There was also a powerful 'proto-trade-union' Ideological State Apparatus, if I may venture such an anachronistic term (the powerful merchants' and bankers' guilds and the journeymen's associations, etc.). Publishing and Communications, even, saw an indisputable development, as did the theatre; initially both were integral parts of the Church, then they became more and more independent of it.

In the pre-capitalist historical period which I have examined extremely broadly, it is absolutely clear that *there was one dominant Ideological State Apparatus, the Church*, which concentrated within it not only religious functions, but also educational ones, and a large proportion of the functions of communications and 'culture'. It is no accident that all ideological struggle, from the sixteenth to the eighteenth century, starting with the first shocks of the Reformation, was *concentrated* in an anti-clerical and anti-religious struggle; rather this is a function precisely of the dominant position of the religious ideological State apparatus.

The foremost objective and achievement of the French Revolution was not just to transfer State power from the feudal aristocracy to the merchant-capitalist bourgeoisie, to break part of the former repressive State apparatus and replace it with a new one (e.g., the national popular Army)—but also to attack the number-one Ideological State Apparatus: the Church. Hence the civil constitution of the clergy, the confiscation of ecclesiastical wealth, and the creation of new ideological State apparatuses to replace the religious ideological State apparatus in its dominant role.

* * *

I believe that the ideological State apparatus which has been installed in the *dominant* position in mature capitalist social formations as a result of a violent political and ideological class struggle against the old dominant ideological State apparatus, is the *educational ideological apparatus*.

4. The *Villes*: a system instituted under Napoleon in 1799 that divided the country into districts administered by a central government. The Estates General: the three groups holding distinct political powers in France: the clergy, nobility, and commoners. When convened by Louis XVI to stave off social unrest in 1789, they instead created their own assembly, the *Parlement*, which was overthrown in 1792 during the French Revolution and replaced briefly by a radical commune.

* * *

Why is the educational apparatus in fact the dominant ideological State apparatus in capitalist social formations, and how does it function?

For the moment it must suffice to say:

1. All ideological State apparatuses, whatever they are, contribute to the same result: the reproduction of the relations of production, i.e. of capitalist relations of exploitation.

2. Each of them contributes towards this single result in the way proper to it. The political apparatus by subjecting individuals to the political State ideology, the 'indirect' (parliamentary) or 'direct' (plebiscitary or fascist) 'democratic' ideology. The communications apparatus by cramming every 'citizen' with daily doses of nationalism, chauvinism, liberalism, moralism, etc., by means of the press, the radio and television. The same goes for the cultural apparatus (the role of sport in chauvinism is of the first importance), etc. The religious apparatus by recalling in sermons and the other great ceremonies of Birth, Marriage and Death, that man is only ashes, unless he loves his neighbour to the extent of turning the other cheek to whoever strikes first. The family apparatus . . . but there is no need to go on.

3. This concert is dominated by a single score, occasionally disturbed by contradictions (those of the remnants of former ruling classes, those of the proletarians and their organizations): the score of the Ideology of the current ruling class which integrates into its music the great themes of the Humanism of the Great Forefathers,[5] who produced the Greek Miracle even before Christianity, and afterwards the Glory of Rome, the Eternal City, and the themes of Interest, particular and general, etc. nationalism, moralism and economism.

4. Nevertheless, in this concert, one ideological State apparatus certainly has the dominant role, although hardly anyone lends an ear to its music: it is so silent! This is the School.

It takes children from every class at infant-school age, and then for years, the years in which the child is most 'vulnerable', squeezed between the family State apparatus and the educational State apparatus, it drums into them, whether it uses new or old methods, a certain amount of 'know-how' wrapped in the ruling ideology (French, arithmetic, natural history, the sciences, literature) or simply the ruling ideology in its pure state (ethics, civic instruction, philosophy). Somewhere around the age of sixteen, a huge mass of children are ejected 'into production': these are the workers or small peasants. Another portion of scholastically adapted youth carries on: and, for better or worse, it goes somewhat further, until it falls by the wayside and fills the posts of small and middle technicians, white-collar workers, small and middle executives, petty bourgeois of all kinds. A last portion reaches the summit, either to fall into intellectual semi-employment, or to provide, as well as the 'intellectuals of the collective labourer', the agents of exploitation (capitalists, managers), the agents of repression (soldiers, policemen, politicians, administrators, etc.) and the professional ideologists (priests of all sorts, most of whom are convinced 'laymen').

5. That is, privileging the concept of "Man" and idealizing the achievements of the ancient Greeks as well as Christianity and the Catholic Church.

Each mass ejected *en route* is practically provided with the ideology which suits the role it has to fulfil in class society: the role of the exploited (with a 'highly-developed' 'professional', 'ethical', 'civic', 'national' and a-political consciousness); the role of the agent of exploitation (ability to give the workers orders and speak to them: 'human relations'), of the agent of repression (ability to give orders and enforce obedience 'without discussion', or ability to manipulate the demagogy of a political leader's rhetoric), or of the professional ideologist (ability to treat consciousnesses with the respect, i.e. with the contempt, blackmail, and demagogy they deserve, adapted to the accents of Morality, of Virtue, of 'Transcendence', of the Nation, of France's World Role, etc.).

Of course, many of these contrasting Virtues (modesty, resignation, submissiveness on the one hand, cynicism, contempt, arrogance, confidence, self-importance, even smooth talk and cunning on the other) are also taught in the Family, in the Church, in the Army, in Good Books, in films and even in the football[6] stadium. But no other ideological State apparatus has the obligatory (and not least, free) audience of the totality of the children in the capitalist social formation, eight hours a day for five or six days out of seven.

But it is by an apprenticeship in a variety of know-how wrapped up in the massive inculcation of the ideology of the ruling class that *the relations of production* in a capitalist social formation, i.e. the relations of exploited to exploiters and exploiters to exploited, are largely reproduced. The mechanisms which produce this vital result for the capitalist regime are naturally covered up and concealed by a universally reigning ideology of the School, universally reigning because it is one of the essential forms of the ruling bourgeois ideology: an ideology which represents the School as a neutral environment purged of ideology (because it is . . . lay), where teachers respectful of the 'conscience' and 'freedom' of the children who are entrusted to them (in complete confidence) by their 'parents' (who are free, too, i.e. the owners of their children) open up for them the path to the freedom, morality and responsibility of adults by their own example, by knowledge, literature and their 'liberating' virtues.

I ask the pardon of those teachers who, in dreadful conditions, attempt to turn the few weapons they can find in the history and learning they 'teach' against the ideology, the system and the practices in which they are trapped. They are a kind of hero. But they are rare and how many (the majority) do not even begin to suspect the 'work' the system (which is bigger than they are and crushes them) forces them to do, or worse, put all their heart and ingenuity into performing it with the most advanced awareness (the famous new methods!). So little do they suspect it that their own devotion contributes to the maintenance and nourishment of this ideological representation of the School, which makes the School today as 'natural', indispensable-useful and even beneficial for our contemporaries as the Church was 'natural', indispensable and generous for our ancestors a few centuries ago.

In fact, the Church has been replaced today *in its role as the dominant Ideological State Apparatus* by the School. It is coupled with the Family just as the Church was once coupled with the Family. We can now claim that the unprecedentedly deep crisis which is now shaking the education system

6. Soccer.

of so many States across the globe, often in conjunction with a crisis (already proclaimed in the *Communist Manifesto*) shaking the family system, takes on a political meaning, given that the School (and the School-Family couple) constitutes the dominant Ideological State Apparatus, the Apparatus playing a determinant part in the reproduction of the relations of production of a mode of production threatened in its existence by the world class struggle.

From *On Ideology*

When I put forward the concept of an Ideological State Apparatus, when I said that the ISAs 'function by ideology', I invoked a reality which needs a little discussion: ideology.

* * *

Ideology Has No History

One word first of all to expound the reason in principle which seems to me to found, or at least to justify, the project of a theory of ideology *in general*, and not a theory of particular ideolog*ies*, which, whatever their form (religious, ethical, legal, political), always express *class positions*.

It is quite obvious that it is necessary to proceed towards a theory of ideolog*ies* in the two respects I have just suggested. It will then be clear that a theory of ideolog*ies* depends in the last resort on the history of social formations, and thus of the modes of production combined in social formations, and of the class struggles which develop in them. In this sense it is clear that there can be no question of a theory of ideolog*ies in general*, since ideolog*ies* (defined in the double respect suggested above: regional and class) have a history, whose determination in the last instance is clearly situated outside ideologies alone, although it involves them.

On the contrary, if I am able to put forward the project of a theory of ideology *in general*, and if this theory really is one of the elements on which theories of ideolog*ies* depend, that entails an apparently paradoxical proposition which I shall express in the following terms: *ideology has no history*.

As we know, this formulation appears in so many words in a passage from *The German Ideology*.[7] Marx utters it with respect to metaphysics, which, he says, has no more history than ethics (meaning also the other forms of ideology).

In *The German Ideology*, this formulation appears in a plainly positivist[8] context. Ideology is conceived as a pure illusion, a pure dream, i.e. as nothingness. All its reality is external to it. Ideology is thus thought as an imaginary construction whose status is exactly like the theoretical status of the dream among writers before Freud.[9] For these writers, the dream was

7. "The phantoms formed in the human brain are also, necessarily, sublimates of their material life-processes, which is empirically verifiable and bound to material premises. Morality, religion, metaphysics, all the rest of ideology and their corresponding forms of consciousness, thus no longer retain the semblance of independence. They have no history, no development; but men, developing their material production and their material intercourse, alter, along with their real existence, their thinking and the products of their thinking." *The German Ideology* (1846), in *The Marx-Engels Reader*, ed. Robert C. Tucker, 2d ed. (New York: Norton, 1978), pp. 154–55.

8. Taking knowledge and meaning to derive solely from what can be empirically observed.

9. Sigmund Freud (1856–1939), Austrian founder of psychoanalysis; *The Interpretation of Dreams* (1900) was his seminal work.

the purely imaginary, i.e. null, result of 'day's residues', presented in an arbitrary arrangement and order, sometimes even 'inverted', in other words, in 'disorder'. For them, the dream was the imaginary, it was empty, null and arbitrarily 'stuck together' (*bricolé*), once the eyes had closed, from the residues of the only full and positive reality, the reality of the day. This is exactly the status of philosophy and ideology (since in this book philosophy is ideology *par excellence*) in *The German Ideology*.

Ideology, then, is for Marx an imaginary assemblage (*bricolage*),[1] a pure dream, empty and vain, constituted by the 'day's residues' from the only full and positive reality, that of the concrete history of concrete material individuals materially producing their existence. It is on this basis that ideology has no history in *The German Ideology*, since its history is outside it, where the only existing history is the history of concrete individuals, etc. In *The German Ideology*, the thesis that ideology has no history is therefore a purely negative thesis, since it means both:

1. ideology is nothing insofar as it is a pure dream (manufactured by who knows what power: if not by the alienation of the division of labour, but that, too, is a *negative* determination);
2. ideology has no history, which emphatically does not mean that there is no history in it (on the contrary, for it is merely the pale, [illegible]ty and inverted reflection of real history) but that it has no history *of* [illegible]

Now, while the thesis I wish to defend formally speaking adopt[illegible]s of *The German Ideology* ('ideology has no history'), it is radically [illegible] from the positivist and historicist thesis of *The German Ideology*.

For on the one hand, I think it is possible to hold that ideologies *have* [illegible] *history of their own* (although it is determined in the last instance by the class struggle); and on the other, I think it is possible to hold that ideology *in general has no history*, not in a negative sense (its history is external to it), but in an absolutely positive sense.

This sense is a positive one if it is true that the peculiarity of ideology is that it is endowed with a structure and a functioning such as to make it a non-historical reality, i.e. an *omni-historical* reality, in the sense in which that structure and functioning are immutable, present in the same form throughout what we can call history, in the sense in which the *Communist Manifesto* defines history as the history of class struggles, i.e. the history of class societies.

To give a theoretical reference-point here, I might say that, to return to our example of the dream, in its Freudian conception this time, our proposition: ideology has no history, can and must (and in a way which has absolutely nothing arbitrary about it, but, quite the reverse, is theoretically necessary, for there is an organic link between the two propositions) be related directly to Freud's proposition that the *unconscious is eternal*, i.e. that it has no history.

If eternal means, not transcendent to all (temporal) history, but omnipresent, trans-historical and therefore immutable in form throughout the extent of history, I shall adopt Freud's expression word for word, and write *ideology is eternal*, exactly like the unconscious. And I add that I find this

1. A term associated with the French anthropologist CLAUDE LÉVI-STRAUSS (b. 1908), who employed it to describe the patchwork of tools used in his structuralist methodology.

comparison theoretically justified by the fact that the eternity of the unconscious is not unrelated to the eternity of ideology in general.

That is why I believe I am justified, hypothetically at least, in proposing a theory of ideology *in general*, in the sense that Freud presented a theory of the unconscious *in general*.

To simplify the phrase, it is convenient, taking into account what has been said about ideologies, to use the plain term ideology to designate ideology in general, which I have just said has no history, or, what comes to the same thing, is eternal, i.e. omnipresent in its immutable form throughout history (= the history of social formations containing social classes). For the moment I shall restrict myself to 'class societies' and their history.

Ideology Is a 'Representation' of the Imaginary Relationship of Individuals to Their Real Conditions of Existence

In order to approach my central thesis on the structure and functioning of ideology, I shall first present two theses, one negative, the other positive. The first concerns the object which is 'represented' in the imaginary form of ideology, the second concerns the materiality of ideology.

THESIS I: Ideology represents the imaginary relationship of individuals to their real conditions of existence.

We commonly call religious ideology, ethical ideology, legal ideology, political ideology, etc., so many 'world outlooks'. Of course, assuming that we do not live one of these ideologies as the truth (e.g. 'believe' in God, Duty, Justice, etc. . . .), we admit that the ideology we are discussing from a critical point of view, examining it as the ethnologist examines the myths of a 'primitive society', that these 'world outlooks' are largely imaginary, i.e. do not 'correspond to reality.'

However, while admitting that they do not correspond to reality, i.e. that they constitute an illusion, we admit that they do make allusion to reality, and that they need only be 'interpreted' to discover the reality of the world behind their imaginary representation of that world (ideology = *illusion/allusion*).

There are different types of interpretation, the most famous of which are the *mechanistic* type, current in the eighteenth century (God is the imaginary representation of the real King), and the *'hermeneutic'* interpretation, inaugurated by the earliest Church Fathers, and revived by Feuerbach and the theologico-philosophical school which descends from him, e.g. the theologian Barth[2] (to Feuerbach, for example, God is the essence of real Man). The essential point is that on condition that we interpret the imaginary transposition (and inversion) of ideology we arrive at the conclusion that in ideology 'men represent their real conditions of existence to themselves in an imaginary form'.

Unfortunately, this interpretation leaves one small problem unsettled: why do men 'need' this imaginary transposition of their real conditions of existence in order to 'represent to themselves' their real conditions of existence?

The first answer (that of the eighteenth century) proposes a simple solu-

2. Karl Barth (1886–1968), German theologian; Ludwig Feuerbach (1804–1872), German philosopher to whom Marx responded in "Theses on Feuerbach" (1845), *The German Ideology*, and *The Jewish Question* (1843).

tion: Priests or Despots are responsible. They 'forged' the Beautiful Lies so that, in the belief that they were obeying God, men would in fact obey the Priests and Despots, who are usually in alliance in their imposture, the Priests acting in the interests of the Despots or *vice versa*, according to the political positions of the 'theoreticians' concerned. There is therefore a cause for the imaginary transposition of the real conditions of existence: that cause is the existence of a small number of cynical men who base their domination and exploitation of the 'people' on a falsified representation of the world which they have imagined in order to enslave other minds by dominating their imaginations.

The second answer (that of Feuerbach, taken over word for word by Marx in his Early Works) is more 'profound', i.e. just as false. It, too, seeks and finds a cause for the imaginary transposition and distortion of men's real conditions of existence, in short, for the alienation in the imaginary of the representation of men's conditions of existence. This cause is no longer Priests or Despots, nor their active imagination and the passive imagination of their victims. This cause is the material alienation which reigns in the conditions of existence of men themselves. This is how, in *The Jewish Question* and elsewhere, Marx defends the Feuerbachian idea that men make themselves an alienated (= imaginary) representation of their conditions of existence because these conditions of existence are themselves alienating (in the *1844 Manuscripts*:[3] because these conditions are dominated by the essence of alienated society—*'alienated labour'*).

All these interpretations thus take literally the thesis which they presuppose, and on which they depend, i.e. that what is reflected in the imaginary representation of the world found in an ideology is the conditions of existence of men, i.e. their real world.

Now I can return to a thesis which I have already advanced: it is not their real conditions of existence, their real world, that 'men' 'represent to themselves' in ideology, but above all it is their relation to those conditions of existence which is represented to them there. It is this relation which is at the centre of every ideological, i.e. imaginary, representation of the real world. It is this relation that contains the 'cause' which has to explain the imaginary distortion of the ideological representation of the real world. Or rather, to leave aside the language of causality it is necessary to advance the thesis that it is the *imaginary nature of this relation* which underlies all the imaginary distortion that we can observe (if we do not live in its truth) in all ideology.

To speak in a Marxist language, if it is true that the representation of the real conditions of existence of the individuals occupying the posts of agents of production, exploitation, repression, ideologization and scientific practice, does in the last analysis arise from the relations of production, and from relations deriving from the relations of production, we can say the following: all ideology represents in its necessarily imaginary distortion not the existing relations of production (and the other relations that derive from them), but above all the (imaginary) relationship of individuals to the relations of production and the relations that derive from them. What is represented in ideology is therefore not the system of the real relations which govern the

3. Marx's *Economic and Philosophical Manuscripts of 1844* was not published until 1932.

existence of individuals, but the imaginary relation of those individuals to the real relations in which they live.

If this is the case, the question of the 'cause' of the imaginary distortion of the real relations in ideology disappears and must be replaced by a different question: why is the representation given to individuals of their (individual) relation to the social relations which govern their conditions of existence and their collective and individual life necessarily an imaginary relation? And what is the nature of this imaginariness? Posed in this way, the question explodes the solution by a 'clique'[4], by a group of individuals (Priests or Despots) who are the authors of the great ideological mystification, just as it explodes the solution by the alienated character of the real world. We shall see why later in my exposition. For the moment I shall go no further.

THESIS II: Ideology has a material existence.

I have already touched on this thesis by saying that the 'ideas' or 'representations', etc., which seem to make up ideology do not have an ideal (*idéale* or *idéelle*)[5] or spiritual existence, but a material existence. I even suggested that the ideal (*idéale, idéelle*) and spiritual existence of 'ideas' arises exclusively in an ideology of the 'idea' and of ideology, and let me add, in an ideology of what seems to have 'founded' this conception since the emergence of the sciences, i.e. what the practicians of the sciences represent to themselves in their spontaneous ideology as 'ideas', true or false. Of course, presented in affirmative form, this thesis is unproven. I simply ask that the reader be favourably disposed towards it, say, in the name of materialism. A long series of arguments would be necessary to prove it.

This hypothetical thesis of the not spiritual but material existence of 'ideas' or other 'representations' is indeed necessary if we are to advance in our analysis of the nature of ideology. Or rather, it is merely useful to us in order the better to reveal what every at all serious analysis of any ideology will immediately and empirically show to every observer, however critical.

While discussing the ideological State apparatuses and their practices, I said that each of them was the realization of an ideology (the unity of these different regional ideologies—religious, ethical, legal, political, aesthetic, etc.—being assured by their subjection to the ruling ideology). I now return to this thesis: an ideology always exists in an apparatus, and its practice, or practices. This existence is material.

Of course, the material existence of the ideology in an apparatus and its practices does not have the same modality as the material existence of a paving-stone or a rifle. But, at the risk of being taken for a Neo-Aristotelian (NB Marx had a very high regard for Aristotle),[6] I shall say that 'matter is discussed in many senses', or rather that it exists in different modalities, all rooted in the last instance in 'physical' matter.

Having said this, let me move straight on and see what happens to the 'individuals' who live in ideology, i.e. in a determinate (religious, ethical, etc.) representation of the world whose imaginary distortion depends on their imaginary relation to their conditions of existence, in other words, in the last

4. I use this very modern term deliberately. For even in Communist circles, unfortunately, it is a commonplace to 'explain' some political deviation by the action of a "clique" [Althusser's note].

5. Though the words sound similar in French, *idéale* means "ideal" and *idéelle* means "ideational" or "conceptual."

6. The Greek philosopher ARISTOTLE (384–322 B.C.E.) emphasized the direct observation of nature and insisted on rigorous scientific procedure.

instance, to the relations of production and to class relations (ideology = an imaginary relation to real relations). I shall say that this imaginary relation is itself endowed with a material existence.

Now I observe the following.

An individual believes in God, or Duty, or Justice, etc. This belief derives (for everyone, i.e. for all those who live in an ideological representation of ideology, which reduces ideology to ideas endowed by definition with a spiritual existence) from the ideas of the individual concerned, i.e. from him as a subject with a consciousness which contains the ideas of his belief. In this way, i.e. by means of the absolutely ideological 'conceptual' device (*dispositif*) thus set up (a subject endowed with a consciousness in which he freely forms or freely recognizes ideas in which he believes), the (material) attitude of the subject concerned naturally follows.

The individual in question behaves in such and such a way, adopts such and such a practical attitude, and, what is more, participates in certain regular practices which are those of the ideological apparatus on which 'depend' the ideas which he has in all consciousness freely chosen as a subject. If he believes in God, he goes to Church to attend Mass, kneels, prays, confesses, does penance (once it was material in the ordinary sense of the term) and naturally repents and so on. If he believes in Duty, he will have the corresponding attitudes, inscribed in ritual practices 'according to the correct principles'. If he believes in Justice, he will submit unconditionally to the rules of the Law, and may even protest when they are violated, sign petitions, take part in a demonstration, etc.

Throughout this schema we observe that the ideological representation of ideology is itself forced to recognize that every 'subject' endowed with a 'consciousness' and believing in the 'ideas' that his 'consciousness' inspires in him and freely accepts, must '*act* according to his ideas', must therefore inscribe his own ideas as a free subject in the actions of his material practice. If he does not do so, 'that is wicked'.

Indeed, if he does not do what he ought to do as a function of what he believes, it is because he does something else, which, still as a function of the same idealist scheme, implies that he has other ideas in his head as well as those he proclaims, and that he acts according to these other ideas, as a man who is either 'inconsistent' ('no one is willingly evil') or cynical, or perverse.

In every case, the ideology of ideology thus recognizes, despite its imaginary distortion, that the 'ideas' of a human subject exist in his actions, or ought to exist in his actions, and if that is not the case, it lends him other ideas corresponding to the actions (however perverse) that he does perform. This ideology talks of actions: I shall talk of actions inserted into *practices*. *And* I shall point out that these practices are governed by the *rituals* in which these practices are inscribed, within the *material existence of an ideological apparatus*, be it only a small part of that apparatus: a small mass in a small church, a funeral, a minor match at a sports' club, a school day, a political party meeting, etc.

Besides, we are indebted to Pascal's[7] defensive 'dialectic' for the wonderful

7. Blaise Pascal (1623–1662), French theologian and mathematician; he was influenced by the religious thinking of Bishop Cornelius Jansen (1585–1638), whose posthumously published writings fostered a movement condemned as heretical by the Roman Catholic Church.

formula which will enable us to invert the order of the notional schema of ideology. Pascal says more or less: 'Kneel down, move your lips in prayer, and you will believe.' He thus scandalously inverts the order of things, bringing, like Christ, not peace but strife, and in addition something hardly Christian (for woe to him who brings scandal into the world!)—scandal itself. A fortunate scandal which makes him stick with Jansenist defiance to a language that directly names the reality.

I will be allowed to leave Pascal to the arguments of his ideological struggle with the religious ideological State apparatus of his day. And I shall be expected to use a more directly Marxist vocabulary, if that is possible, for we are advancing in still poorly explored domains.

I shall therefore say that, where only a single subject (such and such an individual) is concerned, the existence of the ideas of his belief is material in that *his ideas are his material actions inserted into material practices governed by material rituals which are themselves defined by the material ideological apparatus from which derive the ideas of that subject.* Naturally, the four inscriptions of the adjective 'material' in my proposition must be affected by different modalities: the materialities of a displacement for going to mass, of kneeling down, of the gesture of the sign of the cross, or of the *mea culpa*, of a sentence, of a prayer, of an act of contrition, of a penitence, of a gaze, of a hand-shake, of an external verbal discourse or an 'internal' verbal discourse (consciousness), are not one and the same materiality. I shall leave on one side the problem of a theory of the differences between the modalities of materiality.

It remains that in this inverted presentation of things, we are not dealing with an 'inversion' at all, since it is clear that certain notions have purely and simply disappeared from our presentation, whereas others on the contrary survive, and new terms appear.

Disappeared: the term *ideas*.

Survive: the terms *subject, consciousness, belief, actions*.

Appear: the terms *practices, rituals, ideological apparatus*.

* * *

But this very presentation reveals that we have retained the following notions: subject, consciousness, belief, actions. From this series I shall immediately extract the decisive central term on which everything else depends: the notion of the *subject*.

And I shall immediately set down two conjoint theses:

1. there is no practice except by and in an ideology;
2. there is no ideology except by the subject and for subjects.

I can now come to my central thesis.

Ideology Interpellates Individuals as Subjects

This thesis is simply a matter of making my last proposition explicit: there is no ideology except by the subject and for subjects. Meaning, there is no ideology except for concrete subjects, and this destination for ideology is only made possible by the subject: meaning, *by the category of the subject* and its functioning.

By this I mean that, even if it only appears under this name (the subject) with the rise of bourgeois ideology, above all with the rise of legal ideology,[8] the category of the subject (which may function under other names: e.g., as the soul in Plato,[9] as God, etc.) is the constitutive category of all ideology, whatever its determination (regional or class) and whatever its historical date—since ideology has no history.

I say: the category of the subject is constitutive of all ideology, but at the same time and immediately I add that *the category of the subject is only constitutive of all ideology insofar as all ideology has the function (which defines it) of 'constituting' concrete individuals as subjects*. In the interaction of this double constitution exists the functioning of all ideology, ideology being nothing but its functioning in the material forms of existence of that functioning.

* * *

At work in this reaction is the ideological *recognition* function which is one of the two functions of ideology as such (its inverse being the function of *misrecognition—méconnaissance*).

To take a highly 'concrete' example, we all have friends who, when they knock on our door and we ask, through the door, the question 'Who's there?', answer (since 'it's obvious') 'It's me'. And we recognize that 'it is him', or 'her'. We open the door, and 'it's true, it really was she who was there'. To take another example, when we recognize somebody of our (previous) acquaintance (*(re)-connaissance*) in the street, we show him that we have recognized him (and have recognized that he has recognized us) by saying to him 'Hello, my friend', and shaking his hand (a material ritual practice of ideological recognition in everyday life—in France, at least; elsewhere, there are other rituals).

In this preliminary remark and these concrete illustrations, I only wish to point out that you and I are *always already* subjects, and as such constantly practice the rituals of ideological recognition, which guarantee for us that we are indeed concrete, individual, distinguishable and (naturally) irreplaceable subjects. The writing I am currently executing and the reading you are currently[1] performing are also in this respect rituals of ideological recognition, including the 'obviousness' with which the 'truth' or 'error' of my reflections may impose itself on you.

But to recognize that we are subjects and that we function in the practical rituals of the most elementary everyday life (the hand-shake, the fact of calling you by your name, the fact of knowing, even if I do not know what it is, that you 'have' a name of your own, which means that you are recognized as a unique subject, etc.)—this recognition only gives us the 'consciousness' of our incessant (eternal) practice of ideological recognition—its consciousness, i.e. its *recognition*—but in no sense does it give us the (scientific) *knowledge* of the mechanism of this recognition. Now it is this knowledge that we have to reach, if you will, while speaking in ideology, and from within

8. Which borrowed the legal category of "subject in law" to make an ideological notion: man is by nature a subject [Althusser's note].
9. In discussing the structure of the ideal city in his *Republic*, the Greek philosopher PLATO (ca. 427—ca. 347 B.C.E.) analyzed the structure of the inhabitants' souls.

1. NB: this double "currently" is one more proof of the fact that ideology is "eternal," since these two "currentlys" are separated by an indefinite interval; I am writing these lines on April 6, 1969, you may read them at any subsequent time [Althusser's note].

ideology we have to outline a discourse which tries to break with ideology, in order to dare to be the beginning of a scientific (i.e. subjectless) discourse on ideology.

Thus in order to represent why the category of the 'subject' is constitutive of ideology, which only exists by constituting concrete subjects as subjects, I shall employ a special mode of exposition: 'concrete' enough to be recognized, but abstract enough to be thinkable and thought, giving rise to a knowledge.

As a first formulation I shall say: *all ideology hails or interpellates concrete individuals as concrete subjects*, by the functioning of the category of the subject.

This is a proposition which entails that we distinguish for the moment between concrete individuals on the one hand and concrete subjects on the other, although at this level concrete subjects only exist insofar as they are supported by a concrete individual.

I shall then suggest that ideology 'acts' or 'functions' in such a way that it 'recruits' subjects among the individuals (it recruits them all), or 'transforms' the individuals into subjects (it transforms them all) by that very precise operation which I have called *interpellation* or hailing, and which can be imagined along the lines of the most commonplace everyday police (or other) hailing: 'Hey, you there!'[2]

Assuming that the theoretical scene I have imagined takes place in the street, the hailed individual will turn round. By this mere one-hundred-and-eighty-degree physical conversion, he becomes a *subject*. Why? Because he has recognized that the hail was 'really' addressed to him, and that 'it was *really him* who was hailed' (and not someone else). Experience shows that the practical telecommunication of hailings is such that they hardly ever miss their man: verbal call or whistle, the one hailed always recognizes that it is really him who is being hailed. And yet it is a strange phenomenon, and one which cannot be explained solely by 'guilt feelings', despite the large numbers who 'have something on their consciences'.

Naturally for the convenience and clarity of my little theoretical theatre I have had to present things in the form of a sequence, with a before and an after, and thus in the form of a temporal succession. There are individuals walking along. Somewhere (usually behind them) the hail rings out: 'Hey, you there!' One individual (nine times out of ten it is the right one) turns round, believing/suspecting/knowing that it is for him, i.e. recognizing that 'it really is he' who is meant by the hailing. But in reality these things happen without any succession. The existence of ideology and the hailing or interpellation of individuals as subjects are one and the same thing.

* * *

Thus ideology hails or interpellates individuals as subjects. As ideology is eternal, I must now suppress the temporal form in which I have presented the functioning of ideology, and say: ideology has always-already interpellated individuals as subjects, which amounts to making it clear that

2. Hailing as an everyday practice subject to a precise ritual takes a quite "special" form in the policeman's practice of "hailing" which concerns the hailing of "suspects" [Althusser's note].

individuals are always-already interpellated by ideology as subjects, which necessarily leads us to one last proposition: *individuals are always-already subjects*. Hence individuals are 'abstract' with respect to the subjects which they always-already are. This proposition might seem paradoxical.

That an individual is always-already a subject, even before he is born, is nevertheless the plain reality, accessible to everyone and not a paradox at all. Freud shows that individuals are always 'abstract' with respect to the subjects they always-already are, simply by noting the ideological ritual that surrounds the expectation of a 'birth', that 'happy event'. Everyone knows how much and in what way an unborn child is expected. Which amounts to saying, very prosaically, if we agree to drop the 'sentiments', i.e. the forms of family ideology (paternal/maternal/conjugal/fraternal) in which the unborn child is expected: it is certain in advance that it will bear its Father's Name, and will therefore have an identity and be irreplaceable. Before its birth, the child is therefore always-already a subject, appointed as a subject in and by the specific familial ideological configuration in which it is 'expected' once it has been conceived. I hardly need add that this familial ideological configuration is, in its uniqueness, highly structured, and that it is in this implacable and more or less 'pathological' (presupposing that any meaning can be assigned to that term) structure that the former subject-to-be will have to 'find' 'its' place, i.e. 'become' the sexual subject (boy or girl) which it already is in advance. It is clear that this ideological constraint and pre-appointment, and all the rituals of rearing and then education in the family, have some relationship with what Freud studied in the forms of the pre-genital and genital 'stages' of sexuality, i.e. in the 'grip' of what Freud registered by its effects as being the unconscious. But let us leave this point, too, on one side.

Let me go one step further. What I shall now turn my attention to is the way the 'actors' in this *mise en scène* of interpellation, and their respective roles, are reflected in the very structure of all ideology.

An Example: The Christian Religious Ideology

As the formal structure of all ideology is always the same, I shall restrict my analysis to a single example, one accessible to everyone, that of religious ideology, with the proviso that the same demonstration can be produced for ethical, legal, political, aesthetic ideology, etc.

Let us therefore consider the Christian religious ideology. I shall use a rhetorical figure and 'make it speak', i.e. collect into a fictional discourse what it 'says' not only in its two Testaments, its Theologians, Sermons, but also in its practices, its rituals, its ceremonies and its sacraments. The Christian religious ideology says something like this:

It says: I address myself to you, a human individual called Peter (every individual is called by his name, in the passive sense, it is never he who provides his own name), in order to tell you that God exists and that you are answerable to Him. It adds: God addresses himself to you through my voice (Scripture having collected the Word of God, Tradition having transmitted it, Papal Infallibility fixing it for ever on 'nice' points). It says: this is who you are: you are Peter! This is your origin, you were created by God for all eternity, although you were born in the 1920th year of Our Lord! This is your place in the world! This is what you must do! By these means, if you observe the 'law of love' you will be saved, you, Peter, and will become part of the Glorious Body of Christ! Etc. . . .

Now this is quite a familiar and banal discourse, but at the same time quite a surprising one.

Surprising because if we consider that religious ideology is indeed addressed to individuals, in order to 'transform them into subjects', by interpellating the individual, Peter, in order to make him a subject, free to obey or disobey the appeal, i.e. God's commandments; if it calls these individuals by their names, thus recognizing that they are always-already interpellated as subjects with a personal identity (to the extent that Pascal's Christ says: 'It is for you that I have shed this drop of my blood!'); if it interpellates them in such a way that the subject responds: *'Yes, it really is me!'* if it obtains from them the *recognition* that they really do occupy the place it designates for them as theirs in the world, a fixed residence: 'It really is me, I am here, a worker, a boss or a soldier!' in this vale of tears; if it obtains from them the recognition of a destination (eternal life or damnation) according to the respect or contempt they show to 'God's Commandments', Law become Love;—if everything does happen in this way (in the practices of the well-known rituals of baptism, confirmation, communion, confession and extreme unction, etc. . . .), we should note that all this 'procedure' to set up Christian religious subjects is dominated by a strange phenomenon: the fact that there can only be such a multitude of possible religious subjects on the absolute condition that there is a Unique, Absolute, *Other Subject*, i.e. God.

It is convenient to designate this new and remarkable Subject by writing Subject with a capital S to distinguish it from ordinary subjects, with a small s.

It then emerges that the interpellation of individuals as subjects presupposes the 'existence' of a Unique and central Other Subject, in whose Name the religious ideology interpellates all individuals as subjects. All this is clearly written in what is rightly called the Scriptures. 'And it came to pass at that time that God the Lord (Yahweh) spoke to Moses in the cloud. And the Lord cried to Moses, "Moses!" And Moses replied "It is (really) I! I am Moses thy servant, speak and I shall listen!" And the Lord spoke to Moses and said to him, "*I am that I am*" '.

God thus defines himself as the Subject *par excellence*, he who is through himself and for himself ('I am that I am'), and he who interpellates his subject, the individual subjected to him by his very interpellation, i.e. the individual named Moses. And Moses, interpellated-called by his Name, having recognized that it 'really' was he who was called by God, recognizes that he is a subject, a subject *of* God, a subject subjected to God, *a subject through the Subject and subjected to the Subject*. The proof: he obeys him, and makes his people obey God's Commandments.

God is thus the Subject, and Moses and the innumerable subjects of God's people, the Subject's interlocutors-interpellates: his *mirrors*, his *reflections*. Were not men made *in the image* of God? As all theological reflection proves, whereas He 'could' perfectly well have done without men, God needs them, the Subject needs the subjects, just as men need God, the subjects need the Subject. Better: God needs men, the great Subject needs subjects, even in the terrible inversion of his image in them (when the subjects wallow in debauchery, i.e. sin).

* * *

Let us decipher into theoretical language this wonderful necessity for the duplication of *the Subject into subjects* and of *the Subject itself into a subject-Subject*.

We observe that the structure of all ideology, interpellating individuals as subjects in the name of a Unique and Absolute Subject is *speculary*, i.e. a mirror-structure, and *doubly* speculary: this mirror duplication is constitutive of ideology and ensures its functioning. Which means that all ideology is *centred*, that the Absolute Subject occupies the unique place of the Centre, and interpellates around it the infinity of individuals into subjects in a double mirror-connexion such that it *subjects* the subjects to the Subject, while giving them in the Subject in which each subject can contemplate its own image (present and future) the *guarantee* that this really concerns them and Him, and that since everything takes place in the Family (the Holy Family: the Family is in essence Holy), 'God will *recognize* his own in it', i.e. those who have recognized God, and have recognized themselves in Him, will be saved.

Let me summarize what we have discovered about ideology in general.

The duplicate mirror-structure of ideology ensures simultaneously:

1. the interpellation of 'individuals' as subjects;
2. their subjection to the Subject;
3. the mutual recognition of subjects and Subject, the subjects' recognition of each other, and finally the subject's recognition of himself;
4. the absolute guarantee that everything really is so, and that on condition that the subjects recognize what they are and behave accordingly, everything will be all right: Amen—'*So be it*'.

Result: caught in this quadruple system of interpellation as subjects, of subjection to the Subject, of universal recognition and of absolute guarantee, the subjects 'work', they 'work by themselves' in the vast majority of cases, with the exception of the 'bad subjects' who on occasion provoke the intervention of one of the detachments of the (repressive) State apparatus. But the vast majority of (good) subjects work all right 'all by themselves', i.e. by ideology (whose concrete forms are realized in the Ideological State Apparatuses). They are inserted into practices governed by the rituals of the ISAs. They 'recognize' the existing state of affairs, that 'it really is true that it is so and not otherwise', and that they must be obedient to God, to their conscience, to the priest, to de Gaulle, to the boss, to the engineer, that thou shalt 'love thy neighbour as thyself', etc. Their concrete, material behaviour is simply the inscription in life of the admirable words of the prayer: '*Amen—So be it*'.

Yes, the subjects 'work by themselves'. The whole mystery of this effect lies in the first two moments of the quadruple system I have just discussed, or, if you prefer, in the ambiguity of the term *subject*. In the ordinary use of the term, subject in fact means: (1) a free subjectivity, a centre of initiatives, author of and responsible for its actions; (2) a subjected being, who submits to a higher authority, and is therefore stripped of all freedom except that of freely accepting his submission. This last note gives us the meaning of this ambiguity, which is merely a reflection of the effect which produces it: the individual *is interpellated as a (free) subject in order that he shall submit freely to the commandments of the Subject, i.e. in order that he shall (freely) accept his subjection*, i.e. in order that he shall make the gestures and actions of his subjection 'all by himself'. *There are no subjects except by and for their subjection.* That is why they 'work all by themselves'.

'*So be it!* . . .' This phrase which registers the effect to be obtained proves that it is not 'naturally' so ('naturally': outside the prayer, i.e. outside the ideological intervention). This phrase proves that it *has* to be so if things are to be what they must be, and let us let the words slip: if the reproduction of the relations of production is to be assured, even in the processes of production and circulation, every day, in the 'consciousness', i.e. in the attitudes of the individual-subjects occupying the posts which the socio-technical division of labour assigns to them in production, exploitation, repression, ideologization, scientific practice, etc. Indeed, what is really in question in this mechanism of the mirror recognition of the Subject and of the individuals interpellated as subjects, and of the guarantee given by the Subject to the subjects if they freely accept their subjection to the Subject's 'commandments'? The reality in question in this mechanism, the reality which is necessarily *ignored (méconnue)* in the very forms of recognition (ideology = misrecognition/ignorance) is indeed, in the last resort, the reproduction of the relations of production and of the relations deriving from them.

January–April 1969

P.S.

* * *

I have suggested that the ideologies were *realized* in institutions, in their rituals and their practices, in the ISAs. We have seen that on this basis they contribute to that form of class struggle, vital for the ruling class, the reproduction of the relations of production. But the point of view itself, however real, is still an abstract one.

In fact, the State and its Apparatuses only have meaning from the point of view of the class struggle, as an apparatus of class struggle ensuring class oppression and guaranteeing the conditions of exploitation and its reproduction. But there is no class struggle without antagonistic classes. Whoever says class struggle of the ruling class says resistance, revolt and class struggle of the ruled class.

* * *

It is only from the point of view of the classes, i.e. of the class struggle, that it is possible to explain the ideolog*ies* existing in a social formation. Not only is it from this starting-point that it is possible to explain the realization of the ruling ideology in the ISAs and of the forms of class struggle for which the ISAs are the seat and the stake. But it is also and above all from this starting-point that it is possible to understand the provenance of the ideologies which are realized in the ISAs and confront one another there. For if it is true that the ISAs represent the *form* in which the ideology of the ruling class must *necessarily* be realized, and the form in which the ideology of the ruled class must *necessarily* be measured and confronted, ideologies are not 'born' in the ISAs but from the social classes at grips in the class struggle: from their conditions of existence, their practices, their experience of the struggle, etc.

1970

PAUL DE MAN
1919–1983

Spurred by the expansion of research universities, American academic literary criticism flourished from the late 1960s through the early 1980s. Ideas from contemporary Continental philosophy, linguistics, psychoanalysis, and criticism surged into its comparatively narrow confines, which had been dominated by the model of close reading practiced by New Critics like CLEANTH BROOKS. Central to these new and avowedly theoretical stances toward literature was the group of critics then at Yale University, including Paul de Man, HAROLD BLOOM, JACQUES DERRIDA, Geoffrey Hartman, J. Hillis Miller, Shoshana Felman, and de Man's student BARBARA JOHNSON. Called the 'Yale School," they revitalized—or, according to antagonists, ruined—American literary criticism by importing Continental theory and, to varying degress, by espousing deconstruction. An erudite and wide-ranging critic of critics as well as a sophisticated reader of literary texts, de Man was the most influential literary theorist of the Yale School, and perhaps of his generation. Complementing Derrida's broader philosophical project, de Man promulgated deconstruction in literary criticism. His essay "Semiology and Rhetoric" (1973) programmatically outlines his model of deconstructive reading, arguing that rhetoric and figural language ultimately undermine determinate interpretation and that texts become allegories of their own interpretive difficulties. Responding to charges that deconstruction threatens literary study, de Man shifts focus in "The Return to Philology" (1982) to offer a defense of theory, grounding it historically in the linguistically oriented tradition of philology and castigating its critics as alarmists.

De Man was a prominent academic figure in the United States in his later life, but his early life in Europe was marked by the events of World War II, the decisive historical event of his generation. He was born and schooled in Antwerp, Belgium, where his father was a manufacturer of medical equipment and his uncle, Hendrik de Man, was a leading figure in the Socialist Party. In 1937 he entered the University of Brussels, first studying engineering and eventually taking degrees in chemistry (1940) and then philosophy (1942). While he was a student, Belgium was invaded by German forces, and it was under German military occupation from 1940 to 1944. De Man tried to flee to Spain in the summer of 1940 but was denied permission to immigrate; he returned to Belgium in the fall. During this period, he published journalism on literature and music; in 1939 he wrote for a democratic, antifascist student paper, and from 1940 to 1942 he regularly wrote for a Belgian newspaper, *Le Soir (The Evening)*, then under German control.

After the war de Man tried his hand at publishing and translating, but in 1948 he emigrated to the United States, where he worked at Doubleday Bookstore in New York and was introduced to prominent New York intellectuals. With the help of the writer Mary McCarthy, in 1949 he took a job as an instructor of French at Bard College, and in 1951 he moved to Boston to teach at the Berlitz language school. In

1952 he entered the graduate program in comparative literature at Harvard University, attaining a prestigious appointment at the Harvard Society of Fellows (1955–58) and working with the New Critic Reuben Brower, for whom he was a teaching assistant. While a lecturer at Harvard, he received his M.A. in 1958 and his Ph.D. in 1960. Though he began his academic career relatively late in life, he quickly rose to prominence, teaching at Cornell University from 1960 to 1967, intermittently at the University of Zurich from 1963 to 1970, and at Johns Hopkins University from 1968 to 1970. In 1970 he moved to Yale University, where he was appointed Sterling Professor of Comparative Literature in 1979. In 1983, at the height of his influence, de Man died of cancer.

It was not until four years after his death that Ortwin de Graef, a Belgian graduate student who was researching a dissertation on de Man, rediscovered his wartime journalism. Although most of it consisted of cerebral literary reviews, one article contained explicitly anti-Semitic statements, to the effect that European literature would not be diminished if there were no Jewish writers; a few other articles were also troubling. These writings were met with shock, for they suggested that de Man had been complicit with Nazi policies. While de Man had been cleared of charges of collaboration by the Belgian postwar military prosecutor investigating those who had worked for *Le Soir*, his wartime writings became a focal point of debate during the late 1980s and early 1990s, diminishing his influence in literary theory.

De Man was ever attuned to the figural contradictions of language, and his own career took many ironic turns. A debunker of the figure of personification in literary and critical language, he came for many to personify both deconstruction and literary theory. Though eschewing personality in teaching—as he sternly remarks in "The Resistance to Theory" (1982), pedagogy is not show business—he had a large following of students and colleagues who carried out his line of deconstruction. While he was persistently skeptical that any method could yield determinable results, his manner of reading became a model for others' critical practice, fulfilling his prediction, in "Semiology and Rhetoric," that "The whole of literature would respond in similar fashion." And although he advocated the priority of linguistic indeterminacy in interpreting historical events, his work was put into question by the discovery of the historical fact of his wartime writings.

Trained both in the European tradition of philosophy, especially phenomenology, at Brussels and in the American New Criticism during his time at Harvard, de Man was well positioned to adapt the developing discourses of Continental theory to American literary criticism. He showed a consistent affinity with the New Critics in his assiduous practice of close reading. As he remarked in an interview, he worked not from larger ideas but "one inch over the text." He also shared the New Critics' disdain for paraphrase, which reductively glosses texts rather than teasing out their complications. However, de Man departed from the New Critics in several key ways: in denying the determinate meaning that they assumed, in stressing allegory as a primary literary mode, and in continually investigating the theoretical bases of reading.

A foundational statement of deconstructive literary analysis, "Semiology and Rhetoric" takes aim at the semiological approaches characteristic of French structuralism, which attempt to develop a grammar of literary structure on the scientific model of linguistics. Using William Butler Yeats's poem "Among Schoolchildren" (1928) as a test case, de Man shows how meaning cannot be determined by grammar but is exceeded by the figural properties of language. Focusing on the poem's famous last line, "How can we know the dancer from the dance?" he adduces two different readings, taking it first as a rhetorical question reinforcing the images of unity in the poem (the standard interpretation) and then as a serious question that culminates in an image of dramatic uncertainty rather than unity. These yield "two entirely coherent but entirely incompatible readings," and thus "the entire scheme set up by the first reading can be undermined, or deconstructed, in terms of the second." Bringing home his point about the limitations of structuralism as well as of hermeneutic approaches, de Man shows how the poem's rhetoric renders interpretation undecidable. He calls this the "rhetorization of grammar."

As a complement to this rhetorical move, de Man also analyzes what he calls the "grammatization of rhetoric." Taking an example from Marcel Proust's *Remembrance of Things Past* (1913–27), de Man traces the sequence of figures in a passage describing the coolness of a room during summer, which seem necessarily linked and unified in "semi-automatic grammatical patterns." However, de Man argues that this link is deceptive and works only associatively, by contiguity; as he points out, a fly's buzz is no more necessarily connected to summer than the man Henry Ford is connected to an automobile. The figural nature of language again undoes the stable pattern that we assume to determine meaning. Although de Man claims that the indeterminacy generated by figuration applies to all linguistic acts, he specifies that it is explicitly foregrounded in literature. He thereby proposes one answer to the perennial question in literary theory of what distinguishes literature from other kinds of discourse, though he at the same time undercuts this distinction by analyzing how the literary occurs in presumably propositional discourses such as criticism and philosophy.

Generalizing from these examples, de Man finds that all literary texts become, in his trademark phrase, "allegories of reading," offering narratives of the problematic nature of language and interpretation. One of de Man's most influential moves was to reconsider the place of allegory, usually associated with schematic forms of medieval literature, notably in his important early essay "The Rhetoric of Temporality" (1969), as well as in his masterwork, *Allegories of Reading* (1979; "Semiology and Rhetoric" was reprinted as its introduction). De Man stresses that his allegorical rendering is not something overlaid on texts as a theoretical template; as he puts it, "The deconstruction is not something we have added to the text but it constituted the text in the first place." Likewise, one does not "deconstruct" texts; rather, one unravels the ways in which language deconstructs its own assertions, a distinction that suggests the impersonality of language and its operation, beyond human control. For de Man, the workings of language have priority over historical or other considerations; in another essay he makes the startling but consistent claim that "the bases for historical knowledge are not empirical facts but written texts, even if these texts masquerade in the guise of wars and revolutions."

Most famous for his techniques of deconstructive reading of literary texts, de Man was equally influential in his readings of other critics, unpacking their theoretical assumptions and drawing out the contradictory implications of their arguments. He viewed criticism in essentially the same terms as literature, closely reading it to tease out its rhetoric as well as its purported claims—or, in his phrasing, its blindnesses as well as its insights. A succinct foray into debates over the value of theory, de Man's "Return to Philology" exemplifies both his "metacritical" perspective and his command of the critical tradition (treated in a polemical style). Defending against the complaints of traditionalists—in particular, the prominent Harvard professor and literary scholar Walter Jackson Bate—that contemporary theory had caused a "crisis in English studies," de Man roots theory in the aesthetic, hermeneutic, and philological traditions of literary study. A deft rhetorician, de Man quells alarmist "cries of doom" by offering a disarming vignette of a Harvard literature course taught by Reuben Brower, Bate's colleague and de Man's teacher, thereby locating the linguistic focus of deconstruction in philology and the New Criticism. As he provides this nonthreatening portrait of theory's heritage, de Man continues to assert the priority of attention to language and its problematic nature over such external concerns as ethics, religion, politics, hermeneutics, and history. He subtly privileges rhetoric and poetics, which properly study language, over the moralizing and optimistic focus of nineteenth- and twentieth-century humanistic critics from SAMUEL TAYLOR COLERIDGE and MATTHEW ARNOLD to I. A. Richards, T. S. ELIOT, and Bate himself—thereby getting the last word against Bate.

Though he touches on the issue of "institutional resistances" in "The Return to

Philology," de Man more forcefully argues for the philosophical inevitability of theory in a related essay from 1982, "The Resistance to Theory," where he countercharges that those who attack it are demonstrating a Freudian anxiety and block ("resistance"). Extending the logic of indeterminacy, he argues that the resistance to theory is "inherent in the theoretical enterprise itself," and that theory "consists in the impossibility of its definition." Rather than discrediting theory, this paradox yields a "negative knowledge about the reliability of linguistic utterance." Deconstruction is the theory of that negative knowledge.

That de Man's work has drawn an unparalleled amount of criticism from both traditionalists and fellow theorists within the academy, as well as from those outside, testifies to his influence. Although he studied a wide range of canonical literary texts, his advocacy of theory led to the accusation that he was an enemy of literature. And despite being an inveterate close reader, he was charged with threatening the foundations of literary criticism because he radically questioned the possibility of meaning. Within the domain of theory, in perhaps the central struggle of the 1980s, de Man—and deconstruction—was pitted against leftist calls that attention be paid to history, society, and politics. The Marxist critic TERRY EAGLETON claimed that de Man had "given up the world entirely for the aporias and unthinkable paradoxes of a text," and that deconstruction was "politically quietistic"; the postcolonial critic EDWARD SAID charged that deconstruction, by its use of overspecialized "camouflaging jargons" that "obscure the social realities," detracted from the social role and mission of criticism. Analyzing de Man's own rhetoric, the critic Frank Lentricchia quipped that de Man's authoritative pronouncements about language seemed the orders of a Mafia boss, contradicting his own theory of indeterminacy. Although de Man's influence waned somewhat after the 1980s, in part because of the discovery of his wartime writings and in part because of the resurgence of historical methods, he remains a pivotal figure in the assimilation of Continental theory, especially deconstruction, to the North American scene.

BIBLIOGRAPHY

De Man's early reputation derived primarily from his essays, which were collected in books published later in his life or posthumously. His first—and for nearly a decade only—book, *Blindness and Insight: Essays in the Rhetoric of Contemporary Criticism* (1971; 2d ed., 1983), surveys a range of important critics and argues that criticism is frequently predicated on a blindness to its own rhetoric, which paradoxically also enables its insight; it includes the important essay "The Rhetoric of Temporality" (1969) and a famous critique of Derrida, "The Rhetoric of Blindness" (1971). His most unified book, *Allegories of Reading: Figural Language in Rousseau, Nietzsche, Rilke, and Proust* (1979), best exemplifies his deconstructive reading methods and has been extremely influential. The remainder of de Man's books, gathering numerous essays, were published after his death; they are *The Rhetoric of Romanticism* (1984); *The Resistance to Theory* (1986); *Critical Writings, 1953–1978*, edited by Lindsay Waters (1989); *Romanticism and Contemporary Criticism: The Gauss Seminars and Other Papers*, edited by E. S. Burt, Kevin Newmark, and Andrzej Warminski (1992); and *Aesthetic Ideology*, edited by Andrzej Warminski (1996). His controversial journalism dating from World War II is included in *Wartime Journalism, 1939–1943*, edited by Werner Hamacher, Neil Hertz, and Thomas Keenan (1988).

As befits his central role in contemporary theory, de Man's work has drawn a large body of scholarship and commentary. Ortwin de Graef's multivolume project, which includes *Serenity in Crisis: A Preface to Paul de Man, 1939–1960* (1993) and *Titanic Light: Paul de Man's Post-Romanticism, 1960–1969* (1995), reviews de Man's intellectual career, though the best biographical recounting is Lindsay Waters's lengthy introduction to *Critical Writings*, "Paul de Man: Life and Works." A useful factual chronology of de Man's early life is offered in *Responses: On Paul de Man's Wartime*

Journalism, edited by Hamacher, Hertz, and Keenan (1989), their companion volume to *Wartime Journalism*; it also includes several essays elaborating the historical situation in Belgium at the time of the wartime writings. Robert Moynihan, "Interview with Paul de Man," *Yale Review* 73 (1984), is accessible and illuminating.

Important early critical responses include Joseph Riddel, "A Miller's Tale," *Diacritics* 5 (1975), which criticizes de Man for elitism and formalism; Frank Lentricchia's critique of de Man's "rhetoric of authority" in *After the New Criticism* (1980); Rodolphe Gasché, "'*Setzung*' and '*Übersetzung*': Notes on Paul de Man," *Diacritics* 11 (1981), which compares de Man's use of deconstruction unfavorably with that of Derrida; and Suzanne Gearhart, "Philosophy *before* Literature: Deconstruction, Historicity, and the Work of Paul de Man," *Diacritics* 13 (1983), which defends de Man against Gasché. *The Yale Critics: Deconstruction in America*, edited by Jonathan Arac, Wlad Godzich, and Wallace Martin (1983), is an important early assessment of the Yale School and its various members. Barbara Johnson's "Gender Theory and the Yale School" (1984), collected in her *World of Difference* (1987), is a feminist critique by someone affiliated with the Yale School.

Immediately after de Man's death, there was a spate of publications largely sympathetic to his work. *Yale French Studies*, no. 69 (1985), was a lengthy special issue devoted to "The Lesson of Paul de Man," with many critical essays as well as memorial tributes. Jacques Derrida's *Mémoires: For Paul de Man* (1986) is a moving meditation on de Man's project, distinguishing his focus on literature and allegory from Derrida's version of deconstruction. Christopher Norris's *Paul de Man: Deconstruction and the Critique of Aesthetic Ideology* (1988), an introductory survey, roots de Man in the Kantian philosophical tradition and speculates on his view of ideology. Jonathan Culler's retrospective assessment, "Paul de Man's Contribution to Literary Criticism and Theory," in *The Future of Literary Theory* (ed. Ralph Cohen, 1989), is a synoptic overview. *Reading de Man Reading*, edited by Lindsay Waters and Wlad Godzich (1989), collects fourteen useful essays on de Man's work; most are within the deconstructive camp. Following the publication of his wartime writings, the criticism on de Man changed markedly. *Responses* (cited above) records the range of debate, from condemnations to defenses, with some sober assessments of the historical situation in Belgium. David Lehman's sometimes glib *Signs of the Times: Deconstruction and the Fall of Paul de Man* (1991) shows how the wartime writings harmed de Man's popular representation.

Other reconsiderations have been more theoretically focused. Fredric Jameson's "Immanence and Nominalism in Postmodern Theoretical Discourse," in *Postmodernism, or the Cultural Logic of Late Capitalism* (1991), traces de Man's philosophical roots. Echoing Gasché, Jeffrey Nealon, in "The Discipline of Deconstruction," *PMLA* 107 (1992), finds the line of "American deconstruction," following de Man, inferior to Derrida's more philosophical version. In "Reflections on Post 'Post-mortem de Man,'" *Minnesota Review*, nos. 41–42 (1994), Tom Cohen argues that contemporary cultural studies employs naive views of representation and would benefit from deconstructive critique. Several of the essays in *Critical Encounters: Reference and Responsibility in Deconstructive Writing*, edited by Cathy Caruth and Deborah Esch (1995), discuss de Man, particularly his unfinished later work on aesthetics and ideology. Gathering contributions by Derrida, Judith Butler, Johnson, and others, *Material Events: Paul de Man and the Afterlife of Theory*, edited by Tom Cohen, Barbara Cohen, J. Hillis Miller, and Andrzej Warminski (2000), proposes new directions for the study of de Man. The 1985 special issue of *Yale French Studies* cited above and de Man's posthumous *Resistance to Theory* provide complete bibliographical lists of his work up to 1985; de Graef lists de Man's publications up to 1983, as well as more recent secondary sources.

Semiology and Rhetoric

To judge from various recent publications, the spirit of the times is not blowing in the direction of formalist and intrinsic criticism.[1] We may no longer be hearing too much about relevance but we keep hearing a great deal about reference, about the nonverbal "outside" to which language refers, by which it is conditioned and upon which it acts. The stress falls not so much on the fictional status of literature—a property now perhaps somewhat too easily taken for granted—but on the interplay between these fictions and categories that are said to partake of reality, such as the self, man, society, "the artist, his culture and the human community," as one critic puts it. Hence the emphasis on hybrid texts considered to be partly literary and partly referential, on popular fictions deliberately aimed towards social and psychological gratification, on literary autobiography as a key to the understanding of the self, and so on. We speak as if, with the problems of literary form resolved once and forever, and with the techniques of structural analysis refined to near-perfection, we could now move "beyond formalism"[2] towards the questions that really interest us and reap, at last, the fruits of the ascetic concentration on techniques that prepared us for this decisive step. With the internal law and order of literature well policed, we can now confidently devote ourselves to the foreign affairs, the external politics of literature. Not only do we feel able to do so, but we owe it to ourselves to take this step: our moral conscience would not allow us to do otherwise. Behind the assurance that valid interpretation is possible, behind the recent interest in writing and reading as potentially effective public speech acts, stands a highly respectable moral imperative that strives to reconcile the internal, formal, private structures of literary language with their external, referential, and public effects.

I want, for the moment, to consider briefly this tendency in itself, as an undeniable and recurrent historical fact, without regard for its truth or falseness or for its value as desirable or pernicious. It is a fact that this sort of thing happens, again and again, in literary studies. On the one hand, literature cannot merely be received as a definite unit of referential meaning that can be decoded without leaving a residue. The code is unusually conspicuous, complex, and enigmatic; it attracts an inordinate amount of attention to itself, and this attention has to acquire the rigor of a method. The structural moment of concentration on the code for its own sake cannot be avoided, and literature necessarily breeds its own formalism. Technical innovations in the methodical study of literature only occur when this kind of attention predominates. It can legitimately be said, for example, that, from a technical point of view, very little has happened in American criticism since the innovative works of New Criticism. There certainly have been numerous excellent books of criticism since, but in none of them have the techniques of description and interpretation evolved beyond the techniques of close

1. The New Critical distinction between "intrinsic" and "extrinsic" criticism derives from the influential handbook *Theory of Literature* (1949), by René Wellek and Austin Warren; they opposed criticism limited to internal, "formal" features of a literary work to that focusing on external concerns such as the author, readers, or history.

2. A reference to *Beyond Formalism: Literary Essays, 1958–1970* (1970), by Geoffrey Hartman, de Man's colleague at Yale University.

reading established in the thirties and the forties. Formalism, it seems, is an all-absorbing and tyrannical muse; the hope that one can be at the same time technically original and discursively eloquent is not borne out by the history of literary criticism.

On the other hand—and this is the real mystery—no literary formalism, no matter how accurate and enriching in its analytic powers, is ever allowed to come into being without seeming reductive. When form is considered to be the external trappings of literary meaning or content, it seems superficial and expendable. The development of intrinsic, formalist criticism in the twentieth century has changed this model: form is now a solipsistic category of self-reflection, and the referential meaning is said to be extrinsic. The polarities of inside and outside have been reversed, but they are still the same polarities that are at play: internal meaning has become outside reference, and the outer form has become the intrinsic structure. A new version of reductiveness at once follows this reversal: formalism nowadays is mostly described in an imagery of imprisonment and claustrophobia: the "prison house of language," "the impasse of formalist criticism,"[3] etc. Like the grandmother in Proust's novel[4] ceaselessly driving the young Marcel out into the garden, away from the unhealthy inwardness of his closeted reading, critics cry out for the fresh air of referential meaning. Thus, with the structure of the code so opaque, but the meaning so anxious to blot out the obstacle of form, no wonder that the reconciliation of form and meaning would be so attractive. The attraction of reconciliation is the elective breeding-ground of false models and metaphors; it accounts for the metaphorical model of literature as a kind of box that separates an inside from an outside, and the reader or critic as the person who opens the lid in order to release in the open what was secreted but inaccessible inside. It matters little whether we call the inside of the box the content or the form, the outside the meaning or the appearance. The recurrent debate opposing intrinsic to extrinsic criticism stands under the aegis of an inside/outside metaphor that is never being seriously questioned.

Metaphors are much more tenacious than facts, and I certainly don't expect to dislodge this age-old model in one short try. I merely wish to speculate on a different set of terms, perhaps less simple in their differential relationships than the strictly polar, binary opposition between inside and outside and therefore less likely to enter into the easy play of chiasmic[5] reversals. I derive these terms (which are as old as the hills) pragmatically from the observation of developments and debates in recent critical methodology.

One of the most controversial among these developments coincides with a new approach to poetics or, as it is called in Germany, poetology, as a branch of general semiotics. In France, a semiology of literature comes about as the outcome of the long-deferred but all the more explosive encounter of

3. The title of one of de Man's own essays published in French in 1956, later translated as "The Dead-End of Formalist Criticism," in his *Blindness and Insight* (2d ed., 1983). "The 'prison house' ": an allusion to *The Prison-House of Language: A Critical Account of Structuralism and Russian Formalism* (1972), by the American Marxist critic FREDRIC JAMESON.

4. *À la recherche du temps perdu* (1913–27, *Remembrance of Things Past*), by the French novelist Marcel Proust (1871–1924). De Man uses this work as an example throughout the essay; its main character is the semi-autobiographical Marcel.

5. Of chiasmus, a rhetorical device in which the elements of the second of two parallel syntactic structures are inverted (e.g., "renowned for conquest, and in counsel skilled").

the nimble French literary mind with the category of form. Semiology, as opposed to semantics, is the science or study of signs as signifiers; it does not ask what words mean but how they mean. Unlike American New Criticism, which derived the internalization of form from the practice of highly self-conscious modern writers, French semiology turned to linguistics for its model and adopted Saussure and Jakobson rather than Valéry[6] or Proust for its masters. By an awareness of the arbitrariness of the sign (Saussure) and of literature as an autotelic statement "focused on the way it is expressed" (Jakobson) the entire question of meaning can be bracketed, thus freeing the critical discourse from the debilitating burden of paraphrase. The demystifying power of semiology, within the context of French historical and thematic criticism, has been considerable. It demonstrated that the perception of the literary dimensions of language is largely obscured if one submits uncritically to the authority of reference. It also revealed how tenaciously this authority continues to assert itself in a variety of disguises, ranging from the crudest ideology to the most refined forms of aesthetic and ethical judgment. It especially explodes the myth of semantic correspondence between sign and referent, the wishful hope of having it both ways, of being, to paraphrase Marx in the *German Ideology*, a formalist critic in the morning and a communal moralist in the afternoon,[7] of serving both the technique of form and the substance of meaning. The results, in the practice of French criticism, have been as fruitful as they are irreversible. Perhaps for the first time since the late eighteenth century, French critics can come at least somewhat closer to the kind of linguistic awareness that never ceased to be operative in its poets and novelists and that forced all of them, including Sainte Beuve,[8] to write their main works "contre Sainte Beuve." The distance was never so considerable in England and the United States, which does not mean, however, that we may be able, in this country, to dispense altogether with some preventative semiological hygiene.

One of the most striking characteristics of literary semiology as it is practiced today, in France and elsewhere, is the use of grammatical (especially syntactical) structures conjointly with rhetorical structures, without apparent awareness of a possible discrepancy between them. In their literary analyses, Barthes, Genette, Todorov, Greimas,[9] and their disciples all simplify and regress from Jakobson in letting grammar and rhetoric function in perfect continuity, and in passing from grammatical to rhetorical structures without difficulty or interruption. Indeed, as the study of grammatical structures is refined in contemporary theories of generative, transformational, and distributive grammar, the study of tropes and of figures (which is how the term *rhetoric* is used here, and not in the derived sense of comment or of eloquence or persuasion) becomes a mere extension of grammatical models,

6. Paul Valéry (1871–1945), major modern French poet and essayist. FERDINAND DE SAUSSURE (1857–1913), Swiss linguist, the founder of structuralism and semiology. ROMAN JAKOBSON (1896–1982), Russian-born American linguist, literary theorist, and semiologist.

7. In his *German Ideology* (1845–46), the German economic and political theorist KARL MARX (1818–1883) notes that the goal of communist society would be to remove alienating regulations of work, so that one could "hunt in the morning, fish in the afternoon . . . [and] criticize after dinner."

8. Charles-Augustin Sainte-Beuve (1804–1869), the leading 19th-century French literary critic and historian. *Contre Sainte-Beuve* (*Against Saint Beuve*) is the title of a critical response by Proust.

9. All French critics: ROLAND BARTHES (1915–1980), major structuralist and poststructuralist; Gérard Genette (b. 1930), French literary critic and author of *Figures III* (1972; trans. 1980 as *Narrative Discourse: An Essay in Method*), mentioned later; TZVETAN TODOROV (b. 1939), Bulgarian-born structuralist; and A. J. Greimas (1917–1992), Lithuanian-born semiologist.

a particular subset of syntactical relations. In the recent *Dictionnaire encyclopédique des sciences du langage*,[1] Ducrot and Todorov write that rhetoric has always been satisfied with a paradigmatic view over words (words substituting for each other), without questioning their syntagmatic relationship (the contiguity of words to each other). There ought to be another perspective, complementary to the first, in which metaphor, for example, would not be defined as a substitution but as a particular type of combination. Research inspired by linguistics or, more narrowly, by syntactical studies, has begun to reveal this possibility—but it remains to be explored. Todorov, who calls one of his books a *Grammar of the Decameron*,[2] rightly thinks of his own work and that of his associates as first explorations in the elaboration of a systematic grammar of literary modes, genres, and also of literary figures. Perhaps the most perceptive work to come out of this school, Genette's studies of figural modes, can be shown to be assimilations of rhetorical transformations or combinations to syntactical, grammatical patterns. Thus a recent study, now printed in *Figures III* and entitled *Metaphor and Metonymy in Proust*, shows the combined presence, in a wide and astute selection of passages, of paradigmatic, metaphorical figures with syntagmatic, metonymic structures. The combination of both is treated descriptively and nondialectically without considering the possibility of logical tensions.

One can ask whether this reduction of figure to grammar is legitimate. The existence of grammatical structures, within and beyond the unit of the sentence, in literary texts is undeniable, and their description and classification are indispensable. The question remains if and how figures of rhetoric can be included in such a taxonomy. This question is at the core of the debate going on, in a wide variety of apparently unrelated forms, in contemporary poetics. But the historical picture of contemporary criticism is too confused to make the mapping out of such a topography a useful exercise. Not only are these questions mixed in and mixed up within particular groups or local trends, but they are often co-present, without apparent contradiction, within the work of a single author.

Neither is the theory of the question suitable for quick expository treatment. To distinguish the epistemology of grammar from the epistemology of rhetoric is a redoubtable task. On an entirely naïve level, we tend to conceive of grammatical systems as tending towards universality and as simply generative, i.e., as capable of deriving an infinity of versions from a single model (that may govern transformations as well as derivations) without the intervention of another model that would upset the first. We therefore think of the relationship between grammar and logic, the passage from grammar to propositions, as being relatively unproblematic: no true propositions are conceivable in the absence of grammatical consistency or of controlled deviation from a system of consistency no matter how complex. Grammar and logic stand to each other in a dyadic relationship of unsubverted support. In a logic of acts rather than of statements, as in Austin's[3] theory of speech acts,

1. Published in 1972; translated as *Encyclopedic Dictionary of the Sciences of Language* (1979). Oswald Ducrot (b. 1930), French linguist. The distinction between *paradigmatic* and *syntagmatic* draws on Saussure.

2. *Grammaire du Décameron* (1969). *The Decameron* (1348–53), a collection of 100 tales, is the best-known work of the Italian writer GIOVANNI BOCCACCIO.

3. J. L. AUSTIN (1911–1960), influential British philosopher of language, especially of speech acts (what we typically perform when we speak). He distinguishes between locutionary acts (saying something meaningful), illocutionary acts (saying

that has had such a strong influence on recent American work in literary semiology, it is also possible to move between speech acts and grammar without difficulty. The performance of what is called illocutionary acts such as ordering, questioning, denying, assuming, etc., within the language is congruent with the grammatical structures of syntax in the corresponding imperative, interrogative, negative, optative sentences. "The rules for illocutionary acts," writes Richard Ohmann in a recent paper, "determine whether performance of a given act is well-executed, in just the same way as *grammatical* rules determine whether the product of a locutionary act—a sentence—is well formed. . . . But whereas the rules of grammar concern the relationships among sound, syntax, and meaning, the rules of illocutionary acts concern relationships among people."[4] And since rhetoric is then conceived exclusively as persuasion, as actual action upon others (and not as an intralinguistic figure or trope), the continuity between the illocutionary realm of grammar and the perlocutionary realm of rhetoric is self-evident. It becomes the basis for a new rhetoric that, exactly as is the case for Todorov and Genette, would also be a new grammar.

Without engaging the substance of the question, it can be pointed out, without having to go beyond recent and American examples, and without calling upon the strength of an age-old tradition, that the continuity here assumed between grammar and rhetoric is not borne out by theoretical and philosophical speculation. Kenneth Burke[5] mentions *deflection* (which he compares structurally to Freudian displacement), defined as "any slight bias or even unintended error," as the rhetorical basis of language, and deflection is then conceived as a dialectical subversion of the consistent link between sign and meaning that operates within grammatical patterns; hence Burke's well-known insistence on the distinction between grammar and rhetoric. Charles Sanders Peirce, who, with Nietzsche[6] and Saussure, laid the philosophical foundation for modern semiology, stressed the distinction between grammar and rhetoric in his celebrated and so suggestively unfathomable definition of the sign. He insists, as is well known, on the necessary presence of a third element, called the interpretant, within any relationship that the sign entertains with its object. The sign is to be interpreted if we are to understand the idea it is to convey, and this is so because the sign is not the thing but a meaning derived from the thing by a process here called representation that is not simply generative, i.e., dependent on a univocal origin. The interpretation of the sign is not, for Peirce, a meaning but another sign; it is a reading, not a decodage, and this reading has, in its turn, to be interpreted into another sign, and so on *ad infinitum*. Peirce calls this process by means of which "one sign gives birth to another" pure rhetoric, as distinguished from pure grammar, which postulates the possibility of unproblematic, dyadic meaning, and pure logic, which postulates the possibility of the universal truth of meanings. Only if the sign engendered meaning in the same way that the object engenders the sign, that is, by representation, would there be no need to distinguish between grammar and rhetoric.

something meaningful for some purpose), and perlocutionary acts (having an effect on those who hear what is said).

4. "Speech, Literature, and the Space in Between," *New Literary History* 4 (autumn 1972): 50 [de Man's note]. OHMANN (b. 1931), American literary and cultural critic.

5. American rhetorician and literary critic (1897–1993; see above); he drew on the work of the Austrian founder of psychoanalysis SIGMUND FREUD (1856–1939), among many others.

6. FRIEDRICH NIETZSCHE (1844–1900), German philosopher. Peirce (1839–1914), American pragmatist philosopher and linguist.

These remarks should indicate at least the existence and the difficulty of the question, a difficulty which puts its concise theoretical exposition beyond my powers. I must retreat therefore into a pragmatic discourse and try to illustrate the tension between grammar and rhetoric in a few specific textual examples. Let me begin by considering what is perhaps the most commonly known instance of an apparent symbiosis between a grammatical and a rhetorical structure, the so-called rhetorical question, in which the figure is conveyed directly by means of a syntactical device. I take the first example from the sub-literature of the mass media: asked by his wife whether he wants to have his bowling shoes laced over or laced under, Archie Bunker[7] answers with a question: "What's the difference?" Being a reader of sublime simplicity, his wife replies by patiently explaining the difference between lacing over and lacing under, whatever this may be, but provokes only ire. "What's the difference" did not ask for difference but means instead "I don't give a damn what the difference is." The same grammatical pattern engenders two meanings that are mutually exclusive: the literal meaning asks for the concept (difference) whose existence is denied by the figurative meaning. As long as we are talking about bowling shoes, the consequences are relatively trivial; Archie Bunker, who is a great believer in the authority of origins (as long, of course, as they are the right origins) muddles along in a world where literal and figurative meanings get in each other's way, though not without discomforts. But suppose that it is a *de*-bunker rather than a "Bunker," and a de-bunker of the arche (or origin), an archie De-bunker such as Nietzsche or Jacques Derrida[8] for instance, who asks the question "What is the Difference"—and we cannot even tell from his grammar whether he "really" wants to know "what" difference is or is just telling us that we shouldn't even try to find out. Confronted with the question of the difference between grammar and rhetoric, grammar allows us to ask the question, but the sentence by means of which we ask it may deny the very possibility of asking. For what is the use of asking, I ask, when we cannot even authoritatively decide whether a question asks or doesn't ask?

The point is as follows. A perfectly clear syntactical paradigm (the question) engenders a sentence that has at least two meanings, of which the one asserts and the other denies its own illocutionary mode. It is not so that there are simply two meanings, one literal and the other figural, and that we have to decide which one of these meanings is the right one in this particular situation. The confusion can only be cleared up by the intervention of an extra-textual intention, such as Archie Bunker putting his wife straight; but the very anger he displays is indicative of more than impatience; it reveals his despair when confronted with a structure of linguistic meaning that he cannot control and that holds the discouraging prospect of an infinity of similar future confusions, all of them potentially catastrophic in their consequences. Nor is this intervention really a part of the mini-text constituted by the figure which holds our attention only as long as it remains suspended and unresolved. I follow the usage of common speech in calling this semiological enigma "rhetorical." The grammatical model of the question becomes rhetorical not when we have, on the one hand, a literal meaning and on the other hand a figural meaning, but when it is impossible to decide by gram-

7. The main character in the popular CBS television series *All in the Family* (1971–79), played by Carroll O'Connor; his wife, Edith, was played by Jean Stapleton.

8. Algerian-born French philosopher and progenitor of deconstruction (b. 1930; see below). "Arche" derives from the Greek *archē* (origin).

matical or other linguistic devices which of the two meanings (that can be entirely incompatible) prevails. Rhetoric radically suspends logic and opens up vertiginous possibilities of referential aberration. And although it would perhaps be somewhat more remote from common usage, I would not hesitate to equate the rhetorical, figural potentiality of language with literature itself. I could point to a great number of antecedents to this equation of literature with figure; the most recent reference would be to Monroe Beardsley's insistence in his contribution to the *Essays* to honor William Wimsatt, that literary language is characterized by being "distinctly above the norm in ratio of implicit [or, I would say rhetorical] to explicit meaning."[9]

Let me pursue the matter of the rhetorical question through one more example. Yeats's poem "Among School Children"[1] ends with the famous line: "How can we know the dancer from the dance?" Although there are some revealing inconsistencies within the commentaries, the line is usually interpreted as stating, with the increased emphasis of a rhetorical device, the potential unity between form and experience, between creator and creation. It could be said that it denies the discrepancy between the sign and the referent from which we started out. Many elements in the imagery and the dramatic development of the poem strengthen this traditional reading; without having to look any further than the immediately preceding lines, one finds powerful and consecrated images of the continuity from part to whole that makes synecdoche into the most seductive of metaphors: the organic beauty of the tree, stated in the parallel syntax of a similar rhetorical question, or the convergence, in the dance, of erotic desire with musical form:

O chestnut-tree, great-rooted blossomer,
Are you the leaf, the blossom or the bole?
O body swayed to music, O brightening glance,
How can we know the dancer from the dance?

A more extended reading, always assuming that the final line is to be read as a rhetorical question, reveals that the thematic and rhetorical grammar of the poem yields a consistent reading that extends from the first line to the last and that can account for all the details in the text. It is equally possible, however, to read the last line literally rather than figuratively, as asking with some urgency the question we asked earlier within the context of contemporary criticism: *not* that sign and referent are so exquisitely fitted to each other that all difference between them is at times blotted out but, rather, since the two essentially different elements, sign and meaning, are so intricately intertwined in the imagined "presence" that the poem addresses, how can we possibly make the distinctions that would shelter us from the error of identifying what cannot be identified? The clumsiness of the paraphrase reveals that it is not necessarily the literal reading which is simpler than the figurative one, as was the case in our first example; here, the figural reading, which assumes the question to be rhetorical, is perhaps naïve, whereas the literal reading leads to greater complication of theme and statement. For it

9. "The Concept of Literature," in *Literary Theory and Structure: Essays in Honor of William K. Wimsatt*, ed. Frank Brady, John Palmer, and Martin Price (New Haven, 1973), p. 37 [de Man's note]. BEARDSLEY (1915–1985), American aesthetic philosopher and Wimsatt's collaborator. WIMSATT (1907–1975), American New Critic based at Yale.

1. First published in *The Tower* (1928), by William Butler Yeats (1865–1939), a leading modernist Irish poet and the subject of de Man's Ph.D. dissertation.

turns out that the entire scheme set up by the first reading can be undermined, or deconstructed, in the terms of the second, in which the final line is read literally as meaning that, since the dancer and the dance are not the same, it might be useful, perhaps even desperately necessary—for the question can be given a ring of urgency, "Please tell me, how *can* I know the dancer from the dance"—to tell them apart. But this will replace the reading of each symbolic detail by a divergent interpretation. The oneness of trunk, leaf, and blossom, for example, that would have appealed to Goethe, would find itself replaced by the much less reassuring Tree of Life from the Mabinogion that appears in the poem "Vacillation," in which the fiery blossom and the earthly leaf are held together, as well as apart, by the crucified and castrated God Attis,[2] of whose body it can hardly be said that it is "not bruised to pleasure soul."[3] This hint should suffice to suggest that two entirely coherent but entirely incompatible readings can be made to hinge on one line, whose grammatical structure is devoid of ambiguity, but whose rhetorical mode turns the mood as well as the mode of the entire poem upside down. Neither can we say, as was already the case in the first example, that the poem simply has two meanings that exist side by side. The two readings have to engage each other in direct confrontation, for the one reading is precisely the error denounced by the other and has to be undone by it. Nor can we in any way make a valid decision as to which of the readings can be given priority over the other; none can exist in the other's absence. There can be no dance without a dancer, no sign without a referent. On the other hand, the authority of the meaning engendered by the grammatical structure is fully obscured by the duplicity of a figure that cries out for the differentiation that it conceals.

Yeats's poem is not explicitly "about" rhetorical questions but about images or metaphors, and about the possibility of convergence between experiences of consciousness such as memory or emotions—what the poem calls passion, piety, and affection—and entities accessible to the senses such as bodies, persons, or icons. We return to the inside/outside model from which we started out and which the poem puts into question by means of a syntactical device (the question) made to operate on a grammatical as well as on a rhetorical level. The couple grammar/rhetoric, certainly not a binary opposition since they in no way exclude each other, disrupts and confuses the neat antithesis of the inside/outside pattern. We can transfer this scheme to the act of reading and interpretation. By reading we get, as we say, *inside* a text that was first something alien to us and which we now make our own by an act of understanding. But this understanding becomes at once the representation of an extra-textual meaning; in Austin's terms, the illocutionary speech act becomes a perlocutionary actual act—in Frege's[4] terms, *Bedeutung* becomes *Sinn*. Our recurrent question is whether this transformation is semantically controlled along grammatical or along rhetorical lines.

2. Greek god of fertility and vegetation (though not crucified, in Greek versions of his myth). Johann Wolfgang von Goethe (1749–1832), German poet, playwright, and novelist, whose works (including writings in botany) reflected an interest in the organic, developing whole. The *Mabinogion* (comp. 14th c.), a collection of medieval Welsh prose tales. "Vacillation" (1932), a poem by Yeats.

3. Earlier in the final stanza of "Among School Children," Yeats wrote, "The body is not bruised to please the soul."

4. Gottlob Frege (1848–1945), German philosopher of language, logic, and mathematics, who distinguishes between a word's reference (in German, *Bedeutung*), or the object it represents, and its sense (*Sinn*), or the thought it expresses.

Does the metaphor of reading really unite outer meaning with inner understanding, action with reflection, into one single totality? The assertion is powerfully and suggestively made in a passage from Proust that describes the experience of reading as such a union. It describes the young Marcel, near the beginning of Combray,[5] hiding in the closed space of his room in order to read. The example differs from the earlier ones in that we are not dealing with a grammatical structure that also functions rhetorically but have instead the representation, the dramatization, in terms of the experience of a subject, of a rhetorical structure—just as, in many other passages, Proust dramatizes tropes by means of landscapes or descriptions of objects. The figure here dramatized is that of metaphor, an inside/outside correspondence as represented by the act of reading. The reading scene is the culmination of a series of actions taking place in enclosed spaces and leading up to the "dark coolness" of Marcel's room.

> I had stretched out on my bed, with a book, in my room which sheltered, tremblingly, its transparent and fragile coolness from the afternoon sun, behind the almost closed blinds through which a glimmer of daylight had nevertheless managed to push its yellow wings, remaining motionless between the wood and the glass, in a corner, poised like a butterfly. It was hardly light enough to read, and the sensation of the light's splendor was given me only by the noise of Camus[6] . . . hammering dusty crates; resounding in the sonorous atmosphere that is peculiar to hot weather, they seemed to spark off scarlet stars; and also by the flies executing their little concert, the chamber music of summer: evocative not in the manner of a human tune that, heard perchance during the summer, afterwards reminds you of it but connected to summer by a more necessary link: born from beautiful days, resurrecting only when they return, containing some of their essence, it does not only awaken their image in our memory; it guarantees their return, their actual, persistent, unmediated presence.
>
> The dark coolness of my room related to the full sunlight of the street as the shadow relates to the ray of light, that is to say it was just as luminous and it gave my imagination the total spectacle of the summer, whereas my senses, if I had been on a walk, could only have enjoyed it by fragments; it matched my repose which (thanks to the adventures told by my book and stirring my tranquility) supported, like the quiet of a motionless hand in the middle of a running brook the shock and the motion of a torrent of activity.[7]

For our present purpose, the most striking aspect of this passage is the juxtaposition of figural and metafigural language. It contains seductive metaphors that bring into play a variety of irresistible objects: chamber music, butterflies, stars, books, running brooks, etc., and it inscribes these objects within dazzling fire- and waterworks of figuration. But the passage also comments normatively on the best way to achieve such effects; in this sense, it is metafigural: it writes figuratively about figures. It contrasts two ways of

5. The title of the second section of the first volume of Proust's *Recherche*; it is the name of the small town where Marcel spent his childhood holidays at his grandparents' house.

6. A servant.

7. *Swann's Way* [*Du côté de chez Swann*] (Paris: Pléiade, 1954), p. 83 [de Man's note and translation].

evoking the natural experience of summer and unambiguously states its preference for one of these ways over the other: the "necessary link" that unites the buzzing of the flies to the summer makes it a much more effective symbol than the tune heard "perchance" during the summer. The preference is expressed by means of a distinction that corresponds to the difference between metaphor and metonymy, necessity and chance being a legitimate way to distinguish between analogy and contiguity. The inference of identity and totality that is constitutive of metaphor is lacking in the purely relational metonymic contact: an element of truth is involved in taking Achilles for a lion but none in taking Mr. Ford[8] for a motor car. The passage is *about* the aesthetic superiority of metaphor over metonymy, but this aesthetic claim is made by means of categories that are the ontological ground of the metaphysical system that allows for the aesthetic to come into being as a category. The metaphor for summer (in this case, the synesthesia[9] set off by the "chamber music" of the flies) guarantees a presence which, far from being contingent, is said to be essential, permanently recurrent and unmediated by linguistic representations or figurations. Finally, in the second part of the passage, the metaphor of presence not only appears as the ground of cognition but as the performance of an action, thus promising the reconciliation of the most disruptive of contradictions. By then, the investment in the power of metaphor is such that it may seem sacrilegious to put it in question.

Yet, it takes little perspicacity to show that the text does not practice what it preaches. A rhetorical reading of the passage reveals that the figural praxis and the metafigural theory do not converge and that the assertion of the mastery of metaphor over metonymy owes its persuasive power to the use of metonymic structures. I have carried out such an analysis in a somewhat more extended context;[1] at this point, we are more concerned with the results than with the procedure. For the metaphysical categories of presence, essence, action, truth, and beauty do not remain unaffected by such a reading. This would become clear from an inclusive reading of Proust's novel or would become even more explicit in a language-conscious philosopher such as Nietzsche who, as a philosopher, has to be concerned with the epistemological consequences of the kind of rhetorical seductions exemplified by the Proust passage. It can be shown that the systematic critique of the main categories of metaphysics undertaken by Nietzsche in his late work, the critique of the concepts of causality, of the subject, of identity, of referential and revealed truth, etc., occurs along the same pattern of deconstruction that was operative in Proust's text; and it can also be shown that this pattern exactly corresponds to Nietzsche's description, in texts that precede *The Will to Power*[2] by more than fifteen years, of the structure of the main rhetorical tropes. The key to this critique of metaphysics, which is itself a recurrent gesture throughout the history of thought, is the rhetorical model of the trope

8. Henry Ford (1863–1947), American innovator of mass production and founder of the Ford Motor Company. Achilles: the greatest of the Greek warriors who fought at Troy. De Man draws on Jakobson's seminal distinction of metaphor (the figurative relation between brave Achilles and a lion) and metonymy (the figurative relation between Ford and one of his cars).

9. Rhetorical figure in which one sense is represented in terms of another; for example, "a loud tie."

1. In a later chapter of *Allegories of Reading: Figural Language in Rousseau, Nietzsche, Rilke, and Proust* (1979); this essay was reprinted to serve as the book's introduction.

2. A late work, drawing on fragments from ca. 1888 (published posthumously in 1901). For the earlier works to which de Man refers, see especially "On Truth and Lying in a Non-Moral Sense" (1873; above).

or, if one prefers to call it that, literature. It turns out that in these innocent-looking didactic exercises we are in fact playing for very sizeable stakes.

It is therefore all the more necessary to know what is linguistically involved in a rhetorically conscious reading of the type here undertaken on a brief fragment from a novel and extended by Nietzsche to the entire text of post-Hellenic thought. Our first examples dealing with the rhetorical questions were rhetorizations of grammar, figures generated by syntactical paradigms, whereas the Proust example could be better described as a grammatization of rhetoric. By passing from a paradigmatic structure based on substitution, such as metaphor, to a syntagmatic structure based on contingent association such as metonymy, the mechanical, repetitive aspect of grammatical forms is shown to be operative in a passage that seemed at first sight to celebrate the self-willed and autonomous inventiveness of a subject. Figures are assumed to be inventions, the products of a highly particularized individual talent, whereas no one can claim credit for the programmed pattern of grammar. Yet, our reading of the Proust passage shows that precisely when the highest claims are being made for the unifying power of metaphor, these very images rely in fact on the deceptive use of semi-automatic grammatical patterns. The deconstruction of metaphor and of all rhetorical patterns such as mimesis, paronomasia,[3] or personification that use resemblance as a way to disguise differences, takes us back to the impersonal precision of grammar and of a semiology derived from grammatical patterns. Such a reading puts into question a whole series of concepts that underlie the value judgments of our critical discourse: the metaphors of primacy, of genetic history, and, most notably, of the autonomous power to will of the self.

There seems to be a difference, then, between what I called the rhetorization of grammar (as in the rhetorical question) and the grammatization of rhetoric, as in the readings of the type sketched out in the passage from Proust. The former end up in indetermination, in a suspended uncertainty that was unable to choose between two modes of reading, whereas the latter seems to reach a truth, albeit by the negative road of exposing an error, a false pretense. After the rhetorical reading of the Proust passage, we can no longer believe the assertion made in this passage about the intrinsic, metaphysical superiority of metaphor over metonymy. We seem to end up in a mood of negative assurance that is highly productive of critical discourse. The further text of Proust's novel, for example, responds perfectly to an extended application of this pattern: not only can similar gestures be repeated throughout the novel, at all the crucial articulations or all passages where large aesthetic and metaphysical claims are being made—the scenes of involuntary memory, the workshop of Elstir, the septette of Vinteuil,[4] the convergence of author and narrator at the end of the novel—but a vast thematic and semiotic network is revealed that structures the entire narrative and that remained invisible to a reader caught in naïve metaphorical mystification. The whole of literature would respond in similar fashion, although the techniques and the patterns would have to vary considerably, of course, from author to author. But there is absolutely no reason why analyses of the

3. Wordplay, especially a pun.
4. Vinteuil, a composer, and Elstir, a painter, are characters in Proust's *Recherche*. "Septette": a septet, a musical composition for 7 performers.

kind here suggested for Proust would not be applicable, with proper modifications of technique, to Milton or to Dante or to Hölderlin.[5] This will in fact be the task of literary criticism in the coming years.

It would seem that we are saying that criticism is the deconstruction of literature, the reduction to the rigors of grammar of rhetorical mystifications. And if we hold up Nietzsche as the philosopher of such a critical deconstruction, then the literary critic would become the philosopher's ally in his struggle with the poets. Criticism and literature would separate around the epistemological axis that distinguishes grammar from rhetoric. It is easy enough to see that this apparent glorification of the critic-philosopher in the name of truth is in fact a glorification of the poet as the primary source of this truth; if truth is the recognition of the systematic character of a certain kind of error, then it would be fully dependent on the prior existence of this error. Philosophers of science like Bachelard or Wittgenstein[6] are notoriously dependent on the aberrations of the poets. We are back at our unanswered question: does the grammatization of rhetoric end up in negative certainty or does it, like the rhetorization of grammar, remain suspended in the ignorance of its own truth or falsehood?

Two concluding remarks should suffice to answer the question. First of all, it is not true that Proust's text can simply be reduced to the mystified assertion (the superiority of metaphor over metonymy) that our reading deconstructs. The reading is not "our" reading, since it uses only the linguistic elements provided by the text itself; the distinction between author and reader is one of the false distinctions that the reading makes evident. The deconstruction is not something we have added to the text but it constituted the text in the first place. A literary text simultaneously asserts and denies the authority of its own rhetorical mode, and by reading the text as we did we were only trying to come closer to being as rigorous a reader as the author had to be in order to write the sentence in the first place. Poetic writing is the most advanced and refined mode of deconstruction; it may differ from critical or discursive writing in the economy of its articulation, but not in kind.

But if we recognize the existence of such a moment as constitutive of all literary language, we have surreptitiously reintroduced the categories that this deconstruction was supposed to eliminate and that have merely been displaced. We have, for example, displaced the question of the self from the referent into the figure of the narrator, who then becomes the *signifé* [7] of the passage. It becomes again possible to ask such naïve questions as what Proust's, or Marcel's, motives may have been in thus manipulating language: was he fooling himself, or was he represented as fooling himself and fooling us into believing that fiction and action are as easy to unite, by reading, as the passage asserts? The pathos of the entire section, which would have been more noticeable if the quotation had been a little more extended, the constant vacillation of the narrator between guilt and well-being, invites such

5. Friedrich Hölderlin (1770–1843), German Romantic poet. John Milton (1608–1674), English poet whose works include *Paradise Lost* (1667). DANTE ALIGHIERI (1265–1321), Italian poet, best known for the *Divine Comedy* (1321).

6. Ludwig Wittgenstein (1889–1951), Austrian-born philosopher. Gaston Bachelard (1884–1962), French philosopher.

7. Signified (French); a term used by Saussure, who divided the sign into the *signified* (the meaning conveyed) and *signifier* (the symbol or sign that conveys that meaning).

questions. They are absurd questions, of course, since the reconciliation of fact and fiction occurs itself as a mere assertion made in a text, and is thus productive of more text at the moment when it asserts its decision to escape from textual confinement. But even if we free ourselves of all false questions of intent and rightfully reduce the narrator to the status of a mere grammatical pronoun, without which the narrative could not come into being, this subject remains endowed with a function that is not grammatical but rhetorical, in that it gives voice, so to speak, to a grammatical syntagm. The term *voice*, even when used in a grammatical terminology as when we speak of the passive or interrogative voice, is, of course, a metaphor inferring by analogy the intent of the subject from the structure of the predicate. In the case of the deconstructive discourse that we call literary, or rhetorical, or poetic, this creates a distinctive complication illustrated by the Proust passage. The reading revealed a first paradox: the passage valorizes metaphor as being the "right" literary figure, but then proceeds to constitute itself by means of the epistemologically incompatible figure of metonymy. The critical discourse reveals the presence of this delusion and affirms it as the irreversible mode of its truth. It cannot pause there however. For if we then ask the obvious and simple next question, whether the rhetorical mode of the text in question is that of metaphor or metonymy, it is impossible to give an answer. Individual metaphors, such as the chiaroscuro effect or the butterfly, are shown to be subordinate figures in a general clause whose syntax is metonymic; from this point of view, it seems that the rhetoric is superseded by a grammar that deconstructs it. But this metonymic clause has as its subject a voice whose relationship to this clause is again metaphorical. The narrator who tells us about the impossibility of metaphor is himself, or itself, a metaphor, the metaphor of a grammatical syntagm whose meaning is the denial of metaphor stated, by antiphrasis,[8] as its priority. And this subject-metaphor is, in its turn, open to the kind of deconstruction to the second degree, the rhetorical deconstruction of psycholinguistics, in which the more advanced investigations of literature are presently engaged, against considerable resistance.

We end up therefore, in the case of the rhetorical grammatization of semiology, just as in the grammatical rhetorization of illocutionary phrases, in the same state of suspended ignorance. Any question about the rhetorical mode of a literary text is always a rhetorical question which does not even know whether it is really questioning. The resulting pathos is an anxiety (or bliss, depending on one's momentary mood or individual temperament) of ignorance, not an anxiety of reference—as becomes thematically clear in Proust's novel when reading is dramatized, in the relationship between Marcel and Albertine,[9] not as an emotive reaction to what language does, but as an emotive reaction to the impossibility of knowing what it might be up to. Literature as well as criticism—the difference between them being delusive—is condemned (or privileged) to be forever the most rigorous and, consequently, the most unreliable language in terms of which man names and transforms himself.

1973, 1979

8. Rhetorical device of using words in a sense opposite to the generally accepted meaning.

9. Marcel's love interest in the novel.

The Return to Philology

The quarrelsome tone that hangs over the debates on the teaching of literature can often be traced back to the advent of contemporary literary theory. This is certainly not surprising. Whenever new approaches or techniques are being advocated, a very understandable ill-humor overcomes those who feel they may have to modify or to reconsider well-established pedagogical habits that served them well until the most recent troublemakers came along. But the polemical response in the case of contemporary theory, and especially of some of its aspects, runs deeper.

It feeds not only on civilized conservatism but on moral indignation. It speaks with an anxiety that is not only that of a disturbed tranquility but of a disturbed moral conscience. Nor is this mood confined to the opponents of theory. Its protagonists, in most cases, are just as nervous. When they appear not to be their self-assurance often seems to be dependent on utopian schemes. The well-established rationale for the professing of literature has come under fire. Small wonder that it chooses to shoot back.

Ever since the teaching of literature became an autonomous academic field (and we are frequently reminded that this is a fairly recent development, going back no further than the late nineteenth century) it has justified itself as a humanistic and historical discipline, allied to yet distinct from the descriptive sciences of philology[1] and rhetoric. Its ambitions, however, go beyond mere description. It not only has its own national and comparative history but, since it deals with a relatively stable canon of specific texts, it should be a model for the other historical sciences whose subject matter is less clearly defined. Moreover, it has the task of determining the meaning of texts and this hermeneutic function establishes its kinship with theology.

Finally, as a depositor of human experience of considerable variety and scope, it gains access to questions of moral philosophy—questions of value and of normative judgment. Its technical and descriptive aspects as a science of language dovetail with its historical, theological and ethical function. The professor of literature has good reasons to feel appeased; his scientific conscience is satisfied by the positive rigor of his linguistic and historical knowledge, while his moral, political and (in the extensive sense) religious conscience is assuaged by the application of this knowledge to the understanding of the world, of society and of the self. The didactics of literature could legitimately hope to be exemplary for interdisciplinary humanistic studies. Neither is this hope incompatible with literary theory and literary criticism: some forms of theory, especially those which continue a tradition of aesthetic speculation that, in the field of English, can be traced back to Coleridge,[2] fully confirm these expectations. This would be the case for such diverse names as those of I. A. Richards, Lionel Trilling, R. P. Blackmur and Northrop Frye.[3]

1. The discipline that studies cultures through historical analyses of their languages.
2. SAMUEL TAYLOR COLERIDGE (1772–1834), English poet and critic.
3. All 20th-century literary critics: Richards (1893–1979), an English critic whose works include *Practical Criticism* (1929); Trilling (1905–1975), a leading New York Intellectual; Blackmur (1904–1965), an American New Critic; and FRYE (1912–1991), a Canadian associated with archetypal criticism.

It would, however, not be quite the same for William Empson or for Kenneth Burke,[4] or, more recently, for some, predominantly French, critics and philosophers whose work takes into account investigations pursued in the field of structural linguistics and who have kindled the ire of their humanistic colleagues. Thus, in an influential article published in the Harvard alumni bulletin, *Harvard Magazine*, September–October 1982, the Distinguished Professor of English Literature, Walter Jackson Bate, author of outstanding books on Keats, Samuel Johnson[5] and the intellectual history of romanticism, denounced the bankruptcy of literary studies. Their increased professionalism and specialization have failed, he claims, to rescue the humanities at a time when they are said to be "in the weakest state they ever suffered—bent on a self-destructive course, through a combination of anger, fear and purblind defensiveness." In a historical overview that traces the gradual decay of literary teaching, Bate sees the increasing concentration on literary theory as the main cause for this decline. It culminates in the final catastrophe of the post-structural era, the invasion of departments of English by French influences that advocate "a nihilistic view of literature, of human communication, and of life itself."

The main culprit, denounced by name, is Jacques Derrida,[6] said to be a "puckish Parisian" (he is neither), "who never turns to the really major philosophers except to snatch at stale pessimisms" (e.g., Nietzsche[7]). The remark suggests that Professor Bate, a careful scholar and brilliant teacher, has this time confined his sources of information to *Newsweek* magazine.

The crisis in the teaching of literature to which Bate alerts us is genuine enough. This does not mean, however, that his diagnosis or his remedies are valid, even less so since these remedies do not take the form of a reasoned discussion but of an appeal to the administrative officers of the universities to deny tenure to teachers who concentrate on theory. The question to Bate's mind is not even in need of discussion. For all people of good will and good sense, the matter has long since been settled once and for all. What is left is a matter of law-enforcement rather than a critical debate. One must be feeling very threatened indeed to become so aggressively defensive.

My own awareness of the critical, even subversive, power of literary instruction does not stem from philosophical allegiances but from a very specific teaching experience. In the 1950s, Bate's colleague at Harvard, Reuben Brower,[8] taught an undergraduate course in General Education entitled "The Interpretation of Literature" (better known on the Harvard campus and in the profession at large as HUM 6) in which many graduate students in English and Comparative Literature served as teaching assistants. No one could be more remote from high-powered French theory than Reuben Brower. He wrote books on Shakespeare and on Pope[9] that are models of sensitive scholarship but not exactly manifestos for critical terrorism. He was

4. American critic (1897–1993; see above). Empson (1906–1984), English critic. Both wrote significant books on rhetorical analysis.
5. English poet, critic, and lexicographer (1709–1784). Bate (1918–1999), American literary scholar who wrote books of critical analysis as well as Pulitzer Prize–winning biographies of JOHNSON and Keats; the article discussed is titled "The Crisis in English Literature." John Keats (1795–1821), English Romantic poet.
6. Algerian-born French philosopher and progenitor of deconstruction (b. 1930; see below).
7. FRIEDRICH NIETZSCHE (1844–1900), German philosopher.
8. American critic affiliated with the New Criticism (1908–1975).
9. ALEXANDER POPE (1688–1744), English poet.

much more interested in Greek and Latin literature than in literary theory. The critics he felt closest to, besides Eliot, were Richards and Leavis,[1] and in both of them he was in sympathy with their emphasis on ethics.

Brower, however, believed in and effectively conveyed what appears to be an entirely innocuous and pragmatic precept, founded on Richards's "practical criticism." Students, as they began to write on the writings of others, were not to say anything that was not derived from the text they were considering. They were not to make any statements that they could not support by a specific use of language that actually occurred in the text. They were asked, in other words, to begin by reading texts closely as texts and not to move at once into the general context of human experience or history. Much more humbly or modestly, they were to start out from the bafflement that such singular turns of tone, phrase, and figure were bound to produce in readers attentive enough to notice them and honest enough not to hide their non-understanding behind the screen of received ideas that often passes, in literary instruction, for humanistic knowledge.

This very simple rule, surprisingly enough, had far-reaching didactic consequences. I have never known a course by which students were so transformed. Some never saw the point of thus restricting their attention to the matter at hand and of concentrating on the way meaning is conveyed rather than on the meaning itself. Others, however, caught on very quickly and, henceforth, they would never be the same. The papers they handed in at the end of the course bore little resemblance to what they produced at the beginning. What they lost in generality, they more than made up for in precision and in the closer proximity of their writing to the original mode. It did not make writing easier for them for they no longer felt free to indulge in any thought that came into their head or to paraphrase any idea they happened to encounter. The profession is littered with the books that the students of Reuben Brower failed to write. Good readers often are spare writers and in the present state of literary studies, that is all to the good.

Here was a course, then, utterly devoid of subversive intentions as well as of theoretical objections. The conceptual and terminological apparatus was kept to a minimum, with only a few ordinary language terms for metalanguage.[2] The entire stance was certainly not devoid of its own ideological and methodological assumptions, yet they managed to remain implicit without interfering with the procedures. Reuben Brower had a rare talent, not out of respect for the delicacy of language, for keeping things as tidy as a philosophical investigation ought to be yet, at the same time, entirely pragmatic. Mere reading, it turns out, prior to any theory, is able to transform critical discourse in a manner that would appear deeply subversive to those who think of the teaching of literature as a substitute for the teaching of theology, ethics, psychology, or intellectual history. Close reading accomplishes this often in spite of itself because it cannot fail to respond to structures of language which it is the more or less secret aim of literary teaching to keep hidden.

Attention to the philological or rhetorical devices of language is not the

1. F. R. Leavis (1895–1978), English critic. T. S. ELIOT (1888–1965), major American-born modernist poet as well as an influential critic.
2. Language about language itself.

same as aesthetic appreciation, although the latter can be a way of access to the former. Perhaps the most difficult thing for students and teachers of literature to realize is that their appreciation is measured by the analytical rigor of their own discourse about literature, a criterion that is not primarily or exclusively aesthetic. Yet it separates the sheep from the goats, the consumers from the *professors* of literature, the chit-chat of evaluation from actual perception.

The personal experience of Reuben Brower's Humanities 6 was not so different from the impact of theory on the teaching of literature over the past ten or fifteen years. The motives may have been more revolutionary and the terminology was certainly more intimidating. But, in practice, the turn to theory occurred as a return to philology, to an examination of the structure of language prior to the meaning it produces. This is so even among the most controversial French theoreticians. Foucault's first major book, *Les mots et les choses,*[3] as its title indicates, has to do with the referential relationship between language and reality, but it approaches the question not in terms of philosophical speculation but, much more pragmatically, as it appears in the methodological innovations of social scientists and philologists. Whereas Derrida's starting point, though more traditionally "philosophical" in appearance, stresses the empirical powers of language over those of intuition and knowledge. His critique of phenomenology in the name of linguistics, by way of Husserl and Saussure,[4] bears this out. Even in the case of Nietzsche, a frequent point of reference for all these writers, the accent falls on Nietzsche the philologist rather than Nietzsche the existential nihilist.

Why, then, the cries of doom and the appeals to mobilization against a common enemy? It appears that the return to philology, whether it occurs casually or as a consequence of highly self-conscious, philosophical mutations, upsets the taken-for-granted assumptions with which the profession of literature has been operating. As a result, the attribution of a reliable, or even exemplary, cognitive and, by extension, ethical function to literature indeed becomes much more difficult. But this is a recurrent philosophical quandary that has never been resolved. The latest version of the question, which still determines our present-day convictions about the aims of literature, goes back to the rise of aesthetics as an independent discipline in the later half of the eighteenth century. The link between literature (as art), epistemology, and ethics is the burden of aesthetic theory at least since Kant.[5] It is because we teach literature as an aesthetic function that we can move so easily from literature to its apparent prolongations in the spheres of self-knowledge, of religion, and of politics.

In its origin and its development, aesthetics has been the province of philosophers of nature and of the self rather than of philosophers of language. Neither has aesthetic theory succeeded in its admirable ambition to unite cognition, desire and morality in one single synthetic judgment. Professor Bate, in the article mentioned before, asserts as a matter of course that it

3. *Words and Things* (1966), translated as *The Order of Things* (1970), an influential book by the French philosopher and historian of ideas MICHEL FOUCAULT (1926–1984).

4. FERDINAND DE SAUSSURE (1857–1913), Swiss linguist and founder of structuralism and semiotics. Edmund Husserl (1859–1938), German phenomenological philosopher.

5. IMMANUEL KANT (1724–1804), German idealist philosopher whose *Critique of Judgment* (1790; see above) is a foundational work of aesthetics.

suffices to "turn to Kant" to lay to rest a linguistically motivated scepticism like that of David Hume.[6] He echoes a generally admitted position among professors of literature rather than among professors of philosophy.

Whether a reading of *The Critique of Judgment*, as distinct from its simplified versions in Schiller[7] and his offspring, would confirm this assertion certainly stands in need of careful examination. Contemporary literary theory has started this long overdue process.

Literary theory raises the unavoidable question whether aesthetic values can be compatible with the linguistic structures that make up the entities from which these values are derived. Such questions never ceased to haunt the consciousness of writers and philosophers. They come to the fore in the ambivalent rejection of rhetoric at the very moment that it was being used and refined as never before, or in the assimilation of the considerable aesthetic charge emanating from rhetorical tropes to the aesthetic neutrality of grammar. It is by no means an established fact that aesthetic values and linguistic structures are incompatible. What is established is that their compatibility, or lack of it, has to remain an open question and that the manner in which the teaching of literature, since its beginning in the later nineteenth century, has foreclosed the question is unsound, even if motivated by the best of intentions. What also ought to be (but is not) established is that the professing of literature ought to take place under the aegis of this question.

From a purely methodological point of view, this would not be difficult to achieve. It would involve a change by which literature, instead of being taught only as a historical and humanistic subject, should be taught as a rhetoric and a poetics prior to being taught as a hermeneutics and a history. The institutional resistances to such a move, however, are probably insurmountable. For one thing, it changes departments of English from being large organizations in the service of everything except their own subject matter into much smaller units, dedicated to the professional specialization that Professor Bate deplores. It also requires a change in the rationale for the teaching of literature, away from standards of cultural excellence that, in the last analysis, are always based on some form of religious faith, to a principle of disbelief that is not so much scientific as it is critical, in the full philosophical sense of the term. One sees easily enough why such changes are not likely to occur.

Yet, with the critical cat now so far out of the bag that one can no longer ignore its existence, those who refuse the crime of theoretical ruthlessness can no longer hope to gain a good conscience. Neither, of course, can the theorists—but, then, they never laid claim to it in the first place.

1982

6. Scottish philosopher and historian (1711–1776; see above).

7. FRIEDRICH VON SCHILLER (1759–1805), German playwright and poet whose most influential work in aesthetics is *On Naive and Sentimental Poetry* (1795–96).

IRVING HOWE
1920–1993

Criticism at its best, Irving Howe observed, is a "personal art" in which "the power of insight counts far more than allegiance to a critical theory or position. . . . No method can give the critic what he needs most: knowledge, disinterestedness, love, insight, style." These words illuminate Howe's conception of his critical approach—perhaps accurately conveying more a tone or a style—especially the personal, independent slant on literature and politics that he sought to maintain. But they may puzzle present-day readers, who typically see him as a key member of a group: the "New York Intellectuals," who exercised much authority and influence in literary and cultural life from the 1930s into the 1960s.

A number of critics centered in New York City in the 1930s aimed to be men of letters on the model of EDMUND WILSON—active, engaged intellectuals writing about and battling over ideas, political positions, and modernism in literature and the arts. Nearly all were in fact men, and most were secularized Jews; they challenged the formalist, text-centered theory and practice of the emerging New Criticism and, in their politics, embraced Marxism but rejected the Soviet Union and assailed those in the United States and abroad who defended or excused Joseph Stalin's murderous policies. The first generation included the literary critic and editor Philip Rahv, the critic and essayist Lionel Trilling, the political journalist and editor Dwight Macdonald, and the art critics Meyer Schapiro, Clement Greenberg, and Harold Rosenberg; the second included Howe, the critic and memoirist Alfred Kazin, the poet-critic Delmore Schwartz, and the novelist Saul Bellow. Combative, ambitious, cocky, keenly aware of one another's work and influence, proud of being part of an intelligentsia but fiercely determined to take radical risks and be brashly provocative in argument, the New York Intellectuals were, in Rosenberg's witty phrase, a "herd of independent minds."

By the 1950s, few of the New York Intellectuals were Marxists any longer; some viewed themselves as democratic socialists or liberal humanists or cosmopolitan intellectuals, while still others in later years grew increasingly conservative on cultural and political issues. The literary criticism of the best of the New York Intellectuals, especially that of Rahv (e.g., the collection *Literature and the Sixth Sense*, 1969) and Trilling (e.g., *The Liberal Imagination*, 1950) remains stimulating. Yet even this work has come to seem dated, for it dramatizes the need that many once felt for a sharp, self-aware integration of literary and political commentary. Now, after the cold war has ended, many younger readers find much of the writing by the New York Intellectuals hard to understand; its fighting tone, edgy rhythms, and political contexts and cultural references are far from their reality.

In his intellectual autobiography, *A Margin of Hope* (1982), Howe describes the nature of the energized, contentious work of these authors and its relationship to their lives as Jewish Americans:

> The New York writers developed a style of brilliance, and a style of brilliance is often hard to bear. At its best this style represented a certain view of the intellectual life: the free-lance dash, peacock strut, knockout synthesis. It celebrated the idea of the intellectual as antispecialist, the writer whose specialty is not to have one. It celebrated the writer as roamer among theories, as dilettante connoisseur, as *luftmensch* [i.e., impractical visionary] of the mind. . . . Our partial assimilation—roots loosed in Jewish soil but still not torn out, roots lowered into American soil but still not fixed—gave us a seemingly endless range of possibilities.

That sense of possibilities led them to embrace radicalism in both politics and modern literature. The New York Intellectuals, particularly at the outset, combined dedication to the Marxist-socialist tradition with an intense response to European writers, philosophers, and theorists (in particular, Dostoyevsky, NIETZSCHE, FREUD) and to avant-garde authors such as T. S. ELIOT, William Butler Yeats, James Joyce, and William Faulkner. They took their stand on the political Left even as they promoted and wrote brilliantly about modernist authors whose explicit politics were conservative, reactionary, or (in the extreme case of Ezra Pound, author of anti-Semitic, pro-Fascist diatribes) far worse. An author, as Rahv wrote of Dostoyevsky, could create art "reactionary in its abstract content" but "radical in sensibility and subversive in performance."

Howe was born in New York City, the son of immigrant Jews from Ukraine. By his early teens, he was already immersed in the tempestuous world of New York radical politics as a staunch anti-Stalinist. Howe received his undergraduate degree in 1940 from the City College of New York, attended graduate school for eighteen months, and then, in 1942, entered the U.S. Army. When the war ended he returned to New York, quickly becoming an incisive critic and journalist writing about politics, society, and literature. His essays appeared in prominent journals and magazines of opinion, especially the *Partisan Review, Commentary*, and the *Nation*.

Though an anti-Communist, Howe stayed loyal to the ideas and ideals of Marxism. As he explained in 1952, "Marxism seems to me the best available method for understanding and making history. Even as its most dogmatic, it proposes a more realistic theory of society than the currently popular liberalism." In 1954 he and Lewis Coser, bucking the tide of conservatism in American politics and intellectual life, founded the radical quarterly *Dissent* to reexamine the history of socialism and Marxism. *Dissent* still publishes the work of many important leftist literary critics, philosophers, and social scientists from the United States and around the world. Howe's political writings in his books and in *Dissent* proved highly controversial, especially during the 1960s and 1970s, when he wrangled bitterly with leaders of the New Left and popular protest movements. Though sharing many of their goals—he was an early opponent of the Vietnam War, for example—he accused the protesters of moral and political extremism that betrayed the values of socialism and democracy.

Howe later expressed some regret for the hostile tone of these polemics. His positions and, as he conceded, the anger in his voice explain in part why Howe, though still productive, was not an important critic for most younger literary scholars and critics during the 1970s and 1980s. By the later stages of his career he was viewed less as an independent intellectual than as a member of the establishment. His claims to be sympathetic to radical, exploratory ideas were viewed with suspicion, for he was dubious about (or else simply uninterested in) feminism, questioned changes in the canon and the curriculum, balked at new developments in literary theory, and disliked postmodern literature. Indeed, like other New York Intellectuals, Howe had in most regards joined the establishment. He held academic appointments at Brandeis University (1953–61), Stanford University (1961–63), and, beginning in 1963, at the City University of New York, where he was awarded the rank of distinguished professor. He received grants and fellowships and won many honors for his work; he published in the best periodicals; he lectured extensively; and he was the author of a best-seller, *World of Our Fathers* (1976), a richly detailed history of the immigrant Jews' journey to and life in America from the 1880s to 1970s.

Howe realized the complexity of his position as a redoubtable critic of the very system that was bestowing privileges on him; to him it indicated a challenge that modern intellectuals in general faced and would be obliged to articulate. In several of his essays, he presented ironic accounts of the ways in which capitalism soothes the alienated consciousness and manages to absorb even its most stringent critics and outsiders. He regarded the university as part of this process of co-option and embourgeoisement: the specialization that it fostered seemed a trap, shutting one away from larger audiences. But his own work kept its independence. Its great merit lies in Howe's sustained effort to respect the autonomy of literature as an art and yet delineate how it is embedded in history. He defined his own principles cogently: "The most glorious vision of the intellectual life is that which is loosely called humanist: the idea of a mind committed yet dispassionate, ready to stand alone, curious, eager, skeptical. The banner of critical independence, ragged and torn though it may be, is still the best we have" ("This Age of Conformity," 1954).

In this humanist engagement with literature, culture, and politics—a politics of the Left—Howe differs from the New Critics (see JOHN CROWE RANSOM and CLEANTH BROOKS), his contemporaries; in Howe's judgment, too often in their work literary texts appear cut off from political, historical, and other contexts. As he notes in *A Margin of Hope*, their analysis "tended to blunt [the] edge of insurgency" of such movements as modernism. Moreover, the New Critics failed to reflect on their own conservative religious and political views, and on how their critical writing and pedagogy promoted such views. Because they "encouraged a preference for the static," they dismissed "that radicalism of voice which forms a major strand within European and American modernism." Howe's commitment to the dialectical relationship between literature and history separates him from later New Historicists and proponents of "cultural studies" as well (see STEPHEN GREENBLATT and STUART HALL). For these later critics, literature dissolves as a category and becomes woven into "discourse" or "textuality"; hence it no longer inhabits the distinctive place as an art that Howe preserved for it.

In "History and the Novel" (1990), our selection, Howe returns to an issue he had treated before—the various, tangled relations between literature and history. As always, he is deeply interested in the power of the novel as a literary form to incorporate history, to delve into the realities of social crisis and strife, while capturing our attention as a discrete fictional work of art. And as always, part of the pleasure of reading Howe comes from his brilliant throwaway ideas (for example, his striking observation that the novel inevitably both represents historical realities and criticizes dominant values, whatever an author's intentions). From one vantage point, Howe is an old-fashioned believer in the novel's capacity to seduce us into its world, where we lose ourselves in the experience of reading. But Howe has no interest in limiting his discussion to these terms. We can, he suggests, distinguish between what is inside and outside a text, but in fact we know that this distinction, however useful, is misleading: the intersections between a novel and history, art and ideology, do not support it. He points out the virtual impossibility of "separat[ing] ideological sentiments from literary judgments, for [we] read as whole persons, with a rush of feeling and idea that is stronger than any recognition of the book's local verisimilitude."

Some readers may find this essay confusing or even contradictory in its love of the special pleasures that literature provides, on the one hand, and in its attentiveness to the saturation of literary texts in politics and history, on the other. But Howe's claims become clearer when one becomes attuned to his dialectical style and remembers the positions he is arguing against. He resists both formalist approaches that cordon off literature from history and cultural approaches that overpoliticize literature and thereby reduce great writers into exponents of an ideology with which we simply agree or disagree.

At the end, Howe's inquiry into literature and history takes an elegiac turn, when he notes how the passage of time affects our responses to the history depicted in novels. In the case of *Mansfield Park*, for example, present-day readers are rightly troubled by passing references to slaveholding and colonialism, which loomed less significantly for Jane Austen's contemporary audience. For writers of the modern period, Howe adds, we encounter a different problem: novelists such as Ernest Hemingway, Ignazio Silone, and Arthur Koestler describe historical periods and address cultural and political issues that no longer resonate with most younger readers. As Howe concedes, the obvious remedy for a lack of historical knowledge is to learn as much as we can about the period in which an author wrote and set the text. But, he acknowledges, even a "historical imagination" is not enough, for we will still be unable to read the text with the "direct, spontaneous response" enjoyed by earlier generations.

The thrilling radical immediacy of modernism in the arts, the shocks and controversies of the cold war—for Howe these remained vivid, but not so for his students, whose lives were bound up with a different history and set of relationships to politics and literature. The passage of time has likewise diminished the political force of Howe's work, yet his literary criticism remains sharp and bracing, bearing witness to the depth of his commitment to the enduring value of the literary imagination.

BIBLIOGRAPHY

Howe was extraordinarily productive, the author or editor of nearly fifty books. He wrote a critical biography of Sherwood Anderson (1951); monographs on William Faulkner (1952, rev. and expanded 1962, 1975) and Thomas Hardy (1967); a provocative study, *Politics and the Novel* (1957), which includes acute appraisals of Stendhal, Dostoyevsky, Conrad, Turgenev, James, and others; and *The American Newness* (1986), a survey of culture and politics in the age of Emerson, Hawthorne, and Thoreau. With Lewis Coser, he wrote a history of the American Communist Party (1957); he also wrote a study of Leon Trotsky (1978) and a history of socialism in America (1985).

Howe published a number of collections of his essays and reviews, including *A World More Attractive* (1963), *Steady Work* (1966), *Decline of the New* (1970), and *The Critical Point* (1973). His valuable work on Yiddish literature and culture included, with Eliezer Greenberg, *A Treasury of Yiddish Poetry* (1969), *Voices from the Yiddish: Essays, Memoirs, Diaries* (1972), and *Ashes out of Hope: Fiction by Soviet-Yiddish Writers* (1977); and, with Ruth R. Wisse and Khone Shmeruk, *The Penguin Book of Modern Yiddish Verse* (1987). See also two collections of Howe's essays and reviews: *Selected Writings, 1950–1990* (1990) and *A Critic's Notebook,* edited by Nicholas Howe (1994). He presented his intellectual autobiography in *A Margin of Hope* (1982).

For a cogent critical assessment of Howe, consult the entry by Mark Krupnick in *Modern American Critics Since 1955*, vol. 67 (ed. Gregory S. Jay, 1988), in the Gale Dictionary of Literary Biography series. Edward Alexander, *Irving Howe—Socialist, Critic, Jew* (1998), is an excellent intellectual biography. Illuminating background and commentary on Howe and the New York Intellectuals are provided by Grant Webster, *The Republic of Letters* (1979); William Barrett, *The Truants* (1982); Alexander Bloom, *Prodigal Sons: The New York Intellectuals and Their World* (1986); Alan M. Wald, *The New York Intellectuals: The Rise and Decline of the Anti-Stalinist Left from the 1930s to the 1980s* (1987); Neil Jumonville, *Critical Crossings: The New York Intellectuals in Postwar America* (1991); Hugh Wilford, *The New York Intellectuals: From Vanguard to Institution* (1995); and Harvey M. Teres, *Renewing the Left: Politics, Imagination, and the New York Intellectuals* (1996). A broader historical perspective is offered in Thomas Bender, *New York Intellect: A History of Intellectual Life in New York City, From 1750 to the Beginnings of Our Own Time* (1987).

History and the Novel

I.

Defoe's Moll Flanders fears that she will sink into London's depths; Balzac's Lucien races toward fame and fortune; Dostoyevsky's Raskolnikov murders at least partly for money; Joyce's Bloom[1] sells advertisements for a newspaper. Except for Moll, these fictional characters also cherish high motives and grand delusions, yet they are constrained by commonplace necessity. They must find a way to earn a living, they are pressed by circumstances quite as most of us are in reality. No such pressures, however, beset Aeneas, Tristan, or Faust[2]—not even the most literal-minded reader can ever have worried about their finances.

In the novel there is no "once upon a time . . ." There is London in the 1840s, Moscow in the 1950s. The clock rules; place helps determine psychic formation; characters reach identity through social role. In the novel a complex of circumstances often emerges as a "slice" of time across the passage of history, since an illusion of historical stoppage is essential for that "thickness" of specification at which many novels aim: Chicago as it looked upon Sister Carrie's arrival, Paris seen through the eyes of Swann.[3]

But the illusion of historical stoppage must also be linked to an illusion of historical flow. How this is done we hardly know, it is a secret of genius. A fictional "world," say, Faulkner's Yoknapatawpha County,[4] is portrayed at more-or-less stationary points, yet the very act of so conceiving it promotes the illusion of historical motion, somewhat the way a series of stills can result in a moving picture. Social circumstance melts into historical process.

II.

Novelists write on the tacit premise of the self-sufficiency of history, the cosmic solitariness of mankind. Beneath heaven's "indifferent blue"[5] we are now freed from the decrees of any external will, as the glow of faith is replaced by the hard light of causality.

It was deism[6] that taught us to accept the pain of historicity. By granting God powers of initiation and then putting him to sleep forever, deism freed the mind from the puzzle of origins and cleared the way for historical consciousness. Without such a tacit premise, the novel could not have gotten very far, since it really has no room for a will superior to natural law. True, great novels have been written by devout Christians, but as writers they were something more or less than devout Christians.

In wrenching free from the dualisms of Christianity, modern novelists improvised historical dualisms of their own. Soon after the Enlightenment, the problem confronting the novelistic imagination was not only the gloom

1. Bloom is the antihero of *Ulysses* (1922), by James Joyce (1882–1941). Moll Flanders: title character in a picaresque novel (1722) by Daniel Defoe (1660–1731). Lucien: a character in *Lost Illusions* (1837–43), a novel by Honoré de Balzac (1799–1850). Raskolnikov: the central character in *Crime and Punishment* (1866), by Fyodor Dostoyevsky (1821–1881).

2. In German legend a magician and alchemist who sells his soul to the devil in exchange for power and knowledge; also the protagonist in several literary works, including *Faust* (1808, 1832) by Johann Wolfgang von Goethe. Aeneas: the Trojan hero of Virgil's epic poem, the *Aeneid* (19 B.C.E.). Tristan: in Arthurian legend, a knight who falls in love with the Irish princess Iseult; this story provided the basis of the opera *Tristan and Isolde* (1865), by Richard Wagner.

3. Charles Swann, a leading character in *Remembrance of Things Past* (1913–27), by Marcel Proust (1871–1922). Sister Carrie: title character of a naturalistic novel (1900) by Theodore Dreiser (1871–1945).

4. The fictional setting in Mississippi for 14 novels and many short stories by William Faulkner (1897–1962).

5. A phrase from "Sunday Morning" (1923), by the American poet Wallace Stevens.

6. The belief, which gained force in the 18th century, that God created the universe but remains separate or distant from it, permitting all creations to govern themselves through natural laws. Deism rejects the supernatural doctrines of Christianity, such as belief in divine revelation in the Bible, and emphasizes the importance of reason and ethical conduct.

of being distanced from heaven; it was also the pain of estrangement from a society taken to be at least as indifferent to men and women as the cosmos was now recognized to be. In many nineteenth-century novels, society figures as more than the sum of its members. It takes on what we call "a life of its own," and that life is not ours, certainly not the portion of life that we cherish most. Society now hovers over mankind like a crushing weight, sometimes with a willful malevolence. It's notable that conflicting visions of society bear a curious similarity to conflicting visions of God—and, for that matter, of God's disappearance. Remove the idea of a wrathful or a loving God, and the distance from a neutral to a malevolent cosmos is not very great. Remove the idea of a naturally ordained social hierarchy, and the distance from a neutral to a malevolent social order is even smaller.

III.

A parallel development can be noticed, I think, with regard to the idea of the self. As a historically liberating hypothesis advanced during the Enlightenment and the age of Romanticism, the self becomes a shadow of our public lives, created within the modern historical moment while often turning upon it as a critical adversary. The self comes to be treasured as a reserve of consciousness, a resource beyond the press of social forms. The child of history, it erects a defense against the assaults of history. The very assumption that we can locate a psychic presence that we call the self, or that it is useful to suppose such a presence exists, implies a separation of inner being from outer behavior—what might be called the dualism of the person.

With time, the notion of the self becomes frayed, breaking into fragments of dissociation and estrangement. In Beckett's[7] novels and plays it ends as a state of nullity, the self erased or reduced to waiting. Perhaps it's a simplification to see the history of the novel—or historical consciousness working through the novel—as a two-sided confrontation with demons of estrangement: those that bear down from without and those that surge up from within. With Kafka,[8] this distinction collapses.

IV.

The historicity of the novel, wrote Georg Lukacs,[9] is shown in its "derivation of the individuality of characters from the historical peculiarities of their age." Versions of morality, styles of sexual behavior, tokens of psychic anxiety: such elements of fictional characterization are shaped by the moment of composition as well as by the individual sensibility that conforms to, or rebels against, that moment. George Eliot's Dorothea[1] strains toward a "heroic" surmounting of circumstance, but not only does circumstance limit her choice of vocation, the very notion she holds of what a heroic aspiration should be is itself flattened out by the circumstances of her life. By now Turgenev's Bazarov[2] may represent the generic figure of the thwarted rebel,

7. Samuel Beckett (1906–1989), Irish-born writer, best known for his play *Waiting for Godot* (1952).
8. Franz Kafka (1883–1924), Austrian writer born in Prague; his fictions often matter-of-factly present grotesque unreality in a pointless world.
9. GYÖRGY LUKÁCS (1885–1971), Hungarian Marxist philosopher and literary critic, author of *The Historical Novel* (1955).
1. The central character in the novel *Middlemarch* (1871–72), by George Eliot (1819–1880).
2. Character in *Fathers and Sons* (1862), by the Russian novelist Ivan Turgenev (1818–1883).

but to gain this status he had first to be deployed as a narrow-minded positivist of a kind that flourished in mid-nineteenth-century Russia. Nor are they ready-made characters "placed" against a given or fixed historical background; they emerge out of the writer's historical awareness, out of a sense of a lived moment. The characters come, so to say, from the writer-in-history.

But only out of historical awareness? Of course not. Individual natures, visions, idiosyncrasies all play a part. Only as a convenience of discourse can we distinguish the historical from the individual. Still, the novel rests on the assumption that man is a consequence of himself, the outcome of a self-initiated activity over stretches of time. And woman, too. The novel thereby refuses, or at least minimizes the claims of, a belief in unalterable human nature.

Ortega y Gasset,[3] in a famous sentence, remarks that "man has no nature; what he has is . . . a history." This is a powerful overstatement. Even if man has only a history, there are constants and continuities within that history that might well come, in their accumulation, to be something like a fixed nature. In the absence of such constants and continuities, we would be unable to make out fictional characters with any degree of intelligibility. So it might be better to say: man has no unchanging nature; what his nature does have is . . . a history. And in most or much fiction, such an assumption prevails.

Most novelists, I'm sure, never bothered their heads about this, but felt their way empirically, sentence by sentence, character by character. But what about those who did hold to an idea of immutable human nature? We can only speculate. Insofar as novelists like Fielding[4] held to a classical view of a fixed human nature, this had to make itself felt, of course, in their work, and many novels bear the imprint of worldviews inherited from both classical Christianity and earlier literary genres (*Tom Jones,* for instance). Yet the fact that a novelist deliberately and frequently wrote out of a conscious belief in immutable human traits—especially useful, by the way, in comedy, where it allows a stable repertoire of habit—does not at all mean that his work is untouched by the signs of history. Again, *Tom Jones*: Fielding's organizing conception of human nature may be suprahistorical, but his treatment of Squire Western and Lady Bellaston[5] reflects an acute historical consciousness. Fielding may see them as universal types, and so they are, but we also see them as peculiarly situated in a specific moment of English life. Even what a writer like Fielding takes to be an immutable human trait may itself be marked by historical mutability.

V.

One of the things we expect from novels is that they answer the question put by Trollope's title *How We Live Now.*[6] Daily existence, with its scatter of contingencies and exhaustion of energies, preoccupies not only the realists; it absorbs even novelists like Proust who reach toward philosophical scope,

3. José Ortega y Gasset (1883–1955), Spanish philosopher and essayist. The quotation is from *Toward a Philosophy of History* (1941).

4. Henry Fielding (1707–1754), English writer whose works include the novel *Tom Jones* (1749).

5. A fashionable lady, one of Tom Jones's paramours. Squire Western: the Tory father of Sophia, Tom's beloved.

6. A novel by the English writer Anthony Trollope (1815–1882), correctly titled *The Way We Live Now* (1875).

or those like Lawrence[7] who search for deeper grounds of existence. And also a writer like Beckett, whose bubbling nausea has a source in dailiness.

Still, we ought not to think of history as a tyrant imposing itself, as if from necessity, upon every novel within reach. As history seeps into the novel, it becomes transformed into something else, into what might be called history-in-the-novel. Nor does history make itself felt simply as a reproduction of the familiar world. For many acceptable novels a sort of moderate mimesis is sufficient, the kind about which we say, "Well, it gives a pretty faithful picture of life in Oklahoma during the Depression years."[8] Still, as modern readers we have come to expect more. Accurate representation seems no longer enough, if only because journalism claims—or pretends—to offer as much. At least since the late nineteenth century we have imposed an enormous cultural burden upon the novel, coming to think of it as an agency of moral criticism, and more remarkably as a creator of values. *How We Live* becomes *How Should We Live?*—and then, *Can We Live?*

During its two greatest periods—the mid-nineteenth and early twentieth centuries—the novel maintained a deeply critical relation, even a subversive relation, to the social milieu in which it thrived. (Is literature "ungrateful," does it bite the hand that feeds it? Perhaps so; but that hand needs an occasional sharp bite, and anyway it does many other things than feed.) What gets "swept" into the novel are not just depictions of how we live now; it also draws upon the line of critical thought, the fund of literary allusions, the play of street sentiment, and sometimes the ideology of revolt. Look, even, at the work of such unrebellious novelists as Thackeray[9] and Trollope, and you will see that there is more in it than acquiescence to standard Victorian precepts. There is also a subterranean critical ferment, sometimes beyond the writer's intention. Once past the sorts of novels written for amusement or shock, a representation of life can rarely be separated from a criticism of values.

Is this true only for the modern epoch, so ruthless in its self-perceptions? I think not. Something about mimesis, the effort honestly to evoke a portion of shared experience, seems to mandate criticism. And probably there is no such thing as a mere record or "slice" of life, since all representations imply perspective and perspective entails criticism, though not necessarily of a type to satisfy critics of a particular kind or moment.

VI.

When you read a novel with a strong political-historical slant, you are faced with the delicate problem of balancing social rhetoric and imaginative representation. In certain novels by Dostoyevsky, Stendhal, and Conrad, the two can hardly be separated, so that there follows among critics, as Joseph Frank[1] remarks, "quarrels over the validity of the images of social life created by novelists." Works like *The Possessed, The Red and the Black,* and *Nostromo*[2] stir deep passions, which make a pure or disinterested literary judgment very hard

7. D. H. Lawrence (1885–1930), English novelist and poet.
8. An allusion to *The Grapes of Wrath* (1939), a novel by John Steinbeck.
9. William Makepeace Thackeray (1811–1863), English novelist and satirist.

1. Literary critic and scholar (b. 1918), author of a much-admired biography of Dostoyevsky.
2. Novel (1904) by Joseph Conrad (1857–1924). *The Possessed* (1871–72), novel by Dostoyevsky. *The Red and the Black* (1830), novel by Stendhal (1783–1842).

In an essay about *The Possessed,* Frank draws upon an extensive knowledge of Russian culture to argue against critics like Philip Rahv[3] and me, who greatly admire Dostoyevsky's novel, recognize that it scores some hits against leftist dogmatism, and still believe that its attack upon Russian radicalism constitutes, on the whole, a historical distortion. Frank argues that Dostoyevsky "does not transgress the bounds of verisimilitude" in *The Possessed;* it follows closely the career of the infamous Nechaev,[4] the nineteenth-century Russian adventurer-revolutionary of iron will and terrorist deceit. Dostoyevsky, continues Frank:

> has been charged with giving a misleading picture . . . of the Russian radical movement as a whole. Nechaev was incontestably an isolated phenomenon among the radical groups of the 1860s, and his systematic Machiavellianism was alien to the other major organizations of the radical intelligentsia. . . . In point of fact . . . Dostoyevsky never tried to give any other impression.

One critic's "point of fact," however, may clash with another's "impression." I would argue that by the populating his radical group with scoundrels and buffoons, and by employing a style of searing ridicule in his treatment of them (laced though it is with a subterranean feeling of kinship), Dostoyevsky *had* to leave another "impression." He was after bigger game than just the little Nechaev group. He was intent upon the showing that the murderous buffoonery, the "systematic Machiavellianism" of Peter Verkhovensky (the fictional double of Nechaev), is inherent in or a logical extension of the more humane and rational brands of radicalism. He wanted the part to be seen as representing the whole.

If, as Frank writes, Dostoyevsky acknowledged that the circle around Peter Verkhovensky was merely "an isolated phenomenon among the radical groups of the 1860s," and if indeed this acknowledgment informed the plot of *The Possessed,* then not only would his novel lose its claim to representativeness, it would shrink into an extended anecdote about a strange fanatic. But *The Possessed* does advance, as any serious novel must, a strong claim to some degree of representativeness, what I'd call a sort of "potential verisimilitude," one in which the story is taken to form an anticipation of things to come.

So there is a disagreement here. To certain kinds of critics the disagreement would be profoundly uninteresting, since they do not regard verisimilitude as a significant factor in the criticism of fiction. But Frank and I do; we both respond to the heavy breath of history upon Dostoyevsky's work. Where we disagree is in estimating the specific relationship between historical event and Dostoyevsky's rendering of it. For my present purposes, it hardly matters which, if either, of us is right, since what interests me here is in trying to locate a critical problem.

We can read works of literature touching on the politics of a distant time in a relaxed fashion: Who feels strongly about, or quite remembers, Dante's

3. Literary critic (1908–1973), a founder of the journal the *Partisan Review* and the author of many essays on the 19th- and 20th-century novel. Howe here refers to Rahv's "Dostoyevsky in *The Possessed*" (1938).

4. Sergei Nechayev (1847–1882), Russian anarchist.

politics?[5] But novels that evoke our deepest biases, as *The Possessed* still can, make the act of reading into a moral risk, entailing what critics of a few decades ago used to call "the problem of belief."[6] (For readers without beliefs, of course, there is no problem.) Readers with strong political opinions are likely to find that in responding to a novel like *The Possessed*, it is all but impossible to separate ideological sentiments from literary judgments, for they read as whole persons, with a rush of feeling and idea that is stronger than any recognition of the book's local verisimilitude.

Let us suppose, then, that Frank and I, sharing a high estimate of *The Possessed*, are not very far apart in our political views. How are we to explain the differences between us? He believes that, in demonstrating the faithfulness of the novel to the actual experience of Nechaev, he has also demonstrated that "the usual accusations against Dostoyevsky [regarding the historical implication of the novel] must be qualified," while I believe that together with brilliant insights Dostoyevsky offered brilliant distortions. My admiration will probably turn out to be more qualified or uneasy than Frank's.

Can we be certain, however, whether these differences are due to political assumptions or literary valuations? Do we really know how to distinguish between them? The one thing that seems reasonably clear is that I respond more intensely to Dostoyevsky's ideological intent than does Frank. But that of course does not mean that I respond more accurately.

I am left with a severe problem (some would say, a confusion). How can you say that *The Possessed* is both a great work of literature and also a work that offers a distorted, even malicious treatment of its subject? I am not at all sure how to answer this question: perhaps by recognizing that the imperatives of literature and history can be at deep variance. In any case, I am entangled in this difficulty, and the tangle is exactly where I want to remain, since I believe it is faithful to the actual experience of reading such novels.

VII.

"Ah," cries an impatient voice, "history, yes, but what about the eternal themes, those recurrent human experiences, those overarching myths that, as Collingwood[7] once wrote, tell readers 'the secrets of their own hearts,' themes like love and death, innocence and experience, goodness and evil, themes linking Helen and Paris to Anna and Vronsky, perhaps to Lily Bart and Selden?[8] Are not these the abiding concerns of literature, reducing to a quite secondary level all reflected changes of historical circumstance? Do we read Dreiser's *An American Tragedy* for his knowledge of hotels, or for his ability to enter the sadly yearning heart of Clyde Griffiths?[9] And what about the archetypal characters through whom the abiding myths are dramatized,

5. The Italian poet DANTE ALIGHIERI (1265–1321) held strong political views.
6. A topic for debate among the New Critics and other modern critics about the degree to which a reader's beliefs affect his or her response to and judgment of a literary work.
7. R. G. Collingwood (1889–1943), English philosopher, aesthetician, and historian.
8. Characters in an unfulfilled relationship in *The House of Mirth* (1905) by Edith Wharton. In Greek mythology, Helen's abduction from her husband's home by Paris is the cause of the Trojan War. Anna and Vronsky: ill-fated lovers in *Anna Karenina* (1875–77) by Leo Tolstoy (1828–1910), Russian novelist and moralist.
9. Social-climbing protagonist of Dreiser's 1925 novel who is executed for murdering his pregnant girlfriend.

do they not survive—Oedipus and Quixote, Clarissa Harlowe and Tess[1]—even into the age of the computer?"

Well, yes; but the point is that if you strip them to bareness, the eternal themes come to seem commonplace, even boring. To affect us, they must take on flesh that will decay, be located in houses that will crumble. Eternity lodges in the temporal. Here is an illuminating passage by William Troy[2] about the scene in Zola's[3] *Germinal* in which Etienne and Catherine are trapped in the mine:

> It brings us back to an atmosphere and a meaning at least as old as the story of Orpheus and Eurydice.[4] For what is the mine itself but a reintegration of the Hades-Hell symbol? The immediate and particular social situation is contained within the larger pattern of a universal recrudescence . . .

I would prefer to say that the "larger pattern" can be fully realized only through "the immediate and particular social situation," that is, that the "Hades-Hell symbol" reaches universality only through the graphic rendering of the mine. But no matter; in Troy's phrasing or in mine, the central position of social circumstance is clear.

Even powerful archetypes get worn down by the workings of time. A few—Oedipus, Hamlet, Faust—do seem to survive a range of historical situations, in part because we assign changing meanings to them. But Tristan: Does he still exert (except perhaps in Wagner's opera) the imaginative hold he once did? As for Richardson's Clarissa, that spotless exemplar of maidenhood, she has surely lost a good part of her authority. And even Oedipus had to be reinvented by Freud[5] in order to maintain his status as archetype.

If we turn to a more modest variety, the sort for which we claim not universal scope but a large role in a particular culture, we find that these can fade quickly. Sinclair Lewis's Babbitt[6] was elevated a few decades ago to a proper noun in the American language, so representative did he seem of petit bourgeois philistinism. Now Lewis's novel is little read, and Babbitt almost forgotten, the name familiar only to the elderly. Archetypes die, too.

VIII.

Simply because it is what it is, the novel can never quite free itself from the shaping pressures of history; but with some novels, history is more than a mere felt presence, it is an all but completely dominant force.

Stendhal, a latecomer in the line of the French Revolution, writes out of an explicit recognition of historical disadvantage. The Revolution has been

1. Main character in *Tess of the d'Urbervilles* (1891) by Thomas Hardy. Oedipus and Quixote: literary characters so famous that adjectives derived from their names have entered the English language. Clarissa Harlowe: main character of the novel *Clarissa* (1747–48) by the English novelist Samuel Richardson.

2. Literary critic (1903–1961).

3. Émile Zola (1840–1902), French naturalist writer and critic; *Germinal* was published in 1885.

4. Orpheus, a musician unrivaled among mortals, almost succeeded in freeing his dead wife, Eurydice, from the Greek underworld, Hades.

5. SIGMUND FREUD (1856–1939), the Austrian founder of psychoanalysis, wrote an influential, much-debated interpretation of Shakespeare's *Hamlet* in terms of the Oedipus complex (1900; see above).

6. George F. Babbitt, main character of *Babbitt*, a 1922 satiric novel by Sinclair Lewis (1885–1951), is a member of the American middle class who narrow-mindedly espouses its social and business ideals.

traduced; liberalism has suffered rout. For people like himself, who admired Napoleon but refused his tyranny, there is nothing to do but wait. In *The Red and the Black* Julien Sorel strains against the confines of history, tries to escape though cunning and ruse, succumbs to values he had despised, and by way of concluding gesture, offers his head in payment. History comes here to form an accumulation of all the rubbish of a detested past as it defiles the present. History batters the spirit, stamps out spontaneity.

Far more oblique, occasionally as farce tinged with a dry sadness, is Stendhal's still greater novel *The Charterhouse of Parma*.[7] Once its protagonist Fabrizio has left the battlefield of Waterloo and come to the mean little duchy of Parma, the story may seem to be some distance from the gross historical pressures weighing upon Julien Sorel. In *The Charterhouse of Parma* the central trio—the worldly politician Mosca, the grand Duchess Sanseverina, the innocently guileful Fabrizio—must live by personal relations, because personal relations are all that history allows in the post-Napoleonic moment. Yet their sense of the skimpiness of a life focused entirely upon personal relations itself is a mark left by history. They have known something better. Now they must submit to the authority of a comic-opera despot and a shriveled church. Resisting as best they can, they try to live out the Nietzschian[8] prescription of "objection, evasion, joyous distrust, and irony," but history is not to be cheated so easily.

In 1908 the young Trotsky[9] confronts Leo Tolstoy with a mixture of admiration and disapproval: "To history [he] grants no recognition; and this provides the basis for all his thinking." A keen remark, but not really accurate; as Isaiah Berlin showed in *The Hedgehog and the Fox*,[1] it's not history as such, but all intellectual formulation claiming to possess a key to history, to which Tolstoy "grants no recognition." Berlin speaks of

> Tolstoy's violently unhistorical and indeed antihistorical rejection of all efforts to explain or justify human actions or characters in terms of social or individual growth, or "roots" in the past; this side by side with an absorbed and lifelong interest in history.

For Tolstoy, adds Berlin, "history does not reveal causes; it presents only a blank succession of unexplained events." Tolstoy alternated between the hedgehog's search for a "single embracing vision" and the fox's "actual experience of actual men and women in their relation to one another and to an actual, three-dimensional, empirically experienced physical environment."

Yet there is no major novel of the last two centuries in which the experience of history—history as pressure, burden, encompassing atmosphere—is so strongly felt as in *War and Peace*:[2] the very same history that Tolstoy believed to be devoid of rational structure or progressive development. History is *there* in all its abundance, felt in Kutuzov's fatalistic submission to the course of battle, in Pierre's epiphany upon being captured by the French, in Prince

7. Stendhal's 1839 novel, set in early-19th-century Italy, focuses on the life of Fabrizio del Dongo, a young aristocrat and admirer of Napoleon.

8. Characteristic of FRIEDRICH NIETZSCHE (1844–1900), German philosopher.

9. LEON TROTSKY (1879–1940), Russian revolutionary leader and theoretician; quotation from "Tolstoy, Poet and Rebel."

1. A study (1953) of Tolstoy's view of history, by Berlin (1909–1997), a Russian-born English political scientist and intellectual historian.

2. A novel (1864–69) by Tolstoy, focusing on the Napoleonic invasion of Russia (1811–12).

Andrei's discovery when wounded that "everything is empty, everything is a delusion except this infinite sky," even in Natasha's single-minded absorption in domesticity.

If one can say with Tolstoy that history is the impenetrable sequence of human experience—that is, history is everything—and being impenetrable, that it cannot order that experience—that is, history is nothing—then one can conclude that in *War and Peace* history is nonetheless everywhere visible as guide and dynamic in the conduct of his characters. The theorist of anti-history becomes the great portraitist of historical shaping. (He also involves himself in some amusing contradictions. Kutuzov is said to be superior to Napoleon because he, Kutuzov, knows that the course of battle cannot be determined in advance—which is to say, that in denying historical determinism Kutuzov understands the history to which Tolstoy had denied rational order.)

The hedgehog searches and the fox portrays, but what the fox portrays is enabled, is provided for, by the hedgehog's search. It is Tolstoy's supreme achievement that, like Stendhal before him, each of his depictions of personal life bears the impress of historical consciousness, with the two quite as inseparable in his fiction as we take them to be in our life.

In García Márquez's *One Hundred Years of Solitude*[3] the elemental life cycles of a Central American country—the haughty decorums and sensualities by which people in the town of Macondo try to relieve the barrenness of their existence—become a power, a salvage that the sterile official history of the country, that sequence of evolutions and coups d'état, cannot quite destroy. García Márquez wishes to capture all that gradually slips out of memory and can perhaps be regained only through myth: he wishes to preserve the subhistorical "history" of his people as they try to preserve themselves in the midst of an endless civil war.

By itself the fabulous narrative of the rise and fall of the Buenda family in *One Hundred Years of Solitude* might come to seem a grandiose evasion, falsely upbeat, a sort of Central American operetta; but what gives this novel its quotient of ferocity is the repeated intrusion of the sterile official history, the often ridiculous politics and civil wars of the country so self-absorbed in its blood and waste as to point up the meaning of García Márquez's title. The sterile official history is juxtaposed to the fertile subhistorical myth, as a sort of comic transcendence. The matriarch who dominates a good part of the novel feels that "time was not passing . . . but it was turning in a circle." The circle of generations and of solitude.

IX.

I come to a disconcerting conclusion. History may be the rock on which the novel rests, but time crumbles that rock into grains of sand. The circumstances forming the matrix of fiction soon turn out to be inaccessible, distant, perhaps no longer arresting: come to seem alloyed by values we can no longer credit; or decline into mere reflexes of social bias.

Mansfield Park,[4] the one novel by Jane Austen that her admirers find trou-

3. A 1967 novel by Gabriel García Márquez (b. 1928), Colombian writer.

4. An 1814 novel by the English writer Austen (1775–1817).

bling, was the subject of an influential essay some years ago by Lionel Trilling,[5] in which he made a case for this most conservative and least lively of Austen's works. Trilling confronted head-on a problem that disturbs modern readers: that when Sir Thomas, head of a solid family in the landed gentry, leaves for the West Indies, his children and their friends decide to amuse themselves by producing an amateur theatrical, and that this project, which to us must seem the height of innocence, comes to be an occasion for moral uneasiness. The characters of firmer or traditional morality, Fanny Price and Edmund Bertram, express grave doubts at the propriety of dramatic impersonation, and Trilling persuasively explains why, in the circumstances, the amateur theatrical could be seen as morally dubious. Not many readers would today "agree" with Sir Thomas's portentous statement that "such a scheme" is marked by "impropriety," but at least we learn to give it enough conditional assent so that the business of the amateur theatrical does not interfere with our enjoyment of the novel.

But there is another historical fact that may cause even greater uneasiness. Sir Thomas, though subject to moral criticism by Austen because of his imperceptive rigidity, is still shown as a respected patriarch. His visit to the West Indies on behalf of his estate occurs at a time when slavery dominated those islands, which means that it is close to a certainty that he was an owner of slaves. Now this occasioned neither criticism from Austen nor comment from Trilling; but it is a serious ground for those discomforts that the passage of time, the flow of history, can cause in the reading of even great or near-great novels.

One common defense of Austen is that the working of the West Indian estate is not central to the action of *Mansfield Park*; and then we have to make discounts, too, for an earlier time, as later times will for ours. In my years as a teacher I would offer this defense to students, but now I wonder. Austen could have sent Sir Thomas on plenty of other trips. The only requirement of the plot was to get him away from home. Yet, with the deliberateness that marks all her work, she clearly meant to write as she did: Sir Thomas profits from the exploitation of black labor and is nevertheless seen as a morally upright if somewhat unimaginative figure. Now I do not mean to suggest that Austen approved of slavery; but she could assign the patriarchal Sir Thomas a plantation in Antigua without it causing her any visible moral uneasiness in the evaluation of his character. I find this much more troubling than the amateur theatricals, which I am content to accept as a convenience of plot.

The kind of problems presented by *Mansfield Park* can be found in many novels of the past. What can we "do" about them? Seek to accommodate ourselves, or make allowances, or offer partially negative judgments. If we are very sophisticated, we tell ourselves that in reading a novel of the past (and the not-so-distant past: say, Rousseau's *Julie* or Fielding's *Amelia*[6]), we ought to have enough "historical imagination" to enter unfamiliar settings and recognize the integrity of other moralities. And we should also make it our business, of course, to learn about distant historical situations: say, those

5. American literary critic (1905–1975); his essay on Austen is included in *The Opposing Self* (1955).
6. A 1751 novel by Henry Fielding. *Julie, or the New Eloise* (1761), epistolary novel by Jean-Jacques Rousseau (1712–1778), Swiss-born French writer and philosopher.

of Manzoni's *The Betrothed* or Cooper's Leatherstocking tales.[7] We should be able to understand, even if not share, the obsession with virginity that courses through Richardson's *Clarissa*—but see how I betray myself, since the very word "obsession" evinces a bias.

It's a splendid thing, this historical imagination, and everyone needs a supply of it, but the mere fact that we need to invoke it testifies to difficulties. We can no longer read some of these novels with a direct, spontaneous response. There must now be a complex act of "mediation" that entails all sorts of mental reserves. By contrast, nothing of the sort is required if we pick up Elsa Morante's *History*,[8] at least nothing for any literate person over fifty. But for a twenty-year-old to whom the Second World War is almost as distant as the French and Indian War? And fifty years from now: introduction, footnotes, chronological table ("The Second World War, which forms the background to Elsa Morante's novel, broke out in 1939, when . . .").

X.

History makes, history unmakes, the novel. And this is true even for novels we love. It is profoundly disconcerting to see them slowly drained of their original power.

In the 1930s *The Sun Also Rises*[9] was a work that many readers felt close to. We may have been irked by Hemingway's anti-intellectualism, or have scorned his macho posturing, and we certainly knew ourselves to be at a distance from his Parisian expatriates. And yet we felt that Hemingway expressed, through this story of lostness and its sad repressed language, a disenchantment that we had inherited from the generation caught up in the First World War. Even if his notion of a "secret community" surviving historical disaster had a self-dramatizing aspect, it still related to our feelings of plight. There is more than one kind of "secret community."

In later years I still found *The Sun Also Rises* a deeply affecting novel, but by the late 1970s a dismaying change of response began to show itself among my students. They found the milieu of the novel merely exotic; they saw its stylizations as an affection, and its tone—this was the worst of all—as self-pitying. A gap had opened between generations, so that the very novel that history had, so to say, pressed against our hearts had now fallen victim to history.

The decades have passed, these writers have died, and even those of us especially fond of, say, Ignazio Silone[1] know that a work of such moral poise as *Bread and Wine* is not likely to stir younger readers as it once stirred readers of my generation. If a few young people do open *Darkness at Noon*,[2] a novel that roused violent argument when it first appeared, they may need explanatory notes about the Moscow trials. When was it that you said the Moscow trials took place? This fascism mentioned in Silone's *Fontamara*—

7. Five novels featuring the frontiersman Natty Bumppo, nicknamed Leatherstocking, by the American novelist James Fenimore Cooper (1789–1851). *The Betrothed* (1825–26), a romantic novel of 17th-century Milan, by the Italian novelist and poet Alessandro Manzoni (1785–1873).

8. A 1974 novel that describes the life of a half-Jewish teacher and her son, born of a rape by a German soldier during World War II; by the Italian novelist, short story writer, and poet (1918–1985).

9. The first novel (1926) by the American writer Ernest Hemingway (1899–1961).

1. Italian writer and political leader (1900–1978), whose works include the novels *Fontamara* (1930) and *Bread and Wine* (1937).

2. A 1941 novel by Arthur Koestler, describing Joseph Stalin's purges of those he viewed as his enemies in the Soviet Union in the 1930s.

what was that again? Should anyone remember? And isn't it wonderful that we have survived all these catastrophes? Yes, it's wonderful, but one's heart also sinks before the ravages of time, before the sheer sadness of the costs.

1990

HANS ROBERT JAUSS
1921–1997

A leading reader-response theorist, Hans Robert Jauss is best known for promoting the importance of reception history in literary interpretation. Countering the assumption that we confront texts as self-sufficient entities, on their own merits and in their own terms—as "verbal icons," in the phrase of the New Critic WILLIAM K. WIMSATT JR.—Jauss stressed how the expectations that we bring to reading govern our response and aesthetic judgment. For example, if assigned James Joyce's *Ulysses* (1922) in a course, a student probably starts with the assumption that it is a literary masterpiece, unlike a bestseller chosen for summer reading. And this hypothetical student might know that Joyce is considered one of the most influential modernist novelists in English and a progenitor of "stream of consciousness." Our present-day experience of *Ulysses* differs from that of Joyce's own day, in part because stream of consciousness has become a familiar technique—what was innovative to his first readers has been assimilated into literary practice. Such expectations—sometimes to be fulfilled, sometimes to be surprised—shape our thinking as we open the pages of *Ulysses*. Jauss, in a famous phrase derived from hermeneutic philosophy, called this phenomenon "the horizon of expectation." A foundational document in contemporary reader-oriented approaches to literature, Jauss's "Literary History as a Challenge to Literary Theory" (1969; rev. 1970), from which our selection is drawn, makes the case for the influence of expectation on interpretation, for its centrality in generating aesthetic judgments, and for its evolving role in literary history.

Jauss was born in Germany, and while a young man he served during World War II as an officer in the German army on the Eastern front. After the war he studied at the University of Heidelberg, where he worked with the leading hermeneutic philosopher Hans-Georg Gadamer, receiving his doctorate in literature in 1957. After holding positions at Heidelberg, Münster University, and the University of Giessen, in 1966 he accepted an appointment as a professor at the University of Constance, where he delivered "Literaturgeschichte als Provokation" (1967, "Literary History as Challenge"), an early version of his similarly titled essay, as his inaugural lecture. Jauss was originally trained as a scholar of French literature primarily of the medieval period, but with this text he first programmatically developed his theory of reception. When it was published in English in 1969, he captured the attention of an international audience, becoming a prominent figure in the rise of contemporary reader-response theory. He also held visiting professorships at the Sorbonne, the University of Zurich, Columbia University, Yale University, the University of California at Berkeley, and UCLA.

At the University of Constance, Jauss formed, with WOLFGANG ISER and other colleagues, what has been called the "Constance School," which promoted the study of *Rezeptionsästhetik* (the aesthetics of reception), investigating in diverse ways the interaction of readers and texts. The school draws on the philosophical traditions of aesthetics inaugurated in eighteenth-century German philosophy by Alexander

Baumgarten, IMMANUEL KANT, and FRIEDRICH VON SCHILLER; of hermeneutics, or the theory of interpretation, propounded in the nineteenth century by FRIEDRICH SCHLEIERMACHER and Wilhelm Dilthey and in the twentieth by MARTIN HEIDEGGER and Gadamer; and of phenomenology, developed by Edmund Husserl (1859–1938), which emphasizes perception and the interaction of subjects and objects. In particular, Jauss's work employs Gadamer's concept of historical "horizons" and the changing nature of interpretation and aesthetic judgment over time. Like Iser, Jauss sees the literary work as an event rather than a fixed object, a view that reflects the influence of phenomenology. However, their emphases differ; Iser, as does the twentieth-century French critic GEORGES POULET, focuses on the response of the individual reader when confronting a text, whereas Jauss stresses the cumulative experience of historical readers.

"Literary History as a Challenge to Literary Theory" aims to revitalize literary study by examining the history of reception. While proclaiming the importance of literary history, Jauss severely criticizes its accepted forms, which center on individual authors, genres, or current ideas. Traditional models of literary history—for instance, those offered by the modernist poet and critic T. S. ELIOT and later the influential contemporary critic HAROLD BLOOM—focus on the genius of individual authors in a lineage of great works. In contrast, Jauss argues for expanding literary history to encompass readers and the background against which a work is received. His particular target is the view of literary works as timeless, sacrosanct objects, as he declares that "a literary work is not an object that stands by itself and that offers the same view to each reader in each period."

Jauss makes the case that our aesthetic views are shaped by literary history, and that those views change over time. For him, it is only through studying the history of a work's reception that one can fully understand it. He presents seven key theses: first, reception history influences both the writing and reading of literary works; second, a literary historian can ascertain a nonsubjective, objectifiable set of expectations that a reader brings to the text; third, these form a "horizon" that determines interpretation; fourth, reception works dialogically, through a process of "question and answer," at each point in time; fifth, expectations change, and literary history properly records this evolution; sixth, literary historians and philologists can look at reception both over time and at one moment; and seventh, literary history constitutes a "special history" that dialogically relates to "general history," largely through the revision of moral ideas.

Jauss borrows from as well as criticizes two specific models of history, Marxism and Russian formalism. He adopts KARL MARX's focus on historical context, but criticizes the orthodox Marxist notion that literary works simply copy reality and reflect their socioeconomic foundations. Instead, Jauss claims, literary works are also "formative of reality." Addressing the perennial problem of the relation of the art to society, Jauss holds that art has a distinctive special history; but he also recognizes that it influences general history—for example, by questioning "ruling morals." From Russian formalism, the literary theory developed during the early twentieth century by BORIS EICHENBAUM and others, Jauss draws on the concept of "literary evolution," the process through which aesthetic forms develop. While he finds this view of literary history superior to others in accounting for change that has no predetermined endpoint, he criticizes it for focusing only on aesthetic innovation. He therefore revises the formalist concept of literary evolution, basing it not on authorial creation but on the history of audience expectations and judgment.

Shifting the focus away from authors and works, Jauss argues that an audience does not receive a literary work simply on its own merits; it "is received and judged against the background of other works of art as well as against the background of the everyday experience of life." This background he terms the "horizon of expectations." Consider again the example of Joyce's *Ulysses*—Jauss himself uses the example of the French novel *Madame Bovary* (1856), by Gustave Flaubert—which was initially considered shocking and banned because of its references to sex and bodily functions, but now seems relatively tame. Jauss calls the space between original audience expectation and its violation or negation by new works "aesthetic distance," which he holds to be the primary measure of aesthetic value; this distance is produced by works recognized as masterpieces. In contrast, works like popular bestsellers usually have little value because they are predictable, conforming to rather than negating expectation.

Jauss notes, however, that such distance changes over time, so that classic works are continually reevaluated. He stresses that literary history is not simply a collection of static monuments, as most critics assume; rather, particular works startle us and alter the background, fostering new horizons of expectation and new perceptions of social norms. Because of our background, we are no longer surprised by *Ulysses* and thus understand it differently than did its readers in 1922. Still, our understanding encompasses our awareness of the controversy it first incited and how it opened literature to treating a wider range of moral topics in novels displaying a wider range of styles. Although we receive the book differently now, we recognize its role in the history of the novel, and that recognition contributes to our judgment of it as a modern "classic." For Jauss, the interaction between expectation and particular works is what generates interpretation, and our readings of works like *Ulysses* are not static but evolve over time.

Jauss views literary history not as a series of unchanging, "objective" facts but as a record of the "transsubjective" experience of readers. He thereby staves off charges that reader-oriented approaches yield merely idiosyncratic, subjective interpretations; interpretation results not from any one reader's experience but from an "objectifiable" set of expectations provided by a consensus of actual historical readers. This defensive move is similar to STANLEY FISH's proposal that interpretation derives from an established consensus of readers joined in "interpretive communities." But while Fish's notion has been criticized as being ahistorical and static, Jauss accounts for the historical construction of and change within such communities. In general, Jauss's grounding in concrete histories of reading differs from other poststructuralist views, such as Fish's, that stress the "writerly" role played by readers in constructing texts.

Though his concept of reception history forestalls charges of relativism, Jauss's work has been condemned by Marxists for focusing primarily on literary rather than social history. His notion of background is largely limited to the field of literary study, and he rarely extends the scope of his research to consider other forces that shape literary judgment—such as the social and professional institutions that RICHARD OHMANN exposes in "The Shaping of a Canon" (1983; see below). Jauss has also been criticized for a ponderous prose style. Whatever their limitations, Jauss's writings have provided important theoretical groundwork for the contemporary study of reception history in evaluating literary texts. His stress on reception has been useful for cultural studies of literature; for instance, in her highly regarded *Sensational Designs* (1985) the reader-response critic JANE TOMPKINS shows how nineteenth-century American sentimental novels were initially received positively but later devalued because of masculinist expectations. Jauss's views of the historical nature of literary evaluation have influenced debates over the literary canon in ways important to feminist, African American, and postcolonial critics; and perhaps his most significant contribution to contemporary theory is his revision of aesthetics, as he bases judgment not on universality and timelessness but on evolving historical horizons.

BIBLIOGRAPHY

Jauss's untranslated works, primarily studies of French literature, include *Zeit und Erinnerung in Marcel Prousts "A la recherche du temps perdu"* (1955, *Time and Memory in Marcel Proust's "Remembrance of Things Past"*); *Untersuchungen zu mittelalterlichen Tierdichtung* (1959, *Investigations into Medieval Beast Literature*); *La*

Genèse de la poésie allegorique française au Moyen-Age (1962, *The Genesis of Medieval French Allegory*); *Kleine Apologie der ästhetischen Erfahrung* (1972, *Short Defense of Aesthetic Experience*); and *Alterität und modernität der mittelalterlichen Literatur* (1977, *Alterity and Modernity of Medieval Literature*). Parts of "Literary History as Challenge" appeared in English in 1969 in the journal *New Literary History*; it was first published in its entirety in German in 1970 as a short monograph, and the present translation is based on that text. Jauss's major books in English are *Aesthetic Experience and Literary Hermeneutics* (1977; trans. 1982), which modifies his view of aesthetic distance and argues against Theodor Adorno's "aesthetics of negativity"; *Toward an Aesthetic of Reception* (1978; trans. 1982), which contains "Literary History as a Challenge to Literary Theory" and other essays; and *Question and Answer: Forms of Dialogic Understanding* (1989), which stresses the dialogic nature of literary response and history.

Two early articles introducing Jauss's work and reception theory to Anglo-American critics are Robert Weimann, " 'Reception Aesthetics' and the Crisis in Literary History," *Clio* 5 (1975), and Peter Uwe Hohendahl, "Introduction to Reception Aesthetics," *New German Critique* 10 (1977). Paul de Man's "Reading and History" (1982), first published as the introduction to Jauss's *Toward an Aesthetic of Reception* and later collected in de Man's *Resistance to Theory* (1986), lays out differences between deconstruction and hermeneutics. Wlad Godzich's introduction to Jauss's *Aesthetic Experience and Literary Hermeneutics* helpfully contextualizes the work. Robert C. Holub's *Reception Theory: A Critical Introduction* (1984) is a useful survey that situates Jauss in the context of hermeneutic philosophy, Marxism, and the Constance School.

From Literary History as a Challenge to Literary Theory[1]

V

In the question thus posed, I see the challenge to literary studies of taking up once again the problem of literary history, which was left unresolved in the dispute between Marxist and Formalist methods.[2] My attempt to bridge the gap between literature and history, between historical and aesthetic approaches, begins at the point at which both schools stop. Their methods conceive the *literary fact* within the closed circle of an aesthetics of production and of representation. In doing so, they deprive literature of a dimension that inalienably belongs to its aesthetic character as well as to its social function: the dimension of its reception and influence. Reader, listener, and spectator—in short, the factor of the audience—play an extremely limited role in both literary theories. Orthodox Marxist aesthetics treats the reader—if at all—no differently from the author: it inquires about his social position

1. Translated by Timothy Bahti, who occasionally inserts English words in brackets for clarification.
2. Here, the methods of the Russian formalists—literary critics and language theorists, including BORIS EICHENBAUM (1886–1959), who considered literature to be a special use of language that could be studied scientifically and could be analyzed in itself. Marxist methods draw on the theory of historical materialism, devised by KARL MARX (1818–1883), which holds that the economic base of a society determines its superstructure of social forms and ideas, including its literature. Jauss ends the previous section with a question: "If on the one hand literary evolution can be comprehended within the historical change of systems, and on the other hand pragmatic history can be comprehended within the processlike linkage of social conditions, must it not then also be possible to place the 'literary series' and the 'nonliterary series' into a relation that comprehends the relationship between literature and history without forcing literature, at the expense of its character as art, into a function of mere copying or commentary?"

or seeks to recognize him in the structure of a represented society. The Formalist school needs the reader only as a perceiving subject who follows the directions in the text in order to distinguish the [literary] form or discover the [literary] procedure. It assumes that the reader has the theoretical understanding of the philologist who can reflect on the artistic devices, already knowing them; conversely, the Marxist school candidly equates the spontaneous experience of the reader with the scholarly interest of historical materialism, which would discover relationships between superstructure and basis in the literary work. However, as Walther Bulst has stated, "no text was ever written to be read and interpreted philologically by philologists,"[3] nor, may I add, historically by historians. Both methods lack the reader in his genuine role, a role as unalterable for aesthetic as for historical knowledge: as the addressee for whom the literary work is primarily destined.

For even the critic who judges a new work, the writer who conceives of his work in light of positive or negative norms of an earlier work, and the literary historian who classifies a work in its tradition and explains it historically are first simply readers before their reflexive relationship to literature can become productive again. In the triangle of author, work, and public the last is no passive part, no chain of mere reactions, but rather itself an energy formative of history. The historical life of a literary work is unthinkable without the active participation of its addressees. For it is only through the process of its mediation that the work enters into the changing horizon-of-experience of a continuity in which the perpetual inversion occurs from simple reception to critical understanding, from passive to active reception, from recognized aesthetic norms to a new production that surpasses them. The historicity of literature as well as its communicative character presupposes a dialogical and at once processlike relationship between work, audience, and new work that can be conceived in the relations between message and receiver as well as between question and answer, problem and solution. The closed circle of production and of representation within which the methodology of literary studies has mainly moved in the past must therefore be opened to an aesthetics of reception and influence if the problem of comprehending the historical sequence of literary works as the coherence of literary history is to find a new solution.

The perspective of the aesthetics of reception mediates between passive reception and active understanding, experience formative of norms, and new production. If the history of literature is viewed in this way within the horizon of a dialogue between work and audience that forms a continuity, the opposition between its aesthetic and its historical aspects is also continually mediated. Thus the thread from the past appearance to the present experience of literature, which historicism had cut, is tied back together.

The relationship of literature and reader has aesthetic as well as historical implications. The aesthetic implication lies in the fact that the first reception of a work by the reader includes a test of its aesthetic value in comparison with works already read. The obvious historical implication of this is that the understanding of the first reader will be sustained and enriched in a chain

3. "Bedenken eines Philologen," *Studium generale* 7 (1954); 321–23 [Jauss's note]. Bulst (1899–1976), German philologist. Philologists study culture through the historical analyses of languages and texts. Some of the author's notes have been edited, and some omitted.

of receptions from generation to generation; in this way the historical significance of a work will be decided and its aesthetic value made evident. In this process of the history of reception, which the literary historian can only escape at the price of leaving unquestioned the presuppositions that guide his understanding and judgment, the reappropriation of past works occurs simultaneously with the perpetual mediation of past and present art and of traditional evaluation and current literary attempts. The merit of a literary history based on an aesthetics of reception will depend upon the extent to which it can take an active part in the ongoing totalization of the past through aesthetic experience. This demands on the one hand—in opposition to the objectivism of positivist[4] literary history—a conscious attempt at the formation of a canon, which, on the other hand—in opposition to the classicism of the study of traditions—presupposes a critical revision if not destruction of the received literary canon. The criterion for the formation of such a canon and the ever necessary retelling of literary history is clearly set out by the aesthetics of reception. The step from the history of the reception of the individual work to the history of literature has to lead to seeing and representing the historical sequence of works as they determine and clarify the coherence of literature, to the extent that it is meaningful for us, as the prehistory of its present experience.[5]

From this premise, the question as to how literary history can today be methodologically grounded and written anew will be addressed in the following seven theses.

VI

Thesis 1. A renewal of literary history demands the removal of the prejudices of historical objectivism and the grounding of the traditional aesthetics of production and representation in an aesthetics of reception and influence. The historicity of literature rests not on an organization of "literary facts" that is established *post festum,*[6] but rather on the preceding experience of the literary work by its readers.

R. G. Collingwood's postulate, posed in his critique of the prevailing ideology of objectivity in history—"History is nothing but the re-enactment of past thought in the historian's mind"[7]—is even more valid for literary history. For the positivistic view of history as the "objective" description of a series of events in an isolated past neglects the artistic character as well as the specific historicity of literature. A literary work is not an object that stands by itself and that offers the same view to each reader in each period. It is not a monument that monologically reveals its timeless essence. It is much more like an orchestration that strikes ever new resonances among its readers and that frees the text from the material of the words

4. Taking knowledge and meaning to derive solely from what can be empirically observed.

5. Correspondingly, Walter Benjamin (1931) formulated: "For it is not a question of representing the written works in relation to their time but of bringing to representation the time that knows them—that is our time—in the time when they originated. Thus literature becomes an organon of history and the task of literary history is to make it this—and not to make written works the material of history" (*Angelus Novus* [Frankfurt, 1966], p. 456) [Jauss's note]. BENJAMIN (1892–1940), German literary and cultural critic.

6. After the feast (Latin); that is, after the fact, too late.

7. R. G. Collingwood, *The Idea of History* (New York, 1956), p. 252 [Jauss's note]. Collingwood (1889–1943), British philosopher of history.

and brings it to a contemporary existence: "words that must, at the same time that they speak to him, create an interlocutor capable of understanding them."[8] This dialogical character of the literary work also establishes why philological understanding can exist only in a perpetual confrontation with the text, and cannot be allowed to be reduced to a knowledge of facts. Philological understanding always remains related to interpretation that must set as its goal, along with learning about the object, the reflection on and description of the completion of this knowledge as a moment of new understanding.

History of literature is a process of aesthetic reception and production that takes place in the realization of literary texts on the part of the receptive reader, the reflective critic, and the author in his continuing productivity. The endlessly growing sum of literary "facts" that winds up in the conventional literary histories is merely left over from this process; it is only the collected and classified past and therefore not history at all, but pseudohistory. Anyone who considers a series of such literary facts as a piece of the history of literature confuses the eventful character of a work of art with that of historical matter-of-factness. The *Perceval* of Chrétien de Troyes, as a literary event, is not "historical" in the same sense as, for example, the Third Crusade,[9] which was occurring at about the same time. It is not a "fact" that could be explained as caused by a series of situational preconditions and motives, by the intent of a historical action as it can be reconstructed, and by the necessary and secondary consequences of this deed. The historical context in which a literary work appears is not a factical, independent series of events that exists apart from an observer. *Perceval* becomes a literary event only for its reader, who reads this last work of Chrétien with a memory of his earlier works and who recognizes its individuality in comparison with these and other works that he already knows, so that he gains a new criterion for evaluating future works. In contrast to a political event, a literary event has no unavoidable consequences subsisting on their own that no succeeding generation can ever escape. A literary event can continue to have an effect only if those who come after it still or once again respond to it—if there are readers who again appropriate the past work or authors who want to imitate, outdo, or refute it. The coherence of literature as an event is primarily mediated in the horizon of expectations of the literary experience of contemporary and later readers, critics, and authors. Whether it is possible to comprehend and represent the history of literature in its unique historicity depends on whether this horizon of expectations can be objectified.

VII

Thesis 2. The analysis of the literary experience of the reader avoids the threatening pitfalls of psychology if it describes the reception and the influence of a work within the objectifiable system of expectations that arises for

8. Gaetan Picon, *Introduction à une esthétique de la littérature* [*Introduction to an Aesthetics of Literature*] (Paris, 1953), p. 34 [Jauss's note].

9. A European campaign (1189–92)—one of a series undertaken between 1095 and 1291—against the Muslims to gain possession of the Holy Land. Chrétien de Troyes (d. ca. 1180), French poet of courtly romances; *Perceval,* left unfinished at his death, is the earliest literary version of the legendary quest for the Holy Grail.

each work in the historical moment of its appearance, from a preunderstanding of the genre, from the form and themes of already familiar works, and from the opposition between poetic and practical language.

My thesis opposes a widespread skepticism that doubts whether an analysis of aesthetic influence can approach the meaning of a work of art at all or can produce, at best, more than a simple sociology of taste. René Wellek in particular directs such doubts against the literary theory of I. A. Richards.[1] Wellek argues that neither the individual state of consciousness, since it is momentary and only personal, nor a collective state of consciousness, as Jan Mukařovský[2] assumes the effect a work of art to be, can be determined by empirical means. Roman Jakobson wanted to replace the "collective state of consciousness" by a "collective ideology" in the form of a system of norms that exists for each literary work as *langue* and that is actualized as *parole*[3] by the receiver—although incompletely and never as a whole. This theory, it is true, limits the subjectivity of the influence, but it still leaves open the question of which data can be used to comprehend the influence of a particular work on a certain public and to incorporate it into a system of norms. In the meantime there are empirical means that had never been thought of before—literary data that allow one to ascertain a specific disposition of the audience for each work (a disposition that precedes the psychological reaction as well as the subjective understanding of the individual reader). As in the case of every actual experience, the first literary experience of a previously unknown work also demands a "foreknowledge which is an element of the experience itself, and on the basis of which anything new that we come across is available to experience at all, i.e., as it were readable in a context of experience."[4]

A literary work, even when it appears to be new, does not present itself as something absolutely new in an informational vacuum, but predisposes its audience to a very specific kind of reception by announcements, overt and covert signals, familiar characteristics, or implicit allusions. It awakens memories of that which was already read, brings the reader to a specific emotional attitude, and with its beginning arouses expectations for the "middle and end," which can then be maintained intact or altered, reoriented, or even fulfilled ironically in the course of the reading according to specific rules of the genre or type of text. The psychic process in the reception of a text is, in the primary horizon of aesthetic experience, by no means only an arbitrary series of merely subjective impressions, but rather the carrying out of specific instructions in a process of directed perception, which can be comprehended according to its constitutive motivations and triggering signals, and which also can be described by a textual linguistics. If, along with W. D. Stempel, one defines the initial horizon of expectations of a text as paradigmatic isotopy, which is transposed into an immanent syntagmatic horizon of expectations to the extent that the utterance grows, then the process of reception

1. English literary critic (1893–1979), a pioneer of analytic criticism focusing on the text itself. Wellek (1903–1995), Czech-born American literary theorist and historian of literary criticism.
2. Czech literary theorist (1891–1975).
3. Speech (French), distinguished by the Swiss linguist FERDINAND DE SAUSSURE (1857–1913) from *langue,* "language" understood in the abstract as the object of linguistics. JAKOBSON (1896–1982), Russian-born American linguist and literary theorist.
4. Gunther Buck, *Lernen und Erfahrung* [*Learning and Experience*] (Stuttgart, 1967), p. 56 [Jauss's note].

becomes describable in the expansion of a semiotic system that accomplishes itself between the development and the correction of a system.[5] A corresponding process of the continuous establishing and altering of horizons also determines the relationship of the individual text to the succession of texts that forms the genre. The new text evokes for the reader (listener) the horizon of expectations and rules familiar from earlier texts, which are then varied, corrected, altered, or even just reproduced. Variation and correction determine the scope, whereas alteration and reproduction determine the borders of a genre-structure. The interpretative reception of a text always presupposes the context of experience of aesthetic perception: the question of the subjectivity of the interpretation and of the taste of different readers or levels of readers can be asked meaningfully only when one has first clarified which transsubjective horizon of understanding conditions the influence of the text.

The ideal cases of the objective capability of such literary-historical frames of reference are works that evoke the reader's horizon of expectations, formed by a convention of genre, style, or form, only in order to destroy it step by step—which by no means serves a critical purpose only, but can itself once again produce poetic effects. Thus Cervantes[6] allows the horizon of expectations of favorite old tales of knighthood to arise out of the reading of *Don Quixote*, which the adventure of his last knight then seriously parodies. Thus Diderot, at the beginning of *Jacques le Fataliste*,[7] evokes the horizon of expectations of the popular novelistic schema of the "journey" (with the fictive questions of the reader to the narrator) along with the (Aristotelian) convention of the romanesque fable[8] and the providence unique to it, so that he can then provocatively oppose to the promised journey- and love-novel a completely unromanesque "vérité de l'histoire":[9] the bizarre reality and moral casuistry of the enclosed stories in which the truth of life continually denies the mendacious character of poetic fiction. Thus Nerval[1] in the *Chimères* cites, combines, and mixes a quintessence of well-known romantic and occult motifs to produce the horizon of expectations of a mythical metamorphosis of the world only in order to signify his renunciation of romantic poetry. The identifications and relationships of the mythic state that are familiar or disclosable to the reader dissolve into an unknown to the same degree as the attempted private myth of the lyrical "I" fails, the law of sufficient information is broken, and the obscurity that has become expressive itself gains a poetic function.

There is also the possibility of objectifying the horizon of expectations in works that are historically less sharply delineated. For the specific disposition

5. Wolf-Dieter Stempel "Pour une description des genres littéraires" ["For a Description of Literary Genres"], in *Beiträge zur Textlinguistik* [*Contributions to Textual Linguistics*], ed. Stempel (Munich, 1970) [Jauss's note]. Stempel (b. 1929), German philologist. "Syntagmatic" and "paradigmatic" are key terms of semiotics, the study of signs (linguistic and other); paradigmatic relationships obtain between items that can be substituted for one another in a given context (here "isotopic," because the same possibilities are presented to any reader at a given time), while syntagmatic relationships form a meaningful whole in a sequence (that here changes over time).

6. Miguel de Cervantes (1547–1616), Spanish novelist, dramatist, and poet; the novel *Don Quixote* (1605, 1615) is his masterpiece.

7. *Jack the Fatalist* (pub. 1796), novel by the French philosopher and encyclopedist Denis Diderot (1713–1784).

8. A romance of the 12th and 13th centuries, featuring elements of heroic adventure and the supernatural as well as love; it is "Aristotelian" insofar as it reflects the view of plot that the Greek philosopher ARISTOTLE (384–322 B.C.E.) offers in his *Poetics* (see above).

9. True history (French).

1. Gérard de Nerval (born Gérard Labrunie, 1808–1855), French writer of verse and prose; *Chimeras* (1854) is a sonnet sequence.

toward a particular work that the author anticipates from the audience can also be arrived at, even if explicit signals are lacking, through three generally presupposed factors: first, through familiar norms or the immanent poetics of the genre; second, through the implicit relationships to familiar works of the literary-historical surroundings; and third, through the opposition between fiction and reality, between the poetic and the practical function of language, which is always available to the reflective reader during the reading as a possibility of comparison. The third factor includes the possibility that the reader of a new work can perceive it within the narrower horizon of literary expectations, as well as within the wider horizon of experience of life. I shall return to this horizontal structure, and its ability to be objectified by means of the hermeneutics of question and answer, in the discussion of the relationship between literature and lived praxis (see XII).

VIII

Thesis 3. Reconstructed in this way, the horizon of expectations of a work allows one to determine its artistic character by the kind and the degree of its influence on a presupposed audience. If one characterizes as aesthetic distance the disparity between the given horizon of expectations and the appearance of a new work, whose reception can result in a "change of horizons" through negation of familiar experiences or through raising newly articulated experiences to the level of consciousness, then this aesthetic distance can be objectified historically along the spectrum of the audience's reactions and criticism's judgment (spontaneous success, rejection or shock, scattered approval, gradual or belated understanding).

The way in which a literary work, at the historical moment of its appearance, satisfies, surpasses, disappoints, or refutes the expectations of its first audience obviously provides a criterion for the determination of its aesthetic value. The distance between the horizon of expectations and the work, between the familiarity of previous aesthetic experience and the "horizonal change"[2] demanded by the reception of the new work, determines the artistic character of a literary work, according to an aesthetics of reception: to the degree that this distance decreases, and no turn toward the horizon of yet-unknown experience is demanded of the receiving consciousness, the closer the work comes to the sphere of "culinary" or entertainment art. This latter work can be characterized by an aesthetics of reception as not demanding any horizonal change, but rather as precisely fulfilling the expectations prescribed by a ruling standard of taste, in that it satisfies the desire for the reproduction of the familiarly beautiful; confirms familiar sentiments; sanctions wishful notions; makes unusual experiences enjoyable as "sensations"; or even raises moral problems, but only to "solve" them in an edifying manner as predecided questions. If, conversely, the artistic character of a work is to be measured by the aesthetic distance with which it opposes the expectations of its first audience, then it follows that this distance, at first experienced as a pleasing or alienating new perspective, can disappear for later readers,

2. A Husserlian concept [Jauss's note]. Edmund Husserl (1859–1938), German philosopher; the founder of phenomenology, which investigates and describes phenomena as consciously experienced.

to the extent that the original negativity of the work has become self-evident and has itself entered into the horizon of future aesthetic experience, as a henceforth familiar expectation. The classical character of the so-called masterworks especially belongs to this second horizonal change;[3] their beautiful form that has become self-evident, and their seemingly unquestionable "eternal meaning" bring them, according to an aesthetics of reception, dangerously close to the irresistibly convincing and enjoyable "culinary" art, so that it requires a special effort to read them "against the grain" of the accustomed experience to catch sight of their artistic character once again (see section X).

The relationship between literature and audience includes more than the facts that every work has its own specific, historically and sociologically determinable audience, that every writer is dependent on the milieu, views, and ideology of his audience, and that literary success presupposes a book "which expresses what the group expects, a book which presents the group with its own image."[4] This objectivist determination of literary success according to the congruence of the work's intention with the expectations of a social group always leads literary sociology into a dilemma whenever later or ongoing influence is to be explained. Thus R. Escarpit wants to presuppose a "collective basis in space or time" for the "illusion of the lasting quality" of a writer, which in the case of Molière[5] leads to an astonishing prognosis: "Molière is still young for the Frenchman of the twentieth century because his world still lives, and a sphere of culture, views, and language still binds us to him. . . . But the sphere becomes ever smaller, and Molière will age and die when the things which our culture still has in common with the France of Molière die" (p. 117). As if Molière had only mirrored the "mores of his time" and had only remained successful through this supposed intention! Where the congruence between work and social group does not exist, or no longer exists as for example with the reception of a work in a foreign language, Escarpit is able to help himself by inserting a "myth" in between: "myths that are invented by a later world for which the reality that they substitute for has become alien" (p. 111). As if all reception beyond the first, socially determined audience for a work were only a "distorted echo," only a result of "subjective myths," and did not itself have its objective a priori once again in the received work as the limit and possibility of later understanding! The sociology of literature does not view its object dialectically enough when it determines the circle of author, work, and audience so one-sidedly. The determination is reversible: there are works that at the moment of their appearance are not yet directed at any specific audience, but that break through the familiar horizon of literary expectations so completely that an audience can only gradually develop for them.[6] When, then, the new horizon

3. See Boris Tomashevsky, in *Théorie de la littérature: Textes des formalistes russes* [*Theory of Literature: Texts of the Russian Formalists*], ed. Tzvetan Todorov (Paris, 1965), p. 306 n. 53: "The appearance of a genius always equals a literary revolution which dethrones the dominant canon and gives power to processes subordinated until then. . . . The epigones repeat a worn-out combination of processes, and as original and revolutionary as it was, this combination becomes stereotypical and traditional. Thus the epigones kill, sometimes for a long time, the aptitude of their contemporaries to sense the aesthetic force of the examples they imitate; they discredit their masters" [Jauss's note].

4. Robert Escarpit, *Das Buch und der Leser: Entwurf einer Literatursoziologie* [*The Book and the Reader: Model for a Sociology of Literature*] (Cologne, 1961), p. 116 [Jauss's note]. Escarpit (b. 1918), French literary critic.

5. Pen name of Jean-Baptiste Poquelin (1622–1673), French playwright.

6. The incomparably more promising literary sociology of Erich Auerbach brought these aspects to light in the variety of epoch-making breaks in the

of expectations has achieved more general currency, the power of the altered aesthetic norm can be demonstrated in that the audience experiences formerly successful works as outmoded, and withdraws its appreciation. Only in view of such horizonal change does the analysis of literary influence achieve the dimension of a literary history of readers, and do the statistical curves of the bestsellers provide historical knowledge.

A literary sensation from the year 1857 may serve as an example. Alongside Flaubert's *Madame Bovary*, which has since become world-famous, appeared his friend Feydeau's *Fanny*,[7] today forgotten. Although Flaubert's novel brought with it a trial for offending public morals, *Madame Bovary* was at first overshadowed by Feydeau's novel: *Fanny* went through thirteen editions in one year, achieving a success the likes of which Paris had not experienced since Chateaubriand's *Atala*.[8] Thematically considered, both novels met the expectations of a new audience that—in Baudelaire's analysis—had foresworn all romanticism, and despised great as well as naive passions equally:[9] they treated a trivial subject, infidelity in a bourgeois and provincial milieu. Both authors understood how to give to the conventional, ossified triangular relationship a sensational twist that went beyond the expected details of the erotic scenes. They put the worn-out theme of jealousy in a new light by reversing the expected relationship between the three classic roles: Feydeau has the youthful lover of the *femme de trente ans*[1] become jealous of his lover's husband despite his having already fulfilled his desires, and perishing over this agonizing situation; Flaubert gives the adulteries of the doctor's wife in the provinces—interpreted by Baudelaire as a sublime form of *dandysme*[2]—the surprise ending that precisely the laughable figure of the cuckolded Charles Bovary takes on dignified traits at the end. In the official criticism of the time, one finds voices that reject *Fanny* as well as *Madame Bovary* as a product of the new school of *réalisme*, which they reproach for denying everything ideal and attacking the ideas on which the social order of the Second Empire[3] was founded. The audience's horizon of expectations in 1857, here only vaguely sketched in, which did not expect anything great from the novel after Balzac's[4] death, explains the different success of the two novels only when the question of the effect of their narrative form is posed. Flaubert's formal innovation, his principle of "impersonal narration" (*impassibilité*)—attacked by Barbey d'Aurevilly[5] with the comparison that if a storytelling machine could be cast of English steel it would function no differently

relationship between author and reader [Jauss's note]. Auerbach (1892–1957), German literary critic.

7. A work by the French novelist Ernest Aimé Feydeau (1821–1873). *Madame Bovary*, by the French novelist Gustave Flaubert (1821–1880), tells the story of Charles Bovary, a country doctor, and of his wife, Emma Bovary, who is unfaithful to him.

8. An unfinished 1801 romance novel by François-René, vicomte de Chateaubriand (1768–1848), French Romantic writer and statesman.

9. In "*Madame Bovary* par Gustave Flaubert" (*Oeuvres complètes* [*Complete Works*], Pléiade ed. [Paris, 1951], p. 998), Charles Baudelaire writes, "The last years of Louis-Philippe witnessed the last explosions of a spirit still excitable by the play of the imagination; but the new novelist found himself faced with a completely worn-out society—worse than worn-out—stupified and gluttonous, with a horror only of fiction, and love only for possession" [Jauss's note]. BAUDELAIRE (1821–1867), French poet. Louis-Philippe (1773–1850), selected king of France (1830–48); under his rule the new middle classes became rich and corrupt.

1. Woman of thirty years (French); that is, an older woman.

2. Dandyism (French), a devotion to fashion and style praised by Baudelaire.

3. The rule (1848–70) of Louis-Napoléon Bonaparte, who was elected constitutional president after the overthrow of Louis-Philippe and who declared himself emperor in 1852.

4. Honoré de Balzac (1799–1850), French novelist.

5. Jules Barbey d'Aurevilly (1808–1889), French Romantic writer of novels, poetry, and literary criticism.

than Monsieur Flaubert—must have shocked the same audience that was offered the provocative contents of *Fanny* in the inviting tone of a confessional novel. It could also find incorporated in Feydeau's descriptions the modish ideals and suppressed desires of a stylish level of society, and could delight without restraint in the lascivious central scene in which Fanny (without suspecting that her lover is watching from the balcony) seduces her husband—for the moral indignation was already diminished for them through the reaction of the unhappy witness. As *Madame Bovary*, however, became a worldwide success, when at first it was understood and appreciated as a turning-point in the history of the novel by only a small circle of connoisseurs, the audience of novel-readers that was formed by it came to sanction the new canon of expectations; this canon made Feydeau's weaknesses—his flowery style, his modish effects, his lyrical-confessional cliches—unbearable, and allowed *Fanny* to fade into yesterday's bestseller.

IX

Thesis 4. The reconstruction of the horizon of expectations, in the face of which a work was created and received in the past, enables one on the other hand to pose questions that the text gave an answer to, and thereby to discover how the contemporary reader could have viewed and understood the work. This approach corrects the mostly unrecognized norms of a classicist or modernizing understanding of art, and avoids the circular recourse to a general "spirit of the age." It brings to view the hermeneutic difference between the former and the current understanding of a work; it raises to consciousness the history of its reception, which mediates both positions; and it thereby calls into question as a platonizing dogma[6] of philological metaphysics the apparently self-evident claims that in the literary text, literature [Dichtung] is eternally present, and that its objective meaning, determined once and for all, is at all times immediately accessible to the interpreter.

The method of historical reception is indispensable for the understanding of literature from the distant past. When the author of a work is unknown, his intent undeclared, and his relationship to sources and models only indirectly accessible, the philological question of how the text is "properly"—that is, "from its intention and time"—to be understood can best be answered if one foregrounds it against those works that the author explicitly or implicitly presupposed his contemporary audience to know. The creator of the oldest branches of the *Roman de Renart*, for example, assumes—as his prologue testifies—that his listeners know romances like the story of Troy and *Tristan*, heroic epics (*chansons de geste*), and verse fables (*fabliaux*),[7] and that they are therefore curious about the "unprecedented war between the

6. That is, a belief, like that of PLATO (ca. 427–ca. 347 B.C.E.), in timeless Forms or Ideas that give meaning to all particular phenomenon.
7. Both the epic poems (literally, "songs of action") depicting legendary and historical figures and the short, comic tales of ordinary life were popular in 12th–14th century France. *Roman de Renart* (*Novel of Renart*): French stories in verse (mid–12th to early 14th c.) whose protagonists are animals (Renard is a fox, and Ysengrin is a wolf). "The story of Troy": the Trojan War, most famously told in Homer's *Iliad* (ca. 8th c. B.C.E.). *Tristan*: a medieval cycle of tales about the doomed romance of Tristan and Iseult (French versions appeared in the late 12th c.).

two barons, Renart and Ysengrin," which is to overshadow everything already known. The works and genres that are evoked are then all ironically touched on in the course of the narrative. From this horizonal change one can probably also explain the public success, reaching far beyond France, of this rapidly famous work that for the first time took a position opposed to all the long-reigning heroic and courtly poetry.

Philological research long misunderstood the originally satiric intention of the medieval *Reineke Fuchs* and, along with it, the ironic-didactic meaning of the analogy between animal and human natures, because ever since Jacob Grimm[8] it had remained trapped within the romantic notion of pure nature poetry and naive animal tales. Thus, to give yet a second example of modernizing norms, one could also rightly reproach French research into the epic since Bédier for living—unconsciously—by the criteria of Boileau's[9] poetics, and judging a nonclassical literature by the norms of simplicity, harmony of part and whole, probability, and still others. The philological-critical method is obviously not protected by its historical objectivism from the interpreter who, supposedly bracketing himself, nonetheless raises his own aesthetic preconceptions to an unacknowledged norm and unreflectively modernizes the meaning of the past text. Whoever believes that the "timelessly true" meaning of a literary work must immediately, and simply through one's mere absorption in the text, disclose itself to the interpreter as if he had a standpoint outside of history and beyond all "errors" of his predecessors and of the historical reception—whoever believes this "conceals the involvement of the historical consciousness itself in the history of influence." He denies "those presuppositions—certainly not arbitrary but rather fundamental—that govern his own understanding," and can only feign an objectivity "that in truth depends upon the legitimacy of the questions asked."[1]

In *Truth and Method* Hans-Georg Gadamer, whose critique of historical objectivism I am assuming here, described the principle of the history of influence, which seeks to present the reality of history in understanding itself, as an application of the logic of question and answer to the historical tradition. In a continuation of Collingwood's thesis that "one can understand a text only when one has understood the question to which it is an answer,"[2] Gadamer demonstrates that the reconstructed question can no longer stand within its original horizon because this historical horizon is always already enveloped within the horizon of the present: "Understanding is always the process of the fusion of these horizons that we suppose to exist by themselves."[3] The historical question cannot exist for itself; it must merge with the question "that the tradition is for us."[4] One thereby solves the question with which René Wellek described the aporia of literary judgment: should the philologist evaluate a literary work according to the perspective of the past, the standpoint of the present, or the "verdict of the ages"?[5] The actual

8. German philologist (1785–1863) and collector of folktales. *Reineke Fuchs: Reynard the Fox* (German); Grimm's *Reinhart Fuchs* was published in 1834.
9. Nicolas Boileau (1636–1711), French critic and poet, author of *The Art of Poetry* (1674). Joseph Bédier (1864–1938), French scholar of medieval literature.
1. Hans-Georg Gadamer, *Truth and Method: Fundamentals of a Philosophical Hermeneutics* (New York, 1975), p. 268 [Jauss's note]. Gadamer (b. 1900), German philosopher.
2. Ibid., p. 333 [Jauss's note].
3. Ibid., p. 273 [Jauss's note].
4. Ibid., p. 337 [Jauss's note].
5. René Wellek, *Concepts of Criticism*, ed. Stephen G. Nichols Jr. (New Haven, 1963), pp. 17–20 [Jauss's note]. "Aporia": difficulty, logical impasse.

standards of a past could be so narrow that their use would only make poorer a work that in the history of its influence had unfolded a rich semantic potential. The aesthetic judgment of the present would favor a canon of works that correspond to modern taste, but would unjustly evaluate all other works only because their function in their time is no longer evident. And the history of influence itself, as instructive as it might be, is as "authority open to the same objections as the authority of the author's contemporaries."[6] Wellek's conclusion—that there is no possibility of avoiding our own judgment; one must only make this judgment as objective as possible in that one does what every scholar does, namely, "isolate the object"—is no solution to the aporia, but rather a relapse into objectivism. The "verdict of the ages" on a literary work is more than merely "the accumulated judgment of other readers, critics, viewers, and even professors";[7] it is the successive unfolding of the potential for meaning that is embedded in a work and actualized in the stages of its historical reception as it discloses itself to understanding judgment, so long as this faculty achieves in a controlled fashion the "fusion of horizons" in the encounter with the tradition.

* * *

X

Thesis 5. The theory of the aesthetics of reception not only allows one to conceive the meaning and form of a literary work in the historical unfolding of its understanding. It also demands that one insert the individual work into its "literary series" to recognize its historical position and significance in the context of the experience of literature. In the step from a history of the reception of works to an eventful history of literature, the latter manifests itself as a process in which the passive reception is on the part of authors. Put another way, the next work can solve formal and moral problems left behind by the last work, and present new problems in turn.

How can the individual work, which positivistic literary history determined in a chronological series and thereby reduced to the status of a "fact," be brought back into its historical-sequential relationship and thereby once again be understood as an "event"? The theory of the Formalist school, as already mentioned, would solve this problem with its principle of "literary evolution," according to which the new work arises against the background of preceding or competing works, reaches the "high point" of a literary period as a successful form is quickly reproduced and thereby increasingly automatized, until finally, when the next form has broken through, the former vegetates on as a used-up genre in the quotidian sphere of literature.

* * *

Criticism has already displayed the weaknesses of the Formalist theory of evolution: mere opposition or aesthetic variation does not suffice to explain the growth of literature; the question of the direction of change of literary forms remains unanswerable; innovation for itself does not alone make up artistic character; and the connection between literary evolution and social

6. Wellek, p. 17 [Jauss's note].

7. Ibid. [Jauss's note].

change does not vanish from the face of the earth through its mere negation. My thesis XII responds to the last question; the problematic of the remaining questions demands that the descriptive literary theory of the Formalists be opened up, through an aesthetics of reception, to the dimension of historical experience that must also include the historical standpoint of the present observer, that is, the literary historian.

* * *

Founding "literary evolution" on an aesthetics of reception thus not only returns its lost direction insofar as the standpoint of the literary historian becomes the vanishing point—but not the goal!—of the process. It also opens to view the temporal depths of literary experience, in that it allows one to recognize the variable distance between the actual and the virtual significance of a literary work. This means that the artistic character of a work, whose semantic potential Formalism reduces to innovation as the single criterion of value, must in no way always be immediately perceptible within the horizon of its first appearance, let alone that it could then also already be exhausted in the pure opposition between the old and the new form. The distance between the actual first perception of a work and its virtual significance, or, put another way, the resistance that the new work poses to the expectations of its first audience, can be so great that it requires a long process of reception to gather in that which was unexpected and unusable within the first horizon. It can thereby happen that a virtual significance of the work remains long unrecognized until the "literary evolution," through the actualization of a newer form, reaches the horizon that now for the first time allows one to find access to the understanding of the misunderstood older form. Thus the obscure lyrics of Mallarmé and his school prepared the ground for the return of baroque poetry, long since unappreciated and therefore forgotten, and in particular for the philological reinterpretation and "rebirth" of Góngora.[8] One can line up the examples of how a new literary form can reopen access to forgotten literature. These include the so-called "renaissances"—so-called, because the word's meaning gives rise to the appearance of an automatic return, and often prevents one from recognizing that literary tradition can not transmit itself alone. That is, a literary past can return only when a new reception draws it back into the present, whether an altered aesthetic attitude willfully reaches back to reappropriate the past, or an unexpected light falls back on forgotten literature from the new moment of literary evolution, allowing something to be found that one previously could not have sought in it.

The new is thus not only an *aesthetic* category. It is not absorbed into the factors of innovation, surprise, surpassing, rearrangement, or alienation, to which the Formalist theory assigned exclusive importance. The new also becomes a *historical* category when the diachronic analysis[9] of literature is pushed further to ask which historical moments are really the ones that first make new that which is new in a literary phenomenon; to what degree this new element is already perceptible in the historical instant of its emergence;

8. Luis de Góngora y Argote (1561–1627), Spanish poet who employed an ornate style. STÉPHANE MALLARMÉ (1842–1898), French poet.

9. Dealing with phenomena as they change over time; in contrast, synchronic analysis concerns the relation of phenomena at a particular moment in time.

which distance, path, or detour of understanding were required for its realization in content; and whether the moment of its full actualization was so influential that it could alter the perspective on the old, and thereby the canonization of the literary past. How the relationship of poetic theory to aesthetically productive praxis is represented in this light had already been discussed in another context.[1] The possibilities of the interaction between production and reception in the historical change of aesthetic attitudes are admittedly far from exhausted by these remarks. Here they should above all illustrate the dimension into which a diachronic view of literature leads when it would no longer be satisfied to consider a chronological series of literary facts as already the historical appearance of literature.

XI

Thesis 6. The achievements made in linguistics through the distinction and methodological interrelation of diachronic and synchronic analysis are the occasion for overcoming the diachronic perspective—previously the only one practiced—in literary history as well. If the perspective of the history of reception always bumps up against the functional connections between the understanding of new works and the significance of older ones when changes in aesthetic attitudes are considered, it must also be possible to take a synchronic cross-section of a moment in the development, to arrange the heterogeneous multiplicity of contemporaneous works in equivalent, opposing, and hierarchical structures, and thereby to discover an overarching system of relationships in the literature of a historical moment. From this the principle of representation of a new literary history could be developed, if further cross-sections diachronically before and after were so arranged as to articulate historically the change in literary structures in its epoch-making moments.

* * *

The problem of selecting that which is important for a new history of literature can be solved with the help of the synchronic perspective in a manner that has not yet been attempted: a horizontal change in the historical process of "literary evolution" need not be pursued only throughout the web of all the diachronic facts and filiations, but can also be established in the altered remains of the synchronic literary system and read out of further cross-sectional analyses. In principle, a representation of literature in the historical succession of such systems would be possible through a series of arbitrary points of intersection between diachrony and synchrony. The historical dimension of literature, its eventful continuity that is lost in traditionalism as in positivism, can meanwhile be recovered only if the literary historian finds points of intersection and brings works to light that articulate the processlike character of "literary evolution" in its moments formative of history as well as its caesurae between periods. But neither statistics nor the subjective willfulness of the literary historian decides on this historical artic-

1. *Poetik und Hermeneutik* 2, ed. Wolfgang Iser (Munich, 1966), esp. pp. 395–418 [Jauss's note]. *Poetics and Hermeneutics*: a publication featuring the work of the Constance School—the group of scholars, including Jauss and ISER (b. 1926), based at the University of Constance, who focused on the role of the reader in interpretation.

ulation, but rather the history of influence: that "which results from the event" and which from the perspective of the present constitutes the coherence of literature as the prehistory of its present manifestation.

XII

Thesis 7. The task of literary history is thus only completed when literary production is not only represented synchronically and diachronically in the succession of its systems, but also seen as "special history" in its own unique relationship to "general history." This relationship does not end with the fact that a typified, idealized, satiric, or utopian image of social existence can be found in the literature of all times. The social function of literature manifests itself in its genuine possibility only where the literary experience of the reader enters into the horizon of expectations of his lived praxis, preforms his understanding of the world, and thereby also has an effect on his social behavior.

* * *

The relationship between literature and reader can actualize itself in the sensorial realm as an incitement to aesthetic perception as well as in the ethical realm as a summons to moral reflection. The new literary work is received and judged against the background of other works of art as well as against the background of the everyday experience of life. Its social function in the ethical realm is to be grasped according to an aesthetics of reception in the same modalities of question and answer, problem and solution, under which it enters into the horizon of its historical influence.

* * *

It follows from all of this that the specific achievement of literature in social existence is to be sought exactly where literature is not absorbed into the function of a *representational* art. If one looks at the moments in history when literary works toppled the taboos of the ruling morals or offered the reader new solutions for the moral casuistry of his lived praxis, which thereafter could be sanctioned by the consensus of all readers in the society, then a still-little-studied area of research opens itself up to the literary historian. The gap between literature and history, between aesthetic and historical knowledge, can be bridged if literary history does not simply describe the process of general history in the reflection of its works one more time, but rather when it discovers in the course of "literary evolution" that properly *socially formative* function that belongs to literature as it competes with other arts and social forces in the emancipation of mankind from its natural, religious, and social bonds.

If it is worthwhile for the literary scholar to jump over his ahistorical shadow for the sake of this task, then it might well also provide an answer to the question: toward what end and with what right can one today still—or again—study literary history?

1969, 1970

RAYMOND WILLIAMS
1921–1988

Arguably the leading literary intellectual in Britain in the later twentieth century, Raymond Williams is best known for espousing the study of culture and society alongside that of literature. A committed socialist and political activist as well as a highly productive scholar throughout his life, he provided a model for those interested in investigating literature in terms of politics, ideology, and social history. He was a literary journalist and novelist; a prominent critic of drama, the novel, culture, and media; and one of the founding figures of British cultural studies and of media studies and communications. Arguing against traditional views that assume the autonomy of literature and its privileged cultural value, Williams analyzes it as a specific historical product, carrying class values.

The son of a railway worker, Williams grew up in a small farming village, Pandy, in Wales. A sense of class and place informs all his work, most visibly his novels, which depict working-class life and politics in Wales. In 1939 he entered Cambridge University on a state scholarship, where he became acutely aware of class distinctions; he was politically active in the Socialist Club and, for a short time, the Communist Party. In 1941 he left to serve in an artillery division of the British Army during World War II. He returned to Cambridge after the war, taking a degree in English in 1945. By that time he was married, with one small child and another on the way; so instead of accepting a postgraduate fellowship, he began teaching evening classes at Oxford in drama and fiction. His experience in adult education and his involvement with the Workers Educational Association helped convince him of the importance of literature's social and political contexts and of the need for a democratic, "permanent education." In 1961 he returned to Cambridge as a lecturer, and in 1974 a professorship of drama was created for him, a position he held until retiring in 1983. At Cambridge Williams not only wrote prolifically but taught a number of students—among them, STUART HALL and TERRY EAGLETON—who would themselves become important figures in literary and cultural studies.

Literary studies in England after World War II were dominated by "Cambridge English," strongly influenced by F. R. Leavis, a longtime professor at Cambridge and the editor of the leading critical journal of its day, *Scrutiny*. Extolling, in his famous phrase, "the Great Tradition," Leavis privileged literature above all other disciplines, as offering a special morally edifying force. In so doing, he followed MATTHEW ARNOLD, who in *Culture and Anarchy* (1869) claimed that the literary canon could provide a civilizing "sweetness and light" to society, in effect assuming the redemptive power previously enjoyed by religion. Williams desacralizes literature by setting it in its historical context and examining its social uses.

While engaging with history, sociology, and politics, Williams characteristically begins with literary analysis, often examining "keywords" of modern culture. In his masterwork *Culture and Society, 1780–1950* (1958), whose title signals its revision of Arnold, Williams unfolds the history of *culture, art, democracy, industry*, and *class*. For example, *culture*, a term originally applied to agriculture, shifted in the eighteenth century to encompass "tending" the human mind, so that one might be a "cultured" or "cultivated" individual. In the course of the nineteenth century, the term came to mean a general classification of the arts and literature, implying a high social value. Williams connects these transformations to the rise of industrial capitalism; he himself adopts a broader definition, arguing in a famous passage that "a culture is not only a body of intellectual and imaginative work; it is also a whole way of life."

Our selection, "Literature," from *Marxism and Literature* (1977), similarly examines *literature*. With the rise of industrial capitalism, a term once applied to any written material began first to designate more specifically works of the imagination, then certain poems, novels, and plays of high cultural and social value. Williams argues that our contemporary sense derives not from the intrinsic, timeless aesthetic value of literary works themselves but from the ongoing capitalist specialization of society, and that literary forms and genres are determined by the social roles they play. He also examines the development of "national" literatures, which further demonstrates how society, culture, and art interconnect and how literature serves the dominant order. Williams thus challenges all idealizing notions of literature.

Williams responds specifically to the state of English studies of his time, but he also raises a perennial problem in literary theory—the definition of literature. Modern literary theorists often look to formal artistic features intrinsic in works, discerning what ROMAN JAKOBSON terms their "literariness" or "poeticity." Williams sees literature instead as a shifting historical product—not a transcendent entity but a complex mutating human product linked with concepts such as literacy, imagination, taste, and beauty, all inflected by sociohistorical conditions. He also notes that *criticism* and its function have similarly mutated to reflect changing social roles.

Williams calls his theoretical approach "cultural materialism," at once invoking the Marxist focus on the economic means of production and emphasizing the role of culture. Stressing the complex interaction of culture and society, he investigates the material, historical factors that inform culture—part of society's "superstructure"—but he also shows how culture shapes society in an ongoing process, often contesting and resisting dominant modes of production.

Although Marxist and radical thought played a significant role in Anglo-American criticism during the 1930s, such approaches were largely shunned during the cold war, particularly in the United States. The New York Intellectuals, for instance, as the title of IRVING HOWE's *Politics and the Novel* (1957) suggests, were like Williams in joining the literary and the social; but they were avowedly anticommunist and anti-Marxist. It was not until the 1970s and 1980s, in part through Williams's influence and example, that Marxist and socialist ideas once again became accepted in literary studies.

Williams's work, as he remarks in *Culture and Society*, "has been classified under headings as various as cultural history, historical semantics, history of ideas, social criticism, literary history and sociology." While some critics complain about Williams's style, which can be murky and ponderous, his disciplinary boundary crossing made him a model for cultural studies. Conversely, his stress on the political significance of literary works was criticized by more traditional scholars for falling outside the purview of literary studies proper. In a career extending the traditional boundaries of literary studies, Williams exemplifies the possibilities for combining literary work with committed politics, and literary criticism with social criticism.

BIBLIOGRAPHY

Raymond Williams published more than thirty books and approximately six hundred articles during his lifetime, spanning a wide range, from drama, poetry, and novel criticism to cultural history and media studies to literary theory and political commentary. Williams's early books include *Reading and Criticism* (1950), *Drama from Ibsen to Eliot* (1952; rev. as *Drama from Ibsen to Brecht*, 1968); and *Drama in Performance* (1954; rev. ed., 1968). He also published a textbook, *Preface to Film*, co-authored with Michael Orrom (1954). *Culture and Society, 1780–1950* (1958), a key text for British cultural studies, is a good place to enter his work. Its sequels include *Keywords: A Vocabulary of Culture and Society* (1976; rev. ed., 1983), originally planned as an appendix, and *The Long Revolution* (1961).

Williams helped pioneer media studies and the emerging discipline of communications with *Communications* (1962; 3d ed., 1976); *Television: Technology and Cultural Form* (1974) is one of the first significant studies of that medium. *Modern Tragedy* (1966; rev. ed., 1979) continued his work in drama. He co-edited *May Day*

Manifesto, a response to the political events of the 1960s (1967; 2d ed., 1968), with his student Stuart Hall. Williams returned to literary criticism with *The English Novel from Dickens to Lawrence* (1970) and *The Country and the City* (1973).

Marxism and Literature (1977) is a good introduction to Williams's more theoretical considerations of culture and society. *Problems in Materialism and Culture: Selected Essays* (1980) elaborates his theory of "cultural materialism," and *Culture* (1981; retitled *The Sociology of Culture*, 1982) is a sequel to *Marxism and Literature*. A lengthy collection of interviews, *Politics and Letters: Interviews with New Left Review* (1979), provides an accessible overview of his thought. His collections of occasional writings include *Writing in Society* (1984); the posthumous *The Politics of Modernism: Against the New Conformists*, edited by Tony Pinkney (1989), which includes a compelling interview of Williams by Edward Said; and *Resources of Hope: Culture, Democracy, Socialism*, edited by Robin Gable (1989), which collects diverse essays. *What I Came to Say* (1990) offers a short political summation.

Williams edited a number of anthologies on literary figures, drama, and communications, and he regularly published fiction throughout his career, including a trilogy of working-class life in Wales, *Border Country* (1960), *Second Generation* (1964), and *The Fight for Manod* (1979). He also wrote short stories, plays, and television scripts.

The secondary literature on Williams's life and work is considerable. A comprehensive biography, Fred Inglis's *Raymond Williams* (1995) presents a detailed and sometimes anecdotal picture of Williams's life. John and Lizzie Eldridge's *Raymond Williams: Making Connections* (1994) is a useful introduction to the many aspects of Williams's work. There are a number of important collections: *Raymond Williams: Critical Perspectives*, edited by his student Terry Eagleton (1989), gathers essays by Stuart Hall, Said, Eagleton, and others, as well as an interview Eagleton conducted with Williams; *Views beyond the Border Country: Raymond Williams and Cultural Politics*, edited by Dennis L. Dworkin and Leslie G. Roman (1993); *Cultural Materialism: On Raymond Williams*, edited by Christopher Prendergast (1995), which presents sophisticated examinations by contemporary critics; and *Raymond Williams Now: Knowledge, Limits, and the Future*, edited by Jeff Wallace, Rod Jones, and Sophie Nield (1997), which looks at Williams's relevance to subsequent theory. The best single-authored account, John Higgins's *Raymond Williams: Literature, Marxism and Cultural Materialism* (1999), covers all Williams's work, from his early interest in drama to his political interventions.

Raymond Williams, edited by Eagleton, appends a chronological bibliography of all of Williams's writing, as well as a selected secondary bibliography. Higgins's *Raymond Williams*, published more recently, also includes a chronological bibliography of his writings and a good listing of secondary sources.

From Marxism and Literature

Part 1, Chapter 3

Literature

It is relatively difficult to see 'literature' as a concept. In ordinary usage it appears to be no more than a specific description, and what is described is then, as a rule, so highly valued that there is a virtually immediate and unnoticed transfer of the specific values of particular works and kinds of work to what operates as a concept but is still firmly believed to be actual and practical. Indeed the special property of 'literature' as a concept is that it claims this kind of importance and priority, in the concrete achievements of many

particular great works, as against the 'abstraction' and 'generality' of other concepts and of the kinds of practice which they, by contrast, define. Thus it is common to see 'literature' defined as 'full, central, immediate human experience', usually with an associated reference to 'minute particulars'. By contrast, 'society' is often seen as essentially general and abstract: the summaries and averages, rather than the direct substance, of human living. Other related concepts, such as 'politics', 'sociology', or 'ideology', are similarly placed and downgraded, as mere hardened outer shells compared with the living experience of literature.

The naïvety of the concept, in this familiar form, can be shown in two ways: theoretically and historically. It is true that one popular version of the concept has been developed in ways that appear to protect it, and in practice do often protect it, against any such arguments. An essential abstraction of the 'personal' and the 'immediate' is carried so far that, within this highly developed form of thought, the whole process of abstraction has been dissolved. None of its steps can be retraced, and the abstraction of the 'concrete' is a perfect and virtually unbreakable circle. Arguments from theory or from history are simply evidence of the incurable abstraction and generality of those who are putting them forward. They can then be contemptuously rejected, often without specific reply, which would be only to fall to their level.

This is a powerful and often forbidding system of abstraction, in which the concept of 'literature' becomes actively ideological.[1] Theory can do something against it, in the necessary recognition (which ought hardly, to those who are really in contact with literature, to need any long preparation) that whatever else 'it' may be, literature is the process and the result of formal composition within the social and formal properties of a language. The effective suppression of this process and its circumstances, which is achieved by shifting the concept to an undifferentiated equivalence with 'immediate living experience' (indeed, in some cases, to more than this, so that the actual lived experiences of society and history are seen as less particular and immediate than those of literature) is an extraordinary ideological feat. The very process that is specific, that of actual composition, has effectively disappeared or has been displaced to an internal and self-proving procedure in which writing of this kind is genuinely believed to be (however many questions are then begged) 'immediate living experience' itself. Appeals to the history of literature, over its immense and extraordinarily various range, from the *Mabinogion* to *Middlemarch*, or from *Paradise Lost* to *The Prelude*,[2] cause a momentary hesitation until various dependent categories of the concept are moved into place: 'myth', 'romance', 'fiction', 'realist fiction', 'epic', 'lyric', 'autobiography'. What from another point of view might reasonably be taken as initial definitions of the processes and circumstances of composition are converted within the ideological concept, to 'forms' of what is still triumphantly defined as 'full, central, immediate human experience'. Indeed when any concept has so profound and complex an internal specializing develop-

1. That is, plays a role in the dominant system of ideas and beliefs of modern class-based societies that, according to Marxism, operates subliminally and makes us compliant subjects.

2. Williams names major works of prose and poetry: the *Mabinogion* (comp. 14th c.), a collection of medieval Welsh tales; *Middlemarch* (1871–72), a novel by George Eliot; *Paradise Lost* (1667), an epic by John Milton; and *The Prelude* (1850), a long, autobiographical poem by WILLIAM WORDSWORTH.

ment, it can hardly be examined or questioned at all from outside. If we are to understand its significance, and the complicated facts it partially reveals and partially obscures, we must turn to examining the development of the concept itself.

In its modern form the concept of 'literature' did not emerge earlier than the eighteenth century and was not fully developed until the nineteenth century. Yet the conditions for its emergence had been developing since the Renaissance. The word itself came into English use in the fourteenth century, following French and Latin precedents; its root was Latin *littera*, a letter of the alphabet. *Litterature*, in the common early spelling, was then in effect a condition of reading: of being able to read and of having read. It was often close to the sense of modern *literacy*, which was not in the language until the late nineteenth century, its introduction in part made necessary by the movement of *literature* to a different sense. The normal adjective associated with literature was *literate*. *Literary* appeared in the sense of reading ability and experience in the seventeenth century, and did not acquire its specialized modern meaning until the eighteenth century.

Literature as a new category was then a specialization of the area formerly categorized as *rhetoric* and *grammar*:[3] a specialization to reading and, in the material context of the development of printing, to the printed word and especially the book. It was eventually to become a more general category than *poetry* or the earlier *poesy*, which had been general terms for imaginative composition, but which in relation to the development of *literature* became predominantly specialized, from the seventeenth century, to metrical composition and especially written and printed metrical composition. But *literature* was never primarily the active composition—the 'making'—which poetry had described.[4] As reading rather than writing, it was a category of a different kind. The characteristic use can be seen in Bacon—"learned in all literature and erudition, divine and humane"—and as late as Johnson—"he had probably more than common literature, as his son addresses him in one of his most elaborate Latin poems".[5] *Literature*, that is to say, was a category of use and condition rather than of production. It was a particular specialization of what had hitherto been seen as an activity or practice, and a specialization, in the circumstances, which was inevitably made in terms of social class. In its first extended sense, beyond the bare sense of 'literacy', it was a definition of 'polite' or 'humane' learning, and thus specified a particular social distinction. New political concepts of the 'nation' and new valuations of the 'vernacular' interacted with a persistent emphasis on 'literature' as reading in the 'classical' languages. But still, in this first stage, into the eighteenth century, *literature* was primarily a generalized social concept, expressing a certain (minority) level of educational achievement. This carried with it a potential and eventually realized alternative definition of *literature* as 'printed books': the objects in and through which this achievement was demonstrated.

It is important that, within the terms of this development, literature nor-

3. Fundamental subjects in classical and medieval education (defined much more broadly than they are today).

4. The word *poetry* is etymologically related to the Greek verb "to make," *poien*.

5. Written of Milton in the *Life of Milton* (1779), by SAMUEL JOHNSON (1709–1784), the English essayist, poet, and lexicographer. "Learned in all literature . . .": a description of King James I in *The Advancement of Learning* (1605), by the English philosopher and statesman Francis Bacon (1561–1626).

mally included all printed books. There was not necessary specialization to 'imaginative' works. Literature was still primarily reading ability and reading experience, and this included philosophy, history, and essays as well as poems. Were the new eighteenth-century novels 'literature'? That question was first approached, not by definition of their mode or content, but by reference to the standards of 'polite' or 'humane' learning. Was drama literature? This question was to exercise successive generations, not because of any substantial difficulty but because of the practical limits of the category. If literature was reading, could a mode written for spoken performance be said to be literature, and if not, where was Shakespeare? (But of course he could now be read; this was made possible, and 'literary', by *texts*.)

At one level the definition indicated by this development has persisted. Literature lost its earliest sense of reading ability and reading experience, and became an apparently objective category of printed works of a certain quality. The concerns of a 'literary editor' or a 'literary supplement' would still be defined in this way. But three complicating tendencies can then be distinguished: first, a shift from 'learning' to 'taste' or 'sensibility' as a criterion defining literary quality; second, an increasing specialization of literature to 'creative' or 'imaginative' works; third, a development of the concept of 'tradition' within national terms, resulting in the more effective definition of 'a national literature'. The sources of each of these tendencies can be discerned from the Renaissance, but it was in the eighteenth and nineteenth centuries that they came through most powerfully, until they became, in the twentieth century, in effect received assumptions. We can look more closely at each tendency.

The shift from 'learning' to 'taste' or 'sensibility' was in effect the final stage of a shift from a para-national scholarly profession, with its original social base in the church and then in the universities, and with the classical languages as its shared material, to a profession increasingly defined by its class position, from which essentially general criteria, applicable in fields other than literature, were derived. In England certain specific features of bourgeois development strengthened the shift; the 'cultivated amateur' was one of its elements, but 'taste' and 'sensibility' were essentially unifying concepts, in class terms, and could be applied over a very wide range from public and private behaviour to (as Wordsworth complained) either wine or poetry. As subjective definitions of apparently objective criteria (which acquire their apparent objectivity from an actively consensual class sense), and at the same time apparently objective definitions of subjective qualities, 'taste' and 'sensibility' are characteristically bourgeois[6] categories.

'Criticism' is an essentially associated concept, in the same development. As a new term, from the seventeenth century, it developed (always in difficult relations with its general and persistent sense of fault-finding) from 'commentaries' on literature, within the 'learned' criterion, to the conscious exercise of 'taste', 'sensibility', and 'discrimination'. It became a significant special form of the general tendency in the concept of literature towards an emphasis on the use or (conspicuous) consumption[7] of works, rather than on their

6. Middle-class (as distinguished from aristocratic, working-class, and unemployed, criminal, etc.).

7. "Conspicuous consumption" is a term applied by the American sociologist Thorstein Veblen in *The Theory of the Leisure Class* (1899) to the lavish spending by the modern leisure class designed to enhance their status.

production. While the habits of use or consumption were still the criteria of a relatively integrated class, they had their characteristic strengths as well as weaknesses. 'Taste' in literature might be confused with 'taste' in everything else, but, within class terms, responses to literature were notably integrated, and the relative integration of the 'reading public' (a characteristic term of the definition) was a sound base for important literary production. The reliance on 'sensibility', as a special form of an attempted emphasis on whole 'human' response, had its evident weaknesses in its tendency to separate 'feeling' from 'thought' (with an associated vocabulary of 'subjective' and 'objective', 'unconscious' and 'conscious', 'private' and 'public'). At the same time it served, at its best, to insist on 'immediate' and 'living' substance (in which its contrast with the 'learned' tradition was especially marked). It was really only as this class lost its relative cohesion and dominance that the weakness of the concepts *as concepts* became evident. And it is evidence of at least its residual hegemony[8] that *criticism*, taken as a new conscious discipline into the universities, to be practised by what became a new paranational profession, retained these founding class concepts, alongside attempts to establish new abstractly objective criteria. More seriously, criticism was taken to be a natural definition of literary studies, themselves defined by the specializing category (printed works of a certain quality) of *literature*. Thus these forms of the concepts of *literature* and *criticism* are, in the perspective of historical social development, forms of a class specialization and control of a general social practice, and of a class limitation of the questions which it might raise.

The process of the specialization of 'literature' to 'creative' or 'imaginative' works is very much more complicated. It is in part a major affirmative response, in the name of an essentially general human 'creativity', to the socially repressive and intellectually mechanical forms of a new social order: that of capitalism and especially industrial capitalism. The practical specialization of work to the wage-labour production of commodities; of 'being' to 'work' in these terms; of language to the passing of 'rational' or 'informative' 'messages'; of social relations to functions within a systematic economic and political order: all these pressures and limits were challenged in the name of a full and liberating 'imagination' or 'creativity'. The central Romantic assertions, which depend on these concepts, have a significantly absolute range, from politics and nature to work and art. 'Literature' acquired, in this period, a quite new resonance, but it was not yet a specialized resonance. That came later as, against the full pressures of an industrial capitalist order, the assertion became defensive and reserving where it had once been positive and absolute. In 'art' and 'literature', the essential and saving *human* qualities must, in the early phase, be 'extended'; in the later phase, 'preserved'.

Several concepts developed together. 'Art' was shifted from its sense of a general human skill to a special province, defined by 'imagination' and 'sensibility'. 'Aesthetic', in the same period, shifted from its sense of general perception to a specialized category of the 'artistic' and the 'beautiful'. 'Fiction' and 'myth' (a new term from the early nineteenth century) might be seen from the dominant class position as 'fancies' or 'lies' but from this alter-

8. Domination; also an allusion to "cultural hegemony," a Marxist concept developed by the Italian philosopher ANTONIO GRAMSCI (1891–1937), which refers to the manufactured consent that legitimates a dominant group and unifies a society.

native position were honoured as the bearers of '*imaginative* truth'. 'Romance' and 'romantic' were given newly specialized positive emphases. 'Literature' moved with all these. The wide general meaning was still available, but a specialized meaning came steadily to predominate, around the distinguishing qualities of the 'imaginative' and the 'aesthetic'. 'Taste' and 'sensibility' had begun as categories of a social condition. In the new specialization, comparable but more elevated qualities were assigned to 'the works themselves', the 'aesthetic objects'.

But there was still one substantial uncertainty: whether the elevated qualities were to be assigned to the 'imaginative' dimension (access to a truth 'higher' or 'deeper' than 'scientific' or 'objective' or 'everyday' reality; a claim consciously substituting itself for the traditional claims of religion) or to the 'aesthetic' dimension ('beauties' of language or style). Within the specialization of literature, alternative schools made one or other of these emphases, but there were also repeated attempts to fuse them, making 'truth' and 'beauty', or 'truth' and 'vitality of language', identical. Under continuing pressure these arguments became not only positive assertions but increasingly negative and comparative, against all other modes: not only against 'science' and 'society'—the abstract and generalizing modes of other 'kinds' of experience—and not only against other kinds of writing—now in their turn specialized as 'discursive' or 'factual'—but, ironically, against much of 'literature' itself—'bad' writing, 'popular' writing, 'mass culture'. Thus the category which had appeared objective as 'all printed books', and which had been given a social-class foundation as 'polite learning' and the domain of 'taste' and 'sensibility', now became a necessarily selective and self-defining area: not all 'fiction' was 'imaginative'; not all 'literature' was 'Literature'. 'Criticism' acquired a quite new and effectively primary importance, since it was now the only way of validating this specialized and selective category. It was at once a *discrimination* of the authentic 'great' or 'major' works, with a consequent grading of 'minor' works and an effective exclusion of 'bad' or 'negligible' works, and a practical realization and communication of the 'major' values. What had been claimed for 'art' and the 'creative imagination' in the central Romantic arguments was now claimed for 'criticism', as the central 'humane' activity and 'discipline'.

This development depended, in the first place, on an elaboration of the concept of 'tradition'. The idea of a 'national literature' had been growing strongly since the Renaissance. It drew on all the positive forces of cultural nationalism and its real achievements. It brought with it a sense of the 'greatness' or 'glory' of the native language, for which before the Renaissance there had been conventional apology by comparison with a 'classical' range.[9] Each of these rich and strong achievements had been actual; the 'national literature' and the 'major language' were now indeed 'there'. But, within the specialization of 'literature', each was re-defined so that it could be brought to identity with the selective and self-defining 'literary values'. The 'national literature' soon ceased to be a history and became a tradition. It was not, even theoretically, all that had been written or all kinds of writing. It was a

9. That is, not simply the works of Greek and Roman writers but the very languages in which they wrote were thought superior to anything that contemporary writers could achieve in the vernacular (defended by such writers as JOACHIM DU BELLAY, ca. 1522–1560).

selection which culminated in, and in a circular way defined, the 'literary values' which 'criticism' was asserting. There were then always local disputes about who and what should be included, or as commonly excluded, in the definition of this 'tradition'. To have been an Englishman and to have written was by no means to belong to the 'English literary tradition', just as to be an Englishman and to speak was by no means to exemplify the 'greatness' of the language—indeed the practice of most English speakers was continually cited as 'ignorance' or 'betrayal' or 'debasement' of just this 'greatness'. Selectivity and self-definition, which were the evident processes of 'criticism' of this kind, were, however, projected as 'literature' itself, as 'literary values' and even finally as 'essential Englishness': the absolute ratification of a limited and specializing consensual process. To oppose the terms of this ratification was to be 'against literature'.

It is one of the signs of the success of this categorization of literature that even Marxism has made so little headway against it. Marx himself, to be sure, hardly tried.[1] His characteristically intelligent and informed incidental discussions of actual literature are now often cited, defensively, as evidence of the humane flexibility of Marxism, when they ought really to be cited (with no particular devaluation) as evidence of how far he remained, in these matters, within the conventions and categories of his time. The radical challenge of the emphasis on 'practical consciousness' was thus never carried through to the categories of 'literature' and 'the aesthetic', and there was always hesitation about the practical application, in this area, of propositions which were held to be central and decisive almost everywhere else.

When such application was eventually made, in the later Marxist tradition, it was of three main kinds: an attempted assimilation of 'literature' to 'ideology', which was in practice little more than banging one inadequate category against another; an effective and important inclusion of 'popular literature'—the 'literature of the people'—as a necessary but neglected part of the 'literary tradition'; and a sustained but uneven attempt to relate 'literature' to the social and economic history within which 'it' had been produced. Each of these last two attempts has been significant. In the former a 'tradition' has been genuinely extended. In the latter there has been an effective reconstitution, over wide areas, of historical social practice, which makes the abstraction of 'literary values' much more problematical, and which, more positively, allows new kinds of reading and new kinds of questions about 'the works themselves'. This has been known, especially, as 'Marxist criticism' (a radical variant of the established bourgeois practice) though other work has been done on quite different bases, from a wider social history and from wider conceptions of 'the people', 'the language', and 'the nation'.

It is significant that 'Marxist criticism' and 'Marxist literary studies' have been most successful, in ordinary terms, when they have worked within the received category of 'literature', which they may have extended or even revalued, but never radically questioned or opposed. By contrast, what looked like fundamental theoretical revaluation, in the attempted assimilation to 'ide-

1. On the literary and aesthetic writings of the social, economic, and political philosopher KARL MARX (1818–1883), see above.

ology', was a disastrous failure, and fundamentally compromised, in this whole area, the status of Marxism itself. Yet for half a century now there have been other and more significant tendencies. Lukács[2] contributed a profound revaluation of 'the aesthetic'. The Frankfurt School,[3] with its special emphasis on art, undertook a sustained re-examination of 'artistic production', centred on the concept of 'mediation'. Goldmann[4] undertook a radical revaluation of the 'creative subject'. Marxist variants of formalism undertook radical redefinition of the processes of writing, with new uses of the concepts of 'signs' and 'texts',[5] and with a significantly related refusal of 'literature' as a category. The methods and problems indicated by these tendencies will be examined in detail later in this book.

Yet the crucial theoretical break is the recognition of 'literature' as a specializing social and historical category. It should be clear that this does not diminish its importance. Just because it is historical, a key concept of a major phase of a culture, it is decisive evidence of a particular form of the social development of language. Within its terms, work of outstanding and permanent importance was done, in specific social and cultural relationships. But what has been happening, in our own century, is a profound transformation of these relationships, directly connected with changes in the basic means of production. These changes are most evident in the new technologies of language, which have moved practice beyond the relatively uniform and specializing technology of print. The principal changes are the electronic transmission and recording of speech and of writing for speech, and the chemical and electronic composition and transmission of images,[6] in complex relations with speech and with writing for speech, and including images which can themselves be 'written'. None of these means cancels print, or even diminishes its specific importance, but they are not simple additions to it, or mere alternatives. In their complex connections and interrelations they compose a new substantial practice in social language itself, over a range from public address and manifest representation to 'inner speech' and verbal thought. For they are always more than new technologies, in the limited sense. They are *means of production*, developed in direct if complex relations with profoundly changing and extending social and cultural relationships: changes elsewhere recognizable as deep political and economic transformations. It is in no way surprising that the specialized concept of 'literature', developed in precise forms of correspondence with a particular social class, a particular organization of learning, and the appropriate particular technology of print, should now be so often invoked in retrospective, nostalgic, or reactionary moods, as a form of opposition to what is correctly seen as a new phase of civilization. The situation is historically comparable to that invocation of the divine and the sacred, and of divine and sacred learning, against the new humanist concept of literature, in the difficult and contested transition from feudal to bourgeois society.

2. GYÖRGY LUKÁCS (1885–1971), Hungarian Marxist literary critic and philosopher.
3. A group of critics associated with the Frankfurt Institute of Social Research in Germany; influenced by Marxism, they focused on social and cultural criticism of modern society. Major members include MAX HORKHEIMER (1895–1973) and THEODOR ADORNO (1903–1969).
4. Lucien Goldmann (1913–1970), French Marxist sociologist and critic; on the "creative subject," see especially *Cultural Creation in Modern Society* (1971).
5. Terms associated with semiotics and with structuralist critics (e.g., ROLAND BARTHES), who expanded the analysis of "texts" beyond what is written.
6. That is, in audio recording, radio, film, and television.

What can then be seen as happening, in each transition, is a historical development of social language itself: finding new means, new forms and then new definitions of a changing practical consciousness. Many of the active values of 'literature' have then to be seen, not as tied to the concept, which came to limit as well as to summarize them, but as elements of a continuing and changing practice which already substantially, and now at the level of theoretical redefinition, is moving beyond its old forms.

1977

FRANTZ FANON
1925–1961

A leading third world intellectual whose work helped inspire the struggle against colonialism and ground theoretically the subsequent growth of postcolonial culture, Frantz Fanon was one of the most influential thinkers of the twentieth century. Though born in the French Antilles, he had particular impact in Africa, where his writings undergird the works of important anticolonial writers, such as Kenya's NGUGI WĂ THIONG'O and Senegal's Ousmane Sembène. During the 1950s and early 1960s, Fanon's various writings, especially *Les Damnés de la terre* (1961; trans. 1963, *The Wretched of the Earth*), elaborated with passion on the historical conditions of anticolonial struggle. Significantly, Fanon articulated the role to be played by intellectuals in this struggle, offering stern (and prescient, as it turned out) warnings of the difficulties that would face emerging African nations once independence had been won.

Born to a middle-class black family on the island of Martinique, then a French colony, Fanon grew up amid descendants of African slaves brought to the Caribbean to work on the island's sugar plantations. As a teenager, he became intellectually attuned to the problems of colonialism and racism. He was politically active, participating in the guerrilla struggle against the supporters of the pro-Nazi French Vichy government. After the Free French forces gained control of Martinique in 1943, Fanon volunteered to go to Europe to fight. He emerged a decorated war hero, and he stayed in France to complete his education and train as a psychiatrist in Paris and Lyons. There he found that his service to the French state made no difference to the whites around him, who regarded black French subjects like himself as the *Other*—as alien and inferior, yet frightening and dangerous. He came to understand that despite his intelligence, high level of education, and mastery of the French language, he was regarded not as a human being, but as a specimen of an exotic and savage race, viewed through stereotypes developed over centuries of racial prejudice.

While in France, Fanon began his writing career, publishing his first book in 1952: *Peau noire, masques blancs* (trans. 1967, *Black Skin, White Masks*). This book includes the important chapter "The Fact of Blackness," which describes Fanon's growing awareness of racism in France. The work, personal and lyrical, shows the strong influence of Fanon's psychiatric training, as he concentrates primarily on the impact of racism and colonialism on the black psyche. It also engages in a critical dialogue with French existentialism, particularly that of JEAN-PAUL SARTRE, and exhibits the influence of the *négritude* movement (which called in the 1940s and 1950s for a distinctive black cultural identity rather than complete assimilation into French culture). Indeed, one of the leaders of that movement, Aimé Césaire, had been

Fanon's teacher and mentor back in Martinique and remained an important influence throughout his life. Fanon movingly describes, with anguish and anger, the various stages of accommodation and alienation that characterize black life in white societies. In particular, Fanon tells of his own struggle to make sense of the white world and to address it on its own rationalist terms, only to be rejected on the basis of his race and driven back by white prejudice to an antirational, primitivist stance. Then, realizing that such primitivism was taken by whites as simply verifying their own stereotypical attitudes toward blacks, Fanon began to explore the cultural achievements of African civilization, finally achieving a dialectical resolution between Western rationalism and Africanist primitivism.

After completing his medical training, in 1953 Fanon was appointed head of the psychiatric department of the Blida-Jonville Hospital in Algeria, a French colony in North Africa. In 1954 the Algerians, led by the National Liberation Front (FLN), revolted against French rule, initiating a period of violent revolutionary struggle that would last until full Algerian independence was gained in 1962. Sympathetic to the revolution from its inception, Fanon resigned his medical post in 1956 to become the editor of the FLN newspaper. He remained involved in the revolution until his death from leukemia five years later, at the age of thirty-six.

Much of Fanon's writing of that period concentrated on the Algerian revolution, including the essays published in *L'An cinq, de la révolution Algérienne* (1959; trans. 1965, *A Dying Colonialism*). Other essays were posthumously collected and published in 1964 as *Pour la révolution Africaine* (trans. 1976, *Toward the African Revolution*). The culmination of his work, however, was the publication of *The Wretched of the Earth*, just weeks before his death. This volume, which featured an impassioned introduction by Sartre, gained widespread recognition and solidified Fanon's reputation as a leading revolutionary thinker of the twentieth century.

Fanon displays a distinctive political vision, centrally informed by the European tradition of Marxist thought in a version heavily modified to reflect third world, anticolonial perspectives. For example, in his conviction that colonialism would be ended only through violent anticolonial struggle, Fanon was very much in accord with the Marxist view of capitalism's inevitable end. However, Fanon's reasons differed; in particular, he stressed that in the anticolonial struggle would counteract the long-term psychological effects of the violence of colonialism itself. In addition, whereas Marx envisioned the European working class, or proletariat, as the crux of the revolution, Fanon felt that in Africa and other colonial regions, the revolution would have to be led by a coalition of peasants and social outcasts, the so-called lumpenproletariat in whom Marx saw little revolutionary potential in Europe.

Perhaps the most important aspect of Fanon's political thought was his insight into the complex interaction in colonies between class and race. Though he was intensely aware of the centrality of racism to European colonialism, Fanon as a Marxist argued that social, economic, and political oppression in the third world was ultimately more a matter of class. He makes this point most forcefully in his influential argument in *The Wretched of the Earth* that postcolonial African nations court disaster if they simply replace their white colonial bourgeois leaders with a black African postcolonial bourgeoisie, while leaving the basic class structure of the societies in place.

In the important chapter "The Pitfalls of National Consciousness" (excerpted below), Fanon explores the pros and cons of nationalist attitudes in the struggle for independence from colonialism. While viewing nationalism as a necessary and important tool, he warns that it threatens to force emerging African nations into molds provided by their European predecessors. He points out that the new African nations will be ruled by a postcolonial bourgeoisie trained by Europeans to approach problems in characteristically European ways—but without the historical energy that had enabled the European bourgeoisie to defeat their feudal-aristocratic predecessors and to assume power across Europe from the seventeenth to the nineteenth centuries. The members of the African bourgeoisie, he argues, are merely decadent imitators of their Western masters and thus can never lead Africa in its difficult struggle to build new postcolonial societies that truly move beyond the legacy of the colonial past.

In the chapter "On National Culture" (excerpted below), Fanon continues his discussion of nationalism, exploring the role played by culture in the development of viable postcolonial identities for emergent African nations. Here he particularly concentrates on the importance of intellectuals in helping to develop cultural identities for emerging postcolonial nations. He urges African intellectuals to join actively in the anticolonial struggle and to place the building of new postcolonial national identities at the very center of their work. At the same time, he warns these intellectuals to remain aware that the new nation must exist within an international community. As they pursue national culture, they should draw their strength from the African masses but eschew isolationist or traditionalist solutions; they must maintain an understanding of and sense of connection to the outside world.

Fanon's work was an inspiration to the black power movement in the United States during the 1960s. At the same time, he was a key theoretical resource for the generation of intellectuals and writers who struggled to create viable postcolonial cultural identities in Africa and elsewhere. Fanon's work was especially important to a number of radical African novelists (including Ngugi and Sembène), and it continues to provide a central framework within which to interpret their work. Indeed, Fanon is arguably the most important theoretical gloss on the work of some contemporary African novelists, such as Ghana's Ayi Kwei Armah and Zimbabwe's Tsitsi Dangarembga, who have been deeply influenced by his ideas. Ngugi has been among the most explicit in pointing to the importance of Fanon to his work, declaring in *Decolonising the Mind* (1992) that it is "impossible to understand what informs African writing" without first reading two books: Lenin's *Imperialism: The Highest Stage of Capitalism* (1917) and Fanon's *Wretched of the Earth*, "mostly the chapter titled 'pitfalls of national consciousness.'"

During the closing decades of the twentieth century, Fanon's work was joined by that of a new wave of scholars, such as EDWARD SAID and HOMI BHABHA, who often drew on poststructuralist theorists in describing the postcolonial condition. Nevertheless, Fanon's logical but passionate arguments, rooted in a Marxist engagement with the material world, have remained a strong force in postcolonial studies.

BIBLIOGRAPHY

Fanon's major works are *Black Skin, White Masks* (1952; trans. 1967), *A Dying Colonialism* (1959; trans. 1965), *The Wretched of the Earth* (1961; trans. 1963), and *Toward the African Revolution* (1964; trans. 1976). For a good, brief introduction to Fanon's life and ideas, see David Caute's *Frantz Fanon* (1970). For more detailed biographies, see Peter Geismar's *Fanon* (1971) and David Macey's *Frantz Fanon: A Life* (2000). Fanon's life is also the subject of the documentary film *Frantz Fanon: Black Skin, White Mask* (1995). For studies that combine biographical detail with critical analysis of Fanon's thought, see Richard C. Onwuanibe, *A Critique of Revolutionary Humanism: Frantz Fanon* (1983), and Hussein Abadilahi Bulhan, *Frantz Fanon and the Psychology of Oppression* (1985).

Other useful critical studies include Irene Gendzier, *Frantz Fanon: A Critical Study* (1973); Renate Zahar, *Frantz Fanon: Colonialism and Alienation* (1969; trans. 1974); Lewis Gordon, *Frantz Fanon and the Crisis of European Man* (1995); and Ato Sekyi-Otu, *Fanon's Dialectic of Experience* (1996). Several essay collections of the 1990s indicate a resurgence of interest in Fanon's thought: see *Frantz Fanon: Critical Perspectives*, edited by Anthony Alessandrini (1999); *Rethinking Fanon: The Continuing Dialogue*, edited by Nigel Gibson (1999); and *Fanon: A Critical Reader*, edited by Lewis Gordon, Denean Sharpley-Whiting, and Renee White (1996). The last of these also includes a particularly extensive bibliography.

From The Wretched of the Earth[1]

From *The Pitfalls of National Consciousness*

History teaches us clearly that the battle against colonialism does not run straight away along the lines of nationalism. For a very long time the native devotes his energies to ending certain definite abuses: forced labor, corporal punishment, inequality of salaries, limitation of political rights, etc. This fight for democracy against the oppression of mankind will slowly leave the confusion of neo-liberal universalism to emerge, sometimes laboriously, as a claim to nationhood. It so happens that the unpreparedness of the educated classes, the lack of practical links between them and the mass of the people, their laziness, and, let it be said, their cowardice at the decisive moment of the struggle will give rise to tragic mishaps.

National consciousness, instead of being the all-embracing crystallization of the innermost hopes of the whole people, instead of being the immediate and most obvious result of the mobilization of the people, will be in any case only an empty shell, a crude and fragile travesty of what it might have been. The faults that we find in it are quite sufficient explanation of the facility with which, when dealing with young and independent nations, the nation is passed over for the race, and the tribe is preferred to the state. These are the cracks in the edifice which show the process of retrogression, that is so harmful and prejudicial to national effort and national unity. We shall see that such retrograde steps with all the weaknesses and serious dangers that they entail are the historical result of the incapacity of the national middle class to rationalize popular action, that is to say their incapacity to see into the reasons for that action.

This traditional weakness, which is almost congenital to the national consciousness of underdeveloped countries, is not solely the result of the mutilation of the colonized people by the colonial regime. It is also the result of the intellectual laziness of the national middle class, of its spiritual penury, and of the profoundly cosmopolitan mold that its mind is set in.

The national middle class which takes over power at the end of the colonial regime is an underdeveloped middle class. It has practically no economic power, and in any case it is in no way commensurate with the bourgeoisie[2] of the mother country which it hopes to replace. In its narcissism, the national middle class is easily convinced that it can advantageously replace the middle class of the mother country. But that same independence which literally drives it into a corner will give rise within its ranks to catastrophic reactions, and will oblige it to send out frenzied appeals for help to the former mother country. The university and merchant classes which make up the most enlightened section of the new state are in fact characterized by the smallness of their number and their being concentrated in the capital, and the type of activities in which they are engaged: business, agriculture, and the liberal professions. Neither financiers nor industrial magnates are to be found within this national middle class. The national bourgeoisie of underdeveloped countries is not engaged in production, nor in invention, nor

1. Translated by Constance Farrington.
2. In Marxist analysis, the ruling class (owners of the means of production) in capitalist society.

building, nor labor; it is completely canalized into activities of the intermediary type. Its innermost vocation seems to be to keep in the running and to be part of the racket. The psychology of the national bourgeoisie is that of the businessman, not that of a captain of industry; and it is only too true that the greed of the settlers and the system of embargoes set up by colonialism have hardly left them any other choice.

Under the colonial system, a middle class which accumulates capital is an impossible phenomenon. Now, precisely, it would seem that the historical vocation of an authentic national middle class in an underdeveloped country is to repudiate its own nature in so far it as it is bourgeois, that is to say in so far as it is the tool of capitalism, and to make itself the willing slave of that revolutionary capital which is the people.

In an underdeveloped country an authentic national middle class ought to consider as its bounden duty to betray the calling fate has marked out for it, and to put itself to school with the people: in other words to put at the people's disposal the intellectual and technical capital that it has snatched when going through the colonial universities. But unhappily we shall see that very often the national middle class does not follow this heroic, positive, fruitful, and just path; rather, it disappears with its soul set at peace into the shocking ways—shocking because anti-national—of a traditional bourgeoisie, of a bourgeoisie which is stupidly, contemptibly, cynically bourgeois.

The objective of nationalist parties as from a certain given period is, we have seen, strictly national. They mobilize the people with slogans of independence, and for the rest leave it to future events. When such parties are questioned on the economic program of the state that they are clamoring for, or on the nature of the regime which they propose to install, they are incapable of replying, because, precisely, they are completely ignorant of the economy of their own country.

This economy has always developed outside the limits of their knowledge. They have nothing more than an approximate, bookish acquaintance with the actual and potential resources of their country's soil and mineral deposits; and therefore they can only speak of these resources on a general and abstract plane. After independence this underdeveloped middle class, reduced in numbers and without capital, which refuses to follow the path of revolution, will fall into deplorable stagnation. It is unable to give free rein to its genius, which formerly it was wont to lament, though rather too glibly, was held in check by colonial domination. The precariousness of its resources and the paucity of its managerial class force it back for years into an artisan economy. From its point of view, which is inevitably a very limited one, a national economy is an economy based on what may be called local products. Long speeches will be made about the artisan class. Since the middle classes find it impossible to set up factories that would be more profit-earning both for themselves and for the country as a whole, they will surround the artisan class with a chauvinistic tenderness in keeping with the new awareness of national dignity, and which moreover will bring them in quite a lot of money. This cult of local products and this incapability to seek out new systems of management will be equally manifested by the bogging down of the national middle class in the methods of agricultural production which were characteristic of the colonial period.

The national economy of the period of independence is not set on a new footing. It is still concerned with the groundnut harvest, with the cocoa crop and the olive yield. In the same way there is no change in the marketing of basic products, and not a single industry is set up in the country. We go on sending out raw materials; we go on being Europe's small farmers, who specialize in unfinished products.

Yet the national middle class constantly demands the nationalization of the economy and of the trading sectors. This is because, from their point of view, nationalization does not mean placing the whole economy at the service of the nation and deciding to satisfy the needs of the nation. For them, nationalization does not mean governing the state with regard to the new social relations whose growth it has been decided to encourage. To them, nationalization quite simply means the transfer into native hands of those unfair advantages which are a legacy of the colonial period.

Since the middle class has neither sufficient material nor intellectual resources (by intellectual resources we mean engineers and technicians), it limits its claims to the taking over of business offices and commercial houses formerly occupied by the settlers. The national bourgeoisie steps into the shoes of the former European settlement: doctors, barristers, traders, commercial travelers, general agents, and transport agents. It considers that the dignity of the country and its own welfare require that it should occupy all these posts. From now on it will insist that all the big foreign companies should pass through its hands, whether these companies wish to keep on their connections with the country, or to open it up. The national middle class discovers its historic mission: that of intermediary.

Seen through its eyes, its mission has nothing to do with transforming the nation; it consists, prosaically, of being the transmission line between the nation and a capitalism, rampant though camouflaged, which today puts on the mask of neo-colonialism. The national bourgeoisie will be quite content with the role of the Western bourgeoisie's business agent, and it will play its part without any complexes in a most dignified manner. But this same lucrative role, this cheap-Jack's[3] function, this meanness of outlook and this absence of all ambition symbolize the incapability of the national middle class to fulfill its historic role of bourgeoisie. Here, the dynamic, pioneer aspect, the characteristics of the inventor and of the discoverer of new worlds which are found in all national bourgeoisies are lamentably absent. In the colonial countries, the spirit of indulgence is dominant at the core of the bourgeoisie; and this is because the national bourgeoisie identifies itself with the Western bourgeoisie, from whom it has learnt its lessons. It follows the Western bourgeoisie along its path of negation and decadence without ever having emulated it in its first stages of exploration and invention, stages which are an acquisition of that Western bourgeoisie whatever the circumstances. In its beginnings, the national bourgeoisie of the colonial countries identifies itself with the decadence of the bourgeoisie of the West. We need not think that it is jumping ahead; it is in fact beginning at the end. It is already senile before it has come to know the petulance, the fearlessness, or the will to succeed of youth.

The national bourgeoisie will be greatly helped on its way toward decadence by the Western bourgeoisies, who come to it as tourists avid for the

3. Dealer in inferior goods.

exotic, for big game hunting, and for casinos. The national bourgeoisie organizes centers of rest and relaxation and pleasure resorts to meet the wishes of the Western bourgeoisie. Such activity is given the name of tourism, and for the occasion will be built up as a national industry. If proof is needed of the eventual transformation of certain elements of the ex-native bourgeoisie into the organizers of parties for their Western opposite numbers, it is worth while having a look at what has happened in Latin America. The casinos of Havana and of Mexico, the beaches of Rio, the little Brazilian and Mexican girls, the half-breed thirteen-year-olds, the ports of Acapulco and Copacabana[4]—all these are the stigma of this depravation of the national middle class. Because it is bereft of ideas, because it lives to itself and cuts itself off from the people, undermined by its hereditary incapacity to think in terms of all the problems of the nation as seen from the point of view of the whole of that nation, the national middle class will have nothing better to do than to take on the role of manager for Western enterprise, and it will in practice set up its country as the brothel of Europe.

Once again we must keep before us the unfortunate example of certain Latin American republics. The banking magnates, the technocrats, and the big businessmen of the United States have only to step onto a plane and they are wafted into subtropical climes, there for a space of a week or ten days to luxuriate in the delicious depravities which their "reserves" hold for them.

The behavior of the national landed proprietors is practically identical with that of the middle classes of the towns. The big farmers have, as soon as independence is proclaimed, demanded the nationalization of agricultural production. Through manifold scheming practices they manage to make a clean sweep of the farms formerly owned by settlers, thus reinforcing their hold on the district. But they do not try to introduce new agricultural methods, nor to farm more intensively, nor to integrate their farming systems into a genuinely national economy.

In fact, the landed proprietors will insist that the state should give them a hundred times more facilities and privileges than were enjoyed by the foreign settlers in former times. The exploitation of agricultural workers will be intensified and made legitimate. Using two or three slogans, these new colonists will demand an enormous amount of work from the agricultural laborers, in the name of the national effort of course. There will be no modernization of agriculture, no planning for development, and no initiative; for initiative throws these people into a panic since it implies a minimum of risk, and completely upsets the hesitant, prudent, landed bourgeoisie, which gradually slips more and more into the lines laid down by colonialism. In the districts where this is the case, the only efforts made to better things are due to the government: it orders them, encourages them, and finances them. The landed bourgeoisie refuses to take the slightest risk, and remains opposed to any venture and to any hazard. It has no intention of building upon sand; it demands solid investments and quick returns. The enormous profits which it pockets, enormous if we take into account the national revenue, are never reinvested. The money-in-the-stocking mentality is dominant in the psychology of these landed proprietors. Sometimes, especially in the years immediately following independence, the bourgeoisie does not hesitate to

4. Resorts in Mexico and Brazil, respectively.

invest in foreign banks the profits that it makes out of its native soil. On the other hand large sums are spent on display: on cars, country houses, and on all those things which have been justly described by economists as characterizing an underdeveloped bourgeoisie.

We have said that the native bourgeoisie which comes to power uses its class aggressiveness to corner the positions formerly kept for foreigners. On the morrow of independence, in fact, it violently attacks colonial personalities: barristers, traders, landed proprietors, doctors, and higher civil servants. It will fight to the bitter end against these people "who insult our dignity as a nation." It waves aloft the notion of the nationalization and Africanization of the ruling classes. The fact is that such action will become more and more tinged by racism, until the bourgeoisie bluntly puts the problem to the government by saying "We must have these posts." They will not stop their snarling until they have taken over everyone.

* * *

When the bourgeoisie's demands for a ruling class made up exclusively of Negroes or Arabs do not spring from an authentic movement of nationalization but merely correspond to an anxiety to place in the bourgeoisie's hands the power held hitherto by the foreigner, the masses on their level present the same demands, confining however the notion of Negro or Arab within certain territorial limits. Between resounding assertions of the unity of the continent and this behavior of the masses which has its inspiration in their leaders, many different attitudes may be traced. We observe a permanent seesaw between African unity, which fades quicker and quicker into the mists of oblivion, and a heartbreaking return to chauvinism in its most bitter and detestable form.

> On the Senegalese side, the leaders who have been the main theoreticians of African unity, and who several times over have sacrificed their local political organizations and their personal positions to this idea, are, though in all good faith, undeniably responsible. Their mistake—our mistake—has been, under pretext of fighting "Balkanization," not to have taken into consideration the pre-colonial fact of territorialism. Our mistake has been not to have paid enough attention in our analyses to this phenomenon, which is the fruit of colonialism if you like, but also a sociological fact which no theory of unity, be it ever so laudable or attractive, can abolish. We have allowed ourselves to be seduced by a mirage: that of the structure which is the most pleasing to our minds; and, mistaking our ideal for reality, we have believed it enough to condemn territorialism, and its natural sequel, micro-nationalism, for us to get the better of them, and to assure the success of our chimerical undertaking.[5]

From the chauvinism of the Senegalese to the tribalism of the Yolofs[6] is not a big step. For in fact, everywhere that the national bourgeoisie has failed to break through to the people as a whole, to enlighten them, and to consider all problems in the first place with regard to them—a failure due to the bourgeoisie's attitude of mistrust and to the haziness of its political tenets—everywhere that national bourgeoisie has shown itself incapable of extending

5. Mamadou Dia, *Nations africaines et solidarité mondiale* [*African Nations and Worldwide Solidarity* (Paris: Presses Universitaires de France, 1960)] [Fanon's note].

6. An ethnic group of Senegal (also spelled *Wolof*).

its vision of the world sufficiently, we observe a falling back toward old tribal attitudes, and, furious and sick at heart, we perceive that race feeling in its most exacerbated form is triumphing. Since the sole motto of the bourgeoisie is "Replace the foreigner," and because it hastens in every walk of life to secure justice for itself and to take over the posts that the foreigner has vacated, the "small people" of the nation—taxi drivers, cake sellers, and bootblacks—will be equally quick to insist that the Dahomans go home to their own country, or will even go further and demand that the Foulbis and the Peuhls[7] return to their jungle or their mountains.

It is from this viewpoint that we must interpret the fact that in young, independent countries, here and there federalism triumphs. We know that colonial domination has marked certain regions out for privilege. The colony's economy is not integrated into that of the nation as a whole. It is still organized in order to complete the economy of the different mother countries. Colonialism hardly ever exploits the whole of a country. It contents itself with bringing to light the natural resources, which it extracts, and exports to meet the needs of the mother country's industries, thereby allowing certain sectors of the colony to become relatively rich. But the rest of the colony follows its path of underdevelopment and poverty, or at all events sinks into it more deeply.

Immediately after independence, the nationals who live in the more prosperous regions realize their good luck, and show a primary and profound reaction in refusing to feed the other nationals. The districts which are rich in groundnuts, in cocoa, and in diamonds come to the forefront, and dominate the empty panorama which the rest of the nation presents. The nationals of these rich regions look upon the others with hatred, and find in them envy and covetousness, and homicidal impulses. Old rivalries which were there before colonialism, old interracial hatreds come to the surface. The Balubas refuse to feed the Luluas; Katanga[8] forms itself into a state; and Albert Kalondji gets himself crowned king of South Kasai.[9]

African unity, that vague formula, yet one to which the men and women of Africa were passionately attached, and whose operative value served to bring immense pressure to bear on colonialism, African unity takes off the mask, and crumbles into regionalism inside the hollow shell of nationality itself. The national bourgeoisie, since it is strung up to defend its immediate interests, and sees no further than the end of its nose, reveals itself incapable of simply bringing national unity into being, or of building up the nation on a stable and productive basis. The national front which has forced colonialism to withdraw cracks up, and wastes the victory it has gained.

This merciless fight engaged upon by races and tribes, and this aggressive anxiety to occupy the posts left vacant by the departure of the foreigner, will equally give rise to religious rivalries. In the country districts and the bush, minor confraternities, local religions, and maraboutic cults[1] will show a new vitality and will once more take up their round of excommunications. In the

7. All African ethnic groups, the Dahomans from Benin and the Foulbis and Peuhls near or in Senegal.

8. A province in the Democratic Republic of the Congo, now called Shaba, that declared its independence from the newly independent nation of the Republic of the Congo (later Zaire) in July 1960; the secession was ended in January 1963. Balubas and Luluas: ethnic groups from the Congo known for their historical animosity toward one another.

9. A province that seceded from the newly independent Republic of the Congo in August 1960; Kalondji declared himself its king and emperor of the Balubas. The central government regained control of the region in December 1961.

1. Cults centered on marabouts, Muslim mystics in French Africa.

big towns, on the level of the administrative classes, we will observe the coming to grips of the two great revealed religions, Islam and Catholicism.

Colonialism, which had been shaken to its very foundations by the birth of African unity, recovers its balance and tries now to break that will to unity by using all the movement's weaknesses. Colonialism will set the African peoples moving by revealing to them the existence of "spiritual" rivalries. In Senegal, it is the newspaper *New Africa* which week by week distills hatred of Islam and of the Arabs. The Lebanese, in whose hands is the greater part of the small trading enterprises on the western seaboard, are marked out for national obloquy. The missionaries find it opportune to remind the masses that long before the advent of European colonialism the great African empires were disrupted by the Arab invasion. There is no hesitation in saying that it was the Arab occupation which paved the way for European colonialism; Arab imperialism is commonly spoken of, and the cultural imperialism of Islam is condemned. Moslems are usually kept out of the more important posts. In other regions the reverse is the case, and it is the native Christians who are considered as conscious, objective enemies of national independence.

Colonialism pulls every string shamelessly, and is only too content to set at loggerheads those Africans who only yesterday were leagued against the settlers. The idea of a Saint Bartholomew[2] takes shape in certain minds, and the advocates of colonialism laugh to themselves derisively when they hear magnificent declarations about African unity. Inside a single nation, religion splits up the people into different spiritual communities, all of them kept up and stiffened by colonialism and its instruments. Totally unexpected events break out here and there. In regions where Catholicism or Protestantism predominates, we see the Moslem minorities flinging themselves with unaccustomed ardor into their devotions. The Islamic feast-days are revived, and the Moslem religion defends itself inch by inch against the violent absolutism of the Catholic faith. Ministers of state are heard to say for the benefit of certain individuals that if they are not content they have only to go to Cairo. Sometimes American Protestantism transplants its anti-Catholic prejudices into African soil, and keeps up tribal rivalries through religion.

Taking the continent as a whole, this religious tension may be responsible for the revival of the commonest racial feeling. Africa is divided into Black and White, and the names that are substituted—Africa South of the Sahara, Africa North of the Sahara—do not manage to hide this latent racism. Here, it is affirmed that White Africa has a thousand-year-old tradition of culture; that she is Mediterranean, that she is a continuation of Europe, and that she shares in Greco-Latin civilization. Black Africa is looked on as a region that is inert, brutal, uncivilized, in a word, savage. There, all day long you may hear unpleasant remarks about veiled women, polygamy, and the supposed disdain the Arabs have for the feminine sex. All such remarks are reminiscent in their aggressiveness of those that are so often heard coming from the settler's lips. The national bourgeoisie of each of these two great regions, which has totally assimilated colonialist thought in its most corrupt

2. Catholic saint whose name is linked to one of history's most famous examples of violent religious persecution. The massacre of St. Bartholomew's Day began on August 24, 1572, with the killing of French Huguenot (Protestant) leaders in Paris; the massacre spread through the country, and by October tens of thousands had been murdered.

form, takes over from the Europeans and establishes in the continent a racial philosophy which is extremely harmful for the future of Africa. By its laziness and will to imitation, it promotes the ingrafting and stiffening of racism which was characteristic of the colonial era. Thus it is by no means astonishing to hear in a country that calls itself African remarks which are neither more nor less than racist, and to observe the existence of paternalist behavior which gives you the bitter impression that you are in Paris, Brussels, or London.

In certain regions of Africa, driveling paternalism with regard to the blacks and the loathsome idea derived from Western culture that the black man is impervious to logic and the sciences reign in all their nakedness. Sometimes it may be ascertained that the black minorities are hemmed in by a kind of semi-slavery which renders legitimate that species of wariness, or in other words mistrust, which the countries of Black Africa feel with regard to the countries of White Africa. It is all too common that a citizen of Black Africa hears himself called a "Negro" by the children when walking in the streets of a big town in White Africa, or finds that civil servants address him in pidgin English.

Yes, unfortunately it is not unknown that students from Black Africa who attend secondary schools north of the Sahara hear their schoolfellows asking if in their country there are houses, if they know what electricity is, or if they practice cannibalism in their families. Yes, unfortunately it is not unknown that in certain regions north of the Sahara Africans coming from countries south of the Sahara meet nationals who implore them to take them "anywhere at all on condition we meet Negroes." In parallel fashion, in certain young states of Black Africa members of parliament, or even ministers, maintain without a trace of humor that the danger is not at all of a reoccupation of their country by colonialism but of an eventual invasion by "those vandals of Arabs coming from the North."

As we see it, the bankruptcy of the bourgeoisie is not apparent in the economic field only. They have come to power in the name of a narrow nationalism and representing a race; they will prove themselves incapable of triumphantly putting into practice a program with even a minimum humanist content, in spite of fine-sounding declarations which are devoid of meaning since the speakers bandy about in irresponsible fashion phrases that come straight out of European treatises on morals and political philosophy. When the bourgeoisie is strong, when it can arrange everything and everybody to serve its power, it does not hesitate to affirm positively certain democratic ideas which claim to be universally applicable. There must be very exceptional circumstances if such a bourgeoisie, solidly based economically, is forced into denying its own humanist ideology. The Western bourgeoisie, though fundamentally racist, most often manages to mask this racism by a multiplicity of nuances which allow it to preserve intact its proclamation of mankind's outstanding dignity.

The Western bourgeoisie has prepared enough fences and railings to have no real fear of the competition of those whom it exploits and holds in contempt. Western bourgeois racial prejudice as regards the nigger and the Arab is a racism of contempt; it is a racism which minimizes what it hates. Bourgeois ideology, however, which is the proclamation of an essential equality between men, manages to appear logical in its own eyes by inviting the sub-men to become human, and to take as their prototype Western humanity as incarnated in the Western bourgeoisie.

* * *

It is all the easier to neutralize this bourgeois class in that, as we have seen, it is numerically, intellectually, and economically weak. In the colonized territories, the bourgeois caste draws its strength after independence chiefly from agreements reached with the former colonial power. The national bourgeoisie has all the more opportunity to take over from the oppressor since it has been given time for a leisurely tête-à-tête with the ex-colonial power. But deep-rooted contradictions undermine the ranks of that bourgeoisie; it is this that gives the observer an impression of instability. There is not as yet a homogeneity of caste. Many intellectuals, for example, condemn this regime based on the domination of the few. In underdeveloped countries, there are certain members of the elite, intellectuals and civil servants, who are sincere, who feel the necessity for a planned economy, the outlawing of profiteers, and the strict prohibition of attempts at mystification. In addition, such men fight in a certain measure for the mass participation of the people in the ordering of public affairs.

In those underdeveloped countries which accede to independence, there almost always exists a small number of honest intellectuals, who have no very precise ideas about politics, but who instinctively distrust the race for positions and pensions which is symptomatic of the early days of independence in colonized countries. The personal situation of these men (breadwinners of large families) or their background (hard struggles and a strictly moral upbringing) explains their manifest contempt for profiteers and schemers. We must know how to use these men in the decisive battle that we mean to engage upon which will lead to a healthier outlook for the nation. Closing the road to the national bourgeoisie is, certainly, the means whereby the vicissitudes of newfound independence may be avoided, and with them the decline of morals, the installing of corruption within the country, economic regression, and the immediate disaster of an anti-democratic regime depending on force and intimidation. But it is also the only means toward progress.

What holds up the taking of a decision by the profoundly democratic elements of the young nation and adds to their timidity is the apparent strength of the bourgeoisie. In newly independent underdeveloped countries, the whole of the ruling class swarms into the towns built by colonialism. The absence of any analysis of the total population induces onlookers to think that there exists a powerful and perfectly organized bourgeoisie. In fact, we know today that the bourgeoisie in underdeveloped countries is non-existent. What creates a bourgeoisie is not the bourgeois spirit, nor its taste or manners, nor even its aspirations. The bourgeoisie is above all the direct product of precise economic conditions.

Now, in the colonies, the economic conditions are conditions of a foreign bourgeoisie. Through its agents, it is the bourgeoisie of the mother country that we find present in the colonial towns. The bourgeoisie in the colonies is, before independence, a Western bourgeoisie, a true branch of the bourgeoisie of the mother country, that derives its legitimacy, its force, and its stability from the bourgeoisie of the homeland. During the period of unrest that precedes independence, certain native elements, intellectuals, and traders, who live in the midst of that imported bourgeoisie, try to identify themselves with it. A permanent wish for identification with the bourgeois representatives of the mother country is to be found among the native intellectuals and merchants.

* * *

From *On National Culture*

* * *

RECIPROCAL BASES OF NATIONAL CULTURE AND THE FIGHT FOR FREEDOM

Colonial domination, because it is total and tends to oversimplify, very soon manages to disrupt in spectacular fashion the cultural life of a conquered people. This cultural obliteration is made possible by the negation of national reality, by new legal relations introduced by the occupying power, by the banishment of the natives and their customs to outlying districts by colonial society, by expropriation, and by the systematic enslaving of men and women.

Three years ago at our first congress[3] I showed that, in the colonial situation, dynamism is replaced fairly quickly by a substantification of the attitudes of the colonizing power. The area of culture is then marked off by fences and signposts. These are in fact so many defense mechanisms of the most elementary type, comparable for more than one good reason to the simple instinct for preservation. The interest of this period for us is that the oppressor does not manage to convince himself of the objective nonexistence of the oppressed nation and its culture. Every effort is made to bring the colonized person to admit the inferiority of his culture which has been transformed into instinctive patterns of behavior, to recognize the unreality of his "nation," and, in the the last extreme, the confused and imperfect character of his own biological structure.

Vis-à-vis this state of affairs, the native's reactions are not unanimous. While the mass of the people maintain intact traditions which are completely different from those of the colonial situation, and the artisanal style solidifies into a formalism which is more and more stereotyped, the intellectual throws himself in frenzied fashion into the frantic acquisition of the culture of the occupying power and takes every opportunity of unfavorably criticizing his own national culture, or else takes refuge in setting out and substantiating the claims of that culture in a way that is passionate but rapidly becomes unproductive.

The common nature of these two reactions lies in the fact that they both lead to impossible contradictions. Whether a turncoat or a substantialist, the native is ineffectual precisely because the analysis of the colonial situation is not carried out on strict lines. The colonial situation calls a halt to national culture in almost every field. Within the framework of colonial domination there is not and there will never be such phenomena as new cultural departures or changes in the national culture. Here and there valiant attempts are sometimes made to reanimate the cultural dynamic and to give fresh

3. The First Congress of Black Writers and Artists (this chapter is derived from an address delivered in 1959 at the Second Congress, in Rome).

impulses to its themes, its forms, and its tonalities. The immediate, palpable, and obvious interest of such leaps ahead is nil. But if we follow up the consequences to the very end we see that preparations are being thus made to brush the cobwebs off national consciousness, to question oppression, and to open up the struggle for freedom.

A national culture under colonial domination is a contested culture whose destruction is sought in systematic fashion. It very quickly becomes a culture condemned to secrecy. This idea of a clandestine culture is immediately seen in the reactions of the occupying power which interprets attachment to traditions as faithfulness to the spirit of the nation and as a refusal to submit. This persistence in following forms of cultures which are already condemned to extinction is already a demonstration of nationality; but it is a demonstration which is a throwback to the laws of inertia. There is no taking of the offensive and no redefining of relationships. There is simply a concentration on a hard core of culture which is becoming more and more shrivelled up, inert, and empty.

By the time a century or two of exploitation has passed there comes about a veritable emaciation of the stock of national culture. It becomes a set of automatic habits, some traditions of dress, and a few broken-down institutions. Little movement can be discerned in such remnants of culture; there is no real creativity and no overflowing life. The poverty of the people, national oppression, and the inhibition of culture are one and the same thing. After a century of colonial domination we find a culture which is rigid in the extreme, or rather what we find are the dregs of culture, its mineral strata. The withering away of the reality of the nation and the death pangs of the national culture are linked to each other in mutual dependence. This is why it is of capital importance to follow the evolution of these relations during the struggle for national freedom. The negation of the native's culture, the contempt for any manifestation of culture whether active or emotional, and the placing outside the pale of all specialized branches of organization contribute to breed aggressive patterns of conduct in the native. But these patterns of conduct are of the reflexive type; they are poorly differentiated, anarchic, and ineffective. Colonial exploitation, poverty, and endemic famine drive the native more and more to open, organized revolt. The necessity for an open and decisive breach is formed progressively and imperceptibly, and comes to be felt by the great majority of the people. Those tensions which hitherto were non-existent come into being. International events, the collapse of whole sections of colonial empires and the contradictions inherent in the colonial system strengthen and uphold the native's combativity while promoting and giving support to national consciousness.

These new-found tensions which are present at all stages in the real nature of colonialism have their repercussions on the cultural plane. In literature, for example, there is relative overproduction. From being a reply on a minor scale to the dominating power, the literature produced by natives becomes differentiated and makes itself into a will to particularism. The intelligentsia, which during the period of repression was essentially a consuming public, now themselves become producers. This literature at first chooses to confine itself to the tragic and poetic style; but later on novels, short stories, and essays are attempted. It is as if a kind of internal organization or law of expression existed which wills that poetic expression become less frequent in proportion as the objectives and the methods of the struggle for liberation become more precise. Themes are completely altered; in fact, we find less and less of bitter, hopeless recrimination and less also of that violent, resounding, florid writing which on the whole serves to reassure the occupying power. The colonialists have in former times encouraged these modes of expression and made their existence possible. Stinging denunciations, the exposing of distressing conditions and passions which find their outlet in expression are in fact assimilated by the occupying power in a cathartic process. To aid such processes is in a certain sense to avoid their dramatization and to clear the atmosphere.

But such a situation can only be transitory. In fact, the progress of national consciousness among the people modifies and gives precision to the literary utterances of the native intellectual. The continued cohesion of the people constitutes for the intellectual an invitation to go further than his cry of protest. The lament first makes the indictment; and then it makes an appeal. In the period that follows, the words of command are heard. The crystallization of the national consciousness will both disrupt literary styles and themes, and also create a completely new public. While at the beginning the native intellectual used to produce his work to be read exclusively by the oppressor, whether with the intention of charming him or of denouncing him through ethnic or subjectivist means, now the native writer progressively takes on the habit of addressing his own people.

It is only from that moment that we can speak of a national literature. Here there is, at the level of literary creation, the taking up and clarification of themes which are typically nationalist. This may be properly called a literature of combat, in the sense that it calls on the whole people to fight for their existence as a nation. It is a literature of combat, because it molds the national consciousness, giving it form and contours and flinging open before it new and boundless horizons; it is a literature of combat because it assumes responsibility, and because it is the will to liberty expressed in terms of time and space.

On another level, the oral tradition—stories, epics, and songs of the people—which formerly were filed away as set pieces are now beginning to change. The storytellers who used to relate inert episodes now bring them alive and introduce into them modifications which are increasingly fundamental. There is a tendency to bring conflicts up to date and to modernize the kinds of struggle which the stories evoke, together with the names of heroes and the types of weapons. The method of allusion is more and more widely used. The formula "This all happened long ago" is substituted with that of "What we are going to speak of happened somewhere else, but it might well have happened here today, and it might happen tomorrow." The example of Algeria[4] is significant in this context. From 1952–53 on, the storytellers, who were before that time stereotyped and tedious to listen to, completely overturned their traditional methods of storytelling and the contents of their tales. Their public, which was formerly scattered, became compact. The epic, with its typified categories, reappeared; it became an authentic form of entertainment which took on once more a cultural value.

4. A department of France in North Africa that began an armed revolt in 1954. Fanon actively participated in the revolution, which led to Algeria's independence from French rule in 1962.

Colonialism made no mistake when from 1955 on it proceeded to arrest these storytellers systematically.

The contact of the people with the new movement gives rise to a new rhythm of life and to forgotten muscular tensions, and develops the imagination. Every time the storyteller relates a fresh episode to his public, he presides over a real invocation. The existence of a new type of man is revealed to the public. The present is no longer turned in upon itself but spread out for all to see. The storyteller once more gives free rein to his imagination; he makes innovations and he creates a work of art. It even happens that the characters, which are barely ready for such a transformation—highway robbers or more or less anti-social vagabonds—are taken up and remodeled. The emergence of the imagination and of the creative urge in the songs and epic stories of a colonized country is worth following. The storyteller replies to the expectant people by successive approximations, and makes his way, apparently alone but in fact helped on by his public, toward the seeking out of new patterns, that is to say national patterns. Comedy and farce disappear, or lose their attraction. As for dramatization, it is no longer placed on the plane of the troubled intellectual and his tormented conscience. By losing its characteristics of despair and revolt, the drama becomes part of the common lot of the people and forms part of an action in preparation or already in progress.

Where handicrafts are concerned, the forms of expression which formerly were the dregs of art, surviving as if in a daze, now begin to reach out. Woodwork, for example, which formerly turned out certain faces and attitudes by the million, begins to be differentiated. The inexpressive or overwrought mask comes to life and the arms tend to be raised from the body as if to sketch an action. Compositions containing two, three, or five figures appear. The traditional schools are led on to creative efforts by the rising avalanche of amateurs or of critics. This new vigor in this sector of cultural life very often passes unseen; and yet its contribution to the national effort is of capital importance. By carving figures and faces which are full of life, and by taking as his theme a group fixed on the same pedestal, the artist invites participation in an organized movement.

If we study the repercussions of the awakening of national consciousness in the domains of ceramics and pottery-making, the same observations may be drawn. Formalism is abandoned in the craftsman's work. Jugs, jars, and trays are modified, at first imperceptibly, then almost savagely. The colors, of which formerly there were but few and which obeyed the traditional rules of harmony, increase in number and are influenced by the repercussion of the rising revolution. Certain ochres and blues, which seemed forbidden to all eternity in a given cultural area, now assert themselves without giving rise to scandal. In the same way the stylization of the human face, which according to sociologists is typical of very clearly defined regions, becomes suddenly completely relative. The specialist coming from the home country and the ethnologist are quick to note these changes. On the whole such changes are condemned in the name of a rigid code of artistic style and of a cultural life which grows up at the heart of the colonial system. The colonialist specialists do not recognize these new forms and rush to the help of the traditions of the indigenous society. It is the colonialists who become the defenders of the native style. We remember perfectly, and the example took on a certain measure of importance since the real nature of colonialism was not involved, the reactions of the white jazz specialists when after the Second World War new styles such as the be-bop took definite shape. The fact is that in their eyes jazz should only be the despairing, broken-down nostalgia of an old Negro who is trapped between five glasses of whiskey, the curse of his race, and the racial hatred of the white men. As soon as the Negro comes to an understanding of himself, and understands the rest of the world differently, when he gives birth to hope and forces back the racist universe, it is clear that his trumpet sounds more clearly and his voice less hoarsely. The new fashions in jazz are not simply born of economic competition. We must without any doubt see in them one of the consequences of the defeat, slow but sure, of the southern world of the United States. And it is not utopian to suppose that in fifty years' time the type of jazz howl hiccuped by a poor misfortunate Negro will be upheld only by the whites who believe in it as an expression of negritude, and who are faithful to this arrested image of a type of relationship.

We might in the same way seek and find in dancing, singing, and traditional rites and ceremonies the same upward-springing trend, and make out the same changes and the same impatience in this field. Well before the political or fighting phase of the national movement, an attentive spectator can thus feel and see the manifestation of new vigor and feel the approaching conflict. He will note unusual forms of expression and themes which are fresh and imbued with a power which is no longer that of invocation but rather of the assembling of the people, a summoning together for a precise purpose. Everything works together to awaken the native's sensibility and to to make unreal and inacceptable the contemplative attitude, or the acceptance of defeat. The native rebuilds his perceptions because he renews the purpose and dynamism of the craftsmen, of dancing and music, and of literature and the oral tradition. His world comes to lose its accursed character. The conditions necessary for the inevitable conflict are brought together.

We have noted the appearance of the movement in cultural forms and we have seen that this movement and these new forms are linked to the state of maturity of the national consciousness. Now, this movement tends more and more to express itself objectively, in institutions. From thence comes the need for a national existence, whatever the cost.

A frequent mistake, and one which is moreover hardly justifiable, is to try to find cultural expressions for and to give new values to native culture within the framework of colonial domination. This is why we arrive at a proposition which at first sight seems paradoxical: the fact that in a colonized country the most elementary, most savage, and the most undifferentiated nationalism  is the most fervent and efficient means of defending national culture. For culture is first the expression of a nation, the expression of its preferences, of its taboos and of its patterns. It is at every stage of the whole of society that other taboos, values, and patterns are formed. A national culture is the sum total of all these appraisals; it is the result of internal and external tensions exerted over society as a whole and also at every level of that society. In the colonial situation, culture, which is doubly deprived of the support of the nation and of the state, falls away and dies. The condition for its existence is therefore national liberation and the renaissance of the state.

The nation is not only the condition of culture, its fruitfulness, its continuous renewal, and its deepening. It is also a necessity. It is the fight for national existence which sets culture moving and opens to it the doors of creation. Later on it is the nation which will ensure the conditions and framework necessary to culture. The nation gathers together the various indispensable elements necessary for the creation of a culture, those elements which alone can give it credibility, validity, life, and creative power. In the same way it is its national character that will make such a culture open to other cultures and which will enable it to influence and permeate other cultures. A non-existent culture can hardly be expected to have bearing on reality, or to influence reality. The first necessity is the re-establishment of the nation in order to give life to national culture in the strictly biological sense of the phrase.

Thus we have followed the breakup of the old strata of culture, a shattering which becomes increasingly fundamental; and we have noticed, on the eve of the decisive conflict for national freedom, the renewing of forms of expression and the rebirth of the imagination. There remains one essential question: what are the relations between the struggle—whether political or military—and culture? Is there a suspension of culture during the conflict? Is the national struggle an expression of a culture? Finally, ought one to say that the battle for freedom however fertile *a posteriori* with regard to culture is in itself a negation of culture? In short, is the struggle for liberation a cultural phenomenon or not?

We believe that the conscious and organized undertaking by a colonized people to re-establish the sovereignty of that nation constitutes the most complete and obvious cultural manifestation that exists. It is not alone the success of the struggle which afterward gives validity and vigor to culture; culture is not put into cold storage during the conflict. The struggle itself in its development and in its internal progression sends culture along different paths and traces out entirely new ones for it. The struggle for freedom does not give back to the national culture its former value and shapes; this struggle which aims at a fundamentally different set of relations between men cannot leave intact either the form or the content of the people's culture. After the conflict there is not only the disappearance of colonialism but also the disappearance of the colonized man.

This new humanity cannot do otherwise than define a new humanism both for itself and for others. It is prefigured in the objectives and methods of the conflict. A struggle which mobilizes all classes of the people and which expresses their aims and their impatience, which is not afraid to count almost exclusively on the people's support, will of necessity triumph. The value of this type of conflict is that it supplies the maximum of conditions necessary for the development and aims of culture. After national freedom has been obtained in these conditions, there is no such painful cultural indecision which is found in certain countries which are newly independent, because the nation by its manner of coming into being and in the terms of its existence exerts a fundamental influence over culture. A nation which is born of the people's concerted action and which embodies the real aspirations of the people while changing the state cannot exist save in the expression of exceptionally rich forms of culture.

The natives who are anxious for the culture of their country and who wish to give to it a universal dimension ought not therefore to place their confidence in the single principle of inevitable, undifferentiated independence written into the consciousness of the people in order to achieve their task. The liberation of the nation is one thing; the methods and popular content of the fight are another. It seems to us that the future of national culture and its riches are equally also part and parcel of the values which have ordained the struggle for freedom.

And now it is time to denounce certain pharisees. National claims, it is here and there stated, are a phase that humanity has left behind. It is the day of great concerted actions, and retarded nationalists ought in consequence to set their mistakes aright. We however consider that the mistake, which may have very serious consequences, lies in wishing to skip the national period. If culture is the expression of national consciousness, I will not hesitate to affirm that in the case with which we are dealing it is the national consciousness which is the most elaborate form of culture.

The consciousness of self is not the closing of a door to communication. Philosophic thought teaches us, on the contrary, that it is its guarantee. National consciousness, which is not nationalism, is the only thing that will give us an international dimension. This problem of national consciousness and of national culture takes on in Africa a special dimension. The birth of national consciousness in Africa has a strictly contemporaneous connection with the African consciousness. The responsibility of the African as regards national culture is also a responsibility with regard to African Negro culture. This joint responsibility is not the fact of a metaphysical principle but the awareness of a simple rule which wills that every independent nation in an Africa where colonialism is still entrenched is an encircled nation, a nation which is fragile and in permanent danger.

If man is known by his acts, then we will say that the most urgent thing today for the intellectual is to build up his nation. If this building up is true, that is to say if it interprets the manifest will of the people and reveals the eager African peoples, then the building of a nation is of necessity accompanied by the discovery and encouragement of universalizing values. Far from keeping aloof from other nations, therefore, it is national liberation which leads the nation to play its part on the stage of history. It is at the heart of national consciousness that international consciousness lives and grows. And this two-fold emerging is ultimately only the source of all culture.

1961

GILLES DELEUZE 1925–1995 / FÉLIX GUATTARI 1930–1992

Alternately hailed or dismissed in North America as the "enfants terribles" of poststructuralist philosophy and psychoanalysis following the publication of their *Anti-Oedipus: Capitalism and Schizophrenia* (1972), Gilles Deleuze and Félix Guattari are known for their antiestablishment thinking in many domains. Trained as a philosopher and a psychoanalyst, respectively, Deleuze and Guattari critique the patterns of knowledge that govern the disciplines in which they were schooled. In the process, they question the dominance of conceptual stability, organization, and unity as such. Their critique is well summed up in their pun on the word "General": knowledge functions like an operation of conquest and mastery, driven by "generality" as if it were a military "General."

Born in Paris to a middle-class family, Deleuze was educated in the French university system and taught philosophy at the University of Paris at Vincennes (now St. Denis) from 1969 until his retirement in 1987. At the time of the 1968 student-worker revolts in France, Deleuze began to write books in his "own" voice, aiming to replace official philosophy with what he called "bastard" philosophy. Deleuze declared that his early writings, such as *Empiricism and Subjectivity: An Essay on Hume's Theory of Nature* (1953) and *Bergsonism* (1966), still too closely resembled those of an "academic bureaucrat." In his *Nietzsche and Philosophy* (1962) but especially in *Difference and Repetition* (1968), *The Logic of Sense* (1969), and *Spinoza: Practical Philosophy* (1970), Deleuze developed a new philosophy of becoming and exteriority—joining an orphan line of metaphysical thinkers that includes Lucretius, Benedict de Spinoza, Gottfried Leibniz, DAVID HUME, FRIEDRICH NIETZSCHE, and Henri Bergson—that his work combines with various other strands of contemporary theory.

In the interdisciplinary mix of French philosophy and theory of the 1960s and 1970s, he came in contact with the person who would become his "intercessor" for many years, Félix Guattari, a practicing psychoanalyst and political activist. Guattari, usually said to be the more "delirious" of the two, was born in the Paris suburb of Colombes and had received an erratic education; never having earned any official degrees, he had worked since the mid-1950s at La Borde, a psychiatric hospital outside Paris known for innovative practices in group therapy. One of JACQUES LACAN's earliest trainees, Guattari quickly took leave of the master. Lacan, he felt, had transformed structural psychoanalysis into a religion devoted to cultivating and initiating followers. Guattari's antihierarchical and anarchic tendencies drew him into an alliance with Deleuze. Together they wrote the polemical *Anti-Oedipus*.

Described by MICHEL FOUCAULT as "an introduction to non-fascist living," *Anti-Oedipus* was an immediate sensation in France and soon thereafter in England, Canada, and the United States, where it became an academic bestseller when its translation appeared in 1983. It was hailed as a productive attack not only on state philosophy but also on the orthodox Marxism and institutional Freudianism that pervaded the postwar years. In the view of Deleuze and Guattari, psychoanalysis combines with capitalism to channel and control desire, not to liberate it. As a negative critique, the book is more interested in freeing the forces that have been constrained than in proposing alternatives.

After this moment of destruction, they experimented with a philosophy of becoming. In another of their books, *Kafka: Toward a Minor Literature* (1975; trans. 1986), from which we have taken our first selection, Deleuze and Guattari claim that Franz Kafka (1883–1924), although writing in a dominant language, introduces into it elements of his own Jewish, minoritarian culture. He thus recombines dominant ways of thinking with elements of a minority culture to produce something entirely different—a minor literature—thereby undermining power. But Deleuze and Guattari make clear that it does not suffice to *be* Jewish. One has to *become* Jewish—or minoritarian—in an ongoing way. The "outside" is never a *given*. Consider SIGMUND FREUD, whose own relation to dominant German culture was similar to Kafka's. Freud considered himself an observer whose distance from the "compact majority" enabled him to explore the hidden forces underlying the culture around him. Yet over time, according to Deleuze and Guattari, those explorations had become hardened into doctrine.

A Thousand Plateaus: Capitalism and Schizophrenia, the sequel to *Anti-Oedipus*, appeared in 1980. The least well received of their books, as Deleuze and Guattari proudly admit, its project is very different from that of its predecessor. It is more a work of art, a positive exercise in the productive desire and affirmative "nomad" thought that *Anti-Oedipus* called for. The book's introductory chapter (or "plateau"), from which our second selection is taken, is titled "Rhizome" and is often cited as an exemplary text of postmodern philosophy.

Deleuze and Guattari claim that state philosophy as practiced in the academy is a form of the representational thought that has dominated the West since PLATO. Representation posits the self-identity of the thinking subject. The subject, the concepts, and the objects in the world are thus presumed to share a self-resemblance essential for maintaining their identity. Representational thought establishes a correspondence between two symmetrical domains. It is analogical: the success of a representation is derived from its accuracy, its closeness to an original, which nevertheless remains more "real." Deleuze and Guattari take the mimetic hierarchy described by Plato and turn it on its side. Whereas the traditional model for knowledge is drawn from plants with "roots" (the ground or origin that leads to the main growth through genealogy or evolution), Deleuze and Guattari draw their metaphor from fungal "rhizomes"—a network of threads that can send up new growths anywhere along their length, not subject to centralized control or structure. This logic (or rather, nonlogic) is exemplified by invasive species such as mushrooms and crabgrass that proliferate without a controlling structure. As Deleuze and Guattari suggest, the same antihierarchical perspective is what may have led Walt Whitman to choose *Leaves of Grass* (1855) as the title for his book of poems. They thus replace the rooted tree (the Western metaphor for knowledge par excellence) with the rhizome, conceived as an adventitious mode of thinking that grows between things and produces offshoots in unforeseen directions. It is striking that FERDINAND DE SAUSSURE (1857–1913) should choose "tree" as his example of a sign—his structural linguistics conform exactly to the static, binary logic that Deleuze and Guattari critique. (See also Lacan's tribute to the importance of the tree in Western culture, above.)

In their difficult yet rewarding texts, Deleuze and Guattari distinguish between the segment—that is, the official, "molar" line that occupies a given social or political position—and another, "molecular" line that begins to separate itself, and to disaggregate, from the first. Thus, for example, in *Anti-Oedipus* Deleuze and Guattari—both married—write "We are heterosexuals statistically or in molar terms, but homosexuals personally, whether we know it or not, and finally transsexuals elementarily, molecularly." Sexuality for them is that experience of desire that breaks through any self-definition; requires a new, temporarily synthesized multiplicity; and yet does not provide a new identity. The de-Oedipalized body becomes a "Body without Organs," a "desiring-machine" not governed by "phases" of development and not organized into "bundles" or knowable "organs."

Rhizomatic thinking promotes becoming, not being. Deleuze and Guattari state—a statement for which they have been much critized—that because of the special relation of women to the man-standard, all becomings (-child, -animal, -vegetal, -intense) begin with the "becoming-woman" of man. But the "becoming-woman" of man may involve the renunciation not only of sexuality as mastery but also of family trees as trees: "family trees" resemble trees only when the patriarchal name is followed, and when one particular generation or individual is the focus. A true map of all lines—male and female, legitimate and illegitimate—even in heterosexual reproduction would resemble a rhizome, not a tree. At the same time, the women who have been invisible in the family tree cannot simply become an alternative to it. Women, as well as homosexuals, Jews, and blacks, according to Deleuze and Guattari, must constantly reinvent themselves as "minoritarian" to avoid becoming a minority as a new state. This way of being in, and open to, the world is called "ethics" by Spinoza; Deleuze and Guattari call it pragmatics. And for them, books themselves are pragmatic assemblages or tool kits for becoming.

The rhizome replaces, or at least complements, history (the story people tell) with geography (the ground they inhabit). A "map," for Deleuze and Guattari, is a drawing that *is* and *transforms* the object it purportedly represents; a "tracing" merely tries to duplicate the object. Yet the rhizomatic process is not pure "dissemination": it is structured, but not organized, by moments of synthesis. Always in movement, a rhizome has neither beginning nor end. Influenced by theories of chaos and complexity, Deleuze and Guattari claim to study subjectivity where it emerges, society where it mutates, and the world where it is re-created. With the development of the Internet and virtual reality, we have already in some ways entered the rhizomatic structures they describe; but there is no guarantee that the logics they critique have therefore disappeared.

In literature, Deleuze and Guattari do not look for meaning. When reading Heinrich von Kleist (1777–1811) or Franz Kafka against alleged state writers such as Johann Wolfgang von Goethe (1749–1832), or when reading HENRY JAMES (1843–1916) or the twentieth-century writers F. Scott Fitzgerald, VIRGINIA WOOLF, or Nathalie Sarraute, they look for the lines of flight by means of which these writers detach themselves—and their texts—from an immobilizing order. In becoming, these writers "deterritorialize" themselves from and within official culture before "reterritorializing" themselves elsewhere.

From the early 1980s up to his death, Deleuze continued to emphasize the need to mesh aesthetics and philosophy. After *A Thousand Plateaus*, he studied the affective potential of color and line in *Francis Bacon, the Logic of Sensation* (1981); in that work he notes the English painter's capacity to affect and to be affected by chromatic vibration. Architecture, logic, and aesthetics are examined as events in *The Fold: Leibniz and the Baroque* (1988), where Deleuze further writes about the world as a set of lines in relations of movement and rest. His two-volume analysis of cinema invents a taxonomy to replace the one underlying linguistic theories of film. The first volume, *The Movement-Image* (1983), projects the lexicon of classical cinema (close-up, medium shot, long shot) into a philosophical field that associates bodily sensation with mobility, whose effect constitutes cinematic events in the first fifty years of cinema's history. In the second, *The Time-Image* (1985), Deleuze analyzes the effect of duration, invention, and the absence of mimesis in films that follow the aftermath of World War II.

Concurrently, Félix Guattari also published on his own. Developing long-standing relations with radical Italian social groups, he collaborated with the philosopher and political activist Toni Negri. It was, for him, a line of flight away from a fashionable intellectual lassitude reigning in France. He loathed postmodern melancholia, which he excoriated repeatedly. In *The Three Ecologies* (1989), one of his most forceful essays, Guattari mobilizes concepts developed elsewhere with Deleuze. Discussing the relations between thought and politics, he clarifies his theoretical and political stance on many contemporary issues, ranging from the exploitation of women to problems of the third world to racism and environmental degradation. He also reemphasizes the importance of literary texts and broaches the difference between militantism and artistic invention in what he calls the converging of aesthetics, ethics, and politics. The slim volume serves as an indication of how Guattari's thought evolved after texts like "Rhizome." Without reverting back to prestructuralism or to phenomenological analyses, Guattari pleaded for a philosophy of becoming (now renamed "ecosophy") in more openly existential terms.

Deleuze's *Negotiations* (1990) records a series of interviews from 1972 to 1990. Emphasis is placed on the urgency of practicing philosophy in view of the controlling discourses of power—namely, religion, capitalism, science, law, television, and public opinion. He too makes a case for philosophy as guerrilla warfare not just in the streets but within subjects themselves. In the same vein, Deleuze and Guattari wrote their last joint work, the compelling *What Is Philosophy?* (1991), which had an impact similar to that of *Anti-Oedipus*. They reiterate their belief in the continued importance of philosophy as a way of thinking and a mode of action. The inseparability of thought from context informs the hybrid nature of all national philosophical and literary traditions.

Affirmation and *action* were key words in the lexicon and the lives of Deleuze and Guattari. In addition to writing on literature and the arts, Guattari unsuccessfully ran for office in the French Green Party, shortly before his untimely death from a heart attack in 1992. In essays written for *Le Monde diplomatique* he stressed the necessity of restructuring social thought and action. In "The Exhausted," an afterword of sorts to Samuel Beckett's *Quad and Other Plays for Television* (1992), Deleuze reflects that the exhausted person—in contrast to the tired person—has exhausted all the possibilities. For the next three years, he nonetheless continued to teach and write while cancer ravaged his body. In 1995 he jumped to his death from the window of his Parisian apartment.

BIBLIOGRAPHY

Deleuze and Guattari are best known for their *Anti-Oedipus* (1972; trans. 1983), *Kafka: Toward a Minor Literature* (1975; trans. 1986), *A Thousand Plateaus* (1980; trans. 1987), and *What Is Philosophy?* (1991; trans. 1994). In addition to the books mentioned above, Gilles Deleuze's writings, most of which are available in English, include *Proust and Signs* (1964; trans. 1972); *Masochism: An Interpretation of Coldness and Cruelty* (1967; trans. 1971); *Kant's Critical Philosophy* (1971; trans. 1984); *Dialogues*, with Claire Parnet (1977; trans. 1987), on the relation between culture and politics; *Foucault* (1986; trans. 1988); *Essays Critical and Clinical* (1993; trans. 1997), with chapters on Alfred Jarry, Herman Melville, and Whitman; and *The Abecedaire of Gilles Deleuze* (1997), a set of taped television interviews. *The Deleuze Reader*, edited and introduced by Constantin V. Boundas, was published in 1993. Félix Guattari's works include, in addition to the titles mentioned above, *Molecular Revolution: Psychiatry and Politics* (1977; trans. 1984); "A Liberation of Desire," in *Homosexualities and French Literature* (ed. George Stambolian and Elaine Marks, 1979); and *Chaosmosis* (1992; trans. 1995). *The Guattari Reader*, edited and introduced by Gary Genosko, was published in 1996.

Brian Massumi's *User's Guide to Capitalism and Schizophrenia: Deviations from Deleuze and Guattari* (1992) is a sprightly, provocative reading that both explains a revolutionary Deleuze and Guattari and deviates from them. Eleanor Kaufman and Kevin Jon Heller's *Deleuze and Guattari: New Mappings in Politics, Philosophy, and Culture* (1998) contains a variety of articles, including Bruno Bosteel's detailed account of Guattari's relation to language and Aden Evens et al.'s cogent discussion of difference and creativity. Charles J. Stivale's *The Two-Fold Thought of Deleuze and Guattari* (1998) is also useful. A three-volume collection of criticism titled *Critical Assessments: Deleuze and Guattari*, edited by Gary Genosko (2000), gives a wide range of responses.

Criticism on Deleuze includes Michael Hardt, *Gilles Deleuze: An Apprenticeship in Philosophy* (1993), which presents a concrete and existential Deleuze, and *Gilles Deleuze and the Theater of Philosophy*, edited by Constantin V. Boundas and Dorothea Olkowski (1994), which is a good sampler of readings of Deleuze's work; it includes a terse analysis by the French philosopher Alain Badiou, who has since published *Deleuze: The Clamor of Being* (1997; trans. 2000). Another collection of criticism can be found in *Deleuze: A Critical Reader*, edited by Paul Patton (1996). A good overview of Deleuze's involvement with film is provided by David Rodowick in *The Time-Machine* (1997). See also Gregory Flaxman's collection *The Brain Is the Screen: Deleuze and the Philosophy of Cinema* (2000). Feminists, who initially rejected Deleuze and Guattari for robbing women of being with their insistence on becoming, are now revising earlier views. An entire volume, *Deleuze and Feminism*, edited by Ian Buchanan and Claire Colebrook (2000), includes a fresh look at Deleuze by a dozen feminists. See also Buchanan's collection *Gilles Deleuze: A Philosopher for Our Century?* (2000). The best bibliographies are Timothy S. Murphy's "Bibliography of the Works of Gilles Deleuze" in Patton's *Deleuze*, cited above, and Genosko's bibliography in *The Guattari Reader*.

From Kafka: Toward a Minor Literature[1]

From *Chapter 3. What Is a Minor Literature?*

* * *

A minor literature doesn't come from a minor language; it is rather that which a minority constructs within a major language. But the first characteristic of minor literature in any case is that in it language is affected with a high coefficient of deterritorialization. In this sense, Kafka[2] marks the impasse that bars access to writing for the Jews of Prague and turns their literature into something impossible—the impossibility of not writing, the impossibility of writing in German, the impossibility of writing otherwise.[3] The impossibility of not writing because national consciousness, uncertain or oppressed, necessarily exists by means of literature ("The literary struggle has its real justification at the highest possible levels"). The impossibility of writing other than in German is for the Prague Jews the feeling of an irreducible distance from their primitive Czech territoriality. And the impossibility of writing in German is the deterritorialization of the German population itself, an oppressive minority that speaks a language cut off from the masses, like a "paper language" or an artificial language; this is all the more true for the Jews who are simultaneously a part of this minority and excluded from it, like "gypsies who have stolen a German child from its crib." In short, Prague German is a deterritorialized language, appropriate for strange and minor uses. (This can be compared in another context to what blacks in America today are able to do with the English language.)

The second characteristic of minor literatures is that everything in them is political. In major literatures, in contrast, the individual concern (familial, marital, and so on) joins with other no less individual concerns, the social milieu serving as a mere environment or a background; this is so much the case that none of these Oedipal intrigues are specifically indispensable or absolutely necessary but all become as one in a large space. Minor literature is completely different; its cramped space forces each individual intrigue to connect immediately to politics. The individual concern thus becomes all the more necessary, indispensable, magnified, because a whole other story is vibrating within it. In this way, the family triangle connects to other triangles—commercial, economic, bureaucratic, juridical—that determine its values. When Kafka indicates that one of the goals of a minor literature is the "purification of the conflict that opposes father and son and the possibility of discussing that conflict," it isn't a question of an Oedipal phantasm[4] but of a political program. "Even though something is often thought through calmly, one still does not reach the boundary where it connects up with similar things, one reaches the boundary soonest in politics, indeed, one even strives to see it before it is there, and often sees this limiting boundary every-

1. Translated by Dana Polan, who occasionally retains the original French in parentheses.
2. Franz Kafka (1883–1924), Jewish Austrian writer who lived much of his life in Prague and wrote in German; his work is here the focus of the process of "becoming-minor."
3. See letter to [Max] Brod, Kafka, *Letters*, June 1921, and commentaries in [Klaus] Wagenbach, *Franz Kafka: Années de jeunesse* [1958] [Deleuze and Guattari's note]. Some of the authors' notes have been omitted. Max Brod (1884–1968), a close friend and biographer of Kafka; he disobeyed the dying Kafka's request to destroy his papers.
4. That is, the Oedipal complex—the desire of a young boy for his mother that makes him view his father as a competitor—described by SIGMUND FREUD (1856–1939).

where. . . . What in great literature goes on down below, constituting a not indispensable cellar of the structure, here takes place in the full light of day, what is there a matter of passing interest for a few, here absorbs everyone no less than as a matter of life and death."[5]

The third characteristic of minor literature is that in it everything takes on a collective value. Indeed, precisely because talent isn't abundant in a minor literature, there are no possibilities for an individuated enunciation that would belong to this or that "master" and that could be separated from a collective enunciation. Indeed, scarcity of talent is in fact beneficial and allows the conception of something other than a literature of masters; what each author says individually already constitutes a common action, and what he or she says or does is necessarily political, even if others aren't in agreement. The political domain has contaminated every statement (*énoncé*).[6] But above all else, because collective or national consciousness is "often inactive in external life and always in the process of break-down," literature finds itself positively charged with the role and function of collective, and even revolutionary, enunciation. It is literature that produces an active solidarity in spite of skepticism; and if the writer is in the margins or completely outside his or her fragile community, this situation allows the writer all the more the possibility to express another possible community and to forge the means for another consciousness and another sensibility; just as the dog of "Investigations"[7] calls out in his solitude to *another science*. The literary machine thus becomes the relay for a revolutionary machine-to-come, not at all for ideological reasons but because the literary machine alone is determined to fill the conditions of a collective enunciation that is lacking elsewhere in this milieu: *literature is the people's concern.*[8] It is certainly in these terms that Kafka sees the problem. The message doesn't refer back to an enunciating subject who would be its cause, no more than to a subject of the statement (*sujet d'énoncé*) who would be its effect. Undoubtedly, for a while, Kafka thought according to these traditional categories of the two subjects, theauthor and the hero, the narrator and the character, the dreamer and the one dreamed of. But he will quickly reject the role of the narrator, just as he will refuse an author's or master's literature, despite his admiration for Goethe. Josephine the mouse[9] renounces the individual act of singing in order to melt into the collective enunciation of "the immense crowd of the heros of [her] people." A movement from the individuated animal to the pack or to a collective multiplicity—seven canine musicians. In "The Investigations of a Dog," the expressions of the solitary researcher tend toward the assemblage (*agencement*) of a collective enunciation of the canine species even if this collectivity is no longer or not yet given. There isn't a subject; *there are only collective assemblages of enunciation*, and literature expresses these acts insofar as they're not imposed from without and insofar as they exist only as diabolical powers to come or revolutionary forces to be constructed. Kafka's solitude opens him up to everything going on in history today. The letter K[1]

5. Kafka, *Diaries*, December 25, 1911 [Deleuze and Guattari's note].
6. *Énoncé* (French) is the statement or content of an utterance; *énonciation* is the act of uttering it.
7. "Investigations of a Dog" is the title of a story by Kafka.
8. Kafka, *Diaries*, December 25, 1911: "[L]iterature is less a concern of literary history, than of the people" [Deleuze and Guattari's note].
9. Title character in "Josephine the Singer, or the Mouse Folk," the last story written by Kafka. Johann Wolfgang von Goethe (1749–1832), magisterial German poet, playwright, and novelist.
1. The hero of *The Castle* (1926), a posthumously published unfinished novel by Kafka, is known only as K.; the hero of *The Trial* (1925), another posthumously published unfinished novel, is Joseph K.

no longer designates a narrator or a character but an assemblage that becomes all the more machine-like, an agent that becomes all the more collective because an individual is locked into it in his or her solitude (it is only in connection to a subject that something individual would be separable from the collective and would lead its own life).

The three characteristics of minor literature are the deterritorialization of language, the connection of the individual to a political immediacy, and the collective assemblage of enunciation. We might as well say that minor no longer designates specific literatures but the revolutionary conditions for every literature within the heart of what is called great (or established) literature. Even he who has the misfortune of being born in the country of a great literature must write in its language, just as a Czech Jew writes in German, or an Ouzbekian writes in Russian. Writing like a dog digging a hole, a rat digging its burrow.[2] And to do that, finding his own point of underdevelopment, his own *patois*, his own third world, his own desert. There has been much discussion of the questions "What is a marginal literature?" and "What is a popular literature, a proletarian literature?" The criteria are obviously difficult to establish if one doesn't start with a more objective concept—that of minor literature. Only the possibility of setting up a minor practice of major language from within allows one to define popular literature, marginal literature, and so on. Only in this way can literature really become a collective machine of expression and really be able to treat and develop its contents. Kafka emphatically declares that a minor literature is much more able to work over its material.[3] Why this machine of expression, and what is it? We know that it is in a relation of multiple deterritorializations with language; it is the situation of the Jews who have dropped the Czech language at the same time as the rural environment, but it is also the situation of the German language as a "paper language." Well, one can go even farther; one can push this movement of deterritorialization of expression even farther. But there are only two ways to do this. One way is to artificially enrich this German, to swell it up through all the resources of symbolism, of oneirism, of esoteric sense, of a hidden signifier. This is the approach of the Prague school, Gustav Meyrink and many others, including Max Brod.[4] But this attempt implies a desperate attempt at symbolic reterritorialization, based in archetypes, Kabbala, and alchemy, that accentuates its break from the people and will find its political result only in Zionism and such things as the "dream of Zion."[5] Kafka will quickly choose the other way, or, rather, he will invent another way. He will opt for the German language of Prague as it is and in its very poverty. Go always farther in the direction of deterritorialization, to the point of sobriety. Since the language is arid, make it vibrate with a new intensity. Oppose a purely intensive usage of language to all symbolic or even significant or simply signifying usages of it. Arrive at a perfect and unformed expression, a materially intense expression. (For these

2. "The Burrow" is a story by Kafka.

3. Kafka, *Diaries*, December 25, 1911: "A small nation's memory is not smaller than the memory of a large one and so can digest the existing material more thoroughly" [Deleuze and Guattari's note].

4. See the excellent chapter "Prague at the Turn of the Century," in Wagenbach, *Franz Kafka*, on the situation of the German language in Czechoslovakia and on the Prague School [Deleuze and Guattari's note]. Meyrink (1868–1932), German author of occult fiction, including the novel *The Golem* (1915).

5. The Jewish homeland in Palestine, sought by Zionism and achieved in the establishment of the State of Israel in 1948. Kabbala: a system of Jewish mysticism, especially the esoteric theosophy of the 13th century and later (also spelled "Cabala").

two possible paths, couldn't we find the same alternatives, under other conditions, in Joyce and Beckett?[6] As Irishmen, both of them live within the genial conditions of a minor literature. That is the glory of this sort of minor literature—to be the revolutionary force for all literature. The utilization of English and of every language in Joyce. The utilization of English and French in Beckett. But the former never stops operating by exhilaration and overdetermination and brings about all sorts of worldwide reterritorializations. The other proceeds by dryness and sobriety, a willed poverty, pushing deterritorialization to such an extreme that nothing remains but intensities.)

How many people today live in a language that is not their own? Or no longer, or not yet, even know their own and know poorly the major language that they are forced to serve? This is the problem of immigrants, and especially of their children, the problem of minorities, the problem of a minor literature, but also a problem for all of us: how to tear a minor literature away from its own language, allowing it to challenge the language and making it follow a sober revolutionary path? How to become a nomad and an immigrant and a gypsy in relation to one's own language? Kafka answers: steal the baby from its crib, walk the tightrope.

* * *

1975

From A Thousand Plateaus: Capitalism and Schizophrenia[1]

From *Introduction: Rhizome*

The two of us wrote *Anti-Oedipus*[2] together. Since each of us was several, there was already quite a crowd. Here we have made use of everything that came within range, what was closest as well as farthest away. We have assigned clever pseudonyms to prevent recognition. Why have we kept our own names? Out of habit, purely out of habit. To make ourselves unrecognizable in turn. To render imperceptible, not ourselves, but what makes us act, feel, and think. Also because it's nice to talk like everybody else, to say the sun rises, when everybody knows it's only a manner of speaking. To reach, not the point where one no longer says I, but the point where it is no longer of any importance whether one says I. We are no longer ourselves. Each will know his own. We have been aided, inspired, multiplied.

A book has neither object nor subject; it is made of variously formed matters, and very different dates and speeds. To attribute the book to a subject is to overlook this working of matters, and the exteriority of their relations. It is to fabricate a beneficent God to explain geological movements. In a book, as in all things, there are lines of articulation or segmentarity, strata and territories; but also lines of flight, movements of deterritorialization and destratification. Comparative rates of flow on these lines produce phenom-

6. Samuel Beckett (1906–1989), Irish-born novelist and playwright who published in both French and English. James Joyce (1882–1941), Irish writer whose fiction is extraordinarily innovative in technique and language.

1. Translated by Brian Massumi, who occasionally retains the original French in parentheses.

2. *Anti-Oedipus: Capitalism and Schizophrenia*, to which this work is a sequel, was published in French in 1972.

ena of relative slowness and viscosity, or, on the contrary, of acceleration and rupture. All this, lines and measurable speeds, constitutes an *assemblage*. A book is an assemblage of this kind, and as such is unattributable. It is a multiplicity—but we don't know yet what the multiple entails when it is no longer attributed, that is, after it has been elevated to the status of a substantive. One side of a machinic assemblage faces the strata, which doubtless make it a kind of organism, or signifying totality, or determination attributable to a subject; it also has a side facing a *body without organs*,[3] which is continually dismantling the organism, causing asignifying particles or pure intensities to pass or circulate, and attributing to itself subjects that it leaves with nothing more than a name as the trace of an intensity. What is the body without organs of a book? There are several, depending on the nature of the lines considered, their particular grade or density, and the possibility of their converging on a "plane of consistency" assuring their selection. Here, as elsewhere, the units of measure are what is essential: *quantify writing*. There is no difference between what a book talks about and how it is made. Therefore a book also has no object. As an assemblage, a book has only itself, in connection with other assemblages and in relation to other bodies without organs. We will never ask what a book means, as signified or signifier;[4] we will not look for anything to understand in it. We will ask what it functions with, in connection with what other things it does or does not transmit intensities, in which other multiplicities its own are inserted and metamorphosed, and with what bodies without organs it makes its own converge. A book exists only through the outside and on the outside. A book itself is a little machine; what is the relation (also measurable) of this literary machine to a war machine, love machine, revolutionary machine, etc.—and an *abstract machine* that sweeps them along? We have been criticized for overquoting literary authors. But when one writes, the only question is which other machine the literary machine can be plugged into, must be plugged into in order to work. Kleist and a mad war machine, Kafka[5] and a most extraordinary bureaucratic machine . . . (What if one became animal or plant *through* literature, which certainly does not mean literarily? Is it not first through the voice that one becomes animal?) Literature is an assemblage. It has nothing to do with ideology. There is no ideology and never has been.

All we talk about are multiplicities, lines, strata and segmentarities, lines of flight and intensities, machinic assemblages and their various types, bodies without organs and their construction and selection, the plane of consistency, and in each case the units of measure. *Stratometers, deleometers,*[6] *BwO units of density, BwO units of convergence*: Not only do these constitute a quantification of writing, but they define writing as always the measure of

3. A way of thinking about bodily experience as an interconnected system of flows and forces rather than a structure of organs. Also referred to as *BwO*, it highlights the difference between the unpredictable live body and the dissectable dead body and sees the body as a ceaseless "desiring-machine."

4. The terms come from the structural theory of language developed by FERDINAND DE SAUSSURE (1857–1913). The division of the "sign" into "signifier" (the material of the sign) and "signified" (the meaning of the sign) mirrors the division between matter and meaning that Deleuze and Guattari aim to displace here.

5. Franz Kafka (1883–1924), Austrian novelist and short story writer who lived much of his life in Prague; he memorably depicted the bureaucratic machine in his unfinished novel *The Castle* (1926). Heinrich von Kleist (1777–1811), German writer of plays and novellas; his play *Prince Friedrich von Homburg* (1811) is concerned with the "war machine."

6. Deleuze and Guattari's coinage: conversions into lines of death.

something else. Writing has nothing to do with signifying. It has to do with surveying, mapping, even realms that are yet to come.

A first type of book is the root-book. The tree is already the image of the world, or the root the image of the world-tree. This is the classical book, as noble, signifying and subjective organic interiority (the strata of the book). The book imitates the world, as art imitates nature: by procedures specific to it that accomplish what nature cannot or can no longer do. The law of the book is the law of reflection, the One that becomes two. How could the law of the book reside in nature, when it is what presides over the very division between world and book, nature and art? One becomes two: whenever we encounter this formula, even stated strategically by Mao[7] or understood in the most "dialectical" way possible, what we have before us is the most classical and well reflected, oldest, and weariest kind of thought. Nature doesn't work that way: in nature, roots are taproots with a more multiple, lateral, and circular system of ramification, rather than a dichotomous one. Thought lags behind nature. Even the book as a natural reality is a taproot, with its pivotal spine and surrounding leaves. But the book as a spiritual reality, the Tree or Root as an image, endlessly develops the law of the One that becomes two, then of the two that become four . . . Binary logic[8] is the spiritual reality of the root-tree. Even a discipline as "advanced" as linguistics retains the root-tree as its fundamental image, and thus remains wedded to classical reflection (for example, Chomsky[9] and his grammatical trees, which begin at a point S and proceed by dichotomy). This is as much as to say that this system of thought has never reached an understanding of multiplicity: in order to arrive at two following a spiritual method it must assume a strong principal unity. On the side of the object, it is no doubt possible, following the natural method, to go directly from One to three, four, or five, but only if there is a strong principal unity available, that of the pivotal taproot supporting the secondary roots. That doesn't get us very far. The binary logic of dichotomy has simply been replaced by biunivocal[1] relationships between successive circles. The pivotal taproot provides no better understanding of multiplicity than the dichotomous root. One operates in the object, the other in the subject. Binary logic and biunivocal relationships still dominate psychoanalysis (the tree of delusion in the Freudian interpretation of Schreber's[2] case), linguistics, structuralism, and even information science.

The radicle-system, or fascicular root,[3] is the second figure of the book, to which our modernity pays willing allegiance. This time, the principal root has aborted, or its tip has been destroyed; an immediate, indefinite multiplicity of secondary roots grafts onto it and undergoes a flourishing devel-

7. Mao Zedong (1893–1976), leader and principal Marxist theorist of China's communist revolution; the phrase "one becomes two" (applied to the birth of children) appears in his *Examples of Dialectics* (1959).
8. The logic of either / or, in which all values come in pairs of opposition.
9. Noam Chomsky (b. 1928), American linguist who devised transformational-generative grammar, which attempts to relate sentences with different structures and account for all the acceptable sentences of a language by differentiating between "deep structures" (innate and unconscious forms that ensure competence) and "surface structures" (the particular sentences into which the deep structures are transformed in performance).
1. Turning to both sides, but only in a prescribed way.
2. Daniel Paul Schreber (1842–1911), German judge whose *Memoirs of My Nervous Illness* (1903) were analyzed by SIGMUND FREUD (1856–1939), Austrian founder of psychoanalysis, in an important 1911 study.
3. A small, secondary root (a *fascicle* is also a division of a book published in parts, and both words share their Latin root with *fascism*).

opment. This time, natural reality is what aborts the principal root, but the root's unity subsists, as past or yet to come, as possible. We must ask if reflexive, spiritual reality does not compensate for this state of things by demanding an even more comprehensive secret unity, or a more extensive totality. Take William Burroughs's[4] cut-up method: the folding of one text onto another, which constitutes multiple and even adventitious roots (like a cutting), implies a supplementary dimension to that of the texts under consideration. In this supplementary dimension of folding, unity continues its spiritual labor. That is why the most resolutely fragmented work can also be presented as the Total Work or Magnum Opus.[5] Most modern methods for making series proliferate or a multiplicity grow are perfectly valid in one direction, for example, a linear direction, whereas a unity of totalization asserts itself even more firmly in another, circular or cyclic, dimension. Whenever a multiplicity is taken up in a structure, its growth is offset by a reduction in its laws of combination. The abortionists of unity are indeed angel makers, *doctores angelici*, because they affirm a properly angelic and superior unity. Joyce's[6] words, accurately described as having "multiple roots," shatter the linear unity of the word, even of language, only to posit a cyclic unity of the sentence, text, or knowledge. Nietzsche's[7] aphorisms shatter the linear unity of knowledge, only to invoke the cyclic unity of the eternal return, present as the nonknown in thought. This is as much as to say that the fascicular system does not really break with dualism, with the complementarity between a subject and an object, a natural reality and a spiritual reality: unity is consistently thwarted and obstructed in the object, while a new type of unity triumphs in the subject. The world has lost its pivot; the subject can no longer even dichotomize, but accedes to a higher unity, of ambivalence or overdetermination, in an always supplementary dimension to that of its object. The world has become chaos, but the book remains the image of the world: radicle-chaosmos rather than root-cosmos. A strange mystification: a book all the more total for being fragmented. At any rate, what a vapid idea, the book as the image of the world. In truth, it is not enough to say, "Long live the multiple," difficult as it is to raise that cry. No typographical, lexical, or even syntactical cleverness is enough to make it heard. The multiple *must be made*, not by always adding a higher dimension, but rather in the simplest of ways, by dint of sobriety, with the number of dimensions one already has available—always $n - 1$ (the only way the one belongs to the multiple: always subtracted). Subtract the unique from the multiplicity to be constituted; write at $n - 1$ dimensions. A system of this kind could be called a rhizome. A rhizome as subterranean stem is absolutely different from roots and radicles. Bulbs and tubers are rhizomes. Plants with roots or radicles may be rhizomorphic in other respects altogether: the question is whether plant life in its specificity is not entirely rhizomatic. Even some animals are, in their pack form. Rats are rhizomes. Burrows are too,

4. American writer of experimental novels (1914–1997); see "The Cut-Up Method of Brion Gysin" in *The Third Mind* (1978) by Burroughs and Gysin.

5. An allusion to the French poet Stéphane Mallarmé (1842–1898), who combined a notoriously fragmentary style with an alchemical dream of the Great Work.

6. James Joyce (1882–1941), Irish writer known for the innovations of technique and inventions of words in his fiction, especially in *Finnegans Wake* (1939), which ends in an unfinished sentence that is completed by the fragment with which the book begins. *Doctores angelici*: angelic teachers (Latin).

7. Friedrich Nietzsche (1844–1900), German philosopher.

in all of their functions of shelter, supply, movement, evasion, and breakout. The rhizome itself assumes very diverse forms, from ramified surface extension in all directions to concretion into bulbs and tubers. When rats swarm over each other. The rhizome includes the best and the worst: potato and couchgrass, or the weed. Animal and plant, couchgrass is crabgrass.

* * *

Let us summarize the principal characteristics of a rhizome: unlike trees or their roots, the rhizome connects any point to any other point, and its traits are not necessarily linked to traits of the same nature; it brings into play very different regimes of signs, and even nonsign states. The rhizome is reducible neither to the One nor the multiple. It is not the One that becomes Two or even directly three, four, five, etc. It is not a multiple derived from the One, or to which One is added ($n + 1$). It is composed not of units but of dimensions, or rather directions in motion. It has neither beginning nor end, but always a middle (*milieu*) from which it grows and which it overspills. It constitutes linear multiplicities with n dimensions having neither subject nor object, which can be laid out on a plane of consistency, and from which the One is always subtracted ($n - 1$). When a multiplicity of this kind changes dimension, it necessarily changes in nature as well, undergoes a metamorphosis. Unlike a structure, which is defined by a set of points and positions, with binary relations between the points and biunivocal relationships between the positions, the rhizome is made only of lines: lines of segmentarity and stratification as its dimensions, and the line of flight or deterritorialization as the maximum dimension after which the multiplicity undergoes metamorphosis, changes in nature. These lines, or lineaments, should not be confused with lineages of the arborescent type, which are merely localizable linkages between points and positions. Unlike the tree, the rhizome is not the object of reproduction: neither external reproduction as image-tree nor internal reproduction as tree-structure. The rhizome is an antigenealogy. It is a short-term memory, or antimemory. The rhizome operates by variation, expansion, conquest, capture, offshoots. Unlike the graphic arts, drawing, or photography, unlike tracings, the rhizome pertains to a map that must be produced, constructed, a map that is always detachable, connectable, reversible, modifiable, and has multiple entryways and exits and its own lines of flight. It is tracings that must be put on the map, not the opposite. In contrast to centered (even polycentric) systems with hierarchical modes of communication and preestablished paths, the rhizome is an acentered, nonhierarchical, nonsignifying system without a General and without an organizing memory or central automaton, defined solely by a circulation of states. What is at question in the rhizome is a relation to sexuality—but also to the animal, the vegetal, the world, politics, the book, things natural and artificial—that is totally different from the arborescent relation: all manner of "becomings."

A plateau is always in the middle, not at the beginning or the end. A rhizome is made of plateaus. Gregory Bateson[8] uses the word "plateau" to designate something very special: a continuous, self-vibrating region of intensities whose development avoids any orientation toward a culmination

8. English anthropologist, biologist, ethnologist, and philosopher (1904–1980).

point or external end. Bateson cites Balinese culture as an example: mother-child sexual games, and even quarrels among men, undergo this bizarre intensive stabilization. "Some sort of continuing plateau of intensity is substituted for [sexual] climax," war, or a culmination point. It is a regrettable characteristic of the Western mind to relate expressions and actions to exterior or transcendent ends, instead of evaluating them on a plane of consistency on the basis of their intrinsic value.[9] For example, a book composed of chapters has culmination and termination points. What takes place in a book composed instead of plateaus that communicate with one another across microfissures, as in a brain? We call a "plateau" any multiplicity connected to other multiplicities by superficial underground stems in such a way as to form or extend a rhizome. We are writing this book as a rhizome. It is composed of plateaus. We have given it a circular form, but only for laughs. Each morning we would wake up, and each of us would ask himself what plateau he was going to tackle, writing five lines here, ten there. We had hallucinatory experiences, we watched lines leave one plateau and proceed to another like columns of tiny ants. We made circles of convergence. Each plateau can be read starting anywhere and can be related to any other plateau. To attain the multiple, one must have a method that effectively constructs it; no typographical cleverness, no lexical agility, no blending or creation of words, no syntactical boldness, can substitute for it. In fact, these are more often than not merely mimetic procedures used to disseminate or disperse a unity that is retained in a different dimension for an image-book. Technonarcissism. Typographical, lexical, or syntactic creations are necessary only when they no longer belong to the form of expression of a hidden unity, becoming themselves dimensions of the multiplicity under consideration; we only know of rare successes in this.[1] We ourselves were unable to do it. We just used words that in turn function for us as plateaus. RHIZOMATICS = SCHIZOANALYSIS = STRATOANALYSIS = PRAGMATICS = MICROPOLITICS. These words are concepts, but concepts are lines, which is to say, number systems attached to a particular dimension of the multiplicities (strata, molecular chains, lines of flight or rupture, circles of convergence, etc.). Nowhere do we claim for our concepts the title of a science. We are no more familiar with scientificity than we are with ideology; all we know are assemblages. And the only assemblages are machinic assemblages of desire and collective assemblages of enunciation. No signifiance,[2] no subjectification: writing to the *n*th power (all individuated enunciation remains trapped within the dominant significations, all signifying desire is associated with dominated subjects). An assemblage, in its multiplicity, necessarily acts on semiotic flows, material flows, and social flows simultaneously (independently of any recapitulation that may be made of it in a scientific or theoretical corpus). There is no longer a tripartite division between a field of reality (the world) and a field of representation (the book) and a field of

9. Gregory Bateson, *Steps toward an Ecology of Mind* (New York: Ballantine Books, 1972), p. 113. It will be noted that the word "plateau" is used in classical studies of bulbs, tubers, and rhizomes: see the entry for "Bulb" in M. H. Baillon, *Dictionnaire de botanique* [*Dictionary of Botany*] (Paris: Hachette, 1876–92) [Deleuze and Guattari's note].

1. For example, Joëlle de La Casinière, *Absolument nécessaire* [*Absolutely Necessary*]: *The Emergency Book* (Paris: Minuit, 1973), a truly nomadic book. In the same vein, see the research in progress at the Montfaucon Research Center [Deleuze and Guattari's note].

2. A term that emphasizes the process of producing meaning (in contrast to *significance*, which emphasizes the result).

subjectivity (the author). Rather, an assemblage establishes connections between certain multiplicities drawn from each of these orders, so that a book has no sequel nor the world as its object nor one or several authors as its subject. In short, we think that one cannot write sufficiently in the name of an outside. The outside has no image, no signification, no subjectivity. The book as assemblage with the outside, against the book as image of the world. A rhizome-book, not a dichotomous, pivotal, or fascicular book. Never send down roots, or plant them, however difficult it may be to avoid reverting to the old procedures. "Those things which occur to me, occur to me not from the root up but rather only from somewhere about their middle. Let someone then attempt to seize them, let someone attempt to seize a blade of grass and hold fast to it when it begins to grow only from the middle."[3] Why is this so difficult? The question is directly one of perceptual semiotics. It's not easy to see things in the middle, rather than looking down on them from above or up at them from below, or from left to right or right to left: try it, you'll see that everything changes. It's not easy to see the grass in things and in words (similarly, Nietzsche said that an aphorism had to be "ruminated"; never is a plateau separable from the cows that populate it, which are also the clouds in the sky).

History is always written from the sedentary point of view and in the name of a unitary State apparatus, at least a possible one, even when the topic is nomads. What is lacking is a Nomadology, the opposite of a history. There are rare successes in this also, for example, on the subject of the Children's Crusades:[4] Marcel Schwob's book multiplies narratives like so many plateaus with variable numbers of dimensions. Then there is Andrzejewski's book, *Les portes du paradis* (The gates of paradise), composed of a single uninterrupted sentence; a flow of children; a flow of walking with pauses, straggling, and forward rushes; the semiotic flow of the confessions of all the children who go up to the old monk at the head of the procession to make their declarations; a flow of desire and sexuality, each child having left out of love and more or less directly led by the dark posthumous pederastic desire of the count of Vendôme; all this with circles of convergence. What is important is not whether the flows are "One or multiple"—we're past that point: there is a collective assemblage of enunciation, a machinic assemblage of desire, one inside the other and both plugged into an immense outside that is a multiplicity in any case. A more recent example is Armand Farrachi's book on the Fourth Crusade,[5] *La dislocation*, in which the sentences space themselves out and disperse, or else jostle together and coexist, and in which the letters, the typography begin to dance as the crusade grows more delirious.[6] These are models of nomadic and rhizomatic

3. *The Diaries of Franz Kafka*, ed. Max Brod, trans. Joseph Kresh (New York: Schocken, 1948), p. 12 [Deleuze and Guattari's note].
4. The attempt of thousands of children to make their way to the Holy Land to reclaim it from the Muslims; the first group set out from Vendôme in the summer of 1212.
5. One of 8 European military expeditions (1095–1291) intended to drive the Muslims from Jerusalem and other Christian holy sites; the Fourth Crusade was putatively targeted at Egypt (a center of Muslim power) but was diverted to conquer the Christian cities of Zara (in Hungary) and Constantinople, which was sacked in 1203.
6. Marcel Schwob, *The Children's Crusade*, trans. Henry Copley (Boston: Small, Maynard, 1898); Jerzy Andrzejewski, *Les Portes du paradis* (Paris: Gallimard, 1949); Armand Farrachi, *La Dislocation* [*Dislocation*] (Paris: Stock, 1974). It was in the context of Schwob's book that Paul Alphandéry remarked that literature, in certain cases, could revitalize history and impose upon it "genuine research directions"; *La Chrétienneté et l'idée de croisade* [*Christianity and the Idea of the Crusade*] (Paris: Albin Michel, 1959), vol. 2, p. 116 [Deleuze and Guattari's note].

writing. Writing weds a war machine and lines of flight, abandoning the strata, segmentarities, sedentarity, the State apparatus. But why is a model still necessary? Aren't these books still "images" of the Crusades? Don't they still retain a unity, in Schwob's case a pivotal unity, in Farrachi's an aborted unity, and in the most beautiful example, *Les portes du paradis*, the unity of the funereal count? Is there a need for a more profound nomadism than that of the Crusades, a nomadism of true nomads, or of those who no longer even move or imitate anything? The nomadism of those who only assemble (*agencent*). How can the book find an adequate outside with which to assemble in heterogeneity, rather than a world to reproduce? The cultural book is necessarily a tracing: already a tracing of itself, a tracing of the previous book by the same author, a tracing of other books however different they may be, an endless tracing of established concepts and words, a tracing of the world present, past, and future. Even the anticultural book may still be burdened by too heavy a cultural load: but it will use it actively, for forgetting instead of remembering, for underdevelopment instead of progress toward development, in nomadism rather than sedentarity, to make a map instead of a tracing. RHIZOMATICS = POP ANALYSIS, even if the people have other things to do besides read it, even if the blocks of academic culture or pseudoscientificity in it are still too painful or ponderous. For science would go completely mad if left to its own devices. Look at mathematics: it's not a science, it's a monster slang, it's nomadic. Even in the realm of theory, especially in the realm of theory, any precarious and pragmatic framework is better than tracing concepts, with their breaks and progress changing nothing. Imperceptible rupture, not signifying break. The nomads invented a war machine in opposition to the State apparatus. History has never comprehended nomadism, the book has never comprehended the outside. The State as the model for the book and for thought has a long history: logos,[7] the philosopher-king, the transcendence of the Idea, the interiority of the concept, the republic of minds, the court of reason, the functionaries of thought, man as legislator and subject. The State's pretension to be a world order, and to root man. The war machine's relation to an outside is not another "model"; it is an assemblage that makes thought itself nomadic, and the book a working part in every mobile machine, a stem for a rhizome (Kleist and Kafka against Goethe[8]).

Write to the *n*th power, the $n-1$ power, write with slogans: Make rhizomes, not roots, never plant! Don't sow, grow offshoots! Don't be one or multiple, be multiplicities! Run lines, never plot a point! Speed turns the point into a line![9] Be quick, even when standing still! Line of chance, line of hips, line of flight. Don't bring out the General in you! Don't have just ideas, just have an idea (Godard)[1] Have short-term ideas. Make maps, not photos or drawings. Be the Pink Panther and your loves will be like the wasp and the orchid, the cat and the baboon. As they say about old man river:

7. Word, speech; discourse, reason (Greek); in the New Testament, logos is often identified with Christ.
8. Johann Wolfgang von Goethe (1749–1832), magisterial German poet, playwright, and novelist.
9. See Paul Virilio, "Véhiculaire," in *Nomades et vagabonds* [*Nomads and Vagabonds*], ed. Jacques Bergue (Paris: Union Générale d'Éditions, 1975), on the appearance of linearity and the disruption of perception by speed [Deleuze and Guattari's note].
1. Jean-Luc Godard (b. 1930), French filmmaker and screenwriter best known for his work of the 1950s and 1960s during the New Wave in France.

He don't plant 'tatos
Don't plant cotton
Them that plants them is soon forgotten
But old man river he just keeps rollin' along[2]

A rhizome has no beginning or end; it is always in the middle, between things, interbeing, *intermezzo*. The tree is filiation, but the rhizome is alliance, uniquely alliance. The tree imposes the verb "to be," but the fabric of the rhizome is the conjunction, "and . . . and . . . and . . ." This conjunction carries enough force to shake and uproot the verb "to be." Where are you going? Where are you coming from? What are you heading for?[3] These are totally useless questions. Making a clean slate, starting or beginning again from ground zero, seeking a beginning or a foundation—all imply a false conception of voyage and movement (a conception that is methodical, pedagogical, initiatory, symbolic . . .). But Kleist, Lenz, and Büchner[4] have another way of traveling and moving: proceeding from the middle, through the middle, coming and going rather than starting and finishing.[5] American literature, and already English literature, manifest this rhizomatic direction to an even greater extent; they know how to move between things, establish a logic of the AND, overthrow ontology, do away with foundations, nullify endings and beginnings. They know how to practice pragmatics. The middle is by no means an average; on the contrary, it is where things pick up speed. *Between* things does not designate a localizable relation going from one thing to the other and back again, but a perpendicular direction, a transversal movement that sweeps one *and* the other away, a stream without beginning or end that undermines its banks and picks up speed in the middle.

1980

2. From "Ol' Man River," an imitation of a Negro spiritual composed by Jerome Kern with lyrics (here slightly misquoted) by Oscar Hammerstein for the musical *Show Boat* (1927).
3. Paul Gauguin (1848–1903), a French painter who became a "nomad" in Tahiti, gave one of his Tahitian paintings these three questions as a title.
4. Georg Büchner (1813–1837), German dramatist. Jakob Lenz (1751–1792), German poet.
5. See Jean-Christopher Bailly's description of movement in German Romanticism, in his introduction to *La Légende dispersée: Anthologie du romantisme allemand* [*The Dispersed Legend: An Anthology of German Romanticism*] (Paris: Union Générale d'Éditions, 1976), pp. 18ff. [Deleuze and Guattari's note].

JEAN-FRANÇOIS LYOTARD
1925–1998

Jean-François Lyotard was at the center of debates about postmodernism during the 1980s and 1990s. His celebrated announcement of the demise of "grand narratives" and of the "incommensurability" of local "language games" made his *Postmodern Condition* (1979; trans. 1984) the most succinct, accessible, and memorable manifesto of the postmodernist position. Lyotard, along with MICHEL FOUCAULT, was labeled a "young conservative" by the German philosopher JÜRGEN HABERMAS—and the battle was joined. The postmodernists contended that "general human emancipation" could not be gained through the universalist strategies characteristic of both liberalism (with its appeal to human rights) and communism (with its goal of a one-class society).

Born in Versailles, Lyotard received the equivalent of a master's degree in philosophy from the Sorbonne in 1949 and spent the 1950s teaching high school, including a two-year stint in Algeria. Following in the footsteps of the phenomenologist Maurice Merleau-Ponty (1908–1961), Lyotard attempts in his early work to reconcile Marxist politics and philosophy. Active in leftist agitation against the French colonial war in Algeria and in the student revolution of 1968, Lyotard, like many French intellectuals, was dismayed by the powerful French Communist Party's less than adequate responses to these two crises. Increasingly, Marxism appeared unable to understand or to support any political action that did not derive from the working class and address specifically economic grievances. Turning first to psychoanalysis (in *Des dispositifs pulsionnels*, 1973; and *Libidinal Economy*, 1974, trans. 1993) and then to the philosophy of Ludwig Wittgenstein (1889–1951) and IMMANUEL KANT (1724–1804), Lyotard tried to reevaluate the "emancipatory" narratives of Marxism and liberalism, and to consider new bases for aesthetic, moral, and political judgment as well as action. He taught philosophy at the University of Paris (1959–66), the University of Nanterre (1966–70), and the University of Paris VIII at Vincennes (1972–87) and held visiting positions at a number of American universities, most notably the University of California at Irvine. During the early 1980s, he was the first president of the prestigious but controversial International College of Philosophy in Paris, which he co-founded.

Our brief selection, "Defining the Postmodern" (1986), captures many of Lyotard's major themes. Modernism in the arts, he argues, partakes of the universal aims of modernity. Thus modernist architecture sought to make everything new, to transform the whole world, to effect a total revolution in how people live together by creating entirely new cities. But we have now—after Auschwitz and the Soviet gulags—come to recognize that such modern dreams of transforming humanity can be pursued only violently, and even then they will not succeed. Allegiance to one universal standard by which all are judged generates murderous hostility to the different, to whatever resists or simply does not desire to go along with the program. Modernist architects and city planners blithely razed old neighborhoods, confident that their plans for "urban renewal" would make for better lives. Instead, they created inhospitable concrete wastelands, unconnected to how people interact in lived space.

Postmodernism attempts to turn its back on this understanding of progress as the whole world marching in lockstep toward the same utopian future. Instead, Lyotard preaches an appreciation and respect for diversity, for local differences, for the plurality of ways in which humans choose to live. In *The Postmodern Condition*, he argues that there is no common measure by which such local differences (which, following Wittgenstein, he calls distinct "language games") can be compared. We cannot confidently declare one way of life or thought superior to another—one more progressive and modern, the other reactionary and residual. Such differences are "incommensurate," like those between apples and oranges. The use of "progress" as a yardstick has been discredited by the unintended side effects (such as ecological damage and weapons of mass destruction) of increasing scientific knowledge and technological innovation. We would do better if we stopped trying to force the world and its inhabitants into one mold and stopped trying to make history move in one direction.

At times, Lyotard recognizes that belief in progress, the notion that "development" is necessarily a good thing, is still very prevalent and must be combated. At other times, he writes as if a general loss of faith in progress has taken over, as if we are all already postmodern and thus skeptical of the "grand narratives" of modernization and its attendant emancipation of the poor, the ignorant, the oppressed, or whomever.

The debates generated by Lyotard's work certainly do not indicate that a postmodern vision prevails. The political objection voiced by Habermas and others focuses on the apparent passivity of Lyotard's position. If we have no way to judge different ways of life, then whatever exists must be tolerated. Moreover, this absence of standards also seems to leave us unable to imagine a future that we can claim would be better than the status quo. Lyotard addresses some of these concerns in *Just Gaming* (1984), in which he argues that violation of another's chosen way of life is a crime that can and should be halted by intervention (by the state or by other agencies). Thus, since the Nazis forcibly prevented people from living in their own chosen way, forceful intervention against the Nazis was justified.

In matters literary and artistic, Lyotard focuses on shifts in style and expression between modernism and postmodernism. Our selection highlights the extent to which he sees postmodernism in the arts manifesting the signs of what psychologists call posttraumatic stress disorder. The postmodern artist, he observes, is haunted by "the sanguinary last two centuries," the massive crimes against humanity and increasingly vicious wars since the French Revolution. The often-noted use in contemporary art of pastiche (the citation or quoting of various previous moments in art or literary history) is a Freudian "working through" of past material in an effort to break the spell of the traumatic past that paralyzes the present moment. "Postmodernism," as the name suggests, is perhaps not a period in its own right but instead is linked to the modernism it tries to shake. Having discovered that the modernist dream of utterly breaking with the past ensures "repeating" that past, postmodernist art strives instead to work through the tradition in order to overcome it.

Though Lyotard is not sure what lies on the other side of that overcoming, he is optimistic that ours is a healthy moment, implicitly critiquing FREDRIC JAMESON's association of postmodern art with schizophrenia, with the fragmentation of the self. For Lyotard, we would be schizophrenic only if we did not reflect on and recast the various fragments from the tradition. But we should not expect that all the incommensurate pieces of our world and of our selves will fit together neatly. Complexity, he insists, cannot be sidestepped by simple visions of right and wrong or by simple models of all-encompassing systems. And he wants an art that is attentive to complexity, that grapples with the multiple meanings of our past and the plural realities of our present.

In *The Postmodern Condition* and subsequent works (especially *Lessons on the Analytic of the Sublime*, 1991), Lyotard links postmodernist art with the sublime. (See above LONGINUS, JOSEPH ADDISON, EDMUND BURKE, and Kant for traditional accounts of this concept.) Art, Lyotard suggests, is one place where that which resists being fully captured within any existing signifying system can make its existence felt. To avoid modernity's persistent tendency to reduce everything back into known terms or (worse) to obliterate everything that resists such reduction, we must cultivate an appreciation of the sublime, of that which exceeds calculation and understanding. If postmodern art can foster such a sensibility, a future where difference exists and even flourishes just might be possible. Only such a future, Lyotard insists, can do justice to the complexity and variety of the world we inhabit.

BIBLIOGRAPHY

Much, but not all, of Lyotard's work has been translated into English (the date of French publication is given first, where appropriate): *Phenomenology* (1954; 1991); *Libidinal Economy* (1974; 1993); *Duchamps's Trans/Formers* (1977; 1990); *The Pacific Wall* (1975; 1990); *The Postmodern Condition* (1979; 1984); *Just Gaming*, with Jean-Loup Thébaud (1979; 1985); *The Differend* (1983; 1988); *The Postmodern Explained* (1986; 1992); *The Inhuman: Reflections on Time* (1988; 1991); *Peregrinations: Law, Form, Event* (1988); *Heidegger and "the jews"* (1988; 1990); *Lessons on the Analytic of the Sublime* (1991; 1994); *Postmodern Fables* (1993; 1997); and *Signed, Malraux* (1996; 1999). There are five collections of work spanning Lyotard's career: *Driftworks*, edited by Roger McKeon (1984); *The Lyotard Reader*, edited by

Andrew Benjamin (1989); *Political Writings*, edited by Bill Readings (1993); *Toward the Postmodern*, edited by Robert Harvey and Mark S. Roberts (1993); and *Music/Ideology: Resisting the Aesthetic*, edited by Adam Krims (1998). The untranslated works are *Discours, figures* (1971; *Discourse, Figures*); *Dérive à partir de Marx et Freud* (1973; *Starting from Marx and Freud*); *Des dispositifs pulsionnels* (1973; *Driving Impulses*); *Instructions païennes* (1977; *Pagan Instructions*); *Récits tremblants* (1977; *Trembling Stories*); *L'Enthousiasme: La critique kantienne de l'historie* (1986; *Enthusiasm: The Kantian Critique of History*); and *La Guerre des Algériens: Écrits 1956–63* (1988; *The Algerian War: Writing 1956–63*). Stuart Sim's *Jean-François Lyotard* (1996) is the best source for biographical information, and it places Lyotard's work in historical and intellectual context.

David Carroll's *Paraesthetics: Foucault, Lyotard, Derrida* (1987) details Lyotard's connections with poststructuralism. Geoffrey Bennington's *Lyotard: Writing the Event* (1988) is the best introductory work, although Bill Readings's *Introducing Lyotard: Art and Politics* (1991) is also excellent. *Judging Lyotard*, edited by Andrew Benjamin (1992), is a superb collection of essays on Lyotard's work. Joan Nordquist's *Jean-François Lyotard: A Bibliography* (1991) includes all of Lyotard's work in both French and English up to that date as well as all English language commentary on his work.

Defining the Postmodern

I should like to make only a small number of observations, in order to point to—and not at all to resolve—some problems surrounding the term 'postmodern'. My aim is not to close the debate, but to open it, to allow it to develop by avoiding certain confusions and ambiguities, as far as this is possible.

There are many debates implied by, and implicated in, the term 'postmodern'. I will distinguish three of them.

First, the opposition between postmodernism and modernism, or the Modern Movement (1910–45), in architectural theory. According to Paolo Portoghesi[1] (*Dopo architettura moderna*), there is a rupture or break, and this break would be the abrogation of the hegemony of Euclidean geometry,[2] which was sublimated in the plastic poetry of the movement known as De Stijl,[3] for example. According to Victorio Grigotti, another Italian architect, the difference between the two periods is characterized by what is possibly a more interesting fissure. There is no longer any close linkage between the architectural project and socio-historical progress in the realization of human emancipation on the larger scale. Postmodern architecture is condemned to generate a multiplicity of small transformations in the space it inherits, and to give up the project of a last rebuilding of the whole space occupied by humanity. In this sense, a perspective is opened in the larger landscape.

In this account there is no longer a horizon of universalization, of general emancipation before the eyes of postmodern man, or in particular, of the postmodern architect. The disappearance of this idea of progress within

1. Italian architect and critic (b. 1931), whose books *After Modern Architecture* (1981) and *Postmodern, the Architecture of the Post-Industrial Society* (1982) offer influential definitions of the distinction between modernist and postmodernist art.
2. Geometry based on ordinary 2- or 3-dimensional space. The reference here is apparently to modernist art's break with perspectival painting, which tries to represent spatial depth realistically on the canvas.
3. A movement of Dutch painters and architects formed in 1917; it called for purity of line and color in art, along with attention to technological progress in modern society.

rationality and freedom would explain a certain tone, style or modus which are specific to postmodern architecture. I would say a sort of *bricolage*:[4] the high frequency of quotations of elements from previous styles or periods (classical or modern), giving up the consideration of environment, and so on.

Just a remark about this aspect. The 'post-', in the term 'postmodernist' is in this case to be understood in the sense of a simple succession, of a diachrony[5] of periods, each of them clearly identifiable. Something like a conversion, a new direction after the previous one. I should like to observe that this idea of chronology is totally modern. It belongs to Christianity, Cartesianism, Jacobinism.[6] Since we are beginning something completely new, we have to re-set the hands of the clock at zero. The idea of modernity is closely bound up with this principle that it is possible and necessary to break with tradition and to begin a new way of living and thinking. Today we can presume that this 'breaking' is, rather, a manner of forgetting or repressing the past. That's to say of repeating it. Not overcoming it.

I would say that the quotation of elements of past architectures in the new one seems to me to be the same procedure as the use of remains coming from past life in the dream-work as described by Freud, in the *Interpretation of Dreams*.[7] This use of repetition or quotation, be it ironical or not, cynical or not, can be seen in the trends dominating contemporary painting, under the name of 'transavantgardism' (Achille Bonito Oliva) or under the name of neo-expressionism.[8] I'll come back to this question in my third point.

The second point. A second connotation of the term 'postmodern', and I admit that I am at least partly responsible for the misunderstanding associated with this meaning.

The general idea is a trivial one. One can note a sort of decay in the confidence placed by the two last centuries in the idea of progress. This idea of progress as possible, probable or necessary was rooted in the certainty that the development of the arts, technology, knowledge and liberty would be profitable to mankind as a whole. To be sure, the question of knowing which was the subject truly victimized by the lack of development—whether it was the poor, the worker, the illiterate—remained open during the 19th and 20th centuries. There were disputes, even wars, between liberals, conservatives and leftists over the very name of the subject we are to help to become emancipated. Nevertheless, all the parties concurred in the same belief that enterprises, discoveries and institutions are legitimate only insofar as they contribute to the emancipation of mankind.

After two centuries, we are more sensitive to signs that signify the contrary.

4. Literally, "tinkering" (French). The anthropologist CLAUDE LÉVI-STRAUSS (b. 1908) uses the term to describe forms of thought or of work that combine elements taken from various sources.

5. Events strung out along a time line, as contrasted to synchrony (events happening at the same time); both terms are associated with structuralism.

6. The philosophy of the most radical group during the French Revolution, the one most determined to make an entirely new world. "Cartesianism": the philosophy of René Descartes (1596–1650), which breaks from the past by starting from a radical doubting of all received truths.

7. Published in 1900 (see above) by SIGMUND FREUD (1856–1939), Austrian founder of psychoanalysis. Throughout this essay, Lyotard sees the work done by postmodern artists as analogous to the psychic memory work that Freud claimed was done in dreams or done by the patient in psychoanalytic therapy.

8. The name given to the work of Julian Schnabel, Anselm Kiefer, and other painters in the early 1980s who returned to earlier abstract and representational styles to "express" psychological and historical material. Art critic Oliva's *Trans-avantgarde International* (1982) describes neo-expressionism as a break from the impersonal experimentation of the avant-grades.

Neither economic nor political liberalism, nor the various Marxisms, emerge from the sanguinary last two centuries free from the suspicion of crimes against mankind. We can list a series of proper names (names of places, persons and dates) capable of illustrating and founding our suspicion. Following Theodor Adorno,[9] I use the name of Auschwitz to point out the irrelevance of empirical matter, the stuff of recent past history, in terms of the modern claim to help mankind to emancipate itself. What kind of thought is able to sublate (*Aufheben*)[1] Auschwitz in a general (either empirical or speculative) process towards a universal emancipation? So there is a sort of sorrow in the *Zeitgeist*. This can express itself by reactive or reactionary attitudes or by utopias, but never by a positive orientation offering a new perspective.

The development of techno-sciences has become a means of increasing disease, not of fighting it. We can no longer call this development by the old name of progress. This development seems to be taking place by itself, by an autonomous force or 'motricity'.[2] It doesn't respond to a demand coming from human needs. On the contrary, human entities (individual or social) seem always to be destabilized by the results of this development. The intellectual results as much as the material ones. I would say that mankind is in the condition of running after the process of accumulating new objects of practice and thought. In my view it is a real and obscure question to determine the reason of this process of complexification. It's something like a destiny towards a more and more complex condition. Our demands for security, identity and happiness, coming from our condition as living beings and even social beings appear today irrelevant in the face of this sort of obligation to complexify, mediate, memorize and synthesize every object, and to change its scale. We are in this techno-scientific world like Gulliver:[3] sometimes too big, sometimes too small, never at the right scale. Consequently, the claim for simplicity, in general, appears today that of a barbarian.

From this point, it would be necessary to consider the division of mankind into two parts: one part confronted with the challenge of complexity; the other with the terrible ancient task of survival. This is a major aspect of the failure of the modern project (which was, in principle, valid for mankind as a whole).

The third argument is more complex, and I shall present it as briefly as possible. The question of postmodernity is also the question of the expressions of thought: art, literature, philosophy, politics. You know that in the field of art for example, and more especially the plastic arts, the dominant idea is that the big movement of avant-gardism is over. There seems to be general agreement about laughing at the avant-gardes,[4] considered as the expression of an obsolete modernity. I don't like the term avant-garde any more than anyone else, because of its military connotations. Nevertheless I

9. German philosopher and cultural critic (1903–1969). ADORNO famously declared that "To write poetry after Auschwitz"—the Nazi's largest concentration camp—"is barbaric."

1. A technical term from the philosophy of GEORG WILHELM FRIEDRICH HEGEL (1770–1831). In Hegel the thesis and its opposite, the antithesis, are "sublated" in the synthesis that joins them together. Here progress, the movement of humanity to its perfection, is met by an antithesis, the murderous acts of Auschwitz.

2. Lyotard's coinage, conveying the sense that the motor of history, its movement, is now out of human control.

3. The narrator-hero of Jonathan Swift's *Gulliver's Travels* (1726), who visits both an island whose inhabitants are 6 inches tall and an island inhabited by giants.

4. What today are designated the modernist or historical avant-gardes were the self-organized and self-named "cutting edge" movements such as surrealism, dadaism, futurism, and constructivism of the high modernist period (1914–30). The term originally meant the advance guard of an army.

would like to observe that the very process of avant-gardism in painting was in reality a long, obstinate and highly responsible investigation of the presuppositions implied in modernity. The right approach, in order to understand the work of painters from, say, Manet to Duchamp or Barnett Newman[5] is to compare their work with the anamnesis[6] which takes place in psychoanalytical therapy. Just as the patient elaborates his present trouble by freely associating the more imaginary, immaterial, irrelevant bits with past situations, so discovering hidden meanings of his life, we can consider the work of Cézanne, Picasso, Delaunay, Kandinsky, Klee, Mondrian, Malevitch[7] and finally Duchamp as a working through—what Freud called *Durcharbeitung*[8]—operated by modernity on itself. If we give up this responsibility, it is certain that we are condemned to repeat, without any displacement, the modern neurosis, the Western schizophrenia, paranoia, and so on. This being granted, the 'post-' of postmodernity does not mean a process of coming back or flashing back, feeding back, but of *ana*-lysing, *ana*-mnesing, of reflecting.[9]

1986

5. American abstract expressionist painter (1905–1970). Edouard Manet (1833–1883), sometimes called the first modern painter, a forerunner of the impressionists. Marcel Duchamp (1887–1968), French (later American) painter and conceptual artist, whose experiments foreshadowed much postmodern art.
6. Remembering.
7. All important modern artists: Paul Cézanne (1839–1906), French impressionist painter and forerunner of cubism; Pablo Picasso (1881–1973), Spanish painter who is the most celebrated modernist artist; Robert Delaunay (1885–1941), French modernist painter Wassily Kandinsky (1866–1944), Russian abstract painter; Paul Klee (1879–1940), Swiss avante-garde painter; Piet Mondrian (1872–1944), Dutch abstract painter and member of De Stijl; Kasimir Malevich (1878–1935), Russian contructivist painter, active during the Russian Revolution and its immediate aftermath.
8. Working through (German), a technical term from Freudian theories of therapy. Only after "working through" various elements in the past not assimilated into self-understanding can the patient get rid of the symptomatic (and/or neurotic) behaviors that have grown out of the repression of the past.
9. *Ana-* literally means "again" or "back" (Greek).

MICHEL FOUCAULT

1926–1984

Michel Foucault is arguably the most influential European writer and thinker of the second half of the twentieth century. His unclassifiable work (is it history? philosophy? cultural theory?) is controversial and has attracted much criticism, but the questions he raised, the topics he addressed, and the positions he took have become central features of today's intellectual landscape. In literary studies, Foucault stands as a major source for poststructuralism, New Historicism, cultural studies, and queer theory, while also fueling the growing interest in literature and medicine, the examination of the institutional bases from which writers and critics operate, and the interest in processes of identity formation.

Foucault was born in Poitiers, France. His father was a doctor, and he (unlike his brother) went against the family's wishes that he study medicine; he eventually became a fierce critic of modern medical practices and institutions. Awkward, bookish, and brilliant, Foucault progressed easily through the elaborate French educational system, with its extremely competitive exams for gaining a place in the multitiered hierarchy. Foucault took his university degree at the nation's top university, the École Normale Supérieure, where he specialized in the philosophy of psychology.

Under the influence of his teacher LOUIS ALTHUSSER, Foucault joined the Communist Party in 1950, quitting three years later. He spent the 1950s teaching in France (briefly) and then abroad—in Sweden, Poland, and Germany. Returning to France in 1960, he defended the graduate thesis that became his first book, *Folie et deraison* (1961; part was translated into English as *Madness and Civilization*). A major theme of this book and its follow-up, *The Birth of the Clinic* (1963), is an attack on the institutions and procedures characteristic of modern medicine. They inaugurate Foucault's lifelong preoccupation with the ways in which individuals are "administered" by the various bureaucratic institutions—hospitals, prisons, the military, schools—that increasingly render selves docile in the modern world.

Foucault's 1966 *Les Mots et les choses* (translated as *The Order of Things*) made his reputation. Recognizably a structuralist history, *The Order of Things* examines how the disciplines of economics, linguistics, and biology emerged, offering along the way a brilliant, if overly schematic, characterization of the three different "epistemes" (deep-rooted, unconscious structures for organizing knowledge) of the Middle Ages, the "classical period" (Foucault's term for the Enlightenment), and modernity. Foucault attempted to explicate and justify the methodology of *The Order of Things* in his next major book, *The Archaeology of Knowledge* (1969).

By 1969 Foucault's focus had shifted away from intellectual history and methodological meditations. The events of May 1968, when a student-led revolt almost toppled the French government before itself collapsing, together with his own involvement in student unrest in Tunisia (where he taught from 1966 to 1968), "radicalized" Foucault. He became politically active—and remained so to the end of his life. His book *Surveiller et punir: Naissance de la prison* (1975, *Discipline and Punish: The Birth of the Prison*) is a direct outgrowth of his work on prison reform. Foucault asks himself in the first chapter of the book why he has written a history of the prison: "Simply because I am interested in the past? No, if one means by that writing a history of the past in terms of the present. Yes, if one means writing the history of the present." He aims at describing the present through an analysis of the forces that created it, a historical and critical undertaking that he follows the nineteenth-century philosopher FRIEDRICH NIETZSCHE in calling "genealogy." From the history of the prison, Foucault turned next to the history of sexuality. Three volumes of his work on that topic were published, although the entire project was incomplete when he died of complications from AIDS at the age of fifty-seven.

From 1970 on, Foucault spent longer and longer stints in North America as a lecturer or visiting professor at various universities—most notably at the University of California at Berkeley, where the New Historicists gathered around STEPHEN GREENBLATT brought Foucault-inspired work directly into literary studies. Tales of Foucault's experimentation with and explorations of drugs and sex were oral legend before being recorded in James Miller's notorious, yet mostly accurate, biography, *The Passion of Michel Foucault* (1993). The relevance of his personal life to the work is debatable, but Foucault's own growing interest in "the care of the self" in his later years suggests that separating private and public is no easy task.

Our selections present work particularly important to literary and cultural studies. The essay "What Is an Author?" (1969) directly questions some of the most fundamental assumptions of literary criticism. Foucault realizes that he had taken the author for granted in *The Order of Things*, and asks himself what it would mean to take seriously "the death of the author" (in ROLAND BARTHES's famous phrase). Foucault's approach to this question is characteristic of much of his work. We must consider, he says, what "functions" the category of "author" fulfills within the "discourse" the historian or critic deploys in the analysis of written texts. The concept *author*, he points out, is an organizing device, permitting us to group certain texts together. More crucially, the concept underwrites a number of interpretive conventions. We ascribe a certain unity and coherence to all the works written by a single author, or at least we feel that an author's drastic changes in style or opinion must be explained. And we assume, at the most fundamental level, that the author is the source of the text. Interpretation moves from the written text (which may be all we know of a writer) back toward the author, searching out an individual's biography, psychology, and intentions. The author thus functions both to organize the vast reservoir of materials that the past bequeaths us and to anchor a certain way of interpreting those materials.

Foucault's ultimate target here is "humanism," the postmedieval understanding of who and what individuals are. He highlights the historical contingency of the belief that we are "individuals" with unique natures, possessing coherent interior identities, motives, desires, and conscious intentions that cause our actions. Humanism claims for each individual the capacities that literary criticism ascribes to authors.

Significantly, the "author function" has not always been deemed necessary to the apprehension and interpretation of texts. Prior to 1500 anonymous texts were the norm. Even today the importance of authors varies from field to field. A contract has no author, nor does the average poster. We barely note the authors of most newspaper articles. Generally speaking, Foucault opines, emphasis on the author is a mark of prestige. "Discourse that possesses an author's name is not to be immediately consumed and forgotten. . . . Rather, its status and its manner of reception are regulated by the culture in which it circulates."

Foucault's essay, then, invites us to examine the ways in which literary criticism approaches its object—the text—and accords it the prestigious title of "literature" partly through the exaltation of the author (as talented, as worthy of honor and study). He also—and we see here his importance to New Historicism—shifts our focus away from the author and toward larger systematic social forces. What if the author is not the cause, the source, of the text? What if author and text are both effects? In that case, the critic's inquiries and scrutiny need to be directed toward their common cause, toward cultural conventions and their inclusions and exclusions, not confined to formal analyses of texts or psychological investigations of writers' lives.

Such questions reveal a persistent Foucauldian preoccupation: the social constitution of the "subject" (structuralism's preferred term for the self or the individual). In "What Is an Author?" he writes that "the subject should not be entirely abandoned. It should be reconsidered, not to restore the theme of an originating subject, but to seize its functions, its intervention in discourse, and its system of dependencies. . . . [W]e should ask: under what conditions and through what forms can an entity like the subject appear in the order of discourse; what position does it occupy; what functions does it exhibit; and what rules does it follow in each type of discourse?" Though antihumanistic "deconstruction of the self" is characteristic of French poststructuralism, Foucault insists on keeping the category of the *subject* as a means to study the historical discourses of power and knowledge that constitute it.

Foucault uses the term *subject* for two reasons. First, he is thinking of the grammatical subject, the subject of a sentence. Following the structuralists, he is influenced by the idea of a "subject position" that exists as a slot in syntax and is then occupied by different actual selves at different times. That selves assume the subject position only tentatively and temporarily is highlighted by grammatical "shifters," whose most dramatic example is the pronoun "I." When I use "I," it means me; when you use "I," it means you. I become "I," the first-person subject of the sentence, only when I am authorized to speak or when I seize that position. Shifters thus indicate that subject positions—created by language—preexist individual selves, and that power enables their use.

Second, Foucault draws on *subject* as a verb. Individuals get to occupy subject positions (the various roles existing within a discourse or an institution) only through a process in which they are "subjected" to power. Indeed, individuals are constituted by power as subjects prior to having any standing as individuals.

Foucault's work from 1969 to 1980 focuses on the processes through which subjects are produced. Later, he writes of *selves*, using a term that might allow individuals an existence apart from their relations to a constituting power. But in the works of his middle period from which our selections are drawn, Foucault turns the usually celebratory narrative of the rise of the individual in modern Western societies on its head by connecting that rise with a tremendous decrease in freedom. Our selection "The Carceral" (the final section of *Discipline and Punish*) presents Foucault's sweeping, bleak, and all-too-convincing portrait of modern society since the 1740s as a series of increasingly prisonlike institutions that aim at "the accumulation and useful administration of men," conceived as docile subjects. The modern individual is produced by a power that individualizes precisely in order to better control. A panoptic (all-seeing) power keeps subjects under constant surveillance. (Foucault takes the term *panoptic* from the early-nineteenth-century English reformer Jeremy Bentham, who designed a circular prison, the Panopticon, in which each inmate was always in view of a single guard in a central tower.)

Foucault argues that premodern power intervened in subjects' lives only intermittently. Unless they broke the law, most premodern persons lived in deep obscurity, unnoticed by various authorities. But modern societies intervene from day one to shape, train, and normalize individuals. Compulsory schooling, public health measures, passports, employment records, family counseling, and the like are all very recent social practices—none more than 250 years old. In each case, an institution molds behavior according to a norm, subordinates individuals to institutional demands, examines and watches over all subjects, and punishes deviants. Such a society, Foucault argues, not only needs prisons because it inevitably produces deviants but also is itself prisonlike, "carceral," from top to bottom. The institutions that administer individuals (schools, factories, the army) use the same strategies and techniques of control that prisons employ.

Alongside this historical argument, Foucault developed—in both *Discipline and Punish* and *The History of Sexuality*, volume 1, *An Introduction* (1976)—an influential account of the interconnections among power, knowledge, and the subject. Two short phrases provide excellent points of entry to Foucault's revision of traditional notions of power. Famously, he writes that "power is exercised, rather than possessed," and he insists that power is not repressive but "productive."

Power in Foucault's account does not belong to anyone, nor does it all emanate from one specific location, such as the state. Rather, power is diffused throughout social institutions, as it is exercised by innumerable, replaceable functionaries. It operates through the daily disciplines and routines to which bodies are subjected. Thus, for example, the teacher exercises power over students, and schools have countless ways of governing students' behavior. But the teacher holds that power only as a function of his or her place in the institution, being subject as a teacher to various rules, incentives, and punishments. Both teacher and students are located (though differently) within the institution, and both go through their paces within a network that guides and oversees their conduct. Foucault stresses modern power's capillary "microtechniques," its ubiquitous reinforcement of the norm at every step, its direct work upon "docile" bodies. Think of how much time is spent making schoolchildren sit still or develop the motor skills required for "good" handwriting. Foucault sees power as decentralized and depersonalized.

The diffusion of power through the "capillaries" of the social system alters the model of political action. In our selection from the interview "Truth and Power," Foucault tells us that the traditional images of revolution are no longer appropriate. KARL MARX and other revolutionary theorists had dreamed of locating both the "universal" voice (the intellectual) and the agent (the proletariat) of humankind's political aspirations. Their combined efforts could successfully confront the massed power of the state and capitalism. But Foucault points out that power operates in innumerable places, taking many different forms that may or may not work in tandem. There is no single privileged place for the political activist to go to work, no locus of power whose removal will bring the whole system tumbling down. He therefore argues that the time of the "universal" intellectual has given way to that of the "specific" intellectual, "situated" (as are all subjects) in social networks. Though no local struggle is necessarily more crucial or more effective than any other, the political agent must start with the local and the specific—not only because of his or her own location but also because "universalist" claims arrogantly (and mistakenly) assume the right to speak and act for others.

The insistence that "power is productive" underwrites Foucault's rejection of "the repressive hypothesis" in our selection from volume 1 of *The History of Sexuality*. Power is traditionally seen as repressing behaviors that it finds unproductive, threatening, or otherwise undesirable. For example, people have various sexual desires (to masturbate or to seek same-sex partners) that are deemed unacceptable, and social power is exerted to repress those desires and the behaviors that follow from them. Foucault argues, however, that modern power produces the very categories, desires, and actions it strives to regulate. Before an act is prohibited, it is not singled out as something separate and identifiable or perhaps even desirable. The enunciation of the category and the law both creates (identifies, designates) certain actions as crimes and affords them a heightened presence.

In keeping with his historical argument that modern power operates through continual classification, surveillance, and intervention, Foucault goes further, proposing that such power names actions as crimes and perversions precisely to increase its opportunities for intervention. This is why he insists that modern society "is in actual fact, and directly, perverse." It produces the very desires and behaviors it claims to abhor, relying largely on discourse. Power can operate physically on bodies, but discursively it carves up the world. Through language various bodies are assigned to various categories (race, gender, IQ, etc.), and various actions are designated in relation to norms as praiseworthy, deviant, punishable, or criminal. A whole new array of identifiable "perverse" sexualities were named in the nineteenth century. Discourse disposes: it puts everything in its place. Modern power penetrates everywhere, giving a specific name to every possible variant of human action so as to master the world and leave nothing unexamined, unknown, uncatalogued. The nineteenth century (with its supposedly repressed Victorians) began this "explosion of discourse," which in the field of sexuality produced extensive new vocabularies and categories for naming desires and actions that could then become subjected to medical, legal, and other institutional and state interventions.

Along with producing subjects, modern power produces sexual (and other) categories that structure the world in certain ways. Here *Discipline and Punish* and volume 1 of *The History of Sexuality* are in accord. (In the later two volumes of *The History of Sexuality*, partly in response to criticism, Foucault examines how selves might act to produce themselves.) Consider Foucault's comment (one of the founding remarks of queer theory) on the medical categorization of homosexuality in 1870: "Homosexuality appeared as one of the forms of sexuality when it was transposed from the practice of sodomy to a kind of interior androgyny, a hermaphrodism of the soul. The sodomite had been a temporary aberration; the homosexual now was a species." Power acts discursively to produce homosexuality when it separates out and labels as *homosexual* certain actions that had previously been included in the grab-bag term *sodomy* (which also included bestiality and some nonreproductive heterosexual acts). The new attempt to be more precise, more "scientific," in categorizing human sexual behavior itself requires that behavior to be scrutinized more carefully than ever before.

Foucault further argues that the way that the courts and sociologists treat criminals and the medical profession and psychologists view homosexuals indicates a dramatic shift in the very form of subjecthood. In modern society, actions begin to be taken as evidence of a deep-rooted and persistent identity. In the premodern world, in contrast, sodomy and other crimes were seen as temporary aberrations, single acts that carried no particular relation to the self who committed them; they certainly were not seen as demonstrating a sexual identity or a criminal nature. The label *sodomite* says nothing beyond pointing to the commission of particular acts. But the homosexual carries his homosexuality within himself at every moment; the act comes to determine identity. Foucault's argument is that through this connection of actions to "being," of what I do to what I am, modern power produces subjects who have identities, thereby enabling its grip on us. Subjects whose identities must be figured out through an interpretation of their actions become "both an object of analysis and a target of intervention."

Foucault is exposing—and questioning—our era's most fundamental assumptions about who and what individuals are. And he argues that these assumptions have been produced by and are the foundational principles of the "social sciences"—what the French call "the human sciences." It is no coincidence that the modern academic disciplines arise during the same period that sees the shift toward disciplinary power. The knowledge produced in psychology, sociology, anthropology, criminology, and medicine is itself an integral part of the discursive ordering and physical management wielded by modern power.

Power/knowledge is the term Foucault uses to indicate how the production of knowledge is wedded to productive power. Modern power requires increasingly narrow categories through which it analyzes, differentiates, identifies, and administers individuals. The human sciences not only provide tools for this sorting process but also legitimate the actions that follow it. The psychological exam, for example, tells us what needs to be done: is this murderer a criminal who must be sent to prison, or an insane person who must be sent to a hospital?

Clearly, power/knowledge undercuts any lofty humanistic narrative of "the life of the mind" or "the disinterested pursuit of knowledge." The intellectual comes to look like power's dupe, or perhaps a privileged insider to power's activities. The university, in particular, serves a dual function. As gatekeeper, it sorts students via grades, exams, course requirements, and so on, thereby limiting access to various cherished places in the social hierarchy, such as medical careers. At the same time the university undertakes funded research, thereby producing the knowledge through which populations are observed and managed.

Not surprisingly, Foucault's thoughts on the knowledge/power nexus have sparked some of the most intense criticisms of his work, and toward the end of his life he did soften some of his more extreme statements. The close of our selection from "Truth and Power" illustrates disturbing consequences that critics of Foucault's view have highlighted. At issue is the relation of knowledge and truth to political action. The modern world has repeatedly seen governments manipulate their populations by outright lies and by cover-ups of the truth. Eastern European dissidents against communist dictatorships and Americans protesting the war in Vietnam saw the strategy of exposing government lies as crucial. Foucault argues, however, that "truth" is *always* a part of a "regime." He uses the same logic that leads him to present the author as a "function" and to refute "the repressive hypothesis." As he says in our selection from *Discipline and Punish*, "there is no outside." Nothing—whether selves, desires, or truth—is external to the productive power/knowledge that creates the categories by which it is known. Thus, the truth to which dissidents appeal is no less a product of interested strategies—in this case, their own—than the truth spoken by the officials whom they oppose. Truths are not all born equal, because some discourses are more powerful than others. But Foucault does not recognize any component of truth separate from power. His position seems to reduce politics to a battle that can be waged only on the field of propaganda. Can I get the people to buy *my* "regime of truth" in place of the one that currently reigns?

Critics of Foucault have often focused on aspects of this lack of any "outside," as everything that might stand apart from power or discourse is swallowed up within them in his work. Disciplinary power is so all-pervasive and triumphant that meaningful resistance and independent agency appear impossible. Foucault insisted repeatedly that there was resistance everywhere throughout the world created by power, but by his own logic such resistance, like everything else, is an offshoot of power. As a result, many activities that may seem to oppose power are, a Foucauldian analysis shows, "complicitous" with it, reinforcing rather than contesting its reign. (Analyses of this sort, preoccupied with trying to differentiate the truly from the apparently oppositional, abound within New Historicism and cultural studies.) Foucault struggled to find ways to escape this compelling logic without returning to naive appeals to "truth" or "selves" that exist independently of the discursive and social networks in which they appear. His efforts in that direction remain fragmentary. Since his death, the ever-increasing pressure on individuals to fit in the bureaucratic slots of a "globalized" world of transnational corporations, international trade alliances and political organizations, and newly prominent nongovernmental organizations (such as the World Trade Organization) makes Foucault's account of a supervising, norm-enforcing, disciplinary power appear even more pertinent.

BIBLIOGRAPHY

Foucault's works are *Madness and Civilization* (1961; trans. 1965); *The Birth of the Clinic* (1963; trans. 1973); *Death and the Labyrinth: The World of Raymond Roussel* (1963; trans. 1986); *The Order of Things* (1966; trans. 1970); *The Archaeology of Knowledge* (1969; trans. 1972); *This Is Not a Pipe* (1973; trans. 1981); *Discipline and Punish: The Birth of the Prison* (1975; trans. 1977); and the three volumes of *The History of Sexuality: An Introduction* (1976; trans. 1978), *The Use of Pleasure* (1984; trans. 1985), and *The Care of the Self* (1984; trans. 1986). Essays and interviews are collected in *Language, Counter-Memory, and Practice: Selected Essays and Interviews*, edited by Daniel Bouchard (1977); *Power/Knowledge*, edited by Colin Gordon (1980); *Foucault Live: Interviews, 1966–1984*, edited by Sylvère Lotringer (1989); *Politics, Philosophy, and Culture: Interviews and Other Writings, 1977–1984*, edited by Lawrence Kritzman (1989); and a three-volume edition of work not published in earlier books, titled *The Essential Works of Michel Foucault, 1954–1984*, edited by Paul Rabinow (1997–99). Foucault also edited two books: *I, Pierre Rivière, Having Slaughtered My Mother, My Sister, and My Brother: A Case of Parricide in the Nineteenth Century* (1975; trans. 1975); and *Heculine Barbin: Being the Recently Discovered Memoirs of a Nineteenth-Century French Hermaphrodite* (1978; trans. 1980). Didier Eribon's sober and reliable biography, *Michel Foucault* (1989; trans. 1991), should be used to balance James Miller's lively and controversial biography *The Passion of Michel Foucault* (1993).

The critical commentary on Foucault is extensive. Barry Smart's *Michel Foucault* (1985) is the best short introduction; it can be supplemented with Gilles Deleuze's idiosyncratic but interesting *Foucault* (1986; trans. 1988). Hubert L. Dreyfus and Paul Rabinow's *Michel Foucault: Beyond Structuralism and Hermeneutics* (2d ed., 1983) is the best comprehensive overview. Jana Sawicki's *Disciplining Foucault: Feminism, Power, and the Body* (1991) is a very useful examination of feminism's mixed reactions to Foucault, while Simon During's *Foucault and Literature: Towards a Genealogy of Literature* (1992) provides a provocative account of the ramifications of Foucault's work for literary studies. One way to start studying Foucault and his impact is to read through the several excellent collections of essays on his work, including *Foucault: A Critical Reader*, edited by David C. Hoy (1986); *Feminism and Foucault: Reflections on Resistance*, edited by Irene Diamond and Lee Quinby (1988); *The Foucault Effect: Studies in Govermentality*, edited by Graham Burchell, Colin Gordon, and Peter Miller (1991); *The Cambridge Companion to Foucault*, edited by Gary Gutting (1994); *Foucault and the Writing of History*, edited by Jan Goldstein (1994); and the very comprehensive *Michel Foucault: Critical Assessments*, edited by Barry Smart (3 vols., 1994).

Michael Clark's *Michel Foucault: An Annotated Bibliography* (1982) is a model of its kind, while Joan Nordquist's *Michel Foucault: A Bibliography* (1986) and *Michel Foucault II* (1992) are more recent. The fairly extensive bibliography in *The Cambridge Companion to Foucault* is well arranged and easy to use.

What Is an Author?[1]

In proposing this slightly odd question, I am conscious of the need for an explanation. To this day, the "author" remains an open question both with respect to its general function within discourse and in my own writings; that is, this question permits me to return to certain aspects of my own work which now appear ill-advised and misleading. In this regard, I wish to propose a necessary criticism and reevaluation.

For instance, my objective in *The Order of Things*[2] had been to analyse verbal clusters as discursive layers which fall outside the familiar categories of a book, a work, or an author. But while I considered "natural history," the "analysis of wealth," and "political economy" in general terms, I neglected a similar analysis of the author and his works; it is perhaps due to this omission that I employed the names of authors throughout this book in a naive and often crude fashion. I spoke of Buffon, Cuvier, Ricardo,[3] and others as well, but failed to realize that I had allowed their names to function ambiguously. This has proved an embarrassment to me in that my oversight has served to raise two pertinent objections.

It was argued that I had not properly described Buffon or his work and that my handling of Marx[4] was pitifully inadequate in terms of the totality of his thought. Although these objections were obviously justified, they ignored the task I had set myself: I had no intention of describing Buffon or Marx or of reproducing their statements or implicit meanings, but, simply stated, I wanted to locate the rules that formed a certain number of concepts and theoretical relationships in their works. In addition, it was argued that I had created monstrous families by bringing together names as disparate as Buffon and Linnaeus or in placing Cuvier next to Darwin[5] in defiance of the most readily observable family resemblances and natural ties. This objection also seems inappropriate since I had never tried to establish a genealogical table of exceptional individuals, nor was I concerned in forming an intellectual daguerreotype of the scholar or naturalist of the seventeenth and eighteenth century. In fact, I had no intention of forming any family, whether holy or perverse. On the contrary, I wanted to determine—a much more modest task—the functional conditions of specific discursive practices.

Then why did I use the names of authors in *The Order of Things*? Why not avoid their use altogether, or, short of that, why not define the manner in which they were used? These questions appear fully justified and I have

1. Translated by Donald F. Bouchard and Sherry Simon.
2. Published in 1966 as *Les Mots et les choses*; in it, Foucault uncovered the epistemic assumptions of the "classical" (Enlightenment) and modern periods by examining the work of natural scientists, political economists, and linguists.
3. David Ricardo (1777–1823), English economist. Georges-Louis Leclerc, comte de Buffon (1707–1788), French naturalist. Georges Cuvier (1769–1832), French anatomist.
4. KARL MARX (1818–1883), German social, political, and economic philosopher.
5. Charles Darwin (1809–1882), English naturalist and theorist of evolution. Carolus Linnaeus: Carl von Linné (1707–1778), Swedish botanist who devised the modern scientific nomenclature of living things.

tried to gauge their implications and consequences in a book that will appear shortly.[6] These questions have determined my effort to situate comprehensive discursive units, such as "natural history" or "political economy," and to establish the methods and instruments for delimiting, analyzing, and describing these unities. Nevertheless, as a privileged moment of individualization in the history of ideas, knowledge, and literature, or in the history of philosophy and science, the question of the author demands a more direct response. Even now, when we study the history of a concept, a literary genre, or a branch of philosophy, these concerns assume a relatively weak and secondary position in relation to the solid and fundamental role of an author and his works.

For the purposes of this paper, I will set aside a sociohistorical analysis of the author as an individual and the numerous questions that deserve attention in this context: how the author was individualized in a culture such as ours; the status we have given the author, for instance, when we began our research into authenticity and attribution; the systems of valorization in which he was included; or the moment when the stories of heroes gave way to an author's biography; the conditions that fostered the formulation of the fundamental critical category of "the man and his work." For the time being, I wish to restrict myself to the singular relationship that holds between an author and a text, the manner in which a text apparently points to this figure who is outside and precedes it.

Beckett supplies a direction: "What matter who's speaking, someone said, what matter who's speaking."[7] In an indifference such as this we must recognize one of the fundamental ethical principles of contemporary writing. It is not simply "ethical" because it characterizes our way of speaking and writing, but because it stands as an immanent rule, endlessly adopted and yet never fully applied. As a principle, it dominates writing as an ongoing practice and slights our customary attention to the finished product. For the sake of illustration, we need only consider two of its major themes. First, the writing of our day has freed itself from the necessity of "expression"; it only refers to itself, yet it is not restricted to the confines of interiority. On the contrary, we recognize it in its exterior deployment. This reversal transforms writing into an interplay of signs, regulated less by the content it signifies than by the very nature of the signifier. Moreover, it implies an action that is always testing the limits of its regularity, transgressing and reversing an order that it accepts and manipulates. Writing unfolds like a game that inevitably moves beyond its own rules and finally leaves them behind. Thus, the essential basis of this writing is not the exalted emotions related to the act of composition or the insertion of a subject into language. Rather, it is primarily concerned with creating an opening where the writing subject endlessly disappears.

The second theme is even more familiar: it is the kinship between writing and death. This relationship inverts the age-old conception of Greek narrative or epic, which was designed to guarantee the immortality of a hero. The hero accepted an early death because his life, consecrated and magnified by death, passed into immortality; and the narrative redeemed his acceptance of death. In a different sense, Arabic stories, and *The Arabian Nights* in

6. *The Archaeology of Knowledge* (1969).
7. Samuel Beckett, *Texts for Nothing* (1974), p. 16 [translators' note]. Beckett (1906–1974), Irish-born French novelist and playwright.

particular, had as their motivation, their theme and pretext, this strategy for defeating death. Storytellers continued their narratives late into the night to forestall death and to delay the inevitable moment when everyone must fall silent. Scheherazade's story is a desperate inversion of murder; it is the effort, throughout all those nights, to exclude death from the circle of existence.[8] This conception of a spoken or written narrative as a protection against death has been transformed by our culture. Writing is now linked to sacrifice and to the sacrifice of life itself; it is a voluntary obliteration of the self that does not require representation in books because it takes place in the everyday existence of the writer. Where a work had the duty of creating immortality, it now attains the right to kill, to become the murderer of its author. Flaubert, Proust, and Kafka[9] are obvious examples of this reversal. In addition, we find the link between writing and death manifested in the total effacement of the individual characteristics of the writer; the quibbling and confrontations that a writer generates between himself and his text cancel out the signs of his particular individuality. If we wish to know the writer in our day, it will be through the singularity of his absence and in his link to death, which has transformed him into a victim of his own writing. While all of this is familiar in philosophy, as in literary criticism, I am not certain that the consequences derived from the disappearance or death of the author[1] have been fully explored or that the importance of this event has been appreciated. To be specific, it seems to me that the themes destined to replace the privileged position accorded the author have merely served to arrest the possibility of genuine change. Of these, I will examine two that seem particularly important.

To begin with, the thesis concerning a work. It has been understood that the task of criticism is not to reestablish the ties between an author and his work or to reconstitute an author's thought and experience through his works and, further, that criticism should concern itself with the structures of a work, its architectonic forms, which are studied for their intrinsic and internal relationships. Yet, what of a context that questions the concept of a work? What, in short, is the strange unit designated by the term, work? What is necessary to its composition, if a work is not something written by a person called an "author"? Difficulties arise on all sides if we raise the question in this way. If an individual is not an author, what are we to make of those things he has written or said, left among his papers or communicated to others? Is this not properly a work? What, for instance, were Sade's papers before he was consecrated as an author?[2] Little more, perhaps, than rolls of paper on which he endlessly unravelled his fantasies while in prison.

Assuming that we are dealing with an author, is everything he wrote and said, everything he left behind, to be included in his work? This problem is both theoretical and practical. If we wish to publish the complete works of Nietzsche,[3] for example, where do we draw the line? Certainly, everything

8. Scheherazade, narrator of *The Arabian Nights* (a collection of traditional tales from several Middle Eastern cultures, codified ca. 1450), tells her stories to avoid the fate of the king's previous brides: execution on the morning after he marries them.
9. Franz Kafka (1883–1924), Austrian novelist, who lived much of his life in Prague. Gustave Flaubert (1821–1880), and Marcel Proust (1871–1922), French novelists.

1. The phrase "death of the author" comes from the French literary critic ROLAND BARTHES (1915–1980).
2. The French author the marquis de Sade (1740–1814) began to write while in prison.
3. FRIEDRICH NIETZSCHE (1844–1900), the German philosopher, was insane the last ten years of his life and left many unpublished works, including wild jottings from his later years.

must be published, but can we agree on what "everything" means? We will, of course, include everything that Nietzsche himself published, along with the drafts of his works, his plans for aphorisms, his marginal notations and corrections. But what if, in a notebook filled with aphorisms, we find a reference, a reminder of an appointment, an address, or a laundry bill, should this be included in his works? Why not? These practical considerations are endless once we consider how a work can be extracted from the millions of traces left by an individual after his death. Plainly, we lack a theory to encompass the questions generated by a work and the empirical activity of those who naively undertake the publication of the complete works of an author often suffers from the absence of this framework. Yet more questions arise. Can we say that *The Arabian Nights*, and *Stromates* of Clement of Alexandria, or the *Lives* of Diogenes Laertes[4] constitute works? Such questions only begin to suggest the range of our difficulties, and, if some have found it convenient to bypass the individuality of the writer or his status as an author to concentrate on a work, they have failed to appreciate the equally problematic nature of the word "work" and the unity it designates.

Another thesis has detained us from taking full measure of the author's disappearance. It avoids confronting the specific event that makes it possible and, in subtle ways, continues to preserve the existence of the author. This is the notion of *écriture*.[5] Strictly speaking, it should allow us not only to circumvent references to an author, but to situate his recent absence. The conception of *écriture*, as currently employed, is concerned with neither the act of writing nor the indications, as symptoms or signs within a text, of an author's meaning; rather, it stands for a remarkably profound attempt to elaborate the conditions of any text, both the conditions of its spatial dispersion and its temporal deployment.

It appears, however, that this concept, as currently employed, has merely transposed the empirical characteristics of an author to a transcendental anonymity. The extremely visible signs of the author's empirical activity are effaced to allow the play, in parallel or opposition, of religious and critical modes of characterization. In granting a primordial status to writing, do we not, in effect, simply reinscribe in transcendental terms the theological affirmation of its sacred origin or a critical belief in its creative nature? To say that writing, in terms of the particular history it made possible, is subjected to forgetfulness and repression, is this not to reintroduce in transcendental terms the religious principle of hidden meanings (which require interpretation) and the critical assumption of implicit significations, silent purposes, and obscure contents (which give rise to commentary)?[6] Finally, is not the conception of writing as absence a transposition into transcendental terms of the religious belief in a fixed and continuous tradition or the aesthetic principle that proclaims the survival of the work as a kind of enigmatic supplement of the author beyond his own death?

This conception of *écriture* sustains the privileges of the author through

4. Greek scholar (ca. early 3d c. C.E.) whose *Lives* is a compilation of the lives and doctrines of the philosophers. Clement of Alexandria (ca. 150–ca. 215 C.E.), early church father and theologian; the *Stromates* (*Miscellanies*) is a collection of notes, full of digressions, on Christian philosophy.

5. Written language or writing (French). In poststructuralist thought, especially that of JACQUES DERRIDA (b. 1930), *écriture* designates that which is required for any particular speech act—whether spoken or written—to take place.

6. Here Foucault is criticizing the writings of Derrida.

the safeguard of the a priori;[7] the play of representations that formed a particular image of the author is extended within a gray neutrality. The disappearance of the author—since Mallarmé,[8] an event of our time—is held in check by the transcendental. Is it not necessary to draw a line between those who believe that we can continue to situate our present discontinuities within the historical and transcendental tradition of the nineteenth century and those who are making a great effort to liberate themselves, once and for all, from this conceptual framework?

It is obviously insufficient to repeat empty slogans: the author has disappeared; God and man died a common death. Rather, we should reexamine the empty space left by the author's disappearance; we should attentively observe, along its gaps and fault lines, its new demarcations, and the reapportionment of this void; we should await the fluid functions released by this disappearance. In this context we can briefly consider the problems that arise in the use of an author's name. What is the name of an author? How does it function? Far from offering a solution, I will attempt to indicate some of the difficulties related to these questions.

The name of an author poses all the problems related to the category of the proper name. (Here, I am referring to the work of John Searle,[9] among others.) Obviously not a pure and simple reference, the proper name (and the author's name as well) has other than indicative functions. It is more than a gesture, a finger pointed at someone; it is, to a certain extent, the equivalent of a description. When we say "Aristotle,"[1] we are using a word that means one or a series of definite descriptions of the type: "the author of the *Analytics*," or "the founder of ontology," and so forth. Furthermore, a proper name has other functions than that of signification: when we discover that Rimbaud[2] has not written *La Chasse spirituelle*, we cannot maintain that the meaning of the proper name or this author's name has been altered. The proper name and the name of an author oscillate between the poles of description and designation,[3] and, granting that they are linked to what they name, they are not totally determined either by their descriptive or designative functions. Yet—and it is here that the specific difficulties attending an author's name appear—the link between a proper name and the individual being named and the link between an author's name and that which it names are not isomorphous and do not function in the same way; and these differences require clarification.

To learn, for example, that Pierre Dupont[4] does not have blue eyes, does not live in Paris, and is not a doctor does not invalidate the fact that the name, Pierre Dupont, continues to refer to the same person; there has been no modification of the designation that links the name to the person. With

7. That is, that which is derived from self-evident propositions (vs. from experience).
8. STÉPHANE MALLARMÉ (1842–1898), French symbolist poet; he was interested in writing techniques that diminished the author's role in the creation of the poem.
9. See John Searle, *Speech Acts: An Essay in the Philosophy of Language* (1969), pp. 162–74 [translators' note]. Searle (b. 1932), American philosopher.
1. Greek philosopher (384–322 B.C.E; see above).
2. Arthur Rimbaud (1854–1891), French poet. The prose poem "La Chasse spirituelle" was published in 1949 as a recovered "lost" work by Rimbaud; its actual authors revealed the hoax shortly after publication.
3. In the philosophy of language, a *description* is a meaningful set of words that refers to a particular object. Hence, "the author of *Great Expectations*" describes "Charles Dickens." In contrast, the name "Charles Dickens" is a *designation* of the person who bears that name.
4. The French equivalent of "John Doe," a random designation of a living person.

the name of an author, however, the problems are far more complex. The disclosure that Shakespeare was not born in the house that tourists now visit would not modify the functioning of the author's name, but, if it were proved that he had not written the sonnets that we attribute to him, this would constitute a significant change and affect the manner in which the author's name functions. Moreover, if we establish that Shakespeare wrote Bacon's *Organon* and that the same author was responsible for both the works of Shakespeare and those of Bacon, we would have introduced a third type of alteration which completely modifies the functioning of the author's name.[5] Consequently, the name of an author is not precisely a proper name among others.

Many other factors sustain this paradoxical singularity of the name of an author. It is altogether different to maintain that Pierre Dupont does not exist and that Homer or Hermes Trismegistes[6] have never existed. While the first negation merely implies that there is no one by the name of Pierre Dupont, the second indicates that several individuals have been referred to by one name or that the real author possessed none of the traits traditionally associated with Homer or Hermes. Neither is it the same thing to say that Jacques Durand, not Pierre Dupont, is the real name of X and that Stendhal's name was Henri Beyle.[7] We could also examine the function and meaning of such statements as "Bourbaki is this or that person," and "Victor Eremita, Climacus, Anticlimacus, Frater Taciturnus, Constantin Constantius, all of these are Kierkegaard."[8]

These differences indicate that an author's name is not simply an element of speech (as a subject, a complement, or an element that could be replaced by a pronoun or other parts of speech). Its presence is functional in that it serves as a means of classification. A name can group together a number of texts and thus differentiate them from others. A name also establishes different forms of relationships among texts. Neither Hermes not Hippocrates existed in the sense that we can say Balzac[9] existed, but the fact that a number of texts were attached to a single name implies that relationships of homogeneity, filiation, reciprocal explanation, authentification, or of common utilization were established among them. Finally, the author's name characterizes a particular manner of existence of discourse. Discourse that possesses an author's name is not to be immediately consumed and forgotten; neither is it accorded the momentary attention given to ordinary, fleeting words. Rather, its status and its manner of reception are regulated by the culture in which it circulates.

We can conclude that, unlike a proper name, which moves from the interior of a discourse to the real person outside who produced it, the name of

5. Some people have argued that the plays of William Shakespeare (1564–1616) were actually written by the English philosopher Francis Bacon (1561–1626), whose *Organon* (1620) is often cited as the founding text of the "scientific method."

6. The god of letters, to whom 42 philosophico-religious works and books on alchemy and astrology, presumed to be the ancient wisdom of Egypt, were attributed. Homer is the traditional author of the *Iliad* and the *Odyssey* (ca. 8th c. B.C.E.); but the question of whether these two poems, originally transmitted orally, were the work of any single author remains open.

7. The real name of the French novelist (1783–1842) who wrote under the pen name Stendahl.

8. Victor Eremita and the other names listed here were all pseudonyms used by the Danish philosopher Søren Kierkegaard (1813–1855) at various times during his career. Nicolas Bourbaki, the allonym for a group of 20th-century algebraists.

9. Honoré de Balzac (1799–1850), French novelist. Hippocrates (469–399 B.C.E.), Greek physician usually considered the father of medicine; though it is unlikely that he wrote any of the books attributed to him, Hippocrates did exist.

the author remains at the contours of texts—separating one from the other, defining their form, and characterizing their mode of existence. It points to the existence of certain groups of discourse and refers to the status of this discourse within a society and culture. The author's name is not a function of a man's civil status, nor is it fictional; it is situated in the breach, among the discontinuities, which gives rise to new groups of discourse and their singular mode of existence. Consequently, we can say that in our culture, the name of an author is a variable that accompanies only certain texts to the exclusion of others: a private letter may have a signatory, but it does not have an author; a contract can have an underwriter, but not an author; and, similarly, an anonymous poster attached to a wall may have a writer, but he cannot be an author. In this sense, the function of an author is to characterize the existence, circulation, and operation of certain discourses within a society.

In dealing with the "author" as a function of discourse, we must consider the characteristics of a discourse that support this use and determine its difference from other discourses. If we limit our remarks to only those books or texts with authors, we can isolate four different features.

First, they are objects of appropriation; the form of property they have become is of a particular type whose legal codification was accomplished some years ago. It is important to notice, as well, that its status as property is historically secondary to the penal code controlling its appropriation. Speeches and books were assigned real authors, other than mythical or important religious figures, only when the author became subject to punishment and to the extent that his discourse was considered transgressive. In our culture—undoubtedly in others as well—discourse was not originally a thing, a product, or a possession, but an action situated in a bipolar field of sacred and profane, lawful and unlawful, religious and blasphemous. It was a gesture charged with risks long before it became a possession caught in a circuit of property values. But it was at the moment when a system of ownership and strict copyright rules were established (toward the end of the eighteenth and beginning of the nineteenth century) that the transgressive properties always intrinsic to the act of writing became the forceful imperative of literature. It is as if the author, at the moment he was accepted into the social order of property which governs our culture, was compensating for his new status by reviving the older bipolar field of discourse in a systematic practice of transgression and by restoring the danger of writing which, on another side, had been conferred the benefits of property.

Secondly, the "author-function" is not universal or constant in all discourse. Even within our civilization, the same types of texts have not always required authors; there was a time when those texts which we now call "literary" (stories, folk tales, epics, and tragedies) were accepted, circulated, and valorized without any question about the identity of their author. Their anonymity was ignored because their real or supposed age was a sufficient guarantee of their authenticity. Texts, however, that we now call "scientific" (dealing with cosmology and the heavens, medicine or illness, the natural sciences or geography) were only considered truthful during the Middle Ages if the name of the author was indicated. Statements on the order of "Hippocrates said . . ." or "Pliny[1] tells us that . . ." were not merely formulas for an argument based on authority; they marked a proven discourse. In the seventeenth and eighteenth centuries, a totally new conception was developed when scientific texts were accepted on their own merits and positioned within an anonymous and coherent conceptual system of established truths and methods of verification. Authentification no longer required reference to the individual who had produced them; the role of the author disappeared as an index of truthfulness and, where it remained as an inventor's name, it was merely to denote a specific theorem or proposition, a strange effect, a property, a body, a group of elements, or pathological syndrome.

At the same time, however, "literary" discourse was acceptable only if it carried an author's name; every text of poetry or fiction was obliged to state its author and the date, place, and circumstance of its writing. The meaning and value attributed to the text depended on this information. If by accident or design a text was presented anonymously, every effort was made to locate its author. Literary anonymity was of interest only as a puzzle to be solved as, in our day, literary works are totally dominated by the sovereignty of the author. (Undoubtedly, these remarks are far too categorical. Criticism has been concerned for some time now with aspects of a text not fully dependent on the notion of an individual creator; studies of genre or the analysis of recurring textual motifs and their variations from a norm other than the author. Furthermore, where in mathematics the author has become little more than a handy reference for a particular theorem or group of propositions, the reference to an author in biology and medicine, or to the date of his research has a substantially different bearing. This latter reference, more than simply indicating the source of information, attests to the "reliability" of the evidence, since it entails an appreciation of the techniques and experimental materials available at a given time and in a particular laboratory.)

The third point concerning this "author-function" is that it is not formed spontaneously through the simple attribution of a discourse to an individual. It results from a complex operation whose purpose is to construct the rational entity we call an author. Undoubtedly, this construction is assigned a "realistic" dimension as we speak of an individual's "profundity" or "creative" power, his intentions or the original inspiration manifested in writing. Nevertheless, these aspects of an individual, which we designate as an author (or which comprise an individual as an author), are projections, in terms always more or less psychological, of our way of handling texts: in the comparisons we make, the traits we extract as pertinent, the continuities we assign, or the exclusions we practice. In addition, all these operations vary according to the period and the form of discourse concerned. A "philosopher" and a "poet" are not constructed in the same manner; and the author of an eighteenth-century novel was formed differently from the modern novelist. There are, nevertheless, transhistorical constants in the rules that govern the construction of an author.

In literary criticism, for example, the traditional methods for defining an author—or, rather, for determining the configuration of the author from existing texts—derive in large part from those used in the Christian tradition

1. Roman writer (23/24–79 C.E.); only his 37-book *Natural History* survives.

to authenticate (or to reject) the particular texts in its possession. Modern criticism, in its desire to "recover" the author from a work, employs devices strongly reminiscent of Christian exegesis when it wished to prove the value of a text by ascertaining the holiness of its author. In *De Viris Illustribus*, Saint Jerome[2] maintains that homonymy is not proof of the common authorship of several works, since many individuals could have the same name or someone could have perversely appropriated another's name. The name, as an individual mark, is not sufficient as it relates to a textual tradition. How, then, can several texts be attributed to an individual author? What norms, related to the function of the author, will disclose the involvement of several authors? According to Saint Jerome, there are four criteria: the texts that must be eliminated from the list of works attributed to a single author are those inferior to the others (thus, the author is defined as a standard level of quality); those whose ideas conflict with the doctrine expressed in the others (here the author is defined as a certain field of conceptual or theoretical coherence); those written in a different style and containing words and phrases not ordinarily found in the other works (the author is seen as a stylistic uniformity); and those referring to events or historical figures subsequent to the death of the author (the author is thus a definite historical figure in which a series of events converge). Although modern criticism does not appear to have these same suspicions concerning authentication, its strategies for defining the author present striking similarities. The author explains the presence of certain events within a text, as well as their transformations, distortions, and their various modifications (and this through an author's biography or by reference to his particular point of view, in the analysis of his social preferences and his position within a class or by delineating his fundamental objectives). The author also constitutes a principle of unity in writing where any unevenness of production is ascribed to changes caused by evolution, maturation, or outside influence. In addition, the author serves to neutralize the contradictions that are found in a series of texts. Governing this function is the belief that there must be—at a particular level of an author's thought, of his conscious or unconscious desire—a point where contradictions are resolved, where the incompatible elements can be shown to relate to one another or to cohere around a fundamental and originating contradiction. Finally, the author is a particular source of expression who, in more or less finished forms, is manifested equally well, and with similar validity, in a text, in letters, fragments, drafts, and so forth. Thus, even while Saint Jerome's four principles of authenticity might seem largely inadequate to modern critics, they, nevertheless, define the critical modalities now used to display the function of the author.

However, it would be false to consider the function of the author as a pure and simple reconstruction after the fact of a text given as passive material, since a text always bears a number of signs that refer to the author. Well known to grammarians, these textual signs are personal pronouns, adverbs of time and place, and the conjugation of verbs. But it is important to note that these elements have a different bearing on texts with an author and on

2. Church father and scholar (ca. 340–420), the first to translate the Bible into Latin. *De Viris Illustribus* (392–93, *Of Illustrious Men*) is a collection of 130 biographies of Christian writers.

those without one. In the latter, these "shifters"[3] refer to a real speaker and to an actual deictic situation, with certain exceptions such as the case of indirect speech in the first person. When discourse is linked to an author, however, the role of "shifters" is more complex and variable. It is well known that in a novel narrated in the first person, neither the first person pronoun, the present indicative tense, nor, for that matter, its signs of localization refer directly to the writer, either to the time when he wrote, or to the specific act of writing; rather, they stand for a "second self" whose similarity to the author is never fixed and undergoes considerable alteration within the course of a single book. It would be as false to seek the author in relation to the actual writer as to the fictional narrator; the "author-function" arises out of their scission—in the division and distance of the two. One might object that this phenomenon only applies to novels or poetry, to a context of "quasi-discourse," but, in fact, all discourse that supports this "author-function" is characterized by this plurality of egos. In a mathematical treatise, the ego who indicates the circumstances of composition in the preface is not identical, either in terms of his position or his function, to the "I" who concludes a demonstration within the body of the text. The former implies a unique individual who, at a given time and place, succeeded in completing a project, whereas the latter indicates an instance and plan of demonstration that anyone could perform provided the same set of axioms, preliminary operations, and an identical set of symbols were used. It is also possible to locate a third ego: one who speaks of the goals of his investigation, the obstacles encountered, its results, and the problems yet to be solved and this "I" would function in a field of existing of future mathematical discourses. We are not dealing with a system of dependencies where a first and essential use of the "I" is reduplicated, as a kind of fiction, by the other two. On the contrary, the "author-function" in such discourses operates so as to effect the simultaneous dispersion of the three egos.

Further elaboration would, of course, disclose other characteristics of the "author-function," but I have limited myself to the four that seemed the most obvious and important. They can be summarized in the following manner: the "author-function" is tied to the legal and institutional systems that circumscribe, determine, and articulate the realm of discourses; it does not operate in a uniform manner in all discourses, at all times, and in any given culture; it is not defined by the spontaneous attribution of a text to its creator, but through a series of precise and complex procedures; it does not refer, purely and simply, to an actual individual insofar as it simultaneously gives rise to a variety of egos and to a series of subjective positions that individuals of any class may come to occupy.

I am aware that until now I have kept my subject within unjustifiable limits; I should also have spoken of the "author-function" in painting, music, technical fields, and so forth. Admitting that my analysis is restricted to the domain of discourse, it seems that I have given the term "author" an excessively narrow meaning. I have discussed the author only in the limited sense of a person to whom the production of a text, a book, or a work can be legitimately attributed. However, it is obvious that even within the realm of

3. Words whose referent changes according to the context in which they specify a person or thing (pronouns), place (adverbs), or time (adverbs, verb tense)—that is, according to the "deictic situation."

discourse a person can be the author of much more than a book—of a theory, for instance, of a tradition or a discipline within which new books and authors can proliferate. For convenience, we could say that such authors occupy a "transdiscursive" position.

Homer, Aristotle,[4] and the Church Fathers played this role, as did the first mathematicians and the originators of the Hippocratic tradition. This type of author is surely as old as our civilization. But I believe that the nineteenth century in Europe produced a singular type of author who should not be confused with "great" literary authors, or the authors of canonical religious texts, and the founders of sciences. Somewhat arbitrarily, we might call them "initiators of discursive practices."

The distinctive contribution of these authors is that they produced not only their own work, but the possibility and the rules of formation of other texts. In this sense, their role differs entirely from that of a novelist, for example, who is basically never more than the author of his own text. Freud[5] is not simply the author of *The Interpretation of Dreams* or of *Wit and its Relation to the Unconscious* and Marx is not simply the author of the *Communist Manifesto* or *Capital*: they both established the endless possibility of discourse. Obviously, an easy objection can be made. The author of a novel may be responsible for more than his own text; if he acquires some "importance" in the literary world, his influence can have significant ramifications. To take a very simple example, one could say that Ann Radcliffe[6] did not simply write *The Mysteries of Udolpho* and a few other novels, but also made possible the appearance of Gothic romances at the beginning of the nineteenth century. To this extent, her function as an author exceeds the limits of her work. However, this objection can be answered by the fact that the possibilities disclosed by the initiators of discursive practices (using the examples of Marx and Freud, whom I believe to be the first and the most important) are significantly different from those suggested by novelists. The novels of Ann Radcliffe put into circulation a certain number of resemblances and analogies patterned on her work—various characteristic signs, figures, relationships, and structures that could be integrated into other books. In short, to say that Ann Radcliffe created the Gothic Romance means that there are certain elements common to her works and to the nineteenth-century Gothic romance: the heroine ruined by her own innocence, the secret fortress that functions as a counter-city, the outlaw-hero who swears revenge on the world that has cursed him, etc. On the other hand, Marx and Freud, as "initiators of discursive practices," not only made possible a certain number of analogies that could be adopted by future texts, but, as importantly, they also made possible a certain number of differences. They cleared a space for the introduction of elements other than their own, which, nevertheless, remain within the field of discourse they initiated. In saying that Freud founded psychoanalysis, we do not simply mean that the concept of libido or the techniques of dream analysis reappear in the writings of Karl Abraham or Melanie Klein,[7] but that he made possible a certain number of

4. Aristotle's encyclopedic writings enormously influenced medieval philosophy and science.
5. SIGMUND FREUD (1856–1939), Austrian founder of psychoanalysis.
6. English novelist (1764–1823); her *Mysteries of Udolpho* (1791) was extremely popular.
7. Austrian-born English psychoanalyst (1882–1960). Abraham (1877–1925), German psychoanalyst.

differences with respect to his books, concepts, and hypotheses, which all arise out of psychoanalytic discourse.

Is this not the case, however, with the founder of any new science or of any author who successfully transforms an existing science? After all, Galileo[8] is indirectly responsible for the texts of those who mechanically applied the laws he formulated, in addition to having paved the way for the production of statements far different from his own. If Cuvier is the founder of biology and Saussure[9] of linguistics, it is not because they were imitated or that an organic concept or a theory of the sign was uncritically integrated into new texts, but because Cuvier, to a certain extent, made possible a theory of evolution diametrically opposed to his own system and because Saussure made possible a generative grammar radically different from his own structural analysis. Superficially, then, the initiation of discursive practices appears similar to the founding of any scientific endeavor, but I believe there is a fundamental difference.

In a scientific program, the founding act is on an equal footing with its future transformations: it is merely one among the many modifications that it makes possible. This interdependence can take several forms. In the future development of a science, the founding act may appear as little more than a single instance of a more general phenomenon that has been discovered. It might be questioned, in retrospect, for being too intuitive or empirical and submitted to the rigors of new theoretical operations in order to situate it in a formal domain. Finally, it might be thought a hasty generalization whose validity should be restricted. In other words, the founding act of a science can always be rechanneled through the machinery of transformations it has instituted.

On the other hand, the initiation of a discursive practice is heterogeneous to its ulterior transformations. To extend psychoanalytic practice, as initiated by Freud, is not to presume a formal generality that was not claimed at the outset; it is to explore a number of possible applications. To limit it is to isolate in the original texts a small set of propositions or statements that are recognized as having an inaugurative value and that mark other Freudian concepts or theories as derivative. Finally, there are no "false" statements in the work of these initiators; those statements considered inessential or "prehistoric," in that they are associated with another discourse, are simply neglected in favor of the more pertinent aspects of the work. The initiation of a discursive practice, unlike the founding of a science, overshadows and is necessarily detached from its later developments and transformations. As a consequence, we define the theoretical validity of a statement with respect to the work of the initiator, where as in the case of Galileo or Newton,[1] it is based on the structural and intrinsic norms established in cosmology or physics. Stated schematically, the work of these initiators is not situated in relation to a science or in the space it defines; rather, it is science or discursive practice that relate to their works as the primary points of reference.

In keeping with this distinction, we can understand why it is inevitable that practitioners of such discourses must "return to the origin." Here, as well, it is necessary to distinguish a "return" from scientific "rediscoveries"

8. Galileo Galilei (1564–1642), Italian astronomer and physicist.
9. FERDINAND DE SAUSSURE (1857–1913), Swiss linguist.
1. Sir Isaac Newton (1642–1727), English physicist and mathematician.

or "reactivations." "Rediscoveries" are the effects of analogy or isomorphism with current forms of knowledge that allow the perception of forgotten or obscured figures. For instance, Chomsky in his book on Cartesian grammar[2] "rediscovered" a form of knowledge that had been in use from Cordemoy to Humboldt.[3] It could only be understood from the perspective of generative grammar because this later manifestation held the key to its construction: in effect, a retrospective codification of an historical position. "Reactivation" refers to something quite different: the insertion of discourse into totally new domains of generalization, practice, and transformations. The history of mathematics abounds in examples of this phenomenon as the work of Michel Serres on mathematical anamnesis shows.[4]

The phrase, "return to," designates a movement with its proper specificity, which characterizes the initiation of discursive practices. If we return, it is because of a basic and constructive omission, an omission that is not the result of accident or incomprehension. In effect, the act of initiation is such, in its essence, that it is inevitably subjected to its own distortions; that which displays this act and derives from it is, at the same time, the root of its divergences and travesties. This nonaccidental omission must be regulated by precise operations that can be situated, analysed, and reduced in a return to the act of initiation. The barrier imposed by omission was not added from the outside; it arises from the discursive practice in question, which gives it its law. Both the cause of the barrier and the means for its removal, this omission—also responsible for the obstacles that prevent returning to the act of initiation—can only be resolved by a return. In addition, it is always a return to a text in itself, specifically, to a primary and unadorned text with particular attention to those things registered in the interstices of the text, its gaps and absences. We return to those empty spaces that have been masked by omission or concealed in a false and misleading plenitude. In these rediscoveries of an essential lack, we find the oscillation of two characteristic responses: "This point was made—you can't help seeing it if you know how to read"; or, inversely, "No, that point is not made in any of the printed words in the text, but it is expressed through the words, in their relationships and in the distance that separates them." It follows naturally that this return, which is a part of the discursive mechanism, constantly introduces modifications that would come to fix itself upon the primary discursivity and redouble it in the form of an ornament which, after all, is not essential. Rather, it is an effective and necessary means of transforming discursive practice. A study of Galileo's works could alter our knowledge of the history, but not the science, of mechanics; whereas, a re-examination of the books of Freud or Marx can transform our understanding of psychoanalysis or Marxism.

A last feature of these returns is that they tend to reinforce the enigmatic link between an author and his works. A text has an inaugurative value precisely because it is the work of a particular author, and our returns are conditioned by this knowledge. The rediscovery of an unknown text by Newton or Cantor[5] will not modify classical cosmology or group theory; at most, it

2. Noam Chomsky, *Cartesian Linguistics* (1966) [translators' note]. Chomsky (b. 1928), American linguist.

3. Karl Wilhelm von Humboldt (1767–1835), German statesman and philologist. Geraud de Cordemoy (d. 1684), French author of *A Philosophical Discourse Concerning Speech* (1668).

4. Michel Serres, *La Communication: Hermes I* (1968), pp. 78–112 [translators' note].

5. Georg Cantor (1845–1918), Russian-born German mathematician.

will change our appreciation of their historical genesis. Bringing to light, however, *An Outline of Psychoanalysis*, to the extent that we recognize it as a book by Freud, can transform not only our historical knowledge, but the field of psychoanalytic theory—if only through a shift of accent or of the center of gravity. These returns, an important component of discursive practices, form a relationship between "fundamental" and mediate authors, which is not identical to that which links an ordinary text to its immediate author.

These remarks concerning the initiation of discursive practices have been extremely schematic, especially with regard to the opposition I have tried to trace between this initiation and the founding of sciences. The distinction between the two is not readily discernible; moreover, there is no proof that the two procedures are mutually exclusive. My only purpose in setting up this opposition, however, was to show that the "author-function," sufficiently complex at the level of a book or a series of texts that bear a definite signature, has other determining factors when analysed in terms of larger entities—groups of works or entire disciplines.

Unfortunately, there is a decided absence of positive propositions in this essay, as it applies to analytic procedures or directions for future research, but I ought at least to give the reasons why I attach such importance to a continuation of this work. Developing a similar analysis could provide the basis for a typology of discourse. A typology of this sort cannot be adequately understood in relation to the grammatical features, formal structures, and objects of discourse, because there undoubtedly exist specific discursive properties or relationships that are irreducible to the rules of grammar and logic and to the laws that govern objects. These properties require investigation if we hope to distinguish the larger categories of discourse. The different forms of relationships (or nonrelationships) that an author can assume are evidently one of these discursive properties.

This form of investigation might also permit the introduction of an historical analysis of discourse. Perhaps the time has come to study not only the expressive value and formal transformations of discourse, but its mode of existence: the modifications and variations, within any culture, of modes of circulation, valorization, attribution, and appropriation. Partially at the expense of themes and concepts that an author places in his work, the "author-function" could also reveal the manner in which discourse is articulated on the basis of social relationships.

Is it not possible to reexamine, as a legitimate extension of this kind of analysis, the privileges of the subject? Clearly, in undertaking an internal and architectonic analysis of a work (whether it be a literary text, a philosophical system, or a scientific work) and in delimiting psychological and biographical references, suspicions arise concerning the absolute nature and creative role of the subject. But the subject should not be entirely abandoned. It should be reconsidered, not to restore the theme of an originating subject, but to seize its functions, its intervention in discourse, and its system of dependencies. We should suspend the typical questions: how does a free subject penetrate the density of things and endow them with meaning; how does it accomplish its design by animating the rules of discourse from within? Rather, we should ask: under what conditions and through what forms can an entity like the subject appear in the order of discourse; what position does it occupy; what functions does it exhibit; and what rules does it follow in each type of discourse? In short, the subject (and its substitutes) must be stripped of its creative role and analysed as a complex and variable function of discourse.

The author—or what I have called the "author-function"—is undoubtedly only one of the possible specifications of the subject and, considering past historical transformations, it appears that the form, the complexity, and even the existence of this function are far from immutable. We can easily imagine a culture where discourse would circulate without any need for an author. Discourses, whatever their status, form, or value, and regardless of our manner of handling them, would unfold in a pervasive anonymity. No longer the tiresome repetitions:

"Who is the real author?"
"Have we proof of his authenticity and originality?"
"What has he revealed of his most profound self in his language?"

New questions will be heard:

"What are the modes of existence of this discourse?"
"Where does it come from; how is it circulated; who controls it?"
"What placements are determined for possible subjects?"
"Who can fulfill these diverse functions of the subject?"

Behind all these questions we would hear little more than the murmur of indifference:

"What matter who's speaking?"

1969

From Discipline and Punish: The Birth of the Prison[1]

The Carceral

Were I to fix the date of completion of the carceral[2] system, I would choose not 1810 and the penal code, nor even 1844, when the law laying down the principle of cellular internment was passed; I might not even choose 1838, when books on prison reform by Charles Lucas, Moreau-Christophe and Faucher were published.[3] The date I would choose would be 22 January 1840, the date of the official opening of Mettray.[4] Or better still, perhaps, that glorious day, unremarked and unrecorded, when a child in Mettray remarked as he lay dying: 'What a pity I left the colony so soon'.[5] This marked the death of the first penitentiary saint. Many of the blessed no doubt went to join him, if the former inmates of the penal colonies are to be believed when, in singing the praises of the new punitive policies of the body, they remarked: 'We preferred the blows, but the cell suits us better'.

1. Translated by Alan Sheridan.
2. Related to the act of incarceration and to institutions that discipline the body, especially prisons.
3. Charles Lucas, *De la réforme des prisons* (1836); L. Moreau-Christophe, *De la mortalité et la folie dans le régime pénitentiaire* (1839); L. Faucher, *De la réforme des prisons* (1838) [Foucault's note].
4. French prison farm for juvenile criminals founded in 1840; it was widely imitated throughout Europe as a model of modern disciplinary techniques.
5. E. Ducpétiaux, *De la condition physique et morale des jeunes ouvriers* (1852), p. 383 [Foucault's note].

Why Mettray? Because it is the disciplinary form at its most extreme, the model in which are concentrated all the coercive technologies of behaviour. In it were to be found 'cloister, prison, school, regiment'. The small, highly hierarchized groups, into which the inmates were divided, followed simultaneously five models: that of the family (each group was a 'family' composed of 'brothers' and two 'elder brothers'); that of the army (each family, commanded by a head, was divided into two sections, each of which had a second in command; each inmate had a number and was taught basic military exercises; there was a cleanliness inspection every day, an inspection of clothing every week; a roll-call was taken three times a day); that of the workshop, with supervisors and foremen, who were responsible for the regularity of the work and for the apprenticeship of the younger inmates; that of the school (an hour or an hour and a half of lessons every day; the teaching was given by the instructor and by the deputy-heads); lastly, the judicial model (each day 'justice' was meted out in the parlour: 'The least act of disobedience is punished and the best way of avoiding serious offences is to punish the most minor offences very severely: at Mettray, a useless word is punishable'; the principal punishment inflicted was confinement to one's cell; for 'isolation is the best means of acting on the moral nature of children; it is there above all that the voice of religion, even if it has never spoken to their hearts, recovers all its emotional power'[6]); the entire parapenal[7] institution, which is created in order not to be a prison, culminates in the cell, on the walls of which are written in black letters: 'God sees you'.

This superimposition of different models makes it possible to indicate, in its specific features, the function of 'training'. The chiefs and their deputies at Mettray had to be not exactly judges, or teachers, or foremen, or non-commissioned officers, or 'parents', but something of all these things in a quite specific mode of intervention. They were in a sense technicians of behaviour: engineers of conduct, orthopaedists[8] of individuality. Their task was to produce bodies that were both docile and capable; they supervised the nine or ten working hours of every day (whether in a workshop or in the fields); they directed the orderly movements of groups of inmates, physical exercises, military exercises, rising in the morning, going to bed at night, walks to the accompaniment of bugle and whistle; they taught gymnastics;[9] they checked cleanliness, supervised bathing. Training was accompanied by permanent observation; a body of knowledge was being constantly built up from the everyday behaviour of the inmates; it was organized as an instrument of perpetual assessment: 'On entering the colony, the child is subjected to a sort of interrogation as to his origins, the position of his family, the offence for which he was brought before the courts and all the other offences that make up his short and often very sad existence. This information is written down on a board on which everything concerning each inmate is noted in turn, his stay at the colony and the place to which he is sent when he leaves'.[1] The modelling of the body produces a knowledge of the individual, the apprenticeship of the techniques induces modes of behaviour and the acquisition of skills is inextricably linked with the establishment of power

6. Ibid., p. 377 [Foucault's note].
7. Closely related to the penal.
8. Those who correct, or set straight, children.
9. "Anything that helps to tire the body helps to expel bad thoughts; so care is taken that games consist of violent exercise. At night, they fall asleep the moment they touch the pillow" (Ducpétiaux, *De la condition physique et morale*, pp. 375–76) [Foucault's note].
1. E. Ducpétiaux, *Des colonies agricoles* (1851), p. 61 [Foucault's note].

relations; strong, skilled agricultural workers are produced; in this very work, provided it is technically supervised, submissive subjects are produced and a dependable body of knowledge built up about them. This disciplinary technique exercised upon the body had a double effect: a 'soul' to be known and a subjection to be maintained. One result vindicated this work of training: in 1848, at a moment when 'the fever of revolution fired the imagination of all, when the schools at Angers, La Flèche, Alfort, even the boarding schools, rose up in rebellion, the inmates of Mettray were calmer than ever'.[2]

Where Mettray was especially exemplary was in the specificity that it recognized in this operation of training. It was related to other forms of supervision, on which it was based: medicine, general education, religious direction. But it cannot be identified absolutely with them. Nor with administration in the strict sense. Heads or deputy-heads of 'families', monitors and foremen, had to live in close proximity to the inmates; their clothes were 'almost as humble' as those of the inmates themselves; they practically never left their side, observing them day and night; they constituted among them a network of permanent observation. And, in order to train them themselves, a specialized school had been organized in the colony. The essential element of its programme was to subject the future cadres to the same apprenticeships and to the same coercions as the inmates themselves: they were 'subjected as pupils to the discipline that, later, as instructors, they would themselves impose'. They were taught the art of power relations. It was the first training college in pure discipline: the 'penitentiary' was not simply a project that sought its justification in 'humanity' or its foundations in a 'science', but a technique that was learnt, transmitted and which obeyed general norms. The practice that normalized by compulsion the conduct of the undisciplined or dangerous could, in turn, by technical elaboration and rational reflection, be 'normalized'. The disciplinary technique became a 'discipline' which also had its school.

It so happens that historians of the human sciences date the birth of scientific psychology at this time: during these same years, it seems, Weber[3] was manipulating his little compass for the measurement of sensations. What took place at Mettray (and in other European countries sooner or later) was obviously of a quite different order. It was the emergence or rather the institutional specification, the baptism as it were, of a new type of supervision—both knowledge and power—over individuals who resisted disciplinary normalization. And yet, in the formation and growth of psychology, the appearance of these professionals of discipline, normality and subjection surely marks the beginning of a new stage. It will be said that the quantitative assessment of sensorial responses could at least derive authority from the prestige of the emerging science of physiology and that for this alone it deserves to feature in the history of the sciences. But the supervision of normality was firmly encased in a medicine or a psychiatry that provided it with a sort of 'scientificity'; it was supported by a judicial apparatus which, directly or indirectly, gave it legal justification. Thus, in the shelter of these two considerable protectors, and, indeed, acting as a link between them, or

2. G. Ferrus, *Des prisonniers* (1850) [Foucault's note]. The Revolution of 1848, against Louis-Philippe, established the short-lived Second Republic (1848–52).

3. Ernst Weber (1795–1878), German physiologist who devised a method of measuring the sensitivity of the skin.

a place of exchange, a carefully worked out technique for the supervision of norms has continued to develop right up to the present day. The specific, institutional supports of these methods have proliferated since the founding of the small school at Mettray; their apparatuses have increased in quantity and scope; their auxiliary services have increased, with hospitals, schools, public administrations and private enterprises; their agents have proliferated in number, in power, in technical qualification; the technicians of indiscipline have founded a family. In the normalization of the power of normalization, in the arrangement of a power-knowledge over individuals, Mettray and its school marked a new era.

But why choose this moment as the point of emergence of the formation of an art of punishing that is still more or less our own? Precisely because this choice is somewhat 'unjust'. Because it situates the 'end' of the process in the lower reaches of criminal law. Because Mettray was a prison, but not entirely; a prison in that it contained young delinquents condemned by the courts; and yet something else, too, because it also contained minors who had been charged, but acquitted under article 66 of the code,[4] and boarders held, as in the eighteenth century, as an alternative to paternal correction. Mettray, a punitive model, is at the limit of strict penality. It was the most famous of a whole series of institutions which, well beyond the frontiers of criminal law, constituted what one might call the carceral archipelago.[5]

Yet the general principles, the great codes and subsequent legislation were quite clear on the matter: no imprisonment 'outside the law', no detention that had not been decided by a qualified judicial institution, no more of those arbitrary and yet widespread confinements. Yet the very principle of extra-penal incarceration was in fact never abandoned. (A whole study remains to be done of the debates that took place during the Revolution[6] concerning family courts, paternal correction and the right of parents to lock up their children.) And, if the apparatus of the great classical form of confinement was partly (and only partly) dismantled, it was very soon reactivated, re-arranged, developed in certain directions. But what is still more important is that it was homogenized, through the mediation of the prison, on the one hand with legal punishments and, on the other, with disciplinary mechanisms. The frontiers between confinement, judicial punishment and institutions of discipline, which were already blurred in the classical age,[7] tended to disappear and to constitute a great carceral continuum that diffused penitentiary techniques into the most innocent disciplines, transmitting disciplinary norms into the very heart of the penal system and placing over the slightest illegality, the smallest irregularity, deviation or anomaly, the threat of delinquency. A subtle, graduated carceral net, with compact institutions, but also separate and diffused methods, assumed responsibility for the arbitrary, widespread, badly integrated confinement of the classical age.

I shall not attempt here to reconstitute the whole network that formed first the immediate surroundings of the prison, then spread farther and far-

4. An article in the French Penal Code that condemned children for acting "sans discernement" (without discretion).
5. An allusion to *The Gulag Archipelago* (1973–75), by the Russian novelist Aleksandr Solzhenitsyn, which dramatized for the West the extensive chain of prison camps in the Soviet Union between 1918 and 1956.
6. That is, the French Revolution of 1789.
7. Foucault's term for (roughly) the period from 1650 to 1789.

ther outwards. However, a few references and dates should give some idea of the breadth and precocity of the phenomenon.

There were agricultural sections in the *maisons centrales*[8] (the first example of which was Gaillon in 1824, followed later by Fontevrault, Les Douaires, Le Boulard); there were colonies for poor, abandoned vagrant children (Petit-Bourg[9] in 1840, Ostwald in 1842); there were almshouses for young female offenders who 'recoiled before the idea of entering a life of disorder', for 'poor innocent girls whose mothers' immorality has exposed to precocious perversity', or for poor girls found on the doorsteps of hospitals and lodging houses. There were penal colonies envisaged by the law of 1850: minors, acquitted or condemned, were to be sent to these colonies and 'brought up in common, under strict discipline, and trained in agricultural work and in the principal industries related to it'; later, they were to be joined by minors sentenced to hard labour for life and 'vicious and insubordinate wards of the Public Assistance'.[1] And, moving still farther away from penality in the strict sense, the carceral circles widen and the form of the prison slowly diminishes and finally disappears altogether: the institutions for abandoned or indigent children, the orphanages (like Neuhof or Mesnil-Firmin), the establishments for apprentices (like the Bethléem de Reims or the Maison de Nancy); still farther away the factory-convents, such as La Sauvagère, Tarare and Jujurieu (where the girl workers entered about the age of thirteen, lived confined for years and were allowed out only under surveillance, received instead of wages pledged payment, which could be increased by bonuses for zeal and good behaviour, which they could use only on leaving). And then, still farther, there was a whole series of mechanisms that did not adopt the 'compact' prison model, but used some of the carceral methods: charitable societies, moral improvement associations, organizations that handed out assistance and also practised surveillance, workers' estates and lodging houses—the most primitive of which still bear the all too visible marks of the penitentiary system.[2] And, lastly, this great carceral network reaches all the disciplinary mechanisms that function throughout society.

We have seen that, in penal justice, the prison transformed the punitive procedure into a penitentiary technique; the carceral archipelago transported this technique from the penal institution to the entire social body. With several important results.

1. This vast mechanism established a slow, continuous, imperceptible gradation that made it possible to pass naturally from disorder to offence and back from a transgression of the law to a slight departure from a rule, an average, a demand, a norm. In the classical period, despite a certain common reference to offence in general,[3] the order of the crime, the order

8. State prisons (French); the 4 named here began to use prisoners to do agricultural labor.

9. Town in Guadeloupe, a French colony in the Caribbean. The other places named are all in France.

1. On all these institutions, cf. H. Gaíllac, *Les Maisons de correction* (1971) [Foucault's note].

2. Cf., for example, the following description of workers' accommodation built at Lille in the mid–19th century: 'Cleanliness is the order of the day. It is the heart of the regulations. There are a number of severe provisions against noise, drunkenness, disorders of all kinds. A serious offence brings expulsion. Brought back to regular habits of order and economy, the workers no longer desert the workshops on Mondays. . . . The children are better supervised and are no longer a cause of scandal. . . . Prizes are given for the upkeep of the dwellings, for good behavior, for signs of devotion and each year these prizes are competed for by a large number of competitors' (Houzé de l'Aulnay, *Des logements ouvriers à Lille* [1863], pp. 13–15) [Foucault's note]. "Estates": public housing projects.

3. Crime was explicitly defined by certain jurists such as P. F. Muyart de Vouglans, *Refutation du Traité des délits et des peines* (1767), p. 108, and *Les Lois criminelles en France* (1780), p. 3; and G. Rousseaud de la Combe, *Traité des matières criminelles* (1741), pp. 1–2 [Foucault's note].

of sin and the order of bad conduct remained separate in so far as they related to separate criteria and authorities (court, penitence, confinement). Incarceration with its mechanisms of surveillance and punishment functioned, on the contrary, according to a principle of relative continuity. The continuity of the institutions themselves, which were linked to one another (public assistance with the orphanage, the reformitory, the penitentiary, the disciplinary battalion, the prison; the school with the charitable society, the workshop, the almshouse, the penitentiary convent; the workers' estate with the hospital and the prison). A continuity of the punitive criteria and mechanisms, which on the basis of a mere deviation gradually strengthened the rules and increased the punishment. A continuous gradation of the established, specialized and competent authorities (in the order of knowledge and in the order of power) which, without resort to arbitrariness, but strictly according to the regulations, by means of observation and assessment hierarchized, differentiated, judged, punished and moved gradually from the correction of irregularities to the punishment of crime. The 'carceral' with its many diffuse or compact forms, its institutions of supervision or constraint, of discreet surveillance and insistent coercion, assured the communication of punishments according to quality and quantity; it connected in series or disposed according to subtle divisions the minor and the serious penalties, the mild and the strict forms of treatment, bad marks and light sentences. You will end up in the convict-ship, the slightest indiscipline seems to say; and the harshest of prisons says to the prisoners condemned to life: I shall note the slightest irregularity in your conduct. The generality of the punitive function that the eighteenth century sought in the 'ideological' technique of representations and signs now had as its support the extension, the material framework, complex, dispersed, but coherent, of the various carceral mechanisms. As a result, a certain significant generality moved between the least irregularity and the greatest crime; it was no longer the offence, the attack on the common interest, it was the departure from the norm, the anomaly; it was this that haunted the school, the court, the asylum or the prison. It generalized in the sphere of meaning the function that the carceral generalized in the sphere of tactics. Replacing the adversary of the sovereign, the social enemy was transformed into a deviant, who brought with him the multiple danger of disorder, crime and madness. The carceral network linked, through innumerable relations, the two long, multiple series of the punitive and the abnormal.

2. The carceral, with its far-reaching networks, allows the recruitment of major 'delinquents'. It organizes what might be called 'disciplinary careers' in which, through various exclusions and rejections, a whole process is set in motion. In the classical period, there opened up in the confines or interstices of society the confused, tolerant, and dangerous domain of the 'outlaw' or at least of that which eluded the direct hold of power: an uncertain space that was for criminality a training ground and a region of refuge; there poverty, unemployment, pursued innocence, cunning, the struggle against the powerful, the refusal of obligations and laws, and organized crime all came together as chance and fortune would dictate; it was the domain of adventure that Gil Blas, Sheppard or Mandrin,[4] each in his own way, inhabited.

4. Louis Mandrin (1724–1755), French highwayman. Gil Blas: rogue hero and title character of a picaresque French novel (1715–35) by Alain René Lesage. Jack Sheppard (1702–1724), famous English robber, the subject of several popular 18th-century plays, ballads, and books.

Through the play of disciplinary differentiations and divisions, the nineteenth century constructed rigorous channels which, within the system, inculcated docility and produced delinquency by the same mechanisms. There was a sort of disciplinary 'training', continuous and compelling, that had something of the pedagogical curriculum and something of the professional network. Careers emerged from it, as secure, as predictable, as those of public life: assistance associations, residential apprenticeships, penal colonies, disciplinary battalions, prisons, hospitals, almshouses. These networks were already well mapped out at the beginning of the nineteenth century: 'Our benevolent establishments presents an admirably coordinated whole by means of which the indigent does not remain a moment without help from the cradle to the grave. Follow the course of the unfortunate man: you will see him born among foundlings; from there he passes to the nursery, then to an orphanage; at the age of six he goes off to primary school and later to adult schools. If he cannot work, he is placed on the list of the charity offices of his district, and if he falls ill he may choose between twelve hospitals . . . Lastly, when the poor Parisian reaches the end of his career, seven almshouses await his age and often their salubrious régime has prolonged his useless days well beyond those of the rich man'.[5]

The carceral network does not cast the unassimilable into a confused hell; there is no outside. It takes back with one hand what it seems to exclude with the other. It saves everything, including what it punishes. It is unwilling to waste even what it has decided to disqualify. In this panoptic[6] society of which incarceration is the omnipresent armature, the delinquent is not outside the law; he is, from the very outset, in the law, at the very heart of the law, or at least in the midst of those mechanisms that transfer the individual imperceptibly from discipline to the law, from deviation to offence. Although it is true that prison punishes delinquency, delinquency is for the most part produced in and by an incarceration which, ultimately, prison perpetuates in its turn. The prison is merely the natural consequences, no more than a higher degree, of that hierarchy laid down step by step. The delinquent is an institutional product. It is no use being surprised, therefore, that in a considerable proportion of cases the biography of convicts passes through all these mechanisms and establishments, whose purpose, it is widely believed, is to lead away from prison. That one should find in them what one might call the index of an irrepressibly delinquent 'character': the prisoner condemned to hard labour was meticulously produced by a childhood spent in a reformatory, according to the lines of force of the generalized carceral system. Conversely, the lyricism of marginality may find inspiration in the image of the 'outlaw', the great social nomad, who prowls on the confines of a docile, frightened order. But it is not on the fringes of society and through successive exiles that criminality is born, but by means of ever more closely placed insertions, under ever more insistent surveillance, by an accumulation of disciplinary coercion. In short, the carceral archipelago assures, in the depths of the social body, the formation of delinquency on the basis of subtle

5. Moreau de Jonnès, quoted in H. du Touquet, *De la condition des classes pauvres* (1846) [Foucault's note].

6. All-seeing. Jeremy Bentham (1748–1832), English philosopher and reformer, designed an ideal circular prison, which he called the Panopticon, in which the prisoners could be kept under constant surveillance by a single guard in a central tower. In an earlier section of *Discipline and Punish*, Foucault presents this prison as a model and summation of disciplinary power.

illegalities, the overlapping of the latter by the former and the establishment of a specified criminality.

3. But perhaps the most important effect of the carceral system and of its extension well beyond legal imprisonment is that it succeeds in making the power to punish natural and legitimate, in lowering at least the threshold of tolerance to penalty. It tends to efface what may be exorbitant in the exercise of punishment. It does this by playing the two registers in which it is deployed—the legal register of justice and the extra-legal register of discipline—against one another. In effect, the great continuity of the carceral system throughout the law and its sentences gives a sort of legal sanction to the disciplinary mechanisms, to the decisions and judgements that they enforce. Throughout this network, which comprises so many 'regional' institutions, relatively autonomous and independent, is transmitted, with the 'prison-form', the model of justice itself. The regulations of the disciplinary establishments may reproduce the law, the punishments imitate the verdicts and penalties, the surveillance repeat the police model; and, above all these multiple establishments, the prison, which in relation to them is a pure form, unadulterated and unimitigated, gives them a sort of official sanction. The carceral, with its long gradation stretching from the convict-ship or imprisonment with hard labour to diffuse, slight limitations, communicates a type of power that the law validates and that justice uses as its favourite weapon. How could the disciplines and the power that functions in them appear arbitrary, when they merely operate the mechanisms of justice itself, even with a view to mitigating their intensity? When, by generalizing its effects and transmitting it to every level, it makes it possible to avoid its full rigour? Carceral continuity and the fusion of the prison-form make it possible to legalize, or in any case to legitimate disciplinary power, which thus avoids any element of excess or abuse it may entail.

But, conversely, the carceral pyramid gives to the power to inflict legal punishment a context in which it appears to be free of all excess and all violence. In the subtle gradation of the apparatuses of discipline and of the successive 'embeddings' that they involve, the prison does not at all represent the unleashing of a different kind of power, but simply an additional degree in the intensity of a mechanism that has continued to operate since the earliest forms of legal punishment. Between the latest institution of 'rehabilitation', where one is taken in order to avoid prison, and the prison where one is sent after a definable offence, the difference is (and must be) scarcely perceptible. There is a strict economy that has the effect of rendering as discreet as possible the singular power to punish. There is nothing in it now that recalls the former excess of sovereign power when it revenged its authority on the tortured body of those about to be executed.[7] Prison continues, on those who are entrusted to it, a work begun elsewhere, which the whole of the society pursues on each individual through innumerable mechanisms of discipline. By means of a carceral continuum, the authority that sentences infiltrates all those other authorities that supervise, transform, correct, improve. It might even be said that nothing really distinguishes them any more except the singularly 'dangerous' character of the delinquents, the grav-

7. In earlier sections of *Discipline and Punish*, Foucault argues that autocratic power prior to 1789 operated directly and theatrically on an offender's body for a short time, as contrasted to the continuous discreet disciplinary work on bodies that is characteristic of modern carceral society.

ity of their departures from normal behaviour and the necessary solemnity of the ritual. But, in its function, the power to punish is not essentially different from that of curing or educating. It receives from them, and from their lesser, smaller task, a sanction from below; but one that is no less important for that, since it is the sanction of technique and rationality. The carceral 'naturalizes' the legal power to punish, as it 'legalizes' the technical power to discipline. In thus homogenizing them, effacing what may be violent in one and arbitrary in the other, attenuating the effects of revolt that they may both arouse, thus depriving excess in either of any purpose, circulating the same calculated, mechanical and discreet methods from one to the other, the carceral makes it possible to carry out that great 'economy' of power whose formula the eighteenth century had sought, when the problem of the accumulation and useful administration of men first emerged.

By operating at every level of the social body and by mingling ceaselessly the art of rectifying and the right to punish, the universality of the carceral lowers the level from which it becomes natural and acceptable to be punished. The question is often posed as to how, before and after the Revolution, a new foundation was given to the right to punish. And no doubt the answer is to be found in the theory of the contract. But it is perhaps more important to ask the reverse question: how were people made to accept the power to punish, or quite simply, when punished, tolerate being so. The theory of the contract[8] can only answer this question by the fiction of a juridical subject giving to others the power to exercise over him the right that he himself possesses over them. It is highly probable that the great carceral continuum, which provides a communication between the power of discipline and the power of the law, and extends without interruption from the smallest coercions to the longest penal detention, constituted the technical and real, immediately material counterpart of that chimerical granting of the right to punish.

4. With this new economy of power, the carceral system, which is its basic instrument, permitted the emergence of a new form of 'law': a mixture of legality and nature, prescription and constitution, the norm. This had a whole series of effects: the internal dislocation of the judicial power or at least of its functioning; an increasing difficulty in judging, as if one were ashamed to pass sentence; a furious desire on the part of the judges to judge, assess, diagnose, recognize the normal and abnormal and claim the honour of curing or rehabilitating. In view of this, it is useless to believe in the good or bad consciences of judges, or even of their unconscious. Their immense 'appetite for medicine' which is constantly manifested—from their appeal to psychiatric experts, to their attention to the chatter of criminology—expresses the major fact that the power they exercise has been 'denatured'; that it is at a certain level governed by laws; that at another, more fundamental level it functions as a normative power; it is the economy of power that they exercise, and not that of their scruples or their humanism, that makes them pass 'therapeutic' sentences and recommend 'rehabilitating' periods of imprisonment. But, conversely, if the judges accept ever more reluc-

8. The "social contract" theory expounded by the political philosophers Thomas Hobbes (1588–1679), John Locke (1632–1704), and Jean-Jacques Rousseau (1712–1778); it explains states' power over individuals by positing an original contract in which those individuals cede power to the state in return for protection.

tantly to condemn for the sake of condemning, the activity of judging has increased precisely to the extent that the normalizing power has spread. Borne along by the omnipresence of the mechanisms of discipline, basing itself on all the carceral apparatuses, it has become one of the major functions of our society. The judges of normality are present everywhere. We are in the society of the teacher-judge, the doctor-judge, the educator-judge, the 'social worker'-judge; it is on them that the universal reign of the normative is based; and each individual, wherever he may find himself, subjects to it his body, his gestures, his behaviour, his aptitudes, his achievements. The carceral network, in its compact or disseminated forms, with its systems of insertion, distribution, surveillance, observation, has been the greatest support, in modern society, of the normalizing power.

5. The carceral texture of society assures both the real capture of the body and its perpetual observation; it is, by its very nature, the apparatus of punishment that conforms most completely to the new economy of power and the instrument for the formation of knowledge that this very economy needs. Its panoptic functioning enables it to play this double role. By virtue of its methods of fixing, dividing, recording, it has been one of the simplest, crudest, also most concrete, but perhaps most indispensable conditions for the development of this immense activity of examination that has objectified human behaviour. If, after the age of 'inquisitorial' justice, we have entered the age of 'examinatory' justice,[9] if, in an even more general way, the method of examination has been able to spread so widely throughout society, and to give rise in part to the sciences of man, one of the great instruments for this has been the multiplicity and close overlapping of the various mechanisms of incarceration. I am not saying that the human sciences emerged from the prison. But, if they have been able to be formed and to produce so many profound changes in the episteme,[1] it is because they have been conveyed by a specific and new modality of power: a certain policy of the body, a certain way of rendering the group of men docile and useful. This policy required the involvement of definite relations of knowledge in relations of power; it called for a technique of overlapping subjection and objectification; it brought with it new procedures of individualization. The carceral network constituted one of the armatures of this power-knowledge that has made the human sciences historically possible. Knowable man (soul, individuality, consciousness, conduct, whatever it is called) is the object-effect of this analytical investment, of this domination-observation.

6. This no doubt explains the extreme solidity of the prison, that slight invention that was nevertheless decried from the outset. If it had been no more than an instrument of rejection or repression in the service of a state apparatus, it would have been easier to alter its more overt forms or to find a more acceptable substitute for it. But, rooted as it was in mechanisms and strategies of power it could meet any attempt to transform it with a great force of inertia. One fact is characteristic: when it is a question of altering the system of imprisonment, opposition does not come from the judicial institutions alone; resistance is to be found not in the prison as penal sanc-

9. Earlier in *Discipline and Punish*, Foucault discusses the development of examination techniques in churches, schools, hospitals, the military, and other institutions.

1. Foucault's term for the unconscious deep structure that undergirds a historical period's conscious beliefs and knowledge.

tion, but in the prison with all its determinations, links and extra-judicial results; in the prison as the relay in a general network of disciplines and surveillances; in the prison as it functions in a panoptic régime. This does not mean that it cannot be altered, nor that it is once and for all indispensable to our kind of society. One may, on the contrary, cite the two processes which, in the very continuity of the processes that make the prison function, are capable of exercising considerable restraint on its use and of transforming its internal functioning. And no doubt these processes have already begun to a large degree. The first is that which reduces the utility (or increases its inconveniences) of a delinquency accommodated as a specific illegality, locked up and supervised; thus the growth of great national or international illegalities directly linked to the political and economic apparatuses (financial illegalities, information services, arms and drugs trafficking, property speculation) makes it clear that the somewhat rustic and conspicuous work force of delinquency is proving ineffective; or again, on a smaller scale, as soon as the economic levy on sexual pleasure is carried out more efficiently by the sale of contraceptives, or obliquely through publications, films or shows, the archaic hierarchy of prostitution loses much of its former usefulness. The second process is the growth of the disciplinary networks, the multiplication of their exchanges with the penal apparatus, the ever more important powers that are given them, the ever more massive transference to them of judicial functions; now, as medicine, psychology, education, public assistance, 'social work' assume an ever greater share of the powers of supervision and assessment, the penal apparatus will be able, in turn, to become medicalized, psychologized, educationalized; and by the same token that turning-point represented by the prison becomes less useful when, through the gap between its penitentiary discourse and its effect of consolidating delinquency, it articulates the penal power and the disciplinary power. In the midst of all these mechanisms of normalization, which are becoming ever more rigorous in their application, the specificity of the prison and its role as link are losing something of their purpose.

If there is an overall political issue around the prison, it is not therefore whether it is to be corrective or not; whether the judges, the psychiatrists or the sociologists are to exercise more power in it than the administrators or supervisors; it is not even whether we should have prison or something other than prison. At present, the problem lies rather in the steep rise in the use of these mechanisms of normalization and the wide-ranging powers which, through the proliferation of new disciplines, they bring with them.

In 1836, a correspondent wrote to *La Phalange*: 'Moralists, philosophers, legislators, flatterers of civilization, this is the plan of your Paris, neatly ordered and arranged, here is the improved plan in which all like things are gathered together. At the centre, and within a first enclosure: hospitals for all diseases, almshouses for all types of poverty, madhouses, prisons, convict-prisons for men, women and children. Around the first enclosure, barracks, courtrooms, police stations, houses for prison warders, scaffolds, houses for the executioner and his assistants. At the four corners, the Chamber of Deputies, the Chamber of Peers, the Institute and the Royal Palace. Outside, there are the various services that supply the central enclosure, commerce, with its swindlers and its bankruptcies; industry and its furious struggles; the press, with its sophisms; the gambling dens; prostitution, the people dying of hunger or wallowing in debauchery, always ready to lend an ear to the voice of the Genius of Revolutions; the heartless rich . . . Lastly the ruthless war of all against all'.[2]

I shall stop with this anonymous text. We are now far away from the country of tortures, dotted with wheels, gibbets, gallows, pillories; we are far, too, from that dream of the reformers, less than fifty years before: the city of punishments in which a thousand small theatres would have provided an endless multicoloured representation of justice in which the punishments, meticulously produced on decorative scaffolds, would have constituted the permanent festival of the penal code. The carceral city, with its imaginary 'geo-politics', is governed by quite different principles. The extract from *La Phalange* reminds us of some of the more important ones: that at the centre of this city, and as if to hold it in place, there is, not the 'centre of power', not a network of forces, but a multiple network of diverse elements—walls, space, institution, rules, discourse; that the model of the carceral city is not, therefore, the body of the king,[3] with the powers that emanate from it, nor the contractual meeting of wills from which a body that was both individual and collective was born, but a strategic distribution of elements of different natures and levels That the prison is not the daughter of laws, codes or the judicial apparatus; that it is not subordinated to the court and the docile or clumsy instrument of the sentences that it hands out and of the results that it would like to achieve; that it is the court that is external and subordinate to the prison. That in the central position that it occupies, it is not alone, but linked to a whole series of 'carceral' mechanisms which seem distinct enough—since they are intended to alleviate pain, to cure, to comfort—but which all tend, like the prison, to exercise a power of normalization. That these mechanisms are applied not to transgressions against a 'central' law, but to the apparatus of production—'commerce' and 'industry'—to a whole multiplicity of illegalities, in all their diversity of nature and origin, their specific role in profit and the different ways in which they are dealt with by the punitive mechanisms. And that ultimately what presides over all these mechanisms is not the unitary functioning of an apparatus or an institution, but the necessity of combat and the rules of strategy. That, consequently, the notions of institutions of repression, rejection, exclusion, marginalization, are not adequate to describe, at the very centre of the carceral city, the formation of the insidious leniencies, unavowable petty cruelties, small acts of cunning, calculated methods, techniques, 'sciences' that permit the fabrication of the disciplinary individual. In this central and centralized humanity, the effect and instrument of complex power relations, bodies and forces subjected by multiple mechanisms of 'incarceration', objects for discourses that are in themselves elements for this strategy, we must hear the distant roar of battle.

At this point I end a book that must serve as a historical background to various studies of the power of normalization and the formation of knowledge in modern society.

1975

2. *La Phalange*, 10 August 1836 [Foucault's note]. "War of all against all": in *Leviathan* (1651), Hobbes described "the condition of man" as "a condition of war of everyone against everyone."

3. The idea of modeling the city on the human body was common in the Renaissance (see especially the *Treatise* of Francesco di Giorgio, 1439–1501/2).

From The History of Sexuality, Volume 1, An Introduction[1]

Part Two: The Repressive Hypothesis

CHAPTER 1.
THE INCITEMENT TO DISCOURSE

The seventeenth century, then, was the beginning of an age of repression emblematic of what we call the bourgeois societies, an age which perhaps we still have not completely left behind. Calling sex by its name thereafter became more difficult and more costly. As if in order to gain mastery over it in reality, it had first been necessary to subjugate it at the level of language, control its free circulation in speech, expunge it from the things that were said, and extinguish the words that rendered it too visibly present. And even these prohibitions, it seems, were afraid to name it. Without even having to pronounce the word, modern prudishness was able to ensure that one did not speak of sex, merely through the interplay of prohibitions that referred back to one another: instances of muteness which, by dint of saying nothing, imposed silence. Censorship.

Yet when one looks back over these last three centuries with their continual transformations, things appear in a very different light: around and apropos of sex, one sees a veritable discursive explosion. We must be clear on this point, however. It is quite possible that there was an expurgation—and a very rigorous one—of the authorized vocabulary. It may indeed be true that a whole rhetoric of allusion and metaphor was codified. Without question, new rules of propriety screened out some words: there was a policing of statements. A control over enunciations as well: where and when it was not possible to talk about such things became much more strictly defined; in which circumstances, among which speakers, and within which social relationships. Areas were thus established, if not of utter silence, at least of tact and discretion: between parents and children, for instance, or teachers and pupils, or masters and domestic servants. This almost certainly constituted a whole restrictive economy, one that was incorporated into that politics of language and speech—spontaneous on the one hand, concerted on the other—which accompanied the social redistributions of the classical period.[2]

At the level of discourses and their domains, however, practically the opposite phenomenon occurred. There was a steady proliferation of discourses concerned with sex—specific discourses, different from one another both by their form and by their object: a discursive ferment that gathered momentum from the eighteenth century onward. Here I am thinking not so much of the probable increase in "illicit" discourses, that is, discourses of infraction that crudely named sex by way of insult or mockery of the new code of decency; the tightening up of the rules of decorum likely did produce, as a countereffect, a valorization and intensification of indecent speech. But more important was the multiplication of discourses concerning sex in the field of exercise of power itself: an institutional incitement to speak about it, and to do so more and more; a determination on the part of the agencies of power

1. Translated by Robert Hurley.
2. Foucault's term for (roughly) the period from 1650 to 1789.

to hear it spoken about, and to cause *it* to speak through explicit articulation and endlessly accumulated detail.

Consider the evolution of the Catholic pastoral and the sacrament of penance after the Council of Trent.[3] Little by little, the nakedness of the questions formulated by the confession manuals of the Middle Ages, and a good number of those still in use in the seventeenth century, was veiled. One avoided entering into that degree of detail which some authors, such as Sanchez or Tamburini,[4] had for a long time believed indispensable for the confession to be complete: description of the respective positions of the partners, the postures assumed, gestures, places touched, caresses, the precise moment of pleasure—an entire painstaking review of the sexual act in its very unfolding. Discretion was advised, with increasing emphasis. The greatest reserve was counseled when dealing with sins against purity: "This matter is similar to pitch, for, however one might handle it, even to cast it far from oneself, it sticks nonetheless, and always soils."[5] And later, Alfonso de' Liguori prescribed starting—and possibly going no further, especially when dealing with children—with questions that were "roundabout and vague."[6]

But while the language may have been refined, the scope of the confession—the confession of the flesh—continually increased. This was partly because the Counter Reformation[7] busied itself with stepping up the rhythm of the yearly confession in the Catholic countries, and because it tried to impose meticulous rules of self-examination; but above all, because it attributed more and more importance in penance—and perhaps at the expense of some other sins—to all the insinuations of the flesh: thoughts, desires, voluptuous imaginings, delectations, combined movements of the body and the soul; henceforth all this had to enter, in detail, into the process of confession and guidance. According to the new pastoral, sex must not be named imprudently, but its aspects, its correlations, and its effects must be pursued down to their slenderest ramifications: a shadow in a daydream, an image too slowly dispelled, a badly exorcised complicity between the body's mechanics and the mind's complacency: everything had to be told. A twofold evolution tended to make the flesh into the root of all evil, shifting the most important moment of transgression from the act itself to the stirrings—so difficult to perceive and formulate—of desire. For this was an evil that afflicted the whole man, and in the most secret of forms: "Examine diligently, therefore, all the faculties of your soul: memory, understanding, and will. Examine with precision all your senses as well. . . . Examine, moreover, all your thoughts, every word you speak, and all your actions. Examine even unto your dreams, to know if, once awakened, you did not give them your consent. And finally, do not think that in so sensitive and perilous a matter as this, there is anything trivial or insignificant."[8] Discourse, therefore, had to trace the meeting line of the body and the soul, following all its meanderings: beneath the

3. Series of meetings (1545–63) at which the Catholic hierarchy developed its response to the Protestant Reformation.

4. Tommaso Tamburini (1591–1675), Italian Jesuit theologian. Francisco Sanchez (ca. 1550–1623), Portuguese physician and philosopher.

5. Paolo Segneri, *L'Instruction du pénitent* (French translation 1695), p. 301 [Foucault's note]. Segneri (1624–1694), Italian Jesuit.

6. Alfonso de' Liguori, *La Pratique des confesseurs* (French translation 1854), p. 140 [Foucault's note]. Liguori (1696–1787), Italian prelate.

7. Effort (beginning with the Council of Trent) to secure the traditions of the Catholic Church against the innovations of the Protestant Reformation.

8. Segneri, *L'Instruction du pénitent*, pp. 301–2 [Foucault's note].

surface of the sins, it would lay bare the unbroken nervure of the flesh. Under the authority of a language that had been carefully expurgated so that it was no longer directly named, sex was taken charge of, tracked down as it were, by a discourse that aimed to allow it no obscurity, no respite.

It was here, perhaps, that the injunction, so peculiar to the West, was laid down for the first time, in the form of a general constraint. I am not talking about the obligation to admit to violations of the laws of sex, as required by traditional penance; but of the nearly infinite task of telling—telling oneself and another, as often as possible, everything that might concern the interplay of innumerable pleasures, sensations, and thoughts which, through the body and the soul, had some affinity with sex. This scheme for transforming sex into discourse had been devised long before in an ascetic and monastic setting. The seventeenth century made it into a rule for everyone. It would seem in actual fact that it could scarcely have applied to any but a tiny elite; the great majority of the faithful who only went to confession on rare occasions in the course of the year escaped such complex prescriptions. But the important point no doubt is that this obligation was decreed, as an ideal at least, for every good Christian. An imperative was established: Not only will you confess to acts contravening the law, but you will seek to transform your desire, your every desire, into discourse. Insofar as possible, nothing was meant to elude this dictum, even if the words it employed had to be carefully neutralized. The Christian pastoral prescribed as a fundamental duty the task of passing everything having to do with sex through the endless mill of speech.[9] The forbidding of certain words, the decency of expressions, all the censorings of vocabulary, might well have been only secondary devices compared to that great subjugation: ways of rendering it morally acceptable and technically useful.

One could plot a line going straight from the seventeenth-century pastoral to what became its projection in literature, "scandalous" literature at that. "Tell everything," the directors would say time and again: "not only consummated acts, but sensual touchings, all impure gazes, all obscene remarks . . . all consenting thoughts."[1] Sade takes up the injunction in words that seem to have been retranscribed from the treatises of spirtual direction: "Your narrations must be decorated with the most numerous and searching details; the precise way and extent to which we may judge how the passion you describe relates to human manners and man's character is determined by your willingness to disguise no circumstances; and what is more, the least circumstance is apt to have an immense influence upon the procuring of that kind of sensory irritation we expect from your stories."[2] And again at the end of the nineteenth century, the anonymous author of *My Secret Life* submitted to the same prescription; outwardly, at least, this man was doubtless a kind of traditional libertine; but he conceived the idea of complementing his life—which he had almost totally dedicated to sexual activity—

9. The reformed pastor also laid down rules, albeit in a more discreet way, for putting sex into discourse. This notion will be developed in the next volume, *The Body and the Flesh* [Foucault's note]. Foucault's plan later changed; the volumes he managed to complete deal instead with sexuality in the ancient world.

1. Alfonso de' Liguori, *Préceptes sur le sixième commandement* (French translation 1835), p. 5 [Foucault's note].

2. Donatien-Alphonse de Sade, *The 120 Days of Sodom*, trans. Austryn Wainhouse and Richard Seaver (New York: Grove Press, 1966), p. 271 [Foucault's note]. Marquis de Sade (1740–1814), French writer best known for his works of sexual fantasy.

with a scrupulous account of every one of its episodes. He sometimes excuses himself by stressing his concern to educate young people, this man who had eleven volumes published, in a printing of only a few copies, which were devoted to the least adventures, pleasures, and sensations of his sex. It is best to take him at his word when he lets into his text the voice of a pure imperative: "I recount the facts, just as they happened, insofar as I am able to recollect them; this is all that I can do"; "a secret life must not leave out anything; there is nothing to be ashamed of . . . one can never know too much concerning human nature."[3] The solitary author of *My Secret Life* often says, in order to justify his describing them, that his strangest practices undoubtedly were shared by thousands of men on the surface of the earth. But the guiding principle for the strangest of these practices, which was the fact of recounting them all, and in detail, from day to day, had been lodged in the heart of modern man for over two centuries. Rather than seeing in this singular man a courageous fugitive from a "Victorianism" that would have compelled him to silence, I am inclined to think that, in an epoch dominated by (highly prolix) directives enjoining discretion and modesty, he was the most direct and in a way the most naïve representative of a plurisecular injunction[4] to talk about sex. The historical accident would consist rather of the reticences of "Victorian puritanism"; at any rate, they were a digression, a refinement, a tactical diversion in the great process of transforming sex into discourse.

This nameless Englishman will serve better than his queen[5] as the central figure for a sexuality whose main features were already taking shape with the Christian pastoral. Doubtless, in contrast to the latter, for him it was a matter of augmenting the sensations he experienced with the details of what he said about them; like Sade, he wrote "for his pleasure alone," in the strongest sense of the expression; he carefully mixed the editing and rereading of his text with erotic scenes which those writer's activities repeated, prolonged, and stimulated. But after all, the Christian pastoral also sought to produce specific effects on desire, by the mere fact of transforming it—fully and deliberately—into discourse: effects of mastery and detachment, to be sure, but also an effect of spiritual reconversion, of turning back to God, a physical effect of blissful suffering from feeling in one's body the pangs of temptation and the love that resists it. This is the essential thing: that Western man has been drawn for three centuries to the task of telling everything concerning his sex; that since the classical age there has been a constant optimization and an increasing valorization of the discourse on sex; and that this carefully analytical discourse was meant to yield multiple effects of displacement, intensification, reorientation, and modification of desire itself. Not only were the boundaries of what one could say about sex enlarged, and men compelled to hear it said; but more important, discourse was connected to sex by a complex organization with varying effects, by a deployment that cannot be adequately explained merely by referring it to a law of prohibition. A censorship of sex? There was installed rather an apparatus for producing an ever greater quantity of discourse about sex, capable of functioning and taking effect in its very economy.

3. Anonymous, *My Secret Life* (New York: Grove Press, 1966) [Foucault's note].
4. That is, an injunction from many parts of the secular (nonreligious) world.
5. Victoria (1819–1901), whose long reign (1838–1901) delimits the age that bears her name.

This technique might have remained tied to the destiny of Christian spirituality if it had not been supported and relayed by other mechanisms. In the first place, by a "public interest." Not a collective curiosity or sensibility; not a new mentality; but power mechanisms that functioned in such a way that discourse on sex—for reasons that will have to be examined—became essential. Toward the beginning of the eighteenth century, there emerged a political, economic, and technical incitement to talk about sex. And not so much in the form of a general theory of sexuality as in the form of analysis, stocktaking, classification, and specification, of quantitative or causal studies. This need to take sex "into account," to pronounce a discourse on sex that would not derive from morality alone but from rationality as well, was sufficiently new that at first it wondered at itself and sought apologies for its own existence. How could a discourse based on reason speak of *that*? "Rarely have philosophers directed a steady gaze to these objects situated between disgust and ridicule, where one must avoid both hypocrisy and scandal."[6] And nearly a century later, the medical establishment, which one might have expected to be less surprised by what it was about to formulate, still stumbled at the moment of speaking: "The darkness that envelops these facts, the shame and disgust they inspire, have always repelled the observer's gaze. . . . For a long time I hesitated to introduce the loathsome picture into this study."[7] What is essential is not in all these scruples, in the "moralism" they betray, or in the hypocrisy one can suspect them of, but in the recognized necessity of overcoming this hesitation. One had to speak of sex; one had to speak publicly and in a manner that was not determined by the division between licit and illicit, even if the speaker maintained the distinction for himself (which is what these solemn and preliminary declarations were intended to show): one had to speak of it as of a thing to be not simply condemned or tolerated but managed, inserted into systems of utility, regulated for the greater good of all, made to function according to an optimum. Sex was not something one simply judged; it was a thing one administered. It was in the nature of a public potential; it called for management procedures; it had to be taken charge of by analytical discourses. In the eighteenth century, sex became a "police" matter—in the full and strict sense given the term at the time: not the repression of disorder, but an ordered maximization of collective and individual forces: "We must consolidate and augment, through the wisdom of its regulations, the internal power of the state; and since this power consists not only in the Republic in general, and in each of the members who constitute it, but also in the faculties and talents of those belonging to it, it follows that the police must concern themselves with these means and make them serve the public welfare. And they can only obtain this result through the knowledge they have of those different assets."[8] A policing of sex: that is, not the rigor of a taboo, but the necessity of regulating sex through useful and public discourses.

A few examples will suffice. One of the great innovations in the techniques of power in the eighteenth century was the emergence of "population" as an economic and political problem: population as wealth, population as man-

6. Condorcet, cited by Jean-Louis Flandrin, *Familles: Parenté, maison, sexualité dans l'ancienne société* (Paris: Hachette, 1976) [Foucault's note]. Marquis de Condorcet (1743–1794), French mathematician and philosopher.

7. Auguste Tardieu, *Étude médico-légale sur les attentats aux moeurs* (1857), p. 114 [Foucault's note].

8. Johann von Justi, *Éléments généraux de police* (French translation 1769), p. 20 [Foucault's note].

power or labor capacity, population balanced between its own growth and the resources it commanded. Governments perceived that they were not dealing simply with subjects, or even with a "people," but with a "population," with its specific phenomena and its peculiar variables: birth and death rates, life expectancy, fertility, state of health, frequency of illnesses, patterns of diet and habitation. All these variables were situated at the point where the characteristic movements of life and the specific effects of institutions intersected: "States are not populated in accordance with the natural progression of propagation, but by virtue of their industry, their products, and their different institutions. . . . Men multiply like the yields from the ground and in proportion to the advantages and resources they find in their labors."[9] At the heart of this economic and political problem of population was sex: it was necessary to analyze the birthrate, the age of marriage, the legitimate and illegitimate births, the precocity and frequency of sexual relations, the ways of making them fertile or sterile, the effects of unmarried life or of the prohibitions, the impact of contraceptive practices—of those notorious "deadly secrets" which demographers on the eve of the Revolution knew were already familiar to the inhabitants of the countryside.

Of course, it had long been asserted that a country had to be populated if it hoped to be rich and powerful; but this was the first time that a society had affirmed, in a constant way, that its future and its fortune were tied not only to the number and the uprightness of its citizens, to their marriage rules and family organization, but to the manner in which each individual made use of his sex. Things went from ritual lamenting over the unfruitful debauchery of the rich, bachelors, and libertines to a discourse in which the sexual conduct of the population was taken both as an object of analysis and as a target of intervention; there was a progression from the crudely populationist arguments of the mercantilist epoch to the much more subtle and calculated attempts at regulation that tended to favor or discourage—according to the objectives and exigencies of the moment—an increasing birthrate. Through the political economy of population there was formed a whole grid of observations regarding sex. There emerged the analysis of the modes of sexual conduct, their determinations and their effects, at the boundary line of the biological and the economic domains. There also appeared those systematic campaigns which, going beyond the traditional means—moral and religious exhortations, fiscal measures—tried to transform the sexual conduct of couples into a concerted economic and political behavior. In time these new measures would become anchorage points for the different varieties of racism of the nineteenth and twentieth centuries. It was essential that the state know what was happening with its citizens' sex, and the use they made of it, but also that each individual be capable of controlling the use he made of it. Between the state and the individual, sex became an issue, and a public issue no less; a whole web of discourses, special knowledges, analyses, and injunctions settled upon it.

The situation was similar in the case of children's sex. It is often said that the classical period consigned it to an obscurity from which it scarcely emerged before the *Three Essays* or the beneficent anxieties of Little Hans.[1]

9. Claude-Jacques Herbert, *Essai sur la police générale des grains* (1753), pp. 320–21 [Foucault's note].

1. SIGMUND FREUD's *Three Essays on Sexuality* was published in 1905; his case study of Little Hans, titled "Analysis of a Phobia of a Five-Year-Old Boy," dates from 1909.

It is true that a longstanding "freedom" of language between children and adults, or pupils and teachers, may have disappeared. No seventeenth-century pedagogue would have publicly advised his disciple, as did Erasmus[2] in his *Dialogues*, on the choice of a good prostitute. And the boisterous laughter that had accompanied the precocious sexuality of children for so long—and in all social classes, it seems—was gradually stifled. But this was not a plain and simple imposition of silence. Rather, it was a new regime of discourses. Not any less was said about it; on the contrary. But things were said in a different way; it was different people who said them, from different points of view, and in order to obtain different results. Silence itself—the things one declines to say, or is forbidden to name, the discretion that is required between different speakers—is less the absolute limit of discourse, the other side from which it is separated by a strict boundary, than an element that functions alongside the things said, with them and in relation to them within over-all strategies. There is no binary division to be made between what one says and what one does not say; we must try to determine the different ways of not saying such things, how those who can and those who cannot speak of them are distributed, which type of discourse is authorized, or which form of discretion is required in either case. There is not one but many silences, and they are an integral part of the strategies that underlie and permeate discourses.

Take the secondary schools of the eighteenth century, for example. On the whole, one can have the impression that sex was hardly spoken of at all in these institutions. But one only has to glance over the architectural layout, the rules of discipline, and their whole internal organization: the question of sex was a constant preoccupation. The builders considered it explicitly. The organizers took it permanently into account. All who held a measure of authority were placed in a state of perpetual alert, which the fixtures, the precautions taken, the interplay of punishments and responsibilities, never ceased to reiterate. The space for classes, the shape of the tables, the planning of the recreation lessons, the distribution of the dormitories (with or without partitions, with or without curtains), the rules for monitoring bedtime and sleep periods—all this referred, in the most prolix manner, to the sexuality of children.[3] What one might call the internal discourse of the institution—the one it employed to address itself, and which circulated among those who made it function—was largely based on the assumption that this sexuality existed, that it was precocious, active, and ever present. But this was not all: the sex of the schoolboy became in the course of the eighteenth century—and quite apart from that of adolescents in general—a public problem. Doctors counseled the directors and professors of educational establishments, but they also gave their opinions to families; educators designed projects which they submitted to the authorities; schoolmasters turned to students, made recommendations to them, and drafted for their

2. Dutch humanist scholar (1466–1536); his *Dialogues* (1516) cover a wide variety of topics.

3. *Règlement de police pour les lycées* (1809), art. 67: "There shall always be, during class and study hours, an instructor watching the exterior, so as to prevent students who have gone out to relieve themselves from stopping and congregating.

art. 68: "After the evening prayer, the students will be conducted back to the dormitory, where the schoolmasters will put them to bed at once.

art. 69: "The masters will not retire except after having made certain that every student is in bed.

art. 70: "The beds shall be separated by partitions two meters in height. The dormitories shall be illuminated during the night" [Foucault's note].

benefit books of exhortation, full of moral and medical examples. Around the schoolboy and his sex there proliferated a whole literature of precepts, opinions, observations, medical advice, clinical cases, outlines for reform, and plans for ideal institutions. With Basedow[4] and the German "philanthropic" movement, this transformation of adolescent sex into discourse grew to considerable dimensions. Salzmann[5] even organized an experimental school which owed its exceptional character to a supervision and education of sex so well thought out that youth's universal sin would never need to be practiced there. And with all these measures taken, the child was not to be simply the mute and unconscious object of attentions prearranged between adults only; a certain reasonable, limited, canonical, and truthful discourse on sex was prescribed for him—a kind of discursive orthopedics.[6] The great festival organized at the Philanthropinum in May of 1776 can serve as a vignette in this regard. Taking the form of an examination, mixed with floral games, the awarding of prizes, and a board of review, this was the first solemn communion of adolescent sex and reasonable discourse. In order to show the success of the sex education given the students, Basedow had invited all the dignitaries that Germany could muster (Goethe[7] was one of the few to decline the invitation). Before the assembled public, one of the professors, a certain Wolke, asked the students selected questions concerning the mysteries of sex, birth, and procreation. He had them comment on engravings that depicted a pregnant woman, a couple, and a cradle. The replies were enlightened, offered without shame or embarrassment. No unseemly laughter intervened to disturb them—except from the very ranks of an adult audience more childish than the children themselves, and whom Wolke severely reprimanded. At the end, they all applauded these cherub-faced boys who, in front of adults, had skillfully woven the garlands of discourse and sex.[8]

It would be less than exact to say that the pedagogical institution has imposed a ponderous silence on the sex of children and adolescents. On the contrary, since the eighteenth century it has multiplied the forms of discourse on the subject; it has established various points of implantation for sex; it has coded contents and qualified speakers. Speaking about children's sex, inducing educators, physicians, administrators, and parents to speak of it, or speaking to them about it, causing children themselves to talk about it, and enclosing them in a web of discourses which sometimes address them, sometimes speak about them, or impose canonical bits of knowledge on them, or use them as a basis for constructing a science that is beyond their grasp—all this together enables us to link an intensification of the intervention of power to a multiplication of discourse. The sex of children and adolescents has become, since the eighteenth century, an important area of contention around which innumerable institutional devices and discursive strategies have been deployed. It may well be true that adults and children themselves were deprived of a certain way of speaking about sex, a mode that was disallowed as being too direct, crude, or coarse. But this was only the counterpart of other discourses, and perhaps the condition necessary in

4. Johann Basedow (1723–1790), German teacher and educational reformer; his model school was the Philanthropinum, at Dessau.
5. Christian Salzmann (1744–1811), German educator.
6. Discourse that corrects children.
7. Johann Wolfgang von Goethe (1749–1832), German poet, dramatist, and novelist.
8. Johann Gottlieb Schummel, *Fritzens Reise nach Dessau* (1776), cited by Auguste Pinloche, *La Réforme de l'éducation en Allemagne au XVIIIe siècle* (1889), pp. 125–29 [Foucault's note].

order for them to function, discourses that were interlocking, hierarchized, and all highly articulated around a cluster of power relations.

One could mention many other centers which in the eighteenth or nineteenth century began to produce discourses on sex. First there was medicine, via the "nervous disorders"; next psychiatry, when it set out to discover the etiology of mental illnesses, focusing its gaze first on "excess," then onanism, then frustration, then "frauds against procreation," but especially when it annexed the whole of the sexual perversions as its own province; criminal justice, too, which had long been concerned with sexuality, particularly in the form of "heinous" crimes and crimes against nature, but which, toward the middle of the nineteenth century, broadened its jurisdiction to include petty offenses, minor indecencies, insignificant perversions; and lastly, all those social controls, cropping up at the end of the last century, which screened the sexuality of couples, parents and children, dangerous and endangered adolescents—undertaking to protect, separate, and forewarn, signaling perils everywhere, awakening people's attention, calling for diagnoses, piling up reports, organizing therapies. These sites radiated discourses aimed at sex, intensifying people's awareness of it as a constant danger, and this in turn created a further incentive to talk about it.

One day in 1867, a farm hand from the village of Lapcourt, who was somewhat simple-minded, employed here then there, depending on the season, living hand-to-mouth from a little charity or in exchange for the worst sort of labor, sleeping in barns and stables, was turned in to the authorities. At the border of a field, he had obtained a few caresses from a little girl, just as he had done before and seen done by the village urchins round about him; for, at the edge of the wood, or in the ditch by the road leading to Saint-Nicolas, they would play the familiar game called "curdled milk." So he was pointed out by the girl's parents to the mayor of the village, reported by the mayor to the gendarmes, led by the gendarmes to the judge, who indicted him and turned him over first to a doctor, then to two other experts who not only wrote their report but also had it published.[9] What is the significant thing about this story? The pettiness of it all; the fact that this everyday occurrence in the life of village sexuality, these inconsequential bucolic pleasures, could become, from a certain time, the object not only of a collective intolerance but of a judicial action, a medical intervention, a careful clinical examination, and an entire theoretical elaboration. The thing to note is that they went so far as to measure the brainpan, study the facial bone structure, and inspect for possible signs of degenerescence the anatomy of this personage who up to that moment had been an integral part of village life; that they made him talk; that they questioned him concerning his thoughts, inclinations, habits, sensations, and opinions. And then, acquitting him of any crime, they decided finally to make him into a pure object of medicine and knowledge—an object to be shut away till the end of his life in the hospital at Maréville, but also one to be made known to the world of learning through a detailed analysis. One can be fairly certain that during this same period the Lapcourt schoolmaster was instructing the little villagers to mind their language and not to talk about all these things aloud. But

9. H. Bonnet and J. Bulard, *Rapport médico-légal sur l'état mental de Ch.-J. Jouy*, January 4, 1868 [Foucault's note].

this was undoubtedly one of the conditions enabling the institutions of knowledge and power to overlay this everyday bit of theater with their solemn discourse. So it was that our society—and it was doubtless the first in history to take such measures—assembled around these timeless gestures, these barely furtive pleasures between simple-minded adults and alert children, a whole machinery for speechifying, analyzing, and investigating.

Between the licentious Englishman, who earnestly recorded for his own purposes the singular episodes of his secret life, and his contemporary, this village halfwit who would give a few pennies to the little girls for favors the older ones refused him, there was without doubt a profound connection: in any case, from one extreme to the other, sex became something to say, and to say exhaustively in accordance with deployments that were varied, but all, in their own way, compelling. Whether in the form of a subtle confession in confidence or an authoritarian interrogation, sex—be it refined or rustic—had to be put into words. A great polymorphous injunction bound the Englishman and the poor Lorrainese peasant alike. As history would have it, the latter was named Jouy.[1]

Since the eighteenth century, sex has not ceased to provoke a kind of generalized discursive erethism.[2] And these discourses on sex did not multiply apart from or against power, but in the very space and as the means of its exercise. Incitements to speak were orchestrated from all quarters, apparatuses everywhere for listening and recording, procedures for observing, questioning, and formulating. Sex was driven out of hiding and constrained to lead a discursive existence. From the singular imperialism that compels everyone to transform their sexuality into a perpetual discourse, to the manifold mechanisms which, in the areas of economy, pedagogy, medicine, and justice, incite, extract, distribute, and institutionalize the sexual discourse, an immense verbosity is what our civilization has required and organized. Surely no other type of society has ever accumulated—and in such a relatively short span of time—a similar quantity of discourses concerned with sex. It may well be that we talk about sex more than anything else; we set our minds to the task; we convince ourselves that we have never said enough on the subject, that, through inertia or submissiveness, we conceal from ourselves the blinding evidence, and that what is essential always eludes us, so that we must always start out once again in search of it. It is possible that where sex is concerned, the most long-winded, the most impatient of societies is our own.

But as this first overview shows, we are dealing less with *a* discourse on sex than with a multiplicity of discourses produced by a whole series of mechanisms operating in different institutions. The Middle Ages had organized around the theme of the flesh and the practice of penance a discourse that was markedly unitary. In the course of recent centuries, this relative uniformity was broken apart, scattered, and multiplied in an explosion of distinct discursivities which took form in demography, biology, medicine, psychiatry, psychology, ethics, pedagogy, and political criticism. More precisely, the secure bond that held together the moral theology of concupiscence and the obligation of confession (equivalent to the theoretical

1. Jouy sounds like the past participle of *jouir*, the French verb meaning to enjoy, to delight in (something), but also to have an orgasm, to come [translator's note].

2. Abnormal irritability or responsiveness to stimulation.

discourse on sex and its first-person formulation) was, if not broken, at least loosened and diversified: between the objectification of sex in rational discourses, and the movement by which each individual was set to the task of recounting his own sex, there has occurred, since the eighteenth century, a whole series of tensions, conflicts, efforts at adjustment, and attempts at retranscription. So it is not simply in terms of a continual extension that we must speak of this discursive growth; it should be seen rather as a dispersion of centers from which discourses emanated, a diversification of their forms, and the complex deployment of the network connecting them. Rather than the uniform concern to hide sex, rather than a general prudishness of language, what distinguishes these last three centuries is the variety, the wide dispersion of devices that were invented for speaking about it, for having it be spoken about, for inducing it to speak of itself, for listening, recording, transcribing, and redistributing what is said about it: around sex, a whole network of varying, specific, and coercive transpositions into discourse. Rather than a massive censorship, beginning with the verbal proprieties imposed by the Age of Reason, what was involved was regulated and polymorphous incitement to discourse.

The objection will doubtless be raised that if so many stimulations and constraining mechanisms were necessary in order to speak of sex, this was because there reigned over everyone a certain fundamental prohibition; only definite necessities—economic pressures, political requirements—were able to lift this prohibition and open a few approaches to the discourse on sex, but these were limited and carefully coded; so much talk about sex, so many insistent devices contrived for causing it to be talked about—but under strict conditions: does this not prove that it was an object of secrecy, and more important, that there is still an attempt to keep it that way? But this often-stated theme, that sex is outside of discourse and that only the removing of an obstacle, the breaking of a secret, can clear the way leading to it, is precisely what needs to be examined. Does it not partake of the injunction by which discourse is provoked? Is it not with the aim of inciting people to speak of sex that it is made to mirror, at the outer limit of every actual discourse, something akin to a secret whose discovery is imperative, a thing abusively reduced to silence, and at the same time difficult and necessary, dangerous and precious to divulge? We must not forget that by making sex into that which, above all else, had to be confessed, the Christian pastoral always presented it as the disquieting enigma: not a thing which stubbornly shows itself, but one which always hides, the insidious presence that speaks in a voice so muted and often disguised that one risks remaining deaf to it. Doubtless the secret does not reside in that basic reality in relation to which all the incitements to speak of sex are situated—whether they try to force the secret, or whether in some obscure way they reinforce it by the manner in which they speak of it. It is a question rather of a theme that forms part of the very mechanics of these incitements: a way of giving shape to the requirement to speak about the matter, a fable that is indispensable to the endlessly proliferating economy of the discourse on sex. What is peculiar to modern societies, in fact, is not that they consigned sex to a shadow existence, but that they dedicated themselves to speaking of it *ad infinitum*, while exploiting it as *the* secret.

CHAPTER 2.
THE PERVERSE IMPLANTATION

A possible objection: it would be a mistake to see in this proliferation of discourses merely a quantitative phenomenon, something like a pure increase, as if what was said in them were immaterial, as if the fact of speaking about sex were of itself more important than the forms of imperatives that were imposed on it by speaking about it. For was this transformation of sex into discourse not governed by the endeavor to expel from reality the forms of sexuality that were not amenable to the strict economy of reproduction: to say no to unproductive activities, to banish casual pleasures, to reduce or exclude practices whose object was not procreation? Through the various discourses, legal sanctions against minor perversions were multiplied; sexual irregularity was annexed to mental illness; from childhood to old age, a norm of sexual development was defined and all the possible deviations were carefully described; pedagogical controls and medical treatments were organized; around the least fantasies, moralists, but especially doctors, brandished the whole emphatic vocabulary of abomination. Were these anything more than means employed to absorb, for the benefit of a genitally centered sexuality, all the fruitless pleasures? All this garrulous attention which has us in a stew over sexuality, is it not motivated by one basic concern: to ensure population, to reproduce labor capacity, to perpetuate the form of social relations: in short, to constitute a sexuality that is economically useful and politically conservative?[3]

I still do not know whether this is the ultimate objective. But this much is certain: reduction has not been the means employed for trying to achieve it. The nineteenth century and our own have been rather the age of multiplication: a dispersion of sexualities, a strengthening of their disparate forms, a multiple implantation of "perversions." Our epoch has initiated sexual heterogeneities.

Up to the end of the eighteenth century, three major explicit codes—apart from the customary regularities and constraints of opinion—governed sexual practices: canonical law, the Christian pastoral, and civil law. They determined, each in its own way, the division between licit and illicit. They were all centered on matrimonial relations: the marital obligation, the ability to fulfill it, the manner in which one complied with it, the requirements and violences that accompanied it, the useless or unwarranted caresses for which it was a pretext, its fecundity or the way one went about making it sterile, the moments when one demanded it (dangerous periods of pregnancy or breast-feeding, forbidden times of Lent or abstinence), its frequency or infrequency, and so on. It was this domain that was especially saturated with prescriptions. The sex of husband and wife was beset by rules and recommendations. The marriage relation was the most intense focus of constraints; it was spoken of more than anything else; more than any other relation, it was required to give a detailed accounting of itself. It was under constant surveillance: if it was found to be lacking, it had to come forward and plead its case before a witness. The "rest" remained a good deal more confused:

3. This paragraph encapsulates the received view against which Foucault will argue.

one only has to think of the uncertain status of "sodomy," or the indifference regarding the sexuality of children.

Moreover, these different codes did not make a clear distinction between violations of the rules of marriage and deviations with respect to genitality. Breaking the rules of marriage or seeking strange pleasures brought an equal measure of condemnation. On the list of grave sins, and separated only by their relative importance, there appeared debauchery (extramarital relations), adultery, rape, spiritual or carnal incest, but also sodomy, or the mutual "caress." As to the courts, they could condemn homosexuality as well as infidelity, marriage without parental consent, or bestiality. What was taken into account in the civil and religious jurisdictions alike was a general unlawfulness. Doubtless acts "contrary to nature" were stamped as especially abominable, but they were perceived simply as an extreme form of acts "against the law"; they were infringements of decrees which were just as sacred as those of marriage, and which had been established for governing the order of things and the plan of beings. Prohibitions bearing on sex were essentially of a juridical nature. The "nature" on which they were based was still a kind of law. For a long time hermaphrodites were criminals, or crime's offspring, since their anatomical disposition, their very being, confounded the law that distinguished the sexes and prescribed their union.

The discursive explosion of the eighteenth and nineteenth centuries caused this system centered on legitimate alliance to undergo two modifications. First, a centrifugal movement with respect to heterosexual monogamy. Of course, the array of practices and pleasures continued to be referred to it as their internal standard; but it was spoken of less and less, or in any case with a growing moderation. Efforts to find out its secrets were abandoned; nothing further was demanded of it than to define itself from day to day. The legitimate couple, with its regular sexuality, had a right to more discretion. It tended to function as a norm, one that was stricter, perhaps, but quieter. On the other hand, what came under scrutiny was the sexuality of children, mad men and women, and criminals; the sensuality of those who did not like the opposite sex; reveries, obsessions, petty manias, or great transports of rage. It was time for all these figures, scarcely noticed in the past, to step forward and speak, to make the difficult confession of what they were. No doubt they were condemned all the same; but they were listened to; and if regular sexuality happened to be questioned once again, it was through a reflux movement, originating in these peripheral sexualities.

Whence the setting apart of the "unnatural" as a specific dimension in the field of sexuality. This kind of activity assumed an autonomy with regard to the other condemned forms such as adultery or rape (and the latter were condemned less and less): to marry a close relative or practice sodomy, to seduce a nun or engage in sadism, to deceive one's wife or violate cadavers, became things that were essentially different. The area covered by the Sixth Commandment[4] began to fragment. Similarly, in the civil order, the confused category of "debauchery," which for more than a century had been one of the most frequent reasons for administrative confinement, came apart. From the debris, there appeared on the one hand infractions against the legislation (or morality) pertaining to marriage and the family, and on the

4. "Thou shalt not commit adultery."

other, offenses against the regularity of a natural function (offenses which, it must be added, the law was apt to punish). Here we have a likely reason, among others, for the prestige of Don Juan,[5] which three centuries have not erased. Underneath the great violator of the rules of marriage—stealer of wives, seducer of virgins, the shame of families, and an insult to husbands and fathers—another personage can be glimpsed: the individual driven, in spite of himself, by the somber madness of sex. Underneath the libertine, the pervert. He deliberately breaks the law, but at the same time, something like a nature gone awry transports him far from all nature; his death is the moment when the supernatural return of the crime and its retribution thwarts the flight into counternature. There were two great systems conceived by the West for governing sex: the law of marriage and the order of desires—and the life of Don Juan overturned them both. We shall leave it to psychoanalysts to speculate whether he was homosexual, narcissistic, or impotent.

Although not without delay and equivocation, the natural laws of matrimony and the immanent rules of sexuality began to be recorded on two separate registers. There emerged a world of perversion which partook of that of legal or moral infraction, yet was not simply a variety of the latter. An entire sub-race race was born, different—despite certain kinship ties—from the libertines of the past. From the end of the eighteenth century to our own, they circulated through the pores of society; they were always hounded, but not always by laws; were often locked up, but not always in prisons; were sick perhaps, but scandalous, dangerous victims, prey to a strange evil that also bore the name of vice and sometimes crime. They were children wise beyond their years, precocious little girls, ambiguous schoolboys, dubious servants and educators, cruel or maniacal husbands, solitary collectors, ramblers with bizarre impulses; they haunted the houses of correction, the penal colonies, the tribunals, and the asylums; they carried their infamy to the doctors and their sickness to the judges. This was the numberless family of perverts who were on friendly terms with delinquents and akin to madmen. In the course of the century they successively bore the stamp of "moral folly," "genital neurosis," "aberration of the genetic instinct," "degenerescence," or "physical imbalance."

What does the appearance of all these peripheral sexualities signify? Is the fact that they could appear in broad daylight a sign that the code had become more lax? Or does the fact that they were given so much attention testify to a stricter regime and to its concern to bring them under close supervision? In terms of repression, things are unclear. There was permissiveness, if one bears in mind that the severity of the codes relating to sexual offenses diminished considerably in the nineteenth century and that law itself often deferred to medicine. But an additional ruse of severity, if one thinks of all the agencies of control and all the mechanisms of surveillance that were put into operation by pedagogy or therapeutics. It may be the case that the intervention of the Church in conjugal sexuality and its rejection of "frauds" against procreation had lost much of their insistence over the previous two hundred years. But medicine made a forceful entry into the pleasures of the

5. Legendary libertine, whose story is variously told in Molière's play (1665), Mozart's opera (1787), Byron's poem (1819–24), and elsewhere.

couple: it created an entire organic, functional, or mental pathology arising out of "incomplete" sexual practices; it carefully classified all forms of related pleasures; it incorporated them into the notions of "development" and instinctual "disturbances"; and it undertook to manage them.

Perhaps the point to consider is not the level of indulgence or the quantity of repression but the form of power that was exercised. When this whole thicket of disparate sexualities was labeled, as if to disentangle them from one another, was the object to exclude them from reality? It appears, in fact, that the function of the power exerted in this instance was not that of interdiction, and that it involved four operations quite different from simple prohibition.

1. Take the ancient prohibitions of consanguine marriages (as numerous and complex as they were) or the condemnation of adultery, with its inevitable frequency of occurrence; or on the other hand, the recent controls through which, since the nineteenth century, the sexuality of children has been subordinated and their "solitary habits" interfered with. It is clear that we are not dealing with one and the same power mechanism. Not only because in the one case it is a question of law and penality, and in the other, medicine and regimentation; but also because the tactics employed is not the same. On the surface, what appears in both cases is an effort at elimination that was always destined to fail and always constrained to begin again. But the prohibition of "incests" attempted to reach its objective through an asymptotic decrease in the thing it condemned, whereas the control of infantile sexuality hoped to reach it through a simultaneous propagation of its own power and of the object on which it was brought to bear. It proceeded in accordance with a twofold increase extended indefinitely. Educators and doctors combatted children's onanism like an epidemic that needed to be eradicated. What this actually entailed, throughout this whole secular campaign that mobilized the adult world around the sex of children, was using these tenuous pleasures as a prop, constituting them as secrets (that is, forcing them into hiding so as to make possible their discovery), tracing them back to their source, tracking them from their origins to their effects, searching out everything that might cause them or simply enable them to exist. Wherever there was the chance they might appear, devices of surveillance were installed; traps were laid for compelling admissions; inexhaustible and corrective discourses were imposed; parents and teachers were alerted, and left with the suspicion that all children were guilty, and with the fear of being themselves at fault if their suspicions were not sufficiently strong; they were kept in readiness in the face of this recurrent danger; their conduct was prescribed and their pedagogy recodified; an entire medico-sexual regime took hold of the family milieu. The child's "vice" was not so much an enemy as a support; it may have been designated as the evil to be eliminated, but the extraordinary effort that went into the task that was bound to fail leads one to suspect that what was demanded of it was to persevere, to proliferate to the limits of the visible and the invisible, rather than to disappear for good. Always relying on this support, power advanced, multiplied its relays and its effects, while its target expanded, subdivided, and branched out, penetrating further into reality at the same pace. In appearance, we are dealing with a barrier system; but in fact, all around the child, indefinite *lines of penetration* were disposed.

2. This new persecution of the peripheral sexualities entailed an *incorporation of perversions* and a new *specification of individuals*. As defined by the ancient civil or canonical codes, sodomy was a category of forbidden acts; their perpetrator was nothing more than the juridical subject of them. The nineteenth-century homosexual became a personage, a past, a case history, and a childhood, in addition to being a type of life, a life form, and a morphology, with an indiscreet anatomy and possibly a mysterious physiology. Nothing that went into his total composition was unaffected by his sexuality. It was everywhere present in him: at the root of all his actions because it was their insidious and indefinitely active principle; written immodestly on his face and body because it was a secret that always gave itself away. It was consubstantial with him, less as a habitual sin than as a singular nature. We must not forget that the psychological, psychiatric, medical category of homosexuality was constituted from the moment it was characterized—Westphal's famous article of 1870[6] on "contrary sexual sensations" can stand as its date of birth—less by a type of sexual relations than by a certain quality of sexual sensibility, a certain way of inverting the masculine and the feminine in oneself. Homosexuality appeared as one of the forms of sexuality when it was transposed from the practice of sodomy onto a kind of interior androgyny, a hermaphrodism of the soul. The sodomite had been a temporary aberration; the homosexual was now a species.

So too were all those minor perverts whom nineteenth-century psychiatrists entomologized by giving them strange baptismal names: there were Krafft-Ebing's zoophiles and zooerasts, Rohleder's auto-monosexualists; and later, mixoscopophiles, gynecomasts, presbyophiles, sexoesthetic inverts, and dyspareunist women.[7] These fine names for heresies referred to a nature that was overlooked by the law, but not so neglectful of itself that it did not go on producing more species, even where there was no order to fit them into. The machinery of power that focused on this whole alien strain did not aim to suppress it, but rather to give it an analytical, visible, and permanent reality: it was implanted in bodies, slipped in beneath modes of conduct, made into a principle of classification and intelligibility, established as a *raison d'être* and a natural order of disorder. Not the exclusion of these thousand aberrant sexualities, but the specification, the regional solidification of each one of them. The strategy behind this dissemination was to strew reality with them and incorporate them into the individual.

3. More than the old taboos, this form of power demanded constant, attentive, and curious presences for its exercise; it presupposed proximities; it proceeded through examination and insistent observation; it required an exchange of discourses, through questions that extorted admissions, and confidences that went beyond the questions that were asked. It implied a physical proximity and an interplay of intense sensations. The medicalization of

6. Carl Westphal, *Archiv für Neurologie*, 1870 [Foucault's note]. Westphal (1833–1890), German neurologist.

7. The scientists named are Richard Krafft-Ebing (1840–1902), a German psychiatrist best known for his study of sexual abnormalities, and Hermann Rohleder (1866–1938), a German physician who wrote extensively on sexual behavior. They and other psychiatrists labeled people who desire sexual contact with animals (zoophiles, zooerasts), people who masturbate but have no sexual contact with other people (auto-monosexualists), people who get sexual pleasure from viewing pictures of animals and humans having sexual intercourse (mixoscopophiles), men with enlarged breasts (gynecomasts), people who are sexually attracted to clergy (presbyophiles), homosexuals who follow the Greek idealization of the young male body (sexoesthetic inverts), and women for whom sexual intercourse is painful (dyspareunist women).

the sexually peculiar was both the effect and the instrument of this. Imbedded in bodies, becoming deeply characteristic of individuals, the oddities of sex relied on a technology of health and pathology. And conversely, since sexuality was a medical and medicalizable object, one had to try and detect it—as a lesion, a dysfunction, or a symptom—in the depths of the organism, or on the surface of the skin, or among all the signs of behavior. The power which thus took charge of sexuality set about contacting bodies, caressing them with its eyes, intensifying areas, electrifying surfaces, dramatizing troubled moments. It wrapped the sexual body in its embrace. There was undoubtedly an increase in effectiveness and an extension of the domain controlled; but also a sensualization of power and a gain of pleasure. This produced a twofold effect: an impetus was given to power through its very exercise; an emotion rewarded the overseeing control and carried it further; the intensity of the confession renewed the questioner's curiosity; the pleasure discovered fed back to the power that encircled it. But so many pressing questions singularized the pleasures felt by the one who had to reply. They were fixed by a gaze, isolated and animated by the attention they received. Power operated as a mechanism of attraction; it drew out those peculiarities over which it kept watch. Pleasure spread to the power that harried it; power anchored the pleasure it uncovered.

The medical examination, the psychiatric investigation, the pedagogical report, and family controls may have the over-all and apparent objective of saying no to all wayward or unproductive sexualities, but the fact is that they function as mechanisms with a double impetus: pleasure and power. The pleasure that comes of exercising a power that questions, monitors, watches, spies, searches out, palpates, brings to light; and on the other hand, the pleasure that kindles at having to evade this power, flee from it, fool it, or travesty it. The power that lets itself be invaded by the pleasure it is pursuing; and opposite it, power asserting itself in the pleasure of showing off, scandalizing, or resisting. Capture and seduction, confrontation and mutual reinforcement: parents and children, adults and adolescents, educator and students, doctors and patients, the psychiatrist with his hysteric and his perverts, all have played this game continually since the nineteenth century. These attractions, these evasions, these circular incitements have traced around bodies and sexes, not boundaries not to be crossed, but *perpetual spirals of power and pleasure*.

4. Whence those *devices of sexual saturation* so characteristic of the space and the social rituals of the nineteenth century. People often say that modern society has attempted to reduce sexuality to the couple—the heterosexual and, insofar as possible, legitimate couple. There are equal grounds for saying that it has, if not created, at least outfitted and made to proliferate, groups with multiple elements and a circulating sexuality: a distribution of points of power, hierarchized and placed opposite to one another; "pursued" pleasures, that is, both sought after and searched out; compartmental sexualities that are tolerated or encouraged; proximities that serve as surveillance procedures, and function as mechanisms of intensification; contacts that operate as inductors. This is the way things worked in the case of the family, or rather the household, with parents, children, and in some instances, servants. Was the nineteenth-century family really a monogamic and conjugal cell? Perhaps to a certain extent. But it was also a network of pleasures and

powers linked together at multiple points and according to transformable relationships. The separation of grown-ups and children, the polarity established between the parents' bedroom and that of the children (it became routine in the course of the century when working-class housing construction was undertaken), the relative segregation of boys and girls, the strict instructions as to the care of nursing infants (maternal breast-feeding, hygiene), the attention focused on infantile sexuality, the supposed dangers of masturbation, the importance attached to puberty, the methods of surveillance suggested to parents, the exhortations, secrets, and fears, the presence—both valued and feared—of servants: all this made the family, even when brought down to its smallest dimensions, a complicated network, saturated with multiple, fragmentary, and mobile sexualities. To reduce them to the conjugal relationship, and then to project the latter, in the form of a forbidden desire, onto the children, cannot account for this apparatus which, in relation to these sexualities, was less a principle of inhibition than an inciting and multiplying mechanism.[8] Educational or psychiatric institutions, with their large populations, their hierarchies, their spatial arrangements, their surveillance systems, constituted, alongside the family, another way of distributing the interplay of powers and pleasures; but they too delineated areas of extreme sexual saturation, with privileged spaces or rituals such as the classroom, the dormitory, the visit, and the consultation. The forms of a nonconjugal, nonmonogamous sexuality were drawn there and established.

Nineteenth-century "bourgeois" society—and it is doubtless still with us—was a society of blatant and fragmented perversion. And this was not by way of hypocrisy, for nothing was more manifest and more prolix, or more manifestly taken over by discourses and institutions. Not because, having tried to erect too rigid or too general a barrier against sexuality, society succeeded only in giving rise to a whole perverse outbreak and a long pathology of the sexual instinct. At issue, rather, is the type of power it brought to bear on the body and on sex. In point of fact, this power had neither the form of the law, nor the effects of the taboo. On the contrary, it acted by multiplication of singular sexualities. It did not set boundaries for sexuality; it extended the various forms of sexuality, pursuing them according to lines of indefinite penetration. It did not exclude sexuality, but included it in the body as a mode of specification of individuals. It did not seek to avoid it; it attracted its varieties by means of spirals in which pleasure and power reinforced one another. It did not set up a barrier; it provided places of maximum saturation. It produced and determined the sexual mosaic. Modern society is perverse, not in spite of its puritanism or as if from a backlash provoked by its hypocrisy; it is in actual fact, and directly, perverse.

In actual fact. The manifold sexualities—those which appear with the different ages (sexualities of the infant or the child), those which become fixated on particular tastes or practices (the sexuality of the invert, the gerontophile,[9] the fetishist), those which, in a diffuse manner, invest relationships (the sexuality of doctor and patient, teacher and student, psychiatrist and mental patient), those which haunt spaces (the sexuality of the home,

8. An oblique critique of Freud's concept of the Oedipus complex.

9. Lover of the old.

the school, the prison)—all form the correlate of exact procedures of power. We must not imagine that all these things that were formerly tolerated attracted notice and received a pejorative designation when the time came to give a regulative role to the one type of sexuality that was capable of reproducing labor power and the form of the family. These polymorphous conducts were actually extracted from people's bodies and from their pleasures; or rather, they were solidified in them; they were drawn out, revealed, isolated, intensified, incorporated, by multifarious power devices. The growth of perversions is not a moralizing theme that obssessed the scrupulous minds of the Victorians. It is the real product of the encroachment of a type of power on bodies and their pleasures. It is possible that the West has not been capable of inventing any new pleasures, and it has doubtless not discovered any original vices. But it has defined new rules for the game of powers and pleasures. The frozen countenance of the perversions is a fixture of this game.

Directly. This implantation of multiple perversions is not a mockery of sexuality taking revenge on a power that has thrust on it an excessively repressive law. Neither are we dealing with paradoxical forms of pleasure that turn back on power and invest it in the form of a "pleasure to be endured." The implantation of perversions is an instrument-effect: it is through the isolation, intensification, and consolidation of peripheral sexualities that the relations of power to sex and pleasure branched out and multiplied, measured the body, and penetrated modes of conduct. And accompanying this encroachment of powers, scattered sexualities rigidified, became stuck to an age, a place, a type of practice. A proliferation of sexualities through the extension of power; an optimization of the power to which each of these local sexualities gave a surface of intervention: this concatenation, particularly since the nineteenth century, has been ensured and relayed by the countless economic interests which, with the help of medicine, psychiatry, prostitution, and pornography, have tapped into both this analytical multiplication of pleasure and this optimization of the power that controls it. Pleasure and power do not cancel or turn back against one another; they seek out, overlap, and reinforce one another. They are linked together by complex mechanisms and devices of excitation and incitement.

We must therefore abandon the hypothesis that modern industrial societies ushered in an age of increased sexual repression. We have not only witnessed a visible explosion of unorthodox sexualities; but—and this is the important point—a deployment quite different from the law, even if it is locally dependent on procedures of prohibition, has ensured, through a network of interconnecting mechanisms, the proliferation of specific pleasures and the multiplication of disparate sexualities. It is said that no society has been more prudish; never have the agencies of power taken such care to feign ignorance of the thing they prohibited, as if they were determined to have nothing to do with it. But it is the opposite that has become apparent, at least after a general review of the facts: never have there existed more centers of power; never more attention manifested and verbalized; never more circular contacts and linkages; never more sites where the intensity of pleasures and the persistency of power catch hold, only to spread elsewhere.

1976

From Truth and Power[1]

* * *

For a long period, the 'left' intellectual spoke and was acknowledged the right of speaking in the capacity of master of truth and justice. He was heard, or purported to make himself heard, as the spokesman of the universal. To be an intellectual meant something like being the consciousness/conscience of us all. I think we have here an idea transposed from Marxism, from a faded Marxism indeed.[2] Just as the proletariat, by the necessity of its historical situation, is the bearer of the universal (but its immediate, unreflected bearer, barely conscious of itself as such), so the intellectual, through his moral, theoretical and political choice, aspires to be the bearer of this universality in its conscious, elaborated form. The intellectual is thus taken as the clear, individual figure of a universality whose obscure, collective form is embodied in the proletariat.

Some years have now passed since the intellectual was called upon to play this role. A new mode of the 'connection between theory and practice' has been established. Intellectuals have got used to working, not in the modality of the 'universal', the 'exemplary', the 'just-and-true-for-all', but within specific sectors, at the precise points where their own conditions of life or work situate them (housing, the hospital, the asylum, the laboratory, the university, family and sexual relations). This has undoubtedly given them a much more immediate and concrete awareness of struggles. And they have met here with problems which are specific, 'non-universal', and often different from those of the proletariat or the masses. And yet I believe intellectuals have actually been drawn closer to the proletariat and the masses, for two reasons. Firstly, because it has been a question of real, material, everyday struggles, and secondly because they have often been confronted, albeit in a different form, by the same adversary as the proletariat, namely the multinational corporations, the judicial and police apparatuses, the property speculators, etc. This is what I would call the 'specific' intellectual as opposed to the 'universal' intellectual.

* * *

Now let's come back to more precise details. We accept, alongside the development of technico-scientific structures in contemporary society, the importance gained by the specific intellectual in recent decades, as well as the acceleration of this process since around 1960. Now the specific intellectual encounters certain obstacles and faces certain dangers. The danger of remaining at the level of conjunctural struggles, pressing demands restricted to particular sectors. The risk of letting himself be manipulated by the political parties or trade union apparatuses which control these local struggles. Above all, the risk of being unable to develop these struggles for lack of a global strategy or outside support; the risk too of not being followed, or only by very limited groups. In France we can see at the moment an

1. Translated by Colin Gordon.
2. The German political philosopher KARL MARX (1818–1883) believed that the proletariat within capitalism embodied the "universal" revolutionary aspirations of the people.

example of this. The struggle around the prisons, the penal system and the police-judicial system, because it has developed 'in solitary', among social workers and ex-prisoners, has tended increasingly to separate itself from the forces which would have enabled it to grow. It has allowed itself to be penetrated by a whole naive, archaic ideology which makes the criminal at once into the innocent victim and the pure rebel—society's scapegoat—and the young wolf of future revolutions. This return to anarchist themes of the late nineteenth century was possible only because of a failure of integration of current strategies. And the result has been a deep split between this campaign with its monotonous, lyrical little chant, heard only among a few small groups, and the masses who have good reason not to accept it as valid political currency, but who also—thanks to the studiously cultivated fear of criminals—tolerate the maintenance, or rather the reinforcement, of the judicial and police apparatuses.

It seems to me that we are now at a point where the function of the specific intellectual needs to be reconsidered. Reconsidered but not abandoned, despite the nostalgia of some for the great 'universal' intellectuals and the desire for a new philosophy, a new world-view. Suffice it to consider the important results which have been achieved in psychiatry: they prove that these local, specific struggles haven't been a mistake and haven't led to a dead end. One may even say that the role of the specific intellectual must become more and more important in proportion to the political responsibilities which he is obliged willy-nilly to accept, as a nuclear scientist, computer expert, pharmacologist, etc. It would be a dangerous error to discount him politically in his specific relation to a local form of power, either on the grounds that this is a specialist matter which doesn't concern the masses (which is doubly wrong: they are already aware of it, and in any case implicated in it), or that the specific intellectual serves the interests of State or Capital (which is true, but at the same time shows the strategic position he occupies), or, again, on the grounds that he propagates a scientific ideology (which isn't always true, and is anyway certainly a secondary matter compared with the fundamental point: the effects proper to true discourses).

The important thing here, I believe, is that truth isn't outside power, or lacking in power: contrary to a myth whose history and functions would repay further study, truth isn't the reward of free spirits, the child of protracted solitude, nor the privilege of those who have succeeded in liberating themselves. Truth is a thing of this world: it is produced only by virtue of multiple forms of constraint. And it induces regular effects of power. Each society has its régime of truth, its 'general politics' of truth: that is, the types of discourse which it accepts and makes function as true; the mechanisms and instances which enable one to distinguish true and false statements, the means by which each is sanctioned; the techniques and procedures accorded value in the acquisition of truth; the status of those who are charged with saying what counts as true.

In societies like ours, the 'political economy' of truth is characterised by five important traits. 'Truth' is centred on the form of scientific discourse and the institutions which produce it; it is subject to constant economic and political incitement (the demand for truth, as much for economic production as for political power); it is the object, under diverse forms, of immense diffusion and consumption (circulating through apparatuses of education and information whose extent is relatively broad in the social body, notwithstanding certain strict limitations); it is produced and transmitted under the control, dominant if not exclusive, of a few great political and economic apparatuses (university, army, writing, media); lastly, it is the issue of a whole political debate and social confrontation ('ideological' struggles).

It seems to me that what must now be taken into account in the intellectual is not the 'bearer of universal values'. Rather, it's the person occupying a specific position—but whose specificity is linked, in a society like ours, to the general functioning of an apparatus of truth. In other words, the intellectual has a three-fold specificity: that of his class position (whether as petty-bourgeois in the service of capitalism or 'organic' intellectual[3] of the proletariat); that of his conditions of life and work, linked to his condition as an intellectual (his field of research, his place in a laboratory, the political and economic demands to which he submits or against which he rebels, in the university, the hospital, etc.); lastly, the specificity of the politics of truth in our societies. And it's with this last factor that his position can take on a general significance and that his local, specific struggle can have effects and implications which are not simply professional or sectoral. The intellectual can operate and struggle at the general level of that régime of truth which is so essential to the structure and functioning of our society. There is a battle 'for truth', or at least 'around truth'—it being understood once again that by truth I do not mean 'the ensemble of truths which are to be discovered and accepted', but rather 'the ensemble of rules according to which the true and the false are separated and specific effects of power attached to the true', it being understood also that it's not a matter of a battle 'on behalf' of the truth, but of a battle about the status of truth and the economic and political role it plays. It is necessary to think of the political problems of intellectuals not in terms of 'science' and 'ideology', but in terms of 'truth' and 'power'. And thus the question of the professionalisation of intellectuals and the division between intellectual and manual labour can be envisaged in a new way.

All this must seem very confused and uncertain. Uncertain indeed, and what I am saying here is above all to be taken as a hypothesis. In order for it to be a little less confused, however, I would like to put forward a few 'propositions'—not firm assertions, but simply suggestions to be further tested and evaluated.

'Truth' is to be understood as a system of ordered procedures for the production, regulation, distribution, circulation and operation of statements.

'Truth' is linked in a circular relation with systems of power which produce and sustain it, and to effects of power which it induces and which extend it. A 'régime' of truth.

This régime is not merely ideological or superstructural; it was a condition of the formation and development of capitalism.[4] And it's this same régime which, subject to certain modifications, operates in the socialist countries (I leave open here the question of China, about which I know little).

The essential political problem for the intellectual is not to criticise the

3. Someone (regardless of profession) who directs the ideas and aspirations of the particular social class to which he or she "organically" belongs, as described by the Italian Marxist ANTONIO GRAMSCI (1891–1937).

4. Foucault reverses Marxist accounts that see "truth" as a superstructural product of the economic base.

ideological contents supposedly linked to science, or to ensure that his own scientific practice is accompanied by a correct ideology, but that of ascertaining the possibility of constituting a new politics of truth. The problem is not changing people's consciousnesses—or what's in their heads—but the political, economic, institutional régime of the production of truth.

It's not a matter of emancipating truth from every system of power (which would be a chimera, for truth is already power) but of detaching the power of truth from the forms of hegemony,[5] social, economic and cultural, within which it operates at the present time.

The political question, to sum up, is not error, illusion, alienated consciousness or ideology; it is truth itself. Hence the importance of Nietzsche.[6]

1977

5. A term from Gramsci; the manufactured consent that legitimates a dominant group and unifies a society. Foucault's régime of truth is a form of hegemonic discourse.

6. FRIEDRICH NIETZSCHE (1844–1900), German philosopher, who viewed truth as the product of "the will to power." Foucault, following Nietzsche, wants the story of truth to be told in a "genealogical" history that uncovers the struggles among contending forces.

WOLFGANG ISER
b. 1926

Reacting against formalist approaches to literature, notably the New Critical prohibition of considering audience response, American literary criticism in the 1970s began to pay renewed attention to the role of the reader in interpretation. Alongside French poststructuralist approaches that asserted, in ROLAND BARTHES's phrase, the "writerly" nature of reading and psychoanalytic views that studied the psychology of reading, the German "Constance School" was most prominent in advocating the investigation of *Rezeptionsästhetik*, or "the aesthetics of reception." Wolfgang Iser is a leading member of the Constance School, and he focuses particularly on the way in which texts are actively constructed by individual readers through the phenomenology of the reading process.

Born in Germany and trained as an undergraduate at the University of Leipzig and the University of Tubingen, Iser earned his Ph.D. in 1950 from the University of Heidelberg, where he studied with the philosopher Hans-Georg Gadamer. Thereafter, Iser held a series of appointments in English literature at the Universities of Glasgow, Heidelberg, Würzburg, and Cologne, settling finally in 1967 in Germany at the newly founded University of Constance as a professor of English and comparative literature. Iser's arrival at Constance, where he joined a research group that included HANS ROBERT JAUSS, proved especially fruitful for the development of his theories of reader response. Since the mid-1980s, Iser has also held an appointment as permanent visiting professor of English at the University of California at Irvine.

The Constance School draws on the philosophical tradition of aesthetics inaugurated in eighteenth-century German philosophy by Alexander Baumgarten, IMMANUEL KANT, and FRIEDRICH VON SCHILLER, and it focuses on the affective as well as the formal dimensions of art. The work of the Constance School has also been influenced by philosophical considerations of hermeneutics, or the theory of interpretation, developed by FRIEDRICH SCHLEIERMACHER (1768–1834), MARTIN HEIDEGGER (1889–1976), and others. In particular, Iser's work draws on the hermeneutic philosophy of Gadamer and the phenomenological literary theory of Roman Ingarden (1893–1970), which examines the processes of cognition through which we understand literary works.

Iser's early work includes two scholarly studies of English literature, his doctoral dissertation on the eighteenth-century novels of Henry Fielding and a book on the aesthetic views of the Victorian critic WALTER PATER. However, it was not until his inaugural lecture at Constance in 1970, "The Affective Structure of the Text," that he articulated his theory of the interactive nature of the reading experience. This was followed by the two of his books that have most influenced Anglo-American literary studies, *The Implied Reader: Patterns of Communication in Prose Fiction from Bunyan to Beckett* (1972; trans. 1974) and *The Act of Reading: A Theory of Aesthetic Response* (1976; trans. 1978). *The Implied Reader* studies a series of English novels from the eighteenth century through the twentieth century, showing how "readers take an active part in the composition of the novel's meaning." According to Iser, literary texts provide the foundation for their interpretation, but they also imply the action of the reader. Reading is not passive or static but a process of discovery; a reader questions, negates, and revises the expectations that the text establishes, filling in what Iser calls "blanks" or "gaps" in the text and continually modifying his or her interpretation.

Iser's concept of "the implied reader" recalls Wayne Booth's notion of "the implied author," elaborated in *The Rhetoric of Fiction* (1961; rev. ed. 1983). Booth argues that although we might not be able to recover an author's intention to determine meaning (acknowledging the New Critical argument against authorial intention codified in W. K. WIMSATT JR. AND MONROE BEARDSLEY's "Intentional Fallacy," 1946; see above), we can infer intention, particularly bearing on ethical views, from the statements of the narrator. The reader, Iser maintains, can similarly infer from a text directions guiding interpretation. To borrow a phrase from the courtroom, texts ask leading questions.

Expanding on the methods in *The Implied Reader, The Act of Reading* offers a more programmatic explanation of the reading experience and the ways in which readers process texts. Iser argues that texts provide "sets of instructions" or a "repertoire" that the reader must assemble, so that interpretation depends on both the text and response. Interpretation does not derive from one or the other, but from their combination and interaction, forming what Iser calls "the virtual text." As Iser describes it, "the text represents a potential effect that is realized in the reading process."

Iser's version of reader response differs from that of Jauss, who deals with the actual reception of a literary work and how that concrete history tempers our expectations and therefore influences our interpretation. We never see a text on its own, but always in the context of its reception by others. Iser focuses on the individual interactive process—the phenomenology or cognition—of the act of reading, rather than the larger literary-historical concerns that Jauss describes. Iser's investigation of response also differs from that of STANLEY FISH, the most prominent advocate of response criticism in the United States, who locates the meaning of literary texts in the protocols of the interpretive communities to which readers belong rather than in the interaction of text and reader.

Reader-response criticism takes particular aim at the once-dominant dictates of the New Criticism, codified in Wimsatt and Beardsley's "Affective Fallacy" (1949; see above), which dismisses considerations of the reader as "a confusion between the poem and its results." Provocatively turning the tables on formalistic, text-based approaches, Fish claims that the affective fallacy is itself a fallacy, since our readings are always governed not by the text but by the personal assumptions and interpretive protocols that we start with. Iser carves out a compromise position between formalist theories of literature that assume a stable object of study (witness the titles of the best-known books of the New Criticism, CLEANTH BROOKS's *Well Wrought Urn* and Wimsatt's *Verbal Icon*) and more radical reader-based approaches, such as Fish's. Iser carefully qualifies his position, insisting that reading depends on the text and that a theory of response, "if it is to carry any weight at all, must have its foundations in literary texts." A text functions in much the same way as a script does for a play. A script guides a performance, but performers enact it in different ways at different times. Just as we might say that one actor's or director's version of a play is his or her interpretation, readings of literary texts depend on the text but are realized through the process of interpretation. Iser's term "the virtual text" encompasses both dimensions, the text and its realization by an actual reader.

Some critics of contemporary reader-response criticism charge that it promotes radical relativism and indeterminacy. By focusing on the role of the reader rather than the textual object, they contend, reader response leaves meaning to the subjective whim of each individual reader, leaving no objective or secure basis for literary interpretation. Further, they accuse reader-based approaches of rendering interpretation indeterminate, because there might be an infinite number of possible readings for every text—as many as there are readers. Iser's analyses of literature do not subscribe to these views. His concept of a textual "repertoire" acknowledges the formal dimensions of literary works and their determinate role in producing the "virtual text."

Our selection, "Interaction between Text and Reader" (1980), summarizes the theoretical argument offered in *The Act of Reading*. Iser stresses that interpretation is neither objective nor subjective, but always a result of the dynamic interaction of text and reader. The structure of the literary text guides the reader, but the reader continually modifies her or his viewpoint, connecting new segments of the text and filling in the "gaps" of what the text does not mention. Meaning is not static but constantly revised in a process that Iser compares to a feedback loop in communication theory, resembling what philosophers call "the hermeneutic circle."

As Stanley Fish remarks in an essay titled "Why No One Is Afraid of Wolfgang Iser," despite the sometimes contentious debates in contemporary literary theory, there has been relatively little criticism of Iser's work. This results, in part, from Iser's middle-ground position between formalism and certain poststructuralist approaches that argue for the ultimate indeterminacy of interpretation. Iser's acknowledgment of the text's repertoire protects against charges of indeterminacy, and his close attention to texts is consonant with close-reading practices common in Anglo-American literary criticism. In addition, Iser deals primarily with canonical English novels, making his work more "user-friendly" for Anglo-American students and critics. Fish himself argues that Iser's terms are vague and contradictory; for instance, to postulate the existence of gaps, one must assume that there are definite givens, and Fish questions whether one can determine the difference between the two. Other criticism has been voiced by those advocating the study of the social dimensions of literature, such as the Marxist critic TERRY EAGLETON, who notes that by solely concentrating on the "aesthetic aspects" of texts, Iser ignores their social and historical dimensions.

Probably because it takes the middle ground, Iser's work has had more influence on pedagogy and applied criticism than on larger debates in contemporary literary theory. Iser does not claim a revolutionary view or one strongly antagonistic toward other approaches, which might gain vehement adherents and detractors. However, his work has been valuable in calling attention to the reading process. It thereby forms part of what Fish has called "the rhetorical turn" in literary criticism, away from the narrow parameters of "the text itself" and toward the effects of texts on audiences and in history. We might speculate that prominent modes of criticism in the past could ignore the role of the reader since they tacitly assumed that there was one kind of reader (i.e., white, male, and the recipient of a privileged education). With the expansion of higher education after World War II, the diversity of those entering literary studies called attention to the variety of possible reading experiences and how the positions of individual readers might affect their interpretations of texts. Feminist literary criticism has pointed to how the literary canon has been shaped by masculinist assumptions (see SANDRA M. GILBERT AND SUSAN GUBAR) and how women might read differently (see ANNETTE KOLODNY). Other contemporary approaches, such as gay and lesbian criticism, race and ethnic studies, and theories of postcolonialism, also note the significance of the identity of the reader in interpretation.

BIBLIOGRAPHY

Iser's early works, *Die Weltanschauung Henry Fieldings* (1952, *Henry Fielding's Worldview*) and *Walter Pater: The Aesthetic Moment* (1960; trans. 1987), are traditional scholarly studies. He first develops his views of reader response in *Die Appellstruktur der Text* (1970, *The Affective Structure of the Text*), *The Implied Reader: Patterns of Communication in Prose Fiction from Bunyan to Beckett* (1972; trans. 1974), and *The Act of Reading: A Theory of Aesthetic Response* (1976; trans. 1978). Thereafter, Iser published *Staging Politics: The Lasting Impact of Shakespeare's Histories* (1988; trans. 1993), *Prospecting: From Reader Response to Literary Anthropology* (1989), and *The Fictive and the Imaginary: Charting Literary Anthropology* (1991; trans. 1993). *Staging Politics* presents a series of lectures on Shakespeare's histories and their politics. *Prospecting*, which gathers a number of essays elaborating his theories of reader response, calls for a "literary anthropology" that studies the human need for fiction. *The Fictive and the Imaginary* departs from Iser's concern with response to concentrate on literary anthropology, explaining "why literature seems to be necessary as a continual patterning of human plasticity."

The standard collections of reader-response criticism are *Reader-Response Criticism: From Formalism to Post-Structuralism*, edited by Jane P. Tompkins (1980), which includes a useful introduction surveying its development and an annotated but dated bibliography, and *The Reader in the Text: Essays on Audience and Interpretation*, edited by Susan R. Suleiman and Inge Crosman (1980). An early, notable response by Stanley Fish, "Why No One Is Afraid of Wolfgang Iser," appeared in *Diacritics* 11 (1981). Steven Mailloux's *Interpretive Conventions: The Reader in the Study of American Fiction* (1982) includes a good discussion of Iser's relation to the New Criticism and a pointed comparison between Iser and Fish. Robert C. Holub's *Reception Theory: A Critical Introduction* (1984) surveys German reception theory from its roots in hermeneutic philosophy to its practice in the Constance School. The collection of essays *Gender and Reading: Essays on Readers, Texts, and Contexts*, edited by Elizabeth A. Flynn and Patrocinio P. Schweickart (1986), draws attention to the question of gender and the identity of the reader, and its selections include relevant discussions of Iser. Elizabeth Freund's *Return of the Reader: Reader-Response Criticism* (1987) narrates the rise of reader-response criticism in the United States, from the New Critics' disavowal of the reader to Iser's avowal of the reading experience. A special issue of *New Literary History* 31 (2000), edited by John Paul Riquelme, reconsiders different aspects of Iser's work.

Interaction between Text and Reader

Central to the reading of every literary work is the interaction between its structure and its recipient. This is why the phenomenological theory of art[1] has emphatically drawn attention to the fact that the study of a literary work should concern not only the actual text but also, and in equal measure, the actions involved in responding to that text. The text itself simply offers "sche-

1. Phenomenological theories of philosophy focus on human consciousness and perception, particularly the interrelation between the perceiving subject and the perceived object (here, audience and work).

matized aspects"[2] through which the aesthetic object of the work can be produced.

From this we may conclude that the literary work has two poles, which we might call the artistic and the aesthetic: the artistic pole is the author's text, and the aesthetic is the realization accomplished by the reader. In view of this polarity, it is clear that the work itself cannot be identical with the text or with its actualization but must be situated somewhere between the two. It must inevitably be virtual in character, as it cannot be reduced to the reality of the text or to the subjectivity of the reader, and it is from this virtuality that it derives its dynamism. As the reader passes through the various perspectives offered by the text, and relates the different views and patterns to one another, he sets the work in motion, and so sets himself in motion, too.

If the virtual position of the work is between text and reader, its actualization is clearly the result of an interaction between the two, and so exclusive concentration on either the author's techniques or the reader's psychology will tell us little about the reading process itself. This is not to deny the vital importance of each of the two poles—it is simply that if one loses sight of the relationship, one loses sight of the virtual work. Despite its uses, separate analysis would only be conclusive if the relationship were that of transmitter and receiver, for this would presuppose a common code, ensuring accurate communication since the message would only be traveling one way. In literary works, however, the message is transmitted in two ways, in that the reader "receives" it by composing it. There is no common code—at best one could say that a common code may arise in the course of the process. Starting out from this assumption, we must search for structures that will enable us to describe basic conditions of interaction, for only then shall we be able to gain some insight into the potential effects inherent in the work.

It is difficult to describe this interaction, not least because literary criticism has very little to go on in the way of guidelines, and, of course, the two partners in the communication process, namely, the text and the reader, are far easier to analyze than is the event that takes place between them. However, there are discernible conditions that govern interaction generally, and some of these will certainly apply to the special reader-text relationship. The differences and similarities may become clear if we briefly examine types of interaction that have emerged from psychoanalytical research into the structure of communication. The findings of the *Tavistock School*[3] will serve us as a model in order to move the problem into focus.

In assessing interpersonal relationships R. D. Laing writes: "I may not actually be able to see myself as others see me, but I am constantly supposing them to be seeing me in particular ways, and I am constantly acting in the light of the actual or supposed attitudes, opinions, needs, and so on the other has in respect of me."[4] Now, the views that others have of me cannot be called "pure" perception; they are the result of interpretation. And this need for interpretation arises from the structure of interpersonal experience. We

2. See Roman Ingarden, *The Literary Work of Art*, trans. George G. Grabowicz (Evanston, Ill., 1973), pp. 276 ff. [Iser's note]. (Some of Iser's notes have been omitted, and some have been edited.) Ingarden (1893–1970), Polish theorist of literary cognition.

3. A British school of psychology, prominent in the 1960s and 1970s, focused on interpersonal relations; its most prominent member was R. D. Laing (1927–1989), a Scottish psychiatrist.

4. R. D. Laing, H. Phillipson, and A. R. Lee, *Interpersonal Perception: A Theory and a Method of Research* (New York, 1966), p. 4 [Iser's note].

have experience of one another insofar as we know one another's conduct; but we have no experience of how others experience us.

In his book, *The Politics of Experience*, Laing pursues this line of thought by saying: "*your experience of me is invisible to me and my experience of you is invisible to you*. I cannot experience your experience. You cannot experience my experience. We are both invisible men. All men are invisible to one another. Experience is man's invisibility to man."[5] It is this invisibility, however, that forms the basis of interpersonal relations—a basis which Laing calls "no-thing.' "That which is really 'between' cannot be named by any things that come between. The between is itself no-thing."[6] In all our interpersonal relations we build upon this "no-thing," for we react as if we knew how our partners experienced us; we continually form views of their views, and then act as if our views of their views were realities. Contact therefore depends upon our continually filling in a central gap in our experience. Thus, dyadic[7] and dynamic interaction comes about only because we are unable to experience how we experience one another, which in turn proves to be a propellant to interaction. Out of this fact arises the basic need for interpretation, which regulates the whole process of interaction. As we cannot perceive without preconception, each percept, in turn, only makes sense to us if it is processed, for pure perception is quite impossible. Hence dyadic interaction is not given by nature but arises out of an interpretative activity, which will contain a view of others and, unavoidably, an image of ourselves.

An obvious and major difference between reading and all forms of social interaction is the fact that with reading there is no *face-to-face-situation*.[8] A text cannot adapt itself to each reader it comes into contact with. The partners in dyadic interaction can ask each other questions in order to ascertain how far their images have bridged the gap of the inexperienceability of one another's experiences. The reader, however, can never learn from the text how accurate or inaccurate are his views of it. Furthermore, dyadic interaction serves specific purposes, so that the interaction always has a regulative context, which often serves as a *tertium comparationis*.[9] There is no such frame of reference governing the text-reader relationship; on the contrary, the codes which might regulate this interaction are fragmented in the text, and must first be reassembled or, in most cases, restructured before any frame of reference *can* be established. Here, then, in conditions and intention, we find two basic differences between the text-reader relationship and the dyadic interaction between social partners.

Now, it is the very lack of ascertainability and defined intention that brings about the text-reader interaction, and here there is a vital link with dyadic interaction. Social communication, as we have seen, arises out of the fact that people cannot experience how others experience them, and not out of the common situation or out of the conventions that join both partners together. The situations and conventions regulate the manner in which gaps are filled, but the gaps in turn arise out of the inexperienceability and, consequently, function as a basic inducement to communication. Similarly, it is

5. R. D. Laing, *The Politics of Experience* (Harmondsworth, 1968), p. 16. Laing's italics [Iser's note].
6. Ibid., p. 34 [Iser's note].
7. Involving two entities.
8. See also E. Goffman, *Interaction Ritual: Essays on Face-to-Face Behavior* (New York, 1967) [Iser's note]. Erving Goffman (1922–1982), Canadian-born American sociologist.
9. Third point of comparison (Latin).

the gaps, the fundamental asymmetry between text and reader, that give rise to communication in the reading process; the lack of a common situation and a common frame of reference corresponds to the "no-thing," which brings about the interaction between persons. Asymmetry and the "no-thing" are all different forms of an indeterminate, constitutive blank, which underlies all processes of interaction. With dyadic interaction, the imbalance is removed by the establishment of pragmatic connections resulting in an action, which is why the preconditions are always clearly defined in relation to situations and common frames of reference. The imbalance between text and reader, however, is undefined, and it is this very indeterminacy that increases the variety of communication possible.

Now, if communication between text and reader is to be successful, clearly the reader's activity must also be controlled in some way by the text. The control cannot be as specific as in a *face-to-face-situation*, equally it cannot be as determinate as a social code, which regulates social interaction. However, the guiding devices operative in the reading process have to initiate communication and to control it. This control cannot be understood as a tangible entity occurring independently of the process of communication. Athough exercised *by* the text, it is not in the text. This is well illustrated by a comment Virginia Woolf made on the novels of Jane Austen:[1]

> Jane Austen is thus a mistress of much deeper emotion than appears upon the surface. She stimulates us to supply what is not there. What she offers is, apparently, a trifle, yet is composed of something that expands in the reader's mind and endows with the most enduring form of life scenes which are outwardly trivial. Always the stress is laid upon character. . . . The turns and twists of the dialogue keep us on the tenterhooks of suspense. Our attention is half upon the present moment, half upon the future. . . . Here, indeed, in this unfinished and in the main inferior story, are all the element of Jane Austen's greatness.[2]

What is missing from the apparently trivial scenes, the gaps arising out of the dialogue—this is what stimulates the reader into filling the blanks with projections. He is drawn into the events and made to supply what is meant from what is not said. What is said only appears to take on significance as a reference to what is not said; it is the implications and not the statements that give shape and weight to the meaning. But as the unsaid comes to life in the reader's imagination, so the said "expands" to take on greater significance than might have been supposed: even trivial scenes can seem surprisingly profound. The "enduring form of life" which Virginia Woolf speaks of is not manifested on the printed page; it is a product arising out of the interaction between text and reader.

Communication in literature, then, is a process set in motion and regulated, not by a given code, but by a mutually restrictive and magnifying interaction between the explicit and the implicit, between revelation and concealment. What is concealed spurs the reader into action, but this action is also controlled by what is revealed; the explicit in its turn is transformed when the implicit has been brought to light. Whenever the reader bridges the gaps, communication begins. The gaps function as a kind of pivot on

1. English novelist (1775–1817). WOOLF (1882–1941), English novelist and essayist.

2. Virginia Woolf, *The Common Reader, First Series* (London, 1957), p. 174 [Iser's note].

which the whole text-reader relationship revolves. Hence, the structured blanks of the text stimulate the process of ideation to be performed by the reader on terms set by the text. There is, however, another place in the textual system where text and reader converge, and that is marked by the various types of negation which arise in the course of the reading. Blanks and negations both control the process of communication in their own different ways: the blanks leave open the connection between textual perspectives, and so spur the reader into coordinating these perspectives and patterns—in other words, they induce the reader to perform basic operations *within* the text. The various types of negation invoke familiar and determinate elements or knowledge only to cancel them out. What is cancelled, however, remains in view, and thus brings about modifications in the reader's attitude toward what is familiar or determinate—in other words, he is guided to adopt a position in *relation* to the text.

In order to spotlight the communication process we shall confine our consideration to how the blanks trigger off and simultaneously control the reader's activity. Blanks indicate that the different segments and patterns of the text are to be connected even though the text itself does not say so. They are the unseen joints of the text, and as they mark off schemata and textual perspectives from one another, they simultaneously prompt acts of ideation on the reader's part. Consequently when the schemata and perspectives have been linked together, the blanks "disappear."

If we are to grasp the unseen structure that regulates but does not formulate the connection or even the meaning, we must bear in mind the various forms in which the textual segments are presented to the reader's viewpoint in the reading process. Their most elementary form is to be seen on the level of the story. The threads of the plot are suddenly broken off, or continued in unexpected directions. One narrative section centers on a particular character and is then continued by the abrupt introduction of new characters. These sudden changes are often denoted by new chapters and so are clearly distinguished; the object of this distinction, however, is not separation so much as a tacit invitation to find the missing link. Furthermore, in each articulated reading moment, only segments of textual perspectives are present to the reader's wandering viewpoint.

In order to become fully aware of the implication, we must bear in mind that a narrative text, for instance, is composed of a variety of perspectives, which outline the author's view and also provide access to what the reader is meant to visualize. As a rule, there are four main perspectives in narration: those of the narrator, the characters, the plot, and the fictitious reader.[3] Although these may differ in order of importance, none of them on its own is identical to the meaning of the text, which is to be brought about by their constant intertwining through the reader in the reading process. An increase in the number of blanks is bound to occur through the frequent subdivisions of each of the textual perspectives; thus the narrator's perspective is often split into that of the implied author's set against that of the author as narrator. The hero's perspective may be set against that of the minor characters. The fictitious reader's perspective may be divided between the explicit position ascribed to him and the implicit attitude he must adopt to that position.

As the reader's wandering viewpoint travels between all these segments,

3. The reader addressed in a text, as distinct from the actual reader.

its constant switching during the time flow of reading intertwines them, thus bringing forth a network of perspectives, within which each perspective opens a view not only of others, but also of the intended imaginary object. Hence no single textual perspective can be equated with this imaginary object, of which it forms only one aspect. The object itself is a product of interconnection, the structuring of which is to a great extent regulated and controlled by blanks.

In order to explain this operation, we shall first give a schematic description of how the blanks function, and then we shall try to illustrate this function with an example. In the time flow of reading, segments of the various perspectives move into focus and are set off against preceding segments. Thus the segments of characters, narrator, plot, and fictitious reader perspectives are not only marshaled into a graduated sequence but are also transformed into reciprocal reflectors. The blank as an empty space between segments enables them to be joined together, thus constituting a field of vision for the wandering viewpoint. A referential field is always formed when there are at least two positions related to and influencing one another—it is the minimal organizational unit in all processes of comprehension,[4] and it is also the basic organizational unit of the wandering viewpoint.

The first structural quality of the blank, then, is that it makes possible the organization of a referential field of interacting textual segments projecting themselves one upon another. Now, the segments present in the field are structurally of equal value, and the fact that they are brought together highlights their affinities and their differences. This relationship gives rise to a tension that has to be resolved, for, as Arnheim has observed in a more general context: "It is one of the functions of the third dimension to come to the rescue when things get uncomfortable in the second."[5] The third dimension comes about when the segments of the referential field are given a common framework, which allows the reader to relate affinities and differences and so to grasp the patterns underlying the connections. But this framework is also a blank, which requires an act of ideation in order to be filled. It is as if the blank in the field of the reader's viewpoint had changed its position. It began as the empty space between perspective segments, indicating their connectability, and so organizing them into projections of reciprocal influence. But with the establishment of this connectability the blank, as the unformulated framework of these interacting segments, now enables the reader to produce a determinate relationship between them. We may infer already from this change in position that the blank exercises significant control over all the operations that occur within the referential field of the wandering viewpoint.

Now we come to the third and most decisive function of the blank. Once the segments have been connected and a determinate relationship established, a referential field is formed which constitutes a particular reading moment, and which in turn has a discernible structure. The grouping of segments within the referential field comes about, as we have seen, by making the viewpoint switch between the perspective segments. The segment on which the viewpoint focuses in each particular moment

4. See Aron Gurwitsch, *The Field of Consciousness* (Pittsburgh, 1964), pp. 309–75 [Iser's note].

5. Rudolf Arnheim, *Toward a Psychology of Art* (Berkeley, 1967), p. 239 [Iser's note]. Arnheim (b. 1904), a pathbreaking German-born theorist of perception in art and film.

becomes the theme. The theme of one moment becomes the background against which the next segment takes on its actuality, and so on. Whenever a segment becomes a theme, the previous one must lose its thematic relevance[6] and be turned into a marginal, thematically vacant position, which can be and usually is occupied by the reader so that he may focus on the new thematic segment.

In this connection it might be more appropriate to designate the marginal or horizontal position as a vacancy and not as a blank; blanks refer to suspended connectability in the text, vacancies refer to nonthematic segments within the referential field of the wandering viewpoint. Vacancies, then, are important guiding devices for building up the aesthetic object, because they condition the reader's view of the new theme, which in turn conditions his view of previous themes. These modifications, however, are not formulated in the text—they are to be implemented by the reader's ideational activity. And so these vacancies enable the reader to combine segments into a field by reciprocal modification, to form positions from those fields, and then to adapt each position to its successor and predecessors in a process that ultimately transforms the textual perspectives, through a whole range of alternating themes and background relationships, into the aesthetic object of the text.

Let us turn now to an example in order to illustrate the operations sparked off and governed by the vacancies in the referential field of the wandering viewpoint. For this reason we shall have a brief look at Fielding's[7] *Tom Jones* and again, in particular, at the characters' perspective: that of the hero and that of the minor characters. Fielding's aim of depicting human nature is fulfilled by way of a repertoire that incorporates the prevailing norms of eighteenth-century thought systems and social systems and represents them as governing the conduct of the most important characters. In general, these norms are arranged in more or less explicitly contrasting patterns; Allworthy (*benevolence*) is set against Squire Western (*ruling passion*); the same applies to the two pedagogues, Square (*the eternal fitness of things*) and Thwackum (*the human mind as a sink of iniquity*), who in turn are also contrasted with Allworthy and so forth.

Thus in the individual situations, the hero is linked up with the norms of latitudinarian morality, orthodox theology, deistic philosophy,[8] eighteenth-century anthropology, and eighteenth-century aristocracy. Contrasts and discrepancies within the perspective of the characters give rise to the missing links, which enable the hero and the norms to shed light upon one another, and through which the individual situations may combine into a referential field. The hero's conduct cannot be subsumed under the norms, and through the sequence of situations the norms shrink to a reified manifestation of human nature. This, however, is already an observation which the reader must make for himself, because such syntheses are rarely given in the text,

6. For a discussion of the problem of changing relevance and abandoned thematic relevance, see Alfred Schütz, *Reflections on the Problem of Relevance*, ed. Richard M. Zaner (New Haven, 1970) [Iser's note].

7. Henry Fielding (1707–1754), English novelist and playwright; *Tom Jones* was published in 1749.

8. Belief in a supreme being as the source of existence of the universe that rejects the supernatural doctrines of Christianity and the influence or revelation of God in the events of the universe, stressing instead the importance of reason and ethical conduct. "Latitudinarian morality": tolerating free thought or a range of opinion, especially on religious questions.

even though they are prefigured in the theme-and-background structure. The discrepancies continually arising between the perspectives of hero and minor characters bring about a series of changing positions, with each theme losing its relevance but remaining in the background to influence and condition its successor. Whenever the hero violates the norms—as he does most of the time—the resultant situation may be judged in one or two different ways: either the norm appears as a drastic reduction of human nature, in which case we view the theme from the standpoint of the hero, or the violation shows the imperfections of human nature, in which case it is the norm that conditions our view.

In both cases, we have the same structure of interacting positions being transformed into a determinate meaning. For those characters that represent a norm—in particular Allworthy, Squire Western, Square, and Thwackum—human nature is defined in terms of one principle, so that all those possibilities which are not in harmony with the principle are given a negative slant. But when the negated possibilities exert their influence upon the course of events, and so show up the limitations of the principle concerned, the norms begin to appear in a different light. The apparently negative aspects of human nature fight back, as it were, against the principle itself and cast doubt upon it in proportion to its limitations.

In this way, the negation of other possibilities by the norm in question gives rise to a virtual diversification of human nature, which takes on a definite form to the extent that the norm is revealed as a restriction on human nature. The reader's attention is now fixed, not upon what the norms represent, but upon what their representation excludes, and so the aesthetic object—which is the whole spectrum of human nature—begins to arise out of what is adumbrated by the negated possibilities. In this way, the function of the norms themselves has changed: they no longer represent the social regulators prevalent in the thought systems of the eighteenth century, but instead they indicate the amount of human experience which they suppress because, as rigid principles, they cannot tolerate any modifications.

Transformations of this kind take place whenever the norms are the foregrounded theme and the perspective of the hero remains the background conditioning the reader's viewpoint. But whenever the hero becomes the theme, and the norms of the minor characters shape the viewpoint, his well-intentioned spontaneity turns into the depravity of an impulsive nature. Thus the position of the hero is also transformed, for it is no longer the standpoint from which we are to judge the norms; instead we see that even the best of intentions may come to nought if they are not guided by *circumspection*, and spontaneity must be controlled by *prudence*[9] if it is to allow a possibility of self-preservation.

The transformations brought about by the theme-and-background interaction are closely connected with the changing position of the vacancy within the referential field. Once a theme has been grasped, conditioned by the marginal position of the preceding segment, a feedback is bound to occur, thus retroactively modifying the shaping influence of the reader's viewpoint. This reciprocal transformation is hermeneutic by nature,[1] even

9. See Henry Fielding, *Tom Jones*, III.7 and XVIII, Chapter the Last (London, 1962), pp. 92, 427 [Iser's note].

1. Hermeneutics is the theory of interpretation; Iser is alluding to what is called the "hermeneutic circle," a model which holds that meaning is not straightforward but continually modified by feedback.

though we may not be aware of the processes of interpretation resulting from the switching and reciprocal conditioning of our viewpoints. In this sense, the vacancy transforms the referential field of the moving viewpoint into a self-regulating structure, which proves to be one of the most important links in the interaction between text and reader, and which prevents the reciprocal transformation of textual segments from being arbitrary.

To sum up, then, the blank in the fictional text induces and guides the reader's constitutive activity. As a suspension of connectability between textual perspective and perspective segments, it marks the need for an equivalence, thus transforming the segments into reciprocal projections, which in turn organize the reader's wandering viewpoint as a referential field. The tension that occurs within the field between heterogeneous perspective segments is resolved by the theme-and-background structure, which makes the viewpoint focus on one segment as the theme, to be grasped from the thematically vacant position now occupied by the reader as his standpoint. Thematically vacant positions remain present in the background against which new themes occur; they condition and influence those themes and are also retroactively influenced by them, for as each theme recedes into the background of its successor, the vacancy shifts, allowing for a reciprocal transformation to take place. As the vacancy is structured by the sequence of positions in the time flow of reading, the reader's viewpoint cannot proceed arbitrarily; the thematically vacant position always acts as the angle from which a selective interpretation is to be made.

Two points need to be emphasized: (1) we have described the structure of the blank in an abstract, somewhat idealized way in order to explain the pivot on which the interaction between text and reader turns; (2) the blank has different structural qualities, which appear to dovetail. The reader fills in the blank in the text, thereby bringing about a referential field; the blank arising in turn out of the referential field is filled in by way of the theme-and-background structure; and the vacancy arising from juxtaposed themes and backgrounds is occupied by the reader's standpoint, from which the various reciprocal transformations lead to the emergence of the aesthetic object. The structural qualities outlined make the blank shift, so that the changing positions of the empty space mark out a definite need for determination, which the constitutive activity of the reader is to fulfill. In this sense, the shifting blank maps out the path along which the wandering viewpoint is to travel, guided by the self-regulatory sequence in which the structural qualities of the blank interlock.

Now we are in a position to qualify more precisely what is actually meant by reader participation in the text. If the blank is largely responsible for the activities described, then participation means that the reader is not simply called upon to "internalize" the positions given in the text, but he is induced to make them act upon and so transform each other, as a result of which the aesthetic object begins to emerge. The structure of the blank organizes this participation, revealing simultaneously the intimate connection between this structure and the reading subject. This interconnection completely conforms to a remark made by Piaget: "In a word, the subject is there and alive, because the basic quality of each structure is the structuring process itself."[2] The

2. Jean Piaget, *Structuralism*, trans. Haninah Maschler (New York, 1970), p. 140 [Iser's note]. Piaget (1876–1980), Swiss psychologist who applied structuralist methods in psychology.

blank in the fictional text appears to be a paradigmatic structure; its function consists in initiating structured operations in the reader, the execution of which transmits the reciprocal interaction of textual positions into consciousness. The shifting blank is responsible for a sequence of colliding images, which condition each other in the time flow of reading. The discarded image imprints itself on its successor, even though the latter is meant to resolve the deficiencies of the former. In this respect the images hang together in a sequence, and it is by this sequence that the meaning of the text comes alive in the reader's imagination.

1980

E. D. HIRSCH JR.
b. 1928

In his famous *Validity in Interpretation* (1967), the American literary critic Eric Donald Hirsch Jr. argues against nearly every contemporary critical practice in order to establish a set of principles for valid textual interpretation grounded primarily in authorial intention. Although his position has been rejected by most critics, no one concerned with methods of interpretation can ignore his controversial project. When he wrote the book, Hirsch was reacting to the formalist views of the New Critics and their followers, whose skills as close readers he admired but who, he said, had failed to explain how critics can identify one reading as right and another wrong. In Hirsch's view the situation became even worse with the arrival from abroad of the new post-structuralist theories of literature and criticism in the late 1960s and 1970s, when theorists such as JACQUES DERRIDA and MICHEL FOUCAULT appeared to disavow altogether the principle of "validity in interpretation"; thus to Hirsch they were "cognitive atheists." Faced with "relativism" on all fronts, Hirsch placed himself in firm opposition not only to respected formalist theories such as those of W. K. WIMSATT JR. AND MONROE BEARDSLEY in "The Intentional Fallacy" (1946; see above), but also to post-structuralist ideas such as those of ROLAND BARTHES in "Death of the Author" (1968; see above).

E. D. Hirsch was born in Memphis, Tennessee. He earned his B.A. at Cornell University in 1950 and both his M.A. and Ph.D. at Yale University (in 1953 and 1957). During his long and distinguished career, he has received numerous research fellowships and honors, including a Guggenheim Fellowship (1964). Hirsch's very early work focused on problems of interpretation in the field of Romanticism, addressing the texts of such prominent figures as WILLIAM WORDSWORTH, Friedrich von Schelling, and William Blake. With the writing of his two major theoretical works, *Validity in Interpretation* and *The Aims of Interpretation* (1976), Hirsch turned his attention toward the general problem of interpretation; he drew primarily on the German traditions of philology, hermeneutics, and phenomenology, especially the work of FRIEDRICH SCHLEIERMACHER (1768–1834), August Boeckh (1785–1867), Wilhelm Dilthey (1833–1911), and Edmund Husserl (1859–1938). After a brief foray into composition theory in *The Philosophy of Composition* (1977), he published *Cultural Literacy: What Every American Needs to Know* (1987); though primarily aimed at improving literacy and influencing the school curriculum, it is also concerned with problems of interpretation. *Cultural Literacy* won national attention, and much of

Hirsch's subsequent work likewise seeks curricular reform—especially at the primary level, where his theories have been influential. In more recent years, Hirsch has entered into policy debates, and his ideas have been tried, tested, and approved in school systems.

Published to much controversy in 1960 in *PMLA* (the journal of the Modern Language Association and later collected as an appendix to *Validity in Interpretation*, "Objective Interpretation," our selection, is a programmatic statement of Hirsch's hermeneutic project, whose overarching goal for interpretation is the imaginative reconstruction of the author's intention as the source of meaning. To begin with, Hirsch insists that an interpreter must distinguish between the "meaning" of a text and its "significance." Textual meaning is permanent, self-identical, and reproducible through interpretation. Significance, in contrast, is variable: the value or relevance of a text always depends on changing historical, social, and personal conditions. For Hirsch the significance of a text is the proper concern of *criticism*, while meaning is the domain of *interpretation*. Problems of objectivity arise, Hirsch argues, when contemporary theorists confuse interpretation and criticism. He then asserts that the meaning of a text can only be the author's meaning. Textual meaning, it seems, is determined by the psychic acts of the author, which produce "intentional objects" or cognitive universals that are mentally reproducible by others independent of individual biases. Adhering to the rationalist tradition of philosophy out of which Husserl's phenomenology emerges, Hirsch believes that the intentional objects of consciousness, including verbal meaning, are "objective" and "constant."

This "suprapersonal" and "sharable" conscious object is properly the concern of interpretation. Hirsch thus distinguishes his theory from the phenomenological hermeneutics of MARTIN HEIDEGGER, who focuses on how language determines and shapes consciousness rather than on how consciousness precedes and manipulates language. Indeed, Heidegger's idea of the linguistic determination of consciousness puts the German philosopher in the camp of the "cognitive atheists" along with the poststructuralists and deconstructors, according to Hirsch, for it too provides no solid basis for objective interpretation. Borrowing FERDINAND DE SAUSSURE's fertile linguistic distinction between *langue* and *parole*, Hirsch explains that a text represents a *parole*, or an individual utterance; it possesses a determinate verbal meaning created by a member of a particular speech community. *Langue* consists of a system of meaning possibilities shared by the speech community. *Parole*, as a particular use or actualization of *langue*, implies the role of conscious choice, determination, will, or intention. As a result, consciousness for Hirsch precedes language and guarantees its meaning; for Heidegger the forms of language and human consciousness are coextensive.

Hirsch realizes, however, that critics rarely have direct access to an author's consciousness. Therefore, he advocates a reconstructive process for determining the "author's horizon"—the historical set of typical expectations, prohibitions, norms, and limits that define the author's intentions as a whole. These ground and sanction inferences about probable textual meaning. For instance, one important element of an author's horizon is genre, which invariably predetermines interpreters' expectations for understanding a text. The goal is a reconstruction of the speaking subject's stance through attention to historical horizon or context. As Hirsch puts it, "The interpreter's primary task is to reproduce in himself the author's 'logic,' his attitudes, his cultural givens, in short his world."

But as Hirsch's critics have noted, the turn toward the author's horizon reintroduces the problems of textual interpretation in its suggestion that more texts (the author's horizon) are required to interpret the text at hand. For instance, in reading Wordsworth's other poetry and prose in order to contextualize his poem "A Slumber Did My Spirit Seal," a critic will find these other texts as difficult to interpret as the primary poem. The critic will thus be forced to contextualize the secondary material as well, a process that will necessarily repeat itself. Inadvertently, Hirsch depicts each text referring to other texts ad infinitum. As a result, his project to establish a consensus about meaning founders on theories of intertextuality (see, for instance, the work of MIKHAIL BAKHTIN and Roland Barthes in this area). In spite of Hirsch's efforts, critics who invoke "intention" as the basis for textual interpretation still end up disagreeing sharply about what this intention is and how it can be isolated.

What worries Hirsch is the "chaos" of conflicting and competing readings of the same text, and he has devised a theory to try to address this concern. But in practice critics still find themselves in disagreement and dispute. Differences of opinion about the interpretation of a text get translated into arguments over the author's true intention. Such contention results in part from the problems that horizon and intertextuality pose, but it also reflects the tendency of Hirsch's central distinctions between meaning and significance, interpretation and criticism, to break down in practice. "Objective Interpretation" has nevertheless proven itself an indispensable, fertile text of interpretation theory. Moreover, in its attempt to establish common criteria for interpretation, it is an important anticipation of Hirsch's later concern with "cultural literacy," which continues to have practical consequences for education in the United States.

BIBLIOGRAPHY

Hirsch's major works include *Wordsworth and Schelling: A Typological Study of Romanticism* (1960), *Innocence and Experience: An Introduction to Blake* (1964), *Validity in Interpretation* (1967), *The Aims of Interpretation* (1976), *The Philosophy of Composition* (1977), *Cultural Literacy* (1987), *The Dictionary of Cultural Literacy* (1988), the seven-volume *Books to Build On: A Grade-by-Grade Resource Guide for Parents and Teachers* (1991–96), and *The Schools We Need and Why We Don't Have Them* (1996).

Studies of Hirsch's theory of interpretation all find fault to some degree. For instance, Richard Palmer's classic study, *Hermeneutics: Interpretation Theory in Schleiermacher, Dilthey, Heidegger, and Gadamer* (1969), argues that Hirsch fails to address the opposing hermeneutic theories of the historical and social nature of understanding; David Hoy's *Critical Circle: Literature, History, and Philosophical Hermeneutics* (1978) criticizes Hirsch's preoccupation with objective interpretation, adopting a more interactive perspective indebted to Martin Heidegger and Hans Georg Gadamer. P. D. Juhl's *Interpretation: An Essay in the Philosophy of Literary Criticism* (1980) presents a more sympathetic, though not uncritical, overview of Hirsch's position. Two widely read leftist cultural assessments of Hirsch's work are offered by Frank Lentricchia's *After the New Criticism* (1980) and William E. Cain's *Crisis in Criticism: Theory, Literature, and Reform in English Studies* (1984). William Ray's *Literary Meaning: From Phenomenology to Deconstruction* (1984) situates Hirsch's work within wide-ranging contemporary theoretical debates on the problem of literary meaning, factoring in as well the arguments of reader-response theory.

Objective Interpretation

The fact that the term "criticism" has now come to designate all commentary on textual meaning reflects a general acceptance of the doctrine that description and evaluation are inseparable in literary study. In any serious confrontation of literature it would be futile, of course, to attempt a rigorous banishment of all evaluative judgment, but this fact does not give us the license to misunderstand or misinterpret our texts. It does not entitle us to use the text as the basis for an exercise in "creativity" or to submit as serious textual commentary a disguised argument for a particular ethical, cultural, or aesthetic viewpoint. Nor is criticism's chief concern—the present relevance of a text—a strictly necessary aspect of textual commentary. That same kind of theory which argues the inseparability of description and evaluation also argues that a text's meaning is simply its meaning "to us, today." Both kinds of argument support the idea that interpretation is criticism and vice versa. But there is clearly a sense in which we can neither evaluate a text nor determine what it means "to us, today" until we have correctly apprehended what it means. Understanding (and therefore interpretation, in the strict sense of the word) is both logically and psychologically prior to what is generally called criticism. It is true that this distinction between understanding and evaluation cannot always show itself in the finished work of criticism—nor, perhaps, should it—but a general grasp and acceptance of the distinction might help correct some of the most serious faults of current criticism (its subjectivism and relativism) and might even make it plausible to think of literary study as a corporate enterprise and a progressive discipline.

No one would deny, of course, that the more important issue is not the status of literary study as a discipline but the vitality of literature—especially of older literature—in the world at large. The critic is right to think that the text should speak to us. The point which needs to be grasped clearly by the critic is that a text cannot be made to speak to us until what it says has been understood. This is not an argument in favor of historicism as against criticism—it is simply a brute ontological fact. Textual meaning is not a naked given like a physical object. The text is first of all a conventional representation like a musical score, and what the score represents may be construed correctly or incorrectly. The literary text (in spite of the semi-mystical claims made for its uniqueness) does not have a special ontological status which somehow absolves the reader from the demands universally imposed by all linguistic texts of every description. Nothing, that is, can give a conventional representation the status of an immediate given. The text of a poem, for example, has to be construed by the critic before it becomes a poem for him. Then it is, no doubt, an artifact with special characteristics. But before the critic construes the poem it is no artifact for him at all, and if he construes it wrongly, he will subsequently be talking about the wrong artifact, not the one represented by the text. If criticism is to be objective in any significant sense, it must be founded on a self-critical construction of textual meaning, which is to say, on objective interpretation.

The distinction I am drawing between interpretation and criticism was one of the central principles in the now vestigial science of hermeneutics. August Boeckh,[1] for example, divided the theoretical part of his *Encyklopädie* into two sections, one devoted to *Interpretation (Hermeneutik)* and the other to *Kritik*. Boeckh's discussion of this distinction is illuminating: interpretation is the construction of textual meaning as such; it explicates (*legt aus*) those meanings, and only those meanings, which the text explicitly or implicitly represents. Criticism, on the other hand, builds on the results of inter-

1. German philologist (1785–1867).

pretation; it confronts textual meaning not as such; but as a component within a larger context. Boeckh defined it as "that philological function through which a text is understood not simply in its own terms and for its own sake, but in order to establish a relationship with something else, in such a way that the goal is a knowledge of this relationship itself."[2] Boeckh's definition is useful in emphasizing that interpretation and criticism confront two quite distinct "objects," for this is the fundamental distinction between the two activities. The object of interpretation is textual meaning in and for itself and may be called the *meaning* of the text. The object of criticism, on the other hand, is that meaning in its bearing on something else (standards of value, present concerns, etc.), and this object may therefore be called the *significance* of the text.

The distinction between the meaning and the significance of a text was first clearly made by Frege in his article "Über Sinn und Bedeutung,"[3] where he demonstrated that although the meanings of two texts may be different, their referent or truth-value may be identical. For example, the statement, "Scott is the author of *Waverley*," is true and yet the meaning of "Scott" is different from that of "the author of *Waverley*." The *Sinn* of each is different, but the *Bedeutung* (or one aspect of *Bedeutung*—the designatum of "Scott" and "author of *Waverley*") is the same. Frege considered only cases where different *Sinne* have an identical *Bedeutung*, but it is also true that the same *Sinn* may, in the course of time, have different *Bedeutungen*. For example, the sentence, "There is a unicorn in the garden," is prima facie false. But suppose the statement were made when there *was* a unicorn in the garden (as happened in Thurber's imaginative world);[4] the statement would be true; its relevance would have shifted. But true or false, the meaning of the proposition would remain the same, for unless its *meaning* remained self-identical, we would have nothing to label true or false. Frege's distinction, now widely accepted by logicians, is a special case of Husserl's[5] general distinction between the inner and outer horizons of any meaning. In section A I shall try to clarify Husserl's concept and to show how it applies to the problems of textual study and especially to the basic assumptions of textual interpretation.

My purpose is primarily constructive rather than polemical. I would not willingly argue that interpretation should be practiced in strict separation from criticism. I shall ignore criticism simply in order to confront the special problems involved in construing the meaning or *Sinn* of a text. For most of my notions I disclaim any originality. My aim is to revive some forgotten insights of literary study and to apply to the theory of interpretation certain other insights from linguistics and philosophy. For although the analytical movement in criticism has permanently advanced the cause of intrinsic literary study, it has not yet paid enough attention to the problem of establishing norms and limits in interpretation. If I display any argumentative intent,

2. *Encyklopädie und Methodologie der philologischen Wissenschaften*, ed. E. Bratuscheck, 2d ed. (Leipzig, 1886), p. 170 [Hirsch's note].

3. Gottlob Frege, "Über Sinn und Bedeutung" [On Sense and Meaning], *Zeitschrift für Philosophie und philosophische Kritik* 100 (1892). The article has been translated, and one English version may be found in H. Feigl and W. Sellars, *Readings in Philosophical Analysis* (New York, 1949) [Hirsch's note]. Frege (1848–1925), German analytical philosopher.

4. A reference to "The Unicorn in the Garden" (1940), a story by the American humorist and cartoonist James Thurber (1894–1961).

5. Edmund Husserl (1859–1938), German philosopher, a founder of phenomenology.

it is not, therefore, against the analytical movement, which I approve, but only against certain modern theories which hamper the establishment of normative principles in interpretation and which thereby encourage the subjectivism and individualism which have for many students discredited the analytical movement. By normative principles I mean those notions which concern the nature of a correct interpretation. When the critic clearly conceives what a correct interpretation is in principle, he possesses a guiding idea against which he can measure his construction. Without such a guiding idea, self-critical or objective interpretation is hardly possible. Current theory, however, fails to provide such a principle. The most influential and representative statement of modern theory is *Theory of Literature* by Wellek and Warren, a book to which I owe much. I ungratefully select it (especially Chap. 12) as a target of attack, both because it is so influential and because I need a specific, concrete example of the sort of theory which requires amendment.[6]

A. The Two Horizons of Textual Meaning

The metaphorical doctrine that a text leads a life of its own is used by modern theorists to express the idea that textual meaning changes in the course of time.[7] This theory of a changing meaning serves to support the fusion of interpretation and criticism and, at the same time, the idea that present relevance forms the basis for textual commentary. But the view should not remain unchallenged, since if it were correct, there could be no objective knowledge about texts. Any statement about textual meaning could be valid only for the moment, and even this temporary validity could not be tested, since there would be no permanent norms on which validating judgments could be based. While the "life" theory does serve to explain and sanction the fact that different ages tend to interpret texts differently, and while it emphasizes the importance of a text's present relevance, it overlooks the fact that such a view undercuts *all* criticism, even the sort which emphasizes present relevance. If the view were correct, criticism would not only lack permanent validity, but could not even claim current validity by the time it got into print. Both the text's meaning and the tenor of the age would have altered. The "life" theory really masks the idea that the reader construes his own, new meaning instead of that represented by the text.

The "life" theory thus implicitly places the principle of change squarely where it belongs, that is, not in textual meaning as such, but in changing generations of readers. According to Wellek, for example, the meaning of the text changes as it passes "through the minds of its readers, critics, and fellow artists."[8] Now when even a few of the norms which determine a text's meaning are allotted to readers and made dependent on their attitudes and concerns, it is evident that textual meaning must change. But is it proper to make textual meaning dependent upon the reader's own cultural givens? It may be granted that these givens change in the course of time, but does this imply that textual meaning itself changes? As soon as the reader's outlook is

6. Wellek and Warren, *Theory of Literature* [New York, 1949], chap. 12. This chapter is by Wellek [Hirsch's note]. This book by the literary critics Austin Warren (1899–1986) and René Wellek (1903–1995) is a classic of New Criticism.

7. See, for example, ibid., p. 31 [Hirsch's note].

8. Ibid., p. 144 [Hirsch's note].

permitted to determine what a text means, we have not simply a changing meaning but quite possibly as many meanings as readers.

Against such a reductio ad absurdum, the proponent of the current theory points out that in a given age many readers will agree in their construction of a text and will unanimously repudiate the accepted interpretation of a former age. For the sake of fair-mindedness, this presumed unanimity may be granted, but must it be explained by arguing that the text's meaning has changed? Recalling Frege's distinction between *Sinn* and *Bedeutung*, the change could be explained by saying that the meaning of the text has remained the same, while the significance of that meaning has shifted.[9] Contemporary readers will frequently share similar cultural givens and will therefore agree about what the text means to them. But might it not be the case that they agree about the text's meaning "to them" because they have first understood its meaning? If textual meaning itself could change, contemporary readers would lack a basis for agreement or disagreement. No one would bother seriously to discuss such a protean object. The significance of textual meaning has no foundation and no objectivity unless meaning itself is unchanging. To fuse meaning and significance, or interpretation and criticism, by the conception of an autonomous, living, changing meaning does not really free the reader from the shackles of historicism; it simply destroys the basis both for any agreement among readers and for any objective study whatever.

The dilemma created by the fusion of *Sinn* and *Bedeutung* in current theory is exhibited as soon as the theorist attempts to explain how norms can be preserved in textual study. The explanation becomes openly self-contradictory: "It could be scarcely denied that there is [in textual meaning] a substantial *identity* of 'structure' which has remained the *same* throughout the ages. This *structure*, however, is dynamic: it *changes* throughout the process of history while passing through the minds of its readers, critics, and fellow artists."[1] First the "structure" is self-identical; then it changes! What is given in one breath is taken away in the next. Although it is a matter of common experience that a text appears different to us than it appeared to a former age, and although we remain deeply convinced that there *are* permanent norms in textual study, we cannot properly explain the facts by equating or fusing what changes with what remains the same. We must distinguish the two and give each its due.

A couplet from Marvell, used by Wellek to suggest how meaning changes, will illustrate my point:[2]

My vegetable love should grow
Vaster than empires and more slow.[3]

Wellek grants that "vegetable" here probably means more or less what we nowadays express by "vegetative," but he goes on to suggest that we cannot avoid associating the modern connotation of "vegetable" (what it means "to us"). Furthermore, he suggests that this enrichment of meaning may even be desirable. No doubt, the associated meaning *is* here desirable (since it

9. It could also be explained, of course, by saying that certain generations of readers tend to misunderstand certain texts [Hirsch's note].
1. Wellek and Warren, p. 144. My italics [Hirsch's note].
2. Ibid., pp. 166–67 [Hirsch's note].
3. "To His Coy Mistress" (1650), by the English poet Andrew Marvell (1621–1678).

supports the mood of the poem), but Wellek could not even make his point unless we could distinguish between what "vegetable" probably means as used in the text and what it commonly means to us. Simply to discuss the issue is to admit that Marvell's poem probably does not imply the modern connotation, for if we could not separate the sense of "vegetative" from the notion of an "erotic cabbage," we could not talk about the difficulty of making the separation. One need not argue that the delight we may take in such new meanings must be ignored. On the contrary, once we have self-critically understood the text, there is little reason to exclude valuable or pleasant associations which enhance its significance. However, it is essential to exclude these associations in the process of interpretation, that is, in the process of understanding what a text means. The way out of the theoretical dilemma is to perceive that the meaning of a text does not change and that the modern, different connotation of a word like "vegetable" belongs, if it is to be entertained at all, to the constantly changing significance of a text's meaning.

It is in the light of the distinction between meaning and significance that critical theories like T. S. Eliot's need to be viewed.[4] Eliot, like other modern critics, insists that the meaning of a literary work changes in the course of time, but, in contrast to Wellek, instead of locating the principle of change directly in the changing outlooks of readers, Eliot locates it in a changing literary tradition. In his view, the literary tradition is a "simultaneous" (as opposed to temporal) order of literary texts which is constantly rearranging itself as new literary works appear on the public scene. Whenever a new work appears it causes a rearrangement of the tradition as a whole, and this brings about an alteration in the meaning of each component literary text. For example, when Shakespeare's *Troilus* entered the tradition, it altered not only the meaning of Chaucer's *Troilus*,[5] but also, to some degree, the meaning of every other text in the literary tradition.

If the changes in meaning Eliot speaks of are considered to be changes in significance, then his conception is perfectly sound. And indeed, by definition, Eliot is speaking of significance rather than meaning, since he is considering the work in relation to a larger realm, as a component rather than a world in itself. It goes without saying that the character of a component considered as such changes whenever the larger realm of which it is a part changes. A red object will appear to have different color qualities when viewed against differently colored backgrounds. The same is true of textual meaning. But the meaning of the text (its *Sinn*) does not change any more than the hue and saturation of the red object changes when seen against different backgrounds. Yet the analogy with colored objects is only partial: I can look at a red pencil against a green blotting pad and perceive the pencil's color in that special context without knowing the hue and saturation of either pencil or blotter. But textual meaning is a construction, not a naked given like a red object, and I cannot relate textual meaning to a larger realm until I have construed it. Before I can judge just how the changed tradition has altered the significance of a text, I must understand its meaning or *Sinn*.

4. ELIOT, "Tradition and the Individual Talent" [Hirsch's note]. This 1919 essay by the American-born English poet is reprinted above.

5. William Shakespeare's play *Troilus and Cressida* (ca. 1601) and Geoffrey Chaucer's poem *Troilus and Creseyde* (ca. 1385) treat the same postclassical story of the Trojan War.

This permanent meaning is, and can be, nothing other than the author's meaning. There have been, of course, several other definitions of textual meaning—what the author's contemporaries would ideally have construed, what the ideal present-day reader construes, what the norms of language permit the text to mean, what the best critics conceive to be the best meaning, and so on. In support of these other candidates, various aesthetic and psychological objections have been aimed at the author: first, his meaning, being conditioned by history and culture, is too confined and simple; second, it remains, in any case, inaccessible to us because we live in another age, or because his mental processes are private, or because he himself did not know what he meant. Instead of attempting to meet each of these objections separately, I shall attempt to describe the general principle for answering all of them and, in doing so, to clarify further the distinction between meaning and significance. The aim of my exposition will be to confirm that the author's meaning, as represented by his text, is unchanging and reproducible. My problem will be to show that, although textual meaning is *determined* by the psychic acts of an author and realized by those of a reader, textual meaning itself must not be *identified* with the author's or reader's psychic acts as such. To make this crucial point, I shall find it useful to draw upon Husserl's analysis of verbal meaning.

In his chief work, *Logische Untersuchungen*,[6] Husserl sought, among other things, to avoid an identification of verbal meaning with the psychic acts of speaker or listener, author or reader, but to do this he did not adopt a strict, Platonic idealism by which meanings have an actual existence apart from meaning experiences. Instead, he affirmed the objectivity of meaning by analyzing the observable relationship between it and those very mental processes in which it is actualized, for in meaning experiences themselves, the objectivity and constancy of meaning are confirmed.

Husserl's point may be grasped by an example from visual experience.[7] When I look at a box, then close my eyes, and then reopen them, I can perceive in this second view the identical box I saw before. Yet, although I perceive the same box, the two acts of seeing are distinctly different—in this case, temporally different. The same sort of result is obtained when I alter my acts of seeing spatially. If I go to another side of the room or stand on a chair, what I actually "see" alters with my change in perspective, and yet I still "perceive" the identical box; I still understand that the *object* of my seeing is the same. Furthermore, if I leave the room and simply recall the box in memory, I still understand that the *object* I remember is identical with the object I saw. For if I did not understand that, how could I insist that I was remembering? The examples are paradigmatic: All events of consciousness, not simply those involving visual perception and memory, are characterized by the mind's ability to make modally and temporally different *acts* of awareness refer to the same *object* of awareness. An object for the mind remains the same even though what is "going on in the mind" is not the same. The mind's object therefore may not be equated with psychic processes

6. *Logical Investigations* (1900).

7. Most of my illustrations in this section are visual rather than verbal since the former may be more easily grasped. If, at this stage, I were to choose verbal examples, I would have to interpret the examples before making my point. I discuss a literary text in sections B and C. The example of a box was suggested to me by Helmut Kuhn, "The Phenomenological Concept of 'Horizon,' " in *Philosophical Essays in Memory of Edmund Husserl*, ed. Marvin Farber (Cambridge, Mass., 1940) [Hirsch's note].

as such; the mental object is self-identical over against a plurality of mental acts.[8]

The relation between an act of awareness and its object Husserl calls "intention," using the term in its traditional philosophical sense, which is much broader than that of "purpose" and is roughly equivalent to "awareness." (When I employ the word subsequently, I shall be using it in Husserl's sense.)[9] This term is useful for distinguishing the components of a meaning experience. For example, when I "intend" a box, there are at least three distinguishable aspects of that event. First, there is the object as perceived by me; second, there is the act by which I perceive the object; and finally, there is (for physical things) the object which exists independently of my perceptual act. The first two aspects of the event Husserl calls "intentional object" and "intentional act" respectively. Husserl's point, then, is that *different* intentional acts (on different occasions) "intend" an *identical* intentional object.

The general term for all intentional objects is meaning. Verbal meaning is simply a special kind of intentional object, and like any other one, it remains self-identical over against the many different acts which "intend" it. But the noteworthy feature of verbal meaning is its supra-personal character. It is not an intentional object for simply one person, but for many—potentially for all persons. Verbal meaning is, by definition, *that aspect of a speaker's "intention" which, under linguistic conventions, may be shared by others*. Anything not sharable in this sense does not belong to the verbal intention or verbal meaning. Thus, when I say, "The air is crisp," I may be thinking, among other things, "I should have eaten less at supper," and "Crisp air reminds me of my childhood in Vermont," and so on. In certain types of utterance such unspoken accompaniments to meaning may be sharable, but in general they are not, and therefore they do not generally belong to verbal meaning. The nonverbal aspects of the speaker's intention Husserl calls "experience" and the verbal ones "content." However, by content he does not mean simply intellectual content, but all those aspects of the intention—cognitive, emotive, phonetic (and in writing, even visual)—which may be conveyed to others by the linguistic means employed.[1]

Husserl's analysis (in my brief exposition) makes the following points then: Verbal meaning, being an intentional object, is unchanging, that is, it may be reproduced by different intentional acts and remains self-identical through all these reproductions. Verbal meaning is the sharable content of the speaker's intentional object. Since this meaning is both unchanging and interpersonal, it may be reproduced by the mental acts of different persons. Husserl's view is thus essentially historical, for even though he insists that verbal meaning is unchanging, he also insists that any particular verbal utter-

8. See Aron Gurwitsch, "On the Intentionality of Consciousness," in *Philosophical Essays*, ed. Farber [Hirsch's note].

9. Although Husserl's term is a standard philosophical one for which there is no adequate substitute, students of literature may unwittingly associate it with the intentional fallacy. The two uses of the word are, however, quite distinct. As used by literary critics the term refers to a purpose which may or may not be realized by a writer. As used by Husserl the term refers to a process of consciousness. Thus in the literary usage, which involves problems of rhetoric, it is possible to speak of an unfulfilled intention, while in Husserl's usage such a locution would be meaningless [Hirsch's note]. For "The Intentional Fallacy" (1946), an influential New Critical essay by WILLIAM K. WIMSATT JR. AND MONROE BEARDSLEY, see above.

1. Edmund Husserl, *Logische Untersuchungen*, vol. 2, *Untersuchungen zur Phänomenologie und Theorie der Erkenntnis* [*Investigations into Phenomenology and Theory of Perception*], pt. 1, 2d ed. (Halle, 1913), pp. 96–97 [Hirsch's note].

ance, written or spoken, is historically determined. That is to say, the meaning is determined once and for all by the character of the speaker's intention.[2]

Husserl's views provide an excellent context for discussing the central problems of interpretation. Once we define verbal meaning as the content of the author's intention (which for brevity's sake I shall call simply the author's "verbal intention"), the problem for the interpreter is quite clear: he must distinguish those meanings which belong to that verbal intention from those which do not belong. This problem may be rephrased, of course, in a way that nearly everyone will accept: the interpreter has to distinguish what a text implies from what it does not imply; he must give the text its full due, but he must also preserve norms and limits. For hermeneutic theory, the problem is to find a *principle* for judging whether various possible implications should or should not be admitted.

I describe the problem in terms of implication, since, for practical purposes, it lies at the heart of the matter. Generally, the explicit meanings of a text can be construed to the satisfaction of most readers; the problems arise in determining inexplicit or "unsaid" meanings. If, for example, I announce, "I have a headache," there is no difficulty in construing what I "say," but there may be great difficulty in construing implications like "I desire sympathy" or "I have a right not to engage in distasteful work." Such implications may belong to my verbal meaning, or they may not belong. This is usually the area where the interpreter needs a guiding principle.

It is often said that implications must be determined by referring to the context of the utterance, which, for ordinary statements like "I have a headache," means the concrete situation in which the utterance occurs. In the case of written texts, however, context generally means verbal context: the explicit meanings which surround the problematical passage. But these explicit meanings alone do not exhaust what we mean by context when we educe implications. The surrounding explicit meanings provide us with a sense of the whole meaning, and it is from this sense of the whole that we decide what the problematical passage implies. We do not ask simply, "Does this implication belong with these other explicit meanings?" but rather, "Does this implication belong with these other meanings *within a particular sort of total meaning*?" For example, we cannot determine whether "root" belongs with or implies "bark" unless we know that the total meaning is "tree" and not "grass." The ground for educing implications is a sense of the whole meaning, and this is an indispensable aspect of what we mean by context.

Previously I defined the whole meaning of an utterance as the author's verbal intention. Does this mean that the principle for admitting or excluding implications must be to ask, "Did the author have in mind such an implication?" If that is the principle, all hope for objective interpretation must be abandoned, since in most cases it is impossible (even for the author himself) to determine precisely what he was thinking of at the time or times he composed his text. But this is clearly not the correct principle. When I say, "I have a headache," I may indeed imply, "I would like some sympathy," and yet I might not have been explicitly conscious of such an implication. The first step, then, in discovering a principle for admitting and excluding impli-

2. Ibid., p. 91 [Hirsch's note].

cations is to perceive the fundamental distinction between the author's verbal intention and the meanings of which he was explicitly conscious. Here again, Husserl's rejection of psychologism is useful. The author's verbal intention (his total verbal meaning) may be likened to my "intention" of a box. Normally, when I perceive a box, I am explicitly conscious of only three sides, and yet I assert with full confidence (although I might be wrong) that I "intend" a box, an object with *six* sides. Those three unseen sides belong to my "intention" in precisely the same way that the unconscious implications of an utterance belong to the author's intention. They belong to the intention taken as a whole.

Most, if not all, meaning experiences or intentions are occasions in which the whole meaning is not explicitly present to consciousness. But how are we to define the manner in which these unconscious meanings are implicitly present? In Husserl's analysis, they are present in the form of a "horizon," which may be defined as a system of typical expectations and probabilities.[3] "Horizon" is thus an essential aspect of what we usually call context. It is an inexplicit sense of the whole, derived from the explicit meanings present to consciousness. Thus, my view of three surfaces, presented in a familiar and typically box-like way, has a horizon of typical continuations; or, to put it another way, my "intention" of a whole box defines the horizon for my view of three visible sides. The same sort of relationship holds between the explicit and implicit meanings in a verbal intention. The explicit meanings are components in a total meaning which is bounded by a horizon. Of the manifold typical continuations within this horizon the author is not and cannot be explicitly conscious, nor would it be a particularly significant task to determine just which components of his meaning the author *was* thinking of. But it is of the utmost importance to determine the horizon which defines the author's intention as a whole, for it is only with reference to this horizon, or sense of the whole, that the interpreter may distinguish those implications which are typical and proper components of the meaning from those which are not.

The interpreter's aim, then, is to posit the author's horizon and carefully exclude his own accidental associations. A word like "vegetable," for example, had a meaning horizon in Marvell's language which is evidently somewhat different from the horizon it has in contemporary English. This is the linguistic horizon of the word, and it strictly bounds its possible implications. But all of these possible implications do not necessarily belong within the horizon of the particular utterance. What the word implies in the particular usage must be determined by asking, "Which implications are typical components of the whole meaning under consideration?" By analogy, when three surfaces are presented to me in a special way, I must know the typical continuations of the surfaces. If I have never encountered a box before, I might think that the unseen surfaces were concave or irregular, or I might simply think there are other sides but have no idea what they are like. The probability that I am right in the way I educe implications depends upon my familiarity with the type of meaning I consider.

That is the reason, of course, that the genre concept is so important in

3. See Edmund Husserl, *Erfahrung und Urteil* [*Experience and Judgment*], ed. L. Landgrebe (Hamburg, 1948), pp. 26–36, and Kuhn, "The Phenomenological Concept of 'Horizon' " [Hirsch's note].

textual study. By classifying the text as belonging to a particular genre, the interpreter automatically posits a general horizon for its meaning. The genre provides a sense of the whole, a notion of typical meaning components. Thus, before we interpret a text, we often classify it as casual conversation, lyric poem, military command, scientific prose, occasional verse, novel, epic, and so on. In a similar way, I have to classify the object I see as a box, a sphere, a tree, and so on before I can deduce the character of its unseen or inexplicit components. But these generic classifications are simply preliminary indications. They give only a rough notion of the horizon for a particular meaning. The aim of interpretation is to specify the horizon as far as possible. Thus, the object I see is not simply a box but a cigarette carton, and not simply that but a carton for a particular brand of cigarettes. If a paint mixer or dyer wants to specify a particular patch of color, he is not content to call it blue; he calls it Williamsburg Blue. The example of a color patch is paradigmatic for all particular verbal meanings. They are not simply *kinds* of meanings, nor are they single meanings corresponding to individual intentional acts (Williamsburg Blue is not simply an individual patch of color); they are *typical* meanings, particular yet reproducible, and the typical *components* of such meanings are similarly specific. The interpreter's job is to specify the text's horizon as far as he is able, and this means, ultimately, that he must familiarize himself with the typical meanings of the author's mental and experiential world.

The importance of the horizon concept is that it defines in principle the norms and limits which bound the meaning represented by the text. But, at the same time, the concept frees the interpreter from the constricting and impossible task of discovering what the author was explicitly thinking of. Thus, by defining textual meaning as the author's meaning, the interpreter does not, as it is so often argued, impoverish meaning; he simply excludes what does not belong to it. For example, if I say, "My car ran out of gas," I imply, typically, "The engine stopped running." Whether I also imply "Life is ironical" depends on the generality of my intention. Some linguistic utterances, many literary works among them, have an extremely broad horizon which at some points may touch the boundaries of man's intellectual cosmos. But whether this is the case is not a matter for a priori discussion; the decision must be based on a knowledgeable inference as to the particular intention being considered.

Within the horizon of a text's meaning, however, the process of explication is unlimited. In this respect Dryden[4] was right; no text is ever fully explicated. For example, if I undertook to interpret my "intention" of a box, I could make explicit unlimited implications which I did not notice in my original intention. I could educe not only the three unseen sides, but also the fact that the surfaces of the box contain twenty-four right angles, that the area of two adjoining sides is less than half the total surface area, and so on. And if someone asked me whether such meanings were implicit in my intention of a box, I must answer affirmatively. In the case of linguistic meanings, where the horizon defines a much more complex intentional object, such determinations are far more difficult to make. But the probability of an interpreter's inference may be judged by two criteria alone—the accuracy with

4. JOHN DRYDEN (1631–1700), English poet, dramatist, and critic.

which he has sensed the horizon of the whole and the typicality of such a meaning within such a whole. Insofar as the inference meets these criteria, it is truly an explication of textual meaning. It simply renders explicit that which was, consciously or unconsciously, in the author's intention.

The horizon which grounds and sanctions inferences about textual meaning is the "inner horizon" of the text. It is permanent and self-identical. Beyond this inner horizon any meaning has an "outer horizon"; that is to say, any meaning has relationships to other meanings; it is always a component in larger realms. This outer horizon is the domain of criticism. But this outer horizon is not only unlimited, it is also changing since the world itself changes. In general, criticism stakes out only a portion of this outer horizon as its peculiar object. Thus, for example, Eliot partitioned off that aspect of the text's outer horizon which is defined by the simultaneous order of literary texts. The simultaneous order at a given point in time is therefore the inner horizon of the meaning Eliot is investigating, and this inner horizon is just as definite, atemporal, and objective as the inner horizon which bounds textual meaning. However, the critic, like the interpreter, must construe correctly the components of his inner horizon, and one major component is textual meaning itself. The critic must first accurately interpret the text. He need not perform a detailed explication, but he needs to achieve (and validate) that clear and specific sense of the whole meaning which makes detailed explication possible.

B. Determinateness of Textual Meaning

In the previous section I defined textual meaning as the verbal intention of the author, and this argues implicitly that hermeneutics must stress a reconstruction of the author's aims and attitudes in order to evolve guides and norms for construing the meaning of his text. It is frequently argued, however, that textual meaning has nothing to do with the author's mind but only with his verbal achievement, that the object of interpretation is not the author but his text. This plausible argument assumes, of course, that the text automatically has a meaning simply because it represents an unalterable sequence of words. It assumes that the meaning of a word sequence is directly imposed by the public norms of language, that the text as a "piece of language" is a public object whose character is defined by public norms.[5] This view is in one respect sound, since textual meaning must conform to public norms if it is in any sense to be verbal (i.e. sharable) meaning; on no account may the interpreter permit his probing into the author's mind to raise private associations (experience) to the level of public implications (content).

However, this basically sound argument remains one-sided, for even though verbal meaning must conform to public linguistic norms (these are highly tolerant, of course), no mere sequence of words can represent an actual verbal meaning with reference to public norms alone. Referred to these alone, the text's meaning remains indeterminate. This is true even of the simplest declarative sentence like "My car ran out of gas" (did my Pullman dash from a cloud of Argon?). The fact that no one would radically

5. The phrase, "piece of language," comes from the first paragraph of William Empson's *Seven Types of Ambiguity* [1930]. It is typical of the critical school Empson founded [Hirsch's note].

misinterpret such a sentence simply indicates that its frequency is high enough to give its usual meaning the apparent status of an immediate given. But this apparent immediacy obscures a complex process of adjudications among meaning possibilities. Under the public norms of language alone no such adjudications can occur, since the array of possibilities presents a face of blank indifference. The array of possibilities only begins to become a more selective system of *probabilities* when, instead of confronting merely a word sequence, we also posit a speaker who very likely means something. Then and only then does the most usual sense of the word sequence become the most probable or "obvious" sense. The point holds true a fortiori, of course, when we confront less obvious word sequences like those found in poetry. A careful exposition of this point may be found in the first volume of Cassirer's[6] *Philosophy of Symbolic Forms*, which is largely devoted to a demonstration that verbal meaning arises from the "reciprocal determination" of public linguistic possibilities and subjective specifications of those possibilities.[7] Just as language constitutes and colors subjectivity, so does subjectivity color language. The author's or speaker's subjective act is formally necessary to verbal meaning, and any theory which tries to dispense with the author as specifier of meaning by asserting that textual meaning is purely objectively determined finds itself chasing will-o'-the-wisps. The burden of this section is, then, an attack on the view that a text is a "piece of language" and a defense of the notion that a text represents the determinate verbal meaning of an author.

One of the consequences arising from the view that a text is a piece of language—a purely public object—is the impossibility of defining in principle the nature of a correct interpretation. This is the same impasse which results from the theory that a text leads a life of its own, and, indeed, the two notions are corollaries since any "piece of language" must have a changing meaning when the changing public norms of language are viewed as the only ones which determine the sense of the text. It is therefore not surprising to find that Wellek subscribes implicitly to the text-as-language theory. The text is viewed as representing not a determinate meaning, but rather a system of meaning potentials specified not by a meaner but by the vital potency of language itself. Wellek acutely perceives the danger of the view:

> Thus the system of norms is growing and changing and will remain, in some sense, always incompletely and imperfectly realized. But this dynamic conception does not mean mere subjectivism and relativism. All the different points of view are by no means equally right. It will always be possible to determine which point of view grasps the subject most thoroughly and deeply. A hierarchy of viewpoints, a criticism of the grasp of norms, is implied in the concept of the adequacy of interpretation.[8]

The danger of the view is, of course, precisely that it opens the door to subjectivism and relativism, since linguistic norms may be invoked to support

6. Ernst Cassirer (1874–1945), German philosopher.

7. Vol. 1, *Language*, trans. R. Manheim (New Haven, 1953). It is ironic that Cassirer's work should be used to support the notion that a text speaks for itself. The realm of language is autonomous for Cassirer only in the sense that it follows an independent development which is reciprocally determined by objective *and* subjective factors. See pp. 69, 178, 213, 249–50, and passim [Hirsch's note].

8. Wellek and Warren, *Theory of Literature*, p. 144 [Hirsch's note].

any verbally possible meaning. Furthermore, it is not clear how one may criticize a grasp of norms which will not stand still.

Wellek's brief comment on the problem involved in defining and testing correctness in interpretation is representative of a widespread conviction among literary critics that the most correct interpretation is the most "inclusive" one. Indeed, the view is so widely accepted that Wellek did not need to defend his version of it (which he calls "Perspectivism") at length. The notion behind the theory is reflected by such phrases as "always incompletely and imperfectly realized" and "grasps the subject most thoroughly." This notion is simply that no single interpretation can exhaust the rich system of meaning potentialities represented by the text. Hence, every plausible reading which remains within public linguistic norms is a correct reading so far as it goes, but each reading is inevitably partial since it cannot realize all the potentialities of the text. The guiding principle in criticism, therefore, is that of the inclusive interpretation. The most "adequate" construction is the one which gives the fullest coherent account of all the text's potential meanings.[9]

Inclusivism is desirable as a position which induces a readiness to consider the results of others, but, aside from promoting an estimable tolerance, it has little theoretical value. Although its aim is to reconcile different plausible readings in an ideal, comprehensive interpretation, it cannot, in fact, either reconcile different readings or choose between them. As a normative ideal, or principle of correctness, it is useless. This point may be illustrated by citing two expert readings of a well-known poem by Wordsworth. I shall first quote the poem and then quote excerpts from two published exegeses to demonstrate the kind of impasse which inclusivism always provokes when it attempts to reconcile interpretations and, incidentally, to demonstrate the very kind of interpretive problem which calls for a guiding principle:

A slumber did my spirit seal;
I had no human fears:
She seemed a thing that could not feel
The touch of earthly years.

No motion has she now, no force;
She neither hears nor sees;
Rolled round in earth's diurnal course,
With rocks, and stones, and trees.[1]

Here are excerpts from two commentaries on the final lines of the poem; the first is by Cleanth Brooks, the second by F. W. Bateson.[2]

> [The poet] attempts to suggest something of the lover's agonized shock at the loved one's present lack of motion—of his response to her utter and horrible inertness. . . . Part of the effect, of course, resides in the fact that a dead lifelessness is suggested more sharply by an object's

9. Every interpretation is necessarily incomplete in the sense that it fails to explicate all a text's implications. But this kind of incomplete interpretation may still carry an absolutely correct system of emphases and an accurate sense of the whole meaning. This kind of incompleteness is radically different from that postulated by the inclusivists, for whom a sense of the whole means a grasp of the various possible meanings which a text can plausibly represent [Hirsch's note].

1. "A Slumber Did My Spirit Seal" (1800), by the English Romantic poet WILLIAM WORDSWORTH (1770–1850).

2. Frederick Wilse Bateson (1901–1978), English critic, founding editor in 1951 of the journal *Essays in Criticism*. BROOKS (1906–1994), American New Critic and educator.

> being whirled about by something else than by an image of the object in repose. But there are other matters which are at work here: the sense of the girl's falling back into the clutter of things, companioned by things chained like a tree to one particular spot, or by things completely inanimate like rocks and stones. . . . [She] is caught up helplessly into the empty whirl of the earth which measures and makes time. She is touched by and held by earthly time in its most powerful and horrible image.

> The final impression the poem leaves is not of two contrasting moods, but of a single mood mounting to a climax in the pantheistic magnificence of the last two lines. . . . The vague living-Lucy of this poem is opposed to the grander dead-Lucy who has become involved in the sublime processes of nature. We put the poem down satisfied, because its last two lines succeed in effecting a reconciliation between the two philosophies or social attitudes. Lucy is actually more alive now that she is dead, because she is now a part of the life of Nature, and not just a human "thing."[3]

If we grant, as I think we must, that both the cited interpretations are permitted by the text, the problem for the inclusivist is to reconcile the two readings.

Three modes of reconciliation are available to the inclusivist: (1) Brooks' reading includes Bateson's; it shows that any affirmative suggestions in the poem are negated by the bitterly ironical portrayal of the inert girl being whirled around by what Bateson calls the "sublime processes of Nature." (2) Bateson's reading includes Brooks'; the ironic contrast between the active, seemingly immortal girl and the passive, inert, dead girl is overcome by a final unqualified affirmation of immortality. (3) Each of the readings is partially right, but they must be fused to supplement one another. The very fact that the critics differ suggests that the meaning is essentially ambiguous. The emotion expressed is ambivalent and comprises both bitter regret and affirmation. The third mode of reconciliation is the one most often employed and is probably, in this case, the most satisfactory. A fourth type of resolution, which would insist that Brooks is right and Bateson wrong (or vice versa), is not available to the inclusivist, since the text, as language, renders both readings plausible.

Close examination, however, reveals that none of the three modes of argument manages to reconcile or fuse the two different readings. Mode 1, for example, insists that Brooks' reading comprehends Bateson's, but although it is conceivable that Brooks implies all the meanings which Bateson has perceived, Brooks also implies a pattern of emphasis which cannot be reconciled with Bateson's reading. While Bateson construes a primary emphasis on life and affirmation, Brooks emphasizes deadness and inertness. No amount of manipulation can reconcile these divergent emphases, since one pattern of emphasis irrevocably excludes other patterns, and, since emphasis is always crucial to meaning, the two constructions of meaning rigorously exclude one another. Precisely the same strictures hold, of course, for the argument that Bateson's reading comprehends that of

3. Cleanth Brooks, "Irony as a Principle of Structure," in *Literary Opinion in America*, ed. M. D. Zabel, 2d ed. (New York, 1951), p. 736. F. W. Bateson, *English Poetry: A Critical Introduction* (London, 1950), pp. 33, 80–81 [Hirsch's note].

Brooks. Nor can mode 3 escape with impunity. Although it seems to preserve a stress both on negation and on affirmation, thereby coalescing the two readings, it actually excludes both readings and labels them not simply partial, but wrong. For if the poem gives equal stress to bitter irony and to affirmation, then any construction which places a primary stress on either meaning is simply incorrect.

The general principle implied by my analysis is very simple. The submeanings of a text are not blocks which can be brought together additively. Since verbal (and any other) meaning is a *structure* of component meanings, interpretation has not done its job when it simply enumerates what the component meanings are. The interpreter must also determine their probable structure and particularly their structure of emphases. Relative emphasis is not only crucial to meaning (perhaps it is the most crucial and problematical element of all), it is also highly restrictive; it excludes alternatives. It may be asserted as a general rule that whenever a reader confronts two interpretations which impose different emphases on similar meaning components, at least one of the interpretations must be wrong. They cannot be reconciled.

By insisting that verbal meaning always exhibits a determinate structure of emphases, I do not, however, imply that a poem or any other text must be unambiguous. It is perfectly possible, for example, that Wordsworth's poem ambiguously implies both bitter irony and positive affirmation. Such complex emotions are commonly expressed in poetry, but if that is the kind of meaning the text represents, Brooks and Bateson would be wrong to emphasize one emotion at the expense of the other. Ambiguity or, for that matter, vagueness is not the same as indeterminateness. This is the crux of the issue. To say that verbal meaning is determinate is not to exclude complexities of meaning but only to insist that a text's meaning is what it is and not a hundred other things. Taken in this sense, a vague or ambiguous text is just as determinate as a logical proposition; it means what it means and nothing else. This is true even if one argues that a text could display shifting emphases like those magic squares which first seem to jut out and then to jut in. With texts of this character (if any exist), one need only say that the emphases shift and must not, therefore, be construed statically. Any static construction would simply be wrong. The fundamental flaw in the "theory of the most inclusive interpretation" is that it overlooks the problem of emphasis. Since different patterns of emphasis exclude one another, inclusivism is neither a genuine norm nor an adequate guiding principle for establishing an interpretation.

Aside from the fact that inclusivism cannot do its appointed job, there are more fundamental reasons for rejecting it and all other interpretive ideals based on the conception that a text represents a system of meaning possibilities. No one would deny that for the interpreter the text is at first the source of numerous possible interpretations. The very nature of language is such that a particular sequence of words can represent several different meanings (that is why public norms alone are insufficient in textual interpretation). But to say that a text *might* represent several structures of meaning does not imply that it does in fact represent all the meanings which a particular word sequence can legally convey. Is there not an obvious distinction between what a text might mean and what it does mean?

According to accepted linguistic theory, it is far more accurate to say that a written composition is not a mere locus of verbal possibilities, but a record (made possible by the invention of writing) of a verbal actuality. The interpreter's job is to reconstruct a determinate actual meaning, not a mere system of possibilities. Indeed, if the text represented a system of possibilities, interpretation would be impossible, since no actual reading could correspond to a mere system of possibilities. Furthermore, if the text is conceived to represent all the *actual* structures of meaning permissible within the public norms of language, then no single construction (with its exclusivist pattern of emphases) could be correct, and any legitimate construction would be just as incorrect as any other. When a text is conceived as a piece of language, a familiar and all too common anarchy follows. But, aside from its unfortunate consequences, the theory contradicts a widely accepted principle in linguistics. I refer to Saussure's[4] distinction between *langue* and *parole*.

Saussure defined *langue* as the system of linguistic possibilities shared by a speech community at a given point in time.[5] This system of possibilities contains two distinguishable levels. The first consists of habits, engrams, prohibitions, and the like derived from past linguistic usage; these are the "virtualities" of the *langue*. Based on these virtualities, there are, in addition, sharable meaning possibilities which have never before been actualized; these are the "potentialities." The two types of meaning possibilities taken together constitute the *langue* which the speech community draws upon. But this system of possibilities must be distinguished from the actual verbal utterances of individuals who draw upon it. These actual utterances are called *paroles*; they are uses of language and actualize some (but never all) of the meaning possibilities constituting the *langue*.

Saussure's distinction pinpoints the issue: does a text represent a segment of *langue* (as modern theorists hold) or a *parole*? A simple test suffices to provide the answer. If the text is composed of sentences, it represents *parole*, which is to say, the determinate verbal meaning of a member of the speech community. *Langue* contains words and sentence-forming principles, but it contains no sentences. It may be represented in writing only by isolated words in disconnection (*Wörter* as opposed to *Worte*).[6] A *parole*, on the other hand, is always composed of sentences, an assertion corroborated by the firmly established principle that the sentence is the fundamental unit of speech.[7] Of course, there are numerous elliptical and one-word sentences, but wherever it can be correctly inferred that a text represents sentences and not simply isolated words, it may also be inferred that the text represents *parole*, which is to say, actual, determinate verbal meaning.

The point is nicely illustrated in a dictionary definition. The letters in boldface at the head of the definition represent the word as *langue*, with all

4. FERDINAND DE SAUSSURE (1857–1913), Swiss linguist. Literally, *langue* and *parole* mean "language" and "spoken word" (French).

5. This is the "synchronic" as opposed to the "diachronic" sense of the term. See Ferdinand de Saussure, *Cours de linguistique générale* [*Course in General Linguistics*] (Paris, 1931). Useful discussions may be found in Stephen Ullman, *The Principles of Semantics* (Glasgow, 1951), and W. v. Wartburg, *Einführung in die Problematik und Methodik der Sprachwissenschaft* [*Problems and Methods in Linguistics*] (Halle, 1943) [Hirsch's note].

6. The distinction drawn, in German, between isolated and connected words.

7. See, for example, Cassirer, *Symbolic Forms*, vol. 1, *Language*, p. 304 [Hirsch's note].

its rich meaning possibilities. But under one of the subheadings, in an illustrative sentence, those same letters represent the word as *parole*, as a particular, selective actualization from *langue*. In yet another illustrative sentence, under another subheading, the very same word represents a different selective actualization. Of course, many sentences, especially those found in poetry, actualize far more possibilities than illustrative sentences in a dictionary. Any pun, for example, realizes simultaneously at least two divergent meaning possibilities. But the pun is nevertheless an actualization from *langue* and not a mere system of meaning possibilities.

The *langue-parole* distinction, besides affirming the determinateness of textual meaning, also clarifies the special problems posed by revised and interpolated texts. With a revised text, composed over a long period of time (*Faust*,[8] for example), how are we to construe the unrevised portions? Should we assume that they still mean what they meant originally or that they took on a new meaning when the rest of the text was altered or expanded? With compiled or interpolated texts, like many books of the Bible, should we assume that sentences from varied provenances retain their original meanings or that these heterogeneous elements have become integral components of a new total meaning? In terms of Saussure's distinction, the question becomes: should we consider the text to represent a compilation of divers *paroles* or a new unitary *parole* "respoken" by the new author or editor? I submit that there can be no definitive answer to the question, except in relation to a specific scholarly or aesthetic purpose, for in reality the question is not, "How are we to interpret the text?" but, "*Which* text are we to interpret?" Is it to be the heterogeneous compilation of past *paroles*, each to be separately considered, or the new, homogeneous *parole*? Both may be represented by the written score. The only problem is to choose, and having chosen, rigorously to refrain from confusing or in any way identifying the two quite different and separate "texts" with one another. Without solving any concrete problems, then, Saussure's distinction nevertheless confirms the critic's right in most cases to regard his text as representing a single *parole*.

Another problem which Saussure's distinction clarifies is that posed by the bungled text, where the author aimed to convey a meaning which his words do not convey to others in the speech community. One sometimes confronts the problem in a freshman essay. In such a case, the question is, does the text mean what the author wanted it to mean or does it mean what the speech community at large takes it to mean? Much attention has been devoted to this problem ever since the publication in 1946 of Wimsatt's and Beardsley's essay on "The Intentional Fallacy."[9] In that essay the position was taken (albeit modified by certain qualifications) that the text, being public, means what the speech community takes it to mean. This position is, in an ethical sense, right (and language, being social, has a strong ethical aspect): if the author has bungled so badly that his utterance will be misconstrued, then it serves him right when people misunderstand him. However, put in linguistic terms, the position becomes unsatisfactory. It implies that the meaning represented by the text is not the *parole* of an author, but rather the *parole* of

8. Goethe published *Faust* in two parts, in 1808 and 1832.

9. See *Sewanee Review* 54 (1946). Reprinted in William K. Wimsatt, Jr., *The Verbal Icon: Studies in the Meaning of Poetry* (Lexington, Ky., 1954) [Hirsch's note].

the speech community. But since only individuals utter *paroles*, a *parole* of the speech community is a nonexistent, or what the Germans call an *Unding*.[1] A text can represent only the *parole* of a speaker or author, which is another way of saying that meaning requires a meaner.

However, it is not necessary that an author's text represent the *parole* he desired to convey. It is frequently the case, when an author has bungled, that his text represents no *parole* at all. Indeed, there are but two alternatives: either the text represents the author's verbal meaning or it represents no determinate verbal meaning at all. Sometimes, of course, it is impossible to detect that the author has bungled, and in that case, even though his text does not represent verbal meaning, we shall go on misconstruing the text as though it did, and no one will be the wiser. But with most bungles we are aware of a disjunction between the author's words and his probable meaning. Eliot, for example, chided Poe for saying "My most immemorial year," when Poe "meant" his most *memorable* year.[2] We all agree that Poe did not mean what speakers of English generally mean by the word "immemorial"—and so the word cannot have the usual meaning. (An author cannot mean what he does not mean.) The only question, then, is: does the word mean more or less what we convey by "never to be forgotten" or does it mean nothing at all? Has Poe so violated linguistic norms that we must deny his utterance verbal meaning or content?

The question probably cannot be answered by fiat, but since Poe's meaning is generally understood, and since the single criterion for verbal meaning is communicability, I am inclined to describe Poe's meaning as verbal.[3] I tend to side with the Poes and Malaprops[4] of the world, for the norms of language remain far more tolerant than dictionaries and critics like Eliot suggest. On the other hand, every member of the speech community, and especially the critic, has a duty to avoid and condemn sloppiness and needless ambiguity in the use of language, simply in order to preserve the effectiveness of the *langue* itself. Moreover, there must be a dividing line between verbal meanings and those meanings which we half-divine by a supra-linguistic exercise of imagination. There must be a dividing line between Poe's successful disregard of normal usage and the incommunicable word sequences of a bad freshman essay. However, that dividing line is not between the author's meaning and the reader's, but rather between the author's *parole* and no *parole* at all.

Of course, theoretical principles cannot directly solve the interpreter's problem. It is one thing to insist that a text represents the determinate verbal meaning of an author, but it is quite another to discover what that meaning is. The very same text could represent numerous different *paroles*, as any ironic sentence discloses ("That's a *bright* idea?" or "That's a bright *idea!*").

1. An impossibility, nonsense (literally, an "unthing").

2. T. S. Eliot, "From Poe to Valéry," *Hudson Review* 2 (1949): 232 [Hirsch's note]. Eliot is referring to EDGAR ALLAN POE's poem "Ulalume" (1847).

3. The word is, in fact, quite effective. It conveys the sense of "memorable" by the component "memorial," and the sense of "never to be forgotten" by the negative prefix. The difference between this and jabberwocky words is that it appears to be a standard word occurring in a context of standard words. Perhaps Eliot is right to scold Poe, but he cannot properly insist that the word lacks a determinate verbal meaning [Hirsch's note]. The words in Lewis Carroll's poem "Jabberwocky" (1871) are effective (e.g., "frabjous") but nonsense.

4. From Mrs. Malaprop in Richard Sheridan's *The Rivals* (1775), whose peculiar speech spawned the term "malapropism," an inappropriate use of one word for another similar-sounding word.

But it should be of some practical consequence for the interpreter to know that he does have a precisely defined task, namely, to discover the author's meaning. It is therefore not only sound but necessary for the interpreter to inquire, "What in all probability did the author mean? Is the pattern of emphases I construe the author's pattern?" But it is both incorrect and futile to inquire, "What does the language of the text say?" That question can have no determinate answer.

C. *Verification*

Since the meaning represented by a text is that of another, the interpreter can never be certain that his reading is correct. He knows furthermore that the norms of *langue* by themselves are far too broad to specify the particular meanings and emphases represented by the text, that these particular meanings were specified by particular kinds of subjective acts on the part of the author, and that these acts, as such, remain inaccessible.[5] A less self-critical reader, on the other hand, approaches solipsism if he assumes that the text represents a perspicuous meaning simply because it represents an unalterable sequence of words. For if this perspicuous meaning is not verified in some way, it will simply be the interpreter's own meaning, exhibiting the connotations and emphases which he himself imposes. Of course, the reader must realize verbal meaning by his own subjective acts (no one can do that for him), but if he remembers that his job is to construe the author's meaning, he will attempt to exclude his own predispositions and to impose those of the author. However, no one can establish another's meaning with certainty. The interpreter's goal is simply this—to show that a given reading is more probable than others. In hermeneutics, verification is a process of establishing relative probabilities.

To establish a reading as probable it is first necessary to show, with reference to the norms of language, that it is possible. This is the criterion of *legitimacy*: the reading must be permissible within the public norms of the *langue* in which the text was composed. The second criterion is that of *correspondence*: the reading must account for each linguistic component in the text. Whenever a reading arbitrarily ignores linguistic components or inadequately accounts for them, the reading may be presumed improbable. The third criterion is that of *generic appropriateness*: if the text follows the conventions of a scientific essay, for example, it is inappropriate to construe the kind of allusive meaning found in casual conversation.[6] When these three preliminary criteria have been satisfied, there remains a fourth criterion which gives significance to all the rest, the criterion of plausibility or *coherence*. The three preliminary norms usually permit several readings, and this is by definition the case when a text is problematical. Faced with alternatives, the interpreter chooses the reading which best meets the criterion of coherence. Indeed, even when the text is not problematical, coherence remains the decisive criterion, since the meaning is "obvious" only because it "make sense." I wish, therefore, to focus attention

5. To recall Husserl's point, a particular verbal meaning depends on a particular species of "intentional act," not on a single, irreproducible act [Hirsch's note].

6. This third criterion is, however, highly presumptive, since the interpreter may easily mistake the text's genre [Hirsch's note].

on the criterion of coherence and shall take for granted the demands of legitimacy, correspondence, and generic appropriateness. I shall try to show that verification by the criterion of coherence, and ultimately, therefore, verification in general, implies a reconstruction of relevant aspects in the author's outlook. My point may be summarized in the paradox that objectivity in textual interpretation requires explicit reference to the speaker's subjectivity.

The paradox reflects the peculiar nature of coherence, which is not an absolute but a dependent quality. The laws of coherence are variable; they depend upon the nature of the total meaning under consideration. Two meanings ("dark" and "bright," for example) which cohere in one context may not cohere in another.[7] "Dark with excessive bright" makes excellent sense in *Paradise Lost*,[8] but if a reader found the phrase in a textbook on plant pathology, he would assume that he confronted a misprint for "dark with excessive blight." Coherence depends on the context, and it is helpful to recall our definition of context: it is a sense of the whole meaning, constituted of explicit partial meanings plus a horizon of expectations and probabilities. One meaning coheres with another because it is typical or probable with reference to the whole (coherence is thus the first cousin of implication). The criterion of coherence can be invoked only with reference to a particular context, and this context may be inferred only by positing the author's horizon, his disposition toward a particular type of meaning. This conclusion requires elaboration.

The fact that coherence is a dependent quality leads to an unavoidable circularity in the process of interpretation. The interpreter posits meanings for the words and word sequences he confronts, and, at the same time, he has to posit a whole meaning or context in reference to which the submeanings cohere with one another. The procedure is thoroughly circular; the context is derived from the submeanings and the submeanings are specified and rendered coherent with reference to the context. This circularity makes it very difficult to convince a reader to alter his construction, as every teacher knows. Many a self-willed student continues to insist that his reading is just as plausible as his instructor's, and, very often, the student is justified; his reading does make good sense. Often, the only thing at fault with the student's reading is that it is probably wrong, not that it is incoherent. The student persists in his opinion precisely because his construction *is* coherent and self-sustaining. In such a case he is wrong because he has misconstrued the context or sense of the whole. In this respect, the student's hardheadedness is not different from that of all self-convinced interpreters. Our readings are too plausible to be relinquished. If we have a distorted sense of the text's whole meaning, the harder we look at it the more certainly we shall find our distorted construction confirmed.

Since the quality of coherence depends upon the context inferred, there is no absolute standard of coherence by which we can adjudicate between different coherent readings. Verification by coherence implies therefore a verification of the grounds on which the reading is coherent. *It is necessary to establish that the context invoked is the most probable context.* Only then,

7. Exceptions to this are the syncategorematic meanings (color and extension, for example) which cohere by necessity regardless of the context [Hirsch's note].

8. John Milton, *Paradise Lost* (1667), 3.380.

in relation to an established context, can we judge that one reading is more coherent than another. Ultimately, therefore, we have to posit the most probable horizon for the text, and it is possible to do this only if we posit the author's typical outlook, the typical associations and expectations which form in part the context of his utterance. This is not only the one way we can test the relative coherence of a reading, but it is also the only way to avoid pure circularity in making sense of the text.

An essential task in the process of verification is, therefore, a deliberate reconstruction of the author's subjective stance to the extent that this stance is relevant to the text at hand.[9] The importance of such psychological reconstruction may be exemplified in adjudicating between different readings of Wordsworth's "A Slumber Did My Spirit Seal." The interpretations of Brooks and Bateson, different as they are, remain equally coherent and self-sustaining. The implications which Brooks construes cohere beautifully with the explicit meanings of the poem within the context which Brooks adumbrates. The same may be said of Bateson's reading. The best way to show that one reading is more plausible and coherent than the other is to show that one context is more probable than the other. The problem of adjudicating between Bateson and Brooks is therefore, implicitly, the problem every interpreter must face when he tries to verify his reading. He must establish the most probable context.

Now when the *homme moyen sensuel*[1] confronts bereavement such as that which Wordsworth's poem explicitly presents, he adumbrates, typically, a horizon including sorrow and inconsolability. These are for him components in the very meaning of bereavement. Sorrow and inconsolability cannot fail to be associated with death when the loved one, formerly so active and alive, is imagined as lying in the earth, helpless, dumb, inert, insentient. And since there is no hint of life in Heaven but only of bodily death, the comforts of Christianity lie beyond the poem's horizon. Affirmations too deep for tears,[2] like those Bateson insists on, simply do not cohere with the poem's explicit meanings; they do not belong to the context. Brooks' reading, therefore, with its emphasis on inconsolability and bitter irony, is clearly justified not only by the text but by reference to universal human attitudes and feelings.

However, the trouble with such a reading is apparent to most Wordsworthians. The poet is not an *homme moyen sensuel*; his characteristic attitudes are somewhat pantheistic. Instead of regarding rocks and stones and trees merely as inert objects, he probably regarded them in 1799 as deeply alive, as part of the immortal life of nature. Physical death he felt to be a return to the source of life, a new kind of participation in nature's "revolving immortality." From everything we know of Wordsworth's typical attitudes during the period in which he composed the poem, inconsolability and bitter irony

9. The reader may feel that I have telescoped a number of steps here. The author's verbal meaning or "verbal intention" is the object of complex "intentional acts." To reproduce this meaning it is necessary for the interpreter to engage in "intentional acts" belonging to the same species as those of the author. (Two different "intentional acts" belong to the same species when they "intend" the same "intentional object.") That is why the issue of "stance" arises. The interpreter needs to adopt sympathetically the author's stance (his disposition to engage in particular kinds of "intentional acts") so that he can "intend" with some degree of probability the same "intentional objects" as the author. This is especially clear in the case of *implicit* verbal meaning, where the interpreter's realization of the author's stance determines the text's horizon [Hirsch's note].

1. The average nonintellectual man (French).

2. An allusion to the final words of Wordsworth's "Ode: Intimations of Immortality" (1807): "To me the meanest flower that blows can give / Thoughts that do often lie too deep for tears."

do not belong in its horizon. I think, however, that Bateson overstates his case and that he fails to emphasize properly the negative implications in the poem ("No motion has she now, no force"). He overlooks the poet's reticence, his distinct unwillingness to express any unqualified evaluation of his experience. Bateson, I would say, has not paid enough attention to the criterion of correspondence. Nevertheless, in spite of this, and in spite of the apparent implausibility of Bateson's reading, it remains, I think, somewhat more probable than that of Brooks. His procedure is also more objective. Even if he had botched his job thoroughly and had produced a less probable reading than that of Brooks, his method would remain fundamentally sound. Instead of projecting his own attitudes (Bateson is presumably not a pantheist) and instead of positing a "universal matrix" of human attitudes (there is none), he has tried to reconstruct the author's probable attitudes so far as these are relevant in specifying the poem's meaning. It is still possible, of course, that Brooks is right and Bateson wrong. A poet's typical attitudes do not always apply to a particular poem, although Wordsworth is, in a given period, more consistent than most poets. Be that as it may, we shall never be certain what any writer means, and since Bateson grounds his interpretation in a conscious construction of the poet's outlook, his reading must be deemed the more probable one until the uncovering of some presently unknown data makes a different construction of the poet's stance appear more valid.

Bateson's procedure is appropriate to all texts, including anonymous ones. On the surface, it would seem impossible to invoke the author's probable outlook when the author remains unknown, but in this limiting case the interpreter simply makes his psychological reconstruction on the basis of fewer data. Even with anonymous texts it is crucial to posit not simply some author or other, but a particular subjective stance in reference to which the construed context is rendered probable. That is why it is important to date anonymous texts. The interpreter needs all the clues he can muster with regard not only to the text's *langue* and genre, but also to the cultural and personal attitudes the author might be expected to bring to bear in specifying his verbal meanings. In this sense, all texts, including anonymous ones, are "attributed." The objective interpreter simply tries to makes his attribution explicit, so that the grounds for his reading are frankly acknowledged. This opens the way to progressive accuracy in interpretation, since it is possible then to test the assumptions behind a reading as well as the coherence of the reading itself.

The fact that anonymous texts may be successfully interpreted does not, however, lead to the conclusion that all texts should be treated as anonymous ones, that they should, so to say, speak for themselves. I have already argued that no text speaks for itself and that every construed text is necessarily attributed. These points suggest strongly that it is unsound to insist on deriving all inferences from the text itself. When we date an anonymous text, for example, we apply knowledge gained from a wide variety of sources which we correlate with data derived from the text. This extrinsic data is not, however, read into the text. On the contrary, it is used to verify that which we read out of it. The extrinsic information has ultimately a purely verificative function.

The same thing is true of information relating to the author's subjective stance. No matter what the source of this information may be, whether it be the text alone or the text in conjunction with other data, this information is extrinsic to verbal meaning as such. Strictly speaking, the author's subjective stance is not part of his verbal meaning even when he explicitly discusses his feelings and attitudes. This is Husserl's point again. The intentional object represented by a text is different from the intentional acts which realize it. When the interpreter posits the author's stance he sympathetically reenacts the author's intentional acts, but although this imaginative act is necessary for realizing meaning, it must be distinguished from meaning as such. In no sense does the text represent the author's subjective stance: the interpreter simply adopts a stance in order to make sense of the text, and, if he is self-critical he tries to verify his interpretation by showing his adopted stance to be, in all probability, the author's.

Of course, the text at hand is the safest source of clues to the author's outlook, since men do adopt different attitudes on different occasions. However, even though the text itself should be the primary source of clues and must always be the final authority, the interpreter should make an effort to go beyond his text wherever possible, since this is the only way he can avoid a vicious circularity. The harder one looks at a text from an incorrect stance, the more convincing the incorrect construction becomes. Inferences about the author's stance are sometimes difficult to make even when all relevant data are brought to bear, and it is self-defeating to make the inferential process more difficult than it need be. Since these inferences are ultimately extrinsic, there is no virtue in deriving them from the text alone. One must not confuse the result of a construction (the interpreter's understanding of the text's *Sinn*) with the *process* of construction or with a validation of that process. The *Sinn* must be represented by and limited by the text alone, but the processes of construction and validation involve psychological reconstruction and should therefore be based on all the data available.

Not only the criterion of coherence but all the other criteria used in verifying interpretations must be applied with reference to a psychological reconstruction. The criterion of legitimacy, for example, must be related to a speaking subject since it is the author's *langue*, as an internal possession, and not the interpreter's which defines the range of meaning possibilities a text can represent. The criterion of correspondence has force only because we presume that the author meant something by each of the linguistic components he employed, and the criterion of generic appropriateness is relevant only so far as generic conventions are possessed and accepted by the author. The fact that these criteria all refer ultimately to a psychological construction is hardly surprising when we recall that to verify a text is simply to establish that the author probably meant what we construe his text to mean. The interpreter's primary task is to reproduce in himself the author's "logic," his attitudes, his cultural givens, in short, his world. Even though the process of verification is highly complex and difficult, the ultimate verificative principle is very simple—the imaginative reconstruction of the speaking subject.[3]

The speaking subject is not, however, identical with the subjectivity of the author as an actual historical person; it corresponds, rather, to a very limited

3. Here I purposefully display my sympathies with Dilthey's concepts, *Sichhineinfühlen* [to empathize] and *Verstehen* [to understand]. In fact, my whole argument may be regarded as an attempt to ground some of Dilthey's hermeneutic principles in Husserl's epistemology and Saussure's linguistics [Hirsch's note]. Wilhelm Dilthey (1833–1911), German philosopher and historian of ideas.

and special aspect of the author's total subjectivity; it is, so to speak, that "part" of the author which specifies or determines verbal meaning.[4] This distinction is quite apparent in the case of a lie. When I wish to deceive, my secret awareness that I am lying is irrelevant to the verbal meaning of my utterance. The only correct interpretation of my lie is, paradoxically, to view it as being a true statement, since this is the only correct construction of my verbal intention. Indeed, it is only when my listener has *understood* my meaning (presented as true) that he can *judge* it to be a lie. Since I adopted a truth-telling stance, the verbal meaning of my utterance would be precisely the same, whether I was deliberately lying or suffering from the erroneous conviction that my statement was true. In other words, an author may adopt a stance which differs from his deepest attitudes in the same way that an interpreter must almost always adopt a stance different from his own.[5] But for the process of interpretation, the author's private experiences are irrelevant. The only relevant aspect of subjectivity is that which determines verbal meaning or, in Husserl's terms, content.

In a sense all poets are, of course, liars, and to some extent all speakers are, but the deliberate lie, spoken to deceive, is a borderline case. In most verbal utterances, the speaker's public stance is not totally foreign to his private attitudes. Even in those cases where the speaker deliberately assumes a role, this mimetic stance is usually not the final determinant of his meaning. In a play, for example, the total meaning of an utterance is not the intentional object of the dramatic character; that meaning is simply a component in the more complex intention of the dramatist. The speaker himself is spoken. The best description of these receding levels of subjectivity was provided by the scholastic philosophers in their distinction between "first intention," "second intention," and so on. Irony, for example, always entails a comprehension of two contrasting stances (intentional levels) by a third and final complex intention. The speaking subject may be defined as the final and most comprehensive level of awareness determinative of verbal meaning. In the case of a lie, the speaking subject assumes that he tells the truth, while the actual subject retains a private awareness of his deception. Similarly, many speakers retain in their isolated privacy a self-conscious awareness of their verbal meaning, an awareness which may agree or disagree, approve or disapprove, but which does not participate in determining their verbal meaning. To interpretation, this level of awareness is as irrelevant as it is inaccessible. In construing and verifying verbal meaning, only the speaking subject counts.

A separate exposition would be required to discuss the problems of psychological reconstruction. I have here simply tried to forestall the current objections to extrinsic biographical and historical information by pointing, on the one hand, to the exigencies of verification and, on the other, to the

4. Spranger aptly calls this the "cultural subject." See Eduard Spranger, "Zur Theorie des Verstehens und zur geisteswissenschaftlichen Psychologie" ["On the Theory of Understanding and Humanistic Psychology"] in *Festschrift Johannes Volkelt zum 70. Geburtstag* [*Festschrift for Johannes Volkelt's 70th Birthday*] (Munich, 1918), p. 369. It should be clear that I am here in essential agreement with the American anti-intentionalists (term used in the ordinary sense). I think they are right to exclude private associations from verbal meaning. But it is of some practical consequence to insist that verbal meaning is that aspect of an author's meaning which is interpersonally communi*cable*. This implies that his verbal meaning is that which, under linguistic norms, one *can* understand, even if one must sometimes work hard to do so [Hirsch's note].

5. Charles Bally calls this "déboublement de la personalité" [splitting of the personality] See his *Linguistique générale et linguistique française* [*General and French Linguistics* (Paris, 1932)], p. 37 [Hirsch's note].

distinction between a speaking subject and a "biographical" person. I shall be satisfied if this part of my discussion, incomplete as it must be, will help revive the half-forgotten truism that interpretation is the construction of *another's* meaning. A slight shift in the way we speak about texts would be highly salutary. It is natural to speak not of what a text says, but of what an author means, and this more natural locution is the more accurate one. Furthermore, to speak in this way implies a readiness (not notably apparent in recent criticism) to put forth a wholehearted and self-critical effort at the primary level of criticism—the level of understanding.

1960

HAYDEN WHITE
b. 1928

A historian by training, Hayden White has since the 1970s been a central figure in literary debates about the nature of history. While literary critics at this time like STEPHEN GREENBLATT began to turn to history to explain the formal structures of literary texts, White was investigating the formal literary structures of history, beginning with his celebrated 1973 book *Metahistory: The Historical Imagination of Nineteenth-Century Europe*, which outlines an ambitious structuralist scheme for describing a "poetics of history." Drawing on NORTHROP FRYE's *Anatomy of Criticism* (1957) to describe the underlying "deep structure" of historical narratives, this project brings together historiography and literary criticism in a broad reflection on narrative and its relation to culture. "To raise the question of the nature of narrative," White writes in *The Content of the Form: Narrative Discourse and Historical Representation* (1987), "is to invite reflection on the very nature of culture and, possibly, even on the nature of humanity itself. So natural is the impulse to narrative, so inevitable is the form of narrative for any report on the way things really happened, that narrativity could appear problematical only in a culture in which it was absent—or, as in some domains of contemporary Western intellectual and artistic culture, programmatically refused." Reacting against the tendency of history as a discipline to seek its models in the sciences, White contends that the literary dimension of history cannot be dismissed as mere decoration; rather, historians deploy the traditional devices of narrative to make sense of raw data, to organize and give meaning to their accounts of the past. Bringing the tools of the literary critic to bear on historical writing, White's analyses are powerful extensions of narrative theory for students and scholars of literature interested in understanding the nature and mechanisms of history as discourse.

White was born in Martin, Tennessee. After attending Wayne State University he did his graduate work in history at the University of Michigan, earning an M.A. in 1952 and a Ph.D. in 1956. He taught first as an instructor at Wayne State (1955–58), then in 1958 was appointed to the history faculty at the University of Rochester, where he served as head of the department from 1962 to 1964. He subsequently taught history at the University of California, Los Angeles (1968–73), served as the director of the Center for Humanities at Wesleyan University in Connecticut (1973–77), and in 1978 became a professor in the History of Consciousness program at the University of California, Santa Cruz. Since formally retiring in 1994, he has been the Bonsall Professor of Comparative Literature at Stanford University.

White, who began his career as a historian of the medieval church and turned to nineteenth-century thought in the 1960s, has always been eclectic in his scholarly interests. With the publication of *Metahistory*, however, his scholarship became explicitly engaged in literary and theoretical issues, as he responded to critics from the disciplines of both history and literature. His book *Tropics of Discourse: Essays in Cultural Criticism* (1978), from which our selection is taken, examines the structuring role of plots and tropes (figures of speech) in the discourse of history. *The Content of Form* explores the contemporary interplay between narrative theory and history in the work of both historians such as MICHEL FOUCAULT and literary theorists such as FREDRIC JAMESON and Paul Ricoeur. And in *Figural Realism: Studies in the Mimesis Effect* (1999), White takes on mimesis—the representation of reality—in history, an issue that has concerned literary critics from PLATO to Erich Auerbach (see *Mimesis: The Representation of Reality in Western Literature*, 1946).

Hayden White has been in the vanguard of the movement among historians, starting in the 1980s, that has come to be known as the "new cultural history." Historians associated with the movement, such as Lynn Hunt, Thomas Laqueur, and, in France, Roger Chartier, began to question the methods and goals of history in general, many turning to literary techniques and approaches to develop new materials and methods of analysis. The influences on this group of historians are varied. They include cultural Marxist approaches developed in the 1980s by British scholars such as E. P. Thompson and RAYMOND WILLIAMS, as well as the French Annales school, founded in the late 1920s by the historians Marc Bloch and Lucien Febvre. The new cultural history has also been strongly influenced by the work of Foucault, by literary theorists such as JACQUES DERRIDA and MIKHAIL BAKHTIN, and, of course, by White himself. Many of the historians associated with the new cultural history have ties with literary practitioners of the New Historicism and cultural studies.

"The Historical Text as Literary Artifact," our selection, provides an accessible and engaging synopsis of White's main arguments in *Metahistory*, beginning with his definition of metahistory as the attempt to "get behind or beneath the presuppositions which sustain a given type of inquiry [in this case historical inquiry]." A key assumption that, according to White, has sustained historical inquiry is the belief that history (judged by its correspondence to reality) and literature (judged as fiction) are two distinct, diametrically opposed, activities, a presupposition shared by practitioners in both disciplines. On the contrary, White argues, because history, like literature, is a verbal structure and the historian, first and foremost, is a writer, the tools that have served literary critics, the tools that compose the linguistic and rhetorical structures of a text, serve the historian as well. The language in which history is written cannot be dismissed as window dressing, as most historians are tempted to do. Language in history is never merely a means to an end; it is neither transparent nor neutral, nor does it disappear to allow the pure truth of history to emerge. In White's view, historical narratives are verbal fictions with invented contexts. He goes beyond Erich Auerbach, arguing that history, because of its claims to represent reality adequately, is the form best suited for a study of the style of narrative "realism."

Histories gain their explanatory power by processing data into stories. Those stories take their shape from what White calls "emplotment," the process through which the facts contained in "chronicles" are encoded as components of plots. Plots are not immanent in events themselves but exist in the minds of historians, who rarely reflect on them. No historical event can itself constitute a story, tragic or ironic: it can only be presented as such from a particular historian's narrative point of view. The event emerges as a plotted story, which takes on meaning when it is combined with other elements in the limited number of generic plot structures by which a series of events can be constituted. Following Northrop Frye's archetypal analysis, White identifies four possible emplotments: tragic, comic, romantic, and ironic. These generic deep-plot structures are shared between historians and their audiences by virtue of their participation in a common culture.

The kind of emplotment historians will employ to give meaning to a series of events, White argues, is determined by the dominant figurative mode of the language they use to describe these events and story elements. Drawing on the eighteenth-century philosopher GIAMBATTISTA VICO and the twentieth-century critic KENNETH BURKE, White identifies four master tropes or modes of figurative representation—metaphor, metonymy, synecdoche, and irony—which correspond to the four types of emplotment. For White, the differences between contending histories of, say, the French Revolution cannot be resolved by recourse to the facts, because the facts—and, more important, the relationships among those facts—do not inhere in the events themselves, but instead are constituted by historians in the linguistic and literary structures they use to identify and describe the events they study. Tropes are ineradicable from discourse, as are plots. Thus history evokes reality: it does not reproduce or represent it.

This analysis of historical narrative makes special sense in the context of the structuralism of the 1970s, when it first caught public attention. Although White does not draw directly on the terminology of structural linguistics, his debts to such modern structuralists as CLAUDE LÉVI-STRAUSS, ROMAN JAKOBSON, and the linguist Noam Chomsky are clear. And his adaptation of Frye's archetypal criticism is structuralist both in its basic argument that history uses a few "deep structures" to generate its "surface structures" and in its broad contention that historians have mistakenly focused their attention only on the surface, while ignoring the underlying deep structures that produce those narratives.

Historians have objected to White's narrowing of history to language, while more poststructuralist-minded literary critics have taken issue with White's structuralist reductionism (only four master plots and tropes). Some critics argue that Frye's archetypal approach to narrative, which White relies on, is too simple, forcing all narratives willy-nilly into abstract and timeless structures without regard to how they might function in particular cultural contexts. Others contend that unlike most structuralists, White imagines plot as a quintessential expression of the historian's personal style and self. Despite these objections, White's skillful dismantling of the opposition between history and literature has paved the way for many productive studies in both fields. Once historians and literary critics no longer believe that history gives its readers a privileged access to the real or the truth, they turn to investigating the grounds of history—its nature and forms, its uses and abuses—as well as its links to other fields of knowledge and to ideologies.

BIBLIOGRAPHY

White has served as the author, editor, or translator of a dozen books on a wide range of topics in history and literature. He was the coauthor, with Wilson H. Coates and J. Selwyn Schapiro, of the two-volume *Emergence of Liberal Humanism: An Intellectual History of Western Europe* (1966–70). He edited *The Uses of History: Essays in Intellectual and Social History* (1968); with Giorgio Tagliacozzo, *Giambattista Vico: An International Symposium* (1969); and with Wilson H. Coates, *The Ordeal of Liberal Humanism* (1970). The following year, he published *The Graeco-Roman Tradition* (1971). *Metahistory: The Historical Imagination in Nineteenth-Century Europe* (1973) was the groundbreaking study that first brought him to the attention of literary critics. His interest in historiography led him to translate from the Italian Carlo Antoni's *From History to Sociology: The Tradition in German Historical Thinking* (1976) and to collect his own 1976 Clark Library lectures into a volume titled *Theories of History* (1978). Since the late 1970s, White's work has become more literary in its focus, including *Tropics of Discourse: Essays in Cultural Criticism* (1978); *Representing Kenneth Burke* (1982), which he edited with Margaret Brose; *The Content of Form: Narrative Discourse and Historical Representation* (1987); and *Figural Realism: Studies in the Mimesis Effect* (1999). For biographical information consult the brief entry in *Contemporary Authors*, vol. 125 (1989).

Two lengthy, thought-provoking reviews of *Metahistory*, Fredric Jameson's "Figural Relativism: or the Poetics of Historiography" and David Carroll's "On Tropology: The Forms of History," appeared in the journal *Diacritics* 6 (1976). The journal *History and Theory* devoted a special issue, *Metahistory: Six Critiques* 19 [1980]), to White's book. Dominick LaCapra, another historian who has written on the linguistic turn in history, offers a sympathetic evaluation in "A Poetics of Historiography: Hayden White's *Tropics of Discourse*," in his *Rethinking Intellectual History: Texts, Contexts, Language* (1983). James M. Mellard's *Doing Tropology: Analysis of Narrative Discourse* (1989) and Hans Kellner's *Language and Historical Representation: Getting the Story Crooked* (1989) examine, critique, and extend White's approach. Russell Jacoby presents a critique of White's work in his article "A New Intellectual History," *American Historical Review* 97 (1992). By the late 1990s much of the writing on White was dominated by debate over the truth claims of history; for instance, Nancy Partner, "Hayden White (and the content and the form and everyone else) at AHA," *History and Theory* 36 (1997), and Chris Lorenz, "Can Histories be Truth? Narrativism, Positivism, and the 'Metaphorical Turn,' " *History and Theory* 37 (1998). Mellard's book (cited above) contains a bibliography that includes books by and about White.

The Historical Text as Literary Artifact[1]

One of the ways that a scholarly field takes stock of itself is by considering its history. Yet it is difficult to get an objective history of a scholarly discipline, because if the historian is himself a practitioner of it, he is likely to be a devotee of one or another of its sects and hence biased; and if he is not a practitioner he is unlikely to have the expertise necessary to distinguish between the significant and the insignificant events of the field's development. One might think that these difficulties would not arise in the field of history itself, but they do and not only for the reasons mentioned above. In order to write the history of any given scholarly discipline or even of a science, one must be prepared to ask questions *about* it of a sort that do not have to be asked in the practice *of* it. One must try to get behind or beneath the presuppositions which sustain a given type of inquiry and ask the questions that can be begged in its practice in the interest of determining why this type of inquiry has been designed to solve the problems it characteristically tries to solve. This is what metahistory seeks to do. It addresses itself to such questions as, What is the structure of a peculiarly *historical* consciousness? What is the epistemological status of historical *explanations*, as compared with other kinds of explanations that might be offered to account for the materials with which historians ordinarily deal? What are the possible *forms* of historical representation and what are their bases? What authority can historical accounts claim as contributions to a secured knowledge of reality in general and to the human sciences in particular?

Now, many of these questions have been dealt with quite competently

1. This essay is a revised version of a lecture given before the Comparative Literature Colloquium of Yale University on 24 January, 1974. In it I have tried to elaborate some of the themes that I originally discussed in an article, "The Structure of Historical Narrative," *Clio* 1 (1972): 5–20. I have also drawn upon the materials of my book *Metahistory: The Historical Imagination in Nineteenth-Century Europe* (Baltimore, 1973), especially the introduction, entitled "The Poetics of History" [White's note].

over the last quarter-century by philosophers concerned to define history's relationships to other disciplines, especially the physical and social sciences, and by historians interested in assessing the success of their discipline in mapping the past and determining the relationship of the past to the present. But there is one problem that neither philosophers nor historians have looked at very seriously and to which literary theorists have given only passing attention. This question has to do with the status of the historical narrative, considered purely as a verbal artifact purporting to be a model of structures and processes long past and therefore not subject to either experimental or observational controls. This is not to say that historians and philosophers of history have failed to take notice of the essentially provisional and contingent nature of historical representations and of their susceptibility to infinite revision in the light of new evidence or more sophisticated conceptualization of problems. One of the marks of a good professional historian is the consistency with which he reminds his readers of the purely provisional nature of his characterizations of events, agents, and agencies found in the always incomplete historical record. Nor is it to say that literary theorists have *never* studied the structure of historical narratives. But in general there has been a reluctance to consider historical narratives as what they most manifestly are: verbal fictions, the contents of which are as much *invented* as *found* and the forms of which have more in common with their counterparts in literature than they have with those in the sciences.

Now, it is obvious that this conflation of mythic and historical consciousness will offend some historians and disturb those literary theorists whose conception of literature presupposes a radical opposition of history to fiction or of fact to fancy. As Northrop Frye has remarked, "In a sense the historical is the opposite of the mythical, and to tell the historian that what gives shape to his book is a myth would sound to him vaguely insulting."[2] Yet Frye himself grants that "when a historian's scheme gets to a certain point of comprehensiveness it becomes mythical in shape, and so approaches the poetic in its structure." He even speaks of different kinds of historical myths: Romantic myths "based on a quest or pilgrimage to a City of God or classless society"; Comic "myths of progress through evolution or revolution"; Tragic myths of "decline and fall, like the works of Gibbon and Spengler"; and Ironic "myths of recurrence or casual catastrophe." But Frye appears to believe that these myths are operative only in such victims of what might be called the "poetic fallacy" as Hegel, Marx, Nietzsche, Spengler, Toynbee, and Sartre[3]—historians whose fascination with the "constructive" capacity of human thought has deadened their responsibility to the "found" data. "The historian works inductively," he says, "collecting his facts and trying to avoid any informing patterns except those he sees, or is honestly convinced he sees, in the facts themselves." He does not work "from" a "unifying form," as the poet does, but "toward" it; and it therefore follows that the historian, like

2. From *Anatomy of Criticism* (1957); White also cites Frye's "New Directions from Old," in *Fables of Identity* (1963). FRYE (1912–1991), Canadian literary critic.

3. French philosopher (1905–1980; see above). Edward Gibbon (1737–1794), English historian, author of *The History of the Decline and Fall of the Roman Empire* (1776–87). Oswald Spengler (1880–1936), German philosopher of history, author of *The Decline of the West* (1918–22). GEORG WILHELM FRIEDRICH HEGEL (1770–1831), German philosopher, author of *The Philosophy of History* (1837). KARL MARX (1818–1883), political and economic theorist whose philosophy of communism draws on Hegel. FRIEDRICH NIETZSCHE (1844–1900), German philosopher. Arnold Toynbee (1889–1975), English historian, author of the 12-volume *Study of History* (1936–61).

any writer of discursive prose, is to be judged "by the truth of what he says, or by the adequacy of his verbal reproduction of his external model," whether that external model be the actions of past men or the historian's own thought about such actions.

What Frye says is true enough as a statement of the *ideal* that has inspired historical writing since the time of the Greeks, but that ideal presupposes an opposition between myth and history that is as problematical as it is venerable. It serves Frye's purposes very well, since it permits him to locate the specifically "fictive" in the space between the two concepts of the "mythic" and the "historical." As readers of Frye's *Anatomy of Criticism* will remember, Frye conceives fictions to consist in part of sublimates of archetypal myth-structures. These structures have been displaced to the interior of verbal artifacts in such a way as to serve as their latent meanings. The fundamental meanings of all fictions, their thematic content, consist, in Frye's view, of the "pre-generic plot-structures" or *mythoi* derived from the corpora of Classical and Judaeo-Christian religious literature. According to this theory, we understand *why* a particular story has "turned out" as it has when we have identified the archetypal myth, or pregeneric plot structure, of which the story is an exemplification. And we see the "point" of a story when we have identified its theme (Frye's translation of *dianoia*[4]), which makes of it a "parable or illustrative fable." "Every work of literature," Frye insists, "has both a fictional and a thematic aspect," but as we move from "fictional projection" toward the overt articulation of theme, the writing tends to take on the aspect of "direct address, or straight discursive writing and cease[s] to be literature." And in Frye's view, as we have seen, history (or at least "proper history") belongs to the category of "discursive writing," so that when the fictional element—or mythic plot structure—is *obviously* present in it, it ceases to be history altogether and becomes a bastard genre, product of an unholy, though not unnatural, union between history and poetry.

Yet, I would argue, histories gain part of their explanatory effect by their success in making stories out of *mere* chronicles; and stories in turn are made out of chronicles by an operation which I have elsewhere called "emplotment." And by emplotment I mean simply the encodation of the facts contained in the chronicle as components of specific *kinds* of plot structures, in precisely the way that Frye has suggested is the case with "fictions" in general.

The late R. G. Collingwood[5] insisted that the historian was above all a story teller and suggested that historical sensibility was manifested in the capacity to make a plausible story out of a congeries of "facts" which, in their unprocessed form, made no sense at all. In their efforts to make sense of the historical record, which is fragmentary and always incomplete, historians have to make use of what Collingwood called "the constructive imagination," which told the historian—as it tells the competent detective—what "must have been the case" given the available evidence and the formal properties it displayed to the consciousness capable of putting the right question to it. This constructive imagination functions in much the same way that Kant[6]

4. Thought (Greek).
5. English historian (1889–1943), author of *The Idea of History* (1946).
6. IMMANUEL KANT (1724–1804), German philosopher. He distinguished between knowledge deduced from self-evident propositions (a priori) and knowledge deduced from empirical observation (a posteriori).

supposed the *a priori* imagination functions when it tells us that even though we cannot perceive both sides of a tabletop simultaneously, we can be certain it has *two* sides if it has one, because the very concept of *one side* entails at least *one other*. Collingwood suggested that historians come to their evidence endowed with a sense of the *possible* forms that different kinds of recognizably human situations *can* take. He called this sense the nose for the "story" contained in the evidence or for the "true" story that was buried in or hidden behind the "apparent" story. And he concluded that historians provide plausible explanations for bodies of historical evidence when they succeed in discovering the story or complex of stories inplicitly contained within them.

What Collingwood failed to see was that no given set of casually recorded historical events can in itself constitute a story; the most it might offer to the historian are story *elements*. The events are *made* into a story by the suppression or subordination of certain of them and the highlighting of others, by characterization, motific repetition, variation of tone and point of view, alternative descriptive strategies, and the like—in short, all of the techniques that we would normally expect to find in the emplotment of a novel or a play. For example, no historical event is *intrinsically tragic*; it can only be conceived as such from a particular point of view or from within the context of a structured set of events of which it is an element enjoying a privileged place. For in history what is tragic from one perspective is comic from another, just as in society what appears to be tragic from the standpoint of one class may be, as Marx purported to show of the 18th Brumaire of Louis Buonaparte,[7] only a farce from that of another class. Considered as potential elements of a story, historical events are value-neutral. Whether they find their place finally in a story that is tragic, comic, romantic, or ironic—to use Frye's categories—depends upon the historian's decision to *con*figure them according to the imperatives of one plot structure or mythos rather than another. The same set of events can serve as components of a story that is tragic or comic, as the case may be, depending on the historian's choice of the plot structure that he considers most appropriate for ordering events of that kind so as to make them into a comprehensible story.

This suggests that what the historian brings to his consideration of the historical record is a notion of the *types* of configurations of events that can be recognized as stories by the audience for which he is writing. True, he can misfire. I do not suppose that anyone would accept the emplotment of the life of President Kennedy as comedy, but whether it ought to be emplotted romantically, tragically, or satirically is an open question. The important point is that most historical sequences can be emplotted in a number of different ways, so as to provide different interpretations of those events and to endow them with different meanings. Thus, for example, what Michelet in his great history of the French Revolution construed as a drama of Romantic transcendence, his contemporary Tocqueville[8] emplotted as an ironic Tragedy. Neither can be said to have had more knowledge of the "facts" contained in the record; they simply had different notions of the kind of story that best fitted the facts they knew. Nor should it be thought that they told

7. Marx, *The Eighteenth Brumaire of Louis Bonaparte* (1848).
8. Alexis de Tocqueville (1805–1859), French historian and author of *The Old Régime and the French Revolution* (1856). Jules Michelet (1798–1874), French historian, author of a 7-volume history of the French Revolution (1847–53).

different stories of the Revolution because they had discovered different *kinds* of facts, political on the one hand, social on the other. They sought out different kinds of facts because they had different kinds of stories to tell. But why did these alternative, not to say mutually exclusive, representations of what was substantially the same set of events appear equally plausible to their respective audiences? Simply because the historians shared with their audiences certain preconceptions about how the Revolution might be emplotted, in response to imperatives that were generally extra historical, ideological, aesthetic, or mythical.

Collingwood once remarked that you could never explicate a tragedy to anyone who was not already acquainted with the kinds of situations that are regarded as "tragic" in our culture. Anyone who has taught or taken one of those omnibus courses usually entitled Western Civilization or Introduction to the Classics of Western Literature will know what Collingwood had in mind. Unless you have some idea of the generic attributes of tragic, comic, romantic, or ironic situations, you will be unable to recognize them as such when you come upon them in a literary text. But historical situations do not have built into them intrinsic meanings in the way that literary texts do. Historical situations are not *inherently* tragic, comic, or romantic. They may all be inherently ironic, but they need not be emplotted that way. All the historian needs to do to transform a tragic into a comic situation is to shift his point of view or change the scope of his perceptions. Anyway, we only think of situations as tragic or comic because these concepts are part of our generally cultural and specifically literary heritage. *How* a given historical situation is to be configured depends on the historian's subtlety in matching up a specific plot structure with the set of historical events that he wishes to endow with a meaning of a particular kind. This is essentially a literary, that is to say fiction-making, operation. And to call it that in no way detracts from the status of historical narratives as providing a kind of knowledge. For not only are the pregeneric plot structures by which sets of events can be constituted as stories of a particular kind limited in number, as Frye and other archetypal critics suggest; but the encodation of events in terms of such plot structures is one of the ways that a culture has of making sense of both personal and public pasts.

We can make sense of sets of events in a number of different ways. One of the ways is to subsume the events under the casual laws which may have governed their concatenation in order to produce the particular configuration that the events appear to assume when considered as "effects" of mechanical forces. This is the way of scientific explanation. Another way we make sense of a set of events which appears strange, enigmatic, or mysterious in its immediate manifestations is to encode the set in terms of culturally provided categories, such as metaphysical concepts, religious beliefs, or story forms. The effect of such encodations is to familiarize the unfamiliar; and in general this is the way of historiography, whose "data" are always immediately strange, not to say exotic, simply by virtue of their distance from us in time and their origin in a way of life different from our own.

The historian shares with his audience *general notions* of the *forms* that significant human situations *must* take by virtue of his participation in the specific processes of sense-making which identify him as a member of one cultural endowment rather than another. In the process of studying a given complex of events, he begins to perceive the *possible* story form that such events *may* figure. In his narrative account of how this set of events took on the shape which he perceives to inhere within it, he emplots his account as a story of a particular kind. The reader, in the process of following the historian's account of those events, gradually comes to realize that the story he is reading is of one kind rather than another: romance, tragedy, comedy, satire, epic, or what have you. And when he has perceived the class or type to which the story that he is reading belongs, he experiences the effect of having the events in the story explained to him. He has at this point not only successfully *followed* the story; he has grasped the point of it, *understood* it, as well. The original strangeness, mystery, or exoticism of the events is dispelled, and they take on a familiar aspect, not in their details, but in their functions as elements of a familiar kind of configuration. They are rendered comprehensible by being subsumed under the categories of the plot structure in which they are encoded as a story of a particular kind. They are familiarized, not only because the reader now has more *information* about the events, but also because he has been shown how the data conform to an *icon* of a comprehensible finished process, a plot structure with which he is familiar as a part of his cultural endowment.

This is not unlike what happens, or is supposed to happen, in psychotherapy. The sets of events in the patient's past which are the presumed cause of his distress, manifested in the neurotic syndrome, have been defamiliarized, rendered strange, mysterious, and threatening and have assumed a meaning that he can neither accept nor effectively reject. It is not that the patient does not *know* what those events were, does not know the facts; for if he did not in some sense know the facts, he would be unable to recognize them and repress them whenever they arise in his consciousness. On the contrary, he knows them all too well. He knows them so well, in fact, that he lives with them constantly and in such a way as to make it impossible for him to see any other facts except through the coloration that the set of events in question gives to his perception of the world. We might say that, according to the theory of psychoanalysis, the patient has overemplotted these events, has charged them with a meaning so intense that, whether real or merely imagined, they continue to shape both his perceptions and his responses to the world long after they should have become "past history." The therapist's problem, then, is not to hold up before the patient the "real facts" of the matter, the "truth" as against the "fantasy" that obsesses him. Nor is it to give him a short course in psychoanalytical theory by which to enlighten him as to the true nature of his distress by cataloguing it as a manifestation of some "complex." This is what the analyst might do in relating the patient's case to a third party, and especially to another analyst. But psychoanalytic theory recognizes that the patient will resist both of these tactics in the same way that he resists the intrusion into consciousness of the traumatized memory traces in the *form* that he obsessively remembers them. The problem is to get the patient to "reemplot" his whole life history in such a way as to change the *meaning* of those events for him and their *significance* for the economy of the whole set of events that make up his life. As thus envisaged, the therapeutic process is an exercise in the refamiliarization of events that have been defamiliarized, rendered alienated from the patient's life-history, by virtue of their overdetermination as causal forces. And we might say that the events are detraumatized by being removed from the plot structure in which they have a dominant place and inserted in another in which they have a subordinate or simply ordinary function as elements of a life shared with all other men.

Now, I am not interested in forcing the analogy between psychotherapy and historiography; I use the example merely to illustrate a point about the fictive component in historical narratives. Historians seek to refamiliarize us with events which have been forgotten through either accident, neglect, or repression. Moreover, the greatest historians have always dealt with those events in the histories of their cultures which are "traumatic" in nature and the meaning of which is either problematical or overdetermined in the significance that they still have for current life, events such as revolutions, civil wars, large-scale processes such as industrialization and urbanization, or institutions which have lost their original function in a society but continue to play an important role on the current social scene. In looking at the ways in which such structures took shape or evolved, historians *re*familiarize them, not only by providing more information about them, but also by showing how their developments conformed to one another of the story types that we conventionally invoke to make sense of our own life-histories.

Now, if any of this is plausible as a characterization of the explanatory effect of historical narrative, it tells us something important about the *mimetic* aspect of historical narratives.[9] It is generally maintained—as Frye said—that a history is a verbal model of a set of events external to the mind of the historian. But it is wrong to think of a history as a model similar to a scale model of an airplane or ship, a map, or a photograph. For we can check the adequacy of this latter kind of model by going and looking at the original and, by applying the necessary rules of translation, seeing in what respect the model has actually succeeded in reproducing aspects of the original. But historical structures and processes are not like these originals; we cannot go and look at them in order to see if the historian has adequately reproduced them in his narrative. Nor should we want to, even if we could; for after all it was the very strangeness of the original as it appeared in the documents that inspired the historian's efforts to make a model of it in the first place. If the historian only did that for us, we should be in the same situation as the patient whose analyst merely told him, on the basis of interviews with his parents, siblings, and childhood friends, what the "true facts" of the patient's early life were. We would have no reason to think that anything at all had been *explained* to us.

This is what leads me to think that historical narratives are not only models of past events and processes, but also metaphorical statements which suggest a relation of similitude between such events and processes and the story types that we conventionally use to endow the events of our lives with culturally sanctioned meanings. Viewed in a purely formal way, a historical narrative is not only a *reproduction* of the events reported in it, but also a *complex of symbols* which gives us directions for finding an *icon* of the structure of those events in our literary tradition.

I am here, of course, invoking the distinctions between sign, symbol, and icon which C. S. Peirce[1] developed in his philosophy of language. I think

9. White explores in history the same problem of mimesis that PLATO explored in poetry in *Republic* 10 (ca. 373 B.C.E.; see above).

1. Charles Sanders Peirce (1839–1914), American philosopher generally credited, along with FERDINAND DE SAUSSURE (1857–1913), with the

that these distinctions will help us to understand what is fictive in all putatively realistic representations of the world and what is realistic in all manifestly fictive ones. They help us, in short, to answer the question, What are historical representations *representations of*? It seems to me that we must say of histories what Frye seems to think is true only of poetry or philosophies of history, namely that, considered as a system of signs, the historical narrative points in two directions simultaneously: *toward* the events described in the narrative and *toward* the story type or mythos which the historian has chosen to serve as the icon of the structure of the events. The narrative itself is not the icon; what it does is *describe* events in the historical record in such a way as to inform the reader *what to take as an icon* of the events so as to render them "familiar" to him. The historical narrative thus mediates between the events reported in it on the one side and pregeneric plot structures conventionally used in our culture to endow unfamiliar events and situation with meanings on the other.

The evasion of the implications of the fictive nature of historical narrative is in part a consequence of the utility of the concept "history" for the definition of other types of discourse. "History" can be set over against "science" by virtue of its want of conceptual rigor and failure to produce the kinds of universal laws that the sciences characteristically seek to produce. Similarly, "history" can be set over against "literature" by virtue of its interest in the "actual" rather than the "possible," which is supposedly the object of representation of "literary" works. Thus, within a long and distinguished critical tradition that has sought to determine what is "real" and what is "imagined" in the novel, history has served as a kind of archetype of the "realistic" pole of representation. I am thinking of Frye, Auerbach, Booth, Scholes and Kellogg,[2] and others. Nor is it unusual for literary theorists, when they are speaking about the "context" of a literary work, to suppose that this context—the "historical milieu"—has a concreteness and an accessibility that the work itself can never have, as if it were easier to perceive the reality of a past world put together from a thousand historical documents than it is to probe the depths of a single literary work that is present to the critic studying it. But the presumed concreteness and accessibility of historical milieux, these contexts of the texts that literary scholars study, are themselves products of the fictive capability of the historians who have studied those contexts. The historical documents are not less opaque than the texts studied by the literary critic. Nor is the world those documents figure more accessible. The one is no more "given" than the other. In fact, the opaqueness of the world figured in historical documents is, if anything, increased by the production of historical narratives. Each new historical work only adds to the number of possible texts that have to be interpreted if a full and accurate picture of a given historical milieu is to be faithfully drawn. The relationship between the past to be analyzed and historical works produced by analysis of the documents is paradoxical; the *more* we know about the past, the more difficult it is to generalize about it.

founding of semiotics, the modern science that studies all types of sign systems. An icon is a sign in which the signifier (the sound or symbol that conveys meaning) resembles or imitates the signified (the meaning conveyed); a symbol is a sign in which the relationship between the two is purely conventional.

2. All those named are authors of key texts of narrative theory. Erich Auerbach (1892–1957), German literary critic and author of *Mimesis: The Representation of Reality in Western Literature* (1946); Wayne Booth (b. 1921), American literary critic and author of *The Rhetoric of Fiction* (1961); and Robert Scholes (b. 1929) and Alfred Latimer Kellogg (1915–1986), American coauthors of *The Nature of Narrative* (1966).

But if the increase in our knowledge of the past makes it more difficult to generalize about it, it should make it easier for us to generalize about the forms in which that knowledge is transmitted to us. Our knowledge of the past may increase incrementally, but our understanding of it does not. Nor does our understanding of the past progress by the kind of revolutionary breakthroughs that we associate with the development of the physical sciences.[3] Like literature, history progresses by the production of classics, the nature of which is such that they cannot be disconfirmed or negated, in the way that the principal conceptual schemata of the sciences are. And it is their nondisconfirmability that testifies to the essentially *literary* nature of historical classics. There is something in a historical masterpiece that cannot be negated, and this nonnegatable element is its form, the form which is its fiction.

It is frequently forgotten or, when remembered, denied that no given set of events attested by the historical record comprises a *story* manifestly finished and complete. This is as true as the events that comprise the life of an individual as it is of an institution, a nation, or a whole people. We do not *live* stories, even if we give our lives meaning by retrospectively casting them in the form of stories. And so too with nations or whole cultures. In an essay on the "mythical" nature of historiography, Lévi-Strauss[4] remarks on the astonishment that a visitor from another planet would feel if confronted by the thousands of histories written about the French Revolution. For in those works, the "authors do not always make use of the same incidents; when they do, the incidents are revealed in different lights. And yet these are variations which have to do with the same country, the same period, and the same events—events whose reality is scattered across every level of a multilayered structure." He goes on to suggest that the criterion of validity by which historical accounts might be assessed cannot depend on their "elements"—that is to say—their putative factual content. On the contrary, he notes, "pursued in isolation, each element shows itself to be beyond grasp. But certain of them derive consistency from the fact that they can be integrated into a system whose terms are more or less credible when set against the overall coherence of the series." But his "coherence of the series" cannot be the coherence of the *chronological* series, that sequence of "facts" organized into the temporal order of their original occurrence. For the "chronicle" of events, out of which the historian fashions his story of "what really happened," already comes preencoded. There are "hot" and "cold" chronologies, chronologies in which more or fewer dates appear to demand inclusion in a full chronicle of what happened. Moreover, the dates themselves come to us already grouped into classes of dates, classes which are constitutive of putative domains of the historical field, domains which appear as problems for the historian to solve if he is to give a full and culturally responsible account of the past.

All this suggests to Lévi-Strauss that, when it is a matter of working up a comprehensive account of the various domains of the historical record in

3. White may be alluding to Thomas Kuhn's celebrated *Structure of Scientific Revolutions* (1962), which characterizes scientific progress as a sequence of abrupt revolutions that overturn existing paradigms, rendering them obsolete.

4. CLAUDE LÉVI-STRAUSS (b. 1908), French anthropologist whose work was influential in the development of structuralism. White cites Lévi-Strauss's *Savage Mind* (1966) and his "Overture to *Le Cru et le cuit*," published in *Structuralism* (ed. Jacques Ehrmann, 1966).

the form of a story, the "alleged historical continuities" that the historian purports to find in the record are "secured only by dint of fraudulent outlines" imposed by the historian on the record. These "fraudulent outlines" are, in his view, a product of "abstraction" and a means of escape from the "threat of an infinite regress" that always lurks at the interior of every complex set of historical "facts." We can construct a comprehensible story of the past, Lévi-Strauss insists, only by a decision to "give up" one or more of the domains of facts offering themselves for inclusion in our accounts. Our *explanations* of historical structures and processes are thus determined more by what we leave out of our representations than by what we put in. For it is in this brutal capacity to exclude certain facts in the interest of constituting others as components of comprehensible stories that the historian displays his tact as well as his understanding. The "overall coherence" of any given "series" of historical facts is the coherence of story, but this coherence is achieved only by a tailoring of the "facts" to the requirements of the story form. And thus Lévi-Strauss concludes: "In spite of worthy and indispensable efforts to bring another moment in history alive and to possess it, a clairvoyant history should admit that it never completely escapes from the nature of myth."

It is this mediative function that permits us to speak of a historical narrative as an extended metaphor. As a symbolic structure, the historical narrative does not *reproduce* the events it describes; it tells us in what direction to think about the events and charges our thought about the events with different emotional valences. The historical narrative does not *image* the things it indicates; it *calls to mind* images of the things it indicates, in the same way that a metaphor does. When a given concourse of events is emplotted as a "tragedy," this simply means that the historian has so described the events as to *remind us* of that form of fiction which we associate with the concept "tragic." Properly understood, histories ought never to be read as unambiguous signs of the events they report, but rather as symbolic structures, extended metaphors, that "liken" the events reported in them to some form with which we have already become familiar in our literary culture.

Perhaps I should indicate briefly what is meant by the *symbolic* and *iconic* aspects of a metaphor. The hackneyed phrase "My love, a rose" is not, obviously, intended to be understood as suggesting that the loved one is *actually* a rose. It is not even meant to suggest that the loved one has the specific attributes of a rose—that is to say, that the loved one is red, yellow, orange, or black, is a plant, has thorns, needs sunlight, should be sprayed regularly with insecticides, and so on. It is meant to be understood as indicating that the beloved shares the *qualities* which the rose has come to *symbolize* in the customary linguistic usages of Western culture. That is to say, considered as a message, the metaphor gives directions for finding an entity that will evoke the images associated *with loved ones and roses alike* in our culture. The metaphor does not *image* the thing it seeks to characterize, *it gives directions* for finding the set of images that are intended to be associated with that thing. It functions as a symbol, rather than as a sign: which is to say that it does not give us either a *description* or an *icon* of the thing it represents, but *tells us* what images to look for in our culturally encoded experience in order to determine how we *should feel* about the thing represented.

So too for historical narratives. They succeed in endowing sets of past events with meanings, over and above whatever comprehension they provide by appeal to putative causal laws, by exploiting the metaphorical similarities between sets of real events and the conventional structures of our fictions. By the very constitution of a set of events in such a way as to make a comprehensible story out of them, the historian charges those events with the symbolic significance of a comprehensible plot structure. Historians may not like to think of their works as translations of fact into fictions; but this is one of the effects of their works. By suggesting alternative emplotments of a given sequence of historical events, historians provide events with all of the possible meanings with which the literary art of their culture is capable of endowing them. The real dispute between the proper historian and the philosopher of history has to do with the latter's insistence that events can be emplotted in one and only one story form. History-writing thrives on the discovery of all the possible plot structures that might be invoked to endow sets of events with different meanings. And our understanding of the past increases precisely in the degree to which we succeed in determining how far that past conforms to the strategies of sense-making that are contained in their purest forms in literary art.

Conceiving historical narratives in this way may give us some insight into the crisis in historical thinking which has been under way since the beginning of our century. Let us imagine that the problem of the historian is to make sense of a hypothetical *set* of events by arranging them in a *series* that is at once chronologically *and* syntactically structured, in the way that any discourse from a sentence all the way up to a novel is structured. We can see immediately that the imperatives of chronological arrangement of the events constituting the set must exist in tension with the imperatives of the syntactical strategies alluded to, whether the latter are conceived as those of logic (the syllogism) or those of narrative (the plot structure).

Thus, we have a set of events

(1) *a, b, c, d, e, ... , n,*

ordered chronologically but requiring description and characterization as elements of plot or argument by which to give them meaning. Now, the series can be emplotted in a number of different ways and thereby endowed with different meanings without violating the imperatives of the chronological arrangement at all. We may briefly characterize some of these emplotments in the following ways:

(2) A, *b, c, d, e, ... , n*

(3) *a,* B, *c, d, e, ... , n*

(4) *a, b,* C, *d, e, ... , n*

(5) *a, b, c,* D, *e, ... , n*

And so on.

The capitalized letters indicate the privileged status given to certain events or sets of events in the series by which they are endowed with explanatory force, either as causes explaining the structure of the whole series or as symbols of the plot structure of the series considered as a story of a specific kind. We might say that any history which endows any putatively original event (*a*) with the status of a decisive factor (*A*) in the structuration of the whole series of events following after it is "deterministic." The emplotments of the history of "society" by Rousseau in his *Second Discourse*, Marx in the *Manifesto*, and Freud in *Totem and Taboo* would fall into this category.[5] So too, any history which endows the last event in the series (*e*), whether real or only speculatively projected, with the force of full explanatory power (*E*) is of the type of all eschatological or apocalyptical histories. St. Augustine's *City of God* and the various versions of the Joachite notion[6] of the advent of a millennium, Hegel's *Philosophy of History*, and, in general, all Idealist histories are of this sort. In between we would have the various forms of historiography which appeal to plot structures of a distinctively "fictional" sort (Romance, Comedy, Tragedy, and Satire) by which to endow the series with a perceivable form and a conceivable "meaning."

If the series were simply recorded in the order in which the events originally occurred, under the assumption that the ordering of the events in their temporal sequence itself provided a kind of explanation of why they occurred when and where they did, we would have the pure form of the *chronicle*. This would be a "naive" form of chronicle, however, inasmuch as the categories of time and space alone served as the informing interpretative principles. Over against the naive form of chronicle we could postulate as a logical possibility its "sentimental" counterpart,[7] the ironic denial that historical series have any kind of larger significance or describe any imaginable plot structure or indeed can even be construed as a story with a discernible beginning, middle, and end. We could conceive such accounts of history as intending to serve as antidotes to their false or overemplotted counterparts (nos. 2, 3, 4, and 5 above) and could represent them as an ironic return to mere chronicle as constituting the only sense which any cognitively responsible history could take. We could characterize such histories thus:

(6) "*a, b, c, d, e . . . . , n*"

with the quotation marks indicating the conscious interpretation of the events as having nothing other than seriality as their meaning.

This schema is of course highly abstract and does not do justice to the possible mixtures of and variations within the types that it is meant to distinguish. But it helps us, I think, to conceive how events might be emplotted in different ways without violating the imperatives of the chronological order of the events (however they are construed) so as to yield alternative, mutually exclusive, and yet, equally plausible interpretations of the set. I have tried to show in *Metahistory* how such mixtures and variations occur in the writings of the master historians of the nineteenth century; and I have suggested in that book that classic historical accounts always represent attempts both to emplot the historical series adequately and implicitly to come to terms with other plausible emplotments. It is this dialectical tension between two or

5. SIGMUND FREUD (1856–1939), Austrian founder of psychoanalysis; *Totem and Taboo* was published in 1918. Jean-Jacques Rousseau (1712–1778), Swiss-born French philosopher and political theorist; his "second" discourse is the *Discourse on the Origin and Bases of Inequality among Men* (1754). Marx and FRIEDRICH ENGELS's *Communist Manifesto* appeared as a pamphlet in 1848.

6. Taken from Joachim of Fiore (1135–1202), an Italian monk who propounded a millenarian theory of history between 1190 and 1195. AUGUSTINE (354–430), early Christian philosopher and theologian.

7. For the opposition of "naive" and "sentimental," see FRIEDRICH VON SCHILLER, *On Naive and Sentimental Poetry* (1795–96).

more possible emplotments that signals the elements of critical self-consciousness present in any historian of recognizably classical stature.

Histories, then, are not only about events but also about the possible sets of relationships that those events can be demonstrated to figure. These sets of relationships are not, however, immanent in the events themselves; they exist only in the mind of the historian reflecting on them. Here they are present as the modes of relationships conceptualized in the myth, fable, and folklore, scientific knowledge, religion, and literary art, of the historian's own culture. But more importantly, they are, I suggest, immanent in the very language which the historian must use to *describe* events prior to a scientific analysis of them or a fictional emplotment of them. For if the historian's aim is to familiarize us with the unfamiliar, he must use figurative, rather than technical, language. Technical languages are familiarizing only *to* those who have been indoctrinated in their uses and only *of* those sets of events which the practitioners of a discipline have agreed to describe in a uniform terminology. History possesses no such generally accepted technical terminology and in fact no agreement on what kind of events make up its specific subject matter. The historian's characteristic instrument of encodation, communication, and exchange is ordinary educated speech. This implies that the only instruments that he has for endowing his data with meaning, of rendering the strange familiar, and of rendering the mysterious past comprehensible, are the techniques of *figurative* language. All historical narratives presuppose figurative characterizations of the events they purport to represent and explain. And this means that historical narratives, considered purely as verbal artifacts, can be characterized by the mode of figurative discourse in which they are cast.

If this is the case, then it may well be that the kind of emplotment that the historian decides to use to give meaning to a set of historical events is dictated by the dominant figurative mode of the language he has used to *describe* the elements of his account *prior* to his composition of a narrative. Geoffrey Hartman[8] once remarked in my hearing, at a conference on literary history, that he was not sure that he knew what historians of literature might want to do, but he did know that to write a history meant to place an event within a context, by relating it as a part to some conceivable whole. He went on to suggest that as far as he knew, there were only two ways of relating parts to wholes, by metonymy and by synecdoche.[9] Having been engaged for some time in the study of the thought of Giambattista Vico,[1] I was much taken with this thought, because it conformed to Vico's notion that the "logic" of all "poetic wisdom" was contained in the relationships which language itself provided in the four principal modes of figurative representation: metaphor, metonymy, synecdoche, and irony. My own hunch—and it is a hunch which I find confirmed in Hegel's reflections on the nature of non-scientific discourse—is that in any field of study which, like history, has not yet become disciplinized to the point of constructing a formal terminological system for describing its objects, in the way that physics and chemistry have,

8. American literary critic and theorist (b. 1929).
9. A figure of speech in which a part is used for the whole (e.g., "all *hands* on deck") or the whole for a part (e.g., "*England* won the World Cup"). "Metonomy": a figure of speech in which one word or phrase is substituted for another with which it is closely associated (e.g., *the stage* meaning "the theater").
1. Italian philosopher and historian (1668–1744), author of *The New Science* (1725; see above).

it is the types of figurative discourse that dictate the fundamental forms of the data to be studied. This means that the *shape* of the *relationships* which will appear to be inherent in the objects inhabiting her field will in reality have been imposed on the field by the investigator in the very *act of identifying and describing* the objects that he finds there. The implication is that historians *constitute* their subjects as possible objects of narrative representation by the very language they use to *describe* them. And if this is the case, it means that the different kinds of historical interpretations that we have of the same set of events, such as the French Revolution as interpreted by Michelet, Tocqueville, Taine,[2] and others, are little more than projections of the linguistic protocols that these historians used to *pre*-figure that set of events prior to writing their narratives of it. It is only a hypothesis, but it seems possible that the conviction of the historian that he has "found" the form of his narrative in the events themselves, rather than imposed it upon them, in the way the poet does, is a result of a certain lack of linguistic self-consciousness which obscures the extent to which descriptions of events *already* constitute interpretations of their nature. As thus envisaged, the difference between Michelet's and Tocqueville's accounts of the Revolution does not reside only in the fact that the former emplotted his story in the modality of a Romance and the latter his in the modality of Tragedy; it resides as well in the tropological mode—metaphorical and metonymic, respectively—with each brought to his apprehension of the facts as they appeared in the documents.

I do not have the space to try to demonstrate the plausibility of this hypothesis, which is the informing principle of my book *Metahistory*. But I hope that this essay may serve to suggest an approach to the study of such discursive prose forms as historiography, an approach that is as old as the study of rhetoric and as new as modern linguistics. Such a study would proceed along the lines laid out by Roman Jakobson[3] in a paper entitled "Linguistics and Poetics," in which he characterized the difference between Romantic poetry and the various forms of nineteenth-century Realistic prose as residing in the essentially metaphorical nature of the former and the essentially metonymical nature of the latter. I think that this characterization of the difference between poetry and prose is too narrow, because it presupposes that complex macrostructural narratives such as the novel are little more than projections of the "selective" (i.e., phonemic) axis of all speech acts. Poetry, and especially Romantic poetry, is then characterized by Jakobson as a projection of the "combinatory" (i.e., morphemic) axis of language. Such a binary theory pushes the analyst toward a dualistic opposition between poetry and prose which appears to rule out the possibility of a metonymical poetry and a metaphorical prose. But the fruitfulness of Jakobson's theory lies in its suggestion that the various forms of both poetry and prose, all of which have their counterparts in narrative in general and therefore in historiography too, can be characterized in terms of the dominant trope which serves as the paradigm, provided by language itself, of all significant relationships conceived to exist in the world by anyone wishing to represent those relationships in language.

2. Hippolyte-Adolphe Taine (1828–1893), French literary and art critic, philosopher, and historian who analyzed art and literature as products of race, environment, and epoch.

3. Russian-born American linguist (1896–1982); for "Linguistics and Poetics" (1960), see above.

Narrative, or the syntagmatic dispersion of events across a temporal series presented as a prose discourse,[4] in such a way as to display their progressive elaboration as a comprehensible form, would represent the "inward turn" that discourse takes when it tries to *show* the reader the true form of things existing behind a merely apparent formlessness. Narrative *style*, in history as well as in the novel, would then be construed as the modality of the movement from a representation of some original state of affairs to some subsequent state. The primary *meaning* of a narrative would then consist of the destructuration of a set of events (real or imagined) originally encoded in one tropological mode and the progressive restructuration of the set in another tropological mode. As thus envisaged, narrative would be a process of decodation and recodation in which an original perception is clarified by being cast in a figurative mode different from that in which it has come encoded by convention, authority, or custom. And the explanatory force of the narrative would then depend on the contrast between the original encodation and the later one.

For example, let us suppose that a set of experiences comes to us as a grotesque, i.e., as unclassified and unclassifiable. Our problem is to identify the modality of the relationships that bind the discernible elements of the formless totality together in such a way as to make of it a whole of some sort. If we stress the similarities among the elements, we are working in the mode of metaphor; if we stress the differences among them, we are working in the mode of metonymy. Of course, in order to make sense of any set of experiences, we must obviously identify both the parts of a thing that appear to make it up and the nature of the shared aspects of the parts that make them identifiable as a totality. This implies that all original characterizations of anything must utilize *both* metaphor and metonymy in order to "fix" it as something about which we can meaningfully discourse.

In the case of historiography, the attempts of commentators to make sense of the French Revolution are instructive. Burke[5] decodes the events of the Revolution which his contemporaries experience as a grotesque by recoding it in the mode of irony; Michelet recodes these events in the mode of synecdoche; Tocqueville recodes them in the mode of metonymy. In each case, however, the movement from code to recode is narratively described, i.e., laid out on a time-line in such a way as to make the interpretation of the events that made up the "Revolution" a kind of drama that we can recognize as Satirical, Romantic, and Tragic, respectively. This drama can be followed by the reader of the narrative in such a way as to be experienced as a progressive revelation of what the *true* nature of the events consists of. The revelation is not experienced, however, as a restructuring of perception so much as an illumination of a field of occurrence. But actually what has happened is that a set of events originally encoded in one way is simply being decoded by being recoded in another. The events themselves are not substantially changed from one account to another. That is to say, the data that are to be analyzed are not significantly different in the different accounts. What is different are the modalities of their relationships. These modalities,

4. In linguistics, *syntagmatic* designates the relationship between items that combine to form a meaningful whole (e.g., the words in a sentence); by extension, the term here refers to the relationships between events in a narrative, their sequence.

5. Edmund Burke (1729–1797), English author of *Reflections on the Revolution in France* (1790).

in turn, although they *may* appear to the reader to be based on different theories of the nature of society, politics, and history, ultimately have their origin in the figurative characterizations of the whole set of events as representing wholes of fundamentally different sorts. It is for this reason that, when it is a matter of setting different interpretations of the same set of historical phenomena over against one another in an attempt to decide which is the best or most convincing, we are often driven to confusion or ambiguity. This is not to say that we cannot distinguish between good and bad historiography, since we can always fall back on such criteria as responsibility to the rules of evidence, the relative fullness of narrative detail, logical consistency, and the like to determine this issue. But it is to say that the effort to distinguish between good and bad interpretations of a historical event such as the Revolution is not as easy as it might at first appear when it is a matter of dealing with alternative interpretations produced by historians of relatively equal learning and conceptual sophistication. After all, a great historical classic cannot be disconfirmed or nullified either by the discovery of some new datum that might call a specific explanation of some element of the whole account into question or by the generation of new methods of analysis which permit us to deal with questions that earlier historians might not have taken under consideration. And it is precisely because great historical classics, such as works by Gibbon, Michelet, Thucydides, Mommsen, Ranke, Burckhardt, Bancroft,[6] and so on, cannot be definitely disconfirmed that we must look to the specifically literary aspects of their work as crucial, and not merely subsidiary, elements in their historiographical technique.

What all this points to is the necessity of revising the distinction conventionally drawn between poetic and prose discourse in discussion of such narrative forms as historiography and recognizing that the distinction, as old as Aristotle,[7] between history and poetry obscures as much as it illuminates about both. If there is an element of the historical in all poetry, there is an element of poetry in every historical account of the world. And this because in our account of the historical world we are dependent, in ways perhaps that we are not in the natural sciences, on the techniques of *figurative language* both for our *characterization* of the objects of our narrative representations and for the *strategies* by which to constitute narrative accounts of the transformations of those objects in time. And this because history has no stipulatable subject matter uniquely its own; it is always written as part of a contest between contending poetic figurations of what the past *might* consist of.

The older distinction between fiction and history, in which fiction is conceived as the representation of the imaginable and history as the representation of the actual, must give place to the recognition that we can only know

6. All prominent historians: Thucydides (ca. 455–ca. 400 B.C.E.), Greek author of *The History of the Peloponnesian Wars*; Theodor Mommsen (1817–1903), German classical scholar and author of *The History of Rome* (1854–55), who received the 1902 Nobel Prize for literature; Leopold von Ranke (1795–1886), German founder of the modern school of history that championed objectivity based on source materials rather than on legend and tradition; Jakob Burckhardt (1818–1897), Swiss historian of art and culture, author of *The Civilization of the Renaissance in Italy* (1860); and George Bancroft (1800–1891), U.S. statesman and author of a 10-volume *History of the United States* (1837–74).

7. See ARISTOTLE (384–322 B.C.E.), *Poetics* 9, 1451b: "The difference [between history and poetry] is that the former relates things that have happened, the latter things that may happen. For this reason poetry is more philosophical and more serious than history; poetry tends to speak of universals, history of particulars."

the *actual* by contrasting it with or likening it to the *imaginable*. As thus conceived, historical narratives are complex structures in which a world of experience is imagined to exist under at least two modes, one of which is encoded as "real," the other of which is "revealed" to have been illusory in the course of the narrative. Of course, it is a fiction of the historian that the various states of affairs which he constitutes as the beginning, the middle, and the end of a course of development are all "actual" or "real" and that he has merely recorded "what happened" in the transition from the inaugural to the terminal phase. But both the beginning state of affairs and the ending one are inevitably poetic constructions, and as such, dependent upon the modality of the figurative language used to give them the aspect of coherence. This implies that all narrative is not simply a recording of "what happened" in the transition from one state of affairs to another, but a progressive *redescription* of sets of events in such a way as to dismantle a structure encoded in one verbal mode in the beginning so as to justify a recoding of it in another mode at the end. This is what the "middle" of all narratives consist of.

All of this is highly schematic, and I know that this insistence on the fictive element in all historical narratives is certain to arouse the ire of historians who believe that they are doing something fundamentally different from the novelist, by virtue of the fact that they deal with "real," while the novelist deals with "imagined," events. But neither the form nor the explanatory power of narrative derives from the different contents it is presumed to be able to accommodate. In point of fact, history—the real world as it evolves in time—is made sense of in the same way that the poet or novelist tries to make sense of it, i.e., by endowing what originally appears to be problematical and mysterious with the aspect of a recognizable, because it is a familiar, form. It does not matter whether the world is conceived to be real or only imagined; the manner of making sense of it is the same.

So too, to say that we make sense of the real world by imposing upon it the formal coherency that we customarily associate with the products of writers of fiction in no way detracts from the status as knowledge which we ascribe to historiography. It would only detract from it if we were to believe that literature did not teach us anything about reality, but was a product of an imagination which was not of this world but of some other, inhuman one. In my view, we experience the "fictionalization" of history as an "explanation" for the same reason that we experience great fiction as an illumination of a world that we inhabit along with the author. In both we recognize the forms by which consciousness both constitutes and colonizes the world it seeks to inhabit comfortably.

Finally, it may be observed that if historians were to recognize the fictive element in their narratives, this would not mean the degradation of historiography to the status of ideology or propaganda. In fact, this recognition would serve as a potent antidote to the tendency of historians to become captive of ideological preconceptions which they do not recognize as such but honor as the "correct" perception of "the way things *really* are." By drawing historiography nearer to its origins in literary sensibility, we should be able to identify the ideological, because it is the fictive, element in our own discourse. We are always able to see the fictive element in those historians with whose interpretations of a given set of events we disagree; we seldom perceive that element in our own prose. So, too, if we recognized the literary or fictive element in every historical account, we would be able to move the teaching of historiography onto a higher level of self-consciousness than it currently occupies.

What teacher has not lamented his inability to give instruction to apprentices in the *writing* of history? What graduate student of history has not despaired at trying to comprehend and imitate the model which his instructors *appear* to honor but the principles of which remain uncharted? If we recognize that there is a fictive element in all historical narrative, we would find in the theory of language and narrative itself the basis for a more subtle presentation of what historiography consists of than that which simply tells the student to go and "find out the facts" and write them up in such a way as to tell "what really happened."

In my view, history as a discipline is in bad shape today because it has lost sight of its origins in the literary imagination. In the interest of *appearing* scientific and objective, it has repressed and denied to itself its own greatest source of strength and renewal. By drawing historiography back once more to an intimate connection with its literary basis, we should not only be putting ourselves on guard against *merely* ideological distortions; we should be by way of arriving at that "theory" of history without which it cannot pass for a "discipline" at all.

1978

JEAN BAUDRILLARD
b. 1929

A prophet crying out in the wilderness of postmodernity, the sociologist Jean Baudrillard made dramatic pronouncements that hit a nerve in the 1980s and 1990s, especially in the international art world. The urge to define our "postmodern condition" has perhaps faded, but the basic tenets of Baudrillard's critique still speak directly to the phenomena of global financial speculation, ever-increasing tourism, and the frenzied stimulation of consumer desire through the media. The obliteration of nature by culture, particularly the replacement of the real by signs, is Baudrillard's great theme. Paradoxically enough, the accuracy of his analysis, its correspondence to what is happening in the contemporary world, secures him a hearing even from those who find his style cryptic and his claims about media simulation of reality hyperbolic.

The son of civil servants and the grandson of peasants, Baudrillard shares the formative experiences of others among his generation of French intellectuals: coming to age in the aftermath of the German Occupation during World War II, when JEAN-PAUL SARTRE's existential Marxism dominated French thought; political radicalization in response to French colonial wars in Indochina and Algeria during the 1950s; opposition to the American war in Vietnam; and involvement, as a young professor, in the "events" of 1968, when French student protesters brought the nation to a standstill for the month of May.

Baudrillard earned his graduate degree in sociology in 1966, and in 1968 he was teaching at Nanterre, one of the new universities at the center of the students' movement. Before getting his degree, he wrote about and translated German literature; he was deeply influenced by the Frankfurt School social theorists MAX HORKHEIMER and THEODOR ADORNO and by the semiotic criticism of ROLAND BARTHES. In the late 1960s he was affiliated with the "Situationists," an international anarchist group that combined Marxist analysis with innovative critiques of consumer society and bourgeois values. After the collapse of the student movement, Baudrillard, like other members of his generation, began to consider what went wrong, starting with his critiques of Marxism (most notably in his *Mirror of Production*, 1973; trans. 1983) and moving toward the issues of media simulation and the hyperreality of consumer society taken up in our selection from *Simulations* (1981; trans. 1983). After becoming a minor cult figure in the 1980s, Baudrillard in 1987 resigned his post at Nanterre and published increasingly experimental texts that abandon consecutive argumentation for impressionistic collages of travel narrative, autobiographical material, social critique, and theoretical musings.

The key to Baudrillard's thought is his reversal of the commonsense understanding of the relation of culture to nature, of sign to thing signified. Conventional thought holds that nature (both human and nonhuman, such as trees, weather, ecological systems, the law of gravity) precedes culture (the human-made), which is built on top of it. Similarly, we think of a thing as existing in the world, and then of a word being invented and used to designate that thing. At times, Baudrillard implies that this commonsense view accurately describes how things used to be, at some unspecified time in the past. In our selection, he speaks of four "successive phases of the image (the sign)."

Baudrillard argues that signs have now taken priority over the things signified. In fact, things have just about disappeared altogether. He links this development to the "death of God" (an event famously heralded in the nineteenth century by FRIEDRICH NIETZSCHE), to the devastation of natural environments, and to Western imperial destruction of all "primitive," non-Western, nonmetropolitan "others." Something has changed in the human relation to the nonhuman that plays itself out in a deadly hostility to all things different. It is, Baudrillard makes clear, a change for the worse, and all attempts to turn back the clock only accelerate the triumph of the sign. We are left yearning for the things we have killed, and "nostalgia assumes its full meaning" as we create ever more signs to simulate those lost things. This is "the vengeance of the dead," who haunt us in their absence.

To designate this new function of signs, Baudrillard chooses the term *simulacrum*, a word that denotes representation but also carries the sense of a counterfeit, sham, or fake. Simulacra seem to have referents (real phenomena they refer to), but they are merely pretend representations that mark the absence, not the existence, of the objects they purport to represent. Baudrillard blames two distinct but related culprits for this change: contemporary consumer culture and imperialistic Western science and philosophy.

In consumer society, natural needs or desires have been buried under, if not totally eliminated by, desires stimulated by cultural discourses (advertising, media, and the rest), which tell us what we want. We are so precoded, so filled from the very start with the images of what we desire, that we process our relation to the world completely through those images. Furthermore, capitalist production in our time proceeds by first creating a demand through marketing and then producing the product to meet that demand. There are no longer natural needs that human work strives to satisfy. Rather, there are culturally produced "hyperreal" needs that are generated to provide work and profits. The world is remade in the image of our desires. The signs (the images of what we want) exist before we create the thing to which the sign refers. Thus, for example, sexual desire is no longer a response to a person whom we meet and know face-to-face. Rather, sexual desire is stimulated by images promulgated by the media, and we strive to remake our bodies to fit those images. The "hyperreality" of the model overwhelms the reality of the people we actually live among. Consumer society provides a "precession of simulacra," a parade of images that project a life that consumers are encouraged to try to live.

The second part of Baudrillard's argument—his view of Western thought and Western science—explains how things lose their reality in the final phase, the phase of the simulacrum. His account here parallels visions of the West found earlier in Nietzsche and later in JACQUES DERRIDA, MICHEL FOUCAULT, and other poststructuralist thinkers. The West, with its compulsions to explore and to know the whole globe, is driven to *name* and to explain each thing it encounters. The name, our knowledge, replaces the thing. For the difference and otherness of the thing, we substitute the signs that translate, account for, and tame it within our own signifying system. This is why Baudrillard insists that signs murder. The ethnologist (the anthropologist) erases the very people being studied by embalming them in his or her categories, replacing their reality with an explanatory, scholarly account. Having killed the real thing by reducing it to scientific terms, the anthropologist provides an embalmed simulation of that thing for display in the natural history museum. Western science, especially since the Enlightenment, has increasingly translated all otherness into its own terms, making it safe for subsequent touristlike encounters with the packaged exotic. We get simulated otherness; the real thing has evaporated.

In claiming that "we all become living specimens under the spectral light of ethnology," Baudrillard suggests that we all live our lives as if within quotation marks, as if playing a part in a movie. The student who is starting college, for example, has so many images of college students (from movies or TV) in mind that his or her way of being a student will inevitably be patterned in response to those preexisting images. The patterning may come from an attempt to resist the stereotype, to play against expectations, but the priority of the image still prevails. As "authentic" experience becomes ever harder to conceive, simulation, willed or not, rules the day.

We sense this loss of the real, according to Baudrillard; and our search for authenticity, often subconscious, has become ever more panicky as a result. He interprets Disneyland as an elaborately artificial land created precisely to convince us that our "real" lives are real. Caught up in the "precession of simulacra" that kills everything real and replaces it with fabricated models, we feel that something is wrong; but we have no satisfactory strategies for overturning the growing dominance of images and signs.

In many ways, Baudrillard's work echoes Horkheimer and Adorno's earlier critique of the culture industry. Like them, he often comes across as a European intellectual appalled by American mass culture, extravagantly pessimistic and overgeneralizing. Los Angeles for these critics stands for a dystopian future whose worst feature is that its inhabitants apparently like it. The passivity of (post)modern consumers in Baudrillard's work leaves little space for hope. Only his apocalyptic rhetoric, with its hints of coming implosions, offers any prospect of change.

Critiques of Baudrillard's work since the 1980s have emerged largely from cultural studies, with its attention to the creative and progressive uses to which resisting audiences put the materials offered to them by the various media. In describing how we as social agents live out prescripted patterns, Baudrillard misses the playful and parodic resignifications emphasized by performative accounts of action like JUDITH BUTLER's. But the power of his work—and its influence—rests in its one-sidedness, the energy with which he presents his vision of a globalized economy of simulacra, of signs gone mad as they dictate all of our lives and obliterate anything that stands outside of them.

BIBLIOGRAPHY

Baudrillard's books in English translation (with the date of the original French given first) are *The System of Objects* (1968; 1996), *The Consumer Society* (1970; 1998),

For a Critique of the Political Economy of the Sign (1972; 1981), *The Mirror of Production* (1973; 1983), *Symbolic Exchange and Death* (1976; 1993), *The Beauborg Effect* (1977; 1982), *Forget Foucault* (1977; 1978), *In the Shadow of the Silent Majorities* (1978; 1983), *Seduction* (1979; 1990), *Simulations* (1981; 1983), *Fatal Strategies* (1983; 1990), *America* (1986; 1988), *The Ecstasy of Communication* (1987; 1988), *Cool Memories, 1980–1985* (1987; 1990), *The Transparency of Evil* (1990; 1993), *Cool Memories II, 1987–1990* (1990; 1996), *The Gulf War Did Not Take Place* (1990; 1995), *The Illusion of the End* (1992; 1994), *The Perfect Crime* (1993; 1996), and *Fragments: Cool Memories III, 1990–1995* (1995; 1997). There are also two selections of Baudrillard's work in translation: *Jean Baudrillard: Selected Writings*, edited by Mark Poster (1988), and *The Revenge of the Crystal: Selected Writings, 1968–1983*, edited by Paul Foss and Julian Pefanis (1990). Two books collect interviews with Baudrillard: *Baudrillard Live: Selected Interviews*, edited by Mike Gane (1993), and *Paroxysm: Interviews with Philip Petit* (1998). The best biographical source is the entry in *Current Biography Yearbook* (1993).

The first books on Baudrillard, Douglas Kellner's *Jean Baudrillard: From Marxism to Postmodernism* (1989) and Mike Gane's two studies, *Baudrillard: Critical and Fatal Theory* (1991) and *Baudrillard's Bestiary* (1991), focused on the postmodernism debates of the 1980s. The reader new to his thought will be better served by three later collections of critical essays by diverse hands: *Forget Baudrillard?*, edited by Chris Rojek and Bryan S. Turner (1993); *Baudrillard: A Critical Reader*, edited by Douglas Kellner (1994); and *Jean Baudrillard: The Disappearance of Art and Politics*, edited by William Stearns and William Chaloupke (1996). Charles Levin's *Jean Baudrillard: A Study in Cultural Metaphysics* (1996) is a judicious overview and a good place to start. Joan Nordquist's *Jean Baudrillard: A Bibliography* (1991) lists all of Baudrillard's work to that date in French and in English translation, along with all the English language commentaries.

From The Precession of Simulacra[1]

> The simulacrum is never that which conceals the truth—it is the truth which conceals that there is none.
> The simulacrum is true.
>
> *Ecclesiastes*[2]

If we were able to take as the finest allegory of simulation the Borges tale[3] where the cartographers of the Empire draw up a map so detailed that it ends up exactly covering the territory (but where the decline of the Empire sees this map become frayed and finally ruined, a few shreds still discernible in the deserts—the metaphysical beauty of this ruined abstraction, bearing witness to an Imperial pride and rotting like a carcass, returning to the substance of the soil, rather as an aging double ends up being confused with the real thing)—then this fable has come full circle for us, and now has nothing but the discrete charm of second-order simulacra.[4]

Abstraction today is no longer that of the map, the double, the mirror or the concept. Simulation is no longer that of a territory, a referential being or a substance. It is the generation by models of a real without origin or reality: a hyperreal. The territory no longer precedes the map, nor survives

1. Translated by Paul Foss and Paul Patton.
2. Baudrillard's epigraph does not appear in Ecclesiastes.
3. "On Exactitude in Science" (1960), by Jorge Luis Borges (1899–1986), Argentinian short story writer and poet.
4. Cf. J. Baudrillard, *Symbolic Exchange and Death* (1976) [Baudrillard's note].

it. Henceforth, it is the map that precedes the territory—**PRECESSION OF SIMULACRA**—it is the map that engenders the territory and if we were to revive the fable today, it would be the territory whose shreds are slowly rotting across the map. It is the real, and not the map, whose vestiges subsist here and there in the deserts which are no longer those of the Empire, but our own. *The desert of the real itself.*

In fact, even inverted, the fable is useless. Perhaps only the allegory of the Empire remains. For it is with the same Imperialism that present-day simulators try to make the real, all the real, coincide with their simulation models. But it is no longer a question of either maps or territory. Something has disappeared: the sovereign difference between them that was the abstraction's charm. For it is the difference which forms the poetry of the map and the charm of the territory, the magic of the concept and the charm of the real. This representational imaginary, which both culminates in and is engulfed by the cartographer's mad project of an ideal coextensivity between the map and the territory, disappears with simulation—whose operation is nuclear and genetic, and no longer specular and discursive. With it goes all of metaphysics.[5] No more mirror of being and appearances, of the real and its concept. No more imaginary coextensivity: rather, genetic miniaturisation is the dimension of simulation. The real is produced from miniaturised units, from matrices, memory banks and command models—and with these it can be reproduced an indefinite number of times. It no longer has to be rational, since it is no longer measured against some ideal or negative instance. It is nothing more than operational. In fact, since it is no longer enveloped by an imaginary, it is no longer real at all. It is a hyperreal, the product of an irradiating synthesis of combinatory models in a hyperspace without atmosphere.

In this passage to a space whose curvature is no longer that of the real, nor of truth, the age of simulation thus begins with a liquidation of all referentials—worse: by their artificial resurrection in systems of signs, a more ductile material than meaning, in that it lends itself to all systems of equivalence, all binary oppositions and all combinatory algebra. It is no longer a question of imitation, nor of reduplication, nor even of parody. It is rather a question of substituting signs of the real for the real itself, that is, an operation to deter every real process by its operational double, a metastable, programmatic, perfect descriptive machine which provides all the signs of the real and short-circuits all its vicissitudes. Never again will the real have to be produced—this is the vital function of the model in a system of death, or rather of anticipated resurrection which no longer leaves any chance even in the event of death. A hyperreal henceforth sheltered from the imaginary, and from any distinction between the real and the imaginary, leaving room only for the orbital recurrence of models and the simulated generation of difference.

The Divine Irreference of Images

To dissimulate is to feign not to have what one has. To simulate is to feign to have what one hasn't. One implies a presence, the other an absence. But

5. The branch of philosophy that deals with the ultimate structures or substance of the real. With the replacement of the real by the sign, there would be nothing left for metaphysics to ponder.

the matter is more complicated, since to simulate is not simply to feign: "Someone who feigns an illness can simply go to bed and make believe he is ill. Some who simulates an illness produces in himself some of the symptoms." (Littre)[6] Thus, feigning or dissimulating leaves the reality principle intact: the difference is always clear, it is only masked; whereas simulation threatens the difference between "true" and "false", between "real" and "imaginary". Since the simulator produces "true" symptoms, is he ill or not? He cannot be treated objectively either as ill, or as not-ill. Psychology and medicine stop at this point, before a thereafter undiscoverable truth of the illness. For if any symptom can be "produced", and can no longer be accepted as a fact of nature, then every illness may be considered as simulatable and simulated, and medicine loses its meaning since it only knows how to treat "true" illnesses by their objective causes. Psychosomatics[7] evolves in a dubious way on the edge of the illness principle. As for psychoanalysis, it transfers the symptom from the organic to the unconscious order: once again, the latter is held to be true, more true than the former—but why should simulation stop at the portals of the unconscious? Why couldn't the "work" of the unconscious be "produced" in the same way as any other symptom in classical medicine? Dreams already are.[8]

The alienist,[9] of course, claims that "for each form of the mental alienation there is a particular order in the succession of symptoms, of which the simulator is unaware and in the absence of which the alienist is unlikely to be deceived." This (which dates from 1865) in order to save at all cost the truth principle, and to escape the spectre raised by simulation—namely that truth, reference and objective causes have ceased to exist. What can medicine do with something which floats on either side of illness, on either side of health, or with the reduplication of illness in a discourse that is no longer true or false? What can psychoanalysis do with the reduplication of the discourse of the unconscious in a discourse of simulation that can never be unmasked, since it isn't false either?[1]

What can the army do with simulators? Traditionally, following a direct principle of identification, it unmasks and punishes them. Today, it can reform an excellent simulator as though he were equivalent to a "real" homosexual, heart-case or lunatic. Even military psychology retreats from the Cartesian clarities[2] and hesitates to draw the distinction between true and false, between the "produced" symptom and the authentic symptom. "If he acts crazy so well, then he must be mad." Nor is it mistaken: in the sense that all lunatics are simulators, and this lack of distinction is the worst form of subversion. Against it classical reason armed itself with all its categories. But it is this today which again outflanks them, submerging the truth principle.

6. Maximilien Paul Littré (1801–1881), French lexicographer and translator of Hippocrates. Baudrillard takes this definition from Littré's dictionary.

7. Bodily symptoms caused by mental or emotional disturbance; these interest Baudrillard as an example of how ideas or images produce a physical reality.

8. That is, patients in therapy have dreams that fit their therapist's style of interpretation, "produced" in response to the therapist's prompting rather than reflective of some "truth" or "reality."

9. Psychologist (a 19th-c. term).

1. And which is not susceptible to resolution in transference. It is the entanglement of these two discourses which makes psychoanalysis interminable [Baudrillard's note]. SIGMUND FREUD (1856–1939), the Austrian founder of psychoanalysis, wrote that therapy, strictly speaking, was "interminable," but that it should end when the "transference"—which involves the patient's repetition of his or her basic problems in the relationship developed with the therapist—was complete and understood by the patient. The therapist uses this repetition as a way of enlightening the patient about the more general patterns of his or her life.

2. The French philosopher René Descartes (1596–1650) proposed a method for discerning "clear" and hence "certain" ideas.

Outside of medicine and the army, favored terrains of simulation, the affair goes back to religion and the simulacrum of divinity: "I forbad any simulacrum in the temples because the divinity that breathes life into nature cannot be represented." Indeed it can. But what becomes of the divinity when it reveals itself in icons, when it is multiplied in simulacra? Does it remain the supreme authority, simply incarnated in images as a visible theology? Or is it volatilized into simulacra which alone deploy their pomp and power of fascination—the visible machinery of icons being substituted for the pure and intelligible Idea of God? This is precisely what was feared by the Iconoclasts, whose millennial quarrel is still with us today.[3] Their rage to destroy images rose precisely because they sensed this omnipotence of simulacra, this facility they have of effacing God from the consciousness of men, and the overwhelming, destructive truth which they suggest: that ultimately there has never been any God, that only the simulacrum exists, indeed that God himself has only ever been his own simulacrum. Had they been able to believe that images only occulted or masked the Platonic Idea[4] of God, there would have been no reason to destroy them. One can live with the idea of a distorted truth. But their metaphysical despair came from the idea that the images concealed nothing at all, and that in fact they were not images, such as the original model would have made them, but actually perfect simulacra forever radiant with their own fascination. But this death of the divine referential has to be exorcised at all cost.

It can be seen that the iconoclasts, who are often accused of despising and denying images, were in fact the ones who accorded them their actual worth, unlike the iconolaters, who saw in them only reflections and were content to venerate God at one remove. But the converse can also be said, namely that the iconolaters were the most modern and adventurous minds, since underneath the idea of the apparition of God in the mirror of images, they already enacted his death and his disappearance in the epiphany of his representations (which they perhaps knew no longer represented anything, and that they were purely a game, but that this was precisely the greatest game—knowing also that it is dangerous to unmask images, since they dissimulate the fact that there is nothing behind them).

This was the approach of the Jesuits,[5] who based their politics on the virtual disappearance of God and on the worldly and spectacular manipulation of consciences—the evanescence of God in the epiphany of power—the end of transcendence, which no longer serves as alibi for a strategy completely free of influences and signs. Behind the baroque of images hides the grey eminence of politics.

Thus perhaps at stake has always been the murderous capacity of images, murderers of the real, murderers of their own model as the Byzantine icons could murder the divine identity.[6] To this murderous capacity is opposed the dialectical capacity of representations as a visible and intelligible mediation of the Real. All of Western faith and good faith was engaged in this wager

3. Cf. M. Perniola, "Icones, Visions, Simulacres," *Traverses/10*, p. 39 [Baudrillard's note].
4. That is, a perfect, immutable, transcendent Form or Idea in whose reality particular phenomena imperfectly participate, as described in the writings of PLATO (ca. 427–ca. 347 B.C.E.).
5. Members of a Roman Catholic religious order founded in response to the Protestant Reformation, who have long had a reputation for being manipulative and unscrupulous in promoting Catholicism over Protestantism.
6. The Byzantine empire, the eastern half of the Roman Empire, was the home of the Greek Orthodox Church, whose lavish icons have been seen by Western commentators, depending on their own attitude toward images of the divine, as examples either of pagan idolatry or of beautiful religious art.

on representation: that a sign could refer to the depth of meaning, that a sign could *exchange* for meaning and that something could guarantee this exchange—God, of course. But what if God himself can be simulated, that is to say, reduced to the signs which attest his existence? Then the whole system becomes weightless, it is no longer anything but a gigantic simulacrum—not unreal, but a simulacrum, never again exchanging for what is real, but exchanging in itself, in an uninterrupted circuit without reference or circumference.

So it is with simulation, insofar as it is opposed to representation. The latter starts from the principle that the sign and the real are equivalent (even if this equivalence is utopian, it is a fundamental axiom). Conversely, simulation starts from the *utopia* of this principle of equivalence, *from the radical negation of the sign as value*, from the sign as reversion and death sentence of every reference. Whereas representation tries to absorb simulation by interpreting it as false representation, simulation envelops the whole edifice of representation as itself a simulacrum.

This would be the successive phases of the image:

—it is the reflection of a basic reality

—it masks and perverts a basic reality

—it masks the *absence* of a basic reality

—it bears no relation to any reality whatever: it is its own pure simulacrum.

In the first case, the image is a *good* appearance—the representation is of the order of sacrament. In the second, it is an *evil* appearance—of the order of malefice.[7] In the third, it *plays at being* an appearance—it is of the order of sorcery. In the fourth, it is no longer in the order of appearance at all, but of simulation.

The transition from signs which dissimulate something to signs which dissimulate that there is nothing, marks the decisive turning point. The first implies a theology of truth and secrecy (to which the notion of ideology still belongs). The second inaugurates an age of simulacra and stimulation, in which there is no longer any God to recognise his own, nor any last judgement to separate true from false, the real from its artificial resurrection, since everything is already dead and risen in advance.

When the real is no longer what it used to be, nostalgia assumes its full meaning. There is a proliferation of myths of origin and signs of reality; of second-hand truth, objectivity and authenticity. There is an escalation of the true, of the lived experience; a resurrection of the figurative where the object and substance have disappeared. And there is a panic-stricken production of the real and the referential, above and parallel to the panic of material production: this is how simulation appears in the phase that concerns us—a strategy of the real, neo-real and hyperreal whose universal double is a strategy of deterrence.

Rameses, or Rose-Coloured Resurrection

Ethnology almost met a paradoxical death that day in 1971 when the Philippino government decided to return the few dozen Tasaday[8] discovered deep

7. An evil deed.

8. A small group of people "discovered" in 1971 living in the high and rain forest in the Philippines; they were acclaimed as an example of a "primitive" tribe untouched by modern life. (By the mid-1980s, many anthropologists were convinced that

in the jungle, where they had lived for eight centuries undisturbed by the rest of mankind, to their primitive state, out of reach of colonists, tourists and ethnologists. This was at the initiative of the anthropologists themselves, who saw the natives decompose immediately on contact, like a mummy in the open air.

For ethnology to live, its object must die. But the latter revenges itself by dying for having been "discovered", and defies by its death the science that wants to take hold of it.

Doesn't every science live on this paradoxical slope to which it is doomed by the evanescence of its object in the very process of its apprehension, and by the pitiless reversal this dead object exerts on it? Like Orpheus it always turns around too soon, and its object, like Eurydice, falls back into Hades.[9]

It was against this hades of paradox that the ethnologists wanted to protect themselves by cordoning off the Tasaday with virgin forest. Nobody now will touch it: the vein is closed down, like a mine. Science loses a precious capital, but the object will be safe—lost to science, but intact in its "virginity". It isn't a question of sacrifice (science never sacrifices itself: it is always murderous), but of the simulated sacrifice of its object in order to save its reality principle. The Tasaday, frozen in their natural element, provide a perfect alibi, an eternal guarantee. At this point begins a persistent anti-ethnology to which Jaulin, Castaneda and Clastres[1] variously belong. In any case, the logical evolution of a science is to distance itself ever further from its object until it dispenses with it entirely: its autonomy evermore fantastical in reaching its pure form.

The Indian thereby driven back into the ghetto, into the glass coffin of virgin forest, becomes the simulation model for all conceivable Indians *before ethnology*. The latter thus allows itself the luxury of being incarnate beyond itself, in the "brute" reality of these Indians it has entirely reinvented—Savages who are indebted to ethnology for still being Savages: what a turn of events, what a triumph for this science which seemed dedicated to their destruction!

Of course, these particular Savages are posthumous: frozen, cryogenised, sterilised, protected *to death*, they have become referential simulacra, and the science itself a pure simulation. Same thing at Creusot[2] where, in the form of an "open" museum exhibition, they have "museumised" on the spot, as historical witnesses to their period, entire working class quarters, living metallurgical zones, a complete culture including men, women and children and their gestures, languages and habits—living beings fossilised as in a snap shot. The museum, instead of being circumscribed in a geometrical location, is now everywhere, like a dimension of life itself. Thus ethnology, now freed

---

the whole episode was a hoax perpetrated by the Philippine government. Opinion remains divided about the "authenticity" of the Tasaday.)

9. In Greek mythology, the poet-singer Orpheus wins back his dead wife, Eurydice, from the underworld—on the condition (which he does not keep) that he not look back at her until they are on the earth's surface.

1. Three revisionist anthropologists of the 1960s and 1970s, especially interested in Native American peoples and their suffering at the hands of the West: the French Robert Jaulin (b. 1928), Mexican American Carlos Castaneda (1931–1998), and French Pierre Clastres (1934–1977).

2. A town in the Burgundy region of central France and home of the historic Schneider iron and steel mills, founded in 1837. In response to the mill's economic troubles and to the decline of coal mining in the region, the town established a museum in the Schneider family mansion, where it stages the work that it once did in earnest.

from its object, will no longer be circumscribed as an objective science but is applied to all living things and becomes invisible, like an omnipresent fourth dimension, that of the simulacrum. *We are all Tasaday*, or Indians who have once more become "what they used to be", or at least that which ethnology has made them—simulacra Indians who proclaim at last the universal truth of ethnology.

We all become living specimens under the spectral light of ethnology, or of anti-ethnology which is only the pure form of triumphal ethnology, under the sign of dead differences, and of the resurrection of differences. It is thus extremely naive to look for ethnology among the Savages or in some Third World—it is here, everywhere, in the metropolis, among the whites, in a world completely catalogued and analysed and then *artificially revived as though real*, in a world of simulation: of the hallucination of truth, of blackmail by the real, of the murder and historical (hysterical) retrospection of every symbolic form—a murder whose first victims were, noblesse oblige, the Savages, but which for a long time now has been extended to all Western societies.

But at the same moment ethnology gives up its final and only lesson, the secret which kills it (and which the savages understood much better): the vengeance of the dead.

The confinement of the scientific object is the same as that of the insane and the dead. And just as the whole of society is hopelessly contaminated by that mirror of madness it has held out for itself, so science can only die contaminated by the death of the object which is its inverse mirror. It is science which ostensibly masters the object, but it is the latter which deeply invests the former, following an unconscious reversion, giving only dead and circular replies to a dead and circular interrogation.

Nothing changes when society breaks the mirror of madness (abolishes asylums, gives speech back to the mad, etc.) nor when science seems to break the mirror of its objectivity (effacing itself before its object, as Castaneda does, etc.) and to bow down before "differences". Confinement is succeeded by an apparatus which assumes a countless and endlessly diffractable, multipliable form. As fast as ethnology in its classical institution collapses, it survives in an anti-ethnology whose task is to reinject fictional difference and Savagery everywhere, in order to conceal the fact that it is this world, our own, which in its way has become savage again, that is to say devastated by difference and death.

It is in this way, under the pretext of saving the original, that the caves of Lascaux[3] have been forbidden to visitors and an exact replica constructed 500 metres away, so that everyone can see them (you glance through a peephole at the real grotto and then visit the reconstituted whole). It is possible that the very memory of the original caves will fade in the mind of future generations, but from now on there is no longer any difference: the duplication is sufficient to render both artificial.

In the same way the whole of science and technology were recently mobilised to save the mummy of Rameses II, after it had been left to deteriorate in the basement of a museum.[4] The West was panic-stricken at the thought

3. Site in southern France of cave paintings from the Upper Paleolithic period.

4. In 1977, at the instigation of a French archaeologist, the mummy of Rameses II (Egyptian pharaoh, 1304–1237 B.C.E.) was brought from Cairo to Paris for restoration. French scientists declared it

of not being able to save what the symbolic order had been able to preserve for 40 centuries, but away from the light and gaze of onlookers. Rameses means nothing to us: only the mummy is of inestimable worth since it is what guarantees that accumulation means something. Our entire linear and accumulative culture would collapse if we could not stockpile the past in plain view. To this end the pharaohs must be brought out of their tombs, and the mummies out of their silence. To this end they must be exhumed and given military honors. They are prey to both science and the worms. Only absolute secrecy ensured their potency throughout the millennia—their mastery over putrefaction, which signified a mastery over the total cycle of exchange with death. *We* know better than to use our science for the *reparation* of the mummy, that is, to restore a *visible* order, whereas embalming was a mythical labor aimed at immortalising a *hidden* dimension.

We need a visible past, a visible continuum, a visible myth of origin to reassure us as to our ends, since ultimately we have never believed in them. Whence that historic scene of the mummy's reception at Orly airport.[5] All because Rameses was a great despot and military figure? Certainly: but above all because the order which our culture dreams of, behind that defunct power it seeks to annex could have had nothing to do with it, and it dreams thus because it has exterminated this order by exhuming it *as if it were our own past.*

We are fascinated by Rameses as Renaissance Christians were by the American Indians: those (human?) beings who had never known the word of Christ. Thus, at the beginning of colonisation, there was a moment of stupor and amazement before the very possibility of escaping the universal law of the Gospel. There were two possible responses: either to admit that this law was not universal, or to exterminate the Indians so as to remove the evidence. In general, it was enough to convert them, or even simply to discover them, to ensure their slow extermination.

Thus it would have been enough to exhume Rameses to ensure his extermination by museumification. For mummies do not decay because of worms: they die from being transplanted from a prolonged symbolic order, which is master over death and putrescence, on to an order of history, science and museums—our own, which is no longer master over anything, since it only knows how to condemn its predecessors to death and putrescence and their subsequent resuscitation by science. An irreparable violence towards all secrets, the violence of a civilisation without secrets. The hatred by an entire civilization for its own foundations.

And just as with ethnology playing at surrendering its object the better to establish itself in its pure form, so museumification is only one more turn in the spiral of artificiality. Witness the cloister of St-Michel de Cuxa, which is going to be repatriated at great expense from the Cloisters in New York to be reinstalled on "its original site".[6] And everyone is supposed to applaud this restitution (as with the "experimental campaign to win back the sidewalks" on the Champs-Elysees!). However, if the exportation of the cornices

cured of all infection and "immunized" for the future after repairing some tissues and sterilizing them with gamma radiation.

5. One of two main airports serving Paris.

6. A 9th-century Benedictine monastery located in the northeast Pyrenees in France. (This cloister has not in fact been removed from the Cloisters, a New York City museum that contains medieval ecclesiastic architecture taken from Europe.)

was in effect an arbitrary act, and if the Cloisters of New York are really an artificial mosaic of all cultures (according to a logic of the capitalist centralisation of value), then reimportation to the original location is even more artificial: it is a total simulacrum that links up with "reality" by a complete circumvolution.

The cloister should have stayed in New York in its simulated environment, which at least would have fooled no one. Repatriation is only a supplementary subterfuge, in order to make out as though nothing had happened and to indulge in a retrospective hallucination.

In the same way Americans flatter themselves they brought the number of Indians back to what it was before their conquest. Everything is obliterated only to begin again. They even flatter themselves they went one better, by surpassing the original figure. This is presented as proof of the superiority of civilisation: it produces more Indians than they were capable of themselves. By a sinister mockery, this overproduction is yet again a way of destroying them: for Indian culture, like all tribal culture, rests on the limitation of the group and prohibiting any of its "unrestricted" growth, as can be seen in case of Ishi.[7] Demographic "promotion", therefore, is just one more step towards symbolic extermination.

We too live in a universe everywhere strangely similar to the original—here things are duplicated by their own scenario. But this double does not mean, as in folklore, the imminence of death—they are already purged of death, and are even better than in life; more smiling, more authentic, in light of their model, like the faces in funeral parlors.

Hyperreal and Imaginary

Disneyland is a perfect model of all the entangled orders of simulation. To begin with it is a play of illusions and phantasms: Pirates, the Frontier, Future World, etc. This imaginary world is supposed to be what makes the operation successful. But what draws the crowds is undoubtedly much more the social microcosm, the miniaturised and *religious* revelling in real America, in its delights and drawbacks. You park outside, queue up inside, and are totally abandoned at the exit. In this imaginary world the only phantasmagoria is in the inherent warmth and affection of the crowd, and in that sufficiently excessive number of gadgets used there to specifically maintain the multitudinous affect. The contrast with the absolute solitude of the parking lot—a veritable concentration camp—is total. Or rather: inside, a whole range of gadgets magnetise the crowd into direct flows—outside, solitude is directed onto a single gadget: the automobile. By an extraordinary coincidence (one that undoubtedly belongs to the peculiar enchantment of this universe), this deep-frozen infantile world happens to have been conceived and realised by a man who is himself now cryogenised: Walt Disney,[8] who awaits his resurrection at minus 180 degrees centigrade.

The objective profile of America, then, may be traced throughout Disney-

7. The last surviving member of the Yahi (d. 1916), a Native American tribe of northern California. "Discovered" in 1911 and famed as "the last Stone Age man," Ishi lived his last five years at the University of California's Museum of Anthropology in Berkeley.

8. The cartoonist and film producer (1901–1966), who opened Disneyland in 1955. Disney is widely (though mistakenly) believed to have had his body cryogenically preserved upon death.

land, even down to the morphology of individuals and the crowd. All its values are exalted here, in miniature and comic strip form. Embalmed and pacified. Whence the possibility of an ideological analysis of Disneyland (L. Marin[9] does it well in *Utopies, jeux d'espaces*): digest of the American way of life, panegyric to American values, idealised transposition of a contradictory reality. To be sure. But this conceals something else, and that "ideological" blanket exactly serves to cover over a *third-order simulation*: Disneyland is there to conceal the fact that it is the "real" country, all of "real" America, which *is* Disneyland (just as prisons are there to conceal the fact that it is the social in its entirety, in its banal omnipresence, which is carceral[1]). Disneyland is presented as imaginary in order to make us believe that the rest is real, when in fact all of Los Angeles and the America surrounding it are no longer real, but of the order of the hyperreal and of simulation. It is no longer a question of a false representation of reality (ideology), but of concealing the fact that the real is no longer real, and thus of saving the reality principle.

The Disneyland imaginary is neither true nor false; it is a deterrence machine set up in order to rejuvenate in reverse the fiction of the real. Whence the debility, the infantile degeneration of this imaginary. It is meant to be an infantile world, in order to make us believe that the adults are elsewhere, in the "real" world, and to conceal the fact that real childishness is everywhere, particularly amongst those adults who go there to act the child in order to foster illusions as to their real childishness.

Moreover, Disneyland is not the only one. Enchanted Village, Magic Mountain, Marine World: Los Angeles is encircled by these "imaginary stations" which feed reality, reality-energy, to a town whose mystery is precisely that it is nothing more than a network of endless, unreal circulation—a town of fabulous proportions, but without space or dimensions. As much as electrical and nuclear power stations, as much as film studios, this town, which is nothing more than an immense script and a perpetual motion picture, needs this old imaginary made up of childhood signals and faked phantasms for its sympathetic nervous system.

* * *

1981

9. Louis Marin (1931–1992), French cultural historian and semiotician, who writes about Disneyland in *Utopics: Spatial Play* (1973).

1. Relating to prisons and imprisonment and incarceration. In his book about prisons, *Discipline and Punish* (1975; see above), MICHEL FOUCAULT claimed that modern society was increasingly "carceral."

JÜRGEN HABERMAS
b. 1929

Committed to completing what he calls "the unfinished project of modernity," Jürgen Habermas is the most important liberal political philosopher of post–World War II Germany. Although steeped in the Marxist tradition of the University of Frankfurt (where he has been a professor of philosophy since 1961), Habermas nonetheless champions the civil liberties and the formal equality before the law guaranteed in modern Western democracies. In particular, he sees the postwar Federal Republic of West Germany as proof that constitutional representative government serves as a necessary, although not always sufficient, bulwark against the abuses of state power characteristic of the Nazis and of the Democratic Republic of East Germany (1945–89). Habermas recognizes the failings of liberal democracies in addressing questions of economic justice and equality, but he usually argues that the welfare state, or what Europeans call "social democracy," has a better track record than socialism or other alternatives in promoting and spreading prosperity. His political views have led him to argue vehemently against the critique of modernity developed by French post-structuralist writers such as MICHEL FOUCAULT, JACQUES DERRIDA, and JEAN-FRANÇOIS LYOTARD. The postmodernism debates initiated in the 1980s often center around Habermas's attempt to defend Enlightenment ideals of universal reason, rights, and justice against the critiques of the poststructuralists.

Born in Düsseldorf, Habermas was just young enough to avoid service in Adolf Hitler's army. He recalls the Nuremberg trials of Nazi war criminals as the formative historical event of his youth, and he insists that Germany must always keep in mind the lessons of its militaristic, totalitarian, and genocidal past; Habermas has strongly criticized the so-called new historians who argue that the Nazis crimes are no worse than Joseph Stalin's murders in Russia. As a student, Habermas worked with and for THEODOR ADORNO at the Frankfurt Institute for Social Research, and his early work, especially *Knowledge and Human Interests* (1968), reveals a Marxist concern with domination, class struggle, and emancipation. While he still refuses to consider the economic sphere a "private" domain that is off-limits to state action and continues to focus on illegitimate power inequities, his battle with poststructuralism and, especially, his defense of a normative ideal of "communicative reason" shape his later work more than Marxism does.

Habermas's first book, *The Structural Transformation of the Public Sphere: An Inquiry into a Category of Bourgeois Society* (1962; trans. 1991), from which our first selection is taken, already indicates the interests in civil society, civil liberties, and public communication that mark his later endorsement of "the project of modernity" in our second selection. Modernity, for Habermas, is largely a product of the Enlightenment dream of a free and just society guided by the light of reason. Western societies have not realized that dream, but it provides the standards by which they can measure and thus strive to remedy the failings of contemporary societies. Of course, modernity is also a product of the economic arrangements of capitalism, of technological advances, and of the formation of nation-states grounded in ethnic and racial nationalisms. Despite his concern about the various forms of domination (economic, political, and bureaucratic) that threaten to make a free and just society impossible, Habermas firmly believes that we can criticize domination only from the standpoint that political and social arrangements are legitimate insofar as they are rational and commited to equality.

Poststructuralists argue that *reason* has often been a term used to exclude, denigrate, or silence opinions that differ from the dominant view. The other side is always "irrational." In particular, nonprivileged social groups such as women, the poor, children, racial minorities, ethnic others, and the disabled are consistently portrayed as unreasonable. And because the standards of reason are held to be uniform and universally applicable, the supposed failure of whole social groups to meet that standard legitimates their being denied civil liberties (rights) that in principle, but not in practice, are to be "universally" enjoyed. These subterfuges of the discourse of reason lead Lyotard, Foucault, and others to believe we might be better off abandoning it altogether.

Habermas disagrees. He admits that those using the language of universal rights have violated as often as honored them, but he still thinks that reason, suitably defined, can serve as the ideal against which actual practice can be judged. Only the existence of such a norm, he insists, frees us from a political world in which might makes right. And he argues that Foucault (in particular) assumes its existence even in attacking reason, since it is the failure of reason to be universal in practice that incites Foucault's ire. Habermas identifies that norm as "the ideal speech situation," on which depends the very possibility of what he calls "communicative action." This focus on pragmatics (the linguistic study of speech performance) makes Habermas especially interesting for literary theorists. He contends that people would be able neither to understand one another nor to coordinate their activities together without some fundamental agreements embedded in every act of communication.

Our first selection is taken from Habermas's *Habilitationsschrift* (a second doctoral dissertation required from German Ph.D.'s who wish to secure university teaching positions). Here, Habermas offers his influential historical account of the genesis of the Enlightenment ideal of reason. Before the emergence of the bourgeoisie (men who commanded considerable wealth *not* based on ownership of land), power and rights in Europe were divided between the monarch and the traditional orders, or "estates"—the nobility (the "first estate"), the clergy (the "second estate"), and the commons (the "third estate"). The monarch and the two privileged minorities ceaselessly jockeyed for advantage. The bourgeoisie, however, gained social but not political power through its accumulation of "private" wealth, that is, wealth unconnected with holding legitimate sway over other people. Within the ancien régime, the bourgeoisie had no way to translate its growing economic and social power into political power. So this new class needed to change the entire political structure. (Habermas is offering his own answer here to the question "What caused the French Revolution?")

The crucial change began with the transformation of the public sphere, the creation of "civil society" in its modern form. Unlike in the court, the aristocratic estate, the cathedral, the family home, or the place of business, in civil society private persons congregate who are not acting in any official capacity when they gather, who do not know each other intimately, and who meet primarily to talk and exchange opinions. Habermas has in mind the face-to-face exchanges of the salon and the coffeehouse, as well as the explosive spread of newspapers and other written expressions of opinion during the eighteenth century. As TERRY EAGLETON puts it in his Habermasian *Function of Criticism* (1984) "Modern criticism was born of a struggle against the absolutist state." Post-Renaissance literary criticism, like other publicly enunciated opinions, signifies the movement of the bourgeoisie out of the "private" realm and onto the public stage.

For Habermas, Enlightenment "standards of 'reason' and . . . forms of the 'law' " emerge from this explosion of speech aimed at persuading others. He is not here making the claim sometimes proffered elsewhere in his writings that some agreement about these standards is reached, but instead is emphasizing that the very grounds of legitimacy have shifted. Governments must now account for their actions in the court of public opinion, and they will win the case only if they can convince significant portions of the population that those actions are "reasonable" and "legal." Absolutist imposition or appeals to traditional authority will no longer do. The transformation of the public sphere is essential to the victory of the bourgeoisie.

Habermas realizes that the public sphere is not unitary. In our second selection, "Modernity—An Incomplete Project" (1980), he argues that this Enlightenment project of basing authority on reason has gone awry because the specialized discourses of economics, of bureaucratic administration, of technological knowledge, and of art have become separated from the "life-world" of everyday moral and practical decisions. As these fields grow increasingly autonomous and professionalized, they become distanced from the needs of the people. Thus, the criticism of modernity and its experts launched by traditional conservatives, neoconservatives, and "young conservative" poststructuralists is understandable, even justified. But

Habermas strongly urges that we not condemn modernity altogether. Instead of rejecting reason and universality, we must strive to fully reintegrate the discourses of modern science, art, and politics with the everyday perspectives of a life-world in which people strive to secure a decent existence for themselves and their loved ones.

Habermas reads modernism in the arts as a failed attempt to rectify on a cultural level "the differentiation of science, morality and art . . . from the hermeneutics of everyday communication" that is characteristic of modern societies. While he scorns neoconservative attempts to blame the arts for the erosions of tradition caused by capitalist transformations, he sees modernist art, even the radical "surrealist attempt to . . . force a reconciliation of art and life," as incapable of reversing the alienations of modernity because confined to "a single cultural sphere." Only a more holistic analysis and action on a wider social terrain might remedy the ills of modernity, though "the chances for this today are not very good." But Habermas notes that the "young conservative" poststructuralists are beholden to a modernity they claim to despise, because they launch their critique from a distanced aesthetic space. They rely on that distance for their antimodernism, not realizing that such distance is both quintessentially modern and modernity's quintessential failing.

It would be hard to overestimate the impact of Habermas's characterization of the poststructuralists as "young conservatives," or of his description of a surprising antimodernity "alliance of postmodernists with premodernists." The argument over the political significance of poststructuralism has been fierce—and inconclusive. Like the contemporaneous debate between Anglo-American and French feminisms, the battle is between two visions of social transformation, both of which are politically left of center. At issue is whether—and how much—the very terms by which political emancipation has been understood since the Enlightenment themselves hinder liberation. "Modernity—An Incomplete Project" has been a major rallying point for artists and critics who believe that liberal ideals of universal rights, equal protection under the law, and economic justice are norms to which our societies should be held answerable and which should be protected from critique.

Not a single claim by Habermas has gone uncontested, from his historical analyses of the eighteenth century to his various accounts of speech pragmatics to his arguments about the necessity of rational norms and of completing the project of modernity. Critics have questioned the possibility of separating out universal norms of "communicative reason" or other liberal ideals from the vastly different situations in which they are embedded. Similarly, the existence of many different public spheres, with distinctive conventions and protocols, makes generalizations about the "ideal speech situation" suspect. In short, norms appear much more context-sensitive than Habermas allows. Partly in response to such criticisms, Habermas's own work has continued to evolve, moving from a focus on communicative reason in the early 1980s to issues of "discourse ethics" in the late 1980s and to questions of law and democracy in recent years.

BIBLIOGRAPHY

Almost all of Habermas's major works have been translated into English (date given after the date of original German publication). For those coming to Habermas for the first time, the interviews with him collected in *Autonomy and Solidarity*, edited by Peter Dews (1986), offer an accessible overview, which can be followed with *The Philosophical Discourse of Modernity* (1985; 1987), an articulation of his basic position against the attacks on reason by Nietzsche, Adorno, Derrida, and Foucault. His other works include *The Structural Transformation of the Public Sphere* (1962; 1991), *On the Logic of the Social Sciences* (1967; 1988), *Knowledge and Human Interests* (1968; 1971), *Legitimation Crisis* (1973; 1975), *Communication and the Evolution of Society* (1976; 1979), *The Theory of Communicative Action* (2 vols., 1981; 1984–

87), *Moral Consciousness and Communicative Action* (1983; 1990), *The New Conservatism* (1985; 1989), *Between Facts and Norms: Contributions to a Discourse Theory of Law and Democracy* (1992; 1996), and *The Inclusion of the Other* (1996; 1998). Three volumes gather English translations of Habermas's essays written at various times: *Postmetaphysical Thinking* (1994), *Justification and Application: Remarks on Discourse Ethics* (1994), and *On the Pragmatics of Communication* (1998). Biographical information can be found in William Outhwaite's *Habermas: A Critical Introduction* (1994).

The Critical Theory of Jürgen Habermas (1978), by Thomas A. McCarthy, one of Habermas's translators, is still valuable, as is Stephen K. White's excellent *The Recent Work of Jürgen Habermas* (1988). David Rasmussen's *Reading Habermas* (1990) is the best short introduction; it can be supplemented with Outhwaite's more skeptical book (cited above). Of the in-depth studies of Habermas, the three best are David Ingram, *Habermas and the Dialectic of Reason* (1987); Maeve Cook, *Language and Reason: A Study of Habermas's Pragmatics* (1994); and J. M. Bernstein, *Recovering Ethical Life: Jürgen Habermas and the Future of Critical Theory* (1995). Especially useful is David Couzens Hoy and Thomas A. McCarthy's *Critical Theory* (1994), which lays out the case for each side in the Habermas-poststructuralist debate.

There are a large number of collections of varied responses to Habermas's work, which often include replies by Habermas. Noteworthy are *Habermas: Critical Debates*, edited by John Thompson and David Held (1982); *Habermas and Modernity*, edited by Richard J. Bernstein (1985); *The Communicative Ethics Controversy*, edited by Seyla Benhabib and Fred Dallmayr (1990); *Habermas and the Public Sphere*, edited by Craig Calhoun (1992), which contains feminist philosopher Nancy Fraser's highly influential essay "Rethinking the Public Sphere: A Contribution to the Critique of Actually Existing Democracy"; *Critique and Power: Recasting the Foucault-Habermas Debate*, edited by Michael Kelly (1994); *The Cambridge Companion to Habermas*, edited by Stephen K. White (1995); *Feminists Read Habermas*, edited by J. Johanna Meehan (1995); *Habermas and the Unfinished Project of Modernity*, edited by Maurizio d'Entrèves and Seyla Benhabib (1997); and *Habermas on Law and Democracy*, edited by Michel Rosenfeld and Andrew Arato (1998). The Bernstein and Calhoun collections have proved particularly influential in shaping the reception of Habermas's work. Joan Nordquist's bibliography, *Jürgen Habermas III* (1998), lists all of Habermas's work in English and German, along with all English-language commentary on that work.

From The Structural Transformation of the Public Sphere: An Inquiry into a Category of Bourgeois Society[1]

From *Part II. Social Structures of the Public Sphere*

SECTION 4. THE BASIC BLUEPRINT

The bourgeois public sphere may be conceived above all as the sphere of private people come together as a public; they soon claimed the public sphere regulated from above against the public authorities themselves, to engage them in a debate over the general rules governing relations in the basically privatized but publicly relevant sphere of commodity exchange and social labor. The medium of this political confrontation was peculiar and without

1. Translated by Thomas Burger with the assistance of Frederick Lawrence; they occasionally include the German in parentheses and add English in brackets for clarification.

historical precedent: people's public use of their reason (*öffentliches Räsonnement*). In our [German] usage this term (i.e., *Räsonnement*) unmistakably preserves the polemical nuances of both sides: simultaneously the invocation of reason and its disdainful disparagement as merely malcontent griping. Hitherto the estates[2] had negotiated agreements with the princes in which from case to case the conflicting power claims involved in the demarcation of estate liberties from the prince's overlordship or sovereignty were brought into balance.[3] Since the thirteenth century this practice first resulted in a dualism of the ruling estates and of the prince; soon the territorial estates alone represented the land, over against which stood the territorial ruler.[4] It is well known that where the prince's power was relatively reduced by a parliament, as in Great Britain, this development took a different course than it did on the continent, where the monarchs mediatized[5] the estates. The third estate broke with this mode of balancing power since it was no longer capable of establishing itself as a *ruling* estate. A division of rule by parcelling out lordly rights (including the "liberties" of the estates) was no longer possible on the basis of a commercial economy, for the power of control over one's own capitalistically functioning property, being grounded in private law, was apolitical. The bourgeois were private persons; as such they did not "rule." Their power claims against the public authority were thus not directed against the concentration of powers of command that ought to be "divided"; instead, they undercut the principle on which existing rule was based. The principle of control that the bourgeois public opposed to the latter—namely, publicity—was intended to change domination as such. The claim to power presented in rational-critical public debate (*öffentliches Räsonnement*), which *eo ipso*[6] renounced the form of a claim to rule, would entail, if it were to prevail, more than just an exchange of the basis of legitimation while domination was maintained in principle (section 7).

The standards of "reason" and the forms of the "law" to which the public wanted to subject domination and thereby change it in substance reveal their sociological meaning only in an analysis of the bourgeois public sphere itself, especially in the recognition of the fact that it was private people who related to each other in it as a public. The public's understanding of the public use of reason was guided specifically by such private experiences as grew out of the audience-oriented (*publikumsbezogen*) subjectivity of the conjugal family's intimate domain (*Intimsphäre*). Historically, the latter was the source of privateness in the modern sense of a saturated and free interiority. The ancient meaning of the "private"—an inevitability imposed by the necessities of life—was banned, or so it appears, from the inner region of the private sphere, from the home, together with the exertions and relations of dependence involved in social labor. To the degree to which commodity exchange burst out of the confines of the household economy, the sphere of the conjugal family became differentiated from the sphere of social reproduction.

2. The classes once formally vested with distinct powers: traditionally, the nobility, clergy, and commoners.

3. Such status contracts, usually concluded on the occasion of a knight's rendering homage to his Lord's successor, are naturally not to be compared to contracts in the sense of modern private law; see Otto Brunner, *Land und Herrschaft* [*Land and Lordship*] (1943), 484ff. [Habermas's note]

4. See W. Naef, "Frühformen des modernen Staates in Spätmittelalten" ["Early Forms of Modern States in the Late Middle Ages"], *Historische Zeitschrift* 171 (1951): 225ff. [Habermas's note].

5. Mediated among (a role played in England by Parliament).

6. By that itself (Latin).

The process of the polarization of state and society was repeated once more within society itself. The status of private man combined the role of owner of commodities with that of head of the family, that of property owner with that of "human being" *per se*. The doubling of the private sphere on the higher plane of the intimate sphere (section 6) furnished the foundation for an identification of those two roles under the common title of the "private"; ultimately, the political self-understanding of the bourgeois public originated there as well.[7]

To be sure, before the public sphere explicitly assumed political functions in the tension-charged field of state-society relations, the subjectivity originating in the intimate sphere of the conjugal family created, so to speak, its own public. Even before the control over the public sphere by public authority was contested and finally wrested away by the critical reasoning of private persons on political issues, there evolved under its cover a public sphere in apolitical form—the literary precursor of the public sphere operative in the political domain. It provided the training ground for a critical public reflection still preoccupied with itself—a process of self-clarification of private people focusing on the genuine experiences of their novel privateness. Of course, next to political economy, psychology arose as a specifically bourgeois science during the eighteenth century. Psychological interests also guided the critical discussion (*Räsonnement*) sparked by the products of culture that had become publicly accessible: in the reading room and the theater, in museums and at concerts. Inasmuch as culture became a commodity and thus finally evolved into "culture" in the specific sense (as something that pretended to exist merely for its own sake), it was claimed as the ready topic of a discussion through which an audience-oriented (*publikumsbezogen*) subjectivity communicated with itself.[8]

The public sphere in the world of letters (*literarische Öffentlichkeit*) was not, of course, autochthonously bourgeois;[9] it preserved a certain continuity with the publicity involved in the representation enacted at the prince's court. The bourgeois avant-garde of the educated middle class learned the art of critical-rational public debate through its contact with the "elegant world." This courtly-noble society, to the extent that the modern state apparatus[1] became independent from the monarch's personal sphere, naturally separated itself, in turn, more and more from the court and became its counterpoise in the town. The "town" was the life center of civil society not only economically; in cultural-political contrast to the court, it designated especially an early public sphere in the world of letters whose institutions were the coffee houses, the *salons*, and the *Tischgesellschaften* (table societies).[2] The heirs of the humanistic-aristocratic society, in their encounter with the bourgeois intellectuals (through sociable discussions that quickly developed

7. E[rich] Auerbach finds the word, in the sense of a theater audience, documented as early as 1629; until then, the use of "public" as a noun referred exclusively to the state or to the public welfare. See *Der französische Publikum des 17. Jahrhunderts* [*The French Public of the 17th Century*] (1933), p. 5 [Habermas's note].

8. Habermas is both tracing a shift in the meaning of the word *public* and contesting the liberal designation of economic activities as "private." Because "the economy" no longer refers to the household, it is becoming "public"—a word that originally referred mainly to matters of state. Thus the modern state (government) looks different from earlier states: it must establish a relationship to "civil society" and "the market," a relationship that is political and public.

9. That is, produced wholly in and by the bourgeoisie.

1. The bureaucratic state, which gains increasing sway over the nation by means of established procedures and salaried permanent functionaries.

2. That is, gatherings of artists and intellectuals who discussed the issues of the day.

into public criticism), built a bridge between the remains of a collapsing form of publicity (the courtly one) and the precursor of a new one: the bourgeois public sphere (section 5).

With the usual reservations concerning the simplification involved in such illustrations, the blueprint of the bourgeois public sphere in the eighteenth century may be presented graphically as a schema of social realms in the diagram:

Private Realm		Sphere of Public Authority
Civil society (realm of commodity exchange and social labor)	Public sphere in the political realm Public sphere in the world of letters (clubs, press)	State (realm of the "police")
Conjugal family's internal space (bourgeois intellectuals)	(market of culture products) "Town"	Court (courtly-noble society)

The line between state and society, fundamental in our context, divided the public sphere from the private realm. The public sphere was coextensive with public authority, and we consider the court part of it. Included in the private realm was the authentic "public sphere," for it was a public sphere constituted by private people. Within the realm that was the preserve of private people we therefore distinguish again between private and public spheres. The private sphere comprised civil society in the narrower sense, that is to say, the realm of commodity exchange and of social labor; imbedded in it was the family with its interior domain (*Intimsphäre*). The public sphere in the political realm evolved from the public sphere in the world of letters; through the vehicle of public opinion it put the state in touch with the needs of society.

1962

Modernity—An Incomplete Project[1]

In 1980, architects were admitted to the Biennial in Venice,[2] following painters and filmmakers. The note sounded at this first Architecture Biennial was one of disappointment. I would describe it by saying that those who exhibited in Venice formed an avant-garde of reversed fronts. I mean that they sacrificed the tradition of modernity in order to make room for a new historicism. Upon this occasion, a critic of the German newspaper, *Frankfurter Allge-*

1. Translated by Seyla Benhabib [and edited by Hal Foster]. This essay was originally delivered as a talk in September 1980 when Habermas was awarded the Theodor W. Adorno prize by the city of Frankfurt. It was subsequently delivered as a James Lecture of the New York Institute for the Humanities at New York University in March 1981 [Foster's note].

2. A prestigious international exhibition of contemporary art, held every two years.

meine Zeitung, advanced a thesis whose significance reaches beyond this particular event; it is a diagnosis of our times: "Postmodernity definitely presents itself as Antimodernity." This statement describes an emotional current of our times which has penetrated all spheres of intellectual life. It has placed on the agenda theories of postenlightenment, postmodernity, even of posthistory.

From history we know the phrase, "The Ancients and the Moderns." Let me begin by defining these concepts. The term "modern" has a long history, one which has been investigated by Hans Robert Jauss.[3] The word "modern" in its Latin form "modernus" was used for the first time in the late 5th century in order to distinguish the present, which had become officially Christian, from the Roman and pagan past. With varying content, the term "modern" again and again expresses the consciousness of an epoch that relates itself to the past of antiquity, in order to view itself as the result of a transition from the old to the new.

Some writers restrict this concept of "modernity" to the Renaissance, but this is historically too narrow. People considered themselves modern during the period of Charles the Great in the 12th century, as well as in France of the late 17th century at the time of the famous "Querelle des Anciens et des Modernes."[4] That is to say, the term "modern" appeared and reappeared exactly during those periods in Europe when the consciousness of a new epoch formed itself through a renewed relationship to the ancients—whenever, moreover, antiquity was considered a model to be recovered through some kind of imitation.

The spell which the classics of the ancient world cast upon the spirit of later times was first dissolved with the ideals of the French Enlightenment. Specifically, the idea of being "modern" by looking back to the ancients changed with the belief, inspired by modern science, in the infinite progress of knowledge and in the infinite advance towards social and moral betterment. Another form of modernist consciousness was formed in the wake of this change. The romantic modernist sought to oppose the antique ideals of the classicists; he looked for a new historical epoch and found it in the idealized Middle Ages. However, this new ideal age, established early in the 19th century, did not remain a fixed ideal. In the course of the 19th century, there emerged out of this romantic spirit that radicalized consciousness of modernity which freed itself from all specific historical ties. This most recent modernism simply makes an abstract opposition between tradition and the present; and we are, in a way, still the contemporaries of that kind of aesthetic modernity which first appeared in the midst of the 19th century. Since then, the distinguishing mark of works which count as modern is "the new" which will be overcome and made obsolete through the novelty of the next style. But, while that which is merely "stylish" will soon become outmoded, that which is modern preserves a secret tie to the classical. Of course, whatever can survive time has always been considered to be a classic. But the emphatically modern document no longer borrows this power of being a

3. German literary historian and critic (b. 1921; see above). See his *Aesthetic Standards and Historical Reflection in the 'Quarrel of the Ancients and the Moderns"* (1964).

4. Quarrel of the Ancients and the Moderns (French), a literary dispute between those arguing for strict adherence to classical (Greek and Latin) models and defenders of modern (contemporary) works. "Charles the Great" may refer to Charlemagne (742–814), though Habermas places him in the wrong century, perhaps intentionally.

classic from the authority of a past epoch; instead, a modern work becomes a classic because it has once been authentically modern. Our sense of modernity creates its own self-enclosed canons of being classic. In this sense we speak, e.g., in view of the history of modern art, of classical modernity. The relation between "modern" and "classical" has definitely lost a fixed historical reference.

The Discipline of Aesthetic Modernity

The spirit and discipline of aesthetic modernity assumed clear contours in the work of Baudelaire.[5] Modernity then unfolded in various avant-garde movements and finally reached its climax in the Café Voltaire of the dadaists and in surrealism.[6] Aesthetic modernity is characterized by attitudes which find a common focus in a changed consciousness of time. This time consciousness expresses itself through metaphors of the vanguard and the avant-garde. The avant-garde understands itself as invading unknown territory, exposing itself to the dangers of sudden, shocking encounters, conquering an as yet unoccupied future. The avant-garde must find a direction in a landscape into which no one seems to have yet ventured.

But these forward gropings, this anticipation of an undefined future and the cult of the new mean in fact the exaltation of the present. The new time consciousness, which enters philosophy in the writings of Bergson,[7] does more than express the experience of mobility in society, of acceleration in history, of discontinuity in everyday life. The new value placed on the transitory, the elusive and the ephemeral, the very celebration of dynamism, discloses a longing for an undefiled, immaculate and stable present.

This explains the rather abstract language in which the modernist temper has spoken of the "past." Individual epochs lose their distinct forces. Historical memory is replaced by the heroic affinity of the present with the extremes of history—a sense of time wherein decadence immediately recognizes itself in the barbaric, the wild and the primitive. We observe the anarchistic intention of blowing up the continuum of history, and we can account for it in terms of the subversive force of this new aesthetic consciousness. Modernity revolts against the normalizing functions of tradition; modernity lives on the experience of rebelling against all that is normative. This revolt is one way to neutralize the standards of both morality and utility. This aesthetic consciousness continuously stages a dialectical play between secrecy and public scandal; it is addicted to a fascination with that horror which accompanies the act of profaning, and yet is always in flight from the trivial results of profanation.

On the other hand, the time consciousness articulated in avant-garde art is not simply ahistorical; it is directed against what might be called a false normativity in history. The modern, avant-garde spirit has sought to use the past in a different way; it disposes those pasts which have been made avail-

5. CHARLES BAUDELAIRE (1821–1867), French poet and critic.
6. An artistic movement, founded in 1924, that grew directly out of dadaism, which began during World War I; both reacted against logic and both intended to revolutionize art and society. Café Voltaire: meeting place (1915–17) in Zurich, Switzerland, of a group of artists identified with dadaism.
7. Henri Bergson (1859–1941), French philosopher who emphasized the notion of lived time (vs. clock or mechanistic time).

able by the objectifying scholarship of historicism, but it opposes at the same time a neutralized history which is locked up in the museum of historicism.

Drawing upon the spirit of surrealism, Walter Benjamin[8] constructs the relationship of modernity to history in what I would call a posthistoricist attitude. He reminds us of the self-understanding of the French Revolution: "The Revolution cited ancient Rome, just as fashion cites an antiquated dress. Fashion has a scent for what is current, whenever this moves within the thicket of what was once." This is Benjamin's concept of the *Jetztzeit*,[9] of the present as a moment of revelation; a time in which splinters of a messianic presence are enmeshed. In this sense, for Robespierre, the antique Rome was a past laden with momentary revelations.[1]

Now, this spirit of aesthetic modernity has recently begun to age. It has been recited once more in the 1960s; after the 1970s, however, we must admit to ourselves that this modernism arouses a much fainter response today than it did fifteen years ago. Octavio Paz,[2] a fellow-traveller of modernity, noted already in the middle of the 1960s that "the avant-garde of 1967 repeats the deeds and gestures of those of 1917. We are experiencing the end of the idea of modern art." The work of Peter Bürger has since taught us to speak of "post-avant-garde" art; this term is chosen to indicate the failure of the surrealist rebellion.[3] But what is the meaning of this failure? Does it signal a farewell to modernity? Thinking more generally, does the existence of a post-avant-garde mean there is a transition to that broader phenomenon called postmodernity?

This is in fact how Daniel Bell,[4] the most brilliant of the American neoconservatives, interprets matters. In his book, *The Cultural Contradictions of Capitalism*, Bell argues that the crises of the developed societies of the West are to be traced back to a split between culture and society. Modernist culture has come to penetrate the values of everyday life; the life-world[5] is infected by modernism. Because of the forces of modernism, the principle of unlimited self-realization, the demand for authentic self-experience and the subjectivism of a hyperstimulated sensitivity have come to be dominant. This temperament unleashes hedonistic motives irreconcilable with the discipline of professional life in society, Bell says. Moreover, modernist culture is altogether incompatible with the moral basis of a purposive, rational conduct of life. In this manner, Bell places the burden of responsibility for the dissolution of the Protestant ethic (a phenomenon which had already disturbed Max Weber[6]) on the "adversary culture." Culture in its modern form stirs up hatred against the conventions and virtues of everyday life, which has become rationalized under the pressures of economic and administrative imperatives.

8. German writer of literary and cultural criticism (1892–1940; see above).
9. Present time (German).
1. See Benjamin, "Theses on the Philosophy of History," *Illuminations*, trans. Harry Zohn (New York: Schocken, 1969), p. 21 [Foster's note]. Maximilien Robespierre (1758–1794), leader of the Jacobins, the most radical party of the French Revolution.
2. Mexican poet (1914–1998).
3. For Paz on the avant-garde see in particular *Children of the Mire: Modern Poetry from Romanticism to the Avant-Garde* (1974), pp. 148–64. For Bürger see *Theory of the Avant-Garde* (1983) [Foster's note]. Bürger (b. 1936), German literary critic.
4. American sociologist (b. 1919); *The Cultural Contradictions of Capitalism* was published in 1976.
5. Ordinary, daily lived experience: Habermas's term to distinguish everyday life from the specialized "systems" of knowledge and procedure that have emerged in complex, modern societies.
6. German sociologist (1864–1920); his best-known work is *The Protestant Ethic and the Spirit of Capitalism* (1905).

I would call your attention to a complex wrinkle in this view. The impulse of modernity, we are told on the other hand, is exhausted; anyone who considers himself avant-garde can read his own death warrant. Although the avant-garde is still considered to be expanding, it is supposedly no longer creative. Modernism is dominant but dead. For the neoconservative the question then arises: how can norms arise in society which will limit libertinism, reestablish the ethic of discipline and work? What new norms will put a brake on the levelling caused by the social welfare state so that the virtues of individual competition for achievement can again dominate? Bell sees a religious revival to be the only solution. Religious faith tied to a faith in tradition will provide individuals with clearly defined identities and existential security.

Cultural Modernity and Societal Modernization

One can certainly not conjure up by magic the compelling beliefs which command authority. Analyses like Bell's, therefore, only result in an attitude which is spreading in Germany no less than in the States: an intellectual and political confrontation with the carriers of cultural modernity. I cite Peter Steinfels, an observer of the new style which the neoconservatives have imposed upon the intellectual scene in the 1970s:

> The struggle takes the form of exposing every manifestation of what could be considered an oppositionist mentality and tracing its "logic" so as to link it to various forms of extremism: drawing the connection between modernism and nihilism . . . between government regulation and totalitarianism, between criticism of arms expenditures and subservience to communism, between Women's liberation or homosexual rights and the destruction of the family . . . between the Left generally and terrorism, anti-semitism, and fascism . . . [7]

The *ad hominem* approach and the bitterness of these intellectual accusations have also been trumpeted loudly in Germany. They should not be explained so much in terms of the psychology of neoconservative writers; rather, they are rooted in the analytical weaknesses of neoconservative doctrine itself.

Neoconservatism shifts onto cultural modernism the uncomfortable burdens of a more or less successful capitalist modernization of the economy and society. The neoconservative doctrine blurs the relationship between the welcomed process of societal modernization on the one hand, and the lamented cultural development on the other. The neoconservative does not uncover the economic and social causes for the altered attitudes towards work, consumption, achievement and leisure. Consequently, he attributes all of the following—hedonism, the lack of social identification, the lack of obedience, narcissism, the withdrawal from status and achievement competition—to the domain of "culture." In fact, however, culture is intervening in the creation of all these problems in only a very indirect and mediated fashion.

7. Peter Steinfels, *The Neoconservatives* (1979), p. 65 [Foster's note]. Steinfels (b. 1941), American editor and journalist.

In the neoconservative view, those intellectuals who still feel themselves committed to the project of modernity are then presented as taking the place of those unanalyzed causes. The mood which feeds neoconservatism today in no way originates from discontent about the antinomian consequences[8] of a culture breaking from the museums into the stream of ordinary life. This discontent has not been called into life by modernist intellectuals. It is rooted in deep-seated reactions against the process of *societal* modernization. Under the pressures of the dynamics of economic growth and the organizational accomplishments of the state, this social modernization penetrates deeper and deeper into previous forms of human existence. I would describe this subordination of the life-worlds under the system's imperatives as a matter of disturbing the communicative infrastructure of everyday life.

Thus, for example, neopopulist protests only express in pointed fashion a widespread fear regarding the destruction of the urban and natural environment and of forms of human sociability. There is a certain irony about these protests in terms of neoconservatism. The tasks of passing on a cultural tradition, of social integration and of socialization require adherence to what I call communicative rationality. But the occasions for protest and discontent originate precisely when spheres of communicative action, centered on the reproduction and transmission of values and norms, are penetrated by a form of modernization guided by standards of economic and administrative rationality—in other words, by standards of rationalization quite different from those of communicative rationality on which those spheres depend. But neoconservative doctrines turn our attention precisely away from such societal processes: they project the causes, which they do not bring to light, onto the plane of a subversive culture and its advocates.

To be sure, cultural modernity generates its own aporias[9] as well. Independently from the consequences of *societal* modernization and within the perspective of *cultural* development itself, there originate motives for doubting the project of modernity. Having dealt with a feeble kind of criticism of modernity—that of neoconservatism—let me now move our discussion of modernity and its discontents into a different domain that touches on these aporias of cultural modernity—issues that often serve only as a pretense for those positions which either call for a postmodernity, recommend a return to some form of premodernity, or throw modernity radically overboard.

The Project of Enlightenment

The idea of modernity is intimately tied to the development of European art, but what I call "the project of modernity" comes only into focus when we dispense with the usual concentration upon art. Let me start a different analysis by recalling an idea from Max Weber. He characterized cultural modernity as the separation of the substantive reason expressed in religion and metaphysics into three autonomous spheres. They are: science, morality and art. These came to be differentiated because the unified world-views of religion and metaphysics fell apart. Since the 18th century, the problems inherited from these older world-views could be arranged so as to fall under

8. That is, the resulting rejection of socially established norms and morality.

9. Difficulties, logical impasses (a term often used in deconstructive criticism to indicate the point in a text where inherent contradictions render interpretation undecidable).

specific aspects of validity: truth, normative rightness, authenticity and beauty. They could then be handled as questions of knowledge, or of justice and morality, or of taste. Scientific discourse, theories of morality, jurisprudence, and the production and criticism of art could in turn be institutionalized. Each domain of culture could be made to correspond to cultural professions in which problems could be dealt with as the concern of special experts. This professionalized treatment of the cultural tradition brings to the fore the intrinsic structures of each of the three dimensions of culture. There appear the structures of cognitive-instrumental, of moral-practical and of aesthetic-expressive rationality, each of these under the control of specialists who seem more adept at being logical in these particular ways than other people are. As a result, the distance grows between the culture of the experts and that of the larger public. What accrues to culture through specialized treatment and reflection does not immediately and necessarily become the property of everyday praxis. With cultural rationalization of this sort, the threat increases that the life-world, whose traditional substance has already been devalued, will become more and more impoverished.

The project of modernity formulated in the 18th century by the philosophers of the Enlightenment consisted in their efforts to develop objective science, universal morality and law, and autonomous art according to their inner logic. At the same time, this project intended to release the cognitive potentials of each of these domains from their esoteric forms. The Enlightenment philosophers wanted to utilize this accumulation of specialized culture for the enrichment of everyday life—that is to say, for the rational organization of everyday social life.

Enlightenment thinkers of the cast of mind of Condorcet[1] still had the extravagant expectation that the arts and sciences would promote not only the control of natural forces but also understanding of the world and of the self, moral progress, the justice of institutions and even the happiness of human beings. The 20th century has shattered this optimism. The differentiation of science, morality and art has come to mean the autonomy of the segments treated by the specialist and their separation from the hermeneutics of everyday communication. This splitting off is the problem that has given rise to efforts to "negate" the culture of expertise. But the problem won't go away: should we try to hold on to the *intentions* of the Enlightenment, feeble as they may be, or should we declare the entire project of modernity a lost cause? I now want to return to the problem of artistic culture, having explained why, historically, aesthetic modernity is only a part of cultural modernity in general.

The False Programs of the Negation of Culture

Greatly oversimplifying, I would say that in the history of modern art one can detect a trend towards ever greater autonomy in the definition and practice of art. The category of "beauty" and the domain of beautiful objects were first constituted in the Renaissance. In the course of the 18th century, literature, the fine arts and music were institutionalized as activities indepen-

1. Marie-Jean-Antoine-Nicolas de Caritat, marquis de Condorcet (1743–1794), French Enlightenment mathematician and philosopher who believed in the ultimate perfectability of men and women.

dent from sacred and courtly life. Finally, around the middle of the 19th century an aestheticist conception of art emerged, which encouraged the artist to produce his work according to the distinct consciousness of art for art's sake. The autonomy of the aesthetic sphere could then become a deliberate project: the talented artist could lend authentic expression to those experiences he had in encountering his own de-centered subjectivity, detached from the constraints of routinized cognition and everyday action.

In the mid-19th century, in painting and literature, a movement began which Octavio Paz finds epitomized already in the art criticism of Baudelaire. Color, lines, sounds and movement ceased to serve primarily the cause of representation; the media of expression and the techniques of production themselves became the aesthetic object. Theodor W. Adorno[2] could therefore begin his *Aesthetic Theory* with the following sentence: "It is now taken for granted that nothing which concerns art can be taken for granted any more: neither art itself, nor art in its relationship to the whole, nor even the right of art to exist." And this is what surrealism then denied: *das Existenzrecht der Kunst als Kunst.*[3] To be sure, surrealism would not have challenged the right of art to exist, if modern art no longer had advanced a promise of happiness concerning its own relationship "to the whole" of life. For Schiller,[4] such a promise was delivered by aesthetic intuition, but not fulfilled by it. Schiller's *Letters on the Aesthetic Education of Man* speaks to us of a utopia reaching beyond art itself. But by the time of Baudelaire, who repeated this *promesse de bonheur*[5] via art, the utopia of reconciliation with society had gone sour. A relation of opposites had come into being; art had become a critical mirror, showing the irreconcilable nature of the aesthetic and the social worlds. This modernist transformation was all the more painfully realized, the more art alienated itself from life and withdrew into the untouchableness of complete autonomy. Out of such emotional currents finally gathered those explosive energies which unloaded in the surrealist attempt to blow up the autarkical sphere of art and to force a reconciliation of art and life.

But all those attempts to level art and life, fiction and praxis, appearance and reality to one plane; the attempts to remove the distinction between artifact and object of use, between conscious staging and spontaneous excitement; the attempts to declare everything to be art and everyone to be an artist, to retract all criteria and to equate aesthetic judgment with the expression of subjective experiences—all these undertakings have proved themselves to be sort of nonsense experiments. These experiments have served to bring back to life, and to illuminate all the more glaringly, exactly those structures of art which they were meant to dissolve. They gave a new legitimacy, as ends in themselves, to appearance as the medium of fiction, to the transcendence of the artwork over society, to the concentrated and planned character of artistic production as well as to the special cognitive status of judgments of taste. The radical attempt to negate art has ended up ironically by giving due exactly to these categories through which Enlightenment aesthetics had circumscribed its object domain. The surrealists waged the most

2. German philosopher and social critic (1903–1969; see above); *Aesthetic Theory* was published in 1970.
3. The right of art to exist as art (German).
4. FRIEDRICH VON SCHILLER (1759–1805), German poet, dramatist, and historian; for his *Letters* (1795), see above.
5. Promise of happiness or fulfillment (French).

extreme warfare, but two mistakes in particular destroyed their revolt. First, when the containers of an autonomously developed cultural sphere are shattered, the contents get dispersed. Nothing remains from a desublimated meaning or a destructured form; an emancipatory effect does not follow.

Their second mistake has more important consequences. In everyday communication, cognitive meanings, moral expectations, subjective expressions and evaluations must relate to one another. Communication processes need a cultural tradition covering all spheres—cognitive, moral-practical and expressive. A rationalized everyday life, therefore, could hardly be saved from cultural impoverishment through breaking open a single cultural sphere—art—and so providing access to just one of the specialized knowledge complexes. The surrealist revolt would have replaced only one abstraction.

In the spheres of theoretical knowledge and morality, there are parallels to this failed attempt of what we might call the false negation of culture. Only they are less pronounced. Since the days of the Young Hegelians,[6] there has been talk about the negation of philosophy. Since Marx,[7] the question of the relationship of theory and practice has been posed. However, Marxist intellectuals joined a social movement; and only at its peripheries were there sectarian attempts to carry out a program of the negation of philosophy similar to the surrealist program to negate art. A parallel to the surrealist mistakes becomes visible in these programs when one observes the consequences of dogmatism and of moral rigorism.

A reified[8] everyday praxis can be cured only by creating unconstrained interaction of the cognitive with the moral-practical and the aesthetic-expressive elements. Reification cannot be overcome by forcing just one of those highly stylized cultural spheres to open up and become more accessible. Instead, we see under certain circumstances a relationship emerge between terroristic activities and the over-extension of any one of these spheres into other domains: examples would be tendencies to aestheticize politics, or to replace politics by moral rigorism or to submit it to the dogmatism of a doctrine. These phenomena should not lead us, however, into denouncing the intentions of the surviving Enlightenment tradition as intentions rooted in a "terroristic reason." Those who lump together the very project of modernity with the state of consciousness and the spectacular action of the individual terrorist are no less short-sighted than those who would claim that the incomparably more persistent and extensive bureaucratic terror practiced in the dark, in the cellars of the military and secret police, and in camps and institutions, is the *raison d'être* of the modern state, only because this kind of administrative terror makes use of the coercive means of modern bureaucracies.

Alternatives

I think that instead of giving up modernity and its project as a lost cause, we should learn from the mistakes of those extravagant programs which have tried to negate modernity. Perhaps the types of reception of art may offer an example which at least indicates the direction of a way out.

6. Early leftist German followers of the German idealist philosopher GEORG WILHELM FRIEDRICH HEGEL (1770–1831).

7. KARL MARX (1818–1883), German social, economic, and political philosopher and revolutionary.

8. Ossified.

Bourgeois art had two expectations at once from its audience. On the one hand, the layman who enjoyed art should educate himself to become an expert. On the other hand, he should also behave as a competent consumer who uses art and relates aesthetic experiences to his own life problems. This second, and seemingly harmless, manner of experiencing art has lost its radical implications exactly because it had a confused relation to the attitude of being expert and professional.

To be sure, artistic production would dry up, if it were not carried out in the form of a specialized treatment of autonomous problems and if it were to cease to be the concern of experts who do not pay so much attention to exoteric questions. Both artists and critics accept thereby the fact that such problems fall under the spell of what I earlier called the "inner logic" of a cultural domain. But this sharp delineation, this exclusive concentration on one aspect of validity alone and the exclusion of aspects of truth and justice, break down as soon as aesthetic experience is drawn into an individual life history and is absorbed into ordinary life. The reception of art by the layman, or by the "everyday expert," goes in a rather different direction than the reception of art by the professional critic.

Albrecht Wellmer[9] has drawn my attention to one way that an aesthetic experience which is not framed around the experts' critical judgments of taste can have its significance altered: as soon as such an experience is used to illuminate a life-historical situation and is related to life problems, it enters into a language game which is no longer that of the aesthetic critic. The aesthetic experience then not only renews the interpretation of our needs in whose light we perceive the world. It permeates as well our cognitive significations and our normative expectations and changes the manner in which all these moments refer to one another. Let me give an example of this process.

This manner of receiving and relating to art is suggested in the first volume of the work *The Aesthetics of Resistance* by the German-Swedish writer Peter Weiss. Weiss describes the process of reappropriating art by presenting a group of politically motivated, knowledge-hungry workers in 1937 in Berlin.[1] These were young people who, through an evening high-school education, acquired the intellectual means to fathom the general and social history of European art. Out of the resilient edifice of this objective mind, embodied in works of art which they saw again and again in the museums in Berlin, they started removing their own chips of stone, which they gathered together and reassembled in the context of their own milieu. This milieu was far removed from that of traditional education as well as from the then existing regime. These young workers went back and forth between the edifice of European art and their own milieu until they were able to illuminate both.

In examples like this which illustrate the reappropriation of the expert's culture from the standpoint of the life-world, we can discern an element which does justice to the intentions of the hopeless surrealist revolts, perhaps even more to Brecht's[2] and Benjamin's interests in how art works, which having lost their aura, could yet be received in illuminating ways. In sum,

9. German philosopher (b. 1933).
1. The reference is to the novel *Die Ästhetik des Widerstands* (3 vols., 1975–81) by the author [1916–1982] perhaps best known in the United States for his 1965 play *Marat / Sade*. The work of art "reappropriated" by the workers is the Pergamon altar, emblem of power, classicism, and rationality [Foster's note].
2. Bertolt Brecht (1898–1956), German Marxist playwright. On the "aura" of the artwork, see Benjamin, "The Work of Art in the Age of Mechanical Reproduction" (1932; see above).

the project of modernity has not yet been fulfilled. And the reception of art is only one of at least three of its aspects. The project aims at a differentiated relinking of modern culture with an everyday praxis that still depends on vital heritages, but would be impoverished through mere traditionalism. This new connection, however, can only be established under the condition that societal modernization will also be steered in a different direction. The life-world has to become able to develop institutions out of itself which set limits to the internal dynamics and imperatives of an almost autonomous economic system and its administrative complements.

If I am not mistaken, the chances for this today are not very good. More or less in the entire Western world a climate has developed that furthers capitalist modernization processes as well as trends critical of cultural modernism. The disillusionment with the very failures of those programs that called for the negation of art and philosophy has come to serve as a pretense for conservative positions. Let me briefly distinguish the antimodernism of the "young conservatives" from the premodernism of the "old conservatives" and from the postmodernism of the neoconservatives.

The "young conservatives" recapitulate the basic experience of aesthetic modernity. They claim as their own the revelations of a decentered subjectivity, emancipated from the imperatives of work and usefulness, and with this experience they step outside the modern world. On the basis of modernistic attitudes they justify an irreconcilable antimodernism. They remove into the sphere of the far-away and the archaic the spontaneous powers of imagination, self-experience and emotion. To instrumental reason they juxtapose in Manichean fashion[3] a principle only accessible through evocation, be it the will to power or sovereignty, Being or the Dionysiac force[4] of the poetical. In France this line leads from Georges Bataille via Michel Foucault to Jacques Derrida.[5]

The "old conservatives" do not allow themselves to be contaminated by cultural modernism. They observe the decline of substantive reason, the differentiation of science, morality and art, the modern world view and its merely procedural rationality, with sadness and recommend a withdrawal to a position *anterior* to modernity. Neo-Aristotelianism, in particular, enjoys a certain success today. In view of the problematic of ecology, it allows itself to call for a cosmological ethic. (As belonging to this school, which originates with Leo Strauss, one can count the interesting works of Hans Jonas and Robert Spaemann.)[6]

Finally, the neoconservatives welcome the development of modern science, as long as this only goes beyond its sphere to carry forward technical progress, capitalist growth and rational administration. Moreover, they rec-

3. That is, as a polar opposite (like the followers of Machaeism, a religion founded in the 3d c. C.E., who saw the world as divided between two opposed forces—good and evil, spirit and matter, etc.).
4. A reference to *The Birth of Tragedy* (1872; see above) by FRIEDRICH NIETZSCHE, who saw in Greek culture a dynamic tension between the gods Apollo (representing form and reason) and Dionysus (representing frenzy and emotion). He also championed the idea of "the will to power."
5. All important French writers: Bataille (1897–1962), librarian and novelist; FOUCAULT (1926–1984), philosopher and historian of ideas; and DERRIDA (b. 1930), deconstructionist philosopher and critic.
6. All philosophers: Strauss (1899–1973), German-born American political philosopher; Jonas (1903–1993), German-born American moral philosopher; and Spaemann (b. 1927), German moral philosopher. Any philosopher who adapts the thought of ARISTOTLE (384–322 B.C.E.) to his or her own times may be called a "neo-Aristotelian"; Strauss argued in particular for the superiority of Aristotle's political science to the behavioralist approach dominant in the United States in the mid–20th century.

ommend a politics of defusing the explosive content of cultural modernity. According to one thesis, science, when properly understood, has become irrevocably meaningless for the orientation of the life-world. A further thesis is that politics must be kept as far aloof as possible from the demands of moral-practical justification. And a third thesis asserts the pure immanence of art, disputes that it has a utopian content, and points to its illusory character in order to limit the aesthetic experience to privacy. (One could name here the early Wittgenstein, Carl Schmitt of the middle period, and Gottfried Benn[7] of the late period.) But with the decisive confinement of science, morality and art to autonomous spheres separated from the life-world and administered by experts, what remains from the project of cultural modernity is only what we would have if we were to give up the project of modernity altogether. As a replacement one points to traditions which, however, are held to be immune to demands of (normative) justification and validation.

This typology is like any other, of course, a simplification, but it may not prove totally useless for the analysis of contemporary intellectual and political confrontations. I fear that the ideas of antimodernity, together with an additional touch of premodernity, are becoming popular in the circles of alternative culture. When one observes the transformations of consciousness within political parties in Germany, a new ideological shift (*Tendenzwende*) becomes visible. And this is the alliance of postmodernists with premodernists. It seems to me that there is no party in particular that monopolizes the abuse of intellectuals and the position of neoconservatism. I therefore have good reason to be thankful for the liberal spirit in which the city of Frankfurt offers me a prize bearing the name of Theodor Adorno, a most significant son of this city, who as philosopher and writer has stamped the image of the intellectual in our country in incomparable fashion, who, even more, has become the very image of emulation for the intellectual.

1980

7. German poet (1886–1956). Ludwig Wittgenstein (1889–1951), Austrian-born English philosopher. Schmitt (1888–1985), German political philosopher.

ADRIENNE RICH
b. 1929

One of the most celebrated poets of her generation, Adrienne Rich has also been a major voice in American feminism since the late 1960s. In her nonfictional prose and in her poetry, she has explored the ways in which patriarchal society oppresses women and the ways in which women have responded to that oppression. While her analysis of "compulsory heterosexuality" will very likely prove her most lasting contribution to literary and social theory, Rich's contributions to feminist thought cover a wide range of topics, from the silencing of women's voices to the history of childbirth and motherhood. Like Elaine Showalter and SUSAN BORDO, Rich links patriarchal oppression to power exerted directly (and often violently) on women's bodies. But her concern with the psychic and social underpinnings of sexual identity also links Rich's work to the queer theory of JUDITH BUTLER and EVE KOSOFSKY SEDGWICK.

Born and raised in a Jewish family in Baltimore, the precocious Rich was chosen by the poet W. H. Auden as a winner of the prestigious Yale Younger Poets Award at the age of twenty-two, the year she graduated from Radcliffe College. She traveled in Europe for the next two years on a Guggenheim Fellowship. On her return, she married Alfred Conrad, an economist who taught at Harvard University. Between 1953 and 1967, she raised three sons while continuing to publish poetry. When the family moved to New York City in 1966, she began teaching at various local colleges and universities. Her husband committed suicide in 1970; Rich has written some poetry about this event, but the reasons for and circumstances surrounding it remain obscure.

Rich became increasingly identified with the women's movement throughout the 1970s, composing poetry with feminist themes but also for the first time writing prose. She published essays and an important historical, theoretical, and first-person study of motherhood, *Of Woman Born: Motherhood as Experience and Institution* (1976). During this decade, *Diving into the Wreck* (1973) won the National Book Award for poetry, solidifying her status as a major literary figure.

By the mid-1970s Rich was openly lesbian, and in her poetry and prose she was exploring all aspects of what she calls in our selection "lesbian experience." Her work in the 1980s and 1990s, while still exploring feminist and lesbian themes, also included new attempts to connect to her Jewishness, her family (especially her father), and the poetic tradition. Rich was a visiting professor at Cornell University from 1981 to 1987, and she taught at Stanford University from 1987 to 1997. Rich has received many honorary doctorates and literary prizes, but such awards do not convey how revered a figure she is. An inspiration especially for lesbian women and feminists, Rich is admired almost universally for her strength of character, staunch integrity, and immense talents as a poet and a writer.

The essay "Compulsory Heterosexuality and Lesbian Existence" (1980) has been widely influential. When it first appeared, it marked (along with several roughly contemporaneous works, many of them cited in Rich's first footnote) the end of "sisterhood" feminism—the assumption that all women were "sisters" in their shared oppression. Rich highlights the presence of both lesbians and heterosexual women in the feminist movement and calls on feminism to acknowledge its fear of lesbians. Because those hostile to feminism often dismiss it as the complaints of a small group of lesbians, many 1970s feminists went out of their way to prove their heterosexuality. Lesbians and the whole topic of lesbian experience became practically taboo within the movement (except in its more radical separatist branches, which the mainstream also held at a distance). Thus Rich's essay, along with the feminist work of women of color and of working-class women, challenged a feminism that purported to speak for all women yet assumed the viewpoint of a heterosexual, middle-class white woman. Much of the feminist work of the 1980s was devoted to considering the ramifications of these differences (of race, class, and sexual orientation) for the category "woman" and to attending to how such differences would strengthen or weaken feminist activism.

Rich's main purpose, however, is not so much to introduce or explore difference as to consider the extent to which heterosexual desire and identity are fundamental to women's oppression. Heterosexuality, she argues, is not natural but social, and it should be analyzed as we would any social institution. Similar arguments are advanced by the lesbian theorists MONIQUE WITTIG and BONNIE ZIMMERMAN. How is heterosexuality established and maintained? What groups resist it? What alternatives must be suppressed for it to prevail? Who benefits from and who is harmed by this institution's dominance? What forms of enforcement underwrite that dominance? Rich argues that heterosexuality is compulsory because only partners of the opposite sex are deemed appropriate, all same-sex desire must be denied or indulged in secret, and various kinds of same-sex bonding (including friendships) are viewed with suspicion. Compulsory heterosexuality functions to ensure that women are sexually accessible to men, with consent or choice on the women's part neither legally nor practically taken into account. In sum, compulsory heterosexuality is an institution that punishes those who are not heterosexual and systematically ensures the power of men over women.

Because compulsory sexuality is central to creating and preserving the inequality between men and women, Rich argues that "the issue feminists have to address is not simple 'gender inequality' nor the domination of culture by males nor mere 'taboos against homosexuality,' but the enforcement of heterosexuality for women as a means of assuring male right of physical, economic, and emotional access." Feminism cannot truly comprehend the sources and system of inequality if it does not analyze the institution of compulsory heterosexuality. In the years since Rich published her essay, feminists have actively investigated the topics suggested by this charge.

Three topics in Rich's essay have been especially important for feminist literary theory: sexualized relations of power within institutions, lesbian experience, and questions of sexual identity. To begin with, Rich argues that women do not simply face the trials and tribulations experienced by all subordinates in hierarchical institutions; they must also present themselves as "attractive" according to dominant standards of heterosexual desirability and be concerned with sexuality in the appropriate ways (e.g., be flirtatious within the proper bounds, be supportive of male superiors). Such expectations, rarely conscious, even more rarely explicit, permeate public male-female relationships. They form part of a larger unwritten set of rules about the relative positions of men and women in society.

Second, *lesbian experience*—and its corollary term, the *lesbian continuum*—challenges the notion that women "need" men by calling attention to all the ways in which women interact with one another, all the activities central to their lives, that do not involve connection to a man. Rich wants to highlight both how hostile to and threatened by women's independent action patriarchal society is *and* the prevalence of such action despite the price (sometimes very high) paid for it. The lesbian continuum encompasses a wide variety of relationships between and among women, ranging from "the sharing of a rich inner life, the bonding against male tyranny, [to] the giving and receiving of practical and political support." By desexualizing the term *lesbian*, Rich calls our attention to the variety of bonds formed between women and to the various functions those bonds play in women's lives.

Finally, Rich's essay looks forward to the queer theory of the 1990s by asking a crucial question: How is sexual identity formed? Through what processes of psychic identification does a self form heterosexual and/or homosexual desires? While Rich is more suspicious of psychoanalytic understandings of these processes than are many subsequent queer theorists (such as Butler), she fully recognizes that the "law of compulsory heterosexuality" plays a crucial role in the formation of selves, even as she notes that the early bond of the girl baby with her mother works against the injunction to be heterosexual. In addition, the notion of the lesbian continuum recognizes that sexuality comes in many forms and results in many different behaviors—a variety badly captured by the simple dichotomy homosexual/heterosexual.

Rich comes very close here to queer theory's later interest in examples that confound received categories, that challenge the terms by which we make the world and our experiences intelligible. However, she is impatient with the poststructuralist and French psychoanalytic theory that stands behind much queer theory; in articulating similar concepts, she uses her own idiom. An uneasy truce has prevailed between Rich and most theoretically minded American feminists, with both sides carefully avoiding direct attacks on the other. Desire, as Rich discovered in her own life, is neither unitary nor fixed once for all. Women especially suffer in a heterosexual regime that ignores the fluidity of desire in favor of channeling that desire toward heterosexual unions in which the needs of the male are primary.

BIBLIOGRAPHY

Rich has published nearly two dozen books of poetry. Her prose is collected in *On Lies, Secrets, and Silence: Selected Prose, 1966–1978* (1979), *Blood, Bread, and Poetry: Selected Prose, 1979–1985* (1986), and *What Is Found There: Notebooks on Poetry and Politics* (1993). Her book on motherhood, *Of Woman Born: Motherhood as Experience and Institution*, was published in 1976. *Adrienne Rich's Poetry and Prose*, edited by Barbara Charlesworth Gelpi and Albert Gelpi (1993), offers selections from the whole span of Rich's career, along with critical essays on her work. The best biographical source remains Wendy Martin's "Adrienne Rich," in *American Writers*, supplement 1, part 2 (1979). For more recent information, see the entry on Rich in *Contemporary Authors*, New Revision Series 53 (1997).

Reading Adrienne Rich: Reviews and ReVisions 1951–1981, edited by Jane Roberta Cooper (1984), is a collection of critical responses to Rich. A book-length treatment of Rich's feminist work is Liz Yorke's *Adrienne Rich: Passion, Politics and the Body* (1997). Alice Templeton's *The Dream and the Dialogue: Adrienne Rich's Feminist Poetics* (1994) focuses primarily on the poetry. Two broader studies that consider Rich's contribution to feminism are noteworthy: Krista Ratcliff's *Anglo-American Feminist Challenges to the Rhetorical Tradition: Virginia Woolf, Mary Daly, Adrienne Rich* (1996) and Sabine Sielke's *Fashioning the Female Subject: The Intertextual Networking of Dickinson, Moore, and Rich* (1997). Both biographical sources noted above also offer good working bibliographies of Rich's own writings and of critical responses to the work.

From Compulsory Heterosexuality and Lesbian Existence[1]

Foreword (1983)

I want to say a little about the way "Compulsory Heterosexuality" was originally conceived and the context in which we are now living. It was written in part to challenge the erasure of lesbian existence from so much of scholarly feminist literature, an erasure which I felt (and feel) to be not just anti-lesbian, but anti-feminist in its consequences, and to distort the experience of heterosexual women as well. It was not written to widen divisions but to encourage heterosexual feminists to examine heterosexuality as a political institution which disempowers women—and to change it. I also hoped that other lesbians would feel the depth and breadth of woman identification and woman bonding that has run like a continuous though stifled theme through the heterosexual experience, and that this would become increasingly a politically activating impulse, not simply a validation of personal lives. I wanted the essay to suggest new kinds of criticism, to incite new questions in classrooms and academic journals, and to sketch, at least, some bridge over the gap between *lesbian* and *feminist*. I wanted, at the very least, for feminists to find it less possible to read, write, or teach from a perspective of unexamined heterocentricity.

Within the three years since I wrote "Compulsory Heterosexuality"—with this energy of hope and desire—the pressures to conform in a society increasingly conservative in mood have become more intense. The New Right's[2]

1. This essay was first published in *Signs: Journal of Women in Culture and Society* (1980). The shorter version printed here originally appeared in *Adrienne Rich's Poetry and Prose*, edited by Barbara Charlesworth Gelpi and Albert Gelpi (1993); the asterisks mark their deletions.

2. Social or cultural conservatives who stress so-called moral and "family" values, and who are often

messages to women have been, precisely, that we are the emotional and sexual property of men, and that the autonomy and equality of women threaten family, religion, and state. The institutions by which women have traditionally been controlled—patriarchal motherhood, economic exploitation, the nuclear family, compulsory heterosexuality—are being strengthened by legislation, religious fiat, media imagery, and efforts at censorship. In a worsening economy, the single mother trying to support her children confronts the feminization of poverty which Joyce Miller of the National Coalition of Labor Union Women has named one of the major issues of the 1980s. The lesbian, unless in disguise, faces discrimination in hiring and harassment and violence in the street. Even within feminist-inspired institutions such as battered-women's shelters and Women's Studies programs, open lesbians are fired and others warned to stay in the closet. The retreat into sameness—assimilation for those who can manage it—is the most passive and debilitating of responses to political repression, economic insecurity, and a renewed open season on difference.

I want to note that documentation of male violence against women—within the home especially—has been accumulating rapidly in this period. At the same time, in the realm of literature which depicts woman bonding and woman identification as essential for female survival, a steady stream of writing and criticism has been coming from women of color in general and lesbians of color in particular—the latter group being even more profoundly erased in academic feminist scholarship by the double bias of racism and homophobia.[3]

There has recently been an intensified debate on female sexuality among feminists and lesbians, with lines often furiously and bitterly drawn, with *sadomasochism* and *pornography* as key words which are variously defined according to who is talking.[4] The depth of women's rage and fear regarding sexuality and its relation to power and pain is real, even when the dialogue sounds simplistic, self-righteous, or like parallel monologues.

Because of all these developments, there are parts of this essay that I would word differently, qualify, or expand if I were writing it today. But I continue

---

self-identified Christians. They played a large role in the U.S. election of President Ronald Reagan in 1980.

3. See, for example, PAULA GUNN ALLEN, *The Sacred Hoop: Recovering the Feminine in American Indian Traditions* (Boston: Beacon, 1986); Beth Brant, ed., *A Gathering of Spirit: Writing and Art by North American Indian Women* (Montpelier, Vt.: Sinister Wisdom Books, 1984); GLORIA ANZALDÚA and Cherríe Moraga, eds., *This Bridge Called My Back: Writings by Radical Women of Color* (Watertown, Mass.: Persephone, 1981; distributed by Kitchen Table/Women of Color Press, Albany, N.Y.); J. R. Roberts, *Black Lesbians: An Annotated Bibliography* (Tallahassee, Fla.: Naiad, 1981); BARBARA SMITH, ed., *Home Girls: A Black Feminist Anthology* (Albany, N.Y.: Kitchen Table/Women of Color Press, 1984). As Lorraine Bethel and Barbara Smith pointed out in *Conditions* 5: *The Black Women's Issue* (1980), a great deal of fiction by Black women depicts primary relationships between women. I would like to cite here the work of Ama Ata Aidoo, Toni Cade Bambara, Buchi Emecheta, Bessie Head, ZORA NEALE HURSTON, Alice Walker. Donna Allegra, Red Jordan Arobateau, Audre Lorde, Ann Allen Shockley, among others, who write directly as Black lesbians. For fiction by other lesbians of color, see Elly Bulkin, ed., *Lesbian Fiction: An Anthology* (Watertown, Mass.: Persephone, 1981).

See also, for accounts of contemporary Jewish-lesbian existence, Evelyn Torton Beck, ed., *Nice Jewish Girls: A Lesbian Anthology* (Watertown, Mass.: Persephone, 1982; distributed by Crossing Press, Trumansburg, N.Y.); Alice Bloch, *Lifetime Guarantee* (Watertown, Mass.: Persephone, 1982); and Melanie Kaye-Kantrowitz and Irena Klepfisz, eds., *The Tribe of Dina: A Jewish Women's Anthology* (Montpelier, Vt.: Sinister Wisdom Books, 1986).

The earliest formulation that I know of heterosexuality as an institution was in the lesbian-feminist paper *The Furies*, founded in 1971. For a collection of articles from that paper, see Nancy Myron and Charlotte Bunch, eds., *Lesbianism and the Women's Movement* (Oakland, Calif.: Diana Press, 1975; distributed by Crossing Press, Trumansburg, N.Y.) [Rich's note].

4. The so-called sex wars within feminism—with the status of sadomasochism a key issue as feminists argued about pornography—flared in the wake of an academic conference, "Toward a Politics of Sexuality," held at Barnard College in April 1982.

to think that heterosexual feminists will draw political strength for change from taking a critical stance toward the ideology which *demands* heterosexuality, and that lesbians cannot assume that we are untouched by that ideology and the institutions founded upon it. There is nothing about such a critique that requires us to think of ourselves as victims, as having been brainwashed or totally powerless. Coercion and compulsion are among the conditions in which women have learned to recognize our strength. Resistance is a major theme in this essay and in the study of women's lives, if we know what we are looking for.

I

> Biologically men have only one innate orientation—a sexual one that draws them to women,—while women have two innate orientations, sexual toward men and reproductive toward their young.[5]

> I was a woman terribly vulnerable, critical, using femaleness as a sort of standard or yardstick to measure and discard men. Yes—something like that. I was an Anna who invited defeat from men without ever being conscious of it. (But I am conscious of it. And being conscious of it means I shall leave it all behind me and become—but what?) I was stuck fast in an emotion common to women of our time, that can turn them bitter, or Lesbian, or solitary. Yes, that Anna during that time was . . .
>
> [Another blank line across the page:][6]

The bias of compulsory heterosexuality, through which lesbian experience is perceived on a scale ranging from deviant to abhorrent or simply rendered invisible, could be illustrated from many texts other than the two just preceding. The assumption made by Rossi, that women are "innately" sexually oriented only toward men, and that made by Lessing, that the lesbian is simply acting out of her bitterness toward men, are by no means theirs alone; these assumptions are widely current in literature and in the social sciences.

I am concerned here with two other matters as well: first, how and why women's choice of women as passionate comrades, life partners, co-workers, lovers, community has been crushed, invalidated, forced into hiding and disguise; and second, the virtual or total neglect of lesbian existence in a wide range of writings, including feminist scholarship. Obviously there is a connection here. I believe that much feminist theory and criticism is stranded on this shoal.

My organizing impulse is the belief that it is not enough for feminist thought that specifically lesbian texts exist. Any theory or cultural/political creation that treats lesbian existence as a marginal or less "natural" phenomenon, as mere "sexual preference," or as the mirror image of either heterosexual or male homosexual relations is profoundly weakened thereby, whatever its other contributions. Feminist theory can no longer afford merely to voice a toleration of "lesbianism" as an "alternative life style" or make

5. Alice Rossi, "Children and Work in the Lives of Women," paper delivered at the University of Arizona, Tucson, February 1976 [Rich's note].

6. Doris Lessing, *The Golden Notebook* (1962; reprint, New York: Bantam, 1977), p. 480 [Rich's note].

token allusion to lesbians. A feminist critique of compulsory heterosexual orientation for women is long overdue. In this exploratory paper, I shall try to show why.

* * *

II

If women are the earliest sources of emotional caring and physical nurture for both female and male children, it would seem logical, from a feminist perspective at least, to pose the following questions: whether the search for love and tenderness in both sexes does not originally lead toward women; *why in fact women would ever redirect that search*; why species survival, the means of impregnation, and emotional/erotic relationships should ever have become so rigidly identified with each other; and why such violent strictures should be found necessary to enforce women's total emotional, erotic loyalty and subservience to men. I doubt that enough feminist scholars and theorists have taken the pains to acknowledge the societal forces which wrench women's emotional and erotic energies away from themselves and other women and from woman-identified values. These forces, as I shall try to show, range from literal physical enslavement to the disguising and distorting of possible options.

I do not assume that mothering by women is a "sufficient cause" of lesbian existence. But the issue of mothering by women has been much in the air of late, usually accompanied by the view that increased parenting by men would minimize antagonism between the sexes and equalize the sexual imbalance of power of males over females. These discussions are carried on without reference to compulsory heterosexuality as a phenomenon, let alone as an ideology. I do not wish to psychologize here, but rather to identify sources of male power. I believe large numbers of men could, in fact, undertake child care on a large scale without radically altering the balance of male power in a male-identified society.

In her essay "The Origin of the Family," Kathleen Gough lists eight characteristics of male power in archaic and contemporary societies which I would like to use as a framework: "men's ability to deny women sexuality or to force it upon them; to command or exploit their labor to control their produce; to control or rob them of their children; to confine them physically and prevent their movements; to use them as objects in male transactions; to cramp their creativeness; or to withhold from them large areas of the society's knowledge and cultural attainments."[7] (Gough does not perceive these power characteristics as specifically enforcing heterosexuality, only as producing sexual inequality.) Below, Gough's words appear in italics; the elaboration of each of her categories, in brackets, is my own.

Characteristics of male power include *the power of men*

1. *to deny women* [their own] *sexuality*—[by means of clitoridectomy and infibulation;[8] chastity belts; punishment, including death, for

7. Kathleen Gough, "The Origin of the Family," in *Toward an Anthropology of Women*, ed. Rayna Reiter (New York: Monthly Review Press, 1975), pp. 60–70 [Rich's note].

8. The stitching together of the vulva after a clitoridectomy, leaving a small opening for the passage of urine and menstrual blood. Clitoridectomy: usually the removal of the clitoris occurs in the context of a cultural rite of passage to womanhood, but at times such surgery has been recommended to curb sexual desire.

female adultery; punishment, including death, for lesbian sexuality; psychoanalytic denial of the clitoris;[9] strictures against masturbation; denial of maternal and postmenopausal sensuality; unnecessary hysterectomy; pseudolesbian images in the media and literature; closing of archives and destruction of documents relating to lesbian existence]

2. *or to force it* [male sexuality] *upon them*—[by means of rape (including marital rape) and wife beating; father-daughter, brother-sister incest; the socialization of women to feel that male sexual "drive" amounts to a right;[1] idealization of heterosexual romance in art, literature, the media, advertising, etc.; child marriage; arranged marriage; prostitution; the harem; psychoanalytic doctrines of frigidity and vaginal orgasm;[2] pornographic depictions of women responding pleasurably to sexual violence and humiliation (a subliminal message being that sadistic heterosexuality is more "normal" than sensuality between women)]
3. *to command or exploit their labor to control their produce*—[by means of the institutions of marriage and motherhood as unpaid production; the horizontal segregation of women in paid employment;[3] the decoy of the upwardly mobile token woman; male control of abortion, contraception, sterilization, and childbirth; pimping; female infanticide, which robs mothers of daughters and contributes to generalized devaluation of women]
4. *to control or rob them of their children*—[by means of father right and "legal kidnapping";[4] enforced sterilization, systematized infanticide; seizure of children from lesbian mothers by the courts; the malpractice of male obstetrics; use of the mother as "token torturer"[5] in genital mutilation or in binding the daughter's feet (or mind) to fit her for marriage]
5. *to confine them physically and prevent their movement*—[by means of rape as terrorism, keeping women off the streets; purdah; foot binding; atrophying of women's athletic capabilities; high heels and "feminine" dress codes in fashions; the veil;[6] sexual harassment on the streets; horizontal segregation of women in employment; prescriptions for "full-time" mothering at home; enforced economic dependence of wives]
6. *to use them as objects in male transactions*—[use of women as "gifts"; bride price; pimping; arranged marriage; use of women as entertain-

9. The persistent medical claim, prior to the 1970s, that women's sexual pleasure derived from stimulation of the clitoris is not a "true" orgasm.
1. Kathleen Barry, *Female Sexual Slavery* (Englewood Cliffs, N.J.: Prentice-Hall, 1979), pp. 216–19 [Rich's note].
2. The notion that orgasm is achieved through vaginal stimulation (not the case for most women).
3. That is, at the lowest levels of wage labor.
4. Anna Demeter, *Legal Kidnapping* (Boston: Beacon, 1979), pp. xx, 126–28 [Rich's note]. Traditionally, fathers have sole rights to their children; and even when mothers win custody, the courts have consistently maintained the father's right of access to children despite a history of abuse or of financial or emotional neglect. Denied access by mothers, fathers have sometimes resorted to kidnappings, later upheld by the courts as legal.
5. Mary Daly, *Gyn/Ecology: The Metaethics of Radical Feminism* (Boston: Beacon, 1978), pp. 139–41, 163–65 [Rich's note]. The practice of foot binding among upper-class women in pre-Communist China was largely aimed at male sexual gratification.
6. Islamic women often wear a veil or *hijab* (sometimes covering their entire body); to "take the veil" in Western countries is to become a nun and traditionally to retire to a convent.

ers to facilitate male deals—e.g., wife-hostess, cocktail waitress required to dress for male sexual titillation, call girls, "bunnies," geisha, *kisaeng*[7] prostitutes, secretaries]

7. *to cramp their creativeness*—[witch persecutions as campaigns against midwives and female healers, and as pogrom against independent, "unassimilated" women;[8] definition of male pursuits as more valuable than female within any culture, so that cultural values become the embodiment of male subjectivity; restriction of female self-fulfillment to marriage and motherhood; sexual exploitation of women by male artists and teachers; the social and economic disruption of women's creative aspirations;[9] erasure of female tradition][1]
8. *to withhold from them large areas of the society's knowledge and cultural attainments*—[by means of noneducation of females; the "Great Silence" regarding women and particularly lesbian existence in history and culture;[2] sex-role tracking which deflects women from science, technology, and other "masculine" pursuits; male social/professional bonding which excludes women; discrimination against women in the professions]

These are some of the methods by which male power is manifested and maintained. Looking at the schema, what surely impresses itself is the fact that we are confronting not a simple maintenance of inequality and property possession, but a pervasive cluster of forces, ranging from physical brutality to control of consciousness, which suggests that an enormous potential counterforce is having to be restrained.

Some of the forms by which male power manifests itself are more easily recognizable as enforcing heterosexuality on women than are others. Yet each one I have listed adds to the cluster of forces within which women have been convinced that marriage and sexual orientation toward men are inevitable—even if unsatisfying or oppressive—components of their lives. The chastity belt; child marriage; erasure of lesbian existence (except as exotic and perverse) in art, literature, film; idealization of heterosexual romance and marriage—these are some fairly obvious forms of compulsion, the first two exemplifying physical force, the second two control of consciousness. While clitoridectomy has been assailed by feminists as a form of woman torture,[3] Kathleen Barry first pointed out that it is not simply a way of turning

7. Appropriated (Korean); that is, women forced into prostitution. "Bunnies": women working at Playboy Clubs.

8. Barbara Ehrenreich and Deirdre English, *Witches, Midwives, and Nurses: A History of Women Healers* (Old Westbury, N.Y.: Feminist Press, 1973); Andrea Dworkin, *Woman Hating* (New York: Dutton, 1974), pp. 118–54; Daly, pp. 178–222 [Rich's note].

9. See VIRGINIA WOOLF *A Room of One's Own* (London: Hogarth, 1929), and *id.*, *Three Guineas* (New York: Harcourt Brace, [1938] 1966); Tillie Olsen, *Silences* (Boston: Delacorte, 1978); Michelle Cliff, "The Resonance of Interruption," *Chrysalis: A Magazine of Women's Culture* 8 (1979): 29–37 [Rich's note]. For *A Room of One's Own*, see above.

1. Mary Daly, *Beyond God the Father* (Boston: Beacon, 1973), pp. 347–51; Olsen, pp. 22–46 [Rich's note].

2. Daly, *Beyond God the Father*, p. 93 [Rich's note].

3. Fran P. Hosken, "The Violence of Power: Genital Mutilation of Females," *Heresies: A Feminist Journal of Art and Politics* 6 (1979): 28–35; Diana Russell and Nicole van de Ven, eds., *Proceedings of the Informational Tribunal of Crimes Against Women* (Millbrae, Calif.: Les Femmes, 1976), pp. 194–95. See especially "Circumcision of Girls," in Nawal El Saadawi, *The Hidden Face of Eve: Women in the Arab World* (Boston: Beacon, 1982), pp. 33–43 [Rich's note].

the young girl into a "marriageable" woman through brutal surgery. It intends that women in the intimate proximity of polygynous marriage will not form sexual relationships with each other, that—from a male, genital-fetishist[4] perspective—female erotic connections, even in a sex-segregated situation, will be literally excised.[5]

The function of pornography as an influence on consciousness is a major public issue of our time, when a multibillion-dollar industry has the power to disseminate increasingly sadistic, women-degrading visual images. But even so-called soft-core pornography and advertising depict women as objects of sexual appetite devoid of emotional context, without individual meaning or personality—essentially as a sexual commodity to be consumed by males. (So-called lesbian pornography, created for the male voyeuristic eye, is equally devoid of emotional context or individual personality.) The most pernicious message relayed by pornography is that women are natural sexual prey to men and love it, that sexuality and violence are congruent, and that for women sex is essentially masochistic, humiliation pleasurable, physical abuse erotic. But along with this message comes another, not always recognized: that enforced submission and the use of cruelty, if played out in heterosexual pairing, is sexually "normal," while sensuality between women, including erotic mutuality and respect, is "queer," "sick," and either pornographic in itself or not very exciting compared with the sexuality of whips and bondage.[6] Pornography does not simply create a climate in which sex and violence are interchangeable; *it widens the range of behavior considered acceptable from men in heterosexual intercourse*—behavior which reiteratively strips women of their autonomy, dignity, and sexual potential, including the potential of loving and being loved by women in mutuality and integrity.

In her brilliant study *Sexual Harassment of Working Women: A Case of Sex Discrimination*, Catharine A. MacKinnon delineates the intersection of compulsory heterosexuality and economics. Under capitalism, women are horizontally segregated by gender and occupy a structurally inferior position in the workplace. This is hardly news, but MacKinnon raises the question why, even if capitalism "requires some collection of individuals to occupy low-status, low-paying positions . . . such persons must be biologically female," and goes on to point out that "the fact that male employers often do not hire qualified women, *even when they could pay them less than men* suggests that more than the profit motive is implicated" [emphasis added].[7] She cites a wealth of material documenting the fact that women are not only segregated in low-paying service jobs (as secretaries, domestics, nurses, typists, telephone operators, child-care workers, waitresses), but that "sexualization of the woman" is part of the job. Central and intrinsic to the economic realities of women's lives is the requirement that women will "market sexual attractiveness to men, who tend to hold the economic power and position to

4. In the psychoanalytic theory of SIGMUND FREUD, mature sexuality is "genitally organized," while the fetishist takes an object or a nongenital part of the body as the site for a habitual erotic response or fixation. Rich is suggesting instead that male sexuality, fixated on the genitals, is itself fetishistic and thus abnormal.

5. Barry, pp. 163–64 [Rich's note].

6. The issue of "lesbian sadomasochism" needs to be examined in terms of dominant cultures' teachings about the relation of sex and violence. I believe this to be another example of the "double life" of women [Rich's note].

7. Catharine A. MacKinnon, *Sexual Harassment of Working Women: A Case of Sexual Discrimination* (New Haven: Yale University Press, 1979), pp. 15–16 [Rich's note].

enforce their predilections." And MacKinnon documents that "sexual harassment perpetuates the interlocked structure by which women have been kept sexually in thrall to men at the bottom of the labor market. Two forces of American society converge: men's control over women's sexuality and capital's control over employees' work lives."[8] Thus, women in the workplace are at the mercy of sex as power in a vicious circle. Economically disadvantaged, women—whether waitresses or professors—endure sexual harassment to keep their jobs and learn to behave in a complaisantly and ingratiatingly heterosexual manner because they discover this is their true qualification for employment, whatever the job description. And, MacKinnon notes, the woman who too decisively resists sexual overtures in the workplace is accused of being "dried up" and sexless, or lesbian. This raises a specific difference between the experiences of lesbians and homosexual men. A lesbian, closeted on her job because of heterosexist prejudice, is not simply forced into denying the truth of her outside relationships or private life. Her job depends on her pretending to be not merely heterosexual, but a heterosexual *woman* in terms of dressing and playing the feminine, deferential role required of "real" women.

MacKinnon raises radical questions as to the qualitative differences between sexual harassment, rape, and ordinary heterosexual intercourse. ("As one accused rapist put it, he hadn't used 'any more force than is usual for males during the preliminaries.' ") She criticizes Susan Brownmiller[9] for separating rape from the mainstream of daily life and for her unexamined premise that "rape is violence, intercourse is sexuality," removing rape from the sexual sphere altogether. Most crucially she argues that "taking rape from the realm of 'the sexual,' placing it in the realm of 'the violent,' allows one to be against it without raising any questions about the extent to which the institution of heterosexuality has defined force as a normal part of 'the preliminaries.' "[1] "Never is it asked whether, under conditions of male supremacy, the notion of 'consent' has any meaning."[2]

The fact is that the workplace, among other social institutions, is a place where women have learned to accept male violation of their psychic and physical boundaries as the price of survival; where women have been educated—no less than by romantic literature or by pornography—to perceive themselves as sexual prey. A woman seeking to escape such casual violations along with economic disadvantage may well turn to marriage as a form of hoped-for protection, while bringing into marriage neither social nor economic power, thus entering that institution also from a disadvantaged position. MacKinnon finally asks:

> What if inequality is built into the social conceptions of male and female sexuality, of masculinity and femininity, of sexiness and heterosexual attractiveness? Incidents of sexual harassment suggest that male sexual desire itself may be aroused by female vulnerability. . . . Men feel they

8. Ibid., p. 174 [Rich's note].
9. Susan Brownmiller, *Against Our Will: Men, Women, and Rape* (New York: Simon and Schuster, 1975) [Rich's note].
1. MacKinnon, p. 219. Susan Schecter writes: "The push for heterosexual union at whatever cost is so intense that . . . it has become a cultural force of its own that creates battering. The ideology of romantic love and its jealous possession of the partner as property provide the masquerade for what can become severe abuse." (*Aegis: Magazine on Ending Violence against Women* [July–August, 1979]: 50–51) [Rich's note].
2. MacKinnon, p. 298 [Rich's note].

> can take advantage, so they want to, so they do. Examination of sexual harassment, precisely because the episodes appear commonplace, forces one to confront the fact that sexual intercourse normally occurs between economic (as well as physical) unequals . . . the apparent legal requirement that violations of women's sexuality appear out of the ordinary before they will be punished helps prevent women from defining the ordinary conditions of their own consent.[3]

Given the nature and extent of heterosexual pressures—the daily "eroticization of women's subordination," as MacKinnon phrases it[4]—I question the more or less psychoanalytic perspective (suggested by such writers as Karen Horney, H. R. Hayes, Wolfgang Lederer, and, most recently, Dorothy Dinnerstein)[5] that the male need to control women sexually results from some primal male "fear of women" and of women's sexual insatiability. It seems more probable that men really fear not that they will have women's sexual appetites forced on them or that women want to smother and devour them, but that women could be indifferent to them altogether, that men could be allowed sexual and emotional—therefore economic—access to women *only* on women's terms, otherwise being left on the periphery of the matrix.

The means of assuring male sexual access to women have recently received searching investigation by Kathleen Barry.[6] She documents extensive and appalling evidence for the existence, on a very large scale, of international female slavery, the institution once known as "white slavery" but which in fact has involved, and at this very moment involves, women of every race and class. In the theoretical analysis derived from her research, Barry makes the connection between all enforced conditions under which women live subject to men: prostitution, marital rape, father-daughter and brother-sister incest, wife beating, pornography, bride price, the selling of daughters, purdah, and genital mutilation. She sees the rape paradigm—where the victim of sexual assault is held responsible for her own victimization—as leading to the rationalization and acceptance of other forms of enslavement where the woman is presumed to have "chosen" her fate, to embrace it passively, or to have courted it perversely through rash or unchaste behavior. On the contrary, Barry maintains, "female sexual slavery is present in ALL situations where women or girls cannot change the conditions of their existence; where regardless of how they got into those conditions, e.g., social pressure, economic hardship, misplaced trust or the longing for affection, they cannot get out; and where they are subject to sexual violence and exploitation."[7] She provides a spectrum of concrete examples, not only as to the existence of a widespread international traffic in women, but also as to how this operates—whether in the form of a "Minnesota pipeline" funneling blonde, blue-eyed midwestern runaways to Times Square, or the purchasing of young women

3. Ibid., p. 220 [Rich's note].
4. Ibid., p. 221 [Rich's note].
5. Dinnerstein's *The Mermaid and the Minotaur* (1976) focuses on women's child-bearing and child-caring capacities and argues that a more balanced involvement of the male and female parents in child-rearing will greatly improve relations between the sexes. In *Feminine Psychology* (1967), Horney rejects the Freudian notion of "penis envy," arguing that men are afraid of women because of women's procreative abilities. Hayes's *The Dangerous Sex: The Myth of the Feminine* (1964) and Lederer's *The Fear of Women* (1968) make similar arguments.
6. Barry, op. cit. [Rich's note]. [A.R., 1986: See also Kathleen Barry, Charlotte Bunch, and Shirley Castley, eds., *International Feminism: Networking against Female Sexual Slavery* (New York: International Women's Tribune Center, 1984).]
7. Barry, p. 33 [Rich's note].

out of rural poverty in Latin America or Southeast Asia, or the providing of *maisons d'abattage*[8] for migrant workers in the eighteenth arrondissement of Paris. Instead of "blaming the victim" or trying to diagnose her presumed pathology, Barry turns her floodlights on the pathology of sex colonization itself, the ideology of "cultural sadism" represented by the pornography industry and by the overall identification of women primarily as "sexual beings whose responsibility is the sexual service of men."[9]

Barry delineates what she names a "sexual domination perspective" through whose lens sexual abuse and terrorism of women by men has been rendered almost invisible by treating it as natural and inevitable. From its point of view, women are expendable as long as the sexual and emotional needs of the male can be satisfied. To replace this perspective of domination with a universal standard of basic freedom for women from gender-specific violence, from constraints on movement, and from male right of sexual and emotional access is the political purpose of her book. Like Mary Daly in *Gyn/Ecology*, Barry rejects structuralist and other cultural-relativist rationalizations[1] for sexual torture and anti-woman violence. In her opening chapter, she asks of her readers that they refuse all handy escapes into ignorance and denial. "The only way we can come out of hiding, break through our paralyzing defenses, is to know it all—the full extent of sexual violence and domination of women. . . . In *knowing*, in facing directly, we can learn to chart our course out of this oppression, by envisioning and creating a world which will preclude sexual slavery."[2]

"Until we name the practice, give conceptual definition and form to it, illustrate its life over time and in space, those who are its most obvious victims will also not be able to name it or define their experience."

But women are all, in different ways and to different degrees, its victims; and part of the problem with naming and conceptualizing female sexual slavery is, as Barry clearly sees, compulsory heterosexuality.[3] Compulsory heterosexuality simplifies the task of the procurer and pimp in world-wide prostitution rings and "eros centers," while, in the privacy of the home, it leads the daughter to "accept" incest/rape by her father, the mother to deny that it is happening, the battered wife to stay on with an abusive husband. "Befriending or love" is a major tactic of the procurer, whose job it is to turn the runaway or the confused young girl over to the pimp for seasoning. The ideology of heterosexual romance, beamed at her from childhood out of fairy tales, television, films, advertising, popular songs, wedding pageantry, is a tool ready to the procurer's hand and one which he does not hesitate to use, as Barry documents. Early female indoctrination in "love" as an emotion may be largely a Western concept; but a more universal ideology concerns the primacy and uncontrollability of a male sexual drive. This is one of many insights offered by Barry's work:

8. Houses for beating or battering (French). The 18th arrondissement is a district where many Algerians and other North African immigrants to France live.

9. Barry, p. 103 [Rich's note].

1. Structural anthropology in most cases tries to be value-neutral, simply describing the practices and structures of various cultures, without claiming any one culture is superior to another or morally reprehensible in some way.

2. Barry, p. 5 [Rich's note].

3. Ibid., p. 100 [Rich's note].

[A.R., 1986: This statement has been taken as claiming that "all women are victims" purely and simply, or that "all heterosexuality equals sexual slavery." I would say, rather, that all women are affected, though differently, by dehumanizing attitudes and practices directed at women as a group.]

> As sexual power is learned by adolescent boys through the social experience of their sex drive, so do girls learn that the locus of sexual power is male. Given the importance placed on the male sex drive in the socialization of girls as well as boys, early adolescence is probably the first significant phase of male identification in a girl's life and development. . . . As a young girl becomes aware of her own increasing sexual feelings . . . she turns away from her heretofore primary relationships with girlfriends. As they become secondary to her, recede in importance in her life, her own identity also assumes a secondary role and she grows into male identification.[4]

We still need to ask why some women never, even temporarily, turn away from "heretofore primary relationships" with other females. And why does male identification—the casting of one's social, political, and intellectual allegiances with men—exist among lifelong sexual lesbians? Barry's hypothesis throws us among new questions, but it clarifies the diversity of forms in which compulsory heterosexuality presents itself. In the mystique of the overpowering, all-conquering male sex drive, the penis-with-a-life-of-its-own, is rooted the law of male sex right to women, which justifies prostitution as a universal cultural assumption on the one hand, while defending sexual slavery within the family on the basis of "family privacy and cultural uniqueness" on the other.[5] The adolescent male sex drive, which, as both young women and men are taught, once triggered cannot take responsibility for itself or take no for an answer, becomes, according to Barry, the norm and rationale for adult male sexual behavior: a condition of *arrested sexual development*. Women learn to accept as natural the inevitability of this "drive" because they receive it as dogma. Hence, marital rape; hence, the Japanese wife resignedly packing her husband's suitcase for a weekend in the *kisaeng* brothels of Taiwan; hence, the psychological as well as economic imbalance of power between husband and wife, male employer and female worker, father and daughter, male professor and female student.

The effect of male identification means

> internalizing the values of the colonizer and actively participating in carrying out the colonization of one's self and one's sex. . . . Male identification is the act whereby women place men above women, including themselves, in credibility, status, and importance in most situations, regardless of the comparative quality the women may bring to the situation. . . . Interaction with women is seen as a lesser form of relating on every level.[6]

What deserves further exploration is the doublethink many women engage in and from which no woman is permanently and utterly free: However woman-to-woman relationships, female support networks, a female and feminist value system are relied on and cherished, indoctrination in male credibility and status can still create synapses in thought, denial of feeling, wishful thinking, a profound sexual and intellectual confusion.[7] I quote here

4. Ibid., p. 218 [Rich's note].
5. Ibid., p. 140 [Rich's note].
6. Ibid., p. 172 [Rich's note].
7. Elsewhere I have suggested that male identification has been a powerful source of white women's racism and that it has often been women already seen as "disloyal" to male codes and systems who have actively battled against it (Adrienne Rich, "Disloyal to Civilization: Feminism, Racism, Gynephobia," in *On Lies, Secrets, and Silence: Selected Prose, 1966–1978* [New York: W. W. Norton, 1979]) [Rich's note].

from a letter I received the day I was writing this passage: "I have had very bad relationships with men—I am now in the midst of a very painful separation. I am trying to find my strength through women—without my friends, I could not survive." How many times a day do women speak words like these or think them or write them, and how often does the synapse reassert itself?

Barry summarizes her findings:

> Considering the arrested sexual development that is understood to be normal in the male population, and considering the numbers of men who are pimps, procurers, members of slavery gangs, corrupt officials participating in this traffic, owners, operators, employees of brothels and lodging and entertainment facilities, pornography purveyors, associated with prostitution prostitution, wife beaters, child molesters, incest perpetrators, johns (tricks) and rapists, one cannot but be momentarily stunned by the enormous male population engaging in female sexual slavery. The huge number of men engaged in these practices should be cause for declaration of an international emergency, a crisis in sexual violence. But what should be cause for alarm is instead accepted as normal sexual intercourse.[8]

Susan Cavin, in a rich and provocative, if highly speculative, dissertation, suggests that patriarchy becomes possible when the original female band, which includes children but ejects adolescent males, becomes invaded and outnumbered by males; that not patriarchal marriage, but the rape of the mother by the son, becomes the first act of male domination. The entering wedge, or leverage, which allows this to happen is not just a simple change in sex ratios; it is also the mother-child bond, manipulated by adolescent males in order to remain within the matrix past the age of exclusion. Maternal affection is used to establish male right of sexual access, which, however, must ever after be held by force (or through control of consciousness)since the original deep adult bonding is that of woman for woman.[9] I find this hypothesis extremely suggestive, since one form of false consciousness which serves compulsory heterosexuality is the maintenance of a mother-son relationship between women and men, including the demand that women provide maternal solace, nonjudgmental nurturing, and compassion for their harassers, rapists, and batterers (as well as for men who passively vampirize them).

But whatever its origins, when we look hard and clearly at the extent and elaboration of measures designed to keep women within a male sexual purlieu, it becomes an inescapable question whether the issue feminists have to address is not simple "gender inequality" nor the domination of culture by males nor mere "taboos against homosexuality," but the enforcement of heterosexuality for women as a means of assuring male right of physical, economic, and emotional access.[1] One of many means of enforcement is, of course, the rendering invisible of the lesbian possibility, an engulfed continent which rises fragmentedly into view from time to time only to become

8. Barry, p. 220 [Rich's note].

9. Susan Cavin, "Lesbian Origins" (Ph.D. diss., Rutgers University, 1978), unpublished, chap. 6 [Rich's note]. [A.R., 1986: This dissertation was recently published as *Lesbian Origins* (San Francisco: Ism Press, 1986).]

1. For my perception of heterosexuality as an economic institution I am indebted to Lisa Leghorn and Katherine Parker, who allowed me to read the unpublished manuscript of their book *Woman's Worth: Sexual Economics and the World of Women* (London and Boston: Routledge and Kegan Paul, 1981) [Rich's note].

submerged again. Feminist research and theory that contribute to lesbian invisibility or marginality are actually working against the liberation and empowerment of women as a group.[2] The assumption that "most women are innately heterosexual" stands as a theoretical and political stumbling block for feminism. It remains a tenable assumption partly because lesbian existence has been written out of history or catalogued under disease, partly because it has been treated as exceptional rather than intrinsic, partly because to acknowledge that for women heterosexuality may not be a "preference" at all but something that has had to be imposed, managed, organized, propagandized, and maintained by force is an immense step to take if you consider yourself freely and "innately" heterosexual. Yet the failure to examine heterosexuality as an institution is like failing to admit that the economic system called capitalism or the caste system of racism is maintained by a variety of forces, including both physical violence and false consciousness.[3] To take the step of questioning heterosexuality as a "preference" or "choice" for women—and to do the intellectual and emotional work that follows—will call for a special quality of courage in heterosexually identified feminists, but I think the rewards will be great: a freeing-up of thinking, the exploring of new paths, the shattering of another great silence, new clarity in personal relationships.

III

I have chosen to use the terms *lesbian existence* and *lesbian continuum* because the word *lesbianism* has a clinical and limiting ring. *Lesbian existence* suggests both the fact of the historical presence of lesbians and our continuing creation of the meaning of that existence. I mean the term *lesbian continuum* to include a range—through each woman's life and throughout history—of woman-identified experience, not simply the fact that a woman has had or consciously desired genital sexual experience with another woman. If we expand it to embrace many more forms of primary intensity between and among women, including the sharing of a rich inner life, the bonding against male tyranny, the giving and receiving of practical and political support, if we can also hear it in such associations as *marriage resistance* and the "haggard" behavior identified by Mary Daly (obsolete meanings: "intractable," "willful," "wanton," and "unchaste," "a woman reluctant to yield to wooing"),[4] we begin to grasp breadths of female history and psy-

2. I would suggest that lesbian existence has been most recognized and tolerated where it has resembled a "deviant" version of heterosexuality—e.g., where lesbians have, like Stein and Toklas, played heterosexual roles (or seemed to in public) and have been chiefly identified with male culture. See also Claude E. Schaeffer, "The Kuterai Female Berdache: Courier, Guide, Prophetess and Warrior," *Ethnohistory* 12, no. 3 (summer 1965): 193–236. (Berdache: "an individual of a definite physiological sex [m. or f.] who assumes the role and status of the opposite sex and who is viewed by the community as being of one sex physiologically but as having assumed the role and status of the opposite sex" [Schaeffer, p. 231].) Lesbian existence has also been relegated to an upper-class phenomenon, an elite decadence (as in the fascination with Paris salon lesbians such as Renée Vivien and Natalie Clifford Barney), to the obscuring of such "common women" as Judy Grahn depicts in her *The Work of a Common Woman* (Oakland, Calif.: Diana Press, 1978) and *True to Life Adventure Stories* (Oakland, Calif.: Diana Press, 1978) [Rich's note]. Stein and Toklas: the American writer Gertrude Stein (1874–1946) lived from 1909 on with Alice B. Toklas (1877–1967), who in many respects acted like the "wife" of a "genius."

3. A Marxist term referring to an individual's tendency to view reality in ways congruent with the interests of the dominant orthodoxy rather than in ways that reflect his or her own class interest.

4. Daly, *Gyn/Ecology*, p. 15 [Rich's note].

chology which have lain out of reach as a consequence of limited, mostly clinical, definitions of *lesbianism*.

Lesbian existence comprises both the breaking of a taboo and the rejection of a compulsory way of life. It is also a direct or indirect attack on male right of access to women. But it is more than these, although we may first begin to perceive it as a form of naysaying to patriarchy, an act of resistance. It has, of course, included isolation, self-hatred, breakdown, alcoholism, suicide, and intrawoman violence; we romanticize at our peril what it means to love and act against the grain, and under heavy penalties; and lesbian existence has been lived (unlike, say, Jewish or Catholic existence) without access to any knowledge of a tradition, a continuity, a social underpinning. The destruction of records and memorabilia and letters documenting the realities of lesbian existence must be taken very seriously as a means of keeping heterosexuality compulsory for women, since what has been kept from our knowledge is joy, sensuality, courage, and community, as well as guilt, self-betrayal, and pain.[5]

Lesbians have historically been deprived of a political existence through "inclusion" as female versions of male homosexuality. To equate lesbian existence with male homosexuality because each is stigmatized is to erase female reality once again. Part of the history of lesbian existence is, obviously, to be found where lesbians, lacking a coherent female community, have shared a kind of social life and common cause with homosexual men. But there are differences: women's lack of economic and cultural privilege relative to men; qualitative differences in female and male relationships—for example, the patterns of anonymous sex among male homosexuals, and the pronounced ageism in male homosexual standards of sexual attractiveness. I perceive the lesbian experience as being, like motherhood, a profoundly *female* experience, with particular oppressions, meanings, and potentialities we cannot comprehend as long as we simply bracket it with other sexually stigmatized existences. Just as the term *parenting* serves to conceal the particular and significant reality of being a parent who is actually a mother, the term *gay* may serve the purpose of blurring the very outlines we need to discern, which are of crucial value for feminism and for the freedom of women as a group.[6]

As the term *lesbian* has been held to limiting, clinical associations in its patriarchal definition, female friendship and comradeship have been set apart from the erotic, thus limiting the erotic itself. But as we deepen and broaden the range of what we define as lesbian existence, as we delineate a lesbian continuum, we begin to discover the erotic in female terms: as that which is unconfined to any single part of the body or solely to the body itself; as an energy not only diffuse but, as Audre Lorde has described it, omnipresent in "the sharing of joy, whether physical, emotional, psychic," and in

5. "In a hostile world in which women are not supposed to survive except in relation with and in service to men, entire communities of women are simply erased. History tends to bury what it seeks to reject" (Blanche W. Cook, " 'Women Alone Stir My Imagination': Lesbianism and the Cultural Tradition," *Signs: Journal of Women in Culture and Society* 4, no. 4 [summer 1979]: 719–20). The Lesbian Herstory Archives in New York City is one attempt to preserve contemporary documents on lesbian existence—a project of enormous value and meaning, working against the continuing censorship and obliteration of relationships, networks, communities in other archives and elsewhere in the culture [Rich's note].

6. [A.R., 1986: The shared historical and spiritual "crossover" functions of lesbians and gay men in cultures past and present are traced by Judy Grahn in *Another Mother Tongue: Gay Words, Gay Worlds* (Boston: Beacon Press, 1984). I now think we have much to learn both from the uniquely female aspects of lesbian existence and from the complex "gay" identity we share with gay men.].

the sharing of work; as the empowering joy which "makes us less willing to accept powerlessness, or those other supplied states of being which are not native to me, such as resignation, despair, self-effacement, depression, self-denial."[7] In another context, writing of women and work, I quoted the autobiographical passage in which the poet H.D. described how her friend Bryher[8] supported her in persisting with the visionary experience which was to shape her mature work:

> I knew that this experience, this writing-on-the-wall before me, could not be shared with anyone except the girl who stood so bravely there beside me. This girl said without hesitation, "Go on." It was she really who had the detachment and integrity of the Pythoness of Delphi. But it was I, battered and dissociated . . . who was seeing the pictures, and who was reading the writing or granted the inner vision. Or perhaps, in some sense, we were "seeing" it together, for without her, admittedly, I could not have gone on.[9]

If we consider the possibility that all women—from the infant suckling at her mother's breast, to the grown woman experiencing orgasmic sensations while suckling her own child, perhaps recalling her mother's milk smell in her own, to two women, like Virginia Woolf's Chloe and Olivia, who share a laboratory,[1] to the woman dying at ninety, touched and handled by women—exist on a lesbian continuum, we can see ourselves as moving in and out of this continuum, whether we identify ourselves as lesbian or not.

We can then connect aspects of woman identification as diverse as the impudent, intimate girl friendships of eight or nine year olds and the banding together of those women of the twelfth and fifteenth centuries known as Beguines who "shared houses, rented to one another, bequeathed houses to their room-mates . . . in cheap subdivided houses in the artisans' area of town," who "practiced Christian virtue on their own, dressing and living simply and not associating with men," who earned their livings as spinsters, bakers, nurses, or ran schools for young girls, and who managed—until the Church forced them to disperse—to live independent both of marriage and of conventual restrictions.[2] It allows us to connect these women with the more celebrated "Lesbians" of the women's school around Sappho[3] of the seventh century B.C., with women the secret sororities and economic networks reported among African women, and with the Chinese marriage-resistance sisterhoods—communities of women who refused marriage or who, if married, often refused to consummate their marriages and soon left their husbands, the only women in China who were not footbound and who, Agnes Smedley[4] tells us, welcomed the births of daughters and organized

7. Audre Lorde, "Uses of the Erotic: The Erotic as Power," in *Sister Outsider* (Trumansburg, N.Y.: Crossing Press, 1984) [Rich's note].

8. English writer, born Winifred Ellerman (1894–1983), who lived with H.D. (Hilda Doolittle, 1886–1961) for much of the 1920s to 1940s; a wealthy woman, she supported the American poet financially as well as emotionally.

9. Adrienne Rich, "Conditions for Work: The Common World of Women," in *On Lies, Secrets, and Silence*, p. 209; H.D., *Tribute to Freud* (Oxford: Carcanet, 1971), pp. 50–54 [Rich's note]. Pythoness of Delphi: oracular priestess of the Greek god Apollo.

1. Woolf, *A Room of One's Own*, p. 126 [Rich's note].

2. Gracia Clark, "The Beguines: A Mediaeval Women's Community," *Quest: A Feminist Quarterly* 1, no. 4 (1975): 73–80 [Rich's note].

3. Greek lyric poet (b. ca. 612 B.C.E.) who lived on the island of Lesbos. Because some of Sappho's poems express love for women, both *lesbian* and *sapphic* are used to refer to female homosexuality. (The tradition that she had a "school" is not reliable.)

4. American journalist (1892–1950), who spent much time in and wrote about China.

successful women's strikes in the silk mills.[5] It allows us to connect and compare disparate individual instances of marriage resistance: for example, the strategies available to Emily Dickinson, a nineteenth-century white woman genius, with the strategies available to Zora Neale Hurston, a twentieth-century Black woman genius. Dickinson never married, had tenuous intellectual friendships with men, lived self-convented in her genteel father's house in Amherst, and wrote a lifetime of passionate letters to her sister-in-law Sue Gilbert and a smaller group of such letters to her friend Kate Scott Anthon. Hurston married twice but soon left each husband, scrambled her way from Florida to Harlem to Columbia University to Haiti and finally back to Florida, moved in and out of white patronage and poverty, professional success, and failure; her survival relationships were all with women, beginning with her mother. Both of these women in their vastly different circumstances were marriage resisters, committed to their own work and selfhood, and were later characterized as "apolitical." Both were drawn to men of intellectual quality; for both of them women provided the ongoing fascination and sustenance of life.

If we think of heterosexuality as *the* natural emotional and sexual inclination for women, lives such as these are seen as deviant, as pathological, or as emotionally and sensually deprived. Or, in more recent and permissive jargon, they are banalized as "life styles." And the work of such women, whether merely the daily work of individual or collective survival and resistance or the work of the writer, the activist, the reformer, the anthropologist, or the artist—the work of self-creation—is undervalued, or seen as the bitter fruit of "penis envy" or the sublimation of repressed eroticism or the meaningless rant of a "man-hater." But when we turn the lens of vision and consider the degree to which and the methods whereby heterosexual "preference" has actually been imposed on women, not only can we understand differently the meaning of individual lives and work, but we can begin to recognize a central fact of women's history: that women have always resisted male tyranny. A feminism of action, often though not always without a theory, has constantly re-emerged in every culture and in every period. We can then begin to study women's struggle against powerlessness, women's radical rebellion, not just in male-defined "concrete revolutionary situations"[6] but in all the situations male ideologies have not perceived as revolutionary—for example, the refusal of some women to produce children, aided at great risk by other women;[7] the refusal to produce a higher standard of living and leisure for men (Leghorn and Parker show how both are part of women's unacknowledged, unpaid, and ununionized economic contribu-

5. See Denise Paulmé, ed., *Women of Tropical Africa* (Berkeley: University of California Press, 1963), pp. 7, 266–67. Some of these sororities are described as "a kind of defensive syndicate against the male element," their aims being "to offer concerted resistance to an oppressive patriarchate," "independence in relation to one's husband and with regard to motherhood, mutual aid, satisfaction of personal revenge.' See also Audre Lorde, "Scratching the Surface: Some Notes on Barriers to Women and Loving," in *Sister Outsider*, pp. 45–52; Marjorie Topley, "Marriage Resistance in Rural Kwangtung," in *Women in Chinese Society*, ed. M. Wolf and R. Witke (Stanford, Calif.: Stanford University Press, 1978), pp. 67–89; Agnes Smedley, *Portraits of Chinese Women in Revolution*, ed. J. MacKinnon and S. MacKinnon (Old Westbury, N.Y.: Feminist Press, 1976), pp. 103–10 [Rich's note].

6. See Rosalind Petchesky, "Dissolving the Hyphen: A Report on Marxist-Feminist Groups 1–5," in *Capitalist Patriarchy and the Case for Socialist Feminism*, ed. Zillah Eisenstein (New York: Monthly Review Press, 1979), p. 387 [Rich's note].

7. [A.R., 1986: See Angela Davis, *Women, Race, and Class* (New York: Random House, 1981), p. 102; Orlando Patterson, *Slavery and Social Death: A Comparative Study* (Cambridge: Harvard University Press, 1982), p. 133.]

tion). We can no longer have patience with Dinnerstein's view that women have simply collaborated with men in the "sexual arrangements" of history. We begin to observe behavior, both in history and in individual biography, that has hitherto been invisible or misnamed, behavior which often constitutes, given the limits of the counterforce exerted in a given time and place, radical rebellion. And we can connect these rebellions and the necessity for them with the physical passion of woman for woman which is central to lesbian existence: the erotic sensuality which has been, precisely, the most violently erased fact of female experience.

* * *

IV

Woman identification is a source of energy, a potential springhead of female power, curtailed and contained under the institution of heterosexuality. The denial of reality and visibility to women's passion for women, women's choice of women as allies, life companions, and community, the forcing of such relationships into dissimulation and their disintegration under intense pressure have meant an incalculable loss to the power of all women *to change the social relations of the sexes, to liberate ourselves and each other*. The lie of compulsory female heterosexuality today afflicts not just feminist scholarship, but every profession, every reference work, every curriculum, every organizing attempt, every relationship or conversation over which it hovers. It creates, specifically, a profound falseness, hypocrisy, and hysteria in the heterosexual dialogue, for every heterosexual relationship is lived in the queasy strobe light of that lie. However we choose to identify ourselves, however we find ourselves labeled, it flickers across and distorts our lives.[8]

The lie keeps numberless women psychologically trapped, trying to fit mind, spirit, and sexuality into a prescribed script because they cannot look beyond the parameters of the acceptable. It pulls on the energy of such women even as it drains the energy of "closeted" lesbians—the energy exhausted in the double life. The lesbian trapped in the "closet," the woman imprisoned in prescriptive ideas of the "normal" share the pain of blocked options, broken connections, lost access to self-definition freely and powerfully assumed.

The lie is many-layered. In Western tradition, one layer—the romantic—asserts that women are inevitably, even if rashly and tragically, drawn to men; that even when that attraction is suicidal (e.g., *Tristan and Isolde*, Kate Chopin's *The Awakening*),[9] it is still an organic imperative. In the tradition of the social sciences it asserts that primary love between the sexes is "normal"; that women *need* men as social and economic protectors, for adult sexuality, and for psychological completion; that the heterosexually constituted family is the basic social unit; that women who do not attach their primary intensity to men must be, in functional terms, condemned to an even more devastating outsiderhood than their outsiderhood as women. Small wonder that lesbians are reported to be a more hidden population than male homosexuals. The

8. See Russell and van de Ven, p. 40: "Few heterosexual women realize their lack of free choice about their sexuality, and a few realize how and why compulsory heterosexuality is also a crime against them" [Rich's note].

9. *The Awakening* (1899), by the American fiction writer Chopin (1851–1904), records the heroine's sexual awakening through an adulterous liaison and ends with her suicide. *Tristan and Isolde*: the 1859 opera by Richard Wagner, with its celebratory mingling of love and death, retells the medieval legend of a doomed adulterous love.

Black lesbian-feminist critic Lorraine Bethel, writing on Zora Neale Hurston, remarks that for a Black woman—already twice an outsider—to choose to assume still another "hated identity" is problematic indeed. Yet the lesbian continuum has been a life line for Black women both in Africa and the United States.

> Black women have a long tradition of bonding together . . . in a Black/women's community that has been a source of vital survival information, psychic and emotional support for us. We have a distinct Black woman-identified folk culture based on our experiences as Black women in this society; symbols, language and modes of expression that are specific to the realities of our lives. . . . Because Black women were rarely among those Blacks and females who gained access to literary and other acknowledged forms of artistic expression, this Black female bonding and Black woman-identification has often been hidden and unrecorded except in the individual lives of Black women through our own memories of our particular Black female tradition.[1]

Another layer of the lie is the frequently encountered implication that women turn to women out of hatred for men. Profound skepticism, caution, and righteous paranoia about men may indeed be part of any healthy woman's response to the misogyny of male-dominated culture, to the forms assumed by "normal" male sexuality, and to *the failure even of "sensitive" or "political" men to perceive or find these troubling*. Lesbian existence is also represented as mere refuge from male abuses, rather than as an electric and empowering charge between women. One of the most frequently quoted literary passages on lesbian relationship is that in which Colette's[2] Renée, in *The Vagabond*, describes "the melancholy and touching image of two weak creatures who have perhaps found shelter in each other's arms, there to sleep and weep, safe from man who is often cruel, and there to taste *better than any pleasure, the bitter happiness of feeling themselves akin, frail and forgotten* [emphasis added]."[3] Colette is often considered a lesbian writer. Her popular reputation has, I think, much to do with the fact that she writes about lesbian existence as if for a male audience; her earliest "lesbian" novels, the Claudine series, were written under compulsion for her husband and published under both their names. At all events, except for her writings on her mother, Colette is a less reliable source on the lesbian continuum than, I would think, Charlotte Brontë,[4] who understood that while women may, indeed must, be one another's allies, mentors, and comforters in the female struggle for survival, there is quite extraneous delight in each other's company and attraction to each others' minds and character, which attend a recognition of each others' strengths.

By the same token, we can say that there is a *nascent* feminist political

1. Lorraine Bethel, " 'This Infinity of Conscious Pain': Zora Neale Hurston and the Black Female Literary Tradition," in *All the Women Are White, All the Blacks Are Men, But Some of Us Are Brave*, ed. Gloria T. Hull, Patricia Bell Scott, and Barbara Smith (Old Westbury, N.Y.: Feminist Press, 1982), pp. 176–88 [Rich's note].

2. Pen name of Sidonie Gabrielle Claudine Colette (1873–1954), prolific French novelist; *The Vagabond* was published in 1910.

3. Dorothy Dinnerstein, the most recent writer to quote this passage, adds ominously: "But what has to be added to her account is that these 'women enlaced' are sheltering each other not just from what men want to do to them, but also from what they want to do to each other" (Dinnerstein, *The Mermaid and the Minotaur: Sexual Arrangements and the Human Malaise* [New York: Harper and Row, 1976], p. 103). The fact is, however, that woman-to-woman violence is a minute grain in the universe of male-against-female violence perpetuated and rationalized in every social institution [Rich's note].

4. English novelist (1816–1855).

content in the act of choosing a woman lover or life partner in the face of institutionalized heterosexuality.[5] But for lesbian existence to realize this political content in an ultimately liberating form, the erotic choice must deepen and expand into conscious woman identification—into lesbian feminism.

The work that lies ahead, of unearthing and describing what I call here "lesbian existence," is potentially liberating for all women. It is work that must assuredly move beyond the limits of white and middle-class Western Women's Studies to examine women's lives, work, and groupings within every racial, ethnic, and political structure. There are differences, moreover, between "lesbian existence" and the "lesbian continuum," differences we can discern even in the movement of our own lives. The lesbian continuum, I suggest, needs delineation in light of the "double life" of women, not only women self-described as heterosexual but also of self-described lesbians. We need a far more exhaustive account of the forms the double life has assumed. Historians need to ask at every point how heterosexuality as institution has been organized and maintained through the female wage scale, the enforcement of middle-class women's "leisure," the glamorization of so-called sexual liberation, the withholding of education from women, the imagery of "high art" and popular culture, the mystification of the "personal" sphere, and much else. We need an economics which comprehends the institution of heterosexuality, with its doubled workload for women and its sexual divisions of labor, as the most idealized of economic relations.

The question inevitably will arise: Are we then to condemn all heterosexual relationships, including those which are least oppressive? I believe this question, though often heartfelt, is the wrong question here. We have been stalled in a maze of false dichotomies which prevents our apprehending the institution as a whole: "good" versus "bad" marriages; "marriage for love" versus arranged marriage; "liberated" sex versus prostitution; heterosexual intercourse versus rape; *Liebeschmerz*[6] versus humiliation and dependency. Within the institution exist, of course, qualitative differences of experience; but the absence of choice remains the great unacknowledged reality, and in the absence of choice, women will remain dependent upon the chance or luck of particular relationships and will have no collective power to determine the meaning and place of sexuality in their lives. As we address the institution itself, moreover, we begin to perceive a history of female resistance which has never fully understood itself because it has been so fragmented, miscalled, erased. It will require a courageous grasp of the politics and economics, as well as the cultural propaganda, of heterosexuality to carry us beyond individual cases or diversified group situations into the complex kind of overview needed to undo the power men everywhere wield over women, power which has become a model for every other form of exploitation and illegitimate control.

1980, 1986

5. Conversation with Blanche W. Cook, New York City, March 1979 [Rich's note].

6. The sorrow or pain of love (German).

CHINUA ACHEBE
b. 1930

In the wake of global realignments after World War II, many African, Asian, and other countries sought political independence from European colonial rule. The struggle for cultural recognition was an important part of this political process, and the 1960s and 1970s witnessed a profusion of writing from formerly colonial cultures. Arguably the most prominent African writer of his generation, Chinua Achebe brought to the English-speaking world highly regarded novelistic portraits of Nigeria. Alongside his fiction, he has also published influential criticism exposing colonialist biases in English fiction and criticism and arguing for an indigenous African literature. Indicting the view of Africa in Joseph Conrad's classic *Heart of Darkness* (1902) as a reflection of European racist assumptions of the "darkness" or inferiority of Africans, Achebe's "Image of Africa: Racism in Conrad's *Heart of Darkness*" (1977) is a touchstone of anticolonialist—or what has come to be called postcolonial—criticism.

Born in the village of Ogidi in eastern Nigeria, Achebe experienced the world of colonialism firsthand. Nigeria was a construction of European colonial powers; its disparate African tribes and territories were placed under British control from 1906 until 1960, when it achieved independence. His father was a churchman in an evangelical Protestant mission, but as a boy Achebe was also exposed to traditional Igbo culture. He was selected to attend a prestigious colonial secondary school, the Government College at Umuahia, and in 1948 went on to receive his undergraduate training at the newly formed University College in Ibadan, then an affiliate of the University of London. After graduating in 1953, he worked as a producer for the Nigerian Broadcasting Company, later founding and directing the Voice of Nigeria from 1961 to 1966.

Achebe caught the attention of the literary world with the publication of his first novel, *Things Fall Apart* (1958). Depicting traditional Igbo culture and its clash with European culture, it has been an international success, translated into nearly fifty languages and selling millions of copies. Achebe became a senior research fellow at the University of Nigeria in 1967, a professor of English in 1976, and professor emeritus in 1985. He has taught at various U.S. schools, including the University of Massachusetts, the University of Virginia, UCLA, and Bard College, and has won numerous prizes and honors. He has also been actively involved in publishing ventures to promote African writing; most notably, from 1962 through 1987 he was founding editor of the British publisher Heinemann's African Writers Series, which has issued several hundred titles. In addition, Achebe has been an outspoken public figure, especially during the Nigerian Civil War (1967–70), when he supported the independence of Biafra from the Nigerian federation.

Achebe's fiction and criticism present, as one African critic notes, "exemplary texts of nationalist contestation of colonialist myths and distortions of Africans and Africa." Achebe himself, in his influential essay "Colonialist Criticism" (1975), shows how colonialist biases permeate even sophisticated critical commentary on fiction representing Africa. This is the theme of "An Image of Africa," in which Achebe argues that Conrad's *Heart of Darkness*, however critical of the European imperialist mission, presents Africans as savage, subhuman, and incapable of speech. While allowing for the novel's artistry, he unequivocally condemns this view as "offensive and deplorable." Significantly, he focuses much of his attack not on Conrad but on the critical position of Conrad's text in the Western canon as a masterpiece, a position largely forgiving of or blind to its racism. Thus its critical reception—up to the present day—unthinkingly perpetuates racist stereotypes.

Although focused on the racism inherent in the specific case of *Heart of Darkness*,

Achebe's argument broaches large theoretical debates about the canon and about the moral and social values of art. It poses a difficult question: how should we respond to classic works that exhibit racist or other condemnable views? Achebe answers with an emphatic ethical judgment. In dismissing the aestheticist view that art is solely for art's sake or that we should merely appreciate and analyze the aesthetic or linguistic skill of a work, Achebe presupposes a social theory of art, holding that art reflects and propagates social views and values. He does not fully justify this position in "An Image of Africa," but in a central early statement of his views, "The Novelist as Teacher" (1965), he underscores literature's pedagogical mission and its ethical and political responsibilities.

Since its publication, "An Image of Africa" has set the terms of debate about one of the most read and taught books in the English curriculum. Some scholars maintain that Conrad disdainfully opposes European imperialism, which was at its height in 1900, and exhibits sympathy for the plight of Africans. Others argue that *Heart of Darkness* represents not a real Africa but an allegory of an individual psychological descent or of a decontextualized battle between good and evil. Critics heeding Achebe's angry battle cry find texts such as *Heart of Darkness* irretrievably flawed in their racism and limited in that they depict Africa only through Western eyes. More moderate historicist critics have tried to mend fences; while agreeing that *Heart of Darkness* exhibits racist views, they point out that it represents relatively progressive views for its time and conclude that Conrad is not particularly blameworthy, noting that any condemnation would be unfairly based on anachronistic criteria.

Beyond its impact on Conrad criticism, Achebe's denunciation of Conrad assumed a larger significance in the so-called culture wars of the 1980s and 1990s. Traditionalists have taken it as a prime example of "political correctness," an attempt to impose moralistic and political standards on classic works of literature. They claim that canonical works exhibit high aesthetic value, proven by the test of time, and thus should be esteemed. On the other side, a range of theorists—postcolonial, African American, feminist, queer, and so on—contest a literary canon that carries racist, orientalist, sexist, homophobic, and other negative values. This debate seems intractable, in part because both groups argue at cross-purposes; it is doubtful that a traditionalist critic would advocate racism, or that a progressive critic would dispense with aesthetic appreciation. Rather, their disagreement rests on their differing theories of art: traditionalist critics claim priority for formal aesthetic properties, while progressive critics claim priority for art's social—or in Achebe's terms, pedagogical—value.

Along with the Kenyan novelist and critic NGUGI WĂ THIONG'O and others, Achebe has called for representations of imperialism to shift from European perspectives to the perspectives of those colonized. As he remarks in a 1989 interview, "The moment I realized in reading *Heart of Darkness* that I was not supposed to be part of Marlow's crew sailing down the Congo to a bend in the river, but I was one of those on the shore, jumping and clapping and making faces and so on, then I realized that was not me, and that that story had to be told again." This call, advocating a distinctive indigenous voice to represent its own experience, has been influential for the developing field of postcolonial studies, as well as for African American literature and criticism. Achebe's analysis of the West's imagination of Africa as a negative projection of itself draws on the psychoanalytic model of colonialism proposed by FRANTZ FANON, which argues that European depictions of colonies as the "Other" are symptomatic of the West's own cultural neuroses. This analysis of the literary and cultural representation of non-Western cultures has received its fullest treatment in the work of EDWARD SAID, who labels Western projections onto the Eastern Other "Orientalism" (see below). In "An Image of Africa," Achebe simply calls it racism.

BIBLIOGRAPHY

Called "the father of the African novel," Chinua Achebe is best known for his fiction foregrounding the political struggles of Nigeria. His novels to date are *Things Fall Apart* (1958), *No Longer at Ease* (1960), *Arrow of God* (1964), *A Man of the People* (1966), and *Anthills of the Savannah* (1987). He has also published two short story collections, an award-winning volume of poetry, four works of juvenile literature, and four edited collections of African literature. *Morning Yet on Creation Day: Essays* (1975) and *Hopes and Impediments: Selected Essays, 1965–1987* (1988) are overlapping collections of his literary criticism, primarily dealing with the role of the African writer in society. Both include "An Image of Africa." His other criticism includes the slim volumes *A Tribute to James Baldwin* (1989) and *Home and Exile* (2000), and three volumes directly addressing Nigerian politics: *The Trouble with Nigeria* (1983), *The World of the Ogbanje* (1986), and *The University and the Leadership Factor in Nigerian Politics* (1988).

The large secondary literature on Achebe deals primarily with his career as a novelist. Ezenwa-Ohaeto's *Chinua Achebe: A Biography* (1997) is a detailed account of Achebe's life and travels. Catherine Innes's *Chinua Achebe* (1990) offers the best critical survey of his novels as well as his other writings. Though focused on Achebe's novels, Simon Gikandi's *Reading Chinua Achebe: Language and Ideology in Fiction* (1991) examines them in relation to the critical essays. *Chinua Achebe: A Celebration* edited by Kirsten Peterson and Anna Rutherford (1991), offers tributes to Achebe.

There are many entries in the debate over "An Image of Africa": defenders of Conrad include Caribbean writer Wilson Harris in "The Frontier on Which *Heart of Darkness* Stands," *Research on African Literatures* 12 (1981); and Hunt Hawkins, "The Issue of Racism in *Heart of Darkness*," *Conradiana* (1982); following Achebe is Frances B. Singh, "The Colonialistic Bias of *Heart of Darkness*," *Conradiana* 10 (1978); and compromise views are offered by the postcolonial critic Benita Parry in *Conrad and Imperialism* (1983); and Patrick Brantlinger, "*Heart of Darkness*: Anti-Imperialism, Racism, or Impressionism?" *Criticism* 27 (1985). Later updates include Sandya Shetty, "*Heart of Darkness*: Out of Africa Some New Thing Never Comes," *Journal of Modern Literature* 15 (1989), and Hunt Hawkins, "Conrad's *Heart of Darkness*: Politics and History," *Conradiana* 24 (1992). Ezenwa-Ohaeto's *Chinua Achebe* (cited above) contains a useful bibliography of his writing and of selected secondary sources, and Innes's *Chinua Achebe* (cited above) includes a comprehensive bibliography.

An Image of Africa: Racism in Conrad's *Heart of Darkness*[1]

In the fall of 1974 I was walking one day from the English Department at the University of Massachusetts to a parking lot. It was a fine autumn morning such as encouraged friendliness to passing strangers. Brisk youngsters were hurrying in all directions, many of them obviously freshmen in their first flush of enthusiasm. An older man going the same way as I turned and remarked to me how very young they came these days. I agreed. Then he asked me if I was a student too. I said no, I was a teacher. What did I teach? African literature. Now that was funny, he said, because he knew a fellow who taught the same thing, or perhaps it was African *history*, in a certain community college not far from here. It always surprised him, he went on

1. This is an amended version of the second Chancellor's Lecture at the University of Massachusetts, Amherst, February 1975 [Achebe's note].

to say, because he never had thought of Africa as having that kind of stuff, you know. By this time I was walking much faster. "Oh well," I heard him say finally, behind me: "I guess I have to take your course to find out."

A few weeks later I received two very touching letters from high school children in Yonkers, New York, who—bless their teacher—had just read *Things Fall Apart*.[2] One of them was particularly happy to learn about the customs and superstitions of an African tribe.

I propose to draw from these rather trivial encounters rather heavy conclusions which at first sight might seem somewhat out of proportion to them. But only, I hope, at first sight.

The young fellow from Yonkers, perhaps partly on account of his age, but I believe also for much deeper and more serious reasons, is obviously unaware that the life of his own tribesmen in Yonkers, New York, is full of odd customs and superstitions and, like everybody else in his culture, imagines that he needs a trip to Africa to encounter those things.

The other person being fully my own age could not be excused on the grounds of his years. Ignorance might be a more likely reason; but here again I believe that something more wilful than a mere lack of information was at work. For did not that erudite British historian and Regius Professor at Oxford, Hugh Trevor-Roper,[3] also pronounce that African history did not exist?

If there is something in these utterances more than youthful inexperience, more than a lack of factual knowledge, what is it? Quite simply it is the desire—one might indeed say the need—in Western psychology to set Africa up as a foil to Europe, as a place of negations at once remote and vaguely familiar, in comparison with which Europe's own state of spiritual grace will be manifest.

This need is not new; which should relieve us all of considerable responsibility and perhaps make us even willing to look at this phenomenon dispassionately. I have neither the wish nor the competence to embark on the exercise with the tools of the social and biological sciences but do so more simply in the manner of a novelist responding to one famous book of European fiction: Joseph Conrad's *Heart of Darkness*,[4] which better than any other work that I know displays that Western desire and need which I have just referred to. Of course there are whole libraries of books devoted to the same purpose but most of them are so obvious and so crude that few people worry about them today. Conrad, on the other hand, is undoubtedly one of the great stylists of modern fiction and a good story-teller into the bargain. His contribution therefore falls automatically into a different class—permanent literature—read and taught and constantly evaluated by serious academics. *Heart of Darkness* is indeed so secure today that a leading Conrad scholar has numbered it "among the half-dozen greatest short novels in the English language."[5] I will return to this critical opinion in due course because it may

2. Achebe's first and best-known novel (published 1958); it depicts a traditional Nigerian society from an African rather than European perspective.
3. English historian (b. 1914) known for his studies of World War II and the Elizabethan period; formerly Regius professor of modern history (1957–80).
4. The best-known work (1902) of Conrad (1857–1924), the Polish-born English novelist. In it, a ship captain named Marlow retells his journey down the Congo River on behalf of a Belgian company in search of their chief ivory agent, Kurtz.
5. Albert J. Guerard, introduction to *Heart of Darkness and the Secret Sharer*, by Joseph Conrad (New York: New American Library, 1950), p. 9 [Achebe's note].

seriously modify my earlier suppositions about who may or may not be guilty in some of the matters I will now raise.

Heart of Darkness projects the image of Africa as "the other world," the antithesis of Europe and therefore of civilization, a place where man's vaunted intelligence and refinement are finally mocked by triumphant bestiality. The book opens on the River Thames, tranquil, resting peacefully "at the decline of day after ages of good service done to the race that peopled its banks."[6] But the actual story will take place on the River Congo, the very antithesis of the Thames. The River Congo is quite decidedly not a River Emeritus. It has rendered no service and enjoys no old-age pension. We are told that "going up that river was like travelling back to the earliest beginning of the world."

Is Conrad saying then that these two rivers are very different, one good, the other bad? Yes, but that is not the real point. It is not the differentness that worries Conrad but the lurking hint of kinship, of common ancestry. For the Thames too "has been one of the dark places of the earth." It conquered its darkness, of course, and is now in daylight and at peace. But if it were to visit its primordial relative, the Congo, it would run the terrible risk of hearing grotesque echoes of its own forgotten darkness, and falling victim to an avenging recrudescence of the mindless frenzy of the first beginnings.

These suggestive echoes comprise Conrad's famed evocation of the African atmosphere in *Heart of Darkness*. In the final consideration, his method amounts to no more than a steady, ponderous, fake-ritualistic repetition of two antithetical sentences, one about silence and the other about frenzy. We can inspect samples of this on pages 103 and 105 of the New American Library edition: (a) "It was the stillness of an implacable force brooding over an inscrutable intention" and (b) "The steamer toiled along slowly on the edge of a black and incomprehensible frenzy." Of course, there is a judicious change of adjective from time to time, so that instead of "inscrutable," for example, you might have "unspeakable," even plain "mysterious," etc., etc.

The eagle-eyed English critic F. R. Leavis[7] drew attention long ago to Conrad's "adjectival insistence upon inexpressible and incomprehensive mystery." That insistence must not be dismissed lightly, as many Conrad critics have tended to do, as a mere stylistic flaw; for it raises serious questions of artistic good faith. When a writer while pretending to record scenes, incidents, and their impact is in reality engaged in inducing hypnotic stupor in his readers through a bombardment of emotive words and other forms of trickery, much more has to be at stake than stylistic felicity. Generally, normal readers are well armed to detect and resist such underhand activity. But Conrad chose his subject well—one which was guaranteed not to put him in conflict with the psychological predisposition of his readers or raise the need for him to contend with their resistance. He chose the role of purveyor of comforting myths.

The most interesting and revealing passages in *Heart of Darkness* are, however, about people. I must crave the indulgence of my reader to quote almost a whole page from about the middle of the story when representatives

6. Conrad, p. 66 [Achebe's note].

7. Influential modern literary critic (1895–1978); the following quotation is from *The Great Tradition: George Eliot, Henry James, and Joseph Conrad* (1948; reprint, New York: New York University Press, 1960), p. 177.

of Europe in a steamer going down the Congo encounter the denizens of Africa:

> We were wanderers on a prehistoric earth, on an earth that wore the aspect of an unknown planet. We could have fancied ourselves the first of men taking possession of an accursed inheritance, to be subdued at the cost of profound anguish and of excessive toil. But suddenly, as we struggled round a bend, there would be a glimpse of rush walls, of peaked grass-roofs, a burst of yells, a whirl of black limbs, a mass of hands clapping, of feet stamping, of bodies swaying, of eyes rolling, under the droop of heavy and motionless foliage. The steamer toiled along slowly on the edge of the black and incomprehensible frenzy. The prehistoric man was cursing us, praying to us, welcoming us—who could tell? We were cut off from the comprehension of our surroundings; we glided past like phantoms, wondering and secretly appalled, as sane men would be before an enthusiastic outbreak in a madhouse. We could not understand because we were too far and could not remember because we were travelling in the night of first ages, of those ages that are gone, leaving hardly a sign—and no memories.
>
> The earth seemed unearthly. We are accustomed to look upon the shackled form of a conquered monster, but there—there you could look at a thing monstrous and free. It was unearthly, and the men were—No, they were not inhuman. Well, you know, that was the worst of it—this suspicion of their not being inhuman. It would come slowly to one. They howled and leaped, and spun, and made horrid faces; but what thrilled you was just the thought of their humanity—like yours—the thought of your remote kinship with this wild and passionate uproar. Ugly. Yes, it was ugly enough; but if you were man enough you would admit to yourself that there was in you just the faintest trace of a response to the terrible frankness of that noise, a dim suspicion of there being a meaning in it which you—you so remote from the night of first ages—could comprehend.[8]

Herein lies the meaning of *Heart of Darkness* and the fascination it holds over the Western mind: "What thrilled you was just the thought of their humanity—like yours . . . Ugly."

Having shown us Africa in the mass, Conrad then zeros in, half a page later, on a specific example, giving us one of his rare descriptions of an African who is not just limbs or rolling eyes:

> And between whiles I had to look after the savage who was fireman. He was an improved specimen; he could fire up a vertical boiler. He was there below me, and, upon my word, to look at him was as edifying as seeing a dog in a parody of breeches and a feather hat, walking on his hind legs.[9] A few months of training had done for that really fine chap. He squinted at the steam gauge and at the water gauge with an evident effort of intrepidity—and he had filed his teeth, too, the poor devil, and

8. Conrad, pp. 105–6 [Achebe's note].
9. An allusion to a famous remark of Samuel Johnson (1709–1784), who described a woman's preaching as "like a dog's walking on his hinder legs. It is not done well; but you are surprised to find it done at all" (quoted by James Boswell in his *Life of Johnson*, 1791).

> the wool of his pate shaved into queer patterns, and three ornamental scars on each of his cheeks. He ought to have been clapping his hands and stamping his feet on the bank, instead of which he was hard at work, a thrall to strange witchcraft, full of improving knowledge.[1]

As everybody knows, Conrad is a romantic on the side. He might not exactly admire savages clapping their hands and stamping their feet but they have at least the merit of being in their place, unlike this dog in a parody of breeches. For Conrad, things being in their place is of the utmost importance.

"Fine fellows—cannibals—in their place," he tells us pointedly. Tragedy begins when things leave their accustomed place, like Europe leaving its safe stronghold between the policeman and the baker to take a peep into the heart of darkness

Before the story takes us into the Congo basin proper we are given this nice little vignette as an example of things in their place:

> Now and then a boat from the shore gave one a momentary contact with reality. It was paddled by black fellows. You could see from afar the white of their eyeballs glistening. They shouted, sang; their bodies streamed with perspiration; they had faces like grotesque masks—these chaps; but they had bone, muscle, a wild vitality, an intense energy of movement, that was as natural and true as the surf along their coast. They wanted no excuse for being there. They were a great comfort to look at.[2]

Towards the end of the story Conrad lavishes a whole page quite unexpectedly on an African woman who has obviously been some kind of mistress to Mr. Kurtz and now presides (if I may be permitted a little liberty) like a formidable mystery over the inexorable imminence of his departure:

> She was savage and superb, wild-eyed and magnificent. . . . She stood looking at us without a stir and like the wilderness itself, with an air of brooding over an inscrutable purpose.[3]

This Amazon is drawn in considerable detail, albeit of a predictable nature, for two reasons. First, she is in her place and so can win Conrad's special brand of approval; and second, she fulfils a structural requirement of the story; a savage counterpart to the refined, European woman who will step forth to end the story:

> She came forward, all in black with a pale head, floating toward me in the dusk. She was in mourning . . . She took both my hands in hers and murmured, "I had heard you were coming" . . . She had a mature capacity for fidelity, for belief, for suffering.[4]

The difference in the attitude of the novelist to these two women is conveyed in too many direct and subtle ways to need elaboration. But perhaps the most significant difference is the one implied in the author's bestowal of human expression to the one and the withholding of it from the other. It is clearly not part of Conrad's purpose to confer language on the "rudimentary souls" of Africa. In place of speech they made "a violent babble of uncouth

1. Conrad, p. 106 [Achebe's note].
2. Ibid., p. 78 [Achebe's note].
3. Ibid., pp. 136–37.
4. Ibid., p. 153.

sounds." They "exchanged short grunting phrases" even among themselves. But most of the time they were too busy with their frenzy. There are two occasions in the book, however, when Conrad departs somewhat from his practice and confers speech, even English speech, on the savages. The first occurs when cannibalism gets the better of them:

> "Catch 'im," he snapped, with a bloodshot widening of his eyes and a flash of sharp white teeth—"catch 'im. Give 'im to us." "To you, eh?" I asked; "what would you do with them?" "Eat 'im!" he said curtly.[5]

The other occasion was the famous announcement: "Mistah Kurtz—he dead."[6]

At first sight these instances might be mistaken for unexpected acts of generosity from Conrad. In reality they constitute some of his best assaults. In the case of the cannibals the incomprehensible grunts that had thus far served them for speech suddenly proved inadequate for Conrad's purpose of letting the European glimpse the unspeakable craving in their hearts. Weighing the necessity for consistency in the portrayal of the dumb brutes against the sensational advantages of securing their conviction by clear, unambiguous evidence issuing out of their own mouths, Conrad chose the latter. As for the announcement of Mr. Kurtz's death by the "insolent black head in the doorway," what better or more appropriate *finis* could be written to the horror story of that wayward child of civilization who willfully had given his soul to the powers of darkness and "taken a high seat amongst the devils of the land" than the proclamation of his physical death by the forces he had joined?

It might be contended, of course, that the attitude to the African in *Heart of Darkness* is not Conrad's but that of his fictional narrator, Marlow, and that far from endorsing it Conrad might indeed be holding it up to irony and criticism. Certainly, Conrad appears to go to considerable pains to set up layers of insulation between himself and the moral universe of his story. He has, for example, a narrator behind a narrator. The primary narrator is Marlow, but his account is given to us through the filter of a second, shadowy person. But if Conrad's intention is to draw a cordon sanitaire between himself and the moral and psychological *malaise* of his narrator, his care seems to me totally wasted because he neglects to hint, clearly and adequately, at an alternative frame of reference by which we may judge the actions and opinions of his characters. It would not have been beyond Conrad's power to make that provision if he had thought it necessary. Conrad seems to me to approve of Marlow, with only minor reservations—a fact reinforced by the similarities between their two careers.

Marlow comes through to us not only as a witness of truth, but one holding those advanced and humane views appropriate to the English liberal tradition which required all Englishmen of decency to be deeply shocked by atrocities in Bulgaria or the Congo of King Leopold[7] of the Belgians or wherever.

Thus, Marlow is able to toss out such bleeding-heart sentiments as these:

5. Ibid., p. 111.
6. Ibid., p. 148.
7. Leopold II (1835–1909: reigned 1865–1909), an ardent imperialist advocating the colonial development of the Congo region, which was then the private holding of a group of investors headed by Leopold and later (1908–60) a colonial possession of Belgium. "Atrocities in Bulgaria": after an unsuccessful Bulgarian rebellion against Turkish rule, in 1876 the Ottomans massacred some 30,000 Bulgarian men, women, and children.

> They were all dying slowly—it was very clear. They were not enemies, they were not criminals, they were nothing earthly now—nothing but black shadows of disease and starvation, lying confusedly in the greenish gloom. Brought from all the recesses of the coast in all the legality of time contracts, lost in uncongenial surroundings, fed on unfamiliar food, they sickened, became inefficient, and were then allowed to crawl away and rest.[8]

The kind of liberalism espoused here by Marlow/Conrad touched all the best minds of the age in England, Europe and America. It took different forms in the minds of different people but almost always managed to sidestep the ultimate question of equality between white people and black people. That extraordinary missionary Albert Schweitzer,[9] who sacrificed brilliant careers in music and theology in Europe for a life of service to Africans in much the same area as Conrad writes about, epitomizes the ambivalence. In a comment which has often been quoted Schweitzer says: "The African is indeed my brother but my junior brother." And so he proceeded to build a hospital appropriate to the needs of junior brothers with standards of hygiene reminiscent of medical practice in the days before the germ theory of disease came into being. Naturally he became a sensation in Europe and America. Pilgrims flocked, and I believed still flock even after he has passed on, to witness the prodigious miracle in Lambaréné, on the edge of the primeval forest.

Conrad's liberalism would not take him quite as far as Schweitzer's, though. He would not use the word "brother" however qualified; the farthest he would go was "kinship." When Marlow's African helmsman falls down with a spear in his heart he gives his white master one final disquieting look:

> And the intimate profundity of that look he gave me when he received his hurt remains to this day in my memory—like a claim of distant kinship affirmed in a supreme moment.[1]

It is important to note that Conrad, careful as ever with his words, is concerned not so much about "distant kinship" as about someone *laying a claim* on it. The black man lays a claim on the white man which is well-nigh intolerable. It is the laying of this claim which frightens and at the same time fascinates Conrad, "the thought of their humanity—like yours . . . Ugly."

The point of my observations should be quite clear by now, namely that Joseph Conrad was a thoroughgoing racist. That this simple truth is glossed over in criticisms of his work is due to the fact that white racism against Africa is such a normal way of thinking that its manifestations go completely unremarked. Students of *Heart of Darkness* will often tell you that Conrad is concerned not so much with Africa as with the deterioration of one European mind caused by solitude and sickness. They will point out to you that Conrad is, if anything, less charitable to the Europeans in the story than he is to the natives, that the point of the story is to ridicule Europe's civilizing

8. Conrad, p. 82 [Achebe's note].
9. Alsatian theologian, philosopher, and physician (1875–1965), who in 1913 founded a hospital in Lambaréné, a city in the Gabon province of French Equatorial Africa. In 1952 he was awarded the Nobel Peace Prize for his humanitarian efforts in Africa.
1. Conrad, p. 124 [Achebe's note].

mission in Africa. A Conrad student informed me in Scotland that Africa is merely a setting for the disintegration of the mind of Mr. Kurtz.

Which is partly the point. Africa as setting and backdrop which eliminates the African as human factor. Africa as a metaphysical battlefield devoid of all recognizable humanity, into which the wandering European enters at his peril. Can nobody see the preposterous and perverse arrogance in thus reducing Africa to the role of props for the break-up of one petty European mind? But that is not even the point. The real question is the dehumanization of Africa and Africans which this age-long attitude has fostered and continues to foster in the world. And the question is whether a novel which celebrates this dehumanization, which depersonalizes a portion of the human race, can be called a great work of art. My answer is: No, it cannot. I do not doubt Conrad's great talents. Even *Heart of Darkness* has its memorably good passages and moments:

> The reaches opened before us and closed behind, as if the forest had stepped leisurely across the water to bar the way for our return.[2]

Its exploration of the minds of the European characters is often penetrating and full of insight. But all that has been more than fully discussed in the last fifty years. His obvious racism has, however, not been addressed. And it is high time it was!

Conrad was born in 1857, the very year in which the first Anglican missionaries were arriving among my own people in Nigeria. It was certainly not his fault that he lived his life at a time when the reputation of the black man was at a particularly low level. But even after due allowances have been made for all the influences of contemporary prejudice on his sensibility, there remains still in Conrad's attitude a residue of antipathy to black people which his peculiar psychology alone can explain. His own account of his first encounter with a black man is very revealing:

> A certain enormous buck nigger encountered in Haiti fixed my conception of blind, furious, unreasoning rage, as manifested in the human animal to the end of my days. Of the nigger I used to dream for years afterwards.[3]

Certainly Conrad had a problem with niggers. His inordinate love of that word itself should be of interest to psychoanalysts. Sometimes his fixation on blackness is equally interesting, as when he gives us this brief description: "A black figure stood up, strode on long black legs, waving long black arms"[4]—as though we might expect a black figure striding along on black legs to wave white arms! But so unrelenting is Conrad's obsession.

As a matter of interest, Conrad gives us in *A Personal Record* what amounts to a companion piece to the buck nigger of Haiti. At the age of sixteen Conrad encountered his first Englishman in Europe. He calls him "my unforgettable Englishman" and describes him in the following manner:

> [his] calves exposed to the public gaze . . . dazzled the beholder by the splendour of their marble-like condition and their rich tone of young

2. Ibid., pp. 104–5.
3. Qtd. in Jonah Raskin, *The Mythology of Imperialism* (New York: Random House, 1971), p. 143 [Achebe's note].
4. Conrad, p. 142 [Achebe's note].

> ivory . . . The light of a headlong, exalted satisfaction with the world of men . . . illumined his face . . . and triumphant eyes. In passing he cast a glance of kindly curiosity and a friendly gleam of big, sound, shiny teeth . . . his white calves twinkled sturdily.[5]

Irrational love and irrational hate jostling together in the heart of that talented, tormented man. But whereas irrational love may at worst engender foolish acts of indiscretion, irrational hate can endanger the life of the community. Naturally, Conrad is a dream for psychoanalytic critics. Perhaps the most detailed study of him in this direction is by Bernard C. Meyer, M.D. In his lengthy book, Dr. Meyer follows every conceivable lead (and sometime inconceivable ones) to explain Conrad. As an example, he gives us long disquisitions on the significance of hair and hair-cutting in Conrad. And yet not even one word is spared for his attitude to black people. Not even the discussion of Conrad's antisemitism was enough to spark off in Dr. Meyer's mind those other dark and explosive thoughts. Which only leads one to surmise that Western psychoanalysts must regard the kind of racism displayed by Conrad as absolutely normal despite the profoundly important work done by Frantz Fanon[6] in the psychiatric hospitals of French Algeria.

Whatever Conrad's problems were, you might say he is now safely dead. Quite true. Unfortunately, his heart of darkness plagues us still. Which is why an offensive and deplorable book can be described by a serious scholar as "among the half-dozen greatest short novels in the English language." And why it is today perhaps the most commonly prescribed novel in twentieth-century literature courses in English departments of American universities.

There are two probable grounds on which what I have said so far may be contested. The first is that it is no concern of fiction to please people about whom it is written. I will go along with that. But I am not talking about pleasing people. I am talking about a book which parades in the most vulgar fashion prejudices and insults from which a section of mankind has suffered untold agonies and atrocities in the past and continues to do so in many ways and many places today. I am talking about a story in which the very humanity of black people is called in question.

Secondly, I may be challenged on the grounds of actuality. Conrad, after all, did sail down the Congo in 1890 when my own father was still a babe in arms. How could I stand up more than fifty years after his death and purport to contradict him? My answer is that as a sensible man I will not accept just any traveller's tales solely on the grounds that I have not made the journey myself. I will not trust the evidence even of a man's very eyes when I suspect them to be as jaundiced as Conrad's. And we also happen to know that Conrad was, in the words of his biographer, Bernard C. Meyer, "notoriously inaccurate in the rendering of his own history."[7]

But more important by far is the abundant testimony about Conrad's savages which we could gather if we were so inclined from other sources and which might lead us to think that these people must have had other occupations besides merging into the evil forest or materializing out of it simply

5. Qtd. in Bernard C. Meyer, *Joseph Conrad: A Psychoanalytic Biography* (Princeton: Princeton University Press, 1967), p. 30 [Achebe's note]. Meyer (1910–1988), an American psychiatrist as well as a psychoanalytic literary critic.

6. Black West Indian psychoanalyst and social critic (1925–1961; see above), who was an influential proponent of the national liberation of colonial peoples.

7. Meyer, p. 30 [Achebe's note].

to plague Marlow and his dispirited band. For as it happened, soon after Conrad had written his book an event of far greater consequence was taking place in the art world of Europe. This is how Frank Willett, a British art historian, describes it:

> Gauguin had gone to Tahiti, the most extravagant individual act of turning to a non-European culture in the decades immediately before and after 1900 when European artists were avid for new artistic experiences, but it was only about 1904–5 that African art began to make its distinctive impact. One piece is still identifiable; it is a mask that had been given to Maurice Vlaminck in 1905. He records that Derain was "speechless" and "stunned" when he saw it, bought it from Vlaminck and in turn showed it to Picasso and Matisse, who were also greatly affected by it. Ambroise Vollard then borrowed it and had it cast in bronze . . . The revolution of twentieth century art was under way![8]

The mask in question was made by other savages living just north of Conrad's River Congo. They have a name too: the Fang people, and are without a doubt among the world's greatest masters of the sculptured form. The event Frank Willett is referring to marked the beginning of cubism and the infusion of new life into European art that had run completely out of strength.

The point of all this is to suggest that Conrad's picture of the peoples of the Congo seems grossly inadequate even at the height of their subjection to the ravages of King Leopold's International Association for the Civilization of Central Africa.[9]

Travellers with closed minds can tell us little except about themselves. But even those not blinkered, like Conrad, with xenophobia, can be astonishingly blind. Let me digress a little here. One of the greatest and most intrepid travellers of all time, Marco Polo, journeyed to the Far East from the Mediterranean in the thirteenth century and spent twenty years in the court of Kublai Khan[1] in China. On his return to Venice he set down in his book entitled *Description of the World* his impressions of the peoples and places and customs he had seen. But there were at least two extraordinary omissions in his account. He said nothing about the art of printing, unknown as yet in Europe but in full flower in China. He either did not notice it at all or, if he did, failed to see what use Europe could possibly have for it. Whatever the reason, Europe had to wait another hundred years for Gutenberg.[2] But even more spectacular was Marco Polo's omission of any reference to the Great Wall of China, nearly four thousand miles long and already more than one thousand years old at the time of his visit. Again, he may not have seen it; but the Great Wall of China is the only structure built by man which is visible from the moon! Indeed, travellers can be blind.

As I said earlier Conrad did not originate the image of Africa which we

8. Frank Willett, *African Art* (New York: Praeger, 1971), pp. 35–36 [Achebe's note]. Willett (b. 1925), English art historian who focused on works from Africa. Willett names the important French modern painters Paul Gauguin (1848–1903), Maurice de Vlaminck (1876–1958), André Derian (1880–1954), and Henri Matisse (1869–1954), as well as the great Spanish modernist Pablo Picasso (1881–1973). Vollard (1867–1939) was an influential French art dealer and publisher who supported modern art.

9. An international group of explorers, geographers, and scientists, founded by Leopold II; it was first convened in Brussels in 1876.

1. Great Mongol ruler and emperor of China (1216–1294). Polo (1254–1324), Venetian merchant and traveler who is said to have spent years in the Khan's service; his writings about the court and Asia made him famous.

2. Johannes Gutenberg (ca. 1397–1468), the German printer credited with inventing movable type, which revolutionized book production.

find in his book. It was and is the dominant image of Africa in the Western imagination and Conrad merely brought the peculiar gifts of his own mind to bear on it. For reasons which can certainly use close psychological inquiry, the West seems to suffer deep anxieties about the precariousness of its civilization and to have a need for constant reassurance by comparison with Africa. If Europe, advancing in civilization, could cast a backward glance periodically at Africa trapped in primordial barbarity it could say with faith and feeling: There go I but for the grace of God. Africa is to Europe as the picture is to Dorian Gray[3]—a carrier on to whom the master unloads his physical and moral deformities so that he may go forward, erect and immaculate. Consequently, Africa is something to be avoided just as the picture has to be hidden away to safeguard the man's jeopardous integrity. Keep away from Africa, or else! Mr. Kurtz of *Heart of Darkness* should have heeded that warning and the prowling horror in his heart would have kept its place, chained to its lair. But he foolishly exposed himself to the wild irresistible allure of the jungle and lo! the darkness found him out.

In my original conception of this essay I had thought to conclude it nicely on an appropriately positive note in which I would suggest from my privileged position in African and Western cultures some advantages the West might derive from Africa once it rid its mind of old prejudices and began to look at Africa not through a haze of distortions and cheap mystifications but quite simply as a continent of people—not angels, but not rudimentary souls either—just people, often highly gifted people and often strikingly successful in their enterprise with life and society. But as I thought more about the stereotype image, about its grip and pervasiveness, about the wilful tenacity with which the West holds it to its heart; when I thought of the West's television and cinema and newspapers, about books read in its schools and out of school, of churches preaching to empty pews about the need to send help to the heathen in Africa, I realized that no easy optimism was possible. And there was in any case something totally wrong in offering bribes to the West in return for its good opinion of Africa. Ultimately the abandonment of unwholesome thoughts must be its own and only reward. Although I have used the word "wilful" a few times here to characterize the West's view of Africa, it may well be that what is happening at this stage is more akin to reflex action than calculated malice. Which does not make the situation more but less hopeful.

The *Christian Science Monitor*, a paper more enlightened than most, once carried an interesting article written by its Education Editor on the serious psychological and learning problems faced by little children who speak one language at home and then go to school where something else is spoken. It was a wide-ranging article taking in Spanish-speaking children in America, the children of migrant Italian workers in Germany, the quadrilingual phenomenon in Malaysia and so on. And all this while the article speaks unequivocally about language. But then out of the blue sky comes this:

> In London there is an enormous immigration of children who speak Indian or Nigerian dialects, or some other native language.[4]

3. The title character of *The Picture of Dorian Gray* (1890), by the Irish author OSCAR WILDE; he does not age while his portrait changes, reflecting his moral disintegration.

4. *Christian Science Monitor*, November 25, 1974, p. 11 [Achebe's note].

I believe that the introduction of "dialects," which is technically erroneous in the context, is almost a reflex action caused by an instinctive desire of the writer to downgrade the discussion to the level of Africa and India. And this is quite comparable to Conrad's withholding of language from his rudimentary souls. Language is too grand for these chaps; let's give them dialects!

In all this business a lot of violence is inevitably done not only to the image of despised peoples but even to words, the very tools of possible redress. Look at the phrase "native language" in the *Christian Science Monitor* excerpt. Surely the only *native* language possible in London is Cockney English. But our writer means something else—something appropriate to the sounds Indians and Africans make!

Although the work of redressing which needs to be done may appear too daunting, I believe it is not one day too soon to begin. Conrad saw and condemned the evil of imperial exploitation but was strangely unaware of the racism on which it sharpened its iron tooth. But the victims of racist slander who for centuries have had to live with the inhumanity it makes them heir to have always known better than any casual visitor, even when he comes loaded with the gifts of a Conrad.

1975 1977

HAROLD BLOOM
b. 1930

Cantankerous rebel and staunch traditionalist, Harold Bloom embodies the tensions he depicts between tradition and innovation. The tradition of great writers is both a blessing and a curse, Bloom tells us. But most of all, it is an inescapable fact. Bloom thus finds himself fighting on two major fronts, seeking to deny tame visions of what the tradition offers *and* to shore up the primacy of the "strong" poets against those who wish to dismantle or stand aside from the tradition. This double fight has made Bloom that oddity more common in England than North America: a conservative rebel, addicted to sweeping condemnations of those who challenge the canon while carrying on his own revisionary battle with the received order.

The burden of Bloom's argument is that we are belated sons who will never be as great as our fathers, but it is death for us to admit that we are inferior. Bloom's basic model is SIGMUND FREUD's Oedipal conflict between sons and fathers—a masculinist paradigm that requires the use of the male pronoun throughout this headnote. There is no denying Bloom's originality or his learning. His vision of our necessarily ambivalent relation to literary ancestors—"the anxiety of influence"—has itself been very influential, while his broad historical generalizations and strong judgments can be counted on to stimulate debate.

Educated at Cornell and Yale Universities, Bloom has taught at Yale and New York University since receiving his Ph.D. in 1955. Legend has it that Bloom read English before he spoke it, and he unquestionably has much of English poetry memorized; like SAMUEL TAYLOR COLERIDGE and John Ruskin, he quotes from memory in his books, disdaining footnotes. In the 1970s, when the so-called Yale School (which included PAUL DE MAN, J. Hillis Miller, Geoffrey Hartman, and BARBARA JOHNSON) helped bring French literary theory to North American literature departments, Bloom was sometimes linked to deconstruction. After devoting much of the 1980s to massive editing projects (over 200 volumes of literary criticism edited for Chelsea House alone), Bloom wrote a number of best-sellers in the 1990s, gaining a general audience. His allegiance to the cult of genius and to the transcendentally great masterpiece, along with his antipathy to ideological criticism, made him one of the most prominent enemies of "cultural studies." In *The Western Canon* (1994), for example, he attacks the revisionist work on the literary canon performed by what he calls "the school of resentment" (all those who question the assumed greatness of received masterpieces).

For Bloom as for the Romantic poet William Blake, one of his heroes, energy is the only life; and both poetry and criticism for him are matters of life and death. In our selection from *The Anxiety of Influence* (1973), Bloom describes the "strong" poet as engaged in a "fight to the end" against both nature and previous poets. "Every poet begins . . . by rebelling more strongly against the consciousness of death's necessity than all other men and women do." In his impossible quest to achieve immortality, the strong poet strives to replace nature with art and previous poems with his own work, thereby declaring himself self-created and the master of his own fate.

But a basic Oedipal ambivalence complicates the "ephebe's" (newcomer's) relation to his forebears. Even as a poet's world and aims are shaped by the words of the precursors he most admires, the project of self-creation requires the denial of all influence, a "misprision" (misunderstanding) of his actual sources. So too each child enters a world he did not create, is named by others (usually his parents), and is initiated into his culture's traditions. We are all "belated," arriving late into a cultural landscape already created by others, and given a preexisting language to express our selves. Most people fit themselves into typical roles, using common idioms; many try to make the world better fit their needs. But the "strong poet" attains a heightened individuality through a radical re-vision of tradition.

The striving for originality necessarily involves aggression, but this struggle with the past is disguised in what Bloom labeled "six revisionary ratios." Each represents a strategy enabling the latecomer to revise the previous poet while either denying influence or professing reverence. If the newcomer only faithfully repeated the words of the past, he would never attain selfhood or originality. Thus, "to imagine [a poem and a self] is to misinterpret, which makes all poems antithetical to their precursors." Every poem rewrites earlier poems; every poem is an interpretation. Only misinterpretation of precursors affords the poet his own voice, his own distinctive existence.

In *The Anxiety of Influence*'s "Manifesto of Antithetical Criticism," Bloom denies any categorical distinction between what poets do and what critics of poetry do: "Poets' misinterpretations or poems are more drastic than critics' misinterpretations or criticism, but there is only a difference in degree and not at all in kind." In other words, Bloom asserts that every critical act alters the text it interprets even when insisting on its faithfulness or accuracy. It is primarily this connection of criticism to misreading that prompted the association of Bloom with deconstructive theory. But while poststructuralists reject the humanist self, Bloom's version of "intertextuality" is placed in service of the psychological struggle to achieve selfhood. Bloom obviously admires those "strong" writers who most fully gain individuality, and he clearly aspires to write a strong, creative criticism that will overcome and outdo his own precursors, especially RALPH WALDO EMERSON, KENNETH BURKE, and NORTHROP FRYE.

Bloom's psychoanalytic model, like Freud's, stresses competition, aggression, and self-assertion in ways that seem stereotypically male. From a feminist perspective, SANDRA M. GILBERT AND SUSAN GUBAR stress more collaborative, nurturing, and cooperative relationships between writers and their precursors, between individuals and the tradition. Other critics have denied the unity that Bloom claims for the tradition (he makes Shakespeare and Milton the origin of all subsequent English poetry, Emerson and Whitman of American), pointing instead to the hybridity and pluralism of cultural life and arguing that poets are in dialogue with a wide variety of materials, both verbal and nonverbal. Finally, Bloom's work suffers from the ahistoricism of

Freud's Oedipal complex, which is presented as (but not proved to be) true for all families at all times and in all places.

In response, Bloom insists that the tradition is so fully written into us that we delude ourselves if we think we can evade it. We must "consciously know" and accept that we are "latecomers." To gain access to images and ideas that we do not immediately recognize as our own, we need "antithetical texts"—which, paradoxically, are precisely the great works that constitute the Western tradition and us (*Paradise Lost* is Bloom's favorite example). That tradition is both endlessly conflicted and remarkably unitary. It continually produces a "we" that is mostly stable and similar, with the occasional genius possessing distinctive strength and individuality—recognized only in contrast to other voices in the tradition.

Bloom sees all poets as seeking "divination," or to be counted among the immortals. His view of readers (and their reasons for reading) is similarly narrow: they are all would-be poets, locked in the revisionary struggle with previous writers and striving for greatness.

This reverence for greatness shapes Bloom's style of argumentation. Greatness is conferred and confirmed by Time, transcending the nattering of literary critics. (In our selection, Bloom casually asserts the futility of all the existing types of criticism in one quick sentence.) But because it can be obscured in a particular era, it needs a spokesman (to tell us, for example, that T. S. ELIOT and Robert Lowell are negligible poets). Greatness for Bloom is both nowhere, off in misty Platonic regions of the transcendent or embodied in Bloom, the one critic faithful to the long view amid "dying generations at their song" who perversely insist on wasting their time with lesser talents. Either way, the authority of greatness is beyond the reach of mere argument and brooks no disagreement.

BIBLIOGRAPHY

Bloom began as a critic of Romantic poetry, with *Shelley's Mythmaking* (1959), *The Visionary Company: A Reading of English Romantic Poetry* (1961; rev. ed., 1971), *Blake's Apocalypse: A Study in Poetic Argument* (1963), *Yeats* (1970), *Romanticism and Consciousness: Essays in Criticism* (1970), and *The Ringers in the Tower: Studies in Romantic Tradition* (1971). *The Anxiety of Influence: A Theory of Poetry* (1973; 2d ed., 1997) introduced his theoretical view of the poet's struggle with tradition, which was elaborated in *A Map of Misreading* (1975), *Kabbalah and Criticism* (1975), *Poetry and Repression: Revisionism from Blake to Stevens* (1976), *Figures of Capable Imagination* (1976), and *Agon: Towards a Theory of Revisionism* (1982). Other books are *Wallace Stevens: The Poems of Our Climate* (1977), the novel *The Flight to Lucifer: A Gnostic Fantasy* (1979), *The Breaking of the Vessels* (1982), *Ruin the Sacred Truths: Poetry and Belief from the Bible to the Present* (1989), *The Book of J* (1990), *The American Religion: The Emergence of a Post-Christian Nation* (1992), *The Western Canon: The Books and School of the Ages* (1994), *Omens of Millennium: The Gnosis of Angels, Dreams, and Resurrection* (1996), *Shakespeare: The Invention of the Human* (1998), and *How to Read and Why* (2000). A biographical sketch can be found in *Modern American Critics Since 1955*, vol. 67 of the *Dictionary of Literary Biography* (ed. Gregory S. Jay, 1988).

Susan Handleman's *Slayers of Moses: The Emergence of Rabbinic Interpretation in Modern Literary Theory* (1982) links Bloom's work to ancient Jewish interpretive traditions and contemporary deconstruction. David Fite's *Harold Bloom: The Rhetoric of Romantic Vision* (1985) is especially helpful on the relation of Bloom's work to other critical paradigms. Peter de Bolla's *Harold Bloom: Towards Historical Rhetorics* (1988) is a good short introduction, while Graham Allen's *Harold Bloom: A Poetics of Conflict* (1994) offers a "stronger" and theoretical overview of Bloom's whole career. Two interesting examinations of Bloom in a wider context are Rael Meyerowitz's *Transferring to American: Jewish Interpretations of American Dreams* (1995), which situates Bloom alongside two contemporary U.S. critics, Stanley Cavell and

Sacvan Bercovitch; and Lars Ole Sauerberg's *Versions of the Past, Visions of the Future: The Canonical in the Criticism of T. S. Eliot, F. R. Leavis, Northrop Frye, and Harold Bloom* (1997). Allen's *Harold Bloom* (cited above) offers the best available bibliography, although it is not complete.

From The Anxiety of Influence

Introduction. A Meditation upon Priority, and a Synopsis

This short book offers a theory of poetry by way of a description of poetic influence, or the story of intra-poetic relationships. One aim of this theory is corrective: to de-idealize our accepted accounts of how one poet helps to form another. Another aim, also corrective, is to try to provide a poetics that will foster a more adequate practical criticism.

Poetic history, in this book's argument, is held to be indistinguishable from poetic influence, since strong poets make that history by misreading one another, so as to clear imaginative space for themselves.

My concern is only with strong poets, major figures with the persistence to wrestle with their strong precursors, even to the death. Weaker talents idealize; figures of capable imagination[1] appropriate for themselves. But nothing is got for nothing, and self-appropriation involves the immense anxieties of indebtedness, for what strong maker desires the realization that he has failed to create himself? Oscar Wilde,[2] who knew he had failed as a poet because he lacked strength to overcome his anxiety of influence, knew also the darker truths concerning influence. *The Ballad of Reading Gaol* becomes an embarrassment to read, directly one recognizes that every lustre it exhibits is reflected from *The Rime of the Ancient Mariner*;[3] and Wilde's lyrics anthologize the whole of English High Romanticism. Knowing this, and armed with his customary intelligence, Wilde bitterly remarks in *The Portrait of Mr. W. H.* that: "Influence is simply a transference of personality, a mode of giving away what is most precious to one's self, and its exercise produces a sense, and, it may be, a reality of loss. Every disciple takes away something from his master." This is the anxiety of influencing, yet no reversal in this area is a true reversal. Two years later, Wilde refined this bitterness in one of Lord Henry Wotton's elegant observations in *The Picture of Dorian Gray*, where he tells Dorian that all influence is immoral:

> Because to influence a person is to give him one's own soul. He does not think his natural thoughts, or burn with his natural passions. His virtues are not real to him. His sins, if there are such things as sins, are borrowed. He becomes an echo of someone else's music, an actor of a part that has not been written for him.

To apply Lord Henry's insight to Wilde, we need only read Wilde's review of Pater's[4] *Appreciations*, with its splendidly self-deceptive closing observa-

1. A phrase from the poem "Mrs. Alfred Uruguay" (1940) by Wallace Stevens (1879–1955), whom Bloom considers the greatest American poet of the twentieth century.
2. Irish-born playwright and critic (1854–1900; see above). His works mentioned by Bloom are *The Ballad of Reading Gaol* (1898), a poem on his experiences in prison; *The Portrait of Mr. W. H.* (1889), an essay on Shakespeare's sonnets; and *The Picture of Dorian Gray* (1890), a novel.
3. A 1798 poem by SAMUEL TAYLOR COLERIDGE (1772–1834), English Romantic poet and critic.
4. WALTER PATER (1839–1894), English critic who was one of Wilde's teachers at Oxford University; *Appreciations* (1889) is a collection of critical essays.

tion that Pater "has escaped disciples." Every major aesthetic consciousness seems peculiarly more gifted at denying obligation as the hungry generations go on treading one another down. Stevens, a stronger heir of Pater than even Wilde was, is revealingly vehement in his letters:

> While, of course, I come down from the past, the past is my own and not something marked Coleridge, Wordsworth,[5] etc. I know of no one who has been particularly important to me. My reality-imagination complex is entirely my own even though I see it in others.

He might have said: "particularly because I see it in others," but poetic influence was hardly a subject where Stevens' insights could center. Towards the end, his denials became rather violent, and oddly humored. Writing to the poet Richard Eberhart,[6] he extends a sympathy all the stronger for being self-sympathy:

> I sympathize with your denial of any influence on my part. This sort of thing always jars me because, in my own case, I am not conscious of having been influenced by anybody and have purposely held off from reading highly mannered people like Eliot and Pound[7] so that I should not absorb anything, even unconsciously. But there is a kind of critic who spends his time dissecting what he reads for echoes, imitations, influences, as if no one was ever simply himself but is always compounded of a lot of other people. As for W. Blake,[8] I think that this means Wilhelm Blake.

This view, that poetic influence scarcely exists, except in furiously active pedants, is itself an illustration of one way in which poetic influence is a variety of melancholy or an anxiety-principle. Stevens was, as he insisted, a highly individual poet, as much an American original as Whitman or Dickinson, or his own contemporaries: Pound, Williams, Moore.[9] But poetic influence need not make poets less original; as often it makes them more original, though not therefore necessarily better. The profundities of poetic influence cannot be reduced to source-study, to the history of ideas, to the patterning of images. Poetic influence or as I shall more frequently term it, poetic misprision[1] is necessarily the study of the life-cycle of the poet-as-poet. When such study considers the context in which that life-cycle is enacted, it will be compelled to examine simultaneously the relations between poets as cases akin to what Freud called the family romance,[2] and as chapters in the history of modern revisionism, "modern" meaning here post-Enlightenment. The modern poet, as W. J. Bate[3] shows in *The Burden of the Past and the English Poet*, is the inheritor of a melancholy engendered in the mind of the Enlightenment by its skepticism of its own double heritage

5. WILLIAM WORDSWORTH (1770–1850), English Romantic poet.
6. American poet and critic (b. 1904).
7. Ezra Pound (1885–1972), American poet and critic. T. S. ELIOT (1888–1965), American-born English poet and critic.
8. William Blake (1757–1827), Romantic poet, mystic, and artist.
9. Bloom names first 19th- and then 20th-century American poets: Emily Dickinson (1830–1886), Walt Whitman (1819–1892), Marianne Moore (1887–1972), and William Carlos Williams (1883–1963).
1. Error, misinterpretation.
2. The son's sexual desire for his mother and aggression toward his father, according to SIGMUND FREUD (1856–1939), the Austrian founder of psychoanalysis; a term also applied to the child's fantasy that these are not his true parents.
3. Walter Jackson Bate (1918–1999), American literary critic whose 1970 book traces the role of influence in English poetry.

of imaginative wealth, from the ancients and from the Renaissance masters. In this book I largely neglect the area Bate has explored with great skill, in order to center upon intra-poetic relationships as parallels of family romance. Though I employ these parallels, I do so as a deliberate revisionist of some of the Freudian emphases.

Nietzsche[4] and Freud are, so far as I can tell, the prime influences upon the theory of influence presented in this book. Nietzsche is the prophet of the antithetical, and his *Genealogy of Morals* is the profoundest study available to me of the revisionary and ascetic strains in the aesthetic temperament. Freud's investigations of the mechanisms of defense and their ambivalent functionings provide the clearest analogues I have found for the revisionary ratios[5] that govern intra-poetic relations. Yet, the theory of influence expounded here is un-Nietzschean in its deliberate literalism, and in its Viconian[6] insistence that priority in divination is crucial for every strong poet, lest he dwindle merely into a latecomer. My theory rejects also the qualified Freudian optimism that happy substitution is possible, that a second chance can save us from the repetitive quest for our earliest attachments. Poets as poets cannot accept substitutions, and fight to the end to have their initial chance alone. Both Nietzsche and Freud underestimated poets and poetry, yet each yielded more power to phantasmagoria[7] than it truly possesses. They too, despite their moral realism, over-idealized the imagination. Nietzsche's disciple, Yeats and Freud's disciple, Otto Rank,[8] show a greater awareness of the artist's fight against art, and of the relation of this struggle to the artist's antithetical battle against nature.

Freud recognized sublimation as the highest human achievement, a recognition that allies him to Plato[9] and to the entire moral traditions of both Judaism and Christianity. Freudian sublimation involves the yielding-up of more primordial for more refined modes of pleasure, which is to exalt the second chance above the first. Freud's poem, in the view of this book, is not severe enough, unlike the severe poems written by the creative lives of the strong poets. To equate emotional maturation with the discovery of acceptable substitutes may be pragmatic wisdom, particularly in the realm of Eros, but this is not the wisdom of the strong poets. The surrendered dream is not merely a phantasmagoria of endless gratification, but is the greatest of all human illusions, the vision of immortality. If Wordsworth's *Ode: Intimations of Immortality from Recollections of Early Childhood* possessed only the wisdom found also in Freud, then we could cease calling it "the Great Ode."[1] Wordsworth too saw repetition or second chance as essential for development, and his ode admits that we can redirect our needs by substitution or sublimation. But the ode plangently also awakens into failure, and into the creative mind's protest against time's tyranny. A Wordsworthian critic, even one as loyal to Wordsworth as Geoffrey Hartman,[2] can insist upon clearly

4. FRIEDRICH NIETZSCHE (1844–1900), German philosopher; *On the Genealogy of Morals* was published in 1887.
5. Relationships.
6. Like GIAMBATTISTA VICO (1668–1744), the Italian historian and philosopher who claimed that the first language was poetry and was of divine origin.
7. The fantasies and illusions produced by the mind.
8. Austrian psychoanalyst (1884–1939). William Butler Yeats (1865–1939), Irish poet.
9. Greek philosopher (ca. 427–ca. 347 B.C.E.; see above).
1. Wordworth's so-called "Intimations Ode" (1804) traces the decline of human creativity from childhood (when we still have "intimations" of our divine origin) to adulthood.
2. American literary critic (b. 1929), a colleague of Bloom's at Yale University; his books include *Wordsworth's Poetry, 1787–1814* (1964).

distinguishing between *priority*, as a concept from the natural order, and *authority*, from the spiritual order, but Wordsworth's ode declines to make this distinction. "By seeking to overcome priority," Hartman wisely says, "art fights nature on nature's own ground, and is bound to lose." The argument of this book is that strong poets are condemned to just this unwisdom; Wordsworth's Great Ode fights nature on nature's own ground, and suffers a great defeat, even as it retains its greater dream. That dream, in Wordsworth's ode, is shadowed by the anxiety of influence, due to the greatness of the precursor-poem, Milton's[3] *Lycidas*, where the human refusal wholly to sublimate is even more rugged, despite the ostensible yielding to Christian teachings of sublimation.

For every poet begins (however "unconsciously") by rebelling more strongly against the consciousness of death's necessity than all other men and women do. The young citizen of poetry, or ephebe[4] as Athens would have called him, is already the anti-natural or antithetical man, and from his start as a poet he quests for an impossible object, as his precursor quested before him. That this quest encompasses necessarily the diminishment of poetry seems to me an inevitable realization, one that accurate literary history must sustain. The great poets of the English Renaissance are not matched by their Enlightened descendants, and the whole tradition of the post-Enlightenment, which is Romanticism, shows a further decline in its Modernist and post-Modernist heirs. The death of poetry will not be hastened by any reader's broodings, yet it seems just to assume that poetry in our tradition, when it dies, will be self-slain, murdered by its own past strength. An implied anguish throughout this book is that Romanticism, for all its glories, may have been a vast visionary tragedy, the self-baffled enterprise not of Prometheus but of blinded Oedipus, who did not know that the Sphinx was his Muse.[5]

Oedipus, blind, was on the path to oracular godhood, and the strong poets have followed him by transforming their blindness towards their precursors into the revisionary insights of their own work. The six revisionary movements that I will trace in the strong poet's life-cycle could as well be more, and could take quite different names than those I have employed. I have kept them to six, because these seem to be minimal and essential to my understanding of how one poet deviates from another. The names, though arbitrary, carry on from various traditions that have been central in Western imaginative life, and I hope can be useful.

The greatest poet in our language is excluded from the argument of this book for several reasons. One is necessarily historical; Shakespeare[6] belongs to the giant age before the flood, before the anxiety of influence became central to poetic consciousness. Another has to do with the contrast between dramatic and lyric form. As poetry has become more subjective, the shadow

3. John Milton (1608–1674), English poet; *Lycidas* (1637) is an elegy for a college classmate.

4. A young man (from *ephēbos*, Greek); here, more particularly, an initiate or trainee. Wallace Stevens uses the term in "Notes toward a Supreme Fiction" (1947).

5. That is, source of inspiration. Prometheus: the Titan punished for stealing fire from the gods and giving it to humans (by some accounts, he was their creator); he was a favorite figure of Romantic poets. Oedipus: in Greek mythology, the tragic hero whose correct answer to the riddle of the Sphinx—a monster with a woman's face and lion's body—led to his becoming king of Thebes and to his self-blinding after he realized he had unknowingly married his own mother and earlier killed his father, King Laius, in a fight at a crossroads.

6. William Shakespeare (1564–1616), English poet and playwright, wrote before the Enlightenment.

cast by the precursors has become more dominant. The main cause, though, is that Shakespeare's prime precursor was Marlowe,[7] a poet very much smaller than his inheritor. Milton, with all his strength, yet had to struggle, subtly and crucially, with a major precursor in Spenser,[8] and this struggle both formed and malformed Milton. Coleridge, ephebe of Milton and later of Wordsworth, would have been glad to find his Marlowe in Cowper (or in the much weaker Bowles),[9] but influence cannot be willed. Shakespeare is the largest instance in the language of a phenomenon that stands outside the concern of this book: the absolute absorption of the precursor. Battle between strong equals, father and son as mighty opposites, Laius and Oedipus at the crossroads; only this is my subject here, though some of the fathers, as will be seen, are composite figures. That even the strongest poets are subject to influences not poetical is obvious even to me, but again my concern is only with *the poet in a poet*, or the aboriginal poetic self.

A change like the one I propose in our ideas of influence should help us read more accurately any group of past poets who were contemporary with one another. To give one example, as misinterpreters of Keats,[1] *in their poems*, the Victorian disciples of Keats most notably include Tennyson, Arnold, Hopkins, and Rossetti.[2] That Tennyson triumphed in his long, hidden contest with Keats, no one can assert absolutely, but his clear superiority over Arnold, Hopkins, and Rossetti is due to his relative victory or at least holding of his own in contrast to their partial defeats. Arnold's elegiac poetry uneasily blends Keatsian style with anti-Romantic sentiment, while Hopkins' strained intensities and convolutions of diction and Rossetti's densely inlaid art are also at variance with the burdens they seek to alleviate in their own poetic selves. Similarly, in our time we need to look again at Pound's unending match with Browning;[3] as at Stevens' long and largely hidden civil war with the major poets of English and American Romanticism—Wordsworth, Keats, Shelley, Emerson,[4] and Whitman. As with the Victorian Keatsians, these are instances among many, if a more accurate story is to be told about poetic history.

This book's main purpose is necessarily to present one reader's critical vision, in the context both of the criticism and poetry of his own generation, where their current crises most touch him, and in the context of his own anxieties of influence. In the contemporary poems that most move me, like the *Corsons Inlet* and *Saliences* of A. R. Ammons and the *Fragment* and *Soonest Mended* of John Ashbery,[5] I can recognize a strength that battles against the death of poetry, yet also the exhaustions of being a late-comer. Similarly, in the contemporary criticism that clarifies for me my own evasions, in books like *Allegory* by Angus Fletcher, *Beyond Formalism* by Geoffrey Hartman, and *Blindness and Insight* by Paul de Man,[6] I am made aware

7. Christopher Marlowe (1564–1593), English poet and playwright.
8. Edmund Spenser (1552–1599), English poet.
9. Thomas Bowles (1694–1773), English scholar and poet. William Cowper (1731–1800), English poet.
1. John Keats (1795–1821), English Romantic poet.
2. All English poets: Alfred, Lord Tennyson (1809–1892); MATTHEW ARNOLD (1822–1888); Gerard Manley Hopkins (1844–1889); and Dante Gabriel Rossetti (1828–1882).
3. Robert Browning (1812–1889), English Victorian poet.
4. RALPH WALDO EMERSON (1803–1882), American essayist and poet. PERCY BYSSHE SHELLEY (1792–1822), English Romantic poet.
5. Ammons (1926–2001) and Ashbery (b. 1927) are American poets.
6. Belgian-born American literary theorist and critic (1919–1983; see above), author of *Blindness and Insight: Essays into the Rhetoric of Contemporary* (1971). Fletcher (b. 1930), American literary critic, author of *Allegory: The Theory of a Symbolic*

of the mind's effort to overcome the impasse of Formalist criticism, the barren moralizing that Archetypal criticism has come to be, and the anti-humanistic plain dreariness of all those developments in European criticism[7] that have yet to demonstrate that they can aid in reading any one poem by any poet whatsoever. My Interchapter,[8] proposing a more antithetical practical criticism than any we now have, is my response in this area of the contemporary.

A theory of poetry that presents itself as a severe poem, reliant upon aphorism, apothegm, and a quite personal (though thoroughly traditional) mythic pattern, still may be judged, and may ask to be judged, as argument. Everything that makes up this book—parables, definitions, the working-through of the revisionary ratios as mechanisms of defense—intends to be part of a unified meditation on the melancholy of the creative mind's desperate insistence upon priority. Vico, who read all creation as a severe poem, understood that priority in the natural order and authority in the spiritual order had been one and had to remain one, *for poets*, because only this harshness constituted Poetic Wisdom. Vico reduced both natural priority and spiritual authority to property, a Hermetic reduction that I recognize as the *Ananke*,[9] the dreadful necessity still governing the Western imagination.

Valentinus,[1] second-century Gnostic speculator, came out of Alexandria to teach the Pleroma, the Fullness of thirty Aeons, manifold of Divinity: "It was a great marvel that they were in the Father without knowing Him." To search for where you already are is the most benighted of quests, and the most fated. Each strong poet's Muse, his Sophia,[2] leaps as far out and down as can be, in a solipsistic passion of quest. Valentinus posited a Limit, at which quest ends, but no quest ends, if its context is Unconditioned Mind, the cosmos of the greatest post-Miltonic poets. The Sophia of Valentinus recovered, wed again within the Pleroma, and only her Passion or Dark Intention was separated out into our world, beyond the Limit. Into this Passion, the Dark Intention that Valentinus called "strengthless and female fruit," the ephebe must fall. If he emerges from it, however crippled and blinded, he will be among the strong poets.

SYNOPSIS: SIX REVISIONARY RATIOS

1. *Clinamen*, which is poetic misreading or misprision proper; I take the word from Lucretius,[3] where it means a "swerve" of the atoms so as to make change possible in the universe. A poet swerves away from his precursor, by

Mode (1964). *Beyond Formalism: Literary Essays, 1958–1970* was published in 1970.

7. Structuralist and poststructuralist criticism, which began to influence North American critics in the 1960s and 1970s; it is "anti-humanist" in ignoring the individual. Formalist criticism: criticism focusing on the literary work itself, primarily practiced by New Critics, who stressed "close reading" (e.g., Bloom's Yale colleagues CLEANTH BROOKS and WILLIAM K. WIMSATT JR.). Archetypal criticism: criticism focusing on mythological patterns in texts (most prominently, the work of NORTHROP FRYE).

8. "A Manifesto for Antithetical Criticism" (see below), which appears between chapters 3 and 4 of Bloom's 6-chapter book.

9. Necessity (Greek). Hermetic: occult; specifically, of or relating to the Gnostic writings or teachings attibuted to Hermes Trismegistus. Gnosticism, an early Christian heresy, radically rejected the visible world and especially the body as evil; Gnostic rituals emphasized ways to access the hidden knowledge of the spirit.

1. Best known of the Gnostic teachers (d. ca. 160 C.E.).

2. Wisdom (Greek); this personification (usually as the supreme female principle) played an important role in most Gnostic systems.

3. Roman poet and Epicurean philosopher (ca. 94–55 B.C.E.); see *On the Nature of Things* 2.292.

so reading his precursor's poem as to execute a *clinamen* in relation to it. This appears as a corrective movement in his own poem, which implies that the precursor poem went accurately up to a certain point, but then should have swerved, precisely in the direction that the new poem moves.

2. *Tessera*, which is completion and antithesis; I take the word not from mosaic-making, where it is still used, but from the ancient mystery cults, where it meant a token of recognition, the fragment say of a small pot which with the other fragments would re-constitute the vessel. A poet antithetically "completes" his precursor, by so reading the parent-poem as to retain its terms but to mean them in another sense, as though the precursor had failed to go far enough.

3. *Kenosis*, which is a breaking-device similar to the defense mechanisms our psyches employ against repetition compulsions; *kenosis* then is a movement towards discontinuity with the precursor. I take the word from St. Paul,[4] where it means the humbling or emptying-out of Jesus by himself, when he accepts reduction from divine to human status. The later poet, apparently emptying himself of his own afflatus, his imaginative godhood, seems to humble himself as though he were ceasing to be a poet, but this ebbing is so performed in relation to a precursor's poem-of-ebbing that the precursor is emptied out also, and so the later poem of deflation is not as absolute as it seems.

4. *Daemonization*, or a movement towards a personalized Counter-Sublime, in reaction to the precursor's Sublime; I take the term from general Neo-Platonic usage,[5] where an intermediary being, neither divine nor human, enters into the adept to aid him. The later poet opens himself to what he believes to be a power in the parent-poem that does not belong to the parent proper, but to a range of being just beyond that precursor. He does this, in his poem, by so stationing its relation to the parent-poem as to generalize away the uniqueness of the earlier work.

5. *Askesis*, or a movement of self-purgation which intends the attainment of a state of solitude; I take the term, general as it is, particularly from the practice of pre-Socratic shamans like Empedocles.[6] The later poet does not, as in *kenosis*, undergo a revisionary movement of emptying, but of curtailing; he yields up part of his own human and imaginative endowment, so as to separate himself from others, including the precursor, and he does this in his poem by so stationing it in regard to the parent-poem as to make that poem undergo an *askesis* too; the precursor's endowment is also truncated.

6. *Apophrades*, or the return of the dead; I take the word from the Athenian dismal or unlucky days upon which the dead returned to reinhabit the houses in which they had lived. The later poet, in his own final phase, already burdened by an imaginative solitude that is almost a solipsism, holds his own poem so open again to the precursor's work that at first we might believe the wheel has come full circle, and that we are back in the later poet's flooded apprenticeship, before his strength began to assert itself in the revisionary ratios. But the poem is now *held* open to the precursor, where once it *was*

4. Early Christian leader and writer (d. ca. 67 C.E.); see Philippians 2.6–7.

5. On Neoplatonic thought, see PLOTINUS (ca. 204/5–270 C.E.), who sought ways to move through matter toward an apprehension of spirit.

6. Greek philosopher and poet (ca. 493–ca. 433 B.C.E.).

open, and the uncanny effect is that the new poem's achievement makes it seem to us, not as though the precursor were writing it, but as though the later poet himself had written the precursor's characteristic work.

Interchapter. A Manifesto for Antithetical Criticism

If to imagine is to misinterpret, which makes all poems antithetical to their precursors, then to imagine after a poet is to learn his own metaphors for his acts of reading. Criticism then necessarily becomes antithetical also, a series of swerves after unique acts of creative misunderstanding.

The first swerve is to learn to read a great precursor poet as his greater descendants compelled themselves to read him.

The second is to read the descendants as if we were their disciples, and so compel ourselves to learn where we must revise them if we are to be found by our own work, and claimed by the living of our own lives.

Neither of these quests is yet Antithetical Criticism.

That begins when we measure the first *clinamen* against the second. Finding just what the accent of deviation is, we proceed to apply it as corrective to the reading of the first but not the second poet or group of poets. To practice Antithetical Criticism on the more recent poet or poets becomes possible only when they have found disciples not ourselves. But these can be critics, and not poets.

It can be objected against this theory that we never read a poet as poet, but only read one poet in another poet, or even into another poet. Our answer is manifold: we deny that there is, was or ever can be a poet as poet—to a reader. Just as we can never embrace (sexually or otherwise) a single person, but embrace the whole of her or his family romance, so we can never read a poet without reading the whole of his or her family romance as poet. The issue is reduction and how best to avoid it. Rhetorical, Aristotelian, phenomenological, and structuralist criticisms[7] all reduce, whether to images, ideas, given things, or phonemes. Moral and other blatant philosophical or psychological criticisms all reduce to rival conceptualizations. We reduce—if at all—to another poem. The meaning of a poem can only be another poem. This is not a tautology, not even a deep tautology, since the two poems are not the same poem, any more than two lives can be the same life. The issue is true history or rather the true use of it, rather than the abuse of it, both in Nietzsche's sense. True poetic history is the story of how poets as poets have suffered other poets, just as any true biography is the story of how anyone suffered his own family—or his own displacement of family into lovers and friends.

Summary—Every poem is a misinterpretation of a parent poem. A poem is not an overcoming of anxiety, but is that anxiety. Poets' misinterpretations or poems are more drastic than critics' misinterpretations or criticism, but this is only a difference in degree and not at all in kind. There are no interpretations but only misinterpretations, and so all criticism is prose poetry.

7. Again, Bloom lists the types of criticism prevalent in 1973. Rhetorical criticism considers the relation of text to audience (e.g., see KENNETH BURKE). Aristotelian criticism combines interest in genre with a focus on rhetoric (associated with the University of Chicago). Phenomenological criticism highlights the experience of the reader (e.g., see GEORGES POULET and WOLFGANG ISER). Structuralist criticism identifies the general patterns underlying the surface words of the text; it derives from the structuralist linguistics of FERDINAND DE SAUSSURE (1857–1913).

Critics are more or less valuable than other critics only (precisely) as poets are more or less valuable than other poets. For just as a poet must be found by the opening in a precursor poet, so must the critic. The difference is that a critic has more parents. His precursors are poets and critics. But—in truth—so are a poet's precursors, often and more often as history lengthens.

Poetry is the anxiety of influence, is misprision, is a disciplined perverseness. Poetry is misunderstanding, misinterpretation, misalliance.

Poetry (Romance) is Family Romance. Poetry is the enchantment of incest, disciplined by resistance to that enchantment.

Influence is *Influenza*—an astral disease.[8]

If influence were health, who could write a poem? Health is stasis.

Schizophrenia is bad poetry, for the schizophrenic has lost the strength of perverse, wilful, misprision.

Poetry is thus both contraction and expansion; for all the ratios of revision are contracting movements, yet making is an expansive one. Good poetry is a dialectic of revisionary movement (contraction) and freshening outward-going-ness.

The best critics of our time remain Empson and Wilson Knight,[9] for they have misinterpreted more antithetically than all others.

When we say that the meaning of a poem can only be another poem, we may mean a range of poems:

> The precursor poem or poems.
> The poem we write as our reading.
> A rival poem, son or grandson of the same precursor.
> A poem that never got written—that is—the poem that should have been written by the poet in question.
> A composite poem, made up of these in some combination.

A poem is a poet's melancholy at his lack of priority. The failure to have begotten oneself is not the cause of the poem, for poems arise out of the illusion of freedom, out of a sense of priority being possible. But the poem—unlike the mind in creation—is a made thing, and as such is an achieved anxiety.

How do we understand an anxiety? By ourselves being anxious. Every deep reader is an Idiot Questioner. He asks, "Who wrote my poem?" Hence Emerson's insistence that: "In every work of genius we recognize our own rejected thoughts—they come back to us with a certain alienated majesty."[1]

Criticism is the discourse of the deep tautology—of the solipsist who knows that what he means is right, and yet that what he says is wrong. Criticism is the art of knowing the hidden roads that go from poem to poem.

1973

8. Epidemics (such as those associated with influenza) were once thought to be influenced by the stars.
9. William Empson (1906–1984) and George Wilson Knight (1897–1985), English literary critics.
1. Emerson, "Self-Reliance" (1841).

PIERRE BOURDIEU
1930–2002

French sociologist Pierre Bourdieu explores the connection between aesthetic taste and social status. His influential book *Distinction: A Social Critique of the Judgement of Taste* (1979; trans. 1984) is nothing less than an attempt to rewrite IMMANUEL KANT'S landmark *Critique of Judgment* (1790; see above). Bourdieu challenges Kant's claim that our judgments about art are disinterested, arguing instead that cultivated sensibilities both derive from and produce a "cultural capital" that is tied to economic and social advantages. Literary theorists have found Bourdieu's work congenial to their own questioning of aesthetic theories that make art a realm entirely separate from worldly concerns.

Bourdieu came from the provincial petite bourgeoisie (lower middle class); he was born in the village of Denguin, in the Pyrénées district of southwestern France, where his father was the village postmaster. A star rugby player in school, he was also a scholarship student; he received his degree in philosophy from the École normale superiéure, perhaps the most elite university in France (JACQUES DERRIDA was a classmate). After a year teaching high school, Bourdieu was drafted into the army and served for two years in Algeria during the bloody and controversial war between France and Algerians seeking their independence. Returning to France in 1960, Bourdieu began to study anthropology and sociology, and he joined the faculty of the École pratique des hautes études in 1964. He became director of the Centre de Sociologie Européenne in 1968, a position he retained until his death. In 1981 Bourdieu was appointed to the prestigious chair of sociology at the Collège de France.

Kant's *Critique of Judgment* is the founding text of modern aestheticism, and much of Bourdieu's work is devoted to revealing the pernicious social consequences of modern aestheticism's exaltation of art and of those who appreciate art. For Bourdieu, aesthetic judgment (the ability to distinguish between good and bad art, to appreciate the truly fine as opposed to the vulgar) is a sorting process through which modern societies both produce and legitimate economic and status inequalities. The concepts grounding Kant's work—disinterestedness, taste, and autonomy—point toward an effort to shelter art and its reception from worldly concerns. "Disinterestedness"—especially prominent in both Kant and MATTHEW ARNOLD, but found throughout the modern tradition—insists that art is adulterated if mundane purposes influence either artist or audience. Only aesthetic concerns (defined circularly as concerns having to do only with art) are legitimate; otherwise, the artist is corrupted by material considerations and the audience's judgments of artistic value are clouded. Art, then, is to exist in its own autonomous realm.

Bourdieu insists that aesthetic disinterestedness and autonomy are class-based notions impossible to achieve. All acts of aesthetic production and consumption, like all other human actions, take place within social fields and their performance has consequences for the agents' social standing. In modern societies, Bourdieu argues, there are two distinct systems of social hierarchization operating side by side. The first is economic, with position and power determined by the capital (money and property) one commands. The second, whose logic he seeks to describe, is cultural, with status determined by how much "cultural capital" one possesses. We might think of certain contemporary business moguls, who, for all their economic power, will always be deemed "vulgar." No amount of money can buy them respect from the cultural elites.

Bourdieu argues that modern aestheticism is central to the cultural elite's self-understanding and to the general willingness of society to grant it authority and prestige. Though the elite is produced, this process of production is obscured so that the elite's existence is taken as a natural fact. Particularly mystified is the marker of the cultural elite: "taste," its "natural" endowment. That taste (as the faculty of judgment) is notoriously difficult to define and to impart to others is made clear by the earlier works of DAVID HUME and EDMUND BURKE. But we do speak of "acquired tastes," and Bourdieu is determined to show quite specifically how taste is acquired, how it is socially produced in connection with very concrete material goals, and how spectators and readers respond in coded, habitual ways.

Setting aside those who inherit significant economic capital, we can make a rough distinction between those who do some kind of physical labor and those who receive their salaries for mental work and require a university degree to secure their position. Bourdieu favors calling the latter "intellectuals" and memorably designates them "the dominated fraction of the dominant class" because they remain dependent on economic capital for their salaries but have a semiautonomous source of social prestige and power in their possession of cultural capital.

The vast differences in wages and employment opportunities in modern society are justified as meritocratic, the rise of the best and brightest to the top. Bourdieu aims to explode the myth of merit. The two great predictors of success in contemporary society are the socioeconomic status of one's parents and one's success in school. There is not a level playing field, Bourdieu insists. And he argues that taste, an acquired "cultural competence," is used to legitimate social and economic inequalities. How does the rule that "taste classifies, and it classifies the classifier" come to be accepted?

The answer, Bourdieu believes, is aesthetic ideology, which both mystifies taste and makes its possession prestigious. His argument is complex because of the way that aestheticism turns the economic world upside down. Taste is revealed through an (acquired) appreciation for everything that is nonmaterial: mind over body, muted over gaudy, nonpopular over commercial, and, crucially, form over content, "the mode of representation over the object of representation." Prestigious taste's pursuit of disinterestedness and purity leads it to shun everything that might appeal to "lower," popular appetites. That taste secures very concrete economic advantages is thus masked by taste's attachment to artworks esteemed precisely for their apparent unconcern for commercial success. The rarity of taste is ensured because it works against nature; it depends on "sublimating primary needs and impulses."

Since taste functions to make social "distinctions" (hence the title of Bourdieu's book), intellectuals are driven by the desire to stay ahead of the crowd, to distinguish themselves by appreciating works often unknown or even offensive to the many. The shifts in reputation of various artists and various artworks reflect the continual jockeying by groups or individuals for position, prestige, and status. Those who command incomes by virtue of their mental work must keep proving their right to such work by continually demonstrating their good taste. Modern culture's preference for the immaterial and the pure is encoded in the aesthetic ideology and helps explain why mental labor is so much more highly paid than the physical labor that is often more difficult, more dangerous, and more necessary. Cultural capital, acquired through schooling and maintained through a hierarchization of tastes and pleasures, plays an important role in securing the privileges of the upper classes in modern societies.

The major objection to Bourdieu's work—as to much materialist work—is that he is "reductionist," oversimplifying a complex phenomenon by taking part of the picture as the whole. Few would deny that issues of social prestige and status influence judgments of artworks, but we might argue that a variety of desires and motives enter into our responses to art. We regularly distinguish those who value a work only for the social standing linked to such appreciation from those who have other reasons, and many people cling to frowned-on pleasures and tastes in defiance of the social costs. A different objection is that while Bourdieu's picture of idealist aestheticism connects to high modernism, it has much less relevance now that the clear markers between high and low have dissolved. In the more mixed forms of postmodernism, bodily pleasures are not outlawed and outright commercial ambitions on the part of artists do not lead to immediate condemnation by the elites.

Objections aside, Bourdieu's work participates in the general crisis of the aesthetic as category and value that began in the late twentieth century, when the existence of any unique, autonomous quality adhering to the artwork came sharply under question. This crisis has certainly proved among the most persistent features of postmodernism (see JEAN-FRANÇOIS LYOTARD and FREDRIC JAMESON). Bourdieu's linking of aesthetic value to economic and social value has also proved influential among critics who challenge the traditional literary canon (see BARBARA HERRNSTEIN SMITH).

BIBLIOGRAPHY

Bourdieu's published works (almost all of which are available in English; the date of the original French is given first) fall into two groups: his work in sociological and anthropological theory, and his work on art, intellectuals, and the school system. In the first group, the major texts are *Outline of a Theory of Practice* (1972; 1977); *The Logic of Practice* (1980; 1990); *Sociology in Question* (1980; 1993); *In Other Words: Essays toward a Reflexive Sociology* (1987; 1990); *The Political Ontology of Martin Heidegger* (1988; 1991); *An Invitation to Reflexive Sociology*, with Loic Wacquant (1992); and *Practical Reason: On the Theory of Action* (1994; 1998). On intellectuals and art, the major books are *Photography: A Middle-brow Art*, with others (1965; 1996); *Reproduction in Education, Society, and Culture*, with Jean-Claude Passeron (1970; 1977); *Distinction: A Social Critique of the Judgement of Taste* (1979; 1987), *Language and Symbolic Power* (1982; 1991); *Academic Discourse: Linguistic Misunderstanding and Professorial Power*, with Jean-Claude Passeron and Monique de Saint Martin (1984; 1994); *Homo Academicus* (1984; 1988); *The State Nobility: Elite Schools in the Field of Power* (1989; 1996); *The Rules of Art: Genesis and Structure of the Literary Field* (1992; 1995); *Free Exchange*, with Hans Haacke (1994; 1995); *On Television* (1996; 1998); and *Acts of Resistance: Against the New Myths of Our Time* (1998; 1999). An important collection of translated essays is *The Field of Cultural Production*, edited by Randal Johnson (1993).

The best biographical source is Richard Jenkins's *Pierre Bourdieu* (1992), which is also an excellent general introduction. *An Introduction to the Work of Pierre Bourdieu*, edited by Richard Harker, Chellen Mahar, and Chris Wilkes (1990); *Bourdieu: Critical Perspectives*, edited by Craig Calhoun, Edward LiPuma, and Moishe Postone (1993); and *Bourdieu: A Critical Reader*, edited by Richard Shusterman (1999), all collect essays on various issues raised by Bourdieu. More advanced studies are offered in Bridget Fowler's *Pierre Bourdieu and Cultural Theory* (1997) and David Swartz's *Culture and Power* (1997). John Guillory's *Cultural Capital: The Problem of Literary Canon Formation* (1993) addresses the issue of canons and of the institutionalization of literary theory in ways that creatively employ and expand Bourdieu's work. Joan Nordquist's *Pierre Bourdieu: A Bibliography* (1997) lists the works in French, the available translations, and the commentaries in English.

From Distinction: A Social Critique of the Judgement of Taste[1]

Introduction

> You said it, my good knight! There ought to be laws to protect the body of acquired knowledge.
>
> Take one of our good pupils, for example: modest and diligent, from his earliest grammar classes he's kept a little notebook full of phrases.
>
> After hanging on the lips of his teachers for twenty years, he's managed to build up an intellectual stock in trade; doesn't it belong to him as if it were a house, or money?
>
> Paul Claudel,[2] *Le soulier de satin*, Day III, Scene ii

There is an economy of cultural goods, but it has a specific logic. Sociology endeavors to establish the conditions in which the consumers of cultural goods, and their taste for them, are produced, and at the same time to describe the different ways of appropriating such of these objects as are regarded at a particular moment as works of art, and the social conditions of the constitution of the mode of appropriation that is considered legitimate. But one cannot fully understand cultural practices unless 'culture', in the restricted, normative sense of ordinary usage, is brought back into 'culture' in the anthropological sense, and the elaborated taste for the most refined objects is reconnected with the elementary taste for the flavors of food.

Whereas the ideology of charisma regards taste in legitimate culture as a gift of nature, scientific observation shows that cultural needs are the product of upbringing and education: surveys establish that all cultural practices (museum visits, concert-going, reading etc.), and preferences in literature, painting or music, are closely linked to educational level (measured by qualifications or length of schooling) and secondarily to social origin.[3] The relative weight of home background and of formal education (the effectiveness and duration of which are closely dependent on social origin) varies according to the extent to which the different cultural practices are recognized and taught by the educational system, and the influence of social origin is strongest—other things being equal—in 'extra-curricular' and avant-garde culture. To the socially recognized hierarchy of the arts, and within each of them, of genres, schools or periods, corresponds a social hierarchy of the consumers. This predisposes tastes to function as markers of 'class'. The manner in which culture has been acquired lives on in the manner of using it: the importance attached to manners can be understood once it is seen that it is these imponderables of practice which distinguish the different—and ranked—modes of culture acquisition, early or late, domestic or scholastic, and the classes of individuals which they characterize (such as 'pedants' and *mondains*[4]). Culture also has its titles of nobility—awarded by the educational system—and its pedigrees, measured by seniority in admission to the nobility.

The definition of cultural nobility is the stake in a struggle which has gone on unceasingly, from the seventeenth century to the present day, between

1. Translated by Richard Nice, who occasionally retains the original French in parentheses.
2. French poet (1868–1955).
3. Bourdieu et al., *Photography: A Middle-brow Art* (1965); P. Bourdieu and A. Darbel, *The Love of Art: European Art Museums and Their Public* (1969) [Bourdieu's note].
4. Sophisticated, fashionable people (French).

groups differing in their ideas of culture and of the legitimate relation to culture and to works of art, and therefore differing in the conditions of acquisition of which these dispositions are the product.[5] Even in the classroom, the dominant definition of the legitimate way of appropriating culture and works of art favours those who have had early access to legitimate culture, in a cultured household, outside of scholastic disciplines, since even within the educational system it devalues scholarly knowledge and interpretation as 'scholastic' or even 'pedantic' in favour of direct experience and simple delight.

The logic of what is sometimes called, in typically 'pedantic' language, the 'reading' of a work of art, offers an objective basis for this opposition. Consumption is, in this case, a stage in a process of communication, that is, an act of deciphering, decoding, which presupposes practical or explicit mastery of a cipher or code. In a sense, one can say that the capacity to see (*voir*) is a function of the knowledge (*savoir*), or concepts, that is, the words, that are available to name visible things, and which are, as it were, programmes for perception. A work of art has meaning and interest only for someone who possesses the cultural competence, that is, the code, into which it is encoded. The conscious or unconscious implementation of explicit or implicit schemes of perception and appreciation which constitutes pictorial or musical culture is the hidden condition for recognizing the styles characteristic of a period, a school or an author, and, more generally, for the familiarity with the internal logic of works that aesthetic enjoyment presupposes. A beholder who lacks the specific code feels lost in a chaos of sounds and rhythms, colours and lines, without rhyme or reason. Not having learnt to adopt the adequate disposition, he stops short at what Erwin Panofsky[6] calls the 'sensible properties', perceiving a skin as downy or lace-work as delicate, or at the emotional resonances aroused by these properties, referring to 'austere' colours or a 'joyful' melody. He cannot move from the 'primary stratum of the meaning we can grasp on the basis of our ordinary experience' to the 'stratum of secondary meanings', i.e., the 'level of the meaning of what is signified', unless he possesses the concepts which go beyond the sensible properties and which identify the specifically stylistic properties of the work.[7] Thus the encounter with a work of art is not 'love at first sight' as is generally supposed, and the act of empathy, *Einfühlung*,[8] which is the art-lover's pleasure, presupposes an act of cognition, a decoding operation, which implies the implementation of a cognitive acquirement, a cultural code.[9]

This typically intellectualist theory of artistic perception directly contradicts the experience of the art-lovers closest to the legitimate definition; acquisition of legitimate culture by insensible familiarization within the family circle tends to favour an enchanted experience of culture which implies forgetting the acquisition.[1] The 'eye' is a product of history reproduced by

5. The word *disposition* seems particularly suited to express what is covered by the concept of habitus (defined as a system of dispositions)—used later in this chapter. It expresses first the *result of an organizing action*, with a meaning close to that of words such as structure; it also designates a way of being, a habitual state (especially of the body) and, in particular, a *predisposition, tendency, propensity* or *inclination*. P. Bourdieu, *Outline of a Theory of Practice* (1977), p. 214, n. 1 [Bourdieu's note].

6. German-born American art historian and theorist (1892–1968).

7. E. Panofsky, "Iconography and Iconology: An Introduction to the Study of Renaissance Art," in *Meaning in the Visual Arts* (1955), p. 28 [Bourdieu's note].

8. Empathy (German).

9. It will be seen that this internalized code called culture functions as cultural capital owing to the fact that, being unequally distributed, it secures profits of distinction [Bourdieu's note].

1. The sense of familiarity in no way excludes the ethnocentric misunderstanding which results from

education. This is true of the mode of artistic perception now accepted as legitimate, that is, the aesthetic disposition, the capacity to consider in and for themselves, as form rather than function, not only the works designated for such apprehension, i.e., legitimate works of art, but everything in the world, including cultural objects which are not yet consecrated—such as, at one time, primitive arts, or, nowadays, popular photography or kitsch—and natural objects. The 'pure' gaze is a historical invention linked to the emergence of an autonomous field of artistic production, that is, a field capable of imposing its own norms on both the production and the consumption of its products.[2] An art which, like all Post-Impressionist painting,[3] is the product of an artistic intention which asserts the primacy of the mode of representation over the object of representation demands categorically an attention to form which previous art only demanded conditionally.

The pure intention of the artist is that of a producer who aims to be autonomous, that is, entirely the master of his product, who tends to reject not only the 'programmes' imposed a priori by scholars and scribes, but also—following the old hierarchy of doing and saying—the interpretations superimposed a posteriori on his work. The production of an 'open work', intrinsically and deliberately polysemic,[4] can thus be understood as the final stage in the conquest of artistic autonomy by poets and, following in their footsteps, by painters, who had long been reliant on writers and their work of 'showing' and 'illustrating'. To assert the autonomy of production is to give primacy to that of which the artist is master, i.e., form, manner, style, rather than the 'subject', the external referent, which involves subordination to functions—even if only the most elementary one, that of representing, signifying, saying something. It also means a refusal to recognize any necessity other than that inscribed in the specific tradition of the artistic discipline in question: the shift from an art which imitates nature to an art which imitates art, deriving from its own history the exclusive source of its experiments and even of its breaks with tradition. An art which ever increasingly contains reference to its own history demands to be perceived historically; it asks to be referred not to an external referent, the represented or designated 'reality', but to the universe of past and present works of art. Like artistic production, in that it is generated in a field, aesthetic perception is necessarily historical, inasmuch as it is differential, relational, attentive to the deviations (*éscarts*) which make styles. Like the so-called naive painter who, operating outside the field and its specific traditions, remains external to the history of the art, the 'naive' spectator cannot attain a specific grasp of works of art which only have meaning—or value—in relation to the specific history of an artistic tradition. The aesthetic disposition demanded by the products of a highly autonomous field of production is inseparable from a specific cultural com-

applying the wrong code. Thus, Michael Baxandall's work in historical ethnology enables us to measure all that separates the perceptual schemes that now tend to be applied to Quattrocento [14th-c. Italian] paintings and those which their immediate addresses applied. The "moral and spiritual eye" of Quattrocento man, that is, the set of cognitive and evaluative dispositions which were the basis of his perception of the world and his perception of pictorial representation of the world, differs radically from the "pure" gaze (purified, first of all, from all reference to economic value) with which the modern cultivated spectator looks at works of art.*** M. Baxandall, *Painting and Experience in Fifteenth-Century Italy: A Primer in the Social History of Pictorial Style* (1972) [Bourdieu's note].

2. See P. Bourdieu, "The Market of Symbolic Goods" and "Outline of a Sociological Theory of Art Perception" in *The Field of Cultural Production* (1993) [Bourdieu's note].

3. Styles developed in the last two decades of the 19th century, especially by Paul Cézanne, Paul Gauguin, and Vincent van Gogh.

4. Having many meanings.

petence. This historical culture functions as a principle of pertinence which enables one to identify, among the elements offered to the gaze, all the distinctive features and only these, by referring them, consciously or unconsciously, to the universe of possible alternatives. This mastery is, for the most part, acquired simply by contact with works of art—that is, through an implicit learning analogous to that which makes it possible to recognize familiar faces without explicit rules or criteria—and it generally remains at a practical level; it is what makes it possible to identify styles, i.e., modes of expression characteristic of a period, a civilization or a school, without having to distinguish clearly, or state explicitly, the features which constitute their originality. Everything seems to suggest that even among professional valuers, the criteria which define the stylistic properties of the 'typical works' on which all their judgments are based usually remain implicit.

The pure gaze implies a break with the ordinary attitude towards the world, which, given the conditions in which it is performed, is also a social separation. Ortega y Gasset[5] can be believed when he attributes to modern art a systematic refusal of all that is 'human', i.e., generic, common—as opposed to distinctive, or distinguished—namely, the passions, emotions and feelings which 'ordinary' people invest in their 'ordinary' lives. It is as if the 'popular aesthetic' (the quotation marks are there to indicate that this is an aesthetic 'in itself' not 'for itself')[6] were based on the affirmation of the continuity between art and life, which implies the subordination of form to function. This is seen clearly in the case of the novel and especially the theatre, where the working-class audience refuses any sort of formal experimentation and all the effects which, by introducing a distance from the accepted conventions (as regards scenery, plot etc.), tend to distance the spectator, preventing him from getting involved and fully identifying with the characters (I am thinking of Brechtian 'alienation' or the disruption of plot in the *nouveau roman*[7]). In contrast to the detachment and disinterestedness which aesthetic theory regards as the only way of recognizing the work of art for what it is, i.e., autonomous, *selbständig*,[8] the 'popular aesthetic' ignores or refuses the refusal of 'facile' involvement and 'vulgar' enjoyment, a refusal which is the basis of the taste for formal experiment. And popular judgments of paintings or photographs spring from an 'aesthetic' (in fact it is an ethos) which is the exact opposite of the Kantian aesthetic.[9] Whereas, in order to grasp the specificity of the aesthetic judgment, Kant strove to distinguish that which pleases from that which gratifies and, more generally, to distinguish disinterestedness, the sole guarantor of the specifically aesthetic quality of contemplation, from the interest of reason which defines the Good, working-class people expect every image to explicitly perform a function, if only that of a sign, and their judgements make reference, often explicitly, to the norms

5. José Ortega y Gassett (1883–1955), Spanish philosopher and social critic.

6. Terms derived from GEORG WILHELM FRIEDRICH HEGEL's "Master-Slave dialectic" in *Phenomenology of Spirit* (1807; see above). The "in itself" exists passively as a material embodiment of an entity, while the "for itself" self-consciously shapes its identity as a particular kind of entity.

7. New novel (French). The "new novel" of Alain Robbe-Grillet and other French novelists of the 1950s and 1960s disoriented readers by using narrative techniques that made time, place, and narrative point of view difficult to discern. "Brechtian alienation": the German playwright Bertolt Brecht (1898–1956) advocated a political theater that prevented audiences from "identifying" with the characters or taking the events on stage as real, favoring instead a method that "alienated" or distanced spectators from what they were viewing.

8. Self-standing, self-sufficient (German).

9. The highly influential view of art and its appreciation put forward by German philosopher IMMANUEL KANT (1724–1804) in his *Critique of Judgment* (1790; see above).

of morality or agreeableness. Whether rejecting or praising, their appreciation always has an ethical basis.

Popular taste applies the schemes of the ethos, which pertain in the ordinary circumstances of life, to legitimate works of art, and so performs a systematic reduction of the things of art to the things of life. The very seriousness (or naivety) which this taste invests in fictions and representations demonstrates *a contrario*[1] that pure taste performs a suspension of 'naive' involvement which is one dimension of a 'quasi-ludic' relationship with the necessities of the world. Intellectuals could be said to believe in the representation—literature, theatre, painting—more than in the things represented, whereas the people chiefly expect representations and the conventions which govern them to allow them to believe 'naively' in the things represented. The pure aesthetic is rooted in an ethic, or rather, an ethos of elective distance from the necessities of the natural and social world, which may take the form of moral agnosticism (visible when ethical transgression becomes an artistic *parti pris*[2]) or of an aestheticism which presents the aesthetic disposition as a universally valid principle and takes the bourgeois denial of the social world to its limit. The detachment of the pure gaze cannot be dissociated from a general disposition towards the world which is the paradoxical product of conditioning by negative economic necessities—a life of ease—that tends to induce an active distance from necessity.

Although art obviously offers the greatest scope to the aesthetic disposition, there is no area of practice in which the aim of purifying, refining and sublimating primary needs and impulses cannot assert itself, no area in which the stylization of life, that is, the primacy of forms over function, of manner over matter, does not produce the same effects. And nothing is more distinctive, more distinguished, than the capacity to confer aesthetic status on objects that are banal or even 'common' (because the 'common' people make them their own, especially for aesthetic purposes), or the ability to apply the principles of a 'pure' aesthetic to the most everyday choices of everyday life, e.g., in cooking, clothing or decoration, completely reversing the popular disposition which annexes aesthetics to ethics.

In fact, through the economic and social conditions which they presuppose, the different ways of relating to realities and fictions, of believing in fictions and the realities they simulate, with more or less distance and detachment, are very closely linked to the different possible positions in social space and, consequently, bound up with the systems of dispositions (habitus)[3] characteristic of the different classes and class fractions. Taste classifies, and it classifies the classifier. Social subjects, classified by their classifications, distinguish themselves by the distinctions they make, between the beautiful and the ugly, the distinguished and the vulgar, in which their position in the objective classifications is expressed or betrayed. And statistical analysis does indeed show that oppositions similar in structure to those found in cultural practices also appear in eating habits. The antithesis between quantity and quality, substance and form, corresponds to the

1. By way of contrast (Italian).
2. A preconceived opinion or bias; a position (French).
3. A key term in Bourdieu's work, defined elsewhere by him as "a system of acquired dispositions functioning on the practical level as categories of perception and assessment . . . as well as being the organizing principles of action." In other words, habitus names the cultural categories through which individuals process the world and make decisions about what to do.

opposition—linked to different distances from necessity—between the taste of necessity, which favours the most 'filling' and most economical foods, and the taste of liberty—or luxury—which shifts the emphasis to the manner (of presenting, serving, eating etc.) and tends to use stylized forms to deny function.

The science of taste and of cultural consumption begins with a transgression that is in no way aesthetic: it has to abolish the sacred frontier which makes legitimate culture a separate universe, in order to discover the intelligible relations which unite apparently incommensurable 'choices', such as preferences in music and food, painting and sport, literature and hairstyle. This barbarous reintegration of aesthetic consumption into the world of ordinary consumption abolishes the opposition, which has been the basis of high aesthetic since Kant, between the 'taste of sense' and the 'taste of reflection', and between facile pleasure, pleasure reduced to a pleasure of the senses, and pure pleasure, pleasure purified of pleasure, which is predisposed to become a symbol of moral excellence and a measure of the capacity for sublimation which defines the truly human man. The culture which results from this magical division is sacred. Cultural consecration does indeed confer on the objects, persons and situations it touches, a sort of ontological promotion akin to a transubstantiation. Proof enough of this is found in the two following quotations, which might almost have been written for the delight of the sociologist:

'What struck me most is this: nothing could be obscene on the stage of our premier theatre, and the ballerinas of the Opera, even as naked dancers, sylphs, sprites or Bacchae, retain an inviolable purity.'[4]

'There are obscene postures: the simulated intercourse which offends the eye. Clearly, it is impossible to approve, although the interpolation of such gestures in dance routines does give them a symbolic and aesthetic quality which is absent from the intimate scenes the cinema daily flaunts before its spectators' eyes . . . As for the nude scene, what can one say, except that it is brief and theatrically not very effective? I will not say it is chaste or innocent, for nothing commercial can be so described. Let us say it is not shocking, and that the chief objection is that it serves as a box-office gimmick. . . . In *Hair*, the nakedness fails to be symbolic.'[5]

The denial of lower, coarse, vulgar, venal, servile—in a word, natural—enjoyment, which constitutes the sacred sphere of culture, implies an affirmation of the superiority of those who can be satisfied with the sublimated, refined, disinterested, gratuitous, distinguished pleasures forever closed to the profane. That is why art and cultural consumption are predisposed, consciously and deliberately or not, to fulfil a social function of legitimating social differences.

1979

4. O. Merlin, "Mlle Thibon dans la vision de Marguerite," *Le Monde*, 9 December 1965 [Bourdieu's note]. Bacchae: female worshippers of Bacchus, often represented as maddened by wine.

5. F. Chenique, "*Hair* est-il immoral?" *Le Monde*, 28 January 1970 [Bourdieu's note]. The anti–Vietnam War rock musical *Hair* (1967), by Gerome Ragni, James Rado, and Galt MacDermot, was a long-running Broadway hit.

JACQUES DERRIDA
1930–2004

The name of the French philosopher Jacques Derrida is synonymous with deconstruction, a French word (*déconstruction*) he revived but did not invent. Often described as a "method" of "analysis," a "type" of "critique," an "act" of "reading," of a "way" of "writing," deconstruction as a broad phenomenon has become all of those things. But in the writings of Derrida, the words here set in quotation marks are themselves the starting points of a deconstructive reading, not simply its description. Derridean deconstruction thus makes use of—and *at the same time* puts in question (at once uses, puts "under erasure," and does not erase)—the toolbox of classical Western philosophy. Those words have all functioned as philosophical terms, and Derrida, as a historian of philosophy, read them as such. All the gestures of certainty that allow philosophers to say *what something is*, especially when that something is itself an intellectual operation ("concept," "method," "structure," "system," "deconstruction"), become objects of particular critical attention for Derridean deconstruction.

What has been seen—both positively and negatively—as revolutionary about Derrida's work for both philosophy and literary studies is the particular way it attends to language. Not only do the key terms as *terms* belong to a linguistic, and not some purely mental, domain, but that domain or object of inquiry *from the beginning* contains multiple languages. It cannot be traced back to one original language, "full presence," or "living present" that would function as the origin or the end of the multiplicity of languages. The biblical story of the tower of Babel, which recounts humanity's loss of an original universal language, is a powerful myth, but the need for such a myth is not evidence for its validity. Existing languages constantly try, and constantly fail, to present the "truth" or "Being" that is assumed to be behind or beyond language. Derrida thus investigated questions of *translation* that are at the very heart of what other philosophers have called "truth." As he wrote to Toshiko Izutsu, his Japanese translator, "the question of deconstruction is also through and through *the* question of translation." Since we have been conditioned to think of translation as a secondary activity that presupposes a primary text, this reversal—as what we have conceived of as primary simply disappears—changes everything. Language is not merely a vehicle for something that preexists it.

Born in Algeria to French-speaking Jewish parents, Derrida began life in an environment that was both multilingual and culturally complex. Like other Algerian Jews, he experienced firsthand the shifting borderlines of Frenchness: he was excluded from school as non-French during the Vichy government's collaboration with the Nazis in World War II, but in the following decade he was considered *too* French by the Arab and Berber population during the war for Algerian independence from France. He was the third of five children (four boys, one girl); the second and fourth sons died in infancy, the former just before his birth. In his autobiographical meditation called *Circumfessions* (1991)—which is, among other things, a sustained engagement with the *Confessions* of AUGUSTINE, another North African by birth—Derrida writes about the ghosts of his two dead brothers and about the unremembered circumcision that marks his Jewishness, knowing perfectly well that some readers will draw connections between his life and his work. But he leaves it to them to speculate whether certain preoccupations (with ghosts, substitutes, bodily inscriptions, the mobile border between the inside and the outside) are causes or effects of his writing. In any event, he explores precisely the relationship between "life" and "writing."

The pull between literature and philosophy that characterizes Derrida's work was there from the beginning: in high school in Algiers, he imagined writing and teaching literature and, after passing the *baccalauréat* in 1948, he enrolled in the demanding two-year program preparatory to entering one of the prestigious French Grandes Écoles. While reading, he began to be "awed" by philosophers (especially by Søren Kierkegaard and MARTIN HEIDEGGER); he took his first trip to Paris and there enrolled at the famous Lycée Louis-le-Grand. After a difficult period in which he suffered health problems, writer's block, examination failures, and depression, in 1952 he was admitted to the prestigious École Normale Supérieure. In 1956 he passed the *agrégation* (a highly competitive nationwide exam that guarantees successful candidates a teaching job for life). A grant from Harvard University enabled him to work in Cambridge on what in 1962 became his first book: a translation from German of, and a long introduction to, "Questions as to the Origin of Geometry" by the phenomenologist Edmund Husserl (1859–1938). While at Harvard, he also read the works of James Joyce and, in June 1957, married Marguerite Aucouturier (with whom he would have two sons).

During the Algerian War, Derrida was expected to perform his obligatory military service, a requirement he satisfied by spending more than two years in Algeria as a civilian teacher of French and English. Although he condemned French colonialism, he hoped his parents would be able to remain in an independent Algeria; when that proved to be impossible, his whole family moved to Nice, in the south of France.

After several teaching jobs in *lycées* and at the Sorbonne, Derrida was invited in 1955 to become a *maître-assistant* at the École Normale Supérieure, where he taught the history of philosophy for twenty years, and where his seminars became legendary. In 1966, along with a number of other French intellectuals—notably ROLAND BARTHES, JACQUES LACAN, GEORGES POULET, and Lucien Goldmann—he spoke at a landmark conference, "The Languages of Criticism and the Sciences of Man," at Johns Hopkins University. That conference helped shape how structuralism and poststructuralism began to influence literary studies in the United States. Derrida's own talk, an extension but also a critique of structuralism titled "Structure, Sign, and Play in the Discourse of the Human Sciences," was fundamental in articulating what was later seen as the "break" between the two schools.

In 1967 Derrida published his first three books: *La Voix et le phénomène* (*Speech and Phenomena*), a critique of Husserl's concept of the sign; *De la grammatologie* (*Of Grammatology*) an introduction to the necessity and impossibility of a science of writing (from which we draw our first selection); and *L'Écriture et la différence* (*Writing and Difference*) a collection of essays on authors that include MICHEL FOUCAULT (1926–1984), SIGMUND FREUD (1856–1939), G. W. F. HEGEL (1770–1831), and Emmanuel Levinas (1906–1995). He was involved in yet ambivalent about the forces mobilized in the French strikes of May 1968, but his philosophy was crucial to the intellectual upheavals that took place at that time. Derrida published three more books in 1972: *La Dissémination* (*Dissemination*), a collection of four long essays, from which our selection titled "Plato's Pharmacy" is taken; *Marges de la philosophie* (*Margins of Philosophy*) another collection of essays; and *Positions*, the texts of three interviews (the first of many he granted over the years). These early books are touchstones for deconstructive literary criticism; many others followed.

In 1975 Derrida was invited to teach a few weeks a year at Yale University, where he was soon considered a member of the so-called Yale School (along with PAUL DE MAN, J. Hillis Miller, Geoffrey Hartman, and HAROLD BLOOM). From then on, his career was split between two countries, as his role became embattled and marginalized in France and increasingly active and important in the United States. In 1980 he submitted his published works as a *thèse d'état* (advanced doctoral thesis). In 1983 he was elected to the École des Hautes Études en Sciences Sociales (the School for Advanced Study in the Social Sciences). In addition, he regularly offered seminars at several universities in the United States—most notably, at the University of California at Irvine. Derrida died of cancer in Paris at the age of 74.

Our first excerpt from *Of Grammatology*, titled "Exergue," is meant to function as an epigraph (one of the meanings of *exergue*) to Derrida's overall project of investigating the "science of writing." The first thing he notices is that Western discussions of writing tend to make two claims, presenting an *ethnocentric* argument that phonetic writing is the most advanced kind and a *logocentric* argument (a coinage from the Greek word *logos*, meaning "reason, logic, word") that spoken language is superior to written language. Thus, the form of writing that most closely approximates speech is best, and speech itself is considered primary. The consequences of these two assumptions, and the covert or overt forms they take, constitute what Derrida calls "Western metaphysics." To the extent that science itself is modeled on the logic (also from *logos*) of speech, grammatology or a *science of writing*, is itself a contradiction in terms (combining *grammata-*, "writing," and *logy*, "speech"). But Derrida's project is to read rigorously and systematically those moments in the Western tradition where the *text* "speaks" about writing.

Derrida is first and foremost an extraordinary critical reader. Whether he reads writings by philosophers or poets, autobiographers or anthropologists, linguists or psychoanalysts, he pulls out the threads that give the texts coherence and, at the same time, unravel them. His use of the figure of the *web* (well before the existence of but anticipating the World Wide Web) unpacks the appearance of unity presented by a book to reveal an articulation of conflicting messages woven together within it. Yet both forces—the unifying and unraveling—operate in what Derrida calls a "text." If Plato's written "dialogues" mark the beginning of the "age of writing," the writings of Derrida, perhaps, signal its end.

Philosophy, like literature, is the study of things that can matter only to creatures that possess language, even—or especially—when they are attempting to get "beyond" it. That "beyond" is what philosophy calls "metaphysics." Instead of simply getting rid of metaphysics, as American neopragmatists like Richard Rorty try to do, Derrida analyzes the metaphysical residues that cling to the very gesture of going beyond metaphysics, whether it is made in philosophical language, literary language, or the language of everyday life. In a much-misunderstood sentence from our second excerpt from *Of Grammatology* ("The Exorbitant. Question of Method"), Derrida makes the claim that "il n'y a pas de hors-texte," a phrase sometimes translated, not incorrectly, as "there is nothing outside the text." But this translation maintains the inside/outside opposition that the statement in fact aims to overturn. The text is *already* an attempt to include its own outside. There is no outside of *that*.

Though Derrida is known for his neologisms, the terms most closely associated with him are almost never his invention. He instead finds them already in the works he is reading, where they draw his attention by articulating the text in some way that has generally been overlooked. Take, for example, the word *supplément*, which in French means both "substitute" and "addition": in the late-eighteenth-century *Confessions* of Jean-Jacques Rousseau, it is used consciously in only one of its senses at a time, but it necessarily always carries in it the other, thereby drawing together some threads in the text in ways that Rousseau seems not to have intended. As Derrida explains, "the reading must always aim at a certain relationship, unperceived by the writer, between what he commands and what he does not command of the patterns of the language that he uses. The relationship is not a certain quantitative distribution of shadow and light, of weakness or of force, but a signifying structure that critical reading should *produce*."

Derrida is famous for producing such critical readings, which have come to be called "deconstructions." His readings go beyond the mere accuracy of "doubling commentary" ("this indispensable guardrail has always only *protected*, it has never *opened*, a reading"), but they nevertheless remain "intrinsic" to the text. Instead of rushing to expound the text's presumed content, meaning, or referent, they try to remain at the point and within the logic that renders the leap to an outside so tempting. Instead of choosing *between* incompatible or contradictory readings, Derrida attempts to understand the double binds and tensions that are articulated in the text. Rousseau, standing between the Enlightenment and Romanticism, is a figure whose writings are symptomatic of the fissures in the logocentric system that he both reproduces and resists.

In order to see a relationship in a particular language between patterns one commands and patterns one does not command, Derrida worked within the space between the *signified* (what is meant) and the *signifier* (the vehicle for conveying that meaning). The noncoincidence of the two sides of the sign can never be overcome: indeed, we detect a signified when a signifier doesn't quite coincide with it. The signifier, for Derrida, thus functions as a "trace" that gives the impression that a signified was prior to it, even though the only evidence for that signified is the trace itself.

The Swiss linguist FERDINAND DE SAUSSURE, who split the sign into signifier and signified, revolutionized the understanding of language by seeing it as a system (internally as well as externally articulated) and not as a nomenclature (a simple aggregation of names). According to Saussure, language does not arise cumulatively from either things or ideas but instead produces things or ideas out of a structure of differences. "Language is a system of differences," he says in *Course in General Linguistics* (1916), "*without positive terms.*" Derrida takes this concept of difference from Saussure and adds to it the dimension of temporality that Saussure's static (or synchronic) structure does not allow. In doing so, Derrida uncovers a significant contradiction in Saussure: although Saussure *thinks* he can eliminate writing as secondary and keep speech as essential, he treats language as fixed in time and thus as if it were a dead language—a language that we can only know *in writing*.

To mark the combination of such synchronic and diachronic differences, Derrida juxtaposes two grammatical extensions of the verb *différer* (translated into English by two different verbs, "to differ" and "to defer"): *différence*, a noun that implies synchronic comparison, and *différance*, a noun of identical pronunciation that invokes a *process*—the temporal process of deferring or postponing. The structure of language in real time—always changing, and always changing in more than one way—involves both of these senses. But, ironically, a difference (between "e" and "a") meant to be perceived only in writing has become, in English, recognizable in speech: "Derridean *différance*" (pronounced with the French nasal found in "*Vive la différence!*") does not escape the privileging of voice that it was designed to counteract.

Derrida makes the counterintuitive claim that writing is more fundamental than speech. This has often been misunderstood or taken literally. It is as though Derrida is not aware of the fact that babies learn to speak before they learn to write, or that some societies have oral cultures on which writing (Western and imperialistic) has been imposed. Indeed, critics say, hasn't the existence of a written tradition been used to demonstrate Western culture's superiority, and hasn't orality been dismissed as primitive? Why does Derrida say that "Western metaphysics" privileges speech—Logos—and represses writing? Isn't the case just the opposite?

Yes and no. Western culture has always been able to have it both ways; starting with PLATO, who condemned writing *in writing* in his *Phaedrus* (ca. 370 B.C.E.; see above). Our selection from *Dissemination*—excerpts from "Plato's Pharmacy"—offers an analysis of that phenomenon. In his writing, Plato idealized speech as the living emanation of the word, as if it erased the gap between signifier and signified. This idealization of the *logos* (speech, presence, truth, reason) requires that it belong not to any actual language but only to God. And, paradoxically, such an idea of speech is *claimed only in writing*—a writing that pretends it doesn't exist, or is simply a tool that effaces itself in the final moment of truth. This pretence is what Derrida calls "the repression of writing."

In *Phaedrus*, Plato repeats an ancient story of the origin and judgment of writing. The inventor of writing, Theuth, presents it to King Thamus of Egypt as a remedy for forgetfulness. The king rejects his invention on the grounds that it will *induce* forgetfulness, not remedy the condition. The word that they use for writing, *pharmakon* (drug), means "remedy" as well as "poison." Though translators of Plato have chosen one rendering or the other, according to the context, the word contains both meanings; its translations thus dismember it into a *subsequent* either/or structure. Derrida here analyzes the crucial role of translation in the reception of the dialogues of Plato, in the nature of "Platonism," and indeed in the history of philosophy itself.

Derrida shows how the effort to fit everything into binary oppositions (speech and writing, good and bad, true and false, philosophy and literature, etc.) depends on a distinguishability that does not exist within the word *pharmakon*. The translations suggest that it names one side or the other of an existing polarity, but the word is the *medium* and not a result of the split into either/or. A logic prior to that split, however, is almost impossible to think. It risks seeming like sophistry—and after Plato, the distinction between philosophy and sophistry becomes the either/or split on which all the others (and philosophy itself) depend. The distinction Plato makes between sophistry and philosophy *is* philosophy, argues Derrida; philosophy is not merely one counterbalancing term (as Plato, but perhaps not Plato's *text*, seems to believe). Derrida reads Plato's *Phaedrus* as outlining the paradoxical logic of that claim.

In focusing on words—*supplément* in Rousseau, *pharmakon* in Plato (even the word *déconstruction* was originally chosen to translate Heidegger's *Destruktion*, bringing out the sense of "taking apart" rather than "blowing up")—Derrida does not fashion a theoretical metalanguage of concepts designed to support discriminations and generalizations. Each word is found in a text, not made to account for it or for other texts. Such terms are useful because they enable a rereading of the text in which they occur. Derrida is at pains not to separate out a set of terms and define them as "theory," aiming instead to read each new text and find *its* "exorbitant" terms. What these "undecidables" (as Derrida sometimes calls them) have in common is their displacement of what is normally taken for granted as the ground rules for a reading. In that sense, the logics they make visible and functional are generalizible—but they are not logics, if logic is understood as something separable from the text and generalizable apart from it. They are threads *in* it.

Derrida is most successful at making the work of language perceptible at all times within processes of thinking, reading, and writing when he departs from the transparency readers expect—when he draws criticism for the stylistic obscurity he has worked so hard to achieve. In his delays, wordplays, digressions, etymologies, grammatical and syntactical gymnastics, and apparent changes of subject, Derrida doesn't so much transgress rules as stretch them beyond the point where other writers would stop. Some of his sentences are indeed "unspeakable," refusing to correspond to the rhythm of breath, the sounds of emphasis that shape writing as a silent version of what could be spoken out loud. But more than resisting the clarity that every reader, in order to read at all, necessarily continues to seek, Derrida's writings analyze, make visible, and denaturalize the assumptions that have gone into the formation of what counts as clarity in the first place.

BIBLIOGRAPHY

Derrida's analysis of the nontransparency of writing did not slow publication by him or by those inspired (or incensed) by his writing. Derrida's first published book was a translation with a lengthy introduction, *Edmund Husserl's "Origin of Geometry": An Introduction* (1962; trans. 1978). In 1967 Derrida published three books: *La Voix et le phénomène* (trans. 1973, *Speech and Phenomena*), *De la grammatologie* (trans. 1976, *Of Grammatology*; corrected ed., 1998), and *L'Écriture et la différence* (trans. 1978, *Writing and Difference*). In 1972 he published three more books: *La Dissémi-*

nation (trans. 1981, *Dissemination*), *Positions* (trans. 1981, *Positions*), and *Marges—de la philosophie* (trans. 1982, *Margins of Philosophy*).

Glas (1974; trans. 1986, *Glas*), a huge book written in two columns broken up in various ways on the page, discusses the works of the German philosopher Hegel and the transgressive French playwright and novelist Jean Genet; one of the translators, John P. Leavey Jr., published an accompanying volume, *Glassary* (1986). *Éperons: Les Styles de Nietzsche* (1976, 1978; trans. 1979, *Spurs: Nietzsche's Styles*), in which Derrida analyzes how certain philosophers have used concepts of sexual difference, has had a major impact on feminist criticism. In *La Vérité en peinture* (1978; trans. 1987, *The Truth in Painting*), he discusses Heidegger, Kant, Van Gogh, and art criticism. *La Carte postale de Socrate à Freud et au-delà* (1980; trans. 1987, *The Post Card*) continues the discussions of Plato and Socrates, speech and writing, that Derrida began in "Plato's Pharmacy" and includes a groundbreaking reading of Freud's *Beyond the Pleasure Principle*; it also contains "Le facteur de la vérité" ("The Purveyor of Truth"; *facteur* means "mailman" as well as "factor"), Derrida's famous critical reading of Jacques Lacan's seminar on "The Purloined Letter" by Edgar Allan Poe.

Derrida's next publication, *Signéponge/Signsponge* (1983), was a bilingual study of the work of Francis Ponge in which he unpacked the French poet's signature ("anagrammatically") from the poet's works. *Memoires: For Paul de Man*, a collection of lectures that appeared in English in 1986, was revised in 1989 to comment on de Man's wartime journalism.

To simplify the increasingly complex publication history of the 1980s and 1990s, only the English titles of Derrida's important works are given hereafter, unless they appeared in French under a different title. In 1988 Gerald Graff edited *Limited, Inc.*, in which appeared an exchange between Derrida and the philosopher John Searle (first collected in the journal *Glyph* in 1977) about the nature of performative language, with additional texts by Derrida. "Declarations of Independence," *New Political Science* 15 (1986), an influential reading of the American Declaration of Independence, first appeared in French in *Otobiographies: L'enseignement de Nietzsche et la politique du nom propre* (1984). Many individually translated essays on Heidegger, Roland Barthes, Emmanuel Levinas, and Paul de Man and on such topics as racism, translation, and metaphor were first published in *Psyche: Inventions de l'autre* (1987). Derrida's thesis defense, "The Time of a Thesis: Punctuations," in *Philosophy in France Today* (ed. Alan Montefiore, 1983), was published among other texts addressing the institutions of philosophy in France in *Du droit à la philosophie* (1990). *The Other Heading: Reflections on Today's Europe* (1991; trans. 1992) took up political issues, as did Derrida's long-awaited engagement with the texts of Karl Marx, *Specters of Marx: The State of the Debt, the Work of Mourning, and the New International* (1993; trans. 1994).

His meditations on the *gift* and *givenness* and can be found in his *Given Time: I, Counterfeit Money* (1991; trans. 1992), which focuses on Baudelaire and Heidegger, and *The Gift of Death* (1992; trans. 1995), one of Derrida's most explicit discussions of religion. In 1995 three short works (*Passions, Sauf le nom,* and *Khôra*) were translated under the title *On the Name*. *Archive Fever: A Freudian Impression* (1995; trans. 1996), on Freud's *Moses and Monotheism*, was followed by *The Politics of Friendship* (1994; trans. 1997). And two translations appeared in 1998: *Monolingualism of the Other, or, The Prosthesis of Origin* (1996) and *Resistances of Psychoanalysis* (1996). Three readers in English provide useful starting points: *A Derrida Reader: Between the Blinds*, edited by Peggy Kamuf (1991) gives a good overall sample of his writing; *Acts of Literature*, edited by Derek Attridge (1992), and *The Derrida Reader: Writing Performances*, edited by Julian Wolfreys (1998), are more explicitly geared toward literature.

The best source of biographical information is *Jacques Derrida*, coauthored by Geoffrey Bennington and Jacques Derrida (1991; trans. 1993, rev. 1999). Bennington's exposition of Derrida's work, titled "Derridabase," is at the top of each page; Derrida's autobiographical commentary, "Circumfession," is at the bottom. The book also provides photographs, a chronology, and a good bibliography. In addition to the early interviews published as *Positions* (1972; trans. 1981), a later informative collection of interviews, edited by Elisabeth Weber, is available in *Points de suspension, Entretiens* (1992; trans. 1995, *Points . . .*).

Christopher Norris's *Derrida* (1987) remains the best introduction to Derrida's work. *Working through Derrida*, edited by Gary B. Madison (1993), presents very well the divisions around Derrida in Anglo-American philosophy, from John Searle's critique to explications and extensions of Derrida by the leading philosophers Barry Allen, John D. Caputo, and Drucilla Cornell, with Nancy Fraser and Richard Rorty falling somewhere in between. Another collection, *Deconstruction and the Possibility of Justice*, edited by Drucilla Cornell, Michel Rosenfeld, and David Gray Carlson (1992), considers his work's political implications; it begins with an essay by Derrida. Three recent books on Derrida deserve notice: Rodolphe Gasché, *Inventions of Difference: On Jacques Derrida* (1994), which takes seriously Derrida's philosophical critique of reflexivity and specularity and distinguishes between Derrida's deconstruction and American deconstructive literary criticism; Marion Hobson, *Jacques Derrida: Opening Lines* (1998), a difficult but worthwhile reading of the inseparability of Derrida's writing strategies from his arguments; and Christina Howells, *Derrida: Deconstruction from Phenomenology to Ethics* (1999), a very readable introduction to Derrida, with particular attention to the parallel writings of Jean-Paul Sartre.

Two constant critical engagements with deconstruction have come from feminism and Marxism. See, in particular, Diane Elam, *Feminism and Deconstruction: Ms. en Abyme* (1994); *Feminist Interpretations of Jacques Derrida*, edited by Nancy J. Holland (1997); and *Derrida and Feminism: Recasting the Question of Woman*, edited by Ellen K. Feder, Mary C. Rawlinson, and Emily Zakin (1997). The response from Marxism has been divided: in *Marxism and Deconstruction: A Critical Articulation* (1982), Michael Ryan discusses analytical strategies common to Marx and Derrida as inheritors of Hegel; Terry Eagleton, in contrast, attacks deconstruction in his *Literary Theory: An Introduction* (1983; 2d ed., 1996) for not being political. Bill Martin, in *Humanism and Its Aftermath: The Shared Fate of Deconstruction and Politics* (1995), argues that deconstruction *is* political but doesn't go as far as it could. And after Derrida published *Specters of Marx*, Michael Sprinkler organized a symposium around the work, "Ghostly Demarcations," whose proceedings were published under the same title (1999). For critiques of deconstruction from a more traditional standpoint, see John Ellis, *Against Deconstruction* (1989); David H. Hirsch, *The Deconstruction of Literature: Criticism after Auschwitz* (1991); and M. C. Dillon, *Semiological Reductionism: A Critique of the Deconstructionist Movement in Postmodern Thought* (1995).

Studies that extend Derrida's writings in various directions include Jasper Neel, *Plato, Derrida, and Writing* (1988), which investigates the relevance of Derrida's reading of Plato to composition theory; *Writing the Politics of Difference*, edited by Hugh J. Silverman (1991); Jonathan Loesberg, *Aestheticism and Deconstruction: Pater, Derrida, and de Man* (1991); Simon Critchley, *The Ethics of Deconstruction: Derrida and Levinas* (1992; 2d ed., 1999); Morag Patrick, *Derrida, Responsibility, and Politics* (1997); Joseph G. Kronick, *Derrida and the Future of Literature* (1999); Christine van Boheemen-Saaf, *Joyce, Derrida, Lacan, and the Trauma of History: Reading, Narrative, and Postcolonialism* (1999); and Peter Pericles Trifonas, *The Ethics of Writing: Derrida, Deconstruction, and Pedagogy* (2000).

William Schultz's *Jacques Derrida: An Annotated Primary and Secondary Bibliography* (1992) is useful up to 1992. *Jacques Derrida (II): A Bibliography*, compiled by Joan Nordquist (1995), goes up to 1995.

From Of Grammatology[1]

Exergue[2]

1. The one who will shine in the science of writing will shine like the sun. A scribe (EP,[3] p. 87)

O Samas (sun-god), by your light you scan the totality of lands as if they were cuneiform signs (ibid.).

2. These three ways of writing correspond almost exactly to three different stages according to which one can consider men gathered into a nation. The depicting of objects is appropriate to a savage people; signs of words and of propositions, to a barbaric people; and the alphabet to civilized people. J.-J. Rousseau, *Essai sur l'origine des langues.*[4]

3. Alphabetic script is in itself and for itself the most intelligent. Hegel, *Enzyklopädie.*[5]

This triple exergue is intended not only to focus attention on the *ethnocentrism* which, everywhere and always, had controlled the concept of writing. Nor merely to focus attention on what I shall call *logocentrism*: the metaphysics of phonetic writing[6] (for example, of the alphabet) which was fundamentally—for enigmatic yet essential reasons that are inaccessible to a simple historical relativism—nothing but the most original and powerful ethnocentrism, in the process of imposing itself upon the world, controlling in one and the same *order*:

1. *the concept of writing* in a world where the phoneticization of writing must dissimulate its own history as it is produced;

2. *the history of* (the only) *metaphysics*, which has, in spite of all differences, not only from Plato to Hegel (even including Leibniz) but also, beyond these apparent limits, from the pre-Socratics, to Heidegger,[7] always assigned the origin of truth in general to the logos: the history of truth, of the truth of truth, has always been—except for a metaphysical diversion that we shall have to explain—the debasement of writing, and its repression outside "full" speech.

3. *the concept of science* or the scientificity of science—what has always been determined as *logic*—a concept that has always been a philosophical concept, even if the practice of science has constantly challenged its imperialism of the logos, by invoking, for example, from the beginning and ever increasingly, nonphonetic writing. No doubt this subversion has always been

1. Translated by Gayatri Chakravorty Spivak, who sometimes retains the original French in brackets.
2. Epigraph; inscription on a coin; heading (French).
3. *L'Écriture et la psychologie des peuples* (*Writing and Folk Psychology*) (Paris, 1963), the proceedings of a colloquium.
4. *Essay on the Origin of Languages* (written 1761; pub. 1781), by the Swiss-born French philosopher Jean-Jacques Rousseau (1712–1778).
5. *Encyclopedia of the Philosophical Sciences* (1817), by the German philosopher GEORG WILHELM FRIEDRICH HEGEL (1770–1831).
6. Writing modeled on spoken sounds. "Logocentrism": the privileging of *logos*, of "word, speech, story, reason" (Greek). Derrida applies the term to knowledge assumed to be organized around a central truth (e.g., Being, Presence, the Living Voice, or the Word of God).
7. MARTIN HEIDEGGER (1889–1976), German philosopher. PLATO (ca. 427–ca. 347 B.C.E.), Greek philosopher whose dialogues present the oral teachings of Socrates (469–399 B.C.E.). Gottfried Wilhelm Leibniz (1646–1716), German philosopher and mathematician. Pre-Socratics: Greek philosophers of the 6th and 5th centuries B.C.E., whose thought was generally concerned with the natural world and with practical human conduct.

contained within a system of direct address [*système allocutoire*] which gave birth to the project of science and to the conventions of all nonphonetic characteristics.[8] It could not have been otherwise. Nonetheless, it is a peculiarity of our epoch that, at the moment when the phoneticization of writing—the historical origin and structural possibility of philosophy as of science, the condition of the *epistémé*[9]—begins to lay hold on world culture,[1] science, in its advancements, can no longer be satisfied with it. This inadequation had always already begun to make its presence felt. But today something lets it appear as such, allows it a kind of takeover without our being able to translate this novelty into clear cut notions of mutation, explication, accumulation, revolution, or tradition. These values belong no doubt to the system whose dislocation is today presented as such, they describe the styles of an historical movement which was meaningful—like the concept of history itself—only within a logocentric epoch.

By alluding to a science of writing reined in by metaphor, metaphysics, and theology,[2] this exergue must not only announce that the science of writing—grammatology[3]—shows signs of liberation all over the world, as a result of decisive efforts. These efforts are necessarily discreet, dispersed, almost imperceptible; that is a quality of their meaning and of the milieu within which they produce their operation. I would like to suggest above all that, however fecund and necessary the undertaking might be, and even if, given the most favorable hypothesis, it did overcome all technical and epistemological obstacles as well as all the theological and metaphysical impediments that have limited it hitherto, such a science of writing runs the risk of never being established as such and with that name. Of never being able to define the unity of its project or its object. Of not being able to either write its discourse on method[4] or to describe the limits of its field. For essential rea-

8. Cf., for example, the notions of "secondary elaboration" or "symbolism of second intention" in Edmond Ortigues, *Le discours et le symbole* [*Discourse and Symbol*] (Aubier, 1962) pp. 62 and 171. "Mathematical symbolism is a convention of writing, a scriptural symbolism. It is only by an abuse of vocabulary or by analogy that one speaks of a 'mathematical language.' Algorithm is actually a 'characteristics,' it is composed of written characters. It does not speak, except through the intermediary of a language which furnishes not only the phonetic expression of the characters but also the formulation of axioms permitting the determination of the value of these characters. It is true that at a pinch one could decipher unknown characters, but that always supposes an acquired knowledge, a thought already formed by the usage of speech. Therefore, in all hypothesis, mathematical symbolism is the fruit of a secondary elaboration, supposing preliminarily the usage of discourse and the possibility of conceiving explicit conventions. It is nevertheless true that mathematical algorithm will express the formal laws of symbolization, of syntactic structures, independent of particular means of expression." On these problems, cf. also Gilles Gaston Granger, *Pensée formelle et sciences de l'homme* (Paris, 1960), pp. 38f. and particularly pp. 43 and 50f. (on the "Reversal of Relationships between the Spoken Language and Writing") [Derrida's note].

9. Knowledge; professional skill, profession (Greek).

1. All works on the history of writing devote space to the problem of the introduction of phonetic writing in the cultures that did not practice it previously. Cf. e.g., *EP*, pp. pp. 44f. or "La Réforme de l'écriture chinoise," *Linguistique: Recherches internationales à la lumière du marxisme* 7 (May–June 1958) [Derrida's note].

2. Here I do not merely mean those "theological prejudices" which, at an identifiable time and place, inflected or repressed the theory of the written sign in the 17th and 18th centuries. I shall speak of them later in connection with Madeleine V.-David's book [*Debates about Writing and Hieroglyphics in the 17th and 18th Centuries*, 1965]. These prejudices are nothing but the most clearsighted and best circumscribed, historically determined manifestation of a constitutive and permanent presupposition essential to the history of the West, therefore to metaphysics in its entirety, even when it professes to be atheist [Derrida's note].

3. *Grammatology:* "A treatise upon Letters, upon the alphabet, syllabation, reading, and writing," Littré [standard French dictionary]. To my knowledge and in our time, this word has only been used by I. J. Gelb to designate the project of a modern science in *A Study of Writing: The Foundations of Grammatology* (Chicago, 1952) (the subtitle disappears in the 1963 edition). In spite of a concern for systematic or simplified classification, and in spite of the controversial hypotheses on the monogenesis or polygenesis of scripts, this book follows the classical model of histories of writing [Derrida's note].

4. *The Discourse on Method* (1637) is a foundational work of the French philosopher René Descartes.

sons: the unity of all that allows itself to be attempted today through the most diverse concepts of science and of writing, is, in principle, more or less covertly yet always, determined by an historico-metaphysical epoch of which we merely glimpse the *closure*. I do not say the *end*. The idea of science and the idea of writing—therefore also of the science of writing—is meaningful for us only in terms of an origin and within a world to which a certain concept of the sign (later I shall call it *the* concept of sign) and a certain concept of the relationships between speech and writing, have *already* been assigned. A most determined relationship, in spite of its privilege, its necessity, and the field of vision that it has controlled for a few millennia, especially in the West, to the point of being now able to produce its own dislocation and itself proclaim its limits.

Perhaps patient meditation and painstaking investigation on and around what is still provisionally called writing, far from falling short of a science of writing or of hastily dismissing it by some obscurantist reaction, letting it rather develop its positivity as far as possible, are the wanderings of a way of thinking that is faithful and attentive to the ineluctable world of the future which proclaims itself at present, beyond the closure of knowledge. The future can only be anticipated in the form of an absolute danger. It is that which breaks absolutely with constituted normality and can only be proclaimed, *presented*, as a sort of monstrosity. For that future world and for that within it which will have put into question the values of sign, word, and writing, for that which guides our future anterior, there is as yet no exergue.

* * *

The Exorbitant. Question of Method

"For me there has never been an intermediary between everything and nothing." The intermediary is the mid-point and the mediation, the middle term between total absence and the absolute plenitude of presence. It is clear that mediacy is the name of all that Rousseau wanted opinionatedly to efface.[5] This wish is expressed in a deliberate, sharp, thematic way. It does not have to be deciphered. Jean-Jacques recalls it here at the very moment when he is spelling out the supplements that are linked together to replace a mother or a Nature. And here the supplement occupies the middle point between total absence and total presence. The play of substitution fills and marks a determined lack. But Rousseau argues as if the recourse to the supplement—here to Thérèse[6]—was going to appease his impatience when confronted with the intermediary: "From that moment I was alone; for me there has never been an intermediary between everything and nothing. I found in Thérèse the substitute that I needed." The virulence of this concept is thus appeased, as if one were able to *arrest it*, domesticate it, tame it.

This brings up the question of the usage of the word "supplement":[7] of Rousseau's situation within the language and the logic that assures to this word or this concept sufficiently *surprising* resources so that the presumed

5. In omitted text, Derrida has just sketched out a reading of Rousseau's *Confessions* (written 1766–70; pub. 1781–88), focusing on the contradictory claims Rousseau makes about the truth of his own self-portrait.

6. Thérèse Le Vasseur, a working-class woman who accompanied Rousseau for most of his life and had five children with him.

7. In French, *supplément* means both "substitute" and "addition." Both senses are in play in this analysis, articulating a logic that describes the relation between language and the world.

subject of the sentence might always say, through using the "supplement," more, less, or something other than what he *would mean* [*voudrait dire*]. This question is therefore not only of Rousseau's writing but also of our reading. We should begin by taking rigorous account of this *being held within* [*prise*] or this *surprise*: the writer writes *in* a language and *in* a logic whose proper system, laws, and life his discourse by definition cannot dominate absolutely. He uses them only by letting himself, after a fashion and up to a point, be governed by the system. And the reading must always aim at a certain relationship, unperceived by the writer, between what he commands and what he does not command of the patterns of the language that he uses. This relationship is not a certain quantitative distribution of shadow and light, of weakness or of force, but a signifying structure that critical reading should *produce*.

What does produce mean here? In my attempt to explain that, I would initiate a justification of my principles of reading. A justification, as we shall see, entirely negative, outlining by exclusion a space of reading that I shall not fill here: a task of reading.

To produce this signifying structure obviously cannot consist of reproducing, by the effaced and respectful doubling of commentary, the conscious, voluntary, intentional relationship that the writer institutes in his exchanges with the history to which he belongs thanks to the element of language. This moment of doubling commentary should no doubt have its place in a critical reading. To recognize and respect all its classical exigencies is not easy and requires all the instruments of traditional criticism. Without this recognition and this respect, critical production would risk developing in any direction at all and authorize itself to say almost anything. But this indispensable guardrail has always only *protected*, it has never *opened*, a reading.

Yet if reading must not be content with doubling the text, it cannot legitimately transgress the text toward something other than it, toward a referent (a reality that is metaphysical, historical, psychobiographical, etc.) or toward a signified outside the text whose content could take place, could have taken place outside of language, that is to say, in the sense that we give here to that word, outside of writing in general. That is why the methodological considerations that we risk applying here to an example are closely dependent on general propositions that we have elaborated above; as regards the absence of the referent or the transcendental signified.[8] *There is nothing outside of the text* [there is no outside-text; *il n'y a pas de hors-texte*].[9] And that is neither because Jean-Jacques' life, or the existence of Mamma or Thérèse *themselves*, is not of prime interest to us, nor because we have access to their so-called "real" existence only in the text and we have neither any means of altering this, nor any right to neglect this limitation. All reasons of this type would already be sufficient, to be sure, but there are more radical reasons. What we have tried to show by following the guiding line of the "dangerous supplement," is that in what one calls the real life of these exis-

8. The ultimate meaning. The sign was divided into *signified* (the meaning conveyed) and *signifier* (the symbol or sound that conveys that meaning) by the Swiss linguist FERDINAND DE SAUSSURE (1857–1913), who argued that in language, the relation between the two is arbitrary.

9. The translation "there is nothing outside the text," while not incorrect, is misleading because it implies an inside/outside barrier whose existence Derrida is precisely putting in question. A text is *constituted* by the attempt to represent what is outside it: every attempt to get outside of *that* ends up repeating, not transcending, the structure.

tences "of flesh and bone," beyond and behind what one believes can be circumscribed as Rousseau's text, there has never been anything but writing; there have never been anything but supplements, substitutive significations which could only come forth in a chain of differential references, the "real" supervening, and being added only while taking on meaning from a trace and from an invocation of the supplement, etc. And thus to infinity, for we have read, *in the text*, that the absolute present, Nature, that which words like "real mother" name, have always already escaped, have never existed; that what opens meaning and language is writing as the disappearance of natural presence.

Although it is not commentary, our reading must be intrinsic and remain within the text. That is why, in spite of certain appearances, the locating of the word *supplement* is here not at all psychoanalytical, if by that we understand an interpretation that takes us outside of the writing toward a psychobiographical signified, or even toward a general psychological structure that could rightly be separated from the signifier. This method has occasionally been opposed to the traditional doubling commentary; it could be shown that it actually comes to terms with it quite easily. *The security with which the commentary considers the self-identity of the text, the confidence with which it carves out its contour, goes hand in hand with the tranquil assurance that leaps over the text toward its presumed content, in the direction of the pure signified.*[1] And in effect, in Rousseau's case, psychoanalytical studies like those of Dr. Laforgue[2] transgress the text only after having read it according to the most current methods. The reading of the literary "symptom" is most banal, most academic, most naive. And once one has thus blinded oneself to the very tissue of the "symptom," to its proper texture, one cheerfully exceeds it toward a psychobiographical signified whose link with the literary signifier[3] then becomes perfectly extrinsic and contingent. One recognizes the other aspect of the same gesture when, in general works on Rousseau, in a package of classical shape that gives itself out to be a synthesis that faithfully restores, through commentary and compilation of themes, the totality of the work and the thought, one encounters a chapter of biographical and psychoanalytical cast on the "problem of sexuality in Rousseau," with a reference in an Appendix to the author's medical case-history.

If it seems to us in principle impossible to separate, through interpretation or commentary, the signified from the signifier, and thus to destroy writing by the writing that is yet reading, we nevertheless believe that this impossibility is historically articulated. It does not limit attempts at deciphering in the same way, to the same degree, and according to the same rules. Here we must take into account the history of the text in general. When we speak of the writer and of the encompassing power of the language to which he is subject, we are not only thinking of the writer in literature. The philosopher, the chronicler, the theoretician in general, and at the limit everyone writing, is thus taken by surprise. But, in each case, the person writing is inscribed in a determined textual system. Even if there is never a pure signified, there are different relationships as to that which, from the signifier, *is presented* as the irreducible stratum of the signified. For example, the philosophical

1. Pure meaning.
2. See, in particular, Dr. René Laforgue's "Étude sur J.-J. Rousseau," *Revue française de psychanalyse*, I, ii (1927), and *Psychopathologie de l'échec* (1944) [Derrida's note].
3. The words present in a text.

text, although it is in fact always written includes, precisely as its philosophical specificity, the project of effacing itself in the face of the signified content which it transports and in general teaches. Reading should be aware of this project, even if, in the last analysis, it intends to expose the project's failure. The entire history of texts, and within it the history of literary forms in the West, should be studied from this point of view. With the exception of a thrust or a point of resistance which has only been very lately recognized as such, literary writing has, almost always and almost everywhere, according to some fashions and across very diverse ages, lent itself to this *transcendent* reading, in that search for the signified which we here put in question, not to annull it but to understand it within a system to which such a reading is blind. Philosophical literature is only one example within this history but it is among the most significant. And it interests us particularly in Rousseau's case. Who at the same time and for profound reasons produced a philosophical literature to which belong *The Social Contract* and *La nouvelle Héloise*,[4] and chose to live by literary writing; by a writing which would not be exhausted by the message—philosophical or otherwise—which it could, so to speak, deliver. And what Rousseau has said, as philosopher or as psychologist, of writing in general, cannot be separated from the system of his own writing. We should be aware of this.

This poses formidable problems. Problems of outlining in particular. Let me give three examples.

1. If the course I have followed in the reading of the "supplement" is not merely psychoanalytical, it is undoubtedly because the habitual psychoanalysis of literature begins by putting the literary signifier as such within parentheses. It is no doubt also because psychoanalytic theory itself is for me a collection of texts belonging to my history and my culture. To that extent, if it marks my reading and the writing of my interpretation, it does not do so as a principle or a truth that one could abstract from the textual system that I inhabit in order to illuminate it with complete neutrality. In a certain way, I am *within* the history of psychoanalysis as I am *within* Rousseau's text. Just as Rousseau drew upon a language that was already there—and which is found to be somewhat our own, thus assuring us a certain minimal readability of French literature—in the same way we operate today within a certain network of significations marked by psychoanalytic theory, even if we do not master it and even if we are assured of never being able to master it perfectly.

But it is for another reason that this is not even a somewhat inarticulate psychoanalysis of Jean-Jacques Rousseau. Such a psychoanalysis is already obliged to have located all the structures of appurtenance within Rousseau's text, all that is not unique to it—by reason of the encompassing power and the already-thereness of the language or of the culture—all that could be inhabited rather than produced by writing. Around the irreducible point of originality of this writing an immense series of structures, of historical totalities of all orders, are organized, enveloped, and blended. Supposing that psychoanalysis can by rights succeed in outlining them and their interpretations, supposing that it takes into account the entire history of metaphysics—the history of that Western metaphysics that entertains relationships of cohabitation with Rousseau's text, it would still be necessary

4. *The New Eloise* (1761), an enormously popular epistolary novel by Rousseau; *The Social Contract* (1762) is his best-known work of political philosophy.

for this psychoanalysis to elucidate the law of its own appurtenance to metaphysics and Western culture. Let us not pursue this any further. We have already measured the difficulty of the task and the element of frustration in our interpretation of the supplement. We are sure that something irreducibly Rousseauist is captured there but we have carried off, at the same time, a yet quite unformed mass of roots, soil, and sediments of all sorts.

2. Even supposing that Rousseau's text can be rigorously isolated and articulated within history in general, and then within the history of the sign "supplement," one must still take into consideration many other possibilities. Following the appearance of the word "supplement" and of the corresponding concept or concepts, we traverse a certain path within Rousseau's text. To be sure, this particular path will assure us the economy of a synopsis. But are other paths not possible? And as long as the totality of paths is not effectively exhausted, how shall we justify this one?

3. In Rousseau's text, after having indicated—by anticipation and as a prelude—the function of the sign "supplement," I now prepare myself to give special privilege, in a manner that some might consider exorbitant, to certain texts like the *Essay on the Origin of Languages* and other fragments on the theory of language and writing. By what right? And why these short texts, published for the most part after the author's death, difficult to classify, of uncertain date and inspiration?

To all these questions and within the logic of their system, there is no satisfying response. In a certain measure and in spite of the theoretical precautions that I formulate, my choice is in fact *exorbitant.*

But what is the exorbitant?

I wished to reach the point of a certain exteriority in relation to the totality of the age of logocentrism. Starting from this point of exteriority, a certain deconstruction of that totality which is also a traced path, of that orb (*orbis*) which is also orbitary (*orbita*[5]), might be broached. The first gesture of this departure and this deconstruction, although subject to a certain historical necessity, cannot be given methodological or logical intra-orbitary assurances. Within the closure, one can only judge its style in terms of the accepted oppositions. It may be said that this style is empiricist[6] and in a certain way that would be correct. The *departure* is radically empiricist. It proceeds like a wandering thought on the possibility of itinerary and of method. It is affected by nonknowledge as by its future and it *ventures out* deliberately. I have myself defined the form and the vulnerability of this empiricism. But here the very concept of empiricism destroys itself. To *exceed* the metaphysical orb is an attempt to get out of the orbit (*orbita*), to think the entirety of the classical conceptual oppositions, particularly the one within which the value of empiricism is held: the opposition of philosophy and nonphilosophy, another name for empiricism, for this incapability to sustain on one's own and to the limit the coherence of one's own discourse, for being produced as truth at the moment when the value of truth is shattered, for escaping the internal contradictions of skepticism, etc. *The thought of this historical opposition between philosophy and empiricism is not simply empirical and it cannot be thus qualified without abuse and misunderstanding.*

5. Track or rut; circuit (Latin). *Orbis*: orb, circle (Latin).

6. Reliant on experience. Empiricism holds that there is no genuine a priori knowledge of the world.

Let us make the diagram more specific. What is exorbitant in the reading of Rousseau? No doubt Rousseau, as I have already suggested, has only a very relative privilege in the history that interests us. If we merely wished to situate him within this history, the attention that we accord him would be clearly disproportionate. But that is not our intention. We wish to identify a decisive articulation of the logocentric epoch. For purposes of this identification Rousseau seems to us to be most revealing. That obviously supposes that we have already prepared the exit, determined the repression of writing as the fundamental operation of the epoch, read a certain number of texts but not all of them, a certain number of Rousseau's texts but not all of them. This avowal of empiricism can sustain itself only by the strength of the question. The opening of the question, the departure from the closure of a self-evidence, the putting into doubt of a system of oppositions, all these movements necessarily have the form of empiricism and of errancy. At any rate, they cannot be described, *as to past norms*, except in this form. No other trace is available, and as these errant questions are not absolute beginnings in every way, they allow themselves to be effectively reached, on one entire surface, by this description which is also a criticism. We must begin *wherever we are* and the thought of the trace, which cannot not take the scent into account, has already taught us that it was impossible to justify a point of departure absolutely. *Wherever we are*: in a text where we already believe ourselves to be.

Let us narrow the arguments down further. In certain respects, the theme of supplementarity is certainly no more than one theme among others. It is in a chain, carried by it. Perhaps one could substitute something else for it. *But it happens that this theme describes the chain itself, the being-chain of a textual chain, the structure of substitution, the articulation of desire and of language, the logic of all conceptual oppositions taken over by Rousseau*, and particularly the role and the function, in his system, of the concept of Nature. It tells us in a text what a text is, it tells us in writing what writing it, in Rousseau's writing it tells us Jean-Jacques' desire, etc. If we consider, according to the axial proposition of this essay, that there is nothing outside the text, our ultimate justification would be the following: the concept of the supplement and the theory of writing designate textuality itself in Rousseau's text in an indefinitely multiplied structure—*en abyme* [*in an abyss*][7]—to employ the current phrase. And we shall see that this abyss is not a happy or unhappy accident. An entire theory of the structural necessity of the abyss will be gradually constituted in our reading; the indefinite process of supplementarity has always already *infiltrated* presence, always already inscribed there the space of repetition and the splitting of the self. Representation *in the abyss* of presence is not an accident of presence; the desire of presence is, on the contrary, born from the abyss (the indefinite multiplication) of representation, from the representation of representation, etc. The supplement itself is quite exorbitant, in every sense of the word.

Thus Rousseau inscribes textuality in the text. But its operation is not simple. It tricks with a gesture of effacement, and strategic relations like the relationships of force among the two movements form a complex design.

7. That is, *mise en abyme*: literally, "setting in an abyss" (French). As a literary technique, this is a mininarrative that encapsulates the narrative containing it, in a kind of mirroring of representation.

This design seems to us to be represented in the handling of the concept of the supplement. Rousseau cannot utilize it at the same time in all the virtualities of its meaning. The way in which he determines the concept and, in so doing, lets himself be determined by that very thing that he excludes from it, the direction in which he bends it, here as addition, there as substitute, now as the positivity and exteriority of evil, now as a happy auxiliary, all this conveys neither a passivity nor an activity, neither an unconsciousness nor a lucidity on the part of the author. Reading should not only abandon these categories—which are also, let us recall in passing, the founding categories of metaphysics—but should produce the law of this relationship to the concept of the supplement. It it certainly a production, because I do not simply duplicate what Rousseau thought of this relationship. The concept of the supplement is a sort of blind spot in Rousseau's text, the not-seen that opens and limits visibility. But the production, if it attempts to make the not-seen accessible to sight, does not leave the text. It has moreover only believed it was doing so by illusion. It is contained in the transformation of the language it designates, in the regulated exchanges between Rousseau and history. We know that these exchanges only take place by way of the language and the text, in the infrastructural sense that we now give to that word. And what we call production is necessarily a text, the system of a writing and of a reading which we know is ordered around its own blind spot. We know this a priori, but only now and with a knowledge that is not a knowledge at all.

1967

From Dissemination[1]

From *Plato's Pharmacy*

A text is not a text unless it hides from the first comer, from the first glance, the law of its composition and the rules of its game. A text remains, moreover, forever imperceptible. Its law and its rules are not, however, harbored in the inaccessibility of a secret; it is simply that they can never be booked, in the *present*, into anything that could rigorously be called a perception.

And hence, perpetually and essentially, they run the risk of being definitively lost. Who will ever know of such disappearances?

The dissimulation of the woven texture can in any case take centuries to undo its web: a web that envelops a web, undoing the web for centuries; reconstituting it too as an organism, indefinitely regenerating its own tissue behind the cutting trace, the decision of each reading. There is always a surprise in store for the anatomy or physiology of any criticism[2] that might think it has mastered the game, surveyed all the threads at once, deluding itself, too, in wanting to look at the text without touching it, without laying a hand on the "object," without risking—which is the only chance of entering into the game, by getting a few fingers caught—the addition of some new thread. Adding, here, is nothing other than giving to read. One must manage

1. Translated by Barbara Johnson, who occasionally retains the original French in brackets.
2. Perhaps a reference to *Anatomy of Criticism* (1957), the best-known book by the Canadian critic NORTHROP FRYE.

to think this out: that it is not a question of embroidering upon a text, unless one considers that to know how to embroider still means to have the ability to follow the given thread. That is, if you follow me, the hidden thread. If reading and writing are one, as is easily thought these days, if reading *is* writing, this oneness designates neither undifferentiated (con)fusion nor identity at perfect rest; the *is* that couples reading with writing must rip apart.

One must then, in a single gesture, but doubled, read and write. And that person would have understood nothing of the game who, at this [*du coup*][3] would feel himself authorized merely to add on; that is, to add any old thing. He would add nothing: the seam wouldn't hold. Reciprocally, he who through "methodological prudence," "norms of objectivity," or "safeguards of knowledge" would refrain from committing anything of himself, would not read at all. The same foolishness, the same sterility, obtains in the "not serious" as in the "serious." The reading or writing supplement must be rigorously prescribed, but by the necessities of a *game*, by the logic of *play*, signs to which the system of all textual powers must be accorded and attuned.

I

To a considerable degree, we have already said all we *meant to say*. Our lexicon at any rate is not far from being exhausted. With the exception of this or that supplement, our questions will have nothing more to name but the texture of the text, reading and writing, mastery and play, the paradoxes of supplementarity, and the graphic relations between the living and the dead: within the textual, the textile, and the histological. We will keep within the limits of this *tissue*; between the metaphor of the *histos*[4] and the question of the *histos* of metaphor.

Since we have already said everything, the reader must bear with us if we continue on awhile. If we extend ourselves by force of play. If we then *write* a bit: on Plato,[5] who already said in the *Phaedrus* that writing can only repeat (itself), that it "always signifies (*sēmainei*) the same" and that it is a "game" (*paidia*).

1. PHARMACIA

Let us begin again. Therefore the dissimulation of the woven texture can in any case take centuries to undo its web. The example we shall propose of this will not, seeing that we are dealing with Plato, be the *Statesman*, which will have come to mind first, no doubt because of the paradigm of the weaver, and especially because of the paradigm of the paradigm, the example of the example—writing—which immediately precedes it.[6] We will come back to that only after a long detour.

We will take off here from the *Phaedrus*.[7] We are speaking of the *Phaedrus*

3. At this blow (French).
4. "*Histos: anything set upright*, hence: I. *mast*. II. *beam* of a loom, which stood upright, instead of lying hoizontal as in our looms (except in the weaving methods used by the Gobelins and in India), to which the threads of the warp are attached, hence: 1. *loom*; 2. *the warp fixed to the loom*, hence, *the woof*; 3. *woven cloth, piece of canvas*; 4. by anal. *spider web*; or *honeycomb of bees*. III. *rod, wand, stick*. IV. by anal. *shinbone, leg*" [Derrida's note]. Derrida defines the word as used in classical Greek; in modern medicine, it refers to tissues (e.g., "histology"). Some of the author's notes are omitted.
5. Greek philosopher (ca. 427–ca. 347 B.C.E.; see above), many of whose dialogues are referred to by Derrida. He here quotes *Phaedrus* 275d, 276d (see above).
6. In a note, Derrida quotes *Statesman* 277d–e.
7. As a rule, translations of Plato are taken from *The Collected Dialogues of Plato*, ed. Edith Hamilton and Huntington Cairns, Bollingen Series 71 (Princeton: Princeton University Press, 1961), supplemented by other renderings. In addition, I

that was obliged to wait almost twenty-five centuries before anyone gave up the idea that it was a badly composed dialogue. It was at first believed that Plato was too young to do the thing right, to construct a well-made object. Diogenes Laertius[8] records this "they say" (*logos* [sc. *esti*], *legetai*) according to which the *Phaedrus* was Plato's first attempt and thus manifested a certain juvenile quality (*meirakiōdēs ti*).[9] Schleiermacher[1] thinks this legend can be corroborated by means of a ludicrous argument: an aging writer would not have condemned writing as Plato does in the *Phaedrus*. This argument is not merely suspect in itself: it lends credit to the Laertian legend by basing itself on a second legend. Only a blind or grossly insensitive reading could indeed have spread the rumor that Plato was *simply* condemning the writer's activity. Nothing here is of a single piece and the *Phaedrus* also, in its own writing, plays at saving writing—which also means causing it to be lost—as the best, the noblest game. As for the stunning hand Plato has thus dealt himself, we will be able to follow its incidence and its payoff later on.

In 1905, the tradition of Diogenes Laertius was reversed, not in order to bring about a recognition of the excellent composition of the *Phaedrus* but in order to attribute its faults this time to the senile impotence of the author: "The *Phaedrus* is badly composed. This defect is all the more surprising since it is precisely there that Socrates[2] defines the work of art as a living being. But the inability to accomplish what has been well conceived is precisely a proof of old age."[3]

We are no longer at that point. The hypothesis of a rigorous, sure, and subtle form is naturally more fertile. It discovers new chords, new concordances; it surprises them in minutely fashioned counterpoint, within a more secret organization of themes, of names, of words. It unties a whole *sumplokē*[4] patiently interlacing the arguments. What is magisterial about the demonstration affirms itself and effaces itself at once, with suppleness, irony, and discretion.

This is, in particular, the case—and this will be our supplementary thread—with the whole last section (274*b* ff.), devoted, as everyone knows, to the origin, history, and value of writing. That entire hearing of the *trial of writing* should some day cease to appear as an extraneous mythological fantasy, an appendix the organism could easily, with no loss, have done without. In truth, it is rigorously called for from one end of the *Phaedrus* to the other.

Always with irony. But what can be said of irony here? What is its major sign? The dialogue contains the only "rigorously original Platonic myths: the fable of the cicadas in the *Phaedrus*, and the story of Theuth in the same

have occasionally modified the wording or word order of the Platonic texts in order to bring them into line with the parenthetical Greek inserts. Some minor adjustments have also been made when it seemed necessary to achieve a closer parallel to the French version with which Derrida is working [translator's note, edited].

8. Greek author (ca. early 3d c. C.E.) of a 10-volume compendium on the lives of Greek philosophers.

9. On the history of interpretations of the *Phaedrus* and the problem of its composition, a rich, detailed account can be found in L. Robin's *La Théorie platonicienne de l'amour* [*The Platonic Theory of Love*], 2d ed. (Paris: Presses Universitaires de France, 1964), and in the same author's introduction to the Budé edition of the *Phaedrus* [Derrida's note].

1. Friedrich Schleiermacher (1768–1834), German theologian and philosopher.

2. Greek philosopher (469–399 B.C.E.), whose teachings are known to us only through the writings of others—particularly Plato, who makes him the leading figure in the dialogues.

3. H. Raeder, *Platons philosophische Entwickelung* [*Plato's Philosophical Development*] (Leipzig, 1905). A critique of this view, "Sur la composition du *Phèdre*" ["On the Composition of the *Phaedrus*"], by E. Bourguet, appeared in the *Revue de Métaphysique et de Morale*, 1919, p. 335 [Derrida's note].

4. Intertwining; rhetorical interweaving (Greek).

dialogue."[5] Interestingly, Socrates' first words, in the opening lines of the conversation, had concerned "not bothering about" mythologemes[6] (229*c*–230*a*). Not in order to reject them absolutely, but, on the one hand, not bothering them, leaving them alone, making room for them, in order to free them from the heavy serious naïveté of the scientific "rationalists," and on the other, not bothering *with* them, in order to free *oneself* for the relation with oneself and the pursuit of self-knowledge.

To give myths a send-off: a salute, a vacation, a dismissal; this fine resolution of the *khairein,*[7] which means all that at once, will be twice interrupted in order to welcome these "two Platonic myths," so "rigorously original." Both of these myths arise, moreover, in the opening of a question about the status of writing. This is undoubtedly less obvious—has anyone ever picked up on it?—in the case of the cicada story.[8] But it is no less certain. Both myths follow upon the same question, and they are only separated by a short space, just time enough for a detour. The first, of course, does not answer the question; on the contrary, it leaves it hanging, marks time for a rest, and makes us wait for the reprise that will lead us to the second.

Let us read this more closely. At the precisely calculated center of the dialogue—the reader can count the lines—the question of *logography*[9] is raised (257*c*). Phaedrus reminds Socrates that the citizens of greatest influence and dignity, the men who are the most free, feel ashamed (*aiskhunontai*) at "speechwriting" and at leaving *sungrammata*[1] behind them. They fear the judgment of posterity, which might consider them "sophists"[2] (257*d*). The logographer, in the strict sense, is a *ghost writer* who composes speeches for use by litigants, speeches which he himself does not pronounce, which he does not attend, so to speak, in person, and which produce their effects in his absence. In writing what he does not speak, what he would never say and, in truth, would probably never even think, the author of the written speech is already entrenched in the posture of the sophist: the man of non-presence and of non-truth. Writing is thus already on the scene. The incompatibility between the *written* and the *true* is clearly announced at the moment Socrates starts to recount the way in which men are carried out of themselves by pleasure, become absent from themselves, forget themselves and die in the thrill of song (259*c*).

But the issue is delayed. Socrates still has a neutral attitude: writing is not in itself a shameful, indecent, infamous (*aiskhron*) activity. One is dishonored only if one writes in a dishonorable manner. But what does it mean to write in a dishonorable manner? and, Phaedrus also wants to know, what does it mean to write beautifully (*kalōs*)? This question sketches out the central nervure, the great fold that divides the dialogue. Between this question and the answer that takes up its terms in the last section ("But there remains the question of propriety and impropriety in writing, that is to say the conditions which make it proper or improper. Isn't that so?" 274*b*), the

5. P. Frutiger, *Les Mythes de Platon* [*The Myths of Plato*] (Paris: Alcan, 1930) [Derrida's note].
6. Constituent elements of mythology.
7. To rejoice at, to welcome, to bid farewell; or, rejoicing at, welcoming, bidding farewell (Greek).
8. In *Phaedrus* 259, Socrates explains that cicadas once were men who so loved the Muses (9 daughters of Memory who preside over the arts and all intellectual pursuits) that they stopped eating and drinking. They eventually turned into the race of cicadas, who now report to the goddesses which mortals especially honor each Muse.
9. Speechwriting (in Greek, *logographia*).
1. Written compositions (Greek).
2. Those who taught rhetoric and devised arguments for money; the term later became synonymous with fallacious reasoners.

thread remains solid, if not easily visible, all through the fable of the cicadas and the themes of psychagogy,[3] rhetoric, and dialectics.

Thus Socrates begins by sending myths off; and then, twice stopped before the question of writing, he invents two of them—not, as we shall see, entirely from scratch, but more freely and spontaneously than anywhere else in his work. Now, the *khairein*, in the *Phaedrus*' opening pages, *takes place in the name of truth*. We will reflect upon the fact that the myths come back from vacation at the time and in the name of writing.

The *khairein* takes place *in the name of truth*: that is, in the name of knowledge of truth and, more precisely, of truth in the knowledge of the self. This is what Socrates explains (230*a*). But this imperative of self-knowledge is not first felt or dictated by any transparent immediacy of self-presence. It is not perceived. Only interpreted, read, deciphered. A hermeneutics[4] *assigns* intuition. An inscription, the *Delphikon gramma*,[5] which is anything but an oracle, prescribes through its silent cipher; it signifies as one signifies an order—autoscopy and autognosis.[6] The very activities that Socrates thinks can be contrasted to the hermeneutic adventure of myths, which he leaves to the sophists (229*d*).

And the *khairein* takes *place* in the name of truth. The *topoi*[7] of the dialogue are never indifferent. The themes, the topics, the (common-)places, in a rhetorical sense, are strictly inscribed, comprehended each time within a significant site. They are dramatically staged, and in this theatrical geography, unity of place corresponds to an infallible calculation or necessity. For example, the fable of the cicadas would not have taken place, would not have been recounted, Socrates would not have been incited to tell it, if the heat, which weighs over the whole dialogue, had not driven the two friends out of the city, into the countryside, along the river Ilissus. Well before detailing the genealogy of the genus cicada, Socrates had exclaimed, "How welcome and sweet the fresh air is, resounding with the summer chirping of the cicada chorus" (230*c*). But this is not the only counterpoint-effect required by the space of the dialogue. The myth that serves as a pretext for the *khairein* and for the retreat into autoscopy can itself only arise, during the first steps of this excursion, at the sight of the Ilissus. Isn't this the spot, asks Phaedrus, where Boreas, according to tradition, carried off Orithyia?[8] This riverbank, the diaphanous purity of these waters, must have welcomed the young virgins, or even drawn them like a spell, inciting them to play here. Socrates then mockingly proposes a learned explanation of the myth in the rationalistic, physicalist style of the *sophoi*:[9] it was while she was playing with Pharmacia (*sun Pharmakeiai paizousan*) that the boreal wind (*pneuma Boreou*) caught Orithyia up and blew her into the abyss, "down from the rocks hard by," "and having thus met her death was said to have been seized by Boreas . . . For my part, Phaedrus, I regard such theories as attractive no doubt, but as the invention of clever, industrious people who are not exactly to be envied" (229*d*).

3. Training of the soul.
4. Art of interpretation.
5. Delphic inscription (Greek); that is, the famous inscription at Apollo's temple at Delphi, "know thyself" (see *Phaedrus* 229e).
6. Self-knowledge. "Autoscopy": self-examination.
7. Places, topics (Greek).
8. Daughter of the king of Thrace; Boreas, the personification of the north wind, fell in love with her.
9. Wise or learned men (Greek).

This brief evocation of Pharmacia at the beginning of the *Phaedrus*—is it an accident? An hors d'œuvre? A fountain, "perhaps with curative powers," notes Robin,[1] was dedicated to Pharmacia near the Ilissus. Let us in any case retain this: that a little spot, a little stitch or mesh (*macula*[2]) woven into the back of the canvas, marks out for the entire dialogue the scene where that *virgin* was cast into the abyss, surprised by death *while playing with Pharmacia*. Pharmacia (*Pharmakeia*) is also a common noun signifying the administration of the *pharmakon*, the drug: the medicine and/or poison. "Poisoning" was not the least usual meaning of "pharmacia." Antiphon[3] has left us the logogram of an "accusation of poisoning against a mother-in-law" (*Pharmakeias kata tēs mētryias*). Through her games, Pharmacia has dragged down to death a virginal purity and an unpenetrated interior.

Only a little further on, Socrates compares the written texts Phaedrus has brought along to a drug (*pharmakon*). This *pharmakon*, this "medicine," this philter, which acts as both remedy and poison, already introduces itself into the body of the discourse with all its ambivalence. This charm, this spellbinding virtue, this power of fascination, can be—alternately or simultaneously—beneficent or maleficent. The *pharmakon* would be a *substance*—with all that that word can connote in terms of matter with occult virtues, cryptic depths refusing to submit their ambivalence to analysis, already paving the way for alchemy—if we didn't have eventually to come to recognize it as antisubstance itself: that which resists any philosopheme,[4] indefinitely exceeding its bounds as nonidentity, nonessence, nonsubstance; granting philosophy by that very fact the inexhaustible adversity of what funds it and the infinite absence of what founds it.

Operating through seduction, the *pharmakon* makes one stray from one's general, natural, habitual paths and laws. Here, it takes Socrates out of his proper place and off his customary track. The latter had always kept him inside the city. The leaves of writing act as a *pharmakon* to push or attract out of the city the one who never wanted to get out, even at the end, to escape the hemlock.[5] They take him out of himself and draw him onto a path that is properly an *exodus*:[6]

> *Phaedrus*: Anyone would take you, as you say, for a foreigner being shown the country by a guide, and not a native—you never leave town to cross the frontier nor even, I believe, so much as set foot outside the walls.
>
> *Socrates*: You must forgive me, dear friend; I'm a lover of learning, and trees and open country won't teach me anything, whereas men in the town do. Yet you seem to have discovered a drug[7] for getting me out (*dokeis moi tēs emēs exodou to pharmakon hēurēkenai*). A hungry animal can be driven by dangling a carrot or a bit of greenstuff in front of it; similarly if you proffer me speeches bound in books (*en bibliois*) I don't doubt you can cart me all round Attica, and any-

1. Léon Robin (1866–1947), French translator of the *Phaedrus*.
2. Spot, stain (Latin).
3. Greek orator (ca. 480–411 B.C.E.).
4. Constituent element of philosophy.
5. The poison drunk by Socrates after an Athenian court condemned him to death for impiety and corrupting the youth.
6. A way out (Greek).
7. Translated by others as "recipe" and "remedy" [translator's note, edited].

> where else you please. Anyhow, now that we've got here I propose for the time being to lie down, and you can choose whatever posture you think most convenient for reading, and proceed. (230*d–e*)

It is at this point, when Socrates has finally stretched out on the ground and Phaedrus has taken the most comfortable position for handling the text or, if you will, the *pharmakon*, that the discussion actually gets off the ground. A spoken speech—whether by Lysias[8] or by Phaedrus in person—a speech proffered *in the present, in the presence* of Socrates, would not have had the same effect. Only the *logoi en bibliois*, only words that are deferred, reserved, enveloped, rolled up, words that force one to wait for them in the form and under cover of a solid object, letting themselves be desired for the space of a walk, only hidden letters can thus get Socrates moving. If a speech could be purely present, unveiled, naked, offered up in person in its truth, without the detours of a signifier foreign to it, if at the limit an undeferred *logos*[9] were possible, it would not seduce anyone. It would not draw Socrates, as if under the effects of a *pharmakon*, out of his way. Let us get ahead of ourselves. Already: writing, the *pharmakon*, the going or leading astray.

In our discussion of this text we have been using an authoritative French translation of Plato, the one published by Guillaume Budé. In the case of the *Phaedrus*, the translation is by Léon Robin. We will continue to refer to it, inserting the Greek text in parentheses, however, whenever it seems opportune or pertinent to our point. Hence, for example, the word *pharmakon*. In this way we hope to display in the most striking manner the regular, ordered polysemy[1] that has, through skewing, indetermination, or overdetermination, but without mistranslation, permitted the rendering of the same word by "remedy," "recipe," "poison," "drug," "philter," etc. It will also be seen to what extent the malleable unity of this concept, or rather its rules and the strange logic that links it with its signifier,[2] has been dispersed, masked, obliterated, and rendered almost unreadable not only by the imprudence or empiricism of the translators, but first and foremost by the redoubtable, irreducible difficulty of translation. It is a difficulty inherent in its very principle, situated less in the passage from one language to another, from one philosophical language to another, than already, as we shall see, in the tradition between Greek and Greek; a violent difficulty in the transference of a nonphilosopheme into a philosopheme. With this problem of translation we will thus be dealing with nothing less than the problem of the very passage into philosophy.

The *biblia* that will draw Socrates out of his reserve and out of the space in which he is wont to learn, to teach, to speak, to dialogue—the sheltered enclosure of the city—these *biblia* contain a text written by "the ablest writer of our day" (*deinotatos ōn nun graphein*). His name is Lysias. Phaedrus is keeping the text or, if you will, the *pharmakon*, hidden under his cloak. He needs it because he has not learned the speech by heart. This point is important for what follows, the problem of writing being closely linked to the problem of "knowing by heart." Before Socrates had stretched out on the

8. Greek speechwriter (ca. 459–ca. 380 B.C.E.), who taught rhetoric and was one of the masters of classical oratory.

9. Word, speech, story, reason (Greek).

1. Possession of multiple meanings.

2. The symbol or sound that conveys meaning (the signified), a term introduced by the Swiss linguist FERDINAND DE SAUSSURE (1857–1913).

ground and invited Phaedrus to take the most comfortable position, the latter had offered to reconstitute, without the help of the text, the reasoning, argument, and design of Lysias' speech, its *dianoia*. Socrates stops him short: "Very well, my dear fellow, but you must first show me what it is that you have in your left hand under your cloak, for I surmise that it is the actual discourse (*ton logon auton*)" (228*d*). Between the invitation and the start of the reading, while the *pharmakon* is wandering about under Phaedrus' cloak, there occurs the evocation of Pharmacia and the send-off of myths.

Is it after all by chance or by harmonics[3] that, even before the overt presentation of writing as a *pharmakon* arises in the middle of the myth of Theuth, the connection between *biblia* and *pharmaka* should already be mentioned in a malevolent or suspicious vein? As opposed to the true practice of medicine, founded on science, we find indeed, listed in a single stroke, empirical practice, treatments based on recipes learned by heart, mere bookish knowledge, and the blind usage of drugs. All that, we are told, springs out of *mania*: "I expect they would say, 'the man is mad; he thinks he has made himself a doctor by picking up something out of a book (*ek bibliou*), or coming across a couple of ordinary drugs (*pharmakiois*), without any real knowledge of medicine'" (268*c*).

This association between writing and the *pharmakon* still seems external; it could be judged artificial or purely coincidental. But the intention and intonation are recognizably the same: one and the same suspicion envelops in a single embrace the book and the drug, writing and whatever works in an occult, ambiguous manner open to empiricism and chance, governed by the ways of magic and not the laws of necessity. Books, the dead and rigid knowledge shut up in *biblia*, piles of histories, nomenclatures, recipes and formulas learned by heart, all this is as foreign to living knowledge and dialectics as the *pharmakon* is to medical science. And myth to true knowledge. In dealing with Plato, who knew so well on occasion how to treat myth in its archeo-logical or paleo-logical capacity, one can glimpse the immensity and difficulty of this last opposition. The extent of the difficulty is marked out—this is, among a hundred others, the example that retains us here—in that the truth—the original truth—about writing as a *pharmakon* will at first be left up to a myth. The myth of Theuth, to which we now turn.

Up to this point in the dialogue, one can say that the *pharmakon* and the grapheme[4] have been beckoning to each other from afar, indirectly sending back to each other, and, as if by chance, appearing and disappearing together on the same line, for yet uncertain reasons, with an effectiveness that is quite discrete and perhaps after all unintentional. But in order to lift this doubt and on the supposition that the categories of the voluntary and the involuntary still have some absolute pertinence in a reading—which we don't for a minute believe, at least not on the textual level on which we are now advancing—let us proceed to the last phase of the dialogue, to the point where Theuth appears on the scene.

This time it is without indirection, without hidden mediation, without secret argumentation, that writing is proposed, presented, and asserted as a *pharmakon* (274*e*).

In a certain sense, one can see how this section could have been set apart

3. Design, rhythm.

4. Constituent element of writing.

as an appendix, a superadded supplement. And despite all that calls for it in the preceding steps, it is true that Plato offers it somewhat as an amusement, an hors d'œuvre or rather a dessert. All the subjects of the dialogue, both themes and speakers, seem exhausted at the moment the supplement, writing, or the *pharmakon*, are introduced: "Then we may feel that we have said enough both about the art of speaking and about the lack of art (*to men tekhnēs te kai atekhnias logōn*)"[5] (274*b*). And yet it is at this moment of general exhaustion that the question of writing is set out.[6] And, as was foreshadowed earlier by the use of the word *aiskhron* (or the adverb *aiskhrōs*[7]), the question of writing opens as a question of morality. It is truly *morality* that is at stake, both in the sense of the opposition between good and evil, or good and bad, and in the sense of mores, public morals and social conventions. It is a question of knowing what is done and what is not done. This moral disquiet is in no way to be distinguished from questions of truth, memory, and dialectics.[8] This latter question, which will quickly be engaged as *the* question of writing, is closely associated with the morality theme, and indeed develops it by affinity of essence and not by superimposition. But within a debate rendered very real by the political development of the city, the propagation of writing and the activity of the sophists and speechwriters, the primary accent is naturally placed upon political and social proprieties. The type of arbitration proposed by Socrates plays within the opposition between the values of seemliness and unseemliness (*euprepeia/aprepeia*): "But there remains the question of propriety and impropriety in writing, that is to say the conditions which make it proper or improper. Isn't that so?" (274*b*).

Is writing seemly? Does the writer cut a respectable figure? Is it proper to write? Is it done?

Of course not. But the answer is not so simple, and Socrates does not immediately offer it on his own account in a rational discourse or *logos*. He lets it be heard by delegating it to an *akoē*,[9] to a well-known rumor, to hearsay evidence, to a fable transmitted from ear to ear: "I can tell you what our forefathers have said about it, but the truth of it is only known by tradition. However, if we could discover that truth for ourselves, should we still be concerned with the fancies of mankind?" (274*c*).

The truth of writing, that is, as we shall see, (the) nontruth, cannot be discovered in ourselves by ourselves. And it is not the object of a science, only of a history that is recited, a fable that is repeated. The link between writing and myth becomes clearer, as does its opposition to knowledge, notably the knowledge one seeks in oneself, by oneself. And at the same time, through writing or through myth, the genealogical break and the estrange-

5. Here, when it is a question of *logos*, Robin translates *tekhnē* by "art." Later, in the course of the indictment, the same word, this time pertaining to writing, will be rendered by "technical knowledge" [*connaissance technique*] [Derrida's note].

6. While Saussure, in his *Course in General Linguistics* [1916], excludes or settles the question of writing in a sort of preliminary excursus or hors d'œuvre, the chapter Rousseau devotes to writing in the *Essay on the Origin of Languages* [written 1761; pub. 1781] is also presented, despite its actual importance, as a sort of somewhat contingent supplement, a makeup criterion, "another means of comparing languages and of judging their relative antiquity." The same operation is found in Hegel's *Encyclopedia* [1817]; cf. "Le Puits et la pyramide" (1968), in *Hegel et la pensée moderne* (Paris: Presses Universitaires de France, 1970, coll. "Epiméthée") [Derrida's note]. Translated by Alan Bass as "The Pit and the Pyramid: Introduction to Hegel's Semiology," in Derrida's *Margins of Philosophy* (Chicago: University of Chicago Press, 1982). Jean-Jacques Rousseau (1712–1778), Swiss-born French philosopher. GEORG WILHELM FRIEDRICH HEGEL (1770–1831), German idealist philosopher.

7. Shamefully (Greek).

8. The pursuit of truth, philosophy.

9. Something heard (Greek).

ment from the origin are sounded. One should note most especially that what writing will later be accused of—repeating without knowing—here defines the very approach that leads to the statement and determination of its status. One thus begins by repeating without knowing—through a myth—the definition of writing, which is to repeat without knowing. This kinship of writing and myth, both of them distinguished from *logos* and dialectics, will only become more precise as the text concludes. Having just repeated without knowing that writing consists of repeating without knowing, Socrates goes on to base the demonstration of his indictment, of his *logos*, upon the premises of the *akoē*, upon structures that are readable through a fabulous genealogy of writing. As soon as the myth has struck the first blow, the *logos* of Socrates will demolish the accused.

2. THE FATHER OF LOGOS

The story begins like this:

> *Socrates*: Very well, I heard, then, that at Naucratis in Egypt there lived one of the old gods of that country, the one whose sacred bird is called the ibis; and the name of the divinity was Theuth. It was he who first invented numbers and calculation, geometry and astronomy, not to speak of draughts and dice, and above all writing (*grammata*). Now the King of all Egypt at that time was Thamus who lived in the great city of the upper region which the Greeks call the Egyptian Thebes; the god himself they call Ammon. Theuth came to him and exhibited his arts and declared that they ought to be imparted to the other Egyptians. And Thamus questioned him about the usefulness of each one; and as Theuth enumerated, the King blamed or praised what he thought were the good or bad points in the explanation. Now Thamus is said to have had a good deal to remark on both sides of the question about every single art (it would take too long to repeat it here); but when it came to writing, Theuth said, "This discipline (*to mathēma*), my King, will make the Egyptians wiser and will improve their memories (*sophōterous kai mnēmonikōterous*): my invention is a recipe (*pharmakon*) for both memory and wisdom." But the King said . . . etc. (274*c–e*)

Let us cut the King off here. He is faced with the *pharmakon*. His reply will be incisive.

Let us freeze the scene and the characters and take a look at them. Writing (or, if you will, the *pharmakon*) is thus presented to the King. Presented: like a kind of present offered up in homage by a vassal to his lord (Theuth is a demigod speaking to the king of the gods), but above all as a finished work submitted to his appreciation. And this work is itself an art, a capacity for work, a power of operation. This artefactum is an art. But the value of this gift is still uncertain. The value of writing—or of the *pharmakon*—has of course been spelled out to the King, but it is the King who will give it its value, who will set the price of what, in the act of receiving, he constitutes or institutes. The king or god (Thamus represents[1] Ammon, the king of the

1. For Plato, Thamus is doubtless another name for Ammon, whose figure (that of the sun king and of the father of the gods) we shall sketch out later for its own sake. On this question and the debate to which it has given rise, see Frutiger, *Mythes*, p. 233 n. 2, and notably R. Eisler, "Platon und das

gods, the king of kings, the god of gods. Theuth says to him: *Ō basileu*[2]) is thus the other name for the origin of value. The value of writing will not be itself, writing will have no value, unless and to the extent that god-the-king approves of it. But god-the-king nonetheless experiences the *pharmakon* as a product, an *ergon*,[3] which is not his own, which comes to him from outside but also from below, and which awaits his condescending judgment in order to be consecrated in its being and value. God the king does not know how to write, but that ignorance or incapacity only testifies to his sovereign independence. He has no need to write. He speaks, he says, he dictates, and his word suffices. Whether a scribe from his secretarial staff then adds the supplement of a transcription or not, that consignment is always in essence secondary.

From this position, without rejecting the homage, the god-king will depreciate it, pointing out not only its uselessness but its menace and its mischief. Another way of not receiving the offering of writing. In so doing, god-the-king-that-speaks is acting like a father. The *pharmakon* is here presented to the father and is by him rejected, belittled, abandoned, disparaged. The father is always suspicious and watchful toward writing.

Even if we did not want to give in here to the easy passage uniting the figures of the king, the god, and the father, it would suffice to pay systematic attention—which to our knowledge has never been done—to the permanence of a Platonic schema that assigns the origin and power of speech, precisely of *logos*, to the paternal position. Not that this happens especially and exclusively in Plato. Everyone knows this or can easily imagine it. But the fact that 'Platonism," which sets up the whole of Western metaphysics in its conceptuality, should not escape the generality of this structural constraint, and even illustrates it with incomparable subtlety and force, stands out as all the more significant.

Not that logos *is* the father, either. But the origin of logos is *its father*. One could say anachronously that the "speaking subject" is the *father* of his speech. And one would quickly realize that this is no metaphor, at least not in the sense of any common, conventional effect of rhetoric. *Logos* is a son, then, a son that would be destroyed in his very *presence* without the present *attendance* of his father. His father who answers. His father who speaks for him and answers for him. Without his father, he would be nothing but, in fact, writing. At least that is what is said by the one who says: it is the father's thesis. The specificity of writing would thus be intimately bound to the absence of the father. Such an absence can of course exist along very diverse modalities, distinctly or confusedly, successively or simultaneously: to have lost one's father, through natural or violent death, through random violence or patricide; and then to solicit the aid and attendance, possible or impossible, of the paternal presence, to solicit it directly or to claim to be getting along without it, etc. The reader will have noted Socrates' insistence on the misery, whether pitiful or arrogant, of a *logos* committed to writing: ". . . It always needs its father to attend to it, being quite unable to defend itself or attend to its own needs" (275*e*).

ägyptische Alphabet" ["Plato and the Egyptian Alphabet"], *Archiv für Geschichte der Philosophie* (1922); Pauly-Wissowa, *Real-Encylopädie der classischen Altertumswissenschaft* (s.v. "Ammon"); Roscher, *Lexikon der griechischen und römischen Mythologie* (s.v. "Thamus") [Derrida's note].

2. O king (Greek).
3. Work (Greek).

This misery is ambiguous: it is the distress of the orphan, of course, who needs not only an attending presence but also a presence that will attend to its needs; but in pitying the orphan, one also makes an accusation against him, along with writing, for claiming to do away with the father, for achieving emancipation with complacent self-sufficiency. From the position of the holder of the scepter, the desire of writing is indicated, designated, and denounced as a desire for orphanhood and patricidal subversion. Isn't this *pharmakon* then a criminal thing, a poisoned present?[4]

The status of this orphan, whose welfare cannot be assured by any attendance or assistance, coincides with that of a *graphein*[5] which, being nobody's son at the instant it reaches inscription, scarcely remains a son at all and no longer *recognizes* its origins, whether legally or morally. In contrast to writing, living *logos* is alive in that it has a living father (whereas the orphan is already half dead), a father that is *present, standing* near it, behind it, within it, sustaining it with his rectitude, attending it in person in his own name. Living *logos*, for its part, recognizes its debt, lives off that recognition, and forbids itself, thinks it can forbid itself patricide. But prohibition and patricide, like the relations between speech and writing, are structures surprising enough to require us later on to articulate Plato's text between a patricide prohibited and a patricide proclaimed. The deferred murder of the father and rector.

The *Phaedrus* would already be sufficient to prove that the responsibility for *logos*, for its meaning and effects, goes to those who attend it, to those who are present with the presence of a father. These "metaphors" must be tirelessly questioned. Witness Socrates, addressing Eros:[6] "If in our former speech Phaedrus or I said anything harsh against you, blame Lysias, the father of the subject (*ton tou logou patera*)" (275*b*). *Logos*—"discourse"—has the meaning here of argument, line of reasoning, guiding thread animating the spoken discussion (the *Logos*). To translate it by "subject" [*sujet*], as Robin does, is not merely anachronistic. The whole intention and the organic unity of signification is destroyed. For only the "living" discourse, only a spoken word (and not a speech's theme, object, or subject) can have a father; and, according to a necessity that will not cease to become clearer to us from now on, the *logoi* are the children. Alive enough to protest on occasion and to let themselves be questioned; capable, too, in contrast to written things, of responding when their father is there. They are their father's responsible presence.

Some of them, for example, descend from Phaedrus, who is sometimes called upon to sustain them. Let us refer again to Robin, who translates *logos* this time not by "subject" but by "argument," and disrupts in a space of ten lines the play on the *tekhnē tōn logōn*.[7] (What is in question is the *tekhnē* the sophists and rhetors had or pretended to have at their disposal, which was at once an art and an instrument, a recipe, an occult but transmissible "treatise," etc. Socrates considers the then classical problem in terms of the opposition between persuasion [*peithō*] and truth [*alētheia*] [260*a*].)

> *Socrates*: I agree—if, that is, the arguments (*logoi*) that come forward to speak for oratory should give testimony that it is an art (*tekhnē*).

4. A multilingual pun: in English, *gift* means "present"; in German, *Gift* means "poison."
5. To write; writing (Greek).
6. The personification of love.
7. The art of the arguments (Greek).

Now I seem, as it were, to hear some arguments advancing to give their evidence that it tells lies, that it is not an art at all, but an artless routine. "Without a grip on truth," says the Spartan, "there can be no genuine art of speaking (*tou de legein*) either now or in the future."

Phaedrus: Socrates, we need these arguments (*Toutōn dei tōn logōn, ō Sōkrates*). Bring the witnesses here and let's find out what they have to say and how they'll say it (*ti kai pōs legousin*).

Socrates: Come here, then, noble brood (*gennaia*), and convince Phaedrus, father of such fine children (*kallipaida te Phaidron*), that if he doesn't give enough attention to philosophy, he will never become a competent speaker on any subject. Now let Phaedrus answer. (260*e*–261*a*)

It is again Phaedrus, but this time in the *Symposium*, who must speak first because he is both "head of the table" and "father of our subject" (*patēr tou logou*) (177*d*).

What we are provisionally and for the sake of convenience continuing to call a metaphor thus in any event belongs to a whole system. If *logos* has a father, if it is a *logos* only when attended by its father, this is because it is always a being (*on*) and even a certain species of being (the *Sophist*, 260*a*), more precisely a *living* being. *Logos* is a *zōon*. An animal that is born, grows, belongs to the *phusis*.[8] Linguistics, logic, dialectics, and zoology are all in the same camp.

In describing *logos* as a *zōon*, Plato is following certain rhetors and sophists before him who, as a contrast to the cadaverous rigidity of writing, had held up the living spoken word, which infallibly conforms to the necessities of the situation at hand, to the expectations and demands of the interlocutors present, and which sniffs out the spots where it ought to produce itself, feigning to bend and adapt at the moment it is actually achieving maximum persuasiveness and control.[9]

Logos, a living, animate creature, is thus also an organism that has been engendered. An *organism*: a differentiated body *proper*, with a center and extremities, joints, a head, and feet. In order to be "proper," a written discourse *ought* to submit to the laws of life just as a living discourse does. Logographical necessity (*anangkē logographikē*) ought to be analogous to biological, or rather zoological, necessity. Otherwise, obviously, it would have neither head nor tail. Both *structure* and *constitution* are in question in the risk run by *logos* of losing through writing both its tail and its head:

Socrates: And what about the rest? Don't you think the different parts of the speech (*ta tou logou*) are tossed in hit or miss? Or is there really a cogent reason for starting his second point in the second place? And is that the case with the rest of the speech? As for myself, in my ignorance, I thought that the writer boldly set down whatever

8. Nature; natural world (Greek).

9. The association *logos-zōon* appears in the discourse of Isocrates, *Against the Sophists*, and in that of Alcidamas, *On the Sophists*. Cf. also W. Süss, who compares these two discourses line by line with the *Phaedrus*, in *Ethos: Studien zur älteren greichischen Rhetorik* (Leipzig, 1910), pp. 34ff., and A. Diès, "Philosophie et rhétorique," in *Autour de Platon* (Paris: Gabriel Beauchesne, 1927), 1:103 [Derrida's note]. Isocrates (436–338 B.C.E.), Athenian orator; a student of both GORGIAS and Socrates, he was an important teacher of rhetoric. Alcidamas (4th c. B.C.E.), rhetorician and sophist; he was chief among Gorgias's orthodox followers.

happened to come into his head. Can you explain his arrangement of the topics in the order he has adopted as the result of some principle of composition, some logographic necessity?

Phaedrus: It's very kind of you to think me capable of such an accurate insight into his methods.

Socrates: But to this you will surely agree: every discourse (*logon*), like a living creature (*ōsper zōon*), should be so put together (*sunestanai*) that it has its own body and lacks neither head nor foot, middle nor extremities, all composed in such a way that they suit both each other and the whole. (264*b–c*)

The organism thus engendered must be well born, of noble blood: "*gennaia*," we recall, is what Socrates called the *logoi*, those "noble creatures." This implies that the organism, having been engendered, must have a beginning and an end. Here, Socrates' standards become precise and insistent: a speech must have a beginning and an end, it must begin with the beginning and end with the end: "It certainly seems as though Lysias, at least, was far from satisfying our demands: it's from the end, not the beginning, that he tries to swim (on his back!) upstream through the current of his discourse. He starts out with what the lover ought to say at the very end to his beloved!" (264*a*). The implications and consequences of such a norm are immense, but they are obvious enough for us not to have to belabor them. It follows that the spoken discourse behaves like someone attended in origin and present in person. *Logos: "Sermo tanquam persona ipse loquens,"*[1] as one Platonic Lexicon puts it.[2] Like any person, the *logos-zōon* has a father.

But what is a father?

Should we consider this known, and with this term—the known—classify the other term within what one would hasten to classify as a metaphor? One would then say that the origin or cause of *logos* is being compared to what we know to be the cause of a living son, his father. One would understand or imagine the birth and development of *logos* from the standpoint of a domain foreign to it, the transmission of life or the generative relation. But the father is not the generator or procreator in any "real" sense prior to or outside all relation to language.[3] In what way, indeed, is the father/son relation distinguishable from a mere cause/effect or generator/engendered relation, if not by the instance of logos? Only a power of speech can have a father. The father is always father to a speaking/living being. In other words, it is precisely *logos* that enables us to perceive and investigate something like paternity. If there were a simple metaphor in the expression "father of logos," the first word, which seemed the more *familiar*, would nevertheless receive more meaning *from* the second than it would transmit *to* it. The first familiarity is always involved in a relation of cohabitation with *logos*. Living-beings, father and son, are announced to us and related to each other within the household of *logos*. From which one does not escape, in spite of appearances, when one is transported, by "metaphor,"[4] to a foreign territory where one

1. Talk, just as if a person himself [were] speaking (Latin).
2. Fr. Ast, *Lexique platonicien*. Cf. also B. Parain, *Essai sur le logos platonicien* (Paris: Gallimard, 1942), p. 211; and P. Louis, *Les Métaphores de Platon* (Paris: Les Belles Lettres, 1945), pp. 43–44 [Derrida's note].
3. Until the advent of DNA testing and surrogate mothering, only maternity was considered certain. Paternity was thus always dependent on language (the mother's word, the father's name).
4. *Metaphor* derives from the Greek verb that means "to bear or carry across" (i.e., "transport").

meets fathers, sons, living creatures, all sorts of beings that come in handy for explaining to anyone that doesn't know, by comparison, what *logos*, that strange thing, is all about. Even though this hearth is the heart of all metaphoricity, "father of logos" is not a simple metaphor. To have simple metaphoricity, one would have to make the statement that some living creature incapable of language, if anyone still wished to believe in such a thing, has a father. One must thus proceed to undertake a general reversal of all metaphorical directions, no longer asking whether *logos* can have a father but understanding that what the father claims to be the father of cannot go without the essential possibility of *logos*.

A *logos indebted* to a father, what does that mean? At least how can it be read within the stratum of the Platonic text that interests us here?

The figure of the father, of course, is also that of the good (*agathon*). Logos *represents* what it is indebted to: the father who is also chief, capital, and good(s). Or rather *the* chief, *the* capital, *the* good(s). *Patēr* in Greek means all that at once. Neither translators nor commentators of Plato seem to have accounted for the play of these schemes. It is extremely difficult, we must recognize, to respect this play in a translation, and the fact can at least be explained in that no one has ever raised the question. Thus, at the point in the *Republic* where Socrates backs away from speaking of the good in itself (VI, 506*e*), he immediately suggests replacing it with its *ekgonos*, its son, its offspring:

> . . . let us dismiss for the time being the nature of the good in itself, for to attain to my present surmise of that seems a pitch above the impulse that wings my flight today. But what seems to be the offspring (*ekgonos*) of the good and most nearly made in its likeness I am willing to speak if you too wish it, and otherwise to let the matter drop.
>
> Well, speak on, he said, for you will duly pay me the tale of the parent another time.
>
> I could wish, I said, that I were able to make and you to receive the payment, and not merely as now the interest (*tokous*). But at any rate receive this interest and the offspring of the good (*tokon te kai ekgonon autou tou agathou*).

Tokos, which is here associated with *ekgonos*, signifies production and the product, birth and the child, etc. This word functions with this meaning in the domains of agriculture, of kinship relations, and of fiduciary operations. None of these domains, as we shall see, lies outside the investment and possibility of a *logos*.

As product, the *tokos* is the child, the human or animal brood, as well as the fruits of the seed sown in the field, and the interest on a capital investment: it is a *return* or *revenue*. The distribution of all these meanings can be followed in Plato's text. The meaning of *patēr* is sometimes even inflected in the exclusive sense of financial capital. In the *Republic* itself, and not far from the passage we have just quoted. One of the drawbacks of democracy lies in the role that capital is often allowed to play in it: "But these money-makers with down-bent heads, pretending not even to see the poor, but inserting the sting of their money into any of the remainder who do not resist, and harvesting from them in interest as it were a manifold progeny of the parent sum (*tou patros ekgonous tokous pollaplasious*), foster the drone and pauper element in the state" (555*e*).

Now, about this father, this capital, this good, this origin of value and of appearing beings, it is not possible to speak simply or directly. First of all because it is no more possible to look them in the face than to stare at the sun. On the subject of this bedazzlement before the face of the sun, a rereading of the famous passage of the *Republic* (VII, 515c ff) is strongly recommended here.

Thus will Socrates evoke only the visible sun, the son that resembles the father, the *analogon*[5] of the intelligible sun: "It was the sun, then, that I meant when I spoke of that offspring of the Good (*ton tou agathou ekgonon*), which the Good has created in its own image (*hon tagathon egennēsen analogon heautōi*), and which stands in the visible world in the same relation to vision and visible things as that which the good itself bears in the intelligible world to intelligence and to intelligible objects" (508*c*).

How does *Logos* intercede in this *analogy* between the father and the son, the *nooumena* and the *horōmena?*[6]

The Good, in the visible-invisible figure of the father, the sun, or capital, is the origin of all *onta*,[7] responsible for their appearing and their coming into *logos*, which both assembles and distinguishes them: "We predicate 'to be' of many beautiful things and many good things, saying of them severally that they *are*, and so define them in our speech (*einai phamen te kai diorizomen tōi logōi*)" (507*b*).

The good (father, sun, capital) is thus the hidden illuminating, blinding source of *logos*. And since one cannot speak of that which enables one to speak (being forbidden to speak of it or to speak to it face to face), one will speak only of that which speaks and of things that, with a single exception, one is constantly speaking of. And since an account or reason cannot be given of what *logos* (account or reason: *ratio*) is accountable or owing *to*, since the capital cannot be counted nor the chief looked in the eye, it will be necessary, by means of a discriminative, diacritical[8] operation, to count up the plurality of interests, returns, products, and offspring: "Well, speak on (*lege*), he said, for you will duly pay me the tale of the parent another time—I could wish, I said, that I were able to make and you to receive the payment, and not merely as now the interest. But at any rate receive this interest and the offspring of the good. Have a care, however, lest I deceive you unintentionally with a false reckoning (*ton logon*) of the interest (*tou tokou*)" (507*a*).

From the foregoing passage we should also retain the fact that, along with the account (*logos*) of the supplements (to the father-good-capital-origin, etc.), along with what comes above and beyond the One in the very movement through which it absents itself and becomes invisible, thus requiring that its place be supplied, along with differance[9] and diacriticity, Socrates introduces or discovers the ever open possibility of the *kibdēlon*, that which is falsified, adulterated, mendacious, deceptive, equivocal. Have a care, he

5. Analogue (Greek).
6. The intelligible and the visible (Plato's terms in *Republic* 508c).
7. Beings (Greek).
8. Differentiating, separating.
9. Temporal and spatial differentiating or deferral. *Différance* is Derrida's grammatical invention; like *différence*, which sounds the same and refers to synchronic comparison, it derives from *différer*, which means both "to differ" and "to defer, postpone."

says, lest I deceive you with a false reckoning of the interest (*kibdēlon apodidous ton logon tou tokou*). *Kibdēleuma* is fraudulent merchandise. The corresponding verb (*kibdēleuō*) signifies "to tamper with money or merchandise, and, by extension, to be of bad faith."

This recourse to *logos,* from fear of being blinded by any direct intuition of the face of the father, of good, of capital, of the origin of being in itself, of the form of forms, etc., this recourse to logos as that which *protects us from the sun*, protects us under it and from it, is proposed by Socrates elsewhere, in the *analogous* order of the sensible or the visible. We shall quote at length from that text. In addition to its intrinsic interest, the text, in its official Robin translation, manifests a series of slidings, as it were, that are highly significant.[1] The passage in question is the critique, in the *Phaedo*, of "physicalists":

> Socrates proceeded:—I thought that as I had failed in the contemplation of true existence (*ta onta*), I ought to be careful that I did not lose the eye of my soul; as people may injure their bodily eye by observing and gazing on the sun during an eclipse, unless they take the precaution of only looking at the image (*eikona*) reflected in the water, or in some analogous medium. So in my own case, I was afraid that my soul might be blinded altogether if I looked at things with my eyes or tried to apprehend them with the help of the senses. And I thought that I had better have recourse to the world of theory (*en logois*) and seek there the truth of things. . . . So, basing myself in each case on the idea (*logon*) that I judged to be the strongest . . . (99*d*–100*a*)

Logos is a thus a *resource*. One must *turn* to it, and not merely when the solar source is *present* and risks burning the eyes if stared at; one has also to turn away toward *logos* when the sun seems to withdraw during its eclipse. Dead, extinguished, or hidden, that star is more dangerous than ever.

We will let these yarns of suns and sons spin on for a while. Up to now we have only followed this line so as to move from *logos* to the father, so as to tie speech to the *kurios,* the master, the lord, another name given in the *Republic* to the good-sun-capital-father (508*a*). Later, within the same tissue, within the same texts, we will draw on other filial filaments, pull the same strings once more, and witness the weaving or unraveling of other designs.

* * *

4. THE PHARMAKON

Let us return to the text of Plato, assuming we have ever really left it.[2] The word *pharmakon* is caught in a chain of significations. The play of that chain seems systematic. But the system here is not, simply, that of the intentions of an author who goes by the name of Plato. The system is not primarily that of what someone *meant-to-say* [*un vouloir-dire*]. Finely regulated communications are established, through the play of language, among diverse functions of the word and, within it, among diverse strata or regions of culture. These communications or corridors of meaning can sometimes be declared

1. I am indebted to the friendship and alertness of Francine Markovits for having brought this to my attention. This text should of course be placed alongside those of books 6 and 7 of the *Republic* [Derrida's note].

2. In section 3 (omitted here), Derrida has outlined the genealogy of the myth of Theuth.

or clarified by Plato when he plays upon them "voluntarily," a word we put in quotation marks because what it designates, to content ourselves with remaining within the closure of these oppositions, is only a mode of "submission" to the necessities of a given "language." None of these concepts can translate the relation we are aiming at here. Then again, in other cases, Plato can *not* see the links, can leave them in the shadow or break them up. And yet these links go on working of themselves. In spite of him? thanks to him? in *his* text? *outside* his text? but then where? between his text and the language? for what reader? at what moment? To answer such questions in principle and in general will seem impossible; and that will give us the suspicion that there is some malformation in the question itself, in each of its concepts, in each of the oppositions it thus accredits. One can always choose to believe that if Plato did not put certain possibilities of passage into practice, or even interrupted them, it is because he perceived them but left them in the impracticable. This formulation is possible only if one avoids all recourse to the difference between conscious and unconscious, voluntary and involuntary, a very crude tool for dealing with relations in and to language. The same would be true of the opposition between speech—or writing—and language if that opposition, as is often the case, harked back to the above categories.

This reason alone should already suffice to prevent us from reconstituting the entire chain of significations of the *pharmakon*. No absolute privilege allows us absolutely to master its textual system. This limitation can and should nevertheless be displaced to a certain extent. The possibilities and powers of displacement are extremely diverse in nature, and, rather than enumerating here all their titles, let us attempt to produce some of their effects as we go along, as we continue our march through the Platonic problematic of writing.[3]

We have just sketched out the correspondence between the figure of Theuth in Egyptian mythology and a certain organization of concepts, philosophemes, metaphors, and mythemes picked up from what is called the Platonic text. The word *pharmakon* has seemed to us extremely apt for the task of tying all the threads of this correspondence together. Let us now reread, in a rendering derived from Robin, this sentence from the *Phaedrus*: "Here, O King, says Theuth, is a discipline (*mathēma*) that will make the Egyptians wiser (*sophōterous*) and will improve their memories (*mnēmonikōterous*): both memory (*mnēmē*) and instruction (*sophia*) have found their remedy (*pharmakon*)."

The common translation of *pharmakon* by *remedy* [*remède*]—a beneficent drug—is not, of course, inaccurate. Not only can *pharmakon* really mean *remedy* and thus erase, on a certain surface of its functioning, the ambiguity of its meaning. But it is even quite obvious here, the stated intention of Theuth being precisely to stress the worth of his product, that he *turns* the word on its strange and invisible pivot, presenting it from a single one, the most reassuring, of its *poles*.[4] This medicine is beneficial; it repairs and produces, accumulates and remedies, increases knowledge and reduces forget-

3. I take the liberty of referring the reader, in order to give him a preliminary, indicative direction, to the "Question of Method" proposed in *De la grammatologie* [1967, *Of Grammatology*]. With a few precautions, one could say that *pharmakon* plays a role *analogous*, in this reading of Plato, to that of *supplément* in the reading of Rousseau [Derrida's note]. For "The Exorbitant. Question of Method," see above.

4. Derrida is making a link between the tipping of the earth (on one of its poles) and the privileging of one side of a polarity.

fulness. Its translation by "remedy" nonetheless erases, in going outside the Greek language, the other pole reserved in the word *pharmakon*. It cancels out the resources of ambiguity and makes more difficult, if not impossible, an understanding of the context. As opposed to "drug" or even "medicine," *remedy* says the transparent rationality of science, technique, and therapeutic causality, thus excluding from the text any leaning toward the magic virtues of a force whose effects are hard to master, a dynamics that constantly surprises the one who tries to manipulate it as master and as subject.

Now, *on the one hand*, Plato is bent on presenting writing as an occult, and therefore suspect, power. Just like painting, to which he will later compare it, and like optical illusions and the techniques of *mimēsis*[5] in general. His mistrust of the mantic and magic, of sorcerers and casters of spells, is well attested.[6] In the *Laws*, in particular, he reserves them terrible punishments. According to an operation we will have cause to remember later, he recommends that they be excluded—expelled or cut off—from the social arena. Expulsion and ostracism can even be accomplished at the same time, by keeping them in prison, where they would no longer be visited by free men but only by the slave that would bring them their food; then by depriving them of burial: "At death he shall be cast out beyond the borders without burial, and if any free citizen has a hand in his burial, he shall be liable to a prosecution for impiety at the suit of any who cares to take proceedings" (X, 909*b*–*c*).

On the other hand, the King's reply presupposes that the effectiveness of the *pharmakon* can be reversed: it can worsen the ill instead of remedy it. Or rather, the royal answer suggests that Theuth, by ruse and/or naïveté, has exhibited the reverse of the true effects of writing. In order to vaunt the worth of his invention, Theuth would thus have denatured the *pharmakon*, said the opposite (*tounantion*) of what writing is capable of. He has passed a poison off as a remedy. So that in translating *pharmakon* by *remedy*, what one respects is not what Theuth intended, nor even what Plato intended, but rather what the King says Theuth has said, effectively deluding either the King or himself. If Plato's text then goes on to give the King's pronouncement as the truth of Theuth's production and his speech as the truth of writing, then the translation *remedy* makes Theuth into a simpleton or a flimflam artist, *from the sun's point of view*. From that viewpoint, Theuth has no doubt played on the word, interrupting, for his own purposes, the communication between the two opposing values. But the King restores that communication, and the translation takes no account of this. And all the while the two interlocutors, whatever they do and whether or not they choose, remain within the unity of the same signifier. Their discourse plays within it, which is no longer the case in translation. *Remedy* is the rendition that, more than "medicine" or "drug" would have done, obliterates the virtual, dynamic references to the other uses of the same word in Greek. The effect of such a translation is most importantly to destroy what we will later call Plato's anagrammatic writing,[7] to destroy it by interrupting the relations interwoven among differ-

5. Imitation, representation (Greek).
6. Cf. in particular *Republic* 2.364ff.; Letter 7, 333e. The problem is raised with copious and useful references in E. Moutsopoulos, *La Musique dans l'œuvre de Platon* (*Music in the Work of Plato*) (Paris: Presses Universitaires de France, 1959), pp. 13ff. [Derrida's note].
7. Patterns formed by rearranging letters or words. Generalizing from writings (not published until in the 1960s) of Ferdinand de Saussure, who thought he found proper names "anagrammatically" encoded in Latin poetry, many scholars, Derrida

ent functions of the same word in different places, relations that are virtually but necessarily "citational." When a word inscribes itself as the citation of another sense of the same word, when the textual center-stage of the word *pharmakon*, even while it means *remedy*, cites, re-cites, and makes legible that which *in the same word* signifies, in another spot and on a different level of the stage, *poison* (for example, since that it not the only other thing *pharmakon* means), the choice of only one of these renditions by the translator has as its first effect the neutralization of the citational play, of the "anagram," and, in the end, quite simply of the very textuality of the translated text. It could no doubt be shown, and we will try to do so when the time comes, that this blockage of the passage among opposing values is itself already an effect of "Platonism," the consequence of something already at work in the translated text, in the relation between "Plato" and his "language." There is no contradiction between this proposition and the preceding one. Textuality being constituted by differences and by differences from differences, it is by nature absolutely heterogeneous and is constantly composing with the forces that tend to annihilate it.

One must therefore accept, follow, and analyze the composition of these two forces or of these two gestures. That composition is even, in a certain sense, the single theme of this essay. On the one hand Plato decides in favor of a logic that does not tolerate such passages between opposing senses of the same word, all the more so since such a passage would reveal itself to be something quite different from simple confusion, alternation, or the dialectic of opposites. And yet, on the other hand, the *pharmakon*, if our reading confirms itself, constitutes the original medium of that decision, the element that precedes it, comprehends it, goes beyond it, can never be reduced to it, and is not separated from it by a single word (or signifying apparatus), operating within the Greek and Platonic text. All translations into languages that are the heirs and depositaries of Western metaphysics thus produce on the *pharmakon* an *effect of analysis* that violently destroys it, reduces it to one of its simple elements by interpreting it, paradoxically enough, in the light of the ulterior developments it itself has made possible. Such an interpretative translation is thus as violent as it is impotent: it destroys the *pharmakon* but at the same time forbids itself access to it, leaving it untouched in its reserve.

The translation by "remedy" can thus be neither accepted nor simply rejected. Even if one intended thereby to save the "rational" pole and the laudatory intention, the idea of the *correct* use of the *science* or *art* of medicine, one would still run every risk of being deceived by language. Writing is no more valuable, says Plato, as a remedy than as a poison. Even before Thamus has let fall his pejorative sentence, the remedy is disturbing in itself. One must indeed be aware of the fact that Plato is suspicious of the *pharmakon* in general, even in the case of drugs used exclusively for therapeutic ends, even when they are wielded with good intentions, and even when they are as such effective. There is no such thing as a harmless remedy. The *pharmakon* can never be simply beneficial.

For two different reasons, and at two different depths. First of all because the beneficial essence or virtue of a *pharmakon* does not prevent it from

included, saw all texts as potentially tissues of anagrams—relations that, regardless of the author's conscious intentions, might reveal something fundamental to writing.

hurting. The *Protagoras* classes the *pharmaka* among the things that can be both good (*agatha*) and painful (*aniara*) (354*a*). The *pharmakon* is always caught in the mixture (*summeikton*) mentioned in the *Philebus* (46*a*), examples of which are *hubris*, that violent, unbounded excess of pleasure that makes the profligate cry out like a madman (45*e*), and "relieving an itch by rubbing, and anything that can be treated by such a remedy (*ouk allēs deomena pharmaxeōs*)." This type of painful pleasure, linked as much to the malady as to its treatment, is a *pharmakon* in itself. It partakes of both good and ill, of the agreeable and the disagreeable. Or rather, it is within its mass that these oppositions are able to sketch themselves out.

Then again, more profoundly, even beyond the question of pain, the pharmaceutical remedy is essentially harmful because it is artificial. In this, Plato is following Greek tradition and, more precisely, the doctors of Cos.[8] The *pharmakon* goes against natural life: not only life unaffected by any illness, but even sick life, or rather the life of the sickness. For Plato believes in the natural life and normal development, so to speak, of disease. In the *Timaeus*, natural disease, like *logos* in the *Phaedrus*, is compared to a living organism which must be allowed to develop according to its own norms and forms, its specific rhythms and articulations. In disturbing the normal and natural progress of the illness, the *pharmakon* is thus the enemy of the living in general, whether healthy or sick. One must bear this in mind, and Plato invites us to do so, when writing is proposed as a *pharmakon*. Contrary to life, writing—or, if you will, the *pharmakon*—can only *displace* or even *aggravate* the ill. Such will be, in its logical outlines, the objection the king raises to writing: under pretext of supplementing memory, writing makes one even more forgetful; far from increasing knowledge, it diminishes it. Writing does not answer the needs of memory, it aims to the side, does not reinforce the *mnēmē*, but only *hypomnēsis*.[9] And if, in the two texts we are now going to look at together, the formal structure of the argument is indeed the same, if in both cases what is supposed to produce the positive and eliminate the negative does nothing but *displace* and at the same time *multiply* the effects of the negative, leading the lack that was its cause to proliferate, the necessity for this is inscribed in the *sign pharmakon*, which Robin (for example) dismembers, here as remedy, there as drug. We expressly said the *sign pharmakon*, intending thereby to mark that what is in question is *indissociably* a signifier and a concept signified.

A) In the *Timaeus*, which spreads itself out, from its opening pages, in the space between Egypt and Greece as in that between writing and speech ("You Hellenes are never anything but children, and there is not an old man among you," whereas in Egypt "everything has been written down by us of old": *panta gegrammena* [22*b*, 23*a*]), Plato demonstrates that, among all the body's movements, the best is natural motion, which spontaneously, from within, "is produced in a thing by itself":

> Now of all motions that is the best which is produced in a thing by itself, for it is most akin to the motion of thought and of the universe, but that motion which is caused by others is not so good, and worst of all is that

8. That is, the followers of Hippocrates (ca. 460–ca. 377 B.C.E.), the most celebrated physician in antiquity, who was born on the island of Cos.
9. A reminding (Greek).

> which moves the body, when at rest, in parts only and by some agency alien to it. Wherefore of all modes of purifying and reuniting the body the best is gymnastics; the next best is a surging motion, as in sailing or any other mode of conveyance which is not fatiguing; the third sort of motion may be of use in a case of extreme necessity, but in any other will be adopted by no man of sense—I mean the purgative treatment (*tēs pharmakeutikēs katharseōs*) of physicians; for diseases unless they are very dangerous should not be irritated by medicines (*ouk erethisteon pharmakeiais*), since every form of disease is in a manner akin to the living being (*tēi tōn zōōn phusei*), whose complex frame (*sustasis*) has an appointed term of life. For not the whole race only, but each individual—barring inevitable accidents—comes into the world having a fixed span. . . . And this holds also of the constitution of diseases; if anyone regardless of the appointed time tries to subdue them by medicine (*pharmakeiais*), he only aggravates and multiplies them. Wherefore we ought always to manage them by regimen, as far as a man can spare the time, and not provoke a disagreeable enemy by medicines (*pharmakeuonta*). (89*a–d*)

The reader will have noted that:

1. The noxiousness of the *pharmakon* is indicted at the precise moment the entire context seems to authorize its translation by "remedy" rather than poison.

2. The natural illness of the living is defined in its essence as an *allergy*,[1] a reaction to the aggression of an alien element. And it is necessary that the most general concept of disease should be allergy, from the moment the natural life of the body ought only to follow its own endogenous motions.

3. Just as health is auto-nomous and auto-matic, "normal" disease demonstrates its autarky by confronting the pharmaceutical aggression with *metastatic* reactions which displace the site of the disease, with the eventual result that the points of resistance are reinforced and multiplied. "Normal" disease defends itself. In thus escaping the supplementary constraints, the superadded pathogeny[2] of the *pharmakon*, the disease continues to follow its own course.

4. This schema implies that the living being is finite (and its malady as well): that it can have a relation with its other, then, in the allergic reaction, that it has a limited lifetime, that death is already inscribed and prescribed within its structure, in its "constitutive triangles." ("The triangles in us are originally framed with the power to last for a certain time beyond which no man can prolong his life." Ibid.) The immortality and perfection of a living being would consist in its having no relation at all with any outside. That is the case with God (cf. *Republic* II, 381*b–a*). God has no allergies. Health and virtue (*hugieia kai aretē*), which are often associated in speaking of the body and, analogously, of the soul (cf. *Gorgias*, 479*b*), always proceed from within. The *pharmakon* is that which, always springing up from without, acting like the outside itself, will never have any definable virtue of its own. But how can this supplementary parasite be excluded by maintaining the boundary, or, let us say, the triangle?

1. A word coined from the Greek words *allos* (other) and *ergon* (work).

2. Power to cause disease.

B) The system of these four features is reconstituted when, in the *Phaedrus*, King Thamus depresses and depreciates the *pharmakon* of writing, a word that should thus not too hastily be considered a metaphor, unless the metaphorical possibility is allowed to retain all its power of enigma. Perhaps we can now read the King's response:

> But the king said, "Theuth, my master of arts (*Ō tekhnikōtate Theuth*), to one man it is given to create the elements of an art, to another to judge the extent of harm and usefulness it will have for those who are going to employ it. And now, since you are father of written letters (*patēr ōn grammatōn*), your paternal goodwill has led you to pronounce the very opposite (*tounantion*) of what is their real power. The fact is that this invention will produce forgetfulness in the souls of those who have learned it because they will not need to exercise their memories (*lēthēn men en psuchais parexei mnēmēs ameletēsiai*), being able to rely on what is written, using the stimulus of external marks that are alien to themselves (*dia pistin graphēs exōthen hup' allotriōn tupōn*) rather than, from within, their own unaided powers to call things to mind (*ouk endothen autous huph' hautōn anamimnēiskomenous*). So it's not a remedy for memory, but for reminding, that you have discovered (*oukoun mnēmēs, alla hupomnēseōs, pharmakon hēures*). And as for wisdom (*sophias de*), you're equipping your pupils with only a semblance (*doxan*) of it, not with truth (*alētheian*). Thanks to you and your invention, your pupils will be widely read without benefit of a teacher's instruction; in consequence, they'll entertain the delusion that they have wide knowledge, while they are, in fact, for the most part incapable of real judgment. They will also be difficult to get on with since they will be men filled with the conceit of wisdom (*doxosophoi*), not men of wisdom (*anti sophōn*)." (274*e*–275*b*)

The king, the father of speech, has thus asserted his authority over the father of writing. And he has done so with severity, without showing the one who occupies the place of his son any of that paternal good will exhibited by Theuth toward his own children, his "letters." Thamus presses on, multiplies his reservations, and visibly wants to leave Theuth no hope.

In order for writing to produce, as he says, the "opposite" effect from what one might expect, in order for this *pharmakon* to show itself, with use, to be injurious, its effectiveness, its power, its *dunamis*[3] must, of course, be ambiguous. As is said of the *pharmakon* in the *Protagoras*, the *Philebus*, the *Timaeus*. It is precisely this ambiguity that Plato, through the mouth of the King, attempts to master, to dominate by inserting its definition into simple, clear-cut oppositions: good and evil, inside and outside, true and false, essence and appearance. If one rereads the reasons adduced by the royal sentence, one will find this series of oppositions there. And set in place in such a way that the *pharmakon*, or, if you will, writing, can only go around in circles: writing is only apparently good for memory, seemingly able to help it from within, through its own motion, to know what is true. But in truth, writing is essentially bad, external to memory, productive not of science but of belief, not of truth but of appearances. The *pharmakon* produces a play of appearances which enable it to pass for truth, etc.

3. Power (Greek).

But while, in the *Philebus* and the *Protagoras*, the *pharmakon*, because it is painful, seems bad whereas it is beneficial, here, in the *Phaedrus* as in the *Timaeus*, it is passed off as a helpful remedy whereas it is in truth harmful. Bad ambiguity is thus opposed to good ambiguity, a deceitful intention to a mere appearance. Writing's case is grave.

It is not enough to say that writing is conceived out of this or that series of oppositions. Plato thinks of writing, and tries to comprehend it, to dominate it, on the basis of *opposition* as such. In order for these contrary values (good/evil, true/false, essence/appearance, inside/outside, etc.) to be in opposition, each of the terms must be simply *external* to the other, which means that one of these oppositions (the opposition between inside and outside) must already be accredited as the matrix of all possible opposition. And one of the elements of the system (or of the series) must also stand as the very possibility of systematicity or seriality in general. And if one got to thinking that something like the *pharmakon*—or writing—far from being governed by these oppositions, opens up their very possibility without letting itself be comprehended by them; if one got to thinking that it can only be out of something like writing—or the *pharmakon*—that the strange difference between inside and outside can spring; if, consequently, one got to thinking that writing as a *pharmakon* cannot simply be assigned a site within what it situates, cannot be subsumed under concepts whose contours it draws, leaves only its ghost to a logic that can only seek to govern it insofar as logic arises from it—one would then have to *bend* [*plier*][4] into strange contortions what could no longer even simply be called logic or discourse. All the more so if what we have just imprudently called a *ghost* can no longer be distinguished, with the same assurance, from truth, reality, living flesh, etc. One must accept the fact that here, for once, to leave a ghost behind will in a sense be to salvage nothing.

This little exercise will no doubt have sufficed to warn the reader: to come to an understanding with Plato, as it is sketched out in this text, is already to slip away from the recognized models of commentary, from the genealogical or structural reconstitution of a system, whether this reconstitution tries to corroborate or refute, confirm or "overturn," mark a return-to-Plato or give him a "send-off" in the quite Platonic manner of the *khairein*. What is going on here is something altogether different. That too, of course, but still completely other. If the reader has any doubt, he is invited to reread the preceding paragraph. Every model of classical reading is exceeded there at some point, precisely at the point where it attaches to the inside of the series—it being understood that this excess is not a *simple* exit *out* of the series, since that would obviously fall under one of the categories of the series. The excess—but can we still call it that?—is only a *certain* displacement of the series. And a certain *folding back* [*repli*]—which will later be called a *re-mark*—of opposition within the series, or even within its dialectic. We cannot qualify it, name it, comprehend it under a simple concept without immediately being off the mark. Such a functional displacement, which concerns differences (and, as we shall see, "simulacra") more than any conceptual identities signified, is a real and necessary challenge. It writes itself. One must therefore begin by reading it.

4. The French *plier* anticipates Derrida's later reading in *Dissemination* of the French poet STÉPHANE MALLARMÉ (1892–1898), who often uses the word to describe a poem's way of doubling back on itself (*plier* means "to fold"; *repli*, a "folding back").

If writing, according to the king and under the sun, produces the opposite effect from what is expected, if the *pharmakon* is pernicious, it is because, like the one in the *Timaeus*, it doesn't come from around here. It comes from afar, it is external or alien: to the living, which is the right-here of the inside, to *logos* as the *zōon* it claims to assist or relieve. The imprints (*tupoi*) of writing do not inscribe themselves this time, as they do in the hypothesis of the *Theaetetus*, in the wax of the soul *in intaglio*,[5] thus corresponding to the spontaneous, autochthonous motions of psychic life. Knowing that he can always leave his thoughts outside or check them with an external agency, with the physical, spatial, superficial marks that one lays flat on a tablet, he who has the *tekhnē* of writing at his disposal will come to rely on it. He will know that he himself can leave without the *tupoi*'s going away, that he can forget all about them without their leaving his service. They will represent him even if he forgets them; they will transmit his word even if he is not there to animate them. Even if he is dead, and only a *pharmakon* can be the wielder of such power, *over* death but also in cahoots with it. The *pharmakon* and writing are thus always involved in questions of life and death.

Can it be said without conceptual anachronism—and thus without serious interpretive error—that the *tupoi* are the representatives, the *physical* surrogates of the *psychic* that is absent? It would be better to assert that the written traces no longer even belong to the order of the *phusis*, since they are not alive. They do not grow; they grow no more than what could be sown, as Socrates will say in a minute, with a reed (*kalamos*). They do violence to the natural, autonomous organization of the *mnēmē*, in which *phusis* and *psuchē*[6] are not opposed. If writing does belong to the *phusis*, wouldn't it be to that moment of the *phusis*, to that necessary movement through which its truth, the production of its appearing, tends, says Heraclitus,[7] to take shelter in its crypt? "Cryptogram" thus condenses in a single word a pleonastic proposition.

If one takes the king's word for it, then, it is this life of the memory that the *pharmakon* of writing would come to hypnotize: fascinating it, taking it out of itself by putting it to sleep in a monument. Confident of the permanence and independence of its *types* (*tupoi*), memory will fall asleep, will not keep itself up, will no longer keep to keeping itself alert, present, as close as possible to the truth of what is. Letting itself get stoned [*médusée*][8] by its own signs, its own guardians, by the types committed to the keeping and surveillance of knowledge, it will sink down into *lēthē*, overcome by nonknowledge and forgetfulness.[9] Memory and truth cannot be separated. The movement of *alētheia*[1] is a deployment of *mnēmē* through and through. A deployment of living memory, of memory as psychic life in its self-presentation to itself. The powers of *lēthē* simultaneously increase the domains of death, of nontruth, of nonknowledge. This is why writing, at least

5. That is, with an imprint left in relief.
6. Soul (Greek).
7. Greek natural philosopher (active ca. 500 B.C.E.), who viewed the universe as a ceaseless conflict of opposites. Derrida alludes to fragment 123, "Nature loves to hide [itself]."
8. Fascinated (French). The word combines Medusa's power to turn those who see her to stone with a drug's power to carry people out of themselves.
9. We would here like to refer the reader in particular to the extremely rich text by Jean-Pierre Vernant (who deals with these questions with quite different intentions): "Aspects mythiques de la mémoire et du temps," in *Mythe et pensée chez les Grecs* (Paris: Maspéro, 1965). On the word *tupos*, its relations with *perigraphē* and *paradeigma*, cf. A. von Blumenthal, *Tupos und Paradeigma*, quoted by P. M. Schuhl, in *Platon et l'art de son temps* [*Plato and the Art of His Time*, 2d ed.] (Paris: Presses Universitaires de France, 1952), p. 18 n. 4 [Derrida's note].
1. That is, truth's movement away from forgetfulness (*lēthē*).

insofar as it sows "forgetfulness in the soul," turns us toward the inanimate and toward nonknowledge. But it cannot be said that its essence simply and *presently* confounds it with death or nontruth. For writing *has* no essence or value of its own, whether positive or negative. It plays within the simulacrum. It is in its type the mime of memory, of knowledge, of truth, etc. That is why men of writing appear before the eye of God not as wise men (*sophoi*) but in truth as fake or self-proclaimed wise men (*doxosophoi*).

This is Plato's definition of the sophist. For it is above all against sophistics[2] that this diatribe against writing is directed: it can be inscribed within the interminable trial instituted by Plato, under the name of philosophy, against the sophists. The man who relies on writing, who brags about the knowledge and powers it assures him, this simulator unmasked by Thamus has all the features of a sophist: "the imitator of him who knows," as the *Sophist* puts it (*mimētēs tou sophou*, 268c). He whom we would call the graphocrat is as much like the sophist Hippias[3] as a brother. Like the Hippias we see in the *Lesser Hippias*, he boasts about knowing and doing all. And mainly—which Socrates twice, in two different dialogues, ironically pretends he has forgotten to include in his list—about having a better understanding than anyone else of mnemonics and mnemotechnics.[4] This is indeed the power he considers his pride and joy:

> *Socrates*: Then in astronomy also, the same man will be true and false?
>
> *Hippias*: It would seem so.
>
> *Socrates*: And now, Hippias, consider the question at large about all the sciences, and see whether the same principle does not always hold. I know that in most arts you are the wisest (*sophōtatos*) of men, as I have heard you boasting in the Agora at the tables of the money-changers, when you were setting forth the great and enviable stores of your wisdom. . . . Moreover, you told us that you had brought with you poems, epic, tragic, and dithyrambic,[5] as well as prose writings of the most various kinds, and you said that your skill was also pre-eminent in the arts which I was just now mentioning, and in the true principles of rhythm and harmony and of orthography. And, if I remember rightly, there were a great many other accomplishments in which you excelled. I have forgotten to mention your art of memory, which you regard as your special glory, and I dare say that I have forgotten many other things, but, as I was saying, only look to your own arts—and there are plenty of them—and to those of others, and tell me, having regard to the admissions which you and I have made, whether you discover any department of art or any description of wisdom or cunning, whichever name you use, in which the true and false are different and not the same. Tell me, if you can, of any. But you cannot.
>
> *Hippias*: Not without consideration, Socrates.
>
> *Socrates*: Nor will consideration help you, Hippias, as I believe, but then if I am right, remember what the consequence will be.
>
> *Hippias*: I do not know what you mean, Socrates.

2. In French, *la sophistique*; the translation links "dialectics" and "sophistics" as Derrida's two faces of philosophy and avoids dismissing the work of the sophists as mere "sophistry" (Socrates' claim).
3. Very successful Greek teacher and orator (ca. 485–415 B.C.E.).
4. Arts and techniques of memory.
5. Choral poetry originally sung in honor of Dionysus and later associated with highly excited music and impassioned language.

> *Socrates*: I suppose that you are not using your art of memory. . . . (368*a–d*)

The sophist thus sells the signs and insignia of science: not memory itself (*mnēmē*), only monuments (*hupomnēmata*), inventories, archives, citations, copies, accounts, tales, lists, notes, duplicates, chronicles, genealogies, references. Not memory but memorials. He thus answers the demands of the wealthy young men, and that is where he is most warmly applauded. After admitting that his young admirers cannot stand to hear him speak of the greater part of his knowledge (*Greater Hippias*, 285*c–d*), the sophist must tell Socrates all:

> *Socrates*: What then are the subjects on which they listen to you with pleasure and applause? Pray enlighten me; I cannot see.
>
> *Hippias*: They delight in the genealogies of heroes and of men and in stories of the foundations of cities in olden times, and, to put it briefly, in all forms of antiquarian lore, so that because of them I have been compelled to acquire a thorough comprehension and mastery of all that branch of learning.
>
> *Socrates*: Bless my soul, you have certainly been lucky that the Lacedaemonians do not want to hear a recital of the list of our archons, from Solon[6] downward; you would have had some trouble learning it.
>
> *Hippias*: Why? I can repeat fifty names after hearing them once.
>
> *Socrates*: I am sorry, I quite forgot about your mnemonic art. . . . (285*d–e*)

In truth, the sophist only pretends to know everything; his "polymathy" (*The Sophist*, 232*a*) is never anything but pretense. Insofar as writing *lends a hand* to hypomnesia and not to live memory, it, too, is foreign to true science, to anamnesia[7] in its properly psychic motion, to truth in the process of (its) presentation, to dialectics. Writing can only *mime* them. (It could be shown, but we will spare ourselves the development here, that the problematic that today, and in this very spot, links writing with the (putting in) question of truth—and of thought and speech, which are informed by it—must necessarily exhume, without remaining at that, the conceptual monuments, the vestiges of the battlefield [*champ de bataille*], the signposts marking out the battle lines between sophistics and philosophy, and, more generally, all the buttresses erected by Platonism. In many ways, and from a viewpoint that does not cover the entire field, we are today on the eve of Platonism. Which can also, naturally, be thought of as the morning after Hegelianism. At that specific point, the *philosophia*, the *epistēmē* are not "overturned," "rejected," "reined in," etc., in the name of something like writing; quite the contrary. But they are, according to a relation that philosophy would call *simulacrum*, according to a more subtle excess of truth, assumed and at the same time displaced into a completely different field, where one can still, but that's all, "mime absolute knowledge," to use an expression coined by Bataille,[8] whose name will enable us here to dispense with a whole network of references.)

6. Athenian statesman and poet (ca. 638–559 B.C.E.), chief archon (state magistrate; 9 were elected each year) in 594/3 and author of economic, legal, and constitutional reforms.

7. Recollection. "Hypomnesia": remembrance via a reminder.

8. The French novelist and theorist Georges Bataille (1897–1962).

The front line that is violently inscribed between Platonism and its closest other, in the form of sophistics, is far from being unified, continuous, as if stretched between two homogeneous areas. Its design is such that, through a systematic indecision, the parties and the party lines frequently exchange their respective places, imitating the forms and borrowing the paths of the opponent. These permutations are therefore possible, and if they are obliged to inscribe themselves within some common territory, the dissension no doubt remains internal and casts into absolute shadow some entirely-other of *both* sophistics *and* Platonism, some resistance having no common denominator with this whole commutation.

Contrary to what we have indicated earlier, there are also good reasons for thinking that the diatribe against writing is not aimed first and foremost at the sophists. On the contrary: sometimes it seems to proceed *from* them. Isn't the stricture that one should exercise one's memory rather than entrust traces to an outside agency the imperious and classical recommendation of the sophists? Plato would thus be appropriating here, once again, as he so often does, one of the sophists' argumentations. And here again, he will use it against them. And later on, after the royal judgment, Socrates' whole discourse, which we will take apart stitch by stitch, is woven out of schemes and concepts that issue from sophistics.

One must thus minutely recognize the crossing of the border. And be fully cognizant that this reading of Plato is at no time spurred on by some slogan or password of a "back-to-the-sophists" nature.

Thus, in both cases, on both sides, writing is considered suspicious and the alert exercise of memory prescribed. What Plato is attacking in sophistics, therefore, is not simply recourse to memory but, within such recourse, the substitution of the mnemonic device for live memory, of the prosthesis for the organ; the perversion that consists of replacing a limb by a thing, here, substituting the passive, mechanical "by-heart" for the active reanimation of knowledge, for its reproduction in the present. The boundary (between inside and outside, living and nonliving) separates not only speech from writing but also memory as an unveiling (re-)producing a presence from re-memoration as the mere repetition of a monument; truth as distinct from its sign, being as distinct from types. The "outside" does not begin at the point where what we now call the psychic and the physical meet, but at the point where the *mnēmē*, instead of being present to itself in its life as a movement of truth, is supplanted by the archive, evicted by a sign of re-memoration or of com-memoration. The space of writing, space *as* writing, is opened up in the violent movement of this surrogation, in the difference between *mnēmē* and *hypomnēsis*. The outside is already *within* the work of memory. The evil slips in within the relation of memory to itself, in the general organization of the mnesic[9] activity. Memory is finite by nature. Plato recognizes this in attributing life to it. As in the case of all living organisms, he assigns it, as we have seen, certain limits. A limitless memory would in any event be not memory but infinite self-presence. Memory always therefore already needs signs in order to recall the non-present, with which it is necessarily in relation. The movement of dialectics bears witness to this. Memory is thus contaminated by its first substitute: *hypomnēsis*. But what Plato *dreams* of is a memory with no sign. That is, with no supplement. A *mnēmē*

9. Having to do with memory.

with no *hypomnēsis*, no *pharmakon*. And this at the very moment and for the very reason that he calls *dream* the confusion between the hypothetical and the anhypothetical[1] in the realm of mathematical intelligibility (*Republic*, 533*b*).

Why is the surrogate or supplement dangerous? It is not, so to speak, dangerous in itself, in that aspect of it that can present itself as a thing, as a being-present. In that case it would be reassuring. But here, the supplement *is* not, is not a being (*on*). It is nevertheless not a simple nonbeing (*mē on*), either. Its slidings slip it out of the simple alternative presence/absence. *That* is the danger. And that is what enables the type always to pass for the original. As soon as the supplementary outside is opened, its structure implies that the supplement itself can be "typed," replaced by its double, and that a supplement to the supplement, a surrogate for the surrogate, is possible and necessary. Necessary because this movement is not a sensible, "empirical" accident: it is linked to the ideality of the *eidos*[2] as the possibility of the repetition of the same. And writing appears to Plato (and after him to all of philosophy, which is as such constituted in this gesture) as that process of redoubling in which we are fatally (en)trained:[3] the supplement of a supplement, the signifier, the representative of a representative. (A series whose first term or rather whose first structure does not yet—but we will do it later—have to be *kicked up* [*faire sauter*] and its irreducibility made apparent.) The structure and history of *phonetic* writing have of course played a decisive role in the determination of writing as the doubling of a sign, the sign of a sign. The signifier of a phonic signifier. While the phonic signifier would remain in animate proximity, in the living presence of *mnēmē* or *psuchē*, the graphic signifier, which reproduces it or imitates it, goes one degree further away, falls outside of life, entrains life out of itself and puts it to sleep in the type of its double. Whence the *pharmakon*'s two misdeeds: it dulls the memory, and if it is of any assistance at all, it is not for the *mnēmē* but for *hypomnēsis*. Instead of quickening life in the original, "in person," the *pharmakon* can at best only restore its monuments. It is a debilitating poison for memory, but a remedy or tonic for its external signs, its *symptoms*, with everything that this word can connote in Greek: an empirical, contingent, superficial event, generally a fall or collapse, distinguishing itself like an index from whatever it is pointing to. Your writing cures only the symptom, the King has already said, and it is from him that we know the unbridgable difference between the essence of the symptom and the essence of the signified; and that writing belongs to the order and exteriority of the symptom.

Thus, even though writing is external to (internal) memory, even though hypomnesia is not in itself memory, it affects memory and hypnotizes it in its very inside. That is the effect of this *pharmakon*. If it were purely external, writing would leave the intimacy or integrity of psychic memory untouched. And yet, just as Rousseau and Saussure will do in response to the same necessity, yet without discovering *other* relations between the intimate and the alien, Plato maintains *both* the exteriority of writing *and* its power of

1. Not hypothetical (the Greek prefix *a-* or *an-* means "without" or "not").
2. Form, shape (Greek); in Plato, one of the perfect and immutable transcendent Forms that, imperfectly recollected, are the source of all knowledge (see, e.g., *Meno* 81d; *Phaedo* 75b–e).
3. The French verb is *entraîner*, which means both "to carry away," or "to entrain," and "to exercise in," or "to train."

maleficent penetration, its ability to affect or infect what lies deepest inside. The *pharmakon* is that dangerous supplement[4] that breaks into the very thing that would have liked to do without it yet lets itself *at once* be breached, roughed up, fulfilled, and replaced, completed by the very trace through which the present increases itself in the act of disappearing.

If, instead of meditating on the structure that makes such supplementarity possible, if above all instead of meditating on the reduction by which "Plato-Rousseau-Saussure" try in vain to master it with an odd kind of "reasoning," one were to content oneself with pointing to the "logical contradiction," one would have to recognize here an instance of that kind of "kettle-logic" to which Freud turns in the *Traumdeutung*[5] in order to illustrate the logic of dreams. In his attempt to arrange everything in his favor, the defendant piles up contradictory arguments: 1. The kettle I am returning to you is brand new; 2. The holes were already in it when you lent it to me; 3. You never lent me a kettle, anyway. Analogously: 1. Writing is rigorously exterior and inferior to living memory and speech, which are therefore undamaged by it. 2. Writing is harmful to them because it puts them to sleep and infects their very life which would otherwise remain intact. 3. Anyway, if one has resorted to hypomnesia and writing at all, it is not for their intrinsic value, but because living memory is finite, it already has holes in it before writing ever comes to leave its traces. Writing has no effect on memory.

The opposition between *mnēmē* and *hypomnēsis* would thus preside over the meaning of writing. This opposition will appear to us to form a system with all the great structural oppositions of Platonism. What is played out at the boundary line between these two concepts is consequently something like the major decision of philosophy, the one through which it institutes itself, maintains itself, and contains its adverse deeps.

Nevertheless, between *mnēmē* and *hypomnēsis*, between memory and its supplement, the line is more than subtle; it is hardly perceptible. On both sides of that line, it is a question of *repetition*. Live memory repeats the presence of the *eidos*, and truth is also the possibility of repetition through recall. Truth unveils the *eidos*, or the *ontōs on*,[6] in other words, that which can be imitated, reproduced, repeated in its identity. But in the anamnesic movement of truth, what is repeated must present itself as such, as what it is, in repetition. The true is repeated; it is what is repeated in the repetition, what is represented and present in the representation. It is not the repeater in the repetition, nor the signifier in the signification. The true is the presence of the *eidos* signified.

Sophistics—the deployment of hypomnesia—as well as dialectics—the deployment of anamnesia—both presuppose the possibility of repetition. But sophistics this time keeps to the other side, to the other face, as it were, of repetition. And of signification. What is repeated is the repeater, the imitator,

4. The expression "that dangerous supplement," used by Rousseau in his *Confessions* [written 1766–70; pub. 1781–88] to describe masturbation, is the title of that chapter in *Of Grammatology* in which Derrida follows the consequences of the way in which the word *supplément*'s two meanings in French—"addition" and "replacement"—complicate the logic of Rousseau's treatment of sex, education, and writing. Writing, pedagogy, masturbation, and the *pharmakon* share the property of being—with respect to speech, nature, intercourse, and living memory—at once something secondary, external, and compensatory, and something that substitutes, violates, and usurps [translator's note].

5. The *Interpretation of Dreams* (1900) by SIGMUND FREUD (1856–1939), the Austrian founder of psychoanalysis.

6. The really real; what really exists (Greek).

the signifier, the representative, in the absence, as it happens, of *the thing itself*, which these appear to reedit, and without psychic or mnesic animation, without the living tension of dialectics. Writing would indeed be the signifier's capacity to repeat itself by itself, mechanically, without a living soul to sustain or attend it in its repetition, that is to say, without truth's *presenting itself* anywhere. Sophistics, hypomnesia, and writing would thus only be separated from philosophy, dialectics, anamnesis, and living speech by the invisible, almost nonexistent, thickness of that *leaf* between the signifier and the signified.[7] The "leaf": a significant metaphor, we should note, or rather one taken from the signifier face of things, since the leaf with its recto and verso first appears as a surface and support for writing. But by the same token, doesn't the unity of this leaf, of the system of this difference between signified and signifier, also point to the inseparability of sophistics and philosophy? The difference between signifier and signified is no doubt the governing pattern within which Platonism institutes itself and determines its opposition to sophistics. In being inaugurated in this manner, philosophy and dialectics are determined in the act of determining their other.

This profound complicity in the break has a first consequence: the argumentation against writing in the *Phaedrus* is able to borrow all its resources from Isocrates or Alcidamas at the moment it turns their own weapons, "transposing" them,[8] against the sophists. Plato imitates the imitators in order to restore the truth of what they imitate: namely, truth itself. Indeed, only truth as the presence (*ousia*) of the present (*on*) is here discriminative. And its power to discriminate, which commands or, as you will, is commanded by the difference between signified and signifier, in any case remains systematically inseparable from that difference. And this discrimination itself becomes so subtle that eventually it separates nothing, in the final analysis, but the same from itself, from its perfect, almost indistinguishable double. This is a movement that produces itself entirely within the structure of ambiguity and reversibility of the *pharmakon*.

How indeed does the dialectician simulate him whom he denounces as a simulator, as the simulacrum-man? On the one hand, the sophists advised, as does Plato, the exercise of memory. But, as we have seen, it was in order to enable themselves to speak without knowing, to recite without judgment, without regard for truth, in order to give signs. Or rather in order to sell them. Through this economy of signs, the sophists are indisputably men of writing at the moment they are protesting they are not. But isn't Plato one, too, through a symmetrical effect of reversal? Not only because he is actually a writer (a banal argument we will specify later on) and cannot, whether *de facto* or *de jure*, explain what dialectics is without recourse to writing; not only because he judges that the repetition of the same is necessary in anamnesis; but also because he judges it indispensable as an inscription in the type. (It is notable that *tupos* applies with equal pertinence to the graphic impression and to the *eidos* as model. Among many other examples, cf. *Republic*, 402*d*.) This necessity belongs to the order of the law and is posited by the *Laws*. In this instance, the immutable, petrified identity of writing is not simply added to the signified law or prescribed rule like a mute, stupid

7. In his *Course in General Linguistics* (see above), Saussure uses the image of a *leaf* to describe the relation between the signifier and the signified; sophistry and philosophy are as closely connected—and as far apart—as the signifier and the signified.

8. We are here using Auguste Diès's word, referring to his study of *La Transposition platonicienne*, more precisely to his first chapter, "La Transposition de la rhétorique," in *Autour de Platon*, 2:400 [Derrida's note].

simulacrum: it assures the law's permanence and identity with the vigilance of a guardian.[9] As another sort of guardian of the laws, writing guarantees the means of returning at will, as often as necessary, to that ideal object called the law. We can thus scrutinize it, question it, consult it, make it talk, without altering its identity. All this, even in the same words (notably *boētheia*[1]), is the other side, exactly opposite, of Socrates' speech in the *Phaedrus*.

> *Clinias*: And, mark you, such argument will be a most valuable aid to intelligent legislation (*nomothesia*), because legal prescriptions (*prostagmata*), once put into writing (*en grammasi tethenta*), remain always on record, as though to challenge the question of all time to come. Hence we need feel no dismay if they should be difficult on a first hearing, since even the dull student may return to them for reiterated scrutiny. Nor does their length, provided they are beneficial, make it less irrational than it is impious, in my opinion at least, for any man to refuse such discourse his heartiest support (*to mē ou boēthein toutois tois logois*). (X, 891*a*. I am still quoting from an authorized translation,[2] including the Greek where pertinent, and leaving the reader to appreciate the usual effects of translation. On the relation between written and unwritten laws, see notably VII, 793*b–c*.)

The italicized Greek words amply demonstrate it: the *prostagmata* of the law can be *posited* only in writing (*en grammasi tethenta*). *Nomothesia* is engrammatical. The legislator is a writer. And the judge a reader. Let us skip to book XII: "He that would show himself a righteously equal judge must keep these matters before his eyes; he must procure books (*grammata*) on the subject, and must make them his study. There is, in truth, no study whatsoever so potent as this of law, if the law be what it should be, to make a better man of its student" (975*c*).

Inversely, symmetrically, the rhetors had not waited around for Plato in order to *translate writing into judgment*. For Isocrates, for Alcidamas, *logos* was also a living thing (*zōon*) whose vigor, richness, agility, and flexibility were limited and constrained by the cadaverous rigidity of the written sign. The type does not adapt to the changing givens of the present situation, to what is unique and irreplaceable about it each time, with all the subtlety required. While *presence* is the general form of what is, the *present*, for its part, is always different. But writing, in that it repeats itself and remains identical in the type, cannot flex itself in all senses, cannot bend with all the differences among presents, with all the variable, fluid, furtive necessities of psychagogy. He who speaks, in contrast, is not controlled by any preestablished pattern; he is better able to conduct his signs; he is there to accentuate them, inflect them, retain them, or set them loose according to the demands of the moment, the nature of the desired effect, the hold he has on the listener. In attending his signs in their operation, he who acts by vocal means penetrates more easily into the soul of his disciple, producing effects that are always unique, leading the disciple, as though lodged within him, to the

9. "Guardian" (*phulax*) is what Plato calls the rulers of his ideal city in the *Republic*.
1. Help, aid (Greek).
2. Derrida is quoting from Diès; I am quoting from A. E. Taylor. Interestingly, another of these "effects of translation" is precisely the difficulty involved in translating a discussion of effects of translation [translator's note].

intended goal. It is thus not its pernicious violence but its breathless impotence that the sophists held against writing. In contrast to this blind servant with its haphazard, clumsy movements, the Attic school (Gorgias, Isocrates, Alcidamas) extolled the force of living *logos,* the great master, the great power: *logos dunastēs megas estin,*[3] says Gorgias in his *Encomium of Helen.* The dynasty of speech may be just as violent as that of writing, but its infiltration is more profound, more penetrating, more diverse, more assured. The only ones who take refuge in writing are those who are no better speakers than the man in the street. Alcidamas recalls this in his treatise "on those who write speeches" and "on the Sophists." Writing is considered a consolation, a compensation, a remedy for sickly speech.

Despite these similarities, the condemnation of writing is not engaged in the same way by the rhetors as it is in the *Phaedrus.* If the written word is scorned, it is not as a *pharmakon* coming to corrupt memory and truth. It is because *logos* is a more effective *pharmakon.* This is what Gorgias calls it. As a *pharmakon, logos* is at once good and bad; it is not at the outset governed exclusively by goodness or truth. It is only within this ambivalence and this mysterious indetermination of *logos,* and after these have been recognized, that Gorgias *determines* truth as a *world,* a structure or order, the counterpart (*kosmos*) of *logos.* In so doing he no doubt prefigures the Platonic gesture. But before such a determination, we are in the ambivalent, indeterminate space of the *pharmakon,* of that which in *logos* remains potency, potentiality, and is not yet the transparent language of knowledge. If one were justified in trying to capture it in categories that are subsequent to and dependent upon the history thus opened up, categories arising precisely *in the aftermath of decision,* one would have to speak of the "irrationality" of living *logos,* of its spellbinding powers of enchantment, mesmerizing fascination, and alchemical transformation, which make it kin to witchcraft and magic. Sorcery (*goēteia*), psychagogy, such are the "facts and acts" of speech, the most fearsome of *pharmaka.* In his *Encomium of Helen,* Gorgias used these very words to qualify the power of speech.

> Sacred incantations sung with words (*hai gar entheoi dia logōn epōidai*) are bearers of pleasure and banishers of pain, for, merging with opinion in the soul, the power of incantation is wont to beguile it (*ethelxe*) and persuade it and alter it by witchcraft (*goēteiai*). There have been discovered two arts of witchcraft and magic: one consists of errors of soul and the other of deceptions of opinion. . . . What cause then prevents the conclusion that Helen similarly, against her will, might have come under the influence (*humnos*) of speech, just as if ravished by the force of the mighty? . . . For speech constrained the soul, persuading it which it persuaded, both to believe the things said and to approve the things done. The persuader, like a constrainer, does the wrong and the persuaded, like the constrained, in speech is wrongly charged.[4]

Persuasive eloquence (*peithō*) is the power to break in, to carry off, to seduce internally, to ravish invisibly. It is furtive force per se. But in showing

3. *Logos* is a great lord (Greek). For the *Encomium* (ca. 400 B.C.E.), a defense of Helen of Troy (whose abduction from Greece by a Trojan prince led to the Trojan War), see above.

4. On this passage of the *Encomium,* on the relations of *thelgō* and *peithō,* of charm and persuasion, on their use in Homer, Aeschylus, and Plato, see Diès, pp. 116–17 [Derrida's note]. English translation by George Kennedy, in the *The Older Sophists,* ed. R. K. Sprague (Columbia: University of South Carolina Press, 1972), pp. 50–54 [translator's note].

that Helen gave in to the violence of speech (would she have yielded to a letter?), in disculpating[5] this victim, Gorgias indicts *logos* in its capacity to lie. "By introducing some reasoning (*logismon*) into speech (*tōi logōi*)," he wishes "to free the accused of blame and, having reproved her detractors as prevaricators and proved the truth, to free her from their ignorance."

But before being reined in and tamed by the *kosmos* and order of truth, *logos* is a wild creature, an ambiguous animality. Its magical "pharmaceutical" force derives from this ambivalence, which explains the disproportion between the strength of that force and the inconsiderable thing speech seems to be:

> But if it was speech which persuaded her and deceived her heart, not even to this is it difficult to make an answer and to banish blame as follows. Speech is a powerful lord, which by means of the finest and most invisible body effects the divinest words: it can stop fear and banish grief and create joy and nurture pity.

Such persuasion entering the soul through speech is indeed a *pharmakon*, and that is precisely what Gorgias calls it:

> The effect of speech (*tou logou dunamis*) upon the condition of the soul (*pros tēn tēs psuchēs taxin*) is comparable (*ton auton de logon*) to the power of drugs (*tōn pharmakōn taxis*) over the nature of bodies (*tēn tōn somatōn phusin*). For just as different drugs dispel different secretions from the body, and some bring an end to disease and others to life, so also in the case of speeches, some distress, others delight, some cause fear, others make the hearers bold, and some drug and bewitch the soul with a kind of evil persuasion (*tēn psuchēn epharmakeusan kai exegoēteusan*).

The reader will have paused to reflect that the relation (the analogy) between the *logos*/soul relation and the *pharmakon*/body relation is itself designated by the term *logos*. The name of the relation is the same as that of one of its terms. The *pharmakon* is *comprehended* in the structure of *logos*. This comprehension is an act of both *domination* and *decision*.

5. THE PHARMAKEUS

> For if there were nothing any more to hurt us, we should have no need whatever of any assistance. And thus you see it would then be made apparent that it was only on account of evil that we felt regard and affection for good (*tagathon*), as we considered good to be a medicine (*pharmakon*) for evil, and evil to be a disease. But where there is no disease, there is, we are aware, no need of medicine (*ouden dei pharmakou*). This, then, it appears, is the nature of good. . . .
>
> —Yes, he said, that would seem to be true.
>
> —*Lysis*, 220c–d

But if this is the case, and if *logos* is already a penetrating supplement, then isn't Socrates, "he who does not write," also a master of the *pharmakon*? And in that way isn't he the spitting image of a sophist? a *pharmakeus*? a magician? a sorcerer? even a poisoner? and even one of those impostors

5. Clearing from blame.

denounced by Gorgias? The threads of these complicities are almost impossible to disentangle.

Socrates in the dialogues of Plato often has the face of a *pharmakeus*. That is the name given by Diotima[6] to Eros. But behind the portrait of Eros, one cannot fail to recognize the features of Socrates, as though Diotima, in looking at him, were proposing to Socrates the portrait of Socrates (*Symposium*, 203*c, d, e*). Eros, who is neither rich, nor beautiful, nor delicate, spends his life philosophizing (*philosophōn dia pantos tou biou*); he is a fearsome sorcerer (*deinos goēs*), magician (*pharmakeus*), and sophist (*sophistēs*). A being that no "logic" can confine within a noncontradictory definition, an individual of the demonic species, neither god nor man, neither immortal nor mortal, neither living nor dead, he forms "the medium of the prophetic arts, of the priestly rites of sacrifice, initiation, and incantation, of divination and of sorcery (*thusias-teletas-epōidas-manteian*)" (202*e*).

In that same dialogue, Agathon accuses Socrates of trying to bewitch him, to cast a spell over him (*Pharmattein boulei me, ō Sōkrates*, 194*a*). The portrait of Eros by Diotima is placed between this exclamation and the portrait of Socrates by Alcibiades.[7]

Who reminds us that Socrates' brand of magic is worked through *logos* without the aid of any instrument, through the effects of a voice without accessories, without the flute of the satyr[8] Marsyas:

> And aren't you a piper as well? I should think you were—and a far more wonderful piper than Marsyas, who had only to put his flute to his lips to bewitch mankind. . . . His tunes will still have a magic power, and by virtue of their own divinity they will show which of us are fit subjects for divine initiation. Now the only difference, Socrates, between you and Marsyas is that you can get just the same effect without any instrument at all (*aneu organōn*)—with nothing but a few simple words (*psilois logois*[9]). . . ."(215*c–d*)

When confronted with this simple, organless voice, one cannot escape its penetration by stopping up one's ears, like Ulysses[1] trying to block out the Sirens (216*a*).

The Socratic *pharmakon* also acts like venom, like the bite of a poisonous snake (217–18). And Socrates' bite is worse than a snake's since its traces invade the soul. What Socrates' words and the viper's venom have in common, in any case, is their ability to penetrate and make off with the most concealed interiority of the body or soul. The demonic speech of this thaumaturge (en)trains the listener in dionysian frenzy[2] and philosophic *mania*

6. The woman who, in Plato's *Symposium*, gives Socrates instruction about love.
7. Athenian general and statesman (ca. 450–404 B.C.E), who praises Socrates at the end of the *Symposium*. Agathon (d. ca. 401 B.C.E.), Greek tragic poet; the *Symposium* represents a feast in honor of his victory (tragedies were presented in a competition, as part of a religious festival).
8. In Greek mythology, an attendant (often represented as part goat) of Dionysus, god of wine; Marsyas had such confidence in his flute playing that he challenged Apollo, god of music, to a musical contest (and was flayed alive when he lost).
9. "Bare, ungarnished voice, etc."; *psilos logos* also has the sense of abstract argument or simple affirmation without proof (cf. *Theaetetus* 165e) [Derrida's note].
1. Odysseus, Greek king of Ithaca, whose efforts to return home after the Trojan War are recounted in Homer's *Odyssey* (ca. 8th c. B.C.E.); he ordered his crew to fill their ears with wax and tie him to the mast of his ship so that he might safely hear the Sirens—mythical monsters, half woman and half bird, whose singing so entranced passing sailors that the listeners forgot to eat, and died (*Odyssey* 12.173–200).
2. The ecstatic enthusiasm of the worshippers of Dionysus; on the creative force of this frenzy (connected with music), see FRIEDRICH NIETZSCHE, *The Birth of Tragedy* (1872; above).

(218*b*). And when they don't act like the venom of a snake, Socrates' pharmaceutical charms provoke a kind of *narcosis*, benumbing and paralyzing into aporia,[3] like the touch of a sting ray (*narkē*):

> *Meno*: Socrates, even before I met you they told me that in plain truth you are a perplexed man yourself and reduce others to perplexity. At this moment I feel you are exercising magic and witchcraft upon me and positively laying me under your spell until I am just a mass of helplessness (*goēteueis me kai pharmatteis kai atekhnōs ketepaideis, hōste meston aporias gegonenai*). If I may be flippant, I think that not only in outward appearance (*eidos*) but in other respects as well you are exactly like the flat stringray (*narkē*) that one meets in the sea. Whenever anyone comes into contact with it, it numbs him, and that is the sort of thing that you seem to be doing to me now. My mind and my lips are literally numb, and I have nothing to reply to you. . . . In my opinion you are well advised not to leave Athens and live abroad. If you behaved like this as a foreigner in another country, you would most likely be arrested as a wizard (*goēs*). (*Meno*, 80*a–b*)

Socrates arrested as a wizard (*goēs* or *pharmakeus*): that will have to wait. What can be said about this *analogy* that ceaselessly refers the socratic *pharmakon* to the sophistic *pharmakon* and, proportioning them to each other, makes us go back indefinitely from one to the other? How can they be distinguished?

Irony does not consist in the dissolution of a sophistic charm or in the dismantling of an occult substance or power through analysis and questioning. It does not consist in undoing the charlatanesque confidence of a *pharmakeus* from the vantage point of some obstinate instance of transparent reason or innocent *logos*. Socratic irony precipitates out one *pharmakon* by bringing it in contact with another *pharmakon*. Or rather, it reverses the *pharmakon*'s powers and turns *its* surface over[4]—thus taking effect, being recorded and dated, in the act of *classing* the *pharmakon*, through the fact that the *pharmakon* properly consists in a certain inconsistency, a certain impropriety, this nonidentity-with-itself always allowing it to be turned against itself.

What is at stake in this overturning is no less than science and death. Which are consigned to a single type in the structure of the *pharmakon*, the one and only name for that portion that must be awaited. And even, in Socrates' case, deserved.

3. Difficulty, logical impasse (a term often used in deconstructive criticism to indicate the point in a text where inherent contradictions render interpretation undecidable).

4. Alternately and/or all at once, the Socratic *pharmakon* petrifies and vivifies, anesthetizes and sensitizes, appeases and anguishes. Socrates is a benumbing stingray but also an animal that needles: we recall the bee in the *Phaedo* (91c); later we will open the *Apology* at the point where Socrates compares himself precisely to a gadfly. This whole Socratic configuration thus composes a bestiary. It is surprising that the demonic inscribes itself in a bestiary? It is on the basis of this zoo-pharmaceutical ambivalence and of that other Socratic *analogy* that the contours of the *anthrōpos* [human] are determined [Derrida's note].

II

* * *

FROM 9. PLAY: FROM THE PHARMAKON TO THE LETTER AND FROM BLINDNESS TO THE SUPPLEMENT

It has been thought that Plato simply condemned play. And by the same token the art of *mimēsis* which is only a type of play.[5] But in all questions involving play and its "opposite," the "logic" will necessarily be baffling. Play and art are lost by Plato as he saves them, and his logos is then subject to that untold constraint that can no longer even be called "logic." Plato does very well speak of play. He speaks in praise of it. But he praises play "in the best sense of the word," if this can be said without eliminating play beneath the reassuring silliness of such a precaution. The best sense of play is play that is supervised and contained within the safeguards of ethics and politics. This is play comprehended under the innocent, innocuous category of "fun." Amusement: however far off it may be, the common translation of *paidia* by *pastime* [*divertissement*] no doubt only helps consolidate the Platonic repression of play.

The opposition *spoudē/paidia*[6] will never be one of simple symmetry. *Either* play is *nothing* (and that is its only *chance*); either it can give place to no activity, to no discourse worthy of the name—that is, one charged with truth or at least with meaning—and then it is *alogos* or *atopos*. *Or else* play begins to *be* something and its very presence lays it open to some sort of dialectical confiscation. It takes on meaning and works in the service of seriousness, truth and ontology. Only *logoi peri ontōn*[7] can be taken seriously. As soon as it comes into being and into language, play *erases itself as such*. Just as writing must erase itself as such before truth, etc. The point is that there *is* no *as such* where writing or play are concerned. Having no essence, introducing difference as the condition for the presence of essence, opening up the possibility of the double, the copy, the imitation, the simulacrum—the game and the *graphē*[8] are constantly disappearing as they go along. They cannot, in classical affirmation, be affirmed without being negated.

Plato thus plays at taking play seriously. That is what we earlier called the stunning hand Plato has dealt himself. Not only are his writings defined as games,[9] but human affairs in general do not in his eyes need to be taken seriously. One thinks of the famous passage in the *Laws*. Let us reread it despite its familiarity, so as to follow the theological assumption of play into games, the progressive neutralization of the *singularity* of play:

> To be sure, man's life is a business which does not deserve to be taken too seriously (*megalēs men spoudēs ouk axia*); yet we cannot help being in earnest with it, and there's the pity. Still, as we are here in this world, no doubt, for us the becoming thing is to show this earnestness in a suitable way (*hēmin summetron*). . . . I mean we should keep our seri-

5. Cf. *Republic* 10.602a–b; *Statesman* 288c–d; *Sophist* 234b–c; *Laws* 2.667e–668a; *Epinomis* 975d, etc. [Derrida's note].
6. Seriousness/play (Greek).
7. Words about real things (Greek).
8. Writings; indictment (Greek).
9. Cf. *Parmenides* 137b; *Statesman* 268d; *Timaeus* 59c–d. On the context and historical background of this problematic of play, cf. notably Schuhl, *Platon et l'art de son temps*, pp. 61–63 [Derrida's note].

> ousness for serious things, and not waste it on trifles, and that, while God is the real goal of all beneficent serious endeavor (*makariou spoudēs*), man, as we said before,[1] has been constructed as a toy (*paignion*) for God, and this is, in fact, the finest thing about him. All of us, then, men and women alike, must fall in with our role and spend life in making our *play* as perfect as possible—to the complete inversion of current theory. . . . It is the current fancy that our serious work should be done for the sake of our play; thus it is held that war is serious work which ought to be well discharged for the sake of peace. But the truth is that in war we do not find, and we never shall find, either any real play or any real education worth the name, and *these* are the things I count supremely serious for such creatures as ourselves. Hence it is peace in which each of us should spend most of his life and spend it best. What, then, is our right course? We should pass our lives in the playing of games—*certain* games, that is, sacrifice, song, and dance—with the result of ability to gain heaven's grace, and to repel and vanquish an enemy when we have to fight him. . . . (803*b*–*e*)

Play is always lost when it seeks salvation in games. We have examined elsewhere, in "Rousseau's era,"[2] this disappearance of play into games. This (non)logic of play and of writing enables us to understand what has always been considered so baffling:[3] why Plato, while subordinating or condemning writing and play, should have written so much, presenting his writings, *from out of Socrates' death*, as games, *indicting* writing in writing, lodging against it that complaint (*graphē*) whose reverberations even today have not ceased to resound.

What law governs this "contradiction," this opposition to itself of what is said against writing, of a dictum that pronounces itself against itself as soon as it finds its way into writing, as soon as it writes down its self-identity and carries away what is proper to it *against* this ground of writing? This "contradiction," which is nothing other than the relation-to-self of diction as it opposes itself to scription, as it *chases* itself (away) in hunting down what is properly its *trap*—this contradiction is not contingent. In order to convince ourselves of this, it would already suffice to note that what seems to inaugurate itself in Western literature with Plato will not fail to re-edit itself at least in Rousseau, and then in Saussure. In these three cases, in these three "eras" of the repetition of Platonism, which give us a new thread to follow and other knots to recognize in the history of *philosophia* or the *epistēmē*, the exclusion and the devaluation of writing must somehow, in their very affirmation, come to terms with:

1. Cf. *Laws* 1.644d–e: "Let us look at the whole matter in some such light as this. We may imagine that each of us living creatures is a puppet made by gods, possibly as a plaything (*hōs paignion*) or possibly with some more serious purpose (*hōs spoudēi tini*). That, indeed, is more than we can tell, but one thing is certain. These interior states are, so to say, the cords, or strings, by which we are worked; they are opposed to one another, and pull us with opposite tensions in the direction of opposite actions, and therein lies the division of virtue from vice. In fact, so says our argument (*logos*), a man must always yield to one of these tensions without resistance, but pull against all the other strings—must yield, that is, to that golden and hallowed drawing of judgments (*tēn tou logismou agōgēn khrusēn kai hieran*) which goes by the name of the public law of the city. The others are hard and ironlike, it soft, as befits gold, whereas they resemble very various substances." Let us henceforth keep hold of this rein called *khrusos* [gold] or *chrysology* [Derrida's note].

2. Cf. *Of Grammatology* [Derrida's note].

3. The principal references are collected in Robin's *La Théorie platonicienne de l'amour*, pp. 54–59 [Derrida's note].

1. a generalized sort of writing and, along with it,

2. a "contradiction": the written proposal of logocentrism; the simultaneous affirmation of the being-outside of the outside and of its injurious intrusion into the inside;

3. the construction of a "literary" work. Before Saussure's *Anagrams*, there were Rousseau's; and Plato's work, outside and independent of its logocentric "content," which is then only one of its inscribed "functions," can be read in its anagrammatical texture.

Thus it is that the "linguistics" elaborated by Plato, Rousseau, and Saussure must both put writing out of the question and yet nevertheless borrow from it, for fundamental reasons, all its demonstrative and theoretical resources. As far as the Genevans[4] are concerned, we have tried to show this elsewhere. The case is at least equally clear for Plato.

Plato often uses the example of letters of the alphabet in order to come to grips with a problem. They give him a better grip on things; that is, he can use them to explain dialectics—but he never "comes to grips with" the writing he uses. His intentions are always apparently didactic and analogical. But they conform to a constant necessity, which is never thematized as such: what always makes itself apparent is the law of difference, the irreducibility of structure and relation, of proportionality, within analogy.

We noted earlier that *tupos* can designate with equal pertinence the graphic unit and the eidetic model. In the *Republic*, even before he uses the word *tupos* in the sense of model-form (*eidos*) Plato finds it necessary to turn to the example of the letter, still for apparently pedagogical ends, as a model that must be known before one can recognize its copies or icons reflected in water or in a mirror:

> It is, then, said I, as it was when we learned our letters and felt that we knew them sufficiently only when the separate letters did not elude us, appearing as a few elements in all the combinations that convey them, and when we did not disregard them in small things or great and think it unnecessary to recognize them, but were eager to distinguish them everywhere, in the belief that we should never be literate and letter-perfect till we could do this. . . . And is it not also true that if there are any likeness of letters (*eikonas grammatōn*) reflected in water or mirrors, we shall never know them until we know the originals, but such knowledge belongs to the same art and discipline? (402*a*–*b*)

We have no doubt already been warned by the *Timaeus*: in all these *comparisons* with writing, we are not supposed to take the letters *literally*. The *stoikheia tou pantos*, the elements (or letters) of the whole are not assembled like syllables (48*c*). "They cannot reasonably be compared by a man of any sense even to syllables."[5] And yet, in the *Timaeus*, not only is the entire mathematical play of proportionalities based on a *logos* that can do without voice, God's calculation (*logismos theou*) (34*a*) being able to express itself in the silence of numbers; but, in addition, the introduction of the *different* and the *blend* (35*a*), the problematic of the *moving* cause and the *place*—the

4. Rousseau and Saussure.

5. As for the use of letters, in the context of a comparison between the *Timaeus* and the *Jafr*, the Islamic science of letters as a science of "permutation," cf. notably H. Corbin, *Histoire de la philosophie islamique* (Paris: Nouvelle Revue Française), pp. 204ff. [Derrida's note]. The quotation is from *Timaeus* 48b–c.

third irreducible class—the duality of paradigms (49*a*), all these things "require" (49*a*) that we define the origin of the world as a *trace*, that is, a receptacle. It is a matrix, womb, or receptacle that is never and nowhere offered up in the form of presence, or in the presence of form, since both of these already presuppose an inscription within the mother. Here, in any case, the turns of phrase that are somewhat awkwardly called "Plato's metaphors" are exclusively and irreducibly scriptural. Let us, for example, point to a sign of this awkwardness in a certain preface to the *Timaeus*: "In order to conceive of place, one must always, through a process of abstraction that is almost unrealizable in practice, separate or detach an object from the 'place' it occupies. This abstraction, however difficult, is nevertheless imposed upon us by the very fact of change, since two different objects cannot coexist in the same place, and since, without changing place, a same object can become 'other.' But then, we find ourselves unable to represent 'place' itself except by metaphors. Plato used several quite different ones, which have greatly confused modern readers. The 'Place,' the 'locus,' 'that in which' things appear, 'that upon which' they manifest themselves, the 'receptacle,' the 'matrix,' the 'mother,' the 'nurse'—all these expressions make us think of space, which contains things. But later on it is a question of the 'impression-bearer,' the formless 'base,' the completely inodorous substance on which the perfume-maker can fix the scent, the soft gold on which the jeweller can impress many diverse figures" (Rivaud, Budé edition, p. 66). Here is the passage beyond all "Platonic" oppositions, toward the aporia of the originary inscription:

> . . . Then we made two classes; now a third must be revealed. The two sufficed for the former discussion. One, we assumed, was a pattern (*paradeigmatos*) intelligible and always the same, and the second was only the imitation of the pattern, generated and visible. There is also a third kind which we did not distinguish at the time, conceiving that the two would be enough. But now the argument seems to require that we should set forth in words another kind, which is difficult of explanation and dimly seen. What nature are we to attribute to this new kind of being? We reply that it is the receptacle, and in a manner the nurse (*hupodokhēn autēn hoion tithēnēn*), of all generation (*pasēs geneseōs*). . . . [This nurse] must be always called the same, for, inasmuch as she always receives all things, she never departs at all from her own nature and never, in any way or at any time, assumes a form like that of any of the things which enter into her; she is the natural recipient of all impressions (*ekmageion*), and is stirred and informed by them, and appears different from time to time by reason of them. But the forms which enter into and go out of her are the likeness of eternal realities (*tōn ontōn aei mimēmata*) modeled within her after their patterns (*tupōthenta*) in a wonderful and mysterious manner, which we will hereafter investigate. For the present we have only to conceive of three natures: first, that which is in process of generation; secondly, that in which the generation takes place; and thirdly, that of which the thing generated is a resemblance naturally produced. And we may liken the receiving principle to a mother, and the source or spring to a father, and the intermediate nature to a child, and may remark further that if the model is to take

> every variety of form, then the matter in which the model is fashioned will not be duly prepared unless it is formless and free from the impress of any of those shapes which it is hereafter to receive from without. . . . Wherefore the mother and receptacle of all created and visible and in any way sensible things is not to be termed earth or air or fire or water, or any of their compounds, or any of the elements from which these are derived, but is an invisible and formless being which receives all things and in some mysterious way partakes of the intelligible, and is most incomprehensible. (48*e*–51*b*; The *khōra*[6] is big with everything that is disseminated here. We will go into that elsewhere.)

Whence the recourse to dream a bit further on, as in that text of the *Republic* (533*b*) where it is a question of "seeing" what cannot simply be conceived in terms of the opposition between sensible and intelligible, hypothetical and anhypothetical, a certain *bastardy* whose notion (*nothos*) was probably not unknown to Democritus[7] (cf. Rivaud; *Le Problème du devenir et la notion de la matière*[8] . . . p. 310, n. 744):

> And there is a third nature, which is space and is eternal, and admits not of destruction and provides a home for all created things, and is apprehended, when all sense is absent, by a kind of spurious reason (*logismōi tini nothōi*: *bastard* reasoning), and is hardly real—which we, beholding as in a dream, say of all existence that it must of necessity be in some place and occupy a space, but that what is neither in heaven nor in earth has no existence. Of these and other things of the same kind, relating to the true and waking reality of nature, we have only this dreamlike sense, and we are unable to cast off sleep and determine the truth about them. (52*b*–*c*)

Inscription is thus the *production of the son* and at the same time the constitution of *structurality*.[9] The link between structural relations of proportionality on the one hand and literality on the other does not appear only in cosmogonic discourse. It can also be seen in political discourse, and in the discourse of linguistics.

In the political order, structure is a sort of writing. At the moment of ultimate difficulty, when no other pedagogical resource is available, when theoretical discourse cannot find any other way of formulating the order, the world, the *cosmos* of politics, Socrates turns to the grammatical "metaphor." The analogy of the "large letters" and "small letters" comes up in the famous text of the *Republic* (368*c*–*e*) at the point where "keen vision" is necessary, and where it seems to be lacking. Structure is read as a form of writing in an instance where the intuition of sensible or intelligible presence happens to fail.

The same thing occurs in the domain of linguistics. As in Saussure's *Course in General Linguistics*, the scriptural reference becomes absolutely

6. A Greek word (literally, "space") often translated "receptacle" in this passage. In *Khôra* (1992; trans. in *On the Name*, ed. Thomas Dutoit [Stanford: Stanford University Press, 1995]), Derrida treats it as proper name rather than a concept.

7. Greek philosopher (ca. 460—ca. 370 B.C.E.), who argued that the physical world is made up of eternal and invisible atoms, which are in constant motion.

8. A. Rivaud, *Le Problème du devenir et la notion de la matière dans la philosophie grecque depuis les origines jusqu'à Theophraste* [*The Problem of Becoming and the Notion of Matter in Greek Philosophy from Its Origins to Theophrastus*] (Paris: F. Alcan, 1906).

9. Biological (organic) generation and structural (mathematical or linguistic) generation, which are often seen as completely different, thus turn out to be interdependent: the *son* cannot be recognized as such without the whole apparatus of symbolization.

indispensable at the point at which the principle of difference and diacriticity in general must be accounted for as the very condition of signification.[1] This is how Theuth comes to make his second appearance on the Platonic scene. In the *Phaedrus*, the inventor of the *pharmakon* gave a long speech in person and presented his letters as credentials to the king. More concise, more indirect, more allusive, his other intervention seems to us just as philosophically remarkable. It occurs in the name not of the invention of graphics but of grammar, of the science of grammar as a science of differences. It is in the beginning of the *Philebus*: the debate is open on the relations between pleasure (*khairein*) and intelligence or prudence (*phronein*) (11*d*). The discussion soon founders on the problem of *limits*. And hence, as in the *Timaeus*, on the composition of the same and the other, the one and the multiple, the finite and the infinite. ". . . the men of old, who were better than ourselves and dwelt nearer the gods, passed on this gift in the form of a saying. All things, as it ran, that are ever said to be consist of a one and a many, and have in their nature a conjunction (*en hautois sumphuton*) of limit and unlimitedness (*peras de kai apeirian*)." Socrates opposes dialectics, the art of respecting the intermediate forms (*ta mesa*), to eristic, which immediately leaps toward the infinite (16*c*–17*a*). This time, in contrast to what happens in the *Phaedrus*, letters are charged with the task of introducing clarity (*saphēneia*) into discourse:

> *Protarchus*: I think I understand, more or less, part of what you say, Socrates, but there are some points I want to get further cleared up.
>
> *Socrates*: My meaning, Protarchus, is surely clear in the case of the alphabet; so take the letters of your school days as illustrating it.
>
> *Protarchus*: How do you mean?
>
> *Socrates*: The sound (*phōnē*) that proceeds through our mouths, yours and mine and everybody's, is one, isn't it, and also an unlimited variety?
>
> *Protarchus*: To be sure.
>
> *Socrates*: And we have no real understanding if we stop short at knowing it either simply as an unlimited variety, or simply as one. What makes a man "lettered" is knowing the number and the kinds of sounds. (17*a*–*b*)

After a detour through the example of musical intervals (*distēmata*), Socrates goes back to letters in an effort to explain phonic intervals and differences:

> *Socrates*: . . . We might take our letters again to illustrate what I mean now. . . . The unlimited variety of sound was once discerned by some god, or perhaps some godlike man; you know the story that there was some such person in Egypt called Theuth. He it was who originally discerned the existence, in that unlimited variety, of the vowels (*ta phōnēenta*)—not "vowel" in the singular but "vowels" in the plural—and then of other things which, though they could not be called articulate sounds, yet were noises of a kind. There were a number of them, too, not just one, and as a third class he discriminated what we now call the mutes (*aphōna*). Having done that, he

1. Compare Saussure's famous statement that "In language there are only differences *without positive terms*."

> divided up the noiseless ones or mutes (*aphthonga kai aphōna*) until he got each one by itself, and did the same thing with the vowels and the intermediate sounds; in the end he found a number of the things, and affixed to the whole collection, as to each single member of it, the name "letters" (*stoikheion*). It was because he realized that none of us could get to know one of the collection all by itself, in isolation from all the rest, that he conceived of "letter" as a kind of bond of unity (*desmon*) uniting as it were all these sounds into one, and so he gave utterance to the expression "art of letters," implying that there was one art that dealt with the sounds. (18*b–d*)

The scriptural "metaphor" thus crops up every time difference and relation are irreducible, every time otherness introduces determination and puts a system in circulation. The play of the other within being must needs be designated "writing" by Plato in a discourse which would like to think of itself as spoken in essence, in truth, and which nevertheless is written. And if it is written *from out of the death of Socrates*, this is no doubt the profound reason for it. From out of Socrates' death—that is, it would here be just as well to say, from out of the parricide in the *Sophist*. Without that violent eruption against the venerable paternal figure of Parmenides,[2] against his thesis of the unity of being; without the disruptive intrusion of otherness and nonbeing, of nonbeing as other in the unity of being, writing and its play would not have been necessary. Writing is parricidal. Is it by chance that, for the Stranger in the *Sophist*, the necessity and inevitability of parricide, "plain enough, as they say, for even the blind (*tuphlōi*) to see" (one ought to say, *especially* for the blind to see), are the condition of possibility of a discourse on the false, the idol, the icon, the mimeme,[3] the phantasm, and "the arts concerned with such things"? And thus, of writing? Writing is not named at this point but that does not prevent—on the contrary—its relation with all the aforementioned concepts from remaining systematic, and we have recognized it as such:

> *Stranger*: We shall find it necessary in self-defense to put to the question that pronouncement of father Parmenides (*Ton tou patros Parmenidou logon*), and establish by main force that what is not (*mē on*), in some respect has a being, and conversely that what is (*on*), in a way is not.
>
> *Theaetetus*:[4] It is plain that the course of the argument requires us to maintain that at all costs (*Phainetai to toiouton diamakheteon en tois logois*).
>
> *Stranger*: Plain enough even for the blind to see, as they say. Unless these propositions are either refuted or accepted, anyone who talks of false statements or false judgment as being images or likenesses or copies or semblances, or of any of the arts concerned with such things, can hardly escape becoming a laughingstock by being forced to contradict himself.
>
> *Theaetetus*: Quite true.

2. Greek philosopher (b. ca. 515 B.C.E.), whose didactic poem *On Nature* explores the nature of being. His philosophy is discussed in Plato's *Parmenides*.

3. Constituent element of mimesis.

4. Athenian mathematician (ca. 414–369 B.C.E.), a friend and pupil of Plato's.

Stranger: That is why we must now dare to lay unfililial hands on that paternal pronouncement (*tōi patrikōi logōi*), or else, if some scruple holds us back, drop the matter entirely.

Theaetetus: As for that, we must let no scruple hinder us. (241*d*–242*a*)

This parricide, which opens up the play of difference and writing, is a frightening decision. Even for an anonymous Stranger. It takes superhuman strength. And one runs the risk of madness or of being considered mad in the well-behaved, sane, sensible society of grateful sons.[5] So the Stranger is still afraid of not having the strength, not only to play the fool, but also to maintain a discourse that might—for real—be without head or tail; or, to put it another way, to set off on a path where he might not be able to avoid ending up walking on his head. In any event, this parricide will be just as decisive, cutting, and redoubtable as capital punishment. With no hope of return. One lays one's head, as well as one's chief, on the line. Thus, after having begged Theaetetus, without illusions, not to consider him a patricide (*patraloian*), the Stranger asks another favor:

Stranger: In that case, for the third time, I have a small favor to ask.

Theaetetus: You have only to mention it.

Stranger: I believe I confessed just now that on this point the task of refutation has always proved too much for my powers, and still does so.

Theaetetus: You did say that.

Stranger: Well, that confession, I am afraid, may make you think me scatterbrained (*manikos*) when at every turn I shift my position to and fro (*para poda metabalōn emauton anō kai katō*). (242*a*–*b*)

The discourse, then, is off. Paternal *logos* is upside down. Is it then by chance if, once "being" has appeared as a *triton ti*, a third irreducible to the dualisms of classical ontology, it is again necessary to turn to the example of grammatical science and of the relations among letters in order to explain the interlacing that weaves together the system of differences (solidarity-exclusion), of kinds and forms, the *sumplokē tōn eidōn*[6] to which "any discourse we can have owes its existence" (*ho logos gegonen hēmin*) (259*e*)? The *sumplokē*, too, of being and nonbeing (240*c*)? As far as the rules of concordance and discordance, of union and exclusion among different things are concerned, this *sumplokē* "might be said to be in the same case with the letters of the alphabet" (253*a*; cf. the *Statesman* where the "paradigm" of the *sumplokē* is equally *literal*, 278*a*–*b*).[7]

5. It would be interesting to articulate that passage from the *Laws* (8.836b–c), in which a *pharmakon* is sought as a "protection (*diaphugēn*) against this peril," namely, pederasty. The Athenian wonders, without holding out much hope, what would happen "were one to follow the guidance of nature and adopt the law of the old days before Laius (*tēi phusei thēsei ton pro tou Laiou nomon*)—I mean, to pronounce it wrong that male should have to do carnally with youthful male as with female. . . ." Laius, to whom the oracle had predicted that he would be killed by his son, was also the representative of unnatural love. Cf. "*Oedipe*," in Marie Delcourt, *Légendes et cultes de héros en Grèce* [*Legends and Hero Cults in Greece*] (Paris: Presses Universitaires de France, 1942), p. 103.

We also know that according to the *Laws*, there is no greater crime or sacrilege than the murder of the parents: such a murderer should be put to "repeated deaths" (9.869b). And even receive punishment worse than death, which is not the ultimate chastisement. "Hence we must make the chastisements for such crime here is this present life, if we can, no less stern than those of the life to come" (881b) [Derrida's note]. Laius: the father of Oedipus; when they met as strangers at a crossroads, Oedipus killed him.

6. Intertwining or combination of the forms (Greek).

7. On the problem of the letters of the alphabet, particularly as it is treated in the *Statesman*, cf. V. Goldschmidt, *Le Paradigme dans la dialectique Platonicienne* (Paris: Presses Universitaires de France, 1947), pp. 61–67 [Derrida's note].

Grammatical science is doubtless not in itself dialectics. Plato indeed explicitly subordinates the former to the latter (253*b–c*). And, to him, this distinction can be taken for granted; but what, in the final analysis, justifies it? Both are in a sense sciences of language. For dialectics is also the science that guides us "*dia tōn logōn*,"[8] on the voyage through discourses or arguments (253*b*). At this point, what distinguishes dialectics from grammar appears twofold: on the one hand, the linguistic units it is concerned with are larger than the word (*Cratylus*, 385*a*–393*d*); on the other, dialectics is always guided by an intention of *truth*. It can only be satisfied by the presence of the *eidos*, which is here both the signified and the referent: the thing itself. The distinction between grammar and dialectics can thus only in all rigor be established at the point where truth is fully present and fills the *logos*. But what the parricide in the *Sophist* establishes is not only that any *full, absolute* presence of what *is* (of the being-present that most truly "is": the good or the sun that can't be looked in the face) is impossible; not only that any full intuition of truth, any truth-filled intuition, is impossible; but that the very condition of discourse—*true or false*—is the diacritical principle of the *sumplokē*. If truth is the presence of the *eidos*, it must always, on pain of mortal blinding by the sun's fires, come to terms with relation, nonpresence, and thus nontruth. It then follows that the absolute precondition for a rigorous difference between grammar and dialectics (or ontology) cannot in principle be fulfilled. Or at least, it can perhaps be fulfilled *at the root of the principle*, at the point of arche-being or arche-truth,[9] but that point has been crossed out by the necessity of parricide. Which means, by the very necessity of *logos*. And that is the difference that prevents there being *in fact* any difference between grammar and ontology.

But now, what *is* the impossibility of any truth or of any full presence of being, of any fully-being? Or inversely, since such truth would be death as the absolute form of blindness, what is death as truth? Not *what is?* since the form of that question is produced by the very thing it questions, but how is the impossible plenitude of any absolute presence of the *ontōs on* written? How is it inscribed? How is the necessity of the multiplicity of genres and ideas, of relation and difference, prescribed? How is dialectics traced?

The absolute invisibility of the origin of the visible, of the good-sun-father-capital, the unattainment of presence or beingness in any form, the whole surplus Plato calls *epekeina tēs ousias* (beyond beingness or presence), gives rise to a structure of replacements such that all presences will be supplements substituted for the absent origin, and all differences, within the system of presence, will be the irreducible effect of what remains *epekeina tēs ousias*.

Just as Socrates supplements and replaces the father, as we have seen, dialectics supplements and replaces the impossible *noēsis*,[1] the forbidden intuition of the face of the father (good-sun-capital). The withdrawal of that face both opens and limits the exercise of dialectics. It welds it irremediably to its "inferiors," the mimetic arts, play, grammar, writing, etc. The disappearance of that face is the movement of difference which violently opens writing or, if one prefers, which opens itself to writing and which writing opens for itself. All these "movements," in all these "senses," belong to the

8. Through the words (Greek).
9. "Arche-" derives from the Greek *archē*, meaning "beginning, origin."
1. Intelligence, understanding (Greek).

same "system." Also belonging to that same system are the proposition in the *Republic*, describing in nonviolent terms the inaccessibility of the father *epekeina tēs ousias*, and the patricidal proposal which, proffered by the Stranger, threatens the paternal *logos*. And which by the same token threatens the domestic, hierarchical interiority of the pharmacy, the proper order and healthy movement of goods, the lawful prescription of its controlled, classed, measured, labeled products, rigorously divided into remedies and poisons, seeds of life and seeds of death, good and bad traces, the unity of metaphysics, of technology, of well computed binarism. This philosophical, dialectical mastery of the *pharmaka* that should be handed down from legitimate father to well-born son is constantly put in question by a family scene that constitutes and undermines at once the passage between the pharmacy and the house. "Platonism" is both the general *rehearsal* of this family scene and the most powerful effort to master it, to prevent anyone's ever hearing of it, to conceal it by drawing the curtains over the dawning of the West. How can we set off in search of a different guard, if the pharmaceutical "system" contains not only, in a single stranglehold, the scene in the *Phaedrus*, the scene in the *Republic*, the scene in the *Sophist*, and the dialectics, logic, and mythology of Plato, but also, it seems, certain non-Greek structures of mythology? And if it is not certain that there are such things as non-Greek "mythologies"—the opposition *mythos/logos* being only authorized *following* Plato—into what general, unnamable necessity are we thrown? In other words, what does Platonism signify as repetition?

To repeat: the disappearance of the good-father-capital-sun is thus the precondition of discourse, taken this time as a moment and not as a principle of *generalized* writing. That writing (is) *epekeina tēs ousias*. The disappearance of truth as presence, the withdrawal of the present origin of presence, is the condition of all (manifestation of) truth. Nontruth is the truth. Nonpresence is presence. Difference, the disappearance of any originary presence, is *at once* the condition of possibility *and* the condition of impossibility of truth. At once. "At once" means that the being-present (*on*) in its truth, in the presence of its identity and in the identity of its presence, *is doubled* as soon as it appears, as soon as it presents itself. *It appears, in its essence, as* the possibility of its own most proper non-truth, of its pseudo-truth reflected in the icon, the phantasm, or the simulacrum. What is is not what it is, identical and identical to itself, unique, unless it *adds to itself* the possibility of being *repeated* as such. And its identity is hollowed out by that addition, withdraws itself in the supplement that presents it.

The disappearance of the Face or the structure of repetition can thus no longer be dominated by the value of truth. On the contrary, the opposition between the true and the untrue is entirely comprehended, *inscribed*, within this structure or this generalized writing. The true and the untrue are both species of repetition. And there is no repetition possible without the *graphics of supplementarity*, which supplies, for the lack of a full unity, another unit that comes to relieve it, being enough the same and enough other so that it can replace by addition. Thus, on the one hand, repetition is that without which there would be no truth: the truth of being in the intelligible form of ideality discovers in the *eidos* that which can be repeated, being the same, the clear, the stable, the identifiable in its equality with itself. And only the *eidos* can give rise to repetition as anamnesis or maieutics,[2] dialectics or didactics. Here repetition gives itself out to be a repetition of life. Tautology is life only going out of itself to come home to itself. Keeping close to itself through *mnēmē, logos*, and *phōnē*. But on the other hand, repetition is the very movement of non-truth: the presence of what is gets lost, disperses itself, multiplies itself through mimemes, icons, phantasms, simulacra, etc. Through phenomena, already. And this type of repetition is the possibility of becoming-perceptible-to-the-senses: nonideality. This is on the side of non-philosophy, bad memory, hypomnesia, writing. Here, tautology is life going out of itself beyond return. Death rehearsal. Unreserved spending. The irreducible excess, through the play of the supplement, of any self-intimacy of the living, the good, the true.

These two types of repetition relate to each other according to the graphics of supplementarity. Which means that one can no more "separate" them from each other, think of either one apart from the other, "label" them, than one can in *the pharmacy* distinguish the medicine from the poison, the good from the evil, the true from the false, the inside from the outside, the vital from the mortal, the first from the second, etc. Conceived within this original reversibility, the *pharmakon* is the *same* precisely because it has no identity. And the same (is) as supplement. Or in differance. In writing.[3] If he had *meant* to say something, such would have been the speech of Theuth making of writing as a *pharmakon* a singular present to the King.

But Theuth, it should be noted, spoke not another word.

The great god's sentence went unanswered.

....

After closing the pharmacy, Plato went to retire, to get out of the sun. He took a few steps in the darkness toward the back of his reserves, found himself leaning over the *pharmakon*, decided to analyze.

Within the thick, cloudy liquid, trembling deep inside the drug, the whole pharmacy stood reflected, repeating the abyss of the Platonic phantasm.

The analyst cocks his ears, tries to distinguish between two repetitions.

He would like to isolate the good from the bad, the true from the false.

He leans over further: they repeat each other.

Holding the *pharmakon* in one hand, the calamus[4] in the other, Plato mutters as he transcribes the play of formulas. In the enclosed space of the pharmacy, the reverberations of the monologue are immeasurably amplified. The walled-in voice strikes against the rafters, the words come apart, bits and pieces of sentences are separated, disarticulated parts begin to circulate through the corridors, become fixed for a round or two, translate each other, become rejoined, bounce off each other, contradict each other, make trouble, tell on each other, come back like answers, organize their exchanges, protect each other, institute an internal commerce, take themselves for a dialogue. Full of meaning. A whole story. An entire history. All of philosophy.

* * *

1972

2. The Socratic midwifery by means of which the student gives birth to the truth.

3. Derrida has here analyzed the inexorable logic (or rather, graphic)—and not just the contingent metaphoricity—that leads Socrates to call *logos* "writing in the soul." In Section 8 of Part II of "Plato's Pharmacy" ("The Heritage of the Pharmakon: Family Scene" [omitted here]), he quotes from *Phaedrus* Socrates' definition of the discourse of truth: "The sort that goes together with knowledge, and is *written in the soul of the learner*, that can defend itself, and knows to whom it should speak and to whom it should say nothing" (276a; emphasis added).

4. Reed, pen.

RICHARD OHMANN
b. 1931

Few contemporary debates in the humanities have incited as much controversy as those over the literary canon. Deemed "the best that is known and thought" by MATTHEW ARNOLD and his intellectual progeny, the traditional literary canon has been critiqued, attacked, defended, and revised in recent years. The problem, say many literary theorists and critics, is that the canon has been shaped not by eternal or universal standards, but instead by unacknowledged gender, racial, ethnic, and class biases, traditionally favoring, in a memorable phrase, "dead white European males." These critics—feminist, African American, postcolonial, and other—have argued for "opening" the canon to include previously suppressed voices, especially women and people of color. Joining the fray, conservative political figures such as William Bennett and Lynne Cheney, along with academic allies such as Allan Bloom, E. D. HIRSCH JR., and HAROLD BLOOM, blame efforts to revise the canon for a loss of traditionally revered Western cultural values and a fracturing of a unified culture. In "The Shaping of a Canon: U.S. Fiction, 1960–1975" (1983), Richard Ohmann, a leading contemporary critic of the institution of literature, takes a step back and investigates the preliminary material, historical, and institutional processes that form the literary canon.

Born in Cleveland, Ohmann received his B.A. from Oberlin College in 1952 and his Ph.D. in English literature from Harvard University in 1960. He taught at Wesleyan University in Connecticut from 1961 until his retirement in 1998; he also served in various administrative positions, including associate provost, chancellor, and director of the Humanities Center. His initial scholarly work focused on literary style and traditional literary figures, like George Bernard Shaw (1856–1960), but through the 1960s he explored new theoretical approaches imported from linguistics; he was one of the first American scholars to introduce speech act theory (developed in the 1950s by the English philosopher of language J. L. AUSTIN) to literary criticism. In the late 1960s his work again shifted, as he began to examine social and political issues involved in the study of literature. He was deeply influenced by the social unrest and leftist politics of the time, and his later work, most notably his landmark book *English in America: A Radical View of the Profession* (1976), arises out of that era's "ruthless critique of all things existing."

English in America is a pioneering study of the social functions of literary study. While we normally justify the teaching of English as developing an appreciation of language and good writing through the study of great works of literature, Ohmann points out less publicized functions of English studies: "We train young people, and those who train young people, in the skills required by a society most of whose work is done on paper and through talk, not by physical labor. We also discipline the young to do assignments, on time, to follow instructions, to turn out uniform products, to observe the etiquette of verbal communication." In other words, university training in English is concerned not just with literary works but with inculcating the values and skills of white-collar work. Ohmann goes on to describe the class bias of English, arguing that despite the ideology of equal opportunity, "we eliminate the less adapted, the ill-trained, the city youth with bad verbal manners, blacks with the wrong dialect . . . and the rebellious of all shapes and sizes." In short, he produces a damning radical critique of the institution of English, which functions as an "instrument" to "maintain social and economic inequalities." Ohmann concludes *English in America* with a critique of the modern American university overall, detailing its connections to business and the military; he argues that universities are not "ivory towers" operating to produce "pure" knowledge, but the instruments of industrial and military research.

"The Shaping of a Canon: American Fiction, 1960–1975" turns from English departments and the university to investigate institutions involved in the material production and distribution of literature, such as publishing houses, advertising firms, and book reviewing outlets, which are usually considered peripheral to discussions of the value and attributes of literary works. Judgments about literature are typically assumed to be a matter for literary critics, who read, criticize, and evaluate it on its autonomous artistic merits. Countering received opinion, Ohmann demonstrates how influential these institutions in fact are in determining merit and the canon.

As a test case, Ohmann examines a group of contemporary U.S. novels published in the 1960s and early 1970s, inspecting normally overlooked aspects of their distribution and consumption, including agenting, editing, marketing, advertising, and reviewing. He argues that this complex set of institutional channels determines which books receive attention, preselecting which texts are ordained as "precanonical," or potential entrants into the canon. The primary criterion of value for these institutions is the capitalist one of marketability rather than abstract aesthetic merit. In particular, Ohmann demonstrates the large role of advertising in determining value and shaping the canon. As he concludes from the evidence compiled, "if a novel did not become a best-seller within three or four weeks of publication, it was unlikely to reach a large readership later on." While not denying that such works might have aesthetic value, Ohmann shows that aesthetic judgments are inflected by capitalist criteria.

Significantly, Ohmann examines the class character of those who work in the institutions of literature. He notes that they are members of the "professional-managerial" class—those who do intellectual rather than blue-collar work—and that their class position informs their judgments of value. They thus attribute value to books that speak to their lives and ideologies, and he speculates that they favor "illness stories," or works that depict the alienation of white-collar life. Continuing his argument that aesthetic judgments are not simply a matter of abstract, artistic value, Ohmann points out that they are shaped by the class divisions of modern capitalism: those in positions of relative power have more influence in determining which books are considered to have literary merit.

Determining the value of artworks is a perennial problem in aesthetic theory, and contemporary debates over the canon pivot on conflicting theories of value. Those who defend the canon typically see its value as universal and timeless, whereas those who attack it generally see it as politically motivated and historically constructed. The eighteenth-century German philosopher IMMANUEL KANT, a founder of aesthetic theory, posited that aesthetic judgments are necessarily universal and disinterested, distinguishing them from the exercise of individual taste. Ohmann dispels just this sense of universality and disinterest through his analysis of the judgments rendered on contemporary U.S. fiction, which testify to specific class interests and are influenced by elements of the capitalist mode of production.

In his analysis of the social construction of aesthetic judgment, Ohmann has affinities with contemporary theorists such as PIERRE BOURDIEU and BARBARA HERRNSTEIN SMITH. In *Distinction* (1979; see above), Bourdieu conducts a sociological study of contemporary French culture, showing how taste is determined by class. Drawing on the aesthetic theory of the eighteenth-century Scottish philosopher DAVID HUME and of Bourdieu, and the contemporary pragmatist philosophy of Richard Rorty, Smith argues in *Contingencies of Value* (1988; see below) that judgments of value and taste are not universal and timeless, but historically contingent. Ohmann's "Shaping of a Canon" offers a concrete counterpart to Smith's more explicitly theoretical considerations of aesthetic value, providing a case study replete with a "thick description" of historical events illustrating the processes of aesthetic judgment.

Given its focus on class and the social and economic determinants of literary culture, Ohmann's work has been characterized as Marxist and therefore criticized for overstressing material factors and for advocating the radicalization of the profession. Ohmann explains in an interview, however, that he had read few of the Marxist classics at the time he wrote *English in America*; his work arose instead from the collective, radical "Movement" of the 1960s and from his participation in leftist groups such as the Radical Caucus of the Modern Language Association (the central professional organization of academic literary scholars in North America). In his independent leftism, Ohmann resembles his contemporary Noam Chomsky, the famous American linguist and independent radical intellectual, who has also critiqued the university and its complicity with the military-industrial complex. Yet in his focus on thick, historical description conjoined with a critique of capitalism, he resembles Marxists from British cultural studies, like STUART HALL. Ohmann's innovative work in developing a cultural studies approach to literary practices make him somewhat idiosyncratic in an era when most American critics have been more absorbed in debates over poststructuralist theory. "The Shaping of a Canon" remains a distinctive and groundbreaking case study of the actual institutions of literature.

BIBLIOGRAPHY

Richard Ohmann's early work includes *Shaw: The Style and the Man* (1962); the edited collection *The Making of Myth* (1962); two coauthored textbooks on rhetoric and composition; and several influential essays employing speech act theory to analyze the style of literary works. After the late 1960s, he turned to focus on the politics of the profession and the socioinstitutional context of literature, publishing the path-breaking study *English in America: A Radical View of the Profession* (1976; reissued in 1996 with a foreword by Gerald Graff and a new introduction by Ohmann) and a series of essays collected in *Politics of Letters* (1987), which includes "The Shaping of a Canon." Expanding his research to more general issues of literary culture, Ohmann's *Selling Culture: Magazines, Markets, and Class at the Turn of the Century* (1996), a prominent work of American cultural studies, examines the correlated rise of popular literary magazines and advertising in the late nineteenth and early twentieth century in the United States. In a related effort, Ohmann edited the collection *Making and Selling Culture* (1996), which includes essays by publishers and filmmakers as well as academics. From 1966 through 1978, Ohmann also edited the influential journal *College English*, sponsoring innovative issues on feminism, gay studies, and other topics. His collection co-edited with W. B. Coley, *Ideas for English 101: Teaching Writing in College* (1975), derives from *College English*. "English in America Updated: An Interview with Richard Ohmann," conducted by Jeffrey Williams, *Minnesota Review*, ns., 45–46 (1996), recounts Ohmann's career and his embrace of radical politics.

Notable responses to Ohmann include Gerald Graff's criticism of the radical assumptions of *English in America* in *Literature against Itself: Literary Ideas in Modern Society* (1979). In *Doing What Comes Naturally: Change, Rhetoric, and the Practice of Theory in Literary and Legal Studies* (1989), Stanley Fish finds a self-contradictory antiprofessional strand in Ohmann's critique of the profession. "The Shaping of a Canon" has provided a model for subsequent reception studies of the contemporary American canon and the "book market." In "Courses and Canons: The Post-1945 U.S. Novel," *Critique: Studies in Contemporary Fiction* 31 (1990), Raymond Mazurek expands on Ohmann's account to survey the recent canon taught in university courses, while noting the limitations of the category of "illness stories." John Unsworth's "Book Market," in *The Columbia History of the American Novel* (ed. Emory Elliot, 1991), updates Ohmann's survey of publishing culture. Taking Ohmann's seminal essay as a starting point, Jim Neilson's "Commercial Literary Culture," *Minnesota Review*, ns., 48–49 (1997), criticizes the political control inherent in recent commercial publishing and reviewing.

From The Shaping of a Canon: U.S. Fiction, 1960–1975

Categorical names such as The English Novel, The Modern American Novel, and American Literature often turn up in catalogues as titles of college courses, and we know from them pretty much what to expect. They also have standing in critical discourse, along with allied terms unlikely to serve as course titles: *good writing, great literature, serious fiction, literature* itself. The awareness has grown in recent years that such concepts pose problems, even though we use them with easy enough comprehension when we talk or write to others who share our cultural matrix.

Lately, critics like Raymond Williams[1] have been reminding us that the categories change over time (just as *literature* used to mean all printed books but has come to mean only certain poems, plays, novels, etc.) and that at any given moment categories embody complex social relations and a continuing historical process. That process deeply invests all terms with value: since not everyone's values are the same, the negotiating of such concepts is, among other things, a struggle for dominance—whether between adults and the young, professors and their students, one class and another, or men and women. One doesn't usually notice the power or the conflict, except when some previously weak or silent group seeks a share of the power: for example, when, in the 1960s, American blacks and their supporters insisted that black literature be included in school and college curricula, or when they openly challenged the candidacy of William Styron's *Confessions of Nat Turner*[2] for inclusion in some eventual canon.[3] But the gradual firming up of concepts like, say, postwar American fiction is always a contest for cultural hegemony,[4] even if in our society it is often muted—carried on behind the scenes or in the seemingly neutral marketplace.

Not only do the concepts change, in both intension and extension, but the process of their formation also changes. The English, who had power to do so, admitted *Great Expectations* to the canon by means very different from those used to admit the *Canterbury Tales*[5] by earlier generations of tastemakers. Again, the process may differ from genre to genre even in a particular time and place. For instance, profit and the book market are relatively unimportant in deciding what will be considered modern American poetry, by contrast with their function in defining modern American fiction. As a result, in order to work toward a serviceable theory of canon formation, it is necessary to look at a variety of these processes and at how they impinge on one another.

Here, I attempt to sketch out one of them, the process by which novels

1. Welsh literary and cultural critic (1921–1988), whose "Literature" (1977; see above) discusses the historical change that Ohmann refers to.
2. This 1967 novel by Styron (b. 1925) depicts a slave rebellion before the American Civil War. It won a Pulitzer Prize but generated controversy because some questioned whether Styron, a southern-born white author, could authentically represent African Americans.
3. See John Henrik Clarke, ed., *William Styron's Nat Turner: Ten Black Writers Respond* (Boston, 1968) [Ohmann's note]. Some of the author's notes have been edited, and some omitted.
4. The manufactured consent that legitimates a dominant group and unifies a society; a Marxist concept articulated by the Italian theorist ANTONIO GRAMSCI (1891–1937).
5. Middle English poem (ca. 1386–1400) by Geoffrey Chaucer, one of the great works of the Middle Ages. *Great Expectations* (1861), English novel by Charles Dickens.

written by Americans from about 1960 to 1975 have been sifted and assessed, so that a modest number of them retain the kind of attention and respect that eventually makes them eligible for canonical status.[6] I am going to argue that the emergence of these novels has been a process saturated with class values and interests, a process inseparable from the broader struggle for position and power in our society, from the institutions that mediate that struggle, as well as from legitimation of and challenges to the social order. I will then try to be more specific about the representation of those values and interests in the fiction itself.

Reading and the Book Market

People read books silently, and often in isolation, but reading is nonetheless a social act. As one study concludes:

> Book reading in adult life is sustained . . . by interpersonal situations which minimize the individual's isolation from others. To persist over the years, the act of book reading must be incorporated . . . into a social context. Reading a book becomes meaningful when, after completion, it is shared with others. . . . Social integration . . . sustains a persistent engagement with books. Social isolation, in contrast, is likely to lead to the abandonment of books.[7]

Simone Beserman found, in her study of best-sellers around 1970, that frequent reading of books correlated highly with social interaction—in particular, with the desire to rise in society. Upwardly mobile second- and third-generation Americans were heavy readers of best-sellers.[8]

As you would expect, given the way reading is embedded in and reinforced by social relations, networks of friends and family also contributed in determining which books would be widely read. In her survey, Beserman found that 58 percent of those who read a particular best-seller did so upon recommendation of a friend or relative. Who were these people, so crucial to a book's success? Beserman found that they were of better-than-average education (most had finished college), relatively well-to-do, many of them professionals, in middle life, upwardly mobile, living near New York or oriented, especially through the *New York Times*,[9] to New York cultural life.

These people were responsive to novels where they discovered the values

6. I make no large claims for my boundaries. They mark off, crudely, the time when publishing had become part of big business but before subsidiary rights had completely overshadowed hardbound novel publishing. My boundaries also mark the time when people born to one side or the other of 1930 attained cultural dominance and could most strongly advance their reading of the postwar experience. These years roughly enclose the rise and decline of the 1960s movements as well as economic boom and the U.S. intervention in Southeast Asia. Anyhow, things have changed since 1975, both in the great world and in fiction publishing; accordingly I use the past tense when describing the process of canon-formation, even though many of my generalizations still hold true [Ohmann's note].

7. Jan Hajda, "An American Paradox: People and Books in a Metropolis" (Ph.D. diss., University of Chicago, 1963), p. 218, as cited in Elizabeth Warner McElroy, "Subject Variety in Adult Book Reading" (M.A. thesis, University of Chicago, 1967) [Ohmann's note].

8. See Simone Beserman, "Le Best-seller aux États-Unis de 1961 à 1970: Étude littéraire et sociologique" (Ph.D. diss., University of Paris, 1975), pp. 280–95. Surprisingly, neither this audience nor the ways it integrated novel reading into its social existence seem all that different from their counterparts in early 18th-century England, as described, for example, in chap. 2 of Ian Watt, *The Rise of the Novel: Studies in Defoe, Richardson, and Fielding* (Berkeley, 1957) [Ohmann's note].

9. Arguably the most respected newspaper in the United States.

in which they believed or where they found needed moral guidance when shaken in their own beliefs. Saul Bellow's remark, "What Americans want to learn from their writers is how to live,"[1] finds support in Philip H. Ennis's study, *Adult Book Reading in the United States*. Ennis determined that three of the main interests people carried into their reading were a "search for personal meaning, for some kind of map to the moral landscape"; a need to "reinforce or to celebrate beliefs already held, or, when shaken by events, to provide support in some personal crisis"; and a wish to keep up "with the book talk of friends and neighbors."[2]

The values and beliefs of a small group of people played a disproportionate role in deciding what novels would be widely read in the United States. (Toward the end of this essay, I will turn to those values in some detail.) To underscore their influence, consider two other facts about the book market. First, if a novel did not become a best-seller within three or four weeks of publication, it was unlikely to reach a large readership later on. In the 1960s, only a very few books that were slow starters eventually became best-sellers (in paperback, not hardback). I know of three: *Catch-22, Call It Sleep*, and *I Never Promised You a Rose Garden*, to which we may add the early novels of Vonnegut, which were not published in hard covers, and—if we count its 1970s revival in connection with the film—*One Flew over the Cuckoo's Nest.*[3] To look at the process the other way around, once a new book did make the *New York Times* best-seller list, many other people bought it (and store managers around the country stocked it) *because* it was a best-seller. The process was cumulative. So the early buyers of hardcover books exercised a crucial role in selecting the books that the rest of the country's readers would buy.

Second, best-sellerdom was much more important than suggested by the figures for hardbound sales through bookstores. *Love Story*,[4] for instance, the leading best-seller (in all forms) of the decade sold 450,000 hardback copies in bookstores but more than 700,000 through book clubs, 2.5 million through the *Reader's Digest*, 6.5 million in the *Ladies' Home Journal*,[5] and more than 9,000,000 in paperback—not to mention library circulation or the millions of people who saw the film. Books were adopted by clubs, paperback publishers, film producers, and so forth, in large part because they were best-sellers or because those investing in subsidiary rights thought them likely to become best-sellers. As Victor Navasky rather wryly said:

> Publishers got out of the business of *selling* hardcover books ten or fifteen years ago. The idea now is to publish hardcover books so that they

1. Saul Bellow, in Jason Epstein's interview, "Saul Bellow of Chicago," *New York Times Book Review*, May 9, 1971, p. 16 [Ohmann's note]. Bellow (b. 1915), Canadian-born American novelist; he won the Nobel Prize for literature in 1976.

2. Philip H. Ennis, *Adult Book Reading in the United States*, National Opinion Research Center (University of Chicago, 1965), p. 25. Other main needs were (1) "escape," which also implies a relationship between reading a book and the rest of one's social life (what one is escaping *from*), and (2) information, which I suspect is a need less often fulfilled by novels now than in the time of Defoe and Richardson [Ohmann's note]. Daniel Defoe (1660–1731) and Samuel Richardson (1689–1761) were among the earliest English novelists.

3. A 1962 novel by Ken Kesey (b. 1935), made into an Academy Award–winning film (1975, dir. Milos Forman). *Catch-22* (1961), by Joseph Heller (1923–1999). *Call It Sleep* (1934; reissued 1960), by Henry Roth (1906–1995), Ukrainian-born American novelist. *I Never Promised You a Rose Garden* (1964), by Joanne Greenberg (b. 1932). Kurt Vonnegut (b. 1922), American novelist whose early works include *The Sirens of Titan* (1959), *Mother Night* (1962), and *Cat's Cradle* (1963).

4. A 1970 novel by Erich Segal (b. 1937), published by Harper and Row and made into a movie (dir. Arthur Hiller) that same year.

5. Popular mass-market magazines.

can be reviewed or promoted on television in order to sell paperback rights, movie rights, book club rights, serialization rights, international satellite rights, Barbie doll rights, etc.[6]

The phenomenon of the hardbound best-seller had only modest economic and cultural significance in itself but great significance in triggering reproduction and consumption of the story in other forms.

A small group of relatively homogeneous readers, then, had a great deal of influence at this preliminary stage. But of course these people did not make *their* decisions freely among the thousands of novels completed each year. They chose among the smaller number actually published. This fact points to an important role in canon formation for literary agents and for editors at the major houses, who belong to the same social stratum as the buyers of hardbound books, and who—as profitability in publishing came to hinge more and more on the achievement of best-sellerdom for a few books—increasingly earned their keep by spotting (and pushing) novels that looked like best-sellers. Here we have a nearly closed circle of marketing and consumption, the simultaneous exploitation and creation of taste, familiar to anyone who has examined marketplace culture under monopoly capitalism.

But, it is clear, influential readers chose not among all novels published but among the few that came to their attention in an urgent or attractive way. How did that happen? As a gesture toward the kind of answer that question requires, I will consider the extraordinary role of the *New York Times*. The *New York Times Book Review* had about a million and a half readers, several times the audience of any other literary periodical. Among them were most bookstore managers, deciding what to stock, and librarians, deciding what to buy, not to mention the well-to-do, well-educated east-coasters who led in establishing hardback best-sellers. The single most important boost a novel could get was a prominent review in the Sunday *New York Times*—better a favorable one than an unfavorable one, but better an unfavorable one than none at all.

Ads complemented the reviews, or perhaps the word is *inundated*: two-thirds of the space in the *Times Book Review* went to ads. According to Richard Kostelanetz, most publishers spent more than half their advertising budgets for space in that journal.[7] They often placed ads in such a way as to reinforce a good *Times* review or offset a bad one with favorable quotations from reviews in other periodicals. And of course reviews and ads were further reinforced by the *Times* best-seller list itself, for the reason already mentioned. Apparently, the publishers' faith in the *Times* was not misplaced. Beserman asked early readers of *Love Story* where they had heard of the book. Most read it on recommendation of another person; Beserman then

6. Victor Navasky, 'Studies in Animal Behavior," *New York Times Book Review*, February 20, 1973, p. 2 [Ohmann's note]. Navasky (b. 1932), American cultural critic and longtime editor of the liberal-left magazine the *Nation*.

7. See Richard Kostelanetz, *The End of Intelligent Writing: Literary Politics in America* (New York, 1974), p. 207. Kostelanetz's estimate was confirmed by some of Beserman's interviews. Allan Green, who handled advertising for a number of publishers, including Viking, told her in 1971 that on the average, 50 to 60 percent of the budget went to the *New York Times Book Review* and another 10 to 20 percent to the daily *New York Times*. M. Stuart Harris, head of publicity at Harper, said he ordinarily channeled 90 percent into the *Times* at the outset, though once a book's success was assured, he distributed advertising more broadly (see Beserman, p. 120) [Ohmann's note].

spoke to *that* person, and so on back to the beginning of the chain of verbal endorsements. At the original source, in more than half the instances, she found the *Times.*[8] (This in spite of the quite unusual impact, for that time, of Segal's appearance on the "Today" show[9] the day of publication—Barbara Walters said the book made her cry all night; Harper was immediately swamped with orders—and of the novel's appearance in the *Ladies' Home Journal* just before book publication.)

The influence of the *Times Book Review* led publicity departments to direct much of their prepublication effort toward persuading the *Book Review's* editors that a particular novel was important. It is hard to estimate the power of this suasion, but one thing can be measured: the correlation between advertising in the *Book Review* and being reviewed there. A 1968 study concluded, perhaps unsurprisingly, that the largest advertisers got disproportionately large amounts of review space. Among the large advertisers were, for instance:

	Pages of ads	*Pages of reviews*
Random House	74	58
Harper	29	22
Little, Brown	29	21
And the smaller ones:		
Dutton	16	4
Lippincott	16	4
Harvard	9	"negligible"

During the same year Random House (including Knopf and Pantheon) had nearly three times as many books mentioned in the feature "New and Recommended" as Doubleday or Harper, both of which published as many books as the Random House group.[1]

To summarize: a small group of book buyers formed a screen through which novels passed on their way to commercial success; a handful of agents and editors picked the novels that would compete for the notice of those buyers; and a tight network of advertisers and reviewers, organized around the *New York Times Book Review*, selected from these a few to be recognized as compelling, important, "talked-about."

The Next Stage

So far I have been speaking of a process that led to a mass readership for a few books each year. But most of these were never regarded as serious literature and did not live long in popularity or memory. Books like *Love Story, The Godfather, Jonathan Livingston Seagull*, and the novels of Susann, Robbins, Wouk, Wallace, and Uris[2] would run a predictable course. They had large hardback sales for a few months, tapering off to a trickle in a year

8. See Beserman, p. 168 [Ohmann's note].
9. The *Today Show*, a popular television show on NBC, debuted in 1952; Walters (b. 1931), television reporter and celebrity, was one of its hosts from 1964 to 1976.
1. See Kostelanetz, p. 209 [Ohmann's note].
2. Jacqueline Susann (1921–1974), Harold Robbins (1916–1997), Herman Wouk (b. 1915), Irving Wallace (1916–1990) and Leon Uris (b. 1924) were well-known, best-selling authors of the period. *The Godfather* (1969) by Mario Puzo and *Jonathan Livingston Seagull* (1970) by Richard Bach were best-selling American novels.

or so. Meanwhile, they were reprinted in paper covers and enjoyed two or three years of popularity (often stoked by a film version). After that they disappeared or remained in print to be bought in smaller numbers by, for instance, newly won fans of Wallace who wanted to go back and read his earlier books. There was a similar pattern for mysteries, science fiction, and other specialized genres.

But a few novels survived and continued (in paper covers) to attract buyers and readers for a longer time, and they still do. Why? To answer that the *best* novels survive is to beg the question. Excellence is a constantly changing, socially chosen value. Who attributed it to only some novels, and how? I hope now to hint at the way such a judgment took shape.

First, one more word about the *New York Times Book Review*. I have argued that it led in developing a broad audience for fiction. It also began, I believe, the process of distinguishing between ephemeral popular novels and those to be taken seriously over a longer period of time. There was a marked difference in impact between, say, Martin Levin's favorable but mildly condescending (and brief) review of *Love Story* and the kind of front-page review by an Alfred Kazin or an Irving Howe[3] that asked readers to regard a new novel as literature, and that so often helped give the stamp of highbrow approval to books by Bellow, Malamud, Updike, Roth, Doctorow,[4] and so forth. Cultural leaders read the *Times Book Review* too: not only professors but (according to Julie Hoover and Charles Kadushin) 75 percent of our elite intellectuals.[5] By reaching these circles, a major *Times* review could help put a novel on the cultural agenda and ensure that other journals would have to take it seriously.

Among those others, a few carried special weight in forming cultural judgments. In a survey of leading intellectuals, just eight journals—the *New York Review of Books*, the *New Republic*, the *New York Times Book Review*, the *New Yorker, Commentary, Saturday Review, Partisan Review*, and *Harpers*—received almost half the participants' "votes" in response to various questions about influence and importance.[6] In effect, these periodicals were both a communication network among the influentials (where they reviewed one another's books) and an avenue of access to a wider cultural leadership. The elite, writing in these journals, largely determined which books would be seriously debated and which ones permanently valued, as well as what ideas were kept alive, circulated, discussed. Kadushin and his colleagues concluded, from their studies of our intellectual elite and influential journals, that the "top intellectual journals constitute the American equivalent of an Oxbridge establishment, and have served as one of the main gatekeepers for new talent and new ideas."[7]

A novel had to win at least the divided approval of these arbiters in order

3. Kazin (1915–1998) and HOWE (1920–1993), were both highly regarded American literary critics affiliated with the New York Intellectuals. Levin, American writer and columnist.

4. All respected "serious" American novelists: Bernard Malamud (1914–1986), John Updike (b. 1932), Philip Roth (b. 1933) and E. L. Doctorow (b. 1931).

5. See Julie Hoover and Charles Kadushin, "Influential Intellectual Journals: A Very Private Club," *Change*, March 1972, p. 41 [Ohmann's note].

6. See Charles Kadushin, Julie Hoover, and Monique Tichy, "How and Where to Find the Intellectual Elite in the United States," *Public Opinion Quarterly*, spring 1971, pp. 1–18. For the method used to identify an intellectual elite, see Kadushin, "Who Are the Elite Intellectuals?" *Public Interest*, fall 1972, pp. 109–25 [Ohmann's note].

7. Kadushin, Hoover, and Tichy, p. 17 [Ohmann's note]. "Oxbridge establishment": English intellectual elite (assumed to be graduates of Oxford or Cambridge University).

to remain in the universe of cultural discourse, once past the notoriety of best-sellerdom. The career of *Love Story* is a good example of failure to do so. After some initial favorable reviews (and enormous publicity on television and other media), the intellectuals began cutting it down to size. In the elite journals, it was either panned or ignored. Styron and the rest of the National Book Award[8] fiction panel threatened to quit if it were not removed from the list of candidates. And who will read it tomorrow, except on an excursion into the archives of mass culture?

In talking about the *New York Times Book Review*, I suggested a close alliance between reviewing and profit, literary and monetary values. The example of the *New York Review of Books* shows that a similar alliance can exist on the higher ramparts of literary culture. This journal, far and away the most influential among intellectuals (in answer to Kadushin's questions, it was mentioned almost twice as often as the *New Republic*, its nearest competitor), was founded by Jason Epstein, a vice president of Random House, and coedited by his wife, Barbara Epstein.[9] It may be more than coincidental that in 1968 almost one-fourth of the books granted full reviews in the *New York Review* were published by Random House (again, including Knopf and Pantheon)—more than the combined total of books from Viking, Grove, Holt, Harper, Houghton Mifflin, Oxford, Doubleday, Macmillan, and Harvard so honored; or that in the same year one-fourth of the *reviewers* had books in print with Random House and that a third of those were reviewing other Random House books, mainly favorably; or that over a five-year period more than half the regular reviewers (ten or more appearances) were Random House authors.[1] This is not to deny the intellectual strength of the *New York Review*—only to suggest that it sometimes deployed that strength in ways consistent with the financial interest of Random House. One need not subscribe to conspiracy theories in order to see, almost everywhere one looks in the milieu of publishing and reviewing, linkages of fellowship and common interest. Together these networks make up a cultural establishment, inseparable from the market, both influencing and influenced by it.

If a novel was certified in the court of the prestigious journals, it was likely to draw the attention of academic critics in more specialized and academic journals like *Contemporary Literature* and by this route make its way into college curricula, where the very context—course title, academic setting, methodology—gave it de facto recognition as literature. This final step was all but necessary: the college classroom and its counterpart, the academic journal, have become in our society the final arbiters of literary merit, and even of survival. It is hard to think of a novel more than twenty-five years old, aside from specialist fiction and *Gone with the Wind*,[2] that still commands a large readership outside of school and college.

I am suggesting that novels moved toward a canonical position only if they attained both large sales (usually, but not always, concentrated enough to place them among the best-sellers for a while) and the right kind of critical attention. On the one side, this hypothesis conflicts with the one most vigorously advanced by Leslie A. Fiedler—that intellectuals are, in the long run,

8. A prestigious annual book prize, awarded in different genres.
9. Jason Epstein (b. 1928) and Barbara Epstein (b. 1928), influential American literary figures.

1. See Kostelanetz, pp. 107–8 [Ohmann's note].
2. One of the most popular American novels of all time, published in 1936 by Margaret Mitchell.

outvoted by the sorts of readers who keep liking *Gone with the Wind*.[3] On the other side, it collides with the hopes or expectations of critics such as Kostelanetz and Jerome Klinkowitz, who promote an avant-garde fiction called postmodernist, postcontemporary, antinovel, or whatever.[4]

Clearly, I need an independent measure of precanonical status, or my argument closes into a circle. Unfortunately, I don't have a very good one, in part, because it is still too early to settle the issue. But let me offer two scraps of pertinent information. First, the editors of *Wilson Quarterly* polled forty-four professors of American literature (in 1977 or 1978, apparently), asking them to rank in order the ten "most important" novels published in the United States after World War II.[5] The editors printed a list of the twenty-one novels rated highest in this survey; eleven of them were published in or after 1960. In rank order, they are *Catch-22, Gravity's Rainbow, Herzog, An American Dream, The Sotweed Factor, Second Skin, Portnoy's Complaint, The Armies of the Night, V, Rabbit Run,*[6] and *One Flew over the Cuckoo's Nest*. All easily meet the criterion of attention from intellectuals. (Again, it doesn't matter that Norman Podhoretz[7] *hates* Updike's novels, so long as he takes them seriously enough to argue with his peers about them.) As for broad readership, all of the novels except *Second Skin* and perhaps *The Sotweed Factor* have sold over half a million copies—and one may be sure that many of those sales occurred through adoption in college courses.[8]

My second cast of the net is much broader. *Contemporary Literary Criticism* abstracts commentary on recent world literature, mainly by American professors and intellectuals. Its coverage includes critical books, respected academic journals, taste-forming magazines, quarterlies, and little magazines. It claims to excerpt from criticism of "work by well-known creative writers," "writers of considerable public interest," who are alive or who died after January 1, 1960. So it constitutes a sampling of the interests of those who set literary standards, and it monitors the intermediate stage in canon formation. During the ten years and twenty-two volumes of its publication, up through 1982, it has run four or more entries (maximum, nine; and the average entry includes excerpts from four or five critical sources) for forty-eight American novelists of the period in question:[9]

3. See, for instance, Leslie A. Fiedler, *The Inadvertent Epic: From "Uncle Tom's Cabin" to "Roots"* (New York, 1979). Fiedler's *What Was Literature? Class Culture and Mass Society* (New York, 1982) argues again for the primacy of people over professors [Ohmann's note].

4. As Jerome Klinkowitz states in his preface: "For even the well and intelligently read, 'contemporary American fiction' suggests Ken Kesey, Joseph Heller, John Barth, and Thomas Pynchon at best—and at worst Updike, Roth, Bellow, and Malamud." He contends that such a list misses "the direction which fiction will take, and is taking, as the future unfolds before us" (*Literary Disruptions: The Making of a Post-Contemporary American Fiction*, 2d ed. [Urbana, Ill., 1980] p. ix) [Ohmann's note].

5. Twenty-six of the forty-four responded. The survey accompanies an article by Melvin J. Friedman, "To 'Make It New': The American Novel since 1945," *Wilson Quarterly*, winter 1978, pp. 136–37. I don't know how the professors were selected or who they were, but almost every novel on this list was written by a white male with an elite educational background [Ohmann's note].

6. With their authors, in order: *Gravity's Rainbow* (1973), by Thomas Pynchon (b. 1937); *Herzog* (1964), by Bellow; *An American Dream* (1965), by Norman Mailer (b. 1923); *The Sotweed Factor* (1960), by John Barth (b. 1930); *Second Skin* (1964), by John Hawkes (b. 1925); *Portnoy's Complaint* (1969), by Philip Roth; *The Armies of the Night* (1968), by Mailer; *V* (1963), by Pynchon; and *Rabbit, Run* (1960), by Updike.

7. American essayist and editor (b. 1930).

8. John Hawkes is the outstanding example of a novelist whose work has consistently impressed critics and professors, without ever appealing to a wider audience. Should any of us be around to witness the outcome, it will be interesting to see if any of his books has a place in the canon 40 or 50 years from now [Ohmann's note].

9. I omit novelists still alive in 1960, but whose possibly canonical work belongs to an earlier time—Steinbeck, Dos Passos, Hemingway, etc. I *include* those of an older generation (Porter, McCarthy) who did not publish a precanonical novel until the 1960s. I exclude novelists of foreign origin (Asimov, Kosinski, Nabokov) and writers mainly

Auchincloss
Baldwin
Barth
Barthelme
Bellow
Berger
Bradbury
Brautigan
Burroughs
Capote
Cheever
Condon
de Vries
Dickey
Didion
Doctorow
Elkin
Gaddis
Gardner
Gass
Hawkes
Heller
Higgins
Jong
Kesey
R. MacDonald
Mailer
Malamud
McCarthy
McMurtry
Oates
Percy
Piercy
Plath
Porter
Pynchon
Rechy
Reed
Roth
Salinger
Selby
Sorrentino
Styron
Theroux
Updike
Vidal
Vonnegut
Walker[1]

Most of these meet my two criteria. All but a few (Bradbury, Condon, MacDonald, perhaps Auchincloss and Higgins) have received ample consideration by influential critics. Yet most novelists promoted by postcontemporary advocates such as Klinkowitz (Sloan, Coover, Wurlitzer, Katz, Federman, Sukenick,[2] etc.) are missing, while the list includes only a few writers who have had elite approval but small readerships (Elkin, Hawkes, Sorrentino, maybe two or three others). In fact, at least thirty-one of these novelists published one book or more between 1960 and 1975 that was a best-seller in hard or paper covers.[3] On the other hand, the list excludes the overwhelming majority of the writers who regularly produced large best-sellers: Puzo, Susann, Wouk, West, Robbins, Wallace, Michener, Krantz, Forsyth, Crichton,[4] and so on and on. I conclude that both the *Contemporary Literary Criticism* selection and the *Wilson Quarterly* survey give modest support to my thesis. Canon formation during this period took place in the interaction between large audiences and gatekeeper intellectuals.

known for their poetry, plays, or criticism, unless (as with Dickey and Plath) they also produced a precanonical novel during this period [Ohmann note].

1. Novelists whose dates have not already been given: Louis Auchinloss (b. 1917), James Baldwin (1924–1987), Donald Barthelme (1931–1989), Thomas Berger (b. 1924), Ray Bradbury (b. 1920), Richard Brautigan (1933–1984), William Burroughs (1914–1997), Truman Capote (1924–1984), John Cheever (1912–1982), Richard Condon (1915–1996), Peter de Vries (1910–1993), James Dickey (1923–1997), Joan Didion (b. 1934), Stanley Elkin (1930–1995), William Gaddis (1922–1998), John Gardner (1933–1982), William Gass (b. 1924), George Higgins (1939–1999), Erica Jong (b. 1942), Ross MacDonald (1915–1983), Mary McCarthy (1912–1989), Larry McMurtry (b. 1936), Joyce Carol Oates (b. 1938), Walker Percy (1916–1990), Marge Piercy (b. 1936), Sylvia Plath (1932–1963), Katherine Anne Porter (1890–1980), John Rechy (b. 1934), Ishmael Reed (b. 1938), J. D. Salinger (b. 1919), Hubert Selby Jr. (b. 1928), Gilbert Sorrentino (b. 1929), Paul Theroux (b. 1941), Gore Vidal (b. 1925), and Margaret Walker (1915–1998).

2. American critics and novelists: James Park Sloan Jr. (b. 1944), Robert Coover (b. 1932), Rudolph Wurlitzer (b. 1938), Steve Katz (b. 1935), Raymond Federman (b. 1928), and Ronald Sukenick (b. 1932).

3. I got this count by surveying the hardback and paperback best-seller lists in the *New York Times* from 1969 through 1975 and by checking the annual summaries in Alice Payne Hackett and James Henry Burke, *Eighty Years of Best Sellers, 1895–1975* (New York, 1977) for the rest of the 1960s [Ohmann's note].

4. American authors: Paul West (b. 1930), born in England; James Michener (1907–1997); Judith Krantz (b. 1927); Frederick Forsyth (b. 1938), born in England; and Michael Crichton (b. 1942).

Class and the Canon

To return to the main theme, then: I have drawn a sketch of the course a novel had to run in order to lodge itself in our culture as precanonical—as "literature," at least for the moment. It was selected, in turn, by an agent, an editor, a publicity department, a review editor (especially the one at the Sunday *New York Times Book Review*), the New York metropolitan book buyers whose patronage was necessary to commercial success, critics writing for gatekeeper intellectual journals, academic critics, and college teachers. Obviously, the sequence was not rigid, and some steps might on occasion be omitted entirely (as I have indicated with respect to *Catch-22* and *One Flew over the Cuckoo's Nest*). But one would expect the pattern to have become more regular through this period, as publishing was increasingly drawn into the sphere of monopoly capital (with RCA acquiring Random House; ITT, Howard Sams; Time, Inc., Little, Brown; CBS, Holt, Rinehart & Winston; Xerox, Ginn; and so on throughout almost the whole industry). For monopoly capital changed this industry much as it has changed the automobile and the toothpaste industries: by placing much greater emphasis on planned marketing and predictability of profits.[5]

This shift brought publishing into the same arena as many other cultural processes. In fact, the absorption of culture began almost as soon as monopoly capitalism itself, with the emergence of the advertising industry (crucial to planned marketing) in the 1880s and 1890s, and simultaneously with mass-circulation magazines as the main vehicle of national brand advertising.[6] With some variations, cinema, radio, music, sports, newspapers, television, and many lesser forms have followed this path, with books among the last to do so. The change has transformed our culture and the ways we participate in it. It demands rethinking, not only of bourgeois ideas about culture but of central marxian oppositions like base and superstructure, production and reproduction.[7] Culture cannot, without straining, be understood as a reflex of basic economic activity, when culture is itself a core industry and a major source of capital accumulation. Nor can we bracket culture as reproduction, when it is inseparable from the making and selling of commodities. We have at present a relatively new and rapidly changing cultural process that calls for new and flexible ways of thinking about culture.

My account may, however, have made it sound as if in one respect nothing has changed. Under monopoly capital, even more than when Marx and Engels[8] wrote *The German Ideology*, the "class which has the means of material production at its disposal, has control at the same time over the means

5. See the analysis in Paul A. Baran and Paul M. Sweezy, *Monopoly Capital: An Essay on the American Economic and Social Order* (New York, 1966). In publishing, the ascendancy of media packaging over simple book publishing has continued apace in recent years. See Thomas Whiteside, *The Blockbuster Complex: Conglomerates, Show Business, and Book Publishing* (Middletown, Conn., 1981). The practices Whiteside describes, along with the growth of national bookstore chains, have further altered the dynamic of publishing, thereby providing another reason for terminating this study somewhere around 1975 [Ohmann's note]. According to Marxist analysis, capitalism inevitably leads to greater monopolistic control and less competition.

6. See Ohmann's later study *Selling Culture: Magazines, Markets, and Class at the Turn of the Century* (New York: Verso, 1996).

7. See, for instance, Raymond Williams, "Base and Superstructure in Marxist Cultural Theory," *New Left Review* 82 (1973): 3–16 [Ohmann's note]. The base is the economic structure of society, which provides the foundation for the superstructure of forms of social consciousness (legal, political, artistic, etc.).

8. KARL MARX (1818–1883) and FRIEDRICH ENGELS (1820–1895), German social, economic, and political theorists; they wrote *The German Ideology* (see above) in 1845–46.

of mental production." But does it still follow that, "thereby, generally speaking, the ideas of those who lack the means of mental production are subject to" the ruling class?[9] The theory can explain contemporary reality only with an expanded and enriched understanding of "control" and "subject to." For although our ruling class owns the media and controls them formally, it does not exercise direct control over their content—does not now use them in the instrumental and ideological way that Marx and Engels identified 140 years ago. Mobil[1] "idea ads" are the exception, not the rule.

To return to the instance at hand: neither the major stockholders of ITT and Xerox and RCA nor their boards of directors played a significant role in deciding which novels of the 1960s and early 1970s would gain acceptance as literature, and they certainly established no house rules—printing only those books that would advance their outlook on the world. (If they had done so, how could they have allowed, e.g., the Pantheon division of Random House virtually to enlist in the New Left?) They exercised control over publishing in the usual abstract way: they sought a good return on investment and cared little whether it came from a novel by Bellow or by Krantz, or for that matter from novels or computer chips. And very few of the historical actors who did make critical decisions about fiction were members of the haute bourgeoisie.[2] Was class then irrelevant to the early shaping of a canon of fiction? Alternatively, did the working class make its own culture in this sphere?

My argument points toward a conclusion different from both of these, one that still turns upon class but not just upon the two great traditional classes. Intuitively, one can see that literary agents, editors, publicity people, reviewers, buyers of hardbound novels, taste-making intellectuals, critics, professors, most of the students who took literary courses, and, in fact, the writers of the novels themselves, all had social affinities. They went to the same colleges, married one another, lived in the same neighborhoods, talked about the same movies, had to work for their livings (but worked with their minds more than with their hands), and earned pretty good incomes. I hold that they belonged to a common class, one that itself emerged and grew up only with monopoly capitalism. Following Barbara and John Ehrenreich, I call it the professional-managerial class.[3] I characterize it by the affinities just mentioned; by its conflicted relation to the ruling class (intellectuals managed that class's affairs and many of its institutions, and they derived benefits from this position, but they also strove for autonomy and for a somewhat different vision of the future); by its equally mixed relation to the working class (it dominated, supervised, taught, and planned for them, but even in doing so it also served and augmented capital); and by its own marginal position with respect to capital (its members didn't have the wealth to sit back and clip

9. *The Marx-Engels Reader*, ed. Robert C. Tucker (New York, 1972), p. 136 [Ohmann's note].
1. The oil company Mobil Corporation (now Exxon Mobil Corporation).
2. The upper middle class (French).
3. See Barbara and John Ehrenreich, "The Professional-Managerial Class," in Pat Walker, ed., *Between Labor and Capital* (Boston, 1979). Methodologically, I join the Ehrenreichs in holding that the point is not to "define" classes in some ahistorical way and that a notion of class is validated or invalidated by its power in theory, empirical explanation, and political practice. Hence I do not mean to be appropriating a preexisting definition of class in this essay and "applying" it to a particular situation and problem. Rather, I intend my argument and my evidence to help *develop* a more adequate picture of the way class has worked and works in the social process [Ohmann's note]. Barbara Ehrenreich (b. 1941), American social critic and journalist. John Ehrenreich (b. 1943), American sociologist.

coupons, but they had ready access to credit and most could choose—at least at an early stage in their careers—between working for themselves and selling their labor power to others).

People in the professional-managerial class shared one relation to the bourgeoisie and another to the working class: they had many common social experiences and acted out similar styles of life. I hold that they also had—with of course many complexities and much variation—a common understanding of the world and their place in it. In the remainder of this essay, I will look at some of the values, beliefs, and interests that constituted that class perspective, by considering the novels given cultural currency by those class members who produced, marketed, read, interpreted, and taught fiction. My claim is that the needs and values of the professional-managerial class permeate the general form of these novels, as well as their categories of understanding and their means of representation.

For my examples I will draw upon such works as *Franny and Zooey, One Flew over the Cuckoo's Nest, The Bell Jar, Herzog, Portnoy's Complaint*, and Updike's *Rabbit* series.[4] But what I say of these books is true of many other novels from the postwar period that have as yet a chance of becoming canonical. To glance ahead for a moment: these novels told stories of people trying to live a decent life in contemporary social settings, people represented as analogous to "us," rather than as "cases" to be examined and understood from a clinical distance, as in an older realistic convention. They are unhappy people, who move toward happiness, at least a bit, by the ends of their stories.

A premise of this fiction—nothing new to American literature but particularly salient in this period—is that individual consciousness, not the social or historical field, is the locus of significant happening. In passing, note that on the level of style this premise authorizes variety, the pursuit of a unique and personal voice. But on the levels of conceptualization and story, the premise of individual autonomy has an opposite effect: it gives these fictions a common problem and drives their material into narratives that, seen from the middle distance, look very similar. I suggest that much precanonical fiction of this period expresses, in Williams's term, a particular structure of feeling,[5] that that structure of feeling was a common one for the class in question, and that novelists explored its contours before it was articulated in books of social commentary like Philip Slater's *The Pursuit of Loneliness* (1970) and Charles Reich's *The Greening of America* (1970), or in films like *The Graduate*,[6] and certainly, before that structure of feeling informed a broad social movement or entered conversational cliché, in phrases like "a sick society," "the establishment," and "the system." (More avant-garde writers, outside the circuit of best-sellers, had given it earlier expression: the Beats, Mailer in *Advertisements for Myself*, Barth in *The End of the Road*,[7] etc.)

This structure of feeling gathered and strengthened during the postwar

4. The sequels to *Rabbit, Run* are *Rabbit Redux* (1971), *Rabbit Is Rich* (1981), and (after the publication of Ohmann's essay) *Rabbit at Rest* (1990). Novels not already mentioned: *Franny and Zooey* (1961), by J. D. Salinger; *The Bell Jar* (1963), by Sylvia Plath.

5. Williams has used this concept since writing *Culture and Society, 1780–1950* (New York, 1958). Its most exact theoretical formulation is in his *Marxism and Literature* (New York, 1977) [Ohmann's note].

6. An Academy Award–winning film (1967, dir. Mike Nichols), whose somewhat aimless title character is unsure of his career and life plans after college graduation.

7. A novel published in 1958. The Beats: members of a literary and social movement of the 1950s who stressed unconventionality and rebelled against

period. It became rather intense by the early 1960s. After 1965 it exploded into the wider cultural and political arena, when black rebellions, the student movement, the antiwar movement, and later the women's movement made it clear, right there in the headlines and on television, that not everyone considered ours an age of only "happy problems."[8]

In retrospect it is easy to understand some of the forces that generated this consciousness. To chart the connection, I will take a broad and speculative look at the historical experience of the class that endowed fiction with value and suggest how that experience shaped that class's concerns and needs, before I turn at greater length to the fiction that its members wrote, published, read, and preserved.

Like everyone in the society, people in the professional-managerial class lived through a time when the United States was enjoying the spoils of World War II. It altogether dominated the "free world" for two decades, militarily, politically, and economically. Its power sufficed to give it dominance among its allies and to prevent defections from the capitalist sphere, though the "loss" of China and Cuba[9] gave cause for worried vigilance. Its products and its capital flowed freely through most parts of the world (its very money was the currency of capitalism after the Bretton Woods and Dumbarton Oaks agreements[1]). U.S. values also flowed freely, borne by advertising, television shows, and the *Reader's Digest* more than by propaganda. The confidence one would expect to find in the metropolis of such an empire strengthened the feeling of righteousness that came from having defeated one set of enemies in war and having held at bay another set in peace. Both the war and the cold war fostered a chauvinistic and morally polarized conception of the world. *They* were totalitarian monsters; *we* were an open society of free citizens pursuing a way of life superior to any other, past or present.

Furthermore, that way of life generated a material prosperity that was historically unprecedented and that increased from one year to the next. The pent-up buying power of the war period (never before or since has the broad working class had so much money in the bank) eased the conversion from war production to production for consumers by providing capitalists with an enormous and secure domestic market, and they responded with rapid investment and a flow of old and new products. Affluence, like victory in war, made people confident that they and their society were doing things right.

On top of that, social conflict became muted. Inequality remained as pronounced as it had been before, but no more so, and the working class participated in the steady growth of total product.[2] Though workers could not

"square" middle-class life. *Advertisements for Myself* (1959), a collection of Mailer's fiction, nonfiction, poems, and plays.

8. For a sampling of this consciousness, see Herbert Gold's "The Age of Happy Problems" (1956; rpt. in a book of the same title, New York, 1962) [Ohmann's note].

9. That is, the institution in those countries of communist forms of government in 1949 and 1959, respectively.

1. Proposals drawn up in 1944 (at what was then a private estate in Washington, D.C.) that provided the basic plan for the United Nations, chartered the following year. Bretton Woods: at the United Nations Monetary and Financial Conference at Bretton Woods, N.H., in 1944, the International Monetary Fund and the International Bank for Reconstruction and Development (the World Bank) were created; headquartered in Washington, D.C., they are intended to expand international trade by stabilizing exchange rates and promoting investment, respectively. All calculations at the UN, IMF, and World Bank are based in dollars.

2. For instance, the poorest 40 percent of families in the country received 16.8 percent of the income in 1947 and 16.9 percent in 1960, while the percentage going to the richest 5 percent went from 17.2 percent to 16.8 percent. The top 1 percent owned 23.3 percent of the nation's *wealth* in 1945

see any narrowing of the divide between themselves and higher classes, the postwar generation experienced an absolute gain, both from year to year and by comparison with the 1930s; many *perceived* this gain as a softening of class lines. The sense of economic well-being that results from such an experience of history promoted allegiance to the social order, as did the tightening bonds between unions and management, amounting to a truce in class conflict within the assumptions of the welfare state. Cold war propaganda helped make it possible—especially for those who managed the new arrangements and lived in suburbs—to see our society as a harmonious collaboration.

Developments in business additionally gave support to this image of harmony. There was a rapid growth and sophistication of advertising, which not only sold products but continued to shape people into masses, for the purpose of selling those products and advancing a whole way of life whose cornerstones were the suburban home, the family, and the automobile. Leisure and social life became more private, drained of class feeling and even of the feeling of interdependence.

Politics seemed nearly irrelevant to such a life. Moreover, the boundaries of respectable political debate steadily closed in through the 1950s. On one side, socialism was pushed off the agenda by union leaders almost as vigorously as by Truman, McCarthy, the blacklisters, the FBI.[3] On the other side, businessmen gradually abandoned the tough old capitalist principles of laissez-faire and espoused a more benign program of cooperation with labor and government. The spectrum of discussable ideas reached only from corporate liberalism to welfare-state liberalism; no wonder some thought they were witnessing the end of ideology.[4]

Consider the experience of the class that creates the canon of fiction in such an environment. Not only were its numbers and its prosperity growing rapidly along with its institutions but every public voice seemed to be saying to intellectuals, professionals, technical elites, and managers: "History is over, though progress continues. There is no more poverty. Everyone is middle class. The state is a friendly power, capable of smoothing out the abrasions of the economic system, solving its problems one by one through legislation that itself is the product of your ideas and values. You have brought a neutral and a humane rationality to the supervision of public life (exemplified beautifully by that parade of Harvard intellectuals to Washington in 1961[5]). Politics is for experts, not ideologues. You are, therefore, the favored people, the peacemakers, the technicians of an intelligent society, justly rewarded with quick promotions, respect, and adequate incomes. So carry forward this valued social mission, which in no way conflicts with indi-

and 27.4 percent in 1962. These figures come from tables compiled by Frank Ackerman and Andrew Zimbalist, "Capitalism and Inequality in the United States," in Richard C. Edwards, Michael Reich, and Thomas E. Weisskopf, eds., *The Capitalist System: A Radical Analysis of American Society*, 2d ed. (Englewood Cliffs, N.J., 1978), pp. 298, 301 [Ohmann's note].

3. Representative figures of the cold war: Harry S. Truman (1884–1972), as U.S. president (1945–53), strongly opposed the spread of communist forms of government in the world; Joseph McCarthy (1908–1957), U.S. senator from Wisconsin (1947–57), made largely unsubstantiated charges of Communist infiltration in American government and industry in the early 1950s; "the blacklisters" refused to hire those in the entertainment industry accused of having some connection to communism, following public congressional hearings by the House Committee on Un-American Activities that began in 1947; the Federal Bureau of Investigation secretly and sometimes illegally gathered information about American citizens who were alleged to be subversives.

4. See Daniel Bell, *The End of Ideology* (Glencoe, Ill.: Free Press, 1960).

5. During the presidency of John F. Kennedy (1917–1963; president, 1961–63), many intellectuals from Harvard University and elsewhere were appointed to positions in government.

vidual achievement. Enjoy your prestige and comforts. Fulfill yourselves on the terrain of private life."

But because the economic underpinnings of this consciousness were of course *not* unchanging and free of conflict, because material interdependence was an ever more pervasive fact,[6] whether perceived or not, because society cannot be wished away, because freedom on such terms is an illusion—for all these reasons, the individual pursuit of happiness continued to be a problem. Yet myth, ideology, and experience assured the professional-managerial class that no real barriers would prevent personal satisfaction, so it was easy to nourish the suspicion that any perceived lack was one's own fault. If unhappy, one must be personally maladjusted, perhaps even neurotic. I am suggesting that for the people who wrote, read, promoted, and preserved fiction, social contradictions were easily displaced into images of personal illness.[7]

* * *

What I hope to have accomplished * * * is to have given concrete enough form to the following powerful yet vague ideas about culture and value, so that they may be criticized and perhaps developed. (1) A canon—a shared understanding of what literature is worth preserving—takes shape through a troubled historical process. (2) It emerges through specific institutions and practices, not in some historically invariant way. (3) These institutions are likely to have a rather well-defined class base. (4) Although the ruling ideas and myths may indeed be, in every age, the ideas and myths of the ruling class, the ruling class in advanced capitalist societies does not advance its ideas directly through its control of the means of mental production. Rather, a subordinate but influential class shapes culture in ways that express its own interests and experience and that sometimes turn on ruling-class values rather critically—yet in a nonrevolutionary period end up confirming root elements of the dominant ideology, such as the premise of individualism. I hope, in short, to have given a usable and attackable account of the hegemonic process and to have added content to the claim that aesthetic value arises from class conflict.

1983

6. That is, people relied on others, through the intermediary of the market, for more and more goods and services. In an ordinary day's "consuming," each of us depends on the past and present labor of hundreds of millions of workers worldwide. But of course this is easy to forget, since that loaf of bread magically appears on the store shelf and the only labor we *see* is that of the checker and the bagger [Ohmann's note].

7. In the closing section of the essay, omitted here, Ohmann documents specific examples of what he calls "illness stories," such as *The Bell Jar*, *Franny and Zooey*, and *One Flew over the Cuckoo's Nest*, arguing that their depictions of mental illness represent the social fragmentation wrought by modern U.S. capitalism.

STUART HALL
b. 1932

The career of Stuart Hall, perhaps the single most prominent and influential theorist of British cultural studies, exemplifies the theoretical and political trajectory of late-twentieth-century intellectuals from the New Left of the 1960s through the engagement with poststructuralism in the 1970s to the cultural politics of the 1980s and 1990s. Born in Jamaica in 1932, Hall came to Britain as a Rhodes Scholar in 1951 and has never left. As he explains it, a combination of vexed family relations and his own intense involvement in the formation of Britain's New Left made him miss the moment when he might have returned to the Caribbean. Instead, his racial and national difference as a black colonial subject rendered him a "familiar stranger" in his adopted home, occupying a "diasporic" position of knowing two "places intimately" (Jamaica and England), while being "not wholly of either place."

Hall's work within New Left circles, including his position as a founding editor of the influential *New Left Review*, kept him from completing his graduate work at Oxford University. The British New Left strove to create a non-Stalinist, noncommunist socialism that could influence Labour Party policies and move intellectual and political paradigms from a sole focus on economic factors to a more complex understanding of the multiple determinants of people's allegiances, attitudes, and beliefs. Interested in popular culture (as were those who laid the groundwork for British cultural studies, E. P. Thompson, RAYMOND WILLIAMS, and Richard Hoggart), Hall worked with the Education Department of the British Film Institute in the early sixties, which in 1961 led to his appointment at the University of London as the first "lecturer in film and mass media studies" in Britain. He moved to the University of Birmingham in 1964 to join Hoggart's newly formed Centre for Contemporary Cultural Studies, remaining there until 1979 and serving as the center's director during much of that time. He spent the years from 1979 until his retirement in 1998 at the Open University.

The Birmingham years have become legendary, with his work done at the Open University only slightly less so. Many figures later important in cultural studies (for instance, DICK HEBDIGE, Hazel Carby, Angela McRobbie, Paul Gilroy, and Larry Grossberg) were students or co-workers of Hall's at some point. Collaborative work was the norm at both places; this founding work in cultural studies characteristically came to the world in the form of edited volumes in which eight to twelve authors address a topic, arguing with each other but also moving toward an overarching delineation of the factors that need to be considered if the topic is to be adequately analyzed.

Hall, like PAUL DE MAN, was a charismatic teacher, and his immense influence is only partially captured in his written work. An essayist, he has produced no single distillation of his views, and his pieces are scattered in journals and edited volumes that are often hard to find. But the essay form is suited to his intellectual temperament, which is self-consciously nondogmatic, restless, and open to new ideas and changing social conditions.

To some extent, Hall's intellectual stance bedevils cultural studies, especially as it becomes institutionalized in American universities. The dialogic, multivoiced inception of cultural studies makes it a moving target, engaged in a series of debates with various formalized intellectual paradigms (notably Marxism, anthropological and sociological functionalism, and aestheticist literary criticism), all the while avoiding definitive statements of its own position. Hall advocates a "cultural studies . . . that is always self-reflectively deconstructing itself. . . . Let me put it this way: you have to be sure about a position to teach a class, but you have to be open-minded enough to know that you are going to change your mind by the time you teach it next week."

Over the years, Hall's work has been influenced by Western Marxism, poststructuralism (especially MICHEL FOUCAULT), critical race theory, and feminism, as he makes clear in our selection. Such openness has been characterized by some critics of cultural studies as its willingness and ability to absorb anything, a kind of academic imperialism that lacks intellectual or disciplinary boundaries or values.

Hall's wariness about a codification of cultural studies comes through in our selection, "Cultural Studies and Its Theoretical Legacies" (1992), although certain traits typical of British cultural studies can be identified. The primary feature is a commitment to the political relevance of intellectual work. British cultural studies is an outgrowth of leftist politics, born of the theoretical need for alternatives to a vulgar Marxism that is rooted in class politics and economic determinism. As an offshoot of Marxism, this cultural studies is aligned with ANTONIO GRAMSCI against the more pessimistic visions of the Frankfurt School (see MAX HORKHEIMER AND THEODOR W. ADORNO) and LOUIS ALTHUSSER. Adapting Gramsci's crucial notion of hegemony, Hall emphasizes the ways in which the power of ruling elites is constituted and reconstituted within a complex cultural scene that affords various possibilities for action. Rather than stressing the ways that power, through ideology, imposes a mode of life on passive social subjects, he uses the concept of hegemony to provide a more dynamic vision of ongoing struggles among all members of society, with only temporary and always fragile victories by any particular group. Hall's interest in connecting intellectuals "organically" to these political struggles also follows Gramsci's lead. But such Gramscian elements in Hall are elaborated through an engagement with Foucault, as he details power's dispersion through a whole social order, the processes of subject formation, and the power/knowledge produced by intellectual discourses.

What has confused—and sometimes infuriated—many academics about cultural studies is its refusal to declare a prevailing methodology and a designated object of study, two features required of traditional academic disciplines. Cultural studies strives to analyze the hegemonic practices by which social groups are bound (institutionally, intellectually, emotionally, and economically) to dominant social forms. And it examines how forces of resistance creatively intervene in those practices. Since hegemony works through and on every social site and practice, cultural studies has deemed anything a potential object of study and has adapted any disciplinary methodology that might prove useful, ranging from surveys, case studies, and personal observation to textual explication, institutional analysis, and political critique. Partly in response to intellectual elitism, partly by happenstance, and partly as a form of leftist populism, much cultural studies work has focused on popular, as contrasted to high, culture. But any activity through which people negotiate their relationship to society and to the disparate forces and institutions in their lives is fair game for its attention.

The absence of a prevailing methodology does not mean that cultural studies lacks a theory. Hall's scattered essays have addressed a wide array of theoretical issues and, when taken together, delineate a comprehensive overview of the driving questions and angles of approach followed by many cultural studies practitioners. Processes of identity formation are central, as are the concepts of "conjuncture" and "articulation." Hall, like most Marxists, is a "conflict theorist": one who views the social field as a dynamic site of numerous contending forces. Within that field, he refuses to recognize any stable identities—either group (like class) or personal (like ethnicity). Identity for him is always in the process of being constituted by prevailing social norms, institutions, and subject positions, as well as by particular struggles against those would-be determinants. Identity, in other words, is a battleground, where the meaning of social life is being forged and contested. Here as elsewhere, Hall relies on the concept of "conjuncture," the idea that everything exists simultaneously amid specific historical forces in process and amid specific determinant structures. The elements within any conjuncture and the relations of force among them are differently "articulated" at different times and places. Each conjuncture has its own configuration. Social groups, including intellectuals, will work to make their "articulation" of a given constellation of elements prevail.

For Hall, no dominant order can ever provide a seamless, synthetic, permanent vision. All hegemonies must be continually produced by very specific acts of public articulation. Cultural studies is interested in mapping the particular constellation of identities and hegemonic articulations at various social sites; it often focuses on dynamic tensions between mainstream norms and marginalized groups, studying how cultural materials are creatively resignified to fit the nonstandard purposes of such resistant groups. Typical counterhegemonic materials might include a punk 'zine, women's shop floor gossip, romance novels, and rap poetry. A typical cultural studies research project might examine the circuits of production, distribution, and consumption through which such "discourses" pass.

Critics of Hall's work are divided between traditional leftists who object that he overemphasizes a cultural politics of resistance at the expense of a socioeconomic politics focused on systematic inequalities and poststructuralist opponents who see the concept of hegemony as aspiring to a totalized vision that misses the irreducible heterogeneity of the social field. Nevertheless, Hall's—and cultural studies'—importance for contemporary literary studies rests most crucially perhaps on his insistence in "Cultural Studies and Its Theoretical Legacies" that "textuality is never enough." That is to say, Hall insists on linking literary theory's understanding of meaning production and textual interpretation with social theory's delineation of conflicting forces within the social field. If a literary critic believes that any interpretation of a literary text must consider both the social forces that contribute to the text's production *and* the hegemonic work that the text does, then he or she has taken up the concerns and questions that characterize cultural studies.

BIBLIOGRAPHY

Finding Hall's work (scattered in numerous journals and edited volumes) can be difficult. The only volume that collects some of those essays is his *Hard Road to Renewal* (1988). *Stuart Hall: Critical Dialogues in Cultural Studies*, edited by David Morley and Kuan-Hsing Chen (1996), collects several key essays by Hall along with some responses to his work. The most influential collaborative texts done by various British cultural studies groups working with Hall (volumes that usually contain essays by Hall) are *The Popular Arts*, edited by Stuart Hall and Paddy Whannel (1964); *Resistance through Rituals: Youth Subcultures in Post-War Britain*, edited by Stuart Hall and Tony Jefferson (1976); *Policing the Crisis: Mugging, the State, and Law and Order*, edited by Stuart Hall et al. (1978); *Culture, Media, Language: Working Papers in Cultural Studies*, edited by Stuart Hall et al. (1980); *New Times: The Changing Face of Politics in the 1990s*, edited by Stuart Hall and Martin Jacques (1990); *Questions of Cultural Identity*, edited by Stuart Hall and Paul du Gay (1996); and *Representation: Cultural Representations and Signifying Practices*, edited by Stuart Hall (1997). *Women Take Issue: Aspects of Women's Subordination*, edited by the Women's Studies Group, Centre for Contemporary Cultural Studies (1978), and *The Empire Strikes Back: Race and Racism in 70s Britain*, edited by the Centre for Contemporary Cultural Studies (1982), are important early collections that extend cultural studies into studies of gender, race, and postcolonialism. The best biographical sources are two interviews: the first (titled "The Formation of the Diasporic Intellectual") is in the Morley and Chen volume cited above, and the second, Caryl Phillips's "Interview with Stuart Hall," is in *Bomb*, no. 58 (1997).

The excellent set of essays in the Morley and Chen volume is the best place to start for critical responses to Hall. Graeme Turner's *British Cultural Studies: An Introduction* (2d ed., 1996) and Dennis Dworkin's *Cultural Marxism in Postwar Britain History, the New Left, and the Origins of Cultural Studies* (1997) usefully locate Hall's work in its intellectual and institutional contexts. On the intersection of Hall's postcolonial identity with his theoretical work, see Grant Farred, "You Can Go Home Again, You Just Can't Stay: Stuart Hall and the Caribbean Diaspora," *Research in African Literatures* 27.4 (1996). The Morley and Chen volume has a complete bibliography of Hall's published work.

Cultural Studies and Its Theoretical Legacies

This Conference[1] provides us with an opportunity for a moment of self-reflection on cultural studies as a practice, on its institutional positioning, and what Lidia Curti[2] so effectively reminds us is both the marginality and the centrality of its practitioners as critical intellectuals. Inevitably, this involves reflecting on, and intervening in, the project of cultural studies itself.

My title, "Cultural Studies and Its Theoretical Legacies," suggests a look back to the past, to consult and think about the Now and the Future of cultural studies by way of a retrospective glance. It does seem necessary to do some genealogical and archaeological work on the archive. Now the question of the archives is extremely difficult for me because, where cultural studies is concerned, I sometimes feel like a *tableau vivant*,[3] a spirit of the past resurrected, laying claim to the authority of an origin. After all, didn't cultural studies emerge somewhere at that moment when I first met Raymond Williams, or in the glance I exchanged with Richard Hoggart?[4] In that moment, cultural studies was born; it emerged full grown from the head![5] I do want to talk about the past, but definitely not in that way. I don't want to talk about British cultural studies (which is in any case a pretty awkward signifier for me) in a patriarchal way, as the keeper of the conscience of cultural studies, hoping to police you back into line with what it really was if only you knew. That is to say, I want to absolve myself of the many burdens of representation which people carry around—I carry around at least three: I'm expected to speak for the entire black race on all questions theoretical, critical, etc., and sometimes for British politics, as well as for cultural studies. This is what is known as the black person's burden,[6] and I would like to absolve myself of it at this moment.

That means, paradoxically, speaking autobiographically. Autobiography is usually thought of as seizing the authority of authenticity. But in order not to be authoritative, I've got to speak autobiographically. I'm going to tell you about my own take on certain theoretical legacies and moments in cultural studies, not because it is the truth or the only way of telling the history. I myself have told it many other ways before; and I intend to tell it in a different way later. But just at this moment, for this conjuncture, I want to take a position in relation to the "grand narrative"[7] of cultural studies for the pur-

1. "Cultural Studies Now and in the Future," held in April 1990 at the University of Illinois at Urbana-Champaign.
2. Italian academic working in cultural studies (b. 1947).
3. Living picture (French).
4. Hoggart (b. 1918) and WILLIAMS (1921–1988), both British academics and early practitioners of cultural studies.
5. That is, like Athena (goddess of wisdom) born from the head of Zeus (king of the gods), in Greek mythology.
6. An allusion to "The White Man's Burden" (1899), a poem by Rudyard Kipling that paints imperialism as the duty of the "advanced" peoples.
7. JEAN-FRANÇOIS LYOTARD (1925–1998) defined postmodernism as a skepticism toward any "grand narrative" that offers an all-encompassing vision of history's trajectory.

poses of opening up some reflections on cultural studies as a practice, on our institutional position, and on its project. I want to do that by referring to some theoretical legacies or theoretical moments, but in a very particular way. This is not a commentary on the success or effectiveness of different theoretical positions in cultural studies (that is for some other occasion). It is an attempt to say something about what certain theoretical moments in cultural studies have been like for me, and from that position, to take some bearings about the general question of the politics of theory.

Cultural studies is a discursive formation, in Foucault's[8] sense. It has no simple origins, though some of us were present at some point when it first named itself in that way. Much of the work out of which it grew, in my own experience, was already present in the work of other people. Raymond Williams has made the same point, charting the roots of cultural studies in the early adult education movement in his essay on "The Future of Cultural Studies" (1989). "The relation between a project and a formation is always decisive," he says, because they are "different ways of materializing . . . then of describing a common disposition of energy and direction." Cultural studies has multiple discourses; it has a number of different histories. It is a whole set of formations; it has its own different conjunctures and moments in the past. It included many different kinds of work. I want to insist on that! It always was a set of unstable formations. It was "centered" only in quotation marks, in a particular kind of way which I want to define in a moment. It had many trajectories; many people had and have different trajectories through it; it was constructed by a number of different methodologies and theoretical positions, all of them in contention. Theoretical work in the Centre for Contemporary Cultural Studies[9] was more appropriately called theoretical noise. It was accompanied by a great deal of bad feeling, argument, unstable anxieties, and angry silences.

Now, does it follow that cultural studies is not a policed disciplinary area? That it is whatever people do, if they choose to call or locate themselves within the project and practice of cultural studies? I am not happy with that formulation either. Although cultural studies as a project is open-ended, it can't be simply pluralist in that way. Yes, it refuses to be a master discourse or a meta-discourse of any kind. Yes, it is a project that is always open to that which it doesn't yet know, to that which it can't yet name. But it does have some will to connect; it does have some stake in the choices it makes. It does matter whether cultural studies is this or that. It can't be just any old thing which chooses to march under a particular banner. It is a serious enterprise, or project, and that is inscribed in what is sometimes called the "political" aspect of cultural studies. Not that there's one politics already inscribed in it. But there is something *at stake* in cultural studies, in a way that I think, and hope, is not exactly true of many other very important intellectual and critical practices. Here one registers the tension between a refusal to close the field, to police it and, at the same time, a determination to stake out some positions within it and argue for them. That is the tension—the dialogic approach to theory—that I want to try to speak to in a number of different ways in the course of this paper. I don't believe knowl-

8. MICHEL FOUCAULT (1926–1984), French philosopher and historian of ideas.
9. Founded at the University of Birmingham by Richard Hoggart in 1964; Hall served as the center's director from 1968 to 1979.

edge is closed, but I do believe that politics is impossible without what I have called "the arbitrary closure"; without what Homi Bhabha[1] called social agency as an arbitrary closure. That is to say, I don't understand a practice which aims to make a difference in the world, which doesn't have some points of difference or distinction which it has to stake out, which really matter. It is a question of positionalities. Now, it is true that those positionalities are never final, they're never absolute. They can't be translated intact from one conjuncture to another; they cannot be depended on to remain in the same place. I want to go back to that moment of "staking out a wager" in cultural studies, to those moments in which the positions began to matter.

This is a way of opening the question of the "worldliness" of cultural studies, to borrow a term from Edward Said.[2] I am not dwelling on the secular connotations of the metaphor of worldliness here, but on the worldliness of cultural studies. I'm dwelling on the "dirtiness" of it: the dirtiness of the semiotic game, if I can put it that way. I'm trying to return the project of cultural studies from the clean air of meaning and textuality and theory to the something nasty down below. This involves the difficult exercise of examining some of the key theoretical turns or moments in cultural studies.

The first trace that I want to deconstruct has to do with a view of British cultural studies which often distinguishes it by the fact that, at a certain moment, it became a Marxist critical practice. What exactly does that assignation of cultural studies as a Marxist critical theory mean? How can we think cultural studies at that moment? What moment is it we are speaking of? What does that mean for the theoretical legacies, traces, and aftereffects which Marxism continues to have in cultural studies? There are a number of ways of telling that history, and let me remind you that I'm not proposing this as the only story. But I do want to set it up in what I think may be a slightly surprising way to you.

I entered cultural studies from the New Left, and the New Left always regarded Marxism as a problem, as trouble, as danger, not as a solution. Why? It had nothing to do with theoretical questions as such or in isolation. It had to do with the fact that my own (and its own) political formation occurred in a moment historically very much like the one we are in now—which I am astonished that so few people have addressed—the moment of the disintegration of a certain kind of Marxism. In fact, the first British New Left emerged in 1956 at the moment of the disintegration of an entire historical/political project.[3] In that sense I came into Marxism backwards: against the Soviet tanks in Budapest, as it were. What I mean by that is certainly not that I wasn't profoundly, and that cultural studies then wasn't from the beginning, profoundly influenced by the questions that Marxism as a theoretical project put on the agenda: the power, the global reach and history-making capacities of capital; the question of class; the complex relationships between power, which is an easier term to establish in the discourses of culture than exploitation, and exploitation; the question of a general theory which could, in a critical way, connect together in a critical reflection different domains of life, politics and theory, theory and practice,

1. Indian postcolonial theorist and critic (b. 1949); BHABHA makes this point in "The Postcolonial and the Postmodern: A Question of Agency," in *The Location of Culture* (1994).

2. Palestinian-born American literary and cultural critic and social activist (b. 1935); for SAID's discussion of "worldliness," see chapter 1 of *The World, the Text, and the Critic* (1983).

3. That is, when Soviet troops suppressed a short-lived anti-Communist and anti-Soviet rebellion in Hungary in October 1956.

economic, political, ideological questions, and so on; the notion of critical knowledge itself and the production of critical knowledge as a practice. These important, central questions are what one meant by working within shouting distance of Marxism, working on Marxism, working against Marxism, working with it, working to try to develop Marxism.

There never was a prior moment when cultural studies and Marxism represented a perfect theoretical fit. From the beginning (to use this way of speaking for a moment) there was always-already the question of the great inadequacies, theoretically and politically, the resounding silences, the great evasions of Marxism—the things that Marx did not talk about or seem to understand which were our privileged object of study: culture, ideology, language, the symbolic.[4] These were always-already, instead, the things which had imprisoned Marxism as a mode of thought, as an activity of critical practice—its orthodoxy, its doctrinal character, its determinism, its reductionism, its immutable law of history, its status as a metanarrative. That is to say, the encounter between British cultural studies and Marxism has first to be understood as the engagement with a problem—not a theory, not even a problematic. It begins, and develops through the critique of a certain reductionism and economism, which I think is not extrinsic but intrinsic to Marxism; a contestation with the model of base and superstructure, through which sophisticated and vulgar Marxism alike had tried to think the relationships between society, economy, and culture. It was located and sited in a necessary and prolonged and as yet unending contestation with the question of false consciousness. In my own case, it required a not-yet-completed contestation with the profound Eurocentrism of Marxist theory. I want to make this very precise. It is not just a matter of where Marx happened to be born, and of what he talked about, but of the model at the center of the most developed parts of Marxist theory, which suggested that capitalism evolved organically from within its own transformations. Whereas I came from a society where the profound integument of capitalist society, economy, and culture had been imposed by conquest and colonization. This is a theoretical, not a vulgar critique. I don't blame Marx because of where he was born; I'm questioning the theory for the model around which it is articulated: its Eurocentrism.

I want to suggest a different metaphor for theoretical work: the metaphor of struggle, of wrestling with the angels. The only theory worth having is that which you have to fight off, not that which you speak with profound fluency. I mean to say something later about the astonishing theoretical fluency of cultural studies now. But my own experience of theory—and Marxism is certainly a case in point—is of wrestling with the angels—a metaphor you can take as literally as you like. I remember wrestling with Althusser.[5] I remember looking at the idea of "theoretical practice" in *Reading Capital* and thinking, "I've gone as far in this book as it is proper to go." I felt, I will not give an inch to this profound misreading, this super-structuralist mistranslation, of classical Marxism, unless he beats me down, unless he defeats me in the spirit. He'll have to march over me to convince me. I warred with him, to the death. A long, rambling piece I wrote (Hall, 1974)[6] on Marx's

4. On the writings of the German economic and political philosopher KARL MARX (1818–1883) pertaining to culture, see above.

5. LOUIS ALTHUSSER (1918–1990), French philosopher. *Reading Capital* was published in 1965.

6. Stuart Hall, "Marx's Notes on Method: A 'Reading' of the 1857 Introduction," *Working Papers in Cultural Studies* 6 (1974) [Hall's note].

1857 Introduction to *The Grundrisse*, in which I tried to stake out the difference between structuralism in Marx's epistemology and Althusser's, was only the tip of the iceberg of this long engagement. And that is not simply a personal question. In the Centre for Contemporary Cultural Studies, for five or six years, long after the anti-theoreticism or resistance to theory of cultural studies had been overcome, and we decided, in a very un-British way, we had to take the plunge into theory, we walked right around the entire circumference of European thought, in order not to be, in any simple capitulation to the *zeitgeist*, Marxists. We read German idealism, we read Weber upside down, we read Hegelian idealism,[7] we read idealistic art criticism. (I've written about this in the article called "The Hinterland of Science: Sociology of Knowledge" [1980] as well as in "Cultural Studies and the Centre: Some Problems and Problematics" [1980].)[8]

So the notion that Marxism and cultural studies slipped into place, recognized an immediate affinity, joined hands in some teleological or Hegelian moment of synthesis, and there was the founding moment of cultural studies, is entirely mistaken. It couldn't have been more different from that. And when, eventually, in the seventies, British cultural studies did advance—in many different ways, it must be said—within the problematic of Marxism, you should hear the term problematic in a genuine way, not just in a formalist-theoretical way: as a problem; as much about struggling against the constraints and limits of that model as about the necessary questions it required us to address. And when, in the end, in my own work, I tried to learn from and work with the theoretical gains of Gramsci,[9] it was only because certain strategies of evasion had forced Gramsci's work, in a number of different ways, to respond to what I can only call (here's another metaphor for theoretical work) the conundrums of theory, the things which Marxist theory couldn't answer, the things about the modern world which Gramsci discovered remained unresolved within the theoretical framework of grand theory—Marxism—in which he continued to work. At a certain point, the questions I still wanted to address in short were inaccessible to me except via a detour through Gramsci. Not because Gramsci resolved them but because he at least addressed many of them. I don't want to go through what it is I personally think cultural studies in the British context, in a certain period, learned from Gramsci: immense amounts about the nature of culture itself, about the discipline of the conjunctural, about the importance of historical specificity, about the enormously productive metaphor of hegemony, about the way in which one can think questions of class relations only by using the displaced notion of ensemble and blocs. These are the particular gains of the "detour" via Gramsci, but I'm not trying to talk about that. I want to say, in this context, about Gramsci, that while Gramsci belonged and belongs to the problematic of Marxism, his importance for this moment of British cultural studies is precisely the degree to which he radically *displaced* some of the inheritances of Marxism in cultural studies. The radical character of Gramsci's "displacement" of Marxism has not yet been under-

7. In some respects, Marx's materialism was a reaction against the idealist philosophy of GEORG WILHELM FRIEDRICH HEGEL (1770–1831). Max Weber (1864–1920), German social theorist and a founder of sociology as an academic discipline.

8. "The Hinterland of Science" is in *On Ideology* (1980). "Cultural Studies and the Centre" is in *Culture, Media, Language*, edited by S. Hall et al. (1980) [Hall's note].

9. ANTONIO GRAMSCI (1891–1937), Italian Marxist theorist and cultural critic.

stood and probably won't ever be reckoned with, now we are entering the era of post-Marxism. Such is the nature of the movement of history and of intellectual fashion. But Gramsci also did something else for cultural studies, and I want to say a little bit about that because it refers to what I call the need to reflect on our institutional position, and our intellectual practice.

I tried on many occasions, and other people in British cultural studies and at the Centre especially have tried, to describe what it is we thought we were doing with the kind of intellectual work we set in place in the Centre. I have to confess that, though I've read many, more elaborated and sophisticated, accounts, Gramsci's account still seems to me to come closest to expressing what it is I think we were trying to do. Admittedly, there's a problem about his phrase "the production of organic intellectuals."[1] But there is no doubt in my mind that we were trying to find an institutional practice in cultural studies that might produce an organic intellectual. We didn't know previously what that would mean, in the context of Britain in the 1970s, and we weren't sure we would recognize him or her if we managed to produce it. The problem about the concept of an organic intellectual is that it appears to align intellectuals with an emerging historic movement and we couldn't tell then, and can hardly tell now, where that emerging historical movement was to be found. We were organic intellectuals without any organic point of reference; organic intellectuals with a nostalgia or will or hope (to use Gramsci's phrase from another context) that at some point we would be prepared in intellectual work for that kind of relationship, if such a conjuncture ever appeared. More truthfully, we were prepared to imagine or model or simulate such a relationship in its absence: "pessimism of the intellect, optimism of the will."[2]

But I think it is very important that Gramsci's thinking around these questions certainly captures part of what we were about. Because a second aspect of Gramsci's definition of intellectual work, which I think has always been lodged somewhere close to the notion of cultural studies as a project, has been his requirement that the "organic intellectual" must work on two fronts at one and the same time. On the one hand, we had to be at the very forefront of intellectual theoretical work because, as Gramsci says, it is the job of the organic intellectual to know more than the traditional intellectuals do: really know, not just pretend to know, not just to have the facility of knowledge, but to know deeply and profoundly. So often knowledge for Marxism is pure recognition—the production again of what we have always known! If you are in the game of hegemony you have to be smarter than "them." Hence, there are no theoretical limits from which cultural studies can turn back. But the second aspect is just as crucial: that the organic intellectual cannot absolve himself or herself from the responsibility of transmitting those ideas, that knowledge, through the intellectual function, to those who do not belong, professionally, in the intellectual class. And unless those two fronts are operating at the same time, or at least unless those two ambitions are part of the project of cultural studies, you can get enormous theoretical advance without any engagement at the level of the political project.

I'm extremely anxious that you should not decode what I'm saying as an

1. That is the thinking element that guides their particular class; Gramsci sets organic intellectuals against "traditional intellectuals" (e.g., scientists and academics).

2. Quoted from Gramsci's *Prison Notebooks* (1948–51).

anti-theoretical discourse. It is not anti-theory, but it does have something to do with the conditions and problems of developing intellectual and theoretical work as a political practice. It is an extremely difficult road, not resolving the tensions between those two requirements, but living with them. Gramsci never asked us to resolve them, but he gave us a practical example of how to live with them. We never produced organic intellectuals (would that we had) at the Centre. We never connected with that rising historic movement; it was a metaphoric exercise. Nevertheless, metaphors are serious things. They affect one's practice. I'm trying to redescribe cultural studies as theoretical work which must go on and on living with that tension.

I want to look at two other theoretical moments in cultural studies which interrupted the already-interrupted history of its formation. Some of these developments came as it were from outer space: they were not at all generated from the inside, they were not part of an inner-unfolding general theory of culture. Again and again, the so-called unfolding of cultural studies was interrupted by a break, by real ruptures, by exterior forces; the interruption, as it were, of new ideas, which decentered what looked like the accumulating practice of the work. There's another metaphor for theoretical work: theoretical work as interruption.

There were at least two interruptions in the work of the Centre for Contemporary Cultural Studies: The first around feminism, and the second around questions of race. This is not an attempt to sum up the theoretical and political advances and consequences for British cultural studies of the feminist intervention; that is for another time, another place. But I don't want, either, to invoke that moment in an open-ended and casual way. For cultural studies (in addition to many other theoretical projects), the intervention of feminism was specific and decisive. It was ruptural. It reorganized the field in quite concrete ways. First, the opening of the question of the personal as political, and its consequences for changing the object of study in cultural studies, was completely revolutionary in a theoretical and practical way. Second, the radical expansion of the notion of power, which had hitherto been very much developed within the framework of the notion of the public, the public domain, with the effect that we could not use the term power—so key to the earlier problematic of hegemony—in the same way. Third, the centrality of questions of gender and sexuality to the understanding of power itself. Fourth, the opening of many of the questions that we thought we had abolished around the dangerous area of the subjective and the subject, which lodged those questions at the center of cultural studies as a theoretical practice. Fifth, the "re-opening" of the closed frontier between social theory and the theory of the unconscious—psychoanalysis. It's hard to describe the import of the opening of that new continent in cultural studies, marked out by the relationship—or rather, what Jacqueline Rose[3] has called the as yet "unsettled relations"—between feminism, psychoanalysis, and cultural studies, or indeed how it was accomplished.

We know it was, but it's not known generally how and where feminism first broke in. I use the metaphor deliberately. As the thief in the night, it broke in; interrupted, made an unseemly noise, seized the time, crapped on

3. British feminist literary critic (b. 1948).

the table of cultural studies. The title of the volume in which this dawn-raid was first accomplished—*Women Take Issue*[4]— is instructive: for they "took issue" in both senses—took over that year's book and initiated a quarrel. But I want to tell you something else about it. Because of the growing importance of feminist work and the early beginnings of the feminist movement outside in the very early 1970s, many of us in the Centre—mainly, of course, men—thought it was time there was good feminist work in cultural studies. And we indeed tried to buy it in, to import it, to attract good feminist scholars. As you might expect, many of the women in cultural studies weren't terribly interested in this benign project. We were opening the door to feminist studies, being good, transformed men. And yet, when it broke in through the window, every single unsuspected resistance rose to the surface—fully installed patriarchal power, which believed it had disavowed itself. There are no leaders here, we used to say; we are all graduate students and members of staff together, learning how to practice cultural studies. You can decide whatever you want to decide, etc. And yet, when it came to the question of the reading list . . . Now that's where I really discovered about the gendered nature of power. Long, long after I was able to pronounce the words, I encountered the reality of Foucault's profound insight into the individual reciprocity of knowledge and power. Talking about giving up power is a radically different experience from being silenced. That is another way of thinking, and another metaphor for theory: the way feminism broke, and broke into, cultural studies.

Then there is the question of race in cultural studies. I've talked about the important "extrinsic" sources of the formation of cultural studies—for example, in what I called the moment of the New Left, and its original quarrel with Marxism—out of which cultural studies grew. And yet, of course, that was a profoundly English or British moment. Actually getting cultural studies to put on its own agenda the critical questions of race, the politics of race, the resistance to racism, the critical questions of cultural politics, was itself a profound theoretical struggle, a struggle of which *Policing the Crisis*,[5] was, curiously, the first and very late example. It represented a decisive turn in my own theoretical and intellectual work, as well as in that of the Centre. Again, it was only accomplished as the result of a long, and sometimes bitter—certainly bitterly contested—internal struggle against a resounding but unconscious silence. A struggle which continued in what has since come to be known, but only in the rewritten history, as one of the great seminal books of the Centre for Cultural Studies, *The Empire Strikes Back*.[6] In actuality, Paul Gilroy[7] and the group of people who produced the book found it extremely difficult to create the necessary theoretical and political space in the Centre in which to work on the project.

I want to hold to the notion, implicit in both these examples, that movements provoke theoretical moments. And historical conjunctures insist on theories: they are real moments in the evolution of theory. But here I have

4. *Women Take Issue: Aspects of Women's Subordination*, edited by the Women's Studies Group, Centre for Contemporary Cultural Studies (1978).
5. *Policing the Crisis: Mugging, the State, and Law and Order*, edited by Stuart Hall et al. (1978).
6. *The Empire Strikes Back: Race and Racism in 70s Britain*, edited by the Centre for Contemporary Cultural Studies (1982), an important early text in postcolonial theory and criticism.
7. British/Caribbean cultural theorist and critic (b. 1955).

to stop and retrace my steps. Because I think you could hear, once again, in what I'm saying a kind of invocation of a simple-minded anti-theoretical populism, which does not respect and acknowledge the crucial importance, at each point in the moves I'm trying to renarrativize, of what I would call the necessary delay or detour through theory. I want to talk about that "necessary detour" for a moment. What decentered and dislocated the settled path of the Centre for Contemporary Cultural Studies certainly, and British cultural studies to some extent in general, is what is sometimes called "the linguistic turn": the discovery of discursivity, of textuality. There are casualties in the Centre around those names as well. They were wrestled with, in exactly the same way I've tried to describe earlier. But the gains which were made through an engagement with them are crucially important in understanding how theory came to be advanced in that work. And yet, in my view, such theoretical "gains" can never be a self-sufficient moment.

Again, there is no space here to do more than begin to list the theoretical advances which were made by the encounters with structuralist, semiotic, and poststructuralist work: the crucial importance of language and of the linguistic metaphor to *any* study of culture; the expansion of the notion of text and textuality, both as a source of meaning, and as that which escapes and postpones meaning; the recognition of the heterogeneity, of the multiplicity of meanings, of the struggle to close arbitrarily the infinite semiosis beyond meaning; the acknowledgment of textuality and cultural power, of representation itself, as a site of power and regulation; of the symbolic as a source of identity. These are enormous theoretical advances, though of course, it had always attended to questions of language (Raymond Williams's work, long before the semiotic revolution, is central there). Nevertheless, the refiguring of theory, made as a result of having to think questions of culture through the metaphors of language and textuality, represents a point beyond which cultural studies must now always necessarily locate itself. The metaphor of the discursive, of textuality, instantiates a necessary delay, a displacement, which I think is *always* implied in the concept of culture. If you work on culture, or if you've tried to work on some other really important things and you find yourself driven back to culture, if culture happens to be what seizes hold of your soul, you have to recognize that you will always be working in an area of displacement. There's always something decentered about the medium of culture, about language, textuality, and signification, which always escapes and evades the attempt to link it, directly and immediately, with other structures. And yet, at the same time, the shadow, the imprint, the trace, of those other formations, of the intertextuality of texts in their institutional positions, of texts as sources of power, of textuality as a site of representation and resistance, all of those questions can never be erased from cultural studies.

The question is what happens when a field, which I've been trying to describe in a very punctuated, dispersed, and interrupted way, as constantly changing directions, and which is defined as a political project, tries to develop itself as some kind of coherent theoretical intervention? Or, to put the same question in reverse, what happens when an academic and theoretical enterprise tries to engage in pedagogies which enlist the active engagement of individuals and groups, tries to make a difference in the institutional world in which it is located? These are extremely difficult issues to resolve, because what is asked of us is to say "yes" and "no" at one and the same time. It asks us to assume that culture will always work through its textualities—and at the same time that textuality is never enough. But never enough of what? Never enough for what? That is an extremely difficult question to answer because, philosophically, it has always been impossible in the theoretical field of cultural studies—whether it is conceived either in terms of texts and contexts, of intertextuality, or of the historical formations in which cultural practices are lodged—to get anything like an adequate theoretical account of culture's relations and its effects. Nevertheless I want to insist that until and unless cultural studies learns to live with this tension, a tension that all textual practices must assume—a tension which Said describes as the study of the text in its affiliations with "institutions, offices, agencies, classes, academies, corporations, groups, ideologically defined parties and professions, nations, races, and genders"[8]—it will have renounced its "worldly" vocation. That is to say, unless and until one respects the necessary displacement of culture, and yet is always irritated by its failure to reconcile itself with other questions that matter, with other questions that cannot and can never be fully covered by critical textuality in its elaborations, cultural studies as a project, an intervention, remains incomplete. If you lose hold of the tension, you can do extremely fine intellectual work, but you will have lost intellectual practice as a politics. I offer this to you, not because that's what cultural studies ought to be, or because that's what the Centre managed to do well, but simply because I think that, overall, is what defines cultural studies as a project. Both in the British and the American context, cultural studies has drawn the attention itself, not just because of its sometimes dazzling internal theoretical development, but because it holds theoretical and political questions in an ever irresolvable but permanent tension. It constantly allows the one to irritate, bother, and disturb the other, without insisting on some final theoretical closure.

I've been talking very much in terms of a previous history. But I have been reminded of this tension very forcefully in the discussions on AIDS. AIDS is one of the questions which urgently brings before us our marginality as critical intellectuals in making real effects in the world. And yet it has often been represented for us in contradictory ways. Against the urgency of people dying in the streets, what in God's name is the point of cultural studies? What is the point of the study of representations, if there is no response to the question of what you say to someone who wants to know if they should take a drug and if that means they'll die two days later or a few months earlier? At that point, I think anybody who is into cultural studies seriously as an intellectual practice, must feel, on their pulse, its ephemerality, its insubstantiality, how little it registers, how little we've been able to change anything or get anybody to do anything. If you don't feel that as one tension in the work that you are doing, theory has let you off the hook. On the other hand, in the end, I don't agree with the way in which this dilemma is often posed for us, for it is indeed a more complex and displaced question than just people dying out there. The question of AIDS is an extremely important terrain of struggle and contestation. In addition to the people we know who are dying, or have died, or will, there are the many people dying who are

8. Said, *The World, the Text, and the Critic*, chap. 1.

never spoken of. How could we say that the question of AIDS is not also a question of who gets represented and who does not? AIDS is the site at which the advance of sexual politics is being rolled back. It's a site at which not only people will die, but desire and pleasure will also die if certain metaphors do not survive, or survive in the wrong way. Unless we operate in this tension, we don't know what cultural studies can do, can't, can never do; but also, what it has to do, what it alone has a privileged capacity to do. It has to analyze certain things about the constitutive and political nature of representation itself, about its complexities, about the effects of language, about textuality as a site of life and death. Those are the things cultural studies can address.

I've used that example, not because it's a perfect example, but because it's a specific example, because it has a concrete meaning, because it challenges us in its complexity, and in so doing has things to teach us about the future of serious theoretical work. It preserves the essential nature of intellectual work and critical reflection, the irreducibility of the insights which theory can bring to political practice, insights which cannot be arrived at in any other way. And at the same time, it rivets us to the necessary modesty of theory, the necessary modesty of cultural studies as an intellectual project.

I want to end in two ways. First I want to address the problem of the institutionalization of these two constructions: British cultural studies and American cultural studies. And then, drawing on the metaphors about theoretical work which I tried to launch (not I hope by claiming authority or authenticity but in what inevitably has to be a polemical, positional, political way), to say something about how the field of cultural studies has to be defined.

I don't know what to say about American cultural studies. I am completely dumfounded by it. I think of the struggles to get cultural studies into the institution in the British context, to squeeze three or four jobs for anybody under some heavy disguise, compared with the rapid institutionalization which is going on in the U.S. The comparison is not only valid for cultural studies. If you think of the important work which has been done in feminist history or theory in Britain and ask how many of those women have ever had full-time academic jobs in their lives or are likely to, you get a sense of what marginality is really about. So the enormous explosion of cultural studies in the U.S., its rapid professionalization and institutionalization, is not a moment which any of us who tried to set up a marginalized Centre in a university like Birmingham could, in any simple way, regret. And yet I have to say, in the strongest sense, that it reminds me of the ways in which, in Britain, we are always aware of institutionalization as a moment of profound danger. Now, I've been saying that dangers are not places you run away from but places that you go towards. So I simply want you to know that my own feeling is that the explosion of cultural studies along with other forms of critical theory in the academy represents a moment of extraordinarily profound danger. Why? Well, it would be excessively vulgar to talk about such things as how many jobs there are, how much money there is around, and how much pressure that puts on people to do what they think of as critical political work and intellectual work of a critical kind while also looking over their shoulders at the promotions stakes and the publication stakes, and so on. Let me instead return to the point that I made before: my astonishment at what I called the theoretical fluency of cultural studies in the United States.

Now, the question of theoretical fluency is a difficult and provoking metaphor, and I want only to say one word about it. Some time ago, looking at what one can only call the deconstructive deluge (as opposed to deconstructive turn) which had overtaken American literary studies, in its formalist mode, I tried to distinguish the extremely important theoretical and intellectual work which it had made possible in cultural studies from a mere repetition, a sort of mimicry or deconstructive ventriloquism which sometimes passes as a serious intellectual exercise.[9] My fear at that moment was that if cultural studies gained an equivalent institutionalization in the American context, it would, in rather the same way, formalize out of existence the critical questions of power, history, and politics. Paradoxically, what I mean by theoretical fluency is exactly the reverse. There is no moment now, in American cultural studies, where we are *not* able, extensively and without end, to theorize power—politics, race, class, and gender, subjugation, domination, exclusion, marginality, Otherness, etc. There is hardly anything in cultural studies which isn't so theorized. And yet, there is the nagging doubt that this overwhelming textualization of cultural studies' own discourses somehow constitutes power and politics as exclusively matters of language and textuality itself. Now, this is not to say that I don't think that questions of power and the political have to be and are always lodged within representations, that they are always discursive questions. Nevertheless, there are ways of constituting power as an easy floating signifier which just leaves the crude exercise and connections of power and culture altogether emptied of any signification. That is what I take to be the moment of danger in the institutionalization of cultural studies in this highly rarified and enormously elaborated and well-funded professional world of American academic life. It has nothing whatever to do with cultural studies making itself more like British cultural studies, which is, I think, an entirely false and empty cause to try to propound. I have specifically tried not to speak of the past in an attempt to police the present and the future. But I do want to extract, finally, from the narrative I have constructed of the past some guidelines for my own work and perhaps for some of yours.

I come back to the deadly seriousness of intellectual work. It is a deadly serious matter. I come back to the critical distinction between intellectual work and academic work: they overlap, they abut with one another, they feed off one another, the one provides you with the means to do the other. But they are not the same thing. I come back to the difficulty of instituting a genuine cultural and critical practice, which is intended to produce some kind of organic intellectual political work, which does not try to inscribe itself in the overarching metanarrative of achieved knowledges, within the institutions. I come back to theory and politics, the politics of theory. Not theory as the will to truth, but theory as a set of contested, localized, conjunctural knowledges, which have to be debated in a dialogical way. But also

9. See Stuart Hall, "In Defence of Theory," in *People's History and Socialist Theory*, edited by Ralph Samuels (1981)

as a practice which always thinks about its intervention in a world in which it would make some difference, in which it would have some effect. Finally, a practice which understands the need for intellectual modesty. I do think there is all the difference in the world between understanding the politics of intellectual work and substituting intellectual work for politics.

1990 1992

BARBARA HERRNSTEIN SMITH
b. 1932

In writings that have a direct impact on debates about the literary canon, Barbara Herrnstein Smith examines the processes through which artistic value is conferred. Smith's work diverges from that of many academics whose goal is to "open up" the canon. Not focused on the marginalized voices of stigmatized groups, Smith instead explores the general logic of categories such as "aesthetic," "value," "taste," and "masterpiece." Like PIERRE BOURDIEU, she concerns herself with philosophical aesthetics (what she calls "aesthetic axiology"), a set of themes she traces back to DAVID HUME and IMMANUEL KANT. Against the Kantian dictum that art should be disinterested, Smith firmly links art to the purposes that shape our relation to it, while insisting that all aesthetic evaluations hinge on complex, unpredictable, and "contingent" social processes.

Originally from New York City, Smith received her degrees from Brandeis University, with a Ph.D. in English literature in 1965. She began as a chemistry major and an interest in science, along with a refusal to accept any firm distinction between science and the arts, informs all her work. She has taught at Bennington College, the University of Pennsylvania, and Duke University, and she served in 1988 as president of the Modern Language Association, the leading scholarly organization in North America for professors of languages and literature.

Philosophical aesthetics aims to identify the "essential" or "intrinsic" properties that make an object "art." In establishing the universally binding rules that determine whether something is art or not, traditional aesthetics has stressed properties inhering in the object itself—properties distinct from "exchange value" (worth in economic transactions) and "use value" (worth for practical and mundane needs). By definition, the art object transcends commerce and the everyday. Art is "disinterested," appreciated "for its own sake" (not for any other good or advantage it might gain the artist or audience); it appeals to higher mental faculties in elevating form over content. In the repeated attempts to differentiate representations of the nude in painting, sculpture, and art photography from those held to be pornographic, we can see these principles applied. A work is art, and not pornography, we are told, when its focus is on form instead of content, and when its aim is disinterested, meaning that the artist and spectator do not intend or seek titillation.

Smith deploys a number of arguments against this traditional aestheticist position. First and foremost, she insists that no set of universally binding principles can or will be found, that everything is contingent. That is, all definitions of art and all evaluations of specific "artworks" depend on a complex set of changing variables, whose interactions cannot be known in advance and will constantly change. The very attempt to designate stable principles must be understood as a reaction against, a denial of, and attempted solution to the permanent condition of unfixity. Furthermore, the enunciation of essentialist definitions of art obscures the dynamic processes through which definitions and values are produced, transmitted, enforced, and contested. Here, like Bourdieu, Smith follows the logic of KARL MARX's observations on commodity fetishism. By locating value in the object itself (the artwork), we blind ourselves to the social processes and social relations that are the real creators of value.

Smith, however, is not a Marxist, believing that Marxists generally displace objectivity from things onto systems of social relations. She denies objectivity altogether, if by *objectivity* we mean sets of properties intrinsic to certain entities that allow us to predict their effects. Smith's is an interactionist model, derived from the pragmatism of William James (1842–1910) and John Dewey (1859–1952), that sees entities and values as constituted by their dynamic involvement with other entities (notably but not exclusively human agents). The results of such interactions are never predictable in advance, and no party involved is so dominant as to be able to dictate the results. (This neopragmatist line is also taken by, among other contemporary theorists, Richard Rorty, STANLEY FISH, and STEVEN KNAPP AND WALTER BENN MICHAELS.) Of course, any analysis must take into account the relative power wielded by the different parties to the specific interaction. But power differentials, like everything else, are contingent and in flux. Dominance today does not guarantee dominance tomorrow, though we may expect that today's dominant player will act in ways calculated to retain dominance. Hence Smith's interest in institutions, which might be defined as organizations of cultural power through rules, procedures, and exclusionary mechanisms meant to safeguard that power.

To clarify how this neopragmatist theoretical framework translates into the evaluation of a literary work, let's consider a decision about whether to teach *Waiting for Godot* in a sophomore drama class. The main thing to note is that the choice is "situated": it occurs in an institutional context. The instructor takes into account the nature of the audience, the goals of the course, general institutional ideals and guidelines about education, and his or her own desires to read and teach the play again (or for the first time). The list could go on; but even in brief it highlights that the instructor's decision does not rest absolutely on whether Beckett's play is good or not. Good for what? Good as a text in a specific educational setting? Good because it illustrates certain themes or techniques the teacher wants to emphasize? Good because various secondary materials are readily available to students? Good because knowledge of works by Nobel Prize winners is part of being well-educated? Good because the instructor studied Beckett during his or her own college years and hence can readily draw on models of how to go about teaching this play?

In short, Smith insists that judgments of aesthetic value are always made in relation to the purposes we are pursuing. "To exist is to evaluate," she states, because we are always embedded in situations in which we must choose how to respond, what to do, while taking into account both external circumstances and internal goals. Such a viewpoint might seem obvious to the point of being trivial if it were not also clear that the aesthetic tradition has long been dedicated to denying it. Kant and other aesthetic theorists have worked hard to separate art from purposes; they have tried to judge the artwork's goodness without considering any uses to which it might contribute.

In denying that such purposelessness is possible, Smith draws on two somewhat related claims. First, she argues that attempts to characterize the distinctive quality of the aesthetic are circular: they always begin by assuming some quality or experience that exists outside of purposes. In fact, she argues, if purposes are removed, there is nothing left. The aesthetic turns out to be vacuous, an "I know not what it is" that is called, in reverent tones, "art." Second, she insists that the aesthetic as a distinct category cannot be maintained. Every effect that traditional aesthetics attributes to art objects can be plausibly attributed to other kinds of objects or experiences that the tradition would not deem aesthetic. As a result, Smith is emphatically "nominalistic" when it comes to art: something is art because some community agrees to call it art. Nothing in the object itself guarantees that naming, which can and will be contested. Attempts at enforcement are rampant precisely because such namings are so subject to flux (hence always insecure) and, crucially, because the term *art* carries so much value within our tradition. The very battles over art attest to its social values.

In focusing on value—both the inevitability of evaluation in relation to purposes (or interests) and the specific values (economic, educational, prestige, and other) enjoyed by art in our culture—Smith questions the separation of academic literary criticism from evaluation. During the 1950s, both the New Critics and NORTHROP FRYE believed that "objective," scholarly work should avoid entanglement in the messy business of judging whether the text being studied is good or not; the critic should simply interpret or explain the literary text. This effort to secure the rigorous, even quasi-scientific, character of criticism by detaching it from evaluation was also made in some structuralist and early poststructuralist theory. But in insisting that evaluation is unavoidable, Smith does not bestow on critics some special authority to make aesthetic judgments. All readers evaluate, and all evaluations are tied to the reader's interests and purposes.

Smith's emphasis on interest is supplemented by her reliance on evolutionary models and her interest in psychology. In the long run we'll all be dead, the economist John Maynard Keynes (1883–1946) famously said. But it was the Roman philosopher Seneca who told us that art is long even if life is brief. In considering why some works of art endure over the long run, Smith moves from focusing on the interested actions of individual human agents to stressing the accumulation of social and cultural power by the works themselves. The key moment comes when rather than being chosen (to be read, to be studied, to be taught) by individuals seeking to fulfill their own purposes, the literary text acts "to *shape and create* the culture in which its value is produced and transmitted and, for that very reason, to perpetuate the conditions of its own flourishing." In other words, certain texts—by virtue of their repeated citation, their inclusion in the standard curriculum, their constantly reinforced cultural authority—constitute the very foundational meanings and understandings that orient individuals in this world. Hence when readers wish to reinforce their worldview, their ideology, they return to these works, which embody the tradition because they largely created it. To question the canonical status of such texts, to lessen the likelihood of their being read, seems more threatening if we understand their relation to the tradition in this foundational, creative way. No wonder the battles on campuses and in the media over changes in the curriculum have been so heated.

Smith's psychological interests shed light on all that heat, and her work since *Contingencies of Value* (1988) has taken the sources and strategies of intellectual controversies as a major focus. In our selection, which is taken from *Contingencies of Value*, she points out that "temperament" and "moods" influence our evaluations, while also noting the persistent "asymmetry" that describes one's own "true" beliefs as reasonable and "the Other's" "false" beliefs as deluded. Smith's later work considers the dynamics of belief formation and how we argue with ourselves as well as with others. Because no person's beliefs are ever completely consistent or completely stable, our encounters with other viewpoints are both terrifying and potentially transformative. In thinking through the variety of ways in which we respond to and engage with others, Smith's work connects back to the fundamental concerns of those critics and teachers who have opened up the classroom to new voices.

BIBLIOGRAPHY

Smith's books are *Poetic Closure* (1969), *On the Margins of Discourse: The Relation of Literature to Language* (1978), *Contingencies of Value: Alternative Perspectives for Critical Theory* (1988), and *Belief and Resistance: Dynamics of Contemporary Intellectual Controversy* (1997). She has prepared an edition of *Shakespeare's Sonnets* (1969) and has co-edited two collections of essays: with Darryl J. Gless, *The Politics of Liberal Education* (1992), and, with Arkady Plotnitsky, *Mathematics, Science, and Postclassical Theory* (1995).

An exchange between Smith and Martin Mueller titled "Endurance and Contingency," *Salmagundi*, nos. 88–89 (1990), is the best place to start for responses to *Contingencies of Value*. Steven Connor's *Theory and Cultural Value* (1992) offers an extended and illuminating discussion of Smith, focusing on the common complaints against her "relativism" and the less common complaint that her "third-person" account fails to describe value for the agent who is making a decision and whose values thus serve as motives or rules. In *Cultural Capital: The Problem of Literary Canon Formation* (1993), John Guillory strongly criticizes Smith for failing to see that value, far from being contingent, is the overdetermined product of quite specific—and specifiable—social forces.

From Contingencies of Value

Chapter 3. Contingencies of Value

CONTINGENCY AND INTERDEPENDENCE

All value is radically contingent, being neither a fixed attribute, an inherent quality, or an objective property of things but, rather, an effect of multiple, continuously changing, and continuously interacting variables or, to put this another way, the product of the dynamics, of a system, specifically an *economic* system. It is readily granted, of course, that it is in relation to such a system that commodities such as gold, bread, and paperback editions of *Moby-Dick*[1] acquire the value indicated by their market prices. It is traditional, however, both in economic and aesthetic theory as well as in informal discourse, to distinguish sharply between the value of an entity in that sense (that is, its *exchange value*) and some other type of value that may be referred to as its *utility* or *use value* or, especially with respect to so-called nonutilitarian objects such as artworks or works of literature, as its *intrinsic value*. Thus, it might be said that whereas the fluctuating price of a particular paperback edition of *Moby-Dick* is a function of such variables as supply and demand, production and distribution costs, the publisher's calculation of corporate profits, and so forth, these factors do not affect the value of *Moby-Dick* as experienced by an individual reader or its intrinsic value "as a work of literature." These distinctions, however, are not as clear-cut as they may appear.

Like its price in the marketplace, the value of an entity to an individual subject is *also* the product of the dynamics of an economic system: specifically, the personal economy constituted by the subject's needs, interests, and resources—biological, psychological, material, experiential, and so forth. Like any other economy, moreover, this too is a continuously fluctuating or shifting system, for our individual needs, interests, and resources are themselves functions of our continuously changing states in relation to an environment that may be relatively stable but is never absolutely fixed. The two kinds of economic system described here are, it should be noted, not only analogous but also interactive and interdependent, for part of our environment *is* the market economy and, conversely, the market economy is composed, in part, of the diverse personal economies of individual producers, distributors, consumers, and so forth. At the same time, it must be empha-

1. Herman Melville's 1851 work is often regarded as the greatest American novel of the 19th century.

sized that any particular subject's "self"—or that in behalf of which he or she may be said to act with "self-interest"—is also variable, being multiply and differently configurable in terms of different roles, relationships, and, in effect, identities (citizen, parent, woman, property owner, teacher, terrestrial organism, mortal being, etc.), in relation to which different needs and interests acquire priority (and, as may happen, come into conflict) under different conditions.

The traditional discourse of value—including a number of terms I have used here, such as "subject," "object," "needs," "interests," and indeed "value" itself—reflects an arbitrary arresting, segmentation, and hypostasization[2] of the continuous process of our interactions with our environments or what could also be described as the continuous interplay among multiply configurable systems. While it would be difficult to devise (and perhaps impossible to sustain) a truly Heraclitean discourse[3] that did *not* reflect such conceptual operations, we may nevertheless recognize that, insofar as such terms project images of discrete acts, agents and entities, fixed attributes, unidirectional forces, and simple causal and temporal relationships, they obscure the dynamics of value and reinforce dubious concepts of noncontingency: that is, concepts such as "intrinsic," "objective," "absolute," "universal," and "transcendent." It is necessary, therefore, to emphasize a number of other interactive relationships and forms of interdependence that are fragmented by our language and commonly ignored in critical theory and aesthetic axiology.[4]

First, as I have already suggested, a subject's experience of an entity is always a function of his or her personal economy: that is, the specific "existence" of an object or event, its integrity, coherence, and boundaries, the category of entities to which it "belongs," and its specific "features," "qualities," or "properties" are all the variable products of the subject's engagement with his or her environment under a particular set of conditions. Not only is an entity always experienced under more or less different conditions, but the various experiences do not yield a simple cumulative (corrected, improved, deeper, more thorough or complete) knowledge of the entity because they are not additive. Rather, each experience of an entity frames it in a different role and constitutes it as a different configuration, with different "properties" foregrounded and repressed. Moreover, the subject's experiences of an entity are not discrete or, strictly speaking, successive, because recollection and anticipation always overlay perception, and the units of what we call "experience" themselves vary and overlap.

Second, what we speak of as a subject's "needs," "interests," and "purposes" are not only always changing, but they are also not altogether independent of or prior to the entities that satisfy or implement them; that is, entities also produce the needs and interests they satisfy and evoke the purposes they implement. Moreover, because our purposes are continuously

2. The act of attributing real identity to a concept.
3. That is, a discourse offering a new word for each new experience and thing as time unfolded. The pre-Socratic Greek philosopher Heraclitus (active ca. 500 B.C.E.) viewed the world as a place of constant flux.
4. For related discussion of the linguistic and intellectual history of the term/concept "value," see Barbara Herrnstein Smith, "Value/Evaluation," in *Critical Terms for Literary Study*, ed. Frank Lentricchia and Thomas McLaughlin (Chicago, 1995) [Smith's note]. "Aesthetic axiology": traditional philosophies or definitions of art that hold the art object's value to be unchanging and inherent in the object itself.

transformed and redirected by the objects we produce in the very process of implementing them, and because of the complex interrelations among human needs, technological production, and cultural practices, there is a continuous process of mutual modification between our desires and our universe.[5]

Of particular significance for the value of "works of art" and "literature" is the interactive relation between the *classification* of an entity and the functions it is expected or desired to perform. In perceiving an object or artifact in terms of some category—*as*, for example, "a clock," "a dictionary," "a doorstop," "a curio"—we implicitly isolate and foreground certain of its possible functions and typically refer its value to the extent to which it performs those functions more or less effectively. But the relation between function and classification also operates in reverse: thus, under conditions that produce the "need" for a doorstopping object or an "interest" in Victorian artifacts, certain properties and possible functions of various objects in the neighborhood will be foregrounded and both the classification and value of those objects will follow accordingly. As we commonly put it, one will "realize" the value of the dictionary *as* a doorstop or "appreciate" the value of the clock *as* a curio.[6] (The mutually defining relations among classification, function, and value are nicely exhibited in the *OED*'s[7] definition of "curio" as "an object of art, piece of bric-a-brac, etc. valued as a curiosity," which is, of course, something like—and no less accurate than—defining *clock* as "an object valued as a clock.") It may be relevantly noted here that human beings have evolved as distinctly opportunistic creatures and that our survival, both as individuals and as a species, continues to be enhanced by our ability and inclination to reclassify objects and to "realize" and "appreciate" novel and alternate functions for them—which is also to "misuse" them and to fail to respect their presumed purposes and conventional generic classifications.

The various forms of interdependence emphasized here have considerable bearing on what may be recognized as the economics of literary and aesthetic value. The traditional—idealist, humanist, genteel—tendency to isolate or protect certain aspects of life and culture, among them works of art and literature, from consideration in economic terms has had the effect of mystifying the nature—or, more accurately, the dynamics—of their value. In view of the arbitrariness of the exclusion, it is not surprising that the languages of aesthetics and economics nevertheless tend to drift toward each other and that their segregation must be constantly patrolled.[8] (Thus, an

5. The interrelations among human "needs and wants," cultural practices, and economic production are examined in Marshall Sahlins, *Culture and Practical Reason* (Chicago, 1976); Mary Douglas, *The World of Goods* (New York, 1979); Jean Baudrillard, *For a Critique of the Political Economy of the Sign* (Paris, 1972), trans. Charles Levin (St. Louis, 1981); and Pierre Bourdieu, *Distinction: A Social Critique of the Judgement of Taste* (Paris, 1979), trans. Richard Nice (Cambridge, Mass., 1984). Although Baudrillard's critique of the concept of "use value" and, with it, of "sign value" is of considerable interest, his effort to develop "as a basis for the practical overthrow of political economy" (p. 122) a theory of a value "beyond value" (created out of what he calls "symbolic exchange") is less successful, partly because of its utopian anthropology and partly because the value in question does not escape economic accounting [Smith's note]. For the French sociologists BAUDRILLARD (b. 1929) and BOURDIEU (b. 1930), see above.

6. For an excellent analysis of the relation between classification and value, see Michael Thompson, *Rubbish Theory: The Creation and Destruction of Value* (Oxford, 1979), esp. pp. 13–56. The phenomenology and transformations of these classifications are also examined by Susan Stewart in *On Longing: Narratives of the Miniature, the Gigantic, the Souvenir, the Collection* (Baltimore, 1984) [Smith's note].

7. *Oxford English Dictionary*.

8. The magnetism or recurrent mutually metaphoric relation between economic and aesthetic—especially literary—discourse is documented and discussed by Marc Shell in *The Economy of Liter-*

aesthetician deplores a pun on "appreciation" appearing in an article on art investment and warns of the dangers of confusing "the uniqueness of a painting that gives it scarcity value . . . with its unique value as a work of art.")[9] To those for whom terms such as "utility," "effectiveness," and "function" suggest gross pragmatic instrumentality, crass material desires, and the satisfaction of animal needs, a concept such as use value will be seen as irrelevant to or clearly to be distinguished from aesthetic value. There is, however, no good reason to confine the domain of the utilitarian to objects that serve only immediate, specific, and unexalted ends or, for that matter, to assume that the value of artworks has altogether nothing to do with pragmatic instrumentality or animal needs.[1] The recurrent impulse and effort to define aesthetic value by contradistinction to all forms of utility or as the negation of all other nameable sources of interests or forms of value—hedonic, practical, sentimental, ornamental, historical, ideological, and so forth—is, in effect, to define it out of existence; for when all such utilities, interests, and other particular sources of value have been subtracted, nothing remains. Or, to put this in other terms: the "essential value" of an artwork consists of everything from which it is usually distinguished.

To be sure, various candidates have been proposed for a pure, nonutilitarian, interest-free, and, in effect, value-free source of aesthetic value, such as the eliciting of "intrinsically rewarding" intellectual, sensory, or perceptual activities, or Kant's "free play of the cognitive faculties."[2] The question remains, however, whether a strict accounting of any of these seemingly gratuitous activities would not bring us, sooner or later, to their interest, utility, and thus value in some—and perhaps many—senses for those who pursue them.

Three points may be made here. First, in speaking of certain objects and activities as "intrinsically rewarding" or done "for their own sake," what we usually mean is that the rewards involved (a) are not predictable or quantifiable; (b) are likely to be heterogeneous and ongoing rather than specific and terminal; and, in the case of an object (for example, a painting or a child), (c) are produced more or less uniquely by that object as distinct from any other of its kind. Of course, the provision of a variety of ongoing satisfactions is itself a contingent utility, and uniqueness is itself contingent (not everyone would derive irreplaceable satisfaction from that painting or that child). Second, although we may be individually motivated to engage in various ludic, aesthetic, or artistic activities only for the sake of the ongoing pleasure they provide (or other, less readily nameable or specifiable, ongoing satisfactions), our doing so may nevertheless yield a long-term profit in

ature (Baltimore, 1978), and by Kurt Heinzelman in *The Economics of the Imagination* (Amherst, Mass., 1980) [Smith's note].

9. Andrew Harrison, *Making and Thinking* (Indianapolis, 1978), p. 100 [Smith's note].

1. See George J. Stigler and Gary S. Becker, "De Gustibus non est disputandum," *American Economics Review* 67 (March 1977): 76–90, for an ingenious and influential attempt (at the opposite extreme, perhaps, of Baudrillard's) to demonstrate that differences and changes of behavior (including aesthetic behavior) that appear to be matters of "taste" and, as such, beyond explanation in economic terms can be accounted for (a) as functions of subtle forms of "price" and "income" and (b) on the usual economistic assumption that we always behave, all things considered, so as to maximize utility. As Stigler and Becker acknowledge, however, recent experimental studies of "choice behavior" in human (and other) subjects suggest that this latter assumption itself requires modification [Smith's note].

2. The *Critique of Judgment* (1790; see above), by IMMANUEL KANT (1724–1804), is a major source of modern conceptions of art, especially the notion that art is "disinterested"—in other words, "free" of all connection to mundane and material needs, desires, or purposes.

enhanced cognitive development, behavioral flexibility, or other kinds of advantage for survival, and our general tendency to *find* pleasure in such activities may, accordingly, be the product or by-product of our evolutionary development.[3] Third, the occasioning of "intrinsically rewarding" activities (or "experiences") obviously cannot be confined to "works of art" and therefore cannot, without circularity, be said to constitute the defining "aesthetic function" of the objects so labeled.[4] Indeed, since there are no functions performed by artworks that may be specified as generically unique and also no way to distinguish the "rewards" provided by art-related experiences or behavior from those provided by innumerable other kinds of experience and behavior, any distinctions drawn between "aesthetic" and "nonaesthetic" (or "extra-aesthetic") value must be regarded as fundamentally problematic.

It should be noted in passing that, except for allusions to other usages, "art" and "aesthetic" in the present study are equivalent, respectively, to "that which is *called* 'art' in the indicated discourse(s)" and "that which is *related* to that which is called 'art' (etc.)." Their use here is, in short, thoroughly nominalistic. Indeed, the point needs some emphasis in view of the fact that essentialist[5] and circular usages of these terms are key operators in contemporary aesthetic axiology.

"Aesthetic" has, of course, a number of currently viable senses in addition to the nominalistic one just noted. For example, following Baumgarten[6] and early nineteenth-century usage as influenced by Kant, it can also indicate a certain type of cognitive activity and/or sensory experience, specifically the type elicited by artworks either uniquely or among other things. At the same time, it can indicate a certain type of property of any object: specifically, the type of "purely formal" property which, according to Kant's analysis, uniquely elicits the sorts of experiences which, if all else is in order, constitute genuine judgments of taste. A combination or conflation of these three senses issues in the familiar recursive use of the term to name certain types of experience *and* certain types of objects *and* certain types of properties of objects, so that "aesthetic" comes to be roughly equivalent to "relating to certain cognitive/sensory experiences, these being the ones elicited by objects that have certain formal properties, these being the ones that identify objects as artworks, these being the kinds of works that elicit certain cognitive/sensory experiences, these being . . . ," and so forth around again.[7] The academic aesthetician trained to flourish in this sort of circle can spend his or her professional career describing (a) the nature of the "experiences" that are produced by those objects that are readily identifiable as works of art by virtue of their

3. See Robert Fagen, *Animal Play Behavior* (Oxford, 1981), pp. 248–358, for an extensive analysis of "intrinsically rewarding" physical activities and a suggestive account of the kinds of evolutionary mechanisms that could produce and sustain them [Smith's note].

4. See the related discussion of "cognitive play" in Barbara Herrnstein Smith, *On the Margins of Discourse* (Chicago, 1978), pp. 116–24 [Smith's note].

5. Relying on the philosophical position that some essential, shared feature unites a set of objects into a single category. "Nominalistic": relying on the philosophical position that universals exist only in language. Here "art" has meaning only insofar as a speech community uses the word to designate certain objects or experiences as art.

6. Alexander Baumgarten (1714–1762), German philosopher, often cited as the first philosopher of aesthetics.

7. Monroe Beardsley's "instrumentalist" theory of aesthetic value in *Aesthetics: Problems in the Philosophy of Criticism* (New York, 1958), pp. 524–76, and Mukařovský's otherwise quite subtle explorations of these questions in *Aesthetic Function, Norm and Value as Social Facts* (Prague, 1936), trans. Mark E. Suino (Ann Arbor, Mich., 1970), do not altogether escape the confinements and circularities of formalist conceptions of, respectively, "aesthetic experience" and "aesthetic function" [Smith's note]. BEARDSLEY (1915–1985), American New Critic. Jan Mukařovský (1891–1975), Czech structuralist.

having the properties that elicit such experiences, and (b) the nature of the "properties," unquestionably possessed by what are unquestionably works of art, that elicit the experiences that only artworks can elicit. (This is a parody, but not by much.)

In addition to the circularities thus generated, these academic exercises also perpetuate a thoroughly unproblematized conception of art, which is to say an essentialist definition of the *label* "art." The aesthetician who takes for granted the identity of those objects—"works of art"—that exemplify the possession of "aesthetic properties," or, in an only slightly more sophisticated move, who acknowledges the fact of historical and variable usage only to dismiss its force with an appeal to some "core" of examples "that would be acknowledged as works of art by everyone," thereby effaces both the historicity and cultural specificity of the term "art" and also the institutionally and otherwise contingent variability of the honorific labeling of cultural productions. Since the "core" examples cited will always be drawn from the Western academic canon (typically a handful of classic forms, works, and figures recurrently invoked in just these discourses: for example, sculpture, tragedy, symphony; Homer, Rembrandt, Mozart; *King Lear, Don Giovanni*, and, to indicate that there are modern masterpieces too, *Guernica*), and will also typically be attended by the tacit presumption of canonical audiences experiencing those works under canonical conditions plus the tacit exclusion of noncanonical (that is, non-Western, nonacademic, nonadult, or non-high-culture) *audiences* and noncanonical (for example, folk, tribal, or mass-mediated) *conditions of production and reception*, it is no surprise that "essentially aesthetic experiences" always conform to those typical of the Western or Western-educated consumer of high culture and that "essentially aesthetic properties" and "essential aesthetic value" always turn out to be located in all the old familiar places and masterpieces.

MATTERS OF TASTE

Suggestions of the historical or cultural contingency of aesthetic value are commonly countered by evidence of apparent noncontingent value: the endurance, for example, of certain classic canonical works (the invocation of Homer being a topos of the critical tradition) and, if not quite Pope's "gen'ral chorus of mankind,"[8] then at least the convergent sentiments of all people of education and discrimination. Certainly any theory of aesthetic value must be able to account for continuity, stability, and apparent consensus as well as for drift, shift, and diversity in matters of taste. The tendency throughout formal aesthetic axiology, however, has been to explain each in a quite different way: specifically, to explain the constancies of value and convergences of taste by the inherent qualities of certain objects and/or some set of presumed human universals, and to explain the variabilities of value and divergences of taste by historical accident, cultural distortion, and the defects and deficiencies of individual subjects.

This *asymmetrical* type of explanation recalls—and is, in intellectual history, of a piece with—the tendency in traditional philosophy of science to explain the credibility of so-called rational or true beliefs (for example, that

8. From *An Essay on Criticism* (1711; see above), line 188, by ALEXANDER POPE (1688–1744). The English poet championed the (Greek and Latin) classics; here he addresses the question of their endurance over time.

the earth revolves around the sun) by the fact that they *are* rational or true, and the credibility of other beliefs (for example, that the sun revolves around the earth) by special historical, institutional, social, psychological, or otherwise "external" factors. I appropriate here the characterization of this tendency by two of its critics, Barry Barnes and David Bloor, who offer in opposition to it a postulate for historians and sociologists of science that states, in part, that "the incidence of all beliefs without exception . . . must be accounted for by finding the specific, local causes of their credibility."[9]

The classic development of this account of *taste* is found in Hume's essay "Of the Standard of Taste," where the "catholic and universal beauty" is seen to be the result of

> the relation which nature has placed between the form and the sentiment . . . We shall be able to ascertain its influence . . . from the durable admiration which attends those works that have survived all the caprices of mode and fashion, all the mistakes of ignorance and envy.
>
> The same Homer who pleased at Athens two thousand years ago, is still admired at Paris and London. All the changes of climate, government, religion and language have not been able to obscure his glory . . .
>
> It appears then, that amidst all the variety and caprice of taste, there are certain general principles of approbation and blame, whose influence a careful eye may trace in all the operations of the mind. Some particular forms or qualities, from the original structure of the internal fabric, are calculated to please, and others to displease; *and if they fail of their effect in any particular instance, it is from some apparent defect or imperfection in the organ.*
>
> Many and frequent are the defects . . . which prevent or weaken the influence of those general principles.[1]

We shall return to this passage in the next chapter, where, together with Kant's *Critique of Judgment*, Hume's essay will be examined in connection with the general structure of axiological argumentation. For the present, we may observe that two linked notions are central to the account of tastes in traditional aesthetic axiology: first, the idea that certain objects or forms please us "naturally" by virtue of certain human universals; and second, the belief that a *norm* and thus "standard" of correct and defective taste can be derived accordingly. This set of notions obliged—or, rather, permitted—Hume, as it did and still does many others, to conclude that, in matters of taste, most people in the world are substandard or deviant. Perhaps, from a certain perspective, they are. But that still leaves us with a very peculiar sort of norm, and perhaps it can be seen otherwise.

Before turning to that alternative conceptualization, we may recall here I. A. Richards's remarkable explanation of how the very fact that someone is capable of taking pleasure in a sonnet by Ella Wheeler Wilcox[2] is evidence of that person's inability to survive in a complex environment and therefore

9. Barry Barnes and David Bloor, "Relativism, Rationalism, and the Sociology of Knowledge," in *Rationality and Relativism*, ed. Martin Hollis and Steven Lukes (Cambridge, Mass., 1982), pp. 25–26 [Smith's note].

1. *"Of the Standard of Taste" and Other Essays*, ed. John W. Lenz (Indianapolis, 1965), pp. 8–10, emphasis added [Smith's note]. DAVID HUME (1711–1776), Scottish philosopher and historian; for this 1757 essay, see above.

2. American writer (1850–1910) whose syndicated columns and poetry appeared in many daily newspapers. Richards (1893–1979), English literary critic and an important early figure in both New Criticism and reader-response theory.

of his or her biological unfitness (and note as well the general observations on popular culture and the mass media to which Richards is led):

> Those who have adequate impulses . . . are not appeased [by the sonnet's conclusion]. Only for those who make certain conventional, stereotyped maladjustments instead does the magic work.
>
> . . . At present bad literature, bad art, the cinema [*sic*], etc. are an influence of the first importance in fixing immature and actually inapplicable attitudes toward most things . . .
>
> . . . The strongest objection to, let us say, the sonnet we have quoted is that a person who enjoys it, through the very organization of his responses which enables him to enjoy it, is debarred from appreciating many things which, if he could appreciate them, he would prefer.[3]

We can readily recognize the familiar moves of axiologic logic in Richard's proposal, set forth here with egregious circularity, that the Other's enjoyment of his bad meat is possible only because of something suboptimal about his physiology, some problem in the organization of his responses that keeps him from "appreciating" certain "things"—really or objectively good meat, presumably, though Richards avoids saying so explicitly—that he would prefer if his responses were properly organized. Whether the debility is attributed to defective "organs" or defective "organization," to innate deficiencies or the "influence" of popular culture and the mass media, the privileging of the self through the pathologizing of the Other remains the key move and defining objective of axiology.

An alternative view of these matters is, however, possible. Specifically, the array of individual preferences that Hume and Richards regarded as reflecting the proper operation of healthy organs of taste and also the individual preferences that they interpreted as so many instances of personal pathology could *both* be seen as functions of interactions among the following variables:

a) various psychophysiological structures, mechanisms, and tendencies that are *relatively* uniform among human beings;

b) other psychophysiological structures, mechanisms, and tendencies that vary quite widely among individuals;

c) such more or less obvious particulars of personal identity and history as gender, age, the particular physical and social environment into which one was born, ethnic and national culture, formal and informal education, and so forth;

d) other more subtle, volatile, and, accordingly, less readily specifiable or measurable particulars of personal identity, including individual "temperament," "mood" on any given occasion, and current "interests"—each of which, it might be noted, is itself a product of the interactions of the other variables listed here; and, finally,

e) innumerable social, cultural, institutional, and contextual variables operating at every level of analysis, from broad through culturally specific ways of classifying objects to the most subtle and minute contextually specific circumstances of individual encounters with them.

The traditional axiological tendency, noted above, to provide two different kinds of explanation for human preferences—one for canonical tastes and

3. I. A. Richards, *Principles of Literary Criticism* (1924; London, 1960), pp. 202–5 [Smith's note].

the stability of preferences (convergence on an objective norm, the intrinsic value of certain objects) and another for deviant tastes and the mutability of preferences (defective organs, mists, mistakes, the "whirligig of fashion," and so forth)—would be replaced by a single account that explained all these phenomena symmetrically. That is, in accord with such an account, evaluative divergences and the exhibition of so-called bad taste would be seen as the product of the *same* dynamics—the playing out of the same *kinds* of variables, but with different specific values—that produce evaluative convergences and the exhibition of so-called good taste. These points can be elaborated further with regard to human preferences generally—that is, "tastes" for anything, from artworks to lifestyles and from types of food to types of explanation or even types of logic.

Within a particular community, the tastes and preferences of subjects will sometimes be conspicuously *divergent* or indeed idiosyncratic; that is, members of the community will tend to find more satisfaction of a certain kind (aesthetic, erotic, consummatory, or whatever) in quite *different* items from some array of comparable items and will also tend to select among them accordingly. This occurs when and to the extent that the satisfactions in question are themselves functions of types of needs, interests, and resources that vary individually along a relatively *wide* spectrum, are relatively *resistant*—if not altogether intractable—to cultural channeling, and are especially *responsive* to differences of circumstantial context. Conversely, their tastes and preferences will tend to be *convergent*—that is, they will tend to find satisfactions of certain kinds in the *same* items or types of items and to select them accordingly—to the extent that the satisfactions in question are functions of types of needs, interests, and resources that vary individually within a relatively *narrow* spectrum, are relatively *tractable* to cultural channeling, and remain fairly *stable* under a variety of conditions.

Insofar as satisfactions (again, "aesthetic" or any other: erotic, for example) with regard to some array of objects are functions of needs, interests, and resources of the *first* kind, individual preferences for those objects will appear "subjective," "eccentric," "stubborn," and "capricious." Insofar as they are functions of the *second*, preferences will seem so obvious, "natural," and "rational" as not to appear to be matters of taste at all. Indeed, it is precisely under these latter conditions that the value of particular objects will appear to be inherent, that distinctions or gradations of value among them will appear to reduce to differences in the "properties" or "qualities" of the objects themselves, and that explicit judgments of their value will appear to be—and for many, but not all, purposes *will* be—"objective." In short, here as elsewhere, *a co-incidence of contingencies among individual subjects who interact as members of some community will operate for them as noncontingency and be interpreted by them accordingly.*

Because we are speaking here not of two opposed sets of discrete determinants (or "constraints" or "forces") but of the possibility of widely differing specifications for a large number of complexly interacting *variables*, we may expect to find a continuous exhibition of every degree of divergence and convergence among the subjects in a particular community over the course of its history, depending in each instance on the extent of the disparity and uniformity of each of the relevant contingencies and on the strength of various social practices and cultural institutions that control the exhibition of extreme "deviance."[4] It may be noted in passing that the normative mechanisms within a community that suppress divergence—and thereby obscure as well as deny the contingency of value—will always have, as their counterpart, a *counter*mechanism that permits a recognition of that contingency and a more or less genial acknowledgment of the inevitability of divergence: hence the ineradicabilty, in spite of the efforts of establishment axiology, of what might be called folk-relativism: "*Chacun a son goût*," "*De gustibus* . . ."[5] "One man's meat is another's poison," and so forth.

As the preceding account suggests, the prevailing structure of tastes and preferences within some community (and consequent illusion of a consensus based on objective value) will always be implicitly threatened or directly challenged by the divergent tastes and preferences of some subjects within the community (for example, those not yet adequately acculturated, such as the young, and others with "uncultivated" tastes, such as provincials and social upstarts), as well as by most subjects who are outside it or, more significantly, on its periphery and who thus have occasion to interact with its members (for example, exotic visitors, immigrants, colonials, and members of various minority or marginalized groups). Consequently, institutions of evaluative authority will be called upon repeatedly to devise arguments and procedures that validate the community's established tastes and preferences, thereby warding off barbarism and the constant apparition of an imminent collapse of standards and also justifying the exercise of their own normative authority.

Both informally, as in the drawingrooms of men of cultivation and discrimination or in the classrooms of the literary academy, and formally, as in Hume's essay and throughout the central tradition of Western critical theory, that validation typically takes the twofold form of, first, *privileging absolutely*—that is, "standard"-izing, making a standard out of—not simply the preferences of the members of the group but, more significantly and also more powerfully because more invisibly, *the particular contingencies that govern their preferences*; and, second but simultaneously, *discounting or pathologizing* not merely other people's tastes but, again more significantly and effectively, *all other contingencies*.

Thus, it is assumed or maintained:

a) that the particular *functions* that the established members of the group expect and desire the class of objects in question (for example, "works of art" or "literature") to perform are their proper or intrinsic functions, all other expected, desired, or emergent functions being inappropriate, irrelevant, and extrinsic—abuses of the true nature of those objects or violations of their authorially intended or generically intrinsic purposes;

b) that the particular *conditions* (circumstantial, technological, institutional, and so forth) under which the members of the group typically interact with those objects are suitable, standard, or necessary-for-their-proper-appreciation, all other conditions being exceptional, peculiar, irregular, unsuitable, or substandard; and, most significantly of course,

4. See Morse Peckham, *Explanation and Power: The Control of Human Behavior* (New York, 1979), for an account of deviance (or what he calls "the delta effect") as the product of the relation between cultural practices and the *randomness* of behavior and, more generally, for a highly original discussion of the processes and institutions of cultural channeling [Smith's note].

5. That is, *De gustibus non est disputandum*: there is no disputing about taste (Latin). *Chacun a son goût*: to each his own taste (French).

c) that the particular *subjects* who constitute the established and authorized members of the group are of sound mind and body, duly trained and informed, and generally competent, all other subjects being defective, deficient, or deprived: suffering from crudeness of sensibility, diseases and distortions of perception, weaknesses of character, impoverishment of background-and-education, cultural or historical biases, ideological or personal prejudices and/or undeveloped, corrupted, or jaded tastes.

A few points deserve special notice here. The first is that communities (and drawingrooms) come in all sizes and that, insofar as the provincials, colonials, and other marginalized groups mentioned above—including the young—constitute social communities in themselves, they also tend to have prevailing structures of tastes and may be expected to control them in much the same ways as do more obviously "establishment" groups. ("Folk-relativism" is neither confined to the folk nor always exhibited by them.)

Second, with regard to (c) above, we may recall the familiar specifications of the "ideal" critic as one who, in addition to possessing various exemplary natural endowments and cultural competencies, has, through exacting feats of self-liberation, freed himself of all forms of particularity and individuality, all special interests (or, as in Kant, all interests whatsoever), and thus of all bias—which is to say, one who is "free" of everything in relation to which any experience or judgment of value occurs. In these respects, it may be added, the ideal critic of aesthetic axiology is the exact counterpart of the "ideal reader" of literary hermeneutics.[6]

Finally, we may note that the privileging of a particular set of *functions* for artworks or works of literature (cf. (a), above) is often itself justified on the ground that the performance of such functions serves some higher individual, social, or transcendent good, such as the psychic health of the reader, the brotherhood of mankind, the glorification of God, the project of human emancipation, or the survival of Western civilization. Any selection from among these alternate—and clearly to some extent mutually exclusive—higher goods however, would itself require justification in terms of some yet *higher* good, and there is no absolute stopping point for this theoretically infinite regress of judgments and justifications. This is not to say that certain functions of artworks do not serve higher (or at least more general, comprehensive, or longer-range) goods better than others. It is to say, however, that our selection among higher goods, like our selection among any array of goods, will always be contingent.

PROCESSES OF EVALUATION

It follows from the conception of value outlined above that evaluations are not discrete acts or episodes punctuating experience but indistinguishable from the very processes of acting and experiencing themselves. In other words, for a responsive creature, to exist is to evaluate. We are always, so to speak, calculating how things "figure" for us—always pricing them, so to speak, in relation to the total economy of our personal universe. Throughout our lives, we perform a continuous succession of what are, in effect, rapid-fire cost-benefit analyses, estimating the probable "worthwhileness" of alter-

6. The science of interpretation.

nate courses of action in relation to our always limited resources of time and energy, assessing, reassessing, and classifying entities with respect to their probable capacity to satisfy our current needs and desires, and to serve our emergent interests and long-range plans and purposes. We tend to become most conscious of our own evaluative behavior when the need to select among an array of alternate "goods" and/or to resolve an internal "contest of sentiments"[7] moves us to specifically verbal or other symbolic forms of accounting: thus we draw up our lists of pros and cons, lose sleep, and bore our friends by overtly rehearsing our options, estimating the risks and probable outcomes of various actions, and so forth. Most of these "calculations," however, are performed intuitively and inarticulately, and many of them are so recurrent that the habitual arithmetic becomes part of our personality and comprises the very style of our being and behavior, forming what we may call our principles or tastes—and what others may call our biases and prejudices.

I have been speaking up to this point of the evaluations we make for ourselves. We do not, however, move about in a raw universe. Not only are the objects we encounter always to some extent pre-interpreted and pre-classified for us by our particular cultures and languages; they are also pre-evaluated, bearing the marks and signs of their prior valuating and evaluations by our fellow creatures. Indeed, pre-classification is itself a form of pre-evaluation, for the labels or category names under which we encounter objects not only, as I suggested earlier, foreground certain of their possible functions, but also operate as signs—in effect, as culturally certified endorsements—of their more or less effective performance of those functions.

Like all other objects, works of art and literature bear the marks of their own evaluation history, signs of value that acquire their force by virtue of various social and cultural practices and, in this case, certain highly specialized and elaborated institutions. The labels "art" and "literature" are, of course, commonly signs of membership in distinctly honorific categories. The particular functions that may be endorsed by these labels, however, are, unlike those of "doorstops" and "clocks," neither narrowly confined nor readily specifiable but, on the contrary, exceptionally heterogeneous, mutable, and elusive. To the extent—always limited—that the relation between these labels and a particular set of expected and desired functions is stabilized within a community, it is largely through the normative activities of various institutions: most significantly, the literary and aesthetic academy which, among other things, develops pedagogic and other acculturative mechanisms directed at maintaining at least (and, commonly, at most) a *sub*population of the community whose members "appreciate the value" of works of art and literature "as such." That is, by providing them with "necessary backgrounds," teaching them "appropriate skills," "cultivating their interests," and generally "developing their tastes," the academy produces generation after generation of subjects for whom the objects and texts thus labeled do indeed perform the functions thus privileged, thereby ensuring the continuity of mutually defining canonical works, canonical functions, and canonical audiences.[8]

7. The 18th-century phrase here anticipates the discussion of David Hume's essay "Of the Standard of Taste" in Chapter 4 and is intended to suggest a structural/dynamic homology between individual and social conflicts of preference [Smith's note].

8. Pierre Macherey and Étienne Balibar analyze some aspects of this process in "Literature as an

Artistic Creation as a Paradigm of Evaluative Activity

It will be instructive at this point (and also for later analysis) to consider the very beginning of a work's valuational history—that is, its initial evaluation by the artist (here, the author)—for it is not only a prefiguration of all the subsequent acts of evaluation of which the work will become the subject but is also a model or paradigm of all evaluative activity generally. I refer here not merely to that ultimate gesture of authorial judgment that must exhibit itself negatively—that is, in the author's either letting the work stand or ripping it up—but to the thousand individual acts of approval and rejection, preference and assessment, trial and revision, that constitute the entire process of literary composition. The work we receive is not so much the achieved consummation of that process as its enforced abandonment: "abandonment" not because the author's techniques are inadequate to her goals, but because the goals themselves are inevitably multiple, mixed, mutually competing and thus mutually constraining, and also because they are inevitably unstable, changing their nature and relative potency and priority during the very course of composition. The completed work is thus always, in a sense, a temporary truce among contending forces, achieved at the point of exhaustion, that is, the literal depletion of the author's current resources or, given the most fundamental principle of the economics of existence, at the point when she simply has something else—more worthwhile—to do: when, in other words, the time and energy she would have to give to further tinkering, testing, and adjustment are no longer compensated for by an adequately rewarding sense of continuing interest in the process or increased satisfaction in the product.

It is for comparable reasons that we, as readers of the work, will later let our own experience of it stand: not because we have "fully appreciated" the work, not because we have exhausted all its possible sources of interest and hence of value, but because we, too, ultimately have something else—more worthwhile—to do. The reader's experience of the work is pre-figured—that is, both calculated and pre-enacted—by the author in other ways as well: for, in selecting this word, adjusting that turn of phrase, preferring this rhyme to that, she is all the while testing the local and global effectiveness of each decision by impersonating in advance her various presumptive audiences, who thereby themselves participate in shaping the work they will later read. Every literary work—and, more generally, artwork—is thus the product of a complex evaluative feedback loop that embraces not only the ever-shifting economy of the artist's own interest and resources as they evolve during and in reaction to the process of composition, but also all the shifting economies of her assumed and imagined audiences, including those who do not yet exist but those whose emergent interests, variable conditions of encounter, and rival sources of gratification she will attempt to predict—or will intuitively surmise—and to which, among other things, her own sense of the fittingness of each decision will be responsive.[9]

The inevitable evaluative and prefigurative aspects of literary composition, or of what is commonly referred to as "the creative process" in relation spe-

Ideological Form: Some Marxist Propositions," trans. James Kavanagh, *Praxis* 5 (1981): 43–58. See also Bourdieu *Distinction*, pp. 230–44, for a related analysis of what he refers to as "the quasi-miraculous correspondence" between "goods production and taste production" [Smith's note].

9. For a description of some of the specific constraints that shape both the process and its termination and, more generally, for a useful account of the ways in which artworks are "produced" by social networks, see Howard Becker, *Art Worlds* (Berkeley, 1982), pp. 198–209 [Smith's note].

cifically to aesthetic/cultural production, mark significant continuities not only between "creative" and "critical" activities but also between "artistic" and "scientific" production, and thereby make quite problematic the traditional effort to maintain clear distinctions among any of these. I shall return in Chapter 5 to the relation between the simultaneously critical and productive processes of artistic composition and some characteristic aspects of scientific activity.[1]

The description, above, of the evaluative process of the author and, analogously, the individual reader, may be extended even further. For it also describes all the other diverse forms of evaluation by which the work will be subsequently marked and its value reproduced and transmitted: that is, the innumerable implicit acts of evaluation performed by those who, as may happen, publish the work, purchase, preserve, display, quote, cite, translate, perform, allude to, and imitate it; the more explicit but causal judgments made, debated, and negotiated in informal contexts by readers and by all those others in whose personal economies the work, in some way, "figures"; and the highly specialized institutionalized forms of evaluation exhibited in the more or less professional activities of scholars, teachers, and academic or journalistic critics: not only their full-dress reviews and explicit rank-orderings, evaluations, and revaluations, but also such activities as the awarding of literary prizes, the commissioning and publishing of articles about certain works, the compiling of anthologies, the writing of introductions, the construction of department curricula, and the drawing up of class reading lists. All these forms of evaluation, whether overt or covert, verbal or inarticulate, and whether performed by the common reader, professional reviewer, big-time bookseller, or small-town librarian, have functions and effects that are significant in the production and maintenance or destruction of literary value, both reflecting and contributing to the various economies in relation to which a work acquires value. And each of the evaluative acts mentioned, like those of the author and the individual reader, represents a set of individual economic decisions, an adjudication among competing claims for limited resources of time, space, energy, attention—or, of course, money—and also, insofar as the evaluation is a socially responsive act or part of a social transaction, a set of surmises, assumptions, or predictions regarding the personal economies of other people.

Although it is important to recognize that the evaluation of texts is not confined to the formal critical judgments issued within the rooms of the literary academy or upon the pages of its associated publications, the activities of the academy certainly figure significantly in the production of literary value. For example, the repeated inclusion of a particular work in literary anthologies not only promotes the value of that work but goes some distance toward creating its value, as does also its repeated appearance on reading lists or its frequent citation or quotation by professors, scholars, and academic critics. For, as noted in Chapter 1, all these institutional acts have the effect, at the least, of drawing the work into the orbit of attention of a pop-

1. For a related discussion of the continuities among theoretical, critical, and aesthetic activities, see Barbara Herrnstein Smith, "Masters and Servants: Theory in the Literary Academy," in *Explorations in Music, the Arts, and Ideas: A Festschrift for Leonard B. Meyer*, ed. Eugene Narmour (New York, 1989) [Smith's note].

ulation of potential readers; and, by making it more accessible to the interests of those readers while at the same time shaping and supplying the very interests in relation to which they will experience the work, they make it more likely both that the work will be experienced at all and also that it will be experienced as valuable.

The converse side to this process is well known. Those who are in positions to edit anthologies and prepare reading lists are obviously those who occupy positions of some cultural power; and their acts of evaluation—represented in what they exclude as well as in what they include—constitute not merely recommendations of value, but, for the reasons just mentioned, also determinants of value. Moreover, since they will usually exclude not only what they take to be inferior literature but also what they take to be nonliterary, subliterary, or paraliterary, their selections not only imply certain "criteria" of literary value, which may in fact be made explicit, but, more significantly, they produce and maintain certain definitions of "literature" and, thereby, certain assumptions about the desired and expected functions of the texts so classified and about the interests of their appropriate audiences, all of which are usually not explicit and, for that reason, less likely to be questioned, challenged, or even noticed. Thus the privileging power of evaluative authority may be very great, even when it is manifested inarticulately.[2] The academic activities described here, however, are only a small part of the complex process of literary canonization.

THE DYNAMICS OF ENDURANCE

When we consider the cultural re-production of value on a larger time-scale, the model of evaluative dynamics outlined above suggests that both (a) the "survival" or "endurance" of a text and, it may be, (b) its achievement of high canonical status not only as a "work of literature" but as a "classic" are the product neither of the objectively (in the Marxist sense) conspiratorial force of establishment institutions nor of the continuous appreciation of the timeless virtues of a fixed object by succeeding generations of isolated readers but, rather, of a series of continuous interactions among a variably constituted object, emergent conditions, and mechanisms of cultural selection and transmission. These interactions are, in certain respects, analogous to those by virtue of which biological species evolve and survive and also analogous to those through which artistic choices evolve and are found "fit" or fitting by the individual artist. The operation of these cultural-historical dynamics may be briefly indicated here in quite general terms.

At a given time and under the contemporary conditions of available materials and technology or techniques, a particular object—let us say a verbal artifact or text—may perform certain desired/able[3] functions quite well for

2. For a well-documented illustration of the point, see Nina Baym "Melodramas of Beset Manhood: How Theories of American Fiction Exclude Women Authors," *American Quarterly* 31 (summer 1981): 125–39. In addition to anthologies, Baym mentions historical studies, psychological and sociological theories of literary production, and particular methods of literary interpretation [Smith's note].

3. Here and throughout this study the term "desired/able" indicates that the valued effect in question need not have been specifically desired (sought, wanted, imagined or intended) as such by any subject. In other words, its value for certain subjects may have emerged independent of any specific human intention or agency and, indeed, may have been altogether a product of the chances of history or, as we say, a matter of luck [Smith's note].

some set of subjects. It will do so by virtue of certain of its "properties" as they have been specifically constituted—framed, foregrounded, and configured—by those subjects under those conditions and in accord with their particular needs, interests, and resources—and also perhaps largely as prefigured by the artist who, as described earlier, in the very process of producing the work and continuously evaluating its fitness and adjusting it accordingly, will have multiply and variably constituted it.

Two related points need emphasis here. One is that the current value of a work—that is, its effectiveness in performing desired/able functions for some set of subjects—is by no means independent of *authorial* design, labor, and skill. To be sure, the artist does not have absolute control over that value, nor can its dimensions be simply equated with the dimensions of his artistic skill or genius. But the common anxiety that attention to the cultural determinants of aesthetic value makes the artist or artistic labor *irrelevant* is simply unfounded. The second point is that what may be spoken of as the "properties" of a work—its "structure," "features," "qualities," and of course its "meanings"—are not fixed, given, or inherent in the work "itself" but are at every point the variable products of particular *subjects'* interactions with it. Thus, it is never "the *same* Homer."[4] This is not to deny that some aspect, or perhaps many aspects, of a work may be constituted in similar ways by numerous different subjects, *among whom we may include the author*: to the extent that this duplication occurs, however, it will be because the subjects who do the constituting are themselves similar, not only or simply in being human creatures (and thereby, as it is commonly supposed, "sharing an underlying humanity" and so on) but in occupying a particular universe that may be, for them, in many respects recurrent or relatively continuous and stable, and/or in inheriting from one another, through mechanisms of cultural transmission, certain ways of interacting with texts and "works of literature."

To continue, however, the account of the cultural-historical dynamics of endurance. An object or artifact that performs certain desired/able functions particularly well at a given time for some community of subjects, being perhaps not only "fit" but exemplary—that is, "the best of its kind"—under those conditions, will have an immediate survival advantage; for, relative to (or in competition with) other comparable objects or artifacts available at that time, it will not only be better protected from physical deterioration but will also be more frequently used or widely exhibited and, if it is a text or verbal artifact, more frequently read or recited, copied or reprinted, translated, imitated, cited, commented upon, and so forth—in short, culturally reproduced—and thus will be more readily available to perform those or other functions for other subjects at a subsequent time.

Two possible trajectories ensue:

1. If, on the one hand, under the changing and emergent conditions of that subsequent time, the functions for which the text was earlier valued are no longer desired/able or if, in competition with comparable works (including, now, those newly produced with newly available materials and techniques), it no longer performs those original functions particularly well, it

4. For a careful neo-Marxist analysis of the continuous historical "rewriting" of the Homeric texts, see John Frow, *Marxism and Literary History* (Cambridge, Mass., 1986), pp. 172–82 [Smith's note].

will, accordingly, be less well maintained and less frequently cited, recited, etc., so that its visibility as well as interest will fade and it will survive, if at all, simply as a physical relic. It may, of course, be subsequently valued specifically *as* a relic (for its archeological or "historical" interest), in which case it *will* be performing desired/able functions and pursue the trajectory described below. It may also be subsequently "rediscovered" as an "unjustly neglected masterpiece," either when the functions it had originally performed are again desired/able or, what is more likely, when different of its properties and possible functions become foregrounded by a new set of subjects with emergent interests and purposes.

2. If, on the other hand, under changing conditions and in competition with newly produced and other re-produced works, it continues to perform *some* desired/able functions particularly well, even if not the same ones for which it was initially valued (and, accordingly, by virtue of *other* newly foregrounded or differently framed or configured properties—including, once again, emergent "meanings"), it will continue to be cited and recited, continue to be visible and available to succeeding generations of subjects, and thus continue to be culturally re-produced. A work that has in this way survived for some time can always move into a trajectory of extinction through the sudden emergence or gradual conjunction of unfavorable conditions of the kind described above. There are, however, a number of reasons why, once it has achieved canonical status, it will be more secure from that risk.

For one thing, when the value of a work is seen as unquestionable, those of its features that would, in a noncanonical work, be found alienating—for example, technically crude, philosophically naïve, or narrowly topical—will be glozed over or backgrounded. In particular, features that conflict intolerably with the interests and ideologies of subsequent subjects (and, in the West, with those generally benign "humanistic" values for which canonical works are commonly celebrated)—for example, incidents or sentiments of brutality, bigotry, and racial, sexual, or national chauvinism—will be repressed or rationalized, and there will be a tendency among humanistic scholars and academic critics to "save the text" by transferring the locus of its interest to more formal or structural features and/or by allegorizing its potentially alienating ideology to some more general ("universal") level where it becomes more tolerable and also more readily interpretable in terms of contemporary ideologies. Thus we make texts timeless by suppressing their temporality. (It may be added that to those scholars and critics for whom those features are not only palatable but for whom the value of the canonical works consists precisely in their "embodying" and "preserving" such "traditional values," the transfer of the locus of value to formal properties will be seen as a descent into formalism and "aestheticism," and the tendency to allegorize it too generally or to interpret it too readily in terms of "modern values" will be seen not as saving the text but as betraying it.)

Second, in addition to whatever various and perhaps continuously differing functions a work performs for succeeding generations of individual subjects, it will also begin to perform certain characteristic cultural functions by virtue of the very fact that it *has* endured—that is, the functions of a canonical work as such—and be valued and preserved accordingly: as a witness to lost innocence, former glory, and/or apparently persistent communal interests and "values" and thus a banner of communal identity; as a reservoir of images, archetypes, and topoi[5]—characters and episodes, passages and verbal tags—repeatedly invoked and recurrently applied to new situations and circumstances; and as a stylistic and generic exemplar that will energize the production of subsequent works and texts (upon which the latter will be modeled and by which, as a normative "touchstone,"[6] they will be measured). In these ways, the canonical work begins increasingly not merely to *survive within* but to *shape and create* the culture in which its value is produced and transmitted and, for that very reason, to perpetuate the conditions of its own flourishing. Nothing endures like endurance.

To the extent that we develop within and are formed by a culture that is itself constituted in part *by* canonical texts, it is not surprising that those texts seem, as Hans-Georg Gadamer puts it, to "speak" to us "directly" and even "specially": "The classical is what is preserved precisely because it signifies and interprets itself; [that is,] that which speaks in such a way that it is not a statement about what is past, as mere testimony to something that needs to be interpreted, but says something to the present as if it were said specially to us . . . This is just what the word 'classical' means, that the duration of the power of a work to speak directly is fundamentally unlimited."[7] It is hardly, however, as Gadamer implies here, because such texts are uniquely self-mediated or unmediated and hence not needful of interpretation but, rather, because they have already been so thoroughly mediated—evaluated as well as interpreted—*for* us by the very culture and cultural institutions through which they have been preserved and by which we ourselves have been formed.

What is commonly referred to as "the test of time" (Gadamer, for example, characterizes "the classical" as "a notable mode of 'being historical,' that historical process of preservation that through the constant proving of itself sets before us something that is true")[8] is not, as the figure implies, an impersonal and impartial mechanism; for the cultural institutions through which it operates (schools, libraries, theaters, museums, publishing and printing houses, editorial boards, prize-awarding commissions, state censors, and so forth) are, of course, all managed by *persons* (who, by definition, are those with cultural power and commonly other forms of power as well); and, since the texts that are selected and preserved by "time" will always tend to be those which "fit" (and, indeed, have often been *designed* to fit) *their* characteristic needs, interests, resources, and purposes, that testing mechanism has its own built-in partialities accumulated in and thus *intensified* by time. For example, the characteristic resources of the culturally dominant members of a community include access to specific training and the opportunity and occasion to develop not only competence in a large number of cultural codes but also a large number of diverse (or "cosmopolitan") interests. The works that are differentially reproduced, therefore, will tend to be those that gratify the exercise of such competencies and engage interests of that kind: specifically, works that are structurally complex and, in the technical sense, information-rich—and which, by virtue of those qualities, may be especially

5. Traditional or conventional themes or topics.
6. A term closely linked to MATTHEW ARNOLD, who argued in "The Study of Poetry" (1880) that poetry is best judged by testing it against "lines and expressions of the great masters," kept as a "touchstone" in one's mind.
7. *Truth and Method* (New York, 1982), pp. 257–58 [Smith's note]. Gadamer (b. 1900), German philosopher whose most influential work was on hermeneutics.
8. Ibid., p. 255 [Smith's note].

amendable to multiple re-configuration, more likely to enter into relation with the emergent interests of various subjects, and thus more readily adaptable to emergent conditions. Also, as is often remarked, since those with cultural power tend to be members of socially, economically, and politically established classes (or to serve them and identify their own interests with theirs), the texts that survive will tend to be those that appear to reflect and reinforce establishment ideologies. However much canonical works may be seen to "question" secular vanities such as wealth, social position, and political power, "remind" their readers of more elevated values and virtues, and oblige them to "confront" such hard truths and harsh realities as their own mortality and the hidden griefs of obscure people, they would not be found to please long and well if they were seen *radically* to undercut establishment interests or *effectively* to subvert the ideologies that support them. (Construing them to the latter ends, of course, is one of the characteristic ways in which those with anti-establishment interests participate in the cultural re-production of canonical texts and thus in their endurance as well.)

Two final points should be added here. First, it should be noted that "structural complexity" and "information-richness" are, of course, subject-relative as "qualities" and also experientially subject-variable. Since we differ individually in our tolerance for complexity in various sensory/perceptual modalities and also in our ability to process information in different codes, what is interestingly complex and engagingly information-rich to one subject may be intolerably chaotic to another and slickly academic to yet a third. Moreover, these tolerances and competences are themselves the complex and variable products of culturally specific conditions. For these reasons, and *pace* the more naïvely ambitious claims of "empirical aesthetics,"[9] such features cannot operate as "objective" measures of aesthetic value.

Second, it is clear that the needs, interests, and purposes of culturally and otherwise dominant members of a community do not exclusively or totally determine which works survive. The antiquity and longevity of domestic proverbs, popular tales, children's verbal games, and the entire phenomenon of what we call "folklore," which occurs through the same or corresponding mechanisms of cultural selection and re-production as those described above specifically for "texts," demonstrate that the "endurance" of a verbal artifact (if not its achievement of *academic* canonical status as a "work of literature"—many folkloric works do, however, perform all the functions described above as characteristic of canonical works *as such*) may be more or less independent of institutions controlled by those with political power. Moreover, the interests and purposes of the latter must always operate in interaction with non- or antiestablishment interests and purposes as well as with various other contingencies and "accidents of time" over which they have limited, if any, control, from the burning of libraries to political and social revolution, religious iconoclasms, and shifts of dominance among entire languages and cultures.

As the preceding discussion suggests, the value of a literary work is continuously produced and re-produced by the very acts of implicit and explicit

9. The scientific attempt to measure or analyze the features of art objects by assessing their impacts on audiences.

evaluation that are frequently invoked as "reflecting" its value and therefore as being evidence of it. In other words, what are commonly taken to be the *signs* of literary value are, in effect, its *springs*. The endurance of a classic canonical author such as Homer, then, owes not to the alleged transcultural or universal value of his works but, on the contrary, to the continuity of their circulation in a particular culture. Repeatedly cited and recited, translated, taught and imitated, and thoroughly enmeshed in the network of intertextuality that continuously *constitutes* the high culture of the orthodoxly educated population of the West (and the Western-educated population of the rest of the world), that highly variable entity we refer to as "Homer" recurrently enters our experience in relation to a large number and variety of our interests and thus can perform a large number of various functions for us and obviously has performed them for many of us over a good bit of the history of our culture. It is well to recall, however, that there are many people in the world who are not—or are not yet, or choose not to be—among the orthodoxly educated population of the West: people who do not encounter Western classics at all or who encounter them under cultural and institutional conditions very different from those of American and European college professors and their students. The fact that Homer, Dante, and Shakespeare do not figure significantly in the personal economies of these people, do not perform individual or social functions that gratify their interests, *do not have value for them*, might properly be taken as qualifying the claims of transcendent universal value made for such works. As we know, however, it is routinely taken instead as evidence or confirmation of the cultural deficiency—or, more piously, "deprivation"—of such people. The fact that other verbal artifacts (not necessarily "works of literature" or even "texts") and other objects and events (not necessarily "works of art" or even artifacts) have performed and do perform for them the various functions that Homer, Dante, and Shakespeare perform for us and, moreover, that the possibility of performing the totality of such functions is always distributed over the totality of texts, artifacts, objects, and events—a possibility continuously realized and thus a value continuously "appreciated"—commonly cannot be grasped or acknowledged by the custodians of the Western canon.

1988

FREDRIC JAMESON
b. 1934

Although it flourished during the 1930s, Marxist aesthetics and literary criticism all but vanished from critical discourse in the United States after World War II. The cold war consensus stigmatized everything associated with communism, and the dominant methods of the New Criticism practiced by CLEANTH BROOKS and others focused on internal features of works rather than external connections with society, politics, and history. Even when radical cultural criticism revived in the social tumult of the 1960s, its main roots were not in Marxism but in new social movements such as feminism, black power, and environmentalism. Against this current, Fredric Jameson almost single-handedly revived Marxist literary studies within the American academy, principally with *Marxism and Form* (1971), which recovered major figures in the Western Marxist tradition, and with his landmark *The Political Unconscious: Narrative as a Socially Symbolic Act* (1981), which outlined his methods for a Marxist literary criticism. An ambitious synthesis of contemporary structuralist theory and Marxism, *The Political Unconscious*, from which we take our first selection, argues that political and economic history form the subtexts and allegorical meanings of literary works. Jameson broadened his focus to examine contemporary culture, and "Postmodernism and Consumer Society" (1988), our second selection, encapsulates his widely influential views on postmodernism, in particular on the relation of art to present-day capitalist production.

Born in Cleveland, Ohio, Jameson was educated at Haverford College, receiving his B.A. in 1954, and at Yale University, where he earned a doctorate in French and comparative literature in 1959. He also spent a formative year in Germany on a Fulbright Fellowship at the Universities of Munich and Berlin (1956–57). After teaching at Harvard University from 1959 to 1967, Jameson moved to the newly created University of California at San Diego, where he encountered Herbert Marcuse, guru for many student radicals and a surviving figure from the Frankfurt School (of which THEODOR ADORNO was a central member). Thereafter Jameson held positions at Yale University (1976–83) and the University of California at Santa Cruz (1983–85), settling at Duke University in 1986 as distinguished professor of comparative literature and director of the graduate program in literature and of the Center for Critical Theory.

By the mid-1970s, Jameson and TERRY EAGLETON were being hailed as the most significant Marxist literary critics and theorists in the Anglophone world, but it was not until the publication of *The Political Unconscious* that the originality of Jameson's project became clear. Opening with the famous exhortation "Always historicize!" he sets out the methodological approach he calls "metacommentary," which provides a theoretically sophisticated answer to the perennial question of the relation of aesthetics to social history. In contrast to those practicing more conventional forms of historical criticism, Jameson not only situates cultural texts in relation to their immediate historical context but also approaches them from the vantage point of hermeneutics, exploring the interpretive strategies that shape how we understand individual works. Unlike other modern theories of interpretation, such as the reception theory of HANS ROBERT JAUSS, Jameson's stresses that its object is a Marxist analysis of ideology and that Marxism encompasses all other interpretive strategies, showing that their explanations of a text's meaning are only partial.

Jameson holds that a critic wishing to decipher the meaning of a text must proceed through a series of distinct phases, embodied in the text and uncovered through systematic decoding. He draws on a wide array of twentieth-century theoretical sources to do this, from NORTHROP FRYE's four levels of interpretation (which ultimately derive from the medieval interpretive schema of THOMAS AQUINAS), to JACQUES LACAN's theory of the unconscious, to LOUIS ALTHUSSER's account of ideology. Jameson sees Marxist criticism not as exclusionary or separatist but as comprehensive, assimilating a compendium of sources and thereby achieving greater "semantic richness." The critic should examine in turn the political history to which a text refers, social history (conceived in traditional Marxist terms as the history of class struggles), and the history of modes of production. These approaches do not displace but are embedded in each other, building to higher levels of generality and deeper layers of historical causation.

To interpret a text within the horizon of political history, Jameson, borrowing from KENNETH BURKE's theory of symbolic action, focuses on "the individual work . . . grasped essentially as a *symbolic act*." For instance, one can read Shakespeare's *Macbeth* (ca. 1606) as a presentation of the burning political issue of its historical moment, royal succession. Shakespeare's contemporaries would have recognized this both as the play's obvious theme (Macbeth as the murderous usurper; Malcolm as the legitimate but feckless heir) and as a matter of immediate political concern—the play was performed at court not long after James VI of Scotland had assumed the English throne as James I, a Stuart supplanting the Tudor dynasty. Details of plot, character, and thought are in this reading understood as allegorical signs referring to historical figures and to Renaissance doctrines about royal power and its legitimacy.

For the second phase of interpretation, the object of investigation is "the *ideologeme*, that is, the smallest intelligible unit of the essentially antagonistic collective discourses of social classes." To take another example from Shakespeare, in a number of the history plays, such as the two parts of *Henry IV* (ca. 1597, 1599), as well as in several of the tragedies, such as *Hamlet* (ca. 1600) and *King Lear* (ca. 1605), the dramatic struggle between the major characters stages the ideological conflict between older, medieval ideals of kingship and the state and the modernizing tendencies of an emergent absolutist power that advances the interests of the bourgeoisie against the prerogatives of powerful feudal landlords. This sociological interpretation does not cancel out the first; one can still recognize the political allegory in *Henry IV*, which justifies Tudor rule by showing the superiority of the modernizing Tudors (embodied in Prince Hal) over both the rebellious English barons and the effeminate French monarchy.

The outermost circle of interpretation, "the ideology of form," links the literary work with the mode of production (characterized, according to KARL MARX, as tribal hordes, Neolithic kinship societies, Oriental despotism, ancient slaveholding societies, feudalism, capitalism, and finally communism). This criticism subsumes prior levels, probing what Jameson calls "the symbolic messages transmitted to us by the coexistence of various sign systems which are themselves traces or anticipations of modes of production." Thus Hamlet's "problems" (famously elaborated by T. S. ELIOT) do not indicate Shakespeare's dramatic failure (as Eliot argued) but rather signify a historical tension between the feudal ideals embodied in Hamlet's father, ideals to which Hamlet owes one sort of allegiance, and the modern habits imbibed by the prince through his university education at Wittenberg. These latter include Hamlet's tendency toward obsessive individualistic reflection, which prevents his carrying out the revenge that his father decreed against the usurping Claudius. This conflict is visible in the play's dramatic form, which overlays a modern psychological drama onto its older source material governed by the conventions of revenge tragedy (a popular form in Shakespeare's day). The play stands, thematically and formally, on the cusp of a major historical transformation—the transition from feudalism to capitalism. Hamlet's fatal actions at the end do not resolve the play's ideological and formal contradictions because no resolution was imaginable in 1600; the triumph of capitalism over feudalism in Britain would not be achieved until near the end of the seventeenth century, with remnants of feudal ideologies persisting long after.

The imaginative limits imposed on an author or a text by its historical moment reveal the operation of history itself, which "sets inexorable limits to individual as well as collective praxis." And though its causes might not be immediately apparent, we can apprehend history in its effects, which are "inaccessible to us except in textual form." Here Jameson espouses a distinctly poststructuralist view, that—as articulated by PAUL DE MAN—"the bases for historical knowledge are not empirical facts but written texts, even if these texts masquerade in the guise of wars or revolutions"; however, he departs from de Man in stressing the text's ideological over its linguistic import.

In "Postmodernism and Consumer Society," which anticipates his magisterial study *Postmodernism, or, The Cultural Logic of Late Capitalism* (1991), Jameson expands his consideration of the ideology of form, moving beyond the literary canon to contemporary culture—including film, experimental poetry, popular fiction, art, and architecture. He identifies two causal conditions for postmodernism across the arts:

first, its products "emerge as specific reactions against the established forms of high modernism"; and second, it results from the "erosion of the older distinction between high culture and so-called mass or popular culture." These essentially aesthetic determinations, however, are not postmodernism's ultimate cause. In classically Marxist fashion, Jameson looks to the underlying economic formation: postmodernism "expresses the inner truth of that newly emergent social order of late capitalism," sometimes also called consumer, postindustrial, or multinational capitalism, which arose in the immediate aftermath of World War II and reached both its fulfillment and a moment of crisis during the 1960s. For Jameson, "postmodernism" names a historical period, not just a new style or aesthetic. As modernism was a result of the imperial stage of capitalism, so postmodernism is the distinctive "ideology of form" of the contemporary period of consumer capitalism.

Postmodern works exhibit a range of distinctive formal features, such as pastiche, simulation, and in architecture, what Jameson terms "hyperspace." Focusing on what he calls "the nostalgia mode," Jameson describes the peculiar dehistoricized depthlessness of certain postmodern works, such as the popular film *American Graffiti* (1973) and novels like E. L. Doctorow's *Ragtime* (1975). In a postmodern world, we "seem condemned to seek the historical past through our own pop images and stereotypes about the past, which itself remains forever out of reach." Jameson goes on to analyze one of the exemplary monuments of postmodern architecture, John Portman's Bonaventure Hotel (1977) in downtown Los Angeles. Showing how space is configured in disorienting new ways by Portman's structure, Jameson argues that postmodern architecture—emblematic of other postmodern arts—embodies an objectively new kind of bewildering hyperspace, which we lack the necessary perceptual and cognitive tools to understand. He concludes by returning to the contrast between high modernist and postmodern works, reemphasizing modernism's oppositional stance toward the dominant culture of the bourgeoisie. About postmodernism, Jameson is more tentative; he suggests that it may be more than the reflection or reproduction of consumer society or late capitalism, but he ultimately declines to answer the question he has posed about its critical potential.

Recognized as the leading contemporary Marxist critic in the United States as well as a major practitioner of poststructuralist theory, Jameson has drawn both a large following and a great deal of criticism. Some have charged that his writing is overly difficult, obscure, and inaccessible. Theoretically attuned critics have variously questioned his "totalizing" allegorical method of interpretation, his eclectic borrowing from diverse theories, his reductive scheme of historical periods leading to postmodernism, his disregard of feminism and gender dynamics, and his lack of concrete attention to ongoing political struggles. From the Marxist Left, Terry Eagleton questions the connection between theory and politics, pointedly asking of one of Jameson's readings in *The Political Unconscious*: "How is a Marxist-structuralist analysis of a minor novel of Balzac to help shake the foundations of capitalism?" Although Eagleton allows, quoting Althusser, that it contributes to the "class struggle at the level of theory," he concludes that the relation is unclear. Jameson himself answers in an interview that his intention is to make Marxism a central concern in intellectual circles, as well as to redefine it in light of contemporary thought. Though his work may not immediately translate to concrete political practices and policies, Jameson has been a tireless analyst of "the ideology of form" in literary and cultural works, and he is arguably the most influential proponent of Marxism in contemporary criticism.

BIBLIOGRAPHY

Largely focused on stylistics rather than Jean-Paul Sartre's Marxist politics, Jameson's first book, *Sartre: The Origins of a Style* (1961), a revision of his doctoral dissertation, offered scant indication of his subsequent work. The two major studies of the early

1970s, *Marxism and Form: Twentieth-Century Dialectical Theories of Literature* (1971) and *The Prison-House of Language: A Critical Account of Structuralism and Russian Formalism* (1972), respectively introduced the work of the Frankfurt School and other European Marxists and the work of the Russian formalists and early French structuralists to the English-speaking world before much of it was available in translation. After writing a short book on the English modernist Wyndham Lewis, *Fables of Aggression: Wyndham Lewis, the Modernist as Fascist* (1979), Jameson captured the attention of Anglophone intellectual circles with *The Political Unconscious: Narrative as a Socially Symbolic Act* (1981), which solidified his position as the leading representative of Marxist theory. It was followed by a two-volume collection of previously published pieces, *The Ideologies of Theory: Essays, 1971–1986* (1988), which includes his succinct "Metacommentary" (1971) and his programmatic reflections on historical method, "Marxism and Historicism" (1980). *Late Marxism: Adorno, or, the Persistence of the Dialectic* (1990) extends his survey of Marxist figures begun in *Marxism and Form*.

In the 1990s Jameson turned increasingly to film and popular culture. *Signatures of the Visible* (1990) collects writings on film, concluding with an important essay theorizing its development from the silent era onward. *Postmodernism, or, The Cultural Logic of Late Capitalism* (1991) has had wide influence in defining the postmodern era and its art. There followed a collection of essays on the capitalist world system as represented in contemporary cinema, *The Geopolitical Aesthetic: Cinema and Space in the World System* (1992). Jameson also published two books assembled from lectures: *The Seeds of Time* (Wellek Library Lectures, 1994), and *Theory of Culture: Lectures at Rikkyo* (1994). The useful collection *The Cultural Turn: Selected Writings on the Postmodern, 1983–98* (1998), which includes "Postmodernism and Consumer Society," records his developing views on postmodernism. *Brecht and Method* (1998) takes the German dramatist Bertolt Brecht (rather than Adorno) as an exemplary figure for reviving Marxism in the era of late capitalism. Jameson also edited an anthology with Masao Miyoshi, *The Cultures of Globalization* (1998). *The Jameson Reader*, edited by Michael Hardt and Kathi Weeks (2000), provides an excellent selection of work spanning Jameson's career.

Jameson's writings have drawn a substantial though uneven body of criticism. For an interesting early response from Kenneth Burke, see "Methological Repression and / or Strategies of Containment," *Critical Inquiry* 5 (1978). Perhaps the best early accounts are by Terry Eagleton, "The Idealism of American Criticism" (1981) and "Frederic Jameson: The Politics of Style" (1982), both collected in his *Against the Grain: Selected Essays* (1986). Two critical journals devoted special issues to *The Political Unconscious: Diacritics* 12 (1982), which includes essays by the historian Hayden White, Eagleton (cited above), and others, and an illuminating interview with Jameson; and *New Orleans Review* 11 (1984), which includes a response by Jean-François Lyotard, "The Unconscious, History, and Phrases: Notes on *The Political Unconscious*." In "Fredric Jameson's Marxist Hermeneutics," *Boundary* 2 11 (1982–83), the African American social critic Cornel West points to Jameson's roots in the work of György Lukács. Mike Davis offers a celebrated challenge to Jameson's account of postmodern architecture in "Urban Renaissance and the Spirit of Postmodernism," *New Left Review*, no. 151 (1985). *Imaginary Relations: Aesthetics and Ideology in the Theory of Historical Materialism* (1987) by the Marxist critic Michael Sprinker offers a useful analysis of Jameson's historicism. *Postmodernism / Jameson / Critique*, edited by Douglas Kellner (1989), gathers diverse essays as well as Jameson's response to his critics. A famous riposte, Aijaz Ahmad's "Jameson's Rhetoric of Otherness and the 'National Allegory' " (1987), polemically critiques Jameson's notion of third world literature; it has been reprinted in Ahmad's *In Theory: Classes, Nations, Literatures* (1992). Perry Anderson's *Origins of Postmodernity* (1998) is an excellent guide, covering the breadth of Jameson's career. Steven Helmling, in *The Success and Failure of Fredric Jameson: Writing, the Sublime, and the Dialectic of*

Critique (2000), traces Jameson's thought, focusing on his work from *The Political Unconscious* on.

Sean Homer, *Fredric Jameson: Marxism, Hermeneutics, Postmodernism* (1998), is a useful introduction, and contains a bibliography of primary and selected secondary texts. *The Jameson Reader* includes a comprehensive bibliography of Jameson's writings.

From The Political Unconscious: Narrative as a Socially Symbolic Act

Preface

Always historicize! This slogan—the one absolute and we may even say "transhistorical" imperative of all dialectical thought[1]—will unsurprisingly turn out to be the moral of *The Political Unconscious* as well. But, as the traditional dialectic teaches us, the historicizing operation can follow two distinct paths which only ultimately meet in the same place: the path of the object and the path of the subject, the historical origins of the things themselves and that more intangible historicity of the concepts and categories by which we attempt to understand those things. In the area of culture, which is the central field of the present book, we are thus confronted with a choice between study of the nature of the "objective" structures of a given cultural text (the historicity of its forms and of its content, the historical moment of emergence of its linguistic possibilities, the situation-specific function of its aesthetic) and something rather different which would instead foreground the interpretive categories or codes through which we read and receive the text in question. For better or for worse, it is this second path we have chosen to follow here: *The Political Unconscious* accordingly turns on the dynamics of the act of interpretation and presupposes, as its organizational fiction, that we never really confront a text immediately, in all its freshness as a thing-in-itself. Rather, texts come before us as the always-already-read; we apprehend them through sedimented layers of previous interpretations, or—if the text is brand-new—through the sedimented reading habits and categories developed by those inherited interpretive traditions. This presupposition then dictates the use of a method (which I have elsewhere termed the "metacommentary"[2]) according to which our object of study is less the text itself than the interpretations through which we attempt to confront and to appropriate it. Interpretation is here construed as an essentially allegorical act, which consists in rewriting a given text in terms of a particular interpretive master code. The identification of the latter will then lead to an evaluation of such codes or, in other words, of the "methods" or approaches current in American literary and cultural study today. Their juxtaposition with a dialectical or totalizing, properly Marxist ideal of understanding will be used to demonstrate the structural limitations of the other interpretive codes, and in particular to show the "local" ways in which they construct their objects

1. In Marxist theory, thought that links ideas and cultural forms to their economic foundations.

2. See "Metacommentary" (1971), included in Jameson's *Ideologies of Theory: Essays, 1971–1986*, vol. 1, *Situations of Theory* (Minneapolis: University of Minnesota Press, 1988).

of study and the "strategies of containment" whereby they are able to project the illusion that their readings are somehow complete and self-sufficient.

The retrospective illusion of the metacommentary thus has the advantage of allowing us to measure the yield and density of a properly Marxist interpretive act against those of other interpretive methods—the ethical, the psychoanalytic, the myth-critical, the semiotic, the structural, and the theological—against which it must compete in the "pluralism" of the intellectual marketplace today. I will here argue the priority of a Marxian interpretive framework in terms of semantic richness. Marxism cannot today be defended as a mere substitute for such other methods, which would then triumphalistically be consigned to the ashcan of history; the authority of such methods springs from their faithful consonance with this or that local law of a fragmented social life, this or that subsystem of a complex and mushrooming cultural superstructure.[3] In the spirit of a more authentic dialectical tradition, Marxism is here conceived as that "untranscendable horizon" that subsumes such apparently antagonistic or incommensurable critical operations, assigning them an undoubted sectoral validity within itself, and thus at once canceling and preserving them.

Because of the peculiar focus of this retrospective organization, however, it may be worth warning the reader what *The Political Unconscious* is not. The reader should not, in the first place, expect anything like that exploratory projection of what a vital and emergent political culture should be and do which Raymond Williams[4] has rightly proposed as the most urgent task of a Marxist cultural criticism. There are, of course, good and objective historical reasons why contemporary Marxism has been slow in rising to this challenge: the sorry history of Zhdanovite prescription[5] in the arts is one, the fascination with modernisms and "revolutions" in form and language is another, as well as the coming of a whole new political and economic "world system," to which the older Marxist cultural paradigms only imperfectly apply. A provisional conclusion to the present work will spell out some of the challenges Marxist interpretation must anticipate in conceiving those new forms of collective thinking and collective culture which lie beyond the boundaries of our own world. The reader will there find an empty chair reserved for some as yet unrealized, collective, and decentered cultural production of the future, beyond realism and modernism alike.

If this book, then, fails to propose a political or revolutionary aesthetic, it is equally little concerned to raise once again the traditional issues of philosophical aesthetics: the nature and function of art, the specificity of poetic language and of the aesthetic experience, the theory of the beautiful, and so forth. Yet the very absence of such issues may serve as an implicit commentary on them; I have tried to maintain an essentially historicist perspective, in which our readings of the past are vitally dependent on our experience of the present, and in particular on the structural peculiarities of what is sometimes called the *société de consommation* (or the "disaccumulative" moment of late monopoly or consumer or multinational capitalism), what Guy

3. According to the German social and political philosopher KARL MARX (1818–1883), all social, political, and cultural forms are part of a society's superstructure, which interacts with but ultimately depends on its economic base.
4. British literary and cultural critic (1921–1988; see above).
5. The censorship by Andrey Zhdanov (1896–1948), a Bolshevik leader during the Russian Revolution who later, as a member of the Soviet Politburo, tightened the guidelines for cultural activities.

Debord[6] calls the society of the image or of the spectacle. The point is that in such a society, saturated with messages and with "aesthetic" experiences of all kinds, the issues of an older philosophical aesthetics themselves need to be radically historicized, and can be expected to be transformed beyond recognition in the process.

Nor, although literary history is here everywhere implied, should *The Political Unconscious* be taken as paradigmatic work in this discursive form or genre, which is today in crisis. Traditional literary history was a subset of representational narrative, a kind of narrative "realism" become as problematic as its principal exemplars in the history of the novel. The second chapter of the present book, which is concerned with genre criticism, will raise the theoretical problem of the status and possibility of such literary-historical narratives, which in *Marxism and Form* I termed "diachronic[7] construct"; the subsequent readings of Balzac, Gissing, and Conrad[8] project a diachronic framework—the construction of the bourgeois subject in emergent capitalism and its schizophrenic disintegration in our own time—which is, however, here never fully worked out. Of literary history today we may observe that its task is at one with that proposed by Louis Althusser[9] for historiography in general: not to elaborate some achieved and lifelike simulacrum of its supposed object, but rather to "produce" the latter's "concept." This is indeed what the greatest modern or modernizing literary histories—such as Erich Auerbach's *Mimesis*[1]—have sought to do in their critical practice, if not in their theory.

Is it at least possible, then, that the present work might be taken as an outline or projection of a new kind of critical method? Indeed it would seem to me perfectly appropriate to recast many of its findings in the form of a methodological handbook, but such a manual would have as its object *ideological analysis*, which remains, I believe, the appropriate designation for the critical "method" specific to Marxism. For reasons indicated above, this book is not that manual, which would necessarily settle its accounts with rival "methods" in a far more polemic spirit. Yet the unavoidably Hegelian[2] tone of the retrospective framework of *The Political Unconscious* should not be taken to imply that such polemic interventions are not of the highest priority for Marxist cultural criticism. On the contrary, the latter must necessarily also be what Althusser has demanded of the practice of Marxist philosophy proper, namely "class struggle within theory."

For the non-Marxist reader, however, who may well feel that this book is quite polemic enough, I will add what should be unnecessary and underline my debt to the great pioneers of narrative analysis. My theoretical dialogue with them in these pages is not merely to be taken as yet another specimen of the negative critique of "false consciousness"[3] (although it is that too, and,

6. French critic (1931–1994), author of *The Society of the Spectacle* (1967), in which he coins these phrases. *Société de consommation*: consumer society (French).

7. Dealing with change over time (a term common in structuralist linguistics, and often paired with the *synchronic*, which focuses on phenomena at one moment of time). *Marxism and Form* was published in 1971.

8. Joseph Conrad (1857–1924), Polish-born English novelist. Honoré de Balzac (1799–1850), French novelist. George Gissing (1857–1903), English novelist.

9. French Marxist philosopher (1918–1990; see above).

1. *Mimesis: The Representation of Reality in Western Literature* (1946), by the German literary critic Auerbach (1892–1957).

2. Characteristic of GEORG WILHELM FRIEDRICH HEGEL (1770–1831), German idealist philosopher.

3. A Marxist term referring to an individual's tendency to view reality in ways congruent with the interests of the dominant orthodoxy rather than in ways that reflect his or her own class interest.

indeed, in the Conclusion I will deal explicitly with the problem of the proper uses of such critical gestures as demystification and ideological unmasking). It should meanwhile be obvious that no work in the area of narrative analysis can afford to ignore the fundamental contributions of Northrop Frye, the codification by A. J. Greimas of the whole Formalist and semiotic traditions, the heritage of a certain Christian hermeneutics, and above all, the indispensable explorations by Freud of the logic of dreams, and by Claude Lévi-Strauss[4] of the logic of "primitive" storytelling and *pensée sauvage*, not to speak of the flawed yet monumental achievements in this area of the greatest Marxist philosopher of modern times, Georg Lukács.[5] These divergent and unequal bodies of work are here interrogated and evaluated from the perspective of the specific critical and interpretive task of the present volume, namely to restructure the problematics of ideology, of the unconscious and of desire, of representation, of history, and of cultural production, around the all-informing process of *narrative*, which I take to be (here using the shorthand of philosophical idealism) the central function or *instance* of the human mind. This perspective may be reformulated in terms of the traditional dialectical code as the study of *Darstellung*:[6] that untranslatable designation in which the current problems of *representation* productively intersect with the quite different ones of *presentation*, or of the essentially narrative and rhetorical movement of language and writing through time.

Last but not least, the reader may well be puzzled as to why a book ostensibly concerned with the interpretive act should devote so little attention to issues of interpretive validity, and to the criteria by which a given interpretation may be faulted or accredited. I happen to feel that no interpretation can be effectively disqualified on its own terms by a simple enumeration of inaccuracies or omissions, or by a list of unanswered questions. Interpretation is not an isolated act, but takes place within a Homeric battlefield, on which a host of interpretive options are either openly or implicitly in conflict. If the positivistic conception of philological accuracy be the only alternative, then I would much prefer to endorse the current provocative celebration of strong misreadings over weak ones.[7] As the Chinese proverb has it, you use one ax handle to hew another: in our context, only another, stronger interpretation can overthrow and practically refute an interpretation already in place.

I would therefore be content to have the theoretical sections of this book judged and tested against its interpretive practice. But this very antithesis marks out the double standard and the formal dilemma of all cultural study today, from which *The Political Unconscious* is scarcely exempt: an uneasy struggle for priority between models and history, between theoretical speculation and textual analysis, in which the former seeks to transform the latter into so many mere examples, adduced to support its abstract propositions, while the latter continues insistently to imply that the theory itself was just

4. French structuralist anthropologist (b. 1908; see above), whose works include *La Penseé sauvage* (1962, *The Savage Mind*). FRYE (1912–1991), Canadian literary critic associated with archetypal criticism. Greimas (1912–1992), Lithuanian-born French semiotician. SIGMUND FREUD (1859–1939), Austrian founder of psychoanalysis and author of *The Interpretation of Dreams* (1900).

5. GYÖRGY LUKÁCS (1885–1971), Hungarian literary critic and philosopher.

6. Representation (German).

7. A reference to the theory of literary influence presented by the American critic HAROLD BLOOM in such works as *The Anxiety of Influence* (1973; see above) and *A Map of Misreading* (1975).

so much methodological scaffolding, which can readily be dismantled once the serious business of practical criticism is under way. These two tendencies—theory and literary history—have so often in Western academic thought been felt to be rigorously incompatible that it is worth reminding the reader, in conclusion, of the existence of a third position which transcends both. That position is, of course, Marxism, which, in the form of the dialectic, affirms a primacy of theory which is at one and the same time a recognition of the primacy of History itself.

From *Chapter 1. On Interpretation: Literature as a Socially Symbolic Act*

* * *

III

At this point it might seem appropriate to juxtapose a Marxist method of literary and cultural interpretation with those just outlined, and to document its claims to greater adequacy and validity. For better or for worse, however, as I warned in the Preface, this obvious next step is not the strategy projected by the present book, which rather seeks to argue the perspectives of Marxism as necessary preconditions for adequate literary comprehension. Marxist critical insights will therefore here be defended as something like an ultimate *semantic* precondition for the intelligibility of literary and cultural texts. Even this argument, however, needs a certain specification: in particular we will suggest that such semantic enrichment and enlargement of the inert givens and materials of a particular text must take place within three concentric frameworks, which mark a widening out of the sense of the social ground of a text through the notions, first, of political history, in the narrow sense of punctual event and a chroniclelike sequence of happenings in time; then of society, in the now already less diachronic and time-bound sense of a constitutive tension and struggle between social classes; and, ultimately, of history now conceived in its vastest sense of the sequence of modes of production[8] and the succession and destiny of the various human social formations, from prehistoric life to whatever far future history has in store for us.

These distinct semantic horizons are, to be sure, also distinct moments of the process of interpretation, and may in that sense be understood as dialectical equivalents of what Frye has called the successive "phases" in our reinterpretation—our rereading and rewriting—of the literary text. What we must also note, however, is that each phase or horizon governs a distinct reconstruction of its object, and construes the very structure of what can now only in a general sense be called "the text" in a different way.

Thus, within the narrower limits of our first, narrowly political or historical, horizon, "the text," the object of study, is still more or less construed as coinciding with the individual literary work or utterance. The difference between the perspective enforced and enabled by this horizon, however, and

8. In the Marxist schema, human history progresses through tribal hordes, Neolithic kinship societies, Oriental despotism, ancient slaveholding societies, feudalism, capitalism, and finally to communism.

that of ordinary *explication de texte*, or individual exegesis, is that here the individual work is grasped essentially as a *symbolic act*.

When we pass into the second phase, and find that the semantic horizon within which we grasp a cultural object has widened to include the social order, we will find that the very object of our analysis has itself been thereby dialectically transformed, and that it is no longer construed as an individual "text" or work in the narrow sense, but has been reconstituted in the form of the great collective and class discourses of which a text is little more than an individual *parole* or utterance.[9] Within this new horizon, then, our object of study will prove to be the *ideologeme*, that is, the smallest intelligible unit of the essentially antagonistic collective discourses of social classes.

When finally, even the passions and values of a particular social formation find themselves placed in a new and seemingly relativized perspective by the ultimate horizon of human history as a whole, and by their respective positions in the whole complex sequence of the modes of production, both the individual text and its ideologemes know a final transformation, and must be read in terms of what I will call the *ideology of form*, that is, the symbolic messages transmitted to us by the coexistence of various sign systems which are themselves traces or anticipations of modes of production.

The general movement through these three progressively wider horizons will largely coincide with the shifts in focus of the final chapters in this book, and will be felt, although not narrowly and programmatically underscored, in the methodological transformations determined by the historical transformations of their textual objects, from Balzac to Gissing to Conrad.

We must now briefly characterize each of these semantic or interpretive horizons. We have suggested that it is only in the first narrowly political horizon—in which history is reduced to a series of punctual events and crises in time, to the diachronic agitation of the year-to-year, the chroniclelike annals of the rise and fall of political regimes and social fashions, and the passionate immediacy of struggles between historical individuals—that the "text" or object of study will tend to coincide with the individual literary work or cultural artifact. Yet to specify this individual text as a symbolic act is already fundamentally to transform the categories with which traditional *explication de texte* (whether narrative or poetic) operated and largely still operates.

The model for such an interpretive operation remains the readings of myth and aesthetic structure of Claude Lévi-Strauss as they are codified in his fundamental essay "The Structural Study of Myth."[1] These suggestive, often sheerly occasional readings and speculative glosses immediately impose a basic analytical or interpretive principle: the individual narrative, or the individual formal structure, is to be grasped as the imaginary resolution of a real contradiction. Thus, to take only the most dramatic of Lévi-Strauss's analyses—the "interpretation" of the unique facial decorations of the Caduveo Indians[2]—the starting point will be an immanent description of the formal and structural peculiarities of this body art; yet it must be a description

9. Structural linguistics follows the distinction first made by the Swiss linguist FERDINAND DE SAUSSURE (1857–1913), often retaining his French terms, between the speech of an individual language user (*parole*) and language as an abstract system (*langue*).

1. Claude Lévi-Strauss, *Structural Anthropology*, trans. C. Jacobson and B. G. Schoepf (New York: Basic, 1963), pp. 206–31 [Jameson's note]. Some of the author's notes have been edited, and some omitted.

2. A South American indigenous people residing in Argentina, Paraguay, and Brazil.

already pre-prepared and oriented toward transcending the purely formalistic, a movement which is achieved not by abandoning the formal level for something extrinsic to it—such as some inertly social "content"—but rather immanently, by construing purely formal patterns as a symbolic enactment of the social within the formal and the aesthetic. Such symbolic functions are, however, rarely found by an aimless enumeration of random formal and stylistic features; our discovery of a text's symbolic efficacity must be oriented by a formal description which seeks to grasp it as a determinate structure of still properly formal *contradictions*. Thus, Lévi-Strauss orients his still purely visual analysis of Caduveo facial decorations toward this climactic account of their contradictory dynamic: "the use of a design which is symmetrical but yet lies across an oblique axis . . . a complicated situation based upon two contradictory forms of duality, and resulting in a compromise brought about by a secondary opposition between the ideal axis of the object itself [the human face] and the ideal axis of the figure which it represents."[3] Already on the purely formal level, then, this visual text has been grasped as a contradiction by way of the curiously provisional and asymmetrical resolution it proposes for that contradiction.

Lévi-Strauss's "interpretation" of this formal phenomenon may now, perhaps overhastily, be specified. Caduveo are a hierarchical society, organized in three endogamous groups[4] or castes. In their social development, as in that of their neighbors, this nascent hierarchy is already the place of the emergence, if not of political power in the strict sense, then at least of relations of domination: the inferior status of women, the subordination of youth to elders, and the development of a hereditary aristocracy. Yet whereas this latent power structure is, among the neighboring Guana and Bororo,[5] masked by a division into moieties which cuts across the three castes, and whose exogamous exchange[6] appears to function in a nonhierarchical, essentially egalitarian way, it is openly present in Caduveo life, as surface inequality and conflict. The social institutions of the Guana and Bororo, on the other hand, provide a realm of appearance, in which real hierarchy and inequality are dissimulated by the reciprocity of the moieties, and in which, therefore, "asymmetry of class is balanced . . . by symmetry of 'moieties.' " As for the Caduveo,

> they were never lucky enough to resolve their contradictions, or to disguise them with the help of institutions artfully devised for that purpose. On the social level, the remedy was lacking . . . but it was never completely out of their grasp. It was within them, never objectively formulated, but present as a source of confusion and disquiet. Yet since they were unable to conceptualize or to live this solution directly, they began to dream it, to project it into the imaginary. . . . We must therefore interpret the graphic art of Caduveo women, and explain its mysterious charm as well as its apparently gratuitous complication, as the fantasy production of a society seeking passionately to give symbolic expression to the institutions it might have had in reality, had not interest and superstition stood in the way.[7]

3. Claude Lévi-Strauss, *Tristes Tropiques*, trans. John Russell (New York: Atheneum, 1971), p. 176 [Jameson's note].
4. Groups whose members intermarry.
5. Other indigenous peoples of the upper Paraguay River.
6. Marriages outside the group.
7. Lévi-Strauss, *Tristes Tropiques*, pp. 179–80 [Jameson's note].

In this fashion, then, the visual text of Caduveo facial art constitutes a symbolic act, whereby real social contradictions, insurmountable in their own terms, find a purely formal resolution in the aesthetic realm.

This interpretive model thus allows us a first specification of the relationship between ideology and cultural texts or artifacts: a specification still conditioned by the limits of the first, narrowly historical or political horizon in which it is made. We may suggest that from this perspective, ideology is not something which informs or invests symbolic production; rather the aesthetic act is itself ideological, and the production of aesthetic or narrative form is to be seen as an ideological act in its own right, with the function of inventing imaginary or formal "solutions" to unresolvable social contradictions.

Lévi-Strauss's work also suggests a more general defense of the proposition of a political unconscious than we have hitherto been able to present, insofar as it offers the spectacle of so-called primitive peoples perplexed enough by the dynamics and contradictions of their still relatively simple forms of tribal organization to project decorative or mythic resolutions of issues that they are unable to articulate conceptually. But if this is the case for pre-capitalist and even pre-political societies, then how much more must it be true for the citizen of the modern *Gesellschaft*,[8] faced with the great constitutional options of the revolutionary period, and with the corrosive and tradition-annihilating effects of the spread of a money and market economy, with the changing cast of collective characters which oppose the bourgeoisie, now to an embattled aristocracy, now to an urban proletariat, with the great fantasms of the various nationalisms, now themselves virtual "subjects of history" of a rather different kind, with the social homogenization and psychic constriction of the rise of the industrial city and its "masses," the sudden appearance of the great transnational forces of communism and fascism, followed by the advent of the superstates and the onset of that great ideological rivalry between capitalism and communism, which, no less passionate and obsessive than that which, at the dawn of modern times, seethed through the wars of religion, marks the final tension of our now global village? It does not, indeed, seem particularly farfetched to suggest that these texts of history, with their fantasmatic collective "actants,"[9] their narrative organization, and their immense charge of anxiety and libidinal investment, are lived by the contemporary subject as a genuine politico-historical *pensée sauvage* which necessarily informs all of our cultural artifacts, from the literary institutions of high modernism all the way to the products of mass culture. Under these circumstances, Lévi-Strauss's work suggests that the proposition whereby all cultural artifacts are to be read as symbolic resolutions of real political and social contradictions deserves serious exploration and systematic experimental verification. It will become clear in later chapters of this book that the most readily accessible formal articulation of the operations of a political *pensée sauvage* of this kind will be found in what we will call the structure of a properly political *allegory*, as it develops from networks of topical allusion in Spenser or Milton or Swift[1] to the symbolic narratives of

8. Society of impersonal associations (German); often contrasted with *Gemeinschaft* (a community of organic social relationships).

9. Fundamental factors, such as subject and object, that generate narrative plot (a technical term introduced by Greimas).

1. All canonical English authors whose works sometimes include topical political references:

class representatives or "types" in novels like those of Balzac. With political allegory, then, a sometimes repressed ur-narrative[2] or master fantasy about the interaction of collective subjects, we have moved to the very borders of our second horizon, in which what we formerly regarded as individual texts are grasped as "utterances" in an essentially collective or class discourse.

We cannot cross those borders, however, without some final account of the critical operations involved in our first interpretive phase. We have implied that in order to be consequent, the will to read literary or cultural texts as symbolic acts must necessarily grasp them as resolutions of determinate contradictions; and it is clear that the notion of contradiction is central to any Marxist cultural analysis, just as it will remain central in our two subsequent horizons, although it will there take rather different forms. The methodological requirement to articulate a text's fundamental contradiction may then be seen as a test of the completeness of the analysis: this is why, for example, the conventional sociology of literature or culture, which modestly limits itself to the identification of class motifs or values in a given text, and feels that its work is done when it shows how a given artifact "reflects" its social background, is utterly unacceptable. Meanwhile, Kenneth Burke's[3] play of emphases, in which a symbolic act is on the one hand affirmed as a genuine *act*, albeit on the symbolic level, while on the other it is registered as an act which is "merely" symbolic, its resolutions imaginary ones that leave the real untouched, suitably dramatizes the ambiguous status of art and culture.

Still, we need to say a little more about the status of this external reality, of which it will otherwise be thought that it is little more than the traditional notion of "context" familiar in older social or historical criticism. The type of interpretation here proposed is more satisfactorily grasped as the rewriting of the literary text in such a way that the latter may itself be seen as the rewriting or restructuration of a prior historical or ideological *subtext*, it being always understood that that "subtext" is not immediately present as such, not some common-sense external reality, nor even the conventional narratives of history manuals, but rather must itself always be (re)constructed after the fact. The literary or aesthetic act therefore always entertains some active relationship with the Real;[4] yet in order to do so, it cannot simply allow "reality" to persevere inertly in its own being, outside the text and at distance. It must rather draw the Real into its own texture, and the ultimate paradoxes and false problems of linguistics, and most notably of semantics, are to be traced back to this process, whereby language manages to carry the Real within itself as its own intrinsic or immanent subtext. Insofar, in other words, as symbolic action—what Burke will map as "dream," "prayer," or "chart"[5]—is a way of doing something to the world, to that degree what we are calling "world" must inhere within it, as the content it has to take up into itself in order to submit it to the transformations of form. The symbolic act therefore begins by generating and producing its own context in the same moment of emergence in which it steps back from it, taking its measure with a view

Edmund Spenser (1552–1599), John Milton (1608–1674), and Jonathan Swift (1667–1745).
2. Prototypical or originary story.
3. American literary critic and rhetorician (1897–1993; see above).
4. A technical term from the theory of the French psychoanalyst JACQUES LACAN (1901–1981); the Real can be studied only in its effects on the Symbolic (and the Imaginary).
5. Kenneth Burke, *The Philosophy of Literary Form* (Berkeley: University of California Press, 1973), pp. 5–6 [Jameson's note].

toward its own projects of transformation. The whole paradox of what we have here called the subtext may be summed up in this, that the literary work or cultural object, as though for the first time, brings into being that very situation to which it is also, at one and the same time, a reaction. It articulates its own situation and textualizes it, thereby encouraging and perpetuating the illusion that the situation itself did not exist before it, that there is nothing but a text, that there never was any extra- or con-textual reality before the text itself generated it in the form of a mirage. One does not have to argue the reality of history: necessity, like Dr. Johnson's stone,[6] does that for us. That history—Althusser's "absent cause," Lacan's "Real"—is *not* a text, for it is fundamentally non-narrative and nonrepresentational; what can be added, however, is the proviso that history is inaccessible to us except in textual form, or in other words, that it can be approached only by way of prior (re)textualization. Thus, to insist on either of the two inseparable yet incommensurable dimensions of the symbolic act without the other: to overemphasize the active way in which the text reorganizes its subtext (in order, presumably, to reach the triumphant conclusion that the "referent" does not exist); or on the other hand to stress the imaginary status of the symbolic act so completely as to reify its social ground, now no longer understood as a subtext but merely as some inert given that the text passively or fantasmatically "reflects"—to overstress either of these functions of the symbolic act at the expense of the other is surely to produce sheer ideology, whether it be, as in the first alternative, the ideology of structuralism, or, in the second, that of vulgar materialism.

Still, this view of the place of the "referent" will be neither complete nor methodologically usable unless we specify a supplementary distinction between several types of subtext to be (re)constructed. We have implied, indeed, that the social contradiction addressed and "resolved" by the formal prestidigitation of narrative must, however reconstructed, remain an absent cause, which cannot be directly or immediately conceptualized by the text. It seems useful, therefore, to distinguish, from this ultimate subtext which is the place of social *contradiction*, a secondary one, which is more properly the place of ideology, and which takes the form of the *aporia* or the *antinomy*:[7] what can in the former be resolved only through the intervention of praxis here comes before the purely contemplative mind as logical scandal or double bind, the unthinkable and the conceptually paradoxical, that which cannot be unknotted by the operation of pure thought, and which must therefore generate a whole more properly narrative apparatus—the text itself—to square its circles and to dispel, through narrative movement, its intolerable closure. Such a distinction, positing a system of antinomies as the symptomatic expression and conceptual reflex of something quite different, namely a social contradiction, will now allow us to reformulate that coordination between a semiotic and a dialectical method, which was evoked in the preceding section. The operational validity of semiotic analysis, and in particular of the Greimassian semiotic rectangle,[8] derives, as was sug-

6. That is, the stone famously kicked by the English critic, essayist, and lexicographer SAMUEL JOHNSON (1709–1784) to refute the theory of the nonexistence of matter espoused by George Berkeley.

7. A contradiction between two statements of apparently equal validity. "Aporia": difficulty, logical impasse (a term often used in deconstructive criticism to indicate the point in a text where inherent contradictions render interpretation undecidable).

8. Dialectical sets of oppositions through which, Greimas theorizes, narratives generate meaning and which he diagrams in a rectangle. Throughout

gested there, not from its adequacy to nature or being, nor even from its capacity to map all forms of thinking or language, but rather from its vocation specifically to model ideological closure and to articulate the workings of binary oppositions, here the privileged form of what we have called the antinomy. A dialectical reevaluation of the findings of semiotics intervenes, however, at the moment in which this entire system of ideological closure is taken as the symptomatic projection of something quite different, namely of social contradiction.

We may now leave this first textual or interpretive model behind, and pass over into the second horizon, that of the social. The latter becomes visible, and individual phenomena are revealed as social facts and institutions, only at the moment in which the organizing categories of analysis become those of social class. I have in another place described the dynamics of ideology in its constituted form as a function of social class:[9] suffice it only to recall here that for Marxism classes must always be apprehended relationally, and that the ultimate (or ideal) form of class relationship and class struggle is always dichotomous. The constitutive form of class relationships is always that between a dominant and a laboring class: and it is only in terms of this axis that class fractions (for example, the petty bourgeoisie) or ec-centric or dependent classes (such as the peasantry) are positioned. To define class in this way is sharply to differentiate the Marxian model of classes from the conventional sociological analysis of society into strata, subgroups, professional elites and the like, each of which can presumably be studied in isolation from one another in such a way that the analysis of their "values" or their "cultural space" folds back into separate and independent *Weltanschauungen,*[1] each of which inertly reflects its particular "stratum." For Marxism, however, the very content of a class ideology is relational, in the sense that its "values" are always actively in situation with respect to the opposing class, and defined against the latter: normally, a ruling class ideology will explore various strategies of the *legitimation* of its own power position, while an oppositional culture or ideology will, often in covert and disguised strategies, seek to contest and to undermine the dominant "value system."

This is the sense in which we will say, following Mikhail Bakhtin, that within this horizon class discourse—the categories in terms of which individual texts and cultural phenomena are now rewritten—is essentially *dialogical* in its structure.[2] As Bakhtin's (and Voloshinov's) own work in this field is relatively specialized, focusing primarily on the heterogeneous and explosive pluralism of moments of carnival or festival (moments, for example, such as the immense resurfacing of the whole spectrum of the religious or political sects in the English 1640s or the Soviet 1920s) it will be necessary to add the qualification that the normal form of the dialogical is essentially an *antagonistic* one, and that the dialogue of class struggle is one in which

The Political Unconscious, Jameson frequently uses Greimassian rectangles in analyzing novels.

9. See my *Marxism and Form: Twentieth-Century Dialectical Theories of Literature* (Princeton: Princeton University Press, 1971), pp. 376–82. The most authoritative contemporary Marxist statement of this view of social class is to be found in E. P. Thompson, *The Making of the English Working Classes* (New York: Vintage, 1966), pp. 9–11 [Jameson's note].

1. Worldviews (German).

2. Mikhail Bakhtin, *Problems of Dostoyevsky's Poetics,* trans. R. W. Rotsel (Ann Arbor: Ardis, 1973), pp. 153–69. See also Bakhtin's important book on linguistics, written under the name of V. N. Voloshinov, *Marxism and the Philosophy of Language,* trans. L. Matejka and I. R. Titunik (New York: Seminar Press, 1973), pp. 83–98 [Jameson's note]. On the Russian theorist BAKHTIN (1895–1975) and the "dialogical" nature of the novel and discourse, see above. Some believe that to circumvent the suppression of his writings, he published some of his books under the name of a colleague, Valentin N. Volosinov (1895–1936).

two opposing discourses fight it out within the general unity of a shared code. Thus, for instance, the shared master code of religion becomes in the 1640s in England the place in which the dominant formulations of a hegemonic theology are reappropriated and polemically modified.[3]

Within this new horizon, then, the basic formal requirement of dialectical analysis is maintained, and its elements are still restructured in terms of *contradiction* (this is essentially, as we have said, what distinguishes the rationality of a Marxist class analysis from static analysis of the sociological type). Where the contradiction of the earlier horizon was univocal, however, and limited to the situation of the individual text, to the place of a purely individual symbolic resolution, contradiction here appears in the form of the dialogical as the irreconcilable demands and positions of antagonistic classes. Here again, then, the requirement to prolong interpretation to the point at which this ultimate contradiction begins to appear offers a criterion for the completeness or insufficiency of the analysis.

Yet to rewrite the individual text, the individual cultural artifact, in terms of the antagonistic dialogue of class voices is to perform a rather different operation from the one we have ascribed to our first horizon. Now the individual text will be refocused as a *parole*, or individual utterance, of that vaster system, or *langue*, of class discourse. The individual text retains its formal structure as a symbolic act: yet the value and character of such symbolic action are now significantly modified and enlarged. On this rewriting, the individual utterance or text is grasped as a symbolic move in an essentially polemic and strategic ideological confrontation between the classes, and to describe it in these terms (or to reveal it in this form) demands a whole set of different instruments.

For one thing, the illusion or appearance of isolation or autonomy which a printed text projects must now be systematically undermined. Indeed, since by definition the cultural monuments and masterworks that have survived tend necessarily to perpetuate only a single voice in this class dialogue, the voice of a hegemonic class, they cannot be properly assigned their relational place in a dialogical system without the restoration or artificial reconstruction of the voice to which they were initially opposed, a voice for the most part stifled and reduced to silence, marginalized, its own utterances scattered to the winds, or reappropriated in their turn by the hegemonic culture.

This is the framework in which the reconstruction of so-called popular cultures must properly take place—most notably, from the fragments of essentially peasant cultures: folk songs, fairy tales, popular festivals, occult or oppositional systems of belief such as magic and witchcraft. Such reconstruction is of a piece with the reaffirmation of the existence of marginalized or oppositional cultures in our own time, and the reaudition of the oppositional voices of black or ethnic cultures, women's and gay literature, "naive" or marginalized folk art, and the like. But once again, the affirmation of such nonhegemonic cultural voices remains ineffective if it is limited to the merely "sociological" perspective of the pluralistic rediscovery of other isolated social groups: only an ultimate rewriting of these utterances in terms of their essentially polemic and subversive strategies restores them to their proper place in the dialogical system of the social classes. Thus, for instance,

3. See Christopher Hill, *The World Turned Upside Down* (London: Temple Smith, 1972) [Jameson's note].

Bloch's[4] reading of the fairy tale, with its magical wish-fulfillments and its Utopian fantasies of plenty and the *pays de Cocagne*, restores the dialogical and antagonistic content of this "form" by exhibiting it as a systematic deconstruction and undermining of the hegemonic aristocratic form of the epic, with its somber ideology of heroism and baleful destiny; thus also the work of Eugene Genovese on black religion restores the vitality of these utterances by reading them, not as the replication of imposed beliefs, but rather as a process whereby the hegemonic Christianity of the slave-owners is appropriated, secretly emptied of its content and subverted to the transmission of quite different oppositional and coded messages.[5]

Moreover, the stress on the dialogical then allows us to reread or rewrite the hegemonic forms themselves; they also can be grasped as a process of the reappropriation and neutralization, the cooptation and class transformation, the cultural universalization, of forms which originally expressed the situation of "popular," subordinate, or dominated groups. So the slave religion of Christianity is transformed into the hegemonic ideological apparatus of the medieval system; while folk music and peasant dance find themselves transmuted into the forms of aristocratic or court festivity and into the cultural visions of the pastoral; and popular narrative from time immemorial—romance, adventure story, melodrama, and the like—is ceaselessly drawn on to restore vitality to an enfeebled and asphyxiating "high culture." Just so, in our own time, the vernacular and its still vital sources of production (as in black language) are reappropriated by the exhausted and media-standardized speech of a hegemonic middle class. In the aesthetic realm, indeed, the process of cultural "universalization" (which implies the repression of the oppositional voice, and the illusion that there is only one genuine "culture") is the specific form taken by what can be called the process of legitimation in the realm of ideology and conceptual systems.

Still, this operation of rewriting and of the restoration of an essentially dialogical or class horizon will not be complete until we specify the "units" of this larger system. The linguistic metaphor (rewriting texts in terms of the opposition of a *parole* to a *langue*) cannot, in other words, be particularly fruitful until we are able to convey something of the dynamics proper to a class *langue* itself, which is evidently, in Saussure's sense, something like an ideal construct that is never wholly visible and never fully present in any one of its individual utterances. This larger class discourse can be said to be organized around minimal "units" which we will call *ideologemes*. The advantage of this formulation lies in its capacity to mediate between conceptions of ideology as abstract opinion, class value, and the like, and the narrative materials with which we will be working here. The ideologeme is an amphibious formation, whose essential structural characteristic may be described as its possibility to manifest itself either as a pseudoidea—a conceptual or belief system, an abstract value, an opinion or prejudice—or as a protonarrative, a kind of ultimate class fantasy about the "collective characters" which are the classes in opposition. This duality means that the basic requirement for the full description of the ideologeme is already given in

4. Ernst Bloch (1885–1977), German philosopher, a Marxist whose "philosophy of hope" sees history ending in utopia, which he calls the *pays de Cocagne* ("land of plenty"; French).

5. Eugene Genovese, *Roll, Jordan, Roll: The World the Slaves Made* (New York: Vintage, 1976), pp. 161–284 [Jameson's note]. Genovese (b. 1930), American historian.

advance: as a construct it must be susceptible to both a conceptual description and a narrative manifestation all at once. The ideologeme can of course be elaborated in either of these directions, taking on the finished appearance of a philosophical system on the one hand, or that of a cultural text on the other; but the ideological analysis of these finished cultural products requires us to demonstrate each one as a complex work of transformation on that ultimate raw material which is the ideologeme in question. The analyst's work is thus first that of the identification of the ideologeme, and, in many cases, of its initial naming in instances where for whatever reason it had not yet been registered as such. The immense preparatory task of identifying and inventorying such ideologemes has scarcely even begun, and to it the present book will make but the most modest contribution: most notably in its isolation of that fundamental nineteenth-century ideologeme which is the "theory" of *ressentiment*,[6] and in its "unmasking" of ethics and the ethical binary opposition of good and evil as one of the fundamental forms of ideological thought in Western culture. However, our stress here and throughout on the fundamentally narrative character of such ideologemes (even where they seem to be articulated only as abstract conceptual beliefs or values) will offer the advantage of restoring the complexity of the transactions between opinion and protonarrative or libidinal fantasy. Thus we will observe, in the case of Balzac, the generation of an overt and constituted ideological and political "value system" out of the operation of an essentially narrative and fantasy dynamic; the chapter on Gissing, on the other hand, will show how an already constituted "narrative paradigm" emits an ideological message in its own right without the mediation of authorial intervention.

This focus or horizon, that of class struggle and its antagonistic discourses, is, as we have already suggested, not the ultimate form a Marxist analysis of culture can take. The example just alluded to—that of the seventeenth-century English revolution, in which the various classes and class fractions found themselves obliged to articulate their ideological struggles through the shared medium of a religious master code—can serve to dramatize the shift whereby these objects of study are reconstituted into a structurally distinct "text" specific to this final enlargement of the analytical frame. For the possibility of a displacement in emphasis is already given in this example: we have suggested that within the apparent unity of the theological code, the fundamental difference of antagonistic class positions can be made to emerge. In that case, the inverse move is also possible, and such concrete semantic differences can on the contrary be focused in such a way that what emerges is rather the all-embracing unity of a single code which they must share and which thus characterizes the larger unity of the social system. This new object—code, sign system, or system of the production of signs and codes—thus becomes an index of an entity of study which greatly transcends those earlier ones of the narrowly political (the symbolic act), and the social (class discourse and the ideologeme), and which we have proposed to term the historical in the larger sense of this word. Here the organizing unity will be what the Marxian tradition designates as a *mode of production*.

I have already observed that the "problematic" of modes of production is

6. Resentment (French); this theory was developed by the German philosopher FRIEDRICH NIETZSCHE (1844–1900).

the most vital new area of Marxist theory in all the disciplines today; not paradoxically, it is also one of the most traditional, and we must therefore, in a brief preliminary way, sketch in the "sequence" of modes of production as classical Marxism, from Marx and Engels to Stalin,[7] tended to enumerate them.[8] These modes, or "stages" of human society, have traditionally included the following: primitive communism or tribal society (the horde), the *gens* or hierarchical kinship societies (neolithic society), the Asiatic mode of production (so-called Oriental despotism), the *polis* or an oligarchical slaveholding society (the ancient mode of production), feudalism, capitalism, and communism (with a good deal of debate as to whether the "transitional" stage between these last—sometimes called "socialism"—is a genuine mode of production in its own right or not). What is more significant in the present context is that even this schematic or mechanical conception of historical "stages" (what the Althusserians have systematically criticized under the term "historicism") includes the notion of a cultural dominant or form of ideological coding specific to each mode of production. Following the same order these have generally been conceived as magic and mythic narrative, kinship, religion or the sacred, "politics" according to the narrower category of citizenship in the ancient city state, relations of personal domination, commodity reification, and (presumably) original and as yet nowhere fully developed forms of collective or communal association.

Before we can determine the cultural "text" or object of study specific to the horizon of modes of production, however, we must make two preliminary remarks about the methodological problems it raises. The first will bear on whether the concept of "mode of production" is a synchronic one, while the second will address the temptation to use the various modes of production for a classifying or typologizing operation, in which cultural texts are simply dropped into so many separate compartments.

Indeed, a number of theorists have been disturbed by the apparent convergence between the properly Marxian notion of an all-embracing and all-structuring mode of production (which assigns everything within itself—culture, ideological production, class articulation, technology—a specific and unique place), and non-Marxist visions of a "total system" in which the various elements or levels of social life are programmed in some increasingly constricting way. Weber's dramatic notion of the "iron cage" of an increasingly bureaucratic society,[9] Foucault's image of the gridwork of an ever more

7. Jameson suggests that "classical Marxism," or a Marxism relying on definite descriptions of classes, class struggle, and so on, was at its height between the time of Marx and his collaborator FRIEDRICH ENGELS (1820–1895) and that of Joseph Stalin (1879–1953), 2d leader of the U.S.S.R. (1924–53).

8. The "classical" texts on modes of production, besides Lewis Henry Morgan's *Ancient Society* (1877), are Karl Marx, *Pre-Capitalist Economic Formations*, a section of the *Grundrisse* (1857–58), and Friedrich Engels, *The Family, Private Property, and the State* (1884). An important recent contribution to the mode of production debate is Étienne Balibar's "The Basic Concepts of Historical Materialism," in Louis Althusser and Balibar, *Reading Capital*, trans. Ben Brewster (London: New Left Books, 1970), pp. 199–308 [Jameson's note]. Balibar (b. 1942), French political philosopher.

9. "The Puritan wanted to work in a calling; we are forced to do so. For when asceticism was carried out of monastic cells into everyday life, and began to dominate worldly morality, it did its part in building the tremendous cosmos of the modern economic order. This order is now bound to the technical and economic conditions of machine production which today determine the lives of all the individuals who are born into this mechanism, not only those directly concerned with economic acquisition, with irresistible force. Perhaps it will so determine them until the last ton of fossilized coal is burnt. In [one] view the care for external goods should only lie on the shoulders of the saint 'like a light cloak, which can be thrown aside at any moment.' But fate decreed that the cloak should become an iron cage." Max Weber, *The Protestant Ethic and the Spirit of Capitalism*, trans. T. Parsons (New York: Scribners, 1958), p. 181

pervasive "political technology of the body,"[1] but also more traditional "synchronic" accounts of the cultural programming of a given historical "moment," such as those that have variously been proposed from Vico and Hegel to Spengler and Deleuze[2]—all such monolithic models of the cultural unity of a given historical period have tended to confirm the suspicions of a dialectical tradition about the dangers of an emergent "synchronic" thought, in which change and development are relegated to the marginalized category of the merely "diachronic," the contingent or the rigorously nonmeaningful (and this, even where, as with Althusser, such models of cultural unity are attacked as forms of a more properly Hegelian and idealistic "expressive causality"). This theoretical foreboding about the limits of synchronic thought can perhaps be most immediately grasped in the political area, where the model of the "total system" would seem slowly and inexorably to eliminate any possibility of the *negative* as such, and to reintegrate the place of an oppositional or even merely "critical" practice and resistance back into the system as the latter's mere inversion. In particular, everything about class struggle that was anticipatory in the older dialectical framework, and seen as an emergent space for radically new social relations, would seem, in the synchronic model, to reduce itself to practices that in fact tend to reinforce the very system that foresaw and dictated their specific limits. This is the sense in which Jean Baudrillard[3] has suggested that the "total-system" view of contemporary society reduces the options of resistance to anarchist gestures, to the sole remaining ultimate protests of the wildcat strike, terrorism, and death. Meanwhile, in the framework of the analysis of culture also, the latter's integration into a synchronic model would seem to empty cultural production of all its antisystemic capacities, and to "unmask" even the works of an overtly oppositional or political stance as instruments ultimately programmed by the system itself.

It is, however, precisely the notion of a series of enlarging theoretical horizons proposed here that can assign these disturbing synchronic frameworks their appropriate analytical places and dictate their proper use. This notion projects a long view of history which is inconsistent with concrete political action and class struggle only if the specificity of the horizons is not respected; thus, even if the concept of a mode of production is to be considered a synchronic one (and we will see in a moment that things are somewhat more complicated than this), at the level of historical abstraction at which such a concept is properly to be used, the lesson of the "vision" of a total system is for the short run one of the structural limits imposed on praxis rather than the latter's impossibility.

The theoretical problem with the synchronic systems enumerated above lies elsewhere, and less in their analytical framework than in what in a Marxist perspective might be called their infrastructural regrounding. Historically,

[Jameson's note]. Weber (1864–1920), German sociologist who helped found the discipline.

1. Michel Foucault, *Discipline and Punish: The Birth of the Prison,* trans. Alan Sheridan (New York: Vintage, 1979), pp. 26ff. [Jameson's note]. FOUCAULT (1926–1984), French philosopher and historian of ideas.

2. All philosophers who made large claims about historical change: the Italian GIAMBATTISTA VICO (1668–1744) viewed historical change as a cycle; Hegel proposed a dialectical model of thesis, antithesis, and synthesis; the German Oswald Spengler (1880–1936) saw a pattern of decline; and the French GILLES DELEUZE (1925–1995) argued for a Nietzchean repetition modified for differences.

3. French sociologist (b. 1929; see above), who argues that in postmodern society we deal only with simulations of reality (simulacra), not representations.

such systems have tended to fall into two general groups, which one might term respectively the hard and soft visions of the total system. The first group projects a fantasy future of a "totalitarian" type in which the mechanisms of domination—whether these are understood as part of the more general process of bureaucratization, or on the other hand derive more immediately from the deployment of physical and ideological force—are grasped as irrevocable and increasingly pervasive tendencies whose mission is to colonize the last remnants and survivals of human freedom—to occupy and organize, in other words, what still persists of Nature objectively and subjectively (very schematically, the Third World and the Unconscious).

This group of theories can perhaps hastily be associated with the central names of Weber and Foucault; the second group may then be associated with names such as those of Jean Baudrillard and the American theorists of a "post-industrial society."[4] For this second group, the characteristics of the total system of contemporary world society are less those of political domination than those of cultural programming and penetration: not the iron cage, but rather the *société de consommation* with its consumption of images and simulacra, its free-floating signifiers and its effacement of the older structures of social class and traditional ideological hegemony. For both groups, world capitalism is in evolution toward a system which is not socialist in any classical sense, on the one hand the nightmare of total control and on the other the polymorphous or schizophrenic intensities of some ultimate counterculture (which may be no less disturbing for some than the overtly threatening characteristics of the first vision). What one must add is that neither kind of analysis respects the Marxian injunction of the "ultimately determining instance" of economic organization and tendencies: for both, indeed, economics (or political economy) of that type is in the new total system of the contemporary world at an end, and the economic finds itself in both reassigned to a secondary and nondeterminant position beneath the new dominant of political power or of cultural production respectively.

There exist, however, within Marxism itself precise equivalents to these two non-Marxian visions of the contemporary total system: rewritings, if one likes, of both in specifically Marxian and "economic" terms. These are the analyses of late capitalism in terms of *capitalogic*[5] and of *disaccumulation*,[6] respectively; and while this book is clearly not the place to discuss such theories at any length, it must be observed here that both, seeing the originality of the contemporary situation in terms of systemic tendencies *within* capitalism, reassert the theoretical priority of the organizing concept of the mode of production which we have been concerned to argue.

We must therefore now turn to the second related problem about this third and ultimate horizon, and deal briefly with the objection that cultural

4. The most influential statement of the American version of this "end of ideology" / consumer society position is, of course, that of Daniel Bell: see his *Coming of Post-Industrial Society* (New York: Basic, 1973) and *The Cultural Contradictions of Capitalism* (New York: Basic, 1976) [Jameson's note].

5. See, for a review and critique of the basic literature, Stanley Aronowitz, "Marx, Braverman, and the Logic of Capital," *Insurgent Sociologist* 8, nos. 2 / 3 (fall 1978): 126–46 [Jameson's note].

6. The basic texts on "disaccumulation theory" are Martin J. Sklar, "On the Proletarian Revolution and the End of Political-Economic Society," *Radical America* 3, no. 3 (May–June 1969): 1–41; Jim O'Connor, "Productive and Unproductive Labor," *Politics and Society* 5 (1975): 297–336; Fred Block and Larry Hirschhorn, "New Productive Forces and the Contradictions of Contemporary Capitalism," *Theory and Society* 7 (1979): 363–95; and Stanley Aronowitz, "The End of Political Economy," *Social Text*, no. 2 (1980): 3–52 [Jameson's note].

analysis pursued within it will tend toward a purely typological or classificatory operation, in which we are called upon to "decide" such issues as whether Milton is to be read within a "precapitalist" or a nascent capitalist context, and so forth. I have insisted elsewhere on the sterility of such classificatory procedures, which may always, it seems to me, be taken as symptoms and indices of the repression of a more genuinely dialectical or historical practice of cultural analysis. This diagnosis may now be expanded to cover all three horizons at issue here, where the practice of homology, that of a merely "sociological" search for some social or class equivalent, and that, finally, of the use of some typology of social and cultural systems, respectively, may stand as examples of the misuse of these three frameworks. Furthermore, just as in our discussion of the first two we have stressed the centrality of the category of contradiction for any Marxist analysis (seen, within the first horizon, as that which the cultural and ideological artifact tries to "resolve," and in the second as the nature of the social and class conflict within which a given work is one act or gesture), so too here we can effectively validate the horizon of the mode of production by showing the form contradiction takes on this level, and the relationship of the cultural object to it.

Before we do so, we must take note of more recent objections to the very concept of the mode of production. The traditional schema of the various modes of production as so many historical "stages" has generally been felt to be unsatisfactory, not least because it encourages the kind of typologizing criticized above, in political quite as much as in cultural analysis. (The form taken in political analysis is evidently the procedure which consists in "deciding" whether a given conjuncture[7] is to be assigned to a moment within feudalism—the result being a demand for bourgeois and parliamentary rights—or within capitalism—with the accompanying "reformist" strategy—or, on the contrary, a genuine "revolutionary" moment—in which case the appropriate revolutionary strategy is then deduced.)

On the other hand, it has become increasingly clear to a number of contemporary theorists that such classification of "empirical" materials within this or that abstract category is impermissible in large part because of the level of abstraction of the concept of a mode of production: no historical society has ever "embodied" a mode of production in any pure state (nor is *Capital*[8] the description of a historical society, but rather the construction of the abstract concept of capitalism). This has led certain contemporary theorists, most notably Nicos Poulantzas,[9] to insist on the distinction between a "mode of production" as a purely theoretical construction and a "social formation" that would involve the description of some historical society at a certain moment of its development. This distinction seems inadequate and even misleading, to the degree that it encourages the very empirical thinking which it was concerned to denounce, in other words, subsuming a particular or an empirical "fact" under this or that corresponding "abstraction." Yet one feature of Poulantzas' discussion of the "social formation" may be retained: his suggestion that every social formation or

7. Moment in social development at which various antagonistic and sometimes contradictory forces and trends combine.
8. See Marx, *Capital*, vol. 1 (1867).
9. Nicos Poulantzas, *Political Power and Social Classes*, trans. T. O'Hagan (London: New Left Books, 1973), pp. 13–16 [Jameson's note]. Poulantzas (b. 1936), Greek political theorist.

historically existing society has in fact consisted in the overlay and structural coexistence of *several* modes of production all at once, including vestiges and survivals of older modes of production, now relegated to structurally dependent positions within the new, as well as anticipatory tendencies which are potentially inconsistent with the existing system but have not yet generated an autonomous space of their own.

But if this suggestion is valid, then the problems of the "synchronic" system and of the typological temptation are both solved at one stroke. What is synchronic is the "concept" of the mode of production; the moment of the historical coexistence of several modes of production is not synchronic in this sense, but open to history in a dialectical way. The temptation to classify texts according to the appropriate mode of production is thereby removed, since the texts emerge in a space in which we may expect them to be crisscrossed and intersected by a variety of impulses from contradictory modes of cultural production all at once.

Yet we have still not characterized the specific object of study which is constructed by this new and final horizon. It cannot, as we have shown, consist in the concept of an individual mode of production (any more than, in our second horizon, the specific object of study could consist in a particular social class in isolation from the others). We will therefore suggest that this new and ultimate object may be designated, drawing on recent historical experience, as *cultural revolution*, that moment in which the coexistence of various modes of production becomes visibly antagonistic, their contradictions moving to the very center of political, social, and historical life. The incomplete Chinese experiment with a "proletarian" cultural revolution[1] may be invoked in support of the proposition that previous history has known a whole range of equivalents for similar processes to which the term may legitimately be extended. So the Western Enlightenment may be grasped as part of a properly bourgeois cultural revolution, in which the values and the discourses, the habits and the daily space, of the *ancien régime*[2] were systematically dismantled so that in their place could be set the new conceptualities, habits and life forms, and value systems of a capitalist market society. This process clearly involved a vaster historical rhythm than such punctual historical events as the French Revolution or the Industrial Revolution, and includes in its *longue durée*[3] such phenomena as those described by Weber in *The Protestant Ethic and the Spirit of Capitalism*—a work that can now in its turn be read as a contribution to the study of the bourgeois cultural revolution, just as the corpus of work on romanticism is now repositioned as the study of a significant and ambiguous moment in the resistance to this particular "great transformation," alongside the more specifically "popular" (precapitalist as well as working-class) forms of cultural resistance.

But if this is the case, then we must go further and suggest that all previous modes of production have been accompanied by cultural revolutions specific to them of which the neolithic "cultural revolution," say, the triumph of

1. That is, the 1966–76 Cultural Revolution, an attempt to stamp out "bourgeois values" that caused great social and economic disruption in China.

2. That is, the aristocracy.

3. Long duration (French), a phrase used by the French historian Fernand Braudel (1902–1985), whose work emphasized large-scale, long-term changes.

patriarchy over the older matriarchal or tribal forms, or the victory of Hellenic "justice" and the new legality of the *polis* over the vendetta system are only the most dramatic manifestations. The concept of cultural revolution, then—or more precisely, the reconstruction of the materials of cultural and literary history in the form of this new "text" or object of study which is cultural revolution—may be expected to project a whole new framework for the humanities, in which the study of culture in the widest sense could be placed on a materialist basis.

This description is, however, misleading to the degree to which it suggests that "cultural revolution" is a phenomenon limited to so-called "transitional" periods, during which social formations dominated by one mode of production undergo a radical restructuration in the course of which a different "dominant" emerges. The problem of such "transitions" is a traditional crux of the Marxian problematic of modes of production, nor can it be said that any of the solutions proposed, from Marx's own fragmentary discussions to the recent model of Etienne Balibar, are altogether satisfactory, since in all of them the inconsistency between a "synchronic" description of a given system and a "diachronic" account of the passage from one system to another seems to return with undiminished intensity. But our own discussion began with the idea that a given social formation consisted in the coexistence of various synchronic systems or modes of production, each with its own dynamic or time scheme—a kind of metasynchronicity, if one likes—while we have now shifted to a description of cultural revolution which has been couched in the more diachronic language of systemic transformation. I will therefore suggest that these two apparently inconsistent accounts are simply the twin perspectives which our thinking (and our presentation or *Darstellung* of that thinking) can take on this same vast historical object. Just as overt revolution is no punctual event either, but brings to the surface the innumerable daily struggles and forms of class polarization which are at work in the whole course of social life that precedes it, and which are therefore latent and implicit in "prerevolutionary" social experience, made visible as the latter's deep structure only in such "moments of truth"—so also the overtly "transitional" moments of cultural revolution are themselves but the passage to the surface of a permanent process in human societies, of a permanent struggle between the various coexisting modes of production. The triumphant moment in which a new systemic dominant gains ascendency is therefore only the diachronic manifestation of a constant struggle for the perpetuation and reproduction of its dominance, a struggle which must continue throughout its life course, accompanied at all moments by the systemic or structural antagonism of those older and newer modes of production that resist assimilation or seek deliverance from it. The task of cultural and social analysis thus construed within this final horizon will then clearly be the rewriting of its materials in such a way that this perpetual cultural revolution can be apprehended and read as the deeper and more permanent constitutive structure in which the empirical textual objects know intelligibility.

Cultural revolution thus conceived may be said to be beyond the opposition between synchrony and diachrony, and to correspond roughly to what Ernst Bloch has called the *Ungleichzeitigkeit* (or "nonsynchronous devel-

opment") of cultural and social life.[4] Such a view imposes a new use of concepts of periodization, and in particular of that older schema of the "linear" stages which is here preserved and canceled all at once. We will deal more fully with the specific problems of periodization in the next chapter: suffice it to say at this point that such categories are produced within an initial diachronic or narrative framework, but become usable only when that initial framework has been annulled, allowing us now to coordinate or articulate categories of diachronic origin (the various distinct modes of production) in what is now a synchronic or metasynchronic way.

We have, however, not yet specified the nature of the textual object which is constructed by this third horizon of cultural revolution, and which would be the equivalent within this dialectically new framework of the objects of our first two horizons—the symbolic act, and the ideologeme or dialogical organization of class discourse. I will suggest that within this final horizon the individual text or cultural artifact (with its appearance of autonomy which was dissolved in specific and original ways within the first two horizons as well) is here restructured as a field of force in which the dynamics of sign systems of several distinct modes of production can be registered and apprehended. These dynamics—the newly constituted "text" of our third horizon—make up what can be termed *the ideology of form*, that is, the determinate contradiction of the specific messages emitted by the varied sign systems which coexist in a given artistic process as well as in its general social formation.

What must now be stressed is that at this level "form" is apprehended as content. The study of the ideology of form is no doubt grounded on a technical and formalistic analysis in the narrower sense, even though, unlike much traditional formal analysis, it seeks to reveal the active presence within the text of a number of discontinuous and heterogeneous formal processes. But at the level of analysis in question here, a dialectical reversal has taken place in which it has become possible to grasp such formal processes as sedimented content in their own right, as carrying ideological messages of their own, distinct from the ostensible or manifest content of the works; it has become possible, in other words, to display such formal operations from the standpoint of what Louis Hjelmslev[5] will call the "content of form" rather than the latter's "expression," which is generally the object of the various more narrowly formalizing approaches. The simplest and most accessible demonstration of this reversal may be found in the area of literary genre.

4. Ernst Bloch, "Nonsynchronism and Dialectics," *New German Critique*, no. 11 (spring 1977): 22–38. The "nonsynchronous" use of the concept of the mode of production outlined above is in my opinion the only way to fulfill Marx's well-known program for dialectical knowledge "of rising from the abstract to the concrete" (1857 Introduction, *Grundrisse*, ed. Eric Hobsbawm [New York: International, 1965], p. 101). Marx there distinguished three stages of knowledge: (1) the notation of the particular (this would correspond to something like empirical history, the collection of data and descriptive materials on the variety of human societies); (2) the conquest of abstraction, the coming into being of a properly "bourgeois" science or of what Hegel called the categories of the Understanding; (3) the transcendence of abstraction by the dialectic, the "rise to the concrete," the setting in motion of hitherto static and typologizing categories by their reinsertion in a concrete historical situation (in the present context, this is achieved by moving form a classificatory use of the categories of modes of production to a perception of their dynamic and contradictory coexistence in a given cultural moment). Althusser's own epistemology, incidentally, is a gloss on this same fundamental passage of the 1857 Introduction, but one which succeeds only too well in eliminating its dialectical spirit (*For Marx*, trans. Ben Brewster [London: Verso, 1990], pp. 183ff.) [Jameson's note].

5. Danish linguist (1899–1965).

Our next chapter, indeed, will model the process whereby generic specification and description can, in a given historical text, be transformed into the detection of a host of distinct generic messages—some of them objectified survivals from older modes of cultural production, some anticipatory, but all together projecting a formal conjuncture through which the "conjuncture" of coexisting modes of production at a given historical moment can be detected and allegorically articulated.

Meanwhile, that what we have called the ideology of form is something other than a retreat from social and historical questions into the more narrowly formal may be suggested by the relevance of this final perspective to more overtly political and theoretical concerns; we may take the much debated relation of Marxism to feminism as a particularly revealing illustration. The notion of overlapping modes of production outlined above has indeed the advantage of allowing us to short-circuit the false problem of the priority of the economic over the sexual, or of sexual oppression over that of social class. In our present perspective, it becomes clear that sexism and the patriarchal are to be grasped as the sedimentation and the virulent survival of forms of alienation specific to the oldest mode of production of human history, with its division of labor between men and women, and its division of power between youth and elder. The analysis of the ideology of form, properly completed, should reveal the formal persistence of such archaic structures of alienation—and the sign systems specific to them—beneath the overlay of all the more recent and historically original types of alienation—such as political domination and commodity reification—which have become the dominants of that most complex of all cultural revolutions, late capitalism, in which all the earlier modes of production in one way or another structurally coexist. The affirmation of radical feminism, therefore, that to annul the patriarchal is the most *radical* political act—insofar as it includes and subsumes more partial demands, such as the liberation from the commodity form—is thus perfectly consistent with an expanded Marxian framework, for which the transformation of our own dominant mode of production must be accompanied and completed by an equally radical restructuration of all the more archaic modes of production with which it structurally coexists.

With this final horizon, then, we emerge into a space in which History itself becomes the ultimate ground as well as the untranscendable limit of our understanding in general and our textual interpretations in particular. This is, of course, also the moment in which the whole problem of interpretive priorities returns with a vengeance, and in which the practitioners of alternate or rival interpretive codes—far from having been persuaded that History is an interpretive code that includes and transcends all the others—will again assert "History" as simply one more code among others, with no particularly privileged status. This is most succinctly achieved when the critics of Marxist interpretation, borrowing its own traditional terminology, suggest that the Marxian interpretive operation involves a thematization and a reification of "History" which is not markedly different from the process whereby the other interpretive codes produce their own forms of thematic closure and offer themselves as absolute methods.

It should by now be clear that nothing is to be gained by opposing one reified theme—History—by another—Language—in a polemic debate as to ultimate priority of one over the other. The influential forms this debate has taken in recent years—as in Jürgen Habermas' attempt to subsume the "Marxist" model of production beneath a more all-embracing model of "communication" or intersubjectivity,[6] or in Umberto Eco's assertion of the priority of the Symbolic in general over the technological and productive systems which it must organize as *signs* before they can be used as *tools*[7]—are based on the misconception that the Marxian category of a "mode of production" is a form of technological or "productionist" determinism.

It would seem therefore more useful to ask ourselves, in conclusion, how History as a ground and as an absent cause can be conceived in such a way as to resist such thematization or reification, such transformation back into one optional code among others. We may suggest such a possibility obliquely by attention to what the Aristotelians would call the generic satisfaction specific to the form of the great monuments of historiography,[8] or what the semioticians might call the "history-effect" of such narrative texts. Whatever the raw material on which historiographic form works (and we will here only touch on that most widespread type of material which is the sheer chronology of fact as it is produced by the rote-drill of the history manual), the "emotion" of great historiographic form can then always be seen as the radical restructuration of that inert material, in this instance the powerful reorganization of otherwise inert chronological and "linear" data in the form of Necessity: why what happened (at first received as "empirical" fact) had to happen the way it did. From this perspective, then, causality is only one of the possible tropes by which this formal restructuration can be achieved, although it has obviously been a privileged and historically significant one. Meanwhile, should it be objected that Marxism is rather a "comic" or "romance" paradigm, one which sees history in the salvational perspective of some ultimate liberation, we must observe that the most powerful realizations of a Marxist historiography—from Marx's own narratives of the 1848 revolution[9] through the rich and varied canonical studies of the dynamics of the Revolution of 1789 all the way to Charles Bettelheim's[1] study of the Soviet revolutionary experience—remain visions of historical Necessity in the sense evoked above. But Necessity is here represented in the form of the inexorable logic involved in the determinate failure of all the revolutions that have taken place in human history: the ultimate Marxian presupposition—that socialist revolution can only be a total and worldwide process (and that this in turn presupposes the completion of the capitalist "revolution" and of the process of commodification on a global scale)—is the perspective in which the failure or the blockage, the contradictory reversal or functional inversion, of this or that local revolutionary process is grasped as "inevitable," and as the operation of objective limits.

History is therefore the experience of Necessity, and it is this alone which

6. See Jürgen Habermas, *Knowledge and Human Interests*, trans. J. Shapiro (Boston: Beacon, 1971), esp. Part I [Jameson's note]. HABERMAS (b. 1929), German philosopher.

7. Umberto Eco, *A Theory of Semiotics* (Bloomington: Indiana University Press, 1976), pp. 21–26 [Jameson's note]. Eco (b. 1932), Italian semiotician and novelist.

8. That is, emphasizing, as does ARISTOTLE in his *Poetics* (ca. 330 B.C.E.; see above), the importance of form.

9. The uprising in France that overthrew the constitutional monarchy of Louis-Philippe; Marx wrote about it in a series of articles in 1849–50 published together as *Class Struggles in France* (1895).

1. French economist and social scientist (b. 1913), who wrote *Class Struggles in the USSR* (3 vols., 1974–83).

can forestall its thematization or reification as a mere object of representation or as one master code among many others. Necessity is not in that sense a type of content, but rather the inexorable *form* of events; it is therefore a narrative category in the enlarged sense of some properly narrative political unconscious which has been argued here, a retextualization of History which does not propose the latter as some new representation or "vision," some new content, but as the formal effects of what Althusser, following Spinoza,[2] calls an "absent cause." Conceived in this sense, History is what hurts, it is what refuses desire and sets inexorable limits to individual as well as collective praxis, which its "ruses" turn into grisly and ironic reversals of their overt intention. But this History can be apprehended only through its effects, and never directly as some reified force. This is indeed the ultimate sense in which History as ground and untranscendable horizon needs no particular theoretical justification: we may be sure that its alienating necessities will not forget us, however much we might prefer to ignore them.

1981

Postmodernism and Consumer Society[1]

The concept of postmodernism is not widely accepted or even understood today. Some of the resistance to it may come from the unfamiliarity of the works it covers, which can be found in all the arts: the poetry of John Ashbery,[2] for instance, but also the much simpler talk poetry that came out of the reaction against complex, ironic, academic modernist poetry in the 1960s; the reaction against modern architecture and in particular against the monumental buildings of the International Style, the pop buildings and decorated sheds celebrated by Robert Venturi in his manifesto, *Learning from Las Vegas;*[3] Andy Warhol and Pop art, but also the more recent Photorealism;[4] in music, the moment of John Cage but also the later synthesis of classical and 'popular' styles found in composers like Philip Glass and Terry Riley, and also punk and new-wave rock with such groups as the Clash, Talking Heads and the Gang of Four;[5] in film, everything that comes out of Godard[6]—contemporary vanguard film and video—but also a whole new style of commercial or fiction films, which has its equivalent in contemporary

2. Benedict de Spinoza (1632–1677), Dutch rationalist philosopher.

1. The present text combines elements of two previously published essays: "Postmodernism and Consumer Society," in *The Anti-Aesthetic* (Port Townsend, Wash.: Bay Press, 1983), and "Postmodernism: The Cultural Logic of Late Capitalism," in *New Left Review*, no. 146 (1984) [Jameson's note].

2. American poet (b. 1927) whose work is often obscure and demanding.

3. Published in 1972, by the American eclectic postmodern architect Venturi (b. 1925), Denise Scott Brown, and Steven Izenour. International Style: an architectural style, developed in Europe and the United States during the 1920s and 1930s and dominant by midcentury, characterized by rectilinear forms without ornamentation and by construction in glass and steel.

4. An art movement that flourished in the 1970s; it was an outgrowth of pop art, which came to prominence in the 1960s and also focused on everyday subjects from consumer and popular culture, such as the Campbell's Soup cans depicted by Warhol (1928–1987), its best-known American proponent.

5. Jameson names avant-garde musicians: the American composers Cage (1912–1992), Glass (b. 1937), and Riley (b. 1935); and the British punk band the Clash, the American art rock band Talking Heads, and the British Marxist band the Gang of Four, all of whom released debut albums in the late 1970s.

6. Jean-Luc Godard (b. 1930), French film director.

novels as well, where the works of William Burroughs, Thomas Pynchon and Ishmael Reed[7] on the one hand, and the French new novel[8] on the other, are also to be numbered among the varieties of what can be called postmodernism.

This list would seem to make two things clear at once: first, most of the postmodernisms mentioned above emerge as specific reactions against the established forms of high modernism, against this or that dominant high modernism which conquered the university, the museum, the art gallery network, and the foundations. Those formerly subversive and embattled styles—Abstract Expressionism;[9] the great modernist poetry of Pound, Eliot or Wallace Stevens; the International Style (Le Corbusier, Frank Lloyd Wright, Mies); Stravinsky; Joyce, Proust and Mann[1]—felt to be scandalous or shocking by our grandparents are, for the generation which arrives at the gate in the 1960s, felt to be the establishment and the enemy—dead, stifling, canonical, the reified monuments one has to destroy to do anything new. This means that there will be as many different forms of postmodernism as there were high modernisms in place, since the former are at least initially specific and local reactions *against* those models. That obviously does not make the job of describing postmodernism as a coherent thing any easier, since the unity of this new impulse—if it has one—is given not in itself but in the very modernism it seeks to displace.

The second feature of this list of postmodernisms is the effacement in it of some key boundaries or separations, most notably the erosion of the older distinction between high culture and so-called mass or popular culture. This is perhaps the most distressing development of all from an academic standpoint, which has traditionally had a vested interest in preserving a realm of high or elite culture against the surrounding environment of philistinism,[2] of schlock and kitsch, of TV series and *Reader's Digest* culture, and in transmitting difficult and complex skills of reading, listening and seeing to its initiates. But many of the newer postmodernisms have been fascinated precisely by that whole landscape of advertising and motels, of the Las Vegas strip, of the late show and Grade-B Hollywood film, of so-called paraliterature with its airport paperback categories of the gothic and the romance, the popular biography, the murder mystery and the science fiction or fantasy novel. They no longer 'quote' such 'texts' as a Joyce might have done, or a Mahler;[3] they incorporate them, to the point where the line between high art and commercial forms seems increasingly difficult to draw.

A rather different indication of this effacement of the older categories of genre and discourse can be found in what is sometimes called contemporary

7. All American authors of avant-garde fiction: Burroughs (1914–1997), Pynchon (b. 1937), and Reed (b. 1938).
8. A French literary movement that began in the 1950s and sought to frustrate conventional expectations of plot, character, and dialogue.
9. School of abstract painting that emerged in the United States, during the 1940s, characterized by attention to surface qualities, huge canvases, and the attempt to express pure emotion.
1. All prominent representatives of high modernism: in poetry, Ezra Pound (1885–1972), T. S. ELIOT (1888–1965), and Stevens (1879–1955), all Americans; in architecture, the French Le Corbusier (Charles Édouard Jeanneret, 1887–1965), the American Wright (1867–1959), and the German Louis Mies van der Rohe (1886–1969); in music, the Russian composer Igor Stravinsky (1882–1971); and in the novel, the Irish James Joyce (1882–1941), the French Marcel Proust (1871–1922), and the German Thomas Mann (1875–1955).
2. Middle-class materialism (a term coined by MATTHEW ARNOLD in "The Function of Criticism at the Present Time," 1864; see above).
3. Gustav Mahler (1860–1911), Austrian composer.

theory. A generation ago there was still a technical discourse of professional philosophy—the great systems of Sartre or the phenomenologists, the work of Wittgenstein[4] or analytical or common language philosophy—alongside which one could still distinguish that quite different discourse of the other academic disciplines—of political science, for example, or sociology or literary criticism. Today, increasingly, we have a kind of writing simply called 'theory' which is all or none of those things at once. This new kind of discourse, generally associated with France and so-called French theory, is becoming widespread and marks the end of philosophy as such. Is the work of Michel Foucault,[5] for example, to be called philosophy, history, social theory or political science? It's undecidable, as they say nowadays; and I will suggest that such 'theoretical discourse' is also to be numbered among the manifestations of postmodernism.

Now I must say a word about the proper use of this concept: it is not just another word for the description of a particular style. It is also, at least in my use, a periodizing concept whose function is to correlate the emergence of new formal features in culture with the emergence of a new type of social life and a new economic order—what is often euphemistically called modernization, postindustrial or consumer society, the society of the media or the spectacle, or multinational capitalism. This new moment of capitalism can be dated from the postwar boom in the United States in the late 1940s and early 1950s or, in France, from the establishment of the Fifth Republic in 1958.[6] The 1960s are in many ways the key transitional period, a period in which the new international order (neocolonialism, the Green Revolution,[7] computerization and electronic information) is at one and the same time set in place and is swept and shaken by its own internal contradictions and by external resistance. I want here to sketch a few of the ways in which the new postmodernism expresses the inner truth of that newly emergent social order of late capitalism, but will have to limit the description to only two of its significant features, which I will call pastiche and schizophrenia; they will give us a chance to sense the specificity of the postmodernist experience of space and time respectively.

Pastiche Eclipses Parody

One of the most significant features or practices in postmodernism today is pastiche. I must first explain this term, which people generally tend to confuse with or assimilate to that related verbal phenomenon called parody. Both pastiche and parody involve the imitation or, better still, the mimicry of other styles and particularly of the mannerisms and stylistic twitches of other styles. It is obvious that modern literature in general offers a very rich field for parody, since the great modern writers have all been defined by the

4. Ludwig Wittgenstein (1889–1951), Austrian-born English philosopher whose early work was analytic and whose later work explored the nature of language. JEAN-PAUL SARTRE (1905–1980), French existentialist philosopher, novelist, and dramatist. "Phenomenologists": philosophers who focus introspectively on the contents of consciousness.

5. French philosopher and historian of ideas (1926–1984; see above).

6. The government established under a new constitution, written in response to the crisis brought on by France's colonial war in Algeria; Charles de Gaulle (1890–1970) became its first president in 1959.

7. The enormous increase in third world agricultural production (especially in India and Pakistan) in the 1960s made possible by new high-yield varieties of wheat and rice, the use of chemical fertilizers and pesticides, irrigation, and mechanization.

invention or production of rather unique styles: think of the Faulknerian long sentence or of D. H. Lawrence's characteristic nature imagery; think of Wallace Stevens's peculiar way of using abstractions; think also of the mannerisms of the philosophers, of Heidegger for example, or Sartre; think of the musical styles of Mahler or Prokofiev.[8] All of these styles, however different from each other, are comparable in this: each is quite unmistakable; once one is learned, it is not likely to be confused with something else.

Now parody capitalizes on the uniqueness of these styles and seizes on their idiosyncrasies and eccentricities to produce an imitation which mocks the original. I won't say that the satiric impulse is conscious in all forms of parody. In any case, a good or great parodist has to have some secret sympathy for the original, just as a great mimic has to have the capacity to put himself / herself in the place of the person imitated. Still, the general effect of parody is—whether in sympathy or with malice—to cast ridicule on the private nature of these stylistic mannerisms and their excessiveness and eccentricity with respect to the way people normally speak or write. So there remains somewhere behind all parody the feeling that there is a linguistic norm in contrast to which the styles of the great modernists can be mocked.

But what would happen if one no longer believed in the existence of normal language, of ordinary speech, of the linguistic norm (the kind of clarity and communicative power celebrated by Orwell in his famous essay,[9] say)? One could think of it in this way; perhaps the immense fragmentation and privatization of modern literature—its explosion into a host of distinct private styles and mannerisms—foreshadows deeper and more general tendencies in social life as a whole. Supposing that modern art and modernism—far from being a kind of specialized aesthetic curiosity—actually anticipated social developments along these lines; supposing that in the decades since the emergence of the great modern styles society has itself begun to fragment in this way, each group coming to speak a curious private language of its own, each profession developing its private code or idiolect, and finally each individual coming to be a kind of linguistic island, separated from everyone else? But then in that case, the very possibility of any linguistic norm in terms of which one could ridicule private languages and idiosyncratic styles would vanish, and we would have nothing but stylistic diversity and heterogeneity.

That is the moment at which pastiche appears and parody has become impossible. Pastiche is, like parody, the imitation of a peculiar or unique style, the wearing of a stylistic mask, speech in a dead language: but it is a neutral practice of such mimicry, without parody's ulterior motive, without the satirical impulse, without laughter, without that still latent feeling that there exists something *normal* compared to which what is being imitated is rather comic. Pastiche is blank parody, parody that has lost its sense of humor: pastiche is to parody what that curious thing, the modern practice of a kind of blank irony, is to what Wayne Booth[1] calls the stable and comic ironies of, say, the eighteenth century.

8. All innovators of modernism: the American novelist William Faulkner (1897–1962), the English novelist and poet Lawrence (1880–1930), the German philosopher MARTIN HEIDEGGER (1889–1976), and the Russian composer Sergei Prokofiev (1891–1953).

9. "Politics and the English Language" (1946), by the English novelist and essayist George Orwell (pen name of Eric Arthur Blair, 1903–1950).

1. American literary critic (b. 1921), author of *The Rhetoric of Irony* (1974).

The Death of the Subject

But now we need to introduce a new piece into this puzzle, which may help to explain why classical modernism is a thing of the past and why postmodernism should have taken its place. This new component is what is generally called the 'death of the subject'[2] or, to say it in more conventional language, the end of individualism as such. The great modernisms were, as we have said, predicated on the invention of a personal, private style, as unmistakable as your fingerprint, as incomparable as your own body. But this means that the modernist aesthetic is in some way organically linked to the conception of a unique self and private identity, a unique personality and individuality, which can be expected to generate its own unique vision of the world and to forge its own unique, unmistakable style.

Yet today, from any number of distinct perspectives, the social theorists, the psychoanalysts, even the linguists, not to speak of those of us who work in the area of culture and cultural and formal change, are all exploring the notion that that kind of individualism and personal identity is a thing of the past; that the old individual or individualist subject is 'dead'; and that one might even describe the concept of the unique individual and the theoretical basis of individualism as ideological. There are in fact two positions on all this, one of which is more radical than the other. The first one is content to say: yes, once upon a time, in the classic age of competitive capitalism, in the heyday of the nuclear family and the emergence of the bourgeoisie as the hegemonic social class, there was such a thing as individualism, as individual subjects. But today, in the age of corporate capitalism, of the so-called organization man,[3] of bureaucracies in business as well as in the state, of demographic explosion—today, that older bourgeois individual subject no longer exists.

Then there is a second position, the more radical of the two, what one might call the poststructuralist position. It adds: not only is the bourgeois individual subject a thing of the past, it is also a myth; it *never* really existed in the first place; there have never been autonomous subjects of that type. Rather, this construct is merely a philosophical and cultural mystification which sought to persuade people that they 'had' individual subjects and possessed this unique personal identity.

For our purposes, it is not particularly important to decide which of these positions is correct (or rather, which is more interesting and productive). What we have to retain from all this is rather an aesthetic dilemma: because if the experience and the ideology of the unique self, an experience and ideology which informed the stylistic practice of classical modernism, is over and done with, then it is no longer clear what the artists and writers of the present period are supposed to be doing. What is clear is merely that the older models—Picasso,[4] Proust, T. S. Eliot—do not work any more (or are positively harmful), since nobody has that kind of unique private world and style to express any longer. And this is perhaps not merely a 'psychological' matter: we also have to take into account the immense weight of seventy or eighty years of classical modernism itself. There is another sense in which

2. Compare ROLAND BARTHES, "Death of the Author" (1968; see above).
3. See William Whyte, *The Organization Man* (1956).
4. Pablo Picasso (1881–1973), Spanish painter and a pioneer of modernist art, especially cubism.

the writers and artists of the present day will no longer be able to invent new styles and worlds—they've already been invented; only a limited number of combinations are possible; the unique ones have been thought of already. So the weight of the whole modernist aesthetic tradition—now dead—also 'weighs like a nightmare on the brains of the living', as Marx said in another context.[5]

Hence, once again, pastiche: in a world in which stylistic innovation is no longer possible, all that is left is to imitate dead styles, to speak through the masks and with the voices of the styles in the imaginary museum. But this means that contemporary or postmodernist art is going to be about art itself in a new kind of way; even more, it means that one of its essential messages will involve the necessary failure of art and the aesthetic, the failure of the new, the imprisonment in the past.

The Nostalgia Mode

As this may seem very abstract, I want to give a few examples, one of which is so omnipresent that we rarely link it with the kinds of developments in high art discussed here. This particular practice of pastiche is not high-cultural but very much within mass culture, and it is generally known as the 'nostalgia film' (what the French neatly call *la mode rétro*—retrospective styling). We must conceive of this category in the broadest way: narrowly, no doubt, it consists merely of films about the past and about specific generational moments of that past. Thus, one of the inaugural films in this new 'genre' (if that's what it is) was Lucas's *American Graffiti*, which in 1973 set out to recapture all the atmosphere and stylistic peculiarities of the 1950s United States, the United States of the Eisenhower era. Polanski's great film *Chinatown* does something similar for the 1930s, as does Bertolucci's *The Conformist* for the Italian and European context of the same period, the fascist era in Italy;[6] and so forth. We could go on listing these films for some time: why call them pastiche? Are they not rather work in the more traditional genre known as the historical film—work which can more simply be theorized by extrapolating that other well-known form which is the historical novel?

I have my reasons for thinking that we need new categories for such films. But let me first add some anomalies: supposing I suggested that *Star Wars*[7] is also a nostalgia film. What could that mean? I presume we can agree that this is not a historical film about our own intergalactic past. Let me put it somewhat differently: one of the most important cultural experiences of the generations that grew up from the 1930s to the 1950s was the Saturday afternoon serial of the Buck Rogers[8] type—alien villains, true American heroes, heroines in distress, the death ray or the doomsday box, and the cliffhanger at the end whose miraculous resolution was to be witnessed next Saturday afternoon. *Star Wars* reinvents this experience in the form of a

5. See *The Eighteenth Brumaire of Louis Napoleon* (1852) by the German social and political philosopher KARL MARX (1818–1883).
6. All films of the 1970s, set in the relatively recent past: *American Graffiti* (1973), directed by George Lucas (b. 1945), an American; *Chinatown* (1974), directed by Roman Polanski (b. 1933), raised in Poland; and *The Conformist* (1970), written and directed by Bernardo Bertolucci (b. 1941), an Italian.
7. A 1977 film, written and directed by Lucas.
8. Hero of a comic strip created in 1929 featuring science fiction adventures, later popularized in movie serials.

pastiche: that is, there is no longer any point to a parody of such serials since they are long extinct. *Star Wars*, far from being a pointless satire of such now dead forms, satisfies a deep (might I even say repressed?) longing to experience them again: it is a complex object in which on some first level children and adolescents can take the adventures straight, while the adult public is able to gratify a deeper and more properly nostalgic desire to return to that older period and to live its strange old aesthetic artifacts through once again. This film is thus *metonymically*[9] a historical or nostalgia film: unlike *American Graffiti*, it does not reinvent a picture of the past in its lived totality; rather, by reinventing the feel and shape of characteristic art objects of an older period (the serials), it seeks to reawaken a sense of the past associated with those objects. *Raiders of the Lost Ark*,[1] meanwhile, occupies an intermediary position here: on some level it is *about* the 1930s and 1940s, but in reality it too conveys that period metonymically through its own characteristic adventure stories (which are no longer ours).

Now let me discuss another interesting anomaly which may take us further towards understanding nostalgia film in particular and pastiche generally. This one involves a recent film called *Body Heat*,[2] which, as has abundantly been pointed out by the critics, is a kind of distant remake of *The Postman Always Rings Twice* or *Double Indemnity*. (The allusive and elusive plagiarism of older plots is, of course, also a feature of pastiche.) Now *Body Heat* is technically not a nostalgia film, since it takes place in a contemporary setting, in a little Florida village near Miami. On the other hand, this technical contemporaneity is most ambiguous indeed: the credits—always our first cue—are lettered and scripted in a 1930s Art-Deco style which cannot but trigger nostalgic reactions (first to *Chinatown*, no doubt, and then beyond it to some more historical referent). Then the very style of the hero himself is ambiguous: William Hurt is a new star but has nothing of the distinctive style of the preceding generation of male superstars like Steve McQueen or even Jack Nicholson, or rather, his persona here is a kind of mix of their characteristics with an older role of the type generally associated with Clark Gable.[3] So here too there is a faintly archaic feel to all this. The spectator begins to wonder why this story, which could have been situated anywhere, is set in a small Florida town, in spite of its contemporary reference. One begins to realize after a while that the small town setting has a crucial strategic function: it allows the film to do without most of the signals and references which we might associate with the contemporary world, with consumer society—the appliances and artifacts, the high rises, the object world of late capitalism. Technically, then, its objects (its cars, for instance) are 1980s products, but everything in the film conspires to blur that immediate contemporary reference and to make it possible to receive this too as nostalgia work—as a narrative set in some indefinable nostalgic past, an eternal 1930s, say, beyond history. It seems to me exceedingly symptomatic to find the very style of nostalgia films invading and colonizing even those movies today which

9. Through association, not through resemblance.
1. A 1981 film, directed by Steven Spielberg; the story is by Lucas.
2. This 1981 film, starring William Hurt (b. 1950), follows the same seduction-murder plot line as the films noir named, *The Postman Always Rings Twice* (1946) and *Double Indemnity* (1944).
3. Gable (1901–1960), like McQueen (1930–1980) and Nicholson (b. 1937), an American leading man.

have contemporary settings: as though, for some reason, we were unable today to focus our own present, as though we have become incapable of achieving aesthetic representations of our own current experience. But if that is so, then it is a terrible indictment of consumer capitalism itself—or, at the very least, an alarming and pathological symptom of a society that has become incapable of dealing with time and history.

So now we come back to the question of why nostalgia film or pastiche is to be considered different from the older historical novel or film. (I should also include in this discussion the major literary example of all this, to my mind: the novels of E. L. Doctorow[4]—*Ragtime*, with its turn-of-the-century atmosphere, and *Loon Lake*, for the most part about our 1930s. But these are, in my opinion, historical novels in appearance only. Doctorow is a serious artist and one of the few genuinely left or radical novelists at work today. It is no disservice to him, however, to suggest that his narratives do not represent our historical past so much as they represent our ideas or cultural stereotypes about that past.) Cultural production has been driven back inside the mind, within the monadic subject: it can no longer look directly out of its eyes at the real world for the referent but must, as in Plato's cave,[5] trace its mental images of the world on its confining walls. If there is any realism left here, it is a 'realism' which springs from the shock of grasping that confinement and of realizing that, for whatever peculiar reasons, we seem condemned to seek the historical past through our own pop images and stereotypes about that past, which itself remains forever out of reach.

Postmodernism and the City

Now, before I try to offer a somewhat more positive conclusion, I want to sketch the analysis of a full-blown postmodern building—a work which is in many ways uncharacteristic of that postmodern architecture whose principal names are Robert Venturi, Charles Moore, Michael Graves, and more recently Frank Gehry,[6] but which to my mind offers some very striking lessons about the originality of postmodernist space. Let me amplify the figure which has run through the preceding remarks, and make it even more explicit: I am proposing the notion that we are here in the presence of something like a mutation in built space itself. My implication is that we ourselves, the human subjects who happen into this new space, have not kept pace with that evolution; there has been a mutation in the object, unaccompanied as yet by any equivalent mutation in the subject; we do not yet possess the perceptual equipment to match this new hyperspace, as I will call it, in part because our perceptual habits were formed in that older kind of space I have called the space of high modernism. The newer architecture therefore—like many of the other cultural products I have evoked in the preceding

4. American novelist (b. 1931), who published *Ragtime* in 1975 and *Loon Lake* in 1980.

5. That is, the allegory of the cave that opens book 7 of *Republic* (see above), by the Greek philosopher PLATO (ca. 427–ca. 347 B.C.E.); it describes the majority of humanity as trapped in a cave, seeing only the shadows cast by the representations of real objects (the "real" being the Forms or Ideas of things, located outside the cave). This view is echoed in the argument of the French theorist JEAN BAUDRILLARD (b. 1927) that in postmodernity we deal only with simulations of things (their simulacra), not with the things themselves or even with their representations.

6. All prominent American architects: Moore (1925–1993), Graves (b. 1934), and Gehry (b. 1929).

remarks—stands as something like an imperative to grow new organs to expand our sensorium and our body to some new, as yet unimaginable, perhaps ultimately impossible, dimensions.

The Bonaventure Hotel

The building whose features I will very rapidily enumerate in the next few moments is the Bonaventure Hotel, built in the new Los Angeles downtown by the architect and developer John Portman,[7] whose other works include the various Hyatt Regencies, the Peachtree Center in Atlanta, and the Renaissance Center in Detroit, I have mentioned the populist aspect of the rhetorical defence of postmodernism against the elite (and utopian) austerities of the great architectural modernisms: it is generally affirmed, in other words, that these newer building are popular works on the one hand; and that they respect the vernacular of the American city fabric on the other, that is to say, that they no longer attempt, as did the masterworks and monuments of high modernism, to insert a different, a distinct, an elevated, a new utopian language into the tawdry and commercial sign-system of the surrounding city, but rather, on the contrary, seek to speak that very language, using its lexicon and syntax as that has been emblematically 'learned from Las Vegas'.

On the first of these counts, Portman's Bonaventure fully confirms the claim: it is a popular building, visited with enthusiasm by locals and tourists alike (although Portman's other buildings are even more successful in this respect). The populist insertion into the city fabric is, however, another matter, and it is with this that we will begin. There are three entrances to the Bonaventure, one from Figueroa, and the other two by way of elevated gardens on the other side of the hotel, which is built into the remaining slope of the former Beacon Hill. None of these is anything like the old hotel marquee, or the monumental *porte-cochère*[8] with which the sumptuous buildings of yesteryear were wont to stage your passage from city street to the older interior. The entryways of the Bonaventure are as it were lateral and rather backdoor affairs: the gardens in the back admit you to the sixth floor of the towers, and even there you must walk down one flight to find the elevator by which you gain access to the lobby. Meanwhile, what one is still tempted to think of as the front entry, on Figueroa, admits you, baggage and all, onto the second-story balcony, from which you must take an escalator down to the main registration desk. More about these elevators and escalators in a moment. What I first want to suggest about these curiously unmarked ways-in is that they seem to have been imposed by some new category of closure governing the inner space of the hotel itself (and this over and above the material constraints under which Portman had to work). I believe that, with a certain number of other characteristic postmodern buildings, such as the Beaubourg in Paris, or the Eaton Centre in Toronto, the Bonaventure aspires to being a total space, a complete world, a kind of miniature city (and I would want to add that to this new total space corresponds a new collective practice, a new mode in which individuals move and congregate, something like the practice of a new and historically original kind of hyper-crowd). In this sense,

7. Influential American architect (b. 1924).
8. Coach doorway (French); now, a porch roof extending from an entrance over a driveway.

then, ideally the mini-city of Portman's Bonaventure ought not to have entrances at all, since the entryway is always the seam that links the building to the rest of the city that surrounds it: for it does not wish to be a part of the city, but rather its equivalent and its replacement or substitute. That is, however, obviously not possible or practical, whence the deliberate downplaying and reduction of the entrance function to its bare minimum. But this disjunction from the surrounding city is very different from that of the great monuments of the International Style: there, the act of disjunction was violent, visible, and had a very real symbolic significance—as in Le Corbusier's great *pilotis*[9] whose gesture radically separates the new utopian space of the modern from the degraded and fallen city fabric which it thereby explicitly repudiates (although the gamble of the modern was that this new utopian space, in the virulence of its Novum,[1] would fan out and transform that eventually by the power of its new spatial language). The Bonaventure, however, is content to 'let the fallen city fabric continue to be in its being' (to parody Heidegger[2]); no further effects, no larger protopolitical utopian transformation, is either expected or desired.

This diagnosis is to my mind confirmed by the great reflective glass skin of the Bonaventure, whose function I will now interpret rather differently that I did a moment ago when I saw the phenomenon of reflexion generally as developing a thematics of reproductive technology (the two readings are however not incompatible). Now one would want rather to stress the way in which the glass skin repels the city outside; a repulsion for which we have analogies in those reflector sunglasses which make it impossible for your interlocutor to see your own eyes and thereby achieve a certain aggressivity towards and power over the Other. In a similar way, the glass skin achieves a peculiar and placeless dissociation of the Bonaventure from its neighborhood: it is not even an exterior, inasmuch as when you seek to look at the hotel's outer walls you cannot see the hotel itself, but only the distorted images of everything that surrounds it.

Now I want to say a few words about escalators and elevators: given their very real pleasures in Portman, particularly these last, which the artist has termed 'gigantic kinetic sculptures' and which certainly account for much of the spectacle and the excitement of the hotel interior, particularly in the Hyatts, where like great Japanese lanterns or gondolas they ceaselessly rise and fall—given such a deliberate marking and foregrounding in their own right, I believe one has to see such 'people movers' (Portman's own term, adapted from Disney[3]) as something a little more than mere functions and engineering components. We know in any case that recent architectural theory has begun to borrow from narrative analysis in other fields, and to attempt to see our physical trajectories through such buildings as virtual narratives or stories as dynamic paths and narrative paradigms which we as visitors are asked to fulfill and to complete with our own bodies and movements. In the Bonaventure, however, we find a dialectical heightening of this process: it seems to me that the escalators and elevators here henceforth replace move-

9. Pilings (French), pillars that support a building and make bearing walls unnecessary; Le Corbusier used them to leave the ground floor open.
1. New thing, novelty (Latin).
2. Jameson echoes language often used by Heidegger in *Being and Time* (1927).
3. Walt Disney (1901–1966), American animator and filmmaker who planned the amusement parks Disneyland and Disney World; they included escalators and monorails, which Disney called "people movers."

ment but also and above all designate themselves as new reflexive signs and emblems of movement proper (something which will become evident when we come to the whole question of what remains of older forms of movement in this building, most notably walking itself). Here the narrative stroll has been underscored, symbolized, reified and replaced by a transportation machine which becomes the allegorical signifier of that older promenade we are no longer allowed to conduct on our own: and this is a dialectical intensification of the autoreferentiality of all modern culture, which tends to turn upon itself and designate its own cultural production as its content.

I am more at a loss when it comes to conveying the thing itself, the experience of space you undergo when you step off such allegorical devices into the lobby or atrium, with its great central column, surrounded by a miniature lake, the whole positioned between the four symmetrical residential towers with their elevators, and surrounded by rising balconies capped by a kind of greenhouse roof at the sixth level. I am tempted to say that such space makes it impossible for us to use the language of volume of volumes any longer, since these last are impossible to seize. Hanging streamers indeed suffuse this empty space in such a way as to distract systematically and deliberately from whatever form it might be supposed to have; while a constant busyness gives the feeling that emptiness is here absolutely packed, that it is an element within which you yourself are immersed, without any of that distance that formerly enabled the perception of perspective or volume. You are in this hyperspace up to your eyes and your body; and if it seemed to you before that that suppression of depth I spoke of in postmodern painting or literature would necessarily be difficult to achieve in architecture itself, perhaps you may now be willing to see this bewildering immersion as the formal equivalent in the new medium.

Yet escalator and elevator are also in this context dialectical opposites; and we may suggest that the glorious movement of the elevator gondolas is also a dialectical compensation for this filled space of the atrium—it gives us the chance at a radically different, but complementary, spatial experience, that of rapidly shooting up through the ceiling and outside, along one of the four symmetrical towers, with the referent, Los Angeles itself, spread out breathtakingly and even alarmingly before us. But even this vertical movement is contained: the elevator lifts you to one of those revolving cocktail lounges, in which you, seated, are again passively rotated about and offered a contemplative spectacle of the city itself, now transformed into its own images by the glass windows through which you view it.

Let me quickly conclude all this by returning to the central space of the lobby itself (with the passing observation that the hotel rooms are visibly marginalized: the corridors in the residential sections are low-ceilinged and dark, most depressingly functional indeed: while one understands that the rooms are in the worst of taste). The descent is dramatic enough, plummeting back down through the roof to splash down in the lake; what happens when you get there is something else, which I can only try to characterize as milling confusion, something like the vengeance this space takes on those who still seek to walk through it. Given the absolute symmetry of the four towers, it is quite impossible to get your bearings in this lobby; recently, colour coding and directional signals have been added in a pitiful and revealing, rather desperate attempt to restore the coordinates of an older space. I will take as the most dramatic practical result of this spatial mutation the notorious dilemma of the shopkeepers on the various balconies: it has been obvious, since the very opening of the hotel in 1977, that nobody could ever find any of these stores, and even if you located the appropriate boutique, you would be most unlikely to be as fortunate a second time; as a consequence, the commercial tenants are in despair and all the merchandise is marked down to bargain prices. When you recall that Portman is a businessman as well as an architect, and a millionaire developer, an artist who is at one and the same time a capitalist in his own right, you cannot but feel that here too something of a 'return of the repressed' is involved.

So I come finally to my principal point here, that this latest mutation in space—postmodern hyperspace—has finally succeeded in transcending the capacities of the individual human body to locate itself, to organize its immediate surroundings perceptually, and cognitively to map its position in a mappable external world. And I have already suggested that this alarming disjunction point between the body and its built environment—which is to the initial bewilderment of the older modernism as the velocities of spacecraft are to those of the automobile—can itself stand as the symbol and analog of that even sharper dilemma which is the incapacity of our minds, at least at present, to map the great global multinational and decentered communicational network in which we find ourselves caught as individual subjects.

The New Machine

But as I am anxious that Portman's space not be perceived as something either exceptional or seemingly marginalized and leisure-specialized on the order of Disneyland, I would like in passing to juxtapose this complacent and entertaining (although bewildering) leisure-time space with its analog in a very different area, namely the space of postmodern warfare, in particular as Michael Herr evokes it in his great book on the experience of Vietnam, called *Dispatches*.[4] The extraordinary linguistic innovations of this work may still be considered postmodern, in the eclectic way in which its language impersonally fuses a whole range of contemporary collective idiolects, most notably rock language and black language: but the fusion is dictated by problems of content. This first terrible postmodernist war cannot be told in any of the traditional paradigms of the war novel or movie—indeed that breakdown of all previous narrative paradigms is, along with the breakdown of any shared language through which a veteran might convey such experience, among the principal subjects of the book and may be said to open up the place of a whole new reflexivity. Benjamin's account of Baudelaire,[5] and of the emergence of modernism from a new experience of city technology which transcends all the older habits of bodily perception, is both singularly relevant here, and singularly antiquated, in the light of this new and virtually unimaginable quantum leap in technological alienation:

> He was a moving-target-survivor subscriber, a true child of the war, because except for the rare times when you were pinned or stranded the

4. A memoir published in 1977; Herr (b. 1940) is an American journalist.
5. CHARLES BAUDELAIRE (1821–1867), French poet; the German critic WALTER BENJAMIN (1892–1940) discusses him and 19th-century Paris in his unfinished *Arcades Project* (1983; trans. 1999), part of which was published earlier as *Charles Baudelaire: A Lyric Poet in the Era of High Capitalism* (1969; trans. 1973).

> system was geared to keep you mobile, if that was what you thought you wanted. As a technique for staying alive it seemed to make as much sense as anything, given naturally that you were there to begin with and wanted to see it close; it started out sound and straight but it formed a cone as it progressed, because the more you moved the more you saw, the more you saw the more besides death and mutilation you risked, and the more you risked of that the more you would have to let go of one day as a 'survivor'. Some of us moved around the war like crazy people until we couldn't see which way the run was taking us anymore, only the war all over its surface with occasional, unexpected penetration. As long as we could have choppers like taxis it took real exhaustion or depression near shock or a dozen pipes of opium to keep us even apparently quiet, we'd still be running around inside our skins like something was after us, ha, ha, La Vida Loca.[6] In the months after I got back the hundreds of helicopters I'd flown in begin to draw together until they'd formed a collective meta-chopper, and in my mind it was the sexiest thing going; saver-destroyer, provider-waster, right hand-left hand, nimble, fluent, canny and human; hot steel, grease, jungle-saturated canvas webbing, sweat cooling and warming up again, cassette rock and roll in one ear and door-gun fire in the other, fuel, heat, vitality and death, death itself, hardly an intruder.[7]

In this new machine, which does not, like the older modernist machinery of the locomotive or the airplane, represent motion, but which can only be represented *in motion*, something of the mystery of the new postmodernist space is concentrated.

The Aesthetic of Consumer Society

Now I must try very rapidly in conclusion to characterize the relationship of cultural production of this kind to social life in this country today. This will also be the moment to address the principal objection to concepts of postmodernism of the type I have sketched here: namely that all the features we have enumerated are not new at all but abundantly characterized modernism proper or what I call high modernism. Was not Thomas Mann, after all, interested in the idea of pastiche, and are not certain chapters of *Ulysses* its most obvious realization? Can Flaubert, Mallarmé and Gertrude Stein[8] not be included in an account of postmodernist temporality? What is so new about all of this? Do we really need the concept of *post*modernism?

One kind of answer to this question would raise the whole issue of periodization and of how a historian (literary or other) posits a radical break between two henceforth distinct periods. I must limit myself to the suggestion that radical breaks between periods do not generally involve complete changes of content but rather the restructuring of a certain number of elements already given: features that in an earlier period or system were subordinate now become dominant, and features that had been dominant

6. The Crazy Life (Spanish).
7. Michael Herr, *Dispatches* (New York: Knopf, 1977), pp. 8–9 [Jameson's note].
8. American modernist (1874–1946), who was innovative in poetry and prose. *Ulysses* (1922), Joyce's landmark modernist novel. Gustave Flaubert (1821–1880), French novelist. STÉPHANE MALLARMÉ (1842–1898), French poet.

again become secondary. In this sense, everything we have described here can be found in earlier periods and most notably within modernism proper: my point is that until the present day those things have been secondary or minor features of modernist art, marginal rather than central, and that we have something new when they become the central features of cultural production.

But I can argue this more concretely by turning to the relationship between cultural production and social life generally. The older or classical modernism was an oppositional art; it emerged within the business society of the gilded age[9] as scandalous and offensive to the middle-class public—ugly, dissonant, bohemian, sexually shocking. It was something to make fun of (when the police were not called in to seize the books or close the exhibitions): an offense to good taste and to common sense, or, as Freud and Marcuse[1] would have put it, a provocative challenge to the reigning reality- and performance-principles of early twentieth-century middle-class society. Modernism in general did not go well with over-stuffed Victorian furniture, with Victorian moral taboos, or with the conventions of polite society. This is to say that whatever the explicit political content of the great high modernisms, the latter were always in some mostly implicit ways dangerous and explosive, subversive within the established order.

If then we suddenly return to the present day, we can measure the immensity of the cultural changes that have taken place. Not only are Joyce and Picasso no longer weird and repulsive, they have become classics and now look rather realistic to us. Meanwhile, there is very little in either the form or the content of contemporary art that contemporary society finds intolerable and scandalous. The most offensive forms of this art—punk rock, say, or what is called sexually explicit material—are all taken in stride by society, and they are commercially successful, unlike the productions of the older high modernism. But this means that even if contemporary art has all the same formal features as the older modernism, it has still shifted its position fundamentally within our culture. For one thing, commodity production and in particular our clothing, furniture, buildings and other artifacts are now intimately tied in with styling changes which derive from artistic experimentation; our advertising, for example, is fed by postmodernism in all the arts and inconceivable without it. For another, the classics of high modernism are now part of the so-called canon and are taught in schools and universities—which at once empties them of any of their older subversive power. Indeed, one way of marking the break between the periods and of dating the emergence of postmodernism is precisely to be found there: in the moment (the early 1960s, one would think) in which the position of high modernism and its dominant aesthetics become established in the academy and are henceforth felt to be academic by a whole new generation of poets, painters and musicians.

But one can also come at the break from the other side, and describe it in terms of periods of recent social life. As I have suggested, non-Marxists and

9. Era in late-19th-century America of rapid industrial expansion, burgeoning wealth for some, and gaudy materialism (the name is taken from an 1873 novel by Mark Twain and Charles Dudley Warner).

1. Herbert Marcuse (1898–1979), German-born American philosopher and social critic. SIGMUND FREUD (1856–1939), Austrian founder of psychoanalysis.

Marxists alike have come around to the general feeling that at some point following World War II a new kind of society began to emerge (variously described as postindustrial society, multinational capitalism, consumer society, media society and so forth). New types of consumption; planned obsolescence; an ever more rapid rhythm of fashion and styling changes; the penetration of advertising, television and the media generally to a hitherto unparalleled degree throughout society; the replacement of the old tension between city and country, center and province, by the suburb and by universal standardization; the growth of the great networks of superhighways and the arrival of automobile culture—these are some of the features which would seem to mark a radical break with that older prewar society in which high modernism was still an underground force.

I believe that the emergence of postmodernism is closely related to the emergence of this new moment of late, consumer or multinational capitalism. I believe also that its formal features in many ways express the deeper logic of that particular social system. I will only be able, however, to show this for one major theme: namely the disappearance of a sense of history, the way in which our entire contemporary social system has little by little begun to lose its capacity to retain its own past, has begun to live in a perpetual present and in a perpetual change that obliterates traditions of the kind which all earlier social formations have had in one way or another to preserve. Think only of the media exhaustion of news: of how Nixon and, even more so, Kennedy[2] are figures from a now distant past. One is tempted to say that the very function of the news media is to relegate such recent historical experiences as rapidly as possible into the past. The informational function of the media would thus be to help us forget, to serve as the very agents and mechanisms for our historical amnesia.

But in that case the two features of postmodernism on which I have dwelt here—the transformation of reality into images, the fragmentation of time into a series of perpetual presents—are both extraordinarily consonant with this process. My own conclusion here must take the form of a question about the critical value of the newer art. There is some agreement that the older modernism functioned against its society in ways which are variously described as critical, negative, contestatory, subversive, oppositional and the like. Can anything of the sort be affirmed about postmodernism and its social moment? We have seen that there is a way in which postmodernism replicates or reproduces—reinforces—the logic of consumer capitalism; the more significant question is whether there is also a way in which it resists that logic. But that is a question we must leave open.

1988

2. John F. Kennedy (1917–1963), 35th U.S. president (1961–63). Richard Nixon (1913–1994), 37th U.S. president (1969–74), who lost to Kennedy in the 1960 election.

GERALD VIZENOR
b. 1934

With the refrain "This portrait is not an Indian," Gerald Vizenor dissects the images of Native Americans usually presented in literature, history, and popular culture. Written in the associative style of pastiche, juxtaposing cultural commentary with postmodern theory ranging from poststructuralist critiques of representation to postcolonialist critiques of the dominance of the West, Vizenor's "Postindian Warriors," the opening section of his *Manifest Manners: Postindian Warriors of Survivance* (1994), is a declaration of his theory of the "postindian." Along with PAULA GUNN ALLEN, Vizenor is one of the strongest voices in contemporary literary studies demanding that attention be paid to distorted representations of Native American history and culture.

Vizenor was born in Minneapolis to a Swedish American mother and a French Anishinaabe ("Chippewa") father who was from the White Earth reservation in northern Minnesota. After his father's murder when he was less than two years old, Vizenor lived at various times with his paternal grandmother's family, his mother, and foster families. Dropping out of high school, he enlisted in the U.S. Army in 1952 and was stationed in Japan in 1953 as a tank commander and as a scriptwriter in an entertainment unit. There he earned a high school equivalency diploma and discovered an interest in writing, especially in haiku, a form he found similar to Anishinaabe dream songs. Back in civilian life, Vizenor completed his B.A. at the University of Minnesota in 1960. He worked as a social worker at the Minnesota State Reformatory, returned to the University of Minnesota for graduate study, and from 1964 to 1968 was director of the American Indian Employment and Guidance Center in Minneapolis. At a time of increasing Native American political activism in the United States in the late 1960s and 1970s, he reported and wrote essays on Native issues for the Minneapolis *Tribune*. Beginning in 1970 Vizenor has held a series of academic jobs, teaching first at Lake Forest College, then in Minnesota, China, California, and Oklahoma; since 1992 he has been a professor at the University of California at Berkeley.

Like others subjected to European colonialism, Native peoples have commonly been represented as "primitives," lacking legitimate political structures and histories. They have also been treated as one monolithic group, despite their heterogeneity. Native peoples often remain absent even from progressive contemporary analyses of colonialism and identity. Vizenor aims to counteract this ignorance: his early work transcribes material from Native oral traditions and reports on the political situation of present-day Native peoples, his novels represent Native culture, and his later work creates a hybrid theoretical discourse to dispel the false stereotypes of Native peoples.

In "Postindian Warriors," Vizenor creatively spins out a series of neologisms, mixing contemporary Euro-American theory and Native intellectual traditions to defamiliarize common notions of Native Americans. His key terms include *manifest manners, survivance,* and *postindian. Manifest manners* describes the spread of literary and cultural representations much as the historical subjection of Native peoples was explained as *manifest destiny*, a phrase coined in 1845 by John L. O'Sullivan, the editor of the *United States Magazine and Democratic Review*. O'Sullivan wrote that it was "the fulfillment of our manifest destiny to overspread the continent allotted by Providence." This ideology justifying the violence done Native peoples was supported not only by divine preordination but also by cultural and scholarly knowledge, which "proved" the inherent inferiority of Native peoples and warranted their surveillance and control, as well as their "natural" extinction.

Nineteenth-century American novelists and historians participated in the discourse of manifest manners. James Fenimore Cooper, for example, frequently portrays noble as well as evil savages in his popular Leatherstocking Tales, but all his representations reinforce the idea of Indians' inevitable, providential disappearance. Vizenor argues that manifest manners continue to flourish in present-day "simulations" of Native culture. Thus, examining the popular, award-winning film *Dances with Wolves* (1990), an ostensibly sympathetic depiction of Native Americans, he notes that it presents only the perspective of the white characters and their cultural anxieties; it offers no sense of actual tribal culture, whose death in fact is elegaically assumed. Vizenor sees the contemporary discourse of victimhood and sympathy as a "treacherous and elusive" mode still perpetuating Euro-American dominance of Native peoples.

Coining the term *survivance*, which infuses *survival* with a more active sense of resistance, Vizenor turns the image of the Native American from romanticized victim to a figure of strength and endurance: the result is what he calls the "postindian," the postmodern Native person who has an awareness of and manipulates conventional images of the "Indian." Vizenor urges Native people to become "postindian warriors of simulations" and engage in "trickster hermeneutics," using invention in language and the shifting and contingent nature of meaning to replace simulations with a more valid "tribal consciousness."

Vizenor takes his own advice throughout "Postindian Warriors," juxtaposing an eclectic mix of concepts and mannerisms from contemporary poststructuralist and postmodern theory. His playfully neologistic style mimics and parodies that of the deconstructive philosopher JACQUES DERRIDA. From JEAN BAUDRILLARD he borrows the concept of simulation, or the belief that in postmodern life, we are so far from real things and experiences that we can only simulate them, not represent them. While Baudrillard finds simulation characteristic of postmodernity, Vizenor attempts to reclaim a sense of real Native peoples and cultures. He also draws on the writings both of MICHEL FOUCAULT, who has analyzed the link between the production of knowledge and the possession of power by dominant groups, and of EDWARD W. SAID, who has exposed how the Western discourse and discipline of orientalism constructs an imaginary yet enduring "Orient," which reflects the West's own prejudices and enforces control of foreign "others." In Vizenor's words, the Indian is an "occidental invention." He points out the pervasiveness and endurance of "knowledge" about Native peoples that Europeans continue to invoke—often unwittingly, in academic disciplines such as anthropology and literary criticism, in governmental policies, and in popular culture—to justify and maintain their political authority.

Although Vizenor has been a tireless advocate of Native American studies, Native critics have taken him to task for his use of academic theory and language—one critic calls it a "mudbath of jargon"—which they claim duplicates Western dominance. Defenders rebut that he deploys theory ironically as a mocking trickster. This dispute highlights a perennial theoretical problem of authenticity and assimilation, particularly in studies related to racial, ethnic, and national identity. Some scholars call for the rigorous self-representation of minority and colonized peoples and culture, exclusively in their own languages rather than in the "master's tongue." Others, such as HENRY LOUIS GATES JR. in African American studies and HOMI BHABHA in postcolonial studies, argue that minorities adopt the critical tools at hand to make their interventions, changing dominant discourse in the process. Like JANE TOMPKINS and other critics who in recent years have practiced alternative forms of criticism, Vizenor freely employs creative techniques and an informal, essayistic style instead of standard academic argument. Perhaps frustrating for traditional theorists because it juxtaposes a range of sources without developing a consistent theoretical strand, but appealing for those who seek a new mode of critical writing, "Postindian Warriors" is a unique, sometimes eclectic, and distinctive intervention in contemporary theory.

BIBLIOGRAPHY

Vizenor's prolific writings include poetry, fiction, journalism, oral history, autobiography, essays, criticism, and what have been called "mixed-genre" works. Influenced by his time in Japan, he published five books of haiku poetry in the 1960s, collected in *Matushima: Pine Islands* (1984) and later *Cranes Arise: Haiku Scenes* (1998). He also edited three compilations of Anishinaabe oral literature in the 1960s, collected in *Summer in the Spring: Anishinaabe Lyric Poems and Stories* (1993), and three compilations of Chippewa and Ojibwe tribal history and lore. To draw attention to Native American literary tradition he edited a textbook anthology, *Native American Literature: A Brief Introduction and Anthology* (1995). Through the 1980s and 1990s Vizenor became best known for his six novels, notably *The Heirs of Columbus* (1991), and he also published two collections of short stories, a film script, and a play.

Vizenor's experience as a journalist reporting on Native American issues led to *Escorts to White Earth, 1868–1968, One Hundred Years on a Reservation* (1968), *Thomas James White Hawk* (1968), *Tribal Scenes and Ceremonies* (1976; rev. as *Crossbloods: Bone Courts, Bingo, and Other Reports*, 1990), and the mixed-genre *Earthdivers: Tribal Narratives on Mixed Descent* (1983). With his edited collection *Narrative Chance: Postmodern Discourse on Native American Indian Literature* (1989) and his own essay in that collection, "Trickster Discourse: Comic Holotropes and Language Games," Vizenor turned to postmodern and poststructuralist theory. His later critical-theoretical works on the "postindian" include *Manifest Manners: Postindian Warriors of Survivance* (1994), from which our selection "Postindian Warriors" is taken, and *Fugitive Poses: Native American Scenes of Absence and Presence* (1998). A good sample of the range of Vizenor's writing can be found in the collection *Shadow Distance: A Gerald Vizenor Reader*, edited by A. Robert Lee (1994). For Vizenor's biography, consult his autobiography, *Interior Landscapes: Autobiographical Myths and Metaphors* (1990). The collection of interviews with A. Robert Lee, *Postindian Conversations* (1999), provides an excellent overview of Vizenor's career, recounting his life and writing in his own words; it also includes a useful introduction by Lee that fills out Vizenor's biography and summarizes the variety of his work.

For critical examinations of Vizenor's methods, see Elaine Jahner, "Allies in the World Wars: Vizenor's Uses of Contemporary Critical Theory," *Studies in American Indian Literatures* 9 (1985); A. LaVonne Ruoff, "Woodland Word Warrior: An Introduction to the Works of Gerald Vizenor," *Melus* 13 (1986); and David Murray, "Crossblood Strategies in the Writings of Gerald Vizenor," *Yearbook of English Studies* 24 (1994). Ward Churchill criticizes Vizenor's "cliquish obscurantism" in a sharp review of *Manifest Manners* in *American Indian Culture and Research Journal* 18 (1994). In *The Turn of the Native: Studies in Criticism and Culture* (1996), Arnold Krupat discusses Vizenor's writing in relation to postcolonialism. The one book devoted to his work, Kimberly M. Blaeser's *Gerald Vizenor: Writing in the Oral Tradition* (1996), places it in the context of Native oral traditions. A special issue of the journal *Studies in American Indian Literatures*, edited by Louis Owens (9 [1997]), features essays on Vizenor's diverse body of writing.

Blaeser's *Gerald Vizenor* includes an extensive bibliography, and both *Shadow Distance* and *Postindian Conversations* (cited above) offer good selected bibliographies. The best source documenting the criticism of his work is "Gerald Vizenor: An Annotated Bibliography of Criticism," *Studies in American Indian Literature* 11 (1999).

From Manifest Manners: Postindian Warriors of Survivance

From *Chapter 1. Postindian Warriors*

* * *

Manifest Destiny[1] would cause the death of millions of tribal people from massacres, diseases, and the loneliness of reservations. Entire cultures have

1. A 19th-century doctrine that the United States had the divine right and duty to expand its territory and influence throughout North America.

been terminated in the course of nationalism. These histories are now the simulations[2] of dominance, and the causes of the conditions that have become manifest manners in literature. The postindian simulations are the core of survivance,[3] the new stories of tribal courage. The simulations of manifest manners are the continuance of the surveillance and domination of the tribes in literature. Simulations are the absence of the tribal real; the postindian conversions are in the new stories of survivance over dominance. The natural reason of the tribes anteceded by thousands of generations the invention of the Indian. The postindian ousts the inventions with humor, new stories, and the simulations of survivance.

Standing Bear, for instance, had graduated from the government school and he was working at John Wanamaker's department store in Philadelphia when he read in the newspaper that Sitting Bull,[4] the Lakota healer, was scheduled to lecture in the city. "The paper stated that he was the Indian who killed General Custer! The chief and his people had been held prisoners of war, and now here they were to appear" in a theater. "On the stage sat four Indian men, one of whom was Sitting Bull. There were two women and two children with them. A white man came on the stage and introduced Sitting Bull as the man who had killed General Custer," which was not true.

Sitting Bull "addressed the audience in the Sioux tongue" and then the white man, the interpreter, misconstrued his speech in translation. "My friends, white people, we Indians are on our way to Washington to see the Grandfather, or President of the United States," and more was translated as the story of the massacre of General Custer at the Little Big Horn. "He told so many lies I had to smile."

Standing Bear visited Sitting Bull at the hotel. "He wanted his children educated in the white man's way, because there was nothing left for the Indian." The interpreter was in the room, so "I did not get a chance to tell Sitting Bull how the white man had lied about him on the stage. And that was the last time I ever saw Sitting Bull alive."

The postindian warriors hover at last over the ruins of tribal representations and surmount the scriptures of manifest manners with new stories; these warriors counter the surveillance and literature of dominance with their own simulations of survivance. The postindian arises from the earlier inventions of the tribes only to contravene the absence of the real with theatrical performances; the theater of tribal consciousness is the recreation of the real, not the absence of the real in the simulations of dominance.

Manifest manners are the simulations of dominance; the notions and misnomers that are read as the authentic and sustained as representations of Native American Indians. The postindian warriors are new indications of a

2. A term borrowed from the French theorist Jean Baudrillard (b. 1929), who argues that in postmodern society we "simulate" rather than "represent" reality; see *Simulacra and Simulation* (1981).
3. Vizenor's coinage, combining *survival* and *resistance*. "Postindian": the Native person who overcomes false views of Indians by means of other simulations, truth, and humor.
4. Principal chief (ca. 1831–1890) of the Sioux after 1867; he led the alliance of western tribes that defeated George Custer (1839–1876) and the Seventh Cavalry in June 1876 at the Battle of the Little Bighorn. Starvation forced their surrender in 1881. In 1885–86 Sitting Bull toured with the Wild West Show of William Frederick "Buffalo Bill" Cody. Luther Standing Bear (1868–1939), a Lakota who was born on the Pine Ridge Reservation in South Dakota and attended boarding school in Pennsylvania; he worked as a clerk, teacher, minister, and movie actor, later becoming an activist for Native people.

narrative recreation, the simulations that overcome the manifest manners of dominance.

The once bankable simulations of the savage as an impediment to developmental civilization, the simulations that audiences would consume in Western literature and motion pictures, protracted the extermination of tribal cultures.

Michael Blake[5] must have been cued to continue the simulations in his novel, *Dances with Wolves*. "There were Pawnee, the most terrible of all the tribes," he wrote. "They saw with unsophisticated but ruthlessly efficient eyes. . . . And if it was determined that the object should cease to live, the Pawnee saw to its death with psychotic precision."

The motion picture with the same name counts on the bankable manifest manners of the audience to associate with the adventures and discoveries of an errant cavalry officer who counters the simulations of savagism in *his* stories. The tiresome tantivy of tried and true horses with no shadows, and the Western tune of manifest manners, is the most serious deliverance of civilization ever concocted in the movies or literature. The Civil War has become one of those simulations in movies that abates the loathsome memories of more recent wars, and hastens the disabused heroes to discover their honorable pluck with native warriors. *Dances with Wolves*, for instance, must have been inspired by the men who heard the cicerones of *Broken Arrow* and *Little Big Man*.[6] Manifestly, movies have never been the representations of tribal cultures; at best, movies are the deliverance of an unsure civilization.

Simulations are the absence of the tribes; that absence was wiser in the scenes of silence, richer in costumes, and more courageous on a ride beside simulated animals. Western movies are the muse of simulations, and the absence of humor and real tribal cultures.

"The absence of Indians in Western movies, by which I mean the lack of their serious presence as individuals, is so shocking once you realize it that, even for someone acquainted with outrage, it's hard to admit," wrote Jane Tompkins in *West of Everything*.[7] "My unbelief at the travesty of native peoples that Western films afford kept me from scrutinizing what was there. I didn't want to see. I stubbornly expected the genre to be better than it was, and when it wasn't, I dropped the subject. . . . I never cried at anything I saw in a Western, but I cried when I realized this: that after the Indians had been decimated by disease, removal, and conquest, and after they had been caricatured and degraded in Western movies, I had ignored them too."

The Western movies, of course, are not cultural visions, but the vicious encounters with the antiselves of civilization, the invented savage. Since the national encounters over the war in Vietnam, however, the Indian is a new contrivance and encounter of the antiselves in postwestern movies. The new scenes of postwestern simulations are the melancholy antiselves in the ruins of representation; the tribal others are now embraced, a romance with silence and visions. The tragic wisdom that was once denied is now a new invention in such postwestern movies as *Dances with Wolves*.

5. American novelist (b. 1943); his 1988 novel was made in 1990 into an Academy Award–winning movie directed by and starring Kevin Costner.

6. Two westerns: in *Broken Arrow* (dir. Delmer Daves, 1950), Apaches are depicted relatively sympathetically; in the comedy *Little Big Man* (dir. Arthur Penn, 1970), the main character is a white survivor of Little Bighorn.

7. *West of Everything: The Inner Life of Westerns* (1992). TOMPKINS (b. 1940), American literary and cultural critic.

The postindian is the new simulation in the postwestern salvation of the antiselves in the movies; the landscape, overrun to be sure, has turned even richer in postwestern movies with the rescue of natural reason and romance over the ministrations of antitribal mercantilism.

Wallace Stegner[8] has ushered the postwestern landscape into a new theater of literary salvation and dominance; alas, he has no obvious need to be *seen* with the tribal others as survivance. "Being a Westerner is not simple," he wrote in his recent collections of essays, *Where the Bluebird Sings to the Lemonade Springs*. He observes that "ethnic and cultural confusion exists not only in Los Angeles but in varying proportions in every western city and many towns. Much of the adaptation that is going on is adaptation to an uncertain reality or to a reality whose past and present do not match. The western culture and western character with which it is easiest to identify exist largely in the West of make-believe, where they can be kept simple."

Thomas Jefferson, James Fenimore Cooper, Francis Parkman, George Bancroft,[9] and other masters of manifest manners in the nineteenth century, and earlier, represented tribal cultures as the other; to them "language did the capturing, binding Indian society to a future of certain extinction," wrote Larzer Ziff in *Writing in the New Nation*.[1] "Treating living Indians as sources for a literary construction of a vanished way of life rather than as members of a vital continuing culture, such writers used words to replace rather than to represent Indian reality."

The simulations of manifest manners are treacherous and elusive in histories; how ironic that the most secure simulations are unreal sensations, and become the real without a referent to an actual tribal remembrance. Tribal realities are superseded by simulations of the unreal, and tribal wisdom is weakened by those imitations, however sincere. The pleasures of silence, natural reason, the rights of consciousness, transformations of the marvelous, and the pleasure of trickster stories are misconstrued in the simulations of dominance; manifest manners are the absence of the real in the ruins of tribal representations.

Those who "memorialized rather than perpetuated" a tribal presence and wrote "Indian history as obituary" were unconsciously collaborating "with those bent on physical extermination," argued Ziff. "The process of literary annihilation would be checked only when Indian writers began representing their own culture."

Andrew McLaughlin and Claude Van Tyne, authors of a high school history textbook published by Appleton and Company a generation after the Wounded Knee[2] Massacre, resisted the inclusion of more than about half a

8. American novelist (1909–1993), many of whose works are set in the American West; *Where the Bluebird Sings to the Lemonade Springs: Living and Writing in the West* (1992) is a volume of memoirs.

9. All Americans who played major roles in shaping perceptions of the West: Jefferson (1743–1826), 3rd U.S. president (1801–09), whose views on Indians and treaties are expressed in *Notes on the State of Virginia* (1787); Parkman (1823–1893), historian who often focused on U.S. expansion; Cooper (1789–1851), novelist whose Leatherstocking Tales were enormously popular; and Bancroft (1800–1891), historian often called the father of American history.

1. *Writing in the New Nation: Prose, Print, and Politics in the Early United States* (1991). Ziff (b. 1927), American literary scholar.

2. Site in South Dakota within the Pine Ridge Reservation where more than 200 Lakota men, women, and children were massacred on December 29, 1890; followers of Sitting Bull had been pursued to the encampment after a gunfight erupted when troops and tribal police attempted to arrest the chief, killing Sitting Bull and 12 others. McLaughlin and Tyne published *A History of the United States for Schools* in 1911.

page on Indians. Manifest manners and the simulations of dominance are the annihilation, not the survivance of tribal stories.

"Simulation is no longer that of a territory, a referential being or a substance," wrote Jean Baudrillard in *Simulacra and Simulation*. "It is the generation by models of a real without origin or reality: a hyperreal. The territory no longer precedes the map, nor survives it."

Americans, moreover, pursue a "more to come" consumer simulation, wrote Umberto Eco[3] in *Travels in Hyperreality*. "This is the reason for this journey into hyperreality, in search of instances where the American imagination demands the real thing, and, to attain it, must fabricate the absolute fake." Indians, in this sense, must be the simulations of the "absolute fakes" in the ruins of representation, or the victims in literary annihilation.

* * *

The attention to manifest manners and the romance of the land would annihilate tribal names, languages, oral stories, and natural reason. Larzer Ziff argued that literary "annihilation, in which the representation offers itself as the only aspect of the represented that is still extant, is not, of course, physical extermination." However, in "order to conquer the savage one had to outdo him in savagery," and "the wild man within was purged even as the wild man without was exterminated."

The word Indian, and most other tribal names, are simulations in the literature of dominance. Chippewa, for instance, is defined as *otchipwe*, and the invented word Indian is defined as *anishinabe* in *A Dictionary of the Otchipwe Language* by Bishop Baraga.[4] This first dictionary of the language published more than a century ago defined *anishinabe* as a man, woman, child, of the *anishinabe* tribe, but the simulated names, not the names in tribal languages, were sustained by manifest manners in literature.

Cognation and certain loan words can be traced to the earliest use in the literature of dominance. *Canoe*, for instance, was "picked up from the Indians in the West Indies by Columbus's sailors," observed H. L. Mencken in *The American Language*.[5] "It was taken without change into Spanish where it remains as *canoa* to this day." *Maize* is another loan word that came into Spanish and then English from the West Indies. The word *Indian*, however, is a colonial enactment, not a loan word, and the dominance is sustained by the simulation that has superseded the real tribal names.

The Indian was an occidental invention that became a bankable simulation; the word has no referent in tribal languages or cultures. The postindian is the absence of the invention, and the end of representation in literature; the closure of that evasive melancholy of dominance. Manifest manners are the simulations of bourgeois decadence and melancholy.

The postindian warrior is the simulation of survivance in new stories. Indians, and other simulations, are the absence of tribal intimation; the mere

3. Italian semiotician and novelist (b. 1932); *Travels in Hyperreality* was published in 1986.

4. Frederic Baraga (1797–1868), Austrian-born first bishop of Marquette, Michigan; he began his Indian mission in 1831, and published the first Chippewa grammar (1850) and then dictionary: *A Dictionary of the Otchipwe Language, Explained in English. This language is spoken by the Chippewa Indians, and also by the Otawas, Potawatamis and Alogonquins, with little difference. For the use of missionaries, and other persons living among the above mentioned Indians* (1853).

5. *The American Language: An Inquiry into the Development of English in the United States* (1919; 4th ed., 1936). Mencken (1880–1956), American journalist, editor, and critic.

mention of blunders in navigation undermines the significance of discoveries and the melancholy of dominance. The contrivance of names, however, endures in the monologues of manifest manners and literature of dominance. The postindian warriors ensnare the contrivances with their own simulations of survivance.

Russell Means,[6] for instance, launched a new simulation of the name. There is "some confusion about the word *Indian*, a mistaken belief that it refers somehow to the country, India," he wrote in *Mother Jones*. "Columbus called the tribal people he met 'Indio,' from the Italian *in dio*, meaning 'in God.'"

The postindian warriors bear their own simulations and revisions to contend with manifest manners, the "authentic" summaries of ethnology, and the curse of racialism and modernism in the ruins of representation. The wild incursions of the warriors of survivance undermine the simulations of the unreal in the literature of dominance.

Postindian simulations arise from the silence of heard stories, or the imagination of oral literature in translation, not the absence of the real in simulated realities; the critical distinction is that postindian warriors create a new tribal presence in stories. The simulations of manifest manners are dominance, the scriptures of a civilization in paradise. The counteractions of postindian warriors are the simulations of survivance.

The postindian encounters with manifest manners and the simulations of the other are established in names and literature. This is a continuous turn in tribal narratives, the oral stories are dominated by those narratives that are translated, published, and read at unnamed distances. Stories that arise in silence are the sources of a tribal presence. The simulations of dominance and absence of the other are the concern of manifest manners. The simulations of survivance are heard and read stories that mediate and undermine the literature of dominance.

The names of the postindian warriors are new, but their encounters are consistent with the warriors who tread the manifest manners of past missions in tribal communities. The warriors of simulations, then and now, uncover the absence of the real and undermine the comparative poses of tribal traditions.

The warrior modes and postindian interpretations, in this instance, at the closure of the colonial inventions of the tribes in literature; the warriors, then and now, observe postmodern situations, theories of simulation, deconstruction, postindian encounters, silence, remembrance, and other themes of survivance that would trace the inventions of tribal cultures by missionaries and ethnologists to the truancies and cruelties of a melancholy civilization.

The postindian warriors and the missionaries of manifest manners are both responsible for simulations; even that resemblance is a simulation that ends in silence, or the presence of an original referent to tribal survivance. The warriors of simulation are entitled to tease the absence of remembrance in the ruins of representation, and in the tribal performance of heard stories. Simulations in oral stories arise from silence not inscriptions. The causal

6. Lakota activist, writer, film actor, and recording artist (b. 1939); in the late 1960s and early 1970s. Means gained prominence as a spokesman for the American Indian Movement (founded 1968; disbanded nationally in 1978).

narratives of missionaries and ethnologists are terminal simulations of dominance, not survivance.

"But the matter is more complicated, since to simulate is not simply to feign," continued Jean Baudrillard in *Simulacra and Simulation*. "Someone who feigns an illness can simply go to bed and make believe he is ill. Someone who simulates an illness produces in himself some of the symptoms." Hence, "feigning or dissimulating leaves the realty principle intact: the difference is always clear, it is only masked; whereas simulation threatens the difference between 'true' and 'false,' between 'real' and 'imaginary.' Since the simulator produces 'true' symptoms, is he ill or not?"

Jamake Highwater[7] simulated his tribal descent, to be sure, and with such assurance that others feigned their own identities in his presence. Jack Anderson,[8] the investigative columnist, reported that Highwater "fabricated much of the background that made him famous." He was more answerable as a simulation than others were to their own real crossblood identities.

How are we to understand the common attributions of tribal descent in the simulations of postindian identities? Some postindian warriors feign the sources of their own crossblood identities, the masks of a real tribal presence. Others, the wannabes, posers, and the missionaries of manifest manners, would threaten the remembrance of tribal identities with their surveillance and terminal simulations; the scriptures of dominance are the absence of tribal realities not the sources of a presence. The simulations of manifest manners have never been the masks of civilization or even the historical ironies of tribal cultures.

The Indian is the simulation of the absence, an unreal name; however, the misnomer has a curious sense of legal standing. Some of the definitions are ethnological, racial, literary, and juristic sanctions. "To be considered an Indian for federal purposes, an individual must have some Indian blood," wrote Stephen Pevar in *The Rights of Indian Tribes*.[9] "Some federal laws define an Indian as anyone of Indian descent, while other laws require one-fourth or one-half Indian blood in order to be considered as an Indian for purposes of those laws. Still other federal laws define Indian as anyone who has been accepted as a member of a 'federally recognized' Indian tribe." Clearly, the simulations of tribal names, the absence of a presence in a mere tribal misnomer, cannot be sustained by legislation or legal maneuvers.

Postindian autobiographies, the averments of tribal descent, and the assertions of crossblood identities, are simulations in literature; that names, nicknames, and the shadows of ancestors are stories is an invitation to new theories of tribal interpretation.

The sources of natural reason and tribal consciousness are doubt and wonder, not nostalgia or liberal melancholy for the lost wilderness; comic not tragic, because melancholy is cultural boredom, and the tragic is causal, the closure of natural reason. The shimmers of imagination are reason and the simulations are survivance, not dominance; an aesthetic restoration of

7. Choreographer and dance director, journalist, and travel writer (b. 1930); since the mid-1970s, a self-appointed spokesperson for Native people. Highwater has claimed at various times to be Blackfoot, Cree, and Cherokee, and the authenticity of his Indian ancestry has been questioned.

8. American journalist (b. 1922).

9. *The Rights of Indians and Tribes: The Basic ACLU Guide to Indian and Tribal Rights* (2d ed., 1992).

trickster hermeneutics, the stories of liberation and survivance without the dominance of closure. Tribal consciousness is wonder, chance, coincidence, not the revisions of a pedate[1] paradise; even so, for curious reasons some would hear confessions and the conversions of criminals as the evidence of a new tribal awareness.

Trickster hermeneutics is the interpretation of simulations in the literature of survivance, the ironies of descent and racialism, transmutation, third gender, and themes of transformation in oral tribal stories and written narratives. Trickster stories arise in silence, not scriptures, and are the *holotropes* of imagination; the manifold turns of scenes, the brush of natural reason, characters that liberate the mind and never reach a closure in stories.[2] Trickster stories are the postindian simulations of tribal survivance.

The trickster is reason and mediation in stories, the original translator of tribal encounters; the name is an intimation of transformation, men to women, animals to birds, and more than mere causal representation in names. Tricksters are the translation of creation; the trickster creates the tribe in stories, and pronounces the moment of remembrance as the trace of liberation. The animals laughed, birds cried, and there were worried hearts over the everlasting humor that would liberate the human mind in trickster stories. Trickster stories are the translation of liberation, and the shimmer of imagination is the liberation of the last trickster stories.

Trickster hermeneutics is access to trickster stories, and the shimmer of a tribal presence in simulations; this new course of tribal interpretation arises from the postindian turns in literature, the reach of tribal shadows, postmodern conditions of translation, the traces of deconstruction, and the theories of representation and simulation. Trickster hermeneutics is survivance, not closure, and the discernment of tragic wisdom in tribal experiences. The tribes bear the simulations of pathos and the tragic without the wisdom of chance and natural miseries of the seasons. Simulation of the tragic has been sustained by the literature of dominance. Natural reason teases the sense that nature is precarious; however, the realities of chance, fate, and tragic wisdom were denied in the literature of dominance.

"Some say that tragedy teaches us the power of chance, of the force of contingency in determining whether the virtuous thrive," wrote Amélie Oksenberg Rorty in *Essays on Aristotle's Poetics*.[3] "While tragedy does indeed focus on what can go wrong in the actions of the best of men, its ethical lessons are not primarily about the place of accident and fortune in the unfolding of human life." She observed that many "tragedies represent a tale with which the audience is likely to be familiar." The tragic tribal tales, in this sense, are simulations for an audience familiar with manifest manners and the literature of dominance. Decidedly, the stories that turn the tribes tragic are not their own stories.

Manifest manners are scriptural simulations, the causal narratives of racialism, the denial of tragic wisdom, and the cultural leases of objectivism; otherwise, the mere mention of the transitive other, the antiselves in the absence of remembrance, would end in silence. The postindian warriors hear stories that arise in natural silence. Listen, oral stories are the best

1. Having feet.
2. Vizenor plays on Baudrillard's commentary on holograms, a three-dimensional projection of an object, in *Simulacra and Simulation*.
3. See "The Psychology of Aristotelian Tragedy," in *Essays on Aristotle's Poetics*, ed. Rorty (1992). Rorty (b. 1932), Belgian-born American philosopher.

performance of simulations, because the reference is in the performance.

Performance and human silence are strategies of survivance. Nature is a simulation without silence. The presence of human silence and death have no simulations. The absence and the presence of death are mortal performances. "Death actually discloses the imposture of reality, not only in that the absence of duration gives the lie to it, but above all because death is the great affirmer," wrote Georges Bataille[4] in *Theory of Religion*. "But death suddenly shows that the real society was lying. Then it is not the loss of the thing, of the useful member, that is taken into consideration. What the real society has lost is not a member but rather its truth."

Native American Indians have endured the lies and wicked burdens of discoveries, the puritanical destinies of monotheism, manifest manners, and the simulated realities of dominance, with silence, traces of natural reason, trickster hermeneutics, the interpretation of tribal figurations, and the solace of heard stories.

The various translations, interpretations, and representations of the absence of tribal realities have been posed as the verities of certain cultural traditions. Moreover, the closure of heard stories in favor of scriptural simulations as authentic representations denied a common brush with the shimmer of humor, the sources of tribal visions, and tragic wisdom; tribal imagination and creation stories were obscured without remorse in national histories and the literature of dominance.

"One of the greatest paradoxes of contemporary culture is that at a time when the image reigns supreme the very notion of a creative human imagination seems under mounting threat," wrote Richard Kearney in *The Wake of Imagination*.[5] "The imminent demise of imagination is clearly a postmodern obsession. Postmodernism undermines the modernist belief in the image as an *authentic* expression."

In other words, the postindian warriors of postmodern simulations would undermine and surmount, with imagination and the performance of new stories, the manifest manners of scriptural simulations and "authentic" representations of the tribes in the literature of dominance.

Russell Means, for instance, posed with other radical leaders of the American Indian Movement at the occupation of Wounded Knee and landed in motion pictures and a laudable postindian simulation, a studio production of a silk screen portrait by Andy Warhol.

"How about the *American Indian* series?" asked Patrick Smith[6] in *Warhol: Conversations about the Artist*. "Was that any particular Indian?"

"Yeah. That was Russell Means," said Ronnie Cultrone who was, at the time, a studio production assistant to Andy Warhol. "He was involved with the Wounded Knee Massacre,[7] which I don't really know too much about, to tell you the truth. But I think he's still in court. I don't know. Something like that." Indeed, the studio production is a simulation in three dimensions,

4. Influential French writer and critic (1897–1962); his *Theory of Religion* was published in 1974 (trans. 1989).

5. *The Wake of Imagination: Ideas of Creativity in Western Culture* (1988). Kearney (b. 1954), Irish philosopher.

6. American art critic (b. 1949), who published *Warhol* in 1988. Warhol (ca. 1928–1987), famous American artist and leader of the pop art movement; he created the *American Indian* series in 1976.

7. In one of the best-known actions of the American Indian Movement (AIM), which sought in the late 1960s and 1970s to improve the lives of Native people, armed members seized Wounded Knee on February 27, 1973, demanding that the U.S. Senate investigate treaty and other grievances. A siege with federal marshals lasted 70 days; individuals on both sides were wounded in exchanges of gunfire, and 2 Native Americans died.

the absence, presence, and portrait of the militant leader of the American Indian Movement.

This portrait is not an Indian.

René Magritte inscribed "*Ceci n'est pas une pipe*, This is not a pipe," across his painting of an obvious pipe.[8] This ambiguous critique "exemplifies the penetration of discourse into the form of things; it reveals discourse's ambiguous power to deny and to redouble," wrote Michel Foucault in *This Is Not a Pipe*.

Magritte said, "Sometimes the name of an object takes the place of an image. A word can take the place of an object in reality. An image can take the place of a word in a proposition."

Russell Means, with all that, is not a portrait of an Indian. The portrait of an Indian, the silk screen acrylic image of the *American Indian* by Andy Warhol, is denied by the assertion, "This is not an Indian." The portraiture is the absence; the assertion is an ambiguous discourse on simulations and the sources of tribal identities.

* * *

1994

8. *The Treachery of Images* (1935; first version, 1929), by the Belgian surrealist painter Magritte (1898–1967). The inscription became the title of a 1973 book by the French philosopher and historian of ideas FOUCAULT (1926–1984).

EDWARD W. SAID
1935–2003

One of the most prominent public intellectuals of recent decades, Edward W. Said was an influential literary critic and theorist as well as a significant political figure, especially as an advocate of the rights of Palestinians. His early critical work provided groundbreaking considerations of emerging poststructuralist theorists, such as JACQUES DERRIDA and MICHEL FOUCAULT, alongside reconsiderations of earlier philosophers and critics, including GIAMBATTISTA VICO (1668–1744). Arguing for a socially engaged criticism against both linguistically oriented theories like deconstruction and ideologically dogmatic positions, he promoted a "worldly," "secular criticism." Beginning with his landmark *Orientalism* (1978), which is often regarded as having established the field of postcolonial studies, his work focused particularly on imperialism and the interplay between the dominant West (the "Occident") and the Middle and Far East (the "Orient"). In the introduction to *Orientialism*, our selection, Said discusses how European and U.S. literary and cultural representations, academic disciplines, and public perceptions foster biases against non-Western peoples, casting them as oriental Others.

Of Palestinian heritage but educated in British and American colonial schools in Cairo and later in U.S. universities, Said experienced firsthand the complicated relations between the East and Western imperialism. He was born in Jerusalem, Palestine, which had been controlled by Great Britain since 1922 (with a mandate from the League of Nations to help establish a Jewish national home); but in 1947, in the aftermath of World War II, the United Nations divided Palestine into Arab and Jewish territories and placed the city of Jerusalem under its control. The resulting political tension and fighting within Palestine led Said's family to emigrate to Cairo at the end of 1947. When the British mandate expired in 1948, Jewish authorities declared the establishment of the State of Israel, on which all the neighboring Arab countries immediately declared war; hundreds of thousands of Arabs fled what had been Palestine. Though the creation of Israel is celebrated in the West as the restoration of a Jewish homeland, Palestinians call it the *nakbah*, or "disaster"; Said comments, "Israel was established; Palestine was destroyed."

Said's father, Wadie Said, was a prosperous businessman who sold office equipment in Cairo and elsewhere, and Said himself, in the midst of political turmoil, received an elite education. He attended St. George's, an Anglican preparatory school; the American School in Cairo, whose student body was composed primarily of children of U.S. diplomats; and Victoria College, a secondary school where his classmates included the future King Hussein of Jordan. After Said was expelled from school for disciplinary reasons in 1951, his father sent him to Mount Hermon, a preparatory school in Massachusetts, to complete high school and to gain U.S. citizenship. (His father had emigrated to the United States in the 1910s and served in the army in World War I, becoming a naturalized U.S. citizen.) Said became a naturalized citizen in 1953 and attended Princeton University, receiving his B.A. degree in 1957. After a year in Cairo helping with his father's business, he returned to the United States to do doctoral work in English and comparative literature at Harvard University, where he worked with the prominent scholar Harry Levin, earning an M.A. in 1960 and a Ph.D. in 1964.

The academic career of Said was remarkably successful; after joining the faculty at Columbia University in 1963 he quickly ascended the ladder of academic rank, eventually being appointed to several prestigious chairs. He also held distinguished visiting professorships and fellowships at Harvard, Yale, Princeton, Stanford, and elsewhere, and his books garnered a long list of honors, among them a National Book Critics Circle Award nomination for *Orientalism*. At the same time, Said gained political prominence, translating Yasir Arafat's first address to the General Assembly of the United Nations in 1974, serving as a member of the Palestine National Council from 1977 to 1991 (helping to draft its declaration of Palestinian statehood in 1988), and advocating Palestinian national rights in international news media. While often criticizing Israel's and the United States' refusal to recognize a Palestinian state, he also criticized the leadership and policies of the Palestinian Liberation Organization.

In some sense, Said fulfilled the definition of an "organic intellectual"—to use the phrase of the Italian Marxist philosopher ANTONIO GRAMSCI, one of Said's intellectual heroes—developing his criticism of Western representations of Arab culture and his advocacy for the rights of Palestinians out of his personal roots. As he remarked in an interview, however, he always experienced his identity as complicated—as a U.S. citizen as well as a Palestinian, as an "Oriental" as well as a Western scholar educated in the British tradition, and as a renowned academic figure as well as an often dissenting political spokesperson. He felt, as he titled his memoir, "out of place"; this sense of homelessness defined for him the proper stance of the intellectual, who should remain independent of fixed theoretical, disciplinary, professional, and national loyalties, yet always be attentive to social injustice and what he calls the "brute reality" of history.

Said first gained the attention of scholars with the publication of *Beginnings: Intention and Method* (1975), a pioneering comparison of Foucault's method of historical "archaeology" and Derrida's deconstructive critique of language, ultimately favoring Foucault's focus on social forces. A dense meditation on literary "beginnings" and influences, it also conducted an erudite examination of figures from the Western humanistic tradition—Vico, Erich Auerbach, Ernst Robert Curtius, Leo Spitzer, and others. Though already well known in literary circles, Said attained wider prominence both across the academic disciplines and among the general public with the publication of his next book, *Orientalism*. Appearing as conflicts in the Middle East were escalating, it provided a timely—and controversial—critical overview of the history of Western understandings of Arab culture. In particular, it voiced a strong dissent against largely pro-Israeli U.S. policies that operated at the expense of Arab peoples.

With *Orientalism* Said turned to examine more directly the political dimensions of literature and culture. Many critics see this turn as a decisive shift in Said's focus from academic literary theory to actual politics, but in fact his writings display a number of commonalities: a consistent grounding in the literary canon; an appreciation of philology and the long humanistic tradition of criticism; research across disciplines, especially history; an overarching concern, influenced by Foucault, with the complex interrelation of culture and the operation of political power; a belief in the value of individual achievements in literature, criticism, and politics; and an assertion of the independent role of the intellectual as someone who eschews orthodoxies both theoretical and political. For Said, literary, philological, and critical texts are always "in the world" and have social resonances.

In our selection, Said propounds a broad definition of Orientalism, encompassing both Western academic scholarship in disciplines whose field of study is the "Orient"—such as anthropology, philology, history, and area studies—and the general Western image of the "Orient" depicted in novels, political accounts, and contemporary media. Employing the techniques of close literary analysis, he shows how Western writers, archaeologists, linguists, historians, and politicians from the eighteenth century to the present day have "discovered" and in a sense invented the Orient. According to Said, Orientalism reveals more about the West and its fantasies than it does about the actual people, culture, and history of the East; not simply a myth, it is "more particularly valuable as a sign of European-Atlantic power over the Orient than it is as a veridic discourse about the Orient." In effect, the various literary, cultural, and historical discourses of Orientalism participate in the conquest and continuing subjugation of the East. Furthermore, Said's analysis is a sharp warning to scholars and intellectuals, showing how scholarship is sometimes informed by racism and how intellectuals have been complicit in the administration of imperial power.

This examination of Orientalism is particularly indebted to the work of Foucault, as Said adopts Foucault's method of archival research, his focus on cultural and historical knowledges as constituting a system of "discourse," and his tracing of the complex interrelation of power and knowledge. But for Said, the disciplinary institutions of knowledge are not simply embedded in the overarching Foucauldian category of "power": they directly serve the historical interests of European imperialism. Said also diverges from Foucault's generalized, impersonal sense of "discourse," instead retaining a humanistic belief in "the determining imprint of individual writers" and intellectuals. Another important poststructuralist influence is Derrida's critique of concepts such as *center* and *margin* and *self* and *Other*. For Said, the "margin" of the East helps define the colonial center of the West, and the Oriental "Other" is a projection of the Western view that constructs it. These and related terms have played a crucial role in the development of postcolonial studies. Said criticizes Derrida's linguistic focus, however, and extends poststructuralist theory to examine its implications for real-world politics—especially in the British rule of India, the European partitioning of the Middle East, and the U.S. intervention in Vietnam.

A less often recognized influence on Said's work is that of RAYMOND WILLIAMS, the British literary and cultural critic. Said praised the work of Williams, particularly his disregard for such traditional academic boundaries as the distinction between literature and history, and followed Williams in his concern with the societal effects of literature and culture. Although Said's *Culture and Imperialism* (1993) is often taken as a riposte to MATTHEW ARNOLD's *Culture and Anarchy* (1869) in showing how culture does not helpfully stave off anarchy but operates in the service of imperialism, its direct forebear is Williams's *Culture and Society* (1958). Especially in *The World, the Text, and the Critic* (1983), perhaps his most important statement on contemporary criticism, Said insists on the need to analyze the relation of art and criticism to society; he attacks critics who promote a "disinfected" textuality, without reference to and therefore "camouflaging" the social network in which texts are embedded. Although unnamed, his primary target is deconstruction, particularly the influential work of PAUL DE MAN, and Said came to represent a counterpoint to the deconstructive modes of criticism prevalent during the 1970s and 1980s.

While Said acknowledged sympathies with the Left, he also offered some sharp criticism of leftist literary criticism, such as U.S. Marxism, that he viewed as "principally an academic, not a political, commitment," and he disavowed critical systems that prescribe their results in advance. He believed that the critic should retain autonomy as a kind of gadfly. He called for a consistently "oppositional criticism," which "is reducible neither to a doctrine nor to a political position," and which is "life-enhancing and constitutively opposed to every form of tyranny, domination, and abuse; its social goals are noncoercive knowledge produced in the interests of human freedom" (introduction to *The World, the Text, and the Critic*). He named this "secular criticism"; it shuns party-line thinking and dogma, whether stemming from religion, politics, or one's professional discipline or specialization.

Said's work exerted considerable influence, especially in the development of postcolonial studies. *Orientalism* was immediately recognized as a critical classic, with an impact not only on literary studies but also on anthropology, history, international studies, and the discipline known as Orientalism. Said himself was praised as an exemplary intellectual, having crossed the boundary between the academic world and the public sphere and speaking out on contemporary politics. His advocacy on behalf of a Palestinian state provoked attacks, sometimes vehement. Within the field of literary studies, various scholars criticized different aspects of his work: his residual humanism and belief in individual will, his liberal rather than radical views, his eschewal of professionalism for amateurism, his inattention to feminism, and his primary focus on the high Western literary tradition. However, most critics acknowledge his pivotal role in contemporary theory and his success in forging a path for crossing disciplinary boundaries and in combining political commitment and intellectual work. As demonstrated in *Orientalism*, he persistently underscored the relation of literary study to the world, especially the relation of culture to the "brute reality" of imperialism.

BIBLIOGRAPHY

Said's first book, *Joseph Conrad and the Fiction of Autobiography* (1966), an outgrowth of his doctoral dissertation, is a literary study of Conrad's life and fiction. The groundbreaking *Beginnings: Intention and Method* (1975) established Said as a central figure in the leftist poststructuralist literary theory then emerging. *Orientalism* (1978), his most famous book, extended Said's influence to other disciplines and established him as a major contemporary public intellectual. See also his retrospective comments, "Orientalism Reconsidered," in *Literature, Politics and Theory* (ed. Francis Barker et al., 1986), and the afterword to the 1995 edition of *Orientalism*. Said next published three books more directly addressing politics and the Middle East: *Reaction and Counterrevolution in the Contemporary Arab World* (1978), a brief exposé; *The Question of Palestine* (1979), a history of the status of Palestine; and *Covering Islam: How the Media and the Experts Determine How We See the Rest of the World* (1981), an analysis of popular media representations. The latter two, directed at nonacademic audiences, form a trilogy with *Orientalism*. Returning to the field of contemporary theory, *The World, the Text, and the Critic* (1983) gathers many important essays and provides perhaps the best introduction to Said's views on criticism. *After the Last Sky: Palestinian Lives* (1986) offers his personal, poetic reflections on Palestine alongside photographs (by Jean Mohr). Said also co-edited (with Christopher Hitchens) and contributed three essays to the collection *Blaming the Victims: Spurious Scholarship and the Palestinian Question* (1988), which attacks stereotypes of Arabs (as terrorists, for instance).

Said has performed as a concert pianist and has written an occasional column on music for the *Nation; Musical Elaborations* (1991) gathers his writings in this area. *Culture and Imperialism* (1993) is a capstone of his investigation into literary and cultural representations of imperialism. *Representations of the Intellectual: The 1993 Reith Lectures* (1994), a succinct and accessible survey of the role of the intellectual, culminates in Said's call for an independent intellectual who "speaks truth to power." Several later collections gather his diverse commentary on politics in the Middle East: *The Politics of Dispossession: The Struggle for Palestinian Self-Determination, 1969–1994* (1994), *The Pen and the Sword: Conversations with David Barsamian* (1994), *Peace and Its Discontents: Essays on Palestine in the Middle East Peace Process* (1998), and *End of the Peace: Oslo and After* (2000). *The Edward Said Reader*, edited by Moustafa Bayoumi and Andrew Rubin (2000), presents a range of selections covering his career. *Reflections on Exile and Other Essays* (2001), a companion to *The World, the Text, and the Critic*, gathers his later critical essays. *Out of Place: A Memoir* (1999) is an illuminating biographical account, covering Said's early life in Palestine and Cairo through his college years at Princeton University.

From almost the beginning of his career, Said has attracted a large body of criticism. A special issue of the theory journal *Diacritics* 6 (1976) is devoted to *Beginnings*; it also contains an illuminating interview with Said. In *Intellectuals in Power: A Genealogy of Critical Humanism* (1986), Paul A. Bové analyzes Said's relation to the humanistic tradition. Jim Merod, in *The Political Responsibility of the Critic* (1987), sees Said rather than such more academically oriented figures as Fredric Jameson as an exemplary politically engaged critic. *The Predicament of Culture: Twentieth-Century Ethnography, Literature, and Art* (1988), by the anthropologist James Clifford, contains a noted critique of *Orientalism*. In *White Mythologies: Writing History and the West* (1990), Robert Young assigns Said a central role in establishing postcolonial studies. John McGowan, in *Postmodernism and Its Critics* (1991), explores the problem of freedom in Said's concept of exile. *Edward Said: A Critical Reader*, edited by Michael Sprinker (1992), contains an excellent selection of essays examining the range of Said's work, as well as an informative interview with Said.

The Marxist critic Aijaz Ahmad, in his *In Theory: Classes, Nations, Literatures* (1992), severely criticizes Said's relation to postcolonial studies, taking him to task for his focus on the humanistic Western tradition and for his liberal politics. That attack was followed by a special issue of *Public Culture* 12 (1993) debating Ahmad's and Said's merits. Bruce Robbins, in *Secular Vocations: Intellectuals, Professionalism, Culture* (1993), analyzes Said's ambivalent views toward professionalism. In "Jane Austen and Edward Said: Gender, Culture, and Imperialism," *Critical Inquiry* 21 (1995), Susan Fraiman criticizes Said's lack of attention to gender and to texts by women. Jeffrey Williams, "Edward Said's Romance of the Amateur Intellectual," *Review of Education* 17 (1995), surveys Said's career, arguing that his claim for the amateur independent intellectual contradicts his own position as an eminent professional literary critic. Bill Ashcroft and Pal Ahlumwalia's *Edward Said: The Paradox of Identity* (1999) is a useful overview. *Edward Said and the Work of the Critic: Speaking Truth to Power*, edited by Paul A. Bové (2000), gathers a range of essays on Said and two interviews with him. Timothy Brennan, "The Illusion of a Future: *Orientalism* as Traveling Theory," *Critical Inquiry* 26 (2000), provides a retrospective account of the influence of *Orientalism*, arguing that it critiques rather than follows Foucault.

From Orientalism

Introduction

I

On a visit to Beirut during the terrible civil war of 1975–1976 a French journalist wrote regretfully of the gutted downtown area that "it had once seemed to belong to . . . the Orient of Chateaubriand and Nerval."[1] He was right about the place, of course, especially so far as a European was concerned. The Orient was almost a European invention, and had been since antiquity a place of romance, exotic beings, haunting memories and landscapes, remarkable experiences. Now it was disappearing; in a sense it had happened, its time was over. Perhaps it seemed irrelevant that Orientals themselves had something at stake in the process, that even in the time of Chateaubriand and Nerval Orientals had lived there, and that now it was they who were suffering; the main thing for the European visitor was a European representation of the Orient and its contemporary fate, both of which had a privileged communal significance for the journalist and his French readers.

Americans will not feel quite the same about the Orient, which for them is much more likely to be associated very differently with the Far East (China and Japan, mainly). Unlike the Americans, the French and the British—less so the Germans, Russians, Spanish, Portuguese, Italians, and Swiss—have had a long tradition of what I shall be calling *Orientalism*, a way of coming to terms with the Orient that is based on the Orient's special place in European Western experience. The Orient is not only adjacent to Europe; it is also the place of Europe's greatest and richest and oldest colonies, the source of its civilizations and languages, its cultural contestant, and one of its deepest and most recurring images of the Other. In addition, the Orient has helped to define Europe (or the West) as its contrasting image, idea, personality, experience. Yet none of this Orient is merely imaginative. The Orient is an integral part of European *material* civilization and culture. Orientalism expresses and represents that part culturally and even ideologically as a mode of discourse with supporting institutions, vocabulary, scholarship, imagery, doctrines, even colonial bureaucracies and colonial styles. In contrast, the American understanding of the Orient will seem considerably less dense, although our recent Japanese, Korean, and Indochinese adventures[2] ought now to be creating a more sober, more realistic "Oriental" awareness. Moreover, the vastly expanded American political and economic role in the Near East (the Middle East) makes great claims on our understanding of that Orient.

It will be clear to the reader (and will become clearer still throughout the many pages that follow) that by Orientalism I mean several things, all of them, in my opinion, interdependent. The most readily accepted designation

1. Thierry Desjardins, *Le Martyre du Liban* (Paris: Plon, 1976), p. 14 [Said's note]. François-René, vicomte de Chateaubriand (1768–1848), French writer and statesman. Gérard de Nerval (1808–1855), French poet and journalist; he wrote an account of a journey to the Middle East, *Le Voyage en Orient* (1851).

2. That is, the Pacific Theater of World War II (1941–45), the Korean War (1950–53), and the Vietnam War (1964–75), respectively.

for Orientalism is an academic one, and indeed the label still serves in a number of academic institutions. Anyone who teaches, writes about, or researches the Orient—and this applies whether the person is an anthropologist, sociologist, historian, or philologist—either in its specific or its general aspects, is an Orientalist, and what he or she does is Orientalism. Compared with *Oriental studies* or *area studies*, it is true that the term *Orientalism* is less preferred by specialists today, both because it is too vague and general and because it connotes the high-handed executive attitude of nineteenth-century and early-twentieth-century European colonialism. Nevertheless books are written and congresses held with "the Orient" as their main focus, with the Orientalist in his new or old guise as their main authority. The point is that even if it does not survive as it once did, Orientalism lives on academically through its doctrines and theses about the Orient and the Oriental.

Related to this academic tradition, whose fortunes, transmigrations, specializations, and transmissions are in part the subject of this study, is a more general meaning for Orientalism is a style of thought based upon an ontological and epistemological distinction[3] made between "the Orient" and (most of the time) "the Occident." Thus a very large mass of writers, among whom are poets, novelists, philosophers, political theorists, economists, and imperial administrators, have accepted the basic distinction between East and West as the starting point for elaborate theories, epics, novels, social descriptions, and political accounts concerning the Orient, its people, customs, "mind," destiny, and so on. *This* Orientalism can accommodate Aeschylus, say, and Victor Hugo, Dante and Karl Marx.[4] A little later in this introduction I shall deal with the methodological problems one encounters in so broadly construed a "field" as this.

The interchange between the academic and the more or less imaginative meanings of Orientalism is a constant one, and since the late eighteenth century there has been a considerable, quite disciplined—perhaps even regulated—traffic between the two. Here I come to the third meaning of Orientalism, which is something more historically and materially defined than either of the other two. Taking the late eighteenth century as a very roughly defined starting point Orientalism can be discussed and analyzed as the corporate institution for dealing with the Orient—dealing with it by making statements about it, authorizing views of it, describing it, by teaching it, settling it, ruling over it: in short, Orientalism as a Western style for dominating, restructuring, and having authority over the Orient. I have found it useful here to employ Michel Foucault's notion of a discourse, as described by him in *The Archaeology of Knowledge* and in *Discipline and Punish*,[5] to identify Orientalism. My contention is that without examining Orientalism as a discourse one cannot possibly understand the enormously systematic discipline by which European culture was able to manage—and even produce—the Orient politically, sociologically, militarily, ideologically, scientifically, and imaginatively during the post-Enlightenment period. Moreover,

3. That is, a difference in their essential being and how they are known.

4. Said names writers not generally viewed as treating the "Oriental": Aeschylus (525–456 B.C.E.), Greek tragedian; Hugo (1802–1885), French Romantic poet, novelist, and dramatist; DANTE ALIGHIERI (1265–1321), Italian poet; and MARX (1818–1883), German economic, social, and political philosopher.

5. Books published in 1969 and 1975, respectively, by FOUCAULT (1926–1984), French philosopher and historian of ideas, who explores the connections among knowledge, discourse, and power.

so authoritative a position did Orientalism have that I believe no one writing, thinking, or acting on the Orient could do so without taking account of the limitations on thought and action imposed by Orientalism. In brief, because of Orientalism the Orient was not (and is not) a free subject of thought or action. This is not to say that Orientalism unilaterally determines what can be said about the Orient, but that it is the whole network of interests inevitably brought to bear on (and therefore always involved in) any occasion when that peculiar entity "the Orient" is in question. How this happens is what this book tries to demonstrate. It also tries to show that European culture gained in strength and identity by setting itself off against the Orient as a sort of surrogate and even underground self.

Historically and culturally there is a quantitative as well as a qualitative difference between the Franco-British involvement in the Orient and—until the period of American ascendancy after World War II—the involvement of every other European and Atlantic power. To speak of Orientalism therefore is to speak mainly, although not exclusively, of a British and French cultural enterprise, a project whose dimensions take in such disparate realms as the imagination itself, the whole of India and the Levant,[6] the Biblical texts and the Biblical lands, the spice trade, colonial armies and a long tradition of colonial administrators, a formidable scholarly corpus, innumerable Oriental "experts" and "hands," an Oriental professorate, a complex array of "Oriental" ideas (Oriental despotism, Oriental splendor, cruelty, sensuality), many Eastern sects, philosophies, and wisdoms domesticated for local European use—the list can be extended more or less indefinitely. My point is that Orientalism derives from a particular closeness experienced between Britain and France and the Orient, which until the early nineteenth century had really meant only India and the Bible lands. From the beginning of the nineteenth century until the end of World War II France and Britain dominated the Orient and Orientalism; since World War II America has dominated the Orient, and approaches it as France and Britain once did. Out of that closeness, whose dynamic is enormously productive even if it always demonstrates the comparatively greater strength of the Occident (British, French, or American), comes the large body of texts I call Orientalist.

It should be said at once that even with the generous number of books and authors that I examine, there is a much larger number that I simply have had to leave out. My argument, however, depends neither upon an exhaustive catalogue of texts dealing with the Orient nor upon a clearly delimited set of texts, authors, and ideas that together make up the Orientalist canon. I have depended instead upon a different methodological alternative—whose backbone in a sense is the set of historical generalizations I have so far been making in this Introduction—and it is these I want now to discuss in more analytical detail.

II

I have begun with the assumption that the Orient is not an inert fact of nature. It is not merely *there*, just as the Occident itself is not just *there* either. We must take seriously Vico's[7] great observation that men make their

6. The countries bordering the eastern coast of the Mediterranean Sea from Turkey to Egypt, including present-day Syria, Lebanon, and Israel.

7. GIAMBATTISTA VICO (1668–1744), Italian philosopher and historian.

own history; that what they can know is what they have made, and extend it to geography: as both geographical and cultural entities—to say nothing of historical entities—such locales, regions, geographical sectors as "Orient" and "Occident" are man-made. Therefore as much as the West itself, the Orient is an idea that has a history and a tradition of thought, imagery, and vocabulary that have given it reality and presence in and for the West. The two geographical entities thus support and to an extent reflect each other.

Having said that, one must go on to state a number of reasonable qualifications. In the first place, it would be wrong to conclude that the Orient was *essentially* an idea, or a creation with no corresponding reality. When Disraeli said in his novel *Tancred*[8] that the East was a career, he meant that to be interested in the East was something bright young Westerners would find to be an all-consuming passion; he should not be interpreted as saying that the East was *only* a career for Westerners. There were—and are—cultures and nations whose location is in the East, and their lives, histories, and customs have a brute reality obviously greater than anything that could be said about them in the West. About that fact this study of Orientalism has very little to contribute, except to acknowledge it tacitly. But the phenomenon of Orientalism as I study it here deals principally, not with a correspondence between Orientalism and Orient, but with the internal consistency of Orientalism and its ideas about the Orient (the East as career) despite or beyond any correspondence, or lack thereof, with a "real" Orient. My point is that Disraeli's statement about the East refers mainly to that created consistency, that regular constellation of ideas as the pre-eminent thing about the Orient, and not to its mere being, as Wallace Stevens's[9] phrase has it.

A second qualification is that ideas, cultures, and histories cannot seriously be understood or studied without their force, or more precisely their configurations of power, also being studied. To believe that the Orient was created—or, as I call it, "Orientalized"—and to believe that such things happen simply as a necessity of the imagination, is to be disingenuous. The relationship between Occident and Orient is a relationship of power, of domination, of varying degrees of a complex hegemony, and is quite accurately indicated in the title of K. M. Panikkar's classic *Asia and Western Dominance*.[1] The Orient was Orientalized not only because it was discovered to be "Oriental" in all those ways considered commonplace by an average  nineteenth-century European, but also because it *could be*—that is, submitted to being—*made* Oriental. There is very little consent to be found, for example, in the fact that Flaubert's[2] encounter with an Egyptian courtesan produced a widely influential model of the Oriental woman; she never spoke of herself, she never represented her emotions, presence, or history. *He* spoke for and represented her. He was foreign, comparatively wealthy, male, and these were historical facts of domination that allowed him not only to possess Kuchuk Hanem physically but to speak for her and tell his readers in what way she was "typically Oriental." My argument is that Flaubert's situation of strength in relation to Kuchuk Hanem was not an isolated

8. An 1847 novel whose hero leaves 19th-century England for the East, by Benjamin Disraeli (1804–1881), English politician and novelist.

9. American poet (1879–1955); one of his poems is titled "Of Mere Being."

1. K. M. Panikkar, *Asia and Western Dominance* (London: Allen and Unwin, 1959) [Said's note].

2. Gustave Flaubert (1821–1880), French novelist; his travels in Egypt and the Orient are recounted in his letters, and his novel *Salammbô* (1862) is set in ancient Carthage (in modern-day Tunisia).

instance. It fairly stands for the pattern of relative strength between East and West, and the discourse about the Orient that it enabled.

This brings us to a third qualification. One ought never to assume that the structure of Orientalism is nothing more than a structure of lies or of myths which, were the truth about them to be told, would simply blow away. I myself believe that Orientalism is more particularly valuable as a sign of European-Atlantic power over the Orient than it is as a veridic discourse about the Orient (which is what, in its academic or scholarly form, it claims to be). Nevertheless, what we must respect and try to grasp is the sheer knitted-together strength of Orientalist discourse, its very close ties to the enabling socio-economic and political institutions, and its redoubtable durability. After all, any system of ideas that can remain unchanged as teachable wisdom (in academies, books, congresses, universities, foreign-service institutes) from the period of Ernest Renan[3] in the late 1840s until the present in the United States must be something more formidable than a mere collection of lies. Orientalism, therefore, is not an airy European fantasy about the Orient, but a created body of theory and practice in which, for many generations, there has been a considerable material investment. Continued investment made Orientalism, as a system of knowledge about the Orient, an accepted grid for filtering through the Orient into Western consciousness, just as that same investment multiplied—indeed, made truly productive—the statements proliferating out from Orientalism into the general culture.

Gramsci[4] has made the useful analytic distinction between civil and political society in which the former is made up of voluntary (or at least rational and noncoercive) affiliations like schools, families, and unions, the latter of state institutions (the army, the police, the central bureaucracy) whose role in the polity is direct domination. Culture, of course, is to be found operating within civil society, where the influence of ideas, of institutions, and of other persons works not through domination but by what Gramsci calls consent. In any society not totalitarian, then, certain cultural forms predominate over others, just as certain ideas are more influential than others; the form of this cultural leadership is what Gramsci has identified as *hegemony*, an indispensable concept for any understanding of cultural life in the industrial West. It is hegemony, or rather the result of cultural hegemony at work, that gives Orientalism the durability and the strength I have been speaking about so far. Orientalism is never far from what Denys Hay has called the idea of Europe,[5] a collective notion identifying "us" Europeans as against all "those" non-Europeans, and indeed it can be argued that the major component in European culture is precisely what made that culture hegemonic both in and outside Europe: the idea of European identity as a superior one in comparison with all the non-European peoples and cultures. There is in addition the hegemony of European ideas about the Orient, themselves reiterating European superiority over Oriental backwardness, usually overriding the possibility that a more independent, or more skeptical, thinker might have had different views on the matter.

In a quite constant way, Orientalism depends for its strategy on this flex-

3. French historian (1823–1892), who wrote on the Oriental origins of Christianity.
4. ANTONIO GRAMSCI (1891–1937), Italian Marxist whose concept of cultural hegemony has been highly influential.
5. Denys Hay, *Europe: The Emergence of an Idea*, 2d ed. (Edinburgh: Edinburgh University Press, 1968) [Said's note].

ible *positional* superiority, which puts the Westerner in a whole series of possible relationships with the Orient without ever losing him the relative upper hand. And why should it have been otherwise, especially during the period of extraordinary European ascendancy from the late Renaissance to the present? The scientist, the scholar, the missionary, the trader, or the soldier was in, or thought about, the Orient because he *could be there*, or could think about it, with very little resistance on the Orient's part. Under the general heading of knowledge of the Orient, and within the umbrella of Western hegemony over the Orient during the period from the end of the eighteenth century, there emerged a complex Orient suitable for study in the academy, for display in the museum, for reconstruction in the colonial office, for theoretical illustration in anthropological, biological, linguistic, racial, and historical theses about mankind and the universe, for instances of economic and sociological theories of development, revolution, cultural personality, national or religious character. Additionally, the imaginative examination of things Oriental was based more or less exclusively upon a sovereign Western consciousness out of whose unchallenged centrality an Oriental world emerged, first according to general ideas about who or what was an Oriental, then according to a detailed logic governed not simply by empirical reality but by a battery of desires, repressions, investments, and projections. If we can point to great Orientalist works of genuine scholarship like Silvestre de Sacy's *Chrestomathie arabe* or Edward William Lane's *Account of the Manners and Customs of the Modern Egyptians*, we need also to note that Renan's and Gobineau's[6] racial ideas came out of the same impulse, as did a great many Victorian pornographic novels (see the analysis by Steven Marcus of "The Lustful Turk"[7]).

And yet, one must repeatedly ask oneself whether what matters in Orientalism is the general group of ideas overriding the mass of material—about which who could deny that they were shot through with doctrines of European superiority, various kinds of racism, imperialism, and the like, dogmatic views of "the Oriental" as a kind of ideal and unchanging abstraction?—or the much more varied work produced by almost uncountable individual writers, whom one would take up as individual instances of authors dealing with the Orient. In a sense the two alternatives, general and particular, are really two perspectives on the same material: in both instances one would have to deal with pioneers in the field like William Jones,[8] with great artists like Nerval or Flaubert. And why would it not be possible to employ both perspectives together, or one after the other? Isn't there an obvious danger of distortion (of precisely the kind that academic Orientalism has always been prone to) if either too general or too specific a level of description is maintained systematically?

My two fears are distortion and inaccuracy, or rather the kind of inaccuracy produced by too dogmatic a generality and too positivistic a localized focus. In trying to deal with these problems I have tried to deal with three

6. Joseph Arthur, comte de Gobineau (1816–1882), French diplomat and author of *Essay on the Inequality of the Human Races* (1853–55). The French Orientalist Antoine-Isaac Silvestre de Sacy (1758–1838) published his *Arab Chrestomathy* in 1806; Lane (1801–1876), an English scholar of Arabic, published his *Account* in 1836.

7. Steven Marcus, *The Other Victorians: A Study of Sexuality and Pornography in Mid-Nineteenth-Century England* (New York: Bantam, 1967), pp. 200–219 [Said's note].

8. English philologist and judge (1746–1794); he was the first to observe the close resemblance of Sanskrit to Greek and Latin.

main aspects of my own contemporary reality that seem to me to point the way out of the methodological or perspectival difficulties I have been discussing, difficulties that might force one, in the first instance, into writing a coarse polemic on so unacceptably general a level of description as not to be worth the effort, or in the second instance, into writing so detailed and atomistic a series of analyses as to lose all track of the general lines of force informing the field, giving it its special cogency. How then to recognize individuality and to reconcile it with its intelligent, and by no means passive or merely dictatorial, general and hegemonic context?

III

I mentioned three aspects of my contemporary reality: I must explain and briefly discuss them now, so that it can be seen how I was led to a particular course of research and writing.

1. *The distinction between pure and political knowledge.* It is very easy to argue that knowledge about Shakespeare or Wordsworth[9] is not political whereas knowledge about contemporary China or the Soviet Union is. My own formal and professional designation is that of "humanist," a title which indicates the humanities as my field and therefore the unlikely eventuality that there might be anything political about what I do in that field. Of course, all these labels and terms are quite unnuanced as I use them here, but the general truth of what I am pointing to is, I think, widely held. One reason for saying that a humanist who writes about Wordsworth, or an editor whose specialty is Keats,[1] is not involved in anything political is that what he does seems to have no direct political effect upon reality in the everyday sense. A scholar whose field is Soviet economics works in a highly charged area where there is much government interest, and what he might produce in the way of studies or proposals will be taken up by policymakers, government officials, institutional economists, intelligence experts. The distinction between "humanists" and persons whose work has policy implications, or political significance, can be broadened further by saying that the former's ideological color is a matter of incidental importance to politics (although possibly of great moment to his colleagues in the field, who may object to his Stalinism[2] or fascism or too easy liberalism), whereas the ideology of the latter is woven directly into his material—indeed, economics, politics, and sociology in the modern academy are ideological sciences—and therefore taken for granted as being "political."

Nevertheless the determining impingement on most knowledge produced in the contemporary West (and here I speak mainly about the United States) is that it be nonpolitical, that is, scholarly, academic, impartial, above partisan or small-minded doctrinal belief. One can have no quarrel with such an ambition in theory, perhaps, but in practice the reality is much more problematic. No one has ever devised a method for detaching the scholar from the circumstances of life, from the fact of his involvement (conscious or unconscious) with a class, a set of beliefs, a social position, or from the

9. WILLIAM WORDSWORTH (1770–1850), English Romantic poet.
1. John Keats (1795–1821), English Romantic poet.
2. That is, hard-line authoritarianism similar to that of the oppressive Soviet regime (1924–53) of Joseph Stalin (1879–1953).

mere activity of being a member of a society. These continue to bear on what he does professionally, even though naturally enough his research and its fruits do attempt to reach a level of relative freedom from the inhibitions and the restrictions of brute, everyday reality. For there is such a thing as knowledge that is less, rather than more, partial than the individual (with his entangling and distracting life circumstances) who produces it. Yet this knowledge is not therefore automatically nonpolitical.

Whether discussions of literature or of classical philology are fraught with—or have unmediated—political significance is a very large question that I have tried to treat in some detail elsewhere.[3] What I am interested in doing now is suggesting how the general liberal consensus that "true" knowledge is fundamentally nonpolitical (and conversely, that overtly political knowledge is not "true" knowledge) obscures the highly if obscurely organized political circumstances obtaining when knowledge is produced. No one is helped in understanding this today when the adjective "political" is used as a label to discredit any work for daring to violate the protocol of pretended suprapolitical objectivity. We may say, first, that civil society recognizes a gradation of political importance in the various fields of knowledge. To some extent the political importance given a field comes from the possibility of its direct translation into economic terms; but to a greater extent political importance comes from the closeness of a field to ascertainable sources of power in political society. Thus an economic study of long-term Soviet energy potential and its effect on military capability is likely to be commissioned by the Defense Department, and thereafter to acquire a kind of political status impossible for a study of Tolstoi's[4] early fiction financed in part by a foundation. Yet both works belong in what civil society acknowledges to be a similar field, Russian studies, even though one work may be done by a very conservative economist, the other by a radical literary historian. My point here is that "Russia" as a general subject matter has political priority over nicer distinctions such as "economics" and "literary history," because political society in Gramsci's sense reaches into such realms of civil society as the academy and saturates them with significance of direct concern to it.

I do not want to press all this any further on general theoretical grounds: it seems to me that the value and credibility of my case can be demonstrated by being much more specific, in the way, for example, Noam Chomsky has studied the instrumental connection between the Vietnam War and the notion of objective scholarship as it was applied to cover state-sponsored military research.[5] Now because Britain, France, and recently the United States are imperial powers, their political societies impart to their civil societies a sense of urgency, a direct political infusion as it were, where and whenever matters pertaining to their imperial interests abroad are concerned. I doubt that it is controversial, for example, to say that an Englishman in India or Egypt in the later nineteenth century took an interest in those countries that was never far from their status in his mind as British colonies. To say this may seem quite different from saying that all academic

3. See my *The World, the Text, and the Critic* (Cambridge, Mass.: Harvard University Press, 1983) [Said's note].

4. Leo Tolstoy (1828–1910), Russian novelist.

5. Principally in his *American Power and the New Mandarins: Historical and Political Essays* (New York: Pantheon, 1969) and *For Reasons of State* (New York: Pantheon, 1973) [Said's note]. Chomsky (b. 1928), American linguist and radical social critic.

knowledge about India and Egypt is somehow tinged and impressed with, violated by, the gross political fact—and yet *that is what I am saying* in this study of Orientalism. For if it is true that no production of knowledge in the human sciences can ever ignore or disclaim its author's involvement as a human subject in his own circumstances, then it must also be true that for a European or American studying the Orient there can be no disclaiming the main circumstances of *his* actuality: that he comes up against the Orient as a European or American first, as an individual second. And to be a European or an American in such a situation is by no means an inert fact. It meant and means being aware, however dimly, that one belongs to a power with definite interests in the Orient, and more important, that one belongs to a part of the earth with a definite history of involvement in the Orient almost since the time of Homer.

Put in this way, these political actualities are still too undefined and general to be really interesting. Anyone would agree to them without necessarily agreeing also that they mattered very much, for instance, to Flaubert as he wrote *Salammbô*, or to H. A. R. Gibb as he wrote *Modern Trends in Islam*.[6] The trouble is that there is too great a distance between the big dominating fact, as I have described it, and the details of everyday life that govern the minute discipline of a novel or a scholarly text as each is being written. Yet if we eliminate from the start any notion that "big" facts like imperial domination can be applied mechanically and deterministically to such complex matters as culture and ideas, then we will begin to approach an interesting kind of study. My idea is that European and then American interest in the Orient was political according to some of the obvious historical accounts of it that I have given here, but that it was the culture that created that interest, that acted dynamically along with brute political, economic, and military rationales to make the Orient the varied and complicated place that it obviously was in the field I call Orientalism.

Therefore, Orientalism is not a mere political subject matter or field that is reflected passively by culture, scholarship, or institutions; nor is it a large and diffuse collection of texts about the Orient; nor is it representative and expressive of some nefarious "Western" imperialist plot to hold down the "Oriental" world. It is rather a *distribution* of geopolitical awareness into aesthetic, scholarly, economic, sociological, historical, and philological texts; it is an *elaboration* not only of a basic geographical distinction (the world is made up of two unequal halves, Orient and Occident) but also of a whole series of "interests" which, by such means as scholarly discovery, philological reconstruction, psychological analysis, landscape and sociological description, it not only creates but also maintains; it *is*, rather than expresses, a certain *will* or *intention* to understand, in some cases to control, manipulate, even to incorporate, what is a manifestly different (or alternative and novel) world; it is, above all, a discourse that is by no means in direct, corresponding relationship with political power in the raw, but rather is produced and exists in an uneven exchange with various kinds of power, shaped to a degree by the exchange with power political (as with a colonial or imperial establishment), power intellectual (as with reigning sciences like comparative linguistics or anatomy, or any of the modern policy sciences), power cultural

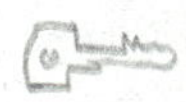

6. Published in 1947; Gibb (1895–1971) was an English scholar of Arabic language and history.

(as with orthodoxies and canons of taste, texts, values), power moral (as with ideas about what "we" do and what "they" cannot do or understand as "we" do). Indeed, my real argument is that Orientalism is—and does not simply represent—a considerable dimension of modern political-intellectual culture, and as such has less to do with the Orient than it does with "our" world.

Because Orientalism is a cultural and a political fact, then, it does not exist in some archival vacuum; quite the contrary, I think it can be shown that what is thought, said, or even done about the Orient follows (perhaps occurs within) certain distinct and intellectually knowable lines. Here too a considerable degree of nuance and elaboration can be seen working as between the broad superstructural pressures and the details of composition, the facts of textuality. Most humanistic scholars are, I think, perfectly happy with the notion that texts exist in contexts, that there is such a thing as intertextuality, that the pressures of conventions, predecessors, and rhetorical styles limit what Walter Benjamin once called the "overtaxing of the productive person in the name of . . . the principle of 'creativity,' " in which the poet is believed on his own, and out of his pure mind, to have brought forth his work.[7] Yet there is a reluctance to allow that political, institutional, and ideological constraints act in the same manner on the individual author. A humanist will believe it to be an interesting fact to any interpreter of Balzac that he was influenced in the *Comédie humaine*[8] by the conflict between Geoffroy Saint-Hilaire and Cuvier,[9] but the same sort of pressure on Balzac of deeply reactionary monarchism is felt in some vague way to demean his literary "genius" and therefore to be less worth serious study. Similarly—as Harry Bracken[1] has been tirelessly showing—philosophers will conduct their discussions of Locke, Hume, and empiricism[2] without ever taking into account that there is an explicit connection in these classic writers between their "philosophic" doctrines and racial theory, justifications of slavery, or arguments for colonial exploitation.[3] These are common enough ways by which contemporary scholarship keeps itself pure.

Perhaps it is true that most attempts to rub culture's nose in the mud of politics have been crudely iconoclastic; perhaps also the social interpretation of literature in my own field has simply not kept up with the enormous technical advances in detailed textual analysis. But there is no getting away from the fact that literary studies in general, and American Marxist theorists in particular, have avoided the effort of seriously bridging the gap between the superstructural and the base levels in textual, historical scholarship; on another occasion I have gone so far as to say that the literary-cultural establishment as a whole has declared the serious study of imperialism and culture off limits.[4] For Orientalism brings one up directly against that question—

7. Walter Benjamin, *Charles Baudelaire: A Lyric Poet in the Era of High Capitalism*, trans. Harry Zohn (London: New Left Books, 1973), p. 71 [Said's note]. BENJAMIN (1892–1940), German literary and cultural critic.

8. *The Human Comedy*, the title given to the totality of his short stories and novels by the French novelist Honoré de Balzac (1799–1850); most portray contemporary French society and many are linked by recurring characters.

9. A debate on comparative anatomy in 1830 between the prominent French zoologists Étienne Geoffroy Saint-Hilaire (1772–1844) and Georges Cuvier (1769–1832).

1. American philosopher (b. 1926).

2. The view, held by British philosophers John Locke (1632–1704) and DAVID HUME (1711–1776), that all knowledge derives from sensory experience.

3. Harry Bracken, "Essence, Accident, and Race," *Hermathena* 116 (winter 1973): 81–96 [Said's note].

4. In an interview published in *Diacritics* 6, no. 3 (fall 1976): 38 [Said's note]. The terms *superstructure* and *base* allude to the Marxist view that all aspects of a society—literature, arts, politics, and

that is, to realizing that political imperialism governs an entire field of study, imagination, and scholarly institutions—in such a way as to make its avoidance an intellectual and historical impossibility. Yet there will always remain the perennial escape mechanism of saying that a literary scholar and a philosopher, for example, are trained in literature and philosophy respectively, not in politics or ideological analysis. In other words, the specialist argument can work quite effectively to block the larger and, in my opinion, the more intellectually serious perspective.

Here it seems to me there is a simple two-part answer to be given, at least so far as the study of imperialism and culture (or Orientalism) is concerned. In the first place, nearly every nineteenth-century writer (and the same is true enough of writers in earlier periods) was extraordinarily well aware of the fact of empire: this is a subject not very well studied, but it will not take a modern Victorian specialist long to admit that liberal cultural heroes like John Stuart Mill, Arnold, Carlyle, Newman, Macaulay, Ruskin, George Eliot, and even Dickens[5] had definite views on race and imperialism, which are quite easily to be found at work in their writing. So even a specialist must deal with the knowledge that Mill, for example, made it clear in *On Liberty* and *Representative Government* that his views there could not be applied to India (he was an India Office functionary for a good deal of his life, after all) because the Indians were civilizationally, if not racially, inferior. The same kind of paradox is to be found in Marx, as I try to show in this book. In the second place, to believe that politics in the form of imperialism bears upon the production of literature, scholarship, social theory, and history writing is by no means equivalent to saying that culture is therefore a demeaned or denigrated thing. Quite the contrary: my whole point is to say that we can better understand the persistence and the durability of saturating hegemonic systems like culture when we realize that their internal constraints upon writers and thinkers were *productive*, not unilaterally inhibiting. It is this idea that Gramsci, certainly, and Foucault and Raymond Williams in their very different ways have been trying to illustrate. Even one or two pages by Williams on "the uses of the Empire" in *The Long Revolution* tell us more about nineteenth-century cultural richness than many volumes of hermetic textual analyses.[6]

Therefore I study Orientalism as a dynamic exchange between individual authors and the large political concerns shaped by the three great empires—British, French, American—in whose intellectual and imaginative territory the writing was produced. What interests me most as a scholar is not the gross political verity but the detail, as indeed what interests us in someone like Lane or Flaubert or Renan is not the (to him) indisputable truth that Occidentals are superior to Orientals, but the profoundly worked over and modulated evidence of his detailed work within the very wide space opened up by that truth. One need only remember that Lane's *Manners and Customs*

so on—depend on its economic form of production.

5. All major Victorian writers and thinkers: Mill (1806–1873), philosopher and social reformer, who published *On Liberty* in 1859 and *Considerations on Representative Government* in 1861; MATTHEW ARNOLD (1822–1888), poet and critic; Thomas Carlyle (1795–1881), historian and essayist; John Henry Newman (1801–1890), prelate and theologian; Thomas Babington Macaulay (1800–1859), historian and statesman; John Ruskin (1819–1900), art critic; Eliot (pen name of Marian Evans, 1819–1880), novelist; and Charles Dickens (1812–1870), novelist.

6. Raymond Williams, *The Long Revolution* (London: Chatto and Windus, 1961), pp. 66–67 [Said's note]. WILLIAMS (1921–1988), British Marxist literary critic.

of the Modern Egyptians is a classic of historical and anthropological observation because of its style, its enormously intelligent and brilliant details, not because of its simple reflection of racial superiority, to understand what I am saying here.

The kind of political questions raised by Orientalism, then, are as follows: What other sorts of intellectual, aesthetic, scholarly, and cultural energies went into the making of an imperialist tradition like the Orientalist one? How did philology, lexicography, history, biology, political and economic theory, novel-writing, and lyric poetry come to the service of Orientalism's broadly imperialist view of the world? What changes, modulations, refinements, even revolutions take place within Orientalism? What is the meaning of originality, of continuity, of individuality, in this context? How does Orientalism transmit or reproduce itself from one epoch to another? In fine, how can we treat the cultural, historical phenomenon of Orientalism as a kind of *willed human work*—not of mere unconditioned ratiocination—in all its historical complexity, detail, and worth without at the same time losing sight of the alliance between cultural work, political tendencies, the state, and the specific realities of domination? Governed by such concerns a humanistic study can responsibly address itself to politics *and* culture. But this is not to say that such a study establishes a hard-and-fast rule about the relationship between knowledge and politics. My argument is that each humanistic investigation must formulate the nature of that connection in the specific context of the study, the subject matter, and its historical circumstances.

2. *The methodological question.* In a previous book I gave a good deal of thought and analysis to the methodological importance for work in the human sciences of finding and formulating a first step, a point of departure, a beginning principle.[7] A major lesson I learned and tried to present was that there is no such thing as a merely given, or simply available, starting point: beginnings have to be made for each project in such a way as to *enable* what follows from them. Nowhere in my experience has the difficulty of this lesson been more consciously lived (with what success—or failure—I cannot really say) than in this study of Orientalism. The idea of beginning, indeed the act of beginning, necessarily involves an act of delimitation by which something is cut out of a great mass of material, separated from the mass, and made to stand for, as well as be, a starting point, a beginning; for the student of texts one such notion of inaugural delimitation is Louis Althusser's idea of the *problematic*, a specific determinate unity of a text, or group of texts, which is something given rise to by analysis.[8] Yet in the case of Orientalism (as opposed to the case of Marx's texts, which is what Althusser studies) there is not simply the problem of finding a point of departure, or problematic, but also the question of designating which texts, authors, and periods are the ones best suited for study.

It has seemed to me foolish to attempt an encyclopedic narrative history of Orientalism, first of all because if my guiding principle was to be "the European idea of the Orient" there would be virtually no limit to the material I would have had to deal with; second, because the narrative model itself did

7. In my *Beginnings: Intention and Method* (New York: Basic, 1975) [Said's note].

8. Louis Althusser, *For Marx*, trans. Ben Brewster (New York: Pantheon Books, 1969), pp. 65–67 [Said's note]. ALTHUSSER (1918–1990), French Marxist philosopher.

not suit my descriptive and political interests; third, because in such books as Raymond Schwab's *La Renaissance orientale*, Johann Fück's *Die Arabischen Studien in Europa bis in den Anfang des 20. Jahrhunderts*, and more recently, Dorothee Metlitzki's *The Matter of Araby in Medieval England*[9] there already exist encyclopedic works on certain aspects of the European-Oriental encounter such as make the critic's job, in the general political and intellectual context I sketched above, a different one.

There still remained the problem of cutting down a very fat archive to manageable dimensions, and more important, outlining something in the nature of an intellectual order within that group of texts without at the same time following a mindlessly chronological order. My starting point therefore has been the British, French, and American experience of the Orient taken as a unit, what made that experience possible by way of historical and intellectual background, what the quality and character of the experience has been. For reasons I shall discuss presently I limited that already limited (but still inordinately large) set of questions to the Anglo-French-American experience of the Arabs and Islam, which for almost a thousand years together stood for the Orient. Immediately upon doing that, a large part of the Orient seemed to have been eliminated—India, Japan, China, and other sections of the Far East—not because these regions were not important (they obviously have been) but because one could discuss Europe's experience of the Near Orient, or of Islam, apart from its experience of the Far Orient. Yet at certain moments of that general European history of interest in the East, particular parts of the Orient like Egypt, Syria, and Arabia cannot be discussed without also studying Europe's involvement in the more distant parts, of which Persia and India are the most important; a notable case in point is the connection between Egypt and India so far as eighteenth- and nineteenth-century Britain was concerned. Similarly the French role in deciphering the Zend-Avesta, the pre-eminence of Paris as a center of Sanskrit studies during the first decade of the nineteenth century, the fact that Napoleon's[1] interest in the Orient was contingent upon his sense of the British role in India: all these Far Eastern interests directly influenced French interest in the Near East, Islam, and the Arabs.

Britain and France dominated the Eastern Mediterranean from about the end of the seventeenth century on. Yet my discussion of that domination and systematic interest does not do justice to (*a*) the important contributions to Orientalism of Germany, Italy, Russia, Spain, and Portugal and (*b*) the fact that one of the important impulses toward the study of the Orient in the eighteenth century was the revolution in Biblical studies stimulated by such variously interesting pioneers as Bishop Lowth, Eichhorn, Herder, and Michaelis.[2] In the first place, I had to focus rigorously upon the British-

9. Raymond Schwab, *La Renaissance orientale* [*The Oriental Renaissance*, French] (Paris: Payot, 1950); Johann W. Fück, *Die Arabischen Studien in Europa bis in den Anfang des 20. Jahrhunderts* [*Arabic Studies in Europe from Its Origins through the Twentieth Century*, German] (Leipzig: Otto Harrassowitz, 1955); Dorothee Metlitzki, *The Matter of Araby in Medieval England* (New Haven: Yale University Press, 1977) [Said's note].

1. Napoléon Bonaparte (1769–1821), general and emperor of France (1804–15), who campaigned in Egypt (1798–99) in an attempt to damage Britain's trade with India. The Zend-Vesta: the Vesta, a book of sacred writings from eastern Iran (begun ca. 600 B.C.E., fixed in form ca. 4th–6th c. C.E.) that collects the teachings of the religious leader and prophet Zoroaster.

2. Johann David Michaelis (1717–1791), German theologian. Robert Lowth (1710–1787), English grammarian and biblical translator. Johann Gottfried Eichhorn (1752–1827), German biblical scholar and professor of Oriental languages. Johann Gottfried Herder (1744–1803), German critic and philologist.

French and later the American material because it seemed inescapably true not only that Britain and France were the pioneer nations in the Orient and in Oriental studies, but that these vanguard positions were held by virtue of the two greatest colonial networks in pre-twentieth-century history; the American Oriental position since World War II has fit—I think, quite self-consciously—in the places excavated by the two earlier European powers. Then too, I believe that the sheer quality, consistency, and mass of British, French, and American writing on the Orient lifts it above the doubtless crucial work done in Germany, Italy, Russia, and elsewhere. But I think it is also true that the major steps in Oriental scholarship were first taken in either Britain and France, then elaborated upon by Germans. Silvestre de Sacy, for example, was not only the first modern and institutional European Orientalist, who worked on Islam, Arabic literature, the Druze religion, and Sassanid Persia; he was also the teacher of Champollion and of Franz Bopp,[3] the founder of German comparative linguistics. A similar claim of priority and subsequent pre-eminence can be made for William Jones and Edward William Lane.

In the second place—and here the failings of my study of Orientalism are amply made up for—there has been some important recent work on the background in Biblical scholarship to the rise of what I have called modern Orientalism. The best and the most illuminatingly relevant is E. S. Shaffer's impressive *"Kubla Khan" and The Fall of Jerusalem*,[4] an indispensable study of the origins of Romanticism, and of the intellectual activity underpinning a great deal of what goes on in Coleridge, Browning,[5] and George Eliot. To some degree Shaffer's work refines upon the outlines provided in Schwab, by articulating the material of relevance to be found in the German Biblical scholars and using that material to read, in an intelligent and always interesting way, the work of three major British writers. Yet what is missing in the book is some sense of the political as well as ideological edge given the Oriental material by the British and French writers I am principally concerned with; in addition, unlike Shaffer I attempt to elucidate subsequent developments in academic as well as literary Orientalism that bear on the connection between British and French Orientalism on the one hand and the rise of an explicitly colonial-minded imperialism on the other. Then too, I wish to show how all these earlier matters are reproduced more or less in American Orientalism after the Second World War.

Nevertheless there is a possibly misleading aspect to my study, where, aside from an occasional reference, I do not exhaustively discuss the German developments after the inaugural period dominated by Sacy. Any work that seeks to provide an understanding of academic Orientalism and pays little attention to scholars like Steinthal, Müller, Becker, Goldziher, Brockelmann, Nöldeke[6]—to mention only a handful—needs to be reproached, and

3. German philologist and Sanskrit scholar (1791–1867). Druze: a Muslim sect (founded in the early 11th c.) whose members live mainly in the mountains of Lebanon and southern Syria. Sassanid Persia: an empire (224–651) founded by Ardashir I, who made Zoroastrianism the official religion. Jean-François Champollion (1790–1823), French founder of Egyptology, who deciphered the hieroglyphs on the Rosetta Stone.

4. E. S. Shaffer, *"Kubla Khan" and the Fall of Jerusalem: The Mythological School in Biblical Criticism and Secular Literature, 1770–1880* (Cambridge: Cambridge University Press, 1975) [Said's note].

5. Robert Browning (1812–1889), English poet. SAMUEL TAYLOR COLERIDGE (1772–1834), English Romantic poet and critic; his works include "Kubla Khan" (written 1797; published 1816).

6. Except for the Hungarian Goldziher (who also wrote in German), all those named are German:

I freely reproach myself. I particularly regret not taking more account of the great scientific prestige that accrued to German scholarship by the middle of the nineteenth century, whose neglect was made into a denunciation of insular British scholars by George Eliot. I have in mind Eliot's unforgettable portrait of Mr. Casaubon in *Middlemarch*. One reason Casaubon cannot finish his Key to All Mythologies is, according to his young cousin Will Ladislaw, that he is unacquainted with German scholarship. For not only has Casaubon chosen a subject "as changing as chemistry: new discoveries are constantly making new points of view": he is undertaking a job similar to a refutation of Paracelsus because "he is not an Orientalist, you know."[7]

Eliot was not wrong in implying that by about 1830, which is when *Middlemarch* is set, German scholarship had fully attained its European preeminence. Yet at no time in German scholarship during the first two-thirds of the nineteenth century could a close partnership have developed between Orientalists and a protracted, sustained *national* interest in the Orient. There was nothing in Germany to correspond to the Anglo-French presence in India, the Levant, North Africa. Moreover, the German Orient was almost exclusively a scholarly, or at least a classical, Orient: it was made the subject of lyrics, fantasies, and even novels, but it was never actual, the way Egypt and Syria were actual for Chateaubriand, Lane, Lamartine, Burton,[8] Disraeli, or Nerval. There is some significance in the fact that the two most renowned German works on the Orient, Goethe's *Westöstlicher Diwan* and Friedrich Schlegel's *Über die Sprache und Weisheit der Indier*,[9] were based respectively on a Rhine journey and on hours spent in Paris libraries. What German Oriental scholarship did was to refine and elaborate techniques whose application was to texts, myths, ideas, and languages almost literally gathered from the Orient by imperial Britain and France.

Yet what German Orientalism had in common with Anglo-French and later American Orientalism was a kind of intellectual *authority* over the Orient within Western culture. This authority must in large part be the subject of any description of Orientalism, and it is so in this study. Even the name *Orientalism* suggests a serious, perhaps ponderous style of expertise; when I apply it to modern American social scientists (since they do not call themselves Orientalists, my use of the word is anomalous), it is to draw attention to the way Middle East experts can still draw on the vestiges of Orientalism's intellectual position in nineteenth-century Europe.

There is nothing mysterious or natural about authority. It is formed, irradiated, disseminated; it is instrumental, it is persuasive; it has status, it establishes canons of taste and value; it is virtually indistinguishable from certain

Heymann Steinthal (1823–1899), philologist; Friedrich Max Müller (1823–1900), philologist and scholar of Hinduism and Buddhism; Carl Heinrich Becker (1876–1933), politician and scholar of Islamic civilization; Ignác Goldziher (1850–1921), scholar of Islamic civilization; Carl Brockelmann (1868–1956), scholar of Semitic languages and Arabic literature; and Theodor Nöldeke (1836–1930), scholar of Semitic languages and Arabic history.

7. George Eliot, *Middlemarch: A Study of Provincial Life* [1871–72] (Boston: Houghton Mifflin, 1956), p. 164 [Said's note]. Paracelsus: pseudonym of Theophrastus Bombastus von Hohenheim (1493–1541), German physician and chemist who was obsessed with alchemy.

8. Sir Richard Francis Burton (1821–1890), English explorer and linguist who made a pilgrimage to Mecca in disguise and translated *Arabian Nights* (1885–88). Alphonse de Lamartine (1790–1869), French Romantic poet, historian, and statesman.

9. *On the Language and Wisdom of India* (1808) by the German Romantic critic Friedrich von Schlegel (1772–1829). *West-Eastern Divan* (1819), a volume of lyric poems by the German poet and dramatist Johann Wolfgang von Goethe (1749–1832).

ideas it dignifies as true, and from traditions, perceptions, and judgments it forms, transmits, reproduces. Above all, authority can, indeed must, be analyzed. All these attributes of authority apply to Orientalism, and much of what I do in this study is to describe both the historical authority in and the personal authorities of Orientalism.

My principal methodological devices for studying authority here are what can be called *strategic location*, which is a way of describing the author's position in a text with regard to the Oriental material he writes about, and *strategic formation*, which is a way of analyzing the relationship between texts and the way in which groups of texts, types of texts, even textual genres, acquire mass, density, and referential power among themselves and thereafter in the culture at large. I use the notion of strategy simply to identify the problem every writer on the Orient has faced: how to get hold of it, how to approach it, how not to be defeated or overwhelmed by its sublimity, its scope, its awful dimensions. Everyone who writes about the Orient must locate himself vis-à-vis the Orient; translated into his text, this location includes the kind of narrative voice he adopts, the type of structure he builds, the kinds of images, themes, motifs that circulate in his text—all of which add up to deliberate ways of addressing the reader, containing the Orient, and finally, representing it or speaking in its behalf. None of this takes place in the abstract, however. Every writer on the Orient (and this is true even of Homer[1]) assumes some Oriental precedent, some previous knowledge of the Orient, to which he refers and on which he relies. Additionally, each work on the Orient *affiliates* itself with other works, with audiences, with institutions, with the Orient itself. The ensemble of relationships between works, audiences, and some particular aspects of the Orient therefore constitutes an analyzable formation—for example, that of philological studies, of anthologies of extracts from Oriental literature, of travel books, of Oriental fantasies—whose presence in time, in discourse, in institutions (schools, libraries, foreign services) gives it strength and authority.

It is clear, I hope, that my concern with authority does not entail analysis of what lies hidden in the Orientalist text, but analysis rather of the text's surface, its exteriority to what it describes. I do not think that this idea can be overemphasized. Orientalism is premised upon exteriority, that is, on the fact that the Orientalist, poet or scholar, makes the Orient speak, describes the Orient, renders its mysteries plain for and to the West. He is never concerned with the Orient except as the first cause of what he says. What he says and writes, by virtue of the fact that it is said or written, is meant to indicate that the Orientalist is outside the Orient, both as an existential and as a moral fact. The principal product of this exteriority is of course representation: as early as Aeschylus's play *The Persians*[2] the Orient is transformed from a very far distant and often threatening Otherness into figures that are relatively familiar (in Aeschylus's case, grieving Asiatic women). The dramatic immediacy of representation in *The Persians* obscures the fact that the audience is watching a highly artificial enactment of what a non-Oriental has made into a symbol for the whole Orient. My analysis of the Orientalist text therefore places emphasis on the evidence, which is by no means invis-

1. Homer's *Iliad* (ca. 8th c. B.C.E.) takes place at Troy, in northwestern Asia Minor (present-day Turkey).

2. A tragedy originally staged in 472 B.C.E. that portrays the return of Xerxes, king of Persia, to his capital after his defeat by the Greeks in the second Persian War (482–478).

ible, for such representations *as representations*, not as "natural" depictions of the Orient. This evidence is found just as prominently in the so-called truthful text (histories, philological analyses, political treatises) as in the avowedly artistic (i.e., openly imaginative) text. The things to look at are style, figures of speech, setting, narrative devices, historical and social circumstances, *not* the correctness of the representation nor its fidelity to some great original. The exteriority of the representation is always governed by some version of the truism that if the Orient could represent itself, it would; since it cannot, the representation does the job, for the West, and *faute de mieux*,[3] for the poor Orient. "Sie können sich nicht vertreten, sie müssen vertreten werden,"[4] as Marx wrote in *The Eighteenth Brumaire of Louis Bonaparte*.

Another reason for insisting upon exteriority is that I believe it needs to be made clear about cultural discourse and exchange within a culture that what is commonly circulated by it is not "truth" but representations. It hardly needs to be demonstrated again that language itself is a highly organized and encoded system, which employs many devices to express, indicate, exchange messages and information, represent, and so forth. In any instance of at least written language, there is no such thing as a delivered presence, but a *re-presence*, or a representation. The value, efficacy, strength, apparent veracity of a written statement about the Orient therefore relies very little, and cannot instrumentally depend, on the Orient as such. On the contrary, the written statement is a presence to the reader by virtue of its having excluded, displaced, made supererogatory any such *real thing* as "the Orient." Thus all of Orientalism stands forth and away from the Orient: that Orientalism makes sense at all depends more on the West than on the Orient, and this sense is directly indebted to various Western techniques of representation that make the Orient visible, clear, "there" in discourse about it. And these representations rely upon institutions, traditions, conventions, agreed-upon codes of understanding for their effects, not upon a distant and amorphous Orient.

The difference between representations of the Orient before the last third of the eighteenth century and those after it (that is, those belonging to what I call modern Orientalism) is that the range of representation expanded enormously in the later period. It is true that after William Jones and Anquetil-Duperron,[5] and after Napoleon's Egyptian expedition, Europe came to know the Orient more scientifically, to live in it with greater authority and discipline than ever before. But what mattered to Europe was the expanded scope and the much greater refinement given its techniques for receiving the Orient. When around the turn of the eighteenth century the Orient definitively revealed the age of its languages—thus outdating Hebrew's divine pedigree—it was a group of Europeans who made the discovery, passed it on to other scholars, and preserved the discovery in the new science of Indo-European philology. A new powerful science for viewing the linguistic Orient was born, and with it, as Foucault has shown in *The Order of Things*,[6] a whole web of related scientific interests. Similarly William Beckford, Byron,[7] Goethe, and

3. For want of anything better (French).
4. "They cannot represent themselves; they must be represented" (German). *Eighteenth Brumaire* was published in 1852. This quotation is also the epigraph of the entire book.
5. The reference is to Abraham-Hyacinthe Anquetil-Duperron (1731–1805), French scholar of Oriental languages who translated the Avesta into French in 1771.
6. Published in 1966 (titled *Les Mots et les choses*, or *The Words and the Things*).
7. George Gordon, Lord Byron (1788–1824), English Romantic poet whose works include such "Eastern tales" as *The Giaour* (1814). Beckford

Hugo restructured the Orient by their art and made its colors, lights, and people visible through their images, rhythms, and motifs. At most, the "real" Orient provoked a writer to his vision; it very rarely guided it.

Orientalism responded more to the culture that produced it than to its putative object, which was also produced by the West. Thus the history of Orientalism has both an internal consistency and a highly articulated set of relationships to the dominant culture surrounding it. My analyses consequently try to show the field's shape and internal organization, its pioneers, patriarchal authorities, canonical texts, doxological[8] ideas, exemplary figures, its followers, elaborators, and new authorities; I try also to explain how Orientalism borrowed and was frequently informed by "strong" ideas, doctrines, and trends ruling the culture. Thus there was (and is) a linguistic Orient, a Freudian Orient, a Spenglerian Orient, a Darwinian Orient,[9] a racist Orient—and so on. Yet never has there been such a thing as a pure, or unconditional, Orient; similarly, never has there been a nonmaterial form of Orientalism, much less something so innocent as an "idea" of the Orient. In this underlying conviction and in its ensuing methodological consequences do I differ from scholars who study the history of ideas. For the emphases and the executive form, above all the material effectiveness, of statements made by Orientalist discourse are possible in ways that any hermetic history of ideas tends completely to scant. Without those emphases and that material effectiveness Orientalism would be just another idea, whereas it is and was much more than that. Therefore I set out to examine not only scholarly works but also works of literature, political tracts, journalistic texts, travel books, religious and philological studies. In other words, my hybrid perspective is broadly historical and "anthropological," given that I believe all texts to be worldly and circumstantial in (of course) ways that vary from genre to genre, and from historical period to historical period.

Yet unlike Michel Foucault, to whose work I am greatly indebted, I do believe in the determining imprint of individual writers upon the otherwise anonymous collective body of texts constituting a discursive formation like Orientalism. The unity of the large ensemble of texts I analyze is due in part to the fact that they frequently refer to each other: Orientalism is after all a system for citing works and authors. Edward William Lane's *Manners and Customs of the Modern Egyptians* was read and cited by such diverse figures as Nerval, Flaubert, and Richard Burton. He was an authority whose use was an imperative for anyone writing or thinking about the Orient, not just about Egypt: when Nerval borrows passages verbatim from *Modern Egyptians* it is to use Lane's authority to assist him in describing village scenes in Syria, not Egypt. Lane's authority and the opportunities provided for citing him discriminately as well as indiscriminately were there because Orientalism could give his text the kind of distributive currency that he acquired. There is no way, however, of understanding Lane's currency without also understanding the peculiar features of *his* text; this is equally true of Renan, Sacy,

(1759–1844), English travel writer and art collector who also wrote the Gothic novel *Vathek, an Arabian Tale* (1786).

8. Expressing praise to God in established ways.

9. That is, an Orient as perceived through the lenses of the psychological theory of SIGMUND FREUD (1856–1939), Austrian founder of psychoanalysis; the historical theory of Oswald Spengler (1880–1936), German historian who argued in *The Decline of the West* (1918–22) that cultures grow and decay in a natural cycle (the Eastern having given way to the Western, which he believed was itself in its last stage); and the evolutionary theory of Charles Darwin (1809–1882), English naturalist.

Lamartine, Schlegel, and a group of other influential writers. Foucault believes that in general the individual text or author counts for very little; empirically, in the case of Orientalism (and perhaps nowhere else) I find this not to be so. Accordingly my analyses employ close textual readings whose goal is to reveal the dialectic between individual text or writer and the complex collective formation to which his work is a contribution.

Yet even though it includes an ample selection of writers, this book is still far from a complete history or general account of Orientalism. Of this failing I am very conscious. The fabric of as thick a discourse as Orientalism has survived and functioned in Western society because of its richness: all I have done is to describe parts of that fabric at certain moments, and merely to suggest the existence of a larger whole, detailed, interesting, dotted with fascinating figures, texts, and events. I have consoled myself with believing that this book is one installment of several, and hope there are scholars and critics who might want to write others. There is still a general essay to be written on imperialism and culture; other studies would go more deeply into the connection between Orientalism and pedagogy, or into Italian, Dutch, German, and Swiss Orientalism, or into the dynamic between scholarship and imaginative writing, or into the relationship between administrative ideas and intellectual discipline. Perhaps the most important task of all would be to undertake studies in contemporary alternatives to Orientalism, to ask how one can study other cultures and peoples from a libertarian, or a nonrepressive and nonmanipulative, perspective. But then one would have to rethink the whole complex problem of knowledge and power. These are all tasks left embarrassingly incomplete in this study.

The last, perhaps self-flattering, observation on method that I want to make here is that I have written this study with several audiences in mind. For students of literature and criticism, Orientalism offers a marvelous instance of the interrelations between society, history, and textuality; moreover, the cultural role played by the Orient in the West connects Orientalism with ideology, politics, and the logic of power, matters of relevance, I think, to the literary community. For contemporary students of the Orient, from university scholars to policymakers, I have written with two ends in mind: one, to present their intellectual genealogy to them in a way that has not been done; two, to criticize—with the hope of stirring discussion—the often unquestioned assumptions on which their work for the most part depends. For the general reader, this study deals with matters that always compel attention, all of them connected not only with Western conceptions and treatments of the Other but also with the singularly important role played by Western culture in what Vico called the world of nations. Lastly, for readers in the so-called Third World,[1] this study proposes itself as a step towards an understanding not so much of Western politics and of the non-Western world in those politics as of the *strength* of Western cultural discourse, a strength too often mistaken as merely decorative or "superstructural." My hope is to illustrate the formidable structure of cultural domination and, specifically for formerly colonized peoples, the dangers and temptations of employing this structure upon themselves or upon others.

The three long chapters and twelve shorter units into which this book is

1. The "underdeveloped" countries, many of them former colonies, now dominated by highly industrialized "first world" (largely Western) nations in a global economy.

divided are intended to facilitate exposition as much as possible. Chapter One, "The Scope of Orientalism," draws a large circle around all the dimensions of the subject, both in terms of historical time and experiences and in terms of philosophical and political themes. Chapter Two, "Orientalist Structures and Restructures," attempts to trace the development of modern Orientalism by a broadly chronological description, and also by the description of a set of devices common to the work of important poets, artists, and scholars. Chapter Three, "Orientalism Now," begins where its predecessor left off, at around 1870. This is the period of great colonial expansion into the Orient, and it culminates in World War II. The very last section of Chapter Three characterizes the shift from British and French to American hegemony; I attempt there finally to sketch the present intellectual and social realities of Orientalism in the United States.

3. *The personal dimension*. In the *Prison Notebooks* Gramsci says: "The starting-point of critical elaboration is the consciousness of what one really is, and is 'knowing thyself' as a product of the historical process to date, which has deposited in you an infinity of traces, without leaving an inventory." The only available English translation inexplicably leaves Gramsci's comment at that, whereas in fact Gramsci's Italian text concludes by adding, "therefore it is imperative at the outset to compile such an inventory."[2]

Much of the personal investment in this study derives from my awareness of being an "Oriental" as a child growing up in two British colonies. All of my education, in those colonies (Palestine and Egypt) and in the United States, has been Western, and yet that deep early awareness has persisted. In many ways my study of Orientalism has been an attempt to inventory the traces upon me, the Oriental subject, of the culture whose domination has been so powerful a factor in the life of all Orientals. This is why for me the Islamic Orient has had to be the center of attention. Whether what I have achieved is the inventory prescribed by Gramsci is not for me to judge, although I have felt it important to be conscious of trying to produce one. Along the way, as severely and as rationally as I have been able, I have tried to maintain a critical consciousness, as well as employing those instruments of historical, humanistic, and cultural research of which my education has made me the fortunate beneficiary. In none of that, however, have I ever lost hold of the cultural reality of, the personal involvement in having been constituted as, "an Oriental."

The historical circumstances making such a study possible are fairly complex, and I can only list them schematically here. Anyone resident in the West since the 1950s, particularly in the United States, will have lived through an era of extraordinary turbulence in the relations of East and West. No one will have failed to note how "East" has always signified danger and threat during this period, even as it has meant the traditional Orient as well as Russia. In the universities a growing establishment of area-studies programs and institutes has made the scholarly study of the Orient a branch of national policy. Public affairs in this country include a healthy interest in the Orient, as much for its strategic and economic importance as for its traditional exoticism. If the world has become immediately accessible to a

2. Antonio Gramsci, *The Prison Notebooks: Selections*, trans. and ed. Quintin Hoare and Geoffrey Nowell Smith (New York: International Publishers, 1971), p. 324 [Said's note].

Western citizen living in the electronic age, the Orient too has drawn nearer to him, and is now less a myth perhaps than a place crisscrossed by Western, especially American, interests.

One aspect of the electronic, postmodern world is that there has been a reinforcement of the stereotypes by which the Orient is viewed. Television, the films, and all the media's resources have forced information into more and more standardized molds. So far as the Orient is concerned, standardization and cultural stereotyping have intensified the hold of the nineteenth-century academic and imaginative demonology of "the mysterious Orient." This is nowhere more true than in the ways by which the Near East is grasped. Three things have contributed to making even the simplest perception of the Arabs and Islam into a highly politicized, almost raucous matter: one, the history of popular anti-Arab and anti-Islamic prejudice in the West, which is immediately reflected in the history of Orientalism; two, the struggle between the Arabs and Israeli Zionism,[3] and its effects upon American Jews as well as upon both the liberal culture and the population at large; three, the almost total absence of any cultural position making it possible either to identify with or dispassionately to discuss the Arabs or Islam. Furthermore, it hardly needs saying that because the Middle East is now so identified with Great Power politics, oil economics, and the simple-minded dichotomy of freedom-loving, democratic Israel and evil, totalitarian, and terroristic Arabs, the chances of anything like a clear view of what one talks about in talking about the Near East are depressingly small.

My own experiences of these matters are in part what made me write this book. The life of an Arab Palestinian in the West, particularly in America, is disheartening. There exists here an almost unanimous consensus that politically he does not exist, and when it is allowed that he does, it is either as a nuisance or as an Oriental. The web of racism, cultural stereotypes, political imperialism, dehumanizing ideology holding in the Arab or the Muslim is very strong indeed, and it is this web which every Palestinian has come to feel as his uniquely punishing destiny. It has made matters worse for him to remark that no person academically involved with the Near East—no Orientalist, that is—has ever in the United States culturally and politically identified himself wholeheartedly with the Arabs; certainly there have been identifications on some level, but they have never taken an "acceptable" form as has liberal American identification with Zionism, and all too frequently they have been radically flawed by their association either with discredited political and economic interests (oil-company and State Department Arabists, for example) or with religion.

The nexus of knowledge and power creating "the Oriental" and in a sense obliterating him as a human being is therefore not for me an exclusively academic matter. Yet it is an *intellectual* matter of some very obvious importance. I have been able to put to use my humanistic and political concerns for the analysis and description of a very worldly matter, the rise, development, and consolidation of Orientalism. Too often literature and culture are presumed to be politically, even historically innocent; it has regularly seemed otherwise to me, and certainly my study of Orientalism has convinced me

3. A political movement, originating in central and eastern Europe in the late 19th century, to reestablish and maintain a Jewish national state in Palestine.

(and I hope will convince my literary colleagues) that society and literary culture can only be understood and studied together. In addition, and by an almost inescapable logic, I have found myself writing the history of a strange, secret sharer of Western anti-Semitism. That anti-Semitism and, as I have discussed it in its Islamic branch, Orientalism resemble each other very closely is a historical, cultural, and political truth that needs only to be mentioned to an Arab Palestinian for its irony to be perfectly understood. But what I should like also to have contributed here is a better understanding of the way cultural domination has operated. If this stimulates a new kind of dealing with the Orient, indeed if it eliminates the "Orient" and "Occident" altogether, then we shall have advanced a little in the process of what Raymond Williams has called the "unlearning" of "the inherent dominative mode."[4]

1978

4. Raymond Williams, *Culture and Society, 1780–1950* (London: Chatto and Windus, 1958), p. 376 [Said's note].

MONIQUE WITTIG
b. 1935

When the French writer and radical lesbian theorist Monique Wittig concluded "The Straight Mind," her 1978 presentation at the Modern Language Association convention in New York, with the statement that "lesbians are not women," she was greeted with stunned silence. Not all feminists, or all lesbians, were ready to abandon a division between the sexes that has seemed so natural and inevitable. Most feminists, as Wittig notes in "One Is Not Born a Woman," "still believe that the basis of women's oppression is biological as well as historical." But for a lesbian like Wittig to refuse to be heterosexual means that she refuses to become a "man" or a "woman"—categories that she regards as political, not as natural givens. For this reason, she has been a central figure in the debate between those feminists who see "woman" as a transhistorical and eternal essence (see, for instance, HÉLÈNE CIXOUS) and those who believe that the idea of "woman" is a social construct (see, for instance, JUDITH BUTLER). Although Wittig is better known for her fiction than her theoretical writing, her fiction frequently blurs the distinction between literature and theory. Feminists have read her second novel, *Les Guérillères* (1969), which describes a postholocaust world where Amazon fighters attempt to create a new society, as an important and inspiring source of theory about language and women's writing.

Wittig was born in Alsace, France, and studied Oriental languages, literatures, history, and philosophy at the Sorbonne in Paris. She won the Prix Medici for her first novel, *L'Opoponax* (1964). Her political views were shaped by the left-wing French intellectual milieu of Paris in the 1950s and 1960s; her participation in the May 1968 student-worker uprisings partly inspired *Les Guérillères*. Active in the French women's movement from its inception, Wittig was a co-founder of the Movement de libération des femmes (MLF, the Women's Liberation Movement), the founder of the Féministes Révolutionaires in 1970, and an active member of Gouines rouges (Red Dykes) in 1971. In 1976 she relocated to the United States, though she continued to explore her materialist theories of lesbianism as a member of the Parisian

Marxist-feminist editorial collective Questions Féministes from 1977 until 1980. She received a Ph.D. in literary languages from the Sorbonne in 1986, and she has taught at the University of California at Berkeley, the University of Southern California, Vassar College, Duke University, New York University, and the University of Arizona. Wittig served from 1980 to 1991 on the advisory board of *Feminist Issues*, where she published many of her influential essays, including our selection, "One Is Not Born a Woman" (1981).

With a nod toward the best-known work of France's most famous feminist, SIMONE DE BEAUVOIR, "One Is Not Born a Woman" rejects biological explanations for inequalities and differences between the sexes. The "immediate given," "the sensible given," even those physical features that appear to constitute the standard categories of sex or race are not, in fact, the result of direct physical perception, as we might intuit; rather they are "mythic constructions," which "reinterpret physical features . . . through the network of relationships in which they are perceived." For this reason, Wittig is critical of feminist speculations about prehistorical matriarchies in which women were the creators of civilization (see, for instance, PAULA GUNN ALLEN). This approach, she argues, only further imprisons women within the category of sex. From a lesbian vantage point, matriarchy and patriarchy are equally oppressive because equally heterosexist.

All "naturalizing" explanations for the differences between men and women, according to Wittig, presume that the foundation of sex difference is heterosexuality, which she redefines as a tacit, unquestioned, and forced social contract. Because lesbians are not dependent on men, they cannot be "real" women; but because they lack economic, ideological, and political privilege, they cannot be men. Like ADRIENNE RICH, Wittig argues that the very existence of lesbians—a class of individuals who are "not-woman, not-man"—refutes the naturalized division between the sexes that supports institutionalized heterosexuality, thereby exposing the artificiality of the ruling sex/gender system. For this reason, "One Is Not Born a Woman" became a foundational text both for gay and lesbian studies and for queer theory in the 1990s.

The Marxist analysis of class offers, for Wittig, at least a starting point for a nonessentialist feminism in which socioeconomic relations, rather than biological necessity, provide the common ground for political struggle. The Marxist model, however, is not without problems of its own, and Wittig identifies two. First, Marx's analysis of the proletariat (industrial workers) as a class itself depends on an already naturalized sexual division of labor that obscures the class conflict between men and women (constituted not as natural categories but on the basis of their different relations to the economic foundations of society). The subordination of women cannot simply be subsumed under the class conflict between the bourgeoisie and the proletariat; it must rather be understood as an independent, if related, historical development. Second, Marxism has failed to develop a model of subjectivity that might enable women and other oppressed groups to constitute themselves as individual historical subjects. While Marxism allows for class consciousness, it has rejected as idealist the "transcendental subject" of Western philosophy. Wittig sets feminism the difficult task of defining the individual subject of feminist struggle in materialist terms, though she is less clear about how to coordinate the various—sometimes conflicting—class identifications that women have (different races, social classes, nationalities). Just as Marxism occludes the different investments of men and women in economic class, feminism runs the risk of obscuring the different ways in which women of different races and classes experience gender. Yet despite its problems, Wittig's challenging essay remains a central document in the essentialism debate within feminism that has continued since the 1980s.

BIBLIOGRAPHY

Wittig is the author of four novels that have been influential for feminist theorists: *The Opoponax* (1964; trans. 1966); *The Guérillères* (1969; trans. 1971); *The Lesbian Body* (1973; trans. 1975); and *Across the Acheron* (1985; trans. 1987). She also published with Sande Zeig *Lesbian Peoples: Material for a Dictionary* (1976; trans. 1987). *The Straight Mind and Other Essays*, a collection of Wittig's essays (mostly written in English for *Feminist Issues*), was published in 1992. Excerpts of Wittig's early works are included in *The New French Feminisms* (ed. Elaine Marks and Isabelle de Courtivron, 1980).

For biographical information on Wittig, see the useful entry by Jeannelle Laillou Savona in *Feminist Writers* (ed. Pamela Kester-Shelton, 1996). Most critical writing on Wittig has focused on her fiction. Alice Jardine's "Pre-Texts for the Transatlantic Feminist," *Yale French Studies* 62 (1981), and Hélène Vivienne Wenzel's "The Text as Body/Politics: An Appreciation of Monique Wittig's Writings in Context," *Feminist Studies* 7 (1981), are two of the earliest theoretical considerations of Wittig's work to appear in English. Teresa de Lauretis examines Wittig's lesbian materialism in "Sexual Indifference and Lesbian Representation," *Theatre Journal* 40 (1988). Diana Fuss's chapter on Monique Wittig in *Essentially Speaking: Feminism, Nature, and Difference* (1989) and Judith Butler's in *Gender Trouble: Feminism and the Subversion of Identity* (1990) include important discussions of Wittig's contribution to the essentialism debate. Erika Ostrovsky's *Constant Journey: The Fiction of Monique Wittig* (1991) charts the relationship between fiction and theory in Wittig's writing. For an analysis of Wittig as a lesbian theorist, see Dianne Chisholm's "Lesbianizing Love's Body: Interventions and Imaginings of Monique Wittig," in *Reimagining Women: Representations of Women in Culture* (ed. Shirley Neuman and Glennis Stephenson, 1993), and Renate Gunther, "Are Lesbians Women? The Relationship between Lesbianism and Feminism in the Works of Luce Irigaray and Monique Wittig," in *Gay Signatures: Gay and Lesbian Theory, Fiction, and Film in France, 1945–1995* (ed. Owen Heathcote, Alex Hughes, and James S. Williams, 1998). For a bibliography of works by and about Wittig, see *French Feminist Thought: Michèle Le Doeuff, Monique Wittig, Catherine Clément: A Bibliography*, edited by Joan Nordquist (1993).

One Is Not Born a Woman

A materialist feminist[1] approach to women's oppression destroys the idea that women are a "natural group": "a racial group of a special kind, a group perceived *as natural*, a group of men considered as materially specific in their bodies."[2] What the analysis accomplishes on the level of ideas, practice makes actual at the level of facts: by its very existence, lesbian society destroys the artificial (social) fact constituting women as a "natural group." A lesbian society[3] pragmatically reveals that the division from men of which women have been the object is a political one and shows that we have been ideologically rebuilt into a "natural group." In the case of women, ideology goes far since our bodies as well as our minds are the product of this manip-

1. Christine Delphy, "Pour un féminisme matérialiste," *L'Arc* 61 (1975). Translated as "For a Materialist Feminism," *Feminist Issues* 1, no. 2 (winter 1981) [except as indicated, all notes are Wittig's].
2. Colette Guillaumin, "Race et Nature: Système des marques, idée de groupe naturel et rapports sociaux," *Pluriel*, no. 11 (1977). Translated as "Race and Nature: The System of Marks, the Idea of a Natural Group and Social Relationships," *Feminist Issues* 8, no. 2 (fall 1988).
3. I use the word *society* with an extended anthropological meaning; strictly speaking, it does not refer to societies, in that lesbian societies do not exist completely autonomously from heterosexual social systems.

ulation. We have been compelled in our bodies and in our minds to correspond, feature by feature, with the *idea* of nature that has been established for us. Distorted to such an extent that our deformed body is what they call "natural," what is supposed to exist as such before oppression. Distorted to such an extent that in the end oppression seems to be a consequence of this "nature" within ourselves (a nature which is only an *idea*). What a materialist analysis does by reasoning, a lesbian society accomplishes practically: not only is there no natural group "women" (we lesbians are living proof of it), but as individuals as well we question "woman," which for us, as for Simone de Beauvoir, is only a myth. She said: "One is not born, but becomes a woman. No biological, psychological, or economic fate determines the figure that the human female presents in society: it is civilization as a whole that produces this creature, intermediate between male and eunuch, which is described as feminine."[4]

However, most of the feminists and lesbian-feminists in America and elsewhere still believe that the basis of women's oppression *is biological as well as* historical. Some of them even claim to find their sources in Simone de Beauvoir.[5] The belief in mother right and in a "prehistory" when women created civilization (because of a biological predisposition) while the coarse and brutal men hunted (because of a biological predisposition) is symmetrical with the biologizing interpretation of history produced up to now by the class of men. It is still the same method of finding in women and men a biological explanation of their division, outside of social facts. For me this could never constitute a lesbian approach to women's oppression, since it assumes that the basis of society or the beginning of society lies in heterosexuality. Matriarchy is no less heterosexual than patriarchy: it is only the sex of the oppressor that changes. Furthermore, not only is this conception still imprisoned in the categories of sex (woman and man), but it holds onto the idea that the capacity to give birth (biology) is what defines a woman. Although practical facts and ways of living contradict this theory in lesbian society, there are lesbians who affirm that "women and men are different species or races (the words are used interchangeably): men are biologically inferior to women; male violence is a biological inevitability . . ."[6] By doing this, by admitting that there is a "natural" division between women and men, we naturalize history, we assume that "men" and "women" have always existed and will always exist. Not only do we naturalize history, but also consequently we naturalize the social phenomena which express our oppression, making change impossible. For example, instead of seeing giving birth as a forced production, we see it as a "natural," "biological" process, forgetting that in our societies births are planned (demography), forgetting that we ourselves are programmed to produce children, while this is the only social activity "short of war"[7] that presents such a great danger of death. Thus, as long as we will be "unable to abandon by will or impulse a lifelong and centuries-old commitment to childbearing as *the* female creative act,"[8] gaining control of the production of children will mean much more than the

4. Simone de Beauvoir, *The Second Sex* [trans. H. M. Parshley] (New York: Bantam, 1952), p. 249. [BEAUVOIR (1908–1986), French novelist, philosopher, and feminist—editor's note.]
5. Redstockings, *Feminist Revolution* (New York: Random House, 1978), p. 18.
6. Andrea Dworkin, "Biological Superiority: The World's Most Dangerous and Deadly Idea," *Heresies* 6 (1989): 46.
7. Ti-Grace Atkinson, *Amazon Odyssey* (New York: Links Books, 1974), p. 15.
8. Dworkin, op. cit.

mere control of the material means of this production: women will have to abstract themselves from the definition "woman" which is imposed upon them.

A materialist feminist approach shows that what we take for the cause or origin of oppression is in fact only the *mark*[9] imposed by the oppressor: the "myth of woman,"[1] plus its material effects and manifestations in the appropriated consciousness and bodies of women. Thus, this mark does not predate oppression: Colette Guillaumin[2] has shown that before the socioeconomic reality of black slavery, the concept of race did not exist, at least not in its modern meaning, since it was applied to the lineage of families. However, now, race, exactly like sex, is taken as an "immediate given," a "sensible given," "physical features," belonging to a natural order. But what we believe to be a physical and direct perception is only a sophisticated and mythic construction, an "imaginary formation,"[3] which reinterprets physical features (in themselves as neutral as any others but marked by the social system) through the network of relationships in which they are perceived. (They are seen as *black*, therefore they *are* black; they are seen as *women*, therefore, they *are* women. But before being *seen* that way, they first had to be *made* that way.) Lesbians should always remember and acknowledge how "unnatural," compelling, totally oppressive, and destructive being "woman" was for us in the old days before the women's liberation movement. It was a political constraint, and those who resisted it were accused of not being "real" women. But then we were proud of it, since in the accusation there was already something like a shadow of victory: the avowal by the oppressor that "woman" is not something that goes without saying, since to be one, one has to be a "real" one. We were at the same time accused of wanting to be men. Today this double accusation has been taken up again with enthusiasm in the context of the women's liberation movement by some feminists and also, alas, by some lesbians whose political goal seems somehow to be becoming more and more "feminine." To refuse to be a woman, however, does not mean that one has to become a man. Besides, if we take as an example the perfect "butch," the classic example which provokes the most horror, whom Proust[4] would have called a woman/man, how is her alienation different from that of someone who wants to become a woman? Tweedledum and Tweedledee.[5] At least for a woman, wanting to become a man proves that she has escaped her initial programming. But even if she would like to, with all her strength, she cannot become a man. For becoming a man would demand from a woman not only a man's external appearance but his consciousness as well, that is, the consciousness of one who disposes by right of at least two "natural" slaves during his life span. This is impossible, and one feature of lesbian oppression consists precisely of making women out of reach for us, since women belong to men. Thus a lesbian *has* to be something else, a not-woman, a not-man, a product of society, not a product of nature, for there is no nature in society.

9. Guillaumin, op. cit.
1. Beauvoir, op. cit.
2. French sociologist and feminist theorist (b. 1934), author of *Racism, Sexism, Power, and Ideology* (1995) [editor's note].
3. Guillaumin, "Race and Nature."
4. Marcel Proust (1871–1922), French novelist [editor's note].
5. Proverbial names for indistinguishable entities, personified as two brothers in Lewis Carroll's *Through the Looking-Glass* (1872) [editor's note].

The refusal to become (or to remain) heterosexual always meant to refuse to become a man or a woman, consciously or not. For a lesbian this goes further than the refusal of the *role* "woman." It is the refusal of the economic, ideological, and political power of a man. This, we lesbians, and nonlesbians as well, knew before the beginning of the lesbian and feminist movement. However, as Andrea Dworkin emphasizes, many lesbians recently "have increasingly tried to transform the very ideology that has enslaved us into a dynamic, religious, psychologically compelling celebration of female biological potential."[6] Thus, some avenues of the feminist and lesbian movement lead us back to the myth of woman which was created by men especially for us, and with it we sink back into a natural group. Having stood up to fight for a sexless society,[7] we now find ourselves entrapped in the familiar deadlock of "woman is wonderful." Simone de Beauvoir underlined particularly the false consciousness[8] which consists of selecting among the features of the myth (that women are different from men) those which look good and using them as a definition for women. What the concept "woman is wonderful" accomplishes is that it retains for defining women the best features (best according to whom?) which oppression has granted us, and it does not radically question the categories "man" and "woman," which are political categories and not natural givens. It puts us in a position of fighting within the class "women" not as the other classes do, for the disappearance of our class, but for the defense of "woman" and its reenforcement. It leads us to develop with complacency "new" theories about our specificity: thus, we call our passivity "nonviolence," when the main and emergent point for us is to fight our passivity (our fear, rather, a justified one). The ambiguity of the term "feminist" sums up the whole situation. What does "feminist" mean? Feminist is formed with the word "femme," "woman," and means: someone who fights for women. For many of us it means someone who fights for women as a class and for the disappearance of this class. For many others it means someone who fights for woman and her defense—for the myth, then, and its reenforcement. But why was the word "feminist" chosen if it retains the least ambiguity? We chose to call ourselves "feminists" ten years ago, not in order to support or reenforce the myth of woman, nor to identify ourselves with the oppressor's definition of us, but rather to affirm that our movement had a history and to emphasize the political link with the old feminist movement.

It is, then, this movement that we can put in question for the meaning that it gave to feminism. It so happens that feminism in the last century could never resolve its contradictions on the subject of nature/culture, woman/society. Women started to fight for themselves as a group and rightly considered that they shared common features as a result of oppression. But for them these features were natural and biological rather than social. They went so far as to adopt the Darwinist theory of evolution. They did not believe like Darwin, however, "that women were less evolved than men, but they did believe that male and female natures had diverged in the course of evolutionary development and that society at large reflected this polarization."[9]

6. Dworkin, op. cit. [Dworkin (b. 1946), American feminist writer known for opposition to pornography and claim that there is no such thing as consensual (heterosexual) sex—editor's note.]
7. Atkinson, p. 6: "If feminism has any logic at all, it must be working for a sexless society."
8. Marxist term referring to the tendency to view reality in ways congruent with the interests of the dominant orthodoxy rather than in ways that reflect an individual's class interest [editor's note].
9. Rosalind Rosenberg, "In Search of Woman's Nature," *Feminist Studies* 3, nos. 1/2 (1975): 144. [Charles Darwin (1809–1892), English naturalist—editor's note.]

"The failure of early feminism was that it only attacked the Darwinist charge of female inferiority, while accepting the foundations of this charge—namely, the view of woman as 'unique.' "[1] And finally it was women scholars—and not feminists—who scientifically destroyed this theory. But the early feminists had failed to regard history as a dynamic process which develops from conflicts of interests. Furthermore, they still believed as men do that the cause (origin) of their oppression lay within themselves. And therefore after some astonishing victories the feminists of this first front found themselves at an impasse out of a lack of reasons to fight. They upheld the illogical principle of "equality in difference," an idea now being born again. They fell back into the trap which threatens us once again: the myth of woman.

Thus it is our historical task, and only ours, to define what we call oppression in materialist terms, to make it evident that women are a class, which is to say that the category "woman" as well as the category "man" are political and economic categories not eternal ones. Our fight aims to suppress men as a class, not through a genocidal, but a political struggle. Once the class "men" disappears, "women" as a class will disappear as well, for there are no slaves without masters. Our first task, it seems, is to always thoroughly dissociate "women" (the class within which we fight) and "woman," the myth. For "woman" does not exist for us: it is only an imaginary formation, while "women" is the product of a social relationship. We felt this strongly when everywhere we refused to be called a "*woman's* liberation movement." Furthermore, we have to destroy the myth inside and outside ourselves. "Woman" is not each one of us, but the political and ideological formation which negates "women" (the product of a relation of exploitation). "Woman" is there to confuse us, to hide the reality "women." In order to be aware of being a class and to become a class we first have to kill the myth of "woman" including its most seductive aspects (I think about Virginia Woolf[2] when she said the first task of a woman writer is to kill "the angel in the house"). But to become a class we do not have to suppress our individual selves, and since no individual can be reduced to her/his oppression we are also confronted with the historical necessity of constituting ourselves as the individual subjects of our history as well. I believe this is the reason why all these attempts at "new" definitions of woman are blossoming now. What is at stake (and of course not only for women) is an individual definition as well as a class definition. For once one has acknowledged oppression, one needs to know and experience the fact that one can constitute oneself as a subject (as opposed to an object of oppression), that one can become *someone* in spite of oppression, that one has one's own identity. There is no possible fight for someone deprived of an identity, no internal motivation for fighting, since, although I can fight only with others, first I fight for myself.

The question of the individual subject is historically a difficult one for everybody. Marxism, the last avatar of materialism, the science which has politically formed us, does not want to hear anything about a "subject." Marxism has rejected the transcendental subject, the subject as constitutive of

1. Ibid., p. 146.
2. English writer (1882–1941). The reference is to WOOLF's "Professions for Women" (lecture, 1931; published 1942); the "Angel" is the Victorian ideal of self-sacrificing womanhood [editor's note].

knowledge, the "pure" consciousness. All that thinks per se, before all experience, has ended up in the garbage can of history, because it claimed to exist outside matter, prior to matter, and needed God, spirit, or soul to exist in such a way. This is what is called "idealism." As for individuals, they are only the product of social relations, therefore their consciousness can only be "alienated." (Marx,[3] in *The German Ideology*, says precisely that individuals of the dominating class are also alienated, although they are the direct producers of the ideas that alienate the classes oppressed by them. But since they draw visible advantages from their own alienation they can bear it without too much suffering.) There exists such a thing as class consciousness, but a consciousness which does not refer to a particular subject, except as participating in general conditions of exploitation at the same time as the other subjects of their class, all sharing the same consciousness. As for the practical class problems—outside of the class problems as traditionally defined—that one could encounter (for example, sexual problems), they were considered "bourgeois" problems that would disappear with the final victory of the class struggle. "Individualistic," "subjectivist," "petit bourgeois," these were the labels given to any person who had shown problems which could not be reduced to the "class struggle" itself.

Thus Marxism has denied the members of oppressed classes the attribute of being a subject. In doing this, Marxism, because of the ideological and political power this "revolutionary science" immediately exercised upon the workers' movement and all other political groups, has prevented all categories of oppressed peoples from constituting themselves historically as subjects (subjects of their struggle, for example). This means that the "masses" did not fight for themselves but for *the* party or its organizations. And when an economic transformation took place (end of private property, constitution of the socialist state), no revolutionary change took place within the new society, because the people themselves did not change.

For women, Marxism had two results. It prevented them from being aware that they are a class and therefore from constituting themselves as a class for a very long time, by leaving the relation "women/men" outside of the social order, by turning it into a natural relation, doubtless for Marxists the only one, along with the relation of mothers to children, to be seen this way, and by hiding the class conflict between men and women behind a natural division of labor (*The German Ideology*). This concerns the theoretical (ideological) level. On the practical level, Lenin,[4] *the* party, all the communist parties up to now, including all the most radical political groups, have always reacted to any attempt on the part of women to reflect and form groups based on their own class problem with an accusation of divisiveness. By uniting, we women are dividing the strength of the people. This means that for the Marxists women *belong* either to the bourgeois class or to the proletariat class, in other words, to the men of these classes. In addition, Marxist theory does not allow women any more than other classes of oppressed people to constitute themselves as historical subjects, because Marxism does not take into account the fact that a class also consists of individuals one by one.

3. KARL MARX (1818–1883), German economic, social, and political philosopher; *The German Ideology* was written in 1845–46 and published in 1932 [editor's note].

4. V. I. Lenin (1870–1924), Marxist revolutionary leader and theorist of the Bolshevik revolution and first head of the new Soviet government [editor's note].

Class consciousness is not enough. We must try to understand philosophically (politically) these concepts of "subject" and "class consciousness" and how they work in relation to our history. When we discover that women are the objects of oppression and appropriation, at the very moment that we become able to perceive this, we become subjects in the sense of cognitive subjects, through an operation of abstraction. Consciousness of oppression is not only a reaction to (fight against) oppression. It is also the whole conceptual reevaluation of the social world, its whole reorganization with new concepts, from the point of view of oppression. It is what I would call the science of oppression created by the oppressed. This operation of understanding reality has to be undertaken by every one of us: call it a subjective, cognitive practice. The movement back and forth between the levels of reality (the conceptual reality and the material reality of oppression, which are both social realities) is accomplished through language.

It is we who historically must undertake the task of defining the individual subject in materialist terms. This certainly seems to be an impossibility since materialism and subjectivity have always been mutually exclusive. Nevertheless, and rather than despairing of ever understanding, we must recognize the *need* to reach subjectivity in the abandonment by many of us to the myth "woman" (the myth of woman being only a snare that holds us up). This real necessity for everyone to exist as an individual, as well as a member of a class, is perhaps the first condition for the accomplishment of a revolution, without which there can be no real fight or transformation. But the opposite is also true; without class and class consciousness there are no real subjects, only alienated individuals. For women to answer the question of the individual subject in materialist terms is first to show, as the lesbians and feminists did, that supposedly "subjective," "individual," "private" problems are in fact social problems, class problems; that sexuality is not for women an individual and subjective expression, but a social institution of violence. But once we have shown that all so-called personal problems are in fact class problems, we will still be left with the question of the subject of each singular woman—not the myth, but each one of us. At this point, let us say that a new personal and subjective definition for all humankind can only be found beyond the categories of sex (woman and man) and that the advent of individual subjects demands first destroying the categories of sex, ending the use of them, and rejecting all sciences which still use these categories as their fundamentals (practically all social sciences).

To destroy "woman" does not mean that we aim, short of physical destruction, to destroy lesbianism simultaneously with the categories of sex, because lesbianism provides for the moment the only social form in which we can live freely. Lesbian is the only concept I know of which is beyond the categories of sex (woman and man), because the designated subject (lesbian) is *not* a woman, either economically, or politically, or ideologically. For what makes a woman is a specific social relation to a man, a relation that we have previously called servitude,[5] a relation which implies personal and physical obligation as well as economic obligation ("forced residence,"[6] domestic cor-

5. In an article published in *L'Idiot International* (mai 1970), whose original title was "Pour un mouvement de libération des femmes" (For a Woman's Liberation Movement).

6. Christiane Rochefort, *Les stances à Sophie* (Paris: Grasset, 1963).

vée, conjugal duties, unlimited production of children, etc.), a relation which lesbians escape by refusing to become or to stay heterosexual. We are escapees from our class in the same way as the American runaway slaves were when escaping slavery and becoming free. For us this is an absolute necessity; our survival demands that we contribute all our strength to the destruction of the class of women within which men appropriate women. This can be accomplished only by the destruction of heterosexuality as a social system which is based on the oppression of women by men and which produces the doctrine of the difference between the sexes to justify this oppression.

1981

SANDRA M. GILBERT b. 1936 — SUSAN GUBAR b. 1944

Sandra M. Gilbert and Susan Gubar's *Madwoman in the Attic* (1979) is a landmark of 1970s American feminism. The book encapsulates both the strengths and limitations of that first decade of "second-wave feminism." (First-wave feminism produced the Declaration of Women's Rights of 1848 and culminated in the ultimately successful campaign for female suffrage during the early twentieth century.) An outgrowth of the civil rights and student protest movements of the 1960s, second-wave feminism has proved to be among the most durable of the sixties' legacies. In its initial phase, contemporary feminists were pulled between its separatist and assimilationist tendencies. They debated whether women were better off disavowing the given order altogether, choosing instead to form their own communities, or striving for equal treatment within patriarchal institutions while working to reform them. *The Madwoman in the Attic* reflects the pressures from both sides. All parties to the dispute, however, assumed that every woman shares a set of similar experiences and that patriarchy—the male-dominated social order—is everywhere essentially the same. These assumptions became problematic later on, and they have been challenged by feminists such as BARBARA SMITH, BELL HOOKS, GLORIA ANZALDÚA, and JUDITH BUTLER.

Born in New York City, Sandra M. Gilbert attended Cornell University, where she was active in undergraduate literary circles. She received her M.A. from New York University and her Ph.D. in English literature from Columbia University. The author of six books of poetry along with her literary criticism, Gilbert has taught at California State University at Hayward, Indiana University, Princeton University, and the University of California at Davis. She and Susan Gubar (who was also born in New York City, and received her Ph.D. from the University of Iowa in 1972) met in 1973; both were young professors at Indiana University, where Gubar continues to teach. *The Madwoman in the Attic* grew out of the course in women's literature that the two team-taught. Gilbert and Gubar have continued to collaborate, while also writing single-authored books. They were jointly named *Ms.* magazine's "Woman of the Year" in 1986 for their work as editors of *The Norton Anthology of Literature by Women*.

Building on the earlier 1970s feminist books by Ellen Moers and Elaine Showalter, *The Madwoman in the Attic* develops the notion that women writers can be understood as a group—and understood as "participat[ing] in a quite different literary subculture from that inhabited by male writers." Such separation is ambiguous: "exhilarating" at its best, "profoundly debilitating" at its worst. Gilbert and

Gubar argue that the influential Oedipal model developed by HAROLD BLOOM to describe the relation of post-Enlightenment male writers to each other does not fit the entirely different situation of women in a male-dominated literary tradition. The female "anxiety of authorship" described by Gilbert and Gubar was an "isolation that felt like illness, [an] alienation that felt like madness" as women writers of the eighteenth and nineteenth centuries wielded their pens in defiance of the social injunction that writing was not women's work. Each women writer had to steal (at great risk and great cost to herself) a right to write that society extended only to men—and she looked to earlier women writers to see how such a theft could be pulled off. These "eighteenth- and nineteenth-century foremothers" enable the work of "contemporary women [who] . . . attempt the pen with energy and authority."

For the aggression and competitiveness found in Bloom's account of the relation between male authors, Gilbert and Gubar thus substitute "the secret sisterhood" of role models who show that women can write. (Their own collaboration breaks with the model of the isolated, individual scholar.) The connection remains "secret" because the early women writers they discuss still "fear . . . the antagonism of male readers" and "dread" assuming "the patriarchal authority of art." But the tradition of women writers does provide resources for each new woman author.

Gilbert and Gubar famously make evident the high costs women writers pay for success. The madwoman in the attic (a reference to Bertha, Rochester's hidden first wife, in Charlotte Brontë's *Jane Eyre*) stands for everything the woman writer must try to repress—though never with complete success—in order to write books acceptable by male standards. In detailing the various illnesses that women suffer, Gilbert and Gubar open up questions of bodily experience and mainstream medicine that are also pursued by Elaine Showalter, MICHEL FOUCAULT, and SUSAN BORDO. Employing a psychological approach to literature, they focus on the psychic cost of repression and on bodily symptoms that are interpreted as responses to societal oppression. For Gilbert and Gubar, women need to speak and write, but they must do so in a world that strives to keep them silent. The woman who speaks out is branded "an active monster"; the woman who remains silent risks madness.

As feminism moved into the 1980s, Gilbert and Gubar's approach was sometimes derided as "Anglo-American" or "liberal" feminism, defined as the effort to achieve equal status for women within existing social institutions. Their treatment of "woman" as a unitary category was also challenged. In placing Anne Sexton, an American poet of the 1960s, alongside Charlotte Brontë, a Victorian novelist, they looked historically naive, while their omission of nonwhite women writers seemed to point to an additional blind spot. Differences of race, class, sexual orientation, ethnicity, and historical period not only meant that not all women had the same fundamental experiences but also suggested that women writers could not be judged and valued according to one universal standard. The intensified exploration of difference challenged the notion of "sisterhood," the heady 1970s assumption that all woman shared certain basic similarities and would gain political unity through their common experience of being oppressed.

But we should not consign *The Madwoman in the Attic* to a now-surpassed moment of feminism, as is sometimes done. Gilbert and Gubar attend to the strategies woman have adopted to survive in a male-dominated society, thus focusing on the world that most women inhabit. The recovery of women's histories and the celebration of women's successes within that male world have proven useful. Traditions are constructed, not discovered, and Gilbert and Gubar offer one remarkable example of how feminist critics can create a usable past, can uncover the achievements and resistances unrecorded by official histories. By being alert both to what women writers have so gloriously done *and* to the high costs paid for those successes, Gilbert and Gubar offer a nuanced view of what it means to dwell in relatively powerless positions within a world one did not make.

BIBLIOGRAPHY

Gilbert and Gubar have co-edited *Shakespeare's Sisters: Feminist Essays on Women Poets* (1979), *The Norton Anthology of Literature by Women: The Traditions in English* (1985; 2d ed., 1996), and *The Female Imagination and the Modernist Aesthetic* (1986). They also coauthored a three-volume sequel to *Madwoman in the Attic* on women and modernism, titled *No Man's Land: The Place of the Woman Writer in the Twentieth Century*, containing *The War of the Words* (1988); *Sexchanges* (1989), and *Letters from the Front* (1994). Paying more attention than *Madwoman in the Attic* did to the historical and ideological context of literary works and focusing less on masterpieces by great writers, *No Man's Land* reflects the changes in feminism and prevailing critical models during the 1980s. Gilbert and Gubar's satire of contemporary academic critical schools and movements, *Masterpiece Theatre: An Academic Melodrama*, was published in 1995. Interestingly, a second edition of *Madwoman in the Attic* (with a new introduction) will be published in 2001.

Sandra M. Gilbert's works to date are *Acts of Attention: The Poems of D. H. Lawrence* (1973); the nonfiction account of the death of her husband, *Wrongful Death: A Medical Tragedy* (1995); and six books of poetry: *In the Fourth World* (1978), *Summer Kitchen* (1983), *Emily's Bread* (1984), *Blood Pressure* (1988), *Ghost Volcano* (1995), and *Kissing the Bread* (2000). Biographical information can be found in *The Dictionary of Literary Biography*, vol. 120 (ed. R. S. Gwynn, 1992).

Susan Gubar has co-edited *For Adult Users Only: The Dilemmas of Violent Pornography* (1989), with Joan Hoff; and *English Inside and Out: The Places of Literary Criticism* (1992), with Jonathan Kamholtz. She is the author of *Racechanges: White Skin, Black Face in American Culture* (1997) and *Critical Condition: Feminism at the Turn of the Century* (2000). Biographical information can be found in *Contemporary Authors, New Revision Series* 70 (1999).

Toril Moi's famous critique of *Madwoman in the Attic* in her *Sexual/Textual Politics* (1985) encapsulates the "French feminist" objections to Gilbert and Gubar's work. Elizabeth Rosdeitcher's "Interview with Sandra M. Gilbert and Susan Gubar," *Critical Texts* 6.1 (1989), is a good place to start in studying their work. A range of critical responses can be traced in Laura E. Donaldson, "The Miranda Complex: Colonialism and the Question of Feminist Reading," *Diacritics* 18.3 (1988); Jane Marcus, "The Asylums of Antaeus: Women, War, and Madness," in *The New Historicism* (ed. H. Aram Veeser, 1989); and *Making Feminist History: The Literary Scholarship of Sandra M. Gilbert and Susan Gubar*, edited by William E. Cain (1994).

From The Madwoman in the Attic: The Woman Writer and the Nineteenth-Century Literary Imagination

From Chapter 2. Infection in the Sentence: The Woman Writer and the Anxiety of Authorship

> The man who does not know sick women does not know women
>
> —S. Weir Mitchell

> I try to describe this long limitation, hoping that with such power as is now mine, and such use of language as is within that power, this will convince any one who cares about it that this "living" of mine had been done under a heavy handicap. . . .
>
> —Charlotte Perkins Gilman

> A Word dropped careless on a Page
> May stimulate an eye
> When folded in perpetual seam
> The Wrinkled Maker lie

Infection in the sentence breeds
We may inhale Despair
At distances of Centuries
From the Malaria—
—Emily Dickinson

I stand in the ring
in the dead city
and tie on the red shoes
. . . .
They are not mine,
they are my mother's,
her mother's before,
handed down like an heirloom
but hidden like shameful letters.
—Anne Sexton[1]

What does it mean to be a woman writer in a culture whose fundamental definitions of literary authority are, as we have seen, both overtly and covertly patriarchal? If the vexed and vexing polarities of angel and monster, sweet dumb Snow White and fierce mad Queen, are major images literary tradition offers women, how does such imagery influence the ways in which women attempt the pen? If the Queen's looking glass speaks with the King's voice,[2] how do its perpetual kingly admonitions affect the Queen's own voice? Since his is the chief voice she hears, does the Queen try to sound like the King, imitating his tone, his inflections, his phrasing, his point of view? Or does she "talk back" to him in her own vocabulary, her own timbre, insisting on her own viewpoint? We believe these are basic questions feminist literary criticism—both theoretical and practical—must answer, and consequently they are questions to which we shall turn again and again, not only in this chapter but in all our readings of nineteenth-century literature by women.

That writers assimilate and then consciously or unconsciously affirm or deny the achievements of their predecessors is, of course, a central fact of literary history, a fact whose aesthetic and metaphysical implications have been discussed in detail by theorists as diverse as T. S. Eliot, M. H. Abrams, Erich Auerbach, and Frank Kermode.[3] More recently, some literary theorists have begun to explore what we might call the psychology of literary history—the tensions and anxieties, hostilities and inadequacies writers feel when they confront not only the achievements of their predecessors but the traditions of genre, style, and metaphor that they inherit from such "forefathers." Increasingly, these critics study the ways in which, as J. Hillis Miller has put

1. Epigraphs: *Doctor on Patient* (Philadelphia: Lippincott, 1888), quoted in Ilza Veith, *Hysteria: The History of a Disease* (Chicago: University of Chicago Press, 1965), pp. 219–20; *The Living of Charlotte Perkins Gilman* (1935; reprint, New York: Harper and Row, 1975), p. 104; J. 1261 in *The Poems of Emily Dickinson*, ed. Thomas Johnson, 3 vols. (Cambridge, Mass.: Belknap Press of Harvard University Press, 1955); "The Red Shoes," in *The Book of Folly* (Boston: Houghton Mifflin, 1972), pp. 28–29 [Gilbert and Gubar's note; except as indicated, all subsequent notes are theirs]. Mitchell (1829–1914), American physician and author, specializing in nervous diseases. Gilman (1860–1935), American feminist author and lecturer who underwent and strongly criticized Mitchell's "rest cure." Dickinson (1830–1886), American poet. Sexton (1928–1974), American feminist poet.

2. Gilbert and Gubar make this argument in chapter 1 of *Madwoman in the Attic*, "The Queen's Looking Glass" [editor's note].

3. In "Tradition and the Individual Talent" [1919], Eliot of course considers these matters; in *Mimesis* [1946] Auerbach traces the ways in which the realist includes what has been previously excluded from art; and in *The Sense of an Ending* [1967] Frank Kermode shows how poets and novelists lay bare the literariness of their predecessors' forms in order to explore the dissonance between fiction and reality. [ELIOT (1888–1965), American-born English poet and critic; for "Tradition and the Individual talent," see above. Abrams (b. 1912), American literary critic. Auerbach (1892–1957), German critic. Kermode (b. 1919), English literary critic—editor's note.]

it, a literary text "is inhabited . . . by a long chain of parasitical presences, echoes, allusions, guests, ghosts of previous texts."[4]

As Miller himself also notes, the first and foremost student of such literary psychohistory has been Harold Bloom.[5] Applying Freudian structures to literary genealogies, Bloom has postulated that the dynamics of literary history arise from the artist's "anxiety of influence," his fear that he is not his own creator and that the works of his predecessors, existing before and beyond him, assume essential priority over his own writings. In fact, as we pointed out in our discussion of the metaphor of literary paternity, Bloom's paradigm of the sequential historical relationship between literary artists is the relationship of father and son, specifically that relationship as it was defined by Freud. Thus Bloom explains that a "strong poet" must engage in heroic warfare with his "precursor," for, involved as he is in a literary Oedipal struggle, a man can only become a poet by somehow invalidating his poetic father.

Bloom's model of literary history is intensely (even exclusively) male, and necessarily patriarchal. For this reason it has seemed, and no doubt will continue to seem, offensively sexist to some feminist critics. Not only, after all, does Bloom describe literary history as the crucial warfare of fathers and sons, he sees Milton's fiercely masculine fallen Satan as *the* type of the poet in our culture, and he metaphorically defines the poetic process as a sexual encounter between a male poet and his female muse. Where, then, does the female poet fit in? Does she want to annihilate a "forefather" or a "foremother"? What if she can find no models, no precursors? Does she have a muse, and what is its sex? Such questions are inevitable in any female consideration of Bloomian poetics.[6] And yet, from a feminist perspective, their inevitability may be just the point; it may, that is, call our attention not to what is wrong about Bloom's conceptualization of the dynamics of Western literary history, but to what is right (or at least suggestive) about his theory.

For Western literary history *is* overwhelmingly male—or, more accurately, patriarchal—and Bloom analyzes and explains this fact, while other theorists have ignored it, precisely, one supposes, because they assumed literature had to be male. Like Freud, whose psychoanalytic postulates permeate Bloom's literary psychoanalyses of the "anxiety of influence," Bloom has defined processes of interaction that his predecessors did not bother to consider because, among other reasons, they were themselves so caught up in such processes. Like Freud, too, Bloom has insisted on bringing to consciousness assumptions readers and writers do not ordinarily examine. In doing so, he has clarified the implications of the psychosexual and sociosexual contexts by which every literary text is surrounded, and thus the meanings of the "guests" and "ghosts" which inhabit texts themselves. Speaking of Freud, the feminist theorist Juliet Mitchell has remarked that "psychoanalysis is not a recommendation *for* a patriarchal society, but an analysis of one."[7] The same sort of statement could be made about Bloom's model of literary history, which is not a recommendation for but an analysis of the

4. J. Hillis Miller, "The Limits of Pluralism, III: The Critic as Host," *Critical Inquiry* 3, no. 3 (spring 1977): 446.

5. American literary critic (b. 1930; see above), author of *The Anxiety of Influence* (1972). On SIGMUND FREUD (1856–1939), the Austrian founder of psychoanalysis, see above [editor's note].

6. For a discussion of the woman writer and her place in Bloomian literary history, see Joanne Feit Diehl, " 'Come Slowly—Eden': An Exploration of Women Poets and Their Muse," *Signs* 3, no. 3 (spring 1978): 572–87. See also the responses to Diehl in *Signs* 4, no. 1 (autumn 1978): 188–96. [For John Milton's Satan, see *Paradise Lost* (1667)—editor's note.]

7. Juliet Mitchell, *Psychoanalysis and Feminism* (New York: Vintage, 1975), p. xiii.

patriarchal poetics (and attendant anxieties) which underlie our culture's chief literary movements.

For our purposes here, however, Bloom's historical construct is useful not only because it helps identify and define the patriarchal psychosexual context in which so much Western literature was authored, but also because it can help us distinguish the anxieties and achievements of female writers from those of male writers. If we return to the question we asked earlier—where does a woman writer "fit in" to the overwhelmingly and essentially male literary history Bloom describes?—we find we have to answer that a woman writer does *not* "fit in." At first glance, indeed, she seems to be anomalous, indefinable, alienated, a freakish outsider. Just as in Freud's theories of male and female psychosexual development there is no symmetry between a boy's growth and a girl's (with, say, the male "Oedipus complex" balanced by a female "Electra complex")[8] so Bloom's male-oriented theory of the "anxiety of influence" cannot be simply reversed or inverted in order to account for the situation of the woman writer.

Certainly if we acquiesce in the patriarchal Bloomian model, we can be sure that the female poet does not experience the "anxiety of influence" in the same way that her male counterpart would, for the simple reason that she must confront precursors who are almost exclusively male, and therefore significantly different from her. Not only do these precursors incarnate patriarchal authority (as our discussion of the metaphor of literary paternity argued), they attempt to enclose her in definitions of her person and her potential which, by reducing her to extreme stereotypes (angel, monster) drastically conflict with her own sense of her self—that is, of her subjectivity, her autonomy, her creativity. On the one hand, therefore, the woman writer's male precursors symbolize authority; on the other hand, despite their authority, they fail to define the ways in which she experiences her own identity as a writer. More, the masculine authority with which they construct their literary personae, as well as the fierce power struggles in which they engage in their efforts of self-creation, seem to the woman writer directly to contradict the terms of her own gender definition. Thus the "anxiety of influence" that a male poet experiences is felt by a female poet as an even more primary "anxiety of authorship"—a radical fear that she cannot create, that because she can never become a "precursor" the act of writing will isolate or destroy her.

This anxiety is, of course, exacerbated by her fear that not only can she not fight a male precursor on "his" terms and win, she cannot "beget" art upon the (female) body of the muse. As Juliet Mitchell notes, in a concise summary of the implications Freud's theory of psychosexual development has for women, both a boy and a girl, "as they learn to speak and live within society, want to take the father's [in Bloom's terminology the precursor's] place, and *only the boy will one day be allowed to do so*. Furthermore both sexes are born into the desire of the mother, and as, through cultural heritage, what the mother desires is the phallus-turned-baby, *both* children

8. In Greek mythology, Electra wishes to avenge the death of her father, Agamemnon, whom her mother, Clytemnestra, has helped to murder on his return from leading the Greek armies in the Trojan War. Some psychologists have argued that a girl has an Electra complex that parallels the boy's Oedipus complex, meaning that she feels aggressive toward her mother and desires her father [editor's note].

desire to be the phallus for the mother. Again, *only the boy can fully recognize himself in his mother's desire*. Thus *both* sexes repudiate the implications of femininity," but the girl learns (in relation to her father) "that her subjugation to the law of the father entails her becoming the representative of 'nature' and 'sexuality,' a chaos of spontaneous, intuitive creativity."[9]

Unlike her male counterpart, then, the female artist must first struggle against the effects of a socialization which makes conflict with the will of her (male) precursors seem inexpressibly absurd, futile, or even—as in the case of the Queen in "Little Snow White"—self-annihilating. And just as the male artist's struggle against his precursor takes the form of what Bloom calls revisionary swerves, flights, misreadings, so the female writer's battle for self-creation involves her in a revisionary process. Her battle, however, is not against her (male) precursor's reading of the world but against his reading of *her*. In order to define herself as an author she must redefine the the terms of her socialization. Her revisionary struggle, therefore, often becomes a struggle for what Adrienne Rich has called "Re-vision—the act of looking back, of seeing with fresh eyes, of entering an old text from a new critical direction . . . an act of survival."[1] Frequently, moreover, she can begin such a struggle only by actively seeking a *female* precursor who, far from representing a threatening force to be denied or killed, proves by example that a revolt against patriarchal literary authority is possible.

For this reason, as well as for the sound psychoanalytic reasons Mitchell and others give, it would be foolish to lock the woman artist into an Electra pattern matching the Oedipal structure Bloom proposes for male writers. The woman writer—and we shall see women doing this over and over again—searches for a female model not because she wants dutifully to comply with male definitions of her "femininity" but because she must legitimize her own rebellious endeavors. At the same time, like most women in patriarchal society, the woman writer does experience her gender as a painful obstacle, or even a debilitating inadequacy; like most patriarchally conditioned women, in other words, she is victimized by what Mitchell calls "the inferiorized and 'alternative' (second sex) psychology of women under patriarchy."[2] Thus the loneliness of the female artist, her feelings of alienation from male predecessors coupled with her need for sisterly precursors and successors, her urgent sense of her need for a female audience together with her fear of the antagonism of male readers, her culturally conditioned timidity about self-dramatization, her dread of the patriarchal authority of art, her anxiety about the impropriety of female invention—all these phenomena of "inferiorization" mark the woman writer's struggle for artistic self-definition and differentiate her efforts at self-creation from those of her male counterpart.

As we shall see, such sociosexual differentiation means that, as Elaine Showalter has suggested, women writers participate in a quite different literary subculture from that inhabited by male writers, a subculture which has its own distinctive literary traditions, even—though it defines itself *in relation to* the "main," male-dominated, literary culture—a distinctive history.[3]

9. Mitchell, *Psychoanalysis and Feminism*, pp. 404–5.
1. Adrienne Rich, "When We Dead Awaken: Writing as Re-Vision," in *Adrienne Rich's Poetry*, ed. Barbara Charlesworth Gelpi and Albert Gelpi (New York: Norton, 1975), p. 90. [RICH (b. 1929), feminist poet and essayist—editor's note.]
2. Mitchell, *Psychoanalysis and Feminism*, p. 402.
3. See Elaine Showalter, *A Literature of Their Own* (Princeton: Princeton University Press, 1977). [Showalter (b. 1941), American feminist literary critic—editor's note.]

At best, the separateness of this female subculture has been exhilarating for women. In recent years, for instance, while male writers seem increasingly to have felt exhausted by the need for revisionism which Bloom's theory of the "anxiety of influence" accurately describes, women writers have seen themselves as pioneers in a creativity so intense that their male counterparts have probably not experienced its analog since the Renaissance, or at least since the Romantic era. The son of many fathers, today's male writer feels hopelessly belated; the daughter of too few mothers, today's female writer feels that she is helping to create a viable tradition which is at last definitively emerging.

There is a darker side of this female literary subculture, however, especially when women's struggles for literary self-creation are seen in the psychosexual context described by Bloom's Freudian theories of patrilineal literary inheritance. As we noted above, for an "anxiety of influence" the woman writer substitutes what we have called an "anxiety of authorship," an anxiety built from complex and often only barely conscious fears of that authority which seems to the female artist to be by definition inappropriate to her sex. Because it is based on the woman's socially determined sense of her own biology, this anxiety of authorship is quite distinct from the anxiety about creativity that could be traced in such male writers as Hawthorne or Dostoevsky. Indeed, to the extent that it forms one of the unique bonds that link women in what we might call the secret sisterhood of their literary subculture, such anxiety in itself constitutes a crucial mark of that subculture.

In comparison to the "male" tradition of strong, father-son combat, however, this female anxiety of authorship is profoundly debilitating. Handed down not from one woman to another but from the stern literary "fathers" of patriarchy to all their "inferiorized" female descendants, it is in many ways the germ of a dis-ease or, at any rate, a disaffection, a disturbance, a distrust, that spreads like a stain throughout the style and structure of much literature by women, especially—as we shall see in this study—throughout literature by women before the twentieth century. For if contemporary women do now attempt the pen with energy and authority, they are able to do so only because their eighteenth- and nineteenth-century foremothers struggled in isolation that felt like illness, alienation that felt like madness, obscurity that felt like paralysis to overcome the anxiety of authorship that was endemic to their literary subculture. Thus, while the recent feminist emphasis on positive role models has undoubtedly helped many women, it should not keep us from realizing the terrible odds against which a creative female subculture was established. Far from reinforcing socially oppressive sexual stereotyping, only a full consideration of such problems can reveal the extraordinary strength of women's literary accomplishments in the eighteenth and nineteenth centuries.

Emily Dickinson's acute observations about "infection in the sentence," quoted in our epigraphs, resonate in a number of different ways, then, for women writers, given the literary woman's special concept of her place in literary psychohistory. To begin with, the words seem to indicate Dickinson's keen consciousness that, in the purest Bloomian or Millerian sense, pernicious "guests" and "ghosts" inhabit all literary texts. For any reader, but especially for a reader who is also a writer, every text can become a "sentence" or weapon in a kind of metaphorical germ warfare. Beyond this, however, the fact that "infection in the sentence *breeds*" suggests Dickinson's recognition that literary texts are coercive, imprisoning, fever-inducing; that, since literature usurps a reader's interiority, it is an invasion of privacy. Moreover, given Dickinson's own gender definition, the sexual ambiguity of her poem's "Wrinkled Maker" is significant. For while, on the one hand, "we" (meaning especially women writers) "may inhale Despair" from all those patriarchal texts which seek to deny female autonomy and authority, on the other hand "we" (meaning especially women writers) "may inhale Despair" from all those "foremothers" who have both overtly and covertly conveyed their traditional authorship anxiety to their bewildered female descendants. Finally, such traditional, metaphorically matrilineal anxiety ensures that even the maker of a text, when she is a woman, may feel imprisoned within texts—folded and "wrinkled" by their pages and thus trapped in their "perpetual seam[s]" which perpetually tell her how she *seems*.

Although contemporary women writers are relatively free of the infection of this "Despair" Dickinson defines (at least in comparison to their nineteenth-century precursors), an anecdote recently related by the American poet and essayist Annie Gottlieb summarizes our point about the ways in which, for all women, "Infection in the sentence breeds":

> When I began to enjoy my powers as a writer, I dreamt that my mother had me sterilized! (Even in dreams we still blame our mothers for the punitive choices our culture forces on us.) I went after the mother-figure in my dream, brandishing a large knife; on its blade was writing. I cried, "Do you know what you are doing? You are destroying my femaleness, my *female power*, which is important to me *because of you*!"[4]

Seeking motherly precursors, says Gottlieb, as if echoing Dickinson, the woman writer may find only infection, debilitation. Yet still she must seek, not seek to subvert, her "*female power*, which is important" to her because of her lost literary matrilineage. In this connection, Dickinson's own words about mothers are revealing, for she alternately claimed that "I never had a mother," that "I always ran Home to Awe as a child. . . . He was an awful Mother but I liked him better than none," and that "a mother [was] a miracle."[5] Yet, as we shall see, her own anxiety of authorship was a "Despair" inhaled not only from the infections suffered by her own ailing physical mother, and her many tormented literary mothers, but from the literary fathers who spoke to her—even "lied" to her—sometimes near at hand, sometimes "at distances of Centuries," from the censorious looking glasses of literary texts.

It is debilitating to be *any* woman in a society where women are warned that if they do not behave like angels they must be monsters. Recently, in fact, social scientists and social historians like Jessie Bernard, Phyllis Chesler, Naomi Weisstein, and Pauline Bart have begun to study the ways in which patriarchal socialization literally makes women sick, both physically and mentally.[6] Hysteria, the disease with which Freud so famously began his

4. Annie Gottlieb, "Feminists Look at Motherhood," *Mother Jones*, November 1976, p. 53.
5. *The Letters of Emily Dickinson*, ed. Thomas Johnson, 3 vols. (Cambridge, Mass: Belknap Press of Harvard University Press, 1958), 2:475, 518.
6. See Jessie Bernard, "The Paradox of the Happy Marriage," Pauline B. Bart, "Depression in Middle-Aged Women," and Naomi Weisstein, "Psychology Constructs the Female," all in Vivian Gornick and Barbara K. Moran, eds., *Woman in Sexist Society* (New York: Basic Books, 1971). See also Phyllis Chesler, *Women and Madness* (New

investigations into the dynamic connections between *psyche* and *soma*,[7] is by definition a "female disease," not so much because it takes its name from the Greek word for womb, *hyster* (the organ which was in the nineteenth century supposed to "cause" this emotional disturbance), but because hysteria did occur mainly among women in turn-of-the-century Vienna, and because throughout the nineteenth century this mental illness, like many other nervous disorders, was thought to be caused by the female reproductive system, as if to elaborate upon Aristotle's notion that femaleness was in and of itself a deformity.[8] And, indeed, such diseases of maladjustment to the physical and social environment as anorexia and agoraphobia did and do strike a disproportionate number of women. Sufferers from anorexia—loss of appetite, self-starvation—are primarily adolescent girls. Sufferers from agoraphobia—fear of open or "public" places—are usually female, most frequently middle-aged housewives, as are sufferers from crippling rheumatoid arthritis.[9]

Such diseases are caused by patriarchal socialization in several ways. Most obviously, of course, any young girl, but especially a lively or imaginative one, is likely to experience her education in docility, submissiveness, selflessness as in some sense sickening. To be trained in renunciation is almost necessarily to be trained to ill health, since the human animal's first and strongest urge is to his/her *own* survival, pleasure, assertion. In addition, each of the "subjects" in which a young girl is educated may be sickening in a specific way. Learning to become a beautiful object, the girl learns anxiety about—perhaps even loathing of—her own flesh. Peering obsessively into the real as well as metaphoric looking glasses that surround her, she desires literally to "reduce" her own body. In the nineteenth century, as we noted earlier, this desire to be beautiful and "frail" led to tight-lacing and vinegar-drinking. In our own era it has spawned innumerable diets and "controlled" fasts, as well as the extraordinary phenomenon of teenage anorexia.[1] Similarly, it seems inevitable that women reared for, and conditioned to, lives of privacy, reticence, domesticity, might develop pathological fears of public places and unconfined spaces. Like the comb, stay-laces, and apple which the Queen in "Little Snow White" uses as weapons against her hated step-

York: Doubleday, 1972), and—for a summary of all these matters—Barbara Ehrenreich and Deirdre English, *Complaints and Disorders: The Sexual Politics of Sickness* (Old Westbury, N.Y.: Feminist Press, 1973).

7. Body (Greek) [editor's note].

8. In *Hints on Insanity* (1861) John Millar wrote that "Mental derangement frequently occurs in young females from Amenorrhoea, especially in those who have any strong hereditary predisposition to insanity," adding that "an occasional warm hipbath or leeches to the pubis will . . . be followed by complete mental recovery." In 1873, Henry Mauldsey wrote in *Body and Mind* that "the monthly activity of the ovaries . . . has a notable effect upon the mind and body; wherefore it may become an important cause of mental and physical derangement." See especially the medical opinions of John Millar, Henry Maudsley, and Andrew Wynter in *Madness and Morals: Ideas on Insanity in the Nineteenth Century*, ed. Vieda Skultans (London: Routledge and Kegan Paul, 1975), pp. 230–35. [See ARISTOTLE (384–322 B.C.E.), *On the Generation of Animals*—editor's note.]

9. See Marlene Boskind-Lodahl, "Cinderella's Stepsisters: A Feminist Perspective on Anorexia Nervosa and Bulimia," *Signs* 2, no. 2 (winter 1976): 342–56; Walter Blum, "The Thirteenth Guest" (on agoraphobia), in *California Living, The San Francisco Sunday Examiner and Chronicle*, 17 April 1977, pp. 8–12; Joan Arehart-Treichel, "Can Your Personality Kill You?" (on female rheumatoid arthritis, among other diseases), *New York* 10, no. 48 (28 November 1977): 45: "According to studies conducted in recent years, four out of five rheumatoid victims are women, and for good reason: The disease appears to arise in those unhappy with the traditional female-sex role."

1. More recent discussions of the etiology and treatment of anorexia are offered in Hilde Bruch, M.D., *The Golden Cage: The Enigma of Anorexia Nervosa* (Cambridge, Mass.: Harvard University Press, 1978), and in Salvador Minuchin, Bernice L. Rosman, and Lester Baker, *Psychosomatic Families: Anorexia Nervosa in Context* (Cambridge, Mass.: Harvard University Press, 1978). [Gilbert and Gubar discuss "tight-lacing and vinegar-drinking" in chapter 1—editor's note.]

daughter, such afflictions as anorexia and agoraphobia simply carry patriarchal definitions of "femininity" to absurd extremes, and thus function as essential or at least inescapable parodies of social prescriptions.

In the nineteenth century, however, the complex of social prescriptions these diseases parody did not merely urge women to act in ways which would cause them to become ill; nineteenth-century culture seems to have actually admonished women to *be* ill. In other words, the "female diseases" from which Victorian women suffered were not always byproducts of their training in femininity; they were the goals of such training. As Barbara Ehrenreich and Deirdre English have shown, throughout much of the nineteenth century "Upper- and upper-middle-class women were [defined as] 'sick' [frail, ill]; working-class women were [defined as] 'sickening' [infectious, diseased]." Speaking of the "lady," they go on to point out that "Society agreed that she was frail and sickly," and consequently a "cult of female invalidism" developed in England and America. For the products of such a cult, it was, as Dr. Mary Putnam Jacobi wrote in 1895, "considered natural and almost laudable to break down under all conceivable varieties of strain—a winter dissipation, a houseful of servants, a quarrel with a female friend, not to speak of more legitimate reasons. . . . Constantly considering their nerves, urged to consider them by well-intentioned but short-sighted advisors, [women] pretty soon become nothing but a bundle of nerves."[2]

Given this socially conditioned epidemic of female illness, it is not surprising to find that the angel in the house of literature frequently suffered not just from fear and trembling but from literal and figurative sickness unto death.[3] Although her hyperactive stepmother dances herself into the grave, after all, beautiful Snow White has just barely recovered from a catatonic trance in her glass coffin. And if we return to Goethe's Makarie, the "good" woman of *Wilhelm Meister's Travels* whom Hans Eichner has described as incarnating her author's ideal of "contemplative purity," we find that this "model of selflessness and of purity of heart . . . this embodiment of *das Ewig-Weibliche*, suffers from migraine headaches."[4] Implying ruthless self-suppression, does the "eternal feminine" necessarily imply illness? If so, we may have found yet another meaning for Dickinson's assertion that "Infection in the sentence breeds." The despair we "inhale" even "at distances of centuries" may be the despair of a life like Makarie's, a life that "*has no story*."

At the same time, however, the despair of the monster-woman is also real, undeniable, and infectious. The Queen's mad tarantella is plainly unhealthy and metaphorically the result of too much storytelling. As the Romantic poets feared, too much imagination may be dangerous to anyone, male or female, but for women in particular patriarchal culture has always assumed mental exercises would have dire consequences. In 1645 John Winthrop, the governor of the Massachusetts Bay Colony, noted in his journal that Anne

2. Quoted in Ehrenreich and English, *Complaints and Disorders*, p. 19.

3. *Fear and Trembling* (1843) and *The Sickness unto Death* (1849) are works on religious faith and despair by the Danish philosopher Søren Kierkegaard; "the angel in the house" is the heroine of the long poem of that title (1854–63), celebrating domesticity, by Coventry Patmore and is the fictional figure whom VIRGINIA WOOLF, in her talk "Professions for Women" (1931; published 1942), declared that she had to kill in order to be free to write [editor's note].

4. Eichner, "The Eternal Female," in *Faust*, ed. Cyrus Hamlin, Norton Critical Edition (New York: W. W. Norton, 1976), p. 620. [Johann Wolfgang von Goethe (1749–1832), German poet, novelist, and playwright, author of *Faust* (1808, 1832) and *Wilhelm Meister's Travels* (1829). *Das Ewig-Weibliche*: the eternal feminine (German)—editor's note.]

Hopkins "has fallen into a sad infirmity, the loss of her understanding and reason, which had been growing upon her divers years, by occasion of her giving herself wholly to reading and writing, and had written many books," adding that "if she had attended her household affairs, and such things as belong to women . . . she had kept her wits."[5] And as Wendy Martin has noted

> in the nineteenth century this fear of the intellectual woman became so intense that the phenomenon . . . was recorded in medical annals. A thinking woman was considered such a breach of nature that a Harvard doctor reported during his autopsy on a Radcliffe graduate he discovered that her uterus had shrivelled to the size of a pea.[6]

If, then, as Anne Sexton suggests (in a poem parts of which we have also used here as an epigraph), the red shoes passed furtively down from woman to woman are the shoes of art, the Queen's dancing shoes, it is as sickening to be a Queen who wears them as it is to be an angelic Makarie who repudiates them. Several passages in Sexton's verse express what we have defined as "anxiety of authorship" in the form of a feverish dread of the suicidal tarantella of female creativity:

> And those girls,
> who wore red shoes,
> each boarded a train that would not stop.
> . . . .
> They tore off their ears like safety pins.
> Their arms fell off them and became hats.
> Their heads rolled off and sang down the street.
> And their feet—oh God, their feet in the market place—
> . . . the feet went on.
> The feet could not stop.
> . . . .
> They could not listen.
> They could not stop.
> What they did was the death dance.
> What they did would do them in.

Certainly infection breeds in these sentences, and despair: female art, Sexton suggests, has a "hidden" but crucial tradition of uncontrollable madness. Perhaps it was her semi-conscious perception of this tradition that gave Sexton herself "a secret fear" of being "a reincarnation" of Edna Millay,[7] whose reputation seemed based on romance. In a letter to DeWitt Snodgrass she confessed that she had "a fear of writing as a woman writes," adding, "I wish I were a man—I would rather, write the way a man writes."[8] After all, dancing the death dance, "all those girls / who wore the red shoes" dismantle their own bodies, like anorexics renouncing the guilty weight of their female flesh.

5. John Winthrop, *The History of New England from 1630 to 1649*, ed. James Savage (Boston, 1826), 2:216.
6. Wendy Martin, "Anne Bradstreet's Poetry: A Study of Subversive Piety," in *Shakespeare's Sisters*, ed. Sandra M. Gilbert and Susan Gubar (Bloomington: Indiana University Press, 1979), pp. 19–31.
7. Edna St. Vincent Millay (1892–1950), American poet [editor's note].
8. "The Uncensored Poet: Letters of Anne Sexton," *Ms.* 6, no. 5 (November 1977): 53.

But if their arms, ears, and heads fall off, perhaps their wombs, too, will "shrivel" to "the size of a pea"?

In this connection, a passage from Margaret Atwood's[9] *Lady Oracle* acts almost as a gloss on the conflict between creativity and "femininity" which Sexton's violent imagery embodies (or dis-embodies). Significantly, the protagonist of Atwood's novel is a writer of the sort of fiction that has recently been called "female gothic," and even more significantly she too projects her anxieties of authorship into the fairy-tale metaphor of the red shoes. Stepping in glass, she sees blood on her feet, and suddenly feels that she has discovered

> The real red shoes, the feet punished for dancing. You could dance, or you could have the love of a good man. But you were afraid to dance, because you had this unnatural fear that if you danced they'd cut your feet off so you wouldn't be able to dance. . . . Finally you overcame your fear and danced, and they cut your feet off. The good man went away too, because you wanted to dance.[1]

Whether she is a passive angel or an active monster, in other words, the woman writer feels herself to be literally or figuratively crippled by the debilitating alternatives her culture offers her, and the crippling effects of her conditioning sometimes seem to "breed" like sentences of death in the bloody shoes she inherits from her literary foremothers.

Surrounded as she is by images of disease, traditions of disease, and invitations both to disease and to dis-ease, it is no wonder that the woman writer has held many mirrors up to the discomforts of her own nature. As we shall see, the notion that "Infection in the sentence breeds" has been so central a truth for literary women that the great artistic achievements of nineteenth-century novelists and poets from Austen and Shelley to Dickinson and Barrett Browning[2] are often both literally and figuratively concerned with disease, as if to emphasize the effort with which health and wholeness were won from the infectious "vapors" of despair and fragmentation. Rejecting the poisoned apples her culture offers her, the woman writer often becomes in some sense anorexic, resolutely closing her mouth on silence (since—in the words of Jane Austen's Henry Tilney—"a woman's only power is the power of refusal"[3]), even while she complains of starvation. Thus both Charlotte and Emily Brontë[4] depict the travails of starved or starving anorexic heroines, while Emily Dickinson declares in one breath that she "had been hungry, all the Years," and in another opts for "Sumptuous Destitution." Similarly, Christina Rossetti[5] represents her own anxiety of authorship in the split between one heroine who longs to "suck and suck" on goblin fruit and another who locks her lips fiercely together in a gesture of silent and passionate renunciation. In addition, many of these literary women become in

9. Canadian novelist and poet (b. 1939) [editor's note].

1. Margaret Atwood, *Lady Oracle* (New York: Simon and Schuster, 1976), p. 335.

2. Elizabeth Barrett Browning (1806–1861), English poet. Jane Austen (1775–1818), English novelist. Mary Shelley (1797–1851), English novelist [editor's note].

3. See *Northanger Abbey* [1818], chapter 10: "You will allow, that in both [matrimony and dancing], man has the advantage of choice, woman only the power of refusal."

4. English poet and novelist (1818–1848). Charlotte Brontë (1816–1855), English novelist [editor's note].

5. English poet (1830–1894) [editor's note].

one way or another agoraphobic. Trained to reticence, they fear the vertiginous openness of the literary marketplace and rationalize with Emily Dickinson that "Publication—is the Auction/Of the Mind of Man" or, worse, punningly confess that "Creation seemed a mighty Crack—/ To make me visible."[6]

As we shall also see, other diseases and dis-eases accompany the two classic symptoms of anorexia and agoraphobia. Claustrophobia, for instance, agoraphobia's parallel and complementary opposite, is a disturbance we shall encounter again and again in women's writing throughout the nineteenth century. Eye "troubles," moreover, seem to abound in the lives and works of literary women, with Dickinson matter-of-factly noting that her eye got "put out," George Eliot[7] describing patriarchal Rome as "a disease of the retina," Jane Eyre and Aurora Leigh[8] marrying blind men, Charlotte Brontë deliberately writing with her eyes closed, and Mary Elizabeth Coleridge writing about "Blindness" that came because "Absolute and bright, / The Sun's rays smote me till they masked the Sun."[9] Finally, aphasia and amnesia—two illnesses which symbolically represent (and parody) the sort of intellectual incapacity patriarchal culture has traditionally required of women—appear and reappear in women's writings in frankly stated or disguised forms. "Foolish" women characters in Jane Austen's novels (Miss Bates in *Emma*, for instance) express Malapropish confusion about language, while Mary Shelley's monster[1] has to learn language from scratch and Emily Dickinson herself childishly questions the meanings of the most basic English words: "Will there really be a 'Morning'?/Is there such a thing as 'Day'?"[2] At the same time, many women writers manage to imply that the reason for such ignorance of language—as well as the reason for their deep sense of alienation and inescapable feeling of anomie—is that they have *forgotten* something. Deprived of the power that even their pens don't seem to confer, these women resemble Doris Lessing's[3] heroines, who have to fight their internalization of patriarchal strictures for even a faint trace memory of what they might have become.

"Where are the songs I used to know, / Where are the notes I used to sing?" writes Christina Rossetti in "The Key-Note," a poem whose title indicates its significance for her. "I have forgotten everything / I used to know so long ago."[4] As if to make the same point, Charlotte Brontë's Lucy Snowe[5] conveniently "forgets" her own history and even, so it seems, the Christian name of one of the central characters in her story, while Brontë's orphaned Jane Eyre seems to have lost (or symbolically "forgotten") her family heritage.

6. See Dickinson, *Poems*, J. 579 ("I had been hungry, all the Years"), J. 709 ("Publication—is the Auction"), and J. 891 ("To my quick ear the Leaves—conferred"); see also Christina Rossetti, "Goblin Market" [1862].

7. English novelist (pen name of Mary Ann Evans, 1819–1880) [editor's note].

8. Heroine of Elizabeth Barrett Browning's "novel in verse" *Aurora Leigh* (1856). Jane Eyre: heroine of Charlotte Brontë's novel *Jane Eyre* (1847) [editor's note].

9. See Dickinson, *Poems*, J. 327 ("Before I got my eye put out), George Eliot, *Middlemarch* [1871–72], book 2, chapter 20, and M. E. Coleridge, "Doubt," in *Poems by Mary E. Coleridge* (London: Elkin Mathews, 1908), p. 40. [Coleridge (1861–1907), English poet and novelist—editor's note.]

1. That is, the monster created in Shelley's novel *Frankenstein* (1818). Malapropish: like Mrs. Malaprop, a character in Richard Sheridan's comic play *The Rivals* (1775), who humorously and unintentionally misuses language [editor's note].

2. See Dickinson, *Poems*, J. 101.

3. Rhodesian and later English novelist (b. 1919) [editor's note].

4. *The Poetical Works of Christina Rossetti*, 2 vols. (Boston: Little, Brown, 1909), 2:11.

5. The heroine of Charlotte Brontë's novel *Villette* (1853) [editor's note].

Similarly, too, Emily Brontë's Heathcliff[6] "forgets" or is made to forget who and what he was; Mary Shelley's monster is "born" without either a memory or a family history; and Elizabeth Barrett Browning's Aurora Leigh is early separated from—and thus induced to "forget"—her "mother land" of Italy. As this last example suggests, however, what all these characters and their authors really fear they have forgotten is precisely that aspect of their lives which has been kept from them by patriarchal poetics: their matrilineal heritage of literary strength, their "female power" which, as Annie Gottlieb wrote, is important to them *because of* (not in spite of) their mothers. In order, then, not only to understand the ways in which "Infection in the sentence breeds" for women but also to learn how women have won through disease to artistic health we must begin by redefining Bloom's seminal definitions of the revisionary "anxiety of influence." In doing so, we will have to trace the difficulty paths by which nineteenth-century women overcame their "anxiety of authorship," repudiated debilitating patriarchal prescriptions, and recovered or remembered the lost foremothers who could help them find their distinctive female power.

* * *

1979

6. The dark hero of Emily Brontë's novel *Wuthering Heights* (1847) [editor's note].

HÉLÈNE CIXOUS
b. 1937

"I have nothing to write except what I don't know," says Hélène Cixous in her essay "Coming to Writing" (1977). And in her autobiographical *Rootprints* (1994), she declares: "No sooner do I write . . . it is not true. And yet, I write hanging on to Truth." Like Socrates, Cixous claims to know only that she does not know. Unlike Socrates, she *writes* what she does not know. Transgressing the laws of genre, Cixous's writing defies categorization, but it nevertheless reinvigorates and reexamines many of the conventions of critical essays, novels, plays, and memoirs. In both form and content, Cixous has attempted to put in practice the freedom from any *givenness* that such radical ignorance ("uncovery") entails.

Cixous (pronounced "seek-soo") is known in the English-speaking world primarily as a mid-1970s feminist theorist, a leading practitioner of what is called *écriture féminine*—feminine writing. The word *féminine* has been subject to energetic debates among feminists, nonfeminists, and antifeminists ever since Cixous first published her celebrated manifesto, "The Laugh of the Medusa," in 1975 in a special issue of *L'Arc* magazine devoted to SIMONE DE BEAUVOIR and the women's movement (Cixous's text was translated in a 1976 issue of *Signs: Journal of Women in Culture and Society*, and has been reprinted many times since). Those debates, central to feminist criticism, will be summarized below. But with all the interrogation of the word *féminine*, one sometimes forgets that in France in the late 1960s, it was the word *écriture* (writing) that was the common denominator for a wide range of explosive new practices and publications.

Écriture may be the best name for what distinguishes contemporary "French theory" from "German idealism" or "Anglo-American pragmatism." It describes everything about writing that can neither be subsumed into an idea nor made to correspond exactly to empirical reality. In the late 1960s, a number of important thinkers in France—JACQUES DERRIDA, JULIA KRISTEVA, and ROLAND BARTHES among them—began to investigate what would happen to Western thought if the fact that it exists mainly in *writing* were taken seriously. Philippe Sollers, editor of the journal *Tel Quel*, proclaimed that a new "science of *écriture*," concentrating on the "textuality" of all discourses and inflected by Marxism, promised revolutionary change. The year was 1968, a time of social and political revolt on all levels of French society.

Hélène Cixous, a young English professor, was at the very heart of the intellectual and institutional ferment. Born in Oran, Algeria, to a multicultural, diasporic Jewish family that spoke German and French, she was surrounded by Spanish and Arabic, experienced anti-Semitism during the Vichy regime of the early 1940s, and saw French colonialism firsthand from a position neither French nor Arab. When her father died in 1948, her mother (appropriately named Eve) studied to become a midwife, and was often accompanied by her daughter as she performed her tasks. Hélène, married at eighteen to Guy Berger, with whom she had two children and whom she divorced in 1964, moved to Paris during the Algerian War of Independence, in which her husband was conscripted on the French side while her brother fought for the Algerian side. Pursuing her studies in English, a language not spoken in her family, she became *agrégée* (received the advanced teaching degree) in 1959 and started to teach at the University of Bordeaux, while beginning work on a doctoral dissertation on James Joyce.

Joyce's late style is perhaps the closest thing in the English tradition to *écriture*. As Cixous was writing her dissertation (published in 1969; trans. 1976, *The Exile of James Joyce*), she often discussed Joyce with Derrida, whom she had met in 1962, and with JACQUES LACAN, who was looking for a tutor on Joyce. She went on to teach at the Sorbonne, and then obtained a chair in English literature at the University of Nanterre near Paris, all before having completed her doctorate.

When protests and strikes erupted both within and outside the university in May 1968, Cixous was charged by the minister of education to head a committee to create an experimental branch of the University of Paris (so-called Paris VIII) in the outlying Bois de Vincennes. Many of the country's most innovative writers and thinkers in literature and philosophy came to teach there, including TZVETAN TODOROV, MICHEL FOUCAULT, and GILLES DELEUZE. The first department of psychoanalysis in France was also established there (a department in which the psychoanalytic feminist Luce Irigaray taught until 1974, when she was expelled by the Lacanians for her book *Speculum of the Other Woman*). With Gérard Genette and Todorov, Cixous created the influential journal *Poétique*. At the University of Paris VIII, first at Vincennes and then at St. Denis, she went on to create and run the only doctoral program in France in *Études Féminines* (Women's Studies), a program that was abolished in the late 1970s by the Barre government and reestablished in the 1980s by the Socialists. But in 1968, she was in the process of completing her *doctorat d'état* in English. She became the youngest "doctor" in France.

So what was this *écriture* that was so much a part of the 1968 moment, and how did it lead to *écriture féminine*?

Ever since Socrates (who did not write) was described in the works of PLATO (who did), writing had been considered a secondary notation of a primary activity, speech. The theory of *écriture*—developed especially in Derrida's *Of Grammatology* (1967) and *Writing and Difference* (1967), where it has come to be known as deconstruction—did not simply reverse the hierarchy between speech and writing; it redefined the terms of that hierarchy. Whereas "speech" had been made to stand for immediacy, presence, truth, Logos (i.e., the "Word"), God, and Oneness (and "writing" had stood for deferral, difference, absence, lack, lawlessness, multiplicity, and heterogeneity),

Derrida argued that speech itself had never actually manifested Truth directly; instead, like writing, it was structured through the difference, first named by FERDINAND DE SAUSSURE (1857–1913), between the signifier (the word) and the signified (the meaning). In any act of language, there was a lag, a discrepancy, between a sign and what it meant. To the extent that there was meaning at all, the two things could not be the same. Thus, to the extent that philosophy existed in language (spoken *or* written), it was structured like "writing." No actual language could achieve the simultaneity of signifier and signified, an idealization that was a consequence of the way in which Platonism and Christianity characterized the divine.

Western philosophy after Plato was centered around the impossible but irresistible search for a fundamental Truth or Logos. Derrida calls this search "logocentrism." Brought to clearest conceptualization in the philosophical work of G. W. F. HEGEL in the early nineteenth century, logocentric structures were organized through a series of binary oppositions (mind/matter, light/darkness, presence/absence, nature/culture, good/evil, etc.), the first term of each being desirable and the other shunned. KARL MARX had already claimed to turn Hegel on his head by reversing the relations between materiality and spirituality. But language was neither exactly material nor exactly spiritual. Theorists of *écriture* thus had to find new ways of making readable everything that had been repressed, obscured, or unacknowledged in Western thought.

In the course of that project, many male writers made use of figures of femininity to bring out what had been marginalized from traditional philosophical discourse. These *figures*—veils, shadows, enigmas, figurative language itself—represented resistance to the One, the Light, the Truth, and, implicitly, the idealization of the Male itself. In a way, therefore, we could say that all *écriture* was already *écriture féminine*—it was just being theorized mainly by men.

In part, Hélène Cixous aimed at rendering literal the figures of femininity in the theory of *écriture* and exploring the consequences of that literalization. She did not simply privilege the "female" half of an existing binary opposition between "male" and "female"; like other theorists of *écriture*, she questioned the very adequacy of either/or logics to name the complexity of cultural realities. But while Derrida did so by demystifying the "metaphysics of presence" involved in the notion of "voice," Cixous did so by describing the physical (as opposed to metaphysical) sensations of a woman who is speaking for the first time in public. Structuralism had analyzed the fundamental importance of binary oppositions; it now seemed urgent for poststructuralists to analyze all the things that those oppositions had obscured—and not only to analyze them but also to perform them, to transform them.

The real scandal of Cixous's work lay in her insistence on its two incompatible logics. On the one hand, she claimed that *écriture féminine* was characterized by the explicitly female body parts that had been repressed by traditional discourse and were being ex-pressed by the woman writer: "There is always within her at least a little of that good mother's milk. She writes in white ink." Yet on the other hand, she claimed that both men and women could write *écriture féminine*. How can both claims be true at the same time?

The binary logic that structures the opposition between "male" and "female" is set up as a relation not between "A" and "B" but between "A" and "not-A." SIGMUND FREUD's geometrical concept of castration, refined but not substantially changed by Lacan, defines "woman" not in terms of what she *has* but in terms of what she *lacks*—that is, a penis. "Is the fact that Logocentrism subjects thought—all concepts, codes, and values—to a binary system, related to 'the' couple, man/woman?" Cixous asks in "Sorties," published the same year as "The Laugh of the Medusa." Yes, she answers, and the consequences for the structure of *all* thought, not just thought having to do with sexual difference, are far-reaching. One half of the opposition is essentially destroyed for the other half to make "sense." If this is so, then *both* sides of an opposition are defined in terms of *one* of its elements. Thus anyone simply trying to unrepress the obscured term—here, the feminine—is likely to reproduce the very structures he or she is resisting. This is why Cixous declares, "I am not a feminist." Feminism, for her, participates in the same logic of opposition as traditional logocentrism or its companion, phallocentrism (the description of sexual difference as a difference between *having* and *lacking* the phallus).

Nonetheless, she acknowledges, the female body *has* been repressed. Indeed, *any* transgressive, desiring body—and perhaps *the body itself*—has been repressed. But maybe there is no "body itself," only bodies that have had power and bodies that haven't. Granted, power and authority and law have presupposed the male body—but on the condition that no actual body be represented at all. Thus, both men and women would have everything left to say about the body, and that "everything" would no longer fall neatly into any given category. By writing *as if* the female body could be asserted, Cixous's *écriture féminine* frees it from invisibility and, at the same time, does *not* make it into a new model for the universal human being. The new opposition is not between male and female, but between a logic of the One and a logic of heterogeneity and multiplicity.

The incompatibility between *écriture féminine* as assertion of the female body and *écriture féminine* as capable of being written by men creates an impossible logic that is *écriture féminine*. Such a writing practice is bound to seem outrageous almost all the time. Responding mainly to "The Laugh of the Medusa," many Anglo-American feminists have accused Cixous of promoting "essentialism"—that is, of equating female writing with an idealized and unhistoricized "femininity." And by making such claims as "women are multiple," "women are open to the other," "women write in white ink," she does seem to be affirming some sort of "essence" of woman. It could be argued that these claims are mythic, performative, and critical rather than descriptive. In her puns (*voler* as "steal" and "fly," *dépenser* as "spend" and "unthink," and *blanc* as both "white" and "blank"), she works on and in language, not in the empirical world. "Essentialism" or "anatomical destiny" is in one sense exactly what Cixous is arguing against.

BIBLIOGRAPHY

In 1969 Cixous won the prestigious Medici Prize for her first novel, *Dedans* (trans. 1986, *Inside*), and she has published many writings since, first called novels, then called fictions, then often not characterized; among those available in English are *Angst* (1977; trans. 1985), *The Book of Promethea* (1983; trans. 1991), and *Manna, for the Mandelstams for the Mandelas* (1988; trans. 1993). These are part mythic autobiography, part meditation, part philosophy, and part poetry, and the mobility of her style gives pronouns and structures of address a range far beyond any person or character. She has written a number of plays as well, including *Portrait of Dora* (1976; trans. 1979) and two historical dramas, one on Cambodia and one on India, which she wrote in collaboration with Ariane Mnouchkine's celebrated Théâtre du Soleil. Cixous is the author of more than fifty books.

"The Laugh of the Medusa" forms part of a larger project Cixous was working on in 1975, another part of which ("Sorties") she published in collaboration with the more historicist feminist Catherine Clément as *La Jeune née* (trans. 1986, *The Newly Born Woman*). These are the texts in which Cixous speaks most explicitly about *écriture féminine*, and they are the best-known works by her in English. In addition to *The Exile of James Joyce* (1969; trans. 1976), she has also written a book on the contemporary Brazilian writer Clarice Lispector, translated as *Reading with Clarice Lispector* (1989; trans. 1990). Two volumes of her other literary criticism and theory have been published as *Coming to Writing and Other Essays*, edited by Deborah Jenson (1991), and *Readings: The Poetics of Blanchot, Joyce, Kleist, Kafka, Lispector, and Tsvetayeva*, edited by Verena Andermatt Conley (1991). Her essay in *The Future of Literary Theory* (ed. Ralph Cohen, 1989), titled "From the Scene of the Unconscious to the Scene of History," gives a good overview of Cixous's own poetics. A collection, *The Hélène Cixous Reader*, with a preface by Cixous and a foreword by Derrida, was edited in 1994 by Susan Sellers. It consists of short extracts from a large number of works, mainly "fictional." Although there is no full-length biography, Cixous has written a partly autobiographical text, complete with family histories and photographs, with Mireille Calle-Gruber called *Hélène Cixous, Photos de racines* (1994; trans. 1997, *Hélène Cixous, Rootprints: Memory and Life Writing*).

There are many critical studies devoted to the work of Cixous. Two books by Verena Andermatt Conley, *Hélène Cixous: Writing the Feminine* (1984) and *Hélène Cixous* (1992), provide excellent introductions. *Hélène Cixous: A Politics of Writing* (1991) by Morag Shiach presents a somewhat critical assessment but discusses aspects of Cixous's work not often mentioned in Anglo-American theory, while Susan Sellers's *Hélène Cixous: Authorship, Autobiography, and Love* (1996) presents a more admiring view. Discussions of Cixous in the context of other "French feminists" (a designation that exists only in English) began with the 1981 anthology called *New French Feminisms*, painstakingly and far-reachingly edited by Elaine Marks and Isabelle de Courtivron. Alice Jardine's *Gynesis: Configurations of Women and Modernity* (1985) analyzes how poststructuralist male theorists in France made use of the figure of woman in their attempts to articulate what had been marginalized from traditional philosophical discourse. Susan Sellers, in her *Language and Sexual Difference: Feminist Writing in France* (1991), sees Cixous as the central theorist of feminine writing. And in a larger study of French thought around 1968, *Logics of Failed Revolt: French Theory after May '68* (1995), Peter Starr sees Cixous as the theorist of a "hysteria" that might be politically enabling. For bibliographies, see the entry on Cixous by Verena Andermatt Conley in *French Women Writers: A Bio-Bibliographic Source Book* (ed. Eva Martin Sartori and Dorothy Wynne Zimmerman, 1991) and *French Feminist Theory (III): Luce Irigaray and Hélène Cixous: A Bibliography* (1996), by Joan Nordquist.

The Laugh of the Medusa[1]

I shall speak about women's writing: about *what it will do*. Woman must write her self: must write about women and bring women to writing, from which they have been driven away as violently as from their bodies—for the same reasons, by the same law, with the same fatal goal. Woman must put herself into the text—as into the world and into history—by her own movement.

The future must no longer be determined by the past. I do not deny that the effects of the past are still with us. But I refuse to strengthen them by repeating them, to confer upon them an irremovability the equivalent of destiny, to confuse the biological and the cultural. Anticipation is imperative.

Since these reflections are taking shape in an area just on the point of being discovered, they necessarily bear the mark of our time—a time during which the new breaks away from the old, and, more precisely, the (feminine) new from the old (*la nouvelle de l'ancien*).[2] Thus, as there are no grounds for establishing a discourse, but rather an arid millennial ground to break,

1. Translated by Keith Cohen and Paula Cohen, who occasionally include the original French in parentheses.

2. In French *la nouvelle* (the new, the news) is grammatically feminine, while *l'ancien* (the old, the former) is masculine.

what I say has at least two sides and two aims: to break up, to destroy; and to foresee the unforeseeable, to project.

I write this as a woman, toward women. When I say "woman," I'm speaking of woman in her inevitable struggle against conventional man; and of a universal woman subject who must bring women to their senses and to their meaning in history. But first it must be said that in spite of the enormity of the repression that has kept them in the "dark"—that dark which people have been trying to make them accept as their attribute—there is, at this time, no general woman, no one typical woman. What they have *in common* I will say. But what strikes me is the infinite richness of their individual constitutions: you can't talk about a female sexuality, uniform, homogeneous, classifiable into codes—any more than you can talk about one unconscious resembling another. Women's imaginary is inexhaustible, like music, painting, writing: their stream of phantasms is incredible.

I have been amazed more than once by a description a woman gave me of a world all her own which she had been secretly haunting since early childhood. A world of searching, the elaboration of a knowledge, on the basis of a systematic experimentation with the bodily functions, a passionate and precise interrogation of her erotogeneity. This practice, extraordinarily rich and inventive, in particular as concerns masturbation, is prolonged or accompanied by a production of forms, a veritable aesthetic activity, each stage of rapture inscribing a resonant vision, a composition, something beautiful. Beauty will no longer be forbidden.

I wished that that woman would write and proclaim this unique empire so that other women, other unacknowledged sovereigns, might exclaim: I, too, overflow; my desires have invented new desires, my body knows unheard-of songs. Time and again I, too, have felt so full of luminous torrents that I could burst—burst with forms much more beautiful than those which are put up in frames and sold for a stinking fortune. And I, too, said nothing, showed nothing; I didn't open my mouth, I didn't repaint my half of the world. I was ashamed. I was afraid, and I swallowed my shame and my fear. I said to myself: You are mad! What's the meaning of these waves, these floods, these outbursts? Where is the ebullient, infinite woman who, immersed as she was in her naiveté, kept in the dark about herself, led into self-disdain by the great arm of parental-conjugal phallocentrism,[3] hasn't been ashamed of her strength? Who, surprised and horrified by the fantastic tumult of her drives (for she was made to believe that a well-adjusted normal woman has a . . . divine composure), hasn't accused herself of being a monster? Who, feeling a funny desire stirring inside her (to sing, to write, to dare to speak, in short, to bring out something new), hasn't thought she was sick? Well, her shameful sickness is that she resists death, that she makes trouble.

And why don't you write? Write! Writing is for you, you are for you; your body is yours, take it. I know why you haven't written. (And why I didn't write before the age of twenty-seven.) Because writing is at once too high, too great for you, it's reserved for the great—that is, for "great men"; and it's

3. The psychoanalytic system in which sexual difference is defined as the difference between having and lacking the phallus; the term has come to refer to the patriarchal cultural system as a whole insofar as that system privileges the phallus as the symbol and source of power. It is closely related to *logocentrism*, a term coined by the French philosopher JACQUES DERRIDA (b. 1930); the two are sometimes combined as *phallogocentrism*.

"silly." Besides, you've written a little, but in secret. And it wasn't good, because it was in secret, and because you punished yourself for writing, because you didn't go all the way; or because you wrote, irresistibly, as when we would masturbate in secret, not to go further, but to attenuate the tension a bit, just enough to take the edge off. And then as soon as we come, we go and make ourselves feel guilty—so as to be forgiven; or to forget, to bury it until the next time.

Write, let no one hold you back, let nothing stop you: not man; not the imbecilic capitalist machinery, in which publishing houses are the crafty, obsequious relayers of imperatives handed down by an economy that works against us and off our backs; and not *yourself*. Smug-faced readers, managing editors, and big bosses don't like the true texts of women—female-sexed texts. That kind scares them.

I write woman: woman must write woman. And man, man. So only an oblique consideration will be found here of man; it's up to him to say where his masculinity and femininity are at: this will concern us once men have opened their eyes and seen themselves clearly.[4]

Now women return from afar, from always: from "without," from the heath where witches are kept alive; from below, from beyond "culture"; from their childhood which men have been trying desperately to make them forget, condemning it to "eternal rest." The little girls and their "ill-mannered" bodies immured, well-preserved, intact unto themselves, in the mirror. Frigidified. But are they ever seething underneath! What an effort it takes—there's no end to it—for the sex cops to bar their threatening return. Such a display of forces on both sides that the struggle has for centuries been immobilized in the trembling equilibrium of a deadlock.

Here they are, returning, arriving over and again, because the unconscious is impregnable. They have wandered around in circles, confined to the narrow room in which they've been given a deadly brainwashing. You can incarcerate them, slow them down, get away with the old Apartheid[5] routine, but for a time only. As soon as they begin to speak, at the same time as they're taught their name, they can be taught that their territory is black: because you are Africa, you are black. Your continent is dark. Dark is dangerous. You can't see anything in the dark, you're afraid. Don't move, you might fall. Most of all, don't go into the forest. And so we have internalized this horror of the dark.

Men have committed the greatest crime against women. Insidiously, violently, they have led them to hate women, to be their own enemies, to mobi-

4. Men still have everything to say about their sexuality, and everything to write. For what they have said so far, for the most part, stems from the opposition activity/passivity, from the power relation between a fantasized obligatory virility meant to invade, to colonize, and the consequential phantasm of woman as a "dark continent" to penetrate and to "pacify." (We know what "pacify" means in terms of scotomizing the other and misrecognizing the self.) Conquering her, they've made haste to depart from her borders, to get out of sight, out of body. The way man has of getting out of himself and into her whom he takes not for the other but for his own, deprives him, he knows, of his own bodily territory. One can understand how man, confusing himself with his penis and rushing in for the attack, might feel resentment and fear of being "taken" by the woman, of being lost in her, absorbed, or alone [Cixous's note]. "Dark continent": a metaphor used by SIGMUND FREUD in his essay "The Question of Lay Analysis" (1926) to describe woman as unexplored and mysterious. "Scotomizing": forming a mental blind spot about (a psychoanalytic term).

5. Apartness (Afrikaans), the former official policy of racial segregation and discrimination in South Africa (1948–93).

lize their immense strength against themselves, to be the executants of their virile needs. They have made for women an antinarcissism! A narcissism which loves itself only to be loved for what women haven't got! They have constructed the infamous logic of antilove.

We the precocious, we the repressed of culture, our lovely mouths gagged with pollen, our wind knocked out of us, we the labyrinths, the ladders, the trampled spaces, the bevies—we are black and we are beautiful.[6]

We're stormy, and that which is ours breaks loose from us without our fearing any debilitation. Our glances, our smiles, are spent; laughs exude from all our mouths; our blood flows and we extend ourselves without ever reaching an end; we never hold back our thoughts, our signs, our writing; and we're not afraid of lacking.[7]

What happiness for us who are omitted, brushed aside at the scene of inheritances; we inspire ourselves and we expire without running out of breath, we are everywhere!

From now on, who, if we say so, can say no to us? We've come back from always.

It is time to liberate the New Woman from the Old by coming to know her—by loving her for getting by, for getting beyond the Old without delay, by going out ahead of what the New Woman will be, as an arrow quits the bow with a movement that gathers and separates the vibrations musically, in order to be more than her self.

I say that we must, for, with a few rare exceptions, there has not yet been any writing that inscribes femininity; exceptions so rare, in fact, that, after plowing through literature across languages, cultures, and ages,[8] one can only be startled at this vain scouting mission. It is well known that the number of women writers (while having increased very slightly from the nineteenth century on) has always been ridiculously small. This is a useless and deceptive fact unless from their species of female writers we do not first deduct the immense majority whose workmanship is in no way different from male writing, and which either obscures women or reproduces the classic representations of women (as sensitive—intuitive—dreamy, etc.).[9]

Let me insert here a parenthetical remark. I mean it when I speak of male writing. I maintain unequivocally that there is such a thing as *marked* writing; that, until now, far more extensively and repressively than is ever suspected or admitted, writing has been run by a libidinal and cultural—hence political, typically masculine—economy;[1] that this is a locus where the repression of women has been perpetuated, over and over, more or less consciously, and

6. A reference to the Song of Solomon (1.5) and, perhaps, to a slogan of the U.S. black power movement of the 1960s.

7. A reference to the reinterpretation of Freud's theory of sexual difference by the French psychoanalyst JACQUES LACAN (1901–1981). For Freud, men have a penis, and women don't. For Lacan, men and women are both structured through a fundamental "lack," but that lack is first perceived on the body of the mother.

8. I am speaking here only of the place "reserved" for women by the Western world [Cixous's note].

9. Which works, then, might be called feminine? I'll just point out some examples: one would have to give them full readings to bring out what is pervasively feminine in their significance. Which I shall do elsewhere. In France (have you noted our infinite poverty in this field?—the Anglo-Saxon countries have shown resources of distinctly greater consequence), leafing through what's come out of the 20th century—and it's not much—the only inscriptions of femininity that I have seen were by Colette, Marguerite Duras, . . . and Jean Genet [Cixous's note]. Genet (1910–1986), male French novelist and playwright. Sidonie Gabrielle Colette (1873–1954), French novelist. Duras (pseudonym of Marguerite Donnadieu, 1914–1996), French novelist, screenwriter, playwright, and film director.

1. The "libidinal economy" is the system of exchanges having to do with sexual desire (libido), which Freud characterized as inherently masculine to the extent that it was active, not passive; in this view, only one desire can function at a time.

in a manner that's frightening since it's often hidden or adorned with the mystifying charms of fiction; that this locus has grossly exaggerated all the signs of sexual opposition (and not sexual difference), where woman has never *her* turn to speak—this being all the more serious and unpardonable in that writing is precisely *the very possibility of change*, the space that can serve as a springboard for subversive thought, the precursory movement of a transformation of social and cultural structures.

Nearly the entire history of writing is confounded with the history of reason, of which it is at once the effect, the support, and one of the privileged alibis. It has been one with the phallocentric tradition. It is indeed that same self-admiring, self-stimulating, self-congratulatory phallocentrism.

With some exceptions, for there have been failures—and if it weren't for them, I wouldn't be writing (I-woman, escapee)—in that enormous machine that has been operating and turning out its "truth" for centuries. There have been poets who would go to any lengths to slip something by at odds with tradition—men capable of loving love and hence capable of loving others and of wanting them, of imagining the woman who would hold out against oppression and constitute herself as a superb, equal, hence "impossible" subject, untenable in a real social framework. Such a woman the poet could desire only by breaking the codes that negate her. Her appearance would necessarily bring on, if not revolution—for the bastion was supposed to be immutable—at least harrowing explosions. At times it is in the fissure caused by an earthquake, through that radical mutation of things brought on by a material up-heaval when every structure is for a moment thrown off balance and an ephemeral wildness sweeps order away, that the poet slips something by, for a brief span, of woman. Thus did Kleist[2] expend himself in his yearning for the existence of sister-lovers, maternal daughters, mother-sisters, who never hung their heads in shame. Once the palace of magistrates is restored, it's time to pay: immediate bloody death to the uncontrollable elements.

But only the poets—not the novelists, allies of representationalism. Because poetry involves gaining strength through the unconscious and because the unconscious, that other limitless country, is the place where the repressed manage to survive: women, or as Hoffmann[3] would say, fairies.

She must write her self, because this is the invention of a *new insurgent* writing which, when the moment of her liberation has come, will allow her to carry out the indispensable ruptures and transformations in her history, first at two levels that cannot be separated.

a) Individually. By writing her self, woman will return to the body which has been more than confiscated from her, which has been turned into the uncanny stranger on display—the ailing or dead figure, which so often turns out to be the nasty companion, the cause and location of inhibitions. Censor the body and you censor breath and speech at the same time.

Write your self. Your body must be heard. Only then will the immense resources of the unconscious spring forth. Our naphtha[4] will spread,

2. Heinrich von Kleist (1777–1811), German dramatist and poet.

3. E. T. A. Hoffmann (1776–1822), German writer known especially for his fantastic tales (Freud discusses "The Sandman" in his influential 1919 essay "The 'Uncanny' "; see above).

4. A volatile petroleum product; the term was used by alchemists to refer to liquids with low boiling points.

throughout the world, without dollars—black or gold—nonassessed values that will change the rules of the old game.

To write. An act which will not only "realize" the decensored relation of woman to her sexuality, to her womanly being, giving her access to her native strength; it will give her back her goods, her pleasures, her organs, her immense bodily territories which have been kept under seal; it will tear her away from the superegoized structure[5] in which she has always occupied the place reserved for the guilty (guilty of everything, guilty at every turn: for having desires, for not having any; for being frigid, for being "too hot"; for not being both at once; for being too motherly and not enough; for having children and for not having any; for nursing and for not nursing . . .)—tear her away by means of this research, this job of analysis and illumination, this emancipation of the marvelous text of her self that she must urgently learn to speak. A woman without a body, dumb, blind, can't possibly be a good fighter. She is reduced to being the servant of the militant male, his shadow. We must kill the false woman who is preventing the live one from breathing. Inscribe the breath of the whole woman.

b) An act that will also be marked by woman's *seizing* the occasion to *speak*, hence her shattering entry into history, which has always been based *on her suppression*. To write and thus to forge for herself the antilogos weapon. To become *at will* the taker and initiator, for her own right, in every symbolic system, in every political process.

It is time for women to start scoring their feats in written and oral language.

Every woman has known the torment of getting up to speak. Her heart racing, at times entirely lost for words, ground and language slipping away—that's how daring a feat, how great a transgression it is for a woman to speak—even just open her mouth—in public. A double distress, for even if she transgresses, her words fall almost always upon the deaf male ear, which hears in language only that which speaks in the masculine.

It is by writing, from and toward women, and by taking up the challenge of speech which has been governed by the phallus, that women will confirm women in a place other than that which is reserved in and by the symbolic,[6] that is, in a place other than silence. Women should break out of the snare of silence. They shouldn't be conned into accepting a domain which is the margin or the harem.

Listen to a woman speak at a public gathering (if she hasn't painfully lost her wind). She doesn't "speak," she throws her trembling body forward; she lets go of herself, she flies; all of her passes into her voice, and it's with her body that she vitally supports the "logic" of her speech. Her flesh speaks true. She lays herself bare. In fact, she physically materializes what she's thinking; she signifies it with her body. In a certain way she *inscribes* what she's saying, because she doesn't deny her drives the intractable and impassioned part they have in speaking. Her speech, even when "theoretical" or political, is

5. The superego, according to Freud, is the part of the psyche that develops through the incorporation of the moral standards of the child's parents and community.

6. A reference to Lacan's theory of the psyche. "The Symbolic" is the dimension of language, law, and the father; in contrast, "the Imaginary" is modeled on the mother-child dyad, or on the relation between an infant and its mirror image.

never simple or linear or "objectified," generalized: she draws her story into history.

There is not that scission, that division made by the common man between the logic of oral speech and the logic of the text, bound as he is by his antiquated relation—servile, calculating—to mastery. From which proceeds the niggardly lip service which engages only the tiniest part of the body, plus the mask.

In women's speech, as in their writing, that element which never stops resonating, which, once we've been permeated by it, profoundly and imperceptibly touched by it, retains the power of moving us—that element is the song: first music from the first voice of love which is alive in every woman. Why this privileged relationship with the voice? Because no woman stockpiles as many defenses for countering the drives as does a man. You don't build walls around yourself, you don't forego pleasure as "wisely" as he. Even if phallic mystification has generally contaminated good relationships, a woman is never far from "mother" (I mean outside her role functions: the "mother" as nonname and as source of goods). There is always within her at least a little of that good mother's milk. She writes in white ink.

Woman for women.—There always remains in woman that force which produces/is produced by the other—in particular, the other woman. *In* her, matrix, cradler; herself giver as her mother and child; she is her own sister-daughter. You might object, "What about she who is the hysterical offspring of a bad mother?" Everything will be changed once woman gives woman to the other woman. There is hidden and always ready in woman the source; the locus for the other. The mother, too, is a metaphor. It is necessary and sufficient that the best of herself be given to woman by another woman for her to be able to love herself and return in love the body that was "born" to her. Touch me, caress me, you the living no-name, give me my self as myself. The relation to the "mother," in terms of intense pleasure and violence, is curtailed no more than the relation to childhood (the child that she was, that she is, that she makes, remakes, undoes, there at the point where, the same, she others herself). Text: my body—shot through with streams of song; I don't mean the overbearing, clutchy "mother" but, rather, what touches you, the equivoice that affects you, fills your breast with an urge to come to language and launches your force; the rhythm that laughs you; the intimate recipient who makes all metaphors possible and desirable; body (body? bodies?), no more describable than god, the soul, or the Other; that part of you that leaves a space between yourself and urges you to inscribe in language your woman's style. In women there is always more or less of the mother who makes everything all right, who nourishes, and who stands up against separation; a force that will not be cut off but will knock the wind out of the codes. We will rethink womankind beginning with every form and every period of her body. The Americans remind us, "We are all Lesbians";[7] that is, don't denigrate woman, don't make of her what men have made of you.

Because the "economy" of her drives is prodigious, she cannot fail, in seizing the occasion to speak, to transform directly and indirectly *all* systems

7. Compare the American feminist slogan attributed to Ti-Grace Atkinson (b. 1939), "Feminism is the theory, lesbianism is the practice"; see also the opening of the Radicalesbians' manifesto, "The Woman-Identified Woman" (1970): "A lesbian is the rage of all women condensed to the point of explosion."

of exchange based on masculine thrift. Her libido will produce far more radical effects of political and social change than some might like to think.

Because she arrives, vibrant, over and again, we are at the beginning of a new history, or rather of a process of becoming in which several histories intersect with one another. As subject for history, woman always occurs simultaneously in several places. Woman un-thinks[8] the unifying, regulating history that homogenizes and channels forces, herding contradictions into a single battlefield. In woman, personal history blends together with the history of all women, as well as national and world history. As a militant, she is an integral part of all liberations. She must be farsighted, not limited to a blow-by-blow interaction. She foresees that her liberation will do more than modify power relations or toss the ball over to the other camp; she will bring about a mutation in human relations, in thought, in all praxis: hers is not simply a class struggle, which she carries forward into a much vaster movement. Not that in order to be a woman-in-struggle(s) you have to leave the class struggle or repudiate it; but you have to split it open, spread it out, push it forward, fill it with the fundamental struggle so as to prevent the class struggle, or any other struggle for the liberation of a class or people, from operating as a form of repression, pretext for postponing the inevitable, the staggering alteration in power relations and in the production of individualities. This alteration is already upon us—in the United States, for example, where millions of night crawlers are in the process of undermining the family and disintegrating the whole of American sociality.

The new history is coming; it's not a dream, though it does extend beyond men's imagination, and for good reason. It's going to deprive them of their conceptual orthopedics,[9] beginning with the destruction of their enticement machine.

It is impossible to *define* a feminine practice of writing, and this is an impossibility that will remain, for this practice can never be theorized, enclosed, coded—which doesn't mean that it doesn't exist. But it will always surpass the discourse that regulates the phallocentric system; it does and will take place in areas other than those subordinated to philosophico-theoretical domination. It will be conceived of only by subjects who are breakers of automatisms, by peripheral figures that no authority can ever subjugate.

Hence the necessity to affirm the flourishes of this writing, to give form to its movement, its near and distant byways. Bear in mind to begin with (1) that sexual opposition, which has always worked for man's profit to the point of reducing writing, too, to his laws, is only a historico-cultural limit. There is, there will be more and more rapidly pervasive now, a fiction that produces irreducible effects of femininity. (2) That it is through ignorance that most readers, critics, and writers of both sexes hesitate to admit or deny outright the possibility or the pertinence of a distinction between feminine and masculine writing. It will usually be said, thus disposing of sexual difference: either that all writing, to the extent that it materializes, is feminine; or, inversely—but it comes to the same thing—that the act of writing is equiv-

8. "*Dé-pense*," a neologism formed on the verb *penser* [to think], hence "unthinks," but also "spends" (from *dépenser*) [translator's note].

9. An allusion to Lacan's term *orthopedic*, which refers to any training process that "corrects" the infant's imagination.

alent to masculine masturbation (and so the woman who writes cuts herself out a paper penis); or that writing is bisexual, hence neuter, which again does away with differentiation. To admit that writing is precisely working (in) the in-between, inspecting the process of the same and of the other without which nothing can live, undoing the work of death—to admit this is first to want the two, as well as both, the ensemble of the one and the other, not fixed in sequences of struggle and expulsion or some other form of death but infinitely dynamized by an incessant process of exchange from one subject to another. A process of different subjects knowing one another and beginning one another anew only from the living boundaries of the other: a multiple and inexhaustible course with millions of encounters and transformations of the same into the other and into the in-between, from which woman takes her forms (and man, in his turn; but that's his other history).

In saying "bisexual, hence neuter," I am referring to the classic conception of bisexuality, which, squashed under the emblem of castration fear[1] and along with the fantasy of a "total" being (though composed of two halves), would do away with the difference experienced as an operation incurring loss, as the mark of dreaded sectility.

To this self-effacing, merger-type bisexuality, which would conjure away castration (the writer who puts up his sign: "bisexual written here, come and see," when the odds are good that it's neither one nor the other), I oppose the *other bisexuality* on which every subject not enclosed in the false theater of phallocentric representationalism has founded his/her erotic universe. Bisexuality; that is, each one's location in self (*répérage en soi*) of the presence—variously manifest and insistent according to each person, male or female—of both sexes, nonexclusion either of the difference or of one sex, and, from this "self-permission," multiplication of the effects of the inscription of desire, over all parts of my body and the other body.

Now it happens that at present, for historico-cultural reasons, it is women who are opening up to and benefiting from this vatic bisexuality which doesn't annul differences but stirs them up, pursues them, increases their number. In a certain way, "woman is bisexual";[2] man—it's a secret to no one—being poised to keep glorious phallic monosexuality in view. By virtue of affirming the primacy of the phallus and of bringing it into play, phallocratic ideology has claimed more than one victim. As a woman, I've been clouded over by the great shadow of the scepter and been told: idolize it, that which you cannot brandish. But at the same time, man has been handed that grotesque and scarcely enviable destiny (just imagine) of being reduced to a single idol with clay balls. And consumed, as Freud and his followers note, by a fear of being a woman! For, if psychoanalysis was constituted from woman, to repress femininity (and not so successful a repression at that—men have made it clear), its account of masculine sexuality is now hardly refutable; as with all the "human" sciences, it reproduces the masculine view, of which it is one of the effects.

Here we encounter the inevitable man-with-rock, standing erect in his old

1. The fear that Freud attributes to every male child imagining the punishment for desiring his mother; more generally, the fear of losing something, of not being "whole," that leads men to cling to masculinity for fear of becoming "castrated" like women.

2. Freud claimed that because the mother was the first object of desire for both sexes, women (who had to change their object of desire) were more inherently bisexual than men.

Freudian realm, in the way that, to take the figure back to the point where linguistics is conceptualizing it "anew," Lacan preserves it in the sanctuary of the phallos (ϕ)[3] "sheltered" from *castration's lack*! Their "symbolic" exists, it holds power—we, the sowers of disorder, know it only too well. But we are in no way obliged to deposit our lives in their banks of lack, to consider the constitution of the subject in terms of a drama manglingly restaged, to reinstate again and again the religion of the father. Because we don't want that. We don't fawn around the supreme hole. We have no womanly reason to pledge allegiance to the negative. The feminine (as the poets suspected) affirms: ". . . And yes," says Molly, carrying *Ulysses* off beyond any book and toward the new writing; "I said yes, I will Yes."[4]

The Dark Continent is neither dark nor unexplorable.[5]—It is still unexplored only because we've been made to believe that it was too dark to be explorable. And because they want to make us believe that what interests us is the white continent, with its monuments to Lack. And we believed. They riveted us between two horrifying myths: between the Medusa[6] and the abyss. That would be enough to set half the world laughing, except that it's still going on. For the phallologocentric sublation[7] is with us, and it's militant, regenerating the old patterns, anchored in the dogma of castration. They haven't changed a thing: they've theorized their desire for reality! Let the priests tremble, we're going to show them our sexts![8]

Too bad for them if they fall apart upon discovering that women aren't men, or that the mother doesn't have one. But isn't this fear convenient for them? Wouldn't the worst be, isn't the worst, in truth, that women aren't castrated, that they have only to stop listening to the Sirens[9] (for the Sirens were men) for history to change its meaning? You only have to look at the Medusa straight on to see her. And she's not deadly. She's beautiful and she's laughing.

Men say that there are two unrepresentable things: death and the feminine sex. That's because they need femininity to be associated with death; it's the jitters that gives them a hard-on! for themselves! They need to be afraid of us. Look at the trembling Perseuses moving backward toward us, clad in apotropes.[1] What lovely backs! Not another minute to lose. Let's get out of here.

Let's hurry: the continent is not impenetrably dark. I've been there often. I was overjoyed one day to run into Jean Genet. It was in *Pompes funèbres*.[2]

3. The symbol (the Greek letter phi) representing the phallic function, in Lacanian terminology.
4. The final words of James Joyce's *Ulysses* (1922), spoken by Molly Bloom.
5. Qualities suggested by Freud, who also saw female sexuality (the "dark continent") as a "riddle" (see "Femininity," 1932).
6. In Greek mythology, the most famous of the monstrous Gorgon sisters; her head was covered with snakes, and anyone who looked at her was turned to stone (Perseus looked at her reflection in his shield to decapitate her). Freud, in his short essay "Medusa's Head" (1922), associates Medusa with castration (= decapitation) and analyzes the ambiguity of the image: the snakes on her head are a denial of the castration she represents, while the notion of being turned to stone represents both castration and arousal. Cixous may also be referring to Lacan as Perseus, capable only of looking at things in a mirror (see above his famous essay "The Mirror Stage," 1949).
7. The standard English translation of *Aufhebung*, a term used by the German philosopher GEORG WILHELM FRIEDRICH HEGEL (1770–1831) to refer to the dialectical progression from a contradiction to a higher synthesis. Here, "woman" has been sublated into the general category "man," and "man," at first *opposed* to "woman," has risen up to become the generic name for all of humankind.
8. In redescribing Medusa as beautiful rather than horrible, Cixous is revising the notion of femininity itself. And "showing our sexts" represents a new articulation of sex and text (as does *écriture féminine*), as women who no longer repress their sexuality can talk about everything.
9. In Greek mythology, nymphs with a woman's head and a bird's body who lived on an island surrounded by rocks; the Sirens' enchanting song lured sailors to their death.
1. Charms with the power to turn away evil.
2. Jean Genet, *Pompes funèbres* [*Funeral Rites*] (Paris, 1948), p. 185 [Cixous's note].

He had come there led by his Jean. There are some men (all too few) who aren't afraid of femininity.

Almost everything is yet to be written by women about femininity: about their sexuality, that is, its infinite and mobile complexity, about their eroticization, sudden turn-ons of a certain minuscule-immense area of their bodies; not about destiny, but about the adventure of such and such a drive, about trips, crossings, trudges, abrupt and gradual awakenings, discoveries of a zone at one time timorous and soon to be forthright. A woman's body, with its thousand and one thresholds of ardor—once, by smashing yokes and censors, she lets it articulate the profusion of meanings that run through it in every direction—will make the old single-grooved mother tongue reverberate with more than one language.

We've been turned away from our bodies, shamefully taught to ignore them, to strike them with that stupid sexual modesty; we've been made victims of the old fool's game: each one will love the other sex. I'll give you your body and you'll give me mine. But who are the men who give women the body that women blindly yield to them? Why so few texts? Because so few women have as yet won back their body. Women must write through their bodies, they must invent the impregnable language that will wreck partitions, classes, and rhetorics, regulations and codes, they must submerge, cut through, get beyond the ultimate reserve-discourse, including the one that laughs at the very idea of pronouncing the word "silence," the one that, aiming for the impossible, stops short before the word "impossible" and writes it as "the end."

Such is the strength of women that, sweeping away syntax, breaking that famous thread (just a tiny little thread, they say) which acts for men as a surrogate umbilical cord, assuring them—otherwise they couldn't come—that the old lady is always right behind them,[3] watching them make phallus, women will go right up to the impossible.

When the "repressed" of their culture and their society returns, it's an explosive, *utterly* destructive, staggering return, with a force never yet unleashed and equal to the most forbidding of suppressions. For when the Phallic period comes to an end, women will have been either annihilated or borne up to the highest and most violent incandescence. Muffled throughout their history, they have lived in dreams, in bodies (though muted), in silences, in aphonic[4] revolts.

And with such force in their fragility; a fragility, a vulnerability, equal to their incomparable intensity. Fortunately, they haven't sublimated; they've saved their skin, their energy. They haven't worked at liquidating the impasse of lives without futures. They have furiously inhabited these sumptuous bodies: admirable hysterics who made Freud succumb to many voluptuous moments impossible to confess, bombarding his Mosaic statue[5] with their carnal and passionate body words, haunting him with their inaudible and

3. An allusion to two Greek myths: the story of Theseus, led out of the Minotaur's labyrinth by Ariadne's thread, and the story of the poet Orpheus, who won the release of his dead wife from the underworld on the condition (which he does not keep) that he not turn around and look at her as they ascended.

4. Speechless; an allusion to Freud's patient Dora, one of whose symptoms was aphonia (loss of voice); she is often considered an exemplary case of the misunderstood hysterical woman (Dora left Freud before the end of the analysis).

5. Michelangelo's statue of Moses (ca. 1515), which fascinated Freud, who here stands as the patriarchal Lawgiver himself.

thundering denunciations, dazzling, more than naked underneath the seven veils of modesty. Those who, with a single word of the body, have inscribed the vertiginous immensity of a history which is sprung like an arrow from the whole history of men and from biblico-capitalist society, are the women, the supplicants of yesterday, who come as forebears of the new women, after whom no intersubjective relation will ever be the same. You, Dora, you the indomitable, the poetic body, you are the true "mistress" of the Signifier.[6] Before long your efficacity will be seen at work when your speech is no longer suppressed, its point turned in against your breast, but written out over against the other.

In body.—More so than men who are coaxed toward social success, toward sublimation, women are body. More body, hence more writing. For a long time it has been in body that women have responded to persecution, to the familial-conjugal enterprise of domestication, to the repeated attempts at castrating them. Those who have turned their tongues 10,000 times seven times before not speaking are either dead from it or more familiar with their tongues and their mouths than anyone else. Now, I-woman am going to blow up the Law: an explosion henceforth possible and ineluctable; let it be done, right now, *in* language.

Let us not be trapped by an analysis still encumbered with the old automatisms. It's not to be feared that language conceals an invincible adversary, because it's the language of men and their grammar. We mustn't leave them a single place that's any more theirs alone than we are.

If woman has always functioned "within" the discourse of man, a signifier that has always referred back to the opposite signifier which annihilates its specific energy and diminishes or stifles its very different sounds, it is time for her to dislocate this "within," to explode it, turn it around, and seize it; to make it hers, containing it, taking it in her own mouth, biting that tongue with her very own teeth to invent for herself a language to get inside of. And you'll see with what ease she will spring forth from that "within"—the "within" where once she so drowsily crouched—to overflow at the lips she will cover the foam.

Nor is the point to appropriate their instruments, their concepts, their places, or to begrudge them their position of mastery. Just because there's a risk of identification doesn't mean that we'll succumb. Let's leave it to the worriers, to masculine anxiety and its obsession with how to dominate the way things work—knowing "how it works" in order to "make it work." For us the point is not to take possession in order to internalize or manipulate, but rather to dash through and to "fly."[7]

Flying is woman's gesture—flying in language and making it fly. We have all learned the art of flying and its numerous techniques; for centuries we've been able to possess anything only by flying; we've lived in flight, stealing away, finding, when desired, narrow passageways, hidden crossovers. It's no accident that *voler* has a double meaning, that it plays on each of them and thus throws off the agents of sense. It's no accident: women take after birds

6. The capitalization of the term, coined by the Swiss linguist FERDINAND DE SAUSSURE (1857–1913) to explain the functioning of signs (divided into *signifier*, the form a sign takes, and *signified*, the concept it represents), indicates that Cixous is here referring specifically to Lacan's designation of the phallus as privileged Signifier within the field of sexuality.

7. Also, "to steal." Both meanings of the verb *voler* are played on, as the text itself explains in the following paragraph [translator's note].

and robbers just as robbers take after women and birds. They (*illes*)[8] go by, fly the coop, take pleasure in jumbling the order of space, in disorienting it, in changing around the furniture, dislocating things and values, breaking them all up, emptying structures, and turning propriety upside down.

What woman hasn't flown/stolen? Who hasn't felt, dreamt, performed the gesture that jams sociality? Who hasn't crumbled, held up to ridicule, the bar of separation?[9] Who hasn't inscribed with her body the differential, punctured the system of couples and opposition? Who, by some act of transgression, hasn't overthrown successiveness, connection, the wall of circumfusion?

A feminine text cannot fail to be more than subversive. It is volcanic; as it is written it brings about an upheaval of the old property crust, carrier of masculine investments; there's no other way. There's no room for her if she's not a he. If she's a her-she, it's in order to smash everything, to shatter the framework of institutions, to blow up the law, to break up the "truth" with laughter.

For once she blazes *her* trail in the symbolic, she cannot fail to make of it the chaosmos[1] of the "personal"—in her pronouns, her nouns, and her clique of referents. And for good reason. There will have been the long history of gynocide.[2] This is known by the colonized peoples of yesterday, the workers, the nations, the species off whose backs the history of men has made its gold; those who have known the ignominy of persecution derive from it an obstinate future desire for grandeur; those who are locked up know better than their jailers the taste of free air. Thanks to their history, women today know (how to do and want) what men will be able to conceive of only much later. I say woman overturns the "personal," for if, by means of laws, lies, blackmail, and marriage, her right to herself has been extorted at the same time as her name, she has been able, through the very movement of mortal alienation, to see more closely the inanity of "propriety," the reductive stinginess of the masculine-conjugal subjective economy, which she doubly resists. On the one hand she has constituted herself necessarily as that "person" capable of losing a part of herself without losing her integrity. But secretly, silently, deep down inside, she grows and multiplies, for, on the other hand, she knows far more about living and about the relation between the economy of the drives and the management of the ego than any man. Unlike man, who holds so dearly to his title and his titles, his pouches of value, his cap, crown, and everything connected with his head, woman couldn't care less about the fear of decapitation (or castration), adventuring, without the masculine temerity, into anonymity, which she can merge with without annihilating herself: because she's a giver.

I shall have a great deal to say about the whole deceptive problematic of the gift.[3] Woman is obviously not that woman Nietzsche dreamed of who

8. *Illes* is a fusion of the masculine pronoun *ils*, which refers back to birds and robbers, with the feminine pronoun *elles*, which refers to women [translator's note].

9. An allusion to Lacan's revision of Saussure in "The Agency of the Letter in the Unconscious" (1957; see above): the "bar" between signifier and signified is identical with the structuring function of civilization.

1. A coinage blending *chaos* and *cosmos*.

2. The killing of women.

3. As explored by the French anthropologist Marcel Mauss in *Essay on the Gift* (1924). A key concept in Cixous's critique of ownership, property, and exchange, the gift functions as excess, as spending, and as abundance—which all become, for Cixous, women's attributes.

gives only in order to.[4] Who could ever think of the gift as a gift-that-takes? Who else but man, precisely the one who would like to take everything?

If there is a "propriety of woman," it is paradoxically her capacity to depropriate unselfishly: body without end, without appendage, without principal "parts." If she is a whole, it's a whole composed of parts that are wholes, not simple partial objects but a moving, limitlessly changing ensemble, a cosmos tirelessly traversed by Eros, an immense astral space not organized around any one sun that's any more of a star than the others.

This doesn't mean that she's an undifferentiated magma, but that she doesn't lord it over her body or her desire. Though masculine sexuality gravitates around the penis, engendering that centralized body (in political anatomy) under the dictatorship of its parts, woman does not bring about the same regionalization which serves the couple head/genitals and which is inscribed only within boundaries. Her libido is cosmic, just as her unconscious is worldwide. Her writing can only keep going, without ever inscribing or discerning contours, daring to make these vertiginous crossings of the other(s) ephemeral and passionate sojourns in him, her, them, whom she inhabits long enough to look at from the point closest to their unconscious from the moment they awaken, to love them at the point closest to their drives; and then further, impregnated through and through with these brief, identificatory embraces, she goes and passes into infinity. She alone dares and wishes to know from within, where she, the outcast, has never ceased to hear the resonance of fore-language. She lets the other language speak—the language of 1,000 tongues which knows neither enclosure nor death. To life she refuses nothing. Her language does not contain, it carries; it does not hold back, it makes possible. When id[5] is ambiguously uttered—the wonder of being several—she doesn't defend herself against these unknown women whom she's surprised at becoming, but derives pleasure from this gift of alterability. I am spacious, singing flesh, on which is grafted no one knows which I, more or less human, but alive because of transformation.

Write! and your self-seeking text will know itself better than flesh and blood, rising, insurrectionary dough kneading itself, with sonorous, perfumed ingredients, a lively combination of flying colors, leaves, and rivers plunging into the sea we feed. "Ah, there's her sea," he will say as he holds out to me a basin full of water from the little phallic mother[6] from whom he's inseparable. But look, our seas are what we make of them, full of fish or not, opaque or transparent, red or black, high or smooth, narrow or bankless; and we are ourselves sea, sand, coral, seaweed, beaches, tides, swimmers, children, waves. . . . More or less wavily sea, earth, sky—what matter would rebuff us? We know how to speak them all.

Heterogeneous, yes. For her joyous benefit she is erogenous; she is the

4. Reread Derrida's text, "Le Style de la femme," in *Nietzsche aujourd'hui* (Paris: Union Générale d'Editions, Coll. 10/18, [1973]), where the philosopher can be seen operating an *Aufhebung* of all philosophy in its systematic reducing of woman to the place of seduction: she appears as the one who is taken for; the bait in person, all veils unfurled, the one who doesn't give but who gives only in order to (take) [Cixous's note]. Translated in Jacques Derrida, *Spurs: Nietzsche's Styles* (1978). FRIEDRICH NIETZSCHE (1844–1900), German philosopher.

5. The first of three components of the infant's psyche (the others being the ego and superego), as theorized by Freud; it is governed by the most primitive unconscious urges for gratification, ruled by no laws of logic, and unconstrained by external reality.

6. The child's fantasy of what the mother must have been like before she was castrated, theorized by both Freud and Lacan.

erotogeneity of the heterogeneous: airborne swimmer, in flight, she does not cling to herself; she is dispersible, prodigious, stunning, desirous and capable of others, of the other woman that she will be, of the other woman she isn't, of him of you.

Woman be unafraid of any other place, of any same, or any other. My eyes, my tongue, my ears, my nose, my skin, my mouth, my body-for-(the)-other—not that I long for it in order to fill up a hole, to provide against some defect of mine, or because, as fate would have it, I'm spurred on by feminine "jealousy"; not because I've been dragged into the whole chain of substitutions that brings that which is substituted back to its ultimate object. That sort of thing you would expect to come straight out of "Tom Thumb," out of the *Penisneid*[7] whispered to us by old grandmother ogresses, servants to their father-sons. If they believe, in order to muster up some self-importance, if they really need to believe that we're dying of desire, that we are this hole fringed with desire for their penis—that's their immemorial business. Undeniably (we verify it at our own expense—but also to our amusement), it's their business to let us know they're getting a hard-on, so that we'll assure them (we the maternal mistresses of their little pocket signifier) that they still can, that it's still there—that men structure themselves only by being fitted with a feather.[8] In the child it's not the penis that the woman desires, it's not that famous bit of skin around which every man gravitates. Pregnancy cannot be traced back, except within the historical limits of the ancients, to some form of fate, to those mechanical substitutions brought about by the unconscious of some eternal "jealous woman"; not to penis envies; and not to narcissism or to some sort of homosexuality linked to the ever-present mother! Begetting a child doesn't mean that the woman or the man must fall ineluctably into patterns or must recharge the circuit of reproduction. If there's a risk there's not an inevitable trap: may women be spared the pressure, under the guise of consciousness-raising, of a supplement of interdictions. Either you want a kid or you don't—*that's your business.*[9] Let nobody threaten you; in satisfying your desire, let not the fear of becoming the accomplice to a sociality succeed the old-time fear of being "taken." And man, are you still going to bank on everyone's blindness and passivity, afraid lest the child make a father and, consequently, that in having a kid the woman land herself more than one bad deal by engendering all at once child—mother—father—family? No; it's up to you to break the old circuits. It will be up to man and woman to render obsolete the former relationship and all its consequences, to consider the launching of a brand-new subject, alive, with defamilialization. Let us demater-paternalize rather than deny woman, in an effort to avoid the co-optation of procreation, a thrilling era of the body. Let us defetishize. Let's get away from the dialectic which has it that the only good father is a dead one, or that the child is the death of his parents. The child is the other, but the other without violence, bypassing loss, struggle. We're fed up with the reuniting of bonds forever to be severed,

7. Penis envy (German); Freud's name for the lifelong wish to have a penis, which he attributed to women. "Tom Thumb": the old nursery tale featuring the diminutive hero of the same name.

8. In the French *s'empenner*, "to sprout feathers": a reference to PLATO's description of the soul's return to its original perfection by regrowing its lost wings; see *Phaedrus* (ca.370 B.C.E.), 246–252a.

9. Abortion was legalized in France in 1974, a year before this essay was published.

with the litany of castration that's handed down and genealogized. We won't advance backward anymore; we're not going to repress something so simple as the desire for life. Oral drive, anal drive, vocal drive—all these drives are our strengths, and among them is the gestation drive—just like the desire to write: a desire to live self from within, a desire for the swollen belly, for language, for blood. We are not going to refuse, if it should happen to strike our fancy, the unsurpassed pleasures of pregnancy which have actually been always exaggerated or conjured away—or cursed—in the classic texts. For if there's one thing that's been repressed here's just the place to find it: in the taboo of the pregnant woman. This says a lot about the power she seems invested with at the time, because it has always been suspected, that, when pregnant, the woman not only doubles her market value, but—what's more important—takes on intrinsic value as a woman in her own eyes and, undeniably, acquires body and sex.

There are thousands of ways of living one's pregnancy; to have or not to have with that still invisible other a relationship of another intensity. And if you don't have that particular yearning, it doesn't mean that you're in any way lacking. Each body distributes in its own special way, without model or norm, the nonfinite and changing totality of its desires. Decide for yourself on your position in the arena of contradictions, where pleasure and reality embrace. Bring the other to life. Women know how to live detachment; giving birth is neither losing nor increasing. It's adding to life an other. Am I dreaming? Am I mis-recognizing? You, the defenders of "theory," the sacrosanct yes-men of Concept, enthroners of the phallus (but not of the penis):

Once more you'll say that all this smacks of "idealism," or what's worse, you'll splutter that I'm a "mystic."

And what about the libido? Haven't I read the "Signification of the Phallus"?[1] And what about separation, what about that bit of self for which, to be born, you undergo an ablation—an ablation, so they say, to be forever commemorated by your desire?

Besides, isn't it evident that the penis gets around in my texts, that I give it a place and appeal? Of course I do. I want all. I want all of me with all of him. Why should I deprive myself of a part of us? I want all of us. Woman of course has a desire for a "loving desire" and not a jealous one. But not because she is gelded; not because she's deprived and needs to be filled out, like some wounded person who wants to console herself or seek vengeance: I don't want a penis to decorate my body with. But I do desire the other for the other,[2] whole and entire, male or female; because living means wanting everything that is, everything that lives, and wanting it alive. Castration? Let others toy with it. What's a desire originating from a lack? A pretty meager desire.

The woman who still allows herself to be threatened by the big dick, who's still impressed by the commotion of the phallic stance, who still leads a loyal master to the beat of the drum: that's the woman of yesterday. They still exist, easy and numerous victims of the oldest of farces: either they're cast in the original silent version in which, as titanesses lying under the mountains they make with their quivering, they never see erected that theoretic

1. A 1958 essay by Jacques Lacan (see above).
2. The non-me, the non-self. In *The Second Sex* (1949), SIMONE DE BEAUVOIR was the first to analyze how society positions woman as man's other.

monument to the golden phallus looming, in the old manner, over their bodies. Or, coming today out of their *infans*[3] period and into the second, "enlightened" version of their virtuous debasement, they see themselves suddenly assaulted by the builders of the analytic empire and, as soon as they've begun to formulate the new desire, naked, nameless, so happy at making an appearance, they're taken in their bath by the new old men, and then, whoops! Luring them with flashy signifiers, the demon of interpretation—oblique, decked out in modernity—sells them the same old handcuffs, baubles, and chains. Which castration do you prefer? Whose degrading do you like better, the father's or the mother's? Oh, what pwetty eyes, you pwetty little girl. Here, buy my glasses and you'll see the Truth-Me-Myself[4] tell you everything you should know. Put them on your nose and take a fetishist's look (you are me, the other analyst—that's what I'm telling you) at your body and the body of the other. You see? No? Wait, you'll have everything explained to you, and you'll know at last which sort of neurosis you're related to. Hold still, we're going to do your portrait, so that you can begin looking like it right away.

Yes, the naives to the first and second degree are still legion. If the New Women, arriving now, dare to create outside the theoretical, they're called in by the cops of the signifier, fingerprinted, remonstrated, and brought into the line of order that they are supposed to know; assigned by force of trickery to a precise place in the chain that's always formed for the benefit of a privileged signifier. We are pieced back to the string which leads back, if not to the Name-of-the-Father, then, for a new twist, to the place of the phallic-mother.[5]

Beware, my friend, of the signifier that would take you back to the authority of a signified! Beware of diagnoses that would reduce your generative powers. "Common" nouns are also proper nouns that disparage your singularity by classifying it into species. Break out of the circles; don't remain within the psychoanalytic closure. Take a look around, then cut through!

And if we are legion, it's because the war of liberation has only made as yet a tiny breakthrough. But women are thronging to it. I've seen them, those who will be neither dupe nor domestic, those who will not fear the risk of being a woman; will not fear any risk, any desire, any space still unexplored in themselves, among themselves and others or anywhere else. They do not fetishize, they do not deny, they do not hate. They observe, they approach, they try to see the other woman, the child, the lover—not to strengthen their own narcissism or verify the solidity or weakness of the master, but to make love better, to invent.

Other love.—In the beginning are our differences. The new love dares for the other, wants the other, makes dizzying, precipitous flights between knowledge and invention. The woman arriving over and over again does not stand still; she's everywhere, she exchanges, she is the desire-that-gives. (Not enclosed in the paradox of the gift that takes nor under the illusion of unitary

3. Incapable of speech (Latin). Lacan uses the word to describe the child at the mirror stage.
4. A reference to Lacan, who had written in his essay "The Freudian Thing" (1955), "Moi, la vérité, je parle" (I, the Truth, speak). "My glasses" alludes to the sinister eyeglass salesman in Hoffmann's "Sandman" (1816) whom Freud analyzes in "The 'Uncanny'."
5. In his seminars of the 1970s, Lacan had attempted to demonstrate the relations among the Imaginary, the Symbolic, and the Real by means of knots made of string. Name-of-the-Father: the Lacanian term for the function of the father in the Symbolic.

fusion. We're past that.) She comes in, comes-in-between herself me and you, between the other me where one is always infinitely more than one and more than me, without the fear of ever reaching a limit; she thrills in our becoming. And we'll keep on becoming! She cuts through defensive loves, motherages, and devourations: beyond selfish narcissism, in the moving, open, transitional space, she runs her risks. Beyond the struggle-to-the-death that's been removed to the bed, beyond the love-battle that claims to represent exchange, she scorns at an Eros dynamic that would be fed by hatred. Hatred: a heritage, again, a remainder, a duping subservience to the phallus. To love, to watch-think-seek the other in the other, to despecularize, to unhoard. Does this seem difficult? It's not impossible, and this is what nourishes life—a love that has no commerce with the apprehensive desire that provides against the lack and stultifies the strange; a love that rejoices in the exchange that multiplies. Wherever history still unfolds as the history of death, she does not tread. Opposition, hierarchizing exchange, the struggle for mastery which can end only in at least one death (one master—one slave, or two nonmasters ≠ two dead)[6]—all that comes from a period in time governed by phallocentric values. The fact that this period extends into the present doesn't prevent woman from starting the history of life somewhere else. Elsewhere, she gives. She doesn't "know" what she's giving, she doesn't measure it; she gives, though, neither a counterfeit impression nor something she hasn't got. She gives more, with no assurance that she'll get back even some unexpected profit from what she puts out. She gives that there may be life, thought, transformation. This is an "economy" that can no longer be put in economic terms. Wherever she loves, all the old concepts of management are left behind. At the end of a more or less conscious computation, she finds not her sum but her differences. I am for you what you want me to be at the moment you look at me in a way you've never seen me before: at every instant. When I write, it's everything that we don't know we can be that is written out of me, without exclusions, without stipulation, and everything we will be calls us to the unflagging, intoxicating, unappeasable search for love. In one another we will never be lacking.

1975, 1976

6. In the Master-Slave dialectic described by Hegel in *Phenomenology of Spirit* (1807; see above), the master is the one who is willing to fight to the death for freedom; the slave chooses life.

GERALD GRAFF
b. 1937

In "Taking Cover in Coverage" (1986), Gerald Graff views the university itself through the lens of critical theory, asking hard questions about the institutional structures within English departments. Why divide literature into separate fields? How do subspecialties affect the way professors work and students learn in literature departments? Worried, as he declares in *Literature against Itself* (1979), that contemporary approaches to literature within English departments have undermined "the power of language to connect us with the world," Graff recommends a novel and subsequently influential method for bringing coherence to what he sees as an increasingly disjointed curriculum, a method he calls "teaching the conflicts."

Born in Chicago, Graff received his B.A. from the University of Chicago in 1959. He did graduate work at Stanford University, where he studied with the New Critic Ivor Winters and the New York Intellectual IRVING HOWE, receiving his Ph.D. in 1963. He taught at the University of New Mexico from 1963 to 1966, then returned to Illinois to teach at Northwestern University (1966–91) and at the University of Chicago (1991–98), where he was appointed to the Pullman professorship formerly held by the narrative and rhetorical theorist Wayne Booth. In 1999 he took a deanship at the University of Illinois–Chicago to develop undergraduate curricula and coordinate teacher education programs.

In his writing, Graff is an iconoclast. While he has been a prominent participant in debates on contemporary theory, he does not readily fit into any definable camp. He is also an unapologetic polemicist, persistently arguing against literary criticism's disconnection from society. In his early work, he attacked the New Critical axiom that "a poem, as a poem, does not say anything about the world." In his provocative *Literature against Itself: Literary Ideas in Modern Society*, Graff turned his sights on a range of contemporary theories and claimed that their excessive focus on language fostered the ineffectuality of literary intellectuals. Overall, Graff shows a consistent concern with the social dimensions of intellectual work, but he does so in a pluralistic way, advocating no particular approach and avoiding orthodoxy.

"Taking Cover in Coverage" looks at the ways in which the university institutionally and historically has shaped intellectual work. Graff begins with a defense of theory. His argument is tacitly directed at antitheorists, ranging from traditionalists who believe, in the phrase of the New Critic René Wellek, that contemporary theory is "destroying literary studies" to neopragmatists, such as STEVEN KNAPP AND WALTER BENN MICHAELS, who claim that theory is inconsequential. Despite Graff's earlier rough handling of theory, he here sees it as enriching our thought and thus advocates putting it at the center of the curriculum. Although Graff had been an opponent of deconstruction, his defense of theory parallels that in PAUL DE MAN's "Resistance to Theory" (1982), which similarly responds to antitheorists and argues for the importance of theory. However, Graff takes to task much contemporary theory for failing to reflect on its own institutional location, willing to "apply theory within the existing structure but . . . fail[ing] to make a theoretical examination of the structure itself."

Moving to his main topic, Graff gives thumbnail sketches of the history of U.S. English departments (born in the late nineteenth and early twentieth centuries) and the "field coverage" model on which they rely. Specialized fields both engender disconnections and insularities that thwart intellectual community and encourage efficiency, innovation and autonomy—the benefits that led to the model's success. While institutional structures in English departments have given faculty a relative degree of freedom to pursue new topics (including contemporary theory), they have also essentially quarantined individual scholars in their particular fields; as a result, there is no common ground for discussion, conflicts are suppressed, the curriculum is incoherent, and students lose out. Graff's recommendation to faculty, which has since become something of a slogan, is to "teach the conflicts" and make such divisions the organizing basis of curriculum.

Throughout his argument, Graff shows a concern for how the divisions wrought by field coverage have harmed not just scholars and professors but students as well. Though pedagogy has been discussed by many in other fields, Graff's consistent attention to teaching is unusual among contemporary theorists. His writing style also sets "Taking Cover in Coverage" apart. Graff argues for theory in an accessible, plain, and colloquial language (using sentences like "literature departments should stop kidding themselves") rarely seen in contemporary theory. In the 1990s a number of other critics, notably Michael Bérubé in his book *Public Access: Literary Theory and Amer-*

ican Cultural Politics (1994), called for an accessible criticism directed to a public rather than a narrowly academic audience.

Graff fleshed out his argument about English departments and field coverage in an important book, *Professing Literature: An Institutional History* (1987), which traces the discipline's history from the nineteenth century to the 1980s. He sees contemporary conflicts over theory as part of a historical process often alternating between traditionalism and new approaches. In the 1990s Graff focused increasingly on pedagogy. He has responded to public debates over the canon, theory, and "political correctness" by extolling their potential as a resource for teaching. Continuing his argument from "Taking Cover in Coverage," particularly in his popular *Beyond the Culture Wars: How Teaching the Conflicts Can Revitalize Higher Education* (1992), Graff advocates foregrounding critical controversies in the classroom rather than hiding them from students. Citing his own experience as a student, he admits that class discussions of literature bored him until he discovered that literature was something to argue over.

Although Graff's conflictual model has been widely accepted as a productive teaching method and as a useful account of theoretical change, several critics have noted its limitations. Some criticize Graff's nostalgia for a vibrant literary culture outside the university, even as he supplies prescriptions that apply only to the academy. Others note the reductiveness of seeing all change in terms of a repeated conflict between tradition and new movements. From a feminist perspective, Graff's conflictual model is precisely what JANE TOMPKINS criticizes in "Me and My Shadow" (1987; see below). Though she joins Graff's attack on the isolation fostered by English departments, Tompkins calls for cooperation rather than confrontation and would see Graff's embrace of conflict as reflecting a masculinist bias—perhaps making the discipline akin to a contact sport. From a postcolonial perspective, critics like NGUGI WĂ THIONG'O argue that "English" departments propagate imperialism, and therefore call for their abolition. Graff mentions that the division of departments by language is arbitrary, but he does not continue this analysis to critique the nationalistic origins and purposes of English departments. Nevertheless, Graff's history of English departments is a pathbreaking investigation showing how our institutions shape literary thought and proposing how they might be changed.

BIBLIOGRAPHY

Stemming from his doctoral dissertation (for which Irving Howe was an adviser), Graff's first book, *Poetic Statement and Critical Dogma* (1970), attacks the lack of social concern evinced by the New Criticism and other approaches. *Literature against Itself: Literary Ideas in Modern Society* (1979) extends his polemic to contemporary theory. Through the 1980s Graff turned his attention more concertedly to the university, in 1985 co-editing (with Reginald Gibbons) a collection, *Criticism in the University*, that deals with the twentieth-century shift from literary journalism to an academic criticism largely divorced from the world. Drawing on nineteenth- and twentieth-century documentary sources, Graff's *Professing Literature: An Institutional History* (1987) is regarded as the standard history of the discipline. In a related work, Graff compiled (with Michael Warner) a collection of historical documents, *The Origins of Literary Studies in America: A Documentary History* (1988). *Beyond the Culture Wars: How Teaching the Conflicts Can Revitalize Higher Education* (1992) presents his program for "teaching the conflicts." Graff has also contributed a substantial history of contemporary American criticism, "Criticism since 1940" (coauthored with Evan Carton), to *The Cambridge History of American Literature*, vol. 8, *Poetry and Criticism, 1940–1995* (ed. Sacvan Bercovitch, 1996); it characteristically foregrounds the cycle of conflicts in and the "academicization" of criticism. He also has edited two casebooks deploying his conflictual model, *Adventures of Huckleberry Finn: A Case Study in Critical Controversy* (co-edited with James Phelan, 1995) and *The Tempest: A Case Study in Contemporary Controversy* (1999).

Graff's views of the English department have been widely discussed. A special issue of the journal *Critical Exchange* (23 [1987]) devotes itself to them and includes an interview with Graff; in particular, Nick Visser's "Criticism and Liberal Reason" criticizes Graff's nostalgia for preacademic literary culture. A leading critic of professionalism, Bruce Robbins, in *Minnesota Review*, n.s., 30–31 (1988), judges Graff's institutional account to be "sociologically thin" in attending only to English departments. The collection *Teaching the Conflicts: Gerald Graff, Curricular Reform, and the Culture Wars*, edited by William E. Cain (1994), gathers eleven useful essays assessing Graff's work, especially in relation to curriculum. Cain's introduction provides an excellent survey, and the volume contains a response and three short essays by Graff (including "Taking Cover in Coverage"). Brook Thomas's "Teaching the Conflicts in the Humanities Core Course at University of California, Irvine," *College Literature* 21 (1994), reports on Graff's method in practice. In *University in Ruins* (1996), Bill Readings assimilates Graff's conflictual model in recommending that the university be a community of "dissensus," but he argues that Graff's model itself becomes "a unified object of professional discourse." Don Bialostosky, in "Is Gerald Graff Machiavellian?" *Style* 33 (1999), provocatively compares Graff's notion of the productive uses of conflict with Machiavelli's prescriptions for power. That Graff's conflictual model has inspired a textbook series, Case Studies in Critical Controversy, published by Belford Books, further testifies to his influence.

Taking Cover in Coverage

In addressing the topic "The Value of Theory in English Studies,"[1] I want to say at the outset that the antagonism usually presumed to exist between literary theory and humanistic tradition has been exaggerated. It is perfectly possible to defend the infusion of theory into the curriculum on traditional grounds, namely, that students need theoretical frameworks in order to conceptualize, and talk about, literature. Until recently, in fact, it was traditionalists like Irving Babbitt and Norman Foerster[2] who called for more "theory," in opposition to the disconnected empircisim of positivist literary history and formalist explication, where the faith seemed to be that "the facts, once in, would of themselves mean something."[3] Most scholars "have left virtually uninspected the theory upon which their practice rests" or have proceeded "as if that theory were an absolute good for all time."[4] While a great deal of current theory does radically attack the premises and values of traditional literary humanism, that attack revives the kinds of questions about literature and its cultural functions that used to concern traditional humanistic critics.

The real enemy of tradition has been the established form of literary study, which has neglected traditional theoretical questions about the ends and social functions of literature and criticism. There is something strange about the belief that we are being traditional when we isolate literary works from their contexts and explicate them in a vacuum or with a modicum of background information. Matthew Arnold[5] would have recognized little tradi-

1. The essay was originally presented at a 1986 seminar run by the Association of Departments of English on this topic.
2. Literary critics and Harvard University professors who espoused the humanistic value of studying literature: Foerster (1887–1972) was a protégé of Babbitt's (1865–1933).
3. Norman Foerster, "The Study of Letters," in *Literary Scholarship: Its Aims and Methods*, by Norman Foerster et al. (Chapel Hill: University of North Carolina Press, 1941), 11–12 [Graff's note].
4. Norman Foerster et al., introduction, in ibid., v [Graff's note].
5. Leading Victorian poet and critic (1822–1888; see above), whose engagement with contemporary society is clear in such works as *Culture and Anarchy* (1869).

tional or humanistic in these established forms of pedagogy. Obviously I am not saying that recent literary theory is nothing more than the application of Arnoldian culture by other means. What I am saying is that recent theory has reawakened some of the large questions that Arnold raised, while rejecting the Arnoldian answers as no longer sufficient.

In fact, it was the breakdown of agreement on the Arnoldian answers that inspired the current popularity of theory and ensures, I think, that this interest will not be a passing fad. By one definition that seems to me valid, "literary theory" is simply the kind of discourse that is generated when presuppositions that were once tacitly shared about literature, criticism, and culture become open to question. Theory is what breaks out when agreement about such terms as *text, reading, history, interpretation, tradition*, and *literature* can no longer be taken for granted, so that their meanings have to be formulated and debated. Admittedly, the term *theory* is used here in a very broad sense, denoting an examination of legitimating presuppositions, beliefs, and ideologies. By this definition, even antitheorists like Arnold and F. R. Leavis[6] qualify as theorists, having theorized about the premises of literature and culture and the place of literature and culture in modern societies. And in this sense all teachers of literature operate on theories, whether they choose to examine these theories or not.

Clearly, we need to reserve another sense of *theory* to denote the technical, abstruse, and systematic speculation typical of recent Continental thought. But here is another misconception—that theory is necessarily obscure, technical and abstruse, and therefore too advanced or esoteric for the average college or high school student of literature. This belief fails to recognize that all teaching involves popularization and that even the most difficult current theories are not intrinsically more resistant to popularization than the New Criticism, which had its own abstruse conceptual origins in Kant, Coleridge, and Croce.[7]

It is the average-to-poor student who suffers most from the established curriculum's poverty of theory, for such a student lacks command of the conceptual contexts that make it possible to integrate perceptions and generalize from them. All the close concentration in the world on the particularities of literary texts will not help a student make sense of these particularities without the categories that give them meaning.

Current antitheorists have things exactly backward when they oppose theory to tradition and to close literary analysis and demand that we minister to the ills of literary studies by desisting from theoretical chatter and getting back to teaching literature itself. It was the isolation of "literature itself" in a conceptual vacuum that stranded students without a context for talking about literature and that still forces many of them to resort to *Cliffs Notes* and other such cribs. It is easy to disdain these cribs, but marketing pressures have actually forced their producers to think through the problems facing the average literature student more realistically than have many department

6. Influential English literary critic (1895–1978; see above), who extolled "the great tradition.".

7. Three important and sometimes abstruse writers on aesthetics: IMMANUEL KANT (1724–1804), a German philosopher; SAMUEL TAYLOR COLERIDGE (1772–1834), a British Romantic poet and theorist; and Benedetto Croce (1866–1952), an Italian philosopher and literary critic. The New Criticism: an approach (championed by CLEANTH BROOKS, WILLIAM K. WIMSATT JR., and others) that emphasizes close reading of the text considered as an autonomous whole; it has greatly influenced teaching from the mid–20th century onward.

curricular planners. *Cliffs Notes* supply students with the generalized things to say about literary works that the literature program takes for granted they will somehow get on their own.

The irony of the current cry of "back to literature itself" is that it was the exclusive concentration on literature itself that helped create a situation in which the *Cliffs Notes* on given works of literature are more readily available in campus bookstores than are the works themselves. Perhaps I am naive to suggest that a more theoretically contextualized curriculum would cause such cribs to wither away. I can certainly imagine a *Cliffs Notes* on deconstruction, supplementing the ones on Keats and Dickens.[8] But for the moment I think we should view this eventuality as a possibility to be recognized and avoided rather than as an inevitability.

These opening reflections will probably persuade only those who agree with them. My purpose here, however, is not to make a case for theory in the literature program but to point up some difficulties that arise once we have decided that such a goal is desirable. In addressing the pedagogical uses of recent literary theory, we tend to treat the issue as if it were primarily a matter of figuring out how to integrate this theory into individual classrooms. We form conference "workshops," which concentrate on technical questions like how to use reader-response criticism to teach *Hamlet*, or poststructuralist theory to teach the romantic lyric, or feminist critiques of the established canon to restructure the nineteenth-century-novel course. Such reforms can be useful and necessary, but if we do not go beyond them we will limit theory to its instrumental uses, making it into a means of sprucing up ritualized procedures of explication. We will apply theory within the existing structure but will fail to make a theoretical examination of the structure itself.

I want to suggest that one of the first things we need to do with literary theory is to train it on the literature department itself, particularly on the way that the department and other departments and the university are organized. Insofar as a literature department represents a certain organization of literature, it is itself a kind of theory, though it has been largely an incoherent theory, and this incoherence in fact has reinforced the impression that the department has no theory.

In deciding to call ourselves departments of English, French, and German—rather than of literature, cultural studies, or something else—and in subdividing these national units into periods and genres, we have already made significant theoretical choices. But we do not see these choices as choices, much less as theoretical ones, because the categories that mark them—English, eighteenth century, poetry, novel—operate as administrative conveniences and eventually as facts of nature that we can take for granted. We need to recognize that the way we organize and departmentalize literature is not only a crucial theoretical choice but one that largely determines our professional activity and the way students and the laity see it or fail to see it.

To make this statement is not to agree with those who think that the departmentalization of literature itself was a kind of original sin and who look back nostalgically to the days before the creative imagination was

8. Charles Dickens (1812–1870), Victorian novelist. John Keats (1795–1821), English Romantic poet.

bureaucratized. Anyone seriously committed to the idea of democratic mass education has to acknowledge the obvious necessity for some form of bureaucratic departmental organization and the specialized division of labor that that entails. But the form that organization takes is neither self-evident nor inevitable, and it will have a lot to do with considerations of theory.

I use the term field coverage as a convenient description of the model of organization that has governed literature departments since the dawn of the modern university, in the last two decades of the nineteenth century. According to the field-coverage model, a department considers itself adequately staffed when it has acquired the personnel to "cover" an adequate number of designated fields of literature, and it assumes that the core of the curriculum will consist of the student's coverage of some portion of those fields. The field-coverage model arose as an adaptation to the modern university's ideal of research specialization, for dividing the territory of literature into fields supervised by specialists imitated the organizational form that had made the sciences efficient in producing advanced research. But the field-coverage principle had a humanistic justification as well, the argument that a student who covered the fields represented by the average department would get a reasonably balanced exposure to the literary-humanistic tradition.

It was the operational advantages, however, that made the field-coverage model irresistible, especially in a newly expanding university where short-term expediency rarely afforded leisure for discussion of first principles and where first principles in any case were becoming increasingly open to dispute. One of the most conspicuous operational advantages was the way field coverage made the department virtually self-regulating. By assigning instructors the roles predetermined by their literary fields, the model created a system in which the job of instruction could proceed as if on automatic pilot, with no need for instructors to confer with their peers or superiors. Assuming that individual instructors had been competently trained—and by about 1900 or so the American system of graduate study had matured sufficiently to see to that—they could be left on their own to carry out their teaching and research jobs without elaborate supervision and management.

A second advantage of the field-coverage model was that it made the department immensely flexible to innovation. By making individuals functionally independent of one another in carrying out their tasks, the model enabled the department to assimilate new subjects, ideas, and methodologies without risking the conflicts that would otherwise have had to be debated and worked through. It thus allowed the modern university to overcome the chronic stagnation that had beset the old nineteenth-century college, where new ideas that challenged the established Christian orthodoxy were usually excluded or suppressed. The coverage model solved the problem of how to make the university open to innovation and diverse viewpoints without incurring paralyzing conflicts.

Unfortunately, these advantages came at a severe cost that we have been paying ever since. The same arrangements that allowed instructors to do their jobs efficiently and independently also relieved them of the need to discuss and reflect on the values and implications of their practices. This form of organization left literature departments without any need to discuss matters of fundamental direction either with their own members or with members of other departments, and it is a rule of bureaucratic organizations that whatever these organizations are not structurally required to do they will tend not to do. Moral exhortation unaccompanied by structural change will be largely wasted. The department was open to innovation as the college had not been before, but under circumstances that were almost as effective in muffling the confrontations provoked by innovation as the old system of repressive control had been. Previously there had been little open debate over first principles because dissenters had been excluded. Now dissenters were invited in, but the departmental structure kept them too isolated from their colleagues for open debate to take place.

Vigorous controversy did arise, but usually only behind the scenes of education, in specialized journals, department meetings, or private gossip—all places where students derived little benefit from it, usually knew nothing of its existence, and certainly did not participate in it. Instructors were freer than they had been from administrative tyranny, but at the sacrifice of certain possibilities of intellectual community.

To put it another way, the field-coverage model solved the problem of theory. Departmental organization took the place of theory, for the presence of an ordered array of fields, fully staffed, made it unnecessary for anyone to have a theory about what the department should do to permit the work of teaching and research to go on. The theoretical choices had already been taken care of in the grid of periods, genres, and other catalog rubrics, which embodied a clear and seemingly uncontroversial conceptualization of what the department was about. With literature courses ranged in periods and genres, instructors did not need to ask what "period" or "genre" meant or what justified the established demarcations. The connections and contrasts between periods and genres, so important for understanding these categories, fell between the cracks, as did other large issues in the university, such as the relation between the sciences and the humanities, which was the responsibility of neither the sciences nor the humanities.

Latent conflicts of method and ideology that had divided the faculty from the outset and the cultural conflicts that these often exemplified did not have to be confronted and taught. Fundamental disagreements over the study of literature were embodied, for example, in the conflict between the research "scholar," who adhered to a positivistic methodology, and the generalist man or woman of letters, who scorned this methodology, and, later, in the conflict between both these types and the hyperanalytical New Critic. But while the department enacted these conflicts, it did not explicitly foreground and engage them. As long as scholars, generalists, and critics covered their turfs within self-enclosed classrooms, the average student did not need to be aware of the clashes of principle, much less use them as a larger context for literary study.

This explanation accounts for the otherwise inexplicable persistence of the fiction of shared humanistic values and purposes during a period when conflicts in method and ideology were becoming progressively more frequent and antagonistic. Since the official premise that humanistic values governed the department did not have to be theorized or subjected to periodical review and discussion, there was no particular reason to acknowledge that the premise was wearing increasingly thin. Not only did the structure provide no necessary occasion for questioning the content of that humanism which, according to the catalog, theoretically held the diverse and conflicting viewpoints of departments together, but the illusion could be maintained that nobody even had a theory.

And of course it was true that the department did not have *a* theory, for it harbored many theories without any clear way to integrate them. Here we arrive at the central problem: How does a department institutionalize theory when there is no agreement on what the theory is to be? The question becomes unanswerable, however, only if it is assumed that a department must achieve theoretical *consensus* before it can achieve theoretical coherence.

The perennial assumption seems to have been that professional and cultural conflicts have to be *resolved* before they can be presented to the students: students, apparently, must be exposed only to the results of the conflicts dividing their teachers, not to the process of conflict itself, which presumably would confuse or demoralize them. Surely one reason why we tend, as I noted earlier, to reduce pedagogical questions to questions about workshop techniques for individual courses is that we doubt the possibility of agreement on larger collective goals. Our doubts are well founded in experience, but why need we assume that we have to agree in order to integrate our activities? Must we have consensus to have coherence?

The unfortunate thing is not that our conflicts of method and ideology have often proved unresolvable but that we have been able to exploit so little of the potential educational value of our unresolved conflicts. Part of the reason stems from the literary mind's temperamental resistance to airing differences; the old-fashioned version of this attitude held that open debate is unseemly, while the more up-to-date version holds that there are no privileged metalanguages, or no fact-of-the-matter outside interpretations, or no "decidable" answers to questions, so that there is nothing to argue about anyway. But even if these sources of resistance to debate were to disappear, there would remain a problem of structure. Our structure prevents exemplary differences of method, ideology, and value from emerging into view even when we want them to.

The literature curriculum mirrors and reproduces the evasion of conflict characteristic of the departmental structure. Hypothetically, the curriculum expresses a unified humanistic tradition, yet anyone who looks at it can see that in every era down to the present it has never expressed a unity of humanistic values but always a set of political trade-offs and compromises among competing professional factions. We need not enter into the now disputed question of whether the curriculum can or should be determined by any more lofty principle than political trade-offs, for again this is precisely the type of theoretical and cultural question that does not have to be resolved in order to play an effective part in education. If the curriculum is going to continue to express political trade-offs, as it seems likely to do unless one faction in the current disciplinary conflict can wholly liquidate its opposition, then why not bring students in on whatever may be instructive in the conflict of political principles involved?

Instead of confronting such conflicts and building them into the curriculum, however, the department (and the university at large) has always responded to pressures by adding new subjects and keeping them safely sealed off from one another. This practice can be justified educationally only on the increasingly hollow pretense that exposure to an aggregate of teachers, periods, genres, methods, and points of view figures to come together in the student's mind as a coherent humanistic experience. The tacit faith is that students will make sense of the aggregate even if their instructors cannot. The surprising thing is that some students manage to do just that, but most do not. Recognition of this failure stimulates further curricular innovation, which in turn, however, is assimilated to the cycle of accretion and marginalization. So we beat on, boats against the current,[9] etc., etc.

Over the hundred-year span of our institutional history we have had a succession of methodological models, each with a corresponding pedagogy, from linguistic philology to positivist literary history to New Critical explication, all of which now remain as geological strata overlaid by the new theories and methodologies. Each of these revisions has marked a paradigm shift in which the conception of what counts as "literature," "scholarship," and "criticism" altered radically. Yet, as I attempt to show in a forthcoming institutional history of academic literary studies in the United States,[1] the one constant through all this change has been the field-coverage model. The contents have been radically reshuffled, but the envelope has remained the same, and with it the method of assimilating innovation. Arguably the changes represent considerable progress in critical sophistication and cultural range, but if I am correct the benefits for the average student have been less than they might have been.

Nor is it just the students who have paid a price under the field-coverage system, it is the faculty as well. The principles of selection for amassing a literature faculty have systematically screened out intellectual commonality and programmed professional loneliness. A self-destructive principle is built into the mighty effort departments make to achieve a balanced spread of interests. If the interests of candidate X overlap those of faculty member Y, their shared ground is an argument for not hiring X—"We already have Y who does that." The calculus of needs determining appointment priorities thus tends to preselect exactly those instructors who have the least basis for talking to one another. In compensation the department gets a salutary diversity, but the potential benefits of diversity are not really exploited. Nor is the problem merely abstract: the recent proliferation of humanities conferences and symposia suggests that these gatherings have become substitutes for the kind of general discussion that does not take place at home.

The moral is that if the introduction of theory is to make a real difference at the average student's level, we must find some way to modify the field-coverage model, if not to scrap it entirely. Otherwise, theory will be institutionalized as yet another field, equivalent to literary periods and genres—which is to say, it will become one more option that can safely be ignored. We will lose theory's potential for drawing the disconnected parts of the literature curriculum into relation and providing students with the needed contexts. So, I would argue, the real threat that theory faces today comes not from its outright opponents, some of whom are at least willing to argue with it, but from those who are perfectly willing to grant theory an honored place in the scheme of departmental coverage so that they can then forget about it.

This pattern seems to be establishing itself now, as departments clamor

9. The last sentence of *The Great Gatsby* (1925), by F. Scott Fitzgerald (it ends, "borne ceaselessly into the past").

1. *Professing Literature: An Institutional History* (Chicago: University of Chicago Press, 1987).

to hire theorists to get the new field covered, after which they sit back and assume that the relation of theory to the interests of the rest of the department will take care of itself. In practice, this policy passes the buck to the students, leaving them to figure out how theory courses correlate with the others. And of course as long as theory is conceived as a special field, the rest of the department can go on thinking that its work has no connection with theory.

Offering students doses of theory in individual courses without helping them make the requisite connections and relations between courses will tend to produce a confused response, which antitheorists will quickly take as proof that theory is inherently over the head of the average student. For the average student to profit from theory, especially from recent theory, the courses that incorporate it must be not only linked with other courses, both theoretical and untheoretical, but also positioned to operate as a central means of correlation and contextualization.

In other words, literature departments should stop kidding themselves. They should stop pretending that, as long as individual courses are reasonably well conceived and well taught, the aggregate can be counted on to take care of itself. If they are serious about incorporating theory, they should not let it remain an option but should make it central to all their activities, not by putting theory specialists in charge but by recognizing that all their members are theorists.

To put it another way, introducing more theory will only compound our problems unless we rethink the assumption that the essential unit of all teaching has to be the single, self-sufficient course that the students correlate with other courses on their own. We can fail just as badly teaching a new canon in a theoretical way as we have failed in teaching an old canon in a nontheoretical way. Unless literature teachers change their means of connecting institutionally with one another, I am afraid that even the most radical theories and canon revisions will not significantly affect the way most students take in what is put before them.

To close, then, I offer a few schematic suggestions:

1. In relation to other courses in the department, theory courses should be central, not peripheral; their function should be to contextualize and pull together the students' work in other courses (outside as well as inside the literature department). Wherever possible, therefore, they should be required courses rather than electives.
2. In taking stock of its strengths, a department should evaluate not just how well it is covering standard fields and approaches but also what potential conflicts of ideological and methodological perspectives it harbors; it should then ask itself what curricular arrangements might exploit these conflicts. There need be no single way of doing this—but one idea (suggested by Brook Thomas[2]) is to couple courses to bring out conceptual relations and contrasts—between, say, views of literature in earlier and modern literary periods or between competing and complementary methodologies of interpretation.
3. A department harboring a conflict between theorists and antitheorists

2. American New Historicist critic (b. 1947).

should look for ways to build this conflict into its courses, so that students can situate themselves in relation to the controversy and eventually participate in it. The department should also look for ways such disputes can be used to complicate and challenge period and genre distinctions without necessarily eliminating them.

4. A department should consider the unit of teaching to be the issue or context, not the isolated text; texts to be taught should be chosen not only for their intrinsic value but for their usefulness in illustrating exemplary problems and issues.
5. As a means of accomplishing goal 4 on a structural scale, the university should subsume literary studies under cultural studies and cultural history, conceived not as a privileged approach but as a framework that encourages ideological dialectic while retaining enough chronological structure to keep focus and continuity from being lost.

The point is that theory is not only a field to be covered, though it is that at one level. It is something that all teachers of literature and all readers practice and that all have a stake in. The worst thing we could do would be to institutionalize theory in a compartmentalized way that would keep theorists and antitheorists from having to hear what they are saying about each other—and would keep students from observing and joining in the battle.

1986

STANLEY E. FISH
b. 1938

One of the most controversial figures in contemporary literary theory, Stanley Fish has been pivotal to theory's development in the American academy. The leading critic of John Milton of his generation, the self-proclaimed inventor of reader-response theory, the progenitor of antifoundationalism and neopragmatism in literary studies, a pioneer of critical legal studies, and through the 1990s a spirited defender of the humanities amid public attacks over political correctness, Fish is perhaps best known for the brio of his intellectual style, which he practices with the intensity of a contact sport. The feminist theorist Nancy Miller once remarked in an interview, "I've seen Stanley Fish, for instance, go through an amazingly brutal exchange of assaults and then walk off, and it's as if he'd played a squash game and then went home to take a shower." Debunking standard notions of interpretation, Fish's essay "Interpreting the *Variorum*" (1976; rev. 1980) introduces his seminal concept, "interpretive communities," which radically revises interpretive theory by locating meaning not in texts but in readers, not in individual response but in the protocols of communities.

Fish was born in Providence, Rhode Island, where his father was a plumbing contractor. The first in his family to go to college, he attended the University of Pennsylvania, receiving his B.A. in 1959. He went on to do graduate work at Yale University, then the bastion of the American New Critics (such as CLEANTH BROOKS and WILLIAM K. WIMSATT JR.), quickly completing an M.A. and Ph.D., in 1960 and 1962. He taught at the University of California at Berkeley from 1962 to 1974 and published two books before he was thirty, most notably a touchstone of Milton criticism, *Surprised by Sin: The Reader in "Paradise Lost"* (1967; rev. ed., 1999). While at Berkeley, he also wrote *Self-Consuming Artifacts: The Experience of Seventeenth-Century Literature* (1972), which was nominated for a National Book Award. From 1974 to 1985 he was Kenan Professor of English at the Johns Hopkins University, publishing another pioneering reader-response work, *Is There a Text in This Class? The Authority of Interpretive Communities* (1980). Concerned with interpretation and its consequences, at Johns Hopkins he also began to teach in the law school, pursuing an interest in legal theory that became more central to his work through the next two decades.

In 1985 Fish moved to Duke University as Arts and Sciences Distinguished Professor of English and Law and as chair of the English department. As chair, he was instrumental in building the most famous—if sometimes controversial—department of its time; he gathered scholars such as EVE KOSOFSKY SEDGWICK, BARBARA HERRNSTEIN SMITH, and his spouse, JANE TOMPKINS, among others, who represented new theoretical approaches. After stepping down as chair in 1993, he became executive director of the Duke University Press, serving through 1998, when he took a position as dean of Arts and Sciences at the University of Illinois–Chicago. In part because he was both an administrator and a prominent critic, through the 1990s Fish was a public spokesperson for the humanities, frequently debating Dinesh D'Souza, a neoconservative critic of affirmative action, over political correctness; writing opinion pieces in the *New York Times;* and occasionally appearing on television. Meanwhile he also published several notable books on theory, professionalism, law, and politics.

A formative factor of Fish's work was his response to the New Criticism. Like other theorists who were trained under its auspices, he rebelled against its belief in the iconic status of the text and its sole focus on literary form and language. HAROLD BLOOM, for instance, asserted the centrality of the author and the author's "anxiety of influence" in the face of the New Critical prohibition of the "intentional fallacy"; STEPHEN GREENBLATT, who like Fish and Bloom received his graduate training at Yale University, asserted the significance of historical context against the New Critical view of texts as self-sufficient "verbal icons." Countering Wimsatt and MONROE BEARDSLEY's declaration in "The Affective Fallacy" (1949; see above) that the audience of a literary work is irrelevant, Fish declared that referring to affectiveness as a fallacy was a fallacy itself. An abiding concern throughout Fish's work is the rhetorical force of texts and their effects on readers.

In *Surprised by Sin*, Fish focuses on the experience of the reader as he or she encounters Milton's *Paradise Lost*. He upends conventional interpretations of Milton, arguing that the poem's meaning is located not in our final assessment but in the process of struggling through Milton's difficult grammar and rhetoric, which didactically makes readers repeat the Fall. He summarizes this argument in "Interpreting the *Variorum*": those who believe in formal unity refuse to acknowledge "the extraordinary number of adjustments required of readers who would negotiate these lines"; instead, the "difficulty we experience in the act of reading" is "what the lines *mean*." Fish extended his views of response in *Self-Consuming Artifacts*, showing how seventeenth-century writers such as Thomas Browne and John Donne establish but then demolish the reader's expectations. Arguing, as would the deconstructive theorist PAUL DE MAN, that literature is largely about its own failures of signification, Fish asserted that these texts thus become "self-consuming artifacts" rather than what Cleanth Brooks termed "well wrought urns."

Though he continued to write about literature (and Milton remained a constant point of reference), through the late 1970s and 1980s Fish engaged in broader theoretical speculations on interpretation and rhetoric, exemplified by *Is There a Text in This Class?*, which includes the revised version of our selection, "Interpreting the *Variorum*." He questions the existence of the freestanding literary text and argues for meaning as a process rather than a formal product. While stressing reading, Fish distances himself from simple, subjectivist views of reader response. There are many possible interpretations, but, as he observes, agreement for the most part prevails. Fish's explanation is that we derive our interpretations not from texts but from the codes and protocols of "the interpretive community." With this key concept, he attempts to stave off the criticism that reader-response theory promotes a radical relativism, or that in interpretation, anything goes.

"Interpreting the *Variorum*" epitomizes Fish's stance and style. It characteristically uses Milton as a test case, attacks accepted beliefs in authorial intention and textual autonomy, and proposes the provocative thesis that texts are empty in themselves and made only by the reader. However, in the second section, "Undoing the Case for Reader-Response Analysis," Fish critiques his earlier assumption of an individual, informed reader. In a sense, his own essay acts as a self-consuming artifact. Correcting his claims that certain lines "generate a pressure for judgment" and that their "speaker is struggling with his agitated thoughts," he asserts that no text can generate any pressure and that any speaker is a fiction constructed by the poem's reader. "I did what critics always do," Fish confesses, "I 'saw' what my interpretive principles permitted or directed me to see, and then I turned around and attributed what I had 'seen' to a text and an intention."

Those interpretive principles—or, as Fish came to prefer, strategies—derive from the educational and professional communities in which we receive training and have membership. These communities, rather than texts, govern and generate interpretation. Emphasizing in the last section of the essay the generative power of "interpretive communities," Fish proposes that they "are made up of those who share interpretive strategies not for reading (in the conventional sense) but for writing texts." In seeing reading as a form of writing, he parallels poststructuralist views of the "death of the author" and of the writerly text (as expressed by ROLAND BARTHES, for example). As proof of the existence of interpretive communities, Fish cites the history of Milton criticism, amassed in the *Variorum* edition of Milton's works, which demonstrates that consensus is the rule within the community of Milton scholars. While changes of consensus present a problem for Fish, his inventive concept of the interpretive community foregrounds the professional and institutional dimensions of literary criticism.

In his later work Fish takes on the perennial problem of the relation of theory to practice. He persistently attacks the assumption that we generate our interpretations from the principles or theories we hold. Instead, in a trademark reversal, he argues that theory stems from our practices, occurs only after the fact, and has no consequences. Like "strategies," practices determine our interpretations. Extending this notion to law, Fish makes a characteristically provocative claim that judges do not derive their decisions from legal principles, such as the doctrine of free speech, but accrue legal precedents to justify their practical judgments. This view is called antifoundationalism: the denial that practice derives from a predetermined foundation of theory or principle. In advocating antifoundationalism in literary and legal studies, Fish complements RICHARD RORTY's celebrated pragmatist critique of the philosophical tradition (*pragma* is the Greek word for "practice"). His argument about the inconsequentiality of theory helped inject neopragmatism into literary studies, providing the catalyst for the influential argument of STEVEN KNAPP AND WALTER BENN MICHAELS in "Against Theory" (1982; see below).

Probably because of his contrarian style as well as the nature of his claims, Stanley Fish has been one of the most cited literary critics of his generation, prompting both admiration and ire. Traditionalists have denounced him as a relativist who believes in nothing. Leftist critics have attacked him for espousing a circular position that makes principled political action impossible. Defenders of theory have countered that Fish's argument itself has consequences in delegitimating the study of theory in the academy. Critics of his concept of interpretive communities note that it does not explain one's entrance into or departure from a particular community; there are social and political factors that influence what community one might enter. Within the reader-response camp itself, WOLFGANG ISER poses the question: "It is quite true that membership of the community helps to prevent arbitrary ideation, but if there is no subjectivist element in reading, how on earth does Professor Fish account for different interpretations of one and the same text?" Rather than troubling Fish, such rebuttals spur his further argument. His work has indelibly marked contemporary literary theory, especially the concept of interpretation.

BIBLIOGRAPHY

Grounded in the study of seventeenth-century literature, Fish's early books are *John Skelton's Poetry* (1965), *Surprised by Sin: The Reader in Paradise Lost* (1967; 2d ed., 1999), *Self-Consuming Artifacts: The Experience of Seventeenth-Century Literature* (1972), and *The Living Temple: George Herbert and Catechizing* (1978). *Is There a Text in This Class? The Authority of Interpretive Communities* (1980) expands his early consideration of the reader to more general discussions of interpretation and theory. Thereafter Fish broadened his field of inquiry to encompass law, pragmatism, and professionalism, as well as literature and literary theory, in three collections of essays: *Doing What Comes Naturally: Change, Rhetoric, and the Practice of Theory in Literary and Legal Studies* (1989), *There's No Such Thing as Free Speech . . . and It's a Good Thing, Too* (1994), and *The Trouble with Principle* (1999). Fish's *Professional Correctness: Literary Studies and Political Change* (1995), composed of his Clarendon lectures at Oxford University, argues that the political claims of much contemporary academic criticism are empty. *The Stanley Fish Reader*, edited by H. Aram Veeser (1999), offers a diverse selection of his work and includes brief headnotes by different hands, although it unfortunately does not include a bibliography.

The critical response to Fish is wide and varied, traversing the many topics he addresses. The famous debate between Fish and Wolfgang Iser on reader-response theory appeared in *Diacritics* 11 (1981). The best discussion of Fish's concept of interpretive communities is Steven Mailloux's *Interpretive Conventions: The Reader in the Study of American Fiction* (1982). Perhaps the first and finest leftist assessment of Fish is Mary Louise Pratt, "Interpretive Strategies/Strategic Interpretation: On Anglo-American Reader Response Criticism," *Boundary 2* 2.11 (1982/83). Elizabeth A. Meese's "Sexual Politics and Critical Judgment," in *After Strange Texts: The Role of Theory in the Study of Literature* (ed. Gregory S. Jay and David L. Miller, 1985), offers a feminist critique of interpretive communities. Important critiques of Fish on interpretation include Gerald Graff's "Interpretation on Tlon: A Response to Stanley Fish," *Critical Inquiry* 17 (1985), and a chapter in Ellen Rooney's *Seductive Reasoning: Pluralism as the Problematic of Contemporary Literary Theory* (1989). In *The Return of the Reader: Reader-Response Criticism* (1987), Elizabeth Freund provides a good overview and usefully places Fish in the field of response criticism.

The later commentary on Fish primarily deals with his antifoundationalism. Much of it appears in law journals, but Christopher Norris's *What's Wrong with Postmodernism: Critical Theory and the Ends of Philosophy* (1990) includes a representative critique of the circularity of the "no consequences" argument for literary theory. Some of the response to Fish seems ad hominem, such as "The Estate Agent," *London Review of Books*, March 2, 2000, by the Marxist critic Terry Eagleton, who calls Fish "a brash, noisy entrepreneur of the intellect" and criticizes the apolitical outcome of Fish's "no consequences" argument.

Interpreting the *Variorum*

[This essay was written in three stages and, as it finally stands, is something of a self-consuming artifact.[1] The original version was prepared in 1973 for a Modern Language Association forum organized by Fredric Jameson[2] and was intended as a brief for reader-oriented criticism. I seized upon the publication of the Milton *Variorum*[3] because it greatly facilitated what had long since become my method, the surveying of the critical history of a work in order to find disputes that rested upon a base of agreement of which the disputants were unaware. I then identified that base with the experience of a work, and argued that formalist criticism,[4] because it is spatial rather than temporal in its emphasis, either ignored or suppressed what is really happening in the act of reading. Thus, in the case of three sonnets by Milton, what is really happening depends upon a moment of hesitation or syntactic slide, when a reader is invited to make a certain kind of sense only to discover (at the beginning of the next line) that the sense he has made is either incomplete or simply wrong. "In a formalist analysis," I complain, "that moment will disappear, either because it has been flattened out and made into an (insoluble) crux or because it has been eliminated in the course of a procedure that is incapable of finding value in temporal phenomena."

What I did not then see is that the moment that disappears in a formalist analysis is the moment that has been made to appear in another kind of analysis, the kind of analysis I was urging in this essay. This is the point of the second stage of the essay, which begins by declaring that formal features do not exist independently of the reader's experience and ends by admitting that my account of the reader's experience is itself the product of a set of interpretive assumptions. In other words, the facts that I cite as ones ignored by a formalist criticism (premature conclusions, double syntax, misidentification of speakers) are not discovered but *created* by the criticism I was myself practicing. The indictment of the first two sections—that a bad (because spatial) model had suppressed what was really happening—loses its force because of my realization that the notion "really happening" is just one more interpretation. This realization immediately presented me with the problem that led me in the fall of 1975 to write the final section, the problem of accounting for the agreement readers often reach and for the principled ways in which they disagree. It was at this point that I elaborated the notion of interpretive communities as an explanation both for the difference we see—and, by seeing, make—and for the fact that those differences are not random or idiosyncratic but systematic and conventional. The essay thus concludes with a perspective that is not at all the perspective with which it

1. A reference to Fish's own book, *Self-Consuming Artifacts: The Experience of Seventeenth-Century Literature* (1972).

2. A leading American Marxist cultural critic (b. 1934; see above). The annual convention of the Modern Language Association, the primary professional organization for North American college and university teachers and scholars in literature and languages, features hundreds of panels.

3. *A Variorum Commentary on the Poems of John Milton*, general ed. Merritt Y. Hughes, 4 vols. (New York: Columbia University Press, 1970–75). A "variorum" edition includes all variants of particular passages. Among the poems by John Milton (1608–1674) are the epic *Paradise Lost* (1667), the paired poems "L'Allegro" and "Il Penseroso" (1631–32), the elegy *Lycidas* (1637), the masque *Comus* (1637), and sonnets, mentioned by Fish.

4. Particularly the American New Criticism, which focuses on the work itself, regarded as an autonomous whole.

began, and it is from that perspective that the essays subsequent to this one are written.]

The Case for Reader-Response Analysis

The first two volumes of the Milton *Variorum Commentary* have now appeared, and I find them endlessly fascinating. My interest, however, is not in the questions they manage to resolve (although these are many) but in the theoretical assumptions which are responsible for their occasional failures. These failures constitute a pattern, one in which a host of commentators—separated by as much as two hundred and seventy years but contemporaries in their shared concerns—are lined up on either side of an interpretive crux. Some of these are famous, even infamous: what is the two-handed engine in *Lycidas*? what is the meaning of Haemony in *Comus?* Others, like the identity of whoever or whatever comes to the window in *L'Allegro*, line 46, are only slightly less notorious. Still others are of interest largely to those who make editions: matters of pronoun referents, lexical ambiguities, punctuation. In each instance, however, the pattern is consistent: every position taken is supported by wholly convincing evidence—in the case of *L'Allegro* and the coming to the window there is a persuasive champion for every proper noun within a radius of ten lines—and the editorial procedure always ends either in the graceful throwing up of hands or in the recording of a disagreement between the two editors themselves. In short, these are problems that apparently cannot he solved, at least not by the methods traditionally brought to bear on them. What I would like to argue is that they are not *meant* to be solved but to be experienced (they signify), and that consequently any procedure that attempts to determine which of a number of readings is correct will necessarily fail. What this means is that the commentators and editors have been asking the wrong questions and that a new set of questions based on new assumptions must be formulated. I would like at least to make a beginning in that direction by examining some of the points in dispute in Milton's sonnets. I choose the sonnets because they are brief and because one can move easily from them to the theoretical issues with which this paper is finally concerned.

Milton's twentieth sonnet—"Lawrence of virtuous father virtuous son"—has been the subject of relatively little commentary. In it the poet invites a friend to join him in some distinctly Horatian[5] pleasures—a neat repast intermixed with conversation, wine, and song, a respite from labor all the more enjoyable because outside the earth is frozen and the day sullen. The only controversy the sonnet has inspired concerns its final two lines:

Lawrence[6] of virtuous father virtuous son,
  Now that the fields are dank, and ways are mire,
  Where shall we sometimes meet, and by the fire
  Help waste a sullen day; what may be won
From the hard season gaining; time will run
  On smoother, till Favonius[7] reinspire

5. Of HORACE (65–8 B.C.E.), a Roman poet whose *Odes* and *Epistles* often praise the simple pleasures of friendship, country life, and uncomplicated food and drink. Poems inviting a friend to dinner made up one genre of Latin poetry.

6. Probably Edward Lawrence, whose father, Henry Lawrence, was a political ally of Milton's.

7. The Roman personification of the west wind, which blows in the spring.

The frozen earth; and clothe in fresh attire
The lily and rose, that neither sowed nor spun.[8]
What neat repast shall feast us, light and choice,
Of Attic taste, with wine, whence we may rise
To hear the lute well touched, or artful voice
Warble immortal notes and Tuscan[9] air?
He who of those delights can judge, and spare
To interpose them oft, is not unwise.[1]

The focus of the controversy is the word "spare," for which two readings have been proposed: leave time for and refrain from. Obviously the point is crucial if one is to resolve the sense of the lines. In one reading "those delights" are being recommended—he who can leave time for them is not unwise; in the other, they are the subject of a warning—he who knows when to refrain from them is not unwise. The proponents of the two interpretations cite as evidence both English and Latin syntax, various sources and analogues, Milton's "known attitudes" as they are found in his other writings, and the unambiguously expressed sentiments of the following sonnet on the same question. Surveying these arguments, A. S. P. Woodhouse roundly declares: "It is plain that all the honours rest with" the meaning "refrain from" or "forbear to." This declaration is followed immediately by a bracketed paragraph initialled D. B. for Douglas Bush, who, writing presumably after Woodhouse has died, begins "In spite of the array of scholarly names the case for 'forbear to' may be thought much weaker, and the case for 'spare time for' much stronger, than Woodhouse found them."[2] Bush then proceeds to review much of the evidence marshaled by Woodhouse and to draw from it exactly the opposite conclusion. If it does nothing else, this curious performance anticipates a point I shall make in a few moments: evidence brought to bear in the course of formalist analyses—that is, analyses generated by the assumption that meaning is embedded in the artifact—will always point in as many directions as there are interpreters; that is, not only will it prove something, it will prove anything.

It would appear then that we are back at square one, with a controversy that cannot be settled because the evidence is inconclusive. But what if that controversy is *itself* regarded as evidence, not of an ambiguity that must be removed, but of an ambiguity that readers have always experienced? What, in other words, if for the question "what does 'spare' mean?" we substitute the question "what does the fact that the meaning of 'spare' has always been an issue mean"? The advantage of this question is that it can be answered. Indeed it has already been answered by the readers who are cited in the *Variorum Commentary*. What these readers debate is the judgment the poem makes on the delights of recreation; what their debate indicates is that the judgment is blurred by a verb that can be made to participate in contradictory readings. (Thus the important thing about the evidence surveyed in the *Variorum* is not how it is marshaled but that it could be marshaled at all, because it then becomes evidence of the equal availability of both interpretations.)

8. Compare Matthew 6.28: "Consider the lilies of the field, how they grow; they toil not, neither do they spin."
9. That is, of Tuscany, in Italy.
1. All references are to *The Poems of John Milton*, ed. John Carey and Alistair Fowler (London: Longmans, Green, 1968) [Fish's note].
2. *Variorum Commentary*, vol. 2, pt. 2, p. 275 [Fish's note]. The American scholars Woodhouse (1895–1964) and Bush (1896–1983) are two of the editors of the *Variorum* volumes.

In other words, the lines first generate a pressure for judgment—"he who of those delights can judge"—and then decline to deliver it; the pressure, however, still exists, and it is transferred from the words on the page to the reader (the reader is "he who"), who comes away from the poem not with a statement but with a responsibility, the responsibility of deciding when and how often—if at all—to indulge in "those delights" (they remain delights in either case). This transferring of responsibility from the text to its readers is what the lines ask us to do—it is the essence of their experience—and in my terms it is therefore what the lines *mean*. It is a meaning the *Variorum* critics attest to even as they resist it, for what they are laboring so mightily to do by fixing the sense of the lines is to give the responsibility back. The text, however, will not accept it and remains determinedly evasive, even in its last two words, "not unwise." In their position these words confirm the impossibility of extracting from the poem a moral formula, for the assertion (certainly too strong a word) they complete is of the form, "He who does such and such, of him it cannot be said that he is unwise"; but of course neither can it be said that he is wise. Thus what Bush correctly terms the "defensive" "not unwise" operates to prevent us from attaching the label "wise" to any action, including *either* of the actions—leaving time for or refraining from—represented by the ambiguity of "spare." Not only is the pressure of judgment taken off the poem, it is taken off the activity the poem at first pretended to judge. The issue is finally not the moral status of "those delights"—they become in seventeenth-century terms "things indifferent"—but on the good or bad uses to which they can be put by readers who are left, as Milton always leaves them, to choose and manage by themselves.

Let us step back for a moment and see how far we've come. We began with an apparently insoluble problem and proceeded, not to solve it, but to make it signify, first by regarding it as evidence of an experience and then by specifying for that experience a meaning. Moreover, the configurations of that experience, when they are made available by a reader-oriented analysis, serve as a check against the endlessly inconclusive adducing of evidence which characterizes formalist analysis. That is to say, any determination of what "spare" means (in a positivist or literal sense) is liable to be upset by the bringing forward of another analogue, or by a more complete computation of statistical frequencies, or by the discovery of new biographical information, or by anything else; but if we first determine that everything in the line before "spare" creates the expectation of an imminent judgment then the ambiguity of "spare" can be assigned a significance in the context of that expectation. (It disappoints it and transfers the pressure of judgment to us.) That context is experiential, and it is within its contours and constraints that significances are established (both in the act of reading and in the analysis of that act). In formalist analyses the only constraints are the notoriously open-ended possibilities and combination of possibilities that emerge when one begins to consult dictionaries and grammars and histories; to consult dictionaries, grammars, and histories is to assume that meanings can be specified independently of the activity of reading; what the example of "spare" shows is that it is in and by that activity that meanings—experiential, not positivist—are created.

In other words, it is the structure of the reader's experience rather than any structures available on the page that should be the object of description.

In the case of Sonnet 20, that experiential structure was uncovered when an examination of formal structures led to an impasse; and the pressure to remove that impasse led to the substitution of one set of questions for another. It will more often be the case that the pressure of a spectacular failure will be absent. The sins of formalist-positivist analysis are primarily sins of omission, not an inability to explain phenomena but an inability to see that they are there because its assumptions make it inevitable that they will be overlooked or suppressed. Consider, for example, the concluding lines of another of Milton's sonnets, "Avenge O Lord thy slaughtered saints."

Avenge O Lord thy slaughtered saints,[3] whose bones
  Lie scattered on the Alpine mountains cold,
  Even them who kept thy truth so pure of old
  When all our fathers worshipped stocks and stones,
Forget not: in thy book record their groans
  Who were thy sheep and in their ancient fold
  Slain by the bloody Piedmontese that rolled
  Mother with infant down the rocks. Their moans
The vales redoubled to the hills, and they
  To heaven. Their martyred blood and ashes sow
  O'er all the Italian fields where still doth sway
The triple Tyrant: that from these may grow
  A hundredfold, who having learnt thy way
  Early may fly the Babylonian woe.

In this sonnet, the poet simultaneously petitions God and wonders aloud about the justice of allowing the faithful—"Even them who kept thy truth"—to be so brutally slaughtered. The note struck is alternately one of plea and complaint, and there is more than a hint that God is being called to account for what has happened to the Waldensians. It is generally agreed, however, that the note of complaint is less and less sounded and that the poem ends with an affirmation of faith in the ultimate operation of God's justice. In this reading, the final lines are taken to be saying something like this: From the blood of these martyred, O God, raise up a new and more numerous people, who, by virtue of an early education in thy law, will escape destruction by fleeing the Babylonian woe. Babylonian woe has been variously glossed;[4] but whatever it is taken to mean it is always read as part of a statement that specifies a set of conditions for the escaping of destruction or punishment; it is a warning to the reader as well as a petition to God. As a warning, however, it is oddly situated since the conditions it seems to specify were in fact met by the Waldensians, who of all men most followed God's laws. In other words, the details of their story would seem to undercut the affirmative moral the speaker proposes to draw from it. It is further undercut by a reading that is fleetingly available, although no one has acknowledged it because it

3. Here the Waldensians, a heretical sect of Christians professing a creed akin to Protestantism that arose in the 12th century. Their strongholds were in the valleys of northern Italy (the "Piedmont") and southern France, and many were killed.

4. It is first of all a reference to the city of iniquity from which the Hebrews are urged to flee in Isaiah and Jeremiah. In Protestant polemics Babylon is identified with the Roman Church whose destruction is prophesied in the book of Revelation. And in some Puritan tracts Babylon is the name for Augustine's earthly city, from which the faithful are to flee inwardly in order to escape the fate awaiting the unregenerate. See *Variorum Commentary*, pp. 440–41 [Fish's note]. AUGUSTINE (354–430), early Christian philosopher and theologian.

is a function not of the words on the page but of the experience of the reader. In that experience, line 13 will for a moment be accepted as a complete sense unit and the emphasis of the line will fall on "thy way" (a phrase that has received absolutely no attention in the commentaries). At this point "thy way" can refer only to the way in which God has dealt with the Waldensians. That is, "thy way" seems to pick up the note of outrage with which the poem began, and if we continue to so interpret it, the conclusion of the poem will be a grim one indeed: since by this example it appears that God rains down punishment indiscriminately, it would be best perhaps to withdraw from the arena of his service, and thereby hope at least to be safely out of the line of fire. This is not the conclusion we carry away, because as line 14 unfolds, another reading of "thy way" becomes available, a reading in which "early" qualifies "learnt" and refers to something the faithful should do (learn thy way at an early age) rather than to something God has failed to do (save the Waldensians). These two readings are answerable to the pulls exerted by the beginning and ending of the poem: the outrage expressed in the opening lines generates a pressure for an explanation, and the grimmer reading is answerable to that pressure (even if it is also disturbing); the ending of the poem, the forward and upward movement of lines 10–14, creates the expectation of an affirmation, and the second reading fulfills that expectation. The criticism shows that in the end we settle on the more optimistic reading—it feels better—but even so the other has been a part of our experience, and because it has been a part of our experience, it *means*. What it means is that while we may be able to extract from the poem a statement affirming God's justice, we are not allowed to forget the evidence (of things seen) that makes the extraction so difficult (both for the speaker and for us). It is a difficulty we experience in the act of reading, even though a criticism which takes no account of that act has, as we have seen, suppressed it.

In each of the sonnets we have considered, the significant word or phrase occurs at a line break where a reader is invited to place it first in one and then in another structure of syntax and sense. This moment of hesitation, of semantic or syntactic slide, is crucial to the experience the verse provides, but in a formalist analysis that moment will disappear, either because it has been flattened out and made into an (insoluble) interpretive crux or because it has been eliminated in the course of a procedure that is incapable of finding value in temporal phenomena. In the case of "When I consider how my light is spent," these two failures are combined.

> When I consider how my light is spent,
> Ere half my days, in this dark world and wide,
> And that one talent which is death to hide,
> Lodged with me useless, though my soul more bent
> To serve therewith my maker, and present
> My true account, lest he returning chide,
> Doth God exact day-labour, light denied,
> I fondly ask; but Patience to prevent
> That murmur, soon replies, God doth not need
> Either man's work or his own gifts, who best
> Bear his mild yoke, they serve him best, his state
> Is kingly. Thousands at his bidding speed

And post o'er land and ocean without rest:
They also serve who only stand and wait.

The interpretive crux once again concerns the final line: "They also serve who only stand and wait." For some this is an unqualified acceptance of God's will, while for others the note of affirmation is muted or even forced. The usual kinds of evidence are marshaled by the opposing parties, and the usual inconclusiveness is the result. There are some areas of agreement. "All the interpretations," Woodhouse remarks, "recognize that the sonnet commences from a mood of depression, frustration [and] impatience."[5] The object of impatience is a God who would first demand service and then take away the means of serving, and the oft noted allusion to the parable of the talents[6] lends scriptural support to the accusation the poet is implicitly making: you have cast the wrong servant into unprofitable darkness. It has also been observed that the syntax and rhythm of these early lines, and especially of lines 6–8, are rough and uncertain; the speaker is struggling with his agitated thoughts and he changes directions abruptly, with no regard for the line as a unit of sense. The poem, says one critic, "seems almost out of control."[7]

The question I would ask is "whose control?" For what these formal descriptions point to (but do not acknowledge) is the extraordinary number of adjustments required of readers who would negotiate these lines. The first adjustment is the result of the expectations created by the second half of line 6—"lest he returning chide." Since there is no full stop after "chide," it is natural to assume that this will be an introduction to reported speech, and to assume further that what will be reported is the poet's anticipation of the voice of God as it calls him, to an unfair accounting. This assumption does not survive line 7—"Doth God exact day-labour, light denied"—which, rather than chiding the poet for his inactivity, seems to rebuke him for having expected that chiding. The accents are precisely those heard so often in the Old Testament when God answers a reluctant Gideon, or a disputatious Moses, or a self-justifying Job: do you presume to judge my ways or to appoint my motives? Do you think I would exact day labor, light denied? In other words, the poem seems to turn at this point from a questioning of God to a questioning of that questioning; or, rather, the reader turns from the one to the other in the act of revising his projection of what line 7 will say and do. As it turns out, however, that revision must itself be revised because it had been made within the assumption that what we are hearing is the voice of God. This assumption falls before the very next phrase, "I fondly ask," which requires not one but two adjustments. Since the speaker of line 7 is firmly identified as the poet, the line must be reinterpreted as a continuation of his complaint—Is that the way you operate, God, denying light, but exacting labor?—but even as that interpretation emerges, the poet withdraws from it by inserting the adverb "fondly," and once again the line slips out of the reader's control.

In a matter of seconds, then, line 7 has led four experiential lives, one as we anticipate it, another as that anticipation is revised, a third when we retroactively identify its speaker, and a fourth when that speaker disclaims

5. *Variorum Commentary*, p. 469 [Fish's note].

6. See Matthew 25.14–30: the servant who hides the one talent he was given (his lord's money) is "cast . . . into outer darkness."

7. *Variorum Commentary*, p. 457 [Fish's note].

it. What changes in each of these lives is the status of the poet's murmurings—they are alternately expressed, rejected, reinstated, and qualified—and as the sequence ends, the reader is without a firm perspective on the question of record: does God deal justly with his servants?

A firm perspective appears to be provided by Patience, whose entrance into the poem, the critics tell us, gives it both argumentative and metrical stability. But in fact the presence of Patience in the poem finally assures its continuing instability by making it impossible to specify the degree to which the speaker approves, or even participates in, the affirmation of the final line: "They also serve who only stand and wait." We know that Patience to prevent the poet's murmur soon replies (not soon enough however to prevent the murmur from registering), but we do not know when that reply ends. Does Patience fall silent in line 12, after "kingly"? or at the conclusion of line 13? or not at all? Does the poet appropriate these lines or share them or simply listen to them, as we do? These questions are unanswerable, and it is because they remain unanswerable that the poem ends uncertainly. The uncertainty is not in the statement it makes—in isolation line 14 is unequivocal—but in our inability to assign that statement to either the poet or to Patience. Were the final line marked unambiguously for the poet, then we would receive it as a resolution of his earlier doubts; and were it marked for Patience, it would be a sign that those doubts were still very much in force. It is marked for neither, and therefore we are without the satisfaction that a firmly conclusive ending (in *any* direction) would have provided. In short, we leave the poem unsure, and our unsureness is the realization (in our experience) of the unsureness with which the affirmation of the final line is, or is not, made. (This unsureness also operates to actualize the two possible readings of "wait": wait in the sense of expecting, that is waiting for an opportunity to serve actively; or wait in the sense of waiting *in* service, a waiting that is itself fully satisfying because the impulse to self-glorifying action has been stilled.)

The question debated in the *Variorum Commentary* is, how far from the mood of frustration and impatience does the poem finally move? The answer given by an experiential analysis is that you can't tell, and the fact that you can't tell is responsible for the uneasiness the poem has always inspired. It is that uneasiness which the critics inadvertently acknowledge when they argue about the force of the last line, but they are unable to make analytical use of what they acknowledge because they have no way of dealing with or even recognizing experiential (that is, temporal) structures. In fact, more than one editor has eliminated those structures by punctuating them out of existence: first by putting a full stop at the end of line 6 and thereby making it unlikely that the reader will assign line 7 to God (there will no longer be an expectation of reported speech), and then by supplying quotation marks for the sestet in order to remove any doubts one might have as to who is speaking. There is of course no warrant for these emendations, and in 1791 Thomas Warton had the grace and honesty to admit as much. "I have," he said, "introduced the turned commas both in the question and answer, not from any authority, but because they seem absolutely necessary to the sense."[8]

8. *Poems upon Several Occasions, English, Italian, and Latin, with Translations, by John Milton*, ed. Thomas Warton (London, 1791), p. 352 [Fish's note]. Warton (1728–1790), English poet, critic, and literary historian.

Undoing the Case for Reader-Response Analysis

Editorial practices like these are only the most obvious manifestations of the assumptions to which I stand opposed: the assumption that there *is* a sense, that it is embedded or encoded in the text, and that it can be taken in at a single glance. These assumptions are, in order, positivist,[9] holistic, and spatial, and to have them is to be committed both to a goal and to a procedure. The goal is to settle on a meaning, and the procedure involves first stepping back from the text, and then putting together or otherwise calculating the discrete units of significance it contains. My quarrel with this procedure (and with the assumptions that generate it) is that in the course of following it through the reader's activities are at once ignored and devalued. They are ignored because the text is taken to be self-sufficient—everything is *in* it—and they are devalued because when they are thought of at all, they are thought of as the disposable machinery of extraction. In the procedures I would urge, the reader's activities are at the center of attention, where they are regarded not as leading to meaning but as *having* meaning. The meaning they have is a consequence of their not being empty; for they include the making and revising of assumptions, the rendering and regretting of judgments, the coming to and abandoning of conclusions, the giving and withdrawing of approval, the specifying of causes, the asking of questions, the supplying of answers, the solving of puzzles. In a word, these activities are interpretive—rather than being preliminary to questions of value, they are at every moment settling and resettling questions of value—and because they are interpretive, a description of them will also be, and without any additional step, an interpretation, not after the fact but of the fact (of experiencing). It will be a description of a moving field of concerns, at once wholly present (not waiting for meaning but constituting meaning) and continually in the act of reconstituting itself.

As a project such a description presents enormous difficulties, and there is hardly time to consider them here;[1] but it should be obvious from my brief examples how different it is from the positivist-formalist project. Everything depends on the temporal dimension, and as a consequence the notion of a mistake, at least as something to be avoided, disappears. In a sequence where a reader first structures the field he inhabits and then is asked to restructure it (by changing an assignment of speaker or realigning attitudes and positions) there is no question of priority among his structurings; no one of them, even if it is the last, has privilege; each is equally legitimate, each equally the proper object of analysis, because each is equally an event in his experience.

The firm assertiveness of this paragraph only calls attention to the questions it avoids. Who is this reader? How can I presume to describe his experiences, and what do I say to readers who report that they do not have the experiences I describe? Let me answer these questions or rather make a beginning at answering them in the context of another example, this time

9. Taking knowledge and meaning to derive solely from what can be empirically observed.

1. See chapters 2, 3, and 5 in *Is There a Text in This Class?* (where this essay was reprinted), as well as *Surprised by Sin: The Reader in Paradise Lost* (1967) and *Self-Consuming Artifacts* [Fish's note, edited].

from Milton's *Comus*. In line 46 of *Comus* we are introduced to the villain by way of a genealogy:

> Bacchus that first from out the purple grape,
> Crushed the sweet poison of misused wine.

In almost any edition of this poem, a footnote will tell you that Bacchus is the god of wine. Of course most readers already know that, and because they know it, they will be anticipating the appearance of "wine" long before they come upon it in the final position. Moreover, they will also be anticipating a negative judgment on it, in part because of the association of Bacchus with revelry and excess, and especially because the phrase "sweet poison" suggests that the judgment has already been made. At an early point then, we will have both filled in the form of the assertion and made a decision about its moral content. That decision is upset by the word "misused"; for what "misused" asks us to do is transfer the pressure of judgment from wine (where we have already placed it) to the abusers of wine, and therefore when "wine" finally appears, we must declare it innocent of the charges we have ourselves made.

This, then, is the structure of the reader's experience—the transferring of a moral label from a thing to those who appropriate it. It is an experience that depends on a reader for whom the name Bacchus has precise and immediate associations; another reader, a reader for whom those associations are less precise will not have that experience because he will not have rushed to a conclusion in relation to which the word "misused" will stand as a challenge. Obviously I am discriminating between these two readers and between the two equally real experiences they will have. It is not a discrimination based simply on information, because what is important is not the information itself, but the action of the mind which its possession makes possible for one reader and impossible for the other. One might discriminate further between them by noting that the point at issue—whether value is a function of objects and actions or of intentions—is at the heart of the seventeenth-century debate over "things indifferent." A reader who is aware of that debate will not only *have* the experience I describe; he will recognize at the end of it that he has been asked to take a position on one side of a continuing controversy; and that recognition (also a part of his experience) will be part of the disposition with which he moves into the lines that follow.

It would be possible to continue with this profile of the optimal reader, but I would not get very far before someone would point out that what I am really describing is the intended reader, the reader whose education, opinions, concerns, linguistic competences, and so on make him capable of having the experience the author wished to provide. I would not resist this characterization because it seems obvious that the efforts of readers are always efforts to discern and therefore to realize (in the sense of becoming) an author's intention. I would only object if that realization were conceived narrowly, as the single act of comprehending an author's purpose, rather than (as I would conceive it) as the succession of acts readers perform in the continuing assumption that they are dealing with intentional beings. In this view discerning an intention is no more or less than understanding, and understanding includes (is constituted by) all the activities which make up what I call the structure of the reader's experience. To describe that experience is therefore to describe the reader's efforts at understanding, and to describe the reader's efforts at understanding is to describe his realization (in two senses) of an author's intention. Or to put it another way, what my analyses amount to are descriptions of a succession of decisions made by readers about an author's intention—decisions that are not limited to the specifying of purpose but include the specifying of every aspect of successively intended worlds, decisions that are precisely the shape, because they are the content, of the reader's activities.

Having said this, however, it would appear that I am open to two objections. The first is that the procedure is a circular one. I describe the experience of a reader who in his strategies is answerable to an author's intention, and I specify the author's intention by pointing to the strategies employed by that same reader. But this objection would have force only if it were possible to specify one independently of the other. What is being specified from either perspective are the conditions of utterance, of what could have been understood to have been meant by what was said. That is, intention and understanding are two ends of a conventional act, each of which necessarily stipulates (includes, defines, specifies) the other. To construct the profile of the informed or at-home reader is at the same time to characterize the author's intention and vice versa, because to do either is to specify the *contemporary* conditions of utterance, to identify, by becoming a member of, a community made up of those who share interpretive strategies.

The second objection is another version of the first: if the content of the reader's experience is the succession of acts he performs in search of an author's intentions, and if he performs those acts at the bidding of the text, does not the text then produce or contain everything—intention *and* experience—and have I not compromised my antiformalist position? This objection will have force only if the formal patterns of the text are assumed to exist independently of the reader's experience, for only then can priority be claimed for them. Indeed, the claims of independence and priority are one and the same; when they are separated it is so that they can give circular and illegitimate support to each other. The question "do formal features exist independently?" is usually answered by pointing to their priority: they are "in" the text before the reader comes to it. The question "are formal features prior?" is usually answered by pointing to their independent status: they are "in" the text before the reader comes to it. What looks like a step in an argument is actually the spectacle of an assertion supporting itself. It follows then that an attack on the independence of formal features will also be an attack on their priority (and vice versa), and I would like to mount such an attack in the context of two short passages from *Lycidas*.

The first passage (actually the second in the poem's sequence) begins at line 42:

> The willows and the hazel copses green
> Shall now no more be seen,
> Fanning their joyous leaves to thy soft lays.

It is my thesis that the reader is always making sense (I intend "making" to have its literal force), and in the case of these lines the sense he makes will involve the assumption (and therefore the creation) of a completed assertion after the word "seen," to wit, the death of Lycidas has so affected the willows and the hazel copses green that, in sympathy, they will wither and die (will no more be seen by *anyone*). In other words, at the end of line 43 the reader will have hazarded an interpretation, or performed an act of perceptual closure, or made a decision as to what is being asserted. I do not mean that he has done four things, but that he has done one thing the description of which might take any one of four forms—making sense, interpreting, performing perceptual closure, deciding about what is intended. (The importance of this point will become clear later.) Whatever he has done (that is, however we characterize it), he will undo it in the act of reading the next line, for here he discovers that his closure, or making of sense, was premature and that he must make a new one in which the relationship between man and nature is exactly the reverse of what was first assumed. The willows and the hazel copses green will in fact be seen, but they will not be seen by Lycidas. It is he who will be no more, while they go on as before, fanning their joyous leaves to someone else's soft lays (the whole of line 44 is now perceived as modifying and removing the absoluteness of "seen"). Nature is not sympathetic, but indifferent, and the notion of her sympathy is one of those "false surmises" that the poem is continually encouraging and then disallowing.

The previous sentence shows how easy it is to surrender to the bias of our critical language and begin to talk as if poems, not readers or interpreters, did things. Words like "encourage" and "disallow" (and others I have used in this essay) imply agents, and it is only "natural" to assign agency first to an author's intentions and then to the forms that assumedly embody them. What really happens, I think, is something quite different: rather than intention and its formal realization producing interpretation (the "normal" picture), interpretation creates intention and its formal realization by creating the conditions in which it becomes possible to pick them out. In other words, in the analysis of these lines from *Lycidas* I did what critics always do: I "saw" what my interpretive principles permitted or directed me to see, and then I turned around and attributed what I had "seen" to a text and an intention. What my principles direct me to "see" are readers performing acts; the points at which I find (or to be more precise, declare) those acts to have been performed become (by a sleight of hand) demarcations *in* the text; those demarcations are then available for the designation "formal features," and as formal features they can be (illegitimately) assigned the responsibility for producing the interpretation which in fact produced them. In this case, the demarcation my interpretation calls into being is placed at the end of line 42; but of course the end of that (or any other) line is worth noticing or pointing out only because my model *demands* (the word is not too strong) perceptual closures and therefore locations at which they occur; in that model this point will be one of those locations, although (1) it need not have been (not every line ending occasions a closure) and (2) in another model, one that does not give value to the activities of readers, the possibility of its being one would not have arisen.

What I am suggesting is that formal units are always a function of the interpretative model one brings to bear; they are not "in" the text, and I would make the same argument for intentions. That is, intention is no more embodied "in" the text than are formal units; rather an intention, like a formal unit, is made when perceptual or interpretive closure is hazarded; it is verified by an interpretive act, and I would add, it is not verifiable in any other way. This last assertion is too large to be fully considered here, but I can sketch out the argumentative sequence I would follow were I to consider it: intention is known when and only when it is recognized; it is recognized as soon as you decide about it; you decide about it as soon as you make a sense; and you make a sense (or so my model claims) as soon as you can.

Let me tie up the threads of my argument with a final example from *Lycidas*:

> He must not float upon his wat'ry bier
> Unwept . . . (13–14)

Here the reader's experience has much the same career as it does in lines 42–44: at the end of line 13 perceptual closure is hazarded, and a sense is made in which the line is taken to be a resolution bordering on a promise: that is, there is now an expectation that something will be done about this unfortunate situation, and the reader anticipates a call to action, perhaps even a program for the undertaking of a rescue mission. With "Unwept," however, that expectation and anticipation are disappointed, and the realization of that disappointment will be inseparable from the making of a new (and less comforting) sense: nothing will be done; Lycidas will continue to float upon his wat'ry bier, and the only action taken will be the lamenting of the fact that no action will be efficacious, including the actions of speaking and listening to this lament (which in line 15 will receive the meretricious and self-mocking designation "melodious tear"). Three "structures" come into view at precisely the same moment, the moment when the reader having resolved a sense unresolves it and makes a new one; that moment will also be the moment of picking out a formal pattern or unit, end of line/beginning of line, and it will also be the moment at which the reader, having decided about the speaker's intention, about what is meant by what has been said, will make the decision again and in so doing will make another intention.

This, then, is my thesis: that the form of the reader's experience, formal units, and the structure of intention are one, that they come into view simultaneously, and that therefore the questions of priority and independence do not arise. What does arise is another question: what produces *them?* That is, if intention, form, and the shape of the reader's experience are simply different ways of referring to (different perspectives on) the same interpretive act, what is that act an interpretation *of*? I cannot answer that question, but neither, I would claim, can anyone else, although formalists try to answer it by pointing to patterns and claiming that they are available independently of (prior to) interpretation. These patterns vary according to the procedures that yield them: they may be statistical (number of two-syllable words per hundred words), grammatical (ratio of passive to active constructions, or of right-branching to left-branching sentences,[2] or of anything else); but whatever they are I would argue that they do not lie innocently in the world but are themselves constituted by an interpretive act, even if, as is often the case, that act is unacknowledged. Of course, this is as true of my analyses as it is of anyone else's. In the examples offered here I appropriate the notion "line ending" and treat it as a fact of nature; and one might conclude that as a

2. Different patterns of modifying clauses: in the left-branching sentence, the modifying clause begins the sentence; in the right-branching, it ends the sentence.

fact it is responsible for the reading experience I describe. The truth I think is exactly the reverse: line endings exist by virtue of perceptual strategies rather than the other way around. Historically, the strategy that we know as "reading (or hearing) poetry" has included paying attention to the line as a unit, but it is precisely that attention which has made the line as a unit (either of print or of aural duration) available. A reader so practiced in paying that attention that he regards the line as a brute fact rather than as a convention will have a great deal of difficulty with concrete poetry;[3] if he overcomes that difficulty, it will not be because he has learned to ignore the line as a unit but because he will have acquired a new set of interpretive strategies (the strategies constitutive of "concrete poetry reading") in the context of which the line as a unit no longer exists. In short, what is noticed is what has been *made* noticeable, not by a clear and undistorting glass, but by an interpretive strategy.

This may be hard to see when the strategy has become so habitual that the forms it yields seem part of the world. We find it easy to assume that alliteration as an effect depends on a "fact" that exists independently of any interpretive "use" one might make of it, the fact that words in proximity begin with the same letter. But it takes only a moment's reflection to realize that the sameness, far from being natural, is enforced by an orthographic convention; that is to say, it is the product of an interpretation. Were we to substitute phonetic conventions for orthographic ones (a "reform" traditionally urged by purists), the supposedly "objective" basis for alliteration would disappear because a phonetic transcription would require that we distinguish between the initial sounds of those very words that enter into alliterative relationships; rather than conforming to those relationships, the rules of spelling make them. One might reply that, since alliteration is an aural rather than a visual phenomenon when poetry is heard, we have unmediated access to the physical sounds themselves and hear "real" similarities. But phonological "facts" are no more uninterpreted (or less conventional) than the "facts" of orthography; the distinctive features that make articulation and reception possible are the product of a system of differences that must be *imposed* before it can be recognized; the patterns the ear hears (like the patterns the eye sees) are the patterns its perceptual habits make available.

One can extend this analysis forever, even to the "facts" of grammar. The history of linguistics is the history of competing paradigms, each of which offers a different account of the constituents of language. Verbs, nouns, cleft sentences, transformations, deep and surface structures, semes, rhemes, tagmemes[4]—now you see them, now you don't, depending on the descriptive apparatus you employ. The critic who confidently rests his analyses on the bedrock of syntactic descriptions is resting on an interpretation; the facts he points to *are* there, but only as a consequence of the interpretive (man-made) model that has called them into being.

The moral is clear: the choice is never between objectivity and interpretation but between an interpretation that is unacknowledged as such and an

3. Poetry, especially of the 1950s and 1960s, in which the visual shape of the words and letters on the page is part of its meaning.

4. Fish lists technical linguistic terms: a seme is a basic unit of meaning, a rheme is a rhetorical unit comparable to the predicate of a sentence, and a tagmene is a unit of construction (e.g., "noun-is-subject"). Cleft sentences: simple sentences divided into 2 clauses, so that a particular word (and thus idea) is emphasized.

interpretation that is at least aware of itself. It is this awareness that I am claiming for myself, although in doing so I must give up the claims implicitly made in the first part of this essay. There I argue that a bad (because spatial) model had suppressed what was really happening, but by my own declared principles the notion "really happening" is just one more interpretation.

Interpretive Communities

It seems then that the price one pays for denying the priority of either forms or intentions is an inability to say how it is that one ever begins. Yet we do begin, and we continue, and because we do there arises an immediate counterobjection to the preceding pages. If interpretive acts are the source of forms rather than the other way around, why isn't it the case that readers are always performing the same acts or a sequence of random acts, and therefore creating the same forms or a random succession of forms? How, in short, does one explain these two "facts" of reading? (1) The same reader will perform differently when reading two "different" (the word is in quotation marks because its status is precisely what is at issue) texts; and (2) different readers will perform similarly when reading the "same" (in quotes for the same reason) text. That is to say, both the stability of interpretation among readers and the variety of interpretation in the career of a single reader would seem to argue for the existence of something independent of and prior to interpretive acts, something which produces them. I will answer this challenge by asserting that both the stability and the variety are functions of interpretive strategies rather than of texts.

Let us suppose that I am reading *Lycidas*. What is it that I am doing? First of all, what I am not doing is "simply reading," an activity in which I do not believe because it implies the possibility of pure (that is, disinterested) perception. Rather, I am proceeding on the basis of (at least) two interpretive decisions: (1) that *Lycidas* is a pastoral and (2) that it was written by Milton. (I should add that the notions "pastoral" and "Milton" are also interpretations; that is, they do not stand for a set of indisputable, objective facts; if they did, a great many books would not now be getting written.) Once these decisions have been made (and if I had not made these I would have made others and they would be consequential in the same way), I am immediately predisposed to perform certain acts, to "find," by looking for, themes (the relationship between natural processes and the careers of men, the efficacy of poetry or of any other action), to confer significances (on flowers, streams, shepherds, pagan deities), to mark out "formal" units (the lament, the consolation, the turn, the affirmation of faith, and so on). My disposition to perform these acts (and others; the list is not meant to be exhaustive) constitutes a set of interpretive strategies, which, when they are put into execution, become the large act of reading. That is to say, interpretive strategies are not put into execution after reading (the pure act of perception in which I do not believe); they are the shape of reading, and because they are the shape of reading, they give texts their shape, making them rather than, as it is usually assumed, arising from them. Several important things follow from this account:

(1) I did not have to execute this particular set of interpretive strategies because I did not have to make those particular interpretive (pre-reading)

decisions. I could have decided, for example, that *Lycidas* was a text in which a set of fantasies and defenses find expression. These decisions would have entailed the assumption of another set of interpretive strategies (perhaps like that put forward by Norman Holland[5] in *The Dynamics of Literary Response*) and the execution of that set would have made another text.

(2) I could execute this same set of strategies when presented with texts that did not bear the title (again a notion which is itself an interpretation) *Lycidas, a Pastoral Monody*. I could decide (it is a decision some have made) that *Adam Bede*[6] is a pastoral written by an author who consciously modeled herself on Milton (still remembering that "pastoral" and "Milton" are interpretations, not facts in the public domain); or I could decide, as Empson[7] did, that a great many things not usually considered pastoral were in fact to be so read; and either decision would give rise to a set of interpretive strategies, which, when put into action, would *write* the text I write when reading *Lycidas*. (Are you with me?)

(3) A reader other than myself who, when presented with *Lycidas*, proceeds to put into execution a set of interpretive strategies similar to mine (how he could do so is a question I will take up later), will perform the same (or at least a similar) succession of interpretive acts. He and I then might be tempted to say that we agree about the poem (thereby assuming that the poem exists independently of the acts either of us performs); but what we really would agree about is the way to write it.

(4) A reader other than myself who, when presented with *Lycidas* (please keep in mind that the status of *Lycidas* is what is at issue), puts into execution a different set of interpretive strategies will perform a different succession of interpretive acts. (I am assuming, it is the article of my faith, that a reader will always execute some set of interpretive strategies and therefore perform some succession of interpretive acts.) One of us might then be tempted to complain to the other that we could not possibly be reading the same poem (literary criticism is full of such complaints) and he would be right; for each of us would be reading the poem he had made.

The large conclusion that follows from these four smaller ones is that the notions of the "same" or "different" texts are fictions. If I read *Lycidas* and *The Waste Land*[8] differently (in fact I do not), it will not be because the formal structures of the two poems (to term them such is also an interpretive decision) call forth different interpretive strategies but because my predisposition to execute different interpretive strategies will *produce* different formal structures. That is, the two poems are different because I have decided that they will be. The proof of this is the possibility of doing the reverse (that is why point 2 is so important). That is to say, the answer to the question "why do different texts give rise to different sequences of interpretive acts?" is that *they don't have to*, an answer which implies strongly that "they" don't exist. Indeed, it has always been possible to put into action interpretive strategies designed to make all texts one, or to put it more accurately, to be forever making the same text. Augustine urges just such a strategy, for example, in

5. American reader-response critic (b. 1927), who employs psychoanalyis: *Dynamics* was published in 1968.
6. An 1859 novel by the English writer George Eliot.
7. William Empson (1906–1984), English critic and poet, whose works include *Some Versions of Pastoral* (1935).
8. A 1922 poem by the American-born poet and critic T. S. ELIOT.

On Christian Doctrine where he delivers the "rule of faith" which is of course a rule of interpretation.[9] It is dazzlingly simple: everything in the Scriptures, and indeed in the world when it is properly read, points to (bears the meaning of) God's love for us and our answering responsibility to love our fellow creatures for His sake. If only you should come upon something which does not at first seem to bear this meaning, that "does not literally pertain to virtuous behavior or to the truth of faith," you are then to take it "to be figurative" and proceed to scrutinize it "until an interpretation contributing to the reign of charity is produced." This then is both a stipulation of what meaning there is and a set of directions for finding it, which is of course a set of directions—of interpretive strategies—for making it, that is, for the endless reproduction of the same text. Whatever one may think of this interpretive program, its success and ease of execution are attested to by centuries of Christian exegesis. It is my contention that any interpretive program, any set of interpretive strategies, can have a similar success, although few have been as spectacularly successful as this one. (For some time now, for at least three hundred years, the most successful interpretive program has gone under the name "ordinary language.")[1] In our own discipline programs with the same characteristic of always reproducing one text include psychoanalytic criticism, Robertsonianism[2] (always threatening to extend its sway into later and later periods), numerology (a sameness based on the assumption of innumerable fixed differences).

The other challenging question—"why will different readers execute the same interpretive strategy when faced with the 'same' text?"—can be handled in the same way. The answer is again that *they don't have to*, and my evidence is the entire history of literary criticism. And again this answer implies that the notion "same text" is the product of the possession by two or more readers of similar interpretive strategies.

But why should this ever happen? Why should two or more readers ever agree, and why should regular, that is, habitual, differences in the career of a single reader ever occur? What is the explanation on the one hand of the stability of interpretation (at least among certain groups at certain times) and on the other of the orderly variety of interpretation if it is not the stability and variety of texts? The answer to all of these questions is to be found in a notion that has been implicit in my argument, the notion of *interpretive communities*. Interpretive communities are made up of those who share interpretive strategies not for reading (in the conventional sense) but for writing texts, for constituting their properties and assigning their intentions. In other words, these strategies exist prior to the act of reading and therefore determine the shape of what is read rather than, as is usually assumed, the other way around. If it is an article of faith in a particular community that there are a variety of texts, its members will boast a repertoire of strategies for making them. And if a community believes in the existence of only one text, then the single strategy its members employ will be forever writing it. The first community will accuse the members of the second of being reduc-

9. For *On Christian Doctrine* (ca. 395 C.E.), see above.

1. The study of how everyday language is used. Strictly speaking, this is a 20th-century movement started by the Austrian-born philosopher Ludwig Wittgenstein (1889–1941), though it is rooted in the work of the English empiricist John Locke (1632–1704).

2. That is, the scripturally based criticism inspired by D. W. Robertson Jr. (1914–92), a critic of medieval literature.

tive, and they in turn will call their accusers superficial. The assumption in each community will be that the other is not correctly perceiving the "true text," but the truth will be that each perceives the text (or texts) its interpretive strategies demand and call into being. This, then, is the explanation both for the stability of interpretation among different readers (they belong to the same community) and for the regularity with which a single reader will employ different interpretive strategies and thus make different texts (he belongs to different communities). It also explains why there are disagreements and why they can be debated in a principled way: not because of a stability in texts, but because of a stability in the makeup of interpretive communities and therefore in the opposing positions they make possible. Of course this stability is always temporary (unlike the longed for and timeless stability of the text). Interpretive communities grow larger and decline, and individuals move from one to another; thus, while the alignments are not permanent, they are always there, providing just enough stability for the interpretive battles to go on, and just enough shift and slippage to assure that they will never be settled. The notion of interpretive communities thus stands between an impossible ideal and the fear which leads so many to maintain it. The ideal is of perfect agreement and it would require texts to have a status independent of interpretation. The fear is of interpretive anarchy, but it would only be realized if interpretation (text making) were completely random. It is the fragile but real consolidation of interpretive communities that allows us to talk to one another, but with no hope or fear of ever being able to stop.

In other words interpretive communities are no more stable than texts because interpretive strategies are not natural or universal, but learned. This does not mean that there is a point at which an individual has not yet learned any. The ability to interpret is not acquired; it is constitutive of being human. What is acquired are the ways of interpreting and those same ways can also be forgotten or supplanted, or complicated or dropped from favor ("no one reads that way anymore"). When any of these things happens, there is a corresponding change in texts, not because they are being read differently, but because they are being written differently.

The only stability, then, inheres in the fact (at least in my model) that interpretive strategies are always being deployed, and this means that communication is a much more chancy affair than we are accustomed to think it. For if there are no fixed texts, but only interpretive strategies making them, and if interpretive strategies are not natural, but learned (and are therefore unavailable to a finite description), what is it that utterers (speakers, authors, critics, me, you) do? In the old model utterers are in the business of handing over ready-made or prefabricated meanings. These meanings are said to be encoded, and the code is assumed to be in the world independently of the individuals who are obliged to attach themselves to it (if they do not they run the danger of being declared deviant). In my model, however, meanings are not extracted but made and made not by encoded forms but by interpretive strategies that call forms into being. It follows then that what utterers do is give hearers and readers the opportunity to make meanings (and texts) by inviting them to put into execution a set of strategies. It is presumed that the invitation will be recognized, and that presumption rests on a projection on the part of a speaker or author of the moves *he* would make if confronted by the sounds or marks he is uttering or setting down.

It would seem at first that this account of things simply reintroduces the old objection; for isn't this an admission that there is after all a formal encoding, not perhaps of meanings, but of the directions for making them, for executing interpretive strategies? The answer is that they will only *be* directions to those who already have the interpretive strategies in the first place. Rather than producing interpretive acts, they are the product of one. An author hazards his projection, not because of something "in" the marks, but because of something he assumes to be in his reader. The very existence of the "marks" is a function of an interpretive community, for they will be recognized (that is, made) only by its members. Those outside that community will be deploying a different set of interpretive strategies (interpretation cannot be withheld) and will therefore be making different marks.

So once again I have made the text disappear, but unfortunately the problems do not disappear with it. If everyone is continually executing interpretive strategies and in that act constituting texts, intentions, speakers, and authors, how can any one of us know whether or not he is a member of the same interpretive community as any other of us? The answer is that he can't, since any evidence brought forward to support the claim would itself be an interpretation (especially if the "other" were an author long dead). The only "proof" of membership is fellowship, the nod of recognition from someone in the same community, someone who says to you what neither of us could ever prove to a third party: "we know." I say it to you now, knowing full well that you will agree with me (that is, understand) only if you already agree with me.

1976, 1980

NGUGI WA THIONG'O b. 1938 — TABAN LO LIYONG b. 1939

HENRY OWUOR-ANYUMBA 1932–1992

Though it is hard to imagine a university in the English-speaking world without an English department, English departments are a relatively recent historical development, arising only in the late nineteenth and early twentieth century. Before that, academic literary study centered on the Greek and Latin classics and focused on elements of rhetoric and philology. During the Victorian era in England, as TERRY EAGLETON points out in the first chapter of *Literary Theory* (1983; see below), English arose as a discipline to foster an appreciation for culture in the less educated classes, who were not trained in Greek and Latin. But as Eagleton also argues, English was enmeshed with nationalism and designed to instill national pride—hence the subject was "English" rather than simply "literature"—particularly in the face of European conflicts (such as those leading up to World War I) and competition for colonies. Moreover, the teaching of English language and literature was a prominent part of the administration of the British Empire in its many colonies around the globe—in

India, Africa, and elsewhere. "On the Abolition of the English Department" (1968), our selection here, stages a revolt against this vestige of British colonial rule: it depicts English not as a neutral or natural subject but as an instrument of imperialism, and promotes the study of indigenous national literatures and languages. Originally a university memorandum, it today is seen as an important inaugural statement of postcolonial literary criticism.

Its lead author, Ngugi wă Thiong'o (James Ngugi), is an internationally renowned novelist, dramatist, and critic. Born in Kenya, which was under British rule from 1895 until 1963, Ngugi witnessed the effects of colonialism firsthand. He attended an independent mission school where the teachers were native Kenyans; but in 1954, in response to the Mau Mau uprising against colonial rule, the British government took control of it and made instruction in English mandatory. In the political turmoil leading to independence, one of his stepbrothers was killed and his mother tortured, and an older brother joined the Mau Mau rebellion. In 1959 Ngugi entered Makerere University in Uganda, receiving his B.A. in 1964; there he also began his writing career, publishing the acclaimed novel *Weep Not, Child* (1964) about the Mau Mau war and East African culture. After attending Leeds University on a British council scholarship (1964–67), he returned to Africa to take a position at Nairobi University, but soon resigned in protest over governmental interference in the university. He rejoined the faculty in 1971, becoming in 1973 head of the Department of Literature, newly formed in response to his and his colleagues' criticism of English. He also renounced his anglicized name, James Ngugi, which he held to be a sign of colonialism; taking his name in his native Kikuyu language, he thereafter wrote first in Kikuyu and then translated his own work into English. In 1977 he was arrested by Kenyan police after the production of one of his plays that was critical of the government. Protests from international literary groups led to his release after he had been imprisoned for a year without being charged. Ngugi eventually left the country; since 1992 he has held the Erich Maria Remarque Chair in Languages at New York University.

Born in northern Uganda, which was under British rule from 1896 until 1962, Taban lo Liyong received his B.A. from the Ugandan National Teachers College in 1962. He traveled to the United States to study political science, but changed paths in 1965 to attend the prestigious writers' workshop at the University of Iowa; in 1968 he became its first African graduate. He was an important early critic of the paucity of African literature, attributing it to British colonial rule: "I blame the British. The education they came to offer was aimed at recruiting candidates for a Christian Heaven" and at "produc[ing] clerks, teachers, servants"—a point made less critically a century earlier by the English historian and politician Thomas Babington Macaulay in "Minute on Indian Education" (1835). In 1968 he returned to Africa on a fellowship offered by the Institute for African Studies at Nairobi University, where he also lectured in the English department and joined forces with Ngugi and Owuor-Anyumba. Since 1978 he has been a member of the Faculty of Literature at Juba in the Sudan.

Born in Kenya, Henry Owuor-Anyumba received a degree in education from the University of East Africa and his B.A. from Cambridge University in 1966. Thereafter he taught at Nairobi University until his retirement in the early 1990s. Less widely known than his coauthors, he was a historian of African music, documenting its distinctive traditions.

After World War II, almost all of the many colonies of the European powers gained their national independence, sometimes through negotiation and sometimes through revolt and war. But political independence did not necessarily entail economic or cultural autonomy, and the effects of colonialism lingered in language, education, and religion, as well as in economic and political structures. The residual effects of imperialism are variously called "postcolonial," "neo-colonial" (the term that Ngugi most frequently uses), or simply "colonial" (the term favored by the celebrated Nigerian novelist CHINUA ACHEBE). Inaugurated as a critique of the results of decolonization, postcolonial studies addresses the perennial theoretical issue of the relation of culture and society, particularly the role that culture—notably language, literature, and education—plays in furthering imperialism. In "Literature and Society" (1973), Ngugi spells out a direct connection between culture and politics, viewing the influence of a dominant culture as a central vehicle for continued colonial control, or "cultural imperialism," "which during classical colonialism supplemented direct military and political occupation [but now] becomes the major agency of control under neo-colonialism."

"On the Abolition of the English Department" deals with how literary education and academic institutions have helped implement cultural imperialism in Africa. Literature is not neutral nor does it merely impart truth and beauty; instead, as Ngugi elaborates in "Literature and Society," "the content of our literature syllabus, its presentation, the machinery for determining the choice of texts and their interpretation were all an integral part of imperialism and domination in the colonial phase, and they are today an integral part of the imperialism and domination in the neo-colonial phase." To remedy this, "On the Abolition of the English Department" offers a straightforward set of proposals for African universities: first, dismantle departments centered on English language and literature; second, create departments centered on the study of indigenous African languages and literature, as well as relevant foreign ones; third, study neglected topics such as the African oral tradition; and, finally, study modern African literature, which includes Caribbean and African American literature. Ngugi, Liyong, and Owuor-Anyumba are careful not to discredit English or European literature, but argue for the benefits of opening literary study to wider currents. Within the debate over the literary canon, they take an expansionist position, recommending that the canon encompass more texts from different cultures rather than be artificially limited, and that we study representative rather than "classic" texts.

A contentious issue among writers and critics during the early days of decolonization was whether to write in native languages or in the dominant colonial language, usually English or French. European authors similarly had to grapple with the status of vernacular languages in the early Renaissance, when Latin was the dominant language of learning (for example, see JOACHIM DU BELLAY, above). In his other work, Ngugi argues for the primary use of native traditions and languages; in contrast, his coauthor Liyong contends that African writers must write in a European language to capture a wide readership—with the qualification that "we will not have to stick to Queen's English[;] . . . we have to tame the shrew and naturalize her," a point also made by Achebe.

Since the 1980s postcolonial and cultural critics have questioned the nationalistic character of such struggles for independence, arguing that nationalism participates in the logic of imperialism and that it rests on a fictive construct, an "imagined community," without an essential core. Set amid debates over decolonization and Afrocentrism, "On the Abolition of the English Department" provides a glimpse into the political effects of literature and the seemingly neutral institutions of education. Ngugi challenges us to consider such questions more closely, declaring, "Every writer is a writer in politics. The only question is what and whose politics."

BIBLIOGRAPHY

Ngugi wă Thiong'o has published numerous critical essays on African literature, education, and politics, collected in *Homecoming: Essays on African and Caribbean Literature, Culture and Politics* (1973), which includes "On the Abolition of the English Department"; *Writers in Politics: Essays* (1981; rev. ed., 1997); *Education for a National Culture* (1981); *Barrel of a Pen: Resistance to Repression in Neo-Colonial Kenya* (1983); *Decolonising the Mind: The Politics of Language in African*

Literature (1986); *Moving the Centre: The Struggle for Cultural Freedom* (1993); and *Penpoints, Gunpoints, and Dreams: Towards a Critical Theory of the Arts and the State of Africa* (1998). *Detained: A Writer's Prison Diary* (1981), written during his year under arrest, is a biographical reflection on his career and politics. Ngugi also has an international reputation as a novelist depicting twentieth-century Kenya; his best-known novels are *Weep Not, Child* (1964), *The River Between* (1965), and *A Grain of Wheat* (1967).

Published primarily in Africa, Taban lo Liyong is a prolific writer of poetry, short stories, and criticism. His most notable books in English are *The Last Word: Cultural Synthesism* (1969), the first book of literary criticism specifically focused on African literature, and *Fixions* (1968), a collection of short stories that contain elements of African oral tradition. Other works include *Eating Chiefs: Lwo Culture from Lolwe to Malkal* (1970), *Thirteen Offensives: Against Our Enemies* (1973), and *Meditations in Limbo* (1978). Henry Owuor-Anyumba's publications in English include a collection, *Kikuyu Folktales,* co-edited with Rose N. Gecau (1970); the monograph *A Musical Profile of Some Kalenjin Songs* (1973); and an article, "Contemporary Lyres in Eastern Africa," *African Musicology* 1 (1983).

There is a great deal of scholarship on Ngugi's work, especially his fiction. *Ngugi wă Thiong'o* (2000) by Oliver Lovesey provides biographical information as well as an overview of Ngugi's work. David Cook and Michael Okenimkpe's *Ngugi wă Thiong'o: An Exploration of His Writings* (1983), a survey, concludes with a chapter on his social criticism. *Ngugi wă Thiong'o: The Making of a Rebel: A Source Book in Kenyan Literature and Resistance,* edited by Carol Sicherman (1989), is a helpful reference work. Simon Gikandi, *Ngugi wă Thiong'o* (2000), is a useful comprehensive study. *Ngugi wă Thiong'o: A Bibliography of Primary and Secondary Works, 1957–1987,* compiled by Carol Sicherman (1991), offers a comprehensive bibliography. More recently, Lovesey's *Ngugi wă Thiong'o* contains a good bibliography. There is to date little criticism and bibliography on Liyong or Owuor-Anyumba.

On the Abolition of the English Department[1]

1. This is a comment on the paper presented by the Acting Head of the English Department at the University of Nairobi[2] to the 42nd meeting of the Arts Faculty Board on the 20th September, 1968.

2 (*a*) That paper was mainly concerned with possible developments within the Arts Faculty and their relationship with the English Department, particularly:

(i) The place of modern languages, especially French;
(ii) The place and role of the Department of English;
(iii) The emergence of a Department of Linguistics and Languages;
(iv) The place of African languages, especially Swahili.

(*b*) In connection with the above, the paper specifically suggested that a department of Linguistics and Languages, to be closely related to English, be established.

1. This debate resulted in the establishment of two departments: Languages and Literature. In both, African languages and literature were to form the core. In the case of the Literature Department, Caribbean and black American literature were to be emphasized. It thus represents a radical departure in the teaching of literature in Africa [Ngugi, Liyong, and Owuor-Anyumba's note].

2. A focal point of the political tension that continued to beset Kenya after independence was gained in 1964.

(*c*) A remote possibility of a Department of African literature, or alternatively, that of African literature and culture, was envisaged.

3. The paper raised important problems. It should have been the subject of a more involved debate and discussion, preceding the appointment of a committee with specific tasks, because it raises questions of value, direction and orientation.

4. For instance, the suggestions, as the paper itself admits, question the role and status of an English Department in an African situation and environment. To quote from his paper:

> The English Department has had a long history at this College and has built up a strong syllabus which by its study of the *historic continuity of a single culture throughout the period of emergence of the modern west*, makes it an important companion to History and to Philosophy and Religious Studies. However, *it is bound to become less 'British', more open to other writing in English (American, Caribbean, African, Commonwealth) and also to continental writing, for comparative purposes.*

5. Underlying the suggestions is a basic assumption that the English tradition and the emergence of the modern west is the central root of our consciousness and cultural heritage. Africa becomes an extension of the west, an attitude which, until a radical reassessment, used to dictate the teaching and organization of History in our University.[3] Hence, in fact, the assumed centrality of English Department, into which other cultures can be admitted from time to time, as fit subjects for study, or from which other satellite departments can spring as time and money allow. A small example is the current, rather apologetic attempt to smuggle African writing into an English syllabus in our three colleges.

6. Here then, is our main question: If there is need for a 'study of the historic continuity of a single culture', why can't this be African? Why can't African literature be at the centre so that we can view other cultures in relationship to it?

This is not mere rhetoric: already African writing, with the sister connections in the Caribbean and the Afro-American literatures, has played an important role in the African renaissance, and will become even more and more important with time and pressure of events. Just because for reasons of political expediency we have kept English as our official language, there is no need to substitute a study of English culture for our own. We reject the primacy of English literature and culture.

7. The aim, in short, should be to orientate ourselves towards placing Kenya, East Africa, and then Africa in the centre. All other things are to be considered in their relevance to our situation, and their contribution towards understanding ourselves.

8. We therefore suggest:

A. That the English Department be abolished;
B. That a Department of African Literature and Languages be set up in its place.

3. Then the University of East Africa with three constituent colleges at Makerere, Dar es Salaam, and Nairobi. Since then the three have become autonomous universities [Ngugi, Liyong, and Owuor: Anyumba's note]. Makerere is in Uganda; Dar es Salaam is the capital of Tanzania.

The primary duty of any literature department is to illuminate the spirit animating a people, to show how it meets new challenges, and to investigate possible areas of development and involvement.

In suggesting this name, we are not rejecting other cultural streams, especially the western stream. We are only clearly mapping out the directions and perspectives the study of culture and literature will inevitably take in an African university.

9. We know that European literatures constitute one source of influence on modern African literatures in English, French, and Portuguese; Swahili,[4] Arabic, and Asian literatures constitute another, an important source, especially here in East Africa; and the African tradition, a tradition as active and alive as ever, constitutes the third and the most significant. This is the stuff on which we grew up, and it is the base from which we make our cultural take-off into the world.

10. Languages and linguistics should be studied in the department because in literature we see the principles of languages and linguistics in action. Conversely, through knowledge of languages and linguistics we can get more from literature. For linguistics not to become eccentric, it should be studied in the Department of African Literature and Languages.

In addition to Swahili, French, and English, whenever feasible other languages such as Arabic, Hindustani, Kikuyu, Luo, Akamba,[5] etc., should be introduced into the syllabus as optional subjects.

11. On the literature side, the Department ought to offer roughly:

(a) The oral tradition, which is our primary root;
(b) Swahili literature (with Arabic and Asian literatures): this is another root, especially in East Africa;
(c) A selected course in European literature: yet another root;
(d) Modern African literature.

For the purposes of the Department, a knowledge of Swahili, English, and French should be compulsory. The largest body of writing by Africans is now written in the French language. Africans writing in the French language have also produced most of the best poems and novels. In fact it makes no sense to talk of modern African literature without French.

12. *The Oral Tradition*

The Oral tradition is rich and many-sided. In fact 'Africa is littered with Oral Literature'. But the art did not end yesterday; it is a living tradition. Even now there are songs being sung in political rallies, in churches, in night clubs by guitarists, by accordion players, by dancers, etc. Another point to be observed is the interlinked nature of art forms in traditional practice. Verbal forms are not always distinct from dance, music, etc. For example, in music there is close correspondence between verbal and melodic tones; in 'metrical lyrics' it has been observed that poetic text is inseparable from tune; and the 'folk tale' often bears an 'operatic' form, with sung refrain as an integral part. The distinction between prose and poetry is absent or very fluid.

Though tale, dance, song, myth, etc. can be performed for individual aes-

4. One of the official languages of Kenya and Tanzania.

5. Some of the diverse languages of the different ethnic groups in and around Kenya.

thetic enjoyment, they have other social purposes as well. Dance, for example, has been studied 'as symbolic expression of social reality reflecting and influencing the social, cultural and personality systems of which it is a part'. The oral tradition also comments on society because of its intimate relationship and involvement.

The study of the oral tradition at the University should therefore lead to a multi-disciplinary outlook: literature, music, linguistics, Sociology, Anthropology, History, Psychology, Religion, Philosophy. Secondly, its study can lead to fresh approaches by making it possible for the student to be familiar with art forms different in kind and historical development from Western literary forms. Spontaneity and liberty of communication inherent in oral transmission—openness to sounds, sights, rhythms, tones, in life and in the environment—are examples of traditional elements from which the student can draw. More specifically, his familiarity with oral literature could suggest new structures and techniques; and could foster attitudes of mind characterized by the willingness to experiment with new forms, so transcending 'fixed literary patterns' and what that implies—the preconceived ranking of art forms.

The study of the Oral Tradition would therefore supplement (not replace) courses in Modern African Literature. By discovering and proclaiming loyalty to indigenous values, the new literature would be on the one hand be set in the stream of History to which it belongs and so be better appreciated; and on the other be better able to embrace and assimilate other thoughts without losing its roots.

13. *Swahili Literature*

There is a large amount of oral and written classical Swahili Literature of high calibre. There is also a growing body of modern Swahili literature: both written and oral.

14. *European Literature*

Europe has influenced Africa, especially through English and French cultures. In our part of Africa there has been an over-concentration on the English side of European life. Even the French side, which is dominant in other countries of Africa, has not received the importance it deserves. We therefore urge for freedom of choice so that a more representative course can be drawn up. We see no reason why English literature should have priority over and above other European literatures where we are concerned. The Russian novel of the nineteenth century should and must be taught. Selections from American, German, and other European literatures should also be introduced. In other words English writings will be taught in their European context and only for their relevance to the East African perspective.

15. *Modern African Literature*

The case for the study of Modern African Literature is self-evident. Its possible scope would embrace:

(a) The African novel written in French and English;
(b) African poetry written in French and English, with relevant translations of works written by Africans in Portuguese and Spanish;
(c) The Caribbean novel and poetry: the Caribbean involvement with Africa can never be over-emphasized. A lot of writers from the West

Indies have often had Africa in mind. Their works have had a big impact on the African renaissance—in politics and literature. The poetry of Negritude[6] indeed cannot be understood without studying its Caribbean roots. We must also study Afro-American literature.

16. *Drama*

Since drama is an integral part of literature, as well as being its extension, various dramatic works should be studied as parts of the literature of the people under study. Courses in play-writing, play-acting, directing, lighting, costuming, etc. should be instituted.

17. *Relationship with other Departments*

From things already said in this paper, it is obvious that African Oral and Modern literatures cannot be fully understood without some understanding of social and political ideas in African history. For this, we propose that either with the help of other departments, or within the department, or both, courses on mutually relevant aspects of African thought be offered. For instance, an introductory course on African art—sculpture, painting—could be offered in co-operation with the Department of Design and Architecture.

18. The 3.1.1[7] should be abolished. We think an undergraduate should be exposed to as many general ideas as possible. Any specialization should come in a graduate school where more specialized courses can be offered.

19. In other words we envisage an active Graduate School will develop, which should be organized with such department as the Institute for Development studies.

20. *Conclusion*

One of the things which has been hindering a radical outlook in our study of literature in Africa is the question of literary excellence; that only works of undisputed literary excellence should be offered. (In this case it meant virtually the study of disputable 'peaks' of English literature.) The question of literary excellence implies a value judgment as to what is literary and what is excellence, and from whose point of view. For any group it is better to study representative works which mirror their society rather than to study a few isolated 'classics', either of their own or of a foreign culture.

To sum up, we have been trying all along to place values where they belong. We have argued the case for the abolition of the present Department of English in the College, and the establishment of a Department of African Literature and Languages. This is not a change of names only. We want to establish the centrality of Africa in the department. This, we have argued, is justifiable on various grounds, the most important one being that education is a means of knowledge about ourselves. Therefore, after we have examined ourselves, we radiate outwards and discover peoples and worlds around us. With Africa at the centre of things, not existing as an appendix or a satellite of other countries and literatures, things must be seen from the African perspective. The dominant object in that perspective is African literature, the major branch of African culture. Its roots go back to past African liter-

6. A literary movement of the 1930s through 1950s that began in Paris among black French-speaking African and Caribbean writers; protesting French colonist rule and assimilationist policies, they declared the value of black African identity, culture, and traditions.

7. This is a course for those who want to specialize in literature: 1st year—three subjects; 2d and 3d years—literature only [Ngugi, Liyong, and Owuor-Anyumba's note].

atures, European literatures, and Asian literatures. These can only be studied meaningfully in a Department of African Literature and Languages in an African University.

We ask that this paper be accepted in principle; we suggest that a representative committee be appointed to work out the details and harmonize the various suggestions into an administratively workable whole.

1968

TZVETAN TODOROV
b. 1939

A central figure in French structuralism, Tzvetan Todorov is best known for advocating the scientific study of narrative, modeled on linguistics, for which he coined the now-standard term *narratology*. He was responsible for renewing attention to the narrative theory put forth earlier in the twentieth century by the Russian formalists, such as BORIS EICHENBAUM and Viktor Shklovsky, and for an effort, with his mentor ROLAND BARTHES to establish a universal "grammar" of narrative. In "Structural Analysis of Narrative' (1969), Todorov presents a condensed manifesto for the narratological approach.

Born in Bulgaria, Todorov emigrated to France in 1963 to study literature and language at University of Paris, where he did his doctoral dissertation under the direction of Barthes. Since 1968 he has held an appointment at the Centre National de la Recherche Scientifique (National Center of Scientific Research) in Paris. His writing has been prolific and varied. From the late 1960s through the 1970s, he focused on questions of literary structure; he later turned to questions of interpretation and larger issues of contemporary culture.

The 1960s witnessed a flourishing of structuralism in fields as diverse as anthropology, psychology, philosophy, and literature. Influenced by FERDINAND DE SAUSSURE (1857–1913) as well as by contemporary linguists, structuralists applied the scientific mode of linguistics to other aspects of human culture, seeking to chart their underlying structures and rules. For instance, fashion or courtship rituals might be seen as operating according to their own distinctive codes. The Saussurean model treats words and other minimal linguistic elements not as freestanding units but as components of a larger, abstract system; the overall system of language rather than individual speech utterances thus becomes the primary object of analysis. The anthropologist CLAUDE LÉVI-STRAUSS became famous for applying structuralist methods to the analysis of the myths and rituals of the primitive societies he observed, and his "Structural Analysis of Myth" (1958) provided an influential early example for work in literary studies. Defining literary study as one of the "human sciences" instead of a humanistic pursuit, structuralist critics aimed to describe and categorize the systematic operation of literature, whose general codes were exhibited and instantiated in individual literary works.

Encapsulating the tenets of Todorov's books *Grammaire du Décaméron* (1969, *Grammar of the Decameron*) and *Poetics of Prose* (1971; trans. 1977), "Structural Analysis of Narrative" seeks to develop a "poetics" or a theoretical study of literary techniques and categories. Todorov is quick to distinguish his version of structural analysis from the New Criticism, the predominant Anglo-American critical approach of the mid–twentieth century. While both focus on internal literary features of works rather than on external concerns such as historical context, he notes that the New Criticism deals only with the individual work itself. The structuralist method proposes instead to understand the overall system in which the work is a part. In his analyses of BOCCACCIO's *Decameron* (1351–53), for example, Todorov's interest is not in any individual tale, but in the general and abstract plot structures that govern all the tales. For Todorov, the New Critical method results only in paraphrase and thus does not create new knowledge; the structuralist method, in contrast, charts the systematic laws and patterns that generate literary works. It therefore yields a scientific knowledge of literature, as physics yields a scientific knowledge of the laws of nature or as linguistics yields a scientific knowledge of the laws of language.

Calling his approach a "poetics," Todorov harkens back to ARISTOTLE's originary division of scientific disciplines, poetics being the study of human-made rather than natural artifacts—specifically, of verbal artifacts, such as epics and tragedies. Following Aristotle's view of plot as the prime category of tragedy, Todorov (and narratology in general) takes plot as the central abstract structure of narrative, analyzing the hundred tales in the *Decameron* on the basis of the similarity of their plots. They lead him to the insight that plot moves from an equilibrium to a disequilibrium—hence the action of the narrative—and concludes in a new equilibrium, which displays either "avoided punishment" or "conversion." As he states, "All of the stories of the *Decameron* can be entered into this very broad schema." In privileging and schematizing plot, Todorov also shows the influence of the Russian formalists, particularly the folklorist Vladimir Propp, whose *Morphology of the Folktale* (1928) charts basic plot motifs or patterns common to folktales. Todorov designates the specific elements of each plot, on the model of the sentence, as subject, predicate, and adjective. In an effort to adopt the technical precision of linguistics, he discerns the "grammar" rather than semantic meaning of narrative.

With the powerful critiques of structuralism and the development of poststructuralism by thinkers such as JACQUES DERRIDA through the 1970s, structuralism waned as a vanguard theoretical approach. However, the structuralist theory of narrative has been less discredited than displaced, supplanted by more socially engaged approaches—among them, Marxism, feminism, the New Historicism, and cultural studies. The interest of those studying narrative in recent decades seems to have shifted to hermeneutic interpretation rather than poetic description, and to issues of culture and society. Todorov's own work broadened to consider larger cultural and interpretive issues, as did that of Barthes, who in the 1970s became a leading proponent of poststructuralist literary criticism, extolling the richness of textual interpretation. Yet as Todorov notes in "Structural Study of Narrative," poetics does not deny "the relation between literature and . . . social life"; therefore it does not contradict "external" approaches, but serves a different purpose. Narratology remains an active though technical subfield in literary studies, and Todorov's work is still regarded as foundational.

BIBLIOGRAPHY

Todorov's work falls into three periods. The first and best-known to English-speaking critics is his structuralist phase; books include *Grammar of the Decameron* (1969); *The Fantastic: A Structural Approach to a Literary Genre* (1970; trans. 1973); *The Poetics of Prose* (1971; trans. 1977), which gathers many important essays on narrative; the *Encyclopedic Dictionary of the Sciences of Language*, coauthored with the philosopher of language Oswald Ducrot (1972; trans. 1979); and *Introduction to Poetics* (1973; trans. 1981), a good starting point in reading Todorov. In addition, he translated into French and edited an influential collection, *Théorie de la littérature: Textes des formalistes russes* (1965, *Theory of Literature: Texts of the Russian Formalists*), which introduced central writings of important Russian formalists to the French scene.

In his second phase, Todorov turned from questions of structure to those of interpretation, publishing *Theories of the Symbol* (1977; trans. 1982), *Symbolism and Interpretation* (1978; trans. 1982), *Genres in Discourse* (1978; abridged trans., 1990), and *Mikhail Bakhtin: The Dialogical Principle* (1981; trans. 1984). He also edited the anthology *French Literary Theory Today: A Reader* (1982). In his third phase, Todorov took up broad issues of cultures, ethics, and history in books including *The Conquest of America: The Question of the Other* (1984; trans. 1992), the retrospective *Literature and Its Theorists: A Personal View of Twentieth-Century Criticism* (1984; trans. 1987), *On Human Diversity: Nationalism, Racism, and Exoticism in French Thought* (1989; trans. 1993), *The Morals of History* (1991; trans. 1995), *Facing the Extreme: Moral Life in the Concentration Camps* (1991; trans. 1996), *Life in Common: An Essay in General Anthropology* (1995; trans. 2000), and *A Passion for Democracy: Benjamin Constant* (1997; trans. 1999). The autobiography *L'Homme dépaysé* (1996, *Man without a Country*) gives an account of his life and travels.

Todorov's "grammar" of plot remains a touchstone for narrative theory. Gérard Genette's seminal *Narrative Discourse: An Essay in Method* (1972; trans. 1980) builds on some of Todorov's narratological categories. In his useful overview, Jonathan Culler in *Structuralist Poetics: Structuralism, Linguistics, and the Study of Literature* (1975) discusses Todorov as a primary representative of the structural approach to fiction. Gerald Prince's *Narratology: The Form and Functioning of Narrative* (1982) is indebted to Todorov, though it notes the limitations of the grammatical approach. Todorov is a significant actor in François Dosse's *History of Structuralism* (1992; trans. 1997), an excellent account of the major figures and events of the movement. Emma Kafalenos expands on the Propp-Todorov definition of narrative as a disruption of equilibrium; see her contribution to *Narratologies: New Perspectives on Narrative Analysis* (ed. David Herman, 1999). For a comprehensive bibliography of Todorov's work, see David Gorman, "Tzvetan Todorov: An Anglo-French Checklist to 1995," *Style* 31 (1997).

Structural Analysis of Narrative[1]

The theme I propose to deal with is so vast that the few pages which follow will inevitably take the form of a resumé. My title, moreover, contains the word "structural," a word more misleading than enlightening today. To avoid misunderstandings as much as possible, I shall proceed in the following fashion. First, I shall give an abstract description of what I conceive to be the structural approach to literature. This approach will then be illustrated by a concrete problem, that of narrative, and more specifically, that of plot. The examples will all be taken from the *Decameron* of Boccaccio.[2] Finally, I shall attempt to make several general conclusions about the nature of narrative and the principles of its analysis.

First of all, one can contrast two possible attitudes toward literature: a theoretical attitude and a descriptive attitude. The nature of structural analysis will be essentially theoretical and non-descriptive; in other words, the aim of such a study will never be the description of a concrete work. The work will be considered as the manifestation of an abstract structure, merely one of its possible realizations; an understanding of that structure will be the real goal of structural analysis. Thus, the term "structure" has, in this case, a logical rather than spatial significance.

1. Translated by Arnold Weinstein.
2. GIOVANNI BOCCACCIO (1313–1375), Italian writer; the *Decameron* (1351–53), his major achievement, is a collection of 100 tales.

Another opposition will enable us to focus more sharply on the critical position which concerns us. If we contrast the internal approach to a literary work with the external one, structural analysis would represent an internal approach. This opposition is well known to literary critics, and Wellek and Warren have used it as the basis for their *Theory of Literature*.[3] It is necessary, however, to recall it here, because, in labeling all structural analysis "theoretical," I clearly come close to what is generally termed an "external" approach (in imprecise usage, "theoretical" and "external," on the one hand, and "descriptive" and "internal," on the other, are synonyms). For example, when Marxists or psychoanalysts deal with a work of literature, they are not interested in a knowledge of the work itself, but in the understanding of an abstract structure, social or psychic, which manifests itself through that work. This attitude is therefore both theoretical and external. On the other hand, a New Critic[4] (imaginary) whose approach is obviously internal, will have no goal other than an understanding of the work itself; the result of his efforts will be a paraphrase of the work, which is supposed to reveal the meaning better than the work itself.

Structural analysis differs from both of these attitudes. Here we can be satisfied neither by a pure description of the work nor by its interpretation in terms that are psychological or sociological or, indeed, philosophical. In other words, structural analysis coincides (in its basic tenets) with theory, with poetics of literature. Its object is the literary discourse rather than works of literature, literature that is virtual rather than real. Such analysis seeks no longer to articulate a paraphrase, a rational resumé of the concrete work, but to propose a theory of the structure and operation of the literary discourse, to present a spectrum of literary possibilities, in such a manner that the existing works of literature appear as particular instances that have been realized.

It must immediately be added that, in practice, structural analysis will also refer to real works: the best stepping-stone toward theory is that of precise, empirical knowledge. But such analysis will discover in each work what it has in common with others (study of genres, of periods, for example), or even with all other works (theory of literature); it would be unable to state the individual specificity of each work. In practice, it is always a question of going continually back and forth, from abstract literary properties to individual works and vice versa. Poetics and description are in fact two complementary activities.

On the other hand, to affirm the internal nature of this approach does not mean a denial of the relation between literature and other homogeneous series, such as philosophy or social life. It is rather a question of establishing a hierarchy: literature must be understood in its specificity, as literature, before we seek to determine its relation with anything else.

It is easily seen that such a conception of literary analysis owes much to the modern notion of science. It can be said that structural analysis of literature is a kind of propaedeutic[5] for a future science of literature. This term

3. First published in 1949 and for decades a standard introduction to literary criticism; the coauthors, Austrian-born René Wellek (1903–1995) and Austin Warren (1899–1986), were two American literary critics.

4. An adherent of the dominant Anglo-American academic approach to literary study in the mid–20th century, which focuses on the text itself and stresses close reading. Prominent New Critics include CLEANTH BROOKS (1906–1994) and WILLIAM K. WIMSATT JR. (1907–1975); Warren and Wellek were loosely associated with the movement.

5. Analysis preliminary to some other study.

"science," used with regard to literature, usually raises a multitude of protests. It will therefore perhaps be fitting to try to answer some of those protests right now.

Let us first of all reread that page from Henry James's[6] famous essay on "The Art of Fiction," which already contains several criticisms: "Nothing, for instance, is more possible than that he [the novelist] be of a turn of mind for which this odd, literal opposition of description and dialogue, incident and description, has little meaning and light. People often talk of these things as if they had a kind of internecine distinctness, instead of melting into each other at every breath, and being intimately associated parts of one general effort of expression. I cannot imagine composition existing in a series of blocks, nor conceive, in any novel worth discussing at all, of a passage of description that is not in its intention narrative, a passage of dialogue that is not in its intention descriptive, a touch of truth of any sort that does not partake of the nature of incident, or an incident that derives its interest from any other source than the general and only source of the success of a work of art—that of being illustrative. A novel is a living thing, all one and continuous, like any other organism, and in proportion as it lives will it be found, I think, that in each of the parts there is something of each of the other parts. The critic who over the close texture of a finished work shall pretend to trace a geography of items will mark some frontiers as artificial, I fear, as any that have been known to history."

In this excerpt, the critic who uses such terms as "description," "narration," "dialogue," is accused by Henry James of committing two sins. First, there will never be found, in a real text, a pure dialogue, a pure description, and so on. Secondly, the very use of these terms is unnecessary, even harmful, since the novel is "a living thing, all one and continuous."

The first objection loses all its weight as soon as we put ourselves in the perspective of structural analysis; although it does aim at an understanding of concepts like "description" or "action," there is no need to find them in a pure state. It seems rather natural that abstract concepts cannot be analyzed directly, at the level of empirical reality. In physics, for example, we speak of a property such as temperature although we are unable to isolate it by itself and are forced to observe it in bodies possessing many other qualities also, like resistance and volume. Temperature is a theoretical concept, and it does not need to exist in a pure state; such is also true for description.

The second objection is still more curious. Let us consider the already dubious comparison between a work and a living thing. We all know that any part of our body will contain blood, nerves, muscles—all at the same time; we nonetheless do not require the biologist to abandon these misleading abstractions, designated by the words: blood, nerves, muscles. The fact that we find them together does not prevent us from distinguishing them. If the first argument of James had a positive aspect (it indicated that our objective should be composed of abstract categories and not concrete works), the second represents an absolute refusal to recognize the existence of abstract categories, of whatever is not visible.

There is another very popular argument against the introduction of scientific principles in literary analysis. We are told in this instance that science must be objective, whereas the interpretation of literature is always subjec-

6. American novelist and critic (1843–1916); for his programmatic "Art of Fiction" (1884), see above.

tive. In my opinion this crude opposition is untenable. The critic's work can have varying degrees of subjectivity; everything depends on the perspective he has chosen. This degree will be much lower if he tries to ascertain the properties of the work rather than seeking its significance for a given period or milieu. The degree of subjectivity will vary, moreover, when he is examining different strata of the same work. There will be very few discussions concerning the metrical or phonic scheme of a poem; slightly more concerning the nature of its images; still more with regard to the more complex semantic patterns.

On the other hand there is no social science (or science whatsoever) which is totally free of subjectivity. The very choice of one group of theoretical concepts instead of another presupposes a subjective decision; but if we do not make this choice, we achieve nothing at all. The economist, the anthropologist, and the linguist must be subjective also; the only difference is that they are aware of it and they try to limit this subjectivity, to make allowance for it within the theory. One can hardly attempt to repudiate the subjectivity of the social sciences at a time when even the natural sciences are affected by it.

It is now time to stop these theoretical speculations and to give an example of the structural approach to literature. This example will serve as illustration rather than proof: the theories which I have just exposed will not be necessarily contested if there are some imperfections in the concrete analysis based on them.

The abstract literary concept I would like to discuss is that of plot. Of course, that does not mean that literature, for me, is reduced to plot alone. I do think, however, that plot is a notion that critics undervalue and, hence, often disregard. The ordinary reader, however, reads a book above all as the narration of a plot; but this naive reader is uninterested in theoretical problems. My aim is to suggest a certain number of useful categories for examining and describing plots. These categories can thus implement the meager vocabulary at our command with regard to the analysis of narrative; it consists of such terms as action, character, recognition.

The literary examples that I shall use are taken from the *Decameron* of Boccaccio. I do not intend, however, to give an analysis of the *Decameron*: these stories will be used only to display an abstract literary structure, that is, plot. I shall begin by stating the plots of several of the tales.

A monk introduces a young girl into his cell and makes love to her. The abbot detects this misbehavior and plans to punish him severely. But the monk learns of the abbot's discovery and lays a trap for him by leaving his cell. The abbot goes in and succumbs to the charms of the girl, while the monk tries his turn at watching. At the end when the abbot intends to punish him, the monk points out that he has just committed the same sin. Result: the monk is not punished (I,4).[7]

Isabetta, a young nun, is with her lover in her cell. Upon discovering this, the other nuns become jealous and go to wake up the abbess and have Isabetta punished. But the abbess was in bed with an abbot; because she has to come out quickly, she puts the under-shorts of the abbot on her head instead of her coif. Isabetta is led into the church; as the abbess begins to

7. There are 10 characters in the *Decameron*, and each in turn tells one story a day for 10 days; "I,4" refers to the 4th story on the 1st day.

lecture her, Isabetta notices the garment on her head. She brings this evidence to everyone's attention and thus escapes punishment (IX,2).

Peronnella receives her lover while her husband, a poor mason, is absent. But one day he comes home early. Peronnella hides the lover in a cask; when the husband comes in, she tells him that somebody wanted to buy the cask and that this somebody is now in the process of examining it. The husband believes her and is delighted with the sale. The lover pays and leaves with the cask (VII,2).

A married woman meets her lover every night in the family's country house, where she is usually alone. But one night the husband returns from town; the lover has not come yet; he arrives a little later and knocks at the door. The wife asserts that this is a ghost who comes to annoy her every night and must be exorcised. The husband pronounces the formula which the wife has improvised; the lover figures out the situation and leaves, pleased with the ingenuity of his mistress (VII,1).

It is easy to recognize that these four plots (and there are many others like them in the *Decameron*) have something in common. In order to express that, I shall use a schematic formulation which retains only the common elements of these plots. The sign → will indicate a relation of entailment between two actions.

X violates a law → Y must punish X → X tries to avoid being punished →
→ { Y violates a law / Y believes that X is not violating the law } →Y does not punish X

This schematic representation requires several explanations.

1. We first notice that the minimal schema of the plot can be shown naturally by a clause. Between the categories of language and those of narrative there is a profound analogy which must be explored.

2. Analysis of this narrative clause leads us to discover the existence of two entities which correspond to the "parts of speech." a) The agents, designated here by X and Y, correspond to proper nouns. They serve as subject or object of the clause; moreover, they permit identification of their reference without its being described. b) The predicate, which is always a verb here: violate, punish, avoid. The verbs have a semantic characteristic in common: they denote an action which modifies the preceding situation. c) An analysis of other stories would have shown us a third part of narrative speech, which corresponds to quality and does not alter the situation in which it appears: the adjective. Thus in I,8: at the beginning of the action Ermino is stingy, whereas Guillaume is generous. Guillaume finds a way to ridicule Ermino's stinginess, and since then Ermino is "the most generous and pleasant of gentlemen." The qualities of the two characters are examples of adjectives.

3. Actions (violate, punish) can have a positive or a negative form; thus, we shall also need the category of status, negation being one possible status.

4. The category of modality[8] is also relevant here. When we say "X must punish Y," we denote thereby an action which has not yet taken place (in the imaginary universe of the story) but which is nonetheless present in a virtual state. André Jolles[9] suggested that entire genres could be character-

8. That is, the determination of whether a sentence expresses a fact, a command, a wish, and so on, as set by the form (the mood) of the verb and its auxiliaries.

9. Dutch literary and art historian (1874–1946); the reference is to his *Einfache Formen* (1930, *Simple Forms*).

ized by their mood; legends would be the genre of the imperative, to the extent that they offer us an example to follow; the fairy tale is, as is often said, the genre of the optative, of the fulfilled wish.

5. When we write "Y believes that X is not violating the law," we have an example of a verb ("believe") which differs from the others. It is not a question of a different action here but of a different perception of the same action. We could therefore speak of a kind of "point of view" which refers not only to the relation between reader and narrator, but also to the characters.

6. There are also relations between the clauses; in our example this is always a causal relation; but a more extensive study would distinguish at least between entailment and presupposition (for example, the relation introducing modal punishment). Analysis of other stories shows that there are also purely temporal relations (succession) and purely spatial ones (parallelism).

7. An organized succession of clauses forms a new syntagmatic pattern,[1] sequence. Sequence is perceived by the reader as a finished story; it is the minimal narrative in a completed form. This impression of completion is caused by a modified repetition of the initial clause; the first and the last clause will be identical but they will either have a different mood or status, for instance, or they will be seen from different points of view. In our example it is punishment which is repeated: first changed in modality, then denied. In a sequence of temporal relations, repetition can be total.

8. We might also ask: is there a way back? How does one get from the abstract, schematic representation to the individual tale? Here, there are three answers:

a) The same kind of organization can be studied at a more concrete level: each clause of our sequence could be rewritten as an entire sequence itself. We would not thereby change the nature of the analysis, but rather the level of generality.

b) It is also possible to study the concrete actions that incorporate our abstract pattern. For instance, we may point out the different laws that become violated in the stories of the *Decameron* or the different punishments that are meted out. That would be a thematic study.

c) Finally, we can examine the verbal medium which composes our abstract patterns. The same action can be expressed by means of dialogue or description, figurative or literal discourse; moreover, each action can be seen from a different point of view. Here we are dealing with a rhetorical study.

These three directions correspond to the three major categories of narrative analysis: study of narrative syntax, study of theme, study of rhetoric.

At this point we may ask: what is the purpose of all this? Has this analysis taught us anything about the stories in question? But that would be a bad question. Our goal is not a knowledge of the *Decameron* (although such analysis will also serve that purpose), but rather an understanding of literature or, in this specific instance, of plot. The categories of plot mentioned here will permit a more extensive and precise description of other plots. The

1. The relationship between linguistic items that combine to form a meaningful whole (e.g., the words in a given sentence); in contrast, paradigmatic relationships obtain between items that can be substituted for one another in a given context (e.g., two adverbs).

object of our study must be narrative mood, or point of view, or sequence, and not this or that story in and for itself.

From such categories we can move forward and inquire about the possibility of a typology of plots. For the moment it is difficult to offer a valid hypothesis; therefore I must be content to summarize the results of my research on the *Decameron*.

The minimal complete plot can be seen as the shift from one equilibrium to another. This term "equilibrium," which I am borrowing from genetic psychology, means the existence of a stable but not static relation between the members of a society; it is a social law, a rule of the game, a particular system of exchange. The two moments of equilibrium, similar and different, are separated by a period of imbalance, which is composed of a process of degeneration and a process of improvement.

All of the stories of the *Decameron* can be entered into this very broad schema. From that point, however, we can make a distinction between two kinds of stories. The first can be labeled "avoided punishment"; the four stories I mentioned at the beginning are examples of it. Here we follow a complete cycle: we begin with a state of equilibrium which is broken by a violation of the law. Punishment would have restored the initial balance; the fact that punishment is avoided establishes a new equilibrium.

The other type of story is illustrated by the tale about Ermino (I,8), which we may label "conversion." This story begins in the middle of a complete cycle, with a state of imbalance created by a flaw in one of the characters. The story is basically the description of an improvement process—until the flaw is no longer there.

The categories which help us to describe these types tell us much about the universe of a book. With Boccaccio, the two equilibriums symbolize (for the most part) culture and nature,[2] the social and the individual; the story usually consists in illustrating the superiority of the second term over the first.

We could also seek even greater generalizations. It is possible to contrast a specific plot typology with a game typology and to see them as two variants of a common structure. So little has been done in this direction that we do not even know what kinds of questions to ask.

I would like to return now to the beginning argument and to look at the initial question again: what is the object of structural analysis of literature (or, if you wish, of poetics)? At first glance, it is literature or, as Jakobson[3] would have said, literariness. But let us look more closely. In our discussion of literary phenomena, we have had to introduce a certain number of notions and to create an image of literature; this image constitutes the constant preoccupation of all research on poetics. "Science is concerned not with things but with the system of signs it can substitute for things," wrote Ortega y Gasset.[4] The virtualities which make up the object of poetics (as of all other sciences), these abstract qualities of literature exist only in the discourse of poetics itself. From this perspective, literature becomes only a mediator, a language, which poetics uses for dealing with itself.

2. The opposition between nature and culture is foundational in structuralism, notably in the work of the French anthropologist CLAUDE LÉVI-STRAUSS (b. 1908).

3. ROMAN JAKOBSON (1896–1982), Russian-born American linguist and literary theorist.

4. José Ortega y Gasset (1883–1955), Spanish philosopher and critic.

We must not, however, conclude that literature is secondary for poetics or that it is not, in a certain sense, the object of poetics. Science is characterized precisely by this ambiguity concerning its object, an ambiguity that need not be resolved, but rather used as the basis for analysis. Poetics, like literature, consists of an uninterrupted movement back and forth between the two poles: the first is auto-reference, preoccupation with itself; the second is what we usually call its object.

There is a practical conclusion to be drawn from these speculations. In poetics as elsewhere, discussions of methodology are not a minor area of the larger field, a kind of accidental by-product: they are rather its very center, its principal goal. As Freud[5] said, "The important thing in a scientific work is not the nature of the facts with which it is concerned, but the rigor, the exactness of the method which is prior to the establishment of these facts, and the research of a synthesis as large as possible."

1969

5. SIGMUND FREUD (1856–1939), Austrian founder of psychoanalysis.

PAULA GUNN ALLEN
b. 1939

"What I'm really attempting to do is affect feminist thinking," Paula Gunn Allen remarked in an interview for *MELUS* in 1982. In this she joins African American theorists like BELL HOOKS and third-world feminist critics like GLORIA ANZALDÚA in criticizing a feminist movement that has been predominantly white and middle class: "my white sisters—and they have influenced the Black and Asian and Chicano sisters—have given the impression that women have always been held down, have always been weak, and have always been persecuted by men, but I know that's not true. I come from a people that that is not true of." Allen approaches feminist theory from the unique perspective of Native American culture; her speculations about the existence of woman-centered societies, societies that were matrilocal, matrifocal, matrilineal, and egalitarian, supplement feminism's focus on women's oppression. More important, however, her rigorous and imaginative critique of Eurocentric critical methods, especially as they are applied to the transmission, translation, and interpretation of Native American oral texts, highlights the difficulties of reading Native American literature in a white European context without either trivializing or romanticizing the culture that produced it.

Paula Gunn Allen was born in Cubero, New Mexico, a Spanish land-grant town near Laguna Pueblo. Allen's mother is Laguna-Sioux; her father is Lebanese American. Both are natives of New Mexico. As a child Allen received her education from mission and convent schools. She received a B.A. in English literature in 1966 and an M.F.A. in creative writing in 1968, both from the University of Oregon. She did not intend to enter the field of Native American studies, but she was asked to teach in the newly formed Native American Studies Program at the University of New Mexico; there she earned her Ph.D. in American Indian studies (1975). After holding a postdoctoral fellowship at the University of California at Los Angeles, she moved to the University of California at Berkeley, where she received a fellowship to research the oral tradition in Native American literature. She has taught at numerous schools, including San Diego State University, San Francisco State University, the University of New Mexico, and the University of California at Berkeley. She now teaches English and Native American studies at UCLA.

"Kochinnenako in Academe: Three Approaches to Interpreting a Keres Indian Tale," our selection from Allen's *Sacred Hoop: Recovering the Feminine in American Indian Traditions* (1986), is a revealing investigation of the effects that cultural expectations have on translation, narrative structures, and interpretive strategies. In exploring the translation made by her mother's uncle, John M. Gunn, of a traditional oral Kochinnenako (or Yellow Woman) story of the Laguna Acoma Keres, Allen demonstrates that translations are never innocent: they are invariably marked by cultural biases so ingrained as to be virtually unconscious. Acting as an anthropologist recording the oral traditions of a foreign culture, John Gunn was anything but a neutral observer simply recording what his informants told him. His translation imposes on the Keres tale a formal plot structure that it lacks. This narrative structure, Allen argues, is necessary to make the tale coherent for a European audience, but it adds sexist, racist, and violent plot details that distort the original, transforming the tale from a ritual enactment of the metamorphosis of winter into spring into a conflict-centered patriarchal narrative involving the familiar rivalry of two powerful men over possession of a woman (the sort of triangle EVE KOSOFSKY SEDGWICK describes in *Between Men*, 1985, as characteristic of Western narrative).

Allen offers three revisionary readings of John Gunn's tale, all of which shed light on contemporary debates about the status of interpretation. The first is a traditional tribal interpretation in which the tale is not a narrative at all, but a ritual enacted every year to represent the transformation of winter into summer through the agency of a woman (Yellow Woman). This ritual was a traditional mechanism for balancing and exchanging political power between two divisions—or moieties—of the tribe. The second reading is a feminist interpretation that, while it is also distorted by Eurocentric assumptions about native cultures, reads the tale as an allegory of colonialism: the defeat of the aggressive white colonizer by the rebel (Miochin) who acts in the best interests of the people. This reading exhorts women to become involved in the struggle to overthrow colonial powers. In a third reading, which attempts to synthesize the other two, Allen offers a "tribal-feminist" account that both reveals the Western colonial context of the tale and underscores the central role played by women in the life of the tribe.

A reader's allegiance to a particular mode of interpretation, she argues, shapes the formal structure of the tale and either asserts or denies women's agency within tribal culture. Allen demonstrates that the formal tools and strategies developed for reading European narrative are inadequate guides to understanding Native American literature. While she is no interpretive pluralist, Allen explores in this essay the ways in which "interpretive communities," especially cultural communities, shape readers' understanding of narrative, a topic also examined by STANLEY FISH.

The most salient influence on Allen's criticism is her own tribal heritage, and in this regard she has affinities with Native American critics like GERALD VIZENOR. But she also draws from and interrogates several other influential critical approaches, including ethnographic studies of Native American tales such as those of the anthropologists Franz Boas (1858–1942) and Ruth Benedict (1887–1948). In addition, she writes with and against feminist theory—drawing on feminist insights, for instance, about the difference between men's and women's art, but criticizing the movement's Eurocentrism, a position she shares with theorists of colonialism and postcolonialism (see GAYATRI CHAKRAVORTY SPIVAK and HOMI BHABHA). "Kochinnenako in Academe" develops a subtle critique of the structuralist assumptions of anthropological critics like CLAUDE LÉVI-STRAUSS (b. 1908), who claims that there are universal structures of narrative on which all mythologies draw. Instead, Allen argues, formal narrative structures depend on specific historical contexts. Whatever universality structuralist critics impute to Native American tales results from the imposition of familiar narrative structures that enable colonial readers to understand the colonized culture.

Ironically, however, Allen seems to be claiming a kind of universality when she argues that women writers share with tribal cultures a common "female" approach to narrative that is accretive, achronological, and "dependent on harmonizing relationships of all elements within a field of perception." She appears to be describing in this statement a kind of *écriture féminine*, a feminine or female writing (see HÉLÈNE CIXOUS), that the rest of her essay belies. While it is possible (and even productive) to argue that some female arts, such as quilting, rely on artistic values that differ from those of elite European art, it is hard to see how Allen can claim that women share a narrative style different from that of elite Western men without arguing for biological essentialism or a common oppression—yet she explicitly denies both. Such an assertion of commonality would obscure European women's complicity in the appropriation of tribal cultures under colonialism. Despite this apparent contradiction, "Kochinnenako in Academe" provides feminist criticism with a pointed critique of certain key Eurocentric assumptions that sustain most narrative theory (including feminist theories of narrative).

BIBLIOGRAPHY

Allen is the author of five volumes of poetry and a novel. Her literary criticism includes *Studies in American Indian Literature: Critical Essays and Course Designs* (1983), which was among the first texts on the teaching of Native American literature, and *The Sacred Hoop: Recovering the Feminine in American Indian Traditions* (1986), a collection of seventeen essays on topics ranging from the status of lesbians in Native American culture to the relationship between narrative structure and ritual in Native American tales. In 1989 she edited *Spider Woman's Granddaughters: Traditional Tales and Contemporary Writing by Native American Women*. A number of interviews with Allen that have appeared in print shed light on her life and work: in *MELUS* 10 (1983); in a collection titled *Survival This Way: Interviews with American Indian Poets* (ed. Joseph Bruchac, 1987); in *North Dakota Quarterly* 57 (1989); and in *Studies in American Indian Literature* 9.3 (1997). Elizabeth I. Hanson's monograph *Paula Gunn Allen* (1990) is a useful introduction to Allen's fiction and critical writing. AnaLouise Keating examines the relationships among Allen and two other ethnic American women writers in *Women Reading Women Writing: Self-Invention in Paula Gunn Allen, Gloria Anzaldúa, and Audre Lord* (1993). Bibliographical and biographical information can be found in Annette VanDyke's essay on Allen in *Contemporary Lesbian Writers of the United States: A Bio-Bibliographic Critical Sourcebook* (ed. Sandra Pollack and Denise D. Knight, 1993).

Kochinnenako in Academe: Three Approaches to Interpreting a Keres Indian Tale

I became engaged in studying feminist thought and theory when I was first studying and teaching American Indian literature in the early 1970s. Over the ensuing fifteen years, my own stances toward both feminist and American Indian life and thought have intertwined as they have unfolded. I have always included feminist content and perspectives in my teaching of American Indian subjects, though at first the mating was uneasy at best. My determination that both areas were interdependent and mutually significant to a balanced pedagogy of American Indian studies led me to grow into an approach to both that is best described as tribal-feminism or feminist-tribalism. Both terms are applicable: if I am dealing with feminism, I approach it from a strongly tribal posture, and when I am dealing with American Indian literature, history, culture, or philosophy I approach it from a strongly feminist one.

A feminist approach to the study and teaching of American Indian life and thought is essential because the area has been dominated by paternalistic, male-dominant modes of consciousness since the first writings about American Indians in the fifteenth century. This male bias has seriously skewed our understanding of tribal life and philosophy, distorting it in ways that are sometimes obvious but are most often invisible.

Often what appears to be a misinterpretation caused by racial differences is a distortion based on sexual politics. When the patriarchal paradigm that characterizes western thinking is applied to gynecentric[1] tribal modes, it transforms the ideas, significances, and raw data into something that is not only unrecognizable to the tribes but entirely incongruent with their philosophies and theories. We know that materials and interpretations amassed by the white intellectual establishment are in error, but we have not pinpointed the major sources of that error. I believe that a fundamental source has been male bias and that feminist theory, when judiciously applied to the field, makes the error correctible, freeing the data for reinterpretation that is at least congruent with a tribal perceptual mode.

To demonstrate the interconnections between tribal and feminist approaches as I use them in my work, I have developed an analysis of a traditional Kochinnenako, or Yellow Woman story of the Laguna-Acoma Keres, as recast by my mother's uncle John M. Gunn in his book *Schat Chen*.[2] My analysis utilizes three approaches and demonstrates the relationship of context to meaning, illuminating three consciousness styles and providing students with a traditionally tribal, nonracist, feminist understanding of traditional and contemporary American Indian life.

Some Theoretical Considerations

Analyzing tribal cultural systems from a mainstream feminist point of view allows an otherwise overlooked insight into the complex interplay of factors that have led to the systematic loosening of tribal ties, the disruption of tribal cohesion and complexity, and the growing disequilibrium of cultures that were anciently based on a belief in balance, relationship, and the centrality of women, particularly elder women. A feminist approach reveals not only the exploitation and oppression of the tribes by whites and white government but also areas of oppression within the tribes and the sources and nature of

1. Woman-centered [editor's note; except as indicated, all notes are Allen's].

2. John M. Gunn, *Schat Chen: History, Traditions and Narratives of the Queres Indians of Laguna and Acoma* (1917 reprint, New York: AMS, 1977). Gunn, my mother's uncle, lived among the Lagunas all his adult life. He spoke Laguna (Keres) and gathered information in somewhat informal ways while sitting in the sun visiting with older people. He married Meta Atseye, my great-grandmother, years after her husband (John Gunn's brother) died and may have taken much of his information from her stories or explanations of Laguna ceremonial events. She had a way of "translating" terms and concepts from Keres into English and from a Laguna conceptual framework into an American one, as she understood it. For example, she used to refer to the Navajo people as "gypsies," probably because they traveled in covered wagons and the women wear long, full skirts and head scarves and both men and women wear a great deal of jewelry.

that oppression. To a large extent, such an analysis can provide strategies for ameliorating the effects of patriarchal colonialism enabling many of the tribes to reclaim their ancient gynarchical,[3] egalitarian, and sacred traditions.

At the present time, American Indians in general are not comfortable with feminist analysis or action within the reservation or urban Indian enclaves. Many Indian women are uncomfortable with feminism because they perceive it (correctly) as white-dominated. They (not so correctly) believe it is concerned with issues that have little bearing on their own lives. They are also uncomfortable with it because they have been reared in an anglophobic world that views white society with fear and hostility. But because of their fear of and bitterness toward whites and their consequent unwillingness to examine the dynamics of white socialization, American Indian women often overlook the central areas of damage done to tribal tradition by white Christian and secular patriarchal dominance. Militant and "progressive" American Indian men are even more likely to quarrel with feminism; they have benefited in certain ways from white male-centeredness, and while those benefits are of real danger to the tribes, the individual rewards are compelling.

It is within the context of growing violence against women and the concomitant lowering of our status among Native Americans that I teach and write. Certainly I could not locate the mechanisms of colonization that have led to the virulent rise of woman-hating among American Indian men (and, to a certain extent, among many of the women) without a secure and determined feminism. Just as certainly, feminist theory applied to my literary studies clarifies a number of issues for me, including the patriarchal bias that has been systematically imposed on traditional literary materials and the mechanism by which that bias has affected contemporary American Indian life, thought, and culture.

The oral tradition is more than a record of a people's culture. It is the creative source of their collective and individual selves. When that wellspring of identity is tampered with, the sense of self is also tampered with; and when that tampering includes the sexist and classist assumptions of the white world within the body of an Indian tradition, serious consequences necessarily ensue.

The oral tradition is a living body. It is in continuous flux, which enables it to accommodate itself to the real circumstances of a people's lives. That is its strength, but it is also its weakness, for when a people finds itself living within a racist, classist, and sexist reality, the oral tradition will reflect those values and will thus shape the people's consciousness to include and accept racism, classism and sexism, and they will incorporate that change, hardly noticing the shift. If the oral tradition is altered in certain subtle, fundamental ways, if elements alien to it are introduced so that its internal coherence is disturbed, it becomes the major instrument of colonization and oppression.

Such alterations have occurred and are still occurring. Those who translate or "render" narratives make certain crucial changes, many unconscious. The cultural bias of the translator inevitably shapes his or her perception of the materials being translated, often in ways that he or she is unaware of. Culture

3. In a system where all persons in power are called Mother Chief and where the supreme deity is female, and social organization is matrilocal, matrifocal, and matrilineal, gynarchy is happening. However, it does not imply domination of men by women as patriarchy implies domination by ruling class males of all aspects of a society.

is fundamentally a shaper of perception, after all, and perception is shaped by culture in many subtle ways. In short, it's hard to see the forest when you're a tree. To a great extent, changes in materials translated from a tribal to a western language are a result of the vast difference in languages; certain ideas and concepts that are implicit in the structure of an Indian language are not possible in English. Language embodies the unspoken assumptions and orientations of the culture it belongs to. So while the problem is one of translation, it is not simply one of word equivalence. The differences are perceptual and contextual as much as verbal.

Sometimes the shifts are contextual; indeed, both the context and content usually are shifted, sometimes subtly, sometimes blatantly. The net effect is a shifting of the whole axis of the culture. When shifts of language and context are coupled with the almost infinite changes occasioned by Christianization, secularization, economic dislocation from subsistence to industrial modes, destruction of the wilderness and associated damage to the biota, much that is changed goes unnoticed or unremarked by the people being changed. This is not to suggest that Native Americans are unaware of the enormity of the change they have been forced to undergo by the several centuries of white presence, but much of that change is at deep and subtle levels that are not easily noted or resisted.

John Gunn received the story I am using here from a Keres-speaking informant and translated it himself. The story, which he titles "Sh-ah-cock and Miochin or the Battle of the Seasons," is in reality a narrative version of a ritual. The ritual brings about the change of season and of moiety among the Keres.[4] Gunn doesn't mention this, perhaps because he was interested in stories and not in religion or perhaps because his informant did not mention the connection to him.

What is interesting about his rendering is his use of European, classist, conflict-centered patriarchal assumptions as plotting devices. These interpolations dislocate the significance of the tale and subtly alter the ideational context of woman-centered, largely pacifist people whose ritual story this is. I have developed three critiques of the tale as it appears in his book, using feminist and tribal understandings to discuss the various meanings of the story when it is read from three different perspectives.

In the first reading, I apply tribal understanding to the story. In the second, I apply the sort of feminist perspective I applied to traditional stories, historical events, traditional culture, and contemporary literature when I began developing a feminist perspective. The third reading applies what I call a feminist-tribal perspective. Each analysis is somewhat less detailed than it might be; but as I am interested in describing modes of perception and their impact on our understanding of cultural artifacts (and by extension our understanding of people who come from different cultural contexts than our own) rather than critiquing a story, they are adequate.

Yellow Woman Stories

The Keres of Laguna and Acoma Pueblos in New Mexico have stories that are called Yellow Woman stories. The themes and to a large extent the motifs

4. Native American tribes that are matrilineal and matrifocal are politically organized into two principal classes called *moieties* (further divided into clans and families, which in turn share primacy of power) [editor's note].

of these stories are always female-centered, always told from Yellow Woman's point of view. Some older recorded versions of Yellow Woman tales (as in Gunn) make Yellow Woman the daughter of the hocheni. Gunn translates *hocheni* as "ruler." But Keres notions of the hocheni's function and position are as cacique or Mother Chief, which differ greatly from Anglo-European ideas of rulership. However, for Gunn to render *hocheni* as "ruler" is congruent with the European folktale tradition.[5]

Kochinnenako, Yellow Woman, is in some sense a name that means Woman-Woman because among the Keres, yellow is the color for women (as pink and red are among Anglo-European Americans), and it is the color ascribed to the Northwest. Keres women paint their faces yellow on certain ceremonial occasions and are so painted at death so that the guardian at the gate of the spirit world, Naiya Iyatiku (Mother Corn Woman), will recognize that the newly arrived person is a woman. It is also the name of a particular Irriaku, Corn Mother (sacred corn-ear bundle), and Yellow Woman stories in their original form detail rituals in which the Irriaku figures prominently.

Yellow Woman stories are about all sorts of things—abduction, meeting with happy powerful spirits, birth of twins, getting power from the spirit worlds and returning it to the people, refusing to marry, weaving, grinding corn, getting water, outsmarting witches, eluding or escaping from malintentioned spirits, and more. Yellow Woman's sisters are often in the stories (Blue, White, and Red Corn) as is Grandmother Spider and her helper Spider Boy, the Sun God or one of his aspects, Yellow Woman's twin sons, witches, magicians, gamblers, and mothers-in-law.

Many Yellow Woman tales highlight her alienation from the people: she lives with her grandmother at the edge of the village, for example, or she is in some way atypical, maybe a woman who refuses to marry, one who is known for some particular special talent, or one who is very quick-witted and resourceful. In many ways Kochinnenako is a role model, though she possesses some behaviors that are not likely to occur in many of the women who hear her stories. She is, one might say, the Spirit of Woman.

The stories do not necessarily imply that difference is punishable; on the contrary, it is often her very difference that makes her special adventures possible, and these adventures often have happy outcomes for Kochinnenako and for her people. This is significant among a people who value conformity and propriety above almost anything. It suggests that the behavior of women, at least at certain times or under certain circumstances, must be improper or nonconformist for the greater good of the whole. Not that all the stories are graced with a happy ending. Some come to a tragic conclusion, some-

5. His use of the term may reflect the use by his informants, who were often educated in Carlisle or Menaul Indian schools, in their attempt to find an equivalent term that Gunn could understand to signify the deep respect and reverence accorded the hocheni tyi'a'muni. Or he might have selected the term because he was writing a book for an anonymous non-Keres audience, which included himself. Since he spoke Laguna Keres, I think he was doing the translations himself, and his renderings of words (and contexts) was likely influenced by the way Lagunas themselves rendered local terms into English. I doubt, however, that he was conscious of the extent to which his renderings reflected European traditions and simultaneously distorted Laguna-Acoma ones.

Gunn was deeply aware of the importance and intelligence of the Keresan tradition, but he was also unable to grant it independent existence. His major impulse was to link the western Keres with the Sumerians, to in some strange way demonstrate the justice of his assessment of their intelligence. An unpublished manuscript in my possession written by John Gunn after *Schat Chen* is devoted to his researches and speculations into this idea.

times resulting from someone's inability to follow the rules or perform a ritual in the proper way.

Other Kochinnenako stories are about her centrality to the harmony, balance, and prosperity of the tribe. "Sh-ah-cock and Miochin" is one of these stories. John Gunn prefaces the narrative with the comment that while the story is about a battle, war stories are rarely told by the Keres because they are not "a war like people" and "very rarely refer to their exploits in war."

Sh-ah-cock and Miochin or the Battle of the Seasons

In the Kush-kut-ret-u-nah-tit (white village of the north) was once a ruler by the name of Hut-cha-mun-Ki-uk (the broken prayer stick), one of whose daughters, Ko-chin-ne-nako, became the bride of Sh-ah-cock (the spirit of winter), a person of very violent temper. He always manifested his presence by blizzards of snow or sleet or by freezing cold, and on account of his alliance with the ruler's daughter, he was most of the time in the vicinity of Kush-kut-ret, and as these manifestations continued from month to month and year to year, the people of Kush-kut-ret found that their crops would not mature, and finally they were compelled to subsist on the leaves of the cactus.

On one occasion Ko-chin-ne-nako had wandered a long way from home in search of the cactus and had gathered quite a bundle and was preparing to carry home by singeing off the thorns, when on looking up she found herself confronted by a very bold but handsome young man. His attire attracted her gaze at once. He wore a shirt of yellow woven from the silks of corn, a belt made from the broad green blades of the same plant, a tall pointed hat made from the same kind of material and from the top which waved a yellow corn tassel. He wore green leggings woven from kow-e-nuh, the green stringy moss that forms in springs and ponds. His moccasins were beautifully embroidered with flowers and butterflies. In his hand he carried an ear of green corn.

His whole appearance proclaimed him a stranger and as Ko-chin-ne-nako gaped in wonder, he spoke to her in a very pleasing voice asking her what she was doing. She told him that on account of the cold and drouth, the people of Kush-kut-ret were forced to eat the leaves of the cactus to keep from starving.

"Here," said the young man, handing her the ear of green corn. "Eat this and I will go and bring more that you may take home with you."

He left her soon and disappeared going towards the south. In a short time he returned bringing with him a big load of green corn. Ko-chin-ne-nako asked him where he had gathered corn and if it grew near by. "No," he replied, "it is from my home far away to the south, where the corn grows and the flowers bloom all the year around. Would you not like to accompany me back to my country?" Ko-chin-ne-nako replied that his home must be very beautiful, but that she could not go with him because she was the wife of Sh-ah-cock. And then she told him of her alliance with the Spirit of Winter, and admitted that her husband was very cold and disagreeable and that she did not love him. The strange young man urged her to go with him to the warm land of the south, saying that he did not fear Sh-ah-cock. But Ko-chin-ne-nako would not consent. So the stranger directed her to return to her home with the corn he had brought and cautioned her not to throw away any of the husks out of the door. Upon leaving he said to her, "you must meet me at this place tomorrow. I will bring more corn for you."

Ko-chin-ne-nako had not proceeded far on her homeward way ere she met her sisters who, having become uneasy because of her long absence, had come in search of her. They were greatly surprised at seeing her with an armful of corn instead of cactus. Ko-chin-ne-nako told them the whole story of how she had obtained it, and thereby only added wonderment to their surprise. They helped her to carry the corn home; and there she again had to tell her story to her father and mother.

When she had described the stranger even from his peaked hat to his butterfly moccasins, and had told them that she was to meet him again on the day following, Hut-cha-mun Ki-uk, the father, exclaimed:

"It is Mi-o-chin!"

"It is Mi-o-chin! It is Mi-o-chin!," echoed the mother. "Tomorrow you must bring him home with you."

The next day Ko-chin-ne-nako went again to the spot where she had met Mi-o-chin, for it was indeed Mi-o-chin, the Spirit of Summer. He was already there, awaiting her coming. With him he had brought a huge bundle of corn.

Ko-chin-ne-nako pressed upon him the invitation of her parents to accompany her home, so together they carried the corn to Kush-kut-ret. When it had been distributed there was sufficient to feed all the people of the city. Amid great rejoicing and thanksgiving, Mi-o-chin was welcomed at the Hotchin's (ruler's) house.

In the evening, as was his custom, Sh-ah-cock, the Spirit of the Winter, returned to his home. He came in a blinding storm of snow and hail and sleet, for he was in a boisterous mood. On approaching the city, he felt within his bones that Mi-o-chin was there, so he called in a loud and blustering voice:

"Ha! Mi-o-chin, are you here?"

For answer, Mi-o-chin advanced to meet him.

Then Sh-ah-cock, beholding him, called again,

"Ha! Mi-o-chin, I will destroy you."

"Ha! Sh-ah-cock, I will destroy you," replied Mi-o-chin, still advancing.

Sh-ah-cock paused, irresolute. He was covered from head to foot with frost (skah). Icycles [*sic*] (ya-pet-tu-ne) draped him round. The fierce, cold wind proceeded from his nostrils.

As Mi-o-chin drew near, the wintry wind changed to a warm summer breeze. The frost and icycles melted and displayed beneath them, the dry, bleached bulrushes (ska-ra-ru-ka) in which Sh-ah-cock was clad.

Seeing that he was doomed to defeat, Sh-ah-cock cried out:

"I will not fight you now, for we cannot try our powers. We will make ready, and in four days from this time, we will meet here and fight for supremacy. The victor shall claim Ko-chin-ne-nako for his wife."

With this, Sh-ah-cock withdrew in rage. The wind again roared and shook the very houses; but the people were warm within them, for Mi-o-chin was with them.

The next day Mi-o-chin left Kush-kut-ret for his home in the south. Arriving there, he began to make his preparations to meet Sh-ah-cock in battle.

First he sent an eagle as a messenger to his friend, Ya-chun-ne-ne-moot (kind of shaley rock that becomes very hot in the fire), who lived in the west, requesting him to come and help to battle Sh-ah-cock. Then he called together the birds and the four legged animals—all those that live in sunny climes. For his advance guard and shield he selected the bat (pickikke), as its tough skin would best resist the sleet and hail that Sh-ah-cock would hurl at him.

Meantime Sh-ah-cock had gone to his home in the north to make his preparations for battle. To his aid he called all the winter birds and all of the four legged animals of the wintry climates. For his advance guard and shield he selected Shro-ak-ah (a magpie).

When these formidable forces had been mustered by the rivals, they advanced Mi-o-chin from the south and Sh-ah-cock from the north, in battle array.

Ya-chun-ne-ne-moot kindled his fires and piled great heaps of resinous fuel upon them until volumes of steam and smoke ascended, forming enormous clouds that hurried forward toward Kush-kut-ret and the battle ground. Upon these clouds rode Mi-o-chin, the Spirit of Summer, and his vast army. All the animals of the army, encountering the smoke from Ya-chun-ne-ne-moot's fires, were colored by the smoke so that, from that day, the animals from the south have been black or brown in color.

Sh-ah-cock and his army came out of the north in a howling blizzard and borne forward on black storm clouds driven by a freezing wintry wind. As he came on, the lakes and rivers over which he passed were frozen and the air was filled with blinding sleet.

When the combatants drew near to Kush-kut-ret, they advanced with fearful rapidity. Their arrival upon the field was marked by fierce and terrific strife.

Flashes of lightning darted from Mi-o-chin's clouds. Striking the animals of Sh-ah-cock, they singed the hair upon them, and turned it white, so that, from that day, the animals from the north have worn a covering of white or have white markings upon them.

From the south, the black clouds still rolled upward, the thunder spoke again and again. Clouds of smoke and vapor rushed onward, melting the snow and ice weapons of Sh-ah-cock and compelling him, at length, to retire from the field. Mi-o-chin, assured of victory, pursued him. To save himself from total defeat and destruction, Sh-ah-cock called for armistice.

This being granted on the part of Mi-o-chin, the rivals met at Kush-kut-ret to arrange the terms of the treaty. Sh-ah-cock acknowledged himself defeated. He consented to give up Ko-chin-ne-nako to Mi-o-chin. This concession was received with rejoicing by Ko-chin-ne-nako and all the people of Kush-kut-ret.

> It was then agreed between the late combatants that, for all time thereafter, Mi-o-chin was to rule at Kush-kut-ret during one-half of the year, and Sh-ah-cock was to rule during the remaining half, and that neither should molest the other.[6]

John Gunn's version has a formal plot structure that makes the account seem to be a narrative. But had he translated it directly from the Keres, even in "narrative" form, as in a storytelling session, its ritual nature would have been clearer.

I can only surmise about how the account might go if it were done that way, basing my ideas on renderings of Keres rituals in narrative forms I am acquainted with. But a direct translation from the Keres would have sounded more like the following than like Gunn's rendition of it:

> Long ago. Eh. There in the North. Yellow Woman. Up northward she went. Then she picked burrs and cactus. Then here went Summer. From the south he came. Above there he arrived. Thus spoke Summer. "Are you here? How is it going?" said Summer. "Did you come here?" thus said Yellow Woman. Then answered Yellow Woman. "I pick these poor things because I am hungry." "Why do you not eat corn and melons?" asked Summer. Then he gave her some corn and melons. "Take it!" Then thus spoke Yellow Woman, "It is good. Let us go. To my house I take you." "Is not your husband there?" "No. He went hunting deer. Today at night he will come back."
>
> Then in the north they arrived. In the west they went down. Arrived then they in the east. "Are you here?" Remembering Prayer Sticks said. "Yes" Summer said. "How is it going?" Summer said. Then he said, "Your daughter Yellow Woman, she brought me here." "Eh. That is good." Thus spoke Remembering Prayer Sticks.

The story would continue, with many of the elements contained in Gunn's version but organized along the axis of directions, movement of the participants, their maternal relationships to each other (daughter, mother, mother chief, etc.), and events sketched in only as they pertained to directions and the division of the year into its ritual/ceremonial segments, one belonging to the Kurena (summer supernaturals or powers who are connected to the summer people or clans) and the other belonging to the Kashare, perhaps in conjunction with the Kopishtaya, the Spirits.

Summer, Miochin, is the Shiwana who lives on the south mountain, and Sh-ah-cock is the Shiwana who lives on the north mountain.[7] It is interesting to note that the Kurena wear three eagle feathers and ctc'otika' feathers (white striped) on their heads, bells, and woman's dress and carry a reed flute, which perhaps is connected with Iyatiku's sister, Istoakoa, Reed Woman.

6. Gunn, *Schat Chen*, pp. 217–22.

7. Franz Boas, *Keresan Texts*, Publications of the American Ethnological Society, vol. 8, pt. 1 (New York: American Ethnological Society, 1928), writes, "The second and the fourth of the shiwana appear in the tale of summer and winter . . . Summer wears a shirt of buckskin with squash ornaments, shoes like moss to which parrot feathers are tied. His face is painted with red mica and flowers are tied on to it . . . Winter wears a shirt of icicles and his shoes are like ice. His shirt is shiny and to its end are tied turkey feathers and eagle feathers" (p. 284).

A KERES INTERPRETATION

When a traditional Keres reads the tale of Kochinnenako, she listens with certain information about her people in mind: she knows, for example, that Hutchamun Kiuk (properly it means Remembering Prayer Sticks, though Gunn translates it as Broken Prayer Sticks)[8] refers to the ritual (sacred) identity of the cacique and that the story is a narrative version of a ceremony related to the planting of corn. She knows that Lagunas and Acomas don't have rulers in the Anglo-European sense of monarchs, lords, and such (though they do, in recent times, have elected governors, but that's another matter), and that a person's social status is determined by her mother's clan and position in it rather than by her relationship to the cacique as his daughter. (Actually, in various accounts, the cacique refers to Yellow Woman as his mother, so the designation of her as his daughter is troublesome unless one is aware that relationships in the context of their ritual significance are being delineated here.)

In any case, our hypothetical Keres reader also knows that the story is about a ritual that takes place every year and that the battle imagery refers to events that take place during the ritual; she is also aware that Kochinnenako's will, as expressed in her attraction to Miochin, is a central element of the ritual. She knows further that the ritual is partly about the coming of summer and partly about the ritual relationship and exchange of primacy between the two divisions of the tribe, that the ritual described in the narrative is enacted by men, dressed as Miochin and Sh-ah-cock, and that Yellow Woman in her Corn Mother aspect is the center of this and other sacred rites of the Kurena, though in this ritual she may also be danced by a Kurena mask dancer. (Gunn includes a drawing of this figure, made by a Laguna, and titled "Ko-chin-ne-nako—In the Mask Dances.")

The various birds and animals along with the forces such as warm air, fire, heat, sleet, and ice are represented in the ritual; Hutchamun Kiuk, the timekeeper or officer who keeps track of the ritual calendar (which is intrinsically related to the solstices and equinoxes), plays a central role in the ritual. The presence of Kochinnenako and Hutchamun Kiuk and the Shiwana Miochin and Sh-ah-cock means something sacred is going on for the Keres.

The ritual transfers the focus of power, or the ritual axis, held in turn by two moieties whose constitution reflects the earth's bilateral division between summer and winter, from the winter to the summer people. Each moiety's right to power is confirmed by and reflective of the seasons, as it is reflective of and supported by the equinoxes. The power is achieved through the Iyani (ritual empowerment) of female Power,[9] embodied in Kochinne-

8. Boas, *Keresan Texts*, p. 288. Boas says he made the same mistake at first, having misheard the word they used.

9. When my sister Carol Lee Sanchez spoke to her university Women's Studies class about the position of centrality women hold in our Keres tradition, one young woman, a self-identified radical feminist, was outraged. She insisted that Sanchez and other Laguna women had been brainwashed into believing that we had power over our lives. After all, she knew that no woman anywhere has ever had that kind of power; her feminist studies had made that fact quite plain to her. The kind of cultural chauvinism that has been promulgated by well-intentioned but culturally entranced feminists can lead to serious misunderstandings such as this and in the process become a new racism based on what becomes the feminist canon. Not that feminists can be faulted entirely on this—they are, after all, reflecting the research and interpretation done in a patriarchal context, by male-biased researchers and scholars, most of whom would avidly support the young radical feminist's strenuous position. It's too bad, though, that feminists fall into the patriarchal trap!

nako as mask dancer and/or Irriaku. Without her empowering mediatorship among the south and north *Shiwana*, the *cacique*, and the village, the season and the moiety cannot change, and balance cannot be maintained.

Unchanging supremacy of one moiety/season over the other is unnatural and therefore undesirable because unilateral dominance of one aspect of existence and of society over another is not reflective of or supported by reality at meteorological or spiritual levels. Sh-ah-cock, is the Winter Spirit or Winter Cloud, a *Shiwana* (one of several categories of supernaturals), and as such is cold and connected to sleet, snow, ice, and hunger. He is not portrayed as cold because he is a source of unmitigated evil (or of evil at all, for that matter).

Half of the people (not numerically but mystically, so to speak) are Winter, and in that sense are Sh-ah-cock; and while this aspect of the group psyche may seem unlovely when its time is over, that same half is lovely indeed in the proper season. Similarly, Miochin will also age—that is, pass his time—and will then give way for his "rival," which is also his complement. Thus balance and harmony are preserved for the village through exchange of dominance, and thus each portion of the community takes responsibility in turn for the prosperity and well-being of the people.

A Keres is of course aware that balance and harmony are two primary assumptions of Keres society and will not approach the narrative wondering whether the handsome Miochin will win the hand of the unhappy wife and triumph over the enemy, thereby heroically saving the people from disaster. The triumph of handsome youth over ugly age or of virile liberality over withered tyranny doesn't make sense in a Keres context because such views contradict central Keres values.

A traditional Keres is satisfied by the story because it reaffirms a Keres sense of rightness, of propriety. It is a tale that affirms ritual understandings, and the Keres reader can visualize the ritual itself when reading Gunn's story. Such a reader is likely to be puzzled by the references to rulers and by the tone of heroic romance but will be reasonably satisfied by the account because in spite of its westernized changes, it still ends happily with the orderly transfer of focality between the moieties and seasons accomplished in seasonal splendor as winter in New Mexico blusters and sleets its way north and summer sings and warms its way home. In the end, the primary Keres values of harmony, balance, and the centrality of woman to maintain them have been validated, and the fundamental Keres principal of proper order is celebrated and affirmed once again.

A MODERN FEMINIST INTERPRETATION

A non-Keres feminist, reading this tale, is likely to wrongly suppose that this narrative is about the importance of men and the use of a passive female figure as a pawn in their bid for power. And, given the way Gunn renders the story, a modern feminist would have good reason to make such an inference. As Gunn recounts it, the story opens in classic patriarchal style and implies certain patriarchal complications: that Kochinnenako has married a man who is violent and destructive. She is the ruler's daughter, which might suggest that the traditional Keres are concerned with the abuses of power of the wealthy. This in turn suggests that the traditional Keres social system, like the traditional Anglo-European ones, suffer from oppressive class structures in which the rich and powerful bring misery to the people, who in the tale are reduced to bare subsistence seemingly as a result of Kochinnenako's unfortunate alliance. A reader making the usual assumptions western readers make when enjoying folk tales will think she is reading a sort of Robin Hood story, replete with a lovely maid Marian, an evil Sheriff, and a green-clad agent of social justice with the Indian name Miochin.

Given the usual assumptions that underlie European folktales, the Western romantic view of the Indian, and the usual antipatriarchal bias that characterizes feminist analysis, a feminist reader might assume that Kochinnenako has been compelled to make an unhappy match by her father the ruler, who must be gaining some power from the alliance. Besides, his name is given as Broken Prayer Stick, which might be taken to mean that he is an unholy man, remiss in his religious duties and weak spiritually.

Gunn's tale does not clarify these issues. Instead it proceeds in a way best calculated to confirm a feminist's interpretation of the tale as only another example of the low status of women in tribal cultures. In accordance with this entrenched American myth, Gunn makes it clear that Kochinnenako is not happy in her marriage; she thinks Sh-ah-cock is "cold and disagreeable, and she cannot love him." Certainly, contemporary American women will read that to mean that Sh-ah-cock is an emotionally uncaring, perhaps cruel husband and that Kochinnenako is forced to accept a life bereft of warmth and love. A feminist reader might imagine that Kochinnenako, like many women, has been socialized into submission. So obedient is she, it seems, so lacking in spirit and independence, that she doesn't seize her chance to escape a bad situation, preferring instead to remain obedient to the patriarchal institution of marriage. As it turns out (in Gunn's tale), Kochinnenako is delivered from the clutches of her violent and unwanted mate by the timely intervention of a much more pleasant man, the hero.

A radical feminist is likely to read the story for its content vis à vis racism and resistance to oppression. From a radical perspective, it seems politically significant that Sh-ah-cock is white. That is, winter is white. Snow is white. Blizzards are white. Clearly, while the story does not give much support to concepts of a people's struggles, it could be construed to mean that the oppressor is designated white in the story because the Keres are engaged in serious combat with white colonial power and, given the significance of storytelling in tribal cultures, are chronicling that struggle in this tale. Read this way, it would seem to acknowledge the right and duty of the people in overthrowing the hated white dictator, who by this account possesses the power of life and death over them.

Briefly, in this context, the story can be read as a tale about the nature of white oppression of Indian people, and Kochinnenako then becomes something of a revolutionary fighter through her collusion with the rebel Miochin in the overthrow of the tyrant Sh-ah-cock. In this reading, the tale becomes a cry for liberation and a direct command to women to aid in the people's struggle to overthrow the colonial powers that drain them of life and strength, deprive them of their rightful prosperity, and threaten them with extinction. An activist teacher could use this tale to instruct women in their obligation to the revolutionary struggle. The daughter, her sisters, and the mother are, after all, implicated in the attempt to bring peace and prosperity to the people; indeed, they are central to it. Such a teacher could, by so using the story, appear to be incorporating culturally diverse materials in the classroom while at the same time exploiting the romantic and moral appeal Native Americans have for other Americans.

When read as a battle narrative, the story as Gunn renders it makes clear that the superiority of Miochin rests as much in his commitment to the welfare of the people as in his military prowess and that because his attempt to free the people is backed up by their invitation to him to come and liberate them, he is successful. Because of his success he is entitled to the hand of the ruler's daughter, Kochinnenako, one of the traditional Old World spoils of victory. Similarly, Sh-ah-cock is defeated not only because he is violent and oppressive but because the people, like Kochinnenako, find that they cannot love him.

A radical lesbian separatist might find herself uncomfortable with the story even though it is so clearly correct in identifying the enemy as white and violent. But the overthrow of the tyrant is placed squarely in the hands of another male figure, Miochin. This rescue is likely to be viewed with a jaundiced eye by many feminists (though more romantic women might be satisfied with it, since it's a story about an Indian woman of long ago), as Kochinnenako has to await the coming of a handsome stranger for her salvation, and her fate is decided by her father and the more salutary suitor Miochin. No one asks Kochinnenako what she wants to do; the reader is informed that her marriage is not to her liking when she admits to Miochin that she is unhappy. Nevertheless, Kochinnenako acts like any passive, dependent woman who is exploited by the males in her life, who get what they want regardless of her own needs or desires.

Some readers (like myself) might find themselves wondering hopefully whether Miochin isn't really female, disguised by males as one of them in order to buttress their position of relative power. After all, this figure is dressed in yellow and green, the colors of corn, a plant always associated with Woman. Kockinnenako and her sisters are all Corn Women and her mother is, presumably, the head of the Corn Clan; and the Earth Mother of the Keres, Iyatiku, is Corn Woman herself. Alas, I haven't yet found evidence to support such a wishful notion, except that the mask dancer who impersonates Kochinnenako is male, dressed female, which is sort of the obverse side of the wish.

A FEMINIST-TRIBAL INTERPRETATION

The feminist interpretation I have sketched—which is a fair representation of one of my early readings from what I took to be a feminist perspective—proceeds from two unspoken assumptions: that women are essentially powerless and that conflict is basic to human existence. The first is a fundamental feminist position, while the second is basic to Anglo-European thought; neither, however, is characteristic of Keres thought. To a modern feminist, marriage is an institution developed to establish and maintain male supremacy; because she is the ruler's daughter, Kochinnenako's choice of a husband determines which male will hold power over the people and who will inherit the throne.[1]

1. For a detailed exposition of what this dynamic consists of, see Adrienne Rich, "Compulsory Heterosexuality and Lesbian Existence," *Signs: Journal of Women in Culture and Society*, vol. 5, no. 4 (summer 1980): 630–61. [For this essay by RICH, see above—editor's note.]

When Western assumptions are applied to tribal narratives, they become mildly confusing and moderately annoying from any perspective.[2] Western assumptions about the nature of human society (and thus of literature) when contextualizing a tribal story or ritual must necessarily leave certain elements unclear. If the battle between Summer Spirit and Winter Spirit is about the triumph of warmth, generosity, and kindness over coldness, miserliness, and cruelty, supremacy of the good over the bad, why does the hero grant his antagonist rights over the village and Kochinnenako for half of each year?

The contexts of Anglo-European and Keres Indian life differ so greatly in virtually every assumption about the nature of reality, society, ethics, female roles, and the sacred importance of seasonal change that simply telling a Keres tale within an Anglo-European narrative context creates a dizzying series of false impressions and unanswerable (perhaps even unposable) questions.

For instance, marriage among traditional Keres is not particularly related to marriage among Anglo-European Americans. As I explain in greater detail in a later essay,[3] paternity is not an issue among traditional Keres people; a child belongs to its mother's clan, not in the sense that she or he is owned by the clan, but in the sense that she or he belongs within it. Another basic difference is the attitude toward conflict; the Keres can best be described as a conflict-phobic people, while Euro-American culture is conflict-centered. So while the orderly and proper annual transference of power from Winter to Summer people through the agency of the Keres central female figure is the major theme of the narrative from a Keres perspective, the triumph of good over evil becomes its major theme when it is retold by a white man.

Essentially what happens is that Summer (a mask dancer dressed as Miochin) asks Kochinnenako permission, in a ritual manner, to enter the village. She (who is either a mask dancer dressed as Yellow Woman, or a Yellow Corn Irriaku) follows a ritual order of responses and actions that enable Summer to enter. The narrative specifies the acts she must perform, the words she must say, and those that are prohibited, such as the command that she not "throw any of the husks out of the door." This command establishes both the identity of Miochin and constitutes his declaration of his ritual intention and his ritual relationship to Kochinnenako.

Agency is Kochinnenako's ritual role here; it is through her ritual agency that the orderly, harmonious transfer of primacy between the Summer and

2. Elaine Jahner, a specialist in Lakota language and oral literature, has suggested that the western obsession with western plot in narrative structure led early informant George Sword to construct narratives in the western fashion and tell them as Lakota traditional stories. Research has shown that Sword's stories are not recognized as Lakota traditional stories by Lakotas themselves; but the tribal narratives that are so recognized are loosely structured and do not exhibit the reliance on central theme or character that is so dear to the hearts of western collectors. As time has gone by, the Sword stories have become a sort of model for later Lakota storytellers who, out of a desire to convey the tribal tales to western collectors, have changed the old structures to ones more pleasing to American and European ears. Personal conversations with Elaine Jahner.

Education in western schools, exposure to mass media, and the need to function in a white-dominated world have subtly but perhaps permanently altered the narrative structures of the old tales and, with them, the tribal conceptual modes of tribal people. The shift has been away from associative, synchronistic, event-centered narrative and thought to a linear, foreground-centered one. Concurrently, tribal social organization and interpersonal relations have taken a turn toward authoritarian, patriarchal, linear, and misogynist modes—hence the rise of violence against women, an unthinkable event in older, more circular, and tribal times.

3. Paula Gunn Allen, "Hwame, Koshkalaka, and the Rest: Lesbians in American Indian Cultures," in *The Sacred Hoop: Recovering the Feminine in American Indian Traditions* (Boston: Beacon Press, 1986), pp. 245–61 [editor's note].

Winter people is accomplished. This transfer takes place at the time of the year that Winter goes north and Summer comes to the pueblo from the south, the time when the sun moves north along the line it makes with the edge of the sun's house as ascertained by the hocheni calendar keeper who determines the proper solar and astronomical times for various ceremonies. Thus, in the proper time, Kochinnenako empowers Summer to enter the village. Kochinnenako's careful observance of the ritual requirements together with the proper conduct of her sisters, her mother, the priests (symbolized by the title Hutchamun Kiuk, whom Gunn identifies as the ruler and Yellow Woman's father, though he could as properly—more properly, actually—be called her mother), the animals and birds, the weather, and the people at last brings summer to the village, ending the winter and the famine that accompanies winter's end.

A feminist who is conscious of tribal thought and practice will know that the real story of Sh-ah-cock and Miochin underscores the central role that woman plays in the orderly life of the people. Reading Gunn's version, she will be aware of the vast gulf between the Lagunas and John Gunn in their understanding of the role of women in a traditional gynecentric society such as that of the western Keres. Knowing that the central role of woman is harmonizing spiritual relationships between the people and the rest of the universe by empowering ritual activities, she will be able to read the story for its western colonial content, aware that Gunn's version reveals more about American consciousness when it meets tribal thought than it reveals about the tribe. When the story is analyzed within the context to which it rightly belongs, its feminist content becomes clear, as do the various purposes to which industrialized patriarchal people can put a tribal story.

If she is familiar with the ritual color code of this particular group of Native Americans, a feminist will know that white is the color of Shipap, the place where the four rivers of life come together and where our Mother Iyatiku lives. Thus she will know that it is appropriate that the Spirit of Woman's Power/Being (Yellow Woman) be "married" (that is, ritually connected in energy-transferring gestalts) first with Winter who is the power signified by the color white, which informs clouds, the Mountain Tse-pina, Shipap, originating Power, Koshare, the north and northwest, and that half of the year, and then with Summer, whose color powers are yellow and green, which inform Kurena, sunrise, the growing and ripening time of Mother Earth, and whose direction is south and southeast and that portion of the year.

A feminist will know that the story is about how the Mother Corn Iyatiku's "daughter," that is, her essence in one of its aspects, comes to live as Remembering Prayer Sticks' daughter first with the Winter people and then with the Summer people, and so on.

The net effect of Gunn's rendition of the story is the unhappy wedding of the woman-centered tradition of the western Keres to patriarchal Anglo-European tradition and thus the dislocation of the central position of Keres women by their assumption under the rule of the men. When one understands that the hocheni is the person who tells the time and prays for all the people, even the white people, and that the Hutchamun Kiuk is the ruler only in the sense that the Constitution of the United States is the ruler of the citizens and government of the United States, then the Keres organization of women, men, spirit folk, equinoxes, seasons, and clouds into a balanced and integral dynamic will be seen reflected in the narrative. Knowing this, a feminist will also be able to see how the interpolations of patriarchal thinking distort all the relationships in the story and, by extension, how such impositions of patriarchy on gynocracy disorder harmonious social and spiritual relationships.

A careful feminist-tribal analysis of Gunn's rendition of a story that would be better titled "The Transfer of Ianyi (ritual power, sacred power) from Winter to Summer" will provide a tribally conscious feminist with an interesting example of how colonization works, however consciously or unconsciously, to misinform both the colonized and the colonizer. She will be able to note the process by which the victim of the translation process, the Keres woman who reads the tale, is misinformed because she reads Gunn's book. Even though she knows that something odd is happening in the tale, she is not likely to apply sophisticated feminist analysis to the rendition; in the absence of real knowledge of the colonizing process of story-changing, she is all too likely to find bits of the Gunn tale sticking in her mind and subtly altering her perception of herself, her role in her society, and her relationship to the larger world.

The hazard to male Keres readers is, of course, equally great. They are likely to imagine that the proper relationship of women to men is subservience. And it is because of such a shockingly untraditional modern interpretation, brought on as much by reading Gunn as by other, perhaps more obvious societal mechanisms, that the relationships between men and women are so severely disordered at Laguna that wife-abuse, rape, and battery of women there has reached frightening levels in recent years.

Political Implications of Narrative Structure

The changes Gunn has made in the narrative are not only changes in content; they are structural as well. One useful social function of traditional tribal literature is its tendency to distribute value evenly among various elements, providing a model or pattern for egalitarian structuring of society as well as literature. However, egalitarian structures in either literature or society are not easily "read" by hierarchically inclined westerners.

Still, the tendency to equal distribution of value among all elements in a field, whether the field is social, spiritual, or aesthetic (and the distinction is moot when tribal materials are under discussion), is an integral part of tribal consciousness and is reflected in tribal social and aesthetic systems all over the Americas. In this structural framework, no single element is foregrounded, leaving the others to supply "background." Thus, properly speaking, there are no heroes, no villains, no chorus, no setting (in the sense of inert ground against which dramas are played out). There are no minor characters, and foreground slips along from one focal point to another until all the pertinent elements in the ritual conversation have had their say.

In tribal literatures, the timing of the foregrounding of various elements is dependent on the purpose the narrative is intended to serve. Tribal art functions something like a forest in which all elements coexist, where each is integral to the being of the others. Depending on the season, the interplay of various life forms, the state of the overall biosphere and psychosphere, and the woman's reason for being there, certain plants will leap into focus on certain occasions. For example, when tribal women on the eastern seaboard went out to gather sassafras, what they noticed, what stood out sharply in their attention, were the sassafras plants. But when they went out to get maple sugar, maples became foregrounded. But the foregrounding of sassafras or maple in no way lessens the value of the other plants or other features of the forest. When a woman goes after maple syrup, she is aware of the other plant forms that are also present.

In the same way, a story that is intended to convey the importance of the Grandmother Spirits will focus on grandmothers in their interaction with grandchildren and will convey little information about uncles. Traditional tales will make a number of points, and a number of elements will be present, all of which will bear some relationship to the subject of the story. Within the time the storyteller has alloted to the story, and depending on the interests and needs of her audience at the time of the storytelling, each of these elements will receive its proper due.

Traditional American Indian stories work dynamically among clusters of loosely interconnected circles. The focus of the action shifts from one character to another as the story unfolds. There is no "point of view" as the term is generally understood, unless the action itself, the story's purpose, can be termed "point of view." But as the old tales are translated and rendered in English, the western notion of proper fictional form takes over the tribal narrative. Soon there appear to be heroes, point of view, conflict, crisis, and resolution, and as western tastes in story crafting are imposed on the narrative structure of the ritual story, the result is a western story with Indian characters. Mournfully, the new form often becomes confused with the archaic form by the very people whose tradition has been re-formed.

The story Gunn calls "Sh-ah-cock and Mi-o-chin or The Battle of the Seasons" might be better termed "How Kochinnenako Balanced the World," though even then the title would be misleading to American readers, for they would see Kochinnenako as the heroine, the foreground of the story. They would see her as the central figure of the action, and of course that would be wrong. There is no central figure in the tale, though there is a central point. The point is concerned with the proper process of a shift in focus, not the resolution of a conflict. Kochinnenako's part in the process is agency, not heroics; even in Gunn's version, she does nothing heroic. A situation presents itself in the proper time, and Yellow Woman acts in accordance with the dictates of timing, using proper ritual as her mode. But the people cannot go from Winter into Summer without conscious acceptance of Miochin, and Yellow Woman's invitation to him, an acceptance that is encouraged and supported by all involved, constitutes a tribal act.

The "battle" between Summer and Winter is an accurate description of seasonal change in central New Mexico during the spring. This comes through in the Gunn rendition, but because the story is focused on conflict rather than on balance, the meteorological facts and their intrinsic relationship to human ritual are obscured. Only a non-Indian mind, accustomed to interpreting events in terms of battle, struggle, and conflict, would assume that the process of transfer had to occur through a battle replete with protagonist, antagonist, a cast of thousands, and a pretty girl as the prize. For who but an industrialized patriarch would think that winter can be vanquished? Winter and Summer enjoy a relationship based on complementarity, mutuality, and this is the moral significance of the tale.

Tribal Narratives and Women's Lives

Reading American Indian traditional stories and songs is not an easy task. Adequate comprehension requires that the reader be aware that Indians never think like whites and that any typeset version of traditional materials is distorting.

In many ways, literary conventions, as well as the conventions of literacy, militate against an understanding of traditional tribal materials. Western technological-industrialized minds cannot adequately interpret tribal materials because they are generally trained to perceive their entire world in ways that are alien to tribal understandings.

This problem is not exclusive to tribal literature. It is one that all ethnic writers who write out of a tribal or folk tradition face, and one that is also shared by women writers, who, after all, inhabit a separate folk tradition. Much of women's culture bears marked resemblance to tribal culture. The perceptual modes that women, even those of us who are literate, industrialized, and reared within masculinist academic traditions, habitually engage in more closely resemble inclusive-field perception than excluding foreground-background perceptions.

Women's traditional occupations, their arts and crafts, and their literature and philosophies are more often accretive than linear, more achronological than chronological, and more dependent on harmonious relationships of all elements within a field of perception than western culture in general is thought to be. Indeed, the patchwork quilt is the best material example I can think of to describe the plot and process of a traditional tribal narrative, and quilting is a non-Indian woman's art, one that Indian women have taken to avidly and that they display in their ceremonies, rituals, and social gatherings as well as in their homes.

It is the nature of woman's existence to be and to create background. This fact, viewed with unhappiness by many feminists, is of ultimate importance in a tribal context. Certainly no art object is bereft of background. Certainly the contents and tone of one's background will largely determine the direction and meaning of one's life and, therefore, the meaning and effect of one's performance in any given sphere of activity.

Westerners have for a long time discounted the importance of background. The earth herself, which is our most inclusive background, is dealt with summarily as a source of food, metals, water, and profit, while the fact that she is the fundamental agent of all planetary life is blithely ignored. Similarly, women's activities—cooking, planting, harvesting, preservation, storage, homebuilding, decorating, maintaining, doctoring, nursing, soothing, and healing, along with the bearing, nurturing, and rearing of children—are devalued as blithely. An antibackground bias is bound to have social costs that have so far remained unexplored, but elite attitudes toward workers, nonwhite races, and women are all part of the price we pay for overvaluing the foreground.

In the western mind, shadows highlight the foreground. In contrast, in the tribal view the mutual relationships among shadows and light in all their varying degrees of intensity create a living web of definition and depth, and significance arises from their interplay. Traditional and contemporary tribal arts and crafts testify powerfully to the importance of balance among all elements in tribal perception, aesthetics, and social systems.

Traditional peoples perceive their world in a unified-field fashion that is very different from the single-focus perception that generally characterizes western masculinist, monotheistic modes of perception. Because of this, tribal cultures are consistently misperceived and misrepresented by nontribal folklorists, ethnographers, artists, writers, and social workers. A number of scholars have recently addressed this issue, but they have had little success because the demands of type and of analysis are, after all, linear and fixed, while the requirements of tribal literatures are accretive and fluid. The one is unidimensional, monolithic, excluding, and chronological while the other is multidimensional, achronological, and including.

How one teaches or writes about the one perspective in terms of the other is problematic. This essay itself is a pale representation of a tribal understanding of the Kochinnenako tale. I am acutely aware that much of what I have said is likely to be understood in ways I did not intend, and I am also aware of how much I did not say that probably needed to be said if the real story of the transfer of responsibility from one segment of the tribe to the other is to be made clear.

In the end, the tale I have analyzed is not about Kochinnenako or Sh-ah-cock and Miochin. It is about the change of seasons and it is about the centrality of woman as agent and empowerer of that change. It is about how a people engage themselves as a people within the spiritual cosmos and in an ordered and proper way that bestows the dignity of each upon all with careful respect, folkish humor, and ceremonial delight. It is about how everyone is part of the background that shapes the meaning and value of each person's life. It is about propriety, mutuality, and the dynamics of socio-environmental change.

1986

JANE TOMPKINS
b. 1940

In recent years many prominent American academic critics have published autobiographies, memoirs, and what has been called "personal criticism," often distancing themselves from the dense theoretical language and investigations of their earlier work. An inaugural manifesto of this trend, Jane Tompkins's "Me and My Shadow" (1987; rev. 1989) turns away from contemporary theory, critiquing it as bereft of feeling and as participating in masculine forms of competition and aggressiveness; her essay illustrates instead a more personally invested form of critical writing.

Tompkins received a B.A. from Bryn Mawr College in 1961 and a Ph.D. from Yale University in 1966, during the heyday of the New Critics (CLEANTH BROOKS and WILLIAM K. WIMSATT JR. were prominent Yale professors). Their motto, as she recalls in her memoir, *A Life in School: What the Teacher Learned* (1996), was "Stay close to the text." Her initial forays in criticism were in keeping with the close textual analysis of the New Criticism. After graduating from Yale, she held a series of academic jobs at institutions ranging from Hartford (Conn.) Community College to Temple University; there in 1976 she attained a tenured professorship, which she held until 1983. As she explains in *A Life in School*, her uneven career path was the direct result of being a woman; male job candidates, through the 1960s and after, often were favored.

Tompkins's real intellectual awakening, in her recounting, occurred in the late 1970s when she was introduced to the new poststructuralist theories of interpretation. She became an influential exponent of the developing field of reader-response criticism, editing a landmark anthology, *Reader-Response Criticism: From Formalism to Post-Structuralism* (1980). She followed this with an influential book, *Sensational Designs: The Cultural Work of American Fiction, 1790–1860* (1985), which combined feminism, reception history, and cultural studies to argue for a revision of the nineteenth-century canon of American literature. In 1985 she and her spouse, the reader-response theorist STANLEY FISH, moved to Duke University, where she was later part of a famous writing group that explored alternative forms of critical writing. She taught at Duke until 1998, when she took a professorship in education at the University of Illinois–Chicago.

Drawing on the disciplines of philosophy, linguistics, and structural anthropology, literary theory in the 1970s and 1980s adopted an impersonal style and technical language, much like that used in the social sciences. In the 1960s many prominent theorists—particularly those affiliated with French structuralism, such as ROLAND BARTHES and TZVETAN TODOROV—had cast the study of literature as one domain of the "human sciences" (specifically a "science of signs," or semiology), rather than a humanistic pursuit. In the 1990s and early 2000s, however, a number of prominent critics, including the Marxist Frank Lentricchia, the feminist Nancy K. Miller, the African Americanist HENRY LOUIS GATES JR., the queer theorist EVE KOSOFSKY SEDGWICK, and the scholar of the novel LENNARD DAVIS, published their autobiographies or memoirs. Many of these figures had established themselves as leading proponents of the theoretical movements of the 1970s and 1980s; yet their personal explorations seemed surprising departures from their earlier avowedly theoretical works.

While gaining attention for its moments of personal exposure, "Me and My Shadow" critiques conventional modes of academic argument that, Tompkins points out, are deeply competitive and are often forms of veiled aggression rather than intellectual collaboration. In a mock response to Ellen Messer-Davidow's "Philosophical Bases of Feminist Literary Criticisms" (1987), she demonstrates how criticism regularly delivers a rhetorical "stab in the entrails." In a related essay, Tompkins calls such critical moves "fighting words" and enjoins critics to unlearn such behavior, which debilitates intellectual community. She presents her views in an informal style mixed with personal asides to avoid the argumentative, "fighting" mode and demonstrate an alternative way to write criticism.

Tompkins's critique does not just focus on writing style but extends to the professional community that fosters such debilitating competition. In her own case, she sees her professional success as having occurred at the expense of her emotional life, creating two separate selves: one who "writes for professional journals, the other in diaries." "Me and My Shadow" attempts to join those split spheres, not only for her own good but as a prescription for others who work in the profession of literature. For Tompkins, the anxiety induced by the profession applies especially to women, and her critique is a feminist one. She roots the competitive mode of criticism in "a male standard of rationality that militates against women's being recognized as culturally legitimate sources of knowledge." In achieving professional success, as she explains in an interview, "I'd had to become a man to do what I'd done." Just as she argues for the value of sentiment in the literary tradition in *Sensational Designs* and blames its exclusion on masculinist bias, she argues here for the value of personal feeling in criticism.

"Me and My Shadow" explicitly targets the philosophical "apparatus" of poststructuralist theory as a "straitjacket," and it thus in some ways parallels contemporaneous arguments reacting against theory's dominance, such as STEVEN KNAPP AND WALTER

BENN MICHAELS's manifesto "Against Theory" (1982; see below) and BARBARA CHRISTIAN's "The Race for Theory" (1987; see below). However, we would be wrong to see Tompkins's argument as nontheoretical, since it not only is rife with references to various theorists but also joins in theoretical conversations on poststructuralism, feminism, professionalism, and subjectivity. It continues her emphasis on subjective rather than objective approaches to literature, evident in her work on reader-response theory, and it is grounded in the feminist concern with the personal and how, in the familiar slogan, the personal is the political.

In *Getting Personal: Feminist Occasions and Other Autobiographical Acts* (1991), Nancy K. Miller named the form of criticism Tompkins advocates "personal criticism," thereby stressing that it does not solely offer autobiographical narrative but combines both personal reflection and critical argument. This form of criticism has also been called "autobiographical literary criticism," "confessional criticism," "intimate critique," and "the new belletrism," and it has incited a great deal of debate. Part of the debate stems from its tendency to include personal details usually left unmentioned, such as Tompkins's reference to waiting to go to the bathroom or Frank Lentricchia's analogy between his penis and a chainsaw in *The Edge of Night: A Confession* (1994). Because it reveals these sometimes sensationalistic details, personal criticism has been attacked as self-indulgent, narcissistic, and participating in gossip worthy of *People* magazine. More measured responses question whether it produces legitimate literary knowledge. David Simpson's *The Academic Postmodern and the Rule of Literature: A Report on Half-Knowledge* (1995) suggests that it is returning to Romantic notions of literature, reinvoking WILLIAM WORDSWORTH's claim that literature arises from a "spontaneous overflow of powerful feelings." Simpson also situates this approach within a larger movement in contemporary literary criticism toward "localism" and a stress on individual identity, which, he argues, occurs at the expense of larger community.

Though personal criticism opens the door to charges of subjectivism, Tompkins goes beyond advocating the expression of emotion to foreground the effects of the professional codes and institutional structures of literary study. She presents a cogent—and often moving—critique of the sometimes personally debilitating results of higher education and professional literary study, which promote competition and isolation rather than community and cooperation. Tompkins ultimately holds out hope for an improved way to study literature, one that does not repress or damage one's emotional life but fosters it alongside the pursuit of theoretical knowledge.

BIBLIOGRAPHY

Tompkins's first book, an edited collection, was *Twentieth Century Interpretations of The Turn of the Screw and Other Tales: A Collection of Critical Essays* (1970). After embracing new theoretical work, she became a prominent exponent of reader-reponse theory, editing *Reader-Response Criticism: From Formalism to Post-Structuralism* (1980), one of the first anthologies to establish this new mode. It includes eleven influential essays by a range of theorists, including Wolfgang Iser, Stanley Fish, and Norman Holland, as well as an excellent introduction, concluding chapter, and annotated bibliography by Tompkins. A celebrated critique of the canon of American literature, Tompkins's next book, *Sensational Designs: The Cultural Work of American Fiction, 1790–1860* (1985), argues for the value of sentimental, "feminine," literature.

"Me and My Shadow," *New Literary History* 19 (1987), announced a departure from her earlier work; it has been reprinted in an expanded version in several anthologies. Our selection is taken from *Gender and Theory: Dialogues on Feminist Criticism* (ed. Linda Kauffman, 1989), which also includes the Messer-Davidow article and a response to Tompkins by Gerald M. MacLean. Employing a hybrid of personal style, literary and cultural analysis, and feminist criticism, *West of Everything: The Inner*

Life of Westerns (1992) extends Tompkins's investigation of sentiment to works of popular culture by men, examining how Western novels and movies depict masculinity. The best biographical source is Tompkins's own *A Life in School: What the Teacher Learned* (1996), which recounts her life from early schooling through her time as a professor at Duke University.

Nancy K. Miller's *Getting Personal: Feminist Occasions and Other Autobiographical Acts* (1991) is a balanced consideration of Tompkins and the turn to personal criticism, examining its roots in feminism and autobiography. Olivia Frey's "Beyond Literary Darwinism: Women's Voices and Critical Discourse," in *The Intimate Critique: Autobiographical Literary Criticism* (ed. Diane P. Freedman, Olivia Frey, and Frances Murphy Zauhar, 1993), focuses on personal criticism as a form of women's writing and sees Tompkins's work as path-breaking; the same anthology collects "Me and My Shadow" and offers many perspectives on "intimate critique." "Writing in Concert: An Interview with Cathy Davidson, Alice Kaplan, Jane Tompkins, and Marianna Torgovnick," conducted by Jeffrey Williams, *Minnesota Review*, n.s., 41–42 (1994), is a revealing account of alternative modes of criticism in the words of Tompkins and her writing-group colleagues at Duke University. In *The Academic Postmodern and the Rule of Literature: A Report on Half-Knowledge* (1995), David Simpson incisively critiques the trend toward subjective approaches, tracing their genesis to nineteenth-century Romanticism. Charles Altieri's "What Is at Stake in Confessional Criticism," in *Confessions of the Critics* (ed. H. Aram Veeser, 1996), assesses some of the benefits and problems of confessional criticism, arguing that personal details constitute more a "clever theoretical gesture" than a distinctive revelation; the anthology also gathers criticisms of the personal turn as well as examples of it, including an essay by Tompkins. Jeffrey Williams's "The New Belletrism," *Style* 33 (1999), sees the turn toward the personal as part of a larger shift toward more traditional belletristic modes of criticism.

Me and My Shadow

I wrote this essay in answer to Ellen Messer-Davidow's 'The philosophical bases of feminist literary criticism' which appeared in the Fall 1987 issue of *New Literary History* along with several replies, including a shorter version of this one.[1] As if it weren't distraction enough that my essay depends on someone else's, I want, before you've even read it, to defend it from an accusation. Believing that my reply, which turns its back on theory, constituted a return to the 'rhetoric of presence', to an 'earlier, naive, untheoretical feminism', someone, whom I'll call the unfriendly reader, complained that I was making the 'old patriarchal gesture of representation' whose effect had been to marginalize women, thus 'reinforcing the very stereotypes women and minorities have fought so hard to overcome.' I want to reply to this objection because I think it is mistaken and because it reproduces exactly the way I used to feel about feminist criticism when it first appeared in the late 1960s.

I wanted nothing to do with it. It was embarrassing to see women, with whom one was necessarily identified, insisting in print on the differences between mens and women's experience, focusing obsessively on women

1. This expanded version of "Me and My Shadow" is taken from *Gender and Theory: Dialogues on Feminist Criticism*, ed. Linda Kauffman (New York: Basil Blackwell, 1989), which also includes Ellen Messer-Davidow's essay (the version cited below); both originally appeared in *New Literary History* 19 (1987).

authors, women characters, women's issues. How pathetic, I thought, to have to call attention to yourself in that way. And in such bad taste. It was the worst kind of special pleading, an admission of weakness so blatant it made me ashamed. What I felt then, and what I think my unfriendly reader feels now, is a version of what women who are new to feminism often feel: that if we don't call attention to ourselves *as* women, but just shut up about it and do our work, no one will notice the difference and everything will be OK.

Women who adopt this line are, understandably, afraid. Afraid of being confused with the weaker sex, the sex that goes around whining and talking about itself in an unseemly way, that can't or won't do what the big boys do ('tough it out') and so won't ever be allowed to play in the big boys' games. I am sympathetic with this position. Not long ago, as organizer of an MLA[2] session entitled 'Professional politics: women and the institution', I urged a large roomful of women to 'get theory' because I thought that doing theory would admit us to the big leagues and enable us at the same time to argue a feminist case in the most unimpeachable terms—those that men had supplied. I busily took my own advice, which was good as far as it went. But I now see that there has been a price for this, at least there has been for me; it is the subject of my reply to Ellen. I now tend to think that theory itself, at least as it is usually practiced, may be one of the patriarchal gestures women *and* men ought to avoid.

There are two voices inside me answering, answering to, Ellen's essay. One is the voice of a critic who wants to correct a mistake in the essay's view of epistemology. The other is the voice of a person who wants to write about her feelings (I have wanted to do this for a long time but have felt too embarrassed). This person feels it is wrong to criticize the essay philosophically, and even beside the point: because a critique of the kind the critic has in mind only insulates academic discourse further from the issues that make feminism matter. That make *her* matter. The critic, meanwhile, believes such feelings, and the attitudes that inform them, are soft-minded, self-indulgent, and unprofessional.

These beings exist separately but not apart. One writes for professional journals, the other in diaries, late at night. One uses words like 'context' and 'intelligibility', likes to win arguments, see her name in print, and give graduate students hardheaded advice. The other has hardly ever been heard from. She had a short story published once in a university literary magazine, but her works exist chiefly in notebooks and manila folders labelled 'Journal' and 'Private'. This person talks on the telephone a lot to her friends, has seen psychiatrists, likes cappuccino, worries about the state of her soul. Her father is ill right now, and one of her friends recently committed suicide.

The dichotomy drawn here is false—and not false. I mean in reality there's no split. It's the same person who feels and who discourses about epistemology. The problem is that you can't talk about your private life in the course of doing your professional work. You have to pretend that epistemology, or whatever you're writing about, has nothing to do with your life, that

2. The Modern Language Association, the main professional organization for literary scholars and critics in North America; at its annual conventions, papers are presented at hundreds of "sessions." Tompkins's panel was organized in 1980.

it's more exalted, more important, because it (supposedly) *transcends* the merely personal. Well, I'm tired of the conventions that keep discussions of epistemology, or James Joyce,[3] segregated from meditations on what is happening outside my window or inside my heart. The public-private dichotomy, which is to say, the public-private *hierarchy*, is a founding condition of female oppression. I say to hell with it. The reason I feel embarrassed at my own attempts to speak personally in a professional context is that I have been conditioned to feel that way. That's all there is to it.

I think people are scared to talk about themselves, that they haven't got the guts to do it. I think readers want to know about each other. Sometimes, when a writer introduces some personal bit of story into an essay, I can hardly contain my pleasure. I love writers who write about their own experience. I feel I'm being nourished by them, that I'm being allowed to enter into a personal relationship with them. That I can match my own experience up with theirs, feel cousin to them, and say, yes, that's how it is.

> When he casts his leaves forth upon the wind [said Hawthorne], the author addresses, not the many who will fling aside his volume, or never take it up, but the few who will understand him. . . . As if the printed book, thrown at large on the wide world, were certain to find out the divided segment of the writer's own nature, and complete his circle of existence by bringing him into communion with it. . . . And so as thoughts are frozen and utterance, benumbed unless the speaker stand in some true relation with this audience—it may be pardonable to imagine that a friend, a kind and apprehensive, though not the closest friend, is listening to our talk.[4]

Hawthorne's sensitivity to the relationship that writing implies is rare in academic prose, even when the subject would seem to make awareness of the reader inevitable. Alison Jaggar[5] gave a lecture recently that crystallized the problem. Western epistemology, she argued, is shaped by the belief that emotion should be excluded from the process of attaining knowledge. Because women in our culture are not simply encouraged but *required* to be the bearers of emotion, which men are culturally conditioned to repress, an epistemology which excludes emotions from the process of attaining knowledge radically undercuts women's epistemic authority. The idea that the conventions defining legitimate sources of knowledge overlapped with the conventions defining appropriate gender behavior (male) came to me as a blinding insight. I saw that I had been socialized from birth to feel and act in ways that automatically excluded me from participating in the culture's most valued activities. No wonder I felt so uncomfortable in the postures academic prose forced me to assume; it was like wearing men's jeans.

Ellen Messer-Davidow's essay participates—as Jaggar's lecture and my précis of it did—in the conventions of Western rationalism. It adopts the impersonal, technical vocabulary of the epistemic ideology it seeks to dislocate. The political problem posed by my need to reply to the essay is this: to

3. Irish modernist writer (1882–1941), much of whose fiction is considered difficult.

4. Nathaniel Hawthorne [1804–1864], "The Custom House," *The Scarlet Letter*, in *The Scarlet Letter and Other Tales of the Puritans*, ed. Harry Levin (Boston: Houghton Mifflin, 1960), pp. 5–6 [Tompkins's note]. Some of the author's notes have been edited.

5. American feminist philosopher (b. 1942); the lecture was published as "Love and Knowledge: Emotion in Feminist Epistemology," *Inquiry* 32 (1989).

adhere to the conventions is to uphold a male standard of rationality that militates against women's being recognized as culturally legitimate sources of knowledge. To break with the convention is to risk not being heard at all.

This is how I would reply to Ellen's essay if I were to do it in the professionally sanctioned way.

The essay provides feminist critics with an overarching framework for thinking about what they do, both in relation to mainstream criticism and in relation to feminist work in other fields. It allows the reader to see women's studies as a whole, furnishing useful categories for organizing a confusing and miscellaneous array of materials. It also provides excellent summaries of a wide variety of books and essays that readers might not otherwise encounter. The enterprise is carried out without pointed attacks on other theorists, without creating a cumbersome new vocabulary, without exhibitionistic displays of intellect or esoteric learning. Its practical aim—to define a field within which debate can take place—is fulfilled by *New Literary History*'s decision to publish it, and to do so in a format which includes replies.

(Very nice, Jane. You sound so reasonable and generous. But, as anybody can tell, this is just the obligatory pat on the back before the stab in the entrails).

The difficulty with the essay from a philosophical, as opposed to a practical, point of view is that the theory it offers as a basis for future work stems from a confused notion of what an epistemology is. The author says: 'An epistemology . . . consists of assumptions that knowers make about the entities and processes in a domain of study, the relations that obtain among them, and the proper methods for investigating them.'[6] I want to quarrel with this definition. Epistemology, strictly speaking, is a *theory* about the origins and nature of knowledge. As such, it is a set of ideas explicitly held and consciously elaborated, and thus belongs to the practice of a sub-category of philosophy called epistemology. The fact that there is a branch of philosophy given over to the study of what knowledge is and how it is acquired is important, because it means that such theories are generated not in relation to this or that 'domain of study' but in relation to one another: that is, within the context of already existing epistemological theories. They are rarely based upon a study of the practices of investigators within a particular field.

An epistemology does not consist of 'assumptions that knowers make' in a particular field; it is a theory about how knowledge is acquired which makes sense, chiefly, in relation to other such theories. What Messer-Davidow offers as the 'epistemology' of traditional literary critics is not *their* epistemology, if in fact they have one, but her description of what she assumes their assumptions are, a description which may or may not be correct. Moreover, if literary critics should indeed elaborate a theory of how they got their beliefs, that theory would have no privileged position in relation to their actual assumptions. It would simply be another theory. This distinction—between actual assumptions and an observer's description of them (even when one is observing one's own practice)—is crucial because it points to an all-important fact about the relation of epistemology to what really gets done in a given domain of study, namely this: that epistemology, a theory

6. Messer-Davidow, "Philosophical Bases," p. 87 [Tompkins's note].

about how one gets one's knowledge, in no way determines the particular knowledge that one has.

This fact is important because Messer-Davidow assumes that if we change our epistemology, our practice as critics will change, too. Specifically, she wants us to give up the subject-object theory, in which 'knowledge is an abstract representation of objective existence,' for a theory which says that what counts as knowledge is a function of situation and perspective. She believes that it follows from this latter theory that knowledge will become more equitable, more self-aware, and more humane.

I disagree. Knowing that my knowledge is perspectival, language-based, culturally constructed, or what have you, does not change in the slightest the things I believe to be true. All that it changes is what I think about how we get knowledge. The insight that my ideas are all products of the situation I occupy in the world applies to all of my ideas equally (including the idea that knowledge is culturally based); and to all of everybody else's ideas as well. So where does this get us? Right back to where we were before, mainly. I still believe what I believe and, if you differ with me, think that you are wrong. If I want to change your mind I still have to persuade you that I am right by using evidence, reasons, chains of inference, citations of authority, analogies, illustrations, and so on. Believing that what I believe comes from my being in a particular cultural framework does not change my relation to my beliefs. I still believe them just as much as if I thought they came from God, or the laws of nature, or my autonomous self.

Here endeth the epistle.

But while I think Ellen is wrong in thinking that a change of epistemology can mean a change in the kinds of things we think, I am in sympathy with the ends she has in view. This sympathy prompts me to say that my professionally correct reply is not on target. Because the target, the goal, rather, is not to be fighting over these questions, trying to beat the other person down. (What the goal is, it is harder to say.) Intellectual debate, if it were in the right spirit, would be wonderful. But I don't know how to be in the right spirit, exactly, can't make points without sounding rather superior and smug. Most of all, I don't know how to enter the debate without leaving everything else behind—the birds outside my window, my grief over Janice, just myself as a person sitting here in stockinged feet, a little bit chilly because the windows are open, and thinking about going to the bathroom. But not going yet.

I find that when I try to write in my 'other' voice, I am immediately critical of it. It wobbles, vacillates back and forth, is neither this nor that. The voice in which I write about epistemology is familiar, I know how it ought to sound. This voice, though, I hardly know. I don't even know if it has anything to say. But if I never write in it, it never will. So I have to try. (That is why, you see, this doesn't sound too good. It isn't a practiced performance, it hasn't got a surface. I'm asking you to bear with me while I try, hoping that this, what I write, will express something you yourself have felt or will help you find a part of yourself that you would like to express.)

The thing I want to say is that I've been hiding a part of myself for a long time. I've known it was there but I couldn't listen because there was no place for this person in literary criticism. The criticism I would like to write would always take off from personal experience. Would always be in some way a chronicle of my hours and days. Would speak in a voice which can talk about everything, would reach out to a reader like me and touch me where I want to be touched. Susan Griffin's voice in 'The way of all ideology'.[7] I want to speak in what Ursula LeGuin,[8] at the Bryn Mawr College commencement in 1986, called the 'mother tongue'. This is LeGuin speaking:

> The dialect of the father tongue that you and I learned best in college . . . only lectures . . . Many believe this dialect—the expository and particularly scientific discourse—is the *highest* form of language, the true language, of which all other uses of words are primitive vestiges . . . And it is indeed a High Language . . . Newton's *Principia* was written in it in Latin . . . and Kant wrote German in it, and Marx, Darwin, Freud, Boas, Foucault,[9] all the great scientists and social thinkers wrote it. It is the language of thought that seeks objectivity.
>
> . . . The essential gesture of the father tongue is not reasoning, but distancing—making a gap, a space, between the subject or self and the object or other. . . . Everywhere now everybody speaks [this] language in laboratories and government buildings and headquarters and offices of business . . . The father tongue is spoken from above. It goes one way. No answer is expected, or heard.
>
> . . . The mother tongue, spoken or written, expects an answer. It is conversation, a word the root of which means 'turning together.' The mother tongue is language not as mere communication, but as relation, relationship. It connects . . . Its power is not in dividing but in binding . . . We all know it by heart. John have you got your umbrella I think it's going to rain. Can you come play with me? If I told you once I told you a hundred times. . . . O what am I going to do? . . . Pass the soy sauce please. Oh, shit . . . You look like what the cat dragged in. . . .[1]

Much of what I'm saying elaborates or circles around these quotes from LeGuin. I find that having released myself from the duty to say things I'm not interested in, in a language I resist, I feel free to entertain other people's voices. Quoting them becomes a pleasure of appreciation rather than the obligatory giving of credit, because when I write in a voice that is not struggling to be heard through the screen of a forced language, I no longer feel that it is not I who am speaking, and so, there is more room for what others have said.

One sentence in Ellen's essay stuck out for me the first time I read it and the second and the third: 'In time we can build a synchronous account of our subject matters as we glissade among them and turn upon ourselves.'[2]

7. "The Way of All Ideology," in *Made from the Earth: An Anthology of Writings* (New York: Harper and Row, 1982), pp. 161–82 [Tompkins's note]. Griffin (b. 1943), American feminist poet, essayist, and critic.

8. American science fiction writer (b. 1929).

9. LeGuin names major Western thinkers, in roughly chronological order: Sir Isaac Newton (1642–1727), mathematician and physicist, whose *Principia Mathematica* (1687) expounded the theory of gravitation; IMMANUEL KANT (1724–1804), German idealist philosopher; KARL MARX (1818–1883), German social, political, and economic theorist; Charles Darwin (1809–1882), English naturalist and originator of the theory of evolution; SIGMUND FREUD (1856–1939), Austrian founder of psychoanalysis; Franz Boas (1858–1942), German-born American anthropologist; and MICHEL FOUCAULT (1926–1984), French philosopher and historian of ideas.

1. Ursula LeGuin, "The Mother Tongue," *Bryn Mawr Alumnae Bulletin*, summer 1986, pp. 3–4 [Tompkins's note].

2. Messer-Davidow, "Philosophical Bases," p. 79 [Tompkins's note].

What attracted me to the sentence was the 'glissade'. Fluidity, flexibility, versatility, mobility. Moving from one thing to another without embarrassment. It is a tenet of feminist rhetoric that the personal is political, but who in the academy acts on this where language is concerned? We all speak the father tongue, which is impersonal, while decrying the fathers' ideas. All of what I have written so far is in a kind of watered-down expository prose. Not much imagery. No description of concrete things. Only that one word, 'glissade'.

Like black swallows swooping and gliding
in a flurry of entangled loops and curves . . .[3]

Two lines of a poem I memorized in high school are what the word 'glissade' called to mind. Turning upon ourselves. Turning, weaving, bending, unbending, moving in loops and curves.

I don't believe we can ever turn upon ourselves in the sense Ellen intends. You can't get behind the thing that casts the shadow. *You* cast the shadow. As soon as you turn, the shadow falls in another place. It is still your shadow. You have not got 'behind' yourself. That is why self-consciousness is not the way to make ourselves better than we are.

Just me and my shadow, walkin' down the avenue.

It is a beautiful day here in North Carolina. The first day that is both cool and sunny all summer. After a terrible summer, first drought, then heat-wave, then torrential rain, trees down, flooding. Now, finally, beautiful weather. A tree outside my window just brushed by red, with one fully red leaf. (This is what I want you to see. A person sitting in stockinged feet looking out of her window—a floor to ceiling rectangle filled with green, with one red leaf. The season poised, sunny and chill, ready to rush down the incline into autumn. But perfect, and still. Not going yet.)

My response to this essay is not a response to something Ellen Messer-Davidow has written; it is a response to something within myself. As I read the opening pages I feel myself being squeezed into a straitjacket; I wriggle, I will not go in. As I read the list 'subject matters, methods of reasoning, and epistemology', the words will not go down. They belong to a debate whose susurrus hardly reaches my ears.

The liberation Ellen promises from the straitjacket of a subject-object epistemology is one I experienced some time ago. Mine didn't take the form she outlines, but it was close enough. I discovered, or thought I discovered, that the post-structuralist way of understanding language and knowledge enabled me to say what I wanted about the world. It enabled me to do this because it pointed out that the world I knew was a construct of ways of thinking about it, and as such, had no privileged claim on the truth. Truth in fact would always be just such a construction, and so, one could offer another, competing, description and so help to change the world that was.

The catch was that anything I might say or imagine was itself the product of an already existing discourse. Not something 'I' had made up but a way of constructing things I had absorbed from the intellectual surround. Post-structuralism's proposition about the constructed nature of things held good, but that did not mean that the world could be changed by an act of will. For,

3. From "The Skaters," by the American poet John Gould Fletcher (1886–1950).

as we are looking at this or that phenomenon and re-seeing it, re-thinking it, the rest of the world, that part of it from which we do the seeing, is still there, in place, real, irrefragable as a whole, and making visible what we see, though changed by it, too.

This little lecture pretends to something I no longer want to claim. The pretense is in the tone and level of the language, not in what it says about post-structuralism. The claim being made by the language is analogous to what Barthes[4] calls the reality effect of historical writing, whose real message is not that this or that happened but that reality exists. So the claim of this language I've been using (and am using right now) lies in its implicit deification of the speaker. Let's call it the 'authority effect'. I cannot describe the pretense except to talk about what it ignores: the human frailty of the speaker, his body, his emotions, his history; the moment of intercourse with the reader—acknowledgment of the other person's presence, feelings, needs. This 'authoritative' language speaks as though the other person weren't there. Or perhaps more accurately, it doesn't bother to imagine who, as Hawthorne said, is listening to our talk.

How can we speak personally to one another and yet not be self-centered? How can we be part of the great world and yet remain loyal to ourselves?

It seems to me that I am trying to write out of my experience without acknowledging any discontinuity between this and the subject matter of the profession I work in. And at the same time find that I no longer want to write about that subject matter, as it appears in Ellen's essay. I am, on the one hand, demanding a connection between literary theory and my own life, and asserting, on the other, that there is no connection.

But here is a connection. I learned what epistemology I know from my husband.[5] I think of it as more his game than mine. It's a game I enjoy playing but which I no longer need or want to play. I want to declare my independence of it, of him. (Part of what is going on here has to do with a need I have to make sure I'm not being absorbed in someone else's personality.) What I am breaking away from is both my conformity to the conventions of a male professional practice and my intellectual dependence on my husband. How can I talk about such things in public? How can I *not*.

Looking for something to read this morning, I took three books down from my literary theory shelf, in order to prove a point. The first book was Félix Guattari's *Molecular Revolution*.[6] I find it difficult to read, and therefore have read very little of it, but according to a student who is a disciple of Deleuze[7] and Guattari, 'molecular revolution' has to do with getting away from ideology and enacting revolution within daily life. It is specific, not programmed—that is, it does not have a 'method', nor 'steps', and is neither psychoanalytic nor marxist, although its discourse seems shaped by those discourses, antithetically. From this kind of revolution, said I to myself, disingenuously, one would expect some recognition of the personal. A revolution that started with daily life would have to begin, or at least would have

4. ROLAND BARTHES (1915–1980), French writer and critic.
5. The well-known reader-response theorist STANLEY FISH (b. 1938).
6. Félix Guattari, *Molecular Revolution: Psychiatry and Politics*, trans. Rosemary Sheed (New York: Penguin, 1984) [Tompkins's note]. GUATTARI (1930–1992), French poststructuralist psychiatrist and philosopher.
7. GILLES DELEUZE (1925–1995), French poststructuralist philosopher and coauthor of several books with Guattari, most notably *Anti-Oedipus: Capitalism and Schizophrenia* (1972).

sometimes to reside, at home. So I open at a section entitled 'Towards a new vocabulary', looking for something in the mother tongue, and this is what I find:

> The distinction I am proposing between machine and structure is based solely on the way we use the words; we may consider that we are merely dealing with a 'written device' of the kind one has to invent for dealing with a mathematical problem, or with an axiom that may have to be reconsidered at a particular stage of development, or again with the kind of machine we shall be talking about here.
>
> I want therefore to make it clear that I am putting into parentheses the fact that, in reality, a machine is inseparable from its structural articulations and conversely, that each contingent structure is dominated (and this is what I want to demonstrate) by a system of machines, or at the very least by one logic machine.[8]

At this point, I start to skip, reading only the first sentence of each paragraph.

> 'We may say of structure that it positions its elements . . .'
>
> 'The agent of action, whose definition here does not extend beyond this principle of reciprocal determination . . .'
>
> 'The machine, on the other hand remains essentially remote . . .'
>
> 'The history of technology is dated . . .'
>
> 'Yesterday's machine, today's and tomorrow's, are not related in their structural determinations . . .'

I find this language incredibly alienating. In fact, the paragraph after the one I stopped at begins: 'The individual's relation to the machine has been described by sociologists following Friedmann[9] as one of fundamental alienation.' I will return to this essay some day and read it. I sense that it will have something interesting to say. But the effort is too great now. What strikes me now is the incredibly distancing effect of this language. It is totally abstract and impersonal. Though the author uses the first person ('The distinction I am proposing', 'I want therefore to make it clear'), it quickly became clear to me that he had no interest whatsoever in the personal, or in concrete situations as I understand them—a specific person, at a specific machine, somewhere in time and space, with something on his/her mind, real noises, smells, aches and pains. He has no interest in his own experience of machines, or in explaining why he is writing about them, what they mean to him personally. I take down the next book: *Poetry and Repression* by Harold Bloom.[1]

This book should contain some reference to the self, to the author's self, to ourselves, to how people feel, to how the author feels, since its subject is psychological: repression. I open the book at page 1 and read:

> Jacques Derrida[2] asks a central question in his essay on 'Freud and the Scene of Writing': 'What is a text, and what must the psyche be if it can be represented by a text?' My narrow concern with poetry prompts the

8. Guattari, *Molecular Revolution*, p. 111 [Tompkins's note].
9. Georges Friedmann (1902–1977), French sociologist.
1. American literary critic (b. 1930; see above), author of *Poetry and Repression: Revision from Blake to Stevens* (New Haven: Yale University Press, 1976).
2. French philosopher, proponent of deconstruction (b. 1930; see above).

> contrary question: 'What is a psyche, and what must a text be if it can be represented by a psyche?' Both Derrida's question and my own require exploration of three terms: 'psyche,' 'text,' 'represented.'
>
> 'Psyche' is ultimately from the Indo-European root . . .

—and I stop reading.

The subject of poetry and repression will involve the asking and answering of questions about 'a text'—a generalized, non-particular object that has been the subject of endless discussion for the past twenty years—and about an equally disembodied 'psyche' in relation to the thing called 'a text'—not, to my mind, or rather in view of my desires, a very promising relation in which to consider it. Answering these questions, moreover, will 'require' (on whose part, I wonder?) the 'exploration' of 'three terms'. Before we get to the things themselves—psyches, texts—we shall have to spend a lot of time looking at them *as words*. With the beginning of the next paragraph, we get down to the etymology of 'psyche'. With my agenda, I get off the bus here.

But first I look through the book. Bloom is arguing against canonical readings (of some very canonical poems) and for readings that are not exactly personal, but in which the drama of a self is constantly being played out on a cosmic stage—lots of references to God, kingdom, Paradise, the fall, the eternal—a biblical stage on which, apparently, only men are players (God, Freud, Christ, Nietzsche,[3] and the poets). It is a drama that, although I can see how gripping Bloom can make it, will pall for me because it isn't *my* drama.

Book number three, Michel Foucault's *History of Sexuality*, is more promising. Section One is entitled 'We "other Victorians" '. So Foucault is acknowledging his and our implication in the object of the study. This book will in some way be about 'ourselves', which is what I want. It begins:

> For a long time, the story goes, we supported a Victorian regime, and we continue to be dominated by it even today. Thus the image of the imperial prude is emblazoned on our restrained, mute, and hypocritical sexuality.[4]

Who, exactly, are 'we'? Foucault is using the convention in which the author establishes common ground with his reader by using the first person plural—a presumptuous, though usually successful, move. Presumptuous because it presumes that we are really like him, and successful because, especially when an author is famous, and even when he isn't, 'our' instinct (I criticize the practice and engage in it too) is to want to cooperate, to be included in the circle the author is drawing so cosily around 'us'. It is chummy, this 'we'. It feels good, for a little while, until it starts to feel coercive, until 'we' are subscribing to things that 'I' don't believe.

There is no specific reference to the author's self, no attempt to specify himself. It continues:

> At the beginning of the seventeenth century . . .

3. FRIEDRICH NIETZSCHE (1844–1900), German philosopher.
4. Michel Foucault, *The History of Sexuality*, vol. 1, *An Introduction*, trans. Robert Hurley (New York: Vintage, 1978), p. 3 [Tompkins's note].

I know now where we are going. We are going to history. 'At the beginning of the seventeenth century a certain frankness was still common, it would seem.' Generalizations about the past, though pleasantly qualified ('a certain frankness', 'it would seem'), are nevertheless disappointingly magisterial. Things continue in a generalizing vein—'It was a time of direct gestures, shameless discourse, and open transgressions.' It's not so much that I don't believe him as that I am uncomfortable with the level or the mode of discourse. It is everything that, I thought, Foucault was trying to get away from, in *The Archaeology of Knowledge*.[5] The primacy of the subject as the point of view from which history could be written, the bland assumption of authority, the taking over of time, of substance, of event, the imperialism of description from a unified perspective. Even though the subject matter interests me—sex, hypocrisy, whether or not our view of Victorianism and of ourselves in relation to it is correct—I am not eager to read on. The point of view is discouraging. It will march along giving orders, barking out commands. I'm not willing to go along for the march, not even on Foucault's say-so (I am, or have been, an extravagant admirer of his).

So I turn to 'my' books. To the women's section of my shelves. I take down, unerringly, an anthology called *The Powers of Desire* edited by Christine Stansell, Ann Snitow, and Sharon Thompson. I turn, almost as unerringly, to an essay by Jessica Benjamin entitled 'Master and slave: the fantasy of erotic domination', and begin to read:

> This essay is concerned with the violence of erotic domination. It is about the strange union of rationality and violence that is made in the secret heart of our culture and sometimes enacted in the body. This union has inspired some of the holiest imagery of religious transcendence and now comes to light at the porno newsstands, where women are regularly depicted in the bonds of love. But the slave of love is not always a woman, not always a heterosexual; the fantasy of erotic domination permeates all sexual imagery in our culture.[6]

I am completely hooked, I am going to read this essay from beginning to end and proceed to do so. It gets better, much better, as it goes along. In fact, it gets so good, I find myself putting it down and straying from it because the subject is *so* close to home, and therefore so threatening, that I need relief from it, little breathers, before I can go on. I underline vigorously and often. Think of people I should give it to to read (my husband, this colleague, that colleague).

But wait a minute. There is no personal reference here. The author deals, like Foucault, in generalities. In even bigger ones than his: hers aren't limited to the seventeenth century or the Victorian era. She generalizes about religion, rationality, violence. Why am I not turned off by this as I was in Foucault's case? Why don't I reject this as a grand drama in the style of Bloom? Why don't I bridle at the abstractions as I did when reading Guattari? Well?

The answer is, I see the abstractions as concrete and the issues as personal. They are already personal for me without being personal*ized* because they

5. An influential 1969 book.

6. Jessica Benjamin, "Master and Slave: The Fantasy of Erotic Domination," in *The Powers of Desire: The Politics of Sexuality*, ed. Ann Snitow, Christine Stansell, and Sharon Thompson (New York: Monthly Review Press, 1983), p. 281 [Tompkins's note]. Benjamin (b. 1946), American psychoanalyst.

concern things I've been thinking about for some time, struggling with, trying to figure out for myself. I don't need the author to identify her own involvement, I don't need her to concretize, because these things are already personal and concrete for me. The erotic is already eroticized.

Probably, when Guattari picks up an article whose first sentence has the words 'machine', 'structure', and 'determination', he cathects[7] it immediately. Great stuff. Juicy, terrific. The same would go for Bloom on encountering multiple references to Nietzsche, representation, God the father, and the Sublime.[8] But isn't erotic domination, as a subject, surer to arouse strong feeling than systems of machines or the psyche that can be represented as a text? Clearly, the answer depends on the readership. The people at the convenience store where I stop to get gas and buy milk would find all these passages equally baffling. Though they *might* have uneasy stirrings when they read Jessica Benjamin. 'Erotic domination', especially when coupled with 'porno newsstands', does call some feelings into play almost no matter who you are in this culture.

But I will concede the point. What is personal is completely a function of what is perceived as personal. And what is perceived as personal by men, or rather, what is gripping, significant, 'juicy', is different from what is felt to be that way by women. For what we are really talking about is not the personal as such, what we are talking about is what is important, answers one's needs, strikes one as immediately *interesting*. For women, the personal is such a category.

In literary criticism, we have moved from the New Criticism, which was anti-personal and declared the personal off-limits at every turn—the intentional fallacy, the affective fallacy[9]—to structuralism, which does away with the self altogether—at least as something unique and important to consider—to deconstruction, which subsumes everything in language and makes the self non-self-consistent, ungraspable, a floating signifier, and finally to new historicism which re-institutes the discourse of the object—'In the seventeenth century'—with occasional side glances at how the author's 'situatedness' affects his writing.

The female subject *par excellence*, which is her self and her experiences, has once more been elided by literary criticism.

The question is, why did this happen? One might have imagined a different outcome. The 1960s paves the way for a new personalism in literary discourse by opening literary discussion up to politics, to psychology, to the 'reader', to the effects of style. What happened to deflect criticism into the impersonal labyrinths of 'language', 'discourse', 'system', 'network', and now, with Guattari, 'machine'?

I met Ellen Messer-Davidow last summer at the School of Criticism and Theory[1] where she was the undoubted leader of the women who were there.

7. Attaches to; from the psychoanalytic term *cathexis*, the attachment of psychic energy to an idea or person.

8. A category of aesthetics especially prominent among the Romantics.

9. These are "fallacies," the New Critics WILLIAM K. WIMSATT JR. AND MONROE C. BEARDSLEY argue in essays with these titles (1946, 1949; see above), because the author's intention and the affective response of the audience are irrelevant to interpretation.

1. A prestigious yearly summer program in the United States at which leading theorists give seminars for doctoral students and faculty; Tompkins refers to the 1985 program.

She organized them, led them (I might as well say us, since, although I was on the faculty as a visiting lecturer, she led me, too). At the end of the summer we put on a symposium, a kind of teach-in on feminist criticism and theory, of which none was being offered that summer. I thought it really worked. Some people, eager to advertise their intellectual superiority, murmured disappointment at the 'level' of discussion (code for, 'my mind is finer and more rigorous than yours'). One person who spoke out at the closing session said he felt bulldozed: a more honest and useful response. The point is that Ellen's leadership affected the experience of everyone at the School that summer. What she offered was not an intellectual performance calculated to draw attention to the quality of her mind, but a sustained effort of practical courage that changed the situation we were in. I think that the kind of thing Ellen did should be included in our concept of criticism: analysis that is not an end in itself but pressure brought to bear on a situation.

Now it's time to talk about something that's central to everything I've been saying so far, although it doesn't *show*, as we used to say about the slips we used to wear. If I had to bet on it I would say that Ellen Messer-Davidow was motivated last summer, and probably in her essay, by anger (forgive me, Ellen, if I am wrong), anger at her, our, exclusion from what was being studied at the School, our exclusion from the discourse of 'Western man'. I interpret her behavior this way because anger is what fuels my engagement with feminist issues; an absolute fury that has never even been tapped, relatively speaking. It's time to talk about this now, because it's so central, at least for me. I hate men for the way they treat women, and pretending that women aren't there is one of the ways I hate most.

Last night I saw a movie called *Gunfight at the OK Corral*,[2] starring Burt Lancaster and Kirk Douglas. The movie is patently about the love-relationship between the characters these men play—Wyatt Earp and Doc Holliday. The women in the movie are merely pawns that serve in various ways to reflect the characters of the men, and to advance the story of their relationship to one another. There is a particularly humiliating part, played by Jo Van Fleet, the part of Doc Holliday's mistress—Kate Fisher—whom he treats abominably (everybody in the movie acknowledges this, it's not just me saying so). This woman is degraded over and over again. She is a whore, she is a drunkard, she is a clinging woman, she betrays the life of Wyatt Earp in order to get Doc Holliday back, she is *no longer young* (perhaps this is her chief sin). And her words are always in vain, they are chaff, less than nothing, another sign of her degradation.

Now Doc Holliday is a similarly degraded character. He used to be a dentist and is now a gambler, who lives to get other people's money away from them; he is a drunk, and he abuses the woman who loves him. But his weaknesses, in the perspective of the movie, are glamorous. He is irresistible, charming, seductive, handsome, witty, commanding; it's no wonder Wyatt Earp falls for him, who wouldn't? The degradation doesn't stick to Kirk Douglas; it is all absorbed by his female counterpart, the 'slut', Jo Van Fleet. We are embarrassed every time she appears on the screen, because every time, she is humiliated further.

What enrages me is the way women are used as extensions of men, mirrors

2. Dir. John Sturges (1957).

of men, devices for showing men off, devices for helping men get what they want. They are never there in their own right, or rarely. The world of the Western contains no women.

Sometimes I think *the world* contains no women.

Why am I so angry?

My anger is partly the result of having been an only child who caved in to authority very early on. As a result I've built up a huge storehouse of hatred and resentment against people in authority over me (mostly male). Hatred and resentment and attraction.

Why should poor men be made the object of this old pent-up anger? (Old anger is the best anger, the meanest, the truest, the most intense. Old anger is pure because it's been dislocated from its source for so long, has had the chance to ferment, to feed on itself for so many years, so that it is nothing but anger. All cause, all relation to the outside world, long since sloughed off, withered away. The rage I feel inside me now is the distillation of forty-six years. It has had a long time to simmer, to harden, to become adamantine, a black slab that glows in the dark.)

Are all feminists fueled by such rage? Is the molten lava of millennia of hatred boiling below the surface of every essay, every book, every syllabus, every newsletter, every little magazine? I imagine that I can open the front of my stomach like a door, reach in, and pluck from memory the rooted sorrow, pull it out, root and branch. But where, or rather, who, would I be then? I am attached to this rage. It is a source of identity for me. It is a motivator, an explainer, a justifier, a no-need-to-say-more greeter at the door. If I were to eradicate this anger somehow, what would I do? Volunteer work all day long?

A therapist once suggested to me that I blamed on sexism a lot of stuff that really had to do with my own childhood. Her view was basically the one articulated in Alice Miller's *The Drama of the Gifted Child*, in which the good child has been made to develop a false self by parents who cathect the child narcissistically. My therapist meant that if I worked out some of my problems—as she understood them, on a psychological level—my feminist rage would subside.

Maybe it would, but that wouldn't touch the issue of female oppression. Here is what Miller says about this:

> Political action can be fed by the unconscious anger of children who have been . . . misused, imprisoned, exploited, cramped, and drilled . . . If, however, disillusionment and the resultant mourning can be lived through . . . , then social and political disengagement do not usually follow, but the patient's actions are freed from the compulsion to repeat.[3]

According to Miller's theory, the critical voice inside me, the voice I noticed butting in, belittling, doubting, being wise, is 'the contemptuous introject'. The introjection of authorities who manipulated me, without necessarily meaning to. I think that if you can come to terms with your 'contemptuous introjects', learn to forgive and understand them, your anger will go away.

3. Alice Miller, *The Drama of the Gifted Child* (New York: Basic Books, 1983), p. 101 [Tompkins's note]. Miller (b. 1923), Swiss psychoanalyst.

But if you're not angry, can you still act? Will you still care enough to write the letters, make the phone calls, attend the meetings? You need to find another center within yourself from which to act. A center of outgoing, outflowing, giving feelings. Love instead of anger. I'm embarrassed to say words like these because I've been taught they are mushy and sentimental and smack of cheap popular psychology. I've been taught to look down on people who read M. Scott Peck and Leo Buscaglia and Harold Kushner,[4] because they're people who haven't very much education, and because they're mostly women. Or if not women, then people who take responsibility for learning how to deal with their feelings, who take responsibility for marriages that are going bad, for children who are in trouble, for friends who need help, for themselves. The disdain for popular psychology and for words like 'love' and 'giving' is part of the police action that academic intellectuals wage ceaselessly against feeling, against women, against what is personal. The ridiculing of the 'touchy-feely', of the 'Mickey Mouse', of the sentimental (often associated with teaching that takes students' concerns into account), belongs to the tradition Alison Jaggar rightly characterized as founding knowledge in the denial of emotion. It is looking down on women, with whom feelings are associated, and on the activities with which women are identified: mother, nurse, teacher, social worker, volunteer.

So for a while I can't talk about epistemology. I can't deal with the philosophical bases of feminist literary criticisms. I can't strap myself psychically into an apparatus that will produce the right gestures when I begin to move. I have to deal with the trashing of emotion, and with my anger against it.

This one time I've taken off the straitjacket, and it feels so good.

1987, 1989

4. Authors of popular self-help books, the best known of which are (respectively) *The Road Less Traveled* (1979), *Loving Each Other* (1984), and *When Bad Things Happen to Good People* (1981).

ANNETTE KOLODNY
b. 1941

Feminist literary critic and activist Annette Kolodny represents—in her work and her career—the struggle, aspirations, and accomplishments of post-1960s women in the U.S. academy. Her essay "Dancing through the Minefield" has been called "the most reprinted essay of American feminist literary criticism." It both summarizes the achievements of feminist literary criticism after its first full decade, the 1970s, and attempts to provide a theoretical underpinning for future feminist work.

Born in New York City, Kolodny did her undergraduate work at Brooklyn College, after which she went to work for *Newsweek* in 1962. She returned to graduate school in 1964, earning her Ph.D. in American literature from the University of California at Berkeley in 1969. Active in the students' movement during her Berkeley years, Kolodny left her first teaching position (at Yale University) after only a year to join her husband in Canada, where he fled when his draft board rejected his application for conscientious objector status during the Vietnam War. She taught at the University of British Columbia before returning to the United States in 1974 to take a position at the University of New Hampshire.

Despite publishing a much-admired work of feminist criticism, *The Lay of the Land: Metaphor as Experience and History in American Life and Letters* (1975), Kolodny was denied tenure at New Hampshire, partly as a response to her continued activism, including her work to establish a program in women's studies. She sued on the basis of sexual discrimination and the violation of academic freedom. A founding member of the National Women's Studies Association (NWSA), Kolodny donated much of the cash settlement to establish the Legal Fund of the NWSA's Task Force on Discrimination. She also served as a director of the task force from 1980 to 1985. Kolodny taught at the University of Maryland and Rensselaer Polytechnic Institute before moving to the University of Arizona in 1983, where she became dean of the Faculty of Humanities. Although this trajectory illustrates the improving status of women in American universities, Kolodny's book *Failing the Future: A Dean Looks at Higher Education in the Twenty-First Century* (1998) details the extent to which women and nonwhite students are still outsiders on American campuses.

Kolodny's first two books—*The Lay of the Land* and *The Land before Her: Fantasy and Experience of the American Frontiers, 1630–1860* (1984)—are major scholarly studies, both in their breadth and in their revision of dominant themes in American studies. But her reputation rests largely on two essays—"Dancing through the Minefield" (*Feminist Studies*, spring 1980) and "A Map of Reading: Gender and the Interpretation of Texts" (*New Literary History*, spring 1980). Although "Dancing," our selection, slights psychoanalytically informed feminist work, it continues to serve as a helpful guide to feminist concerns and methodologies.

What comes through strongest in the essay is feminism's persistent commitment to what is often called "social constructionism," although Kolodny in 1980 did not use that term. Social constructivists argue that things in the world—selves, texts, bodies, behaviors—are the products of ongoing social processes of interaction, and thus do not have fixed or inherent meanings. Entities are always dynamic, always in process; their identities change over time as they establish new relations with various other elements in the social scene. Kolodny's primary example in her essay is the "canon" of literary works deemed "great" and worthy of study. (PIERRE BOURDIEU and BARBARA HERRNSTEIN SMITH also address questions of aesthetic value from a social constructivist position.) She insists that the "aesthetic value" of literary works is "determined not so much by the work itself as by the critical technique or aesthetic criteria through which it is . . . read." The critic's interpretation is a product of the interaction between reader and text. And we must understand that *how* any critic reads is also a social product: "reading is a highly socialized—or learned—activity." Just as there is no pure text offering its meanings untouched by conventions and social relations, so there is no pure reader, unshaped by prevailing habits and assumptions. Readers and texts are both made—and they are continually being remade. To deny these social constructions and the changes they cause, Kolodny argues, is to use a claim of fixity to silence debates over values and purposes before such arguments can even begin.

Kolodny believes, then, that feminist criticism should "discover how aesthetic value is assigned in the first place" and "evaluate the imputed norms and normative reading patterns that, in part, led to those pronouncements." Here is a key theoretical moment of her essay. Having become embroiled in value disagreements, feminism should consider the processes underlying value judgments. Kolodny does not believe this theoretical ground will be free of conflict, but she identifies a three-part "theoretical core" that she believes "most current feminist literary criticism" assumes. Her crucial first axiom is that "literary history . . . is a fiction": that is, any narrative which tells the story of literature, indicating the "major" and "minor" works while ignoring others altogether, is constructed by specific individuals within specific institutions and with specific assumptions and aims. Such narratives and the canons they create can—and should—be contested.

Where Kolodny says "fictions," we might today substitute "social constructions," if only because "fictions" can sound inconsequential and arbitrary. Fictions of the sort Kolodny describes have real effects as well as real causes. Literary criticism matters to feminists because they insist that literature embodies social beliefs, conventions, attitudes, and ideologies that operate powerfully throughout the whole of society. Just as feminism for Kolodny embeds judgments of aesthetic values within social processes, so feminists embed the aesthetic within larger "ideological codes" and "value systems." Not just the aesthetic but language itself is deeply and persistently implicated in "establishing, reflecting, and maintaining an asymmetrical relationship between women and men."

Kolodny's essay becomes more problematic—and has attracted criticism—when she moves to theorizing the social embedding of readers. The second of her three explicit axioms is that "we" readers "engage . . . not texts but paradigms." Her point is that texts are encountered by readers from within a certain mind-set, a point most famously made by STANLEY FISH. For Kolodny, "we appropriate meaning from a text according to what we need (or desire) or, in other words, according to the critical assumptions or predispositions (conscious or not) that we bring to it. . . . For most readers, this is a fairly unconscious process." This formulation raises many questions. Most troubling is that Kolodny's own values—as enunciated in the remainder of the essay—appear to run counter to the theoretical claim.

Kolodny's third axiom—"we must reexamine . . . the inherent biases and assumptions informing the critical methods which (in part) shape our aesthetic responses"—strives to undo the unconsciousness of readers identified in axiom two. But a problem arises: Kolodny does not consider the social forces that work against readers' movement from unconsciousness to critical awareness. Failing to pay enough attention to ideology (the ways subjects apprehend the world through culture's filter), she does not recognize the seismic transformation that would be required before selves would be capable of naming their biases and assumptions. Kolodny's critics say that she underestimates power—the social power that establishes and maintains the "fictions" of her first axiom—when she envisions that critics can make a deliberate "choice . . . between having some awareness of what constitutes . . . the bases of our aesthetic responses and going without such an awareness."

In advocating a feminist "pluralism," Kolodny partly responds to such criticism. There are multiple interpretations of various texts, and pluralism recognizes the possible validity and "usefulness" of various readings in terms of different contexts and purposes. Moreover, the fact of different interpretations shows that no single ideology or "fiction" ever reigns supreme. By examining the logic and arguments of different critical approaches, we can move toward the kind of broad critical awareness that Kolodny wishes to promote.

The last paragraph of her essay illustrates certain limits and strengths of Kolodny's understanding of feminist politics. On the one hand, she accords "ideology" the "power" to order "the *sum* of our actions" and tells us "that ideas . . . determine the ways we live"; yet on the other hand she asserts that a "consciously ideologically premised criticism" will be up to the task of undoing that power. Less debatable perhaps is her insistence that women live and work within institutions that are not likely to wither away. She will not let dreams of total revolution distract us from the daily struggles to survive and prosper in the world before us. And she insists that individual success for some women is not enough. Feminism is committed to improving the conditions of all women as they negotiate their way through hierarchies (academic, corporate, political, familial) that have kept them subordinate. Kolodny remains resolutely focused on the work to be done that is right in front of her, while holding on to the larger vision of what that mundane work is striving to accomplish in the long run.

BIBLIOGRAPHY

Kolodny's books to date are *The Lay of the Land: Metaphor as Experience and History in American Life and Letters* (1975), *The Land before Her: Fantasy and Experience of the American Frontiers, 1630–1860* (1984), and *Failing the Future: A Dean Looks at Higher Education in the Twenty-First Century* (1998). *The Dictionary of Literary Biography*, vol. 67 (ed. Gregory S. Jay, 1988), contains a useful entry on Kolodny, which can be supplemented with Mark Lussier and Peggy McCormack's "Interview with Annette Kolodny," *New Orleans Review* 13.4 (1986).

Judith Kegan Gardiner, Elly Bulkin, Rena Patterson, and Annette Kolodny, "An Interchange on Feminist Criticism," *Feminist Studies* 8.3 (1982), is the best place to begin for responses to Kolodny's work. Toril Moi's *Sexual/Textual Politics* (1985) discusses Kolodny as an example of the Anglo-American feminism against which Moi argues. Jane Marcus, "Storming the Toolshed," *Signs* 7.2 (1985), and Tania Modleski, "Feminism and the Power of Interpretation," in *Feminist Studies/Critical Studies* (ed. Teresa de Lauretis, 1986), offer more sympathetic, albeit still critical, evaluations of Kolodny.

Dancing through the Minefield: Some Observations on the Theory, Practice, and Politics of a Feminist Literary Criticism

Had anyone the prescience, ten years ago, to pose the question of defining a "feminist" literary criticism, she might have been told, in the wake of Mary Ellmann's *Thinking About Women*,[1] that it involved exposing the sexual stereotyping of women in both our literature and our literary criticism and, as well, demonstrating the inadequacy of established critical schools and methods to deal fairly or sensitively with works written by women. In broad outline, such a prediction would have stood well the test of time, and, in fact, Ellmann's book continues to be widely read and to point us in useful directions. What could not have been anticipated in 1969, however, was the catalyzing force of an ideology that, for many of us, helped to bridge the gap between the world as we found it and the world as we wanted it to be. For those of us who studied literature, a previously unspoken sense of exclusion from authorship, and a painfully personal distress at discovering whores, bitches, muses, and heroines dead in childbirth where we had once hoped to discover ourselves, could—for the first time—begin to be understood as more than "a set of disconnected, unrealized private emotions."[2] With a renewed courage to make public our otherwise private discontents, what had once been "felt individually as personal insecurity" came at last to be "viewed collectively as structural inconsistency"[3] within the very disciplines we studied. Following unflinchingly the full implications of Ellmann's percipient observations, and emboldened by the liberating energy of feminist ideology—in all its various forms and guises—feminist criticism very quickly moved beyond merely "expos[ing] sexism in one work of lit-

1. Mary Ellmann, *Thinking about Women* (New York: Harcourt Brace Jovanovich, Harvest, 1968). [Except as indicated, all notes are Kolodny's.]
2. See Clifford Geertz, "Ideology as a Cultural System," in his *The Interpretation of Cultures: Selected Essays* (New York: Basic Books, 1973), p. 232.
3. Ibid., p. 204.

erature after another,"[4] and promised, instead, that we might at last "begin to record new choices in a new literary history."[5] So powerful was that impulse that we experienced it, along with Adrienne Rich, as much "more than a chapter in cultural history": it became, rather, "an act of survival."[6] What was at stake was not so much literature or criticism as such, but the historical, social, and ethical consequences of women's participation in, or exclusion from, either enterprise.

The pace of inquiry these last ten years has been fast and furious—especially after Kate Millett's 1970 analysis of the sexual politics of literature[7] added a note of urgency to what had earlier been Ellmann's sardonic anger—while the diversity of that inquiry easily outstripped all efforts to define feminist literary criticism as either a coherent system or a unified set of methodologies. Under its wide umbrella, everything has been thrown into the question: our established canons, our aesthetic criteria, our interpretative strategies, our reading habits, and, most of all, ourselves as critics and as teachers. To delineate its full scope would require nothing less than a book—a book that would be outdated even as it was being composed. For the sake of brevity, therefore, let me attempt only a summary outline.

Perhaps the most obvious success of this new scholarship has been the return to circulation of previously lost or otherwise ignored works by women writers. Following fast upon the initial success of the Feminist Press in reissuing gems such as Rebecca Harding Davis's 1861 novella, *Life in the Iron Mills*, and Charlotte Perkins Gilman's 1892 *The Yellow Wallpaper*, published in 1972 and 1973 respectively,[8] commercial trade and reprint houses vied with one another in the reprinting of anthologies of lost texts and, in some cases, in the reprinting of whole series. For those of us in American literature especially, the phenomenon promised a radical reshaping of our concepts of literary history and, at the very least, a new chapter in understanding the development of women's literary traditions. So commercially successful were these reprintings, and so attuned were the reprint houses to the political attitudes of the audiences for which they were offered, that many of us found ourselves wooed to compose critical introductions which would find in the pages of nineteenth-century domestic and sentimental fictions some signs of either muted rebellions or overt radicalism, in anticipation of the current wave of "new feminism." In rereading with our students these previously lost works, we inevitably raised perplexing questions as to the reasons for their disappearance from the canons of "major works," and we worried over the aesthetic and critical criteria by which they had been accorded diminished status.

This increased availability of works by women writers led, of course, to an

4. Lillian S. Robinson, "Cultural Criticism and the *Horror Vacui*," *College English* 33, no. 1 (1972); reprinted as "The Critical Task" in her *Sex, Class, and Culture* (Bloomington: Indiana University Press, 1978), p. 51.

5. Elaine Showalter, *A Literature of Their Own: British Women Novelists from Brontë to Lessing* (Princeton: Princeton University Press, 1977), p. 36.

6. ADRIENNE RICH, "When We Dead Awaken: Writing as Re-Vision," *College English* 34, no. 1 (October 1972); reprinted in *Adrienne Rich's Poetry*, ed. Barbara Charlesworth Gelpi and Albert Gelpi (New York: W. W. Norton, 1975), p. 90.

7. Kate Millett, *Sexual Politics* (Garden City, N.Y.: Doubleday, 1970).

8. Rebecca Harding Davis, *Life in the Iron Mills*, originally published in *The Atlantic Monthly*, April 1861; reprinted with "A Biographical Interpretation" by Tillie Olsen (Old Westbury, N.Y.: Feminist Press, 1972). Charlotte Perkins Gilman, *The Yellow Wallpaper*, originally published in *The New England Magazine*, May 1892; reprinted with an afterword by Elaine R. Hedges (Old Westbury, N.Y.: Feminist Press, 1973).

increased interest in what elements, if any, might comprise some sort of unity or connection among them. The possibility that women had developed either a unique, or at least a related tradition of their own, especially intrigued those of us who specialized in one national literature or another, or in historical periods. Nina Baym's recent *Woman's Fiction: A Guide to Novels by and about Women in America, 1820–1870*[9] demonstrates the Americanists' penchant for examining what were once the "best sellers" of their day, the ranks of the popular fiction writers, among which women took a dominant place throughout the nineteenth century, while the feminist studies of British literature emphasized instead of the wealth of women writers who have been regarded as worthy of canonization. Not so much building upon one another's work as clarifying, successively, the parameters of the questions to be posed, Sydney Janet Kaplan, Ellen Moers, Patricia Meyer Spacks, and Elaine Showalter, among many others, concentrated their energies on delineating an internally consistent "body of work" by women that might stand as a female counter-tradition. For Kaplan, in 1975, this entailed examining women writers' various attempts to portray feminine consciousness and self-consciousness, not as a psychological category, but as a stylistic or rhetorical device.[1] That same year, arguing essentially that literature publicizes the private, Spacks placed her consideration of a "female imagination" within social and historical frames, to conclude that "for readily discernible historical reasons women have characteristically concerned themselves with matters more or less peripheral to male concerns," and she attributed to this fact an inevitable difference in the literary emphases and subject matters of female and male writers.[2] The next year, Moers's *Literary Women: The Great Writers* focused on the pathways of literary influence that linked the English novel in the hands of women.[3] And, finally, in 1977, Showalter took up the matter of a "female literary tradition in the English novel from the generation of the Brontës[4] to the present day" by arguing that, because women in general constitute a kind of "subculture within the framework of a larger society," the work of women writers, in particular, would thereby demonstrate a unity of "values, conventions, experiences, and behaviors impinging on each individual" as she found her sources of "self-expression relative to a dominant [and, by implication, male] society."[5]

At the same time that women writers were being reconsidered and reread, male writers were similarly subjected to a new feminist scrutiny. The continuing result—to put ten years of difficult analysis into a single sentence—has been nothing less than an acute attentiveness to the ways in which certain power relations—usually those in which males wield various forms of influence over females—are inscribed in the texts (both literary and critical) that we have inherited, not merely as subject matter, but as the unques-

9. Nina Baym, *Woman's Fiction: A Guide to Novels by and about Women in America, 1820–1870* (Ithaca: Cornell University Press, 1978).
1. In her *Feminine Consciousness in the Modern British Novel* (Urbana: University of Illinois Press, 1975), p. 3, Sydney Janet Kaplan explains that she is using the term "feminine consciousness" "not simply as some general attitude of women toward their own femininity, and not as something synonymous with a particular sensibility among female writers. I am concerned with it as a literary device: a method of characterization of females in fiction."
2. Patricia Meyer Spacks, *The Female Imagination* (New York: Avon Books, 1975), p. 6.
3. Ellen Moers, *Literary Women: The Great Writers* (Garden City, N.Y.: Doubleday, 1976).
4. The sisters Charlotte (1816–1855), Emily (1818–1848), and Anne (1820–1849) Brontë all published novels [editor's note].
5. Showalter, *A Literature of Their Own*, p. 11.

tioned, often unacknowledged *given* of the culture. Even more important than the new interpretations of individual texts are the probings into the consequences (for women) of the conventions that inform those texts. For example, in surveying selected nineteenth- and early twentieth-century British novels which employ what she calls "the two suitors convention," Jean E. Kennard sought to understand why and how the structural demands of the convention, even in the hands of women writers, inevitably work to imply "the inferiority and necessary subordination of women." Her 1978 study, *Victims of Convention*, points out that the symbolic nature of the marriage which conventionally concludes such novels "indicates the adjustment of the protagonist to society's values, a condition which is equated with her maturity." Kennard's concern, however, is with the fact that the structural demands of the form too often sacrifice precisely those "virtues of independence and individuality," or, in other words, the very "qualities we have been invited to admire in" the heroines.[6] Kennard appropriately cautions us against drawing from her work any simplistically reductive thesis about the mimetic relations between art and life. Yet her approach nonetheless suggests that what is important about a fiction is not whether it ends in a death or a marriage, but what the symbolic demands of that particular conventional ending imply about the values and beliefs of the world that engendered it.

Her work thus participates in a growing emphasis in feminist literary study on the fact of literature as a social institution, embedded not only within its own literary traditions, but also within the particular physical and mental artifacts of the society from which it comes. Adumbrating Millett's 1970 decision to anchor her "literary reflections" to a preceding analysis of the historical, social, and economic contexts of sexual politics,[7] more recent work—most notably Lillian Robinson's—begins with the premise that the process of artistic creation "consists not of ghostly happenings in the head but of a matching of the states and processes of symbolic models against the states and processes of the wider world."[8] The power relations inscribed in the form of conventions within our literary inheritance, these critics argue, reify the encodings of those same power relations in the culture at large. And the critical examination of rhetorical codes becomes, in their hands, the pursuit of ideological codes, because both embody either value systems or the dialectic of competition between value systems. More often than not, these critics also insist upon examining not only the mirroring of life in art, but also the normative impact of art on life. Addressing herself to the popular art available to working women, for example, Robinson is interested in understanding not only "the forms it uses," but, more importantly, "the myths it creates, the influence it exerts." "The way art helps people to order, interpret, mythologize, or dispose of their own experience," she declares, may be "complex and often ambiguous, but it is not impossible to define."[9]

Whether its focus be upon the material or the imaginative contexts of literary invention; single texts or entire canons; the relations between authors, genres, or historical circumstances; lost authors or well-known

6. Jean E. Kennard, *Victims of Convention* (Hamden, Conn.: Archon Books, 1978), pp. 164, 18, 14.
7. See Millett, *Sexual Politics*, pt. 3, "The Literary Reflection," pp. 235–361.
8. The phrase is Geertz's, "Ideology as a Cultural System," p. 214.
9. Lillian Robinson, "Criticism—and Self-Criticism," *College English* 36, no. 4 (1974), and "Criticism: Who Needs It?" in *The Uses of Criticism*, ed. A. P. Foulkes (Bern and Frankfurt: Lang, 1976); both reprinted in *Sex, Class, and Culture*, pp. 67, 80.

names, the variety and diversity of all feminist literary criticism finally coheres in its stance of almost defensive rereading. What Adrienne Rich had earlier called "re-vision," that is, "the act of looking back, of seeing with fresh eyes, of entering an old text from a new critical direction,"[1] took on a more actively self-protective coloration in 1978, when Judith Fetterley called upon the woman reader to learn to "resist" the sexist designs a text might make upon her—asking her to identify against herself, so to speak, by manipulating her sympathies on behalf of male heroes, but against female shrew or bitch characters.[2] Underpinning a great deal of this critical rereading has been the not-unexpected alliance between feminist literary study and feminist studies in linguistics and language-acquisition. Tillie Olsen's commonsense observation of the danger of "perpetuating—by continued usage—entrenched, centuries-old oppressive power realities, early-on incorporated into language,"[3] has been given substantive analysis in the writings of feminists who study "language as a symbolic system closely tied to a patriarchal social structure." Taken together, their work demonstrates "the importance of language in establishing, reflecting, and maintaining an asymmetrical relationship between women and men."[4]

To consider what this implies for the fate of women who essay the craft of language is to ascertain, perhaps for the first time, the real dilemma of the poet who finds her most cherished private experience "hedged by taboos, mined with false-namings."[5] It also examines the dilemma of the male reader who, in opening the pages of a woman's book, finds himself entering a strange and unfamiliar world of symbolic significance. For if, as Nelly Furman insists, neither language use nor language acquisition are "gender-neutral," but are, instead, "imbued with our sex-inflected cultural values";[6] and if, additionally, reading is a process of "sorting out the structures of signification"[7] in any text, then male readers who find themselves outside of and unfamiliar with the symbolic systems that constitute female experience in women's writings will necessarily dismiss those systems as undecipherable, meaningless, or trivial. And male professors will find no reason to include such works in the canons of "major authors." At the same time, women writers, coming into a tradition of literary language and conventional forms already appropriated, for centuries, to the purposes of male expression, will be forced virtually to "wrestle" with that language in an effort "to remake it as a language adequate to our conceptual processes."[8] To all of this, feminists concerned with the politics of language and style have been acutely attentive. "Language conceals an invincible adversary," observes French critic Hélène Cixous, "because it's the language of men and their grammar."[9] But equally

1. Rich, "When We Dead Awaken," p. 90.
2. Judith Fetterley, *The Resisting Reader: A Feminist Approach to American Fiction* (Bloomington: Indiana University Press, 1978).
3. Tillie Olsen, *Silences* (New York: Delacorte Press/Seymour Lawrence, 1978), pp. 239–40.
4. See Cheris Kramer, Barrie Thorne, and Nancy Henley, "Perspectives on Language and Communication," review essay in *Signs* 3, no. 3 (summer 1978): 646.
5. See Adrienne Rich's discussion of the difficulty in finding authentic language for her experience as a mother in her *Of Woman Born* (New York: W. W. Norton, 1976), p. 15.
6. Nelly Furman, "The Study of Women and Language: Comment on Vol. 3, no. 3," *Signs* 4, no. 1 (autumn 1978): 184.
7. Again, my phrasing comes from Geertz, "Thick Description: Toward an Interpretive Theory of Culture" in his *Interpretation of Cultures: Selected Essays* (New York: Basic Books, 1972), p. 9.
8. Julia Penelope Stanley and Susan W. Robbins, "Toward a Feminist Aesthetic," *Chrysalis*, no. 6 (1977): 63.
9. Hélène Cixous, "The Laugh of the Medusa," trans. Keith Cohen and Paula Cohen, *Signs* 1, no. 4 (summer 1976): 87. [For this essay, see above—editor's note.]

insistent, as in the work of Sandra M. Gilbert and Susan Gubar, has been the understanding of the need for *all* readers—male and female alike—to learn to penetrate the otherwise unfamiliar universes of symbolic action that comprise women's writings, past and present.[1]

To have attempted so many difficult questions and to have accomplished so much—even acknowledging the inevitable false starts, overlapping, and repetition—in so short a time, should certainly have secured feminist literary criticism an honored berth on that ongoing intellectual journey which we loosely term in academia, "critical analysis." Instead of being welcomed onto the train, however, we've been forced to negotiate a minefield. The very energy and diversity of our enterprise have rendered us vulnerable to attack on the grounds that we lack both definition and coherence; while our particular attentiveness to the ways in which literature encodes and disseminates cultural value systems calls down upon us imprecations echoing those heaped upon the Marxist critics of an earlier generation. If we are scholars dedicated to rediscovering a lost body of writings by women, then our finds are questioned on aesthetic grounds. And if we are critics, determined to practice revisionist readings, it is claimed that our focus is too narrow, and our results are only distortions or, worse still, polemical misreadings.

The very vehemence of the outcry, coupled with our total dismissal in some quarters,[2] suggests not our deficiencies, however, but the potential magnitude of our challenge. For what we are asking be scrutinized are nothing less than shared cultural assumptions so deeply rooted and so long ingrained that, for the most part, our critical colleagues have ceased to recognize them as such. In other words, what is really being bewailed in the claims that we distort texts or threaten the disappearance of the great Western literary tradition itself[3] is not so much the disappearance of either text or tradition but, instead, the eclipse of that particular *form* of the text, and that particular *shape* of the canon, which previously reified male readers' sense of power and significance in the world. Analogously, by asking whether, as readers, we ought to be "really satisfied by the marriage of Dorothea Brooke to Will Ladislaw? of Shirley Keeldar to Louis Moore?" or whether, as Kennard suggests, we must reckon with the ways in which "the qualities we have been invited to admire in these heroines [have] been sacrificed to structural neat-

1. In *The Madwoman in the Attic: The Woman Writer and the Nineteenth-Century Literary Imagination* (New Haven: Yale University Press, 1979), SANDRA M. GILBERT and SUSAN GUBAR suggest that women's writings are in some sense "palimpsestic" in that their "surface designs conceal or obscure deeper, less accessible (and less socially acceptable) levels of meaning" (p. 73). It is, in their view, an art designed "both to express and to camouflage" (p. 81).

2. Consider, for example, Paul Boyer's reductive and inaccurate generalization that "what distinguishes ordinary books and articles about women from feminist writing is the feminist insistence on asking the same questions of every work and demanding ideologically satisfactory answers to those questions as a means of evaluating it," in his "A Case against Feminist Criticism," *Partisan Review* 43, no. 4 (1976): 602. It is partly as a result of such misconceptions that we have the paucity of feminist critics who are granted a place in English departments which otherwise pride themselves on the variety of their critical orientations.

3. Ambivalent though he is about the literary continuity that begins with Homer, HAROLD BLOOM nonetheless somewhat ominously prophesies "that the first true break . . . will be brought about in generations to come, if the burgeoning religion of Liberated Woman spreads from its clusters of enthusiasts to dominate the West," in his *A Map of Misreading* (New York: Oxford University Press, 1975), p. 33. On p. 36, he acknowledges that while something "as violent [as] a quarrel would ensue if I expressed my judgment" on Robert Lowell and Norman Mailer, "it would lead to something more intense than quarrels if I expressed my judgment upon . . . the 'literature of Women's Liberation.' " [Lowell (1917–1977), Amercan poet. Mailer (b. 1923), American writer of novels and nonfiction—editor's note.]

ness,"[4] is to raise difficult and profoundly perplexing questions about the ethical implications of our otherwise unquestioned aesthetic pleasures. It is, after all, an imposition of high order to ask the viewer to attend to Ophelia's sufferings in a scene where, before, he'd always so comfortably kept his eye fixed firmly on Hamlet. To understand all this, then, as the real nature of the challenge we have offered and, in consequence, as the motivation for the often overt hostility we've aroused, should help us learn to negotiate the minefield, if not with grace, then with at least a clearer comprehension of its underlying patterns.

The ways in which objections to our work are usually posed, of course, serve to obscure their deeper motivations. But this may, in part, be due to our own reticence at taking full responsibility for the truly radicalizing premises that lie at the theoretical core of all we have so far accomplished. It may be time, therefore, to redirect discussion, forcing our adversaries to deal with the substantive issues and pushing ourselves into a clearer articulation of what, in fact, we are about. Up until now, I fear, we have only piecemeal dealt with the difficulties inherent in challenging the authority of established canons and then justifying the excellence of women's traditions, sometimes in accord with standards to which they have no intrinsic relation.

At the very point at which we must perforce enter the discourse—that is, claiming excellence or importance for our "finds"—all discussion has already, we discover, long ago been closed. "If Kate Chopin[5] were *really* worth reading," an Oxford-trained colleague once assured me, "she'd have lasted—like Shakespeare"; and he then proceeded to vote against the English department's crediting a women's studies seminar I was offering in American women writers. The canon, for him, conferred excellence: Chopin's exclusion demonstrated only her lesser worth. As far as he was concerned, I could no more justify giving English department credit for the study of Chopin than I could dare publicly to question Shakespeare's genius. Through hindsight, I've now come to view that discussion as not only having posed fruitless oppositions, but also as having entirely evaded the much more profound problem lurking just beneath the surface of our disagreement. That is, that the fact of canonization puts any work beyond questions of establishing its merit and, instead, invites students to offer only increasingly more ingenious readings and interpretations, the purpose of which is to validate the greatness already imputed by canonization.

Had I only understood it for what it was then, into this circular and self-serving set of assumptions I might have interjected some statement of my right to question why *any* text is revered and my need to know what it tells us about "how we live, how we have been living, how we have been led to imagine ourselves, [and] how our language has trapped as well as liberated us."[6] The very fact of our critical training within the strictures imposed by an established canon of major works and authors, however, repeatedly deflects us from such questions. Instead, we find ourselves endlessly responding to the *riposte* that the overwhelmingly male presence among

4. Kennard, *Victims of Convention*, p. 14. [Dorothea Brooke, the heroine of George Eliot's *Middlemarch* (1871–72), marries Will Ladislaw at the novel's end; Shirley Keeldar, the heroine of Charlotte Brontë's *Shirley* (1849), marries Louis Moore—editor's note.]

5. American fiction writer (1851–1904) whose once-neglected work is now often taught in American literature classes [editor's note].

6. Rich, "When We Dead Awaken," p. 90.

canonical authors was only an accident of history—and never intentionally sexist—coupled with claims to the "obvious" aesthetic merit of those canonized texts. It is, as I say, a fruitless exchange, serving more to obscure than to expose the territory being protected and dragging us, again and again, through the minefield.

It is my contention that current hostilities might be transformed into a true dialogue with our critics if we at last made explicit what appear, to this observer, to constitute the three crucial propositions to which our special interests inevitably give rise. They are, moreover, propositions which, if handled with care and intelligence, could breathe new life into now moribund areas of our profession: (1) Literary history (and with that, the historicity of literature) is a fiction; (2) insofar as we are taught how to read, what we engage are not texts but paradigms; and, finally, (3) since the grounds upon which we assign aesthetic value to texts are never infallible, unchangeable, or universal, we must reexamine not only our aesthetics but, as well, the inherent biases and assumptions informing the critical methods which (in part) shape our aesthetic responses. For the sake of brevity, I won't attempt to offer the full arguments for each but, rather, only sufficient elaboration to demonstrate what I see as their intrinsic relation to the potential scope of and present challenge implied by feminist literary study.

1. *Literary history (and, with that, the historicity of literature) is a fiction.* To begin with, an established canon functions as a model by which to chart the continuities and discontinuities, as well as the influences upon and the interconnections between works, genres, and authors. That model we tend to forget, however, is of our own making. It will take a very different shape, and explain its inclusions and exclusions in very different ways, if the reigning critical ideology believes that new literary forms result from some kind of ongoing internal dialectic within preexisting styles and traditions or if, by contrast, the ideology declares that literary change is dependent upon societal development and thereby determined by upheavals in the social and economic organization of the culture at large.[7] Indeed, whenever in the previous century of English and American literary scholarship one alternative replaced the other, we saw dramatic alterations in canonical "wisdom."

This suggests, then, that our sense of a "literary history" and, by extension, our confidence in a "historical" canon, is rooted not so much in any definitive understanding of the past, as it is in our need to call up and utilize the past on behalf of a better understanding of the present. Thus, to paraphrase David Couzens Hoy, it becomes "necessary to point out that the understanding of art and literature is such an essential aspect of the present's self-understanding that this self-understanding conditions what even gets taken" as comprising that artistic and literary past. To quote Hoy fully, "this continual reinterpretation of the past goes hand in hand with the continual reinterpretation by the present of itself."[8] In our own time, uncertain as to which, if any, model truly accounts for our canonical choices or accurately explains literary history, and pressured further by the feminists' call for some

7. The first is a proposition currently expressed by some structuralists and formalist critics; the best statement of the second probably appears in Georg Lukács, *Writer and Critic* (New York: Grosset and Dunlap, 1970), p. 119. [On the Hungarian Marxist critic GYÖRGY LUKÁCS, see above—editor's note.]

8. David Couzens Hoy, "Hermeneutic Circularity, Indeterminacy, and Incommensurability," *New Literary History* 10, no. 1 (autumn 1978): 166–67.

justification of the criteria by which women's writings were largely excluded from both that canon and history, we suffer what Harold Bloom has called "a remarkable dimming" of "our mutual sense of canonical standards."[9]

Into this apparent impasse, feminist literary theorists implicitly introduce the observation that our choices and evaluations of current literature have the effect either of solidifying or of reshaping our sense of the past. The authority of any established canon, after all, is reified by our perception that current work seems to grow, almost inevitably, out of it (even in opposition or rebellion), and is called into question when what we read appears to have little or no relation to what we recognize as coming before. So, were the larger critical community to begin to seriously attend to the recent outpouring of fine literature by women, this would surely be accompanied by a concomitant researching of the past, by literary historians, in order to account for the present phenomenon. In that process, literary history would itself be altered: works by seventeenth-, eighteenth-, or nineteenth-century women, to which we had not previously attended, might be given new importance, as "precursors" or as prior influences upon present-day authors; while selected male writers might also be granted new prominence as figures whom the women today, or even yesterday, needed to reject. I am arguing, in other words, that the choices we make in the present inevitably alter our sense of the past that led to them.

Related to this is the feminist challenge to that patently mendacious critical fallacy that we read the "classics" in order to reconstruct the past "the way it really was," and that we read Shakespeare and Milton in order to apprehend the meanings that they intended. Short of time machines or miraculous resurrections there is simply no way to know, precisely or surely, what "really was," what Homer intended when he sang, or Milton when he dictated.[1] Critics more acute than I have already pointed up the impossibility of grounding a reading in the imputation of authorial intention because the further removed the author is from us, so too must be her or his systems of knowledge and belief, points of view, and structures of vision (artistic and otherwise).[2] (I omit here the difficulty of finally either proving or disproving the imputation of intentionality because, inescapably, the only appropriate authority is unavailable: deceased.) What we have really come to mean when we speak of competence in reading historical texts,[3] therefore, is the ability to recognize literary conventions which have survived through time—so as to remain operational in the mind of the reader—and, where these are lacking, the ability to translate (or perhaps transform?) the text's ciphers into more current and recognizable shapes. But we never really reconstruct the

9. Bloom, *Map of Misreading*, p. 36.
1. When John Milton (1608–1674) composed his great epic, *Paradise Lost* (1667), he was blind; he therefore dictated the poem to his daughters (whose work as his amanuenses has struck some feminist critics as emblematic). The epics attributed to Homer (ca. 8th c. B.C.E.) are the oldest surviving works of Greek literature [editor's note].
2. John Dewey offered precisely this argument in 1934 when he insisted that a work of art "is re-created every time it is esthetically experienced. . . . It is absurd to ask what an artist 'really' meant by his product: he himself would find different meanings in it at different days and hours and in different stages of his own development." Further, he explained, "It is simply an impossibility that any one today should experience the Parthenon as the devout Athenian contemporary citizen experienced it, any more than the religious statuary of the twelfth century can mean, esthetically, even to a good Catholic today just what it meant to the worshipers of the old period," in *Art as Experience* (New York: Capricorn Books, 1958), pp. 108–9.
3. In his very influential *Structuralist Poetics* (1975), Jonathan Culler described the "competent" reader as one versed in the literary conventions and other cultural background knowledge that inform the production and reception of literary texts [editor's note].

past in its own terms. What we gain when we read the "classics," then, is neither Homer's Greece nor George Eliot's England *as they knew it* but, rather, an approximation of an already fictively imputed past made available, through our interpretive strategies, for present concerns. Only by understanding this can we put to rest that recurrent delusion that the "continuing relevance" of the classics serves as "testimony to perennial features of human experience."[4] The only "perennial feature" to which our ability to read and reread texts written in previous centuries testifies is our inventiveness—in the sense that all of literary history is a fiction which we daily recreate as we reread it. What distinguishes feminists in this regard is their desire to alter and extend what we take as historically relevant from out of that vast storehouse of our literary inheritance and, further, feminists' recognition of the storehouse for what it really is: a resource for remodeling our literary history, past, present, and future.

2. *Insofar as we are taught how to read, what we engage are not texts but paradigms.* To pursue the logical consequences of the first proposition leads, however uncomfortably, to the conclusion that we appropriate meaning from a text according to what we need (or desire) or, in other words, according to the critical assumptions or predispositions (conscious or not) that we bring to it. And we appropriate different meanings, or report different gleanings, at different times—even from the same text—according to our changed assumptions, circumstances, and requirements. This, in essence, constitutes the heart of the second proposition. For insofar as literature is itself a social institution, so, too, reading is a highly socialized—or learned—activity. What makes it so exciting, of course, is that it can be constantly relearned and refined, so as to provide either an individual or an entire reading community, over time, with infinite variations of the same text. It *can* provide that, but, I must add, too often it does not. Frequently our reading habits become fixed, so that each successive reading experience functions, in effect, normatively, with one particular kind of novel stylizing our expectations of those to follow, the stylistic devices of any favorite author (or group of authors) alerting us to the presence or absence of those devices in the works of others, and so on. "Once one has read his first poem," Murray Krieger has observed, "he turns to his second and to the others that will follow thereafter with an increasing series of preconceptions about the sort of activity in which he is indulging. In matters of literary experience, as in other experiences," Krieger concludes, "one is a virgin but once."[5]

For most readers, this is a fairly unconscious process, and not unnaturally, what we are taught to read well and with pleasure, when we are young, predisposes us to certain specific kinds of adult reading tastes. For the professional literary critic, the process may be no different, but it is at least more conscious. Graduate schools, at their best, are training grounds for competing interpretive paradigms or reading techniques: affective stylistics, structuralism, and semiotic analysis, to name only a few of the more recent entries. The delight we learn to take in the mastery of these interpretive strategies is then often mistakenly construed as our delight in reading spe-

4. Charles Altieri, "The Hermeneutics of Literary Indeterminacy: A Dissent from the New Orthodoxy," *New Literary History* 10, no. 1 (autumn 1978): 90.

5. Murray Krieger, *Theory of Criticism: A Tradition and Its System* (Baltimore: Johns Hopkins University Press, 1976), p. 6.

cific texts, especially in the case of works that would otherwise be unavailable or even offensive to us. In my own graduate career, for example, with superb teachers to guide me, I learned to take great pleasure in *Paradise Lost*, even though as both a Jew and a feminist, I can subscribe neither to its theology nor to its hierarchy of sexual valuation. If, within its own terms (as I have been taught to understand them), the text manipulates my sensibilities and moves me to pleasure—as I will affirm it does—then, at least in part, that must be because, in spite of my real-world alienation from many of its basic tenets, I have been able to enter that text through interpretive strategies which allow me to displace less comfortable observations with others to which I have been taught pleasurably to attend. Though some of my teachers may have called this process "learning to read the text properly," I have now come to see it as learning to effectively manipulate the critical strategies which they taught me so well. Knowing, for example, the poem's debt to epic conventions, I am able to discover in it echoes and reworkings of both lines and situations from Virgil[6] and Homer; placing it within the ongoing Christian debate between Good and Evil, I comprehend both the philosophic and the stylistic significance of Satan's ornate rhetoric as compared to God's majestic simplicity in Book III. But, in each case, an interpretative model, already assumed, had guided my discovery of the evidence for it.[7]

When we consider the implications of these observations for the processes of canon formation and for the assignment of aesthetic value, we find ourselves locked in a chicken-and-egg dilemma, unable easily to distinguish as primary the importance of *what* we read as opposed to *how* we have learned to read it. For, simply put, we read well, and with pleasure, what we already know how to read; and what we know how to read is to a large extent dependent upon what we have already read (works from which we've developed our expectations and learned our interpretive strategies). What we then choose to read—and, by extension, teach and thereby "canonize"—usually follows upon our previous reading. Radical breaks are tiring, demanding, uncomfortable, and sometimes wholly beyond our comprehension.

Though the argument is not usually couched in precisely these terms, a considerable segment of the most recent feminist rereadings of women writers allows the conclusion that, where those authors have dropped out of sight, the reason may be due not to any lack of merit in the work but, instead, to an incapacity of predominantly male readers to properly interpret and appreciate women's texts—due, in large part, to a lack of prior acquaintance. The fictions which women compose about the worlds they inhabit may owe a debt to prior, influential works by other women or, simply enough, to the daily experience of the writer herself or, more usually, to some combination of the two. The reader coming upon such fiction, with knowledge of neither its informing literary traditions nor its real-world contexts, will thereby find himself hard-pressed, though he may recognize the words on the page, to competently decipher its intended meanings. And this is what makes the recent studies by Spacks, Moers, Showalter, Gilbert and Gubar, and others so crucial. For, by attempting to delineate the connections and interrelations

6. Roman poet (70–19 B.C.E.); his *Aeneid* is an epic on the legendary origins of the Roman people [editor's note].

7. See STANLEY E. FISH, "Normal Circumstances, Literal Language, Direct Speech Acts, the Ordinary, the Everyday, the Obvious, What Goes without Saying, and Other Special Cases," *Critical Inquiry* 4, no. 4 (summer 1978): 627–28.

that make for a female literary tradition, they provide us invaluable aids for recognizing and understanding the unique literary traditions and gender-related contexts out of which women write.

The (usually male) reader who, both by experience and by reading, has never made acquaintance with those contexts—historically, the lying-in room, the parlor, the nursery, the kitchen, the laundry, and so on—will necessarily lack the capacity to fully interpret the dialogue or action embedded therein; for, as every good novelist knows, the meaning of any character's action or statement is inescapably a function of the specific situation in which it is embedded.[8] Virginia Woolf therefore quite properly anticipated the male reader's dispostion to write off what he could not understand, abandoning women's writings as offering "not merely a difference of view, but a view that is weak, or trivial, or sentimental because it differs from his own." In her 1929 essay on "Women and Fiction," Woolf grappled most obviously with the ways in which male writers and male subject matter had already preempted the language of literature. Yet she was also tacitly commenting on the problem of (male) audience and conventional reading expectations when she speculated that the woman writer might well "find that she is perpetually wishing to alter the established values [in literature]—to make serious what appears insignificant to a man, and trivial what is to him important."[9] "The competence' necessary for understanding [a] literary message . . . depends upon a great number of codices," after all; as Cesare Segre has pointed out, to be competent, a reader must either share or at least be familiar with, "in addition to the code language . . . the codes of custom, of society, and of conceptions of the world"[1] (what Woolf meant by "values"). Males ignorant of women's "values" or conceptions of the world will necessarily, thereby, be poor readers of works that in any sense recapitulate their codes.

The problem is further exacerbated when the language of the literary text is largely dependent upon figuration. For it can be argued, as Ted Cohen has shown, that while "in general, and with some obvious qualifications . . . all literal use of language is accessible to all whose language it is . . . figurative use can be inaccessible to all but those who share information about one another's knowledge, beliefs, intentions, and attitudes.[2] There was nothing fortuitous, for example, in Charlotte Perkins Gilman's decision to situate the progressive mental breakdown and increasing incapacity of the protagonist of *The Yellow Wallpaper* in an upstairs room that had once served as a nursery (with barred windows, no less). But the reader unacquainted with the ways in which women traditionally inhabited a household might not have taken the initial description of the setting as semantically relevant; and the progressive infantilization of the adult protagonist would thereby lose some of its symbolic implications. Analogously, the contemporary poet who declares, along with Adrienne Rich, the need for "a whole new poetry beginning here" is acknowledging that the materials available for symbolization and figuration from women's contexts will necessarily differ from those that men have traditionally utilized:

8. Ibid., p. 642.

9. VIRGINIA WOOLF, "Women and Fiction," in her *Granite and Rainbow: Essays* (London: Hogarth, 1958), p. 81.

1. Cesare Segre, "Narrative Structures and Literary History," *Critical Inquiry* 3, no. 2 (winter 1976): 272–73.

2. Ted Cohen, "Metaphor and the Cultivation of Intimacy," *Critical Inquiry* 5, no.1 (autumn 1978): 9.

Vision begins to happen in such a life
as if a woman quietly walked away
from the argument and jargon in a room
and sitting down in the kitchen, began turning in her lap
bits of yam, calico and velvet scraps,
....
pulling the tenets of a life together
with no mere will to mastery,
only care for the many-lived, unending
forms in which she finds herself.[3]

What, then, is the fate of the woman writer whose competent reading community is composed only of members of her own sex? And what, then, the response of the male critic who, on first looking into Virginia Woolf or Doris Lessing,[4] finds all of the interpretative strategies at his command inadequate to a full and pleasurable deciphering of their pages? Historically, the result has been the diminished status of women's products and their consequent absence from major canons. Nowadays, however, by pointing out that the act of "interpreting language is no more sexually neutral than language use or the language system itself," feminist students of language, like Nelly Furman, help us better understand the crucial linkage between our gender and our interpretive, or reading, strategies. Insisting upon "the contribution of the . . . reader [in] the active attribution of significance to formal signifiers,"[5] Furman and others promise to shake us all—female and male alike—out of our canonized and conventional aesthetic assumptions.

3. *Since the grounds upon which we assign aesthetic value to texts are never infallible, unchangeable, or universal, we must reexamine not only our aesthetics but, as well, the inherent biases and assumptions informing the critical methods which (in part) shape our aesthetic responses.* I am, on the one hand, arguing that men will be better readers, or appreciators, of women's books when they have read more of them (as women have always been taught to become astute readers of men's texts). On the other hand, it will be noted, the emphasis of my remarks shifts the act of critical judgment from assigning aesthetic valuations to texts and directs it, instead, to ascertaining the adequacy of any interpretative paradigm to a full reading of both female and male writing. My third proposition—and, I admit, perhaps the most controversial—thus calls into question that recurrent tendency in criticism to establish norms for the evaluation of literary works when we might better serve the cause of literature by developing standards for evaluating the adequacy of our critical methods.[6] This does not mean that I wish to discard aesthetic valuation. The choice, as I see it, is not between retaining or discarding aesthetic values; rather, the choice is between having some awareness of what constitutes (at least in part) the bases of our aesthetic responses

3. From Adrienne Rich's "Transcendental Etude," in her *The Dream of a Common Language: Poems, 1974–1977* (New York: W. W. Norton, 1978), pp. 76–77.

4. Kolodny echoes here John Keats's 1819 sonnet "On First Looking into Chapman's Homer," which describes the "new worlds" that "swim" into view as Keats reads George Chapman's translation of Homer's poetry. Lessing (b. 1919), English novelist, orginally from Rhodesia, whose *Golden Notebook* (1962) is a feminist landmark [editor's note].

5. Furman, "The Study of Women and Language," p. 184.

6. "A recurrent tendency in criticism is the establishment of false norms for the evaluation of literary works," notes Robert Scholes in his *Structuralism in Literature: An Introduction* (New Haven: Yale University Press, 1974), p. 131.

and going without such an awareness. For it is my view that insofar as aesthetic responsiveness continues to be an integral aspect of our human response system—in part spontaneous, in part learned and educated—we will inevitably develop theories to help explain, formalize, or even initiate those responses.

In challenging the adequacy of received critical opinion or the imputed excellence of established canons, feminist literary critics are essentially seeking to discover how aesthetic value is assigned in the first place, where it resides (in the text or in the reader), and, most importantly, what validity may really be claimed by our aesthetic "judgments." What ends do those judgments serve, the feminist asks; and what conceptions of the world or ideological stances do they (even if unwittingly) help to perpetuate? In so doing, she points out, among other things, that any response labeled "aesthetic" may as easily designate some immediately experienced moment or event as it may designate a species of nostalgia, a yearning for the components of a simpler past, when the world seemed known or at least understandable. Thus the value accorded an opera or a Shakespeare play may well reside in the viewer's immediate viewing pleasure, or it may reside in the play's nostalgic evocation of a once-comprehensible and ordered world. At the same time, the feminist confronts, for example, the reader who simply cannot entertain the possibility that women's worlds are symbolically rich, the reader who, like the male characters in Susan Glaspell's 1917 short story, "A Jury of Her Peers," has already assumed the innate "insignificance of kitchen things."[7] Such a reader, she knows, will prove himself unable to assign significance to fictions that attend to "kitchen things" and will, instead, judge such fictions as trivial and as aesthetically wanting. For her to take useful issue with such a reader, she must make clear that what appears to be a dispute about aesthetic merit is, in reality, a dispute about the *contexts of judgment*; and what is at issue, then, is the adequacy of the prior assumptions and reading habits brought to bear on the text. To put it bluntly: we have had enough pronouncements of aesthetic valuation for a time; it is now our task to evaluate the imputed norms and normative reading patterns that, in part, led to those pronouncements.

By and large, I think I've made my point. Only to clarify it do I add this coda: when feminists turn their attention to the works of male authors which have traditionally been accorded high aesthetic value and, where warranted, follow Olsen's advice that we assert our "right to say: this is surface, this falsifies reality, this degrades,"[8] such statements do not necessarily mean that we will end up with a diminished canon. To question the source of the aesthetic pleasures we've gained from reading Spenser,[9] Shakespeare, Milton, and so on, does not imply that we must deny those pleasures. It means only that aesthetic response is once more invested with epistemological, ethical, and moral concerns. It means, in other words, that readings of *Paradise Lost* which analyze its complex hierarchal structures but fail to note the implications of gender within that hierarchy; or which insist upon the inher-

7. For a full discussion of the Glaspell short story which takes this problem into account, please see my "A Map for Re-Reading: Or, Gender and the Interpretation of Literary Texts," forthcoming in a special issue on narrative, *New Literary History* (1980). [Glaspell (1876–1948), American playwright, who also wrote fiction. In the story mentioned, it is women's attention to "kitchen things" that enables them to solve a murder—editor's note.]

8. Olsen, *Silences*, p. 45.

9. English poet (1552–1599) [editor's note].

ent (or even inspired) perfection of Milton's figurative language but fail to note the consequences, for Eve, of her specifically gender-marked weakness, which, like the flowers to which she attends, requires "propping up";[1] or which concentrate on the poem's thematic reworking of classical notions of martial and epic prowess into Christian (moral) heroism but fail to note that Eve is stylistically edited out of that process—all such readings, however useful, will no longer be deemed wholly adequate. The pleasures we had earlier learned to take in the poem will not be diminished thereby, but they will become part of an altered reading attentiveness.

These three propositions I believe to be at the theoretical core of most current feminist literary criticism, whether acknowledged as such or not. If I am correct in this, then that criticism represents more than a profoundly skeptical stance toward all other preexisting and contemporaneous schools and methods, and more than an impassioned demand that the variety and variability of women's literary expression be taken into full account, rather than written off as caprice and exception, the irregularity in an otherwise regular design. It represents that locus in literary study where, in unceasing effort, female self-consciousness turns in upon itself, attempting to grasp the deepest conditions of its own unique and multiplicitous realities, in the hope, eventually, of altering the very forms through which the culture perceives, expresses, and knows itself. For, if what the larger women's movement looks for in the future is a transformation of the structures of primarily male power which now order our society, then the feminist literary critic demands that we understand the ways in which those structures have been—and continue to be—reified by our literature and by our literary criticism. Thus, along with other "radical" critics and critical schools, though our focus remains the power of the word to both structure and mirror human experience, our overriding commitment is to a radical alteration—an improvement, we hope—in the nature of that experience.

What distinguishes our work from those similarly oriented "social consciousness" critiques, it is said, is its lack of systematic coherence. Pitted against, for example, psychoanalytic or Marxist readings, which owe a decisive share of their persuasiveness to their apparent internal consistency as a system, the aggregate of feminist literary criticism appears woefully deficient in system, and painfully lacking in program. It is, in fact, from all quarters, the most telling defect alleged against us, the most explosive threat in the minefield. And my own earlier observation that, as of 1976, feminist literary criticism appeared "more like a set of interchangeable strategies than any coherent school or shared goal orientation," has been taken by some as an indictment, by others as a statement of impatience. Neither was intended. I felt then, as I do now, that this would "prove both its strength *and* its weakness,"[2] in the sense that the apparent disarray would leave us vulnerable to the kind of objection I've just alluded to; while the fact of our diversity would finally place us securely where, all along, we should have been: camped out, on the far side of the minefield, with the other pluralists and pluralisms.

In our heart of hearts, of course, most critics are really structuralists[3]

1. See *Paradise Lost* 9.424–33 [editor's note].
2. Annette Kolodny, "Literary Criticism," review essay in *Signs* 2, no. 2 (winter 1976): 420.
3. Kolodny uses this term "structuralist" loosely here to refer to critical efforts to uncover the "deep" structures and forms underlying surface

(whether or not they accept the label) because what we are seeking are patterns (or structures) that can order and explain the otherwise inchoate; thus, we invent, or believe we discover, relational patternings in the texts we read which promise transcendence from difficulty and perplexity to clarity and coherence. But, as I've tried to argue in these pages, to the imputed "truth" or "accuracy" of these findings, the feminist must oppose the painfully obvious truism that what is attended to in a literary work, and hence what is reported about it, is often determined not so much by the work itself as by the critical technique or aesthetic criteria through which it is filtered or, rather, read and decoded. All the feminist is asserting, then, is her own equivalent right to liberate new (and perhaps different) significances from these same texts; and, at the same time, her right to choose which features of a text she takes as relevant because she is, after all, asking new and different questions of it. In the process, she claims neither definitiveness nor structural completeness for her different readings and reading systems, but only their usefulness in recognizing the particular achievements of woman-as-author and their applicability in conscientiously decoding woman-as-sign.

That these alternate foci of critical attentiveness will result in alternate readings or interpretations of the same text—even among feminists—should be no cause for alarm. Such developments illustrate only the pluralist contention that, "in approaching a text of any complexity . . . the reader must choose to emphasize certain aspects which seem to him crucial" and that, "in fact, the variety of readings which we have for many works is a function of the selection of crucial aspects made by the variety of readers." Robert Scholes, from whom I've been quoting, goes so far as to assert that "there is no single 'right' reading for any complex literary work," and, following the Russian formalist school, he observes that "we do not speak of readings that are simply true or false, but of readings that are more or less rich, strategies that are more or less appropriate."[4] Because those who share the term "feminist" nonetheless practice a diversity of critical strategies, leading, in some cases, to quite different readings, we must acknowledge among ourselves that sister critics, "having chosen to tell a different story, may in their interpretation identify different aspects of the meanings conveyed by the same passage."[5]

Adopting a "pluralist" label does not mean, however, that we cease to disagree; it means only that we entertain the possibility that different readings, even of the same text, may be differently useful, even illuminating, within different contexts of inquiry. It means, in effect, that we enter a dialectical process of examining, testing, even trying out the contexts—be they prior critical assumptions or explicitly stated ideological stances (or some combination of the two)—that led to the disparate readings. Not all will be equally acceptable to every one of us, of course, and even those prior

expressions of meaning. Such structures are thought to "generate" the more chaotic (or "inchoate") words and organizations of actual statements [editor's note].

4. Scholes, *Structuralism in Literature*, pp. 144–45. These comments appear within his explication of Tzvetan Todorov's theory of reading. [On the Bulgarian-born French theorist TODOROV, see above—editor's note.]

5. I borrow this concise phrasing of pluralistic modesty from M. H. Abrams's "The Deconstructive Angel," *Critical Inquiry* 3, no. 3 (spring 1977): 427. Indications of the pluralism that was to mark feminist inquiry were to be found in the diversity of essays collected by Susan Koppelman Cornillon for her early and groundbreaking anthology, *Images of Women in Fiction: Feminist Perspectives* (Bowling Green, Ohio: Bowling Green University Popular Press, 1972).

assumptions or ideologies that are acceptable may call for further refinement and/or clarification. But, at the very least, because we will have grappled with the assumptions that led to it, we will be better able to articulate *why* we find a particular reading or interpretation adequate or inadequate. This kind of dialectical process, moreover, not only makes us more fully aware of what criticism is, and how it functions; it also gives us access to its future possibilities, making us conscious, as R. P. Blackmur put it, "of what we have done," "of what can be done next, or done again,"[6] or, I would add, of what can be done differently. To put it still another way: just because we will no longer tolerate the specifically sexist omissions and oversights of earlier critical schools and methods does not mean that, in their stead, we must establish our own "party line."

In my view, our purpose is not and should not be the formulation of any single reading method or potentially procrustean set of critical procedures nor, even less, the generation of prescriptive categories for some dreamed-of nonsexist literary canon.[7] Instead, as I see it, our task is to initiate nothing less than a playful pluralism responsive to the possibilities of multiple critical schools and methods, but captive of none, recognizing that the many tools needed for our analysis will necessarily be largely inherited and only partly of our own making. Only by employing a plurality of methods will we protect ourselves from the temptation to so oversimplify any text—and especially those particularly offensive to us—that we render ourselves unresponsive to what Scholes has called "its various systems of meaning and their interaction."[8] Any text we deem worthy of our critical attention is usually, after all, a locus of many and varied kinds of (personal, thematic, stylistic, structural, rhetorical, etc.) relationships. So, whether we tend to treat a text as a *mimesis,* in which words are taken to be recreating or representing viable worlds; or whether we prefer to treat a text as a kind of equation of communication, in which decipherable messages are passed from writers to readers; and whether we locate meaning as inherent in the text, the act of reading, or in some collaboration between reader and text—whatever our predilection, let us not generate from it a straitjacket that limits the scope of possible analysis. Rather, let us generate an ongoing dialogue of competing potential possibilities—among feminists and, as well, between feminist and nonfeminist critics.

The difficulty of what I describe does not escape me. The very idea of pluralism seems to threaten a kind of chaos for the future of literary inquiry while, at the same time, it seems to deny the hope of establishing some basic conceptual model which can organize all data—the hope which always begins any analytical exercise. My effort here, however, has been to demonstrate the essential delusions that inform such objections: If literary inquiry has historically escaped chaos by establishing canons, then it has only substituted one mode of arbitrary action for another—and, in this

6. R. P. Blackmur, "A Burden for Critics," *Hudson Review* 1 (1948): 171. Blackmur, of course, was referring to the way in which criticism makes us unconscious of how art functions; I use his wording here because I am arguing that that same awareness must also be focused on the critical act itself. "Consciousness," he avers, "is the way we feel the critic's burden." [Blackmur (1904–1965), American New Critic—editor's note.]

7. I have earlier elaborated my objection to prescriptive categories for literature in "The Feminist as Literary Critic," critical response in *Critical Inquiry* 2, no. 4 (summer 1976): 827–28.

8. Scholes, *Structuralism in Literature,* pp. 151–52.

case, at the expense of half the population. And if feminists openly acknowledge ourselves as pluralists, then we do not give up the search for patterns of opposition and connection—probably the basis of thinking itself; what we give up is simply the arrogance of claiming that our work is either exhaustive or definitive. (It is, after all, the identical arrogance we are asking our nonfeminist colleagues to abandon.) If this kind of pluralism appears to threaten both the present coherence of and the inherited aesthetic criteria for a canon of "greats," then, as I have earlier argued, it is precisely that threat which, alone, can free us from the prejudices, the strictures, and the blind spots of the past. In feminist hands, I would add, it is less a threat than a promise.

What unites and repeatedly invigorates feminist literary criticism, then, is neither dogma nor method but, as I have indicated earlier, an acute and impassioned *attentiveness* to the ways in which primarily male structures of power are inscribed (or encoded) within our literary inheritance; the consequences of that encoding for women—as characters, as readers, and as writers; and, with that, a shared analytic *concern* for the implications of that encoding not only for a better understanding of the past, but also for an improved reordering of the present and future as well. If that *concern* identifies feminist literary criticism as one of the many academic arms of the larger women's movement, then that *attentiveness*, within the halls of academe, poses no less a challenge for change, generating, as it does, the three propositions explored here. The critical pluralism that inevitably follows upon those three propositions, however, bears little resemblance to what Robinson has called "the greatest bourgeois theme of all, the myth of pluralism, with its consequent rejection of ideological commitment as 'too simple' to embrace the (necessarily complex) truth."[9] Only ideological commitment could have gotten us to enter the minefield, putting in jeopardy our careers and our livelihood. Only the power of ideology to transform our conceptual worlds, and the inspiration of that ideology to liberate long-suppressed energies and emotions, can account for our willingness to take on critical tasks that, in an earlier decade, would have been "abandoned in despair or apathy."[1] The fact of differences among us proves only that, despite our shared commitments, we have nonetheless refused to shy away from complexity, preferring rather to openly disagree than to give up either intellectual honesty or hard-won insights.

Finally, I would argue, pluralism informs feminist literary inquiry not simply as a description of what already exists but, more importantly, as the only critical stance consistent with the current status of the larger women's movement. Segmented and variously focused, the different women's organizations neither espouse any single system of analysis nor, as a result, express any wholly shared, consistently articulated ideology. The ensuing loss in effective organization and political clout is a serious one, but it has not been paralyzing; in spite of our differences, we have united to *act* in areas of clear mutual concern (the push for the Equal Rights Amendment is probably the most

9. Lillian Robinson, "Dwelling in Decencies: Radical Criticism and the Feminist Perspective," *College English* 32, no. 8 (May 1971);' reprinted in *Sex, Class, and Culture,* p. 11.

1. "Ideology bridges the emotional gap between things as they are and as one would have them be, thus insuring the performance of roles that might otherwise be abandoned in despair or apathy," comments Geertz in "Ideology as a Cultural System," p. 205.

obvious example).[2] The trade-off, as I see it, has made possible an ongoing and educative dialectic of analysis and preferred solutions, protecting us thereby from the inviting traps of reductionism and dogma. And so long as this dialogue remains active, both our politics and our criticism will be free of dogma—but never, I hope, of feminist ideology, in all its variety. For, "whatever else ideologies may be—projections of unacknowledged fears, disguises for ulterior motives, phatic expressions of group solidarity" (and the women's movement, to date, has certainly been all of these, and more)—whatever ideologies express, they are, as Geertz astutely observes, "most distinctively, maps of problematic social reality and matrices for the creation of collective conscience." And despite the fact that "ideological advocates . . . tend as much to obscure as to clarify the true nature of the problems involved," as Geertz notes, "they at least call attention to their existence and, by polarizing issues, make continued neglect more difficult. Without Marxist attack, there would have been no labor reform; without Black Nationalists, no deliberate speed."[3] Without Seneca Falls, I would add, no enfranchisement of women, and without "consciousness raising,"[4] no feminist literary criticism nor, even less, women's studies.

Ideology, however, only truly manifests its power by ordering the *sum* of our actions.[5] If feminist criticism calls anything into question, it must be that dog-eared myth of intellectual neutrality. For, what I take to be the underlying spirit, or message, of any consciously ideologically premised criticism—that is, that ideas are important *because* they determine the ways we live, or want to live, in the world—is vitiated by confining those ideas to the study, the classroom, or the pages of our books. To write chapters decrying the sexual stereotyping of women in our literature, while closing our eyes to the sexual harassment of our women students and colleagues; to display Katharine Hepburn and Rosalind Russell[6] in our courses on "The Image of the Independent Career Women in Film," while managing not to notice the paucity of female administrators on our own campus; to study the women who helped make universal enfranchisement a political reality, while keeping silent about our activist colleagues who are denied promotion or tenure; to include segments on "Women in the Labor Movement" in our American studies or women's studies courses, while remaining willfully ignorant of the department secretary fired for her efforts to organize a clerical workers' union; to glory in the delusions of "merit," "privilege," and "status" which accompany campus life in order to insulate ourselves from the millions of women who labor in poverty—all this is not merely hypocritical; it destroys both the spirit and the meaning of what we are about. It puts us, however

2. The Equal Rights Amendment, passed by the U.S. Congress in 1972, failed to become part of the Constitution when fewer than the required 38 states ratified it by the 1982 deadline [editor's note].

3. Geertz, "Ideology as a Cultural System," pp. 220, 205.

4. The aim of the group meetings at which women discussed their grievances and plans in the late 1960s and early 1970s; these meetings were the origin of "second wave" feminism, the name given to the revival of feminist activism between 1968 and 1975. Seneca Falls: the 1848 Women's Convention that met in Seneca Falls, N.Y., produced a "Declaration of Sentiments" (modeled on the Declaration of Independence) that served as a crucial founding document of "first wave" feminism [editor's note].

5. I here follow FREDRIC JAMESON's view in *The Prison-House of Language: A Critical Account of Structuralism and Russian Formalism* (Princeton: Princeton University Press, 1974), p. 107: "Ideology would seem to be that grillwork of form, convention, and belief which orders our actions."

6. Hepburn (b. 1907) and Russell (1907–1976), both American movie stars, played career women in a number of films [editor's note].

unwittingly, in the service of those who laid the minefield in the first place. In my view, it is a fine thing for many of us, individually, to have traversed the minefield; but that happy circumstance will only prove of lasting importance if, together, we expose it for what it is (the male fear of sharing power and significance with women) and deactivate its components, so that others, after us, may literally dance through the minefield.

1980

JULIA KRISTEVA
b. 1941

Linguist, literary critic, cultural theorist, and psychoanalyst, Julia Kristeva has been one of the central figures of French intellectual life in the late twentieth and early twenty-first century. Kristeva's main contribution to contemporary theory resides in her elucidation of the processes by which preverbal experience—bodily drives and affects—enters into language and activates creative, transformative, and at times revolutionary modes of cultural production. Like other structuralist and poststructuralist theorists—most notably JACQUES LACAN, ROLAND BARTHES, and JACQUES DERRIDA—Kristeva has a long-standing interest in the relationship of subjectivity to language, in how the speaking subject is both constituted through and threatened by the logic of signification. But Kristeva diverges from other contemporary theorists in her insistence on the corporeal origins of subjectivity and of artistic practice. In contrast to the Saussurean linguistic models of Lacanian psychoanalysis, for instance, Kristeva has emphasized the importance of prelinguistic, instinctual, and sensory components of both subjectivity and signification. Indeed, while Kristeva's thinking has undergone major transformations over the past three decades, progressively moving away from abstract linguistics and toward more classically psychoanalytic concerns, her writings nevertheless exhibit a remarkable degree of continuity insofar as they have consistently sought to articulate—without completely departing from language—the force of the body and its drives.

Born in Bulgaria in 1941, Kristeva arrived in France on a doctoral research fellowship in December 1965. Since her francophone parents were not members of Bulgaria's ruling Communist Party, she had been excluded from the foreign-language schools available to the children of the "red bourgeoisie." Nevertheless, she acquired a French as well as a Bulgarian education from an early age by attending two schools—Bulgarian in the morning and French in the afternoon. In Paris she became a student of Roland Barthes and quickly established herself as a major participant in the lively avant-garde milieu of the late 1960s. By the spring of 1967, Kristeva's articles were being published in such leading journals as *Critique, Langages*, and *Tel Quel*, and in 1970 she was appointed to the editorial board of *Tel Quel*, the intellectual venue for the young generation of structuralist and poststructuralist theorists. *Tel Quel* was edited by the charismatic writer and theorist Philippe Sollers, whom she later married and with whom she had a son. In 1974 she was appointed professor of linguistics at the University of Paris VII, where she continues to teach.

Besides Barthes, Lucien Goldmann (an influential sociological critic), and CLAUDE LÉVI-STRAUSS, who were her teachers, Kristeva acknowledges intellectual debts to other twentieth-century figures: MIKHAIL BAKHTIN, Émile Benveniste (an important linguist), Jacques Lacan, Melanie Klein (a theorist of pre-Oedipal development), and, of course, SIGMUND FREUD. With TZVETAN TODOROV, Kristeva brought the work of Bakhtin into prominence in the French context. In 1970 she published an introduction to the French translation of Bakhtin's work on Dostoyevsky, and she combined his concept of "dialogism" (the idea that a text contains language from more than one "world") with FERDINAND DE SAUSSURE's notebooks on anagrams in poetry (which had recently been discovered and were being published by Jean Starobinski in *Tel Quel*) into a general theory of "intertextuality."

The intertextual sense of the multiplicity of origins and meanings in language informs the theory of the sign set forth in Kristeva's first book, *Σημειωτιχὴ (Séméiótiké): Recherches pour une Sémanalyse* (1969, *Research toward a Sem-analysis*, where *sem-* is from the Greek word for "sign"). This was followed in 1974 by *Revolution in Poetic Language*, Kristeva's doctoral dissertation, in which she developed a theory of poetic language based on the writings of STÉPHANE MALLARMÉ (1842–1898) and Isidore Ducasse (better known as the comte de Lautréamont, 1846–1870). We print several sections from this book as our selection, below. The "revolution" in poetic language Kristeva analyzed in the work of these late-nineteenth-century French poets quickly became a revolution brought about by Kristeva herself in the *analysis* of poetic language as such.

Kristeva finds two forces competing for expression in the language of poetry: the symbolic and the semiotic. The *symbolic* is that aspect of language that allows it to *refer*. It is systematic, propositional, rule-bound, tied to the social order, dependent on a functional separation between the subject and the object, and capable of existing independently of its referent. The linguistics of Saussure focused on this dimension, treating language as a theoretical fiction studied in the absence of any particular speaker. The *semiotic* dimension of language—which cannot be known except in the moments where it breaks through the symbolic—is that aspect that bears the trace of the language user's own body and of the mother's protolinguistic presence—the babbling of the infant who tries out the vocal repertoire before he or she learns to speak, for instance, or the mother's voice prior to the baby's acquisition of language: poetic language in this sense has been called "babble, doodle, and riddle." The "music" of poetry (and indeed prosody itself), Kristeva contends, arises out of this dimension. It is important to avoid two possible misunderstandings of Kristeva's use of these terms. Her "symbolic" is similar to Lacan's, insofar as it is not symbolic *of* anything—not a collection of meaning-filled symbols as, say, CARL JUNG, might conceive it—but is a *structure*. And "the semiotic" is not the same as *semiotics*, which is the study of the functioning of signs.

In *Revolution in Poetic Language*, Kristeva thus maintains that all signification entails the dialectical interaction of the symbolic and the semiotic. The semiotic represents the discharge of pre-Oedipal instinctual energies and drives within language; it is associated with what Kristeva, following PLATO, designates as the *chora* (literally, "space"; Greek)—receptacle, space, womb. This semiotic *chora*, which "precedes and underlies figuration," is, in turn, connected to the maternal body, to the feminine in general, and to what remains mysterious, unintelligible, and unsignifiable. Kristeva's thesis is that the eruption of the semiotic within the symbolic is what provides the creative and innovative impulse of modern poetic language. Ordinary language use depends on a *thetic* or positing structure (Kristeva borrows the term from the German phenomenologist Edmund Husserl, 1859–1938): that is, it is positional and propositional. Artistic practice, capable of transgressing the thetic boundary between the symbolic and the semiotic, fractures and disrupts established modes of signification so as to retrieve the surmounted semiotic energies and thus create an opening for new, polyvalent cultural meanings. This thetic rupture, then, is profoundly subversive, not only implying an upheaval of art forms (such as that effected by Mallarmé and Lautréamont, according to Kristeva, on traditional literary discourse) but also calling for a reconfiguration of the notion of subjectivity. Distinguishing between the *genotext* (the energies that bring a text about) and the *phenotext* (the linguistic structure that results), Kristeva tries to capture the trace of what in a subject brings a text into being, not just what the text signifies. The genotext corresponds roughly to Freud's primary (unconscious) processes—a dream's "latent content." But while a dream's "manifest content" obeys only the rule of representability, a text is shaped by all the linguistic and social structures of the symbolic order.

The "revolution" of Kristeva's title therefore both refers to a transformation in poetic practice and heralds the emergence of what Kristeva, throughout her writings, refers to as the *sujet-en-procès. Procès*, in French, means both "process" and "trial." Hence, this expression can be translated "subject in process" or "subject on trial." The phrase itself expresses what Kristeva sees as the double bind of subjecthood: it combines the incompatible forces of constant change and constant judgment. The subject both *cannot* and *must* present itself in stasis. The semiotic dimension frees the subject from stasis and, according to Kristeva, "gives us a vision of the human venture as a venture of innovation, of creation, of opening, of renewal" (*Interviews*, 1996).

But the breakthroughs of the semiotic have their dark as well as their playful side. The theories of psychoanalysis have enabled Kristeva—who completed her training as a psychoanalyst in 1979—to analyze in more detail the consequences of those breakthroughs for life and writing. Her many book-length studies—treating horror, anti-Semitism, melancholy, and abjection—attend to the destructive as well as the creative consequences of breaking through the symbolic, which is the repository of civilization in both its repressive and its protective guises. Indeed, for Kristeva psychoanalysis is the *practice* of the difficulty in tearing apart the two "sides." The *abject*, for instance, is as important to the constitution of the "subject" as its "object." The abject is what the subject's consciousness has to expel or disregard in order to create the proper separation between subject and object. The mother splits into two parts: she is the prototype of subsequent objects that the subject will desire or hate, but she is also the despised ground of infantile dependency and bodily need. Another way of putting this is that the abject is still unconsciously desired and thereby transformed into something undesirable, filthy, and disgusting, like the bodily processes for which it stands. Both matter and mother are *abjects* for the fantasy of self-creation.

Kristeva's publications after 1979 thus take an explicitly psychoanalytic approach to what she calls "the maladies of the soul." *Powers of Horror: An Essay on Abjection* (1980; trans. 1982), *Tales of Love* (1983; trans. 1987), *Black Sun: Depression and Melancholia* (1987; trans. 1989), and *New Maladies of the Soul* (1993; trans. 1995) often feature case studies from her clinical practice. At the same time, Kristeva began enlarging and loosening her compact, difficult, and rather abstract style to attempt new kinds of writing. In a special 1977 issue of *Tel Quel* titled *Recherches féminines* (*Research by and about Women*), she published a celebrated essay about motherhood ("Héréthique de l'amour" or "Love's Herethics"; later translated as "Stabat Mater") written in two columns juxtaposed irregularly on the page. She went on to write several novels, the first of which, *The Samurai* (1990), is a thinly disguised account of the *Tel Quel* milieu. Its Japanese title is a wink at the Chinese title used by SIMONE DE BEAUVOIR (an important precursor for Kristeva) for a similar roman à clef, *The Mandarins* (1954).

Kristeva has published more explicitly political writings as well, from her early *About Chinese Women* (1974)—based on a trip to China taken by several members of *Tel Quel* during its period of interest in Maoism—to the later *Strangers to Ourselves* (1989) and *Nations without Nationalism* (1990). In *Strangers to Ourselves*, Kristeva rediscovers Freud's notion of the "uncanny" in the context of the encounter between the self and the "foreigner": by recognizing that the foreignness lies *within* the self, it might be possible, she suggests, to avoid the violence entailed by its projection outward onto others.

"Women's Time" (1979; trans. 1981), a synthesis of Kristeva's analysis of language, the social contract, and feminism, has been much reprinted. It addresses the question of female subjectivity by interrogating the position that women are said to occupy in the social structure. If, according to Lévi-Strauss, women are circulated on the marriage market between men of different groups like the words of a system of communication, what happens when women are seen not as the *objects* but as the *subjects* of communication? If women have had to bear the sacrificial weight of the social contract in patriarchy, does that mean that lifting the weight of patriarchy would provide free, unfettered enjoyment and fulfillment for women? It is Kristeva's contention that a liberating change in the social order, however necessary and desirable, would nevertheless not give access to the fulfillment whose attainment appears to be blocked by specific structures of subjectivity. The fantasy of wholeness is a function of those obstacles, not something beyond them. Kristeva's ideal could be said to be postfeminist in the sense that it implies the demolition of "Woman" as an identifiable social category. To the extent that feminism depends on the difference between men and women conceived as an *opposition*, she has resisted being called a "feminist." This has estranged her from some feminists committed to an oppositional notion of political action. When asked what constitutes her distinctiveness, however, she responds by calling herself "a female intellectual," committed to exploring the oxymoronic exclusiveness inherent in the traditional understanding of those categories but refusing to conceive of either one as an "identity."

The attempt to bridge the gap between French and Anglo-American feminisms has contributed to the introduction and dissemination of Kristeva's work to the English-speaking world—see, notably, Toril Moi's *Sexual/Textual Politics: Feminist Literary Theory* (1985)—but Kristeva herself tends to view institutionalized forms of feminism (like all institutionalized groups) as totalizing, at times even as totalitarian, forms of cultural discourse. In "Women's Time" she wonders whether feminism is not in the process of becoming a sort of religion; and she remains highly critical of any feminist politics based on universalist or essentialist notions of femininity. Although Kristeva, in Anglo-American writings, frequently gets grouped together with HÉLÈNE CIXOUS and Luce Irigaray as a representative of "French feminism," the three writers are really very different, united only by the extent to which each is influenced by the 1968 upheaval in French society. Yet Kristeva's rich and provocative writings—particularly her reflections on love, abjection, melancholy, maternity, and the preverbal semiotic—are directly relevant to feminist theorists and continue to generate a sizable body of criticism.

Drawing together linguistics, psychoanalysis, political science, and feminism, Julia Kristeva's work has repeatedly revealed aspects of textuality that literary theory is in danger of glossing over. In insisting that the speaking subject's investment in language is neither transcendental nor entirely conscious, she has enlarged, enriched, and complicated our sense of what goes on in a literary text.

BIBLIOGRAPHY

Kristeva's writings first became widely available in English through the publication of the 1980 collection *Desire in Language*, edited by Leon S. Roudiez (who was also responsible for inviting Kristeva to be a regular visitor at Columbia University) and translated by Thomas Gora, Alice Jardine, and Roudiez. This collection, which does not correspond to any book in French, contains essays from her *Séméiótikè* (1969) and from *Polylogue* (1977). Margaret Waller's English translation of *Revolution in Poetic Language* (1984) reproduces the first half of the original 1974 French text. The best-known translation of "Women's Time" is by Alice Jardine and Harry Blake, and was originally published in the journal *Signs* 7 (1981). Another translation, slightly updated by Kristeva, was produced by Ross Mitchell Guberman for the English translation of *New Maladies of the Soul* (1995). All of the work that derives from Kristeva's "psychoanalytic" period is deeply literary as well, grappling with such authors as Louis-Ferdinand Céline (1894–1961), Gérard de Nerval (1808–1855), Plotinus (ca. 204/5–ca. 270), and Charles Baudelaire (1821–1867). *Powers of Horror*

(1980; trans. 1982), *Tales of Love* (1983; trans. 1987), and *Black Sun* (1987; trans. 1989) have been influential in literary studies. Among her other writings are *Language: The Unknown* (1981; trans. 1989) and *Time and Sense: Proust and the Experience of Literature* (1994; trans. 1996). Kristeva has also written a number of novels and a series of reflections on the limits of psychoanalysis. Toril Moi's *Kristeva Reader* (1986) and Kelly Oliver's *Portable Kristeva* (1997) present good selections and substantial introductions to Kristeva's writings. Two books contain biographical information: *Julia Kristeva: Interviews*, edited by Ross Mitchell Guberman (1996), and, with a grain of salt, *The Samurai* (1990; trans. 1992).

There exist a number of helpful explications of Kristeva's work. Elizabeth Grosz's *Sexual Subversions: Three French Feminists* (1989) places Kristeva in the context of French philosophy and feminism, and Michael Payne's *Reading Theory: An Introduction to Lacan, Derrida, and Kristeva* (1993) has a chapter devoted to *Revolution in Poetic Language*. John Lechte, *Julia Kristeva* (1990); Kelly Oliver, *Reading Kristeva: Unraveling the Double-Bind* (1993); Anna Smith, *Julia Kristeva: Readings of Exile and Estrangement* (1996); and Anne-Marie Smith, *Julia Kristeva: Speaking the Unspeakable* (1998), all provide overviews of Kristeva's main arguments and concepts. The critical literature on Kristeva is represented in numerous collections of essays, the most notable of which include *Abjection, Melancholia, and Love: The Work of Julia Kristeva*, edited by John Fletcher and Andrew Benjamin (1990); *Body/Text in Julia Kristeva: Religion, Women, and Psychoanalysis*, edited by David Crownfield (1992); *Ethics, Politics, and Difference in Julia Kristeva's Writing*, edited by Kelly Oliver (1993); and *After the Revolution: On Kristeva*, edited by John Lechte and Mary Zournazi (1998).

French Feminist Criticism: Women, Language, and Literature by Elissa D. Gelfand and Virginia Thorndike Hules (1985), contains a dated but well-annotated bibliography of the early Kristeva. Joan Nordquist's *Julia Kristeva: A Bibliography* (1995) provides a comprehensive list of Kristeva's books and essays as well as of relevant critical literature published in English.

From Revolution in Poetic Language[1]

From *Part I. The Semiotic and the Symbolic*

2. THE SEMIOTIC *CHORA* ORDERING THE DRIVES

We understand the term "semiotic"[2] in its Greek sense: σημεῖον = distinctive mark, trace, index, precursory sign, proof, engraved or written sign, imprint, trace, figuration. This etymological reminder would be a mere archaeological embellishment (and an unconvincing one at that, since the term ultimately encompasses such disparate meanings), were it not for the fact that the preponderant etymological use of the word, the one that implies a *distinctiveness*, allows us to connect it to a precise modality in the signifying process. This modality is the one Freudian psychoanalysis points to in postulating not only the *facilitation* and the structuring *disposition* of drives, but also the so-called *primary processes*[3] which displace and condense both energies and their inscription. Discrete quantities of energy move through the body of the

1. Translated by Margaret Waller, who occasionally inserts the original French in brackets.
2. In Kristeva's usage, pre-Oedipal—that is, before the infant's discovery of sexual difference—preverbal drives and affects.
3. The most primitive of unconscious mechanisms, according to SIGMUND FREUD (1856–1939), Austrian founder of psychoanalysis. "Facilitation" (French *frayage*, from Freud's German *Bahnung*) and "disposition" are the processes that shape habits of desire.

subject who is not yet constituted as such and, in the course of his development, they are arranged according to the various constraints imposed on this body—always already involved in a semiotic process—by family and social structures. In this way the drives, which are "energy" charges as well as "psychical" marks, articulate what we call a *chora*: a nonexpressive totality formed by the drives and their stases in a motility that is as full of movement as it is regulated.

We borrow the term *chora*[4] from Plato's *Timaeus*[5] to denote an essentially mobile and extremely provisional articulation constituted by movements and their ephemeral stases. We differentiate this uncertain and indeterminate *articulation* from a *disposition* that already depends on representation, lends itself to phenomenological, spatial intuition,[6] and gives rise to a geometry. Although our theoretical description of the *chora* is itself part of the discourse of representation that offers it as evidence, the *chora*, as rupture and articulations (rhythm), precedes evidence, verisimilitude, spatiality, and temporality. Our discourse—all discourse—moves with and against the *chora* in the sense that it simultaneously depends upon and refuses it. Although the *chora* can be designated and regulated, it can never be definitively posited: as a result, one can situate the *chora* and, if necessary, lend it a topology, but one can never give it axiomatic form.[7]

The *chora* is not yet a position that represents something for someone (i.e., it is not a sign); nor is it a *position* that represents someone for another position (i.e., it is not yet a signifier either[8]); it is, however, generated in order to attain to this signifying position. Neither model nor copy, the *chora* precedes and underlies figuration and thus specularization, and is analogous only to vocal or kinetic rhythm. We must restore this motility's gestural and vocal play (to mention only the aspect relevant to language) on the level of the socialized body in order to remove motility from ontology and amorphousness[9] where Plato confines it in an apparent attempt to conceal it from

4. The term "*chora*" has recently been criticized for its ontological essence by Jacques Derrida, *Positions*, trans. and annot. Alan Bass (Chicago: University of Chicago Press, 1981), pp. 75, 106 n. 39 [Kristeva's note]. Some of the author's notes have been omitted. DERRIDA (b. 1930), French philosopher.

5. One of the later dialogues by the Greek philosopher PLATO (ca. 427–ca. 347 B.C.E.).

6. Phenomenology is a philosophical method restricted to analyzing the intellectual processes of which we are introspectively aware (while ignoring external objects, the question of whose existence is "bracketed").

7. Plato emphasizes that the receptacle (ὑποδοχεῖον), which is also called space (χώρα) vis-à-vis reason, is necessary—but not divine since it is unstable, uncertain, ever changing and becoming; it is even unnameable, improbable, bastard: "Space,which is everlasting, not admitting destruction; providing a situation for all things that come into being, but itself apprehended without the senses by a sort of bastard reasoning, and hardly an object of belief. This, indeed, is that which we look upon as in a dream and say that anything that is must needs be in some place and occupy some room . . ." (*Timaeus*, trans. Francis M. Cornford, 52a–b). Is the receptacle a "thing" or a mode of language? Plato's hesitation between the two gives the receptacle an even more uncertain status. It is one of the elements that antedate not only the *universe* but also *names* and even *syllables*: "We speak . . . positing them as original principles, elements (as it were, letters) of the universe; whereas one who has ever so little intelligence should not rank them in this analogy even so low as syllables" (48b). "It is hard to say, with respect to any one of these, which we ought to call really water rather than fire, or indeed which we should call by any given name rather than by all the names together or by each severally, so as to use language in a sound and trustworthy way. . . . Since, then, in this way no one of these things ever makes its appearance as the *same* thing, which of them can we steadfastly affirm to be *this*—whatever it may be—and not something else, without blushing for ourselves? It cannot be done" (49b–d) [Kristeva's note].

8. A reference to the statement by the French psychoanalyst JACQUES LACAN (1901–1981) that "a signifier represents a subject for another signifier"; see Seminar XI (1964), *The Four Fundamental Concepts of Psychoanalysis* (1973; trans. 1977).

9. There is a fundamental ambiguity: on the one hand, the receptacle is mobile and even contradictory, without unity, separable and divisible: presyllable, pre-word. Yet, on the other hand, because this separability and divisibility antecede numbers and forms, the space or receptacle is called *amorphous*; thus its suggested rhythmicity will in a cer-

Democritean rhythm.[1] The theory of the subject proposed by the theory of the unconscious will allow us to read in this rhythmic space, which has no thesis and no position, the process by which signifiance[2] is constituted. Plato himself leads us to such a process when he calls this receptacle or *chora* nourishing and maternal,[3] not yet unified in an ordered whole because deity is absent from it. Though deprived of unity, identity, or deity, the *chora* is nevertheless subject to a regulating process [*réglementation*], which is different from that of symbolic law but nevertheless effectuates discontinuities by temporarily articulating them and then starting over, again and again.

The *chora* is a modality of signifiance in which the linguistic sign is not yet articulated as the absence of an object and as the distinction between real and symbolic. We emphasize the regulated aspect of the *chora*: its vocal and gestural organization is subject to what we shall call an objective *ordering* [*ordonnancement*], which is dictated by natural or socio-historical constraints such as the biological difference between the sexes or family structure. We may therefore posit that social organization, always already symbolic, imprints its constraint in a mediated form which organizes the *chora* not according to a *law* (a term we reserve for the symbolic) but through an *ordering*.[4] What is this mediation?

---

tain sense be erased, for how can one think an articulation of what is not yet singular but is nevertheless necessary? All we may say of it, then, to make it intelligible, is that it is amorphous but that it "is of such and such a quality," not even an index or something in particular ("this" or "that"). Once named, it immediately becomes a container that takes the place of infinitely repeatable separability. This amounts to saying that this repeated separability is "ontologized" the moment a *name* or a *word* replaces it, making it intelligible: "Are we talking idly whenever we say that there is such a thing as an intelligible Form of anything? Is this nothing more than a word?" (*Timaeus* 51c). Is the Platonic *chora* the "nominability" of rhythm (of repeated separation)?

Why then borrow an ontologized term in order to designate an articulation that antecedes positing? First, the Platonic term makes explicit an insurmountable problem for discourse: once it has been named, that functioning, even if it is presymbolic, is brought back into a symbolic position. All discourse can do is differentiate, by means of a "bastard reasoning," the receptacle from the motility, which, by contrast, is not being posited as being "a *certain* something" ["une *telle*"]. Second, this motility is the precondition for symbolicity, heterogeneous to it, yet indispensable. Therefore what needs to be done is to try and differentiate, always through a "bastard reasoning," the specific arrangements of this motility, without seeing them as recipients of accidental singularities, or a *Being* always posited in itself, or a projection of the *One*. Moreover, Plato invites us to differentiate in this fashion when he describes this, while gathering it into the receiving membrane: "But because it was filled with powers that were neither alike nor evenly balanced, there was no equipoise in any region of it; but it was everywhere swayed unevenly and shaken by these things, and its motion shook them in turn. And they, being thus moved, were perpetually being separated and carried in different directions; just as when things are shaken and winnowed by means of winnowing baskets and other instruments for cleaning corn . . . it separated the most unlike kinds farthest apart from one another, and thrust the most alike closest together; whereby the different kinds came to have different regions, even before the ordered whole consisting of them came to be . . . but were altogether in such a condition as we should expect for anything when deity is absent from it" (52d–53b). Indefinite "conjunctions" and "disjunctions" (functioning, devoid of Meaning), the *chora* is governed by a necessity that is not God's law [Kristeva's note]. "Corn": wheat.

1. That is, the eternal motion of atoms in haphazard collision postulated by the Greek philosopher Democritus (ca. 460–ca. 370 B.C.E.), a concept here presented as a precursor of the semiotic.
2. Kristeva's coinage: the fact or process of signification, encompassing both the symbolic and the semiotic.
3. The Platonic space or receptacle is a mother and wet nurse: "Indeed we may fittingly compare the Recipient to a mother, the model to a father, and the nature that arises between them to their offspring" (*Timaeus* 50d); "Now the wet nurse of Becoming was made watery and fiery, received the characters of earth and air, and was qualified by all the other affections that go with these . . ." (52d; translation modified) [Kristeva's note].
4. "Law," which derives etymologically from *lex* [Latin], necessarily implies the act of judgment whose role in safeguarding society was first developed by the Roman law courts. "Ordering," on the other hand, is closer to the series "rule," "norm" (from the Greek γνώμων, meaning "discerning" [adj.], "carpenter's square" [noun]), etc., which implies a numerical or geometrical necessity. On normativity in linguistics, see Alain Rey, "Usages, judgments et prescriptions linguistiques" [Linguistic Usage, Judgment, and Prescription], *Langue Française* (December 1972), 16:5. But the temporary ordering of the *chora* is not yet even a *rule*: the arsenal of geometry is posterior to the *chora*'s motility; it fixes the *chora* in place and reduces it [Kristeva's note].

According to a number of psycholinguists, "concrete operations" precede the acquisition of language, and organize preverbal semiotic space according to logical categories, which are thereby shown to precede or transcend language. From their research we shall retain not the principle of an operational state[5] but that of a preverbal functional state that governs the connections between the body (in the process of constituting itself as a body proper), objects, and the protagonists of family structure.[6] But we shall distinguish this functioning from symbolic operations that depend on language as a sign system—whether the language [*langue*][7] is vocalized or gestural (as with deaf-mutes). The kinetic functional stage of the *semiotic* precedes the establishment of the sign; it is not, therefore, cognitive in the sense of being assumed by a knowing, already constituted subject. The genesis of the *functions* organizing the semiotic process can be accurately elucidated only within a theory of the subject that does not reduce the subject to one of understanding, but instead opens up within the subject this other scene of pre-symbolic functions. The Kleinian theory[8] expanding upon Freud's positions on the drives will momentarily serve as a guide.

Drives involve pre-Oedipal semiotic functions and energy discharges that connect and orient the body to the mother. We must emphasize that "drives" are always already ambiguous, simultaneously assimilating and destructive; this dualism, which has been represented as a tetrad[9] or as a double helix, as in the configuration of the DNA and RNA molecule,[1] makes the semiotized body a place of permanent scission. The oral and anal drives,[2] both of which are oriented and structured around the mother's body,[3] dominate this sensorimotor organization. The mother's body is therefore what mediates the symbolic law organizing social relations and becomes the ordering principle of the semiotic *chora*,[4] which is on the path of destruction, aggressivity, and

5. Operations are, rather, an act of the subject of understanding [Kristeva's note]. Hans G. Furth, in *Piaget and Knowledge: Theoretical Foundations* (Englewood Cliffs, N.J.: Prentice-Hall, 1969), offers the following definition of "concrete operations": "Characteristic of the first stage of operational intelligence. A concrete operation implies underlying general systems or 'groupings' such as classification, seriation, number. Its applicability is limited to objects considered as real (concrete)" (p. 260) [translator's note].

6. Piaget stresses that the roots of sensorimotor operations precede language and that the acquisition of thought is due to the symbolic function, which, for him, is a notion separate from that of language per se. See Jean Piaget, "Language and Symbolic Operations," in *Piaget and Knowledge*, pp. 121–30 [Kristeva's note].

7. That is, language as an abstract system, as distinguished from the speech or hand signs of any particular language user (*parole*)—a distinction first drawn by the Swiss linguist FERDINAND DE SAUSSURE (1857–1913).

8. The theory of mother-child relations held by Melanie Klein (1882–1960), Austrian-born English psychoanalyst.

9. Such a position has been formulated by Lipot Szondi, *Experimental Diagnostic of Drives*, trans. Gertrude Aull (New York: Grune and Stratton, 1952) [Kristeva's note]. "Tetrad": group of four.

1. See James D. Watson, *The Double Helix: A Personal Account of the Discovery of the Structure of DNA* (London: Weidenfeld and Nicolson, 1968) [Kristeva's note].

2. The first and second phases of Freud's discussion of infantile sexuality; the "oral" is associated with sucking, the "anal" with the start of toilet training.

3. Throughout her writings, Melanie Klein emphasizes the "pre-Oedipal" phase, i.e., a period of the subject's development that precedes the "discovery" of castration and the positing of the superego, which itself is subject to (paternal) Law. The processes she describes for this phase correspond, *but on a genetic level*, to what we call the semiotic as opposed to the symbolic, which underlies and conditions the semiotic. Significantly, these pre-Oedipal processes are organized through projection onto the mother's body, for girls as well as for boys: "at this stage of development children of both sexes believe that it is the body of their mother which contains all that is desirable, especially their father's penis." *The Psycho-analysis of Children*, trans. Alix Strachey (London: Hogarth Press, 1932), p. 269. Our own view of this stage is as follows: Without "believing" or "desiring" any "object" whatsoever, the subject is in the process of constituting himself vis-à-vis a non-object. He is in the process of separating from this non-object so as to make that non-object "one" and posit himself as "other": the mother's body is the not-yet-one that the believing and desiring subject will imagine as a "receptacle" [Kristeva's note].

4. As for what situates the mother in symbolic space, we find the phallus again (see Jacques Lacan, "La Relation d'objet et les structures freu-

death. For although drives have been described as disunited or contradictory structures, simultaneously "positive" and "negative," this doubling is said to generate a dominant "destructive wave" that is drive's most characteristic trait: Freud notes that the most instinctual drive is the death drive.[5] In this way, the term "drive" denotes waves of attack against stases, which are themselves constituted by the repetition of these charges; together, charges and stases lead to no identity (not even that of the "body proper") that could be seen as a result of their functioning. This is to say that the semiotic *chora* is no more than the place where the subject is both generated and negated, the place where his unity succumbs before the process of charges and stases that produce him. We shall call this process of charges and stases a *negativity* to distinguish it from negation, which is the act of a judging subject (see below, part II).

Checked by the constraints of biological and social structures, the drive charge thus undergoes stases. Drive facilitation, temporarily arrested, marks *discontinuities* in what may be called the various material supports [*matériaux*] susceptible to semiotization: voice, gesture, colors. Phonic (later phonemic), kinetic, or chromatic units and differences are the marks of these stases in the drives. Connections or *functions* are thereby established between these discrete marks which are based on drives and articulated according to their resemblance or opposition, either by slippage or by condensation. Here we find the principles of metonymy and metaphor[6] indissociable from the drive economy underlying them.

Although we recognize the vital role played by the processes of displacement and condensation in the organization of the semiotic, we must also add to these processes the relations (eventually representable as topological spaces) that connect the zones of the fragmented body to each other and also to "external" "objects" and "subjects," which are not yet constituted as such. This type of relation makes it possible to specify the *semiotic* as a psychosomatic modality of the signifying process; in other words, not a symbolic modality but one articulating (in the largest sense of the word) a continuum: the connections between the (glottal and anal) sphincters in (rhythmic and intonational) vocal modulations, or those between the sphincters and family protagonists, for example.

diennes" [Object Relations and Freudian Structures], *Bulletin de Psychologie*, April 1957, pp. 426–30), represented by the mother's father, i.e., the subject's maternal grandfather (see Marie-Claire Boons, "Le Meurtre du Père chez Freud" [Killing the Father in Freud], *L'Inconscient*, January–March 1968, 5: 101–29) [Kristeva's note].

5. Though disputed and inconsistent, the Freudian theory of drives is of interest here because of the predominance Freud gives to the death drive in both "living matter" and the "human being." The death drive is transversal to identity and tends to disperse "narcissisms" whose constitution ensures the link between structures and, by extension, life. But at the same time and conversely, narcissism and pleasure are only temporary positions from which the death drive blazes new paths [*se fraye de nouveaux passages*]. Narcissism and pleasure are therefore inveiglings and realizations of the death drive. The semiotic *chora*, converting drive discharges into stases, can be thought of both as a delaying of the death drive and as a possible realization of this drive, which tends to return to a homeostatic state. This hypothesis is consistent with the following remark: "at the beginning of mental life," writes Freud, "the struggle for pleasure was far more intense than later but not so unrestricted: it had to submit to frequent interruptions." *Beyond the Pleasure Principle*, in *The Standard Edition of the Complete Psycho-Analytic Works of Sigmund Freud*, ed. James Strachey (London: Hogarth Press, 1953), 18:63 [Kristeva's note].

6. Two figures (dependent on resemblance and association, respectively), most influentially discussed by the Russian-born American linguist ROMAN JAKOBSON in "Two Aspects of Language and Two Types of Aphasic Disturbances" (1956; see above); Lacan (in "The Agency of the Letter in the Unconscious," 1957; see above) and others connected them to Freud's dream-work processes of condensation and displacement, as described in *The Interpretation of Dreams* (1900; see above).

All these various processes and relations, anterior to sign and syntax, have just been identified from a genetic perspective as previous and necessary to the acquisition of language, but not identical to language. Theory can "situate" such processes and relations diachronically within the process of the constitution of the subject precisely because *they function synchronically within the signifying process of the subject himself*, i.e., the subject of *cogitatio*.[7] Only in *dream* logic, however, have they attracted attention, and only in certain signifying practices, such as the *text*, do they dominate the signifying process.

It may be hypothesized that certain semiotic articulations are transmitted through the biological code or physiological "memory" and thus form the inborn bases of the symbolic function. Indeed, one branch of generative linguistics asserts the principle of innate language universals. As it will become apparent in what follows, however, the *symbolic*—and therefore syntax and all linguistic categories—is a social effect of the relation to the other, established through the objective constraints of biological (including sexual) differences and concrete, historical family structures. Genetic programmings are necessarily semiotic: they include the primary processes such as displacement and condensation, absorption and repulsion, rejection and stasis, all of which function as innate preconditions, "memorizable" by the species, for language acquisition.

Mallarmé[8] calls attention to the semiotic rhythm within language when he speaks of "The Mystery in Literature" ["Le Mystère dans les lettres"]. Indifferent to language, enigmatic and feminine, this space underlying the written is rhythmic, unfettered, irreducible to its intelligible verbal translation; it is musical, anterior to judgment, but restrained by a single guarantee: syntax. As evidence, we could cite "The Mystery in Literature" in its entirety.[9] For now, however, we shall quote only those passages that ally the functioning of that "air or song beneath the text" with woman:

> And the instrument of Darkness, whom they have designated, will not set down a word from then on except to deny that she must have been the enigma; lest she settle matters with a wisk of her skirts; 'I don't get it!'
>
> ....
>
> —They [the critics] play their parts disinterestedly or for a minor gain: leaving our Lady and Patroness exposed to show her dehiscence or lacuna, with respect to certain dreams, as though this were the standard to which everything is reduced.[1]

To these passages we add others that point to the "mysterious" functioning of literature as a rhythm made intelligible by syntax: "Following the instinct for rhythms that has chosen him, the poet does not deny seeing a lack of proportion between the means let loose and the result." "I know that there are those who would restrict Mystery to Music's domain; when writing aspires to it."[2]

7. Thinking (Latin).
8. STÉPHANE MALLARMÉ (1842–1898), French poet.
9. Mallarmé, *Oeuvres complètes* [*Complete Works*] (Paris: Gallimard, 1945), pp. 382–87 [Kristeva's note].
1. Ibid., p. 383 [Kristeva's note].
2. Ibid., pp. 383, 385 [Kristeva's note].

> What pivot is there, I mean within these contrasts, for intelligibility? a guarantee is needed—
>
> Syntax—
>
> . . . an extraordinary appropriation of structure, limpid, to the primitive lightning bolts of logic. A stammering, what the sentence seems, here repressed [. . .]
>
> ....
>
> The debate—whether necessary average clarity deviates in a detail—remains one for grammarians.[3]

Our positing of the semiotic is obviously inseparable from a theory of the subject that takes into account the Freudian positing of the unconscious. We view the subject in language as decentering the transcendental ego,[4] cutting through it, and opening it up to a dialectic in which its syntactic and categorical understanding is merely the liminary moment of the process, which is itself always acted upon by the relation to the other dominated by the death drive and its productive reiteration of the "signifier." We will be attempting to formulate the distinction between *semiotic* and *symbolic* within this perspective, which was introduced by Lacanian analysis, but also within the constraints of a practice—the *text*—which is only of secondary interest to psychoanalysis.

5. THE THETIC: RUPTURE AND/OR BOUNDARY

We shall distinguish the semiotic (drives and their articulations) from the realm of signification, which is always that of a proposition or judgment, in other words, a realm of *positions*. This positionality, which Husserlian phenomenology orchestrates through the concepts of *doxa, position,* and *thesis,* is structured as a break in the signifying process, establishing the *identification* of the subject and its object as preconditions of propositionality. We shall call this break, which produces the positing of signification, a *thetic*[5] phase. All enunciation, whether of a word or of a sentence, is thetic. It requires an identification; in other words, the subject must separate from and through his image, from and through his objects. This image and objects must first be posited in a space that becomes symbolic because it connects the two separated positions, recording them or redistributing them in an open combinatorial system.

The child's first so-called holophrastic enunciations include gesture, the object, and vocal emission. Because they are perhaps not yet sentences (NP-VP),[6] generative grammar is not readily equipped to account for them. Nevertheless, they are already thetic in the sense that they separate an object from the subject, and attribute to it a semiotic fragment, which thereby becomes a signifier. That this attribution is either metaphoric or metonymic ("woof-woof" says the dog, and all animals become "woof-woof") is logically secondary to the fact that it constitutes an *attribution,* which is to say, a

3. Ibid., pp 385–86 [Kristeva's note].

4. The autonomous, abstract subject implicit in perception and cognition, as defined by the German philosopher Edmund Husserl (1859–1938), a founder of phenomenology.

5. Propositional (from *thesis*), also a term from Husserl.

6. Noun-phrase, verb-phrase; nomenclature from the generative and transformational grammar of the American linguist Noam Chomsky (b. 1928).

positing of identity or difference, and that it represents the nucleus of judgment or proposition.

We shall say that the thetic phase of the signifying process is the "deepest structure" of the possibility of enunciation, in other words, of signification and the proposition. Husserl theologizes this deep logic of signification by making it a productive *origin* of the "free spontaneity" of the Ego:

> Its *free spontaneity and activity* consists in positing, positing on the strength of this or that, positing as an antecedent or a consequent, and so forth; it does not live within the theses as a passive indweller; the theses radiate from it as from a primary source of generation [*Erzeugungen*]. Every thesis begins with a *point of insertion* [*Einsatzpunkt*] with a point at which *the positing has its origin* [*Ursprungssetzung*]; so it is with the first thesis and with each further one in the synthetic nexus. This 'inserting' even belongs to the thesis as such, as a remarkable modus of original actuality. It somewhat resembles the *fiat*,[7] the point of insertion of will and action.[8]

In this sense, *there exists only one signification*, that of the thetic phase, which contains the object as well as the proposition, and the complicity between them. There is no sign that is not thetic and every sign is already the germ of a "sentence," attributing a signifier to an object through a "copula"[9] that will function as a signified. Stoic semiology, which was the first to formulate the matrix of the sign, had already established *this complicity between sign and sentence,* making them proofs of each other.

Modern philosophy recognizes that the right to represent the founding *thesis* of signification (sign and/or proposition) devolves upon the transcendental ego. But only since Freud have we been able to raise the question not of the origin of this thesis but rather of the process of its production. To brand the thetic as the foundation of metaphysics is to risk serving as an antechamber for metaphysics—unless, that is, we specify the way the thetic is produced. In our view, the Freudian theory of the unconscious and its Lacanian development show, precisely, that thetic signification is a stage attained under certain precise conditions during the signifying process, and that it constitutes the subject without being reduced to this process precisely because it is the threshold of language. Such a standpoint constitutes neither a reduction of the subject to the transcendental ego, nor a denial [*dénégation*] of the thetic phase that establishes signification.

12. GENOTEXT AND PHENOTEXT

In light of the distinction we have made between the semiotic *chora* and the symbolic, we may now examine the way texts function. What we shall call a *genotext* will include semiotic processes but also the advent of the symbolic. The former includes drives, their disposition, and their division of the body, plus the ecological and social system surrounding the body, such as objects

7. Literally "let there be" (Latin); this is the form of God's creative pronouncements in Genesis, in the Vulgate Bible.

8. Edmund Husserl, *Ideas: General Introduction to Pure Phenomenology*, trans. W. R. Boyce Gibson (London: Allen and Unwin, 1969), p. 342 [Kristeva's note].

9. Linking verb (which joins the subject and predicate).

and pre-Oedipal relations with parents. The latter encompasses the emergence of object and subject, and the constitution of nuclei of meaning involving categories semantic and categorial fields. Designating the genotext in a text requires pointing out the transfers of drive energy that can be detected in phonematic devices (such as the accumulation and repetition of phonemes[1] or rhyme) and melodic devices (such as intonation or rhythm), in the way semantic and categorial fields are set out in syntactic and logical features, or in the economy of mimesis (fantasy, the deferment of denotation, narrative, etc). The genotext is thus the only transfer of drive energies that organizes a space in which the subject is not *yet* a split unity that will become blurred, giving rise to the symbolic. Instead, the space it organizes is one in which the subject will be *generated* as such by a process of facilitations[2] and marks within the constraints of the biological and social structure.

In other words, even though it can be seen in language, the genotext is not linguistic (in the sense understood by structural or generative linguistics). It is, rather, a *process*, which tends to articulate structures that are ephemeral (unstable, threatened by drive charges, "quanta" rather than "marks") and nonsignifying (devices that do not have a double articulation).[3] It forms these structures out of: a) instinctual dyads, b) the corporeal and ecological continuum, c) the social organism and family structures, which convey the constraints imposed by the mode of production, and d) matrices of enunciation, which give rise to discursive "genres" (according to literary history), "psychic structures" (according to psychiatry and psychoanalysis), or various arrangements of "the participants in the speech event" (in Jakobson's notion of the linguistics of discourse).[4] We may posit that the matrices of enunciation are the result of the repetition of drive charges (a) within biological, ecological, and socio-familial constraints (b and c), and the stabilization of their facilitation into stases whose surrounding structure accommodates and leaves its mark on symbolization.

The genotext can thus be seen as language's underlying foundation. We shall use the term *phenotext* to denote language that serves to communicate, which linguistics describes in terms of "competence" and "performance."[5] The phenotext is constantly split up and divided, and is irreducible to the semiotic process that works through the genotext. The phenotext is a structure (which can be generated, in generative grammar's sense); it obeys rules of communication and presupposes a subject of enunciation and an addressee. The genotext, on the other hand, is a process; it moves through zones that have relative and transitory borders and constitutes a *path* that is not restricted to the two poles of univocal information between two full-fledged subjects. If these two terms—genotext and phenotext—could be translated into a metalanguage that would convey the difference between

1. Units of sound. The translator previously noted: " 'Device' is Kristeva's own choice for the translation of *dispositif*: something devised or constructed for a particular purpose."
2. The translation of Freud's German *Bahnungen*. According to Freud, it was easier to repeat an experience than to have a new one; repetition thus lays down or "facilitates" a pattern for future experiences.
3. To signify something else, language must both link the sign to the thing (referent) and articulate the two parts of the sign (signifier and signifier).
4. See "Shifters, Verbal Categories, and the Russian Verb," in Roman Jakobson, *Selected Writings*, 2 vols. (The Hague: Mouton, 1971), 2:130–47 [Kristeva's note].
5. Chomsky's terms, corresponding roughly to Saussure's *langue* and *parole*: "competence" is knowledge of language as a system; "performance" involves linguistic acts by particular speakers.

them, one might say that the genotext is a matter of topology, whereas the phenotext is one of algebra.[6] This distinction may be illustrated by a particular signifying system: written and spoken Chinese, particularly classical Chinese. Writing represents-articulates the signifying process into specific networks or spaces; *speech* (which may correspond to that writing) restores the diacritical elements necessary for an exchange of meaning between two subjects (temporality, aspect, specification of the protagonists, morpho-semantic identifiers, and so forth).[7]

The signifying process therefore includes both the genotext and the phenotext; indeed it could not do otherwise. For it is in language that all signifying operations are realized (even when linguistic material is not used), and it is on the basis of language that a theoretical approach may attempt to perceive that operation.

In our view, the process we have just described accounts for the way all signifying practices are generated.[8] But every signifying practice does not encompass the infinite totality of that process. Multiple constraints—which are ultimately sociopolitical—stop the signifying process at one or another of the theses that it traverses; they knot it and lock it into a given surface or structure; they discard *practice* under fixed, fragmentary, symbolic *matrices*, the tracings of various social constraints that obliterate the infinity of the process: the phenotext is what conveys these obliterations. Among the capitalist mode of production's numerous signifying practices only certain literary texts of the avant-garde (Mallarmé, Joyce[9]) manage to cover the infinity of the process, that is, reach the semiotic *chora*, which modifies linguistic structures. It must be emphasized, however, that this total exploration of the signifying process generally leaves in abeyance the theses that are characteristic of the social organism, its structures, and their political transformation: the text has a tendency to dispense with political and social signifieds.

It has only been in very recent years or in revolutionary periods that signifying practice has inscribed within the phenotext the plural, heterogeneous, and contradictory process of signification encompassing the flow of drives, material discontinuity, political struggle, and the pulverization of language.[1]

Lacan has delineated four types of discourse in our society: that of the hysteric, the academic, the master, and the analyst.[2] Within the perspective just set forth, we shall posit a different classification, which, in certain respects, intersects these four Lacanian categories, and in others, adds to them. We shall distinguish between the following signifying practices: narrative, metalanguage, contemplation, and text-practice.

6. That is, the genotext is the shape taken by existing space, while the phenotext translates the relations discovered into a formal language.

7. See Joseph Needham, *Science and Civilisation in China*, 4 vols. (Cambridge: Cambridge University Press, 1960), vol. 1 [Kristeva's note].

8. From a similar perspective, Edgar Morin writes: "We can think of magic, mythologies, and ideologies both as mixed systems, making affectivity rational and rationality affective, and as outcomes of combining: a) fundamental drives, b) the chancy play of fantasy, and c) logico-constructive systems. (To our mind, the theory of myth must be based on triunic syncretism rather than unilateral logic.)" He adds, in a note, that "myth does not have a single logic but a synthesis of three kinds of logic." "Le Paradigme perdu: La Nature humaine" [Paradigm Lost: Human Nature], paper presented at the "Invariants biologiques et universaux culturels" [Biological Invariants and Cultural Universals] Colloquium, Royaumont, September 6–9, 1972 [Kristeva's note].

9. James Joyce (1882–1941), Irish writer known for his innovations in the form and language of the novel.

1. An allusion to *Le Poème pulvérisé* (1947, *The Pulverized Poem*), a volume of prose poems by the French poet René Char.

2. Lacan presented this typology of discourse at his 1969 and 1970 seminars [Kristeva's note].

Let us state from the outset that this distinction is only provisional and schematic, and that although it corresponds to actual practices, it interests us primarily as a didactic implement [*outil*]—one that will allow us to specify some of the modalities of signifying dispositions. The latter interest us to the extent that they give rise to different practices and are, as a consequence, more or less coded in modes of production. Of course narrative and contemplation could also be seen as devices stemming from (hysterical and obsessional) transference neurosis; and metalanguage and the text as practices allied with psychotic (paranoid and schizoid) economies.[3]

1974

3. Suggesting parallels between creativity and madness, Kristeva connects narrative with hysteria, contemplation with obsession, metalanguage with paranoia, and textuality with schizophrenia.

LAURA MULVEY
b. 1941

Writer and filmmaker Laura Mulvey is widely regarded as one of the most challenging and incisive contemporary feminist cultural theorists. Belonging to the 1970s generation of British film theorists and independent filmmakers, she came to prominence with "Visual Pleasure and Narrative Cinema," a foundational text in feminist film criticism. This essay, published in 1975 in the vanguard British film journal *Screen* and frequently anthologized since, was groundbreaking as one of the earliest pieces of feminist criticism to go beyond cataloguing images of women in films. Extending the psychoanalytic insights of both SIGMUND FREUD and JACQUES LACAN, Mulvey describes how sexual difference and inequality are inscribed not only in the content or subject matter of a film but in its formal visual apparatus—its characteristic ways of looking—as well.

Born in Oxford, England, Mulvey received a B.A. in history from Oxford University in 1963. In 1972, with Claire Johnston and Linda Myles, she organized the women's events at the Edinburgh Film Festival. She has taught classes at Bulmershe College in Reading, England; the London Institute; the University of East Anglia; Cornell University; the University of California at Davis; and the British Film Institute. She has co-directed several avant-garde films with her husband, Peter Wollen, including *Penthesileia: Queen of the Amazons* (1974), *Riddles of the Sphinx* (1977), *Amy!* (1980), *Crystal Gazing* (1982), and *The Bad Sister* (1983), all of which attempt to undermine conventional cinematic methods of filming women. In addition, her essays on a wide variety of subjects have been published in *Visual and Other Pleasures* (1989) and *Fetishism and Curiosity* (1996).

In 1975 Mulvey's essay on visual pleasure and narrative cinema was revolutionary. It was written at a time when feminist literary criticism was beginning to establish itself as a field of study in many English departments and when women's studies programs were just getting off the ground. Few of the works now considered canonical in feminist literary criticism had been written. Anglo-American feminists, documenting images of women in literature, focused mainly on the content rather than the form of the texts they examined. Furthermore, many were hostile toward psychoanalysis, though a few were already exploring the potential connections between Freud and feminism. In France the theorists who would come to be known in the

United States as the French feminists—JULIA KRISTEVA, HÉLÈNE CIXOUS, and Luce Irigaray—were using psychoanalytic theory as a means of exploring sexual difference and inequality, but their work would not begin to have a significant impact on American feminism until the 1980s.

"Visual Pleasure and Narrative Cinema" describes the manner in which the traditional visual apparatus of mainstream Hollywood "narrative" film looks at women as passive objects subordinated to the male gaze. Using a dense but illuminating psychoanalytic framework, Mulvey explores how the male unconscious shapes the erotic pleasures involved in looking. While she concedes that psychoanalysis might not offer a way out of the inequalities between the sexes or the oppression of women, she argues that it does provide a useful political tool for illustrating the mechanisms of pleasure on which the cinematic objectification of women depends.

According to Mulvey, the visual techniques of cinema afford viewers two contradictory pleasures. First, through the process Freud terms *scopophilia* (pleasure in looking), we enjoy making others the object of a controlling gaze. Second, through a process of identification that parallels Lacan's famous mirror stage (theorized in "The Mirror Stage," 1949; see above), we derive pleasure from identifying with an ideal image on the screen. Both have their origins in infantile processes by which we learned to separate ourselves from others. As described to this point, the two processes seem to structure the visual pleasure of men and women in the same way. However, Mulvey argues that because the male viewer cannot bear the burden of sexual objectification, he (the viewer is specifically male) deflects the tension by splitting his gaze between spectacle and narrative. A woman on-screen typically functions as the primary erotic object for both screen characters and audience members, becoming the object of the dominant, male gaze; as such, she exists outside the narrative illusions of time and space the film creates. At the same time, spectators identify with the male protagonist, who acts within the parameters of time and space—the diegesis—created by the film's story line.

The visual apparatus of mainstream film is further complicated because the process of gazing on the female object of desire is both pleasurable and threatening. While film creates an illusionistic world that allows for the free play of desire, in actuality the viewer is never free from the circumstances that gave rise to those desires within the symbolic social order, especially from the castration complex. The female object of the gaze, because she lacks a penis, is associated with the primordial fear of castration; although that threat initiates the male subject's integration into the symbolic social order, it also creates considerable anxiety. For this reason, the controlling male ego must attempt to escape the threat of castration evoked by the very gaze that gives it pleasure. Mulvey maintains that the male unconscious has two means of disarming the threat. The first is a form of voyeurism—investigating the female, demystifying her, and either denouncing, punishing, or saving her. The second is male disavowal, achieved by the substitution of a fetish object that becomes reassuring rather than dangerous. She examines these processes in the films of the directors Josef von Sternberg (1894–1969) and Alfred Hitchcock (1899–1980).

Before the pleasures of mainstream film can be challenged, Mulvey argues, viewers must be able to break down the cinematic codes that create the controlling male gaze and the illusionistic world that satisfies the desires it invokes. The cinema depends on three looks: that of the camera, that of the audience, and that of the film's characters. It achieves its illusion of truth and reality (mimesis) by denying or downplaying the first two (the material process of recording and the critical reading of the viewer) and by emphasizing the last. Only by disrupting the seamlessness of this whole visual illusion can women's subordination to the male gaze be defied.

The visual dynamics described in "Visual Pleasure and Narrative Cinema" have been widely applied not only to film but to other media as well, including photography, advertising, painting, and television, making this essay a landmark text for visual culture and media studies generally. But Mulvey's description of the male gaze has not been without its critics—feminists included—who have pointed out its limitations. For many, the spatial logic of the male gaze limits the ways in which vision (and visual pleasure) can be understood. Because the masculine gaze is always posited as the site of mastery and control, while the feminine is marked by submission to the gaze, little room is left within mainstream narrative cinema for resistances or alternative practices. Nor does avant-garde cinema, where Mulvey locates the alternative to the male gaze, offer much evidence of being any more responsive to feminist critique than Hollywood filmmaking. Others argue that her paradigm locks the activity of looking into a traditional Oedipal heterosexuality. Moreover, theories drawing on a visual apparatus based on a gendered split between female object and male voyeur cannot describe the visual pleasure of female viewers, or account for the male gaze at another male. Mulvey herself has recognized the validity of such objections, attempting to address many of them in a later essay, "Afterthoughts on 'Visual Pleasure and Narrative Cinema' Inspired by King Vidor's *Duel in the Sun*" (1981). Despite such criticism, Mulvey's 1975 essay continues to inspire important work in feminist film studies.

BIBLIOGRAPHY

Laura Mulvey has published three books: *Visual and Other Pleasures* (1989) collects her essays on a wide range of topics, *Citizen Kane* (1992) explores what is perhaps the most celebrated American film, and *Fetishism and Curiosity* (1996) examines how the concept of fetishism as it has been developed by Karl Marx and Freud relates to artistic texts. For biographical information on Mulvey, consult the interviews by Jacqueline Suter and Sandy Flitterman, "Textual Riddles: Women as Enigma or Site of Social Meanings? An Interview with Laura Mulvey," *Discourse* 1 (1979), and by Juan Suarez and Millicent Manglis, "Cinema, Gender, and the Topographies of Enigmas: A Conversation with Laura Mulvey," *Cinefocus* 3 (1995).

A great deal of feminist film criticism since 1975 has been written in response to Mulvey's essay. Among the most notable analyses are E. Ann Kaplan, *Women and Film: Both Sides of the Camera* (1983); *Re-vision: Essays in Feminist Film Criticism*, edited by Mary Ann Doane, Patricia Mellencamp, and Linda Williams (1984); Kaplan, *Rocking around the Clock: Music Television, Postmodernism, and Consumer Culture* (1987), which examines MTV and the popular music video, in another extension and critique of Mulvey's argument; and Mary Ann Doane, *The Desire to Desire: The Woman's Film of the 1940s* (1987). An anthology that demonstrates Mulvey's considerable influence on feminist film criticism is *Female Spectators: Looking at Film and Television*, edited by E. Deidre Pribram (1988). Several major psychoanalytic books on film assess Mulvey's contributions, including Kaja Silverman, *The Acoustic Mirror: The Female Voice in Psychoanalysis and Cinema* (1988); *Psychoanalysis and Cinema*, edited by E. Ann Kaplan (1990); and *Femmes Fatales: Feminism, Film Theory, Psychoanalysis*, edited by Mary Ann Doane (1991).

Visual Pleasure and Narrative Cinema

I Introduction

(A) A POLITICAL USE OF PSYCHOANALYSIS

This paper intends to use psychoanalysis to discover where and how the fascination of film is reinforced by pre-existing patterns of fascination already at work within the individual subject and the social formations that have moulded him. It takes as its starting-point the way film reflects, reveals and even plays on the straight, socially established interpretation of sexual difference which controls images, erotic ways of looking and spectacle. It is helpful to understand what the cinema has been, how its magic has worked in the past, while attempting a theory and a practice which will challenge this cinema of the past. Psychoanalytic theory is thus appropriated here as a political weapon, demonstrating the way the unconscious of patriarchal society has structured film form.

The paradox of phallocentrism[1] in all its manifestations is that it depends on the image of the castrated women to give order and meaning to its world. An idea of woman stands as linchpin to the system: it is her lack that produces the phallus as a symbolic presence, it is her desire to make good the lack that the phallus signifies. Recent writing in *Screen*[2] about psychoanalysis and the cinema has not sufficiently brought out the importance of the representation of the female form in a symbolic order[3] in which, in the last resort, it speaks castration and nothing else. To summarise briefly: the function of woman in forming the patriarchal unconscious is twofold: she firstly symbolises the castration threat by her real lack of a penis and secondly thereby raises her child into the symbolic. Once this has been achieved, her meaning in the process is at an end. It does not last into the world of law and language except as a memory, which oscillates between memory of maternal plenitude and memory of lack. Both are posited on nature (or on anatomy in Freud's famous phrase[4]). Woman's desire is subjugated to her image as bearer of the bleeding wound; she can exist only in relation to castration and cannot transcend it. She turns her child into the signifier of her own desire to possess a penis (the condition, she imagines, of entry into the symbolic). Either she must gracefully give way to the word, the name of the father and the law, or else struggle to keep her child down with her in the half-light of the imaginary. Woman then stands in patriarchal culture as a signifier[5] for the male other, bound by a symbolic order in which man can live out his fantasies and obsessions through linguistic command by imposing them on the silent image of woman still tied to her place as bearer, not maker, of meaning.

There is an obvious interest in this analysis for feminists, a beauty in its exact rendering of the frustration experienced under the phallocentric order. It gets us nearer to the roots of our oppression, it brings closer an articulation of the problem, it faces us with the ultimate challenge: how to fight the unconscious structured like a language (formed critically at the moment of arrival of language) while still caught within the language of the patriarchy?

1. The psychoanalytic system in which sexual difference is defined as the difference between having and lacking the phallus; the term has come to refer to the patriarchal cultural system as a whole insofar as that system privileges the phallus as the symbol and source of power. Because of that privilege, women suffer "penis envy" and men suffer the "castration complex" (the fear of every male child that his desire for his mother will be punished by castration by his father; more generally, the fear of becoming "castrated" like women that leads men to cling to masculinity); both terms are originally from the theories of SIGMUND FREUD (1856–1939).

2. Vanguard British film journal, founded in 1969 by the British Society for Education in Film and Television.

3. In the theories of the psyche put forward by the French psychoanalyst JACQUES LACAN (1901–1981), the Symbolic is the dimension of language, law, and the father; in contrast, the Imaginary is modeled on the preverbal mother-child dyad, or on the relation between an infant and its mirror image.

4. That is, "anatomy is destiny" ("The Dissolution of the Oedipus Complex," 1924).

5. Term used by structuralist and poststructuralist theorists that was coined by the Swiss linguist FERDINAND DE SAUSSURE (1857–1913) to explain the functioning of signs, which he divided into a *signifier* (the form a sign takes) and a *signified* (the concept it represents).

There is no way in which we can produce an alternative out of the blue, but we can begin to make a break by examining patriarchy with the tools it provides, of which psychoanalysis is not the only but an important one. We are still separated by a great gap from important issues for the female unconscious which are scarcely relevant to phallocentric theory: the sexing of the female infant and her relationship to the symbolic, the sexually mature woman as non-mother, maternity outside the signification of the phallus, the vagina. But, at this point, psychoanalytic theory as it now stands can at least advance our understanding of the *status quo*, of the patriarchal order in which we are caught.

(B) DESTRUCTION OF PLEASURE AS A RADICAL WEAPON

As an advanced representation system, the cinema poses questions about the ways the unconscious (formed by the dominant order) structures ways of seeing and pleasure in looking. Cinema has changed over the last few decades. It is no longer the monolithic system based on large capital investment exemplified at its best by Hollywood in the 1930s, 1940s and 1950s. Technological advances (16mm and so on) have changed the economic conditions of cinematic production, which can now be artisanal as well as capitalist. Thus it has been possible for an alternative cinema to develop. However self-conscious and ironic Hollywood managed to be, it always restricted itself to a formal *mise en scène*[6] reflecting the dominant ideological concept of the cinema. The alternative cinema provides a space for the birth of a cinema which is radical in both a political and an aesthetic sense and challenges the basic assumptions of the mainstream film. This is not to reject the latter moralistically, but to highlight the ways in which its formal preoccupations reflect the psychical obsessions of the society which produced it and, further, to stress that the alternative cinema must start specifically by reacting against these obsessions and assumptions. A politically and aesthetically avant-garde cinema is now possible, but it can still only exist as a counterpoint.

The magic of the Hollywood style at its best (and of all the cinema which fell within its sphere of influence) arose, not exclusively, but in one important aspect, from its skilled and satisfying manipulation of visual pleasure. Unchallenged, mainstream film coded the erotic into the language of the dominant patriarchal order. In the highly developed Hollywood cinema it was only through these codes that the alienated subject, torn in his imaginary memory by a sense of loss, by the terror of potential lack in fantasy, came near to finding a glimpse of satisfaction: through its formal beauty and its play on his own formative obsessions. This article will discuss the interweaving of that erotic pleasure in film, its meaning and, in particular, the central place of the image of woman. It is said that analysing pleasure, or beauty, destroys it. That is the intention of this article. The satisfaction and reinforcement of the ego[7] that represent the high point of film history hitherto must be attacked. Not in favour of a reconstructed new pleasure, which cannot exist in the abstract, nor of intellectualised unpleasure, but to make

6. In film, everything within the frame of a shot, including actors, settings, costumes, action, and lighting.

7. The part of the psyche, as described by Freud, that is conscious, controls behavior, and is in touch with external reality.

way for a total negation of the ease and plenitude of the narrative fiction film. The alternative is the thrill that comes from leaving the past behind without simply rejecting it, transcending outworn or oppressive forms, and daring to break with normal pleasurable expectations in order to conceive a new language of desire.

II Pleasure in Looking/Fascination with the Human Form

A The cinema offers a number of possible pleasures. One is scopophilia (pleasure in looking). There are circumstances in which looking itself is a source of pleasure, just as, in the reverse formation, there is pleasure in being looked at. Originally, in his *Three Essays on Sexuality*, Freud isolated scopophilia as one of the component instincts of sexuality which exist as drives quite independently of the erotogenic zones. At this point he associated scopophilia with taking other people as objects, subjecting them to a controlling and curious gaze. His particular examples centre on the voyeuristic activities of children, their desire to see and make sure of the private and forbidden (curiosity about other people's genital and bodily functions, about the presence or absence of the penis and, retrospectively, about the primal scene[8]). In this analysis scopophilia is essentially active. (Later, in 'Instincts and Their Vicissitudes', Freud developed his theory of scopophilia further, attaching it initially to pre-genital auto-eroticism, after which, by analogy, the pleasure of the look is transferred to others. There is a close working here of the relationship between the active instinct and its further development in a narcissistic form.) Although the instinct is modified by other factors, in particular the constitution of the ego, it continues to exist as the erotic basis for pleasure in looking at another person as object. At the extreme, it can become fixated into a perversion, producing obsessive voyeurs and Peeping Toms whose only sexual satisfaction can come from watching, in an active controlling sense, an objectified other.

At first glance, the cinema would seem to be remote from the undercover world of the surreptitious observation of an unknowing and unwilling victim. What is seen on the screen is so manifestly shown. But the mass of mainstream film, and the conventions within which it has consciously evolved, portray a hermetically sealed world which unwinds magically, indifferent to the presence of the audience, producing for them a sense of separation and playing on their voyeuristic fantasy. Moreover the extreme contrast between the darkness in the auditorium (which also isolates the spectators from one another) and the brilliance of the shifting patterns of light and shade on the screen helps to promote the illusion of voyeuristic separation. Although the film is really being shown, is there to be seen, conditions of screening and narrative conventions give the spectator an illusion of looking in on a private world. Among other things, the position of the spectators in the cinema is blatantly one of repression of their exhibitionism and projection of the repressed desire onto the performer.

B The cinema satisfies a primordial wish for pleasurable looking, but it also goes further, developing scopophilia in its narcissistic aspect. The conven-

8. The scene of the child's parents engaged in sexual intercourse. Freud published *Three Essays on the Theory of Sexuality* in 1905 and "Instincts and Their Vicissitudes" in 1915.

tions of mainstream film focus attention on the human form. Scale, space, stories are all anthropomorphic. Here, curiosity and the wish to look intermingle with a fascination with likeness and recognition: the human face, the human body, the relationship between the human form and its surroundings, the visible presence of the person in the world. Jacques Lacan has described how the moment when a child recognises its own image in the mirror is crucial for the constitution of the ego.[9] Several aspects of this analysis are relevant here. The mirror phase occurs at a time when children's physical ambitions outstrip their motor capacity, with the result that their recognition of themselves is joyous in that they imagine their mirror image to be more complete, more perfect than they experience in their own body. Recognition is thus overlaid with misrecognition: the image recognised is conceived as the reflected body of the self, but its misrecognition as superior projects this body outside itself as an ideal ego, the alienated subject which, re-introjected[1] as an ego ideal, prepares the way for identification with others in the future. This mirror moment predates language for the child.

Important for this article is the fact that it is an image that constitutes the matrix of the imaginary, of recognition/misrecognition and identification, and hence of the first articulation of the I, of subjectivity. This is a moment when an older fascination with looking (at the mother's face, for an obvious example) collides with the initial inklings of self-awareness. Hence it is the birth of the long love affair/despair between image and self-image which has found such intensity of expression in film and such joyous recognition in the cinema audience. Quite apart from the extraneous similarities between screen and mirror (the framing of the human form in its surroundings, for instance), the cinema has structures of fascination strong enough to allow temporary loss of ego while simultaneously reinforcing it. The sense of forgetting the world as the ego has come to perceive it (I forgot who I am and where I was) is nostalgically reminiscent of that pre-subjective moment of image recognition. While at the same time, the cinema has distinguished itself in the production of ego ideals, through the star system for instance. Stars provide a focus or centre both to screen space and screen story where they act out a complex process of likeness and difference (the glamorous impersonates the ordinary).

C Sections A and B have set out two contradictory aspects of the pleasurable structures of looking in the conventional cinematic situation. The first, scopophilic arises from pleasure in using another person as an object of sexual stimulation through sight. The second, developed through narcissism and the constitution of the ego, comes from identification with the image seen. Thus, in film terms, one implies a separation of the erotic identity of the subject from the object on the screen (active scopophilia), the other demands identification of the ego with the object on the screen through the spectator's fascination with and recognition of his like. The first is a function of the sexual instincts, the second of ego libido.[2] This dichotomy was crucial for Freud. Although he saw the two as interacting and overlaying each other,

9. Lacan, in "The Mirror Stage" (1949; see above), describes the development of selfhood in children between 6 and 18 months old.

1. A psychoanalytic term; *introjection* is the unconscious process by which the outside world is taken into the self and represented in its internal structure.

2. Narcissistic libido, a pleasure derived from idealizing the self.

the tension between instinctual drives and self-preservation polarises in terms of pleasure. But both are formative structures, mechanisms without intrinsic meaning. In themselves they have no signification, unless attached to an idealisation. Both pursue aims in indifference to perceptual reality, and motivate eroticised phantasmagoria that affect the subject's perception of the world to make a mockery of empirical objectivity.

During its history, the cinema seems to have evolved a particular illusion of reality in which this contradiction between libido and ego has found a beautifully complementary fantasy world. In *reality* the fantasy world of the screen is subject to the law which produces it. Sexual instincts and identification processes have a meaning within the symbolic order which articulates desire. Desire, born with language, allows the possibility of transcending the instinctual and the imaginary, but its point of reference continually returns to the traumatic moment of its birth: the castration complex. Hence the look, pleasurable in form, can be threatening in content, and it is woman as representation/image that crystallises this paradox.

III Woman as Image, Man as Bearer of the Look

A In a world ordered by sexual imbalance, pleasure in looking has been split between active/male and passive/female. The determining male gaze projects its fantasy onto the female figure, which is styled accordingly. In their traditional exhibitionist role women are simultaneously looked at and displayed, with their appearance coded for strong visual and erotic impact so that they can be said to connote *to-be-looked-at-ness*. Woman displayed as sexual object is the *leitmotif* of erotic spectacle: from pin-ups to striptease, from Ziegfeld to Busby Berkeley,[3] she holds the look, and plays to and signifies male desire. Mainstream film neatly combines spectacle and narrative. (Note, however, how in the musical song-and-dance numbers interrupt the flow of the diegesis.[4]) The presence of woman is an indispensable element of spectacle in normal narrative film, yet her visual presence tends to work against the development of a story-line, to freeze the flow of action in moments of erotic contemplation. This alien presence then has to be integrated into cohesion with the narrative. As Budd Boetticher[5] has put it:

> What counts is what the heroine provokes, or rather what she represents. She is the one, or rather the love or fear she inspires in the hero, or else the concern he feels for her, who makes him act the way he does. In herself the woman has not the slightest importance.

(A recent tendency in narrative film has been to dispense with this problem altogether; hence the development of what Molly Haskell[6] has called the 'buddy movie', in which the active homosexual eroticism of the central male figures can carry the story without distraction.) Traditionally, the woman displayed has functioned on two levels: as erotic object for the characters within the screen story, and as erotic object for the spectator within the

3. American choreographer and film director (1895–1976), famous for his musical productions. Florenz Ziegfeld (1869–1932), American theatrical producer, best known for extravagant revues featuring showgirls.
4. The ongoing story or narrative.
5. American film director (b. 1916), best known for his westerns.
6. American film critic (b. 1939); she discusses "buddy movies" in *From Reverence to Rape: The Treatment of Women in the Movies* (1974).

auditorium, with a shifting tension between the looks on either side of the screen. For instance, the device of the show-girl allows the two looks to be unified technically without any apparent break in the diegesis. A woman performs within the narrative; the gaze of the spectator and that of the male characters in the film are neatly combined without breaking narrative verisimilitude. For a moment the sexual impact of the performing woman takes the film into a no man's land outside its own time and space. Thus Marilyn Monroe's first appearance in *The River of No Return* and Lauren Bacall's songs in *To Have and Have Not*.[7] Similarly, conventional close-ups of legs (Dietrich, for instance) or a face (Garbo)[8] integrate into the narrative a different mode of eroticism. One part of a fragmented body destroys the Renaissance space, the illusion of depth demanded by the narrative; it gives flatness, the quality of a cut-out or icon, rather than verisimilitude, to the screen.

B An active/passive heterosexual division of labour has similarly controlled narrative structure. According to the principles of the ruling ideology and the psychical structures that back it up, the male figure cannot bear the burden of sexual objectification. Man is reluctant to gaze at his exhibitionist like. Hence the split between spectacle and narrative supports the man's role as the active one of advancing the story, making things happen. The man controls the film fantasy and also emerges as the representative of power in a further sense: as the bearer of the look of the spectator, transferring it behind the screen to neutralise the extra-diegetic[9] tendencies represented by woman as spectacle. This is made possible through the processes set in motion by structuring the film around a main controlling figure with whom the spectator can identify. As the spectator identifies with the main male protagonist, he projects his look onto that of his like, his screen surrogate, so that the power of the male protagonist as he controls events coincides with the active power of the erotic look, both giving a satisfying sense of omnipotence. A male movie star's glamorous characteristics are thus not those of the erotic object of the gaze, but those of the more perfect, more complete, more powerful ideal ego conceived in the original moment of recognition in front of the mirror. The character in the story can make things happen and control events better than the subject/spectator, just as the image in the mirror was more in control of motor co-ordination.

In contrast to woman as icon, the active male figure (the ego ideal of the identification process) demands a three-dimensional space corresponding to that of the mirror recognition, in which the alienated subject internalised his own representation of his imaginary existence. He is a figure in a landscape. Here the function of film is to reproduce as accurately as possible the so-called natural conditions of human perception. Camera technology (as exemplified by deep focus in particular) and camera movements (determined by the action of the protagonist), combined with invisible editing (demanded by realism), all tend to blur the limits of screen space. The male protagonist is free to command the stage, a stage of spatial illusion in which he articu-

7. The 1944 American film (dir. Howard Hawks) that was the film debut of the actress Bacall (b. 1924). *River of No Return* (dir. Otto Preminger, 1954), American film that stars the actress Monroe (1926–1962) as a beautiful saloon singer.

8. Greta Garbo (1905–1990), Swedish-born American film actress. Marlene Dietrich (1901–1992), German-born American actress.

9. Outside the story or the frame of the camera.

lates the look and creates the action. (There are films with a woman as main protagonist, of course. To analyse this phenomenon seriously here would take me too far afield. Pam Cook and Claire Johnston's study of *The Revolt of Mamie Stover*[1] in Phil Hardy (ed.), *Raoul Walsh* (Edinburgh, 1974), shows in a striking case how the strength of this female protagonist is more apparent than real.)

C1 Sections III A and B have set out a tension between a mode of representation of woman in film and conventions surrounding the diegesis. Each is associated with a look: that of the spectator in direct scopophilic contact with the female form displayed for his enjoyment (connoting male fantasy) and that of the spectator fascinated with the image of his like set in an illusion of natural space, and through him gaining control and possession of the woman within the diegesis. (This tension and the shift from one pole to the other can structure a single text. Thus both in *Only Angels Have Wings*[2] and in *To Have and Have Not*, the film opens with the woman as object of the combined gaze of spectator and all the male protagonists in the film. She is isolated, glamorous, on display, sexualised. But as the narrative progresses she falls in love with the main male protagonist and becomes his property, losing her outward glamorous characteristics, her generalised sexuality, her show-girl connotations; her eroticism is subjected to the male star alone. By means of identification with him, through participation in his power, the spectator can indirectly possess her too.)

But in psychoanalytic terms, the female figure poses a deeper problem. She also connotes something that the look continually circles around but disavows: her lack of a penis, implying a threat of castration and hence unpleasure. Ultimately, the meaning of woman is sexual difference, the visually ascertainable absence of the penis, the material evidence on which is based the castration complex essential for the organisation of entrance to the symbolic order and the law of the father. Thus the woman as icon, displayed for the gaze and enjoyment of men, the active controllers of the look, always threatens to evoke the anxiety it originally signified. The male unconscious has two avenues of escape from this castration anxiety: preoccupation with the re-enactment of the original trauma (investigating the woman, demystifying her mystery), counterbalanced by the devaluation, punishment or saving of the guilty object (an avenue typified by the concerns of the *film noir*[3]); or else complete disavowal of castration by the substitution of a fetish object or turning the represented figure itself into a fetish so that it becomes reassuring rather than dangerous (hence overvaluation, the cult of the female star).

This second avenue, fetishistic scopophilia, builds up the physical beauty of the object, transforming it into something satisfying in itself. The first avenue, voyeurism, on the contrary, has associations with sadism: pleasure lies in ascertaining guilt (immediately associated with castration), asserting control and subjugating the guilty person through punishment or forgiveness. This sadistic side fits in well with narrative. Sadism demands a story, depends on making something happen, forcing a change in another person,

1. A 1956 American film (dir. Raoul Walsh), starring Jane Russell in the title role.
2. A 1939 American film (dir. Howard Hawks); the female "object" is Jean Arthur.
3. Literally, "black film" (French), a postwar genre characterized by dark settings, by shady or disturbed characters who are alienated and isolated, and by a view of society from its underside.

a battle of will and strength, victory/defeat, all occurring in a linear time with a beginning and an end. Fetishistic scopophilia, on the other hand, can exist outside linear time as the erotic instinct is focused on the look alone. These contradictions and ambiguities can be illustrated more simply by using works by Hitchcock and Sternberg,[4] both of whom take the look almost as the content or subject matter of many of their films. Hitchcock is the more complex, as he uses both mechanisms. Sternberg's work, on the other hand, provides many pure examples of fetishistic scopophilia.

C2 Sternberg once said he would welcome his films being projected upside-down so that story and character involvement would not interfere with the spectator's undiluted appreciation of the screen image. This statement is revealing but ingenuous: ingenuous in that his films do demand that the figure of the woman (Dietrich, in the cycle of films with her, as the ultimate example) should be identifiable; but revealing in that it emphasises the fact that for him the pictorial space enclosed by the frame is paramount, rather than narrative or identification processes. While Hitchcock goes into the investigative side of voyeurism, Sternberg produces the ultimate fetish, taking it to the point where the powerful look of the male protagonist (characteristic of traditional narrative film) is broken in favour of the image in direct erotic rapport with the spectator. The beauty of the woman as object and the screen space coalesce; she is no longer the bearer of guilt but a perfect product, whose body, stylised and fragmented by close-ups, is the content of the film and the direct recipient of the spectator's look.

Sternberg plays down the illusion of screen depth; his screen tends to be one-dimensional, as light and shade, lace, steam, foliage, net, streamers and so on reduce the visual field. There is little or no mediation of the look through the eyes of the main male protagonist. On the contrary, shadowy presences like La Bessière in *Morocco*[5] act as surrogates for the director, detached as they are from audience identification. Despite Sternberg's insistence that his stories are irrelevant, it is significant that they are concerned with situation, not suspense, and cyclical rather than linear time, while plot complications revolve around misunderstanding rather than conflict. The most important absence is that of the controlling male gaze within the screen scene. The high point of emotional drama in the most typical Dietrich films, her supreme moments of erotic meaning, take place in the absence of the man she loves in the fiction. There are other witnesses, other spectators watching her on the screen, their gaze is one with, not standing in for, that of the audience. At the end of *Morocco*, Tom Brown has already disappeared into the desert when Amy Jolly kicks off her gold sandals and walks after him. At the end of *Dishonoured*,[6] Kranau is indifferent to the fate of Magda. In both cases, the erotic impact, sanctified by death, is displayed as a spectacle for the audience. The male hero misunderstands and, above all, does not see.

In Hitchcock, by contrast, the male hero does see precisely what the audi-

4. Josef von Sternberg (1894–1969), Austrian-born American film director; he brought the actress Marlene Dietrich to the United States and featured her in a number of films in the early 1930s. Alfred Hitchcock (1899–1980), English film director known as a master of suspense; many of his most important films were made in Hollywood.

5. A 1930 American film directed by Sternberg; La Bessière is played by Adolphe Menjou, Tom Brown by Gary Cooper, and Amy Jolly by Dietrich.

6. A 1931 American film directed by Sternberg; Kranau is played by Victor McLaglen and Marie (not "Magda"), a spy, by Dietrich.

ence sees. However, although fascination with an image through scopophilic eroticism can be the subject of the film, it is the role of the hero to portray the contradictions and tensions experienced by the spectator. In *Vertigo* in particular, but also in *Marnie* and *Rear Window*,[7] the look is central to the plot, oscillating between voyeurism and fetishistic fascination. Hitchcock has never concealed his interest in voyeurism, cinematic and non-cinematic. His heroes are exemplary of the symbolic order and the law—a policeman (*Vertigo*), a dominant male possessing money and power (*Marnie*)—but their erotic drives lead them into compromised situations. The power to subject another person to the will sadistically or to the gaze voyeuristically is turned onto the woman as the object of both. Power is backed by a certainty of legal right and the established guilt of the woman (evoking castration, psychoanalytically speaking). True perversion is barely concealed under a shallow mask of ideological correctness—the man is on the right side of the law, the woman on the wrong. Hitchcock's skillful use of identification processes and liberal use of subjective camera from the point of view of the male protagonist draw the spectators deeply into his position, making them share his uneasy gaze. The spectator is absorbed into a voyeuristic situation within the screen scene and diegesis, which parodies his own in the cinema.

In an analysis of *Rear Window*, Douchet[8] takes the film as a metaphor for the cinema. Jeffries is the audience, the events in the apartment block opposite correspond to the screen. As he watches, an erotic dimension is added to his look, a central image to the drama. His girlfriend Lisa had been of little sexual interest to him, more or less a drag, so long as she remained on the spectator side. When she crosses the barrier between his room and the block opposite, their relationship is reborn erotically. He does not merely watch her through his lens, as a distant meaningful image, he also sees her as a guilty intruder exposed by a dangerous man threatening her with punishment, and thus finally giving him the opportunity to save her. Lisa's exhibitionism has already been established by her obsessive interest in dress and style, in being a passive image of visual perfection; Jeffries's voyeurism and activity have also been established through his work as a photo-journalist, a maker of stories and captor of images. However, his enforced inactivity, binding him to his seat as a spectator, puts him squarely in the fantasy position of the cinema audience.

In *Vertigo*, subjective camera predominates. Apart from one flashback from Judy's point of view, the narrative is woven around what Scottie sees or fails to see.[9] The audience follows the growth of his erotic obsession and subsequent despair precisely from his point of view. Scottie's voyeurism is blatant: he falls in love with a woman he follows and spies on without speaking to. Its sadistic side is equally blatant: he has chosen (and freely chosen, for he had been a successful lawyer) to be a policeman, with all the attendant possibilities of pursuit and investigation. As a result, he follows, watches and falls in love with a perfect image of female beauty and mystery. Once he actually confronts her, his erotic drive is to break her down and force her *to tell* by persistent cross-questioning.

7. Three American films directed by Hitchcock: *Vertigo* (1958), *Marnie* (1964), and *Rear Window* (1954).

8. Jean Douchet, French film director and critic, author of *Alfred Hitchcock* (1967). Jeffries, temporarily immobilized by a broken leg, is played by James Stewart; Lisa is played by Grace Kelly.

9. Scottie (James Stewart) is hired to watch Madeleine (Kim Novak), a wealthy man's wife; he becomes obsessed with her, and after her suicide, he finds another woman who resembles her (Judy, also played by Novak).

In the second part of the film, he re-enacts his obsessive involvement with the image he loved to watch secretly. He reconstructs Judy as Madeleine, forces her to conform in every detail to the actual physical appearance of his fetish. Her exhibitionism, her masochism, make her an ideal passive counterpart to Scottie's active sadistic voyeurism. She knows her part is to perform, and only by playing it through and then replaying it can she keep Scottie's erotic interest. But in the repetition he does break her down and succeeds in exposing her guilt. His curiosity wins through; she is punished.

Thus, in *Vertigo*, erotic involvement with the look boomerangs: the spectator's own fascination is revealed as illicit voyeurism as the narrative content enacts the processes and pleasures that he is himself exercising and enjoying. The Hitchcock hero here is firmly placed within the symbolic order, in narrative terms. He has all the attributes of the patriarchal superego.[1] Hence the spectator, lulled into a false sense of security by the apparent legality of his surrogate, sees through his look and finds himself exposed as complicit, caught in the moral ambiguity of looking. Far from being simply an aside on the perversion of the police, *Vertigo* focuses on the implications of the active/looking, passive/looked-at split in terms of sexual difference and the power of the male symbolic encapsulated in the hero. Marnie, too, performs for Mark Rutland's gaze and masquerades as the perfect to-be-looked-at image.[2] He, too, is on the side of the law until, drawn in by obsession with her guilt, her secret, he longs to see her in the act of committing a crime, make her confess and thus save her. So he, too, becomes complicit as he acts out the implications of his power. He controls money and words; he can have his cake and eat it.

IV Summary

The psychoanalytic background that has been discussed in this article is relevant to the pleasure and unpleasure offered by traditional narrative film. The scopophilic instinct (pleasure in looking at another person as an erotic object) and, in contradistinction, ego libido (forming identification processes) act as formations, mechanisms, which mould this cinema's formal attributes. The actual image of woman as (passive) raw material for the (active) gaze of man takes the argument a step further into the content and structure of representation, adding a further layer of ideological significance demanded by the patriarchal order in its favourite cinematic form—illusionistic[3] narrative film. The argument must return again to the psychoanalytic background: women in representation can signify castration, and activate voyeuristic or fetishistic mechanisms to circumvent this threat. Although none of these interacting layers is intrinsic to film, it is only in the film form that they can reach a perfect and beautiful contradiction, thanks to the possibility in the cinema of shifting the emphasis of the look. The place of the look defines cinema, the possibility of varying it and exposing it. This is what makes cinema quite different in its voyeuristic potential from, say, striptease theatre, shows and so on. Going far beyond highlighting a woman's to-be-looked-at-ness, cinema builds the way she is to be looked at into the

1. The part of the psyche, as described by Freud, that develops through the incorporation of the moral standards of the parents and community.
2. In *Marnie*, the title character (Tippi Hedren) is a habitual thief and liar who steals from her employers and then changes her identity; Rutland (Sean Connery) hires her despite recognizing her.
3. Relying on illusion to convey realism.

spectacle itself. Playing on the tension between film as controlling the dimension of time (editing, narrative) and film as controlling the dimension of space (changes in distance, editing), cinematic codes create a gaze, a world and an object, thereby producing an illusion cut to the measure of desire. It is these cinematic codes and their relationship to formative external structures that must be broken down before mainstream film and the pleasure it provides can be challenged.

To begin with (as an ending), the voyeuristic-scopophilic look that is a crucial part of traditional filmic pleasure can itself be broken down. There are three different looks associated with cinema: that of the camera as it records the pro-filmic event, that of the audience as it watches the final product, and that of the characters at each other within the screen illusion. The conventions of narrative film deny the first two and subordinate them to the third, the conscious aim being always to eliminate intrusive camera presence and prevent a distancing awareness in the audience. Without these two absences (the material existence of the recording process, the critical reading of the spectator), fictional drama cannot achieve reality, obviousness and truth. Nevertheless, as this article has argued, the structure of looking in narrative fiction film contains a contradiction in its own premises: the female image as a castration threat constantly endangers the unity of the diegesis and bursts through the world of illusion as an intrusive, static, one-dimensional fetish. Thus the two looks materially present in time and space are obsessively subordinated to the neurotic needs of the male ego. The camera becomes the mechanism for producing an illusion of Renaissance space, flowing movements compatible with the human eye, an ideology of representation that revolves around the perception of the subject; the camera's look is disavowed in order to create a convincing world in which the spectator's surrogate can perform with verisimilitude. Simultaneously, the look of the audience is denied an intrinsic force: as soon as fetishistic representation of the female image threatens to break the spell of illusion, and the erotic image on the screen appears directly (without mediation) to the spectator, the fact of fetishisation, concealing as it does castration fear, freezes the look, fixates the spectator and prevents him from achieving any distance from the image in front of him.

This complex interaction of looks is specific to film. The first blow against the monolithic accumulation of traditional film conventions (already undertaken by radical film-makers) is to free the look of the camera into its materiality[4] in time and space and the look of the audience into dialectics[5] and passionate detachment. There is no doubt that this destroys the satisfaction, pleasure and privilege of the 'invisible guest', and highlights the way film has depended on voyeuristic active/passive mechanisms. Women, whose image has continually been stolen and used for this end, cannot view the decline of the traditional film form with anything much more than sentimental regret.

1973 1975

4. Actual mechanisms.

5. Analysis of interaction.

GAYATRI CHAKRAVORTY SPIVAK

b. 1942

Gayatri Chakravorty Spivak is an unsettling voice in literary theory and, especially, postcolonial studies. She has described herself as a "practical deconstructionist feminist Marxist" and as a "gadfly." She uses deconstruction to examine "how truth is constructed" and to deploy the assertions of one intellectual and political position (such as Marxism) to "interrupt" or "bring into crisis" another (feminism, for example). In her work, she combines passionate denunciations of the harm done to women, non-Europeans, and the poor by the privileged West with a persistent questioning of the grounds on which radical critique takes its stand.

Her continual interrogation of assumptions can make Spivak difficult to read. But her restless critiques connect directly to her ethical aspiration for a "politics of the open end," in which deconstruction acts as a "safeguard" against the repression or exclusion of "alterities"—that is, people, events, or ideas that are radically "other" to the dominant worldview. She writes against the "epistemic violence" done by discourses of knowledge that carve up the world and condemn to oblivion the pieces that do not easily fit. Characteristically, she does not claim to avoid such violence herself; rather, she self-consciously explores structures of violence without assuming a final, settled position.

Spivak was born in Calcutta, India, and received her B.A. from the University of Calcutta. She came to the United States and completed her M.A. and Ph.D. in English literature at Cornell University, where PAUL DE MAN was one of her mentors. She has taught at various American universities, including the University of Iowa, the University of Texas, the University of Pittsburgh, and Columbia University. Her earliest important work was her introduction to and translation of JACQUES DERRIDA's *Of Grammatology* (1977), the first of his major books to be rendered in full into English. Spivak played a key role in introducing French "theory" into North American and British literature departments between 1975 and 1982. Almost from the start, she emphasized how deconstruction's interest in the "violence" of traditional hierarchical binary oppositions (between male and female, the West and the rest, etc.) afforded a passage from literary theory to radical politics. Spivak joined feminism's interest in silenced women to a Marxist global concern with the political, economic, and cultural oppression of nonwhite people. The result was a series of highly influential essays that helped set the agenda for feminism and for postcolonial theory in the 1980s and 1990s.

"Can the Subaltern Speak?" may be Spivak's best-known essay; it is certainly her most controversial. First given as a lecture in 1983 and published in different versions in 1985 and 1988, Spivak offers a greatly expanded revision (more than one hundred pages) in her *Critique of Postcolonial Reason* (1999). Our selection offers three sections from this revised version, beginning with the sentence in which Spivak poses a central concern: "the possibility that the intellectual is complicit in the persistent constitution of the Other as the Self's shadow." Her essay insists "on marking [critics'] positionality as investigating subjects." Postcolonial critics, like many feminists, want to give silenced others a voice. But Spivak worries that even the most benevolent effort merely repeats the very silencing it aims to combat. After all, colonialists often thought of themselves as well-intentioned. Spivak points to the British outlawing of *sati*, the Hindu practice of burning a widow on her husband's funeral pyre. While this intervention saved some lives and may have given women a modicum of free choice, it also served to secure British power in India and to underscore the asserted difference between British "civilization" and Indian "barbarism." Hindu culture was driven underground, written out of law, denied any legitimacy. Can today's intellectuals avoid a similar condescension when they represent the oppressed?

Spivak articulates her reasons for her worries in the first part of our selection, applying MICHEL FOUCAULT's understanding of "epistemic violence" to the "remotely orchestrated, far-flung, and heterogeneous project to constitute the colonial subject as Other." Foucault views intellectual power as functioning discursively to produce the very subject over which it then exercises mastery. Of course, no discourse succeeds in obliterating all alternative discourses. Intellectuals have frequently tried to create counterdiscourses that contest the dominant discourses, with the hope of connecting with the oppressed's own acts of resistance. Spivak sees postcolonial studies as a new instance of this attempt to liberate the other and to enable that other to experience and articulate those parts of itself that fall outside what the dominant discourse has constituted as its subjecthood. She asks whether such work can succeed. Can—with or without the intervention of well-intentioned intellectuals—the "subaltern" speak? Her blunt answer is no.

A subaltern, according to the dictionary, is a person holding a subordinate position, originally a junior officer in the British army. But Spivak draws on the term's nuances. It has particularly rich connotations for the Indian subcontinent because the Anglo-Indian writer Rudyard Kipling (1865–1936) so often viewed imperialism from the ambivalent position of the subaltern functionary in the complex colonial hierarchy, caught between detested superiors and feared "natives." The Italian Marxist theorist ANTONIO GRAMSCI later applied the term to the unorganized masses that must be politicized for the workers' revolution to succeed. In the 1980s the Subaltern Studies Group (a collective of radical historians in India with whom Spivak maintains ties) appropriated the term, focusing their attention on the disenfranchised peoples of India. The "subaltern" always stands in an ambiguous relation to power—subordinate to it but never fully consenting to its rule, never adopting the dominant point of view or vocabulary as expressive of its own identity. "One must nevertheless insist that the colonized subaltern *subject* is irretrievably heterogeneous," declares Spivak. Can this difference be articulated? And if so, by whom?

Because subalterns exist, to some extent, outside power, theorists and advocates of political transformation have consistently looked to them as a potential source of change. Marxists speak of and for the proletariat, feminists of and for oppressed women, and anticolonialists of and for third world peoples. In part, Spivak is reacting against the persistent tendency of radical political movements to romanticize the other, especially against the notion that third world peoples must lead the fight against multinational global capitalism. To assign them that role is to repeat colonialism's basic violence, which views non-Europeans as important only insofar as they follow Western scripts. Furthermore, when most of the power resides in the West, why should the least powerful of those caught up in globalization be responsible for halting its advance? Finally, Spivak points out that the suggestion that all third world peoples stand in the same relation to global capitalism and should respond to it in the same way is "essentialist."

Essentialism names the belief that certain people or entities share some essential, unchanging "nature" that secures their membership in a category. In the 1980s, essentialism was the target of much feminist criticism because activists recognized that generalizations about "woman" inevitably exclude some women. One response was "difference feminism," which stressed alliances among women across their differences and hoped to replace a solidarity based on shared essential qualities and experiences. Spivak's landmark contribution to this debate was the concept of "strategic essentialism." In some instances, she argued, it was important *strategically* to make essentialist claims, even while one retained an awareness that those claims were, at best, crude political generalizations. For example, feminists must publicize "the feminization of poverty"—the ways in which employment practices and wages, divorce law and settlements, and social policies ensure that in many societies women make up the majority of poor adults. Of course, many women are not poor, and poverty has causes other than an individual's sex, but to battle effectively against the poverty of some women requires the strategic essentialism of highlighting the gendered nature of economic inequality.

Leftist intellectuals who romanticize the oppressed, Spivak argues, essentialize the subaltern and thus replicate the colonialist discourses they purport to critique. To replace this leftist fantasy of an untouched or essential purity lodged in a particular group, Spivak reminds us (citing Ranajit Guha, a founding member of the Subaltern Studies Group) that a person's or group's identity is relational, a function of its place in a system of differences. There is no true or pure other; instead, the other always already exists in relation to the discourse that would name it as other.

But does the differential position of otherness afford it some resources it can use to articulate its singularity, its nonidentity with power? Spivak seems doubtful; her historical and political analysis describes Western capitalism and colonialism as triumphant. The whole world is now organized economically, politically, and culturally along the lines of Western discourses. Although those discourses are not perfectly aligned, their multiplicity generally reinforces rather than undercuts the marginalization of nonwhite peoples and the dual marginalization of nonwhite women. Given this bleak picture, Spivak turns (in the second part of our selection) to SIGMUND FREUD in an effort to develop an appropriate model of intellectual work.

Freud furthers the analysis of colonialism by helping us see how the very identity of whiteness itself is created in part through the self-proclaimed benevolence of colonial action. More important, he implicitly cautions us against scapegoating or, conversely, creating saviors. Spivak's "sentence"—"White men are saving brown women from brown men"—serves to justify colonial interventions if white men are taken as saviors and brown men are scapegoated as oppressors (of brown women). A postcolonialist discourse could just as easily scapegoat white men, with the inevitable consequence of presenting either brown men or brown women as the saviors. Spivak thinks that Freud (as both a positive and a negative example, since he himself didn't always avoid scapegoating) can aid us to keep the "sentence" open, to explore the dynamics of the unfolding human relationships without foreclosing narratives by assigning determinate roles. She remains leery of any attempt to fix and celebrate the subaltern's distinctive voice by claims that the subaltern occupies the position of victim, abjected other, scapegoat, savior, and so on. The critic must remain attentive to the fluidity of possible relations and actions. Spivak's discussion of Freud is offered not "as a solution" but "in acknowledgment of these dangers" of interpreting and representing the other.

Neither Freud nor Spivak is silent. They each make various determinate claims and, Spivak says, reveal their "political interests" in those claims. As intellectuals, both are at home (although their belonging is qualified by Freud's being Jewish and Spivak's being a nonwhite women) within the dominant discourse. The subaltern is not similarly privileged, and does not speak in a vocabulary that will get a hearing in institutional locations of power. The subaltern enters official and intellectual discourse only rarely and usually through the mediating commentary of someone more at home in those discourses. If the problematic is understood this way, it is hard to see how the subaltern can be capable of speaking.

In the third part of our selection, Spivak offers yet a further twist. She tells the story of Bhubaneswari Bhaduri's suicide not as an example of the Indian woman's inability to speak within Western discourse, but to show that Indian discourse has been so battered by the storms of (colonial) history that it, too, offers no resources for successful communication. Bhubaneswari's suicide is misunderstood by everyone, including her own family—and no one in India seems interested in Spivak's return to and reinterpretation of the event. "Unnerved by this failure of communication," Spivak wrote her "passionate lament: the subaltern cannot speak!" Fifteen years later, Spivak comments: "It was an inadvisable remark."

What scraps of comfort has Spivak unearthed in the meantime to challenge her first, despairing conclusion? She has reminded herself that "speaking" always occurs within the nexus of actions that include listening, responding, interpreting, and qualifying. One's words can be taken up in any number of possible ways. The ongoing effects of an utterance, not its singular expression or any one response, produces its character as a speech act. Much of the point of revisionist history, of returning to scenes of domination and oppression, is to reactivate attempts at speaking that other forces tried to obliterate and keep from having effects. In revisiting Bhubaneswari's suicide, Spivak makes it speak in new ways. To deny that this retelling is a form of speaking would be to hold on to a criterion of "authenticity" that runs counter to Spivak's whole argument about identity. The historian who tries to recover the past should sketch "the itinerary of the trace" that the silenced subaltern has left, should mark the sites where the subaltern was effaced, and should delineate the discourses that did the effacing.

Spivak remains wary of all representations, even while accepting that the opening of "a line of communication" is "to be desired" and "allows us to take pride in our work without making missionary claims." On theoretic and ethical grounds, she insists that any system, any discourse, inevitably excludes something, and she will "reserve" the word *subaltern* to point toward "the sheer heterogeneity of decolonized space." She very much wants the "traces" of those exclusions to haunt us. In every utterance, she urges us to hear the faint whisper of what could not be said. And she asks us to be ready to change our current discourse for a new one that would get closer to what the old one leaves unspoken—although the new discourse will have its own silences. This attunement to the unheard is what Spivak, following the philosopher Bimal Krishna Matilal, calls "moral love."

A persistent complaint against Spivak, aside from her difficult style, is that she leaves us no place to stand. Her political pronouncements are unambiguous, but she steadfastly refuses to advocate solutions beyond an openness to the other that can appear vague, undiscriminating, and indeed theatrical. To continually dismantle one's own assumptions seems itself an act of privilege, a deconstructionist's luxury that few can afford, especially those who have to make decisions here and now (a point somewhat conceded by Spivak in her concept of "strategic essentialism"). As an antidote to complacency, however, Spivak's work is exemplary. She never lets anyone, including herself, smugly assume that he or she is on the side of the angels. Her restless probing is unsettling, but invigorating. Like the stranger whose name is "trouble," she shakes things up and gets them moving. No topic is ever quite the same or quite so easy after Spivak has come through town.

BIBLIOGRAPHY

Spivak's first book was *Myself I Must Remake: The Life and Poetry of W. B. Yeats* (1974). Her later theoretical works include *In Other Worlds: Essays in Cultural Politics* (1987), *Outside in the Teaching Machine* (1993), and *A Critique of Postcolonial Reason* (1999). *The Post-Colonial Critic: Interviews, Strategies, Dialogues*, edited by Sarah Harasym (1990), provides a useful collection of interviews with Spivak; it is perhaps the best place to begin an engagement with her work and contains some biographical information as well. *The Spivak Reader*, edited by Donna Landry and Gerald MacLean (1995), is a one-volume collection of some of Spivak's most influential essays. Spivak is the translator (and author of substantial introductions in both volumes) of Jacques Derrida's *Of Grammatology* (1977) and of the Indian woman writer Mahasweta Devi's *Imaginary Maps: Three Stories* (1995). She is the co-editor, with Ranajit Guha, of *Selected Subaltern Studies* (1988).

Substantial critical analyses of Spivak's work can be found in Robert J. Young, *White Mythologies: Writing History and Writing the West* (1990); Sangeeta Ray, "Shifting Subjects Shifting Ground: The Names and Spaces of the Postcolonial," *Hypatia* 7.2 (1992); Benita Parry, "Problems in Current Theories of Colonial Discourse," in *The Post-Colonial Studies Reader* (ed. Bill Ashcroft, Gareth Griffiths, and

Helen Tiffin, 1995); Asha Varasharajan, *Exotic Parodies: Subjectivity in Adorno, Said, and Spivak* (1995); and Bart Moore-Gilbert, *Postcolonial Theory: Contexts, Practices, Politics* (1997). A bibliography of Spivak's published work appears in *The Spivak Reader*, mentioned above.

From A Critique of Postcolonial Reason

From *Chapter 3. History*

[CAN THE SUBALTERN SPEAK?]

* * *

In the face of the possibility that the intellectual is complicit in the persistent constitution of the Other as the Self's shadow, a possibility of political practice for the intellectual would be to put the economic "under erasure," to see the economic factor as irreducible as it reinscribes the social text, even as it is erased, however imperfectly, when it claims to be the final determinant or the transcendental signified.[1]

Until very recently, the clearest available example of such epistemic violence[2] was the remotely orchestrated, far-flung, and heterogeneous project to constitute the colonial subject as Other. This project is also the asymmetrical obliteration of the trace of that Other in its precarious Subject-ivity. It is well known that Foucault locates one case of epistemic violence, a complete overhaul of the episteme, in the redefinition of madness at the end of the European eighteenth century.[3] But what if that particular redefinition was only a part of the narrative of history in Europe as well as in the colonies? What if the two projects of epistemic overhaul worked as dislocated and unacknowledged parts of a vast two-handed engine? Perhaps it is no more than to ask that the subtext of the palimpsestic narrative of imperialism be recognized as "subjugated knowledge," "a whole set of knowledges that have been disqualified as inadequate to their task or insufficiently elaborated: naive knowledges, located low down on the hierarchy, beneath the required level of cognition or scientificity."[4]

This is not to describe "the way things really were" or to privilege the

1. This argument is developed further in Spivak, "Scattered Speculations on the Question of Value," in *In Other Worlds: Essays in Cultural Politics* (New York: Methuen, 1987), pp. 154–75. Once again, the *Anti-Oedipus* did not ignore the economic text, although the treatment was perhaps too allegorical. In this respect, the move from schizo- to rhyzo-analysis in *A Thousand Plateaus* was not, perhaps salutary [Spivak's note]. Some of the author's notes have been edited, and some omitted. Spivak here argues against regarding the economic as all-powerful *or* as negligible; instead, the economic factor has a discernible impact on society and its discourses (the "social text"). In *A Thousand Plateaus* (1980), the French philosopher GILLES DELEUZE (1925–1995) and the French psychoanalyst FÉLIX GUATTARI (1930–1992) argue for a model of knowledge patterned not on plants with roots (as is traditional) but on fungal rhizomes, which lack centralized control or structure; their earlier *Anti-Oedipus: Capitalism and Schizophrenia* (1972) critiques both orthodox Marxism and institutional Freudianism. Earlier in her book, Spivak faults them for ignoring sociohistorical specificities, an omission that leads them to posit an essentialized psychological "subject of desire" in place of a historically constituted subject.

2. That is, the forcible replacement of one structure of beliefs with another; the term is borrowed from the writings of the French philosopher and historian of ideas MICHEL FOUCAULT (1926–1984), who meant by *episteme* (literally, "knowledge"; Greek) the underlying structure of knowledge and beliefs during a historical period.

3. See Foucault, *Madness and Civilization: A History of Insanity in the Age of Reason*, trans. Richard Howard (New York: Pantheon, 1965), pp. 251, 262, 269 [Spivak's note].

4. Foucault, *Power/Knowledge: Selected Interviews and Other Writings, 1972–1977*, ed. Colin Gordon (New York: Pantheon, 1980), p. 82 [Spivak's note].

narrative of history as imperialism as the best version of history. It is, rather, to continue the account of how *one* explanation and narrative of reality was established as the normative one. A comparable account in the case(s) of Central and Eastern Europe is soon to be launched. To elaborate on this, let us consider for the moment and briefly the underpinnings of the British codification of Hindu Law.

Once again, I am not a South Asianist. I turn to Indian material because I have some accident-of-birth facility there.

Here, then, is a schematic summary of the epistemic violence of the codification of Hindu Law. If it clarifies the notion of epistemic violence, my final discussion of widow-sacrifice[5] may gain added significance.

At the end of the eighteenth century, Hindu Law, insofar as it can be described as a unitary system, operated in terms of four texts that "staged" a four-part episteme defined by the subject's use of memory: *sruti* (the heard), *smriti* (the remembered), *sāstra* (the calculus), and *vyavahāra* (the performance). The origins of what had been heard and what was remembered were not necessarily continuous or identical. Every invocation of *sruti* technically recited (or reopened) the event of originary "hearing" or revelation. The second two texts—the learned and the performed—were seen as dialectically continuous. Legal theorists and practitioners were not in any given case certain if this structure described the body of law or four ways of settling a dispute. The legitimation, through a binary vision, of the polymorphous structure of legal performance, "internally" noncoherent and open at both ends, is the narrative of codification I offer as an example of epistemic violence.[6]

Consider the often-quoted programmatic lines from Macaulay's infamous "Minute on Indian Education" (1835):

> We must at present do our best to form a class who may be interpreters between us and the millions whom we govern; a class of persons, Indian in blood and colour, but English in taste, in opinions, in morals, and in intellect. To that class we may leave it to refine the vernacular dialects of the country, to enrich those dialects with terms of science borrowed from the Western nomenclature, and to render them by degrees fit vehicles for conveying knowledge to the great mass of the population.[7]

The education of colonial subjects complements their production in law. One effect of establishing a version of the British system was the development of an uneasy separation between disciplinary formation in Sanskrit studies and the native, now alternative, tradition of Sanskirt "high culture." In the first section, I have suggested that within the former, the cultural explanations generated by authoritative scholars matched the epistemic violence of the legal project.[8]

Those authorities would be *the very best* of the sources for the nonspecialist

5. Suttee (from the Hindu *satī*, literally "devoted woman"), the Hindu custom of a widow's being cremated on the funeral pyre of her husband.

6. That is, the British Empire's imposition of "binary vision" in place of the existing set of beliefs, the "polymorphous" Hindu Law.

7. Thomas Babington Macaulay, "Minute on Indian Education," in *Selected Writings*, ed. John Clive and Thomas Pinney (Chicago: University of Chicago Press, 1972), p. 249 [Spivak's note]. Macaulay (1800–1859), English historian and statesman.

8. In suggesting that the organization and production of knowledge within academic disciplines acts with and reinforces more overtly political and legal accumulations of power, Spivak follows Foucault.

French intellectual's entry into the civilization of the Other.[9] I am, however, not referring to intellectuals and scholars of colonial production, like Shastri,[1] when I say that the Other as Subject is inaccessible to Foucault and Deleuze. I am thinking of the general nonspecialist, nonacademic population across the class spectrum, for whom the episteme operates its silent programming function. Without considering the map of exploitation,[2] on what grid of "oppression" would they place this motley crew?

Let us now move to consider the margins (one can just as well say the silent, silenced center) of the circuit marked out by this epistemic violence, men and women among the illiterate peasantry, Aboriginals, and the lowest strata of the urban subproletariat. According to Foucault and Deleuze (in the First World,[3] under the standardization and regimentation of socialized capital, though they do not seem to recognize this) and mutatis mutandis the metropolitan[4] "third world feminist" only interested in resistance within capital logic, the oppressed, if given the chance (the problem of representation cannot be bypassed here), and on the way to solidarity through alliance politics (a Marxist thematic is at work here) *can speak and know their conditions.* We must now confront the following question: On the other side of the international division of labor from socialized capital, inside *and* outside the circuit of the epistemic violence of imperialist law and education supplementing an earlier economic text, *can the subaltern speak?*

We have already considered the possibility that, given the exigencies of the inauguration of colonial records, the instrumental woman (the Rani of Sirmur) is not fully written.[5]

Antonio Gramsci's[6] work on the "subaltern classes" extends the class-position / class-consciousness argument isolated in *The Eighteenth Brumaire.*[7] Perhaps because Gramsci criticizes the vanguardistic position of the Leninist intellectual,[8] he is concerned with the intellectual's rôle in the subaltern's cultural and political movement into the hegemony. This movement

9. I have discussed this issue in greater detail with reference to Julia Kristeva's *About Chinese Women*, trans. Anita Barrows (New York: Urizen, 1977), in "French Feminism in an International Frame," in *In Other Worlds*, pp. 136–41 [Spivak's note]. KRISTEVA (b. 1941), Bulgarian-born French philosopher and psychoanalyst.

1. Mahamahopadhyaya Shastri (active 1920s), described by Spivak earlier in the chapter as a "learned Indianist, [and] brilliant representative of the indigenous elite within colonial production."

2. That is, the map of the colonized non-Western world, a map absent from Western thought.

3. The highly industrialized (largely Western) nations in a global economy, which dominate the "underdeveloped" countries of the "third world," many of which are former colonies.

4. Of or pertaining to the "mother country," as distinguished from its colony.

5. In an earlier chapter, Spivak discusses at length how the British in 1815 prevented the widow-suicide of the widow of the deposed leader of the province of Sirmur, arguing that their intervention was based on a misunderstanding of Hindu practice, served the British's administrative needs in Sirmur, was conducted with an almost parodic British reverence for "legality," and completely obscured the Rani's motives and wishes.

6. Italian Marxist (1891–1937; see above), best-known for his notions of "cultural hegemony" (the manufactured consent that legitimates a dominant group and unifies a society) and the "organic intellectual" (someone, regardless of profession, who directs the ideas and aspirations of the particular social class to which he or she "organically" belongs). In his *Prison Notebooks* (published 1948–51), he applies the word *subaltern* to the proletariat.

7. *The Eighteenth Brumaire of Louis Napoleon* (1852), an analysis by the German social, economic, and political theorist KARL MARX (1818–1883) of the dictatorship (later emperorship) declared by President Louis Bonaparte of France in 1851. Spivak argued earlier in her text that Marx explores the "gap" between "class-position" (a group's location in the economic relations of production) and "class-consciousness" (a group's ability to represent to itself the interests that stem from its class position).

8. That is, the position of the Russian revolutionary V. I. Lenin (1870–1924), contrary to Marx's own theory, that the proletarian revolution must be led by a vanguard (i.e., the Bolsheviks).

must be made to determine the production of history as narrative (of truth).[9] In texts such as *The Southern Question,* Gramsci considers the movement of historical-political economy in Italy within what can be seen as an allegory of reading taken from or prefiguring an international division of labor.[1] Yet an account of the phased development of the subaltern is thrown out of joint when his cultural macrology[2] is operated, however remotely, by the epistemic interference with legal and disciplinary definitions accompanying the imperialist project. When I move, at the end of this essay, to the question of woman as subaltern, I will suggest that the possibility of collectivity itself is persistently foreclosed through the manipulation of female agency.[3]

The first part of my proposition—that the phased development of the subaltern is complicated by the imperialist project—is confronted by the "Subaltern Studies" group.[4] They *must* ask, Can the subaltern speak? Here we are within Foucault's own discipline of history and with people who acknowledge his influence. Their project is to rethink Indian colonial historiography from the perspective of the discontinuous chain of peasant insurgencies during the colonial occupation. This is indeed the problem of "the permission to narrate" discussed by Said.[5] As Ranajit Guha, the founding editor of the collective, argues,

> The historiography of Indian nationalism has for a long time been dominated by elitism—colonialist elitism and bourgeois-nationalist elitism . . . shar[ing] the prejudice that the making of the Indian nation and the development of the consciousness—nationalism—which confirmed this process were exclusively or predominantly elite achievements. In the colonialist and neo-colonialist historiographies these achievements are credited to British colonial rulers, administrators, policies, institutions, and culture; in the nationalist and neo-nationalist writings—to Indian elite personalities, institutions, activities and ideas.[6]

Certain members of the Indian elite are of course native informants for first-world intellectuals interested in the voice of the Other. But one must nevertheless insist that the colonized subaltern *subject* is irretrievably heterogeneous.

Against the indigenous elite we may set what Guha calls "the *politics* of the people," both outside ("this was an *autonomous* domain, for it neither originated from elite politics nor did its existence depend on the latter") and inside ("it continued to operate vigorously in spite of [colonialism], adjusting itself to the conditions prevailing under the Raj[7] and in many respects developing entirely new strains in both form and content") the circuit of colonial

9. That is, a way of seeing the world shared by those individuals won over to the hegemonic view.
1. Antonio Gramsci, *The Southern Question*, trans. Pasquale Verdicchio (West Lafayette, Ind.: Bordighera, 1995) [Spivak's note].
2. Prolonged discourse.
3. That is, by colonial and postcolonial economic and political arrangements that place women and men at odds with one another.
4. A group of radical historians in India—in particular, the editorial collective of the annual publication *Subaltern Studies* (founded in 1982)—who worked to recover the struggles of the poor independent of elite nationalism and to reconstruct peasant consciousness.
5. Edward W. Said, "Permission to Narrate," *London Review of Books*, February 16, 1984 [Spivak's note]. SAID (b. 1935), Palestinian-born American theorist of postcolonialism and political activist.
6. Ranajit Guha, *Subaltern Studies* 1 (1982): 1 [Spivak's note].
7. British colonial rule in India.

production. I cannot entirely endorse this insistence of determinate vigor and full autonomy, for practical historiographic exigencies will not allow such endorsements to privilege subaltern consciousness. Against the possible charge that his approach is essentialist, Guha constructs a definition of the people (the place of that essence) that can be only an identity-in-differential. He proposes a dynamic stratification grid describing colonial social production at large. Even the third group on the list, the buffer group, as it were, between the people and the great macro-structural dominant groups, is itself defined as a place of in-betweenness. The classification falls into: "dominant foreign groups," and "dominant indigenous groups at the all-India and at the regional and local levels" representing the elite; and "[t]he social groups and elements included in [the terms "people" and "subaltern classes"] represent[ing] *the demographic difference between the total Indian population and all those whom we have described as the "elite."*[8]

"The task of research" projected here is "to investigate, identify and measure the *specific* nature and degree of the *deviation* of [the] elements [constituting item 3] from the ideal and situate it historically." "Investigate, identify, and measure the specific": a program could hardly be more essentialist and taxonomic. Yet a curious methodological imperative is at work. I have argued that, in the Foucault-Deleuze conversation, a post-representationalist vocabulary[9] hides an essentialist agenda. In subaltern studies, because of the violence of imperialist epistemic, social, and disciplinary inscription, a project understood in essentialist terms[1] must traffic in a radical textual practice of differences. The object of the group's investigation, in this case not even of the people as such but of the floating buffer zone of the regional elite—is a *deviation* from an *ideal*—the people or subaltern—which is itself defined as a difference from the elite. It is toward this structure that the research is oriented, a predicament rather different from the self-diagnosed transparency of the first-world radical intellectual. What taxonomy can fix such a space? Whether or not they themselves perceive it—in fact Guha sees his definition of "the people" within the master-slave dialectic[2]—their text articulates the difficult task of rewriting its own conditions of impossibility as the conditions of its possibility. "At the regional and local levels [the dominant indigenous groups] . . . if belonging to social strata hierarchically inferior to those of the dominant all-Indian groups *acted in the interests of the latter and not in conformity to interests corresponding truly to their own social being.*"[3] When these writers speak, in their essentializing language, of a gap between interest and action in the intermediate group, their conclusions are closer to Marx than to the self-conscious naivete of Deleuze's pronouncement on the issue. Guha, like Marx, speaks of interest in terms of the social rather than the libidinal being. The Name-of-the-Father imagery in *The Eighteenth Brumaire* can help to emphasize that, on the level of class or group

8. Guha, pp. 4, 8 [Spivak's note].
9. That is, a vocabulary that champions difference and the undecidable.
1. In terms of a search for the "true" or "essential" voice of Indian resistance to the British.
2. As set forth by the German philosopher GEORG WILHELM FRIEDRICH HEGEL in *Phenomenology of Spirit* (1807; see above): he tells of two self-consciousnesses that confront each other and fight for mutual recognition. One wins the battle and the other loses, but each gets recognition and thereby identifies him- or herself through the eyes of the other.
3. Guha, 1 [Spivak's note].

action, "true correspondence to own being" is as artificial or social as the patronymic.[4]

It is to this intermediate group that the second woman in this chapter belongs.[5] The pattern of domination is here determined mainly by gender rather than class. The subordinated gender following the dominant within the challenge of nationalism while remaining caught within gender oppression is not an unknown story.

For the (gender-unspecified) "true" subaltern group, whose identity is its difference, there is no unrepresentable subaltern subject that can know and speak itself; the intellectual's solution is not to abstain from representation. The problem is that the subject's itinerary[6] has not been left traced so as to offer an object of seduction to the representing intellectual. In the slightly dated language of the Indian group, the question becomes, How can we touch the consciousness of the people, even as we investigate their politics? With what voice-consciousness can the subaltern speak?

My question about how to earn the "secret encounter" with the contemporary hill women of Sirmur[7] is a practical version of this. The woman of whom I will speak in this section was not a "true" subaltern, but a metropolitan middle-class girl. Further, the effort she made to write or speak her body was in the accents of accountable reason, the instrument of self-conscious responsibility. Still her Speech Act[8] was refused. She was made to unspeak herself posthumously, by other women. In an earlier version of this chapter, I had summarized this historical indifference and its results as: the subaltern cannot speak.

The critique by Ajit K. Chaudhury, a West Bengali Marxist, of Guha's search for the subaltern consciousness can be taken as representative of a moment of the production process that includes the subaltern.[9] Chaudhury's perception that the Marxist view of the transformation of consciousness involves the knowledge of social relations seems, in principle, astute. Yet the heritage of the positivist ideology[1] that has appropriated orthodox Marxism obliges him to add this rider: "This is not to belittle the importance of understanding peasants' consciousness or workers' consciousness *in its pure form*. This enriches our knowledge of the peasant and the worker and, possibly, throws light on how a particular mode takes on different forms in different regions, *which is considered a problem of second order importance in classical Marxism*."[2]

This variety of "internationalist Marxism," which believes in a pure, retrievable form of consciousness only to dismiss it, thus closing off what

4. That is, the Name-of-the-Father, a term used by the French psychoanalyst JACQUES LACAN (1901–1981) to refer to the father in the Symbolic realm (not a biological entity), which marks the child's entrance into language-based experience.

5. Bhunaneswari Bhaduri, discussed later in this selection.

6. That is, the history of its constitution as a subject—and hence the erasure of its heterogeneity—by epistemically violent discourses.

7. That is, the contemporary equivalents of the Rani of Sirmur.

8. An allusion to the speech act theory of the English philosopher J. L. AUSTIN (1911–1960), who considered all the actions typically performed in speaking (here the reverse is suggested: an action serves as an utterance).

9. Since then, in the disciplinary fallout after the serious electoral and terrorist augmentation of Hindu nationalism in India, more alarming charges have been leveled at the group. See Aijaz Ahmad, *In Theory: Classes, Nations, Literature* (London: Verso, 1992), pp. 68, 194, 207–11; and Sumit Sarkar, "The Fascism of the Sangh Parivar," *Economic and Political Weekly*, January 30, 1993, pp. 163–67 [Spivak's note].

1. The sociopolitical program that takes knowledge and meaning to derive solely from what can be empirically observed.

2. Ajit K. Chaudhury, "New Wave Social Science," *Frontier* 16.24 (January 28, 1984), p. 10. Emphasis mine [Spivak's note].

in Marx remain moments of productive bafflement, can at once be the occasion for Foucault's and Deleuze's rejection of Marxism *and* the source of the critical motivation of the subaltern studies groups. All three are united in the assumption that there *is* a pure form of consciousness. On the French scene, there is a shuffling of signifiers: "the unconscious" or "the subject-in-oppression" clandestinely fills the space of "the pure form of consciousness." In orthodox "internationalist" intellectual Marxism, whether in the First World or the Third, the pure form of consciousness remains, paradoxically, a material effect, and therefore a second-order problem. This often earns it the reputation of racism and sexism. In the subaltern studies group it needs development according to the unacknowledged terms of its own articulation.

Within the effaced itinerary of the subaltern subject, the track of sexual difference is doubly effaced.[3] The question is not of female participation in insurgency, or the ground rules of the sexual division of labor, for both of which there is "evidence." It is, rather, that, both as object of colonialist historiography and as subject of insurgency, the ideological construction of gender keeps the male dominant. If, in the contest of colonial production, the subaltern has no history and cannot speak, the subaltern as female is even more deeply in shadow.

In the first part of this chapter we meditate upon an elusive female figure called into the service of colonialism. In the last part we will look at a comparable figure in anti-colonialist nationalism. The regulative psychobiography of widow self-immolation will be pertinent in both cases. In the interest of the invaginated spaces[4] of this book, let us remind ourselves of the gradual emergence of the new subaltern in the New World Order.[5]

* * *

I am generally sympathetic with the call to make U.S. feminism more "theoretical." It seems, however, that the problem of the muted subject of the subaltern woman, though not solved by an "essentialist" search for lost origins, cannot be served by the call for more theory in Anglo-America either.

That call is often given in the name of a critique of "positivism," which is seen here as identical with "essentialism." Yet Hegel, the modern inaugurator of "the work of the negative," was not a stranger to the notion of essences. For Marx, the curious persistence of essentialism within the dialectic was a profound and productive problem. Thus, the stringent binary opposition between positivism / essentialism (read, U.S.) and "theory" (read, French or Franco-German via Anglo-American) may be spurious. Apart from repressing the ambiguous complicity between essentialism and critiques of positivism (acknowledged by Derrida in "Of Grammatology as a Positive Science"[6]), it also errs by implying that positivism is not a theory. This move allows the emergence of a proper name, a positive essence, Theory. And once again,

3. I do not believe that the recent trend of romanticizing anything written by the Aboriginal or outcaste intellectual has lifted the effacement [Spivak's note].
4. An allusion to the *écriture féminine* (feminine writing) championed by the French feminist HÉLÈNE CIXOUS (b. 1937) and a description of Spivak's method, which folds together various arguments rather than laying them out in a linear progression.
5. A phrase coined by George Bush (b. 1924; 41st U.S. president, 1989–93) to describe what was needed after the collapse of communism in Eastern Europe to replace East-West cold war rivalries.
6. A section of *Of Grammatology* (1967; trans. 1977 by Spivak), by the French deconstructive philosopher JACQUES DERRIDA (b. 1930).

the position of the investigator remains unquestioned. If and when this territorial debate turns toward the Third World, no change in the question of method is to be discerned. This debate cannot take into account that, in the case of the woman as subaltern, rather few ingredients for the constitution of the itinerary of the trace of a sexed subject (rather than an anthropological object) can be gathered to locate the possibility of dissemination.[7]

Yet I remain generally sympathetic to aligning feminism with the critique of positivism and the defetishization of the concrete. I am also far from averse to learning from the work of Western theorists, though I have learned to insist on marking their positionality as investigating subjects. Given these conditions, and as a literary critic, I tactically confronted the immense problem of the consciousness of the woman as subaltern. I reinvented the problem in a sentence and transformed it into the object of a simple semiosis.[8] What can such a transformation mean?

This gesture of transformation marks the fact that knowledge of the other subject is theoretically impossible. Empirical work in the discipline constantly performs this transformation tacitly. It is a transformation from a first-second person performance to the constatation in the third person.[9] It is, in other words, at once a gesture of control and an acknowledgement of limits. Freud provides a homology[1] for such positional hazards.

Sarah Kofman has suggested that the deep ambiguity of Freud's use of women as a scapegoat may be read as a reaction-formation to an initial and continuing desire to give the hysteric a voice, to transform her into the *subject* of hysteria.[2] The masculine-imperialist ideological formation that shaped that desire into "the daughter's seduction"[3] is part of the same formation that constructs the monolithic "third-world woman." No contemporary metropolitan investigator is not influenced by that formation. Part of our "unlearning" project is to articulate our participation in that formation—by *measuring* silences, if necessary—into the *object* of investigation. Thus, when confronted with the questions, Can the subaltern speak? and Can the subaltern (as woman) speak? our efforts to give the subaltern a voice in history will be doubly open to the dangers run by Freud's discourse. It is in acknowledgment of these dangers rather than as solution to a problem that I put together the sentence "White men are saving brown women from brown men," a sentence that runs like a red thread through today's "gender and development." My impulse is not unlike the one to be encountered in Freud's investigation of the sentence "A child is being beaten."[4]

7. An allusion to Derrida, one of whose important works is titled *Dissemination* (1972).

8. Process of meaning making, of producing signs. The "sentence," given below, is "White men are saving brown women from brown men."

9. In speech act theory, an utterance that describes a condition, fact, or state of affairs; in contrast, a performative utterance does something (e.g., saying, "I promise to . . ." makes a promise). By writing in the 3d person, Western scholars hide the performative nature of their work, which creates a particular way of seeing the "facts."

1. An example of similarity in structure due to similar development; like the scholars, the psychoanalyst SIGMUND FREUD (1856–1939) turned the performatives of his own 1st-person claims and his patients' appropriated 2d-person accounts into 3d-personal "empirical" statements of scientific "fact."

2. Sarah Kofman, *The Enigma of Woman: Woman in Freud's Writings*, trans. Catherine Porter (Ithaca, N.Y.: Cornell University Press, 1985) [Spivak's note].

3. A reference both to Freud's work on female hysteria (viewed as a symptom of frustrated sexual desire for a male authority figure) and to *The Daughter's Seduction* (1982), a book by Jane Gallop that describes feminist appropriations of Freud.

4. Freud, " 'A Child Is Being Beaten': A Contribution to the Study of the Origin of Sexual Perversion," in *The Standard Edition of the Complete Psychological Works of Sigmund Freud*, ed. James

The use of Freud here does not imply an isomorphic analogy between subject-formation and the behavior of social collectives, a frequent practice, often accompanied by a reference to Reich,[5] in the conversation between Deleuze and Foucault. I am, in other words, not suggesting that "White men are saving brown women from brown men" is a sentence indicating a *collective* fantasy symptomatic of a *collective* itinerary of sadomasochistic repression in a *collective* imperialist enterprise. There is a satisfying symmetry in such an allegory, but I would rather invite the reader to consider it a problem in "wild psychoanalysis" than a clinching solution.[6] Just as Freud's insistence on making the woman the scapegoat in "A child is being beaten" and elsewhere discloses his political interests, however imperfectly, so my insistence on imperialist subject-production as the occasion for this sentence discloses a politics that I cannot step around.

* * *

A young woman of sixteen or seventeen, Bhubaneswari Bhaduri, hanged herself in her father's modest apartment in North Calcutta in 1926. The suicide was a puzzle since, as Bhubaneswari was menstruating at the time, it was clearly not a case of illicit pregnancy. Nearly a decade later, it was discovered, in a letter she had left for her elder sister, that she was a member of one of the many groups involved in the armed struggle for Indian independence. She had been entrusted with a political assassination. Unable to confront the task and yet aware of the practical need for trust, she killed herself.

Bhubaneswari had known that her death would be diagnosed as the outcome of illegitimate passion. She had therefore waited for the onset of menstruation. While waiting, Bhubaneswari, the *brahmacārini*[7] who was no doubt looking forward to good wifehood, perhaps rewrote the social text of *sati*-suicide in an interventionist way. (One tentative explanation of her inexplicable act had been a possible melancholia brought on by her father's death and her brother-in-law's repeated taunts that she was too old to be not-yet-a-wife.) She generalized the sanctioned motive for female suicide by taking immense trouble to displace (not merely deny), in the physiological inscription of her body, its imprisonment within legitimate passion by a single male. In the immediate context, her act became absurd, a case of delirium rather than sanity. The displacing gesture—waiting for menstruation—is at first a reversal of the interdict against a menstruating widow's right to immolate herself; the unclean widow must wait, publicly, until the cleansing bath of the fourth day, when she is no longer menstruating, in order to claim her dubious privilege.

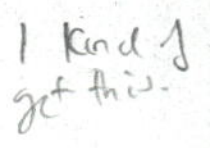

In this reading, Bhubaneswari Bhaduri's suicide is an unemphatic, ad hoc,

Strachey, 24 vols. (London: Hogarth, 1953–74), 17:175–204. For a list of ways in which Western criticism constructs "third world women," see Chandra Talpade Mohanty, "Under Western Eyes: Feminist Scholarship and Colonial Discourses," in *Third World Women and the Politics of Feminism*, ed. Mohanty et al. (Bloomington: Indiana University Press, 1991), pp. 51–80 [Spivak's note].

5. Wilhelm Reich (1897–1957), Austrian psychoanalyst whose *Mass Psychology of Fascism* (1933) exemplifies a radical attempt to psychoanalyze a whole society.

6. Freud, "'Wild' Psycho-Analysis," in *Standard Edition*, 11:221–27. A good deal of psychoanalytic social critique would fit this description [Spivak's note]. Freud warns against "wild" psychoanalysis that jumps to conclusions without the slow accumulation of information and the relationship between patient and therapist necessary for psychoanalytic treatment.

7. Female member of the Brahmin (upper) caste (Hindi).

subaltern rewriting of the social text of *sati*-suicide as much as the hegemonic account of the blazing, fighting, familial Durga.[8] The emergent dissenting possibilities of that hegemonic account of the fighting mother are well documented and popularly well remembered through the discourse of the male leaders and participants in the Independence movement. The subaltern as female cannot be heard or read.

I know of Bhubaneswari's life and death through family connections. Before investigating them more thoroughly, I asked a Bengali woman, a philosopher and Sanskritist whose early intellectual production is almost identical to mine, to start the process. Two responses: (a) Why, when her two sisters, Saileswari and Raseswari, led such full and wonderful lives, are you interested in the hapless Bhubaneswari? (b) I asked her nieces. It appears that it was a case of illicit love.

I was so unnerved by this failure of communication that, in the first version of this text, I wrote, in the accents of passionate lament: the subaltern cannot speak! It was an inadvisable remark.

In the intervening years between the publication of the second part of this chapter in essay form and this revision, I have profited greatly from the many published responses to it. I will refer to two of them here: "Can the Subaltern Vote?" and "Silencing Sycorax."[9]

As I have been insisting, Bhubaneswari Bhaduri was not a "true" subaltern. She was a woman of the middle class, with access, however clandestine, to the bourgeois movement for Independence. Indeed the Rani of Sirmur, with her claim to elevated birth, was not a subaltern at all. Part of what I seem to have argued in this chapter is that woman's interception of the claim to subalternity can be staked out across strict lines of definition by virtue of their muting by heterogeneous circumstances. Gulari[1] cannot speak to us because indigenous patriarchal "history" would only keep a record of her funeral and colonial history only needed her as an incidental instrument. Bhubaneswari attempted to "speak" by turning her body into a text of woman / writing. The immediate passion of my declaration "the subaltern cannot speak," came from the despair that, in her own family, among women, in no more than fifty years, her attempt had failed. I am not laying the blame for the muting on the *colonial* authorities here, as Busia seems to think: "Gayatri Spivak's 'Can the Subaltern Speak?'—section 4 of which is a compelling explication of this role of disappearing in the case of Indian women in British legal history."[2]

I am pointing, rather, at her silencing by her own more emancipated granddaughters: a new mainstream. To this can be added two newer groups: one, the liberal multiculturalist metropolitan academy, Susan Barton's[3] great-granddaughters; as follows:

8. In Hindu mythology and religion, one of the many forms of Devi (the divine mother goddess). She is a warrior, often represented with 8 or 10 arms; each hand holds the special weapon of the other gods.
9. Leerom Medovoi et al., "Can the Subaltern Vote?" *Socialist Review* 20.3 (July–September 1990): 133–49; and Abena Busia, "Silencing Sycorax: On African Colonial Discourse and the Unvoiced Female," *Cultural Critique*, no. 14 (winter 1989–90): 81–104 [Spivak's note]. Spivak's original essay was "Can the Subaltern Speak?" in *Marxism and the Interpretation of Culture*, ed. Cary Nelson and Lawrence Grossberg (Urbana: University of Illinois Press, 1988), pp. 271–313.
1. The family name of the Rani of Sirmur.
2. Busia, "Silencing Sycorax," p. 102 [Spivak's note].
3. The daughter whose mother refuses to acknowledge her as her own in Daniel Defoe's

As I have been saying all along, I think it is important to acknowledge our complicity in the muting, in order precisely to be more effective in the long run. Our work cannot succeed if we always have a scapegoat. The postcolonial migrant investigator is touched by the colonial social formations. Busia strikes a positive note for further work when she points out that, after all, I am able to read Bhubaneswari's case, and therefore she *has* spoken in some way. Busia is right, of course. All speaking, even seemingly the most immediate, entails a distanced decipherment by another, which is, at best, an interception. That is what speaking is.

I acknowledge this theoretical point, and also acknowledge the practical importance, for oneself and others, of being upbeat about future work. Yet the moot decipherment by another in an academic institution (willy-nilly a knowledge-production factory) many years later must not be too quickly identified with the "speaking" of the subaltern. It is not a mere tautology to say that the colonial or postcolonial subaltern is defined as the being on the other side of difference, or an epistemic fracture, even from other groupings among the colonized. What is at stake when we insist that the subaltern speaks?

In "Can the Subaltern Vote?" the three authors apply the question of stakes to "political speaking." This seems to me to be a fruitful way of extending my reading of subaltern speech into a collective arena. Access to "citizenship" (civil society) by becoming a voter (in the nation) is indeed the symbolic circuit of the mobilizing of subalternity into hegemony. This terrain, ever negotiating between national liberation and globalization, allows for examining the casting of the vote itself as a performative convention given as constative "speech" of the subaltern subject. It is part of my current concerns to see how this set is manipulated to legitimize globalization; but it is beyond the scope of this book. Here let us remain confined to the field of academic prose, and advance three points:

1. Simply by being postcolonial or the member of an ethnic minority, we are not "subaltern." That word is reserved for the sheer heterogeneity of decolonized space.
2. When a line of communication is established between a member of subaltern groups and the circuits of citizenship or institutionality, the subaltern has been inserted into the long road to hegemony. Unless we want to be romantic purists or primitivists about "preserving subalternity"—a contradiction in terms—this is absolutely to be desired. (It goes without saying that museumized or curricularized access to ethnic origin—another battle that must be fought—is not identical with preserving subalternity.) Remembering this allows us to take pride in our work without making missionary claims.
3. This trace-structure (effacement in disclosure) surfaces as the tragic emotions of the political activist, springing not out of superficial utopianism, but out of the depths of what Bimal Krishna Matilal has called "moral

novel *Roxana: The Fortunate Mistress* (1724). The South African writer J. M. Coetzee uses Susan Barton as the narrator for much (but not all) of his retelling of the Robinson Crusoe story in his novel *Foe* (1987), a retelling that Spivak discusses at length in chapter 2 of *A Critique of Postcolonial Reason*.

love." Mahasweta Devi,[4] herself an indefatigable activist, documents this emotion with exquisite care in "Pterodactyl, Puran Sahay, and Pirtha."

And finally, the third group: Bhubaneswari's elder sister's eldest daughter's eldest daughter's eldest daughter is a new U.S. immigrant and was recently promoted to an executive position in a U.S.-based transnational. She will be helpful in the emerging South Asian market precisely because she is a well-placed Southern diasporic.

> For Europe, the time when the new capitalism *definitely* superseded the old can be established with fair precision: it was the beginning of the twentieth century . . . [With t]he boom at the end of the nineteenth century and the crisis of 1900–03 . . . [c]artels become one of the foundations of the whole of economic life. Capitalism has been transformed into imperialism.[5]

Today's program of global financialization carries on that relay. Bhubaneswari had fought for national liberation. Her great-grandniece works for the New Empire. This too is a historical silencing of the subaltern. When the news of this young woman's promotion was broadcast in the family amidst general jubilation I could not help remarking to the eldest surviving female member: "Bhubaneswari"—her nickname had been Talu—"hanged herself in vain," but not too loudly. Is it any wonder that this young woman is a staunch multiculturalist, believes in natural childbirth, and wears only cotton?

1983 — 1988, 1999

4. Indian author (b. 1925), who writes in Bengali; some of her work has been translated into English by Spivak. Matilal (1935–1991), Indian philosopher who taught at Oxford University for many years.

5. V. I. Lenin, *Imperialism: The Highest Stage of Capitalism: A Popular Outline* (London: Junius: Chicago: Pluto, 1996), pp. 15, 17 [Spivak's note].

GLORIA ANZALDÚA
1942–2004

Mexican American writer and activist Gloria Anzaldúa self-consciously embodied the longings, critical consciousness, and contradictions of so-called identity politics. She both spoke from her perspective as a lesbian Mexican American *and* contradicted any simple categorization of individuals through their ethnic origins or sexual orientation. We are all mixtures, she insisted, and she called for a new *mestiza* (mixed or hybrid) consciousness to replace "the policy of racial purity that white America practices." Her work simultaneously celebrates and explores the difficulties of multicultural identity.

Anzaldúa came from a seventh-generation Mexican American family that settled in the Rio Grande Valley in southern Texas. After her father died when she was fifteen, she worked as a farm laborer for a time to help support her family. The only member of her family with any education beyond high school, she received her B.A. from Pan-American University in 1969 and an M.A. in English and education from the University of Texas at Austin in 1972. After teaching at a high school for migrant workers in Indiana, Anzaldúa returned to Texas to pursue a Ph.D. in comparative literature, but quit when she met resistance to her desire to focus on Chicano (Mexican American) studies. She subsequently did additional graduate work at the University of California at Santa Cruz while teaching at both San Francisco State University and Santa Cruz, where she once again found herself at odds with academic proprieties. Apart from occasional visiting positions at universities, in her later years she devoted herself primarily to writing and social activism. She received a National Endowment for the Arts Fiction Award as well as the 1991 Lesbian Rights Award.

Anzaldúa's work is important—and has been widely read and taught—not only because she effectively articulates the radical understandings and aspirations of the ethnic, feminist, and gay liberation movements born in the late 1960s and early 1970s, but also because she faced the ambivalences and contradictions of these movements. For literary studies, the most obvious result of such liberation efforts (often referred to as "the new social movements") has been the overt politicization of teaching and criticism. To the bafflement of many and the outrage of some, reading lists and teaching methods in literature classes have been opened to political scrutiny. A formerly vague and innocuous idea—culture—is now a battleground. At stake is "identity"—especially the relative status accorded different identities within a multiethnic society. The new social movements demand not just equal rights and economic opportunity but also respect and recognition. They aim at affirming racial, sexual, and class identities in all their difference from prevailing norms. Anzaldúa's writings speak to this call for affirmation and acknowledgement.

The political energies of the new social movements interacted with developments in literary studies in three especially salient ways. First, the new interest in different identities within American culture arose at the same time that French poststructuralism arrived in literature departments. Although distinct from the "multiculturalist" emphasis on inter- and intracultural differences, the poststructuralist concept of "difference" (especially in the work of JACQUES DERRIDA) provided a favorable theoretical environment for exploring the heterogeneity of identity. In particular, the poststructuralist questioning of boundaries and of the integrity of defined entities encouraged the interest in mixed, hybrid identities found in ethnic theory like Anzaldúa's.

The second conjunction of the new social movements with developments in literary studies centered around the term *voice*. Mid-twentieth-century New Criticism tried to sever the content expressed in literary works from the intention and voice of the author through an insistence on the "intentional fallacy" (see WILLIAM K. WIMSATT JR. AND MONROE C. BEARDSLEY), which states that the narrator in a novel or the speaker in a lyric poem is always a mask, a "persona," never the author. With the increasing interest of the 1960s in the personal (culminating in feminism's declaration that "the personal is political") and the growing desire to recover lost and oppressed "voices" in American history, the new social movements stressed the voices of testimony and experience at the exact time when literary critics were striving to reconnect literary expressions to their authors. "Recovery work," which resurrected neglected or forgotten works by nonwhite, nonmale, and nonheterosexual authors, was combined with a new valuing of narratives of personal experience in both historical and contemporary texts. Anzaldúa's text, in our selection taken from her book *Borderlands/ La Frontera* (1987), mixes cultural analysis with history, private memories, poems, and politics, demonstrating the stylistic possibilities opened up by the new interest in personal voice. Furthermore, her preoccupation with the difficulties faced by writers who use the "master's tongue" (in her case, English) resonates with similar concerns in postcolonial theory. Anzaldúa wants to combat the suppression of Spanish in America by creating a space for Spanish voices within American literature and culture, but she also recognizes that she must use English to reach the widest possible audience. So her literary voice mixes languages as well as genres.

Third, and finally, the dual focus of the new social movements on "identity" and "culture" coincides with the general shift in literary studies after 1965 from text to context, a movement partly reflected in the broad (and often loosely used) term "cultural studies." The literary work is studied as a product or symptom of its culture or of its author's identity and not as a self-enclosed unit of purely aesthetic elements. In addition, the writing and reading (interpreting) of literary texts are understood as dynamic processes through which identities and cultures are produced, reproduced, maintained, and transformed. Cultural representations are the very stuff of which identities are made, and literature is one crucial arena in which that making is done. As Anzaldúa put it, "culture" is a "story to explain the world and our participation in it, a . . . value system with images and symbols to connect us to each other and to the planets." She saw her cultural work as the production of a "new" culture, a new story with new images.

Cultural representations, such as the stereotypes that undergird contempt for others who are different, can hurt. They are powerful in every sense of that word, coming to us invested with authority and upheld by the social institutions that promulgate them. Those representations, those images, occupy us; they are ours, they are us. That's what it means to be immersed in a culture. For that reason, Anzaldúa insists that the primary political work is "inner." "The struggle," she writes, "has always been inner, and is played out in outer terrains. Awareness of our situation must come before inner changes, which in turn come before changes in society. Nothing happens in the 'real' world unless it first happens in our heads." This focus on changing images and representations is sometimes called "cultural politics," which means emphasizing the transformation of values and beliefs more than changes in elected officials, laws, or working conditions.

It is not surprising that Anzaldúa and other literary people would put their energy and faith into cultural politics. Words and images are their stock-in-trade, what most influences them, and where they have some chance of wielding influence. But cultural politics in the late-twentieth-century United States was also a direct response to the civil rights movement, which succeeded in changing the laws and institutional structures of a legally racist society. People discovered, however, that abolishing the legality of racism was hardly the same thing as creating a nonracist society. Cultural politics is often criticized as vague, as nonconcrete, as ignoring bread-and-butter issues. But a cultural politics like Anzaldúa's is developed to foreground and contest the nebulous quality of racism and sexism in her America, prejudices that often do not manifest themselves in overt ways yet have persistent concrete effects in the continued poverty of and the differential opportunities in housing, education, and employment available to nonwhites and women.

Anzaldúa's work, then, is largely concerned with conveying what it feels like for a nonwhite, nonheterosexual woman to live in post–civil rights movement North America. She explores the ambiguities and ambivalences lived by a "hyphenated" Mexican American. The United States both is obsessed with this presence of nonwhites in its midst and acts as if they do not exist. On one level, she simply calls for recognition, for the acknowledgment by the culture at large, and Anglos in particular, that she and her people—part Native American, part European, part American—exist. They have been here a long time and are going to be here even longer; meanwhile, "the dominant white culture is killing us slowly with its ignorance." Anzaldúa calls our attention to the 20 million Mexican Americans in the United States.

But on another level, Anzaldúa is arguing that our whole understanding of identity has to be revised. The old notion that we can know who we are by tracing our roots, by referring back to some stable point of origin, has to be abandoned. There is no pure, single source. All identities are hybrids, formed over time through the interaction of multiple cultures and constantly being transformed by new encounters in the "borderlands" between one culture and another. Anzaldúa's work here parallels contemporary postcolonial criticism, particularly that of HOMI K. BHABHA. The nostalgic demand for unitary, isolated cultures can only do harm in a world in which each of us is always already a mixture and we constantly come into contact with, and must live among, others who are mixed in different ways.

Identity politics is often criticized for its contradictions, especially for joining a celebration of difference with simplistic notions of group solidarity. Anzaldúa's work addresses the complex emotional core of identity politics: the deep desire felt throughout the contemporary world for an identity that can be asserted, recognized, affirmed, and respected in the public sphere. In addition, she describes the very forces of cultural mixing and powerful blindnesses that make an unambiguous, clear identity so attractive, especially to those who are least visible within the current order. In trying to negotiate these contrary pressures and achieve a coherent identity in the face of the myriad cultural influences that shape us, Anzaldúa necessarily becomes a writer of ambiguity and ambivalence. "It makes us crazy constantly," she writes, "but if the center holds, we've made some kind of evolutionary step forward."

BIBLIOGRAPHY

Anzaldúa's books include *Speaking in Tongues: A Letter to Third World Women Writers* (1983), *Borderlands/La Frontera: The New Mestiza* (1987), *Towards a New Consciousness* (1990), and two children's books, *Friends from the Other Side/Amigos del otro lado* (1993) and *Prietita and the Ghost Woman/Prietita y la Llorona* (1996). She is also the co-editor (with Cherríe Moraga) of *This Bridge Called My Back: Writings by Radical Women of Color* (1981) and editor of *Making Face, Making Soul: Creative and Critical Perspectives by Women of Color* (1990), two highly influential collections. The biographical information in Juanita Ramos, "Gloria Anzaldúa," in *Contemporary Lesbian Writers of the United States: A Bio-Bibliographical Critical Sourcebook* (ed. Sandra Pollack, Denise D. Knight, and Pamela Farley Tucker, 1993), can be augmented by the autobiographical reflections found in Gloria Anzaldúa, *Interviews/Entrevistas*, edited by Analouise Keating (2000).

Anzaldúa's work has generated numerous responses that address issues of ethnicity, sexuality, feminism, and identity politics. Recommended are Yvonne Yarbro Bejarano's "Gloria Anzaldúa's *Borderlands/La Frontera*: Cultural Studies, 'Difference,' and the Non-Unitary Subject," *Cultural Critique* 28 (1994); Analouise Keating's *Women Reading Women Writing: Self-Invention in Paula Gunn Allen, Gloria Anzaldúa, and Audre Lorde* (1996); and the three essays on Anzaldúa, by Jennifer Browdy de Hernandez, Dionne Espinoza, and Analouise Keating, in *Other Sisterhoods: Literary Theory and U.S. Women of Color* (ed. Sandra Kumamoto Stanley, 1998). A good, although not complete, bibliography of Anzaldúa's work and responses to it can be found in Ramos's biographical essay cited above.

From Borderlands/*La Frontera*: The New Mestiza

Chapter 7.
La conciencia de la mestiza: *Towards a New Consciousness*

Por la mujer de mi raza
hablará el espíritu.

José Vascocelos, Mexican philosopher, envisaged *una raza mestiza, una mezcla de razas afines, una raza de color—la primera raza síntesis del globo.*

He called it a cosmic race, *la raza cósmica*, a fifth race embracing the four major races of the world.[1] Opposite to the theory of the pure Aryan, and to the policy of racial purity that white America practices, his theory is one of inclusivity. At the confluence of two or more genetic streams, with chromosomes constantly "crossing over," this mixture of races, rather than resulting in an inferior being, provides hybrid progeny, a mutable, more malleable species with a rich gene pool. From this racial, ideological, cultural and biological cross-pollinization, an "alien" consciousness is presently in the making—a new *mestiza* consciousness, *una conciencia de mujer*. It is a consciousness of the Borderlands.

UNA LUCHA DE FRONTERAS/A STRUGGLE OF BORDERS

Because I, a *mestiza*,
continually walk out of one culture
and into another,
because I am in all cultures at the same time,
alma entre dos mundos, tres, cuatro,
me zumba la cabeza con lo contradictorio.
Estoy norteada por todas las voces que me hablan
simultáneamente.

The ambivalence from the clash of voices results in mental and emotional states of perplexity. Internal strife results in insecurity and indecisiveness. The *mestiza*'s dual or multiple personality is plagued by psychic restlessness.

In a constant state of mental nepantilism, an Aztec[2] word meaning torn between ways, *la mestiza* is a product of the transfer of the cultural and spiritual values of one group to another. Being tricultural, monolingual, bilingual, or multilingual, speaking a patois, and in a state of perpetual transition, the *mestiza* faces the dilemma of the mixed breed: which collectivity does the daughter of a darkskinned mother listen to?

El choque de un alma atrapado entre el mundo del espíritu y el mundo de la técnica a veces la deja entullada. Cradled in one culture, sandwiched between two cultures, straddling all three cultures and their value systems, *la mestiza* undergoes a struggle of flesh, a struggle of borders, an inner war. Like all people, we perceive the version of reality that our culture communicates. Like others having or living in more than one culture, we get multiple, often opposing messages. The coming together of two self-consistent but habitually incomparable frames of reference[3] causes *un choque*, a cultural collision.

Within us and within *la cultura chicana*,[4] commonly held beliefs of the white culture attack commonly held beliefs of the Mexican culture, and both

1. This is my own "take off" on José Vasconcelos' idea. José Vasconcelos, *La Raza Cósmica: Misión de la Raza Ibero-Americana* (Mexico City: Aguilar S.A. de Ediciones, 1961) [Anzaldúa's note].
2. One of the major native groups in Mexico before the arrival of Europeans.
3. Arthur Koestler termed this "bisociation." Albert Rothenberg, *The Creative Process in Art, Science, and Other Fields* (Chicago: University of Chicago Press, 1979), 12 [Anzaldúa's note]. Koestler (1905–1983), Hungarian-born English novelist, journalist, and critic.
4. Chicanos are portrayed by Anzaldúa as existing between Anglo (white European) U.S. culture and the indigenous Native American culture of both Mexico and the United States.

attack commonly held beliefs of the indigenous culture. Subconsciously, we see an attack on ourselves and our beliefs as a threat and we attempt to block with a counterstance.

But it is not enough to stand on the opposite river bank, shouting questions, challenging patriarchal, white conventions. A counterstance locks one into a duel of oppressor and oppressed; locked in mortal combat, like the cop and the criminal, both are reduced to a common denominator of violence. The counterstance refutes the dominant culture's views and beliefs, and, for this, it is proudly defiant. All reaction is limited by, and dependent on, what it is reacting against. Because the counterstance stems from a problem with authority—outer as well as inner—it's a step towards liberation from cultural domination. But it is not a way of life. At some point, on our way to a new consciousness, we will have to leave the opposite bank, the split between the two mortal combatants somehow healed so that we are on both shores at once and, at once, see through serpent and eagle eyes. Or perhaps we will decide to disengage from the dominant culture, write it off altogether as a lost cause, and cross the border into a wholly new and separate territory. Or we might go another route. The possibilities are numerous once we decide to act and not react.

A TOLERANCE FOR AMBIGUITY

These numerous possibilities leave *la mestiza* floundering in uncharted seas. In perceiving conflicting information and points of view, she is subjected to a swamping of her psychological borders. She has discovered that she can't hold concepts or ideas in rigid boundaries. The borders and walls that are supposed to keep the undesirable ideas out are entrenched habits and patterns of behavior; these habits and patterns are the enemy within. Rigidity means death. Only by remaining flexible is she able to stretch the psyche horizontally and vertically. *La mestiza* constantly has to shift out of habitual formations; from convergent thinking, analytical reasoning that tends to use rationality to move toward a single goal (a Western mode), to divergent thinking,[5] characterized by movement away from set patterns and goals and toward a more whole perspective, one that includes rather than excludes.

The new *mestiza* copes by developing a tolerance for contradictions, a tolerance for ambiguity. She learns to be an Indian in Mexican culture, to be Mexican from an Anglo point of view. She learns to juggle cultures. She has a plural personality, she operates in a pluralistic mode—nothing is thrust out, the good the bad and the ugly, nothing rejected, nothing abandoned. Not only does she sustain contradictions, she turns the ambivalence into something else.

She can be jarred out of ambivalence by an intense, and often painful, emotional event which inverts or resolves the ambivalence. I'm not sure exactly how. The work takes place underground—subconsciously. It is work that the soul performs. That focal point or fulcrum, that juncture where the *mestiza* stands, is where phenomena tend to collide. It is where the possibility

5. In part, I derive my definitions for "convergent" and "divergent" thinking from Rothenberg, 12–13 [Anzaldúa's note].

of uniting all that is separate occurs. This assembly is not one where severed or separated pieces merely come together. Nor is it a balancing of opposing powers. In attempting to work out a synthesis, the self has added a third element which is greater than the sum of its severed parts. That third element is a new consciousness—a *mestiza* consciousness—and though it is a source of intense pain, its energy comes from continual creative motion that keeps breaking down the unitary aspect of each new paradigm.

En unas pocas centurias, the future will belong to the *mestiza*. Because the future depends on the breaking down of paradigms, it depends on the straddling of two or more cultures. By creating a new mythos—that is, a change in the way we perceive reality, the way we see ourselves, and the ways we behave—*la mestiza* creates a new consciousness.

The work of *mestiza* consciousness is to break down the subject-object duality that keeps her a prisoner and to show in the flesh and through the images in her work how duality is transcended. The answer to the problem between the white race and the colored, between males and females, lies in healing the split that originates in the very foundation of our lives, our culture, our languages, our thoughts. A massive uprooting of dualistic thinking in the individual and collective consciousness is the beginning of a long struggle, but one that could, in our best hopes, bring us to the end of rape, of violence, of war.

La encrucijada/The Crossroads

A chicken is being sacrificed
   at a crossroads, a simple mound of earth
a mud shrine for *Eshu*,
   Yoruba[6] god of indeterminacy,
who blesses her choice of path.
   She begins her journey.

Su cuerpo es una bocacalle. La mestiza has gone from being the sacrificial goat to becoming the officiating priestess at the crossroads.

As a *mestiza* I have no country, my homeland cast me out; yet all countries are mine because I am every woman's sister or potential lover. (As a lesbian I have no race, my own people disclaim me; but I am all races because there is the queer of me in all races.) I am cultureless because, as a feminist, I challenge the collective cultural/religious male-derived beliefs of Indo-Hispanics and Anglos; yet I am cultured because I am participating in the creation of yet another culture, a new story to explain the world and our participation in it, a new value system with images and symbols that connect us to each other and to the planet. *Soy un amasamiento*, I am an act of kneading, of uniting and joining that not only has produced both a creature of darkness and a creature of light, but also a creature that questions the definitions of light and dark and gives them new meanings.

6. One of the two largest ethnic groups in Nigeria; many Caribbean and Latin American blacks come from the Yoruba and have retained elements of their ancestral culture.

We are the people who leap in the dark, we are the people on the knees of the gods. In our very flesh, (r)evolution works out the clash of cultures. It makes us crazy constantly, but if the center holds, we've made some kind of evolutionary step forward. *Nuestra alma el trabajo*, the opus, the great alchemical work; spiritual *mestizaje*, a "morphogenesis,"[7] an inevitable unfolding. We have become the quickening serpent movement.

Indigenous like corn, like corn, the *mestiza* is a product of crossbreeding, designed for preservation under a variety of conditions. Like an ear of corn—a female seed-bearing organ—the *mestiza* is tenacious, tightly wrapped in the husks of her culture. Like kernels she clings to the cob; with thick stalks and strong brace roots, she holds tight to the earth—she will survive the crossroads.

Lavando y remojando el maíz en agua de cal, despojando el pellejo. Moliendo, mixteando, amasando, haciendo tortillas de masa.[8] She steeps the corn in lime, it swells, softens. With stone roller on *metate* she grinds the corn, then grinds again. She kneads and moulds the dough, pats the round balls into *tortillas*.

We are the porous rock in the stone *metate*
squatting on the ground
We are the rolling pin, *el maíz y agua,*
la masa harina. Somos el amasijo.
Somos lo molido en el metate.
We are the *comal* sizzling hot,
the hot *tortilla*, the hungry mouth.
We are the coarse rock.
We are the grinding motion,
the mixed potion, *somos el molcajete.*
We are the pestle, the *comino, ajo, pimienta,*
We are the *chile colorado*,
the green shoot that cracks the rock.
We will abide.

EL CAMINO DE LA MESTIZA/THE MESTIZA WAY

Caught between the sudden contraction, the breath sucked in and the endless space, the brown woman stands still, looks at the sky. She decides to go down, digging her way along the roots of trees. Sifting through the bones, she shakes them to see if there is any marrow in them. Then, touching the dirt to her forehead, to her tongue, she takes a few bones, leaves the rest in their burial place

7. To borrow chemist Ilya Prigogine's theory of "dissipative structures." Prigogine [b. 1917] discovered that substances interact not in predictable ways as it was taught in science, but in different and fluctuating ways to produce new and more complex structures, a kind of birth he called "morphogenesis," which created unpredictable innovation Harold Gilliam, "Searching for a New World View," *This World*, January 1981, 23 [Anzaldúa's note].

8. *Tortillas de masa*: corn tortillas are of two types, the smooth uniform ones made in a tortilla press and usually bought at a tortilla factory or supermarket, and *gorditas*, made by mixing *masa* with lard or shortening or butter (my mother sometimes puts in bits of bacon or *chicarrones*) [Anzaldúa's note].

> She goes through her backpack, keeps her journal and address book, throws away the muni-bart metromaps.[9] The coins are heavy and they go next, then the greenbacks flutter through the air. She keeps her knife, can opener and eyebrow pencil. She puts bones, pieces of bark, *hierbas*, eagle feather, snakeskin, tape recorder, the rattle and drum in her pack and she sets out to become the complete *tolteca*.[1]

Her first step is to take inventory. *Despojando, desgranando, quitando paja.* Just what did she inherit from her ancestors? This weight on her back—which is the baggage from the Indian mother, which the baggage from the Spanish father, which the baggage from the Anglo?

Pero es difícil differentiating between *lo heredado, lo adquirido, lo impuesto*. She puts history through a sieve, winnows out the lies, looks at the forces that we as a race, as women, have been a part of. *Luego bota lo que no vale, los desmientos, los desencuentos, el embrutecimiento. Aguarda el juicio, hondo y enraízado, de la gente antigua.* This step is a conscious rupture with all oppressive traditions of all cultures and religions. She communicates that rupture, documents the struggle. She reinterprets history and, using new symbols, she shapes new myths. She adopts new perspectives toward the darkskinned, women and queers. She strengthens her tolerance (and intolerance) for ambiguity. She is willing to share, to make herself vulnerable to foreign ways of seeing and thinking. She surrenders all notions of safety, of the familiar. Deconstruct, construct. She becomes a *nahual*, able to transform herself into a tree, a coyote, into another person. She learns to transform the small "I" into the total Self. *Se hace moldeadora de su alma. Según la concepción que tiene de sí misma, así será.*

QUE NO SE NOS OLVIDE LOS HOMBRES

> "*Tú no sirves pa' nada*—
> you're good for nothing.
> *Eres pura vieja.*"

"You're nothing but a woman" means you are defective. Its opposite is to be *un macho*. The modern meaning of the word "machismo," as well as the concept, is actually an Anglo invention. For men like my father, being "macho" meant being strong enough to protect and support my mother and us, yet being able to show love. Today's macho has doubts about his ability to feed and protect his family. His "machismo" is an adaptation to oppression and poverty and low self-esteem. It is the result of hierarchical male dominance. The Anglo, feeling inadequate and inferior and powerless, displaces or transfers these feelings to the Chicano by shaming him. In the Gringo world, the Chicano suffers from excessive humility and self-effacement, shame of self and self-depreciation. Around Latinos he suffers from a sense of language inadequacy and its accompanying discomfort; with Native Americans he suffers from a racial amnesia which ignores our common blood, and from guilt because the Spanish part of him took their

9. Maps of San Francisco's bus and subway routes.

1. Gina Valdés, *Puentes y Fronteras: Coplas Chicanas* (Los Angeles Castle Lithograph, 1982), 2 [Anzaldúa's note].

land and oppressed them. He has an excessive compensatory hubris when around Mexicans from the other side. It overlays a deep sense of racial shame.

The loss of a sense of dignity and respect in the macho breeds a false machismo which leads him to put down women and even to brutalize them. Coexisting with his sexist behavior is a love for the mother which takes precedence over that of all others. Devoted son, macho pig. To wash down the shame of his acts, of his very being, and to handle the brute in the mirror, he takes to the bottle, the snort, the needle, and the fist.

Though we "understand" the root causes of male hatred and fear, and the subsequent wounding of women, we do not excuse, we do not condone, and we will no longer put up with it. From the men of our race, we demand the admission/acknowledgment/disclosure/testimony that they wound us, violate us, are afraid of us and of our power. We need them to say they will begin to eliminate their hurtful put-down ways. But more than the words, we demand acts. We say to them: We will develop equal power with you and those who have shamed us.

It is imperative that *mestizas* support each other in changing the sexist elements in the Mexican-Indian culture. As long as woman is put down, the Indian and the Black in all of us is put down. The struggle of the *mestiza* is above all a feminist one. As long as *los hombres* think they have to *chingar mujeres* and each other to be men, as long as men are taught that they are superior and therefore culturally favored over *la mujer*, as long as to be a *vieja* is a thing of derision, there can be no real healing of our psyches. We're halfway there—we have such love of the Mother, the good mother. The first step is to unlearn the *puta/virgen* dichotomy and to see *Coatlapopeuh-Coatlicue* in the Mother, *Guadalupe*.[2]

Tenderness, a sign of vulnerability, is so feared that it is showered on women with verbal abuse and blows. Men, even more than women, are fettered to gender roles. Women at least have had the guts to break out of bondage. Only gay men have had the courage to expose themselves to the woman inside them and to challenge the current masculinity. I've encountered a few scattered and isolated gentle straight men, the beginnings of a new breed, but they are confused, and entangled with sexist behaviors that they have not been able to eradicate. We need a new masculinity and the new man needs a movement.

Lumping the males who deviate from the general norm with man, the oppressor, is a gross injustice. *Asombra pensar que nos hemos quedado en ese pozo oscuro donde el mundo encierra a las lesbianas. Asombra pensar que hemos, como femenistas y lesbianas, cerrado nuestros corazónes a los hombres, a nuestros hermanos los jotos, desheredados y marginales como nosotros.* Being the supreme crossers of cultures, homosexuals have strong bonds with the queer white, Black, Asian, Native American, Latino, and with the queer in Italy, Australia and the rest of the planet. We come from

2. Our Lady of Guadalupe, the Virgin Mary (who is said to have appeared to a Native American in that Mexican city in 1531). *Coatlapopeuh-Coatlicue*: Aztec earth goddess who is the mother of the gods.

all colors, all classes, all races, all time periods. Our role is to link people with each other—the Blacks with Jews with Indians with Asians with whites with extraterrestrials. It is to transfer ideas and information from one culture to another. Colored homosexuals have more knowledge of other cultures; have always been at the forefront (although sometimes in the closet) of all liberation struggles in this country; have suffered more injustices and have survived them despite all odds. Chicanos need to acknowledge the political and artistic contributions of their queer. People, listen to what your *jotería* is saying.

The *mestizo* and the queer exist at this time and point on the evolutionary continuum for a purpose. We are a blending that proves that all blood is intricately woven together, and that we are spawned out of similar souls.

SOMOS UNA GENTE

Hay tantísimas fronteras
que dividen a la gente,
pero por cada frontera
existe también un puente.
—Gina Valdés[3]

Divided Loyalties. Many women and men of color do not want to have any dealings with white people. It takes too much time and energy to explain to the downwardly mobile, white middle-class women that it's okay for us to want to own "possessions," never having had any nice furniture on our dirt floors or "luxuries" like washing machines. Many feel that whites should help their own people rid themselves of race hatred and fear first. I, for one, choose to use some of my energy to serve as mediator. I think we need to allow whites to be our allies. Through our literature, art, *corridos*, and folktales we must share our history with them so when they set up committees to help Big Mountain Navajos or the Chicano farmworkers or *los Nicaragüenses*[4] they won't turn people away because of their racial fears and ignorances. They will come to see that they are not helping us but following our lead.

Individually, but also as a racial entity, we need to voice our needs. We need to say to white society: We need you to accept the fact that Chicanos are different, to acknowledge your rejection and negation of us. We need you to own the fact that you looked upon us as less than human, that you stole our lands, our personhood, our self-respect. We need you to make public restitution: to say that, to compensate for your own sense of defectiveness, you strive for power over us, you erase our history and our experience because it makes you feel guilty—you'd rather forget your brutish acts. To say you've split yourself from minority groups, that you disown us, that your dual consciousness splits off parts of yourself, transferring the "negative" parts onto us. (Where there is persecution of minorities, there is shadow projection. Where there is violence and war, there is repression of

3. Valdés, *Puentes y Fronteras*, 2 [Anzaldúa's note].
4. In the 1980s the U.S. government funded soldiers fighting against the Sandinista government of Nicaragua.

shadow.) To say that you are afraid of us, that to put distance between us, you wear the mask of contempt. Admit that Mexico is your double, that she exists in the shadow of this country, that we are irrevocably tied to her. Gringo, accept the doppelganger in your psyche. By taking back your collective shadow the intracultural split will heal. And finally, tell us what you need from us.

BY YOUR TRUE FACES WE WILL KNOW YOU

I am visible—see this Indian face—yet I am invisible. I both blind them with my beak nose and am their blind spot. But I exist, we exist. They'd like to think I have melted in the pot. But I haven't, we haven't.

The dominant white culture is killing us slowly with its ignorance. By taking away our self-determination, it has made us weak and empty. As a people we have resisted and we have taken expedient positions, but we have never been allowed to develop unencumbered—we have never been allowed to be fully ourselves. The whites in power want us people of color to barricade ourselves behind our separate tribal walls so they can pick us off one at a time with their hidden weapons; so they can whitewash and distort history. Ignorance splits people, creates prejudices. A misinformed people is a subjugated people.

Before the Chicano and the undocumented worker and the Mexican from the other side can come together, before the Chicano can have unity with Native Americans and other groups, we need to know the history of their struggle and they need to know ours. Our mothers, our sisters and brothers, the guys who hang out on street corners, the children in the playgrounds, each of us must know our Indian lineage, our afro-*mestisaje*, our history of resistance.

To the immigrant *mexicano* and the recent arrivals we must teach our history. The 80 million *mexicanos* and the Latinos from Central and South America must know of our struggles. Each one of us must know basic facts about Nicaragua, Chile and the rest of Latin America.[5] The Latinoist movement (Chicanos, Puerto Ricans, Cubans and other Spanish-speaking people working together to combat racial discrimination in the market place) is good but it is not enough. Other than a common culture we will have nothing to hold us together. We need to meet on a broader communal ground.

The struggle is inner: Chicano, *indio*, American Indian, *mojado*, *mexicano*, immigrant Latino, Anglo in power, working class Anglo, Black, Asian—our psyches resemble the bordertowns and are populated by the same people. The struggle has always been inner, and is played out in the outer terrains. Awareness of our situation must come before inner changes, which in turn come before changes in society. Nothing happens in the "real" world unless it first happens in the images in our heads.

5. This history includes U.S. government interventions in various Latin and Central American countries from 1950 to 1990, undermining governments thought to be too leftist and supporting right-wing governments.

EL DÍA DE LA CHICANA

I will not be shamed again
Nor will I shame myself.

I am possessed by a vision that we Chicanas and Chicanos have taken back or uncovered our true faces, our dignity and self-respect. It's a validation vision.

Seeing the Chicana anew in light of her history. I seek an exoneration, a seeing through the fictions of white supremacy, a seeing of ourselves in our true guises and not as the false racial personality that has been given to us and that we have given to ourselves. I seek our woman's face, our true features, the positive and the negative seen clearly, free of the tainted biases of male dominance. I seek new images of identity, new beliefs about ourselves, our humanity and worth no longer in question.

Estamos viviendo en la noche de la Raza, un tiempo cuando el trabajo se hace a lo quieto, en el oscuro. El día cuando aceptamos tal y como somos y para en donde vamos y porque—ese día será de la Raza. Yo tengo el conpromiso de expresar mi visión, mi sensibilidad, mi percepión de la revalidación de la gente mexicana, su mérito estimación, honra, aprecio, y validez.

On December 2nd when my sun goes into my first house, I celebrate *el día de la Chicana y el Chicano*. On that day I clean my altars, light my *Coatlalopeuh* candle, burn sage and copal, take *el baño para espantar basura*, sweep my house. On that day I bare my soul, make myself vulnerable to friends and family by expressing my feelings. On that day I affirm who we are.

On that day I look inside our conflicts and our basic introverted racial temperament. I identify our needs, voice them. I acknowledge that the self and the race have been wounded. I recognize the need to take care of our personhood, of our racial self. On that day I gather the splintered and disowned parts of *la gente mexicana* and hold them in my arms. *Todas las partes de nosotros valen.*

On that day I say, "Yes, all you people wound us when you reject us. Rejection strips us of self-worth; our vulnerability exposes us to shame. It is our innate identity you find wanting. We are ashamed that we need your good opinion, that we need your acceptance. We can no longer camouflage our needs, can no longer let defenses and fences sprout around us. We can no longer withdraw. To rage and look upon you with contempt is to rage and be contemptuous of ourselves. We can no longer blame you, nor disown the white parts, the male parts, the pathological parts, the queer parts, the vulnerable parts. Here we are weaponless with open arms, with only our magic. Let's try it our way, the *mestiza* way, the Chicana way, the woman way.

On that day, I search for our essential dignity as a people, a people with a sense of purpose—to belong and contribute to something greater than our *pueblo*. On that day I seek to recover and reshape my spiritual identity. *¡Anímate! Raza, a celebrar el día de la Chicana.*

EL RETORNO

> All movements are accomplished in six stages,
> and the seventh brings return.
> —I Ching[6]

> *Tanto tiempo sin verte casa mía,*
> *mi cuna, mi hondo nido de la huerta.*
> —"Soledad"[7]

I stand at the river, watch the curving, twisting serpent, a serpent nailed to the fence where the mouth of the Rio Grande empties into the Gulf.

I have come back. *Tanto dolor me costó el alejamiento.* I shade my eyes and look up. The bone beak of a hawk slowly circling over me, checking me out as potential carrion. In its wake a little bird flickering its wings, swimming sporadically like a fish. In the distance the expressway and the slough of traffic like an irritated sow. The sudden pull in my gut, *la tierra, los aguaceros.* My land, *el viento soplando la arena, el lagartijo debajo de un nopalito. Me acuerdo como era antes. Una región desértica de vasta llanuras, costeras de baja altura, de escasa lluvia, de chaparrales formados por mesquites y huizaches.* If I look real hard I can almost see the Spanish fathers who were called "the cavalry of Christ" enter this valley riding their burros, see the clash of cultures commence.

Tierra nata. This is home, the small towns in the Valley, *los pueblitos* with chicken pens and goats picketed to mesquite shrubs. *En las colonias on the other side of the tracks, junk cars line the front yards of hot pink and lavender-trimmed houses—Chicano architecture we call it, self-consciously. I have missed the TV shows where hosts speak in half and half, and where awards are given in the category of Tex-Mex music. I have missed the Mexican cemeteries blooming with artificial flowers, the fields of aloe vera and red pepper, rows of sugar cane, of corn hanging on the stalks, the cloud of polvareda* in the dirt roads behind a speeding pickup truck, *el sabor de tamales de rez y venado.* I have missed *la yegua colorada* gnawing the wooden gate of her stall, the smell of horse flesh from Carito's corrals. *He hecho menos las noches calientes sin aire, noches de linternas y lechuzas* making holes in the night.

I still feel the old despair when I look at the unpainted, dilapidated, scrap lumber houses consisting mostly of corrugated aluminum. Some of the poorest people in the U.S. live in the Lower Rio Grande Valley, an arid and semiarid land of irrigated farming, intense sunlight and heat, citrus groves next to chaparral and cactus. I walk through the elementary school I attended so long ago, that remained segregated until recently. I remember how the white teachers used to punish us for being Mexican.

How I love this tragic valley of South Texas, as Ricardo Sánchez[8] calls it;

6. Richard Wilhelm, *The I Ching or Book of Changes*, trans. Cary F. Baynes (Princeton: Princeton University Press, 1950), 98 [Anzaldúa's note].

7. "Soledad" is sung by the group Haciendo Punto and Otto Son [Anzaldúa's note].

8. American poet and critic (1941–1995).

this borderland between the Nueces and the Rio Grande. This land has survived possession and ill-use by five countries: Spain, Mexico, the Republic of Texas, the U.S., the Confederacy, and the U.S. again. It has survived Anglo-Mexican blood feuds, lynchings, burnings, rapes, pillage.

Today I see the Valley still struggling to survive. Whether it does or not, it will never be as I remember it. The borderlands depression that was set off by the 1982 peso devaluation in Mexico resulted in the closure of hundreds of Valley businesses. Many people lost their homes, cars, land. Prior to 1982, U.S. store owners thrived on retail sales to Mexicans who came across the border for groceries and clothes and appliances. While goods on the U.S. side have become 10, 100, 1000 times more expensive for Mexican buyers, goods on the Mexican side have become 10, 100, 1000 times cheaper for Americans. Because the Valley is heavily dependent on agriculture and Mexican retail trade, it has the highest unemployment rates along the entire border region; it is the Valley that has been hardest hit.[9]

"It's been a bad year for corn," my brother, Nune, says. As he talks, I remember my father scanning the sky for a rain that would end the drought, looking up into the sky, day after day, while the corn withered on its stalk. My father has been dead for 29 years, having worked himself to death. The life span of a Mexican farm laborer is 56—he lived to be 38. It shocks me that I am older than he. I, too, search the sky for rain. Like the ancients, I worship the rain god and the maize goddess, but unlike my father I have recovered their names. Now for rain (irrigation) one offers not a sacrifice of blood, but of money.

"Farming is in a bad way," my brother says. "Two to three thousand small and big farmers went bankrupt in this country last year. Six years ago the price of corn was $8.00 per hundred pounds," he goes on. "This year it is $3.90 per hundred pounds." And, I think to myself, after taking inflation into account, not planting anything puts you ahead.

I walk out to the back yard, stare at *los rosales de mamá*. She wants me to help her prune the rose bushes, dig out the carpet grass that is choking them. *Mamagrande Ramona también tenía rosales*. Here every Mexican grows flowers. If they don't have a piece of dirt, they use car tires, jars, cans, shoe boxes. Roses are the Mexican's favorite flower. I think, how symbolic—thorns and all.

Yes, the Chicano and Chicana have always taken care of growing things and the land. Again I see the four of us kids getting off the school bus, changing into our work clothes, walking into the field with Papí and Mamí, all six of us bending to the ground. Below our feet, under the earth lie the watermelon seeds. We cover them with paper plates, putting *terremotes* on

9. Out of the 22 border counties in the four border states, Hidalgo County (named for Father Hidalgo who was shot in 1810 after instigating Mexico's revolt against Spain under the banner of *la Virgen de Guadalupe*) is the most poverty-stricken county in the nation as well as the largest home base (along with Imperial in California) for migrant farm-workers. It was here that I was born and raised. I am amazed that both it and I have survived [Anzaldúa's note].

top of the plates to keep them from being blown away by the wind. The paper plates keep the freeze away. Next day or the next, we remove the plates, bare the tiny green shoots to the elements. They survive and grow, give fruit hundreds of times the size of the seed. We water them and hoe them. We harvest them. The vines dry, rot, are plowed under. Growth, death, decay, birth. The soil prepared again and again, impregnated, worked on. A constant changing of forms, *renacimientos de latierra madre.*

This land was Mexican once
was Indian always
and is.
And will be again.

1987

HOUSTON A. BAKER JR.
b. 1943

Since the late 1960s, Houston A. Baker Jr. has been central to the increasing critical and scholarly attention paid to African American literature. Along with detailed criticism of many notable African American writers, Baker's work provides highly influential theoretical paradigms for the study of "vernacular" literatures. His deep commitment to the specificity of African American culture and the dignity of African American experience is combined with an adventurous willingness to constantly reexamine his own critical stance toward that culture and experience. The result has been a body of work exemplary in its engagement with the material studied, with the shifting theoretical landscape, and with the pressing needs of black Americans.

Baker was born in 1943 and raised in Louisville, Kentucky, when that city, like the rest of the American South, practiced racial segregation. "During [my] youth," he writes, "the town was *dangerously* Southern for black ambitions and enterprise (like walking down the street)." Baker attended an honors high school, where he was one of the few black students, then did his undergraduate work at historically black Howard University in Washington, D.C. He received a Ph.D. in 1968 from the University of California at Los Angeles, with a dissertation on Victorian poetry, but he quickly left nineteenth-century British literature behind. Apart from some early essays, Baker has focused on African American literature. He has also published several volumes of his own poetry. Baker first found his voice and subject in his initial jobs as a professor—at Yale University and then the University of Virginia—when he became an early proponent and teacher of courses on black writers. Hired to direct the Afro-

American Studies Program at the University of Pennsylvania in 1974, he was named the Albert M. Greenfield Professor of Human Relations there in 1982. He joined the faculty at Duke University in 1998. He has served as president of the Modern Language Association, and holds honorary degrees from several universities.

In his work, Baker walks a fine line between validating African American writing for the mainstream, nonblack, academic tradition and insisting on the specific differences that mark African American writing as a distinct tradition of its own. He was one of the first academic critics to argue that the standards of judgment used in evaluating white writing were not suitable for judging black writing. His articulation of appropriate standards explained the value of black literature to a previously indifferent (at best) white academy. Similarly, in our selection as elsewhere in his work, Baker's use of "high" theory—the invocation of concepts drawn from G. W. F. HEGEL, KARL MARX, JACQUES DERRIDA, and FREDRIC JAMESON—has the effect of placing black literature on a par with canonical masterpieces that are deemed worthy of sophisticated analysis and prolonged, intensive attention. His explicit use of theory to study African American texts aligns him with HENRY LOUIS GATES JR. and against BARBARA CHRISTIAN among contemporary black literary critics, who have long debated the relevance of European theory and philosophy to black literary studies.

Baker wants to use theory to highlight "the distinctive, the culturally specific aspects of Afro-American literature," not to assimilate black works to the existing canon. His project mirrors the problem faced by black writers themselves: how to use the language of the dominant white culture to express the different realities of African American life. To complicate matters, Baker adopts the theoretical view that language "speaks" the subject, rather than the other way around. Linguistic and literary forms and meanings precede personal experience and its expression by any particular subject. The very experiences of subjects (including that of their own status as subjects) are shaped and produced by those preexisting discursive forms. Within this theoretical perspective, African American literature can be unique only if it is created within a distinctive culture that "speaks" subjects, constitutes experiences, and generates expressions differently than does mainstream culture.

Baker's argument for this distinct African American culture employs Hegel's concept of "determinate negation," which posits that the definition or determination of identity occurs by excluding entities now understood as not part of the self. The importance of this concept for Baker and for theorists of racial, ethnic, gendered, and other social differences cannot be overstated. Mainstream culture achieves its self-understanding and its coherence through defining itself as "not colored": white America achieves its identity by its negative relation to "colored" America. Given this act of exclusion, black America inevitably had to form its own culture. Baker sees his critical task as the description and analysis of that distinctive black culture.

But Baker does not want the concept of black culture that he delineates to be too rigid or simplistic. His epigraph from Ralph Ellison indicates that black "cultural wholeness" is "always in cacophonic motion." For Baker, "Afro-American culture is a complex, reflexive enterprise which finds its proper figuration in blues conceived as a matrix. . . . The matrix is a point of ceaseless input and output, a web of interacting, crisscrossing impulses always in productive transit." Note here the simultaneous commitment to a single "Afro-American culture" and to dynamic, continually productive and transformative actions within that culture. The shift in terminology from "culture" to "matrix" highlights Baker's efforts to describe a unity, a single framework within which all the singularities are held, without suggesting conformity among the parts.

Baker wants to keep difference alive on two levels—between black and white culture, and within black culture—while staying attuned to structuralist and semiotic theories of powerful, holistic cultural "codes" that produce individual events and subjects according to large-scale patterns. To do so, he relies primarily on the idea of the "vernacular." The term itself derives from the special Latin vocabulary of slavery, meaning a slave who was not bought by the slaveowner but was born into slavery on the master's estate. More generally, it can refer to a nonstandard language or dialect of a place or country. To study the vernacular, for Baker, is to study how a particular language is used by just those speakers who have not been in the social position to use or create the "standard" language. His emphasis on the black vernacular as the dialect of the marginalized, the unheard, connects with similar concerns in contemporary feminist and postcolonial theory, as in the work of HOMI K. BHABHA. How do those whose speech carries no authority and who are usually expected to be silent use the master's language differently than the master himself does? How do they make that language, so often employed to oppress them, serve their own purposes and needs? What resources are to be found within those "nonstandard dialects" created by speakers far from the centers of power?

Baker argues that "the blues" is the vernacular core of black America. In *Blues, Ideology, and Afro-American Literature* (1984), he lyrically details the complex features of this form and then connects particular literary works to its overarching "matrix." For Baker, the vernacular is an expression of the popular as well as the local. "High" art, like "standard" language, understands itself in contrast to "low" forms that exist apart from authoritative institutions such as museums, libraries, and universities. Popular art, like a speech dialect, comes from below and is often anonymous. (We need to distinguish here between "popular art" or "folk art" and the very different "pop culture" produced by the mass media. By their very nature, such media—despite their efforts to capitalize on dialects—cannot produce these localized variants, which are limited to smaller groups.) Jokes, folktales, and traditional songs are good examples of anonymous, popular art forms. Baker wants to activate this popular and anonymous element of the vernacular; he sees the "higher" instances of African American poetry and prose fiction as springing from the fertile ground of an anonymously created blues that serves as a shared vernacular for all African Americans, regardless of class, region, or gender.

What all African Americans share, Baker insists, is the "obdurate 'economics of slavery,' " by which he means the ongoing, centuries-long material, symbolic, and social deprivations suffered by blacks in American society. The blues is a central form of expression created by African Americans as a people in response to racism and its concrete effects. Baker is anxious, however, not to reduce the blues to a simple expression of the experience of oppression. He stresses that any artistic expression, as well as any act of criticism, is "inventive": the raw material of experience is worked on and shaped into artistic form. In the simplest terms, experience doesn't come to us in musical notes. So a translation from experience to art is always part of the process. And because the art forms already exist when a particular artist goes to create a particular blues song, the conventions of the blues to a certain extent shape the forms of experience, rather than raw experience simply dictating its artistic expression.

Baker maintains an allegiance to the concept of "experience"; he does not believe that we perceive only according to established forms. Rather, the meeting of such forms and personal experience is precisely the moment of "invention." Indeed, the artist at times creates new forms; thus Baker's definition of the blues matrix emphasizes the "reflexive." Experience and form mutually influence each other as individual African American artists strive to "achieve a resonant, improvisational, expressive dignity."

Baker's commitments to experience, individual expression, and the unity of African American culture all place him at odds with certain more radical antihumanist versions of poststructuralism, although he invokes the work of such theorists. Like some feminist and postcolonial theorists, Baker retains a stake in the individual subject situated among marginalized groups, a commitment that tempers the usual hostility to the "bourgeois" or "Cartesian" subject found in much poststructuralist work. In addition, Baker's desire to locate a single African American cultural matrix runs athwart work that stresses the nonintegrity of cultural formations. Certainly, his focus on the blues immediately calls to mind other distinctive African American cultural forms, such as the slave narrative, the oral tradition of black preaching, jazz, and "trash talk" within groups of black men. Are these forms of expression all variants of the "blues matrix," or do we need to think of multiple strands of available forms within a varied African American tradition? And how should we think about borrowings between white and black cultures, since the boundaries between the two are continually crossed? Baker's work since *Blues, Ideology, and Afro-American Literature* has taken up some of these questions, as he has examined rap music and the interaction between modernism and the Harlem Renaissance.

During his career, Baker has attempted to negotiate a number of vexed issues, ranging from the status of African American studies in the university to the relation of African American literature to the wider experience, needs, and cultural resources of all African American people. In joining Hegel to the blues singer Robert Johnson, and in celebrating the blues as an artistic form available to African Americans both as evidence of their unique cultural identity and as a means to express that identity, Baker is being, he tells us, inventive. He is working to create a new social position for black Americans through a re-vision of their cultural achievements.

BIBLIOGRAPHY

Baker's critical books to date are *Long Black Song: Essays in Black American Literature and Culture* (1972), *Singers of Daybreak: Studies in Black American Literature* (1974), *A Many-Colored Coat of Dreams: The Poetry of Countee Cullen* (1974), *Paul Laurence Dunbar, an Evaluation* (1974), *The Journey Back: Issues in Black Literature and Criticism* (1980), *Blues, Ideology, and Afro-American Literature: A Vernacular Theory* (1984), *Modernism and the Harlem Renaissance* (1987), *Afro-American Poetics: Revisions of Harlem and the Black Aesthetic* (1988), and *Black Studies, Rap, and the Academy* (1993). He edited one of the first anthologies of African American literature, *Black Literature in America* (1971), and is a co-editor of *The Norton Anthology of African American Literature* (1996). He has also edited or co-edited many collections of critical essays: *Twentieth Century Interpretations of Native Son* (1972); *Reading Black: Essays in the Criticism of African, Caribbean, and Black American Literature* (1976); with Leslie Fiedler, *English Literature: Opening Up the Canon* (1981); *Three American Literatures: Essays on Chicano, Native American, and Asian American Literature for Teachers of American Literature* (1982); with Patricia Redmond, *Afro-American Literary Studies in the 1990s* (1989); with Patricia Redmond and Elizabeth Alexander, *Workings of the Spirit: The Poetics of Afro-American Women's Writing* (1991); and with Manthia Diawara and Ruth H. Lindeborg, *Black British Cultural Studies* (1996). Biographical information can be found in *Contemporary Black Biography*, vol. 6 (1994).

Two interviews offer a convenient place to begin studying Baker's work: Jerry W. Ward Jr.'s "A Black and Crucial Enterprise: An Interview with Houston A. Baker, Jr.," *Black American Literature Forum* 16.2 (1982), and Michael Bérubé's "Hybridity in the Center: An Interview with Houston A. Baker, Jr.," *African American Review* 26.4 (1992). The range of critical responses to Baker's work includes Michael Awkward, "Race, Gender, and the Politics of Reading," *Black American Literature Forum* 22.1 (1988); Andrea Mueller-Hartmann, "Houston A. Baker, Jr.:The Development of a Black Literary Critic," *Literary Griot* 1.2 (1989); Kwame Anthony Appiah, "The Conservation of Race," *Black American Literature Forum* 23.1 (1989); Sandra Adell, "A Function at the Junction," *Diacritics* 20 (1990); Jo-Anne Cornwell Giles, "Afro-American Criticism and Western Consciousness: The Politics of Knowing," *Black American Literature Forum* 24.1 (1990); Michael Bérubé, "Power Surge: Houston Baker's Vernacular Spectacular," *Village Voice Literary Supplement* 109 (October 1992); and Winston Napier, "From the Shadows: Houston Baker's Move toward a Postnationalist Appraisal of the Black Aesthetic," *New Literary History* 25 (1994).

From Blues, Ideology, and Afro-American Literature: A Vernacular Theory

Introduction

> *Vernacular*, adj.: *Of a slave*: That is born on his master's estate; home-born
> *Of arts, or features of these*: Native or peculiar to a particular country or locality

> Other states indicate themselves in their deputies . . . but the genius of the United States is not best or most in its executives or legislatures, nor in its ambassadors or authors or colleges or churches or parlors, nor even in its newspapers or inventors . . . but always most in the common people . . . these . . . are unrhymed poetry. It awaits the gigantic and generous treatment worthy of it.
>
> —Walt Whitman[1]

> If you see me coming, better open up your door,
> If you see me coming, better open up your door,
> I ain't no stranger, I been here before.
>
> —Traditional Blues

> Standing at the crossroads, tried to flag a ride,
> Standing at the crossroads, tried to flag a ride,
> Ain't nobody seem to know me, everybody passed me by.
>
> —Crossroad Blues[2]

> In every case the result of an untrue mode of knowledge must not be allowed to run away into an empty nothing, but must necessarily be grasped as the nothing of *that from which it results*—a result which contains what was true in the preceding knowledge.
>
> —Hegel,[3] *Phenomenology of Spirit*

> So perhaps we shy from confronting our cultural wholeness because it offers no easily recognizable points of rest, no facile certainties as to who, what, or where (culturally or historically) we are. Instead, the whole is always in cacophonic motion.
>
> —Ralph Ellison,[4] "The Little Man at the Chehaw Station"

> . . . maybe one day, you'll find they actually do understand exactly what you are talking about, all these fantasy people. All these blues people.
>
> —Amiri Baraka,[5] *Dutchman*

FROM SYMBOL TO IDEOLOGY

In my book *The Journey Back: Issues in Black Literature and Criticism* (1980),[6] I envisioned the "speaking subject" creating language (a code) to be deciphered by the present-day commentator. In my current study, I envision language (the code) "speaking" the subject. The subject is "decentered." My quest during the past decade has been for the distinctive, the culturally specific aspects of Afro-American literature and culture. I was convinced that I had found such specificity in a peculiar subjectivity, but the objectivity of

1. American poet (1819–1892). From the 1855 preface to *Leaves of Grass*.
2. By Mississippi Delta blues singer Robert Johnson (ca. 1911–1938).
3. GEORG WILHELM FRIEDRICH HEGEL (1770–1831), German philosopher; *Phenomenology of Spirit* was published in 1807.
4. African American novelist (1914–1994); this essay was published in 1978.
5. African American poet and playwright (formerly LeRoi Jones, b. 1934); the play *Dutchman* was published in 1964.
6. Chicago: University of Chicago Press, 1980 [Baker's note].

economics and the sound lessons of poststructuralism arose to reorient my thinking. I was also convinced that the symbolic, and quite specifically the symbolically anthropological, offered avenues to the comprehension of Afro-American expressive culture in its plenitude.[7] I discovered that the symbolic's antithesis—practical reason, or the material—is as necessary for understanding Afro-American discourse as the cultural-in-itself.

My shift from a centered to a decentered subject, from an exclusively symbolic to a more inclusively expressive perspective, was prompted by the curious force of dialectical thought. My access to the study of such thought came from attentive readings of Fredric Jameson, Hayden White, Marshall Sahlins,[8] and others. While profiting from observations by these scholars, I also began to attend meetings of a study group devoted to Hegel's *Phenomenology of Spirit*.

Having journeyed with the aid of symbolic anthropology to what appeared to be the soundest possible observations on Afro-American art, I found myself confronted suddenly by a figure-to-ground reversal. A fitting image for the effect of my reorientation is the gestalt illustration of the Greek hydria (a water vase with curved handles) that transforms itself into two faces in profile. John Keat's "Ode on a Grecian Urn," with its familiar detailing of the economies of "art" and human emotion, can be considered one moment in the shift.[9] Contrasting with Keat's romantic figurations are the emergent faces of a venerable ancestry. The shift from Greek hydrias to ancestral faces is a shift from high art to vernacular expression.

The "vernacular" in relation to human beings signals "a slave born on his master's estate." In expressive terms, vernacular indicates "arts native or peculiar to a particular country or locale." The material conditions of slavery in the United States and the rhythms of Afro-American blues combined and emerged from my revised materialistic perspective as an ancestral matrix that has produced a forceful and indigenous American creativity. The moment of emergence of economic and vernacular concerns left me, as the French say, *entre les deux*:[1] suspended somewhere between symbolic anthropology and analytical strategies that Fredric Jameson calls the "ideology of form."[2]

IDEOLOGY, SEMIOTICS, AND THE MATERIAL

In acknowledging a concern for the ideology of form, however, I do not want to imply that my symbolic-anthropological orientation was untrue, in the

7. Though a great many sources were involved in my reoriented cultural thinking, certainly the terminology employed in my discussion at this point derives from Marshall Sahlins's wonderfully lucid *Culture and Practical Reason* (Chicago: University of Chicago Press, 1976). Sahlins delineates two modes of thinking that have characterized anthropology from its inception. These two poles are "symbolic" and "functionalist." He resolves the dichotomy suggested by these terms through the middle term "cultural proposition," a phrase that he defines as a cultural mediating ground where the material and symbolic, the useful and the ineffable, ceaselessly converge and depart [Baker's note].

8. American anthropologist (b. 1930). JAMESON (b. 1934), American Marxist literary theorist. WHITE (b. 1928), American historian and narrative theorist.

9. "Ode on a Grecian Urn" (1819), by the Romantic poet Keats (1795–1821), contrasts the cold perfection of timeless art with the pain experienced by those who live in time.

1. Between the two (French).

2. The "ideology of form" as a description of Jameson's project derives from the essay "The Symbolic Inference; or, Kenneth Burke and Ideological Analysis," *Critical Inquiry* 4 (1978): 507–23. Surely, though, Jameson's most recent study, *The Political Unconscious: Narrative as a Socially Symbolic Act* (Ithaca, N.Y.: Cornell University Press, 1981), offers the fullest description of his views on ways in which cultural texts formally inscribe material/historical conditions of their production, distribution, and consumption [Baker's note].

sense of deluded or deceived.[3] This symbolic orientation was simply one moment in my experiencing of Afro-American culture—a moment superseded now by a prospect that constitutes its determinate negation.[4] What was true in my prior framework remains so in my current concern for the ideology of form. Certainly the mode of ideological investigation proposed by Jameson is an analysis that escapes all hints of "vulgar Marxism" through its studious attention to modern critiques of political economy, and also through its shrewd incorporation of poststructuralist thought.[5]

In chapters that follow, I too attempt to avoid a naive Marxism.[6] I do not believe, for example, that a fruitful correlation exists when one merely claims that certain black folk seculars are determinate results of agricultural gang labor. Such attributions simply privilege the material as a substrate while failing to provide detailed accounts of processes leading from an apparent substrate to a peculiar expressive form. A faith of enormous magnitude is required to accept such crude formulations as adequate explanations. The "material" is shifty ground, and current critiques of political economy suggest that postulates based on this ground can be understood only in "semiotic" terms. Hence, the employment of ideology as an analytical category begins with the awareness that "production" as well as "modes of production" must be grasped in terms of the sign. An example of a persuasive case for "political economy" as a code existing in a relationship of identity with language can be found in Jean Baudrillard's *For a Critique of the Political Economy of the Sign*. To read economics as a semiotic process leads to the realization that ideological analyses may be as decidedly intertextual as, say, analyses of the relationship between Afro-American vernacular expression and more sophisticated forms of verbal art. If what is normally categorized as *material* (e.g., "raw material," "consumer goods") can be interpreted semiotically, then any collection of such entities and their defining interrelationships may be defined as a text.[7]

In the chapters in this book, however, I do not write about or interpret the *material* in exclusively semiotic terms. Although I am fully aware of insights to be gained from semiotics, my analyses focus directly on the living and laboring conditions of people designated as "the desperate class" by

3. In *The Journey Back*, I define my project as follows: "The phrase ['the anthropology of art'] expresses for me the notion that art must be studied with an attention to the methods and findings of disciplines which enable one to address such concerns as the status of the artistic object, the relationship of art to other cultural systems, and the nature and function of artistic creation and perception in a given society" (p. xvi). The project's privileging of "symbolic anthropology" and "art" under the sign *interdisciplinary* involved exclusions that were ironical and (I now realize) somewhat disabling where a full description of expressive culture is sought [Baker's note].

4. The Hegelian epigraph that marks the beginning of these introductory remarks offers the best definition I know of "determinate negation." The epigraph is taken from the *Phenomenology of Spirit* [Baker's note]. "Determinate negation": the process of defining an entity by indicating what it is not.

5. I have in mind Louis Althusser and Étienne Balibar, *Reading Capital* (London: New Left Books, 1977), and Jean Baudrillard's *For a Critique of the Political Economy of the Sign* (1972; St. Louis: Telos Press, 1981) and *The Mirror of Production* (1973; St. Louis: Telos Press, 1975). By "poststructuralist" thought, I have in mind the universe of discourse constituted by *deconstruction*. Jacques Derrida's *Of Grammatology* (1967; Baltimore: Johns Hopkins University Press, 1976) is perhaps the locus classicus of the deconstructionist project. One of the more helpful accounts of deconstruction is Christopher Norris's *Deconstruction: Theory and Practice* (London: Methuen, 1982). Of course, there is a certain collapsing of poststructuralism and political economy in the sources cited previously [Baker's note]. On the French philosophers ALTHUSSER (1918–1990) and DERRIDA (b. 1930), and the French social critic BAUDRILLARD (b. 1929), see above.

6. That is, a Marxism that sees cultural and political phenomena as direct reflections of economic activities connected to material needs.

7. See Baudrillard, *For a Critique of the Political Economy of the Sign* [Baker's note].

James Weldon Johnson's[8] narrator in *The Autobiography of an Ex-Colored Man*. Such people constitute the vernacular in the United States. Their lives have always been sharply conditioned by an "economics of slavery" as they worked the agricultural rows, searing furnaces, rolling levees, bustling roundhouses, and piney-woods logging camps of America. A sense of "production" and "modes of production" that foregrounds such Afro-American labor seems an appropriate inscription of the material.

THE MATRIX AS BLUES

The guiding presupposition of the chapters that follow is that Afro-American culture is a complex, reflexive enterprise which finds its proper figuration in blues conceived as a matrix. A matrix is a womb, a network, a fossil-bearing rock, a rocky trace of a gemstone's removal, a principal metal in an alloy, a mat or plate for reproducing print or phonograph records. The matrix is a point of ceaseless input and output, a web of intersecting, crisscrossing impulses always in productive transit. Afro-American blues constitute such a vibrant network. They are what Jacques Derrida might describe as the "always already" of Afro-American culture.[9] They are the multiplex, enabling *script* in which Afro-American cultural discourse is inscribed.

First arranged, scored, and published for commercial distribution early in the twentieth century when Hart Wand, Arthur "Baby" Seals, and W. C. Handy[1] released their first compositions, the blues defy narrow definition. For they exist, not as a function of formal inscription, but as a forceful condition of Afro-American inscription itself. They were for Handy a "found" folk signifier, awakening him from (perhaps) a dream of American form in Tutwiler, Mississippi, in 1903.[2] At a railroad juncture deep in the southern night, Handy dozed restlessly as he awaited the arrival of a much-delayed train. A guitar's bottleneck resonance suddenly jolted him to consciousness, as a lean, loose-jointed, shabbily clad black man sang:

Goin' where the Southern cross the Dog.
Goin' where the Southern cross the Dog.
Goin' where the Southern cross the Dog.

This haunting invocation of railroad crossings in bottleneck tones left Handy stupified and inspired. In 1914, he published his own Yellow Dog Blues.

But the autobiographical account of the man who has been called the "Father of the Blues" offers only a simplistic detailing of *a progress*, describing, as it were, the elevation of a "primitive" folk ditty to the status of "art" in America. Handy's rendering leaves unexamined, therefore, myriad corri-

8. African American writer (1871–1938), best known for his fictive autobiography (published anonymously in 1912).

9. In *Of Grammatology*, Derrida defines a problematic in which *writing*, conceived as an iterable *differe(a)nce,* is held to be *always already* instituted (or, in motion) when a traditionally designated *Man* begins to speak. Hence, *script* is anterior to speech, and absence and *differe(a)nce* displace presence and identity (conceived as "Intention") in philosophical discourse [Baker's note].

1. In 1912, within a few months of each other, Wand (a white band leader), Seals (a black vaudeville performer), and Handy (a black composer) published the first transcriptions of blues songs.

2. The story appears in W. C. Handy, *Father of the Blues*, ed. Arna Bontemps (New York: Macmillan Co., 1941), p. 78. Other defining sources of blues include Paul Oliver, *The Story of the Blues* (London: Chilton, 1969); Samuel B. Charters, *The Country Blues* (New York: Rinehart, 1959); Giles Oakley, *The Devil's Music: A History of the Country Blues* (New York: Harcourt Brace Jovanovich, 1976); Amiri Baraka, *Blues People: Negro Music in White America* (New York: William E. Morrow, 1963); Albert Murray, *Stomping the Blues* (New York: McGraw-Hill Book Co., 1976); and William Ferris, *Blues from the Delta* (New York: Anchor Books, 1979) [Baker's note].

dors, mainroads, and way-stations of an extraordinary and elusive Afro-American cultural phenomenon.

DEFINING BLUES

The task of adequately describing the blues is equivalent to the labor of describing a world class athlete's awesome gymnastics. Adequate appreciation demands comprehensive attention. An investigator has to *be* there, to follow a course recommended by one of the African writer Wole Soyinka's[3] ironic narrators to a London landlord: "See for yourself."

The elaborations of the blues may begin in an austere self-accusation; "Now this trouble I'm having, I brought it all on myself." But the accusation seamlessly fades into humorous acknowledgment of duplicity's always duplicitous triumph: "You know the woman that I love, I stoled her from my best friend, / But you know that fool done got lucky and stole her back again." Simple provisos for the troubled mind are commonplace, and drear exactions of crushing manual labor are objects of wry, *in situ* commentary. Numinous invocation punctuates a guitar's resonant back beat with: "Lawd, Lawd, Lawd . . . have mercy on me / Please send me someone, to end this misery." Existential declarations of lack combine with lustily macabre prophecies of the subject's demise. If a "matchbox" will hold his clothes, surely the roadside of much-traveled highways will be his memorial plot: "You can bury my body down by the highway side / So my old devil spirit can catch a Greyhound bus and ride." Conative formulations of a brighter future (sun shining in the back door some day, wind rising to blow the blues away) join with a slow-moving *askesis*[4] of present, amorous imprisonment: "You leavin' now, baby, but you hangin' crepe on my door," or "She got a mortgage on my body, and a lien on my soul." Self-deprecating confession and slack-strumming growls of violent solutions combine: "My lead mule's cripple, you know my off mule's blind / You know I can't drive nobody / Bring me a loaded .39 (I'm go'n pop him, pop that mule!)." The wish for a river of whiskey where if a man were a "divin' duck" he would submerge himself and never "come up" is a function of a world in which "when you lose yo' eyesight, yo' best friend's gone / Sometimes yo' own dear people don't want to fool with you long."

Like a streamlined athlete's awesomely dazzling explosions of prowess, the blues song erupts, creating a veritable playful festival of meaning. Rather than a rigidly personalized form, the blues offer a phylogenetic[5] recapitulation—a nonlinear, freely associative, nonsequential meditation—of species experience. What emerges is not a filled subject, but an anonymous (nameless) voice issuing from the black (w)hole.[6] The blues singer's signatory coda is always *atopic*, placeless: "If anybody ask you who sang this song / Tell 'em

3. Nobel Prize–winning Nigerian writer (b. 1934). The quotation is from his poem "Telephone Conversation."
4. Training, asceticism (Greek).
5. Reflecting its evolutionary history.
6. The description at this point is coextensive with the "decentering" of the subject mentioned at the outset of my introduction. What I wish to effect by noting a "subject" who is not *filled* is a displacement of the notion that knowledge, or "art," or "song," are manifestations of an ever more clearly defined individual consciousness of *Man*. In accord with Michel Foucault's explorations in his *Archaeology of Knowledge* (1969; New York: Harper and Row, 1972), I want to claim that blues is like a discourse that comprises the "already said" of Afro-America. Blues' governing statements and sites are thus vastly more interesting in the process of cultural investigation than either a history of ideas or a history of individual, subjective consciousness vis-à-vis blues. When I move to the "X" of the trace and the body as host, I am invoking Mark Taylor's formulations in a suggestive deconstructive essay toward radical christology called "The Text as Victim," in *Deconstruction and Theology* (New York: Crossroad, 1982), pp. 58–78 [Baker's note]. On the French philosopher and historian FOUCAULT (1926–1987), see above.

X done been here and gone." The "signature" is a space already "X"(ed), a trace of the already "gone"—a fissure rejoined. Nevertheless, the "you" (audience) addressed is always free to invoke the X(ed) spot in the body's absence. For the signature comprises a scripted authentication of "your" feelings. Its mark is an invitation to energizing intersubjectivity. Its implied (in)junction reads: Here is my body meant for (a phylogenetically conceived) you.

The blues are a synthesis (albeit one always synthesizing rather than one already hypostatized). Combining work songs, group seculars, field hollers, sacred harmonies, proverbial wisdom, folk philosophy, political commentary, ribald humor, elegiac lament, and much more, they constitute an amalgam that seems always to have been in motion in America—always becoming, shaping, transforming, displacing the peculiar experiences of Africans in the New World.

BLUES AS CODE AND FORCE

One way of describing the blues is to claim their amalgam as a code radically conditioning Afro-America's cultural signifying. Such a description implies a prospect in which any aspect of the blues—a guitar's growling vamp or a stanza's sardonic boast of heroically back-breaking labor—"stands," in Umberto Eco's words, "for something else" in virtue of a systematic set of conventional procedures.[7] The materiality of any blues manifestation, such as a guitar's walking bass or a French harp's[8] "whoop" of motion seen, is, one might say, enciphered in ways that enable the material to escape into a named or coded, blues signification. The material, thus, slips into irreversible difference. And as phenomena named and set in meaningful relation by a blues code, both the harmonica's whoop and the guitar's bass can recapitulate vast dimensions of experience. For such discrete blues instances are always intertextually related by the blues code as a whole. Moreover, they are involved in the code's manifold interconnections with other codes of Afro-American culture.

A further characterization of blues suggests that they are equivalent to Hegelian "force."[9] In the *Phenomenology*, Hegel speaks of a flux in which there is "only *difference* as a *universal* difference, or as a difference into which the many antitheses have been resolved. This difference, as a *universal* difference, is consequently the *simple element in the play of Force itself* and what is true in it. It is the *law of Force*" (p. 90). Force is thus defined as a relational matrix where *difference* is the law. Finally the blues, employed as an image for the investigation of culture, represents a *force* not unlike electricity. Hegel writes:

> Of course, given positive electricity, negative too is given *in principle*; for the positive is, only as related to a negative, or, the positive is *in its*

7. The definition of "code" is drawn from *A Theory of Semiotics* (Bloomington: Indiana University Press, 1976). All references to Eco refer to this work and are hereafter marked by page numbers in parentheses [Baker's note]. Eco (b. 1932), Italian literary critic and novelist.

8. Harmonica.

9. *The Phenomenology of Spirit*, trans. A. V. Miller (New York: Oxford University Press, 1977). While it is true that the material dimensions of the dialectic are of primary importance to my current study, it is also true that the locus classicus of the dialectic, in and for itself, is the *Phenomenology*. Marx may well have stood Hegel on his feet through a materialist inversion of the *Phenomenology*, but subsequent generations have always looked at that uprighted figure—Hegel himself—as an authentic host [Baker's note]. On the German social, political, and economic theorist KARL MARX (1818–1883), see above.

> *own self* the difference from itself; and similarly with the negative. But that electricity as such should divide itself in this way is not in itself a necessity. Electricity, as *simple Force*, is indifferent to its law—to be positive and negative; and if we call the former its Notion but the latter its being then its Notion is indifferent to its being. It merely *has* this property, which just means that this property is not *in itself* necessary to it . . . It is only with law as law that we are to compare its *Notions* as Notion, or its necessity. But in all these forms, necessity has shown itself to be only an empty word. [p. 93]

Metaphorically extending Hegel's formulation vis-à-vis electricity, one might say that a traditional property of cultural study may well be the kind of dichotomy inscribed in terms like "culture" and "practical reason." But even if such dichotomies are raised to the status of law, they never constitute the necessity or "determinant instances" of cultural study and explanation conceived in terms of *force*—envisioned, that is, in the analytic notion of a blues matrix as force. The blues, therefore, comprise a mediational site where familiar antinomies are resolved (or dissolved) in the office of adequate cultural understanding.

BLUES TRANSLATION AT THE JUNCTION

To suggest a trope for the blues as a forceful matrix in cultural understanding is to summon an image of the black blues singer at the railway junction lustily transforming experiences of a durative (unceasingly oppressive) landscape into the energies of rhythmic song. The railway juncture is marked by transience. Its inhabitants are always travelers—a multifarious assembly in transit. The "X" of crossing roadbeds signals the multidirectionality of the juncture and is simply a single instance in a boundless network that redoubles and circles, makes sidings and ladders, forms Y's and branches over the vastness of hundreds of thousands of American miles. Polymorphous and multidirectional, scene of arrivals and departures, place betwixt and between (ever *entre les deux*), the juncture is the way-station of the blues.

The singer and his production are always at this intersection, this crossing, codifying force, providing resonance for experience's multiplicities. Singer and song never arrest transience—fix it in "transcendent form." Instead they provide expressive equivalence for the juncture's ceaseless flux. Hence, they may be conceived as translators.[1]

Like translators of written texts, blues and its sundry performers offer interpretations of the experiencing of experience. To experience the juncture's ever-changing scenes, like successive readings of ever-varying texts by conventional translators, is to produce vibrantly polyvalent interpretations encoded as blues. The singer's product, like the railway juncture itself (or a

1. Having heard John Felstiner in a session at the 1982 Modern Language Association Convention present a masterful paper defining "translation" as a process of preserving "something of value" by keeping it in motion, I decided that the blues were apt translators of experience. Felstiner, it seemed to me, sought to demonstrate that *translation* was a process equivalent to gift-giving in Mauss's classic definition of that activity. The value of the gift of translation is never fixed because, say, the poem, is always in a transliterational motion, moving from one alphabet to another, always renewing and being *re-newed* in the process. Translation forestalls fixity. It calls attention always to the *translated's* excess—to its complex multivalence [Baker's note]. Marcel Mauss (1872–1950), French anthropologist; in *The Gift* (1925), he outlines gift-exchange as a continual exchange of goods kept in motion by the obligation created to give something in return after one receives a gift.

successful translator's original), constitutes a lively scene, a robust matrix, where endless antinomies are mediated and understanding and explanation find conditions of possibility.

The durative—transliterated as lyrical statements of injustice, despair, loss, absence, denial, and so forth—is complemented in blues performance by an instrumental energy (guitar, harmonica, fiddle, gut-bucket bass, molasses jug, washboard) that employs locomotive rhythms, train bells, and whistles as onomatopoeic references.[2] In *A Theory of Semiotics*, Eco writes:

> Music presents, on the one hand, the problem of a semiotic system without a semantic level (or a content plane): on the other hand, however, there are musical "signs" (or syntagms)[3] with an explicit denotative value (trumpet signals in the army) and there are syntagms or entire "texts" possessing pre-culturalized connotative value ("pastoral" or "thrilling" music, etc.). [p. 111]

The absence of a content plane noted by Eco implies what is commonly referred to as the "abstractness" of instrumental music. The "musical sign," on the other hand, suggests cultural signals that function onomatopoeically by calling to mind "natural" sounds or sounds "naturally" associated with common human situations. Surely, though, it would be a mistake to claim that onomatopoeia is in any sense "natural," for different cultures encode even the "same" natural sounds in varying ways. (A rooster onomatopoeically sounded in Puerto Rican Spanish is phonically unrecognizable in United States English, as a classic Puerto Rican short story[4] makes hilariously clear.)

If onomatopoeia is taken as cultural mimesis, however, it is possible to apply the semiotician's observations to blues by pointing out that the dominant blues syntagm in America is an instrumental imitation of *train-wheels-over-track-junctures*. This sound is the "sign," as it were, of the blues, and it combines an intriguing melange of phonics: rattling gondolas,[5] clattering flatbeds, quilling whistles, clanging bells, rumbling boxcars, and other railroad sounds. A blues text may thus announce itself by the onomatopoeia of the train's whistle sounded on the indrawn breath of a harmonica or a train's bell tinkled on the high keys of an upright piano. The blues stanzas may then roll through an extended meditative repertoire with a steady train-wheels-over-track-junctures guitar back beat as a traditional, syntagmatic complement. If desire and absence are driving conditions of blues performance, the amelioration of such conditions is implied by the onomatopoeic *training* of blues voice and instrument. Only a *trained* voice can sing the blues.[6]

At the junctures, the intersections of experience where roads cross and diverge, the blues singer and his performance serve as codifiers, absorbing and transforming discontinuous experience into formal expressive instances that bear only the trace of origins, refusing to be pinned down to any final, dualistic significance. Even as they speak of paralyzing absence and ineradicable desire, their instrumental rhythms suggest change, movement, action, continuance, unlimited and unending possibility. Like signification itself,

2. Words that refer to an object by imitating the sounds that object makes.
3. Meaningful arrangements or combinations of smaller expressive units.
4. "Peyo Mercé: English Teacher," by Abelardo Díaz Altaro (1917–1999).
5. Railroad cars with fixed sides and no top.
6. One of the most inspiring and intriguing descriptions of the relationship between blues voice and the sounds of the railroad is Albert Murray's lyrical exposition in *Stomping the Blues* [Baker's note].

blues are always nomadically wandering. Like the freight-hopping hobo, they are ever on the move, ceaselessly summing novel experience.

ANTINOMIES AND BLUES MEDIATION

The blues performance is further suggestive if economic conditions of Afro-American existence are brought to mind. Standing at the juncture, or railhead, the singer draws into his repertoire hollers, cries, whoops, and moans of black men and women working in fields without recompense. The performance can be cryptically conceived, therefore, in terms suggested by the bluesman Booker White, who said, "The foundation of the blues is working behind a mule way back in slavery time."[7] As a force, the blues matrix defines itself as a network mediating poverty and abundance in much the same manner that it reconciles durative and kinetic. Many instances of the blues performance contain lyrical inscriptions of both lack and commercial possibility. The performance that sings of abysmal poverty and deprivation may be recompensed by sumptuous food and stimulating beverage at a country picnic, amorous favors from an attentive listener, enhanced Afro-American communality, or Yankee dollars from representatives of record companies traveling the South in search of blues as commodifiable entertainment. The performance, therefore, mediates one of the most prevalent of all antinomies in cultural investigation—creativity and commerce.

As driving force, the blues matrix thus avoids simple dualities. It perpetually achieves its effects as a fluid and multivalent network. It is only when "understanding"—the analytical work of a translator who translates the infinite changes of the blues—converges with such blues "force," however, that adequate explanatory perception (and half-creation) occurs. The matrix effectively functions toward cultural understanding, that is, only when an investigator brings an inventive attention to bear.

THE INVESTIGATOR, RELATIVITY, AND BLUES EFFECT

The blues matrix is a "cultural invention": a "negative symbol" that generates (or obliges one to invent) its own referents.[8] As an inventive trope, this matrix provides for my following chapters the type of image or model that is always present in accounts of culture and cultural products. If the analyses that I provide are successful, the blues matrix will have *taken effect* (and *affect*) through me.

To "take effect," of course, is not identical with to "come into existence" or to "demonstrate serviceability for the first time." Because what I have defined as a blues matrix is so demonstrably anterior to any single instance of its cultural-explanatory employment, my predecessors as effectors are obviously legion. "Take effect," therefore, does not signify discovery in the traditional sense of that word. Rather, it signals the tropological nature[9] of my uses of an already extant matrix.

Ordinarily, accounts of art, literature, and culture fail to acknowledge their

7. Quoted in Oakley *The Devil's Music*, p. 7 [Baker's note]. Booker T. Washington (also called "Bukka") White (1906–1971), blues guitarist and harmonica player.

8. I have appropriated the term "negative symbol" from Roy Wagner's *The Invention of Culture* (Chicago: University of Chicago Press, 1975), p. xvi [Baker's note].

9. Figurative extension.

governing theories; further, they invariably conceal the *inventive* character of such theories. Nevertheless, all accounts of art, expressive culture, or culture in general are indisputably functions of their creators' tropological energies. When such creators talk of "art," for example, they are never dealing with existential givens. Rather, they are summoning objects, processes, or events defined by a model that they have created (by and for themselves) as a picture of art. Such models, or tropes, are continually invoked to constitute and explain phenomena inaccessible to the senses. Any single model, or any complementary set of inventive tropes, therefore, will offer only a selective account of experience—a partial reading, as it were, of the world. While the single account temporarily reduces chaos to ordered plan, all such accounts are eternally troubled by "remainders."

Where literary art is concerned, for example, a single, ordering, investigative model or trope will necessarily exclude phenomena that an alternative model or trope privileges as a definitive artistic instance. Recognizing the determinacy of "invention" in cultural explanation entails the acknowledgement of what might be called a *normative relativity*. To acknowledge relativity in our post-Heisenbergian universe[1] is, of course, far from original. Neither, however, is it an occasion for the skeptics or the conservatives to heroically assume the critical stage.

The assumption of normative relativity, far from being a call to abandonment or retrenchment in the critical arena, constitutes an invitation to speculative explorations that are aware both of their own partiality and their heuristic transitions from suggestive (sometimes dramatic) images to inscribed concepts. The openness implied by relativity enables, say, the literary critic to *re-cognize* his endeavors, presupposing from the outset that such labors are not directed toward independent, observable, empirical phenomena but rather toward processes, objects, and events that he or she half-creates (and privileges as "art") through his or her own speculative, inventive energies and interests.

One axiological[2] extrapolation from these observations on invention and relativity is that no object, process, or single element possesses *intrinsic aesthetic value*. The "art object" as well as its value are selective *constructions* of the critic's tropes and models. A radicalizing uncertainty may thus be said to mark cultural explanation. This uncertainty is similar in kind to the always selective endeavors of, say, the particle physicist.[3]

The physicist is always compelled to choose between velocity and position.[4] Similarly, an investigator of Afro-American expressive culture is cease-

1. That is, a universe governed by the "uncertainty principle" articulated in 1927 by Werner Heisenberg (1901–1976), a Nobel Prize–winning German physicist: it states that one cannot precisely determine both the position and momentum of atomic particles at any one moment. The exact calculations of classical mechanics are thus replaced with statements of probability in quantum mechanics.

2. Pertaining to the branch of philosophy dealing with values.

3. My references to a "post-Heisenbergian universe" and to the "particle physicist" were made possible by a joyful reading of Gary Zukav's *The Dancing Wu Li Masters: An Overview of the New Physics* (New York: William E. Morrow, 1979) [Baker's note].

4. Zukav, ibid., writes: "According to the uncertainty principle, we cannot measure accurately, at the same time, both the position *and* the momentum of a moving particle. The more precisely we determine one of these properties, the less we know about the other. If we precisely determine the position of the particle, then, strange as it sounds, there is *nothing* that we can know about its momentum. If we precisely determine the momentum of the particle, there is no way to determine its position" (p. 111). Briefly, if we bring to bear enough energy actually to "see" the imagined "particle," that energy has always already *moved*

lessly compelled to forgo manifold variables in order to apply intensive energy to a selected array.

Continuing the metaphor, one might say that if the investigator's efforts are sufficiently charged with blues energy,[5] he is almost certain to remodel elements and events appearing in traditional, Anglo-American space-time in ways that make them "jump" several rings toward blackness and the vernacular. The blues-oriented observer (the *trained* critic) necessarily "heats up" the observational space by his or her very presence.[6]

An inventive, tropological, investigative model such as that proposed by *Blues, Ideology, and Afro-American Literature* entails not only awareness of the metaphorical nature of the blues matrix, but also a willingness on my own part to do more than merely hear, read, or see the blues. I must also play (with and on) them. Since the explanatory possibilities of a blues matrix—like analytical possibilities of a delimited set of forces in unified field theory—are hypothetically unbounded, the blues challenge investigative *understanding* to an unlimited play.

BLUES AND VERNACULAR EXPRESSION IN AMERICA

The blues should be privileged in the study of American culture to precisely the extent that inventive understanding successfully converges with blues force to yield accounts that persuasively and playfully refigure expressive geographies in the United States. My own ludic uses of the blues are various, and each figuration implies the valorization of vernacular facets of American culture. The Afro-American writer James Alan McPherson is, I think, the commentator who most brilliantly and encouragingly coalesces blues, vernacular, and cultural geographies of the United States in his introduction to *Railroad: Trains and Train People in American Culture*.[7]

Having described a fiduciary reaction to the steam locomotive by nineteenth-century financiers and an adverse artistic response by such traditional American writers as Melville, Hawthorne, and Thoreau,[8] McPherson details the reaction of another sector of the United States population to the railroad:

> To a third group of people, those not bound by the assumptions of either business or classical traditions in art, the shrill whistle might have spoken of new possibilities. These were the backwoodsmen and Africans and recent immigrants—the people who comprised the vernacular level of American society. To them the machine might have been loud and frightening, but its whistle and its wheels promised movement. And since a commitment to both freedom and movement was the basic prom-

the particle from its *position* (which is one of the aspects of its existence that one attempts to *determine*) when we take our measurement. Indeterminacy thus becomes normative [Baker's note].

5. The "blues force" is my translational equivalent in investigative "energy" for the investigative energy delineated by Heisenberg's formulations [Baker's note].

6. Eco (*A Theory of Semiotics*, p. 29) employs the metaphor of "ecological variation" in his discussion of the semiotic investigations of culture to describe observer effect in the mapping of experience [Baker's note].

7. New York: Random House, 1976. All citations refer to this edition and are hereafter marked by page numbers in parentheses [Baker's note]. McPherson (b. 1943), novelist and short story writer.

8. All canonical authors of mid-nineteenth-century American literature: Herman Melville (1819–1891), Nathaniel Hawthorne (1804–1864), and Henry David Thoreau (1817–1862).

ise of democracy, it was probable that such people would view the locomotive as a challenge to the integrative powers of their imaginations. [p. 6]

Afro-Americans—at the bottom even of the vernacular ladder in America—responded to the railroad as a "meaningful symbol offering both economic progress and the possibility of aesthetic expression" (p. 9). This possibility came from the locomotive's drive and thrust, its promise of unrestrained mobility and unlimited freedom. The blues musician at the crossing, as I have already suggested, became an expert at reproducing or translating these locomotive energies. With the birth of the blues, the vernacular realm of American culture acquired a music that had "wide appeal because it expressed a toughness of spirit and resilience, a willingness to transcend difficulties which was strikingly familiar to those whites who remembered their own history" (p. 16). The signal expressive achievement of blues, then, lay in their translation of technological innovativeness, unsettling demographic fluidity, and boundless frontier energy into expression which attracted avid interest from the American masses. By the 1920s, American financiers had become aware of commercial possibilities not only of railroads but also of black music deriving from them.

A "race record" market flourished during the twenties. Major companies issued blues releases under labels such as Columbia, Vocalion, Okeh, Gennett, and Victor. Sometimes as many as ten blues releases appeared in a single week; their sales (aided by radio's dissemination of the music) climbed to hundreds of thousands. The onset of the Great Depression ended this phenomenal boom. During their heyday, however, the blues unequivocally signified a ludic predominance of the vernacular with that sassy, growling, moaning, whooping confidence that marks their finest performances.

McPherson's assessment seems fully justified. It serves, in fact, as a suggestive play in the overall project of refiguring American expressive geographies. Resonantly complementing the insights of such astute commentators as Albert Murray, Paul Oliver, Samuel Charters, Amiri Baraka, and others, McPherson's judgments highlight the value of a blues matrix for cultural analysis in the United States.

In harmony with other brilliant commentators on the blues already noted, Ralph Ellison selects the railroad way-station (the "Chehaw Station") as his topos for the American "little man."[9] In "The Little Man at the Chehaw Station,"[1] he autobiographically details his own confirmation of his Tuskegee music teacher's observation that in the United States

> You must *always* play your best, even if it's only in the waiting room at Chehaw Station, because in this country there'll always be a little man hidden behind the stove . . . and he'll know the *music*, and the *tradition*, and the standards of *musicianship* required for whatever you set out to perform. [p. 25]

When Hazel Harrison made this statement to the young Ellison, he felt that she was joking. But as he matured and moved through a diversity of

9. The Chehaw Station is a whistle-stop near Tuskegee, Alabama. It was a feature of the landscape of Tuskegee Institute, where Ellison studied music (and much else) [Baker's note].

1. *American Scholar* 47 (1978): 24–48. All citations refer to this version and are hereafter marked by page numbers in parentheses [Baker's note].

American scenes, Ellison realized that the inhabitants of the "drab, utilitarian structure" of the American vernacular do far more than respond in expressive ways to "blues-echoing, train-whistle rhapsodies blared by fast express trains as they thundered past" the junction. At the vernacular level, according to Ellison, people possess a "cultivated taste" that asserts its "authority out of obscurity" (p. 26). The "little man" finally comes to represent, therefore, "that unknown quality which renders the American audience far more than a receptive instrument that may be dominated through a skillful exercise of the sheerly 'rhetorical' elements—the flash and filigree—of the artist's craft" (p. 26).

From Ellison's opening gambit and wonderfully illustrative succeeding examples, I infer that the vernacular (in its expressive adequacy and adept critical facility) always *absorbs* "classical" elements of American life and art. Indeed, Ellison seems to imply that expressive performers in America who ignore the judgments of the vernacular are destined to failure.

Although his injunctions are intended principally to advocate a traditional "melting pot" ideal in American "high art," Ellison's observations ultimately valorize a comprehensive, vernacular expressiveness in America. Though he seldom loses sight of the possibilities of a classically "transcendent" American high art, he derives his most forceful examples from the vernacular: Blues seem implicitly to comprise the *All* of American culture.

BLUES MOMENTS IN AFRO-AMERICAN EXPRESSION

In the chapters that follow, I attempt to provide suggestive accounts of moments in Afro-American discourse when personae, protagonists, autobiographical narrators, or literary critics successfully negotiate an obdurate "economics of slavery" and achieve a resonant, improvisational, expressive dignity. Such moments and successful analyses of them provide cogent examples of the blues matrix at work.

The expressive instances that I have in mind occur in passages such as the conclusion of the *Narrative of the Life of Frederick Douglass*.[2] Standing at a Nantucket convention, riffing (in the "break" suddenly confronting him) on the *personal* troubles he has seen and successfully negotiated in a "prisonhouse of American bondage," Douglass achieves a profoundly dignified blues voice. Zora Neale Hurston's[3] protagonist Janie in the novel *Their Eyes Were Watching God*—as she lyrically and idiomatically relates a tale of personal suffering and triumph that begins in the sexual exploitations of slavery—is a blues artist par excellence. Her wisdom might well be joined to that of Amiri Baraka's Walker Vessels[4] (a "locomotive container" of blues?), whose chameleon code-switching from academic philosophy to blues insight makes him a veritable incarnation of the absorptively vernacular. The narrator of Richard Wright's[5] *Black Boy* inscribes a black blues life's lean desire (as I shall demonstrate in chapter 3) and suggests yet a further instance of the blues matrix's expressive energies. Ellison's invisible man and Baraka's narrator in *The System of*

2. The 1845 autobiography of the African American antislavery activist and writer (1818–1895).
3. African American novelist and anthropologist (1891–1960; see above); *Their Eyes Were Watching God* was published in 1937.
4. A character in Baraka's play *The Slave* (1962).
5. African American novelist (1908–1960); *Black Boy*, an autobiography, was published in 1945.

Dante's Hell[6] (whose blues book produces dance) provide additional examples. Finally, Toni Morrison's[7] Milkman Dead in *Song of Solomon* discovers through "Sugarman's" song that an awesomely expressive blues response may well consist of improvisational and serendipitous surrender to the air: "As fleet and bright as a lodestar he wheeled toward Guitar and it did not matter which one of them would give up his ghost in the killing arms of his brother. For now he knew what Shalimar knew: If you surrendered to the air, you could *ride* it."[8]

Such blues moments are but random instances of the blues matrix at work in Afro-American cultural expression. In my study as a whole, I attempt persuasively to demonstrate that a blues matrix (as a vernacular trope for American cultural explanation in general) possesses enormous force for the study of literature, criticism, and culture. I know that I have appropriated the vastness of the vernacular in the United States to a single matrix. But I trust that my necessary selectivity will be interpreted, not as a sign of myopic exclusiveness, but as an invitation to inventive play. The success of my efforts would be effectively signaled in the following chapters, I think, by the transformation of my "I" into a juncture where readers could freely improvise their own distinctive tropes for cultural explanation. A closing that in fact opened on such inventive possibilities (like the close of these introductory remarks) would be appropriately marked by the crossing sign's inviting "X."

1984

6. A 1965 novel. The novel *Invisible Man* (1952) is Ellison's best-known work.
7. Nobel Prize–winning African American novelist (b. 1931).
8. *Song of Solomon* (New York: Alfred A. Knopf, 1977), p. 337 [Baker's note].

TERRY EAGLETON
b. 1943

Satirically paraphrasing MATTHEW ARNOLD's influential view of the ennobling power of literature and culture, Terry Eagleton writes: "If the masses are not thrown a few novels, they may react by throwing up a few barricades." In *Culture and Anarchy* (1869), Arnold claims that art, literature, and culture confer "greatness and a noble spirit" on those who appreciate them, and furthermore are the means to avoid anarchy. In "The Rise of English" (1983), Eagleton argues that literature concerns not simply beauty and spiritual uplift, but the social control of the middle and working classes. Answering a perennial question in literary theory about the role of literature in society, Eagleton bluntly asserts that the discipline of literature, like formal religion, is deeply involved in the reproduction of the dominant social order.

A student of the Marxist literary and cultural critic RAYMOND WILLIAMS, Eagleton has been the foremost Marxist commentator on literary theory in England since the 1980s, as well as a literary journalist, novelist, and playwright. Born in a working-class community in Salford, England, he attended Cambridge University on a scholarship, receiving his B.A. in 1964 and his Ph.D. in 1968. He taught at Cambridge for a year, but since 1969 he has held various appointments at Oxford University, becoming Thomas Warton Professor of English and Literature in 1992. During the politically vibrant late 1960s, Eagleton was active in the Catholic Left—among other things, he helped found a journal, *Slant*—and he published three books before he was thirty. It was not until the mid-1970s, however, that he established himself as a leading expositor of Marxism within the emerging field of contemporary literary theory, most notably with *Criticism and Ideology: A Study in Marxist Literary Theory* (1976). Extending LOUIS ALTHUSSER's theory of ideology to literature, it propounds a Marxist theory of the text. Against traditional, aestheticist views that literature primarily produces beauty and pleasure, as well as the conventional Marxist view, espoused by LEON TROTSKY, that texts directly reflect social reality, Eagleton argues that texts actively produce ideology rather than merely reflect it.

While his later work frequently returns to questions of aesthetics and ideology, Eagleton subsequently turned away from the pursuit of an overarching theoretical model, or what the American sociologist C. Wright Mills (1916–1962) termed "Grand Theory." As he remarked in a 1990 interview, "I think that back in the seventies we used to suffer from a certain fetishism of method; we used to think that we have to get a certain kind of systematic method right, and this would be *the* way of proceeding. I think some of my early work, certainly *Criticism and Ideology*, would fall within that general approach." Rather than dispensing with Marxism, however, he distinguishes between theoretical methods and political goals: "[A] Marxist has to define certain urgent political goals and allow, as it were, those to determine questions of method rather than the other way around." In eschewing large-scale theoretical models, Eagleton resembles the twentieth-century neopragmatists Richard Rorty, STANLEY FISH, AND STEVEN KNAPP AND WALTER BENN MICHAELS, who insist that method cannot be determined in advance but derives from practice. But whereas they argue that literary studies are politically ineffectual, Eagleton advocates a political focus.

Another element of Eagleton's turn from Grand Theory is his style, which is lively, witty, clear, and frequently opinionated, combining theory and literary journalism. Eagleton unabashedly states his opinions—often in audacious one-liners, such as "deconstruction is the death drive at the level of theory"—and injects humor into his writing. For instance, he concludes his collection of essays, *Against the Grain, Essays 1975–1985* (1986), with a comic song:

> Chaucer was a class traitor
> Shakespeare hated the mob
> Donne sold out a bit later
> Sidney was a nob.
>
> . . . .
>
> There are only three names
> To be plucked from this dismal set
> Milton Blake and Shelley
> Will smash the ruling class yet.

However whimsical, Eagleton's song memorably reinforces his argument for the class orientation of literature, valuing the socially revolutionary rather than the purely aesthetic.

In his *Function of Criticism: From the "Spectator" to Post-Structuralism* (1984), Eagleton declares that contemporary criticism has lost its social purpose and become marginalized through the technocratic fetishizing of Grand Theory. Drawing on the twentieth-century German philosopher JÜRGEN HABERMAS's concept of the public sphere, he notes that modern criticism arose in the eighteenth century in opposition to the absolutist state, and he calls for the renewed oppositional role of criticism in the public sphere. To that end, Eagleton became known as the foremost popularizer of contemporary literary theory in the 1980s. His *Literary Theory: An Introduction* (1983; 2d ed., 1996), from which "The Rise of English" is drawn, was an academic bestseller and probably the most influential introduction to contemporary theory for students and curious readers. It conducts a knowledgeable but fast-paced, readable, and pithy survey of reader-response and reception theory, structuralism, deconstruction, and psychoanalysis. Rather than presenting a dispassionate history, *Literary Theory* bluntly states Eagleton's preferences and value judgments. Finding fault with most contemporary theories for their lack of attention to politics, he praises Marxist and feminist criticism for their concern with the political effects of literature.

Accessible and polemical, "The Rise of English" illustrates Eagleton's trademark style. Developing some of the concerns of Raymond Williams's "Literature" (1977; see above), this survey of the discipline combines broad historical overview and ideological analysis. Eagleton sees English, which became an academic subject only in the late nineteenth century, as an outgrowth of nationalism as well as a replacement for religion as a crucial ideological apparatus. While lacking nuance, Eagleton's analysis succinctly answers a major theoretical question, proposing that literature has social significance not simply as an innocent, pleasurable entertainment but as a primary means of reinforcing the dominant social order.

In part because of his popularizations of theory, and in part because of the often sweeping, polemical nature of his arguments, Eagleton has occasionally been dismissed by specialist commentators on theory. His influence among theorists is much less pronounced than that of FREDRIC JAMESON, the most prominent U.S. Marxist critic. However, Eagleton has made theory accessible to students and nonspecialists, persistently reminding readers of its social role in the public sphere. He has provided a model for younger literary critics who self-consciously choose to write in a more journalistic mode, turning from the dense language and specialist focus of Grand Theory to address a larger public in discussing cultural issues. The tension in criticism between specialization and accessibility, which itself became a central theoretical issue in the 1990s, mirrors a perennial debate in literary studies—whether literature demonstrates special qualities available only to connoisseurs who have expert knowledge of the tradition, as articulated by the modernist T. S. ELIOT, or whether literature can reach the common reader, in what the Romantic poet WILLIAM WORDSWORTH calls "the real language of men."

BIBLIOGRAPHY

Eagleton has been prolific, writing more than twenty critical books, scores of pieces of literary journalism, several plays, and a novel. In this he follows the model of his teacher Raymond Williams, though he has focused primarily on literary criticism and theory rather than cultural and media studies. Eagleton's early books include *Shakespeare and Society: Critical Studies in Shakespearean Drama* (1967), *Exiles and Emigres: Studies in Modern Literature* (1970), and *The Body as Language: Outline of a "New Left" Theology* (1970). He also edited collections that reflect his involvement in the Catholic Left, including *Directions: Pointers for the Post-Conciliar Church* (1968) and, with Brian Wicker, *From Culture to Revolution: The "Slant" Symposium, 1967* (1968). In the 1970s and early 1980s he published three works of Marxist theory: *Marxism and Literary Criticism* (1976), a superb short survey of major Marxist critics and debates; the influential *Criticism and Ideology: A Study in Marxist Literary Theory* (1976); and *Walter Benjamin; or, Towards a Revolutionary Criticism* (1981), reassessing Benjamin as a model for Marxist criticism. He also published two works of literary criticism, *Myths of Power: A Marxist Study of the Brontës* (1975; 2d ed., 1988) and *The Rape of Clarissa: Writing, Sexuality, and Class Struggle in Samuel Richardson* (1982), which is notable for its engagement with feminism.

In the mid-1980s Eagleton published the popular overview *Literary Theory: An Introduction* (1983; 2d ed., 1996) and a short history, *The Function of Criticism: From the "Spectator" to Post-Structuralism* (1984), which is perhaps the best place to start reading his work. He also published a short critical introduction, *William Shakespeare* (1986); a collection of his essays, *Against the Grain: Essays, 1975–1985* (1986); and a fine edited collection assessing the influence of his teacher, *Raymond Williams:*

A Critical Reader (1989). In the 1990s, Eagleton published several critical histories, including *The Ideology of the Aesthetic* (1990), an engaging and ambitious account of aesthetic theory from David Hume to Theodor Adorno; the slim *Significance of Theory* (1990), which gathers two lectures and an interesting interview commenting on contemporary theory; *Ideology: An Introduction* (1991), an accessible tour of the development of the concept of ideology; and *The Illusions of Postmodernism* (1996), an attack on key tendencies of contemporary theory. Of Irish ancestry, Eagleton has also shown an interest in Irish culture, especially in *Heathcliff and the Great Hunger: Studies in Irish Culture* (1995) and *Crazy John and the Bishop and Other Essays on Irish Culture* (1998). He continued his lucid expositions of key theoretical ideas in two short volumes, *Marx* (1999) and *The Idea of Culture* (2000). Alongside his own books, he co-edited with Drew Milne a useful anthology, *Marxist Literary Theory: A Reader* (1996). His creative work includes the novel *Saints and Scholars* (1987); a script, *Wittgenstein: The Terry Eagleton Script, the Derek Jarman Film* (1993); and plays, *Saint Oscar and Other Plays* (1997). *The Eagleton Reader*, edited by Stephen Regan (1998), provides an excellent sampler spanning all of Eagleton's work.

Notable comments on Eagleton's views of English and theory include Elaine Showalter's "Critical Cross-Dressing: Male Feminists and the Woman of the Year," *Raritan* 3.2 (1983), which applauds his attention to feminism; Jonathan Culler's review of *Literary Theory*, in *Poetics Today* 5 (1984), which praises Eagleton's efficient history of theory but criticizes his simplistic sense of historical causality; Richard Aczel's "Eagleton and English," *New Left Review* 154 (1985), which usefully situates his work up to *The Function of Criticism*; Steven Helming's "Marxist Pleasure: Jameson and Eagleton," in *Essays in Postmodern Culture* (ed. Eyal Amiran and John Unsworth, 1993), which interestingly compares the two prominent Marxist critics; and R. Boffin's "Used Books," *Critical Quarterly* 37 (1995), which contests Eagleton's claim for "the centrality of literature" as an ideology, reasoning that "if literature was as central to the social order as Eagleton claims, the massive success of his own book [*Literary Theory*] should presage some extraordinary transformation of the social order." *The Eagleton Reader* contains the definitive bibliography of both Eagleton's writings and commentary on his work up to 1996.

From Literary Theory: An Introduction

From *Chapter 1. The Rise of English*

* * *

To speak of 'literature and ideology' as two separate phenomena which can be interrelated is, as I hope to have shown, in one sense quite unnecessary. Literature, in the meaning of the word we have inherited, *is* an ideology.[1] It has the most intimate relations to questions of social power. But if the reader is still unconvinced, the narrative of what happened to literature in the later nineteenth century might prove a little more persuasive.

If one were asked to provide a single explanation for the growth of English studies in the later nineteenth century, one could do worse than reply: 'the failure of religion'. By the mid-Victorian period, this traditionally reliable, immensely powerful ideological form was in deep trouble. It was no longer winning the hearts and minds of the masses, and under the twin impacts of

1. That is, a system of specific class beliefs, images, values, and practices that functions to reproduce the dominant social order.

scientific discovery and social change its previous unquestioned dominance was in danger of evaporating. This was particularly worrying for the Victorian ruling class, because religion is for all kinds of reasons an extremely effective form of ideological control. Like all successful ideologies, it works much less by explicit concepts or formulated doctrines than by image, symbol, habit, ritual and mythology. It is affective and experiential, entwining itself with the deepest unconscious roots of the human subject; and any social ideology which is unable to engage with such deep-seated a-rational fears and needs, as T. S. Eliot[2] knew, is unlikely to survive very long. Religion, moreover, is capable of operating at every social level: if there is a doctrinal inflection of it for the intellectual elite, there is also a pietistic brand of it for the masses. It provides an excellent social 'cement', encompassing pious peasant, enlightened middle-class liberal and theological intellectual in a single organization. Its ideological power lies in its capacity to 'materialize' beliefs as practices: religion is the sharing of the chalice and the blessing of the harvest, not just abstract argument about consubstantiation or hyperdulia.[3] Its ultimate truths, like those mediated by the literary symbol, are conveniently closed to rational demonstration, and thus absolute in their claims. Finally religion, at least in its Victorian forms, is a *pacifying* influence, fostering meekness, self-sacrifice and the contemplative inner life. It is no wonder that the Victorian ruling class looked on the threatened dissolution of this ideological discourse with something less than equanimity.

Fortunately, however, another remarkably similar discourse lay to hand: English literature. George Gordon,[4] early Professor of English Literature at Oxford, commented in his inaugural lecture that 'England is sick, and . . . English literature must save it. The Churches (as I understand) having failed, and social remedies being slow, English literature has now a triple function: still, I suppose, to delight and instruct us, but also, and above all, to save our souls and heal the State.'[5] Gordon's words were spoken in our own century, but they find a resonance everywhere in Victorian England. It is a striking thought that had it not been for this dramatic crisis in mid-nineteenth-century ideology, we might not today have such a plentiful supply of Jane Austen casebooks and bluffer's guides to Pound.[6] As religion progressively ceases to provide the social 'cement', affective values and basic mythologies by which a socially turbulent class-society can be welded together, 'English' is constructed as a subject to carry this ideological burden from the Victorian period onwards. The key figure here is Matthew Arnold,[7] always preternaturally sensitive to the needs of his social class, and engagingly candid about being so. The urgent social need, as Arnold recognizes, is to 'Hellenize' or cultivate the philistine middle class, who have proved unable to underpin

2. American-born English poet, critic, and dramatist (1888–1965; see above).
3. The particular veneration of the Virgin Mary by Roman Catholics "Consubstantiation": the Lutheran doctrine that the body and blood of Christ coexist with the elements of bread and wine during Holy Communion (a point of argument with the Roman Catholic belief in transubstantiation, the literal transformation of the consecrated bread and wine into the body and blood of Christ).
4. Oxford professor and critic (1881–1942).
5. Quoted by Chris Baldick, *The Social Mission of English Criticism, 1848–1932* (Oxford, 1983), p. 105 [Eagleton's note]. "To delight and instruct" are the traditional functions of literature; see HORACE, *Ars Poetica* (ca. 10 B.C.E.), lines 343–44, above.
6. Ezra Pound (1885–1972), American poet, editor, and critic, notable for his difficulty and abstruse range of literary references. Austen (1775–1817), English novelist.
7. English critic, poet, and school inspector (1822–1888; see above), who greatly influenced modern views of literature. In *Culture and Anarchy* (1869; see above) he divided England into Barbarians (the aristocracy), Philistines (the materialist middle classes), and the Populace; he also opposed "Hellenism" to "Hebraism," favoring the former (and classical Greek culture generally).

their political and economic power with a suitably rich and subtle ideology. This can be done by transfusing into them something of the traditional style of the aristocracy, who as Arnold shrewdly perceives are ceasing to be the dominant class in England, but who have something of the ideological wherewithal to lend a hand to their middle-class masters. State-established schools, by linking the middle class to 'the best culture of their nation', will confer on them 'a greatness and a noble spirit, which the tone of these classes is not of itself at present adequate to impart'.[8]

The true beauty of this manoeuvre, however, lies in the effect it will have in controlling and incorporating the working class:

> It is of itself a serious calamity for a nation that its tone of feeling and grandeur of spirit should be lowered or dulled. But the calamity appears far more serious still when we consider that the middle classes, remaining as they are now, with their narrow, harsh, unintelligent, and unattractive spirit and culture, will almost certainly fail to mould or assimilate the masses below them, whose sympathies are at the present moment actually wider and more liberal than theirs. They arrive, these masses, eager to enter into possession of the world, to gain a more vivid sense of their own life and activity. In this their irrepressible development, their natural educators and initiators are those immediately above them, the middle classes. If these classes cannot win their sympathy or give them their direction, society is in danger of falling into anarchy.[9]

Arnold is refreshingly unhypocritical: there is no feeble pretence that the education of the working class is to be conducted chiefly for their own benefit, or that his concern with their spiritual condition is, in one of his own most cherished terms, in the least 'disinterested'. In the even more disarmingly candid words of a twentieth-century proponent of this view: 'Deny to working-class children any common share in the immaterial, and presently they will grow into the men who demand with menaces a communism of the material'.[1] If the masses are not thrown a few novels, they may react by throwing up a few barricades.

Literature was in several ways a suitable candidate for this ideological enterprise. As a liberal, 'humanizing' pursuit, it could provide a potent antidote to political bigotry and ideological extremism. Since literature, as we know, deals in universal human values rather than in such historical trivia as civil wars, the oppression of women or the dispossession of the English peasantry, it could serve to place in cosmic perspective the petty demands of working people for decent living conditions or greater control over their own lives, and might even with luck come to render them oblivious of such issues in their high-minded contemplation of eternal truths and beauties. English, as a Victorian handbook for English teachers put it, helps to 'promote sympathy and fellow feeling among all classes'; another Victorian writer speaks of literature as opening a 'serene and luminous region of truth where all may meet and expatiate in common', above 'the smoke and stir, the din and turmoil of man's lower life of care and business and debate'.[2] Literature

8. "The Popular Education of France," in *Democratic Education*, ed. R. H. Super (Ann Arbor, 1962), p. 22 [Eagleton's note].
9. Ibid., p. 26 [Eagleton's note].
1. George Sampson, *English for the English* (1921), quoted by Baldick, *The Social Mission of English Criticism*, p. 103 [Eagleton's note].
2. H. G. Robinson, "On the Use of English Classical Literature in the Work of Education," *Macmillan's Magazine* 11 (1860), quoted by Baldick, *The Social Mission of English Criticism*, p. 66 [Eagleton's note].

would rehearse the masses in the habits of pluralistic thought and feeling, persuading them to acknowledge that more than one viewpoint than theirs existed—namely, that of their masters. It would communicate to them the moral riches of bourgeois civilization, impress upon them a reverence for middle-class achievements, and, since reading is an essentially solitary, contemplative activity, curb in them any disruptive tendency to collective political action. It would give them a pride in their national language and literature: if scanty education and extensive hours of labour prevented them personally from producing a literary masterpiece, they could take pleasure in the thought that others of their own kind—English people—had done so. The people, according to a study of English literature written in 1891, 'need political culture, instruction, that is to say, in what pertains to their relation to the State, to their duties as citizens; and they need also to be impressed sentimentally by having the presentation in legend and history of heroic and patriotic examples brought vividly and attractively before them'.[3] All of this, moreover, could be achieved without the cost and labour of teaching them the Classics: English literature was written in their own language, and so was conveniently available to them.

Like religion, literature works primarily by emotion and experience, and so was admirably well-fitted to carry through the ideological task which religion left off. Indeed by our own time literature had become effectively identical with the opposite of analytical thought and conceptual enquiry: whereas scientists, philosophers and political theorists are saddled with these drably discursive pursuits, students of literature occupy the more prized territory of feeling and experience. Whose experience, and what kinds of feeling, is a different question. Literature from Arnold onwards is the enemy of 'ideological dogma', an attitude which might have come as a surprise to Dante, Milton and Pope;[4] the truth or falsity of beliefs such as that blacks are inferior to whites is less important than what it feels like to experience them. Arnold himself had beliefs, of course, though like everybody else he regarded his own beliefs as reasoned positions rather than ideological dogmas. Even so, it was not the business of literature to communicate such beliefs directly—to argue openly, for example, that private property is the bulwark of liberty. Instead, literature should convey *timeless* truths, thus distracting the masses from their immediate commitments, nurturing in them a spirit of tolerance and generosity, and so ensuring the survival of private property. Just as Arnold attempted in *Literature and Dogma* and *God and the Bible*[5] to dissolve away the embarrassingly doctrinal bits of Christianity into poetically suggestive sonorities, so the pill of middle-class ideology was to be sweetened by the sugar of literature.

There was another sense in which the 'experiential' nature of literature was ideologically convenient. For 'experience' is not only the homeland of ideology, the place where it takes root most effectively; it is also in its literary form a kind of vicarious self-fulfillment. If you do not have the money and leisure to visit the Far East, except perhaps as a soldier in the pay of British imperialism, then you can always 'experience' it at second hand by reading

3. J. C. Collins, *The Study of English Literature* (1891), quoted by Baldick, *The Social Mission of English Criticism*, pp. 64–65 [Eagleton's note].

4. All three major poets—the Italian DANTE ALIGHIERI (1265–1321) and the English John Milton (1608–1674) and ALEXANDER POPE (1688–1744)—held strong political views.

5. Published in 1873 and 1875, respectively.

Conrad or Kipling.[6] Indeed according to some literary theories this is even more real than strolling round Bangkok. The actually impoverished experience of the mass of people, an impoverishment bred by their social conditions, can be supplemented by literature: instead of working to change such conditions (which Arnold, to his credit, did more thoroughly than almost any of those who sought to inherit his mantle), you can vicariously fulfil someone's desire for a fuller life by handing them *Pride and Prejudice*.[7]

It is significant, then, that 'English' as an academic subject was first institutionalized not in the Universities, but in the Mechanics' Institutes, working men's colleges and extension lecturing circuits.[8] English was literally the poor man's Classics—a way of providing a cheapish 'liberal' education for those beyond the charmed circles of public school and Oxbridge.[9] From the outset, in the work of 'English' pioneers like F. D. Maurice and Charles Kingsley,[1] the emphasis was on solidarity between the social classes, the cultivation of 'larger sympathies', the instillation of national pride and the transmission of 'moral' values. This last concern—still the distinctive hallmark of literary studies in England, and a frequent source of bemusement to intellectuals from other cultures—was an essential part of the ideological project; indeed the rise of 'English' is more or less concomitant with an historic shift in the very meaning of the term 'moral', of which Arnold, Henry James and F. R. Leavis[2] are the major critical exponents. Morality is no longer to be grasped as a formulated code or explicit ethical system: it is rather a sensitive preoccupation with the whole quality of life itself, with the oblique, nuanced particulars of human experience. Somewhat rephrased, this can be taken as meaning that the old religious ideologies have lost their force, and that a more subtle communication of moral values, one which works by 'dramatic enactment' rather than rebarbative abstraction, is thus in order. Since such values are nowhere more vividly dramatized than in literature, brought home to 'felt experience' with all the unquestionable reality of a blow on the head, literature becomes more than just a handmaiden of moral ideology: it *is* moral ideology for the modern age, as the work of F. R. Leavis was most graphically to evince.

The working class was not the only oppressed layer of Victorian society at whom 'English' was specifically beamed. English literature, reflected a Royal Commission witness in 1877, might be considered a suitable subject for 'women . . . and the second- and third-rate men who [. . .] become schoolmasters.'[3] The 'softening' and 'humanizing' effects of English, terms recurrently used by its early proponents, are within the existing ideological stereotypes of gender clearly feminine. The rise of English in England ran parallel to the gradual, grudging admission of women to the institutions of higher education; and since English was an untaxing sort of affair, concerned

6. Both these English writers—the Polish-born novelist Joseph Conrad (1857–1924) and the short story writer, poet, and novelist Rudyard Kipling (1865–1936)—often set their works in places under colonial rule (though not usually the Far East).

7. Jane Austen's best-known novel (published 1813).

8. See Lionel Gossman, "Literature and Education," *New Literary History* 13.2 (1982): 341–71. See also D. J. Palmer, *The Rise of English Studies* (London, 1965) [Eagleton's note].

9. Oxford and Cambridge Universities; both date to the 12th century. "Public school": in Great Britain, endowed boarding schools, whose curriculum traditionally has been largely classical.

1. English clergyman, social reformer, and novelist (1819–1875). Maurice (1805–1872), English theologian, clergyman, and writer.

2. English literary critic (1895–1978) and editor of the influential journal *Scrutiny*. JAMES (1843–1916), American novelist and critic.

3. Quoted by Gossman, "Literature and Education," pp. 341–42 [Eagleton's note].

with the finer feelings rather than with the more virile topics of *bona fide* academic 'disciplines', it seemed a convenient sort of non-subject to palm off on the ladies, who were in any case excluded from science and the professions. Sir Arthur Quiller Couch,[4] first Professor of English at Cambridge University, would open with the word 'Gentlemen' lectures addressed to a hall filled largely with women. Though modern male lecturers may have changed their manners, the ideological conditions which make English a popular University subject for women to read have not.

If English had its feminine aspect, however, it also acquired a masculine one as the century drew on. The era of the academic establishment of English is also the era of high imperialism in England. As British capitalism became threatened and progressively outstripped by its younger German and American rivals, the squalid, undignified scramble of too much capital chasing too few overseas territories, which was to culminate in 1914 in the first imperialist world war, created the urgent need for a sense of national mission and identity. What was at stake in English studies was less English *literature* than *English* literature: our great 'national poets' Shakespeare and Milton, the sense of an 'organic' national tradition and identity to which new recruits could be admitted by the study of humane letters. The reports of educational bodies and official enquiries into the teaching of English, in this period and in the early twentieth century, are strewn with nostalgic back-references to the 'organic' community of Elizabethan England[5] in which nobles and groundlings found a common meeting-place in the Shakespearian theatre, and which might still be reinvented today. It is no accident that the author of one of the most influential Government reports in this area, *The Teaching of English in England* (1921), was none other than Sir Henry Newbolt,[6] minor jingoist poet and perpetrator of the immortal line 'Play up! play up! and play the game!' Chris Baldick has pointed to the importance of the admission of English literature to the Civil Service examinations in the Victorian period: armed with this conveniently packaged version of their own cultural treasures, the servants of British imperialism could sally forth overseas secure in a sense of their national identity, and able to display that cultural superiority to their envying colonial peoples.[7]

It took rather longer for English, a subject fit for women, workers and those wishing to impress the natives, to penetrate the bastions of ruling-class power in Oxford and Cambridge. English was an upstart, amateurish affair as academic subjects went, hardly able to compete on equal terms with the rigours of Greats or philology;[8] since every English gentleman read his own literature in his spare time anyway, what was the point of submitting it to systematic study? Fierce rearguard actions were fought by both ancient Universities against this distressingly dilettante subject: the definition of an academic subject was what could be examined, and since English was no more than idle gossip about literary taste it was difficult to know how to make it unpleasant enough to qualify as a proper academic pursuit. This, it might be said, is one of the few problems associated with the study of English which have since been effectively resolved. The frivolous contempt for his subject

4. English critic (1863–1944).
5. That is, England during the reign (1558–1603) of Queen Elizabeth I (1533–1603), the period during which Shakespeare wrote many of his plays.
6. English poet, historian, and novelist (1862–1938); Eagleton quotes "Vitaï Lampada" from *The Island Race* (1898).
7. See Baldick, *The Social Mission of English Criticism*, pp. 70–72 [Eagleton's note].
8. The study of cultures through historical analyses of their languages. "Greats": studies of Greek and Latin literature, history, and philosophy.

displayed by the first really 'literary' Oxford professor, Sir Walter Raleigh, has to be read to be believed.[9] Raleigh held his post in the years leading up to the First World War; and his relief at the outbreak of the war, an event which allowed him to abandon the feminine vagaries of literature and put his pen to something more manly—war propaganda—is palpable in his writing. The only way in which English seemed likely to justify its existence in the ancient Universities was by systematically mistaking itself for the Classics; but the classicists were hardly keen to have this pathetic parody of themselves around.

If the first imperialist world war more or less put paid to Sir Walter Raleigh, providing him with an heroic identity more comfortingly in line with that of his Elizabethan namesake,[1] it also signalled the final victory of English studies at Oxford and Cambridge. One of the most strenuous antagonists of English—philology—was closely bound up with Germanic influence; and since England happened to be passing through a major war with Germany, it was possible to smear classical philology as a form of ponderous Teutonic nonsense with which no self-respecting Englishman should be caught associating.[2] England's victory over Germany meant a renewal of national pride, an upsurge of patriotism which could only aid English's cause; but at the same time the deep trauma of the war, its almost intolerable questioning of every previously held cultural assumption, gave rise to a 'spiritual hungering', as one contemporary commentator described it, for which poetry seemed to provide an answer. It is a chastening thought that we owe the University study of English, in part at least, to a meaningless massacre. The Great War, with its carnage of ruling-class rhetoric, put paid to some of the more strident forms of chauvinism on which English had previously thrived: there could be few more Walter Raleighs after Wilfred Owen.[3] English Literature rode to power on the back of wartime nationalism; but it also represented a search for spiritual solutions on the part of an English ruling class whose sense of identity had been profoundly shaken, whose psyche was ineradicably scarred by the horrors it had endured. Literature would be at once solace and reaffirmation, a familiar ground on which Englishmen could regroup both to explore, and to find some alternative to, the nightmare of history.

* * *

1983

9. See Baldick, *The Social Mission of English Criticism* pp. 76–79 [Eagleton's note]. Raleigh (1861–1922), English scholar, essayist, and critic.

1. The soldier, courtier and poet Sir Walter Ralegh (1552–1618).

2. See Francis Mulhern, *The Moment of "Scrutiny"* (London, 1979), pp. 20–22 [Eagleton's note].

3. English poet (1893–1918) who wrote about his experiences as a soldier in World War I; he died in combat.

STEPHEN GREENBLATT
b. 1943

The leading proponent of "New Historicism," Stephen Greenblatt became a key figure in the shift from literary to cultural poetics and from textual to contextual interpretation in U.S. English departments in the 1980s and 1990s. Inspired by MICHEL FOUCAULT's historical investigations of medical and penal institutions and his theoretical understanding of power, the New Historicists see the literary work as a vessel tossed in a social sea of competing interests, antagonistic values, and contradictions. For Greenblatt, literary works are "fields of force, places of dissension and shifting interests, occasions for the jostling of orthodox and subversive impulses."

Greenblatt was born in Cambridge, Massachusetts, in 1943 and did his undergraduate and graduate work at Yale University, gaining his Ph.D. in 1969. For more than twenty years, he taught at the University of California at Berkeley, where he was one of the founders of *Representations*, the journal in which much pathbreaking New Historicist work first appeared. He moved to Harvard University in the mid-1990s.

New Historicism, as our selection suggests, begins its quest to be political by denying that any social world is stable and that artworks are separated from the power struggles constituting social reality. The literary work is a player in the competition among various groups to gain their ends, a competition that takes place on many levels. New Historicism accepts Foucault's insistence that power operates through myriad capillary channels; these include not just direct coercion and governmental action but also, crucially, daily routines and language. Because discourse organizes perception of the world by its categorical groupings and because symbols bind social agents emotionally to institutions and practices, conflicts over images resonate throughout the social order. Thus the New Historicist not only pays attention to such discursive disputes in particular texts but also examines how particular texts are addressed to other texts, other discursive orders, in the wider culture. A "cultural poetics" tries to identify the key images—and the values, beliefs, practices, and social structures that those images point toward—of a particular cultural moment. Unlike the old historicist, the New Historicist does not expect that cultural moment to be unified, with the literary text simply reflecting or embodying that unity. Rather, the text is a dynamic interweaving of multiple strands from a culture that is itself an unstable field of contending forces.

Any given text for the New Historicist is an attempted intervention in the ongoing struggle to influence or even dominate the cultural field. The critic's own work intervenes in his or her own present, responding to and striving to alter contemporary configurations of power. To explain how Shakespeare's *Richard II* is implicated in the power struggles of its time is both to write a history of the consolidation of power prior to our moment and to awaken today's reader to the conflicts that define our moment. The New Historicists, again following Foucault, often construct narratives in which dispersed and disputed power becomes more insidious, and dominance grows more dominant. They want to emphasize history's contingencies, its fluidity in any given moment, but they also emphasize how history reveals the growth of forms of power that continuously affect subjects' lives.

The tendency to tell similar historical tales of power's expanding reach, coupled with fairly blunt evaluations of literary works as either complicitous with or resistant to power, has opened New Historicism to criticism. Historians have objected that these literary critics read a few nonliterary texts, juxtapose them with plays or novels, and think they are doing history. But such complaints, even when justified in individual cases, largely miss the point. New Historicism is part of a broader sea change in literary studies—and in history as well. Instead of asking what a particular text means in and of itself, New Historicists ask what it *does* within the ensemble of social relations in which it is embedded. Rather than focusing on the masterpiece or on the author of masterpieces, these critics attempt to understand the lived social reality of the era being studied. And just as New Historicism and cultural studies were beginning to emerge in departments of literature, history departments also were changing. During the late twentieth century, new prominence was given to both social and cultural history, which shift the historians' gaze away from famous actors or grand historical events to ordinary people and their mundane routines. A whole new relation to texts, which were now being read to gain insight into the society from which they sprang, along with a new definition of the goal of historical investigation, has increasingly blurred the disciplinary lines between English and history. As literary critics have become more familiar with this paradigm, they have grown accustomed to delving as deeply into archives as historians; and some historians have begun to adopt the more linguistically nuanced interpretations of sources characteristic of literary critics.

Greenblatt's work, along with that of Louis Adrian Montrose, Stephen Mullaney, Jonathan Dollimore, Catherine Belsey, and numerous other literary critics, has ensured that English Renaissance studies and New Historicism have become inextricably linked. But New Historicists work has also been highly influential in studies of other historical periods, especially nineteenth-century American and British literature. Jerome McGann, for example, though not influenced so directly by Foucault as are members of the *Representations* group, has brought a New Historicist concern with social context to the criticism of British Romantic poetry. By the late 1990s, literary critics seldom explicitly identified themselves as New Historicists, but the emphasis on context over text still prevailed in literary studies.

BIBLIOGRAPHY

Greenblatt's books to date are *Three Modern Satirists: Waugh, Orwell, and Huxley* (1965), *Sir Walter Ralegh: The Renaissance Man and His Roles* (1973), *Renaissance Self-Fashioning From More to Shakespeare* (1980), *Shakespearian Negotiations: The Circulation of Social Energy in Renaissance England* (1988), *Learning to Curse: Essays in Early Modern Culture* (1990), and *Marvelous Possessions: The Wonder of the New World* (1991). He has also edited important collections of New Historicist work: *Allegory and Representation* (1981), *The Power of Forms in the English Renaissance* (1982), *Representing the English Renaissance* (1988), *New World Encounters* (1993), and, with Catherine Gallagher, *Practicing the New Historicism* (2000). He co-edited, with Giles Gunn, *Redrawing the Boundaries: The Transformation of English and American Literary Studies* (1992), is general editor of *The Norton Shakespeare* (1997), and is a co-editor of *The Norton Anthology of English Literature* (7th ed., 1999).

For a wide range of critical responses to Greenblatt's work, see Donald Pease, "Toward a Sociology of Literary Knowledge: Greenblatt, Colonialism, and the New Historicism," in *Consequences of Theory* (ed. Jonathan Arac and Barbara Johnson, 1991); Anne D Hall, "The Political Wisdom of Cultural Poetics," *Modern Philology* 93 (1994); James J. Paxson, "The Green(blatt)ing of America," *Minnesota Review*, n.s., 41–42 (1994); and Simon During, "Post-Foucauldian Criticism: Government, Death, Mimesis," in *Genealogy and Literature* (ed. Lee Quinby, 1995).

Introduction to *The Power of Forms in the English Renaissance*

"I am Richard II. Know ye not that?" exclaimed Queen Elizabeth on August 4, 1601, in the wake of the abortive Essex rising.[1] On the day before the rising, someone had paid the Lord Chamberlain's Men forty shillings to

1. An attempt against the court of Queen Elizabeth I (1523–1603; reigned 1558–1603) in February 1601, led by Robert Devereux (1566–1601), the 2d earl of Essex. When the citizens of London failed to come to his small army's aid, Essex and his followers fled; Essex was executed for treason.

revive their old play about the deposing and killing of Richard II.[2] As far as we know, the play—almost certainly Shakespeare's—was performed only once at the Globe, but in Elizabeth's bitter recollection the performance has metastisized: "this tragedy was played 40tie times in open streets and houses."[3]

The Queen enjoyed and protected the theater; against moralists who charged that it was a corrupting and seditious force, she evidently sided with those who replied that it released social tensions, inculcated valuable moral lessons, and occupied with harmless diversion those who might otherwise conspire against legitimate authority. But there were some in the Essex faction who saw in the theater the power to subvert, or rather the power to wrest legitimation from the established ruler and confer it on another. This power, notwithstanding royal protection, censorship, and the players' professions of unswerving loyalty, could be purchased for forty shillings.

The story of Richard II was obviously a highly charged one in a society where political discussion was conducted, as in parts of the world today, with Aesopian indirection.[4] Clearly it is not the text alone—over which the censor had some control—that bears the full significance of Shakespeare's play, or of any version of the story. It is rather the story's full situation—the genre it is thought to embody, the circumstances of its performance, the imaginings of its audience—that governs its shifting meanings. "40tie times in open streets and houses": for the Queen the repeatability of the tragedy, and hence the numbers of people who have been exposed to its infection, is part of the danger, along with the fact (or rather her conviction) that the play had broken out of the boundaries of the playhouse, where such stories are clearly marked as powerful illusions, and moved into the more volatile zone—the zone she calls "open"—of the streets. In the streets the story begins to lose the conventional containment of the playhouse where audiences are kept at a safe distance both from the action on stage and from the world beyond the walls. And in the wake of this subversive deregulation, the terms that mark the distinction between the lucid and the real become themselves problematical: are the "houses" to which Elizabeth refers public theaters or private dwellings where her enemies plot her overthrow? can "tragedy" be a strictly literary term when the Queen's own life is endangered by the play?[5]

Modern historical scholarship has assured Elizabeth that she had nothing to worry about: *Richard II* is not at all subversive but rather a hymn to Tudor[6] order. The play, far from encouraging thoughts of rebellion, regards the deposition of the legitimate king as a "sacrilegious" act that drags the country down into "the abyss of chaos"; "that Shakespeare and his audience regarded Bolingbroke as a usurper," declares J. Dover Wilson, "is incontestable."[7] But

2. *Richard II* (ca. 1595). The Lord Chamberlain's Men: Shakespeare's theater company.

3. Elizabeth was speaking to William Lambarde the antiquary; see the Arden edition of Shakespeare's *King Richard II*, ed. Peter Ure (1956), pp. lvii–lxii [Greenblatt's note]. "Metastisized": grown (a word usually applied to cancers).

4. Aesop's fables make their point by way of story rather than by direct statement.

5. The ambiguity is intensified by the Queen's preceding comment, according to Lambarde: *"Her Majestie.* 'He that will forget God, will also forget his benefactors; this tragedy was played 40tie times in open streets and houses' " (Ure, p. lix) [Greenblatt's note].

6. The English royal dynasty that begins with Henry VII (1457–1509) in 1485 and ends with Elizabeth I.

7. John Dover Wilson, "The Political Background of Shakespeare's *Richard II* and *Henry IV*," *Shakespeare-Jahrbuch* 75 (1939): 47. The condemnation of Bolingbroke is "evident," we are told, "from the whole tone and emphasis of *Richard II*" (p. 48) [Greenblatt's note]. Bolingbroke: the name of Henry IV (1367–1415) before he deposed his cousin Richard II (1367–1400; reigned, 1377–99) in 1399. Bolingbroke's violent rise to power is the subject of Shakespeare's *Richard II*.

in 1601 neither Queen Elizabeth nor the Earl of Essex were so sure: after all, someone on the eve of a rebellion thought the play sufficiently seditious to warrant squandering two pounds on the players, and the Queen understood the performance as a threat. Moreover, even before the Essex rising, the actual disposition scene (IV.i. 154–318 in the Arden edition) was carefully omitted from the first three quartos[8] of Shakespeare's play and appears for the first time only after Elizabeth's death.

How can we account for the discrepancy between Dover Wilson's historical reconstruction and the anxious response of the figures whose history he purports to have accurately reconstructed? The answer lies at least in part in the difference between a conception of art that has no respect whatsoever for the integrity of the text ("I am Richard II. Know ye not that?") and one that hopes to find, through historical research, a stable core of meaning within the text, a core that unites disparate and even contradictory parts into an organic whole. That whole may provide a perfectly orthodox celebration of legitimacy and order, as measured by homilies, royal pronouncements, and official propaganda, but the Queen is clearly responding to something else: to the presence of *any* representation of deposition, whether regarded as sacrilegious or not; to the choice of this particular story at this particular time; to the place of the performance; to her own identity as it is present in the public sphere and as it fuses with the figure of the murdered king. Dover Wilson is not a New Critic:[9] he does not conceive of the text as an iconic object whose meaning is perfectly contained within its own formal structure. Yet for him historical research has the effect of conferring autonomy and fixity upon the text, and it is precisely this fixity that is denied by Elizabeth's response.

Dover Wilson's work is a distinguished example of the characteristic assumptions and methods of the mainstream literary history practiced in the first half of our century, and a further glance at these may help us to bring into focus the distinctive assumptions and methods exemplified in the essays collected in this volume.[1] To be sure, these essays are quite diverse in their concerns and represent no single critical practice; a comparative glance, for example, at the brilliant pieces by Franco Moretti and John Traugott[2] will suggest at once how various this work is. Yet diverse as they are, many of the present essays give voice, I think, to what we may call the new historicism, set apart from both the dominant historical scholarship of the past and the formalist criticism that partially displaced this scholarship in the decades after World War Two. The earlier historicism tends to be monological; that is, it is concerned with discovering a single political vision, usually identical to that said to be held by the entire literate class or indeed the entire population ("In the eyes of the later middle ages," writes Dover Wilson, Richard II "represented the type and exemplar of royal martyrdom" [p. 50]). This vision, most often presumed to be internally coherent and consistent, though

8. The earliest printed versions of individual plays by Shakespeare; the 1st quarto of *Richard II* appeared in 1597, and 2 more in 1598 (the 4th, printed in 1608, contained the deposition scene).

9. A close reader who focuses exclusively on the text as an autonomous whole. See, for example, JOHN CROWE RANSOM and CLEANTH BROOKS (above).

1. An anthology of critical essays on English Renaissance literature.

2. Moretti, " 'A Huge Eclipse': Tragic Form and the Deconsecration of Sovereignty"; and Traugott, "Creating a Rational Rinaldo: A Study in the Mixture of the Genres of Comedy and Romance in *Much Ado About Nothing*."

occasionally analyzed as the fusion of two or more elements, has the status of an historical fact. It is not thought to be the product of the historian's interpretation, nor even of the particular interests of a given social group in conflict with other groups. Protected then from interpretation and conflict, this vision can serve as a stable point of reference, beyond contingency, to which literary interpretation can securely refer. Literature is conceived to mirror the period's beliefs, but to mirror them, as it were, from a safe distance.

The new historicism erodes the firm ground of both criticism and literature. It tends to ask questions about its own methodological assumptions and those of others: in the present case, for example, it might encourage us to examine the ideological situation not only of *Richard II* but of Dover Wilson on *Richard II*. The lecture from which I have quoted—"The Political Background of Shakespeare's *Richard II* and *Henry IV*"—was delivered before the German Shakespeare Society, at Weimar, in 1939. We might, in a full discussion of the critical issues at stake here, look closely at the relation between Dover Wilson's reading of *Richard II*—a reading that discovers Shakespeare's fears of chaos and his consequent support for legitimate if weak authority over the claims of ruthless usurper—and the eerie occasion of his lecture ("these plays," he concludes, "should be of particular interest to German students at this moment of that everlasting adventure which we call history" [p. 51]).

Moreover, recent criticism has been less concerned to establish the organic unity of literary works and more open to such works as fields of force, places of dissension and shifting interests, occasions for the jostling of orthodox and subversive impulses. "The Elizabethan playhouse, playwright, and player," writes Louis Adrian Montrose in a brilliant recent essay, "exemplify the contradictions of Elizabethan society and make those contradictions their subject. If the world is a theatre and the theatre is an image of the world, then by reflecting upon its own artifice, the drama is holding the mirror up to nature."[3] As the problematizing of the mirror metaphor suggests, Renaissance literary works are no longer regarded either as a fixed set of texts that are set apart from all other forms of expression and that contain their own determinate meanings or as a stable set of reflections of historical facts that lie beyond them. The critical practice represented in this volume challenges the assumptions that guarantee a secure distinction between "literary foreground" and "political background" or, more generally, between artistic production and other kinds of social production. Such distinctions do in fact exist, but they are not intrinsic to the texts; rather they are made up and constantly redrawn by artists, audiences, and readers. These collective social constructions on the one hand define the range of aesthetic possibilities within a given representational mode and, on the other, link that mode to the complex network of institutions, practices, and beliefs that constitute the culture as a whole. In this light, the study of genre is an exploration of the poetics of culture.

1982

3. "The Purpose of Playing: Reflections on a Shakespearean Anthropology," *Helio*, n.s., 7 (1980): 57 [Greenblatt's note].

BARBARA CHRISTIAN
1943–2000

"How does one respond to a language that is tonality, dance, to these voices without mutilating them and turning them into logical progressions, mere intellectual concepts? How does one shimmy back to forms that soar beyond philosophical discourse or jargon?" Writing in "Being the Subject and the Object: Reading African-American Women's Novels" (1990), Barbara Christian poses a series of questions that interrogate not only the utility of theory to the project of African American literature but also the very nexus of literature and philosophy that has occupied literary criticism and theory since PLATO banished the poets from his ideal Republic (see above). While Plato preferred the "truths" of philosophy to the lies of the poets, Christian would seem to agree with SIR PHILIP SIDNEY that literature is superior to philosophy because it offers more dynamic and complex representations of the world. At the same time, Christian rejects the beliefs of "neutral humanists" who would characterize literature as pure expression or as a disinterested search for truth. Because she speaks for an African American literary tradition that has been devalued and excluded from the Western literary canon, she is sensitive to the roles that power and privilege play in determining literary value. The complex interplay between an appreciation of literature as "hieroglyph"—"a figure which is both sensual and abstract"—and a realist's understanding of the politics of literary work characterizes Christian's critical writing.

Born on St. Thomas in the Virgin Islands, Christian attended a Catholic mission school and went on to earn an A.B. cum laude from Marquette University in 1963; from Columbia University she received an M.A. in 1964 and a Ph.D. with distinction in 1970. From 1971 until her death in 2000, she taught English, African American studies, and women's studies at the University of California at Berkeley, where she was the first black woman to receive tenure. She served on the editorial boards of several journals, including *Feminist Studies* (1984–92), *Black American Literature Forum* (1985–90), *Sage* (1987–89), and *Contentions* (1990–2000). Her scholarly honors include the 1994 MELUS award for her contributions to ethnic studies.

In our selection "The Race for Theory" (1988), Christian deplores the influence that contemporary theory has exerted over the study of literature, especially the study of African American literature. "Theory," by which she means primarily the poststructuralist theories of JACQUES DERRIDA, popularized in the 1980s by such Yale Critics as PAUL DE MAN, purportedly attempts to fix ideas, to prescribe a "set method" for interpreting literary texts. She thus equates theorists with philosophers. But critics—especially critics of the "energetic emergent literatures" by women, African Americans, and third world writers—need to read without preconceived ideas, remaining open to the complex intersections of language, class, race, and gender. More negatively than BELL HOOKS, Christian questions why the elitist jargon and opaque style of postmodern theory, with its proclamation of the death of the author, should become prominent at the same moment when the works of black men and women are just gaining recognition. But unlike hooks, who sees in postmodernism a means of exploring black experience without becoming mired in reductive notions of authentic blackness, Christian fears that theory, because of its abstracting tendencies, will lead to precisely the kinds of monolithic formulations about authenticity that marred the U.S. Black Arts Movements and black cultural nationalism of the 1960s.

Christian identifies herself with an earlier twentieth-century tradition of African American literary critics, who were keenly interested in the practice of literature. Though not immersed in the abstract logic of Western philosophy, these critics—including ZORA NEALE HURSTON, Ralph Ellison, Richard Wright, and LANGSTON

HUGHES—do theorize; but for them, theory is a dynamic rather than static activity, embedded in stories, riddles, proverbs, and play with language (HENRY LOUIS GATES JR. addresses this argument differently and in more detail). Without naming them, Christian sets herself in opposition to critics such as Gates, HOUSTON A. BAKER JR., and hooks, who have defended theory as useful for understanding African American literature. Among theorists she quickly became a symbol of the widespread reaction against the rise of theory in the 1970s.

Christian's critique is related to feminist criticism of theory in the 1980s and 1990s (see ANNETTE KOLODNY). "The Race for Theory" similarly reserves its harshest criticism for poststructuralist French theorists such as HÉLÈNE CIXOUS and JULIA KRISTEVA, who, by the late 1980s, had achieved a kind of authoritative status among academic feminists. Christian questions whether this kind of feminist theory, culled from the practices of first world white women, can be at all relevant to the experiences of nonwhite and non-Western women.

While "The Race for Theory" can be, and has been, criticized for its vagueness, its tendency to tar a disparate set of theoretical discourses with the same brush, and its refusal to engage with the specifics of any particular theory, it does evince a keen understanding of the power relations that structure contemporary academic literary studies. Theory is not simply one literary discourse among others; it is not a neutral, value-free set of ideas. Christian recognizes that postmodern theory is both an ideology and a commodity within academic literary studies—one highly valued in the 1980s and 1990s, endowing a few elite theorists with substantial influence within the academic profession. She attacks the "race for theory" because, as the metaphor implies, it has become an end in itself rather than a means to an end, a way of advancing in the profession rather than a means of understanding literature. "The Race for Theory" stands as a challenge to feminist critics, African American critics, and critics of other "emergent" literatures to understand what might be at stake in their involvement with contemporary literary theory.

BIBLIOGRAPHY

Christian's interest in the development of multiethnic curricula is evidenced by her work as co-editor of the prizewinning *In Search of Our Past: Six Units for the Teaching of a Multi-Ethnic Women's History* (1980). Much of her literary criticism is concerned with delineating and examining a tradition of African American women writers. Her published works include *Black Women Novelists: The Development of a Tradition, 1892–1976* (1980), *Black Feminist Criticism: Perspectives on Black Women Writers* (1985), and *From the Inside Out: African-American Women's Literary Tradition and the State* (1987). Christian was also the editor of *"Everyday Use," Alice Walker: A Casebook* (1994), editor of the contemporary section of the *Norton Anthology of African-American Literature* (1996), and one of three editors of *Female Subjects in Black and White: Race, Psychoanalysis, Feminism* (1997).

In "Kinship and Resemblances: Women on Women," *Feminist Studies* 11.1 (1985), Hortense J. Spillers writes insightfully about Christian's literary criticism, as does JoAnne Cornwell-Giles in "Afro-American Criticism and Western Consciousness: The Politics of Knowing," *Black American Literature Forum* 24.1 (1990). Michael Awkward responds to Christian's critique of theory in "Appropriative Gestures: Theory and Afro-American Literary Criticism," in *Gender and Theory: Dialogues in Feminist Criticism* (ed. Linda Kaufmann, 1989). For useful bibliographic and biographical information on Barbara Christian, see the entry by Nancy Rage Tarcher in *Feminist Writers* (ed. Pamela Kester-Shelton, 1996).

The Race for Theory

I have seized this occasion to break the silence among those of us, critics, as we are now called, who have been intimidated, devalued by what I call the race for theory. I have become convinced that there has been a takeover in the literary world by Western philosophers from the old literary élite, the neutral humanists. Philosophers have been able to effect such a takeover because so much of the literature of the West has become pallid, laden with despair, self-indulgent, and disconnected. The New Philosophers, eager to understand a world that is today fast escaping their political control, have redefined literature so that the distinctions implied by that term, that is, the distinctions between everything written and those things written to evoke feeling as well as to express thought, have been blurred. They have changed literary critical language to suit their own purposes as philosophers, and they have reinvented the meaning of theory.

My first response to this realization was to ignore it. Perhaps, in spite of the egocentrism of this trend, some good might come of it. I had, I felt, more pressing and interesting things to do, such as reading and studying the history and literature of black women, a history that had been totally ignored, a contemporary literature bursting with originality, passion, insight, and beauty. But unfortunately it is difficult to ignore this new takeover, since theory has become a commodity which helps determine whether we are hired or promoted in academic institutions—worse, whether we are heard at all. Due to this new orientation, works (a word which evokes labor) have become texts.[1] Critics are no longer concerned with literature, but with other critics' texts, for the critic yearning for attention has displaced the writer and has conceived of himself as the center. Interestingly in the first part of this century, at least in England and America, the critic was usually also a writer of poetry, plays, or novels. But today, as a new generation of professionals develops, he or she is increasingly an academic. Activities such as teaching or writing one's response to specific works of literature have, among this group, become subordinated to one primary thrust, that moment when one creates a theory, thus fixing a constellation of ideas for a time at least, a fixing which no doubt will be replaced in another month or so by somebody else's competing theory as the race accelerates. Perhaps because those who have effected the takeover have the power (although they deny it) first of all to be published, and thereby to determine the ideas which are deemed valuable, some of our most daring and potentially radical critics (and by *our* I mean black, women, third world) have been influenced, even coopted, into speaking a language and defining their discussion in terms alien to and opposed to our needs and orientation. At least so far, the creative writers I study have resisted this language.

For people of color have always theorized—but in forms quite different from the Western form of abstract logic. And I am inclined to say that our theorizing (and I intentionally use the verb rather than the noun) is often in narrative forms, in the stories we create, in riddles and proverbs, in the play with language, since dynamic rather than fixed ideas seem more to our liking.

1. See, e.g., ROLAND BARTHES, "From Work to Text" (1971; above).

How else have we managed to survive with such spiritedness the assault on our bodies, social institutions, countries, our very humanity? And women, at least the women I grew up around, continuously speculated about the nature of life through pithy language that unmasked the power relations of their world. It is this language, and the grace and pleasure with which they played with it, that I find celebrated, refined, critiqued in the works of writers like Morrison and Walker.[2] My folk, in other words, have always been a race for theory—though more in the form of the hieroglyph, a written figure which is both sensual and abstract, both beautiful and communicative. In my own work I try to illuminate and explain these hieroglyphs, which is, I think, an activity quite different from the creating of the hieroglyphs themselves. As the Buddhists would say, the finger pointing at the moon is not the moon.

In this discussion, however, I am more concerned with the issue raised by my first use of the term, *the race for theory*, in relation to its academic hegemony,[3] and possibly of its inappropriateness to the energetic emerging literatures in the world today. The pervasiveness of this academic hegemony is an issue continually spoken about—but usually in hidden groups, lest we, who are disturbed by it, appear ignorant to the reigning academic élite. Among the folk who speak in muted tones are people of color, feminists, radical critics, creative writers, who have struggled for much longer than a decade to make their voices, their various voices, heard, and for whom literature is not an occasion for discourse among critics but is necessary nourishment for their people and one way by which they come to understand their lives better. Clichéd though this may be, it bears, I think, repeating here.

The race for theory, with its linguistic jargon, its emphasis on quoting its prophets, its tendency towards "Biblical" exegesis, its refusal even to mention specific works of creative writers, far less contemporary ones, its preoccupations with mechanical analyses of language, graphs, algebraic equations, its gross generalizations about culture, has silenced many of us to the extent that some of us feel we can no longer discuss our own literature, while others have developed intense writing blocks and are puzzled by the incomprehensibility of the language set adrift in literary circles. There have been, in the last year, any number of occasions on which I had to convince literary critics who have pioneered entire new areas of critical inquiry that they did have something to say. Some of us are continually harassed to invent wholesale theories regardless of the complexity of the literature we study. I, for one, am tired of being asked to produce a black feminist literary theory as if I were a mechanical man. For I believe such theory is prescriptive—it ought to have some relationship to practice. Since I can count on one hand the number of people attempting to be black feminist literary critics in the world today, I consider it presumptuous of me to invent a theory of how we *ought* to read. Instead, I think we need to read the works of our writers in our various ways and remain open to the intricacies of the intersection of language, class, race, and gender in the literature. And it would help if we share our process, that is, our practice, as much as possible since, finally, our work *is* a collective endeavor.

2. Alice Walker (b. 1944), African American writer. Toni Morrison (b. 1931), African American novelist and winner of the 1993 Nobel Prize in literature.

3. That is, theory's dominance over the world's emerging literatures.

The insidious quality of this race for theory is symbolized for me by the very name of this special issue—Minority Discourse[4]—a label which is borrowed from the reigning theory of the day and is untrue to the literatures being produced by our writers, for many of our literatures (certainly Afro-American literature) are central, not minor, and by the titles of many of the articles, which illuminate language as an assault on the other, rather than as possible communication, and play with, or even affirmation of another. I have used the passive voice in my last sentence construction, contrary to the rules of Black English, which like all languages has a particular value system, since I have not placed responsibility on any particular person or group. But that is precisely because this new ideology has become so prevalent among us that it behaves like so many of the other ideologies with which we have had to contend. It appears to have neither head nor center. At the least, though, we can say that the terms "minority" and "discourse" are located firmly in a Western dualistic or "binary" frame which sees the rest of the world as minor, and tries to convince the rest of the world that it *is* major, usually through force and then through language, even as it claims many of the ideas that we, its "historical" other, have known and spoken about for so long. For many of us have never conceived of ourselves only as somebody's *other*.

Let me not give the impression that by objecting to the race for theory I ally myself with or agree with the neutral humanists who see literature as pure expression and will not admit to the obvious control of its production, value, and distribution by those who have power, who deny, in other words, that literature is, of necessity, political. I am studying an entire body of literature that has been denigrated for centuries by such terms as *political*. For an entire century Afro-American writers, from Charles Chestnutt in the nineteenth century through Richard Wright in the 1930s, Imamu Baraka[5] in the 1960s, Alice Walker in the 1970s, have protested the literary hierarchy of dominance which declares when literature is literature, when literature is great, depending on what it thinks is to its advantage. The Black Arts Movement[6] of the 1960s, out of which Black Studies, the Feminist Literary Movement of the 1970s, and Women's Studies grew, articulated precisely those issues, which came *not* from the declarations of the New Western philosophers but from these groups' reflections on their own lives. That Western scholars have long believed their ideas to be universal has been strongly opposed by many such groups. Some of my colleagues do not see black critical writers of previous decades as eloquent enough. Clearly they have not *read* Wright's "Blueprint for Negro Writing," Ellison's *Shadow and Act*, Chestnutt's resignation from being a writer, or Alice Walker's "Search for Zora Neale Hurston."[7] There are two reasons for this general ignorance of

4. This essay was originally published in *Cultural Critique* with other papers written for a conference at the University of California at Berkeley titled "Minority Discourse," held May 29–31, 1986.

5. Novelist, poet, and playwright (born LeRoi Jones, 1934). Chesnutt (1858–1932), writer of short fiction and novels. Wright (1908–1960), novelist.

6. U.S. social and literary movement that began in the mid-1960s and ended in the early 1970s; it extended the concerns of the civil rights and black power movements into literature, academia, and the arts.

7. Walker's "Looking for Zora" (1975) was crucial in the "rediscovery" of HURSTON (1891–1960), African American novelist and anthropologist. Both *Shadow and Act* (1964) by the novelist and essayist Ralph Ellison (1914–1997) and "Blueprint for Negro Writing" (1937) by Wright are important pieces of African American criticism.

what our writer-critics have said. One is that black writing has been generally ignored in this country. Since we, as Toni Morrison has put it, are seen as a discredited people, it is no surprise, then, that our creations are also discredited, but this is also due to the fact that until recently dominant critics in the Western World have also been creative writers who have had access to the upper middle class institutions of education and until recently our writers have decidedly been excluded from these institutions and in fact have often been opposed to them. Because of the academic world's general ignorance about the literature of black people and of women, whose work too has been discredited, it is not surprising that so many of our critics think that the position arguing that literature is political begins with these New Philosophers. Unfortunately, many of our young critics do not investigate the reasons *why* that statement—literature is political—is now acceptable when before it was not; nor do we look to our own antecedents for the sophisticated arguments upon which we can build in order to change the tendency of any established Western idea to become hegemonic.

For I feel that the new emphasis on literary critical theory is as hegemonic as the world which it attacks. I see the language it creates as one which mystifies rather than clarifies our condition, making it possible for a few people who know that particular language to control the critical scene—that language surfaced, interestingly enough, just when the literature of peoples of color, of black women, of Latin Americans, of Africans began to move to "the center." Such words as *center* and *periphery* are themselves instructive. *Discourse, canon, texts*, words as latinate as the tradition from which they come, are quite familiar to me. Because I went to a Catholic Mission school in the West Indies I must confess that I cannot hear the word "canon" without smelling incense, that the word "text" immediately brings back agonizing memories of Biblical exegesis, that "discourse" reeks for me of metaphysics forced down my throat in those courses that traced *world* philosophy from Aristotle through Thomas Aquinas to Heidegger.[8] "Periphery" too is a word I heard throughout my childhood, for if anything was seen as being at the periphery, it was those small Caribbean islands which had neither land mass nor military power. Still I noted how intensely important this periphery was, for U.S. troops were continually invading one island or another if any change in political control even seemed to be occurring. As I lived among folk for whom language was an absolutely necessary way of validating our existence, I was told that the minds of the world lived only in the small continent of Europe. The metaphysical language of the New Philosophy, then, I must admit, is repulsive to me and is one reason why I raced from philosophy to literature, since the latter seemed to me to have the possibilities of rendering the world as large and as complicated as I experienced it, as sensual as I knew it was. In literature I sensed the possibility of the integration of feeling/knowledge, rather than the split between the abstract and the emotional in which Western philosophy inevitably indulged.

Now I am being told that philosophers are the ones who write literature, that authors are dead, irrelevant, mere vessels through which their narratives ooze, that they do not work nor have they the faintest idea what they are

8. MARTIN HEIDEGGER (1888–1976), German philosopher. ARISTOTLE (384–322 B.C.E.), Greek philosopher. THOMAS AQUINAS (1225–1274), Italian philosopher and theologian.

doing; rather they produce texts as disembodied as the angels. I am frankly astonished that scholars who call themselves Marxists or post-Marxists could seriously use such metaphysical language even as they attempt to deconstruct the philosophical tradition from which their language comes. And as a student of literature, I am appalled by the sheer ugliness of the language, its lack of clarity, its unnecessarily complicated sentence constructions, its lack of pleasurableness, its alienating quality. It is the kind of writing for which composition teachers would give a freshman a resounding F.

Because I am a curious person, however, I postponed readings of black women writers I was working on and read some of the prophets of this new literary orientation. These writers did announce their dissatisfaction with some of the cornerstone ideas of their own tradition, a dissatisfaction with which I was born. But in their attempt to change the orientation of Western scholarship, they, as usual, concentrated on themselves and were not in the slightest interested in the worlds they had ignored or controlled. Again I was supposed to know *them*, while they were not at all interested in knowing *me*. Instead they sought to "deconstruct" the tradition to which they belonged even as they used the same forms, style, language of that tradition, forms which necessarily embody its values. And increasingly as I read them and saw their substitution of their philosophical writings for literary ones, I began to have the uneasy feeling that their folk were not producing any literature worth mentioning. For they always harkened back to the masterpieces of the past, again reifying the very texts they said they were deconstructing. Increasingly, as *their* way, *their* terms, *their* approaches remained central and became the means by which one defined literary critics, many of my own peers who had previously been concentrating on dealing with the other side of the equation, the reclamation and discussion of past and *present* third world literatures, were diverted into continually discussing the new literary theory.

From my point of view as a critic of contemporary Afro-American women's writing, this orientation is extremely problematic. In attempting to find the deep structures in the literary tradition, a major preoccupation of the new New Criticism,[9] many of us have become obsessed with the nature of reading itself to the extent that we have stopped writing about literature being written today. Since I am slightly paranoid, it has begun to occur to me that the literature being produced *is* precisely one of the reasons why this new philosophical-literary-critical theory of relativity is so prominent. In other words, the literature of blacks, women of South America and Africa, etc., as overtly "political" literature was being preempted by a new Western concept which proclaimed that reality does not exist, that everything is relative, and that every text is silent about something—which indeed it must necessarily be.

There is, of course, much to be learned from exploring how we know what we know, how we read what we read, an exploration which, of necessity, can have no end. But there also has to be a "what," and that "what," when it is even mentioned by the new philosophers, are texts of the past, primarily Western male texts, whose norms are again being transferred onto third

9. An approach (championed by CLEANTH BROOKS, W. K. WIMSATT JR., and others) that emphasizes close reading of the text considered as an autonomous whole; it has greatly influenced teaching from the mid–20th century onward.

world, female texts as theories of reading proliferate. Inevitably a hierarchy has now developed between what is called theoretical criticism and practical criticism, as mind is deemed superior to matter. I have no quarrel with those who wish to philosophize about how we know what we know. But I do resent the fact that this particular orientation is so privileged and has diverted so many of us from doing the first readings of the literature being written today as well as of past works about which nothing has been written. I note, for example, that there is little work done on Gloria Naylor,[1] that most of Alice Walker's works have not been commented on—despite the rage around *The Color Purple*[2]—that there has yet to be an in-depth study of Frances Harper, the nineteenth-century abolitionist poet and novelist. If our emphasis on theoretical criticism continues, critics of the future may have to reclaim the writers we are now ignoring, that is, if they are even aware these artists exist.

I am particularly perturbed by the movement to exalt theory, as well, because of my own adult history. I was an active member of the Black Arts Movement of the sixties and know how dangerous theory can become. Many today may not be aware of this, but the Black Arts Movement tried to create Black Literary Theory and in doing so became prescriptive. My fear is that when Theory is not rooted in practice, it becomes prescriptive, exclusive, élitish.

An example of this prescriptiveness is the approach the Black Arts Movement took towards language. For it, blackness resided in the use of black talk which they defined as hip urban language. So that when Nikki Giovanni reviewed Paule Marshall's[3] *Chosen Place, Timeless People*, she criticized the novel on the grounds that it was not black, for the language was too elegant, too white. Blacks, she said, did not speak that way. Having come from the West Indies where we do, some of the time, speak that way, I was amazed by the narrowness of her vision. The emphasis on *one way* to be black resulted in the works of Southern writers being seen as non-black since the black talk of Georgia does not sound like the black talk of Philadelphia. Because the ideologues, like Baraka, come from the urban centers they tended to privilege their way of speaking, thinking, writing, and to condemn other kinds of writing as not being black enough. Whole areas of the canon were assessed according to the dictum of the Black Arts Nationalist point of view, as in Addison Gayle's[4] *The Way of the New World*, while other works were ignored because they did not fit the scheme of cultural nationalism. Older writers like Ellison and Baldwin[5] were condemned because they saw that the intersection of Western and African influences resulted in a new Afro-American culture, a position with which many of the Black Nationalist ideologues disagreed. Writers were told that writing love poems was not being black. Further examples abound.

It is true that the Black Arts Movements resulted in a necessary and important critique both of previous Afro-American literature and of the white-

1. African American novelist (b. 1950), best known for *The Women of Brewster Place* (1983).
2. Walker's 1982 novel was the subject of much controversy among African American critics because of its negative portrayal of black men.
3. African American novelist (b. 1929); *Chosen Place, Timeless People* was published in 1969. Giovanni (b. 1943), African American poet.
4. African American critic (b. 1932). *The Way of the New World* (1975) treats the African American novel.
5. James Baldwin (1924–1987), African American novelist and essayist.

established literary world. But in attempting to take over power, it, as Ishmael Reed[6] satirizes so well in *Mumbo Jumbo*, became much like its opponent, monolithic and downright repressive.

It is this tendency towards the monolithic, monotheistic, etc., which worries me about the race for theory. Constructs like the *center* and the *periphery* reveal that tendency to want to make the world less complex by organizing it according to one principle, to fix it through an idea which is really an ideal. Many of us are particularly sensitive to monolithism since one major element of ideologies of dominance, such as sexism and racism, is to dehumanize people by stereotyping them, by denying them their variousness and complexity. Inevitably, monolithism becomes a metasystem, in which there is a controlling ideal, especially in relation to pleasure. Language as one form of pleasure is immediately restricted, and becomes heavy, abstract, prescriptive, monotonous.

Variety, multiplicity, eroticism are difficult to control. And it may very well be that these are the reasons why writers are often seen as *persona non grata* by political states, whatever form they take, since writers/artists have a tendency to refuse to give up their way of seeing the world and of playing with possibilities; in fact, their very expression relies on that insistence. Perhaps that is why creative literature, even when written by politically reactionary people, can be so freeing, for in having to embody ideas and recreate the world, writers cannot merely produce "one way."

The characteristics of the Black Arts Movement are, I am afraid, being repeated again today, certainly in the other area to which I am especially tuned. In the race for theory, feminists, eager to enter the halls of power, have attempted their own prescriptions. So often I have read books on feminist literary theory that restrict the definition of what *feminist* means and overgeneralize about so much of the world that most women as well as men are excluded. And seldom do feminist theorists take into account the complexity of life—that women are of many races and ethnic backgrounds with different histories and cultures and that as a rule women belong to different classes that have different concerns. Seldom do they note these distinctions, because if they did they could not articulate a theory. Often as a way of clearing themselves they do acknowledge that women of color, for example, do exist, then go on to do what they were going to do anyway, which is to invent a theory that has little relevance for us.

That tendency towards monolithism is precisely how I see the French feminist theorists.[7] They concentrate on the female body as the means to creating a female language, since language, they say, is male and necessarily conceives of woman as other. Clearly many of them have been irritated by the theories of Lacan[8] for whom language is phallic. But suppose there are peoples in the world whose language was invented primarily in relation to women, who after all are the ones who relate to children and teach language. Some Native American languages, for example, use female pronouns when speaking about non-gender specific activity. Who knows who, according to

6. African American writer (b. 1938). *Mumbo Jumbo* (1972) is one of his best-known novels.
7. The most prominent include HÉLÈNE CIXOUS (b. 1937), Luce Irigaray (b. 1930), and JULIA KRISTEVA (b. 1941).
8. JACQUES LACAN (1901–1981), French psychoanalyst.

gender, created languages. Further, by positing the body as the source of everything French feminists return to the old myth that biology determines everything and ignore the fact that gender is a social rather than a biological construct.

I could go on critiquing the positions of French feminists who are themselves more various in their points of view than the label which is used to describe them, but that is not my point. What I am concerned about is the authority this school now has in feminist scholarship—the way it has become *authoritative discourse*, monologic, which occurs precisely because it does have access to the means of promulgating its ideas. The Black Arts Movement was able to do this for a time because of the political movements of the 1960s—so too with the French feminists who could not be inventing "theory" if a space had not been created by the Women's Movement. In both cases, both groups posited a theory that excluded many of the people who made that space possible. Hence one of the reasons for the surge of Afro-American women's writing during the 1970s and its emphasis on sexism in the black community is precisely that when the ideologues of the 1960s said *black*, they meant *black male*.

I and many of my sisters do not see the world as being so simple. And perhaps that is why we have not rushed to create abstract theories. For we know there are countless women of color, both in America and in the rest of the world to whom our singular ideas would be applied. There is, therefore, a caution we feel about pronouncing black feminist theory that might be seen as a decisive statement about Third World women. This is not to say we are not theorizing. Certainly our literature is an indication of the ways in which our theorizing, of necessity, is based on our multiplicity of experiences.

There is at least one other lesson I learned from the Black Arts Movement. One reason for its monolithic approach had to do with its desire to destroy the power which controlled black people, but it was a power which many of its ideologues wished to achieve. The nature of our context today is such that an approach which desires power singlemindedly must of necessity become like that which it wishes to destroy. Rather than wanting to change the whole model, many of us want to be at the center. It is this point of view that writers like June Jordan and Audre Lorde[9] continually critique even as they call for empowerment, as they emphasize the fear of difference among us and our need for leaders rather than a reliance on ourselves.

For one must distinguish the desire for power from the need to become empowered—that is, seeing oneself as capable of and having the right to determine one's life. Such empowerment is partially derived from a knowledge of history. The Black Arts Movement did result in the creation of Afro-American Studies as a concept, thus giving it a place in the university where one might engage in the reclamation of Afro-American history and culture and pass it on to others. I am particularly concerned that institutions such as Black Studies and Women's Studies, fought for with such vigor and at some sacrifice, are not often seen as important by many of our black or women scholars precisely because the old hierarchy of traditional departments is seen as superior to these "marginal" groups. Yet, it is in this context

9. African American poet and essayist (1934–1992). Jordan (b. 1936), African American poet.

that many others of us are discovering the extent of our complexity, the interrelationships of different areas of knowledge in relation to a distinctly Afro-American or female experience. Rather than having to view our world as subordinate to others, or rather than having to work as if we were hybrids, we can pursue ourselves as subjects.

My major objection to the race for theory, as some readers have probably guessed by now, really hinges on the question, "for whom are we doing what we are doing when we do literary criticism?" It is, I think, the central question today especially for the few of us who have infiltrated the academy enough to be wooed by it. The answer to that question determines what orientation we take in our work, the language we use, the purposes for which it is intended.

I can only speak for myself. But what I write and how I write is done in order to save my own life. And I mean that literally. For me literature is a way of knowing that I am not hallucinating, that whatever I feel/know *is*. It is an affirmation that sensuality is intelligence, that sensual language is language that makes sense. My response, then, is directed to those who write what I read and to those who read what I read—put concretely—to Toni Morrison and to people who read Toni Morrison (among whom I would count few academics). That number is increasing, as is the readership of Walker and Marshall. But in no way is the literature Morrison, Marshall, or Walker create supported by the academic world. Nor given the political context of our society, do I expect that to change soon. For there is no reason, given who controls these institutions, for them to be anything other than threatened by these writers.

My readings do presuppose a need, a desire among folk who like me also want to save their own lives. My concern, then, is a passionate one, for the literature of people who are not in power has always been in danger of extinction or of cooptation, not because we do not theorize, but because what we can even imagine, far less who we can reach, is constantly limited by societal structures. For me, literary criticism is promotion as well as understanding, a response to the writer to whom there is often no response, to folk who need the writing as much as they need anything. I know, from literary history, that writing disappears unless there is a response to it. Because I write about writers who are now writing, I hope to help ensure that their tradition has continuity and survives.

So my "method," to use a new "lit. crit." word, is not fixed but relates to what I read and to the historical context of the writers I read *and* to the many critical activities in which I am engaged, which may or may not involve writing. It is a learning from the language of creative writers, which is one of surprise, so that I might discover what language I might use. For my language is very much based on what I read and how it affects me, that is, on the surprise that comes from reading something that compels you to read differently, as I believe literature does. I, therefore, have no set method, another prerequisite of the new theory, since for me every work suggests a new approach. As risky as that might seem, it is, I believe, what intelligence means—a tuned sensitivity to that which is alive and therefore cannot be known until it is known. Audre Lorde puts it in a far more succinct and sensual way in her essay "Poetry is not a Luxury":

> As they become known to and accepted by us, our feelings and the honest exploration of them become sanctuaries and spawning grounds for the most radical and daring of ideas. They become a safe-house for that difference so necessary to change and the conceptualization of any meaningful action. Right now, I could name at least ten ideas I would have found intolerable or incomprehensible and frightening, except as they came after dreams and poems. This is not idle fantasy, but a disciplined attention to the true meaning of "it feels right to me." We can train ourselves to respect our feelings and to transpose them into a language so they can be shared. And where that language does not yet exist, it is our poetry which helps to fashion it. Poetry is not only dream and vision; it is the skeleton architecture of our lives. It lays the foundations for a future of change, a bridge across our fears of what has never been before.[1]

1988

1. Audre Lorde, *Sister Outsider* (Trumansburg, N.Y.: Crossing Press, 1984), p. 37 [Christian's note].

DONNA HARAWAY
b. 1944

In the introduction to her book *Simians, Cyborgs, and Women: The Reinvention of Nature* (1991), Donna Haraway describes her transformation from a "proper, U.S. socialist feminist, white, female, hominid biologist" into a "multiply marked cyborg feminist" whose writings range freely from primatology to epistemology and on subjects from AIDS to feminist science fiction. Haraway's challenging and innovative theoretical work is part of the cultural studies of science and technology, a thriving subdiscipline interested in the history, sociology, and politics of technoscience. Her best-known text, "A Manifesto for Cyborgs" (1985), has been hailed as the central text of cyberfeminism—a new and often iconoclastic wave of feminist theory and practice that is seeking to reclaim technoscience. As she attempts to understand the place of technology within a postmodern, socialist feminism, Haraway argues that far from being antithetical to the human organism, technology is a material and symbolic apparatus that is already deeply involved in what it means to be human. The old political strategies—Marxist, liberal, and conservative—have become obsolete in the face of a global technoscience that is outpacing the ethical and political mechanisms we have devised for containing it. Her landmark essay is a call for "reconstructing socialist-feminist politics . . . through theory and practice addressed to the social relations of science and technology." In this manifesto, she introduces the mysterious boundary creature and new myth: the cyborg, a "hybrid of machine and organism" that, for Haraway, becomes a metaphor for the "disassembled and reassembled, postmodern collective and personal self" of contemporary cultural theory suited to the West's late capitalist social order.

Haraway's educational history illuminates the broad range of her scholarship. With the aid of a Boettcher Foundation scholarship, she earned a degree in zoology and philosophy in 1966 from Colorado College, where she also fulfilled the requirements for an English major. She studied philosophies of evolution in Paris for a year on a Fulbright scholarship before beginning graduate studies in biology at Yale University;

in 1972 she earned a Ph.D. for an interdisciplinary dissertation on the functions of metaphor in shaping twentieth-century research in developmental biology. She has taught at the University of Hawaii and Johns Hopkins University and has been a professor in the History of Consciousness Program at the University of California at Santa Cruz since 1980, where she teaches feminist theory and science studies. She is also an affiliated faculty member in the Women's Studies, Anthropology, and Environmental Studies Boards at Santa Cruz.

"A Manifesto for Cyborgs" attempts to appropriate the resources of contemporary technoscience as a means of constructing "an ironic political myth faithful to feminism, socialism, and materialism." The positive icon of this new feminist mythology is the cyborg, the hybrid creation of modern science—part human, part machine. Like the feminist theorist GLORIA ANZALDÚA, Haraway is interested in exploring those boundaries, borders, and borderlands where our jumbled personal and collective identities are constructed and contested. By adopting the cyborg as a political myth, feminism, she believes, might be able to initiate effective political action without recourse to essentialism or identity politics; she argues "for *pleasure* in the confusion of boundaries and for *responsibility* in their construction." Identity is multiply configured during postmodern times. While Anzaldúa investigates boundary confusion in geographical space and racial identity, Haraway explores and affirms the breakdowns in three crucial boundaries that have resulted from post–World War II technoscience: those between human and animal, organism and machine, and the physical and nonphysical.

Because they are situated on the boundary between organism and machine, Haraway argues, cyborgs do not participate in the various traditional mythologies that have defined the West. Most pernicious among these are the myths of essential identity and original unity—the myth of the garden of Eden, a belief in a pure, coherent social identity that separates the truly human from animals, machines, and other races and ethnic groups. Haraway joins postmodern feminists such as JUDITH BUTLER and EVE KOSOFSKY SEDGWICK in the critique of essentialism, arguing that totalizing formulations of pure identity often associated with Marxism, the feminism of Catharine MacKinnon, and other movements are based on exclusion and marginalization. Because the cyborg is postgender, post-Western, post-Marxist, and post-Oedipal, it serves as a viable image for a new partial and heterogeneous subjectivity that reconceptualizes identity politics. Cyborgs, being "wary of holism, but needy for connection," offer a new kind of community and politics based not on unity but affinity, not on the party but on the coalition, not on the totalized conception of the category "woman" (central to many feminisms) but on partial explanations based on a careful understanding of difference. Haraway warns that "difference" is not inherently liberating: "some differences are playful; some are poles of world historical systems of domination."

Haraway's post-Marxist call for new political strategies follows from her perception of new forms of political domination. The old forms of domination endemic to an industrial society—to white patriarchal capitalism—are rapidly being rendered obsolete by new technologies. The emerging new networks of power, which she calls the "informatics of domination," are adapted to technoscientific economies based on information systems. Haraway's focus on the metaphor of the cyborg does not, as a few of her critics have unfairly charged, ignore the real material oppression of women worldwide—their poverty and exploitation; it is not a flight away from the "real world" into a poststructuralist utopia, even though her poststructuralist language is very difficult and highly theoretical. Her exploration of the informatics of domination rests on an analysis of the social and material relations of science and technology. These real and frequently oppressive relations include the "homework economy" (that is, the restructuring and feminization of the workplace), encroaching privatization and the loss of public life, growing insecurity even among the well-to-do, cultural impoverishment, and the "failure of subsistence networks for the most vulnerable."

Haraway has been criticized for the exuberance with which she embraces the "monstrous" mixed identity of the cyborg, but her enthusiasm is usually qualified by sobering discussions of the various impacts of modern technoscience on our lives. Her cyborg myth, which recognizes that monsters always mark the limits of community, attempts to integrate women and machines into a new "science" fiction. Writing and language, she argues, are crucial to the new technology and to the new cyborg politics. She advocates, however, not the "dream of a common language" embraced by ADRIENNE RICH or the purified *écriture féminine* (feminine writing) described by HÉLÈNE CIXOUS, but a "powerful infidel heteroglossia," derived from MIKHAIL BAKHTIN, that enables us to theorize the complications of language, the frustrations of communicating experience, and the necessity of negotiating rather than policing boundaries that are becoming increasingly unstable.

BIBLIOGRAPHY

Haraway's dissertation appeared as *Crystals, Fabrics, and Fields: Metaphors of Organicism in Twentieth-Century Developmental Biology* (1976). Her "Manifesto for Cyborgs" (1985), first published in the journal *Socialist Review*, has been reprinted more than fifteen times. *Primate Visions: Gender, Race, and Nature in the World of Modern Science* (1989), Haraway's second book, examines the cultural and ideological ramifications of twentieth-century primatology. In addition, she has published two collections of her essays: *Simians, Cyborgs, and Women: The Reinvention of Nature* (1991) and *Modest_Witness@Second_Millennium.FemaleMan©Meets OncoMouse™* (1997).

Among the earliest evaluations of Haraway's influential work are Istvan Csicsery-Ronay Jr.'s "The SF of Theory: Baudrillard and Haraway," *Science Fiction Studies* 18 (1991), and Allison Fraiberg's "Of AIDS, Cyborgs, and Other indiscretions: Resurfacing the Body in the Postmodern" (1991), published in the online journal *Postmodern Culture* (vol. 1), together with a response by David Porush. A 1993 special issue of the journal *Genders*, titled *Cyberpunk: Technologies of Cultural Identity*, examines the ways in which Haraway's analysis of the cyborg figures in several cyberpunk texts. For more advanced evaluations of Haraway's manifesto, see Chela Sandoval, "Re-Entering Cyberspace: Sciences of Resistance," *Dispositio/n: American Journal of Cultural Histories and Theories* 19 (1994), and Linda Howell, "The Cyborg Manifesto Revisited: Issues and Methods for Technocultural Feminism," in *Postmodern Apocalypse: Theory and Cultural Practice at the End* (ed. Richard Dellamora, 1995). William Grassie offers a reading of Haraway's feminist philosophy in "Cyborgs, Trickster, and Hermes: Donna Haraway's Metatheory of Science and Religion," *Zygon* 31 (1996). Rosi Braidotti's "Cyberfeminism with a Difference," *New Formations* 29 (1996), uses Haraway's notion of the "informatics of domination" to investigate the politics of cyberfeminism. Jonathan Crewe examines Haraway's use of postmodern theory in "Transcoding the World: Haraway's Postmodernism," *Signs* 22 (1997). Csicsery-Ronay returns to his analysis of Haraway in "The Cyborg and the Kitchen Sink; or, The Salvation Story of No Salvation Story," *Science Fiction Studies* 23 (1998). A useful bibliography of writings by and about Haraway can be found in *The Cyborg Handbook*, edited by Chris Hables Gray, with Heidi J. Figuroa-Sarriera and Steven Mentor (1996); it also contains a foreword written by Haraway.

A Manifesto for Cyborgs: Science, Technology, and Socialist Feminism in the 1980s

An Ironic Dream of a Common Language[1] *for Women in the Integrated Circuit*

This essay is an effort to build an ironic political myth faithful to feminism, socialism, and materialism. Perhaps more faithful as blasphemy is faithful, than as reverent worship and identification. Blasphemy has always seemed to require taking things very seriously. I know no better stance to adopt from within the secular-religious, evangelical traditions of United States politics, including the politics of socialist-feminism. Blasphemy protects one from the moral majority within, while still insisting on the need for community. Blasphemy is not apostasy. Irony is about contradictions that do not resolve into larger wholes, even dialectically, about the tension of holding incompatible things together because both or all are necessary and true. Irony is about humor and serious play. It is also a rhetorical strategy and a political method, one I would like to see more honored within socialist feminism. At the center of my ironic faith, my blasphemy, is the image of the cyborg.

A cyborg is a cybernetic organism, a hybrid of machine and organism, a creature of social reality as well as a creature of fiction. Social reality is lived social relations, our most important political construction, a world-changing fiction. The international women's movements have constructed "women's experience," as well as uncovered or discovered this crucial collective object. This experience is a fiction and fact of the most crucial, political kind. Liberation rests on the construction of the consciousness, the imaginative apprehension, of oppression, and so of possibility. The cyborg is a matter of fiction and lived experience that changes what counts as women's experience in the late twentieth century. This is a struggle over life and death, but the boundary between science fiction and social reality is an optical illusion.

Contemporary science fiction is full of cyborgs—creatures simultaneously animal and machine, who populate worlds ambiguously natural and crafted. Modern medicine is also full of cyborgs, of couplings between organism and machine, each conceived as coded devices, in an intimacy and with a power that was not generated in the history of sexuality. Cyborg "sex" restores some of the lovely replicative baroque of ferns and invertebrates (such nice organic prophylactics against heterosexism). Cyborg replication is uncoupled from organic reproduction. Modern production seems like a dream of cyborg colonization of work, a dream that makes the nightmare of Taylorism[2] seem idyllic. And modern war is a cyborg orgy, coded by C^3I, command-control-communication-intelligence, an $84 billion item in 1984's U.S. defense budget. I am making an argument for the cyborg as a fiction mapping our social and bodily reality and as an imaginative resource suggesting some very fruit-

1. A reference to the feminism of ADRIENNE RICH (b. 1929), author of "Compulsory Heterosexuality and Lesbian Existence" (1980; see above) and of a 1978 collection of poetry titled *The Dream of a Common Language*.

2. A system of industrial management, devised by the American inventor and engineer Frederick Taylor (1856–1916), that seeks to maximize workers' efficiency in order to optimize production.

ful couplings. Foucault's biopolitics[3] is a flaccid premonition of cyborg politics, a very open field.

By the late twentieth century, our time, a mythic time, we are all chimeras, theorized and fabricated hybrids of machine and organism; in short, we are cyborgs. The cyborg is our ontology,[4] it gives us our politics. The cyborg is a condensed image of both imagination and material reality, the two joined centers structuring any possibility of historical transformation. In the traditions of "Western" science and politics—the tradition of racist, male-dominant capitalism; the tradition of progress; the tradition of the appropriation of nature as resource for the productions of culture; the tradition of reproduction of the self from the reflections of the other—the relation between organism and machine has been a border war. The stakes in the border war have been the territories of production, reproduction, and imagination. This essay is an argument for *pleasure* in the confusion of boundaries and for *responsibility* in their construction. It is also an effort to contribute to socialist-feminist culture and theory in a post-modernist, non-naturalist mode and in the utopian tradition of imagining a world without gender, which is perhaps a world without genesis, but maybe also a world without end. The cyborg incarnation is outside salvation history.

The cyborg is a creature in a post-gender world; it has no truck with bisexuality, pre-Oedipal symbiosis,[5] unalienated labor,[6] or other seductions to organic wholeness through a final appropriation of all the powers of the parts into a higher unity. In a sense, the cyborg has no origin story in the Western sense; a "final" irony since the cyborg is also the awful apocalyptic *telos* of the "West's" escalating dominations of abstract individuation, an ultimate self untied at last from all dependency, a man in space. An origin story in the "Western," humanist sense depends on the myth of original unity, fullness, bliss and terror, represented by the phallic mother from whom all humans must separate, the task of individual development and of history, the twin potent myths inscribed most powerfully for us in psychoanalysis and Marxism. Hilary Klein has argued[7] that both Marxism and psychoanalysis, in their concepts of labor and of individuation and gender formation, depend on the plot of original unity out of which difference must be produced and enlisted in a drama of escalating domination of woman/nature. The cyborg skips the step of original unity, of identification with nature in the Western sense. This is its illegitimate promise that might lead to subversion of its teleology as star wars.[8]

The cyborg is resolutely committed to partiality, irony, intimacy, and perversity. It is oppositional, utopian, and completely without innocence. No

3. A term used in *The History of Sexuality* (1976) by the French philosopher and cultural historian MICHEL FOUCAULT (1926–1984) to describe the social mechanisms of power that regulate the body, extending the methods of power and knowledge over life itself.

4. The branch of philosophy concerned with the nature of being. Chimera: in Greek mythology, a female monster with a lion's head, a goat's body, and a serpent's tail; more generally, any monster made of incongruous parts.

5. In psychoanalytic theory, a period of maternal dependence, narcissistic identification, and polymorphous erotic drives that occurs during earliest infancy, preceding the Oedipal phase when conflict with the father and the social order emerge. This period of intense attachment to the maternal has been of great interest to contemporary feminist psychoanalytic theorists (e.g., JULIA KRISTEVA and HÉLÈNE CIXOUS).

6. In Marxist theory, labor that does not occur within the exploitative relationships of slavery, feudalism, colonialism, or capitalism.

7. For example, see Klein's "Marxism, Psychoanalysis, and Mother Nature," *Feminist Studies* 15 (1989).

8. The Strategic Defense Initiative, proposed by President Ronald Reagan in 1983, to create a shield against incoming missiles.

longer structured by the polarity of public and private, the cyborg defines a technological polis based partly on a revolution of social relations in the *oikos*, the household. Nature and culture are reworked; the one can no longer be the resource for appropriation or incorporation by the other. The relationships for forming wholes from parts, including those of polarity and hierarchical domination, are at issue in the cyborg world. Unlike the hopes of Frankenstein's monster,[9] the cyborg does not expect its father to save it through a restoration of the garden; i.e., through the fabrication of a heterosexual mate, through its completion in a finished whole, a city and cosmos. The cyborg does not dream of community on the model of the organic family, this time without the Oedipal project.[1] The cyborg would not recognize the Garden of Eden; it is not made of mud and cannot dream of returning to dust. Perhaps that is why I want to see if cyborgs can subvert the apocalypse of returning to nuclear dust in the manic compulsion to name the Enemy. Cyborgs are not reverent; they do not re-member the cosmos. They are wary of holism, but needy for connection—they seem to have a natural feel for united front politics, but without the vanguard party.[2] The main trouble with cyborgs, of course, is that they are the illegitimate offspring of militarism and patriarchal capitalism, not to mention state socialism. But illegitimate offspring are often exceedingly unfaithful to their origins. Their fathers, after all, are inessential.

I will return to the science fiction of cyborgs at the end of this essay, but now I want to signal three crucial boundary breakdowns that make the following political fictional (political scientific) analysis possible. By the late twentieth century in United States scientific culture, the boundary between human and animal is thoroughly breached. The last beachheads of uniqueness have been polluted if not turned into amusement parks—language, tool use, social behavior, mental events, nothing really convincingly settles the separation of human and animal. And many people no longer feel the need of such a separation; indeed, many branches of feminist culture affirm the pleasure of connection of human and other living creatures. Movements for animal rights are not irrational denials of human uniqueness; they are clear-sighted recognition of connection across the discredited breach of nature and culture. Biology and evolutionary theory over the last two centuries have simultaneously produced modern organisms as objects of knowledge and reduced the line between humans and animals to a faint trace re-etched in ideological struggle or professional disputes between life and social sciences. Within this framework, teaching modern Christian creationism should be fought as a form of child abuse.

Biological-determinist ideology is only one position opened up in scientific culture for arguing the meanings of human animality. There is much room for radical political people to contest for the meanings of the breached boundary.[3] The cyborg appears in myth precisely where the boundary

9. That is, the creature constructed in Mary Shelley's novel *Frankenstein* (1818), who begs his creator for a mate.

1. Psychoanalysis describes the task of early childhood—the formation of a distinct ego or identity—as separation from the mother, accomplished through the Oedipal stage in which the paternal figure intervenes between the mother-child dyad.

2. Haraway alludes to Soviet history. Vanguard party: party intended to lead and control the revolution of the workers (e.g., the Bolshevik Party, established during the Russian Revolution). "United front politics": coalitions (e.g., the united fronts set up by the Comintern during the 1930s).

3. Useful references to left and/or feminist radical science movements and theory and to biological/biotechnological issues include: Ruth Bleier, *Science and Gender: A Critique of Biology*

between human and animal is transgressed. Far from signaling a walling off of people from other living beings, cyborgs signal disturbingly and pleasurably tight coupling. Bestiality has a new status in this cycle of marriage exchange.

The second leaky distinction is between animal-human (organism) and machine. Pre-cybernetic machines could be haunted; there was always the specter of the ghost in the machine.[4] This dualism structured the dialogue between materialism and idealism that was settled by a dialectical progeny, called spirit or history, according to taste. But basically machines were not self-moving, self-designing, autonomous. They could not achieve man's dream, only mock it. They were not man, an author to himself, but only a caricature of that masculinist reproductive dream. To think they were otherwise was paranoid. Now we are not so sure. Late-twentieth-century machines have made thoroughly ambiguous the difference between natural and artificial, mind and body, self-developing and externally-designed, and many other distinctions that used to apply to organisms and machines. Our machines are disturbingly lively, and we ourselves frighteningly inert.

Technological determinism is only one ideological space opened up by the reconceptions of machine and organism as coded texts through which we engage in the play of writing and reading the world.[5] "Textualization" of everything in post-structuralist, post-modernist theory has been damned by Marxists and socialist feminists for its utopian disregard for lived relations

---

and Its Themes on Women (New York: Pergamon, 1984); Elizabeth Fee, "Critiques of Modern Science: The Relationship of Feminist and Other Radical Epistemologies," and Evelyn Hammonds, "Women of Color, Feminism, and Science," papers for Symposium on Feminist Perspectives on Science, University of Wisconsin, 11–13 April 1985 (proceedings to be published by Pergamon) [Ruth Bleier, ed., *Feminist Approaches to Science* (New York: Pergamon, 1986)]; Stephen J. Gould, *Mismeasure of Man* (New York: Norton, 1981); Ruth Hubbard, Mary Sue Henifin and Barbara Fried, eds., *Biological Woman, the Convenient Myth* (Cambridge, Mass.: Schenkman, 1982); Evelyn Fox Keller, *Reflections on Gender and Science* (New Haven: Yale University Press, 1985); R. C. Lewontin, Steve Rose, and Leon Kamin, *Not in Our Genes* (New York: Pantheon, 1984); *Radical Science Journal*, 26 Freegrove Road, London N7 9RQ; *Science for the People*, 897 Main St., Cambridge, MA 02139 [Haraway's note]. Haraway's original references are, where appropriate, updated in square brackets.

4. A phrase associated with the dualism of the French philosopher René Descartes (1596–1650), who separated the publicly observable (material, physical) from the private mind (spiritual).

5. Starting points for left and/or feminist approaches to technology and politics include: Ruth Schwartz Cowan, *More Work for Mother: The Ironies of Household Technology from the Open Hearth to the Microwave* (New York: Basic Books, 1983); Joan Rothschild, *Machina ex Dea: Feminist Perspectives on Technology* (New York: Pergamon, 1983); Sharon Traweek, [*Beamtimes and Lifetimes: The World of High Energy Physics* (Cambridge, Mass.: Harvard University Press, 1988)]; R. M. Young and Les Levidov, eds., *Science, Technology, and the Labour Process*, vols. 1–3 (London: CSE Books); Joseph Weizenbaum, *Computer Power and Human Reason* (San Francisco: Freeman, 1976); Langdon Winner, *Autonomous Technology: Technics out of Control as a Theme in Political Thought* (Cambridge, Mass.: MIT Press, 1977); Langdon Winner, [*The Whale and the Reactor* (Chicago: University of Chicago Press, 1986)]; Jan Zimmerman, ed., *The Technological Woman: Interfacing with Tomorrow* (New York: Praeger, 1983); *Global Electronics Newsletter*, 867 West Dana St., #204, Mountain View, CA 94041; *Processed World*, 55 Sutter St., San Francisco, CA 94104; *ISIS*, Women's International Information and Communication Service. P.O. Box 50 (Cornavin), 1211 Geneva 2, Switzerland, and Via Santa Maria dell'Anima 30, 00186 Rome, Italy. Fundamental approaches to modern social studies of science that do not continue the liberal mystification that it all started with Thomas Kuhn, include: Karin Knorr-Cetina, *The Manufacture of Knowledge* (Oxford: Pergamon, 1981); K. D. Knorr-Cetina and Michael Mulkay, eds., *Science Observed: Perspectives on the Social Study of Science* (Beverly Hills, Calif.: Sage, 1983); Bruno Latour and Steve Woolgar, *Laboratory Life: The Social Construction of Scientific Facts* (Beverly Hills, Calif.: Sage, 1979); Robert M. Young, "Interpreting the Production of Science," *New Scientist*, vol. 29 (March 1979), pp. 1026–28. More is claimed than is known about room for contesting productions of science in the mythic/material space of "the laboratory": the 1984 Directory of the Network for the Ethnographic Study of Science, Technology, and Organizations lists a wide range of people and projects crucial to better radical analysis; available from NBSSTO, P.O. Box 11442, Stanford, CA 94305 [Haraway's note]. Kuhn (1922–1996), American historian of science; his book that some view as starting modern social studies of science is *The Structure of Scientific Revolutions* (Chicago: University of Chicago Press, 1962).

of domination that ground the "play" of arbitrary reading.[6] It is certainly true that post-modernist strategies, like my cyborg myth, subvert myriad organic wholes (e.g., the poem, the primitive culture, the biological organism). In short, the certainty of what counts as nature—a source of insight and a promise of innocence—is undermined, probably fatally. The transcendent authorization of interpretation is lost and with it the ontology grounding "Western" epistemology.[7] But the alternative is not cynicism or faithlessness, i.e., some version of abstract existence, like the accounts of technological determinism destroying "man" by the "machine" or "meaningful political action" by the "text." Who cyborgs will be is a radical question; the answers are a matter of survival. Both chimpanzee and artifacts have politics, so why shouldn't we?[8]

The third distinction is a subset of the second: the boundary between physical and non-physical is very imprecise for us. Pop physics books on the consequences of quantum theory and the indeterminacy principle[9] are a kind of popular scientific equivalent to the Harlequin romances as a marker of radical change in American white heterosexuality: they get it wrong, but they are on the right subject. Modern machines are quintessentially microelectronic devices: they are everywhere and they are invisible. Modern machinery is an irreverent upstart god, mocking the Father's ubiquity and spirituality. The silicon chip is a surface for writing; it is etched in molecular scales disturbed only by atomic noise, the ultimate interference for nuclear scores. Writing, power, and technology are old partners in Western stories of the origin of civilization, but miniaturization has changed our experience of mechanism. Miniaturization has turned out to be about power; small is not so much beautiful as pre-eminently dangerous, as in cruise missiles. Contrast

6. Fredric Jameson, "Postmodernism, or, The Cultural Logic of Late Capitalism," *New Left Review*, July/August 1984, pp. 53–94. See Marjorie Perloff, " 'Dirty' Language and Scramble Systems," *Sulfur* 11 (1984), pp. 178–83; Kathleen Fraser, *Something (Even Human Voices) in the Foreground, a Lake* (Berkeley, Calif.: Kelsey St. Press, 1984).

A provocative, comprehensive argument about the policies and theories of "post-modernism" is made by Fredric Jameson, who argues that post-modernism is not an option, a style among others, but a cultural dominant requiring radical reinvention of left politics from within; there is no longer any place from without that gives meaning to the comforting fiction of critical distance. Jameson also makes clear why one cannot be for or against post-modernism, an essentially moralist move. My position is that feminists (and others) need continuous cultural reinvention, post-modernist critique, and historical materialism; only a cyborg would have a chance. The old dominations of white capitalist patriarchy seem nostalgically innocent now: they normalized heterogeneity, e.g., into man and woman, white and black. "Advanced capitalism" and post-modernism release heterogeneity without a norm, and we are flattened, without subjectivity, which requires depth, even unfriendly and drowning depths. It is time to write *The Death of the Clinic*. The clinic's methods required bodies and works; we have texts and surfaces. Our dominations don't work by medicalization and normalization anymore; they work by networking, communications redesign, stress management. Normalization gives way to automation, utter redundancy. Michel Foucault's *Birth of the Clinic* [1963], *History of Sexuality*, and *Discipline and Punish* [1975] name a form of power at its moment of implosion. The discourse of biopolitics gives way to technobabble, the language of the spliced substantive; no noun is left whole by the multinationals. These are their names, listed from one issue of *Science*: Tech-Knowledge, Genentech, Allergen, Hybritech, Compupro, Genen-cor, Syntex, Allelix, Agrigenetics Corp., Syntro, Codon, Repligen, Micro-Angelo from Scion Corp., Percom Data, Inter Systems, Cyborg Corp., Statcom Corp., Intertec. If we are imprisoned by language, then escape from that prison house requires language poets, a kind of cultural restriction enzyme to cut the code; cyborg heteroglossia is one form of radical culture politics [Haraway's note]. On the American Marxist literary critic JAMESON (b. 1934), whose works include *The Prison-House of Language* (1972), see above. "Heteroglossia": an allusion to the highly influential theories of MIKHAIL M. BAKHTIN (1895–1975).

7. The branch of philosophy concerned with ways of knowing.

8. Frans de Waal, *Chimpanzee Politics: Power and Sex among the Apes* (New York: Harper & Row, 1982); Langdon Winner, "Do Artifacts Have Politics?" *Daedalus*, winter 1980 [Haraway's note].

9. That is, the theory formulated in 1927 by the German physicist Werner Heisenberg that one cannot specify both the position and momentum of a particle.

the TV sets of the 1950s or the news cameras of the 1970s with the TV wrist bands or hand-sized video cameras now advertised. Our best machines are made of sunshine; they are all light and clean because they are nothing but signals, electromagnetic waves, a section of a spectrum. And these machines are eminently portable, mobile—a matter of immense human pain in Detroit and Singapore. People are nowhere near so fluid, being both material and opaque. Cyborgs are ether, quintessence.

The ubiquity and invisibility of cyborgs is precisely why these sunshine-belt machines are so deadly. They are as hard to see politically as materially. They are about consciousness—or its simulation.[1] They are floating signifiers moving in pickup trucks across Europe, blocked more effectively by the witch-weavings of the displaced and so unnatural Greenham women,[2] who read the cyborg webs of power very well, than by the militant labor of older masculinist politics, whose natural constituency needs defense jobs. Ultimately the "hardest" science is about the realm of greatest boundary confusion, the realm of pure number, pure spirit, C^3I, cryptography, and the preservation of potent secrets. The new machines are so clean and light. Their engineers are sun-worshipers mediating a new scientific revolution associated with the night dream of post-industrial society. The diseases evoked by these clean machines are "no more" than the minuscule coding changes of an antigen in the immune system, "no more" than the experience of stress. The nimble little fingers of "Oriental" women, the old fascination of little Anglo-Saxon Victorian girls with doll houses, women's enforced attention to the small take on quite new dimensions in this world. There might be a cyborg Alice[3] taking account of these new dimensions. Ironically, it might be the unnatural cyborg women making chips in Asia and spiral dancing in Santa Rita whose constructed unities will guide effective oppositional strategies.

So my cyborg myth is about transgressed boundaries, potent fusions, and dangerous possibilities which progressive people might explore as one part of needed political work. One of my premises is that most American socialists and feminists see deepened dualisms of mind and body, animal and machine, idealism and materialism in the social practices, symbolic formulations, and physical artifacts associated with "high technology" and scientific culture. From *One-Dimensional Man* to *The Death of Nature*,[4] the analytic resources developed by progressives have insisted on the necessary domination of technics and recalled us to an imagined organic body to integrate our resistance. Another of my premises is that the need for unity of people trying to resist worldwide intensification of domination has never been more acute. But a slightly perverse shift of perspective might better enable us to contest for

1. Jean Baudrillard, *Simulations*, trans. P. Foss, P. Patton, P. Beitchman (New York: Semiotext(e), 1983). Jameson ("Postmodernism," p. 66) points out that Plato's definition of the simulacrum is the copy for which there is no original, i.e., the world of advanced capitalism; of pure exchange [Haraway's note]. On the French social critic and theorist BAUDRILLARD (b. 1929) and the Greek philosopher PLATO (ca. 427–ca. 327 B.C.E.), see above.

2. British group that protested the placement of nuclear cruise missiles at the U.S. Air Force base at Greenham Common for nearly two decades, beginning in 1982.

3. A reference to the heroine of *Alice's Adventures in Wonderland* (1865) by Lewis Carroll, who became both very small and very large.

4. Herbert Marcuse, *One-Dimensional Man* (Boston: Beacon, 1964); Carolyn Merchant, *Death of Nature* (San Francisco: Harper & Row, 1980) [Haraway's note].

meanings, as well as for other forms of power and pleasure in technologically-mediated societies.

From one perspective, a cyborg world is about the final imposition of a grid of control on the planet, about the final abstraction embodied in a Star War apocalypse waged in the name of defense, about the final appropriation of women's bodies in a masculinist orgy of war.[5] From another perspective, a cyborg world might be about lived social and bodily realities in which people are not afraid of their joint kinship with animals and machines, not afraid of permanently partial identities and contradictory standpoints. The political struggle is to see from both perspectives at once because each reveals both dominations and possibilities unimaginable from the other vantage point. Single vision produces worse illusions than double vision or many-headed monsters. Cyborg unities are monstrous and illegitimate; in our present political circumstances, we could hardly hope for more potent myths for resistance and recoupling. I like to imagine LAG, the Livermore Action Group,[6] as a kind of cyborg society, dedicated to realistically converting the laboratories that most fiercely embody and spew out the tools of technological apocalypse, and committed to building a political form that actually manages to hold together witches, engineers, elders, perverts, Christians, mothers, and Leninists[7] long enough to disarm the state. Fission Impossible is the name of the affinity group in my town. (Affinity: related not by blood but by choice, the appeal of one chemical nuclear group for another, avidity.)

Fractured Identities

It has become difficult to name one's feminism by a single adjective—or even to insist in every circumstance upon the noun. Consciousness of exclusion through naming is acute. Identities seem contradictory, partial, and strategic. With the hard-won recognition of their social and historical constitution, gender, race, and class cannot provide the basis for belief in "essential" unity. There is nothing about being "female" that naturally binds women. There is not even such a state as "being" female, itself a highly complex category constructed in contested sexual scientific discourses and other social practices. Gender, race, or class consciousness is an achievement forced on us by the terrible historical experience of the contradictory social realities of patriarchy, colonialism, and capitalism. And who counts as "us" in my own rhetoric? Which identities are available to ground such a potent political myth called "us," and what could motivate enlistment in this collectivity? Painful fragmentation among feminists (not to mention among women) along every possible fault line has made the concept of *woman* elusive, an excuse for the matrix of women's dominations of each other. For me—and for many who share a similar historical location in white, professional middle

5. Zoe Sofia, "Exterminating Fetuses," *Diacritics*, vol. 14, no. 2 (summer 1984), pp. 47–59, and "Jupiter Space" (Pomona, Calif.: American Studies Association, 1984) Haraway's note].

6. A group organized to protest the development of nuclear weapons technology at Lawrence Livermore National Laboratory in Livermore, California.

7. Adherents of the militant offshoot of communism associated with Vladimir Lenin (1870–1924), founder of the Russian Bolshevik Party.

class, female, radical, North American, mid-adult bodies—the sources of a crisis in political identity are legion. The recent history for much of the U.S. left and U.S.. feminism has been a response to this kind of crisis by endless splitting and searches for a new essential unity. But there has also been a growing recognition of another response through coalition—affinity, not identity.[8]

Chela Sandoval, from a consideration of specific historical moments in the formation of the new political voice called women of color, has theorized a hopeful model of political identity called "oppositional consciousness," born of the skills for reading webs of power by those refused stable membership in the social categories of race, sex, or class.[9] "Women of color," a name contested at its origins by those whom it would incorporate, as well as a historical consciousness marking systematic breakdown of all the signs of Man in "Western" traditions, constructs a kind of post-modernist identity out of otherness and difference. This post-modernist identity is fully political, whatever might be said about other possible post-modernisms.

Sandoval emphasizes the lack of any essential criterion for identifying who is a woman of color. She notes that the definition of the group has been by conscious appropriation of negation. For example, a Chicana or U.S. black woman has not been able to speak as a woman or as a black person or as a Chicano. Thus, she was at the bottom of a cascade of negative identities, left out of even the privileged oppressed authorial categories called "women and blacks," who claimed to make the important revolutions. The category "woman" negated all non-white women; "black" negated all non-black people, as well as all black women. But there was also no "she," no singularity, but a sea of differences among U.S. women who have affirmed their historical identity as U.S. women of color. This identity marks out a self-consciously constructed space that cannot affirm the capacity to act on the basis of natural identification, but only on the basis of conscious coalition, of affinity, of political kinship.[1] Unlike the "woman" of some streams of the white women's movement in the United States, there is no naturalization of the matrix, or at least this is what Sandoval argues is uniquely available through the power of oppositional consciousness.

Sandoval's argument has to be seen as one potent formulation for feminists out of the worldwide development of anti-colonialist discourse, i.e., discourse dissolving the "West" and its highest product—the one who is not

8. Powerful developments of coalition politics emerge from "third world" speakers, speaking from nowhere, the displaced center of the universe, earth: "We live on the third planet from the sun"—*Sun Poem* by Jamaican writer Edward Kamau Braithwaite, review by Nathaniel Mackey, *Sulfur*, 11 (1984), pp. 200–205. *Home Girls*, ed. Barbara Smith (New York: Kitchen Table, Women of Color Press, 1983), ironically subverts naturalized identities precisely while constructing a place from which to speak called home. See esp. Bernice Reagan, "Coalition Politics, Turning the Century," pp. 356–68 [Haraway's note]. On the African American feminist critic SMITH (b. 1946), see below.

9. Chela Sandoval. "Dis-illusionment and the Poetry of the Future: The Making of Oppositional Consciousness," Ph.D. qualifying essay, UCSC, 1984 [Haraway's note].

1. bell hooks, *Ain't I a Woman?* (Boston: South End Press, 1981); Gloria Hull, Patricia Bell Scott, and Barbara Smith, eds., *All the Women Are White, All the Men Are Black, But Some of Us Are Brave: Black Women's Studies* (Old Westbury, Conn.: Feminist Press, 1982). Toni Cade Bambara, in *The Salt Eaters* (New York: Vintage/Random House, 1981), writes an extraordinary post-modernist novel, in which the women of color theater group, The Seven Sisters, explores a form of unity. Thanks to Elliott Evans's readings of Bambara, Ph.D. qualifying essay, UCSC, 1984 [Haraway's note]. On the African American feminist critic HOOKS (b. 1952), see below.

animal, barbarian, or woman; i.e., man, the author of a cosmos called history. As orientalism is deconstructed politically and semiotically, the identities of the occident destabilize, including those of feminists.[2] Sandoval argues that "women of color" have a chance to build an effective unity that does not replicate the imperializing, totalizing revolutionary subjects of previous Marxisms and feminisms which had not faced the consequences of the disorderly polyphony emerging from decolonization.

Katie King has emphasized the limits of identification and the political/poetic mechanics of identification built into reading "the poem," that generative core of cultural feminism. King criticizes the persistent tendency among contemporary feminists from different "moments" or "conversations" in feminist practice to taxonomize[3] the women's movement to make one's own political tendencies appear to be the *telos* of the whole. These taxonomies tend to remake feminist history to appear to be an ideological struggle among coherent types persisting over time, especially those typical units called radical, liberal, and socialist feminism. Literally, all other feminisms are either incorporated or marginalized, usually by building an explicit ontology and epistemology.[4] Taxonomies of feminism produce epistemologies to police deviation from official women's experience. And of course, "women's culture," like women of color, is consciously created by mechanisms inducing affinity. The rituals of poetry, music, and certain forms of academic practice have been pre-eminent. The politics of race and culture in the U.S. women's movements are intimately interwoven. The common achievement of King and Sandoval is learning how to craft a poetic/political unity without relying on a logic of appropriation, incorporation, and taxonomic identification.

The theoretical and practical struggle against unity-through-domination or unity-through-incorporation ironically not only undermines the justifications for patriarchy, colonialism, humanism, positivism, essentialism, scientism, and other unlamented -isms, but *all* claims for an organic or natural standpoint. I think that radical and socialist/Marxist feminisms have also undermined their/our epistemological strategies and that this is a crucially valuable step in imagining possible unities. It remains to be seen whether all "epistemologies" as Western political people have known them fail us in the task to build effective affinities.

It is important to note that the effort to construct revolutionary standpoints, epistemologies as achievements of people committed to changing the world, has been part of the process showing the limits of identification. The acid tools of post-modernist theory and the constructive tools of ontological

2. On orientalism in feminist works and elsewhere, see Lisa Lowe "Orientation: Representations of Cultural and Sexual 'Others,'" Ph.D. thesis, UCSC; Edward Said, *Orientalism* (New York: Pantheon, 1978 [Haraway's note]. On the Palestinian-born American critic SAID (b. 1935), see above.

3. To categorize or classify.

4. Katie King has developed a theoretically sensitive treatment of the workings of feminist taxonomies as genealogies of power in feminist ideology and polemic: "Prospectus," in *Gender and Genre: Academic Practice and the Making of Criticism* (Santa Cruz, Calif.: University of California, 1984). King examines an intelligent, problematic example of taxonomizing feminisms to make a little machine producing the desired final position: Alison Jaggar, *Feminist Politics and Human Nature* (Totowa, N.J.: Rowman & Allanheld, 1983). My caricature here of socialist and radical feminism is also an example [Haraway's note].

discourse about revolutionary subjects might be seen as ironic allies in dissolving Western selves in the interests of survival. We are excruciatingly conscious of what it means to have a historically constituted body. But with the loss of innocence in our origin, there is no expulsion from the Garden either. Our politics lose the indulgence of guilt with the naïveté of innocence. But what would another political myth for socialist feminism look like? What kind of politics could embrace partial, contradictory, permanently unclosed constructions of personal and collective selves and still be faithful, effective—and, ironically, socialist feminist?

I do not know of any other time in history when there was greater need for political unity to confront effectively the dominations of "race," "gender," "sexuality," and "class." I also do not know of any other time when the kind of unity we might help build could have been possible. None of "us" have any longer the symbolic or material capability of dictating the shape of reality to any of "them." Or at least "we" cannot claim innocence from practicing such dominations. White women, including socialist feminists, discovered (i.e., were forced kicking and screaming to notice) the non-innocence of the category "woman." That consciousness changes the geography of all previous categories; it denatures them as heat denatures a fragile protein. Cyborg feminists have to argue that "we" do not want any more natural matrix of unity and that no construction is whole. Innocence, and the corollary insistence on victimhood as the only ground for insight, has done enough damage. But the constructed revolutionary subject must give late-twentieth-century people pause as well. In the fraying of identities and in the reflexive strategies for constructing them, the possibility opens up for weaving something other than a shroud for the day after the apocalypse that so prophetically ends salvation history.

Both Marxist/socialist feminisms and radical feminisms have simultaneously naturalized and denatured the category "women" and consciousness of the social lives of "women." Perhaps a schematic caricature can highlight both kinds of moves. Marxian socialism is rooted in an analysis of wage labor which reveals class structure. The consequence of the wage relationship is systematic alienation, as the worker is dissociated from his (sic) product. Abstraction and illusion rule in knowledge, domination rules in practice. Labor is the pre-eminently privileged category enabling the Marxist to overcome illusion and find that point of view which is necessary for changing the world. Labor is the humanizing activity that makes man; labor is an ontological category permitting the knowledge of a subject, and so the knowledge of subjugation and alienation.

In faithful filiation, socialist feminism advanced by allying itself with the basic analytic strategies of Marxism. The main achievement of both Marxist feminists and socialist feminists was to expand the category of labor to accommodate what (some) women did, even when the wage relation was subordinated to a more comprehensive view of labor under capitalist patriarchy. In particular, women's labor in the household and women's activity as mothers generally, i.e., reproduction in the socialist feminist sense, entered theory on the authority of analogy to the Marxian concept of labor. The unity of women here rests on an epistemology based on the ontological structure of "labor." Marxist/socialist feminism does not "naturalize" unity; it is a possible achievement based on a possible standpoint rooted in social relations. The essentializing move is in the ontological structure of labor or of its analogue, women's activity.[5] The inheritance of Marxian humanism, with its pre-eminently Western self, is the difficulty for me. The contribution from these formulations has been the emphasis on the daily responsibility of real women to build unities, rather than to naturalize them.

Catharine MacKinnon's version of radical feminism is itself a caricature of the appropriating, incorporating, totalizing tendencies of Western theories of identity grounding action.[6] It is factually and politically wrong to assimilate all of the diverse "moments" or "conversations" in recent women's politics named radical feminism to MacKinnon's version. But the teleological logic[7] of her theory shows how an epistemology and ontology—including their negations—erase or police difference. Only one of the effects of MacKinnon's theory is the rewriting of the history of the polymorphous field called radical feminism. The major effect is the production of a theory of experience, of women's identity, that is a kind of apocalypse for all revolutionary standpoints. That is, the totalization built into this tale of radical feminism achieves its end—the unity of women—by enforcing the experience of and testimony to radical non-being. As for the Marxist/socialist feminist, consciousness is an achievement, not a natural fact. And MacKinnon's theory eliminates some of the difficulties built into humanist revolutionary subjects, but at the cost of radical reductionism.

MacKinnon argues that radical feminism necessarily adopted a different analytical strategy from Marxism, looking first not at the structure of class, but at the structure of sex/gender and its generative relationship, men's constitution and appropriation of women sexually. Ironically, MacKinnon's "ontology" constructs a non-subject, a non-being. Another's desire, not the self's labor, is the origin of "woman." She therefore develops a theory of consciousness that enforces what can count as "women's" experience—any-

5. The feminist standpoint argument is being developed by: Jane Flax, "Political Philosophy and the Patriarchal Unconsciousness," in Sandra Harding and Merrill Hintikka, eds., *Discovering Reality* (Dordrecht: Reidel, 1983); Sandra Harding, "The Contradictions and Ambivalence of a Feminist Science," ms.; Harding and Hintikka, *Discovering Reality*; Nancy Hartsock, *Money, Sex, and Power* (New York: Longman, 1983) and "The Feminist Standpoint: Developing the Ground for a Specifically Feminist Historical Materialism," in Harding and Hintikka, *Discovering Reality;* Mary O'Brien, *The Politics of Reproduction* (New York: Routledge & Kegan Paul, 1981); Hilary Rose, "Hand, Brain, and Heart: A Feminist Epistemology for the Natural Sciences," *Signs*, vol. 9, no. 1 (1983), pp. 73–90; Dorothy Smith, "Women's Perspective as a Radical Critique of Sociology," *Sociological Inquiry* 44 (1974), and "A Sociology of Women," in J. Sherman and E. T. Beck, eds., *The Prism of Sex* (Madison: University of Wisconsin Press, 1979).

The central role of object-relations versions of psychoanalysis and related strong universalizing moves in discussing reproduction, caring work, and mothering in many approaches to epistemology underline their authors' resistance to what I am calling post-modernism. For me, both the universalizing moves and the versions of psychoanalysis make analysis of "women's place in the integrated circuit" difficult and lead to systematic difficulties in accounting or even seeing major aspects of the construction of gender and gender social life [Haraway's note]. Haraway's main target in object-relations theory is Nancy Chodorow's influential book *The Reproduction of Mothering* (1978).

6. Catharine MacKinnon, "Feminism, Marxism, Method, and the State: An Agenda for Theory," *Signs*, vol. 7, no. 3 (1982), pp. 515–44. A critique indebted to MacKinnon, but without the reductionism and with an elegant feminist account of Foucault's paradoxical conservatism on sexual violence (rape), is Teresa de Lauretis, ["The Violence of Rhetoric: Considerations on Representation and Gender," *Semiotica* 54 (1985), pp. 11–31], special issue on "The Rhetoric of Violence," ed. Nancy Armstrong. A theoretically elegant feminist social-historical examination of family violence, that insists on women's, men's, children's complex agency without losing sight of the material structures of male domination, race, and class, is Linda Gordon, [*Heroes of Their Own Lives* (New York: Viking, 1988)] [Haraway's note]. MacKinnon (b. 1946), an American legal theorist, is best known for arguing in favor of local ordinances against pornography.

7. Logic oriented toward an end.

thing that names sexual violation, indeed, sex itself as far as "women" can be concerned. Feminist practice is the construction of this form of consciousness; i.e., the self-knowledge of a self-who-is-not.

Perversely, sexual appropriation in this radical feminism still has the epistemological status of labor, i.e., the point from which analysis able to contribute to changing the world must flow. But sexual objectification, not alienation, is the consequence of the structure of sex/gender. In the realm of knowledge, the result of sexual objectification is illusion and abstraction. However, a woman is not simply alienated from her product, but in a deep sense does not exist as a subject, or even potential subject, since she owes her existence as a woman to sexual appropriation. To be constituted by another's desire is not the same thing as to be alienated in the violent separation of the laborer from his product.

MacKinnon's radical theory of experience is totalizing in the extreme; it does not so much marginalize as obliterate the authority of any other women's political speech and action. It is a totalization producing what Western patriarchy itself never succeeded in doing—feminists' consciousness of the non-existence of women, except as products of men's desire. I think MacKinnon correctly argues that no Marxian version of identity can firmly ground women's unity. But in solving the problem of the contradictions of any Western revolutionary subject for feminist purposes, she develops an even more authoritarian doctrine of experience. If my complaint about socialist/Marxian standpoints is their unintended erasure of polyvocal, unassimilable, radical difference made visible in anti-colonial discourse and practice, MacKinnon's intentional erasure of all difference through the device of the "essential" non-existence of women is not reassuring.

In my taxonomy, which like any other taxonomy is a reinscription of history, radical feminism can accommodate all the activities of women named by socialist feminists as forms of labor only if the activity can somehow be sexualized. Reproduction had different tones of meanings for the two tendencies, one rooted in labor, one in sex, both calling the consequences of domination and ignorance of social and personal reality "false consciousness."[8]

Beyond either the difficulties or the contributions in the argument of any one author, neither Marxist nor radical feminist points of view have tended to embrace the status of a partial explanation; both were regularly constituted as totalities. Western explanation has demanded as much; how else could the "Western" author incorporate its others? Each tried to annex other forms of domination by expanding its basic categories through analogy, simple listing, or addition. Embarrassed silence about race among white radical and socialist feminists was one major, devastating political consequence. History and polyvocality disappear into political taxonomies that try to establish genealogies. There was no structural room for race (or for much else) in theory claiming to reveal the construction of the category woman and social group women as a unified or totalizable whole. The structure of my caricature looks like this:

8. A Marxist term referring to an individual's tendency to view reality in ways congruent with the interests of the dominant orthodoxy rather than in ways that reflect his or her own class interest.

Socialist Feminism—
  structure of class//wage labor//alienation
  labor, by analogy reproduction, by extension sex, by addition race
Radical Feminism—
  structure of gender//sexual appropriation//objectification
  sex, by analogy labor, by extension reproduction, by addition race

In another context, the French theorist Julia Kristeva claimed women appeared as a historical group after World War II, along with groups like youth. Her dates are doubtful; but we are now accustomed to remembering that as objects of knowledge and as historical actors, "race" did not always exist, "class" has a historical genesis, and "homosexuals" are quite junior. It is no accident that the symbolic system of the family of man—and so the essence of woman—breaks up at the same moment that networks of connection among people on the planet are unprecedentedly multiple, pregnant, and complex. 'Advanced capitalism" is inadequate to convey the structure of this historical moment. In the "Western" sense, the end of man is at stake. It is no accident that woman disintegrates into women in our time. Perhaps socialist feminists were not substantially guilty of producing essentialist theory that suppressed women's particularity and contradictory interests. I think we have been, at least through unreflective participation in the logics, languages, and practices of white humanism and through searching for a single ground of domination to secure our revolutionary voice. Now we have less excuse. But in the consciousness of our failures, we risk lapsing into boundless difference and giving up on the confusing task of making partial, real connection. Some differences are playful; some are poles of world historical systems of domination. "Epistemology" is about knowing the difference.

The Informatics of Domination

In this attempt at an epistemological and political position, I would like to sketch a picture of possible unity, a picture indebted to socialist and feminist principles of design. The frame for my sketch is set by the extent and importance of rearrangements in worldwide social relations tied to science and technology. I argue for a politics rooted in claims about fundamental changes in the nature of class, race, and gender in an emerging system of world order analogous in its novelty and scope to that created by industrial capitalism; we are living through a movement from an organic, industrial society to a polymorphous, information system—from all work to all play, a deadly game. Simultaneously material and ideological, the dichotomies may be expressed in the following chart of transitions from the comfortable old hierarchical dominations to the scary new networks I have called the informatics of domination:

Representation	Simulation
Bourgeois novel, realism	Science fiction, post-modernism
Organism	Biotic component
Depth, integrity	Surface, boundary
Heat	Noise
Biology as clinical practice	Biology as inscription

Physiology	Communications engineering
Small group	Subsystem
Perfection	Optimization
Eugenics	Population control
Decadence, *Magic Mountain*	Obsolescence, *Future Shock*[9]
Hygiene	Stress Management
Microbiology, tuberculosis	Immunology, AIDS
Organic division of labor	Ergonomics/cybernetics of labor
Functional specialization	Modular construction
Reproduction	Replication
Organic sex role specialization	Optimal genetic strategies
Biological determinism	Evolutionary inertia, constraints
Community ecology	Ecosystem
Racial chain of being	Neo-imperialism, United Nations humanism
Scientific management in home/fractory	Global factory/Electronic cottage
Family/Market/Factory	Women in the Integrated Circuit
Family wage	Comparable worth[1]
Public/Private	Cyborg citizenship
Nature/Culture	Fields of difference
Cooperation	Communications enhancement
Freud	Lacan[2]
Sex	Genetic engineering
Labor	Robotics
Mind	Artificial Intelligence
World War II	Star Wars
White Capitalist Patriarchy	Informatics of Domination

This list suggests several interesting things.[3] First, the objects on the right-hand side cannot be coded as "natural," a realization that subverts naturalistic coding for the left-hand side as well. We cannot go back ideologically or materially. It's not just that "god" is dead; so is the "goddess." In relation to objects like biotic components, one must think not in terms of essential properties, but in terms of strategies of design, boundary constraints, rates of flows, systems logics, costs of lowering constraints. Sexual reproduction is one kind of reproductive strategy among many, with costs and benefits as

9. A 1970 work of social history, and production by Alvin Toffler. *The Magic Mountain* (1924), a novel by Thomas Mann.

1. The concept that male and female workers holding different jobs that are comparable in difficulty and responsibility should receive equal pay. "Family wage": a wage high enough that a single (usually male) bread winner can support a family.

2. JACQUES LACAN (1901–1981), French psychoanalyst; he argued that the unconscious is structured like a language and claimed to be the intellectual heir of SIGMUND FREUD (1856–1939), the Austrian founder of psychoanalysis.

3. My previous efforts to understand biology as a cybernetic command-control discourse and organisms as "natural-technical objects of knowledge" are: "The High Cost of Information in Post–World War II Evolutionary Biology," *Philosophical Forum*, vol. 13, nos. 2–3 (1979), pp. 206–37; "Signs of Dominance: From a Physiology to a Cybernetics of Primate Society," *Studies in History of Biology* 6 (1983), pp. 129–219; "Class, Race, Sex, Scientific Objects of Knowledge: A Socialist-Feminist Perspective on the Social Construction of Productive Knowledge and Some Political Consequences," in Violet Haas and Carolyn Perucci, eds., *Women in Scientific and Engineering Professions* (Ann Arbor: University of Michigan Press, 1984), pp. 212–29 [Haraway's note].

a function of the system environment. Ideologies of sexual reproduction can no longer reasonably call on the notions of sex and sex role as organic aspects in natural objects like organisms and families. Such reasoning will be unmasked as irrational, and ironically corporate executives reading *Playboy* and anti-porn radical feminists will make strange bedfellows in jointly unmasking the irrationalism.

Likewise for race, ideologies about human diversity have to be formulated in terms of frequencies of parameters, like blood groups or intelligence scores. It is "irrational" to invoke concepts like primitive and civilized. For liberals and radicals, the search for integrated social systems gives way to a new practice called "experimental ethnography" in which an organic object dissipates in attention to the play of writing. At the level of ideology, we see translations of racism and colonialism into languages of development and underdevelopment, rates and constraints of modernization. Any objects or persons can be reasonably thought of in terms of disassembly and reassembly; no "natural" architectures constrain system design. The financial districts in all the world's cities, as well as the export-processing and free-trade zones, proclaim this elementary fact of "late capitalism." The entire universe of objects that can be known scientifically must be formulated as problems in communications engineering (for the managers) or theories of the text (for those who would resist). Both are cyborg semiologies.[4]

One should expect control strategies to concentrate on boundary conditions and interfaces, on rates of flow across boundaries—and not on the integrity of natural objects. "Integrity" or "sincerity" of the Western self gives way to decision procedures and expert systems. For example, control strategies applied to women's capacities to give birth to new human beings will be developed in the languages of population control and maximization of goal achievement for individual decision-makers. Control strategies will be formulated in terms of rates, costs of constraints, degrees of freedom. Human beings, like any other component or subsystem, must be localized in a system architecture whose basic modes of operation are probabilistic, statistical. No objects, spaces, or bodies are sacred in themselves; any component can be interfaced with any other if the proper standard, the proper code, can be constructed for processing signals in a common language. Exchange in this world transcends the universal translation effected by capitalist markets that Marx analyzed so well.[5] The privileged pathology affecting all kinds of components in this universe is stress—communications breakdown.[6] The cyborg is not subject to Foucault's biopolitics; the cyborg simulates politics, a much more potent field of operations.

This kind of analysis of scientific and cultural objects of knowledge which have appeared historically since World War II prepares us to notice some important inadequacies in feminist analysis which has proceeded as if the

4. Studies of sign systems.

5. That is, the translation of individual labor power into commodities. On the German political theorist, economist, and revolutionary KARL MARX (1818–1883), see above.

6. E. Rusten Hogness, "Why Stress? A Look at the Making of Stress, 1936–56," available from the author, 4437 Mill Creek Rd., Healdsburg, CA 95448 [Haraway's note].

organic, hierarchical dualisms ordering discourse in "the West" since Aristotle still ruled. They have been cannibalized, or as Zoe Sofia (Sofoulis) might put it, they have been "techno-digested." The dichotomies between mind and body, animal and human, organism and machine, public and private, nature and culture, men and women, primitive and civilized are all in question ideologically. The actual situation of women is their integration/exploitation into a world system of production/reproduction and communication called the informatics of domination. The home, workplace, market, public arena, the body itself—all can be dispersed and interfaced in nearly infinite, polymorphous ways, with large consequences for women and others—consequences that themselves are very different for different people and which make potent oppositional international movements difficult to imagine and essential for survival. One important route for reconstructing socialist-feminist politics is through theory and practice addressed to the social relations of science and technology, including crucially the systems of myth and meanings structuring our imaginations. The cyborg is a kind of disassembled and reassembled post-modern collective and personal self. This is the self feminists must code.

Communications technologies and biotechnologies are the crucial tools recrafting our bodies. These tools embody and enforce new social relations for women worldwide. Technologies and scientific discourses can be partially understood as formalizations, i.e., as frozen moments, of the fluid social interactions constituting them, but they should also be viewed as instruments for enforcing meanings. The boundary is permeable between tool and myth, instrument and concept, historical systems of social relations and historical anatomies of possible bodies, including objects of knowledge. Indeed, myth and tool mutually constitute each other.

Furthermore, communications sciences and modern biologies are constructed by a common move—*the translation of the world into a problem of coding*, a search for a common language in which all resistance to instrumental control disappears and all heterogeneity can be submitted to disassembly, reassembly, investment, and exchange.

In communications sciences, the translation of the world into a problem in coding can be illustrated by looking at cybernetic (feedback controlled) systems theories applied to telephone technology, computer design, weapons deployment, or data base construction and maintenance. In each case, solution to the key questions rests on a theory of language and control; the key operation is determining the rates, directions, and probabilities of flow of a quantity called information. The world is subdivided by boundaries differentially permeable to information. Information is just that kind of quantifiable element (unit, basis of unity) which allows universal translation, and so unhindered instrumental power (called effective communication). The biggest threat to such power is interruption of communication. Any system breakdown is a function of stress. The fundamentals of this technology can be condensed into the metaphor C³I, command-control-communication-intelligence, the military's symbol for its operations theory.

In modern biologies, the translation of the world into a problem in coding can be illustrated by molecular genetics, ecology, socio-biological evolutionary theory, and immunobiology. The organism has been translated into problems of genetic coding and read-out. Biotechnology, a writing technology, informs research broadly.[7] In a sense, organisms have ceased to exist as objects of knowledge, giving way to biotic components, i.e., special kinds of information processing devices. The analogous moves in ecology could be examined by probing the history and utility of the concept of the ecosystem. Immunobiology and associated medical practices are rich exemplars of the privilege of coding and recognition systems as objects of knowledge, as constructions of bodily reality for us. Biology is here a kind of cryptography. Research is necessarily a kind of intelligence activity. Ironies abound. A stressed system goes awry; its communication processes break down; it fails to recognize the difference between self and other. Human babies with baboon hearts evoke national ethical perplexity—for animal-rights activists at least as much as for guardians of human purity. Gay men, Haitian immigrants, and intravenous drug users[8] are the "privileged" victims of an awful immune-system disease that marks (inscribes on the body) confusion of boundaries and moral pollution.

But these excursions into communications sciences and biology have been at a rarefied level; there is a mundane, largely economic reality to support my claim that these sciences and technologies indicate fundamental transformations in the structure of the world for us. Communications technologies depend on electronics. Modern states, multinational corporations, military power, welfare-state apparatuses, satellite systems, political processes, fabrication of our imaginations, labor-control systems, medical constructions of our bodies, commercial pornography, the international division of labor, and religious evangelism depend intimately upon electronics. Microelectronics is the technical basis of simulacra, i.e., of copies without originals.

Microelectronics mediates the translations of *labor* into robotics and word processing; *sex* into genetic engineering and reproductive technologies; and *mind* into artificial intelligence and decision procedures. The new biotechnologies concern more than human reproduction. Biology as a powerful engineering science for redesigning materials and processes has revolutionary implications for industry, perhaps most obvious today in areas of fermentation, agriculture, and energy. Communications sciences and biology are constructions of natural-technical objects of knowledge in which the difference between machine and organism is thoroughly blurred; mind, body, and tool are on very intimate terms. The "multinational" material organization of the production and reproduction of daily life and the symbolic organization of the production and reproduction of culture and imagination seem equally implicated. The boundary-maintaining images of base and superstructure,[9] public and private, or material and ideal never seemed more feeble.

I have used Rachel Grossman's image of women in the integrated circuit to name the situation of women in a world so intimately restructured through

7. A left entry to the biotechnology debate: *GeneWatch*, a Bulletin of the Committee for Responsible Genetics, 5 Doane St. 4th floor, Boston, MA 02109; Susan Wright, ["Recombinant DNA Technology and Its Social Transformation, 1972–82," *Osiris*, 2d ser., vol. 2 (1996), pp. 303–60] and "Recombinant DNA: The Status of Hazards and Controls," *Environment*, July/August 1982; Edward Yoxen, *The Gene Business* (New York: Harper & Row, 1983) [Haraway's note].

8. These three groups were the focus of medical attention when AIDS was first identified in the 1980s.

9. "Base" and "superstructure" are Marxist terms: a society's base is its economic mode of production, which conditions its superstructure—its social, political, juridical, and intellectual life generally.

the social relations of science and technology.[1] I use the odd circumlocution, "the social relations of science and technology," to indicate that we are not dealing with a technological determinism, but with a historical system depending upon structured relations among people. But the phrase should also indicate that science and technology provide fresh sources of power, that we need fresh sources of analysis and political action.[2] Some of the rearrangements of race, sex, and class rooted in high-tech-facilitated social relations can make socialist feminism more relevant to effective progressive politics.

The Homework Economy

The "new industrial resolution" is producing a new worldwide working class. The extreme mobility of capital and the emerging international division of labor are intertwined with the emergence of new collectivities, and the weakening of familiar groupings. These developments are neither gender- nor race-neutral. White men in advanced industrial societies have become newly vulnerable to permanent job loss, and women are not disappearing from the job rolls at the same rates as men. It is not simply that women in third-world countries are the preferred labor force for the science-based multinationals in the export-processing sectors, particularly in electronics. The picture is more systematic and involves reproduction, sexuality, culture, consumption, and production. In the prototypical Silicon Valley, many women's lives have been structured around employment in electronics-dependent jobs, and their intimate realities include serial heterosexual monogamy, negotiating childcare, distance from extended kin or most other forms of traditional community, a high likelihood of loneliness and extreme economic vulnerability as they age. The ethnic and racial diversity of women in Silicon Valley structures a microcosm of conflicting differences in culture, family, religion, education, language.

Richard Gordon has called this new situation the homework economy.[3] Although he includes the phenomenon of literal homework emerging in con-

1. Starting references for "women in the integrated circuit": Pamela D'Onofrio-Flores and Sheila M. Pfafflin, eds., *Scientific-Technological Change and the Role of Women in Development* (Boulder, Colo.: Westview Press, 1982); Maria Patricia Fernandez-Kelly, *For We Are Sold, I and My People* (Albany, N.Y.: SUNY Press, 1983); Annette Fuentes and Barbara Ehrenreich, *Women in the Global Factory* (Boston: South End Press, 1983), with an especially useful list of resources and organizations; Rachael Grossman, "Women's Place in the Integrated Circuit," *Radical America*, vol. 14, no. 1 (1980), pp. 29–50; June Nash and M. P. Fernandez-Kelly, eds., *Women and Men and the International Division of Labor* (Albany, N.Y.: SUNY Press, 1983); Aihwa Ong, "Japanese Factories, Malay Workers: Industrialization and the Cultural Construction of Gender in West Malaysia," in [Jane Atkinson and Shelly Errington, eds., *Power and Difference: Gender in Island Southeast Asia* (Stanford: Stanford University Press, 1990)]; Science Policy Research Unity, *Microelectronics and Women's Employment in Britain* (University of Sussex, 1982) [Haraway's note].

2. The best example is Bruno Latour, *Les Microbes: Guerre et Paix, suivi de Irréductions* [*Microbes: War and Peace, followed by Irreductions*] (Paris: Métailié, 1984) [Haraway's note].

3. For the homework economy and some supporting arguments: Richard Gordon, "The Computerization of Daily Life, the Sexual Division of Labor, and the Homework Economy," in R. Gordon, ed., *Microelectronics in Transition* (Norwood N.J.: Ablex, 1985); Patricia Hill Collins. "Third World Women in America," and Sara G. Burr, "Woman and Work," in Barbara K. Haber, ed., *The Women's Annual, 1981* (Boston: G. K. Hall, 1982); Judith Gregory and Karen Nussbaum, "Race against Time: Automation of the Office," *Office: Technology and People* 1 (1982), pp. 197–236; Frances Fox Piven and Richard Cloward, *The New Class War: Reagan's Attack on the Welfare State and Its Consequences* (New York: Pantheon, 1982); Microelectronics Group, *Microelectronics: Capitalist Technology and the Working Class* (London: CSE, 1980); Karin Stallard, Barbara Ehrenreich, and Holly Sklar, *Poverty in the American Dream* (Boston: South End Press, 1983), including a useful organization and resource list [Haraway's note].

nection with electronics assembly, Gordon intends "homework economy" to name a restructuring of work that broadly has the characteristics formerly ascribed to female jobs, jobs literally done only by women. Work is being redefined as both literally female and feminized, whether performed by men or women. To be feminized means to be made extremely vulnerable; able to be disassembled, reassembled, exploited as a reserve labor force; seen less as workers than as servers; subjected to time arrangements on and off the paid job that make a mockery of a limited work day; leading an existence that always borders on being obscene, out of place, and reducible to sex. Deskilling is an old strategy newly applicable to formerly privileged workers. However, the homework economy does not refer only to large-scale deskilling, nor does it deny that new areas of high skill are emerging, even for women and men previously excluded from skilled employment. Rather, the concept indicates that factory, home, and market are integrated on a new scale and that the places of women are crucial—and need to be analyzed for differences among women and for meanings for relations between men and women in various situations.

The homework economy as a world capitalist organizational structure is made possible by (not caused by) the new technologies. The success of the attack on relatively privileged, mostly white, men's unionized jobs is tied to the power of the new communications technologies to integrate and control labor despite extensive dispersion and decentralization. The consequences of the new technologies are felt by women both in the loss of the family (male) wage (if they ever had access to this white privilege) and in the character of their own jobs, which are becoming capital-intensive, e.g., office work and nursing.

The new economic and technological arrangements are also related to the collapsing welfare state and the ensuing intensification of demands on women to sustain daily life for themselves as well as for men, children, and old people. The feminization of poverty—generated by dismantling the welfare state, by the homework economy where stable jobs become the exception, and sustained by the expectation that women's wage will not be matched by a male income for the support of children—has become an urgent focus. The causes of various women-headed households are a function of race, class, or sexuality; but their increasing generality is a ground for coalitions of women on many issues. That women regularly sustain daily life partly as a function of their enforced status as mothers is hardly new; the kind of integration with the overall capitalist and progressively war-based economy is new. The particular pressure, for example, on U.S. black women, who have achieved an escape from (barely) paid domestic service and who now hold clerical and similar jobs in large numbers, has large implications for continued enforced black poverty *with* employment. Teenage women in industrializing areas of the third world increasingly find themselves the sole or major source of a cash wage for their families, while access to land is ever more problematic. These developments must have major consequences in the psychodynamics and politics of gender and race.

Within the framework of three major stages of capitalism (commercial/early industrial, monopoly, multinational)—tied to nationalism, imperialism, and multinationalism, and related to Jameson's three dominant aesthetic periods of realism, modernism, and post-modernism—I would argue that specific forms of families dialectically relate to forms of capital and to its political and cultural concomitants. Although lived problematically and unequally, ideal forms of these families might be schematized as (1) the patriarchal nuclear family, structured by the dichotomy between public and private and accompanied by the white bourgeois ideology of separate spheres[4] and nineteenth-century Anglo-American bourgeois feminism; (2) the modern family mediated (or enforced) by the welfare state and institutions like the family wage, with a flowering of a-feminist heterosexual ideologies, including their radical versions represented in Greenwich Village around World War I; and (3) the "family" of the homework economy with its oxymoronic structure of women-headed households and its explosion of feminisms and the paradoxical intensification and erosion of gender itself.

This is the context in which the projections for worldwide structural unemployment stemming from the new technologies are part of the picture of the homework economy. As robotics and related technologies put men out of work in "developed" countries and exacerbate failure to generate male jobs in third-world "development," and as the automated office becomes the rule even in labor-surplus countries, the feminization of work intensifies. Black women in the United States have long known what it looks like to face the structural underemployment ("feminization") of black men, as well as their own highly vulnerable position in the wage economy. It is no longer a secret that sexuality, reproduction, family, and community life are interwoven with this economic structure in myriad ways which have also differentiated the situations of white and black women. Many more women and men will contend with similar situations, which will make cross-gender and race alliances on issues of basic life support (with or without jobs) necessary, not just nice.

The new technologies also have a profound effect on hunger and on food production for subsistence worldwide. Rae Lessor Blumberg estimates that women produce about fifty per cent of the world's subsistence food.[5] Women are excluded generally from benefiting from the increased high-tech commodification of food and energy crops, their days are made more arduous

4. That is, the division of life into the public sphere of work and the private sphere of the home, where authority was said to be held by men and by women, respectively.

5. Rae Lessor Blumberg, "A General Theory of Sex Stratification and Its Application to the Position of Women in Today's World Economy," paper delivered to Sociology Board, UCSC, February 1983. Also Blumberg, *Stratification: Socioeconomic and Sexual Inequality* (Boston; Brown, 1981). See also Sally Hacker, "Doing It the Hard Way: Ethnographic Studies in the Agribusiness and Engineering Classroom," California American Studies Association, Pomona, 1984, forthcoming in *Humanity and Society*; S. Hacker and Lisa Bovit, "Agriculture to Agribusiness: Technical Imperatives and Changing Roles," *Proceedings* of the Society for the History of Technology, Milwaukee, 1981; Lawrence Busch and William Lacy, *Science, Agriculture, and the Politics of Research* (Boulder, Colo.: Westview Press, 1983); Denis Wilfred, "Capital and Agriculture, a Review of Marxian Problematics," *Studies in Political Economy*, no. 7 (1982), pp. 127–54; Carolyn Sachs, *The Invisible Farmers: Women in Agricultural Production* (Totowa, N.J.: Rowman & Allanheld, 1983). Thanks to Elizabeth Bird, "Green Revolution Imperialism," I & II, ms. UCSC, 1984.

The conjunction of the Green Revolution's social relations with biotechnologies like plant genetic engineering makes the pressures on land in the third world increasingly intense. AID's estimates (*New York Times*, 14 October 1984) used at the 1984 World Food Day are that in Africa, women produce about 90 per cent of rural food supplies, about 60–80 per cent in Asia, and provide 40 per cent of agricultural labor in the Near East and Latin America. Blumberg charges that world organizations' agricultural politics, as well as those of multinationals and national governments in the third world, generally ignore fundamental issues in the sexual division of labor. The present tragedy of famine in Africa might owe as much to male supremacy as to capitalism, colonialism, and rain patterns. More accurately, capitalism and racism are usually structurally male dominant [Haraway's note]. The Green Revolution: the Western campaign that introduced high-yield varieties of specific staple crops and promoted pesticides to increase food production in developing countries.

because their responsibilities to provide food do not diminish, and their reproductive situations are made more complex. Green Revolution technologies interact with other high-tech industrial production to alter gender divisions of labor and differential gender migration patterns.

The new technologies seem deeply involved in the forms of "privatization" that Ros Petchesky has analyzed, in which militarization, right-wing family ideologies and policies, and intensified definitions of corporate property as private synergistically interact.[6] The new communications technologies are fundamental to the eradication of "public life" for everyone. This facilitates the mushrooming of a permanent high-tech military establishment at the cultural and economic expense of most people, but especially of women. Technologies like video games and highly miniaturized television seem crucial to production of modern forms of "private life." The culture of video games is heavily oriented to individual competition and extraterrestrial warfare. High-tech, gendered imaginations are produced here, imaginations that can contemplate destruction of the planet and a sci-fi escape from its consequences. More than our imaginations is militarized; and the other realities of electronic and nuclear warfare are inescapable.

The new technologies affect the social relations of both sexuality and of reproduction, and not always in the same ways. The close ties of sexuality and instrumentality, of views of the body as a kind of private satisfaction- and utility-maximizing machine, are described nicely in sociobiological origin stories that stress a genetic calculus and explain the inevitable dialectic of domination of male and female gender roles.[7] These sociobiological stories depend on a high-tech view of the body as a biotic component or cybernetic communications system. Among the many transformations of reproductive situations is the medical one, where women's bodies have boundaries newly permeable to both "visualization" and "intervention." Of course, who controls the interpretation of bodily boundaries in medical hermeneutics is a major feminist issue. The speculum[8] served as an icon of women's claiming their bodies in the 1970s; that hand-craft tool is inadequate to express our needed body politics in the negotiation of reality in the practices of cyborg reproduction. Self-help is not enough. The technologies of visualization recall the important cultural practice of hunting with the camera and the deeply predatory nature of a photographic consciousness.[9] Sex, sexuality, and reproduction are central actors in high-tech myth systems structuring our imaginations of personal and social possibility.

6. Cynthia Enloe. "Women Textile Workers in the Militarization of Southeast Asia," in Nash and Fernandez-Kelly, *Women and Men*; Rosalind Petchesky, "Abortion, Anti-Feminism, and the Rise of the New Right," *Feminist Studies*, vol. 7, no. 2 (1981) [Haraway's note].

7. For a feminist version of this logic, see Sarah Blaffer Hrdy, *The Woman That Never Evolved* (Cambridge, Mass.: Harvard University Press, 1981). For an analysis of scientific women's story-telling practices, especially in relation to sociobiology, in evolutionary debates around child abuse and infanticide, see Donna Haraway, "The Contest for Primate Nature: Daughters of Man the Hunter in the Field, 1960–80," in Mark Kann, ed., *The Future of American Democracy* (Philadelphia: Temple University Press, 1983), pp. 175–208 [Haraway's note].

8. A medical instrument used in vaginal examinations; feminist books such as *Our Bodies, Ourselves* (3 eds. in the 1970s) advocated self-examination.

9. For the moment of transition of hunting with guns to hunting with cameras in the construction of popular meanings of nature for an American urban immigrant public, see Donna Haraway, "Teddy Bear Patriarchy," *Social Text*, [no. 11 (winter 1984–85), pp. 20–64]; Roderick Nash, "The Exporting and Importing of Nature: Nature-Appreciation as a Commodity, 1850–1980," *Perspectives in American History*, vol. 3 (1979), pp. 517–60; Susan Sontag, *On Photography* (New York: Dell, 1977); and Douglas Preston, "Shooting in Paradise," *Natural History*, vol. 93, no. 12 (December 1984), pp. 14–19 [Haraway's note].

Another critical aspect of the social relations of the new technologies is the reformulation of expectations, culture, work, and reproduction for the large scientific and technical work force. A major social and political danger is the formation of a strongly bimodal social structure, with the masses of women and men of all ethnic groups, but especially people of color, confined to a homework economy, illiteracy of several varieties, and general redundancy and impotence, controlled by high-tech repressive apparatuses ranging from entertainment to surveillance and disappearance. An adequate socialist-feminist politics should address women in the privileged occupational categories, and particularly in the production of science and technology that constructs scientific-technical discourses, processes, and objects.[1]

This issue is only one aspect of inquiry into the possibility of a feminist science, but it is important. What kind of constitutive role in the production of knowledge, imagination, and practice can new groups doing science have? How can these groups be allied with progressive social and political movements? What kind of political accountability can be constructed to tie women together across the scientific-technical hierarchies separating us? Might there be ways of developing feminist science/technology politics in alliance with anti-military science facility conversion action groups? Many scientific and technical workers in Silicon Valley, the high-tech cowboys included, do not want to work on military science.[2] Can these personal preferences and cultural tendencies be welded into progressive politics among this professional middle class in which women, including women of color, are coming to be fairly numerous?

Women in the Integrated Circuit

Let me summarize the picture of women's historical locations in advanced industrial societies, as these positions have been restructured partly through the social relations of science and technology. If it was ever possible ideologically to characterize women's lives by the distinction of public and private domains—suggested by images of the division of working-class life into factory and home, of bourgeois life into market and home, and of gender existence into personal and political realms—it is now a totally misleading ideology, even to show how both terms of these dichotomies construct each other in practice and in theory. I prefer a network ideological image, suggesting the profusion of spaces and identities and the permeability of boundaries in the personal body and in the body politic. "Networking" is both a feminist practice and a multinational corporate strategy—weaving is for oppositional cyborgs.

The only way to characterize the informatics of domination is as a massive

1. For crucial guidance for thinking about the political/cultural implications of the history of women doing science in the United States, see: Violet Haas and Carolyn Perucci, eds., *Women in Scientific and Engineering Professions* (Ann Arbor: University of Michigan Press, 1984); Sally Hacker, "The Culture of Engineering: Women, Workplace, and Machine," *Women's Studies International Quarterly*, vol. 4, no. 3 (1981), pp. 341–53; Evelyn Fox Keller, *A Feeling for the Organism* (San Francisco: Freeman, 1983); National Science Foundation, *Women and Minorities in Science and Engineering* (Washington, D.C.: NSF, 1982); Margaret Rossiter, *Women Scientists in America* (Baltimore: John Hopkins University Press, 1982) [Haraway's note].

2. John Markoff and Lenny Siegel, "Military Micros," UCSC Silicon Valley Research Project conference, 1983. High Technology Professionals for Peace and Computer Professionals for Social Responsibility are promising organizations [Haraway's note].

intensification of insecurity and cultural impoverishment, with common failure of subsistence networks for the most vulnerable. Since much of this picture interweaves with the social relations of science and technology, the urgency of a socialist-feminist politics addressed to science and technology is plain. There is much now being done, and the grounds for political work are rich. For example, the efforts to develop forms of collective struggle for women in paid work, like SEIU's District 925,[3] should be a high priority for all of us. These efforts are profoundly tied to technical restructuring of labor processes and reformations of working classes. These efforts also are providing understanding of a more comprehensive kind of labor organization, involving community, sexuality, and family issues never privileged in the largely white male industrial unions.

The structural rearrangements related to the social relations of science and technology evoke strong ambivalence. But it is not necessary to be ultimately depressed by the implications of late-twentieth-century women's relation to all aspects of work, culture, production of knowledge, sexuality, and reproduction. For excellent reasons, most Marxisms see domination best and have trouble understanding what can only look like false consciousness and people's complicity in their own domination in late capitalism. It is crucial to remember that what is lost, perhaps especially from women's points of view, is often virulent forms of oppression, nostalgically naturalized in the face of current violation. Ambivalence toward the disrupted unities mediated by high-tech culture requires not sorting consciousness into categories of "clear-sighted critique grounding a solid political epistemology" versus "manipulated false consciousness," but subtle understanding of emerging pleasures, experiences, and powers with serious potential for changing the rules of the game.

There are grounds for hope in the emerging bases for new kinds of unity across race, gender, and class, as these elementary units of socialist-feminist analysis themselves suffer protean transformations. Intensifications of hardship experienced worldwide in connection with the social relations of science and technology are severe. But what people are experiencing is not transparently clear, and we lack sufficiently subtle connections for collectively building effective theories of experience. Present efforts—Marxist, psychoanalytic, feminist, anthropological—to clarify even "our" experience are rudimentary.

I am conscious of the odd perspective provided by my historical position—a Ph.D. in biology for an Irish Catholic girl was made possible by Sputnik's[4] impact on U.S. national science-education policy. I have a body and mind as much constructed by the post-World War II arms race and cold war as by the women's movements. There are more grounds for hope by focusing on the contradictory effects of politics designed to produce loyal American technocrats, which as well produced large numbers of dissidents, rather than by focusing on the present defeats.

The permanent partiality of feminist points of view has consequences for our expectations of forms of political organization and participation. We do

3. The division of the Service Employees International Union that represents librarians and civic employees.

4. The first artificial satellite, launched by the Soviet Union on October 4, 1957; its launch spurred the United States to invest in science and science education and to begin the space race.

not need a totality in order to work well. The feminist dream of a common language, like all dreams for a perfectly true language, of perfectly faithful naming of experience, is a totalizing and imperialist one. In that sense, dialectics[5] too is a dream language, longing to resolve contradiction. Perhaps, ironically, we can learn from our fusions with animals and machines how not to be Man, the embodiment of Western logos.[6] From the point of view of pleasure in these potent and taboo fusions, made inevitable by the social relations of science and technology, there might indeed be a feminist science.

Cyborgs: A Myth of Political Identity

I want to conclude with a myth about identity and boundaries which might inform late-twentieth-century political imaginations. I am indebted in this story to writers like Joanna Russ, Samuel Delany, John Varley, James Tiptree, Jr., Octavia Butler, Monique Wittig, and Vonda McIntyre.[7] These are our storytellers exploring what it means to be embodied in high-tech worlds. They are theorists for cyborgs. Exploring conceptions of bodily boundaries and social order, the anthropologist Mary Douglas should be credited with helping us to consciousness about how fundamental body imagery is to world view, and so to political language.[8] French feminists like Luce Irigaray and Monique Wittig, for all their differences, know how to write the body, how to weave eroticism, cosmology, and politics from imagery of embodiment, and especially for Wittig, from imagery of fragmentation and reconstitution of bodies.[9]

American radical feminists like Susan Griffin, Audre Lorde, and Adrienne Rich have profoundly affected our political imaginations—and perhaps restricted too much what we allow as a friendly body and political language.[1] They insist on the organic, opposing it to the technological. But their symbolic systems and the related positions of ecofeminism and feminist paganism, replete with organicisms, can only be understood in Sandoval's terms

5. Marxist dialectics relates society's cultural sphere (its politics, arts, philosophy, and religion) directly to its socioeconomic foundations, depicting society—including its apparent contradictions—as a coherent total system.

6. Haraway alludes to the French philosopher JACQUES DERRIDA (b. 1930), who deconstructs Western logos (literally, "word; discourse, reason"; Greek) and its partial conception of "Man."

7. Katie King, The Pleasure of Repetition and the Limits of Identification in Feminist Science Fiction: Reimaginations of the Body after the Cyborg," California American Studies Association, Pomona, 1984. An abbreviated list of feminist science fiction underlying themes of this essay: Octavia Butler, *Wild Seed, Mind of My Mind, Kindred, Survivor*; Suzy McKee Charnas, *Motherlines*; Samuel Delany, *Tales of Neveryon*; Anne McCaffrey, *The Ship Who Sang, Dinosaur Planet*; Vonda McIntyre, *Superluminal, Dreamsnake*; Joanna Russ, *Adventures of Alix, The Female Man*; James Tiptree, Jr., *Star Songs of an Old Primate, Up the Walls of the World*; John Varley, *Titan, Wizard, Demon* [Haraway's note].

8. Mary Douglas, *Purity and Danger* (London: Routledge & Kegan Paul, 1966), *Natural Symbols* (London: Cresset Press, 1970) [Haraway's note].

9. French feminisms contribute to cyborg heteroglossia. Carolyn Burke, "Irigaray through the Looking Glass," *Feminist Studies*, vol. 7, no. 2 (1981), pp. 288–306; Luce Irigaray, *Ce sexe qui n'en est pas un* [The sex which is not one] (Paris: Minuit, 1977); L. Irigaray, *Et l'une ne bouge pas sans l'autre* [One does not move without the other] (Paris: Minuit, 1979); Elaine Marks and Isabelle de Courtivron, eds., *New French Feminisms* (Amherst: University of Massachusetts Press, 1980); *Signs*, vol. 7, no. 1 (1981), special issue on French feminism; Monique Wittig, *The Lesbian Body*, trans. David LeVay (New York: Avon, 1975; *Le corps lesbian*, 1973) [Haraway's note]. On the French writer WITTIG (b. 1935), see above.

1. But all these poets are very complex, not least in treatment of themes of lying and erotic, decentered collective and personal identities. Susan Griffin, *Women and Nature: The Roaring Inside Her* (New York: Harper & Row, 1978); Audre Lorde, *Sister Outsider* (Trumansburg, N.Y.: Crossing Press, 1984); Adrienne Rich, *The Dream of a Common Language* (New York: Norton, 1978) [Haraway's note].

as oppositional ideologies fitting the late twentieth century. They would simply bewilder anyone not preoccupied with the machines and consciousness of late capitalism. In that sense they are part of the cyborg world. But there are also great riches for feminists in explicitly embracing the possibilities inherent in the breakdown of clean distinctions between organism and machine and similar distinctions structuring the Western self. It is the simultaneity of breakdowns that cracks the matrices of domination and opens geometric possibilities. What might be learned from personal and political "technological" pollution? I will look briefly at two overlapping groups of texts for their insight into the construction of a potentially helpful cyborg myth: constructions of women of color and monstrous selves in feminist science fiction.

Earlier I suggested that "women of color" might be understood as a cyborg identity, a potent subjectivity synthesized from fusions of outsider identities. There are material and cultural grids mapping this potential. Audre Lorde captures the tone in the title of her *Sister Outsider*. In my political myth, Sister Outsider is the offshore woman, whom U.S. workers, female and feminized, are supposed to regard as the enemy preventing their solidarity, threatening their security. Onshore, inside the boundary of the United States, Sister Outsider is a potential amidst the races and ethnic identities of women manipulated for division, competition, and exploitation in the same industries. "Women of color" are the preferred labor force for the science-based industries, the real women for whom the worldwide sexual market, labor market, and politics of reproduction kaleidoscope into daily life. Young Korean women hired in the sex industry and in electronics assembly are recruited from high schools, educated for the integrated circuit. Literacy, especially in English, distinguishes the "cheap" female labor so attractive to the multinationals.

Contrary to orientalist stereotypes of the "oral primitive," literacy is a special mark of women of color, acquired by U.S. black women as well as men through a history of risking death to learn and to teach reading and writing. Writing has a special significance for all colonized groups. Writing has been crucial to the Western myth of the distinction of oral and written cultures, primitive and civilized mentalities, and more recently to the erosion of that distinction in "post-modernist" theories attacking the phallogocentrism[2] of the West, with its worship of the monotheistic, phallic, authoritative, and singular word, the unique and perfect name.[3] Contests for the meanings of writing are a major form of contemporary political struggle. Releasing the play of writing is deadly serious. The poetry and stories of U.S. women of color are repeatedly about writing, about access to the power to signify; but this time that power must be neither phallic nor innocent. Cyborg writing must not be about the Fall, the imagination of a once-upon-a-time wholeness before language, before writing, before Man. Cyborg writing is about the power to survive, not on the basis of original innocence, but on the basis of seizing the tools to mark the world that marked them as other.

2. A Derridean term applied to the male-centered values and mode of reasoning—philosophy—characteristic of Western culture from ancient Greek times to the present.

3. Jacques Derrida, *Of Grammatology*, trans. and introd. G. C. Spivak (Baltimore: Johns Hopkins University Press, 1976), esp. part II, "Nature, Culture, Writing"; Claude Lévi-Strauss, *Tristes Tropiques*, trans. John Russell (New York: Criterion Books, 1961), esp. "The Writing Lesson" [Haraway's note]. For this text by the French structural anthropologist LÉVI-STRAUSS (b. 1908), see above.

The tools are often stories, retold stories, versions that reverse and displace the hierarchical dualisms of naturalized identities. In retelling origin stories, cyborg authors subvert the central myths of origin of Western culture. We have all been colonized by those origin myths, with their longing for fulfillment in apocalypse. The phallogocentric origin stories most crucial for feminist cyborgs are built into the literal technologies—technologies that write the world, biotechnology and microelectronics—that have recently textualized our bodies as code problems on the grid of C^3I. Feminist cyborg stories have the task of recoding communication and intelligence to subvert command and control.

Figuratively and literally, language politics pervade the struggles of women of color; and stories about language have a special power in the rich contemporary writing by U.S. women of color. For example, retellings of the story of the indigenous woman Malinche, mother of the mestizo "bastard" race of the new world, master of languages, and mistress of Cortés[4] carry special meaning for Chicana constructions of identity. Cherríe Moraga in *Loving in the War Years* explores the themes of identity when one never possessed the original language, never told the original story, never resided in the harmony of legitimate heterosexuality in the garden of culture, and so cannot base identity on a myth or a fall from innocence and right to natural names, mother's or father's.[5] Moraga's writing, her superb literacy, is presented in her poetry as the same kind of violation as Malinche's mastery of the conquerer's language—a violation, an illegitimate production, that allows survival. Moraga's language is not "whole"; it is self-consciously spliced, a chimera of English and Spanish, both conqueror's languages. But it is this chimeric monster, without claim to an original language before violation, that crafts the erotic, competent, potent identities of women of color. Sister Outsider hints at the possibility of world survival not because of her innocence, but because of her ability to live on the boundaries, to write without the founding myth of original wholeness, with its inescapable apocalypse of final return to a deathly oneness that Man has imagined to be the innocent and all-powerful Mother, freed at the End from another spiral of appropriation by her son. Writing marks Moraga's body, affirms it as the body of a woman of color, against the possibility of passing into the unmarked category of the Anglo father or into the orientalist myth of "original illiteracy" of a mother that never was. Malinche was mother here, not Eve before eating the forbidden fruit. Writing affirms Sister Outsider,

4. Hernán Cortés (1485–1547), Spanish explorer who conquered Mexico. Malinche: an Aztec chieftain's daughter who was Cortés's interpreter as well as his mistress.

5. Cherríe Moraga, *Loving in the War Years* (Boston: South End Press, 1983). The sharp relation of women of color to writing as theme and politics can be approached through: "The Black Woman and the Diaspora: Hidden Connections and Extended Acknowledgments," an International Literary Conference, Michigan State University, October 1985; Mari Evans, ed., *Black Women Writers: A Critical Evaluation* (Garden City. N.Y.: Doubleday/Anchor, 1984); Dexter Fisher, ed., *The Third Woman: Minority Women Writers of the United States* (Boston: Houghton Mifflin, 1980); several issues of *Frontiers*, esp. vol. 5 (1980), "Chicanas en el Ambiente Nacional," and vol. 7 (1983), "Feminisms in the Non-Western World"; Maxine Hong Kingston, *China Men* (New York: Knopf, 1977); Gerda Lerner, ed., *Black Women in White America: A Documentary History* (New York: Vintage, 1971); Cherríe Moraga and Gloria Anzaldúa, eds., *This Bridge Called My Back: Writings by Radical Women of Color* (Watertown, Mass.: Persephone, 1981); Robin Morgan, ed., *Sisterhood Is Global* (Garden City, N.Y.: Anchor/Doubleday, 1984). The writing of white women has had similar meanings: Sandra Gilbert and Susan Gubar, *The Madwoman in the Attic* (New Haven: Yale University Press, 1979); Joanna Russ, *How to Suppress Women's Writing* (Austin: University of Texas Press, 1983) [Haraway's note]. For the American critics ANZALDÚA (b. 1942), GILBERT (b. 1936), and GUBAR (b. 1944), see above.

not the Woman-before-the-Fall-into-Writing needed by the phallogocentric Family of Man.

Writing is pre-eminently the technology of cyborgs, etched surfaces of the late twentieth century. Cyborg politics is the struggle for language and the struggle against perfect communication, against the one code that translates all meaning perfectly, the central dogma of phallogocentrism. That is why cyborg politics insist on noise and advocate pollution, rejoicing in the illegitimate fusions of animal and machine. These are the couplings which make Man and Woman so problematic, subverting the structure of desire, the force imagined to generate language and gender, and so subverting the structure and modes of reproduction of "Western" identity, of nature and culture, of mirror and eye, slave and master, body and mind. "We" did not originally choose to be cyborgs, but choice grounds a liberal politics and epistemology that imagines the reproduction of individuals before the wider replications of "texts."

From the perspective of cyborgs, freed of the need to ground politics in "our" privileged position of the oppression that incorporates all other dominations, the innocence of the merely violated, the ground of those closer to nature, we can see powerful possibilities. Feminisms and Marxisms have run aground on Western epistemological imperatives to construct a revolutionary subject from the perspective of a hierarchy of oppressions and/or a latent position of moral superiority, innocence, and greater closeness to nature. With no available original dream of a common language or original symbiosis promising protection from hostile "masculine" separation, but written into the play of a text that has no finally privileged reading or salvation history, to recognize "oneself" as fully implicated in the world, frees us of the need to root politics in identification, vanguard parties, purity, and mothering. Stripped of identity, the bastard race teaches about the power of the margins and the importance of a mother like Malinche. Women of color have transformed her from the evil mother of masculinist fear into the originally literate mother who teaches survival.

This is not just literary deconstruction, but liminal transformation. Every story that begins with original innocence and privileges the return to wholeness imagines the drama of life to be individuation, separation, the birth of the self, the tragedy of autonomy, the fall into writing, alienation; i.e., war, tempered by imaginary respite in the bosom of the Other. These plots are ruled by a reproductive politics—rebirth without flaw, perfection, abstraction. In this plot women are imagined either better or worse off, but all agree they have less selfhood, weaker individuation, more fusion to the oral, to Mother, less at stake in masculine autonomy. But there is another route to having less at stake in masculine autonomy, a route that does not pass through Woman, Primitive, Zero, the Mirror Stage and its imaginary.[6] It passes through women and other present-tense, illegitimate cyborgs, not of Woman born, who refuse the ideological resources of victimization so as to have a real life. These cyborgs are the people who refuse to disappear on

6. Haraway alludes to Lacan's "Mirror Stage" (1966; see above), which describes the stages of identity formation during childhood; the "Imaginary," modeled on the relation between an infant and its mirror image, precedes entrance into the "Symbolic" (the dimension of language, law, and the father).

cue, no matter how many times a "Western" commentator remarks on the sad passing of another primitive, another organic group done in by "Western" technology, by writing.[7] These real-life cyborgs, e.g., the Southeast Asian village women workers in Japanese and U.S. electronics firms described by Aihwa Ong, are actively rewriting the texts of their bodies and societies. Survival is the stakes in this play of readings.

To recapitulate, certain dualisms have been persistent in Western traditions; they have all been systemic to the logics and practices of domination of women, people of color, nature, workers, animals—in short, domination of all constituted as *others*, whose task is to mirror the self. Chief among these troubling dualisms are self/other, mind/body, culture/nature, male/female, civilized/primitive, reality/appearance, whole/part, agent/resource, maker/made, active/passive, right/wrong, truth/illusion, total/partial, God/man. The self is the One who is not dominated, who knows that by the service of the other; the other is the one who holds the future, who knows that by the experience of domination, which gives the lie to the autonomy of the self. To be One is to be autonomous, to be powerful, to be God; but to be One is to be an illusion, and so to be involved in a dialectic of apocalypse with the other. Yet to be other is to be multiple, without clear boundary, frayed, insubstantial. One is too few, but two are too many.

High-tech culture challenges these dualisms in intriguing ways. It is not clear who makes and who is made in the relation between human and machine. It is not clear what is mind and what body in machines that resolve into coding practices. Insofar as we know ourselves in both formal discourse (e.g., biology) and in daily practice (e.g., the homework economy in the integrated circuit), we find ourselves to be cyborgs, hybrids, mosaics, chimeras. Biological organisms have become biotic systems, communications devices like others. There is no fundamental, ontological separation in our formal knowledge of machine and organism, of technical and organic.

One consequence is that our sense of connection to our tools is heightened. The trance state experienced by many computer users has become a staple of science-fiction film and cultural jokes. Perhaps paraplegics and other severely handicapped people can (and sometimes do) have the most intense experiences of complex hybridization with other communication devices. Anne McCaffrey's *The Ship Who Sang*[8] explored the consciousness of a cyborg, hybrid of girl's brain and complex machinery, formed after the birth of a severely handicapped child. Gender, sexuality, embodiment, skill: all were reconstituted in the story. Why should our bodies end at the skin, or include at best other beings encapsulated by skin? From the seventeenth century till now, machines could be animated—given ghostly souls to make them speak or move or to account for their orderly development and mental capacities. Or organisms could be mechanized—reduced to body understood as resource of mind. These machine/organism relationships are obsolete, unnecessary. For us, in imagination and in other practice, machines can be

7. James Clifford argues persuasively for recognition of continuous cultural reinvention, the stubborn non-disappearance of those "marked" by Western imperializing practices; see "On Ethnographic Allegory" [in James Clifford and George E. Marcus, eds., *Writing Culture: The Poetics and Polities of Ethnography* (Berkeley: University of California Press, 1986), pp. 98–121] and "On Ethnographic Authority," *Representations*, vol. 1, no. 2 (1983), pp. 118–46 [Haraway's note].

8. A 1969 novel by McCaffrey (b. 1926).

prosthetic devices, intimate components, friendly selves. We don't need organic holism to give impermeable wholeness, the total woman and her feminist variants (mutants?). Let me conclude this point by a very partial reading of the logic of the cyborg monsters of my second group of texts, feminist science fiction.

The cyborgs populating feminist science fiction make very problematic the statuses of man or woman, human, artifact, member of a race, individual identity, or body. Katie King clarifies how pleasure in reading these fictions is not largely based on identification. Students facing Joanna Russ for the first time, students who have learned to take modernist writers like James Joyce or Virginia Woolf[9] without flinching, do not know what to make of *The Adventures of Alyx* or *The Female Man*,[1] where characters refuse the reader's search for innocent wholeness while granting the wish for heroic quests, exuberant eroticism, and serious politics. *The Female Man* is the story of four versions of one genotype, all of whom meet, but even taken together do not make a whole, resolve the dilemmas of violent moral action, nor remove the growing scandal of gender. The feminist science fiction of Samuel Delany, especially *Tales of Neveryon*,[2] mocks stories of origin by redoing the neolithic revolution, replaying the founding moves of Western civilization to subvert their plausibility. James Tiptree, Jr.,[3] an author whose fiction was regarded as particularly manly until her "true" gender was revealed, tells tales of reproduction based on non-mammalian technologies like alternation of generations or male brood pouches and male nurturing. John Varley constructs a supreme cyborg in his arch-feminist exploration of Gaea, a mad goddess–planet–trickster–old woman–technological device on whose surface an extraordinary array of post-cyborg symbioses are spawned.[4] Octavia Butler writes of an African sorceress pitting her powers of transformation against the genetic manipulations of her rival (*Wild Seed*), of time warps that bring a modern U.S. black woman into slavery where her actions in relation to her white master-ancestor determine the possibility of her own birth (*Kindred*), and of the illegitimate insights into identity and community of an adopted cross-species child who came to know the enemy as self (*Survivor*).[5]

Because it is particularly rich in boundary transgressions, Vonda McIntyre's *Superluminal*[6] can close this truncated catalogue of promising monsters who help redefine the pleasures and politics of embodiment and feminist writing. In a fiction where no character is "simply" human, human status is highly problematic. Orca, a genetically altered diver, can speak with killer whales and survive deep ocean conditions, but she longs to explore space as a pilot, necessitating bionic implants jeopardizing her kinship with the divers and cetaceans. Transformations are effected by virus vectors carrying a new developmental code, by transplant surgery, by implants of microelectronic devices, by analogue doubles, and other means. Laenea becomes

9. English novelist and critic (1882–1941), author of *A Room of One's Own* (1929; see above). Joyce (1882–1941), Irish writer whose novels *Ulysses* (1922) and *Finnegans Wake* (1939) are famously abstruse.
1. Works by Russ (b. 1937) published in 1983 and 1975, respectively.
2. A 1979 collection of stories by Delany (b. 1942).
3. Pen name of Alice Sheldon (ca. 1915–1987).
4. Haraway describes the setting of *Titan* (1979), *Wizard* (1980), and *Demon* (1984), a trilogy by Varley (b. 1947).
5. Novels by Butler (b. 1947) published in 1980, 1979, and 1978, respectively.
6. A 1983 novel by McIntyre (b. 1948).

a pilot by accepting a heart implant and a host of other alterations allowing survival in transit at speeds exceeding that of light. Radu Dracul survives a virus-caused plague on his outerworld planet to find himself with a time sense that changes the boundaries of spatial perception for the whole species. All the characters explore the limits of language, the dream of communicating experience, and the necessity of limitation, partiality, and intimacy even in this world of protean transformation and connection.

Monsters have always defined the limits of community in Western imaginations. The Centaurs and Amazons[7] of ancient Greece established the limits of the centered polis of the Greek male human by their disruption of marriage and boundary pollutions of the warrior with animality and woman. Unseparated twins and hermaphrodites were the confused human material in early modern France who grounded discourse on the natural and supernatural, medical and legal, portents and diseases—all crucial to establishing modern identity.[8] The evolutionary and behavioral sciences of monkeys and apes have marked the multiple boundaries of late-twentieth-century industrial identities. Cyborg monsters in feminist science fiction define quite different political possibilities and limits from those proposed by the mundane fiction of Man and Woman.

There are several consequences to taking seriously the imagery of cyborgs as other than our enemies. Our bodies, ourselves; bodies are maps of power and identity. Cyborgs are no exceptions. A cyborg body is not innocent; it was not born in a garden; it does not seek unitary identity and so generate antagonistic dualisms without end (or until the world ends); it takes irony for granted. One is too few, and two is only one possibility. Intense pleasure in skill, machine skill, ceases to be a sin, but an aspect of embodiment. The machine is not an *it* to be animated, worshiped and dominated. The machine is us, our processes, an aspect of our embodiment. We can be responsible for machines; *they* do not dominate or threaten us. We are responsible for boundaries; we are they. Up till now (once upon a time), female embodiment seemed to be given, organic, necessary; and female embodiment seemed to mean skill in mothering and its metaphoric extensions. Only by being out of place could we take intense pleasure in machines, and then with excuses that this was organic activity after all, appropriate to females. Cyborgs might consider more seriously the partial, fluid, sometimes aspect of sex and sexual embodiment. Gender might not be global identity after all.

The ideologically charged question of what counts as daily activity, as experience, can be approached by exploiting the cyborg image. Feminists have recently claimed that women are given to dailiness, that women more than men somehow sustain daily life, and so have a privileged epistemological position potentially. There is a compelling aspect to this claim, one that makes visible unvalued female activity and names it as the ground of life. But *the* ground of life? What about all the ignorance of women, all the exclusions and failures of knowledge and skill? What about men's access to daily

7. In Greek mythology, female warriors. Centaurs: creatures with the body of a horse and the torso and upper body of a man.

8. Page DuBois, *Centaurs and Amazons* (Ann Arbor: University of Michigan Press, 1982); Lorraine Daston and Katharine Park, "Hermaphrodites in Renaissance France," ms., n.d.; Katharine Park and Lorraine Daston, "Unnatural Conceptions: The Study of Monsters in 16th and 17th Century France and England," *Past and Present*, no. 92 (August 1981), pp. 20–54 [Haraway's note].

competence, to knowing how to build things, to take them apart, to play? What about other embodiments? Cyborg gender is a local possibility taking a global vengeance. Race, gender, and capital require a cyborg theory of wholes and parts. There is no drive in cyborgs to produce total theory, but there is an intimate experience of boundaries, their construction and deconstruction. There is a myth system waiting to become a political language to ground one way of looking at science and technology and challenging the informatics of domination.

One last image: organisms and organismic, holistic politics depend on metaphors of rebirth and invariably call on the resources of reproductive sex. I would suggest that cyborgs have more to do with regeneration and are suspicious of the reproductive matrix and of most birthing. For salamanders, regeneration after injury, such as the loss of a limb, involves regrowth of structure and restoration of function with the constant possibility of twinning or other odd topographical productions at the site of former injury. The regrown limb can be monstrous, duplicated, potent. We have all been injured, profoundly. We require regeneration, not rebirth, and the possibilities for our reconstitution include the utopian dream of the hope for a monstrous world without gender.

Cyborg imagery can help express two crucial arguments in this essay: (1) the production of universal, totalizing theory is a major mistake that misses most of reality, probably always, but certainly now; (2) taking responsibility for the social relations of science and technology means refusing an anti-science metaphysics, a demonology of technology, and so means embracing the skillful task of reconstructing the boundaries of daily life, in partial connection with others, in communication with all of our parts. It is not just that science and technology are possible means of great human satisfaction, as well as a matrix of complex dominations. Cyborg imagery can suggest a way out of the maze of dualisms in which we have explained our bodies and our tools to ourselves. This is a dream not of a common language, but of a powerful infidel heteroglossia. It is an imagination of a feminist speaking in tongues to strike fear into the circuits of the super-savers of the new right. It means both building and destroying machines, identities, categories, relationships, spaces, stories. Though both are bound in the spiral dance, I would rather be a cyborg than a goddess.

1985

BARBARA SMITH
b. 1946

A pioneer of black feminist and lesbian criticism, Barbara Smith was an early voice calling attention to black women's writing. Despite the achievements of the women's liberation movement and the civil rights movement during the politically vibrant 1960s, critics soon began to point out limitations: the feminist movement seemed to speak primarily from the perspective of white, middle-class, heterosexual women, and the civil rights movement for black men. Charging in her famous 1977 essay "Toward a Black Feminist Criticism" that "All segments of the literary world—whether establishment, progressive, Black, female, or lesbian—do not know, or at least act as if they do not know, that Black women writers and Black lesbian writers exist," Smith assumed the task of establishing a distinctive tradition of black women's writing and a specifically black feminist and lesbian criticism.

Barbara Smith was born in Cleveland, where she became involved in the civil rights movement as a high school student in the 1960s. After earning a B.A. from Mount Holyoke College in 1969 and an M.A. from the University of Pittsburgh in 1971, she was active in the emerging black feminist movement; in 1974 she became one of the founding members of Boston's Combahee River Collective, a black feminist group named after Harriet Tubman's guerrilla campaign of 1863 that freed more than 750 slaves. Smith taught as an instructor at the University of Massachusetts (1976–81) and has held several visiting professorships, but she has primarily worked outside the academy, as a writer, editor, publisher, and activist. In 1980, with the poet Audre Lorde, she co-founded Kitchen Table/Women of Color Press, the first publishing collective organized by women of color. She was the director of the press from 1984 through 1995, when she left to write full-time. During the 1990s, she held fellowships at the Schomburg Center for Research in Black Culture, the Bunting Institute at Radcliffe College, and the Center for Lesbian and Gay Studies at the City University of New York.

The 1970s were an especially rich time for black women's writing, witnessing the beginning of the careers of a generation of writers of prose and poetry that includes Toni Morrison, Toni Cade Bambara, Alice Walker, Audre Lorde, and June Jordan; the formation of organizations such as the Combahee River Collective, which provided an alternative to mainstream feminism; and the recovery of earlier writers, such as ZORA NEALE HURSTON (1891–1960). This renaissance of black women's literature inspired the black women's liberation movement. Its members held a wide range of views but agreed that women of color experience oppressions different from those of white women and black men, because of their race, sex, sexuality, and economic status. They were thus committed to the liberation of black women from racism, sexism, heterosexism, and classism in culture as well as politics.

In "Toward a Black Feminist Criticism," Smith points out the glaring absence of scholarship on black women's writing, which she links to black women's invisibility in the mainstream feminist movement. Feminists initially tried to create a sense of solidarity by emphasizing the universality of women's experiences and the bond forged by their differences from men. To correct the limitations of this universalizing assumption, Smith calls for a redefinition of the goals of the women's movement and for an autonomous black feminist movement. Surveying the treatment of black women authors by book reviewers and literary critics, Smith accrues evidence of black women's invisibility. She quotes from both black and white male critics who ignore or denigrate black women's literary accomplishments, and points out that even feminists such as Elaine Showalter and Patricia Meyers Spacks omitted women writers of color from the influential studies they published in the 1970s.

In addition to faulting critical practices, Smith enumerates principles for a black feminist approach that would show more positively "the profound subtleties of this particular body of literature." A black feminist critic should (1) explore both sexual and racial politics in black women's writing; (2) assume that there is an identifiable literary tradition; (3) decipher the common themes, motifs, and concepts in black women's literature that derive from writers' political, social, and economic experiences; (4) examine the specific black female language in this literature; (5) demonstrate an existing tradition that does "not try to graft the ideas or methodology of white/male literary thought upon the precious materials of Black women's art"; (6) try to be innovative and daring, following the model of black women's literature; and, perhaps most important, (7) assert the political implications of a literary work and its connections to the situation of black women.

Drawing upon these principles, Smith devotes a substantial portion of the essay to a reading of Toni Morrison's novel *Sula* (1973) from the new perspective of black lesbian feminism, focusing on the relationships between women. It is regarded as a pioneering analysis of the novel, though some scholars criticized what they saw as a fabrication of lesbian themes. Deborah McDowell, in her influential overview "New Directions for Black Feminist Criticism" (1980), praises Smith but faults her definition of lesbianism as vague and reductive, overlooking *Sula*'s "density and complexity." However, Smith is careful to note that Morrison did not intend readers to view the relationship between the two main characters, Sula and Nel, as lesbian, and that her reading of the lesbian overtones in their relationship exemplifies how a black lesbian feminist perspective might deepen our understanding of the nuances and political possibilities of a text.

In the years following the essay's publication, diverse feminists have taken up Smith's challenge to build their own literary and political traditions. Smith provided a model for later writers who stressed the differences among women, including the black feminist Deborah McDowell, the white lesbian feminist BONNIE ZIMMERMAN, the Native American feminist PAULA GUNN ALLEN, and the third world feminist GLORIA ANZALDÚA. In "What Has Never Been: An Overview of Lesbian Feminist Criticism" (1981; see below), Zimmerman cites "Toward a Black Feminist Criticism" as one of the origins of lesbian feminist literary criticism, and McDowell accords it a prominent place in inaugurating black feminist criticism.

In more recent years, a key debate in feminism has concerned essentialism, with most feminists opposing the view that gender, ethnic, and racial identities are determined by biological essences rather than by cultural differences. Some have criticized Smith's insistence on a separate literature and criticism for black women as "essentialist." Smith has met this charge with some impatience, dismissing it as a narrow academic debate resulting from "the new scholasticism" and "obscurantist academic theory," and arguing that regardless of the issue of essentialism, she "share[s] an objective *political* status with other Black females in this country, a political status that is not substantially altered by economic or educational variables." Intended as a consciousness-raising piece to call attention to the common ground black women share, "Toward a Black Feminist Criticism" combines groundbreaking scholarship and a commitment to black feminist activism.

BIBLIOGRAPHY

"Toward a Black Feminist Criticism" was first published in 1977 in the lesbian feminist literary magazine *Conditions*, and it has since been widely anthologized. In 1981 Smith co-edited (with Gloria T. Hull and Patricia Bell Scott) a pioneering anthology of black feminism, *All the Women Are White, All the Blacks Are Men, but Some of Us Are Brave*. Drawing on a later issue of *Conditions*, Smith edited, with Lorraine Bethel, a pioneering anthology of black lesbian feminist writings, *Home Girls: A Black Feminist Anthology* (1983). In 1984, she coauthored (with Elly Bulkin and Minnie Bryce Pratt) *Yours in Struggle: Three Feminist Perspectives on Anti-Semitism and Racism*. Smith's *The Truth That Never Hurts: Writings on Race, Gender, and Freedom* (1998) collects a wide array of her writings from the 1970s through the 1990s, including well-known critical essays such as "Toward a Black Feminist Tradition" and "The Truth That Never Hurts: Black Lesbians in Fiction in the 1980s," essays on race politics in the United States, and her firsthand accounts of "working for liberation."

Deborah McDowell's influential survey "New Directions for Black Feminist Criticism" (1980), an important early response to Smith, praises Smith's pathbreaking work while noting its limitations. Hazel Carby, in *Reconstructing Womanhood: The Emergence of the Afro-American Woman Novelist* (1987), acknowledges the importance of Smith's essay as a manifesto but criticizes its belief in "an essential black female experience and an exclusive black female language." Though disagreeing on the necessity of theory, Barbara Christian's "But What Do We Think We're Doing Anyway: The State of Black Feminist Criticism(s) or My Version of a Little Bit of History" credits Smith's role in establishing black women's literature; the essay is included in the anthology *Changing Our Own Words: Essays on Criticism, Theory, and Writing by Black Women* (ed. Cheryl A. Wall, 1989), which is dedicated "To the community of black women writing and to Barbara Smith for pointing 'towards a black feminist criticism.' " In an argument against Barbara Christian's "Race for Theory" (1987; see above), Michael Awkward's "Appropriative Gestures: Theory and Afro-American Literary Criticism," in *Gender and Theory: Dialogues on Feminist Criticism* (ed. Linda Kaufman, 1989), invokes Smith's essay as demonstrating the importance of theory, proposing that it might be improved by engaging reader-response theory. An interesting update examining Smith's continuing relevance is Deborah G. Chay's "Rereading Barbara Smith: Black Feminist Criticism and the Category of Experience," *New Literary History* 24 (1993), which also includes a short response from Smith.

Toward a Black Feminist Criticism

For all my sisters, especially Beverly and Demita

I do not know where to begin. Long before I tried to write this I realized that I was attempting something unprecedented, something dangerous, merely by writing about Black women writers from a feminist perspective and about Black lesbian writers from any perspective at all. These things have not been done. Not by white male critics, expectedly. Not by Black male critics. Not by white women critics who think of themselves as feminists. And most crucially not by Black women critics, who, although they pay the most attention to Black women writers as a group, seldom use a consistently feminist analysis or write about Black lesbian literature. All segments of the literary world—whether establishment, progressive, Black, female, or lesbian—do not know, or at least act as if they do not know, that Black women writers and Black lesbian writers exist.

For whites, this specialized lack of knowledge is inextricably connected to their not knowing in any concrete or politically transforming way that Black women of any description dwell in this place. Black women's existence, experience, and culture and the brutally complex systems of oppression which shape these are in the "real world" of white and/or male consciousness beneath consideration, invisible, unknown.

This invisibility, which goes beyond anything that either Black men or white women experience and tell about in their writing, is one reason it is so difficult for me to know where to start. It seems overwhelming to break such a massive silence. Even more numbing, however, is the realization that so many of the women who will read this have not yet noticed us missing either from their reading matter, their politics, or their lives. It is galling that ostensible feminists and acknowledged lesbians have been so oblivious to the implications of any womanhood that is not white womanhood and that they have yet to struggle with the deep racism in themselves that is at the source of their ignorance.

I think of the thousands and thousands of books, magazines, and articles which have been devoted, by this time, to the subject of women's writing and

I am filled with rage at the fraction of those pages that mention Black and other Third World women. I finally do not know how to begin because in 1977 I want to be writing this for a Black feminist publication, for Black women who know and love these writers as I do and who, if they do not yet know their names, have at least profoundly felt the pain of their absence.

The conditions that coalesce into the impossibilities of this essay have as much to do with politics as with the practice of literature. Any discussion of Afro-American writers can rightfully begin with the fact that for most of the time we have been in this country we have been categorically denied not only literacy but the most minimal possibility of a decent human life. In her landmark essay, "In Search of Our Mothers' Gardens," Alice Walker discloses how the political, economic, and social restrictions of slavery and racism have historically stunted the creative lives of Black women.[1]

At the present time I feel that the politics of feminism have a direct relationship to the state of Black women's literature. A viable, autonomous Black feminist movement in this country would open up the space needed for the exploration of Black women's lives and the creation of consciously Black woman-identified art. At the same time a redefinition of the goals and strategies of the white feminist movement would lead to much-needed change in the focus and content of what is now generally accepted as women's culture.

I want to make in this essay some connections between the politics of Black women's lives, what we write about, and our situation as artists. In order to do this I will look at how Black women have been viewed critically by outsiders, demonstrate the necessity for Black feminist criticism, and try to understand what the existence or nonexistence of Black lesbian writing reveals about the state of Black women's culture and the intensity of *all* Black women's oppression.

The role that criticism plays in making a body of literature recognizable and real hardly needs to be explained here. The necessity for nonhostile and perceptive analysis of works written by persons outside the "mainstream" of white/male cultural rule has been proven by the Black cultural resurgence of the 1960s and 1970s and by the even more recent growth of feminist literary scholarship. For books to be real and remembered they have to be talked about. For books to be understood they must be examined in such a way that the basic intentions of the writers are at least considered. Because of racism Black literature has usually been viewed as a discrete subcategory of American literature, and there have been Black critics of Black literature who did much to keep it alive long before it caught the attention of whites. Before the advent of specifically feminist criticism in this decade, books by white women, on the other hand, were not clearly perceived as the cultural manifestation of an oppressed people. It took the surfacing of the second wave of the North American feminist movement[2] to expose the fact that these works contain a stunningly accurate record of the impact of patriarchal values and practice upon the lives of women, and more significantly, that literature by women provides essential insights into female experience.

1. Alice Walker, "In Search of Our Mothers' Gardens," *Ms.*, May 1974 [Smith's note]. Some of the author's notes have been edited. Walker (b. 1994), African American novelist, poet, and activist.

2. That is, feminists of the 1960s and later; the "first wave" was made up of feminists engaged in the battles for women's suffrage, education, and legal autonomy in the 19th century.

In speaking about the current situation of Black women writers, it is important to remember that the existence of a feminist movement was an essential precondition to the growth of feminist literature, criticism, and women's studies, which focused at the beginning almost entirely upon investigations of literature. The fact that a parallel Black feminist movement has been much slower in evolving cannot help but have impact upon the situation of Black women writers and artists and explains in part why during this very same period we have been so ignored.

There is no political movement to give power or support to those who want to examine Black women's experience through studying our history, literature, and culture. There is no political presence that demands a minimal level of consciousness and respect from those who write or talk about our lives. Finally, there is not a developed body of Black feminist political theory whose assumptions could be used in the study of Black women's art. When Black women's books are dealt with at all, it is usually in the context of Black literature, which largely ignores the implications of sexual politics. When white women look at Black women's works they are of course ill equipped to deal with the subtleties of racial politics. A Black feminist approach to literature that embodies the realization that the politics of sex as well as the politics of race and class are crucially interlocking factors in the works of Black women writers is an absolute necessity. Until a Black feminist criticism exists we will not even know what these writers mean. The citations from a variety of critics which follow prove that without a Black feminist critical perspective not only are books by Black women misunderstood, they are destroyed in the process.

Jerry H. Bryant, *The Nation's* white male reviewer of Alice Walker's *In Love and Trouble: Stories of Black Women*, wrote in 1973:

> The subtitle of the collection, "Stories of Black Women," is probably an attempt by the publisher to exploit not only black subjects but feminine ones. There is nothing feminist about these stories, however.[3]

Blackness and feminism are to his mind mutually exclusive and peripheral to the act of writing fiction. Bryant of course does not consider that Walker might have titled the work herself, nor did he apparently read the book, which unequivocally reveals the author's feminist consciousness.

In *The Negro Novel in America*, a book that Black critics recognize as one of the worst examples of white racist pseudoscholarship, Robert Bone cavalierly dismisses Ann Petry's classic, *The Street*.[4] He perceives it to be "a superficial social analysis" of how slums victimize their Black inhabitants. He further objects:

> It is an attempt to interpret slum life in terms of *Negro* experience, when a larger frame of reference is required. As Alain Locke has observed, "*Knock on Any Door* is superior to *The Street* because it designates class and environment, rather than mere race and environment, as its antagonist."[5]

3. Jerry H. Bryant, "The Outskirts of a New City," *Nation*, November 12, 1973, p. 502 [Smith's note].
4. The best-known book (1944) by the American novelist Petry (1908–1997). Bone (b. 1924), American literary critic specializing in African American literature.
5. Robert Bone, *The Negro Novel in America* (New Haven: Yale University Press, 1958), p. 180. *Knock on Any Door* is a novel by Black writer Willard Motley [Smith's note]. Locke (1886–1954), influential black philosopher and critic.

Neither Robert Bone nor Alain Locke, the Black male critic he cites, can recognize that *The Street* is one of the best delineations in literature of how sex, race, *and* class interact to oppress Black women.

In her review of Toni Morrison's *Sula*[6] for the *New York Times Book Review* in 1973, putative feminist Sara Blackburn makes similarly racist comments:

> Toni Morrison is far too talented to remain only a marvelous recorder of the black side of provincial American life. If she is to maintain the large and serious audience she deserves, she is going to have to address a riskier contemporary reality than this beautiful but nevertheless distanced novel. *And if she does this, it seems to me that she might easily transcend that early and unintentionally limiting classification "black woman writer" and take her place among the most serious, important and talented American novelists now working.*[7] (Italics mine)

Recognizing Morrison's exquisite gift, Blackburn unashamedly asserts that Morrison is "too talented" to deal with mere Black folk, particularly those double nonentities, Black women. In order to be accepted as "serious," "important," "talented," and "American," she must obviously focus her efforts upon chronicling the doings of white men.

The mishandling of Black women writers by whites is paralleled more often by their not being handled at all, particularly in feminist criticism. Although Elaine Showalter[8] in her review essay on literary criticism for *Signs* states that "the best work being produced today [in feminist criticism] is exacting and cosmopolitan," her essay is neither. If it were, she would not have failed to mention a single Black or Third World woman writer, whether "major" or "minor," to cite her questionable categories. That she also does not even hint that lesbian writers of any color exist renders her purported overview virtually meaningless. Showalter obviously thinks that the identities of being Black and female are mutually exclusive, as this statement illustrates:

> Furthermore, there are other literary subcultures (black American novelists, for example) whose history offers a precedent for feminist scholarship to use.[9]

The idea of critics like Showalter *using* Black literature is chilling, a case of barely disguised cultural imperialism. The final insult is that she footnotes the preceding remark by pointing readers to works on Black literature by white males Robert Bone and Roger Rosenblatt![1]

Two recent works by white women, Ellen Moers's *Literary Women: The Great Writers* and Patricia Meyer Spacks's *The Female Imagination*, evidence the same racist flaw.[2] Moers includes the names of four Black and one Puertorriqueña writer in her seventy pages of bibliographical notes and does not deal at all with Third World women in the body of her book. Spacks refers to a comparison between Negroes (*sic*) and women in Mary Ellmann's *Think-*

6. The second novel (1973) by Morrison (b. 1931), who in 1993 became the first black woman to be awarded the Nobel Prize in literature.
7. Sara Blackburn, "You Still Can't Go Home Again," *New Yorks Times Book Review*, December 30, 1973, p. 3 [Smith's note].
8. Prominent American feminist literary critic (b. 1941), who in *A Literature of Their Own* (1977) defined a specifically female tradition of the English novel.
9. Elaine Showalter, "Literary Criticism," *Signs* 1 (1975): 460, 445 [Smith's note].
1. American critic and journalist (b. 1940).
2. Ellen Moers, *Literary Women: The Great Writers* (Garden City, N.Y.: Anchor Books, 1977); Patricia Meyer Spacks, *The Female Imagination* (New York: Avon Books, 1976) [Smith's note]. These books by the American feminist critics Moers (1928–1979) and Spacks (b. 1929) were pioneering works in establishing a canon of women's writing.

ing about Women[3] under the index entry "blacks, women and." "*Black Boy* (Wright)" is the preceding entry. Nothing follows. Again there is absolutely no recognition that Black and female identity ever coexist, specifically in a group of Black women writers. Perhaps one can assume that these women do not know who Black women writers are, that like most Americans they have little opportunity to learn about them. Perhaps. Their ignorance seems suspiciously selective, however, particularly in the light of the dozens of truly obscure white women writers they are able to unearth. Spacks was herself employed at Wellesley College at the same time that Alice Walker was there teaching one of the first courses on Black women writers in the country.

I am not trying to encourage racist criticism of Black women writers like that of Sara Blackburn, to cite only one example. As a beginning I would at least like to see in print white women's acknowledgment of the contradictions of who and what are being left out of their research and writing.[4]

Black male critics can also *act* as if they do not know that Black women writers exist and are, of course, hampered by an inability to comprehend Black women's experience in sexual as well as racial terms. Unfortunately there are also those who are as virulently sexist in their treatment of Black women writers as their white male counterparts. Darwin Turner's discussion of Zora Neale Hurston in his *In a Minor Chord: Three Afro-American Writers and Their Search for Identity* is a frightening example of the near assassination of a great Black woman writer.[5] His descriptions of her and her work as "artful," "coy," "irrational," "superficial," and "shallow" bear no relationship to the actual quality of her achievements. Turner is completely insensitive to the sexual political dynamics of Hurston's life and writing.

In a recent interview the notoriously misogynist writer Ishmael Reed[6] comments in this way upon the low sales of his newest novel:

> But the book only sold 8000 copies. I don't mind giving out the figure: 8000. Maybe if I was one of those young *female* Afro-American writers that are so hot now, I'd sell more. You know, fill my books with ghetto women who can *do no wrong*. . . . But come on, I think I could have sold 8000 copies by myself.[7]

The politics of the situation of Black women are glaringly illuminated by this statement. Neither Reed nor his white male interviewer has the slightest compunction about attacking Black women in print. They need not fear widespread public denunciation since Reed's statement is in perfect agreement with the values of a society that hates Black people, women, and Black women. Finally the two of them feel free to base their actions on the premise that Black women are powerless to alter either their political or their cultural oppression.

3. An early (1968) work of second-wave literary criticism, by Ellmann (1921–1989). *Black Boy* (1945) is the autobiography of the African American novelist Richard Wright (1908–1960).

4. An article by Nancy Hoffman, "White Women, Black Women: Inventing an Adequate Pedagogy," *Women's Studies Newsletter* 5 (spring 1977): 21–24, gives valuable insights into how white women can approach the writing of Black women [Smith's note].

5. Darwin T. Turner, *In a Minor Chord: Three Afro-American Writers and Their Search for Identity* (Carbondale: Southern Illinois University Press, 1971) [Smith's note]. HURSTON (1891–1960), writer of fiction and folklore whose works were long neglected.

6. African American novelist (b. 1938), known for his satirical and experimental fiction.

7. John Domini, "Roots and Racism: An Interview with Ishmael Reed," *Boston Phoenix*, April 5, 1977, p. 20 [Smith's note].

In her introduction to "A Bibliography of Works Written by American Black Women" Ora Williams quotes some of the reactions of her colleagues toward her efforts to do research on Black women:

> Others have reacted negatively with such statements as, "I really don't think you are going to find very much written," "Have 'they' written anything that is any good?" and, "I wouldn't go overboard with this woman's lib thing." When discussions touched on the possibility of teaching a course in which emphasis would be on the literature by Black women, one response was. "Ha, ha. That will certainly be the most nothing course ever offered!"[8]

A remark by Alice Walker capsulizes what all the preceding examples indicate about the position of Black women writers and the reasons for the damaging criticism about them. She responds to her interviewer's question, "Why do you think that the black woman writer has been so ignored in America? Does she have even more difficulty than the black male writer, who perhaps has just begun to gain recognition?" Walker replies:

> There are two reasons why the black woman writer is not taken as seriously as the black male writer. One is that she's a woman. Critics seem unusually ill-equipped to intelligently discuss and analyze the works of black women. Generally, they do not even make the attempt; they prefer, rather, to talk about the lives of black women writers, not about what they write. And, since black women writers are not—it would seem—very likable—until recently they were the least willing worshippers of male supremacy—comments about them tend to be cruel.[9]

A convincing case for Black feminist criticism can obviously be built solely upon the basis of the negativity of what already exists. It is far more gratifying, however, to demonstrate its necessity by showing how it can serve to reveal for the first time the profound subtleties of this particular body of literature.

Before suggesting how a Black feminist approach might be used to examine a specific work, I will outline some of the principles that I think a Black feminist critic could use. Beginning with a primary commitment to exploring how both sexual and racial politics and Black and female identity are inextricable elements in Black women's writings, she would also work from the assumption that Black women writers constitute an identifiable literary tradition. The breadth of her familiarity with these writers would have shown her that not only is theirs a verifiable historical tradition that parallels in time the tradition of Black men and white women writing in this country, but that thematically, stylistically, aesthetically, and conceptually Black women writers manifest common approaches to the act of creating literature as a direct result of the specific political, social, and economic experience they have been obliged to share. The way, for example, that Zora Neale Hurston, Margaret Walker[1] Toni Morrison, and Alice Walker incorporate the traditional

8. Ora Williams, "A Bibliography of Works Written by American Black Women," *College Language Association Journal* 15 (1972): 355. There is an expanded book-length version of this bibliography: *American Black Women in the Arts and Social Sciences: A Bibliographic Survey* (Metuchen; N.J.: Scarecrow Press, 1973) [Smith's note]. Williams (b. 1926), an African American professor of English, published a revised and expanded edition in 1978.

9. John O'Brien, ed., *Interviews with Black Writers* (New York: Liveright, 1973), p. 201 [Smith's note].

1. African American poet and novelist (1915–1998).

Black female activities of root-working, herbal medicine, conjure, and midwifery into the fabric of their stories is not mere coincidence, nor is their use of specifically Black female language to express their own and their characters' thoughts accidental. The use of Black women's language and cultural experience in books *by* Black women *about* Black women results in a miraculously rich coalescing of form and content and also takes their writing far beyond the confines of white/male literary structures. The Black feminist critic would find innumerable commonalities in works by Black women.

Another principle which grows out of the concept of a tradition and which would also help to strengthen this tradition would be for the critic to look first for precedents and insights in interpretation within the works of other Black women. In other words she would think and write out of her own identity and not try to graft the ideas or methodology of white/male literary thought upon the precious materials of Black women's art. Black feminist criticism would by definition be highly innovative, embodying the daring spirit of the works themselves. The Black feminist critic would be constantly aware of the political implications of her work and would assert the connections between it and the political situation of all Black women. Logically developed, Black feminist criticism would owe its existence to a Black feminist movement while at the same time contributing ideas that women in the movement could use.

Black feminist criticism applied to a particular work can overturn previous assumptions about it and expose for the first time its actual dimensions. At the "Lesbians and Literature" discussion at the 1976 Modern Language Association convention Bertha Harris[2] suggested that if in a woman writer's work a sentence refuses to do what it is supposed to do, if there are strong images of women and if there is a refusal to be linear, the result is innately lesbian literature. As usual, I wanted to see if these ideas might be applied to the Black women writers that I know and quickly realized that many of their works were, in Harris's sense, lesbian. Not because women are "lovers," but because they are the central figures, are positively portrayed and have pivotal relationships with one another. The form and language of these works are also nothing like what white patriarchal culture requires or expects.

I was particularly struck by the way in which Toni Morrison's novels *The Bluest Eye* and *Sula*[3] could be explored from this new perspective. In both works the relationships between girls and women are essential, yet at the same time physical sexuality is overtly expressed only between men and women. Despite the apparent heterosexuality of the female characters, I discovered in rereading *Sula* that it works as a lesbian novel not only because of the passionate friendship between Sula and Nel but because of Morrison's consistently critical stance toward the heterosexual institutions of male-female relationships, marriage, and the family. Consciously or not, Morrison's work poses both lesbian and feminist questions about Black women's autonomy and their impact upon each other's lives.

Sula and Nel find each other in 1922 when each of them is twelve, on the brink of puberty and the discovery of boys. Even as awakening sexuality

2. American lesbian novelist (b. 1937). The Modern Language Association: the primary North American professional organization for scholars in English and foreign literatures; at its annual convention, papers are presented in hundreds of panels.

3. Toni Morrison, *The Bluest Eye* (1970; reprint, New York: Pocket Books, 1976) and *Sula* (New York: Alfred A. Knopf, 1973). All subsequent references to *Sula* will be designated in the text [Smith's note].

"clotted their dreams," each girl desires "a someone" obviously female with whom to share her feelings. Morrison writes:

> For it was in dreams that the two girls had met. Long before Edna Finch's Mellow House opened, even before they marched through the chocolate halls of Garfield Primary School . . . they had already made each other's acquaintance in the delirium of their noon dreams. They were solitary little girls whose loneliness was so profound it intoxicated them and sent them stumbling into Technicolored visions that always included a presence, a someone who, quite like the dreamer, shared the delight of the dream. When Nel, an only child, sat on the steps of her back porch surrounded by the high silence of her mother's incredibly orderly house, feeling the neatness pointing at her back, she studied the poplars and fell easily into a picture of herself lying on a flower bed, tangled in her own hair, waiting for some fiery prince. He approached but never quite arrived. But always, watching the dream along with her, were some smiling sympathetic eyes. Someone as interested as she herself in the flow of her imagined hair, the thickness of the mattress of flowers, the voile sleeves that closed below her elbows in gold-threaded cuffs.
>
> Similarly, Sula, also an only child, but wedged into a household of throbbing disorder constantly awry with things, people, voices and the slamming of doors, spent hours in the attic behind a roll of linoleum galloping through her own mind on a gray-and-white horse tasting sugar and smelling roses in full view of someone who shared both the taste and the speed.
>
> So when they met, first in those chocolate halls and next through the ropes of the swing, they felt the ease and comfort of old friends. Because each had discovered years before that they were neither white nor male, and that all freedom and triumph was forbidden to them, they had set about creating something else to be. Their meeting was fortunate, for it let them use each other to grow on. Daughters of distant mothers and incomprehensible fathers (Sula's because he was dead; Nel's because he wasn't), they found in each other's eyes the intimacy they were looking for. (pp. 51–52)

As this beautiful passage shows, their relationship, from the very beginning, is suffused with an erotic romanticism. The dreams in which they are initially drawn to each other are actually complementary aspects of the same sensuous fairy tale. Nel imagines a "fiery prince" who never quite arrives while Sula gallops like a prince "on a gray-and-white horse."[4] The "real world" of patriarchy requires, however, that they channel this energy away from each other to the opposite sex. Lorraine Bethel explains this dynamic in her essay "Conversations with Ourselves: Black Female Relationships in Toni Cade Bambara's[5] *Gorilla, My Love* and Toni Morrison's *Sula*":

> I am not suggesting that Sula and Nel are being consciously sexual, or that their relationship has an overt lesbian nature. I am suggesting, however, that there is a certain sensuality in their interactions that is rein-

4. My sister, Beverly Smith, pointed out this connection to me [Smith's note.].
5. African American writer of fiction and screenplays (1939–1995) as well as activist; the short story collection *Gorilla, My Love* was published in 1972.

> forced by the mirror-like nature of their relationship. Sexual exploration and coming of age is a natural part of adolescence. Sula and Nel discover men together, and though their flirtations with males are an important part of their sexual exploration, the sensuality that they experience in each other's company is equally important.[6]

Sula and Nel must also struggle with the constrictions of racism upon their lives. The knowledge that "they were neither white nor male" is the inherent explanation of their need for each other. Morrison depicts in literature the necessary bonding that has always taken place between Black women for the sake of barest survival. Together the two girls can find the courage to create themselves.

Their relationship is severed only when Nel marries Jude, an unexceptional young man who thinks of her as "the hem—the tuck and fold that hid his raveling edges" (p. 83). Sula's inventive wildness cannot overcome social pressure or the influence of Nel's parents who "had succeeded in rubbing down to a dull glow any sparkle or splutter she had" (p. 83). Nel falls prey to convention while Sula escapes it. Yet at the wedding which ends the first phase of their relationship, Nel's final action is to look past her husband toward Sula,

> a slim figure in blue, gliding, with just a hint of a strut, down the path towards the road. . . . Even from the rear Nel could tell that it was Sula and that she was smiling; that something deep down in that litheness was amused. (p. 85)

When Sula returns ten years later, her rebelliousness full blown, a major source of the town's suspicions stems from the fact that although she is almost thirty, she is still unmarried. Sula's grandmother, Eva, does not hesitate to bring up the matter as soon as she arrives. She asks:

> "When you gone to get married? You need to have some babies. It'll settle you. . . . Ain't no woman got no business floatin' around without no man." (p. 92)

Sula replies: "I don't want to make somebody else. I want to make myself" (p. 92). Self-definition is a dangerous activity for any woman to engage in, especially a Black one, and it expectedly earns Sula pariah status in Medallion.

Morrison clearly points out that it is the fact that Sula has not been tamed or broken by the exigencies of heterosexual family life which most galls the others:

> Among the weighty evidence piling up was the fact that Sula did not look her age. She was near thirty and, unlike them, had lost no teeth, suffered no bruises, developed no ring of fat at the waist or pocket at the back of her neck. (p. 115)

In other words she is not a domestic serf, a woman run down by obligatory childbearing or a victim of battering. Sula also sleeps with the husbands of

6. Lorraine Bethel, "Conversations with Ourselves: Black Female Relationships in Toni Cade Bambara's *Gorilla, My Love* and Toni Morrison's *Sula*," unpublished paper written at Yale University, 1976 [Smith's note].

the town once and then discards them, needing them even less than her own mother did for sexual gratification and affection. The town reacts to her disavowal of patriarchal values by becoming fanatically serious about their own family obligations, as if in this way they might counteract Sula's radical criticism of their lives.

Sula's presence in her community functions much like the presence of lesbians everywhere to expose the contradictions of supposedly "normal" life. The opening paragraph of the essay "The Woman-Identified Woman" has amazing relevance as an explanation of Sula's position and character in the novel. It asks:

> What is a lesbian? A lesbian is the rage of all women condensed to the point of explosion. She is the woman who, often beginning at an extremely early age, acts in accordance with her inner compulsion to be a more complete and freer human being than her society—perhaps then, but certainly later—cares to allow her. These needs and actions, over a period of years, bring her into painful conflict with people, situations, the accepted ways of thinking, feeling and behaving, until she is in a state of continual war with everything around her, and usually with herself. She may not be fully conscious of the political implications of what for her began as personal necessity, but on some level she has not been able to accept the limitations and oppression laid on her by the most basic role of her society—the female role.[7]

The limitations of the *Black* female role are even greater in a racist and sexist society, as is the amount of courage it takes to challenge them. It is no wonder that the townspeople see Sula's independence as imminently dangerous.

Morrison is also careful to show the reader that despite their years of separation and their opposing paths, Nel and Sula's relationship retains its primacy for each of them. Nel feels transformed when Sula returns and thinks:

> It was like getting the use of an eye back, having a cataract removed. Her old friend had come home. Sula. Who made her laugh, who made her see old things with new eyes, in whose presence she felt clever, gentle and a little raunchy. (p. 95)

Laughing together in the familiar "rib-scraping" way, Nel feels "new, soft and new" (p. 98). Morrison uses here the visual imagery which symbolizes the women's closeness throughout the novel.

Sula fractures this closeness, however, by sleeping with Nel's husband, an act of little import according to her system of values. Nel, of course, cannot understand. Sula thinks ruefully:

> Nel was the one person who had wanted nothing from her, who had accepted all aspects of her. Now she wanted everything, and all because of *that*. Nel was the first person who had been real to her, whose name she knew, who had seen as she had the slant of life that made it possible to stretch it to its limits. Now Nel was one of *them*. (pp. 119–120)

7. New York Radicalesbians, "The Woman-Identified Woman," in *Lesbians Speak Out* (Oakland: Women's Press Collective, 1974), p. 87 [Smith's note].

Sula also thinks at the realization of losing Nel about how unsatisfactory her relationships with men have been and admits:

> She had been looking all along for a friend, and it took her a while to discover that a lover was not a comrade and could never be—for a woman. (p. 121)

The nearest that Sula comes to actually loving a man is in a brief affair with Ajax and what she values most about him is the intellectual companionship he provides, the brilliance he "allows" her to show.

Sula's feelings about sex with men are also consistent with a lesbian interpretation of the novel. Morrison writes:

> She went to bed with men as frequently as she could. It was the only place where she could find what she was looking for: *misery and the ability to feel deep sorrow*. . . . During the lovemaking she found and needed to find the cutting edge. When she left off cooperating with her body and began to assert herself in the act, particles of strength gathered in her like steel shavings drawn to a spacious magnetic center, forming a tight cluster that nothing, it seemed, could break. *And there was utmost irony and outrage in lying under someone, in a position of surrender, feeling her own abiding strength and limitless power*. . . . When her partner disengaged himself, she looked up at him in wonder trying to recall his name . . . waiting impatiently for him to turn away . . . *leaving her to the postcoital privateness in which she met herself, welcomed herself, and joined herself in matchless harmony*. (pp. 122–123; italics mine)

Sula uses men for sex which results, not in communion with them, but in her further delving into self.

Ultimately the deepest communion and communication in the novel occurs between two women who love each other. After their last painful meeting, which does not bring reconciliation, Sula thinks as Nel leaves her:

> "So she will walk on down that road, her back so straight in that old green coat . . . thinking how much I have cost her and never remember the days when we were two throats and one eye and we had no price." (p. 147)

It is difficult to imagine a more evocative metaphor for what women can be to each other, the "pricelessness" they achieve in refusing to sell themselves for male approval, the total worth that they can only find in each other's eyes.

Decades later the novel concludes with Nel's final comprehension of the source of the grief that has plagued her from the time her husband walked out:

> "All that time, I thought I was missing Jude." And the loss pressed down on her chest and came up into her throat. "We was girls together," she said as though explaining something. "O Lord, Sula," she cried, "girl, girl, girlfriend."
>
> It was a fine cry—loud and long—but it had no bottom and it had no top, just circles and circles of sorrow. (p. 174)

Again Morrison exquisitely conveys what women, Black women, mean to each other. This final passage verifies the depth of Sula and Nel's relationship and its centrality to an accurate interpretation of the work.

Sula is an exceedingly lesbian novel in the emotions expressed, in the definition of female character, and in the way that the politics of heterosexuality are portrayed. The very meaning of lesbianism is being expanded in literature, just as it is being redefined through politics. The confusion that many readers have felt about *Sula* may well have a lesbian explanation. If one sees Sula's inexplicable "evil" and nonconformity as the evil of not being male-identified, many elements in the novel become clear. The work might be clearer still if Morrison had approached her subject with the consciousness that a lesbian relationship was at least a possibility for her characters. Obviously Morrison did not *intend* the reader to perceive Sula and Nel's relationship as inherently lesbian. However, this lack of intention only shows the way in which heterosexist assumptions can veil what may logically be expected to occur in a work. What I have tried to do here is not to prove that Morrison wrote something that she did not, but to point out how a Black feminist critical perspective at least allows consideration of this level of the novel's meaning.

In her interview in *Conditions: One* Adrienne Rich[8] talks about unconsummated relationships and the need to reevaluate the meaning of intense yet supposedly nonerotic connections between women. She asserts:

> We need a lot more documentation about what actually happened: I think we can also imagine it, because we know it happened—we know it out of our own lives.[9]

Black women are still in the position of having to "imagine," discover, and verify Black lesbian literature because so little has been written from an avowedly lesbian perspective. The near nonexistence of Black lesbian literature which other Black lesbians and I so deeply feel has everything to do with the politics of our lives, the total suppression of identity that all Black women, lesbian or not, must face. This literary silence is again intensified by the unavailability of an autonomous Black feminist movement through which we could fight our oppression and also begin to name ourselves.

In a speech, "The Autonomy of Black Lesbian Women," Wilmette Brown comments upon the connection between our political reality and the literature we must invent:

> Because the isolation of Black lesbian women, given that we are superfreaks, given that our lesbianism defies both the sexual identity that capital gives us and the racial identity that capital gives us, the isolation of Black lesbian women from heterosexual Black women is very profound. Very profound. I have searched throughout Black history, Black literature, whatever, looking for some women that I could see were somehow lesbian. Now I know that in a certain sense they were all lesbian. But that was a very painful search.[1]

Heterosexual privilege is usually the only privilege that Black women have. None of us have racial or sexual privilege, almost none of us have class privilege; maintaining "straightness" is our last resort. Being out, particularly out in print, is the final renunciation of any claim to the crumbs of "toler-

8. American poet, essayist, and lesbian feminist. (b. 1929; see above).
9. Elly Bulkin, "An Interview with Adrienne Rich: Part I," *Conditions: One* 1 (1977): 62 [Smith's note].
1. Wilmette Brown, "The Autonomy of Black Lesbian Women," manuscript of speech delivered July 24, 1976, in Toronto, Canada [Smith's note].

ance" that nonthreatening "ladylike" Black women are sometimes fed. I am convinced that it is our lack of privilege and power in every other sphere that allows so few Black women to make the leap that many white women, particularly writers, have been able to make in this decade, not merely because they are white or have economic leverage, but because they have had the strength and support of a movement behind them.

As Black lesbians we must be out not only in white society but in the Black community as well, which is at least as homophobic. That the sanctions against Black lesbians are extremely high is well illustrated in this comment by Black male writer Ishmael Reed. Speaking about the inroads that whites make into Black culture, he asserts:

> In Manhattan you find people actively trying to impede intellectual debate among Afro-Americans. The powerful "liberal/radical/existentialist" influences of the Manhattan literary and drama establishment speak through tokens, like for example that ancient notion of the *one* black ideologue (who's usually a Communist), the *one* black poetess (who's usually a feminist lesbian).[2]

To Reed, "feminist" and "lesbian" are the most pejorative terms he can hurl at a Black woman and totally invalidate anything she might say regardless of her actual politics or sexual identity. Such accusations are quite effective for keeping in line Black women writers who are writing with integrity and strength from any conceivable perspective, but especially ones who are actually feminist and lesbian. Unfortunately Reed's reactionary attitude is all too typical. A community which has not confronted sexism, because a widespread Black feminist movement has not required it to, has likewise not been challenged to examine its heterosexism. Even at this moment I am not convinced that one can write explicitly as a Black lesbian and live to tell about it.

Yet there are a handful of Black women who have risked everything for truth. Audre Lorde, Pat Parker, and Ann Allen Shockley have at least broken ground in the vast wilderness of works that do not exist.[3] Black feminist criticism will again have an essential role not only in creating a climate in which Black lesbian writers can survive, but in undertaking the total reassessment of Black literature and literary history needed to reveal the Black woman-identified women that Wilmette Brown and so many of us are looking for.

Although I have concentrated here upon what does not exist and what needs to be done, a few Black feminist critics have already begun this work. Gloria T. Hull at the University of Delaware has discovered in her research on Black women poets of the Harlem Renaissance[4] that many of the women

2. Domini, "Roots and Racism," p. 18 [Smith's note].

3. Audre Lorde, *New York Headshop and Museum* (Detroit: Broadside Press, 1974); *Coal* (New York: Norton, 1976); *Between Our Selves* (Point Reyes, Calif.: Eidolon Editions, 1976); *The Black Unicorn* (New York: Norton, 1978). Pat Parker, *Child of Myself* (Oakland: Women's Press Collective, 1972); *Pit Stop* (Oakland: Women's Press Collective, 1973); *Womanslaughter* (Oakland: Diana Press, 1978); *Movement in Black* (Oakland: Diana Press, 1978). Ann Allen Shockley, *Loving Her* (Indianapolis: Bobbs-Merrill, 1974) [Smith's note]. All Americans: Lorde (1934–1992), poet and essayist; Parker (1944–1989), poet; and Shockley (b. 1927), novelist.

4. Vibrant movement of the 1920s and early 1930s encompassing literature and the visual and performing arts; Harlem in New York City was then the cultural capital of black America. Major literary figures of the Harlem Renaissance include Alain Locke, LANGSTON HUGHES, and Hurston. Hull (b. 1944), scholar and poet, a pioneer in African American feminist studies.

who are considered "minor" writers of the period were in constant contact with each other and provided both intellectual stimulation and psychological support for each other's work. At least one of these writers, Angelina Weld Grimké,[5] wrote many unpublished love poems to women. Lorraine Bethel, a recent graduate of Yale College, has done substantial work on Black women writers, particularly in her senior essay, "This Infinity of Conscious Pain: Blues Lyricism and Hurston's Black Female Folk Aesthetic and Cultural Sensibility in *Their Eyes Were Watching God*," in which she brilliantly defines and uses the principles of Black feminist criticism. Elaine Scott at the State University of New York at Old Westbury is also involved in highly creative and politically resonant research on Hurston and other writers.

The fact that these critics are young and, except for Hull, unpublished merely indicates the impediments we face. Undoubtedly there are other women working and writing whom I do not even know, simply because there is no place to read them. As Michele Wallace states in her article "A Black Feminist's Search for Sisterhood":

> We exist as women who are Black who are feminists, each stranded for the moment, working independently because there is not yet an environment in this society remotely congenial to our struggle—[or our thoughts].[6]

I only hope that this essay is one way of breaking our silence and our isolation, of helping us to know each other.

Just as I did not know where to start I am not sure how to end. I feel that I have tried to say too much and at the same time have left too much unsaid. What I want this essay to do is lead everyone who reads it to examine *everything* that they have ever thought and believed about feminist culture and to ask themselves how their thoughts connect to the reality of Black women's writing and lives. I want to encourage in white women, as a first step, a sane accountability to all the women who write and live on this soil. I want most of all for Black women and Black lesbians somehow not to be so alone. This last will require the most expansive of revolutions as well as many new words to tell us how to make this revolution real. I finally want to express how much easier both my waking and my sleeping hours would be if there were one book in existence that would tell me something specific about my life. One book based in Black feminist and Black lesbian experience, fiction or nonfiction. Just one work to reflect the reality that I and the Black women whom I love are trying to create. When such a book exists then each of us will not only know better how to live, but how to dream.

1977

5. Poet and dramatist (1880–1958); few of her works were published in her lifetime.
6. Michele Wallace, "A Black Feminist's Search for Sisterhood," *Village Voice*, July 28, 1975, p. 7 [Smith's note]. Wallace (b. 1952), African American critic.

BARBARA JOHNSON
b. 1947

Barbara Johnson is known as a translator in various senses of the word. She is the celebrated translator of JACQUES DERRIDA's *Dissemination* (1972; trans. 1981); and she is also one of the earliest and most interesting translators of structuralist and poststructuralist theory into literary insights. Often praised for her "lucidity" and "clarity," she has nevertheless emphasized, again and again, the unavoidability and necessity of linguistic complexity and difficulty in formulating intractable problems. For her, language cannot be extricated from what is problematic; language is not simply *about* problems, it *participates in* them.

Born in 1947 near Boston, she was the first of four children. Her father was a school principal and her mother a librarian. She attended Oberlin College (1965–69), majoring in French, and completed a Ph.D. in French at Yale University in 1977. Her studies at Yale took place at a complicated intersection of politics and criticism; while the effects of the 1969 student strike against the Vietnam War and the trial of Black Panther Bobby Seale in New Haven lingered, the "Yale School" of academic literary theory was developing, and, around 1968, there had exploded onto the scene "French Theory"—a shorthand designation for structuralism and poststructuralism in many fields. The "Yale School" was the label by which the academic and popular press referred to a group of male literary critics (PAUL DE MAN, HAROLD BLOOM, Geoffrey Hartman, J. Hillis Miller) who were all interested in Romanticism and who often incorporated structuralist and poststructuralist perspectives in their work. At the same time, the works of Derrida, JACQUES LACAN, and other French theorists were gaining recognition, but because most had not yet been translated into English, French departments provided one of the first points of entry into the American academy for their revolutionary ideas. The challenge of translating between one context and another thus itself became part of the theoretical enterprise.

Johnson's work has been profoundly engaged with and by the work of a number of teachers and colleagues, both at Yale, where she taught French and comparative literature from 1977 to 1983, and at Harvard University, where she has taught French, comparative literature, and English since 1983: in particular, Paul de Man (her thesis director at Yale) and colleagues Shoshana Felman (at Yale), HENRY LOUIS GATES JR. (at both Yale and Harvard), and Marjorie Garber (at Harvard). Her first book, published in France in 1979, examined the prose poems of the nineteenth-century French writers CHARLES BAUDELAIRE and STÉPHANE MALLARMÉ. Titled *Défigurations du language poétique: la seconde révolution baudelairienne* (*Disfigurations of Poetic Langage: The Second Baudelairean Revolution*), it analyzed the significance of Baudelaire's turn to prose after the publication of his one book of lyric verse, *Les Fleurs du mal* (*Flowers of Evil*). Johnson's second book, *The Critical Difference: Essays in the Contemporary Rhetoric of Reading* (1980), which ranged more widely over theory, quickly followed. The word *difference* in the title is meant to name two different conceptions of difference and the tension between them: binary difference in its traditional sense (prose and poetry, male and female, etc.); and Derridean *différance*, a nonidentity within each term that is concealed or repressed in the process of establishing opposition. Johnson named these "the difference between" and "the difference within," terms that have entered the critical lexicon.

The Critical Difference collected what might be called Johnson's first "allegories of theory": the essays focused on the process of finding in literary texts preoccupations that have become newly readable through new theoretical perspectives. Rather than viewing theory as something applied to the text, she contends that theoretical questions already inhabit the text. The theory can draw them out, and, perhaps, provide the means of analyzing the text's resistances to the very theory that illuminates it.

Theory thus becomes a subset of literature: a process of formulating a knowledge the literary text is presumed to store. The key words of the theory are themselves *words*; they are therefore subject to the same play, seriousness, and instability that literary texts can give to all words. What constitutes "literature," however, is not fixed but constantly changing, a function of the kinds of questions asked of it: what is "stored" in the text both is and isn't in it. As the text and the theory interact, the two constantly shift ground. Johnson's reading of Hermann Melville's *Billy Budd*, our selection, sees Melville's short novel as deeply preoccupied by the same issues about language that occupied FERDINAND DE SAUSSURE (1857–1913) and J. L. AUSTIN (1911–1960). *Billy Budd* is a particularly good example of a text fissured by conflicting assumptions about words: the final revision was never finished by Melville, and competing versions of it have been published posthumously. Another well-known essay from *The Critical Difference*, "The Frame of Reference," examines the influential analyses, by Lacan and Derrida, of EDGAR ALLAN POE's story "The Purloined Letter" (1844) and meditates explicitly on the structure of mutual framing between text and theory.

In 1981 Johnson published her translation of Derrida's *Dissemination*, with a much-cited introduction. In 1982 she edited an issue of *Yale French Studies* titled *The Pedagogical Imperative: Teaching as a Literary Genre*. In this collection of essays, such authors as Derrida, de Man, Felman, Jane Gallop, and JEAN-FRANÇOIS LYOTARD explored not how to teach literary texts but how literature depicts teaching, and how "the literary" and "the pedagogical" are linked.

In 1980 a student introduced Johnson to the work of ZORA NEALE HURSTON (1891–1960); aided by a series of conversations with Henry Louis Gates Jr., Johnson became one of the first scholars to apply French literary theory to African American texts. Hurston was a particularly productive novelist for this enterprise, since her rhetorical virtuosity and folkloric imagination were at odds with the kinds of realist texts that dominated the canon of African American literature. Feminists, prompted by the writer Alice Walker's essays of the mid-1970s about Hurston's importance to the literary tradition of black women, were beginning to rethink both the canon and canonical aesthetics through Hurston's novels and folktales. The resultant boom in Hurston studies contributed to a change in African American studies itself, epitomized by Gates's *The Signifying Monkey: A Theory of Afro-American Literary Criticism* (1988). Johnson's two essays on Hurston appear in her collection *A World of Difference* (1987), a book in which she attempts to think deconstructively about a wide set of questions. For example, the often-reprinted essay "Apostrophe, Animation, and Abortion," which ends the book, brings together in striking ways literature (lyric poetry) and law (the abortion debates).

In 1991 Johnson co-edited a volume titled *Consequences of Theory*, whose contributors attempted to refute the notorious assertion, made by STANLEY FISH in his *Doing What Comes Naturally: Change, Rhetoric, and the Practice of Theory in Literary and Legal Studies* (1989), that theory has no consequences. There followed in 1993 *Freedom and Interpretation*, Johnson's edited volume of the Oxford Amnesty Lectures of 1992, part of a project designed to raise money for Amnesty International. The lecturers invited to Oxford that year had been asked by the organizers to address what happens to the idea of "human rights" in an age of the "deconstruction of the subject." Johnson's introduction attempts to analyze what is at stake in the question, especially when its two elements are viewed as not simply opposed. This volume belongs to the larger investigation of the relations between deconstruction and politics, a topic hotly debated at the time.

Johnson's own lectures on literary theory given at Bucknell University yielded *The Wake of Deconstruction* (1994), in which she discusses the questions deconstruction had both awakened and left in its wake, especially after the double "death" of Paul de Man (his literal death in 1983, followed by the revelation in 1987 of his collaborationist journalism). The two lectures, "Double Mourning and the Public Sphere" and "Women and Allegory," analyze the conflation of deconstruction, political correctness, and identity politics, which had all become strangely and wrongly linked in the public mind.

In the late 1990s, a series of attacks on feminism and on women's studies programs led Johnson to write about the status of ambivalence within oppositional movements. She argues in the introduction to *The Feminist Difference* (1998) that the trap of unanimity, even when called forth by a common target, is ultimately impoverishing except on specific and strategic occasions. The debates within feminism—among black and white feminists, among lesbians and heterosexuals, among women from different classes or different countries—had revealed that the strength of the feminist movement lay not in unity but in the ability to face differences and conflicts and still go on, and that it was the continued functioning of the powers being contested (even *within* feminists themselves) that made going on so difficult. The essays in *The Feminist Difference* take up the issues raised in the book's subtitle—*Literature, Psychoanalysis, Race, and Gender*—and are loosely structured around paired texts.

Our selection, from "Melville's Fist: The Execution of *Billy Budd*" (1979), weaves together Melville's writing strategies with the tale he is telling. In addition, it examines the early critical literature surrounding Melville's text, which can be seen to act out the problems found within the work. The problem brought to crisis by the plot—Billy Budd's murder of John Claggart—is an outgrowth of issues of representation exemplified by the two characters. "Handsome is as handsome does," the saying applied to Billy, presupposes the ideal of an absolute correspondence (Saussure calls it "motivation") between a sign and its meaning, a signifier and a signified. In contrast, "His portrait I essay, but shall never hit it," the narrator's admission about his representation of John Claggart, presupposes an unbridgeable gap between the two parts of the sign. Captain Vere, whose role is to judge ("read") the resulting confrontation, must negotiate between these two theories of the sign—the "motivated" versus the "arbitrary"—in relation to the legal "forms" or conventions under which he is obliged to operate. Johnson frames the tale in the context not only of linguistic theory but also of relations between literature and law. For Captain Vere cannot pronounce upon the "text" before him without at the same time, as J. L. Austin would put it, "doing things with words."

"Melville's Fist" is a good example of what we might call the literary life of theory. The essay both provides an intricate close reading of a text and discovers, within the text, questions the theory is attempting to discuss. It is all too easy to think of theory as a body of knowledge rather than as an approach to insoluble problems. By uncovering general preoccupations that are "in" the text even though they could *not*, in the same form, have been "in" Melville's mind, Johnson explores the questions that the text and the theory implicitly share—questions about motivation, intention, action, and law. In finding Saussure and Austin already impossibly within Melville, she suggests that a reader can achieve a closeness to texts that is based not on accuracy (as measured against some fixed standard or truth) but on intimacy (as results from getting to know how something works).

In describing the processes by which forces of uncertainty are institutionalized as certainties—and thus, as theories—Johnson once lamented that "nothing fails like success" (*A World of Difference*). The "linguistic turn" in the human sciences during the twentieth century has in some ways been superseded and critiqued, but Johnson remains unconvinced that the project of accounting for the role of language can ever really become outmoded. We need to find, she implies, not something "beyond the linguistic turn" but a way to keep being surprised by it.

At Harvard University, Johnson has been named the Fredric Wertham Professor of Law and Psychiatry in Society, a title reflective of her ongoing interdisciplinary work. Like SAMUEL TAYLOR COLERIDGE's Ancient Mariner, whom she cites as a model teacher, she seems determined to repeat the story of the importance of language in widely differing contexts. But the lesson she derives from the Mariner about pedagogy is not simple: "Teaching," she writes in her introduction to *The Pedagogical Imperative*, "is a compulsion to repeat what one has not yet understood."

BIBLIOGRAPHY

Barbara Johnson is the author of *Défigurations du langage poétique* (1979), *The Critical Difference* (1980), *A World of Difference* (1987), *The Wake of Deconstruction* (1994), and *The Feminist Difference* (1998). She edited *The Pedagogical Imperative* (1982); with Jonathan Arac, *Consequences of Theory* (1990); and *Freedom and Interpretation* (1993), and in 1981 she translated Jacques Derrida's *Dissemination*. Johnson is currently engaged in two large projects. "Moses and Intertextuality: Sigmund Freud, Zora Neale Hurston, and the Bible," an essay from the first—"Moses and Multiculturalism"—has been published in *Poetics of the Americas* (ed. Bainard Cowan and Jefferson Humphries, 1997). Two essays from the second, "Persons & Things," have been published: "Anthropomorphism in Lyric and Law," *Yale Journal of Law and the Humanities* 10.2 (1998), and "Using People: Kant with Winnicott," in *The Turn to Ethics* (ed. Marjorie Garber, Beatrice Hanssen, and Rebecca L. Walkowitz, 2000).

Johnson's *The Wake of Deconstruction* contains introductory essays by Harold Schweizer and Michael Payne on her work, as well as the text of an interview. An earlier interview was published by Imre Salusinszky in *Criticism in Society* (1987). There is a detailed (though unannotated) bibliography in *The Wake of Deconstruction*.

From Melville's Fist: The Execution of *Billy Budd*

The Plot against the Characters

The plot of Melville's *Billy Budd*[1] is well known, and, like its title character, appears entirely straightforward and simple. It is a tale of three men in a boat: the innocent, ignorant foretopman, handsome Billy Budd; the devious, urbane master-at-arms, John Claggart; and the respectable, bookish commanding officer, Captain the Honorable Edward Fairfax ("Starry") Vere. Falsely accused by Claggart of plotting mutiny aboard the British man-of-war *Bellipotent*, Billy Budd, his speech impeded by a stutter, strikes his accuser dead in front of the Captain, and is condemned, after a summary trial, to hang.

In spite of the apparent straightforwardness of the facts of the case, however, there exists in the critical literature on *Billy Budd* a notable range of disagreement over the ultimate meaning of the tale. For some, the story constitutes Melville's "testament of acceptance,"[2] his "ever-lasting yea,"[3] his "acceptance of tragedy,"[4] or at least his "recognition of necessity."[5] For others, Melville's "final stage" is, on the contrary, "irony":[6] *Billy Budd* is consid-

1. Herman Melville, *Billy Budd* [a posthumous, unfinished, much-revised novella first published in 1924], in *"Billy Budd, Sailor," and Other Stories*, ed. H. Beaver (New York: Penguin Books, 1967). Unless otherwise indicated, all references to *Billy Budd* are to this edition, which reprints the Hayford and Sealts Reading Text [except as indicated, all notes are Johnson's]. [Melville (1819–1891), American writer of fiction and poetry—editor's note.]

2. E. L. Grant Watson, "Melville's Testament of Acceptance," *New England Quarterly* 6 (1933): 319–27.

3. The expression appears in both J. Freeman, *Herman Melville* (New York: Macmillan, 1926), p. 136, and in R. M. Weaver, *The Shorter Novels of Herman Melville* (New York: Liveright, 1928), p. li.

4. W. E. Sedgwick, *Herman Melville: The Tragedy of Mind* (Cambridge, Mass.: Harvard University Press, 1944), pp. 231–49.

5. F. B. Freeman, *Melville's Billy Budd* (Cambridge, Mass.: Harvard University Press, 1948), pp. 115–24.

6. J. Schiffman, "Melville's Final Stage: Irony," *American Literature* 22 (1950): 128–36.

ered a "testament of resistance,"[7] "ironic social criticism,"[8] or the last vituperation in Melville's "quarrel with God."[9] More recently, critical attention has devoted itself to the fact of ambiguity itself in the story, sometimes deploring it,[1] sometimes revelling in it,[2] and sometimes simply listing it.[3] The ambiguity is attributed to various causes: the unfinished state of the manuscript, Melville's change of heart toward Vere, Melville's unreconciled ambivalence toward authority or his guilt about paternity, or the incompatibility between the "plot" and the "story."[4]

* * *

Most studies of the story tend to begin, after a few general remarks about the nature of good and evil, with a delineation of the three main characters: Billy, Claggart, and Vere. As Charles Weir puts it, "The purely physical action of the story is clear enough, and about its significant details there is never any doubt. . . . It is, therefore, with some consideration of the characters of the three principal actors that any analysis must begin."[5] "Structurally," writes F. B. Freeman, "the three characters *are* the novel" (p. 73).

Melville goes to great lengths to describe both the physical and the moral characteristics of his protagonists. Billy Budd, a twenty-one-year-old "novice in the complexities of factitious life," is remarkable for his "significant personal beauty," his "reposeful good nature," his "straightforward simplicity," and his "unconventional rectitude." But Billy's intelligence ("such as it was," says Melville) is as primitive as his virtues are pristine. He is illiterate, he cannot understand ambiguity, and he stutters.

Claggart, on the other hand, is presented as the very image of urbane, intellectualized, articulate evil. Although "of no ill figure upon the whole," something in Claggart's pallid face consistently inspires uneasiness and mistrust. He is a man, writes Melville, "in whom was the mania of an evil nature, not engendered by vicious training or corrupting books or licentious living, but born with him and innate, in short, 'a depravity according to nature' " (p. 354). The mere sight of Billy Budd's rosy beauty and rollicking innocence does not fail to provoke in such a character "an antipathy spontaneous and profound."

The third man in the drama, the one who has inspired the greatest critical dissent, is presented in less vivid but curiously more contradictory terms. The *Bellipotent*'s captain is described as both unaffected and pedantic, dreamy and resolute, irascible and undemonstrative, "mindful of the welfare of his men, but never tolerating an infraction of discipline," "intrepid to the verge of temerity, though never injudiciously so" (p. 338). While Billy and Claggart are said to owe their characters to "nature," Captain Vere is shaped mainly by his fondness for books:

7. P. Withim, "*Billy Budd:* Testament of Resistance," *Modern Language Quarterly* 20 (1959): 115–27.

8. K. E. Zink, "Herman Melville and the Forms—Irony and Social Criticism in *Billy Budd,*" *Accent* 12 (1952): 131–39.

9. L. Thompson, *Melville's Quarrel with God* (Princeton: Princeton University Press, 1952).

1. K. Ledbetter, "The Ambiguity of *Billy Budd,*" *Texas Studies in Literature and Language* 4 (1962): 130–34.

2. S. E. Hyman, quoted in R. H. Fogle, "*Billy Budd*—Acceptance of Irony," *Tulane Studies in English* 8 (1958):107.

3. E. M. Cifelli, "*Billy Budd*: Boggy Ground to Build On," *Studies in Short Fiction* 13 (1976): 463–69.

4. L. T. Lemon, "*Billy Budd*: The Plot against the Story," *Studies in Short Fiction* 2 (1964): 32–43. [The larger story is that of the French and English wars following the time of the French Revolution, in which *Billy Budd* is set—editor's note.]

5. Charles Weir Jr., "Malice Reconciled," in *Critics on Melville*, ed. Theodore Rountree (Coral Gables: University of Miami Press, 1972), p. 121.

> He loved books, never going to sea without a newly replenished library, compact but of the best. . . . With nothing of that literary taste which less heeds the thing conveyed than the vehicle, his bias was toward those books to which every serious mind of superior order occupying any active post of authority in the world naturally inclines: books treating of actual men and events no matter of what era—history, biography, and unconventional writes like Montaigne,[6] who, free from cant and convention, honestly and in the spirit of common sense philosophize upon realities. (p. 340)

Vere, then, is an honest, serious reader, seemingly well suited for the role of judge and witness that in the course of the story he will come to play.

No consideration of the nature of character in *Billy Budd*, however, can fail to take into account the fact that the fate of each of the characters is the direct reverse of what one is led to expect from his "nature." Billy is sweet, innocent, and harmless, yet he kills. Claggart is evil, perverted, and mendacious, yet he dies a victim. Vere is sagacious and responsible, yet he allows a man whom he feels to be blameless to hang. It is this discrepancy between character and action that gives rise to the critical disagreement over the story: readers tend either to save the plot and condemn Billy ("acceptance," "tragedy," or "necessity"), or to save Billy and condemn the plot ("irony," "injustice," or "social criticism").

In an effort to make sense of this troubling incompatibility between character and plot, many readers are tempted to say of Billy and Claggart, as does W. Y. Tindall, that "each is more important for what he is than what he does. . . . Good and bad, they occupy the region of good and evil."[7] This reading effectively preserves the allegorical values suggested by Melville's opening chapters, but it does so only by denying the importance of the plot. It ends where the plot begins: with the identification of the moral natures of the characters. One may therefore ask whether the allegorical interpretation (good vs. evil) depends as such on this sort of preference for "being" over "doing," and, if so, what effect the incompatibility between character and action may have on the allegorical functioning of *Billy Budd*.

Interestingly enough, Melville himself both invites an allegorical reading and subverts the very terms of its consistency when he writes of the murder: "Innocence and guilt personified in Claggart and Budd in effect changed places" (p. 380). Allowing for the existence of personification but reversing the relation between personifier and personified, positioning an opposition between good and evil only to make each term take on the properties of its opposite, Melville thus sets up his plot in the form of a chiasmus:[8]

This story, which is often read as a retelling of the story of Christ, is thus literally a cruci-fiction—a fiction structured in the shape of a cross. At the moment of the reversal, an instant before his fist shoots out, Billy's face

6. Michel de Montaigne (1533–1592), French essayist [editor's note].

7. "The Ceremony of Innocence," in *Great Moral Dilemmas in Literature, Past and Present*, ed. R. M. McIver (New York: Harper and Row, 1956), p. 75.

8. A rhetorical figure in which the elements of the second of two parallel clauses are inverted, forming a kind of *X*, or Greek chi (e.g., "Eat to live, don't live to eat") [editor's note].

seems to mark out the point of crossing, bearing "an expression which was as a crucifixion to behold" (p. 376). Innocence and guilt, criminal and victim, change places through the mute expressiveness of Billy's inability to speak.

If *Billy Budd* is indeed an allegory, it is thus an allegory of the questioning of the traditional conditions of allegorical stability. The fact that Melville's plot requires that the good act out the evil designs of the bad while the bad suffer the unwarranted fate of the good indicates that the real opposition with which Melville is preoccupied here is less the static opposition between evil and good than the dynamic opposition between a man's "nature" and his acts, or, in Tyndall's terms, the relation between human "being" and human "doing."

Curiously enough, it is precisely this question of "being" versus "doing" that is brought up by the only sentence we ever see Claggart directly address to Billy Budd. When Billy accidentally spills his soup across the path of the master-at-arms, Claggart playfully replies, "Handsomely done, my lad! And handsome *is* as handsome *did* it, too!" (p. 350; emphasis mine). The proverbial expression "handsome *is* as handsome *does*," from which this exclamation springs, posits the possibility of a continuous, predictable, transparent relationship between "being" and "doing." It supposes that the inner goodness of Billy Budd is in harmonious accord with his fair appearance, that, as Melville writes of the stereotypical "Handsome Sailor" in the opening pages of the story, "the moral nature" is not "out of keeping with the physical make" (p. 322). But it is precisely this continuity between the physical and the moral, between appearance and action, or between "being" and "doing," that Claggart questions in Billy Budd. He warns Captain Vere not to be taken in by Billy's physical beauty: "You have but noted his fair cheek. A mantrap may be under the ruddy-tipped daisies" (p. 372). Claggart indeed soon finds his suspicions confirmed with a vengeance: when he repeats his accusation in front of Billy, he is struck down dead. It would thus seem that to question the continuity between character and action cannot be done with impunity, that fundamental questions of life and death are always surreptitiously involved.

In an effort to examine what it is that is at stake in Claggart's accusation, it might be helpful to view the opposition between Billy and Claggart as an opposition not between innocence and guilt but between two conceptions of language, or between two types of reading. Billy seemingly represents the perfectly *motivated* sign; that is, his inner self (the signified) is considered transparently readable from the beauty of his outer self (the signifier).[9] His "straightforward simplicity" is the very opposite of the "moral obliquities" or "crookedness of heart" that characterizes "citified" or rhetorically sophisticated man. "To deal in double meanings and insinuations of any sort," writes Melville, "was quite foreign to his nature" (p. 327). In accordance with this "nature," Billy reads everything at face value, never questioning the meaning of appearances. He is dumbfounded at the Dansker's suggestion, "incomprehensible to a novice," that Claggart's very pleasantness can be interpreted as its opposite, as a sign that he is "down on" Billy Budd. To Billy, "the

9. The sign was divided into *signified* (the meaning conveyed) and *signifier* (the symbol or sound that conveys that meaning) by the Swiss linguist FERDINAND DE SAUSSURE (1857–1913), who argued that in language, the relation between the two is *arbitrary*; to the extent that the signified determines the signifier, the sign is *motivated* [editor's note].

occasional frank air and pleasant word *went for what they purported to be*, the young sailor never having heard as yet of the 'too fair-spoken man' " (pp. 365–66; emphasis mine). As a reader, then, Billy is symbolically as well as factually illiterate. His literal-mindedness is represented by his illiteracy because, in assuming that language can be taken at face value, he excludes the very functioning of *difference* that makes the act of reading both indispensable and undecidable.

Claggart, on the other hand, is the very image of difference and duplicity, both in his appearance and in his character. His face is not ugly, but it hints of something defective or abnormal. He has no vices, yet he incarnates evil. He is an intellectual, but uses reason as "an ambidexter implement for effecting the irrational" (p. 354). Billy inspires in him both "profound antipathy" and a "soft yearning." In the incompatibility of his attributes, Claggart is thus a personification of ambiguity and ambivalence, of the distance between signifier and signified, of the separation between being and doing: "apprehending the good, but powerless to be it, a nature like Claggart's, . . . what recourse is left to it but to recoil upon itself" (p. 356). As a reader, Claggart has learned to "exercise a distrust keen in proportion to the fairness of the appearance" (p. 364). He is properly an ironic reader, who, assuming the sign to be arbitrary and unmotivated, reverses the value signs of appearances and takes a daisy for a mantrap and an unmotivated accidental spilling of soup for an intentional sly escape of antipathy. Claggart meets his downfall, however, when he attempts to master the arbitrariness of the sign for his own ends, precisely by falsely (that is, arbitrarily) accusing Billy of harboring arbitrariness, of hiding a mutineer beneath the appearance of a baby.

Such a formulation of the Budd/Claggart relationship enables one to take a new look not only at the story itself, but at the criticism as well. For, curiously enough, it is precisely this opposition between the literal reader (Billy) and the ironic reader (Claggart) that is reenacted in the critical readings of *Billy Budd* in the opposition between the "acceptance" school and the "irony" school. Those who see the story as a "testament of acceptance" tend to take Billy's final benediction of Vere at face value: as Lewis Mumford puts it, "As Melville's own end approached, he cried out with Billy Budd: God Bless Captain Vere! In this final affirmation Herman Melville died."[1] In contrast, those who read the tale ironically tend to take Billy's sweet farewell as Melville's bitter curse. Joseph Schiffman writes: "At heart a kind man, Vere, strange to say, makes possible the depraved Claggart's wish—the destruction of Billy. 'God bless Captain Vere!' Is this not piercing irony? As innocent Billy utters these words, does not the reader gag?" (p. 133) But since the acceptance/irony dichotomy is already contained within the story, since it is obviously one of the things the story is *about*, it is not enough to try to decide which of the readings is correct. What the reader of *Billy Budd* must do is to analyze what is at stake in the very opposition between literality and irony. This question, crucial for an understanding of *Billy Budd* not only as a literary but also as a critical phenomenon, will be taken up again in the final pages of the present study, but first let us examine further the linguistic implications of the murder itself.

1. *Herman Melville* (New York: Harcourt, Brace, and World, 1929), p. 357.

The Fiend That Lies Like Truth

If Claggart's accusation that Billy is secretly plotting mutiny is essentially an affirmation of the possibility of a discontinuity between being and doing, of an arbitrary, nonmotivated relation between signifier and signified, then Billy's blow must be read as an attempt violently to deny that discontinuity or arbitrariness. The blow, as a denial, functions as a substitute for speech, as Billy, during his trial, explains: "I did not mean to kill him. Could I have used my tongue I would not have struck him. But he foully lied to my face and in presence of my captain, and I had to say something, and I could only say it with a blow" (p. 383). But in striking a blow in defense of the sign's motivation, Billy, paradoxically enough, actually personifies the very *absence* of motivation: "I did not mean. . . ." His blow is involuntary, accidental, properly unmotivated. He is a sign that does not mean to mean. Billy, who cannot understand ambiguity, who takes pleasant words at face value and then obliterates Claggart for suggesting that one could do otherwise, whose sudden blow is a violent denial of any discrepancy between his being and his doing, thus ends up radically illustrating the very discrepancy he denies.

The story thus takes place between the postulate of continuity between signifier and signified ("handsome is as handsome does") and the postulate of their discontinuity ("a mantrap may be under the ruddy-tipped daisies"). Claggart, whose accusations of incipient mutiny are apparently false and therefore illustrate the very doublefacedness which they attribute to Billy, is negated for proclaiming the very lie about Billy which Billy's act of negation paradoxically proves to be the truth.

This paradox can also be stated in another way, in terms of the opposition between the performative and the constative functions of language.[2] Constative language is language used as an instrument of cognition—it describes, reports, speaks *about* something other than itself. Performative language is language which itself functions as an act, not as a report of one. Promising, betting, swearing, marrying, and declaring war, for example, are not descriptions of acts but acts in their own right. The proverb "handsome is as handsome does" can thus also be read as a statement of the compatibility between the constative ("being") and the performative ("doing") dimensions of language. But what Billy's act dramatizes is precisely their radical *incompatibility*—Billy performs the truth of Claggart's report to Vere only by means of his absolute and blind denial of its cognitive validity. If Billy had understood the truth, he would not have performed it. Handsome cannot both be and do its own undoing. The knowledge that being and doing are incompatible cannot know the ultimate performance of its own confirmation.

Melville's chiasmus thus creates a reversal not only between the places of guilt and innocence, but between the postulate of continuity and the postulate of discontinuity between doing and being, performance and cognition. When Billy's fist strikes Claggart's forehead, it is no longer possible for knowing and doing to meet. Melville's story not only reports the occurrence of a particularly deadly performative utterance; it itself *performs* the radical incompatibility between knowledge and acts.

All this, we recall, is triggered by a stutter, a linguistic defect. No analysis

2. The distinction between *constative* and *performative* language was developed by the English philosopher J. L. Austin (1911–1960) [editor's note].

of the story's dramatization of linguistic categories can be complete without careful attention to this glaring infelicity. Billy's "vocal defect" is presented and explained in the story in the following terms:

> There was just one thing amiss in him . . . , an occasional liability to a vocal defect. Though in the hour of elemental uproar or peril he was everything that a sailor should be, yet under sudden provocation of strong heart-feeling his voice, otherwise singularly musical, as if expressive of the harmony within, was apt to develop an organic hesitancy, in fact more or less of a stutter or even worse. In this particular Billy was a striking instance that the arch interferer, the envious marplot of Eden, still has more or less to do with every human consignment to this planet of Earth. In every case, one way or another he is sure to slip in his little card, as much as to remind us—I too have a hand here. (pp. 331–332)

It is doubtless this Satanic "hand" that shoots out when Billy's speech fails him. Billy is all too literally a "*striking* instance" of the workings of the "envious marplot."

Melville's choice of the word "marplot" to characterize the originator of Billy's stutter deserves special note. It seems logical to understand that the stutter "mars" the plot in that it triggers the reversal of roles between Billy and Claggart. Yet in another sense this reversal does not *mar* the plot, it *constitutes* it. Here as in the story of Eden, what the envious marplot mars is not the plot, but the state of plotlessness that exists "in the beginning." What both the Book of Genesis and *Billy Budd* narrate is thus not the story of a fall, but a fall into story.

In this connection, it is not irrelevant to recall what it is that Claggart falsely accuses Billy of: precisely of instigating a *plot*, of stirring up mutiny against the naval authorities. What Claggart is in a sense doing by positing this fictitious plot, then, is trying desperately to scare up a plot for the story. And it is Billy's very act of denial of his involvement in any plot that finally brings him *into* the plot. Billy's involuntary blow is an act of mutiny not only against the authority of his naval superiors, but also against the authority of his own conscious intentions. Perhaps it is not by chance that the word "plot" can mean both "intrigue" and "story": if all plots somehow tell the story of their own marring, then perhaps it could be said that all plots are plots against authority, that authority is precisely that which creates the sense of its own destruction, that all stories necessarily recount by their very existence the subversion of the father, of the gods, of consciousness, of order, of expectations, or of meaning.

But is Billy truly as "plotless" as he appears? Does his "simplicity" hide no division, no ambiguity? As many critics have remarked, Billy's character seems to result mainly from his exclusion of the negative. When informed that he is being arbitrarily impressed for service on a man-of-war, Billy "makes no demur" (p. 323). When invited to a clandestine meeting by a mysterious stranger, Billy acquiesces through his "incapacity of plumply saying *no*" (p. 359). But it is interesting to note that although Billy thus seems to be "just a boy who cain't say no,"[3] almost all the words used to describe him are negative in form: in-nocent, un-conventional, il-literate, un-

3. A reference to the song "I Cain't Say No," from the Richard Rodgers and Oscar Hammerstein II musical *Oklahoma!* (1943; film, 1955) [editor's note].

sophisticated, un-adulterate, etc. And although he denies any discrepancy between what is said and what is meant, he does not prove to be totally incapable of lying. When asked about the shady visit of the afterguardsman, he distorts his account in order to edit out anything that indicates any incompatibility with the absolute maintenance of authority. He neglects to report the questionable proposition even though "it was his duty as a loyal blue jacket" (p. 362) to do so. In thus shrinking from "the dirty work of a telltale" (p. 362), Billy maintains his "plotlessness" not spontaneously but through a complex act of filtering. Far from being simply and naturally pure, he is obsessed with maintaining his own irreproachability in the eyes of authority. After witnessing a flogging, he is so horrified that he resolves "that never through remissness would he make himself liable to such a visitation or do or omit aught that might merit even verbal reproof" (p. 346). Billy does not simply exclude the negative: he represses it. His reaction to questionable behavior of any sort (Red Whiskers, the afterguardsman, Claggart) is to obliterate it. He retains his "*blank* ignorance" (p. 363) only by a vigorous act of erasing. As Melville says of Billy's reaction to Claggart's petty provocations, "the ineffectual speculations into which he was led were so disturbingly alien to him that *he did his best to smother them*" (p. 362; emphasis mine).

> In his *disgustful recoil* from an overture which, though he but ill comprehended, he *instinctively knew* must involve evil of some sort, Billy Budd was like a young horse fresh from the pasture suddenly inhaling a vile whiff from some chemical factory, and by repeated snortings trying to *get it out* of his nostrils and lungs. This frame of mind *barred all desire* of holding further parley with the fellow, even were it but for the purpose of gaining some enlightenment as to his design in approaching him. (p. 361; emphasis mine)

Billy maintains his purity only through constant, though unconscious, censorship. "Innocence," writes Melville, "was his blinder" (p. 366).

It is interesting to note that while the majority of readers see Billy as a personification of goodness and Claggart as a personification of evil, those who do not tend to read from a psychoanalytical point of view.[4] Much has been made of Claggart's latent homosexuality, which Melville clearly suggests. Claggart, like the hypothetical "X—," "is a nut not to be cracked by the tap of a lady's fan" (p. 352). The "unobserved glance" he sometimes casts upon Billy contains "a touch of soft yearning, as if Claggart could even have loved Billy but for fate and ban" (p. 365). The spilling of the soup and Claggart's reaction to it are often read symbolically as a sexual exchange, the import of which, of course, is lost on Billy, who cannot read.

* * *

The Deadly Space Between

While Billy thus stands as a performative riddle (are his actions motivated or accidental?), John Claggart is presented as an enigma for cognition, a man "who for reasons of his own was keeping *incog*" (p. 343; emphasis mine).

4. See especially Rollo May, *Power and Innocence* (1972), and, more recently, EVE KOSOFSKY SEDGWICK, *Epistemology of the Closet* (1990) [editor's note].

Repeatedly referred to as a "mystery," Claggart, it seems, is difficult, even perilous, to describe:

> For the adequate comprehending of Claggart by a normal nature these hints are insufficient. To pass from a normal nature to him one must cross "the deadly space between." And this is best done by indirection. (p. 352)

Between Claggart and a "normal nature," there exists a gaping cognitive chasm. In a literal sense, this image of crossing a "deadly space" in order to reach Claggart can be seen almost as an ironic prefiguration of the murder. Billy does indeed "cross" the "space" between himself and Claggart by means of a "deadly" blow. The phrase "space between" recurs, in fact, just after the murder, to refer to the physical separation between the dead Claggart and the condemned Billy:

> Aft, and on either side, was a small stateroom, the one now temporarily a jail and the other a dead-house, and a yet smaller compartment, leaving a *space between* expanding forward. (p. 382; emphasis mine)

It is by means of a deadly chiasmus that the spatial chasm is crossed.

But physical separation is obviously not the only kind of "deadly space" involved here. The expression "deadly space between" refers primarily to a gap in cognition, a boundary beyond which ordinary understanding does not normally go. This sort of space, which stands as a limit to comprehension, seems to be an inherent feature of the attempt to describe John Claggart. From the very beginning, Melville admits: "His portrait I essay, but shall never hit it" (p. 342). What Melville says he will *not* do here is precisely what Billy Budd *does* do: hit John Claggart. It would seem that speaking and killing are thus mutually exclusive: Billy Budd kills because he cannot speak, while Melville, through the very act of speaking, does not kill. Billy's fist crosses the "deadly space" *directly*; Melville's crossing, "done by indirection," leaves its target intact.

This state of affairs, reassuring as it sounds on a moral level, is, however, rather unsettling if one examines what it implies about Melville's writing. For how reliable can a description be if it does not hit its object? What do we come to know of John Claggart if what we learn is that his portrait is askew? If to describe perfectly, to refer adequately, would be to "hit" the referent and thus annihilate it; if to know completely would be to obliterate the very object known; if the perfect fulfillment of the constative, referential function of language would consist in the total obliteration of the object of that function; then language can retain its "innocence" only by giving up its referential validity. Melville can avoid murder only by grounding his discourse in ineradicable error. If to cross a space by indirection—that is, by rhetorical displacement—is to escape deadliness, that crossing can succeed only on the condition of radically losing its way.

* * *

The cognitive spaces marked out by these eclipses of meaning are important not because they mark the limits of interpretation but because they function as its *cause*. The gaps in understanding are never directly perceived as such by the characters in the novel; those gaps are themselves taken as interpretable signs and triggers for interpretation. The lack of knowledge of Claggart's past, for example, is seen as a sign that he has something to hide:

> Nothing was known of his former life. . . . Among certain grizzled sea gossips of the gun decks and forecastle went a rumor perdue[5] that the master-at-arms was a *chevalier* [Melville's italics] who had volunteered into the King's navy by way of compounding for some mysterious swindle whereof he had been arraigned at the King's Bench. *The fact that nobody could substantiate this report was, of course, nothing against its secret currency*. . . . Indeed a man of Claggart's accomplishments, without prior nautical experience entering the navy at mature life, as he did, and necessarily allotted at the start to the lowest grade in it; a man too who never made allusion to his previous life ashore; these were circumstances which *in the dearth of exact knowledge* as to his true antecedents opened to the invidious *a vague field for unfavorable surmise*. (p. 343; emphasis mine)

In other words, it is precisely the absence of knowledge that here leads to the propagation of tales. The fact that nothing is known of Claggart's origins is not a simple, contingent, theoretically remediable lack of information; it is the very *origin* of his "evil nature." Interestingly, in Billy's case, an equal lack of knowledge leads some readers to see his origin as divine. Asked who his father is, Billy replies, "God knows." The divine and the satanic can thus be seen as metaphysical interpretations of discontinuities in knowledge. In *Billy Budd*, a stutter and a tautology serve to mark the spot from which evil springs.

Evil, then, is essentially the misreading of discontinuity through the attribution of meaning to a space or division in language. But the fact that stories of Claggart's evil arise out of a seemingly meaningless gap in knowledge is hardly a meaningless or innocent fact in itself, either in its causes or in its consequences. Claggart's function is that of a policeman "charged among other matters with the duty of preserving order on the populous lower gun decks" (p. 342). As Melville points out, "no man holding his office in a man-of-war can ever hope to be popular with the crew" (p. 345). The inevitable climate of resentment surrounding the master-at-arms might itself be sufficient to turn the hypothesis of depravity into a self-fulfilling prophecy. As Melville puts it, "The point of the present story *turn[s] on the hidden nature* of the master-at-arms" (p. 354). The entire plot of *Billy Budd* could conceivably be seen as a consequence not of what Claggart *does*, but of what he *does not say*.

It is thus by means of the misreading of gaps in knowledge and of discontinuities in action that the plot of *Billy Budd* takes shape. But because Melville describes both the spaces and the readings they engender, his concentration on the vagaries of interpretive error open up within the text the possibility of substantiating quite a number of "inside narratives" different from the one with which we are explicitly presented. What Melville's tale tells is the snowballing of tale-telling. It is possible, indeed, to retell the story

5. Unattributable [editor's note].

from a point of view that fully justifies Claggart's suspicions, merely by putting together a series of indications already available in the narrative:

1. As Billy is being taken from the merchant ship to the warship, he shouts in farewell, "And good-bye to you too, old *Rights-of-Man*." Lt. Ratcliffe, who later recounts the incident to Claggart (as is shown by the latter's referring to it in making his accusation to Vere), interprets this as "a sly slur at impressment in general, and that of himself in especial" (p. 327). The first information Claggart is likely to have gleaned on Billy Budd has thus passed through the filter of the Lieutenant's interpretation that the handsome recruit's apparent gaiety conceals resentment.

2. When Billy resolves, after seeing the flogging of another novice, "never to merit reproof," his "punctiliousness in duty" (p. 346) is laughed at by his topmates. Billy tries desperately to make his actions coincide with his desire for perfect irreproachability, but he nevertheless finds himself "getting into petty trouble" (p. 346). Billy's "unconcealed anxiety" is considered "comical" by his fellows (p. 347). It is thus Billy's obsessive concern with his own perfection that starts a second snowball rolling, since Claggart undertakes a subtle campaign of petty persecutions "to try the temper of the man" (p. 358). The instrument used by Claggart to set "little traps for the worriment of the foretopman" is a corporal called "Squeak," who, "having naturally enough concluded that his master could have no love for the sailor, made it his business, faithful understrapper that he was, to foment the ill blood by perverting to his chief certain innocent frolics of the good-natured foretopman, besides inventing for his mouth sundry contumelious epithets he claimed to have overheard him let fall" (p. 357). Again, Claggart perceives Billy only through the distortion of an unfavorable interpretation.

3. With this impression of Billy already in his mind, Claggart proceeds to take Billy's spilling of the soup across his path "not for the mere accident it assuredly was, but for the sly escape of a spontaneous feeling on Billy's part more or less answering to the antipathy of his own" (p. 356). If this is an over-reading, it is important to note that the critical tendency to see sexual or religious symbolism in the soup scene operates on exactly the same assumption as that made by Claggart: that what appears to be an accident is actually motivated and meaningful. Claggart's spontaneous interpretation, hidden behind his playful words ("Handsomely done . . ."), is not only legitimate enough on its own terms, but receives unexpected confirmation in Billy's naive outburst: "There now, who says that Jemmy Legs is down on me!" This evidence of a preexisting context in which Claggart, referred to by his disrespectful nickname, has been discussed by Billy with others—apparently a number of others, although in fact it is only one person—provides all the support Claggart needs to substantiate his suspicions. And still, he is willing to try another test.

4. Claggart sends an afterguardsman to Billy at night with a proposition to join a mutinous conspiracy of impressed men. Although Billy rejects the invitation, he does not report it as loyalty demands. He is thus protecting

the conspirators. Claggart's last test has been completed: Billy is a danger to the ship. In his function as chief of police, it is Claggart's duty to report the danger. . . .

This "reversed" reading is no more—but certainly no less—legitimate than the ordinary "good vs. evil" interpretation. But its very possibility—evoked not only by these behind-the-scenes hints and nuances but also by the "garbled" newspaper report—can be taken as a sign of the centrality of the *question of reading* posed not only *by* but also *in* the text of *Billy Budd*. Far from recounting an unequivocal "clash of opposites"[6] the confrontation between Billy and Claggart is built by a series of minute gradations and subtle insinuations. The opposites that clash here are not two *characters* but two *readings*.

Three Readings of Reading

It is no doubt significant that the character around whom the greatest critical dissent has revolved is neither the good one nor the evil one but the one who is explicitly presented as a *reader*, Captain Vere. On some level, readers of *Billy Budd* have always testified to the fact that it is reading, as much as killing, that is at the heart of Melville's story. But how is the act of reading being manifested? And what, precisely, are its relations with the deadliness of the spaces it attempts to comprehend?

As we have noted, critical readings of *Billy Budd* have generally divided themselves into two opposing groups, the "testament of acceptance" school on the one hand and the "testament of resistance" or "irony" school on the other. The first is characterized by its tendency to take at face value the narrator's professed admiration of Vere's sagacity and the final benediction of Vere uttered by Billy. The second group is characterized by its tendency to distance the reader's point of view from that of any of the characters, including the narrator, so that the injustice of Billy's execution becomes perceptible through a process of reversal of certain explicit pronouncements within the tale. This opposition between "acceptance" and "irony" quite strikingly mirrors, as we mentioned earlier, the opposition within the story between Billy's naiveté and Claggart's paranoia. We will therefore begin our analysis of Melville's study of the nature of reading with an examination of the way in which the act of reading is manifested in the confrontation between these two characters.

It seems evident that Billy's reading method consists in taking everything at face value, while Claggart's consists in seeing a mantrap under every daisy. Yet in practice, neither of these methods is rigorously upheld. The naive reader is not naive enough to forget to edit out information too troubling to report. The instability of the space between sign and referent, normally denied by the naive reader, is called upon as an *instrument* whenever that same instability threatens to disturb the *content* of meaning itself. Billy takes every sign as transparently readable as long as what he reads is consistent with transparent peace, order, and authority. When this is not so, his reading

6. J. M. Murry, "Herman Melville's Silence," *Times Literary Supplement*, July 10, 1924, p. 433.

clouds accordingly. And Claggart, for whom every sign can be read as its opposite, neglects to doubt the transparency of any sign that tends to confirm his own doubts: "the master-at-arms *never suspected the veracity*" (p. 357) of Squeak's reports. The naive believer thus refuses to believe any evidence that subverts the transparency of his beliefs, while the ironic doubter forgets to suspect the reliability of anything confirming his own suspicions.

* * *

But what of the third reader in the drama, Captain Vere? What can be said of a reading whose task is precisely to read the *relation* between naiveté and paranoia, acceptance and irony, murder and error?

* * *

In order to analyze what is at stake in Melville's portrait of Vere, let us first examine the ways in which Vere's reading differs from those of Billy Budd and John Claggart:

1. While the naive/ironic dichotomy was based on a symmetry between *individuals*, Captain Vere's reading takes place within a social *structure*: the rigidly hierarchical structure of a British warship. While the naive reader (Billy) destroys the other in order to defend the self, and while the ironic reader (Claggart) destroys the self by projecting aggression onto the other, the third reader (Vere) subordinates both self and other, and ultimately sacrifices both self and other, for the preservation of a political order.

2. The apparent purpose of both Billy's and Claggart's readings was to determine *character*: to preserve innocence or to prove guilt. Vere, on the other hand, subordinates character to action, being to doing: "A martial court," he tells his officers, "must needs in the present case confine its attention to the *blow's consequence*, which consequence justly is to be deemed not otherwise than as the *striker's deed*" (p. 384).

3. In the opposition between the metaphysical and the psychoanalytical readings of Billy's deed, the deciding question was whether the blow should be considered accidental or (unconsciously) motivated. But in Vere's courtroom reading, both these alternatives are irrelevant: "Budd's intent or non-intent is nothing to the purpose" (p. 389). What matters is not the cause but the consequences of the blow.

4. The naive or literal reader takes language at face value and treats signs as *motivated*; the ironic reader assumes that the relation between sign and meaning can be *arbitrary* and that appearances are made to be reversed. For Vere, the functions and meanings of signs are neither transparent nor reversible but fixed by socially determined *convention*. Vere's very character is determined not by a relation between his outward appearance and his inner being but by the "buttons" that signify his position in society. While both Billy and Claggart are said to owe their character to "Nature," Vere sees his actions and being as meaningful only within the context of a contractual allegiance:

> Do these buttons that we wear attest that our allegiance is to Nature? No, to the King. Though the ocean, which is inviolate Nature primeval, though this be the element where we move and have our being as sailors, yet as the King's officers lies our duty in a sphere correspondingly natural? So little is that true, that in receiving our commissions we in the most important regards ceased to be natural free agents. When war is declared are we the commissioned fighters previously consulted? We fight at command. If our judgments approve the war, that is but coincidence. (p. 387)

Judgment is thus for Vere a function neither of individual conscience nor of absolute justice but of "the rigor of martial law" (p. 387) operating *through* him.

5. While Billy and Claggart read spontaneously and directly, Vere's reading often makes use of precedent (historical facts, childhood memories), allusions (to the Bible, to various ancient and modern authors), and analogies (Billy is like Adam, Claggart is like Ananias[7]). Just as both Billy and Claggart have no known past, they read without memory; just as their lives end with their reading, they read without foresight. Vere, on the other hand, interrogates both past and future for interpretative guidance.

6. While Budd and Claggart thus oppose each other directly, without regard for circumstance or consequence, Vere reads solely in function of the attending historical situation: the Nore and Spithead mutinies[8] have created an atmosphere "critical to naval authority" (p. 380), and, since an engagement with the enemy fleet is possible at any moment, the *Bellipotent* cannot afford internal unrest.

The fundamental factor that underlies the opposition between the metaphysical Budd/Claggart conflict on the one hand and the reading of Captain Vere on the other can be summed up in a single word: history. While the naive and the ironic readers attempt to impose upon language the functioning of an absolute, timeless, universal law (the sign as *either* motivated *or* arbitrary), the question of *martial* law arises within the story precisely to reveal the law as a *historical* phenomenon, to underscore the element of contextual mutability in the conditions of any act of reading. Arbitrariness and motivation, irony and literality, are parameters between which language constantly fluctuates, but only historical context determines which proportion of each is perceptible to each reader.

* * *

There is still another reason for the uncertainty over Vere's final status, however: the unfinished state of the manuscript at Melville's death. According to editors Hayford and Sealts,[9] it is the "late pencil revisions" that cast the greatest doubt upon Vere; Melville was evidently still fine-tuning the

7. A man who is struck down dead in front of Peter for lying to God (Acts 5.3–5) [editor's note].

8. Uprisings in the British fleet in 1797. Spithead is an anchorage off Portsmouth's harbor (south England); the Nore is a sandbank at the mouth of the Thames River [editor's note].

9. Editor's introduction, *Billy Budd, Sailor* (Chicago: University of Chicago Press, 1962); see esp. pp. 34–35.

text's attitude toward its third reader when he died. The ultimate irony in the tale is thus that our final judgment of the very reader who takes history into consideration is made problematic precisely by the intervention of history: by the historical accident of the author's death. History here affects interpretation not only within the content of the narration but also within the very production of the narrative. And what remains suspended by this historical accident is nothing less than the exact signifying value of history itself. Clearly, the meaning of "history" as a feature distinguishing Vere's reading from those of Claggart and Budd can in no way be taken for granted.

Judgment as Political Performance

In the final analysis, the question is not: what did Melville really think of Captain Vere? but rather: What is at stake in his way of presenting him? What can we learn from him about the act of judging? Melville seems to be presenting us less with an *object* for judgment than with an *example* of judgment. And the very vehemence with which the critics tend to praise or condemn the justice of Vere's decision indicates that it is judging, not murdering, that Melville is asking us to judge.

And yet Vere's judgment *is* an act of murder. Captain Vere is a reader who kills, not, like Billy, *instead* of speaking, but rather, precisely *by means of* speaking. While Billy kills through verbal impotence, Vere kills through the very potency and sophistication of rhetoric. Judging, in Vere's case, is nothing less than the wielding of the power of life and death through language. In thus occupying the point at which murder and language meet, Captain Vere positions himself precisely astride the "deadly space between." While Billy's performative force occupies the vanishing point of utterance and cognition, and while the validity of Claggart's cognitive perception is realized only through the annihilation of the perceiver, Captain Vere's reading mobilizes both power and knowledge, performance and cognition, error and murder. Judgment is precisely cognition functioning as an act. It is this combination of performance and cognition that defines Vere's reading not merely as historical but as *political*. If politics is defined as the attempt to reconcile action with understanding, then Melville's story offers an exemplary context in which to analyze the interpretive and performative structures that make politics so problematic.

That the alliance between knowledge and action is by no means an easy one is amply demonstrated in Melville's story. Vere indeed has often been seen as the character in the tale who experiences the greatest suffering: his understanding of Billy's character and his military duty are totally at odds. On the one hand, cognitive exactitude requires that "history" be taken into consideration. Yet what constitutes "knowledge of history"? How are "circumstances" to be defined? What sort of causality does "precedent" imply? And what is to be done with overlapping but incompatible "contexts"? Before deciding upon innocence and guilt, Vere must define and limit the frame of reference within which his decision is to be possible. He does so by choosing the "legal" context over the "essential" context:

> In a *legal view* the apparent victim of the tragedy was he who had sought to victimize a man blameless; and the indisputable deed of the latter,

> *navally regarded*, constituted the most heinous of military crimes. Yet more. The *essential right and wrong* involved in the matter, the clearer that might be, so much the worse for the responsibility of a loyal sea commander, inasmuch as he was not authorized to determine the matter on that *primitive* basis. (p. 380; emphasis mine)

Yet it is precisely this determination of the proper frame of reference that dictates the outcome of the decision: once Vere has defined his context, he has also in fact reached his verdict. The very choice of the *conditions* of judgment itself constitutes a judgment. But what are the conditions of choosing the conditions of judgment?

* * *

If Vere names the Absolute—as opposed to the martial—by means of quotations and allusions, does this not suggest that the two alternative frames of reference within which judgment is possible are not Nature and the King, but rather two types of textual authority: the Bible and the Mutiny Act?[1] This is not to say that Vere is "innocently" choosing one text over another, but that the nature of "Nature" in a legal context cannot be taken for granted. Even Thomas Paine,[2] who is referred to by Melville in his function as proponent of "natural" human rights, cannot avoid grounding his concept of nature in Biblical myth. In the very act of rejecting the authority of antiquity, he writes:

> The fact is, that portions of antiquity, by proving every thing, establish nothing. It is authority against authority all the way, till we come to the divine origin of the rights of man, at the Creation. Here our inquiries find a resting-place, and our reason a home.[3]

The final frame of reference is neither the heart nor the gun, neither Nature nor the King, but the authority of a Sacred Text. Authority seems to be nothing other than the vanishing-point of textuality. And Nature is authority whose textual origins have been forgotten. Even behind the martial order of the world of the man-of-war, there lies a religious referent: the *Bellipotent's* last battle is with a French ship called the *Athée*.[4]

Judgment, then, would seem to ground itself in a suspension of the opposition between textuality and referentiality, just as politics can be seen as that which makes it impossible to draw the line between "language" and "life." Vere, indeed, is presented precisely as a reader who does not recognize the "frontier" between "remote allusions" and current events:

> In illustrating of any point touching the stirring personages and events of the time he would be as apt to cite some historic character or incident of antiquity as he would be to cite from the moderns. He seemed unmindful of the circumstance that to his bluff company such remote allusions, however pertinent they might really be, were altogether alien to men whose reading was mainly confined to the journals. But consid-

1. An act first passed in 1689, which in fact applied only to the army; even the Articles of War of 1749, to which Vere also and more appropriately alludes, give him more latitude than he claims [editor's note].

2. English-born American revolutionary and political theorist (1737–1809) [editor's note].

3. Thomas Paine, *The Rights of Man* (Garden City, N.Y.: Anchor Press, 1973), p. 303.

4. Atheist (French) [editor's note].

> erateness in such matters is not easy to natures constituted like Captain Vere's. Their honesty prescribes to them directness, sometimes far-reaching like that of a migratory fowl that in its flight never heeds when it crosses a frontier. (p. 341)

Yet it is precisely by inviting Billy Budd and John Claggart to "cross" the "frontier" between their proper territory and their superior's cabin, between the private and the political realms, that Vere unwittingly sets up the conditions for the narrative chiasmus he must judge.

As was noted earlier, Captain Vere's function, according to many critics, is to insert "ambiguity" into the story's "oversimplified" allegorical opposition. Yet at the same time, it is precisely Captain Vere who inspires the most vehement critical oppositions. Captain Vere, in other words, seems to mobilize simultaneously the seemingly contradictory forces of ambiguity and polarity.

In his median position between the Budd/Claggart opposition and the acceptance/irony opposition, Captain Vere functions as a focus for the *conversion* of polarity into ambiguity and back again. Interestingly, he plays exactly the same role in the progress of the plot. It is Vere who brings together the "Innocent" Billy and the "guilty" Claggart in order to test the validity of Claggart's accusations, but he does so in such a way as to effect not a clarification but a reversal of places between guilt and innocence. Vere's fatherly words to Billy are precisely what triggers the ambiguous deed upon which Vere must pronounce a verdict of "condemn *or* let go." Just as Melville's readers, faced with the ambiguity they themselves recognize as being provided by Vere, are quick to pronounce the Captain vicious *or* virtuous, evil *or* just; so, too, Vere, who clearly perceives the "mystery" in the "moral dilemma" confronting him, must nevertheless reduce the situation to a binary opposition.

It would seem, then, that the function of judgment is to convert an ambiguous situation into a decidable one. But it does so by converting a difference *within* (Billy as divided between conscious submissiveness and unconscious hostility, Vere as divided between understanding father and military authority) into a difference *between* (between Claggart and Billy, between Nature and the King, between authority and criminality). A difference *between* opposing forces presupposes that the entities in conflict be knowable. A difference *within* one of the entities in question is precisely what problematizes the very *idea* of an entity in the first place, rendering the "legal point of view" inapplicable. In studying the plays of both ambiguity and binarity, Melville's story situates *its* critical difference neither within nor between, but precisely in the very question of the *relation between the two* as the fundamental question of all human politics. The political context in *Billy Budd* is such that on all levels the differences *within* (mutiny on the warship, the French revolution as a threat to "lasting institutions," Billy's unconscious hostility) are subordinated to differences *between* (the *Bellipotent* vs. the *Athée*, England vs. France, murderer vs. victim). This is why Melville's choice of historical setting is so significant: the war between France and England at the time of the French Revolution is as striking an example of the simultaneous functioning of differences within and between as is the confrontation between Billy and Claggart in relation to their own internal divisions.

War, indeed, is the absolute transformation of *all* differences into *binary* differences.

It would seem, then, that the maintenance of political authority requires that the law function as a set of rules for the regular, predictable misreading of the "difference within" as a "difference between." Yet if * * * law is thus defined in terms of its repression of ambiguity, then it is itself an overwhelming example of an entity based on a "difference within." Like Billy, the law, in attempting to eliminate its own "deadly space," can only inscribe itself in a space of deadliness.

* * *

But if judging is always a *partial* reading (in both senses of the word), is there a place for reading beyond politics? Are we, as Melville's readers, outside the arena in which power and fees are exchanged? If law is the forcible transformation of ambiguity into decidability, is it possible to read ambiguity *as such*, without that reading functioning as a political act?

Even about this, Melville has something to say. For there is a fourth reader in *Billy Budd*, one who "never interferes in aught and never gives advice" (p. 363): the old Dansker. A man of "few words, many wrinkles," and "the complexion of an antique parchment" (p. 347), the Dansker is the very picture of one who understands and emits ambiguous utterances. When asked by Billy for an explanation of his petty troubles, the Dansker says only, "Jemmy Legs [Claggart] is down on you" (p. 349). This interpretation, entirely accurate as a reading of Claggart's ambiguous behavior, is handed down to Billy without further explanation:

> Something less unpleasantly oracular he tried to extract; but the old sea Chiron, thinking perhaps that for the nonce he had sufficiently instructed his young Achilles,[5] pursed his lips, gathered all his wrinkles together, and would commit himself to nothing further. (p. 349)

As a reader who understands ambiguity yet refuses to "commit himself," the Dansker thus dramatizes a reading that attempts to be as cognitively accurate and as performatively neutral as possible. Yet however neutral he tries to remain, the Dansker's reading does not take place outside the political realm: it is his very refusal to participate in it, whether by further instruction or by direct intervention, that leads to Billy's exclamation in the soup episode ("There now, who says Jemmy Legs is down on me?"). The transference of knowledge is not any more innocent than the transference of power. For it is precisely through the impossibility of finding a spot from which knowledge could be all-encompassing that the plays of political power proceed.

Just as the attempt to "know" without "doing" can itself function as a deed, the fact that judgment is always explicitly an act adds a further insoluble problem to its cognitive predicament. Since, as Vere points out, no judgment can take place in the *Last* Assizes,[6] no judge can ever pronounce a Last Judgment. In order to reach a verdict, Vere must determine the consequences not only of the fatal blow, but also precisely of his own verdict.

5. In Greek mythology, the greatest of the Greek warriors at Troy and the hero of Homer's *Iliad* (ca. 8th c. B.C.E.); Chiron, a centaur, was his teacher [editor's note].

6. Session of the superior court in English counties [editor's note].

Judgment is an act not only because it kills, but because it is in turn open to judgment:

> "Can we not convict and yet mitigate the penalty?" asked the sailing master. . . .
>
> "Gentlemen, were that clearly lawful for us under the circumstances, consider the consequences of such clemency. . . . To the people the foretopman's deed, however it be worded in the announcement, will be plain homicide committed in a flagrant act of mutiny. What penalty for that should follow, they know. But it does not follow. *Why?* They will ruminate. You know what sailors are. Will they not revert to the recent outbreak at the Nore?" (p. 389)

The danger is not only one of repeating the Nore mutiny, however. It is also one of forcing Billy, for all his innocence, to repeat his crime. Billy is a politically charged object from the moment he strikes his superior. He is no longer, and can never again be, plotless. If he were set free, he himself would be unable to explain why. As a focus for the questions and intrigues of the crew, he would be even less capable of defending himself than before, and would surely strike again. The political reading, as cognition, attempts to understand the past; as performance, it attempts to eliminate from the future any necessity for its own recurrence.

What this means is that every judge is in the impossible position of having to include the effects of his own act of judging within the cognitive context of his decision. The question of the nature of the type of historical causality that would govern such effects can neither be decided nor ignored. Because of his official position, Vere cannot choose to read in such a way that his reading would not be an act of political authority. But what Melville shows in *Billy Budd* is that authority consists precisely in the impossibility of containing the effects of its own application.

As a political allegory, Melville's *Billy Budd* is thus much more than a study of good and evil, justice and injustice. It is a dramatization of the twisted relations between knowing and doing, speaking and killing, reading and judging, which make political understanding and action so problematic. In the subtle creation of Claggart's "evil" out of a series of spaces in knowledge, Melville shows that gaps in cognition, far from being mere absences, take on the performative power of true acts. The *force* of what is not known is all the more effective for not being perceived as such. The crew, which does not understand that it does not know, is no less performative a reader than the Captain, who clearly perceives and represses the presence of "mystery." The legal order, which attempts to submit "brute force" to "forms, measured forms," can only eliminate violence by transforming violence into the final authority. And cognition, which perhaps begins as a power play against the play of power, can only increase, through its own elaboration, the range of what it tries to dominate. The "deadly space" or "difference" that runs through *Billy Budd* is not located *between* knowledge and action, performance and cognition: it is that which, within cognition, functions as an act; it is that which, within action, prevents us from ever knowing whether what we hit coincides with what we understand. And this is what makes the meaning of Melville's last work so . . . *striking*.

1979

BONNIE ZIMMERMAN
b. 1947

"Beginning with nothing," Bonnie Zimmerman announces in "What Has Never Been: An Overview of Lesbian Feminist Criticism" (1981), "this generation quickly began to expand the limitations of literary scholarship by pointing to what had been for decades 'unspeakable'—lesbian existence." Arising out of the social and cultural movements of the 1960s, feminist criticism by the late 1970s was a controversial but widely recognized practice in contemporary literary criticism and theory. As it gained institutional recognition, however, many within the feminist movement began to question the assumption of a monolithic feminism based on the commonality of women's experience. In particular, lesbian-identified women and women of color, such as Bonnie Zimmerman, BARBARA SMITH, and GLORIA ANZALDÚA, argued that the Anglo-American feminist movement spoke largely from the standpoint of white, heterosexual, middle-class women, tending to take that perspective as universal while ignoring differences in race, sexuality, or class. Aiming to remedy this limitation, Zimmerman's "What Has Never Been" is a defining document of lesbian-focused literary criticism, staking out a new area of feminist scholarship.

Born in Chicago, Zimmerman studied philosophy at Indiana University, earning a B.A. in 1968, and English at the State University of New York at Buffalo, where she earned her Ph.D. in 1974. She held several temporary academic positions in the Chicago area, but since 1978 she has taught at San Diego State University, where she was active in establishing a women's studies major, then a rare offering in the curriculum; she has frequently served as chair of the women's studies department. Zimmerman was also one of the first openly lesbian professors in the American academy, and, linking her politics and scholarship, she pioneered the development of interdisciplinary courses studying lesbian literature, history, and theory.

While the feminist and sexual liberation movements of the 1960s seemed to dispel negative biases against alternative sexualities, lesbian theory and literary criticism were still marginalized a decade later in course offerings and in academic scholarship. As Zimmerman laments in "What Has Never Been," even feminist forums were reluctant to acknowledge the worth of lesbian theory; when not condemned, it usually received only token mentions. Although the essay begins with this criticism, "What Has Never Been" embraces the opportunity to establish a new field and to bring lesbian studies out of the "closet." For Zimmerman, this scholarly transformation has political as well as professional consequences, fostering a sense of lesbian identity and community.

Grounded in encyclopedic research, "What Has Never Been" traces the origins of lesbian feminist literary criticism, reviews definitions of lesbianism, inventories a lesbian literary canon, and suggests a "lesbian aesthetic." Looking to the future, it also assesses the difficulties, outlines the tasks, and anticipates the challenges that face lesbian feminist literary critics. One of the main challenges that Zimmerman identifies is "heterosexism"—the assumption in mainstream feminism and in culture at large that heterosexuality is the one natural way to express sexual or affectional attachment. She details the heterosexist assumptions that dominate feminist literary anthologies, journals, and books of literary criticism, in particular faulting such prominent feminists as Elaine Showalter, SANDRA M. GILBERT, and SUSAN GUBAR, whose well-known studies of women writers fail to note female companions and lesbian attachments. Further, she claims that anthologies ignore prominent lesbian writers, that surveys omit lesbianism as a theme or perspective, and that analyses either disregard or vilify lesbian characters and themes in literature. To overcome heterosexist biases, she calls for lesbian theorists to develop their own resources to build a canon and a critical approach.

In building a distinctive canon and criticism, Zimmerman sees a central theoretical problem in the definition of "lesbian" and whom that term includes or excludes. Some modern critics, like Catherine Stimpson, lean toward a narrow definition predicated on sexual intimacy, while others, like the feminist poet and critic ADRIENNE RICH, advocate a more expansive category. Rich's concept of a "lesbian continuum" encompasses all women who have intense women-identified bonds, which might be social or political rather than sexual. This problem of definition mirrors a perennial one in theory, particularly in those studies based on identity: if they are exclusive, then such definitions might reproduce biases and static categories of thought; whereas if they are too expansive, then they might gradually erase meaningful distinctions. Although Zimmerman admires the flexibility of Rich's "continuum," she ultimately cautions against it, arguing that it diminishes a sense of lesbian difference and specificity; instead, she advocates Lillian Faderman's definition that identifies as lesbian those women who have affectionate attachments with other women, usually in a romantic couple.

Once the lesbian critic has settled this theoretical problem, her primary responsibilities, according to Zimmerman, are to identify lesbian texts and to build a literary tradition. This first involves a task of recovery, because many lesbians were historically constrained to write in "code" to avoid public ostracism. As an example of building a canon, Zimmerman cites Barbara Smith's famous lesbian reading (see above) of the African American novelist Toni Morrison's *Sula* (1973), arguing against the need for biographical evidence or proof of authorial intention. Once a canon is established, she hopes lesbian critics can go on to analyze the images and stereotypes of lesbians in literature and to examine the stylistics of lesbian writing, culminating in defining a specifically lesbian aesthetic. In some ways, Zimmerman's template for developing lesbian criticism parallels the course of early feminist criticism, which in the 1970s worked to construct a canon of women's writing (or what Elaine Showalter called a "literature of their own") and to critique literary stereotypes of women, and in the 1980s moved to examine specific characteristics of *écriture féminine* (female/feminine writing or style), in the phrase of the French feminist HÉLÈNE CIXOUS.

Zimmerman concludes by anticipating problems that might face lesbian critics. Although she celebrates the radical edge of lesbian separatism and its resistance to dominant hierarchies, she also foresees that lesbian criticism must be flexible and pluralistic to avoid stagnation and dogmatism. Another problem is naiveté about the universality of the lesbian experience. Much as critics challenged mainstream feminism of the 1970s for representing as universal an experience that excluded lesbians and women of color, Zimmerman challenges the new lesbian criticism to allow for specificity and diversity, especially in recognizing race and class differences. Despite these caveats, she closes on a hopeful note, finding that lesbian studies constitutes one of the most exciting areas of contemporary theory because of its exploration of "what has never been."

While "What Has Never Been" has been widely praised for helping to establish the field of lesbian literary criticism, some critics have offered emendations of specific points, such as Zimmerman's compromise definition of what qualifies as lesbian literature. In a later book, *The Safe Sea of Women: Lesbian Fiction, 1969–1989* (1990), Zimmerman herself narrows its scope, asserting that although some leeway must be granted in identifying lesbian fiction of the nineteenth and early twentieth centuries, contemporary fiction should be classified as "lesbian" if it has (1) an author who has declared herself as a lesbian, (2) a main character who acknowledges her lesbian orientation, or (3) a story that puts love between women at its center. Lillian Faderman argues that this set of rigid criteria excludes many contemporary novels that might also be productively considered lesbian literature.

Although, as Zimmerman surmises in a 1992 essay, "Lesbian theory is much more evident throughout current literary criticism than it was in 1981," in recent years a new debate has surfaced: its relation to queer theory. Drawing on poststructuralist and psychoanalytic critiques of subjectivity and identity, proponents of queer theory, such as JUDITH BUTLER, argue that lesbian feminist criticism assumes a tacit essentialism—the belief that identity derives from a determinate essence, rather than from cultural circumstances and conventions. Updating her defense of a distinctive lesbian criticism, Zimmerman argues against subsuming lesbian studies within gay or queer studies, cautioning that such a theoretical move dissolves the ties between lesbianism and feminism and obliterates the specificity of lesbian identity and a lesbian aesthetic. "What Has Never Been" remains a landmark call for developing a distinctively lesbian feminist criticism.

BIBLIOGRAPHY

First published in 1981 in the influential journal *Feminist Studies*, "What Has Never Been: An Overview of Lesbian Feminist Literary Criticism" has since been widely anthologized. In *The Safe Sea of Women: Lesbian Fiction, 1969–1989* (1990), Zimmerman constructs a canon of contemporary lesbian fiction written during the gay liberation movement, analyzing its symbols and stereotypes. She has published many articles and also edited two influential collections and one reference work solidying the field of lesbian studies: *Professions of Desire: Lesbian and Gay Studies in Literature*, co-edited with George Haggerty (1995); *The New Lesbian Studies: Into the Twenty-First Century*, co-edited with Toni A. H. McNaron (1996); and *Lesbian Histories and Cultures*, the first of the two-volume *Encyclopedia of Lesbian and Gay Histories and Cultures*, co-edited with George Haggerty (2000). In *Around 1981: Feminist Literary Theory* (1992), Jane Gallop assesses the place of "What Has Never Been" in the development of feminist criticism. Lillian Faderman, in "What Is Lesbian Literature? Forming a Historical Canon," in *The New Lesbian Studies* (cited above), modifies Zimmerman's definition of the lesbian novel. In " 'Gone Are the Days': Bisexual Perspectives on Lesbian/Feminist Literary Theory," *Feminist Studies* 61 (1999), Ann Kaloski Naylor discusses Zimmerman's negotiation between essentialism and deconstruction. A brief biography and bibliography of Zimmerman appear in *Gay and Lesbian Literature* (ed. Sharon Malinowski, 1994).

What Has Never Been: An Overview of Lesbian Feminist Literary Criticism

In the 1970s, a generation of lesbian feminist literary critics came of age. Some, like the lesbian professor in Lynn Strongin's poem, "Sayre,"[1] had been closeted in the profession; many had "come out" as lesbians in the women's liberation movement. As academics and as lesbians, we cautiously began to plait together the strands of our existence: teaching lesbian literature, establishing networks and support groups, and exploring assumptions about a lesbian-focused literary criticism. Beginning with nothing, as we thought, this generation quickly began to expand the limitations of literary scholarship by pointing to what had been for decades "unspeakable"—lesbian existence—thus phrasing, in novelist June Arnold's words, "what has never been."[2] Our process has paralleled the development of feminist literary criticism—and,

1. Lynn Strongin, "Sayre," in *Rising Tides: Twentieth Century American Women Poets*, ed. Laura Chester and Sharon Barba (New York: Washington Square Press, 1973), p. 317 [Zimmerman's note]. Some of the author's notes have been edited, and some omitted.

2. June Arnold, "Lesbian Fiction," in *Lesbian Writing and Publishing*, special issue of *Sinister Wisdom* 2 (fall 1976): 28 [Zimmerman's note]. Arnold (1926–1982), American novelist and publisher who founded a lesbian feminist press, Daughters Inc., in 1972.

indeed, pioneering feminist critics and lesbian critics are often one and the same. As women in a male-dominated academy, we explored the way we write and read from a different or "other" perspective. As lesbians in a heterosexist academy, we have continued to explore the impact of "otherness," suggesting dimensions previously ignored and yet necessary to understand fully the female condition and the creative work born from it.

Lesbian critics, in the 1980s, may have more questions than answers, but the questions are important not only to lesbians, but to all feminists teaching and criticizing literature. Does a woman's sexual and affectional preference influence the way she writes, reads, and thinks? Does lesbianism belong in the classroom and in scholarship? Is there a lesbian aesthetic distinct from a feminist aesthetic? What should be the role of the lesbian critic? Can we establish a lesbian "canon" in the way in which feminist critics have established a female canon? Can lesbian feminists develop insights into female creativity that might enrich all literary criticism? Different women, of course, answer these questions in different ways, but one set of assumptions underlies virtually all lesbian criticism: that a woman's identity is not defined only by her relation to a male world and male literary tradition (as feminist critics have demonstrated), that powerful bonds between women are a crucial factor in women's lives, and that the sexual and emotional orientation of a woman profoundly affects her consciousness and thus her creativity. Those critics who have consciously chosen to read as lesbians argue that this perspective can be uniquely liberating and can provide new insights into life and literature because it assigns the lesbian a specific vantage point from which to criticize and analyze the politics, language, and culture of patriarchy:

> We have the whole range of women's experience and the other dimension too, which is the unique viewpoint of the dyke.[3] This extra dimension puts us a step outside of so-called normal life and lets us see how gruesomely abnormal it is. . . . [This perspective] can issue in a world-view that is distinct in history and uniquely liberating.[4]

The purpose of this essay is to analyze the current state of lesbian scholarship, to suggest how lesbians are exercising this unique world view, and to investigate some of the problems, strengths, and future needs of a developing lesbian feminist literary criticism.[5]

One way in which this unique world view takes shape is as a "critical consciousness about heterosexist assumptions."[6] Heterosexism is the set of values and structures that assumes heterosexuality to be the only natural form of sexual and emotional expression, "*the* perceptual screen provided by our [patriarchal] cultural conditioning."[7] Heterosexist assumptions abound

3. A disparaging term for a lesbian, reclaimed by lesbians as a positive self-description.
4. Sandy Boucher, "Lesbian Artists," in *Lesbian Art and Artists*, a special issue of *Heresies* 3 (fall 1977): 48 [Zimmerman's note].
5. This survey is limited to published and unpublished essays in literary criticism that present a perspective either sympathetic to lesbianism or those explicitly lesbian in orientation. It is limited to *literature* and to theoretical articles (not book reviews). The sexual preference of the authors is, for the most part, irrelevant; this is an analysis of lesbian feminist *ideas*, not authors. Although the network of lesbian critics is well developed, some major unpublished papers may have escaped my attention [Zimmerman's note].
6. Elly Bulkin, " 'Kissing against the Light': A Look at Lesbian Poetry," *Radical Teacher* 10 (1978): 8. This article was reprinted in *College English* and *Women's Studies Newsletter* [Zimmerman's note].
7. Julia Penelope [Stanley], "The Articulation of Bias: Hoof in Mouth Disease," paper presented at the convention of the National Council of Teachers of English, San Francisco, November 1979 [Zimmerman's note].

in literary texts, such as feminist literary anthologies, that purport to be open-minded about lesbianism. When authors' biographies make special note of husbands, male mentors, and male companions, even when that author was primarily female-identified, but fail to mention the female companions of prominent lesbian writers—that is heterosexism. When anthologists ignore historically significant lesbian writers such as Renée Vivien and Radclyffe Hall[8]—that is heterosexism. When anthologies include only the heterosexual or nonsexual works of a writer like Katherine Philips or Adrienne Rich[9] who is celebrated for her lesbian or homo-emotional poetry—that is heterosexism. When a topically organized anthology includes sections on wives, mothers, sex objects, young girls, aging women, and liberated women, but not lesbians—that is heterosexism. Heterosexism in feminist anthologies—like the sexism of androcentric[1] collections—serves to obliterate lesbian existence and maintain the lie that women have searched for emotional and sexual fulfillment only through men—or not at all.

Lesbians have also expressed concern that the absence of lesbian material in women's studies journals such as *Feminist Studies, Women's Studies*, and *Women and Literature* indicates heterosexism either by omission or by design. Only in 1979 did lesbian-focused articles appear in *Signs* and *Frontiers*.[2] Most lesbian criticism first appeared in alternative, non-establishment lesbian journals, particularly *Sinister Wisdom* and *Conditions*,[3] which are unfamiliar to many feminist scholars. For example, *Signs'* first review article on literary criticism by Elaine Showalter[4] (1975) makes no mention of lesbianism as a theme or potential critical perspective, not even to point out its absence. Annette Kolodny, in the second review article in *Signs* (1976), does call Jane Rule's *Lesbian Images* "a novelist's challenge to the academy and its accompanying critical community," and further criticizes the homophobia in then-current biographies, calling for "candor and sensitivity" in future work.[5] However, neither this nor subsequent review articles familiarize the reader with "underground" sources of lesbian criticism, some of which had appeared by this time, nor do they explicate lesbianism as a literary theme or critical perspective. Ironically, more articles on lesbian literature have appeared in traditional literary journals than in the women's studies press, just as for years only male critics felt free to mention lesbianism. Possibly, feminist critics continue to feel that they will be identified as "dykes," thus invalidating their work.

The perceptual screen of heterosexism is also evident in most of the acclaimed works of feminist literary criticism. None of the current collections of essays—such as *The Authority of Experience* or *Shakespeare's Sis-*

8. English poet and novelist (1880–1943), whose work is openly lesbian; her best-known novel is *The Well of Loneliness* (1928), which was banned in England as obscene. Vivien (1877–1909), born Pauline Tarn, in London; French writer of poetry and prose.

9. Contemporary American lesbian feminist poet and critic (b. 1929; see above). Philips (1623–1664), English poet who celebrates female love and equality.

1. Male-centered.

2. Leading feminist scholarly journals; all began publication in the 1970s.

3. Founded in 1976 and 1977, respectively.

4. A leading American feminist literary critic (b. 1941); Showalter's pioneering *A Literature of Their Own: British Women Novelists from Brontë to Lessing* (1977) was instrumental in establishing a female canon.

5. Annette Kolodny, "Literary Criticism: Review Essay," *Signs* 2 (1976): 416, 419 [Zimmerman's note]. Kolodny (b. 1941), influential American feminist literary critic. Rule (b. 1931), American-born Canadian novelist; *Lesbian Images*, a collection of essays, was published in 1975.

ters[6]—includes even a token article from a lesbian perspective. Ellen Moers' *Literary Women*,[7] germinal work as it is, is homophobic as well as heterosexist. Lesbians, she points out, appear as monsters, grotesques, and freaks in works by Carson McCullers, Djuna Barnes (her reading of *Nightwood* is at the very least questionable), and Diane Arbus,[8] but she seems to concur in this identification rather than call it into question or explain its historical context. Although her so-called defense of unmarried women writers against the "charge" of lesbianism does criticize the way in which this word has been used as a slur, she neither condemns such antilesbianism nor entertains the possibility that some women writers were, in fact, lesbians. Her chapter on "Loving Heroinism" is virtually textbook heterosexism, assuming as it does that women writers only articulate love for men. Perceptual blinders also mar *The Female Imagination* by Patricia Meyers Spacks which never uses the word "lesbian" (except in the index) or "lover" to describe either the "sexual ambiguity" of the bond between Jane and Helen in *Jane Eyre*,[9] nor Margaret Anderson's relationship with a "beloved older woman." Furthermore, Spacks claims that Gertrude Stein, "whose life lack[ed] real attachments" (a surprise to Alice B. Toklas), also "denied whatever is special to women" (which lesbianism is not?).[1] This latter judgment is particularly ominous because heterosexuals often have difficulty accepting that a lesbian, especially a role-playing "butch," is in fact a woman. More care is demonstrated by Elaine Showalter who, in *A Literature of Their Own*, uncovers the attitudes toward lesbianism held by nineteenth-century writers Eliza Lynn Linton and Mrs. Humphrey Ward.[2] However, she does not integrate lesbian issues into her discussion of the crucial generation of early twentieth-century writers (Virginia Woolf, Vita Sackville-West, Dorothy Richardson, and Rosamond Lehmann[3] among others; Radclyffe Hall is mentioned, but not *The Well of Loneliness*), all of whom wrote about sexual love between women. Her well-taken point that modern British novelists avoid lesbianism might have been balanced, however, by a mention of Maureen Duffy, Sybille Bedford, or Fay Weldon.[4] Finally, Sandra Gilbert and Susan Gubar's *The Madwoman in the Attic* does not even index lesbian-

6. Edited by the influential feminist literary critics and collaborators SANDRA M. GILBERT (b. 1936) and SUSAN GUBAR (b. 1944) (1979). *The Authority of Experience* (1977), edited by Arlyn Diamond and Lee R. Edwards.

7. *Literary Women: The Great Writers* (1976), pioneering feminist work by Moers (1928–1979).

8. American photographer (1923–1971). McCullers (1917–1967), American novelist and short story writer. Barnes (1892–1982), American journalist and novelist best known for her novel *Nightwood* (1936).

9. The 1847 novel by Charlotte Brontë (1816–1855); Helen and the young Jane meet at boarding school (where Helen dies).

1. Spacks, *The Female Imagination* (New York: Avon Books, 1975), pp. 89, 214, 363 [Zimmerman's note]. Anderson (1886–1973), American editor, publisher, and writer; the "older woman" was the French actress and singer Georgette Leblanc (d. 1941), with whom she had a 20-year relationship. In 1907 the American modernist poet and novelist Stein (1874–1946) met the American Toklas (1877–1967) in Paris, where they lived together for the rest of her life.

2. Both women were successful English novelists; while Linton (1822–1898) caricatured women working toward suffrage as lesbians, Ward (1851–1920), who was also antisuffrage, in her fiction valorized intimate friendships between women.

3. All English novelists: WOOLF (1882–1941) and Sackville-West (1892–1962) had a romantic relationship in the late 1920s; the lifework of Richardson (1873–1957) was a 13-volume novel sequence, *Pilgrimage* (1915–38), that attempted to convey feminine consciousness in a feminine style (to which the description "stream of consciousness" was first applied); and Lehmann (1901–1990) in her first novel, *Dusty Answer* (1927), portrayed an adolescent lesbian relationship.

4. English novelist, playwright, and critic (b. 1931). Duffy (b. 1933), English lesbian novelist, poet, and playwright and socialist activist. Bedford (b. 1911), German-born English novelist and biographer.

ism; the lone reference made in the text is to the possibility that "Goblin Market" describes "a covertly (if ambiguously) lesbian world."[5] The authors' tendency to interpret all pairs of female characters as aspects of the self sometimes serves to mask a relationship that a lesbian reader might interpret as bonding or love between women.

Lesbian critics, who as feminists owe much to these critical texts, have had to turn to other resources, first to develop a lesbian canon, and then to establish a lesbian critical perspective. Barbara Grier who, as Gene Damon, reviewed books for the pioneering lesbian journal *The Ladder*, laid the groundwork for this canon with her incomparable, but largely unknown *The Lesbian in Literature: A Bibliography.*[6] Equally obscure was Jeannette Foster's[7] *Sex Variant Women in Literature*, self-published in 1956 after having been rejected by a university press because of its subject matter. An exhaustive chronological account of every reference to love between women from Sappho and Ruth[8] to the fiction of the fifties, *Sex Variant Women* has proven to be an invaluable starting point for lesbian readers and scholars. Out of print almost immediately after its publication and lost to all but a few intrepid souls, it was finally reprinted by Diana Press in 1975. A further resource and gathering point for lesbian critics was the special issue on lesbian writing and publishing in *Margins*, a review of small press publications, which appeared in 1975, the first issue of a literary journal devoted entirely to lesbian writing. In 1976, its editor, Beth Hodges, produced a second special issue, this time in *Sinister Wisdom*. Along with the growing visibility and solidarity of lesbians within the academic profession, and the increased availability of lesbian literature from feminist and mass-market presses, these two journal issues propelled lesbian feminist literary criticism to the surface.[9]

The literary resources available to lesbian critics form only part of the story, for lesbian criticism is equally rooted in political ideology. Although not all lesbian critics are activists, most have been strongly influenced by the politics of lesbian feminism. These politics travel the continuum from civil rights advocacy to separatism; however, most, if not all, lesbian feminists assume that lesbianism is a healthy lifestyle chosen by women in virtually all eras and all cultures, and thus strive to eliminate the stigma historically attached to lesbianism. One way to remove this stigma is to associate lesbian-

5. Gilbert and Gubar, *The Madwoman in the Attic: The Woman Writer and the Nineteenth-Century Literary Imagination* (New Haven: Yale University Press, 1979), p. 567 [Zimmerman's note]. In "Goblin Market" (1862), a long children's poem by the English poet Christina Rossetti, one sister who sickens after eating the forbidden fruits offered by goblin men is saved when the other—pelted with fruit by the men—allows her to take the pulp from her body.

6. Gene Damon, Jan Watson, and Robin Jordan, *The Lesbian in Literature: A Bibliography* (1967; rpt., Reno: Naiad Press, 1975) [Zimmerman's note]. Grier (b. 1933), American publisher and editor, who in 1973 co-founded the lesbian feminist Naiad Press.

7. American writer, teacher, and librarian (1895–1981).

8. The biblical figure who swore she would be parted from her mother-in-law, Naomi, only by death (Ruth 1.15–17). Sappho (b. ca. 612 B.C.E.), Greek lyric poet who was at the center of a band of women who worshipped Aphrodite and the Muses; it is because of the intensity of the feelings for her companions, expressed in her poems, that the English word for female homosexual was coined from the name of her home island, Lesbos.

9. In addition, networks of lesbian critics, teachers, and scholars were established through panels at the Modern Language Association's annual convention and at the Lesbian Writer's Conference in Chicago, which began in 1974 and continued for several years. Currently, networking continues through conferences, journals, and other institutionalized outlets [Zimmerman's note]. The MLA is the primary North American professional organization for literary scholars in English and foreign languages; its annual convention includes hundreds of panels, which are forums at which academic papers are presented.

ism with positive and desirable attributes, to divert women's attention away from male values and toward an exclusively female communitas. Thus, the influential Radicalesbians' essay, "The Woman-Identified Woman," argues that lesbian feminism assumes "the primacy of women relating to women, of women creating a new consciousness of and with each other. . . . We see ourselves as prime, find our centers inside of ourselves."[1] Many lesbian writers and critics have also been influenced profoundly by the politics of separatism which provides a critique of heterosexuality as a political institution rather than a personal choice, "because relationships between men and women are essentially political, they involve power and dominance."[2] As we shall see, the notion of "woman-identification," that is, the primacy of women bonding with women emotionally and politically, as well as the premises of separatism, that lesbians have a unique and critical place at the margins of patriarchal society, are central to much current lesbian literary criticism.

Unmasking heterosexist assumptions in feminist literary criticism has been an important but hardly primary task for lesbian critics. We are more concerned with the development of a unique lesbian feminist perspective or, at the very least, determining whether or not such a perspective is possible. In order to do so, lesbian critics have had to begin with a special question: "When is a text a 'lesbian text' or its writer a 'lesbian writer' "?[3] Lesbians are faced with this special problem of definition: presumably we know when a writer is a "Victorian writer" or a "Canadian writer." To answer this question, we have to determine how inclusively or exclusively we define "lesbian." Should we limit this appellation to those women for whom sexual experience with other women can be proven? This is an almost impossible historical task, as many have noted, for what constitutes proof? Women have not left obvious markers in their private writings. Furthermore, such a narrow definition "names" lesbianism as an exclusively sexual phenomenon which, many argue, may be an inadequate construction of lesbian experience, both today and in less sexually explicit eras. This sexual definition of lesbianism also leads to the identification of literature with life, and thus can be an overly defensive and suspect strategy.

Nevertheless, lesbian criticism continues to be plagued with the problem of definition. One perspective insists that

> desire must be there and at least somewhat embodied. . . . That carnality distinguishes it from gestures of political sympathy for homosexuals and from affectionate friendships in which women enjoy each other, support each other, and commingle their sense of identity and well-being.[4]

1. Radicalesbians, "The Woman-Identified Woman," in *Radical Feminism*, ed. Anne Koedt, Ellen Levine, and Anita Rapone (New York: Quadrangle, 1973), and extensively reprinted in women's studies anthologies [Zimmerman's note]. Radicalesbians: American group of lesbian separatists, formed in 1970 largely in reaction to discrimination against lesbians within the women's movement (particularly the National Organization for Women), which cast lesbianism as a political choice (defining a lesbian as "the rage of all women condensed to the point of explosion"); members included the novelist and poet Rita Mae Brown and the writer and activist Karla Jay.
2. Charlotte Bunch, "Lesbians in Revolt," in *Lesbianism and the Women's Movement*, ed. Nancy Myron and Charlotte Bunch (Baltimore: Diana Press, 1975), p. 30 [Zimmerman's note].
3. Susan Snaider Lanser, "Speaking in Tongues: *Ladies Almanack* and the Language of Celebration," *Frontiers* 4, no. 3 (1979): 39 [Zimmerman's note].
4. Catharine R. Stimpson, "Zero Degree Deviancy: A Study of the Lesbian Novel," unpublished

A second perspective, which might be called a school, claims, on the contrary, that "the very meaning of lesbianism is being expanded in literature, just as it is being redefined through politics."[5] An articulate spokeswoman for this "expanded meaning" school of criticism is Adrienne Rich, who offers a compelling inclusive definition of lesbianism:

> I mean the term *lesbian continuum* to include a range—through each woman's life and throughout history—of woman-identified experience; not simply the fact that a woman has had or consciously desired genital experience with another woman. If we expand it to embrace many more forms of primary intensity between and among women, including the sharing of a rich inner life, the bonding against male tyranny, the giving and receiving of practical and political support . . . we begin to grasp breadths of female history and psychology which have lain out of reach as a consequence of limited, mostly clinical, definitions of 'lesbianism.'[6]

This definition has the virtue of deemphasizing lesbianism as a static entity and of suggesting interconnections among the various ways in which women bond together. However, all inclusive definitions of lesbianism risk blurring the distinctions between lesbian relationships and non-lesbian female friendships, or between lesbian identity and female-centered identity. Some lesbian writers would deny that there are such distinctions, but this position is reductive and of mixed value to those who are developing lesbian criticism and theory and who may need limited and precise definitions. In fact, reductionism is a serious problem in lesbian ideology. Too often, we identify lesbian and woman, or feminist: we equate lesbianism with any close bonds between women or with political commitment to women. These identifications can be fuzzy and historically questionable, as, for example, in the claim that lesbians have a unique relationship with nature or (as Rich also has claimed) that all female creativity is lesbian. By so reducing the meaning of lesbian, we have in effect eliminated lesbianism as a meaningful category.

A similar problem arises when lesbian theorists redefine lesbianism politically, equating it with strength, independence, and resistance to patriarchy. This new political definition then influences the interpretation of literature: "If in a woman writer's work a sentence refuses to do what it is supposed to do, if there are strong images of women and if there is a refusal to be linear, the result is innately lesbian literature."[7] The concept of an "innately" lesbian perspective or aesthetic allows the critic to separate lesbianism from biographical content, which is an essential development in lesbian critical theory. Literary interpretation will, of course, be supported by historical and biographical evidence, but perhaps lesbian critics should borrow a few insights from New Criticism.[8] If a text lends itself to a lesbian reading, then

paper [Zimmerman's note]. Later published as "Zero Degree Deviancy: The Lesbian Novel in English," *Critical Inquiry* 8 (winter 1981): 363–80.

5. Barbara Smith, "Toward a Black Feminist Criticism," *Conditions: Two* 1, no. 2 (1977): 39. It is sometimes overlooked that Smith's pathbreaking article on black feminist criticism is also a lesbian feminist analysis [Zimmerman's note]. SMITH (b. 1946), pioneering black and lesbian feminist critic; for this essay, see above.

6. Adrienne Rich, "Compulsory Heterosexuality and Lesbian Existence," *Signs* 5, no. 4 (1980): 648–49 [Zimmerman's note]. For this essay, see above.

7. Bertha Harris, qtd. by Smith, "Toward a Black Feminist Criticism," p. 33 [Zimmerman's note].

8. A formalist approach (championed by CLEANTH BROOKS, WILLIAM K. WIMSATT JR., and others) that emphasizes close reading of the text considered as an autonomous whole; it has greatly influenced teaching from the mid–20th century onward.

no amount of biographic "proof" ought to be necessary to establish it as a lesbian text. Barbara Smith, for example, interprets Toni Morrison's *Sula*[9] as a lesbian novel, regardless of the author's affectional preference. But we need to be cautious about what we call "innately" lesbian. Why is circularity or strength limited to lesbians, or, similarly, why is love of nature or creativity? It is certainly not evident that women, let alone lesbians, are "innately" anything. And, although it might require a lesbian perspective to stress the dominant relationship between Nel and Sula ("All that time, all that time, I thought I was missing Jude"), it is difficult to imagine a novel so imbued with heterosexuality as lesbian.

Almost midway between the inclusive and exclusive approaches to a definition of lesbianism lies that of Lillian Faderman in her extraordinary overview, *Surpassing the Love of Man: Romantic Friendship and Love Between Women From the Renaissance to the Present*. Faderman's precise definition of lesbianism provides a conceptual framework for the four hundred years of literary history explored by the text:

> "Lesbian" describes a relationship in which two women's strongest emotions and affections are directed toward each other. Sexual contact may be a part of the relationship to a greater or lesser degree, or it may be entirely absent. By preference the two women spend most of their time together and share most aspects of their lives with each other.[1]

Broader than the exclusive definition of lesbianism—for Faderman argues that not all lesbian relationships may be fully embodied—but narrower than Rich's "lesbian continuum," this definition is both specific and discriminating. The book is slightly marred by a defensive, overexplanatory tone, caused, no doubt, by her attempt to neutralize the "intense charge of the word *lesbian*"; note, for example, that this charged word is omitted from the title.[2] Furthermore, certain problems remain with her framework, as with any that a lesbian critic or historian might establish. The historical relationship between genital sexuality and lesbianism remains unclear, and we cannot identify easily lesbianism outside a monogamous relationship. Nevertheless, despite problems in definition that may be inherent in lesbian studies, the strength of *Surpassing the Love of Men* is partially the precision with which Faderman defines her topic and chooses her texts and subjects.

This problem of definition is exacerbated by the problem of silence. One of the most pervasive themes in lesbian criticism is that woman-identified writers, silenced by a homophobic and misogynistic society, have been forced to adopt coded and obscure language and internal censorship. Emily Dickinson[3] counseled us to "tell all the truth / but tell it slant," and critics are now calculating what price we have paid for slanted truth. The silences of heterosexual women writers may become lies for lesbian writers, as Rich warns: "a life 'in the closet' . . . [may] spread into private life, so that lying

9. A 1973 novel by Morrison (b. 1931), African American novelist and winner of the Nobel Prize for literature.

1. Lillian Faderman, *Surpassing the Love of Men: Romantic Friendship and Love between Women from the Renaissance to the Present* (New York: William Morrow, 1981), pp. 17–18 [Zimmerman's note]. Faderman (b. 1940), American lesbian critic and historian.

2. Adrienne Rich, "It Is the Lesbian in Us . . ." in *On Lies, Secrets, and Silence* (New York: Norton, 1979), p. 202 [Zimmerman's note].

3. American poet (1830–1886); Zimmerman quotes (with misplaced line break) poem J. 1129.

(described as *discretion*) becomes an easy way to avoid conflict or complication."[4] Gloria T. Hull recounts the moving story of just such a victim of society, the black lesbian poet Angelina Weld Grimké, whose "convoluted life and thwarted sexuality" marked her slim output of poetry with images of self-abnegation, diminution, sadness, and the wish for death. The lesbian writer who is working class or a woman of color may be particularly isolated, shackled by conventions and, ultimately, silenced "with [her] real gifts stifled within."[5] What does a lesbian writer do when the words cannot be silenced? Critics are pointing to the codes and strategies for literary survival adopted by many women. For example, Willa Cather[6] may have adopted her characteristic male persona in order to express safely her emotional and erotic feelings for other women. Thus, a writer some critics call antifeminist or at least disappointing may be better appreciated when her lesbianism is taken into account. Similarly, many ask whether Gertrude Stein cultivated obscurity, encoding her lesbianism in order to express hidden feelings and evade potential enemies. Or, on the other hand, Stein may have been always a declared lesbian, but a victim of readers' (and scholars') unwillingness or inability to pay her the close and sympathetic attention she requires.[7]

The silence of "Shakespeare's [lesbian] sister"[8] has meant that modern writers have had little or no tradition with which to nurture themselves. Feminist critics such as Moers, Showalter, and Gilbert and Gubar have demonstrated the extent and significance of a female literary tradition, but the lesbian writer developed her craft alone (and perhaps this is the significance of the title of the lesbian novel about novel writing, *The Well of Loneliness*). Elly Bulkin's much-reprinted article on lesbian poetry points out that lesbian poets "have their work shaped by the simple fact of their having begun to write without knowledge of such history and with little or no hope of support from a woman's and/or lesbian writing community."[9] If white women can at least imagine a lesbian literature, the black lesbian writer, as Barbara Smith demonstrates, is even more hampered by the lack of tradition: "Black women are still in the position of having to 'imagine,' discover and verify Black lesbian literature because so little has been written from an avowedly lesbian perspective."[1] Blanche Wiesen Cook points out further that all lesbians are affected by this absence of tradition and role models, or the limiting of role models to Hall's Stephen Gordon. She also reminds us that our lesbian foremothers and networks were not simply lost and forgotten; rather, our past has been "erased," obliterated by the actions of a hostile society.[2]

It would appear then that lesbian critics are faced with a set of problems that make our work particularly delicate and problematic, requiring caution,

4. Rich, "Women and Honor: Some Notes on Lying (1975)," in *On Lies, Secrets, and Silence*, p. 190 [Zimmerman's note].

5. Gloria T. Hull, "'Under the Days': The Buried Life and Poetry of Angelina Weld Grimké," *Conditions: Five* 2, no. 2 (1979): 23, 20 [Zimmerman's note]. Grimké (1880–1958), writer of poetry, plays, and short stories.

6. American novelist (1873–1947).

7. Two male critics—Edmund Wilson and Robert Bridgman—first suggested the connection between Stein's obscurity and her lesbianism [Zimmerman's note]. WILSON (1895–1972), American literary and social critic and novelist.

8. A reference to "Judith Shakespeare," imagined by Woolf in *A Room of One's Own* (1929; see above) to illustrate the debilitating obstacles faced by women who wish to write.

9. Bulkin, "'Kissing against the Light,'" p. 8 [Zimmerman's note].

1. Smith, "Toward a Black Feminist Criticism," p. 39 [Zimmerman's note].

2. Blanche Wiesen Cook, "'Women Alone Stir My Imagination': Lesbianism and the Cultural Tradition," *Signs* 4, no. 4 (1979): 718–39 [Zimmerman's note]. Gordon is the protagonist of Hall's *Well of Loneliness* (and is herself a novelist). Cook (b. 1941), American historian and activist.

sensitivity, and flexibility as well as imagination and risk. Lesbian criticism begins with the establishment of the lesbian text: the creation of language out of silence. The critic must first define the term "lesbian" and then determine its applicability to both writer and text, sorting out the relation of literature to life. Her definition of lesbianism will influence the texts she identifies as lesbian, and, except for the growing body of literature written from an explicit lesbian perspective since the development of a lesbian political movement, it is likely that many will disagree with various identifications of lesbian texts. It is not only *Sula* that may provoke controversy, but even the "coded" works of lesbian writers like Gertrude Stein. The critic will need to consider whether a lesbian text is one written by a lesbian (and if so, how do we determine who is a lesbian?), one written about lesbians (which might be by a heterosexual woman or a man), or one that expresses a lesbian "vision" (which has yet to be satisfactorily outlined). But despite the problems raised by definition, silence and coding, and absence of tradition, lesbian critics have begun to develop a critical stance. Often this stance involves peering into shadows, into the spaces between words, into what has been unspoken and barely imagined. It is a perilous critical adventure with results that may violate accepted norms of traditional criticism, but which may also transform our notions of literary possibility.

One of the first tasks of this emerging lesbian criticism has been to provide lesbians with a tradition, even if a retrospective one. Jane Rule, whose *Lesbian Images* appeared about the same time as *Literary Women*, first attempted to establish this tradition. Although her text is problematic, relying overly much on biographical evidence and derivative interpretations and including some questionable writers (such as Dorothy Baker[3]) while omitting others, *Lesbian Images* was a milestone in lesbian criticism. Its importance is partially suggested by the fact that it took five years for another complete book—Faderman's—to appear on lesbian literature. In a review of *Lesbian Images*, I questioned the existence of a lesbian "great tradition" in literature, but now I think I was wrong.[4] Along with Rule, Dolores Klaich in *Woman Plus Woman* and Louise Bernikow in the introduction to *The World Split Open* have explored the possibility of a lesbian tradition,[5] and recent critics such as Faderman and Cook in particular have begun to define that tradition, who belongs to it, and what links the writers who can be identified as lesbians. Cook's review of lesbian literature and culture in the early twentieth century proposes "to analyze the literature and attitudes out of which the present lesbian feminist works have emerged, and to examine the continued denials and invalidation of the lesbian experience."[6] Focusing on the recognized lesbian networks in France and England that included Virginia Woolf, Vita Sackville-West, Ethel Smyth, Gertrude Stein, Radclyffe Hall, Natalie Barney, and Romaine Brooks,[7] Cook provides an important outline of a les-

3. American novelist (1907–1968).

4. Bonnie Zimmerman, "The New Tradition," *Sinister Wisdom* 2 (1976): 34–41 [Zimmerman's note]. "The great tradition," a phrase made famous by the English critic F. R. Leavis's use of it to title his 1948 study of the English novel, designates the canon of English literature (composed almost entirely of works by men).

5. Dolores Klaich, *Woman Plus Woman: Attitudes toward Lesbianism* (New York: William Morrow, 1974); Louise Bernikow, *The World Split Open: Four Centuries of Women Poets in England and America, 1552–1950* (New York: Vintage Books, 1974) [Zimmerman's note].

6. Cook, " 'Women Alone Stir My Imagination,' " p. 720 [Zimmerman's note].

7. American painter (1874–1970). Smyth (1858–1944), English composer and campaigner for

bian cultural tradition and an insightful analysis of the distortions and denials of homophobic scholars, critics, and biographers.

Faderman's *Surpassing the Love of Men*, like her earlier critical articles, ranges more widely through a literary tradition of romantic love between women (whether or not one calls that "lesbian") from the sixteenth to the twentieth centuries. Her thesis is that passionate love between women was labeled neither abnormal nor undesirable—probably because women were perceived to be asexual—until the sexologists led by Krafft-Ebing and Havelock Ellis[8] "morbidified" female friendship around 1900.

Although she does not always clarify the dialectic between idealization and condemnation that is suggested in her text, Faderman's basic theory is quite convincing. Most readers, like myself, will be amazed at the wealth of information about women's same-sex love that Faderman has uncovered. She rescues from heterosexual obscurity Mary Wollstonecraft, Mary Wortley Montagu, Anna Seward, Sarah Orne Jewett, Edith Somerville, "Michael Field," and many others, including the Scottish school-mistresses whose lesbian libel suit inspired Lillian Hellman's *The Children's Hour*.[9] Faderman has also written on the theme of same-sex love and romantic friendship in poems and letters of Emily Dickinson; in novels by Henry James, Oliver Wendell Holmes, and Henry Wadsworth Longfellow;[1] and in popular magazine fiction of the early twentieth century.[2]

Faderman is preeminent among those critics who are attempting to establish a lesbian tradition by rereading writers of the past previously assumed to be heterosexual or "spinsters." As songwriter Holly Near expresses it: "Lady poet of great acclaim / I have been misreading you / I never knew your poems were meant for me."[3] It is in this area of lesbian scholarship that the most controversy—and some of the most exciting work—occurs. Was Mary Wollstonecraft's passionate love for Fanny Blood, recorded in *Mary, A Fiction*,[4] lesbian? Does Henry James dissect a lesbian relationship in *The Bostonians*? Did Emily Dickinson address many of her love poems to a woman, not a man? How did Virginia Woolf's relationship with Vita Sackville-West and Ethel Smyth affect her literary vision? Not only are some lesbian critics increasingly naming such women and relationships "lesbian," they are also

---

women's suffrage. Barney (1876–1972), American lesbian writer whose Paris salon attracted famous writers and artists for 60 years.

8. English physician (1859–1939), pioneer of the field of "sexology" and coauthor of *Sexual Inversion* (1897). Baron Richard von Krafft-Ebing (1840–1902), German neurologist whose *Psychopathia Sexualis* (1876) detailed sexual "perversions."

9. A 1934 play by the American playwright and memoirist Hellman (1905–1984). WOLLSTONECRAFT (1759–1797), English writer best known for *A Vindication of the Rights of Woman* (1792; see above). Montagu (1689–1762), English poet and essayist. Seward (1747–1809), English poet. Jewett (1849–1909), American novelist and short story writer. Somerville (1858–1949), Irish novelist who frequently collaborated with her cousin Violet Martin. "Michael Field": the pseudonym of the English poets Katharine Harris Bradley (1846–1914) and her niece, Edith Emma Cooper (1862–1913), who wrote and lived together.

1. Popular 19th-century American poet (1807–1882). JAMES (1843–1916), American writer of fiction and criticism; his novels include *The Bostonians* (1886), which focuses in large part on the relation between a Boston feminist and the woman whom she hopes to persuade to join her in fighting for women's rights. Holmes (1809–1894), American physician, poet, and essayist.

2. See Lillian Faderman's articles: "The Morbidification of Love between Women by Nineteenth-Century Sexologists," *Journal of Homosexuality* 4, no. 1 (1978): 73–90; "Emily Dickinson's Letters to Sue Gilbert," *Massachusetts Review* 18, no. 2 (1977): 197–225; "Emily Dickinson's Homoerotic Poetry," *Higginson Journal* 18 (1978): 19–27; "Female Same-Sex Relationships in Novels by Longfellow, Holmes, and James," *New England Quarterly* 60, no. 3 (1978): 309–32; and "Lesbian Magazine Fiction in the Early Twentieth Century," *Journal of Popular Culture* 11, no. 4 (1978): 800–817 [Zimmerman's note].

3. Holly Near, "Imagine My Surprise," on *Imagine My Surprise!* (Redwood Records, 1978) [Zimmerman's note].

4. A 1788 novel by Wollenstonecraft; Fanny (Frances) Blood (1757–1785) had died in childbirth.

suggesting that criticism cannot fail to take into account the influence of sexual and emotional orientation on literary expression.

In the establishment of a self-conscious literary tradition, certain writers have become focal points both for critics and for lesbians in general, who affirm and celebrate their identity by "naming names," establishing a sense of historical continuity and community through the knowledge that incontrovertibly great women were also lesbians. Foremost among these heroes (or "heras") are the women who created the first self-identified lesbian feminist community in Paris during the early years of the twentieth century. With Natalie Barney at its hub, this circle included such notable writers as Colette,[5] Djuna Barnes, Radclyffe Hall, Renée Vivien, and, peripherally, Gertrude Stein. Contemporary lesbians—literary critics, historians, and layreaders—have been drawn to their mythic and mythmaking presence, seeing in them a vision of lesbian society and culture that may have existed only once before on the original island of Lesbos. More interest, however, has been paid to their lives so far than to their art. Barnes's portraits of decadent, tormented lesbians and homosexuals in *Nightwood* and silly, salacious ones in *The Ladies Almanack*[6] often prove troublesome to lesbian readers and critics. However, Elaine Marks's perceptive study of French lesbian writers traces a tradition and how it has changed, modified by circumstance and by feminism, from the Sappho of Renée Vivien to the amazons of Monique Wittig.[7]

The problems inherent in reading lesbian literature primarily for role modeling is most evident with Hall—the most notorious of literary lesbians—whose archetypal "butch," Stephen Gordon, has bothered readers since the publication of *The Well of Loneliness*. Although one critic praises it as "the standard by which all subsequent similar works are measured," most contemporary lesbian feminists would, I believe, agree with Faderman's harsh condemnation that it "helped to wreak confusion in young women."[8] Such an extraliterary debate is not limited to lesbian novels and lesbian characters; I am reminded of the intense disappointment expressed by many feminists over George Eliot's[9] disposal of Dorothea Brooke in *Middlemarch*. In both cases, the cry is the same: why haven't these writers provided us with appropriate role models? Cook may be justified in criticizing Hall for creating a narrow and debilitating image for lesbians who follow, but my reading of the novel (and that of Catherine Stimpson in an excellent study of the lesbian novel) convinces me that both Hall's hero and message are highly complex.[1] In looking to writers for a tradition, we need to recognize that the tradition may not always be a happy one. Women like Stephen Gordon exist alongside characters like Molly Bolt, in Rita Mae Brown's *Rubyfruit Jungle*,[2] but lesbians may also question whether or not the incarnation of a "politically cor-

5. Sidonie Gabrielle Colette (1873–1954), French novelist.
6. A 1928 novel parodying Barney's lesbian salon.
7. Elaine Marks, "Lesbian Intertextuality," in *Homosexualities and French Literature*, ed. George Stambolian and Elaine Marks (Ithaca, N.Y.: Cornell University Press, 1979), pp. 353–77 [Zimmerman's note]. WITTIG (b 1935), French lesbian feminist writer and activist whose experimental prose works include *Les Guérillères* (1969) and *Le Corps lesbien* (1973, *The Lesbian Body*). Vivien translated Sappho.
8. Lillian Faderman and Ann Williams, "Radclyffe Hall and the Lesbian Image," *Conditions: One* 1, no. 1 (1977): 40 [Zimmerman's note].
9. English novelist (pseudonym of Marian Evans, 1819–1880); in *Middlemarch* (1871–72), the vision and yearnings of her protagonist are frustrated.
1. Stimpson, "Zero Degree Deviancy," pp. 8–17 [Zimmerman's note].
2. This 1973 novel was one of the earliest to portray lesbian love positively.

rect" but elusive and utopian mythology provides our only appropriate role model.

As with Hall, many readers and critics are strongly antipathetic to Stein, citing her reactionary and antifeminist politics and her role-playing relationship with Alice B. Toklas. However, other critics, by carefully analyzing Stein's actual words, establish, convincingly to my reading, that she did have a lesbian and feminist perspective, calling into question assumptions about coding and masculine role playing. Cynthia Secor, who is developing an exciting lesbian feminist interpretation of Stein, argues that her novel *Ida* attempts to discover what it means to be a female person, and that the author profited from her position on the boundaries of patriarchal society: "Stein's own experience as a lesbian gives her a critical distance that shapes her understanding of the struggle to be one's self. Her own identity is not shaped as she moves into relation with a man."[3] Similarly, Elizabeth Fifer points out that Stein's situation encouraged her to experiment with parody, theatricality, role playing, and "the diversity of ways possible to look at homosexual love and at her love object."[4] Deirdre Vanderlinde finds in *Three Lives* "one of the earliest attempts to find a new language in which to say, 'I, woman-loving woman, exist.' "[5] Catharine Stimpson places more critical emphasis on Stein's use of masculine pronouns and conventional language, but despite what may have been her compromise, Stimpson feels that female bonding in Stein provides her with a private solution to woman's mind-body split.[6]

Along with Stein, Dickinson's woman-identification has drawn the most attention from recent critics, and has generated considerable controversy between lesbian and other feminist critics. Faderman insists that Dickinson's love for women must be considered homosexual, and that critics must take into account her sexuality (or affectionality). Like most critics who accept this lesbian identification of Dickinson, she points to Susan Gilbert Dickinson as Emily's primary romantic and sexual passion. Both Faderman and Bernikow thus argue that Dickinson's "muse" was sometimes a female figure as well as a male.[7] Some of this work can be justifiably criticized for too closely identifying literature with life; however, by altering our awareness of what is *possible*—namely, that Dickinson's poetry was inspired by her love for a woman—we also can transform our response to the poetry. Paula Bennett daringly suggests that Dickinson's use of crumbs, jewels, pebbles, and similar objects was an attempt to create "clitoral imagery."[8] In a controversial paper on the subject, Nadean Bishop argues forcefully that the poet's marriage poems must be reread in light of what she considers to have been Dickinson's consummated sexual relationship with her sister-in-law.[9]

3. Cynthia Secor, "*Ida*, a Great American Novel," *Twentieth Century Literature* 24, no. 1 (1978): 99 [Zimmerman's note]. *Ida: A Novel* (1941) is a late work by Stein.

4. Elizabeth Fifer, "Is Flesh Advisable? The Interior Theater of Gertrude Stein," *Signs* 4, no. 3 (1979): 478 [Zimmerman's note].

5. Deirdre Vanderlinde, "Gertrude Stein: *Three Lives*," paper presented at the MLA convention, San Francisco, December 1979 [Zimmerman's note]. In *Three Lives* (1909), her first novel, Stein depicts the lives of three working-class women in minimalist, plain language.

6. Catharine Stimpson, "The Mind, and Body, and Gertrude Stein," *Critical Inquiry* 3, no. 3 (1977): 489–506 [Zimmerman's note].

7. Lillian Faderman and Louise Bernikow, "Comment on Joanne Feit Diehl's " 'Come Slowly—Eden,' " *Signs* 4, no. 1 (1978): 188–95 [Zimmerman's note]. Gilbert, who met and became a close friend of Dickinson in the late 1840s, married the poet's brother, Austin, in 1856; the women then lived next door to one another.

8. Paula Bennett, "The Language of Love: Emily Dickinson's Homoerotic Poetry," *Gai Saber* 1, no. 1 (1977): 13–17; and "Emily Dickinson and the Value of Isolation," *Dickinson Studies* 36 (1979): 13–17 [Zimmerman's note].

9. Nadean Bishop, "Renunciation in the Bridal Poems of Emily Dickinson," paper presented at the

The establishment of a lesbian literary tradition, a "canon," as my lengthy discussion suggests, has been the primary task of critics writing from a lesbian feminist perspective. But it is not the only focus to emerge. For example, lesbian critics, like feminist critics in the early seventies, have begun to analyze the images, stereotypes, and mythic presence of lesbians in fiction by or about lesbians. Bertha Harris, a major novelist as well as a provocative and trailblazing critic, considers the lesbian to be the prototype of the monster and "the quintessence of all that is female; and female enraged . . . a lesbian is . . . that which has been unspeakable about women."[1] Harris offers this monstrous lesbian as a female archetype who subverts traditional notions of female submissiveness, passivity, and virtue. Her "tooth-and-claw" image of the lesbian is ironically similar to that of Ellen Moers, although from a lesbian rather than heterosexual point of view. But the very fact that Moers presents the lesbian-as-monster in a derogatory context and Harris in a celebratory one suggests that there is an important dialectic between how the lesbian articulates herself and how she is articulated and objectified by others. Popular culture, in particular, exposes the objectifying purpose of the lesbian-as-monster image, such as the lesbian vampire first created by Joseph Sheridan LeFanu's 1871 ghost story, "Carmilla," and revived in early 1970s "B" films as a symbolic attack on women's struggle for self-identity.[2] Other critics also have analyzed the negative symbolic appearance of the lesbian in literature. Ann Allen Shockley, reviewing black lesbian characters in American fiction, notes that "within these works exists an undercurrent of hostility, trepidation, subtlety, shadiness, and in some instances, ignorance culling forth homophobic stereotypes."[3] Homophobic stereotypes are also what Judith McDaniel and Maureen Brady find in abundance in recent commercial fiction (such as *Kinflicks, A Sea Change, Some Do* and *How to Save Your Own Life*[4]) by avowedly feminist novelists. Although individuals might disagree with McDaniel and Brady's severe criticism of specific novels, their overall argument is unimpeachable. Contemporary feminist fiction, by perpetuating stereotyped characters and themes (such as the punishment theme so dear to prefeminist lesbian literature), serves to "disempower the lesbian."[5] Lesbian, as well as heterosexual, writers present the lesbian as Other, as Julia Penelope Stanley discovered in prefeminist fiction: "the lesbian character creates for herself a mythology of darkness, a world in which she moves through dreams and shadows."[6] Lesbian critics may wish to avoid this analysis of the lesbian as Other because we no longer wish to dwell upon the cultural violence done against us. Yet this area must be explored until we strip these stereotypes of their inhibiting and dehumanizing presence in our popular culture and social mythology.

National Women's Studies Association Conference, Bloomington, Indiana, May 1980 [Zimmerman's note].

1. Bertha Harris, "*What we mean to say*: Notes toward Defining the Nature of Lesbian Literature," *Heresies* 3 (1977): 7–8 [Zimmerman's note].

2. Bonnie Zimmerman, "Daughters of Darkness': Lesbian Vampires," *Jump Cut*, nos. 24–25 (1981): 23–24 [Zimmerman's note]. Le Fanu (1814–1873), Irish writer best known for his ghost stories and mysteries.

3. Ann Allen Shockley, "The Black Lesbian in American Literature: An Overview," *Conditions: Five* 2, no. 2 (1979): 136 [Zimmerman's note].

4. All American novels of the 1970s: *Kinflicks* (1975), by Lisa Alther; *A Sea Change* (1976), by Lois Gould; *Some Do* (1978), by Jane DeLynn; and *How to Save Your Own Life* (1977), by Erica Jong.

5. Maureen Brady and Judith McDaniel, "Lesbians in the Mainstream: Images of Lesbians in Recent Commercial Fiction," *Conditions: Six* 2, no. 3 (1980): 83 [Zimmerman's note].

6. Julia Penelope Stanley, "Uninhabited Angels: Metaphors for Love," *Margins* 23 (1975): 8. The "Other": that against which members of a dominant group define themselves in opposition.

Lesbian critics have also delved into the area of stylistics and literary theory. If we have been silenced for centuries and speak an oppressor's tongue, then liberation for the lesbian must begin with language. Some writers may have reconciled their internal censor with their speech by writing in code, but many critics maintain that modern lesbian writers, because they are uniquely alienated from the patriarchy, experiment with its literary style and form. Julia Penelope Stanley and Susan Wolfe, considering such diverse writers as Virginia Woolf, Gertrude Stein, Kate Millett, and Elana Dykewoman,[7] claim that "a feminist aesthetic, as it emerges out of women's evolution, grounds itself in female consciousness and in the unrelenting language of process and change."[8] In this article, the authors do not call their feminist aesthetic a lesbian feminist aesthetic, although all the writers they discuss are, in fact, lesbians. Susan Wolfe later confronted this fact: "Few women who continue to identify with men can risk the male censure of 'women's style,' and few escape the male perspective long enough to attempt it."[9] Through examples from Kate Millett, Jill Johnston,[1] and Monique Wittig, she illustrates her contention that lesbian literature is characterized by the use of the continuous present, unconventional grammar and neologism; and that it breaks boundaries between art and the world, between events and our perceptions of them, and between past, present, and the dream world. It is, as even the proponents of this theory admit, highly debatable that all lesbian writers are modernists, or that all modernists are lesbians. If Virginia Woolf wrote in nonlinear, stream-of-consciousness style because she was a lesbian (or "woman-identified") how does one explain Dorothy Richardson whose *Pilgrimage*, despite one lesbian relationship, is primarily heterosexual? If both Woolf and Richardson can be called "feminist" stylists, then how does one explain the nonlinear experimentation of James Joyce or Alain Robbe-Grillet,[2] for example? The holes that presently exist in this theory should not, however, detract from the highly suggestive overlap between experimental and lesbian writers. Nor should we ignore the clear evidence that many contemporary, self-conscious lesbian writers (such as Wittig, Johnston, Bertha Harris and June Arnold) are choosing an experimental style as well as content.

This development of a self-conscious lesbian literature and literary theory in recent years has led a number of critics to investigate the unifying themes and values of current literature. Such an attempt has been made by Elly Bulkin, who traces the various sources of contemporary lesbian poetry, analyzes "the range of lesbian voices," and advises feminist teachers how to teach lesbian poetry. Mary Carruthers, in asking why so much contemporary feminist poetry is also lesbian, observes that the "lesbian love celebrated in contemporary women's poetry requires an affirmation of the value of femaleness, women's bodies, women's sexuality—in women's language."[3] Jane Gurko and

7. American lesbian separatist writer and activist (b. 1949). Millett (b. 1934), American feminist critic, novelist, and artist.
8. Julia Penelope Stanley and Susan J. Wolfe, "Toward a Feminist Aesthetic," *Chrysalis*, no. 6, p. 66 [Zimmerman's note].
9. Susan J. Wolfe, "Stylistic Experimentation in Millett, Johnston, and Wittig," paper presented at the MLA convention, New York, December 1978 [Zimmerman's note].

1. English-born American dancer, critic, and activist (b. 1929), author of *Lesbian Nation* (1973).
2. French novelist and theoretician (b. 1922), best known for developing the experimental "New Novel" in the 1950s and 1960s. Joyce (1882–1941), Irish modernist whose most experimental use of language and form appears in *Ulysses* (1922) and *Finnegans Wake* (1939).
3. Mary Carruthers, "Imagining Women: Notes toward a Feminist Poetic," *Massachusetts Review*

Sally Gearhart compare contemporary lesbian and gay male literature, attempting to discern to what extent one or the other transforms heterosexual ideology. They claim that, unlike gay male literature, lesbian literature "does express a revolutionary model of sexuality which in its structure, its content, and its practice defies the fundamental violent assumptions of patriarchal culture."[4] There is a danger in this attempt to establish a characteristic lesbian vision or literary value system, one that is well illustrated by this article. In an attempt to say *this* is what defines a lesbian literature, we are easily tempted to read selectively, omitting what is foreign to our theories. Most contemporary lesbian literature does embrace a rhetoric of nonviolence, but this is not universally true; for example, M. F. Beal's *Angel Dance*[5] is a lesbian hard-boiled detective novel and Monique Wittig's *Le Corps lesbien* is infused with a violent eroticism that is, nonetheless, intensely nonpatriarchal. Violence, role playing, disaffection, unhappiness, suicide, and self-hatred, to name a few "taboo" subjects, all exist within the lesbian culture, and a useful criticism will have to effectively analyze these as *lesbian* themes and issues, regardless of ideological purity.

Lesbian feminist criticism faces a number of concerns that must be addressed as it grows in force and clarity. Among these concerns is the fact that this criticism is dominated by the politics of lesbian separatism. This is exemplified by the following statement from *Sinister Wisdom*, a journal that has developed a consistent and articulate separatist politics,

> 'lesbian consciousness' is really a point of view, a view from the boundary. And in a sense every time a woman draws a circle around her psyche, saying 'this is a room of *my own*.' and then writes from within that 'room,' she's inhabiting lesbian consciousness.[6]

The value of separatism which, I believe, has always provided the most exciting theoretical developments in lesbian ideology, is precisely this marginality: lesbian existence "on the periphery of patriarchy."[7] Separatism provides criticism, as it did for lesbian politics, a cutting edge and radical energy that keeps us moving forward rather than backward either from fear or complacency. Those critics who maintain a consciously chosen position on the boundaries (and not one imposed by a hostile society) help to keep lesbian and feminist criticism radical and provocative, preventing both from becoming another arm of the established truth. At the same time, however, it is essential that separatist criticism does not itself become an orthodoxy, and thus repetitive, empty, and resistant to change. Lesbian criticism, as Kolodny has argued about feminist criticism, has more to gain from resisting dogma than from monotheism.[8] Understandably, those critics and scholars willing to identify themselves publicly as lesbians also have tended to hold radical politics of marginality. Exposing one's self to public scrutiny as a lesbian may

20, no. 2 (1979): 301 [Zimmerman's note].

4. Jane Gurko and Sally Gearhart, "The Sword and the Vessel versus the Lady on the Lake: A Lesbian Model of Nonviolent Rhetoric," paper presented at the 1979 MLA convention [Zimmerman's note].

5. A 1977 novel by the American writer Beal (b. 1937).

6. Harriet Desmoines, "Notes for a Magazine II," *Sinister Wisdom* 1, no. 1 (1976): 29 [Zimmerman's note].

7. Wolfe, "Stylistic Experimentation," p. 16 [Zimmerman's note].

8. Annette Kolodny, "Dancing through the Minefield: Some Observations on the Theory, Practice, and Politics of a Feminist Literary Criticism," *Feminist Studies* 6, no. 1 (1980): 1–25 [Zimmerman's note]. For this essay, see above.

in fact entail marginality through denial of tenure or loss of job, and those lesbians willing to risk these consequences usually have a political position that justifies their risk. However, to me it seems imperative that lesbian criticism develop diversity in theory and approach. Much as lesbians, even more than heterosexual feminists, may mistrust systems of thought developed by and associated with men and male values, we may, in fact, enrich our work through the insights of Marxist, structuralist, semiotic, or even psychoanalytic criticism. Perhaps "male" systems of thought are incompatible with a lesbian literary vision, but we will not know until we attempt to integrate these ideas into our work.

Similarly, lesbian criticism and cultural theory in general can only gain by developing a greater specificity, historically and culturally. We have tended to write and act as if lesbian experience—which is perceived as that of a contemporary, white middle-class feminist—is universal and unchanging. Although most lesbians know that this is not the case, we too often forget to apply rigorous historical and cross-cultural tools to our scholarship. Much of this ahistoricity occurs around the shifting definitions of lesbianism from one era and one culture to another. To state simply that Wollstonecraft "was" a lesbian because she passionately loved Fanny Blood, or Susan B. Anthony was a lesbian because she wrote amorous letters to Anna Dickinson,[9] without accounting for historical circumstances, may serve to distort or dislocate the actual meaning of these women's lives (just as it is distorting to *deny* their love for women). There are also notable differences among the institution of the *berdache* (the adoption by one sex of the opposite gender role) in Native American tribes; *faute de mieux*[1] lesbian activity tolerated in France (as in Colette's *Claudine* novels); idyllic romantic friendships (such as that of the famous Ladies of Llangollen[2]); and contemporary self-conscious lesbianism. I do believe that there is a common structure—a lesbian "essence"—that may be located in all these specific historical existences, just as we may speak of a widespread, perhaps universal, structure of marriage or the family. However, in each of these cases—lesbianism, marriage, the family—careful attention to history teaches us that differences are as significant as similarities, and vital information about female survival may be found in the different ways in which women have responded to their historical situation. This tendency toward simplistic universalism is accompanied by what I see as a dangerous development of biological determinism and a curious revival of the nineteenth-century feminist notion of female (now lesbian) moral superiority—that women are uniquely caring and superior to inherently violent males. Although only an undertone in some criticism and literature, any such sociobiological impulse should be questioned at every appearance.

The denial of meaningful differences among women is being challenged, particularly around the issue of racism. Bulkin has raised criticisms about the racism of white lesbian feminist theory. She has written that

> if I can put together—or think someone else can put together—a viable piece of feminist criticism or theory whose base is the thought and writ-

9. American orator, playwright, and abolitionist (1842–1932), who had a romantic friendship with Anthony (1820–1906), American abolitionist who became a leader of the women's suffrage movement.

1. For want of anything better (French).

2. Nickname of Lady Eleanor Butler (1739–1829) and Sarah Ponsonby (1755–1831), two English women who in 1778 defied their families' wishes to live together in Llangollen Vale, in north Wales, where they received visits from many distinguished writers (including WILLIAM WORDSWORTH).

> ing of white women/lesbians and expect that an analysis of racism can be tacked on or dealt with later as a useful addition, it is a measure of the extent to which I partake of that white privilege.[3]

Implicit in the criticism of Bulkin and other antiracist writers is the belief that lesbians, because of our experience of stigma and exclusion from the feminist mainstream, ought to be particularly sensitive to the dynamic between oppression and oppressing. White lesbians who are concerned about eradicating racism in criticism and theory have been greatly influenced as well by the work of several black lesbian feminist literary critics, such as Gloria T. Hull, Barbara Smith, and Lorraine Bethel. Such concern is not yet present over the issue of class, although the historical association of lesbianism with upper-class values has often been used by left-wing political groups and governments to deny legitimacy to homosexual rights and needs. Lesbian critics studying the Barney circle, for example, might analyze the historical connections between lesbianism and class status. Lesbian critics might also develop comparisons among the literature of various nationalities because the lesbian canon is of necessity cross-national. We have barely explored the differences between American, English, French, and German lesbian literature (although *Surpassing the Love of Men* draws some distinctions), let alone non-Western literature. The paucity of lesbian scholars trained in these literatures has so far prevented the development of a truly international lesbian literary canon.

As lesbian criticism matures, we may anticipate the development of ongoing and compelling political and practical concerns. At this time, for example, lesbians are still defining and discovering texts. We are certainly not as badly off as we were in the early seventies when the only lesbian novels in print were *The Well of Loneliness*, *Rubyfruit Jungle*, and Isabel Miller's *Patience and Sarah*.[4] However, texts published prior to 1970 are still difficult to find, and even *The Well of Loneliness* is intermittently available at the whim of publishers. Furthermore, the demise of Diana Press and the apparent slowdown of Daughters (two of the most active lesbian publishing houses) leaves many major works unavailable, possibly forever. As the boom in gay literature subsides, teachers of literature will find it very difficult to unearth teachable texts. Scholars have the excellent Arno Press series, *Homosexuality: Lesbians and Gay Men in Society, History, and Literature*, but, as Faderman's monumental scholarship reveals, far more lesbian literature exists than anyone has suspected. This literature needs to be unearthed, analyzed, explicated, perhaps translated, and made available to readers.

As lesbian critics, we also need to address the exclusion of lesbian literature from not merely the traditional, but also the feminist canon. Little lesbian literature has been integrated into the mainstream of feminist texts, as evidenced by what is criticized, collected, and taught. It is a matter of serious concern that lesbian literature is omitted from anthologies or included in mere token amounts, or that critical works and Modern Language Association panels still exclude lesbianism. It may as yet be possible for heterosexual feminists to claim ignorance about lesbian literature; however, lesbian critics

3. Elly Bulkin, "Racism and Writing: Some Implications for White Lesbian Critics," *Sinister Wisdom* 13 (1980): 16 [Zimmerman's note].

4. A 1969 novel, first published as *A Place for Us* (retitled in 1972), by Alma Routsong (b. 1924) under the pseudonym Isabel Miller.

should make it impossible for that claim to stand much longer. Lesbianism is still perceived as a minor and somewhat discomforting variation within the female life cycle, when it is mentioned at all. Just as we need to integrate lesbian material and perspectives into the traditional and feminist canons, we might also apply lesbian theory to traditional literature. Feminists have not only pointed out the sexism in many canonical works, but have also provided creative and influential rereadings of these works; similarly lesbians might contribute to the rereading of the classics. For example, *The Bostonians*, an obvious text, has been reread often from a lesbian perspective, and we could reinterpret D. H. Lawrence's antifeminism or Doris Lessing's[5] compromised feminism (particularly in *The Golden Notebook*) by relating these attitudes to their fear of or discomfort with lesbianism. Other texts or selections of texts—such as Rossetti's "Goblin Market" or the relationship between Lucy Snowe and Ginevra Fanshawe in *Villette*[6]—might reveal a subtext that could be called lesbian. Just as few texts escape a feminist revision, few might evade a lesbian transformation.

This last point—that there is a way in which we might "review" literature as lesbians—brings me to my conclusion. In a brief period of a few years, critics have begun to demonstrate the existence of a distinct lesbian aesthetic, just as feminists have outlined elements of a female aesthetic. Certain components of this aesthetic or critical perspective are clear:

> Perhaps lesbian feminist criticism [or literature, I would add] is a political or thematic perspective, a kind of imagination that can see beyond the barriers of heterosexuality, role stereotypes, patterns of language and culture that may be repressive to female sexuality and expression.[7]

A lesbian artist very likely would express herself differently about sexuality, the body, and relationships. But are there other—less obvious—unifying themes, ideas, and imagery that might define a lesbian text or subtext? How, for example, does the lesbian's sense of outlaw status affect her literary vision? Might lesbian writing, because of the lesbian's position on the boundaries, be characterized by a particular sense of freedom and flexibility or, rather, by images of violently imposed barriers, the closet? Or, in fact, is there a dialectic between freedom and imprisonment unique to lesbian writing? Do lesbians have a special perception of suffering and stigma, as so much prefeminist literature seems to suggest? What about the "muse," the female symbol of literary creativity: do women writers create a lesbian relationship with their muse as May Sarton[8] asserts? If so, do those writers who choose a female muse experience a freedom from inhibition because of that fact, or might there be a lack of creative tension in such a figurative same-sex relationship? I feel on solid ground in asserting that there are certain topics and themes that define lesbian culture, and that we are beginning to define a lesbian symbolism. Lesbian literature may present a unified tradition of thematic concerns such as that of unrequited longing, a longing of almost cosmic totality because the love object is denied not by circumstance or

5. English novelist (b. 1919), originally from Rhodesia; *The Golden Notebook* (1962) is her novel most often viewed as feminist. Lawrence (1885–1930), English poet and novelist.
6. An 1853 novel by Charlotte Brontë; Lucy Snowe teaches in a boarding school where Ginevre Fanshawe is a pupil.
7. Judith McDaniel, "Lesbians and Literature," *Sinister Wisdom* 2 (1976): 2 [Zimmerman's note].
8. American poet, novelist, and essayist (1912–1995).

chance, but by necessity. The tension between romantic love and genital sexuality takes a particular form in woman-to-woman relationships, often articulated through musings of the difference between purity and impurity (culminating in Colette's study of variant sexuality, *The Pure and the Impure*[9]). Lesbian literature approaches the theme of development or the quest in a manner different from that of men or heterosexual women. Lesbian literature, as lesbian culture in general, is particularly flexible on issues of gender and role identification; even *The Well of Loneliness* hints at the tragedy of rigid gender roles. Because of this flexibility, lesbian artists and writers have always been fascinated with costuming, because dress is an external manifestation of gender roles lesbians often reject. As we read and reread literature from a lesbian perspective, I am confident we will continue to expand our understanding of the lesbian literary tradition and a lesbian aesthetic.

This essay has suggested the vigor of lesbian criticism and its value to all feminists in raising awareness of entrenched heterosexism in existing texts, clarifying the lesbian traditions in literature through scholarship and reinterpretation, pointing out barriers that have stood in the way of free lesbian expression, explicating the recurring themes and values of lesbian literature, and exposing the dehumanizing stereotypes of lesbians in our culture. Many of the issues that face lesbian critics—resisting dogma, expanding the canon, creating a non-racist and non-classist critical vision, transforming our readings of traditional texts, and exploring new methodologies—are the interests of all feminist critics. Because feminism concerns itself with the removal of limitations and impediments in the way of female imagination, and lesbian criticism helps to expand our notions of what is *possible* for women, then all women would grow by adopting for themselves a lesbian vision. Disenfranchised groups have had to adopt a double vision for survival; one of the political transformations of recent decades has been the realization that enfranchised groups—men, whites, heterosexuals, the middle class—would do well to adopt that double vision for the survival of us all. Lesbian literary criticism simply restates what feminists already know, that one group cannot name itself "humanity" or even "woman": "We're not trying to become part of the old order misnamed 'universal' which has tabooed us; we are transforming the meaning of 'universality.' "[1] Whether lesbian criticism will survive depends as much upon the external social climate as it does upon the creativity and skill of its practitioners. If political attacks on gay rights and freedom grow; if the so-called Moral Majority[2] wins its fight to eliminate gay teachers and texts from the schools (it would be foolhardy to believe they will exempt universities); and if the academy, including feminist teachers and scholars, fails to support lesbian scholars, eradicate heterosexist values and assumptions, and incorporate the insights of lesbian scholarship into the mainstream; then current lesbian criticism will probably suffer the same fate as did Jeannette Foster's *Sex Variant Women* in the fifties. Lesbian or heterosexual, we will all suffer from that loss.

1981

9. Published in French in 1941.
1. Elly Bulkin, "An Interview with Adrienne Rich: Part II," *Conditions: Two* 1, no. 2 (1977): 58 [Zimmerman's note].
2. A conservative political organization founded in 1979 by the Baptist evangelist Jerry Falwell; it had considerable influence in U.S. politics in the 1980s and early 1990s.

SUSAN BORDO
b. 1947

Susan Bordo epitomizes feminist efforts to detail the oppression of women and the resources available for resistance. Although strongly influenced by MICHEL FOUCAULT, Bordo is wary of theory and the academy. She advocates a politically active feminism. Writing in a steely, lucid prose that reaches out to nonacademic audiences, she works against both cultural self-congratulation ("you've come a long way, baby") and the abstractions of French feminism. She insists on the practical consequences for women's daily lives of feminism's analyses of contemporary culture. Bordo's work on the physical shaping of women's bodies by cultural forces introduces a crucial gendered element into contemporary literary and cultural theory's interest in the processes involved in the formation of social subjects.

Bordo was educated at Carleton College and the State University of New York at Stony Brook, from which she received her Ph.D. in 1982. She has taught at Le Moyne College and the University of Kentucky. Trained as a philosopher, she now describes her work as "gender studies," which is "part of cultural studies." "But neither gender studies nor cultural studies," she writes, "can be of much significance unless they reach outside the academic world." She calls the "slow unlearning" of the "language" and "arrogance" of the academy her "second and ongoing education."

Bordo's early work explored the exclusionary use of terms such as "rationality" and "objectivity" in the philosophical tradition. Like others studying what came to be called "feminist epistemology," she argued that knowledge is not something achieved by a pure mind that "distances" itself from the object it studies. Rather, knowledge is "embodied," produced from a "standpoint" by a body that is located as a material entity among other material entities. Her work participates in an emerging field called "body studies."

Not all bodies are alike. Different bodies are assigned to different locations, are represented differently in prevailing cultural codes, and are accorded different authority as producers of knowledge. One crucial way to differentiate bodies is, of course, gender. Bordo turns her attention to the ways in which the body is a "text of culture." Prevailing and enforced cultural notions of gender differences are inscribed on the body, as it shapes itself to fit conventions of proper appearance, deportment, and physical activity.

Psychoanalytic feminists tend to discuss the shaping of the girl's body and of her relation to it in generalized terms that posit a triangular familial relation (mother–father–daughter) and an overarching patriarchal Law (the law of the father, compulsory heterosexuality, or the incest taboo). Bordo eschews this focus on the family, contending instead that a variety of social forces converge in the shaping of bodies—and that this constellation of forces shifts over time and from one society to another. The decline in hysteria and the recent rise in anorexia and bulimia point to changes in the cultural nexus within which bodies are produced. Like others who adopt a "social constructivist" position, Bordo argues that the body does not have a fixed and enduring nature; bodies are plastic and change in response to the social demands placed on them.

Bordo follows other contemporary feminists (such as Elaine Showalter, and SANDRA M. GILBERT and SUSAN GUBAR) in noting that women over the past two hundred years are more prone than men to suffer from a number of illnesses that occupy an ill-defined terrain between the physical and the psychological. In our selection from her book *Unbearable Weight* (1993), Bordo focuses on three such illnesses: hysteria (extreme emotional excitability), anorexia (inability or refusal to eat), and agoraphobia (inability to enter public places). She strives to demonstrate that these "pathologies of resistance" mark the ways individual women *both* insert their bodies into "the network of practices, institutions, and technologies" within which bodies are produced *and* struggle against those very networks.

Her analysis of anorexia provides an example of this doubleness. Contemporary women in the United States, Bordo argues, are pulled in multiple directions as competing demands are made on them. The anorectic's refusal to eat is tied directly to the peculiar "double bind" in which today's young woman is placed. She is expected to emulate the impossibly thin body that is presented as the ideal in countless media images, while she is also urged—in a kind of demonic parody of feminism—to take control of her own life, to be strong, to become a superwoman. The conflicting message is that only one ideal is acceptable, but you are supposed to be your own woman. Anorexia for Bordo is not solely, as in some popular accounts, the result of an obsession with thinness; it is also, crucially, a comprehensible response to powerlessness. The young woman dramatically enacts her powerlessness by playing the female role to its extreme, making its destructive underpinnings obvious. Paradoxically, this strategy also secures for her a modicum of power as she gains control over her appetite and directly resists (albeit in a self-destructive way) the family, friends, and therapists who urge her to eat.

Bordo is careful to say that cultural images are not everything. "Anorexia," she writes, "clearly contains a dimension of physical addiction to the biochemical effects of starvation." But like Foucault, she focuses on the discourses through which society produces, understands, defines, and interprets the female body. Social codings of beauty, of motherhood, of sexual modesty or its opposite place the individual woman in relation to the prevailing images and conventions. Even if that relation is one of negation and resistance, the power of the categories is still felt as the individual struggles against them. Every body is marked by its relation to the "constitutive mechanisms" of a "power" that "shapes." Femininity, for Bordo, is ideology (a culture's dominant notions of the feminine) inscribed on the body.

In presenting anorexia as a parodic demonstration of the destructive energy stored in our cultural categories, Bordo appears close to JUDITH BUTLER's influential discussion of how homosexual cross-dressing "troubles" gender categories. But Bordo has been sharply critical of Butler because she believes that Butler vastly underestimates the suffering the parodic body endures and vastly overestimates the cultural or political effectiveness of parody. Anorexia, as analyzed by Bordo, may be an eloquent bodily articulation of the unreasonable demands our society places on women, but that articulation through parody can hardly be celebrated or encouraged when its practical effects "utterly defeat rebellion and subvert protest." Anorexia is self-destructive and does nothing in itself to alter the cultural order that calls it forth. Action, Bordo insists, must come on other fronts, especially those of feminist critique and feminist political activism. In this respect, Bordo self-consciously looks back to the feminism of the late 1960s and early 1970s as a model.

The fundamental dispute between Bordo and Butler, or more widely between Anglo-American and French-oriented feminisms, rests on the question of how political and cultural transformation should be attempted. Bordo honors "female praxis": individual and collective action with clear, conscious goals that are pursued through a series of purposive strategies. Similarly, she aims for subjects who are reasonably at home in their bodies, who can experience their bodies as aligned with their purposes and aspirations in life. The anorectic demonstrates how difficult American culture makes it for women to achieve such selfhood and such a relation to their bodies, but the example of the anorectic does not lead Bordo to think the basic goal unattainable. French feminists and those influenced by them believe that such desires for self-unity are themselves symptoms of the repressive patriarchal cultural order of intelligibilty that must be transformed. All ideals of coherence, of unity, of conscious control must be problematized if we are not to repeat endlessly the enforcement of differences that characterizes existing male cultural domination. The two sides share the conviction that cultural codings are powerful and that feminism begins with an analysis of how those codings exercise power, especially over the ongoing social construction of bodies. Their disagreements over the site of the most effective cultural and political interventions continue to resonate throughout feminist theory.

BIBLIOGRAPHY

Bordo is the author of *The Flight to Objectivity: Essays on Cartesianism and Culture* (1987), *Unbearable Weight: Feminism, Western Culture, and the Body* (1993), and *Twilight Zones: The Hidden Life of Cultural Images from Plato to O.J.* (1997). She edited, with Alison M. Jaggar, *Gender/Body/Knowledge: Feminist Reconstructions of Being and Knowing* (1989). Representative reviews of *Unbearable Weight* can be found in the *New York Times Book Review*, September 26, 1993; the *London Review of Books*, March 10, 1994; and *Hypatia* 10.4 (1995). Ellen Rooney, "What Can the Matter Be?" *American Literary History* 8.4 (1995), offers a fuller engagement with Bordo's work.

From Unbearable Weight: Feminism, Western Culture, and the Body

Chapter 5. The Body and the Reproduction of Femininity

RECONSTRUCTING FEMINIST DISCOURSE ON THE BODY

The body—what we eat, how we dress, the daily rituals through which we attend to the body—is a medium of culture. The body, as anthropologist Mary Douglas has argued, is a powerful symbolic form, a surface on which the central rules, hierarchies, and even metaphysical commitments of a culture are inscribed and thus reinforced through the concrete language of the body.[1] The body may also operate as a metaphor for culture. From quarters as diverse as Plato and Hobbes to French feminist Luce Irigaray,[2] an imagination of body morphology has provided a blueprint for diagnosis and/or vision of social and political life.

The body is not only a *text* of culture. It is also, as anthropologist Pierre Bourdieu and philosopher Michel Foucault[3] (among others) have argued, a *practical*, direct locus of social control. Banally, through table manners and toilet habits, through seemingly trivial routines, rules, and practices, culture is "*made* body," as Bourdieu puts it—converted into automatic, habitual activity. As such it is put "beyond the grasp of consciousness . . . [untouchable] by voluntary, deliberate transformations."[4] Our conscious politics, social commitments, strivings for change may be undermined and betrayed by the life of our bodies—not the craving, instinctual body imagined by Plato, Augustine, and Freud,[5] but what Foucault calls the "docile body," regulated by the norms of cultural life.[6]

1. Mary Douglas, *Natural Symbols* (New York: Pantheon, 1982) and *Purity and Danger* (London: Routledge and Kegan Paul, 1966) [except as indicated, all notes are Bordo's].
2. French feminist theorist (b. 1930). PLATO (ca. 427–347 B.C.E.), Greek philosopher. Thomas Hobbes (1588–1679), English political philosopher [editor's note].
3. French philosopher and historian of ideas (1926–1984; see above). BOURDIEU (b. 1930), French social theorist [editor's note].
4. Pierre Bourdieu, *Outline of a Theory of Practice* (Cambridge: Cambridge University Press, 1977), p. 94 (emphasis in original).
5. SIGMUND FREUD (1856–1939), Austrian founder of psychoanalysis. AUGUSTINE (354–430), Christian theologian. The three thinkers all evidenced a disgust with the body, especially the female body [editor's note].
6. On docility, see Michel Foucault, *Discipline and Punish* (New York: Vintage, 1979), pp. 135–69. For a Foucauldian analysis of feminine practice, see Sandra Bartky, "Foucault, Femininity, and the Modernization of Patriarchal Power," in

Throughout his later "genealogical" works (*Discipline and Punish, The History of Sexuality*), Foucault constantly reminds us of the primacy of practice over belief. Not chiefly through ideology, but through the organization and regulation of the time, space, and movements of our daily lives, our bodies are trained, shaped, and impressed with the stamp of prevailing historical forms of selfhood, desire, masculinity, femininity. Such an emphasis casts a dark and disquieting shadow across the contemporary scene. For women, as study after study shows, are spending more time on the management and discipline of our bodies than we have in a long, long time. In a decade marked by a reopening of the public arena to women, the intensification of such regimens appears diversionary and subverting. Through the pursuit of an ever-changing, homogenizing, elusive ideal of femininity—a pursuit without a terminus, requiring that women constantly attend to minute and often whimsical changes in fashion—female bodies become docile bodies—bodies whose forces and energies are habituated to external regulation, subjection, transformation "improvement." Through the exacting and normalizing disciplines of diet, makeup, and dress—central organizing principles of time and space in the day of many women—we are rendered less socially oriented and more centripetally focused on self-modification. Through these disciplines, we continue to memorize on our bodies the feel and conviction of lack, of insufficiency, of never being good enough. At the farthest extremes, the practices of femininity may lead us to utter demoralization, debilitation, and death.

Viewed historically, the discipline and normalization of the female body—perhaps the only gender oppression that exercises itself, although to different degrees and in different forms, across age, race, class, and sexual orientation—has to be acknowledged as an amazingly durable and flexible strategy of social control. In our own era, it is difficult to avoid the recognition that the contemporary preoccupation with appearance, which still affects women far more powerfully than men, even in our narcissistic and visually oriented culture, may function as a backlash phenomenon, reasserting existing gender configurations against any attempts to shift or transform power relations.[7] Surely we are in the throes of this backlash today. In newspapers and magazines we daily encounter stories that promote traditional gender relations and prey on anxieties about change: stories about latch-key children, abuse in day-care centers, the "new woman's" troubles with men, her lack of marriageability, and so on. A dominant visual theme in teenage magazines involves women hiding in the shadows of men, seeking solace in their arms,

her *Femininity and Domination* (New York: Routledge, 1990); see also Susan Brownmiller, *Femininity* (New York: Ballantine, 1984).

7. During the late 1970s and 1980s, male concern over appearance undeniably increased. Study after study confirms, however, that there is still a large gender gap in this area. Research conducted at the University of Pennsylvania in 1985 found men to be generally satisfied with their appearance, often, in fact, "distorting their perceptions [of themselves] in a positive, self-aggrandizing way" ("Dislike of Own Bodies Found Common among Women," *New York Times*, March 19, 1985, p. C1). Women, however, were found to exhibit extreme negative assessments and distortions of body perception. Other studies have suggested that women are judged more harshly than men when they deviate from dominant social standards of attractiveness. Thomas Cash et al., in "The Great American Shape-Up," *Psychology Today*, April 1986, p. 34, report that although the situation for men has changed, the situation for women has more than proportionally worsened. Citing results from 30,000 responses to a 1985 survey of perceptions of body image and comparing similar responses to a 1972 questionnaire, they report that the 1985 respondents were considerably more dissatisfied with their bodies than the 1972 respondents, and they note a marked intensification of concern among men. Among the 1985 group, the group most dissatisfied of all with their appearance, however, were teenage women. Women today constitute by far the largest number of consumers of diet products, attenders of spas and diet centers, and subjects of intestinal by-pass and other fat-reduction operations.

willingly contracting the space they occupy. The last, of course, also describes our contemporary aesthetic ideal for women, an ideal whose obsessive pursuit has become the central torment of many women's lives. In such an era we desperately need an effective political discourse about the female body, a discourse adequate to an analysis of the insidious, and often paradoxical, pathways of modern social control.

Developing such a discourse requires reconstructing the feminist paradigm of the late 1960s and early 1970s, with its political categories of oppressors and oppressed, villains and victims. Here I believe that a feminist appropriation of some of Foucault's later concepts can prove useful. Following Foucault, we must first abandon the idea of power as something possessed by one group and leveled against another; we must instead think of the network of practices, institutions, and technologies that sustain positions of dominance and subordination in a particular domain.

Second, we need an analytics adequate to describe a power whose central mechanisms are not repressive, but *constitutive*: "a power bent on generating forces, making them grow, and ordering them, rather than one dedicated to impeding them, making them submit, or destroying them." Particularly in the realm of femininity, where so much depends on the seemingly willing acceptance of various norms and practices, we need an analysis of power "from below," as Foucault puts it; for example, of the mechanisms that shape and proliferate—rather than repress—desire, generate and focus our energies, construct our conceptions of normalcy and deviance.[8]

And, third, we need a discourse that will enable us to account for the subversion of potential rebellion, a discourse that, while insisting on the necessity of objective analysis of power relations, social hierarchy, political backlash, and so forth, will nonetheless allow us to confront the mechanisms by which the subject at times becomes enmeshed in collusion with forces that sustain her own oppression.

This essay will not attempt to produce a general theory along these lines. Rather, my focus will be the analysis of one particular arena where the interplay of these dynamics is striking and perhaps exemplary. It is a limited and unusual arena, that of a group of gender-related and historically localized disorders: hysteria, agoraphobia, and anorexia nervosa.[9] I recognize that these disorders have also historically been class- and race-biased, largely (although not exclusively) occurring among white middle- and upper-middle-class women. Nonetheless, anorexia, hysteria, and agoraphobia may provide

8. Michel Foucault, *The History of Sexuality*, vol. 1, *An Introduction* (New York: Vintage, 1980), pp. 136, 94.

9. On the gendered and historical nature of these disorders: the number of female to male hysterics has been estimated at anywhere from 2:1 to 4:1, and as many as 80 percent of all agoraphobics are female (Annette Brodsky and Rachel Hare-Mustin, *Women and Psychotherapy* [New York: Guilford Press, 1980], pp. 116, 122). Although more cases of male eating disorders have been reported in the late eighties and early nineties, it is estimated that close to 90 percent of all anorectics are female (Paul Garfinkel and David Garner, *Anorexia Nervosa: A Multidimensional Perspective* [New York: Brunner/Mazel, 1982], pp. 112–13). For a sophisticated account of female psychopathology, with particular attention to nineteenth-century disorders but, unfortunately, little mention of agoraphobia or eating disorders, see Elaine Showalter, *The Female Malady: Women, Madness and English Culture*, 1830–1980 (New York: Pantheon, 1985). For a discussion of social and gender issues in agoraphobia, see Robert Seidenberg and Karen DeCrow, *Women Who Marry Houses: Panic and Protest in Agoraphobia* (New York: McGraw-Hill, 1983). On the history of anorexia nervosa, see Joan Jacobs Brumberg, *Fasting Girls: The Emergence of Anorexia Nervosa as a Modern Disease* (Cambridge: Harvard University Press, 1988). ["Hysteria": a psychoneurosis marked by emotional excitability. The word derives from the Greek word for womb; it was thought that such ailments were peculiar to women and caused by disturbances of the uterus—editor's note.]

a paradigm of one way in which potential resistance is not merely undercut but *utilized* in the maintenance and reproduction of existing power relations.[1]

The central mechanism I will describe involves a transformation (or, if you wish, duality) of meaning, through which conditions that are objectively (and, on one level, experientially) constraining, enslaving, and even murderous, come to be experienced as liberating, transforming, and life-giving. I offer this analysis, although limited to a specific domain, as an example of how various contemporary critical discourses may be joined to yield an understanding of the subtle and often unwitting role played by our bodies in the symbolization and reproduction of gender.

THE BODY AS A TEXT OF FEMININITY

The continuum between female disorder and "normal" feminine practice is sharply revealed through a close reading of those disorders to which women have been particularly vulnerable. These, of course, have varied historically: neurasthenia[2] and hysteria in the second half of the nineteenth century; agoraphobia and, most dramatically, anorexia nervosa and bulimia in the second half of the twentieth century. This is not to say that anorectics did not exist in the nineteenth century—many cases were described, usually in the context of diagnoses of hysteria[3]—or that women no longer suffer from classical hysterical symptoms in the twentieth century. But the taking up of eating disorders on a mass scale is as unique to the culture of the 1980s as the epidemic of hysteria was to the Victorian era.[4]

The symptomatology of these disorders reveals itself as textuality. Loss of mobility, loss of voice, inability to leave the home, feeding others while starving oneself, taking up space, and whittling down the space one's body takes up—all have symbolic meaning, all have *political* meaning under the varying rules governing the historical construction of gender. Working within this framework, we see that whether we look at hysteria, agoraphobia, or anorexia, we find the body of the sufferer deeply inscribed with an ideological construction of femininity emblematic of the period in question. The construction, of course, is always homogenizing and normalizing, erasing racial, class, and other differences and insisting that all women aspire to a coercive, standardized ideal. Strikingly, in these disorders the construction of femininity is written in disturbingly concrete, hyperbolic terms: exaggerated, extremely literal, at times virtually caricatured presentations of the ruling feminine mystique. The bodies of disordered women in this way offer themselves as an aggressively graphic text for the interpreter—a text that insists, actually demands, that it be read as a cultural statement, a statement about gender.

1. In constructing such a paradigm I do not pretend to do justice to any of these disorders in its individual complexity. My aim is to chart some points of intersection, to describe some similar patterns, as they emerge through a particular reading of the phenomenon—a political reading, if you will.
2. An emotional and psychic disorder characterized by easy fatigability and often by lack of motivation, as well as feelings of inadequacy [editor's note].
3. Showalter, *The Female Malady*, pp. 128–29.
4. On the epidemic of hysteria and neurasthenia, see Showalter, *The Female Malady*; Carroll Smith-Rosenberg, "The Hysterical Woman: Sex Roles and Role Conflict in Nineteenth-Century America," in her *Disorderly Conduct: Visions of Gender in Victorian America* (Oxford: Oxford University Press, 1985).

Both nineteenth-century male physicians and twentieth-century feminist critics have seen, in the symptoms of neurasthenia and hysteria (syndromes that became increasingly less differentiated as the century wore on), an exaggeration of stereotypically feminine traits. The nineteenth-century "lady" was idealized in terms of delicacy and dreaminess, sexual passivity, and a charmingly labile and capricious emotionality.[5] Such notions were formalized and scientized in the work of male theorists from Acton and Krafft-Ebing[6] to Freud, who described "normal," mature femininity in such terms.[7] In this context, the dissociations, the drifting and fogging of perception, the nervous tremors and faints, the anesthesias,[8] and the extreme mutability of symptomatology associated with nineteenth-century female disorders can be seen to be concretizations of the feminine mystique of the period, produced according to rules that governed the prevailing construction of femininity. Doctors described what came to be known as the hysterical personality as "impressionable, suggestible, and narcissistic; highly labile, their moods changing suddenly, dramatically, and seemingly for inconsequential reasons . . . egocentric in the extreme . . . essentially asexual and not uncommonly frigid"[9]—all characteristics normative of femininity in this era. As Elaine Showalter points out, the term *hysterical* itself became almost interchangeable with the term *feminine* in the literature of the period.[1]

The hysteric's embodiment of the feminine mystique of her era, however, seems subtle and ineffable compared to the ingenious literalism of agoraphobia and anorexia. In the context of our culture this literalism makes sense. With the advent of movies and television, the rules for femininity have come to be culturally transmitted more and more through standardized visual images. As a result, femininity itself has come to be largely a matter of constructing, in the manner described by Erving Goffman, the appropriate surface presentation of the self.[2] We are no longer given verbal descriptions or exemplars of what a lady is or of what femininity consists. Rather, we learn the rules directly through bodily discourse: through images that tell us what clothes, body shape, facial expression, movements, and behavior are required.

In agoraphobia and, even more dramatically, in anorexia, the disorder presents itself as a virtual, though tragic, parody of twentieth-century constructions of femininity. The 1950s and early 1960s, when agoraphobia first began to escalate among women, was a period of reassertion of domesticity and

5. Martha Vicinus, "Introduction: The Perfect Victorian Lady," in Martha Vicinus, ed., *Suffer and Be Still: Women in the Victorian Age* (Bloomington: Indiana University Press, 1972), pp. x–xi.
6. Richard von Kraft-Ebing (1840–1902), German physician who wrote about sexual behavior, especially sexual "pathologies." William Acton (1813–1875), English doctor and civil servant who wrote physician's manuals on sexuality that codify Victorian stereotypes [editor's note].
7. See Carol Nadelson and Malkah Notman, *The Female Patient* (New York: Plenum, 1982), p. 5; E. M. Sigsworth and T. J. Wyke, "A Study of Victorian Prostitution and Venereal Disease," in Vicinus, *Suffer and Be Still*, p. 82. For more general discussions, see Peter Gay, *The Bourgeois Experience: Victoria to Freud*, vol. 1, *Education of the Senses* (New York: Oxford University Press, 1984), esp. pp. 109–68; Showalter, *The Female Malady*, esp. pp. 121–44. The delicate lady, an ideal that had very strong class connotations (as does slenderness today), is not the only conception of femininity to be found in Victorian cultures. But it was arguably the single most powerful ideological representation of femininity in that era, affecting women of all classes, including those without the material means to realize the ideal fully. See Helena Mitchie, *The Flesh Made Word* (New York: Oxford University Press, 1987), for discussions of the control of female appetite and Victorian constructions of femininity.
8. Losses of feeling in various parts of the body [editor's note].
9. Smith-Rosenberg, *Disorderly Conduct*, p. 203.
1. Showalter, *The Female Malady*, p. 129.
2. Erving Goffman, *The Presentation of Self in Everyday Life* (Garden City, N.Y.: Anchor Doubleday, 1959).

dependency as the feminine ideal. *Career woman* became a dirty word, much more so than it had been during the war, when the economy depended on women's willingness to do "men's work." The reigning ideology of femininity, so well described by Betty Friedan and perfectly captured in the movies and television shows of the era, was childlike, nonassertive, helpless without a man, "content in a world of bedroom and kitchen, sex, babies and home."[3] The housebound agoraphobic lives this construction of femininity literally. "You want me in this home? You'll have me in this home—with a vengeance!" The point, upon which many therapists have commented, does not need belaboring. Agoraphobia, as I. G. Fodor has put it, seems "the logical—albeit extreme—extension of the cultural sex-role stereotype for women" in this era.[4]

The emaciated body of the anorectic, of course, immediately presents itself as a caricature of the contemporary ideal of hyperslenderness for women, an ideal that, despite the game resistance of racial and ethnic difference, has become the norm for women today. But slenderness is only the tip of the iceberg, for slenderness itself requires interpretation. "C'est le sens qui fait vendre," said Barthes, speaking of clothing styles—it is meaning that makes the sale.[5] So, too, it is meaning that makes the body admirable. To the degree that anorexia may be said to be "about" slenderness, it is about slenderness, as a citadel of contemporary and historical meaning, not as an empty fashion ideal. As such, the interpretation of slenderness yields multiple readings, some related to gender, some not. For the purposes of this essay I will offer an abbreviated, gender-focused reading. But I must stress that this reading illuminates only partially, and that many other currents not discussed here—economic, psychosocial, and historical, as well as ethnic and class dimensions—figure prominently.[6]

We begin with the painfully literal inscription, on the anorectic's body, of the rules governing the construction of contemporary femininity. That construction is a double bind[7] that legislates contradictory ideals and directives. On the one hand, our culture still widely advertises domestic conceptions of femininity, the ideological moorings for a rigorously dualistic sexual division of labor that casts woman as chief emotional and physical nurturer. The rules for this construction of femininity (and I speak here in a language both symbolic and literal) require that women learn to feed others, not the self, and to construe any desires for self-nurturance and self-feeding as greedy and excessive.[8] Thus, women must develop a totally other-oriented emotional

3. Betty Friedan, *The Feminine Mystique* (New York: Dell, 1962), p. 36. The theme song of one such show ran, in part: "I married Joan . . . What a girl . . . what a whirl . . . what a life! I married Joan . . . What a mind . . . love is blind . . . what a wife!" [From *I Married Joan*, an NBC sitcom (1952–55)—editor's note.]

4. See I. G. Fodor, "The Phobic Syndrome in Women," in V. Franks and V. Burtle, eds., *Women in Therapy* (New York: Brunner/Mazel, 1974), p. 119; see also Kathleen Brehony, "Women and Agoraphobia," in Violet Franks and Esther Rothblum, eds., *The Stereotyping of Women* (New York: Springer, 1983).

5. In Jonathan Culler, *Roland Barthes* (New York: Oxford University Press, 1983), p. 74. [BARTHES (1915–1980), French literary critic—editor's note.]

6. For other interpretive perspectives on the slenderness ideal, see "Reading the Slender Body" in *Unbearable Weight* (1993); Kim Chernin, *The Obsession: Reflections on the Tyranny of Slenderness* (New York: Harper and Row, 1981); Susie Orbach, *Hunger Strike: The Anorectic's Struggle as a Metaphor for Our Age* (New York: W. W. Norton, 1985).

7. A psychological predicament in which a person receives from a single source conflicting messages that allow no appropriate response. First coined in 1956 by the Scottish psychologist R. D. Laing in his study of schizophrenic children, the term is now used more broadly [editor's note].

8. See my "Hunger as Ideology" in *Unbearable Weight* for a discussion of how this construction of femininity is reproduced in contemporary commercials and advertisements concerning food, eating, and cooking.

economy. In this economy, the control of female appetite for food is merely the most concrete expression of the general rule governing the construction of femininity: that female hunger—for public power, for independence, for sexual gratification—be contained, and the public space that women be allowed to take up be circumscribed, limited. * * * [S]lenderness, set off against the resurgent muscularity and bulk of the current male body-ideal, carries connotations of fragility and lack of power in the face of a decisive male occupation of social space. On the body of the anorexic woman such rules are grimly and deeply etched.

On the other hand, even as young women today continue to be taught traditionally "feminine" virtues, to the degree that the professional arena is open to them they must also learn to embody the "masculine" language and values of that arena—self-control, determination, cool, emotional discipline, mastery, and so on. Female bodies now speak symbolically of this necessity in their slender spare shape and the currently fashionable men's-wear look. * * * Our bodies, too, as we trudge to the gym every day and fiercely resist both our hungers and our desire to soothe ourselves, are becoming more and more practiced at the "male" virtues of control and self-mastery. * * * The anorectic pursues these virtues with single-minded, unswerving dedication. "Energy, discipline, my own power will keep me going," says ex-anorectic Aimee Liu, recreating her anorexic days. "I need nothing and no one else. . . . I will be master of my own body, if nothing else, I vow."[9]

The ideal of slenderness, then, and the diet and exercise regimens that have become inseparable from it offer the illusion of meeting, through the body, the contradictory demands of the contemporary ideology of femininity. Popular images reflect this dual demand. In a single issue of *Complete Woman* magazine, two articles appear, one on "Feminine Intuition," the other asking, "Are You the New Macho Woman?" In *Vision Quest*,[1] the young male hero falls in love with the heroine, as he says, because "she has all the best things I like in girls and all the best things I like in guys," that is, she's tough and cool, but warm and alluring. In the enormously popular *Aliens*, the heroine's personality has been deliberately constructed, with near–comic book explicitness, to embody traditional nurturant femininity alongside breathtaking macho prowess and control; Sigourney Weaver, the actress who portrays her, has called the character "Rambolina."[2]

In the pursuit of slenderness and the denial of appetite the traditional construction of femininity intersects with the new requirement for women to embody the "masculine" values of the public arena. The anorectic, as I have argued, embodies this intersection, this double bind, in a particularly painful and graphic way.[3] I mean *double bind* quite literally here. "Mascu-

9. Aimee Liu, *Solitaire* (New York: Harper and Row, 1979), p. 123.

1. A 1985 film directed by Harold Becker [editor's note].

2. That is, a feminine version of the excessively masculine hero (played by Sylvester Stallone) of the popular Rambo movies: *First Blood* (1982), *Rambo: First Blood Part II* (1985), and *Rambo III* (1988). *Aliens* (1986), a film directed by James Cameron [editor's note].

3. Striking, in connection with this, is Catherine Steiner-Adair's 1986 study of high-school women, which reveals a dramatic association between problems with food and body image and emulation of the cool, professionally "together" and gorgeous superwoman. On the basis of a series of interviews, the high schoolers were classified into two groups: one expressed skepticism over the superwoman ideal, the other thoroughly aspired to it. Later administrations of diagnostic tests revealed that 94 percent of the pro-superwoman group fell into the eating-disordered range of the scale. Of the other group, 100 percent fell into the noneating-disordered range. Media images notwithstanding, young women today appear to sense, either consciously or through their bodies, the

linity" and "femininity," at least since the nineteenth century and arguably before, have been constructed through a process of mutual exclusion. One cannot simply add the historically feminine virtues to the historically masculine ones to yield a New Woman, a New Man, a new ethics, or a new culture. Even on the screen or on television, embodied in created characters like the *Aliens* heroine, the result is a parody. Unfortunately, in this image-bedazzled culture, we find it increasingly difficult to discriminate between parodies and possibilities for the self. Explored as a possibility for the self, the "androgynous" ideal ultimately exposes its internal contradiction and becomes a war that tears the subject in two—a war explicitly thematized, by many anorectics, as a battle between male and female sides of the self.[4]

PROTEST AND RETREAT IN THE SAME GESTURE

In hysteria, agoraphobia, and anorexia, then, the woman's body may be viewed as a surface on which conventional constructions of femininity are exposed starkly to view, through their inscription in extreme or hyperliteral form. They are written, of course, in languages of horrible suffering. It is as though these bodies are speaking to us of the pathology and violence that lurks just around the corner, waiting at the horizon of "normal" femininity. It is no wonder that a steady motif in the feminist literature on female disorder is that of pathology as embodied *protest*—unconscious, inchoate, and counterproductive protest without an effective language, voice, or politics, but protest nonetheless.

American and French feminists[5] alike have heard the hysteric speaking a language of protest, even or perhaps especially when she was mute. Dianne Hunter interprets Anna O.'s[6] aphasia, which manifested itself in an inability to speak her native German, as a rebellion against the linguistic and cultural rules of the father and a return to the "mother-tongue": the semiotic babble of infancy, the language of the body. For Hunter, and for a number of other feminists working with Lacanian categories, the return to the semiotic level is both regressive and, as Hunter puts it, an "expressive" communication "addressed to patriarchal thought," "a self-repudiating form of feminine discourse in which the body signifies what social conditions make it impossible to state linguistically."[7] "The hysterics are accusing; they are pointing," writes Catherine Clément in *The Newly Born Woman*; they make a "mockery of culture."[8] In the same volume, Hélène Cixous speaks of "those wonderful hysterics, who subjected Freud to so many voluptuous moments too shameful to mention, bombarding his mosaic statute/law of Moses with their carnal, passionate body-words, haunting him with their inaudible thundering

impossibility of simultaneously meeting the demands of two spheres whose values have been historically defined in utter opposition to each other.

4. See my "Anorexia Nervosa" in *Unbearable Weight*.

5. That is, feminists whose approach is primarily sociological ("American") and feminists whose orientation is more psychoanalytic ("French") [editor's note].

6. The pseudonym for the hysteric patient discussed in Freud's first published case history (cowritten with Joseph Breuer) [editor's note].

7. Dianne Hunter, "Hysteria, Psychoanalysis and Feminism," in Shirley Garner, Claire Kahane, and Madelon Sprengnether, eds., *The (M)Other Tongue* (Ithaca: Cornell University Press, 1986), p. 42. [Lacanian: derived from the work of the French psychoanalyst JACQUES LACAN (1901–1981). Semiotic level: a mother-oriented use of language postulated by the French feminist JULIA KRISTEVA (b. 1941)—editor's note.]

8. Catherine Clément and Hélène Cixous, *The Newly Born Woman*, trans. Betsy Wing (Minneapolis: University of Minnesota Press, 1986), p. 42.

denunciations." For Cixous, Dora, who so frustrated Freud, is "the core example of the protesting force in women."[9]

The literature of protest includes functional as well as symbolic approaches. Robert Seidenberg and Karen DeCrow, for example, describe agoraphobia as a "strike" against "the renunciations usually demanded of women" and the expectations of housewifely functions such as shopping, driving the children to school, accompanying their husband to social events.[1] Carroll Smith-Rosenberg presents a similar analysis of hysteria, arguing that by preventing the woman from functioning in the wifely role of caretaker of others, of "ministering angel" to husband and children, hysteria "became one way in which conventional women could express—in most cases unconsciously—dissatisfaction with one or several aspects of their lives."[2] A number of feminist writers, among whom Susie Orbach is the most articulate and forceful, have interpreted anorexia as a species of unconscious feminist protest. The anorectic is engaged in a "hunger strike," as Orbach calls it, stressing that this is a political discourse, in which the action of food refusal and dramatic transformation of body size "expresses with [the] body what [the anorectic] is unable to tell us with words"—her indictment of a culture that disdains and suppresses female hunger, makes women ashamed of their appetites and needs, and demands that women constantly work on the transformation of their body.[3]

The anorectic, of course, is unaware that she is making a political statement. She may, indeed, be hostile to feminism and any other critical perspectives that she views as disputing her own autonomy and control or questioning the cultural ideals around which her life is organized. Through embodied rather than deliberate demonstration she exposes and indicts those ideals, precisely by pursuing them to the point at which their destructive potential is revealed for all to see.

The same gesture that expresses protest, moreover, can also signal retreat; this, indeed, may be part of the symptom's attraction. Kim Chernin, for example, argues that the debilitating anorexic fixation, by halting or mitigating personal development, assuages this generation's guilt and separation

9. Clément and Cixous, *The Newly Born Woman*, p. 95. [Dora: the pseudonym of the patient discussed in Freud's *Dora: An Analysis of a Case of Hysteria* (1904). The case has attracted much feminist attention because Freud discounts what seems the fairly obvious sexual abuse of the young Dora by several older men in her circle while imputing various deviant sexual desires to Dora herself. The French feminist CIXOUS (b. 1937) wrote a play about Dora—editor's note.]

1. Seidenberg and DeCrow, *Women Who Marry Houses*, p. 31.

2. Smith-Rosenberg, *Disorderly Conduct*, p. 208.

3. Orbach, *Hunger Strike*, p. 102. When we look into the many autobiographies and case studies of hysterics, anorectics, and agoraphobics, we find that these are indeed the sorts of women one might expect to be frustrated by the constraints of a specified female role. Sigmund Freud and Joseph Breuer, in *Studies on Hysteria* (New York: Avon, 1966), and Freud, in the later *Dora: An Analysis of a Case of Hysteria* (New York: Macmillan, 1963), constantly remark on the ambitiousness, independence, intellectual ability, and creative strivings of their patients. We know, moreover, that many women who later became leading social activists and feminists of the nineteenth century were among those who fell ill with hysteria and neurasthenia. It has become a virtual cliché that the typical anorectic is a perfectionist, driven to excel in all areas of her life. Though less prominently, a similar theme runs throughout the literature on agoraphobia.

One must keep in mind that in drawing on case studies, one is relying on the perceptions of other acculturated individuals. One suspects, for example, that the popular portrait of the anorectic as a relentless overachiever may be colored by the lingering or perhaps resurgent Victorianism of our culture's attitudes toward ambitious women. One does not escape this hermeneutic problem by turning to autobiography. But in autobiography one is at least dealing with social constructions and attitudes that animate the subject's own psychic reality. In this regard the autobiographical literature on anorexia, drawn on in a variety of places in *Unbearable Weight*, is strikingly full of anxiety about the domestic world and other themes that suggest deep rebellion against traditional notions of femininity.

anxiety over the prospect of surpassing our mothers, of living less circumscribed, freer lives.[4] Agoraphobia, too, which often develops shortly after marriage, clearly functions in many cases as a way to cement dependency and attachment in the face of unacceptable stirrings of dissatisfaction and restlessness.

Although we may talk meaningfully of protest, then, I want to emphasize the counterproductive, tragically self-defeating (indeed, self-deconstructing) nature of that protest. Functionally, the symptoms of these disorders isolate, weaken, and undermine the sufferers; at the same time they turn the life of the body into an all-absorbing fetish, beside which all other objects of attention pale into unreality. On the symbolic level, too, the protest collapses into its opposite and proclaims the utter capitulation of the subject to the contracted female world. The muteness of hysterics and their return to the level of pure, primary bodily expressivity have been interpreted, as we have seen, as rejecting the symbolic order of the patriarchy and recovering a lost world of semiotic, maternal value. But *at the same time*, of course, muteness is the condition of the silent, uncomplaining woman—an ideal of patriarchal culture. Protesting the stifling of the female voice through one's own voicelessness—that is, employing the language of femininity to protest the conditions of the female world—will always involve ambiguities of this sort. Perhaps this is why symptoms crystallized from the language of femininity are so perfectly suited to express the dilemmas of middle-class and upper-middle-class women living in periods poised on the edge of gender change, women who have the social and material resources to carry the traditional construction of femininity to symbolic excess but who also confront the anxieties of new possibilities. The late nineteenth century, the post–World War II period, and the late twentieth century are all periods in which gender becomes an issue to be discussed and in which discourse proliferates about "the Woman Question," "the New Woman," "What Women Want," "What Femininity Is."

COLLUSION, RESISTANCE, AND THE BODY

The pathologies of female protest function, paradoxically, as if in collusion with the cultural conditions that produce them, reproducing rather than transforming precisely that which is being protested. In this connection, the fact that hysteria and anorexia have peaked during historical periods of cultural backlash against attempts at reorganization and redefinition of male and female roles is significant. Female pathology reveals itself here as an extremely interesting social formation through which one source of potential for resistance and rebellion is pressed into the service of maintaining the established order.

In our attempt to explain this formation, objective accounts of power relations fail us. For whatever the objective social conditions are that create a pathology, the symptoms themselves must still be produced (however unconsciously or inadvertently) by the subject. That is, the individual must invest the body with meanings of various sorts. Only by examining this productive process on the part of the subject can we, as Mark Poster has put it, "illuminate the mechanisms of domination in the processes through which mean-

4. Kim Chernin, *The Hungry Self: Women, Eating, and Identity* (New York: Harper and Row, 1985), esp. pp. 41–93.

ing is produced in everyday life"; that is, only then can we see how the desires and dreams of the subject become implicated in the matrix of power relations.[5]

Here, examining the context in which the anorexic syndrome is produced may be illuminating. Anorexia will erupt, typically, in the course of what begins as a fairly moderate diet regime, undertaken because someone, often the father, has made a casual critical remark. Anorexia *begins in*, emerges out of, what is, in our time, conventional feminine practice. In the course of that practice, for any number of individual reasons, the practice is pushed a little beyond the parameters of moderate dieting. The young woman discovers what it feels like to crave and want and need and yet, through the exercise of her own will, to triumph over that need. In the process, a new realm of meanings is discovered, a range of values and possibilities that Western culture has traditionally coded as "male" and rarely made available to women: an ethic and aesthetic of self-mastery and self-transcendence, expertise, and power over others through the example of superior will and control. The experience is intoxicating, habit-forming.

At school the anorectic discovers that her steadily shrinking body is admired, not so much as an aesthetic or sexual object, but for the strength of will and self-control it projects. At home she discovers, in the inevitable battles her parents fight to get her to eat, that her actions have enormous power over the lives of those around her. As her body begins to lose its traditional feminine curves, its breasts and hips and rounded stomach, begins to feel and look more like a spare, lanky male body, she begins to feel untouchable, out of reach of hurt, "invulnerable, clean and hard as the bones etched into my silhouette," as one student described it in her journal. She despises, in particular, all those parts of her body that continue to mark her as female. "If only I could eliminate [my breasts]," says Liu, "cut them off if need be."[6] For her, as for many anorectics, the breasts represent a bovine, unconscious, vulnerable side of the self. Liu's body symbolism is thoroughly continuous with dominant cultural associations. Brett Silverstein's studies on the "Possible Causes of the Thin Standard of Bodily Attractiveness for Women"[7] testify empirically to what is obvious from every comedy routine involving a dramatically shapely woman: namely, our cultural association of curvaceousness with incompetence. The anorectic is also quite aware, of course, of the social and sexual vulnerability involved in having a female body; many, in fact, were sexually abused as children.

Through her anorexia, by contrast, she has unexpectedly discovered an entry into the privileged male world, a way to become what is valued in our culture, a way to become safe, to rise above it all—for her, they are the same thing. She has discovered this, paradoxically, by pursuing conventional feminine behavior—in this case, the discipline of perfecting the body as an object—to excess. At this point of excess, the conventionally feminine deconstructs, we might say, into its opposite and opens onto those values our culture has coded as male. No wonder the anorexia is experienced as liberating and that she will fight family, friends, and therapists in an effort

5. Mark Poster, *Foucault, Marxism, and History* (Cambridge: Polity Press, 1984), p. 28.
6. Liu, *Solitaire*, p. 99.
7. Brett Silverstein, "Possible Causes of the Thin Standard of Bodily Attractiveness for Women," *International Journal of Eating Disorders* 5 (1986): 907–16.

to hold onto it—fight them to the death, if need be. The anorectic's experience of power is, of course, deeply and dangerously illusory. To reshape one's body into a male body is *not* to put on male power and privilege. To *feel* autonomous and free while harnessing body and soul to an obsessive body-practice is to serve, not transform, a social order that limits female possibilities. And, of course, for the female to become male is only for her to locate herself on the other side of a disfiguring opposition. The new "power look" of female body-building, which encourages women to develop the same hulk-like, triangular shape that has been the norm for male body-builders, is no less determined by a hierarchical, dualistic construction of gender than was the conventionally "feminine" norm that tyrannized female body-builders such as Bev Francis for years.

Although the specific cultural practices and meanings are different, similar mechanisms, I suspect, are at work in hysteria and agoraphobia. In these cases too, the language of femininity, when pushed to excess—when shouted and asserted, when disruptive and demanding—deconstructs into its opposite and makes available to the woman an illusory experience of power previously forbidden to her by virtue of her gender. In the case of nineteenth-century femininity, the forbidden experience may have been the bursting of fetters—particularly moral and emotional fetters. John Conolly, the asylum reformer, recommended institutionalization for women who "want that restraint over the passions without which the female character is lost."[8] Hysterics often infuriated male doctors by their lack of precisely this quality. S. Weir Mitchell described these patients as "the despair of physicians," whose "despotic selfishness wrecks the constitution of nurses and devoted relatives, and in unconscious or half-conscious self-indulgence destroys the comfort of everyone around them."[9] It must have given the Victorian patient some illicit pleasure to be viewed as capable of such disruption of the staid nineteenth-century household. A similar form of power, I believe, is part of the experience of agoraphobia.

This does not mean that the primary reality of these disorders is not one of pain and entrapment. Anorexia, too, clearly contains a dimension of physical addiction to the biochemical effects of starvation. But whatever the physiology involved, the ways in which the subject understands and thematizes her experience cannot be reduced to a mechanical process. The anorectic's ability to live with minimal food intake allows her to feel powerful and worthy of admiration in a "world," as Susie Orbach describes it, "from which at the most profound level [she] feels excluded" and unvalued.[1] The literature on both anorexia and hysteria is strewn with battles of will between the sufferer and those trying to "cure" her; the latter, as Orbach points out, very rarely understand that the psychic values she is fighting for are often more important to the woman than life itself.

TEXTUALITY, PRAXIS, AND THE BODY

The "solutions" offered by anorexia, hysteria, and agoraphobia, I have suggested, develop out of the practice of femininity itself, the pursuit of which is still presented as the chief route to acceptance and success for women in

8. Showalter, *The Female Malady*, p. 48.
9. Smith-Rosenberg, *Disorderly Conduct*, p. 207.
1. Orbach, *Hunger Strike*, p. 103.

our culture. Too aggressively pursued, that practice leads to its own undoing, in one sense. For if femininity is, as Susan Brownmiller has said, at its core a "tradition of imposed limitations,"[2] then an unwillingness to limit oneself, even in the pursuit of femininity, breaks the rules. But, of course, in another sense the rules remain fully in place. The sufferer becomes wedded to an obsessive practice, unable to make any effective change in her life. She remains, as Toril Moi has put it, "gagged and chained to [the] feminine role," a reproducer of the docile body of femininity.[3]

This tension between the psychological meaning of a disorder, which may enact fantasies of rebellion and embody a language of protest, and the practical life of the disordered body, which may utterly defeat rebellion and subvert protest, may be obscured by too exclusive a focus on the symbolic dimension and insufficient attention to praxis. As we have seen in the case of some Lacanian feminist readings of hysteria, the result of this can be a one-sided interpretation that romanticizes the hysteric's symbolic subversion of the phallocentric[4] order while confined to her bed. This is not to say that confinement in bed has a transparent, univocal meaning—in powerlessness, debilitation, dependency, and so forth. The "practical" body is no brute biological or material entity. It, too, is a culturally mediated form; its activities are subject to interpretation and description. The shift to the practical dimension is not a turn to biology or nature, but to another "register," as Foucault puts it, of the cultural body, the register of the "useful body" rather than the "intelligible body."[5] The distinction can prove useful, I believe, to feminist discourse.

The intelligible body includes our scientific, philosophic, and aesthetic representations of the body—our cultural *conceptions* of the body, norms of beauty, models of health, and so forth. But the same representations may also be seen as forming a set of *practical* rules and regulations through which the living body is "trained, shaped, obeys, responds," becoming, in short, a socially adapted and "useful body."[6] Consider this particularly clear and appropriate example: the nineteenth-century hourglass figure, emphasizing breasts and hips against a wasp waist, was an intelligible *symbolic* form, representing a domestic, sexualized ideal of femininity. The sharp cultural contrast between the female and the male form, made possible by the use of corsets and bustles, reflected, in symbolic terms, the dualistic division of social and economic life into clearly defined male and female spheres. At the same time, to achieve the specified look, a particular feminine *praxis* was required—straitlacing, minimal eating, reduced mobility—rendering the female body unfit to perform activities outside its designated sphere. This, in Foucauldian terms, would be the "useful body" corresponding to the aesthetic norm.

The intelligible body and the useful body are two arenas of the same discourse; they often mirror and support each other, as in the above illustration. Another example can be found in the seventeenth-century philosophic conception of the body as a machine, mirroring an increasingly more automated

2. Brownmiller, *Femininity*, p. 14.
3. Toril Moi, "Representations of Patriarchy: Sex and Epistemology in Freud's *Dora*," in Charles Bernheimer and Claire Kahane, eds., *In Dora's Case: Freud—Hysteria—Feminism* (New York: Columbia University Press, 1985), p. 192.
4. Patriarchal; specifically, characterized by the authority of the phallus in the primal family made up of the dominant father and the subordinate mother and child [editor's note].
5. Foucault, *Discipline and Punish*, p. 136.
6. Foucault, *Discipline and Punish*, p. 136.

productive machinery of labor. But the two bodies may also contradict and mock each other. A range of contemporary representations and images, as noted earlier, have coded the transcendence of female appetite and its public display in the slenderness ideal in terms of power, will, mastery, the possibilities of success in the professional arena. These associations are carried visually by the slender superwomen of prime-time television and popular movies and promoted explicitly in advertisements and articles appearing routinely in women's fashion magazines, diet books, and weight-training publications. Yet the thousands of slender girls and women who strive to embody these images and who in that service suffer from eating disorders, exercise compulsions, and continual self-scrutiny and self-castigation are anything *but* the "masters" of their lives.

Exposure and productive cultural analysis of such contradictory and mystifying relations between image and practice are possible only if the analysis includes attention to and interpretation of the "useful" or, as I prefer to call it, the practical body. Such attention, although often in inchoate and theoretically unsophisticated form, was central to the beginnings of the contemporary feminist movement. In the late 1960s and early 1970s the objectification of the female body was a serious political issue. All the cultural paraphernalia of femininity, of learning to please visually and sexually through the practices of the body—media imagery, beauty pageants, high heels, girdles, makeup, simulated orgasm—were seen as crucial in maintaining gender domination.

Disquietingly, for the feminists of the present decade, such focus on the politics of feminine praxis, although still maintained in the work of individual feminists, is no longer a centerpiece of feminist cultural critique.[7] On the popular front, we find *Ms.* magazine[8] presenting issues on fitness and "style," the rhetoric reconstructed for the 1980s to pitch "self-expression" and "power." Although feminist theory surely has the tools, it has not provided a critical discourse to dismantle and demystify this rhetoric. The work of French feminists has provided a powerful framework for understanding the inscription of phallocentric, dualistic culture on gendered bodies, but it has offered very little in the way of concrete analyses of the female body as a locus of practical cultural control. Among feminist theorists in this country, the study of cultural representations of the female body has flourished, and it has often been brilliantly illuminating and instrumental to a feminist rereading of culture.[9] But the study of cultural representations alone, divorced from consideration of their relation to the practical lives of bodies, can obscure and mislead.

Here, Helena Mitchie's significantly titled *The Flesh Made Word* offers a striking example. Examining nineteenth-century representations of women,

7. A focus on the politics of sexualization and objectification remains central to the anti-pornography movement (e.g., in the work of Andrea Dworkin, Catharine MacKinnon). Feminists exploring the politics of appearance include Sandra Bartky, Susan Brownmiller, Wendy Chapkis, Kim Chernin, and Susie Orbach. And a developing feminist interest in the work of Michel Foucault has begun to produce a poststructuralist feminism oriented toward practice; see, for example, Irene Diamond and Lee Quinby, *Feminism and Foucault: Reflections on Resistance* (Boston: Northeastern University Press, 1988).

8. At first a mass-market magazine (founded 1972) that also took a fairly consistent feminist approach, *Ms.* became more and more like a traditional "woman's magazine" before folding in 1989. It was revived in an advertising-free form closer to its original in 1990 [editor's note].

9. See, for example, Susan Suleiman, ed., *The Female Body in Western Culture* (Cambridge: Harvard University Press, 1986).

appetite, and eating, Mitchie draws fascinating and astute metaphorical connections between female eating and female sexuality. Female hunger, she argues, and I agree, "figures unspeakable desires for sexuality and power."[1] The Victorian novel's "representational taboo" against depicting women eating (an activity, apparently, that only "happens offstage," as Mitchie puts it) thus functions as a "code" for the suppression of female sexuality, as does the general cultural requirement, exhibited in etiquette and sex manuals of the day, that the well-bred woman eat little and delicately. The same coding is drawn on, Mitchie argues, in contemporary feminist "inversions" of Victorian values, inversions that celebrate female sexuality and power through images exulting in female eating and female hunger, depicting it explicitly, lushly, and joyfully.

Despite the fact that Mitchie's analysis centers on issues concerning women's hunger, food, and eating practices, she makes no mention of the grave eating disorders that surfaced in the late nineteenth century and that are ravaging the lives of young women today. The practical arena of women dieting, fasting, straitlacing, and so forth is, to a certain extent, implicit in her examination of Victorian gender ideology. But when Mitchie turns, at the end of her study, to consider contemporary feminist literature celebrating female eating and female hunger, the absence of even a passing glance at how women are *actually* managing their hungers today leaves her analysis adrift, lacking any concrete social moorings. Mitchie's sole focus is on the inevitable failure of feminist literature to escape "phallic representational codes."[2] But the feminist celebration of the female body did not merely deconstruct on the written page or canvas. Largely located in the feminist counterculture of the 1970s, it has been culturally displaced by a very different contemporary reality. Its celebration of female flesh now presents itself in jarring dissonance with the fact that women, feminists included, are starving themselves to death in our culture.

This is not to deny the benefits of diet, exercise, and other forms of body management. Rather, I view our bodies as a site of struggle, where we must *work* to keep our daily practices in the service of resistance to gender domination, not in the service of docility and gender normalization. This work requires, I believe, a determinedly skeptical attitude toward the routes of seeming liberation and pleasure offered by our culture. It also demands an awareness of the often contradictory relations between image and practice, between rhetoric and reality. Popular representations, as we have seen, may forcefully employ the rhetoric and symbolism of empowerment, personal freedom, "having it all." Yet female bodies, pursuing these ideals, may find themselves as distracted, depressed, and physically ill as female bodies in the nineteenth century were made when pursuing a feminine ideal of dependency, domesticity, and delicacy. The recognition and analysis of such contradictions, and of all the other collusions, subversions, and enticements through which culture enjoins the aid of our bodies in the reproduction of gender, require that we restore a concern for female praxis to its formerly central place in feminist politics.

1989, 1993

1. Mitchie, *The Flesh Made Word*, p. 13.

2. Mitchie, *The Flesh Made Word*, p. 149.

HOMI K. BHABHA
b. 1949

A prominent figure in postcolonial studies, Homi K. Bhabha has infused thinking about nationality, ethnicity, and politics with poststructuralist theories of identity and indeterminacy. Drawing on a wide range of theorists, particularly the deconstructive philosopher JACQUES DERRIDA, Bhabha's essay "The Commitment to Theory" (1989) revises conventional notions of nationality and the colonial subject, showing how both are shifting, hybrid cultural constructions. It also provides a powerful argument for the importance of theory, for the indelible link between theory and politics, and for the use of poststructuralist theory in the tacitly anti-imperialist cause of postcolonial studies.

Bhabha was born two years after India gained national independence from British colonial rule, and his life exemplifies some of the hybrid subject positions of the postcolonial world. He was raised in the Parsi community of Bombay, India, where his father was an important constitutional lawyer. After receiving a B.A. from Bombay University, he traveled to England to earn his M.A., M.Phil., and D.Phil. from Oxford University. Beginning in 1978, he taught at Sussex University for sixteen years; he also held visiting appointments in the United States at Princeton University and the University of Pennsylvania during the late 1980s and early 1990s. In 1994 he became Chester D. Tripp Professor in the Humanities at the University of Chicago, moving in 2001 to Harvard University.

Postcolonial criticism arose in the wake of the turbulent struggles for national independence of many African, Asian, and Latin American countries that were under the rule of European colonial empires through the middle of the twentieth century. Many early anticolonialist critics promoted autonomous, nationalistic literary traditions to counteract the cultural as well as material domination of imperialism. Later, postcolonial theorists turned to analyze the ideological bases of colonial domination. Perhaps the two most influential figures in this development of contemporary postcolonial theory were EDWARD W. SAID and GAYATRI CHAKRAVORTY SPIVAK. In *Orientalism* (1978; see above), a foundational text of postcolonial studies, Said diagnosed the paths of cultural domination that projected non-Western people as the "Other." In "Can the Subaltern Speak?" (1988; see above), Spivak argued that postcolonial subjects have no voice under the dominant regime of colonial discourse.

Extending the work of Said and Spivak, Bhabha starts with a deconstructive critique of the dichotomies of the West and the Orient, the center and the periphery, the empire and the colonized, the oppressor and the oppressed, and the self and the other. He borrows but adapts Derrida's analysis of how binary oppositions structure Western thought, arguing that such dichotomies are too reductive because they imply that any national culture is unitary, homogeneous, and defined by "fixity" or an essential core. Instead, Bhabha proposes that nationalities, ethnicities, and identities are dialogic, indeterminate, and characterized by "hybridity"—one of his key terms. In "The Commitment to Theory," he defines hybridity as what "is new, *neither the one nor the other*," which emerges from a "Third Space." To reinforce this fluid sense of nationality and identity, Bhabha employs a vocabulary of process-oriented terms, including *dialogic, translation, negotiation, in-between, cross-reference*, and *ambivalence*.

Although "the wit and wisdom of Jacques Derrida" (as he calls it in another essay) is fundamental to his work, Bhabha draws on a wide array of twentieth-century theorists throughout "The Commitment to Theory." Building on the influential concept of nations set forth by Benedict Anderson in *Imagined Communities* (1983), Bhabha stresses how nationality is narratively produced, rather than arising from an intrinsic essence. From MIKHAIL BAKHTIN, he takes the concept of dialogue to stress that colonialism is not a one-way street but entails an interaction between colonizer and colonized. Regarding identity, he draws on FRANTZ FANON's psychoanalytic model of colonialism and JACQUES LACAN's concepts of "mimicry" and the split subject, arguing that there is always an "excess" in the cultural imitation that the colonial subject is forced to produce. This mimicry in turn both revises colonial discourse and creates a new, hybrid identity for the colonial subject.

The goal of Bhabha's theorizing of hybridity is not simply to modify the terms of debate in postcolonial studies but to make a political intervention. In general, Bhabha contends that theory is not separate from or opposed to political activism, but works hand in hand with it. Employing a deconstructive reversal of the opposition between textuality and the world, Bhabha claims that political events—he uses the example of a famous British strike—are in fact textual and discursive, often generated and spurred by "oppositional *cultural* practices." More specifically, the concept of hybridity militates against "restrictive notions of cultural identity" that result in political separatism, as seen in nationalistic movements or in identity politics. For Bhabha, hybridity fosters the larger goal of "socialist community" while acknowledging cultural differences. Such socialist community arises from the solidarity of different groups and movements working in coalition to create a new, progressive hegemony, as STUART HALL similarly urges.

Although preoccupied with postcolonialism, "The Commitment to Theory" also addresses another field of critical debate. In its unabashed advocacy of poststructuralist theory, Bhabha tacitly responds to many critics of the 1980s and 1990s. Their attacks came both from within the academy—epitomized by STEVEN KNAPP AND WALTER BENN MICHAELS's "Against Theory" (1982; see below) and BARBARA CHRISTIAN's "Race for Theory" (1988; see above)—and from outside, in claims that theory was too obscure, detracted from literature, and represented a solipsistic academic pursuit. Like PAUL DE MAN's "Resistance to Theory" (1982), which asserts theory's philosophical inevitability, "The Commitment to Theory" offers a staunch defense; but unlike de Man, Bhabha argues for theory's political relevance.

While rooted in contemporary debates, "The Commitment to Theory" also takes part in the larger tradition of defenses of literary practices, which starts with ARISTOTLE's defense of poetry in the *Poetics* (see above) and extends to nineteenth- and twentieth-century defenses of criticism, such as OSCAR WILDE's claims for the artistic value of criticism, "The Critic as Artist" (1890; see above), and JOHN CROWE RANSOM's argument for the value of professional criticism, "Criticism, Inc." (1938; see above). Such works shield literature and criticism against accusations that they lack utility, social relevance, and moral good. Bhabha updates the tradition by declaring the political efficacy of literary theory.

This debate continues to the present day, and Bhabha has frequently been criticized for his embrace of theory at the expense of practice, his dense jargon, and his copiously allusive writing style. His sharpest critics have come from the Left, taking to task his view of politics as textual. In particular, the Marxist critic Aijaz Ahmad has criticized him for detaching politics from specific locations and political situations. Ahmad also upbraids him for ignoring class and caste, charging that Bhabha's concept of hybridity applies more aptly to privileged postcolonial intellectuals who have gained success in the Western world, like Bhabha himself, than to those in colonial situations. Other commentators, more concerned with theoretical consistency, have noted that the notion of a hybrid identity is too broad and amorphous, applying ultimately to all identities. But within the context of debates in postcolonial studies, the concept of hybridity has decisively altered static thinking about nations and identities.

BIBLIOGRAPHY

Bhabha's reputation primarily rests on his essays, many of which are collected in his book *The Location of Culture* (1994), which includes "The Commitment to Theory." He has also edited an influential anthology on the cultural construction of nationality,

Nation and Narration (1990). In a different register from his academic work, he writes on art and culture as a regular contributor to *Artforum* and to the British public radio network.

Bhabha is the subject of a growing body of criticism. Robert Young's "The Ambivalence of Bhabha," in *White Mythologies: Writing History and the West* (1990), is a useful discussion of Bhabha's overall project. From the left, Aijaz Ahmad's "The Politics of Literary Postcoloniality," *Race and Class* 36.3 (1995), sternly criticizes Bhabha's philosophical conception of politics and his elision of the concrete structural relations of class and caste. Bart Moore-Gilbert, in *Postcolonial Theory: Contexts, Practices, Politics* (1997), situates Bhabha's work among that of other prominent postcolonial theorists and comments on its "babelian" or many-voiced performance. Anthony Easthope's "Bhabha, Hybridity, and Identity," *Textual Practice* 12.2 (1998), uncovering its Derridean roots, criticizes the amorphous nature of "hybridity." The collection *Hybridity and Postcolonialism: Twentieth-Century Indian Literature*, edited by Monika Fludernik (1998), assesses the varying uses of "hybridity" and includes a useful chapter by Fludernik on "The Constitution of Hybridity."

The Commitment to Theory

I

There is a damaging and self-defeating assumption that theory is necessarily the elite language of the socially and culturally privileged. It is said that the place of the academic critic is inevitably within the Eurocentric archives of an imperialist or neo-colonial West. The Olympian realms of what is mistakenly labelled 'pure theory' are assumed to be eternally insulated from the historical exigencies and tragedies of the wretched of the earth.[1] Must we always polarize in order to polemicize? Are we trapped in a politics of struggle where the representation of social antagonisms and historical contradictions can take no other form than a binarism of theory vs politics? Can the aim of freedom of knowledge be the simple inversion of the relation of oppressor and oppressed, centre and periphery, negative image and positive image? Is our only way out of such dualism the espousal of an implacable oppositionality or the invention of an originary counter-myth of radical purity? Must the project of our liberationist aesthetics be forever part of a totalizing Utopian vision of Being and History that seeks to transcend the contradictions and ambivalences that constitute the very structure of human subjectivity and its systems of cultural representation?

Between what is represented as the 'larceny' and distortion of European 'metatheorizing and the radical, engaged, activist experience of Third World creativity,[2] one can see the mirror image (albeit reversed in content and intention) of that ahistorical nineteenth-century polarity of Orient and Occident which, in the name of progress, unleashed the exclusionary imperialist ideologies of self and other. This time round, the term 'critical theory', often

1. An allusion to *The Wretched of the Earth* (1961; see above), by the Martinique-born French psychoanalyst and postcolonial theorist FRANTZ FANON (1925–1961).

2. See C. Taylor, "Eurocentrics vs. New Thought at Edinburgh," *Framework* 34 (1987), for an illustration of this style of argument. See particularly footnote 1 (p. 148) for an exposition of his use of "larceny" ("the judicious distortion of African truths to fit western prejudices") [Bhabha's note]. Third World: "underdeveloped" nations, many of which were formerly colonies of "First World" nations (countries of the industrialized West).

untheorized and unargued, is definitely the Other, an otherness that is insistently identified with the vagaries of the depoliticized Eurocentric critic. Is the cause of radical art or critique best served, for instance, by a fulminating professor of film who announces, at a flashpoint in the argument, 'We are not artists, we are political activists?' By obscuring the power of his own practice in the rhetoric of militancy, he fails to draw attention to the specific value of a politics of cultural production; because it makes the surfaces of cinematic signification the grounds of political intervention, it gives depth to the language of social criticism and extends the domain of 'politics' in a direction that will not be entirely dominated by the forces of economic or social control. Forms of popular rebellion and mobilization are often most subversive and transgressive when they are created through oppositional *cultural* practices.

Before I am accused of bourgeois voluntarism, liberal pragmatism, academicist pluralism and all the other '-isms' that are freely bandied about by those who take the most severe exception to 'Eurocentric' theoretic*ism* (Derrideanism, Lacanianism,[3] poststructuralism . . .), I would like to clarify the goals of my opening questions. I am convinced that, in the language of political economy, it is legitimate to represent the relations of exploitation and domination in the discursive division between the First and Third World, the North and the South. Despite the claims to a spurious rhetoric of 'internationalism' on the part of the established multinationals and the networks of the new communications technology industries, such circulations of signs and commodities as there are, are caught in the vicious circuits of surplus value that link First World capital to Third World labour markets through the chains of the international division of labour, and national comprador[4] classes. Gayatri Spivak is right to conclude that it is 'in the interest of capital to preserve the comprador theatre in a state of relatively primitive labour legislation and environmental regulation'.[5]

I am equally convinced that, in the language of international diplomacy, there is a sharp growth in a new Anglo-American nationalism which increasingly articulates its economic and military power in political acts that express a neo-imperialist disregard for the independence and autonomy of peoples and places in the Third World. Think of America's 'backyard' policy towards the Caribbean and Latin America, the patriotic gore and patrician lore of Britain's Falklands Campaign or, more recently, the triumphalism of the American and British forces during the Gulf War.[6] I am further convinced that such economic and political domination has a profound hegemonic influence on the information orders of the Western world, its popular media and its specialized institutions and academics. So much is not in doubt.

3. The influential poststructuralist lines of thinking inspired by, respectively, the French deconstructive philosopher JACQUES DERRIDA (b. 1930) and the French psychoanalyst JACQUES LACAN (1901–1981).

4. Native intermediary employed by a European business to supervise native employees.

5. G. C. Spivak, *In Other Worlds* (London: Methuen, 1987), pp. 166–67 [Bhabha's note]. GAYATRI CHAKRAVORTY SPIVAK (b. 1942), U.S.-based Indian postcolonial theorist.

6. The international conflict (1990–91) triggered by Iraq's August 1990 invasion of oil-rich Kuwait; a U.S.-led coalition decisively defeated the Iraqi forces. The Falklands Campaign: a brief, undeclared war in 1982 between Great Britain and Argentina over control of the Falkland Islands (off the coast of Argentina), occupied and administered by the British since 1833; the ignominious defeat of the Argentine forces led to a landslide victory for Prime Minister Margaret Thatcher's Conservative Party in that year's parliamentary elections in Britain (and to the fall of the military government in Argentina the following year).

What does demand further discussion is whether the 'new' languages of theoretical critique (semiotic, poststructuralist, deconstructionist and the rest) simply reflect those geopolitical divisions and their spheres of influence. Are the interests of 'Western' theory necessarily collusive with the hegemonic role of the West as a power bloc? Is the language of theory merely another power ploy of the culturally privileged Western elite to produce a discourse of the Other that reinforces its own power–knowledge equation?

A large film festival in the West—even an alternative or counter-cultural event such as Edinburgh's 'Third Cinema' Conference[7]—never fails to reveal the disproportionate influence of the West as cultural forum, in all three senses of that word: as place of public exhibition and discussion, as place of judgement, and as market-place. An Indian film about the plight of Bombay's pavement-dwellers wins the Newcastle Festival[8] which then opens up distribution facilities in India. The first searing exposé of the Bhopal disaster is made for Channel Four.[9] A major debate on the politics and theory of Third Cinema first appears in *Screen*, published by the British Film Institute. An archival article on the important history of neo-traditionalism and the 'popular' in Indian cinema sees the light of day in *Framework*.[1] Among the major contributors to the development of the Third Cinema as precept and practice are a number of Third World film-makers and critics who are exiles or *émigrés* in the West and live problematically, often dangerously, on the 'left' margins of a Eurocentric, bourgeois liberal culture. I don't think I need to add individual names or places, or detail the historical reasons why the West carries and exploits what Bourdieu[2] would call its symbolic capital. The condition is all too familiar, and it is not my purpose here to make those important distinctions between different national situations and the disparate political causes and collective histories of cultural exile. I want to take my stand on the shifting margins of cultural displacement—that confounds any profound or 'authentic' sense of a 'national' culture or an 'organic' intellectual[3]—and ask what the function of a committed theoretical perspective might be, once the cultural and historical hybridity of the postcolonial world is taken as the paradigmatic place of departure.

Committed to what? At this stage in the argument, I do not want to identify any specific 'object' of political allegiance—the Third World, the working class, the feminist struggle. Although such an objectification of political activity is crucial and must significantly inform political debate, it is not the only option for those critics or intellectuals who are committed to progressive

7. A showcase for films by Latin American, African, Middle Eastern, and Asian filmmakers at the Edinburgh International Film Festival; Bhabha is referring to the 40th festival (August 11–13, 1986).
8. Arts festival in northeastern England.
9. A British commercially supported network, created in 1982 and intended to increase the representation of minorities on television; it is known for high-quality dramas and documentaries. "Bhopal disaster": the leakage of tons of poisonous gas in December 1984 from a pesticide plant in central India owned by Union Carbide, a U.S. multinational, which was one of the worst industrial disasters in history; thousands died and tens (perhaps hundreds) of thousands were injured.
1. See T. H. Gabriel "Teaching Third World Cinema," and Julianne Burton, "The Politics of Aesthetic Distance—Sao Bernando," both in *Screen* 24.2 (1983), and A. Rajadhyaksha, "Neo-traditionalism: Film as Popular Art in India," *Framework*, nos. 32 / 33 (1986) [Bhabha's note].
2. PIERRE BOURDIEU (b. 1930), French sociologist; one of his key terms is "symbolic capital," the tools used by individuals and institutions within a given environment to gain dominance and thus to reproduce themselves over time.
3. Someone (regardless of profession) who directs the ideas and aspirations of the particular social class to which he or she "organically" belongs, as described by the Italian Marxist theorist ANTONIO GRAMSCI (1891–1937). "National culture": a term associated with Fanon.

political change in the direction of a socialist society. It is a sign of political maturity to accept that there are many forms of political writing whose different effects are obscured when they are divided between the 'theoretical' and the 'activist'. It is not as if the leaflet involved in the organization of a strike is short on theory, while a speculative article on the theory of ideology ought to have more practical examples or applications. They are both forms of discourse and to that extent they produce rather than reflect their objects of reference. The difference between them lies in their operational qualities. The leaflet has a specific expository and organizational purpose, temporally bound to the event; the theory of ideology makes its contribution to those embedded political ideas and principles that inform the right to strike. The latter does not justify the former; nor does it necessarily precede it. It exists side by side with it—the one as an enabling part of the other—like the recto and verso of a sheet of paper, to use a common semiotic analogy in the uncommon context of politics.

My concern here is with the process of 'intervening ideologically', as Stuart Hall describes the role of 'imagining' or representation in the practice of politics in his response to the British election of 1987.[4] For Hall, the notion of hegemony implies a politics of *identification* of the imaginary.[5] This occupies a discursive space which is not exclusively delimited by the history of either the right or the left. It exists somehow in-between these political polarities, and also between the familiar divisions of theory and political practice. This approach, as I read it, introduces us to an exciting, neglected moment, or movement, in the 'recognition' of the relation of politics to theory; and confounds the traditional division between them. Such a movement is initiated if we see that relation as determined by the rule of repeatable materiality, which Foucault describes as the process by which statements from one institution can be transcribed in the discourse of another.[6] Despite the schemata of use and application that constitute a field of stabilization for the statement, any change in the statement's conditions of use and reinvestment, any alteration in its field of experience or verification, or indeed any difference in the problems to be solved, can lead to the emergence of a new statement: the difference of the same.

In what hybrid forms, then, may a politics of the theoretical statement emerge? What tensions and ambivalences mark this engimatic place from which theory speaks? Speaking in the name of some counter-authority or horizon of 'the true' (in Foucault's sense of the strategic effects of any apparatus or *dispositif*[7]), the theoretical enterprise has to represent the adversarial authority (of power and / or knowledge) which, in a doubly inscribed move, it simultaneously seeks to subvert and replace. In this complicated formulation I have tried to indicate something of the boundary and location of the event of theoretical critique which does not *contain* the truth (in polar opposition to totalitarianism, 'bourgeois liberalism' or whatever is supposed to repress it). The 'true' is always marked and informed by the ambivalence of

4. S. Hall, "Blue Election, Election Blues," *Marxism Today*, July 1987, pp. 30–35 [Bhabha's note]. HALL (b. 1932), a leading figure in British cultural studies.

5. The notion of hegemony—the manufactured consent that legitimates a dominant group and unifies a society—derives from Gramsci.

6. M. Foucault, *The Archaeology of Knowledge*, [trans. A. M. Sheridan] (London: Tavistock, 1972), pp. 102–5 [Bhabha's note]. MICHEL FOUCAULT (1926–1984), French philosopher and historian of ideas

7. Apparatus, device (French).

the process of emergence itself, the productivity of meanings that construct counter-knowledges *in medias res*,[8] in the very act of agonism, within the terms of a negotiation (rather than a negation) of oppositional and antagonistic elements. Political positions are not simply identifiable as progressive or reactionary, bourgeois or radical, prior to the act of *critique engagée*,[9] or outside the terms and conditions of their discursive address. It is in this sense that the historical moment of political action must be thought of as part of the history of the form of its writing. This is not to state the obvious, that there is no knowledge—political or otherwise—outside representation. It is to suggest that the dynamics of writing and textuality require us to rethink the logics of causality and determinacy through which we recognize the 'political' as a form of calculation and strategic action dedicated to social transformation.

'What is to be done?'[1] must acknowledge the force of writing, its metaphoricity and its rhetorical discourse, as a productive matrix which defines the 'social' and makes it available as an objective of and for, action. Textuality is not simply a second-order ideological expression or a verbal symptom of a pre-given political subject. That the political subject—as indeed the subject of politics—is a discursive event is nowhere more clearly seen than in a text which has been a formative influence on Western democratic and socialist discourse—Mill's essay 'On Liberty'.[2] His crucial chapter, 'On The Liberty of Thought and Discussion', is an attempt to define political judgement as the problem of finding a form of *public rhetoric* able to represent different and opposing political 'contents' not as a priori preconstituted principles but as a dialogical discursive exchange; a negotiation of terms in the on-going present of the enunciation of the political statement. What is unexpected is the suggestion that a crisis of identification is initiated in the textual performance that displays a certain 'difference' *within* the signification of any single political system, prior to establishing the substantial differences *between* political beliefs. A knowledge can only become political through an agonistic process: dissensus, alterity and otherness are the discursive conditions for the circulation and recognition of a politicized subject and a public 'truth':

> [If] opponents of all important truths do not exist, it is indispensable to imagine them . . . [He] must feel the whole force of the difficulty which the true view of the subject has to encounter and dispose of; *else he will never really possess himself of the portion of truth which meets and removes that difficulty*. . . . Their conclusion may be true, but it might be false for anything they know: they have never thrown themselves into the *mental position* of those who think differently from them . . . and consequently they do not, in any proper sense of the word, *know the doctrine which they themselves profess*.[3] (My emphases)

It is true that Mill's 'rationality' permits, or requires, such forms of contention and contradiction in order to enhance his vision of the inherently pro-

8. In the middle of things (Latin); usually, in the midst of a narrative.
9. Engaged criticism (French), a term associated with the French philosopher, playwright, and political activist JEAN-PAUL SARTRE (1905–1980).
1. The title of a famous 1902 pamphlet by the Russian Marxist revolutionary V. I. Lenin.
2. Published in 1859 by the English philosopher and social reformer John Stuart Mill (1806–1873).
3. J. S. Mill, "On Liberty," in *Utilitarianism, Liberty, Representative Government* (London: Dent and Sons, 1972), pp. 93–94 [Bhabha's note].

gressive and evolutionary bent of *human* judgement. (This makes it possible for contradictions to be resolved and also generates a sense of the 'whole truth' which reflects the natural, organic bent of the human mind.) It is also true that Mill always reserves, in society as in his argument, the unreal neutral space of the Third Person as the representative of the 'people', who witnesses the debate from an 'epistemological distance' and draws a reasonable conclusion. Even so, in his attempt to describe the political as a form of debate and dialogue—as the process of public rhetoric—that is crucially mediated through this ambivalent and antagonistic faculty of a political 'imagination', Mill exceeds the usual mimetic sense of the battle of ideas. He suggests something much more dialogical: the realization of the political idea at the ambivalent point of textual address, its emergence through a form of political projection.

Rereading Mill through the stategies of 'writing' that I have suggested, reveals that one cannot passively follow the line of argument running through the logic of the opposing ideology. The textual process of political antagonism initiates a contradictory process of reading between the lines; the agent of the discourse becomes, in the same time of utterance, the inverted, projected object of the argument, turned against itself. It is, Mill insists, only by effectively assuming the mental position of the antagonist and working through the displacing and decentring force of that discursive difficulty that the politicized 'portion of truth' is produced. This is a different dynamic from the ethic of tolerance in liberal ideology which has to imagine opposition in order to contain it and demonstrate its enlightened relativism or humanism. Reading Mill, against the grain, suggests that politics can only become representative, a truly public discourse, through a splitting in the signification of the subject of representation; through an ambivalence at the point of the enunciation of a politics.

I have chosen to demonstrate the importance of the space of writing, and the problematic of address, at the very heart of the liberal tradition because it is here that the myth of the 'transparency' of the human agent and the reasonableness of political action is most forcefully asserted. Despite the more radical political alternatives of the right and the left, the popular, common-sense view of the place of the individual in relation to the social is still substantially thought and lived in ethical terms moulded by liberal beliefs. What the attention to rhetoric and writing reveals is the discursive ambivalence that makes 'the political' possible. From such a perspective, the problematic of political judgement cannot be represented as an epistemological problem of appearance and reality or theory and practice or word and thing. Nor can it be represented as a dialectical problem or a symptomatic contradiction constitutive of the materiality of the 'real'. On the contrary, we are made excruciatingly aware of the ambivalent juxtaposition, the dangerous interstitial relation of the factual and the projective, and, beyond that, of the crucial function of the textual and the rhetorical. It is those vicissitudes of the movement of the signifier,[4] in the fixing of the factual and the closure of the real, that ensure the efficacy of stategic thinking in the discourses of *Realpolitik*. It is this to-and-fro, this *fort / da*[5] of the symbolic

4. The symbol or sound that conveys meaning (what is conveyed is the signified), as described in the analysis of signs by the Swiss linguist FERDINAND DE SAUSSURE (1857–1913).

5. Gone / here (German). In *Beyond the Pleasure Principle* (1920), SIGMUND FREUD describes how

process of political negotiation, that constitutes a politics of address. Its importance goes beyond the unsettling of the essentialism or logocentricism of a received political tradition, in the name of an abstract free play of the signifier.[6]

A critical discourse does not yield a *new* political object, or aim, or knowledge, which is simply a mimetic reflection of an a priori political principle or theoretical commitment. We should not demand of it a pure teleology of analysis whereby the prior principle is simply augmented, its rationality smoothly developed, its identity as socialist or materialist (as opposed to neo-imperialist or humanist) consistently confirmed in each oppositional stage of the argument. Such identikit[7] political idealism may be the gesture of great individual fervour, but it lacks the deeper, if dangerous, sense of what is entailed by the *passage* of history in theoretical discourse. The language of critique is effective not because it keeps forever separate the terms of the master and the slave,[8] the mercantilist and the Marxist, but to the extent to which it overcomes the given grounds of opposition and opens up a space of translation: a place of hybridity, figuratively speaking, where the construction of a political object that is new, *neither the one nor the other*, properly alienates our political expectations, and changes, as it must, the very forms of our recognition of the moment of politics. The challenge lies in conceiving of the time of political action and understanding as opening up a space that can accept and regulate the differential structure of the moment of intervention without rushing to produce a unity of the social antagonism or contradiction. This is a sign that history is *happening*—within the pages of theory, within the systems and structures we construct to figure the passage of the historical.

When I talk of *negotiation* rather than *negation*, it is to convey a temporality that makes it possible to conceive of the articulation of antagonistic or contradictory elements: a dialectic without the emergence of a teleological or transcendent History,[9] and beyond the prescriptive form of symptomatic reading where the nervous tics on the surface of ideology reveal the 'real materialist contradiction' that History embodies. In such a discursive temporality, the event of theory becomes the *negotiation* of contradictory and antagonistic instances that open up hybrid sites and objectives of struggle, and destroy those negative polarities between knowledge and its objects, and between theory and practical-political reason.[1] If I have argued against a

his 18-month-old nephew would throw a spool tied to a piece of yarn, saying "Fort," and then pull it back in, saying "Da"; for Freud this game was a way for the child to work out his anxiety about his mother's absence. In "The Mirror Stage" (1949; see above), Lacan argues that the game is about the child's entry into the Symbolic (the structure of language itself).

6. "The free play of the signifier," like "logocentrism" (the privileging of speech, the assumption that knowledge is organized around some central Truth), is a concept developed by Jacques Derrida in *Of Grammatology* (1967; see above).

7. Likeness of a person's face constructed from descriptions (used by the police to help identify a suspect).

8. An allusion to the Master-Slave dialectic developed by the German philosopher GEORG FRIEDRICH WILHELM HEGEL in *Phenomenology of Spirit* (1807; see above), which describes two self-consciousnesses that confront each other and fight for mutual recognition; each identifies him- or herself through the eyes of the other as ruler and ruled.

9. That is, a process of change through contest of opposites that—unlike in the systems of Hegel or KARL MARX (1818–1883), in which the dialectic plays a key role—does not necessarily lead to a predetermined end.

1. For a significant elaboration of a similar argument, see E. Laclau and C. Mouffe, *Hegemony and Socialist Strategy*, [trans. W. Moore and P. Cammack] (London: Verso, 1985), chap. 3 [Bhabha's note]. Ernesto Laclau (b. 1935), Argentine political theorist, and Chantal Mouffe (b. 1943), Colombian political theorist, are known for their elaboration of "post-Marxism."

primordial and previsionary division of right or left, progressive or reactionary, it has been only to stress the fully historical and discursive *différance*[2] between them. I would not like my notion of negotiation to be confused with some syndicalist sense of reformism because that is not the political level that is being explored here. By negotiation I attempt to draw attention to the structure of *iteration*[3] which informs political movements that attempt to articulate antagonistic and oppositional elements without the redemptive rationality of sublation or transcendence.[4]

The temporality of negotiation or translation, as I have sketched it, has two main advantages. First, it acknowledges the historical connectedness between the subject and object of critique so that there can be no simplistic, essentialist opposition between ideological miscognition and revolutionary truth. The progressive reading is crucially determined by the adversarial or agonistic situation itself; it is effective because it uses the subversive, messy mask of camouflage and does not come like a pure avenging angel speaking the truth of a radical historicity and pure oppositionality. If one is aware of this heterogeneous emergence (not origin) of radical critique, then—and this is my second point—the function of theory within the political process becomes double-edged. It makes us aware that our political referents and priorities—the people, the community, class struggle, anti-racism, gender difference, the assertion of an anti-imperialist, black or third perspective—are not there in some primordial, naturalistic sense. Nor do they reflect a unitary or homogeneous political object. They make sense as they come to be constructed in the discourse of feminism or Marxism or the Third Cinema or whatever, whose objects of priority—class or sexuality or 'the new ethnicity'—are always in historical and philosophical tension, or cross-reference with other objectives.

Indeed, the whole history of socialist thought which seeks to 'make it new and better' seems to be a different process of articulating priorities whose political objects can be recalcitrant and contradictory. Within contemporary Marxism, for example, witness the continual tension between the English, humanist, labourist faction and the 'theoreticist', structuralist, new left tendencies. Within feminism, there is again a marked difference of emphasis between the psychoanalytic / semiotic tradition and the Marxist articulation of gender and class through a theory of cultural and ideological interpellation.[5] I have presented these differences in broad brush-strokes, often using the language of polemic to suggest that each position is always a process of translation and transference of meaning. Each objective is constructed on the trace of that perspective that it puts under erasure; each political object is determined in relation to the other, and displaced in that critical act. Too often these theoretical issues are peremptorily transposed into organizational terms and represented as sectarianism. I am suggesting that such contradictions and conflicts, which often thwart political intentions and make the

2. Derrida's term, drawing on the two senses of the French verb *différer*, that combines spatial difference and temporal deferral.

3. Repetition; Derrida applies the term to the repetitious structure of signification.

4. For a philosophical underpinning of some of the concepts I am proposing here see R. Gasché, *The Tain of the Mirror* (Cambridge, Mass.: Harvard University Press, 1986) [Bhabha's note]. "Sublation": in Hegel, the negation but partial incorporation of an element in the dialectic process.

5. The term used by the French Marxist philosopher LOUIS ALTHUSSER (1918–1990) to refer to how ideology "hails" or creates individuals as subjects, in "Ideology and Ideological State Apparatuses" (1970; see above).

question of commitment complex and difficult, are rooted in the process of translation and displacement in which the object of politics is inscribed. The effect is not stasis or a sapping of the will. It is, on the contrary, the spur of the negotiation of socialist democratic politics and policies which demand that questions of organization are theorized and socialist theory is 'organized', *because there is no given community or body of the people whose inherent, radical historicity emits the right signs.*

This emphasis on the representation of the political, on the construction of discourse, is the radical contribution of the translation of theory. Its conceptual vigilance never allows a simple identity between the political objective and its means of representation. This emphasis on the necessity of heterogeneity and the double inscription of the political objective is not merely the repetition of a general truth about discourse introduced into the political field. Denying an essentialist logic and a mimetic referent to political representation is a strong, principled argument against political separatism of any colour, and cuts through the moralism that usually accompanies such claims. There is literally, and figuratively, no space for the unitary or organic political objective which would offend against the sense of a socialist *community* of interest and articulation.

In Britain, in the 1980s, no political struggle was fought more powerfully, and sustained more poignantly, on the values and traditions of a socialist community than the miners' strike of 1984–5.[6] The battalions of monetarist figures and forecasts on the profitability of the pits were starkly ranged against the most illustrious standards of the British labour movement, the most cohesive cultural communities of the working class. The choice was clearly between the dawning world of the new Thatcherite city gent and a long history of the working man, or so it seemed to the traditional left and the new right. In these class terms the mining women involved in the strike were applauded for the heroic supporting role they played, for their endurance and initiative. But the revolutionary impulse, it seemed, belonged securely to the working-class male. Then, to commemorate the first anniversary of the strike, Beatrix Campbell,[7] in the *Guardian*, interviewed a group of women who had been involved in the strike. It was clear that their experience of the historical struggle, their understanding of the historic choice to be made, was startlingly different and more complex. Their testimonies would not be contained simply or singly within the priorities of the politics of class or the histories of industrial struggle. Many of the women began to question their roles within the family and the community—the two central institutions which articulated the meanings and mores of the *tradition* of the labouring classes around which ideological battle was enjoined. Some challenged the symbols and authorities of the culture they fought to defend. Others disrupted the homes they had struggled to sustain. For most of them there was no return, no going back to the 'good old days'. It would be simplistic to suggest either that this considerable social change was a spin-off from the class struggle or that it was a repudiation of the politics of class

6. A yearlong struggle, sometimes violent, between the U.K.'s Conservative government and the National Union of Mineworkers, which went on strike after the government announced that it would close uneconomic coal pits; the union defeat capped Margaret Thatcher's efforts, begun when she became prime minister in 1979, to impose legal restrictions on British unions.

7. English journalist, feminist, and socialist (b. 1947); the *Guardian* is a major daily newspaper in England.

from a socialist-feminist perspective. There is no simple political or social truth to be learned, for there is no unitary representation of a political agency, no fixed hierarchy of political values and effects.

My illustration attempts to display the importance of the hybrid moment of political change. Here the transformational value of change lies in the rearticulation, or translation, of elements that are *neither the One* (unitary working class) *nor the Other* (the politics of gender) *but something else besides*, which contests the terms and territories of both. There is a negotiation between gender and class, where each formation encounters the displaced, differentiated boundaries of its group representation and enunciative sites in which the limits and limitations of social power are encountered in an agonistic relation. When it is suggested that the British Labour Party should seek to produce a socialist alliance among progressive forces that are widely dispersed and distributed across a range of class, culture and occupational forces—without a unifying sense of the class for itself—the kind of hybridity that I have attempted to identify is being acknowledged as a historical necessity. We need a little less pietistic articulation of political principle (around class and nation); a little more of the principle of political *negotiation*.

This seems to be the theoretical issue at the heart of Stuart Hall's arguments for the construction of a counter-hegemonic power bloc through which a socialist party might construct its majority, its constituency; and the Labour Party might (in)conceivably improve its image. The unemployed, semi-skilled and unskilled, part-time workers, male and female, the low paid, black people, underclasses: these signs of the fragmentation of class and cultural consensus represent both the historical experience of contemporary social divisions, and a structure of heterogeneity upon which to construct a theoretical and political alternative. For Hall, the imperative is to construct a new social bloc of different constituencies, through the production of a form of symbolic identification that would result in a collective will. The Labour Party, with its desire to reinstate its traditionalist image—white, male, working class, trade union based—is not hegemonic enough, Hall writes. He is right; what remains unanswered is whether the rationalism and intentionality that propel the collective will are compatible with the language of symbolic image and fragmentary identification that represents, for Hall and for 'hegemony'/'counter-hegemony', the fundamental political issue. Can there ever be hegemony enough, except in the sense that a two-thirds majority will elect us a socialist government?

It is by intervening in Hall's argument that the necessities of negotiation are revealed. The interest of Hall's position lies in his acknowledgement, remarkable for the British left, that, though influential, 'material interests on their own have no necessary class belongingness.[8] This has two significant effects. It enables Hall to see the agents of political change as discontinuous, divided subjects caught in conflicting interests and identities. Equally, at the historical level of a Thatcherite population, he asserts that divisive rather than solidary forms of identification are the rule, resulting in undecidabilities and aporia[9] of political judgement. What does a working woman put first? Which of her identities is the one that determines her political choices? The

8. Hall, "Blue Election," p. 33 [Bhabha's note].

9. Difficulty, logical impasse (a term often used in deconstructive criticism to indicate the point in a text where inherent contradictions render interpretation undecidable).

answers to such questions are defined, according to Hall, in the ideological definition of materialist interests; a process of symbolic identification achieved through a political technology of imaging that hegemonically produces a social bloc of the right or the left. Not only is the social bloc heterogeneous, but, as I see it, the work of hegemony is itself the process of iteration and differentiation. It depends on the production of alternative or antagonistic images that are always produced side by side and in competition with each other. It is this side-by-side nature, this partial presence, or metonymy of antagonism, and its effective significations, that give meaning (quite literally) to a politics of struggle *as the struggle of identifications* and the war of positions. It is therefore problematic to think of it as sublated into an image of the collective will.

Hegemony requires iteration and alterity to be effective, to be productive of politicized populations: the (non-homogeneous) symbolic–social bloc needs to represent itself in a solidary collective will—a modern image of the future—if those populations are to produce a progressive government. Both may be necessary but they do not easily follow from each other, for in each case the mode of representation and its temporality are different. The contribution of negotiation is to display the 'in-between' of this crucial argument; it is *not* self-contradictory but significantly performs, in the process of its discussion, the problems of judgement and identification that inform the political space of its enunciation.

For the moment, the act of negotiation will only be interrogatory. Can such split subjects and differentiated social movements, which display ambivalent and divided forms of identification, be represented in a collective will that distinctively echoes Gramsci's enlightenment inheritance and its rationalism?[1] How does the language of the will accommodate the vicissitudes of its representation, its construction through a symbolic majority where the have-nots identify themselves from the position of the haves? How do we construct a politics based on such a displacement of affect or strategic elaboration (Foucault), where political positioning is ambivalently grounded in an acting-out of political fantasies that require repeated passages across the differential boundaries between one symbolic bloc *and an other*, and the positions available to each? If such is the case, then how do we fix the counter-image of socialist hegemony to reflect the divided will, the fragmented population? If the policy of hegemony is, quite literally, *unsignifiable* without the metonymic representation of its agonistic and ambivalent structure of articulation, then how does the collective will stabilize and unify its address as an agency of *representation*, as representative of a people? How do we avoid the mixing or overlap of images, the split screen, the failure to synchronize sound and image? Perhaps we need to change the ocular language of the image in order to talk of the social and political identifications or representations of a people. It is worth noting that Laclau and Mouffe have turned to the language of textuality and discourse, to *différance* and enunciative modalities, in attempting to understand the structure of hegemony.[2] Paul Gilroy also refers to Bakhtin's theory of narrative when he describes the performance of black expressive cultures as an attempt to transform the relationship between performer and crowd 'in *dialogic* rituals so

1. I owe this point to Martin Thom [Bhabha's note].

2. Laclau and Mouffe, *Hegemony and Socialist Strategy*, chap. 3 [Bhabha's note].

that spectators acquire the active role of participants in collective processes which are sometimes cathartic and which may symbolize or even create a community' (my emphasis).[3]

Such negotiations between politics and theory make it impossible to think of the place of the theoretical as a metanarrative claiming a more total form of generality. Nor is it possible to claim a certain familiar epistemological distance between the *time and place* of the intellectual and the activitist, as Fanon suggests when he observes that 'while politicians situate their action in actual present-day events, men of culture take their stand in the field of history'.[4] It is precisely that popular binarism between theory and politics, whose foundational basis is a view of knowledge as totalizing generality and everyday life as experience, subjectivity or false consciousness,[5] that I have tried to erase. It is a distinction that even Sartre subscribes to when he describes the committed intellectual as the theoretician of practical knowledge whose defining criterion is rationality and whose first project is to combat the irrationality of ideology.[6] From the perspective of negotiation and translation, *contra* Fanon and Sartre, there can be no final discursive *closure* of theory. It does not foreclose on the political, even though battles for power-knowledge[7] may be won or lost to great effect. The corollary is that there is no first or final act of revolutionary social (or socialist) transformation.

I hope it is clear that this erasure of the traditional boundary between theory / politics, and my resistance to the en-*closure* of the theoretical, whether it is read negatively as elitism or positively as radical supra-rationality, do not turn on the good or bad faith of the activist agent or the intellectual *agent provocateur*. I am primarily concerned with the conceptual structuring of the terms—the theoretical / the political—that inform a range of debates around the place and time of the committed intellectual. I have therefore argued for a certain relation to knowledge which I think is crucial in structuring our sense of what the *object* of theory may be in the act of determining our specific political *objectives*.

II

What is at stake in the naming of critical theory as 'Western'? It is, obviously, a designation of institutional power and ideological Eurocentricity. Critical theory often engages with texts within the familiar traditions and conditions of colonial anthropology either to universalize their meaning within its own cultural and academic discourse, or to sharpen its internal critique of the Western logocentric sign, the idealist subject, or indeed the illusions and delusions of civil society. This is a familiar manoeuvre of theoretical knowledge, where, having opened up the chasm of cultural difference, a mediator or metaphor of otherness must be found to contain the effects of difference.

3. P. Gilroy, *There Ain't No Black in the Union Jack* (London: Hutchinson, 1987), p. 214 [Bhabha's note]. MIKHAIL M. BAKHTIN (1895–1975), Russian literary theorist and philosopher of language, associated with the "dialogic."
4. F. Fanon, *The Wretched of the Earth* (Harmondsworth: Penguin, 1967), p. 168 [Bhabha's note].
5. A Marxist term referring to an individual's tendency to view reality in ways congruent with the interests of the dominant orthodoxy rather than in ways that reflect his or her own class interest.
6. J.-P. Sartre, *Politics and Literature*, [trans. J. A. Underwood, J. Calder] (London: Calder and Boyars, 1973), pp. 16–17 [Bhabha's note].
7. An allusion to the work of Foucault, which investigates the interrelation of political power and disciplines of knowledge.

In order to be institutionally effective as a discipline, the knowledge of cultural difference must be made to foreclose on the Other; difference and otherness thus become the fantasy of a certain cultural space or, indeed, the certainty of a form of theoretical knowledge that deconstructs the epistemological 'edge' of the West.

More significantly, the site of cultural difference can become the mere phantom of a dire disciplinary struggle in which it has no space or power. Montesquieu's Turkish Despot, Barthes's Japan, Kristeva's China, Derrida's Nambikwara Indians, Lyotard's Cashinahua pagans[8] are part of this strategy of containment where the Other text is forever the exegetical horizon of difference, never the active agent of articulation. The Other is cited, quoted, framed, illuminated, encased in the shot / reverse-shot strategy of a serial enlightenment. Narrative and the *cultural* politics of difference become the closed circle of interpretation. The Other loses its power to signify, to negate, to initiate its historic desire, to establish its own institutional and oppositional discourse. However impeccably the content of an 'other' culture may be known, however anti-ethnocentrically it is represented, it is its *location* as the closure of grand theories, the demand that, in analytic terms, it be always the good object of knowledge, the docile body of difference, that reproduces a relation of domination and is the most serious indictment of the institutional powers of critical theory.

There is, however, a distinction to be made between the institutional history of critical theory and its conceptual potential for change and innovation. Althusser's critique of the temporal structure of the Hegelian-Marxist expressive totality, despite its functionalist limitations, opens up the possibilities of thinking the relations of production in a time of differential histories. Lacan's location of the signifier of desire, on the cusp of language and the law, allows the elaboration of a form of social representation that is alive to the ambivalent structure of subjectivity and sociality. Foucault's archaeology of the emergence of modern, Western man as a problem of finitude, inextricable from its afterbirth, its Other, enables the linear, progressivist claims of the social sciences—the major imperializing discourses—to be confronted by their own historicist limitations. These arguments and modes of analysis can be dismissed as internal squabbles around Hegelian causality, psychic representation or sociological theory. Alternatively, they can be subjected to a translation, a transformation of value as part of the questioning of the project of modernity in the great, revolutionary tradition of C. L. R. James—*contra* Trotsky[9] or Fanon, *contra* phenomenology and existentialist psychoanalysis. In 1952, it was Fanon who suggested that an oppositional, differential reading of Lacan's Other might be more relevant for the colonial condition than the Marxisant[1] reading of the master-slave dialectic.

It may be possible to produce such a translation or transformation if we

8. Bhabha gives examples of cultural others used by French cultural critics and philosophers to further their own arguments: Charles-Louis de Secondat, baron de la Brède et de Montesquieu (1689–1755) employs the "Turkish Despot" in his *Persian Letters* (1721), which satirizes French society; his observations on Japan, presented in *Empire of Signs* (1970), convinced ROLAND BARTHES (1915–1980) that some signs have no signified; JULIA KRISTEVA (b. 1941) treats China in *About Chinese Women* (1974); in *Of Grammatology*, Derrida finds in CLAUDE LÉVI-STRAUSS's anthropological descriptions of Brazil's Nambikwara in *Tristes Tropiques* (1955; see above) evidence of internal resistance to coercive naming practices; and JEAN-FRANÇOIS LYOTARD (1925–1998) discusses the storytelling of the tribal Cashinahua of Peru in *The Postmodern Condition* (1979).

9. LEON TROTSKY (1879–1940), Russian Marxist revolutionary and theorist. James (1901–1989), Trinidadian political activist and critic of colonialism.

1. Marxism-influenced. Bhabha is referring to Fanon's *Black Skin, White Masks* (1952).

understand the tension within critical theory between its institutional containment and its revisionary force. The continual reference to the horizon of other cultures which I have mentioned earlier is ambivalent. It is a site of citation, but it is also a sign that such critical theory cannot forever sustain its position in the academy as the adversarial cutting edge of Western idealism. What is required is to demonstrate another territory of translation, another testimony of analytical argument, a different engagement in the politics of and around cultural domination. What this other site for theory might be will become clearer if we first see that many poststructuralist ideas are themselves opposed to Enlightenment humanism and aesthetics. They constitute no less than a deconstruction of the moment of the modern, its legal values, its literary tastes, its philosophical and political categorical imperatives. Secondly, and more importantly, we must rehistoricize the moment of 'the emergence of the sign', or 'the question of the subject', or the 'discursive construction of social reality' to quote a few popular topics of contemporary theory. This can only happen if we relocate the referential and institutional demands of such theoretical work in the field of cultural difference—*not cultural diversity*.

Such a reorientation may be found in the historical texts of the colonial moment in the late eighteenth and early nineteenth centuries. For at the same time as the question of cultural difference emerged in the colonial text, discourses of civility were defining the doubling moment of the emergence of Western modernity. Thus the political and theoretical genealogy of modernity lies not only in the origins of the *idea* of civility, but in this history of the colonial moment. It is to be found in the resistance of the colonized populations to the Word of God and Man—Christianity and the English language. The transmutations and translations of indigenous traditions in their opposition to colonial authority demonstrate how the desire of the signifier, the indeterminacy of intertextuality, can be deeply engaged in the postcolonial struggle against dominant relations of power and knowledge. In the following words of the missionary master we hear, quite distinctly, the oppositional voices of a culture of resistance; but we also hear the uncertain and threatening process of cultural transformation. I quote from A. Duff's[2] influential *India and India Missions* (1839):

> Come to some doctrine which you believe to be peculiar to Revelation; tell the people that they must be regenerated or born again, else they can never 'see God'. Before you are aware, they may go away saying, 'Oh, there is nothing new or strange here; our own Shastras[3] tell us the same thing; we know and believe that we must be born again; it is our fate to be so.' But what do they understand by the expression? It is that they are to be born again and again, in some other form, agreeably to their own system of transmigration or reiterated births. To avoid the appearance of countenancing so absurd and pernicious a doctrine, you vary your language, and tell them that there must be a second birth—that they must be twice-born. Now it so happens that this, and all similar phraseology, is preoccupied. The sons of a Brahman have to undergo

2. Alexander Duff (1806–1878), Scottish missionary to India from the Free Church of Scotland.
3. Sutras, or precepts summarizing Vedic teachings; the Vedas are the sacred literature of Hinduism.

various purificatory and initiatory ceremonial rites, before they attain to full Brahmanhood. The last of these is the investiture with the sacred thread; which is followed by the communication of the Gayatri, or most sacred verse in the Vedas. This ceremonial constitutes, 'religiously and metaphorically, their second birth'; henceforward their distinctive and peculiar appellation is that of the twice-born, or regenerated men. *Hence it is your improved language might only convey the impression that all must become perfect Brahmans, ere they can 'see God'.*[4] (My emphasis)

The grounds of evangelical certitude are opposed not by the simple assertion of an antagonistic cultural tradition. The process of translation is the opening up of another contentious political and cultural site at the heart of colonial representation. Here the word of divine authority is deeply flawed by the assertion of the indigenous sign, and in the very practice of domination the language of the master becomes hybrid—neither the one thing nor the other. The incalculable colonized subject—half acquiescent, half oppositional, always untrustworthy—produces an unresolvable problem of cultural difference for the very address of colonial cultural authority. The 'subtile system of Hinduism', as the missionaries in the early nineteenth century called it, generated tremendous policy implications for the institutions of Christian conversion. The written authority of the Bible was challenged and together with it a postenlightenment notion of the 'evidence of Christianity' and its historical priority, which was central to evangelical colonialism. The Word could no longer be trusted to carry the truth when written or spoken in the colonial world by the European missionary. Native catechists therefore had to be found, who brought with them their own cultural and political ambivalences and contradictions, often under great pressure from their families and communities.

This revision of the history of critical theory rests, I have said, on the notion of cultural difference, not cultural diversity. Cultural diversity is an epistemological object—culture as an object of empirical knowledge—whereas cultural difference is the process of the *enunciation* of culture as 'knowledge*able*', authoritative, adequate to the construction of systems of cultural identification. If cultural diversity is a category of comparative ethics, aesthetics or ethnology, cultural difference is a process of signification through which statements *of* culture or *on* culture differentiate, discriminate and authorize the production of fields of force, reference, applicability and capacity. Cultural diversity is the recognition of pre-given cultural contents and customs; held in a time-frame of relativism it gives rise to liberal notions of multiculturalism, cultural exchange or the culture of humanity. Cultural diversity is also the representation of a radical rhetoric of the separation of totalized cultures that live unsullied by the intertextuality of their historical locations, safe in the Utopianism of a mythic memory of a unique collective identity. Cultural diversity may even emerge as a system of the articulation and exchange of cultural signs in certain early structuralist accounts of anthropology.

Through the concept of cultural difference I want to draw attention to the common ground and lost territory of contemporary critical debates. For they

4. Rev. A. Duff, *India and India Missions: Including Sketches of the Gigantic System of Hinduism* (Edinburgh: John Johnstone; London: John Hunter, 1839), p. 560 [Bhabha's note].

all recognize that the problem of cultural interaction emerges only at the significatory boundaries of cultures, where meanings and values are (mis)read or signs are misappropriated. Culture only emerges as a problem, or a problematic, at the point at which there is a loss of meaning in the contestation and articulation of everyday life, between classes, genders, races, nations. Yet the reality of the limit or limit-text of culture is rarely theorized outside of well-intentioned moralist polemics against prejudice and stereotype, or the blanket assertion of individual or institutional racism—that describe the effect rather than the structure of the problem. The need to think the limit of culture as a problem of the enunciation of cultural difference is disavowed.

The concept of cultural difference focuses on the problem of the ambivalence of cultural authority: the attempt to dominate in the *name* of a cultural supremacy which is itself produced only in the moment of differentiation. And it is the very authority of culture as a knowledge of referential truth which is at issue in the concept and moment of *enunciation*. The enunciative process introduces a split in the performative present of cultural identification; a split between the traditional culturalist demand for a model, a tradition, a community, a stable system of reference, and the necessary negation of the certitude in the articulation of new cultural demands, meanings, strategies in the political present, as a practice of domination, or resistance. The struggle is often between the historicist teleological or mythical time and narrative of traditionalism—of the right or the left—and the shifting, strategically displaced time of the articulation of a historical politics of negotiation which I suggested above. The time of liberation is, as Fanon powerfully evokes, a time of cultural uncertainty, and, most crucially, of significatory or representational undecidability:

> But [native intellectuals] forget that the forms of thought and what [they] feed . . . on, together with modern techniques of information, language and dress, have dialectically reorganized the people's intelligences and *the constant principles (of national art)* which acted as safeguards during the colonial period are now undergoing extremely radical changes. . . . [We] must join the people in that fluctuating movement which they are *just* giving a shape to . . . which will be the signal for everything to be called into question . . . it is to the zone of *occult instability* where the people dwell that we must come.[5] (My emphases)

The enunciation of cultural difference problematizes the binary division of past and present, tradition and modernity, at the level of cultural representation and its authoritative address. It is the problem of how, in signifying the present, something comes to be repeated, relocated and translated in the name of tradition, in the guise of a pastness that is not necessarily a faithful sign of historical memory but a strategy of representing authority in terms of the artifice of the archaic. That iteration negates our sense of the origins of the struggle. It undermines our sense of the homogenizing effects of cultural symbols and icons, by questioning our sense of the authority of cultural synthesis in general.

This demands that we rethink our perspective on the identity of culture.

5. Fanon, *The Wretched of the Earth*, pp. 182–83 [Bhabha's note].

Here Fanon's passage—somewhat reinterpreted—may be helpful. What is implied by his juxtaposition of the constant national principles with his view of culture-as-political-struggle, which he so enigmatically and beautifully describes as 'the zone of occult instability where the people dwell'? These ideas not only help to explain the nature of colonial struggle; they also suggest a possible critique of the positive aesthetic and political values we ascribe to the unity or totality of cultures, especially those that have known long and tyrannical histories of domination and misrecognition. Cultures are never unitary in themselves, nor simply dualistic in the relation of Self to Other. This is not because of some humanistic nostrum that beyond individual cultures we all belong to the human culture of mankind; nor is it because of an ethical relativism which suggests that in our cultural capacity to speak of and judge others we necessarily 'place ourselves in their position', in a kind of relativism of distance of which Bernard Williams has written at length.[6]

The reason a cultural text or system of meaning cannot be sufficient unto itself is that the act of cultural enunciation—the *place of utterance*—is crossed by the *différance* of writing. This has less to do with what anthropologists might describe as varying attitudes to symbolic systems within different cultures than with the structure of symbolic representation itself—not the content of the symbol or its social function, but the structure of symbolization. It is this difference in the process of language that is crucial to the production of meaning and ensures, at the same time, that meaning is never simply mimetic and transparent.

The linguistic difference that informs any cultural performance is dramatized in the common semiotic account of the disjuncture between the subject of a proposition (*énoncé*) and the subject of enunciation, which is not represented in the statement but which is the acknowledgement of its discursive embeddedness and address, its cultural positionality, its reference to a present time and a specific space. The pact of interpretation is never simply an act of communication between the I and the You designated in the statement. The production of meaning requires that these two places be mobilized in the passage through a Third Space, which represents both the general conditions of language and the specific implication of the utterance in a performative and institutional strategy of which it cannot 'in itself' be conscious. What this unconscious relation introduces is an ambivalence in the act of interpretation. The pronominal I of the proposition cannot be made to address—in its own words—the subject of enunciation, for this is not personable, but remains a spatial relation within the schemata and strategies of discourse. The meaning of the utterance is quite literally neither the one nor the other. This ambivalence is emphasized when we realize that there is no way that the content of the proposition will reveal the structure of its positionality; no way that context can be mimetically read off from the content.

The implication of this enunciative split for cultural analysis that I especially want to emphasize is its temporal dimension. The splitting of the subject of enunciation destroys the logics of synchronicity and evolution which traditionally authorize the subject of cultural knowledge. It is often taken for

6. B. Williams, *Ethics and the Limits of Philosophy* (London: Fontana, 1985), chap. 9 [Bhabha's note].

granted in materialist and idealist problematics that the value of culture as an object of study, and the value of any analytic activity that is considered cultural, lie in a capacity to produce a cross-referential, generalizable unity that signifies a progression or evolution of ideas-in-time, as well as a critical self-reflection on their premisses or determinants. It would not be relevant to pursue the detail of this argument here except to demonstrate—via Marshall Sahlins's *Culture and Practical Reason*—the validity of my general characterization of the Western expectation of culture as a disciplinary practice of writing. I quote Sahlins at the point at which he attempts to define the difference of Western bourgeois culture:

> We have to do not so much with functional dominance as with structural—with different structures of symbolic *integration*. And to this gross difference in design correspond differences in symbolic performance: between an *open, expanding* code, responsive by *continuous* permutation to events it has itself staged, and an apparently *static* one that seems to know not events, but only its own preconceptions. The gross distinction between 'hot' societies and 'cold', development and underdevelopment, societies with and without history—and so between large societies and small, expanding and self-contained, colonizing and colonized.[7] (My emphases)

The intervention of the Third Space of enunciation, which makes the structure of meaning and reference an ambivalent process, destroys this mirror of representation in which cultural knowledge is customarily revealed as an integrated, open, expanding code. Such an intervention quite properly challenges our sense of the historical identity of culture as a homogenizing, unifying force, authenticated by the originary Past, kept alive in the national tradition of the People. In other words, the disruptive temporality of enunciation displaces the narrative of the Western nation which Benedict Anderson so perceptively describes as being written in homogeneous, serial time.[8]

It is only when we understand that all cultural statements and systems are constructed in this contradictory and ambivalent space of enunciation, that we begin to understand why hierarchical claims to the inherent originality or 'purity' of cultures are untenable, even before we resort to empirical historical instances that demonstrate their hybridity. Fanon's vision of revolutionary cultural and political change as a 'fluctuating movement' of occult instability could not be articulated as cultural *practice* without an acknowledgement of this indeterminate space of the subject(s) of enunciation. It is that Third Space, though unrepresentable in itself, which constitutes the discursive conditions of enunciation that ensure that the meaning and symbols of culture have no primordial unity or fixity; that even the same signs can be appropriated, translated, rehistoricized and read anew.

Fanon's moving metaphor—when reinterpreted for a theory of cultural signification—enables us to see not only the necessity of theory, but also the restrictive notions of cultural identity with which we burden our visions of political change. For Fanon, the liberatory people who initiate the productive instability of revolutionary cultural change are themselves the bearers of a

7. M. Sahlins, *Culture and Practical Reason* (Chicago: University of Chicago Press, 1976), p. 211 [Bhabha's note].

8. B. Anderson, *Imagined Communities* (London: Verso, 1983), chap. 1 [Bhabha's note].

hybrid identity. They are caught in the discontinuous time of translation and negotiation, in the sense in which I have been attempting to recast these words. In the moment of liberatory struggle, the Algerian people destroy the continuities and constancies of the nationalist tradition which provided a safeguard against colonial cultural imposition. They are now free to negotiate and translate their cultural identities in a discontinuous intertextual temporality of cultural difference. The native intellectual who identifies the people with the true national culture will be disappointed. The people are now the very principle of 'dialectical reorganization' and they construct their culture from the national text translated into modern Western forms of information technology, language, dress. The changed political and historical site of enunciation transforms the meanings of the colonial inheritance into the liberatory signs of a free people of the future.

> I have been stressing a certain void or misgiving attending every assimilation of contraries—I have been stressing this in order to expose what seems to me a fantastic mythological congruence of elements. . . . And if indeed therefore any real sense is to be made of material change it can only occur with an acceptance of a concurrent void and with a willingness to descend into that void wherein, as it were, one may begin to come into confrontation with a spectre of invocation whose freedom to participate in an alien territory and wilderness has become a necessity for one's reason or salvation.[9]

This meditation by the great Guyanese writer Wilson Harris on the void of misgiving in the textuality of colonial history reveals the cultural and historical dimension of that Third Space of enunciations which I have made the precondition for the articulation of cultural difference. He sees it as accompanying the 'assimilation of contraries' and creating that occult instability which presages powerful cultural changes. It is significant that the productive capacities of this Third Space have a colonial or postcolonial provenance. For a willingness to descend into that alien territory—where I have led you—may reveal that the theoretical recognition of the split-space of enunciation may open the way to conceptualizing an *inter*national culture, based not on the exoticism of multiculturalism or the *diversity* of cultures, but on the inscription and articulation of culture's *hybridity*. To that end we should remember that it is the 'inter'—the cutting edge of translation and negotiation, the *in-between* space—that carries the burden of the meaning of culture. It makes it possible to begin envisaging national, anti-nationalist histories of the 'people'. And by exploring this Third Space, we may elude the politics of polarity and emerge as the others of our selves.

1989

9. W. Harris, *Tradition, the Writer, and Society* (London: New Beacon, 1973), pp. 60–63 [Bhabha's note].

LENNARD J. DAVIS
b. 1949

A pioneer of disability studies, Lennard Davis broke theoretical ground in 1995 with his book *Enforcing Normalcy: Disability, Deafness, and the Body*, calling attention to an aspect of identity that until then had "been relegated to a sideshow, a freak show at that, far away from the academic midway of progressive ideas and concerns." The son of deaf parents, Davis melded personal experience and contemporary theoretical training to cast new light on representations of disability and on the concepts of normalcy that buttress those representations. "Visualizing the Disabled Body: The Classical Nude and the Fragmented Torso," a chapter from *Enforcing Normalcy*, criticizes mainstream images of the ideal and the normal body, showing their dependence on the fragmented and monstrous body of early childhood fantasy.

Davis was born in the Bronx, New York, to immigrant, working-class Jewish parents. He attended Columbia University, where he was involved in the student rebellion in 1968, receiving a B.A. in 1970 and a Ph.D. in 1976. He wrote his doctoral dissertation under the supervision of EDWARD W. SAID and also attended courses in the early 1970s at the École Pratique des Hautes Études in Paris, where he studied with ROLAND BARTHES. Davis taught at Columbia from 1977 to 1985 and held several visiting posts until 1992, when he gained a professorship at Binghamton University of the State University of New York. In 2000 he moved to the University of Illinois at Chicago to become head of the English department and one of the architects of a new program, the first of its kind, in disability studies. Davis published his first two books on the history and theory of the novel, but his research interests shifted in the early 1990s when he became a member of CODA (Children of Deaf Adults). Thereafter he focused on deafness and disability, co-founding the Modern Language Association's Committee on Disability Issues in the Profession and writing on these topics in academic venues as well as more popular ones such as the *Nation* and the *New York Times*.

Like the studies of gender, sexuality, race, and ethnicity that have become prominent in recent decades, disability studies focuses on identity, the way that identity relates to the body, and the social constructions of marginality and normality. It draws on a wide array of twentieth-century theoretical sources, including psychoanalysis, cultural studies, feminism, and especially body studies. Beginning with the work of MICHEL FOUCAULT, who examined the disciplining and medicalization of the body as a form of social control, the body has emerged as one of the central theoretical categories of recent years, often replacing the concern with subjectivity that was prominent in the 1970s and 1980s. In particular, feminist theorists such as HÉLÈNE CIXOUS and SUSAN BORDO have exposed the frequently negative body images enforced on women. In a different vein, DONNA HARAWAY's "Manifesto for Cyborgs" (1985; see above) has also influenced disability studies by promoting a postmodern view of the body as a technologically constructed "cyborg."

Demonstrating how the body is a social construction rather than a universal constant, Davis—and disability studies—starts with a critique of "normalcy," which functions to stigmatize as abnormal those with different or limited abilities. In *Enforcing Normalcy*, he traces the history of the idea of the normal, which was born in the eighteenth century with eugenics and statistics, mandating that people fit within the limits of a "normal curve." Before that time, Davis argues, the "ideal" was the primary model in Western culture; this concept assumed that all bodies were less than ideal, and there was less stigma attached to disability. Some disability theorists trace the emphasis on the normal body to industrial capitalism, which required a standardized body for factory work and labeled the disabled body as abnormal, relegating it to marginal status. In our own era we have seen the rise of the "normal ideal," especially in Hollywood movies, which depict ideal bodies as normal and less-than-ideal bodies as abnormal.

"Visualizing the Disabled Body" analyzes the depiction of disability and normalcy in art, literature, and film. Beginning with a striking comparison between a famous Greek statue, the Venus de Milo, and a contemporary woman with disabilities, Davis questions our aesthetic and social preconceptions that lead us to think an armless statue beautiful and a living woman without arms ugly, deformed, and de-eroticized. He looks at the ideal body in the classical art form of the nude and considers the interplay between the ideal Venus and the monstrous Medusa in Greek mythology. After deconstructing this dichotomy, he investigates the images of disability prevalent in a range of works of art and literature, including Mary Shelley's novel *Frankenstein* (1818), the photography of Diane Arbus (1923–1971) and others, and films such as *Frankenstein* (1931) and *Born on the Fourth of July* (1989). Davis finds that the "visual arts have done a magnificent job of centralizing normalcy and of marginalizing different bodies," and hence excel at their socially coercive role of "enforcing" normalcy.

Turning to psychoanalysis, Davis draws on JACQUES LACAN's notion of the primordial "fragmented body" to understand the persistent creation of disabled bodies. The abnormal body suggests that one's coherent identity is actually a dreamlike construction that merely conceals the fundamentally fragmentary nature of identity. As Davis puts it, "wholeness is in fact a hallucination." In particular, Davis considers *Frankenstein* in terms of the fragmented, grotesque body. In an innovative reading, he sees the scientist's creation as representing a person with disabilities. The creature is horrible because he is a composite made from disparate body parts, thereby literalizing the notion we hold from early infancy of the primordial, fragmented body.

Disability theorists like Davis aim not only at making a theoretical intervention but at changing community views of disability and removing its social stigma. Just as feminism, queer studies, and African American studies arose out of political movements, so disability studies is connected with a political movement, one that seeks greater rights for people with disabilities. Part of its goal is to redefine disabled people as a minority group. As Davis passionately argues, "people with disabilities have been an oppressed and repressed group. People with disabilities have been isolated, incarcerated[,] . . . institutionalized, and controlled to a degree probably unequal to that experienced by any other minority group. As fifteen percent of the population, people with disabilities make up the largest physical minority within the United States." Construed as one among many minority groups, disabled people can demand equal treatment as a matter of human rights whose denial is a form of unjust discrimination.

One problematic question for disability theorists is that of definition. The central critique launched by disability studies aims to break down the dichotomy of abled / disabled and normal / abnormal, offering instead a broad conceptual continuum encompassing persons of varying abilities. At the same time, disability is cast as a specific identity defined narrowly enough that most people (e.g., the nearsighted) are not considered disabled. This second tactic invokes "the disabled" as a category designed to convey minority status and legal rights. The tension between wide and narrow definitions of disability mirrors a tension in other identity-based studies—whether focusing on race, ethnicity, gender, or sexuality—between deconstructing conventional categories that marginalize them and asserting a separate status to remedy losses of rights. Perhaps it reflects less a contradiction than a two-pronged strategy, at once aiming ideologically to dispel prejudice and pragmatically asserting the rights of those injured by prejudice. In concentrating on these tasks, Davis's work and disability studies compellingly reconfigure concepts of identity, the body, and normalcy.

BIBLIOGRAPHY

Lennard Davis's writings on the novel include *Factual Fictions: The Origins of the Novel* (1983; rpt. 1997), a study of the origin of the novel in relation to other genres, such as journalism and history, and *Resisting Novels: Ideology and Fiction* (1987), which examines the ideological suasion of fiction. He also co-edited with his spouse, M. Bella Mirabella, *Left Politics and the Literary Profession* (1990). Davis's *Enforcing Normalcy: Disability, Deafness, and the Body* (1995) and his edited anthology *The Disability Studies Reader* (1997) both stake out the field of disability studies. Davis also edited his parents' correspondence, published as *"Shall I Say a Kiss?": Courtship Letters of a Deaf Couple, 1936–38* (1999), which conveys the experience of two deaf people in England just before World War II. In addition to his academic work, he has published articles in mainstream magazines, including the *Nation*, the *New York Times, McCall's, Redbook*, and *Parents*. The best biographical source about Davis is his autobiography, *My Sense of Silence: Memoir of a Childhood with Deafness* (2000), which explores the political and psychological issues surrounding disability.

Davis's investigation of the origin of the novel has received significant attention, most notably a feminist expansion in Catherine Gallagher's *Nobody's Story: The Vanishing Act of Women Writers in the Marketplace, 1679–1820* (1995). Surveying the emergence of the field, Rachel Adams's "Enabling Differences: New York in Disability Studies," *Michigan Quarterly Review* 37 (1998), praises Davis's critique of normalcy but criticizes his "overwhelming accumulation of examples" and theoretical sources, finding that he insufficiently bridges the "differences between deafness and other forms of physical impairment." Focusing on deafness, Brenda Jo Brueggeman draws on Davis's work in *Lend Me Your Ear: Rhetorical Constructions of Deafness* (1999) and " 'Writing Insight': Deafness and Autobiography," *American Quarterly* 52 (2000).

From Enforcing Normalcy: Disability, Deafness, and the Body

From *Visualizing the Disabled Body: The Classical Nude and the Fragmented Torso*

> A human being who is first of all an invalid is *all* body, therein lies his inhumanity and his debasement. In most cases he is little better than a carcass—.
>
> —Thomas Mann, *The Magic Mountain*[1]

> . . . the female is as it were a deformed male.
>
> —Aristotle, *Generation of Animals*[2]

> When I begin to wish I were crippled—even though I am perfectly healthy—or rather that I would have been better off crippled, that is the first step towards *butoh*.
>
> —Tatsumi Hijikata,[3] co-founder of the Japanese performance art / dance form *butoh*.

She has no arms or hands, although the stump of her upper right arm extends just to her breast. Her left foot has been severed, and her face is badly scarred, with her nose torn at the tip, and her lower lip gouged out. Fortunately, her facial mutilations have been treated and are barely visible, except

1. The 1924 masterpiece, set in a tuberculosis sanatorium, by the German novelist Mann (1875–1955).
2. One of the zoological works of the Greek philosopher (384–322 B.C.E.; see above), whose works set the course of Western science for centuries.
3. Japanese dancer, teacher, and choreographer (1928–1986); his style featured dancers with distorted, emaciated bodies, shaved heads, and white-plastered faces.

for minor scarring visible only up close. The big toe of her right foot has been cut off, and her torso is covered with scars, including a particularly large one between her shoulder blades, one that covers her shoulder, and one covering the tip of her breast where her left nipple was torn out.

Yet she is considered one of the most beautiful female figures in the world. When the romantic poet Heinrich Heine saw her he called her 'Notre-Dame de la Beauté.'[4]

He was referring to the Venus de Milo.[5]

Consider too Pam Herbert, a quadriplegic with muscular dystrophy, writing her memoir by pressing her tongue on a computer keyboard, who describes herself at twenty-eight years old:

> I weigh about 130 pounds; I'm about four feet tall. It's pretty hard to get an accurate measurement on me because both of my knees are permanently bent and my spine is curved, so 4' is an estimate. I wear size two tennis shoes and strong glasses; my hair is dishwater blonde and shoulder length.[6]

In this memoir, she describes her wedding night:

> We got to the room and Mark laid me down on the bed because I was so tired from sitting all day. Anyway, I hadn't gone to the bathroom all day so Mark had to catheterize me. I had been having trouble going to the bathroom for many years, so it was nothing new to Mark, he had done it lots of times before.
>
> It was time for the biggest moment of my life, making love. Of course, I was a little nervous and scared. Mark was very gentle with me. He started undressing me and kissing me. We tried making love in the normal fashion with Mark on top and me on the bottom. Well, that position didn't work at all, so then we tried laying on our sides coming in from behind. That was a little better. Anyway, we went to sleep that night a little discouraged because we didn't have a very good lovemaking session. You would have thought that it would be great, but sometimes things don't always go the way we want them to. We didn't get the hang of making love for about two months. It hurt for a long time.[7]

I take the liberty of bringing these two women's bodies together. Both have disabilities. The statue is considered the ideal of Western beauty and eroticism, although it is armless and disfigured. The living woman might be considered by many 'normal' people to be physically repulsive, and certainly without erotic allure. The question I wish to ask is why does the impairment of the Venus de Milo in no way prevent 'normal' people from considering her beauty, while Pam Herbert's disability becomes the focal point for horror and pity?

In asking this question, I am really raising a complex issue. On a social level, the question has to do with how people with disabilities are seen and

4. Our Lady of Beauty (French). Heine (1797–1856), German Romantic poet and journalist.

5. Famous classical statue of Aphrodite, Greek goddess of love (2d c. B.C.E. copy of a 4th c. original), found on the island of Melos in 1820; it is now displayed in the Louvre, the national art museum of France. The Romans called this goddess Venus.

6. In S. E. Browne, D. Connors, and N. Stern, eds., *With the Power of Each Breath: A Disabled Women's Anthology* (Pittsburgh: Cleis Press, 1985), p. 147 [Davis's note]. Some of the author's notes have been edited, and some omitted.

7. Ibid., p. 155 [Davis's note].

why, by and large, they are de-eroticized. If, as I mentioned earlier, disability is a cultural phenomenon rooted in the senses, one needs to inquire how a disability occupies a field of vision, of touch, of hearing; and how that disruption or distress in the sensory field translates into psycho-dynamic representations. This is more a question about the nature of the subject than about the qualities of the object, more about the observer than the observed. The 'problem' of the disabled has been put at the feet of people with disabilities for too long.

Normalcy, rather than being a degree zero of existence, is more accurately a location of bio-power, as Foucault[8] would use the term. The 'normal' person (clinging to that title) has a network of traditional ableist assumptions and social supports that empowers the gaze[9] and interaction. The person with disabilities, until fairly recently, had only his or her own individual force or will. Classically, the encounter has been, and remains, an uneven one. Anne Finger describes it in strikingly visual terms by relating an imagined meeting between Rosa Luxemburg and Antonio Gramsci,[1] each of whom was a person with disabilities, although Rosa is given the temporary power of the abled gaze:

> We can measure Rosa's startled reaction as she glimpses him the misshapen dwarf limping towards her in a second-hand black suit so worn that the cuffs are frayed and the fabric is turning green with age, her eye immediately drawn to this disruption in the visual field; the unconscious flinch; the realization that she is staring at him, and the too-rapid turning away of the head. And then, the moment after, the consciousness that the quick aversion of the gaze was as much of an insult as the stare, so she turns her head back but tries to make her focus general, not a sharp gape. Comrade Rosa, would you have felt a slight flicker of embarrassment? shame? revulsion? dread? of a feeling that can have no name?[2]

In this encounter what is suppressed, at least in this moment, is the fact that Rosa Luxemburg herself is physically impaired (she walked with a limp for her whole life). The emphasis then shifts from the cultural norm to the deviation; Luxemburg, now the gazing subject, places herself in the empowered position of the norm, even if that position is not warranted.

Disability, in this and other encounters, is a disruption in the visual, auditory, or perceptual field as it relates to the power of the gaze. As such, the disruption, the rebellion of the visual, must be regulated, rationalized, contained. Why the modern binary—normal / abnormal—must be maintained is a complex question. But we can begin by accounting for the desire to split bodies into two immutable categories: whole and incomplete, abled and disabled, normal and abnormal, functional and dysfunctional.

In the most general sense, cultures perform an act of splitting (*Spaltung*,[3]

8. MICHEL FOUCAULT (1926–1984), French philosopher and historian of ideas; the study of bio-power (as a political technology for manipulating the body) is a major theme in his work.

9. A term associated with the psychoanalytic theory of JACQUES LACAN (1901–1981) and, more specifically, with Lacan-influenced film studies (e.g., LAURA MULVEY's 1975 "Visual Pleasure and Narrative Cinema," above).

1. Italian Marxist philosopher (1891–1937; see above). Luxemburg (1871–1919), German Marxist revolutionary.

2. Anne Finger, "Comrade Luxemburg and Comrade Gramsci Pass Each Other at a Congress of the Second International in Switzerland on the 10th of March, 1912," unpublished manuscript, 1994 [Davis's note].

3. Crack; splitting, division (German). The term is used by SIGMUND FREUD (1856–1939) in discussing psychosis and fetishism, especially in "Splitting of the Ego in the Process of Defense" (1940) and "Fetishism" (1927; see above); more important for

to use Freud's term). These violent cleavages of consciousness are as primitive as our thought processes can be. The young infant splits the good parent from the bad parent—although the parent is the same entity. When the child is satisfied by the parent, the parent is the good parent; when the child is not satisfied, the parent is bad. As a child grows out of the earliest phases of infancy, she learns to combine those split images into a single parent who is sometimes good and sometimes not. The residue of *Spaltung* remains in our inner life, personal and collective, to produce monsters and evil stepmothers as well as noble princes and fairy godmothers.

In this same primitive vein, culture tends to split bodies into good and bad parts. Some cultural norms are considered good and others bad. Everyone is familiar with the 'bad' body: too short or tall, too fat or thin, not masculine or feminine enough, not enough or too much hair on the head or other parts of the body, penis or breasts too small or (excepting the penis) too big. Furthermore, each individual assigns good and bad labels to body parts—good: hair, face, lips, eyes, hands; bad: sexual organs, excretory organs, underarms.

The psychological explanation may provide a reason why it is imperative for society at large to engage in *Spaltung*. The divisions whole / incomplete, able / disabled neatly cover up the frightening writing on the wall that reminds the hallucinated whole being that its wholeness is in fact a hallucination, a developmental fiction. *Spaltung* creates the absolute categories of abled and disabled, with concomitant defenses against the repressed fragmented body.

But a psychological explanation alone is finally insufficient. Historical specificity makes us understand that disability is a social process with an origin. So, why certain disabilities are labeled negatively while others have a less negative connotation is a question tied to complex social forces (some of which I have tried to lay out in earlier chapters). It is fair to say, in general, that disabilities would be most dysfunctional in postindustrial countries, where the ability to perambulate or manipulate is so concretely tied to productivity, which in itself is tied to production. The body of the average worker as we have seen, becomes the new measure of man and woman. Michael Oliver, citing Ryan and Thomas (1980), notes:

> With the rise of the factory . . . [during industrialization] many more disabled people were excluded from the production process for 'The speed of factory work, the enforced discipline, the time-keeping and production norms—all these were a highly unfavorable change from the slower, more self-determined and flexible methods of work into which many handicapped people had been integrated.'[4]

Both industrial production and the concomitant standardization of the human body have had a profound impact on how we split up bodies.

We tend to group impairments into the categories either of 'disabling' (bad) or just 'limiting' (good). For example, wearing a hearing aid is seen as much more disabling than wearing glasses, although both serve to amplify a deficient sense. But loss of hearing is associated with aging in a way that

the point made here Lacan makes the concept fundamental to subjectivity itself. Other psychoanalysts who developed Freud's notion of *Spaltung* in the directions suggested by Davis include Melanie Klein (the child's splitting of objects) and Bruno Bettelheim (the link between the split and fairy tales).

4. J. Ryan and F. Thomas, *The Politics of Mental Handicap* (Harmondsworth: Penguin, 1980), ctd. in Michael Oliver, *The Politics of Disablement: A Sociological Approach* (New York: St. Martin's, 1990), p. 27 [Davis's note].

nearsightedness is not. Breast removal is seen as an impairment of femininity and sexuality, whereas the removal of a foreskin is not seen as a diminution of masculinity. The coding of body parts and the importance attached to their selective function or dysfunction is part of a much larger system of signs and meanings in society, and is constructed as such.

'Splitting' may help us to understand one way in which disability is seen as part of a system in which value is attributed to body parts. The disabling of the body part or function is then part of a removal of value. The gradations of value are socially determined, but what is striking is the way that rather than being incremental or graduated, the assignment of the term 'disabled,' and the consequent devaluation are total. That is, the concept of disabled seems to be an absolute rather than a gradient one. One is either disabled or not. Value is tied to the ability to earn money. If one's body is productive, it is not disabled. People with disabilities continue to earn less than 'normal' people and, even after the passage of the Americans with Disabilities Act, 69 percent of Americans with disabilities were unemployed.[5] Women and men with disabilities are seen as less attractive, less able to marry and be involved in domestic production.

The ideology of the assigning of value to the body goes back to preindustrial times. Myths of beauty and ugliness have laid the foundations for normalcy. In particular, the Venus myth is one that is dialectically linked to another. This embodiment of beauty and desire is tied to the story of the embodiment of ugliness and repulsion. So the appropriate mythological character to compare the armless Venus with is Medusa.[6] Medusa was once a beautiful sea goddess who, because she had sexual intercourse with Poseidon at one of Athene's temples, was turned by Athene into a winged monster with glaring eyes, huge teeth, protruding tongue, brazen claws, and writhing snakes for hair. Her hideous appearance has the power to turn people into stone, and Athene eventually completes her revenge by having Perseus kill Medusa. He finds Medusa by stealing the one eye and one tooth shared by the Graiae until they agree to help him. Perseus then kills Medusa by decapitating her while looking into his brightly polished shield, which neutralizes the power of her appearance; he then puts her head into a magic wallet that shields onlookers from its effects. When Athene receives the booty, she uses Medusa's head and skin to fashion her own shield.

In the Venus tradition, Medusa is a poignant double. She is the necessary counter in the dialectic of beauty and ugliness, desire and repulsion, wholeness and fragmentation. Medusa is the disabled woman to Venus's perfect body. The story is a kind of allegory of a 'normal' person's intersection with the disabled body. This intersection is marked by the power of the visual. The 'normal' person sees the disabled person and is turned to stone, in some

5. *New York Times*, October 27, 1994, A22 [Davis's note]. The Americans with Disabilities Act was passed in 1990.

6. The pairing of beauty with ugliness is further carried out in Venus's marriage to Vulcan, who is himself both ugly and disabled by his lameness. Lameness tends also be associated in an ableist way with impotence—as it is, for example, in W. Somerset Maugham's [1915 novel] *Of Human Bondage* [Davis's note]. Davis gives one version of the myth. In most accounts, Medusa is one of three monstrous sisters, the Gorgons; because she is the only mortal among them, the hero Perseus (the son of Zeus and Danaë) is able to kill her, once he has obtained supernatural aids—winged sandals and the wallet into which he could put Medusa's head—with the unwilling help of the Graiae, the Gorgons' sisters. Poseidon is the Greek god of the sea; Athene (Athena), the Greek goddess of war, the arts and crafts, and wisdom. Vulcan is an Italian fire-god, identified with the Greek Hephaestus, god of fire and especially the forge.

sense, by the visual interaction. In this moment, the normal person suddenly feels self-conscious, rigid, unable to look but equally drawn to look. The visual field becomes problematic, dangerous, treacherous. The disability becomes a power derived from its otherness, its monstrosity, in the eyes of the 'normal' person. The disability must be decapitated and then contained in a variety of magic wallets. Rationality, for which Athene stands, is one of the devices for containing, controlling, and reforming the disabled body so that it no longer has the power to terrorize. And the issue of mutilation comes up as well because the disabled body is always the reminder of the whole body about to come apart at the seams. It provides a vision of, a caution about, the body as a construct held together willfully, always threatening to become its individual parts—cells, organs, limbs, perceptions—like the fragmented, shared eye and tooth that Perseus ransoms back to the Graiae.

In order to understand better how normalcy is bred into ways of viewing the body, it might be productive to think about the body as it appears in art, photography, and the other visual media. There has been a powerful tradition in Western art of representing the body in a way that serves to solidify, rather early on in history, a preferred mode of envisioning the body. This tradition, identified by Kenneth Clark, has been most clearly articulated in the 'nude.' The nude, as Clark makes clear, is not a literal depiction of the human body but rather a set of conventions about the body: 'the nude is not the subject of art, but a form of art.' Or, as he says, the nude is 'the body re-formed.'[7] If that is the case then the nude is really part of the development of a set of idealized conventions about the way the body is supposed to look.

While some nudes may be male, when people talk about 'the nude' they most often mean the female nude. Lynda Nead, in a feminist correction of Clark, points out that 'more than any other subject, the female nude connotes "Art." '[8] And in that tradition, the Venus becomes the vortex for thinking about the female body. The Venus is, rather than a subject, a masculine way of fashioning the female body, or of remaking it into a conceptual whole.

I emphasize the word 'whole,' because the irony of the Venus tradition is that virtually no Venuses have been preserved intact from antiquity. Indeed, one of the reasons for the popularity of the Venus de Milo was that from the time it was discovered in 1820 until 1893 when Furtwängler's[9] scholarship revealed otherwise, the statue was, according to Clark, 'believed to be an original of the fifth century and the only free-standing figure of a woman that had come down from the great period with the advantage of a head.'[1]

The mutilation of the statues is made more ironic by the fact that their headless and armless state is usually overlooked by art historians—barely referred to at all by Clark, for example, in the entirety of his book. The art historian does not *see* the absence and so fills the absence with a presence. This compensation leads us to understand that in the discourse of the nude, one is dealing not simply with art history but with the reception of disability, the way that the 'normal' observer compensates or defends against the presence of difference. This is a 'way of seeing' not often discussed in art criti-

7. Kenneth Clark, *The Nude: A Study in Ideal Form* (New York: Pantheon, 1964), pp. 5, 3 [Davis's note]. Clark (1903–1983), English art historian.

8. Lynda Nead, *The Female Nude: Art, Obscenity, and Sexuality* (London: Routledge, 1992), p. i [Davis's note].

9. Adolf Furtwängler (1853–1907), German classical archaeologist.

1. Clark, *The Nude*, p. 89 [Davis's note].

cism. Of course, one can consider that art historians are really just making the best of a bad situation, but it is possible to make a number of further observations.

First of all, the headlessness and armlessness of Venuses link them, structurally, with the Medusa tradition. Many of these Venuses have in effect been decapitated. There seems to be a reciprocal relationship between the decapitations of Medusa in myth and of Venus in reality. It seems that the Venus is really only made possible in coordination with the Medusa—that Aphrodite can romp because Medusa can kill. So it is a fitting dialectic that Medusa's beheading is contained within every broken Venus. The speechlessness of the art historian about the mutilation of his objects of beauty and desire is the effect of his metaphoric transformation to stone. This lapsus[2] in speech is really an avoidance, a wish to avoid the castrating, terrifying vision of Medusa—the disabled, the monster, who is also the disabler. In a larger sense, as Nead suggests, all visions of the female nude, particularly in the Venus tradition, are attempts by male artists and critics to gird themselves against the irrationality and chaos of the body—particularly the female body:

> It begins to speak of a deep-seated fear and disgust of the female body and of femininity within patriarchal culture and of a construction of masculinity around the related fear of the contamination and dissolution of the male ego.[3]

In thinking about disability, one can extend this argument and say that the fear of the unwhole body, of the altered body, is kept at bay by depictions of whole, systematized bodies—the nudes of Western art. The unwhole body is the unholy body. Or as Kaja Silverman points out[4] about images of the body in film, society creates a 'protective shield' that insulates it against the possibility of mutilation, fragmentation, castration.

Indeed, the systematization of the body by artist and critic suggests a linearity, a regularity, a completeness that belie the fragmentary, explosive way the body is constitutively experienced. Clark exemplifies this systematic approach in discussing the Esquiline Venus of the fifth century, the first embodiment of these conventions.

> But she is solidly desirable, compact, proportionate; and, in fact, her proportions have been calculated on a simple mathematical scale. The unit of measurement is her head. She is seven heads tall; there is the length of one head between her breasts, one from breast to navel, and one from the navel to the division of the legs . . . fundamentally this is the architecture of the body that will control the observations of classically minded artists till the end of the nineteenth century.[5]

The amnesia of art historians to the subject of mutilation and decapitation (the Esquiline Venus has no head) is not accidental. The most we get from

2. A falling, slip (Latin); slips of the tongue are discussed by Freud in *The Psychopathology of Everyday Life* (1901).
3. Nead, *The Female Nude*, pp. 17–18 [Davis's note].
4. Kaja Silverman, "Historical Trauma and Male Subjectivity," in *Psychoanalysis and Cinema*, ed. E. Ann Kaplan (New York: Routledge, 1990), p. 14 [Davis's note].
5. Clark, *The Nude*, p. 75 [Davis's note].

Clark in his entire book is one wistful mention of a Greco-Roman depiction of the three graces as 'a relief in the Louvre, headless, alas.'[6] The 'alas' speaks volumes. This amnesia, this looking away from incompleteness, an averting of the attention, a sigh, is the tip of a defensive mechanism that allows the art historian still to see the statue as an object of desire. So the critic's aim is to restore the damage, bring back the limbs, through an act of imagination.[7] This phenomenon is not unlike the experience of 'phantom limb,' the paradoxical effect that amputees experience of sensing their missing limb. In the case of the art historian, the statue is seen as complete with phantom limbs and head. The art historian does not see the lack, the presence of an impairment, but rather mentally reforms the outline of the Venus so that the historian can return the damaged woman in stone to a pristine origin of wholeness. His is an act of reformation of the visual field, a sanitizing of the disruption in perception.

This is the same act of imagination, or one might say control, that bans from the nude the representation of normal biological processes. For example, there are no pregnant Venuses, there are no paintings of Venuses who are menstruating, micturating, defecating—lactating and lacrimating[8] being the only recognized activities of idealized women. There are no old Venuses (with the exception of a Diana by Rembrandt[9]). One might think of a pregnant Venus as a temporarily disabled woman, and as such banned from the reconstruction of the body we call 'the nude.' Clark distinguishes between prehistoric fertility goddesses, like the Willendorf Venus,[1] images of fertility and pregnancy, and the differently ideal Grecian versions which are never pregnant. As Nead notes, 'Clark alludes to this image of the female body [the Willendorf Venus] as undisciplined, out of control; it is excluded from the proper concerns of art in favor of the smooth, uninterrupted line of the Cycladic [Greek] figure.'[2] As artists and art historians shun the fluids and changes in shape that are incompatible with the process of forming the 'regular' body, the evidentiary record of mutilated Venuses must be repressed by a similar process.

A cautionary word must be said on the decapitated and armless Venuses. While it is true that male statues equally are truncated, the incompleteness of the female statues suggests another obvious point that has been repressed for so long—violence. Did all these statues lose their arms and heads by sheer accident, were the structurally fragile head and limbs more likely to deteriorate than the torso, were there random acts of vandalism, or was a particular kind of symbolic brutality committed on these stone women? Did

6. Ibid., p. 91 [Davis's note]. The Graces: daughters of Zeus, they personified beauty and grace, and were the constant attendants of Aphrodite / Venus.

7. This phenomenon corresponds to the filmgoer's experience of watching stories of disability. As Martin Norden points out, when disability is depicted in film, there is a strong tendency to erase or fix the "problem" by the end of the film (*Cinema of Isolation: A History of Physical Disability in the Movies* [New Brunswick, N.J.: Rutgers University Press, 1994], pp. 59ff.). For instance, no one recalls that Luke Skywalker in *Star Wars* [*The Empire Strikes Back*, 1980] lost his lower arm in a battle with his father, Darth Vader. At the end of the film, a techno-intensive prosthesis is fitted on his stump, and for the sequels he acts as if his hand had grown back. No short-circuits or balky fingers are ever a problem in the sequels [Davis's note].

8. Weeping.

9. Rembrandt van Rijn (1606–1669), Dutch painter. Diana: a Roman goddess identified with the Greek Artemis, goddess of the hunt.

1. A 4" limestone statue of a woman (ca. 25,000 B.C.E.), found near the Austrian town of Willendorf in 1903.

2. Nead, *The Female Nude*, p. 19 [Davis's note].

vandals, warriors, and adolescent males amuse themselves by committing focused acts of violence, of sexual bravado and mockery on these embodiments of desire? An armless woman is a symbol of sexual allure without the ability to resist, a headless nude captures a certain kind of male fantasy of submission without the complication of the individuality and the authority granted by a face, even an idealized one. We do not know and will probably never know what happened to these statues, although the destruction of the Parthenon[3] figures has been documented as done by occupying soldiers. The point is that the violence against the body, the acts of hacking, mutilation and so on, have to be put in the context we have been discussing. An act of violence against a female statue is constitutively different from that against a male statue—and these are acts that can be placed in a range of terrorist acts against women during war. Such acts create disabled people, and so, in a sense, these Venuses are the disabled women of art. To forget that is again to commit acts of omission of a rather damning nature.

Of course, a statue is not a person. But as representations of women, the Venus statues carry a powerful cultural signification. The reaction to such statues, both by critics and other viewers, tells much about the way in which we consider the body both as a whole and as incomplete. One point to note is that the art historian, like Clark, tends to perform a complex double act. On the one hand, the critic sees the incomplete statue as whole, imagines the phantom limbs in order to defend against incompleteness, castration, the chaotic or 'grotesque body,' as Peter Stallybrass and Allon White have, using Bakhtinian terminology, called it.[4] On the other hand (if indeed our standard is *two* hands), the critic and the artist are constantly faced with the fragmentary nature of the body, analyzing parts, facing the gaze of the missing part that must be argued into existence.

The model for the fragmentary nature of the nude is best illustrated by the famous story of Zeuxis, as told by Pliny.[5] When Zeuxis painted his version of Aphrodite, he constructed her from the parts of five beautiful young women of his town of Kroton. His vision of the wholeness of Aphrodite was really an assemblage of unrelated parts. Likewise, the critic in regarding the whole nude must always be speaking of parts: 'their torsos have grown so long that the distance from the breasts to the division of the legs is three units instead of two, the pelvis is wide, the thighs are absurdly short.'[6] The whole can only be known by the sum of its parts—even when those parts are missing. John Barrell has detailed the reactions of eighteenth-century men to the Venus dei Medici, and noted how they tended to examine every detail of the statue.[7] Edward Wright, for example, tells observers to 'strictly examine every part' and a typical account read thus:

3. The chief temple to Athena, built (447–432 B.C.E.) on Athens' Acropolis; the Acropolis was seized by the Turks in 1458, and during a Venetian bombardment in 1687 the explosion of a powder magazine in the temple destroyed the center of the building. Many sculptures decorated the structure.
4. See Peter Stallybrass and Allon White, *The Politics and Poetics of Transgression* (Chicago: University of Chicago Press, 1987) [Davis's note]. The Russian theorist MIKHAIL BAKHTIN (1895–1975) discusses the "carnivalesque" and the "grotesque body" in *Rabelais and His World* (1965).
5. Pliny the Elder (23/4–79 C.E.), Roman historian and scientific encyclopedist; he gave this account of the Greek painter Zeuxis (active in Athens ca. 400 B.C.E.) in his *Natural History* 35.36.
6. Clark, *The Nude*, p. 91 [Davis's note].
7. John Barrell, " 'The Dangerous Goddess': Masculinity, Prestige, and the Aesthetic in Early Eighteenth-Century Britain," *Cultural Critique* 12 (1989): 101–31 [Davis's note]. Venus de' Medici: a Roman copy (1st c. B.C.E.) of a Greek original (4th c. B.C.E.), discovered in Rome in the 16th century (now in the Uffizi, Florence).

> One might very well insist on the beauty of the breasts. . . . They are small, distinct, and delicate to the highest degree; with an idea of softness. . . . And yet with all that softness, they have a firmness too. . . . From her breasts, her shape begins to diminish gradually down to her waist; . . . Her legs are neat and slender; the small of them is finely rounded; and her feet are little, white, and pretty.[8]

Another carped:

> The head is something too little for the Body, especially for the Hips and Thighs; the Fingers excessively long and taper, and no match for the Knuckles, except for the little Finger of the Right-Hand.[9]

These analyses perform a juggling act between the fragmentation of the body and its reunification into an hallucinated erotic whole.[1] In imagining the broken statues, the critic must mentally replace the arms and the head, then criticize any other restoration, as does Clark in attacking the reconstruction of the Venus of Arles: 'the sculptor Girardon[2] . . . not only added the arms and changed the angle of the head, but smoothed down the whole body, since the King was offended by the sight of ribs and muscles.'[3] The point here is that the attempt of the critic to keep the body in some systematic whole is really based on a repression of the fragmentary nature of the body.

One might also want to recall that for the Greeks these statues, while certainly works of art, were also to be venerated, since they were representations of deities. For the Greeks, Aphrodite was not a myth; she was a goddess whose domain was desire. It somehow seems appropriate that the ritualistic or reverential attitude toward these statues, pointed out by Walter Benjamin,[4] indeed their very appearance in stone (which Page duBois sees as a cultic representation of the bones of the female spirits[5]), has been reproduced in the attitude of that most secular of worshippers, the art critic. For the Venus has a double function: she is both a physical and a spiritual incarnation of desire. In that double sense, the critic must emphasize her spiritual existence by going beyond her physical incarnation in fallible stone, and her mutilations, to the essential body, the body of Desire, the body of the Other.

We can put this paradox in Lacanian terms. For Lacan, the most primitive, the earliest experience of the body is actually of the fragmented body (*corps morcelé*).[6] The infant experiences his or her body as separate parts or pieces, as 'turbulent movements.' For the infant, rather than a whole, the body is an assemblage of arms, legs, surfaces. These representations / images of frag-

8. Ctd. in ibid., p. 127 [Davis's note].
9. Ibid. [Davis's note].
1. The Medici Venus had been reconstructed, so the 18th-century men did not have to face the incompleteness of their erotic ideal [Davis's note].
2. François Girardon (1628–1715), French sculptor. Venus of Arles: a Roman copy of a Greek original (ca. 350–340 B.C.E.) by Praxiteles (now in the Louvre).
3. Clark, *The Nude* p. 87 [Davis's note].
4. See "The Work of Art in the Age of Mechanical Reproduction" (1936) [Davis's note]. BENJAMIN (1892–1940), German theorist and aesthetician; for this essay, see above.
5. See Page duBois, *Sowing the Body: Psychoanalysis and Ancient Representations of Women* (Chicago: University of Chicago Press, 1988) [Davis's note].
6. The term *corps morcelé* is a bit more vivid than "fragmented body," the now-standard translation of the term into English. *Morceler* is defined as "to divide up into pieces." It more actively carries the concept of chopping, cutting, or hacking. Thus the *corps morcelé* might more accurately be called "the cut-up body." However, I will retain the standard usage, for the sake of uniformity [Davis's note].

mented body parts Lacan calls *imagos* because they are 'constituted for the "instincts" themselves.'

> Among these *imagos* are some that represent the elective vectors of aggressive intentions, which they provide with an efficacity that might be called magical. These are the images of castration, mutilation, dismemberment, dislocation, evisceration, devouring, bursting open of the body, in short, the *imagos* that I have grouped together under the apparently structural term of *imagos of the fragmented body*.[7]

The process that builds a self involves the enforced unifying of these fragments through the hallucination of a whole body, 'a Gestalt, that is to say, in an exteriority,' as Lacan has pointed out. The process 'extends from a fragmented body-image to a form of its totality . . . and, lastly, to the assumption of the armour of an alienating identity.'[8] When the child points to an image in the mirror—at that stage Lacan calls 'the mirror phase'—the child recognizes (actually misrecognizes) that unified image as his or her self. That identification is really the donning of an identity, an 'armor' against the chaotic or fragmentary body.

In this sense, the disabled body is a direct *imago* of the repressed fragmented body. The disabled body causes a kind of hallucination of the mirror phase gone wrong. The subject looks at the disabled body and has a moment of cognitive dissonance, or should we say a moment of cognitive resonance with the earlier state of fragmentation. Rather than seeing the whole body in the mirror, the subject sees the repressed fragmented body; rather than seeing the object of desire, as controlled by the Other, the subject sees the true self of the fragmented body. For Lacan, because the child first saw its body as a 'collection of discrete part-objects, adults can never perceive their bodies in a complete fashion in later life.'[9] This repressed truth of self-perception revolves around a prohibited central, specular moment—of seeing the disabled body—in which the 'normal' person views the Medusa image, in which the Venus-nude cannot be sustained as a viable armor. In Lacanian terms, the *moi*[1] is threatened with a breaking-up, literally, of its structure, is threatened with a reminder of its incompleteness. In a specular, face-to-face moment, the ego is involved in what J. B. Pontalis calls 'death work,' which involves the 'fundamental process of unbinding [of the ego], of fragmentation, of breaking up, of separation, of bursting.'[2] Thus the specular moment between the armored, unified self and its repressed double—the fragmented body—is characterized by a kind of death-work, repetition compulsion in which the unified self continuously sees itself undone—castrated, mutilated, perforated, made partial. In this context, it is worth noting that the Venus tradition involves castration at its very origin. Aphrodite is said to have been born from the foam of Uranus's genitals which Cronus threw into the sea after castrating his father.[3] The dynamic is clear. Male mutilation is

7. Lacan, "The Mirror Stage" [see above], in *Écrits: A Selection*, trans. Alan Sheridan (New York: Norton, 1977), pp. 2, 11 [Davis's note].
8. Lacan, "The Mirror Stage," pp. 2, 4 [Davis's note].
9. Ellie Ragland-Sullivan, *Jacques Lacan and the Philosophy of Psychoanalysis* (Urbana: University of Illinois Press, 1987), p. 21 [Davis's note].

1. Me (French), a Lacanian term for the self.
2. Ctd. in Ragland-Sullivan, *Jacques Lacan*, p. 70 [Davis's note]. Pontalis (b. 1924), French psychoanalyst.
3. Robert Graves, *The Greek Myths* (New York: Penguin, 1957), p. 49 [Davis's note]. Uranus (literally "Sky" in Greek), the first ruler of the world, was born from Gaia (Earth); Cronus was the youn-

mitigated by the creation of the desirable female body. The disabled body is corrected by the wholeness of the constructed body of the nude. But, as has been noted, the emphasis on wholeness never entirely erases the foundation of the Venus tradition in the idea of mutilation, fragmented bodies, decapitation, amputation.

If we follow these terms, the disabled Venus serves as an unwanted reminder that the 'real' body, the 'normal body,' the observer's body, is in fact always already a 'fragmented body.' The linking together of all the disparate bodily sensations and locations is an act of will, a hallucination that always threatens to fall apart. The mutilated Venus and the disabled person, particularly the disabled person who is missing limbs or body parts, will become in fantasy visual echoes of the primal fragmented body—a signifier of castration and lack of wholeness. Missing senses, blindness, deafness, aphasia, in that sense, will point to missing bodily parts or functions. The art historian in essence dons or retains the armor of identity, needs the armor as does Perseus who must see Medusa through the polished shield. The art historian's defense is that mirror-like shield that conjures wholeness through a misrecognition linking the parts into a whole.

What this analysis tells us is that the 'disabled body' belongs to no one, just as the normal body, or even the 'phallus' belongs to no one. Even a person who is missing a limb, or is physically 'different,' still has to put on, assume, the disabled body and identify with it.[4] The disabled body, far from being the body of some small group of 'victims,' is an entity from the earliest of childhood instincts, a body that is common to all humans, as Lacan would have it. The 'normal' body is actually the body we develop later. It is in effect a Gestalt—and therefore in the realm of what Lacan calls the Imaginary. The realm of the 'Real' in Lacanian terms is where the fragmented body is found because it is the body that precedes the ruse of identity and wholeness. Artists often paint this vision, and it often appears in dreams 'in the form of disjointed limbs, or of those organs represented in exoscopy . . . the very same that the visionary Hieronymus Bosch has fixed for all time.'[5]

In understanding this point, we can perhaps see how the issue of disability transcends the rather narrow category to which it has been confined. Just as, I claim, we readers are all deaf, participating in a deafened moment, likewise, we all—first and foremost—have fragmented bodies. It is in tracing our tactical and self-constructing (deluding) journeys away from that originary self that we come to conceive and construct that phantom goddess of wholeness, normalcy, and unity—the nude.

One might even add that the element of repulsion and fear associated with fragmentation and disability may in fact come from the very act of repressing

gest of their children (and was himself overthrown by Zeus).

4. Irving Kenneth Zola pointed out that people with disabilities are mostly born into "normal" families. Thus they are socialized into an ableist culture and have to adopt their disabled identity. "We think of ourselves in the shadows of the external world. The very vocabulary we use to describe ourselves is borrowed from the society. We are *de*-formed, *dis*-eased, *dis*-abled, *dis*-ordered, *ab*-normal, and most telling of all an *in*-valid" ("Communication Barriers between 'the Able-Bodied' and 'the Handicapped,'" in *Psychological and Social Impact of Physical Disability*, ed. Robert P. Marinelli and Arthur E. Dell Orto [New York: Springer, 1984], p. 144) [Davis's note].

5. Lacan, "The Mirror Stage," p. 4 [Davis's note]. "Exoscopy": a view from the outside. Bosch (ca. 1460–1516), Dutch painter whose best-known works feature grotesque figures that sometimes combine human, animal, vegetable, and inanimate parts.

the primal fragmentariness of the body. As Freud wrote, 'the uncanny is in reality nothing new or foreign, but something familiar and old-established in the mind that has been estranged only [in] the process of repression.'[6] The feelings of repulsion associated with the uncanny, *das Unheimlich*, the unfamiliar, are not unlike the emotions of the 'normal' when they are visualizing the disabled. The key to the idea of the uncanny is in its relation to the normal. *Heimlich* is a word associated with the home, with familiarity—and with the comfortable predictability of the home. The disabled body is seen as *unheimlich* because it is the familiar gone wrong. Disability is seen as something that does not belong at home, not to be associated with the home. Freud notes that the terror or repulsion of the uncanny is ambivalent, is found precisely in its relation to and yet deviance from the familiar. That the uncanny can be related to disability is made clear when Freud cites specifically 'dismembered limbs, a severed head, a hand cut off at the wrist' as *unheimlich*.[7] What is uncanny about dismemberment seems to be the familiarity of the body part that is then made *unheimlich* by its severing. As Freud wrote, 'the *unheimlich* is what was once *heimisch*, homelike, familiar; the prefix "un" is the token of repression.'[8]

But in this equation I think Freud is actually missing the earlier repression of the inherently fragmentary nature of the original body *imago*. The homeyness of the body, its familiarity as whole, complete, contained, is based on a dynamic act of repression. Freud is assuming that the whole body is an *a priori* given, as he had done with the concept of the ego. But as Lacan has shown more than adequately, the ego is a multifaceted structure to be understood in its philosophical complexity. Likewise the ground of the body, its materiality given by Freud, needs a re-analysis. The route of disability studies allows for this revisioning. In this process, the *heimisch* body becomes the *unheimlich* body, and the fragment, the disabled parts, can be seen as the originary, familiar, body made unfamiliar by repression. Dominant culture has an investment in seeing the disabled, therefore, as uncanny, as something found outside the home, unfamiliar, while in fact where is the disabled body found if not at home?

I have been concentrating on the physical body, but it is worth considering for a moment the issue of madness. While mental illness is by definition not related to the intactness of the body, nevertheless, it shows up as a disruption in the visual field. We 'see' that someone is insane by her physical behavior, communication, and so on. Yet the fear is that the mind is fragmenting, breaking up, falling apart, losing itself—all terms we associate with becoming mad. With the considerable information we have about the biological roots of mental illness, we begin to see the disease again as a breaking up of 'normal' body chemistry: amino acid production gone awry, depleted levels of certain polypeptide chains or hormones. Language production can become fragmentary, broken, in schizophrenic speech production. David Rothman[9] points out that in eighteenth- and nineteenth-century America, insanity was seen as being caused by the fragmented nature of 'modern' life—particularly the pressures brought to bear on people by a society in which economic boundaries were disappearing. This fragmenting of society pro-

6. Freud, "The Uncanny" [see above], in *Studies in Parapsychology* (New York: Collier, 1963), p. 47 [Davis's note].

7. Ibid., p. 49 [Davis's note].

8. Ibid., p. 51 [Davis's note].

9. American historian (b. 1937).

duced a fragmentation of the individual person. So the asylums that sprung up during this period recommended a cure that involved a removal from the urban, alienated, fragmented environment to rural hospitals in which order and precision could be restored. 'A precise schedule and regular work became the two characteristics of the best private and public institutions. . . . The structure of the mental hospital would counteract the debilitating influences of the community.' As Rothman notes, 'Precision, certainty, regularity, order' were the words that were seen as embodying the essence of cure.[1] The mind would be restored to 'wholeness' by restoring the body through manual labor. However, needless to add, one had to have a whole body to have a whole mind. The general metaphor here continues to be a notion of wholeness, order, clean boundaries, as opposed to fragmentations, disordered bodies, messy boundaries.

If people with disabilities are considered anything, they are or have been considered creatures of disorder—monsters, monstrous. Leslie Fiedler has taken some pains to show this in his book *Freaks.*[2] If we look at Mary Shelley's *Frankenstein,*[3] we find some of the themes we have been discussing emerge in novelistic form. First, we might want to note that we have no name for the creation of Dr Frankenstein other than 'monster.' (This linguistic lapsus is usually made up for in popular culture by referring to the creature itself as 'Frankenstein,' a terminology that confuses the creator with the created.) In reading the novel, or speaking about it, we can only call the creature 'the monster.' This linguistic limitation is worth noting because it encourages the reader to consider the creature a monster rather than a person with disabilities.

We do not often think of the monster in Mary Shelley's work as disabled, but what else is he? The characteristic of his disability is a difference in appearance. He is more than anything a disruption in the visual field. There is nothing else different about him—he can see, hear, talk, think, ambulate, and so on. It is worth noting that in popular culture, largely through the early film versions of the novel, the monster is inarticulate, somewhat mentally slow, and walks with a kind of physical impairment.[4] In addition, the film versions add Ygor, the hunchbacked criminal who echoes the monster's disability in his own. Even in the recent film version by Kenneth Branagh, the creature walks with a limp and speaks with an impediment.[5] One cannot dismiss this filtering of the creature through the lens of multiple disability. In order for the audience to fear and loathe the creature, he must be made to transcend the pathos of a single disability. Of course, it would be unseemly for a village to chase and torment a paraplegic or a person with acromegaly. Disabled people are to be pitied and ostracized; monsters are to be destroyed; audiences must not confuse the two.

1. David J. Rothman, *The Discovery of the Asylum: Social Order and Disorder in the Early Republic* (Boston: Little Brown, 1971), pp. 144, 145 [Davis's note].
2. *Freaks: Myths and Images of the Secret Self* (New York: Simon and Schuster, 1978); Fiedler (b. 1917) is an American literary and cultural critic.
3. The 1818 tale of horror by Mary Shelley (1797–1851), English novelist and wife of PERCY BYSSHE SHELLEY.
4. According to Norden, Robert Florey, a writer who contributed to the original *Frankenstein* script, came up with the idea of having Dr. Frankenstein's assistant Fritz break into a medical school to steal a brain. He finds the "normal" brain the doctor wanted but then drops it and takes one marked "abnormal" instead [Davis's note]. The French-born writer and director Florey (1900–1979) worked on the best-known (though not earliest) film version, directed by James Whale (1931).
5. *Mary Shelley's Frankenstein* (1994), which also starred the Irish director Branagh (b. 1960) as Victor Frankenstein.

In the novel, it is clear that Dr Frankenstein cannot abide his creation for only one reason—its hideous appearance. Indeed, the creature's only positive human contact is with the blind old man De Lacey, who cannot see the unsightly features. When De Lacey's family catches a glimpse of the creature, the women faint or run, and the men beat and pursue him. His body is a zone of repulsion; the reaction he evokes is fear and loathing. The question one wants to ask is why does a physical difference produce such a profound response?

The answer, I believe, is twofold. First, what is really hideous about the creature is not so much his physiognomy as what that appearance suggests. The *corps morcelé* makes its appearance immediately in the construction of the monster. Ironically, Dr Frankenstein adapts Zeuxis's notion of taking ideal parts from individuals to create the ideal whole body. As he says, 'I collected bones from charnel houses. . . . The dissecting room and the slaughter-house furnished many of my materials.'[6] From these fragments, seen as loathsome and disgusting, Frankenstein assembles what he wishes to create—a perfect human. It is instructive in this regard to distinguish the Boris Karloff incarnation of the creature[7]—with the bolt through his neck—or Branagh's grotesquely sewn creature, from the image that Mary Shelley would have us imagine. Dr Frankenstein tells us:

> His limbs were in proportion, and I had selected his features as beautiful. Beautiful—Great God! His yellow skin scarcely covered the work of muscles and arteries beneath; his hair was of a lustrous black and flowing; his teeth of a pearly whiteness; but these luxuriances only formed a more horrid contrast with his watery eyes, that seemed almost of the same colour as the dun white sockets in which they were set, his shrivelled complexion and straight black lips.[8]

What then constitutes the horror? If we add up the details, what we see is a well-proportioned man with long black hair, pearly white teeth, whose skin is somewhat deformed—resulting in jaundice and perhaps a tightness or thinness of the skin, a lack of circulation perhaps causing shriveling, watery eyes and darkened lips. This hardly seems to constitute horror rather than, say, pathos.[9]

What is found to be truly horrifying about Frankenstein's creature is its composite quality, which is too evocative of the fragmented body. Frankenstein's reaction to this living *corps morcelé* is repulsion: 'the beauty of the dream vanished, and breathless horror and disgust filled my heart.'[1] Frankenstein attempted to create a unified nude, an object of beauty and har-

6. Mary Shelley, *Frankenstein, or The Modern Prometheus* (Oxford: Oxford University Press, 1990), pp. 54–55 [Davis's note]. Prometheus, the Titan punished for giving mortals fire stolen from the gods, is sometimes also credited with creating the human race from mud.

7. In *Frankenstein* (1931), *Bride of Frankenstein* (1935), and *Son of Frankenstein* (1939); the English actor Karloff (born William Henry Pratt, 1887–1969) is best remembered for his roles in these and other horror films.

8. Shelley, *Frankenstein*, p. 57 [Davis's note].

9. Indeed, one could argue that this function of horror films is to remove the element of pity in the visual transaction between "normal" viewer and disabled object. In the place of pity, pure repulsion is made allowable by turning the object with a disability into a criminal, a horror, a monstrosity. While everyone may enjoy a good horror movie now and then, there is a case to be made that horror films involving physically disabled characters are in fact the equivalent of racist films. The counterbalanced compassionate films showing people with disabilities triumphing over their disability is just the other moment of the same dialectic [Davis's note].

1. Shelley, *Frankenstein*, p. 57 [Davis's note].

mony—a Venus, in effect. He ended up with a Medusa whose existence reveals the inhering and enduring nature of the archaic fragmented body, endlessly repressed but endlessly reappearing.

Why does the appearance of the monster produce so powerful an affect? Routinely, one might view a deformed person, even a multiply deformed one, without desiring to kill that person. Here we see a man whose skin is strange or unnatural being transposed into the category 'monster.' The element of skin reminds us that the monster as a disturbance in the visual field is linked to the tactile field. The disruption in the skin's surface immediately translates into a threat of touching, of being touched. The idea of touch always initiates a dialectic of attraction and repulsion, of fear, hatred, or erotic attraction. Indeed, from a psychoanalytic viewpoint there is not much difference between these choices. So, inevitably, the disabled body becomes a site of the erotic, as instantly it is perceived in either the Venus or the Medusa scenarios.[2] In Shelley's novel, after the creation, Dr Frankenstein has rather a peculiar response—he goes to sleep and has a dream about his fiancée:

> I thought I saw Elizabeth, in the bloom of health, walking in the streets of Ingolstadt. Delighted and surprised, I embraced her, but as I imprinted the first kiss on her lips, they became livid with the hue of death; her features appeared to change, and I thought that I held the corpse of my dead mother in my arms; a shroud enveloped her form, and I saw the grave-worms crawling in the folds of the flannel.[3]

The rather incredible set of associations made by Dr Frankenstein would take pages to explore thoroughly, but what we might want to note here is that the immediate flight from the Medusa image of the monster's fragmented body leads immediately to the Venus body of Elizabeth, seen as frankly erotic. However, upon the first sexual contact the Venus myth immediately deconstructs, and Elizabeth's body initially changes to a corpse, then to the decomposing corpse of Frankenstein's dead mother. The visual leads to the tactile, which then contaminates the normal body. And all these moments lead back to the decomposing, fragmenting body. Later in the novel, when the creature demands a spouse, Frankenstein again creates the fragmented, now female, body. But at the last minute 'trembling with passion, [I] tore to pieces the thing on which I was engaged.'[4] Frankenstein's explicit reason for failing to give the monster a mate is fear that a race of deformed creatures would populate the earth and threaten the human race.[5] Thus the risk of the erotic touch, of the frankly erotic agenda for the creature, is seen as a contaminating danger to 'normal' people. So, the fragmented body is hacked up, exploded, into the fragments that make it up.

The work of Didier Anzieu, a psychoanalyst, might help to amplify how touch and skin contribute to the concept of the disabled body. Frankenstein's creation is driven out largely because of the nature of his skin, his covering,

2. Women with disabilities are often the target of sexual or physical abuse; children with disabilities or Deaf children are often the victims of child abuse. This impulse to touch is unfortunately seen quite dramatically in these situations [Davis's note].

3. Shelley, *Frankenstein*, p. 58 [Davis's note].

4. Ibid., p. 168 [Davis's note].

5. Later in the century Alexander Graham Bell would raise the same specter in regard to a deaf race taking over should deaf people be allowed to marry each other [Davis's note]. Bell (1847–1922), the Scottish-born American inventor best known for producing the first telephone, was keenly interested in the education of the deaf and in eugenics; Davis is referring to his *Memoirs upon the Formation of a Deaf Variety of the Human Race* (1884).

made hideous by its color, texture, and incompleteness. Anzieu postulates that skin is in effect an *imago* of the ego. As such, when the infant hallucinates the whole body, he or she actually uses the concept and the reality of skin as a metaphor for wholeness, completeness, total enveloping of a unitary self. The skin is in effect a 'narcissistic envelope.' As Anzieu notes:

> the boundaries of the body image (or the image of the body's boundaries) are acquired in the course of the child's detaching itself from its mother and they are to some degree analogous to the Ego boundaries which Federn has shown as being de-cathected in the process of depersonalization.[6]

For Anzieu, the skin is the metaphor and the reality of the intact ego. Any perforation or alteration of the skin's entirety signals the deconstruction of the concept of unity, of envelopment.

> In my view, the skin that has been torn from the body, if it is preserved whole, represents the protective envelope, the shield, which one must take from the other in phantasy either simply to have it for oneself or to duplicate and reinforce one's own skin.[7]

The disabled body presents in both visual and tactile terms the rupture of the skin-ego, whether that disruption is lack of limbs or dysfunction of sensory organs. Indeed, seeing is related to touching, as Freud has noted, as is hearing—each of which connects an observer to an object that may be out of range of touch. Anzieu tries to account for a prohibition on touching in Western culture, citing biblical injunctions, Christ's *noli me tangere*,[8] incest and masturbation prohibitions, and even Freud's renunciation of touching as a therapeutic technique. The point to be made is that touching involves the contact of one's ego, literally in this case, with the ego of the object. In the case of the perceptual realms involved in the disability transaction between subject and object, the specular moment leads to the tactile moment. Thus, touching represents an opening up of the ego, a kind of risk that the envelope may fail to contain the subject because of the moment of contact. 'The prohibition on touching separates the region of the familiar, a protected and protective region, from that of the strange, which is troubling and dangerous.'[9] Our touch is familiar, but the touch of the Other is *unheimlich*; so the disabled touch is seen as both contagious and erotic.

That this touch is eroticized and connected with the Oedipal moment is significant.

> The most primitive form of the tactile prohibition seems to run: do not stay clinging to the body of your parents . . . [but] the Oedipal prohibition reverses the elements of the prohibition on touching: what is familiar, in the first sense of familial, becomes dangerous . . .[1]

6. Didier Anzieu, *The Skin Ego*, [trans. Chris Turner] (New Haven: Yale University Press, 1989), pp. 39, 32 [Davis's note]. "Being de-cathected": having suffered the withdrawal of psychic energy or investment.

7. Ibid., p. 50 [Davis's note].

8. Do not touch me (Latin), a quotation from the Vulgate. These are the words of Jesus to Mary Magdalene after his resurrection (John 20.17).

9. Anzieu, *The Skin Ego*, p. 146 [Davis's note].

1. Ibid., pp. 146–67 [Davis's note]. Oedipal moment: the point at which, in Freud's schema, the boy internalizes the prohibition against incest (fearing castration as the potential punishment); the name is borrowed from the Greek myth of Oedipus, who, ignorant of their identities, killed his father and married his mother.

Around the Oedipal moment swirl the images of castration, mutilation, and a general prohibition against 'generalized contact, i.e. on the embracing, conjoining and confusing of bodies.' Touch represents a fragmenting of the body, a threat of mutilation, and a fear of losing one's boundaries, one's bodily integrity. In this sense, touching the creature, touching the disabled body, is both an erotic lure and a self-destroying gesture.

We can return, again, to the Venus, neatly enclosed in its marmoreal skin and thus representing an unperforated body, despite the mutilations that have disfigured it. Most of the visual arts eschew disability and disabled images, except perhaps for the romanticized images around madness. The work of Mary Duffy, a contemporary artists without arms, provides one notable exception to this reluctance to think of Venuses without arms as the equivalent of Medusa. In the first plate of a photographic series entitled *Cutting the Ties that Bind*, we see a standing figure draped entirely in white cloth against a dark background so that the figure beneath the drapery is not visible. In the second plate, the drapery is partially removed so that it covers mainly the thighs and legs revealing to us a female body, the artist's, without arms. The figure is clearly meant to reproduce the Venus de Milo in the flesh. The third picture in the series shows the figure stepping away from the drapery with a triumphant smile. The work serves to show how the female disabled body can be reappropriated by the artist herself. Duffy writes:

> By confronting people with my naked body, with its softness, its roundness and its threat I wanted to take control, redress the balance in which media representations of disabled women [are] usually tragic, always pathetic. I wanted to hold up a mirror to all those people who had stripped me bare previously . . . the general public with naked stares, and more especially the medical profession.[2]

The Medusa gaze is rerouted so that it comes not from the object of horror, the monstrous woman, but from the gaze of the normal observer. It is the 'normal' gaze that is seen as naked, as dangerous. And unlike Perseus slaying Medusa by holding up a mirror, it is now the 'object of horror' who holds the mirror up to the 'normal' observer.

This reappropriation of the normal gaze was further carried out by the photographer Jo Spence. Recognizing the inherent and unstated pose of normalcy imposed by the camera and by the photographic session, Spence revisioned her photography to be capable of representing the nude model as a person with disabilities. Her work, detailed in many shows and in her book *Putting Myself in the Picture: A Political, Personal, and Photographic Autobiography* (1986), partly focuses on her mastectomy. Spence links this operative and post-operative process to an understanding and participating gaze that seeks to touch, not recoil from, bodily changes. In addition to the simple fact of the partial mastectomy, Spence includes in her work photographs and texts that question assumptions about age and beauty. Her body is middle-aged, irregular, and defies the canons of ideal feminine beauty. Her work is involved with 'explaining my experience as a patient and the contradictions between ways in which the medical profession controls women's bodies and the "imaginary bodies" we inhabit as women.'[3]

2. Ctd. in Nead, *The Female Nude*, p. 78 [Davis's note].
3. Jo Spence, *Putting Myself in the Picture: A Political, Personal, and Photographic Autobiography* (London: Camden House, 1986), p. 156 [Davis's note].

The visual arts have done a magnificent job of centralizing normalcy and of marginalizing different bodies. As we have seen, initially the impulse came from a move to idealize the body and make up the perfect body out of perfect sub-units. Then with the rise of hegemonic normalcy, the impulse veered from ideal to normalizing representations. Either of these paradigms pushes the ordinary body, the abnormal body, out of the picture. Photographer David Hevey has written about the paucity of images of the disabled in photographic anthologies. He concludes that 'disabled people are represented but almost exclusively as symbols of "otherness" placed within equations which take their non-integration as a natural by-product of their impairment.'[4] When he looked for any images of disabled people, he found either medical photographs in which the 'patients' appear 'passive and stiff and "done to", the images bear a bizarre resemblance to colonial pictures where "the blacks" stand frozen and curious, while "whitey" lounges confident and sure,'[5] or images like those of Diane Arbus[6] that show the disabled as 'grotesque.' Ungrotesque, routine pictures of disabled people in advertising, 'art' photography, films and so on are hard to find. With the same regularity that bodies of color were kept out of the mainstream (and even the avant-garde) media in the years before the civil rights movement, so too are disabled bodies disqualified from representing universality.

One of the ways that visual images of the disabled have been appropriated into the modernist and postmodernist aesthetic is through the concept of the 'grotesque.' The word was used by Bakhtin to describe the aesthetic of the Middle Ages, which reveled in presenting the body in its nonidealized form. The grotesque, for Bakhtin, was associated with the common people, with a culture that periodically turned the established order upside down through the carnival and the carnivalesque. Gigantic features, scatological references, inverse political power were all hallmarks of the grotesque—an aesthetic that ultimately was displaced by humanistic notions of order, regularity, and of course power during the Renaissance.

While the term 'grotesque' has had a history of being associated with this counterhegemonic notion of people's aesthetics and the inherent power of the masses, what the term has failed to liberate is the notion of actual bodies as grotesque. There is a thin line between the grotesque and the disabled. Hevey examines, for example, how critics have received Diane Arbus's photographs of the disabled. Susan Sontag[7] writes that Arbus's 'work shows people who are pathetic, pitiable, as well as repulsive, but it does not arouse any compassionate feelings.' Later she adds, 'Do they see themselves, the viewer wonders, like *that*? Do they know how grotesque they are?'[8] The grotesque, in this sense, is seen as a concept without the redeeming sense of class rebellion in Bakhtin's formulation. Here it is simply the ugly, what makes us wince, look away, feel pity—more allied with its dictionary definition of 'hideous,' 'monstrous,' 'deformed,' 'gnarled.' Though artists and writers may use the grotesque, they rarely write about that state from the subject position of the disabled. The grotesque, as with disability in general, is used as a meta-

4. David Hevey, *The Creatures Time Forgot: Photography and Disability Imagery* (London: Routledge, 1992), p. 54 [Davis's note].
5. Ibid., p. 53 [Davis's note].
6. American photographer (1923–1971), whose best-known portraits emphasize the grotesqueness or abnormality of their subjects.
7. American cultural critic and novelist (b. 1933).
8. Ctd. in Hevey, *The Creatures Time Forgot*, p. 57 [Davis's note].

phor for otherness, solitude, tragedy, bitterness, alterity. The grotesque is defined in this sense as a disturbance in the normal visual field, not as a set of characteristics through which a fully constituted subject views the world. One problem with terms like 'disability' and 'the grotesque' is that they disempower the object of observation. The body is seen through a set of cultural default settings arrived at by the wholesale adoption of ableist cultural values.

In no area is this set of cultural values related to the visual more compelling than in film. Film is a medium whose main goal, one might say, is the construction and reconstruction of the body. The abnormal body plays a major role in the defining of the normal body, and so one might assume that film would be concerned with the issue of disability. Martin F. Norden has recently published the most complete account to date of disability in the film industry, *The Cinema of Isolation: A History of Physical Disability in the Movies* (1994). The remarkable thing about this book is the staggering number of films that have been made about the issue of disability. When I first began to consider the issue of how the disabled body is depicted in film, I came up with my own list of twenty or so films, and I thought that I would mention the occasional way in which the disabled were included in a film industry that mainly focused on the normal body. In other words, I thought I was dealing with a parallel situation to, say, the depiction in cinema of African-Americans—a marginalized group who rarely appeared in Hollywood films until recently and, if they did, played mainly minor characters or supernumerary roles.

But the facts about the depiction of disability are quite the opposite of what I had thought. The film industry has been obsessed with the depiction of the disabled body from the earliest silent films. The blind, the deaf, the physically disabled were singled out from the very beginning of cinema. Norden finds movies about disability from as early as 1898, and the earliest one-reeler silent films of the period 1902–1909 include such representative titles as *Deaf Mute Girl Reciting 'Star Spangled Banner'* (1902), *Deaf Mutes' Ball* (1907), *The Invalid's Adventure* (1907), *The Legless Runner* (1907), *The One-legged Man* (1908), *The Hunchback Brings Luck* (1908), *The Little Cripple* (1908), *A Blind Woman's Story* (1908), *The Blind Boy* (1908), *The Cripple's Marriage* (1909), *The Electrified Humpback* (1909), to name only a few. Later multi-reeler silent films routinely told the stories of the disabled. D. W. Griffith made a few disability-related films, culminating his efforts in the famous *Orphans of the Storm* (1921) in which two hapless sisters (Lillian and Dorothy Gish),[9] one of whom is blind, try to survive on the streets of Paris. But the noteworthy fact about this film is not merely its disability-related content but that Griffith's version was the *fifth* filmic remake of the 1874 French play *Les Deux Orphelines*.[1] With film only in its infancy, this particular disability story had been told afresh approximately once every four years from 1900 through 1921.

Norden's book lists about six hundred disability-related films in its index, a far cry from my twenty or so. And if one stops and thinks about the subject, one realizes that films concerning people with disabilities are almost always

9. The American sisters Lillian (1896–1993) and Dorothy Gish (1898–1968), who had long careers in film and on stage, were important actresses in early motion pictures—especially the silent films of the pioneering American director Griffith (1875–1948).

1. *The Two Orphans*, by Adolphe d'Ennery and Eugène Cormon.

playing at any given time. For example, at the moment I write this sentence on 5 January 1995, I can go see movies about the deaf Beethoven in *Immortal Beloved*, the linguistically deprived girl in Jodie Foster's *Nell*, the emotionally impaired monarch in *The Madness of King George*, and of course the lovable, mentally challenged *Forrest Gump*. In recent years films like *My Left Foot, Lorenzo's Oil, Rainman, Children of a Lesser God, Elephant Man, Mask, Awakenings, Stanley and Iris,* to name only a few better-known films, have become major hits. In addition to films centrally about disabled people, there are hundreds of films in which characters, mainly evil, are depicted as using wheelchairs, missing limbs or eyes, walking with a limp, stuttering, and so on.

The point that Norden's book made clear to me is that the cinematic experience, far from including disabilities in an ancillary way, is powerfully arranged around the management and deployment of disabled and 'normal' bodies. Disabled stories, stories of people's bodies or minds going wrong, make compelling tales. But more than that, as with any obsession, there has to be an underlying reason why films are drawn obsessively to the topic of disability. In order to understand why film makers routinely incorporate disabled bodies into films, it might be relevant to ask what else routinely appears in films. The answer is more than obvious: sex and violence. While it is fashionable for liberals to decry the violent content of films, and conservatives to decry the sexual, it might be more accurate for them to think of films as vehicles for the delivery of images of the body in extreme circumstances. The inherent voyeuristic nature of film makes it a commodity that works by visualizing for viewers the body in attitudes that it is otherwise difficult to see. Few people in quotidian life see couples making love on a regular basis, but that is a routine experience to filmgoers. Likewise, most middle-class citizens rarely see dead, mutilated, bleeding bodies, but the average viewer has no shortage of such images.

So films, one could say, are a streamlined delivery system that produces dramatically these bodily images in exchange for a sum of money (as the Coca-Cola industry can be said to be a system for delivering caffeine and sugar, or as cigarettes are really time-release delivery systems for nicotine administration). As novels were seen to be mechanisms for the cultural production of normativity, so films have to be seen in the same regard, with the addition that the phantasm of the body is particularly subject to these normativizing activities.

Films enforce the normal body, but through a rather strange process. The normal body, invented in the nineteenth century as a departure from the ideal body, has shifted over to a new concept: the normal ideal. This normal ideal body is the one we see on the screen. It is the commodified body of the eroticized male or female star. This body is not actually the norm, but it is the fantasized, hypostatized body of commodified desire. In order to generate this body and proliferate its images, films have constantly to police and to regulate the variety of bodily differences. These bodies are the modern equivalents of the nude Venuses, and to keep them viable, to think on and obsess about them, the Medusa body has constantly to be shown, reshown, placed, categorized, itemized, and anatomized. In short, we cannot have Sharon Stone without Linda Hunt; we cannot have Tom Cruise without Ron Kovic;[2] we cannot have the fantasy of the erotic *femme fatale*'s body without having the sickened, disabled, deformed person's story testifying to the universal power of the human spirit to overcome adversity. As Norden points out, when films about disabled people are made, more often than not the disabled characters get cured by the end of the film.[3] The tension between the whole and the fragmented body, between the erotic, complete body and the uncanny, incomplete body, must be constantly deployed and resolved through films.

* * *

Throughout this chapter, I have tried to show that the concept of disability is a crucial part of the very way we conceive of and live in our bodies. In art, photography, film, and other media in which the body is represented, the 'normal' body always exists in a dialectical play with the disabled body. Indeed, our representations of the body are really investigations of and defenses against the notion that the body is anything but a seamless whole, a complete, unfragmented entity. In addition to the terms of race, class, gender, sexual preference and so on—all of which are factors in the social construction of the body—the concept of disability adds a background of somatic concerns. But disability is more than a background. It is in some sense the basis on which the 'normal' body is constructed: disability defines the negative space the body must not occupy, it is the Manichean binary[4] in contention with normality. But this dialectic is one that is enforced by a set of social conditions and is not natural in any sense. Only when disability is made visible as a compulsory term in a hegemonic process, only when the binary is exposed and the continuum acknowledged, only when the body is seen apart from its existence as an object of production or consumption—only then will normalcy cease being a term of enforcement in a somatic judicial system.

1995

2. The paraplegic veteran (b. 1946) of the Vietnam War whose autobiography, *Born on the Fourth of July* (1984), was made into a 1989 film (dir. Oliver Stone) starring Cruise (b. 1962), one of the biggest box-office draws of his generation. Stone (b. 1958), 5' 8" and thin, is known for sexy leading roles, while the 4' 10" Hunt (b. 1945) is a "character" actor.

3. Norden, *The Cinema of Isolation*, p. 59 [Davis's note].

4. The converse in a dualistic worldview; Manichaeism saw the world as divided between good and evil, light and darkness, spirit and matter.

HENRY LOUIS GATES JR.

b. 1950

A prolific and tireless advocate of African American literature and culture, Henry Louis Gates Jr. has played a vital part in establishing an African American literary canon and in creating a distinctive African American literary theory that simultaneously combines deconstructive criticism with African literary tradition. One of the most protean of contemporary critics, he has also helped build institutional structures to study African American literature and has disseminated his views of race and culture through mainstream media, writing for such magazines as *Newsweek* and the *New Yorker* and frequently appearing on television. His diverse roles have made him one of the best-known academic critics in America. "Talking Black: Critical Signs of the Times" (1988) sets out his credo for present-day African American literary theory, which borrows from but revises mainstream theory with infusions of African American modes of thought and vernacular discourse.

Gates was born and raised in Keyser, West Virginia. After high school, he attended Potomac State Community College but was encouraged by an English instructor to transfer to Yale University, from which he received his B.A. in 1973. While an undergraduate (1970–71), Gates traveled to Africa on a fellowship, visiting fifteen countries and learning about African culture. On his return to the United States he worked as a director of student affairs for the West Virginia gubernatorial campaign of John D. Rockefeller IV, later writing his senior honors thesis on the campaign. He received Mellon and Ford Foundation fellowships that enabled him to undertake graduate study at Cambridge University, where he earned his M.A. in 1974 and Ph.D. in 1979. At Cambridge he worked with the Nigerian writer Wole Soyinka, who exposed him to Yoruba myths and interpretive modes. While in England he also began a journalistic career, working as a London correspondent for *Time* magazine from 1973 to 1975. In 1975 he returned to the United States, attending Yale Law School for a month before changing paths to pursue literary studies. He began teaching at Yale in 1976 as a lecturer in English; by the time he left, in 1985, he had become a full professor and had received several prestigious awards, including a 1981 MacArthur Fellowship. After teaching at Cornell University (1985–90), where he was appointed the Du Bois Professor of Literature in 1988, and a year at Duke University, in 1991 he moved to Harvard University as professor of English and as W. E. B. Du Bois Professor of the Humanities, chair of the department of Afro-American studies, and director of the W. E. B. Du Bois Institute for Afro-American Research. The institute, where he has gathered a remarkable faculty of black scholars from several disciplines, has provided the institutional base for his many projects.

Gates's work shows the influence of the two poles of his education: the sophisticated reading practices and deconstructive literary theories of the critics affiliated with Yale University in the 1970s, such as PAUL DE MAN, JACQUES DERRIDA, and Geoffrey Hartman, and the indigenous African tradition of literature and interpretation introduced to him by Soyinka. His early critical writing draws on an array of contemporary theory, from sources as diverse as MIKHAIL M. BAKHTIN, NORTHROP FRYE, and Derrida, which he applies to readings of African American literature in an attempt to revalue it and to construct a canon. In his innovative book *The Signifying Monkey: A Theory of African-American Literary Criticism* (1988), he melds the poststructuralist theory of signification rooted in the linguistics of FERDINAND DE SAUSSURE with the African vernacular tradition of "signifyin(g)," deriving from Yoruba oral literature. The latter tradition is evident in present-day practices such as "the dozens" (a game of verbal one-upsmanship) and jazz improvisation. Gates stresses that he uses theory provisionally; his intention is "to develop theories of criticism indigenous to our literatures" by drawing on "black textual tradition." His deployment of poststructuralism enables him to define race as a function of linguistic and cultural differences rather than as a natural or essential property. In literature, he explains in *Signifying Monkey*, "blackness" is not a transcendental property but is "produced in the text itself only through a complex process of signification."

By blending contemporary Euro-American theory with African tradition, Gates positions himself as an intermediary between dominant Anglo-American and minority African American literary cultures. In advocating theory alongside the black tradition, his work parallels that of the African American critic HOUSTON A. BAKER JR., although Baker primarily draws on African American rather than African sources. Against the conservative view that African American literature lacks aesthetic merit and is valuable only as a social report, Gates urges us to gauge it on its own aesthetic terms, within the vernacular black tradition. Using these criteria, he establishes an African American canon. Against radical black separatist arguments for the exclusive study of African American literature, or Afrocentrism, Gates argues instead for "cultural tolerance," and he freely makes use of mainstream literary theory as a means to specific ends. Between traditionalists and radicals, between assimilationists and separatists, and between antitheorists and theorists, Gates negotiates a middle path. His ultimate goal is institutional as well as theoretical. As he puts it in our selection, he aims to forge a place for black writing and criticism in "the broader, larger institution of literature."

"Talking Black" exemplifies Gates's intermediary role, drawing on two competing poles in African American cultural politics—assimilationist and separatist—as well as asserting the status of black writing in mainstream literary culture. Characteristically, Gates calls for simultaneously using critical theory and injecting African American tradition. He foregrounds the example of the early African American intellectual and religious leader Alexander Crummell (1819–1898), who advocated studying classical languages and obtaining a traditional white education. Most African American critics view this position as overly accommodating, and Gates distances himself from it, stressing that his amalgam of contemporary theoretical approaches and black tradition transforms the theory it employs. "Talking Black," which originally appeared in the New York–based weekly the *Village Voice*, also exemplifies Gates's efforts to bridge the gap between the specialized sphere of academic criticism and the public sphere of journalism, efforts that have been remarkably successful.

This middle-of-the-road position has helped win Gates a high degree of public visibility and success, but it has also generated much criticism. Traditionalists believe that the effort to create a separate African American canon degrades the Western canon, whose value, they argue, has been confirmed over time. Some dedicated theorists see Gates's mainstream writings as a watering-down of his scholarship. On the other hand, some African American critics consider his use of sophisticated theory to be elitist—an argument made by BARBARA CHRISTIAN in "The Race for Theory" (1988; see above). At a further extreme, separatist Afrocentrist critics consider it a means of accommodating white culture, in effect claiming that Gates has become a latter-day Crummell. Other radical critics judge that he focuses too exclusively on literature and culture rather than on the material conditions of African Americans. Gates unapologetically defines his role as that of a literary critic and argues that attention to black literary tradition and heritage carries an implicit politics, fostering greater cultural recognition for African Americans. Ironically, Gates's intermediary position, both intellectual and stylistic, fuels his popular influence as well as the attacks of his most cogent detractors.

BIBLIOGRAPHY

Gates first had an impact on literary studies through his editorial work: he rediscovered the earliest novel by an African American, Harriet E. Wilson's *Our Nig: Or, Sketches from the Life of a Free Black, in a Two Story White House, North* (1983), which had been privately printed in 1859. He also edited three important anthologies of contemporary criticism: *Black Literature and Literary Theory* (1984), which opens with an important introduction by Gates, "Criticism in the Jungle," that assesses the state of African American literary criticism; *"Race," Writing, and Difference* (1986), which includes an influential introduction on the importance of race and the concept of difference in literary studies; and *Reading Black, Reading Feminist: A Critical Anthology* (1990). Gates's first two books of his own, *Figures in Black: Words, Signs, and the "Racial" Self* (1987), a collection of essays, and *The Signifying Monkey: A Theory of African-American Literary Criticism* (1988), which won the 1989 American Book Award, innovatively combine poststructuralist literary theory and indigenous African literary sources.

Gates's writing then shifted to address larger, more mainstream, audiences, as exemplified by the essays collected in *Loose Canons: Notes on the Culture Wars* (1992), which includes "Talking Black." In 1994 he published an informative autobiography focusing on his childhood, *Colored People: A Memoir*. He next published a dialogue with the African American philosopher and critic Cornel West, *The Future of the Race* (1996), which examines the social possibilities for African Americans in the late twentieth century. *Thirteen Ways of Looking at a Black Man* (1997) gathers a series of Gates's essays on significant contemporary African American figures, such as Harry Belafonte and General Colin Powell. In 1999 he wrote and narrated the six-part television series *Wonders of the African World*, which was accompanied by a book of the same title (1999).

One of Gates's major goals is to increase the institutional presence of African American writers; thus he and Nellie Y. McKay were general editors of *The Norton Anthology of African American Literature* (1997). He is the editor of the Schomburg Library of Nineteenth-Century Black Women Writers, the Amistad Critical Studies in African American Literature (with K. Anthony Appiah), and the Black Periodical Literature Project, and he has edited or co-edited more than twenty volumes of African American writing and criticism on African American literature and culture. He also oversaw the rebirth of the pioneering journal *Transition*.

Joyce A. Joyce's " 'Who the Cap Fit': Unconsciousness and Unconscionableness in the Criticism of Houston A. Baker, Jr., and Henry Louis Gates, Jr.," *New Literary History* 18 (1987), charges Gates with elitism; it drew a sharp answer from Gates, distinguishing the different voices he uses in academic and public forums and contending that Joyce exhibits what de Man labeled "the resistance to theory." In "Henry Louis Gates, Jr. and African American Literary Discourse," *New England Quarterly* 62 (1989), Wahneema Lubiano offers a balanced assessment of Gates's theory, which she defines as "precisely a theory of literary history" and argues against the charge that it is apolitical. Kenneth W. Warren's "Delimiting America: The Legacy of Du Bois," *American Literary History* 1 (1989), criticizes Gates's reliance on the image of professionalistic pluralism "to establish some non-political notion of black unity." Ronald Judy, in *(Dis)forming the American Canon: African-Arabic Slave Narratives and the Vernacular* (1993), revises Gates's concept of "signifyin(g)," rerouting the tradition through Arabic and other sources. Sandra Adell, in *Double-Consciousness / Double Bind: Theoretical Issues in Twentieth-Century Black Literature* (1994), relevantly compares Gates and Baker. A severe political critique comes from Adolph L. Reed, in *W. E. B. Du Bois and American Political Thought: Fabianism and the Color Line* (1997); Reed castigates Gates, especially in his later work, as a center-right apologist and a "representative Negro" in the manner of Booker T. Washington.

Talking Black: Critical Signs of the Times

> For a language acts in diverse ways, upon the spirit of a people; even as the spirit of a people acts with a creative and spiritualizing force upon a language.
>
> —ALEXANDER CRUMMELL,[1] 1860

> A new vision began gradually to replace the dream of political power—a powerful movement, the rise of another ideal to guide the unguided, another pillar of fire by night after a clouded day. It was the ideal of "book-learning"; the curiosity, born of compulsory ignorance, to know and test the power of the cabalistic letters of the white man, the longing to know. Here at last seemed to have been

1. African American Episcopalian minister (1819–1898), who earned a degree from Cambridge University (1853) and cultivated scholarship among young blacks.

> discovered the mountain path to Canaan; longer than the highway of Emancipation and law, steep and rugged, but straight, leading to heights high enough to overlook life.
>
> —W. E. B. DU BOIS,[2] 1903

> The knowledge which would teach the white world was Greek to his own flesh and blood . . . and he could not articulate the message of another people.
>
> —W. E. B. DU BOIS, 1903

Alexander Crummell, a pioneering nineteenth-century Pan-Africanist,[3] statesman, and missionary who spent the bulk of his creative years as an Anglican minister in Liberia, was also a pioneering intellectual and philosopher of language, founding the American Negro Academy[4] in 1897 and serving as the intellectual godfather of W. E. B. Du Bois. For his first annual address as president of the academy, delivered on December 28, 1897, Crummell selected as his topic "The Attitude of the American Mind Toward the Negro Intellect." Given the occasion of the first annual meeting of the great intellectuals of the race, he could not have chosen a more timely or appropriate subject.

Crummell wished to attack, he said, "the denial of intellectuality in the Negro; the assertion that he was not a human being, that he did not belong to the human race." He argued that the desire "to becloud and stamp out the intellect of the Negro" had led to the enactment of "laws and Statutes, closing the pages of every book printed to the eyes of Negroes; barring the doors of every school-room against them!" This, he concluded, "was the systematized method of the intellect of the South, to stamp out the brains of the Negro!"—a program that created an "almost Egyptian darkness[5] [which] fell upon the mind of the race, throughout the whole land."

Crummell next shared with his audience a conversation between two Boston lawyers which he had overheard when he was "an errand boy in the Anti-slavery office in New York City" in 1833 or 1834:

> While at the Capitol they happened to dine in the company of the great John C. Calhoun,[6] then senator from South Carolina. It was a period of great ferment upon the question of Slavery, States' Rights, and Nullification; and consequently the Negro was the topic of conversation at the table. One of the utterances of Mr. Calhoun was to this effect—"That if he could find a Negro who knew the Greek syntax, he would then believe that the Negro was a human being and should be treated as a man."

"Just think of the crude asininity," Crummell concluded rather generously, "of even a great man!"

The salient sign of the black person's humanity—indeed, the only sign for

2. African American historian and sociologist (1868–1963; see above), co-founder of the NAACP and the foremost voice of black protest in the early 20th century. Both his epigraphs are from chapter 1 of *The Souls of Black Folk* (1903).

3. A believer in the innate unity of all black Africans and their overseas descendants; more especially, one active in the movement for the unity and independence of African states (as was Du Bois, beginning in 1900 with the Pan-African Congress in London).

4. A learned society for African Americans that promoted civil rights through scholarly work on African American culture and history.

5. An allusion to one of the plagues said to have been brought by God against the Egyptians who were holding the Israelites in slavery (Exodus 10.21–23).

6. Prominent American political leader (1782–1850) and the 7th U.S. vice president (1825–32); he was a strong advocate of states' rights and of slavery.

Calhoun—would be the mastering of the very essence of Western civilization, of the very foundation of the complex fiction upon which white Western culture had been constructed. It is likely that "Greek syntax," for John C. Calhoun, was merely a hyperbolic figure of speech, a trope of virtual impossibility; he felt driven to the hyperbolic mode, perhaps, because of the long racist tradition in Western letters of demanding that black people *prove* their full humanity. We know this tradition all too well, dotted as it is with the names of the great intellectual Western racialists, such as Francis Bacon, David Hume, Immanuel Kant, Thomas Jefferson, and G. W. F. Hegel.[7] Whereas each of these figures demanded that blacks write poetry to prove their humanity, Calhoun—writing in a post–Phillis Wheatley[8] era—took refuge in, yes, Greek syntax.

In typical African-American fashion, a brilliant black intellectual accepted Calhoun's challenge. The anecdote Crummell shared with his fellow black academicians turned out to be his shaping scene of instruction. For Crummell himself jumped on a boat, sailed to England, and matriculated at Queens' College, Cambridge, where he mastered the intricacies of Greek syntax. Calhoun, we suspect, was not impressed.

Crummell never stopped believing that mastering the master's tongue was the sole path to civilization, intellectual freedom, and social equality for the black person. It was Western "culture," he insisted, that the black person "must claim as his rightful heritage, as a man—not stinted training, not a caste education, not," he concluded prophetically, "a Negro curriculum." As he argued so passionately in his speech of 1860, "The English Language in Liberia," the acquisition of the English language, along with Christianity, is the wonderful sign of God's providence encoded in the nightmare of African enslavement in the racist wilderness of the New World. English, for Crummell, was "the speech of Chaucer and Shakespeare, of Milton and Wordsworth, of Bacon and Burke, of Franklin and Webster,"[9] and its potential mastery was "this one item of compensation" that "the Almighty has bestowed upon us" in exchange for "the exile of our fathers from their African homes to America." In the English language are embodied "the noblest theories of liberty" and "the grandest ideas of humanity." If black people master the master's tongue, these great and grand ideas will become African ideas, because "ideas conserve men, and keep alive the vitality of nations."

In dark contrast to the splendors of the English language, Crummell set the African vernacular languages, which, he wrote, have "definite marks of inferiority connected with them all, which place them at the widest distances from civilized languages." Any effort to render the master's discourse in our own black tongue is an egregious error, for we cannot translate sublime utterances "in[to] broken English—a miserable caricature of their noble

7. Major thinkers who generally (save the slave-holding Jefferson) are not thought of as "racialist": Bacon (1561–1626), English philosopher, scientist, and statesman; HUME (1711–1776), Scottish philosopher and historian; KANT (1724–1804), German idealist philosopher; Jefferson (1743–1826), drafter of the Declaration of Independence, Founding Father, and 3d president (1801–09) of the United States; HEGEL (1770–1831), German idealist philosopher.

8. The first black American woman poet in the United States (ca. 1753–1784), born probably in Senegal and sold as a slave to a Boston family.

9. Crummell names English and American men famed for their skill with words: the English poet Geoffrey Chaucer (ca. 1343–1400) and the poet/dramatist William Shakespeare (1564–1616); two poets, John Milton (1608–1674) and WILLIAM WORDSWORTH (1770–1850); two philosopher/statesmen, Bacon and EDMUND BURKE (1727–1797); and two American politicians, the popular author, inventor, and ambassador Benjamin Franklin (1706–1790) and the great orator Daniel Webster (1782–1852).

tongue." We must abandon forever both indigenous African vernacular languages and the neo-African vernacular languages that our people have produced in the New World:

> All low, inferior, and barbarous tongues are, doubtless, but the lees and dregs of noble languages, which have gradually, as the soul of a nation has died out, sunk down to degradation and ruin. We must not suffer this decay on these shores, in this nation. We have been made, providentially, the deposit of a noble trust; and we should be proud to show our appreciation of it. Having come to the heritage of this language we must cherish its spirit, as well as retain its letter. We must cultivate it among ourselves; we must strive to infuse its spirit among our reclaimed and aspiring natives.

I cite the examples of John C. Calhoun and Alexander Crummell as metaphors for the relation between the critic of black writing and the broader, larger institution of literature. Learning the master's tongue, for our generation of critics, has been an act of empowerment, whether that tongue be New Criticism, humanism, structuralism, Marxism, poststructuralism, feminism, new historicism,[1] or any other "ism." Each of these critical discourses arises from a specific set of texts within the Western tradition. At least for the past decade, many of us have busied ourselves with the necessary task of learning about these movements in criticism, drawing upon their modes of reading to explicate the texts in our own tradition.

This is an exciting time for critics of Afro-American literature. More critical essays and books are being produced than ever before, and there have never been more jobs available teaching Afro-American literature in white colleges and universities. In a few years, we shall at last have our very own Norton anthology,[2] a sure sign that the teaching of Afro-American literature is being institutionalized. Our pressing question now becomes this. In what languages shall we choose to speak, and write, our own criticisms? What are we now to do with the enabling masks of empowerment that we have donned as we have practiced one mode of formal criticism or another?

There is a long history of resistance to (white) theory in the (black) tradition. Unlike almost every other, the Afro-American literary tradition was generated as a response to allegations that its authors did not, and *could not* create literature, considered the signal measure of a race's innate "humanity." The African living in Europe or in the New World seems to have felt compelled to create a literature not only to demonstrate that blacks did indeed possess the intellectual ability to create a written art, but also to indict the several social and economic institutions that delimited the "humanity" of all black people in Western cultures.

So insistent did these racist allegations prove to be, at least from the eighteenth to the early twentieth century, that it is fair to describe the subtext of the history of black letters in terms of the urge to refute them. Even as late as 1911, when J. E. Casely-Hayford[3] published *Ethiopia Unbound* (the "first" African novel), he felt it necessary to address this matter in the first two

1. Major critical schools of 20th-century U.S. literary studies.
2. *The Norton Anthology of African American Literature* (1997), whose general editors were Gates and Nellie Y. McKay.
3. Ghanaian lawyer, writer, and advocate of African nationalism (1866–1930).

paragraphs of this text. "At the dawn of the twentieth century," the novel opens, "men of light and leading both in Europe and in America had not yet made up their minds as to what place to assign to the spiritual aspirations of the black man." Few literary traditions have begun with such a complex and curious relation to criticism: allegations of an absence led directly to a presence, a literature often inextricably bound in a dialogue with its harshest critics.

Black literature and its criticism, then, have been put to uses that were not primarily aesthetic; rather, they have formed part of a larger discourse on the nature of the black, and of his or her role in the order of things. The relation among theory, tradition, and integrity within black culture has not been, and perhaps cannot be, a straightforward matter.

Despite the fact that critics of black literature are often attacked for using theory and that some black readers respond to their work by remarking that it's all Greek to them, it is probably true that critics of Afro-American literature are more concerned with the complex relation between literature and theory than ever before. There are many reasons for this, not the least of which is our increasingly central role in "the profession" precisely when our colleagues are engulfed in their own extensive debates about the intellectual merit of so much theorizing. Theory, as a second-order reflection upon a primary gesture, has *always* been viewed with suspicion by scholars who find it presumptuous and even decadent when criticism claims the right to stand on its own: theoretical texts breed equally "decadent" theoretical responses in a creative process that can be very far removed from a poem or a novel.

For the critic of Afro-American literature, this process is even more perilous because most of the contemporary literary theory derives from critics of Western European languages and literatures. Is the use of theory to write about Afro-American literature merely another form of intellectual indenture, a mental servitude as pernicious in its intellectual implications as any other kind of enslavement? The key word implied in this panel discussion[4] is *integrity*. To quote the *Oxford English Dictionary*'s definition of the word, does theorizing about a text or a literary tradition "mar," "violate," "impair," or "corrupt" the "soundness" of an "original perfect state" of a black text or of the black tradition? To argue that it does is to align oneself with the New Critics[5]—who often seem not to have cared particularly for, or about, the writing of Afro-Americans—and with their view that texts are "organic wholes" in the first place. This is a critical error.

The sense of "integrity" as it seems to arise in the Afro-American tradition is more akin to the notion of "ringing true," or to Houston Baker's[6] concept of "sounding." (One of the most frequently used critical judgments in the African-American tradition is "That just don't sound right," or, as Alice Walker puts it in *The Color Purple*,[7] "Look like to me only a fool would want to talk in a way that feel peculiar to your mind.") That is the sense that black nationalists[8] call on here, without understanding how problematic this can

4. The panel "Integrity and the Black Tradition," where this essay was originally presented at the 1987 convention of the Modern Language Association (the primary North American professional organization for scholars in English and foreign languages and literatures).

5. Those literary interpreters (CLEANTH BROOKS, WILLIAM K. WIMSATT JR., etc.) who emphasize close reading of the text as an autonomous ("organic") whole; they dominated Anglo-American criticism in the mid-20th century.

6. A leading African American literary theorist (b. 1943; see above).

7. A 1982 novel by Walker (b. 1944), African American novelist and poet.

8. Those who advocate a separatist black culture and political organization, a stance associated with the black power and Black Arts movements of the 1960s through mid-1970s.

be. Doubleness, alienation, equivocality—since the turn of the century at least, these have been recurrent tropes for the black tradition.

To be sure, this matter of criticism and "integrity" has a long and rather tortured history in black letters. It was David Hume, after all, who called Francis Williams,[9] the Jamaican poet of Latin verse, "a parrot who merely speaks a few words plainly." Phillis Wheatley, too, has long suffered from the spurious attacks of black and white critics alike for being the *rara avis*[1] of a school of so-called mockingbird poets, whose use of European and American literary conventions has been considered a corruption of a "purer" black expression, found in forms such as the blues, signifying, spirituals, and Afro-American dance. Can we, as critics, escape a "mockingbird" relation to theory? And can we escape the racism of so many critical theorists, from Hume and Kant through the Southern Agrarians and the Frankfurt school?[2]

Only recently have some scholars attempted to convince critics of black literature that we can. Perhaps predictably, a number of these attempts share a concern with that which has been most repressed in the received tradition of Afro-American criticism: close readings of the texts themselves. My advocacy of theory's value for such readings is meant as a prelude to the definition of critical principles peculiar to the black literary traditions, related to contemporary theory generally and yet, as Robert Farris Thompson[3] puts it, "indelibly black." I have tried to work through contemporary theories of literature not to "apply" them to black texts, but to transform by translating them into a new rhetorical realm—to re-create, through revision, the critical theory at hand. As our familiarity with the black tradition and with literary theory expands, we shall invent our own black, text-specific theories, as some of us have begun to do. We must learn to read a black text within a black formal cultural matrix, as well as its "white" matrix.

This is necessary because the existence of a black canon is a historically contingent phenomenon; it is not inherent in the nature of "blackness," not vouchsafed by the metaphysics of some racial essence. The black tradition exists only insofar as black artists enact it. Only because black writers have read and responded to other black writers with a sense of recognition and acknowledgment can we speak of a black literary inheritance, with all the burdens and ironies that has entailed. Race is a text (an array of discursive practices), not an essence. It must be *read* with painstaking care and suspicion, not imbibed.

I have tried to employ contemporary theory to defamiliarize[4] the texts of the black tradition: ironically, it is necessary to create distance between reader and texts in order to go beyond reflexive responses and achieve critical insight into and intimacy with their formal workings, I have done this to respect the "integrity" of these texts, by trying to avoid confusing my experience as an Afro-American with the act of language that defines a black text.

9. Jamaican poet (1700–1770).
1. Rare bird (Latin).
2. German social and aesthetic theorists who gathered at Frankfurt's Institute for Social Research (founded in 1923); prominent members include THEODOR ADORNO AND MAX HORKHEIMER. Southern Agrarians: also known as the Fugitives, a group of Southern poets and critics (many, including JOHN CROWE RANSOM, were associated with Vanderbilt University in the 1920s) who were politically conservative and viewed works of literature as autonomous verbal structures; their manifesto was *I'll Take My Stand: The South and the Agrarian Tradition by Twelve Southerners* (1930).
3. African American art historian (b. 1932).
4. A term from the Russian formalist Viktor Shklovsky (1893–1984); defamiliarization is the process through which an object of art "makes strange" what is familiar, so our response to it is not routine and it can be appreciated not as imitative but as an independent work.

This is the challenge of the critic of black literature in the 1980s: not to shy away from white power—that is, literary theory—but to translate it into the black idiom, *renaming* principles of criticism where appropriate, but especially *naming* indigenous black principles of criticism and applying them to our own texts. *Any* tool that enables the critic to explain the complex workings of the language of a text is appropriate here. For it is language, the black language of black texts, that expresses the distinctive quality of our literary tradition. Once it may have seemed that the only critical implements black critics needed were the pom-pom and the twirled baton; in fact, there is no deeper form of literary disrespect. We will not protect the "integrity" of our tradition by remaining afraid of, or naive about, literary theory; rather, we will inflict upon it the violation of reflexive, stereotypical readings—or non-reading. We are the keepers of the black literary tradition. No matter what theories we embrace, we have more in common with each other than we do with any other critic of any other literature. We write for each other, and for our own contemporary writers. This relation is a critical trust.

It is also *political* trust. How can the demonstration that our texts sustain ever closer and more sophisticated readings *not* be political at a time when all sorts of so-called canonical critics mediate their racism through calls for "purity" of the "tradition," demands as implicitly racist as anything the Southern Agrarians said? How can the deconstruction of the forms of racism itself not be political? How can the use of literary analysis to explicate the racist social text in which we still find ourselves be anything *but* political? To be political, however, does not mean that I have to write at the level of a Marvel comic book. My task, as I see it, is to help guarantee that black and so-called Third World literature[5] is taught to black and Third World and white students by black and Third World and white professors in heretofore white mainstream departments of literature, and to train students to think, to read, and to write clearly, to expose false uses of language, fraudulent claims, and muddled arguments, propaganda, and vicious lies—from all of which our people have suffered just as surely as we have from an economic order in which we were zeros and a metaphysical order in which we were absences. These are the "values" which should be transmitted through critical theory.

In the December 1986 issue of the *Voice Literary Supplement*, in an essay entitled "Cult-Nats Meet Freaky-Deke," Greg Tate[6] argued cogently and compellingly that "black aestheticians need to develop a coherent criticism to communicate the complexities of our culture. There's no periodical on black cultural phenomena equivalent to *The Village Voice* or *Artforum*, no publication that provides journalism on black visual art, philosophy, politics, economics, media, literature, linguistics, psychology, sexuality, spirituality, and pop culture. Though there are certainly black editors, journalists, and academics capable of producing such a journal, the disintegration of the black cultural nationalist movement and the brain-drain of black intellectuals to white institutions have destroyed the vociferous public dialogue that used to exist between them." While I would argue that *Sage, Callaloo,* and *Black American Literature Forum (BALF)* are indeed fulfilling that function for academic critics, I am afraid that the truth of Tate's claim is irresistible.

5. Literature from the "underdeveloped" countries, many of them former colonies, now dominated by highly industrialized "first world" (largely Western) nations in a global economy.

6. African American cultural critic and journalist.

But his most important contribution to the future of black criticism is to be found in his most damning allegation. "What's unfortunate," he writes, "is that while black artists have opened up the entire 'text of blackness' for fun and games, not many black critics have produced writing as fecund, eclectic, and freaky-deke as the art, let alone the culture, itself. . . . For those who prefer exegesis with a polemical bent, just imagine how critics as fluent in black and Western culture as the postliberated artists could strike terror into that bastion of white supremacist thinking, the Western art [and literary] world[s]." To which I can only say, echoing Shug in Alice Walker's *The Color Purple*, "Amen. Amen."

Tate's challenge is a serious one because neither ideology nor criticism nor blackness can exist as entities of themselves, outside the forms of their texts. This is the central theme of Ralph Ellison's *Invisible Man* and Ishmael Reed's *Mumbo Jumbo*,[7] for example. But how can we write or read the text of "Black Theory"? What language(s) do black people use to represent their critical or ideological positions? In what forms of language do we speak or write? Can we derive a valid, integral "black" text or criticism or ideology from borrowed or appropriate forms? Can a black woman's text emerge "authentically" as borrowed, or "liberated," or revised, from the patriarchal forms of the slave narratives, on the one hand, or from the white matriarchal forms of the sentimental novel, on the other, as Harriet Jacobs and Harriet Wilson attempted to do in *Incidents in the Life of a Slave Girl* (1861) and *Our Nig* (1859)?[8] Where lies the liberation in revision, the ideological integrity of defining freedom in the modes and forms of difference charted so cogently by so many poststructural critics of black literature?

For it is in these spaces of difference that black literature has dwelled. And while it is crucial to read these patterns of difference closely, we must understand as well that the quest was lost, in a major sense, before it had even begun, simply because the terms of our own self-representation have been provided by the master. It is not enough for us to show that refutation, negation, and revision exist, and to define them as satisfactory gestures of ideological independence. Our next concern must be to address the black political signified, that is, the cultural vision and the critical language that underpin the search through literature and art for a profound reordering and humanizing of everyday existence. We must urge our writers and critics to undertake the fullest and most ironic exploration of the manner and matter, the content and form, the structure and sensibility so familiar and poignant to us in our most sublime form of art, black music, where ideology and art are one, whether we listen to Bessie Smith or to postmodern and poststructural John Coltrane.[9]

Just as we must urge our writers to meet this challenge, we as critics must turn to our own peculiarly black structures of thought and feeling to develop our own languages of criticism. We must do so by drawing on the black vernacular, the language we use to speak to each other when no outsiders are around. Unless we look to the vernacular to ground our theories and

7. The best-known novel (1972) by Reed (b. 1938), African American novelist and poet. *Invisible Man* (1952) is the masterpiece of Ellison (1914–1994), African American writer of fiction, essays, and criticism.

8. Accounts of slave life by Jacobs (1813–1877) and Wilson (1808–ca. 1870). Jacobs writes of hiding for nearly 7 years in a small, cramped attic; this is the "garret" to which Gates later refers.

9. American jazz saxophonist and composer (1926–1967). Smith (ca. 1898–1937), American blues singer.

modes of reading, we will surely sink in the mire of Nella Larsen's quicksand,[1] remain alienated in the isolation of Harriet Jacob's garret, or masked in the received stereotype of the Black Other helping Huck to return to the raft, singing "China Gate" with Nat King Cole under the Da Nang moon, or reflecting our bald heads in the shining flash of Mr. T's[2] signifying gold chains.

We must redefine theory itself from within out own black cultures, refusing to grant the racist premise that theory is something that white people do, so that we are doomed to imitate our white colleagues, like reverse black minstrel critics done up in whiteface. We are all heirs to critical theory, but critics are also heir to the black vernacular critical tradition as well. We must not succumb, as did Alexander Crummell, to the tragic lure of white power, the mistake of accepting the empowering language of white critical theory as "universal" or as our only language, the mistake of confusing the enabling mask of theory with our own black faces. Each of us has, in some literal or figurative manner, boarded a ship and sailed to a metaphorical Cambridge, seeking to master the master's tools. (I myself, being quite literal-minded, booked passage some fourteen years ago on the *QE2*.[3]) Now we must at last don the empowering mask of blackness and talk *that* talk, the language of black difference. While it is true that we must, as Du Bois said so long ago, "know and test the power of the cabalistic letters of the white man," we must also know and test the dark secrets of a black discursive universe that awaits its disclosure through the black arts of interpretation. For the future of theory, in the remainder of this century, is black indeed.

1988

1. *Quicksand* (1928) was the first novel by the African American writer Larsen (1891–1964).

2. Lawrence Tureaud (b. 1952), popular African American television and film actor of the 1980s, generally seen in a Mohawk haircut and copious gold jewelry. Huck: title character of Mark Twain's *Adventures of Huckleberry Finn* (1884), who is helped by the runaway slave Jim back to the raft traveling down the Mississippi River. Cole (1919–1965), innovative African American pianist and leading popular singer of the 1950s and 1960s, who had a small role (and sang the title song) in the 1957 film *China Gate* (dir. Samuel Fuller), which was set in the last days of the French war in Vietnam; Da Nang, in central Vietnam, later became a major American military base.

3. *Queen Elizabeth* 2, a Cunard liner put into service in 1969; though now used primarily for cruises, it provides the only regularly scheduled luxury passenger service across the Atlantic. Gates pursued his graduate studies at Cambridge University.

EVE KOSOFSKY SEDGWICK
b. 1950

In the 1992 preface to the second edition of *Between Men: English Literature and Male Homosocial Desire* (1985), Eve Sedgwick writes about the emergence in the late 1980s and early 1990s of queer theory, a new paradigm of literary theory that owes its productivity to the "gorgeous generativity, the speculative generosity and daring, the permeability, and the activism that have long been lodged in the multiple histories of queer *reading*." In the aftermath of the famous Stonewall riots, when gay men and lesbians fought back against a police raid on a gay bar in New York City in the summer of 1969, and often under the umbrella of feminist and then gender studies, increasingly vocal gay and lesbian liberation movements took shape. In the 1970s, the work of literary theorists such as ADRIENNE RICH, BONNIE ZIMMERMAN, BARBARA SMITH, GLORIA ANZALDÚA, Louie Crew, and Rictor Norton had begun to define a gay and lesbian studies movement in the academy based on the identity politics that had well served both feminists and civil rights activists. The 1980s, however, saw a reappraisal of political strategies and the emergence of a "highly productive queer community whose explicit basis [was] the criss-crossing of the lines of identification and desire among genders, races and sexual definitions." By the early 1990s, it was possible to talk about queer theory as a vital new area of literary theory, built on the pioneering work of theorists such as MICHEL FOUCAULT, JUDITH BUTLER, MONIQUE WITTIG, and Sedgwick herself; its aim was to expose incoherencies in the supposedly stable definitions of male and female sexuality, to include not only gay and lesbian but also transgendered subjects, and to explore topics such as cross-dressing, gender ambiguity, and transsexuality.

Born in Dayton, Ohio, Sedgwick received her B.A. from Cornell University and went on to earn an M.Phil. and in 1975 a Ph.D. from Yale University. She has taught at a number of colleges and universities; since 1998, she has been a Distinguished Professor of English at the Graduate Center at the City University of New York. She has held major fellowships from the Mellon Foundation (1976–78), the Bunting Institute at Radcliffe College (1983–84), the Guggenheim Foundation (1987–88), and the National Humanities Center (1991–92).

In *Between Men* Sedgwick explores the phenomenon of *homosociality*, a term she applied to the social bonds formed between persons of the same sex. While these bonds can be distinguished from homosexuality—sexual desire between persons of the same sex—they exist on a continuum with it. The structures of male and female homosocial bonds are, Sedgwick argues, quite distinct. The continuum between male homosocial and homosexual desire is disrupted by the often intense homophobia (fear of homosexuality) that marks rituals of male bonding in our culture. But the opposition between homosocial and homosexual is much less pronounced, much less dichotomous, observes Sedgwick, for women than it is for men (see, for instance, Adrienne Rich's famous notion of a "lesbian continuum" in "Compulsory Heterosexuality and Lesbian Existence," above). *Between Men* examines how male homosociality gets constructed and reflected in European literary texts from 1750 to 1850. In particular, Sedgwick is interested in the ways in which homosocial desire is constituted in Western literature between men whose bonding is forged through their rivalry over a woman who mediates their relationship and deflects any taint of homoeroticism. A popular example of this phenomenon might be the triangle formed between Arthur, Guinevere, and Lancelot in Arthurian literature.

In *Epistemology of the Closet* (1990), Sedgwick points out that the versions of modern lesbian and gay history recounted by gay liberation movements following Stonewall were all based on a metaphor of "the closet," which created what she calls the regime of the "open secret" and has dominated lesbian and gay life for more than a century. She suggests that this regime, with its contradictory and constraining rules about privacy and disclosure, public and private, awareness and ignorance, has shaped the way in which many questions of value and epistemology (knowledge) have been conceived and addressed not only in gay subculture but in modern Western society as a whole. In her book's introduction, which she titles "Axiomatic," Sedgwick explores this problem through seven "axioms." The second axiom, included in our selection below, argues that while sexuality and gender may be implicated in one another, they constitute conceptually distinct realms. To treat sexuality as a part of gender perpetuates heterosexist assumptions about sexuality, foreclosing other as yet unarticulated ways of understanding. For Sedgwick, it follows that while lesbian, gay, and antihomophobic scholarship have much to learn from feminism, one cannot assume that the interests of the various actors coincide. Any alliances among movements to end oppression are strategic and political, not necessarily natural.

Sedgwick's criticism exhibits the strong influence of feminist, Foucauldian, and deconstructive (see JACQUES DERRIDA) modes of analysis and, like many poststructuralist critics, she writes in a philosophical prose that is often challenging. Yet while some critics have voiced the familiar complaint about the impenetrability of poststructuralist prose, others have been more concerned with the political stakes involved in her argument. Some fear that queer theory seeks to dissolve familiar identity categories such as gay and lesbian, creating an apolitical movement that ignores the real material conditions of gay life. Others suspect that queer theory will once more render women and lesbians invisible under the guise of a gender-neutral politics. These vexing political issues aside, Sedgwick's groundbreaking theoretical work raises important questions about the limits of identity politics, as it reshapes our understanding of the relationships between literature and sexuality.

BIBLIOGRAPHY

Sedgwick's books of criticism and theory to date are *The Coherence of Gothic Conventions* (1980), *Between Men: English Literature and Male Homosocial Desire* (1985), *Epistemology of the Closet* (1990), *Tendencies* (1993), and *A Dialogue on Love* (1999). She has also published a volume of poetry, *Fat Art, Thin Art* (1994). She has edited *Performativity and Performances* (1994), with Andrew Parker; *Shame and Its Sisters: A Silvan Tomkins Reader* (1995); *Gary in Your Pocket: Stories and Notebooks by Gary Fisher* (1996); and *Novel Gazing: Queer Readings in Fiction* (1997), the first collection of queer criticism of the novel.

One of the earliest critiques of *Between Men* was David Van Leer's "Beast of the Closet: Homosociality and the Pathology of Manhood," *Critical Inquiry* 15 (1989). Another valuable article is Blakey Vermeule's "Is There a Sedgwick School for Girls?" *Qui Parle: Literature, Philosophy, Visual Arts, and History* 5 (1991). A number of interviews with Sedgwick have appeared in print, including Sarah Chinn, Mario DiGangi, and Patrick Horrigan, "A Talk with Eve Kosofsky Sedgwick," *PreText: A Journal of Rhetoric and Theory* 13 (1992), and Jeffrey Williams, "Sedgwick Unplugged (An Interview with Eve Kosofsky Sedgwick)," *Minnesota Review* 40, n.s., (1993). Tim Dean's "On the Eve of a Queer Future," *Raritan* 15 (1995), examines Sedgwick's later writing. For bibliography consult Joan Nordquist, *Queer Theory: A Bibliography* (1997).

From Between Men: English Literature and Male Homosocial Desire

From Introduction

I. HOMOSOCIAL DESIRE

The subject of this book is a relatively short, recent, and accessible passage of English culture, chiefly as embodied in the mid-eighteenth- to mid-nineteenth-century novel. The attraction of the period to theorists of many disciplines is obvious: condensed, self-reflective, and widely influential change in economic, ideological, and gender arrangements. I will be arguing that concomitant changes in the structure of the continuum of male "homosocial desire" were tightly, often causally bound up with the other more visible changes; that the emerging pattern of male friendship, mentorship, entitlement, rivalry, and hetero- and homosexuality was in an intimate and shifting relation to class; and that no element of that pattern can be understood outside of its relation to women and the gender system as a whole.

"Male homosocial desire": the phrase in the title of this study is intended to mark both discriminations and paradoxes. "Homosocial desire," to begin with, is a kind of oxymoron. "Homosocial" is a word occasionally used in history and the social sciences, where it describes social bonds between persons of the same sex; it is a neologism, obviously formed by analogy with "homosexual," and just as obviously meant to be distinguished from "homosexual." In fact, it is applied to such activities as "male bonding," which may, as in our society, be characterized by intense homophobia, fear and hatred of homosexuality.[1] To draw the "homosocial" back into the orbit of "desire," of the potentially erotic, then, is to hypothesize the potential unbrokenness of a continuum between homosocial and homosexual—a continuum whose visibility, for men, in our society, is radically disrupted. It will become clear, in the course of my argument, that my hypothesis of the unbrokenness of this continuum is not a *genetic* one—I do not mean to discuss genital homosexual desire as "at the root of" other forms of male homosociality—but rather a strategy for making generalizations about, and marking historical differences in, the *structure* of men's relations with other men. "Male homosocial desire" is the name this book will give to the entire continuum.

I have chosen the word "desire" rather than "love" to mark the erotic emphasis because, in literary critical and related discourse, "love" is more easily used to name a particular emotion, and "desire" to name a structure; in this study, a series of arguments about the structural permutations of social impulses fuels the critical dialectic. For the most part, I will be using "desire" in a way analogous to the psychoanalytic use of "libido"[2]—not for a particular affective state or emotion, but for the affective or social force, the glue, even when its manifestation is hostility or hatred or something less emotively charged, that shapes an important relationship. How far this force is properly sexual (what, historically, it means for something to be "sexual") will be an active question.

The title is specific about *male* homosocial desire partly in order to acknowledge from the beginning (and stress the seriousness of) a limitation of my subject; but there is a more positive and substantial reason, as well. It is one of the main projects of this study to explore the ways in which the shapes of sexuality, and what *counts* as sexuality, both depend on and affect historical power relationships.[3] A corollary is that in a society where men

1. The notion of "homophobia" is itself fraught with difficulties. To begin with, the word is etymologically nonsensical. A more serious problem is that the linking of fear and hatred in the "-phobia" suffix, and in the word's usage, does tend to prejudge the question of the cause of homosexual oppression: it is attributed to fear, as opposed to (for example) a desire for power, privilege, or material goods. An alternative term that is more suggestive of collective, structurally inscribed, perhaps materially based oppression is "heterosexism." This study will, however, continue to use "homophobia," for three reasons. First, it will be an important concern here to question, rather than to reinforce, the presumptively symmetrical opposition between homo- and heterosexuality, which seems to be implicit in the term "heterosexism." Second, the etiology of individual people's attitudes toward male homosexuality will not be a focus of discussion. And third, the ideological and thematic treatments of male homosexuality to be discussed from the late eighteenth century onward do combine fear and hatred in a way that is appropriately called phobic. For a good summary of social science research on the concept of homophobia, see Stephen M. Morin and Ellen M. Garfinkle, "Male Homophobia," in *Gayspeak: Gay Male and Lesbian Communication*, ed. James W. Chesebro (New York: Pilgrim Press, 1981), pp. 117–29 [except as indicated, all notes are Sedgwick's].

2. Psychic drive or energy associated with the sexual instinct but also inherent in other mental desires and drives [editor's note].

3. For a good survey of the background to this assertion, see Jeffrey Weeks, *Sex, Politics, and Society: The Regulation of Sexuality Since 1800* (London: Longman, 1981), pp. 1–18.

and women differ in their access to power, there will be important gender differences, as well, in the structure and constitution of sexuality.

For instance, the diacritical[4] opposition between the "homosocial" and the "homosexual" seems to be much less thorough and dichotomous for women, in our society, than for men. At this particular historical moment, an intelligible continuum of aims, emotions, and valuations links lesbianism with the other forms of women's attention to women: the bond of mother and daughter, for instance, the bond of sister and sister, women's friendship, "networking," and the active struggles of feminism.[5] The continuum is crisscrossed with deep discontinuities—with much homophobia, with conflicts of race and class—but its intelligibility seems now a matter of simple common sense. However agonistic the politics, however conflicted the feelings, it seems at this moment to make an obvious kind of sense to say that women in our society who love women, women who teach, study, nurture, suckle, write about, march for, vote for, give jobs to, or otherwise promote the interests of other women, are pursuing congruent and closely related activities. Thus the adjective "homosocial" as applied to women's bonds (by, for example, historian Carroll Smith-Rosenberg)[6] need not be pointedly dichotomized as against "homosexual"; it can intelligibly denominate the entire continuum.

The apparent simplicity—the unity—of the continuum between "women loving women" and "women promoting the interests of women," extending over the erotic, social, familial, economic, and political realms, would not be so striking if it were not in strong contrast to the arrangement among males. When Ronald Reagan and Jesse Helms[7] get down to serious logrolling on "family policy," they are men promoting men's interests. (In fact, they embody Heidi Hartmann's definition of patriarchy: "relations between men, which have a material base, and which, though hierarchical, establish or create interdependence and solidarity among men that enable them to dominate women.")[8] Is their bond in any way congruent with the bond of a loving gay male couple? Reagan and Helms would say no—disgustedly. Most gay couples would say no—disgustedly. But why not? Doesn't the continuum between "men-loving-men" and "men-promoting-the-interests-of-men" have the same intuitive force that it has for women?

Quite the contrary: much of the most useful recent writing about patriarchal structures suggests that "obligatory heterosexuality" is built into male-dominated kinship systems, or that homophobia is a *necessary* consequence of such patriarchal institutions as heterosexual marriage.[9] Clearly, however convenient it might be to group together all the bonds that link males to

4. Distinctive; serving as a distinguishing feature [editor's note].

5. Adrienne Rich describes these bonds as forming a "lesbian continuum," in her essay "Compulsory Heterosexuality and Lesbian Existence," *Signs* 5 (1980): 631–60. [Rich (b. 1929), American feminist poet and essayist; for this essay, see above—editor's note.]

6. "The Female World of Love and Ritual," in *A Heritage of Her Own: Toward a New Social History of American Women*, ed. Nancy F. Cott and Elizabeth H. Pleck (New York: Simon and Schuster, 1979), pp. 311–42; usage appears on, e.g., pp. 316, 317.

7. Senator (b. 1921) from North Carolina (1973–). Reagan (b. 1911), 40th president of the United States (1981–89). Both conservative Republicans were well known for their vocal support of "family values" during the 1980s [editor's note].

8. "The Unhappy Marriage of Marxism and Feminism: Toward a More Progressive Union," in *Women and Revolution: A Discussion of the Unhappy Marriage of Marxism and Feminism*, ed. Lydia Sargent (Boston: South End Press, 1981), pp. 1–41; the quotation is from p. 14.

9. See, for example, Gayle Rubin, "The Traffic in Women: Notes toward a 'Political Economy' of Sex," in *Toward an Anthropology of Women*, ed. Rayna Reiter (New York: Monthly Review Press, 1975), pp. 182–83.

males, and by which males enhance the status of males—usefully symmetrical as it would be, that grouping meets with a prohibitive structural obstacle. From the vantage point of our own society, at any rate, it has apparently been impossible to imagine a form of patriarchy that was not homophobic. Gayle Rubin writes, for instance, "The suppression of the homosexual component of human sexuality, and by corollary, the oppression of homosexuals, is . . . a product of the same system whose rules and relations oppress women."[1]

The historical manifestations of this patriarchal oppression of homosexuals have been savage and nearly endless. Louis Crompton makes a detailed case for describing the history as genocidal.[2] Our own society is brutally homophobic; and the homophobia directed against both males and females is not arbitrary or gratuitous, but tightly knit into the texture of family, gender, age, class, and race relations. Our society could not cease to be homophobic and have its economic and political structures remain unchanged.

Nevertheless, it has yet to be demonstrated that, because most patriarchies structurally include homophobia, therefore patriarchy structurally *requires* homophobia. K. J. Dover's recent study, *Greek Homosexuality*, seems to give a strong counterexample in classical Greece. Male homosexuality, according to Dover's evidence, was a widespread, licit, and very influential part of the culture. Highly structured along lines of class, and within the citizen class along lines of age, the pursuit of the adolescent boy by the older man was described by stereotypes that we associate with romantic heterosexual love (conquest, surrender, the "cruel fair," the absence of desire in the love object), with the passive part going to the boy. At the same time, however, because the boy was destined in turn to grow into manhood, the assignment of roles was not permanent.[3] Thus the love relationship, while temporarily oppressive to the object, had a strongly educational function; Dover quotes Pausanias in Plato's *Symposium* as saying "that it would be right for him [the boy] to perform any service for one who improves him in mind and character."[4] Along with its erotic component, then, this was a bond of mentorship; the boys were apprentices in the ways and virtues of Athenian citizenship, whose privileges they inherited. These privileges included the power to command the labor of slaves of both sexes, and of women of any class including their own. "Women and slaves belonged and lived together," Hannah Arendt writes. The system of sharp class and gender subordination was a necessary part of what the male culture valued most in itself: "Contempt for laboring originally [arose] out of a passionate striving for freedom from necessity and a no less passionate impatience with every effort that left no trace, no monument, no great work worthy to remembrance";[5] so the contemptible labor was left to women and slaves.

The example of the Greeks demonstrates, I think, that while heterosexu-

1. Rubin, "Traffic," p. 180.
2. Louis Crompton, "Gay Genocide: From Leviticus to Hitler," in *The Gay Academic*, ed. Louie Crew (Palm Springs, Calif.: ETC Publications, 1978), pp. 67–91; but see chapter 5 [of *Between Men*] for a discussion of the limitations of "genocide" as an understanding of the fate of homosexual men.
3. On this, see Jean Baker Miller, *Toward a New Psychology of Women* (Boston: Beacon Press, 1976), chap. 1.
4. K. J. Dover, *Greek Homosexuality* (New York: Random House–Vintage, 1980), p. 91. [Dover's quotation is from PLATO, *Symposium* 184d—editor's note.]
5. Hannah Arendt, *The Human Condition* (Chicago: University of Chicago Press, 1958), p. 83; quoted in Adrienne Rich, *On Lies, Secrets, and Silence: Selected Prose, 1966–1978* (New York: Norton, 1979), p. 206.

ality is necessary for the maintenance of any patriarchy, homophobia, against males at any rate, is not. In fact, for the Greeks, the continuum between "men loving men" and "men promoting the interests of men" appears to have been quite seamless. It is as if, in our terms, there were no perceived discontinuity between the male bonds at the Continental Baths and the male bonds at the Bohemian Grove[6] or in the board room or Senate cloakroom.

It is clear, then, that there is an asymmetry in our present society between, on the one hand, the relatively continuous relation of female homosocial and homosexual bonds, and, on the other hand, the radically discontinuous relation of male homosocial and homosexual bonds. The example of the Greeks (and of other, tribal cultures, such as the New Guinea "Sambia" studied by G. H. Herdt[7]) shows, in addition, that the structure of homosocial continuums is culturally contingent, not an innate feature of either "maleness" or "femaleness." Indeed, closely tied though it obviously is to questions of male vs. female power, the explanation will require a more exact mode of historical categorization than "patriarchy," as well, since patriarchal power structures (in Hartmann's sense) characterize both Athenian and American societies. Nevertheless, we may take as an explicit axiom that the historically differential shapes of male and female homosociality—much as they themselves may vary over time—will always be articulations and mechanisms of the enduring inequality of power between women and men.

Why should the different shapes of the homosocial continuum be an interesting question? Why should it be a *literary* question? Its importance for the practical politics of the gay movement as a minority rights movement is already obvious from the recent history of strategic and philosophical differences between lesbians and gay men. In addition, it is theoretically interesting partly as a way of approaching a larger question of "sexual politics": What does it mean—what difference does it make—when a social or political relationship is sexualized? If the relation of homosocial to homosexual bonds is so shifty, then what theoretical framework do we have for drawing any links between sexual and power relationships?

1985

From Epistemology of the Closet

From Introduction: Axiomatic

AXIOM 2: THE STUDY OF SEXUALITY IS NOT COEXTENSIVE WITH THE STUDY OF GENDER; CORRESPONDINGLY, ANTIHOMOPHOBIC INQUIRY IS NOT COEXTENSIVE WITH FEMINIST INQUIRY. BUT WE CAN'T KNOW IN ADVANCE HOW THEY WILL BE DIFFERENT.

Sex, gender, sexuality: three terms whose usage relations and analytical relations are almost irremediably slippery. The charting of a space between

6. On the Bohemian Grove, an all-male summer camp for American ruling-class men, see G. William Domhoff, *The Bohemian Grove and Other Retreats: A Study in Ruling-Class Cohesiveness* (New York: Harper and Row, 1974); and a more vivid, although homophobic, account, John van der Zee, *The Greatest Men's Party on Earth: Inside the Bohemian Grove* (New York: Harcourt Brace Jovanovich, 1974). [The Continental Baths: a gay bathhouse/club, very popular in the 1970s, located on Manhattan's Upper West Side—editor's note.]

7. American anthropologist (b. 1949), author of *Guardians of the Flute: Idioms of Masculinity* (1981) [editor's note].

something called "sex" and something called "gender" has been one of the most influential and successful undertakings of feminist thought. For the purposes of that undertaking, "sex" has had the meaning of a certain group of irreducible, biological differentiations between members of the species Homo sapiens who have XX and those who have XY chromosomes. These include (or are ordinarily thought to include) more or less marked dimorphisms of genital formation, hair growth (in populations that have body hair), fat distribution, hormonal function, and reproductive capacity. "Sex" in this sense—what I'll demarcate as "chromosomal sex"—is seen as the relatively minimal raw material on which is then based the social construction of *gender*. Gender, then, is the far more elaborated, more fully and rigidly dichotomized social production and reproduction of male and female identities and behaviors—of male and female *persons*—in a cultural system for which "male / female" functions as a primary and perhaps model binarism affecting the structure and meaning of many, many other binarisms whose apparent connection to chromosomal sex will often be exiguous or nonexistent. Compared to chromosomal sex, which is seen (by these definitions) as tending to be immutable, immanent in the individual, and biologically based, the meaning of gender is seen as culturally mutable and variable, highly relational (in the sense that each of the binarized genders is defined primarily by its relation to the other), and inextricable from a history of power differentials between genders. This feminist charting of what Gayle Rubin refers to as a "sex / gender system,"[1] the system by which chromosomal sex is turned into, and processed as, cultural gender, has tended to minimize the attribution of people's various behaviors and identities to chromosomal sex and to maximize their attribution to socialized gender constructs. The purpose of that strategy has been to gain analytic and critical leverage on the female-disadvantaging social arrangements that prevail at a given time in a given society, by throwing into question their legitimative ideological grounding in biologically based narratives of the "natural."

"Sex" is, however, a term that extends indefinitely beyond chromosomal sex. That its history of usage often overlaps with what might, now, more properly be called "gender" is only one problem. ("I can only love someone of my own sex." Shouldn't "sex" be "gender" in such a sentence? "M. saw that the person who approached was of the opposite sex." Genders—insofar as there are two and they are defined in contradistinction to one another—may be said to be opposite; but in what sense is XX the opposite of XY?) Beyond chromosomes, however, the association of "sex," precisely through the physical body, with reproduction and with genital activity and sensation keeps offering new challenges to the conceptual clarity or even possibility of sex / gender differentiation. There is a powerful argument to be made that a primary (or *the* primary) issue in gender differentiation and gender struggle is the question of who is to have control of women's (biologically) distinctive reproductive capability. Indeed, the intimacy of the association between several of the most signal forms of gender oppression and "the facts" of women's bodies and women's reproductive activity has led some radical feminists to question, more or less explicitly, the usefulness of insisting on a sex / gender distinction. For these reasons, even usages involving the "sex / gender sys-

1. Gayle Rubin, "The Traffic in Women: Notes toward a 'Political Economy' of Sex," in *Toward an Anthropology of Women*, ed. Rayna Reiter (New York: Monthly Review Press, 1975), pp. 157–210 [except as indicated, all notes are Sedgwick's].

tem" within feminist theory are able to use "sex / gender" only to delineate a problematical *space* rather than a crisp distinction. My own loose usage in this book will be to denominate that problematized space of the sex / gender system, the whole package of physical and cultural distinctions between women and men, more simply under the rubric "gender." I do this in order to reduce the likelihood of confusion between "sex" in the sense of "the space of differences between male and female" (what I'll be grouping under "gender") and "sex" in the sense of sexuality.

For meanwhile the whole realm of what modern culture refers to as "sexuality" and *also* calls "sex"—the array of acts, expectations, narratives, pleasures, identity-formations, and knowledges, in both women and men, that tends to cluster most densely around certain genital sensations but is not adequately defined by them—that realm is virtually impossible to situate on a map delimited by the feminist-defined sex / gender distinction. To the degree that it has a center or starting point in certain physical sites, acts, and rhythms associated (however contingently) with procreation or the potential for it, "sexuality" in this sense may seem to be of a piece with "chromosomal sex": biologically necessary to species survival, tending toward the individually immanent, the socially immutable, the given. But to the extent that, as Freud argued and Foucault[2] assumed, the distinctively sexual nature of human sexuality has to do precisely with its excess over or potential difference from the bare choreographies of procreation, "sexuality" might be the very opposite of what we originally referred to as (chromosomal-based) sex: it could occupy, instead, even more than "gender" the polar position of the relational, the social / symbolic, the constructed, the variable, the representational (see Figure 1). To note that, according to these different findings, *something* legitimately called sex or sexuality is all over the experiential and conceptual map is to record a problem less resolvable than a necessary

Biological Essential Individually immanent	Cultural Constructed Relational

Constructivist Feminist Analysis

chromosomal sex ———————————— gender
gender inequality

Radical Feminist Analysis

chromosomal sex
reproductive relations ———————— reproductive relations
sexual inequality ———————— sexual inequality

Foucault-influenced Analysis

chromosomal sex ———————— reproduction ———————— sexuality

Figure 1. Some Mappings of Sex, Gender, and Sexuality

2. MICHEL FOUCAULT (1926–1984), French philosopher and historian of ideas. SIGMUND FREUD (1856–1939), Austrian founder of psychoanalysis [editor's note].

choice of analytic paradigms or a determinate slippage of semantic meaning; it is rather, I would say, true to quite a range of contemporary worldviews and intuitions to find that sex / sexuality *does* tend to represent the full spectrum of positions between the most intimate and the most social, the most predetermined and the most aleatory, the most physically rooted and the most symbolically infused, the most innate and the most learned, the most autonomous and the most relational traits of being.

If all this is true of the definitional nexus between sex and sexuality, how much less simple, even, must be that between sexuality and gender. It will be an assumption of this study that there is always at least the potential for an analytic distance between gender and sexuality, even if particular manifestations or features of particular sexualities are among the things that plunge women and men most ineluctably into the discursive, institutional, and bodily enmeshments of gender definition, gender relation, and gender inequality. This, too, has been posed by Gayle Rubin:

> I want to challenge the assumption that feminism is or should be the privileged site of a theory of sexuality. Feminism is the theory of gender oppression. . . . Gender affects the operation of the sexual system, and the sexual system has had gender-specific manifestations. But although sex and gender are related, they are not the same thing.[3]

This book will hypothesize, with Rubin, that the question of gender and the question of sexuality, inextricable from one another though they are in that each can be expressed only in the terms of the other, are nonetheless not the same question, that in twentieth-century Western culture gender and sexuality represent two analytic axes that may productively be imagined as being as distinct from one another as, say, gender and class, or class and race. Distinct, that is to say, no more than minimally, but nonetheless usefully.

Under this hypothesis, then, just as one has learned to assume that every issue of racial meaning must be embodied through the specificity of a particular class position—and every issue of class, for instance, through the specificity of a particular gender position—so every issue of gender would necessarily be embodied through the specifity of a particular sexuality, and vice versa; but nonetheless there could be use in keeping the analytic axes distinct.

An objection to this analogy might be that gender is *definitionally* built into determinations of sexuality, in a way that neither of them is definitionally intertwined with, for instance, determinations of class or race. It is certainly true that without a concept of gender there could be, quite simply, no concept of homo- or heterosexuality. But many other dimensions of sexual choice (auto- or alloerotic,[4] within or between generations, species, etc.) have no such distinctive, explicit definitional connection with gender; indeed, some dimensions of sexuality might be tied, not to gender, but *instead* to differences or similarities of race or class. The definitional narrowing-down in this century of sexuality as a whole to a binarized calculus of *homo-*

3. Gayle Rubin, "Thinking Sex: Notes for a Radical Theory of the Politics of Sexuality," in *Pleasure and Danger: Exploring Female Sexuality*, ed. Carole S. Vance (Boston: Routledge & Kegan Paul, 1984), pp. 307–8.

4. Based in eroticism focused on the other. "Autoerotic": based in eroticism focused on the self [editor's note].

or *hetero*sexuality is a weighty fact but an entirely historical one. To use that fait accompli as a reason for analytically conflating sexuality per se with gender would obscure the degree to which the fact itself requires explanation. It would also, I think, risk obscuring yet again the extreme intimacy with which all these available analytic axes do after all mutually constitute one another: to assume the distinctiveness of the *intimacy* between sexuality and gender might well risk assuming too much about the definitional *separability* of either of them from determinations of, say, class or race.

It may be, as well, that a damaging bias toward heterosocial[5] or heterosexist assumptions inheres unavoidably in the very concept of gender. This bias would be built into any gender-based analytic perspective to the extent that gender definition and gender identity are necessarily relational between genders—to the extent, that is, that in any gender system, female identity or definition is constructed by analogy, supplementarity, or contrast to male, or vice versa. Although many gender-based forms of analysis do involve accounts, sometimes fairly rich ones, of intragender behaviors and relations, the ultimate definitional appeal in many gender-based analysis must necessarily be to the diacritical[6] frontier between different genders. This gives heterosocial and heterosexual relations a conceptual privilege of incalculable consequence. Undeniably, residues, markers, tracks, signs referring to that diacritical frontier between genders are everywhere, as well, internal to and determinative of the experience of each gender and its intragender relations; gender-based analysis can never be dispensed with in even the most purely intragender context. Nevertheless it seems predictable that the analytic bite of a purely gender-based account will grow less incisive and direct as the distance of its subject from a social interface between different genders increases. It is unrealistic to expect a close, textured analysis of same-sex relations through an optic calibrated in the first place to the coarser stigmata of gender difference.[7] The development of an alternative analytic axis—call it sexuality—might well be, therefore, a particularly urgent project for gay / lesbian and antihomophobic inquiry.

It would be a natural corollary to Axiom 2 to hypothesize, then, that gay / lesbian and antihomophobic inquiry still has a lot to learn from asking questions that feminist inquiry has learned to ask—but only so long as we don't demand to receive the same answers in both interlocutions. In a comparison of feminist and gay theory as they currently stand, the newness and consequent relative underdevelopment of gay theory are seen most clearly in two manifestations. First, we are by now very used to asking as feminists what we aren't yet used to asking as antihomophobic readers: how a variety of forms of oppression intertwine systemically with each other; and especially how the person who is disabled through one set of oppressions may *by the same positioning* be enabled through others. For instance, the understated demeanor of educated women in our society tends to mark both their def-

5. A term used to described social bonds between persons of different genders, by analogy with *homosocial*, the notion Sedgwick explores in *Between Men* (1985; see above) [editor's note].

6. Distinctive; serving as a distinguishing feature [editor's note].

7. For valuable related discussions, see Katie King, "The Situation of Lesbianism as Feminism's Magical Sign: Contests for Meaning and the US Women's Movement, 1968–1972," *Communication* 9 (1986): 65–91, special issue, "Feminist Critiques of Popular Culture," ed. Paula A. Treichler and Ellen Wartella; and Teresa de Lauretis, "Sexual Indifference and Lesbian Representation," *Theatre Journal* 40 (May 1988): 155–77.

erence to educated men and their expectation of deference from women and men of lower class. Again, a woman's use of a married name makes graphic at the same time her subordination as a woman and her privilege as a presumptive heterosexual. Or, again, the distinctive vulnerability to rape of women of all races has become in this country a powerful tool for the racist enforcement by which white people, including women, are privileged at the expense of Black people of both genders. That one is *either* oppressed *or* an oppressor, or that if one happens to be both, the two are not likely to have much to do with each other, still seems to be a common assumption, however, in at any rate male gay writing and activism,[8] as it hasn't for a long time been in careful feminist work.

Indeed, it was the long, painful realization, *not* that all oppressions are congruent, but that they are *differently* structured and so much intersect in complex embodiments that was the first great heuristic[9] breakthrough of socialist-feminist thought and of the thought of women of color.[1] This realization has as its corollary that the comparison of different axes of oppression is a crucial task, not for any purpose of ranking oppressions, but to the contrary because each oppression is likely to be in a uniquely indicative relation to certain distinctive nodes of cultural organization. The *special* centrality of homophobic oppression in the twentieth century, I will be arguing, has resulted from its inextricability from the question of knowledge and the processes of knowing in modern Western culture at large.

The second and perhaps even greater heuristic leap of feminism has been the recognition that categories of gender and, hence, oppressions of gender can have a structuring force for nodes of thought, for axes of cultural discrimination, whose thematic subject isn't explicitly gendered at all. Through a series of developments structured by the deconstructive understandings and procedures sketched above, we have now learned as feminist readers that dichotomies in a given text of culture as opposed to nature, public as

8. Gay male–centered work that uses more complex models to investigate the intersection of different oppressions includes Gay Left Collective, eds., *Homosexuality: Power and Politics* (London: Allison & Busby, 1980); Paul Hoch, *White Hero Black Beast: Racism, Sexism, and the Mask of Masculinity* (London: Pluto, 1979); Guy Hocquenghem, *Homosexual Desire*, trans. Daniella Dangoor (London: Allison & Busby, 1978); Mario Mieli, *Homosexuality and Liberation: Elements of a Gay Critique*, trans. David Fernbach (London: Gay Men's Press, 1980); D. A. Miller, *The Novel and the Police* (Berkeley: University of California Press, 1988); Michael Moon, " 'The Gentle Boy from the Dangerous Classes': Pederasty, Domesticity, and Capitalism in Horatio Alger," *Representations*, no. 19 (summer 1987): 87–110; Michael Moon, *Disseminating Whitman* (Cambridge: Harvard University Press, 1990); and Jeffrey Weeks, *Sexuality and Its Discontents: Meanings, Myths, and Modern Sexualities* (London: Longman, 1980).

9. Explanatory, serving as an aid to problem solving [editor's note].

1. The influential socialist-feminist investigations have included Michèle Barrett, *Women's Oppression Today: Problems in Marxist Feminist Analysis* (London: Verso, 1980); Zillah Eisenstein, ed., *Capitalist Patriarchy and the Case for Socialist Feminism* (New York: Monthly Review Press, 1979); and Juliet Mitchell, *Women's Estate* (New York: Vintage, 1973). On the intersections of racial with gender and sexual oppressions, see, for example, Elly Bulkin, BARBARA SMITH, and Minnie Bruce Pratt, *Yours in Struggle: Three Feminist Perspectives on Anti-Semitism and Racism* (New York: Long Haul Press, 1984); BELL HOOKS [Gloria Watkins], *Feminist Theory: From Margin to Center* (Boston: South End Press, 1984); Katie King, "Audre Lorde's Lacquered Layerings: The Lesbian Bar as a Site of Literary Production," *Cultural Studies* 2, no. 3 (1988): 321–42; Audre Lorde, *Sister Outsider: Essays and Speeches* (Trumansburg, N.Y.: Crossing Press, 1984); Cherríe Moraga, *Loving in the War Years: Lo que nunca paso por sus labios* (Boston: South End Press, 1938); Cherrié Moraga and GLORIA ANZALDÚA, eds., *This Bridge Called My Back: Writings by Radical Women of Color* (Watertown: Persephone, 1981; rpt. ed., New York: Kitchen Table, Women of Color Press, 1983); and Barbara Smith, ed., *Home Girls: A Black Feminist Anthology* (New York: Kitchen Table, Women of Color Press, 1983). Good overviews of several of these intersections as they relate to women and in particular to lesbians, can be found in Ann Snitow, Christine Stansell, and Sharon Thompson, eds., *The Powers of Desire: The Politics of Sexuality* (New York: Monthly Review/New Feminist Library, 1983); Vance, *Pleasure and Danger*; and de Lauretis, "Sexual Indifference."

opposed to private, mind as opposed to body, activity as opposed to passivity, etc. etc., are, under particular pressures of culture and history, likely places to look for implicit allegories of the relations of men to women; more, that to fail to analyze such nominally ungendered constructs in gender terms can itself be a gravely tendentious move in the gender politics of reading. This has given us ways to ask the question of gender about texts even where the culturally "marked" gender (female) is not present as either author or thematic.

The dichotomy heterosexual / homosexual, as it has emerged through the last century of Western discourse, would seem to lend itself peculiarly neatly to a set of analytic moves learned from this deconstructive moment in feminist theory. In fact, the dichotomy heterosexual / homosexual fits the deconstructive template much more neatly than male / female itself does, and hence, importantly differently. The most dramatic difference between gender and sexual orientation—that virtually all people are publicly and unalterably assigned to one or the other gender, and from birth—seems if anything to mean that it is, rather, sexual orientation, with its far greater potential for rearrangement, ambiguity, and representational doubleness, that would offer the apter deconstructive object. An essentialism of sexual object-choice is far less easy to maintain, far more visibly incoherent, more visibly stressed and challenged at every point in the culture than any essentialism of gender. This is not an argument for any epistemological or ontological privileging of an axis of sexuality over an axis of gender; but it is a powerful argument for their potential distinctness one from the other.

Even given the imperative of constructing an account of sexuality irreducible to gender, however, it should already be clear that there are certain distortions necessarily built into the relation of gay / lesbian and antihomophobic theory to a larger project of conceiving a theory of sexuality as a whole. The two can after all scarcely be coextensive. And this is true not because "gay / lesbian and antihomophobic theory" would fail to cover heterosexual as well as same-sex object-choice (any more than "feminist theory" would fail to cover men as well as women), but rather because, as we have noted, sexuality extends along so many dimensions that aren't well described in terms of the gender of object-choice at all. Some of these dimensions are habitually condensed under the rubrics of object-choice, so that certain discriminations of (for instance) *act* or of (for another instance) *erotic localization* come into play, however implicitly and however incoherently, when categories of object-choice are mobilized. One used, for instance, to hear a lot about a high developmental stage called "heterosexual genitality," as though cross-gender object-choice automatically erased desires attaching to mouth, anus, breasts, feet, etc.; a certain anal-erotic salience of male homosexuality is if anything increasingly strong under the glare of heterosexist AIDS-phobia; and several different historical influences have led to the de-genitalization and bodily diffusion of many popular, and indeed many lesbian, understandings of lesbian sexuality. Other dimensions of sexuality, however, distinguish object-choice quite differently (e.g., human / animal, adult / child, singular / plural, autoerotic / alloerotic) or are not even about object choice (e.g., orgasmic / nonorgasmic, noncommercial / commercial, using bodies only / using manufactured objects, in private / in public, spontaneous / scripted).[2] Some of these other dimensions of sexuality have had high diacritical importance in different historical contexts (e.g., human / animal, autoerotic / alloerotic). Others, like adult / child object choice, visibly do have such importance today, but without being very fully subsumed under the hetero / homosexual binarism. Still others, including a host of them I haven't mentioned or couldn't think of, subsist in this culture as nondiacritical differences, differences that seem to make little difference beyond themselves—except that the hyperintensive structuring of sexuality in our culture sets several of them, for instance, at the exact border between legal and illegal. What I mean at any rate to emphasize is that the implicit condensation of "sexual theory" into "gay / lesbian and antihomophobic theory," which corresponds roughly to our by now unquestioned reading of the phrase "sexual orientation" to mean "gender of object-choice," is at the very least damagingly skewed by the specificity of its historical placement.

1990

2. This list owes something to Rubin, "Thinking Sex," esp. pp. 281–82.

DICK HEBDIGE
b. 1951

Dick Hebdige combines sharp yet sympathetic analysis of youth subcultures with lucid articulations of the theoretical and political commitments of cultural studies. Cultural studies can sometimes seem to include almost anything; Hebdige's work—along with that of STUART HALL—exemplifies the approach in its British incarnation. In his hands, a specific relation to the Marxist tradition, a fundamental grounding in semiotics, and an attention to marginalized subcultures combine to generate an analysis that is distinct both from sociological investigations of deviance and from mainstream literary criticism of printed texts.

From a London working-class family, Hebdige studied at the celebrated University of Birmingham Centre for Contemporary Cultural Studies. He taught at Goldsmith's College of the University of London from 1984 to 1992 before moving to the United States to become dean of Critical Studies at the California Institute of the Arts.

The title of our selection, "From Culture to Hegemony" (1979), summarizes the historical and theoretical trajectory that created British cultural studies. As Hebdige relates, British intellectuals RAYMOND WILLIAMS and Richard Hoggart began in the late 1950s to search out redeeming cultural resources to set against what they deplored in contemporary society. They built on the idea, which Williams traces back to nineteenth-century social critics such as SAMUEL TAYLOR COLERIDGE and MATTHEW ARNOLD, that culture provides a repository of values and ideals against which the present can be judged. Williams especially was eager to expand this cultural repository to include the communal practices, values, and beliefs of ordinary people. As Williams came to realize, an anthropological notion of culture as "a whole way of life" and an artistic notion of culture as the works that embody the tradition's highest achievement coexist in a sometimes productive but often confusing tension.

Realizing that this tension arises because both Williams and Hoggart continue to use culture as a standard of excellence, Hebdige substitutes the semiotic analysis of culture that he derives from ROLAND BARTHES for their moral project. Thus culture in the Arnoldian sense of identifying the best or the highest drops out of the picture. And because culture refers primarily to the semiotic element of all human activities, the term is not hopelessly vague. The basic claim of semiotics is that every object, practice, and relation within human societies is enmeshed in a systematic web of codes and conventions that constitute the specific item's value and meaning. Different societies vary not just in what they do, but in how they understand and value what they do. Cultural studies attends to the significance attached to various objects and activities in a particular society *and* to the linguistic and symbolic processes through which significance is produced in that society.

There are two other important consequences of this semiotic turn. First, literary texts and other artworks tend now to be neither more nor less important than any other cultural artifact or practice. The emphasis on *how* cultural meanings are produced renders moot the question of their intrinsic interest or aesthetic value. This merger of literature into the wider cultural field explains the widespread perception that cultural studies poses a threat to literary criticism. Second, the turn connects British cultural studies to French poststructuralism, especially in elevating social codes to a position of importance over individual speakers. Meanings are assigned within language, not by selves but systems, and things come to us already laden with meanings.

Many British cultural studies writers, however, retain a Marxist populism that wants to celebrate the creative and resistant political agency of ordinary men and women. As a result, Hebdige is less ready than are some French theorists to jettison all faith in small-scale action and choice. Hence his focus on "subcultural style," which can be defined as the creative variations that come into existence as marginal groups put into actual practice the meanings made available by preexisting dominant codes. In the terms of FERDINAND DE SAUSSURE's influential linguistic theory, style is *parole*, the individualized utterances of actual speakers: though they use the words and grammatical structures of the already-existing *langue* (language system), they still have considerable latitude in how they combine its elements at any particular moment.

The concept of ideology within the Marxist tradition provides a theoretical account of the social production of significances. As our selection makes clear, British cultural studies retains the Marxist insistence that the prevailing ideas, beliefs, and values in society are those of the dominant class. But this definition of ideology is now recast through the encounter with French theory. From Roland Barthes, Hebdige takes the idea that ideology "naturalizes," making dominant beliefs, habits, practices, and social structures seem inevitable. From LOUIS ALTHUSSER, British cultural studies takes the notion that ideology is the "lived relation" of the subject to social institutions (the family, school, law, etc.).

Depicted as fundamental and unconscious, as a set of routines and rituals reproduced by daily life and enforced by social institutions, ideology could easily be seen as all-powerful, susceptible to neither contestation nor revision. British cultural studies responded to this tendency with its most significant theoretical contribution: recourse to the concept of hegemony. *Hegemony*, a term first used in this context by the Italian Marxist ANTONIO GRAMSCI, introduces contestation, power differentials, and collective action into the social and cultural fields traversed by ideology. Our selection provides Hebdige's very influential account of hegemony, which subsequent writers have modified in various ways.

For Gramsci, hegemony is "manufactured consent." Different groups compete for power, and success in ruling always depends in part on the assent of large parts of the population to the dominant group's legitimacy. To win that assent, competing groups must produce overarching visions of society that explain their particular group's place, the place of other groups, and the goals and goods that underwrite their use of power—visions produced much more consciously than either traditional or revisionist notions of ideology allow. The existence of competing groups—organized not solely according to class, as traditional Marxism insists, but also according to such variables as ethnicity, race, gender, region, and religion—ensures that there are always various hegemonic visions in circulation, enjoying different degrees of consent among different groups.

Hebdige highlights three components of hegemony. First, though the theory of hegemony underscores that brute power cannot ensure long-lasting dominance, the necessary consent from the governed is won by all other means, fair and foul: arguments, emotional appeals, images, and symbols. Thus, any analysis of cultural meanings must consider where and how such meanings were produced in relation to various groups' bids for dominance at a particular time.

Second, hegemony is a site of struggle at the level of social language. Hebdige combines the Marxist emphasis on conflict with the semiotic focus on the ongoing production of meaning to argue that "the struggle between different discourses, different definitions and meanings . . . is therefore always, at the same time, a struggle within signification: a struggle for possession of the sign which extends to even the most mundane areas of everyday life." Thus, even a hegemonic vision that has acquired relative dominance is always "a moving equilibrium," keeping its balance only by shifting continually to meet its various challengers.

Third and finally—here we find another hallmark of British cultural studies—Hebdige uses this conflictual model of hegemony to emphasize the mobility of signs. The same object—a safety pin, for example—can acquire an entirely new meaning when it is placed through a teenager's earlobe instead of through an infant's diaper. "Commodities can be symbolically 'repossessed' in everyday life, and endowed with implicitly oppositional meanings." Cultural studies scholars see not passive consumers or silent majorities but opposition and resistance in contemporary populations, as they focus on the creative "resignification" of received commodities, practices, institutions, and values.

Yet, as Hebdige notes, such symbolic repossessions are not in themselves acts of political resistance. Though "implicitly" oppositional, they do not directly challenge the powers that be. In particular, the challenges made by youth subcultures, notably punks, are "expressed obliquely, in style." (For Hebdige, youth *style* encompasses slang, dress, music, and dance.) He suggests that the disenchanted young can become effective political agents only if they are given some self-understanding of the larger social field.

More pessimistically, Hebdige hints at one moment that the styles of youth subcultures themselves impede political action. "The objections [to the dominant culture] are lodged, the contradictions displayed (and, as we shall see, 'magically resolved') at the profoundly superficial level of appearances: that is, at the level of signs." This view of symbolic resolution as foreclosing the desire for "real" action—which derives directly from CLAUDE LÉVI-STRAUSS's theory of myth—is also found in FREDRIC JAMESON's influential book *The Political Unconscious* (1981), but has fallen into disfavor since the 1980s. It seems odd for Hebdige to dismiss resolutions on the level of the sign as somehow not real, as not addressing contradictions on a level that truly matters, when most of his chapter argues for the importance of signs. Moreover, an uneasiness at viewing the activities of consumers as either inchoate or misplaced resistance, requiring the intellectual to transform them into something truly political, has significantly affected the development of cultural studies, especially in North America. To be sure, simply celebrating a group's creativity and its acts of resistance leaves everything as it is within a contemporary scene that hardly appears transformed by various acts of "symbolic repossession." Yet we should also wonder at this point just how we would be able to detect social transformation at all. What yardstick would differentiate "real" or "substantial" from "superficial" changes? Hebdige has no answers to this key question. At issue is the relation of the aesthetic to the political. A concern with style is, after all, a traditional aesthetic concern. To what extent is style—or any kind of artistic expression—an articulation of a political position or, more dramatically, a potentially transformative political act?

BIBLIOGRAPHY

Hebdige's books to date are *Subculture: The Meaning of Style* (1979), *Cut 'n' Mix: Culture, Identity, and Caribbean Music* (1987), and *Hiding in the Light: On Images and Things* (1988).

In a series of essays responding to and growing out of Hebdige's work, Angela McRobbie has questioned the male focus of the subcultures Hebdige describes and has pondered the political effectiveness of subcultural resistance. See her "Settling Accounts with Subcultures: A Feminist Critique," *Screen Education* 34 (1980); "Postmodernism and Popular Culture," *Journal of Communication Inquiry* 10 (1986); and "New Times in Cultural Studies," *New Formations* 13 (1991). Further reactions to Hebdige's work can be found in Anne Beezer's "Dick Hebdige, *Subculture*," in *Reading into Cultural Studies* (ed. Martin Barker and Anne Beezer, 1992); Vincent B. Leitch, *Cultural Criticism, Literary Theory, Poststructuralism* (1992); and Neil Nehring, *Flowers in the Dustbin: Culture, Anarchy, and Postwar England* (1993).

From Subculture: The Meaning of Style

Chapter 1.
From Culture to Hegemony

CULTURE

> Culture: cultivation, tending, in Christian authors, worship; the action or practice of cultivating the soil; tillage, husbandry; the cultivation or rearing of certain animals (e.g. fish); the artificial development of microscopic organisms, organisms so produced; the cultivating or development (of the mind, faculties, manners), improvement or refinement by education and training; the condition of being trained or refined; the intellectual side of civilization; the prosecution or special attention or study of any subject or pursuit. (*Oxford English Dictionary*)

Culture is a notoriously ambiguous concept as the above definition demonstrates. Refracted through centuries of usage, the word has acquired a number of quite different, often contradictory, meanings. Even as a scientific term, it refers both to a process (artificial development of microscopic organisms) and a product (organisms so produced). More specifically, since the end of the eighteenth century, it has been used by English intellectuals and literary figures to focus critical attention on a whole range of controversial issues. The 'quality of life', the effects in human terms of mechanization, the division of labour and the creation of a mass society have all been discussed within the larger confines of what Raymond Williams has called the 'Culture and Society' debate.[1] It was through this tradition of dissent and criticism that the dream of the 'organic society'—of society as an integrated, meaningful whole—was largely kept alive. The dream had two basic trajectories.

1. Raymond Williams, *Culture and Society* (Penguin, 1961) [Hebdige's note]. WILLIAMS (1921–1988), British Marxist literary critic.

One led back to the past and to the feudal ideal of a hierarchically ordered community. Here, culture assumed an almost sacred function. Its 'harmonious perfection' was posited against the Wasteland of contemporary life.[2]

The other trajectory, less heavily supported, led towards the future, to a socialist Utopia where the distinction between labour and leisure was to be annulled. Two basic definitions of culture emerged from this tradition, though these were by no means necessarily congruent with the two trajectories outlined above. The first—the one which is probably most familiar to the reader—was essentially classical and conservative. It represented culture as a standard of aesthetic excellence: 'the best that has been thought and said in the world,'[3] and it derived from an appreciation of 'classic' aesthetic form (opera, ballet, drama, literature, art). The second, traced back by Williams to Herder and the eighteenth century,[4] was rooted in anthropology. Here the term 'culture' referred to a

> . . . particular way of life which expresses certain meanings and values not only in art and learning, but also in institutions and ordinary behaviour. The analysis of culture, from such a definition, is the clarification of the meanings and values implicit and explicit in a particular way of life, a particular culture.[5]

This definition obviously had a much broader range. It encompassed, in T. S. Eliot's words,

> . . . all the characteristic activities and interests of a people. Derby Day, Henley Regatta, Cowes, the 12th of August, a cup final, the dog races, the pin table, the dart-board, Wensleydale cheese, boiled cabbage cut into sections, beetroot in vinegar, 19th Century Gothic churches, the music of Elgar. . . .[6]

As Williams noted, such a definition could only be supported if a new theoretical initiative was taken. The theory of culture now involved the 'study of relationships between elements in a whole way of life.'[7] The emphasis shifted from immutable to historical criteria, from fixity to transformation:

> . . . an emphasis [which] from studying particular meanings and values seeks not so much to compare these, as a way of establishing a scale, but by studying their modes of change to discover certain general causes or 'trends' by which social and cultural developments as a whole can be better understood.[8]

Williams was, then, proposing an altogether broader formulation of the relationships between culture and society, one which through the analysis of

2. Matthew Arnold, *Culture and Anarchy* (1868) [Hebdige's note]. ARNOLD (1822–1888), English poet and critic.
3. Ibid.
4. Raymond Williams, *Keywords* (Fontana Books, 1976) [Hebdige's note]. Johann Gottfried von Herder (1744–1803), German historian and philosopher who was one of the first writers to use the term "culture" to designate the distinctive ways of life of different peoples.
5. Raymond Williams, *The Long Revolution* (Penguin, 1965) [Hebdige's note].
6. T. S. Eliot, *Notes toward a Definition of Culture* (Faber and Faber, 1963) [Hebdige's note]. ELIOT (1888–1965), American-born English poet and literary critic. Derby Day: the day of the Derby Stakes, a major horse race in England run every May. Henley Regatta: annual amateur rowing races held near Oxford, which begin in June. Cowes: Cowes Week, annual yacht races held off the Isle of Wight in late July. 12th of August: opening of grouse-hunting season. "Cup": major soccer tournament. "Pin table": pinball machine. Edward Elgar (1857–1934), English composer.
7. Williams, *The Long Revolution* [Hebdige's note].
8. Ibid. [Hebdige's note].

'particular meanings and values' sought to uncover the concealed fundamentals of history; the 'general causes' and broad social 'trends' which lie behind the manifest appearances of an 'everyday life'.

In the early years, when it was being established in the Universities, Cultural Studies sat rather uncomfortably on the fence between these two conflicting definitions—culture as a standard of excellence, culture as a 'whole way of life'—unable to determine which represented the most fruitful line of enquiry. Richard Hoggart[9] and Raymond Williams portrayed working-class culture sympathetically in wistful accounts of pre-scholarship boyhoods (Leeds for Hoggart, a Welsh mining village for Williams[1]) but their work displayed a strong bias towards literature and literacy[2] and an equally strong moral tone. Hoggart deplored the way in which the traditional working-class community—a community of tried and tested values despite the dour landscape in which it had been set—was being undermined and replaced by a 'Candy Floss[3] World' of thrills and cheap fiction which was somehow bland *and* sleazy. Williams tentatively endorsed the new mass communications but was concerned to establish aesthetic and moral criteria for distinguishing the worthwhile products from the 'trash'; the jazz—'a real musical form'—and the football—'a wonderful game'—from the 'rape novel, the Sunday strip paper and the latest Tin Pan drool.'[4] In 1966 Hoggart laid down the basic premises upon which Cultural Studies were based:

> First, without appreciating good literature, no one will really understand the nature of society, second, literary critical analysis can be applied to certain social phenomena other than 'academically respectable' literature (for example, the popular arts, mass communications) so as to illuminate their meanings for individuals and their societies.[5]

The implicit assumption that it still required a literary sensibility to 'read' society with the requisite subtlety, and that the two ideas of culture could be ultimately reconciled was also, paradoxically, to inform the early work of the French writer, Roland Barthes, though here it found validation in a method—semiotics—a way of reading signs.[6]

BARTHES: MYTHS AND SIGNS

Using models derived from the work of the Swiss linguist Ferdinand de Saussure[7] Barthes sought to expose the *arbitrary* nature of cultural phenomena,

9. English literary critic (b. 1918) and a founding figure of cultural studies at the University of Birmingham in England.
1. Richard Hoggart, *The Uses of Literacy* (Penguin, 1958); Raymond Williams, *Border Country* (Penguin, 1960) [Hebdige's note].
2. Although Williams had posited a new, broader definition of culture, he intended this to complement rather than contradict earlier formulations: "It seems to me that there is value in each of these kinds of definition. . . . the degree to which we depend, in our knowledge of many past societies and past stages of our own, on the body of intellectual and imaginative work which has retained its major communicative power, makes the description of culture in these terms if not complete, then at least reasonable . . . there are elements in the 'ideal' definition which . . . seem to me valuable" (*The Long Revolution*) [Hebdige's note].
3. Cotton candy.
4. Williams, *The Long Revolution* [Hebdige's note].
5. Richard Hoggart, "Literature and Society," *American Scholar*, spring 1966 [Hebdige's note].
6. Terrence Hawkes, *Structuralism and Semiotics* (Methuen, 1977) [Hebdige's note]. BARTHES (1915–1980), semiotician and literary critic.
7. In his *Course in General Linguistics*, Saussure stressed the arbitrary nature of the linguistic sign. For Saussure, language is a system of mutually related values, in which arbitrary "signifiers" (e.g. words) are linked to equally arbitrary "signifieds" ("concepts . . . negatively defined by their relations with other terms in the system") to form signs. These signs together constitute a system. Each element is defined through its position within the relevant system—its relation to other elements—through the dialectics of identity and difference. Saussure postulated that other systems of significance (e.g. fashion, cookery) might be studied in a similar way, and that eventually linguistics would

to uncover the latent meanings of an everyday life which, to all intents and purposes, was 'perfectly natural'. Unlike Hoggart, Barthes was not concerned with distinguishing the good from the bad in modern mass culture, but rather with showing how *all* the apparently spontaneous forms and rituals of contemporary bourgeois societies are subject to a systematic distortion, liable at any moment to be dehistoricized, 'naturalized', converted into myth:

> The whole of France is steeped in this anonymous ideology: our press, our films, our theatre, our pulp literature, our rituals, our Justice, our diplomacy, our conversations, our remarks about the weather, a murder trial, a touching wedding, the cooking we dream of, the garments we wear, everything in everyday life is dependent on the representation which the bourgeoisie *has and makes us have* of the relations between men and the world.[8]

Like Eliot, Barthes' notion of culture extends beyond the library, the opera-house and the theatre to encompass the whole of everyday life. But this everyday life is for Barthes overlaid with a significance which is at once more insidious and more systematically organized. Starting from the premise that 'myth is a type of speech', Barthes set out in *Mythologies* to examine the normally hidden set of rules, codes and conventions through which meanings particular to specific social groups (i.e. those in power) are rendered universal and 'given' for the whole of society. He found in phenomena as disparate as a wrestling match, a writer on holiday, a tourist-guide book, the same artificial nature, the same ideological core. Each had been exposed to the same prevailing rhetoric (the rhetoric of common sense) and turned into myth, into a mere element in a 'second-order semiological system.'[9] (Barthes uses the example of a photograph in *Paris-Match* of a Negro soldier saluting the French flag, which has a first and second order connotation: (1) a gesture of loyalty, but also (2) 'France is a great empire, and all her sons, without colour discrimination, faithfully serve under her flag'.)

Barthes' application of a method rooted in linguistics to other systems of discourse outside language (fashion, film, food, etc.) opened up completely new possibilities for contemporary cultural studies. It was hoped that the invisible seam between language, experience and reality could be located and prised open through a semiotic analysis of this kind: that the gulf between the alienated intellectual and the 'real' world could be rendered meaningful and, miraculously, at the same time, be made to disappear. Moreover, under Barthes' direction, semiotics promised nothing less than the reconciliation of the two conflicting definitions of culture upon which Cultural Studies was so ambiguously posited—a marriage of moral conviction (in this case, Barthes' Marxist beliefs) and popular themes: the study of a society's total way of life.

This is not to say that semiotics was easily assimilable within the Cultural Studies project. Though Barthes shared the literary preoccupations of Hoggart and Williams, his work introduced a new Marxist 'problematic'[1] which

---

form part of a more general science of signs—a semiology [Hebdige's note].

SAUSSURE (1857–1913), founder of structuralist linguistics. His *Course* was first published in 1916.

8. Roland Barthes, *Mythologies* (Paladin, 1972) [Hebdige's note].

9. Ibid. [Hebdige's note].

1. The fashionable status of this word has in recent years contributed to its indiscriminate use. I intend here the very precise meaning established by Louis Althusser: "the *problematic* of a word or concept consists of the theoretical or ideological framework within which that word or concept can be used to establish, determine and discuss a particular range of issues and a particular kind of problem" (Louis Althusser and Étienne Balibar,

was alien to the British tradition of concerned and largely untheorized 'social commentary'. As a result, the old debate seemed suddenly limited. In E. P. Thompson's[2] words it appeared to reflect the parochial concerns of a group of 'gentlemen amateurs'. Thompson sought to replace Williams' definitions of the theory of culture as 'a theory of relations between elements in a whole way of life' with his own more rigorously Marxist formulation: 'the study of relationships in a whole way of *conflict*'. A more analytical framework was required; a new vocabulary had to be learned. As part of this process of theorization, the word 'ideology' came to acquire a much wider range of meanings than had previously been the case. We have seen how Barthes found an 'anonymous ideology' penetrating every possible level of social life, inscribed in the most mundane of rituals, framing the most casual social encounters. But how can ideology be 'anonymous', and how can it assume such a broad significance? Before we attempt any reading of subcultural style, we must first define the term 'ideology' more precisely.

IDEOLOGY: A *LIVED* RELATION

In the *German Ideology*,[3] Marx shows how the basis of the capitalist economic structure (surplus value, neatly defined by Godelier as 'Profit . . . is unpaid work'[4]) is hidden from the consciousness of the agents of production. The failure to see through appearances to the real relations which underlie them does not occur as the direct result of some kind of masking operation consciously carried out by individuals, social groups or institutions. On the contrary, ideology by definition thrives *beneath* consciousness. It is here, at the level of 'normal common sense', that ideological frames of reference are most firmly sedimented and most effective, because it is here that their ideological nature is most effectively concealed. As Stuart Hall puts it:

> It is precisely its 'spontaneous' quality, its transparency, its 'naturalness', its refusal to be made to examine the premises on which it is founded, its resistance to change or to correction, its effect of instant recognition, and the closed circle in which it moves which makes common sense, at one and the same time, 'spontaneous', ideological and *unconscious*. You cannot learn, through common sense, *how things are*: you can only discover *where they fit* into the existing scheme of things. In this way, its very taken-for-grantedness is what establishes it as a medium in which its own premises and presuppositions are being rendered *invisible* by its apparent transparency.[5]

Since ideology saturates everyday discourse in the form of common sense, it cannot be bracketed off from everyday life as a self-contained set of 'political opinions' or 'biased views'. Neither can it be reduced to the abstract

Reading Capital [New Left Books, 1968]; see also Tony Bennett, *Formalism and Marxism* [Methuen, 1979]) [Hebdige's note]. ALTHUSSER (1918–1990), French Marxist philosopher.

2. English leftist historian (1924–1993), whose emphasis on cultural history and the agency of the people in his classic *The Making of the English Working Class* (1963) strongly influenced British cultural studies.

3. For KARL MARX and FRIEDRICH ENGELS's *German Ideology* (written 1845–46; pub. 1932), see above.

4. M. Godelier, "Structure and Contradiction in 'Capital,'" in M. Lane, ed., *Structuralism: A Reader* (Jonathan Cape, 1970) [Hebdige's note].

5. Stuart Hall, "Culture, the Media, and the 'Ideological Effect,'" in J. Curran et al., eds., *Mass Communication and Society* (Edward Arnold, 1977) [Hebdige's note]. HALL (b. 1932), leading figure in British cultural studies.

dimensions of a 'world view' or used in the crude Marxist sense to designate 'false consciousness'.[6] Instead, as Louis Althusser has pointed out:

> . . . ideology has very little to do with 'consciousness'. . . . It is profoundly *unconscious*. . . . Ideology is indeed a system of representation, but in the majority of cases these representations have nothing to do with 'consciousness': they are usually images and occasionally concepts, but it is above all as *structures* that they impose on the vast majority of men, not via their 'consciousness'. They are perceived-accepted-suffered cultural objects and they act functionally on men via a process that escapes them.[7]

Although Althusser is here referring to structures like the family, cultural and political institutions, etc., we can illustrate the point quite simply by taking as our example a physical structure. Most modern institutions of education, despite the apparent neutrality of the materials from which they are constructed (red brick, white tile, etc.) carry within themselves implicit ideological assumptions which are literally structured into the architecture itself. The categorization of knowledge into arts and sciences is reproduced in the faculty system which houses different disciplines in different buildings, and most colleges maintain the traditional divisions by devoting a separate floor to each subject. Moreover, the hierarchical relationship between teacher and taught is inscribed in the very lay-out of the lecture theatre where the seating arrangements—benches rising in tiers before a raised lectern—dictate the flow of information and serve to 'naturalize' professorial authority. Thus, a whole range of decisions about what is and what is not possible within education have been made, however unconsciously, before the content of individual courses is even decided.

These decisions help to set the limits not only on what is taught but on *how* it is taught. Here the buildings literally *reproduce* in concrete terms prevailing (ideological) notions about what education *is* and it is through this process that the educational structure, which can, of course, be altered, is placed beyond question and appears to us as a 'given' (i.e. as immutable). In this case, the frames of our thinking have been translated into actual bricks and mortar.

Social relations and processes are then appropriated by individuals only through the forms in which they are represented to those individuals. These forms are, as we have seen, by no means transparent. They are shrouded in a 'common sense' which simultaneously validates and mystifies them. It is precisely these 'perceived-accepted-suffered cultural objects' which semiotics sets out to 'interrogate' and decipher. All aspects of culture possess a semiotic value, and the most taken-for-granted phenomena can function as signs: as elements in communication systems governed by semantic rules and codes which are not themselves directly apprehended in experience. These signs are, then, as opaque as the social relations which produce them and which they re-present. In other words, there is an ideological dimension to every signification:

6. A Marxist term referring to an individual's tendency to view reality in ways congruent with the interests of the dominant orthodoxy rather than in ways that reflect his or her own class interest.

7. Louis Althusser, *For Marx* (Vintage, 1970) [Hebdige's note].

> A sign does not simply exist as part of reality—it reflects and refracts another reality. Therefore it may distort that reality or be true to it, or may perceive it from a special point of view, and so forth. Every sign is subject to the criteria of ideological evaluation. . . . The domain of ideology coincides with the domain of signs. They equate with one another. Whenever a sign is present, ideology is present too. Everything ideological possesses a semiotic value.[8]

To uncover the ideological dimension of signs we must first try to disentangle the codes through which meaning is organized. 'Connotative' codes are particularly important. As Stuart Hall has argued, they ' . . . cover the face of social life and render it classifiable, intelligible, meaningful.'[9] He goes on to describe these codes as 'maps of meaning' which are of necessity the product of selection. They cut across a range of potential meanings, making certain meanings available and ruling others out of court. We tend to live inside these maps as surely as we live in the 'real' world: they 'think' us as much as we 'think' them, and this in itself is quite 'natural'. All human societies *reproduce* themselves in this way through a process of 'naturalization'. It is through this process—a kind of inevitable reflex of all social life—that *particular* sets of social relations, *particular* ways of organizing the world appear to us as if they were universal and timeless. This is what Althusser means when he says that 'ideology has no history' and that ideology in this general sense will always be an 'essential element of every social formation.'[1]

However, in highly complex societies like ours, which function through a finely graded system of divided (i.e. specialized) labour, the crucial question has to do with which specific ideologies, representing the interests of which specific groups and classes will prevail at any given moment, in any given situation. To deal with this question, we must first consider how power is distributed in our society. That is, we must ask which groups and classes have how much say in defining, ordering and classifying out the social world. For instance, if we pause to reflect for a moment, it should be obvious that access to the means by which ideas are disseminated in our society (i.e. principally the mass media) is *not* the same for all classes. Some groups have more say, more opportunity to make the rules, to organize meaning, while others are less favourably placed, have less power to produce and impose their definitions of the world on the world.

Thus, when we come to look beneath the level of 'ideology-in-general' at the way in which specific ideologies work, how some gain dominance and others remain marginal, we can see that in advanced Western democracies the ideological field is by no means neutral. To return to the 'connotative' codes to which Stuart Hall refers we can see that these 'maps of meaning' are charged with a potentially explosive significance because they are traced and re-traced along the lines laid down by the *dominant* discourses about reality, the *dominant* ideologies. They thus tend to represent, in however

8. V. N. Volosinov, *Marxism and the Philosophy of Language* (Seminar Press, 1973) [Hebdige's note]. Valentin N. Volosinov (1895–?), a critic in Leningrad during the 1920s and a colleague of MIKHAIL BAKHTIN (1895–1975). Scholars disagree about the authorship of *Marxism and the Philosophy of Language* (first published in 1927 under Volosinov's name); some argue that the book is really by Bakhtin, others by Volosinov (who is believed to have died in the purges of the 1930s).

9. Hall, "Culture, the Media, and the 'Ideological Effect' " [Hebdige's note].

1. Louis Althusser, *Lenin and Philosophy* (New Left Books, 1971); Althusser and Balibar, *Reading Capital* [Hebdige's note].

obscure and contradictory a fashion, the interests of the *dominant* groups in society.

To understand this point we should refer to Marx:

> The ideas of the ruling class are in every epoch the ruling ideas, i.e. the class which is the ruling *material* force of society is at the same time its ruling *intellectual* force. The class which has the means of material production at its disposal, has control at the same time over the means of mental production, so that generally speaking, the ideas of those who lack the means of mental production are subject to it. The ruling ideas are nothing more than the ideal expression of the dominant material relationships grasped as ideas; hence of the relationships which make the one class the ruling class, therefore the ideas of its dominance.[2]

This is the basis of Antonio Gramsci's[3] theory of *hegemony* which provides the most adequate account of how dominance is sustained in advanced capitalist societies.

HEGEMONY: THE MOVING EQUILIBRIUM

> 'Society cannot share a common communication system so long as it is split into warring classes' (Brecht,[4] *A Short Organum for the Theatre*).

The term hegemony refers to a situation in which a provisional alliance of certain social groups can exert 'total social authority' over other subordinate groups, not simply by coercion or by the direct imposition of ruling ideas, but by 'winning and shaping consent so that the power of the dominant classes appears both legitimate and natural.'[5] Hegemony can only be maintained so long as the dominant classes 'succeed in framing all competing definitions within their range',[6] so that subordinate groups are, if not controlled, then at least contained within an ideological space which does not seem at all 'ideological': which appears instead to be permanent and 'natural', to lie outside history, to be beyond particular interests.[7]

This is how, according to Barthes, 'mythology' performs its vital function of naturalization and normalization and it is in his book *Mythologies* that Barthes demonstrates most forcefully the full extension of these normalized forms and meanings. However, Gramsci adds the important proviso that hegemonic power, precisely *because* it requires the consent of the dominated majority, can never be permanently exercised by the same alliance of 'class fractions'. As has been pointed out, 'Hegemony . . . is not universal and "given" to the continuing rule of a particular class. It has to be won, reproduced, sustained. Hegemony is, as Gramsci said, a "moving equilibrium" containing relations of forces favourable or unfavorable to this or that tendency.'[8]

2. Karl Marx and Friedrich Engels, *The German Ideology* (Lawrence and Wishart, 1970) [Hebdige's note].
3. Italian Marxist (1891–1937; see above).
4. Bertolt Brecht (1898–1956), German Marxist playwright. "A Short Organum" was published in 1948.
5. Hall, "Culture, the Media, and the 'Ideological Effect.' " [Hebdige's note].
6. Ibid. [Hebdige's note].
7. See *Social Trends*, no. 6, 1975 [Hebdige's note].
8. S. Hall et al., eds., *Resistance through Rituals* (Hutchinson, 1976) [Hebdige's note]. This is one of many collections of essays published by members of the Birmingham Centre for Contemporary Cultural Studies in the 1970s and 1980s.

In the same way, forms cannot be permanently normalized. They can always be deconstructed, demystified, by a 'mythologist' like Barthes. Moreover, commodities can be symbolically 'repossessed' in everyday life, and endowed with implicitly oppositional meanings, by the very groups who originally produced them. The symbiosis in which ideology and social order, production and reproduction, are linked is then neither fixed nor guaranteed. It can be prised open. The consensus can be fractured, challenged, overruled, and resistance to the groups in dominance cannot always be lightly dismissed or automatically incorporated. Although, as Lefebvre has written, we live in a society where '. . . objects in practice become signs and signs objects and a second nature takes the place of the first—the initial layer of perceptible reality,' there are, as he goes on to affirm, always 'objections and contradictions which hinder the closing of the circuit' between sign and object, production and reproduction.[9]

We can now return to the meaning of youth subcultures, for the emergence of such groups has signalled in a spectacular fashion the breakdown of consensus in the post-war period. In the following chapters we shall see that it is precisely objections and contradictions of the kind which Lefebvre has described that find expression in subculture. However, the challenge to hegemony which subcultures represent is not issued directly by them. Rather it is expressed obliquely, in style. The objections are lodged, the contradictions displayed (and, as we shall see, 'magically resolved') at the profoundly superficial level of appearances: that is, at the level of signs. For the sign-community, the community of myth-consumers, is not a uniform body. As Volosinov has written, it is cut through by class:

> Class does not coincide with the sign community, i.e. with the totality of users of the same set of signs of ideological communication. Thus various different classes will use one and the same language. As a result, differently oriented accents intersect in every ideological sign. Sign becomes the arena of the class struggle.[1]

The struggle between different discourses, different definitions and meanings within ideology is therefore always, at the same time, a struggle within signification: a struggle for possession of the sign which extends to even the most mundane areas of everyday life. To turn once more to the examples used in the Introduction, to the safety pins and tubes of vaseline,[2] we can see that such commodities are indeed open to a double inflection: to 'illegitimate' as well as 'legitimate' uses. These 'humble objects' can be magically appropriated; 'stolen' by subordinate groups and made to carry 'secret' meanings: meanings which express, in code, a form of resistance to the order which guarantees their continued subordination.

Style in subculture is, then, pregnant with significance. Its transformations go 'against nature', interrupting the process of 'normalization'. As such, they are gestures, movements towards a speech which offends the 'silent majority', which challenges the principle of unity and cohesion, which contradicts the myth of consensus. Our task becomes, like Barthes', to discern the hidden

9. Henri Lefebvre, *Everyday Life in the Modern World* (Allen Lane, 1971).

1. Volosinov, *Marxism and the Philosophy of Language*.

2. Safety pins, as Hebdige points out in his introduction, can be used for body piercings; and vaseline can be used during sexual activities.

messages inscribed in code on the glossy surfaces of style, to trace them out as 'maps of meaning' which obscurely re-present the very contradictions they are designed to resolve or conceal.

Academics who adopt a semiotic approach are not alone in reading significance into the loaded surfaces of life. The existence of spectacular subcultures continually opens up those surfaces to other potentially subversive readings. Jean Genet, the archetype of the 'unnatural' deviant, again exemplifies the practice of resistance through style. He is as convinced in his own way as is Roland Barthes of the ideological character of cultural signs. He is equally oppressed by the seamless web of forms and meanings which encloses and yet excludes him. His reading is equally partial. He makes his own list and draws his own conclusions:

> I was astounded by so rigorous an edifice whose details were united against me. Nothing in the world is irrelevant: the stars on a general's sleeve, the stock-market quotations, the olive harvest, the style of the judiciary, the wheat exchange, the flower-beds, . . . Nothing. This order . . . had a meaning—my exile.[3]

It is this alienation from the deceptive 'innocence' of appearances which gives the teds, the mods, the punks[4] and no doubt future groups of as yet unimaginable 'deviants' the impetus to move from man's second 'false nature'[5] to a genuinely expressive artifice; a truly subterranean style. As a symbolic violation of the social order, such a movement attracts and will continue to attract attention, to provoke censure and to act, as we shall see, as the fundamental bearer of significance in subculture.

No subculture has sought with more grim determination than the punks to detach itself from the taken-for-granted landscape of normalized forms, nor to bring down upon itself such vehement disapproval. We shall begin therefore with the moment of punk and we shall return to that moment throughout the course of this book. It is perhaps appropriate that the punks, who have made such large claims for illiteracy, who have pushed profanity to such startling extremes, should be used to test some of the methods for 'reading' signs evolved in the centuries-old debate on the sanctity of culture.

1979

3. Jean Genet, *The Thief's Journal* (Penguin, 1967) [Hebdige's note]. The French writer of novels and plays (1910–1986) was marked as "deviant" as a homosexual and a convicted thief.

4. Three phases in British youth subcultures of the postwar era. The teddy boys of the middle 1950s to early 1960s joined an Elvis Presley–style appropriation of black rhythm-and-blues with highly artificial, almost Edwardian, clothes. The mods of the 1960s were "working-class dandies," symbolized by the Carnaby Street look of 1965–66. The punks of the late 1970s aggressively staged their position as alienated outcasts, with rough music, deliberately nonglamorous clothes, and piercings, hair dyes, and tattoos that assaulted prevailing notions of bodily beauty.

5. Barthes, *Mythologies* [Hebdige's note].

STEVEN KNAPP b. 1951 | WALTER BENN MICHAELS b. 1948

"The whole enterprise of critical theory is misguided and should be abandoned," declared Steven Knapp and Walter Benn Michaels stunningly, in their famous essay "Against Theory" (1982). While the advent of structuralist and poststructuralist theory in the late 1960s was attacked by traditionalists who bemoaned the loss of a proper focus on literature, by the 1980s "theory" had become a dominant mode in literary studies, spurring a renaissance of critical writing. "Against Theory" announced doubts within the ranks of a generation of younger critics about the impending establishment of theory, asserting a revisionary attitude that came to be called "neopragmatism." To some extent, it represented a struggle within theory between the deconstructive approach promoted by the "Yale School" (particularly PAUL DE MAN, whom Knapp and Michaels discuss at length), arguably the most influential theoretical approach through the late 1970s and early 1980s, and newly developing approaches such as New Historicism, represented by Knapp and Michaels's then-colleague at Berkeley, STEPHEN GREENBLATT. Although it did not put a stop to work in theory, "Against Theory" set off one of the most vibrant debates of the 1980s and augured the shift to critical methods with a more practical focus—notably, New Historicism and cultural studies—that became prominent from the late 1980s onward.

"Against Theory" appeared early in the academic careers of both its authors. At the time of its publication, Knapp was a beginning assistant professor of English at the University of California at Berkeley, having received his B.A. from Yale University in 1973 and Ph.D. from Cornell University in 1981. Michaels had been in the English Department at Berkeley only a few years longer; he received his B.A. in 1970 and Ph.D. in 1975 from the University of California at Santa Barbara. Each subsequently published two books and took positions at Johns Hopkins University: Michaels, who became an influential practitioner of New Historicist approaches to American literature, joined Hopkins's Department of English in 1987, and Knapp was appointed dean of the School of Arts and Sciences in 1994 and provost and vice president for academic affairs in 1996.

Before poststructuralism changed the Anglo-American critical landscape, literary theory was dominated by New Criticism; perhaps its most programmatic and influential statement was WILLIAM K. WIMSATT JR. AND MONROE C. BEARDSLEY's "Intentional Fallacy" (1946; see above). Wimsatt and Beardsley made the case that critics should not concern themselves with the "intentions" of authors (including their beliefs, personal attitudes, and life histories) but should focus on the literary work itself. Their polemical goal was to displace the biographical, historical, and impressionistic criticism prevalent during the early part of the century. "Against Theory" is similarly intended to articulate a new conception of literary study. Like "The Intentional Fallacy," it attempts to clear the ground for a better kind of literary study by refuting a fallacy that threatens to distract critics from their proper function. It argues against what might be called "the theoretical fallacy": the assumption that arguments about abstract principles and general methods, once resolved, will reliably guide the practice of literary criticism. According to Knapp and Michaels, criticism is an activity that cannot be governed by transcendent principles; rather, it is a "practice," prior to and not determined by any guiding theory.

Knapp and Michaels draw especially on the critique of interpretation developed by STANLEY FISH. Although Fish himself is criticized at the end of "Against Theory," his perceived error is the failure to be fully consistent with his own argument about the inconsequentiality of theory. This position is usually called *antifoundationalism*, and it draws on the American philosophical tradition of pragmatism. Pragmatism has never been precisely defined, but its adherents generally assert that theoretical concepts (such as meaning and truth) derive their substance or content from actual human practices, not logical principles. Fish's and Knapp and Michaels's revision of pragmatism inspired a movement called "the new pragmatism" or "neopragmatism." "Against Theory," arguing the pointlessness of any theoretical formulation of the practical activity of literary interpretation into abstract dichotomies like meaning and intention, is one of its key manifestos.

"Against Theory" has two primary targets that Knapp and Michaels take to represent contemporary theory: hermeneutics, exemplified by E. D. HIRSCH JR., and deconstruction, exemplified by Paul de Man. Knapp and Michaels set them at different ends of the same spectrum: Hirsch is seen as advocating a positive theory of interpretation, which holds that discovering authorial intention provides a key to meaning, whereas de Man argues for a negative theory of interpretation, which holds that intention is never available and thus reliable interpretation can never be obtained. For Knapp and Michaels, both Hirsch and de Man falsely separate intention and meaning, concepts embedded in each other and impossible to discuss in isolation.

A significant feature of "Against Theory" is the forcefulness and clarity of its writing, which seemed to invite a direct response (and implicitly to reproach the sometimes difficult prose of much poststructuralist theorizing); indeed, counterarguments were soon launched, and nine were gathered in *Against Theory: Literary Studies and the New Pragmatism* (1985). With some outrage, the American critic Daniel T. O'Hara claims that Knapp and Michaels jeopardized the advances literary study had made under the auspices of theory, "only to return us to [the world] of our grandfathers, the world of the New Critics and the gentlemen-scholars of literary history," who narrowly concern themselves with practical readings. Arguing that theory serves a purpose as "a heuristic or regulative ideal of critical activity," O'Hara warns of the dangerous institutional consequence of "Against Theory": "by clearing the air of theory [it has] also taken away from students the means necessary to do criticism at all."

In a more sympathetic response, the leading American pragmatist philosopher Richard Rorty endorses Knapp and Michaels's critique of theory as providing a foundation for practice but disagrees with their call to "eliminate the 'career option' of writing and teaching theory." Like O'Hara, Rorty believes that such a move would harm English departments, and he notes that theory provides "an opportunity to discuss philosophy books—as well as novels, poems, critical essays, and so forth—with literature students." Stanley Fish agrees that "it is time to admit what everyone knows: theory has consequences; not, however, because it stands apart from and can guide practice but because it is itself a form of practice," with "all the political and institutional consequences of other practices."

One of the central problems of "Against Theory" is its use of the word *theory*. At key points Knapp and Michaels carefully define what they mean by the term—any attempt to guide or regulate critical practice by general principles standing outside or above human interests, beliefs, and practices. They oppose this kind of theory but acknowledge the value of certain noninterpretive theoretical approaches, such as the technical, formally focused field of narratology. At other moments, however, they seem to dismiss wholesale any version of theory. This rejection is troublesome, since, as some critics have noted, it would be difficult to see Knapp and Michaels's essay itself as anything other than what is commonly called theory.

Whatever the limitations of Knapp and Michael's argument, "Against Theory" codifies some assumptions of its authors' generation. As "The Intentional Fallacy" marked a turn from biographical, historical, and impressionistic approaches to literature, so "Against Theory" signals a turn away from dense philosophical considerations toward practical, cultural criticism. In its wake, the production of "theory," as Knapp and Michaels narrowly define it, has lessened—the result not of theory's inadequacy but (ironically) of its success, as it has become commonplace in the discourse of almost all contemporary criticism. While Knapp and Michaels provide a salutary reminder not to overvalue theory, the debate over whether they overreacted in dismissing theory from critical practice continues.

BIBLIOGRAPHY

Knapp is best known for his "antitheory" argument; his other work includes *Personification and the Sublime: Milton to Coleridge* (1985) and *Literary Interest: The Limits of Anti-Formalism* (1993). Both books are based in practical criticism and readings of literary works, but each addresses what might be considered theoretical topics—allegory and the definition of literature, respectively. Michaels, after gaining attention with "Against Theory," has become one of the most prominent Americanists of his generation, examining the historical context of late-nineteenth-century American literature in *The Gold Standard and the Logic of Naturalism: American Literature at the Turn of the Century* (1987) and provocatively considering modernism and multiculturalism in *Our America: Nativism, Modernism, and Pluralism* (1995). He also edited, with Donald E. Pease, the collection *The American Renaissance Reconsidered* (1985).

"Against Theory" precipitated a cascade of responses, rejoinders by Knapp and Michaels, and follow-ups. It originally appeared in the leading theory journal *Critical Inquiry* 8.4 (1982). A set of responses, "For and Against Theory," with contributions by E. D. Hirsch Jr. and six others, appeared in *Critical Inquiry* 9.4 (1983), along with "A Reply to Our Critics" by Knapp and Michaels. A further symposium, "Pragmatism and Literary Theory," appeared in *Critical Inquiry* 11.3 (1985), composed of Stanley Fish's "Consequences," Richard Rorty's "Philosophy without Principles," and Knapp and Michaels's "Reply to Richard Rorty: What Is Pragmatism?" All these essays were reprinted as a book, *Against Theory: Literary Studies and the New Pragmatism*, edited by W. J. T. Mitchell (1985). Subsequently, Knapp and Michaels published a sequel, "Against Theory 2: Hermeneutics and Deconstruction," *Critical Inquiry* 14.1 (1987). Notable later responses to Knapp and Michaels are mainly by philosophers: Stanley Cavell, "The Division of Talent," *Critical Inquiry* 11.4 (1985); George M. Wilson, "Again, Theory: On Speaker's Meaning, Linguistic Meaning, and the Meaning of a Text," *Critical Inquiry* 19.1 (1992), with Knapp and Michaels's "Reply to George Wilson"; David Couzen Hoy, "Intentions and Law: Defending Hermeneutics," with a rejoinder by Knapp and Michaels, in *Legal Hermeneutics: History, Theory, and Practice* (ed. Gregory Leyh, 1992); and John Searle, "Literary Theory and Its Discontents," *New Literary History* 25.3 (1994), with Knapp and Michaels's "Reply to John Searle," plus Searle's "Structure and Intention in Language: A Reply to Knapp and Michaels."

Against Theory

1

By "theory" we mean a special project in literary criticism: the attempt to govern interpretations of particular texts by appealing to an account of interpretation in general. The term is sometimes applied to literary subjects with no direct bearing on the interpretation of individual works, such as narratology, stylistics, and prosody.[1] Despite their generality, however, these subjects seem to us essentially empirical, and our argument against theory will not apply to them.

Contemporary theory has taken two forms. Some theorists have sought to ground the reading of literary texts in methods designed to guarantee the

1. The specialized study of narrative structure, literary style, and versification, respectively.

objectivity and validity of interpretations. Others, impressed by the inability of such procedures to produce agreement among interpreters, have translated that failure into an alternative mode of theory that denies the possibility of correct interpretation. Our aim here is not to choose between these two alternatives but rather to show that both rest on a single mistake, a mistake that is central to the notion of theory per se. The object of our critique is not a particular way of doing theory but the idea of doing theory at all.

Theory attempts to solve—or to celebrate the impossibility of solving—a set of familiar problems: the function of authorial intention, the status of literary language, the role of interpretive assumptions, and so on. We will not attempt to solve these problems, nor will we be concerned with tracing their history or surveying the range of arguments they have stimulated. In our view, the mistake on which all critical theory rests has been to imagine that these problems are real. In fact, we will claim such problems only seem real—and theory itself only seems possible or relevant—when theorists fail to recognize the fundamental inseparability of the elements involved.

The clearest example of the tendency to generate theoretical problems by splitting apart terms that are in fact inseparable is the persistent debate over the relation between authorial intention and the meaning of texts. Some theorists have claimed that valid interpretations can only be obtained through an appeal to authorial intentions. This assumption is shared by theorists who, denying the possibility of recovering authorial intentions, also deny the possibility of valid interpretations. But once it is seen that the meaning of a text is simply identical to the author's intended meaning, the project of *grounding* meaning in intention becomes incoherent. Since the project itself is incoherent, it can neither succeed nor fail; hence both theoretical attitudes toward intention are irrelevant. The mistake made by theorists has been to imagine the possibility or desirability of moving from one term (the author's intended meaning) to a second term (the text's meaning), when actually the two terms are the same. One can neither succeed nor fail in deriving one term from the other, since to have one is already to have them both.

In the following two sections we will try to show in detail how theoretical accounts of intention always go wrong. In the fourth section we will undertake a similar analysis of an influential account of the role interpretive assumptions or beliefs play in the practice of literary criticism. The issues of belief and intention are, we think, central to the theoretical enterprise; our discussion of them is thus directed not only against specific theoretical arguments but against theory in general. Our examples are meant to represent the central mechanism of all theoretical arguments, and our treatment of them is meant to indicate that all such arguments will fail and fail in the same way. If we are right, then the whole enterprise of critical theory is misguided and should be abandoned.

2. *Meaning and Intention*

The fact that what a text means is what its author intends is clearly stated by E. D. Hirsch when he writes that the meaning of a text "is, and can be, nothing other than the author's meaning" and "is determined once and for all by the character of the speaker's intention."[2] Having defined meaning as the author's intended meaning, Hirsch goes on to argue that all literary interpretation "must stress a reconstruction of the author's aims and attitudes in order to evolve guides and norms for construing the meaning of his text." Although these guides and norms cannot guarantee the correctness of any particular reading—nothing can—they nevertheless constitute, he claims, a "fundamentally sound" and "objective" method of interpretation (pp. 224, 240).

What seems odd about Hirsch's formulation is the transition from definition to method. He begins by defining textual meaning as the author's intended meaning and then suggests that the best way to find textual meaning is to look for authorial intention. But if meaning and intended meaning are already the same, it's hard to see how looking for one provides an objective method—or any sort of method—for looking for the other; looking for one just *is* looking for the other. The recognition that what a text means and what its author intends it to mean are identical should entail the further recognition that any appeal from one to the other is useless. And yet, as we have already begun to see, Hirsch thinks the opposite; he believes that identifying meaning with the expression of intention has the supreme theoretical usefulness of providing an objective method of choosing among alternative interpretations.

Hirsch, however, has failed to understand the force of his own formulation. In one moment he identifies meaning and intended meaning; in the next moment he splits them apart. This mistake is clearly visible in his polemic against formalist critics who deny the importance of intention altogether. His argument against these critics ends up invoking their account of meaning at the expense of his own. Formalists, in Hirsch's summary, conceive the text as a " 'piece of language,' " a "public object whose character is defined by public norms." The problem with this account, according to Hirsch, is that "no mere sequence of words can represent an actual verbal meaning with reference to public norms alone. Referred to these alone, the text's meaning remains indeterminate." Hirsch's example, "My car ran out of gas," is, as he notes, susceptible to an indeterminate range of interpretations. There are no public norms which will help us decide whether the sentence means that my automobile lacks fuel or "my Pullman dash[ed] from a cloud of Argon." Only by assigning a particular intention to the words "My car ran out of gas" does one arrive at a determinate interpretation. Or, as Hirsch himself puts it, "The array of possibilities only begins to become a more selective system of *probabilities* when, instead of confronting merely a word sequence, we also posit a speaker who very likely means something" (p. 225).

This argument seems consistent with Hirsch's equation of meaning and intended meaning, until one realizes that Hirsch is imagining a moment of

2. E. D. Hirsch Jr., *Validity in Interpretation* (New Haven, Conn., 1967), pp. 216, 219. Our remarks on Hirsch are in some ways parallel to criticism offered by P. D. Juhl in the second chapter of his *Interpretation: An Essay in the Philosophy of Literary Criticism* (Princeton, N.J., 1980). Juhl's position will be discussed in the next section. All further citations to these works will be included in the text [Knapp and Michaels's note]. Some of the authors' notes have been edited, and some omitted. HIRSCH (b. 1928), American literary theorist and cultural commentator. Juhl (b. 1946), American literary theorist.

interpretation before intention is present. This is the moment at which the text's meaning "remains indeterminate," before such indeterminacy is cleared up by the *addition* of authorial intention. But if meaning and intention really are inseparable, then it makes no sense to think of intention as an ingredient that needs to be added; it must be present from the start. The issue of determinacy or indeterminacy is irrelevant. Hirsch thinks it's relevant because he thinks, correctly, that the movement from indeterminacy to determinacy involves the addition of information, but he also thinks, incorrectly, that adding information amounts to adding intention. Since intention is already present, the only thing added, in the movement from indeterminacy to determinacy, is information *about* the intention, not the intention itself. For a sentence like "My car ran out of gas" even to be recognizable as a sentence, we must already have posited a speaker and hence an intention. Pinning down an interpretation of the sentence will not involve adding a speaker but deciding among a range of possible speakers. Knowing that the speaker inhabits a planet with an atmosphere of inert gases and on which the primary means of transportation is railroad will give one interpretation; knowing that the speaker is an earthling who owns a Ford will give another. But even if we have none of this information, as soon as we attempt to interpret at all we are already committed to a characterization of the speaker as a speaker of language. We know, in other words, that the speaker intends to speak; otherwise we wouldn't be interpreting. In this latter case, we have less information about the speaker than in the other two (where we at least knew the speaker's planetary origin), but the relative lack of information has nothing to do with the presence or absence of intention.

This mistake no doubt accounts for Hirsch's peculiar habit of calling the proper object of interpretation the "author's meaning" and, in later writings, distinguishing between it and the "reader's meaning."[3] The choice between these two kinds of meaning becomes, for Hirsch, an ethical imperative as well as an "operational" necessity. But if all meaning is always the author's meaning, then the alternative is an empty one, and there is no choice, ethical or operational, to be made. Since theory is designed to help us make such choices, all theoretical arguments on the issue of authorial intention must at some point accept the premises of anti-intentionalist accounts of meaning. In debates about intention, the moment of imagining intentionless meaning constitutes the theoretical moment itself. From the standpoint of an argument against critical theory, then, the only important question about intention is whether there can in fact be intentionless meanings. If our argument against theory is to succeed, the answer to this question must be no.

The claim that all meanings are intentional is not, of course, an unfamiliar one in contemporary philosophy of language. John Searle, for example, asserts that "there is no getting away from intentionality," and he and others have advanced arguments to support this claim.[4] Our purpose here is not to add another such argument but to show how radically counterintuitive the alternative would be. We can begin to get a sense of this simply by noticing how difficult it is to imagine a case of intentionless meaning.

Suppose that you're walking along a beach and you come upon a curious

3. See Hirsch, *The Aims of Interpretation* (Chicago, 1976), p. 8 [Knapp and Michaels's note].

4. John R. Searle, "Reiterating the Differences: A Reply to Derrida," *Glyph* 1 (1977): 202 [Knapp and Michaels's note]. Searle (b. 1932), American philosopher of mind and of language.

sequence of squiggles in the sand. You step back a few paces and notice that they spell out the following words:

A slumber did my spirit seal;
  I had no human fears:
She seemed a thing that could not feel
  The touch of earthly years.[5]

This would seem to be a good case of intentionless meaning: you recognize the writing as writing, you understand what the words mean, you may even identify them as constituting a rhymed poetic stanza—and all this without knowing anything about the author and indeed without needing to connect the words to any notion of an author at all. You can do all these things without thinking of anyone's intention. But now suppose that, as you stand gazing at this pattern in the sand, a wave washes up and recedes, leaving in its wake (written below what you now realize was only the first stanza) the following words:

No motion has she now, no force;
  She neither hears nor sees;
Rolled round in earth's diurnal course,
  With rocks, and stones, and trees.

One might ask whether the question of intention still seems as irrelevant as it did seconds before. You will now, we suspect, feel compelled to explain what you have just seen. Are these marks mere accidents, produced by the mechanical operation of the waves on the sand (through some subtle and unprecedented process of erosion, percolation, etc.)? Or is the sea alive and striving to express its pantheistic faith? Or has Wordsworth, since his death, become a sort of genius[6] of the shore who inhabits the waves and periodically inscribes on the sand his elegiac sentiments? You might go on extending the list of explanations indefinitely, but you would find, we think, that all the explanations fall into two categories. You will either be ascribing these marks to some agent capable of intentions (the living sea, the haunting Wordsworth, etc.), or you will count them as nonintentional effects of mechanical processes (erosion, percolation, etc.). But in the second case—where the marks now seem to be accidents—will they still seem to be words?

Clearly not. They will merely seem to *resemble* words. You will be amazed, perhaps, that such an astonishing coincidence could occur. Of course, you would have been no less amazed had you decided that the sea or the ghost of Wordsworth was responsible. But it's essential to recognize that in the two cases your amazement would have two entirely different sources. In one case, you would be amazed by the identity of the author—who would have thought that the sea can write poetry? In the other case, however, in which you accept the hypothesis of natural accident, you're amazed to discover that what you thought was poetry turns out not to be poetry at all. It isn't poetry because it isn't language; that's what it means to call it an accident. As long as you thought the marks were poetry, you were assuming their intentional character. You had no idea who the author was, and this may have tricked you into thinking that positing an author was irrelevant to your ability to read

5. "A Slumber Did My Spirit Seal" (1799), by the English Romantic poet WILLIAM WORDSWORTH (1770–1850)—an example used by Hirsch in *Validity in Interpretation*.

6. Pervading spirit.

the stanza. But in fact you had, without realizing it, already posited an author. It was only with the mysterious arrival of the second stanza that your tacit assumption (e.g., someone writing with a stick) was challenged and you realized that you had made one. Only now, when positing an author seems impossible, do you genuinely imagine the marks as authorless. But to deprive them of an author is to convert them into accidental likenesses of language. They are not, after all, an example of intentionless meaning; as soon as they become intentionless they become meaningless as well.

The arrival of the second stanza made clear that what had seemed to be an example of intentionless language was either not intentionless or not language. The question was whether the marks counted as language; what determined the answer was a decision as to whether or not they were the product of an intentional agent. If our example has seemed farfetched, it is only because there is seldom occasion in our culture to wonder whether the *sea* is an intentional agent. But there *are* cases where the question of intentional agency might be an important and difficult one. Can computers speak? Arguments over this question reproduce exactly the terms of our example. Since computers are machines, the issue of whether they can speak seems to hinge on the possibility of intentionless language. But our example shows that there is no such thing as intentionless language; the only real issue is whether computers are capable of intentions. However this issue may be decided—and our example offers no help in deciding it—the decision will not rest on a theory of meaning but on a judgment as to whether computers can be intentional agents. This is not to deny that a great deal—morally, legally, and politically—might depend on such judgments. But no degree of practical importance will give these judgments theoretical force.

The difference between theoretical principle and practical or empirical judgments can be clarified by one last glance at the case of the wave poem. Suppose, having seen the second stanza wash up on the beach, you have decided that the "poem" is really an accidental effect of erosion, percolation, and so on and therefore not language at all. What would it now take to change your mind? No theoretical argument will make a difference. But suppose you notice, rising out of the sea some distance from the shore, a small submarine, out of which clamber a half dozen figures in white lab coats. One of them trains his binoculars on the beach and shouts triumphantly, "It worked! It worked! Let's go down and try it again." Presumably, you will now once again change your mind, not because you have a new account of language, meaning, or intention but because you now have new evidence of an author. The question of authorship is and always was an empirical question; it has now received a new empirical answer. The theoretical temptation is to imagine that such empirical questions must, or should, have theoretical answers.

Even a philosopher as committed to the intentional status of language as Searle succumbs to this temptation to think that intention is a theoretical issue. After insisting, in the passage cited earlier, on the inescapability of intention, he goes on to say that "in serious literal speech the sentences are precisely the realizations of the intentions" and that "there need be no *gulf* at all between the illocutionary intention and its expression."[7] The point, however, is not that there *need* be no gulf between intention and the meaning

7. Searle, "Reiterating," p. 202 [Knapp and Michaels's note].

of its expression but that there *can* be no gulf. Not only in serious literal speech but in *all* speech what is intended and what is meant are identical. In separating the two Searle imagines the possibility of expression without intention and so, like Hirsch, misses the point of his own claim that when it comes to language "there is no getting away from intentionality." Missing this point, and hence imagining the possibility of two different *kinds* of meaning, is more than a theoretical mistake; it is the sort of mistake that makes theory possible. It makes theory possible because it creates the illusion of a choice between alternative methods of interpreting.

To be a theorist is only to think that there is such a choice. In this respect intentionalists and anti-intentionalists are the same. They are also the same in another respect: neither can really escape intention. But this doesn't mean the intentionalists win, since what intentionalists want is a guide to valid interpretation; what they get, however, is simply a description of what everyone always does. In practical terms, then, the stakes in the battle over intention are extremely low—in fact, they don't exist. Hence it doesn't matter who wins. In theoretical terms, however, the stakes are extremely high, and it still doesn't matter who wins. The stakes are high because they amount to the existence of theory itself; it doesn't matter who wins because as long as one thinks that a position on intention (either for or against) makes a difference in achieving valid interpretations, the ideal of theory itself is saved. Theory wins. But as soon as we recognize that there are no theoretical choices to be made, then the point of theory vanishes. Theory loses.

3. *Language and Speech Acts*

We have argued that what a text means and what its author intends it to mean are identical and that their identity robs intention of any theoretical interest. A similar account of the relation between meaning and intention has recently been advanced by P. D. Juhl. According to Juhl, "there is a logical connection between statements about the meaning of a literary work and statements about the author's intention such that a statement about the meaning of a work *is* a statement about the author's intention." Juhl criticizes Hirsch, as we do, for believing that critics "*ought* to . . . try to ascertain the author's intention," when in fact, Juhl argues, "they are necessarily doing so already" (*Interpretation*, p. 12). But for Juhl, these claims serve in no way to discredit theory; rather, they themselves constitute a theory that "makes us aware of what we as critics or readers are doing in interpreting literature" and, more crucially, "provides the basis for a principled acceptance or rejection of an interpretation of a literary work" (p. 10). How is it that Juhl derives a theory from arguments which seem to us to make theory impossible?

What makes this question particularly intriguing is the fact that Juhl's strategy for demonstrating the centrality of intention is apparently identical to ours; it consists "in contrasting statements about the meaning of a literary work created by a person with statements about the meaning of a text produced by chance, such as a computer poem" (p. 13).[8] But Juhl's treatment

8. In fact, Juhl employs the same poem we do—Wordsworth's "A Slumber Did My Spirit Seal"—in his own treatment of accidental "language" (*Interpretation*, pp. 70–82). The device of contrasting intentional speech acts with marks produced by chance is a familiar one in speech-act theory [Knapp and Michaels's note]. "Speech-act theory": that branch of philosophy, pioneered by the English philosopher J. L. AUSTIN (1911–1960), that focuses on the actions performed in linguistic

of examples like our wave poem reveals that his sense of the relation between language and intention is after all radically different from ours. Like Hirsch, but at a further level of abstraction, Juhl ends up imagining the possibility of language prior to and independent of intention and thus conceiving intention as something that must be added to language to make it work. Like Hirsch, and like theorists in general, Juhl thinks that intention is a matter of choice. But where Hirsch recommends that we choose intention to adjudicate among interpretations, Juhl thinks no recommendation is necessary—not because we need never choose intention but only because our concept of a literary work is such that to read literature is already to have chosen intention.

Discussing the case of a "poem" produced by chance ("marks on [a] rock" or "a computer poem"), Juhl points out that there is "something odd about *interpreting* [such a] 'text.' " However one might understand this text, one could not understand it as a representation of "the meaning of a particular utterance." We agree with this—if it implies that the random marks mean nothing, are not language, and therefore cannot be interpreted at all. But for Juhl the implications are different. He thinks that one *can* interpret the random marks, though only in the somewhat specialized sense "in which we might be said to 'interpret' a sentence when we explain its meaning to a foreigner, by explaining to him what the individual words mean, how they function in the sentence, and thus how the sentence *could* be used or what it *could* be used to express or convey" (pp. 84–86).

Our point is that marks produced by chance are not words at all but only resemble them. For Juhl, the marks remain words, but words detached from the intentions that would make them utterances. Thus he can argue that when a "parrot utters the words 'Water is pouring down from the sky,' " one can understand that "the words mean 'It is raining' " but deny that the " 'parrot *said* that it is raining' " (p. 109). It is clear that, for Juhl, the words continue to mean even when devoid of intention. They mean *"in abstracto"* and thus constitute the condition of language prior to the addition of intention, that is, prior to "a speaker's utterance or speech act." In literary interpretation, this condition of language is never operative because, Juhl claims, "our notion of the meaning of a literary work" is "like our notion of the meaning of a person's speech act," not "like our notion of the meaning of a word in a language" (p. 41).

Implicit in Juhl's whole treatment of meaning and intention is the distinction made here between language and speech acts. This distinction makes possible a methodological prescription as strong as Hirsch's, if more general: when confronted with a piece of language, read it as a speech act. The prescriptive force of Juhl's argument is obscured by the fact that he has pushed the moment of decision one step back. Whereas Hirsch thinks we have to add intentions to *literature* in order to determine what a text means, Juhl thinks that adding intentions to *language* gives us speech acts (such as literary works) whose meaning is already determinate. Juhl recognizes that as soon as we think of a piece of language as literature, we already regard it as a speech act and hence the product of intention; his prescription tells us

exchanges; Austin distinguished the locutionary act (saying something meaningful), illocutionary act (employing this language for some purpose), and perlocutionary act (having an effect on listeners or readers).

how to get from language in general to a specific utterance, such as a literary work.

But this prescription only makes sense if its two terms (language and speech acts) are not already inseparable in the same way that meaning and intention are. Juhl is right of course to claim that marks without intention are not speech acts, since the essence of a speech act is its intentional character. But we have demonstrated that marks without intention are not language either. Only by failing to see that linguistic meaning is always identical to expressed intention can Juhl imagine language without speech acts. To recognize the identity of language and speech acts is to realize that Juhl's prescription—when confronted with language, read it as a speech act—can mean nothing more than: when confronted with language, read it as language.

For Hirsch and Juhl, the goal of theory is to provide an objectively valid method of literary interpretation. To make method possible, both are forced to imagine intentionless meanings or, in more general terms, to imagine a separation between language and speech acts. The method then consists in adding speech acts to language; speech acts bring with them the particular intentions that allow interpreters to clear up the ambiguities intrinsic to language as such. But this separation of language and speech acts need not be used to establish an interpretive method; it can in fact be used to do just the opposite. For a theorist like Paul de Man,[9] the priority of language to speech acts suggests that all attempts to arrive at determinate meanings by adding intentions amount to a violation of the genuine condition of language. If theory in its positive or methodological mode rests on the choice of speech acts over language, theory in its negative or antimethodological mode tries to preserve what it takes to be the purity of language from the distortion of speech acts.

The negative theorist's hostility to method depends on a particular account of language, most powerfully articulated in de Man's "The Purloined Ribbon." The essay concerns what de Man sees as a crucial episode in Rousseau's *Confessions*,[1] in which Rousseau attempts to interpret, and thereby to justify, a particularly incriminating speech act. While working as a servant, he had stolen a ribbon from his employers. When accused of the theft, he blamed it on a fellow servant, Marion. In the passage that interests de Man, Rousseau is thus concerned with two crimes, the theft itself and the far more heinous act of excusing himself by accusing an innocent girl. This second act, the naming of Marion, is the one that especially needs justifying.

Rousseau offers several excuses, each an explanation of what he meant by naming Marion. But the explanation that intrigues de Man is the surprising one that Rousseau perhaps meant nothing at all when he said "Marion." He was merely uttering the first sound that occurred to him: "Rousseau was making whatever noise happened to come into his head; he was saying nothing at all."[2] Hence, de Man argues, "In the spirit of the text, one should resist all temptation to give any significance whatever to the sound 'Marion.' " The

9. Influential Belgian-born American literary critic (1919–1983; see above), a theorist of deconstruction.

1. The 12-book autobiography (1776–70, pub. 1781–88) by the Swiss-born French philosopher and social theorist Jean-Jacques Rousseau (1712–1778).

2. Paul de Man, "The Purloined Ribbon," *Glyph* 1 (1977): 39; all further citations to this work will be included in the text [Knapp and Michaels's note].

claim that "Marion" was meaningless gives Rousseau his best defense: "For it is only if . . . the utterance of the sound 'Marion' is truly without any conceivable motive that the total arbitrariness of the action becomes the most effective, the most efficaciously performative excuse of all" (p. 37). Why? Because, "if the essential non-signification of the statement had been properly interpreted, if Rousseau's accusers had realized that Marion's name was 'le premier objet qui s'offrit,'[3] they would have understood his lack of guilt as well as Marion's innocence" (p. 40).

But de Man is less interested in the efficacy of the "excuse" than he is in what it reveals about the fundamental nature of language. The fact that the sound "Marion" can mean nothing reminds us that language consists of inherently meaningless sounds to which one adds meanings—in other words, that the relation between signifier and signified is arbitrary.[4] Why does de Man think this apparently uncontroversial description of language has any theoretical interest? The recognition that the material condition of language is inherently meaningless has no theoretical force in itself. But de Man thinks that the material condition of language is not simply meaningless but is also already "linguistic," that is, sounds are signifiers even before meanings (signifieds) are added to them. As a collection of "pure signifier[s]," in themselves "devoid of meaning and function," language is primarily a meaningless structure to which meanings are secondarily (and in de Man's view illegitimately) added (p. 32). Thus, according to de Man, Rousseau's accusers mistakenly added a meaning to the signifier "Marion"—hearing a speech act where they should have heard only language. This separation of language and speech act is the precondition for de Man's version of the theoretical choice.

De Man's separation of language and speech acts rests on a mistake. It is of course true that sounds in themselves are meaningless. It is also true that sounds become signifiers when they function in language. But it is not true that sounds in themselves are signifiers; they become signifiers only when they acquire meanings, and when they lose their meanings they stop being signifiers. De Man's mistake is to think that the sound "Marion" remains a signifier even when emptied of all meaning. The fact is that the meaningless noise "Marion" only *resembles* the signifier "Marion," just as accidentally uttering the sound "Marion" only *resembles* the speech act of naming Marion. De Man recognizes that the accidental emission of the sound "Marion" is not a speech act (indeed, that's the point of the example), but he fails to recognize that it s not language either. What reduces the signifier to noise and the speech act to an accident is the absence of intention. Conceiving linguistic activity as the accidental emission of phonemes, de Man arrives at a vision of "the absolute randomness of language, prior to any figuration or meaning": "There can be no use of language which is not, within a certain perspective thus radically formal, i.e. mechanical, no matter how deeply this aspect may be concealed by aesthetic, formalistic delusions" (pp. 44, 41).

By conceiving language as essentially random and mechanical, de Man gives a new response to the dilemma of the wave poem and suggests a fuller account of why that dilemma is central to theory in general. Our earlier

3. The first object that presented itself (French).
4. The sign was divided into *signified* (the meaning conveyed) and *signifier* (the symbol or sound that conveys that meaning) by the Swiss linguist FERDINAND DE SAUSSURE (1857–1913), who argued that in language, the relation between the two is *arbitrary* (to the extent that the signified determines the signified, the sign is *motivated*).

discussion of the wave poem was intended to show how counterintuitive it is to separate language and intention. When the second stanza washed up on the beach, even the theorist should have been ready to admit that the poem was not a poem because the marks were not language. But our subsequent discussions of Juhl and de Man have revealed that theory precisely depends on not making this admission. For Juhl, the accidental marks remain language, but language *in abstracto* and hence inherently ambiguous. The wave poem thus presents a positive theorist like Juhl with a choice between the multiple meanings of intentionless marks and the determinate meaning of an intentional speech act. Since the point of positive theory is to ground the practice of determining particular meanings, the positive theorist chooses to read the marks as an intentional act. But when a negative theorist like de Man encounters the second (accidental) stanza, it presents him with a slightly different version of the same choice. For de Man the marks are not multiply meaningful but essentially meaningless, and the choice is not between one intentional meaning and many intentionless meanings but between intentional meaning and no meaning at all. Since, in de Man's view, all imputations of meaning are equally groundless, the positive theorist's choice of intention seems to him pointless. In apparent hostility to interpretive method, the negative theorist chooses the meaningless marks. But the negative theorist's choice in fact provides him with a positive methodology, a methodology that grounds the practice of interpretation in the single decisive truth about language. The truth about language is its accidental and mechanical nature: any text, "properly interpreted," will reveal its "essential nonsignification" (p. 40). For both Juhl and de Man, proper interpretation depends upon following a methodological prescription. Juhl's prescription is: when confronted with language, read it as a speech act. De Man's prescription is: when confronted with what seems to be a speech act, read it as language.

The wave poem, as encountered by a theorist, presents a choice between two kinds of meaning or, what comes to the same thing, two kinds of language. The issue in both cases is the presence or absence of intention; the positive theorist adds intention, the negative theorist subtracts it.[5] In our view, however, the relation between meaning and intention or, in slightly different terms, between language and speech acts is such that intention can neither be added nor subtracted. Intention cannot be added to or subtracted from meaning because meanings are always intentional; intention cannot be added to or subtracted from language because language consists of speech acts, which are also always intentional. Since language has intention already built into it, no recommendation about what to do with intention has any bearing on the question of how to interpret any utterance or text. For the nontheorist, the only question raised by the wave poem is not *how* to interpret but *whether* to interpret. Either the marks are a poem and hence a speech act, or they are not a poem and just happen to resemble a speech act. But once this empirical question is decided, no further judgments—and

5. At least this is true of the present generation of theorists. For earlier theorists such as W. K. Wimsatt and Monroe C. Beardsley, the objective meanings sought by positive theory were to be acquired precisely by *subtracting* intention and relying on the formal rules and public norms of language. This, of course, is the view they urge in "The Intentional Fallacy" [Knapp and Michaels's note]. "The Intentional Fallacy" (1946; see above) is a programmatic theoretical statement by the American New Critics WIMSATT (1907–1975) AND BEARDSLEY (1915–1985).

therefore no theoretical judgments—about the status of intention can be made.

4. *Theory and Practice*

Our argument so far has concerned what might be called the ontological side of theory—its peculiar claims about the nature of its object. We have suggested that those claims always take the form of generating a difference where none in fact exists, by imagining a mode of language devoid of intention—devoid, that is, of what makes it language and distinguishes it from accidental or mechanical noises and marks. But we have also tried to show that this strange ontological project is more than a spontaneous anomaly; it is always in the service of an epistemological goal.[6] That goal is the goal of method, the governance of interpretive practice by some larger and more principled account. Indeed, theoretical controversy in the Anglo-American tradition has more often taken the form of arguments about the epistemological situation of the interpreter than about the ontological status of the text. If the ontological project of theory has been to imagine a condition of language before intention, its epistemological project has been to imagine a condition of knowledge before interpretation.

The aim of theory's epistemological project is to base interpretation on a direct encounter with its object, an encounter undistorted by the influence of the interpreter's particular beliefs. Several writers have demonstrated the impossibility of escaping beliefs at any stage of interpretation and have concluded that theory's epistemological goal is therefore unattainable. Some have gone on to argue that the unattainability of an epistemologically neutral stance not only undermines the claims of method but prevents us from ever getting any correct interpretations. For these writers the attack on method thus has important practical consequences for literary criticism, albeit negative ones.[7]

But in discussing theory from the ontological side, we have tried to suggest that the impossibility of method has no practical consequences, positive or negative. And the same conclusion has been reached from the epistemological side by the strongest critic of theoretical attempts to escape belief, Stanley Fish.[8] In his last essay in *Is There a Text in This Class?*, Fish confronts the "final question" raised by his critique of method, namely, "what implications it has for the practice of literary criticism." His answer is, "none whatsoever":

> That is, it does not follow from what I have been saying that you should go out and do literary criticism in a certain way or refrain from doing it

6. That is, it is governed by a particular theory of knowledge.

7. Negative theory rests on the perception of what de Man calls "an insurmountable obstacle in the way of any reading or understanding" (*Allegories of Reading* [New Haven, Conn., 1979], p. 131). Some theorists (e.g., David Bleich and Norman Holland) understand this obstacle as the reader's subjectivity. Others (like de Man himself and J. Hillis Miller) understand it as the aporia between constative and performative language, between demonstration and persuasion. In all cases, however, the negative theorist is committed to the view that interpretation is, as Jonathan Culler says, "necessary error" (*The Pursuit of Signs* [Ithaca, N.Y., 1981], p. 14 [Knapp and Michaels's note]. Bleich (b. 1940) and Holland (b. 1927) are American reader-response critics; Miller (b. 1928) and Culler (b. 1944) are American deconstructive critics. "Aporia": difficulty, logical impasse (a term often used in deconstructive criticism to indicate the point in a text where inherent contradictions render interpretation undecidable).

8. American literary theorist (b. 1938; see above).

> in other ways. The reason for this is that the position I have been presenting is not one that you (or anyone else) could live by. Its thesis is that whatever seems to you to be obvious and inescapable is only so within some institutional or conventional structure, and that means that you can never operate outside some such structure, even if you are persuaded by the thesis. As soon as you descend from theoretical reasoning about your assumptions, you will once again inhabit them and you will inhabit them without any reservations whatsoever; so that when you are called on to talk about Milton or Wordsworth or Yeats, you will do so from within whatever beliefs you hold about these authors.[9]

At the heart of this passage is the familiar distinction between "theoretical reasoning" and the "assumptions" or "beliefs" that inform the concrete "practice of literary criticism." Where most theorists affirm the practical importance of their theories, Fish's originality lies in his denial that his theory has any practical consequences whatsoever. But once theory gives up all claims to affect practice, what is there left for theory to do? Or, since Fish's point is that there is nothing left for theory to *do*, what is there left for theory to *be*? Understood in these terms, Fish's work displays the theoretical impulse in its purest form. Stripped of the methodological project either to ground or to undermine practice, theory continues to imagine a position outside it. While this retreat to a position outside practice looks like theory's last desperate attempt to save itself, it is really, as we hope to show, the founding gesture of all theoretical argument.

Fish's attack on method begins with an account of belief that is in our view correct. The account's two central features are, first, the recognition that beliefs cannot be grounded in some deeper condition of knowledge and, second, the further recognition that this impossibility does not in any way weaken their claims to be true. "If one believes what one believes," Fish writes, "then one believes that what one believes is *true*, and conversely, one believes that what one doesn't believe is not true" (p. 361). Since one can neither escape one's beliefs nor escape the sense that they are true, Fish rejects both the claims of method and the claims of skepticism. Methodologists and skeptics maintain that the validity of beliefs depends on their being grounded in a condition of knowledge prior to and independent of belief; they differ only about whether this is possible. The virtue of Fish's account is that it shows why an insistence on the inescapability of belief is in no way inimical to the ordinary notions of truth and falsehood implicit in our sense of what knowledge is. The character of belief is precisely what gives us those notions in the first place; having beliefs just *is* being committed to the truth of what one believes and the falsehood of what one doesn't believe. But to say all this is, as Fish asserts, to offer no practical help or hindrance to the task of acquiring true beliefs. We can no more get true beliefs by looking for knowledge than we can get an author's meaning by looking for his or her intention, and for the same reason; knowledge and true belief are the same.

So far, this argument seems to us flawless. But Fish, as it turns out, fails

9. Stanley Fish, *Is There a Text in This Class? The Authority of Interpretive Communities* (Cambridge, Mass., 1980), p. 370; all further citations to this work will be included in the text [Knapp and Michaels's note]. John Milton (1608–1674) and William Butler Yeats (1865–1939) are, like Wordsworth, canonical writers of English poetry.

to recognize the force of his own discussion of belief, and this failure is what makes him a theorist. It commits him, ultimately, to the ideal of knowledge implicit in all epistemological versions of theory, and it leads him to affirm, after all, the methodological value of his theoretical stance. Fish's departure from his account of belief shows up most vividly in his response to charges that his arguments lead to historical relativism. The fear of relativism is a fear that the abandonment of method must make all inquiry pointless. But, Fish rightly says, inquiry never seems pointless; our present beliefs about an object always seem better than any previous beliefs about the same object: "In other words, the idea of progress is inevitable, not, however, because there *is* a progress in the sense of a clearer and clearer sight of an independent object but because the *feeling* of having progressed is an inevitable consequence of the firmness with which we hold our beliefs" (pp. 361–62).

As an account of the inevitable psychology of belief, this is irreproachable. But when he later turns from the general issue of intellectual progress to the particular case of progress in literary criticism, Fish makes clear that he thinks our psychological assurance is unfounded. Our present beliefs only *seem* better than earlier ones; they never really *are*. And, indeed, the discovery of this truth about our beliefs gives us, Fish thinks, a new understanding of the history of literary criticism and a new sense of how to go about studying it. According to what Fish calls the "old model" for making sense of the history of criticism, the work of critics "like Sidney, Dryden, Pope, Coleridge, Arnold"[1] could only be seen as "the record of the rather dismal performances of men . . . who simply did not understand literature and literary values as well as we do." But Fish's new model enables us to "regard those performances not as unsuccessful attempts to approximate our own but as extensions of a literary culture whose assumptions were *not inferior but merely different*" (pp. 367–68; our emphasis).

To imagine that we can see the beliefs we hold as no better than but "merely different" from opposing beliefs held by others is to imagine a position from which we can see our beliefs without really believing them. To be in this position would be to see the truth about beliefs without actually having any—to know without believing. In the moment in which he imagines this condition of knowledge outside belief, Fish has forgotten the point of his own earlier identification of knowledge and true belief.

Once a theorist has reached this vision of knowledge, there are two epistemological ways to go: realism and idealism.[2] A realist thinks that theory allows us to stand outside our beliefs in a neutral encounter with the objects of interpretation; an idealist thinks that theory allows us to stand outside our beliefs in a neutral encounter with our beliefs themselves. The issue in both cases is the relation between objects and beliefs. For the realist, the object exists independent of beliefs, and knowledge requires that we shed our beliefs in a disinterested quest for the object. For the idealist, who insists that we can never shed our beliefs, knowledge means recognizing the role beliefs play in *constituting* their objects. Fish, with his commitment to the primacy of beliefs, chooses idealism: "objects," he thinks, "are made and not

1. Fish names the major English poet-critics up to the 20th century: SIR PHILIP SIDNEY (1554–1586), JOHN DRYDEN (1631–1700), ALEXANDER POPE (1688–1744), SAMUEL TAYLOR COLERIDGE (1772–1834), and MATTHEW ARNOLD (1822–1888).

2. In philosophy, idealism holds that only mental entities are real; perceptual realism holds that material things exist independently of us.

found"; interpretation "is not the art of construing but the art of constructing" (pp. 331, 327). Once he arrives at epistemological idealism, Fish's methodological payoff immediately follows. Knowing that "interpreters do not decode poems" but "make them," "we are free to consider the various forms the literary institution has taken and to uncover the interpretative strategies by which its canons have been produced and understood" (pp. 327, 368). By thinking of the critic as an idealist instead of a realist, Fish is able to place literary criticism at the very center of all literary practice:

> No longer is the critic the humble servant of texts whose glories exist independently of anything he might do; it is what he does, within the constraints embedded in the literary institution, that brings texts into being and makes them available for analysis and appreciation. The practice of literary criticism is not something one must apologize for; it is absolutely essential not only to the maintenance of, but to the very production of, the objects of its attention. [p. 368]

We began this section by noting that Fish, like us, thinks that no general account of belief can have practical consequences. But, as we have just seen, *his* account turns out to have consequences after all. Why, then, is Fish led both to assert that his argument has no practical consequences and to proclaim its importance in providing a new model for critical practice? The answer is that, despite his explicit disclaimers, he thinks a true account of belief must be a *theory* about belief, whereas we think a true account of belief can only be a *belief* about belief.[3] The difference between these two senses of what it means to have a true account of something is the difference between theory and the kind of pragmatist argument we are presenting here. These two kinds of positions conceive their inconsequentiality in two utterly different ways. A belief about the nature of beliefs is inconsequential because it merely tells you what beliefs are, not whether they are true or false in particular or in general. From this point of view, knowing the truth about belief will no more help you in acquiring true beliefs than knowing that meaning is intentional will help you find correct meanings. This is not in the least to say that you can't have true beliefs, only that you can't get them by having a good account of what beliefs are.

Fish's *theory* about beliefs, on the other hand, strives to achieve inconsequentiality by standing outside all the practical commitments that belief entails. It is perfectly true that one can achieve inconsequentiality by going outside beliefs but only because, as Fish himself insists, to be outside beliefs is to be nowhere at all. But of course Fish doesn't think that his theory about beliefs leaves him nowhere at all; he thinks instead that it gives him a way of arriving at truth, not by choosing some beliefs over others but by choosing beliefless knowledge over all beliefs. The truth of knowledge, according to Fish, is that no beliefs are, in the long run, truer than others; all beliefs, in the long run, are equal. But, as we have noted, it is only from the standpoint of a theory about belief which is not itself a belief that this truth can be seen. Hence the descent from "theoretical reasoning" about our beliefs to the actual practice of believing—from neutrality to commitment—demands that

3. Fish calls his account a "general or metacritical belief" (*Is There a Text in This Class?*, p. 359; cf. pp. 368–70) [Knapp and Michaels's note].

we forget the truth theory has told us. Unlike the ordinary methodologist, Fish wants to repudiate the attempt to derive practice from theory, insisting that the world of practice must be founded not on theoretical truth but on the repression of theoretical truth. But the sense that practice can only begin with the repression of theory already amounts to a methodological prescription: when confronted with beliefs, forget that they are not really true. This prescription gives Fish everything theory always wants: knowledge of the truth-value of beliefs and instructions on what to do with them.[4]

We can now see why Fish, in the first passage quoted, says that his position is "not one that you (or anyone else) could live by . . . even if you [were] persuaded" by it. Theory, he thinks, can have no practical consequences; it cannot be lived because theory and practice—the truth about belief and belief itself—can never in principle be united. In our view, however, the only relevant truth about belief is that you can't go outside it, and, far from being unlivable, this is a truth you can't help but live. It has no practical consequences not because it can never be *united* with practice but because it can never be *separated* from practice.

The theoretical impulse, as we have described it, always involves the attempt to separate things that should not be separated: on the ontological side, meaning from intention, language from speech acts; on the epistemological side, knowledge from true belief. Our point has been that the separated terms are in fact inseparable. It is tempting to end by saying that theory and practice too are inseparable. But this would be a mistake. Not because theory and practice (unlike the other terms) really are separate but because theory is nothing else but the attempt to escape practice. Meaning is just another name for expressed intention, knowledge just another name for true belief, but theory is not just another name for practice. It is the name for all the ways people have tried to stand outside practice in order to govern practice from without. Our thesis has been that no one can reach a position outside practice, that theorists should stop trying, and that the theoretical enterprise should therefore come to an end.

1982

4. In one respect Fish's prescription is unusual: it separates the two theoretical goals of grounding practice and reaching objective truth. It tells us what is true and how to behave—but not how to behave in order to find out what is true [Knapp and Michaels's note].

BELL HOOKS

b. Gloria Jean Watkins, 1952

bell hooks first emerged in the 1980s as a trenchant critical voice among African American intellectuals. Her wide-ranging essays about American culture offer critiques on issues ranging from the academy to the environmental crisis, from the media to masculinity, from racism to sexism, while exploring the unique problems and perspectives of black women and the underprivileged. Within feminism, much of her writing has been devoted to articulating the intersections of race, class, and gender oppression. In *Feminist Theory: From Margin to Center* (1984) she writes, "Feminism is the struggle to end sexist oppression. Its aim is not to benefit solely any specific group of women, any particular race or class of women. It does not privilege women over men. It has the power to transform in a meaningful way all our lives."

Born into a rural black working-class family in Hopkinsville, Kentucky, Gloria Jean Watkins suffered a turbulent childhood but found inspiration in books and solace in imagination. When, as an adult, she took the name "bell hooks," it was to honor her outspoken great-grandmother and the legacy of her past. hooks received a B.A. from Stanford University in 1973, an M.A. from the University of Wisconsin in 1976, and, in 1983, a Ph.D. from the University of California, Santa Cruz. She taught African American studies at Yale University and English and women's studies at Oberlin College from 1988 until 1993. Since 1993 she has taught in the English department of the City University of New York Graduate Center.

hooks gained prominence as a social critic with the publication of her first book, *Ain't I a Woman: Black Women and Feminism* (1981), begun when she was only nineteen and published while she was still a graduate student. An extremely prolific writer, she has published more than a dozen books since then on topics as varied as feminist theory, racism, film, art, spirituality, and cultural studies. With the publication of *Bone Black: Memories of Girlhood* (1996) and *Wounds of Passion: A Writing Life* (1997), she turned to the genre of autobiography to explore more fully her interest in capturing "the authority of experience" that she examines in our selection, "Postmodern Blackness." Like Cornel West, with whom she collaborated on *Breaking Bread: Insurgent Black Intellectual Life* (1991), hooks has sought a niche as a public intellectual on the Left, attempting to reach a wider audience outside of academia for her cultural criticism while remaining connected to her underclass black community. As an essayist, she follows in the rich tradition of twentieth-century black intellectuals such as W. E. B. DU BOIS, C. L. R. James and ZORA NEALE HURSTON, although doubtless hooks would also include in any list of intellectual forebears earlier black women such as Anna Cooper (the nineteenth-century author of *A Voice from the South by a Black Woman of the South*) and Sojourner Truth.

In "Postmodern Blackness," which appears in her *Yearning: Race, Gender, and Cultural Politics* (1990), hooks asks why African Americans should have any interest in "postmodern theory." She applies this label to the philosophic critique of modernity that celebrates difference and otherness, that advocates radical liberation and political equality, that finds fault with rigid concepts of identity, and that criticizes so-called master narratives (for example, those about the inevitable progress of human reason, the eventual triumph of the proletariat, or the ending of the world on Judgment Day). For hooks and other cultural critics, postmodernity also evokes late-twentieth-century postindustrial society with its job restructuring, ubiquitous media and popular culture, and new social movements and protest groups. Like BARBARA CHRISTIAN, hooks believes that the abstract philosophical discourse of postmodernism—as defined by French theorists such as JACQUES DERRIDA, JEAN-FRANÇOIS LYOTARD, and JEAN BAUDRILLARD—is dominated by white male intellectuals. These academic elites speak to one another, oblivious to the concerns of black people. Despite its invocation of "difference," she argues, postmodernism is exclusionary: while using the concepts of difference and marginality to legitimate itself in the face of accusations of irrelevance, it seems unwilling to engage the experiences or writings of the truly marginalized—black women, for example. In its celebration of indeterminacy and free play in language and in its focus on deconstructing identity, postmodernism fails to offer useful analyses of the power relations that shape discourse. Without "adequate concrete knowledge" of and contact with oppressed and marginalized groups, white theorists risk impeding rather than supporting "radical liberation struggle."

Because she discerns in those silenced by the "master narratives" of Western culture a "yearning"—what she describes as a "longing for critical voice"—hooks, unlike Christian and some other minority intellectuals, is not willing to abandon postmodernism to the intellectual elites. She identifies the intersection of "identity politics" and the postmodern critique of human essence as a particularly significant site of struggle for African Americans, who, she argues, need to resist outmoded notions of essential blackness in much the same way as feminist critics have contested the idea of the essentially female (see JUDITH BUTLER, MONIQUE WITTIG, and JULIA KRISTEVA). hooks is critical of the concept of essential blackness whether imposed from without as racist stereotype or from within as prescription for an "authentic black identity," an identity that refuses to recognize the multiplicities of black experiences that ground "diverse cultural productions." At the same time, hooks argues, the postmodern critique of essence ought not to be used to dismiss black and feminist identity politics. hooks worries about the potential within postmodernist discourse to deny a critical voice to those who have been "subjected to" colonization or domination. She is suspicious that the postmodern call to dismantle identity comes at a historical moment when subjugated people are beginning to assert their own identity and to act collectively in its name. hooks's solution is to embrace the postmodern critique of essentialism while emphasizing the traditional humanistic "authority of experience."

The dangers hooks exposes in the discourse of postmodernism are real, though it is worth noting that hooks here treats "postmodernism" as a single set of monologic discourses that mean the same thing to everyone. Postmodern theory is a wide-ranging and diverse set of practices, texts, and discourses no more easily reducible to one set of essential meanings than is "blackness." Both terms in hooks's title must be seen as equally under interrogation, and much work remains to be done to understand the relations between them. Greater precision about the complex meanings within postmodern discourse of such terms as *identity, subjectivity*, and *experience* might break the impasse she describes between a desire to reclaim a common black history, culture, and experience and the need to avoid imposing restrictive and damaging stereotypes on diverse experiences. hooks is in agreement with the best "oppositional practices" of postmodernism, however, when she suggests that it is in the gaps, ruptures, and contradictions of Western master narratives that the struggles for liberation and for coalition politics will discover effective forms of resistance and new forms of community.

BIBLIOGRAPHY

hooks's critical writing, mainly essay collections, include, on feminist theory, *Ain't I a Woman: Black Women and Feminism* (1981), *Feminist Theory: From Margin to Center* (1984), *Talking Back: Thinking Feminist, Thinking Black* (1989), and *Sisters of the Yam: Black Women and Self-Recovery* (1993); on race, *Breaking Bread: Insurgent Black Intellectual Life* (with Cornel West, 1991), *Black Looks: Race and Representation* (1992), and *Killing Rage: Ending Racism* (1995); on teaching, *Teaching to Transgress: Education as the Practice of Freedom* (1994); on film, *Reel to Real: Race, Sex, and Class at the Movies* (1996); and on cultural studies, *Yearning: Race, Gender, and Cultural Politics* (1990), *Outlaw Culture: Resisting Representation* (1994), and *Art on My Mind: Visual Politics* (1995). Her memoirs—*Bone Black: Memories of Girlhood* (1996), *Wounds of Passion: A Writing Life* (1997), and *Remembering Rapture: The Writer at Work* (1999)—are good sources of information on her life. For a biographical sketch, see Lara Dieckmann's entry in *Significant Contemporary American Feminists: A Biographical Sourcebook* (1999).

A few critical articles on hooks have appeared. Of most interest to students of literary criticism are Cassie Premo, "When the Difference Becomes Too Great: Images of the Self and Survival in a Postmodern World," *Genre* 28 (1995), and Clive Thomson, "Culture, Identity, and Dialogue: bell hooks and Gayatri Chakravorty Spivak," in *Dialogism and Cultural Criticism* (ed. Thomson and Hans Raj Dau, 1995). hooks's essays about teaching have also been of interest to critics, including Tom Fox, "Literacy and Activism: A Response to bell hooks," *Journal of Advanced Composition*

14 (1994); Joyce Irene Middleton, "bell hooks on Literacy and Teaching: A Response," *Journal of Advanced Composition* 14 (1994); and Gary Olson and Elizabeth Hirsh, "Feminist Praxis and the Politics of Literacy: A Conversation with bell hooks," in *Women Writing Culture* (ed. Olson and Hirsch, 1995). Bibliographical information on hooks may be found in Genevieve Fabre's "Selected Bibliography of Essays on Black Women and Black Feminist Criticism," *Revue Française d'Études Americaines* 24 (1986), as well as in the Schomburg Center for Research in Black Studies' *Bibliographic Guide to Black Studies* (1995).

Postmodern Blackness

Postmodernist discourses are often exclusionary even as they call attention to, appropriate even, the experience of "difference" and "Otherness" to provide oppositional political meaning, legitimacy, and immediacy when they are accused of lacking concrete relevance. Very few African-American intellectuals have talked or written about postmodernism. At a dinner party I talked about trying to grapple with the significance of postmodernism for contemporary black experience. It was one of those social gatherings where only one other black person was present. The setting quickly became a field of contestation. I was told by the other black person that I was wasting my time, that "this stuff does not relate in any way to what's happening with black people." Speaking in the presence of a group of white onlookers, staring at us as though this encounter were staged for their benefit, we engaged in a passionate discussion about black experience. Apparently, no one sympathized with my insistence that racism is perpetuated when blackness is associated solely with concrete gut level experience conceived as either opposing or having no connection to abstract thinking and the production of critical theory. The idea that there is no meaningful connection between black experience and critical thinking about aesthetics or culture must be continually interrogated.

My defense of postmodernism and its relevance to black folks sounded good, but I worried that I lacked conviction, largely because I approach the subject cautiously and with suspicion.

Disturbed not so much by the "sense" of postmodernism but by the conventional language used when it is written or talked about and by those who speak it, I find myself on the outside of the discourse looking in. As a discursive practice it is dominated primarily by the voices of white male intellectuals and/or academic elites who speak to and about one another with coded familiarity. Reading and studying their writing to understand postmodernism in its multiple manifestations, I appreciate it but feel little inclination to ally myself with the academic hierarchy and exclusivity pervasive in the movement today.

Critical of most writing on postmodernism, I perhaps am more conscious of the way in which the focus on "Otherness and difference" that is often alluded to in these works seems to have little concrete impact as an analysis or standpoint that might change the nature and direction of postmodernist theory. Since much of this theory has been constructed in reaction to and against high modernism, there is seldom any mention of black experience or writings by black people in this work, specifically black women (though in more recent work one may see a reference to Cornel West, the black male scholar who has most engaged postmodernist discourse). Even if an aspect of black culture is the subject of postmodern critical writing, the works cited will usually be those of black men. A work that comes immediately to mind is Andrew Ross's chapter "Hip, and the Long Front of Color" in *No Respect: Intellectuals and Popular Culture*;[1] while it is an interesting reading, it constructs black culture as though black women have had no role in black cultural production. At the end of Meaghan Morris' discussion of postmodernism in her collection of essays *The Pirate's Fiancée: Feminism, Reading, Postmodernism*, she provides a bibliography of works by women, identifying them as important contributions to a discourse on postmodernism that offer new insight as well as challenging male theoretical hegemony.[2] Even though many of the works do not directly address postmodernism, they address similar concerns. There are no references to works by black women.

The failure to recognize a critical black presence in the culture and in most scholarship and writing on postmodernism compels a black reader, particularly a black female reader, to interrogate her interest in a subject where those who discuss and write about it seem not to know black women exist or even to consider the possibility that we might be somewhere writing or saying something that should be listened to, or producing art that should be seen, heard, approached with intellectual seriousness. This is especially the case with works that go on and on about the way in which postmodernist discourse has opened up a theoretical terrain where "difference and Otherness" can be considered legitimate issues in the academy. Confronting both the absence of recognition of black female presence that much postmodernist theory re-inscribes and the resistance on the part of most black folks to hearing about real connection between postmodernism and black experience, I enter a discourse, a practice, where there may be no ready audience for my words, no clear listener, uncertain then, that my voice can or will be heard.

During the sixties, the black power movement was influenced by perspectives that could easily be labeled modernist. Certainly many of the ways black folks addressed issues of identity conformed to a modernist universalizing agenda. There was little critique of patriarchy as a master narrative among black militants. Despite the fact that black power ideology reflected a modernist sensibility, these elements were soon rendered irrelevant as militant protest was stifled by a powerful, repressive postmodern state. The period directly after the black power movement was a time when major news magazines carried articles with cocky headlines like "Whatever Happened to Black America?" This response was an ironic reply to the aggressive, unmet demand by decentered, marginalized black subjects who had at least momentarily successfully demanded a hearing, who had made it possible for black liberation to be on the national political agenda. In the wake of the black power movement, after so many rebels were slaughtered and lost, many of these voices were silenced by a repressive state; others became inarticulate. It has become necessary to find new avenues to transmit the messages of black liberation struggle, new ways to talk about racism and other politics of

1. Andrew Ross, *No Respect: Intellectuals and Popular Culture* (New York: Routledge, 1989).
2. Meaghan Morris, *The Pirate's Fiancée: Feminism, Reading, Postmodernism* (London: Verso, 1988).

domination. Radical postmodernist practice, most powerfully conceptualized as a "politics of difference," should incorporate the voices of displaced, marginalized, exploited, and oppressed black people. It is sadly ironic that the contemporary discourse which talks the most about heterogeneity, the decentered subject, declaring breakthroughs that allow recognition of Otherness, still directs its critical voice primarily to a specialized audience that shares a common language rooted in the very master narratives it claims to challenge. If radical postmodernist thinking is to have a transformative impact, then a critical break with the notion of "authority" as "mastery over" must not simply be a rhetorical device. It must be reflected in habits of being, including styles of writing as well as chosen subject matter. Third world nationals, elites, and white critics who passively absorb white supremacist thinking, and therefore never notice or look at black people on the streets or at their jobs, who render us invisible with their gaze in all areas of daily life, are not likely to produce liberatory theory that will challenge racist domination, or promote a breakdown in traditional ways of seeing and thinking about reality, ways of constructing aesthetic theory and practice. From a different standpoint, Robert Storr makes a similar critique in the global issue of *Art in America* when he asserts:

> To be sure, much postmodernist critical inquiry has centered precisely on the issues of "difference" and "Otherness." On the purely theoretical plane the exploration of these concepts has produced some important results, but in the absence of any sustained research into what artists of color and others outside the mainstream might be up to, such discussions become rootless instead of radical. Endless second guessing about the latent imperialism of intruding upon other cultures only compounded matters, preventing or excusing these theorists from investigating what black, Hispanic, Asian and Native American artists were actually doing.[3]

Without adequate concrete knowledge of and contact with the non-white "Other," white theorists may move in discursive theoretical directions that are threatening and potentially disruptive of that critical practice which would support radical liberation struggle.

The postmodern critique of "identity," though relevant for renewed black liberation struggle, is often posed in ways that are problematic. Given a pervasive politic of white supremacy which seeks to prevent the formation of radical black subjectivity, we cannot cavalierly dismiss a concern with identity politics. Any critic exploring the radical potential of postmodernism as it relates to racial difference and racial domination would need to consider the implications of a critique of identity for oppressed groups. Many of us are struggling to find new strategies of resistance. We must engage decolonization as a critical practice if we are to have meaningful chances of survival even as we must simultaneously cope with the loss of political grounding which made radical activism more possible. I am thinking here about the postmodernist critique of essentialism as it pertains to the construction of "identity" as one example.

3. Robert Storr, "The Global Issue: A Symposium," *Art in Amerca* 77 (1989): 88.

Postmodern theory that is not seeking to simply appropriate the experience of "Otherness" to enhance the discourse or to be radically chic should not separate the "politics of difference" from the politics of racism. To take racism seriously one must consider the plight of underclass people of color, a vast majority of whom are black. For African-Americans our collective condition prior to the advent of postmodernism and perhaps more tragically expressed under current postmodern conditions has been and is characterized by continued displacement, profound alienation, and despair. Writing about blacks and postmodernism, Cornel West describes our collective plight:

> There is increasing class division and differentiation, creating on the one hand a significant black middle-class, highly anxiety-ridden, insecure, willing to be co-opted and incorporated into the powers that be, concerned with racism to the degree that it poses contraints on upward social mobility; and, on the other, a vast and growing black underclass, an underclass that embodies a kind of walking nihilism of pervasive drug addiction, pervasive alcoholism, pervasive homicide, and an exponential rise in suicide. Now because of the deindustrialization, we also have a devastated black industrial working class. We are talking here about tremendous hopelessness.

This hopelessness creates longing for insight and strategies for change that can renew spirits and reconstruct grounds for collective black liberation struggle. The overall impact of postmodernism is that many other groups now share with black folks a sense of deep alienation, despair, uncertainty, loss of a sense of grounding even if it is not informed by shared circumstance. Radical postmodernism calls attention to those shared sensibilities which cross the boundaries of class, gender, race, etc., that could be fertile ground for the construction of empathy—ties that would promote recognition of common commitments, and serve as a base for solidarity and coalition.

Yearning is the word that best describes a common psychological state shared by many of us, cutting across boundaries of race, class, gender, and sexual practice. Specifically, in relation to the post-modernist deconstruction of "master" narratives, the yearning that wells in the hearts and minds of those whom such narratives have silenced is the longing for critical voice. It is no accident that "rap" has usurped the primary position of rhythm and blues music among young black folks as the most desired sound or that it began as a form of "testimony" for the underclass. It has enabled underclass black youth to develop a critical voice, as a group of young black men told me, a "common literacy." Rap projects a critical voice, explaining, demanding, urging. Working with this insight in his essay "Putting the Pop Back into Postmodernism," Lawrence Grossberg comments:

> The postmodern sensibility appropriates practices as boasts that announce their own—and consequently our own—existence, like a rap song boasting of the imaginary (or real—it makes no difference) accomplishments of the rapper. They offer forms of empowerment not only in the face of nihilism but precisely through the forms of nihilism itself:

> an empowering nihilism, a moment of positivity through the production and structuring of affective relations.[4]

Considering that it is as subject one comes to voice, then the postmodernist focus on the critique of identity appears at first glance to threaten and close down the possibility that this discourse and practice will allow those who have suffered the crippling effects of colonization and domination to gain or regain a hearing. Even if this sense of threat and the fear it evokes are based on a misunderstanding of the postmodernist political project, they nevertheless shape responses. It never surprises me when black folks respond to the critique of essentialism, especially when it denies the validity of identity politics by saying, "Yeah, it's easy to give up identity, when you got one." Should we not be suspicious of postmodern critiques of the "subject" when they surface at a historical moment when many subjugated people feel themselves coming to voice for the first time? Though an apt and oftentimes appropriate comeback, it does not really intervene in the discourse in a way that alters and transforms.

Criticisms of directions in postmodern thinking should not obscure insights it may offer that open up our understanding of African-American experience. The critique of essentialism encouraged by postmodernist thought is useful for African-Americans concerned with reformulating outmoded notions of identity. We have too long had imposed upon us from both the outside and the inside a narrow, constricting notion of blackness. Postmodern critiques of essentialism which challenge notions of universality and static over-determined identity within mass culture and mass consciousness can open up new possibilities for the construction of self and the assertion of agency.

Employing a critique of essentialism allows African-Americans to acknowledge the way in which class mobility has altered collective black experience so that racism does not necessarily have the same impact on our lives. Such a critique allows us to affirm multiple black identities, varied black experience. It also challenges colonial imperialist paradigms of black identity which represent blackness one-dimensionally in ways that reinforce and sustain white supremacy. This discourse created the idea of the "primitive" and promoted the notion of an "authentic" experience, seeing as "natural" those expressions of black life which conformed to a pre-existing pattern or stereotype. Abandoning essentialist notions would be a serious challenge to racism. Contemporary African-American resistance struggle must be rooted in a process of decolonization that continually opposes re-inscribing notions of "authentic" black identity. This critique should not be made synonymous with a dismissal of the struggle of oppressed and exploited peoples to make ourselves subjects. Nor should it deny that in certain circumstances this experience affords us a privileged critical location from which to speak. This is not a re-inscription of modernist master narratives of authority which privilege some voices by denying voice to others. Part of our struggle for radical black subjectivity is the quest to find ways to construct self and identity that are oppositional and

4. Lawrence Grossberg, "Putting the Pop Back into Postmodernism," in *Universal Abandon: The Politics of Postmodernism*, ed. Andrew Ross (Minneapolis: University of Minnesota Press, 1988), p. 181.

liberatory. The unwillingness to critique essentialism on the part of many African-Americans is rooted in the fear that it will cause folks to lose sight of the specific history and experience of African-Americans and the unique sensibilities and culture that arise from that experience. An adequate response to this concern is to critique essentialism while emphasizing the significance of "the authority of experience."[5] There is a radical difference between a repudiation of the idea that there is a black "essence" and recognition of the way black identity has been specifically constituted in the experience of exile and struggle.

When black folks critique essentialism, we are empowered to recognize multiple experiences of black identity that are the lived conditions which make diverse cultural productions possible. When this diversity is ignored, it is easy to see black folks as falling into two categories: nationalist or assimilationist, black-identified or white-identified. Coming to terms with the impact of postmodernism for black experience, particularly as it changes our sense of identity, means that we must and can rearticulate the basis for collective bonding. Given the various crises facing African-Americans (economic, spiritual, escalating racial violence, etc.), we are compelled by circumstance to reassess our relationship to popular culture and resistance struggle. Many of us are as reluctant to face this task as many non-black postmodern thinkers who focus theoretically on the issue of "difference" are to confront the issue of race and racism.

Music is the cultural product created by African-Americans that has most attracted postmodern theorists. It is rarely acknowledged that there is far greater censorship and restriction of other forms of cultural production by black folks—literary, critical writing, etc. Attempts on the part of editors and publishing houses to control and manipulate the representation of black culture, as well as the desire to promote the creation of products that will attract the widest audience, limit in a crippling and stifling way the kind of work many black folks feel we can do and still receive recognition. Using myself as an example, that creative writing I do which I consider to be most reflective of a postmodern oppositional sensibility, work that is abstract, fragmented, non-linear narrative, is constantly rejected by editors and publishers. It does not conform to the type of writing they think black women should be doing or the type of writing they believe will sell. Certainly I do not think I am the only black person engaged in forms of cultural production, especially experimental ones, who is constrained by the lack of an audience for certain kinds of work. It is important for postmodern thinkers and theorists to constitute themselves as an audience for such work. To do this they must assert power and privilege within the space of critical writing to open up the field so that it will be more inclusive. To change the exclusionary practice of postmodern critical discourse is to enact a postmodernism of resistance. Part of this intervention entails black intellectual participation in the discourse.

In his essay "Postmodernism and Black America," Cornel West suggests that black intellectuals "are marginal—usually languishing at the interface of Black and white cultures or thoroughly ensconced in Euro-American settings." He cannot see this group as potential producers of radical postmod-

5. The title of a 1977 collection of essays of feminist criticism, edited by Arlyn Diamond and Lee R. Edwards.

ernist thought. While I generally agree with this assessment, black intellectuals must proceed with the understanding that we are not condemned to the margins. The way we work and what we do can determine whether or not what we produce will be meaningful to a wider audience, one that includes all classes of black people. West suggests that black intellectuals lack "any organic link with most of Black life" and that this "diminishes their value to Black resistance." This statement bears traces of essentialism. Perhaps we need to focus more on those black intellectuals, however rare our presence, who do not feel this lack and whose work is primarily directed towards the enhancement of black critical consciousness and the strengthening of our collective capacity to engage in meaningful resistance struggle. Theoretical ideas and critical thinking need not be transmitted solely in written work or solely in the academy. While I work in a predominantly white institution, I remain intimately and passionately engaged with black community. It's not like I'm going to talk about writing and thinking about postmodernism with other academics and/or intellectuals and not discuss these ideas with underclass non-academic black folks who are family, friends, and comrades. Since I have not broken the ties that bind me to underclass poor black community, I have seen that knowledge, especially that which enhances daily life and strengthens our capacity to survive, can be shared. It means that critics, writers, and academics have to give the same critical attention to nurturing and cultivating our ties to black community that we give to writing articles, teaching, and lecturing. Here again I am really talking about cultivating habits of being that reinforce awareness that knowledge can be disseminated and shared on a number of fronts. The extent to which knowledge is made available, accessible, etc. depends on the nature of one's political commitments.

Postmodern culture with its decentered subject can be the space where ties are severed or it can provide the occasion for new and varied forms of bonding. To some extent, ruptures, surfaces, contextuality, and a host of other happenings create gaps that make space for oppositional practices which no longer require intellectuals to be confined by narrow separate spheres with no meaningful connection to the world of the everyday. Much postmodern engagement with culture emerges from the yearning to do intellectual work that connects with habits of being, forms of artistic expression, and aesthetics that inform the daily life of writers and scholars as a well as a mass population. On the terrain of culture, one can participate in critical dialogue with the uneducated poor, the black underclass who are thinking about aesthetics. One can talk about what we are seeing, thinking, or listening to; a space is there for critical exchange. It's exciting to think, write, talk about, and create art that reflects passionate engagement with popular culture, because this may very well be "the" central future location of resistance struggle, a meeting place where new and radical happenings can occur.

1990

JUDITH BUTLER
b. 1956

Judith Butler's *Gender Trouble: Feminism and the Subversion of Identity* (1990), arguably the most influential theoretical text of the 1990s, is a founding document of queer theory and a key statement of "performative" accounts of cultural meaning. Butler's work distills forty years of French theory—from pioneer feminist SIMONE DE BEAUVOIR to JULIA KRISTEVA, and from JACQUES LACAN and LOUIS ALTHUSSER to JACQUES DERRIDA and MICHEL FOUCAULT—to explore how gendered identity is socially produced through repetitions of ordinary daily activities. Her goal is to uncover the assumptions that "restrict the meaning of gender to received notions of masculinity and femininity." In opening up "the field of possibility for gender," Butler aims for a feminism that avoids "exclusionary gender norms" in its portrayal of acceptable identities.

Trained in philosophy, Judith Butler received her undergraduate and graduate degrees at Yale University. She has taught in interdisciplinary programs, first at Johns Hopkins University and then at the University of California at Berkeley. *Gender Trouble* made her something between a celebrity and a cult figure, especially in gay and lesbian subcultures, and she has responded by jealously guarding her personal life from public scrutiny.

Key for Butler is the insistence that nothing is natural, not even sexual identity. Feminists have sometimes distinguished between "sex" as the anatomical difference between male and female bodies and "gender" as the meanings attached to those bodily differences in various cultures. Butler argues that even anatomical differences can be experienced only through the categories and expectations set out by the culture's signifying order. Moreover, anatomical differences are mapped to expectations about sexual desire, specifically to society's "compulsory heterosexuality" (a term Butler borrows from ADRIENNE RICH), which posits that there are two sexes and that desire runs from one sex to the other. Our culture's understanding of sexuality is ill-equipped, therefore, to recognize bodies that confound the strict binary division between male and female, or desires that cross, combine, or otherwise fail to conform to a fairly narrow understanding of sex as genital intercourse between two people, one "naturally" female, the other "naturally" male.

Following Foucault's work in *The History of Sexuality* (1976), Butler stresses that modern culture sees sexuality as a fundamental constituent of identity. Our sex and our sexual desires and activities are profound indices of who we are. Butler hopes—like many contemporary critical theorists—to reveal that the seemingly "natural" is actually socially constructed and, thus, contingent. The established and conventional connections between anatomy and desire, and between sexual activities and ascriptions of identity, are not inevitable; they have been different in other cultures and in other historical eras, and they are open to revision or, to use one of Butler's favorite words, "resignification." The meanings and categories by which we understand and live our daily existence can be altered.

Such alteration does not come easily, however. "Those naturalized and reified notions of gender that support masculine hegemony and heterosexist power" are written into our very psyches as well as into the dominant institutions of political and social life. Butler follows the accounts of subject formation found in Foucault and Lacan. For Foucault, discourse (the articulated categories of thought) orders knowledge along lines that produce subjects open to power's control. Such power, he stresses, works at the level of daily routine. For Lacan, individuals achieve an identity, a recognized place in the social order, by passing into the Law (the culture's signifying order)—at the cost of creating the unconscious and establishing a permanent split, an alienation of self from desire, within the subject.

To Foucault's account of power's "micro-physics" and Lacan's description of subject formation, Butler adds Derrida's understanding of "performative speech acts." She believes "the performative" offers her a model of action within theories that often seem to allow subjects no room for resistance to power. Derrida develops his notion of the performative in an essay on J. L. AUSTIN, the twentieth-century Oxford philosopher who invented the term, and in a later debate with the American philosopher John Searle. Austin comes from an Anglo-American tradition (dating back to John Locke) that sees the meaning of language as grounded in the way that words refer to already existing objects. I speak of a certain blue chair, and my words are meaningful and true insofar as they conform to the facts of the matter. But Austin realized that some utterances are creative: they make something come into existence, rather than referring to something that already exists. Anyone who makes a promise, or a judge who sentences someone to prison, creates a fact (the promise, the sentence) through the act of speaking. Such speech acts are performatives.

Surprisingly, as Austin pursues this notion he finds it increasingly difficult to distinguish performatives from referential speech acts. Derrida picks up on this difficulty and adds the concepts of "citation" and "repetition" to the analysis. Every speech act, Derrida argues, succeeds in meaning anything at all only by virtue of its "citing" previous uses of the term it now employs. In other words, language works because the speakers of that language have a prior knowledge of its terms and its prevailing usages (both syntactic and semantic). Every new speech act is a repetition, using old words and structures in this new instance. There are thus fairly strict limits on novelty. An utterance that departs too far from received understandings will be incomprehensible. But exact repetition does not occur very often either. After all, we are using the old words in new contexts. Each separate use of a word tweaks it in this or that direction in relation to a variety of pressures: the context, the audience, conscious or unconscious purposes. Thus, each speech act has a performative dimension; instead of repeating or referring to preexisting meanings in its "citation" of a previously used word, it alters, if always within limits, the meaning of that word. Languages are reproduced, are kept alive and functioning, through innumerable acts of use; but those acts also constantly change the language. Most changes are inadvertent by-products of use, but some may be conscious, such as contemporary efforts to abandon "man" as the generic word referring to all human beings.

Butler proposes that we understand "sex" and "gender" as citational repetitions. Various cultural discourses converge in a prevailing (although never fully homogeneous or monolithic) understanding of what "boy" and "girl," "man" and "woman" signify. Individual actions then "cite" these meanings, playing off them in various ways. Power functions pervasively through these meanings. The little boy learns that his crying is not masculine; he must grow into his masculinity by imitating the behavior designated as "male" to the point that such behavior becomes "second nature." The little girl learns that some ways of acting make her a tomboy, and she is encouraged to dress the part of "femininity." In Butler's view, we feel our way into these roles, slowly establishing (under the watchful eyes of powerful social forces) the way we will occupy them. Given our prevailing categories, we experience this process as discovering our identity. Butler believes identity is a trap, a hardening into rigid, binarized categories of much more fluid and heterogeneous possibilities. She calls for actions that will "resignify" our received meanings—actions that will lead to a "proliferation" of the "constitutive categories" into which all selves are now constrained to fit.

The costs of identity's straitjacket, Butler believes, are high—both for those who fit the categories comfortably and those who don't. "Deviants" (such as homosexuals, bisexuals, hermaphrodites, or other less recognizable nonidentities) are inevitable, according to Butler, although her reasons for this claim are not completely clear. For her, discursive power is never fully effective. It cannot create all individuals in its preferred image, in part because any social field is traversed by various discourses, none of which ever achieves full domination. In any case, compulsory heterosexuality cannot erase all nonheterosexual desires or acts. But the price paid by those labeled deviant for such desires and acts—in internalized guilt and external sanctions—is exorbitant. On the side of "normality," heterosexual identity can be achieved only through the forceful exclusion or "disavowal" of all nonheterosexual desires, in keeping with commonplace obsessional notions of identity as consistent in all places and at all times. Socially, this disavowal is expressed through homophobia and other discourses of "abjection" (Kristeva's famous term) that single out deviants as worthy targets of aggression and punishment.

Butler calls for a loosening of the categories, a relaxation of our fixation on identity. Power uses identity to latch onto us, and normative identity calls for a homogeneity too difficult to live. A change of this type can be seen as therapeutic—and in keeping with SIGMUND FREUD's goal of moderating the strictures of conventional morality and its excessive internal voice, the superego. But Butler's attack on identity also has specifically political dimensions. She believes that feminism has been hurt by its attempt to find an identity that would designate something common to everyone in the movement. She calls instead for a coalitional politics that avoids the fights over purity (of identity, of doctrine, of commitment) that often tear apart movements dependent on complete agreement among members over long periods of time. Thus, while Butler's work grows out of feminism, she is against any "identity politics" that sees political groupings and beliefs as grounded in a shared identity, whether ethnic, racial, sexual, national, or economic. All forms of identity politics, she believes, are prone to aggressions used to enforce rigid consistencies.

How do we begin to loosen the hold of identity, especially at a time when the passions attached to identity and its preservation are fervent and pervasive? An initial step, Butler says, is to make evident identity's construction; it is not inevitable (even if social power hardly leaves us much freedom to choose our ways of being in the world). Identity is not something planted in us to be discovered, but something that is performatively produced by acts that "effectively constitute the identity they are said to express or reveal." At the end of *Gender Trouble*, Butler advocates parody in general and drag performances in particular because such "subversive" performances "destabilize the naturalized categories of identity and desire." It is here that queer theory makes its appearance. Such theory is interested in any and all acts, images, and ideas that "trouble," violate, cross, mix, or otherwise confound established boundaries between male and female, normal and abnormal, self and other. In a limited sense, the goal is to create more space for and recognition of the various actions performed daily in a social landscape blinded and hostile to variety. But the broader goal is a general troubling, an attempted unfixing, of the links between acts, categories, representations, desires, and identities.

The main objections to Butler's position echo the objections often made to poststructuralist work. Key questions focus on agency, power, and ethics, while a difficult style and specialized terminology seem to guarantee a small audience for work that aims to have political consequences. To what extent does Butler believe that conscious, purposive action is possible if she posits an all-encompassing discursive power that shapes us at such a deep, unconscious level? How are we to understand "compulsory heterosexuality," "masculine hegemony," "phallogocentrism" (Derrida's term for the masculine power at the origin of the Law), and other terms by which she designates power? Have there been societies in which these forms of power have not been dominant? Is the formation of subjectivity entirely a matter of the self's relation to power, or do intersubjective relationships have any important role to play? What enables the critical enterprise itself, the ability to describe the processes of subject formation? Within ongoing debates over the details, however, a new interest in violations of received categories and the performative reproduction and transformation of culture attests to Butler's impact on literary studies.

BIBLIOGRAPHY

Butler's first book, *Subjects of Desire: Hegelian Reflections in Twentieth-Century France* (1986), traces French theories of subject formation as influenced by the nineteenth-century German philosopher G. W. F. Hegel. Her books after *Gender Trouble* (1990)—*Bodies That Matter: On the Discursive Limits of "Sex"* (1993), *Excitable Speech: A Politics of the Performative* (1996), and *The Psychic Life of Power: Theories in Subjection* (1997)—address various objections to her work and further develop her performative model of subject formation. Also of interest is Butler's *Antigone's Claim: Kinship between Life and Death* (2000). She has co-edited two important collections: with Joan W. Scott, *Feminists Theorize the Political* (1992); and with Linda Singer, *Erotic Welfare: Sexual Theory and Politics in the Age of Epidemic* (1993). Limited biographical information can be found in "Preface (1999)" in the tenth anniversary edition of *Gender Trouble* (1999).

Two excellent places to start in exploring the responses occasioned by Butler's work are Peter Osborne and Lynne Segal's "Gender as Performance: An Interview with Judith Butler," *Radical Philosophy* 67 (1994), and *Feminist Contentions: A Philosophical Exchange* (1995), which presents a debate among Butler, Seyla Benhabib, Drucilla Cornell, and Nancy Fraser, all leading women philosophers. For a good sampling of other responses to Butler's work, see Susan Bordo, "Postmodern Subjects, Postmodern Bodies," *Feminist Studies* 18.1 (1992); Shane Phelan, "Social Constructionism, Sexuality, and Politics," *Women and Politics* 12.1 (1992); John McGowan, "Thinking about Violence: Feminism, Cultural Politics, and Norms," *Centennial Review* 37.3 (1993); Debra Silverman, "Making a Spectacle: Or, Is There Female Drag?" *Critical Matrix* 7.2 (1993); Biddy Martin, "Sexualities without Gender and Other Queer Utopias," *Diacritics* 24.2–3 (1994); and Pheng Cheah, "Mattering," *Diacritics* 26.1 (1996).

From Gender Trouble

From *Preface*

Contemporary feminist debates over the meanings of gender lead time and again to a certain sense of trouble, as if the indeterminacy of gender might eventually culminate in the failure of feminism. Perhaps trouble need not carry such a negative valence. To make trouble was, within the reigning discourse of my childhood, something one should never do precisely because that would get one *in* trouble. The rebellion and its reprimand seemed to be caught up in the same terms, a phenomenon that gave rise to my first critical insight into the subtle ruse of power: the prevailing law threatened one with trouble, even put one in trouble, all to keep one out of trouble. Hence, I concluded that trouble is inevitable and the task, how best to make it, what best way to be in it. As time went by, further ambiguities arrived on the critical scene. I noted that trouble sometimes euphemized some fundamentally mysterious problem usually related to the alleged mystery of all things feminine. I read Beauvoir[1] who explained that to be a woman within the terms of a masculinist culture is to be a source of mystery and unknowability for men, and this seemed confirmed somehow when I read Sartre[2] for whom all desire, problematically presumed as heterosexual and masculine, was

1. SIMONE DE BEAUVOIR (1908–1986), French existentialist and feminist writer.

2. JEAN-PAUL SARTRE (1905–1980), French existentialist philosopher.

defined as *trouble*. For that masculine subject of desire, trouble became a scandal with the sudden intrusion, the unanticipated agency, of a female "object" who inexplicably returns the glance, reverses the gaze, and contests the place and authority of the masculine position. The radical dependency of the masculine subject on the female "Other" suddenly exposes his autonomy as illusory. That particular dialectical reversal of power, however, couldn't quite hold my attention—although others surely did. Power seemed to be more than an exchange between subjects or a relation of constant inversion between a subject and an Other; indeed, power appeared to operate in the production of that very binary frame for thinking about gender. I asked, what configuration of power constructs the subject and the Other, that binary relation between "men" and "women," and the internal stability of those terms? What restriction is here at work? Are those terms untroubling only to the extent that they conform to a heterosexual matrix for conceptualizing gender and desire? What happens to the subject and to the stability of gender categories when the epistemic regime of presumptive heterosexuality is unmasked as that which produces and reifies these ostensible categories of ontology?

But how can an epistemic/ontological regime be brought into question? What best way to trouble the gender categories that support gender hierarchy and compulsory heterosexuality? Consider the fate of "female trouble," that historical configuration of a nameless female indisposition, which thinly veiled the notion that being female is a natural indisposition. Serious as the medicalization of women's bodies is, the term is also laughable, and laughter in the face of serious categories is indispensable for feminism. Without a doubt, feminism continues to require its own forms of serious play. *Female Trouble* is also the title of the John Waters film that features Divine, the hero/heroine of *Hairspray*[3] as well, whose impersonation of women implicitly suggests that gender is a kind of persistent impersonation that passes as the real. Her/his performance destabilizes the very distinctions between the natural and the artificial, depth and surface, inner and outer through which discourse about genders almost always operates. Is drag the imitation of gender, or does it dramatize the signifying gestures through which gender itself is established? Does being female constitute a "natural fact" or a cultural performance, or is "naturalness" constituted through discursively constrained performative acts that produce the body through and within the categories of sex? Divine notwithstanding, gender practices within gay and lesbian cultures often thematize "the natural" in parodic contexts that bring into relief the performative construction of an original and true sex. What other foundational categories of identity—the binary of sex, gender, and the body—can be shown as productions that create the effect of the natural, the original, and the inevitable?

To expose the foundational categories of sex, gender, and desire as effects of a specific formation of power requires a form of critical inquiry that Foucault, reformulating Nietzsche,[4] designates as "genealogy." A genealogical critique refuses to search for the origins of gender, the inner truth of female

3. *Hairspray* (1988) and *Female Trouble* (1974), films by the independent producer/director John Waters (b. 1946). Divine (born Harris Glenn Milstead, 1945–1988), a 300-pound cross-dresser who starred in many of Waters's films.

4. FRIEDRICH NIETZSCHE (1844–1900), German philosopher. MICHEL FOUCAULT (1926–1984), French philosopher and historian of ideas.

desire, a genuine or authentic sexual identity that repression has kept from view; rather, genealogy investigates the political stakes in designating as an *origin* and *cause* those identity categories that are in fact the *effects* of institutions, practices, discourses with multiple and diffuse points of origin. The task of this inquiry is to center on—and decenter—such defining institutions: phallogocentrism and compulsory heterosexuality.[5]

Precisely because "female" no longer appears to be a stable notion, its meaning is as troubled and unfixed as "women," and because both terms gain their troubled significations only as relational terms, this inquiry takes as its focus gender and the relational analysis it suggests. Further, it is no longer clear that feminist theory ought to try to settle the questions of primary identity in order to get on with the task of politics. Instead, we ought to ask, what political possibilities are the consequence of a radical critique of the categories of identity. What new shape of politics emerges when identity as a common ground no longer constrains the discourse on feminist politics? And to what extent does the effort to locate a common identity as the foundation for a feminist politics preclude a radical inquiry into the political construction and regulation of identity itself?

* * *

From *Chapter 3. Subversive Bodily Acts*

* * *

BODILY INSCRIPTIONS, PERFORMATIVE SUBVERSIONS

> "Garbo 'got in drag' whenever she took some heavy glamour part, whenever she melted in or out of a man's arms, whenever she simply let that heavenly-flexed neck . . . bear the weight of her thrown-back head. . . . How resplendent seems the art of acting! It is all *impersonation*, whether the sex underneath is true or not."
>
> —Parker Tyler, "The Garbo Image,"
> quoted in Esther Newton, *Mother Camp*.[6]

Categories of true sex, discrete gender, and specific sexuality have constituted the stable point of reference for a great deal of feminist theory and politics. These constructs of identity serve as the points of epistemic departure from which theory emerges and politics itself is shaped. In the case of feminism, politics is ostensibly shaped to express the interests, the perspectives, of "women." But is there a political shape to "women," as it were, that precedes and prefigures the political elaboration of their interests and epistemic point of view? How is that identity shaped, and is it a political shaping that takes the very morphology and boundary of the sexed body as the ground, surface, or site of cultural inscription? What circumscribes that site as "the female body"? Is "the body" or "the sexed body" the firm foundation on which

5. A term coined by the American feminist poet ADRIENNE RICH (b. 1929) to indicate society's injunction against all homosexual desires and acts. "Phallogocentrism": a term coined by the French philosopher JACQUES DERRIDA (b. 1930) for the patriarchal dominance of sexuality and the legal system.

6. *Mother Camp: Female Impersonators in America* (Chicago: University of Chicago Press, 1972). Greta Garbo (1905–1990), Swedish-born American film star.

gender and systems of compulsory sexuality operate? Or is "the body" itself shaped by political forces with strategic interests in keeping that body bounded and constituted by the markers of sex?

The sex/gender distinction and the category of sex itself appear to presuppose a generalization of "the body" that preexists the acquisition of its sexed significance. This "body" often appears to be a passive medium that is signified by an inscription from a cultural source figured as "external" to that body. Any theory of the culturally constructed body, however, ought to question "the body" as a construct of suspect generality when it is figured as passive and prior to discourse. There are Christian and Cartesian precedents[7] to such views which, prior to the emergence of vitalistic biologies in the nineteenth century, understand "the body" as so much inert matter, signifying nothing or, more specifically, signifying a profane void, the fallen state: deception, sin, the premonitional metaphorics of hell and the eternal feminine. There are many occasions in both Sartre's and Beauvoir's work where "the body" is figured as a mute facticity, anticipating some meaning that can be attributed only by a transcendent consciousness, understood in Cartesian terms as radically immaterial. But what establishes this dualism for us? What separates off "the body" as indifferent to signification, and signification itself as the act of a radically disembodied consciousness or, rather, the act that radically disembodies that consciousness? To what extent is that Cartesian dualism presupposed in phenomenology[8] adapted to the structuralist frame in which mind/body is redescribed as culture/nature? With respect to gender discourse, to what extent do these problematic dualisms still operate within the very descriptions that are supposed to lead us out of that binarism and its implicit hierarchy? How are the contours of the body clearly marked as the taken-for-granted ground or surface upon which gender significations are inscribed, a mere facticity devoid of value, prior to significance?

Wittig[9] suggests that a culturally specific epistemic *a priori* establishes the naturalness of "sex." But by what enigmatic means has "the body" been accepted as a *prima facie* given that admits of no genealogy? Even within Foucault's essay on the very theme of genealogy, the body is figured as a surface and the scene of a cultural inscription: "the body is the inscribed surface of events."[1] The task of genealogy, he claims, is "to expose a body totally imprinted by history." His sentence continues, however, by referring to the goal of "history"—here clearly understood on the model of Freud's "civilization"—as the "destruction of the body" (148). Forces and impulses with multiple directionalities are precisely that which history both destroys and preserves through the *entstehung* (historical event) of inscription. As "a volume in perpetual disintegration" (148), the body is always under siege, suffering destruction by the very terms of history. And history is the creation of values and meanings by a signifying practice that requires the subjection

7. In the dualistic system of the French philosopher René Descartes (1596–1650), spirit and matter are mutually exclusive.

8. A philosophical method restricted to analyzing the intellectual processes of which we are introspectively aware (while ignoring external objects, the question of whose existence is "bracketed").

9. MONIQUE WITTIG (b. 1935), French feminist novelist.

1. Michel Foucault, "Nietzsche, Genealogy, History," in *Language, Counter-Memory, Practice*, ed. Donald F. Bouchard, trans. Donald F. Bouchard and Sherry Simon (Ithaca: Cornell University Press, 1977), p. 148 [Butler's note]. Some of the author's notes are edited, and some omitted.

of the body. This corporeal destruction is necessary to produce the speaking subject and its significations. This is a body, described through the language of surface and force, weakened through a "single drama" of domination, inscription, and creation (150). This is not the *modus vivendi* of one kind of history rather than another, but is, for Foucault, "history" (148) in its essential and repressive gesture.

Although Foucault writes, "Nothing in man [*sic*]—not even his body—is sufficiently stable to serve as the basis for self-recognition or for understanding other men [*sic*]" (153), he nevertheless points to the constancy of cultural inscription as a "single drama" that acts on the body. If the creation of values, that historical mode of signification, requires the destruction of the body, much as the instrument of torture in Kafka's *In the Penal Colony*[2] destroys the body on which it writes, then there must be a body prior to that inscription, stable and self-identical, subject to that sacrificial destruction. In a sense, for Foucault, as for Nietzsche, cultural values emerge as the result of an inscription on the body, understood as a medium, indeed, a blank page; in order for this inscription to signify, however, that medium must itself be destroyed—that is, fully transvaluated into a sublimated domain of values. Within the metaphorics of this notion of cultural values is the figure of history as a relentless writing instrument, and the body as the medium which must be destroyed and transfigured in order for "culture" to emerge.

By maintaining a body prior to its cultural inscription, Foucault appears to assume a materiality prior to signification and form. Because this distinction operates as essential to the task of genealogy as he defines it, the distinction itself is precluded as an object of genealogical investigation. Occasionally in his analysis of Herculine,[3] Foucault subscribes to a prediscursive multiplicity of bodily forces that break through the surface of the body to disrupt the regulating practices of cultural coherence imposed upon that body by a power regime, understood as a vicissitude of "history." If the presumption of some kind of precategorial source of disruption is refused, is it still possible to give a genealogical account of the demarcation of the body as such as a signifying practice? This demarcation is not initiated by a reified history or by a subject. This marking is the result of a diffuse and active structuring of the social field. This signifying practice effects a social space for and of the body within certain regulatory grids of intelligibility.

Mary Douglas' *Purity and Danger* suggests that the very contours of "the body" are established through markings that seek to establish specific codes of cultural coherence. Any discourse that establishes the boundaries of the body serves the purpose of instating and naturalizing certain taboos regarding the appropriate limits, postures, and modes of exchange that define what it is that constitutes bodies:

> ideas about separating, purifying, demarcating and punishing transgressions have as their main function to impose system on an inherently untidy experience. It is only by exaggerating the difference between within and without, above and below, male and female, with and against, that a semblance of order is created.[4]

2. A 1919 story by Franz Kafka (1883–1924), Austrian writer who was born and lived most of his life in Prague.

3. Herculine Barbin, a 19th-century French hermaphrodite whose memoirs were published in 1978 with an introduction by Foucault (discussed by Butler earlier in this chapter).

4. Mary Douglas, *Purity and Danger* (London: Routledge and Kegan Paul, 1969) p. 4 [Butler's note]. Douglas (1921), Italian-born anthropologist.

Although Douglas clearly subscribes to a structuralist distinction between an inherently unruly nature and an order imposed by cultural means, the "untidiness" to which she refers can be redescribed as a region of *cultural* unruliness and disorder. Assuming the inevitably binary structure of the nature/culture distinction, Douglas cannot point toward an alternative configuration of culture in which such distinctions become malleable or proliferate beyond the binary frame. Her analysis, however, provides a possible point of departure for understanding the relationship by which social taboos institute and maintain the boundaries of the body as such. Her analysis suggests that what constitutes the limit of the body is never merely material, but that the surface, the skin, is systemically signified by taboos and anticipated transgressions; indeed, the boundaries of the body become, within her analysis, the limits of the social *per se*. A poststructuralist appropriation of her view might well understand the boundaries of the body as the limits of the socially *hegemonic*. In a variety of cultures, she maintains, there are

> pollution powers which inhere in the structure of ideas itself and which punish a symbolic breaking of that which should be joined or joining of that which should be separate. It follows from this that pollution is a type of danger which is not likely to occur except where the lines of structure, cosmic or social, are clearly defined.
>
> A polluting person is always in the wrong. He [*sic*] has developed some wrong condition or simply crossed over some line which should not have been crossed and this displacement unleashes danger for someone.[5]

In a sense, Simon Watney has identified the contemporary construction of "the polluting person" as the person with AIDS in his *Policing Desire: AIDS, Pornography, and the Media*.[6] Not only is the illness figured as the "gay disease," but throughout the media's hysterical and homophobic response to the illness there is a tactical construction of a continuity between the polluted status of the homosexual by virtue of the boundary-trespass that *is* homosexuality and the disease as a specific modality of homosexual pollution. That the disease is transmitted through the exchange of bodily fluids suggests within the sensationalist graphics of homophobic signifying systems the dangers that permeable bodily boundaries present to the social order as such. Douglas remarks that "the body is a model that can stand for any bounded system. Its boundaries can represent any boundaries which are threatened or precarious."[7] And she asks a question which one might have expected to read in Foucault: "Why should bodily margins be thought to be specifically invested with power and danger?"[8]

Douglas suggests that all social systems are vulnerable at their margins, and that all margins are accordingly considered dangerous. If the body is synecdochal for the social system *per se* or a site in which open systems converge, then any kind of unregulated permeability constitutes a site of pollution and endangerment. Since anal and oral sex among men clearly establishes certain kinds of bodily permeabilities unsanctioned by the hegemonic order, male homosexuality would, within such a hegemonic point of view, constitute a site of danger and pollution, prior to and regardless of the

5. Ibid., p. 113 [Butler's note].
6. Simon Watney, *Policing Desire: AIDS, Pornography, and the Media* (Minneapolis: University of Minnesota Press, 1988) [Butler's note].
7. Douglas, *Purity and Danger*, p. 115 [Butler's note].
8. Ibid., p. 121 [Butler's note].

cultural presence of AIDS. Similarly, the "polluted" status of lesbians, regardless of their low-risk status with respect to AIDS, brings into relief the dangers of their bodily exchanges. Significantly, being "outside" the hegemonic order does not signify being "in" a state of filthy and untidy nature. Paradoxically, homosexuality is almost always conceived within the homophobic signifying economy as *both* uncivilized and unnatural.

The construction of stable bodily contours relies upon fixed sites of corporeal permeability and impermeability. Those sexual practices in both homosexual and heterosexual contexts that open surfaces and orifices to erotic signification or close down others effectively reinscribe the boundaries of the body along new cultural lines. Anal sex among men is an example, as is the radical re-membering of the body in Wittig's *The Lesbian Body*.[9] Douglas alludes to "a kind of sex pollution which expresses a desire to keep the body (physical and social) intact,"[1] suggesting that the naturalized notion of "the" body is itself a consequence of taboos that render that body discrete by virtue of its stable boundaries. Further, the rites of passage that govern various bodily orifices presuppose a heterosexual construction of gendered exchange, positions, and erotic possibilities. The deregulation of such exchanges accordingly disrupts the very boundaries that determine what it is to be a body at all. Indeed, the critical inquiry that traces the regulatory practices within which bodily contours are constructed constitutes precisely the genealogy of "the body" in its discreteness that might further radicalize Foucault's theory.[2]

Significantly, Kristeva's discussion of abjection in *The Powers of Horror* begins to suggest the uses of this structuralist notion of a boundary-constituting taboo for the purposes of constructing a discrete subject through exclusion.[3] The "abject" designates that which has been expelled from the body, discharged as excrement, literally rendered "Other." This appears as an expulsion of alien elements, but the alien is effectively established through this expulsion. The construction of the "not-me" as the abject establishes the boundaries of the body which are also the first contours of the subject. Kristeva writes:

> *nausea* makes me balk at that milk cream, separates me from the mother and father who proffer it. "I" want none of that element, sign of their desire; "I" do not want to listen, "I" do not assimilate it, "I" expel it. But since the food is not an "other" for "me," who am only in their desire, I expel *myself*, I spit *myself* out, I abject *myself* within the same motion through which "I" claim to establish myself.[4]

9. Published in 1973.
1. Douglas, *Purity and Danger*, p. 140 [Butler's note].
2. Foucault's essay "A Preface to Transgression" (in *Language, Counter-Memory, Practice*) does provide an interesting juxtaposition with Douglas's notion of body boundaries constituted by incest taboos. Originally written in honor of Georges Bataille, this essay explores in part the metaphorical "dirt" of transgressive pleasures and the association of the forbidden orifice with the dirt-covered tomb. See pp. 46–48 [Butler's note]. Bataille (1897–1962), French novelist and philosopher.
3. Kristeva discusses Mary Douglas's work in a short section of *The Powers of Horror: An Essay on Abjection*, trans. Leon Roudiez (New York: Columbia University Press, 1982), originally published as *Pouvoirs de l'horreur* (1980). Assimilating Douglas's insights to her own reformulation of Lacan, Kristeva writes, "Defilement is what is jettisoned from the *symbolic system*. It is what escapes that social rationality, that logical order on which a social aggregate is based, which then becomes differentiated from a temporary agglomeration of individuals and, in short, constitutes a *classification system* or *a structure*" (p. 65) [Butler's note]. JULIA KRISTEVA (b. 1941), French feminist literary critic and psychoanalyst.
4. Ibid., p. 63.

The boundary of the body as well as the distinction between internal and external is established through the ejection and transvaluation of something originally part of identity into a defiling otherness. As Iris Young has suggested in her use of Kristeva to understand sexism, homophobia, and racism, the repudiation of bodies for their sex, sexuality, and/or color is an "expulsion" followed by a "repulsion" that founds and consolidates culturally hegemonic identities along sex/race/sexuality axes of differentiation.[5] Young's appropriation of Kristeva shows how the operation of repulsion can consolidate "identities" founded on the instituting of the "Other" or a set of Others through exclusion and domination. What constitutes through division the "inner" and "outer" worlds of the subject is a border and boundary tenuously maintained for the purposes of social regulation and control. The boundary between the inner and outer is confounded by those excremental passages in which the inner effectively becomes outer, and this excreting function becomes, as it were, the model by which other forms of identity-differentiation are accomplished. In effect, this is the mode by which Others become shit. For inner and outer worlds to remain utterly distinct, the entire surface of the body would have to achieve an impossible impermeability. This sealing of its surfaces would constitute the seamless boundary of the subject; but this enclosure would invariably be exploded by precisely that excremental filth that it fears.

Regardless of the compelling metaphors of the spatial distinctions of inner and outer, they remain linguistic terms that facilitate and articulate a set of fantasies, feared and desired. "Inner" and "outer" make sense only with reference to a mediating boundary that strives for stability. And this stability, this coherence, is determined in large part by cultural orders that sanction the subject and compel its differentiation from the abject. Hence, "inner" and "outer" constitute a binary distinction that stabilizes and consolidates the coherent subject. When that subject is challenged, the meaning and necessity of the terms are subject to displacement. If the "inner world" no longer designates a topos,[6] then the internal fixity of the self and, indeed, the internal locale of gender identity, become similarly suspect. The critical question is not *how* did that identity become *internalized?* as if internalization were a process or a mechanism that might be descriptively reconstructed. Rather, the question is: From what strategic position in public discourse and for what reasons has the trope of interiority and the disjunctive binary of inner/outer taken hold? In what language is "inner space" figured? What kind of figuration is it, and through what figure of the body is it signified? How does a body figure on its surface the very invisibility of its hidden depth?

From Interiority to Gender Performatives

In *Discipline and Punish* Foucault challenges the language of internalization as it operates in the service of the disciplinary regime of the subjection and subjectivation of criminals. Although Foucault objected to what he

5. Iris Marion Young, "Objection and Oppression; Unconscious Dynamics of Racism, Sexism, and Homophobia," paper presented at the Society of Phenomenology and Existential Philosophy Meetings, Northwestern University, 1988. The paper is included as part of a larger chapter [chapter 5] in *Justice and the Politics of Difference* (1990) [Butler's note].

6. Place (Greek).

understood to be the psychoanalytic belief in the "inner" truth of sex in *The History of Sexuality*, he turns to a criticism of the doctrine of internalization for separate purposes in the context of his history of criminology. In a sense, *Discipline and Punish* can be read as Foucault's effort to rewrite Nietzsche's doctrine of internalization in *On the Genealogy of Morals* on the model of *inscription*. In the context of prisoners, Foucault writes, the strategy has been not to enforce a repression of their desires, but to compel their bodies to signify the prohibitive law as their very essence, style, and necessity. That law is not literally internalized, but incorporated, with the consequence that bodies are produced which signify that law on and through the body; there the law is manifest as the essence of their selves, the meaning of their soul, their conscience, the law of their desire. In effect, the law is at once fully manifest and fully latent, for it never appears as external to the bodies it subjects and subjectivates. Foucault writes:

> It would be wrong to say that the soul is an illusion, or an ideological effect. On the contrary, it exists, it has a reality, it is produced permanently *around, on, within*, the body by the functioning of a power that is exercised on those that are punished [my emphasis].[7]

The figure of the interior soul understood as "within" the body is signified through its inscription *on* the body, even though its primary mode of signification is through its very absence, its potent invisibility. The effect of a structuring inner space is produced through the signification of a body as a vital and sacred enclosure. The soul is precisely what the body lacks; hence, the body presents itself as a signifying lack. That lack which *is* the body signifies the soul as that which cannot show. In this sense, then, the soul is a surface signification that contests and displaces the inner/outer distinction itself, a figure of interior psychic space inscribed *on* the body as a social signification that perpetually renounces itself as such. In Foucault's terms, the soul is not imprisoned by or within the body, as some Christian imagery would suggest, but "the soul is the prison of the body."[8]

The redescription of intrapsychic processes in terms of the surface politics of the body implies a corollary redescription of gender as the disciplinary production of the figures of fantasy through the play of presence and absence on the body's surface, the construction of the gendered body through a series of exclusions and denials, signifying absences. But what determines the manifest and latent text of the body politic? What is the prohibitive law that generates the corporeal stylization of gender, the fantasied and fantastic figuration of the body? We have already considered the incest taboo and the prior taboo against homosexuality as the generative moments of gender identity,[9] the prohibitions that produce identity along the culturally intelligible grids of an idealized and compulsory heterosexuality. That disciplinary production of gender effects a false stabilization of gender in the interests of the heterosexual construction and regulation of sexuality within the reproductive domain. The construction of coherence conceals the gender discontinuities that run rampant within heterosexual, bisexual, and gay and lesbian

7. Michel Foucault, *Discipline and Punish: The Birth of the Prison*, trans. Alan Sheridan (New York: Vintage, 1979), p. 29 [Butler's note]. *The History of Sexuality* was published in 1976, *On the Genealogy of Morals* in 1887.
8. Ibid., p. 30 [Butler's note].
9. In chapter 2 of *Gender Trouble*.

contexts in which gender does not necessarily follow from sex, and desire, or sexuality generally, does not seem to follow from gender—indeed, where none of these dimensions of significant corporeality express or reflect one another. When the disorganization and disaggregation of the field of bodies disrupt the regulatory fiction of heterosexual coherence, it seems that the expressive model loses its descriptive force. That regulatory ideal is then exposed as a norm and a fiction that disguises itself as a developmental law regulating the sexual field that it purports to describe.

According to the understanding of identification as an enacted fantasy or incorporation, however, it is clear that coherence is desired, wished for, idealized, and that this idealization is an effect of a corporeal signification. In other words, acts, gestures, and desire produce the effect of an internal core or substance, but produce this *on the surface* of the body, through the play of signifying absences that suggest, but never reveal, the organizing principle of identity as a cause. Such acts, gestures, enactments, generally construed, are *performative* in the sense that the essence or identity that they otherwise purport to express are *fabrications* manufactured and sustained through corporeal signs and other discursive means. That the gendered body is performative suggests that it has no ontological status apart from the various acts which constitute its reality. This also suggests that if that reality is fabricated as an interior essence, that very interiority is an effect and function of a decidedly public and social discourse, the public regulation of fantasy through the surface politics of the body, the gender border control that differentiates inner from outer, and so institutes the "integrity" of the subject. In other words, acts and gestures, articulated and enacted desires create the illusion of an interior and organizing gender core, an illusion discursively maintained for the purposes of the regulation of sexuality within the obligatory frame of reproductive heterosexuality. If the "cause" of desire, gesture, and act can be localized within the "self" of the actor, then the political regulations and disciplinary practices which produce that ostensibly coherent gender are effectively displaced from view. The displacement of a political and discursive origin of gender identity onto a psychological "core" precludes an analysis of the political constitution of the gendered subject and its fabricated notions about the ineffable interiority of its sex or of its true identity.

If the inner truth of gender is a fabrication and if a true gender is a fantasy instituted and inscribed on the surface of bodies, then it seems that genders can be neither true nor false, but are only produced as the truth effects of a discourse of primary and stable identity. In *Mother Camp: Female Impersonators in America*, anthropologist Esther Newton suggests that the structure of impersonation reveals one of the key fabricating mechanisms through which the social construction of gender takes place. I would suggest as well that drag fully subverts the distinction between inner and outer psychic space and effectively mocks both the expressive model of gender and the notion of a true gender identity. Newton writes:

> At its most complex, [drag] is a double inversion that says, "appearance is an illusion." Drag says [Newton's curious personification] "my 'outside' appearance is feminine, but my essence 'inside' [the body] is masculine." At the same time it symbolizes the opposite inversion; "my appearance

'outside' [my body, my gender] is masculine but my essence 'inside' [myself] is feminine."[1]

Both claims to truth contradict one another and so displace the entire enactment of gender significations from the discourse of truth and falsity.

The notion of an original or primary gender identity is often parodied within the cultural practices of drag, cross-dressing, and the sexual stylization of butch/femme identities. Within feminist theory, such parodic identities have been understood to be either degrading to women, in the case of drag and cross-dressing, or an uncritical appropriation of sex-role stereotyping from within the practice of heterosexuality, especially in the case of butch/femme lesbian identities. But the relation between the "imitation" and the "original" is, I think, more complicated than that critique generally allows. Moreover, it gives us a clue to the way in which the relationship between primary identification—that is, the original meanings accorded to gender—and subsequent gender experience might be reframed. The performance of drag plays upon the distinction between the anatomy of the performer and the gender that is being performed. But we are actually in the presence of three contingent dimensions of significant corporeality: anatomical sex, gender identity, and gender performance. If the anatomy of the performer is already distinct from the gender of the performer, and both of those are distinct from the gender of the performance, then the performance suggests a dissonance not only between sex and performance, but sex and gender, and gender and performance. As much as drag creates a unified picture of "woman" (what its critics often oppose), it also reveals the distinctness of those aspects of gendered experience which are falsely naturalized as a unity through the regulatory fiction of heterosexual coherence. *In imitating gender, drag implicitly reveals the imitative structure of gender itself—as well as its contingency.* Indeed, part of the pleasure, the giddiness of the performance is in the recognition of a radical contingency in the relation between sex and gender in the face of cultural configurations of causal unities that are regularly assumed to be natural and necessary. In the place of the law of heterosexual coherence, we see sex and gender denaturalized by means of a performance which avows their distinctness and dramatizes the cultural mechanism of their fabricated unity.

The notion of gender parody defended here does not assume that there is an original which such parodic identities imitate. Indeed, the parody is *of* the very notion of an original; just as the psychoanalytic notion of gender identification is constituted by a fantasy of a fantasy, the transfiguration of an Other who is always already a "figure" in that double sense, so gender parody reveals that the original identity after which gender fashions itself is an imitation without an origin. To be more precise, it is a production which, in effect—that is, in its effect—postures as an imitation. This perpetual displacement constitutes a fluidity of identities that suggests an openness to resignification and recontextualization; parodic proliferation deprives hegemonic culture and its critics of the claim to naturalized or essentialist gender identities. Although the gender meanings taken up in these parodic styles are clearly part of hegemonic, misogynist culture, they are nevertheless

1. Newton, *Mother Camp*, p. 103 [Butler's note].

denaturalized and mobilized through their parodic recontextualization. As imitations which effectively displace the meaning of the original, they imitate the myth of originality itself. In the place of an original identification which serves as a determining cause, gender identity might be reconceived as a personal/cultural history of received meanings subject to a set of imitative practices which refer laterally to other imitations and which, jointly, construct the illusion of a primary and interior gendered self or parody the mechanism of that construction.

According to Fredric Jameson's "Postmodernism and Consumer Society," the imitation that mocks the notion of an original is characteristic of pastiche rather than parody:

> Pastiche is, like parody, the imitation of a peculiar or unique style, the wearing of a stylistic mask, speech in a dead language: but it is a neutral practice of mimicry, without parody's ulterior motive, without the satirical impulse, without laughter, without that still latent feeling that there exists something *normal* compared to which what is being imitated is rather comic. Pastiche is blank parody, parody that has lost its humor.[2]

The loss of the sense of "the normal," however, can be its own occasion for laughter, especially when "the normal," "the original" is revealed to be a copy, and an inevitably failed one, an ideal that no one *can* embody. In this sense, laughter emerges in the realization that all along the original was derived.

Parody by itself is not subversive, and there must be a way to understand what makes certain kinds of parodic repetitions effectively disruptive, truly troubling, and which repetitions become domesticated and recirculated as instruments of cultural hegemony.[3] A typology of actions would clearly not suffice, for parodic displacement, indeed, parodic laughter, depends on a context and reception in which subversive confusions can be fostered. What performance where will invert the inner/outer distinction and compel a radical rethinking of the psychological presuppositions of gender identity and sexuality? What performance where will compel a reconsideration of the *place* and stability of the masculine and the feminine? And what kind of gender performance will enact and reveal the performativity of gender itself in a way that destabilizes the naturalized categories of identity and desire.

If the body is not a "being," but a variable boundary, a surface whose permeability is politically regulated, a signifying practice within a cultural field of gender hierarchy and compulsory heterosexuality, then what language is left for understanding this corporeal enactment, gender, that constitutes its "interior" signification on its surface? Sartre would perhaps have called this act "a style of being," Foucault, "a stylistics of existence." And in my earlier reading of Beauvoir,[4] I suggest that gendered bodies are so many "styles of the flesh." These styles all never fully self-styled, for styles have a history, and those histories condition and limit the possibilities. Consider gender, for instance, as *a corporeal style*, an "act," as it were, which is both intentional

2. Fredric Jameson, "Postmodernism and Consumer Society," in *The Anti-Aesthetic: Essays on Postmodern Culture*, ed. Hal Foster (Port Townshend, Wash.: Bay Press, 1983), p. 114 [Butler's note]. JAMESON (b. 1934), U.S. Marxist literary critic.

3. The manufactured consent that legitimates a dominant group and unifies a society, as theorized by the Italian Marxist ANTONIO GRAMSCI (1891–1937).

4. In chapter 1 of *Gender Trouble*.

and performative, where "*performative*" suggests a dramatic and contingent construction of meaning.

Wittig understands gender as the workings of "sex," where "sex" is an obligatory injunction for the body to become a cultural sign, to materialize itself in obedience to a historically delimited possibility, and to do this, not once or twice, but as a sustained and repeated corporeal project. The notion of a "project," however, suggests the originating force of a radical will, and because gender is a project which has cultural survival as its end, the term *strategy* better suggests the situation of duress under which gender performance always and variously occurs. Hence, as a strategy of survival within compulsory systems, gender is a performance with clearly punitive consequences. Discrete genders are part of what "humanizes" individuals within contemporary culture; indeed, we regularly punish those who fail to do their gender right. Because there is neither an "essence" that gender expresses or externalizes nor an objective ideal to which gender aspires, and because gender is not a fact, the various acts of gender create the idea of gender, and without those acts, there would be no gender at all. Gender is, thus, a construction that regularly conceals its genesis; the tacit collective agreement to perform, produce, and sustain discrete and polar genders as cultural fictions is obscured by the credibility of those productions—and the punishments that attend not agreeing to believe in them; the construction "compels" our belief in its necessity and naturalness. The historical possibilities materialized through various corporeal styles are nothing other than those punitively regulated cultural fictions alternately embodied and deflected under duress.

Consider that a sedimentation of gender norms produces the peculiar phenomenon of a "natural sex" or a "real woman" or any number of prevalent and compelling social fictions, and that this is a sedimentation that over time has produced a set of corporeal styles which, in reified form, appear as the natural configuration of bodies into sexes existing in a binary relation to one another. If these styles are enacted, and if they produce the coherent gendered subjects who pose as their originators, what kind of performance might reveal this ostensible "cause" to be an "effect"?

In what senses, then, is gender an act? As in other ritual social dramas, the action of gender requires a performance that is *repeated*. This repetition is at once a reenactment and reexperiencing of a set of meanings already socially established; and it is the mundane and ritualized form of their legitimation.[5] Although there are individual bodies that enact these significations by becoming stylized into gendered modes, this "action" is a public action. There are temporal and collective dimensions to these actions, and their public character is not inconsequential; indeed, the performance is effected with the strategic aim of maintaining gender within its binary frame—an aim that cannot be attributed to a subject, but, rather, must be understood to found and consolidate the subject.

Gender ought not to be construed as a stable identity or locus of agency from which various acts follow; rather, gender is an identity tenuously constituted in time, instituted in an exterior space through a *stylized repetition*

5. See Victor Turner, *Dramas, Fields, and Metaphors* (Ithaca: Cornell University Press, 1974). See also Clifford Geertz, "Blurred Genres: The Refiguration of Thought," in *Local Knowledge: Further Essays in Interpretive Anthropology* (New York: Basic Books, 1983) [Butler's note].

of acts. The effect of gender is produced through the stylization of the body and, hence, must be understood as the mundane way in which bodily gestures, movements, and styles of various kinds constitute the illusion of an abiding gendered self. This formulation moves the conception of gender off the ground of a substantial model of identity to one that requires a conception of gender as a constituted *social temporality.* Significantly, if gender is instituted through acts which are internally discontinuous, then the *appearance of substance* is precisely that, a constructed identity, a performative accomplishment which the mundane social audience, including the actors themselves, come to believe and to perform in the mode of belief. Gender is also a norm that can never be fully internalized; "the internal" is a surface signification, and gender norms are finally phantasmatic, impossible to embody. If the ground of gender identity is the stylized repetition of acts through time and not a seemingly seamless identity, then the spatial metaphor of a "ground" will be displaced and revealed as a stylized configuration, indeed, a gendered corporealization of time. The abiding gendered self will then be shown to be structured by repeated acts that seek to approximate the ideal of a substantial ground of identity, but which, in their occasional *dis*continuity, reveal the temporal and contingent groundlessness of this "ground." The possibilities of gender transformation are to be found precisely in the arbitrary relation between such acts, in the possibility of a failure to repeat, a de-formity, or a parodic repetition that exposes the phantasmatic effect of abiding identity as a politically tenuous construction.

If gender attributes, however, are not expressive but performative, then these attributes effectively constitute the identity they are said to express or reveal. The distinction between expression and performativeness is crucial. If gender attributes and acts, the various ways in which a body shows or produces its cultural signification, are performative, then there is no preexisting identity by which an act or attribute might be measured; there would be no true or false, real or distorted acts of gender, and the postulation of a true gender identity would be revealed as a regulatory fiction. That gender reality is created through sustained social performances means that the very notions of an essential sex and a true or abiding masculinity or femininity are also constituted as part of the strategy that conceals gender's performative character and the performative possibilities for proliferating gender configurations outside the restricting frames of masculinist domination and compulsory heterosexuality.

Genders can be neither true nor false, neither real nor apparent, neither original nor derived. As credible bearers of those attributes, however, genders can also be rendered thoroughly and radically *incredible*.

1990

STUART MOULTHROP
b. 1957

By the late 1990s almost all American college and university students had access to the Internet, and many schools required incoming students to own a personal computer. The reliance on this technology represents a vast change in education and particularly in the production and transmission of written texts. Many predict that just as the printing press revolutionized writing, thinking, and education, so the spread of electronic media will revolutionize writing, publishing, and our very perception of written texts. Stuart Moulthrop's "You Say You Want a Revolution? Hypertext and the Laws of Media" (1991; rev. 1993) reviews the history and development of hypertext, assesses its possibilities, and sketches some of its links with postmodernist theory.

Born in Baltimore, Maryland, Moulthrop received his B.A. from George Washington University in 1979 and his Ph.D. from Yale University in 1986. He has taught at Yale, the University of Texas at Austin, and the Georgia Institute of Technology; since 1994 he has been on the faculty of the School of Communications Design of the University of Baltimore. He co-edited the innovative online humanities journal *Postmodern Culture* from 1995 to 1999, overseeing a pioneering hypertext special issue of the journal in 1997. In a series of essays written through the 1990s, Moulthrop was among the first analysts of the new electronic media and their relation to literature and theory, and one of the first practitioners of hypertextual fiction.

Hypertexts—a term coined by Theodor Nelson in 1965—are electronic documents connected by links that the reader can activate. The reader uses a software viewer or browser that recognizes links as commands and thus can open the document anchored by the link. These documents can be not only writings but photographs, audio files, drawings, or any other digitized materials; the reader can choose which links to follow, interacting with and activating the work. Hypertext changes the act of reading so that each text includes diverse other texts, promoting a version of what the poststructuralist theorist JULIA KRISTEVA has termed "intertextuality" as a matter of course. Unlike books, hypertexts make possible the juxtaposition of other media and support a mode of connection that does not depend on traditional linear, hierarchical models. In perusing hypertexts, one finds multiple pathways of reading.

Hypertext matured in the 1990s with the advent of the World Wide Web, which expanded the possible links to an incalculable number and held out the promise of new kinds of writing, a revisionary aesthetics of pastiche, new disciplinary arrangements, and a more democratic politics. Several writers, the novelist Robert Coover and Moulthrop himself among them, have explored the possibilities and implications of the medium for fiction. Influenced in part by WALTER BENJAMIN (especially "The Work of Art in the Age of Mechanical Reproduction," 1936; see above) and by the Canadian media critic Marshall McLuhan (1911–1980), who argue that media are not neutral carriers but influence social thought and organization, many intellectuals believe that hypertext heralds a paradigm shift away from the age of the codex or printed documents to a more democratic and interactive way of thinking.

Moulthrop both values the transformative potential of hypertext and criticizes its indiscriminate promotion. For him, particular strengths of hypertext include its ability to constructively disrupt traditional thinking practices, its ability to make visible the assumptions and practices that structure both reading and social life, and its ability to produce more critical readers. Moulthrop's writings invoke the metaphor of a "breakdown" or "crash" to express the arresting power of hypertext, a power founded on structural instability. Cybertexts—texts in virtual writing space—are "structures for breakdown, ways of thinking critically and creatively about all the plausible, deceptive constructions we find in cyberspace," he writes in one essay. Breakdowns violate reader expectations, change the predicted course of reading, and open up possibilities for new paradigm shifts; they promote a radical form of what the Russian formalists (such as BORIS EICHENBAUM) termed "defamiliarization." In another essay, Moulthrop argues that "the act of reading in hypertext is constituted as struggle: a chapter of chances, a chain of detours, a series of revealing failures," a struggle that yields pleasure and counters the centralizing power of the system in which electronic writing takes part. In his own published hypertexts, the medium serves to destabilize the reader's complacency. His *Victory Garden* (1991), focusing on the Gulf War of 1991, uses hypertextual language to engage U.S. political culture. In "Hegirascope" (1995), another attempt to situate the reader in a "structure for breakdown," timed links—that is, links that appear only for a set period of time—construct a world that changes on its own as the reader attempts to control it.

In "You Say You Want a Revolution," our selection, Moulthrop reviews the early history of hypertext and sorts through the disparate views of its possibilities. He does not embrace the claim that hypertext by itself will bring about a revolution in culture or reading; rather, hypertext provides a way of talking about ambiguous impulses in postmodern culture. For Moulthrop, hypertext enhances textuality: it does not displace literacy, as some fear, but works to counter "post-literacy" in the age of television. Surprisingly, it retrieves many elements of typographic culture. Moulthrop notes the possible danger of hypertext's being controlled by large corporations, but he suggests that emerging technology may shatter such constraints.

Relying on a broad range of references, Moulthrop shows how hypertext is linked with contemporary poststructuralist theory, particularly in its promotion of intertextuality and the active engagement of the reader. This engaged reader resembles the one sought by ROLAND BARTHES when he praised the more active "writerly text" over the conventional "readerly" work meant to be passively consumed. Moulthrop also notes a parallel with deconstructive theory in hypertext's disruption of language. And he explains that hypertext realizes JEAN BAUDRILLARD's notion of the simulacrum, because the writing on a computer monitor is not physically "there" in the same way that printed text exists on a page—hypertext is virtual, "always a simulacrum for which no physical instantiation exists." Making another poststructuralist connection, Moulthrop suggests that hypermedia embodies GILLES DELEUZE AND FÉLIX GUATTARI's notion of the rhizome, a sprawling network that has no origin, end point, trajectory, or hierarchy.

While some critics celebrate hypertext for its promise of new paradigms, new art, and new political practice, others decry it for the same reasons. Some lament the loss of print culture and the simple pleasures of reading a book. Neil Postman, an American critic of culture and education, argues that interactive media stupefy the public, displace active writing and thinking, and deny the real social world outside the machine; like most who hold these views, he sees computer-mediated games as exemplifying these points. Others, more hopeful about the technological trend, criticize today's hypermedia as not going far enough in challenging traditional aesthetic and political paradigms. Though it appears to undermine readerly passivity, its openness and interactivity are limited to preset choices determined for the reader. Other critics worry about corporate and government controls on a medium intended to promote free and unlimited exchange. In his self-consciously balanced assessment of hypertext, Moulthrop notes that we should be both hopeful about its future and skeptical—borrowing from postmodern writers, he uses the word "paranoid"—about the ongoing development of hypermedia; as he warns, "it seems equally possible that our engagement with interactive media will follow the path of reaction, not revolution."

BIBLIOGRAPHY

Stuart Moulthrop has written numerous essays on hypertext, among them "Rhizome and Resistance: Hypertext and the Dreams of a New Culture," in a pioneering anthology, *Hyper / Text / Theory* (ed. George Landow, 1994); "Traveling in the Breakdown Lane: A Principle of Resistance for Hypertext," in a special issue of the journal *Mosaic* 28 (1995); "Media Matters: Technologies of Literary Production"; "Decorating the Corpse: Hypertext after the Web," the introduction to a 1997 special issue of *Postmodern Culture* on hypertext that Moulthrop edited; "No War Machine," in the anthology *Reading Matters: Narrative in the New Media Ecology* (ed. Joseph Tabbi and Michael Wutz, 1997); and "Everybody's Elegies," the concluding response to the collection *Passions, Pedagogies, and Twenty-first Century Technologies* (ed. Gail E. Hawisher and Cynthia L. Selfe, 2000). A practitioner of as well as a commentator on hypertext, Moulthrop is the author of some of the earliest hyperfictions, including *Victory Garden* (1991); "Dreamtime" (1992); "Hegirascope" (1995); "The Color of Television," with Sean Cohen (1996); "Hegirascope 2" (1997); and "Reagan Library" (1999).

In "Trivializing or Liberating? The Limitations of Hypertext Theorizing," *Mosaic* 32 (1999), David Miall criticizes Moulthrop and other advocates of hypertext, finding that claims on its behalf have been too universalizing, have too reductively deprecated print literature, and have misunderstood the nature of literary reading. J. Yellowlees Douglas, *The End of Books—Or Books without End? Reading Interactive Narratives* (2000), examines the possible advantages of hypertext over print fiction, noting the multiple openings and endings of Moulthrop's hypertexts. Many sources for hypertext, aptly enough, are on the World Wide Web.

You Say You Want a Revolution? Hypertext and the Laws of Media

1 When this essay first appeared, all of two years ago,[1] very few people outside the information sciences had heard of **hypertext**, a technology for creating electronic documents in which the user's access to information is not constrained, as in books, by linear or hierarchical arrangements of discourse. This obscurity had always seemed strange, since **hypertext** has been around for a long time. Its underlying concept—creating and enacting linkages between stored bits of information—originated in 1945 with Vannevar Bush, science advisor to President Roosevelt, who wanted to build a machine called Memex[2] to help researchers organize disparate sources of knowledge.[3] Bush's design, based on microfilm, rotating spools, and photoelectric cells, proved impractical for the mechanical technologies of the late 1940s. But when electronic computers arrived on the academic scene a few years later, Bush's projections were quickly realized. In a sense, all distributed computing systems are **hypertextual**, since they deliver information dynamically in response to users' demands.[4] Indeed, artificial intelligence researchers cre-

1. In the online humanities journal *Postmodern Culture* 1.3, in 1991. This revised version appeared in print.
2. From "memory extension." Bush (1890–1974), an electrical engineer who designed an early computer, directed the U.S. Office of Scientific Research and Development (1941–45) during the later years of Franklin Delano Roosevelt's (1882–1945) presidency.
3. See Vannevar Bush, "As We May Think," *Atlantic Monthly*, July 1945, pp. 101–8; and George Landow, *Hypertext: The Convergence of Contemporary Critical Theory and Technology* (Baltimore: Johns Hopkins University Press, 1992), pp. 14–15 [Moulthrop's note].
4. Jay Bolter, *Writing Space: The Computer, Hypertext, and the History of Writing* (Fairlawn, N.J.: Erlbaum, 1990), pp. 9–10 [Moulthrop's note].

ated the first **hypertextual** narrative, the computer game called "Adventure," in order to experiment with interactive computing in the early 1960s.[5]

It was about this time that Theodor Holm Nelson,[6] a sometime academic 2
and a dedicated promoter of technology, coined the term "**hypertext**." Nelson offered plans for a worldwide network of information, centrally coordinated through a linking and retrieval system he called Xanadu. In a trio of self-published manifestoes (*Computer Lib, Dream Machines, Literary Machines*), Nelson outlined the structure and function of Xanadu, right down to the franchise arrangements for "Silverstands," the informational equivalent of fast-food outlets where users would go to access the system. (This was long before anyone dreamed of personal computers.) Nelson's ideas got serious consideration from computer scientists, notably Douglas Englebart, one of the pioneers of users interface design. Englebart and Nelson collaborated at Brown University in the early 1970s on a **hypertext** system called FRESS, and a number of academic and industrial experiments followed.[7] To a large extent, however, the idea of **hypertext**—which both Bush and Nelson had envisioned as a dynamic, read / write system in which users could both manipulate and alter the textual corpus—was neglected in favor of more rigidly organized models like distributed databases and electronic libraries, systems that operate mainly in a read-only retrieval mode. To Nelson, **hypertext** and other forms of interactive computing represented a powerful force for social change. "Tomorrow's **hypertext** systems have immense political ramifications," he wrote in *Literary Machines*. Yet no one seemed particularly interested in exploring those ramifications, at least not until the mid-1980s, when the personal computer business went ballistic.

1987: the *annus mirabilis*[8] of **hypertext**. Many strange and wonderful 3
things happened in and around that year. Nelson's underground classics, *Computer Lib* and *Dream Machines*, were published by Microsoft Press; Nelson himself joined Autodesk, an industry leader in software development, which announced plans to support Xanadu as a commercial enterprise; the Association for Computing Machinery sponsored the first of its international conferences on **hypertext**; and most important, Apple Computer began giving away HyperCard, an object-oriented **hypertext** system, to anyone who owned a Macintosh personal computer. HyperCard is the Model T[9] of **hypertext**: relatively cheap (originally free), simple to operate (being largely an extension of the Macintosh's graphical user interface), quite crude compared to more state-of-the-art products, but still enormously powerful. In the late 1980s it seemed plausible that HyperCard and other personal computer applications would usher in a new paradigm for textual communication, the logical step beyond desktop publishing to all-electronic documents containing multiple pathways of expression.

It has now been six years since that great unveiling of **hypertext** and no 4
such "digital revolution" has arrived. At one point, sources in the personal computer industry foresaw a burgeoning market for "stackware" and other **hypertextually** organized products; nothing of the kind has materialized.

5. Steven Levy, *Hackers: Heroes of the Computer Revolution* (New York: Dell, 1984), pp. 140–41 [Moulthrop's note].
6. Nelson (b. 1937) published *Computer Lib and Dream Machines* in 1974 and *Literary Machines* in 1981.
7. See Jeffrey Conklin, "Hypertext: An Introduction and Survey," *Computer* 20 (1987): 17–41 [Moulthrop's note].
8. Year of wonders (Latin).
9. That is, like the first mass-produced automobile, the Model T Ford (1908–27). Containing both data and code (computer instructions), HyperCard enabled its objects (data) to interact.

Instead, the most commercially ambitious application of HyperCard in electronic publishing has been the Voyager Company's line of "Expanded Books," based exclusively on print titles and carefully designed to duplicate the look and function of traditional books.[1] True, the **hypertext** concept has finally received some attention from humanist academics. Jay David Bolter's *Writing Space* (1991) outlines a historical view of **hypertext** as the successor to print technology—and with Nelson's *Literary Machines* is one of the first studies of **hypertext** to be presented in **hypertextual** form. George Landow's ***Hypertext*** (1992) places developments in electronic writing within the context of poststructuralist criticism and postmodern culture (and is also due to appear shortly as a **hypertext**). The spectre of **hypertextual** fiction has even been raised by the novelist Robert Coover in the *New York Times Book Review*.[2] But paradoxically (or as fate would have it), this recognition comes when **hypertext** is no longer what one of my colleagues calls a "bleeding edge" technology. Indeed, much of the cachet seems to have bled out of **hypertext,** which has been bumped from the limelight by hazier and more glamorous obsessions: cyberspace, virtual reality, and the Information Highway.

5 Such changes of fashion seem a regular hazard of the postmodern territory—taking *post modo* at its most literal, to mean "after the now" or *the next thing*. Staring down at our desktop, laptop, or palmtop machines—which we know will be obsolete long before we have paid for them—those of us within what Fred Pfeil calls the "baby-boom professional-managerial class" will always desire *the next thing*.[3] Not for nothing have we updated *Star Trek,* our true space Odyssey, into a "Next Generation."[4] We are the generation (and generators) of nextness. Or so Steve Jobs[5] once assumed, somewhat to his present chagrin. Possibly **hypertext,** like Jobs's sophisticated NeXT computer, represents an idea that hasn't quite come to the mainstream of postmodern culture, a precocious curio destined to be dug up years from now and called "strangely ahead of its time." Unfortunately, as Ted Nelson can testify, **hypertext** has been through this process once before. A certain circularity seems to be in play.

6 Perhaps the problem lies not in our technologies or the things we want to do with them, but in our misunderstanding of technological history. Some of us keep saying, as I note in this essay, that we need a revolution, a paradigm shift, a total uprooting of the old information order: an apocalyptic rupture of "blessed break," as Robert Lowell once put it.[6] And yet that is not what we have received, at least so far. Maybe we suffer this disappointment because we do not understand what we are asking for. What could "revolution" mean in a postmodern context? We might look for answers in Baudrillard, Lyotard, Donna Haraway, or Hakim Bey;[7] but Hollywood, as usual, has

1. Dominic Stansberry, "Hyperfiction: Beyond the Garden of the Forking Paths," *New Media*, May 1993, p. 54 [Moulthrop's note].
2. See Robert Coover, "The End of Books," *New York Times Book Review*, June 21, 1992, 1+ [Moulthrop's note].
3. Fred Pfeil, *Another Tale to Tell* (New York: Verso, 1990), p. 98 [Moulthrop's note].
4. *Star Trek: The Next Generation* (1986–94), a television sequel to *Star Trek* (television series, 1966–69; films, 1979–91), set about 100 years later than the original's 23rd century. "A Space Odyssey" was the subtitle of Stanley Kubrick's science fiction film *2001* (1968).
5. Co-founder of Apple Corporation (b. 1955), who left Apple in 1985 after a power struggle and founded NeXT Corporation, producing a highly advanced computer that was a commercial failure; Jobs returned to Apple in 1996.
6. In "For the Union Dead" (1959), by the American lyric poet Lowell (1917–1977).
7. Moulthrop names theorists of postmodernism: the French philosopher JEAN BAUDRILLARD (b. 1929) argues that in postmodernism, representa-

the best line. J. F. Lawton's screenplay for *Under Siege*,[8] last summer's Steven Seagal vehicle, includes an enlightening exchange between a CIA spymaster (played by Nick Mancuso) and a rebellious terrorist formerly in his employ (Tommy Lee Jones). The spook chides the terrorist, reminding him that the sixties are over, "the Movement is dead." Jones's character replies: "Yes! Of course! Hence the name: 'Movement.' It moves a certain distance, then it stops. Revolution gets its name by always coming back around—*in your face*."

Perhaps **hypertext** is just another movement. On one level, it is hard to 7
discriminate among **hypertext**, virtual reality, and next year's interactive cable systems. All three seem to move in the same general direction, attempting to increase and enrich our consumption of information. But as Andrew Ross has noted, undertakings of this type may have large consequences.[9] Potentially at least, they threaten to upset the stability of language-as-property—a possibility with great political ramifications indeed. It might therefore be dangerous to dismiss **hypertext** as merely a local movement, an initiative as dead as the social agendas of the sixties from which it partly sprang. Considering the vicissitudes of **hypertext**'s history, we might indeed call it a "revolution"—if revolution is something that comes full circle, escaping repression to smack us smartly in the face. Such being the case, however, is this revolution something our culture genuinely wants? When it comes to information technologies, what *do* we want? Why are we moving in circles? What is this figure we are weaving, twice or thrice,[1] and what enchantment or enchantment do we wish to contain?

The original Xanadu (Samuel Taylor Coleridge's) came billed as "A Vision in 8
a Dream," designated doubly unreal and thus easily aligned with our era of "operational simulation" where, strawberry fields,[2] nothing is "real" in the first place, since no place is really "first."[3] But all great dreams invite revisions, and these days we find ourselves perpetually on the re-make. So here is a new Xanadu™, the universal **hypertext** system proposed by Theodor Holm Nelson—a vision which, unlike its legendary precursor, cannot be integrated into the dream park of the hyperreal. Hyperreality, we are told, is a site of collapse or implosion where referential or "grounded" utterance becomes indistinguishable from the self-referential and the imaginary. We construct our representational systems not in serial relation to indisputably

tion has been replaced by a simulation of reality that leads to "hyperreality"; for the French philosopher JEAN-FRANÇOIS LYOTARD (1925–1998), postmodernity is characterized by the collapse of all explanatory master narratives; the American feminist HARAWAY (b. 1944) presents a "cyborg" vision of culture in her best-known essay, "A Manifesto for Cyborgs" (1985; see above); and Hakim Bey (pseudonym of Peter Lamborn Wilson) is a philosopher and radical cultural critic whose influential 'zine publications are collected in *T.A.Z.: The Temporary Autonomous Zone, Ontological Anarchy, Poetic Terrorism* (1991) and elsewhere.

8. Directed by Andrew Davis (1992).

9. Andrew Ross, *Strange Weather: Culture, Science, and Technology in the Age of Limits* (New York: Verso, 1991), p. 38 [Moulthrop's note].

1. An echo of the final lines of "Kubla Khan" (1797, pub. 1816), by the English Romantic poet SAMUEL TAYLOR COLERIDGE (1772–1834): "Weave a circle round him thrice, / And close your eyes with holy dread, / For he on honey-dew hath fed, / And drunk the milk of Paradise." The poem, a "vision" that Coleridge claimed to have written in an opium dream, is set in Xanadu, a mythical place.

2. An allusion to the Beatles' song "Strawberry Fields Forever" (pub. 1967; words and music by John Lennon and Paul McCartney), which tells of a place where "Nothing is real" (the actual Strawberry Field is a park in Liverpool, England). The title of this essay quotes the beginning of their song "Revolution" (1968): "You say you want a revolution / Well, you know / We all want to change the world."

3. Jean Baudrillard, *Simulations*, trans. Paul Foss, Paul Patton, and Philip Beitchman (New York: Semiotext(e), 1983), p. 10 [Moulthrop's note].

"real" phenomena, but rather in recursive and multiple parallel, "mapping on to different co-ordinate systems."[4] Maps derive not from territories but from previous map-making enterprises: all the world's a simulation.

9 This reality implosion brings serious ideological consequences, for some would say it invalidates the informing "master narratives" of modernity, leaving us with a proliferation of incompatible discourses and methods.[5] Such unchecked variation, it has been objected, deprives social critique of a clear agenda.[6] Hyperreality privileges no discourse as absolute or definitive; critique becomes just another form of paralogy,[7] a countermove in the language game that is techno-social construction of reality. The game is all-encompassing, and therein lies a problem. As Linda Hutcheon observes, "the ideology of postmodernism is paradoxical, for it depends upon and draws its power from that which it contests. It is not truly radical; nor is it truly oppositional."[8]

10 This problem of complicity grows especially acute where media and technologies are concerned. Hyperreality is as much a matter of writing practice as it is of textual theory: as Michael Heim points out, "[i]n magnetic code there are no originals."[9] Electronic information may be rapidly duplicated, transmitted, and assembled into new knowledge structures. From word processing to interactive multimedia, postmodern communication systems accentuate what Ihab Hassan calls "immanence" or "the intertextuality of all life. A patina of thought, of signifiers, of 'connections,' now lies on everything the mind touches in its gnostic (noö) sphere . . ."[1] Faced with this infinitely convoluted system of discourse, we risk falling into technological abjection, a sense of being hopelessly abandoned to simulation, lost in "the technico-luminous cinematic space of total spatio-dynamic theatre."[2] If all the world's a simulation, then we are but simulacral subjects cycling through our various iterations, incapable of any "radical" or "oppositional" action that would transform the techno-social matrix. Even supposedly resistant attitudes like "cyberpunk," as Andrew Ross has observed, tend to tail off into cynical interludes where the rules of the game go unquestioned.[3]

11 Of course, this pessimistic or defeatist outlook is hardly universal. We are far more likely to hear technology described as an instrumentality of change or a tool for liberation. Bolter, Drexler, McCorduck, and Zuboff all contend[4] that post modern modes of communication (electronic writing, computer networks, text-linking systems) can destabilize social hierarchies and promote broader definitions of authority in the informational workplace. Heim

4. Thomas Pynchon, *Gravity's Rainbow* (New York: Viking, 1973), p. 159 [Moulthrop's note].
5. Jean-François Lyotard, *The Postmodern Condition: A Report on Knowledge*, trans. Geoff Bennington and Brian Massumi (Minneapolis: University of Minnesota Press, 1984), p. 26 [Moulthrop's note].
6. TERRY EAGLETON [b. 1943], "Capitalism, Modernism, and Postmodernism," *New Left Review*, no. 152 (1985): 63 [Moulthrop's note].
7. An innovative move in a language game, as discussed in Lyotard's *Postmodern Condition*.
8. Linda Hutcheon, *A Poetics of Postmodernism: History, Theory, Fiction* (New York: Routledge, 1988), p. 120 [Moulthrop's note].
9. Michael Heim, *Electric Language: A Philosophical Study of Word Processing* (New Haven: Yale University Press, 1987), p. 162 [Moulthrop's note].
1. Ihab Hassan, *The Postmodern Turn: Essays in Postmodern Theory and Culture* (Columbus: Ohio State University Press, 1987), p. 172 [Moulthrop's note].
2. Baudrillard, *Simulations*, p. 139 [Moulthrop's note].
3. Ross, *Strange Weather*, p. 160 [Moulthrop's note].
4. In Bolter, *Writing Space*; K. Eric Drexler, *Engines of Creation: The Coming of Nanotechnology* (New York: Doubleday, 1987); Pamela McCorduck, *The Universal Machine: Confessions of a Technological Optimist* (New York: McGraw-Hill, 1985); and Shoshana Zuboff, *In the Age of the Smart Machine: The Future of Work and Power* (New York: Basic, 1988) [Moulthrop's note].

points out that under the influence of these technologies "psychic life will be redefined."[5] But if Hutcheon is correct in her observation that postmodernism is non-oppositional, then how will such a reconstruction of order and authority take place? How and by whom is psychic life—and more important, political life—going to be redefined?

These questions must ultimately be addressed not in theory but in practice; which is where the significance of Nelson's new Xanadu lies. With Xanadu, Nelson invalidates technological abjection, advancing an unabashedly millenarian vision of technological renaissance in which the system shall set us free.[6] In its extensive ambitions, Xanadu transcends the hyperreal. It is not an opium vision but something stranger still, a business plan for the development of what Barthes called the "*social* space" of writing,[7] a practical attempt to reconfigure literate culture. Xanadu is the most ambitious project ever proposed for **hypertext** or "non-sequential writing."[8] **Hypertext** systems exploit the interactive potential of computers to reconstruct text not as a fixed series of symbols, but as a variable-access database in which any discursive unit may possess multiple vectors of association.[9] A **hypertext** is a complex network of textual elements. It consists of units or "lexias,"[1] which may be analogous to pages, paragraphs, sections, or volumes. Lexias are connected by "links," which act like dynamic footnotes that automatically retrieve the material to which they refer. Because it is no longer book-bounded, **hypertextual** discourse may be modified at will as reader / writers forge new links within and among documents. Potentially this collectivity of linked text, which Nelson calls the "docuverse," can expand without limit. 12

As Nelson foresees it, Xanadu would embody this textual universe. The system would provide a central repository and distribution network for all writing: it would be the publishing house, communications medium, and great **hypertextual** Library of Babel.[2] Yet for all its radical ambitions, Nelson's design preserves familiar proprieties. Local Xanadu outlets would be Silverstands™, retail access and consulting centers modeled after fast-food franchises and thus integrated with the present economy of information exchange. Xanadu would protect intellectual property through copyright. Users would pay per byte accessed and would receive royalties when others obtained proprietary material they had published in the system. The problems and complexities of this scheme are vast, and at the moment, the fulfilled Xanadu remains a "2020 Vision," a probe into the relatively near future. But it is a future with compelling and important implications for the postmodern present. 13

The future, as Disney and Spielberg have taught us, is a place we must 14

5. Heim, *Electric Language*, p. 164 [Moulthrop's note].
6. See John 8.31–32: "If ye continue in my word, then are ye my disciples indeed; and ye shall know the truth, and the truth shall make you free." "Abjection": repulsion.
7. In "From Work to Text" (1971; see above), by ROLAND BARTHES (1915–1980), French structuralist and poststructuralist literary critic.
8. Nelson, *Dream Machines*, p. 29, and *Literary Machines*, 5/2 [Moulthrop's note].
9. See Michael Joyce, "Siren Shapes: Exploratory and Constructive Hypertexts," *Academic Computing*, November 1988, 11ff.; Landow, *Hypertext*; and John Statin, "Reading Hypertext: Order and Coherence in a New Medium," *College English* 52 (1990): 870–83 [Moulthrop's note].
1. Units of meaning, a term borrowed by George Landow from Roland Barthes's *S/Z* (1970).
2. That is, the library that contains all possible books, as described in the story "Library of Babel" by the Argentine author Jorge Luis Borges (1899–1986). For Babel as the place where unitary human language was split by God into many languages, see Genesis 11.

come "back" to.[3] The American tomorrow will be a heyday of nostalgia, an intensive pursuit of "lost" or "forgotten" values. Xanadu is no exception: Ted Nelson sees the history of writing in the 21st century as an epic of recovery. His "grand hope" lies in "a return to literacy, a cure for television stupor, a new Renaissance of ideas and generalist understanding, a grand posterity that does not lose the details which are the final substance of everything."[4] To a skeptical observer, this vision of Xanadu might suggest another domain of the postmodern theme park. Gentle readers, welcome to Literacyland!

15 But on the other hand, this vision might add up to more than just a sideshow attraction. Nelson foresees a renovation of culture, a unification of discourse, a reader-and-writer's paradise where all writing opens itself to / in the commerce of ideas. This is the world in which all "work" becomes "text," not substance but reference, not containment but connection.[5] The magnitude of the change implied here is enormous. But what about the politics of that change? What community of interpretation—and beyond that, what social order—does this intertextual world presume? With the conviction of a true Enlightenment man, Nelson envisions "a new populitism that can make the deeper understandings of the few at last available to the many."[6]

16 What is *populitism?*—another of Nelson's infamous neologisms (e.g., "hypermedia," "cybercrud," "teledildonics"), in this case a portmanteau combining "populism" with "elite." The word suggests the society-of-text envisioned by theorists like Shoshana Zuboff and Jay David Bolter, a writing space in which traces of authority persist only as local and contingent effects, the social equivalent of the deconstructed author-function.[7] A "populite" culture might mark the first step toward realization of Jean-François Lyotard's "game of perfect information" where all have equal access to the world of data, and where "[g]iven equal competence (no longer in the acquisition of knowledge, but in its production), what extra performativity depends on in the final analysis is 'imagination,' which allows one either to make a new move or change the rules of the game."[8] This is the utopia of information-in-process, the ultimate wetware dream of the clerisy:[9] discourse converted with 100 percent efficiency into capital, the mechanism of that magical process being nomology or rule-making—admittedly a rather specialized form of "imagination."

17 At least two troubles lurk in this paradise. First, the prospect that social / textual order will devolve not unto the many but only to a very few; and more important, that those few will fail to recognize the terms of their splendid isolation. Consider the case of the reluctant computer dick Clifford Stoll, whose memoir, *The Cuckoo's Egg,* nicely illustrates these problems. Stoll excoriates "cyberpunks," electronic vandals who abuse the openness of scientific computing environments. Their unsportsmanlike conduct spoils the

3. As taught by Walt Disney (1901–1966), legendary American cartoonist and film producer whose theme parks Disneyland and Walt Disney World include "nostalgic" visions of the future, and by Steven Spielberg (b. 1946), producer of the film *Back to the Future* (1985; dir. Robert Zemeckis).

4. Theodor Holm Nelson, "How Hypertext (Un)does the Canon," paper delivered at the Modern Language Association Convention, Chicago, December 28, 1990, p. 4 [Moulthrop's note].

5. See Barthes, "From Work to Text"; Landow, *Hypertext*; and Zuboff, *In the Age of the Smart Machine* [Moulthrop's note].

6. Nelson, "How Hypertext (Un)does the Canon," p. 6 [Moulthrop's note].

7. A term coined by the French philosopher and historian of ideas MICHEL FOUCAULT in "What Is an Author?" (1971; see above) to designate the historical circumstances and conception of authorship that make us want to know about the author of a poem and not the author of a contract.

8. Lyotard, *The Postmodern Condition*, p. 52 [Moulthrop's note].

9. Intelligentsia (a term introduced by Coleridge).

information game, necessitating cumbersome restrictions on the free flow of data. But Stoll's definition of informational "freedom" appears murky at best. He repeatedly refers to the mainframe whose system he monitors as "his" computer, likening cybernetic intrusions to burglaries. Digital information, as Stoll sees it, stands in strict analogy to material and private property.

Private in what sense? Stoll professes to believe that scientists must have easy access to research results, but only within their own communities. He is quick to condemn incursions by "unauthorized" outsiders. There is some sense in this argument: Stoll repeatedly points out that the intruder in the Stanford mainframe might have interfered with a lifesaving medical imaging system. But along with this concern comes an ideological danger. Who decides what information "belongs" to whom? Stoll's "popular elite" is restricted to academic scientists, a version of "the people" as *nomenklatura,*[1] those whose need to know is defined by their professional affiliation. More disturbingly, Stoll seems unaware of the way this brotherhood is situated within larger political hierarchies. Describing a meeting with Pentagon brass, he reflects: "How far I'd come. A year ago, I would have viewed these officers as war-mongering puppets of the Wall Street capitalists. This, after all, was what I'd learned in college. Now things didn't seem so black and white. They seemed like smart people handling a serious problem."[2] 18

Here is elite populism at its scariest. Though he protests (too much) his political correctness, Stoll's sense of specialist community shifts to accommodate the demands of the moment. He observes repeatedly over the course of the memoir that he is finally "coming of age" as a working scientist. When in Fort Meade,[3] Stoll does as the natives do, recognizing agents of Air Force Intelligence, the National Security Agency, even the CIA and FBI as brothers-in-craft. After all, they are "smart" (technologically adept) and "serious" (professional). Their immediate goal seems legitimate and laudable. They are just "handling" a problem, tracking down the intruder who has violated the electronic privacy of Stoll's community (and, not coincidentally, their own). They are the good policemen, the ones Who Are Your Friends, not really "Them" after all but just a quaint, braid-shouldered version of "Us." 19

Stoll is not troubled that these boon companions live at the heart of the military-industrial complex. He disregards the fact that they seem aware of domestic communications intercepts—in phone conversations, Stoll's CIA contact refers to the FBI as "the F entity," evidently to thwart a monitoring program.[4] Stoll does task his agency buddies for sowing disinformation and managing dirty wars,[5] but this critique never gets much past the stage of rhetorical questions. In fact Stoll seems increasingly comfortable in the intelligence community. If the data spooks turn out to be less interested in freedom of scientific speech than in quashing a security leak, Stoll has no real objection. His own ideals and interests are conveniently served in the process. 20

What leads to such regrettable blindness, and how might it have been 21

1. Political elite (Russian).
2. Clifford Stoll, *The Cuckoo's Egg: Tracking a Spy through the Maze of Computer Espionage* (New York: Doubleday, 1989), p. 278 [Moulthrop's note].
3. U.S. military and intelligence base in Maryland.
4. Stoll, *The Cuckoo's Egg*, p. 144.
5. Government campaigns against their own citizens.

prevented? These may be especially pertinent questions as we consider entrusting our literate culture to an automated information system. The spooks are not so easily conjured away. It is no longer sufficient to object that scientists and humanists form distinct communities, and that Stoll's seduction could not happen in our own elect company. The old "Two Cultures"[6] paradigm has shifted out from under us, largely through catholic adoption of technologies like data networks and **hypertext**. Networks are networks, and we can assume that most if not all of them will eventually engender closed elites. Fascism, as Deleuze and Guattari instruct, is a matter of all-too-human desire.[7] What can shield humanist networks, or even the "generalist" networks Nelson foresees, from the strategy of divide and co-opt? What might insulate Xanadu from those ancestral voices prophesying war?[8]

22 The answer, as forecasters like Pamela McCorduck, K. Eric Drexler, and Andrew Ross point out, may lie in the **hypertext** concept itself—the operating principle of an open and dynamic medium, a consensual canon with a minimum of hierarchical impedances and a fundamental instability in those hierarchies it maintains. Visionary and problematic as it may seem, Nelson's idea of "populitism" has much to recommend it—not the least of which is its invitation to consider more carefully the likely social impact of advanced communication systems. In fact **hypertext** may well portend social change, a fundamental reshaping of text production and reception. The telos of the electronic society-of-text is anarchy in its true sense: local autonomy based on consensus, limited by a relentless disintegration of global authority. Since information is now virtually an equivalent of capital, and since textuality is our most powerful way of shaping information, it follows that Xanadu might indeed change the world. But to repeat the crucial question, how will this change come about? What actual social processes can translate the pragmatics of Nelson's business plan into the radicalism of a **hypertext** manifesto?

23 The complete answers lie with future history. In one respect, Ted Nelson's insistence that Xanadu become an economically viable enterprise is exemplary. We will discover the full implications of this technology only as we build, manage, and work in **hypertextual** communities, starting within the existing constraints of information capitalism. But while we wait on history, we can try a little augury. In trying to theorize a nascent medium, one is reduced to *playing* medium, eking out predictions with the odd message from the Other Side. Which brings us to the last work of Marshall McLuhan, a particularly important ancestral voice from whom to hear. At his death, McLuhan left behind notes for an enigmatic final project: the fourfold "Laws of Media" which form the framework for a semiotics of technology.[9] The Laws proceed from four basic questions that can be asked about any invention:

6. A phrase coined by the English novelist and physicist C. P. Snow (1905–1980), who saw a clear difference between how those working in the sciences and those working in the humanities think.

7. Gilles Deleuze and Félix Guattari, *Anti-Oedipus: Capitalism and Schizophrenia*, trans. Robert Hurley, Mark Seem, and Helen R. Lane (New York: Viking, 1977), p. 26 [Moulthrop's note]. DELEUZE (1925–1995), French antirationalist philosopher; GUATTARI (1936–1992), French psychiatrist and poststructuralist philosopher.

8. Coleridge, "Kubla Khan," line 40.

9. H. Marshall McLuhan and Eric McLuhan, *The Laws of Media: The New Science* (Toronto: University of Toronto Press, 1988) [Moulthrop's note]. Marshall McLuhan (1911–1980), Canadian cultural historian and influential theorist of media.

- What does it enhance or intensify?
- What does it render obsolete or displace?
- What does it retrieve that was previously obsolete?
- What does it produce or become when taken to its limit?

As McLuhan demonstrates, these questions are particularly instructive when applied to pivotal or transforming technologies like printing or broadcasting. They are intended to discover the ways in which information systems affect the social text, rearranging sense ratios and rewriting theories of cultural value. They reveal the nature of the basic statement, the "uttering or 'outering' " that underlies mechanical extensions of human faculties. If we put Xanadu and **hypertext** to this series of questions, we may discover more about both the potential and the limits of **hypertext** as an agency of change. 24

1. What does **hypertext** enhance or intensify?

According to McLuhan's standard analysis, communications media adjust the balance or "ratio" of the senses by privileging one channel of perception over others. Print promotes sight over hearing, giving us an objectified, perspectival, symbolized world: "an eye for an ear."[1] But this approach needs modification for our purposes. **Hypertext** differs from earlier media in that it is not a new thing at all but a return or *recursion* (of which more later) to an earlier form of symbolic discourse, namely print. The effect of **hypertext** thus falls not simply upon the sense channels but farther along the cognitive chain. As Vannevar Bush pointed out in the very first speculation on informational linking technologies, these mechanisms enhance the fundamental capacity of *pattern recognition.*[2] 25

Hypertext is all about connection, linkage, and affiliation. Formally speaking, its universe is the one Thomas Pynchon had in mind when he defined "paranoia" as "the realization that *everything is connected*, everything in the Creation—not yet blindingly one, but at least connected. . . ."[3] In **hypertext** systems, this ethos of connection is realized in technics; users do not passively rehearse or receive discourse, they explore and construct links.[4] At the kernel of the **hypertext** concept lie ideas of affiliation, correspondence, and resonance. In this, as Nelson has argued from the start, **hypertext** is nothing more than an extension of what literature has always been (at least since "Tradition and the Individual Talent"[5])—a temporally extended network of relations which successive generations of readers and writers perpetually make and unmake. 26

This redefinition of textuality gives rise to a number of questions. What does it mean to enhance our sensitivity to patterns in this shifting matrix, to become sensitized to what Pynchon calls "other orders behind the visible?" Does this mean that **hypertext** will turn us into "paranoids," anxious interpreters convinced that all structures are mysteriously organized against us? What does interpretive "resistance" mean in a **hypertextual** context? Can 27

1. H. Marshall McLuhan, *Understanding Media: The Extensions of Man* (New York: McGraw-Hill, 1964), p. 81 [Moulthrop's note].
2. Qtd. in Nelson, *Literary Machines* 1/50 [Moulthrop's note].
3. Pynchon, *Gravity's Rainbow*, p. 820 [Moulthrop's note].
4. Joyce, "Siren Shapes," p. 12 [Moulthrop's note].
5. Influential 1919 essay (see above) by the American-born English poet and critic T. S. ELIOT (1888–1965).

such a reading strategy be possible after poststructuralism, with the author-function reduced (like Pynchon himself) to a voiceless occasion for deconstructive "writing"?[6] Perverse though it may seem, **hypertext** does increase the agonistic element in reading. Early experience with **hypertext** narrative suggests that its readers may actually be more concerned with prior authority and design than are readers of conventional writing. The apparent "quick-liming of the author" does not dispel the aura of intention in **hypertext.**[7] The constantly repeated ritual of interaction, with its reminder of discursive alternatives, reveals the text as a made thing, not monologic perhaps but hardly indeterminate. The text gestures toward openness—*what options can you imagine?*—but then swiftly forecloses: some options are available but not others, and someone clearly did the defining long before you began interacting. The author persists, undead presence in the literary machine, the inevitable Hand that turns the time. **Hypertextual** writing—at least when considered as read-only or "exploratory" text[8]—may thus emphasize antithetical modes of reading, leading us to regard the deconstructed system-maker much in the way that Leo Bersani describes the author of *Gravity's Rainbow*: as "the enemy text."[9]

28 So perhaps we need a Psychiatrist General's Warning: Interacting With This **Hypertext** Can Make You Paranoid—indeed it must, since the root sense of paranoia, a parallel or parallax gnosis,[1] happens to be a handy way to conceive of the meta-sense of pattern recognition that **hypertext** serves to enhance. But would such a distortion of our cognitive ratios necessarily constitute pathology? In dealing with vast and nebulous information networks—to say nothing of those corporate-sponsored "virtual realities" that may lie in our future—a certain "creative paranoia" may be a definite asset. In fact the paragnosticism implicit in **hypertext** may be the best way to keep the information game clean. Surrounded by filaments and tendrils of a network, the sojourner in Xanadu or other **hypertext** systems will always be reminded of her situation in a fabric of power arrangements. Her ability to build and pursue links should encourage her to subject those arrangements to inquiry. Which brings us to the second of McLuhan's key questions:

2. What does **hypertext** displace or render obsolete?

29 Though it may be tempting to respond, *the book, stupid,* that answer is ineligible. The book is already "dead" (or superseded) if by "alive" you mean that the institution in question is essential to our continued commerce in ideas. True, the cultural indications are ambiguous. Irving Louis Horowitz argues that reports of the book's demise are exaggerated; even

6. Alec McHoul and David Wills, *Writing Pynchon: Strategies in Fictional Analysis* (Urbana: University of Illinois Press, 1990), p. 9 [Moulthrop's note].

7. Jane Yellowlees Douglas, "Wandering through the Labyrinth: Encountering Interactive Fiction," *Computers and Composition* 6 (1989): 100 [Moulthrop's note].

8. See Joyce, "Siren Shapes." [Moulthrop's note]. Joyce distinguishes between "constructive" hypertext, which is interactive, and "exploratory" hypertext, which invites passive reading.

9. Leo Bersani, "Pynchon, Paranoia, and Literature," *Representations*, no. 25 (1989): 108 [Moulthrop's note].

1. Knowledge (Greek). Parallax: the apparent displacement of an object when observed from two points of view. The roots of *paranoia* are the Greek words *para* (near) and *nous* (mind, reason). *Paragnosticism* later in this paragraph is Moulthrop's coinage to denote deep skepticism.

in an age of television and computers, we produce more books each year than ever before.[2] Indeed, our information ecology seems likely to retain a mix of print and electronic media for at least the next century. Yet as Alvin Kernan recently pointed out, the outlook for books in the long run is anything but happy.[3] As the economic and ecological implications of dwindling forests come home, the cost of paper will rise precipitously. At the same time, acidic decay of existing books will enormously increase maintenance costs to libraries. Given these factors, some shift to electronic storage seems inevitable (though Kernan, an analog man to the last, argues for microfilm).

Yet this change in the medium of print does not worry cultural conserva- 30
tives like Kernan, Neil Postman, or E. D. Hirsch nearly so much as the prospect that the decline of the book may terminate the cultural dominance of print. The chief technological culprit in Kernan's "death of literature" is not the smart machine but the idiot box. "Such common culture as we still have," Kernan laments, "comes largely from television."[4] But the idiot box—or to be precise, the boxed idiot—is precisely the intellectual problem that **hypertext** seems excellently suited to address. In answer to McLuhan's second question—what does **hypertext** render obsolete?—the best answer is not *literacy* but rather *post-literacy*. As Nelson foresees, the development of **hypertext** systems implies a revival of typographic culture (albeit in a dynamic, truly paperless environment). That forecast may seem recklessly naive or emptily prophetic, but it is quite likely valid. **Hypertext** means the end of the death of literature.

Here the voice of the skeptic must be heard: *a revival of literacy?—read* 31
my lips: not in a million years. Even the most devoted champion of print is likely to resist the notion of a Gutenberg renaissance.[5] In the West, genuine literacy—cultural, multicultural, or simply functional—can be found only among a well-defined managerial and professional class. At present that class is fairly large, but in the U.S. and U.K., world leaders in laissez-faire education, it is contracting noticeably. So it must seem foolish to imagine, as Ted Nelson does, a mass consumer market for typographic information, a growth industry based on the electronic equivalent of the local library.

Indeed, should Xanadu become a text-only system (which is not intended), 32
its prospects would be poor in the long run. There are however other horizons for interactive textuality—not just **hypertext** but another Nelsonian coinage, "hypermedia." Print is not the only means of communication deliverable in a polysequential format articulated by software links. In trying to imagine the future of **hypertext** culture, we must also consider interactive multimedia "texts" that incorporate voice, music, animated graphics, and video along with alphabetic script.[6] **Hypertext** is about connection—promiscuous, pervasive, and polymorphously perverse connection. It is a writing practice

2. Irving Louis Horowitz, *Communicating Ideas: The Crisis of Publishing in a Post-Industrial Society* (New York: Oxford University Press, 1986), p. 20 [Moulthrop's note]
3. Alvin Kernan, *The Death of Literature* (New Haven: Yale University Press, 1990), pp. 135–43 [Moulthrop's note]
4. Ibid., p. 147 [Moulthrop's note]. Postman (b. 1931), American educational and cultural critic. HIRSCH (b. 1929), American literary critic and theorist.
5. That is, a renaissance matching that sparked by Johannes Gutenberg (1400–1468), the German printer credited with inventing a printing press with movable type cast in molds.
6. Richard Lanham, "The Electronic Word: Literacy Study and the Digital Revolution," *New Literary History* 20 (1989): 287 [Moulthrop's note].

ideally suited to the irregular, the transgressive, and the carnivalesque. Culturally speaking, the *promiscuity* of **hypertext** (in the root sense of "a tendency to seek relations") knows no bounds of form, format, or cultural level. There is no reason to assume that **hypertext** or hypermedia should not support popular as well as elite culture, or indeed that it might not promote a "populite" miscegenation of discourses.

33 But what can this mean—talking books in homeboy jive? Street rap mixed over Eliotic scholia?[7] Nintendo with delusions of cinema? Or worse, could we be thinking of yet more industrial light and magic,[8] the Disneyverse of eyephones and datagloves where YOU (insert userName) ARE IN THE FANTASY? Perhaps, as one critic of the computer industry recently put it, interactive multimedia must inevitably decay to its lowest common denominator, "hyper-MTV."[9] According to this analysis, the linear and objectifying tendencies of any print content in a multimedium text would be overwhelmed by the subjective, irrational, and emotive influence of audio / video. This being the case, **hypertext** could hardly claim to represent "a cure for television stupor."

34 But Nelson's aspiration should not be so easily set aside as merely a vision in a dream. **Hypertext** does indeed have the power to recover print literacy—though not in quite the way that Nelson supposes; which brings us to the third of McLuhan's queries:

3. What does **hypertext** retrieve that was previously obsolete?

35 Xanadu and similar projects could invite large numbers of people to become reacquainted with the cultural power of typographic literacy. To assert this, of course, is to break with McLuhan's understanding of media history. It is hard to dispute the argument of *Understanding Media* and *The Gutenberg Galaxy*[1] that the culture of the printing press has entered into dialectic contention with a different ethos based on the "cool" immediacy of broadcasting. But though that diagnosis remains tremendously important, McLuhan's cultural prognosis for the West holds less value. McLuhan saw clearly the transforming impact of "electric" technologies, but perhaps because he did not live much beyond the onset of the personal computer boom, he failed to recognize the next step—the *recursion* to a new stage of typographic literacy through the syncretic medium of **hypertext**.

36 It is crucial to distinguish recursion from return or simple repetition, because this difference answers the objection that print literacy will be lost or suppressed in multimedia texts. Recursion is self-reference with the possibility of progressive self-modification.[2] Considered for its recursive possibilities, "writing" means something radically different in linked interactive compositions than it does in a codex book or even a conventional electronic document. Literacy in **hypertext** encompasses two domains: the ordinary

7. Marginal commentary (Latin), such as the erudite footnotes that T. S. Eliot provided for his poem "The Waste Land" (1922).
8. Industrial Light and Magic is a company, founded by Steven Spielberg, that creates special effects for movies.
9. Steven Levy, "The End of Literature: Multimedia Is Television's Insidious Offspring," *Macworld*, June 1991, p. 52 [Moulthrop's note].
1. Marshall McLuhan, *The Gutenberg Galaxy: The Making of Typographic Man* (Toronto: University of Toronto Press, 1962).
2. Douglas Hofstadter, *Gödel, Escher, Bach: An Eternal Golden Braid* (New York: Basic, 1979), p. 127 [Moulthrop's note].

grammatical, rhetorical, and tropological space that we now know as "literature," and also a second province, stricter in its formalisms but much greater in its power to shape interactive discourse. This second domain has been called "writing space";[3] a case might be made (with apologies to those who insist that virtual reality is strictly a non-print phenomenon) that it also represents the true meaning of *cyberspace*.

Walter Benjamin observed with some regret that by the 1930's, any literate European could become an author, at least to the extent of publishing a letter or article in the newspapers.[4] With no regrets at all, Ted Nelson envisions a similar extension of amateur literary production in Xanadu, where all readers of the system can potentially become writers, or at least editors and commentators. The First Amendment guarantee of free speech, Nelson points out, is a *personal* liberty: anyone may publish, and in Xanadu everyone can. Nelson bases his prediction of revived literacy on the promise of a broadly popular publishing franchise. 37

This vision is limited in one crucial regard. Nelson treats print essentially as the *content* of his system, which is taking a rather narrow view. In describing Xanadu as a more or less transparent medium for the transmission of text, Nelson overlooks the fact that alphabetic or alphanumeric representation also defines the *form* of Xanadu, and indeed of any **hypertext** system. This neglect is consistent with the generally broad focus of Nelson's vision, which has led him to dismiss details of user-interface design as "front-end functions" to be worked out by the user. 38

Design details, whether anterior or posterior to the system, cannot be passed over so easily. In fact the structure and specifications of the **hypertext** environment are themselves parts of the docuverse, arguably the most important parts. Beneath any **hypertext** document or system there exists a lower layer that we might call the *hypotext*. On this level, in the working implementations of its "protocols," Xanadu is a creature of print. The command structures that govern linkage, display, editing, accounting, and all the other functions of the system exist as digital impulses that may be translated into typographic text. They were written out, first in pseudo-English strings, then in a high-level programming language, finally as binary code. Therefore Xanadu at its most intimate level is governed by all those features of the typographic medium so familiar from McLuhan's analysis: singular sequentiality, objectivity, instrumentality, "left-brained" visual bias, and so on. The wonder of **hypertext** and hypermedia lies in their capacity to escape these limitations by using the microprocessor to turn linear, monologic typography recursively back upon itself—to create linear control structures that militate against absolute linear control. 39

In recognizing the recursive trick behind **hypertextual** writing, we come to a broader understanding of electronic literacy. Literacy under **hypertext** must extend not only to the "content" of a composition but to its hypotextual "form" as well—e.g., the way nodes are divided to accommodate data structures and display strategies, or the types of linkage available and the ways they are apparent to the reader. Practically speaking, this means that users of a **hypertext** system can be expected to understand print not only as the 40

3. Bolter, *Writing Space*, p. 4 [Moulthrop's note].
4. Noted in "The Work of Art in the Age of Mechanical Reproduction" (1936; see above), by BENJAMIN (1892–1940), German literary critic and aesthetician.

medium of traditional literary discourse, but also as a meta-tool, the key to power at the level of the system itself.

41 Ong and McLuhan have argued that television and radio introduce "secondary orality," a recursion to non-print forms of language and an "audile space" of cognition.[5] By analogy, **hypertext** and hypermedia seem likely to instigate a *secondary literacy*—"secondary" in that this approach to reading and writing includes a self-consciousness about the technological mediation of those acts, a sensitivity to the way texts-below-the-text constitute another order behind the visible. This secondary literacy involves both rhetoric and technics: to read at the hypotextual level is to confront (paragnostically) the design of the system; to write at this level is to reprogram, revising the work of the first maker. Thus this secondary literacy opens for its readers a *cyberspace* in the truest sense of the word, meaning a place of command and control where the written word has the power to remake appearances. This space has always been accessible to the programming elite, to system operators like Clifford Stoll and shady operators like his hacker adversary. But Nelson's 2020 Vision puts a Silverstand in every commercial strip right next to McDonald's and Videoland. Vice President Gore's information "Superhighway"[6] would bring cyberspace even closer. If Xanadu succeeds in re-awakening primary literacy as a mass phenomenon, there is reason to believe that it will inculcate secondary literacy as well.

42 But like any grand hope, this technopiate dream of a new literacy ultimately has to confront its man from Porlock.[7] Secondary literacy might well prove culturally disastrous. The idea of a general cyberspace franchise, in which all control structures are truly contingent and "consensual," does summon up visions of informatic chaos. "Chaos," however, is a concept we have recently begun to understand as something other than simply an absence of "order": it is instead a condition of possibility in which new arrangements spontaneously assemble themselves.[8]

43 Taking this neo-chaotic view, we might inquire into the positive effects of secondary literacy in a postmodern political context. In outlining a first move beyond our recent "depthless," ahistorical quiescence, Fredric Jameson calls for an "aesthetic of cognitive mapping," a "pedagogical political culture" in which we would begin to teach ourselves where we stand in the networks of transnational power.[9] At this moment, as the West reconsiders its New World Order in the aftermath of a war for oil reserves,[1] we seem in especially urgent need of such education. But a cultural pedagogy clearly needs something more than the evening war news, especially when

5. Walter Ong, *Orality and Literacy: The Technologizing of the Word* (New York: Methuen, 1982), p. 135; McLuhan, *Laws of Media*, p. 57 [Moulthrop's note].
6. As U.S. vice president (1993–2001), Albert Gore Jr. (b. 1948) helped popularize the term "information superhighway"; as a member of Congress (1977–93), he promoted the Internet.
7. According to Coleridge, his vision of Xanadu was interrupted when a man from Porlock, a nearby town, knocked on his door; "Kubla Khan" is thus an unfinished poem.
8. Ilya Prigogine and Isabelle Stengers, *Order out of Chaos: Man's New Dialogue with Nature* (New York: Bantam, 1984), p. 14 [Moulthrop's note].
9. Fredric Jameson, "Postmodernism, or the Cultural Logic of Late Capitalism," *New Left Review*, no. 146 (1984): 92 [Moulthrop's note]. JAMESON (b. 1934), a leading American Marxist critic.
1. The Persian Gulf War (1990–91), also known as "Operation Desert Shield" and "Desert Storm," which drove Iraqi forces out of oil-rich Kuwait. "New World Order": a phrase coined by George Bush (b. 1924; U.S. president, 1989–93) to describe what was needed to replace East-West cold war rivalries after the collapse of communism in Eastern Europe.

reporters are confined to informational wading pools. We require not only a sensitivity to the complex textuality of power but an ability to intercept and manipulate that text—an advanced creative paranoia. This must ultimately be a human skill, independent of technological "utterance"; but the secondary literacy fostered by **hypertext** could help us at least to begin the enormous task of drawing our own cognitive maps. Here, however, we verge on the main question of **hypertextual** politics, which brings up the last question in the Toronto[2] catechism:

4. What does **hypertext** become when taken to its limit?

Orthodox McLuhanite doctrine holds that "every form, pushed to the limit 44
of its potential, reverses its characteristics."[3] Media evolution, in McLuhan's view, proceeds through sharply punctuated equilibriums. "Hot" media like print tend to increase their routinization and determinism until they reach a limit (say, the prose of the late 19th century). Beyond that point, the overheated medium turns paradoxical, passing almost instantly from hot to supercool, bombarding readers with such a plethora of codings that conventional interpretation collapses. Structure and hierarchy, the distinguishing features of a hot medium, reduce to indeterminacy. The plurality of codes overwhelms hermeneutic certainty, the "figure" of a univocal text reverses into polysemous "ground," and we reach the ultima Thule of Gutenberg culture, *Finnegans Wake*.[4]

But though McLuhan had much to say about the reversal of overheated 45
media, he left the complementary possibility unexplored. What happens to already cool or participatory media when they reach their limits? True to the fourth law, their characteristics reverse, but here the effect is reactionary, not radical. Radio, for instance, begins in interactive orality (two-way transceiving) but decays into the hegemony of commercial broadcasting, where "talk radio" lingers as a reminder of how open the airwaves are not. Television too starts by shattering the rigid hierarchies of the Gutenberg nation-state, promising to bring anyplace into our living rooms; but its version of Global Village turns out to be homogenous and hegemonic, a planetary empire of signs (as we say in Atlanta, "Always Coca-Cola").[5]

Hypertext and hypermedia are also interactively cool, so following this 46
analysis we might conclude that they will undergo a similar implosion, becoming every bit as institutionalized and conservative as broadcast networks. Indeed, it doesn't take McLuhanite media theory to arrive at that forecast. According to the economic logic of late capitalism, wouldn't the Xanadu Operating Company ultimately sell out to Sony, Matsushita, Philips, or some other wielder of multinational leverage?

Such a self-negating "reversal" may not be the only possible outcome, 47
however. What if the corporate shogunate decide not to venture their capital? What if business leaders realize that truly interactive information networks

2. Beginning in 1963, McLuhan was director of the University of Toronto's Centre for Culture and Technology.

3. McCluhan, *Laws of Media*, p. viii [Moulthrop's note].

4. The 1939 novel by Irish writer James Joyce, arguably the most experimental and difficult long work of fiction in Western literature.

5. Coca-Cola was invented in Atlanta, Georgia, in 1886; "Always Coca-Cola" was an advertising slogan. "Global Village": McLuhan's term for the interconnected world that would result from the linking of electronic information media.

do not make wise investments? This conclusion might be supported by memory of the nastiness Sears and IBM stirred up when they tried to curtail user autonomy on their Prodigy videotex system.[6] This scenario of corporate rejection is not just speculative fabulation, but the basis for a proposed modification to McLuhan's fourth law. Media taken to their limits tend to reverse, but not all media reverse in the same way. The case of a complex, syncretic, and fundamentally interactive medium like **hypertext** may involve a "reversal" that does not bring us back to the same-as-it-ever-was—not a reversal in fact but a recursion (*déjà vu*) to a new cultural space.

48 We have entered into a period of change in reading and writing that Richard Lanham calls a "digital revolution."[7] As this revolution proceeds (if it is allowed to do so), its consequences will be enormous. The idea of **hypertext** as a figment of the capitalist imagination, an information franchise in both Nelson's and Lyotard's senses, could well break down. Though Xanadu may in fact open its Silverstands some day, **hypertext** might not long remain a commercial proposition. The type of literacy and the kind of social structure this medium supports stand fundamentally against absolute property and hierarchy. As we have hinted, **hypertext** and hypermedia peel back to reveal not just an aesthetics of cognitive mapping but nothing less than the simulacral map-as-territory itself: the real beginnings of cyberspace in the sense of a *domain of control*.

49 "Cyberspace. A consensual hallucination experienced daily by billions of legitimate operators, in every nation . . . A graphic representation of data abstracted from the banks of every computer in the human system."[8] William Gibson's concept of a cybernetic workspace, laid out in his dystopian novel *Neuromancer*, represents the ultimate shared vision in the global dream of information commerce. For all its advancement beyond the age of nation-state capitalism, Gibson's world remains intensely competitive and hierarchical (for nation-state-substitute the revived *zaibatsu*). *Neuromancer is Nineteen Eighty-Four* updated for 1984, the *future* somewhat gloomily surveyed from Reagan's America.[9]

50 There is accordingly no trace of social "consensus" in Gibson's "consensual" infosphere. In his version of cyberspace, the shape of vision is imposed from without. "They" control the horizontal, "They" control the vertical.[1] Of course there must be some elements of chaos, else Gibson would be out of business as a paperback writer; so he invents the "cyberspace cowboy," a hacker hero who plays the information game by what he likes to call his own rules. But though cowboys may attempt to unsettle the system, their incursions amount at best to harassment and privateering. These forms of enterprise are deemed "illegal," though they are really just business by another

6. See Steven Levy, "In the Realm of the Censor: The Online Service Prodigy Tells Its Users to Shut Up and Shop," *Macworld*, January 1991, 69+ [Moulthrop's note].

7. Lanham, "The Electronic Word," p. 268 [Moulthrop's note].

8. William Gibson, *Neuromancer* (New York: Ace, 1984), p. 51 [Moulthrop's note]. This science fiction novel is often credited with being the first work of "cyberpunk" fiction.

9. That is, the conservative America of the presidency (1981–89) of Ronald Reagan (b. 1911). *Zaibatsu*: family-owned industrial and financial cartels that became powerful in late-19th-century Japan. *Nineteen Eighty-Four* (1949), novel by the English writer George Orwell (Eric Arthur Blair) depicting a totalitarian society.

1. A reference to the television science fiction anthology *The Outer Limits* (1963–64), whose opening voice-over contained the sentences, "We will control the vertical. We will control the horizontal."

name ("biz," in Gibson's parlance), inventiveness and competitive advantage being the only effective principles of operation.

51 Gibson's dark dream is one thing—in effect it is a realization of McLuhan's prophecy of reversal, an empowering technology turned into a mechanism of co-optation and enslavement. But perhaps Ted Nelson's 2020 Vision of **hypertextual literacy** is something else. If not a utopian alternative, Nelson's project may at least provide a heterotopia, an otherplace not zoned in the usual ways for property and performativity. Cyberspace as Gibson and others define it is a Cartesian[2] territory where scientists of control define boundaries and power lines. The Xanadu model lets us conceive instead a decentered space of literacy and empowerment where each subject acts as *kubernetes* or as Timothy Leary says, "reality pilot," steering her way across the intertextual sea.[3]

52 Nelson's visions of the future differ crucially from Gibson's. In Xanadu we find not consensual illusion but genuine, negotiated consensus. The pathways and connections among texts would be created on demand. According to Nelson's plans to date, only the most fundamental "back end" conventions would be strictly determined: users would be free to customize "front end" systems to access information more or less as they like. Xanadu thus possesses virtually no "canons" in the sense of a shelf of classics or a book of laws; the canons of Xanadu might come closer to the musical meaning of the word—congeries of connections and relationships that are recognizably orderly yet inexhaustibly various. The shifting networks of consensus and textual demand (or desire) in Xanadu would be constructed by users and for users. Their very multiplicity and promiscuity, one might argue, would militate powerfully against any slide from populism back toward hierarchy.

53 Nelson's visionary optimism seems vindicated, then. Xanadu as currently conceived—even in its status as Nelson's scheme to get rich very slowly—opens the door to a true social revolution with implications beyond the world of literature or mass entertainment. Xanadu would remove economic and social gatekeeping functions from the current owners of the means of text production (editors, publishers, managers of conglomerates). It would transfer control of cultural work to a broadly conceived population of culture workers: writers, artists, critics, "independent scholars," autodidacts, "generalists," fans, punks, cranks, hacks, hackers, and other non- or quasi-professionals. "Tomorrow's **hypertext** systems have immense political ramifications, and there are many *struggles* to come," Nelson warns.[4] This is an understatement of cosmic proportions.

54 But it would be a mistake to celebrate cybernetic May Day[5] without performing a few reality checks. Along with all those visionary forecasts of "post-hierarchical" information exchange,[6] some hard facts need to be

2. Dualistic; characterized by the strict distinction between mind and body proposed by the French philosopher René Descartes (1596–1650).
3. Timothy Leary, "The Cyberpunk: The Individual as Reality Pilot," in *Storming the Reality Studio: A Casebook of Cyberpunk and Postmodern Fiction*, ed. Larry McCaffery (Durham: Duke University Press, 1992), p. 247 [Moulthrop's note]. Leary (1920–1996), an American psychologist, is best known for promoting the use of hallucinogens. *Kubernetes*: helmsman (Greek), the origin of the word "cybernetics" (and hence all subsequent cyber- coinages).
4. Nelson *Literary Machines* 3/19 [Moulthrop's note].
5. That is, a day celebrating a successful revolution (the Second Socialist International in 1889 designated May Day as a holiday for labor).
6. Zuboff, *In the Age of the Smart Machine*, p. 399 [Moulthrop's note].

acknowledged. The era of the garage-born computer messiah has passed. Directly or indirectly, most development of hardware and software depends on heavily capitalized multinational companies that do a thriving business with the defense establishment. This affiliation clearly influences the development of new media—consider an influential paper on "The Rhetoric of **Hypertext**" which uses the requirements of a military training system to propose general standards of coherence and instrumental effectiveness for this medium.[7] Technological development does not happen in cyberspace, but in the more familiar universe of postindustrial capital. Thus to the clear-headed, any suggestion that computer technology might be anything but an instrument of this system must seem quixotic—or just plain stupid.

55 Before stepping off into cyberspace, we do well to peel off the futurist headgear and listen to some voices in the street. No one wants to read anymore: "books suck, Nintendo rules." Computers are either imperial business machines or head toys for yuppies. Anyone still interested in "mass" culture needs to check out the yawning gap between the rich and the debtpayers, not to mention the incipient splintering of Euro-America into warring ethnicities and "multicultural" tribes. And while we're at it, we might also do some thinking about our most recent global conflict, wargame-as-video-game with realistic third-world blood, a campaign in defense of economic imbalance and the West's right to determine political order in the Middle East. Perhaps we are using the word "revolution" far too loosely. Given the present state of political and cultural affairs, any vision of a "populite" future, or as John Perry Barlow has it, an "electronic frontier,"[8] needs hard scrutiny. Revolution, as Tommy Lee Jones reminds us, is what you find *in your face*.

56 Do we really want a revolution? Are academic and corporate intellectuals truly prepared to dispense with the current means of text production and the advantages they afford in the present information economy? More to the point, *are we capable* of overturning these institutions, assuming we have the will to do so? Looking back from the seventies, Jean Baudrillard criticized the students of Paris '68[9] for assuming control of the national broadcast center only to reinstate one-to-many programming and the obscurantist focus of the "media event." The pre-revolutionary identity of television swiftly reasserted itself in the midst of radical action. The seizure was a sham, Baudrillard concludes: "Only total revolution, theoretical and practical, can restore the symbolic in the demise of the sign and of value. Even signs must burn."[1] Xanadu as Nelson imagines it does promise to immolate certain cultural icons: the entrepreneurial publishing house, the codex book, the idea of text as unified, self-contained utterance. Taken to its limits, **hypertext** could reverse/recourse into a general medium of control, a means of ensuring popular franchise in the new order of virtual space. Public-access Xanadu might be the last hope for consensual democracy in an age of global simulation.

57 Or it might not: we do well to remember that Ted Nelson's vision comes cleverly packaged with assurances that copyright and intellectual property

7. Patricia Carlson, "The Rhetoric of **Hypertext**," *Hypermedia* 2 (1990): 109–31 [Moulthrop's note].

8. See Bruce Sterling, *The Hacker Crackdown: Law and Disorder on the Electronic Frontier* (New York: Bantam, 1992) [Moulthrop's note]. Barlow (b. 1947) is a co-founder of the Electronic Frontier Foundation, which works to protect the rights of those in cyberspace and to encourage the broader spread of computer-based technologies.

9. In May 1968, students and workers in Paris and throughout France staged protests and a general strike that paralyzed the country; it was a turning point in French political culture.

1. Jean Baudrillard, *For a Critique of the Political Economy of the Sign*, trans. Charles Levin (St. Louis: Telos, 1981), p. 163 [Moulthrop's note].

shall not perish from the earth. Some signs would seem to be flame-resistant. The vision of Xanadu as cyberspatial New Jersusalem is conceivable and perhaps eligible, but by no stretch of the imagination is it inevitable. To live in the postmodern condition is to get along without the consolation of providential fictions or theories of historical necessity. This renunciation includes the "Laws of Media," whose force in the final analysis is theoretical and heuristic, not normative. As Linda Hutcheon observes, postmodernism undermines any attempt at binary distinction. To invoke the possibility of a "post-hierarchical" information order, one must assert the fact that all orders are contingent, the product of discursive formations and social contracts. But this postulate generates a fatally recursive paradox: if all order is consensual, then the social consensus may well express itself against revolution and in support of the old order. The term "post-hierarchical" may some day turn out to carry the same nasty irony as the words "postmodern" or "postwar" in the aftermath of Desert Storm: welcome back to the future, same as it ever was.

In the end it is impossible to dismiss Nelson's prophecies of cultural ren- 58
ovation in Xanadu; but it is equally hard to predict their easy fulfillment. Xanadu and the **hypertext** concept in general challenge humanists and information scientists to reconsider fundamental assumptions about the social space of writing. They may in fact open the way to a new textual order and a new politics of knowledge and expression. However, changes of this magnitude cannot come without major upheavals. Responsibility for the evolution of **hypertext** systems as genuine alternatives to the present information economy rests as much with software developers, social scientists, and literary theorists as it does with legislators and capitalists. If anything unites these diverse elites, it might be their allegiance to existing institutions of intellectual authority—the printed word, the book, the library, the university, the publishing house.

It may be, as Linda Hutcheon asserts, that though we are incapable of 59
direct opposition to our native conditions, we can still criticize and undermine them through such postmodern strategies as deconstruction, parody, and pastiche.[2] Secondary literacy might indeed find expression in a perverse turn about or within the primary body of literate culture. But it seems equally possible that our engagement with interactive media will follow the path of reaction, not revolution. The cultural mood at century's end seems anything but radical. Witness President Bush's attacks on cultural diversity (or as he saw it, "political correctness") in higher education. Or consider Camille Paglia's memorable "defense" of polyvalent, post-print ways of knowing, capped off by a bizarre reversal in which she decrees that children of the Tube must be force-fed "the logocentric and Apollonian side of our culture."[3] Given these signs and symptoms, the prospects for populite renaissance do not seem especially rosy. "It is time for the enlightened repression of the children," Paglia declares. Yet in the face of all this we can still find visionary

2. Hutcheon, *A Poetics of Postmodernism*, pp. 120–21 [Moulthrop's note].

3. Neil Postman and Camille Paglia, "She Wants Her MTV! He Wants His Book!" *Harper's*, March 1991, 44ff. [Moulthrop's note]. Apollonian: rational, as opposed by the German philosopher FRIEDRICH NIETZSCHE (1844–1900) to the "Dionysian," or ecstatic. "Logocentric": tending to privilege words and universal reason over other forms of rationality; a term associated with the French philosopher JACQUES DERRIDA (b. 1930), who applies it to the privileging of speech over writing.

souls who say they want a textual, social, cultural, intellectual revolution. In the words of Lennon:

> *Well, you know . . .*
> We all want to change your head.[4]

60 The question remains: which heads do the changing, and which get the change

?

1991, 1993

4. The Beatles, "Revolution."

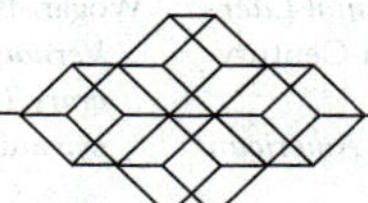

Selected Bibliography of Theory and Criticism

This selected bibliography of theory and criticism consists of six parts: (1) a bibliography of theory and criticism bibliographies; (2) a list of theory anthologies divided into periods; (3) a historically subdivided list of histories of criticism; (4) a short list of theory glossaries, encyclopedias, and handbooks; (5) a brief list of introductions and guides to criticism and theory; and (6) succinct descriptive bibliographies of sixteen contemporary critical schools and movements. All sources are in English.

I. THEORY AND CRITICISM BIBLIOGRAPHIES

Baker, William, and Kenneth Womack. *Recent Works in Critical Theory, 1989–1995: An Annotated Bibliography*. Westport, CT: Greenwood, 1996.

Hall, Vernon. *Literary Criticism: Plato through Johnson*. New York: Appleton-Century-Crofts, 1970.

Irvine, Martin. "A Guide to the Sources of Medieval Theories of Interpretation, Signs, and the Arts of Discourse: Aristotle to Ockham." *Semiotica* 63.1/2 (1987): 89–108.

Marshall, Donald G. *Contemporary Critical Theory: A Selected Bibliography*. New York: MLA, 1993.

Modern Language Association's International Bibliography. Vol. 4, *General Literature and Related Topics*. New York: MLA, published annually.

Orr, Leonard, comp. *Research in Critical Theory since 1965: A Classified Bibliography*. Westport, CT: Greenwood, 1989.

The Year's Work in Critical and Cultural Theory. Ed. Kate McGowan. Oxford: Blackwell, published annually.

II. ANTHOLOGIES OF THEORY AND CRITICISM

General Overviews

Adams, Hazard, ed. *Critical Theory since Plato*. 2d ed. Fort Worth: Harcourt Brace Jovanovich, 1992.

Allen, Gay W., and Harry Hayden Clark, eds. *Literary Criticism: Pope to Croce*. New York: American Book, 1941.

Allot, Miriam Farris, ed. *Novelists on the Novel*. New York: Columbia UP, 1959.

Bate, Walter Jackson, ed. *Criticism: The Major Texts*. Enlarged ed. San Diego: Harcourt Brace Jovanovich, 1970.

Beckson, Karl, ed. *Great Theories in Literary Criticism*. New York: Noonday, 1963.

Brown, Clarence Arthur ed. *The Achievement of American Criticism: Representative Selections from Three Hundred Years of American Criticism*. New York: Ronald, 1954.

Clark, Barrett, ed. *European Theories of the Drama: An Anthology of Dramatic Theory and Criticism from Aristotle to the Present Day*. Rev. Henry Popkin. New York: Crown, 1965.

Davis, Robert Con, and Laurie Finke, eds. *Literary Criticism and Theory: The Greeks to the Present*. New York: Longman, 1989.

Duffield, Holley Gene, ed. *Problems in Criticism of the Arts*. San Francisco: Chandler, 1968.

Foerster, Norman, ed. *American Critical Essays, Nineteenth and Twentieth Centuries*. London: Oxford UP, 1930.

Gilbert, Allen H., ed. *Literary Criticism: Plato to Dryden*. New York: Appleton-Century-Crofts, 1963.

Gross, Laila, ed. *An Introduction to Literary Criticism: An Anthology*. New York: Putnam, 1971.

Hardison, O. B., Jr., ed. *Modern Continental Literary Criticism.* New York: Appleton-Century-Crofts, 1962.

Hutner, Gordon, ed. *American Literature, American Culture.* Oxford: Oxford UP, 1998.

Kaplan, Charles, and William Anderson, eds. *Criticism: The Major Statements.* 4th ed. New York: St. Martin's, 1999.

Lewisohn, Ludwig, ed. *A Modern Book of Criticism.* New York: Boni and Liveright, 1919.

Mueller-Vollmer, Kurt, ed. *The Hermeneutics Reader: Texts of the German Tradition from the Enlightenment to the Present.* New York: Continuum, 1985.

Richter, David, ed. *The Critical Tradition: Classic Texts and Contemporary Trends.* 2d ed. Boston: Bedford, 1998.

Schorer, Mark, Josephine Miles, and Gordon McKenzie, eds. *Criticism: The Foundations of Modern Literary Judgment.* New York: Harcourt Brace, 1948.

Selden, Raman, ed. *The Theory of Criticism from Plato to the Present: A Reader.* New York: Longman, 1988.

Sidnell, Michael, et al., eds. *Sources in Dramatic Theory.* 2 vols. Cambridge: Cambridge UP, 1991.

Singer, Alan, and Allen Dun, eds. *Literary Aesthetics: An Anthology.* Cambridge, MA: Blackwell, 2000.

Smith, James Harry, and Edd Winfield Parks, eds. *The Great Critics: An Anthology of Literary Criticism.* 3d ed. New York: Norton, 1967.

Stevick, Philip, ed. *The Theory of the Novel.* New York: Free P, 1967.

Sutton, Walter, and Richard Foster, eds. *Modern Criticism: Theory and Practice.* New York: Odyssey, 1963.

From Antiquity through the Medieval Period

Benson, Thomas W., and Michael H. Prosser, eds. and trans. *Readings in Classical Rhetoric.* Bloomington: Indiana UP, 1972.

Bloom, Harold, ed. *The Art of the Critic: Literary Theory and Criticism from the Greeks to the Present.* Vol. 1, *Classical and Medieval.* New York: Chelsea House, 1985.

Miller, Joseph M., Michael H. Prosser, and Thomas W. Benson, eds. and trans. *Readings in Medieval Rhetoric.* Bloomington: Indiana UP, 1973.

Minnis, A. J., A. B. Scott, and David Wallace, eds. *Medieval Literary Theory and Criticism, c. 1100–c. 1375: The Commentary Tradition.* Rev. ed. Oxford: Clarendon, 1991.

Preminger, Alex, O. B. Hardison Jr., and Kevin Kerrane, eds. *Classical and Medieval Literary Criticism: Translations and Interpretations.* New York: Ungar, 1974.

Russell, D. A., and M. Winterbottom, eds. *Ancient Literary Criticism: The Principal Texts in New Translations.* Oxford: Clarendon, 1973.

———, eds. *Classical Literary Criticism.* Rev. ed. Oxford: Oxford UP, 1989.

Wogan-Browne, Joycelyn, et al., eds. *The Idea of the Vernacular: An Anthology of Middle English Literary Theory, 1280–1520.* University Park: Pennsylvania State UP, 1999.

From the Renaissance through the Enlightenment

Bloom, Harold, ed. *The Art of the Critic: Literary Theory and Criticism from the Greeks to the Present.* Vol. 2, *Early Renaissance.* New York: Chelsea House, 1986.

———, ed. *The Art of the Critic: Literary Theory and Criticism from the Greeks to the Present.* Vol. 3, *Late Renaissance.* New York: Chelsea House, 1987.

———, ed. *The Art of the Critic: Literary Theory and Criticism from the Greeks to the Present.* Vol. 4, *Enlightenment.* New York: Chelsea House, 1987.

Chapman, G. W., ed. *Literary Criticism in England, 1660–1800.* Englewood Cliffs, NJ: Prentice-Hall, 1966.

Elledge, Scott, ed. *Eighteenth-Century Critical Essays.* 2 vols. Ithaca, NY: Cornell UP, 1961.

Elledge, Scott, and Donald Schier, eds. *The Continental Model: Selected French Critical Essays of the Seventeenth Century, in English Translation.* Ithaca, NY: Cornell UP, 1970.

Folger Collective, ed. *Women Critics, 1660–1820: An Anthology.* Bloomington: Indiana UP, 1995.

Hardison, O. B., Jr., ed. *English Literary Criticism: The Renaissance.* New York: Appleton-Century-Crofts, 1963.

Hynes, Samuel, ed. *English Literary Criticism, Restoration and Eighteenth Century.* New York: Appleton-Century-Crofts, 1963.

Jones, Edmund Davis, ed. *English Critical Essays: Sixteenth–Eighteenth Centuries.* New York: Oxford UP, 1922.

Needham, H. A., ed. *Taste and Criticism in the Eighteenth Century: A Selection of Texts Illustrating the Evolution of Taste and Development of Critical Theory.* London: Harrap, 1952.

Sigworth, Oliver, ed. *Criticism and Aesthetics, 1660–1800.* San Francisco: Rinehart, 1971.

Simon, Irene, ed. *Neo-Classical Criticism, 1600–1800.* Columbia: U of South Carolina P, 1971.

Smith, G. Gregory, ed. *Elizabethan Critical Essays.* 2 vols. Oxford: Clarendon, 1904.

Spingarn, Joel, ed. *Critical Essays of the Seventeenth Century.* Vol. 1, *1605–1650.* Oxford: Clarendon, 1908.

———, ed. *Critical Essays of the Seventeenth Century.* Vol. 2, *1650–1685.* Oxford: Clarendon, 1908.

———, ed. *Critical Essays of the Seventeenth Century.* Vol. 3, *1685–1700.* Oxford: Clarendon, 1909.

Tayler, Edward W., ed. *Literary Criticism of Seventeenth-Century England.* New York: Knopf, 1967.

Vickers, Brian, ed. *English Renaissance Literary Criticism.* Oxford: Clarendon, 1999.

Weinberg, Bernard, ed. *Critical Prefaces of the*

French Renaissance. Evanston, IL: Northwestern UP, 1950.

From Romanticism through the Victorian Period

Bloom, Harold, ed. *The Art of the Critic: Literary Theory and Criticism from the Greeks to the Present*. Vol. 5, *Early Romantics*. New York: Chelsea House, 1988.

———, ed. *The Art of the Critic: Literary Theory and Criticism from the Greeks to the Present*. Vol. 6, *Later Romantics*. New York: Chelsea House, 1988.

———, ed. *The Art of the Critic: Literary Theory and Criticism from the Greeks to the Present*. Vol. 7, *Later Nineteenth Century*. New York: Chelsea House, 1989.

Bromwich, David, ed. *Romantic Critical Essays*. New York: Cambridge UP, 1987.

Hepworth, Brian, ed. *The Rise of Romanticism: Essential Texts*. Manchester: Carcanet New P, 1978.

Hoffman, Daniel C., and Samuel Hynes, eds. *English Literary Criticism, Romantic and Victorian*. New York: Appleton-Century-Crofts, 1963.

Jones, Edmund Davis, ed. *English Critical Essays: Nineteenth Century*. London: Oxford UP, 1916.

Nisbet, H. B., ed. *German Aesthetic and Literary Criticism: Winckelmann, Lessing, Hamann, Herder, Schiller and Goethe*. Cambridge: Cambridge UP, 1985.

Peters, Robert, ed. *Victorians on Literature and Art*. New York: Appleton-Century-Crofts, 1961.

Schulte-Sasse, Jochen, ed. *Theory as Practice: A Critical Anthology of Early German Romantic Writings*. Minneapolis: U of Minnesota P, 1997.

Simpson, David, ed. *German Aesthetic and Literary Criticism: Kant, Fichte, Schelling, Schopenhauer, Hegel*. Cambridge: Cambridge UP, 1984.

———, ed. *The Origins of Modern Critical Thought: German Aesthetics and Literary Criticism from Lessing to Hegel*. Cambridge: Cambridge UP, 1988.

Warner, Eric, ed. *Strangeness and Beauty: An Anthology of Aesthetic Criticism, 1840–1910*. 2 vols. Cambridge: Cambridge UP, 1983.

Wheeler, Kathleen, ed. *German Aesthetic and Literary Criticism: The Romantic Ironists and Goethe*. Cambridge: Cambridge UP, 1984.

Willson, A. Leslie, ed. *German Romantic Criticism*. New York: Continuum, 1982.

The Modern and Contemporary Periods

Adams, Hazard, and Leroy Searle, eds. *Critical Theory since 1965*. Tallahassee: Florida State UP, 1986.

Babbitt, Irving, et al. *Criticism in America: Its Function and Status*. New York: Harcourt Brace, 1924.

Bloom, Harold, ed. *The Art of the Critic: Literary Theory and Criticism from the Greeks to the Present*. Vol. 8, *Early Twentieth Century*. New York: Chelsea House, 1989.

———, ed. *The Art of the Critic: Literary Theory and Criticism from the Greeks to the Present*. Vol. 9, *Middle-Twentieth Century*. New York: Chelsea House, 1989.

———, ed. *The Art of the Critic: Literary Theory and Criticism from the Greeks to the Present*. Vol. 10, *Contemporary*. New York: Chelsea House, 1990.

———, ed. *The Art of the Critic: Literary Theory and Criticism from the Greeks to the Present*. Vol. 11, *Contemporary (Conclusion) with Glossary and Index*. New York: Chelsea House, 1990.

Bowman, James C., ed. *Contemporary American Criticism*. New York: Holt, 1926.

Brooker, Peter, and Peter Widdowson, eds. *A Practical Reader in Contemporary Literary Theory*. New York: Prentice Hall/Harvester Wheatsheaf, 1996.

Burgum, Edwin B., ed. *The New Criticism*. New York: Prentice Hall, 1930.

Cahoone, Lawrence, ed. *From Modernism to Postmodernism: An Anthology*. Cambridge, MA: Blackwell, 1999.

Davis, Robert Con, and Ronald Schleifer, eds. *Contemporary Literary Criticism: Literary and Cultural Studies*. 4th ed. New York: Longman, 1998.

Drake, William A., ed. *American Criticism*. New York: Harcourt, Brace, 1926.

Glicksberg, Charles, ed. *American Literary Criticism, 1900–1950*. New York: Hendricks House, 1952.

Handy, William J., and Max Westbrook, eds. *Twentieth-Century Criticism: The Major Statements*. New York: Free P, 1974.

Hoffman, Michael J., and Patrick D. Murphy, eds. *Essentials of the Theory of Fiction*. 2d ed. Durham, NC: Duke UP, 1996.

Lambropoulos, Vassilis, and David Neal Miller, eds. *Twentieth-Century Literary Theory: An Introductory Anthology*. Albany: State U of New York P, 1987.

Latimer, Dan, ed. *Contemporary Critical Theory*. San Diego: Harcourt Brace Jovanovich, 1989.

Lodge, David, ed. *Modern Criticism and Theory: A Reader*. London: Longman, 1988.

———, ed. *Twentieth-Century Literary Criticism: A Reader*. London: Longman, 1972.

Lucy, Niall, ed. *Postmodern Literary Theory: An Anthology*. Cambridge, MA: Blackwell, 1999.

McKeon, Michael, ed. *Theory of the Novel: A Historical Approach*. Baltimore: Johns Hopkins UP, 2000.

Newton, K. M., ed. *Twentieth-Century Literary Theory: A Reader*. New York: St. Martin's, 1997.

Philipson, Morris, and Paul J. Gudel, eds. *Aesthetics Today*. Rev. ed. New York: Meridian, 1980.

Rice, Phillip, and Patricia Waugh, eds. *Modern Literary Theory: A Reader*. 3d ed. New York: St. Martin's, 1996.

Rivkin, Julie, and Michael Ryan, eds. *Literary Theory: An Anthology*. Cambridge, MA: Blackwell, 1998.

Rylance, Rick, ed. *Debating Texts: Readings in Twentieth-Century Literary Theory and Method*. Toronto: U of Toronto P, 1987.

Stallman, Robert Wooster, ed. *Critiques and Essays in Criticism, 1920–1948*. New York: Ronald, 1949.

Staton, Shirley F., ed. *Literary Theories in Praxis*. Philadelphia: U of Pennsylvania P, 1987.

West, Ray B., ed. *Essays in Modern Literary Criticism*. New York: Rinehart, 1952.

Wolfreys, Julian, ed. *Literary Theories: A Reader and Guide*. New York: New York UP, 1999.

Zabel, Morton Dauwen, ed. *Literary Opinion in America: Essays Illustrating the Status, Methods, and Problems of Criticism in the United States in the Twentieth Century*. 3d ed. New York: Harper and Row, 1962.

III. HISTORIES OF CRITICISM AND THEORY

Covering Multiple Periods

Baldick, Chris. *The Social Mission of English Criticism, 1848–1932*. Oxford: Oxford UP, 1983.

Baym, Max. *A History of Literary Aesthetics in America*. New York: Ungar, 1973.

Beardsley, Monroe C. *Aesthetics from Classical Greece to the Present: A Short History*. New York: Macmillan, 1966.

Bernstein, J. M. *The Fate of Art: Aesthetic Alienation from Kant to Derrida*. Oxford: Polity, 1991.

Blamires, Harry. *A History of Literary Criticism*. New York: St. Martin's, 1991.

Bolgar, R. R. *The Classical Heritage and Its Beneficiaries*. Cambridge: Cambridge UP, 1954.

Bosanquet, Bernard. *A History of Æsthetic*. 2d ed. London: Allen and Unwin, 1904.

Bowie, Andrew. *From Romanticism to Critical Theory: The Philosophy of German Literary Theory*. New York: Routledge, 1996.

Carritt, E. F. *Philosophies of Beauty from Socrates to Robert Bridges*. New York: Oxford UP, 1931.

Cassedy, Steven. *Flight from Eden: The Origins of Modern Criticism and Theory*. Berkeley: U of California P, 1990.

Court, Franklin E. *Institutionalizing English Literature: The Culture and Politics of Literary Study, 1750–1900*. Stanford: Stanford UP, 1992.

Crane, R. S., ed. *Critics and Criticism: Ancient and Modern*. Chicago: U of Chicago P, 1952.

———, ed. *Critics and Criticism: Essays in Method*. Abridged ed. Chicago: U of Chicago P, 1957.

Daiches, David. *Critical Approaches to Literature*. Englewood Cliffs, NJ: Prentice-Hall, 1956.

Day, Gary, ed. *The British Critical Tradition: A Re-Evaluation*. New York: St. Martin's, 1993.

Doležel, Lubomír. *Occidental Poetics: Tradition and Progress*. Lincoln: U of Nebraska P, 1990.

Eagleton, Terry. *The Function of Criticism: From the "Spectator" to Post-Structuralism*. London: Verso, 1984.

———. *The Ideology of the Aesthetic*. Oxford: Blackwell, 1990.

Foerster, Norman. *American Criticism: A Study of Literary Theory from Poe to the Present*. Boston: Houghton Mifflin, 1928.

Fowlie, Wallace. *The French Critic, 1549–1967*. Carbondale: Southern Illinois UP, 1968.

Gilbert, K. E., and Helmut Kuhn. *A History of Esthetics*. 2d ed. Bloomington: Indiana UP, 1953.

Grafton, Anthony. *Defenders of the Text: The Traditions of Scholarship in an Age of Science, 1450–1800*. Cambridge, MA: Harvard UP, 1991.

Guillén, Claudio. *Challenge of Comparative Literature*. Trans. Cola Franzen. Cambridge, MA: Harvard UP, 1993.

Guillory, John. *Cultural Capital: The Problem of Literary Canon Formation*. Chicago: U of Chicago P, 1993.

Hall, Vernon, Jr. *A Short History of Literary Criticism*. New York: New York UP, 1963.

Harland, Richard. *Literary Theory from Plato to Barthes: An Introductory History*. New York: St. Martin's, 1999.

Hayden, John O. *Polestar of the Ancients: The Aristotelian Tradition in Classical and English Literary Criticism*. Newark: U of Delaware P, 1979.

Hohendahl, Peter Uwe, ed. *A History of German Literary Criticism, 1730–1980*. Trans. Franz Blaha et al. Lincoln: U of Nebraska P, 1988.

Mahoney, John L. *The Whole Internal Universe: Imitation and the New Defense of Poetry in British Criticism, 1600–1830*. New York: Fordham UP, 1985.

Marino, Adrian. *The Biography of "the Idea of Literature" from Antiquity to the Baroque*. Albany: State U of New York P, 1996.

Parrinder, Patrick. *Authors and Authority: English and American Criticism, 1750–1990*. New York: Columbia UP, 1991.

Patterson, Warner F. *Three Centuries of French Poetic Theory: A Critical History of the Chief Arts of Poetry in France, 1328–1630*. 2 vols. New York: Russell and Russell, 1966.

Perosa, Sergio. *American Theories of the Novel, 1793–1903*. New York: New York UP, 1983.

Smith, Bernard. *Forces in American Criticism: A Study in the History of American Literary Thought*. New York: Harcourt, 1939.

Stone, P. W. K. *The Art of Poetry, 1750–1820: Theories of Poetic Composition and Style in the Late Neo-Classic and Early Romantic Periods*. New York: Barnes and Noble, 1967.

Stovall, Floyd, ed. *The Development of American Literary Criticism*. Chapel Hill: U of North Carolina P, 1955.

Sychrava, Juliet. *Schiller to Derrida: Idealism in Aesthetics*. Cambridge: Cambridge UP, 1989.

Talmor, Sascha. *The Rhetoric of Criticism from Hobbes to Coleridge*. Oxford: Pergamon, 1984.

Todorov, Tzvetan. *Theories of the Symbol*. Trans. Catherine Porter. Ithaca, NY: Cornell UP, 1982.

Watson, George. *The Literary Critics: A Study of English Descriptive Criticism*. 2d ed. Totowa, NJ: Rowman and Littlefield, 1973.

Williams, Raymond. *Culture and Society, 1780–1950*. London: Penguin, 1958.

Wimsatt, William K., Jr., and Cleanth Brooks. *Literary Criticism: A Short History*. New York: Knopf, 1957.

From Antiquity through the Medieval Period

Allen, Judson Boyce. *The Ethical Poetic of the Later Middle Ages: A Decorum of Convenient Distinction*. Toronto: U of Toronto P, 1982.

Atkins, J. W. H. *English Literary Criticism: The Medieval Phase*. Gloucester, MA: P. Smith, 1934.

———. *Literary Criticism in Antiquity, a Sketch of Its Development*. Vol. 1, *Greek*. Cambridge: Cambridge UP, 1934.

———. *Literary Criticism in Antiquity, a Sketch of Its Development*. Vol. 2, *Graeco-Roman*. Cambridge: Cambridge UP, 1934.

Clogan, Paul, ed. *Medieval Poetics*. Cambridge: Cambridge UP, 1976.

Colish, Marcia. *The Mirror of Language: A Study in the Medieval Theory of Language*. Rev. ed. Lincoln: U of Nebraska P, 1983.

Copeland, Rita. *Rhetoric, Hermeneutics, and Translation in the Middle Ages: Academic Traditions and Vernacular Texts*. Cambridge: Cambridge UP, 1991.

Curtius, Ernst Robert. *European Literature and the Latin Middle Ages*. Trans. Willard R. Trask. Princeton: Princeton UP, 1953.

D'Alton, J. D. F. *Roman Literary Theory and Criticism, a Study in Tendencies*. New York: Longmans, Green, 1931.

Eco, Umberto. *Art and Beauty in the Middle Ages*. Trans. Hugh Bredin. New Haven: Yale UP, 1986.

Eco, Umberto, and Costantino Marmo, eds. *On the Medieval Theory of Signs*. Trans. Shona Kelly. Philadelphia: Benjamins, 1989.

Eden, Kathy. *Hermeneutics and the Rhetorical Tradition: Chapters in the Ancient Legacy and Its Humanist Reception*. New Haven: Yale UP, 1997.

Gellrich, Jesse. *The Idea of the Book in the Middle Ages: Language Theory, Mythology, and Fiction*. Ithaca, NY: Cornell UP, 1985.

Gould, Thomas. *The Ancient Quarrel between Poetry and Philosophy*. Princeton: Princeton UP, 1991.

Greenfield, Concetta C. *Humanist and Scholastic Poetics, 1200–1500*. Lewisburg, PA: Bucknell UP, 1981.

Grube, G. M. A. *The Greek and the Roman Critics*. Toronto: U of Toronto P, 1968.

Haug, Walter. *Vernacular Literary Theory in the Middle Ages: The German Tradition, 800–1300, in Its European Context*. Trans. Joanna M. Catling. Cambridge: Cambridge UP, 1997.

Irvine, Martin. *The Making of Textual Culture: "Grammatica" and Literary Theory, 350–1100*. Cambridge: Cambridge UP, 1994.

Kennedy, George Alexander, ed. *The Cambridge History of Literary Criticism*. Vol. 1, *Classical Criticism*. New York: Cambridge UP, 1989.

Klibansky, Raymond. *The Continuity of the Platonic Tradition during the Middle Ages*. London: Warburg Institute, 1939.

Meijering, Roos. *Literary and Rhetorical Theory in Greek Scholia*. Gronigen: Egbert Forsten, 1987.

Minnis, A. J. *Medieval Theory of Authorship: Scholastic Literary Attitudes in the Later Middle Ages*. 2d ed. Philadelphia: U of Pennsylvania P, 1988.

Montgomery, Robert Langford. *The Reader's Eye: Studies in Didactic Literary Theory from Dante to Tasso*. Berkeley: U of California P, 1979.

Morse, Ruth. *Truth and Convention in the Middle Ages: Rhetoric, Representation, and Reality*. Cambridge: Cambridge UP, 1991.

Purcell, William M. *Ars Poetriae: Rhetorical and Grammatical Invention at the Margin of Literacy*. Columbia: U of South Carolina P, 1996.

Roberts, W. R. *Greek Rhetoric and Literary Criticism*. New York: Longmans, Green, 1928.

Russell, D. A. *Criticism in Antiquity*. Berkeley: U of California P, 1981.

Saintsbury, George. *A History of Criticism and Literary Taste in Europe*. Vol. 1, *Classical and Mediæval Criticism*. Edinburgh: W. Blackwood and Sons, 1900.

Sturges, Robert. *Medieval Interpretation: Models of Reading in Literary Narrative, 1100–1500*. Carbondale: Southern Illinois UP, 1990.

Trimpi, Wesley. *Muses of One Mind: The Literary Analysis of Experience and Its Continuity*. Princeton: Princeton UP, 1983.

Vance, Eugene. *Marvelous Signals: Poetics and Sign Theory in the Middle Ages*. Lincoln: U of Nebraska P, 1986.

Zumthor, Paul. *Toward a Medieval Poetics*. Trans. Philip Bennett. Minneapolis: U of Minnesota P, 1992.

From the Renaissance through the Enlightenment

Atkins, J. W. H. *English Literary Criticism: Seventeenth and Eighteenth Centuries*. London: Methuen, 1951.

———. *English Literary Criticism: The Renascence*. London: Methuen, 1947.

Baldwin, Charles S. *Renaissance Literary Theory and Practice: Classicism in the Rhetoric and Poetic of Italy, France, and England, 1400–1600*. New York: Columbia UP, 1939.

Bate, Walter Jackson. *From Classic to Romantic: The Premises of Taste in Eighteenth-Century England*. Cambridge, MA: Harvard UP, 1946.

Bosker, A. *Literary Criticism in the Age of Johnson*. 2d ed. New York: Hafner, 1953.

Clark, A. F. B. *Boileau and the French Classical Critics in England, 1660–1830*. Paris: E. Champion, 1925.

Coleman, Francis X. J. *The Aesthetic Thought of the French Enlightenment*. Pittsburgh: U of Pittsburgh P, 1971.

Engell, James. *Forming the Critical Mind: Dryden to Coleridge*. Cambridge, MA: Harvard UP, 1989.

Ferguson, Margaret W. *Trials of Desire: Renaissance Defenses of Poetry*. New Haven: Yale UP, 1983.

Hall, Vernon. *Renaissance Literary Criticism: A Study of Its Social Content*. New York: Columbia UP, 1945.

Hardison, O. B., Jr. *The Enduring Monument: A Study of the Idea of Praise in Renaissance Literary Theory and Practice*. Chapel Hill: U of North Carolina P, 1962.

Hathaway, Baxter. *The Age of Criticism: The Late Renaissance in Italy*. Ithaca, NY: Cornell UP, 1962.

———. *Marvels and Commonplaces: Renaissance Literary Criticism*. New York: Random House, 1968.

Hipple, Walter. *The Beautiful, the Sublime, and the Picturesque in Eighteenth-Century British Aesthetic Theory*. Carbondale: Southern Illinois UP, 1957.

Jones, Thora B., and Bernard de B. Nicol. *Neo-Classical Dramatic Criticism, 1560–1770*. Cambridge: Cambridge UP, 1975.

Kinney, Arthur F. *Humanist Poetics: Thought, Rhetoric, and Fiction in Sixteenth-Century England*. Amherst: U of Massachusetts P, 1986.

Marks, Emerson. *The Poetics of Reason: English Neoclassical Criticism*. New York: Random House, 1968.

Mattick, Paul, Jr., ed. *Eighteenth-Century Aesthetics and the Reconstruction of Art*. Cambridge: Cambridge UP, 1993.

Miller, G. M. *The Historical Point of View in English Literary Criticism, 1570–1770*. New York: B. Franklin, 1968.

Monk, Samuel H. *The Sublime: A Study of Critical Theory in Eighteenth-Century England*. New York: Modern Language Association, 1935.

Montgomery, Robert Langford. *Terms of Response: Language and Audience in Seventeenth- and Eighteenth-Century Theory*. University Park: Pennsylvania State UP, 1992.

Nisbet, H. B., and Claude Rawson, eds. *The Cambridge History of Literary Criticism*. Vol. 4, *The Eighteenth Century*. Cambridge: Cambridge UP, 1997.

Norton, Robert E. *The Beautiful Soul: Aesthetic Morality in the Eighteenth Century*. Ithaca, NY: Cornell UP, 1995.

Paulson, Ronald. *The Beautiful, Novel, and Strange: Aesthetics and Heterodoxy*. Baltimore: Johns Hopkins UP, 1996.

———. *Breaking and Remaking: Aesthetic Practice in England, 1700–1820*. New Brunswick, NJ: Rutgers UP, 1989.

Pittock, Joan. *The Ascendancy of Taste*. New York: Routledge, 1973.

Runge, Laura. *Gender and Language in British Literary Criticism, 1660–1790*. Cambridge: Cambridge UP, 1997.

Saintsbury, George. *A History of Criticism and Literary Taste in Europe*. Vol. 2, *From the Renaissance to the Decline of Eighteenth-Century Orthodoxy*. Edinburgh: W. Blackwood and Sons, 1902.

Spingarn, Joel. *History of Literary Criticism in the Renaissance*. 2d ed. New York: Columbia UP, 1908.

Sweeting, Elizabeth J. *Early Tudor Criticism, Linguistic and Literary*. Oxford: Blackwell, 1940.

Weinberg, Bernard. *A History of Literary Criticism in the Italian Renaissance*. 2 vols. Chicago: U of Chicago P, 1961.

Weinsheimer, Joel C. *Eighteenth-Century Hermeneutics: Philosophy of Interpretation in England from Locke to Burke*. New Haven: Yale UP, 1993.

Wellek, René. *A History of Modern Criticism: 1750–1950*. Vol. 1, *The Later Eighteenth Century*. New Haven: Yale UP, 1955.

Zimbardo, Rose A. *A Mirror to Nature: Transformations in Aesthetics and Drama, 1660–1732*. Lexington: UP of Kentucky, 1986.

From Romanticism through the Victorian Period

Abrams, M. H. *The Mirror and the Lamp: Romantic Theory and the Critical Tradition*. New York: Oxford UP, 1953.

Babbitt, Irving. *The Masters of Modern French Criticism*. New York: Houghton Mifflin, 1912.

Behler, Ernst. *German Romantic Literary Theory*. Cambridge: Cambridge UP, 1993.

Brown, Marshall, ed. *The Cambridge History of Literary Criticism*. Vol. 5, *Romanticism*. New York: Cambridge UP, 2000.

Charvat, William. *The Origins of American Critical Thought, 1810–1835*. Philadelphia: U of Pennsylvania P, 1936.

Dale, Peter Allan. *The Victorian Critic and the Idea of History*. Cambridge, MA: Harvard UP, 1977.

Foakes, R. A. *Romantic Criticism, 1800–1850*. London: Edward Arnold, 1968.

Helfer, Martha B. *The Retreat of Representation: The Concept of "Darstellung" in German Critical Discourse*. Albany: State U of New York P, 1996.

Lacoue-Labarthe, Philippe, and Jean-Luc Nancy. *The Literary Absolute: The Theory of Literature in German Romanticism*. Trans. Philip Barnard and Cheryl Lester. Albany: State U of New York P, 1988.

Lehmann, A. G. *The Symbolist Aesthetic in France, 1885–1895*. Oxford: Blackwell, 1950.

Moser, Charles A. *Esthetics as Nightmare: Russian Literary Theory, 1855–70*. Princeton: Princeton UP, 1989.

Murphy, Paul Thomas. *Toward a Working-Class Canon: Literary Criticism in British Working-Class Periodicals, 1818–1858*. Columbus: Ohio State UP, 1994.

Rathbun, John W. *American Literary Criticism, 1800–1860*. Boston: Twayne, 1979.

Rathbun, John W., and Harry H. Clark. *American Literary Criticism, 1860–1905*. Boston: Twayne, 1979.

Saintsbury, George. *A History of Criticism and Lit-*

erary Taste in Europe. Vol. 3, *Modern Criticism*. Edinburgh: W. Blackwood and Sons, 1904.

Stang, Richard. *The Theory of the Novel in England: 1850–1870*. New York: Columbia UP, 1959.

Warren, A. H. *English Poetic Theory, 1825–1865*. Princeton: Princeton UP, 1950.

Wellek, René. *A History of Modern Criticism: 1750–1950*. Vol. 2, *The Romantic Age*. New Haven: Yale UP, 1955.

———. *A History of Modern Criticism: 1750–1950*. Vol. 3, *The Age of Transition*. New Haven: Yale UP, 1965.

———. *A History of Modern Criticism: 1750–1950*. Vol. 4, *The Later Nineteenth Century*. New Haven: Yale UP, 1965.

Woodmansee, Martha. *Author, Art, and the Market: Rereading the History of Aesthetics*. New York: Columbia UP, 1994.

The Modern and Contemporary Periods

Baldick, Chris. *Criticism and Literary Theory, 1890 to the Present*. London: Longman, 1996.

Berman, Art. *From the New Criticism to Deconstruction: The Reception of Structuralism and Post-Structuralism*. Urbana: U of Illinois P, 1988.

Bové, Paul A. *Intellectuals in Power: A Genealogy of Critical Humanism*. New York: Columbia UP, 1986.

Bruss, Elizabeth W. *Beautiful Theories: The Spectacle of Discourse in Contemporary Criticism*. Baltimore: Johns Hopkins UP, 1982.

Cain, William E. *The Crisis in Criticism*. Baltimore: Johns Hopkins UP, 1984.

Carton, Evan, and Gerald Graff. "Criticism Since 1940." *The Cambridge History of American Literature*. Ed. Sacvan Bercovitch. Vol. 8, *Poetry and Criticism, 1940–1995*. Cambridge: Cambridge UP, 1996. 261–535.

Cohen, Ralph, ed. *The Future of Literary Theory*. New York: Routledge, 1989.

Collier, Peter, and Helga Geyer-Ryan, eds. *Literary Theory Today*. Cambridge: Polity, 1990.

Culler, Jonathan. *Framing the Sign: Criticism and Its Institutions*. Norman: U of Oklahoma P, 1988.

Dosse, François. *History of Structuralism*. Vol. 1, *The Rising Sign, 1945–1966*. Trans. Deborah Glassman. Minneapolis: U of Minnesota P, 1997.

———. *History of Structuralism*: Vol. 2, *The Sign Sets, 1967–Present*. Trans. Deborah Glassman. Minneapolis: U of Minnesota P, 1997.

Erlich, Victor. *Russian Formalism: History—Doctrine*. 3d ed. New Haven: Yale UP, 1981.

Fekete, John. *The Critical Twilight: Explorations in the Ideology of Anglo-American Literary Theory from Eliot to McLuhan*. London: Routledge and Kegan Paul, 1977.

Ffrench, Patrick. *The Time of Theory: A History of "Tel Quel" (1960–1983)*. Oxford: Clarendon; New York: Oxford UP, 1995.

Foster, Richard J. *The New Romantics: A Reappraisal of the New Criticism*. Bloomington: Indiana UP, 1962.

Goldsmith, Arnold L. *American Literary Criticism, 1905–1965*. Boston: Twayne, 1979.

Goodheart, Eugene. *The Failure of Criticism*. Cambridge, MA: Harvard UP, 1978.

Graff, Gerald. *Professing Literature: An Institutional History*. Chicago: U of Chicago P, 1987.

Hyman, Stanley Edgar. *The Armed Vision: A Study in the Methods of Modern Literary Scholarship*. 2d ed. New York: Vintage, 1955.

Leitch, Vincent B. *American Literary Criticism from the 1930s to the 1980s*. New York: Columbia UP, 1988.

Lentricchia, Frank. *After the New Criticism*. Chicago: U of Chicago P, 1980.

———. *Criticism and Social Change*. Chicago: U of Chicago P, 1983.

Litz, Walton A., et al., eds. *The Cambridge History of Literary Criticism*. Vol. 7, *Modernism and the New Criticism*. New York: Cambridge UP, 2000.

McGowan, John. *Postmodernism and Its Critics*. Ithaca, NY: Cornell UP, 1991.

Mowitt, John. *Text: The Genealogy of an Anti-Disciplinary Subject*. Durham, NC: Duke UP, 1992.

Mulhern, Francis. *The Moment of "Scrutiny."* London: NLB, 1979.

O'Connor, William Van. *An Age of Criticism, 1900–1950*. Chicago: H. Regnery, 1952.

O'Hara, Daniel T. *The Romance of Interpretation: Visionary Criticism from Pater to de Man*. New York Columbia UP, 1985.

Ohmann, Richard. *English in America*. New York: Oxford UP, 1976.

Pritchard, John Paul. *Criticism in America*. Norman: U of Oklahoma P, 1956.

Ray, William. *Literary Meaning: From Phenomenology to Deconstruction*. New York: Blackwell, 1984.

Selden, Raman, ed. *The Cambridge History of Literary Criticism*. Vol. 8, *From Formalism to Poststructuralism*. New York: Cambridge UP, 1995.

Shumway, David R. *Creating American Civilization: A Genealogy of American Literature as an Academic Discipline*. Minneapolis: U of Minnesota P. 1994.

Simon, John K., ed. *Modern French Criticism from Proust and Valéry to Structuralism*. Chicago: U of Chicago P, 1972.

Sosnoski, James. *Token Professionals and Master Critics: A Critique of Orthodoxy in Literary Studies*. Albany: State U of New York P, 1994.

Sutton, Walter. *Modern American Criticism*. Englewood Cliffs, NJ: Prentice-Hall, 1963.

Todorov, Tzvetan. *Literature and Its Theorists: A Personal View of Twentieth-Century Criticism*. Trans. Catherine Porter. Ithaca, NY: Cornell UP, 1987.

Vanderbilt, Kermit. *American Literature and the Academy: The Roots, Growth, and Maturity of a Profession*. Philadelphia: U of Pennsylvania P, 1986.

Webster, Grant. *The Republic of Letters: A History of Postwar American Literary Opinion*. Baltimore: Johns Hopkins UP, 1979.

Wellek, René. *A History of Modern Criticism: 1750–1950*. Vol. 5, *English Criticism, 1900–1950*. New Haven: Yale UP, 1986.

———. *A History of Modern Criticism: 1750–1950*. Vol. 6, *American Criticism, 1900–1950*. New Haven: Yale UP, 1986.

———. *A History of Modern Criticism: 1750–1950*. Vol. 7, *German, Russian, and Eastern European Criticism, 1900–1950*. New Haven: Yale UP, 1991.

———. *A History of Modern Criticism: 1750–1950*. Vol. 8, *French, Italian, and Spanish Criticism, 1900–1950*. New Haven: Yale UP, 1993.

IV. GLOSSARIES, ENCYCLOPEDIAS, AND HANDBOOKS

Abrams, M. H. *A Glossary of Literary Terms*. 7th ed. Fort Worth: Harcourt Brace, 1999.

Childers, Joseph, and Gary Hentzi, eds. *The Columbia Dictionary of Modern Literary and Cultural Criticism*. New York: Columbia UP, 1995.

Coyle, Martin, Peter Garside, and Malcom Kelsall, eds. *Encyclopedia of Literature and Criticism*. London: Routledge, 1991.

Cuddon, J. A., and C. E. Preston. *A Dictionary of Literary Terms and Literary Theory*. 4th ed. Oxford: Blackwell, 1998.

Ducrot, Oswald, and Tzvetan Todorov. *Encyclopedic Dictionary of the Sciences of Language*. Trans. Catherine Porter. Baltimore: Johns Hopkins UP, 1979.

Groden, Michael, and Martin Kreiswirth, eds. *The Johns Hopkins Guide to Literary Theory and Criticism*. Baltimore: Johns Hopkins UP, 1994.

Harris, William V. *A Dictionary of Concepts in Literary Criticism and Theory*. Westport, CT: Greenwood, 1992.

Holman, C. Hugh, and William Harmon. *A Handbook to Literature*. 8th ed. New York: Macmillan, 1999.

Kelly, Michael, ed. *Encyclopedia of Aesthetics*. 4 vols. Oxford: Oxford UP, 1998.

Lechte, John. *Fifty Key Contemporary Thinkers: From Structuralism to Postmodernity*. London: Routledge, 1994.

Lentricchia, Frank, and Thomas McLaughlin, eds. *Critical Terms for Literary Study*. 2d ed. Chicago: U of Chicago P, 1995.

Makaryk, Irena R., ed. *Encyclopedia of Contemporary Literary Theory: Approaches, Scholars, Terms*. Toronto: U of Toronto P, 1993.

Preminger, Alex, and T. V. F. Brogan, eds. *The New Princeton Encyclopedia of Poetry and Poetics*. Princeton: Princeton UP, 1993.

Williams, Raymond. *Keywords: A Vocabulary of Culture and Society*. 2d ed. New York: Oxford UP, 1983.

V. INTRODUCTIONS AND GUIDES

Barry, Peter. *Beginning Theory: An Introduction to Literary and Cultural Theory*. Manchester: Manchester UP, 1995.

Booker, M. Keith. *A Practical Introduction to Literary Theory and Criticism*. White Plains, NY: Longman, 1996.

Bressler, Charles E. *Literary Criticism: An Introduction to Theory and Practice*. 2d ed. Upper Saddle River, NJ: Prentice Hall, 1999.

Culler, Jonathan. *Literary Theory: A Very Short Introduction*. Oxford: Oxford UP, 1997.

Eagleton, Terry. *Literary Theory: An Introduction*. 2d ed. Minneapolis: U of Minnesota P, 1996.

Hall, Donald E. *Literary and Cultural Theory: From Basic Principles to Advanced Applications*. Boston: Houghton Mifflin, 2001.

Jefferson, Ann, and David Robey, eds. *Modern Literary Theory: A Comparative Introduction*. Totowa, NJ: Barnes and Noble, 1982.

Natoli, Joseph, ed. *Tracing Literary Theory*. Urbana: U of Illinois P, 1987.

Ryan, Michael. *Literary Theory: A Practical Introduction*. Cambridge, MA: Blackwell, 1999.

Selden, Raman, Peter Widdowson, and Peter Brooker. *A Reader's Guide to Contemporary Literary Theory*. 4th ed. New York: Prentice Hall, 1997.

Tyson, Lois. *Critical Theory Today: A User-Friendly Guide*. New York: Garland, 1999.

Wellek, René, and Austin Warren. *Theory of Literature*. 3d ed. New York: Harcourt, 1962.

VI. MODERN AND CONTEMPORARY CRITICAL SCHOOLS AND MOVEMENTS

Each of the following sixteen entries on modern and contemporary critical schools and movements, listed in alphabetical order, follows a set pattern of five paragraphs. The first paragraph identifies groundbreaking and influential texts, while the second covers informative introductions, overviews, and histories. Paragraph three represents the breadth of the school by listing selected anthologies and readers. Where

reference sources such as area-specific bibliographies, handbooks, dictionaries, or encyclopedias exist, they are listed in the fourth paragraph. The final paragraph highlights well-received crossover texts that mark fruitful intersections between schools and movements. Not surprisingly, these five categories of texts overlap. All sources are in English.

African American Criticism and Theory
Asian American Criticism and Theory
Chicano/Chicana Studies
Cultural Studies
Deconstruction and Poststructuralism
Feminist Criticism and Theory
Formalism
Gay and Lesbian Criticism and Queer Theory
Marxism
Native American Studies
New Historicism
Phenomenology and Hermeneutics
Postcolonial Criticism and Theory
Psychoanalytic Theory
Reader-Response Criticism
Structuralism and Semiotics

African American Criticism and Theory

Significant twentieth-century African American criticism and theory begins with the works of the Harlem Renaissance and the related protest tradition, including such texts as James Weldon Johnson's preface to *The Book of American Negro Poetry* (1922), one of the earliest discussions of race and form; Langston Hughes's "Negro Artist and the Racial Mountain" (1926); W. E. B. Du Bois's "Criteria of Negro Art" (1926); and Richard Wright's "Blueprint for Negro Writing" (1937), a seminal point of origin for the vernacular theorizing that culminated in Stephen Henderson's highly influential introduction to *Understanding the New Black Poetry* (1973). Another phase of African American theory and criticism emerges in the 1960s with the Black Arts movement. Groundbreaking characterizations of the Black Aesthetic appear in Amiri Baraka's *Home: Social Essays* (1966), which chronicles Baraka's personal shift from phenomenology to black aesthetics; Hoyt Fuller's "Toward a Black Aesthetic" (1968); and Larry Neal's "Black Arts Movement" (1968). In the late 1970s and 1980s a younger generation of academic intellectuals began to critique the assumptions behind the Black Aesthetic and to incorporate structuralist and poststructuralist insights, as demonstrated in Robert B. Stepto, *From Behind the Veil: A Study of Afro-American Narrative* (1979); *Afro-American Literature: The Reconstruction of Instruction* (1979), edited by Dexter Fisher and Robert B. Stepto; Houston A. Baker Jr., *Blues, Ideology, and Afro-American Literature: A Vernacular Theory* (1984); and Henry Louis Gates Jr., *The Signifying Monkey: A Theory of Afro-American Literary Criticism* (1988). The 1970s and 1980s mark the first appearance of feminist works, including especially Barbara Smith, "Toward a Black Feminist Criticism" (1977); Angela Davis, *Women, Race, and Class* (1981); Alice Walker, *In Search of Our Mother's Garden: Womanist Prose* (1983); bell hooks, *Feminist Theory: From Margin to Center* (1984); Audre Lorde, *Sister Outsider: Essays and Speeches* (1984); and Barbara Christian, *Black Feminist Criticism: Perspectives on Black Women Writers* (1985).

For brief introductions, see two essays by Henry Louis Gates Jr.: "African American Criticism," in *Redrawing the Boundaries: Transformation of English and American Literary Studies* (1992), edited by Stephen Greenblatt and Giles Gunn, and " 'Ethnic and Minority' Studies," in *Introduction to Scholarship in Modern Languages and Literature* (1992), edited by Joseph Gibaldi. *Afro-American Literary Study in the 1990s* (1989), edited by Houston A. Baker Jr. and Patricia Redmond, provides an overview of theoretical issues and problems in the field. Joyce A. Joyce's provocative *Warriors, Conjurers, and Priests: Defining African-Centered Literary Criticism* (1994) can be read as an introduction to the Black Aesthetic and a critique of Eurocentric approaches to African American literature. This book may be profitably read in conjunction with Sandra Adell's *Double Consciousness/Double Bind: Theoretical Issues in Twentieth-Century Black Literature* (1994), which focuses on the extent to which modern and contemporary black literature and criticism are already implicated in the Western tradition of literature and philosophy. For a survey of the pivotal critical writings of the black nationalist movement in the 1960s, see Sandra Hollin Flowers, *African American Nationalist Literature of the 1960s: Pens of Fire* (1996). And for a history of the literary and political debates that have appeared in African American journals and little magazines from 1900 to the early 1970s, see *Propaganda and Aesthetics: The Literary Politics of Afro-American Magazines in the Twentieth Century* (1979), edited by Abby A. Johnson and Ronald M. Johnson.

Two famous early collections of various essays that have had an enduring impact on subsequent black criticism and theory are *The New Negro* (1925), edited by Alain Locke, and *The Negro Caravan* (1941), edited by Sterling A. Brown, Arthur P. Davis, and Ulysses Lee. Anthologies including essays of theory and criticism from the perspective of the Black Arts movement include *Black Fire: An Anthology of Afro-American Writing* (1968), edited by Amiri Baraka and Larry Neal; *Black Expression: Essays by and about Black Americans in the Creation of Art* (1969), edited by Addison Gayle Jr.; and most notably *The Black Aesthetic* (1971), also edited by Gayle. For collections of essays reflecting later poststructuralism-influenced developments, see *Black Literature and Literary Theory* (1984) and *"Race," Writing, and Difference* (1986), both edited by Henry Louis Gates Jr. Among important early collections of feminist essays are *Sturdy Black Bridges: Vision of Black Women in Literature* (1979), edited by Roseann Bell et al.; *All the Women Are White, All the Blacks Are Men, But Some of Us Are Brave* (1981), edited by Gloria Hull, Patricia Bell Scott, and Barbara Smith; *Home Girls: A Black Feminist Anthology* (1983), edited by Barbara Smith; and *Black Women Writers, 1950–1980: A Critical Evaluation* (1984), edited by Mari Evans. Significant feminist collections that address later developments are *Changing Our Own Words: Essays on Criticism, Theory, and Writing by Black Women* (1989), edited by Cheryl A. Wall; *Reading Black, Reading Feminist: A Critical Anthology* (1990), edited by Henry Louis Gates Jr.; *Words of Fire: An Anthology of African American Feminist Thought* (1995), edited by Beverly Guy-Sheftall; the various essays in *Other Sisterhoods: Literary Theory and U.S. Women of Color* (1998), edited by Sandra Kumamoto Stanley; and *The Black Feminist Reader* (2000), edited by Joy James and T. Denean Sharpley-Whiting. For a general anthology with historical scope, see *African-American Literary Criticism, 1773–2000* (1999), edited by Hazel Anneth Ervin. *Within the Circle: An Anthology of African American Literary Criticism from the Harlem Renaissance to the Present* (1994), edited by Angelyn Mitchell, represents the spectrum of twentieth-century African American literary and cultural criticism, while *African American Literary Theory: A Reader* (2000), edited by Winston Napier, provides an extensive range of materials from the last half of the twentieth century, especially the closing decades.

For an annotated bibliography of major theoretical and critical works in African American literary and cultural studies, see A. LaVonne Brown Ruoff et al., "African American Literature," in *Redefining American Literary History* (1990), edited by Ruoff and Jerry W. Ward Jr. A respected resource for information on African American literature, theory, and criticism is *The Oxford Companion to African American Literature* (1997), edited by William Andrews, Frances Smith Foster, and Trudier Harris.

On the intersection of African American theory with Marxism, see, for example, Harold Cruse's famous *The Crisis of the Negro Intellectual* (1967) and *Rebellion or Revolution?* (1968). In *The Journey Back: Issues in Black Literature and Criticism* (1980), Houston A. Baker Jr. combines structuralism with the concerns of African American literary theory. Barbara Christian, *Black Women Novelists: The Development of a Tradition, 1892–1976* (1980); Barbara Smith, *The Truth That Never Hurts: Writing on Race, Gender, and Freedom* (1988); Hazel W. Carby, *Reconstructing Womanhood: The Emergence of the Afro-American Woman Novelist* (1987); and Deborah E. McDowell, *"The Changing Same": Black Women's Literature, Criticism, and Theory* (1995) variously mark the intersections between feminism and African American theory. Michele Wallace's *Black Popular Culture* (1992), edited by Gina Dent, combines African American theory with cultural studies. For exemplary linkings of African American theory with feminism, psychoanalysis, and rhetoric, see Claudia Tate, *Domestic Allegories of Political Desire* (1992) and *Psychoanalysis and Black Novels: Desire and the Protocols of Race* (1998), and Barbara Johnson, *The Feminist Difference: Literature, Psychoanalysis, Race, and Gender* (1998). For texts of black British cultural studies that intersect with the concerns of African American studies, see Paul Gilroy, *The Black Atlantic: Modernity and Double Consciousness* (1993); *Black British Cultural Studies: A Reader* (1996), edited by Houston A. Baker Jr., Manthia Diawara, and Ruth H. Lindeborg; and Kobena Mercer, *Welcome to the Jungle: New Positions in Black Cultural Studies* (1994), which includes lesbian and gay studies, queer theory, psychoanalysis, and postcolonial studies. On the meeting points of African American literary theory, feminism, and postmodern cultural studies, see Michael Awkward, *Negotiating Difference: Race, Gender, and the Politics of Positionality* (1995). Philip Brian Harper's *Are We Not Men? Masculine Anxiety and the Problem of African American Identity* (1996) explores issues of queer theory and gender studies within the context of African American theory. *Female Subjects in Black and White: Race, Psychoanalysis, Feminism* (1997), edited by Elizabeth Abel, Barbara Christian, and Helene Moglen, makes connections between black and white feminists via psychoanalysis.

Asian American Criticism and Theory

The term "Asian American," which came into use in the 1960s as an expression of solidarity and cultural nationalism, covers both Asian immigrants and North America–born people of Asian descent. Asian American literature—a broad and contested category—encompasses writings by Americans whose ancestry is Bangladeshi, Burmese, Cambodian, Chinese, Filipino, Japanese, Korean, Indian, Indonesian, Laotian, Nepali, Pakistani, Sri Lankan, Thai, and Vietnamese. An influential theoretical statement on Asian American literature is the introduction to *Aiiieeeee! An Anthology of Asian-American Writers* (1974), edited by Frank Chin et al. The groundbreaking full-length critical study of Asian American literature as a distinct academic field is Elaine Kim's *Asian American Literature: An Introduction to the Writings and Their Social Contexts* (1982), which treats Chinese, Japanese, Korean, and Filipino literatures. Influential feminist Asian American works of theory and criticism include Trinh T. Minh-ha's *Woman, Native, Other: Writing, Postcoloniality and Feminism* (1989) and Amy Ling's *Between Worlds: Women Writers of Chinese Ancestry* (1990).

Sau-Ling Cynthia Wong's *Reading Asian American Literature: From Necessity to Extravagance* (1993) can be used as a sophisticated theoretical introduction to current issues and problems in the study of Asian American literatures. Also useful as an introduction to theoretical issues is Jeffery Paul Chan et al., "An Introduction to Chinese-American and Japanese-American Literatures," in *Three American Literatures: Essays in Chicano, Native American, and Asian-American Literature for Teachers of American Literature* (1982), edited by Houston A. Baker Jr. For an excellent survey of the field, see King-Kok Cheung, "Re-viewing Asian American Literary Studies," in her edited compendium, *An Interethnic Companion to Asian American Literature* (1997).

Prominent collections of Asian American theory and criticism include *Reading the Literatures of Asian America* (1992), edited by Shirley Geok-Lin Lim and Amy Ling; *Asian Americans: Collages of Identities* (1992), edited by Lee C. Lee; and *Ideas of Home: Literature of Asian Migration* (1997), edited by Geoffrey Kain. For feminist anthologies, see *This Bridge Called My Back: Writings by Radical Women of Color* (1981), edited by Cherríe Moraga and Gloria Anzaldúa, which includes essays by Mitsuye Yamada and Nellie Wong; *Making Waves: An Anthology of Writing by and about Asian American Women* (1989) plus *Making More Waves: New Writing by Asian American Women* (1997), both edited by Asian Women United of California; and *Other Sisterhoods: Literary Theory and U.S. Women of Color* (1998), edited by Sandra Kumamoto Stanley.

For bibliographies of theory and criticism, see King-Kok Cheung and Stan Yogi's *Asian American Literature: An Annotated Bibliography* (1988), as well as the more recent survey by Cheung in her edited *Interethnic Companion*.

On cultural studies and Asian American theory, see the essays in Rey Chow's *Writing Diaspora: Tactics of Intervention in Contemporary Cultural Studies* (1993). King-Kok Cheung's *Articulate Silences: Hisaye Yamamoto, Maxine Hong Kingston, and Joy Kogawa* (1993) combines Asian American criticism with insights from poststructuralism and feminism. For a highly esteemed synthesis of Asian American theory with Marxism, feminism, cultural studies, poststructuralism, and postcolonial theory, see Lisa Lowe's *Immigrant Acts: On Asian American Cultural Politics* (1996), which provides useful frameworks for studying Asian American culture "transnationally." The various essays in *Q & A: Queer in Asian America* (1998), edited by David L. Eng and Alice Y. Hom, explore the interconnections between Asian American theory and gay, lesbian, and queer theory.

Chicano / Chicana Studies

Focused on the literature, history, and culture of Mexican Americans, "Chicano/Chicana" studies is a part of "Hispanic American" studies, which concentrates more broadly on the study of all Spanish-speaking peoples who were born in, or have immigrated to, the United States, including particularly Latinos/Latinas, Cubanos/Cubanas, and Puertorriqueños/Puertorríqueñas. During the specifically Chicano movement of the 1960s, Américo Paredes's seminal study *"With His Pistol in His Hand": A Border Ballad and Its Hero* (1958) emerged as a major critical reference, providing a model of Chicano cultural analysis. An early influential theoretical reflection on literary and historical methods is Joseph Sommers's "From the Critical Premise to the Product: Critical Modes and Their Applications to a Chicano Literary Text" (1977). Sommers, along with Tomás Ybarra-Frausto, edited a significant group of essays focusing on theory and applied analysis, *Modern Chicano Writers: A Collection of Critical Essays* (1979). Cherríe Moraga's *Loving in the War Years: Lo que nunca pasó por sus labios* (1983); *Beyond Stereotypes: The Critical Analysis of Chicana Literature* (1985), edited by Maria Herrera-Sobek; and Gloria Anzaldúa's *Borderlands / La Frontera: The New Mestiza* (1987) are three landmark texts of Chicana feminist theory. Highly influential are two works by José David Saldívar, *Dialectics of Our America: Genealogy, Culture Critique, and Literary History* (1991) and *Border Matters: Remapping American Cultural Studies* (1998), both of which unite a Marxist-poststructuralist strain of Chicano/Chicana studies with issues in cultural studies.

For an overview of Chicano and Hispanic studies as a whole, including literary, historical, and cultural matters as well as research opportunities, see the essays in the first volume of *Recovering the U.S. Hispanic Literary Heritage* (1993), edited by Ramón Gutiérrez and Genaro Padilla, as well as those in the second volume, with the same title (1996), edited by Erlinda Gonzales-Berry and Chuck Tatum. Useful as advanced introductions and surveys are *Three American Literatures: Essays in Chicano, Native American, and Asian-American Literature for Teachers of American Literature* (1982), edited by Houston A. Baker Jr; *Redefining American Literary History* (1990), edited by A. LaVonne Brown Ruoff and Jerry W. Ward Jr.; and *Chicano Cultural Representations: Reframing Critical Discourses*, a special issue of *Cultural Studies* 4 (1990), edited by Angie Chabram and Rosa Linda Fregoso.

For early collections of contemporary Chicano criticism, see the Chicano pieces in *Minority Language and Literature: Retrospective and Perspective* (1977), edited by Dexter Fisher; *New Directions in Chicano Scholarship* (1978), edited by Ricardo Romo and Raymund Paredes; and *The Identification and Analysis of Chicano Literature* (1979), edited by Francisco Jiménez. Important collections of feminist essays include *The Bridge Called My Back: Writings by Radical Women of Color* (1981), edited by Cherríe Moraga and Gloria Anzaldúa, which contains essays by Norma Alarcón, Moraga, and Anzaldúa, among others; *Chicana Voices: Intersections of Class, Race, and Gender* (1986), edited by Teresa Córdova et al.; *Living Chicana Theory* (1998), edited by Carla Trujillo; and the various essays in *Other Sisterhoods: Literary Theory and U.S. Women of Color* (1998), edited by Sandra Kumamoto Stanley. Two useful later collections of Chicano criticism and theory are *Retrospace: Collected Essays on Chicano Literature* (1990), edited by Juan Bruce-Novoa, and the influential *Criticism in the Borderlands: Studies in Chicano Literature, Culture, and Ideology* (1991), edited by Héctor Calderón and José David Saldívar.

For bibliographies of theoretical and critical texts, see Ernestina N. Eger, *A Bibliography of Criticism of Contemporary Chicano Literature* (1982); Roberto G. Trujillo, *Literature Chicana: Creative and Critical Writings through 1984* (1985); Teresa McKenna, "Chicano Literature," in *Redefining American Literary History* (1990); and especially the influential texts of 1991 and 1998 by Saldívar cited at the end of the first paragraph of this section and Calderón and Saldívar's collection, *Criticism in the Borderlands*.

On Chicano criticism in relationship to Marxism and poststructuralism, see Ramón Saldívar's often-cited *Chicano Narrative: The Dialectics of Difference* (1990). José E. Limón's *Mexican Ballads, Chicano Poems: History and Influence in Mexican-American Social Poetics* (1992) links the concerns of Chicano/Chicana studies with those of New Historicism. Essays by various writers on queer theory and Chicano/Chicana studies can be found in *Entiendes? Queer Readings, Hispanic Writings* (1995), edited by Emilie L. Bergmann and Paul Julian Smith. Alfred Arteaga's *Chicano Poetics: Heterotexts and Hybridities* (1997) examines intersections of literary and social forces from the combined perspectives of gender, race, postmodern, and postcolonial studies. The intersections among cultural studies, feminism, and Chicano/Chicana studies are explored in Alviana E. Quintana's *Home Girls: Chicana Literary Voices* (1996), as well as in *Chicana/o Latina/o Cultural Studies: Transnational and Transdisciplinary Movements*, a special issue of *Cultural Studies* 13 (1999), edited by Angie Chabram Dernersesian.

Cultural Studies

Most contemporary cultural studies has its roots both in British cultural studies developed during the 1960s and 1970s and in French structuralism and poststructuralism of the same decades. The founding texts of the British line are Richard Hoggart, *The Uses of Literacy* (1957); Raymond Williams, *Culture and Society, 1780–1950* (1958), which is a history of British cultural criticism from Edmund Burke to George Orwell; and E. P. Thompson, *The Making of the English Working Class* (1963). Also important is the University of Birmingham's famous Centre for Contemporary Cultural Studies (CCCS), a groundbreaking research institute founded by Hoggart in 1963 and administered by Stuart Hall during the 1970s that generated such pioneering works as Dick Hebdige, *Subculture: The Meaning of Style* (1979); Stuart Hall et al., *Culture, Media, Language: Working Papers in Cultural Studies, 1972–1979* (1980); Paul Gilroy, *There Ain't No Black in the Union Jack* (1987); and the belated but landmark manifesto by Richard Johnson, "What Is Cultural Studies Anyway?" *Social Text* 16 (1986–87). Key French contributions include Roland Barthes, *Mythologies* (1957; trans. 1972); Louis Althusser, *For Marx* (1965; trans. 1969); Michel Foucault, *Discipline and Punish* (1975; trans. 1977) and *The History of Sexuality*, vol. 1 (1976; trans. 1978); Pierre Bourdieu, *Distinction: A Social Critique of the Judgment of Taste* (1979; trans. 1984); Jean Baudrillard, *Simulations* (1983); and Michel de Certeau, *The Practice of Everyday Life* (1980; trans. 1984). Much of contemporary cultural studies, especially the British line, is an offshoot of modern Western Marxist theory, which provides many of its founding sources, including especially the work of Antonio Gramsci in his *Prison Notebooks* (written 1929–35; selections trans. 1971) and the various studies of the Frankfurt School, particularly Max Horkheimer and Theodor W. Adorno's *Dialectic of Enlightenment* (1944; trans. 1972). (On Marxist theory and criticism, see below.) Cultural studies in Australia extends the British and French lines in pioneering and productive directions, evident in the sampler *Australian Cultural Studies: A Reader* (1993), edited by John Frow and Meaghan Morris. For a collection of texts of U.S. cultural studies, see *American Cultural Studies: A Reader* (2000), edited by John Hartley and Roberta E. Pearson.

Graeme Turner's *British Cultural Studies: An Introduction* (2d ed., 1996) provides a succinct yet comprehensive introduction to contemporary British cultural studies, including a short history of its development and discussions of its central areas of inquiry. Other wide-ranging introductory treatments include Patrick Brantlinger, *Crusoe's Footprints: Cultural Studies in Britain and America* (1990); Antony Easthope, *Literary into Cultural Studies* (1991); Fred Inglis, *Cultural Studies* (1993); Jere Paul Surber, *Culture and Critique: An Introduction to the Critical Discourses of Cultural Studies* (1998); and Patrick Fuery and Nick Mansfield, *Cultural Studies and Critical Theory* (2d ed., 2000). Martin Barker and Anne Beezer's *Reading into Cultural Studies* (1992) offers a critical overview of the most influential texts in the tradition of cultural studies, and Steven Best and Douglas Kellner's *Postmodern Theory: A Critical Interrogation* (1991) assesses the contributions of the leading French poststructuralist cultural theorists. "Forum: Thirty-Two Letters on the Relation between Cultural Studies and the Literary," published in the journal *PMLA* 112.2 (1997), offers a substantial sampling of North American literature professors' views of how cultural studies relates to literary studies. For detailed histories on the development of British cultural studies, see Ioan Davies, *Cultural Studies and Beyond: Fragments of Empire* (1995); Dennis Dworkin, *Cultural Marxism in Postwar Britain: History, the New Left, and the Origins of Cultural Studies* (1997); and Tom Steele, *The Emergence of Cultural Studies, 1945–1965: Cultural Politics, Adult Education, and the English Question* (1997).

Important anthologies representing the wide-ranging concerns and methods of cultural studies include the pioneering *Culture, Ideology, and Social Process: A Reader* (1981), edited by Tony Bennett et al.; *Cultural Studies* (1992), edited by Lawrence Grossberg, Cary Nelson, and Paula A. Treichler; *English Studies/Cultural Studies: Institutionalizing Dissent* (1994), edited by Isaiah Smithson and Nancy Ruff, which explores the intersection of cultural studies with rhetoric and composition; *Disciplinarity and Dissent in Cultural Studies* (1996), edited by Cary Nelson and Dilip Gaonkar, which tracks the various receptions of cultural studies by academic disciplines; and *The Cultural Studies Reader* (2d ed., 1999), edited by Simon During. Two anthologies focusing on attempts to define cultural studies are *What Is Cultural Studies? A Reader* (1996), edited by John Storey, and *Studying Culture: An Introductory Reader* (2d ed., 1997), edited by Ann Gray and Jim McGuigan. On cultural studies and race in Britain, see *Black British Cultural Studies: A Reader* (1996), edited by Houston A. Baker Jr., Manthia Diawara, and Ruth H. Lindeborg. Among the many early influential CCCS casebooks worth serious consideration are *Resistance Through Rituals: Youth Sub-Cultures in Post-War Britain* (1976), *Policing the Crisis: Mugging, the State, and Law and Order* (1978), *Women Take Issue* (1978), and *The Empire Strikes Back: Race and Racism in 70s Britain* (1982).

Bibliographies of limited scope are available in the anthologies by During and by Gray and McGuigan mentioned in the preceding paragraph. For a more comprehensive bibliography, see Storey's anthology. In *Keywords: A Vocabulary of Culture and Society* (rev. ed., 1983), Raymond Williams provides an influential dictionary.

Cultural studies has served as an inclusive meeting ground for many kinds of critical projects. On specifically Marxist approaches to cultural studies, see Raymond Williams's *Marxism and Literature* (1977) and especially the essays by various hands in *Marxism and the Interpretation of Culture* (1988), edited by Cary Nelson and Lawrence Grossberg. For pioneering postcolonial work in cultural studies, see Edward W. Said's *Orientalism* (1978), as well as Gayatri Chakravorty Spivak's influential postcolonial feminist work in *In Other Worlds: Essays in Cultural Politics* (1987). *Writing Culture: The Poetics and Politics of Ethnography* (1986), edited by James Clifford and George Marcus, develops connections between cultural studies and anthropology, following the trail blazed by Clifford Geertz in *The Interpretation of Cultures: Selected Essays* (1973). On cultural studies and feminism, see especially Meaghan Morris, *The Pirate's Fiancée: Feminism, Reading, Postmodernism* (1988); Janice Radway, *Reading the Romance: Women, Patriarchy, and Popular Literature* (1991); and Anne Balsamo's synoptic "Feminism and Cultural Studies," *Journal of the Midwest MLA* 24.1 (1991). Feminist cultural studies focusing on film in relationship to psychoanalysis—an area of intense study—include Laura Mulvey, *Visual and Other Pleasures* (1989); Kaja Silverman, *The Acoustic Mirror: The Female Voice in Psychoanalysis and Cinema* (1988); and Mary Ann Doane, *Femmes Fatales: Feminism, Film Theory, Psychoanalysis* (1991). More general studies of media, including film and television, are found in *Logics of Television: Essays in Cultural Criticism* (1990), edited by Patricia Mellencamp, and *Technoculture* (1991), edited by Constance Penley and Andrew Ross. On cultural studies approaches to contemporary popular culture, see Andrew Ross, *No Respect: Intellectuals and Popular Culture* (1989); *Rethinking Popular Culture: Contemporary Perspectives in Cultural Studies* (1991), edited by Chandra Mukerji and Michael Schudson; and Lawrence Grossberg, *Dancing in Spite of Myself: Essays in Popular Culture* (1997). For cultural studies and science studies, look to the essays of Donna Haraway, notably those in her *Simians, Cyborgs, and Women: The Reinvention of Nature* (1991). In *The Black Atlantic: Modernity and Double Consciousness* (1993), Paul Gilroy links cultural studies with Afrocentric concerns broadly construed. James J. Sosnoski, *Modern Skeletons in Postmodern Closets: A Cultural Studies Alternative* (1995), develops a view of literary theory inspired by cultural studies. For cultural studies in relationship to feminism, lesbian criticism, and black feminist criticism, see the sizable collection of essays in *Feminist Cultural Studies* (2 vols., 1995), edited by Terry Lovell.

Deconstruction and Poststructuralism

Deconstruction and poststructuralism both emerged in the 1960s and 1970s as critiques of phenomenology and structuralism. Though the terms *deconstruction, poststructuralism*, and sometimes *postmodern theory* are often used interchangeably, they are not synonymous. Whereas deconstruction is a philosophical school initiated by Jacques Derrida, poststructuralism is a broad movement that concerns itself with all of the arts and human sciences, embracing a wide variety of critical projects. If deconstruction can be said to have a clear beginning, it is perhaps best marked by the penultimate essay of Derrida's *Writing and Difference* (1968; trans. 1978), "Structure, Sign, and Play in the Discourse of the Human Sciences," which was originally presented as a paper at a celebrated 1966 Johns Hopkins University conference on structuralism. But more important from the perspective of literary theory and criticism are two other works by Derrida: *Of Grammatology* (1967; trans. 1976), which mounts a wide-ranging critique of structuralism and offers an extended analysis of Jean-Jacques Rousseau, and *Dissemination* (1972; trans. 1981), which provides exemplary textual analyses of Plato, Stéphane Mallarmé, and Philippe Sollers. The early development of deconstruction in the United States occurred in the influential works of the Yale School, notably Harold Bloom, *The Anxiety of Influence* (1973); Paul de Man, *Allegories of Reading: Figural Language in Rousseau, Nietzsche, Rilke, and Proust* (1979); Geoffrey Hartman, *Crit-*

icism in the Wilderness (1980); Barbara Johnson, *The Critical Difference* (1980); numerous articles of the 1970s by J. Hillis Miller, some revised in *Fiction and Repetition: Seven English Novels* (1982); and Shoshana Felman, *Writing and Madness: Literature, Philosophy, Psychoanalysis* (1985). The most influential texts of the groundbreaking phase of French poststructuralism, which often focuses on Marxism and psychoanalysis, include Louis Althusser, *For Marx* (1966; trans. 1969); Jacques Lacan, *Écrits* (1966; trans. 1977); and Gilles Deleuze and Félix Guattari, *Anti-Oedipus: Capitalism and Schizophrenia* (1972; trans. 1977). For exemplary early poststructuralist accounts of literature, see Roland Barthes, *S/Z* (1970; trans. 1974), and Julia Kristeva, *Revolution in Poetic Language* (1974; trans. 1984). Beyond this early phase emerges an influential line of poststructuralist feminism that includes Luce Irigaray, *Speculum of the Other Woman* (1974; trans. 1985), and Hélène Cixous and Catherine Clément, *The Newly Born Woman* (1975; trans. 1986). Finally, one highly influential strand of French poststructuralism foregrounds cultural critique; see Jean Baudrillard, *The Mirror of Production* (1973; trans. 1975); Michel Foucault, *Discipline and Punish* (1975; trans. 1977); and Jean-François Lyotard, *The Postmodern Condition: A Report on Knowledge* (1979; trans. 1984).

For an accessible introduction to deconstruction, see Christopher Norris, *Deconstruction: Theory and Practice* (1982). For more sophisticated introductions, see Jonathan Culler, *On Deconstruction: Theory and Criticism after Structuralism* (1982), and Vincent B. Leitch, *Deconstructive Criticism: An Advanced Introduction* (1983). Steven Best and Douglas Kellner's lucid *Postmodern Theory: Critical Interrogations* (1991) offers a critical introduction to the leading poststructuralist theorists, as does John Sturrock's earlier *Structuralism and Since: From Lévi-Strauss to Derrida* (1979). A useful general introduction to poststructuralism is Madan Sarup's *Introductory Guide to Poststructuralism and Postmodernism* (2d ed., 1993). Toril Moi's celebrated *Sexual/Textual Politics* (1985) critically compares and contrasts French feminist poststructuralism with Anglo-American humanistic feminist criticism, providing an introductory overview in the process. For a historical account of events specifically in England, see Anthony Easthope, *British Post-Structuralism Since 1968* (1988). Eve Tavor Bannet's *Structuralism and the Logic of Dissent* (1988) places French poststructuralism within the historical and social contexts of the 1960s, while Patrick Ffrench's *Time of Theory: A History of "Tel Quel" (1960–1983)* (1995) offers an extensive history of French poststructuralism focusing on members of the *Tel Quel* group and their influential journal, which early on published the work of Kristeva, Barthes, and Derrida, among many others. See also Peter Starr's *Logics of Failed Revolt: French Theory after May '68* (1995) for a discussion of major figures. Art Berman's *From the New Criticism to Deconstruction: The Reception of Structuralism and Post-Structuralism* (1988) presents a historical overview of the U.S. reception of French poststructuralism, chronicling the critical interactions between poststructuralism and American literary criticism.

An important, early collection from the Yale School is Harold Bloom et al.'s *Deconstruction and Criticism* (1979), which gathers essays by Jacques Derrida and the four leading first-generation American members, Bloom, de Man, Hartman, and Miller. See also *A Recent Imagining: Interviews with Harold Bloom, Geoffrey Hartman, J. Hillis Miller, Paul de Man* (1986), edited by Robert Moynihan. *Deconstruction: A Reader* (2000), edited by Martin McQuillan, offers a collection of essential essays representing the range and depth of deconstruction, including nine pieces by Jacques Derrida. For general anthologies of poststructuralist work, see *Textual Strategies: Perspectives in Post-Structuralist Criticism* (1979), edited by Josué Harari; *Untying the Text: A Post-Structuralist Reader* (1981), edited by Robert Young; and *On Signs* (1985), edited by Marshall Blonsky. John P. Muller and William J. Richardson's casebook, *The Purloined Poe: Lacan, Derrida, and Psychoanalytic Reading* (1988), collects celebrated essays by Lacan, Derrida, and Barbara Johnson on reading Edgar Allan Poe. For readers on Derrida, see *A Derrida Reader: Between the Blinds* (1991), edited by Peggy Kamuf; *Acts of Literature* (1992), edited by Derrick Attridge; and *The Derrida Reader: Writing Performances* (1998), edited by Julian Wolfreys. Introductory readers on individual poststructuralists include *A Barthes Reader* (1982), edited by Susan Sontag; *The Foucault Reader* (1984), edited by Paul Rabinow; *The Kristeva Reader* (1986), edited by Toril Moi; *Jean Baudrillard: Selected Writings* (1988), edited by Mark Poster; *The Hélène Cixous Reader* (1994), edited by Susan Sellers; and *The Portable Kristeva* (1997), edited by Kelly Oliver. *The "Tel Quel" Reader* (1998), edited by Patrick Ffrench and Roland-François Lack, presents wide-ranging poststructuralist essays from various members of the *Tel Quel* group.

For early general bibliographies of poststructuralism, see the Harari anthology noted in the preceding paragraph and Joan M. Miller's *French Structuralism: A Multidisciplinary Bibliography with a Checklist of Sources for Louis Althusser, Roland Barthes, Jacques Derrida, Michel Foucault, Lucien Goldmann, Jacques Lacan, and an Update of Works on Claude Lévi-Strauss* (1981).

The developments of deconstruction and poststructuralism involve a very large number of offshoots and hybrids, some of the more influential and interesting of which are mentioned here. Roland Barthes's *Pleasure of the Text* (1973; trans. 1975) offers a poststructuralist approach to reader-response theory, while Michel Foucault's *History of Sexuality*, (vol. 1, 1976; trans. 1978) provides an early pioneering poststructuralist exploration of sexuality and gender. Edward W. Said's landmark *Orientalism* (1978) joins poststructuralism to postcolonial theory, and Fredric Jameson's *Political Unconscious: Narrative as a Socially Symbolic Act* (1981) expounds a Marxian theory of interpretation significantly informed by poststructuralist insights. On the intersection of poststructuralist psychoanalysis and feminism, see the essays by many hands collected in Shoshana Felman's *Literature and Psychoanalysis—The Question of Reading: Otherwise* (1982); Jane Gallop's *Thinking through the Body* (1988) also articulates connections between poststructuralism and feminism, producing an especially influential hybrid. John D. Caputo's *Radical Hermeneutics: Repetition, Deconstruction, and the Hermeneutic Project* (1987) innovatively recasts phenomenological hermeneutics in a deconstructive mode. Gayatri Chakravorty Spivak's *In Other Worlds: Essays in Cultural Politics* (1987) mixes deconstruction together with Marxism, feminism, and postcolonial theory. In *The Signifying Monkey: A Theory of African-American Literary Criticism* (1988), Henry Louis Gates Jr. famously combines African-American literary studies with Yale-style deconstruction. On the institutional and disciplinary implications of deconstruction in relationship to postmodern theory, see Jeffrey T. Nealon, *Double Reading: Postmodernism after Deconstruction* (1993). For the intersections of deconstruction and pragmatism, see the essays collected in Chantal Mouffe's *Deconstruction and Pragmatism* (1996). Judith Butler's landmark *Gender Trouble: Feminism and the Subversion of Identity* (1990) develops new connections among French poststructuralism, feminism, and queer theory; in *The Psychic Life of Power: Theories in Subjection* (1997), she negotiates the vexing problem of subject formation in Nietzsche, Foucault, Althusser, and Freud. *Inside/Out: Lesbian Theories/Gay Theories* (1991), edited by Diana Fuss, offers a wide range of poststructuralist perspectives on sexuality, gender, and queer theory. For especially sophisticated applications of poststructuralist procedures to more recent postcolonial theory, see Homi K. Bhabha, *The Location of Culture* (1994). Diane Elam's *Feminism and Deconstruction: Ms. en Abyme* (1994) memorably highlights the intersections of Derridean philosophy and feminist theories, while Chris Weedon's *Feminist Practice and Poststructuralist Theory* (2d ed., 1996) discusses links among feminism, poststructuralism, and cultural studies.

Feminist Criticism and Theory

For a collection of early modern feminist theory and criticism, see *Women Critics, 1660–1820: An Anthology* (1995), edited by the Folger Collective on Early Women Critics. The beginnings of modern feminist theory are variously marked by such important texts as Virginia Woolf, *A Room of One's Own* (1929); Simone de Beauvoir, *The Second Sex* (1949; trans. 1953); Betty Friedan, *The Feminine Mystique* (1963); and Kate Millett, *Sexual Politics* (1969). Slightly later groundbreaking texts of academic American feminist literary criticism include Ellen Moers, *Literary Women* (1976); Elaine Showalter, *A Literature of Their Own: British Women Novelists from Brontë to Lessing* (1977); Judith Fetterley, *The Resisting Reader: A Feminist Approach to American Fiction* (1978); Lillian Robinson, *Sex, Class, and Culture* (1978); and Sandra M. Gilbert and Susan Gubar, *The Madwoman in the Attic: The Woman Writer and the Nineteenth-Century Literary Imagination* (1979). Important works in the British tradition from this period include Juliet Mitchell, *Psychoanalysis and Feminism: Freud, Reich, Laing, and Women* (1974); Mary Jacobus, *Women Writing and Writing about Women* (1979); and Michèle Barrett, *Women's Oppression Today: Problems in Marxist Feminist Analysis* (1980). Influential short pieces of contemporary French feminist theory from the 1970s appear in the classic *New French Feminism: An Anthology* (1980), edited by Elaine Marks and Isabelle de Courtivron, and important full-length contemporaneous works include Luce Irigaray's *Speculum of the Other Woman* (1974; trans. 1985) and Hélène Cixous and Catherine Clément's *Newly Born Woman* (1975; trans. 1986). For many indispensable feminist contributions from women of color and lesbian authors, see the sections on African American Criticism and Theory, Asian American Criticism and Theory, Chicano/Chicana Studies, Gay and Lesbian Criticism and Queer Theory, Native American Studies, and Postcolonial Criticism and Theory.

For accessible introductions to feminist criticism and theory, see K. K. Ruthven, *Feminist Literary Studies: An Introduction* (1984); *Making a Difference: Feminist Literary Criticism* (1985), edited by Gayle Greene and Coppélia Kahn; and Mary Evans, *Introducing Contemporary Feminist Thought* (1997). A more advanced introduction is Chris Weedon's *Feminist Practice and Poststructuralist Theory* (2d ed., 1996). Toril Moi's *Sexual/Textual Politics: Feminist Literary Theory* (1985) and Jane Gallop's *Around 1981: Academic Feminist Literary Theory* (1992) offer informative accounts of the early stages of contemporary feminist theory's development, while Imelda Whelehan's *Modern Feminist Thought: From the Second Wave to "Post Feminism"* (1995) surveys later trends. Susan Gubar's *Critical Condition: Feminism at the Turn of the Century* (200) casts a skeptical and critical eye on recent developments in feminist theory, focusing in particular on the latter's relationship to African American, postcolonial, and poststructuralist theory.

A widely used comprehensive anthology of feminist literary criticism and theory is *Feminisms: An Anthology of Literary Theory and Criticism* (2d ed., 1997), edited by Robyn R. Warhol and Diane Price Herndl. Wide-ranging retrospective collections tracing the history and development of contemporary feminist theory include *New Feminist Criticism* (1985), edited by Elaine Showalter; *Changing Subjects: The Making of Feminist Literary Criticism* (1993), edited by Gayle Green and Coppélia Kahn; and *The Second Wave: A Reader in Feminist Theory* (1997), edited by Linda Nicholson, which gathers major feminist essays covering a forty-year period. On the various waves of feminism, see *Generations: Academic Feminists in Dialogue* (1998), edited by Devoney Looser and E. Ann Kaplan. The reader *Conflicts in Feminism* (1990), edited by Marianne Hirsch and Evelyn Fox Keller, offers a clear sense of contemporary debates within feminist theory; similar readers include *Destabilizing Theories: Contemporary Feminist Debates* (1992), edited by Michèle Barrett and Anne Phillips; *Feminist Literary Criticism* (2d ed., 1995), edited by Mary Eagleton; and *The Feminist Reader: Essays in Gender and the Politics of Literary Criticism* (2d ed., 1998), edited by Catherine Belsey and Jane Moore. For a provocative dialogue on these debates, see the essays by Judith Butler, Drucilla Cornell, and others in *Feminist Contentions: A Philosophical Exchange* (1995), edited by Seyla Benhabib et al. Essays foregrounding issues of race and gender can be found in *This Bridge Called My Back: Writings by Radical Women of Color* (1981), edited by Cherríe Moraga and Gloria Anzaldúa; *Making Face, Making Soul—Haciendo Caras: Creative and Critical Perspectives by Feminists of Color* (1990), edited by Gloria Anzaldúa; *Reading Black, Reading Feminist* (1990), edited by Henry Louis Gates Jr.; *Other Sisterhoods: Literary Theory and U.S. Women of Color* (1998), edited by Sandra Kumamoto Stanley; and *The Black Feminist Reader* (2000), edited by Joy James and T. Denean Sharpley-Whiting. Important collections focusing on the relationship between feminist theory and politics are *Coming to Terms: Feminism, Theory, Politics* (1989), edited by Elizabeth Weed, and *Feminists Theorize the Political* (1992), edited by Judith Butler and Joan W. Scott. Explorations of the futures of feminist theory are collected in *New Feminist Discourses: Essays in Literature, Criticism, and Theory* (1992), edited by Isobel Armstrong, and *Listening to Silences: New Essays in Feminist Criticism* (1994), edited by Elaine Hedges and Shelley Fisher Fishkin. *Scattered Hegemonies: Postmodernist and Transnational Feminist Practices* (1994), edited by Inderpal Grewal and Caren Kaplan, addresses global concerns of feminism. On feminism, environmentalism, and literary analysis, see *Ecofeminist Literary Criticism: Theory, Interpretation, Pedagogy* (1998), edited by Greta Gaard and Patrick D. Murphy. *French Feminism Reader* (2000), edited by Kelly Oliver, collects selections from the French feminist theory most influential in the English-speaking world.

Useful reference sources on feminist terminology include Elizabeth Wright, *Feminism and Psychoanalysis: A Critical Dictionary* (1992); Maggie Humm, *The Dictionary of Feminist Theory* (2d ed., 1995); and Carol G. Gould, *Key Concepts in Critical Theory: Gender* (1997). For comprehensive treatments of terminology and key figures in feminism, followed by relevant bibliographies, see Elizabeth Kowaleski-Wallace, *Encyclopedia of Feminist Literary Theory* (1997). Among bibliographic resources are Wendy Frost and Michele Valiquette, *Feminist Literary Criticism: A Bibliography of Journal Articles, 1975–1981* (1988); Joan Nordquist, *Feminist Theory: A Bibliography* (1992); and Maggie Humm, *An Annotated Critical Bibliography of Feminist Criticism* (1987) and *A Reader's Guide to Contemporary Feminist Literary Criticism* (1994).

Feminist criticism and theory has productively combined with other schools and movements. In *The Daughter's Seduction: Feminism and Psychoanalysis* (1982), Jane Gallop offers an early U.S. feminist exploration of Lacanian psychoanalysis; a complementary work also drawing race studies into its orbit is *Female Subjects in Black and White: Race, Psychoanalysis, Feminism* (1997), edited by Elizabeth Abel, Barbara Christian, and Helene Moglen. Linking the concerns of feminism with those of queer theory are Eve Kosofsky Sedgwick's *Between Men: English Literature and Male Homosocial Desire* (1985) and the essays in *Feminism Meets Queer Theory* (1997), edited by Elizabeth Weed and Naomi Schor. On the intersections of deconstruction and feminism, see Barbara Johnson, *A World of Difference* (1987), and Diane Elam, *Feminism and Deconstruction: Ms. en Abyme* (1994). Influential interdisciplinary works of feminist film theory and criticism include *Revisions: Essays in Feminist Film Criticism* (1984), edited by Mary Ann Doane et al.; Teresa de Lauretis, *Alice Doesn't: Feminism, Semiotics, Cinema* (1984); *Feminism and Film Theory* (1988), edited by Constance Penley; Kaja Silverman, *The Acoustic Mirror: The Female Voice in Psychoanalysis and Cinema* (1988), and Laura Mulvey, *Visual and Other Pleasures* (1989). *Feminism and Foucault* (1988), edited by Irene Diamond and Lee Quinby, establishes fruitful connections with one of poststructuralism's leading theorists. On the intersection of postmodernism and feminism, see *Feminism / Postmodernism* (1990), edited by Linda J. Nicholson, and *Feminism and Postmodernism* (1994), edited by Margaret Ferguson and Jennifer Wicke. *Men in Feminism* (1987), edited by Alice Jardine and Paul Smith, and *Engendering Men: The Question of Male Feminist Criticism* (1990), edited by Joseph A. Boone and Michael Cadden, both consider the roles of men in feminism. For links between feminism and Marxism, see Rita Felski, *Beyond Feminist Aesthetics: Feminist Literature and Social Change* (1989); *Women, Class, and the Feminist Imagination: A Socialist-Feminist Reader* (1990), edited by Karen Hansen and Ilene Philipson; Teresa Ebert, *Ludic Feminism and After: Postmodernism, Desire, and Labor in Late Capitalism* (1996); and *Materialist Feminism: A Reader in Class, Difference, and Women's Lives* (1997), edited by Rosemary Hennessy and Chrys Ingraham. Pioneering feminist texts by women of color include Barbara Christian, *Black Women Novelists* (1980); bell hooks, *Ain't I a Woman: Black Women and Feminism* (1981); Paula Gunn Allen, *The Sacred Hoop: Recovering the Feminine in American Indian Traditions* (1986); and Gloria Anzaldúa, *Borderlands / La Frontera: The New Mestiza* (1987). *Theorizing Feminism: Parallel Trends in the Humanities and Social Sciences*

(1994), edited by Anne C. Herrmann and Abigail J. Stewart, explores a wide range of interdisciplinary work linking gender studies with race, class, sexuality, and postmodern studies. For influential feminist studies concerned with the sciences, see Sandra Harding, *The Science Question in Feminism* (1986), and Donna J. Haraway, *Simians, Cyborgs, and Women: The Reinvention of Nature* (1991). On the link between feminism and postcolonial studies, see Gayatri Chakravorty Spivak, *In Other Worlds: Essays in Cultural Politics* (1987); Trinh T. Minh-ha, *Woman, Native, Other: Writing, Postcoloniality, and Feminism* (1989); and Julia Emberley, *Thresholds of Difference: Feminist Critique, Native Women's Writings, Postcolonial Theory* (1993). Works exploring autobiographical approaches to feminist theory include *The Private Self: Theory and Practice of Women's Autobiographical Writings* (1988), edited by Shari Benstock; *Life/Lines: Theorizing Women's Autobiography* (1988), edited by Bella Brodzki and Celeste Schenck; Nancy Miller, *Getting Personal: Feminist Occasions and Other Autobiographical Acts* (1991); Lee Gilmore, *Autobiographics: A Feminist Theory of Self-Representation* (1994); and *Women, Autobiography, Theory* (1998), edited by Sidonie Smith and Julia Watson. Judith Butler's often-cited *Bodies That Matter: On the Discursive Limits of "Sex"* (1993) creatively merges feminism, psychoanalysis, poststructuralism, and queer theory. *American Feminist Thought at Century's End: A Reader* (1993), edited by Linda Kauffman, marks the influences of feminist theory on other schools and movements, including sexuality and gender studies, psychoanalytic criticism, postcolonial studies, and cultural studies.

Formalism

The major formalist approaches to literature stem from early- and mid-twentieth-century British, American, and Slavic traditions. The Anglo-American tradition of formalism had as a harbinger T. S. Eliot's "Tradition and the Individual Talent" (1917), which was soon followed by his influential formalist statements in "Hamlet and His Problems" (1919) and "The Metaphysical Poets" (1921). Groundbreaking texts of British formalism include I. A. Richards's *Principles of Literary Criticism* (1924) and William Empson's *Seven Types of Ambiguity* (1930). Landmark texts in the American formalist tradition include John Crowe Ransom's essay "Criticism, Inc." (1937); his subsequent work *The New Criticism* (1941); and Cleanth Brooks's *Well Wrought Urn: Studies in the Structure of Poetry* (1947). Of equal canonical status for American New Criticism is W. K. Wimsatt Jr. and Monroe C. Beardsley's later *The Verbal Icon: Studies in the Meaning of Poetry* (1954). Apart from the New Critics, the Chicago School developed a neo-Aristotelian approach to formalism, which is on display in their collection *Critics and Criticism: Ancient and Modern* (1952), edited by R. S. Crane, as well as in Wayne C. Booth's *Rhetoric of Fiction* (1961). Encompassing the diverse work of the Moscow Linguistic Circle, the Leningrad-based Society for the Study of Poetic Language (OPOYAZ), and, to a certain extent, the Prague Linguistic Circle, the Slavic formalist tradition includes such influential texts as Viktor Shklovsky's "Art as Technique" (1917), Vladimir Propp's *Morphology of the Folktale* (1928; trans. 1958), and early pieces by Roman Jakobson collected in his *Language in Literature* (1987), edited by Krystyna Pomorska and Stephen Rudy. Inspired by structural linguistics, the Slavic tradition eventually turned toward structuralism and semiotics, as exemplified in Jan Mukařovský's "Note on the Czech Translation of Šklovskij's *Theory of Prose*" (1934). The Slavic tradition and the Anglo-American tradition meet for the first time in René Wellek and Austin Warren's celebrated formalist handbook for students, *Theory of Literature* (1949).

For an introduction to the major figures, issues, and problems in Anglo-American formalism, see Murray Krieger, *The New Apologists for Poetry* (1956). On the Southern wing of the New Critics, see Louise Cowan, *The Southern Critics: An Introduction to the Criticism of John Crowe Ransom, Allen Tate, Donald Davidson, Robert Penn Warren, Cleanth Brooks, and Andrew Lytle* (1971), and Mark Jancovich, *The Cultural Politics of the New Criticism* (1993). For a succinct statement of the principles of New Criticism, see Cleanth Brooks, "New Criticism," in *The Princeton Encyclopedia of Poetry and Poetics* (enlarged ed., 1974). Cleanth Brooks and Robert Penn Warren's *Understanding Poetry* (1938) and *Understanding Fiction* (1943), which have gone through many printings, are influential textbooks that introduce New Critical methodologies. Chris Baldick's *Social Mission of English Literary Criticism, 1848–1932* (1983) offers a historical overview of the British formalists, while Grant Webster's *Republic of Letters: A History of Postwar American Literary Opinion* (1979) provides a detailed history of American formalism. Tony Bennett's *Formalism and Marxism* (1979) gives a brief introduction to the Russian formalists. For a more sophisticated introduction, see Peter Steiner, *Russian Formalism: A Metapoetics* (1984). Victor Erlich's *Russian Formalism: History—Doctrine* (3d ed., 1981) is the definitive history of the Russian formalists, while Jurij Striedter's *Literary Structure, Evolution, and Value: Russian Formalism and Czech Structuralism Reconsidered* (1989) provides a useful survey. For a history of the Prague School, see F. W. Galan, *Historic Structures: The Prague School Project, 1928–1946* (1985). A suggestive comparison is developed by Ewa M. Thompson in *Russian Formalism and Anglo-American Criticism* (1971).

The New Criticism and Contemporary Literary Theory: Connections and Continuities (1995), edited by William J. Spurlin and Michael Fischer, assembles a collection of influential essays from first-generation New Critics as well as from their prominent self-proclaimed critics of the 1970s and 1980s; it includes essays reassessing the value of

New Criticism for the 1990s. For representative selections from the Chicago School, see the abridged edition of *Critics and Criticism: Essays in Method* (1957), edited by R. S. Crane. Anthologies of Russian work include *Russian Formalist Criticism: Four Essays* (1965), edited and translated by Lee T. Lemon and Mario J. Reis; *Russian Formalism: A Collection of Articles and Texts in Translation* (1973), edited and translated by Stephen Bann and John E. Bowlt; and *Formalism: History, Comparison, Genre* (1978), edited and translated by L. M. O'Toole and Ann Shukman. *A Prague School Reader on Esthetics, Literary Structure, and Style* (1964), edited and translated by Paul L. Garvin, and *The Prague School: Selected Writings, 1929–1946* (1982), edited by Peter Steiner and translated by various hands, collect definitive works from the Prague School.

Chris Baldick's *Criticism and Literary Theory: 1890 to the Present* (1996) includes detailed individual bibliographies of the major British and American formalists, while Webster's *Republic of Letters* provides in-depth bibliographical profiles of the most influential American formalists. *Profession 82* (1982), edited by Richard I. Brod and Phyllis P. Franklin, offers a bibliographical survey of the Chicago School. For a bibliography of Russian formalism, see Erlich's *Russian Formalism*, and for a bibliography of Prague School work consult Galen's *Historic Structures*.

As a movement concerned with the autonomy of art and with intrinsic criticism, formalism generally does not lend itself to crossover projects. To sample a formalism that expands to interdisciplinary issues, see Kenneth Burke's work, particularly his *Philosophy of Literary Form: Studies in Symbolic Action* (1941). I. A. Richards's *Practical Criticism* (1929) marks a turning of formalist experiment to reader-response theory, whereas René Wellek and Austin Warren's *Theory of Literature* (1949) draws on both the phenomenological tradition and the history of literature. For a polemical engagement with poststructuralism by a latter-day formalist, see Murray Krieger, *Poetic Presence and Illusion: Essays in Critical History and Theory* (1979). Wayne Booth's *Critical Understanding: The Powers and Limits of Pluralism* (1979) is a formalist attempt to lay down pragmatic pluralistic principles by which to negotiate a complex world of contending critical methods, while Steven Knapp's *Literary Interest: The Limits of Anti-Formalism* (1993) is a latter-day defense of formalism.

Gay and Lesbian Criticism and Queer Theory

A pioneering text of gay theory, which emerged from the gay liberation movement of the 1960s, is *Out of the Closets: Voices of Gay Liberation* (1972), edited by Karla Jay and Allen Young. Early gay and lesbian criticism, which often focused on studying affirmative images, includes such texts as the special issue of the journal *College English* 36 (1974) titled *The Homosexual Imagination*, edited by Louie Crew and Rictor Norton; Jane Rule, *Lesbian Images* (1975); Roger Austen, *Playing the Game: The Homosexual Novel in America* (1977); and Vito Russo, *The Celluloid Closet: Homosexuality in the Movies* (1981). Contemporary gay and lesbian criticism and queer theory frequently acknowledge three formative French influences: Guy Hocquenghem, *Homosexual Desire* (1972; trans. 1978); Michel Foucault, *The History of Sexuality* (3 vols., 1976–84; trans. 1978–86), and Monique Wittig, *The Straight Mind* (1980; trans. 1992). Also important are Adrienne Rich's "Compulsory Heterosexuality and Lesbian Existence" (1980) and Marilyn Frye's *Politics of Reality: Essays in Feminist Theory* (1983). The undisputedly groundbreaking text separating early gay-affirmative image studies from a newer, theoretically minded academic movement is the highly regarded *Between Men: English Literature and Male Homosocial Desire* (1985), by Eve Kosofsky Sedgwick. Subsequent influential works include *Men in Feminism* (1987), edited by Alice Jardine and Paul Smith; *AIDS: Cultural Analysis, Cultural Activism* (1988), edited by Douglas Crimp; Sedgwick, *Epistemology of the Closet* (1990); Judith Butler, *Gender Trouble: Feminism and the Subversion of Identity* (1990); and *Queer Theory*, a special issue of the journal *Differences* 3 (1992), edited by Teresa de Lauretis, which offers a pioneering collection devoted to the speculative work of expanding gay and lesbian studies to broader queer horizons.

Annamarie Jagose's *Queer Theory: An Introduction* (1996) makes an accessible starting point, while Lee Edelman's *Homographesis: Essays in Gay Literature and Theory* (1994) may serve as a more advanced introduction. Terry Castle's *Apparitional Lesbian: Female Homosexuality and Modern Culture* (1993) can be read as a theoretical and historical introduction to the lesbian in literature. For a survey of the diverse interests and issues of gay and lesbian criticism, see *Professions of Desire: Lesbian and Gay Studies in Literature* (1995), edited by George E. Haggerty and Bonnie Zimmerman. *The Gay 90s: Disciplinary and Interdisciplinary Formations in Queer Studies* (1997), edited by Thomas Foster, Carol Siegel, and Ellen E. Berry, provides an overview of queer studies. Historical treatments include the pioneering *Gay American History* (1976), by Jonathan Katz, Martin Duberman, and Martha Vicinus; their subsequent continuation, *Lesbian and Gay Almanac* (1983); *Hidden from History: Reclaiming the Gay and Lesbian Past* (1989), by George Chauncey Jr.; and the documentary anthology *We Are Everywhere: A Historical Sourcebook of Gay and Lesbian Politics* (1997), edited by Mark Blasius and Shane Phelan.

The Lesbian and Gay Studies Reader (1993), edited by Henry Abelove, Michèle Aina Barale, and David M. Halperin, is the leading anthology of the field, collecting the most significant English-language work up to its publication date. *Lesbian and Gay Writing: An Anthology of Critical Essays*

(1990), edited by Mark Lilly, focuses on work by gay and lesbian critics on gay/lesbian authors. *Inside/Out: Lesbian Theories, Gay Theories* (1991), edited by Diane Fuss is an influential anthology; others are *Queering the Renaissance* (1994), edited by Jonathan Goldberg and *Negotiating Lesbian and Gay Subjects* (1995), edited by Monica Dorenkamp and Richard Henke, which continues the work of Fuss's anthology. Important women-identified collections include *Lesbian Texts/Contexts: Radical Revisions* (1990), edited by Karla Jay and Joanne Glasgow; *New Lesbian Criticism: Literary and Cultural Readings* (1992) edited by Sally Munt; *Sexual Practice, Textual Theory: Lesbian Cultural Criticism* (1993), edited by Susan J. Wolfe and Julia Penelope; and *The Lesbian Postmodern* (1994), edited by Laura L. Doan. For two readers on the politics of homosexuality and culture, see *Fear of a Queer Planet: Queer Politics and Social Theory* (1993), edited by Michael Warner, and the literary and historically situated *Cultural Politics—Queer Reading* (1994), edited by Alan Sinfield. Activist theoretical perspectives are offered by the contributors to *Activating Theory: Lesbian, Gay, and Bisexual Politics* (1993), edited by Joseph Bristow and Angelia R. Wilson, and to *Playing with Fire: Queer Politics, Queer Theories* (1996), edited by Shane Phelan. For critical applications of queer theory to a wide range of British, French, and American novels, see *Novel Gazing: Queer Readings in Fiction* (1997), edited by Eve Kosofsky Sedgwick.

Bibliographies of gay and lesbian criticism and queer theory are available in Fuss's anthology, *Inside/Out*; Linda Garber, *Lesbian Sources: A Bibliography of Periodical Articles, 1970–1990* (1993); Sharon Malinowski, *Gay and Lesbian Literature* (1995); and Joan Nordquist, *Queer Theory: A Bibliography* (1997). Other useful bibliographical resources include Wayne R. Dynes, *Homosexuality: A Research Guide* (1987); Dolores Maggiore, *Lesbianism: An Annotated Bibliography and Guide to the Literature, 1976–1986* (1988); and Simon Stern, "Lesbian and Gay Studies: A Selective Bibliography," *Yale Journal of Criticism* 3 (1989).

Gay and lesbian criticism and queer theory, like many other contemporary schools and movements, often draw from and advance other theoretical perspectives. To sample such combinations, see, for personal criticism, *Life/Lines: Theorizing Women's Autobiography* (1988), edited by Bella Brodzki and Celeste Schenck; for ethnicity and race studies, *Making Face/Making Soul—Haciendo Caras: Creative and Critical Perspectives by Feminists of Color* (1990), edited by Gloria Anzaldúa; for feminist theory, *Angry Women* (1991), edited by Andrea Juno and V. Vale; for postcolonial criticism, *Nationalisms and Sexualities* (1992), edited by Andrew Parker et al.; for psychoanalytic theory, *Sexuality and Space* (1992), edited by Beatriz Colomina and Jennifer Bloomer; and for cultural studies, *Queer Representations: Reading Lives, Reading Cultures* (1997), edited by Martin Duberman.

Marxism

The history of Marxist criticism includes distinct, sometimes contending, projects and traditions. Marx himself did not compose a work of literary criticism or theory. Important early Russian groundbreaking texts are Georgi Plekhanov's *Art and Society* (1912; trans. 1936) and Leon Trotsky's *Literature and Revolution* (1924; trans. 1925). Influential German contributions to Marxist theory and criticism include the works of the Frankfurt School, especially Max Horkheimer and Theodor Adorno's *Dialectic of Enlightenment* (1944; trans. 1972) and the work of a critic closely associated with the school, Walter Benjamin, particularly *Illuminations* (1968), a posthumous collection of essays. The Chinese tradition of Marxist criticism arises out of the work of Mao Zedong, whose articles, speeches, and reports are collected in *On Literature and Art* (1958). In *The Historical Novel* (1937; trans. 1962), the Hungarian György Lukács famously sets out to develop a socialist aesthetic based on a Hegelian understanding of the European tradition. In the essays collected in *Brecht on Theatre* (1964), Bertolt Brecht opposes the realist approach to aesthetics represented by Lukács, advocating instead avant-garde experimentation. Other landmark texts of Marxist criticism include the British cultural studies texts of Raymond Williams, such as *Culture and Society, 1780–1950* (1958); the psychoanalytical structuralist works of the French philosopher Louis Althusser, particularly *Lenin and Philosophy and Other Essays* (1971); Richard Ohmann's *English in America: A Radical View of the Profession* (1976), which pioneered the critique of the university English department as a hegemonic institution; and the synthesizing theoretical books of the American Marxist literary critic Fredric Jameson, most notably *The Political Unconscious: Narrative as a Socially Symbolic Act* (1981). Much contemporary work in Marxist criticism draws on parts of *The Prison Notebooks* (written 1929–35; selections trans. 1971) of Antonio Gramsci and *The Dialogic Imagination* (1975; trans. 1981) of Mikhail M. Bakhtin, whose initial impact came decades after they were written.

Terry Eagleton's *Marxism and Literary Criticism* (1976) provides a concise introductory overview of key issues in Marxist criticism. Tony Bennett's *Formalism and Marxism* (1979) is a brief critical survey of issues in post-Althusserian criticism, offering also a short history of how a political understanding of aesthetics arises out of the work of the Russian formalists. More advanced introductions to Marxist criticism include Fredric Jameson, *Marxism and Form* (1971); Dave Laing, *The Marxist Theory of Art: An Introductory Survey* (1978); and Pauline Johnson, *Marxist Aesthetics* (1984). Informative histories of Marxist literary theory include Peter Demetz's *Marx, Engels, and the Poets: Origins of Marxist Literary Criticism* (1967) and Henri Arvon's *Marxist Esthetics* (1970; trans. 1973). Perry Anderson's *Considerations on Western Marxism* (1984) is a brief but rich intellectual history of the emergence of a culturally oriented Marxist tradition. In *The Dialectical Imagination: A History of the Frankfurt School* (1973), Martin Jay offers an authoritative history of the Frankfurt School, while Mark Poster's *Existential Marxism in Postwar France* (1975) provides a knowledgeable account of philosophical and cultural developments from Jean-Paul Sartre to Louis Althusser. For other useful historical studies, see Alan A. Wald, *The New York Intellectuals: The Rise and Decline of the Anti-Stalinist Left from the 1930s to the 1980s* (1987), and Ted Benton, *The Rise and Fall of Structural Marxism* (1984).

There are a number of informative anthologies of Marxist criticism. *Marx and Engels on Literature and Art* (1973), edited by Lee Baxandall and Stefan Morawski, gathers many of the most important passages of literary criticism written by Marx and Engels and also provides a theoretical and historical introduction. *Marxism and Art: Writings in Aesthetics and Criticism* (1972), edited by Berel Lang and Forrest Williams, and *Marxism and Art: Essays Classic and Contemporary* (1973), edited by Maynard Solomon, collect numerous important essays that focus, for the most part, on pre-Althusserian critical issues. *Aesthetics and Politics* (1977), edited by the New Left Review, contains a selection of essays by Theodor Adorno, Walter Benjamin, Ernst Bloch, Bertolt Brecht, and György Lukács, as well as commentary in an afterword by Fredric Jameson. Later critical developments are addressed in *An Anthology of Western Marxism: From Lukács and Gramsci to Socialist Feminism* (1989), edited by Roger Gottlieb; *Contemporary Marxist Criticism* (1992), edited by Francis Mulhern; *Marxist Literary Theory: A Reader* (1996), edited by Terry Eagleton and Drew Milne; and *Marxism beyond Marxism* (1996), edited by Saree Makdisi, Cesare Casarino, and Rebecca Karl. Essays presented at two celebrated fin de siècle conferences on Marxism are assembled in *Marxism and the Interpretation of Culture* (1988), edited by Cary Nelson and Lawrence Grossberg, and *Whither Marxism?* (1995), edited by Bernd Magnus and Stephen Cullenberg.

James W. Russell's *Marx-Engels Dictionary* (1980), Jozef Wilczynski's *Encyclopedic Dictionary of Marxism, Socialism, and Communism* (1981), and especially Tom Bottomore's *Dictionary of Marxist Thought* (2d ed., 1991) are useful resources for students unfamiliar with Marxist terminology. Lee Baxandall's *Marxism and Aesthetics* (1973) and Chris Bullock and David Peck's *Guide to Marxist Literary Criticism* (1980) offer substantial bibliographies. Baxandall is international in scope, while Bullock and Peck focus primarily on Britain, the United States, and Canada.

Because Marxist criticism attends to social history, it has proven useful to many contemporary critical schools and movements, ranging from feminism and race studies to postcolonial theory and cultural studies. Conversely, Marxist critics often synthesize other critical movements. V. N. Vološinov's *Marxism and the Philosophy of Language* (1929; trans. 1973), for example, attempts to demonstrate the value of Marxist criticism for linguistics and language theory, while Herbert Marcuse's *Eros and Civilization: A Philosophical Inquiry into Freud* (1955) is one of several important Frankfurt School attempts to wed Marxist cultural criticism and psychoanalysis. Louis Althusser in *For Marx* (1965; trans. 1969) incorporates psychoanalytic and structuralist insights into the Marxist project, as does Fredric Jameson in *The Political Unconscious: Narrative as a Socially Symbolic Act* (1981). Michael Ryan's *Marxism and Deconstruction: A Critical Articulation* (1982) establishes fruitful points of contact between Marx and the deconstructive philosophy of Jacques Derrida. Antonio Negri's *Marx Beyond Marx* (1979; trans. 1984) and Ernesto Laclau and Chantal Mouffe's *Hegemony and Socialist Strategy: Towards a Radical Democratic Politics* (1985) reflect the advent of post-Marxism in their transformation of traditional Marxist concepts. Nancy Hartsock's *Money, Sex, and Power: Toward a Feminist Historical Materialism* (1983) allies feminist and Marxist theory, while Gayatri Chakravorty Spivak's *In Other Worlds: Essays in Cultural Politics* (1987) combines Marxism and feminist studies with deconstruction, postcolonial theory, and cultural studies. Slavoj Žižek's *Sublime Object of Ideology* (1989) is an influential text at the intersection/crossroads of psychoanalysis, philosophy, and Marxist cultural and economic theories. Aijaz Ahmad's *In Theory: Classes, Nations, Literatures* (1992) situates postcolonial studies within Marxist paradigms, as does Ranajit Guha's *Dominance without Hegemony: History and Power in Colonial India* (1997).

Native American Studies

Before the advent of the American Indian literary renaissance during the 1960s, Native American studies was confined largely to anthropological and linguistic research on oral literatures; examples include Daniel G. Brinton, *Aboriginal American Authors and Their Productions* (1883); Franz Boas, *Race, Language, and Culture* (1910); and Paul Radín, *The Trickster: A Study in American Indian Mythology* (1956). Occasionally, literary studies of oral literatures was combined with ethnographic criticism, as in Roy Harvey Pearce's *The Savages of America: A Study of the Indian and the Idea of Civilization* (1953) and Richard Slotkin's later *Regeneration through Violence: The Mythology of the American Frontier, 1600–1860* (1973). In the late 1970s a series of groundbreaking book-length studies emerged that treated the writings of the American Indian literary renaissance as "literature"; among them were Charles R. Larson, *American Indian Fiction* (1978); Alan R. Velie, *Four American Indian Literary Masters: N. Scott Momaday, James Welch, Leslie Marmon Silko, and Gerald Vizenor* (1982); *Studies in American Indian Literature* (1983), edited by Paula Gunn Allen; and Kenneth Lincoln, *Native American Renaissance* (1983). Pioneering revisionist ethnographic approaches also appeared at this time, best exemplified by Dell Hymes's *"In Vain I Tried to Tell You": Essays in Native American Ethnopoetics* (1981). Yet another significant development was the emergence of a line of feminist works; see especially Paula Gunn Allen, *The Sacred Hoop: Recovering the Feminine in American Indian Traditions* (1986).

For general introductions to the field, see A. LaVonne Brown Ruoff, *American Indian Literatures: An Introduction, Bibliographic Review, and Selected Bibliography* (1990), as well as the earlier *Three American Literatures: Essays in Chicano, Native American, and Asian-American Literatures for Teachers of American Literature* (1982), edited by Houston A. Baker Jr. For introductions to the theory of Indian oral literatures, see Dennis Tedlock, *The Spoken Word and the Work of Interpretation* (1983); William Clements, *Native American Verbal Art: Texts and Contexts* (1996); and Karl Kroeber, *Artistry in Native American Myths* (1998). David Murray, *Forked Tongues: Speech, Writing, and Representation in North American Indian Texts* (1991); Louis Owen, *Other Destinies: Understanding the American Indian Novel* (1992); Robert A. Warrior, *Tribal Secrets: Recovering American Indian Intellectual Traditions* (1995); and Jace Weaver, *That the People Might Live: Native American Literatures and Native American Community* (1997) can be read as introductions to the theory of Native American written literatures. An accessible introduction to critical methodology is Greg Sarris's *Keeping Slug Woman Alive: A Holistic Approach to American Indian Texts* (1993). Two works by Arnold Krupat, *The Voice in the Margin: Native American Literature and the Canon* (1989) and *The Turn to the Native: Studies in Criticism and Culture* (1996), serve as wide-ranging introductions to the theoretical debates and issues in the field as a whole, while a third, *Ethnocriticism: Ethnography, History, Literature* (1991), introduces an influential interdisciplinary approach to Native American literature.

For a collection of critical essays on Native American texts from 1620 to 1940, see *Early Native American Writing: New Critical Essays* (1996), edited by Helen Jaskoski. *Literature of the American Indians: Views and Interpretations* (1975), edited by Abraham Chapman, is an important collection of essays covering nearly a hundred years of traditional ethnographic criticism. For various collections of revisionist ethnographic criticism, see *Traditional Literatures of the American Indian: Texts and Interpretations* (1981), edited by Karl Kroeber; *Smoothing the Ground: Essays on Native American Oral Literature* (1983), edited by Brian Swann; *Reading the Fire: Essays in the Traditional Indian Literature of the Far West* (1983), edited by Jarold Ramsey; *Critical Essays on Native American Literature* (1985), edited by Andrew Wiget; and *Recovering the Word: Essays on Native American Literature* (1987), edited by Brian Swann and Arnold Krupat. *Other Sisterhoods: Literary Theory and U.S. Women of Color* (1998), edited by Sandra Kumamoto Stanley, presents a number of feminist essays. Collections that focus largely on literary concerns include the theoretically informed *Narrative Chance: Postmodern Discourse on Native American Indian Literatures* (1993), edited by Gerald Vizenor; *New Voices in Native American Literary Criticism* (1993), edited by Arnold Krupat; *Native American Perspectives on Literature and History* (1995), edited by Alan R. Velie; and *Critical Perspectives on Native American Fiction* (2d ed., 1997), edited by Richard F. Fleck.

Informative bibliographies of theory and criticism include A. LaVonne Brown Ruoff's "American Indian Literature," in *Redefining American Literary History* (1990), edited by Ruoff and Jerry W. Ward Jr., and the more extensive contemporaneous bibliography published in Ruoff's *American Indian Literature*.

For a discussion of Native American studies in relationship to gender studies and gay and lesbian studies, see the essays in *Two-Spirit People: Native American Gender, Identity, Sexuality, and Spirituality* (1997), edited by Sue Ellen Jacobs, Wesley Thomas, and Sabine Lang, as well as Lang's *Men as Women, Women as Men: Changing Gender in Native American Cultures* (1998). Gerald Vizenor's *Fugitive Poses: Native American Indian Scenes of Absence and Presence* (1998) articulates a version of Native American studies connected with a variety of deconstructive and poststructuralist theorists. On Native American studies and feminism, see Kathleen M. Donovan, *Feminist Readings of Native American Literature: Coming to Voice* (1998). For an example of personal criticism focused on the concept of identity, see Louis Owens, *Mixedblood Messages: Literature, Film, Family, Place* (1998).

New Historicism

The term "New Historicism"—a contested phrase from its inception in the 1980s—refers either narrowly to the historical criticism of early modern cultures linked with Stephen Greenblatt and some of his colleagues or, more broadly, to a diverse critical movement concerned (as Greenblatt is) with structuralist and poststructuralist approaches to literary and cultural history inspired by several landmark works, namely Pierre Bourdieu, *Outline of a Theory of Practice* (1972; trans. 1977); Clifford Geertz, *The Interpretation of Cultures* (1973); Hayden White, *Metahistory: The Historical Imagination in Nineteenth-Century Europe* (1974); and Michel Foucault, *Discipline and Punish: The Birth of the Prison* (1975; trans. 1977). Also instrumental in prompting a "turn toward history" in the 1980s are Louis Althusser, *Lenin and Philosophy and Other Essays* (1971); Raymond Williams, *Marxism and Literature* (1977); Edward W. Said, *Orientalism* (1978); Frank Lentricchia, *After the New Criticism* (1980); and Fredric Jameson, *The Political Unconscious: Narrative as a Socially Symbolic Act* (1981). The groundbreaking text of New Historicism, in the narrow sense of the term, is Stephen Greenblatt's *Renaissance Self-Fashioning: From More to Shake-*

speare (1980). Two programmatic statements by Greenblatt on the New Historicism are his introduction to an edited collection, *The Power of Forms in the English Renaissance* (1982), and "Toward a Poetics of Culture" in his *Learning to Curse: Essays in Early Modern Culture* (1991). Regularly cited as authoritative theoretical accounts of New Historicist tenets are two essays by Louis A. Montrose: "Renaissance Literary Studies and the Subject of History" (1986), subsequently revised as "Professing the Renaissance: The Poetics and Politics of Culture" in *The New Historicism* (1989), edited by H. Aram Veeser, and "New Historicism," in *Redrawing the Boundaries* (1992), edited by Giles Gunn and Stephen Greenblatt. Frequently associated with Greenblatt and Montrose, although distinguished by a Marxist materialist component in her work, is Catherine Gallagher, whose book *The Industrial Reformation of English Fiction: Social Discourse and Narrative Form, 1832–1867* (1985) explores post-Romantic topics and texts. In the broader sense of the term, leading early examples of New Historicism emerged during the 1980s in many subdisciplines and fields. In American studies, for instance, "New Americanist" work appeared, including Michael Paul Rogin, *Subversive Genealogy: The Politics and Art of Herman Melville* (1983); Sacvan Bercovitch and Myra Jehlen, *Ideology and Classic American Literature* (1986); Lawrence Buell, *New England Literary Culture from Revolution through Renaissance* (1986); Walter Benn Michaels, *The Gold Standard and the Logic of Naturalism: American Literature at the Turn of the Century* (1987); Eric J. Sundquist, *To Wake the Nations: Race in the Making of American Literature* (1993); and *Revisionary Interventions into the American Canon* (1994), edited by Donald E. Pease. In medieval studies, influential works include Lee Patterson's *Negotiating the Past: The Historical Understanding of Medieval Literature* (1987) and *The New Medievalism* (1991), edited by Marina S. Brownlee, Kevin Brownlee, and Stephen G. Nichols. In Renaissance studies, a radical historicism indebted to Raymond Williams's influential idea of *cultural materialism* developed mainly in Britain, as reflected in the groundbreaking *Political Shakespeare: New Essays in Cultural Materialism* (1985), edited by Jonathan Dollimore and Alan Sinfield. In Romanticism, historicism figured prominently in Jerome McGann's *Romantic Ideology: A Critical Investigation* (1983) and Marjorie Levinson et al.'s *Rethinking Historicism: Critical Readings in Romantic History* (1989).

For a brief introduction, see Paul Hamilton's "New Historicism" in his survey of twentieth-century historical approaches titled *Historicism* (1996). A more extensive introduction is John Brannigan's *New Historicism and Cultural Materialism* (1998). *New Historicism and Renaissance Drama* (1992), edited by Richard Wilson and Richard Dutton, offers a critical survey of New Historicism in relationship to Renaissance studies, while Brook Thomas's *New Historicism and Other Old-Fashioned Topics* (1991) provides a critical account of the general trend toward historicism. For an excellent survey of New Historical developments in the broadest sense of the term, see the essays collected in *New Historical Literary Study: Essays on Reproducing Texts, Representing History* (1993), edited by Jeffrey N. Cox and Larry J. Reynolds. Also useful as a survey on New Historicism broadly conceived is Jeremy Hawthorn's *Cunning Passages: New Historicism, Cultural Materialism, and Marxism in the Contemporary Literary Debate* (1996). Catherine Gallagher and Stephen Greenblatt's *Practicing New Historicism* (2000) provides a sophisticated and readable reflection on the theory, practice, and historical development of New Historicism.

Two standard anthologies are *The New Historicism* (1989) and *The New Historicism Reader* (1994), both edited by H. Aram Veeser. For an earlier collection of essays committed to exploring social and historical dimensions of literary works, see *Historical Studies and Literary Criticism* (1985), edited by Jerome J. McGann. *Historical Criticism and the Challenge of Theory* (1993), edited by Janet Lavarie Smarr, provides a selection of essays that demonstrate self-reflexive historical literary study, while *New Historicism and Cultural Materialism: A Reader* (1996), edited by Kiernan Ryan, collects various essays that focus on the distinctions between the cultural poetics of New Historicism and the materialist critique promoted by British cultural materialism.

For bibliographic assistance, see the 1994 Veeser anthology (*The New Historicism Reader*), as well as the texts mentioned above by Wilson and Dutton (*New Historicism and Renaissance Drama*) and especially by Ryan (*New Historicism and Cultural Materialism*).

The practices of New Historicism lend themselves to many diverse critical projects. Prominent among these are two series of books published by the University of California Press under the titles Representations and The New Historicism: Studies in Cultural Poetics. The first reprints back issues from the leading New Historicist journal *Representations*—for example, *The Making of the Modern Body: Sexuality and Society in the Nineteenth Century* (1987), edited by Catherine Gallagher and Thomas Laqueur. The second series, edited by Stephen Greenblatt, includes a wide-ranging line of books, such as José E. Limón, *Mexican Ballads, Chicano Poems: History and Influence in Mexican-American Social Poetics* (1992); Christopher Craft, *Another Kind of Love: Male Homosexual Desire in English Discourse, 1850–1920* (1994); Catherine Gallagher, *Nobody's Story: The Vanishing Acts of Women Writers in the Marketplace, 1670–1820* (1994); and Frank Lestringant's work in postcolonial theory and criticism, *Cannibals: The Discovery and Representation of the Cannibal from Columbus to Jules Verne* (1994; trans. 1997).

Phenomenology and Hermeneutics

The first major works of phenomenological aesthetics were by Roman Ingarden, *The Literary Work of Art* (1931; trans. 1973) and *The Cognition of the*

Literary Work of Art (1937; trans. 1973). Also groundbreaking for phenomenological theory is Martin Heidegger, "The Origin of the Work of Art" (1935), later collected in his important *Poetry, Language, Thought* (1971). A less theoretical, applied form of phenomenological literary criticism crystallized in the Geneva School, whose most influential works include Marcel Raymond's *From Baudelaire to Surrealism* (1933; trans. 1949) and Georges Poulet's four-volume *Studies in Human Time* (1949–68; 2 vols. trans., 1956–59). U.S. phenomenological criticism is best represented by J. Hillis Miller's *Poets of Reality: Six Twentieth-Century Writers* (1965). Modern philological hermeneutics emerged in the United States with E. D. Hirsch Jr.'s landmark *Validity in Interpretation* (1967) and was developed in his *Aims of Interpretation* (1976). While hermeneutics and phenomenology combined fruitfully in several short sections of Martin Heidegger's *Being and Time* (1927; trans. 1962), the linkage culminated in the work of Hans-Georg Gadamer, in the monumental *Truth and Method* (1960; trans. 1975, rev. 1989) and subsequent writings. Later important combinations of phenomenology and hermeneutics can be found in the writings of the German school of reception aesthetics located at the University of Constance, especially Hans Robert Jauss's *Aesthetic Experience and Literary Hermeneutics* (1977; trans. 1982).

For a brief introductory overview of the Geneva School, see J. Hillis Miller, "The Geneva School: The Criticism of Marcel Raymond, Albert Béguin, Georges Poulet, Jean Rousset, Jean-Pierre Richard, and Jean Starobinski" (1966), collected in his *Theory Now and Then* (1991). A full-length account of Geneva criticism is provided by Sarah Lawall's *Critics of Consciousness: The Existential Structures of Literature* (1968). Georges Poulet's "Phenomenology of Reading," which first appeared in *New Literary History: A Journal of Theory and Interpretation* 1.1 (1969), is an influential theoretical statement. For a more comprehensive introduction to phenomenological criticism in general, including Ingarden and Heidegger as well as the Geneva School, see Robert R. Magliola, *Phenomenology and Literature: An Introduction* (1977). Richard Palmer's *Hermeneutics: Interpretation Theory in Schleiermacher, Dilthey, Heidegger, and Gadamer* (1969) offers a highly regarded historical introduction to hermeneutics, as does Jean Grondin's *Introduction to Philosophical Hermeneutics* (1991; trans. 1994). Other helpful texts include David Couzens Hoy, *The Critical Circle: Literature, History, and Philosophical Hermeneutics* (1978); Roy J. Howard, *Three Faces of Hermeneutics: An Introduction to Current Theories of Understanding* (1982); and William Ray, *Literary Meaning: From Phenomenology to Deconstruction* (1984). For a concise survey of modern hermeneutics with a concluding focus on Gadamer's significance for literary theory, see Joel C. Weinsheimer, *Philosophical Hermeneutics and Literary Theory* (1991). Kathy Eden's *Hermeneutics and the Rhetorical Tradition: Chapters in the Ancient Legacy and Its Humanist Perception* (1997) locates a historical basis for hermeneutics in classical theories of rhetoric. Gerald L. Bruns's *Hermeneutics: Ancient and Modern* (1992) covers a broad spectrum of key figures and topics in the tradition of literary and philosophical hermeneutics.

For a reader in phenomenological criticism, see *The French New Criticism: An Introduction and Sampler* (1967), edited by Laurent Le Sage, and especially *European Literary Theory and Practice: From Existential Phenomenology to Structuralism* (1973), edited by Vernon W. Gras. Useful general readers in hermeneutics include *The Hermeneutic Reader: Texts of the German Tradition from the Enlightenment to the Present* (1985), edited by Kurt Mueller-Vollmer; *The Hermeneutic Tradition: From Ast to Ricoeur* (1990), edited by Gayle L. Ormiston and Alan D. Schrift; and *Rhetoric and Hermeneutics in Our Time: A Reader* (1997), edited by Walter Jost and Michael J. Hyde. A wide-ranging collection of essays by many hands focusing on the implications of Heidegger's postmetaphysical thought for literary studies is *Martin Heidegger and the Question of Literature: Toward a Postmodern Literary Hermeneutics* (1979), edited by William V. Spanos. *Hermeneutics: Questions and Prospects* (1984), edited by Gary Shapiro and Alan Sica, covers contemporary hermeneutics in relationship to philosophy, literature, and social science.

A bibliography of phenomenological and hermeneutical criticism may be found in *The Cambridge History of Literary Criticism*, volume 8, *From Formalism to Poststructuralism* (1995), edited by Raman Selden. Also useful are the earlier bibliographies in Palmer's *Hermeneutics* and Grondin's *Introduction to Philosophical Hermeneutics*, as well as that in *The Existential Coordinates of the Human Condition: Poetic-Epic-Tragic: The Literary Genre* (1984), edited by Anna-Teresa Tymieniecka.

Gaston Bachelard's works, such as *The Poetics of Space* (1958; trans. 1964), offer a unique combination of phenomenology and psychoanalysis. For the intersections of phenomenology and formalism, see René Wellek's essays on the ontology of the literary work in *Concepts of Criticism* (1963), particularly "Concepts of Form and Structure in Twentieth-Century Criticism." Phenomenology and deconstruction meet in Joseph N. Riddel, *The Inverted Bell: Modernism and the Counterpoetics of William Carlos Williams* (1974). In *The Act of Reading: A Theory of Aesthetic Response* (1976; trans. 1978), Wolfgang Iser articulates a theory of reader response indebted to the phenomenological aesthetics of Ingarden. Mario J. Valdés's *Shadows in the Cave: A Phenomenological Approach to Literary Criticism Based on Hispanic Texts* (1982) places phenomenology in dialogue with ethnic studies. Hans Robert Jauss's *Toward an Aesthetic of Reception* (1982) combines hermeneutics with historicist reception theory. For the intersections of hermeneutics, structuralism, and semiotics, see T. K. Seung, *Structuralism and Hermeneutics* (1982) and *Semiotics and Thematics in Hermeneutics* (1982). Paul Ricoeur's *Time and Narrative* (3 vols., 1983–85; trans. 1984–88), particularly volume 2, links hermeneutics and narratology, and John D. Caputo's *Radical Hermeneutics: Repetition, Deconstruction, and the Hermeneutic Project* (1987) crosses hermeneutics with deconstruction. Richard Rorty's *Essays on Heidegger and Others* (1991) explores, among other things, the points of contact between pragmatism and Heideggerian hermeneutics.

Postcolonial Criticism and Theory

The late-twentieth-century emergence of postcolonial criticism and theory out of colonial politics and experience is manifested in such key early texts as Aimé Césaire, *Discourse on Colonialism* (1950; trans. 1972); Frantz Fanon, *Black Skin, White Masks* (1952; trans. 1967) and *The Wretched of the Earth* (1961; trans. 1963); and Ngugi wă Thiong'o, *Homecoming: Essays* (1972). The groundbreaking texts of postcolonial criticism and theory as an academic field are Edward W. Said's *Orientalism* (1978); Gayatri Chakravorty Spivak's *In Other Worlds: Essays in Cultural Politics* (1987), which also makes a significant contribution to feminist theory; and Homi K. Bhabha's essays of the 1980s collected in *The Location of Culture* (1994). Exemplary works focused on reading literature within colonial contexts include Selwyn R. Cudjoe's *Resistance and Caribbean Literature* (1980) and Barbara Harlow's *Resistance Literature* (1987). During the 1990s two notable lines of theoretical inquiry emerged in postcolonial studies. The first, focused on theories of nationalism, includes such founding texts as Benedict Anderson's *Imagined Communities: Reflections on the Origins and Spread of Nationalism* (2d ed., 1991) and Partha Chatterjee's *Nationalist Thought and the Colonial World: A Derivative Discourse* (2d ed., 1993). Theorizing globalization is the central concern of the second line of inquiry; among its most important texts is Arjun Appadurai's *Modernity at Large: Cultural Dimensions of Globalization* (1996).

For introductions to postcolonial theory, see Bill Ashcroft, Gareth Griffiths, and Helen Tiffin, *The Empire Writes Back: Theories and Practices in Post-colonial Literature* (1989); Leela Gandhi, *Postcolonial Theory: A Critical Introduction* (1998); Ania Loomba, *Colonialism/Postcolonialism* (1998); Robert Young, *Postcolonialism: An Historical Introduction* (1999); and *A Companion to Postcolonial Studies* (1999), edited by Sangeeta Ray and Henry Schwarz. A brief introductory statement is provided in Homi K. Bhabha's "Postcolonial Criticism" in *Redrawing the Boundaries* (1992), edited by Stephen Greenblatt and Giles Gunn. An important full-length introduction is Ella Shohat and Robert Stam's *Unthinking Eurocentrism: Multiculturalism and the Media* (1994). Robert Young's *White Mythologies: Writing, History, and the West* (1990) may be read as an advanced introduction and critique of Western historiography. Bart Moore-Gilbert's *Postcolonial Theory: Contexts, Practices, Politics* (1997) provides a critical overview of the three major postcolonial theorists, Said, Spivak, and Bhabha. On the pivotal role of Said's and Spivak's work in postcolonial studies, see *Edward Said: A Critical Reader* (1992), edited by Michael Sprinker, and *The Spivak Reader: Selected Works of Gayatri Chakravorty Spivak* (1996), edited by Donna Landry and Gerald MacLean. For historical background, see *Colonial Discourse and Post-Colonial Theory: A Reader* (1994), edited by Patrick Williams and Laura Chrisman, which gathers critical and theoretical pieces from the 1950s to 1990s that represent the scope of debates in postcolonial studies. More on the history of colonial discourse can be found in three additional respected works: *Europe and Its Others* (2 vols., 1985), edited by Francis Baker et al., which contains some of the founding essays of postcolonial criticism; Eric Hobsbawm, *Age of Empire* (1987); and *After Colonialism: Imperial Histories and Postcolonial Displacements* (1994), edited by Gyan Prakash.

Influential readers and anthologies of postcolonial criticism include *"Race," Writing, and Difference* (1985), edited by Henry Louis Gates Jr., a collection of some major voices in the field; *Nation and Narration* (1990), edited by Homi K. Bhabha, which takes as its touchstone the ambivalence over nationhood; *The Post-Colonial Studies Reader* (1994), edited by Bill Ashcroft, Gareth Griffiths, and Helen Tiffin; and *Colonial Discourse/Postcolonial Theory* (1994), edited by Francis Barker, Peter Hulme, and Margaret Iversen. The later *Contemporary Postcolonial Theory: A Reader* (1996), edited by Padmini Mongia, provides a generous selection of key articles that address central issues in the field, while *Rethinking Postcolonialism: A Critical Reader* (1999), edited by David Theo Goldberg and Ato Quayson, combines new with seminal texts. For readers on the connections between postcolonial theory and practice, see *Third World Women and the Politics of Feminism* (1991), edited by Chandra Talpade Mohanty, Ann Russo, and Lourdes Torres; *The Decolonization of Imagination: Culture, Knowledge, and Power* (1995), edited by Jan Nederveen Pieterse and Bhikhu Parekh; and *The Post-Colonial Question: Common Skies, Divided Horizons* (1996), edited by Iain Chambers and Lidia Curti, which focuses on the key concept of hybridity.

Definitions of theoretical terms and a useful bibliography are provided by Bill Ashcroft, Gareth Griffiths, and Helen Tiffin's *Key Concepts in Post-Colonial Studies* (1998). For other helpful bibliographies, see the following readers cited above: Williams and Chrisman, *Colonial Discourse and Post-Colonial Theory*; Ashcroft, Griffiths, and Tiffin, *The Post-Colonial Studies Reader*; and Mongia, *Contemporary Postcolonial Theory*; see also Gandhi, *Postcolonial Theory*.

As is the case with other contemporary schools and movements, postcolonial theory and criticism contain many crossover or interdisciplinary texts. Said's *Orientalism* and Bhabha's *Location of Culture* develop contrasting poststructural approaches to postcolonial issues, the former employing Foucauldian theory, the latter a Derridean deconstructive methodology. Bhabha's work also possesses a heavy psychoanalytic component. Spivak's *In Other Worlds* weaves Marxism and feminism into postcolonial studies in pioneering ways. For more on the relationship between Marxism and postcolonial studies, see the essays by diverse hands in *Marxist Theories of Imperialism: A Critical Survey* (1980), edited by Anthony Brewer, as well as Raymond Williams's *Politics of Modernism: Against the New Conformists* (1989), which includes a revealing interview with Said. Ashis Nandy's *Intimate Enemy: Loss and Recovery of Self under Colonialism* (1983) is an exemplary text marking the intersection of psychoanalysis and postcolonial studies. Sara Suleri's *Meatless Days* (1989) approaches feminist postcolonial studies from the perspective of personal criticism, as does Trinh T. Minh-ha's *Woman, Native, Other: Writing, Postcoloniality, and Feminism* (1989). A much-debated, resolutely Marxist critical account of postcolonial theory's intersections with various contemporary schools and movements appears in Aijaz Ahmad's *In Theory: Classes, Nations, Literatures* (1992). Anne McClintock's *Imperial Leather: Race, Gender, and Sexuality in the Colonial Conquest* (1994) connects psychoanalytic, feminist, and Marxist discourses. The various essays in the interdisciplinary *Dangerous Liaisons: Gender, Nation, and Postcolonial Perspectives* (1997), edited by Anne McClintock, Aamir Mufti, and Ella Shohat, promote the utility of multiple approaches, especially feminist ones. E. San Juan Jr.'s *Beyond Postcolonial Theory* (1997) takes issue especially with Bhabha and Spivak, arguing for a more politically activist stance.

Psychoanalytic Theory

Sigmund Freud's work is the primary source of psychoanalytic theory for literary intellectuals, followed closely by the work of Jacques Lacan and, to a lesser extent, Carl Gustav Jung. The authoritative English translation of Freud's work was done under the direction of James Strachey, *The Standard Edition of the Complete Psychological Works of Sigmund Freud* (24 vols., 1953–74). English translations of Lacan's most influential works include *Écrits: A Selection* (1977) and *The Four Fundamental Concepts of Psychoanalysis* (1978), both translated by Alan Sheridan; and *Feminine Sexuality: Jacques Lacan and the école freudienne* (1983), translated by Jacqueline Rose, who edited the book with Juliet Mitchell. The standard English translation of Jung's work is by R. F. C. Hull, *The Collected Works of C. G. Jung* (20 vols., 1954–92). Three foundational essays in the psychoanalytic understanding of literature are Freud's "Creative Writers and Daydreaming" (1908), Jung's "On the Relation of Analytical Psychology to Poetry" (1922), and Lacan's "Seminar on Poe's 'Purloined Letter' " (1966).

Robert N. Mullinger's *Psychoanalysis and Literature: An Introduction* (1981) provides an elementary introduction to psychoanalysis and psychoanalytic criticism. For a broad introduction to Freud, see J. N. Isbister, *Freud: An Introduction to His Life and Work* (1985). Malcolm Bowie's *Lacan* (1991) introduces Lacanian theory in a clear, accessible manner, as does Teresa Brennan's *History after Lacan* (1993). For advanced introductions, see Elizabeth Grosz, *Jacques Lacan: A Feminist Introduction* (1990), and Slavoj Žižek, *Looking Awry: An Introduction to Jacques Lacan through Popular Culture* (1991). A basic introduction to Jungian criticism is provided by Bettina L. Knapp's *Jungian Approach to Literature* (1984). For a concise overview of Freud and Lacan, see chapter 4 of Kaja Silverman, *The Subject of Semiotics* (1983); for a critical overview of Freud, Lacan, and Jung, as well as Freud's famous critics Gilles Deleuze and Félix Guattari, see Elizabeth Wright, *Psychoanalytic Criticism: A Reappraisal* (rev. ed., 1998). *Holland's Guide to Psychoanalytic Psychology and Literature-and-Psychology* (1990) by Norman Holland offers a historical overview of psychoanalytic criticism from the perspective of clinical psychoanalysis. For a historical account of the rise and influence of Lacanian theory, see Elisabeth Roudinesco, *Jacques Lacan and Co.: A History of Psychoanalysis in France, 1925–1985* (1990), and Sherry Turkel, *Psychoanalytic Politics: Jacques Lacan and Freud's French Revolution* (2d ed., 1992). An influential critical overview of post-Lacanian French psychoanalytic feminists—Julia Kristeva, Hélène Cixous, and Luce Irigaray—appears in the closing half of Toril Moi's *Sexual/Textual Politics: Feminist Literary Theory* (1985). A broad chronicle is available in Reuben Fine's *History of Psychoanalysis* (1990).

For a Freud reader, see *Writings on Art and Literature* (1997), edited by Neil Hertz. *Literature and Psychoanalysis* (1987), edited by Edith Kurzweil and William Phillips, collects a broad historical range of essays in psychoanalytic criticism, by authors from Freud to Julia Kristeva. Other introductory collections include *Introducing Psychoanalytic Theory* (1982), edited by Sander L. Gilman; *Everything You Wanted to Know about Lacan (But Were Afraid to Ask Hitchcock)* (1992), edited by Slavoj Žižek; and *Psychoanalytic Literary Criticism* (1994), edited by Maud Ellmann. For advanced collections of psychoanalytic criticism, see *Psychoanalysis and the Question of the Text* (1978), edited by Geoffrey Hartman; the Lacanian *Literature and Psychoanalysis: The Question of Reading: Otherwise* (1981), edited by Shoshana Felman; and *Psychoanalytic Criticism: A Reader* (1996), edited by Sue Vice. *The Purloined Poe: Lacan, Derrida, and Psychoanalytic Reading* (1988), edited by John Muller, brings together celebrated essays by Lacan, Jacques Derrida, and Barbara Johnson on interpreting Edgar Allan Poe's "Purloined Letter." For a collection of archetypal criticism written near the close of the twentieth century, see *Jungian Literary Criticism* (1992), edited by Richard Sugg.

Helpful reference sources on the terminology of psychoanalysis include Jean Laplanche and J.-B.

Pontalis, *The Language of Psycho-analysis* (1967; trans. 1973); John P. Muller and William J. Richardson, *Lacan and Language: A Reader's Guide to "Écrits"* (1982); Elizabeth Wright, *Feminism and Psychoanalysis: A Critical Dictionary* (1992); and Dylan Evans, *An Introductory Dictionary of Lacanian Psychoanalysis* (1996). Another resource is John Bristow's *Sexuality* (1997), which focuses on the critical uses and abuses of that concept. Bibliographic assistance is available in Norman Kiell, *Psychoanalysis, Psychology, and Literature: A Bibliography* (2 vols., 1982; suppl., 1990); Joseph P. Natoli and Frederik L. Rusch, *Psychocriticism: An Annotated Bibliography* (1984); and Holland's overview, *Holland's Guide*. On Freud, see Alexander Grinstein, *Sigmund Freud's Writings: A Comprehensive Bibliography* (1977). Bibliographies of Lacan include Joan Nordquist's *Jacques Lacan: A Bibliography* (1987) and Michael Clark's *Jacques Lacan: An Annotated Bibliography* (1988). For a bibliography of Jungian criticism, see Jos Van Meurs, *Jungian Literary Criticism, 1920–1980: An Annotated Critical Bibliography of Works in English (with a Selection of Titles after 1980)* (1988).

Psychoanalytic theory readily combines with other critical methods and approaches. Wide-ranging links between psychoanalysis and feminist theory are developed in several provocative collections: see, for example, *The (M)Other Tongue: Essays in Feminist Psychoanalytic Interpretation* (1985), edited by Shirley Nelson Garner, Claire Kahane, and Madelon Sprengnether; *Feminism and Psychoanalysis* (1989), edited by Richard Feldstein and Judith Roof; and *Between Feminism and Psychoanalysis* (1989), edited by Teresa Brennan. Harold Bloom's earlier *The Anxiety of Influence: A Theory of Poetry* (1973) joined psychoanalysis and Yale School deconstruction. Significant, widely varied Marxist extensions of psychoanalytic theory include Herbert Marcuse, *Eros and Civilization: A Philosophical Inquiry into Freud* (1955); Louis Althusser, *Lenin and Philosophy and Other Essays* (1971); and Fredric Jameson, *The Political Unconscious: Narrative as a Socially Symbolic Act* (1981). Myth criticism, which occupied a prominent place in the interim between the stagnation of the New Criticism and the rise of postformalist theories in the 1960s, derived largely from psychoanalytic theories, most notably in such different classic books as Joseph Campbell, *The Hero with a Thousand Faces* (1949); Northrop Frye, *Anatomy of Criticism: Four Essays* (1957); and Leslie Fiedler, *Love and Death in the American Novel* (1960). Influential early poststructuralist readings of psychoanalysis include Jacques Derrida, "Freud and the Scene of Writing" (1966); Gilles Deleuze and Félix Guattari, *Anti-Oedipus: Capitalism and Schizophrenia* (1972; trans. 1977); Luce Irigaray, *Speculum of the Other Woman* (1974; trans. 1985) and *This Sex Which Is Not One* (1977; trans. 1985); and Julia Kristeva, *Revolution in Poetic Language* (1974; trans. 1984) and *Powers of Horror: An Essay on Abjection* (1980; trans. 1982). For intersections of psychoanalysis and narratology, see the essays in *Lacan and Narrative: The Psychoanalytic Difference in Narrative Theory* (1983), edited by Robert Con Davis, as well as Peter Brooks's *Reading for the Plot: Design and Intention in Narrative* (1984). Psychoanalysis from a postcolonial perspective is most famously presented in Frantz Fanon's *Wretched of the Earth* (1961; trans. 1963), particularly its concluding case studies. Intersections of psychoanalysis and reader-response criticism are explored in Norman Holland's books, most notably *Poems in Persons: An Introduction to the Psychoanalysis of Literature* (1973). Judith Butler's *Gender Trouble: Feminism and the Subversion of Identity* (1990) critically extends psychoanalysis, breaking new ground for poststructuralist feminist queer theory. The broad influence of psychoanalysis on various theoretical schools and movements, particularly feminism, Marxism, and deconstruction, is exhibited in the essays collected by Richard Feldstein and Henry Sussman in *Psychoanalysis and . . .* (1989).

Reader-Response Criticism

Among the influential forerunners of the rise of reader-response criticism in the 1960s and 1970s are I. A. Richards's *Practical Criticism: A Study in Literary Judgment* (1929), Louise Rosenblatt's *Literature as Exploration* (1937), and the phenomenological work of the Geneva School from the 1930s to the 1950s, summed up in Georges Poulet's later "Phenomenology of Reading" (1969). Arising largely in opposition to such formalist notions as the "affective fallacy," the diverse founding texts of U.S. reader-response criticism include Stanley E. Fish, *Surprised by Sin: The Reader in Paradise Lost* (1967); Norman Holland, *The Dynamics of Literary Response* (1968); David Bleich, *Readers and Feelings: An Introduction to Subjective Criticism* (1975); Jonathan Culler, *Structuralist Poetics: Structuralism, Linguistics, and the Study of Literature* (1975); Louise Rosenblatt, *The Reader, the Text, the Poem: The Transactional Theory of the Literary Work* (1978); and Judith Fetterley, *The Resisting Reader: A Feminist Approach to American Fiction* (1979). Particularly important for U.S. reader-response criticism is Fish's essay "Literature in the Reader: Affective Stylistics" (1970). Developed in Germany during the 1960s and 1970s, the Constance School of reception aesthetics gained attention through two books by Wolfgang Iser, *The Implied Reader: Patterns of Communication in Prose Fiction from Bunyan to Beckett* (1972; trans. 1974) and *The Act of Reading: A Theory of Aesthetic Response* (1976; trans. 1978), as well as through Hans Robert Jauss's *Aesthetic Experience and Literary Hermeneutics* (1977; trans. 1982). Influential statements of French poststructuralist reader-response theory appear in Roland Barthes's *S/Z* (1970; trans. 1974) and his *Pleasure of the Text* (1973; trans. 1975).

Steven Mailloux's *Interpretive Conventions: The Reader in the Study of American Fiction* (1982) provides an introductory critical survey of five influential theories of reader response and develops a sociological model of reading. On German reader-oriented criticism, see Robert C. Holub, *Reception Theory: A Critical Introduction* (1984). For more general introductions to reader response, see Elizabeth Freund, *The Return of the Reader: Reader-Response Criticism* (1987), and Richard Beach, *A Teacher's Introduction to Reader-Response Theories* (1993).

Representative collections of works in the tradition of reader-response criticism are available in *New Perspectives in German Literary Criticism* (1979), edited by Richard Armacher and Victor Lange; *Reader-Response Criticism: From Formalism to Post-Structuralism* (1980), edited by Jane Tompkins; and *The Reader in the Text: Essays on Audience and Interpretation* (1980), edited by Susan Suleiman and Inge Crosman.

For bibliographies on reader-response criticism, see the anthologies by Tompkins and by Suleiman and Crosman cited in the previous paragraph, as well as Mailloux's *Interpretive Conventions* and Beach's *Teacher's Introduction*.

Reader-response criticism is a pluralistic and heterogeneous movement, encompassing many different critical projects. For a formalist approach to reader-response, see Wayne Booth, *Rhetoric of Fiction* (1961; 2d ed., 1983). On the links between psychoanalysis and reader-response criticism, see Norman Holland, *Five Readers Reading* (1975). Culler's *Structuralist Poetics* and Michael Riffaterre's *Semiotics of Poetry* (1978) mark the various intersections of reader-response and structuralism, as does Gerald Prince's *Narratology: The Form and Functioning of Narrative* (1982). Semiotics and reader response also combine in Umberto Eco, *The Role of the Reader: Explorations in the Semiotics of Texts* (1979). Paul de Man's *Allegories of Reading: Figural Language in Rousseau, Nietzsche, Rilke, and Proust* (1979) articulates a theory of reading from the point of view of deconstruction. On the relationship of neopragmatism to reader response, see Steven Knapp and Walter Benn Michaels, "Against Theory," *Critical Inquiry*, 8 (1982). Mary Louise Pratt's "Interpretive Strategies/Strategic Interpretations: On Anglo-American Reader-Response Criticism," *Boundary 2* 11 (1982) presents a critique of reader-response theory from a Marxist perspective, while Robert Scholes's *Textual Power: Literary Theory and the Teaching of English* (1985) unites ideological analysis with reader-response and structuralist methods. The intersection of feminism and reader-response criticism is marked by the often-cited *Gender and Reading: Essays on Readers, Texts, and Contexts* (1986), edited by Elizabeth A. Flynn and Patrocinio P. Schweickart. On the application of sociological methods of cultural studies to reception issues, see Janice Radway's celebrated *Reading the Romance: Women, Patriarchy, and Popular Literature* (1984). Robert C. Holub's *Crossing Borders: Reception Theory, Poststructuralism, Deconstruction* (1992) develops connections between poststructuralist theory and reader-response criticism, while Judith Still and Michael Worton's *Textuality and Sexuality: Reading Theories and Practices* (1993) explores links among feminism, gender studies, and reader-response criticism. Steven Mailloux's *Rhetorical Power* (1989) and his *Reception Histories: Rhetoric, Pragmatism, and American Cultural Politics* (1998) represent a latter-day reader-response criticism that intersects with cultural studies.

Structuralism and Semiotics

In Europe the seminal groundbreaking text of structuralism and semiotics is Ferdinand de Saussure's posthumously published collection of lecture notes, *Course in General Linguistics* (1915), which presents the first structuralist approach to language, superseding traditional philological and historical modes of analysis. In America the philosopher Charles Sanders Peirce undertook similar contemporaneous work, as seen particularly in the scattered writings collected in *Peirce on Signs: Writings on Semiotic by Charles Sanders Peirce* (1991), edited by James Hoopes. Early applications of structuralist method to the study of literature were made by the Russian formalists in the 1920s and, more fully, by the Prague School of linguistics between the world wars. Important in this regard are the various essays of Roman Jakobson collected posthumously in *Language in Literature* (1987), as well as the articles by Jan Mukařovský translated into English in *The Word and Verbal Art* (1977) and *Structure, Sign, and Function* (1978). Various highly regarded nonliterary applications of structuralist method include Claude Lévi-Strauss, *Structural Anthropology* (1958; trans. 1963); Louis Althusser, *For Marx* (1965; trans. 1969); and Hayden White, *Metahistory: The Historical Imagination in Nineteenth-Century Europe* (1973). For leading examples of literary theory inspired by structural linguistics, see Jakobson, "Closing Statement: Linguistics and Poetics" (1960); Käte Hamburger, *Logic of Literature* (2d ed., 1968; trans. 1973); and Michael Riffaterre, *Semiotics of Poetry* (1978), all of which can be instructively compared with Northrop Frye's earlier attempt to put literary criticism on a scientific footing in *Anatomy of Criticism: Four Essays* (1957). Important works in the tradition of narratology, the structuralist study of narrative, include Lévi-Strauss, "The Structural Study of Myth" (1955); Tzvetan Todorov, *Poetics of Prose* (1971; trans. 1977); Gérard Genette, *Narrative Discourse: An Essay on Method* (1972; trans. 1980); and A. J. Greimas, *Maupassant: The Semiotics of the Text* (1976; trans. 1988). Roland Barthes's *Mythologies* (1957; trans. 1972) and Bob Hodge and Gunther Kress's *Social Semiotics* (1988) are admired examples of semiotics, the application of structural linguistics to the world of cultural phenomena.

Jonathan Culler's *Ferdinand de Saussure* (rev. ed., 1986) provides a lucid and concise introduction to the basic principles of Saussure's structural linguistics, while his award-winning *Structuralist Poetics: Structuralism, Linguistics, and the Study of Literature* (1975) offers a sophisticated introduction to structuralism and its applications to literary study. A more succinct, basic introduction, Terence Hawkes's *Structuralism and Semiotics* (1977) gives an excellent overview of major trends, schools, and figures. In *The Prison-House of Language: A Critical Account of Structuralism and Russian Formalism* (1972), Fredric Jameson expounds a Marxist critique of structuralism and formalism, while also providing an introduction to their key concepts. *Structuralism: An Introduction* (1973), edited by David Robey, and *Structuralism and Since* (1979), edited by John Sturrock, provide interdisciplinary introductions to structuralism. Robert Scholes's *Structuralism in Literature: An Introduction* (1974) focuses on the role of structuralism in literary studies, while Wallace Martin's *Recent Theories of Narrative* (1986) surveys the field of narratology. A well-known advanced introduction to semiotics is Umberto Eco's *Theory of Semiotics* (1976). For an international overview of semiotics, see R. W. Bailey, *The Sign: Semiotics around the World* (1978). A historical and theoretical account of the Prague School is available in F. W. Galan's *Historic Structures: The Prague School Project, 1928–1946* (1985). Thomas A. Sebeok's brief *Semiotics in the United States* (1991) gives an anecdotal history of American semiotics, while Françoise Dosse's *History of Structuralism* (2 vols., 1991–92; trans. 1997) comprehensively details the history of French structuralism, with considerable attention to the many disciplines involved.

Structuralism: A Reader (1970), edited by Michael Lane, represents the range and depth of structuralist works by providing a collection of multidisciplinary essays, as does the compact classroom favorite, *The Structuralists: From Marx to Lévi-Strauss* (1972), edited by Richard T. and Fernande M. De George. For an influential anthology that simultaneously introduced French structuralism and poststructuralism to many Americans, see *Sciences of Man: The Structuralist Controversy* (1970), edited by Richard Macksey and Eugenio Donato, later reprinted as *The Structuralist Controversy: The Languages of Criticism and the Sciences of Man* (1972). *On Signs: A Semiotic Reader* (1985), edited by Marshall Blonsky, is a well-organized collection of essays on theoretical and practical semiotics, illustrating, among other things, the wide-ranging cultural uses of semiotics. *Semiotics: An Introductory Reader* (1986), edited by Robert E. Innes, collects classic European and American statements on semiotics. Definitive works of the Prague School are collected in *A Prague School Reader on Esthetics, Literary Structure, and Style* (1964), edited by Paul L. Garvin, and *The Prague School: Selected Writings, 1929–1946* (1982), edited by Peter Steiner. For collections of essays from the field of narratology, see *Narrative/Theory* (1996), edited by David H. Richter, and *Narratologies: New Perspectives on Narrative Analysis* (1999), edited by David Herman.

For scholarly definitions of terminology, consult Oswald Ducrot and Tzvetan Todorov, *Encyclopedic Dictionary of the Sciences of Language* (1972; trans. 1979); A. J. Greimas and Joseph Courtés, *Semiotics and Language: An Analytical Dictionary* (1979; trans. 1982); and Paul Bouissac, *Encyclopedia of Semiotics* (1998). For narratological terminology, see Gerald Prince, *A Dictionary of Narratology* (1987), and Mieke Bal, *Narratology: Introduction to the Theory of Narrative* (2d ed., 1997). Vincent Colapietro's *Glossary of Semiotics* (1993) is an elementary source of definitions. Roland Barthes's *Elements of Semiology* (1964; trans. 1968) offers a terse technical exposition of semiotic methods for advanced students. For a bibliography of selected influential French figures in structuralism, see Joan M. Miller, *French Structuralism: A Multidisciplinary Bibliography with a Checklist of Sources for Louis Althusser, Roland Barthes, Jacques Derrida, Michel Foucault, Lucien Goldmann, Jacques Lacan, and an Update of Works on Claude Lévi-Strauss* (1981). Josué Harari's more general bibliography, *Structuralists and Structuralisms: A Selected Bibliography of French Contemporary Thought* (1971), charts the impact of French structuralism on philosophy, anthropology, and psychoanalysis, as well as on literature.

The structuralist method has found applications in many contemporary critical schools and movements. A widely influential structuralist approach to psychoanalysis appears in Jacques Lacan's *Écrits* (1966; trans. 1977) and his *Four Fundamental Concepts of Psychoanalysis* (1973; trans. 1977). On structuralism and Marxism, see Fredric Jameson, *The Political Unconscious: Narrative as a Socially Symbolic Act* (1981). For the New Historicism, Michel Foucault's work, especially *Discipline and Punish: The Birth of the Prison* (1975; trans. 1977), pioneers important structuralist modes of history writing, even though Foucault himself resisted being classified as a structuralist. Also important to the New Historicism in this regard is Hayden White's *Tropics of Discourse: Essays in Cultural Criticism* (1978). Edward W. Said's *Orientalism* (1978) extends Foucault's structuralist methods to postcolonial criticism and theory. Two texts that mark the rich intersections of semiotics, psychoanalysis, and literary theory and criticism are Julia Kristeva's *Desire in Language: A Semiotic Approach to Literature and Art* (1980) and Kaja Silverman's *Subject of Semiotics* (1983). On the relationship between semiotics, Marxism, and psychoanalysis, see Rosalind Coward and John Ellis, *Language and Materialism: Developments in Semiology and the Theory of the Subject* (1977), and Jean-Joseph Goux, *Symbolic Economies: After Marx and Freud* (1990). Elizabeth A. Meese's *(SEM)erotics: Theorizing Lesbian Writing* (1992) links semiotics to lesbian theory and criticism.

PERMISSIONS ACKNOWLEDGMENTS

Chinua Achebe: "An Image of Africa: Racism in Conrad's *Heart of Darkness*" from *The Chancellor's Lecture Series*, 1974–75, Amherst 1976. Reprinted *from The Massachusetts Review*. © 1978 *The Massachusetts Review*, Inc. Reprinted by permission.

Dante Alighieri: "The Letter to Can Grande" from *Literary Criticism of Dante Alighieri*, translated and edited by Robert S. Haller. Reprinted by permission of the University of Nebraska Press. Copyright © 1973 by University of Nebraska Press. "Il Convivio" from *Dante's Il Convivio* (The Banquet), translated by Richard Lansing, © 1990 by Richard H. Lansing. Reprinted by permission of Garland Publishing, Inc.

Paula Gunn Allen: "Kochinnenako in Academe: Three Approaches to Interpreting a Keres Indian Tale" from *The Sacred Hoop*. Copyright © 1986, 1992 by Paula Gunn Allen. Reprinted by permission of Beacon Press, Boston.

Louis Althusser: "A Letter on Art in Reply to André Daspre" and "Ideology and Ideological State Apparatuses" from *Lenin and Philosophy and Other Essays*, translated by Ben Brewster. Copyright © 1971 by Monthly Review Press. Reprinted by permission of Monthly Review Foundation.

Gloria Anzaldúa: "La conciencia de la mestiza: Towards a New Consciousness" from *Borderlands*/ La Frontera: *The New Mestiza*, ©1987 by Gloria Anzaldúa. Reprinted by permission of Aunt Lute Books.

Aristotle: "Poetics" from *Poetics I*, translated by Richard Janko © 1987. Reprinted by permission of Hackett Publishing Company. "Rhetoric" from *On Rhetoric: A Theory of Civic Discourse*, translated by George A. Kennedy, copyright 1992 by George A. Kennedy. Used by permission of Oxford University Press, Inc.

Augustine: From *On Christian Doctrine*, translated by D. W. Robertson Jr. Copyright © 1958. Reprinted by permission of Prentice-Hall, Inc., Upper Saddle River, NJ. "The Trinity," translated by Stephen McKenna, from *Fathers of the Church*, series #45: *St. Augustine: De Trinitate*. Reprinted by permission of The Catholic University Press of America.

J. L. Austin: "Performative Utterances" from *Philosophical Papers*, © 1979. We have made diligent efforts to contact the copyright holder to obtain permission to reprint this selection. If you have information that would help us, please write to W. W. Norton & Company, 500 Fifth Avenue, New York, NY 10110.

Houston A. Baker: "Introduction" from *Blues, Ideology, and Afro-American Literature*, © 1984 by University of Chicago Press. Reprinted by permission.

Mikhail Bakhtin: "Discourse in the Novel" from *The Dialogic Imagination: Four Essays*, edited by Michael Holquist, translated by Caryl Emerson and Michael Holquist. Copyright © 1981. Reprinted by permission of University of Texas Press.

Roland Barthes: "Work to Text" and "The Death of the Author" from *Image, Music, Text*. English translation copyright © 1977 by Stephen Heath. Reprinted by permission of Farrar, Straus & Giroux, LLC. "The Brain of Einstein," "Photography and Electoral Appeal," and "Soap-Powders and Detergents" from *Mythologies*, translated by Annette Lavers. Translation copyright © 1972 by Jonathan Cape. Reprinted by permission of Farrar, Straus & Giroux, LLC, and the publisher, Jonathan Cape. We have made diligent efforts to contact the copyright holder to obtain permission to reprint this selection. If you have information that would help us, please write to W. W. Norton & Company, 500 Fifth Avenue, New York, NY 10110.

Charles Baudelaire: "The Painter of Modern Life" from *The Painter of Modern Life & Other Essays*. Translated by Jonathan Mayne. © 1964 by Phaidon Press Ltd. Reprinted by permission of the publisher.

Jean Baudrillard: "The Precession of Simulacra" from *Simulations*, translated by Paul Foss and Paul Patton. © 1983 Semiotext(e) and Jean Baudrillard. We have made diligent efforts to contact the copyright holder to obtain permission to reprint this selection. If you have information that would help us, please write to W. W. Norton & Company, 500 Fifth Avenue, New York, NY 10110.

Simone de Beauvoir: From *The Second Sex*, translated by H. M. Parshley. Copyright © 1952 and renewed 1980 by Alfred A. Knopf, Inc. Reprinted by permission of the publisher. Also reprinted by permission of the British publisher, Jonathan Cape.

Aphra Behn: "Epistle to the Reader" from *The Dutch Lover* from *The Works of Aphra Behn*, vol. V, and "Preface to *The Lucky Chance*" from *The Works of Aphra Behn*, vol. VII, edited by Janet Todd. © 1996 Ohio State University Press. Reprinted by permission of Ohio State University Press and Pickering & Chatto.

Joachim du Bellay: From *The Defence and Illustration of the French Language*, translated by Gladys M. Turquet. Reprinted by permission of the publisher, J. M. Dent & Sons.

Walter Benjamin: "The Work of Art in the Age of Mechanical Reproduction" from *Illuminations*, copyright © 1955 by Suhrkamp Verlag, Frankfurt. English translation by Harry Zohn, copyright © 1968 and renewed 1996 by Harcourt, Inc., reprinted by permission of Harcourt, Inc., and by the publishers of *Walter Benjamin: Selected Writings* edited by Marcus Bullock and Michael W. Jennings. The Belknap Press of Harvard University Press, copyright © 1998 by the President and Fellows of Harvard College.

Homi K. Bhabha: "The Commitment to Theory" from *The Location of Culture,* © 1994 by Homi K. Bhabha. Reprinted by permission of Routledge.

Harold Bloom: "The Anxiety of Influence" from *The Anxiety of Influence: A Theory of Poetry,* Second Edition, copyright 1997 by Oxford University Press, Inc. Used by permission of Oxford University Press, Inc.

Giovanni Boccaccio: "Genealogy of the Gentile Gods," Book 14, from *Boccaccio on Poetry,* translated by Charles Osgood, © 1956. Reprinted by permission of Prentice-Hall, Inc., Upper Saddle River, NJ.

Susan Bordo: "The Body and the Reproduction of Femininity" from *Unbearable Weight: Feminism, Western Culture, and the Body.* Copyright © 1993 by The Regents of the University of California. Reprinted with the permission of The University of California Press.

Pierre Bourdieu: "Introduction" from *Distinction: A Social Critique of the Judgment of Taste,* translated by Richard Nice, © 1984 by the President and Fellows of Harvard College and Rout- ledge and Kegan Paul Ltd. We have made diligent efforts to contact the copyright holder to obtain permission to reprint this selection. If you have information that would help us, please write to W. W. Norton & Company, 500 Fifth Avenue, New York, NY 10110.

Cleanth Brooks: "The Formalist Critics" first published in *The Kenyon Review* (Winter 1951), OS, vol. XIII, no. 1, copyright *The Kenyon Review.* "The Heresy of Paraphrase" from *The Well Wrought Urn: Studies in the Structure of Poetry,* copyright 1947 and renewed 1975 by Cleanth Brooks. Reprinted by permission of Harcourt, Inc., and Dobson Books Ltd.

Kenneth Burke: "Kinds of Criticism" from *Poetry* 68, no. V, © 1946 by the Modern Poetry Association. Reprinted by permission of *Poetry* and Kenneth Burke's Literary Trust.

Judith Butler: "Preface" and "Subversive Bodily Acts" from *Gender Trouble.* Copyright 1999 by Judith Butler. Reproduced by permission of Taylor & Francis, Inc./Routledge, Inc.

Barbara Christian: "The Race for Theory" from *Cultural Critique* (Spring 1987). © 1987 by The University of Minnesota Press. Reprinted by permission.

Hélène Cixous: "The Laugh of the Medusa" from *The Signs Reader,* translated by Keith and Paula Cohen, edited by Abel & Abel. © 1976 by Hélène Cixous. Reprinted by permission of the author and The University of Chicago Press.

Samuel Taylor Coleridge: "Biographia Literaria" from *The Collected Works of Samuel Taylor Coleridge,* vol. VII. "The Statesman's Manual" from *The Collected Works of Samuel Taylor Coleridge,* vol. VI. Copyright © 1971 by Princeton University Press. Reprinted by permission of Princeton University Press.

Pierre Corneille: "Of the Three Unities of Action, Time, and Place" from *The Continental Model,* edited and translated by D. Schier, edited by S. Elledge. © 1960 by The University of Minnesota Press. Reprinted by permission of The University of Minnesota Press.

Lennard J. Davis: "Visualizing the Disabled Body" from *Enforcing Normalcy.* © 1995 Lennard J. Davis. Reprinted by permission of Verso.

Gilles Deleuze and Félix Guattari: "What is a Minor Literature?" from *Kafka: Toward a Minor Literature,* translated by Dana Polan. Copyright © 1986 by The University of Minnesota. Originally published as *Kafka: Pour une literature mineure.* Copyright 1975 by Les Éditions de Minuit, Paris. "Rhizome" from *A Thousand Plateaus: Capitalism and Schizophrenia,* translated by Brian Massumi. Copyright © 1987 by The University of Minnesota Press. Originally published as *Mille Plateaux,* vol. 2 *of Capitalisme et schizophrenie,* ©1980 by Les Éditions de Minuit, Paris. We have made diligent efforts to contact the copyright holder to obtain permission to reprint this selection. If you have information that would help us, please write to W. W. Norton & Company, 500 Fifth Avenue, New York, NY 10110.

Paul de Man: "Semiology and Rhetoric" from *Diacritics,* © The Johns Hopkins University Press. Reprinted by permission. "The Return to Philology" from *The Times Literary Supplement,* December 10, 1982. © Paul de Man. We have made diligent efforts to contact the copyright holder to obtain permission to reprint this selection. If you have information that would help us, please write to W. W. Norton & Company, 500 Fifth Avenue, New York, NY 10110.

Jacques Derrida: "Exergue" and "The Exorbitant" from *Of Grammatology.* Translated by Gayatri Chakravorty Spivak. © 1998 by The Johns Hopkins University Press. Reprinted with permission of The Johns Hopkins University Press. "Plato's Pharmacy" from *Dissemination.* Translated by Barbara Johnson. ©1981 by The University of Chicago Press. Reprinted by permission.

W. E. B. Du Bois: "Criteria of Negro Art" from *The Crisis,* vol. 32 (October 1926). Reprinted by permission of The Crisis Publishing Company, the publisher of the magazine of the National Association for the Advancement of Colored People.

Terry Eagleton: "The Rise of English" from *Literary Theory: An Introduction,* © 1983 by Terry Eagleton. Reprinted by permission of The University of Minnesota.

Boris Eichenbaum: "The Theory of the 'Formal Method' " from *Russian Formalist Criticism: Four Essays,* translated and with an introduction by Lee T. Lemon and Marion J. Reis. Copyright ©1965 by the University of Nebraska Press. Copyright © renewed 1993 by The University of Nebraska Press. Reprinted by permission of The University of Nebraska Press.

T. S. Eliot: "The Metaphysical Poets" and "Tradition and the Individual Talent" from *Selected Essays*

© 1950 by Harcourt, Inc., and renewed 1978 by Esme Valerie Eliot. Reprinted by permission of the publisher and Faber and Faber Ltd.

Frantz Fanon: "On National Culture" and "The Pitfalls of National Consciousness" from *The Wretched of the Earth*, translated by Constance Farrington. Copyright © 1963 by Presence Africaine. Used by permission of Grove/Atlantic, Inc., and HarperCollins Publishers Ltd. We have made diligent efforts to contact the copyright holder to obtain permission to reprint this selection. If you have information that would help us, please write to W. W. Norton & Company, 500 Fifth Avenue, New York, NY 10110.

Stanley Fish: "Interpreting the Variorum" from *Critical Inquiry* 2.3 (1976). Reprinted by permission of The University of Chicago Press.

Michel Foucault: "The Carceral" from *Discipline and Punish*, translated by Alan Sheridan. Originally published in French as *Surveiller et Punir; Naissance de la Prison* by Éditions Gallimard, Paris. Copyright © 1975 by Éditions Gallimard. Reprinted by permission of Georges Borchardt, Inc., and Penguin Books Ltd. "The Repressive Hypothesis" from *The History of Sexuality,* vol. 1: *An Introduction*, translated by Robert Hurley. Originally published in French as *La Volonte de Savoir* by Éditions Gallimard, Paris. Copyright © 1976 by Éditions Gallimard. Reprinted by permission of Georges Borchardt, Inc., and Penguin Books Ltd. "Truth and Power" from *Power/Knowledge*, edited and translated by Colin Gordon. Copyright © 1972, 1975, 1976, 1977 by Michel Foucault. This collection copyright © 1980 by The Harvester Press. Reprinted by permission of Pantheon Books, a division of Random House, Inc. "What Is an Author?" from *Language, Counter-Memory, Practice: Selected Essays and Interviews*, edited by Donald F. Bouchard. Copyright © 1977 Cornell University. Used by permission of Cornell University Press. We have made diligent efforts to contact the copyright holder to obtain permission to reprint this selection. If you have information that would help us, please write to W. W. Norton & Company, 500 Fifth Avenue, New York, NY 10110.

Sigmund Freud: "Fetishism," "Interpretation of Dreams," and "The Uncanny" from *The Collected Papers*, vol. IV, *of Sigmund Freud*, Authorized translation under the supervision of Joan Riviere. Published by Basic Books, Inc., by arrangement with The Hogarth Press Ltd. and The Institute of Psycho-Analysis, London. Reprinted by permission of Basic Books, a member of Perseus Books, LLC. Permission to quote from *The Standard Edition of the Complete Psychological Works of Sigmund Freud*, translated and edited by James Strachey, granted by the Sigmund Freud Copyrights, The Institute of Psycho-Analysis, and The Hogarth Press.

Northrop Frye: "The Archetypes of Literature" first published in *The Kenyon Review* (Winter 1951), OS, vol. XIII, no 1. Copyright *The Kenyon Review*. Reprinted by permission.

Henry Louis Gates Jr.: "Talking Black" from *Loose Canons: Notes on the Culture Wars.* © 1992 by Henry Louis Gates Jr. First appeared in the *Voice Literary Supplement*, 1998. We have made diligent efforts to contact the copyright holder to obtain permission to reprint this selection. If you have information that would help us, please write to W. W. Norton & Company, 500 Fifth Avenue, New York, NY 10110.

Théophile Gautier: "Preface" to *Mademoiselle de Maupin*, edited and translated by Joanna Richardson, © 1981 Joanna Richardson. We have made diligent efforts to contact the copyright holder to obtain permission to reprint this selection. If you have information that would help us, please write to W. W. Norton & Company, 500 Fifth Avenue, New York, NY 10110.

Geoffrey of Vinsauf: "Poetria Nova" from *Classical and Medieval Literary Criticism*, edited by Alex Preminger. Copyright © 1974 by Frederick Ungar Publishing. Reprinted by permission of Continuum International Publishing Co.

Sandra Gilbert and Susan Gubar: "Infection in the Sentence" from *The Madwoman in the Attic.* © 1979 by Yale University Press, © 1984 by Sandra M. Gilbert and Susan Gubar. Reprinted by permission of Yale University Press.

Giambattista Giraldi (Cinthio): "Discourse on the Composition of Romances" from *Giraldi Cinthio on Romantics*, translated by Henry Snuggs. Copyright © 1968. Reprinted with the permission of The University Press of Kentucky.

Gorgias: "Encomium of Helen" from *Early Greek Political Thought: From Homer to Sophists*, edited by Michael Gagarin and Paul Woodruff. Copyright © 1995. Reprinted with the permission of Cambridge University Press.

Gerald Graff: "Taking Cover in Coverage" from *Profession* 86. Reprinted by permission of the Modern Language Association of America.

Antonio Gramsci: "The Formation of the Intellectuals" from *Selections from the Prison Notebooks*, edited and translated by Quintin Hoare and Geoffrey Nowell Smith. © 1971. Reprinted by permission of the International Publishers Company.

Stephen Greenblatt: "Introduction" to *The Power of Forms in the English Renaissance*. Reprinted by permission of *Genre,* copyright 1982 by the University of Oklahoma.

Jürgen Habermas: "Modernity—An Incomplete Project" from *The Anti-Aesthetic: Essays on Postmodern Culture*, edited by Hal Foster, © 1983 by Bay Press. We have made diligent efforts to contact the copyright holder to obtain permission to reprint this selection. If you have information that would help us, please write to W. W. Norton & Company, 500 Fifth Avenue, New York, NY

10110. Selections from *The Structural Transformation of the Public Sphere,* translated by Thomas Burger. This translation © 1989 by the Massachusetts Institute of Technology. This work originally appeared in German under the title *Strukturwandel der Öffentlicheit,* © 1962 Hermann Luchterhand Verlag, Darmstadt and Neuwied, Federal Republic of Germany. Reprinted by permission of MIT Press and Blackwell Publishers Ltd.

Stuart Hall: "Cultural Studies and Its Theoretical Legacies" from *Cultural Studies* (1992), edited by Lawrence Grossberg, Cary Nelson, and Paula Treichler. Reprinted by permission of Taylor and Francis Ltd.

Donna Haraway: "A Manifesto for Cyborgs: Science, Technology, and Socialist Feminism in the 1980s" from *Socialist Review,* vol. 15, no. 80 (1985). Reprinted by permission of the author.

Dick Hebdige: "From Culture to Hegemony" from *Subculture: The Meaning of Style.* Copyright © 1979 by Dick Hebdige. Reprinted by permission of Routledge.

G. W. F. Hegel: "Lectures on Fine Art" from *Aesthetics: Lectures on Fine Art,* vol. I, translated by T. M. Knox. © Oxford University Press 1975. Reprinted by permission of Oxford University Press. "The Master/Slave Dialectic" from *Phenomenology of Spirit,* translated by A. V. Miller, © Oxford University Press 1977. Reprinted by permission of Oxford University Press.

Martin Heidegger: "Language" from *Poetry, Language, Thought,* translated by Albert Hofstadter. Copyright © 1971 by Martin Heidegger. Reprinted by permission of HarperCollins Publishers, Inc.

E. D. Hirsch Jr.: "Objective Interpretation" from *Validity in Interpretation.* © 1960 by the Modern Language Association. Reprinted by permission of the Modern Language Association of America.

bell hooks: "Postmodern Blackness" from *Yearning = Race, Gender and Cultural Politics.* © 1990 by Gloria Watkins. Reprinted by permission of South End Press.

Horace: "The Art of Poetry" from *Ancient Literary Criticism,* edited by D. A. Russell and M. Winterbottom. © Oxford University Press 1972. Reprinted by permission of Oxford University Press.

Max Horkheimer and Theodor W. Adorno: "The Culture Industry: Enlightenment as Mass Deception" from *Dialectic of Enlightenment,* translated by J. Cumming. © 1972 by Herder and Herder. Reprinted by permission of Continuum International Publishing Group.

Irving Howe: "History and the Novel" from *The New Republic,* September 3, 1990. Reprinted by permission.

Hugh of St. Victor: From *The Didascalicon of Hugh of St. Victor,* translated by Jerome Taylor. © 1961 by Columbia University Press. Reprinted by permission of Columbia University Press.

Langston Hughes: "The Negro Artist and the Racial Mountain" from the June 23, 1926, issue of *The Nation.* Reprinted with permission.

Zora Neale Hurston: "Characteristics of Negro Expression" from *Negro: An Anthology,* edited by Nancy Cunard and Hugh Ford. © 1970 Frederick Ungar Publishing. Reprinted by permission of The Continuum International Publishing Group. "What White Publishers Won't Print" from *I Love Myself When I Am Laughing,* edited by Alice Walker and M. H. Washington, © the Estate of Zora Neale Hurston. Reprinted by permission of the Victoria Sanders Literary Agency.

Wolfgang Iser: "Interaction between Text and Reader" from *The Reader in the Text: Essays on Audience and Interpretation,* edited by Susan Suleiman and I. Crosman. Copyright © 1980 by Princeton University Press. Reprinted by permission of Princeton University Press.

Roman Jakobson: "Linguistics and Politics" and "Two Aspects of Language and Two Types of Aphasic Disturbance" from *Language in Literature,* edited by Krystyna Pomorska and Stephen Rudy. © 1987 by The Jakobson Trust. We have made diligent efforts to contact the copyright holder to obtain permission to reprint this selection. If you have information that would help us, please write to W. W. Norton & Company, 500 Fifth Avenue, New York, NY 10110.

Fredric Jameson: "Preface" and "On Interpretation" from *The Political Unconscious: Narrative as a Socially Symbolic Act.* Copyright © 1981 by Cornell University Press. Used by permission of the publisher, Cornell University Press. "Postmodernism and Consumer Society" from *Postmodernism and Its Discontents, Theories, Practices,* edited by E. Ann Kaplan. © 1988 by Verso. Reprinted by permission.

Hans R. Jauss: "Literary History as a Challenge to Literary Theory" from *Toward an Aesthetic of Reception,* translated by Timothy Bahti. © 1982 by the University of Minnesota. We have made diligent efforts to contact the copyright holder to obtain permission to reprint this selection. If you have information that would help us, please write to W. W. Norton & Company, 500 Fifth Avenue, New York, NY 10110.

Barbara Johnson: "Melville's Fist: The Execution of Billy Budd" from *Studies in Romanticism* 18.4 (Winter 1979). Reprinted by permission.

Samuel Johnson: *The Rambler, Essay* 4, edited by Bate & Strauss. © 1969 by Yale University Press. Reprinted by permission of the publisher.

C. G. Jung: "On the Relation of Analytical Psychology to Poetry" (1922) from *The Spirit in Man, Art, and Literature, The Collected Works of C. G. Jung.* Copyright ©1966 by Princeton University Press. Reprinted by permission of Princeton University Press.

Immanuel Kant: From *Critique of Judgment*, translated by Werner S. Pluhar, © by Werner S. Pluhar 1987. Reprinted by permission of Hackett Publishing Company, Inc.

Steven Knapp and Walter Benn Michaels: "Against Theory" from *Against Theory: Literary Studies and the New Pragmatism*. © 1982 by The University of Chicago Press. Reprinted by permission of the author and the publisher.

Annette Kolodny: "Dancing Through the Minefield: Some Observations on the Theory, Practice, and Politics of a Feminist Literary Criticism" from *Feminist Studies* 6.1 (Spring 1980). Copyright © 1979 by Annette Kolodny. Reprinted by permission of the author.

Julia Kristeva: From *Revolution in Poetic Language*. © 1984 by Columbia University Press. Reprinted by permission of the publisher.

Jacques Lacan: "The Agency of the Letter in the Unconscious," "The Mirror Stage," and "The Signification of the Phallus" from *Ecrits: A Selection by Jacques Lacan*, translated and edited by Alan Sheridan. Copyright © 1966 by Editions du Seuil. English translation © 1977 by Tavistock Publications. Used by permission of W. W. Norton & Company, Inc., and Routledge.

Gotthold E. Lessing: From *Laocoön: An Essay on the Limits of Painting and Poetry*, translated by E. A. McCormick. Copyright © 1962 by The Bobbs-Merrill Company, Inc. © 1984 by The Johns Hopkins University Press. Reprinted by permission of The Johns Hopkins University Press.

Claude Lévi-Strauss: "A Writing Lesson" from *Tristes Tropiques*, translated by John and Doreen Weightman. Copyright © 1955 by Librairie Plon. English translation copyright © 1973 by Jonathan Cape Limited. Reprinted by permission of Georges Borchardt and the publisher, Jonathan Cape.

Longinus: "On Sublimity" from *Ancient Literary Criticism: Principal Texts & New Translations*, edited by D. A. Russell and M. Winterbottom. © Oxford University Press 1972. We have made diligent efforts to contact the copyright holder to obtain permission to reprint this selection. If you have information that would help us, please write to W. W. Norton & Company, 500 Fifth Avenue, New York, NY 10110.

György Lukacs: "Realism in the Balance" from *Aesthetics and Politics*, edited by Ronald Taylor. © Artisjus. Reprinted by permission of Verso.

Jean-François Lyotard: "Defining the Postmodern" from *ICA Documents 4*, 1986. © Jean-François Lyotard. We have made diligent efforts to contact the copyright holder to obtain permission to reprint this selection. If you have information that would help us, please write to W. W. Norton & Company, 500 Fifth Avenue, New York, NY 10110.

Macrobius: From *Commentary on the Dream of Scipio*, translated by William Stahl. Copyright © 1952 by Columbia University Press. Reprinted by permission of Columbia University Press.

Moses Maimonides: From *The Guide of the Perplexed*, translated by Shlomo Pines. © 1963 by The University of Chicago Press. Reprinted by permission of The University of Chicago Press.

Stéphane Mallarmé: "Crise de vers" from *Mallarmé: The Poet and His Circle*, edited by Rosemary Lloyd. © 1999 Cornell University Press. Used by permission of the publisher, Cornell University Press.

Karl Marx and Friedrich Engels: "Letter, Friedrich Engels to Joseph Bloch, Sept. 21–22, 1890," "Economic and Philosophic Manuscripts of 1844," first pub. in German in 1932, "Manifesto of the Communist Party," "Preface to *A Contribution to the Critique of Political Economy*," "The Fetishism of Commodities" from *Capital*, "The German Ideology: Part I," and "The Struggle for a Normal Working-Day" from *The Marx-Engels Reader*, translated by Robert C. Tucker. Copyright © 1978, 1972 by W. W. Norton & Company, Inc. Used by permission of W. W. Norton & Company, Inc. "Grundrisse" from *Foundations of the Critique of Political Economy*, translated by Martin Nicolaus. © 1973 Martin Nicolaus. Reprinted by permission of *New Left Review*.

Giacopo Mazzoni: From *On the Defense of the Comedy of Dante*, translated by Robert Montgomery. © 1983 by Robert L. Montgomery. Reprinted with the permission of the University of Florida.

Stuart Moulthrop: "You Say You Want a Revolution? Hypertext and the Laws of Media" from *Postmodern Culture* 1.3 (1991). © *Postmodern Culture* and The Johns Hopkins University Press. Reprinted by permission.

Laura Mulvey: "Visual Pleasure and Narrative Cinema" from *Visual and Other Pleasures*. Copyright © 1989 by Laura Mulvey. We have made diligent efforts to contact the copyright holder to obtain permission to reprint this selection. If you have information that would help us, please write to W. W. Norton & Company, 500 Fifth Avenue, New York, NY 10110.

Friedrich Nietzsche: "On Truth and Lying in a Non-Moral Sense" and "The Birth of Tragedy" from *The Birth of Tragedy and Other Writings*, translated and edited by Ronald Speirs, and edited by Raymond Geuss. © 1999 by Cambridge University Press. Reprinted with the permission of Cambridge University Press.

Richard Ohmann: "The Shaping of a Canon: U.S. Fiction, 1960–1975" from *Politics of Letters*, ©1987 by Richard Ohmann, Wesleyan University Press. Reprinted by permission, University Press of New England, Hanover, NH.

Walter Pater: From *The Renaissance: Studies in Art and Poetry*, edited by Donald Hill. © 1980 The Regents of The University of California. Reprinted with the permission of The University of California Press.

Christine de Pizan: From *The Book of the City of Ladies*, translated by Earl Jeffrey Richards. Copyright © 1982, 1998 by Persea Books, Inc. Reprinted by permission of Persea Books, Inc.

Plato: "Ion" from *Plato: Complete Works*, edited by John Cooper, 1997. © Hackett Publishing Company. Reprinted by permission of Hackett Publishing Company, Inc. From *Plato's Republic*, translated by Robin Waterfield. We have made diligent efforts to contact the copyright holder to obtain permission to reprint this selection. If you have information that would help us, please write to W. W. Norton & Company, 500 Fifth Avenue, New York, NY 10110.

Plotinus: "On the Intellectual Beauty" from *The Enneads*, translated by Stephen MacKenna. Reprinted by permission of Faber and Faber Ltd.

Alexander Pope: "An Essay on Criticism" from *The Twickenham Edition of The Poems of Alexander Pope*, vol. I. Reprinted by permission of Routledge.

Georges Poulet: "Phenomenology of Reading" from *New Literary History: A Journal of Theory and Interpretation* 1.1 (October 1969). © 1969 The University of Virginia. Reprinted by permission of The Johns Hopkins University Press.

John Crowe Ransom: "Criticism, Inc." from *The World's Body.* Copyright 1938 by Charles Scribner and Sons; copyright renewed © 1966 by John Crowe Ransom. Reprinted with the permission of Scribner, a Division of Simon & Schuster.

Adrienne Rich: "Compulsory Heterosexuality and Lesbian Existence" from *Blood, Bread, and Poetry: Selected Prose 1979–1985*. Copyright © 1986 by Adrienne Rich. Used by permission of the author, W. W. Norton & Company, Inc., and Virago Press.

Pierre de Ronsard: "A Brief on the Art of French Poetry" from *The Great Critics: An Anthology of Literary Criticism*, edited and translated by James Harry Smith and Edd Winfield Parks. Copyright ©1932, 1939, 1951 by W. W. Norton & Company, Inc., renewed © 1967 by James Harry Smith and Edd Winfield Parks. Reprinted by permission of W. W. Norton & Company, Inc.

Edward W. Said: "Introduction" to *Orientalism.* Copyright © 1978 by Edward W. Said. Reprinted by permission of Pantheon Books, a division of Random House, Inc.

Jean-Paul Sartre: "Why Write?" from *What Is Literature? and Other Essays*, edited by Steven Ungar, translated by Bernard Frechtman and J. MacCombie. © 1988 by the President and Fellows of Harvard College. We have made diligent efforts to contact the copyright holder to obtain permission to reprint this selection. If you have information that would help us, please write to W. W. Norton & Company, 500 Fifth Avenue, New York, NY 10110.

Ferdinand de Saussure: From *Course in General Linguistics*, translated by Wade Baskin. © 1966 by the Philosophical Library, NY. Reprinted by permission.

Friedrich Schiller: "Letters 2, 6, 9" from *On the Aesthetic Education of Man*, edited and translated by Elizabeth Wilkinson and L. A. Willoughby. © Oxford University Press 1967. Reprinted by permission of Oxford University Press.

Friedrich Schleiermacher: "Outline of the 1819 Lectures" from *New Literary History* 10 (Autumn 1978), edited by H. Kimmerle, translated by R. Haas. © 1978 by The University of Virginia. Reprinted by permission of The Johns Hopkins University Press.

Eve Kosofsky Sedgwick: "Axiom 2" from "Introduction: Axiomatic" from *Epistemology of the Closet*. Copyright © 1990 The Regents of the University of California. Reprinted with the permission of The University of California Press. "Homosocial Desire" from *Between Men.* Copyright 1985 Columbia University Press. Reprinted by permission of Columbia University Press.

Percy B. Shelley: "A Defence of Poetry" from *Shelley's Poetry and Prose*: A Norton Critical Edition, edited by Donald Reiman and Sharon Powers. Copyright © 1977 by Donald H. Reiman and Sharon B. Powers. Reprinted by permission of W. W. Norton & Company, Inc.

Sir Philip Sidney: "An Apology for Poetry" from *An Apology for Poetry,* edited by Forrest G. Robinson, © 1970. Reprinted by permission of Prentice-Hall, Inc., Upper Saddle River, NJ.

Barbara Smith: "Toward a Black Feminist Criticism" from *The Truth That Never Hurts.* Copyright © 1998 by Barbara Smith. Reprinted by permission of Rutgers University Press.

Barbara H. Smith: From *Contingencies of Value,* copyright © 1988 by the President and Fellows of Harvard College. Reprinted by permission of Harvard University Press.

Gayatri C. Spivak: "History" [Can the Subaltern Speak?] from *A Critique of Postcolonial Reason*, © 1999 Harvard University Press. Used by permission of University of Illinois Press.

Germaine de Stael: "Essays on Fiction" from *An Extraordinary Woman: Selected Writings of Germaine de Stael*, edited by V. Folkenflik. Copyright 1987 by Columbia University Press. Reprinted by permission of the publisher.

Ngugi Wă Thiong'o, Taban Lo Liyong, and Henry Owuor-Anyumba: "On the Abolition of the English Department" from *Homecoming: Essays on African and Caribbean Literature, Culture and Politics.* © 1972 by Ngugi Wă Thiong'o. Granted by permission of Heinemann Educational Books Ltd.

Tzvetan Todorov: "Structural Analysis of Narrative" from *Novel: A Forum on Fiction* 3.1 (Fall 1969), translated by Arnold Weinstein. Copyright NOVEL Corp. © 1969. Reprinted with permission.

Jane Tompkins: "Me and My Shadow" from *New Literary History* 19.1. © 1987 The University of Virginia. Reprinted by permission of The Johns Hopkins University Press.

Leon Trotsky: From *Literature and Revolution*, translated by Rose Strunsky. © 1925 by International Publishers Company, Inc. Reprinted by permission.

Giambattista Vico: From *The New Science of Giambattista Vico: Unabridged Translation of the Third Edition (1744) with the Addition of the "Practice of the New Science,"* translated by Thomas Goddard Bergin and Max Harold Fisch. Copyright 1948 by Cornell University. Revised and abridged edition copyright ©1961 by Thomas Goddard Bergin and Max Harold Fisch. Revised unabridged edition copyright ©1968 by Cornell University. Translation of "Practice of the New Science" copyright 1976 by The Johns Hopkins University Press. Used by permission of the publisher, Cornell University Press.

Gerald Vizenor: "Postindian Warriors" from *Manifest Manners: Postindian Warriors of Survivance.* © 1994 by Gerald Vizenor and reprinted with permission from Wesleyan University Press.

Hayden White: "The Historical Text as Literary Artifact" from *Tropics of Discourse: Essays in Cultural Criticism.* © 1978 by The Johns Hopkins University Press. Reprinted by permission.

Raymond Williams: "Literature" from *Marxism and Literature.* Copyright Oxford University Press 1977. Reprinted by permission of Oxford University Press.

Edmund Wilson: "Marxism and Literature" from *The Triple Thinkers: Twelve Essays on Literary Subjects.* © 1938, 1948 by Edmund Wilson. We have made diligent efforts to contact the copyright holder to obtain permission to reprint this selection. If you have information that would help us, please write to W. W. Norton & Company, 500 Fifth Avenue, New York, NY 10110.

W. K. Wimsatt Jr. and M. C. Beardsley: "The Affective Fallacy" first published in the *Sewanee Review* 57.1 (Winter 1949). Copyright 1949, 1977 by The University of the South. Reprinted with the permission of the editor. "The Intentional Fallacy" first published in the *Sewanee Review* 54.3 (Summer 1946). Copyright 1946, 1974 by The University of the South. Reprinted with the permission of the editor.

Monique Wittig: "One Is Not Born a Woman" from *The Straight Mind.* Copyright © 1992 by Monique Wittig. Reprinted by permission of Beacon Press, Boston.

Mary Wollstonecraft: "Vindication of the Rights of Woman" from *The Vindications*, edited by D. L. Macdonald and Kathleen Scherf. Reprinted by permission of Broadview Press.

Virginia Woolf: From *A Room of One's Own*, copyright 1929 by Harcourt, Inc., and renewed 1957 by Leonard Woolf. Reprinted by permission of the publisher.

Bonnie Zimmerman: "What Has Never Been: An Overview of Lesbian Feminist Criticism." This article is a revised version of an article originally published in *Feminist Studies* 7.3 (Fall 1981). Reprinted by permission of the publisher, Feminist Studies, Inc.

Every effort has been made to contact the copyright holders of each of the selections. Rights holders of any selections not credited should contact W. W. Norton & Company, Inc., 500 Fifth Avenue, New York, NY 10110, in order for a correction to be made in the next reprinting of our work.

Author/Title Index

Subject Index

What follows is a general index of terms, concepts, persons, and works mentioned in the Anthology. If you would like to use a brief index that lists only the authors and pieces represented in the Anthology, turn to page 2561 for the Author/Title Index.